THE COMPLETE WORDSTUDY DICTIONARY
OLD TESTAMENT

The Complete WordStudy Dictionary
Old Testament

Warren Baker, D.R.E.
Eugene Carpenter, Ph.D.

Advancing the Ministries of the Gospel
AMG *Publishers*
God's Word to you is our highest calling.

The Complete Word Study Dictionary: Old Testament

6815 Shallowford Rd.
Chattanooga, Tennessee 37421

ISBN 0-89957-667-2

First printing—October 2003

Cover designed by ImageWright, Inc., Chattanooga, Tennessee
Interior design and typesetting by Warren Baker and Reider Publishing Services, West Hollywood, California

Printed in Canada
09 08 07 06 05 04 03 —T— 8 7 6 5 4 3 2 1

To my wife, DeeAnn P. Baker.
The big things and the little things she has done
to encourage and support me during this project and many
others are my constant joy and rejoicing before God.
I could not have done it without her.

To my wife, Joyce D. Carpenter.
Her patience, support, and encouragement have been
unfailing throughout its production. She graciously spent
many hours checking the accuracy of biblical references.
I could not have done it without her.

Contents

Acknowledgements ix

Preface xi

Books of the Bible xiii

Abbreviations xv

Transliteration Guide xvii

The Complete Word Study Dictionary: Old Testament 1

The Complete Word Study Concordance: Old Testament 1255

Acknowledgments

We would like to thank Dr. Spiros Zodhiates for inspiring us with his vision to make the biblical languages understandable to everyone.

We would like to thank those who have worked with us to complete this dictionary:

The editors: Gracie Black, Dorothy Boyse, Stephen Broyles, Agnes Lawless, Vickie Overcash, Amy Turner, Tim Wehse, and Dennis Wisdom.

The typists: Renee Kaufman, Cheri Mullins, and Connie Stewart.

Preface

The Complete Word Study Dictionary: Old Testament is the final volume in AMG's Word Study Series. These Bible study tools are designed to make the original languages of the Bible accessible to every student of the Word of God. This lexicon is intended as a companion volume to *The Complete Word Study Old Testament*, which identifies the words of the Hebrew text of the Old Testament by the placement of Strong's numbers and grammatical codes over the English text. Together these two volumes represent the Old Testament portion of this series.

This book consists of two parts: The Complete Word Study Dictionary: Old Testament and The Complete Word Study Old Testament Concordance.

The Complete Word Study Dictionary: Old Testament offers definitions and explanations for every word used in the Hebrew Old Testament. Each entry is identified by a number from Strong's Dictionary of the Hebrew Bible, so that readers can make great use of the information that is given about each word, even if they have no working knowledge of the Hebrew language.

The Complete Word Study Old Testament Concordance is also coded to Strong's numbering system. This concordance details every occurrence of every Hebrew and Aramaic word in the Old Testament by book, chapter, and verse.

The special features of this work are as follows:

Subdivided Entries

Entries in both the dictionary and the concordance are subdivided as needed to identify various uses of a word(s). The division of a single entry into A, B, C, etc., represents different uses of the same word. Proper noun entries are subdivided in this manner to identify different places and/or individuals that have the same name. Roman numerals under a single entry number indicate entirely distinct words that Strong identified by the same number.

Key Variants Between English Versions

In the concordance portion of the work especially, we have endeavored to account for important differences between the KJV and the NASB and NIV.

Traditional Hebrew Variants
The reader will also notice references to Qe and Ke. These two abbreviations stand for the Qeri (oral tradition) and Kethiv (written tradition) respectively. The difference is often simply a matter of spelling. In some instances, however, the two readings represent two different words.

Chapter and Verse Differences
Next to some verse references will be others in parentheses (or the next set of enclosures): e.g., (Ps. 49:10[11]). As you may be aware, the division of the books of the Bible into chapters and verses was not done when these books were originally written. In some passages of Scripture, the chapter and verse numbers are different between our English versions and the Hebrew text. The references in parentheses identify the position of the passage according to the text of the Hebrew Old Testament.

Books of the Bible

The Old Testament

Genesis	Gen.	Ecclesiastes	Eccl.
Exodus	Ex.	Song of Solomon	Song
Leviticus	Lev.	Isaiah	Isa.
Numbers	Num.	Jeremiah	Jer.
Deuteronomy	Deut.	Lamentations	Lam.
Joshua	Josh.	Ezekiel	Ezek.
Judges	Judg.	Daniel	Dan.
Ruth	Ruth	Hosea	Hos.
1 Samuel	1 Sam.	Joel	Joel
2 Samuel	2 Sam.	Amos	Amos
1 Kings	1 Kgs.	Obadiah	Obad.
2 Kings	2 Kgs.	Jonah	Jon.
1 Chronicles	1 Chr.	Micah	Mic.
2 Chronicles	2 Chr.	Nahum	Nah.
Ezra	Ezra	Habakkuk	Hab.
Nehemiah	Neh.	Zephaniah	Zeph.
Esther	Esth.	Haggai	Hag.
Job	Job	Zechariah	Zech.
Psalms	Ps.	Malachi	Mal.
Proverbs	Prov.		

The New Testament

Matthew	Matt.	1 Timothy	1 Tim.
Mark	Mark	2 Timothy	2 Tim.
Luke	Luke	Titus	Titus
John	John	Philemon	Phile.
Acts	Acts	Hebrews	Heb.
Romans	Rom.	James	James
1 Corinthians	1 Cor.	1 Peter	1 Pet.
2 Corinthians	2 Cor.	2 Peter	2 Pet.
Galatians	Gal.	1 John	1 John
Ephesians	Eph.	2 John	2 John
Philippians	Phil.	3 John	3 John
Colossians	Col.	Jude	Jude
1 Thessalonians	1 Thess.	Revelation	Rev.
2 Thessalonians	2 Thess.		

General Abbreviations

act. (active)
adj. (adjective, adjectival)
adv. (adverb, adverbial, adverbially)
ant. (antonym)
aor. (aorist [2 aor. for second aorist])
art. (article)
a.t. (author's translation)
attrib. (attributive)
AV (Authorized Version)
cf. (compare, comparison)
chap. (chapter)
Class. Gr. (Classical Greek)
coll. (collective)
com. (common)
conj. (conjunction, conjunctive)
dat. (dative)
def. (definite)
deriv. (derivative[s], derivation)
e.g. (for example)
Eng. (English)
etc. (and so forth)
f. (following)
ff. (following in the plural)
fem. (feminine)
fig. (figuativaly)
fut. (future)
gen. (genitive)
Gr. (Greek)
Hebr. (Hebrew)
ibid. (in the same place)
i.e. (that is)
indef. (indefinite, indefinitely)
inf. (infinitive)
intens. (intensive)
intrans. (intransitive)
KJV (King James Version)
Lat. (Latin)
masc. (masculine)
MS (manuscript)
MSS (manuscripts)
MT (Masoretic text)
NASB (New American Standard Bible)
n.f. (not found in the NT)
NIV (New International Version)
NKJV (New King James Version)
NT (New Testament)
neg. (negative)
nom. (nominative)
obj. (object, objective[ly])
OT (Old Testament)
p. (page), pp. (pages)
part. (participle, participial)
pass. (passive)
pl. (plural)
poss. (possessive)
prep. (preposition)
pres. (present)
priv. (privative)
pron. (pronoun)
RSV (Revised Standard Version)
Sept. (Septuagint)
sing. (singular)
subst. (substantive)
subj. (subject, subjective)
s.v. (under the word)
syn. (synonym, synonymous)
trans. (transitive, transitively)
v. (verse), vv. (verses)
voc. (vocative)
vol. (volume)

GUIDE TO THE TRANSLITERATION OF HEBREW CONSONANTS

Consonant	Hebrew Name	Trans– literation	Phonetic Sound	Example
א	Aleph	ʾ	Silent	Similar to h in honor
בּ	Beth	*b*	*b*	as in boy
ב	Veth	*ḇ*	v	as in vat
גּ	Gimel	*g*	g	as in get
ג	Gimel	*g*	g	as in get
דּ	Daleth	*d*	d	as in do
ד	Daleth	*ḏ*	d	as in do
ה	Hē	*h*	h	as in hat
ו	Waw	*w*	w	as in wait
ז	Zayin	*z*	z	as in zip
ח	Cheth	*ḥ*	ch	Similar to ch in the German *ach*
ט	Teth	*ṭ*	t	as in time
י	Yodh	*y*	y	as in you
כּ	Kaph	*k*	k	as in kit
כ	Chaph	*ḵ*	ch	Similar to ch in the German *ach*
ל	Lamed	*l*	l	as in lit
מ	Mem	*m*	m	as in move
נ	Nun	*n*	n	as in not
ס	Samekh	*s*	s	as in see
ע	Ayin	ʿ	Silent	Similar to h in honor
פּ	Pē	*p*	p	as in put
פ	Phē	*p̱*	f	as in phone
צ	Tsadde	*ṣ*	ts	as in wits
ק	Qoph	*q*	q	as in Qatar
ר	Resh	*r*	r	as in run
שׂ	Sin	*ś*	s	as in see
שׁ	Shin	*š*	sh	as in ship
תּ	Taw	*t*	t	as in time
ת	Thaw	*ṯ*	th	as in this

GUIDE TO THE TRANSLITERATION OF HEBREW VOWELS

Hebrew Vowel	Name	Position	Trans-literation	Sound
ְ	Shewa (Silent)	מְ	*Not transliterated or pronounced*	
ְ	Shewa (Vocal)	מְ	^{e}	u as in but
ַ	Pathah	מַ	*a*	a as in lad
ֲ	Hateph Pathah	מֲ	^{a}	a as in lad
ָ	Qamets	מָ	*ā*	a as in car
ֳ	Hateph Qamets	מֳ	^{o}	a as in car
ֵי	Sere Yodh	מֵי	*ēy*	ey as in prey
ֵ	Sere	מֵ	*ē*	ey as in prey
ֶ	Seghol	מֶ	*e*	e as in set
ֱ	Hateph Seghol	מֱ	^{e}	e as in set
ִי	Hiriq Yodh	מִי	*iy*	i as in machine
ִ	Hiriq	מִ	*i*	i as in pin
ָ	Qamets Qatan	מָ	*o*	o as in hop
ֹ	Holem	מֹ	*ō*	o as in go
וֹ	Holem	מוֹ	*ô*	o as in go
ֻ	Qubbuts	מֻ	*u*	u as in put
וּ	Shureq	מוּ	*û*	u as in tune

The Complete Word Study Dictionary Old Testament

Abbreviated Bibliography:

Abegg, Martin, Jr., Peter Flint and Eugene Ulrich. *The Dead Sea Scrolls Bible.* San Francisco: Harper Collins Publishers, 1999.

Botterweck, G. and H. Ringgren. *Theological Dictionary of the Old Testament.* Translated by John T. Willis. Grand Rapids: Eerdmans, 1974.

Bromiley, Geoffrey W. *The International Standard Bible Encyclopedia.* 4 vols. William B. Eerdmans Publishing Company, 1970–1988.

Brown, F., S. R. Driver, and C. Briggs, eds. *A Hebrew and English Lexicon of the Old Testament.* Oxford: Clarendon Press, 1907.

Carpenter, Eugene E. and Philip Comfort. *Treasury of Key Bible Words.* Nashville, TN: Broadman, 2000.

Harris, R. Laird, Gleason L. Archer, Jr., and Bruce K. Waltke. *Theological Wordbook of the Old Testament.* 2 vols. Chicago: Moody Press, 1980.

Holladay, William L., ed. *A Concise Hebrew and Aramaic Lexicon of the Old Testament.* Leiden: E. J. Brill, 1971.

Jenni, E. and C. Westermann. *Theologisches Handworterbuch zum Alten Testament.* Munchen: Chr. Kaise, 1979.

Jones, Alfred. *Jones' Dictionary of Old Testament Proper Names.* 1856. Reprint edition. Grand Rapids: Kregel, 1990.

Koehler, L., W. Baumgartner, and J. Stamm, eds. *The Hebrew and Aramaic Lexicon of the Old Testament.* Leiden: E. J. Brill, 1996.

Owens, J., ed. *Analytical Key to the Old Testament.* Grand Rapids: Baker, 1990.

Rasmussen, Carl G. *Zondervan NIV Atlas of the Bible.* Grand Rapids, MI: Zondervan Publishing House, 1989.

VanGemeren, W., ed. *New International Dictionary of Old Testament Theology and Exegesis.* Grand Rapids: Zondervan, 1997.

Wood, Leon J. *A Survey of Israel's History.* Rev. ed., David O'Brien. Grand Rapids, MI: Zondervan Publishing House, 1986.

apocalyptic "beast" (Dan. 7:11). See the Hebrew cognate *'āḇaḏ* (6).

8. אֹבֵד *'ōḇēḏ:* An abstract noun meaning destruction. The word is used this way only in Numbers 24:20, 24 where Balaam prophesies the destruction of three nations or areas, one of which is Eber. If Eber refers to the Hebrews, then the destruction is not to be understood as absolute. Other occurrences of this form, although spelled identically, are used differently and are included under *'āḇaḏ* (6).

9. אֲבֵדָה *'aḇēḏāh:* A feminine noun meaning a lost object or possession. The term is employed only in a legal context in the Hebrew Bible (Ex. 22:8; Lev. 6:4[5:23]; Deut. 22:3). To keep a lost item in one's possession and lie about it to the rightful owner is listed among sins, such as deception concerning a deposit or pledge and robbery and fraud (Lev. 6:3[5:22]).

10. אֲבַדֹּה *'aḇaddōh:* A noun referring to the place of the dead, indistinguishable in meaning from *'aḇaddôn* (11). This form occurs only in Proverbs 27:20 where, along with Sheol, it identifies death as a place that can always hold more just as the eyes of humans always want more. This word originally may have been *'aḇēḏāh* (9) or *'aḇaddôn* (11) but was changed in the transmission of the ancient manuscript.

11. אֲבַדּוֹן *'aḇaddôn:* A feminine noun meaning destruction (that is, death). It may also mean a place of destruction. It is used extensively in wisdom literature and connotes the abode of the dead. It commonly forms a word pair with *šᵉ'āl* (7594) (Job 26:6; Prov. 15:11; 27:20) but is also linked with death (Job 28:22) and the grave (Ps. 88:11[12]). See the Hebrew verb *'āḇaḏ* (6).

12. אַבְדָן *'aḇḏān:* A noun, probably masculine, meaning destruction. It occurs only in Esther 9:5 where the Jews striking their enemies with the sword results in slaughter and destruction. A similar form, *'oḇḏān* (13), also meaning destruction, occurs in Esther 8:6 in a similar context: the desire of the Jews' enemies to bring destruction on them. These two forms may be identical.

13. אָבְדָן *'oḇḏān:* A masculine noun meaning destruction. This term conveys the slaughter of the Jews (Esth. 8:6; 9:5). See the Hebrew verb *'āḇaḏ* (6).

14. אָבָה *'āḇāh:* A verb meaning to be willing, to consent, to be acquiescent, to yield, to desire. Its primary meaning is to be positively inclined to respond to some authority or petition. The word is used to signify willingness or desire (Gen. 24:5, 8; Judg. 19:25; 2 Chr. 21:7; Isa. 30:15); agreement in principle (Judg. 11:17; 1 Kgs. 20:8); consent to authority (Job 39:9; Isa. 1:19); yielding, as to sin (Deut. 13:8[9]; Prov. 1:10); and, by extension, to be content (Prov. 6:35; Eccl. 7:8).

15. אָבֶה *ʾāḇeh:* This is a masculine singular noun found in Job 34:36 as an interjection *ʾāḇiy*, indicating the desire of the speaker. It is well rendered as Oh, that! It may rather be a first person singular future verb (*bāyay*), indicating, similarly, the desire of the speaker Elihu.

16. אֵבֶה *ʾēḇeh:* A masculine singular noun meaning reed, papyrus (Job 9:26). The meaning in this context is probably swift, indicating swift ships (NKJV). This thought parallels the lightning fast flight of the eagle. But the meaning could be literal, indicating reed or papyrus boats (NIV, NASB).

17. אֲבוֹי *ʾaḇôy:* An exclamation of anxiety or pain found in Proverbs 23:29. It translates well as woe. It parallels four other words that refer to sorrow, complaints, undeserved wounds, and red eyes.

18. אֵבוּס *ʾēḇûs:* A masculine noun meaning crib or manger. It is associated with a donkey (Isa. 1:3); oxen where it may mean a trough for feeding (Prov. 14:4); and the wild ox (Job 39:9).

19. אִבְחָה *ʾiḇḥāh:* A feminine noun meaning slaughter. In Ezekiel (21:15 [20]), it is the slaughter resulting from the avenging sword of the Lord as it strikes His rebellious and corrupt people.

20. אֲבַטִּיחַ *ʾaḇaṭṭiyaḥ:* A masculine noun meaning melon, watermelon. It is used only in the plural form (Num. 11:5) to refer to Egyptian melons of some kind, along with other Egyptian vegetables and fruits for which the Israelites longed after leaving Egypt.

21. אֲבִי *ʾaḇiy:* A feminine proper noun, Abi (2 Kgs. 18:2). See *ʾaḇiyāāh* (29).

22. אֲבִיאֵל *ʾaḇiyʾēl:* A masculine proper noun designating Abiel.

A. The father of Kish and Ner (1 Sam. 9:1; 14:51).

B. One of David's mighty men (1 Chr. 11:32).

23. אֲבִיאָסָף *ʾaḇiyʾāsāp̄:* A masculine proper noun, Abiasaph (Ex. 6:24).

24. אָבִיב *ʾāḇiyḇ:* A masculine noun used twice in the Old Testament meaning a fresh, ripe ear of barley (Ex. 9:31). As an offering, it could be roasted in fire and presented to the Lord (Lev. 2:14).

25. אֲבִי גִּבְעוֹן *ʾaḇiy giḇʿôn:* A proper noun designating Abi Gibeon (1 Chr. 8:29; 9:35).

26. אֲבִיגַיִל *ʾaḇiygayil:* A proper noun designating Abigail, formed by combining the words for father (*ʾāḇ* [1]) and to be glad (*giyl* [1523]). The name means "my father is glad, joyful."

A. She was a Carmelite (Alebite, 2 Sam. 2:2; 3:3). She was the wife of Nabal, a foolish boorish man, who died because of his insolent anger and behavior (1 Sam. 25:27). Abigail was a beautiful and wise woman. She became one of David's wives after Nabal's death (1 Sam. 27:3). David's second son, Daniel or Chileab (2 Sam. 3:3; 1 Chr. 3:1), was by her (2 Sam. 3:3).

B. Abigal, a proper noun, and shortened form of Abigail (2 Sam. 17:25). She was a sister of David and the mother of Amasa (cf. 1 Chr. 2:16–17), sharing the same mother, a daughter of Nahash or Jesse (cf. 1 Chr. 2:13–17). Nahash in 2 Samuel 17:25 may be another name for Jesse, David's father (cf. Isa. 14:29). Or possibly, the text is corrupt in this reading, a scribal error.

27. אֲבִידָן ***'abiydān:*** A proper noun designating Abidan (Num. 1:11; 2:22; 7:60, 65; 10:24).

28. אֲבִידָע ***'abiydā':*** A proper noun designating Abida (Gen. 25:4; 1 Chr. 1:33).

29. אֲבִיָּה ***'abiyyāh,*** אֲבִיָּהוּ ***'abiyāhû:*** A proper noun designating Abijah, referring to several different Israelite men in the Old Testament and also to two Israelite women. It is made up of *'āb* (1), father, plus *yāh* (3050), Lord or Yah(weh), "my father is Yahweh."

A. It refers to Hezron's wife who bore him Ashur, the father of Tekoa.

B. A descendant of Aaron who served in the priestly services. He also is called Abijam (1 Kgs. 14:31; 15:1, 7–8). He reigned in Judah (913–910 B.C.) and found both censure (1 Kgs. 15:3) and praise from the biblical authors (2 Chr. 13:1—14:1). He won a decisive battle against Jeroboam (2 Chr. 13:19–22).

C. The son of Becher who was the son of Benjamin (1 Chr. 7:6–8).

D. The second son of Samuel (1 Sam. 8:2) bears this name. He served as a judge at Beersheba but was corrupt (1 Sam. 8:1–3).

E. Abijah was the son of Jeroboam I, the apostate first king of Israel (1 Kgs. 14:1–18). He received a positive evaluation from the writer.

F. Abijah is the name of Rehoboam's son by Maacah, daughter (granddaughter?) of Absalom (1 Chr. 3:10; 2 Chr. 11:20—14:1). Rehoboam chose him from among his sons to be king (2 Chr. 11:22).

G. The name of a priest who affirmed and sealed the renewal covenant of Nehemiah (10:7). He returned under Zerubbabel to Jerusalem (Neh. 12:1, 4, 17).

H. The name of Hezekiah's mother. She was the daughter of Zechariah.

30. אֲבִיהוּא ***'abiyhû':*** A proper noun designating Abihu, from *'āb* (1), father, and *hû'* (1931), "he (is)", hence, meaning "he is (my) father." He was Aaron's second son (Ex. 6:23). He ate and drank in the presence of God (Ex. 24:1, 9) on Mount Sinai. He and his brother were later slain before the Lord because they offered "strange fire," "unholy, unapproved fire" (Lev. 10:1–8; cf. Num. 3:4; 26:61; 1 Chr. 24:2) at the Lord's altar.

31. אֲבִיהוּד *ʾabiyhûd:* A proper noun designating Abihud (1 Chr. 8:3).

32. אֲבִיחַיִל *ʾabiyhayil:* The Old Testament describes five individuals by the name Abihail:

A. The father of Zuriel (Num. 3:35).

B. The wife of Abishur (1 Chr. 2:29).

C. A son of Huri (1 Chr. 5:14).

D. The mother-in-law of Rehoboam (2 Chr. 11:18); and the father of Esther (Esth. 2:15; 9:29).

33. אֲבִי הָעֶזְרִי *ʾabiy hāʿezriy:* A proper noun designating Abiezrite (Judg. 6:11, 24; 8:32).

34. אֶבְיוֹן *ʾebyôn:* An adjective meaning poor, needy, signifying that a person is in want or need of material goods. In Israel the poor were often subjected to oppression and abuse by the rich or those in power (Amos 2:6; 4:1; 5:12). Job, a righteous man, cared for these people as a father (Job 29:16; 30:25). However, the poor were not to be favored because they were poor in a case of justice (Ex. 23:6) nor were they to be taken advantage of. During the sabbatical seventh year, they were permitted to eat the produce of the fallow land. The Lord watched over these persons with special care (Job 5:15; Jer. 20:13). The Lord would deliver the poor in times of need (Ps. 9:18[19]; 12:5[6]; 40:17[18]). They became—along with the widow, the orphan, and the oppressed—one of the disadvantaged groups in society for which God was especially concerned (Job 24:4, 14, 21; Jer. 5:28). The oppressed or humble are sometimes equated with the poor (Isa. 29:19).

35. אֲבִיּוֹנָה *ʾabiyyônāh:* A feminine noun meaning desire that is used to describe the failure of desire of an aging person (NKJV, Eccl. 12:5). Some think the word is better translated to indicate the caperberry which had become an ineffective stimulate in old age (NASB, Eccl. 12:5).

36. אֲבִיטוּב *ʾabiyṭûb:* A proper noun designating Abitub (1 Chr. 8:11).

37. אֲבִיטַל *ʾabiyṭal:* A proper noun designating Abital (2 Sam. 3:4; 1 Chr. 3:3).

38. אֲבִיָּם *ʾabiyyām:* A proper noun designating Abijam (1 Kgs. 14:31; 15:1, 7, 8). Abijam is another name for the successor to Rehoboam, see Abijah (24,F).

39. אֲבִימָאֵל *ʾabiymāʾēl:* A proper noun designating Abimael (Gen. 10:28; 1 Chr. 1:22).

40. אֲבִימֶלֶךְ *ʾabiymelek:* A proper noun designating Abimelech.

A. A proper noun depicting four different men in the Old Testament. The name means "my father is king." It may refer to two different kings of the Philistines in Genesis 20:1–18; 21:22–32, dealing with Abraham, and in Genesis 26:1–33, dealing with

Isaac. But some scholars feel the term may be, not a proper noun, but a cognomen of Philistine kings in general.

B. It refers to a son of Gideon born to a concubine from Shechem. He tried to establish a corrupt kingship in Israel but failed. He had slain seventy of his brothers and declared himself king. He died ignominiously as he was besieging a city called Thebez (Judg. 9). Kingship was discredited for the time being.

C. It refers to a son of Abiathar, a priest, if the Masoretic text is correct (cf. 2 Sam. 8:17; 1 Chr. 18:16).

D. In the superscription to Psalm 34, the king of Gath is given the name Abimelech. This could be, however, a general term (see A above) for a Philistine king.

41. אֲבִינָדָב ***ᵃḇiynāḏāḇ:*** A proper noun designating the name Abinadab, which was given to three Israelites.:

A. A levite (1 Sam. 7:1; 2 Sam. 6:3, 4; 1 Chr. 13:7).

B. The second son of Jesse (1 Sam. 16:8; 17:13; 1 Kgs. 4:11; 1 Chr. 2:13).

C. A son of Saul (1 Sam. 31:2; 1 Chr. 8:33; 9:39; 10:2).

42. אֲבִינֹעַם ***ᵃḇiynō'ām:*** A proper noun designating Abinoam, indicating a "father of pleasantness" (*'āḇ* [1], father; *nō'am* [5278], pleasant[ness]). He is, based on context, the father of Barak from Kedesh in Naphtali, a city west of and slightly north of the southern tip of the Sea of Galilee (Judg. 4:6, 12; 5:1, 12). Barak is listed as a faithful hero in the New Testament (Heb. 11:32).

43. אֶבְיָסָף ***'eḇyāsāp̱:*** A proper noun designating Ebiasaph (1 Chr. 6:23(8), 37(22); 9:19).

44. אֲבִיעֶזֶר ***ᵃḇiy'ezer:*** A proper noun designating Abiezer, the name of two individuals in the Old Testament:

A. A Manassite (Josh. 17:2; Judg. 6:34; 8:2; 18).

B. A Benjamite (2 Sam. 23:27; 1 Chr. 11:28; 27:12).

45. אֲבִי עַלְבוֹן ***ᵃḇiy 'alḇôn:*** A proper noun designating Abi-albon (2 Sam. 23:31).

46. אָבִיר ***'āḇiyr:*** An adjective meaning strong, mighty. It functions as a noun for God in Genesis 49:24, meaning the Mighty One (of Jacob) (NASB) or Mighty God of Jacob (NKJV) and similarly in other places (Ps. 132:2, 5; Isa. 1:24, the Mighty One of Israel; Isa. 49:26; 60:16).

47. אַבִּיר ***'abbiyr:*** An adjective meaning mighty or strong. Used frequently as a noun, the word applies to God as the Mighty One (Ps. 132:2, 5; Isa. 1:24). It also designates angels (Ps. 78:25); men (Ps. 76:5); bulls (Ps. 22:12[13]); and horses (Jer. 8:16). When used to describe a person or a person's heart, it normally refers to a strength independent of or opposed to God (Job 34:20; Ps. 76:5[6]; Isa. 46:12). It is used once to mean chief of the shepherds (1 Sam. 21:7[8]).

48. אֲבִירָם *'abiyrām:* A proper designating Abiram, the name of two Israelites. The name means "my father is exalted" (*'āb* [1], father; *rûm*, high):

A. In Numbers 16, he is one of the sons of Eliab, who, along with others, rebelled against Moses' leadership. He was from the line of Reuben.

B. In 1 Kings 16:34, he is the son of Hiel of Bethel who lost Abiram when he laid the foundations to build Jericho (1 Kgs. 16:34) in fulfillment of Joshua 6:26. He was evidently Hiel's firstborn son.

49. אֲבִישַׁג *'abiyšag:* A proper noun designating Abishag (1 Kgs. 1:3, 15; 2:17, 21, 22).

50. אֲבִישׁוּעַ *'abiyšûa':* A proper noun designating Abishua:

A. A son of Phinehas (1 Chr. 6:4(5:30), 5(5:31), 50(35); Ezra 7:5).

B. A son of Bela (1 Chr. 8:4).

51. אֲבִישׁוּר *'abiyšûr:* A proper noun designating Abishur (1 Chr. 2:28, 29).

52. אֲבִישַׁי *'abiyšay:* A proper noun designating Abishai, meaning "father of (a) gift" or perhaps "my father is Jesse" or "my father is (*yēš* [3426], exists)." He was the son of David's sister Zeruiah (1 Sam. 26:6; 2 Sam. 2:18), a brother to Joab and Asahel (1 Chr. 2:16; 11:20). He was loyal and faithful to David and a leader of his mighty men (2 Sam. 23:18), possibly the leader of the second group of three (2 Sam. 23:18). He quelled the rebellion of Sheba against David (2 Sam. 20:6). He took part in several important events (e.g., 2 Sam. 2:18; 3:30). He protected David often and slew the giant Philistine Ishbi-Benob (2 Sam. 21:15–17) when he threatened David.

53. אֲבִישָׁלוֹם *'abiysālôm*, אַבְשָׁלוֹם *'abšālôm:* A proper noun designating Absalom:

A. This son was beloved by David and the people but seemingly for the wrong superficial reasons. While he was handsome and had beautiful hair, he was also violent, passionate, headstrong, and a self-seeking man who was born in Hebron (2 Sam. 3:3). He killed Amnon for raping his half-sister Tamar (2 Sam. 13:20–38). The story of Absalom stretches over chapters 13—20 of 2 Samuel (cf. also 1 Kgs. 1:6; 2:7, 28; 1 Chr. 3:2). He was exiled from Jerusalem for three years (2 Sam. 13:37–38). Upon his return, after an indefinite period, he plotted to overthrow David, his father (2 Sam. 15—18) but was eventually defeated and judged by God. He died an ignominious death (2 Sam. 18:1–33). The third Psalm's superscription sets the psalm in the time when David fled from before Absalom. Absalom's tragic story illustrated well the curse the Lord placed on David's house because of David's affair with Bathsheba and his murder of her husband Uriah (2 Sam. 12:11–12).

B. A proper noun for David's third son by Maacah, daughter of Talmai, king of Geshur. This is another rendering of Absalom (1 Kgs. 15:2, 10). His mother is identified by referring to him as her son.

54. אֶבְיָתָר *'eḇyāṯār:* A proper noun designating Abiathar, a priest who survived Saul's slaughter of the priests at Nob (1 Sam. 22:6–23). His name means "father of excellence or abundance." He was the son of Ahimelech, son of Ahitub, priest of Nob, in the days of Saul (1 Sam. 22:20). His father, Ahimelech, gave holy bread to David and his men to eat during David's flight from Saul (1 Sam. 22:1–9). Abiathar fled to David, who protected him, and he served, along with Zadok, as David's priest (cf. 2 Sam. 15:24; 17:15; 20:25). Abiathar rescued the holy ephod from Nob and used it during David's reign (1 Sam. 23:2, 9, 10). He helped take the ark to Jerusalem (1 Chr. 15:11; 27:34). He, however, backed the wrong person, Adonijah, for king instead of Solomon after David's death (1 Kgs. 1:7, 19, 25). Under Solomon, Zadok was raised above Abiathar in the priesthood. Abiathar is mentioned by Jesus in Mark 2:25, 26 in a general sense as a representative of the priesthood.

55. אָבַךְ *'āḇak:* A verb used in a reflexive sense in Isaiah 9:18 to mean to roll upward, to rise and roll upward. In this context, it refers figuratively to the rolling, rising smoke of briars, thorns, and thickets that have been set on fire by Israel's wickedness.

56. אָבַל *'aḇal:* A verb that means to mourn in its simple verb forms. Those who mourn are persons who mourn for looking at God's coming judgments (Isa. 19:8; Amos 8:8; 9:5). But figuratively, the gates of the city of Zion mourn because of her desolation (Isa. 3:26) as does the earth itself (Isa. 24:4) when God comes in judgment (Isa. 33:9; cf. Amos 1:2). In the reflexive use of the verb, it indicates mourning for the dead (Gen. 37:34); for Jerusalem (Isa. 66:10); over a particular person (1 Sam. 15:35; 16:1); or over sin or judgment (Ex. 33:4; Neh. 8:9). It is also used to indicate that God causes mourning (Lam. 2:8; Ezek. 31:15). In both cases, the word is used in a figurative sense. In the first instance, He causes the deep to mourn over Assyria, and in the second case, He causes the wall of Jerusalem to mourn over the fall of the city which it (the wall) was to surround and protect.

57. אָבֵל *'āḇēl:* An adjective meaning mourning, sorrowing, and, as a noun, mourner(s). It describes Jacob's mourning for Joseph's supposed death (Gen. 37:35). It describes mourning for imminent calamity (Esth. 6:12). It functions as a noun in several passages (Job 29:25; Ps. 35:14; Isa. 57:18; 61:2, 3).

58. אָבֵל *'āḇēl:* A feminine noun meaning plain or meadow (Judg. 11:33). But it may be part of the name of a city (NASB, NKJV).

59. אָבֵל ***'āḇēl:*** A proper noun designating Abel, used of a city and a stone:

A. A proper noun designating a great stone named Abel, "great stone of Abel" (KJV, NIV, "the large rock"; NASB, "the large stone"; the Masoretic text reads rather "the great, large meadows") where the ark was temporarily (1 Sam. 6:18).

B. A proper noun designating a city that was known as a place where proper judgment was rendered (2 Sam. 20:18). Sheba fled there for protection but was executed instead (2 Sam. 20:22).

The word is used in several other proper compound place names as well: e.g., Abel Beth Maacah (1 Kgs. 15:20); Abel Keramim (Judg. 11:33); Abel Meholah (Judg. 7:22); Abel Mizraim (Gen. 50:11).

60. אֵבֶל ***'ēḇel:*** A masculine noun indicating mourning or a period of mourning. The word indicates mourning for the dead (Gen. 27:41) or for calamity (Esth. 4:3; 9:22; Job 30:31). In Isaiah 61:3 and 2 Samuel 14:2, it seems to indicate a garment for mourning, as well as mourning itself. A period of mourning is also depicted by the word (2 Sam. 11:27; Eccl. 7:2, 4).

61. אֲבָל ***'aḇāl:*** An adverb meaning indeed, surely, verily, and in a more adversative sense however, but. The word means indeed, surely in several passages (Gen. 42:21; 2 Sam. 14:5; 1 Kgs. 1:43; 2 Kgs. 4:14). It is more adversative in other verses (Gen. 17:19; 2 Chr. 1:4; 19:3; Ezra 10:13).

62. אָבֵל בֵּית־מַעֲכָה ***'āḇēl bēyṯ-ma'aḵāh:*** A proper noun designating Abel Beth Maacah (2 Sam. 20:14, 15).

63. אָבֵל הַשִּׁטִּים ***'āḇēl haššiṭṭiym:*** A proper noun designating Abel Shittim, the complete name of Shittim (7851,A) (Num. 33:49).

64. אָבֵל כְּרָמִים ***'āḇēl kerāmiym:*** A proper noun designating Abel Keramim (Judg. 11:33).

65. אָבֵל מְחוֹלָה ***'āḇēl meḥôlāh:*** A proper noun designating Abel Meholah (Judg. 7:22; 1 Kgs. 4:12; 19:16).

66. אָבֵל מַיִם ***'āḇēl mayim:*** A proper noun designating Abel Maim (2 Chr. 16:4).

67. אָבֵל מִצְרַיִם ***'āḇēl miṣrayim:*** A proper noun designating Abel Mizraim (Gen. 50:11).

68. אֶבֶן ***'eḇen:*** A feminine noun meaning stone. The word is used often and has both literal and figurative meanings depending upon its context. It is also used as a major source of raw material for all kinds of projects produced by various skilled craftsmen or merchants. Both precious and nonprecious stones are mentioned in Scripture.

In its natural or adapted states, stone was used as a pillow (Gen.

28:11, 18); a cover of a well (29:2, 3, 8); a weapon of opportunity (Ex. 21:18); a weapon of official executions (Lev. 20:2, 27; 24:23; Num. 14:10); sling stones (1 Sam. 17:40, 49); memorial stones (Josh. 4:3, 5–9); sacred pillars (Gen. 28:18). In Joshua 24:26, 27, they are used as witnesses by Joshua.

Various items were made of stone: the tablets of the Ten Commandments (Ex. 31:18; 34:1; Deut. 5:22 [19]); vessels (Ex. 7:19); and pavement (2 Kgs. 16:17). Washed stones are mentioned (Lev. 14:40, 42, 43, 45), and they were used in walls, tombs, and buildings (2 Kgs. 22:6; Neh. 4:2[3:34]; Isa. 14:19). Stones were especially important for use as foundation stones or cornerstones (Job 38:6; Isa. 28:16; Jer. 51:26); and capstones (Zech. 3:9; 4:7).

Many precious stones are noted in various passages (Gen. 2:12; Ex. 28:9–12, 17–21), especially those featured in the breastplate of Israel's high priest. They are also featured in the Garden of Eden as mentioned in Ezekiel 28:13–16.

The word indicates some tools or equipment used by merchants and builders such as weights (Prov. 20:10, 23; 27:3). They were described as plummets or a plumb line (Isa. 34:11) in a literal and figurative sense as well by the biblical writer.

69. אֶבֶן **'eḇen:** An Aramaic feminine noun found only in the Aramaic portions of the Old Testament of Daniel and Ezra. The stones referred to in Ezra (5:8) are heavy or huge stones used to build the second Temple. The word is used as powerful imagery in Daniel (2:34, 35, 45) to refer to the kingdom of God. In Daniel 5:4, 23, stone gods/idols are referred to. In 6:17 (18) a special stone is used to seal the lion's den.

70. אֹבֶן **'ōḇen:** A feminine dual noun used to describe a potter's wheel (Jer. 18:3) and the two stones on which a pregnant woman placed herself in order to deliver her child (Ex. 1:16). The NASB translates the literal Hebrew word "the two stones" as the birthstool while the NKJV renders it as birthstools. A less likely interpretation would render it as the (two) male testicles.

71. אֲבָנָה **ᵃḇānāh:** A proper noun designating Abana (2 Kgs. 5:12).

72. אֶבֶן הָעֵזֶר **'eḇen hā'ēzer:** A proper noun designating Ebenezer:

A. A proper noun referring to a city where Israel was ignominiously defeated by the Philistines twice (1 Sam. 4:1; 5:1). The word means "stone of (the) help." This could be where Samuel placed a stone to commemorate a later victory over the Philistines (see 1 Sam. 7:12). Its exact location is obscure, some placing it near Beth-Shemesh, other placing it about 10 to 12 miles east of Joppa.

B. A proper noun given to a stone erected by Samuel to commemorate an Israelite victory over the Philistines, meaning "stone of (the) help" (1 Sam. 7:12).

73. אַבְנֵט ***'aḇnēṭ:*** A masculine noun meaning girdle or sash. The word refers to the girdle worn by the high priest (Ex. 28:4, 39; 39:29; Lev. 8:7; 16:4) and of priests as well (Ex. 28:40; 29:9; Lev. 8:13). It refers to the Lord's placing of a sash or girdle upon His servant Eliakim, the son of Hilkiah (Isa. 22:21).

74. אֲבִינֵר ,אַבְנֵר ***'aḇnēr, 'ᵃḇiynēr:*** A proper noun designating Abner. Abner served as the captain of Saul's army and was Saul's cousin or uncle (1 Chr. 8:33; 9:39). He continued to support the house of Saul after Saul's death (2 Sam. 3:1), supporting Esh-baal, man of Baal (1 Chr. 8:33); later, Ishbosheth, man of shame (2 Sam. 2:8–17), as king at a city named Mahanaim. Abner tried to come over to David's camp but was killed by Joab, David's captain (cf. 2 Sam. 2:18—3:38). David mourned Abner's death as a great man (2 Sam. 3:6–38, esp. vv. 33, 34).

75. אָבַס ***'āḇas:*** A verb meaning to fatten. The word is a plural passive participle in 1 Kings 4:23 (5:3) and refers to fatted fowl. It is used in the same form in the singular to indicate a fatted ox or calf in Proverbs 15:17 (cf. NASB, NKJV).

76. אֲבַעְבֻּעֹת ***'ᵃḇa'bu'ōt:*** A feminine noun indicating a festering boil or skin eruption, possibly blisters. It refers specifically to the boils that broke out on people and beasts in the sixth plague (Ex. 9:9, 10).

77. אֶבֶץ ***'eḇeṣ:*** A proper noun designating the proper name of Ebez, sometimes spelled Abez (Josh. 19:20).

78. אִבְצָן ***'iḇṣān:*** A proper noun designating Ibzan (Judg. 12:8, 10).

79. אָבַק ***'āḇaq:*** A verb meaning to wrestle and found only in the story of Jacob's contest or wrestling/striving with a mysterious Man by the Jabbok River (Gen. 32:24[25], 25[26]). Jacob's name was subsequently changed to Israel.

80. אָבָק ***'āḇāq:*** A masculine noun meaning dust, especially extremely fine, powdery particles in contrast to the coarser dust or *'āp̱ār* (6083). It is used to signify the dust easily driven by the wind (Isa. 5:24) and dust raised by the hooves of galloping horses (Ezek. 26:10). As a metaphor, it signifies the notion of utter insignificance (Isa. 29:5); conditions of drought (Deut. 28:24); and clouds as the dust of God's feet (Nah. 1:3).

81. אֲבָקָה ***'ᵃḇāqāh:*** A feminine noun meaning spice or powder. It is found only in Song of Solomon 3:6. Both the NKJV and NASB render the word as powder(s). The word clearly indicates some aromatic powder(s).

82. אָבַר ***'āḇar:*** A verb meaning to fly and found only in Job 39:26. The high flight of the hawk and its southward route are understood only by the Creator. The flight of the hawk is orchestrated by the Lord as indicated by the causal aspect of the verb form.

83. אֵבֶר *'ēḇer:* A masculine noun indicating wing or pinion. It is used of the wings of a dove in Psalm 55:6(7) and of an eagle in Isaiah 40:31. The word is used figuratively to describe the wings of the king of Babylon (Nebuchadnezzar), depicted as a huge eagle (Ezek. 17:3).

84. אֶבְרָה *'eḇrāh:* A feminine noun indicating feathers or wings. It describes the wings of an ostrich (Job 39:13); of an eagle spreading its wings to carry its young (Deut. 32:11); as Yahweh carried His people (cf. Ex. 19:4). It is used metaphorically of the wings of protection which the Lord gives those who rest under them (Ps. 91:4). The wings of a dove gilded with gold and silver are descriptive of Israel's prosperity in Psalm 68:13(14).

85. אַבְרָהָם *'aḇrāhām:* The proper name Abraham, bestowed on Abram ("exalted father") after he received the promise of land (Gen. 15:17–21) and progeny from the Lord (Gen. 17:5, 9, 15, 17, 18, 22, 23, 24, 26). His father was Terah in Ur (Gen. 11:26). The Lord appeared to him several times (Gen. 12:7). He received the promises of God (Gen. 12:1–3), the covenant (Gen. 15:6; 15:13–17), and the seal of the covenant of circumcision (Gen. 17:26). He was blessed by God (Gen. 12:1–3). Through him the nations would be blessed. He was born in Ur of the Chaldees but moved at God's call to Haran in Mesopotamia (Gen. 11:26–32). He moved on to Palestine from Haran at God's call (Gen. 12:1, 4). His call and actions prefigured the Exodus event itself. He was the father of the nation of Israel both biologically and, more importantly, spiritually. His faith was especially highlighted when he was willing to sacrifice his son at the Lord's command (Gen. 22), expecting to receive him back (Gen. 22:18), if necessary.

The promise of land included the territory from the great Euphrates River to the River of Egypt, El-Arish, but this promise was not fulfilled until the time of Solomon and/or David. Abraham's promised son, Isaac, became the inheritor of the promises and covenants (Gen. 25:5), not any son from Keturah or Hagar (Gen. 25:1–18). The promises passed on to Jacob and his descendants.

The God of Abraham was the Lord, (Yahweh; Gen. 14:22), the High God, the Creator (Gen. 14:18–20), the God of Moses and Israel (Ex. 3:15; 6:3). In a religious and spiritually true sense, Israel, as well as Isaac, was the "seed of Abraham." Gentile Christians are considered the spiritual (faith) seed of Abraham in the New Testament (cf. Gal. 3:16, 29). Abraham is uniquely considered the "father" of three great religions: Judaism, Christianity, and Islam. He is referred to nearly two hundred times in the Koran.

86. אַבְרֵךְ *'aḇrēḵ:* A verb meaning to bow the knee or make way. The word occurs only in Genesis 41:43. It is possibly a verb of four letters in an imperative form meaning to bow the knee. It designates the homage to be paid toward Joseph in Egypt.

87. אַבְרָם *'abrām:* A proper noun referring to Abram, the biological and spiritual father of Israel. He was born to Terah in Ur of the Chaldees. The name means "exalted father" but was changed to Abraham, "father of a multitude" (Gen. 17:5, 9, 15, 17, 18). He is referred to as Abram in Genesis 12:1–17:5; 1 Chronicles 1:27; Nehemiah 9:7. He was seventy-five years old when God called him (Gen. 12:1–18). He was chosen by God (Neh. 9:7). See entry under Abraham (85).

88. אֹבֹת *'ōbōt:* A proper noun designating Oboth (Num. 21:10, 11; 33:43, 44).

89. אָגֵא *'āgē':* A proper noun designating Agee (2 Sam. 23:11).

90. אֲגַג *ᵃgag:* A proper noun designating Agag:

A. A proper noun referring to an Amalekite king (Num. 24:7). The reference in Numbers 24:7 may be proleptic, or it may have been a common name among the Amalekites, the sworn enemies of the Israelites from the time Israel departed Egypt (Ex. 17:8–16).

B. Perhaps a title like "Pharaoh." The name refers to a specific king in Saul's day (1 Sam. 15:8, 33), who was slain by Samuel. Haman may been a descendant of the Amalekites (Esth. 3; 4; 5; 6:7; 8; 9).

91. אֲגָגִי *ᵃgāgiy:* A proper noun designating Agagite (Esth. 3:1, 10; 8:3, 5; 9:24).

92. אֲגֻדָּה *ᵃguddāh:* A feminine noun designating a bunch, a group, or a bundle. It refers to a bunch of hyssop (Ex. 12:22) but also to a group or band of men (2 Sam. 2:25). In its figurative or metaphorical usage, it refers to wickedness as bands or bonds (Isa. 58:6). In Amos 9:6, it refers to the structures or strata fitted together like a vault, layers, or strata (NASB, NKJV).

93. אֱגוֹז *ᵉgôz:* A masculine noun meaning nuts or nut trees. It is found only in Song of Solomon 6:11 in parallel with other beautiful features of nature.

94. אָגוּר *'āgûr:* A proper noun designating a masculine noun that means nuts or nut trees (Song 6:11).

95. אֲגוֹרָה *ᵃgôrāh:* A feminine noun indicating a piece or payment. It refers to a piece or payment of silver in 1 Samuel 2:36.

96. אֵגֶל *'egel:* A masculine noun meaning a drop. In Job 38:28 it refers to drops of dew.

97. אֶגְלַיִם *'eglayim:* A proper noun designating Eglaim (Isa. 15:8).

98. אֲגַם *ᵃgam:* A masculine noun indicating a pool or pond. It refers to swampy or muddy water (Isa. 14:23) or to any type of pond or pool of water (Ex. 7:19; 8:5[1]; Ps. 107:35; Isa. 41:18). The pools in Exodus are an object of the plagues of blood and frogs. In Jeremiah 51:32, the abstract ending is added to the word, and it refers to a marsh or swamp.

99. אָגֵם *'āgēm:* I. An adjective meaning sick or stagnant. It refers to hired laborers of Egypt in Isaiah 19:10 (KJV). But see II also.

II. A masculine noun meaning grieved, troubled, or sick (NASB, NIV, NKJV, see I., cf. KJV). It refers to laborers or wage earners in Isaiah 19:10.

100. אַגְמוֹן *'agmôn:* A masculine noun referring to a rope, reed, or cord of reeds (Job 41:2[40:26], 20[12]; Isa. 58:5). It is also translated as bulrush (NASB, Isa. 9:14[13]; 19:15). In Isaiah 58:5, it is used figuratively to picture a humble person bowing his or her head as a reed.

101. אַגָּן *'aggān:* A masculine noun designating a bowl, basin, or goblet. It refers to a large, deep bowl (Ex. 24:6; Isa. 22:24). It is used in a simile in Song of Solomon 7:2 (3).

102. אֲגַף *'ᵃgap̱:* A masculine noun meaning troops or bands of soldiers. It refers to troops of Israel whom the Lord will scatter (Ezek. 12:14; 17:21) and to the multitude of troops gathered around Gog whom the Lord will destroy in a great eschatological battle (Ezek. 38:6, 9, 22; 39:4).

103. אָגַר *'āgar:* A verb meaning to gather in crops (Deut. 28:39). In Proverbs, it is used to describe the ant who gathers in its harvest (6:8) and the wise son who gathers in the crops during the summer (10:5).

104. אִגְּרָא *'iggᵉrā':* The Aramaic feminine word refers to a letter or correspondence. In Ezra it describes a letter sent to King Artaxerxes (4:8, 11) and one sent to Darius (5:6). These were high-level letters of correspondence.

105. אֲגַרְטָל *'ᵃgarṭāl:* A masculine noun meaning bowl, basin, or dish. It refers to the thirty gold basins (NKJV) or dishes (NASB) returned to the temple in Jerusalem during the time of Ezra (1:9, 10).

106. אֶגְרֹף *'egrōp̱:* A masculine noun indicating a fist. The fist is used as a weapon (Ex. 21:18) and as a symbol of violence (Isa. 58:4).

107. אִגֶּרֶת *'iggereṯ:* A feminine noun indicating a letter or written correspondence of some kind. There are letters of invitation delivered by couriers of the king (2 Chr. 30:1, 6) and letters granting royal authority to Nehemiah (Neh. 2:7–9). The Feast of Purim is officially established in Esther 9:26, 29 by letters.

108. אֵד *'ēḏ:* A masculine noun meaning some kind of mist. In the beginning, it watered the ground before it had rained (Gen. 2:6). In Job 36:27, it refers to the mist of the clouds from which rain distilled and fell to earth.

109. אָדַב *'āḏaḇ:* A verb meaning to grieve or cause grief. It refers to the grief that Eli would experience at the death of his descendants (1 Sam. 2:33).

110. אַדְבְּאֵל *'aḏbᵉ'ēl:* A proper noun designating Abdeel (Gen. 25:13; 1 Chr. 1:29).

111. אֲדַד *'ᵃḏaḏ:* A proper noun designating Hadad (1 Kgs. 11:17), a variant form of the Hebrew name Hadad (1908,B).

112. אִדּוֹ *'iddô:* A proper noun designating Iddo (Ezra 8:17).

113. אָדוֹן *'āḏôn:* A masculine noun meaning lord or master. The most frequent usage is of a human lord, but it is also used of divinity. Generally, it carries the nuances of authority rather than ownership. When used of humans, it refers to authority over slaves (Gen. 24:9; Judg. 19:11); people (1 Kgs. 22:17); a wife (Gen. 18:12; Amos 4:1); or a household (Gen. 45:8; Ps. 105:21). When used of divinity, it frequently occurs with *yᵉhōwāh* (3068), signifying His sovereignty (Ex. 34:23; Josh. 3:13; Isa. 1:24). See the Hebrew noun *'ᵃḏōnāy* (136).

114. אַדּוֹן *'addôn:* A proper noun designating Addon (Neh. 7:61).

115. אֲדוֹרַיִם *'ᵃḏôrayim:* A proper noun designating Adoraim (2 Chr. 11:9).

116. אֱדַיִן *'ᵉḏayin:* An Aramaic adverb found in the Aramaic portions of Ezra and Daniel. It is rendered quite uniformly as then, thereupon in most translations (Ezra 4:9, 23, 24; 5:2, 4; Dan. 2:14, 15; 3:3, 13; 4:7[4], 19[16]; 5:3, 6; 6:3–6[4–7]; 7:1, 11, 19).

117. אַדִּיר *'addiyr:* An adjective meaning excellent, majestic, lofty, or great. When describing physical objects, it often denotes strength of the waters of the sea (Ex. 15:10; Ps. 93:4); the precious value of a bowl (Judg. 5:25); or both the strength and beauty of trees (Ezek. 17:23; Zech. 11:2). When describing humans, it refers to those who lead, either as rulers or royalty (Jer. 14:3; 25:34–36; 30:21; Nah. 3:18). When describing God, this word describes His majestic power (1 Sam. 4:8; Ps. 8:1[2], 9[10]; Isa. 10:34) that is greater than the breakers of the sea (Ps. 93:4).

118. אֲדַלְיָא *'Aḏalyā':* A proper noun designating Adalia (Esth. 9:8).

119. אָדַם *'āḏam:* A verb meaning to be red, ruddy, dyed red. It is used to describe people: Esau (Gen. 25:25); David (1 Sam. 16:12; 17:42); and princes (Lam. 4:7). As for things, it describes ram skins that were dyed red (Ex. 25:5; 26:14; 35:7) and red wine (Prov. 23:31). Metaphorically, this word describes sin as "red like crimson" (Isa. 1:18).

120. אָדָם *'āḏām:* A masculine noun meaning a male, any human being, or generically the human race.

The word is used to signify a man, as opposed to a woman (Gen. 2:18; Eccl. 7:28); a human (Num. 23:19; Prov. 17:18; Isa. 17:7); the human race in general (Gen. 1:27; Num. 8:17; Ps. 144:3; Isa. 2:17); and the representative embodiment of humanity, as the appellation "son of man" indicates (Ezek. 2:1, 3). The first man used this word as a proper noun, "Adam" (Gen. 2:20).

121. אָדָם *'āḏām:* The proper noun designating Adam:

A. A proper noun or name used of the first human in some cases. It also occurs as a common noun meaning humanity, humankind, etc., depending on its content. Here the discussion centers on its use as a proper noun or name for the first man or humankind.

The word is used in 1 Chronicles 1:1 to refer to the first person and gives him the name Adam, since it stands at the head of a list of proper names. In Genesis 1—5, it is used as a proper name or noun depending on the context. In Genesis 4:25; 5:3–5, the word *'āḏām* refers to a specific person and is a proper name. It seems best to render the Hebrew as "man," a proper noun, in Genesis 5:1, since it echoes Genesis 1:26–28. In all earlier references, it is best rendered as "the man," since it bears the Hebrew article (except for 1:26; 2:5; 2:20). The NIV renders the proper name "Adam" in Genesis 2:20 for the first time (2:20; 3:17, 20, 21; 4:1, 25; 5:3–5). The translations do not agree in detail as to when to render the noun as a proper name or a proper noun ("the man") (NASB, proper name [Gen. 2:20; 3:17, 21; 4:25; 5:1, 3, 4, 5]).

The root or etymology of the word is uncertain, but the biblical author is clearly making a wordplay about Adam's being taken from the ground (cf. *'āḏām* [121]) to *'ᵃḏāmāh* [127]; see Gen. 2:7; 3:19).

B. A proper noun referring to a small town along the east side of the Jordan River. It is the location of a mighty act of God when He stopped the flow of the Jordan so Israel could cross it in flood time (Josh. 3:16).

122. אָדֹם *'āḏōm:* A masculine adjective meaning red, ruddy, the color of blood (red to reddish brown). The meaning of the word is best demonstrated in 2 Kings 3:22, where the Moabites saw the sunrise reflecting off the water which the Lord had miraculously provided. The Moabites thought the water was "as red as blood." This word is also used to describe the color of lentil stew (Gen. 25:30); the health or attractiveness of a man (Song 5:10); the color of garments (Isa. 63:2); the color of animals, like a red heifer (Num. 19:2) or chestnut or bay–colored horses (Zech. 1:8; 6:2).

123. אֱדוֹם *'ᵉḏôm,* אֱדֹם *'ᵉḏōm:* A proper noun designating Edom:

A. A proper noun used as another name for Esau (Gen. 25:30; 36:1, 8, 19, 43). Edom was the firstborn or oldest son of Isaac and Rebekah but lost his birthright when he sold it to Jacob for a pot of "red stuff" (NASB) or "red stew" (Gen. 25:30, NIV). His name came from a root meaning "red" or "ruddy" (Gen. 25:24, 30). He was the twin brother of Jacob, son of Isaac.

B. The name also describes the country or people of Edom, Esau's descendants. His descendants lived in Edom (the land) even in Jacob's day (Gen. 32:3[4]; 36:6–43). They had kings before Israel had any kings (Gen. 36:31–39). The nation existed at the time of the Exodus. They refused to let Israel pass through their land (Num. 20:14–21) even though they were physically related to Israel. Obadiah prophesied against Edom for not helping Israel and for fostering Babylon's destruction of Jerusalem and Judah (Obad. 1:1; Ps. 137:7). David controlled the land in his reign (2 Sam. 8:13–14), but there was tribal warfare against Edom often (1 Kgs. 11:14–16). Sometimes Israel and Edom fought as allies (2 Kgs. 3:4–27). Sela, capital city of Edom, ensconced high in the rocky crags of Edom, was captured in the time of Amaziah of Judah (2 Kgs. 14:7; 2 Chr. 25:11–12). Edom's gods were largely gods or goddesses of fertility. The language of Edom was similar to Hebrew and Moabite. The area of Edom, on the southeast corner of the Dead Sea, featured a reddish sandstone.

124. אֹדֶם ***ʼō<u>d</u>em:*** A feminine noun meaning ruby or sardius. These semiprecious stones are mentioned in Exodus (28:17; 39:10) and Ezekiel (28:13). In Exodus they are mounted on the breastpiece of the high priest, and in Ezekiel they are part of the covering of the mythical satanic being used to represent the king of Tyre.

125. אֲדַמְדָּם ***ʼa<u>d</u>amdām:*** An adjective meaning reddish. This word is used only six times in the Old Testament. It signifies the reddish appearance of leprosy on the skin (Lev. 13:19, 24, 42, 43); the mark of leprosy on a garment (Lev. 13:49); or the mark of leprosy within a house (Lev. 14:37). It is related to the verb *ʼā<u>d</u>am* (119), meaning to be red, and the adjective *ʼā<u>d</u>ōm*, meaning red (122).

126. אַדְמָה ***ʼa<u>d</u>māh:*** A proper noun designating Admah (Gen. 10:19; 14:2, 8; Deut. 29:23[22]; Hos. 11:8).

127. אֲדָמָה ***ʼa<u>d</u>āmāh:*** A feminine noun meaning dirt, ground, earth, clay. In the narrow sense of the word, it signifies the earth or clay God used to form man (Gen. 2:7); dirt put on the head during mourning (2 Sam. 1:2; Neh. 9:1); the ground itself (Ex. 3:5); cultivated land (Gen. 4:2; Zech. 13:5). In a broader sense, it means the inhabited earth (Isa. 24:21; Amos 3:2). The first man, Adam, both came from the ground and was assigned the task of tending the ground (see Gen. 2:7, 15).

128. אֲדָמָה ***ʼa<u>d</u>āmāh:*** A proper noun designating Adamah (Josh. 19:36).

129. אֲדָמִי *ªdāmiy:* A proper noun designating Adami (Josh. 19:33).

130. אֱדֹמִי *ᵉdōmiy:* A proper noun designating Edomite (Deut. 23:7(8); 1 Sam. 21:7(8); 22:9, 18, 22; 1 Kgs. 11:1, 14, 17; 2 Kgs. 16:6; 2 Chr. 25:14; 28:17; Ps. 52:title[2]).

131. אֲדֻמִּים *ªdummiym:* A proper noun designating Adummim (Josh. 15:7; 18:17).

132. אַדְמֹנִי, אַדְמוֹנִי *'admōniy, 'admôniy:* An adjective meaning red, ruddy. Esau is the prime example of someone who was red (Gen. 25:25). The Edomites, or "red ones," descended from Esau. David is the other notable figure whose complexion was characterized as good-looking, bright-eyed, and ruddy (1 Sam. 16:12).

133. אַדְמָתָא *'admātā':* A proper noun designating Admatha (Esth. 1:14).

134. אֶדֶן *'eden:* A masculine noun indicating a base, pedestal, or socket. It was a term used of the construction of various parts of the Tabernacle in Exodus; for example, these sockets served as holders and as a foundation for the hollow boards used to construct the Tabernacle (Ex. 26:19, 21, 25; 35:11; Num. 3:36, 37). It describes the bases of the earth (Job 38:6). And it describes the legs of the lover, set like pillars upon pedestals of gold, in Song of Solomon 5:15.

135. אַדָּן *'addān:* A proper noun designating Addan (Ezra 2:59).

136. אֲדֹנָי *ªdōnāy:* A masculine noun used exclusively of God. An emphatic form of the word *'ādôn* (113), this word means literally "my Lord" (Gen. 18:3). It is often used in place of the divine name *YHWH* (3068), which was held by later Jewish belief to be too holy to utter. This designation points to the supreme authority or power of God (Ps. 2:4; Isa. 6:1). The word was often combined with the divine name to reinforce the notion of God's matchlessness (e.g., Ezek. 20:3; Amos 7:6).

137. אֲדֹנִי בֶזֶק *ªdōniy bezeq:* A proper noun identifying Adoni-Bezek, a Canaanite king. The name means "Lord of Bezek." He was an unjust king towards his conquered people and in the end received "poetic justice" for these misdeeds (Judg. 1:4–7). He was defeated by Simeonites and Judahites (Judg. 1:4) at Bezek. He was mutilated and brought to Jerusalem where he expired. Bezek was located northeast of Shechem (cf. 1 Sam. 11:8).

138. אֲדֹנִיָּה, אֲדֹנִיָּהוּ *ªdōniyyah, ªdōniyyāhû:* A proper noun designating Adonijah:

A. The proper name of David's fourth son by Haggith. His name means "my Lord is Yahweh." He tried unsuccessfully to take the throne upon David's imminent death (1 Kgs. 1:1–53; 2:13–25). Solomon offered to spare Adonijah if he showed loyalty to him, but Adonijah tried to get the inside track on Solomon again and was executed (1 Kgs. 2:13–25).

B. A proper name of a Levite appointed by Jehoshaphat to teach the Book of the Law in all the towns of Judah (2 Chr. 17:7–9).

C. The name also refers to one of the Israelites, a leader in Israel, who sealed Nehemiah's covenant to follow the Law of God (Neh. 10:16–29).

139. אֲדֹנִי צֶדֶק ***ʼadōniy ṣedeq:*** A proper noun designating Adoni-Zedek (Josh. 10:1, 3).

140. אֲדֹנִיקָם ***ʼadōniyqām:*** A proper noun designating Adonikam (Ezra 2:13; 8:13; Neh. 7:18).

141. אֲדֹנִירָם ***ʼadōniyrām:*** A proper noun designating Adoniram (1 Kgs. 4:6; 5:14[28]).

142. אָדַר ***ʼādar:*** A verb meaning to magnify, glorify, or, in the passive sense, to be magnified. Whereas the Hebrew noun *kāḇôḏ* (3519) pictures glory in terms of weight, this word pictures it in terms of size. The Hebrew word is used only three times in the Old Testament: to celebrate God's power and holiness after the deliverance of Israel from Egypt (Ex. 15:6, 11); and to describe the Law given on Sinai as great and glorious (Isa. 42:21).

143. אֲדָר ***ʼadār:*** A proper noun designating Adar, the twelfth month in the Hebrew calendar. It is used in the Book of Esther only and corresponds to February–March. A second Adar month (an intercalary month) was added as necessary to make the seasons of the years uniform. It is the same as entry 144.

144. אֲדָר ***ʼadār:*** The Babylonian proper name Adar used in Ezra 6:15 for the twelfth month in Israel's calendar. It is the same as entry 143.

145. אֶדֶר ***ʼeder:*** A masculine noun that means handsome, great, glorious; a rich robe. In Micah 2:8, the word refers to a rich robe or a splendid garment, while in Zechariah 11:13, it evidently means something like magnificent price (NASB), princely price (NKJV), or handsome price (NIV).

146. אַדָּר ***ʼaddār:*** A proper noun designating Addar:

A. The name of a grandson of Benjamin (1 Chr. 8:3).

B. A city in Judah (Josh. 15:3).

147. אִדַּר ***ʼiddar:*** An Aramaic feminine noun meaning threshing floor. In Daniel 2:35 (NASB, NKJV, NIV), it refers to summer threshing floors.

148. אֲדַרְגָּזֵר ***ʼadargāzēr:*** An Aramaic masculine noun meaning counselor. It is found only in the book of Daniel. When Nebuchadnezzar erected his statue for all to bow down to, he sent a decree to all the important people (i.e., satraps, administrators, counselors) to come for the dedication ceremony (Dan. 3:2, 3).

149. אַדְרַזְדָּא ***'adrazdā':*** An Aramaic adverb meaning diligently, zealously. It is used in Ezra (7:23) to indicate the zeal and diligence exercised in the construction of the new temple.

150. אֲדַרְכֹּן ***'adarkōn:*** A noun meaning monetary value and weight. This word is used only in 1 Chronicles 29:7, where David collected money for the first temple, and in Ezra 8:27, where it tells the weight of gold basins for use in the second temple. The word may refer to the Greek *drachma*, which weighed 4.3 grams, or to the Persian *daric*, which weighed about twice as much.

151. אֲדֹרָם ***'adōrām:*** A proper noun designating Adoram (2 Sam. 20:24; 1 Kgs. 12:18).

152. אַדְרַמֶּלֶךְ ***'adrammelek:*** A proper noun designating Adrammelech.:

A. An idol (2 Kgs. 17:31).

B. A son of Sennacherib (2 Kgs. 19:37; Isa. 37:38).

153. אֶדְרָע ***'edrā':*** An Aramaic noun meaning strength, force, literally, arm. It indicates the threatening way in which the Jews were forced to stop building the new house of God (Ezra 4:23) in the time of Ezra.

154. אֶדְרֶעִי ***'edre'iy:*** A proper noun designating Edrei (Num. 21:33; Deut. 1:4; 3:1, 10; Josh. 12:4; 13:12, 31; 19:37).

155. אַדֶּרֶת ***'adderet:*** A feminine noun indicating a cloak, splendor, robe, or glory. It indicates a fur garment (hairy garment, NKJV, NASB) in Genesis 25:25 to describe Esau's appearance at birth and a prophet's hairy garment (Zech. 13:4). It refers to a beautiful robe (Josh. 7:21, 24) or mantle or an ordinary mantle or robe (1 Kgs. 19:13, 19). It depicts a splendid vine (Ezek. 17:8) or kingly robe (Jon. 3:6). In Zechariah 11:3, it is used figuratively to refer to the glory or wealth of the shepherds' flocks or pasturelands (NASB, cf. NIV).

156. אָדוֹשׁ ***'ādôš:*** A verb meaning to thresh and possibly the infinitive of *duš* (1758). It is translated as to thresh (NASB) in Isaiah 28:28, referring to the threshing of grain for bread.

157. אָהַב ***'āhab:*** A verb meaning to love. The semantic range of the verb includes loving or liking objects and things such as bribes (Isa. 1:23); wisdom (Prov. 4:6); wine (Prov. 21:17); peace, truth (Zech. 8:19); or tasty food (Gen. 27:4, 9, 14). The word also conveys love for other people (Gen. 29:32; Ruth 4:15; 1 Kgs. 11:1); love for God (Ex. 20:6; Ps. 116:1); and also God's love of people (Deut. 4:37; 1 Kgs. 10:9; Hos. 3:1).

158. אַהַב ***'ahab:*** A masculine noun meaning love or lover. Both occurrences of this noun are in the plural. In Proverbs 5:19, it refers to marital love, while in Hosea 8:9, the word refers to Israel's trust in foreign alliances rather than in God. The foreign nations are Israel's hired lovers.

159. אֹהַב **'ōhaḇ:** A masculine noun meaning loved one. It occurs twice in the Hebrew Bible, both times in the plural (Prov. 7:18; Hos. 9:10). Both occurrences are associated with illicit sexual relations.

160. אַהֲבָה **'ahᵃḇāh:** A feminine noun meaning love. The word often signifies a powerful, intimate love between a man and a woman (Gen. 29:20; Song 2:4, 5, 7); love between friends (2 Sam. 1:26); God's love for His people (Isa. 63:9; Hos. 3:1). Frequently, it is associated with forming a covenant, which enjoins loyalty (Deut. 7:8). When used in an abstract way, the word designates a desirable personal quality, which connotes affection and faithfulness (Prov. 15:17; 17:9).

161. אֹהַד **'ōhaḏ:** A proper noun designating A proper noun designating Ohad (Gen. 46:10; Ex. 6:15).

162. אֲהָהּ **'ᵃhāh:** This is an interjection usually rendered ah! oh! or alas! indicating great emotion. It usually indicates despair (Josh. 7:7; Judg. 11:35; Ezek. 11:13) but also a strong sense of marvel with fear (Judg. 6:22). It can indicate a feeling of inability (Jer. 1:6) or confusion (Jer. 4:10; Ezek. 4:14). It may introduce an announcement of the day of the Lord (Joel 1:15).

163. אֲהֲוָא **'ahᵃwā':** A proper noun designating Ahava (Ezra 8:15, 21, 31).

164. אֵהוּד **'ēhûḏ:** A proper noun designating Ehud:

A. A proper noun referring to Israel's second "judge" or deliverer listed in the Book of Judges (3:13–30; 1 Chr. 8:6). He freed Israel from the oppression of the Moabites for eighty years. He was a left-handed man, a fact that helped him carry out the assassination of Eglon, king of Moab.

B. A proper noun identifying this Ehud as a descendant of Benjamin and the son of Bilhan (1 Chr. 7:10).

165. אֱהִי **'ehiy:** I. This is a verb meaning, I will be, in the first person singular from *hāyah*, to be (KJV, NKJV, Hos. 13:10; see II). It is translated as, I will be. However, some authorities consider this an interrogative pronoun.

II. This form is treated as an interrogative pronoun by some (NIV, NASB Hos. 13:10; see I) meaning where? (also 13:14, KJV; see I).

166. אָהַל **'āhal:** This is a verb used one time in the Old Testament meaning to be bright, to shine. In Job 25:5, it clearly means to be bright (NASB, brightness; NIV, is bright; NKJV, does shine).

167. אָהַל **'āhal:** This verb means to pitch a tent. It describes Lot pitching his tent in Sodom while Abraham placed his tent by the oaks of Mamre in Hebron (Gen. 13:12, 18). God's judgment on Babylon would keep the

Arab from pitching his tent there again (Isa. 13:20).

168. אֹהֶל *'ōhel:* A masculine noun meaning tent. It is used literally as a habitation of nomadic peoples and patriarchs (Gen. 9:21; 25:27). It can be used figuratively for a dwelling (Ps. 91:10; 132:3); or a people group (Gen. 9:27; Jer. 35:7; 49:29). As a generic collective, it describes cattle (Gen. 4:20) or wickedness (Job 15:34; Ps. 84:10[11]). The word is also employed in reference to the Tabernacle, the "tent" (Num. 12:5, 10; Ezek. 41:1).

169. אֹהֶל *'ōhel:* A proper noun designating Ohel (1 Chr. 3:20).

170. אָהֳלָה *'oh^olah:* A proper noun designating Oholah (Ezek. 23:4, 5, 36, 44).

171. אָהֳלִיאָב *'oh^oliyāḇ:* A proper noun designating Oholiab (Ex. 31:6; 35:34; 36:1, 2; 38:23).

172. אָהֳלִיבָה *'oh^oliyḇāh:* A proper noun designating Oholibah (Ezek. 23:4, 11, 22, 36, 44).

173. אָהֳלִיבָמָה *'oh^oliyḇāmāh:* A proper noun designating Oholibamah:

A. The name of the wife of Esau (Gen. 36:2, 5, 14, 18, 25).

B. An Edomite chief (Gen. 36:41; 1 Chr. 1:52).

174. אֲהָל *'ahāl:* A masculine noun appearing only in the plural, designating aloes, an aromatic wood. These aloes were a feature of Jacob and Israel's land of inheritance, according to a prophecy by Balaam (Num. 24:6). Aloes were used to scent garments (Ps. 45:8[9]) and by harlots to scent their beds along with myrrh and cinnamon. It is used metaphorically in Song of Solomon 4:14.

175. אַהֲרֹן *'ah^arôn:* A proper noun designating Aaron, Moses' oldest brother and the first high priest in Israel. He was the third descendant of Levi (Ex. 6:16–20; 1 Chr. 6:1–3). He was three years older than Moses (Ex. 7:7). He played important roles in Israel: God used him to welcome and receive Moses back to Egypt (Ex. 4:27), and he served as Moses' spokesman at times (Ex. 4:16; 7:1). He performed, at Moses' bidding, several of the plagues (Ex. 7:9, 10); he was permitted to ascend Sinai and eat and drink in the presence of the Lord (Ex. 24:1–10); he was in charge of the people while Moses was on Sinai, but unfortunately, he succumbed to the desires and threats of the people, fashioned a golden calf, and proclaimed an illegal feast to Yahweh, the Lord (Ex. 32). Moses was strongly rebuked by him (Ex. 32:21–24). God, nevertheless, chose him as Israel's first high priest, an office passed on by divine order to his sons (Ex. 28). He became involved in murmuring against Moses as sole leader of the people for which he was rebuked (Num. 12). He was divinely approved as Israel's high priest (Num. 16—17) when his rod budded and bore fruit while the other rods did not. This is noted in the New

Testament (Heb. 9:4). He and Moses failed to trust God at a key juncture (Meribah) in Israel's wilderness wanderings and were forbidden to enter the Promised Land (Num. 20:12). His death is emphasized to honor him (Num. 20; 33:38, 39; Deut. 10:6). He was buried on Mount Hor. He had four sons through Elisheba, his wife, named Nadab, Abihu, Eleazar and Ithamar (Ex. 6:23). The first two were killed because they offered illegal fire before the Lord's altar (Lev. 10:1–3). Eleazar succeeded Aaron (Num. 20:28; Deut. 10:6). The phrases "sons of Aaron/descendants of Aaron" are found regularly in the Old Testament (e.g., Josh. 21:4, 10; 1 Chr. 6:54).

176. אַו *'aw*, אוֹ *'ô*: I. A noun possibly meaning desire or craving (Prov. 31:4; NASB, NIV). It is also found translated as a negative meaning nor (using the reading *'ey* in KJV, NKJV).

II. A particle conjunction of choice usually meaning or, but also rather, except in some contexts but still in essence meaning or. It can be translated as either when used in conjunction with another *'ô* (Gen. 44:19) or whether (Lev. 5:1; cf. also Gen. 24:55; Ex. 21:31, or if; 1 Sam. 20:10; Isa. 27:5).

177. אוּאֵל *'ûēl*: A proper noun designating Uel (Ezra 10:34).

178. אוֹב *'ôḇ*: A masculine noun meaning a conjured spirit, a medium or necromancer; or a leather bottle. The primary use of the word is connected to the occult practice of necromancy or consulting the dead. It is used to signify a conjurer who professes to call up the dead by means of magic, especially to give revelation about future uncertainties (1 Sam. 28:7; Isa. 8:19); a man or woman who has a familiar spirit (Lev. 20:27; 1 Chr. 10:13; Isa. 29:4); the conjured spirit itself, particularly when speaking through the medium (1 Sam. 28:8; 2 Kgs 21:6; 2 Chr. 33:6). The Israelites were strictly forbidden from engaging in such practices or consulting mediums (Lev. 19:31; Deut. 18:10–12). Interestingly, the word is used once to signify a leather bottle that may burst under pressure (Job 32:19). There is no convincing evidence that this particular reference has any occult connotations. Rather, the connection between the two divergent meanings of this Hebrew word is probably that a medium was seen as a "container" for a conjured spirit.

179. אוֹבִיל *'ôḇiyl*: A proper noun designating Obil (1 Chr. 27:30).

180. אוּבָל *'ûḇāl*, אֻבָל *'uḇāl*: A masculine noun meaning river, canal, waterway. In Daniel 8:2, 3, 6, the word refers to a canal in one of the capital cities of Persia, Susa.

181. אוּד *'ûḏ*: A masculine noun meaning a firebrand or piece of firewood. The word is used metaphorically to refer to Rezin and Remaliah, two powerless, ineffective kings in Syria and Israel, respectively (Isa. 7:4).

In Amos it refers to Israel as a barely burning but faintly alive people whom God rescued (4:11; cf. Zech. 3:2).

182. אוֹדוֹת *'ôḏôṯ*, אֹדוֹת *'ōḏôṯ*: A feminine noun used only in the plural, meaning (be)cause, reason, on account of, concerning; hence, it functions often as a preposition or conjunctive adverb. It means (be)cause in Genesis 21:11, 25; Numbers 12:1 and on account of in Genesis 26:32 and Exodus 18:8. Its meaning as cause or reason is seen emphatically in Jeremiah 3:8.

183. אָוָה *'āwāh*: A verb meaning to desire, to be inclined. This word is used to signify coveting, as in the tenth commandment (Deut. 5:21[18]; but *ḥāmaḏ* [2530] is used in Exodus 20:17). The word may also signify acceptable desires for objects such as food or beauty (Ps. 45:11[12]; Mic. 7:1); as well as for righteousness and God (Isa. 26:9; Mic. 7:1). Both God and humans can be the subject of this word (Ps. 132:13, 14).

184. אָוָה *'āwāh*: A verb meaning to draw or mark out. In Numbers 34:10, the word is used reflexively to indicate drawing out a line (for yourselves) to indicate the eastern border of the land of Israel's inheritance.

185. אַוָּה *'awwāh*: A feminine noun meaning lust, desire, lust after. It refers to hunger for meat (Deut. 12:15, 20, 21), but it also indicates the desire of one's soul in general for something (1 Sam. 23:20). It refers to the mating desire of animals as well (Jer. 2:24), but in Jeremiah it is a symbol of Israel's lustful, uncontrolled behavior. It even refers to God's will or desire (Hos. 10:10).

186. אוּזַי *'ûzay*: A proper noun designating Uzai (Neh. 3:25).

187. אוּזָל *'ûzāl*: A proper noun designating Uzal (Gen. 10:27; 1 Chr. 1:21).

188. אוֹי *'ôy*: An interjection meaning woe! alas! In general its meaning is woe (Num. 21:29). This woe can be directed to oneself (Jer. 4:13; 10:19). It functions as a noun in Proverbs 23:29 indicating woe!

189. אֱוִי *'ewiy*: A proper noun designating Evi (Num. 31:8; Josh 13:21).

190. אוֹיָה *'ôyāh*: An interjection that is the poetic form of *'ôy* (188), meaning woe! alas! It is found in Psalm 120:5, depicting the distress of one who has lived too long among a violent people.

191. אֱוִיל *'ewiyl*: An adjective meaning foolish in the sense of one who hates wisdom and walks in folly, despising wisdom and morality. The adjective is used in Jeremiah 4:22, depicting God's people as a whole, while in Hosea 9:7 God's foolish people call the prophet a fool. The word depicts a simpleton, fool thirteen times in Proverbs (e.g. 1:7; 7:22; 24:7; 29:9). The wise advisors of Pharaoh in

Zoan are ironically called fools (Isa. 19:11).

192. אֱוִיל מְרֹדַךְ ***ᵉwiyl mᵉrōḏaḵ:*** A proper noun designating Evil-Merodach (2 Kgs. 25:27; Jer. 52:31).

193. אוּל ***'ûl:*** I. A masculine noun meaning belly, body, or strength in Psalm 73:4. It is a begrudging assertion of the health and wealth of the arrogant persons the psalmist encounters.

II. A masculine noun indicating a mighty person, leader, or noble in 2 Kings 24:15 (KJV; NIV; NASB; NKJV).

194. אוּלַי, אֻלַי ***'ûlay,*** ***'ulay:*** An adverb or adverbial conjunction meaning peradventure, perhaps, and asserting a note of contingency into a sentence that may express fear, hope, entreaty, or wish (Gen. 16:2; Ex. 32:30; Num. 22:6; 1 Sam. 6:5; Job 1:5; Jer. 20:10). It may be rendered as suppose, what if, in the structure of an expression (cf. KJV, NASB, NIV, NKJV, Gen. 18:24).

195. אוּלַי ***'ûlay:*** A proper noun designating Ulai (Dan. 8:2, 16).

196. אֱוִלִי ***ᵉwiliy:*** An adverb meaning foolish. It describes a foolish shepherd (Zech. 11:15) who does not care for the sheep but rather destroys them.

197. אוּלָם ***'ûlām:*** A masculine noun meaning porch, portico. The most famous porch was located in front of the nave of Solomon's Temple, measuring 20 x 10 cubits (30 feet x 15 feet) (1 Kgs. 6:3; 1 Chr. 28:11; 2 Chr. 3:4; Joel 2:17). Ezekiel's visionary temple had a porch in the gates (Ezek. 40:7–9, 15, 39, 40) and elsewhere (Ezek. 41:15, 25).

198. אוּלָם ***'ûlām:*** A proper noun designating Ulam:

A. The name of a son of Sheresh (1 Chr. 7:16, 17).

B. A son of Eshek (1 Chr. 8:39, 40).

199. אוּלָם ***'ûlām:*** A conjunctive adverb meaning but, however. It is rendered quite uniformly as a strong adversative (Gen. 28:19; Ex. 9:16; Num. 14:21; Job 1:11; Mic. 3:8).

200. אִוֶּלֶת ***'iwweleṯ:*** A feminine noun indicating folly or foolishness. Folly is destructive to the psalmist (Ps. 38:5[6]), and only God can discern our follies (Ps. 69:5[6]). It is used twenty-two times in Proverbs chapters 5—27; (e.g., 5:23; 12:23; 27:22).

201. אוֹמָר ***'ômār:*** A proper noun designating Omar (Gen. 36:11,15; 1 Chr. 1:36).

202. אוֹן ***'ôn:*** A masculine noun meaning strength, manhood, generative power. Reuben was the firstfruit of Jacob's generative power and strength (Gen. 49:3) as is any firstborn (Deut. 21:17). It refers to the fleeting strength of the wicked (Job 18:12); physical strength (Hos. 12:3[4]); and riches as strength (Hos. 12:8[9]).

203. אֹון *'ôn:* A proper noun designating On, the son of Peleth (Num. 16:1).

204. אֹון *'ôn:* A proper noun designating On, a city in Egypt (Gen. 41:45, 50; 46:20; Ezek. 30:17).

205. אָוֶן *'āwen:* A masculine noun meaning nothingness, trouble, sorrow, evil, or mischief. The primary meaning is that of emptiness and vanity. It is used to signify empty or futile pursuits (Prov. 22:8; Isa. 41:29); nothingness, in the sense of utter destruction (Amos 5:5); an empty word, implying falsehood or deceit (Ps. 10:7; Prov. 17:4; Zech. 10:2); wickedness or one who commits iniquity (Num. 23:21; Job 22:15; Ps. 14:4[5]; 36:4; 101:8; Isa. 58:9; Mic. 2:1); evil or calamity (Job 5:6; Prov. 12:21; Jer. 4:15); and great sorrow (Deut. 26:14; Ps. 90:10; Hos. 9:4). In a metaphorical sense, the word is used once to signify an idol, strongly conveying the futility of worshiping an idol, which is, in fact, "nothing" (Isa. 66:3).

206. אָוֶן *'āwen:* A proper noun designating Aven:

A. Another name for the city of On (204) (Ezek. 30:17).

B. The shortened form of Beth-Aven (1007) (Hos. 8:10).

C. A town in the kingdom of Damascus (Amos 1:5).

207. אֹונֹו *'ônô:* A proper noun designating Ono (1 Chr. 8:12; Ezra 2:33; Neh. 6:2; 7:37; 11:35).

208. אֹונָם *'ônām:* A proper noun designating Onam:

A. A son of Shobal (Gen. 36:23; 1 Chr. 1:40).

B. A son of Jerahmeel (1 Chr. 2:26, 28).

209. אֹונָן *'ônān:* A proper noun designating Onan (Gen. 38:4, 8, 9; 46:12; Num. 26:19; 1 Chr. 2:3).

210. אוּפָז *'ûp̄āz:* A proper noun designating Uphaz (Jer. 10:9; Dan. 10:5).

211. אֹופִיר *'ôp̄iyr:* A proper noun designating Ophir:

A. A name describing the area from which Solomon imported great quantities of gold (1 Kgs. 9:28; 10:11; 1 Chr. 29:4). The place was renowned for its fine gold, its major product to the nations (Job 22:24; 28:16; Isa. 13:12). Its exact location is still a puzzle but may have been in the south or southwest part of the Arabian Peninsula.

B. A proper noun describing the son of Yoqtan (Joktan) in Shem's genealogical list (Gen. 10:29; 1 Chr. 1:23).

212. אֹופָן *'ôp̄ān:* A masculine noun meaning wheel (although it is feminine in one usage). God caused the chariot wheels of the Egyptians to come off while they were chasing the Israelites through the Red Sea (Ex. 14:25). This word is also used to describe the movable stands in Solomon's Temple (1 Kgs. 7:30, 32, 33); the wheels of threshing carts

(Prov. 20:26; Isa. 28:27); and the wheels of Ezekiel's chariot that supported the four living creatures (Ezek. 1:15, 16, 19–21).

213. אוּץ ***'ûṣ:*** A verb meaning to hasten, to urge, to insist, or to try. It expresses urgency (Ex. 5:13) directed towards workers by foremen. It is used to describe the failure of the sun to set in Joshua's famous battle in the Valley of Aijalon (Josh. 10:13). It is translated as narrow (cramped), also (Josh. 17:15). It can carry the connotation of to insist upon in its causative usage (Gen. 19:15; Isa. 22:4).

214. אוֹצָר ***'ôṣār:*** A masculine noun meaning treasure or storehouse. Various items were stored up, such as supplies (Neh. 12:44) or treasures of a palace or temple (1 Kgs. 7:51; Jer. 15:13). The Lord also has treasures in the heavens (Deut. 28:12) and in the winds (Jer. 10:13). The word refers to storehouses themselves (Neh. 13:12, 13).

215. אוֹר ***'ôr:*** A verb meaning to give light, to shine, to become light, day. The heavenly bodies provide light (Gen. 1:15, 17), as does fire (Ex. 13:21). Lightning shines forth (Ps. 77:18[19]; 97:4). The presence of the Lord can cause the earth to shine forth (Ezek. 43:2). A lamp or burning wood also gives off light (Ps. 18:28[29]; Isa. 27:11). Metaphorically, the Lord's face may shine on us (Num. 6:25), and His law enlightens our eyes (Ezra 9:8; Ps. 13:3[4]; Prov. 29:13). In a beautiful idiom, it is asserted that wisdom lights up a person's face (Eccl. 8:1).

216. אוֹר ***'ôr:*** A masculine noun meaning light. In a literal sense, it is used primarily to refer to light from heavenly bodies (Jer. 31:35; Ezek. 32:7) but also for light itself (Gen. 1:3; Eccl. 12:2). The pillar of fire was a light for the wandering Israelites (Ex. 13:21). One day God, who is clothed with light (a manifestation of His splendor), will replace the light of the heavens with His own light (Ps. 104:2; Isa. 60:19, 20; cf. Rev. 21:23; 22:5). Light is always used as a positive symbol, such as for good fortune (Job 30:26); victory (Mic. 7:8, 9); justice and righteousness (Isa. 59:9); guidance (Ps. 119:105); and a bearer of deliverance (Isa. 49:6). Expressions involving light include the light of one's face, meaning someone's favor (Ps. 44:3[4]); to see light, meaning to live (Ps. 49:19[20]); and to walk in the light, meaning to live by God's known standards (Isa. 2:5).

217. אוּר ***'ûr:*** A noun meaning fire. It refers to the fire of God's judgment (Isa. 31:9) and God's destruction of the wicked (Ezek. 5:2). In Isaiah 44:16 and 47:14, the noun is used to speak of a form of idol worship.

218. אוּר ***'ûr:*** A proper noun designating Ur:

A. The name of the city which Terah and Abraham left to go to Haran (Gen. 11:28, 31). It is called

"Ur of the Chaldees." It was most likely in southeast Iraq on the Euphrates River. It is probably ancient Tell el-Muqayyar. A few scholars have argued that it is somewhere in northern Mesopotamia or even southeast Turkey. Many ancient tablets have been uncovered there, and the "Law Code" of Ur-Nammu has been found and deciphered. It became the location of the much later neo-Babylonian kings (626–538 B.C.).

B. The father of one of David's mighty men (1 Chr. 11:35).

219. אוֹרָה ***'ôrāh:*** A feminine noun meaning light, brightness, splendor, herbs. The primary stress of the word is on the life-giving properties. It is used to signify light (Ps. 139:12); joyous well-being (Esth. 8:16); vibrant green herbs (2 Kgs. 4:39). The word also conveys the quality of living (Isa. 26:19).

220. אֻוֵרוֹת ***'ᵃwērôṯ:*** A feminine plural noun indicating stalls or pens for cattle (2 Chr. 32:28; NASB, NIV).

221. אוּרִי ***'ûriy:*** A proper noun designating Uri:

A. The name of the father of Bezaleel (Ex. 31:2; 35:30; 38:22; 1 Chr. 2:20; 2 Chr. 1:5).

B. The father of Geber (1 Kgs. 4:19).

C. A gatekeeper (Ezra 10:24).

222. אוּרִיאֵל ***'ûriyēl:*** A proper noun designating Uriel:

A. The name of a levite (1 Chr. 6:24[9]).

B. A levite under David (1 Chr. 15:5, 11).

C. The grandfather of Abijah (2 Chr. 13:2).

223. אוּרִיָּה ***'ûriyyah:*** A proper noun designating Uriah:

A. A Hittite who served in David's army (2 Sam. 11). David eventually had him killed in battle. The name means "light of Yahweh." Bathesheba was his wife. He was a member of David's elite forces (2 Sam. 23:39; 1 Chr. 11:41). He proved himself to be an honorable man before David had him killed (Deut. 23:10, 11; 2 Sam. 11:11).

B. The name of a priest who served as a witness for Isaiah the prophet (Isa. 8:1–4) at God's directions. He would witness a legal action to which he could later bear witness. He served as a priest under King Ahaz (735–715 B.C.) (2 Kgs. 16:10–11). He took part in the construction of an idolatrous altar in Judah (2 Kgs. 16:12–16).

C. The name of a prophet in Judah. He is famous for his prophecies against Jerusalem that were in complete agreement with Jeremiah's prophecies (Jer. 26:20–23). He fled from Jehoiakim but was eventually captured and put to death in Jerusalem (Jer. 26:23; cf. Luke 11:47).

D. The name of a returned exile recorded in Nehemiah 3:4, 21. He was a priest and the father of Meremoth (cf. Ezra 8:33).

E. The name of a returned exile from Babylon. He stood by and supported Ezra's reading of the Law at the Watergate (Neh. 8:4). He may be the Uriah listed in D above.

224. אוּרִים *'ûriym:* A masculine plural noun, which occurs seven times in the Old Testament, usually with "the Thummim." Our knowledge of the Urim and Thummim is limited. They were kept in the breastplate which the high priest wore over his heart (Ex. 28:30; Lev. 8:8) and were given to the Levites as part of Moses' blessing (Deut. 33:8). Some believe they were flat objects which were cast to determine the will of God, one providing a negative answer and the other a positive, much like casting lots. However, that is somewhat conjectural. Joshua received God's revelation by Eleazer's use of the Urim (Num. 27:21). God didn't answer Saul when he consulted the Lord with the use of the Urim (1 Sam. 28:6). The Urim and Thummim were also used to approve priestly qualifications (Ezra 2:63; Neh. 7:65).

225. אוּת *'ûṯ:* A verb meaning to consent, to agree. It is used by Jacob's sons to lure the sons of Shechem to be circumcised (Gen. 34:15). And it indicates agreement or consent to something (2 Kgs. 12:8[9]).

226. אוֹת *'ôṯ:* A masculine noun meaning sign, signal, mark, miracle. This word is used most often to describe awe-inspiring events: God's work to bring the Hebrew people out of Egypt (Ex. 4:8, 9; Num. 14:22; Deut. 7:19; Ps. 78:43; Jer. 32:20, 21); miracles verifying God's message (1 Sam. 2:34; 10:7, 9; Isa. 7:11, 14). Moreover, this word may also denote signs from false prophets (Deut. 13:1[2], 2[3]; Isa. 44:25); circumstances demonstrating God's control (Deut. 28:46; Ps. 86:17). Associate meanings of the word denote physical emblems (Num. 2:2); a promise to remember (Gen. 17:11; Deut. 6:8; Josh. 2:12; 4:6); an event to occur in the future (Isa. 20:3; Ezek. 4:3).

227. אָז *'āz,* מֵאָז *mē'āz:* An adverb meaning then, at that time, or since. This word may introduce something that used to be so (Gen. 12:6); what happened next in a narrative (Ex. 15:1); or what will happen in the future (Isa. 35:5, 6). On occasion, it is also used as a preposition, such as in Ruth 2:7: "Even from the morning" (KJV).

228. אֲזָא *'ᵃzā',* אֲזָה *'ᵃzāh:* An Aramaic verb meaning to make hot, to heat. It is used by Nebuchadnezzar in its infinitive form to order the furnace to be heated seven times hotter than normal (Dan. 3:19, 22).

229. אֶזְבַּי *'ezbay:* A proper noun designating Ezbai (1 Chr. 11:37).

230. אֲזָד *'azāḏ:* An Aramaic verb meaning to be gone, to go forth, promulgate. Some would prefer to designate this an adjective or noun in Daniel 2:5, 8. It designates the word or command that had gone forth from King Nebuchadnezzar.

231. אֵזוֹב ***'ēzôḇ:*** A masculine noun meaning hyssop, a woody plant with aromatic leaves and small flowers. It was used as a brush to sprinkle items used in various purificatory (Lev. 14:4, 6) and other rites in Israel, especially the blood used in the Passover rites (Ex. 12:22). It was used in the ordinance concerning the red heifer (Num. 19:6, 18). It is used literally and figuratively of spiritual cleansing (Ps. 51:7[9]).

232. אֵזוֹר ***'ēzôr:*** A masculine noun meaning belt or girdle. It was the inner piece of clothing (2 Kgs. 1:8; Ezek. 23:15). It could be of skin or linen (Jer. 13:1). It was used figuratively of Israel and Judah's faithfulness to the Lord (Jer. 13:1, 2, 4, 6, 7, 10, 11) and of the Lord's authority over kings (Job 12:18). In Isaiah 11:5, it is a metaphor for righteousness.

233. אֲזַי ***'ᵃzay:*** An adverb meaning then, in that case, or possibly if not . . . then. It is the first word in each line of Psalm 124:3–5 and is closely related in meaning to *'āz* (227), then.

234. אַזְכָּרָה ***'azkārāh:*** A feminine noun indicating a memorial portion offering. It is the portion of the meal offering that was burned (Lev. 2:2, 9: Num. 5:26).

235. אָזַל ***'āzal:*** A verb meaning to disappear, to fail, to go away. God helps His people when their strength is gone (Deut. 32:36). It describes food when it is all used up (1 Sam. 9:7). The word depicts the disappearance of water as it evaporates (Job 14:11) but also the simple departure of a person (Prov. 20:14).

236. אֲזַל ***'ᵃzal:*** An Aramaic verb meaning to go up, go away. It is found in the Aramaic portions of Ezra to depict persons traveling (4:23; 5:8, 15) and in Daniel to describe persons walking from one place to another (2:17, 24; 6:18[19], 19[20]).

237. אֶזֶל ***'ezel:*** A proper noun designating Ezel (1 Sam. 20:19).

238. אָזַן ***'āzan:*** A verb meaning to give an ear, to lend an ear, to listen, to hear. This word is almost always found in poetic texts of the Old Testament and is often found in songs. The Song of Moses begins with an exhortation for the heavens to lend its ear (Deut. 32:1); Jeremiah asked for the people of Israel to listen to his prophecy (Jer. 13:15). God's people commonly asked the Lord to listen to their prayers and petitions; this significant use is found many times throughout the Book of Psalms (Ps. 5:1[2]; 77:1[2]; 80:1[2]).

239. אָזַן ***'āzan:*** A verb meaning to ponder or consider. It describes the Preacher of Ecclesiastes thinking as he attempts to teach the people wisdom (12:9) and as he tries to find the best way to impart his instruction to the people.

240. אָזֵן ***'āzēn:*** This masculine noun indicates a weapon or tool. A tent peg or spade was to be kept among a person's personal tools in order to keep the Lord's camp holy and clean by covering up one's excrement (Deut. 23:13[14]).

241. אֹזֶן *'ōzen:* A masculine noun meaning ear. The word is often used metaphorically as an instrument of obedience (Prov. 25:12) and intellect (Job 12:11; 13:1; Prov. 18:15; Eccl. 1:8). In Jeremiah 6:10, the disobedient or inattentive are said to have uncircumcised ears. The Hebrew idiom for revealing something or making one aware is to open the ears (Ruth 4:4; 1 Sam. 20:2, 12, 13; Isa. 35:5).

242. אֻזֵּן שֶׁאֱרָה *'uzzēn še'erāh:* A proper noun designating Uzzen Sheerah (1 Chr. 7:24).

243. אַזְנוֹת תָּבוֹר *'aznôṯ tāḇôr:* A proper noun designating Aznoth Tabor (Josh. 19:34).

244. אָזְנִי *'ozniy:* A proper noun designating Ozni, a descendant of Ozni (Num. 26:16).

245. אֲזַנְיָה *'azanyāh:* A proper noun designating Azaniah (Neh. 10:9[10]).

246. אֲזִק *'azēq:* A masculine noun meaning chain and used in the plural form in the Old Testament. Jeremiah is freed from his chains (Jer. 40:1, 4) and permitted to go where he wishes.

247. אָזַר *'āzar:* A verb meaning to arm, to gird up, to bind. The soldier must put on his armor and gird up for battle (Jer. 1:17). Elijah bound his leather girdle on his loins (2 Kgs. 1:8). In his distress, Job asserts that his garment binds him (30:18). The word is used metaphorically to describe the girding on of strength. The Lord is said to be girded with strength and might (Ps. 65:6[7]), and He girds up the great Persian king to do His will (Isa. 45:5). Persons can gird themselves (Isa. 8:9) literally or figuratively.

248. אֶזְרוֹעַ *'ezrôa':* A feminine noun meaning arm. It refers to the Lord's outstretched arm (Jer. 32:21) and to Job's pitiful plea concerning his condition (31:22) and his feeble arm.

249. אֶזְרָח *'ezrāḥ:* A masculine noun indicating a native-born person of a land (Ezek. 47:22) as opposed to a stranger (*gēr*) or settler (*tôšaḇ*). These persons had full rights to take part in Israel's rites and festivals (Ex. 12:19, 48, 49; Lev. 16:29; Josh. 8:33). Strangers could be treated as natives in some cases (Ex. 12:48) and were to have, in general, respect and humanitarian treatment just as the natives (Lev. 19:34). They were to be loved. It is used figuratively to describe native soil (Ps. 37:35).

250. אֶזְרָחִי *'ezrāḥiy:* A proper noun designating Ezrahite (1 Kgs. 4:31[5:11]; Ps. 88:title[1]; 89:title[1]).

251. אָח *'āḥ:* A masculine noun meaning brother. The word is used not only of those with common parents but also of those with common ancestors. Thus, the descendants of Israel are brothers (Lev. 19:17; 25:46), as are two nations with common ancestors (Amos 1:11, Obad. 1:10, 12). It further describes a close friend outside the immediate physical family (2 Sam. 1:26).

252. אַח *'aḥ:* An Aramaic masculine noun meaning brother. It occurs only in Ezra 7:18 and is the equivalent of the Hebrew word *'āḥ* (251).

253. אָח *'āḥ:* A particle used as an interjection meaning alas! oh! It indicates pain or grief (Ezek. 6:11; 21:15[20]).

254. אָח *'aḥ:* A feminine noun indicating a brazier or a firepot of metal or clay (Jer. 36:22, 23). This brazier was located in Jehoiakim's winter house where he burned the first draft of Jeremiah's prophecies.

255. אֹחַ *'ōaḥ:* A masculine noun referring to a jackal or owl. After Babylon was destroyed, it would become the haunt of owls and other scavengers (Isa. 13:21).

256. אַחְאָב *'aḥ'āḇ:* A proper noun designating Ahab:

A. The name of an Israelite king, son of Omri, and the seventh king in Israel (ca. 874–852 B.C.). He was notoriously corrupt and infamous for marrying the Sidonian Princess Jezebel through whom idolatry and spiritual harlotry permeated Israel. The priests of Baal filled the land (1 Kgs. 18:19–20). He worshiped the god Baal, setting up a temple for Baal in Samaria, his capital city (1 Kgs. 16:32). He set up Asherah poles representing the goddess of fertility Asherah, who was also the consort of El. Elijah called for a drought for nearly three years as a sign to Ahab (1 Kgs. 17:1; 18:5–6). The Lord also caused it to rain again as a sign to Ahab through Elijah (1 Kgs. 18:44–46). But the Lord also delivered Ahab in battle as a sign to him that the Lord desired to bless him (1 Kgs. 20:13) and to demonstrate who was the true Lord of the land. He fought many battles against the Syrians (1 Kgs. 22:1). But Ahab's corruption and rebellion were displayed even more openly when he had a fellow Israelite, Naboth, killed in order to get his vineyard (1 Kgs. 21:1–19). The Lord destroyed not only Ahab but his entire house (2 Kgs. 9:6–10). Both Ahab and his father Omri became bywords for evil and corruption among the prophets (Mic. 6:16). Ahab died at Romoth-Gilead because he followed his false prophets (1 Kgs. 22:19–38). Ahaziah, his son, reigned after his death.

B. The name of a false prophet, a son of Kolaiah. He was condemned by Jeremiah for prophesying in Yahweh's, the Lord's, name. Jeremiah predicted his death (Jer. 29:21, 22) at the hands of Babylonian forces.

257. אַחְבָּן *'aḥbān:* A proper noun designating Ahban (1 Chr. 2:29).

258. אָחַד ***'āḥaḏ:*** A verb meaning to go one way or the other. It metaphorically describes the actions of the Lord's sword for destruction (Ezek. 21:16[21]).

259. אֶחָד ***'eḥāḏ:*** A numerical adjective meaning one, first, once, the same. It may mean simply one of various things: e.g., place (Gen. 1:9); soul, or person (Lev. 4:27); a person from among many (Gen. 3:22; 42:19; 1 Sam. 26:15). It has the idea of unity or integrity as when it designates one justice for all (Num. 15:16) or actual physical unity (Ex. 36:12). The Lord is one (Deut. 6:4). It expresses agreement or unity among persons (Ex. 24:3) or physical unity (Zeph. 3:9). It may serve as an indefinite article, one man (1 Sam 1:1), or to indicate the first of something, e.g., the first day of the month (Gen. 8:5). The word is pluralized to mean several, few, or a while (Gen. 11:1; 27:44).

260. אָחוּ ***'āḥû:*** A masculine noun meaning reed, papyrus, marsh plant. It is what grows in a marsh (Job 8:11), i.e., papyrus or marsh plant. Cows grazed among the marsh grass in Egypt according to Pharaoh's dream (Gen. 41:2, 18).

261. אֵחוּד ***'ēḥûḏ:*** A proper noun designating Ehud (1 Chr. 8:6).

262. אַחְוָה ***'aḥwāh:*** A feminine noun indicating speech or declaration. It refers to the declaration of Job (13:17).

263. אַחֲוָיָה ***'aḥ^{a}wāyah:*** An Aramaic feminine noun meaning explanation. It refers to the explanation of riddles or enigmas (Dan. 5:12; cf. NIV, explain).

264. אַחֲוָה ***'aḥ^{a}wāh:*** A noun meaning brotherhood. It is used only in Zechariah 11:14 where it signifies the unity between Judah and Israel whose common ancestor is Jacob. The brotherhood is symbolically broken by Zechariah's breaking his staff.

265. אֲחוֹחַ ***'^{a}ḥôaḥ:*** A proper noun designating Ahoah (1 Chr. 8:4).

266. אֲחוֹחִי ***'aḥôḥiy:*** A proper noun designating Ahohite (2 Sam. 23:9, 28; 1 Chr. 11:12, 29; 27:4).

267. אֲחוּמַי ***'^{a}ḥûmay:*** A proper noun designating Ahumai (1 Chr. 4:2).

268. אָחוֹר ***'āḥôr:*** A masculine noun meaning back. It can in general refer to the back or back side of something: of a dwelling (Ex. 26:12, Tabernacle) or of God (Ex. 33:23). It indicates direction, such as before, behind, backward (Gen. 49:17; Ezek. 2:10), or westward (Isa. 9:11, 12). Temporally, it can refer to the future (Isa. 42:23) or mean finally, holding back to the last (Prov. 29:11). Finally, it is used metaphorically, causing wise men to fail or to turn back (Isa. 44:25).

269. אָחוֹת ***'āḥôṯ:*** A feminine noun meaning sister. Besides a biological sister, it also refers to more intimate female relatives. Song of Solomon uses the word to refer to a bride (Song 4:9, 10, 12; 5:1, 2). In Numbers 25:18, it is used as a generic term for female relatives. Poetically, it sometimes refers to a geographical location (Jer. 3:7, 8, 10; Ezek. 16:45, 52). For inanimate objects, it can often be translated as the English word *another* (Ex. 26:3, 5, 6, 17; Ezek. 1:9; 3:13).

270. אָחַז ***'aḥaz:*** A verb indicating to seize, to grasp, hold firmly. This meaning is employed quite uniformly. Someone or a thing can be seized (Gen. 25:26; Ex. 15:14). In its passive usage, it has the idea of being seized or held fast (Gen. 22:13, the ram) or being settled in a land (Gen. 34:10), metaphorically.

271. אָחָז ***'āḥāz:*** A proper noun designating Ahaz:

A. The name of a king of Judah who ruled 735–715 B.C. Ahaz is a shortened name for Jehoahaz. The name means "he has seized." His reign lasted 17 years. He was the son of Jotham, who reigned before him. His most famous son was Hezekiah (2 Kgs. 15:38; 16:1, 2, 5, 7, 8). He did not follow the will of God as David had (2 Kgs. 16), but pursued the practices of the pagan nations (1 Kgs. 16:1–4). He was faithless at crucial times and did not trust the Lord to deliver him and Judah from their enemies (Isa. 7:1–12), especially from Assyria. He brought in pagan altar styles into the Temple area (2 Kgs. 16:10–20). Isaiah prophesied during his reign (Isa. 1:1; 14:28).

B. The name of a Benjamite, a son of Micah. Ahaz fathered Jehoaddah (1 Chr. 8:35–36) and was himself a great-grandson of Saul (1 Chr. 9:39, 42).

272. אֲחֻזָּה ***'ᵃḥuzzāh:*** A feminine noun meaning possession, literally meaning something seized. The word usually refers to the possession of land, especially of the Promised Land (Gen. 48:4; Deut. 32:49). Because the Promised Land is "an everlasting possession," (Gen. 17:8) this word often refers to land that is to pass down within families, never being permanently taken away (Lev. 25; Num. 27:4, 7, Ezek. 46:16–18). The Levites had God, instead of land, as their "possession" (Ezek. 44:28).

273. אַחְזַי ***'aḥzay:*** A proper noun designating Ahzai (Neh. 11:13).

274. אֲחַזְיָהוּ ***'ᵃḥazyāhû,*** אֲחַזְיָה ***'ᵃḥazyāh:*** A proper noun designating Ahaziah. The name means "Yah (Lord) has seized."

A. The name of a king of Israel. He was Ahab's son and ruled in Samaria (1 Kgs. 22:51) while Jehoshaphat ruled in Judah. He reigned two years (853–852 B.C.) and did not follow the Lord. He served Baal-Zebub the Canaanite god (1 Kgs. 22:53), even inquiring of him for health reasons (2 Kgs. 1:2). Because he did this, the Lord caused his death as announced by Elijah (2 Kgs. 1:16–17).

B. The same name was borne by a king of Judah, Ahaziah, also Jehoahaz (2 Chr. 21:17), the son of Jehoram (2 Kgs. 8:24–26), son of Jehoshaphat (2 Kgs. 8:16). He was killed by Jehu (2 Kgs. 9:27–29) in fulfillment of Elijah's prophecies years earlier. He reigned less than one year (841 B.C.). His mother was the wicked Queen Athaliah, Ahab's daughter.

275. אֲחֻזָּם ***ʼaḥuzzām:*** A proper noun designating Ahuzzam (1 Chr. 4:6).

276. אֲחֻזַּת ***ʼaḥuzzaṯ:*** A proper noun designating Ahuzzath (Gen. 26:26).

277. אֲחִי ***ʼaḥiy:*** A proper noun designating Ahi:

A. The name of a Gadite (1 Chr. 5:15).

B. An Asherite (1 Chr. 7:34).

278. אֵחִי ***ʼēḥiy:*** A proper noun designating Ehi (Gen. 46:21).

279. אֲחִיאָם ***ʼaḥiyʼām:*** A proper noun designating Ahiam (2 Sam. 23:33; 1 Chr. 11:35).

280. אֲחִידָה ***ʼaḥiyḏāh:*** An Aramaic feminine noun meaning puzzle or riddle. Daniel was able to deliver explanations to these enigmas (Dan. 5:12) and riddles.

281. אֲחִיָּה ***ʼaḥiyyāh:*** A proper noun designating Ahijah, a name given to at least nine different individuals in the Old Testament. The name means "brother of Yah," Yah being a shortened form of Yahweh, Lord. The name refers to the following persons:

A. A priest who served under Saul and "wore the ephod" (1 Sam. 14:3); he was from the line of high priests. He was in charge of the ark of God (1 Sam. 14:18).

B. An official under Saul who served as recorder or secretary (1 Kgs. 4:3).

C. A prophet of Shiloh where the ark was (1 Kgs. 11:29). he announced the rending of the Southern Kingdom from Jeroboam (1 Kgs. 11:29–31; 12:15); Jeroboam's son Abijah's death (1 Kgs. 14:2, 4–6, 18); and the extinction of Jeroboam's house (1 Kgs. 14:6–16). His written words became a source of events under Solomon (2 Chr. 9:29).

D. The father of King Baasha of Israel. He was from the tribe of Issachar. His son Baasha was a wicked king whose house was eradicated from Israel (1 Kgs. 16:1–7; 2 Kgs. 9:9–10).

E. He is listed as a grandson of Hezron (1 Chr. 2:25), a son of Jerahmeel.

F. He is listed as a descendant of Saul, a son of Ehud (1 Chr. 8:7).

G. The name is borne by one of David's mighty men (1 Chr. 11:36). He is called "the Pelonite."

H. The name is borne by a Levite under David (1 Chr. 26:20) who was in charge of Temple treasuries.

I. He served as a leader of the people of Israel under Nehemiah (Neh.

10:26[27]), who signed and sealed the covenant of renewal.

282. אֲחִיהוּד *'aḥiyhûd:* A proper noun designating Ahihud (Num. 34:27).

283. אַחְיוֹ *'aḥyô:* A proper noun designating Ahio:
A. The name of a son of Abinadab (2 Sam. 6:3, 4; 1 Chr. 13:7).
B. Benjamite (1 Chr. 8:14).
C. Gibeonite (1 Chr. 8:31; 9:37).

284. אֲחִיחָד *'aḥiyhud:* A proper noun designating Ahihud (1 Chr. 8:7).

285. אֲחִיטוּב *'aḥiyṭûḇ:* A proper noun designating Ahitub:
A. A son of Phinehas (1 Sam. 14:3; 22:9, 11, 12, 20).
B. The father of Zadok (2 Sam. 8:17; 1 Chr. 6:7(5:33), 8(5:34), 52(37); 18:16).
C. A priest (1 Chr. 6:11(5:37), 12(5:38); Ezra 7:2).
D. Another priest (1 Chr. 9:11; Neh. 11:11).

286. אֲחִילוּד *'aḥiylûḏ:* A proper noun designating Ahilud:
A. The father of Jehoshaphat (2 Sam. 8:16; 20:24; 1 Kgs. 4:3; 1 Chr. 18:15).
B. The father of Baana (1 Kgs. 4:12).

287. אֲחִימוֹת *'aḥiymôṯ:* A proper noun designating Ahimoth (1 Chr. 6:25[10]).

288. אֲחִימֶלֶךְ *'aḥiymeleḵ:* A proper noun designating Ahimelech. The name means "my brother is king."
A. He served as a priest in Saul's time (1 Sam. 21:1[2], 2[3], 8[9]; 22:9, 11). He was the son of Ahitub. He was priest in Nob and gave David bread when he was fleeing from Saul. Saul had him executed for rebellion.
B. The name refers to a Hittite who served under David before David was crowned king (1 Sam. 26:6).
C. The name refers to the father of Abiathar (1 Sam. 22:20; 23:6; 30:7), but in 2 Samuel 8:17 refers to Ahimelech as son of Abiathar. Generally, it is thought that 2 Sam. 8:17 features a copyist's error.

289. אֲחִימָן *'aḥiyman,* אֲחִימָן *'aḥiymān:* A proper noun designating Ahiman:
A. A son of Anak (Num. 13:22; Josh. 15:14; Judg. 1:10).
B. A levite (1 Chr. 9:17).

290. אֲחִימַעַץ *'aḥiymaʿaṣ:* A proper noun designating Ahimaaz. The name means "wrath is my brother."
A. The name refers to a son of Zadok (2 speedy messenger (2 Sam. 18:27). He helped carry the message of Absalom's defeat and demise to David (2 Sam. 18:19).
B. It refers to Saul's father-in-law who was the father of Ahinoam, Saul's wife (1 Sam. 14:50).
C. It refers to an officer who served under Solomon (1 Kgs. 4:15). He functioned as a district governor

(1 Kgs. 4:7–8) and married Solomon's daughter Basemath.

291. אַחְיָן ***'aḥyān:*** A proper noun designating Ahian (1 Chr. 7:19).

292. אֲחִינָדָב ***'ᵃḥiynāḏāḇ:*** A proper noun designating Ahinadab (1 Kgs. 4:14).

293. אֲחִינֹעַם ***'ᵃḥiynō'am:*** A proper noun designating Ahinoam:

A. The name of Saul's wife, daughter of Ahimaaz. The name means "my brother is pleasant." This is the only reference to any wife of Saul.

B. It refers to one of David's wives, a Jezreelite. She was his first wife (1 Sam. 25:43) and bore his first son, Amnon (2 Sam. 3:2).

294. אֲחִיסָמָךְ ***'ᵃḥiysāmāḵ:*** A proper noun designating Ahisamach (Ex. 31:6; 35:34; 38:23).

295. אֲחִיעֶזֶר ***'ᵃḥiy'ezer:*** A proper noun designating Ahiezer:

A. The name of a man from the tribe of Dan who helped produce a census of the tribes of Israel (Num. 1:12), son of Ammishaddai (Num. 2:25). He also presented the tribe's dedication offering of the Tabernacle (Num. 7:66, 71). He was in charge of the standard of the tribe as well (Num. 10:25).

B. He was a trained warrior who chose to support and help David, although he was related to Saul (1 Chr. 12:3).

296. אֲחִיקָם ***'ᵃḥiyqām:*** A proper noun designating Ahikam (2 Kgs. 22:12, 14; 25:22; 2 Chr. 34:20; Jer. 26:24; 39:14; 40:5–7, 9, 11, 14, 16; 41:1, 2, 6, 10, 16, 18; 43:6).

297. אֲחִירָם ***'ᵃḥiyrām:*** A proper noun designating Ahiram (Num. 26:38).

298. אֲחִירָמִי ***'ᵃḥirāmiy:*** A proper noun designating Ahiramite (Num. 26:38).

299. אֲחִירַע ***'ᵃḥiyra':*** A proper noun designating Ahira (Num. 1:15; 2:29; 7:78, 83; 10:27).

300. אֲחִישָׁחַר ***'ᵃḥiyšaḥar:*** A proper noun designating Ahishahar (1 Chr. 7:10).

301. אֲחִישָׁר ***'ᵃḥiyšār:*** A proper noun designating Ahishar (1 Kgs. 4:6).

302. אֲחִיתֹפֶל ***'ᵃḥiyṯōpel:*** A proper noun designating Ahithophel. He served as chief advisor and counselor to David (2 Sam. 15:12) but joined Absalom, forsaking David during Absalom's rebellion and conspiracy. He was from Gilon. The Lord confounded Ahithophel's counsel at David's request (2 Sam. 15:31, 34). Absalom turned against his advice and followed Hushai the Arkite's counsel (2 Sam. 17:5–22). Ahithophel, ashamed and threatened, committed suicide (2 Sam. 17:23).

303. אַחְלָב ***'aḥlāḇ:*** A proper noun designating Ahlab (Judg. 1:31).

304. אַחְלַי ***'aḥlay:*** A proper noun designating Ahlai:

A. A son of Sheshan (1 Chr. 2:31).

B. The father of one of David's mighty men (1 Chr. 11:41).

305. אַחֲלֵי ***aḥ^{a}lēy***, אַחֲלַי, ***'aḥ^{a}lay:*** An interjection meaning would that! if only! It represents a polite wish or desire (2 Kgs. 5:3) or a mere cry of the soul for integrity and stability (Ps. 119:5).

306. אַחְלָמָה ***'aḥlāmāh:*** A feminine noun indicating a semiprecious stone. It was one of the stones mounted in the third row upon the breastpiece of the high priest (Ex. 28:19; 39:12). It is a jasper or amethyst stone. It had a tribal name engraved on it, so that the high priest represented that tribe before the Lord.

307. אַחְמְתָא ***'aḥm^{e}ṯa':*** A proper noun designating Achmetha, Ecbatana (Ezra 6:2).

308. אֲחַסְבַּי ***'^{a}ḥasbay:*** A proper noun designating Ahasbai (2 Sam. 23:34).

309. אָחַר ***'āḥar:*** A verb meaning to delay or hold back. It means to delay or remain (Gen. 32:4[5]); 2 Sam. 20:5, [K^e]). In its intensive usage, it can mean to hesitate (Ex. 22:29[28]; Judg. 5:28). In its causal stem, it means to come too late (2 Sam. 20:5, [Q^e]).

310. אַחַר ***'aḥar:*** A preposition meaning behind, after, afterwards. The usage is quite uniform, varying slightly according to context. Used more adverbally, it can mean such things as behind someone or something (Gen. 22:13); afterwards or after that (an event) (Gen. 18:5). Used more specifically as a preposition, it means behind (Gen. 37:17); after, such as to pursue something literally or figuratively (Job 39:8); after in a temporal sense, such as when clouds return after the rain (Eccl. 12:2); or after talking ceases (Job 42:7).

311. אַחֲרֵי ***'aḥ^{a}rēy:*** An Aramaic preposition meaning after, afterward. It means the future in Daniel 2:29, 45. It also indicates the temporal sequence of kings and kingdoms (Dan. 7:24). Pronominal suffixes may be attached to it, e.g., *'aḥ^{a}ray*, after me, etc.

312. אַחֵר ***'aḥēr:*** An adjective meaning other, another. Its meaning is nuanced according to its context. It means other (Neh. 7:34) but in context also additional or further offspring (Gen. 4:25) and further or another in the flood story (Gen. 8:10, 12). It can take on a figurative meaning indicating that a person has become another person (1 Sam. 10:9, literally, with another heart). When used with a language, it means a foreign language (Isa. 28:11) or tongue. Its most important theological use is to designate other gods whom Israel was not to worship or serve (Ex.

34:14; Deut. 5:7; in Deut. 19 times and Jer. 18 times).

313. אַחֵר ***'aḥēr:*** A proper noun designating Aher (1 Chr. 7:12).

314. אַחֲרוֹן ***'aḥᵃrôn,*** אַחֲרֹן ***'aḥᵃrōn:*** An adjective meaning last, afterwards, next. Its use is quite consistent, but it is nuanced by its context to mean in second position (Gen. 33:2); or to the west, westward (Deut. 11:24). It is used in a temporal sense to mean latter (Ex. 4:8); future (Deut. 29:22[21]); or present (Ruth 3:10). It also means last (2 Sam. 19:11[12], 12[13]). God is called the first and the last (Isa. 41:4). It takes on the meaning of finally in some contexts (2 Sam. 2:26; 1 Kgs. 17:13).

315. אַחְרַח ***'aḥraḥ:*** A proper noun designating Aharah (1 Chr. 8:1).

316. אֲחַרְחֵל ***ᵃḥarḥēl:*** A proper noun designating Aharhel (1 Chr. 4:8).

317. אָחֳרִי ***'oḥᵒriy:*** An Aramaic adjective meaning other, another. It indicates another or different kingdom arising after Babylon (Dan. 2:39; 7:5) and subsequent kingdoms to that one (Dan. 7:6). Finally, it indicates another or different (in kind?) horn, the little horn of Daniel (7:20).

318. אָחֳרֵין ***'oḥᵒrēyn:*** An Aramaic adverb meaning last, end, finally. It refers to the last person in a series in Daniel (4:8[5]).

319. אַחֲרִית ***'aḥᵃriyṯ:*** A feminine noun meaning the end, last time, latter time (Gen. 49:1; Num. 23:10; 24:14, 20; Deut. 4:30; 8:16; 11:12; 31:29; 32:20, 29; Job 8:7; 42:12; Ps. 37:37, 38; 73:17; 109:13; 139:9; Prov. 5:4, 11; 14:12, 13; 16:25; 19:20; 20:21; 23:18, 32; 24:14, 20; 25:8; 29:21; Eccl. 7:8; 10:13; Isa. 2:2; 41:22; 46:10; 47:7; Jer. 5:31; 12:4; 17:11; 23:20; 29:11; 30:24; 31:17; 48:47; 49:39; 50:12; Lam. 1:9; Ezek. 23:25; 38:8, 16; Dan. 8:19, 23; 10:14; 11:4; 12:8; Hos. 3:5; Amos 4:2; 8:10; 9:1; Mic. 4:1).

320. אַחֲרִית ***'aḥᵃriyṯ:*** An Aramaic feminine noun used to indicate the end time or latter, last time(s). It is rendered as latter days in Daniel (NASB, 2:28).

321. אָחֳרָן ***'oḥᵒrān:*** An Aramaic adjective meaning other, another. It indicates someone with special dream interpretive powers (Dan. 2:11). It also means simply a different person (Dan. 5:17), other gods (Dan. 3:29), or a subsequent king or kingdom (7:24).

322. אֲחֹרַנִּית ***ᵃḥōranniyṯ:*** An adverb that means backward. It indicates backward motion (2 Kgs. 20:10, 11), such as walking backward (Gen. 9:23); or falling backward (1 Sam. 4:18). It is used figuratively to describe a heart turning back to the Lord (1 Kgs. 18:37).

323. אֲחַשְׁדַּרְפַּן ***ᵃḥašdarpan:*** A masculine noun meaning satrap, governor of a Persian province. It occurs as a technical administrative term several times (Ezra 8:36; Esth. 3:12; 8:9; 9:3).

324. אֲחַשְׁדַּרְפַּן ***'ᵃḥašdarpan:*** A Chaldean noun meaning satrap. Satraps were officials who governed large provinces in Persia as representatives of the Persian sovereign. *Peḥāh* (6346) denotes a smaller office within a satrapy. Daniel was one of three rulers over the satraps and became an object of their evil schemes (Dan. 6:1–4[2–5], 6[7], 7[8]; the word also occurs in Dan. 3:2, 3, 27). All occurrences of this Chaldean word are in the book of Daniel, but the Hebrew equivalent (323) is spelled the same and occurs in Ezra and Esther.

325. אֲחַשְׁוֵרוֹשׁ ***'ᵃḥašwērôš:*** A proper noun designating Ahasuerus. A king of Persia, also Xerxes I (Greek, Aramaic), who reigned 485–465 B.C. He was involved in the great Battle of Salamis in Greece in 480 B.C. In Ezra 6:4, he is an opponent to Israel's rebuilding the city walls. He is the king during the events in Esther (1:2; 6:2, etc.). Some scholars argue that in the Book of Esther the king may be Artaxerxes II (404–359 B.C.). He is mentioned as the father of Darius the Mede, who is still not fully identified, although he may be Cyrus (Dan. 9:1).

326. אֲחַשְׁתָּרִי ***'ᵃḥaštāriy:*** A proper noun designating Haahashtari (1 Chr. 4:6).

327. אֲחַשְׁתְּרָן ***'ᵃḥašteᵉrān:*** A masculine noun meaning speedy or royal. The term royal seems to be the better translation, but the idea of speed is probably included in the designation of royal steeds or studs (NASB, Esth. 8:10, 14; NKJV, royal horses).

328. אַט ***'aṭ,*** אִטִּים ***'iṭṭiym:*** An adverb meaning gently, with gentleness. It occurs five times (Gen. 33:14; 2 Sam. 18:5; 1 Kgs. 21:27; Job 15:11; Isa. 8:6).

329. אָטָד ***'āṭāḏ:*** I. A masculine noun meaning bramble, thorn. The bramble or thornbush was considered one of the lowliest of trees and is referred to in Jotham's fable (Judg. 9:14, 15). It was a scraggly bush that produced nothing of value—an apt figure to represent Abimelech.

II. Atad: threshing floor in Transjordan; another name for *'āḇēl miṣrayim* [67].

330. אֵטוּן ***'ēṭûn:*** A masculine noun indicating fine linen. It is translated by some as colored linen (NIV; Prov. 7:16). It was imported from Egypt.

331. אָטַם ***'āṭam:*** A verb meaning to stop up, be narrow, frame. It refers to stopping one's ears (Isa. 33:15) or closing one's mouth (Prov. 17:28). It also indicates a framed, shuttered, or latticed window (1 Kgs. 6:4; Ezek. 40:16).

332. אָטַר ***'āṭar:*** A verb meaning to shut or close. It is used figuratively of a pit shutting its mouth (Ps. 69:15[16]).

333. אָטֵר *'āṭēr:* A proper noun designating Ater (Ezra 2:16, 42; Neh. 7:21, 45; 10:17[18]).

334. אִטֵּר *'iṭṭēr:* An adjective indicating left-handedness. It describes Ehud, a judge in Israel, as a left-handed man. Seven hundred left-handed stone slingers, who were considered especially skilled, are mentioned as part of the tribe of Benjamin (Judg. 20:16).

335. אֵי *'ēy:* An adverb meaning where, whence. Its use is quite uniform. It takes suffixes and can mean where are you? (Gen. 3:9). It takes on the meaning of which, e.g., *'ēy zeh* (2088) *hadderek* which way then? (2 Chr. 18:23). With *min* (4480) on the front, it indicates from where (Gen. 16:8). And it can mean why? (Jer. 5:7).

336. אִי *'iy:* A masculine noun meaning not. It is found in Job 22:30 used to indicate one not innocent (NASB; NKJV, cf. KJV, island).

337. אִי *'iy:* A particle used on an interjection meaning woe! It indicates a cry of warning for both persons and metaphorically a land that has a child for a king (Eccl. 4:10; 10:16).

338. אִי *'iy:* A masculine noun indicating a hyena or jackal. In the desolations left of a destroyed Babylon or other nation, jackals or hyenas prowl about and make their home (Isa. 13:22; 34:14; Jer. 50:39).

339. אִי *'iy:* A masculine noun meaning island or coastland. It depicts the Phoenicians as a coastland (Isa. 20:6; 23:2, 6). Distant islands or shores were designated by this word (Isa. 40:15). In general, the islands, shores, and coastlands of the Mediterranean Sea are indicated.

340. אָיַב *'āyaḇ:* A verb meaning to be an enemy. The Lord asserts that He will be an enemy to the enemy of His people, if His people serve Him (Ex. 23:22).

341. אֹיֵב *'ōyēḇ:* A masculine noun meaning enemy. It is the masculine singular participle of *'āyaḇ*. Its use is uniform, and it refers to all kinds of enemies: a personal enemy (Ex. 23:4); a national enemy (Gen. 22:17); an enemy of God (Ps. 8:2[3]). But God can become the declared enemy of a rebellious people (Isa. 63:10).

342. אֵיבָה *'ēyḇāh:* A feminine noun meaning hostility, animosity, or ill will. It is used to signify acrimony, as between the woman and the serpent (Gen. 3:15); malice that leads to violent acts against another (Num. 35:21); and the lingering hatred between mortal enemies (Ezek. 25:15; 35:5).

343. אֵיד *'ēyḏ:* A masculine noun meaning calamity or disaster. The word refers to a time of trouble when a person is in special need of help (Prov. 27:10); a calamity so severe that men and women should not rejoice or take selfish advantage of those whom the disaster renders helpless before God (Job 31:23; Prov. 17:5; Obad. 1:13). The calamity may result from a deliberate violation of principles (Prov. 1:26) or a more explicit judgment of God (Jer. 18:17). It may even befall a righteous person (2 Sam. 22:19; Ps. 18:18[19]).

344. אַיָּה ***'ayyāh:*** A feminine noun indicating a black kite or falcon. These birds cannot be eaten; they are unclean (Lev. 11:14; Deut. 14:13). They were known for their keen sight (Job 28:7).

345. אַיָּה ***'ayyāh:*** A proper noun designating Aiah:

A. A son of Zibeon (Gen. 36:24; 1 Chr. 1:40).

B. The father of Rizpah (2 Sam. 3:7; 21:8, 10, 11).

346. אַיֵּה ***'ayyēh:*** An adverb indicating where. Its rendering is uniformly, "Where?" (Gen. 18:9; Ex. 2:20; Job 14:10). Combined with *'ēpô'*, it means, "Where then?" (Judg. 9:38). It is used to posit a theological question about God (2 Kgs. 2:14) or His word (Jer. 17:15).

347. אִיּוֹב ***'iyyôḇ:*** A proper noun designating Job. He is the central character of the Book of Job and is the object of testing. By the Lord's permission Satan ("adversary") was permitted to test Job to the limit twice: (1) Job lost all his worldly possessions, riches, and family—yet remained faithful to God; (2) God permitted Satan to afflict Job sorely, almost unto death—yet again Job submitted to the mysterious will of God concerning his suffering (Job 40:1–5; 42:1–6). Even his friends forsook him in his suffering. Job was a non-Israelite of great value in God's eyes who said that Job was blameless, upright, God-fearing, and one who resisted evil (Job 1:1). He was considered a wise man as well. His wealth was legendary (Job 1:1–3). The location of the land of Uz is uncertain, but possibly it was east of Edom (Jer. 25:2; Lam. 4:21). Job is mentioned in the New Testament (Jas. 5:11) and in Ezekiel 14:14, 20 as a wise and righteous man.

348. אִיזֶבֶל ***'iyzeḇel:*** A proper noun designating Jezebel. She was a Sidonian princess who married the Israelite king Ahab. Her father was Ethbaal, king of Tyre and a priest of Baal. She introduced Tyrian Baal worship in Israel and promoted and fostered the priests of Baal (1 Kgs. 16:31). She killed the many prophets of the Lord (1 Kgs. 18:4). She attempted to kill Elijah ("the Lord is God") (1 Kgs. 19:1). She arranged to have Naboth killed (1 Kgs. 21:5–25). Elijah condemned her, and the Lord appointed Jehu to eradicate her and her family from Israel (2 Kgs. 9:6–10; 22–37). She was the queen mother for ten or more years after Ahab died. She died at Jehu's hand in ca. 842 B.C. She is mentioned as a negative symbol of a false prophet in the New Testament (Rev. 2:20).

349. **אֵיךְ** ***'ēyk̲,*** **אֵיכָה** ***'ēyk̲āh,*** **אֵיכָכָה** ***'ēyk̲āk̲āh:*** I. An interrogative adverb meaning How? How! It is translated this way uniformly, but its connotation can be slightly different according to context. It can hint or connote doubt (Gen. 44:8); reproach (Judg. 16:15); mourning (2 Sam. 1:19); assertiveness (Jer. 3:19).

II. An interrogative adverb asking How? How! It is translated uniformly but connotes different shades of meaning. It connotes what? (2 Kgs. 6:15). It functions rhetorically (Deut. 1:12). It further expresses mourning, reproach, where (Isa. 1:21; Jer. 8:8). It functions in some cases as a technical literary word introducing a dirge (Isa. 1:21).

III. This interrogative adverb means, "How?" It is found twice in the Old Testament. It indicates a psychological impossibility (Esth. 8:6; Song 5:3).

350. **אִי־כָבוֹד** ***'iy-k̲āb̲ôd̲:*** A proper noun designating Ichabod. It is the name of the son born of Phinehas, son of Eli, high priest in Israel (1 Sam. 4:21). The name means "the glory has departed," referring to the capture of the ark of God by the Philistines. He was the uncle of Ahijah, the son of his brother Ahitub (1 Sam. 14:3).

351. **אֵיכֹה** ***'ēyk̲ōh:*** An adverb meaning where. It functions as an interrogative (2 Kgs. 6:13) for the whereabouts of Elisha.

352. **אַיִל** ***'ayil:*** I. A masculine noun meaning ram. It is used in general of the rams of sacrifice, the most famous one being the ram God Himself provided in place of Isaac (Gen. 22:13).

II. A masculine noun indicating a gatepost or lintel. It refers to doorposts (1 Kgs. 6:31). It is translated as side pillars as well (NASB, Ezek. 40:9, 10, 16).

III. A masculine noun meaning leader or mighty man, i.e., a strong pillar or post for others to look to. It has this meaning many times. The leaders or mighty men in Moab are described figuratively with this word. It describes the leading men of Israel (2 Kgs. 24:15) or of the nations (Ps. 58:1[2]).

IV. A masculine noun referring to an oak tree or terebinth tree. This sacred fertility tree was associated with pagan worship (Isa. 1:29; 57:5). God's faithful people should rather be oaks of righteousness (NASB, Isa. 61:3). It can refer to especially strong or huge trees (Ezek. 31:14).

353. **אֱיָל** ***'eyāl:*** A masculine noun meaning strength. It refers to strength or energy in Psalm 88:4[5].

354. **אַיָּל** ***'ayyāl:*** A masculine noun meaning deer, hart. It was lawful for the Israelites to slay and eat (Deut. 12:15, 22; 1 Kgs. 4:23[5:3]) this animal. In a beautiful simile, the deer longs for the water brooks as the human soul longs for God (Ps. 42:1[2]). It refers to the beloved in

Song of Solomon 2:9, 17 (NKJV, NIV, NASB, gazelle).

355. אַיָּלָה ***'ayyālāh:*** A feminine noun indicating a doe or female deer. It refers to the beloved in Song of Solomon 2:7; 3:5. Jacob prophesies that Naphtali is a deer let free (Gen. 49:21). The feet of the deer are used as a symbol of swiftness (2 Sam. 22:34; Ps. 18:33[34]; Hab. 3:19). The birth period of the deer was a mystery (Job 39:1), one of the secrets of God.

356. אֵלֹון ***'ēlôn,*** אֵילֹון ***'ēylôn:*** A proper noun designating Elon. The name refers to several different persons:

A. The son of Zebulun by Leah (Gen. 46:14) in Paddan Aram. He headed up a family clan (Num. 26:26).

B. The name of Esau's father-in-law (Gen. 26:34). Elon was a Hittite, a fact that grieved Isaac and Rebekah (Gen. 36:2).

C. A judge/deliverer in Israel raised up by the Lord to lead Israel for ten years. He was from the tribe of Zebulun (Judg. 12:11, 12).

D. A town in the territory allotted to the tribe of Dan (Judg. 19:43; 1 Kgs. 4:9). It was in the coastal area east of Joppa.

357. אַיָּלֹון ***'ayyālôn,*** אַיָלֹון ***'ayālôn:*** A proper noun designating Aijalon. The name refers to two different cities:

A. A city in the territory of Dan (Josh. 19:42) but was not captured by Dan (Judg. 1:35). It was a levitical city (Josh. 21:24), a place where both people of Benjamin and Ephraim lived. It was reinforced by Solomon's son Rehoboam (2 Chr. 11:10). Later, Philistines captured it (2 Chr. 28:18).

B. A city in Zebulun as well (Judg. 12:12). Elon, a judge, was buried in it. Its exact location is unclear.

358. אֵילֹון בֵּית חָנָן ***'ēylôn bēyt ḥānān:*** A proper noun designating Elon Bethhanan (1 Kgs. 4:9), the full name for the city of Elon (356,D).

359. אֵילַת ***'ēylat,*** אֵילֹות ***'ēylôt:*** A proper noun designating Elath (Deut. 2:8; 1 Kgs. 9:26; 2 Kgs. 14:22; 16:6; 2 Chr. 8:17; 26:2).

360. אֱיָלוּת ***'eyālût:*** A feminine abstract noun meaning strength or help. The psalmist pleas that the Lord would be his strength (NASB, help, Ps. 22:19[20]).

361. אֵילָם ***'ēylām:*** A masculine noun indicating a vestibule, porch, or portico. It is used fourteen times in Ezekiel to refer to the portico of the gates of the new temple complex (NKJV, archway(s) often, Ezek. 40:16, 21, 22, 24–26).

362. אֵילִם ***'ēylim:*** A proper noun designating Elim (Ex. 15:27; 16:1; Num. 33:9, 10).

363. אִילָן ***'iylān:*** An Aramaic masculine noun meaning tree. It refers to the huge, powerful tree depicted in Daniel (4:10[7], 11[8], 14[11], 20[17]) which symbolizes the kingdom of Babylon and its king and to God's provision for the whole earth.

364. אֵיל פָּארָן *'ēyl pā'rān:* A proper noun designating El Paran (Gen. 14:6).

365. אַיֶּלֶת *'ayyeleṯ:* I. A feminine noun meaning doe of a fallow deer. The feminine of *'ayyāl*. It is used metaphorically to refer to the wife of one's youth (Prov. 5:19).

II. A proper noun designating Aijeleth (Ps. 22:title[1]).

366. אָיֹם *'āyōm:* An adjective meaning terrible, horrible, dreadful, awesome. It means awesome in an amorous setting (NASB) in Song of Solomon 6:4, 10 (NIV, majestic). It depicts a dreadful or terrible people in Habakkuk 1:7.

367. אֵימָה *'ēymāh:* A feminine noun meaning fear, terror, dread, or horror. The basic meaning is that of fear. It is used to signify the dread of the darkness that fell on Abraham (Gen. 15:12); a fear of hostile opponents (Josh. 2:9; Ezra 3:3); the terror of the Lord's judgment (Ex. 15:16; 23:27; Job 9:34); dread of the wrath of an earthly king (Prov. 20:2); something fierce or fearsome (Job 39:20). In a metaphorical sense, it refers once to pagan idols (Jer. 50:38).

368. אֵימִים *'ēymiym:* A masculine proper noun referring to the Emim, Emites. These people lived in Shaveh-kiriathaim (Gen. 14:5). They are described as an ancient people by the author of Deuteronomy. They no longer existed as a people in the author's day but had been great, numerous, and as tall as the giants, the Anakim. They were also known by some as Rephaim (Deut. 2:10, 11).

369. אַיִן *'ayin:* A particle or semi-verb of negation or nonexistence meaning no, none, nothing. It is used hundreds of times with various negative nuances. It can simply negate something (Ex. 17:7; Ps. 135:17) or assert that something is as nothing in comparison (Isa. 40:17). Used with the preposition *l^e*, it indicates nonpossession (Gen. 11:30; Prov. 13:7; Isa. 27:4; Hos. 10:3). It refers to the lack of a successor (Dan. 9:26). It indicates those who lack strength or power (Isa. 40:29, *ûl^e'ēyn 'ōniym*). When used with an infinitive, it negates the thought of the infinitive (Ps. 32:9). When the preposition *l^e* is added to the negated infinitive (*'eyn* + *l^e* + inf.), it gives the meaning not to permit + the meaning of the particular infinitive (Esth. 4:2). The antonym of *'ayin* is *yeš*, there is, are.

370. אַיִן *'ayin:* An adverb meaning where. It is always connected to *min* (4480), from, and it means from where (Gen. 29:4; 42:7; Num. 11:13). It is used in an indirect question, as in Joshua 2:4 on the lips of Rahab.

371. אִין *'iyn:* This is a negative adverb and may be an alternative form or irregular form for *'ayin* in the construct form. It is found only in 1 Samuel 21:8[9]. The NASB renders it as "is there not" (so also, NKJV, KJV, NIV).

372. אִיעֶזֶר ***'iy'ezer:*** A proper noun designating Iezer (Num. 26:30), a form of Abiezer (44,A).

373. אִיעֶזְרִי ***'iy'ezriy:*** A proper noun designating Iezerite (Num. 26:30).

374. אֵיפָה ***'ēypāh,*** אֵפָה ***'ēpāh:*** A feminine noun of measurement transliterated as ephah. An ephah was a dry measurement and equaled ten omers (Ex. 16:36). The ephah equaled three-fifths of a bushel or in metric measure, twenty-two liters. The omer was two quarts or about two liters. The ephah was a measure used often when preparing sacrificial offerings or foods (Lev. 5:11; 6:20[13]; Num. 5:15; 28:5; Judg. 6:19; 1 Sam. 17:17). It is especially prominent in the sacrificial practices of the new temple vision of Ezekiel (45:10, 11, 13, 24; 46:5, 7, 11, 14). Israel was to keep honest measures as a part of her righteousness. Micah observes that in her rebellious and unrighteous practices, Israel had shortened her ephah (Mic. 6:10). The business practices of God's people were to be based on true weights and measures in the marketplace.

375. אֵיפֹה ***'eypōh:*** An adverb meaning where. It is rendered uniformly as where. It is employed in direct questions (1 Sam. 19:22) and indirect questions (Gen. 37:16). In Judges it means what kind (8:18), "What kind of men?"

376. אִישׁ ***'iyš:*** A masculine noun meaning a man or an individual. It is also used to mean male or husband. This word does not indicate humankind but the male gender in particular. Its feminine counterpart is a woman or wife. In Hosea 2:16[18], this word describes God's special relationship to Israel. He will be their protective husband, not their master. Curiously, the word is also used of animals (Gen. 7:2), referring to a male and his mate.

377. אִישׁ ***'iyš,*** אָשַׁשׁ ***'āšaš:*** I. A verbal root meaning to show oneself a man, to be strong, firm. It is employed in a reflexive form in the text. It is used in Isaiah 46:8 to mean show yourselves men (NKJV, KJV). It is nuanced to mean fix it in mind (NIV) or be assured (NASB). See אִישׁ II.

II. A verb stem meaning to fix in mind (NIV) or to be assured (NASB). It is debatable whether two separate verbal roots are spelled *'iyš* or whether one root has a semantic range covering a larger range of meaning than was earlier thought. It is translated as to fix in mind (NIV) or be assured (NASB) in Isaiah 46:8. The KJV and NKJV render it as to show oneself a man, to be brave and courageous.

378. אִישׁ בֹּשֶׁת ***'iyš bōšet:*** A proper noun designating Ish-Bosheth. The name means "man of shame." It refers to Ish-Bosheth, one of Saul's sons whom Abner put forth as king against David after Saul's death (2 Sam. 2:8, 10, 12, 15). He later offended Abner (2 Sam. 3:8) and was killed (2 Sam. 4:5, 8, 12). David avenged his death by executing his assassins.

379. אִשְׁהוֹד ***'iyšhôd:*** A proper noun designating Ishhod (1 Chr. 7:18).

380. אִישׁוֹן ***'iyšôn,*** אֱשׁוּן ***'ešûn:*** I. A masculine noun meaning pupil or apple of the eye. The eye or pupil of the eye was considered a vital part of life (Prov. 20:20), the lamp or light of life. Israel is depicted lovingly and caringly as the pupil of the Lord's eye (Deut. 32:10). The psalmist cries out for the Lord to consider him as the apple of His eye (Ps. 17:8). Wisdom is to be the apple of the eye of the wise person (Prov. 7:2).

II. A masculine noun indicating the approach of darkness or time of twilight. It describes twilight as the time when harlots go forth to ply their trades (Prov. 7:9).

381. אִישׁ־חַיִל ***'iyš-ḥayil:*** A masculine noun meaning valiant man (1 Sam. 31:12; 2 Sam. 23:20; 24:9; 1 Kgs. 1:42).

382. אִישׁ־טוֹב ***'iyš-ṭôḇ,*** אִישׁ טוֹב ***'iyš ṭôḇ:*** I. Translated by the KJV as the proper name Ish-tob (2 Sam. 10:6, 8).

II. Translated in other versions as the men of Tob, *'iyš* (376) and *ṭôḇ* (2897) (2 Sam. 10:6, 8).

383. אִיתַי ***'iṯay:*** An Aramaic particle meaning there is, there are. It makes an assertion of existence (Dan. 2:28, 30). It is used with *hēn* preceding it to mean whether it is, thus forming a conditional sentence (Ezra 5:17). It can serve as a verb meaning be when placed before a participle or adjective (Dan. 3:17). Compare to Hebrew *yēš* (3426).

384. אִיתִיאֵל ***'iytiy'ēl:*** A proper noun designating Ithiel:

A. A person instructed by Agur (Prov. 30:1).

B. A Benjamite (Neh. 11:7).

385. אִיתָמָר ***'iyṯāmār:*** A proper noun designating Ithamar. He was Aaron's youngest son (Ex. 6:23; Num. 3:2) who served in the newly established priesthood (Ex. 28:1). He was involved in building the Tabernacle and keeping records about it (Ex. 38:21). He was present when Nadab and Abihu were killed (Lev. 10:6–16). He directed the work of the Merarites and Gershonites as they cared for the wagons transporting the Tabernacle (Num. 7:8). One of his descendants, Daniel, returned from the Babylonian Exile under Ezra (8:2).

386. אֵיתָן ***'ēytān:*** A masculine noun indicating strength, permanence, endurance. Figuratively, it describes the usual, constant position of a stream or sea (Ex. 14:27). It indicates the ancient, enduring feature of a nation, such as Babylon (Jer. 5:15).

Literally, it depicts the perennial (constant) watering of a pasture (Jer. 49:19) or the flooding or overflow of a dry river bed (wadi, Deut. 21:4). Used as a noun, it envisions constant overflowing streams (Ps. 74:15).

387. אֵיתָן *'ēyṯān:* A proper noun designating Ethan (1 Kgs. 4:31[5:11]; 1 Chr. 2:6, 8; 6:42[27], 44[29]; 15:17, 19; Ps. 89:title[1]).

388. אֵיתָנִים *'eṯāniym:* A proper noun designating Ethanim, the seventh month in Israel. Solomon dedicated the Temple during this month (1 Kgs. 8:2). It was later named Tishri (September–October).

389. אַךְ *'aḵ:* A particle meaning only, surely, but. Its emphatic use is translated as indeed or surely (Gen. 26:9; 29:14; 1 Kgs. 22:32; Jer. 5:4). It takes on a restrictive meaning and is translated as only (Gen. 7:23; 9:4, NASB) or just as (Gen. 27:13; Judg. 10:15, NASB). Its contrastive sense, but, however, or nevertheless, is also found (Jer. 34:4, NASB).

390. אַכַּד *'akkaḏ:* A proper noun designating Akkad (Gen. 10:10).

391. אַכְזָב *'aḵzāḇ:* An adjective meaning lying, deceptive. It indicates what is not expected, such as a stream that promises water but has none (Jer. 15:18). It is used in a powerful wordplay depicting the city Aczib as a city of deception that will dry up (Mic. 1:14).

392. אַכְזִיב *'aḵziyḇ:* A proper noun designating Achzib:
A. A lowland in Judah (Josh. 15:44; Mic. 1:14).
B. A lowland in Asher (Josh. 19:29; Judg. 1:31).

393. אַכְזָר *'aḵzār:* An adjective meaning cruel or deadly. It refers to the deadly or cruel venom of cobras (Deut. 32:33). Job calls God's actions toward him cruel (Job 30:21), and God accuses His own people of being cruel (Lam. 4:3). It is rendered fierce to describe Leviathan (NASB, NKJV, KJV, NIV, Job 41:10[2]).

394. אַכְזָרִי *'aḵzāriy:* An adjective meaning cruel. It refers to persons (Prov. 5:9; 11:17; 12:10) whose cruelty is often contrasted to the person who is merciful or righteous. It refers to the cruel day of the Lord (Isa. 13:9) which features the savages of the cruel warriors of Babylon (Jer. 6:23; 30:14; 50:42).

395. אַכְזְרִיּוּת *'aḵz^{e}riyyût:* A feminine abstract noun indicating cruelty, fierceness. The word is used to describe wrath or anger (Prov. 27:4).

396. אֲכִילָה *ᵃḵiylāh:* A feminine noun meaning food or meal. It refers to the food Elijah ate or to the eating of a meal (1 Kgs. 19:8).

397. אָכִישׁ *'āḵiyš:* A proper noun designating Achish. He was the king of Gath, son of Maoch (1 Sam. 27:2), to whom David fled when Saul was pursuing him (1 Sam. 21:10[11]).

David feigned madness, and Achish let him be (1 Sam. 21:12–14[13–15]). Achish used David to carry out raids (1 Sam. 27:8–12), even making him his bodyguard (1 Sam. 28:2). However, the Philistine officers distrusted him and would not let David go with them on raids (1 Sam. 29:2–11). Achish was saddened by this turn of events.

398. אָכַל *'āḵal:* A verb meaning to eat, devour, consume. This word has many uses. It is used of humans most often (Gen. 3:6, 11, 18; Ex. 16:35; 34:15; Ruth 2:14). It also means to eat a meal (Gen. 43:25; Ex. 2:20). It is used frequently in a cultic setting. To eat before the Lord is mentioned in the context of offering sacrifice (Deut. 12:7). The burnt offering was consumed by fire into ashes (Lev. 6:10[3]). It is used to describe the feeding of birds or animals and translated often as devour, eat, consume (Gen. 37:20, 33; 1 Kgs. 13:28; 14:11). It describes the feeding of locusts (Joel 1:4; 2:25); moths (Job 13:28); flies (Ps. 78:45); worms (Deut. 28:39).

It is regularly used in a metaphorical sense describing the activity of fire that consumes or devours (Lev. 6:10[3]; Nah. 3:13). The Lord is pictured as a consuming fire of judgment (Deut. 4:24). It describes the action of a consuming sword (Deut. 32:42; 2 Sam. 2:26). It depicts the consuming oppression of the poor (Prov. 30:14; Hab. 3:14). The passive use of *'āḵal* means to be eaten, devoured (Ex. 12:46; Zech. 9:4), or consumed (Neh. 2:3, 13; Isa. 1:20). A causal use of the verb means to cause to eat or feed (Ex. 16:32; Deut. 8:3, 16; 1 Kgs. 22:27).

The word is used in some idioms; one means to eat up space, that is, to lay claim to space (Ezek. 42:5). It refers to the act of an adulterous woman with regard to the sex act (Prov. 30:20), to enjoy love.

399. אֲכַל *'aḵal:* I. An Aramaic verb meaning to eat, consume, or devour. It describes Nebuchadnezzar's devouring grass like an ox (Dan. 4:33[30]) and the voracious acts of destruction enacted by the beasts of Daniel (7:5, 7, 19, 23).

II. Possibly another Aramaic verb meaning to slander. The word is best translated as slander (Dan. 3:8; 6:24[25]). It means literally "to eat their pieces" (3:8) or "to eat/crush their bones" (6:24[25]). It is likely the same as I, but used in an idiomatic phrase.

400. אֹכֶל *'ōḵel:* A masculine noun meaning good. Its use is uniform, but it refers to food for all kinds of living things: humans (Gen. 14:11) and animals (Ps. 104:21, 27). The phrase *'āśa' 'ōḵel* means to make food (Hab. 3:17). *'Ēṯ 'ōkel* indicates mealtime (Ruth 2:14). It refers to flesh (Ps. 78:18, 30; 104:21) as well as to the prey or food of eagles (Job 9:26; 39:29) or wild animals (Ps. 104:21). It is used to modify the store (food) cities where grain was kept (Gen. 41:35; 47:24).

401. אֻכָּל *'ukkāl:* A proper noun designating Ucal (Prov. 30:1).

402. אָכְלָה *'oklāh:* A feminine noun meaning food or that which is eaten (Gen. 9:3; Ex. 16:15; Lev. 25:6; Jer. 12:9; Ezek. 21:32[37]).

403. אָכֵן *'ākēn:* An adverb meaning surely, truly, or yet. It basically gives expression to something or some situation that was unexpected. Jacob was surprised to find the Lord's presence where he had slept (Gen. 28:16), and Moses was amazed to find that Pharaoh knew of his killing an Egyptian (Ex. 2:14; cf. 1 Sam. 15:32). It is used to show contrast with what was expected. Against all odds, the servant of the Lord would receive from the Lord (Isa. 49:4). This use is found several times after the verb to say, *'āmartiy* (Isa. 49:4; 53:4; Jer. 3:20; Zeph. 3:7).

404. אָכַף *'ākap:* A verb meaning to crave, to urge. It depicts the drive or urge to work that hunger creates in the laborer (Prov. 16:26).

405. אֶכֶף *'ekep:* A masculine noun meaning hard, pressure. The NASB translates the Hebrew word as pressure in Job 33:7, while others render the word as hand (NKJV, KJV, NIV) using the Greek translation (LXX) as their source.

406. אִכָּר *'ikār:* A masculine noun meaning plowman or farmworker. The workers labored in the fields (2 Chr. 26:10; Jer. 14:4) as a regular feature of Israel's agricultural community (Jer. 31:24). The farmers would be an important group affected by the judgments of the Lord (Isa. 61:5; Jer. 51:23; Joel 1:11; Amos 5:16).

407. אַכְשָׁף *'akšāp:* A proper noun designating Achshaph (Josh. 11:1; 12:20; 19:25).

408. אַל *'al:* An adverb meaning no, not, without; a basic adverb of negation. It is used consistently with the imperfect form of the verb to render a negative imperative or prohibition (Gen. 15:1; 22:12; 37:27; Ps. 25:2; Jer. 18:18). With the regular imperative, it expresses purpose, such as, that we may not die (1 Sam. 12:19). In poetic sections, it may express the poet's strong emotions (Job 5:22; Ps. 41:2[3]; Prov. 3:25; Isa. 2:9). It is also used without a verb to express simple negation in an imperative mode, as in *'al-ṭal,* let there be no dew (2 Sam. 1:21). It can have the meaning of there is no (Prov. 12:28), i.e., there is no death. It can also function as a noun + l^e meaning something comes to naught, nothing (Job 24:25). Coupled with the particle *nā',* it means please do not or therefore, do not (Gen. 18:3).

409. אַל *'al:* An Aramaic adverb of prohibition meaning do not, let not. It is used as a prohibition in Daniel (2:24; 4:19[16]; 5:10).

410. אֵל *'ēl:* A masculine noun meaning God, god, mighty one, hero. This is one of the most ancient terms for God, god, or deity. It appears most often in Genesis, Job, Psalms, and Isaiah and not at all in some books. The root meaning of the word mighty can be seen in Job 41:25[17] and Micah 2:1. This word is used occasionally of other gods (Ex. 34:14; Deut. 3:24; Ps. 44:20[21]; Mal. 2:11) but is most often used to mean the one true God (Ps. 5:4[5]; Isa. 40:18). It expresses various ideas of deity according to its context. The most common may be noted briefly: the holy God as contrasted to humans (Hos. 11:9); the High God El (Gen. 14:18; 16:13; Ezek. 28:2); the Lord (Yahweh) as a title of Israel according to the Lord's own claim (Gen. 33:20; Isa. 40:18); God or god in general (Ex. 34:14; Deut. 32:21; Mic. 7:8); the God of Israel, the Lord (Num. 23:8; Ps. 118:27); God (Job 5:8).

This word is used with various descriptive adjectives or attributes: *'ēl* is God of gods (Ps. 50:1); God of Bethel (Gen. 35:7); a forgiving God (Ps. 99:8). He is the holy God (Isa. 5:16). Especially significant are the assertions declaring that *'ēl* is with us, Immanuel (Isa. 7:14); and He is the God of our salvation (Isa. 12:2); a gracious God (Neh. 9:31); a jealous God (Ex. 20:5; 34:14). The closeness of this God is expressed in the hand of God (Job 27:11).

In the human realm, the word also designates men of power or high rank (Ezek. 31:11); mighty men (Job 41:25[17]); or mighty warriors (Ezek. 32:21). The word is used to designate superior and mighty things in nature, such as mighty or high mountains (Ps. 36:6[7]), lofty, high cedars, or stars (Ps. 80:10[11]; Isa. 14:13).

In conjunction with other descriptive words, it occurs as *'ēl šaday*, "God Almighty" (7706) (Gen. 17:1; 28:3; Ex. 6:3) or *'ēl 'elyôn*, "God Most High" (5945) (Gen. 14:18, 19; Ps. 78:35). Used with hand (*yād*) in some settings, the word conveys power, strength (Gen. 31:29; Deut. 28:32; Prov. 3:27), or ability.

411. אֵל ***'ēl:*** This is used in the plural as a masculine or feminine demonstrative pronoun meaning these, those. It is found five times and translated uniformly (Gen. 19:8, 25; Deut. 4:42; 1 Chr. 20:8).

412. אֵל ***'ēl:*** An Aramaic plural noun meaning these. It is found in Ezra 5:15 referring to articles of the temple.

413. אֶל ***'ēl,*** אֶל ***'el:*** A preposition meaning to, into, concerning. It has the basic meaning of toward. It is used in all kinds of situations indicating direction (Gen. 2:19; 16:11; 18:7; Lev. 1:16). It is used metaphorically to refer to speaking to someone (Gen. 8:15) or sexual intercourse (Gen. 16:2; Num. 25:1). It indicates direction when things face each other (Num. 12:8). Its use in the idiom *hinn*e*ni 'ēl* indicates motion toward (Gen. 4:8). Other meanings according to context are: as far as (Jer. 51:9); into (Jon. 1:5); to sit at (Gen. 24:11; 1 Kgs. 13:20). Used figuratively, it can mean with regard to something (2 Sam. 1:24). When used with other prepositions, it indicates direction or location according to the preposition it is being combined with (Josh. 15:13; 17:4; 1 Kgs. 8:6; 2 Kgs. 9:18).

It is used in place of or interchangeably for the preposition *'al* and takes on the meaning of upon, on (Josh. 5:14; Judg. 6:37).

414. אֵלָא *'ēlā':* A proper noun designating Ela (1 Kgs. 4:18).

415. אֵל אֱלֹהֵי יִשְׂרָאֵל *'ēl *ᵉ*lōhey yisrā'ēl:* A proper noun designating El Elohe Israel, a name given to the Lord as the "God, the (true) God of Israel" where Jacob set up an altar to him at Shechem, thus identifying also with the God of his fathers (Gen. 22:19–20).

416. אֵל בֵּית אֵל *'ēl bēyṯ 'ēl:* A proper noun designating El Bethel (Gen. 35:7).

417. אֶלְגָּבִישׁ *'elgāḇiyš:* A masculine noun meaning hailstone. It is used only in Ezekiel (13:11, 13; 38:22) where it is a feature of God's judgment upon the inferior work of the false prophets.

418. אַלְגּוּמִּים *'algûmmiym:* A masculine plural noun for algum wood, algum trees or logs. These items were obtained by Solomon from Lebanon for use in constructing the Temple (2 Chr. 2:8[7]; 9:10, 11).

419. אֶלְדָּד *'eldāḏ:* A proper noun designating Eldad (Num. 11:26, 27).

420. אֶלְדָּעָה *'eldā'āh:* A proper noun designating Eldaah (Gen. 25:4; 1 Chr. 1:33).

421. אָלָה *'ālāh:* A verb meaning to lament or to wail. It is used in Joel 1:8 to depict the mournful lament that needs to be made because of the coming devastation of the day of the Lord.

422. אָלָה *'ālāh:* A verb meaning to curse, to put under oath. It is used in many cases of persons bringing curses on themselves if they are guilty of doing wrong (Judg. 17:2). Similarly, *'ālāh* is used to prove someone's guilt or innocence. The person is guilty if the curse occurs but is innocent if the curse does not occur (1 Kgs. 8:31; 2 Chr. 6:22). In 1 Samuel 14:24, the word is used to put someone under an oath. In Hosea, the word refers to a curse placed on a person who makes a covenant or treaty and does not keep his word (Hos. 10:4).

423. אָלָה *'ālāh:* A feminine noun meaning an oath, a sworn covenant, or a curse. The word signifies an oath to testify truthfully (Lev. 5:1; 1 Kgs. 8:31); a sworn covenant, bearing a curse if violated (Deut. 29:19; Neh. 10:29[30]); a curse from God for covenant violations (Deut. 29:20; 2 Chr. 34:24; Dan. 9:11); God's judgment on sin (Deut. 30:7; Isa. 24:6; Zech. 5:3); and that which is accursed because of unfaithfulness, such as an adulterous wife or the erring tribe of Judah (Num. 5:27; Jer. 29:18; 42:18; 44:12).

424. אֵלָה *'ēlāh:* A feminine noun referring to an oak tree or terebinth tree. This was a mighty tree often connected to a cultic setting or activity (Gen. 35:4; 1 Kgs. 13:14; Ezek. 6:13). The angel of the Lord came to it (Judg. 6:11), and Gideon served food under the tree. Absalom's hair caught in one of these trees (2 Sam. 18:9, 10, 14) and led to his death. Saul and his sons were buried under an oak (1 Chr. 10:12). Israel is likened to an oak with falling leaves (Isa. 1:30; cf. 6:13).

425. אֵלָה *'ēlāh:* A proper noun designating Elah. The name means "terebinth" or "oak." It is given to persons or things in the Old Testament:

A. It refers to the head of a clan in Edom (Gen. 36:41; 1 Chr. 1:52). He was a descendant of Esau (Gen. 36:40).

B. It refers to the valley where David slew Goliath (1 Sam. 17:2, 19; 21:9[10]). It corresponds to Wadi es-Sant located 18 miles southwest of Jerusalem. Warring armies could speak to each other across the valley.

C. It designates a son of Baasha, fourth king in Israel (1 Kgs. 16:6, 8, 13, 14). He reigned two years in Tirzah. He is condemned by the biblical writer and pictured as a corrupt, carousing king. Zimri assassinated him (1 Sam. 6:10).

D. It refers to the father of Hoshea, Elah (2 Kgs. 15:30; 17:1; 18:1, 9). He was the last king in Israel and was a puppet king, most likely, to the great Assyrian king Tiglath-pileser III. He reigned 732–722 B.C.

E. The name of a son of Caleb. He also bore a son named Kenaz (1 Chr. 4:15).

F. He was the son of a Benjamite named Uzzi who was a leader or chief of an Israelite tribe (1 Chr. 9:8). He resettled in Judah after the Babylonian Exile (1 Chr. 9:1–2).

426. אֱלָהּ *'elāh:* An Aramaic masculine noun meaning deity, divinity. This word can be used in a general sense to indicate a god (Dan. 3:15) or gods (Dan. 2:11; 3:12, 18, 25). In a specific sense, it signifies the God of Israel, namely, Yahweh (Ezra 5:1, 2, 8; 6:14; 7:15; Dan. 2:20, 28; 3:17).

427. אַלָּה *'allāh:* A feminine noun indicating an oak tree or a terebinth tree. Cultic activity is recorded concerning this tree. Joshua set up a sacred stone under this tree as a witness to the renewed covenant at Shechem (24:26).

428. אֵלֶּה *'ēlleh:* A demonstrative pronoun or adjective meaning these. It usually refers to preceding items and functions as a demonstrative adjective (Gen. 6:9; 15:1; 2 Sam. 23:22). Referring to following items, it functions as a demonstrative pronoun meaning these are (Gen. 6:9; Deut. 27:12, 13; 1 Sam. 4:8).

429. אֵלֶּה *'ēlleh:* An Aramaic plural demonstrative adjective or pronoun meaning these. It refers to items for the temple (Ezra 5:15) and is used in a wordplay of irony concerning the heavens in Jeremiah 10:11.

430. אֱלֹהִים *'elōhiym:* A masculine plural noun meaning God, gods, judges, angels. Occurring more than 2, 600 times in the Old Testament, this word commonly designates the one true God (Gen. 1:1) and is often paired with God's unique name *yehōwāh* (3068) (Gen. 2:4; Ps. 100:3). When the word is used as the generic designation of God, it conveys in Scripture that God is the Creator (Gen. 5:1); the King (Ps. 47:7[8]); the Judge (Ps. 50:6); the Lord (Ps. 86:12); and the Savior (Hos. 13:4). His character is compassionate (Deut. 4:31); gracious (Ps. 116:5); and faithful to His covenant (Deut. 7:9). In fewer instances, this word refers to foreign gods, such as Dagon (1 Sam. 5:7) or Baal (1 Kgs. 18:24). It also might refer to judges (Ex. 22:8[7], 9[8]) or angels as gods (Ps. 97:7). Although the form of this word is plural, it is frequently used as if it were singular—that is, with a singular verb (Gen. 1:1–31; Ex. 2:24). The plural form of this word may be regarded (1) as intensive to indicate God's fullness of power; (2) as majestic to indicate God's kingly rule; or (3) as an allusion to the Trinity (Gen. 1:26). The singular form of this word *'elôah* (433) occurs only in poetry (Ps. 50:22; Isa. 44:8). The shortened form of the word is *'ēl* (410).

431. אֲלוּ *'alû:* An Aramaic interjection meaning behold! lo! It indicates surprise and amazement (Dan. 2:31; 4:10[7], 13[10]; 7:8). It is sometimes left untranslated or implied in the structure of the translation (cf. NIV, NKJV, 7:8).

432. אִלּוּ *'illû:* An interjection meaning but if, yea though. It makes a sentence assert a condition contrary to fact, "if . . ." (Esth. 7:4, NKJV, Had we been . . . ; cf. NASB, Now if we had only . . . ; Eccl. 6:6).

433. אֱלוֹהַּ *'elôah:* A masculine noun meaning god or God. It is thought by some to be the singular of the noun *'elōhiym* (430). This word is used of *yehōwāh* (3068) (Ps. 18:31 [32]) and, with a negative, to describe what is not God (Deut. 32:17). Most occurrences of this word are in the book of Job, where the speakers may not be Israelites and thus use other generic names for God (Job 3:4), of which this is one. It is used once in the name, "God of Jacob" (Ps. 114:7) and once in the phrase, "God of forgiveness" (Neh. 9:17).

434. אֱלוּל *'elûl:* A noun meaning a worthless thing, futility. It designates the deceptive production of false prophets spinning out futile, worthless things, idolatries (NIV) (Jer. 14:14).

435. אֱלוּל ***'ᵉlûl:*** A proper noun designating the month Elul (Neh. 6:15).

436. אֵלוֹן ***'ēlôn:*** A masculine noun meaning oak, great tree (Gen. 12:6; 13:18; 14:13; 18:1; Deut. 11:30; Judg. 4:11; 9:6, 37; 1 Sam. 10:3).

437. אַלּוֹן ***'allôn:*** A masculine noun indicating a great tree, oak. This tree marked the grave site of Deborah, Rebekah's nurse (Gen. 35:8), the oak of weeping (cf. Josh. 19:33; KJV, Allon [438], a proper noun). In the Prophets, it has several uses: it indicates illicit shrines (Hos. 4:13); materials for producing idols (Isa. 44:14); a symbol, i.e., a stump as a devastated Israel (Isa. 6:13). Elsewhere, it indicates strength (Isa. 2:13; Amos 2:9) or it serves as a metaphor for mighty or prominent men (Zech. 11:2).

438. אַלּוֹן ***'allôn:*** A proper noun designating Allon:

A. A city near Kadesh Naphtali (Josh 19:33).

B. The father of Shiphi (1 Chr. 4:37).

439. אַלּוֹן בָּכוּת ***'allôn bāḵûṯ:*** A proper noun designating Allon Bacuth (Gen. 35:8).

440. אֵלֹנִי ***'ēlôniy:*** A proper noun designating Elonite (Num. 26:26).

441. אַלּוּף ***'allûp̄***, אַלֻּף, ***'allup:*** An adjective meaning docile or a masculine noun meaning tame, friend, intimate, chief, captain. Even though the adjectival usage is rare, it is found in the well-known description, "Like a docile lamb to the slaughter" (Jer. 11:19). In the nominal form, this word connotes the closest of companions; such companions can be separated by a whisperer (Prov. 16:28). In another aspect, this term was used to describe a leader of a nation or group. Esau's descendants were listed as chiefs of Edom (Gen. 36:15).

442. אָלוּשׁ ***'ālûš:*** A proper noun designating Alush (Num. 33:13, 14).

443. אֶלְזָבָד ***'elzāḇāḏ:*** A proper noun designating Elzabad:

A. A Gadite (1 Chr. 12:12).

B. A Korahite (1 Chr. 26:7).

444. אָלַח ***'ālaḥ:*** A verb meaning to corrupt, be filthy morally. It describes humankind as corrupt and dependent on evil or iniquity as on water. This state of pollution is strong in the fool (Ps. 14:3) and the godless (Ps. 53:3), who are, in fact, in the same condition.

445. אֶלְחָנָן ***'elḥānān:*** A proper noun designating Elhanan:

A. A son of Jair (2 Sam. 21:19; 1 Chr. 20:5).

B. A son of Dodo (2 Sam. 23:24; 1 Chr. 11:26).

446. אֱלִיאָב ***'ᵉliy'āḇ:*** A proper noun designating Eliab. The name means "God is my father" or "God is father." It was given to several persons in the Old Testament:

A. It referred to a prince of the tribe of Zebulun at the time of the Exodus event (Num. 1:9, etc.). His father was Helon.

B. It depicts the father of Abiram and Dathan, who rebelled against Moses (Num. 16:12–14; 26:8–11) and were destroyed by the Lord. Eliab's father was Pallu (Num. 26:8).

C. It denotes David's oldest brother (1 Sam. 16:6). He despised David at times and considered David self-centered and self-seeking (1 Sam. 17:28). He had a daughter, Abihail. One of Rehoboam's wives was her daughter (2 Chr. 11:18).

D. A Kohathite bore the name. He was a descendant of Samuel (1 Chr. 6:27[12]; cf. Eliel, 1 Chr. 6:34; Elihu, 1 Sam. 1:1).

E. A Gadite bore the name. He was third in command of the Gadites who helped David during his flight from Saul (1 Chr. 12:8–9).

F. A Levitical singer bears the name. He was appointed as part of the worship leaders of the Levites (1 Chr. 15:18), playing the lyre (1 Chr. 15:20).

447. אֱלִיאֵל *ᵉliy'ēl:* A proper noun designating Eliel. The name means "my God is God" or "God is God"—the true God. It was given to several persons in the Old Testament.

A. He is listed as a Kohathite musician in 1 Chronicles 6:34[19], but see also Eliab (1 Chr. 6:27[12]; 1 Sam. 1:1).

B. He served as a family leader or head in Manasseh and was considered a famous man and great warrior (1 Chr. 5:24).

C. It refers to Eliel, a leader and son of Shimei (1 Chr. 8:20, 21), a descendant of Saul of the tribe of Benjamin.

D. It refers to a son of Shashak (1 Chr. 8:22, 25). He was also a leader in the tribe of Benjamin.

E. He was one of the mighty men of David's army (1 Chr. 11:46).

F. One of David's mighty men who did mighty deeds for the Lord and his chosen king (1 Chr. 11:47).

G. He was one of the Gadite warriors who defected from Saul to David and served as leaders (1 Chr. 12:11).

H. He is listed as the leader from Hebron, a descendant of Hebron, who helped David bring the ark to Jerusalem (1 Chr. 15:9, 11).

I. It designates a Levite who helped supervise the preparations of the Temple to receive offerings to its renovation (2 Chr. 31:13).

448. אֱלִיָּתָה *ᵉliyyāṯah*, אֱלִיאָתָה *ᵉliy'āṯah:* A proper noun designating Eliathah (1 Chr. 25:4, 27).

449. אֱלִדָּד *ᵉliḏāḏ:* A proper noun designating Elidad (Num. 34:21).

450. אֶלְיָדָע *'elyāḏā':* A proper noun designating Eliada:

A. A son of David (2 Sam. 5:16; 1 Chr. 3:8).

B. A Benjamite chief (2 Chr. 17:17).

C. An Aramite (1 Kgs. 11:23).

451. אַלְיָה *'alyāh:* A feminine noun describing the fat tail or rump of sheep. This portion of a sheep was used in the cultic sites of Israel. This part of the animal, along with other items, was involved in the wave offering before the Lord (Ex. 29:22; Lev. 8:25), the peace offering (Lev. 3:9), and the trespass offering (Lev. 7:3).

452. אֵלִיָּה *'ēliyyāh,* אֵלִיָּהוּ *'ēliyyāhû:* A proper noun designating Elijah, the name of four Israelites. It means "the Lord is God."

A. The major person is Elijah the Tishbite who was called by God to fight for Yahweh and to eradicate Baalism from Israel. His ministry extended from the time of Ahab (874–853 B.C.) into Jehoram's (2 Chr. 21:4–16). He became, in effect, the covenant prosecutor for the Lord. He challenged Ahab, Jezebel, and the prophets of Baal constantly to make them realize that the Lord is God.

The Lord cared for Elijah miraculously (1 Kgs. 17:1). Elijah called a famine on the land and announced its end (1 Kgs. 17:1–2; 18:16–46). The Lord encouraged him in times of depression (1 Kgs. 19:1–18). Elijah called Elisha, his successor (1 Kgs. 19:19–21). He condemned Ahab's seizing of Naboth's vineyard (1 Kgs. 21:17, 20, 28). He was taken up into the sky by a whirlwind (2 Kgs. 2:11–14). His return or a prophet like him was foretold by Malachi (4:5[3:23]).

B. It identifies a Benjamite (1 Chr. 8:27), a son of Jeroham.

C. It refers to an infamous priest who intermarried with a foreign woman (Ezra 10:21). He descended from Harim.

D. It indicates another unfortunate priest who intermarried with a foreign woman. He descended from Elam (Ezra 10:26).

453. אֱלִיהוּ *'ᵉliyhû,* אֱלִיהוּא *'ᵉliyhû':* A proper noun designating Elihu, which means "my God is He" or "He is God." It was used of the following persons:

A. Elihu is listed as the great-grandfather of Samuel (1 Sam. 1:1). But see also Eliab above. He was an Ephramite.

B. It depicts a military leader in Manasseh who defected to David when David was fleeing from Saul (1 Chr. 12:20).

C. It refers to the youngest speaker in the Book of Job who supposedly speaks "on God's behalf" angrily toward both Job and his other friends (Job 32:2–4). Some of his insights are correct, as he stresses the majesty and sovereignty of God.

D. It refers to a Kohathite who was a gatekeeper and a leader in the service of the Temple (1 Chr. 26:1, 7).

E. He was an officer placed over the tribe of Judah (1 Chr. 27:18), but he was also a brother of David's.

454. אֱלְיְהוֹעֵינַי *'elyᵉhôʿēynay,* אֶלְיוֹעֵינַי *'elyôʿēynay:* A proper noun designating Elioenai. This name means "the Lord, my eyes." It is used several times:

A. He was a gatekeeper at the Temple from the family of Korah, son of Mechelemiah (1 Chr. 26:3).

B. He was a family head or leader who returned from exile under Ezra during the reign of the Persian King Artaxerxes (458 B.C.) (Ezra 8:4).

C. He was a person in the royal line of David, lived after the Exile, and was a son of Neariah (1 Chr. 3:23, 24).

D. It refers to a son of Beker, a Benjamite. He was the leader of a family and/or a warrior (1 Chr. 7:8).

E. It refers to a descendant of Simeon and Shimei, and important family line (1 Chr. 4:36).

F. He was listed as one of the descendants of Pashur who intermarried with foreigners after the exile (Ezra 10:22).

G. He was listed as guilty of intermarriage with foreigners after the exile. He was a son of Zattu and in the priestly line (Ezra 10:22).

H. He was a priest who performed in the worship (choir?) at the second Temple under Nehemiah (Neh. 12:41).

455. אֱלְיַחְבָּא ***'elyaḥbā':*** A proper noun designating Eliahba (2 Sam. 23:32; 1 Chr. 11:33).

456. אֱלִיחֹרֶף ***'eliyḥōrep̱:*** A proper noun designating Elihoreph (1 Kgs. 4:3).

457. אֱלִיל ***'eliyl:*** A masculine noun meaning worthlessness. The term is frequently used to describe false gods and idols (Lev. 19:4; Ps. 96.5; Isa. 2:8; Hab. 2:18). Sometimes, this noun is used in a prepositional phrase, such as in Zechariah 11:17, where the Hebrew literally says "shepherd of worthlessness," and in Job 13:4, "physicians of worthlessness." In those verses, *'eliyl* functions as an adjective.

458. אֱלִימֶלֶךְ ***'eliymelek̲:*** A proper noun designating Elimelech (Ruth 1:2, 3; 2:1, 3; 4:3, 9).

459. אִלֵּין ***'illēyn:*** An Aramaic plural demonstrative pronoun or adjective meaning these, those. It is used only in Daniel meaning these or those (Dan. 2:40, 44; 6:2[3] 6[7]; 7:17).

460. אֶלְיָסָף ***'elyāsāp̱:*** A proper noun designating Eliasaph:

A. Chief of Gad (Num. 1:14; 2:14; 3:24; 7:42, 47; 10:20).

B. Chief of Gershon (Num. 3:24).

461. אֱלִיעֶזֶר ***'eliy'ezer:*** A proper noun designating Eliezer, which means "my God is help." It was applied to various persons in the Old Testament:

A. It designates Abraham's slave born in his household (Gen. 15:3) and, hence, Abraham's potential heir. He may be mentioned in Genesis 24:2. Isaac, of course, became the true heir.

B. One of Moses' sons, mentioned first in Exodus 18:4. He is quoted in 18:4 and listed in the genealogies of Chronicles (1 Chr. 23:15, 17; 26:25).

C. It refers to a Benjamite, a son of Becher (1 Chr. 7:8).

D. It identifies a Reubenite who was a son of Zichri. He was a leader in Reuben during David's reign (1 Chr. 27:16).

E. It is applied to a prophet in the reign of Jehoshaphat in Judah. He condemned the building of ships by the king and told of their destruction (1 Chr. 20:35–37).

F. It describes a priest who helped David bring the ark to Jerusalem from Obed-edom's home (1 Chr. 15:24).

G. It describes a leader under Ezra who helped gather Levites for temple worship (Ezra 8:16).

H. It refers to a priest under Ezra who had intermarried with foreign women (Ezra 10:18).

I. It describes a Levite who had intermarried with foreign women in Ezra's day (Ezra 10:23).

J. It refers to a son of Harim who had intermarried with foreign women in Ezra's day (Ezra 10:31).

462. אֱלִיעֵינַי *eliy'ēynay:* A proper noun designating Elienai (1 Chr. 8:20).

463. אֱלִיעָם *'eliy'ām:* A proper noun designating Eliam:

A. It describes the father of Bathsheba and means "God of (the) people." He is referred to as Ammiel also (1 Chr. 3:5, see entry 5988) by simply reversing the beginning and end of the Hebrew word, possibly a scribal error.

B. It also refers to one of David's thirty mighty men (2 Sam. 23:24). He was son of Ahithophel and possible the same person mentioned in A.

464. אֱלִיפַז *eliypaz:* A proper noun designating Eliphaz:

A. It refers to a son of Esau. He fathered five sons (Gen. 36:4, 10–12, 15, 16; 1 Chr. 1:35, 36) by his wife. He fathered a son by his concubine Tinna named Amalek (Gen. 36:12).

B. He was one of the outspoken and maligners of Job under the claim of helping Job and representing God (Job 2:11; 4:1; 15:1; 22:1). But God condemned him and his two friends and instructed Job to pray for them (Job 42:7–9). At times he could try to be kind (Job 14:12–21), but his "retribution theology" and conviction that Job had sinned controlled his words and actions. He made himself the measure of his theology.

465. אֱלִיפָל *'eliypāl:* A proper noun designating Eliphal (1 Chr. 11:35).

466. אֱלִיפְלֵהוּ *'eliypelēhû:* A proper noun designating Eliphelehu (1 Chr. 15:18, 21).

467. אֱלִיפֶלֶט *'eliypeleṭ*, אֶלְפֶּלֶט *'elpeleṭ:* A proper noun designating Eliphelet. The name is applied to several persons in the Old Testament:

A. A descendant, a son, of David. His mother is not given (2 Sam. 5:16).

B. This is another son of David. His mother is not noted (1 Chr. 3:8; 14:7).

C. The name of a son of Ahasbai, who was himself a Maacathite (2 Sam. 23:34).

D. He is listed as a family chief or head in Jerusalem over Benjamites (1 Chr. 8:39).

E. He was a son of Adonikam. He returned as a family chief under Ezra (Ezra 8:13).

F. He is listed as an Israelite who married a foreign woman. His father was Hashum (Ezra 10:33).

468. אֱלִיצוּר ***ᵉliyṣûr:*** A proper noun designating Elizur (Num. 1:5; 2:10; 7:30, 35; 10:18).

469. אֱלִיצָפָן ***ᵉliyṣāp̱ān***, אֶלְצָפָן ***'elṣāp̱ān:*** A proper noun designating Elizaphan:

A. Chief of the Kohathites (Ex. 6:22; Lev. 10:4; Num. 3:30; 1 Chr. 15:8; 2 Chr. 29:13).

B. Chief of Zebulon (Num. 34:25).

470. אֱלִיקָא ***ᵉliyqā':*** A proper noun designating Elika (2 Sam. 23:25).

471. אֶלְיָקִים ***'elyāqiym:*** A proper noun designating Eliakim. The name is applied to three persons in the Old Testament. It means "God establishes/raises up."

A. It refers to the son of Hilkiah who was the chief in charge of the king's palace under Hezekiah. He served as one of Hezekiah's messengers to King Sennacherib of Assyria and to Isaiah the prophet (2 Kgs. 18:18, 26, 37; 19:2; Isa. 22:20; 36:3, 11, 22; 37:2). He was highly regarded by the Lord (Isa. 22:20).

B. It applies to a son of the great king Josiah (2 Kgs. 23:34; 2 Chr. 36:4) who was made king by Pharaoh Neco after Josiah's death. His name was changed to Jehoiakim. He became an evil king.

C. It refers to a priest in the time of Nehemiah (Neh. 12:41). He helped in the worship services at the Temple.

472. אֱלִישֶׁבַע ***ᵉliyšeḇa':*** A proper noun designating Elisheba (Ex. 6:23).

473. אֱלִישָׁה ***ᵉliyšāh:*** A proper noun designating Elishah (Gen. 10:4; 1 Chr. 1:7; Ezek. 27:7).

474. אֱלִישׁוּעַ ***ᵉliyšûa':*** A proper noun designating Elishua (2 Sam. 5:15; 1 Chr. 14:5).

475. אֶלְיָשִׁיב ***'elyāšiyḇ:*** A proper noun designating Eliashib. Several persons bear this title meaning "God returns":

A. He was a son of Elioenai and, therefore, was listed in the royal line of David's descendants (1 Chr. 3:24). In 1 Chronicles 24:12, the name is listed as a priest , evidently not the same person.

B. The person listed in 1 Chronicles 24:12 was a priest or of the priestly line (see A).

C. It refers to a priest during the time of Nehemiah (Ezra 10:6). He is high priest finally under Nehemiah

(Neh. 3:1; 20, 21). He sinned with respect to Moses' marriage laws with foreigners (Neh. 13:4, 5). He also had a grandson, Joiada, who married the daughter of Sanballat, a Horonite (Neh. 13:28).

D. An Eliashib is mentioned as a singer from the Levites who had intermarried with a foreigner (Ezra 10:24).

E. An Israelite who had intermarried with a foreigner in Ezra's time (Ezra 10:36).

F. An Israelite who had intermarried with a foreigner in Ezra's day (Ezra 10:27).

476. אֱלִישָׁמָע *ᵉliyšāmāʿ*: A proper noun designating Elishama. The name is used by six persons in the Old Testament. The name means "God hears" or "has heard."

A. He was the leading commander of the tribe of Ephraim (Num. 1:10), son of Ammihud (Num. 2:18), grandson of Joshua (1 Chr. 7:26).

B. It refers to a son of David born in Jerusalem (2 Sam. 5:16).

C. It refers to a different son with the same name born to David in Jerusalem (a few mss. read Elishua instead) (1 Chr. 3:6).

D. It indicates a scribe of Jehoiakim, in effect, an ancient term for a keeper of records (Jer. 36:12), an official under the king. He kept the scrolls (Jer. 36:20, 21).

E. It refers to a person listed as one of the royal seed of David who hoped to become king after Gedaliah was assassinated (2 Kgs. 25:25; Jer. 41:1).

F. It refers to a Judaite (1 Chr. 2:41).

G. It refers to a priest under Jehoshaphat, king of Judah, who helped vigorously teach the Book of the Law to all of Judah (2 Chr. 17:8).

477. אֱלִישָׁע *ᵉliyšāʿ*: A proper noun designating Elisha, a great prophet of Israel who worked during the ninth century. His name means "God is salvation." We know little about his background. At some point, he became God's prophet who completed and extended the work of Elijah, who anointed him as his successor (1 Kgs. 19:16). His call was to "put to death" the line of Ahab and Jezebel out of Israel (1 Kgs. 19:17, 19) by his prophetic, "dynamic" word. He was active for nearly fifty years under as many as six kings (Ahab, Ahaziah, Jehoram, Jehu, Jehoahaz, Jehoash). His father was Shaphat. He drove oxen as a living, among other things (1 Kgs. 19:19–21). He was mentioned by Elijah (2 Kgs. 2:1–5), whom Elisha saw go up to heaven in a whirlwind.

He and Elijah were God's prophets who fought against Baalism and restored the "Lord as God" in Israel. Elisha performed many miracles, purifying water (2 Kgs. 2:19–22); providing food and money for a widow (2 Kgs. 4:1–7); restoring the Shunammite's son to life (2 Kgs. 4:32–37); purifying food and feeding many persons miraculously (2 Kgs. 4:38–44). He instructed Naaman about how to be healed (2 Kgs. 5:1–14) and caused an axhead to float (2 Kgs. 6:1–7). He spoke God's prophetic words in the political arena to even pagan kings (2 Kgs. 8:7–15). He anointed Jehu as king who would destroy the line of Ahab (2 Kgs. 9:1–13). Jezebel, Ahab's family line, and the prophets and priests of Baal were killed according to Elisha's prophecy (2 Kgs. 9:30–37; 10). He died soon after counseling Jehoash, king of Israel, concerning his wars with Aram (2 Kgs. 13:10–20). Even his bones retained some kind of honor before the Lord. A dead man was revived by coming into contact with them (2 Kgs. 13:21).

478. אֱלִישָׁפָט ***eliyšāpāṭ:*** A proper noun designating Elishaphat (2 Chr. 23:1).

479. אִלֵּךְ ***'illēk:*** An Aramaic plural demonstrative pronoun meaning these, those. It refers to both persons and walls (Ezra 4:21; 5:9). In Daniel the word points out various groups of persons (3:12, 13; 6:5[6], 11[12]).

480. אַלְלַי ***'allay:*** An interjection meaning woe! alas! It depicts the hopeless emotional outlook of Job before God (10:15). It expresses the anxiety and distress of the prophet Micah (7:1).

481. אָלַם ***'ālam:*** I. A verb meaning to bind. It is used in an agricultural setting of binding sheaves pictured in Joseph's dream (Gen. 37:7).

II. A verb meaning to be bound, to be speechless. It describes being speechless from awe or fright; the servant of the Lord was silent, speechless like a lamb before its shearers (Isa. 53:7); Daniel was speechless in the presence of an awesome divine being (10:15). It is used of a tongue or lips that have been put to silence (Ps. 31:18[19]; 39:9[10]; Ezek. 3:26) and lips that are wisely quiet before the wicked (Ps. 39:2[3]).

482. אֵלֶם ***'ēlem:*** I. A masculine noun referring to oak trees. The word is in the title of Psalm 56 and means oaks in a short phrase meaning according to the tune of the distant oaks (NKJV, distant lands; it is transliterated in the KJV and NASB).

II. A masculine noun (Ps. 56:title) transliterated as part of *Jonath elem rehokim* in the NASB, KJV. See I.

III. A noun meaning congregation, company. The translators vary in their rendering of this word. It has often been rendered as silence or silent one, but there are other possibilities. It means congregation (KJV, Ps. 58:1[2]), but the NASB translates gods, the NKJV silent ones, and the NIV prefers rulers.

483. אִלֵּם ***'illēm:*** An adjective meaning mute, unable to speak, dumb. God makes whom He will dumb or mute (Prov. 31:8). The mute will be able to speak when the Lord's full salvation is realized (Isa. 35:6). The Lord's prophetic spokesmen are not to be mute but to proclaim His will. His Spirit loosens their tongues. One's enemies and fear can make a person like a mute or dumb person (Ps. 38:13[14]). Pagan idols are mute, useless things (Hab. 2:18).

484. אַלְמֻגִּים *'almuggiym:* A masculine plural noun meaning almug trees. Its only usage is found in 1 Kings 10:11, 12. These trees were imported from a distant land named Ophir. They are perhaps red sandalwood or Lebanese trees.

485. אֲלֻמָּה *'ᵃlummah:* A feminine noun meaning sheaf or bundle of stalks. It refers to a bundle of cut stalks of grain or similar growth bound with twine or straw (Ps. 126:6). The word is used to describe some aspects of Joseph's dreams (Gen. 37:7).

486. אַלְמוֹדָד *'almôḏāḏ:* A proper noun designating Almodad (Gen. 10:26; 1 Chr. 1:20).

487. אַלַּמֶּלֶךְ *'allammeleḵ:* A proper noun designating Alammelech (Josh. 19:26).

488. אַלְמָן *'almān:* An adjective meaning forsaken or widowed. It occurs only in Jeremiah 51:5, assuring Israel and Judah that, even in exile, they have not been forsaken by their God. Although this Hebrew word is similar to the Hebrew word for widow, the context of this verse does not support the idea that Israel is pictured as the wife of the Lord.

489. אַלְמֹן *'almōn:* A masculine noun indicating widowhood. It was one of the disasters that could befall a city under judgment by the Lord (Isa. 47:9); the husbands of many women would be killed or captured, leaving the wives without husbands.

490. אַלְמָנָה *'almānāh:* A feminine noun meaning widow. The word occurs many times in the Law and the Prophets, where the well-being and care of the widow are the subject (Deut. 14:29; Isa. 1:17; Jer. 7:6; Zech. 7:10). Israel's concern for the widow was founded in the Lord's own concern (Ps. 68:5[6]; 146:9; Prov. 15:25; Jer. 49:11). Figuratively, the term occurs twice in reference to a devastated city: Jerusalem (Lam. 1:1) and Babylon (Isa. 47:8).

491. אַלְמָנוּת *'almānûṯ:* A feminine abstract noun indicating widowhood. It is used adjectively to describe a widow's garment (Gen. 38:14, 19). It indicates the state of a woman after the death of her husband.

492. אַלְמֹנִי *'almōniy:* A masculine noun serving as an indefinite pronoun meaning so and so, such a one, friend. Its exact meaning is difficult to discern. It indicates an unidentified relative (Ruth 4:1) but also a certain unknown place (1 Sam. 21:2[3]; 2 Kgs. 6:8).

493. אֶלְנַעַם *'elna'am:* A proper noun designating Elnaam (1 Chr. 11:46).

494. אֶלְנָתָן *'elnāṯān:* A proper noun designating Elnathan:

A. The grandfather of Jehoiachin (2 Kgs. 24:8; Jer. 26:22; 36:12, 25).

B. The first of three Levites of the same name mentioned in Ezra 8:16.

C. The second of three Levites of the same name mentioned in Ezra 8:16.

D. The third of three Levites of the same name mentioned in Ezra 8:16.

495. אֶלָּסָר ***'ellāsār:*** A proper noun designating Ellasar (Gen. 14:1, 9).

496. אֶלְעָד ***'el'āḏ:*** A proper noun designating Elead (1 Chr. 7:21).

497. אֶלְעָדָה ***'el'āḏāh:*** A proper noun designating Eladah, also spelled Eleadah (1 Chr. 7:20).

498. אֶלְעוּזַי ***'el'ûzay:*** A proper noun designating Eluzai (1 Chr. 12:5).

499. אֶלְעָזָר ***'el'āzār:*** A proper noun designating Eleazar. The name means "God has helped" or "God helps." It is used of several persons in the Old Testament:

A. Most often, it depicts Eleazar, the third son of Aaron who succeeded him as high priest (Ex. 6:23, 25; 28:1; Lev. 10:6, 12, 16; Num. 20:25–28; Deut. 6:10). He succeeded Aaron because his older brothers Nadab and AbiHu were slain by the Lord(Lev. 10:1–2). He is often featured with Moses or Joshua or both (Num. 26:1; Josh. 14:1). He became an expert in administering the covenantal laws in ancient Israel (Num. 19:3). He, along with Joshua, allotted the land to the tribes (Josh. 14:1–5; 19:51). He gave new rulings for the people as new situations arose (Josh. 17:3–6). His son was Phinehas (Josh. 22:13). He accompanied Aaron to the top of Mount Hor where Aaron died (Num. 20:25–26). He was buried in the area of Ephraim at Gibeah (Josh. 24:33). The term "sons of Eleazar" is found in the postexilic era and describes a major part of the priesthood at that time (1 Chr. 24:1–6).

B. It refers to a son of Abinadab who guarded the ark of the Lord (1 Sam. 7:1).

C. He is listed as one of the exclusive "three" mighty men of David who slew many Philistines (2 Sam. 23:9–10).

D. It refers to a Merarite, a family division of Levites (1 Chr. 23:21, 22). He had only daughters.

E. It names Eleazar, a priest, who served and ministered in the house of God (Neh. 12:42).

F. A priest, a son of Eleazar, who ministered in the rebuilt Temple in Ezra's day (Ezra 8:33).

G. It refers to an Israelite who had intermarried with a foreigner in Ezra's day (Ezra 10:25).

500. אֶלְעָלֵא ***'el'ālē':*** A proper noun designating Elealeh (Num. 32:3, 37; Isa. 15:4; 16:9; Jer. 48:34).

501. אֶלְעָשָׂה ***'el'āśāh:*** A proper noun designating Eleasah:

A. A son of Helez (1 Chr. 2:39, 40).

B. Son of Rapha (1 Chr. 8:37; 9:43).

C. A descendant of Pashhur (Ezra 10:22).

D. Son of Shaphan (Jer. 29:3).

502. אָלַף *'ālap̱:* A verb meaning to learn or, in a causative sense, to teach. The meaning apparently derives from a noun meaning association, familiarity, which leads to learning. This root idea appears in Proverbs 22:25 where association with an angry man causes one to learn his ways. Other usages mean to teach without obvious reference to learning by association (Job 15:5; 33:33; 35:11).

503. אָלַף *'ālap̱:* A masculine verb meaning thousand. It presents the idea of bringing forth thousands or making a thousandfold. It comes from the noun *'elep̱* (505) and is found only once in the Old Testament. The psalmist asked God for his granaries to be filled and his sheep to bring forth thousands (Ps. 144:13).

504. אֶלֶף *'elep̱:* A masculine noun referring to cattle or oxen (Deut. 7:13; 28:4, 18, 51; Ps. 8:7(8); Prov. 14:4; Isa. 30:24).

505. אֶלֶף *'elep̱:* A masculine noun meaning a thousand or clan. The word was commonly used for people, weights (including money), measures, and livestock (Judg. 8:26; 2hough the word is usually literal, sometimes it is used poetically to suggest a large number (Gen. 24:60; Job. 9:3). In a few cases, it carries the sense of an extended family or clan (Judg. 6:15).

506. אֲלַף *'ᵃlap̱:* An Aramaic masculine noun meaning one thousand. This word is found only in the book of Daniel. For example, Belshazzar held a magnificent feast and invited the lords of the land, whose total number was one thousand (Dan. 5:1). Daniel had a dream of people ministering to the Ancient of Days; Daniel called these people the thousand thousands (Dan. 7:10).

507. אֶלֶף *'elep̱:* A proper noun designating Eleph (Josh. 18:28).

508. אֶלְפַּעַל *'elpa'al:* A proper noun designating Elpaal (1 Chr. 8:11, 12, 18).

509. אָלַץ *'ālaṣ:* A verb meaning to urge, to prod. It describes the process Delilah used to wring information out of Samson (Judg. 16:16).

510. אלקום *'alqûm:* I. A masculine noun describing troops, a band of soldiers, army, military levy in Proverbs 30:31. The presence of a royal army or troops causes the king to overflow with pride (NASB, NIV, NKJV; see II).

II. Possibly a compound noun meaning no uprising or no adversary (Prov. 30:31, KJV; see I).

511. אֶלְקָנָה *'elqānāh:* A proper noun designating Elkanah, a common name in the Old Testament meaning "God has purchased/acquired." It is used as follows:

A. It refers to a grandson of Korah in the genealogical line of Moses and Aaron (Ex. 6:24).

B. It refers to the patient and compassionate Elkanah, husband of Hannah, and father of Samuel (1 Chr. 6:27[12], 34[19]).

C. It indicates a descendant of Levi, a Levite (1 Chr. 6:23).

D. It refers to the father of Zophai, a Levite from the same line as C (1 Chr. 6:26).

E. It indicates another Levite who lived in Jerusalem. He had a son named Asa (1 Chr. 9:16).

F. It refers to a warrior of David, from the Benjamites, a Korahite (1 Chr. 12:6).

G. It refers to another Levite who served as a doorkeeper of the ark (1 Chr. 15:23).

H. He was a powerful officer or commander of Ahaz. He was slain in battle by Israelites under King Pekah (2 Chr. 28:7).

512. אֶלְקֹשִׁי ***'elqōšiy:*** A proper noun designating Elkoshite (Nah. 1:1).

513. אֶלְתּוֹלַד ***'eltôlad:*** A proper noun designating Eltolad (Josh. 15:30; 19:4).

514. אֶלְתְּקֵא ***'elt^eqē':*** A proper noun designating Eltekeh (Josh. 19:44; 21:23).

515. אֶלְתְּקֹן ***'elt^eqōn:*** A proper noun designating Eltekon (Josh. 15:59).

516. אַל תַּשְׁחֵת ***'al tašḥēṯ:*** I. This proper name is often interpreted as the title of a tune to which a particular Psalm was to be sung (Ps. 57:title[1]; 58:title[1]; 59:title[1]; 75:title[1]).

II. Some translators interpret it as a tune title translated "Do Not Destroy," though some believe it should be understood as directions to preserve the Psalm and not a tune title (Ps. 57:title[1]; 58:title[1]; 59:title[1]; 75:title[1]).

517. אֵם ***'ēm:*** A feminine noun meaning mother, a woman with children (Ex. 20:12; Ps. 35:14). The word may also signify a female ancestor, animals, or humans in general (Gen. 3:20; 1 Kgs. 15:13). A nation or city is sometimes viewed as the mother of its people. So in that sense, this word is sometimes used to refer to a nation (Isa. 50:1; Hos. 2:2[4], 5[7]).

518. אִם ***'im:*** A particle meaning when, if, whenever. This word introduces conditional sentences capable of being fulfilled regularly, both in legal and everyday settings (Gen. 18:3; 43:4; Ex. 22:2[1]; 1 Sam. 14:9, 10). Some conditions introduced cannot be fulfilled (Gen. 13:16; Num. 22:18). It introduces wishes meaning if only (Ps. 81:8[9]; 95:7; 139:19). It is found in oaths (Num. 14:8; 1 Sam. 3:17); in some cases, it means not, or used with *lô'*, it means indeed, surely (Ps. 89:35[36]; Isa. 5:9). In a few cases, *'im* (518) introduces questions (Gen. 17:17; Josh. 5:13; Judg. 5:8, KJV; 1 Kgs.

1:27) which are direct or indirect (Gen. 18:21; Ex. 22:7[6]). It introduces concessive clauses meaning although or even if (Jer. 15:1). Finally, it combines with other particles or conjunctions: *kî 'im* means unless, rather; *'im lô'* means if not but rather (Gen. 24:38); *biltîy 'im* means except, except if; *raq 'im* means only if. When *'im* is followed with another *'im* in close proximity, it means whether . . . or (Ex. 19:13; Deut. 18:3). It can serve as a prohibition used with the future or imperfect form of the verb (Song 2:7).

519. אָמָה *'āmāh:* A feminine noun indicating a maidservant or slave girl. It depicts a simple maidservant (Gen. 30:3; 31:33; Ex. 2:5; 2 Sam. 6:20). It refers to a girl who is a servant in a legal sense (Ex. 20:10, 17; 21:20; Lev. 25:6; Job 31:13). It is applied to concubines (Gen. 20:17; 21:12; Ex. 23:12). In a figurative or metaphorical sense, it is used to express the humility of any person (Ruth 3:9; 1 Sam. 1:16; 25:24; 2 Sam. 20:17). It is used as a token of submission when addressing God (1 Sam. 1:11; Ps. 86:16; 116:16).

520. אַמָּה *'ammāh:* A feminine noun meaning, measure, cubit. The basic meaning is forearm. It was used to indicate a part of a door or a pivot of doors (Isa. 6:4). The phrase *'ammat 'îyš* was an ordinary cubit (Deut. 3:11; cf. Ezek. 40:5, 13–15 for a cubit one handbreath longer). The ordinary cubit was about 50 centimeters long, 18 inches, and the longer cubit in Ezekiel was about 58 centimeters long, 22 inches. The phrase *'el-'ammāh* means exactly to the cubit (Gen. 6:16).

521. אַמָּה *'ammāh:* An Aramaic feminine noun meaning cubit. It is used twice in the Old Testament (Ezra 6:3; Dan. 3:1). Ezra gives the height and width of the temple as sixty cubits. Ironically, the height of Nebuchadnezzar's image in Daniel was six cubits wide and sixty cubits high.

522. אַמָּה *'ammāh:* I. This is a proper noun referring to Ammah, a hill near the Jordan Valley (2 Sam. 2:24).

II. A feminine noun translated as a mother city (2 Sam. 8:1).

III. This is a proper noun that is part of the name Metheg Ammah (4965,I) (2 Sam. 8:1).

523. אֻמָּה *'ummāh:* A feminine noun meaning tribe, people. This word occurs three times in the Hebrew Bible (Gen. 25:16; Num. 25:15; Ps. 117:1) and is always plural. It is synonymous with *gôy* (1471).

524. אֻמָּה *'ummāh:* An Aramaic feminine noun meaning nation. This word corresponds to the Hebrew word *'ēm* (517) meaning mother, and when carried into the Aramaic, this word shifts to mean mother in a collective sense (i.e., nation). Often a nation is found in the expression "peoples, nations, and languages" (Dan. 3:4, 7; 4:1[3:31]; 5:19; 6:25[26];

7:14; cf. Ezra 4:10). For example, after Shadrach, Meshach, and Abednego came through the fiery furnace, Nebuchadnezzar issued a decree to every people, language, and nation concerning the God of the Hebrews (Dan. 3:29).

525. אָמוֹן ***'āmôn:*** A masculine noun meaning architect or craftsman. The word is used in Proverbs 8:30 as the personification of wisdom. Wisdom is portrayed as a craftsman at God's side, involved in designing the creation.

526. אָמוֹן ***'āmôn:*** A proper noun designating Amon. It refers to at least three persons in the Old Testament:

A. It refers to Amon, governor of Samaria. He imprisoned the prophet Micaiah at the word of King Ahab (1 Kgs. 22:26, 27).

B. It refers to a son of Manasseh, king of Judah, who took the throne at his father's death (2 Kgs. 21:18). He was assassinated after ruling two years. He was a wicked king like his father (2 Kgs. 21:20–22). Josiah, his famous righteous son, was made king in his place (2 Kgs. 21:24).

C. He was descended in the line of Solomon's servants and one who returned from the Babylonian exile under Nehemiah (Neh. 7:59).

527. אָמוֹן ***'āmôn:*** A masculine noun of uncertain derivation, meaning either a skilled craftsman or a throng of people. It is used only twice in the Old Testament. In Proverbs 8:30, the sense is that of a master architect or artisan (525). The other appearance in Jeremiah 52:15 seems to designate a general multitude of people.

528. אָמוֹן ***'āmôn,*** נֹא אָמוֹן ***nō' 'āmôn:*** A masculine noun meaning artisan or master craftsman. The legs of the beloved are said to be the work of an artisan (Song 7:1[2]). This word is also a proper name of an Egyptian god (Jer. 46:25; Nah. 3:8). The Egyptian god was the local deity of Thebes but came to be the supreme god in Egypt.

529. אֵמוּן ***'ēmûn:*** A masculine noun meaning trustworthiness, faithfulness, or dependability. It is used to signify the rare and beneficial quality of trustworthiness in an individual (Prov. 13:17; 14:5; 20:6); the character of a righteous nation (Isa. 26:2); and in a negative sense, a fundamental lack of dependability or faithfulness (Deut. 32:20).

530. אֱמוּנָה ***'ᵉmûnāh:*** A noun meaning truth, faithfulness. It is used to describe God's character and His actions in Deuteronomy 32:4. The psalmists often use this word in their praise of the Lord and His faithfulness (Ps. 33:4; 100:5; 119:90). When people are faithful, good comes their way (2 Chr. 19:9; Prov. 12:22; 28:20). The word *'ᵉmûnāh* is also used with righteousness to describe the character (Prov. 12:17; Isa. 59:4; Jer. 5:1).

531. אָמוֹץ ***'āmôṣ:*** A proper noun designating Amoz (2 Kgs. 19:2, 20; 20:1; 2 Chr. 26:22; 32:20, 32; Isa. 1:1; 2:1; 13:1; 20:2; 37:2, 21; 38:1).

532. אָמִי ***'āmiy:*** A proper noun designating Ami (Ezra 2:57).

533. אַמִּיץ ***'ammiyṣ***, אַמִּץ ***'ammiṣ:*** An adjective meaning mighty, brave, strong. The word is used to describe brave warriors (Amos 2:16) but also is used to depict the strength of God and His might (Job 9:4, 19; Isa. 40:26), as well as His means of bringing judgment on peoples (Isa. 28:2). It is used metaphorically to describe the strength or effectiveness of conspiracy (2 Sam. 15:12).

534. אָמִיר ***'āmiyr:*** A masculine noun indicating the upper or topmost branches. It describes Damascus in a simile as like an olive tree with a few olives left in its topmost branches (Isa. 17:6, 9).

535. אָמַל ***'āmal:*** A verb meaning to languish, be feeble, pine away. The word describes the languishing of a fertile woman with whom God has dealt harshly (1 Sam. 2:5). Metaphorically, it depicts the city gates of Judah languishing, that is, her elders cry out at the cities' gates (Jer. 14:2). The crops of Moab languish in the fields under the Lord's judgment (Isa. 16:8; Joel 1:10, 12). In a striking metaphor, the word depicts the hearts of His people pining away because they have committed spiritual harlotry (Ezek. 16:30).

536. אֻמְלַל ***'umlal:*** An adjective meaning weak, faint. It is used to describe the despair seizing the psalmist in a time of grave trouble (Ps. 6:2[3]).

537. אֲמֵלָל ***'ªmēlāl:*** An adjective meaning weak, feeble. The word describes the supposed weakness of the Jewish people who had returned from exile in Babylon, at least through the eyes of Sanballat (Neh. 4:2[3:34]), as they tried to rebuild the city wall.

538. אֲמָם ***'ªmām:*** A proper noun designating Amam (Josh. 15:26).

539. אָמַן ***'āman:*** A verb meaning to be firm, to build up, to support, to nurture, or to establish. The primary meaning is that of providing stability and confidence, like a baby would find in the arms of a parent. It is used to signify support of a pillar (2 Kgs. 18:16); nurture and nourishment (Num. 11:12; Ruth 4:16; thus, a nurse, 2 Sam. 4:4); cradling in one's arms (Isa. 60:4); a house firmly founded (1 Sam. 2:35; 25:28); a secure nail that finds a solid place to grip (Isa. 22:23); a lasting permanence (Ps. 89:28[29]; with negative particle, Jer. 15:18). Metaphorically, the word conveys the notion of faithfulness and trustworthiness, such that one could fully depend on (Deut. 7:9; Job 12:20; Ps. 19:7[8]; Isa. 55:3; Mic. 7:5). Therefore, the word can also signify certitude or assurance (Deut. 28:66; Job 24:22; Hos. 5:9) and belief, in the sense of receiving something as true and sure

(Gen. 15:6; Ex. 4:5; 2 Chr. 20:20; Ps. 78:22; Isa. 53:1; Jon. 3:5).

540. אֲמַן *'ᵃman:* An Aramaic verb meaning to trust in, to put one's faith in someone or something. This verb occurs only three times in the Hebrew Bible. In Daniel 6:23(24), it states that Daniel trusted in his God. In the other occurrences, the verb is in the form of a passive participle and functions as an adjective meaning trustworthy or faithful: the interpretation of the king's dream is trustworthy (Dan. 2:45); and Daniel is described as a faithful man without negligence or corruption (Dan. 6:4[5]).

541. אָמַן *'āman:* A verb meaning to go to the right or to use the right hand. This word is identical to *yāman* (3231) and is related to the noun *yᵉmāniy* (3233), meaning right hand. In the Old Testament, this word is always used with its opposite, *śāma'l*, meaning to go to the left or to use the left hand. Lot could choose which direction he wanted to go (Gen. 13:9). God would guide Israel where they needed to go (Isa. 30:21). God commanded Ezekiel to go the way God directed him (Ezek. 21:16[21]).

542. אָמָּן *'ommān:* A masculine noun indicating a craftsman, artist. It indicates the person, the artist, who produces a work of skill and beauty (Song 7:1[2]).

543. אָמֵן *'āmēn:* An adverb meaning verily or truly. The word is used more often as the declaration may it be so. It comes from a root meaning to confirm; to support; to be faithful. The major idea behind this word is constancy and reliability. It is used as a declaration to acknowledge affirmation of a statement (1 Kgs. 1:36); acceptance of a curse (Neh. 5:13); affirmation of a prophecy (Jer. 28:6). It is also used in response to worship and praise (1 Chr. 16:36; Neh. 8:6). The English word *amen* comes from this word and means, "I agree; may it be so."

544. אֹמֶן *'ōmen:* A masculine noun meaning truth, faithfulness, full reliability. This word stresses both the truthfulness of something and, therefore, its reliability simultaneously. God's wonders and plans are planned and executed with perfect faithfulness (Isa. 25:1).

545. אָמְנָה *'omnāh:* A feminine noun meaning rearing up or bringing up; under one's care. It describes the care and rearing one receives under another's watchful eye, such as Esther received from Mordecai (Esth. 2:20).

546. אָמְנָה *'omnāh:* An adverb meaning verily, truly, indeed. Abraham used this word to express that he was being truthful when he said Sarah was his sister (Gen. 20:12)—although, in fact, he was lying. When Achan took loot from Jericho, he admitted his sin by saying he had indeed sinned against God (Josh. 7:20).

547. אֹמְנָה *'ōmᵉnāh:* A feminine noun indicating a pillar or doorpost.

Solomon's Temple had pillars or doorposts overlaid with gold (2 Kgs. 18:16).

548. אֲמָנָה *'ᵃmānāh:* A feminine noun meaning agreement, faith, support. It occurs in Nehemiah 9:38[10:1] and 11:23. In Nehemiah 9:38, it is the object of the verb *kāraṯ* (3772), which is also used in the idiom "to make (lit., cut) a covenant," suggesting a possible semantic overlap.

549. אֲמָנָה *'ᵃmānāh:* A proper noun referring to Amana, a region in Anti-Lebanon (Song 4:8).

550. אַמְנוֹן *'amnôn,* אֲמִינוֹן *'amiynôn:* A proper noun designating Amnon:

A. The name identifies David's firstborn son in Hebron (2 Sam. 3:2). He committed a grievous sin in Israel by raping his half-sister Tamar, sister of Absalom, his half-brother (13). Absalom killed him in revenge (2 Sam. 13:23–39). David hated Ammon for this deed but never reprimanded him for it (2 Sam. 13:21).

B. It refers to a son of Shimon in the descendants of the line of Judah (1 Chr. 4:20).

551. אָמְנָם *'omnām:* An adverb meaning admittedly, truly, or surely. The word is used to acknowledge that something is true but not the whole truth. Hezekiah admitted that Assyria destroyed other nations and their gods but claimed that it was because they were false gods (2 Kgs. 19:17; Isa. 37:18). Job admitted the truth of his friends' sayings but claimed that they did not see the whole truth (Job 9:2; 12:2, 19:4, 5). Eliphaz used the word to deny negative statements about God and himself (Job 34:12; 36:4).

552. אֻמְנָם *'umnām:* An interrogative particle meaning verily, truly, indeed. It always occurs in questions. An example is Genesis 18:13, where Sarah doubted that she would have a child, "Shall I of a surety bear a child . . . ?"

553. אָמַץ *'āmaṣ:* A verb meaning to be strong, determined, bold, courageous; conquer. It means to be strong and courageous. This idea is translated by the NKJV as prevailed when referring to men of Judah in war (2 Chr. 13:18; conquered, NASB). A people or nation can be considered strong (Gen. 25:23). The emphatic stem of the verb means to make strong or cause to grow strong (Prov. 8:28; 31:17; Isa. 44:14) of inanimate objects. It is used of human activity in repairing or strengthening a house or building (2 Chr. 24:13). Metaphorically, it means to strengthen or harden one's attitude or heart (Deut. 2:30; 15:7; 2 Chr. 36:13). It also is used in some contexts to mean to show courage or to show or prove oneself strong (Ps. 27:14; 31:24[25]); to persist in an activity (Ruth 1:18); or make haste (1 Kgs. 12:18). With a slight change, it means to be better or superior (2 Chr. 13:7).

554. אָמֹץ ***'āmōṣ:*** An adjective meaning powerful, strong. Some versions render this term as strong steeds (horses) (NKJV, Zech. 6:3), while others prefer powerful (NIV, Zech. 6:3, 7; cf. KJV, bay horses). The basic meaning is strength, power.

555. אֹמֶץ ***'ōmeṣ:*** A masculine noun meaning strength. It refers to a basic strength of character generated by a righteous and clean life (Job 17:9).

556. אַמְצָה ***'amṣāh:*** A feminine noun meaning strength. The word refers to strong support against threats of danger as supplied by those who are living in Jerusalem (Zech. 12:5).

557. אַמְצִי ***'amṣiy:*** A proper noun designating Amzi:

A. A son of Bani (1 Chr. 6:46(31).

B. A son of Zechariah (Neh. 11:12).

558. אֲמַצְיָה ***'amaṣyāh,*** אֲמַצְיָהוּ ***'amaṣyāhû:*** A proper noun designating Amaziah, a name designating several persons in Israel. It means "God is mighty/powerful."

A. He was the son of Joash, a Judean king. He warred against Jehoash of Israel (2 Kgs. 13:12). He reigned twenty-nine years. He served the Lord faithfully during his righteous long reign. He defeated the Edomites (2 Kgs. 14:7) but suffered defeat in Jerusalem at the hands of King Jehoash of Israel (2 Kgs. 14:11–20). His enemies assassinated him in Lachish (2 Kgs. 14:19–20).

B. It refers to an Amaziah of the Simeonites, who had a son, Joshah (1 Chr. 4:34).

C. It refers to a son of Hilkiah of the Merarites who were part of the Temple musicians (1 Chr. 6:45).

D. It indicates a priest of Bethel under King Jeroboam II in Israel (Amos 7:10) who confronted Amos the prophet. He was condemned by Amos.

559. אָמַר ***'āmar:*** A verb meaning to say. It is translated in various ways depending on the context. It is almost always followed by a quotation. In addition to vocal speech, the word refers to thought as internal speech (2 Sam. 13:32; Esth. 6:6). Further, it also refers to what is being communicated by a person's actions along with his words (Ex. 2:14; 2 Chr. 28:13).

560. אֲמַר ***'amar:*** An Aramaic verb meaning to say, to tell, to command. This root carries the same semantic range as its Hebrew cognate, *'āmar* (559) (Ezra 5:3, 15; Dan. 2:4; 3:24–26; 4:7–9[4–6]; 7:23).

561. אֵמֶר ***'ēmer:*** A masculine noun meaning word, speech, saying. The primary meaning is something said. The word is used like *dāḇār* (1697); however, it occurs (with the exception of Joshua 24:27) only in poetry, usually in the plural, often in the phrase "the words of my mouth" (Deut. 32:1; Ps. 19:14[15]). Words are seen as taking from their context qualities such as truth (Prov. 22:21); beauty (Gen.

49:21); deception (Isa. 32:7); knowledge (Prov. 23:12). This word may refer to God's words (Job 6:10; Ps. 138:4) as well as people's words.

562. אֹמֶר ***'ōmer:*** A masculine noun meaning utterance, speech, word. It is used only in poetry in parallel constructions with *dāḇār* (1697), meaning word (Ps. 19:3[4]; Prov. 2:16; 4:10, 20); *millîm* (4405), meaning words (Job 32:12, 14; 33:3; 34:37); *miṣwāh* (4687), meaning commandment (Job 23:12; Prov. 2:1; 7:1).

563. אִמַּר ***'immar:*** An Aramaic masculine noun meaning lamb. It refers to the lambs, along with other animals, supplied by the Persian kings, Darius and Artaxerxes, for the Temple being built in Jerusalem (Ezra 6:9; 7:17). Two hundred such rams were offered at the dedication of the new Temple constructed in Jerusalem in 516 B.C. (Ezra 6:17).

564. אִמֵּר ***'immēr:*** A proper noun designating Immer. The name applies to several people in Israel:

A. It refers to a priest under the governor Zerubbabel who returned from Babylon (Ezra 2:37; 7:40). Some of his descendants intermarried with the people of the land (Ezra 10:20). He had a son, Meshillemoth, among the new residents of Jerusalem (Neh. 11:13).

B. It indicates a priest who is assigned during the time of David (1 Chr. 24:14).

C. It indicates a Babylonian village from which Israelites returned from the Babylonian exile (Ezra 2:59), supposedly descendants of Solomon's servants.

D. It refers to a priest, father of Pashhur, who attacked Jeremiah the prophet and had him constrained (Jer. 20:2).

565. אֶמְרָה ***'emrāh,*** אִמְרָה, ***'imrāh:*** A feminine noun meaning word. This rare poetic term occurs more in Psalm 119 than everywhere else combined. It is used in parallel with teaching, covenant, commandment, and voice (Deut. 32:2; 33:9; Ps. 119:172; Isa. 28:23). This noun most often designates God's Word, which is the psalmist's guide for life and his basis for requesting God's kindness, graciousness, and deliverance (Ps. 119:11, 41, 58, 76, 116, 133, 154, 170). The keeping of God's Word is a frequent topic in Scripture (Deut. 33:9; Ps. 119:67, 158; cf. Isa. 5:24). God's Word is pure, sweeter than honey, and has been magnified with His name (Ps. 119:103; 138:2; Prov. 30:5).

566. אִמְרִי ***'imriy:*** A proper noun designating Imri:

A. A Judaite (1 Chr. 9:4).

B. An assistant to Nehemiah (Neh. 3:2).

567. אֱמֹרִי ***ᵉmōriy:*** A proper noun referring to an Amorite (1 Sam. 7:14; 2 Sam. 21:2; 1 Kgs. 4:19; 9:20; 21:26; 2 Kgs. 21:11).

568. אֲמַרְיָה ***ᵃmaryāh***, אֲמַרְיָהוּ ***ᵃmaryāhû:*** A proper noun designating Amariah, a common name in the Old Testament:

A. It refers to one of Aaron's descendants, a grandfather of Zadok, a high priest in Israel under David (1 Chr. 6:7).

B. A son of Azariah in Aaron's line. His father served as a priest in Jerusalem in Solomon's Temple (1 Chr. 6:10–11[5:37]).

C. The second son of Hebron descended from Kohath (1 Chr. 23:19).

D. The name of a high priest who was over the Levites who were administering the Law of the Lord, in addition to his usual duties (2 Chr. 19:11).

E. It refers to a Levite who assisted Kore in collecting gifts made to the Lord (2 Chr. 31:14–15).

F. The name of a son of Binnui, an Israelite who intermarried with the people of the land in the time of Ezra (Ezra 10:42).

G. It refers to Amariah, a priest who returned under Nehemiah and who sealed Nehemiah's covenant to serve the Lord and keep the Law of God (Neh. 10:3).

H. A son of Shephatiah who resettled in Jerusalem under Nehemiah. He was of the line of Judah (Neh. 11:4).

I. A son of Hezekiah who had a son, Gedaliah. He was an ancestor of Zephaniah (Zeph. 1:1).

569. אַמְרָפֶל ***'amrāpel:*** A proper noun designating Amraphel (Gen. 14:1, 9).

570. אֶמֶשׁ ***'emeš:*** An adverb of time meaning yesterday, last night. It refers to the evening of the previous day (Gen. 19:34; 31:29, 42) but also has the sense of yesterday (2 Kgs. 9:26) or recently. It seems to have the meaning by night in Job (30:3).

571. אֱמֶת ***'emet:*** A feminine noun meaning truth, faithfulness. It is frequently connected with lovingkindness (Prov. 3:3; Hos. 4:1) and occasionally with other terms such as peace (2 Kgs. 20:19); righteousness (Isa. 48:1); and justice (Ps. 111:7). To walk in truth is to conduct oneself according to God's holy standards (1 Kgs. 2:4; 3:6; Ps. 86:11; Isa. 38:3). Truth was the barometer for measuring both one's word (1 Kgs. 22:16; Dan. 11:2) and actions (Gen. 24:49; Josh. 2:14). Accordingly, God's words (Ps. 119:160; Dan. 10:21) and actions (Neh. 9:33) are characterized by this Hebrew term also. Indeed, God is the only God of truth (Ex. 34:6; 2 Chr. 15:3; Ps. 31:5[6]).

572. אַמְתַּחַת ***'amtaḥat:*** A feminine noun meaning sack, bag. It is featured in the Joseph narrative as the container of grain, especially of the money hidden in them by order of Joseph (Gen. 42:27, 28; 43:12, 18; 44:1).

573. אֲמִתַּי ***'amittay:*** A proper noun designating Amittai (2 Kgs. 14:25; Jon. 1:1).

574. אֵימְתָן ***'ēmṯān:*** An Aramaic adjective meaning terrifying, frightful. It is one of the descriptive words describing the fourth beast of Daniel's dream (Dan. 7:7).

575. אָן ***'ān:*** An adverb meaning where, whither. The word is sometimes spelled with the letter ה, *h* on the end to show direction toward, whither. The *h* is not accented. The word can be rendered quite uniformly: with reference to time, it means to what point or how long? (Ex. 16:28; Job 8:2). With the ה of direction added to indicate place, it means to which, whither? (Gen. 16:8; 32:17[18]; 2 Kgs. 6:6; Isa. 10:3). Preceded by *'āneh* it means to any place, whither (1 Kgs. 2:36, 42; 2 Kgs. 5:25).

576. אֲנָא ***'anā'***, אֲנָה, ***'anāh:*** An Aramaic pronoun meaning I, me. It regularly means simply is but is used to reinforce other nouns, pronouns, or suffixes as well. Daniel 7:28 is a case in point: As for me, I, Daniel (cf. Ezra 6:12; 7:21).

577. אָנָּא ***'ānnā'***, אָנָּה ***'ānnāh:*** An interjection of entreaty meaning I beg you, ah now, alas, or oh. The primary use of the word is to intensify the urgency of request or the gravity of a given situation. It is used to signify the pressing desire for forgiveness (Gen. 50:17); the great weight of sin (Ex. 32:31); earnestness in prayer of petition (2 Kgs. 20:3; Neh. 1:5, Jon. 1:14).

578. אָנָה ***'ānāh:*** A verb meaning to mourn, to lament. It describes the despairing response of fishermen toward the loss of water in the Nile (Isa. 19:8). Figuratively, it describes the hopeless reactions of the gates, the elders, of the cities of Judah at the judgment on them from the Lord (Isa. 3:26).

579. אָנָה ***'ānāh:*** A verb meaning to meet, to seek occasion or allow to meet, to happen. It describes any kind of event or occurrence of something in general (Ps. 91:10), such as evil befalling or not befalling someone (Prov. 12:21). It also indicates an occurrence or event that takes place occasioned by God (Ex. 21:13). And it depicts an event or occasion brought about by a person (2 Kgs. 5:7).

580. אֲנוּ ***'anû:*** A pronoun meaning we. It serves as the subject of a participle in Jeremiah 42:6.

581. אִנּוּן ***'innûn***, אִנִּין, ***'inniyn:*** An Aramaic demonstrative pronoun meaning those, they. It regularly means they or those (Dan. 2:44). It also functions as a linking verb meaning were, are (Ezra 5:4). It serves as the object, them, of the verb in Daniel 6:24[25].

582. אֱנוֹשׁ ***'enôš:*** A masculine noun meaning man. In the singular, this word occurs in poetry and prayers (2 Chr. 14:11[10]). This word may derive from *'ānaš* (605), meaning to be weak or sick. In comparison to *'îš* (376), which also means man, *'enôš* often occurs in passages emphasizing man's frailty (Job 7:17; Ps. 8:4[5]; 90:3). However, the plural of *'enôš* serves as the plural of *'îš* and occurs throughout the Old Testament.

583. אֱנוֹשׁ ***'enôš:*** A proper noun designating Enosh (Gen. 4:26; 5:6, 7, 9–11); 1 Chr. 1:1).

584. אָנַח ***'ānaḥ:*** A verb meaning to groan, moan. It indicates a universal response to grave oppression or despair as when Israel was in Egypt (Ex. 2:23). More generally, it is also the response of a people when they are ruled by a wicked government or of persons who are deprived of their pleasures or addictions (Isa. 24:7). Groaning or moaning is the response of a people whom God judges, much as Lebanon (Jer. 22:23), or a desolated city (Lam. 1:4, 8, 11, 21), such as Jerusalem. Even animals moan because of destruction (Joel 1:18). The righteous groan because of injustice and corruption (Ezek. 9:4), and especially God's righteous prophets (Ezek. 21:6[11]) groan over the rebellion of God's people.

585. אֲנָחָה ***'anāḥāh:*** A feminine noun indicating moaning, sighing. This response is brought on by physical (Job 3:24; 23:2), spiritual, or mental despair (Ps. 6:6[7]). It involves both body and soul (Ps. 31:9[10], 10[11]; 38:9[10]). Babylon would be punished because of the groaning she caused to others (Isa. 21:2). But sighing and groaning will be removed from the redeemed of the Lord (Isa. 35:10).

586. אֲנַחְנָא ***'anaḥnā',*** אֲנַחְנָה ***'anaḥnāh:*** An Aramaic plural pronoun meaning we. It is the standard first common plural independent pronoun in biblical Aramaic. In Scripture it is used with a participle (Ezra 4:16; Dan. 3:16, 17) and with the infinitive (Ezra 5:11).

587. אֲנַחְנוּ ***'anaḥnû:*** A first common plural independent pronoun meaning we. Its use is quite uniform in meaning we (Gen. 13:8; 29:4; 37:7; Num. 9:7; Deut. 1:28). It may precede or follow (Gen. 19:13; Num. 10:29; Judg. 19:18) a participle. It can follow a verb for emphasis (Judg. 9:28; 2 Kgs. 10:4). It also can be used in a reflexive construction following a preposition to mean with ourselves (Gen. 13:8, lit., with us, we).

588. אֲנָחֲרַת ***'anāḥarāṯ:*** A proper noun designating Anaharath (Josh. 19:19).

589. אֲנִי ***'aniy:*** A first person common pronoun meaning I, me. It may serve as subject or object. It often serves as a subject of a participle, normally by following it (Gen. 18:17; Judg. 15:3; Jer. 1:12). Following a first person verb, it gives emphasis (Judg. 8:23; 2 Sam. 12:28). In answer to a question, it means I am, yes (Gen. 27:24; Judg. 13:11). With an interrogative Heb. *ha* attached to it, it means do I? (Isa. 66:9). Placed in front of the Lord's name, it serves as an introduction, I am the Lord; so also with Pharaoh, I am Pharaoh (Gen. 41:44; Ex. 6:6). It is synonymous with *'ānōḵî*.

590. אֳנִי *'ᵒniy:* A common noun meaning ships, fleet. These could be of average size (1 Kgs. 9:26, 27) and designated as ships of Solomon. Or possibly they were larger, sea-going vessels bound for Tarshish (1 Kgs. 10:22). Ships propelled by oars are designated in Isaiah 33:21 as galley ships.

591. אֳנִיָּה *'ᵒniyyāh:* A feminine noun meaning ship, boat. The word designates simply a ship (Gen. 49:13; Deut. 28:68; Prov. 30:19). These ships are further designated as a ship sailing to Tarshish (2 Chr. 9:21; Jon. 1:3); merchant ships (Prov. 31:14); swift ships (Job 9:26). Combined with the word for men in the construct form, it designates seamen (1 Kgs. 9:27).

592. אֲנִיָּה *'ᵃniyyāh:* A feminine noun meaning sorrow, mourning. It functions with other words for mourning for emphasis (Isa. 29:2; Lam. 2:5). In each usage, the Lord brings about the mourning over His city, Ariel, or Jerusalem.

593. אֲנִיעָם *'ᵃniy'ām:* A proper noun designating Aniam (1 Chr. 7:19).

594. אֲנָךְ *'ᵃnāḵ:* A masculine noun meaning plumb or plumb line, a line used to determine verticality or straightness. It was employed by the Lord through Amos to test His people (Amos 7:7, 8).

595. אָנֹכִי *'ānōḵiy:* A common independent pronoun meaning I, me. It is used as a formula of introduction when placed before the Lord, I am the Lord (Ex. 20:2). It is used in contrasts with other pronouns, you and I (Hos. 1:9). Placed before a first person verb form, it is emphatic, I myself gave (Hos. 2:8[10]). It is used often as a predicate or verb meaning I am (Gen. 24:34; 1 Sam. 30:13; 2 Sam. 1:8). Sometimes biblical writers preferred to use *'ānōḵīy* and at other times *'anīy*, evidently for poetic or rhythmical reasons.

596. אָנַן *'ānan:* A verb meaning to complain, find fault. It describes the response of the people of Israel who found fault with the food supply they had in the wilderness (Num. 11:1). Complaining is ruled out because of humanity's sins (Lam. 3:39) in the case of the fall of Jerusalem to Babylon.

597. אָנַס *'ānas:* A verb meaning to compel. It refers to the lack of a social or royal compulsion to do something (Esth. 1:8). In Persia such a social or royal custom or decree compelling one to drink could not have been broken without serious consequences. The laws of the Medes and Persians could not be broken.

598. אֲנַס *'ᵃnas:* An Aramaic verb meaning to be difficult, to baffle, to trouble. The verb depicts the inability to solve a mystery or puzzling thing, such as the imagery in a dream (Dan. 4:9[6]).

599. אָנַף *'ānap̱:* A verb meaning to be angry, enraged, or to breathe through the nose. The word derives its meaning from the heavy breathing and snorting typical of anger. It is used solely in reference to God's anger or severe displeasure with His people: Moses (Deut. 1:37; 4:21); Aaron (Deut. 9:20); Solomon (1 Kgs. 11:9); and Israel (Deut. 9:8; 1 Kgs. 8:46; 2 Kgs. 17:18; Ps. 60:1[3]; 79:5) all provoked this divine anger. In Psalm 2:12, this word is used in reference to the Messiah.

600. אֲנַף *'ᵃnap̱:* An Aramaic masculine noun meaning face, facial expression. It is used in a figurative expression to fall on one's face in obeisance (Dan. 2:46), to honor or worship. It also refers literally to a person's face (Dan. 3:19).

601. אֲנָפָה *'ᵃnāp̱āh:* A feminine noun meaning most likely heron, but plover or cormorant are possible translations. This bird was forbidden as food (Lev. 11:19; Deut. 14:18) for God's holy people.

602. אָנַק *'ānaq:* A verb meaning to cry out, to groan, to groan silently. It depicts the cries of the mortally wounded (Jer. 51:52), as well as those who cry out and groan because of the slaughter of war and judgment (Ezek. 26:15). It also describes the groans of those who are devastated and shocked by moral and spiritual atrocities, especially those committed in Jerusalem (Ezek. 9:4). Ezekiel groans, but silently and inwardly, over the death of his wife (Ezek. 24:17).

603. אֲנָקָה *'ᵃnāqāh:* A feminine noun depicting crying or groaning. It describes the cry and expression of those who are needy (Ps. 12:5[6]) or are wrongfully imprisoned (Ps. 79:11; 102:20[21]). Groaning may be misplaced because the one crying out is in the wrong (Mal. 2:13).

604. אֲנָקָה *'ᵃnāqāh:* A feminine noun meaning ferret or gecko. This small animal is classified as unclean, a swarming thing which the Israelites were not permitted to eat (Lev. 11:30, 31).

605. אָנַשׁ *'ānaš:* A verb meaning to be sick, incurable, in poor health. It describes a weakened condition that can lead to death (2 Sam. 12:15; Job 34:6; Isa. 17:11) or an incurable pain or ill health (Jer. 15:18). In its most potent theological usage, it describes the incurably wicked, desperately sick condition of the human heart (Jer. 17:9) that only God knows.

606. אֱנָשׁ *'ᵉnāš:* An Aramaic masculine noun meaning man or mankind. This word is often used to differentiate man from deity. It can also be synonymous with human beings. The most frequent usage occurs in the book of Daniel. It is used in a general, collective sense to mean everyone (Ezra 6:11; Dan. 3:10); and in the phrase "son of man" to mean a human being (Dan. 7:13). See the related Hebrew noun *’ᵉnôš* (582).

607. אַנְתָּה *’antah*, אַנְתְּ *’anᵉt*: An Aramaic independent personal pronoun meaning you. It is used to mean simply you (Dan. 6:16[17]) but is also employed to point out and emphasize, as in, you Ezra (Ezra 7:25). It precedes the expression, O king (Dan. 2:29, 31), regularly as an expression of respect and court demeanor.

608. אַנְתּוּן *’antûn*: An Aramaic independent plural pronoun meaning you. It is found only in Daniel 2:8, referring to the Chaldeans of Babylon.

609. אָסָא *’āsā’*: A proper noun designating Asa:

A. The name of a good king in Judah. The name means, probably, "one who cares, heals." He was the third king in Judah after the monarchy. He was the grandson of Rehoboam. His mother (or grandmother) was Maacah (1 Kgs. 15:9–10). He was evaluated as a good king who followed the Lord. He ruled forty-one years (910–869 B.C.) He did not remove the high places (1 Kgs. 15:9–14). He warred with Baasha, king of Israel but overcame him by making a treaty with Ben-Hadad of Aram (1 Kgs. 15:18–22). He built fortifications in Judah (Jer. 41:9). He was diseased in his feet during his old age (1 Kgs. 15:23–24). Jehoshaphat, his son, succeeded him.

B. A Levite, a son of Elkanah, who returned from exile to Jerusalem (1 Chr. 9:16).

610. אָסוּךְ *’āsûḵ*: A masculine noun referring to a small pot or jar for oil. It is used only once to refer to the jar of oil that belonged to a poor widow (2 Kgs. 4:2). It was made of clay.

611. אָסוֹן *’āsôn*: A masculine noun meaning mischief, evil, harm, hurt, or damage. It signifies potential danger during a journey (Gen. 42:4, 38), bodily harm or personal loss (Ex. 21:22, 23).

612. אֵסוּר *’ēsûr*: A masculine noun meaning a bond, chains binding, or prison. It was used to bind Samson's hands and, evidently, was quite strong (Judg. 15:14). It refers figuratively to hands that are chains or binding (Eccl. 7:26). A house of binding means a prison (Jer. 37:15).

613. אֱסוּר *’ᵉsûr*: An Aramaic masculine noun meaning band, imprisonment. It refers to the act of incarceration (Ezra 7:26). It indicates a strong band made of iron and bronze that could bind up a huge tree stump (Dan. 4:15[12], 23[20]).

614. אָסִיף *’āsiyp̱*, אָסִף *’āsip̱*: A masculine active noun meaning an ingathering, harvest. It refers to an ingathering taken in before the rainy season from either the winepress or threshing floor (Ex. 23:16; 34:22).

615. אָסִיר ***'āsiyr:*** A masculine noun meaning prisoner, captive. It refers to a variety of prisoners or captives: prisoners of war (Isa. 14:17); prisoners held in containment for various reasons (Gen. 39:20); or who had been under taskmasters (Job 3:18). These persons were also the object of God's special concern (Ps. 68:6[7]; 69:33[34]; 79:11). This word describes the freed captives, prisoners from the Babylonian exile, the exiles of Israel (Zech. 9:11). They were prisoners of hope (Zech. 9:12) awaiting their release from captivity in Babylon.

616. אַסִּיר ***'assiyr:*** A masculine noun depicting prisoners, captives (collective noun). It is used to describe captives of war and plunder (Isa. 10:4). In a highly theological usage, it refers to prisoners as those kings of earth and the host of heaven whom the Lord will gather into prison and eventually punish (Isa. 24:22). Equally significant is the spiritual liberation and rescue given to prisoners suffering spiritual captivity. The Servant of the Lord will bring them out, liberating them (Isa. 42:7).

617. אַסִּיר ***'assiyr:*** A proper noun designating Assir:

A. A son of Korah (Ex. 6:24).

B. A son of Ebiasaph (1 Chr. 6:22[7], 23[8], 37[22]).

C. A son of Jeconiah (1 Chr. 3:17).

618. אָסָם ***'āsām:*** A masculine noun meaning storehouse, barn, stores. The word refers to those buildings where the blessing from the Lord in produce was stored (Deut. 28:8). Barns full of plenty were a result of honoring the Lord with one's wealth (Prov. 3:10).

619. אַסְנָה ***'asnāh:*** A proper noun designating Asnah (Ezra 2:50).

620. אָסְנַפַּר ***'osnappar:*** A proper noun designating Osnappar, probably a reference to Ashurbanipal (Ezra 4:10).

621. אָסְנַת ***'ās^{e}naṯ:*** A proper noun designating Asenath (Gen. 41:45, 50; 46:20).

622. אָסַף ***'āsap̱:*** A verb meaning to gather, to take away, to harvest. The meaning of the word varies depending on the context. The word can mean to gather people for different purposes (Gen. 29:22; 42:17; Ex. 3:16; 4:29). It is used of a nation collecting armies for fighting (Num. 21:23; Judg. 11:20; 1 Sam. 17:1; 2 Sam. 10:17); and the Lord taking away Rachel's disgrace of childlessness (Gen. 30:23). Oftentimes it refers to gathering or harvesting food or gathering other objects, such as animals (Jer. 12:9); quail (Num. 11:32); eggs (Isa. 10:14); money (2 Kgs. 22:4; 2 Chr. 24:11). The word also refers to death or burial, literally meaning to be gathered to one's people (Gen. 25:8, 17; 35:29; 49:29, 33); to be gathered to one's fathers (Judg. 2:10); or to be gathered to one's grave (2 Kgs. 22:20; 2 Chr. 34:28).

623. אָסָף *'āsāp̱:* A proper noun designating Asaph, a name applied to several persons in the Old Testament. The name means "gatherer, convener."

A. He was one of David's chief music leaders. Son of Berachiah (1 Chr. 6:39[24]) and a Levite (1 Chr. 15:17). He sounded the bronze cymbals. He ministered before the ark of God (1 Chr. 16:5). His sons were appointed to various duties by David (1 Chr. 25:1). He composed many psalms (Pss. 50, 73—83). The singers at the Temple under Ezra were descendants of Asaph (Ezra 2:41). His descendants helped dedicate the new Temple (Ezra 3:10) and the wall (Neh. 12:35, 36).

B. An Asaph was the father of King Hezekiah's secretary, Joah, an important official position (2 Kgs. 18:17–18).

C. It refers to a Korahite named Asaph who served as a gatekeeper (1 Chr. 26:1).

D. It designates a person who cared for the Persian king's forests. He gave Nehemiah timber for work in Jerusalem (Neh. 2:8–9).

E. It refers to a Levite who lived in Jerusalem on the return from the Babylonian Exile (Neh. 11:17).

624. אָסֹף *'āsōp̱,* אֲסֻפִּים *'ᵃsuppiym:* A masculine noun meaning a collection, treasury, or storehouse. The primary meaning of the root is that which is gathered. It is used three times in the Old Testament to signify the storehouses near the gates of a temple (1 Chr. 26:15, 17; Neh. 12:25).

625. אֹסֶף *'ōsep̱:* A masculine noun meaning a collection, ingathering, harvest. The Hebrew word especially refers to a harvest of summer fruit, as is depicted in Micah 7:1, "Gather the summer fruits" (NKJV). The prophet Isaiah is the other biblical author to use this term. In Isaiah 32:10, he states that the complacent people will be troubled and insecure because "the gathering will not come," but, then in Isaiah 33:4, the prophet uses the same word to refer to the Lord's spoil being collected like "the gathering of the caterpillar."

626. אֲסֵפָה *'ᵃsēp̱āh:* A feminine noun meaning a gathering or a collection. This word is related to *'āsap̱* (622), which means to gather or collect. This particular word occurs only in Isaiah 24:22, "And they will be gathered together, as prisoners are gathered in the pit" (NKJV).

627. אֲסֻפָּה *'ᵃsuppah:* A feminine noun meaning council or assembly. It comes from a root meaning to gather. Although there are many usages of the different forms of the root, this particular word is used only once in the Hebrew Bible, and the usage is plural instead of singular. It is used with the word for master and can be translated as "the gathering of masters"; "the council of scholars"; or "the collected sayings of scholars" (Eccl. 12:11).

628. אֲסַפְסֻף *ʼasapsup:* A masculine noun meaning a gathering or mixed multitude. This word is related to *ʼāsap̱* (622), which means to gather or collect. It occurs only in Numbers 11:4, "And the mixed multitude that was among them fell a lusting" (KJV).

629. אָסְפַּרְנָא *ʼosparnāʼ:* An Aramaic adverb indicating speed or diligence; eagerly, exactly, with care. It reflects the manner in which the new Temple in Jerusalem was being built in the time of Ezra (538–516 B.C.). It describes the speed, diligence, and strictness with which the decrees of Darius and Artaxerxes designating payment for the temple and its worship services were to be carried out (Ezra 6:8, 12, 13; 7:17, 21, 26).

630. אַסְפָּתָא *ʼaspāṯāʼ:* A proper noun designating Aspatha (Esth. 9:7).

631. אָסַר *ʼāsar:* A verb meaning to bind, obligate, imprison, hold captive. The word has several areas of meaning. The word describes tying up or binding animals (Gen. 49:11; 1 Sam. 6:7; 2 Kgs. 7:10; Ps. 118:27). It refers to binding with a cord or fetters, such as the binding of Simeon (Gen. 42:24), Samson (Judg. 15:10; 16:5–8), and Zedekiah (2 Kgs. 25:7). Used figuratively, it means to bind or punish someone (a fool) with discipline or to exercise authority over someone (Ps. 105:22). The beauty of a woman's hair can hold a king captive (Song 7:5[6]). It means to fasten or to gird on something, such as a waistcloth (Neh. 4:18[12]; Job 12:18). As a military term, it means to begin the battle, to attack, to set the battle (1 Kgs. 20:14; 2 Chr. 13:3). Used as a technical legal term, it means to bind oneself to a vow of abstention (Num. 30:2–11[3–12]), using its cognate noun (*ʼissār* [632]) after it (cf. NIV, to obligate). In its passive uses, it means to be bound, taken prisoner, or be imprisoned (Gen. 42:19; Judg. 16:6, 10; Isa. 22:3).

632. אֱסָר *ʼesār,* אִסָּר *ʼissār:* A masculine noun meaning bond, binding obligation, or vow of abstention or agreement. All references to this word are in Numbers (30:2–5[3–6], 7[8], 10–14[11–15]). It is used eleven times, most often with the verb *ʼāsar*, to bind oneself with a vow of abstention or binding obligation (NKJV, agreement; NIV, pledge).

633. אֱסָר *ʼesār:* An Aramaic masculine noun meaning decree, injunction. It refers to a royal decree issued to stop a certain thing or activity, such as Daniel's faithful prayers to the Lord three times daily (Dan. 6:7–9[8–10], 12[13], 13[14], 15[16]).

634. אֵסַרְחַדּוֹן *ʼēsarḥaddôn:* A proper noun designating Esarhaddon, a great Assyrian king who succeeded Sennacherib who tried to destroy Jerusalem (2 Kgs. 19:37). He reigned 681–669 B.C.

635. אֶסְתֵּר *ʼestēr:* The name of the Jewish queen Esther of Persia. Her name means "star." She was raised up by God at the right time and place to bring deliverance to the Jews in Persia (Esth. 4:12–14). An Amalakite, Haman, plotted to destroy God's chosen people, but Esther and Mordecai worked together to thwart the plan (Esth. 3—4). The Persian king Ahasuerus (Xerxes) reigned 486–465 B.C. Her request to slay the enemies of the Jews is not to be followed today, but God's great deliverance of the Jews is still celebrated in the Feast of Purim today (Esth. 10:18–32).

636. אָע *'ā':* An Aramaic masculine noun referring to a wood beam, timber. It refers to the beams used to construct the new Temple in the time of Ezra (5:8) and approved by Cyrus and Darius, kings of Persia (Ezra 6:4, 11). It refers to idols made of wood as well (Dan. 5:4, 23).

637. אַף *'ap:* A particle meaning also, yea, indeed, even. Its main meanings are also, even, or it notes emphasis (Gen. 40:16; Ps. 89:27[28]); contrast (Ps. 44:9[10]). It means yes when used with *kiy* (3588) to introduce a conditional sentence (yes, if . . . , Ezek. 14:21); really, when used before *kīy* to introduce a question (Gen. 3:1). It introduces clauses of time when used before *kīy*, e.g., Nehemiah 9:18, even if.

638. אַף *'ap̱:* An Aramaic conjunction meaning also, even. It indicates that something was said or done or not said or done (Ezra 5:10, 14; Dan. 6:22[23]) or that something is to be continued or added to (Ezra 6:5).

639. אַף *'ap̱:* A masculine noun meaning nose, nostril, and anger. These meanings are used together in an interesting wordplay in Proverbs 30:33. This word may, by extension, refer to the whole face, particularly in the expression, to bow one's face to the ground (Gen. 3:19; 19:1; 1 Sam. 24:8[9]). To have length of nose is to be slow to wrath; to have shortness of nose is to be quick tempered (Prov. 14:17, 29; Jer. 15:14, 15). This Hebrew term is often intensified by being paired with another word for anger or by associating it with various words for burning (Num. 22:27; Deut. 9:19; Jer. 4:8; 7:20). Human anger is almost always viewed negatively with only a few possible exceptions (Ex. 32:19; 1 Sam. 11:6; Prov. 27:4). The anger of the Lord is a frequent topic in the Old Testament. The Old Testament describes how God is reluctant to exercise His anger and how fierce His anger is (Ex. 4:14; 34:6; Ps. 30:5[6]; 78:38; Jer. 51:45).

640. אָפַד *'āp̱aḏ:* A verb meaning to gird, to bind, to tie. It indicates the fastening or tight wrapping of a band around a person (Ex. 29:5; Lev. 8:7). In these references, it indicates that the ephod would be firmly fastened to the high priest.

641. אֵפֹד *'ēp̱ōḏ:* A proper noun designating Ephod (Num. 34:23).

642. אֲפֻדָּה *'apuddāh:* A feminine noun meaning ephod, the woven material design of an ephod, a garment of the priest, or an image. It refers to the special composition of the garment the high priest wore which had the twelve stones representing the twelve tribes of Israel on it. The waistband of the priest was to be made like the *'apuddāh* (Ex. 28:8; 39:5). It also refers to (molten) images covered with gold (Isa. 30:22).

643. אַפֶּדֶן *'appeden:* A masculine noun indicating tent structure, a tent palace, pavilion. It refers to a royal tent or structure that the fierce king of the North will pitch before he is destroyed (Dan. 11:45).

644. אָפָה *'āpāh:* A verb meaning to bake. The word refers to the preparation of items of food, especially unleavened bread (Gen. 19:3; Ex. 12:39); but it also refers to whatever needed to be prepared over fire (Ex. 16:23). The participle of the verb always means baker (Gen. 40:1, 2, 5, 16; 41:10; Jer. 37:21; Hos. 7:4). In its passive form, it means to be baked (Lev. 6:7[10]; 7:9; 23:17).

645. אֵפוֹ *'ēpô*, אֵפוֹא *'ēpô':* A particle meaning then, now. It is sometimes used after an interrogative word (Gen. 27:33; Ex. 33:16) but also before an interrogative word (Gen. 27:37). It is found in wishes meaning would that (Job 19:23) or oh that! It is employed in conditional sentences with *'im* (518) or *'im lô'* meaning if then or if then . . . not (Job 9:24; 24:25). It expresses a logical result, such as know then, know now (2 Kgs. 10:10).

646. אֵפוֹד *'ēpôd*, אֵפֹד *'ēpōd:* A masculine noun meaning ephod, a garment of the high priest. A garment worn around the high priest's upper body that featured twelve semiprecious and precious stones on the front, each one bearing the name of one of the tribes of Israel (Ex. 28:4, 6, 12, 15, 25–28). The breastplate bearing the stones was on the front of the ephod itself. The ephod was made by a skilled workman and had two shoulder pieces which were fastened together to hold it securely. It also bore two stones, one on each of its shoulders that represented the tribes of Israel. Each stone had six of the tribes of Israel engraved on it.

It represents idolatrous cultic objects made by Gideon and Micah (Judg. 8:27; 17:5) and later used to obtain decisions, probably incorrectly (1 Sam. 23:9). The object was probably a sacred robe with some metallic aspect to it. The word refers to a simple linen ephod as well (1 Sam. 2:18, 28).

647. אֲפִיחַ *'apiyah:* A proper noun designating Aphiah (1 Sam. 9:1).

648. אָפִיל *'āpiyl:* An adjective indicating a late ripening. The word refers to wheat and spelt as grains which ripen late. They were not destroyed, therefore, in the plague of hail (Ex. 9:32).

649. אַפַּיִם *'appayim:* A proper noun designating Appaim (1 Chr. 2:30, 31).

650. אָפִיק *'āpiyq:* I. A masculine noun referring to a torrent, a stream channel, ravine; tube. The word is found often in Ezekiel (6:3; 31:12; 32:6; 34:13; 35:8; 36:4, 6) indicating a stream channel. It refers to channels opened in the deep sea waters (2 Sam. 22:16) but also to the wadis or quickly appearing but swiftly vanishing streams in the desert (Job 6:15; Joel 1:20). It also, however, describes smooth flowing streams of peace (Song 5:12). The strength of Behemoth is described by this word (KJV, Job 40:18).

II. An adjective meaning strong, mighty. The word refers to someone or something that is strong, mighty. The word refers to strong persons of great wealth and influence. It describes the tubes, sinews, of the Behemoth (NIV, NASB, Job 40:18).

651. אָפֵל *'āpēl:* An adjective meaning dark or gloomy. This word is related to *'ōpel* (652), which means darkness or gloom. The only time this word occurs in the Old Testament is in Amos 5:20, "Shall not the day of the LORD be darkness, and not light? even very dark, and no brightness in it?" (KJV).

652. אֹפֶל *'ōpel:* A masculine noun, used only in poetry to denote darkness, gloom, especially a thick darkness. Although the term can be used in reference to physical darkness (Job 28:3; Ps. 91:6), it is more often used in a figurative sense to designate things like obscurity (Job 3:6); death (Job 10:22); evil (Job 23:17; 30:26; Ps. 11:2). In Isaiah 29:18, the term has both a literal and a figurative meaning in reference to the blind.

653. אֲפֵלָה *'ªpēlāh:* A feminine noun meaning darkness or gloominess. It signifies physical darkness: the plague of darkness (Ex. 10:22); the naïve walking in darkness (Prov. 7:9); the darkness which causes people to stumble and grope (Prov. 4:19; Deut. 28:29). Metaphorically, it is used to describe the calamity and misfortune that comes to the wicked (Isa. 8:22; Jer. 23:12) or the darkness of the day of the Lord (Joel 2:2; Zeph. 1:15).

654. אֶפְלָל *'eplāl:* A proper noun designating Ephlal (1 Chr. 2:37).

655. אֹפֶן *'ōpen:* A masculine noun meaning right time, right circumstance. The word refers to the proper time for appropriate words to be used (Prov. 25:11).

656. אָפֵס *'āpēs:* A verb indicating coming to an end, being used up, gone. It refers to a depletion of money (Gen. 47:15, 16) or the ending of God's promise (Ps. 77:8[9]). Or it can indicate the completion of the Lord's judgments (Isa. 16:4; 29:20).

657. אֶפֶס *'epes,* אֹפֶס *'ōphes:* I. A masculine noun indicating ceasing, end, extremity, naught. It is used essentially in three ways meaning ceasing, nonexistence, no effect: 1) to cease to exist or effect (Isa. 34:12; 41:29); to act with no effect (Isa. 52:4); 2) a cessation of something, such as until there is no place (Deut. 32:36; 2 Kgs. 14:26; Isa. 45:6; Amos 6:10); 3) the idea of limiting, such as only (Num. 22:35; 23:13) or except that (Num. 13:28; Deut. 15:4; Judg. 4:9). The word is also used to mean ceasing in the sense of end or extremity: the ends of the earth (Deut. 33:17; 1 Sam. 2:10; Prov. 30:4; Jer. 16:19; Mic. 5:4[3]).

II. A masculine noun indicating ankles or soles of the feet. It is used only in the dual, referring to two extremities. In Ezekiel 47:3 it means, therefore, the soles of the feet or ankles.

658. אֶפֶס דַּמִּים *'epes dammiym:* A proper noun designating Ephes-dammim (1 Sam. 17:1).

659. אֶפַע *'epa':* A masculine noun meaning worthlessness, nothing, of no account. It refers to the absolute inability of pagan gods to act as gods (Isa. 41:24). They are of no account (NASB).

660. אֶפְעֶה *'ep'eh:* A masculine noun meaning adder, viper, or snake. This creature is found in the desert (Isa. 30:6). The tongue or (metaphorically) the venom of this snake slays a wicked person (Job 20:16). It refers figuratively to the evil that the rebellious Israelites encounter when they seek help from the wrong source (Isa. 59:5).

661. אָפַף *'āpap:* A verb meaning to entangle, surround, engulf, encompass. Literally, it depicts waves of water enshrouding Jonah (2:5[6]). It refers figuratively to waves of death or evil surrounding and wrapping up the psalmist (212[13]; 116:3).

662. אָפַק *'āpaq:* A verb meaning to hold back, restrain oneself, be compelled. The word depicts self-control (Gen. 43:31; 45:1; Esth. 5:10). It means to make oneself do something (1 Sam. 13:12). It depicts the Lord's self-control (Isa. 42:14; 63:15; 64:12[11]).

663. אֲפִיק *'ᵃpiyq,* אֲפֵק *'ᵃpēq:* A proper noun designating Aphek, a name given to several cities in the Old Testament:

A. It names a city allotted to the tribe of Asher (Josh. 19:30). The tribe was not able to drive out the inhabitants of the city (Judg. 1:31) but intermingled with them. It is located southeast of Acco.

B. It names a city on the border of the Amorites, Sidonian territory, located southeast of Baal-gad in Lebanon (Josh. 13:5).

C. A city in the southeast area of Sharon country near the Jarkon River. Joshua executed its king (Josh. 12:18). Philistines gathered there for two major battles (1 Sam. 4:1; 29:1). It was located northeast of Joppa. Herod the Great built Antipatris, a fortress there in ca. 35 B.C.

D. A city east of the Jordan where Israel and the Arameans battled (1 Kgs. 20:26, 30; 2 Kgs. 13:17). Ben-Hadad was defeated there. Some scholars place it east of Galilee.

664. אֲפֵקָה *'apēqāh:* A proper noun designating Aphekah (Josh. 15:53).

665. אֵפֶר *'ēper:* A masculine noun meaning soil, ashes, dust. It describes loose soil or dirt put on a person's head to indicate mourning (2 Sam. 13:19; Ezek. 27:30). It is used in the phrase sackcloth and ashes (*saq wā'ēpek*, Isa. 58:5; Jon. 3:6). It describes the wicked figuratively as ashes under the feet of the righteous (Ezek. 28:18; Mal. 4:3[3:21]). Humans are mere dust and ashes (Gen. 18:27). It is used to describe the ashes of the red heifer (Num. 19:9, 10) used in a cleansing ritual.

666. אֲפֵר *'apēr:* A. A masculine noun meaning headband, bandage. This word describes something placed over a person's eyes in order to disguise him or her (1 Kgs. 20:38; cf. KJV, ashes).

B. A masculine noun meaning ashes or dust. It describes something used to cover a persons' eyes to disguise him or her (1 Kgs. 20:38; cf. NASB, NIV, NKJV).

667. אֶפְרֹחַ *'eprōah:* A masculine noun indicating a young bird. The word describes young birds still in the nest with their mother. The young birds could be taken, but the mother had to be left (Deut. 22:6). It refers to baby hawks (Job 39:30) and swallows (Ps. 84:3[4]).

668. אַפִּרְיוֹן *'appiryôn:* A masculine noun meaning chariot, carriage, sedan chair. The word describes the carriage or sedan chair in which Solomon rode on his wedding day (Song 3:9).

669. אֶפְרַיִם *'eprayim:* A proper noun designating Ephraim:

A. The second son of Joseph. The name is a dual form and indicates fruitfulness (Gen. 41:52). He was born in Egypt as was Manasseh (Gen. 46:20) by Asenath, the daughter of Potiphera, Priest of On (Heliopolis, "city of the sun"). Jacob recognized the two boys as his by adoption (Gen. 48:5). Jacob blessed Ephraim, the younger, ahead of Manasseh, the elder (Gen. 48:20). His descendants were numerous (Num. 26:28; 1 Chr. 7:20, 22).

B. The name refers to the territory allotted to Ephraim (A above), the tribe formed by his descendants. The tribe became tens of thousands (Deut. 33:17). The location of the tribal land was in central Israel, bordered on the north by Manasseh, the west by Dan, the south by Dan-Benjamin, the east by Manasseh (Josh. 16). The name "Ephraim" became synonymous for Northern Israel. Ephraim and the north broke away from Judah and the line of David after Solomon's death (1 Kgs. 12:12–19). The prophets saw a day when Ephraim would be reunited with David and Judah, one nation—Israel, again (Ezek. 37:15–17; Zech. 9:10, 13; 10:7). The Lord never cast off Ephraim (N. Israel) fully, for he loved them (Hos. 11:8).

670. אֲפָרְסָי ***ᵃpārᵉsāy:*** I. A proper noun referring to Apharsites (Ezra 4:9, KJV).

II. A reference to the men of Persia (Ezra 4:9, NIV).

III. A reference to secretaries (Ezra 4:9, NASB).

671. אֲפַרְסְכָי ***ᵃparsᵉḵāy,*** אֲפַרְסַתְכָי ***ᵃparsatḵāy:*** I. An Aramaic proper noun referring to the Apharsathchites, a people settled in Samaria (KJV, Ezra 4:9; 5:6; 6:6).

II. An Aramaic masculine noun referring to officials, lesser governers (NASB, NIV, Ezra 4:9; 5:6; 6:6).

672. אֶפְרָת ***'eprāṯ,*** אֶפְרָתָה ***'eprāṯāh:*** A proper noun designating Ephrath:

A. It is used as a name for Bethlehem in antiquity. Rachel was buried there (Gen. 35:16, 19; 48:7), and Naomi lived there (Ruth 4:11). David's father, Jesse, came from there (1 Sam. 17:12). It was the territory of David (Ps. 132:6). It was prophesied as the place from which the Ruler over Israel would come, whose origins were mysterious and from ancient times (Mic. 5:2[1]).

B. It refers to the second wife of Caleb, son of Hezron (1 Chr. 2:18, 19).

673. אֶפְרָתִי ***'eprāṯiy:*** A proper noun designating Ephraimite, Ephrathite:

A. A proper noun referring to an Ephraimite, a descendant of Ephraim (Judg. 12:5; 1 Sam. 1:1; 1 Kgs. 11:26).

B. A proper noun referring to an Ephrathite, an inhabitant of Ephratah (Ruth 1:2; 1 Sam. 17:12).

674. אַפְּתֹם ***'appᵉṯōm:*** An Aramaic masculine noun meaning revenue. It refers to the tribute, custom, and tolls that went to Persian kings (Ezra 4:13).

675. אֶצְבּוֹן ***'eṣbôn:*** A proper noun designating Ezbon:

A. A son of Gad (Gen. 46:16).

B. A grandson of Benjamin (1 Chr. 7:7).

676. אֶצְבַּע ***'eṣbaʿ:*** A feminine noun meaning finger, toe. The word designates either fingers (Ex. 29:12; Lev. 4:6, 17) or toes (2 Sam. 21:20; 1 Chr. 20:6). Various functions of the finger are noted. It was an instrument that could be used for good or evil: (1) The forefinger of a priest applied blood or oil in certain rituals (Lev. 4:6, 17, 25; 14:16, 27). (2) it was used figuratively to describe God's act of writing (Ex. 31:18) or intervention (Ex. 8:19[15]). (3) Several fingers were a measure of thickness (Jer. 52:21). (4)

Idols were produced by the work of human fingers (Isa. 2:8).

677. אֶצְבַּע *'eṣba':* An Aramaic feminine noun meaning finger or toe. Used as an anthropomorphism, it describes the fingers and toes on the great image of Daniel (Dan. 2:41, 42) and of the mysterious hand that wrote on the wall of Belshazzar's palace.

678. אָצִיל *'āṣiyl:* A masculine noun designating side, corner, chief. This term can indicate the sides or borders of the earth, thereby referring to its extremities or remotest countries (Isa. 41:9); or it can be used figuratively to mean nobles (Ex. 24:11).

679. אַצִּיל *'aṣṣiyl:* A. A feminine noun meaning joint, armpit, wrist. It refers to the joint of a person's hand or wrist (Ezek. 13:18). It indicates the arm joints or armpits (Jer. 38:12) by which Jeremiah was rescued.

B. A feminine noun meaning great or long. It is used to describe a cubit as long (Ezek. 41:8) or great (KJV).

680. אָצַל *'āṣal:* A verb meaning to reserve, hold back, take part of. It is used of taking away both a blessing and a birthright (Gen. 27:36). It describes removing some of the Spirit of God from Moses to place it on the seventy elders of Israel (Num. 11:17, 25). Its opposite means to give free reign to, not refuse (Eccl. 2:10), e.g., one's eyes. It can be used literally as an architectural term meaning to shorten, be shortened, or to set back (Ezek. 42:6), such as temple chambers.

681. אֵצֶל *'ēṣel:* A masculine noun meaning nearness, beside, next to. It is used only as a preposition. It functions in two ways: (1) to indicate proximity (Gen. 39:10, 15; 41:3) meaning beside something or in a certain locality (Deut. 11:30; 1 Kgs. 1:9; 4:12); (2) to indicate removal from proximity or location when used with *min* (4480), from (1 Sam. 17:30; 20:41; 1 Kgs. 3:20; Ezek. 40:7).

682. אָצֵל *'āṣēl,* אָצַל *'āṣal:* A proper noun designating Azel:

A. A Benjamite (1 Chr. 8:37, 38; 9:43, 44).

B. A city (Zech. 14:5).

683. אֲצַלְיָהוּ *'aṣalyāhû:* A proper noun designating Azaliah (2 Kgs. 22:3; 2 Chr. 34:8).

684. אֹצֶם *'ōṣem:* A proper noun designating Ozem:

A. A brother of David (1 Chr. 2:15).

B. A descendant of Judah (1 Chr. 2:25).

685. אֶצְעָדָה *'eṣ'āḏāh:* A feminine noun meaning armlet, bracelet. This item is mentioned as booty found after Israel defeated Midian and was presented to the high priest (Num. 31:50). It may refer to a "pace chain," a chain between the ankles. Elsewhere it refers to an armlet (2 Sam. 1:10) that clasped the upper arm.

686. אָצַר ***'āṣar:*** A verb meaning to store up or put in charge of stored items. It refers to everything stored in Hezekiah's palace and the temple (2 Kgs. 20:17; Isa. 39:6). It indicates Nehemiah's (13:13) placing certain persons in charge of the tithes kept in the storehouses. It is used figuratively of the wealth, wages, and gains of Tyre, a city of harlotry, which would be destroyed by the Lord. Her wealth would be decimated, not stored up (Isa. 23:18). Amos uses the word to refer to hoarding up evil or violence (3:10).

687. אֵצֶר ***'ēṣer:*** A proper noun designating Ezer (Gen. 36:21, 27, 30; 1 Chr. 1:38, 42).

688. אֶקְדָּח ***'eqdāḥ:*** A masculine noun meaning crystal or sparkling jewel. The word describes the material of the restored gates of Zion, gates of crystal, which the Lord will provide (Isa. 54:12).

689. אַקּוֹ ***'aqqô:*** A masculine noun referring to a wild goat. It is among the animals that the Israelites could eat and still be holy (Deut. 14:5).

690. אֲרָא ***'arā':*** A proper noun designating Ara (1 Chr. 7:38).

691. אֶרְאֵל ***'er'ēl:*** A masculine noun meaning valiant one, brave one. It depicts the brave men of Jerusalem who weep in her streets because of the devastation the city has suffered (Isa. 33:7). These men may be priests, inhabitants of Jerusalem, or heroes.

692. אַרְאֵלִי ***'ar'ēliy:*** A proper noun designating Areli:

A. Areli, son of Gad (Gen. 46:16; Num. 26:17).

B. A masculine plural proper noun referring to the Arelites (Num. 26:17).

693. אָרַב ***'āraḇ:*** A verb meaning to ambush, lie in wait, to lurk. The word describes the activity of the wicked man as he lurks to oppress or destroy the afflicted (Deut. 19:11; Ps. 10:9). It describes lying in ambush as a military tactic with intent to kill (Josh. 8:2, 4, 7). It can mean to put or set up an ambush (Judg. 9:25; 1 Sam. 15:5).

694. אֲרָב ***'arāḇ:*** A proper noun designating Arab (Josh. 15:52).

695. אֶרֶב ***'ereḇ:*** A masculine noun indicating a den or lying in wait. It is the lair or home of the beast lying in wait, as directed by God (Job 37:8; 38:40).

696. אֹרֶב ***'ōreḇ:*** A masculine noun meaning ambush, trap. It is used figuratively to describe the harm and evil that wicked people plan for their own neighbor (Jer. 9:8[7]]). It describes the political intrigue aimed against the king or by the king (Hos. 7:6, NKJV, NASB, KJV translate as a verb, *'āraḇ* [693], to lie in wait, to plot).

697. אַרְבֶּה ***'arbeh:*** A masculine noun indicating locusts or grasshoppers. The word refers to a species of migrating or desert locusts. Infestations of locusts could destroy entire crops (Deut. 28:38). The eighth plague on Egypt was a locust plague of immense destructive proportions (Ex. 10:4, 12–14, 19). A locust plague, real or imagined, was used figuratively to describe the coming devastation of the day of the Lord (Joel 1:4; 2:25). It was, however, included in the Law of Moses among the insects that could be eaten (Lev. 11:22). The locust appeared suddenly and disappeared suddenly (Nah. 3:15, 17). Wise men noted that locusts were a well-organized group, even though they had no king (Prov. 30:27). They could thus be likened to an invading army (Judg. 6:5; 7:12). There were several kinds of locusts or perhaps several phases in the lives of locusts described in Joel 1:4.

698. אָרְבָּה ***'orbāh:*** A feminine noun depicting deceit, trickery, artifice. It refers literally to the tricks of one's hands; in context, it describes the deceit or trickery of Moab's actions (Isa. 25:11).

699. אֲרֻבָּה ***'ᵃrubbāh:*** A feminine noun meaning floodgate, window. It refers generally to windows in a house (Eccl. 12:3), but here possibly to eye sockets. Figuratively, it refers to windows or floodgates of the sky (Gen. 7:11; 8:2) which God controls. In general, it refers to God's ability to provide an abundance of anything (2 Kgs. 7:2, 19) but also to the windows through which God pours judgments from on high (Isa. 24:18). The word refers symbolically to lattices, nests (NASB, NIV), or roosts (KJV, NIV windows) for safety (Isa. 60:8). It also depicts a window in a wall through which smoke escapes (Hos. 13:3).

700. אֲרֻבּוֹת ***'ᵃrubbôṯ:*** A proper noun designating Arubboth (1 Kgs. 4:10).

701. אַרְבִּי ***'arbiy:*** A proper noun designating Arbite (2 Sam. 23:35).

702. אַרְבַּע ***'arba',*** אַרְבָּעָה ***'arbā'āh:*** A common noun meaning four. Used as an ordinal number, it means fourth. Put into its plural form, *'arbā'îm,* it means forty; put into its dual form, *'arbā'ayîm,* fourfold. With the preposition b^e added to it, followed by the month, it means fourth (Zech. 1:7).

703. אַרְבַּע ***'arba':*** An Aramaic common noun meaning four. Followed by m^e*'āh,* hundred, it means four hundred (Ezra 6:17). It is used in Daniel to describe four beasts, four winds, four wings (7:2, 3, 6, 17), and four men (3:25), one of whom was like a son of the gods.

704. אַרְבַּע ***'arba':*** A proper noun designating Arba; see also *qiryaṯ 'arba'* (7153) (Josh. 15:13; 21:11).

705. אַרְבָּעִים ***'arbā'iym:*** A common noun meaning forty, fortieth. It is always in its absolute form. Used alone it means forty of something (Gen. 7:17; Judg. 3:11; 1 Sam. 4:18; 1 Kgs. 19:8; Amos 2:10). It combines with other numbers to give the counting numbers, forty-one (1 Kgs. 14:21; 15:10), etc. With the preposition b^e added, it means fortieth, such as in the fortieth year (Deut. 1:3) or in the forty-first year (2 Chr. 16:13).

706. אַרְבַּעְתַּיִם ***'arba'tayim:*** A noun meaning fourfold. This is the dual form of *'arba'*, four. It is found only once in 2 Samuel 12:6 where it describes fourfold restitution for a lamb.

707. אָרַג ***'ārag:*** A verb meaning to weave, to braid. The verb describes the work of a skilled craftsman, an expert at working materials together. Egyptians were known for their fine woven white cloth (Isa. 19:9). The fringe or binding around the neck of the high priest's robe was the work of a weaver (Ex. 28:32; 35:35; 39:22, 27), as well as other priestly garments. The participle of the verb indicates a weaver (1 Sam. 17:7). It describes the intertwining of human hair (Judg. 16:13) or the production of pagan cult hangings (2 Kgs. 23:7). It is used figuratively to indicate the rolling up of one's life like a weaver (Isa. 38:12) rolls up his equipment.

708. אֶרֶג ***'ereg:*** A masculine noun referring to a loom or weaver's shuttle. It describes a hairpiece or hair loom or web (Judg. 16:14). The speed of the motion of the weaver's shuttle is used metaphorically to refer to the days of Job's life passing by swiftly (Job 7:6).

709. אַרְגֹּב ***'argōḇ:*** A proper noun designating Argob:

A. The name of an area in Basham, east of the Jordan, the land of King Og (Deut. 3:4, 13, 14). Later, it was part of Solomon's lands (1 Kgs. 4:13).

B. He was an administrator or official of Pekahiah, king of Israel who was assassinated by Pekah and his followers (2 Kgs. 15:25–26; so NIV, NASB; KJV seems to indicate that he was an officer to Pekah in the affair).

710. אַרְגְּוָן ***'arg^ewān:*** A masculine noun meaning purple. It is used only once in 2 Chronicles 2:7[6]). It indicates wool dyed purple. Some recent translators prefer to translate this as red purple.

711. אַרְגְּוָן ***'arg^ewān:*** An Aramaic masculine noun meaning purple, scarlet. It was wool dyed purple and was a feature of royal garments (Dan. 5:7, 16, 29).

712. אַרְגָּז ***'argāz:*** A masculine noun indicating a box or chest. It refers to a container holding several gold mice and molds of the tumors the Philistines were suffering from (1 Sam. 6:8, 11, 15).

713. אַרְגָּמָן ***'argāmān:*** A masculine noun indicating purple. This wool dyed purple or red purple was featured in the high priest's clothing (Ex. 28:5, 6, 8, 15) and its decorative features (Ex. 28:33), such as pomegranates. It was the color of a purple cloth which covered the altar when it was cleaned (Num. 4:13). This color was a feature of royal clothing (Judg. 8:26; Esth. 8:15; Jer. 10:9); the hangings and decorations in royal palaces (Esth. 1:6); and even royal couches (Song 3:10).

714. אַרְדְּ ***'ard:*** A proper noun designating Ard (Gen. 46:21; Num. 26:40).

715. אַרְדּוֹן ***'ardôn:*** A proper noun designating Ardon (1 Chr. 2:18).

716. אַרְדִּי ***'ardiy:*** A proper noun designating Ardite (Num. 26:40).

717. אָרָה ***'ārāh:*** A verb meaning to gather, to pluck. It is used figuratively to describe the way the nations had devastated Israel and taken away its strength (Ps. 80:12[13]). It is used to describe the gathering of myrrh (Song 5:1).

718. אֲרוּ ***'arû:*** An Aramaic interjection meaning lo, behold. It describes an expression of emotional surprise and terror (Dan. 7:2, 5–7, 13) at the appearance of strange beasts and the Son of Man carried on clouds in a vision.

719. אַרְוַד ***'arwad:*** A proper noun designating Arvad (Ezek. 27:8, 11).

720. אֲרוֹד ***'arôd:*** A proper noun designating Arod (Num. 26:17).

721. אַרְוָדִי ***'arwādiy:*** A proper noun designating Arvadite (Gen. 10:18; 1 Chr. 1:16).

722. אֲרוֹדִי ***'arôdiy:*** A proper noun designating Arodi:

A. A son of Gad (Gen. 46:16).

B. A son of Arod (Num. 26:17).

723. אֻרְוָה ***'urwāh:*** A feminine noun indicating a stall, pen. The term is used to describe the huge complex of quarters constructed for Solomon's horses. These horses pulled his chariots and provided steeds for his horsemen (1 Kgs. 4:26[5:6]; 2 Chr. 9:25).

724. אֲרוּכָה ***'arûkāh,*** אֲרֻכָה ***'arukāh:*** A feminine noun meaning the healing of a wound, restoration, repair. The intuitive meaning is healing caused by the fleshly covering of a physical wound. It signifies the restoration of Israel, both the need for it (Jer. 8:22) and the reality of it (Isa. 58:8); and also the rebuilding of Jerusalem's walls that had been torn down (Jer. 33:6).

725. אֲרוּמָה ***'arûmāh:*** A proper noun designating Arumah (Judg. 9:41).

726. אֲרוֹמִים ***'arômiym:*** A proper noun designating Aramean and Syrian (2 Kgs. 16:6).

727. אָרוֹן ***'ārôn,*** אָרֹן ***'ārōn:*** A common noun meaning a box, chest, or ark. It is treated as masculine in some passages and as feminine in others. This word refers to the chest for collecting money offerings (2 Kgs. 12:9[10], 10[11]); or the sarcophagus in which the mummy of Joseph was placed (Gen. 50:26). In a sacred or cultic context, the term identifies the ark of the covenant (Num. 10:33), which at one time contained the tablets of the law (Deut. 10:5); a copy of the Law which Moses had written (Deut. 31:26); a pot of manna (Ex. 16:33, 34); Aaron's rod (Num. 17:10). This word is often used with another word to denote the ark of the covenant: "the ark of the LORD your God" (Josh. 4:5); "the ark of God" (1 Sam. 3:3); "the ark of the God of Israel" (1 Sam. 5:7); "the holy ark" (2 Chr. 35:3).

728. אֲרַוְנָה ***ʼarawnāh:*** The name of a Jebusite, Araunah, who owned a threshing floor or building (2 Sam. 24:16, 18, 20–24). A destroying angel of pestilence struck Israel from there. David bought the threshing floor from Araunah to stop the Lord's pestilence and plague upon the land (2 Sam. 24:18–21) because of David's sin.

729. אָרוּז ***ʼārûz:*** A. An adjective meaning made of cedar or possibly a twisted rope. It describes one among several luxury items that Tyre traded with the nations. It is translated as an adjective modifying chest, chests of cedar (KJV, Ezek. 27:24) but also as tightly wound cords (NASB) or twisted cords (NIV).

B. An adjective meaning tightly wound, knotted, twisted cord. It describes one among several luxury items that Tyre traded with the nations. It is translated as wound cords (NASB, Ezek. 27:24), twisted cords (NIV), or as an adjective modifying chests, chests of cedar (KJV).

730. אֶרֶז ***ʼerez:*** A masculine noun meaning cedar, cedar tree. The word occurs quite often (Lev. 14:4, 6; Num. 19:6; Judg. 9:15; 1 Kgs. 4:33[5:13]). It is a species of tree from Lebanon, evidently a cedar tree. Some feel that the word refers to a fir tree, since the cedar has a trunk too short for large construction work. It was considered a tall, stately tree (Judg. 9:15; 2 Kgs. 14:9; Amos 2:9). Solomon contrasted it with the smallest of plants (1 Kgs. 4:33[5:13]). It was considered prime construction material (2 Sam. 7:2, 7; Ezra 3:7; Job 40:17; Song 8:9). It is used to depict the strong but devastated Davidic dynasty in a powerful allegory (Ezek. 17:3).

731. אַרְזָה ***ʼarzāh:*** A feminine noun indicating cedar work or beams of cedar. It describes the cedar construction or furnishings found in the Assyrian palace at Nineveh (Zeph. 2:14), laid bare because of God's destruction of the city. Cedar work was a regular feature of royal buildings or furnishings.

732. אָרַח ***ʼāraḥ:*** A verb meaning to travel, to wander. Figuratively, it refers to sharing or agreeing with another person, good or bad (Job 34:8). The participle of the verb refers to a traveler or wanderer (Judg. 19:17; 2 Sam. 12:4). A wanderer or wayfarer in the desert was a common sight (Jer. 9:2[1]). It refers to the seemingly temporary stay of the Lord with Israel during a time of judgment (Jer. 14:8).

733. אָרַח *'āraḥ:* A proper noun designating Arah:

A. An Asherite (1 Chr. 7:39).

B. Head of a family (Ezra 2:5; Neh. 6:18; 7:10).

734. אֹרַח *'ōraḥ:* A masculine noun meaning path, way, byway, or highway. It describes the literal path one walks on (Judg. 5:6); the path or rank one walks in (Joel 2:7). Figuratively, this word describes the path of an individual or course of life (Job 6:18); the characteristics of a lifestyle, good or evil (Ps. 16:11); righteousness or judgment (Prov. 2:13). It is further used to mean traveler or wayfarer (Job 31:32). In the plural, it means caravans or troops (Job 6:19).

735. אֲרַח *'araḥ':* An Aramaic feminine noun meaning way, manner of life. It describes the just ways of the King of heaven, His manner of dealing with things (Dan. 4:37[34]) but also refers to the ways and manner of life of persons (Dan. 5:23).

736. אֹרְחָה *'ōreḥāh:* A feminine noun meaning caravan, traveling group. It refers to a group of Ishmaelites, merchants, taking their wares to Egypt (Gen. 37:25). Merchant caravans of an Arabian Dedanite tribe are depicted in Isaiah 21:13, that will be attacked by both the Assyrians and Babylonians (cf. Ezek. 27:20; 38:13).

737. אֲרֻחָה *'aruḥāh:* A feminine noun meaning meal, dinner; allowance, portion, provisions. It describes an allowance of food given to Jeremiah (Jer. 40:5) and to Jehoiachin while he was confined in Babylon (2 Kgs. 25:30; Jer. 52:34). The word describes a portion (NASB, dish) of vegetables as a modest meal (Prov. 15:17; NIV, meal; KJV, dinner).

738. אֲרִי *'ariy*, אַרְיֵה *'aryēh:* I. A masculine noun meaning lion. The word refers to an animal (Judg. 14:5, 18; 1 Sam. 17:34, 36; 2 Sam. 23:20). Figuratively, it describes Israel's rise to a powerful nation (Num. 23:24; 24:9) and Israel's destroyers Assyria and Babylon (Jer. 50:17). Jerusalem's kings are depicted as destructive lions (Zeph. 3:3). The strength of lions was celebrated in songs and poetry (2 Sam. 1:23; Prov. 22:13).

II. A feminine noun referring to a lion. The word refers to an animal. It has the same basic function and meaning as I. In addition, it is used in the following ways: Judah and Dan in particular are described as lions or a lion's whelps (Gen. 49:9; Deut. 33:22) using this word. One of the four living beings of Ezekiel's vision has the face of a lion (Ezek. 1:10; 10:14). The Lord roars as a lion (Hos. 11:10; Amos 3:4, 8) as a protector of His people or, if necessary, as a judge of His people.

III. A masculine noun depicting one pierced. The word describes the piercing of the psalmist's hands and feet, a prophetic assertion also applied to Christ (Ps. 22:16[17], KJV, NKJV, NASB, NIV).

739. אֲרִיאֵל *ʼariyʼēl:* A. A masculine proper noun referring to Ariel of Moab, whose two sons were killed by one of David's mighty men (2 Sam. 23:20; 1 Chr. 11:22, NASB). The NKJV renders this as lion-like heroes.

B. A masculine noun indicating a hero warrior, a man of courage. The word means lion of God. The NKJV renders this as lion-like heroes (cf. KJV, lionlike men), while the NIV renders it as best men (2 Sam. 23:20).

740. אֲרִיאֵל *ʼariyʼēl:* A proper noun designating Ariel:

A. It refers to a Jew in exile in Babylon, a leader of his community, who helped Ezra gather Levites to return to Jerusalem. The name means "lioness of God (El)."

B. The name was applied to Jerusalem as the chief stronghold and chosen place of the Lord (Isa. 29:1, 2, 7).

741. אֲרִיאֵל *ʼariyʼēl,* אֲרִאֵל *ʼariʼēl:* A masculine noun meaning altar or hearth. It refers to the hearth of the altar for the new Temple of Ezekiel's vision (Ezek. 43:15, 16; NIV, NASB, altar hearth; KJV, altar).

742. אֲרִידַי *ʼariyday:* A proper noun designating Aridai (Esth. 9:9).

743. אֲרִידָתָא *ʼariydātāʼ:* A proper noun designating Aridatha (Esth. 9:8).

744. אַרְיֵה *ʼaryēh:* An Aramaic masculine noun meaning lion. It is used to describe the den of lions (Dan. 6:7[8], 12[13]) and employed figuratively to depict the first beast of Daniel's apocalyptic dream (7:4), a lion representing Babylon and Nebuchadnezzar.

745. אַרְיֵה *ʼaryēh:* A proper noun designating Arieh (2 Kgs. 15:25).

746. אַרְיוֹךְ *ʼaryôḵ:* A proper noun designating Arioch:

A. A king in Ellasar who warred with three other kings against five kings in the early days of Abraham. The battle was in the Valley of Siddim (Gen. 14:1–4).

B. The name of a Babylonian officer at Nebuchadnezzar's palace in Babylon. He was the overseer of the king's guard who would have been in charge of executing the wise men of Babylon (Dan. 2:1–25).

747. אֲרִיסַי *ʼariysay:* A proper noun designating Arisai (Esth. 9:9).

748. אָרַךְ *ʼāraḵ:* A verb meaning to be long, prolong, draw out, or postpone. In most instances, it refers to the element of time. Most commonly, it bears the causative sense: to prolong one's days (Deut. 5:16); to show continuance (Ex. 20:12); tarry or stay long (Num. 9:19); to survive after (Josh. 24:31); to postpone or defer anger (Isa. 48:9); to draw out (1 Kgs. 8:8). Used literally, it describes the growth of branches (Ezek. 31:5); and as a command, to lengthen one's cords (Isa. 54:2).

749. אֲרִיךְ *'ariyk:* An Aramaic adjective meaning proper, fitting. It indicates a political situation which it is not correct to tolerate or condone (Ezra 4:14).

750. אָרֵךְ *'ārēk:* An adjective meaning long, drawn out, or slow. This word primarily describes feelings pertaining to a person: either being slow of temper or patient. In wisdom literature, the person who is patient and does not anger quickly is extolled as a person of understanding (Prov. 14:29; Eccl. 7:8). When used to describe God, the Hebrew word means slow to anger and is immediately contrasted with God's great love, faithfulness, and power, demonstrating His true nature and His long-suffering (Ex. 34:6). Also, this Hebrew word is used of an eagle's long pinions or feathers (Ezek. 17:3).

751. אֶרֶךְ *'erek:* A proper noun designating Erech (Gen. 10:10).

752. אָרֹךְ *'ārōk:* An adjective meaning long. It occurs only in the feminine singular tense and is used to modify exile (Jer. 29:28); war (2 Sam. 3:1); and God's wisdom (Job 11:9). See the verb *'ārak* (748).

753. אֹרֶךְ *'ōrek:* A masculine noun meaning length, long. It is primarily used in describing physical measurements, for example, Noah's ark (Gen. 6:15) and the land (Gen. 13:17). It is also used for the qualities of patience (forbearance) in Proverbs 25:15 and limitless presence (forever) in Psalm 23:6. In perhaps its most significant theological usage, it speaks of long life or "length of your days" (NASB), a desirable state of existence embodied in the Lord (Deut. 30:20), given to those who walk in obedience (Ps. 91:16; Prov. 3:2) and wisdom (Prov. 3:16). This kind of existence begins in the eternity of God and is granted to those He has chosen.

754. אַרְכָה *'arkāh:* An Aramaic feminine noun meaning lengthening, prolonging. It is used temporally (Dan. 4:27[24]; 7:12).

755. אַרְכֻבָּה *'arkubbāh:* An Aramaic feminine noun meaning knee. The word refers to Belshazzar's knees knocking together because of his terror of the writing on the wall (Dan. 5:6).

756. אַרְכְוָי *'arkᵉwāy:* A proper noun referring to an Archevite, a native of Erech (Ezra 4:9).

757. אַרְכִּי *'arkiy:* A proper noun designating Archite. It refers to a descendant of Ham in the line of Canaan who lived in Arkat. It was located just north of modern Tripoli, It is mentioned in several ancient sources from Egypt and Assyria. Its modern archaeological tell is Tell-'Argal. Joseph's allotment of land passed by it (Josh. 16:2). Hushai was a wise man serving David and was an Arkite (2 Sam. 15:32).

758. אֲרָם *'arām:* Aram is another name for Syria, found often in the Old

Testament as early as Abraham's journeys when he settled in Haran in Aram (Gen. 11:28–32). The name means "Aram of two rivers" in northern Mesopotamia. Balaam, the pagan soothsayer, came from Aram (Num. 23:7). It was often at war with Israel, even in the time of Judges (Judg. 3:10; 2 Sam. 8:5–6). Israel fell prey to the religious intrigues of Syria's gods (Judg. 10:6). Aram's most famous city, its capital, was Damascus (2 Sam. 8:5–6). Their soldiers were often mercenaries (2 Sam. 10:6–7). The Arameans purchased war equipment from Israel in Solomon's day (1 Kgs. 10:29).

Israel's history was closely interwoven with the nation and territory of Aram (Saul, David, Solomon, and later kings, e.g., Ahab). The language of Aram, Aramaic, was at one time the lingua franca of the ancient Near East and left its impression in the Aramaisms of the Old Testament. Elisha the prophet was involved with the kings of Damascus, Hazael and Ben-Hadad (2 Kgs. 8:7–15).

759. אַרְמוֹן *'armôn:* A masculine noun meaning fortress, citadel. Amos frequently equated God's judgment with the destruction of a fortress (Amos 3:11). The word is used in parallel construction with strength (Amos 3:11); siege tower (Isa. 23:13); rampart (Ps. 122:7; citadel, NIV; palace, NASB, NKJV, KJV); fortification (Lam. 2:5; palace, NASB, NKJV, KJV, NIV).

760. אֲרַם צוֹבָה *'aram ṣôḇāh:* A proper noun designating Aram-zobah (Ps. 60:title[1]).

761. אֲרַמִּי *'arammiy:* A gentilic noun (with the ending *iy*) indicating a Syrian or Aramean. It referred to an area between the Tigris and Euphrates Rivers (Gen. 25:9–20). Bethuel, Isaac's father-in-law, was an Aramean. Syrian refers to the same ethnic group. Laban was an Aramean as was Naaman (2 Kgs. 5:20). The origins of the Israelites were tied to them (Deut. 26:5). The Syrians and Israelites were often at war (2 Kgs. 9:15). Manasseh had a concubine from among the Arameans (1 Chr. 7:14).

762. אֲרָמִית *'arāmiyṯ:* A proper noun referring to the Aramaic (Syriac) language. Biblical Aramaic describes the language in Ezra 4:8—6:18; 7:12–26 and Daniel 2:4b—7:28, as well as a few words in Genesis 31:47 and Jeremiah 10:11. It was also spoken by Rabshakeh of Assyria and the leaders of Judah (2 Kgs. 18:26; Isa. 36:11). Official letters were written in it (Ezra 4:7).

The language was named for the people from Aram who spoke it. The Arameans were an influential people but not fully understood yet. Many of the Elephantine Papyri and Dead Sea Scrolls were written in Aramaic. Termed Syriac in the KJV, it is a Semitic language like Hebrew and very similar to Hebrew. The language was at one time the lingua franca (cf.

2 Kgs. 18:26) of the ancient Near East. In a few cases, a few words called "Aramaisms" appear even in the New Testament (e.g. Mark 5:41; John 1:42; Acts 9:36, 40; 1 Cor. 16:22).

763. אֲרַם נַהֲרַיִם ***'aram naharayim:*** The name means "Aram of the (two) rivers" which is equal to Mesopotamia ("between the rivers"). It is bounded by the upper Euphrates on its west and by the Hebur River on the east. Abraham's servant sought a wife for Isaac there (Gen. 24:10), and Balaam came from the area (Deut. 23:4[5]). It was a source of trouble later in the time of the judges and David (Judg. 3:8, 10; 1 Chr. 19:6; Ps. 60:[title]).

764. אַרְמֹנִי ***'armōniy:*** A proper noun designating Armoni (2 Sam. 21:8).

765. אֲרָן ***'arān:*** A proper noun designating Aran (Gen. 36:28; 1 Chr. 1:42).

766. אֹרֶן ***'ōren:*** A masculine noun indicating an ash tree or fir tree. The tree indicated is translated as an ash tree (KJV, Isa. 44:14), fir tree (NASB), and a pine tree (NKJV, NIV). The words depicting ancient trees in Scripture are difficult to decipher with certainty and are still being researched.

767. אֹרֶן ***'ōren:*** A proper noun designating Oren (1 Chr. 2:25).

768. אַרְנֶבֶת ***'arnebeṯ:*** A feminine noun indicating a rabbit or unknown species of animal. It indicates an unclean animal not to be eaten by Israelites (Lev. 11:6; Deut. 14:7; NASB, NIV, rabbit; KJV, NKJV, hare).

769. אַרְנוֹן ***'arnôn:*** A proper noun designating Arnon, a river that bounded Moab on the north and the land of the Amorites on the south (Num. 21:13–15). It was a boundary of Reuben later in Israel's history. It flows west into the Dead Sea almost opposite Ein-Gedi.

770. אַרְנָן ***'arnān:*** A proper noun designating Arnan (1 Chr. 3:21).

771. אָרְנָן ***'ornān*** or ***'ārnān:*** A proper noun designating Ornan. This is a variant reading of Araunah in 1 Chronicles 21:15, 18, 20–25, 28, the Jebusite who owned the "Ornan" threshing floor where the angel of the Lord stopped plaguing Israel.

772. אֲרַע ***'ara':*** An Aramaic, feminine noun meaning earth. Functioning as an adverb, it also carries the idea of downward, below, or towards the earth. This concept appears in Jeremiah 10:11 in conjunction with the phrase "under the heavens" to say that the gods who did not make heaven and earth will perish. It is also used to mean the realm where humans live (Dan. 2:35). The word also occurs twice in Daniel 2:39; in the first instance, it means inferior or less than, and in the second occurrence, it means earth. See the equivalent Hebrew noun *'eres* (776).

773. אַרְעִי *'ar'iy:* An Aramaic feminine noun meaning bottom, floor. The word indicates the bottom of a lions' den, evidently recessed in the ground (Dan. 6:24[25]).

774. אַרְפָּד *'arpāḏ:* A proper noun designating Arpad. It refers to a city in a province in northern Syria conquered by the Assyrians near Hamanth (2 Kgs. 18:34; 19:13). It is Tell Eafad, north of modern Aleppo. It was judged severely by the Lord (Isa. 10:9) and fell to Assyria.

775. אַרְפַּכְשַׁד *'arpaḵšaḏ:* A proper noun designating Arphaxad (Gen. 10:22, 24; 11:10–13; 1 Chr. 1:17, 18, 24).

776. אֶרֶץ *'ereṣ:* A noun meaning the earth, land. It is used almost 2,500 times in the Old Testament. It refers to the whole earth under God's dominion (Gen. 1:1; 14:19; Ex. 9:29; Ps. 102:25[26]; Prov. 8:31; Mic. 4:13). Since the earth was God's possession, He promised to give the land of Canaan to Abraham's descendants (Gen. 12:7; 15:7). The Promised Land was very important to Abraham's descendants and to the nation of Israel that possessed the land (Josh. 1:2, 4). Israel's identity was tied to the land because it signified the fulfillment of God's promise to Abraham. If the Israelites were disobedient, however, they would be cursed by losing the land (Lev. 26:32–34, 36, 38, 39; Deut. 28:63, 64; Jer. 7:7).

777. אַרְצָא *'arṣā':* A proper noun designating Arza (1 Kgs. 16:9).

778. אֲרַק *'ᵃraq:* An Aramaic, feminine noun meaning earth. Related to the Hebrew word *'eres* (776), it corresponds to the term planet. This Aramaic word occurs only once in the Hebrew Bible in Jeremiah 10:11. The English word *earth* occurs twice in this verse, but it does not translate the same Aramaic word. The first is the Aramaic word being defined here; the second is the Aramaic noun *'ᵃra'* (772). Both of these words mean world.

779. אָרַר *'ārar:* A verb generally denoting to inflict with a curse. There are at least five other Hebrew verbs with the same general meaning. This verb, in a more specific sense, means to bind (with a spell); to hem in with obstacles; to render powerless to resist. It is sometimes used as an antonym of *bāraḵ* (1288). In Genesis 3, God renders curses on the serpent, the woman, and the man for their sins in the Garden of Eden. To the serpent, God says, "Cursed are you more than all cattle, and more than every beast of the field" (Gen. 3:14 NASB), meaning that the serpent would be the lowest of all animals. Then to the man, God says, "Cursed is the ground because of you," meaning that he would have difficulties in producing food from the soil. In Numbers 22:6, King Balak of Moab asks Balaam to curse the Israelites. His desire is for the Israelites to be immobilized or rendered impotent so he can defeat them, his superior enemy.

780. אֲרָרַט ***'ᵃrāraṭ:*** A proper noun designating Ararat, the name of the mountain range on which the Noahic ark rested after the flood (Gen. 8:4). It is used to indicate an area, "land of Ararat" (2 Kgs. 19:37; Isa. 37:38). It is in modern Armenia in the area of Lake Van.

781. אָרַשׂ ***'āraś:*** A verb meaning to betroth, pledge in marriage. The word means to become engaged to, to marry a woman (Deut. 20:7). The betrothed was usually accompanied with a bride price (Ex. 22:16[15]; 2 Sam. 3:14) or dowry. It was considered adultery and much more dangerous to seduce a betrothed woman than a virgin (Ex. 22:16[15]; Deut. 22:23, 25, 27, 28). A betrothed woman was bound to marry the man she was engaged to (Deut. 28:30). The word was used figuratively to describe the Lord's betrothal of Israel to Himself (Hos. 2:19[21], 20[22]). Therefore, the relationship with His people was one of personal intimacy at its deepest level.

782. אֲרֶשֶׁת ***'ᵃrešeṯ:*** A feminine noun meaning request, desire. It describes the desire of the king to know the Lord through both the Lord's blessing and gift of life (Ps. 21:2[3]).

783. אַרְתַּחְשַׁסְתְּא ***'artaḥšast',*** אַרְתַּחְשַׁשְׂתָּא ***'artaḥšaśtā':*** The name of the Persian king, Artaxerxes I, who ruled 465–424 B.C. (Ezra 4:7, 8). He stopped the work on the second Temple (Ezra 4:18–23). Ezra returned to Jerusalem in his reign (Ezra 7:1–7) about 458 B.C. Under Ezra Artaxerxes prospered Ezra's work and the Law of God (Ezra 7:13–28). He permitted Nehemiah to return to Jerusalem to build its walls (Neh. 2:1–10) and become governor there (Neh. 5:14). Nehemiah returned to Persia in ca. 433 B.C. for a while (Neh. 13:6).

784. אֵשׁ ***'ēš:*** A common feminine noun meaning fire. The word is used in various ways: It refers to any fire that breaks out and burns up something, whether people, things, or animals (Ex. 22:6[5]). Both idols and the golden calf were burned up by fire (Ex. 32:20; Deut. 7:5, 25; 12:3). It is used as a symbol for God (Gen. 15:17; Ex. 3:2; 13:21, 22; 19:18; Deut. 4:11). It describes the fire made for cooking, roasting, etc. (Ex. 12:8, 9; Lev. 2:14). It was used on the brazen altar to burn offerings (Lev. 1:7; 6:9[2]). In some cases, it was fire from the Lord which consumed sacrifices (Lev. 9:24; 2 Chr. 7:1, 3). It was used to describe strange fire offered before the Lord *'ēš zorāh,* meaning incense not commanded by the Lord (Num. 3:4; 26:61). It was used to depict lightning in the plagues in Egypt (Ex. 9:23, 24; cf. Ps. 18:13[14]). The Lord's anger could be depicted as burning like fire (Ps. 89:46[47]; Ezek. 22:31; 38:19). But great wickedness was also described as consuming like fire (Isa. 9:18[17], 19[18]). The word is used in various short phrases in connection with other words: It is used to depict a torch or flame of fire (Ex. 3:2; Dan. 10:6, *labbaṯ-'ēš*; Joel 2:5). With several other words, it means spark of fire (Job 18:5); oven of fire (Zech. 12:6); flame of or flaming fire (Ps. 104:4); tongue of fire (Isa. 5:24) and a few other combinations.

785. אֶשָּׁא ***'eššā':*** An Aramaic feminine noun meaning fire, flame. It is found in only Daniel 7:11, where the fourth beast of Daniel is burned up by fire.

786. אִשׁ ***'iš:*** An adverb meaning there is one, or is there one? It is used in combination with *'im* (518) meaning if in 2 Samuel 14:19, and the same phrase means if there is, in the sense of either, is there one, or no one (NASB, NIV, NKJV; KJV none). It is coupled with the question word h^a in Micah 6:10 and means is there (NASB) or are there (NKJV, KJV). The phrase is impersonal so that it may be translated as am I (NIV, Mic. 6:10) as well.

787. אֹשׁ ***'ōš:*** An Aramaic masculine noun depicting a foundation. It refers to the new foundation being restored to Jerusalem during the time of Ezra's return (458 B.C.) and later (Ezra 4:12) and the restoring of the foundations of the new Temple (Ezra 5:16; 6:3).

788. אַשְׁבֵּל ***'ašbēl:*** A proper noun designating Ashbel (Gen. 46:21; Num. 26:38; 1 Chr. 8:1).

789. אַשְׁבֵּלִי ***'ašbēliy:*** A proper noun designating Ashbelite (Num. 26:38).

790. אֶשְׁבָּן ***'ešbān:*** A proper noun designating Eshban (Gen. 36:26; 1 Chr. 1:41).

791. אַשְׁבֵּעַ ***'ašbēa':*** A proper noun designating Ashbea (1 Chr. 4:21).

792. אֶשְׁבַּעַל ***'ešba'al:*** A proper noun designating Esh-baal (1 Chr. 8:33; 9:39).

793. אֶשֶׁד ***'āšēḏ:*** A masculine noun meaning slope. It refers to the sloping banks and surrounding area of the temporary streams or wadis in the territory that separated the Moabites and the Amorites from each other (Num. 21:15). The word is found in the poetry of the book of the wars of Yahweh.

794. אֲשֵׁדָה ***'ašēḏāh:*** A feminine noun meaning slope. It is found three times. Twice it refers to the mountain slopes of Mount Pisgah (Deut. 3:17; 4:49). The word is rendered as slopes of the south from which the Lord comes to His people in the remaining usage (NIV, Deut. 33:2). Others prefer to translate this difficult word differently (NASB, flashing lightning; NKJV, KJV, fiery law).

795. אַשְׁדּוֹד ***'ašdôḏ:*** A proper noun designating Ashdod, a Philistine city (Josh. 11:22). Joshua fought against it as one of the five major Philistine cities (Gaza, Ashdod,

Ashkelon, Gath, Ekron [Josh. 13:3]). the ark of God lodged there in Dagon's temple (1 Sam. 5:1–7) but was moved from there because of the Lord's curse on Ashdod (cf. 1 Sam. 6:17). The Assyrians conquered it under Sargon (Isa. 20:1). God judged Ashdod harshly (Jer. 25:20; Amos 1:8; Zeph. 2:4; Zech. 9:6).

796. אַשְׁדּוֹדִי *'ašdôḏiy:* A proper noun designating Ashdodite (Josh. 13:3; 1 Sam. 5:3, 6; Neh. 4:7(1); 13:23).

797. אַשְׁדּוֹדִית *'ašdôḏiyt:* A proper noun designating the language of Ashdod. It refers to the local language (or dialect) spoken in the city of Ashdod on the shore of the Mediterranean Sea. Israelites, through improper marriages with these people, were speaking this language (Neh. 13:24).

798. אַשְׁדּוֹת הַפִּסְגָּה *'ašdôṯ hap-pisgāh:* A proper noun designating Ashdothpisgah (Deut. 3:17; Josh. 12:3; 13:20).

799. אֶשְׁדָּת *'ēšdāṯ:* I. A feminine noun meaning fiery law. To get this meaning, the word is considered a compound word made up of *'ēš,* fire, and *dāṯ,* law (Deut. 33:2, NKJV, KJV).

II. A feminine noun meaning flashing lightning. The word is translated as flashing lightning in the NASB (Deut. 33:2) since the scene at Sinai featured this phenomenon of nature at the appearance (theophany) of the Lord.

III. A feminine noun meaning mountain slope. The NIV prefers to render the word as slopes since it refers to the Lord as coming from the south (*yomin*) down from the mountains (Deut. 33:2).

800. אֶשָּׁה *'eššāh:* A feminine noun referring to fire. This fire consumes or burns up lead. In this case, lead is part of the impurities being burned up to purge God's people, but the process goes on in vain (Jer. 6:29).

801. אִשֶּׁה *'iššeh:* A feminine noun meaning offering made by fire, fire offering. Its usage is highly religious and theological in a ritual context. The word describes how the various offerings were presented to the Lord; that is, they were offerings made by means of fire. This practice gave rise to referring to all the offerings the priests presented as fire offerings; hence, some consider this term a general term that applied to all the sacrifices of the Israelites (Deut. 18:1; 1 Sam. 2:28). The fire was actually not offered. Instead, it was the means by which the various offerings were presented to God. The fire caused the offering to go up in smoke, a fact indicated by the causative form of the Hebrew verb, and that created a pleasant aroma to the Lord. The fire also purified what was offered. In this sense, the offerings could be called fire offerings or offerings made by fire. The other words for sacrifice in the Old Testament are specific and describe a certain sacrifice, although *qorbān* (7133) is used in a general sense a few times. The word *'iššeh* is slightly more specific.

The Levites were put in charge of all the offerings by fire to the Lord (Josh. 13:14). Both animal sacrifices and nonanimal sacrifices were presented to the Lord by fire (Lev. 1:9; 2:10), as well as such items as the sacred bread and frankincense placed in the Holy Place (Lev. 24:7). These offerings by fire cover at least the burnt offering (Lev. 1:3–17; 6:8–13); the grain offering (Lev. 2:1–16; 6:14–23; 7:9, 10); the fellowship or peace offering (Lev. 3:9; 7:11–21, 28–34); the sin offering (Lev. 4:1–35; 5:1–13; 6:24–30); the guilt offering (Lev. 5:14–19; 7:1–10). All of these offerings were the Lord's (Num. 28:2), but the phrase "to the Lord" is explicitly stated most of the time (Ex. 29:18; Lev. 2:11; Num. 28:13). As noted above, the offering by fire produced a pleasing or soothing aroma to the Lord as it ascended (cf. Lev. 1:9; Num. 15:13, 14; 29:13, 36), a phrase indicating that the Lord had accepted the sacrifice.

802. אִשָּׁה *'iššāh:* A feminine noun meaning woman, wife, or female. The origin of this word has been recorded in Genesis 2:23, where Adam said, "She shall be called Woman (*'iššāh* [802]), because she was taken out of Man (*'iyš* [376]) (NASB)." While this word predominantly means woman or wife, it is further used in various ways: those able to bear children (Gen. 18:11); a widow (Ruth 4:5; 1 Sam. 27:3); an adulteress (Prov. 6:26; 7:5); female children (Num. 31:18); or female animals (Gen. 7:2).

803. אָשְׁיָה *'āšyāh:* A feminine noun designating a pillar or support. The word is used both literally and figuratively to depict the strong and mighty supports and pillars constructed in Babylon, which the Lord would destroy (Jer. 50:15).

804. אַשּׁוּר *'aššûr:* A proper noun designating Asshur:

A. The name of a second son of Shem who began the ancient line from which the Assyrians came, with their capital at Asshur (Gen. 10:22; 1 Chr. 1:17).

B. An ancient name for Assyria found in Genesis 2:14. The Tigris River ran by its capital city Asshur. Nimrod is connected with the land in Genesis 10:11 where he built Nineveh, a later capital of Assyria. Asshur (Assyria) is mentioned by Balaam in his final prophecies (Num. 24:22, 24). Assyria/Asshur became a byword for violence and political terror tactics. It conquered and ruled by fear and brutality. Samaria took Northern Israel captive in 722 B.C. In ca. 701 B.C., Sennacherib threatened to besiege and destroy Jerusalem in Hezekiah's reign and during the time of Isaiah the prophet (Isa. 36—37). God delivered the city. Jonah preached repentance to the great city of Nineveh, and the Assyrians repented and experienced the Lord's grace (see Jon. 3:4—4:11). On the other hand, later the prophet

Nahum preached the destruction of the city and rejoiced over its fall, as did the rest of the ancient Near East (Nah. 1—3). Nineveh and the remnants of the Assyrian Empire fell in 612 B.C.

805. אַשּׁוּרִי ***'aššûriy:*** A proper noun designating Asshurite (Gen. 25:3; 2 Sam. 2:9).

806. אַשְׁחוּר ***'ašḥûr:*** A proper noun designating Ashhur (1 Chr. 2:24; 4:5).

807. אֲשִׁימָא ***'ᵃšiymā':*** A masculine proper noun Ashima. It is the name of a god(s) set up and worshiped in the deserted land of Samaria (2 Kgs. 17:30). The people who worshiped this deity came from Hamath and had been resettled in Samaria by the Assyrians.

808. אָשִׁישׁ ***'āšiyš:*** A. A masculine noun meaning foundation; similar to. The word may refer to the foundations of the city Kir-hareseth, a devastated city in Moab (KJV, NKJV, Isa. 16:7). See #803.

B. A masculine noun meaning sacrificial raisin cakes which were produced in Kir-hareseth, a devastated city of Moab (NASB, Isa. 16:7). It is considered to be related to *'ašiyšāh.* See #809.

C. A masculine noun meaning men. It refers to the people destroyed by God's judgment on the city of Kir-hareseth, a city of Moab (NIV, Isa. 16:7). It is considered to be related to *'iyš.* See #376.

809. אֲשִׁישָׁה ***'ᵃšiyšāh:*** A feminine noun referring to raisin cakes. It was a special luxury gift to the people to celebrate the arrival of the ark in Jerusalem (2 Sam. 6:19; 1 Chr. 16:3), where the ark was placed inside a tent. It was a food desired for its energizing qualities (Song 2:5). Raisin cakes were also tied to pagan worship in some cases (Hos. 3:1).

810. אֶשֶׁךְ ***'ešek:*** A masculine noun meaning testicle. Crushed testicles were a defect that disqualified a descendant of Aaron from the priesthood (Lev. 21:20).

811. אֶשְׁכּוֹל ***'eškôl,*** אֶשְׁכֹּל ***'eškōl:*** A masculine noun indicating a cluster of something, often grapes. It may refer to just the stalk of the vine (Gen. 40:10) or the entire cluster of grapes (Num. 13:23, 24; Song 7:8[9]; Mic. 7:1). It also describes a group of henna blossoms (Song 1:14) as like the breasts of the bride (Song 7:7[8]). A cluster could contain new wine (Isa. 65:8).

812. אֶשְׁכֹּל ***'eškōl,*** אֶשְׁכּוֹל ***'eškôl:*** A proper noun designating Ashima (2 Kgs. 17:30).

813. אַשְׁכְּנַז ***'aškᵉnaz:*** A proper noun designating Ashkenaz:

A. The name refers to a descendant of Japheth through Gomer (Gen. 10:3), Japheth being the third son of Noah (Gen. 10:1).

B. It refers to a people from the north, in this case, from the area north of Babylon on the Euphrates.

It probably refers to the Sythians mentioned by the Greek historian Herodotus. Jeremiah calls them to war against and to destroy Babylon (Jer. 51:27).

814. אֶשְׁכָּר ***'eškār:*** A masculine noun meaning gift, payment. It refers to valuable gifts brought to Solomon from the kings of Sheba and Seba (Ps. 72:10). These items are also designated as payment(s) from Rhodes or Dedan to Tyre (Ezek. 27:15).

815. אֶשֶׁל ***'ešel:*** A masculine noun meaning tamarisk tree. This tree has small leaves and survives well in the dry, hot climate of Israel. The word appears only three times in the Old Testament: when Abraham planted a tamarisk tree near the well in Beersheba (Gen. 21:33); the place where Saul and his men gathered (1 Sam. 22:6); and where Saul's bones were buried at Jabesh (1 Sam. 31:13).

816. אָשַׁם ***'āšam,*** אָשֵׁם ***āšēm:*** A verb meaning to be guilty or to do wrong. This word is most often used to describe the product of sin—that is, guilt before God. It may be used of individuals (Lev. 5:2–5; Num. 5:6, 7); congregations (Lev. 4:13); or nations (Ezek. 25:12; Hos. 13:16[14:1]). Because of the close connection between guilt and sin, this word may be used as a synonym for sin (Hos. 4:15; 13:1), while often the idea of punishment for a wrong done is implied (Hos. 10:2; Zech. 11:5). See the related nouns, *'āšām* (817), meaning guilt, and *'ašmāh* (819), meaning guiltiness.

817. אָשָׁם ***'āšām:*** A masculine noun used to express the concept of guilt or offense. It can connote the deeds which bring about guilt (Ps. 68:21[22]). It can also express the condition of being guilty, that is, the results of the actions as shown in Genesis 26:10 (NIV), "You would have brought guilt upon us." This word can also refer to the restitution that the guilty party was to make to the victim in the case of property damage (Num. 5:7). The biblical writer also uses this term to designate the guilt offering, the offering which is presented to the Lord in order to absolve the person guilty of an offense against God or man, which can be estimated and compensated (Lev. 5:6).

818. אָשֵׁם ***'āšēm:*** An adjective meaning guilty. This word comes from the verb *'āšam* (816), meaning to be guilty and is related to the nouns *'āšām* (817), meaning guilt, and *'ašmāh* (819), referring to guiltiness. Thus, the adjective describes one who is in a guilty state. It describes Joseph's brothers, who declared, "Truly we are guilty concerning our brother" (Gen. 42:21, NASB); David in not bringing back Absalom (2 Sam. 14:13); and priests who had married foreign wives (Ezra 10:19).

819. אַשְׁמָה ***'ašmāh:*** A feminine noun suggesting the concept of sin or guilt. It is similar in meaning to *'āšām*

(817). It can represent wrong actions (2 Chr. 24:18); the status of guilt which comes on a person by virtue of his or her wrong actions (Ezra 10:10); the guilt offering itself (Lev. 6:5[5:24]).

820. אַשְׁמָן *’ašmān:* A. A masculine noun indicating desolate (places). It is taken by some translators as a figurative description of desolate places where injustice is rampant (KJV, NKJV, Isa. 59:10).

B. A masculine noun indicating a strong, vigorous (person). It is taken by some translators as a description of vigorous or strong people among whom God's weakened people stumble about (NIV, NASB, Isa. 59:10).

821. אַשְׁמוּרָה *’ašmûrāh,* אַשְׁמֹרֶת *’ašmōreṯ:* A feminine noun indicating a night watch, watch (period of time). It refers to a night watch in general (Judg. 7:19, the middle watch which lasted from 10 p.m. – 2 p.m.; Ps. 90:4). It may point to the last watch (period) of the night (Ex. 14:24; 1 Sam. 11:11), literally, the watch (period) of the morning.

822. אֶשְׁנָב *’ešnāḇ:* A masculine noun designating a window lattice. The word describes the latticed window through which Sisera's mother looked as she waited for her son (Judg. 5:28). It was more or less an empty hole in the wall. It was common in the walls of buildings located within villages (Prov. 7:6).

823. אַשְׁנָה *’ašnāh:* A proper noun designating Ashnah:

A. A city in Judah (Josh. 15:33).

B. Another city in Judah (Josh. 15:43).

824. אֶשְׁעָן *’eš‘ān:* A proper noun designating Eshan (Josh. 15:52).

825. אַשָּׁף *’aššāp̱:* A masculine noun meaning enchanters, conjurers of spirits, necromancers, or astrologers. Found only in the plural, this word is borrowed from the Aramaic language. It is found only in the book of Daniel in relation to wise men or diviners (Dan. 2:2; 5:11).

826. אָשַׁף *’āšap̱:* An Aramaic masculine noun which denotes a conjurer, enchanters, magicians. It is closely related to the Hebrew word *’aššāp̱* (825). This designation, in both the Aramaic and the Hebrew forms, appears only in the book of Daniel. Since no etymology is apparent, its meaning must be determined by its context. The word always occurs in a list with one to three or four other words, whose meanings clearly refer to people with occult knowledge in the practice of divination (Dan. 2:10, 27; 4:7[4]; 5:7, 11, 15).

827. אַשְׁפָּה *’ašpāh:* A feminine noun indicating a quiver or container for arrows. The quiver was a container for arrows; it rested against the sides of warhorses (Job 39:23). To take up the quiver was to prepare for battle (Isa. 22:6). The prophet describes it as being like an open grave (Jer. 5:16) into which Israel would fall. Figuratively, it is pictured as a container for the arrows of the Lord (Lam. 3:13).

828. אַשְׁפְּנַז ***'ašpᵉnaz:*** A proper noun designating Ashpenaz (Dan. 1:3).

829. אֶשְׁפָּר ***'ešpār:*** A masculine noun indicating a piece or portion of something, such as meat, dates, etc. It indicates a cake of dates as a special luxury gift to the Israelites on the arrival of the ark in Jerusalem (NKJV, piece of meat; KJV, piece of flesh; 2 Sam. 6:19; 1 Chr. 16:3).

830. אַשְׁפֹּת ***'ašpōṯ,*** אַשְׁפּוֹת ***'ašpôṯ:*** A masculine noun indicating an ash heap, dung hill, refuse heap, dump. It is used in poetry to describe the condition of the needy (poor) (1 Sam. 2:8; Ps. 113:7). It depicts, most likely, a dump or dung hill during the time of Jeremiah (Lam. 4:5). It describes the Refuse or Dung Gate during the time of Nehemiah (2:13; 3:13, 14).

831. אַשְׁקְלוֹן ***'ašqᵉlôn:*** A proper noun designating Ashkelon, a city taken by the Judahites in the time of the judges (Judg. 1:18). This was one of the five famous Philistine cities (Judg. 1:18; 14:19). Samson visited the city in anger (Judg. 14:19). It is mentioned in the story of the capture of the ark by the Philistines (1 Sam. 6:17–18) and in David's lament for Saul. It was an object of God's wrath (Jer. 25:20).

832. אֶשְׁקְלוֹנִי ***'ešqᵉlôniy:*** A proper noun designating Ashkelonite (Josh. 13:3).

833. אָשַׁר ***'āšar:*** A verb meaning to go straight, to go on, to advance forward, to be called blessed, or to be made happy. Of blessing or happiness, this verb is primarily used causatively: to call one blessed (Ps. 72:17); to pronounce happiness (Gen. 30:13); to be made happy or blessed (Prov. 3:18). Used figuratively, it means to follow a straight path in understanding (Prov. 9:6) or in one's heart (Prov. 23:19). When it is used intensively, it means going straight or advancing (Prov. 4:14).

834. אֲשֶׁר ***'ᵃšer:*** This word functions as (a) a relative pronoun meaning which, who, that or (b) a conjunction meaning that, because, so that, as, so that. The use of the word is determined by its function in the sentence in which it is used. Its basic usage: (a) a relative pronoun (Gen. 21:2; Deut. 1:22; Isa. 5:28; Hos. 3:1); a relative pronoun with a preposition prefixed (Gen. 21:17; Ex. 5:11; 33:12); or with nouns placed before *'ᵃšer* in the construct or "of" state, e.g., Gen. 39:20, "The place where the king's prisoners were confined."

835. אֶשֶׁר ***'ešer:*** A masculine noun meaning a person's state of bliss. This Hebrew word is always used to refer to people and is never used of God. It is almost exclusively poetic and usually exclamatory, "O the bliss of. . . ."

In Proverbs, this blissfulness is frequently connected with wisdom (Prov. 3:13; 8:32, 34). This term is also used to describe a person or nation who enjoys a relationship with God (Deut. 33:29; Job 5:17; Ps. 33:12; 146:5). In some contexts, the word does not seem to have any religious significance (1 Kgs. 10:8; Prov. 14:21; Eccl. 10:17), and at least in one context, it has no religious significance (Ps. 137:8, 9).

836. אָשֵׁר ***ʼāšēr:*** A proper noun designating Asher:

A. The name of Leah's second son to Jacob through Zilpah. the name means "happy, blessed." He then had four sons and a daughter (Gen. 46:17; Num. 26:46 who bore children; 1 Chr. 7:30–40). Jacob blessed Asher and his posterity (Gen. 49:20).

B. The name is applied to the tribe of Asher in Israel, descended from the son of Jacob (see A). There were five chief families in Asher (Num. 26:44ff). Moses blessed the tribe before his demise (Deut. 33:24). The territory of Asher was bounded on the east by the Mediterranean Sea, and much of its land lay in the Plain of Acco. It reached from Mount Carmel on the south to the Litani River in the north. It was bounded by Manasseh (south), Zebulun (southeast), Naphtali (east), Aram/Lebanon (north). In Ezekiel's vision, Asher is named as bordering Dan (Ezek. 48:2, 3, 34), and the New Jerusalem features a western gate bearing Asher's name. The tribe failed to conquer all of its territory (Judg. 1:31–32). Unfortunately, Asher did not aid Deborah and Barak (5:17). They did fight against the Midianites under Gideon (Judg. 6:35; 7:33). Anna, the prophetess in the New Testament, was from this tribe (Luke 2:36).

837. אֹשֶׁר ***ʼōšer:*** A masculine noun meaning happiness. The Hebrew word is found once in the Bible describing a feeling of joy (Gen. 30:13).

838. אָשֻׁר ***ʼoššur,*** אַשֻּׁר ***ʼaššur:*** A feminine noun meaning step, path. The word is often used figuratively to describe a person's walk or manner of life. It describes the path that is pleasing to God (Job 23:11; 31:7; Ps. 17:5) and the steps of a wise or sensible person (Prov. 14:15).

839. אֲשֻׁרִים ***ʼᵃšuriym:*** A masculine plural proper noun referring to Ashurites. The word is taken as a proper noun indicating the Ashurites, a people not mentioned elsewhere (Ezek. 27:6, KJV, NKJV). The NASB, NIV prefer to translate it as boxwood, cypress wood respectively.

840. אֲשַׂרְאֵל ***ʼᵃśar'ēl:*** A proper noun designating Asarel (1 Chr. 4:16).

841. אֲשַׂרְאֵלָה ***ʼᵃśar'ēlāh:*** A proper noun designating Asarelah (1 Chr. 25:2).

842. אֲשֵׁרָה ***ʼᵃšērāh,*** אֲשֵׁירָה ***ʼᵃšēyrāh:*** A feminine noun which signifies the Canaanite fertility goddess believed to be the consort of Baal. Because of this association, the worship of Baal and Asherah was often linked together (Judg. 3:7; 1 Kgs. 18:19; 2 Kgs. 23:4). The noun is most often used for a carved wooden image of the goddess instead of a proper name (Judg. 6:26; 1 Kgs. 14:15). This image was frequently associated with high places and fresh (i.e., green) trees—the latter contributing to the misleading translations of the Septuagint and Vulgate that the word denoted "groves" (Deut. 12:3; 1 Kgs. 14:23; Jer. 17:2). The Israelites were commanded by God to cut down and burn the images (Ex. 34:13; Deut. 12:3), and occasionally the Israelites took steps to eliminate them (1 Kgs. 15:13; 2 Kgs. 23:4, 6, 7). Nevertheless, throughout much of Israel's preexilic history, false worship was a problem, even to the extent that Asherah's image was erected in God's temple itself (2 Kgs. 21:7; Isa. 27:9).

843. אָשֵׁרִי ***'āšēriy:*** A proper noun designating Asherite (Judg. 1:32).

844. אַשְׂרִיאֵל ***'aśriy'ēl:*** A proper noun designating Asriel (Num. 26:31; Josh. 17:2; 1 Chr. 7:14).

845. אַשְׂרִאֵלִי ***'aśri'ēliy:*** A proper noun designating Asrielite (Num. 26:31).

846. אֻשַּׁרְנָא ***'uššarnā':*** An Aramaic masculine noun meaning wall, structure. The word indicates a structure most likely (NASB, NIV, Ezra 5:3, 9) rather than a wall. It occurs in the context of rebuilding the temple.

847. אֶשְׁתָּאוֹל ***'eštā'ôl:*** A proper noun designating Eshtaol. It is a part of Judah's inheritance according to clans. It was located in the western lowlands of the Negev. It was later given to Dan (Josh. 15:33; 19:41; Judg. 18:2, 8, 11). Samson's relatives came from this area (Judg. 13:25; 16:31).

848. אֶשְׁתָּאֻלִי ***'eštā'uliy:*** A proper noun designating Eshtaolite (1 Chr. 2:53).

849. אֶשְׁתַּדּוּר ***'eštaddûr:*** An Aramaic masculine noun meaning revolt, rebellion (Ezra 4:15, 19).

850. אֶשְׁתּוֹן ***'eštôn:*** A proper noun designating Eshton (1 Chr. 4:11, 12).

851. אֶשְׁתְּמוֹעַ ***'eštᵉmôa'***, אֶשְׁתְּמֹה ***'eštᵉmōh:*** A proper noun designating Eshtemoa.

I. A city in Judah (Josh. 15:50; 21:14; 1 Sam. 30:28; 1 Chr. 6:57[42]).

II. A Judaite (1 Chr. 4:17, 19).

852. אָת ***'āṯ:*** An Aramaic masculine noun meaning sign, miraculous sign. The word refers to the dreams and the personal humbling that Nebuchadnezzar had gone through as part of God's righteous judgment on him (Dan. 4:2[3:32], 3[3:33]; 6:27[28]). These signs were communications and messages in various ways that communicated effectively to the king concerning his own life and the history of the world.

853. אֵת *'ēṯ:* This particle points out the definite direct object in a biblical Hebrew sentence. It is usually not translatable. It is normally employed in Hebrew prose but may often be missing in Hebrew poetry. It occurs as *'eṯ, 'eṯ-, or 'ēṯ-*. It may take pronominal suffixes, *'ôṯīy*, me; *'ôṯkā*, you, etc. (1 Sam. 8:7). Used before *mīy, 'eṯ mīy*, it indicates whom. In fact, it is able to point out any kind of accusative in a sentence (cf. 1 Kgs. 15:23). It is used thousands of times in the Old Testament.

854. אֵת *'ēṯ:* A preposition meaning with, against, near, among. It indicates closer proximity than the Hebrew *'im* (5973). It may indicate together with, such as to walk with (2 Sam. 16:17) or simply bunched together, included with (Gen. 6:13; Judg. 1:3; 14:11). It is found often in the phrase "the people who were with him" (*hā'ām 'ᵃšer 'ittô*, Judg. 4:13; 7:1; 1 Sam. 14:20). It indicates one can walk with God as a friend (Gen. 5:22, 24). Verbs of fighting, striving, and similar verbs are followed often by *'ēṯ*, with (Num. 20:13; Prov. 23:11; Isa. 45:9; 50:8). It is used to indicate location, e.g., near or at a place (Judg. 3:19; 4:11; 1 Kgs. 9:26). It also means near one's person, care, or space, i.e., with me (Gen. 27:15; 30:29; Lev. 6:4[5:23]; 19:13). Coupled with *min* (4480), from, it is used often to indicate from or away from proximity with (Gen. 25:10; 42:24; Ex. 25:2; Num. 17:2[17]). It can be used figuratively in this area to indicate rights, obligation, or special benefits from various persons (Gen. 47:22; Ex. 27:21; Num. 3:9; Deut. 18:3).

855. אֵת *'ēṯ:* A masculine noun indicating a plowshare or mattock. It designates an iron farm implement (1 Sam. 13:20, 21). Plowshares would be beaten into swords in Joel's picture of the coming day of the Lord (3:10[4:10]), but in the prophet Micah's vision, this process is reversed (4:3).

856. אֶתְבַּעַל *'eṯba'al:* A proper noun designating Ethbaal (1 Kgs. 16:31).

857. אָתָה *'āṯāh*, אָתָא *'āṯā':* A verb meaning to come, arrive. This verb means to come and is found in various contexts: It indicates people who come to the Lord (Jer. 3:22) but in general for whatever reason (Deut. 33:21; Isa. 41:25). It also describes the coming of a certain time or activity, such as morning (Job 16:22; Isa. 21:12); beasts (Isa. 56:9); calamity (Prov. 1:27; Job 3:25). In its causative stem, it is used to bring something (Jer. 12:9; Isa. 21:14).

858. אֲתָה *ᵃṯāh*, אֲתָא *ᵃṯā':* An Aramaic verb meaning to come, to arrive. The basic meaning is to come (Ezra 4:12; Dan. 3:2). It is used in an active causative sense to mean to bring someone or something (Dan. 3:13; 5:2, 3); and in a passive sense, these same objects are brought (Dan. 3:13; 6:17[18]) into various settings.

859. אַתָּה *'attāh:* A personal pronoun meaning you. It is also written *'attā* in a few places (1 Sam. 24:18[19]; Ps. 6:3[4]). Its basic use is as the independent personal pronoun meaning you (Num. 11:15; Deut. 5:27[24]; 2 Chr. 14:11[10]; Ezek. 28:14). It is used for emphasis before finite verb forms and then may mean you, yourself. It may also be used after (appended) a verb for emphasis (Ex. 18:19; 1 Sam. 17:56; 20:8). Used after a previous suffix referring to you, it is again emphatic (2 Chr. 35:21).

860. אָתוֹן *'āṯôn:* A feminine noun indicating a donkey, she ass. It was a primary means of transportation of persons or products (Gen. 12:16; 45:23; Judg. 5:10) and was property that constituted wealth (Gen. 32:15[16]; Job 1:3, 14; 42:12). The most famous she ass is the talking donkey of Balaam (Num. 22:21–23, 25, 27–30), mentioned fourteen times.

861. אַתּוּן *'attûn:* An Aramaic masculine noun meaning furnace. It designates the huge furnace into which the three Hebrew companions of Daniel were thrown (Dan. 3:6, 11, 15, 17).

862. אַתּוּק *'attûq,* אַתִּיק *'attiyq:* A masculine noun indicating a gallery or porch. It is an architectural term. It may mean a passage or street as well (Ezek. 41:15, 16; 42:3, 5).

863. אִתַּי *'ittay:* A proper noun designating Ittai:

A. The name of one of David's faithful Philistine commanders, a Gittite (2 Sam. 18:2). He chose to stay with David rather than go away in safety while David fled from Absalom (2 Sam. 15:19–22).

B. Also the name given to one of David's select warriors, one of his "thirty" (2 Sam. 23:24–39).

864. אֵתָם *'ēṯām:* A proper noun designating Etham (Ex. 13:20; Num. 33:6–8).

865. אֶתְמוֹל *'eṯmôl,* אֶתְמוּל *'eṯmûl:* An adverb of time indicating yesterday, formerly, recently. It often means yesterday (Ps. 90:4). Used many times before *šilšôm* (8032), it literally means yesterday and the third day, that is, formerly, as formerly (1 Sam. 4:7; 14:21; 2 Sam. 5:2). Used with the preposition *min* (4480), from, it means already (Isa. 30:33; Mic. 2:8).

866. אֶתְנָה *'eṯnāh:* A feminine noun meaning reward, gift, hire paid to a prostitute, wages. It is used figuratively to refer to Israel's vine and fig trees which she had received through her harlotrous dealings with the nations around her (Hos. 2:12[14].

867. אֶתְנִי *'eṯniy:* A proper noun designating Ethni (1 Chr. 6:41[26]).

868. אֶתְנַן *'eṯnan:* A masculine noun indicating the gift or hire for a prostitute. It refers specifically to a harlot's pay (Deut. 23:18[19]). Moses often depicts Israel as playing the harlot (Ezek. 16:31, 34, 41; Hos. 9:1).

Tyre was considered a pagan harlotrous city among the nations (Isa. 23:17, 18). The word refers to expensive idols of Samoa (Mic. 1:7) that led her into more harlotry.

869. אֶתְנָן ***'eṯnān:*** A proper noun designating Ethnan (1 Chr. 4:7).

870. אֲתַר ***ᵃṯar:*** An Aramaic masculine noun indicating a place, site, in place of; after this. It refers to the site of the Temple in Jerusalem in Ezra's day (5:15; 6:3, 5, 7). It seems to mean trace or evidence in Daniel 2:35 (NASB, NKJV, NIV; cf. KJV, place). With *bᵉ* on the front, it means in place of, that is, after this (Dan. 7:6, 7).

871. אֲתָרִים ***ᵃṯāriym:*** I. A masculine plural noun referring to spies (KJV, Num. 21:1).

II. A masculine proper noun referring to the Atharim (NASB, NIV, Num. 21:1).

ב Beth

872. בִּאָה ***bi'āh:*** A. feminine noun indicating an entrance or entranceway. It was an entryway large enough to have the image of jealousy placed in it (Ezek. 8:5). It stood in the northern entrance.

873. בְּאִישׁ ***bi'ysh:*** An Aramaic adjective indicating wicked, evil. Israel's enemies use the word to describe their perception of Jerusalem as a rebellious city and dangerous to the Persian kings (Ezra 4:12).

874. בָּאַר ***bā'ar:*** A verb meaning to declare, expound. It is used to describe Moses' oral exposition of the Law given at Sinai (Deut. 1:5). It also indicates a written process of clarifying and recording a revelation from God (Deut. 27:8; Hab. 2:2; cf. NASB, inscribe).

875. בְּאֵר ***b^{e}'ēr:*** A feminine noun referring to a well or pit. It defines a source of water whether natural (Gen. 16:14, Ex. 2:15) or dug out by workers (Gen. 21:25, 30; 26:15, 18; Num. 21:16–18). It defines a pit which is a source of bitumen (Gen. 14:10). It is used metaphorically to refer to a pit of destruction (Ps. 55:23[24]; NIV, pit of corruption) or in a positive sense to the well of water represented by one's own wife rather than a strange woman (Prov. 5:15). It refers to underground water sources or even the underworld (Ps. 69:15[16]). It refers to a specific desert location (Num. 21:16).

876. בְּאֵר ***b^{e}'ēr:*** A proper noun designating Beer (Num. 21:16; Judg. 9:21).

877. בֹּאר ***bō'r:*** A masculine noun meaning a cistern or well. It refers to a common well for drawing and drinking water; a famous one was located by Bethlehem (2 Sam. 23:15). It is used figuratively to describe broken cisterns (Jer. 2:13). See also #953.

878. בְּאֵרָא ***b^{e}'ērā':*** A proper noun designating Beera (1 Chr. 7:37).

879. בְּאֵר אֵלִים ***b^{e}'ēr 'ēliym:*** A proper noun designating Beer-elim (Isa. 15:8).

880. בְּאֵרָה ***b^{e}'ērāh:*** A proper noun designating Beerah (1 Chr. 5:6).

881. בְּאֵרוֹת ***'b^{e}'ērôṯ:*** A proper noun designating Beeroth (Deut. 10:6; Josh. 9:17; 18:25; 2 Sam. 4:2; Ezra 2:25; Neh. 7:29).

882. בְּאֵרִי ***b^{e}'ēriy:*** A proper noun designating Beeri:
A. A Hittite (Gen. 26:34).
B. Hosea's father (Hos. 1:1).

883. בְּאֵר לַחַי רֹאִי ***b^{e}'ēr laḥay rō'iy:*** A proper noun designating Beer-lahai-roi (Gen. 16:14; 24:62; 25:11).

884. בְּאֵר שֶׁבַע ***bᵉʼēr šeḇaʻ:*** A proper noun designating Beersheba (Gen. 21:14, 31–33; 22:19; 26:23, 33; 28:10; 46:1, 5; Neh. 11:27, 30; Amos 5:5; 8:14).

885. בְּאֵרֹת בְּנֵי־יַעֲקָן ***bᵉʼērōṯ bᵉnēy yaᵃqān:*** A phrase used in Deuteronomy 10:6 to describe a particular location. It is interpreted differently in each translation: as the proper name Beeroth Bene-Jaakan (nasb); as the description of Beeroth of the children of Jaakan (kjv); as the description of the wells of the Jaakanites (niv); and as the description of the wells of Bene Jaakan (NKJV).

886. בְּאֵרֹתִי ***bᵉʼērōṯiy:*** A proper noun designating Beerothite (2 Sam. 4:2, 3, 5, 9; 23:27).

887. בָּאַשׁ ***bāʼaš̱h:*** A verb meaning to stink, to be offensive, to be repulsive. It denotes a bad physical smell, like the reeking odor of blood in the Nile River (Ex. 7:21) or the odor of spoiled manna (Ex. 16:20). In a figurative sense, it speaks of a person who becomes strongly revolting to another, a metaphorical "stench in the nostrils." Jacob worried that his sons' retributive murder of the Shechemites caused him to stink before the people of the land (Gen. 34:30). The Israelites fretted that Moses' preaching caused them to be offensive to Pharaoh (Ex. 5:21), thus risking their lives. The verb also negatively expresses the actions of the wicked (Prov. 13:5); folly (Eccl. 10:1); and the stinking of wounds resulting from God's reproof of sin (Ps. 38:5[6]).

888. בְּאֵשׁ ***bᵉʼēš:*** An Aramaic verb meaning to be displeased, distressed. It is a verb expressing a strong feeling of distress with oneself and external circumstances (Dan. 6:14[15]).

889. בְּאֹשׁ ***bᵉʼōš:*** A masculine noun indicating a stench or foul odor. It is used literally to describe the smell of rotting corpses (Isa. 34:3; Joel 2:20; Amos 4:10) of both Israel's enemies and her own armies.

890. בָּאְשָׁה ***boʼšāh:*** A feminine noun referring to weeds, stinkweeds, darnel. It describes a useless category of weeds. It is some kind of Eurasian grass which some translators render a darnel (cf. KJV, cockle) (Job 31:40).

891. בְּאֻשִׁים ***bāʼuš:*** A masculine noun indicating a useless, worthless thing. The word is used in parallel with (good) grapes but means the opposite of good grapes. So it is bad grapes or bad fruit (NIV, Isa. 5:2, 4). It is rendered worthless ones (grapes) by the NASB.

892. בָּבָה ***bāḇāh:*** A feminine noun indicating the apple [*bᵉḇāḇaṯ*] of the eye. It is used in a figurative sense to describe Israel as the Lord's most prized possession (Zech. 2:8[12]) whom He will defend at all costs.

893. בֵּבַי ***bēḇay:*** A proper noun designating Bebai (Ezra 2:11; 8:11; 10:28; Neh. 7:16; 10:15[16]).

894. בָּבֶל ***bāḇel:*** A proper noun designating Babel or Babylon, a name meaning "confession" and the name of the foreign power most often mentioned in the Old Testament, Babylon. Its beginnings go back to Nimrod, "a mighty warrior" and hunter but also a founder of cities and city-states (Gen. 10:8–12). At Babel the languages of the world became mixed and separated (Gen. 11:9), and there great towers (ziggurats) were built to approach the gods as humankind deemed necessary. God stopped the building of these "towers of hubris" (Gen. 11:5–8), where humankind tried to gather together as one (Gen. 11:1–2). It was a part of the Assyrian Empire for a while (2 Kgs. 17:24, 30). The neo-Babylonian Empire, founded by Nabopolassar (626 B.C.) is often mentioned in the prophets (Isa. Jer., Ezek., Dan., Mic., Zech.). Its greatest king, Nebuchadnezzar, ruled nearly 43 years and is the topic of much of the Book of Daniel (1:1; 2, 3, 4). The Babylonians under Nebuchadnezzar destroyed Jerusalem and took Judah into exile in 587/6 B.C. (2 Kgs. 25:1–28; Jer. 52:3–34). Isaiah the prophet especially denounced the idolatry of Babylon (Isa. 40—66). Israel was exiled in 587/6 to Babylon for seventy years in fulfillment of both the prophet Moses' and Jeremiah's prophecies (Deut. 28; Jer. 25:1–14). They returned in 538 B.C. under Cyrus, king of Persia (2 Chr. 36:20–23; Ezra 1:1–3; Zech. 2:7[11]).

895. בָּבֶל ***bāḇel:*** A proper noun designating Babel or Babylon, an Aramaic word referring to the city or nation of Babylon. The Aramaic word is found only in Ezra and Daniel. See entry 894. The references are to the neo-Babylonian Empire (ca. 626–586 B.C.).

896. בָּבְלָי ***bāḇᵉlāy:*** A proper noun designating Babylonian (Ezra 4:9).

897. בַּג ***bag:*** A masculine noun indicating spoil, booty, plunder. It refers figuratively to Ammon being given to the nations as plunder or spoil (Ezek. 25:7). Most translators render *baz,* which is the suggested reading in the Hebrew text rather than *bāg,* whose meaning is in doubt in this text (NASB, KJV, NKJV, NIV).

898. בָּגַד ***bāgaḏ:*** A verb meaning to deal treacherously with, to be traitorous, to act unfaithfully, to betray. The verb connotes unfaithfulness in relationships like marriage (Ex. 21:8; Jer. 3:20; Mal. 2:14); Israel's covenant with the Lord (Ps. 78:57; 119:158); friendships (Job 6:15; Jer. 3:20; Mal. 2:10); leadership (Judg. 9:23).

899. בֶּגֶד ***begeḏ:*** I. A masculine noun referring to garment, clothes. It describes any type of clothing or garment (Ps. 45:8[9]). But combined with an appropriate qualifying word, it depicts specialized clothing and cultic garments as well, such as a widow's garment or cultic garments (Ex. 28:2–4). It refers to a lap garment or apron used to hold various items placed in it (2 Kgs. 4:39). Hence, it can be translated as a "lap full" (*m^elō'* *biḡdô*). It also describes a covering or wrapping for tabernacle furniture (Num. 4:6–9, 11–13) or even a bed (1 Sam. 19:13).

II. A masculine noun meaning treachery, deceit, fraud. It is always accompanied by the verb *bāgaḏ*, to deal falsely, deceitfully for emphasis (Isa. 24:16; Jer. 12:1). It describes the way of the wicked who deal in deceit or treachery.

900. בֹּגְדוֹת ***bōg^eḏôṯ:*** A feminine plural noun depicting treacherousness, faithlessness. It describes prophets of Israel who deal treacherously (Zeph. 3:4).

901. בָּגוֹד ***bāgôḏ:*** An adjective meaning treacherous, unfaithful. The word describes Judah's attitude and actions, even after she sees Israel's rebellious actions (Jer. 3:7, 10). It contains the idea of false pretense.

902. בִּגְוַי ***bigway:*** A proper noun designating Bigvai:

A. A leader under Zerubbabel (Ezra 2:2, 14; 8:14; Neh. 7:7, 19).

B. A jew (Neh. 10:16[17]).

903. בִּגְתָא ***bigṯā':*** A proper noun designating Bigtha (Esth. 1:10).

904. בִּגְתָן, בִּגְתָנָא ***bigṯān, bigṯānā':*** A proper noun designating Bigthan, Bigthana (Esth. 2:21; 6:2).

905. בַּד ***baḏ:*** I. A word that functions both as an adjective or masculine noun meaning alone, by itself. There are several basic uses: with *l^e* prefixed, it means alone, by itself, apart from, such as five curtains alone (Ex. 26:9; 36:16); him alone (Judg. 7:5; see especially Zech. 12:12–14). This idea is also expressed by putting a suffix on the end of *baḏ* to express being alone (Gen. 2:18; 21:28; 32:16[17]; 2 Sam. 10:8; Ps. 51:4[6]). It limits an idea, such as "by You only" (Eccl. 7:29; Isa. 26:13). Used with *min* (4480) after it, it means apart from, besides (Ex. 12:37; Num. 29:39; Deut. 3:5), as it does when *min* is prefixed to it (Gen. 26:1; 46:26; Lev. 9:17; 23:38).

II. A masculine noun indicating a part, pole. It indicates a part or parts of something such as an amount of an ingredient used to make incense or anointing oil (Ex. 30:34). Or it indicates various parts of objects: persons, animals, trees, parts of a structure, etc. (Ex. 25:13–15; Job 18:13; 41:12[4]; Ezek. 17:6; 19:14). It designates the poles used to carry the ark (Ex. 25:14, 15).

906. בַּד ***baḏ:*** A masculine noun meaning linen. It describes a type of fabric used in the garments of the priests. It is most likely linen (Ex. 28:42; 39:28; Lev. 16:23). It is used to describe the ephod of Samuel and other priests (1 Sam. 2:18; 22:18). It is a feature of the clothing of divine beings mentioned in Ezekiel and Daniel (9:2, 3, 11; 10:2, 6, 7; Dan. 10:5; 12:6, 7).

907. בַּד ***baḏ:*** A masculine noun indicating idle talk, empty talk, lying, boasting, bragging. It describes boasting or vain talk, such as Zophar claimed Job was uttering (Job 11:3). An arrogant nation utters false boasts (NASB, Isa. 16:6; Jer. 48:30; 50:36) as do false prophets (Isa. 44:25).

908. בָּדָא ***bāḏā':*** A verb meaning to devise, make something up, invent. It is used twice in a negative sense. It describes the making of a new illegal feast by Jeroboam I in Northern Israel in the eighth month (1 Kgs. 12:33) and the creation of false accusations against the Jews by Nehemiah's enemies (Neh. 6:8).

909. בָּדַד ***bāḏaḏ:*** A verb meaning to be isolated, alone, lonely. It describes a state of isolation of separation, loneliness. Three subjects are mentioned: a straggling lone soldier of Assyria (Isa. 14:31); Israel depicted as a wild donkey alone by itself (Hos. 8:9); and a lonely bird resembling a broken person before the Lord (Ps. 102:7[8]).

910. בָּדָד ***bāḏāḏ:*** A masculine noun indicating isolation, separation, aloneness, desolation. It describes a state of separation. A leper had to dwell outside the camp (Lev. 13:46) by himself. Any city could be isolated, cut off by itself (Isa. 27:10). It describes the status of Israel dwelling alone among the nations (Num. 23:9), separated unto the Lord religiously and physically (Deut. 33:28; cf. Jer. 49:31). The Lord's unique leadership of Israel is described by this word (Deut. 32:12; Ps. 4:8[9]). It describes the isolation and loneliness of a person seemly cut off from the Lord (Jer. 15:17).

911. בְּדַד ***b***^{e}***ḏaḏ:*** A proper noun designating Bedad (Gen. 36:35; 1 Chr. 1:46).

912. בֵּדְיָה ***bēḏ***^{e}***yāh:*** A proper noun designating Bedeiah (Ezra 10:35).

913. בְּדִיל ***b***^{e}***ḏiyl:*** A masculine noun meaning tin. It describes booty taken from the Midianites (Num. 31:22) that had to be purified by fire. Israel is described as tin that needs to be purified in the furnace of God's judgments (Ezek. 22:18, 20). It is translated as alloy (NASB, NKJV, Isa. 1:25), as impurities (NIV) and as tin (KJV) in a difficult passage to decipher.

914. בָּדַל ***bāḏal:*** A verb meaning to separate, to divide, to detach. This word is used most often of the various words that indicate these ideas. It is used both literally and figuratively in two different stems. The first stem is reflexive or passive in its function, and the second is causative. The reflexive sense of the word is used to express Israel's separation of themselves from intermarriage and the abominations and pollution of the nations around them (Ezra 6:21; 10:11) in order to dedicate themselves to the Lord and His Law (Neh. 10:28[29]). Its passive usage indicates those being set apart for something (1 Chr. 23:13) or, in a negative sense, being excluded from something (e.g., from the community of Israel [Ezra 10:8]).

The verb is used most often in its active causative meanings that are the active counterparts to its passive reflexive meanings. Perhaps the most famous example of this is found in the creation story as God produces a separation between light and darkness (Gen. 1:4). Just as significant is the distinction He makes between His people Israel and the peoples and nations surrounding them (Lev. 20:24). The fact that Moses set aside the Levites to administer and to carry out their holy duties is described by this word (Num. 8:14), as is the exclusion of a person from the Israelite community (Deut. 29:21[20]). In the religious and ritualistic sphere, this word indicates a sharp division between the holy and unholy (profane) and the clean and unclean (Lev. 20:25). It also describes priests dividing sacrificial animals into pieces (Lev. 1:17).

The use of this word by the writer indicates that God desires to make discriminations between this people and the nations, among groups within His own people and within His larger creation, both animate and inanimate. These differences are important to God and are to be observed carefully, especially by His chosen nation.

915. בָּדָל ***bāḏāl:*** A masculine noun meaning a piece. It is used figuratively to refer to Israel's enemies snatching a "piece of an ear" representing Israel during God's judgments on her (Amos 3:12).

916. בְּדֹלַח ***b^e^ḏōlaḥ:*** A masculine noun designating bdellium or aromatic resin. It describes a yellowish gum resin that may look like gold pearls in its hardened stage (Gen. 2:12; Num. 11:7). Manna is said to resemble this material in its appearance (NKJV, KJV, NASB, all render bdellium; NIV, resin).

917. בְּדָן ***b^e^ḏān:*** A proper noun designating Bedan:
A. A judge (1 Sam. 12:11).
B. A Manassite (1 Chr. 7:17).

918. בָּדַק ***bāḏaq:*** A verb meaning to repair, restore. It describes the workmen's cleaning and reparations made on the temple during Josiah's reign (2 Chr. 34:10).

919. בֶּדֶק ***beḏeq:*** A masculine noun indicating breach, seam, damage. The word describes a chink, crack, or rent in the temple (2 Kgs. 12:5–8[6–9], 12[13]; 22:5) that needed to be repaired. It describes a leak or seam in a ship (Ezek. 27:9, 27) that needed to be caulked or repaired.

920. בִּדְקַר ***biḏqar:*** A proper noun designating Bidkar (2 Kgs. 9:25).

921. בְּדַר ***b^e^ḏar:*** An Aramaic verb meaning to scatter. It describes the scattering of the fruit, the people of the earth, from the tree in Nebuchadnezzar's dream (Dan. 4:14[11]).

922. בֹּהוּ ***bōhû:*** A masculine noun indicating void or emptiness. It depicts the state of matter after God had created it but before He had fashioned it for habitation (Gen. 1:2). It, therefore, describes the state of the land or earth after God judges it (Isa. 34:11; Jer. 4:23). It is used in combination with *tōhû,* without form, each time.

923. בַּהַט ***bahaṭ:*** A masculine noun meaning red stone, porphyry. The garden floor of the king's palace in the citadel in Susa was made of porphyry (NASB, NIV, Esth. 1:6; KJV, red (stone); NKJV, alabaster). All of these were precious or semiprecious stones.

924. בְּהִילוּ ***b^ehiylû:*** An Aramaic feminine noun meaning haste. It describes quick travel and response to an urgent situation (Ezra 4:23) by the enemies of the Jews.

925. בָּהִיר ***bāhiyr:*** An adjective meaning bright. It describes the exceeding brightness of the sun right after the wind has cleared the skies following a storm. This is an example of one of God's marvels in the created order (Job. 37:21).

926. בָּהַל ***bāhal:*** A verb meaning to be dismayed or terrified. It is sometimes used when a sudden threat conveys great fear (Ex. 15:15; 1 Sam. 28:21). This word can also mean hasten or to be in a hurry (2 Chr. 26:20; Eccl. 8:3).

927. בְּהַל ***b^ehal:*** An Aramaic verb meaning to be in a hurry; to be troubled, to be disturbed. It occurs only in the book of Daniel, where it is used of someone in a hurry (Dan. 2:25; 3:24; 6:19[20]) or someone who is terrified, frightened, or troubled (Dan. 4:5[2], 19[16]; 5:6, 9; 7:15, 28). In each of these cases, the people are terrified because of a dream or a vision from God.

928. בֶּהָלָה ***behālāh:*** A feminine noun meaning dismay, sudden terror, or fright. One of the curses for not obeying the commands of the Lord is sudden terror (Lev. 26:16). When God makes the new heaven and earth, children will not be doomed to this terror (Isa. 65:23). But the people in Jerusalem will be the object of such terror for not remaining faithful to God (Jer. 15:8).

929. בְּהֵמָה ***b^ehēmāh:*** A feminine noun, usually functioning collectively, meaning animals, beasts, livestock, cattle. It takes on the following meanings in context: animals or beasts in general (Ex. 9:9; 1 Kgs. 4:33[5:13]); wild animals; beasts of the earth (Deut. 28:26; 32:24; 1 Sam. 17:44). Often it refers to cattle or livestock (NIV, NASB, Gen. 1:24–26; 2:20; 8:1; 47:18); beasts of burden (Gen. 34:23); or beasts for riding (Neh. 2:12, 14).

930. בְּהֵמוֹת ***b^ehēmôṯ:*** A masculine noun referring to a very large animal. In Job 40:15, it seems to refer to a hippopotamus or crocodile. Most translators transliterate the word as Behemoth (KJV, NKJV, NASB, NIV).

931. בֹּהֶן ***bōhen:*** A masculine noun indicating a thumb or big toe. It refers to the right thumb and right big toe of the high priest that are smeared with blood as part of his installation ceremony (Ex. 29:20; Lev. 8:23, 24). This process was also part of the cleansing ritual of a leper (Lev. 14:14, 17, 25, 28). It refers to big toes and right thumbs in general (Judg. 1:6, 7).

932. בֹּהַן ***bōhan:*** A proper noun designating Bohan (Josh. 15:6; 18:17).

933. בֹּהַק ***bōhaq:*** A masculine noun referring to a white skin spot, harmless rash, freckle, eczema. This word describes a harmless skin rash (Lev. 13:39) which did not render a person unclean.

934. בַּהֶרֶת ***baheret̲:*** A feminine noun indicating a bright spot, white spot. The spots were potentially dangerous or pathogenic and had to be watched until their natures could be identified more accurately (Lev. 13:2, 4, 19, 23–26; 14:56).

935. בּוֹא ***bô':*** A verb meaning to come, to go, to bring. This word is used often and takes on many nuances of meaning: concerning physical location, it means to go, to come, to bring to a location (Gen. 6:19; 12:11; Josh. 6:1; Judg. 18:18); to a group or person (Ex. 18:19; Esth. 2:12). It is used with the preposition *'el* to mean to have intercourse (Gen. 6:4; 16:2; Deut. 22:13). It bears the meaning of coming or arriving (Gen. 19:22; Prov. 18:3) physically or temporally, such as harvest time (Lev. 25:22). It means to take place, to happen (1 Sam. 9:6). Used with the preposition *b*^{e} and others, it can take on the idea of having dealings with (Josh. 23:7; Ps. 26:4; Prov. 22:24). It has several idiomatic uses: followed by *b*^{e}*dāmīym,* it indicates involvement in bloodguilt (1 Sam. 25:26). With the word "after," it means to be in pursuit of someone or something (Ex. 14:17).

It is used in a causative way to bring something, e.g., an army (2 Sam. 5:1–3) from the battleground, to gather in something (2 Sam. 9:10). It is used idiomatically in several short phrases all headed by *hēbiy'*, to bring: to bring justice (Eccl. 11:9); to bring legal cases (Ex. 18:19); to take something away (*hēbīy* + *mē'aḥar,* Ps. 78:71); to apply one's heart (Prov. 23:12); to understand. In a passive sense, it means to be brought, to be offered or burned, be put into (Gen. 33:11; 43:18; Lev. 6:30[23]; 11:32). In its participial forms, the words may refer to the near future (2 Kgs. 20:17; Isa. 39:6; Jer. 7:32) or to future things to come to pass (Isa. 27:6; 41:22).

936. בּוּז ***bûz:*** A verb meaning to despise, to hold in contempt. It indicates scorn or disrespect for someone or something. Fools especially despise or hold contempt for wisdom (Prov. 1:7; 23:9). Contempt may be aimed at persons (Prov. 6:30; 11:12), but a mother or father are never to be despised (Prov. 23:22; 30:17). God's word or instruction is not to be held in contempt (Prov. 13:13), and love is said to be beyond contempt (Song 8:1, 7).

937. בּוּז ***bûz:*** A masculine noun indicating shame or contempt. Contempt is an attitude of disrespect and scorn toward persons. Contempt may spring from pride or personal wickedness (Job 31:34; Ps. 123:3, 4; Prov. 18:3) but also from pride because of wealth (Job 12:5). It indicates persons who could become the object or laughingstock of contempt (Gen. 38:23). God pours out contempt on the objects of His judgments (Ps. 107:40).

938. בּוּז ***bûz:*** A proper noun designating Buz:

A. The second son of Nahor (Gen. 22:21; Jer. 25:23).

B. A Gadite (1 Chr. 5:14).

939. בּוּזָה ***bûzāh:*** A feminine noun indicating contempt. It indicates an attitude of scorn and disrespect. The Jews had become an object of scorn from Sanballat and his followers during the time of Nehemiah (Neh. 4:4[3:36]).

940. בּוּזִי ***bûziy:*** A proper noun designating Buzite (Job 32:2, 6).

941. בּוּזִי ***bûziy:*** A proper noun designating Buzi (Ezek. 1:3).

942. בַּוַּי ***bawway:*** A proper noun designating Bavvai (Nah. 3:18).

943. בּוּךְ ***bûḵ:*** A verb meaning to be confused, complexed; to mill around, wander aimlessly. It indicates a confused state of mind and activity (Ex. 14:3; Esth. 3:15) because of not knowing what to do. The word describes the endless wandering of animals during the Lord's judgments on His people (Joel 1:18).

944. בּוּל ***bûl:*** A masculine noun indicating food, produce; trunk of a tree, block of wood. It describes the sustenance produced on the mountains for Behemoth (Job 40:20). Speaking of idols, Isaiah refers to a block of wood (NIV, NKJV, NASB, Isa. 44:19; KJV, stock of a tree) and using this wood as part of the idol.

945. בּוּל ***bûl:*** A masculine proper noun, Bul. The word designates the eighth month of the eleventh year of Solomon's reign, which would be 959 B.C. In this month, the Temple was finished (1 Kgs. 6:38[39]).

946. בּוּנָה ***bûnāh:*** A proper noun designating Bunah (1 Chr. 2:25).

947. בּוּס ***bûs:*** A verb that signifies to tread down, to trample underfoot. This term generally has a negative connotation, implying a destructive action (Zech. 10:5). God is often the subject of this verb, when He states that He will trample His enemies (Ps. 60:12[14]); Isa. 14:25; 63:6). It can also be used with people as the subject but with the understanding that they are only God's instruments (Ps. 44:5[6]). This expression can also have a figurative meaning: to reject (Prov. 27:7) and to desecrate (Isa. 63:18).

948. בּוּץ ***bûṣ:*** A masculine noun indicating fine linen. This was a fine, costly white linen. It is used to describe a house where Egyptian linen workers plied their trade (1 Chr. 15:27). Some temple workers were skilled in working with linen (2 Chr. 2:14[13]); it was part of the temple veil (2 Chr. 3:14). It was used to pay for Tyrian imports (Ezek. 27:16).

949. בּוֹצֵץ ***bôṣēṣ:*** A proper noun designating Bozer (1 Sam. 14:4).

950. בּוּקָה ***bûqāh:*** A feminine noun meaning emptiness. The word describes the state of Nineveh after God's judgment on it. The city was bereft of inhabitants and joy (Nah. 2:10[11]).

951. בּוֹקֵר ***bôqēr:*** A masculine noun indicating a shepherd or herdsman. It describes the work of Amos when he was called to be a prophet (Amos 7:14). He tended cattle and sheep and grew figs.

952. בּוּר ***bûr:*** A verb meaning to declare, to explain. It is used to describe the process the preacher of Ecclesiastes (9:1) goes through in his efforts to expound on the puzzles, riddles, and mysteries of life that surround every person under the sun.

953. בּוֹר ***bôr:*** A masculine noun meaning pit, cistern, well. The term can refer to rock-hewn reservoirs or man-made wells. When empty, such cisterns served as perfect prisons (i.e., Joseph [Gen. 37:20, 22, 24, 28, 29] and Jeremiah [Jer. 38:6, 7, 9–11, 13]). The semantic range extends to prisons in general. Joseph refers to Pharaoh's dungeon as *bôr* (Gen. 40:15). Figuratively, it carries positive and negative connotations. Positively, it can signify a man's wife (Prov. 5:15), and Sarah is the cistern of Israel (Isa. 51:1). Negatively, it represents death (Prov. 28:17); Sheol (Ps. 30:3[4]); exile (Zech. 9:11).

954. בּוֹשׁ ***bôš:*** A verb meaning to be ashamed, to act shamefully, or to put to shame. It is both an external and a subjective experience, ranging from disgrace (Hos. 10:6) to guilt (Ezra 9:6). In Genesis 2:25, shame is related to the sexual nature of humans. Moreover, to act shamefully is equivalent to acting unwisely (Prov. 10:5; 14:35). To be ashamed is to experience distress, as farmers with no harvest (Jer. 14:4; Joel 1:11), but the blessing of God means that one will never be put to shame (Ps. 25:20; Joel 2:26, 27).

955. בּוּשָׁה ***bûšāh:*** A feminine noun meaning shame. Although this word is used only four times in the Old Testament, its meaning is clear from an understanding of the verb *bôš* (954) meaning to be ashamed, to act shamefully, or to put to shame. This word refers to the shame that came on David during his distress (Ps. 89:45[46]), as well as the shame associated with the destruction of an enemy (Mic. 7:10); of Edom (Obad. 1:10); and of the people in the land of Israel (Ezek. 7:18).

956. בִּית ***biyṯ:*** An Aramaic verb meaning to pass the night, spend the night. It indicates that someone passes time. Darius passed the night fasting and without sleep or diversions (Dan. 6:18[19]).

957. בַּז ***baz:*** A masculine noun meaning booty, prey, plunder, spoils. The word describes the act of plundering or the objects taken in the process. The temple was despoiled, plundered (Ezek. 7:21; 23:46). Many things were taken as booty: various objects (Isa. 10:6; 33:23; Ezek. 29:19) including human beings (Num. 14:3, 31; Jer. 2:14). Even the Lord's flock, Israel, became prey to evil shepherds as well as foreign enemies (Ezek. 34:8, 22). The word is part of a phrase in Isaiah 8:1 meaning, "Swift is the booty, speedy is the prey" (NASB; cf. NIV, "quick to the plunder, swift to the spoil").

958. בָּזָא ***bāzā':*** A verb meaning to divide, cut through, wash away. The word describes the effect of the Nile River of Egypt and its tributaries or sources in Ethiopia (Isa. 18:2, 7).

959. בָּזָה ***bāzāh:*** A verb meaning to hold in contempt or to despise. The verb means to hold in disdain, to disrespect. It can mean to prefer something more than the thing despised, e.g., Esau's birthright (Gen. 25:34), or not to treat something with proper respect (Ezek. 16:59; 22:8; Mal. 1:6). The psalmist thanks the Lord for not despising a broken and humble heart (Ps. 51:17[19]). The notorious Syrian king, Antiochus Epiphanes, a forerunner of the Antichrist, is depicted as a despicable person who scorns God Himself (Dan. 11:21).

960. בָּזֹה ***bāzōh:*** An adjective meaning despised. The word indicates something or someone scorned or disdained. The Servant in Isaiah is described with this term (Isa. 49:7); the NIV treats the word as a verb, to be despised.

961. בִּזָּה ***bizzāh:*** A feminine noun meaning to loot, to plunder, to despoil. The word refers to objects of plunder. A city was looted for its objects worthy of plundering (2 Chr. 14:14[13]; 25:13). It also refers to the activity of plunder itself (Ezra 9:7; Neh. 4:4[3:36]; Dan. 11:33). It was significant that the Jews did not seize the spoil in the city of Susa (Esth. 9:10, 15, 16).

962. בָּזַז ***bāzaz:*** A verb meaning to loot, to plunder, to spoil, to rob. The word describes this destructive activity taken against cities or places (Gen. 34:27; 2 Kgs. 7:16), people and cattle (Num. 31:9; Isa. 10:2; 11:14). Its passive uses are similar with the meaning of be plundered (Isa. 24:3) or taken as spoil (Jer. 50:37).

963. בִּזָּיוֹן ***bizzāyôn:*** A masculine noun meaning disrespect, contempt.

It means a lack of respect or disrespect in the case of the women of Media and Persia (Esth. 1:14).

964. בִּזְיוֹתְיָה *bizyôṯyāh:* A proper noun designating Biziothiah (Josh. 15:28).

965. בָּזָק *bāzāq:* A masculine noun indicating lightning, a bolt of lightning, or a flash of lightning. The word is used in a figurative sense to describe the movement of the living beings in Ezekiel's chariot vision (Ezek. 1:14).

966. בֶּזֶק *bezeq:* A proper noun designating Bezek (Judg. 1:4, 5; 1 Sam. 11:8).

967. בָּזַר *bāzar:* A verb describing a process of scattering or dispersing. It refers to the dispersal and confusion of peoples who were engaged in warfare (Ps. 68:30[31]). It depicts the dispersal or distribution of booty and plunder to allies in war (Dan. 11:24).

968. בִּזְּתָא *bizzᵉṯā':* A proper noun designating Biztha (Esth. 1:10).

969. בָּחוֹן *bāḥôn:* I. A masculine noun meaning an assayer, tester. It refers to someone who evaluates and sizes up something. Jeremiah was called to be an assayer of the Lord's people (Jer. 6:27).

II. A masculine noun meaning tower or fortification. The word is used figuratively of Jeremiah among God's disobedient people (Jer. 6:27). As a tower or a fortification, he would examine them to see if they would turn to the Lord (NKJV, NASB; NIV, a tester of metals).

970. בָּחוּר *baḥûr:* A masculine noun indicating a young man. It is usually in its plural form. The word refers to an unmarried adult male in his prime (1 Sam. 9:2; Eccl. 11:9; Isa. 62:5). It is used as a collective noun meaning young men (Jer. 15:8). It is used with the word for virgin, *bᵉṯûlāh,* to indicate young men and virgins (Deut. 32:25; 2 Chr. 36:17; Jer. 51:22) and with *zᵉqēniym* to indicate young and old men (Jer. 31:13).

971. בַּחוּן *baḥûn,* בַּחִין *baḥiyn:* A masculine noun designating a siege tower. It depicts an ancient, often-used tool of ancient warfare that was effective in scaling and battering high walls and gates of enemy cities during a time of war (Isa. 23:13).

972. בָּחִיר *bāḥiyr:* An adjective meaning chosen. It depicts a person chosen by God, such as Saul (2 Sam. 21:6). God chose Moses (Ps. 106:23) and David for specific purposes (Ps. 89:3[4]). The Lord chose His special Servant (Isa. 42:1). But God's people as a whole were His chosen as well (1 Chr. 16:13; Ps. 106:5; Isa. 43:20; 65:9, 15, 22). As all of the above contexts indicate, a person chosen by God also had special blessings and promises from the Lord.

973. בָּחַל *bāḥal:* A verb meaning to abhor or to obtain by greed. This word has two different, unrelated meanings. The first meaning is to abhor and comes from a Syriac word meaning to be nauseated by or to experience disgust with. It is used only in Zechariah 11:8 to refer to the flock who abhorred the shepherd. The second meaning, to obtain by greed, comes from an Arabic word with a similar meaning. This word only appears in Proverbs 20:21. However, a textual problem exists, and some people read the verse with the Hebrew word *bāhal* (926), meaning to be in haste.

974. בָּחַן ***bāḥan:*** A verb meaning to examine, to try, to prove. This verb can refer to any type of test. Joseph tested his brothers (Gen. 42:15, 16); while Job and Elihu indicated that the ear tests words as the palate tastes food (Job 12:11; 34:3), thereby indicating that the hearer should be able to vindicate his or her assertions. However, it generally refers to God's testing of humanity. The psalmist acknowledges this fact (Ps. 11:4, 5) and even requests it (Ps. 139:23). The biblical writers sometimes compare God's testing to the refining of precious metals, like gold and silver (Job 23:10; Zech. 13:9). There are also a few passages in which people test God, but these clearly state that this is not normal (Ps. 95:9; Mal. 3:10, 15).

975. בַּחַן ***baḥan:*** A masculine noun indicating a watchtower. It indicates a garrisoned tower from which Israel's watchmen could guard their fields, cities, and nation (Isa. 32:14).

976. בֹּחַן ***bōḥan:*** A masculine noun meaning testing. This word is derived from the verb *bāhan* (974), meaning to examine, try, or prove. The idea is that the testing verifies or authenticates. In Ezekiel 21:13[18], the strength of the sword is verified in its testing. In Isaiah 28:16, the stone is verified in that it has been tested and proved.

977. בָּחַר ***bāḥar:*** A verb whose meaning is to take a keen look at, to prove, to choose. It denotes a choice, which is based on a thorough examination of the situation and not an arbitrary whim. Although this word rarely means to prove, it does communicate that sense in Isaiah 48:10, where it describes the way God tested Israel in order to make a careful choice: "I have tested you in the furnace of affliction." In most contexts, the word suggests the concept to choose or to select. It can designate human choice (Gen. 13:11; Deut. 30:19; Josh. 24:15; Judg. 10:14) or divine choice (Deut. 7:7; 1 Sam. 2:28; Neh. 9:7; Ps. 135:4); however, in either case, it generally has theological overtones. This word can also have the connotations to desire, to like, or to delight in. A good example is Isaiah 1:29, where the word is in synonymous parallelism with *ḥāmad* (2530), meaning to desire or take pleasure in.

978. בַּחֲרוּמִי ***bah̩arûmiy:*** A proper noun designating Baharumite; see also *barḥumiy* (1273) (1 Chr. 11:33).

979. בְּחוּרוֹת ***beḥûrôṯ***, בְּחוּרִים ***beḥûriym:*** A masculine plural abstract noun meaning youth, age, or time of youth. The early years of life were considered times of joy, opportunity, and enjoyment—but above all, a vital time to remember one's Creator (Eccl. 11:9; 12:1). The word refers to one's early years as the time of youth (Num. 11:28).

980. בַּחוּרִים ***baḥûriym***, בַּחֻרִים ***baḥuriym:*** A proper noun designating Bahurim (2 Sam. 3:16; 16:5; 17:18; 19:16[17]; 1 Kgs. 2:8).

981. בָּטָה ***bāṭāh***, בָּטָא ***bāṭā':*** A verb meaning to speak rashly or thoughtlessly, to babble. It connotes a foolish utterance with an oath spoken thoughtlessly or flippantly (Lev. 5:4).

982. בָּטַח ***bāṭaḥ:*** A verb indicating to trust, to be confident. It expresses the feeling of safety and security that is felt when one can rely on someone or something else. It is used to show trust in God (2 Kgs. 18:5; Ps. 4:5[6]; Jer 49:11); in other people (Judg. 9:26; 20:36; Isa. 36:5, 6, 9); or in things (Ps. 44:6[7]; Jer. 7:4; Hab. 2:18). In addition, this expression can also relate to the state of being confident, secure, without fear (Judg. 18:7, 10, 27; Job 11:18; Prov. 28:1).

983. בֶּטַח ***beṭaḥ:*** A masculine noun or adjective meaning security. As a noun, it primarily means security or calm assurance (Gen. 34:25; Isa. 32:17). As an adjective, it means assurance or confidence. It is primarily a positive term: to dwell in safety because of God's protection (Lev. 25:18); to lie down safely or in security (Hos. 2:18[20]); to walk securely or assuredly (Prov. 10:9). In other instances, it is a negative term meaning to be too self-assured or careless (Ezek. 30:9; 39:6).

984. בֶּטַח ***beṭaḥ:*** A proper noun designating Betah (2 Sam. 8:8).

985. בִּטְחָה ***biṭḥāh:*** A feminine noun meaning trust, confidence. It is used only in Isaiah 30:15 where this trust was to characterize the people of God. Used as such, it explicates a key theme of Isaiah's theology: true belief in God should be exhibited by implicit trust (confidence) in Him (cf. Isa. 26:3, 4). The people of God, even in their sinful failure, should glorify Him by quiet trust instead of reliance on self-stratagems and other powers (cf. Isa. 7:4). This confident trust would bring divine strength and salvation. The failure to trust could only provoke judgment (cf. Isa. 31:1). Such trust or confidence as indicative of belief is echoed throughout the Old Testament, particularly in the Psalms.

986. בִּטָּחוֹן ***biṭṭāḥôn:*** A masculine noun meaning trust or hope. It is used to signify Hezekiah's trust in God when Jerusalem was under siege (2 Kgs. 18:19); or the hope that living people possess (Eccl. 9:4).

987. בַּטֻּחוֹת ***baṭṭuḥôṯ:*** A feminine plural noun meaning security, safety. Its only occurrence is Job 12:6.

988. בָּטַל ***bāṭal:*** A verb meaning to cease, stand idle; be inactive. The word describes the inactivity of either the decaying teeth of an elderly person or, literally, those who grind grain using millstones (Eccl. 12:3). It is likely that the writer wants our minds to move back and forth between literal and figurative images in his poetry.

989. בְּטֵל ***beṭēl:*** An Aramaic verb that means to cease, cause to cease, to stop, discontinue; to delay. The word refers to the cessation of work on the temple of the Lord in the days of Artaxerxes and Darius, kings of Persia (Ezra 4:21, 23, 24; 5:5). The word means more properly delay in Ezra 6:8 (NASB; NIV, stop).

990. בֶּטֶן ***beṭen:*** A feminine noun meaning belly, womb, inner body, rounded projection. With perhaps the general meaning of inside, *beṭen* often refers to the physical belly. It also frequently refers to the womb, where it is at times significantly linked with God's sovereign care, comfort, and the calling of His elect (Ps. 22:9[10]; 139:13; Isa. 44:2; 49:1; Jer. 1:5). Defined as womb, the Hebrew word is sometimes used with the word *reḥem*, also meaning womb (7358). First Kings 7:20 uses the word to refer to a rounded projection of a temple pillar. In a figurative sense, *beṭen* means the inner being of a person. Ancient wisdom literature pictured the belly, or inmost part, as the place where thoughts were treasured and the spiritual being expressed itself and was satisfied (Job 32:18; Prov. 20:27).

991. בֶּטֶן ***beṭen:*** A proper noun designating Beten (Josh. 19:25).

992. בָּטְנָה ***boṭnāh:*** A masculine noun depicting a pistachio nut. It was one item among others carried into Egypt by Jacob's sons at his directions (Gen. 43:11; KJV, nuts).

993. בְּטֹנִים ***beṭōniym:*** A proper noun designating Betonim (Josh. 13:26).

994. בִּי ***biy:*** A particle used as an interjection meaning please, excuse me, oh. The particle is intended to express politeness, pardon, deep concern with great respect toward the one spoken to. It is used in addressing noble men, such as Jacob, Joseph, Moses, Eli, Solomon (Gen. 43:20; 44:18; Num. 12:11; 1 Sam. 1:26; 1 Kgs. 3:17, 26); divine beings, the angel of the Lord (Judg. 6:13, 15); but most often the Lord (Ex. 4:10, 13; Josh. 7:8; Judg. 13:8).

995. בִּין ***biyn:*** A verb meaning to discern, to perceive, to observe, to pay attention to, to be intelligent, to be discreet, to understand; in the causative sense, to give understanding, to teach; in the reflexive sense, to consider diligently. People can perceive by means of their senses: eyes (Prov. 7:7); ears (Prov. 29:19); touch (Ps. 58:9[10]); taste (Job 6:30). But actual discerning is not assured. Those who hear do not always understand (Dan. 12:8). In the final analysis, only God gives and conceals understanding (Isa. 29:14).

996. בַּיִן ***bayin:*** A noun used as a preposition to mean between, among, in the midst. It means literally between two things (Gen. 15:17). It is repeated later in a sentence with the two words meaning (between . . . and, *bayin . . . ûbayin;* Gen. 1:4, 6; Isa. 59:2). It indicates that something is within a certain area (Prov. 26:13, in the open square, NASB). Preceded by *'el* and followed by *l^{e}*, it gives location among (Ezek. 10:2), or with *min* (4480) on the front, it indicates from between (Gen. 49:10). In Nehemiah 5:18, it means interval, marking a period of ten days.

997. בֵּין ***bēyn:*** An Aramaic preposition indicating between, among. It is used in two verses in the Old Testament. It indicates position in the middle of the teeth (Dan. 7:5). With respect to more than two items, it describes a position among them (Dan. 7:8), i.e., among the ten horns.

998. בִּינָה ***biynāh:*** A feminine noun meaning understanding, comprehension, discernment, righteous action. The word is found mainly in wisdom literature, the Psalms, in several of the major prophets, and 1 and 2 Chronicles. In nearly all the literary contexts in the Bible where it occurs with these basic meanings, it carries strong moral and religious connotations. In Job 28:28, the act of turning away from evil was said to be understanding and was based on a prior proper discernment of what was evil. A lack of this kind of understanding was morally culpable and resulted in sin and even drove away God's compassion for persons who did not have it (Isa. 27:11). Happily, understanding as a moral or religious entity can be acquired (Prov. 4:5, 7) and even increased (Isa. 29:24) by seeking after it diligently. The understanding that God desires has a cognitive dimension, therefore, as further illustrated when the author of Proverbs spoke of words of "understanding" (Prov. 1:2). The understanding and discernment that is the object of all knowing is the knowledge of the Holy One (Prov. 9:10). Understanding is to mark God's people. It is not surprising, therefore, to learn that by means of understanding, God made all His created order (cf. Ps. 136:5).

God has graciously endowed human beings with the ability of understanding and comprehension, but this faculty is not infallible, and, therefore, we are to ask God for guidance at all times (Prov. 3:5). Our own ability of understanding should, however, function to give us discernment, for instance, in showing a proper attitude toward seeking the riches of this world (Prov. 23:4). Our understanding is also the ability that enables us to understand languages (Isa. 33:19), literature, visions, and dreams (Dan. 1:20). It is the ability that decodes the symbols of communication for us. The writer of Proverbs personifies understanding along with wisdom in the famous wisdom chapter of Proverbs (Prov. 2:3; 8:14).

999. בִּינָה ***biynāh:*** An Aramaic feminine noun meaning understanding. The Hebrew root for this word means to distinguish, to separate, to perceive. Therefore, this word carries the idea of discernment, as one separates the truth from lies (Dan. 2:21).

1000. בֵּיצָה ***bēyṣāh:*** A feminine noun meaning egg. The word indicates the egg of a mother bird (Deut. 22:6); a snake (Isa. 59:5); an ostrich (Job 39:14). It refers to abandoned eggs (Isa. 10:14) gathered by an arrogant Assyrian king.

1001. בִּירָה ***biyrāh:*** An Aramaic feminine noun referring to a citadel, palace, fortress. The word describes a fortified building (Ezra 6:2), which was situated in Ecbatana in the Median province of Persia.

1002. בִּירָה ***biyrāh:*** A feminine noun indicating a citadel, palace, or capitol. The word refers to the Temple built by Solomon (1 Chr. 29:1, 19). It also depicts a fortified building or area (acropolis) (Neh. 7:2; Dan. 8:2). Or its main intent may be to designate a building as the capitol (Neh. 1:1), palace, or citadel of a city or nation (Esth. 1:2, 5; 2:3, 5, 8).

1003. בִּירָנִיּוֹת ***biyrāniyyôṯ:*** A feminine noun depicting a fortress, fortified place. It refers to fortified places used to protect and defend a people or nation. Fortresses were constructed by Jehosaphat (2 Chr. 17:12) and Jotham (2 Chr. 27:4) respectively in Judah.

1004. בַּיִת ***bayiṯ:*** A noun meaning house, dwelling, family, temple, palace. It is used basically to denote a building in which a family lives (Deut. 20:5) but can also refer to the family or household itself (Gen. 15:2; Josh. 7:14; 24:15). It often is used of a clan such as "house of Aaron" (Ps. 115:10, 12; 118:3). Sometimes it means palace or dynasty when employed in the Hebrew phrase "house of the king" (Gen. 12:15; 1 Kgs. 4:6; Jer. 39:8). When the Old Testament speaks of the house of the Lord, it obviously refers to the Temple or Tabernacle (Ex. 23:19; Dan. 1:2). The word is also found in place names: Bethel, meaning "house of God" (Gen. 12:8); Beth-shemesh, meaning "house of the sun" (Josh. 15:10); and Bethlehem, meaning "house of bread" (Gen. 35:19).

1005. בַּיִת ***bayiṯ:*** An Aramaic masculine noun referring to a temple, royal residence, house. It has in mind a palace (Dan. 4:4[1]). In combination with other words, it takes on the meaning of royal treasury (Ezra 6:4); royal residence (Dan. 4:30[27]); banquet hall (Dan. 5:10); treasure house (Ezra 5:17); archives (Ezra 6:1; KJV, house of rolls [scrolls]). It refers to the

Temple often (Ezra 4:24; 7:23; Dan. 5:3, 23) as the house of God.

1006. בַּיִת ***bayiṯ:*** A proper noun designating Bajith (Isa. 15:2).

1007. בֵּית אָוֶן ***bēyṯ 'āwen:*** A proper noun designating Beth Aven (Josh. 7:2; 18:12; 1 Sam. 13:5; 14:23; Hos. 4:15; 5:8; 10:5, 8). See also *'āwen* (206,B).

1008. בֵּית־אֵל ***bēyṯ–'ēl:*** A proper noun designating Bethel:

A. A town situated on the Ephraim-Benjamin border. It is about 15 north of Jerusalem. It means "house of God" and is mentioned often in the Old Testament, next, in fact to Jerusalem. Its archeological name is Beit Beitin. Jacob also called it Luz (Judg. 1:22, 23). Abraham tented near it (Gen. 12:8; 13:3), and Jacob dreamed important dreams there (Gen. 28:19). It was given to the tribe of Benjamin (Josh. 12:16; 18:22). Jeroboam II built an altar there to a golden calf (1 Kgs. 12:29, 32–33). It became a slanderous byword among some prophets (Jer. 48:13; Hos. 10:15; Amos 4:4; 5:5, 6). Amaziah, the priest of Bethel in Amos's day, was soundly rebuked by the prophet (7:10–17). Josiah finally destroyed its corrupt altar and place of worship (2 Kgs. 23:4–19). It was resettled in the time of the return from exile (2 Kgs. 17:28).

B. A town in southern Judah near Beersheba and Ziklag (1 Sam. 30:27).

1009. בֵּית אַרְבֵּאל ***bēyṯ 'arbē'l:*** A proper noun designating Beth Arbel (Hos. 10:14).

1010. בֵּית בַּעַל מְעוֹן ***bēyṯ ba'al me'ôn,*** בֵּית מְעוֹן ***bēyṯ me'ôn:*** A proper noun designating Beth Maal Meon, Beth Meon (Josh. 13:17; Jer. 48:23).

1011. בֵּית בִּרְאִי ***bēyṯ bir'iy:*** A proper noun designating Beth Biri (1 Chr. 4:31).

1012. בֵּית בָּרָה ***bēyṯ bārāh:*** A proper noun designating Beth Barah (Judg. 7:24).

1013. בֵּית־גָּדֵר ***bēyṯ-gāḏēr:*** A proper noun designating Beth Gader (1 Chr. 2:51).

1014. בֵּית גָּמוּל ***bēyṯ gāmûl:*** A proper noun designating Beth Gamul (Jer. 48:23).

1015. בֵּית דִּבְלָתַיִם ***bēyṯ diḇlāṯayim:*** A proper noun designating Beth Diblathaim (Jer. 48:22).

1016. בֵּית־דָּגוֹן ***bēyṯ-dāgôn:*** A proper noun designating Beth Dagon:

A. A town in Judah (Josh. 15:41).

B. A town in Asher (Josh. 19:27).

1017. בֵּית הָאֱלִי ***bēyṯ hā'eliy:*** A proper noun designating Bethelite (1 Kgs. 16:34).

1018. בֵּית הָאֵצֶל ***bēyṯ hā'ēṣel:*** A proper noun designating Beth Ezel (Mic. 1:11).

1019. בֵּית הַגִּלְגָּל ***bēyṯ haggilgāl:*** A proper noun designating Beth Gilgal (Neh. 12:29).

1020. בֵּית הַיְשִׁימוֹת ***bēyṯ hay^{e}šiymôṯ:*** A proper noun designating Beth Jeshimoth (Num. 33:49; Josh. 12:3; 13:20; Ezek. 25:9).

1021. בֵּית הַכֶּרֶם ***bēyṯ hakkerem:*** A proper noun designating Beth Hakkerem (Neh. 3:14; Jer. 6:1).

1022. בֵּית הַלַּחְמִי ***bēyṯ hallaḥmiy:*** A proper noun designating Bethlehemite (1 Sam. 16:1, 18; 17:58; 2 Sam. 21:19).

1023. בֵּית הַמֶּרְחָק ***bēyṯ hammerḥāq:*** A phrase that is listed here by Strong as a proper noun. Most translations treat it as a language phrase (see *bēyṯ* [1004] and *merḥāq* [4801]) meaning last house, outskirts, a place that is far off (2 Sam. 15:17).

1024. בֵּית מַרְכָּבוֹת ***beyṯ markāḇôṯ,*** בֵּית הַמַּרְכָּבוֹת ***beyṯ hammarkāḇôṯ:*** A proper noun designating Beth Marcaboth (Josh. 19:5; 1 Chr. 4:31).

1025. בֵּית הָעֵמֶק ***bēyṯ hā'ēmeq:*** A proper noun designating Beth Emek (Josh. 19:27).

1026. בֵּית הָעֲרָבָה ***bēyṯ hā^{a}rāḇāh:*** A proper noun designating Beth Arabah (Josh. 15:6, 61; 18:18, 22).

1027. בֵּית הָרָם ***bēyṯ hārām:*** A proper noun designating Beth Haram (Josh. 13:27).

1028. בֵּית הָרָן ***bēyṯ hārān:*** A proper noun designating Beth Haran (Num. 32:36).

1029. בֵּית הַשִּׁטָּה ***bēyṯ haššiṭṭah:*** A proper noun designating Beth Shittah (Judg. 7:22).

1030. בֵּית הַשִּׁמְשִׁי ***bēyṯ haššimšiy:*** A proper noun designating Bethshemite (1 Sam. 6:14, 18).

1031. בֵּית חָגְלָה ***bēyṯ ḥoglāh:*** A proper noun designating Beth Hoglah (Josh. 15:6; 18:19, 21).

1032. בֵּית חוֹרוֹן ***bēyṯ ḥôrôn:*** A proper noun designating Beth Horon (Josh. 10:10, 11; 16:3, 5; 18:13, 14; 21:22; 1 Sam. 13:18; 1 Kgs. 9:17; 1 Chr. 6:68(53); 7:24; 2 Chr. 8:5; 25:13).

1033. בֵּית כָּר ***bēyṯ kār:*** A proper noun designating Beth Car (1 Sam. 7:11).

1034. בֵּית לְבָאוֹת ***bēyṯ l^{e}ḇā'ôṯ:*** A proper noun designating Beth Lebaoth (Josh. 19:6).

1035. בֵּית לֶחֶם ***beyṯ leḥem:*** A proper noun designating Bethlehem:

A. A name applied to a village in Judea, south of Bethlehem. The name means "house of food (bread)." It was formerly called Ephrath (Gen. 35:19). Rachel died and was buried there. Elimelech, husband of Naomi, lived there and left to take his family to Moab (Ruth 1:1, 2). Naomi returned there with Ruth (Ruth 1:19, 22).

David's father and family lived in Bethlehem (1 Sam. 16:1–4; 17:11–15). The Philistines controlled the town at certain times (2 Sam. 23:13–14). It was resettled on the return from the Babylonian captivity (Ezra 2:21; Neh. 7:26). The greatest honor and prophecy referring to Bethlehem was given by Micah (5:2[1]) concerning the "ruler of Israel," whose origins were from ancient times.

B. The name was borne by a city in Zebulun (Josh. 19:15). An Israelite judge, Ibzan, came from this city (Judg. 12:8, 10). It is about seven miles west and north of Nazareth.

1036. בֵּית לְעַפְרָה ***beyt l^e'aprāh:*** This phrase in Micah 1:10 is interpreted by some as the proper noun Beth Ophrah (KJV), whereas others translate the phrase house of Aphrah (*bēyt* [1004] with prep. and fem. of *'āpār* [6083], NASB, NIV).

1037. בֵּית מִלּוֹא ***bēyt millô':*** This proper noun is a reference to two locations: one near Shechem and one in Jerusalem. The location near Shechem is mentioned in Judges 9:6, 20 (Beth Millo, NASB, NIV; house of Millo, KJV). The citadel in Jerusalem is mentioned in 2 Kings 12:20(21) (house of Millo, NASB, KJV; Beth Millo, NIV).

1038. בֵּית מַעֲכָה ***bēyt ma'^akāh:*** A proper noun designating Beth Maacah, a shortened form of *'ābēl beyt-ma'^akāh* (62) (2 Sam. 20:14, 15).

1039. בֵּית נִמְרָה ***bēyt nimrāh:*** A proper noun designating Beth Nimrah (Num. 32:36; Josh. 13:27).

1040. בֵּית עֶדֶן ***bēyt 'eden:*** A proper noun designating Beth Eden (Amos 1:5).

1041. בֵּית עַזְמָוֶת ***bēyt 'azmāwet:*** A proper noun designating Beth Azmaveth (Neh. 7:28).

1042. בֵּית עֲנוֹת ***bēyt '^anôt:*** A proper noun designating Beth Anoth (Josh. 15:59).

1043. בֵּית עֲנָת ***bēyt '^anāt:*** A proper noun designating Beth Anath (Josh. 19:38; Judg. 1:33).

1044. בֵּית עֵקֶד ***bēyt 'ēqed:*** A proper noun designating Beth Eked (2 Kgs. 10:12, 14).

1045. בֵּית עַשְׁתָּרוֹת ***bēyt 'aštarôt:*** A proper noun designating the temple of Ashtaroth (1 Sam. 31:10).

1046. בֵּית פֶּלֶט ***bēyt peleṭ:*** A proper noun designating Beth Pelet (Josh. 15:27; Neh. 11:26).

1047. בֵּית פְּעוֹר ***bēyt p^e'ôr:*** A proper noun designating Beth Peor (Deut. 3:29; 4:46; 34:6; Josh. 13:20).

1048. בֵּית פַּצֵּץ ***bēyt paṣṣēṣ:*** A proper noun designating Beth Pazzez (Josh. 19:21).

1049. בֵּית צוּר ***bēyt ṣûr:*** A proper noun designating Beth Zur (Josh.

15:58; 1 Chr. 2:45; 2 Chr. 11:7; Neh. 3:16).

1050. בֵּית רְחוֹב ***bēyt̲ r^eḥôb̲:*** A proper noun designating Beth Rehob (Judg. 18:28; 2 Sam. 10:6).

1051. בֵּית רָפָא ***bēyt̲ rāpā':*** A proper noun designating Beth Rapha (1 Chr. 4:12).

1052. בֵּית שְׁאָן ***bēyt̲ š^e'ān***, בֵּית שָׁן ***bēyt̲ šān:*** A proper noun designating Beth Shean (Josh. 17:11, 16; Judg. 1:27; 1 Sam. 31:10, 12; 2 Sam. 21:12; 1 Kgs. 4:12; 1 Chr. 7:29).

1053. בֵּית שֶׁמֶשׁ ***bēyt̲ šemeš:*** A proper noun designating Beth Shemesh:

A. A city in northwest Judah (Josh. 15:10; 21:16; 1 Sam. 6:9, 12, 13, 15, 19, 20; 1 Kgs. 4:9; 2 Kgs. 14:11, 13; 1 Chr. 6:59[44]; 2 Chr. 25:21, 23; 28:18).

B. A city in Naphtali (Josh. 19:38; Judg. 1:33).

C. A city in Issachar (Josh. 19:22).

D. The Egyptian sacred city of On, also known as Heliopolis (Jer. 43:13).

1054. בֵּית תַּפּוּחַ ***bēyt̲ tappûaḥ:*** A proper noun designating Beth Tappuah (Josh. 15:53).

1055. בִּיתָן ***biyt̲ān:*** A masculine noun meaning palace. It refers to the king's palace in Susa (Esth. 1:5) and is combined with garden *ginnat̲* (1594) to indicate the palace garden (Esth. 7:7, 8).

1056. בָּכָא ***bāk̲ā':*** A proper noun designating Baca (Ps. 84:6[7]).

1057. בָּכָא ***bāk̲ā':*** A masculine noun indicating a balsam tree or baka shrubs. The word refers to valley shrubs or balsam trees in the tops of which the Lord made the presence of His military forces known (2 Sam. 5:23, 24; 1 Chr. 14:14, 15). Balsam trees yield an aromatic resinous substance.

1058. בָּכָה ***bāk̲āh:*** A verb meaning to weep, to wail. The weeping may be because of grief, pain, humiliation, or joy (Gen. 42:24; 43:30; Ex. 2:6; Num. 11:4, 10; Ps. 78:64; Joel 1:5). It is the opposite of laughing (Eccl. 3:4). It depicts weeping in general, or used with modifiers, it indicates bitter, intense weeping (1 Sam. 1:10; Isa. 30:19; Jer. 22:10; Mic. 1:10). It is used to describe a penitent's weeping before the Lord (Deut. 1:45; Judg. 20:23; 2 Kgs. 22:19). Weeping and fasting are mentioned together as an act of mourning (Judg. 20:26; 2 Sam. 12:21, 22).

1059. בֶּכֶה ***bek̲eh:*** A masculine noun indicating weeping. Weeping is described as an act of deep penitence before the Lord, along with confession; praying and prostration (Ezra 10:1).

1060. בְּכוֹר ***b^ek̲ôr***, בְּכֹר ***b^ek̲ōr:*** A masculine noun indicating the firstborn. The word refers to the firstborn of animals (Gen. 4:4), as well as of persons (Gen. 25:13). The firstborn of sons in Israel were redeemed, not sacrificed (Num. 3:40–43; 18:15, 17). The firstborn of clean animals were sacrificed to the Lord (Deut. 12:6, 17), but the firstborn males of unclean animals could be redeemed (Num. 18:15). A donkey, though clean, was redeemed because of its use as a beast of burden (Ex. 13:13; 34:20). It is used metaphorically to refer to Israel as the Lord's firstborn son (Ex. 4:22). In combination with the word death, it means firstborn of death (Job 18:13), indicating a most powerful attack of ill health and death on a person. This is the fate of the wicked. The firstborn son held special privileges called his birthright (Gen. 25:5–6; 27:19–36; 43:33; Deut. 21:15–17). This special standing could be lost (Gen. 25:31–34). Esau is described as despising his birthright (Gen. 25:34) as the firstborn of Isaac.

1061. בִּכּוּרִים ***bikkûriym:*** A masculine plural noun meaning firstfruits. It refers to the yearly first gathering of the ripened produce of the land in honor of the fact that both the land and its produce belonged to the Lord. The produce was presented in a ritual (Ex. 23:16, 19) to the Lord in its harvested state or, in the case of some items, when the product had been properly prepared. The "day of the first fruits" or Pentecost is mentioned (Num. 28:26). At this festival, "bread of the first fruits" was made from the newly harvested grain (Lev. 23:20). Firstfruits were a part of the grain offering ritual (Lev. 2:14; 23:17, 20) and a staple in the support of the priests (Ezek. 44:30). The word refers to Israel as the firstfruits of the Lord's harvest.

1062. בְּכוֹרָה ***b^ek̲ôrāh,*** בְּכֹרָה ***b^ek̲ōrāh:*** A feminine noun meaning birthright, firstborn, right of firstborn. The firstborn son was a symbol and proof of the strength and virility of his parents (Deut. 21:17). The word refers to the rights and privileges of the firstborn (Gen. 25:31–34; 43:33). This right could be sold or forfeited through deception (Gen. 27:36) or grave sin (1 Chr. 5:1, 2). The word also means firstborn in some contexts (Gen. 4:4; Deut. 12:6; Neh. 10:36[37]).

1063. בִּכּוּרָה ***bik̲k̲ûrāh:*** A feminine noun indicating early fruit, firstfruit. It refers to the first early ripe figs (Isa. 28:4) that are picked quickly and eaten at once. The word functions figuratively for the godly person who has perished from the land (Mic. 7:1) and as Israel when God first found her (Hos. 9:10) and was delighted in her. It symbolizes the exiles as good figs whom the Lord will watch over (Jer. 24:2) and Ephraim, Northern Israel, as a people who will soon disappear from the land like a fresh first-ripe fig (Isa. 28:4) that is swallowed in a second once it is picked.

1064. בְּכוֹרַת ***b^ek̲ôrat̲:*** A proper noun designating Becorath (1 Sam. 9:1).

1065. בְּכִי ***b^e^k̲iy:*** A masculine noun meaning tears, weeping. The word describes weeping that expresses various accompanying emotions: It affects one's facial appearance (Job 16:16); it is paralleled only by deep mourning (Esth. 4:3; Jer. 31:9, 15); it expresses humiliation (Isa. 22:12; Joel 2:12); and it is profoundly bitter (Isa. 22:4). It indicates the flow of dribbling streams in mines (Job 28:11).

1066. בֹּכִים ***bōk̲iym:*** A proper noun designating Bochim (Judg. 2:1, 5).

1067. בְּכִירָה ***b^e^k̲iyrāh:*** A feminine noun indicating firstborn daughter. The word always describes firstborn women. Merab was the firstborn of King Saul (1 Sam. 14:49). The firstborn of Lot bore the father of the Moabites (Gen. 19:31, 33, 34, 37). A firstborn daughter was the first one given in marriage (Gen. 29:26).

1068. בְּכִית ***b^e^kiyt̲:*** A feminine noun meaning mourning. It depicts a period of mourning (Gen. 50:3, 4). In the case of Jacob's death, the period may have been as long as 110 days.

1069. בָּכַר ***bāk̲ar:*** A verb meaning to be born first, have the birthright. It means to recognize as firstborn (Deut. 21:16). The word describes animals being born as firstlings or firstborn (Lev. 27:26). It depicts a woman who bears her first son (Jer. 4:31). It also describes fruitful trees bearing fruit every month (Ezek. 47:12).

1070. בֵּכֶר ***bēk̲er:*** A feminine noun meaning a young camel. The word depicts young camels bringing goods and products to a glorified Zion (Isa. 60:6) from Midian and Ephah. These camels were beasts of burden that could cross the deserts quickly.

1071. בֶּכֶר ***bek̲er:*** A proper noun designating Becher:

A. A son of Ephraim (Num. 26:35).

B. A son of Benjamin (Gen. 46:21; 1 Chr. 7:6, 8).

1072. בִּכְרָה ***bik̲rāh:*** A feminine noun indicating a young female camel. The word describes a swift, young she-camel confused and running here and there just as Israel had been doing (Jer. 2:23).

1073. בַּכֻּרוֹת ***bakkûrôt̲:*** A feminine noun meaning first ripe. The word stands for first-ripe figs that are delightful to eat (Jer. 24:2). They symbolize the captives of Judah in Babylonian exile.

1074. בֹּכְרוּ ***bōk̲^e^rû:*** A proper noun designating Bocheru (1 Chr. 8:38; 9:44).

1075. בִּכְרִי ***bik̲riy:*** A proper noun designating Bichri (2 Sam. 20:1, 2, 6, 7, 10, 13, 21, 22).

1076. בַּכְרִי ***bak̲riy:*** A proper noun designating Becherite (Num. 26:35).

1077. בַּל ***bal:*** A negative particle meaning not, cannot; scarcely, hardly. This negative is used in poetry and is a synonym of Hebrew *lô'*. It is often found repeated in certain contexts meaning no, not (Isa. 26:10, 11, 14, 18; 33:20, 21, 23, 24; 44:8, 9). It is used often to negate the verb *môṭ*, to move, to choke, to stagger, to reel, e.g., Psalm 16:8, "I will not be shaken" (NASB) (Job 41:23[15]; Ps. 10:6; 16:8; 21:7[8]; 30:6[7]; Prov. 10:30; 12:3). It means scarcely, hardly, no sooner in Isaiah 40:24, depicting the ephemeral nature of worldly rulers.

1078. בֵּל ***bēl:*** A masculine proper noun meaning Bel. It designates a Babylonian god whose name means lord (Isa. 46:1; Jer. 50:2; 51:44). The Lord is bringing swift judgment on this false pagan god.

1079. בָּל ***bāl:*** An Aramaic noun which means heart, mind. There is only one occurrence of this word in Scripture (Dan. 6:14[15], NKJV), where King Darius "set his heart on Daniel." The phrase expresses the concern the king had for Daniel.

1080. בְּלָא ***b^e^lā':*** An Aramaic verb meaning to oppress, wear down. The word indicates a partially successful attempt to defeat or weary the saints of the Most High (Dan. 7:25).

1081. בַּלְאֲדָן ***bal'^a^ḏān:*** A proper noun designating Baladan (2 Kgs. 20:12; Isa. 39:1).

1082. בָּלַג ***bālag:*** A verb meaning to smile, be cheerful, rejoice; flash forth, flash up; gain strength. The word indicates a recovery of fortune because God turns His anger away (Job 10:20; Ps. 39:13[14]). The word in this context means a recovery of strength and good spirits. It is the opposite of a depressed state of mind (Job 9:27). On the other hand, the word depicts God's swift action in judgment against the strong (Amos 5:9; KJV, "He [God] strengtheneth").

1083. בִּלְגָּה ***bilgāh:*** A proper noun designating Bilgah:

A. A priest (1 Chr. 24:14).
B. A priest (Neh. 12:5, 18).

1084. בִּלְגַּי ***bilgay:*** A proper noun designating Bilgai (Neh. 10:8[9]).

1085. בִּלְדַּד ***bildaḏ:*** A proper noun designating Bildad, the name of one of Job's supposed comforters. It is possible that he may have descended from a son of Abraham (Gen. 25:2). He, along with Eliphaz and Zophar, persisted in condemning Job for his supposed sins. The Lord reprimanded them (Job 42:9). Their retribution argument was simply that since Job was suffering, he must have sinned.

1086. בָּלָה ***bālāh:*** A verb meaning to wear out, grow old, be exhausted; waste away; enjoy. Various things wear out or become used up: clothing (Deut. 8:4; 29:5[4]) is often the subject; figuratively, the heavens and the earth wear out (Ps. 102:26[27]; Isa. 51:6; the bones of a guilty person (Ps.

32:3); persons in general (Gen. 18:12; Job 13:28). In some forms of the verb, it means to cause something to wear out or be wiped out (1 Chr. 17:9; Ps. 49:14[15]; Lam. 3:4). This usage takes on the idea of using something to the full, hence, to enjoy something (Job 21:13; Isa. 65:22).

1087. בָּלֶה ***bāleh:*** An adjective meaning old, worn out. The word refers to old sacks, sandals, and clothing and largely used up food as a part of the deception of the Gibeonites (Josh. 9:4, 5). It describes the corrupt and lewd character of someone worn out by acts of harlotry (Ezek. 23:43). Ezekiel applies it to Israel and Judah.

1088. בָּלָה ***bālāh:*** A proper noun designating Balah (Josh. 19:3, see also *bilhāh* [1090,C]).

1089. בָּלַה ***bālah:*** A verb meaning to terrify, to tremble, to frighten; to deter. It describes an attempt to keep someone from doing something. The enemies of the Jews tried to keep the returned exiles from rebuilding the Temple by diplomatic and threatening words and actions (Ezra 4:4).

1090. בִּלְהָה ***bilhāh:*** A proper noun designating Bilhah:

A. It refers to a handmaid of Rachel. She bore two sons, Dan and Naphtali (Gen. 35:25). Reuben committed a great sin against Jacob (Israel) by sleeping with Bilhah (Gen. 35:22). Dan and Naphtali had a total of five sons as well (Gen. 46:22–25).

B. It refers to a town in which the sons of Shimei and his brothers lived (1 Chr. 4:27–33).

1091. בַּלָּהָה ***ballāhāh:*** A feminine noun indicating terror, calamity. It describes fearful, threatening events or circumstances that beset a wicked person (Job 18:11, 14). God may bring on these calamities (Ezek. 26:21) so that the object is terrified (Ezek. 27:36; 28:19). Various terrors are depicted: the king of terrors (Job 18:14); terrors of deep darkness (Job 24:17); terrors that pursue a person relentlessly (Job 27:20; 30:15); instantaneous, unexpected terrors (Ps. 73:19; Isa. 17:14).

1092. בִּלְהָן ***bilhān:*** A proper noun designating Bilhan:

A. A son of Ezer (Gen. 36:27; 1 Chr. 1:42).

B. A Benjamite (1 Chr. 7:10).

1093. בְּלוֹ ***b^{e}lô:*** An Aramaic masculine noun meaning tribute. It describes a tax or tribute paid in kind (Ezra 4:13, 20; 7:24).

1094. בְּלוֹי ***b^{e}lôy:*** A masculine noun indicating old, worn-out things. The word describes clothes and rags used to pull Jeremiah out of a pit (Jer. 38:11, 12).

1095. בֵּלְטְשַׁאצַּר ***bēlṭ^{e}ša'ṣṣar:*** A proper noun designating Belteshazzar. The babylonian name given to Daniel by a chief official, while Daniel was captive in Babylon. The name means "Bel (Lord), protect (him or his life)" in Babylonian. Daniel did not recognize this pagan god but served the Lord God.

1096. בֵּלְטְשַׁאצַּר ***bēlṭᵉša'ṣṣar:*** A proper noun designating Belteshazzar. The Aramaic name for the Hebrew name in entry 1095. Its meaning is the same. It occurs in the Aramaic portions of Daniel (2:4b—7:28).

1097. בְּלִי ***bᵉliy:*** A negative particle meaning not, without. It is used as a noun with a negative implication often meaning destruction, failure (Ps. 72:7; Isa. 38:17). More often it negates something by interjecting the idea of without, defective: without a name, nameless (Job 30:8); without a place, last place (Isa. 28:8); and often with the meaning without: without water (Job 8:11); without clothing, naked (Job 24:10); without knowledge (Job 35:16; 42:3). It is used to negate an idea put forth in an adjective or participle of a verb (2 Sam. 1:21; Ps. 19:3[4]).

A preposition may be prefixed to *beliy* to mean without (Job 35:16; 36:12, without knowledge; Isa. 5:14; Jer. 2:15). With the preposition *min* (4480) prefixed, this combination expresses causation, because, since (Deut. 9:28; 28:55). Sometimes the same construction means for lack of or for want of (Isa. 5:13; Ezek. 34:5; Hos. 5:6). The Lord's people are being destroyed for lack of knowledge (Hos. 4:6). This combination functions with a following *'ᵃšer* and as a conjunction meaning so that not . . . (Eccl. 3:11). Very rarely, it is used to negate a finite verb form (Gen. 31:20; Isa. 32:10; Job 41:26[18]).

1098. בְּלִיל ***bᵉliyl:*** A masculine noun meaning fodder. It describes a mixed fodder or mash for cattle (Job 6:5; 24:6) or oxen. It was considered a desirable food for oxen and donkeys (Isa. 30:24).

1099. בְּלִימָה ***bᵉliymāh:*** A feminine noun meaning nothingness. The word literally means what is nothing. In poetic language, it describes what God hangs the earth on—nothing (Job. 26:7).

1100. בְּלִיַּעַל ***bᵉliyya'al:*** A masculine noun of unknown origin meaning worthlessness. Often a strong moral component in the context suggests the state of being good for nothing and therefore expresses the concept of wickedness (Job 34:18; Prov. 6:12; Nah. 1:11). It is always used in reference to persons with only two exceptions, once for a disease and once for a nonspecific thing (Ps. 41:8[9]; 101:3). The term is applied to the hard-hearted (Deut. 15:9; 1 Sam. 30:22); perjurers (1 Kgs. 21:13; Prov. 19:28); and those promoting rebellion against a king's authority (2 Sam. 20:1; 2 Chr. 13:7) or God's authority (Deut. 13:13[14]). This word was not treated as a proper name by the Septuagint translators of the Old Testament, but it does appear in its Greek form as a name for the devil in the

Dead Sea scrolls and in the New Testament (cf. 2 Cor. 6:15).

1101. בָּלַל bālal: A verb meaning to mix, to mingle, to tangle, to confuse, to bewilder, to perplex, to anoint. The word is often used in a technical sense to signify the mixing of oil with the fine flour used to bake cakes without yeast that were then presented as grain offerings (Lev. 2:4; 14:21). Similarly, oil was mixed with fine wheat flour to bake wafers without yeast in a sacrificial setting (Ex. 29:2). Sometimes oil was simply mingled with fine flour itself as part of a drink offering (Ex. 29:40). While these food items readily combined with positive results, the verb can also indicate confusion, bewilderment, or perplexity. The language of the whole earth was confused by the Lord at the tower of Babel so that people could not understand each other (Gen. 11:9).

Since the verb could mean to moisten or to dampen when used in the technical sacrificial examples noted above, it is a reasonable extension of that usage to the anointing of a person with oil. This usage is found (Ps. 92:10[11]) where the psalmist rejoiced that he was anointed with fine oils.

The verb is used one time also to indicate the feeding of donkeys, (i.e., providing fodder for the animal to eat [Judg. 19:21]), but in this case, the verb is probably from a different original root.

1102. בָּלַם bālam: A verb meaning to restrain, to hold in, to curb. It means to curb the wild nature of a horse or mule with a bit or bridle (Ps. 32:9). A person should not need this kind of restraint.

1103. בָּלַס bālas: A verb indicating to gather; scratch open; to care for. It describes the process of caring for (NIV; NKJV), gathering (KJV), or growing sycamore figs; the process of scratching or slitting open a sycamore fruit to help it ripen (Amos 7:14). In its participial form (*bôles*), it indicates Amos as one who cared for sycamore fruit and carried out this procedure.

1104. בָּלַע bāla': A verb meaning to swallow or engulf. The literal meaning of this word is to swallow, as a person swallows a fig (Isa. 28:4) or as the great fish swallowed Jonah (Jon. 1:17[2:1]). It further describes how the earth consumed Pharaoh's army (Ex. 15:12) and the rebellious Israelites (Num. 16:32); and a consuming destruction that comes on people (2 Sam. 17:16; Job 2:3; Ps. 21:9[10]); cities (2 Sam. 20:19); or nations (Lam. 2:5).

1105. בֶּלַע bela': A masculine noun meaning what is swallowed or devoured. This word is derived from the verb *bāla'* (1104), meaning to swallow or engulf. It is used only twice in the Old Testament: In Psalm 52:4[6], it speaks of "devouring words." In Jeremiah 51:44, the word is used of the things the god Bel has swallowed. In both cases, the word connotes a destructive action.

1106. בֶּלַע **bela‘:** A proper noun designating Bela:

A. Another name for *ṣō‘ar* (6820) (Gen. 14:2, 8).

B. An Edomite king (Gen. 36:32, 33; 46:21; 1 Chr. 1:43, 44).

C. A son of Benjamin (Num. 26:38, 40; 1 Chr. 7:6, 7; 8:1, 3).

D. A son of Azaz (1 Chr. 5:8).

1107. בַּלְעֲדֵי **bal‘adēy,** בִּלְעֲדֵי **bil‘adēy:** A particle meaning apart from, except for. It is used with pronominal suffixes to mean except for or without, e.g., without your (permission), *bil‘ādeykā* (Gen. 41:44), referring to Joseph. It can mean apart from the person indicated by the attached suffix (Gen. 14:24; 41:16). With a prefixed *min* (4480), the word means except for someone or something (Num. 5:20; 2 Kgs. 18:25). Before a verb form, it may mean with respect to (what I see) (Job 34:32) in the sense of what I do not realize I see (NASB, NIV, NKJV, KJV).

1108. בַּלְעִי **bal‘iy:** A proper noun designating Belaite (Num. 26:38).

1109. בִּלְעָם **bil‘ām:** A proper noun designating Bileam:

A. The Mesopotamian seer, pagan prophet or soothsayer, that Balek, king of Moab, hired to curse Israel because he was afraid of what Israel might do to Moab (Num. 22:5, 7–10). The name may mean something like "swallower of a nation" (Heb. *bāla‘* (1104), "to swallow, to devour, to engulf". The "am" on the end may be an adverb used to intensify the meaning or, *‘am* (5971) may mean "people, nation"). At any rate, Bileam (Balaam in Greek) attempted to curse Israel—an impossible thing according to the biblical writer who shows intricately and with great force how no one—not even a great false prophet—can put a curse on God's people (Josh. 24:9, 10). The Lord made Balaam to utter one of the greatest prophecies of the Old Testament. He predicted a "star" would come from Judah (David). He later tried to curse Israel to commit spiritual and physical harlotry by following after Baal of Peor (Num. 31:8, 16). This name became a byword of evil, corruption, and false religion in the New Testament also (2 Pet. 2:15; Jude 11; Rev. 2:14). Also, one of his prophecies is preserved from about 750 B.C. witnessing to his fame in the ancient Near East. Micah recalls this incident (Mic. 6:5).

The Moabites are cursed because of this incident (Deut. 23:4[5].5[6]). God actually turned Balaam's curse into a blessing. The Israelites later executed Balaam (Josh. 13:22).

B. The name of a city given to the Kohathites by the tribe of Ephraim (1 Chr. 6:70[55]).

1110. בָּלַק **bālaq:** A verb meaning to lay waste, destroy. It describes the devastated state of a city (Nah. 2:10[11]) or the earth itself (Isa. 24:1) brought about by the Lord's acts of judgment.

1111. בָּלָק ***bālāq:*** A proper noun designating Balak, the name of the king of Moab who hired Bileam (Balaam) to curse Israel. He tried to work with the leaders of the Midianites to destroy Israel (Num. 22:4–7). His people were in fact cursed by Israel's God (cf. Gen. 12:1–3). He was unable to curse the people who God had blessed (Josh. 24:9; Mic. 6:5).

1112. בֵּלְשַׁאצַּר ***bēlša'ṣṣar:*** The name of King Belshazzar of Babylon (ca. 551 B.C.) who was the son of Nabonidus, the true king of Babylon. The name means "Bel protects the king." He was killed when Persia under Cyrus took the city of Babylon in 538 B.C. He defiled the holy vessels of the temple of the Lord (Dan. 5:1–4). In his third year, Daniel dreamed a dream that showed the rise and demise of Greece (goat) and Media-Persia. In Belshazzar's first year (ca. 553 B.C.), Daniel had dreamed about the rise and fall of four mighty world empires followed by the establishment of the kingdom of God, which will be ruled by the Son of Man and last forever (Dan. 7:13–28).

1113. בֵּלְשַׁאצַּר ***bēlša'ṣṣar:*** A proper noun designating Belshazzar, the Aramaic name corresponding to the Hebrew name in Daniel 8:1 (see entry 1112).

1114. בִּלְשָׁן ***bilšān:*** A proper noun designating Bilshan (Ezra 2:2; Neh. 7:7).

1115. בִּלְתִּי ***biltiy:*** A negative particle indicating not, except. It is used often to negate an infinitive meaning: not to, plus infinitive, e.g., plus *'āḵal* (398), not to eat (Gen. 3:11; cf. 4:15; 19:21; Deut. 4:21); in order that . . . not, negative purpose, is expressed by this construction (Gen. 4:15; 38:9; Ex. 8:22[18], 29[25]; Deut. 17:12); so that . . . not, negative result, is expressed likewise (Isa. 44:10; Jer. 7:8). It is used after verbs that assert a command or order (Gen. 3:11; 2 Kgs. 17:15; Jer. 35:8, 9, 14); verbs of swearing (Josh. 5:6; Judg. 21:7); agreeing (2 Kgs. 12:8[9]); interceding (Jer. 36:25).

It is used to negate a following noun, such as in the phrase *'âḏ-biltīy šāmayim,* until there be no heavens (Job 14:12; cf. Num. 21:35; Josh. 8:22; 2 Kgs. 10:11); to negate an adjective, he is not clean (1 preceding *'im* (518) (Gen. 47:18; Judg. 7:14). In some cases when it is used alone, it means except (Gen. 43:3; Num. 11:6; Isa. 10:4).

1116. בָּמָה ***bāmāh:*** A feminine noun meaning high place. This word may refer to a physical high place, like a mountain (Ps. 18:33[34]; Hab. 3:19); or a place of worship. Although Samuel conducted sacrifices in these locations (1 Sam. 9:13), they were predominantly places of idol worship, which God hates (Ps. 78:58). These high places became symbolic of the idolatry of the Israelites (2 Kgs. 12:3[4]; 14:4; 15:4; Jer. 19:5).

1117. בָּמָה ***bāmāh:*** A proper noun designating Bamah (Ezek. 20:29).

1118. בִּמְהָל ***bimhāl:*** A proper noun designating Bimhal (1 Chr. 7:33).

1119. בְּמוֹ ***b^emô:*** A preposition meaning in, from, with, by. It serves as a poetic substitute for the common prose preposition *b^e* in Hebrew. It is used to indicate the instrument by which or with which something is done (Job 9:30; 16:4, 5), such as snow, head, mouth. It indicates how something is done (Ps. 11:2; Isa. 25:10; 43:2) or where it is done.

1120. בָּמוֹת, בָּמוֹת בַּעַל ***bāmôṯ, bāmôṯ ba'al:*** A proper noun designating Bamoth. A name describing two locations:

I. Bamoth (Num. 21:19, 20).

II. Bamoth Baal (Num. 22:41; Josh. 13:17).

1121. בֵּן ***bēn:*** A noun meaning son that occurs almost five thousand times in the Old Testament. Although the most basic meaning and general translation is son, the direct male offspring of human parents (Gen. 4:25; 27:32; Isa. 49:15), it is more generally a relational term because of its variety of applications. This word can express an adopted child (Ex. 2:10); children in general, male and female (Gen. 3:16; 21:7; Ex. 21:5); descendants, such as grandsons (Josh. 22:24, 25, 27; 2 Kgs. 10:30); relative age (Gen. 5:32; 17:12; Prov. 7:7; Song 2:3); the male offspring of animals (Lev. 22:28; Deut. 22:6, 7; 1 Sam. 6:7, 10); a member of a guild, order, or class (1 Kgs. 20:35; 1 Chr. 9:30; Ezra 4:1); a person with a certain quality or characteristic (1 Sam. 14:52; 2 Sam. 3:34; 2 Kgs. 14:14). It may also have a gentilic sense and designate a person from a certain place (Gen. 17:12; Ps. 149:2; Ezek. 23:15, 17).

1122. בֵּן ***bēn:*** A proper noun designating Ben (1 Chr. 15:18).

1123. בְּנֵי ***b^enēy:*** A masculine noun meaning son. This is the Aramaic equivalent of the Hebrew word *bēn* (1121), meaning son. Thus, it is only used in the Aramaic sections of the Old Testament (Ezra 4:8—6:18; 7:12–26; Dan. 2:4—7:28; Jer. 10:11). Although it may refer to the offspring of animals (Ezra 6:9), it is used mostly of the sons of particular groups of people: of Israel (Ezra 6:16); of captives (Dan. 2:25; 5:13; 6:13[14]); of kings (Ezra 6:10; 7:23); of those who accused Daniel (Dan. 6:24[25]); of people in general (Dan. 2:38; 5:21).

1124. בְּנָה ***b^enāh,*** בְּנָא ***b^enā':*** An Aramaic verb meaning to build, rebuild, construct. It is used to describe the building of a city (Ezra 4:12, 13, 16, 21; Dan. 4:30[27]) or temple, house of God (Ezra 5:2–4; 6:3, 7).

1125. בֶּן־אֲבִינָדָב ***ben 'a<u>b</u>iynā<u>d</u>ā<u>b</u>:*** A proper noun designating Ben Abinadab (1 Kgs. 4:11).

1126. בֶּן־אוֹנִי ben 'ôniy: A proper noun designating Ben-Oni (Gen. 35:18).

1127. בֶּן־גֶּבֶר ben-geber: A proper noun designating Ben-Geber (1 Kgs. 4:13).

1128. בֶּן־דֶּקֶר ben-deqer: A proper noun designating Ben-Deker (1 Kgs. 4:9).

1129. בָּנָה bānāh: A verb meaning to build, build up, rebuild, construct. The word is used literally to describe the construction of many things. The main areas of its use are: to build a city (Gen. 11:4), house (Gen. 33:17). It describes the construction of the temple of the Lord on earth (1 Kgs. 3:1; 5:18[32]; 6:2; Ps. 78:69), as well as Jerusalem (Ps. 147:2). With a following *mâṣôr,* fortification, it means to build fortified cities (2 Chr. 11:5); to fortify (1 Kgs. 15:22; 16:24). It has the sense of rebuilding something (Josh. 6:26; Amos 9:14). With a following b^e preposition, it means build at or work on (Neh. 4:10[4], 17[11]; Zech. 6:15).

It is used in a figurative sense: Eve is built from Adam's rib, not created separately (Gen. 2:22); used with a following *bayit* l^e, house to, it gives the idea of building a family (Deut. 25:9; Jer. 24:6) or making it possible for one to live on in descendants (Gen. 16:2; Jer. 12:16); it depicts wisdom building her house (Prov. 9:1). It is used to describe the building up of the lovingkindness of the Lord (Ps. 89:2[3]). The Lord built His sanctuary not only on earth but truly in the heavens (Amos 9:6).

Nearly all these meanings and uses are also expressed in the passive use of the verb. The Jews who returned from exile were built up, established (Jer. 12:16; cf. Mal. 3:15). The Lord's lovingkindness will be established (Ps. 89:2[3], noted above). The throne or dynasty of King David is described as being established or built up using this word as was Israel herself after returning from exile (Ps. 89:4[5]: Jer. 24:6; 31:4; 33:7).

1130. בֶּן־הֲדַד ben hadad: A proper noun designating Ben-Hadad:

A. The name of an important king of Syria (Aram) in biblical history. His name means "Son of Hadad." He ruled from Damascus (1 Kgs. 15:18, 20). He was in league with King Asa in Judah against Baasha in Northern Israel. This person was Ben-Hadad I, son of Tabrimmon, son of Hezion, king of Aram. He ruled ca. 893–860 B.C. The references in 1 Kings 20:1–33 are taken to refer to this individual. Ben-Hadad then fought also with Ahab who conquered him (1 Kgs. 20:1–34). But Ahab let Ben-Hadad go free instead of executing him as he should have (1 Kgs. 20:35–43).

B. A second Ben-Hadad II seems to have ruled Aram (Syria) about 860–843 B.C. Some scholars hold that Ben-Hadad I and II are the same person. More believe that the Ben-Hadad of 1 Kings 20:1–33 is a son or grandson of Hadad I. This Ben-Hadad was son of the king of Aram, Hazael, and succeeded him, reigning during the time of Jehoakim in Israel (ca. 814–798 B.C.). Jehoash (798–782 B.C.) son of Jehoahaz, recovered much of what Ben-Hadad II had captured from Jehoahaz. He and his father Hazael are both condemned in Amos 1:4.

1131. בִּנּוּי ***binnûy:*** A proper noun designating Binnui:

A. The father of Noadiah (Ezra 8:33).

B. A son of Pahath-moab (Ezra 10:30).

C. A son of Bani (Ezra 10:38).

D. A son of Henadad (Neh. 3:24; 10:9[10]; 12:8).

E. The head of a family (Neh. 7:15).

1132. בֶּן־זוֹחֵת ***ben zôḥēṯ:*** A proper noun designating Ben-Zoheth (1 Chr. 4:20).

1133. בֶּן־חוּר ***ben ḥûr:*** A proper noun designating Ben-Hur, an officer under Solomon (1 Kgs. 4:8).

1134. בֶּן חַיִל ***ben ḥayil:*** A proper noun designating Ben-Hail (2 Chr. 17:7).

1135. בֶּן־חָנָן ***ben-ḥānān:*** A proper noun designating Ben-Hanan (1 Chr. 4:20).

1136. בֶּן־חֶסֶד ***ben-ḥesed:*** A proper noun designating Ben-Hesed (1 Kgs. 4:10).

1137. בָּנִי ***bāniy:*** A proper noun designating Bani:

A. One of David's mighty men (2 Sam. 23:36).

B. An Aaronite (1 Chr. 6:46[31]).

C. A descendant of Pharez (1 Chr. 9:4; Ezra 2:10; 10:29, 34).

D. A son of Bani (Ezra 10:38).

E. A Levite (Neh. 3:17; 8:7; 9:4, 5; 10:13[14], 14[15]; 11:22).

1138. בּוּנִּי ***bûnniy:*** A proper noun designating Bunni:

A. A Levite (Neh. 11:15).

B. A Levite (Neh. 9:4).

C. A Jewish man or family (Neh. 10:15[16]).

1139. בְּנֵי־בְרַק ***b^enēy b^eraq:*** A proper noun designating Bene Berak (Josh. 19:45).

1140. בִּנְיָה ***binyāh:*** A feminine noun referring to a structure, building. It is a general term used to describe the Temple structure itself apart from the temple inclusive of the court area (Ezek. 41:13).

1141. בְּנָיָה ***b^enāyāh,*** בְּנָיָהוּ ***b^enāyāhû:*** A proper noun designating Benaiah:

A. The commander of David's bodyguard (2 Sam. 8:18; 20:23) made up of foreigners. The name means "the Lord builds up." He was among the "thirty" of David's mighty men (2 Sam. 20:33). After David died, he helped install Solomon as king (1 Kgs. 1:1—2:46) and removed Joab (1 Kgs. 2:34–46). He became a leading official for Solomon (1 Kgs. 4:4).

B. He was one of David's elite "thirty" top warriors and commanders.

The other persons bearing this name are referred to only briefly. Little is known about them:

C. He was a descendant of the brothers of Shimei, a Simeonite (1 Chr. 4:24).

D. Another Beniah was a priest, evidently a gatekeeper from the Levites (1 Chr. 15:18) and also a musician (1 Chr. 15:20, 24; 16:5, 6).

E. He was the father of Jehoiada who succeeded Ahithophel, the wise man to David (1 Chr. 27:34).

F. The grandfather of Jehaziel, a prophet who uttered some famous words to King Jehoshaphat (2 Chr. 20:13–17) that foretold his victory over Moab and Ammon.

G. A Levite who hoped to oversee the renovation of the Temple under King Hezekiah (2 Chr. 31:13).

H. An Israelite, evidently a priest, guilty of intermarrying among foreigners.

I. Another Israelite who had married a foreigner in Ezra's time.

J. A descendant of Bani who had married a non-Israelite.

K. Another priestly Israelite who had married a foreigner in the land.

L. The father of a corrupt leader of Israel named Pelatiah (Ezek. 11:1, 13). He plotted evil and misled the people of Jerusalem.

1142. בְּנֵי יַעֲקָן ***b^e^nēy ya^a^qān:*** A proper noun designating Bene-jaakan (Num. 33:31, 32).

1143. בֵּנַיִם ***bēnayim:*** A masculine dual noun meaning champion, single fighter. The word refers to a giant named Goliath, a Philistine warrior who was over nine feet tall. He stepped forward as their hero, literally, the man of the space between the armies (*'îš bēnayim*). He stood forth to represent them (1 Sam. 17:4, 23) as David represented Israel.

1144. בִּנְיָמִין ***binyāmiyn:*** A proper noun designating Benjamin. The name means "son of my right hand."

A. He was the youngest of Jacob's sons. His mother Rachel died at his birth and called him Benoni, "son of my sorrow" (Gen. 35:18, 24). He was second only to Joseph in his father's affections. Jacob called him a wolf that tears his prey (Gen. 49:27); Moses called him loved by the Lord, one whom God protected (Deut. 33:12). He went to Egypt with his brothers (Ex. 1:3).

B. The name of the tribe descended from Benjamin. It consisted of many descendants and families (Gen. 46:19, 21; cf. 1 Chr. 7:6). The tribe inhabited territory in the center of Israel, bounded by Ephraim (north), Dan (west), Judah (south). The Manasseh, Gad, and Reuben territories touched the north-northeast border of Benjamin. Its border actually extended south of Jerusalem (Josh. 18:11–28). Bethel, Mizpah, and Gibeon were located in its territory, although its borders shifted slightly from time to time. The judge Ehud, a left-handed man, was from Benjamin, as was Saul, Israel's first king (Judg. 3:15; 1 Sam. 9:1). The Benjamites were threatened as a tribe over a Levite's concubine who was raped and killed in Benjamite territory (Judg. 19—21). After the monarchy, Benjamin stayed tied to Judah (1 Kgs. 12:21, 23; 15:16–22). The tribe had a place in Ezekiel's new Temple vision (Ezek. 48:22–32).

C. It refers to a son of Bilham, son of Jediael. He was a head of a family in Benjamin.

D. A son of Harim of the priestly line who had taken a foreign wife (Ezra 10:32).

E. It refers to one or possible two gates in Jerusalem bearing this name (Jer. 20:2; cf. 37:13; Zech. 14:10). Legal matters or business issues were often transacted at these places.

1145. בֶּן־יְמִינִי ***ben-y***^{e}***miyniy:*** A proper noun designating Benjamite. A gentilic noun indicating that a person was associated with or a part of the tribe of Benjamin (see entry 1141). Ehud was a Benjamite (Judg. 3:15), and the people of Gibeah were Benjamites (Judg. 19:16). Saul, the first king in Israel, was a Benjamite (1 Sam. 9:21). Cush, a Benjamite, has a psalm dedicated to him (Ps. 7:1; [title]).

1146. בִּנְיָן ***binyān:*** A masculine noun denoting a building, structure. The word is used to refer to the Temple of Ezekiel's vision (40:5; 42:1, 10) and refers to the back building of the complex as the whole (41:12, 15).

1147. בִּנְיָן ***binyān:*** An Aramaic masculine noun denoting a structure or building. It is identical to its Hebrew counterpart. It refers to the Temple that was to be built by the returned exiles (Ezra 5:4).

1148. בְּנִינוּ ***b***^{e}***niynû:*** A proper noun designating Beninu (Neh. 10:13, 14).

1149. בְּנַס ***b***^{e}***nas:*** An Aramaic verb denoting to be angry. This verb is used often in the Aramaic translations but only once in the Hebrew Bible (Dan. 2:12), where Daniel states that Nebuchadnezzar was angry because his diviners could not reveal to him his dream and its interpretation. It is followed by the phrase *q*^{e}*ṣap̱* (7108) *śaggîʾ* (7690), meaning he was very angry.

1150. בִּנְעָא ***binʿāʾ:*** A proper noun designating Binea (1 Chr. 8:37; 9:43).

1151. בֶּן־עַמִּי ***ben-ʿammiy:*** A proper noun designating Ben-Ammi (Gen. 19:38).

1152. בְּסוֹדְיָה ***b***^{e}***sôḏ***^{e}***yāh:*** A proper noun designating Besodeiah (Neh. 3:6).

1153. בֵּסַי ***bēsay:*** A proper noun designating Besai (Ezra 2:49; Neh. 7:52).

1154. בֶּסֶר ***beser:*** A masculine noun referring to a sour or unripe grape. It is used to depict the distasteful character of the success of the wicked man. His renown and good fortune drop off like a sour or unripe grape at the peak of his success (Job 15:33, KJV, NKJV, NASB, NIV, unripe).

1155. בֹּסֶר *bōser:* A masculine noun depicting a sour grape or unripe grape. It describes the infamous fortune of a wicked man that is quickly gone like a vine casts off unripe or sour grapes (Job 15:33, KJV, NKJV, NASB; NIV, unripe). It is also used of ripening grapes (Isa. 18:5, NASB; KJV, sour grape). The word was used figuratively with the meaning sour grapes to describe something that had a destructive impact upon the descendants of the fathers who ate the sour grapes (Jer. 31:29, 30; Ezek. 18:2).

1156. בְּעָא *b^e'ā':* A verb meaning to ask, seek, or request. An Aramaic word found only in Daniel, it connotes the idea to ask, request, or petition (Dan. 2:18). It also conveys the idea of praying to God or seeking out a person (Dan. 2:13); asking a person for something (Dan. 6:7[8]); making other inquiries (Dan. 7:16); or seeking out a fault (Dan. 6:4[5]).

1157. בַּעַד *ba'ad:* A particle meaning for, through, behind. This particle has many nuanced meanings. The basic renderings are: behind, as in shutting a door behind oneself (Gen. 7:16); surrounding one, shutting a person in (Ps. 3:3[4]; 139:11; Jon. 2:6[7]). Figuratively, it is used after a verb of shutting to indicate (*ba'ad*) the womb (Gen. 20:18). After the verb to pray, it indicates what is prayed for (Gen. 20:7). It indicates stand on behalf (*ba'ad*) of something or someone (2 Sam. 10:12). It is used to indicate looking through (*ba'ad*) something (Gen. 26:8) or to describe motion over something (2 Sam. 20:21). It is used to render the idiom this . . . for that, e.g., skin for (*b^e'ad*) skin (Job 2:4).

1158. בָּעָה *bā'āh:* A verb which means to cause to swell or boil up; to seek, to ask, to request. This verb describes a swelling of water (Isa. 64:2[1]); or a rising of desire or interest (Isa. 21:12). In the latter interpretation, the verb is also used in the passive form, to be searched (out), with the implication of being ransacked or plundered. This meaning is evident by the context and by the synonymous parallelism in the following verse, "But how Esau will be ransacked, his hidden treasures pillaged!" (Obad. 1:6 NIV).

1159. בָּעוּ *ba'û:* A feminine noun meaning petition. An Aramaic term related to *be'ā'* (1156), meaning to ask, seek, or request, this word occurs only twice in Scripture, both times in Daniel. It conveys the idea of petition (Dan. 6:7[8], 13[14]).

1160. בְּעוֹר *b^e'ôr:* A proper noun designating Beor:

A. The father of Balaam (Num. 22:5; 24:3, 15; 31:8; Deut. 23:4(5); Josh. 13:22; 24:9; Mic. 6:5).

B. The father of a king of Edom (Gen. 36:32; 1 Chr. 1:43).

1161. בִּעוּתִים *bi'ûṯiym:* A masculine plural noun denoting terrors, horror. It describes terrifying experiences and impressions from God (Job 6:4) which are devastating and destructive (Ps. 88:16[17]).

1162. בֹּעַז *bō'az:* A. A masculine proper noun transliterated as *bō'az.* Boaz was a kinsman redeemer for Naomi and became the second husband of Ruth. His name may mean quickness, swiftness, or literally, in him, strength (*b^e* plus *'az*). He and Ruth bore Obed, grandfather of David (Ruth 4:13, 21).

B. A masculine proper noun transliterated as *bō'az.* It serves as the name for the north column of two pillars constructed at the porch of Solomon's Temple (1 Kgs. 7:21).

1163. בָּעַט *bā'aṭ:* A verb meaning to kick at, kick out; disdain, scorn. It refers to the disrespectful attitude and unholy actions of the high priest's sons in the time of the birth and maturation of Samuel (1 Sam. 2:29). It refers to a rebellious disposition and action of Israel toward the Lord (Deut. 32:15).

1164. בְּעִי *b^e'iy:* A masculine noun meaning ruin (heap), against a ruin, entreaty; figuratively, a grave. In its only use in Job 30:24, it is probably best interpreted as an occurrence of the preposition *b^e* ("for" or "against") and *'iy* (5856, "ruin"), and should be translated as "against a ruin." However, some have interpreted this word as a derivative of *bā'āh* (1158) and translated it as "entreaty" or "prayer," or in a derived meaning, "grave." Either translation would fit the context, for both communicate that the outstretched hand of God is present in the midst of destruction. This destroying hand has either brought a person (in this case, Job) to utter ruin or is the very thing against which there is no entreaty or prayer. Job is speaking from the shattered depths of utter personal ruin, where he perceives the hand of God as against him.

1165. בְּעִיר *b^e'iyr:* A masculine noun denoting animal, cattle, or livestock; beasts. It refers to beasts of burden (Gen. 45:17); cattle (Ps. 78:48); and grazing animals (Ex. 22:5[4]); to animals or domesticated beasts in general (Num. 20:4). The Lord provided water for the animals as well as for people in the desert (Num. 20:8, 11).

1166. בָּעַל *bā'al:* A verb meaning to marry, have dominion, or to rule over. In relation to marriage, it refers to marrying a woman (Deut. 24:1); or a woman to be married (Prov. 30:23). Figuratively, it is used in connection with God's marriage to Israel (Jer. 3:14), as well as Judah and Israel's marriage to the daughter of a foreign god (Mal. 2:11). Other times, this verb means to have dominion over land (1 Chr. 4:22) or people (Isa.

26:13). Used as a participle, it means to be married to (Gen. 20:3).

1167. בַּעַל ***baʿal:*** A masculine singular noun meaning lord, husband, owner, possessor, the title of a Canaanite deity (Baal). It can also denote rulers and leaders (Isa. 16:8). Commonly, it refers to legally owning something such as an ox or bull (Ex. 21:28); house (Ex. 22:8[7]; or land (Job 31:38). The word can also describe possessing a quality, attribute, or characteristic like anger (Prov. 22:24); wrath (Prov. 29:22); hair (2 Kgs. 1:8); appetite (Prov. 23:2); wisdom (Eccl. 7:12). When Joseph is called a dreamer, he is literally a possessor of dreams (Gen. 37:19). Further, the word can connote husband as used of Abraham (Gen. 20:3) and elsewhere (Ex. 21:3; Deut. 22:22). It often refers to the Canaanite deity, generally known as Baal in the Old Testament and other local manifestations (Num. 25:3). Worship of this deity seems to have been common in the Northern Kingdom which is attested in the preponderance of the Baal theophoric element in many proper nouns. The Lord may also have been referred to with this generic term for "lord." But in light of the worship of Baal in the north, Hosea longed for a time when this usage would cease (Hos. 2:16[18]).

1168. בַּעַל ***baʿal:*** A. A masculine proper noun naming the Canaanite god Baal; lord. Used with the definite article, it means the god Baal served by the Canaanites and Philistines, but Israel was caught up in worshiping this pagan god, too (Judg. 2:11, 13; 6:25; 28, 30; 1 Kgs. 18:18, 19, 21; 19:18; 2 Kgs. 3:2; 10:18–23; Hos. 2:8[10]). The word occurs in the plural, indicating the many manifestations of pagan polytheism (Judg. 2:11; 1 Sam. 7:4; 12:10; 1 Kgs. 18:18; Jer. 2:23; Hos. 11:2). It is used without the definite article as a name indicating, e.g., high places of Baal (Num. 22:41; NIV renders as Bamoth Baal). In construct with a following word, *baʿal berīyṯ*, it means lord of the covenant (Judg. 8:33; 9:4).

B. A proper noun naming a city, Baal. It denoted a border city of the tribe of Simeon (NIV renders as Baalath with a note; 1 Chr. 4:33).

C. A masculine proper name, Baal. The name describes the immediate son of Reaiah but a descendant of Reuben, the firstborn of Jacob (1 Chr. 5:5).

D. A masculine proper name found as a descendant of Benjamin (1 Chr. 8:30) from the line that produced King Saul (1 Chr. 9:36).

1169. בְּעֵל ***beʿēl:*** A masculine Aramaic noun meaning lord, master, overlord, owner. It is used in Ezra 4:8, 9, and 17 as an official title for Rehum, a Persian provincial officer, the "chancellor." It corresponds to the Hebrew word *baʿal* (1167), which also means lord or owner but is used with broader variations in meaning ranging from man, ruler, owner, and husband to the description of false gods.

1170. בַּעַל בְּרִית ***ba'al beriyṯ:*** A masculine proper name. It refers to a Canaanite god. This god had his own temple in Shechem (Judg. 9:4). The name means lord of the covenant (Judg. 8:33; 9:4; cf. 9:46). After Gideon's deliverance and death, Israel again worshiped the baals, lords of the land, specifically setting up Baal-Berith as their chief god.

1171. בַּעַל גָּד ***ba'al gāḏ:*** A proper noun designating the false god Baal-Berith (Judg. 8:33; 9:4).

1172. בַּעֲלָה ***ba'alāh:*** A feminine singular noun meaning lady, owner, or possessor. It is the feminine form of *bā'al* (1167). The word occurs three times in the Bible, and twice it refers to possessing occult abilities: possessor of ghosts (1 Sam. 28:7); and spells (Nah. 3:4).

1173. בַּעֲלָה ***ba'alāh:*** A proper noun designating Baalah (Josh. 15:9–11, 29; 2 Sam. 6:2; 1 Chr. 13:6).

1174. בַּעַל הָמוֹן ***ba'al hāmôn:*** A proper noun designating Baal Hamon (Song 8:11).

1175. בְּעָלוֹת ***be'ālôṯ:*** A proper noun designating Bealoth (Josh. 15:24; 1 Chr. 4:33; 1 Kgs. 4:16).

1176. בַּעַל זְבוּב ***ba'al zeḇûḇ:*** A masculine proper name meaning lord of flies. A Philistine god of the city of Ekron recognized by Ahaziah, king of Israel (Judg. 10:62; Kgs. 1:2, 3, 6, 16).

1177. בַּעַל חָנָן ***ba'al ḥānān:*** A proper noun designating Baal-Hanan:

A. A king of Edom (Gen. 36:38, 39; 1 Chr. 1:49, 50).

B. A Gederite (1 Chr. 27:28).

1178. בַּעַל חָצוֹר ***ba'al ḥāṣôr:*** A proper noun designating Baal Hazor (2 Sam. 13:23).

1179. בַּעַל חֶרְמוֹן ***ba'al ḥermôn:*** A proper noun designating Baal Hermon (Judg. 3:3; 1 Chr. 5:23).

1180. בַּעְלִי ***ba'aliy:*** This masculine proper name for Baali is found in Hos. 2:16(18). The NIV interprets it as the words my master.

1181. בַּעֲלֵי בָמוֹת ***ba'alēy bāmôṯ:*** This masculine noun is used to denote dominant heights, lit., it means lords of the high places (Num. 22:41).

1182. בְּעֶלְיָדָע ***be'elyāḏā':*** A proper noun designating Beeliada (1 Chr. 14:7).

1183. בְּעַלְיָה ***be'alyāh:*** A proper noun designating Bealiah (1 Chr. 12:5).

1184. בַּעֲלֵי יְהוּדָה ***ba'alēy yehûḏāh:*** A proper noun designating Baale Judah (2 Sam. 6:2)), another name for *ba'alāh* (1173).

1185. בַּעֲלִיס ***ba'aliys:*** A proper noun designating Baalis (Jer. 40:14).

1186. בַּעַל מְעוֹן *ba'al me'ôn:* A proper noun designating Baal Meon (Num. 32:38; 1 Chr. 5:8; Ezek. 25:9).

1187. בַּעַל פְּעוֹר *ba'al pe'ôr:* A masculine proper name. It is used once in the Pentateuch (Num. 25:3, 5; Deut. 4:3; Ps. 106:28; Hos. 9:10) and rendered as a proper name Baalpeor (KJV) or as Baal of Peor (NIV, NKJV, NASB), stressing the location of this god's habitation. Peor became a byword for shame along with baal, which is best translated as shame in Hosea. Evidently, the name refers to a Moabite mountain. It was one of the places from which Balaam blessed Israel (Num. 23:28).

1188. בַּעַל פְּרָצִים *ba'al perāṣiym:* A proper noun designating Baal Perazim (Num. 32:38; 1 Chr. 5:8; Ezek. 25:9).

1189. בַּעַל צְפוֹן *ba'al ṣepôn,* בַּעַל צְפֹן *ba'al ṣepōn:* A proper noun designating Baal Zephon (Ex. 14:2, 9; Num. 33:7).

1190. בַּעַל שָׁלִשָׁה *ba'al šālišāh:* A proper noun designating Baal Shalishah (2 Kgs. 4:42).

1191. בַּעֲלָת *ba'alāt:* A proper noun designating Baalath (Josh. 19:44; 1 Kgs. 9:18; 2 Chr. 8:6).

1192. בַּעֲלַת בְּאֵר *ba'alat be'ēr:* A proper noun designating Baalath Beer (Josh. 19:8).

1193. בַּעַל תָּמָר *ba'al tāmār:* A proper noun designating Baal Tamar (Judg. 20:33).

1194. בְּעֹן *be'ōn:* A proper noun designating Beon (Num. 32:3).

1195. בַּעֲנָא *ba'anā':* A proper noun designating Baana:

A. One of Solomon's governors over one of his twelve districts. He had to supply provisions for the king for one month.

B. Another of Solomon's governors and possibly the son of one of David's wise men (cf. 2 Sam. 15:31–37).

C. The father of Zadok, who helped repair the Fish Gate after the captives returned from the Babylonian exile (Neh. 3:3–5).

1196. בַּעֲנָה *ba'anāh:* A proper noun designating Baanah:

A. He served as the commander of Saul's son Ish-bosheth who tried to seize the throne after Saul died. He was assassinated.

B. The father of Heleb. He was a Netophathite (2 Sam. 23:29).

C. A Jew of some standing, he was a leader with whom many exiles returned from Babylon (Ezra 2:2).

D. He is listed as a leader of the people who sealed the covenant of Nehemiah to serve the Lord faithfully.

1197. בָּעַר *bā'ar:* I. A verb meaning to burn, to consume. The verb indicates the process of combustion. It describes fire itself flaming up (Jer. 20:9) or various objects: a burning bush (Ex. 3:2, 3); burning wood (Ps.

83:14[15]). It is used figuratively of the Lord's anger burning and consuming Jacob and Israel (Isa. 6:13; 30:27; 42:25) and the wicked (Ps. 106:18; Jer. 44:6). It describes wickedness consuming persons like a fire (Isa. 9:18[17]).

In some contexts, it means to cause a fire or consume something, such as a field or olive trees (Ex. 22:6[5]) or to burn something to ashes (Nah. 2:13[14]).

II. A verb meaning to remove, to graze, to ruin. It depicts cattle feeding or grazing in a field (Ex. 22:5[4]) or an enemy of Israel being ruined or consumed (Num. 24:22). It describes dung being consumed or perhaps swept away (NASB; cf. NIV, burns; KJV, take away; 1 Kgs. 14:10). In certain contexts, it is best translated as remove, get rid of something, root out (Deut. 13:5[6]; 2 Kgs. 23:34).

III. A verb meaning to be stupid, brutish. This root denotes being deluded, stupid for worshiping idols (Jer. 10:8), being without common religious sense Jer. 10:8, 14) and led astray.

1198. בַּעַר ***ba'ar:*** An adjective meaning senseless, foolish (Ps. 73:22). It refers to a person who is senseless about riches (Ps. 49:10[11]) or a person who will not learn discipline (Prov. 12:1). As a general term, it depicts any person who stands before the unsearchable wisdom of God as stupid (Prov. 30:2, 3).

1199. בַּעֲרָא ***ba'ᵃrā':*** A proper noun designating Baara (1 Chr. 8:8).

1200. בְּעֵרָה ***bᵉ'ērāh:*** A feminine singular noun meaning burning. Its only occurrence is in Exodus 22:6[5] where it connotes burning offerings.

1201. בַּעְשָׁא ***ba'šā':*** A proper noun designating Baasha, a king of northern Israel (908–886) who gained the kingship by assassinating Jeroboam II's son. He reigned in Tirzah. He exterminated the dynasty of Jeroboam (1 Kgs. 16:3–8). He was a thorn in Judah's flesh during his reign. He is roundly condemned as a wicked king (1 Kgs. 15:33) who, ironically, continued the evil policies and practices of Jeroboam I. God sent Jehu as a prophet who announced the eradication of Baasha's house from Israel (1 Kgs. 16:1–7; 21:22).

1202. בַּעֲשֵׂיָה ***ba'ᵃśēyāh:*** A proper noun designating Baaseiah (1 Chr. 6:40[25]).

1203. בְּעֶשְׁתְּרָה ***bᵉ'ešᵉrāh:*** A proper noun designating Be-eshterah (Josh. 21:27).

1204. בָּעַת ***bā'aṯ:*** A verb meaning to fear, to be or to make afraid, to startle. The basic ideas of this word can be summarized as an individual's realization that he or she is less powerful than someone or something else and can be overcome. An evil spirit tormented Saul (1 Sam. 16:14, 15), but God is also accused of making people afraid (Job 7:14; 9:34). It is used of humans, as when Haman was terrified (Esth. 7:6). This word can also mean to fall upon or to overwhelm (Job 3:5; Ps. 18:4[5]).

1205. בְּעָתָה ***beʻāṯāh:*** A feminine noun indicating trouble, terror. It describes a state of illness and destruction brought on by the Lord (Jer. 8:15; 14:19); a time devoid of peace, the opposite of what Judah had hoped for (Jer. 14:19).

1206. בֹּץ ***bōṣ:*** A masculine noun meaning mud, salt, mire. It describes wet, soggy, muddy ground. It is used figuratively in a metaphorical expression to depict the failure of Zedekiah to act and do what Jeremiah was telling him to do. The king thus would be sunk in the mud, unable to act (Jer. 38:22).

1207. בִּצָּה ***biṣṣāh:*** A feminine noun meaning mire, marsh. It refers to the place and type of water and soil conditions needed for the papyrus plant and reeds to grow (Job 8:11; 40:21). It refers to the places around the Salt Sea that will remain salty when the Lord transforms the land (Ezek. 47:11).

1208. בָּצוּר ***bāṣûr,*** בָּצִיר ***bāṣiyr:*** I. An adjective depicting something as inaccessible, thick, impenetrable, dense. It refers to the farmer's thick cedar forests of Lebanon (Zech. 11:2; NKJV, NASB, NIV). The Lord would destroy this forest in judgment.

II. An adjective indicating vintage or time of grape harvest. It is an idiom used to describe the "vintage" forest of the magnificent cedars of Lebanon (Zech. 11:2; KJV).

1209. בֵּצָי ***bēṣāy:*** A proper noun designating Bezai (Ezra 2:17; Neh. 7:23; 10:18[19]).

1210. בָּצִיר ***bāṣiyr:*** A masculine noun indicating the time of grape harvest, vintage. It refers to the time of grape harvesting (Lev. 26:5; Isa. 32:10) or the actual yield of wine or grapes from an area (Judg. 8:2; Jer. 48:32; Mic. 7:1). It implies the thoroughness of a grape harvest (Isa. 24:13) as a metaphor for the extent of God's judgments on the earth. It is used idiomatically to describe the excellence of the cedar forests of Lebanon (Zech. 11:2, KJV; cf. NASB, NKJV, NIV).

1211. בָּצָל ***bāṣāl:*** A masculine noun indicating an onion. It refers to one of the luxury foods that Israel ate in Egypt and for which they longed again as they tracked about in the desert (Num. 11:5).

1212. בְּצַלְאֵל ***beṣal'ēl:*** A proper noun designating Bezalel:

A. An artisan (Ex. 31:2; 35:30; 36:1, 2; 37:1; 38:22; 1 Chr. 2:20; 2 Chr. 1:5).

B. An Israelite (Ezra 10:30).

1213. בַּצְלוּת ***baṣlûṯ:*** A proper noun designating Bazluth (Ezra 2:52; Neh. 7:54).

1214. בָּצַע ***bāṣaʻ:*** A verb meaning to cut off, to gain by violence. Figuratively, it bears the sense of being destroyed or judged (Job 27:8; Isa. 38:12; Jer. 51:13). In some cases, it is used to express the dispensing of the Lord's judgment (Isa. 10:12; Lam. 2:17). The word also describes taking from someone out of greed (Prov. 1:19; Jer. 8:10; Ezek. 22:12).

1215. בֶּצַע ***beṣaʻ:*** A masculine noun denoting profit, gain, dishonest gain, covetousness. The word refers to illegal or unjust gain or profit which God's people were to avoid (Gen. 37:26; Ex. 18:21; 1 Sam. 8:3; Ps. 119:36; Prov. 28:16). It is further qualified in some contexts as gain obtained by violent means (Judg. 5:19; Mic. 4:13) or profit gained with selfish goals in mind (Gen. 37:26; Mal. 3:14).

1216. בָּצַק ***bāṣaq:*** A verb meaning to become swollen. It was used of the failure of the Israelites' feet to swell in their desert marches in Sinai (Deut. 8:4). God's providential kindness and care for His people was recorded and remembered by the exiles returned from Babylon (Neh. 9:21).

1217. בָּצֵק ***bāṣēq:*** A masculine noun referring to dough. The word describes non–fermented dough (Ex. 12:34, 39), which was demanded in the celebration of the Passover or dough made with no restrictive stipulations attached to its makeup (2 Sam. 13:8; Jer. 7:18; Hos. 7:4). It was used in both worshiping the Lord and, in times of rebellion, to present gifts to pagan deities, such as the queen of heaven (Jer. 7:18).

1218. בָּצְקַת ***boṣqaṯ:*** A proper noun designating Bozkath (Josh. 15:39; 2 Kgs. 22:1).

1219. בָּצַר ***bāṣar:*** I. A verb denoting to harvest, to gather. It refers to the process of harvesting grapes (Lev. 25:5, 11; Deut. 24:21). In its participial form, it indicates a grape harvester (Jer. 6:9; 49:9; Obad. 1:5) whose activity illustrates the extent of God's judgments on Israel or her enemies.

II. A verb meaning to humble, to cut off. It describes the power and sovereignty of God over the princes or rulers of the earth (Ps. 76:12[13]).

III. A verb indicating to be inaccessible or make inaccessible, to be thwarted. It describes the possibility of something being done or accomplished or found out (Gen. 11:6). In its passive sense, it describes the impossibility of something being thwarted or frustrated, such as God's counsel or purpose (Job 42:2). Used as a noun, it refers to unattainable knowledge or things, great and mighty things (NASB, Jer. 33:3). It means to strengthen or fortify in the sense of making a city or wall inaccessible (Isa. 22:10; Jer. 51:53).

IV. A verb meaning to test, assay. It is used in an emphatic form of the verb to indicate a tester (Jer. 6:27). In context it depicts someone who will test (KJV, try) God's people using them as the ore.

1220. בֶּצֶר beṣer: I. A masculine noun denoting gold. The word refers to gold (Job 22:24) and then, using a play on the same word, depicts the Almighty as the true gold and silver of His people (Job 22:25; KJV renders this noun as defense).

II. A masculine noun meaning defense. It is found in Job 22:25 describing the Almighty as Job's defense (KJV; NASB, NIV, NKJV render it as a wordplay and translate as gold).

1221. בֶּצֶר beṣer: A proper noun designating Bezer:

A. A city in Reuben (Deut. 4:43; Josh. 20:8; 21:36; 1 Chr. 6:78[63]).

B. A descendant of Asher (1 Chr. 7:37).

1222. בְּצַר b^eṣar: A masculine noun denoting gold (KJV, Job 36:19). The word may be a phrase meaning in distress (b^e + *ṣar* [6862,I]). So, most translators understand the syntax of the verse differently and translate it as "not be in distress" (NIV) or similar renderings (NASB, NKJV).

1223. בָּצְרָה boṣrāh: A feminine noun meaning pen, sheepfold (Mic. 2:12).

1224. בָּצְרָה boṣrāh: A proper noun designating Bozrah:

A. The mountainous capital city of Edom. The name means "fortress." It was where the major caravan highways of Edom ran (Gen. 36:33) and where early kings of Edom reigned. It lay south, southeast of the Salt Sea (Dead Sea). The prophets mention it in prophecies of judgment (Isa. 34:6; 63:1; Jer. 49:1, 13, 22; Amos 1:12).

B. It refers also to a city in Moab (Jer. 48:24). It is mentioned in a prophecy of judgment. It may be the same as Bezer.

1225. בִּצָּרוֹן biṣṣārôn: A masculine noun depicting a fortress or stronghold. It refers to a place of strength and fortification to which the exiles of Judah will return, probably the rebuilt city of Jerusalem as Zion (Zech. 9:12).

1226. בַּצֹּרֶת baṣṣōreṯ: A feminine noun denoting death, drought. It describes a period when rain and, hence, food were scarce in Judah, a judgment on God's people (Jer. 14:1). The person who trusts in the Lord need not fear a devastating year of drought (Jer. 17:8).

1227. בַּקְבּוּק baqbûq: A proper noun designating Bakbuk (Ezra 2:51; Neh. 7:53).

1228. בַּקְבֻּק baqbuq: A masculine noun denoting a jar, bottle. It refers to an earthenware jar, a potter's creation. Jeremiah's breaking of such a jar was an object lesson for Judah, whom the Lord would likewise break so it could not be restored (Jer. 19:1, 10). A similar jar was used to carry honey (1 Kgs. 14:3).

1229. בַּקְבֻּקְיָה baqbuqyāh: A proper noun designating Bakbukiah (Neh. 11:17; 12:9, 25).

1230. בַּקְבַּקַּר ***baqbaqqar:*** A proper noun designating Bakbakkar (1 Chr. 9:15).

1231. בֻּקִּי ***buqqiy:*** A proper noun designating Bukki:

A. A Danite (Num. 34:22).

B. A descendant of Aaron (1 Chr. 6:5(5:31), 51(36); Ezra 7:4).

1232. בֻּקִּיָּהוּ ***buqqiyyāhû:*** A proper noun designating Bukkiah (1 Chr. 25:4, 13).

1233. בָּקִיעַ ***bāqiya':*** A masculine noun meaning a small fragment or break. It refers to a crack or hole in the wall (Isa. 22:9) of the City of David as a future prophetic picture of the fall of that city. It refers to the fragments of the small houses that will be left after the Lord judges His people Israel (Amos 6:11).

1234. בָּקַע ***bāqa':*** A verb indicating to split, break open, divide; to hatch, break into, burst open, burst forth. This word has the basic idea of something splitting or dividing with force. Its main translations include the following: to split, e.g., the sea, especially the Red Sea, or wood (Ex. 14:16, 21; Neh. 9:11; Ps. 78:13; Eccl. 10:9); rip open bodies (2 Kgs. 2:24; 8:12; 15:16; Hos. 13:16[14:1]; Amos 1:13); to hatch eggs (Isa. 34:15; 59:5). It has the meaning of invade or break into (2 Sam. 23:16; 2 Chr. 21:17). It describes the dividing of the Mount of Olives with the Lord standing on it (Zech. 14:4). It describes the breaking or breaching of various other things: wineskins, (Josh. 9:13; Job 32:19); light (Isa. 58:8); tunnels or valleys (Judg. 15:19; Job 28:10; Mic. 1:4). It describes a city being taken by storm or breached (Isa. 7:6; Ezek. 26:10).

1235. בֶּקַע ***beqa':*** A masculine noun indicating half a shekel, a beka. It refers to a weight equal to ten gerahs or 6.1 gm (.22 oz.). It is defined (Ex. 38:26) as half a shekel or the weight of a gold nose ring (Gen. 24:22).

1236. בִּקְעָה ***biq'āh:*** An Aramaic feminine noun referring to a plain. It is used in Daniel 3:1 to describe the location of the plain of Dura where Nebuchadnezzar set a huge obelisk gilded with gold.

1237. בִּקְעָה ***biq'āh:*** A feminine noun denoting a plain. It describes a valley plain, one of the most famous being the plain in the land of Shinar where the Tower of Babel was erected (Gen. 11:2). These areas were created by the will of God (Ps. 104:8). It is used literally and figuratively by the prophet Amos to describe the Valley of Aven, literally, the Valley of Wickedness (1:5). The plain or Valley of Megiddo, a huge sprawling plain, is the traditional place where the last great battles of Gog and Magog will take place (Zech. 12:11).

1238. בָּקַק ***bāqaq:*** I. A verb meaning to empty; lay waste; be laid waste. It described the destroying of land (Isa. 24:1, 3; Jer. 51:2), especially as an act of God. It has the meaning of to deflate or demoralize the spirit of someone (Isa. 19:3) or to break or make void someone's counsel (Jer. 19:7). Israel is described as an empty vine (Hos. 10:1, KJV; cf. NKJV), a vine laid waste.

II. A verb meaning to grow or be luxuriant. The word is rendered with this meaning in Hosea 10:1 (NIV, NASB).

1239. בָּקַר ***bāqar:*** A verb meaning to seek, to look for, to consider, to investigate. It describes the process the priest goes through to see whether someone is unclean (Lev. 13:36) or religious inquiring in general at the bronze altar (2 Kgs. 16:15). It describes concern in general about an issue (Lev. 27:33). The psalmist's greatest desire was the object sought by this verb: to dwell in the house of the Lord (Ps. 27:4). On the other hand, the object the Lord seeks and cares for is His sheep, His people (Ezek. 34:11, 12).

1240. בְּקַר ***b^{e}qar:*** An Aramaic verb meaning to seek, to search for, to investigate, to find out. It refers to a formal search made for official documents (Ezra 4:15, 19; 6:1) and to a formal oral investigation to be made by Ezra at the command of King Artaxerxes (Ezra 7:14).

1241. בָּקָר ***bāqār:*** A common collective noun referring to a herd, cattle, ox, oxen. It refers to female cattle, cows (Gen. 33:13), and is used to describe a herd of cattle or a single animal (Ex. 22:1[21:37]). A *ben-bāqār*, a son of cattle, refers to a calf (Gen. 18:7). These animals were used as beasts of burden or for farming, plowing, etc. (2 Sam. 6:6; 1 Chr. 12:40). The possession of cattle was important and constituted wealth.

1242. בֹּקֶר ***bōqer:*** A masculine noun meaning daybreak, morning. The word indicates the time of arrival of this period of the day (Gen. 29:25; Ex. 10:13; 14:27; Judg. 19:25; Ruth 3:13) and is the opposite of night (Gen. 29:25). It could refer to the time before people can recognize each other (Ruth 3:14). It denotes the coming of sunrise (Judg. 9:33).

To the psalmist, the morning was a time to praise God (Ps. 5:3[4]). Genesis uses the formula: There was evening, and there was morning (Gen. 1:5, 8, 13). The phrase in Dan. 8:14 refers to 2, 300 half-days, literally, until evening–morning. The phrase morning by morning (Ex. 16:21; 30:7; 36:3) is used with the verb šāḵam, to rise early, and means to rise early in the morning (Gen. 19:27; 20:8; 21:14).

1243. בַּקָּרָה ***baqqārāh:*** A feminine noun indicating seeking or caring, care. It indicates the seeking and caring of a shepherd for his flock when they are scattered (Ezek. 34:12). In context, it depicts the Lord's care for His flock at a crucial time.

1244. בִּקֹּרֶת ***biqqōreṯ:*** A feminine noun denoting punishment, reprimanding. It describes a reprimand or punishment in a case of improper sexual relationships (Lev. 19:20).

1245. בָּקַשׁ bāqaš: A verb meaning to seek, to require; to try to obtain. It is used to describe subjects seeking or requiring various things for various reasons: a stolen object (Gen. 31:39); persons (Gen. 37:15, 16); someone's life (Ex. 4:19; 24); evil against someone (1 Sam. 25:26) or good (Neh. 2:10; Ps. 122:9).

It denotes seeking someone's presence, especially the Lord's (1 Kgs. 10:24; Hos. 5:15) or His word (Amos 8:12). Prayer was a means of seeking the Lord's will (Dan. 9:3). In the passive use of the verb, something is sought for (Jer. 50:20; Ezek. 26:21) or is examined (Esth. 2:23).

1246. בַּקָּשָׁה baqqāšāh: A feminine noun meaning request, desire, something sought. It is used to describe a request in general (Ezra 7:6). In its biblical use, it especially refers to requests made to royalty (Esth. 5:3, 6–8; 7:2, 3; 9:12).

1247. בַּר bar: An Aramaic masculine noun denoting son. Sometimes an *n* (*nun*) is found in its spelling instead of *r* (*resh*), especially in the plural form (see #1123). The word refers to sons in general or to specific sons (Ezra 5:1, 2; 6:10; Dan. 5:22; 6:24[25]). In its plural form, it refers to Israelites (Ezra 6:16) or captives, exiles (Ezra 6:16; Dan. 2:25; 5:13). In its singular and plural forms, it is combined with the word for mankind, humankind (*'ᵉnāš*) to denote a human being (Dan. 7:13) in general or people in general (Dan. 2:38; 5:21). In Daniel 7:13 with the preposition *bᵉ* added to bar, it denotes a being "like" a son of man. Combined with the word for god(s), it refers to a divine or angelic creature (Dan. 3:25).

1248. בַּר bar: A masculine noun meaning son. It refers to the specially anointed Son of the Lord to whom the nations will pay homage (Ps. 2:7, 12). But it depicts any son in general who needs to learn wisdom (Prov. 31:2).

1249. בַּר bar: An adjective meaning pure, clean, radiant. This term is extremely rare and occurs only in the poetic books. The word typically means purity or cleanness of heart (Ps. 24:4; 73:1; cf. Job 11:4). This term also describes a clean feeding trough (Prov. 14:4). Radiance is ascribed to both the commandments of the Lord and the Shulamite (Ps. 19:8[9]; Song 6:10). The only other occurrence of this word also applies to the Shulamite and seems to indicate a select status, but this status is probably based on her purity (Song 6:9).

1250. בַּר bar, בָּר bār: A masculine noun meaning corn, grain; field. This staple was one of the blessings the Lord gave to Israel from the land of Canaan (Ps. 65:13[14]; Joel 2:24). It was abundant in Egypt during a time of drought in Israel (Gen. 41:35,

49; 42:3, 25). It was from a source of health and strength (Job 39:4; NASB, NIV, translate as referring to open fields or wilds; Prov. 11:26). It became a cause of judgment when Israel began to covet the wealth that flowed from selling it (Amos 8:5, 6).

1251. בַּר ***bar:*** An Aramaic masculine noun referring to field. It describes the place where beasts live freely (Dan. 2:38; 4:12[9], 15[12], 21[18], 23[20], 25[22], 32[29]). Nebuchadnezzar's kingdom, given to him by God, was figuratively referred to as the location for these fields.

1252. בֹּר ***bōr:*** A masculine noun indicating cleanness, purity. The connotation is a cleanness or pureness in the spiritual sense rather than the physical. Note the synonymous parallelism between this Hebrew word and *ṣed̲eq* (6664), which means righteousness as the basis for divine reward or recompense (2 Sam. 22:21, 25; Ps. 18:20[21], 24[25]). It occurs only once by itself (2 Sam. 22:25). It usually occurs with *yād̲* (3027), meaning hand (2 Sam. 22:21; Ps. 18:20[21], 24[25]), or *kap̲* (3709), meaning palm (Job 9:30; 22:30).

1253. בֹּר ***bōr:*** A masculine noun referring to eye, washing, soda, potash. A substance formed from wood and plant ashes. It was used as a cleansing agent. It parallels the word for soap or snow (Job 9:30) and is described as something with which Job would wash his hands. It was used to remove dross, according to Isaiah (Isa. 1:25).

1254. בָּרָא ***bārā':*** A verb meaning to create. Only God is the subject of this verb. It is used for His creating: heaven and earth (Gen. 1:1); humanity (Gen. 1:27); the heavenly host (Isa. 40:26); the ends of the earth (40:28); north and south (Ps. 89:12[13]); righteousness; salvation (Isa. 45:8); evil (Isa. 45:7). David asked God to "create" in him a clean heart (Ps. 51:10[12]). Isaiah promised that God will create a new heaven and earth (Isa. 65:17).

There are other roots that are spelled the same, but have different meanings. These include: to make fat (1 Sam. 2:29); to clear timber (Josh. 17:15, 18; Ezek. 23:47); and to choose (Ezek. 21:19[24], KJV).

1255. בְּרֹאדַךְ בַּלְאֲדָן ***b^e^rō'd̲ak̲ bal^a^d̲ān:*** A proper noun designating Berodach-baladan (2 Kgs. 20:12).

1256. בְּרָאיָה ***b^e^rā'yāh:*** A proper noun designating. Beraiah (1 Chr. 8:21).

1257. בַּרְבֻּר ***barbur:*** A masculine noun depicting a bird or fowl, choice or fattened fowl. It is described as one item on Solomon's luxurious menu of daily provisions (1 Kgs. 4:23[5:3]).

1258. בָּרַד ***bārad̲:*** A verb meaning to hail. It depicts a devastating storm that would lay a forest low (Isa. 32:19) as part of God's reconstruction program.

1259. בָּרָד ***bārād̲:*** A masculine noun denoting hail or hailstones. The word is used to describe hail that came down as the seventh plague of Egypt (Ex. 9:18, 19, 22–26, 28, 29; Ps. 78:47, 48; 105:32), large enough to kill cattle, plants, and trees, nearly devastating the land (Ex. 10:5, 12, 15). Hailstones were a terrifying weapon of and accompaniment of the Lord's appearances (Josh. 10:11; Ps. 18:12 [13], 13[14]). The Lord stored up these hailstones (Job 38:22) and discharged them at His will (Isa. 28:2, 17; Hag. 2:17) as His teaching and destructive agents.

1260. בֶּרֶד ***bered̲:*** A proper noun designating Bered:

A. A town (Gen. 16:14).

B. An Ephraimite (1 Chr. 7:20).

1261. בָּרֹד ***bārōd̲:*** An adjective referring to something mottled, spotted, speckled, dappled. It refers to male goats and sheep (Gen. 31:10, 12) with this coloring and to horses drawing one of the chariots in Zechariah's vision (6:3, 6). It features either different shades or different colors or both.

1262. בָּרָה ***bārāh:*** I. A verb meaning to eat, to feed. It describes the intake of bread or food (2 Sam. 13:6, 10) or the act of causing someone to eat food (2 Sam. 3:35; 13:5), to feed or to give him or her food. It has a more violent meaning: to devour (Lam. 4:10) human flesh as a result of Israel's destruction and the resulting famine.

II. A verb meaning to select, make a covenant, assign a task. In its sole usage, Goliath uses the word to challenge Israel's army to select or chose a representative for themselves (1 Sam. 17:8).

1263. בָּרוּךְ ***bārûk̲:*** A proper noun designating Baruch:

A. The faithful scribe and friend of Jeremiah. He was the son of Neriah (Jer. 51:59) and brother to Seriah (Jer. 32:12; 51:59). His name means "blessed." He recorded Jeremiah's prophecies twice and also read them to the people (Jer. 36:4–32). He and Jeremiah were both forcefully taken to Egypt (Jer. 43:4–7). According to tradition, they died in Egypt. He was so well respected as a scribe that later apocalypses were given his name (e.g., The Apocalypse of Baruch).

B. The name refers to a priest, a son of Zabbai. He helped Nehemiah rebuild the Jerusalem wall and supported the renewal covenant (Neh. 10:6).

C. It denotes the father of Maaseiah (Neh. 11:5). He was son of Col-Hozeh, son of Hazaiah.

1264. בְּרֹמִים ***b^e^rōmiym:*** A masculine plural noun meaning multicolored or of two colors. It refers to multicolored rugs or carpets (Ezek. 27:24), which were part of Tyre's rich export trade with the Mediterranean world.

1265. בְּרוֹשׁ ***b^e^rôš:*** A masculine noun indicating a tree, possibly fir wood, pinewood, a fir tree. It refers to pine logs (NIV), cypress timber (NASB, NKJV), or fir timber (KJV, 1 Kgs. 5:8[22], 10[24]; 6:15, 34). This wood was used in constructing the Temple, ships (Ezek. 27:5), and even musical instruments (2 Sam. 6:5). Used in a figurative sense, it refers to spear shafts (Nah. 2:3[4]). It is not clear whether the word refers to cypress, fir wood, or timber. This wood became a symbol of stateliness, luxury (Ezek. 31:8), or productiveness (Hos. 14:8[9]). In a time of war, this timber was often cut down (Zech. 11:2). It is personified in Isaiah (14:8), rejoicing over the fall of Assyria (Isa. 37:24), that had devastated forests. When Israel is restored, this tree will be restored (Isa. 41:19).

1266. בְּרוֹת ***b^e rôṯ:*** A masculine noun denoting fir, pine, juniper. It is building material in the house of the lover and the beloved (Song 1:17) because of its beauty and stateliness. It parallels in grandeur the splendid cedars.

1267. בָּרוּת ***bārûṯ:*** A feminine noun meaning food (Ps. 69:21[22]).

1268. בֵּרוֹתָה ***bērôṯāh,*** בֵּרֹתַי ***bērōṯay:*** A proper noun designating Berothai, Berothah (2 Sam. 8:8; Ezek. 47:16).

1269. בִּרְזָוִת ***birzāwiṯ:*** A proper noun designating Birzaith (1 Chr. 7:31).

1270. בַּרְזֶל ***barzel:*** A masculine noun denoting iron, an iron ax head. The word is found in lists detailing various metals (Num. 31:22; Josh. 22:8; Dan. 2:35). It was found in the earth as ore and had to be smelted to purify it (Deut. 8:9; Job 28:2). Many ancient implements of all kinds were made of iron (Gen. 4:22), such as bedsteads (Deut. 3:11); tools (Gen. 4:22; Deut. 27:5; Josh. 8:31; 1 Kgs. 6:7); farming tools (Deut. 28:48; 2 Sam. 12:31). It was used in powerful chariots of war (Josh. 17:16, 18; Judg. 1:19; 4:3). The mention of iron stands out in importance several times: the iron ax head that Elisha caused to float (2 Kgs. 6:5, 6); tools made of iron (Job 19:24; Jer. 17:1); the iron scepter by which the Messiah will reign, indicating a rulership of power and authority (Ps. 2:9). It is used in a figurative sense many times: the sky is made like iron (Lev. 26:19); the limbs and sinews of Leviathan or Behemoth are like iron rods (Job 40:18); iron used to sharpen iron is like a mind sharpening another mind (Prov. 27:17); a horn strong like iron to thresh with (Mic. 4:13).

1271. בַּרְזִלַּי ***barzillay:*** A proper noun designating Barzillai, a name meaning "son of iron." It refers to three different people:

A. A man from Gilead (2 Sam. 17:27; 19:32–40). He was a faithful follower of David.

B. It denotes a priest (Ezra 2:61; Neh. 7:63). He married a daughter of

Barzillai and had, evidently, taken on the name.

C. It refers to a Meholathite (2 Sam. 21:8). His son married Saul's daughter Merab, who bore five sons to him.

1272. בָּרַח ***bāraḥ:*** A verb describing running away, to run away, to flee. It describes the passing of a bar through something (Ex. 26:28; 36:33). Literally, it describes the act of fleeing, eloping, sometimes from a place or person, as when Moses fled from Pharaoh (Ex. 2:15; 1 Sam. 19:12, 18; Jer. 4:29). Figuratively, it depicts days or humans fleeing away, disappearing like a shadow (Job 9:25; 14:2). It carries the idea of coming or going quickly in some contexts (Song 8:14) or of putting to flight (Neh. 13:28; Job 41:28[20]; Prov. 19:26).

1273. בַּרְחֻמִי ***barḥumiy:*** A proper noun designating Barhumite, a transposed form of *baḥ^a^rûmiy* (978) (2 Sam. 23:31).

1274. בְּרִי ***b^e^riy:*** An adjective meaning fat. It is used to modify sheep (Ezek. 34:20) as fat sheep as opposed to lean sheep.

1275. בֵּרִי ***bēriy:*** A proper noun designating Beri (1 Chr. 7:36).

1276. בֵּרִי ***bēriy:*** A proper noun designating Berite (2 Sam. 20:14).

1277. בָּרִיא ***bāriy':*** An adjective denoting something as fat, healthy. It refers to cattle (Gen. 41:4); persons (Judg. 3:17); food (Hab. 1:16); healthy (fat) of flesh (Ps. 73:4; Dan. 1:15) through eating the Jewish diet.

1278. בְּרִיאָה ***b^e^riy'āh:*** A feminine noun indicating something new. In its biblical context, it describes something as the result of divine activity (Num. 16:30) that can serve as a sign.

1279. בִּרְיָה ***biryāh:*** A feminine noun meaning food, diet. It refers to some kind of prepared food delivered to Amnon by Tamar (2 Sam. 13:5, 7, 10).

1280. בְּרִיחַ ***b^e^riyaḥ:*** A masculine noun denoting a bar, bolt, gate; a noble (person). It refers to wooden crossbars used to join wooden frames in the Tabernacle, gates, and doors (Ex. 26:26–29; Judg. 16:3; 1 Sam. 23:7). It refers to eerie features of the depths of the sea, the underworld (Jon. 2:6[7]), and the unseen bolts or restraints God put on the activity of the sea (Job 38:10). Also in a figurative use, it refers to bars of distress, stress (Ps. 107:16), which are broken by the Lord.

1281. בָּרִחַ ***bāriaḥ,*** בָּרִיחַ ***bāriyaḥ:*** A masculine noun indicating one fleeing, a fugitive; crooked. The word describes a serpent, *nahaš,* in Job 26:13 that is escaping or writhing; hence, it is probably best translated as a gliding serpent (NIV) or as a fleeing serpent (NASB, NKJV). The KJV translates the word as crooked, giving more attention to the deceitful character of the serpent.

1282. בָּרִיחַ *bāriyaḥ:* A proper noun designating Bariah (1 Chr. 3:22).

1283. בְּרִיעָה *b^e^riy'āh*, בְּרִעָה *b^e^ri'āh:* A proper noun designating Beriah:

A. A son of Asher (Gen. 46:17; Num. 26:44, 45; 1 Chr. 7:30, 31; 23:10, 11).

B. A son of Ephraim (1 Chr. 7:23).

C. A Benjamite (1 Chr. 8:13, 16).

D. A Levite (1 Chr. 23:10, 11).

1284. בְּרִיעִי *b^e^riy'iy:* A masculine proper noun. The word indicates a nationality of Beriites, of the clan of Berites (Num. 26:44).

1285. בְּרִית *b^e^riyṯ:* A feminine noun meaning covenant, treaty, alliance, agreement. The word is used many times in the Old Testament. Its basic uses are outlined here. It describes covenants, or agreements between and among human beings: between Abraham and the Amorites, Abraham and the Philistines, Jacob and Laban, etc. (Gen. 14:13; 21:27, 32; 31:44). The nations were said to have made a covenant against Israel (Ps. 83:5[6]). It is used figuratively to depict a covenant with death (Isa. 28:15, 18) or with the stones of the field (Job 5:23).

It denotes an alliance, ordinance, or agreement between persons. References to covenants between people included Abraham's military treaty with the Ammorites (Gen. 14:13); Jonathan and David's pledge of friendship (1 Sam. 18:3); David's covenant with Abner (2 Sam. 3:12); the covenant of marriage (Prov. 2:17). The word *b^e^riyṯ* is often preceded by the verb *karaṯ* to express the technical idea of "cutting a covenant."

This word is used to describe God's making a covenant with humankind. It may be an alliance of friendship (Ps. 25:14). The covenants made between God and humans defined the basis of God's character in the Old Testament. They showed the strength of His divine promise from Adam all the way through to the exile and restoration. It is employed many times: God's covenant with Noah (Gen. 9:, 11–13, 15–17; Isa. 54:10) in the form of a promise; with Abraham, Isaac, and Jacob (Gen. 15:18; 17:2, 4, 7, 9–11, 13, 14, 19, 21; Ex. 2:24; Lev. 26:42) to increase their descendants, giving them Canaan and making them a blessing to the nations; with all Israel and Moses at Sinai (Ex. 19:5; 24:7, 8; 34:10; Deut. 29:1 [28:69]) with the stipulations of the Ten Commandments, including the guiding cases in the Book of the Covenant. The words of this covenant (*diḇrēy habb^e^riyṯ*) were kept in the ark in the Holy of Holies (Ex. 34:28; 40:20). A covenant with Phinehas established an everlasting priesthood in Israel (Num. 25:12, 13). It is used to refer to the covenant established with David and his house (Ps. 89:3[4], 28[29]; Jer. 33:21), an eternal covenant establishing David and his descendants as the inheritors of an everlasting kingdom. Jeremiah refers to a new covenant (Jer. 31:31) that God will establish in the future. The concept is personified in a person, a Servant who becomes the covenant of the people (Isa. 42:6; 49:8).

In addition to the verb *kāraṯ* mentioned above, the verb *qûm* is employed with *b^e^riyṯ* meaning to establish a covenant (Gen. 6:18; 9:9; Ex. 6:4) or to confirm a covenant (Lev. 26:9; Deut. 8:18). The word is used with *nāṯan,* to give, meaning to give or make a covenant (Gen. 17:2; Num. 25:12). Five other verbs are used in this way less often (Deut. 29:12[11]; 2 Sam. 23:5; 2 Chr. 15:12; Ps. 50:16; 111:9; Ezek. 16:8. A covenant could be transgressed or violated (Deut. 17:2; Judg. 2:20), but the Lord never broke His covenants; He always remembered a covenant (Gen. 9:15, 16; Ex. 2:24; 6:5; Lev. 26:42).

1286. בְּרִית ***b^e^riyṯ:*** A masculine proper noun Berith. This was the name of a Canaanite god. The word is combined with the term El, god, forming the name of a temple in Shechem, El-Berith, literally, the god of the covenant (Judg. 9:46).

1287. בֹּרִית ***bōriyṯ:*** A feminine noun referring to soap, alkali. This cleaning agent is derived from a soap-bearing plant. It removes external dirt but could not remove the stain from Israel's guilt before God (Jer. 2:22). It is designated as the soap of a person who washes cloth or a fuller (Mal. 3:2) and so would be of high quality.

1288. בָּרַךְ ***bāraḵ:*** A verb meaning to bless, kneel, salute, or greet. The verb derives from the noun knee and perhaps suggests the bending of the knee in blessing. Its derived meaning is to bless someone or something. The verb is used when blessing God (Gen. 9:26) or people (Num. 24:9). God used this verb when He blessed Abraham in the Abrahamic covenant (Gen. 12:3). The word is used intensively when God blesses people or people bless each other (Josh. 17:14). When the word is used reflexively, it describes a person blessing or congratulating himself (Deut. 29:19[20]). Other meanings are to bend the knee (2 Chr. 6:13); and to greet someone with a salutation or friendliness (1 Sam. 25:14).

1289. בְּרַךְ ***b^e^raḵ:*** I. An Aramaic verb meaning to kneel. It describes Daniel's practice of kneeling while he prayed to his God three times daily facing Jerusalem (Dan. 6:10[11]).

II. An Aramaic verb meaning to bless, to praise. It describes Daniel's and Nebuchadnezzar's reverent verbal response to God who had helped them (Dan. 2:19, 20; 3:28; 4:34[31]) in special ways.

1290. בֶּרֶךְ ***bereḵ:*** A feminine noun denoting a knee. It is used with the verb *kāra'*, to bend, meaning to bend the knee. Isaiah declares that every knee will bow before the Lord (Isa. 45:23) in the sense of worshiping and confessing the Lord. Solomon knelt before the Lord at the altar to worship his God (1 Kgs. 8:54; cf. 1 Kgs. 18:42). The phrase "on her knees" designates the lap of a mother (2 Kgs. 4:20 KJV). In Ezekiel's vision, water reached up to his knees (47:4). One of the curses the Lord would lay on a disobedient people was ailing knees (Deut. 28:35). Since the knees were a picture of strength, terror or fasting could weaken them (Job 4:4; Ps. 109:24; Isa. 35:3; Nah. 2:10[11]).

1291. בְּרֵךְ ***b^e rēḵ:*** An Aramaic feminine noun meaning knee. It is combined with the verb *b^e raḵ* to mean to kneel (Dan. 6:10[11]), literally, to kneel on his knees.

1292. בָּרַכְאֵל ***baraḵ'ēl:*** A proper noun designating Barachel (Job 32:2, 6).

1293. בְּרָכָה ***b^e rāḵāh:*** A feminine noun meaning blessing. The general idea of this word is one of good favor bestowed on another. This may be expressed in the giving of a tangible gift (Gen. 33:11; 1 Sam. 25:27) or in the pronouncing of a verbal blessing (Gen. 27:36; 49:28). Most often, however, this word speaks of God's favor on the righteous (Gen. 12:2; Mal. 3:10). It is related to the common verb *bāraḵ* (1288), meaning to bless and is often used to contrast God's blessing and His curse.

1294. בְּרָכָה ***b^e rāḵāh:*** A proper noun designating Beracah:

A. A Benjamite (1 Chr. 12:3).

B. A valley (2 Chr. 20:26).

1295. בְּרֵכָה ***b^e rēḵāh:*** A feminine noun indicating a pool, pond. It refers to a small body of water in Jerusalem called the upper pool (2 Kgs. 18:17; Isa. 36:2) and later a pool called the King's Pool (Neh. 2:14) and the famous Pool of Siloam (Neh. 3:15). The word is used to describe Nineveh as a pool being drained of its resources in its destruction (Nah. 2:8[9]). The cities of Hebron and Gibeon had small pools (2 Sam. 2:13; 4:12). The pools of Heshbon were known for their beauty and stillness (Song 7:4[5]).

1296. בֶּרֶכְיָה ***bereḵyah,*** בֶּרֶכְיָהוּ ***bereḵyāhû:*** A proper noun designating Berechiah, Berkiah:

A. The father of Zechariah (Zech. 1:1, 7).

B. An Ephraimite (2 Chr. 28:12).

C. The father of Asaph (1 Chr. 6:39[24]; 15:17).

D. A son of Zerubbabel (1 Chr. 3:20).

E. A Levite (1 Chr. 9:16; 15:23).

F. A father of Meshullam (Neh. 3:4, 30; 6:18).

1297. בְּרַם ***b^e ram:*** An Aramaic conjunctive adverb meaning but, nevertheless, however. It indicates that something is being done in spite of certain contrary circumstances or expectations (Ezra 5:13; Dan. 4:15[12], 23[20]; 5:17). Daniel receives an answer from the Lord in spite of the impossible situation in which he found himself (Dan. 2:28).

1298. בֶּרַע ***bera':*** A proper noun designating Bera (Gen. 14:2).

1299. בָּרַק ***bāraq:*** A verb indicating casting forth, sending forth, or flashing forth. It refers to a flash of lightning (Ps. 144:6). It is followed by its related noun, *bārāq*, lightning, literally, to flash lightning.

1300. בָּרָק ***bārāq:*** A masculine noun referring to lightning. Its most famous appearance is in the great theophany at Mt. Sinai when God settles on the sacred mountain amid thundering and lightning (Ex. 19:16; Ps. 18:14[15]). The Exodus was accompanied by lightning as well (Ps. 77:18[19]), but this phenomenon witnesses to the presence of God in every storm (Ps. 97:4). The swiftness of lightning is used to describe war chariots (Nah. 2:4[5]), while its blazing brightness describes the face of an angelic being (Dan. 10:6; cf. Ezek. 21:10[15], 15[20], 28[33]).

1301. בָּרָק ***bārāq:*** A proper noun designating Barak. Barak helped Deborah call together Israel's tribes to war against Sisera. His name means "lightning flash." His father was Abinoam. He refused to act alone, which prompted the Lord to deliver Israel from Sisera by the hand of a woman (Judg. 4:9; 6:24–27), Jael, wife of Heber the Kenite. Barak and Deborah together composed and sang the "Song of Deborah" (Judg. 5:1).

1302. בַּרְקוֹס ***barqôs:*** A proper noun designating Barkos (Ezra 2:53; Neh. 7:55).

1303. בַּרְקֳנִים ***barq^{o}niym:*** A masculine plural noun denoting briers. The word denotes the wild desert prickly plants used by Gideon to punish the kings of Midian after catching them (Judg. 8:7, 16).

1304. בָּרֶקֶת ***bāreqet̠,*** בָּרְקַת ***bār^{e}qath:*** A feminine noun denoting an emerald, beryl. The word refers to a semiprecious stone, either a beryl or emerald (Ex. 28:17; 39:10; KJV has carbuncle). It was possibly dark green in color. One of these stones was set in the first row of the breastpiece worn on the ephod by the high priest. It bore one of the names of the tribes of Israel. It was, according to Ezekiel, found in the Garden of Eden (28:13).

1305. בָּרַר ***bārar,*** בָּרוּר ***bārûr:*** A verb signifying to purify, select. God declares that He will purge the rebels from Israel (Ezek. 20:38) and that He will give the people purified lips (Zeph. 3:9). The term can also mean to polish or make shine like polished arrows (Isa. 49:2; Jer. 51:11). Primarily used in the books of Chronicles, it points out that which was choice or select: men (1 Chr. 7:40); gatekeepers (1 Chr. 9:22); musicians (1 Chr. 16:41); sheep (Neh. 5:18). It can also carry the connotation of testing or proving (Eccl. 3:18).

1306. בִּרְשַׁע ***birša':*** A proper noun designating Birsha (Gen. 14:2).

1307. בֵּרֹתִי **bērōṯiy:** A proper noun designating Berothite (1 Chr. 11:39).

1308. בְּשׂוֹר **bᵉsôr:** A proper noun designating Besor (1 Sam. 30:9, 10, 21).

1309. בְּשׂוֹרָה **bᵉśôrāh,** בְּשֹׂרָה **bᵉśōrāh:** A feminine noun indicating news, tidings, message. It indicates a report delivered to someone about something: the report about the death of Saul was reported using this word (2 Sam. 4:10); news of the defeat of David's enemies (2 Sam. 18:20, 25, 27). It is used for either bad news or good news (2 Kgs. 7:9).

1310. בָּשַׁל **bāšal:** A verb meaning to boil, to cook, to roast; to ripen. The word indicates simply cooking without an object (Ezek. 24:5). It describes the preparation of various foods: to bake cakes or bread (2 Sam. 13:8), to cook or boil meat (Deut. 16:7; 1 Kgs. 19:21). In its passive use, it indicates something boiled (Ex. 12:9), a cooking method forbidden in preparing the Passover lamb. It describes the ripening of grapes and fruit of the vine (Gen. 40:10). It is used in a figurative sense to indicate that the harvest, the nations of the world, are ripe and ready to be cut (Joel 3:13[4:13]).

1311. בָּשֵׁל **bāšēl:** An adjective denoting something cooked, boiled. Combined with the verb, to boil, it emphasizes that the Passover lamb must not be boiled (Ex. 12:9). It can refer to a part of a boiled ram (Num. 6:19).

1312. בִּשְׁלָם **bišlām:** A proper noun designating Bishlam (Ezra 4:7).

1313. בָּשָׂם **bāśām:** A masculine noun indicating spice, balsam. The word is used figuratively in Song of Solomon 5:1 to refer to spices, some of the delights of the lover's beloved. The beloved is pictured as the lover's garden of delight.

1314. בֶּשֶׂם **beśem,** בֹּשֶׂם **bōśem:** A masculine noun designating spice, balsam; fragrance, perfume. This item was highly prized. It is mentioned several times in Song of Solomon to describe a fragrance and pleasant aroma (4:10, 14; 5:1, 13; 6:2; 8:14). It is best translated as fragrance in Song of Solomon 4:16 (KJV, NKJV, spices). It was featured in beauty treatments (Esth. 2:12). It was an ingredient in the anointing oil and fragrant incense used in the Tabernacle rituals (Ex. 25:6; 30:23; 35:8, 28). It was one of the gifts to Solomon from the Queen of Sheba and was a feature in the king's storehouses (2 Kgs. 20:13; Isa. 39:2; Ezek. 27:22).

1315. בָּשְׂמַת **bāśᵉmaṯ:** A proper noun designating Bashemath, Basemath:

A. One of the wives of Esau, a daughter of a Hittite (Gen. 26:34).

B. One of the wives of Esau, a daughter of Ishmael (Gen. 36:3, 4, 10, 13, 17).

C. A daughter of Solomon (1 Kgs. 4:15).

1316. בָּשָׁן ***bāšān:*** A proper noun designating Bashan. The name of a region east of the Jordan River ruled by Og, king of Bashan. It was east and north of the Sea of Galilee. The Lord gave it into the hands of Israel (Num. 21:33). It was given to Manasseh as an allotment (Num. 32:33). The Yarmuk River cut across it. Its futile lands were legendary (Deut. 32:14; Ps. 22:12[13]; Isa. 2:13; Ezek. 39:18). Both David and Solomon were in charge of it (1 Kgs. 4:13, 19). It was seized by various foreign powers during the vicissitudes of Israel's history (cf. 2 Kgs. 10:33; 14:25). It was an object of prophetic judgment by Jeremiah (22:20), but its return to Israel is a part of the future hope of the prophets (Jer. 50:19; Mic. 7:14).

1317. בָּשְׁנָה ***bošnāh:*** A feminine noun meaning shame. The word indicates the painful emotion and feeling Israel will experience, along with a sense of guilt, disgrace, and embarrassment, because of her worship of idols (Hos. 10:6). Its calf idol will be packed off to Assyria.

1318. בָּשַׁס ***bāšas:*** A verb meaning to trample, to tread. The word indicates the oppression that the rich and powerful exercised on Israel's poor by treading them down (Amos 5:11). It may mean to effect this abuse literally by levying heavy rent on the poor (NASB).

1319. בָּשַׂר ***bāśar:*** A verb meaning to bring news or to bear tidings. The general idea of this word is that of a messenger announcing a message, which may either be bad news (1 Sam. 4:17, the death of Eli's sons) or good news (Jer. 20:15, the birth of Jeremiah). It is often used within the military setting: a messenger coming from battle lines to report the news (2 Sam. 18:19, 20, 26) or victory (1 Sam. 31:9; 2 Sam. 1:20). When used of God's message, this word conveys the victorious salvation which God provides to His people (Ps. 96:2; Isa. 40:9; 52:7; 61:1).

1320. בָּשָׂר ***bāśār:*** A masculine noun whose basic meaning is flesh. The basic meaning is frequently observed in the Old Testament, especially in the literature concerning sacrificial practices (Lev. 7:17) and skin diseases (Lev. 13). It also is used of the animal body (Gen. 41:2–4, 18, 19); the human body (Isa. 10:18); the penis (Gen. 17:11, 13, 14, 23–25); blood relations (Gen. 2:23, 24; 29:14); and human frailty (Gen. 6:3; Job 10:4). This word is further used in the phrase *kōl* (3605) *bāśār,* meaning all flesh, to indicate all living beings (Gen. 6:17, 19; 7:21); animals (Gen. 7:15, 16; 8:17); humanity (Gen. 6:12, 13).

1321. בְּשַׂר ***b***^{e}***śar:*** A masculine noun meaning flesh. It is an Aramaic word found only in the book of Daniel. When used figuratively, it signifies all flesh or humankind (Dan. 2:11) and all creatures (Dan. 4:12[9]).

It is also used in relation to the devouring of flesh in a literal sense (Dan. 7:5).

1322. בֹּשֶׁת ***bōšet:*** A feminine noun denoting shame, humiliation, disgrace. The word depicts the feelings of guilt, disgrace, and embarrassment persons experience because of unfortunate acts or words committed (1 Sam. 20:30; 2 Chr. 32:21). Humiliation and disgrace was brought on God's people through the exile at the hands of Babylon (Ezra 9:7), but He could also bring shame on one's enemies (Job 8:22). Used with its related verb *bôš*, it could express deep shame (Isa. 42:17); with the word face following, it could express a face of shame (2 Chr. 32:21; Ezra 9:7; Jer. 7:19; Dan. 9:7, 8) meaning their "own shame." To be clothed with shame is a figurative expression of the psalmist (Ps. 35:26; 132:18). The phrase "shame of your youth" (Isa. 54:4) refers to Israel's early indiscretions. The biblical authors would sometimes substitute this word for the word *ba'al* in a person's name, emphasizing the shame of ever recognizing such a pagan god (2 Sam. 2:8; Judg. 6:32). In other places and ways, it replaces the word *ba'al* that became so closely attached to the gods of Canaan (Jer. 3:24; cf. 11:13; Hos. 9:10).

1323. בַּת ***bat:*** A feminine noun meaning daughter. It designates a female child (Gen. 30:21; 34:1; Ex. 1:16, 22; Lev. 12:6). Combined with the phrase the king, it refers to a princess (2 Kgs. 9:34; 2 Chr. 22:11; Dan. 11:6). Properly modified, it can refer to a daughter-in-law (Ruth 1:11–13); sister (Ezek. 22:11); half-sister (Gen. 20:12); cousin (Esth. 2:7); or granddaughter (Gen. 46:7). It is used to address a person politely (Ruth 3:10, 11).

It is used to designate women in various ways: of a certain city, land, or nation (Judg. 21:21; Song 3:11; Isa. 3:16, 17); figuratively, it refers to a city as a daughter, e.g., daughter of Zion (Isa. 1:8; 10:32); villages may be referred to as daughters of a central city (Num. 21:25; Josh. 15:45). In more figurative uses, it depicts the character of a person when modified by the following words: daughter of a strange god (Mal. 2:11); or daughter of a troop, i.e., a city of troops or warriors (Mic. 5:1[4:14]; cf. Eccl. 12:4). The phrase daughter (KJV, apple) of an eye is found (Lam. 2:18, NASB, NIV, NKJV), meaning the pupil of the eye. The leech has two daughters that are never satisfied (Prov. 30:15). In at least one place, it refers to branches of a vine that climb a wall (Gen. 49:22, literally, daughter of walking up a wall).

1324. בַּת ***bat:*** A common noun denoting a liquid measure, bath. It equaled one-tenth of a homer or kor or about twenty-three liquid or twenty dry quarts (Ezek. 45:14). It is mentioned as a liquid measure of oil (Ezek. 45:14); wine (2 Chr. 2:10[9]); and water (1 Kgs. 7:26). Some authorities think another bath existed equaling twice the capacity of the better-known bath.

1325. בַּת ***bat:*** An Aramaic masculine noun meaning bath. This is the same liquid measure discussed under #1324. Six hundred baths of wine would have equaled about 2,300 quarts or about six hundred gallons (Ezra 7:22). King Artaxerxes of Persia ordered this amount of wine to be supplied to Ezra as he requested.

1326. בָּתָה ***bāṯāh:*** A feminine noun indicating a wasteland, devastation, desert, waste. Isaiah prophesied that the Lord would turn Jerusalem into a wasteland because of its failure to produce good fruit (Isa. 5:6).

1327. בַּתָּה ***battāh:*** A feminine noun indicating steep, desolate; precipice, steep ravines. The word describes the ravines or valleys (KJV) as deep or steep where the Assyrians will settle when they come to attack Israel (Isa. 7:19).

1328. בְּתוּאֵל ***beṯû'ēl:*** A proper noun designating Bethuel:

A. He was the son of Nahor, brother of Abraham. He became the father of Rebekah, Isaac's wife. Isaac told Jacob to get a wife from the house of Bethuel for Jacob (Gen. 28:1–2). He was an ancestor of the Arameans (Gen. 22:22, 23; 24:15, 24).

B. The name of a town that the sons of Shimei, a Simeonite, and his brothers inhabited (1 Chr. 4:27–30).

1329. בְּתוּל ***beṯûl:*** A proper noun designating Bethul (Josh. 19:4).

1330. בְּתוּלָה ***beṯûlāh:*** A feminine noun meaning virgin. Some scholars prefer to translate the term loosely as maiden or young woman. Yet in Genesis 24:16, Rebekah is described as a beautiful woman and a *beṯûlāh*. The text states that no man had known Rebekah—that is, had sexual relations with her. Also, Judges 21:12 states that there were "four hundred young *beṯûlāh*, that had known no man by lying with any male." In these verses, this Hebrew word certainly connotes virginity. But in Joel 1:8, the Lord describes the *beṯûlāh* mourning for the husband of her youth. In this case, the word means young woman. Moreover, the word also refers to cities or countries that are personified as females (Isa. 37:22; 47:1; Jer. 18:13; 31:4, 21; Amos 5:2). For further occurrences of this Hebrew word, see Deuteronomy 22:23, 28; Judges 19:24; 2 Samuel 13:2, 18; 1 Kings 1:2; Esther 2:2; Zechariah 9:17.

1331. בְּתוּלִים ***beṯûliym:*** A feminine noun meaning virginity, virgin, or maiden. It is primarily used to describe the sexual purity or chastity of a young woman. Variations on this theme show it is used in contrast to a defiled or impure woman (Deut. 22:14); to signify the virginal state of a woman to be married (Lev. 21:13); or to signify the virginal state of young women in general (Judg. 11:37).

1332. בִּתְיָה ***bityāh:*** A proper noun designating Bithiah (1 Chr. 4:18).

1333. בָּתַק ***bāṯaq:*** A verb meaning to thrust through, cut up, slaughter, cut to pieces. It describes a terrifying treatment of the inhabitants of Jerusalem because of their unfaithfulness toward the Lord and their lewdness with pagan nations (Ezek. 16:40).

1334. בָּתַר ***bāṯar:*** A verb meaning to cut or divide into pieces. The verb implies from its context that Abraham did not cut the dove and young pigeon in half during the covenantal ritual described in Genesis 15:10.

1335. בֶּתֶר ***beṯer:*** A masculine noun indicating a piece cut off, a half cut off. It describes the pieces of sacrificial meat produced when Abraham cut a three-year-old ram and a three-year-old goat in two during a covenantal ritual (Gen. 15:10). It also describes half of a calf cut in two for a pagan ritual (Jer. 34:18) and condemns to death those who took part in the ceremony (Jer. 34:19).

1336. בֶּתֶר ***beṯer:*** This is a masculine proper noun that refers to Bether (Song 2:17, KJV, NASB). Some translators interpret this as a masculine noun meaning rugged (Song 2:17, NIV).

1337. בַּת רַבִּים ***baṯ rabbiym:*** A proper noun designating Bath Rabbim (Song 7:4[5]).

1338. בִּתְרוֹן ***biṯrôn:*** A proper noun designating Bithron (2 Sam. 2:29).

1339. בַּת־שֶׁבַע ***baṯ-šeḇaʻ:*** A proper noun designating Bathsheba, the name of one of David's wives. She bore Solomon as a result of David's adultery. David murdered her husband Uriah (2 Sam. 11:1—12:24). The name means "daughter of an oath." Her father was Eliam (2 Sam. 11:3; cf. 1 Chr. 3:5). Her first son died, after which she bore David four more sons (1 Chr. 3:5). She secured the ascension of her son Solomon to the throne (1 Kgs. 1:1—2:19). She is called Bathshua in 1 Chronicles 3:5.

1340. בַּת שׁוּעַ ***baṯ šûaʻ:*** A proper noun designating Bath-shua:

A. Wife of Judah (1 Chr. 2:3).

B. Alternate spelling for Bathsheba, the wife of David (1 Chr. 3:5).

ג Gimel

1341. גֵּא *gē':* An adjective meaning haughty, prideful. The word describes the character and attitude of Moab toward Israel (16:6). It has the same meaning as *gē'eh* (1343).

1342. גָּאָה *gā'āh:* A verb meaning to rise, to grow up, to exalt, to lift up. It is used physically of a stream in Ezekiel 47:5, "The waters were risen"; and of plants in Job 8:11, "Can the rush grow up without mire?" In a figurative sense, it speaks of a lifting up or exaltation (specifically of God). The verb emphatically describes God's matchless power in Miriam's song (Ex. 15:1, 21). This is the key usage of *gā'āh*: The Lord only is highly exalted. The horse and rider He easily casts into the sea; He alone legitimately lifts up the head, as Job admits in Job 10:16. None can stand before Him. Some Hebrew words derived from this one express an important negative theme—that of lifting up of one's self in wrongful pride against the rightful place of God: *gē'eh* (1343); *ga'awāh* (1346); and *gā'ôn* (1347).

1343. גֵּאֶה *gē'eh:* An adjective meaning proud, haughty. The word describes an attitude of pride in persons that the Lord will judge (Job 40:11, 12; Ps. 94:2; Prov. 15:25) at the right time (Isa. 2:12). A whole nation can be depicted as haughty (Jer. 48:29). These persons set traps and snares for the righteous (Ps. 140:5[6]). The opposite attitude and character trait is humility which is preferred to an arrogant and proud demeanor (Prov. 16:19).

1344. גֵּאָה *gē'āh:* A feminine noun denoting pride, haughtiness. This attitude and character trait is hated by true wisdom along with evil actions, perverted talk, and arrogance (Prov. 8:13).

1345. גְּאוּאֵל *ge'û'ēl:* A proper noun designating Geuel (Num. 13:15).

1346. גַּאֲוָה *ga'awāh:* A feminine noun referring to majesty, pride, arrogance; rage. In a good sense, the word can refer to the exaltation or loftiness of God (Deut. 33:26; Ps. 68:34[35]). It refers figuratively to the pride of Israel, God, as her majesty (Deut. 33:29). It describes the activity of the sea as a raging or swelling of its waters (Ps. 46:3[4]). It describes the haughty, prideful attitude of the wicked (Ps. 10:2; 31:18[19], 23[24]; Isa. 9:9[8]); a pride that destroys them (Prov. 29:23). The warriors of Babylon are termed God's instruments to judge His people and referred to as the Lord's proudly exulting ones (Isa. 13:3; cf. Zeph. 3:11), a pride the Lord used to His purposes.

1347. גָּאוֹן *gā'ôn:* A masculine noun designating pride, majesty, arrogance, excellence. It refers to the exalted majesty or excellence of the Lord (Ex. 15:7; Isa. 24:14; Mic. 5:4[3]) and even to His redeemed people and their pride in Him (Isa. 4:2). It is used in a neutral sense to describe the proud, high waves of the sea (Job 38:11) and the thick growth or thicket around some areas of the Jordan (Jer. 12:5). Israel, Jacob, Judah, and Israel are all depicted as possessing excessive pride (Jer. 13:9; Amos 6:8), or, in some cases, these references may have a positive thrust to them.

1348. גֵּאוּת *gē'ûṯ:* A feminine abstract noun referring to majesty, pride; surging, swelling. The word praises the exaltation of God (Ps. 93:1; Isa. 26:10) and His exalted or excellent works (Isa. 12:5; NIV, glorious). It refers figuratively to the proud crown of Ephraim that will cause her to go into captivity (Isa. 28:1, 3). In a negative sense, it mentions those who speak proudly (Ps. 17:10). It describes the rising, swelling waves of the sea (Ps. 89:9[10]) over which the Lord rules.

1349. גַּאֲיוֹן *ga'ayôn:* An adjective meaning proud, haughty, arrogant. The word refers to those persons who heap contempt and abuse on those who trusted in God (Ps. 123:4), acting arrogantly toward them.

1350. גְּאוּלִים *ge'ûliym*, גָּאַל *gā'al:* A verb meaning to redeem or act as a kinsman-redeemer. The word means to act as a redeemer for a deceased kinsman (Ruth 3:13); to redeem or buy back from bondage (Lev. 25:48); to redeem or buy back a kinsman's possessions (Lev. 25:26); to avenge a kinsman's murder (Num. 35:19); to redeem an object through a payment (Lev. 27:13). Theologically, this word is used to convey God's redemption of individuals from spiritual death and His redemption of the nation of Israel from Egyptian bondage and also from exile (see Ex. 6:6).

1351. גָּאַל *gā'al:* A verb meaning to defile, to pollute, to stain, to make impure. The word means to be defiled, as when one's hands are polluted by blood (Isa. 59:3). God's garments are stained (*gā'al*) by blood from His judgments on nations (Isa. 63:3). Daniel refused to defile himself with unclean food in Babylon (Dan. 1:8). The word is used in a technical sense to define those who were defiled or polluted so that they could not take part in the priesthood (Ezra 2:62; Neh. 7:64). Jerusalem itself became defiled by her rebellious actions (Zeph. 3:1). Defiling the Lord's altar was equivalent to defiling Him (Mal. 1:7, 12).

1352. גֹּאַל *gō'al:* A masculine noun designating defilement, pollution. The word refers to cultic defilement brought about through forbidden marriages with non-Israelites by priests of Israel (Neh. 13:29).

1353. גְּאֻלָּה *ge'ullāh:* A feminine singular noun meaning redemption.

The term is typically used in legal texts denoting who can redeem (Lev. 25:24, 31, 32, 48); what they can redeem (Lev. 25:26); when (Lev. 25:26, 51, 52); and for how much (Lev. 25:26, 51, 52). Redemption was a means by which property remained in families or clans. The best picture of this custom in the Bible is Ruth 4:6, 7.

1354. גַּב *gaḇ:* A masculine noun meaning convex surface, back, mound. The term designates the back of humans (Ps. 129:3) or cherubim (Ezek. 10:12). It denotes a mound used as a forbidden religious high place, a place of worship (Ezek. 16:24, 31, 39). It may be used as a technical term for the height of an altar (Ezek. 43:13, NIV, KJV) or its base molding (NASB). It refers to the thick part or protrusion of a shield (Job 15:26; cf. NIV, NASB, KJV [boss or knob of a shield], NKJV). It describes the eyebrows (Lev. 14:9) or even the rim of a wheel (1 Kgs. 7:33; Ezek. 1:18).

1355. גַּב *gaḇ:* An Aramaic masculine noun denoting side, back. The word occurs once in one of Daniel's visions. It refers to the backside of a leopard where, strangely, four wings were attached (Dan. 7:6).

1356. גֵּב *gēḇ:* I. A masculine noun designating a pit, ditch, well, cistern, trench. It refers figuratively to ditches (2 Kgs. 3:16) dug to receive a deluge of unexpected water predicted by Elisha. It also indicates cisterns (Jer. 14:3; KJV, pits).

II. A masculine noun indicating a beam. It describes a part of the covering structure of the Temple (1 Kgs. 6:9). The beams were made of cedar. Others think it may be a technical architectural term.

1357. גֵּב *gēḇ:* A masculine noun depicting a locust. The word refers to a swarm of locusts used figuratively to describe people engaged in plundering spoil (Isa. 33:4).

1358. גֹּב *gōḇ:* An Aramaic masculine noun meaning den, pit. It describes an enclosed area where lions were kept (Dan. 6:7[8], 12[13]). The entrance to the den could be closed and sealed (Dan. 6:17[18]).

1359. גֹּב *gōḇ*, גּוֹב *gôḇ:* A proper noun designating Gob (2 Sam. 21:18, 19).

1360. גֶּבֶא *geḇe':* A masculine noun referring to a cistern or marsh. It refers to something from which water can be scooped or drawn (Isa. 30:14), either a cistern or a naturally occurring marshy (Ezek. 47:11) area.

1361. גָּבַהּ *gāḇah:* A verb meaning to be high, exalted, arrogant. It describes anything that is literally tall or high, such as a tree or vine (Ezek. 19:11); the heavens (Job 35:5; Ps. 103:11; Isa. 55:9), people (1 Sam. 10:23). It is used figuratively to refer to persons or things of high or great dignity: God (Isa. 5:16); God's ways (Isa. 55:9); the Servant of the Lord will be high and exalted before Him

(Isa. 52:13); kings who are exalted by the Lord (Job 36:7). It refers to pride or being lofty, literally exalted in heart, in either a good sense (2 Chr. 17:6) or more often in a bad sense. One can be lofty or haughty (Ps. 131:1; Prov. 18:12). It has the same meaning without being combined with heart (Isa. 3:16; Jer. 13:15; Ezek. 16:50). In certain uses of the word, it means to make high, raise up, or exalt various things: trees (Ezek. 17:24); a wall (2 Chr. 33:14); a gate (Prov. 17:19), especially to lift up the humble or lowly (Ezek. 21:26[31]) according to God's judgments; flames or sparks of fire (Job 5:7).

1362. גָּבֹהַּ ***gāḇōah:*** An adjective denoting high, proud, lofty. The word describes an attitude of haughtiness or arrogance (Ps. 101:5; Prov. 16:5), which the Lord hates. Patience is better than haughtiness (Eccl. 7:8). It refers to Assyria figuratively as a high tree (Ezek. 31:3).

1363. גֹּבַהּ ***gōḇah:*** A masculine noun referring to height, grandeur, dignity. Used literally, it refers to the tall aspects of something: buildings, trees, persons, heaven (1 Sam. 17:4; Job 11:8; Ezek. 1:18; 19:11; 31:10, 14; Amos 2:9). It is employed figuratively to depict grandeur or dignity (Job 40:10) and in a negative sense excessive pride or arrogance (Ps. 10:4; Prov. 16:18; Jer. 48:29).

1364. גָּבוֹהַּ ***gāḇôah,*** גָּבֹהַּ ***gāḇōah:*** An adjective denoting high, exalted, proud. It is used to denote items that are literally high: mountains (Gen. 7:19); trees (Isa. 10:33); persons (1 Sam. 16:7); or any high or exalted thing (in a figurative sense, too) (Ezek. 21:26[31]). It refers figuratively to haughty persons in the phrase the eyes of the proud (Isa. 5:15) and also denotes a high position in rank or authority (Eccl. 5:8[7]).

1365. גַּבְהוּת ***gaḇhûṯ:*** A feminine noun indicating lofty or arrogant. It is used to refer to the arrogant or proud look of the eyes of persons (Isa. 2:11) whose pride will be humbled by the Lord (Isa. 2:17).

1366. גְּבוּל ***g^e^ḇûl:*** A masculine noun designating a border, boundary, or territory; barrier, wall. It is used to point out the limits or boundaries of territories (1 Sam. 13:18) or borderland of geographical areas (Ps. 78:54). It may refer to the territory enclosed (Gen. 47:21; Ex. 8:2[7:27]; Deut. 19:3; Josh. 13:26). It depicts the limits God set for various aspects of His creation (Ps. 104:9) but also the man-made boundary markers set by people (Deut. 19:14; Prov. 22:28) that were to be respected. As a technical architectural term, it refers to lattice work, a barrier, or a wall (Ezek. 40:12) and also to some kind of border work (Ezek. 43:13, 17, 20). Figuratively, it is used to refer to a territory, a border of darkness, or holiness (Ps. 78:54; Mal. 1:4).

1367. גְּבוּלָה g^ebûlāh: A feminine noun indicating a territory or boundary. The word describes the fixed limits the Lord has set for the entire earth, including its seasonal variations (Ps. 74:17). The word depicts the fixed boundaries of the various nations and boundaries set by God (Isa. 10:13) or a certain territory or area around a city (Num. 32:33). It denotes the boundary lines set up to define an area (Num. 34:2, 12) and sections or rows within a garden for planting various crops (Isa. 28:25).

1368. גִּבּוֹר gibbôr, גִּבֹּר gibbōr: An adjective meaning brave, strong, mighty. The word refers to God Himself as *'el* (413) *gibbôr*, usually rendered as the Mighty God (Isa. 10:21; Jer. 32:18). It is used to describe the Child born to rule and govern God's kingdom as Mighty God (Isa. 9:6[5]). The Lord is depicted as a mighty one for His people Israel, mighty to save (Deut. 10:17; Ps. 24:8; Zeph. 3:17). Angels are depicted as mighty in strength (Ps. 103:20). It describes the might and power of the messianic King (Ps. 45:3[4]).

The word means manly, strong, vigorous, and was a term of approbation (Gen. 10:8, 9; 1 Sam. 14:52; Ps. 112:2). It could be used of animals, such as a lion (Prov. 30:30), the mightiest beast. It refers regularly to warriors, heroes, champions in battle (1 Sam. 17:51; 2 Sam. 20:7; 2 Kgs. 24:16; Isa. 21:17). It could be used in a bad sense to denote heroes at drinking wine (Isa. 5:22).

1369. גְּבוּרָה g^ebûrāh: A feminine noun denoting strength, power, might. The word depicts the nature of God's mighty deeds. It describes the strength of the Lord's right hand that delivers His anointed (Ps. 20:6[7]), meaning all of His powerful acts as well as His power and might in general (Deut. 3:24; 1 Chr. 29:11, 12; Job 26:14; Ps. 65:6[7]; 66:7). It describes the strength of various things: animals (Job 41:12[4]; Ps. 147:10); people (Judg. 8:21; Eccl. 9:16). It indicates the might or power by which the Lord's powerful king reigns (1 Chr. 29:30); or the bravery and valor of the king's warriors (Judg. 8:21; Prov. 8:14; Isa. 3:25). It refers to the strength of persons that may prolong their lives (Ps. 90:10). Its usage is flexible and can refer to the power of the sun (Judg. 5:31); or the strength of an army or military plan (2 Kgs. 18:20).

1370. גְּבוּרָה g^ebûrāh: An Aramaic feminine noun indicating power, might. In context, it refers to God's revelation of His secrets to people. In an important sequence of verses, it is asserted that God's power or strength to reveal His plans are His alone (Dan. 2:20), but He shares it to a limited extent with His servants (Dan. 2:23).

1371. גִּבֵּחַ gibbēaḥ: An adjective meaning bald. It refers to a person's head from which all hair has fallen out (Lev. 13:41). This unnatural condition did not make a person unclean.

1372. גַּבַּחַת ***gabbaḥaṯ:*** A feminine noun depicting a bald forehead, forehead; barrenness. It refers to the baldness of one's forehead, bald at the front (Lev. 13:42, 43). And it indicates a bare spot on something, i.e., a garment, etc. (Lev. 13:55).

1373. גַּבַּי ***gabbay:*** A proper noun designating Gabbai (Neh. 11:8).

1374. גֵּבִים ***gēḇiym:*** A proper noun designating Gebim (Isa. 10:31).

1375. גָּבִיעַ ***gāḇiya‘:*** A masculine noun indicating a cup, bowl. It points to a bowl or drinking cup (Gen. 44:2, 12, 16, 17). And it denotes the golden cups on the lampstand for the Tabernacle (Ex. 25:31, 33; 37:17, 19). It refers to a cup for wine (Jer. 35:5).

1376. גְּבִיר ***g^{e}ḇiyr:*** A masculine noun referring to a lord, ruler, master. It occurs in Isaac's blessing of Jacob, describing Jacob as the future master and lord over his brother Esau and his descendants (Gen. 27:29, 37).

1377. גְּבִירָה ***g^{e}ḇiyrāh:*** A feminine noun depicting a queen, a lady. In general, the word denotes a woman or mistress (Gen. 16:4, 8, 9; 2 Kgs. 5:3). As a more formal term, it means the title of the king's mother, the queen mother (1 Kgs. 15:13; 2 Kgs. 10:13). It is used as the title of Pharaoh's wife in Egypt (1 Kgs. 11:19). Sons of this female were considered full brothers of the king (2 Kgs. 10:13).

1378. גָּבִישׁ ***gāḇiyš:*** A masculine noun denoting a pearl, crystal, jasper. It is a semiprecious stone mentioned in Job 28:18, where it is compared unfavorably with the value of wisdom (NASB, crystal; NIV, jasper; KJV, pearls; NKJV, quartz).

1379. גָּבַל ***gāḇal:*** A verb meaning to set bounds or boundaries, to set limits. It describes the process of setting bounds around something or making a boundary (Ex. 19:12, 23; Deut. 19:14); or it depicts something that bounds or limits an area, such as the Jordan, which served to bound the territory of Benjamin on the east (Josh. 18:20). Used with the preposition b^e, it means to border on some other area or land (Zech. 9:2).

1380. גְּבַל ***g^{e}ḇal:*** A proper noun designating Gebal, a city in Phoenicia (Ezek. 27:9).

1381. גְּבָל ***g^{e}ḇāl:*** A proper noun designating Gebal, an area south of the Dead Sea (Ps. 83:7[8]).

1382. גִּבְלִי ***giḇliy:*** I. A masculine proper noun indicating inhabitants of an area. It refers to the Gebalites, the inhabitants of the city of Gebal, a city not yet conquered in Joshua's day (Josh. 13:5). They were skilled workers with wood and stone (1 Kgs. 5:18[32]).

II. A masculine noun referring to Gebalites who are specifically depicted as excellent craftsmen in stone and timber (1 Kgs. 5:18[32]).

1383. גַּבְלֻת ***gab̲lut̲:*** A feminine noun designating a twisting, braiding. The word describes the way chains of pure gold were joined together or connected for stability and beauty as a part of the high priest's outfit (Ex. 28:22; 39:15). Some suggest that the word means welded together.

1384. גִּבֵּן ***gibbēn:*** A word denoting a hunchback condition. It describes a person with an abnormally curved or hunched back. This condition disqualified a descendant of Aaron from serving at the Lord's altar (Lev. 21:20).

1385. גְּבִינָה ***g^{e}b̲iynāh:*** A feminine noun indicating cheese. It is used figuratively of God curdling Job like cheese as a picture of suffering (Job. 10:10).

1386. גַּבְנֹון ***gab̲nôn:*** A masculine noun meaning high, rugged, high arched. It describes the physical appearance of the mountain of Bashan (Ps. 68:15[16], 16[17]). Some translate it as a high hill (KJV), many peaks (NASB), rugged (NIV), each trying to catch the impression conveyed by the psalmist of this sacred mountain.

1387. גֶּבַע ***geb̲a':*** A proper noun designating Geba (Gaba), a town allotted to Benjamin (Josh. 18:24) which was also appointed as a Levitical city (Josh. 21:17; 1 Chr. 6:60; 8:6). It was situated in northern Judah (2 Kgs. 23:8). The exiles from Babylon resettled the city (Ezra 2:26; Neh. 7:30; 11:31; 12:29). It was about six miles north of Jerusalem. Asa, king of Judah, fortified it. Judah was defined as "from Geba to Beersheba" (2 Kgs. 23:8).

1388. גִּבְעָא ***gib̲'ā':*** A proper noun designating Gibea (1 Chr. 2:49).

1389. גִּבְעָה ***gib̲'āh:*** A feminine noun denoting a hill. It often simply refers to a hill, not a mountain (Ex. 17:9, 10; 2 Sam. 2:25) but often with negative implications that Israel used these natural locations as illicit places of worship of foreign gods (1 Kgs. 14:23; 2 Kgs. 17:10; Jer. 2:20). It often stands poetically in a parallel relationship with Hebrew *hār,* mountain, and means the same thing (Deut. 33:15; Ps. 72:3; 114:4, 6; Isa. 2:2, 14; 30:17, 25; Joel 3:18[4:18]). It is combined with a following word to designate a specific hill: teacher's hill; hill of Moreh (Judg. 7:1); hill of foreskins, Gibeath Haaraloth (Josh. 5:3); hill of God (1 Sam. 10:5; NIV, Gibeah of God). It designates in general the hills where Jerusalem is located (Zeph. 1:10).

1390. גִּבְעָה ***gib̲'āh:*** A proper noun designating Gibeah:

A. A city allotted to Judah located in the hills of Hebron (Josh. 15:57).

B. A location and/or city in the mountains of Ephraim. The name means "hill" and is so translated in a few places. Eleazar, Aaron's son, was buried there (Josh. 24:33). Its exact location is not yet determined.

C. A town allotted to Benjamin (Josh. 18:28). The men of the city raped and killed a Levite's concubine, and the city was practically destroyed because of the act (Judg. 19:20). Isaiah refers to it, as does Hosea (5:8; 9:9; 10:9), each time as an example of wickedness and a picture of the judgment of God on such behavior. However, it also served as the capital for Saul, Israel's first king (1 Sam. 10:10–26; 11:4). It is translated as "hill" (NASB) in 2 Samuel 6:3, 4 by some translations and not at all by the NIV in 2 Samuel 6:4.

1391. גִּבְעוֹן ***gib̲ʿôn:*** A proper noun designating Gibeon. A mighty city inhabited by Hivites (Horites?) who deceived Joshua and Israel into making a treaty of peace with them (Josh. 9:1–27). It was a powerful city (2 Sam. 10:2), and the surrounding peoples attacked it because it had made a treaty with Israel. Joshua and Israel, however, later fought with Gibeon and defeated a powerful coalition of Canaanite kings. God mightily intervened, and the sun "stood still" over Gibeon until their enemies were defeated (Josh. 10:1–15). The city was given to the tribe of Benjamin but became a Levitical city (Josh. 18:25). Several momentous events occurred in the city (2 Sam. 2:12–24; 20:8; 21:1–11). People from the city helped rebuild Jerusalem's walls (Neh. 3:7; 7:25). Jeremiah cursed a false prophet from Gibeon (Jer. 28:1). It is located at El-Jib about 6 miles northwest of Jerusalem.

1392. גִּבְעֹל ***gib̲ʿōl:*** A masculine noun meaning in bud, in bloom. It refers to the crop status of flax. It was in bloom and therefore destroyed during the seventh plague of hail (Ex. 9:31).

1393. גִּבְעֹנִי ***gib̲ʿôniy:*** A proper noun designating Gibeonites (2 Sam. 21:1–4, 9; 1 Chr. 12:4; Neh. 3:7).

1394. גִּבְעַת ***gib̲ʿat̲:*** A proper noun designating Gibeath (Josh. 18:28).

1395. גִּבְעָתִי ***gib̲ʿāt̲iy:*** A proper noun designating Gibeathite (1 Chr. 12:3).

1396. גָּבַר ***gāb̲ar:*** A verb meaning to be strong, to prevail. It may refer to human effort or physical strength (Eccl. 10:10). It is used to indicate superior strength or success over someone else or something, as when Israel prevailed over Amalek (Ex. 17:11). It indicates something is more abundant or superior to something else (Gen. 49:26); it swells and becomes dominant (Gen. 7:18–20; Jer. 9:3[2]). In a temporal sense, it means to remain, to prevail (Gen. 7:24). It is used figuratively to describe the unity and strength of friendship (1 Sam. 1:23), such as David and Jonathan's. The godly prevail or are successful because the Lord strengthens them (1 Sam. 2:9; Zech. 10:6). In Daniel 9:27, it is used in a form of the verb that means to cause a covenant to be established or, possibly, to cause a covenant to prevail (NIV, confirm a covenant; NASB, make a firm covenant; KJV, confirm the covenant).

1397. גֶּבֶר *ge̱ber:* A masculine noun meaning man, mighty (virile) man, warrior. It is used of man but often contains more than just a reference to gender by referring to the nature of a man, usually with overtones of spiritual strength or masculinity, based on the verb *gāḇar* (1396), meaning to be mighty. The word is used to contrast men with women and children (Ex. 10:11) and to denote warrior ability (Jer. 41:16). The fifteen occurrences of the word in Job are significant, presenting a vast contrast between the essence of man (even a good one) and God (Job 4:17; 22:2). This contrast only adds more force to the passage in Zechariah 13:7 where God calls Himself *geḇer.* This passage points to the coming of Jesus—the One who as God would take on sinful human nature. He is the Man (the Shepherd of the sheep).

1398. גֶּבֶר *geḇer:* A proper noun designating Geber (1 Kgs. 4:19).

1399. גְּבַר *g^eḇar:* A masculine noun meaning man. This is the construct of the Hebrew word *geḇer* (1397) and has the same meaning. It is found in the Psalms to describe a male who is upright before the Lord. He is described as a blameless man, literally, a man of no shame (Ps. 18:25[26]).

1400. גְּבַר *g^eḇar:* An Aramaic masculine singular noun meaning man. It occurs ten times. See the word *geḇer* (1397).

1401. גִּבָּר *gibbar:* An Aramaic masculine noun meaning mighty one, warrior, hero. This word is used only once in the Bible, where it is attached to another word meaning strength. It translates as "mighty one" or "strongest soldier" (Dan. 3:20).

1402. גִּבָּר *gibbār:* A proper noun designating Gibbar (Ezra 2:20).

1403. גַּבְרִיאֵל *gaḇriy'ēl:* A proper noun designating Gabriel (Dan. 8:16; 9:21).

1404. גְּבֶרֶת *g^eḇereṯ:* A noun meaning lady, queen, mistress. In many cases, this word refers to either a woman who is a mistress or to the servant of a mistress (Gen. 16:4, 8, 9; 2 Kgs. 5:3; Prov. 30:23). Also, it refers to a lady of a kingdom, that is, the queen (Isa. 47:5, 7).

1405. גִּבְּתוֹן *gibb^eṯôn:* A proper noun designating Gibbethon (Josh. 19:44; 21:23; 1 Kgs. 15:27; 16:15, 17).

1406. גָּג *gāg:* A masculine noun designating a roof, a top. It indicates something that covers the top of a structure. It describes various roofs: a house roof (Deut. 22:8); a flat roof (1 Sam. 9:25, 26); a palace roof (2 Sam. 11:2); or roof of a tower (Judg. 9:51). Persons could walk about and gather on these roofs. Illicit altars were sometimes located on roofs (2 Kgs. 23:12; Jer. 19:13), as in the time of Ahaz, a wicked king. Lamentations and wailing took place on rooftops from where the destruction of a city or village was visible (Isa. 15:3). The corner of a roof depicts a meager and inadequate place to live (Prov. 21:9). It refers to the top of the altar of incense (Ex. 30:3; 37:26).

1407. גַּד gad: A masculine noun referring to coriander seed. It is used in a simile or comparison to describe what manna was like (Ex. 16:31; Num. 11:7). It is an Eurasian aromatic herb. This word refers to its seed as fruit.

1408. גַּד gad: A masculine proper noun denoting fortune, false god. It refers to a deity named Gad but means fortune (Isa. 65:11, NASB, NIV; KJV, troop; NKJV, Gad, meaning idolatrous practices).

1409. גַּד gad: A. A masculine noun meaning good fortune. The word indicates luck or fortune and is therefore given by Leah as the name for her maid's son, Gad (Gen. 30:11, NASB; NIV). Others prefer to render the word as a troop (KJV, NKJV).

B. A masculine noun indicating a troop. It is translated as a troop often (Gen. 30:11, KJV, NKJV); others favor rendering it as good fortune (NASB, NIV). It is rendered as troop in Isaiah 65:11 (KJV); as fortune, a god, (NASB, NIV); or as Gad, meaning idolatrous practices (NKJV). A careful study of the context of its use is necessary to decide which rendering is most likely correct.

1410. גָּד gāḏ: A proper noun designating Gad:

A. The seventh son of Jacob born through Zilpah, Leah's maidservant (Gen. 30:11). The name means "good fortune."

B. The tribe of Gad, the descendants of Jacob's seventh son. He bore many sons himself (Gen. 46:16; 49:19; Ex. 1:4). Jacob prophesied that Gad would be a fighter and prevail against his troublesome opponents (Gen. 49:19). Moses' prophetic blessing echoes this (Deut. 33:20). This tribe, along with Manasseh and Reuben was allotted land on the east side of the Jordan (Transjordan). Its western border was the Jordan River from the southern tip of Galilee almost down to the northern tip of the Dead Sea. Manasseh bounded it on the north, Reuben on the south (Josh. 13:13–28). The vicissitudes of Gad's history saw the tribe and tribal territory change hands numerous times: (2 Sam. 23:31—24:5; 2 Kgs. 15:29; Jer. 49:1–7). Ezekiel's vision of a new Temple has a portion of land for Gad (48:27, 28, 34).

C. A prophet who wrote records of David's reign that are now lost (1 Chr. 29:29). He spoke to David as a prophet several times during his prophetic activity (1 Sam. 22:5; 2 Sam. 24:11–19). He was also active in Temple worship administration (2 Chr. 29:25).

1411. גְּדָבַר ***g^edā<u>b</u>ar:*** An Aramaic masculine noun denoting a treasurer. This is one of the many bureaucratic officials of the royal administrators of Babylon. He was in charge of the monies of the king and the kingdom (Dan. 3:2, 3).

1412. גֻּדְגֹּדָה ***gu<u>d</u>gō<u>d</u>ah:*** A proper noun designating Gudgodah (Deut. 10:7).

1413. גָּדַד ***gā<u>d</u>a<u>d</u>:*** A verb meaning to cut, to crowd together. In some cases, this verb is used to describe cutting the skin in mourning (Jer. 16:6; 41:5; 47:5) or in pagan religious practices (1 Kgs. 18:28). God prohibited such pagan rites (Deut. 14:1). This Hebrew verb also means to gather together, such as troops (Mic. 5:1[4:14]) or a crowd (Jer. 5:7).

1414. גְּדַד ***g^e<u>d</u>a<u>d</u>:*** An Aramaic verb meaning to chop, hew, or cut down. It is used to indicate the act of cutting down the symbolic tree in Nebuchadnezzar's dream (Dan. 4:14[11], 23[20]).

1415. גָּדָה ***gā<u>d</u>āh:*** A feminine noun indicating a riverbank. It refers to the banks of the Jordan River when Israel entered the land of Canaan (Josh. 3:15; 4:18) and at other times when it was in a flood stage (1 Chr. 12:15[16]). It is used to refer to the banks of the Euphrates River in a figurative sense (Isa. 8:7).

1416. גְּדוּד ***g^e<u>d</u>û<u>d</u>:*** A masculine noun meaning a band, a troop. It is used to indicate a marauding band, a raiding party, or a group that makes inroads into enemy territory. It sometimes refers to Israel's military (2 Sam. 4:2; 2 Chr. 22:1), but more often, it refers to the marauding enemies of Israel (Gen. 49:19; 1 Sam. 30:8, 15, 23; 1 Kgs. 11:24; 2 Kgs. 5:2; 6:23; 24:2). In some instances, these marauding bands operate independently and are thus labeled as troops of robbers (Hos. 6:9; 7:1). By extension, the word sometimes refers to the actual raid itself (2 Sam. 3:22). On other occasions, it indicates the army in general (Job 29:25) or some division of troops within the army (1 Chr. 7:4; 2 Chr. 25:9, 10, 13; 26:11; Mic. 5:1[4:14]). It is used figuratively for God's chastisements (Job 19:12) and His attacking forces (Job 25:3).

1417. גְּדוּד ***g^e<u>d</u>û<u>d</u>:*** A masculine noun indicating a furrow, edge of furrow, ridge. It depicts the furrows of fertile earth that God waters abundantly (Ps. 65:10[11]), giving bountiful crops as a sign of His goodness.

1418. גְּדוּדָה ***g^e<u>d</u>û<u>d</u>āh:*** A feminine noun denoting a cutting, slashing, incision. It represents ritualistic incisions or cuts inflicted on the hands of Moabites in their hopeless acts of lamentation and mourning, for they were suffering judgment from the Lord (Jer. 48:37).

1419. גָּדוֹל ***gā<u>d</u>ôl,*** גָּדֹל ***gā<u>d</u>ōl,*** הַגְּדוֹלִים ***hagg^e<u>d</u>ôliym:*** An adjective meaning great. The word emphasizes the importance, size, and significance of something or someone. It is used to attribute theological importance in various ways to things of great significance: God's great acts of redemption are emphasized, His great and awesome things (Deut. 10:21; Ps. 71:19; 106:21); His great acts in nature and in general are recognized (Job 5:9; 9:10; 37:5). It is used to describe the might and greatness of God's arm which brought Israel from Egypt (Ex. 15:16). God's presence and character in power, counsel, compassion, and mercy are described as great (Ps. 145:8; Isa. 54:7; Jer. 32:19; Nah. 1:3). It designates persons as influential, masters, great (Gen. 39:9) or as leading persons (2 Kgs. 10:6). Elisha's miracles are great and influential (2 Kgs. 8:4). The word is used to describe an intensity or extent of fear (Deut. 4:34; Prov. 19:19); weeping (Isa. 38:3); evil or sin (Gen. 4:13; 20:9; 39:9). It is used in general to describe whatever is large, numerous, or intent, such as a sea (Num. 34:6); river (Gen. 15:18); wilderness (Deut. 1:19); number (Gen. 12:2; 2 Kgs. 10:19; Jer. 31:8); sound (Gen. 39:14; Ex. 11:6); or one's age (Gen. 10:21; 27:1; 29:16). A few fixed expressions occur using this word: the great king, referring to the king of Assyria (2 Kgs. 18:19, 28); the great (high) priest (Lev. 21:10); the great sea, meaning the Mediterranean Sea (Num. 34:6); the great river meaning the Euphrates (Deut. 1:7).

1420. גְּדוּלָּה ***g^eḏûllāh,*** גְּדֻלָּה ***g^eḏullāh:*** A feminine noun denoting greatness. It depicts the surpassing deeds and acts of God (Ps. 145:6), including His great act in choosing David and making him king (2 Sam. 7:21, 23; 1 Chr. 17:19, 21). Greatness is ascribed to God Himself because of His actions (1 Chr. 29:11; Ps. 145:3). It is used in this way to refer to honorable persons, such as Mordecai (Esth. 10:2; Ps. 71:21). It depicts the great majesty of kingship (Esth. 1:4). It indicates dignity or recognition given as a reward (Esth. 6:3).

1421. גִּדּוּף ***giddûp̱:*** A masculine noun indicating insult, scorn, revilement. It describes God's rejection and scorn of Israel because of their rebellion and scorn toward Him (Isa. 43:28). It describes the scorn Israel's enemies heap on them (Zeph. 2:8). On the other hand, God's people are to endure and not fear the scorn, rejection, and revilings of others (Isa. 51:7).

1422. גְּדוּפָה ***g^eḏûp̱āh:*** A feminine noun denoting a taunt; a reviling. It designates an address or speech placing scorn and reproach on someone or something before others. Jerusalem would become the object of taunts or revilings (NASB) because of her abominations (Ezek. 5:15).

1423. גְּדִי ***g^eḏiy:*** A masculine noun designating a kid, a young goat, or the young of other animals. Followed by the word for goats (*'izzîm*), it refers almost always to the young of goats (Gen. 27:9, 16; 38:17, 20; 1 Sam.

16:20). It was often used as food or a sacrificial animal (Judg. 6:19; 13:15, 19). It was never to be boiled in the milk of its mother (Ex. 23:19; 34:26; Deut. 14:21).

1424. גָּדִי ***gāḏiy:*** A proper noun designating Gadi (2 Kgs. 15:14, 17).

1425. גָּדִי ***gāḏiy:*** A proper noun designating Gadite, a descendant of Gad (Num. 34:14; Deut. 3:12, 16; 4:43; 29:8[7]; Josh. 1:12; 12:6; 13:8; 22:1; 2 Sam. 23:36; 2 Kgs. 10:33; 1 Chr. 5:18, 26; 12:8, 37; 26:32).

1426. גַּדִּי ***gaddiy:*** A proper noun designating Gaddi (Num. 13:11).

1427. גַּדִּיאֵל ***gaddiy'ēl:*** A proper noun designating Gaddiel (Num. 13:10).

1428. גִּדְיָה ***giḏyāh:*** A feminine noun denoting a bank, river. It refers to the banks of the Jordan River at flood time (1 Chr. 12:15[16]). It is used figuratively of the banks of the Euphrates overflowing with the attacking Assyrians as they inundate Israel and Judah (Isa. 8:7).

1429. גְּדִיָּה ***g^eḏiyyāh:*** A feminine noun indicating a kid, a young goat. It is a tender word referring to the young goats pastured by the young maiden that the lover is describing (Song 1:8).

1430. גָּדִישׁ ***gāḏiyš:*** I. A masculine noun denoting a grain stack, a stack of grain. These stacks were in the harvest fields and were easily ignited by fire (Ex. 22:6[5]). Samson destroyed a whole harvest of the Philistines by burning these stacks (Judg. 15:5). They stood in the field and were used when it was well cured (Job 5:26).

II. A masculine noun indicating a tomb, grave mound. It refers to the tomb or burial mound of an influential but wicked person. His tomb is guarded after his burial (Job 21:32).

1431. גָּדַל ***gāḏal:*** A verb meaning to become great, make great, magnify, grow up, grow; promote. It refers to the natural process of a person's development, a child's growing up (Gen. 21:8, 20; 25:27; Ex. 2:10, 11). It indicates that something or someone becomes great or influential in wealth (Gen. 26:13; Jer. 5:27); value (1 Sam. 26:24); or importance (1 Kgs. 10:23; Eccl. 2:9; Dan. 8:9, 10). It indicates the greatness of the Messiah that extends throughout the earth (Mic. 5:4[3]) or to the importance of Jerusalem (Ezek. 16:7).

The verb asserts the greatness of God (2 Sam. 7:22; Ps. 104:1) and His works (Ps. 92:5[6]). In the sense of magnifying something, it refers to magnifying the Lord Himself (Ps. 35:27; 40:16[17]; 70:4[5]), along with His name (2 Sam. 7:26). In some forms, the word means to cause something to grow, become great: hair (Num. 6:5); plants (Isa. 44:14; Jon. 4:10), but it refers to magnifying or making God great as well (Ps. 34:3[4]). The Lord's acts of salvation are made great by Himself (Ps.

18:50[51]). The Lord promised to make Abraham's name great (Gen. 12:2). It means to promote someone to a higher office or position (Esth. 3:1). Used of children, it may mean to bring them up (Isa. 1:2) or educate them (Dan. 1:5). Used in a reflexive sense, the word means to magnify oneself (Ezek. 38:23) or boast (Isa. 10:15; Dan. 11:36, 37).

1432. גָּדֵל ***gādēl:*** An adjective indicating growing up, becoming great, great. Used with certain verbs (*hālak, hālok*), it means to become greater and greater; that is, to increase in wealth and influence (Gen. 26:13). It indicates growing up or getting older (1 Sam. 2:26), as well as increasing in power and greatness (2 Chr. 17:12). Its use in Ezekiel 16:26 is best translated figuratively as lustful neighbors (NASB, NIV; cf. KJV, literally, great of flesh).

1433. גֹּדֶל ***gōdel:*** A masculine noun indicating majesty or greatness. It is used to describe anything large: a great tree (Ezek. 31:7); persons (Ezek. 31:2); in a figurative sense, God's grace (Num. 14:19) or greatness through His mighty acts (Deut. 3:24) and power (Ps. 79:11). The psalmist calls God's greatness excellent (NASB, KJV) or surpassing (NIV) (Ps. 150:2, literally, abundant). It takes on the meaning of arrogance or bravado (Isa. 9:9[8]]) with respect to Israel's rebellions. It indicates the extreme arrogance of the heart of the great king of Assyria that the Lord would bring down (Isa. 10:12).

1434. גָּדִל ***gādil:*** A masculine noun denoting a tassel, a fastoon. It indicates a tassel on a garment (Deut. 22:12). As an architectural term, it denotes chain-like decorations on the capitals of pillars (1 Kgs. 7:17).

1435. גִּדֵּל ***giddēl:*** A proper noun designating Giddel:

A. The head of a family (Ezra 2:47; Neh. 7:49).

B. A servant of Solomon (Ezra 2:56; Neh. 7:58).

1436. גְּדַלְיָה ***gedalyāh,*** גְּדַלְיָהוּ ***gedalyāhû:*** A proper noun designating Gedaliah.

A. The name means "great is the Lord." It describes the son of Ahikam, whom Nebuchadnezzar appointed as his chief minister in Judea after the fall of Jerusalem (586/87 B.C.; 2 Kgs. 25:22). He was joined by other Israelites including Jeremiah (Jer. 40:5–9; 41:1–18; 43:6). This group remained supportive of the king of Babylon (Jer. 40:5–16). Gedaliah was assassinated by Ishmael (2 Kgs. 25:22–25; Jer. 41:1–4). The remnant fled to Egypt.

B. He was a son of Jeduthun and led in the Temple worship with others (1 Chr. 25:3, 9).

C. A priest who had married a foreign woman in Ezra's day (Ezra 10:18).

D. The father of Cushi, the father of the prophet Zephaniah (Zeph. 1:1).

E. An official of Zedekiah who counseled the king to put Jeremiah to death (Jer. 38:1, 4–5).

1437. גִּדַּלְתִּי ***giddaltiy:*** A proper noun designating Giddalti (1 Chr. 25:4, 29).

1438. גָּדַע ***gāḏa':*** A verb meaning to cut down, cut off, cut in pieces; be cut down. It describes cutting off a hand or arm in the sense of cutting one's family line or one's strength (1 Sam. 2:31; Lam. 2:3). It is further used figuratively to describe the cutting off or shattering of two staffs representing Israel or Judah (Zech. 11:10, 14). It describes the cutting down of pagan idols or objects of worship called Asherim (Deut. 7:5; Ezek. 6:6) and depicts the cutting down of the morning star, Lucifer, symbolic for the king of Babylon (Isa. 14:12). The horns or strength of the wicked are cut off (Ps. 75:10[11]).

1439. גִּדְעוֹן ***giḏ'ôn:*** A proper noun designating Gideon, an important judge who delivered the Israelites from the Midianites and a coalition of other peoples in his day by a small hand-picked group of soldiers (Judg. 7:1–8), singled out by the Lord (Judg. 6—7). The Lord Himself sent fear into the camp of the Midianites (Judg. 7:13–14). Gideon's name means "smiter, hewer." The Israelites sought to make him king after he had slain Zebah and Zalmunna, princes of the Midianite coalition (Judg. 8:6–21). He refused the offer. He made a gold ephod, however, which was later worshiped foolishly by the Israelites (Judg. 8:25–27).

He was given the name Jerub-Baal which means "Let Baal contend/fight" because he had challenged the god Baal (Judg. 6:31–22; 8:29–32). He had seventy sons. A son named Abimelech by a concubine arose after him to claim kingship for himself (Judg. 8:29–31). The Israelites soon began to go after Baal when Gideon died.

1440. גִּדְעֹם ***giḏ'ōm:*** A proper noun designating Gidom (Judg. 20:45).

1441. גִּדְעֹנִי ***giḏ'ōniy:*** A proper noun designating Gideoni (Num. 1:11; 2:22; 7:60, 65; 10:24).

1442. גָּדַף ***gāḏap:*** A verb meaning to revile, to blaspheme. It describes the conscious verbal abuse of a person or God (Num. 15:30; 2 Isa. 37:6; Ezek. 20:27). Punishment for this sin was possible death or at least being cut off from the community of God's people.

1443. גָּדַר ***gāḏar:*** A verb indicating to close off, to wall up. It is used figuratively of false prophets failing to erect a wall of stones of truth and justice to stand in the day of battle (Ezek. 13:5; 22:30) around Israel. It describes, again figuratively, the Lord's action to wall up or repair the breeches in the Davidic dynasty of kings (Amos 9:11). In its participial form, it denotes a mason, one who works with stones (2 Kgs. 12:12[13]). Used ironically, the word describes the Lord's building a wall against His unfaithful people (Hos. 2:6[8]), much as He did, seemingly, against Job (19:8).

1444. גֶּדֶר *geḏer:* A masculine noun referring to a wall, a fence. It depicts a stone wall, broken down by a sluggard's neglect (Prov. 24:31). The eastern wall of Ezekiel's visionary Temple is indicated with this word (Ezek. 42:10).

1445. גֶּדֶר *geḏer:* A proper noun designating Geder (Josh. 12:13).

1446. גְּדוֹר *g^{e}ḏôr:* A proper noun designating Gedor:
A. A son of Jehiel (1 Chr. 8:31; 9:37).
B. A city (Josh. 15:58; 1 Chr. 12:7).
C. A city (1 Chr. 4:39).
D. A son of Penuel (1 Chr. 4:4).
E. A son of Jered (1 Chr. 4:18).

1447. גָּדֵר *gāḏēr:* A common noun meaning wall, fence, hedge. It depicts a stone wall of loose stones (Num. 22:24) but also a city wall (Mic. 7:11) or a wall in general (Eccl. 10:8). It denotes a wall of Ezekiel's Temple (Ezek. 42:7). Used in a figurative sense, it refers to the hedge or wall of the Lord's vineyard (Ps. 80:12[13]; Isa. 5:5), which no one could build up and make firm (Ezek. 22:30). An unstable wall is used to depict threatening persons (Ps. 62:3[4]).

1448. גְּדֵרָה *g^{e}ḏērāh:* A feminine noun designating a wall, a hedge, a sheepfold. It refers to a stone pen or sheepfold (Num. 32:16, 36; 1 Sam. 24:3[4]) but also a city wall (Ps. 89:40[41]) or a temple wall (Ezek. 42:12). The wall served as a major defense or stronghold (Ps. 89:40[41]).

1449. גְּדֵרָה *g^{e}ḏērāh:* A proper noun naming a city, Gederah. It is one of the cities lying within the territory of Judah in the deep south near Edom (Josh. 15:36).

1450. גְּדֵרוֹת *g^{e}ḏērôṯ:* A proper noun designating Gederoth (Josh. 15:41; 2 Chr. 28:18).

1451. גְּדֵרִי *g^{e}ḏēriy:* A proper noun designating Gederite (1 Chr. 27:28).

1452. גְּדֵרָתִי *g^{e}ḏērāṯiy:* A proper noun designating Gederathite (1 Chr. 12:4).

1453. גְּדֵרֹתַיִם *g^{e}ḏērōṯayim:* A proper noun designating Gederothaim (Josh. 15:36).

1454. גֵּה *gēh:* A demonstrative pronoun. It stands undoubtedly for *zeh* (2088), this, the normal demonstrative pronoun. This list begins a description of the boundaries of Ezekiel's land (Ezek. 47:13).

1455. גָּהָה *gāhāh:* A verb meaning to cure. It describes the process of recovery from a serious wound. In context, it indicates the unsuccessful attempt to heal Ephraim's sickness of apostasy (Hos. 5:13).

1456. גֵּהָה *gēhāh:* A feminine noun indicating a cure, medicine. A joyful heart is declared to be a good cure or medicine as opposed to a broken spirit (Prov. 17:22).

1457. גָּהַר *gāhar:* A verb meaning to crouch down, to bend. It is used to describe Elijah's posture in prayer on Mount Carmel as he beseeches the Lord for rain (1 Kgs. 18:42). It describes Elisha's crouching over or stretching himself out on the Shunammite's dead son in order to restore him to life (2 Kgs. 4:34, 35).

1458. גַּו *gaw:* A masculine noun meaning back. It refers to someone's back but is used with the verb to cast away to form idioms meaning to cast behind one's back, that is, to forget, ignore, reject. The idiom indicates rejecting the Lord (1 Kgs. 14:9; Ezek. 23:35) or His laws (Neh. 9:26).

1459. גַּו *gaw:* An Aramaic masculine noun denoting interior, midst, middle. It is always used with the preposition b^e meaning in (Ezra 5:7; Dan. 3:25; 4:10[7]); the preposition l^e meaning into (Dan. 3:6, 11); or the preposition *min* (4480) meaning out from (Dan. 3:26).

1460. גֵּו *gēw:* I. A masculine noun meaning back. It depicts the back of a person's body. A fool's back is for lashes or a rod (Prov. 10:13; 19:29; 26:3) so that he might learn wisdom. In a figure of speech, the Lord casts the sins of repentant persons behind His back (Isa. 38:17). Walking on someone's back means to humiliate and denigrate him or her (Isa. 51:23).

II. A masculine noun meaning midst, community. It indicates the fellowship or the midst of a community of persons (Job 30:5) from which the lowly in society are driven.

1461. גּוּב *gûḇ:* A verb meaning digger, plowman, field worker. It is used in a verb form indicating one who digs or plows the ground, a job filled by the poor of the land at the time Israel was sent to Babylon into exile (2 Kgs. 25:12). In general, it means one who works the ground.

1462. גּוֹב *gôḇ,* גּוֹבַי *gôḇay:* A masculine noun designating locusts. The word depicts a swarm or multitude of locusts as indicative of the multitude of Assyria's military personnel (Nah. 3:17). Amos refers to a locust swarm being gathered to destroy crops (Amos 7:1).

1463. גּוֹג *gôg:* A proper noun designating Gog:

A. The name of a descendant of Reuben, the son of Joel (1 Chr. 5:4).

B. The name occurs often in Ezekiel 38 and 39. Ezekiel puts forth an inspired prophecy against him (38:2). He is pictured as a great enemy against God's people. He is from the land of Magog or possibly "from the land of Gog." The name appears in apocalyptic literature which often is highly symbolic and cryptic in meaning. The Lord, at any rate, sets Himself against Gog (38:2).

Gog will lead a coalition of nations against God's people who are then dwelling securely in the land of Israel (Ezek. 38:14–16). But God, in fact, will bring Gog forth and will destroy him and his people. The Lord shows Himself holy in His actions against Gog (Ezek. 38:16; 39:1–8). The Lord spoke about this through other prophets (Ezek. 38:17–18). The multitudes of Gog will be buried in the Valley of Hamon Gog, that is, "multitudes of Gog" (Ezek. 39:15), while God's people will be liberated from the fear and threat of Gog (39:16–29).

1464. גּוּד ***gûḏ:*** A verb meaning to attack, to overcome, to invade. It is used to describe an enemy's attack on Gad and the response of Gad in return (Gen. 49:19) with a wordplay on the letter *gimel* (ג). It describes Babylon's coming invasion of Judah (Hab. 3:16).

1465. גֵּוָה ***gēwāh:*** A feminine noun denoting back, body. It describes the back portion of the human body between the neck and pelvis. In biblical usage, it refers to the back of the wicked person being pierced by an arrow (Job 20:25).

1466. גֵּוָה ***gēwāh:*** A feminine noun indicating pride, a lifting up. It refers to God's action to help a downhearted person, a lifting up or an injection of confidence (NASB) (Job. 22:29). Jeremiah uses the word to describe pride that separates from God's benefits (Jer. 13:17). It designates something from which God tries to keep a person (Job 33:17).

1467. גֵּוָה ***gēwāh:*** A feminine noun referring to pride. It indicates an arrogant, self-centered evaluation of one's actions and character which God will humble (Dan. 4:37[34]).

1468. גּוּז ***gûz:*** A verb meaning to bring in, to pass away. It is used figuratively of life passing away (Ps. 90:10). Literally, it speaks of wind bringing quail over the land from the sea (Num. 11:31).

1469. גּוֹזָל ***gôzzāl:*** A feminine noun referring to a young pigeon, a young bird. It was one of two birds Abraham used in a covenantal ritual (Gen. 15:9). In Deuteronomy 32:11, it refers specifically to the young of an eagle.

1470. גּוֹזָן ***gôzān:*** A proper noun designating Gozan, a city and its surrounding areas conquered by the Assyrians to which Israelites were exiled by the Assyrians (1 Kgs. 17:6; 18:11; 19:12). It was located on a major route through upper Mesopotamia and situated due east of Haran and modern Aleppo.

1471. גּוֹי ***gôy,*** גּוֹיִם ***gôyim,*** הַגּוֹיִם ***hāggôyim:*** A masculine noun meaning nation, people, Gentiles, country. The word is used to indicate a nation or nations in various contexts and settings: it especially indicates the offspring of Abraham that God made into a nation (Gen. 12:2) and thereby set the stage for Israel's appearance in history as a nation (Gen. 18:18; Ps. 106:5). Israel was to be a holy nation (Ex. 19:6). Even the descendants of Abraham that did not come from the seed of Isaac would develop into nations (Gen. 21:13). God can create a nation, even a holy nation like Israel, through the descendants of the person whom He chooses, as He nearly does in the case of Moses when Israel rebels (Ex. 32:10). Edom refers to Israel and Judah as two separate nations (Ezek. 35:10), but God planned for them to be united forever into one nation (Ezek. 37:22). Then they would become the head of the nations (Deut. 28:12). In this overall literary, theological, and historical context, it is clear that Israel would share common ancestors, and would have a sufficient increase in numbers to be considered a nation. It would have a common place of habitation and a common origin, not only in flesh and blood, but in their religious heritage. It would share a common history, culture, society, religious worship, and purposes for the present and the future.

This noun is used to mean nations other than Israel as well; pagan, Gentile, or heathen nations (Ex. 9:24; 34:10; Ezek. 5:6–8), for all the earth and all the nations belong to God (cf. Ex. 19:5). Israel was to keep herself from the false religions, unclean practices, and views of these nations (Ezra 6:21). In the plural, the noun may indicate the generic humankind (Isa. 42:6). In a few instances, the word refers to a group of people rather than to a nation (2 Kgs. 6:18; Ps. 43:1; Isa. 26:2), although the exact translation is difficult in these cases.

The word is used in a figurative sense to refer to animals or insects, such as in Joel 1:6 where it depicts locusts.

1472. גְּוִיָּה g^ewiyyāh: A feminine noun meaning body, corpse, carcass. Most often, this word is used to depict a dead body, either a human, such as Saul (1 Sam. 31:10), or an animal, such as Samson's lion (Judg. 14:8, 9). In the Bible, this word is used to describe the slaughter of a nation as dead bodies are scattered everywhere (Ps. 110:6; Nah. 3:3). Sometimes the word refers to live bodies. But in these cases, the idea of defeat or humiliation is present (Gen. 47:18; Neh. 9:37). When the experience is visionary, however, the word depicts live beings with no humiliation implied (Ezek. 1:11, 23; Dan. 10:6).

1473. גּוֹלָה gôlāh, גֹּלָה gōlāh: A feminine noun meaning captivity, exile, captives, exiles. This word is the feminine participle of *gālāh* (1540). It most often refers to the Babylonian captivity and its captives (2 Kgs. 24:16; Ezek. 1:1) but is also used of the Assyrian captivity (1 Chr. 5:22) and even of the exiles of foreign nations (Jer. 48:7, 11; Amos 1:15). The phrase, children of the captivity, occurs in Ezra and describes those who returned from the captivity in Babylon (Ezra 4:1; 6:19, 20; 10:7, 16).

1474. גּוֹלָן ***gôlān:*** A proper noun designating Golan (Deut. 4:43; Josh. 20:8; 21:27; 1 Chr. 6:71[56]).

1475. גּוּמָּץ ***gûmmāṣ:*** A masculine noun meaning pit. Although this word is used only once in the Old Testament, its meaning is derived from a related Aramaic word, which means to dig. Thus, a pit is the result of digging. The meaning is clear when it is used in Ecclesiastes 10:8: "He that diggeth a pit shall fall into it" (KJV). Furthermore, this meaning is further verified in a similar passage found in Proverbs 26:27, in which a parallel word, *šaḥaṯ* (7845), meaning pit, is used.

1476. גּוּנִי ***gûniy:*** A proper noun designating Guni:

A. A Naphtalite (Gen. 46:24; Num. 26:48; 1 Chr. 7:13).

B. A Gadite (1 Chr. 5:15).

1477. גּוּנִי ***gûniy:*** A proper noun designating Gunites (Num. 26:48).

1478. גָּוַע ***gāwaʿ:*** A verb meaning to expire, to die. The word is apparently from a root meaning to breathe out. This word is used to describe the death of humans and animals in the flood (Gen. 6:17; 7:21). It is used in a repeated formula (along with *mûṯ* [4191], meaning to die) to describe the death of the patriarchs and Ishmael (Gen. 25:8, 17; 35:29; 49:33). Sometimes the context of the word refers to the root meaning of breathing out (Job 34:14; Ps. 104:29). In Zechariah 13:8, the word is used to predict the deaths of two-thirds of the nation of Israel.

1479. גּוּף ***gûp̄:*** A verb meaning to shut. It indicates shutting a city gate (Neh. 7:3), in this case, the gates of Jerusalem during its reconstruction under Nehemiah.

1480. גּוּפָה ***gûp̄āh:*** A feminine noun meaning dead body, corpse. This word appears only twice in the Old Testament and in the same verse. First Chronicles 10:12 describes Saul and his son's dead bodies. The word has a similar meaning to *g^e^wiyyāh* (1472), meaning body, as is demonstrated when that word is used in a parallel passage, 1 Samuel 31:12.

1481. גּוּר ***gûr:*** A verb meaning to sojourn, to dwell as a foreigner; in the reflexive sense, to seek hospitality with. The term is commonly used of the patriarchs who sojourned in Canaan (Gen. 26:3; 35:27); places outside Canaan (Gen. 12:10; 20:1; 21:23; 32:4[5]; 47:4); Naomi and her family in Moab (Ruth 1:1); the exiles in Babylonia (Jer. 42:15). Metaphorically, the term is used of one who worships in God's temple (Ps. 15:1; 61:4[5]). It is used reflexively with the meaning to seek hospitality with in 1 Kings 17:20.

1482. גּוּר ***gûr:*** A masculine noun designating a lion's cub. It refers to a young, aggressive offspring. It is used literally of the young of jackals (Lam. 4:3). It is employed figuratively to depict the ancestor and tribal character of Judah (Gen. 49:9); Dan (Deut.

33:22); in general of the Israelites (Ezek. 19:2, 3, 5). It refers to the Assyrian capital of Nineveh as the lair of a lioness' cub (Nah. 2:11[12]).

1483. גּוּר gûr: A proper noun designating Gur (2 Kgs. 9:27).

1484. גּוֹר gôr: A common noun depicting a cub. It refers figuratively to Babylonians growling or yelling for food to devour (Jer. 51:38) and to the Assyrians as lion cubs fed by the Assyrian war machine of oppression (Nah. 2:12[13]).

1485. גּוּר־בַּעַל gûr-ba'al: A proper noun designating Gur Baal (2 Chr. 26:7).

1486. גּוֹרָל gôrāl: A masculine noun indicating a portion or lot. A lot was cast, probably a stone or stones, to decide questions or appoint persons for various reasons; for apportioning land (Num. 26:55; 33:54; Josh. 18:6, 11); for assignments of various kinds, such as goats on the Day of Atonement (Lev. 16:8–10); priests, singers, musicians, etc. to their duties (1 Chr. 24:5, 31; 25:8; 26:13); for living in Jerusalem (Neh. 11:1), etc. (Judg. 20:9; Neh. 10:34[35]); for allotting slaves (Joel 3:3[4:3]). Lots were cast to distribute garments (Ps. 22:18[19]). The word also is used to refer to things allotted such as land (Josh. 15:1; 17:1; 21:40[38]) or even the boundary itself of an allotment (Josh. 18:11). It refers figuratively to one's destiny or fortune (Prov. 1:14) but notes an allotted share or portion in the age to come (Dan. 12:13). Finally, it can designate a portion or allotment for someone in the sense of recompense or retribution (Isa. 17:14; Jer. 13:25).

1487. גּוּשׁ gûš: A masculine noun indicating a clod, scab, lump, crust. It refers to a diseased formation, scab, or irritation on the skin (Job 7:5), which in Job's case, is described as festering or broken (NASB, runs).

1488. גֵּז gēz: A masculine noun meaning fleece, mown field, shearing. It refers to wool sheared from sheep (Deut. 18:4) and to clothing made from it (Job 31:20). It designates the object cut or mown, such as a mown field (Ps. 72:6) as well as the act or process of mowing (Amos 7:1).

1489. גִּזְבָּר gizbār: A masculine noun meaning treasurer. It designates a person in charge of the monetary resources and treasures of a king or nation (Ezra 1:8). He was responsible for the safekeeping and dispersement of these things.

1490. גִּזְבַּר gizbar: An Aramaic masculine noun referring to a treasurer. It indicates a person in charge of the monetary resources and treasures of a king or a nation (Ezra 7:21). He was responsible for the safekeeping and dispersement of these things.

1491. גָּזָה gāzāh: A verb meaning to take, to cut. It refers to the cutting of the umbilical cord (Ps. 71:6). Figuratively, it describes God as taking a child from its mother's womb.

1492. גִּזָּה ***gizzāh:*** A feminine noun denoting fleece. It indicates a piece of wool, a fleece of wool (Judg. 6:37–40). Gideon used a fleece to determine the Lord's will in his life.

1493. גִּזוֹנִי ***gizôniy:*** A proper noun designating Gizonite (1 Chr. 11:34).

1494. גָּזַז ***gāzaz:*** A verb meaning to shear, to cut. It indicates the cutting of someone's hair. Jeremiah cut his hair as a sign of mourning (Jer. 7:29) and as a sign of the Lord's rejection of His people. It means to shear sheep (Gen. 31:19), as well as to be cut off or shorn (Nah. 1:12) in a figurative sense as in the destruction of Nineveh.

1495. גָּזֵז ***gāzēz:*** A proper noun designating Gazez (1 Chr. 2:46).

1496. גָּזִית ***gāziyṯ:*** A feminine noun indicating a dressed or cut stone, hewn stone, smooth stone, ashlar. A cut stone used in building the Solomonic Temple (1 Kgs. 5:17[31]; 6:36) and Solomon's palace (1 Kgs. 7:9, 11, 12). It was used in houses constructed for the rich (Amos 5:11). Cut stones dressed out by men were not permitted in a stone altar (Ex. 20:25). But they were permissible in certain parts of Ezekiel's Temple and its supporting components (40:42). It is used figuratively to depict the Lord's hemming in of Jeremiah's ministry and life (Lam. 3:9).

1497. גָּזַל ***gāzal:*** A verb meaning to rob, to take away by force. It is used often figuratively, as evil leaders of Israel pulling off or tearing off the skin of God's people (Mic. 3:2). In another figurative usage, it means to take away or deprive persons of their rights (Isa. 10:2) or for sleep to be taken away (Prov. 4:16). In a literal sense, it describes the seizing of the houses of the oppressed (Mic. 2:2). Other objects are seized or taken away: wells (Gen. 21:25) or women (Gen. 31:31). It means to rob persons of their personal property (Judg. 9:25; Job 24:2) or even children (Job 24:9).

1498. גָּזֵל ***gāzēl:*** A masculine noun indicating something stolen, robbery. It refers to the sin of robbery that can be atoned for by a guilt offering (Lev. 6:2[5:21]; Ps. 62:10[11]). The Lord hates this sin (Isa. 61:8), but it was one of the oppressive sins of Israel (Ezek. 22:29), especially against the poor, the needy, and the sojourners.

1499. גֵּזֶל ***gēzel:*** A masculine noun referring to robbery, stealing, denial. It is a strong word indicating the denial or even violent perversion (KJV) of something such as the robbery of justice (Eccl. 5:8[7]). It can indicate robbing one's relative, doing what is not good but evil (Ezek. 18:18), a characteristic of an unrighteous person.

1500. גְּזֵלָה ***g^ezēlāh:*** A feminine noun indicating robbery, plunder, something stolen. It refers to something taken by robbery. It can be atoned for by a guilt offering (Lev. 6:4[5:23]). Isaiah uses the word in the sense of plunder or spoil taken from the poor (Isa. 3:14). The righteous person avoids this robbery or plunder (Ezek. 18:7), but the evil person engages in it (Ezek. 18:12; 33:15).

1501. גָּזָם ***gāzām:*** A masculine noun indicating a palmerworm, a gnawing locust. It describes a certain kind of locust (NASB, gnawing locust; NIV, locust swarm; KJV, palmerworm) which normally does not totally devour a crop (Joel 1:4; 2:25). This locust was sent by God as judgment on His people (Amos 4:9).

1502. גַּזָּם ***gazzām:*** A proper noun designating Gazzam (Ezra 2:48; Neh. 7:51).

1503. גֶּזַע ***geza':*** A masculine noun referring to a stem, a trunk. It indicates a tree stump left in the ground (Job 14:8) which can still revive if watered. Isaiah pictures a righteous branch springing from this kind of stump (Isa. 11:1). It is used figuratively of the brief establishment of the "roots" of earthly rulers before they wither away (Isa. 40:24).

1504. גָּזַר ***gāzar:*** A verb meaning to cut, to divide, to separate. The basic meaning of this word can be seen in Solomon's command to divide the baby in two pieces (1 Kgs. 3:25, 26); in the act of cutting down trees (2 Kgs. 6:4); or when God divided the Red Sea (Ps. 136:13). The word also describes a person separated from God's temple (2 Chr. 26:21); from God's caring hand (Ps. 88:5[6]); or from life itself (Isa. 53:8). So great may be the separation that destruction may occur (Lam. 3:54; Ezek. 37:11; Hab. 3:17). In a few instances, this word means to decree (Esth. 2:1; Job 22:28). The meaning is related to the Hebrew idiom, to cut a covenant, which means to make a covenant. In that idiom, the synonym *kārat̲* (3772), meaning to cut, is used.

1505. גְּזַר ***g***^{e}***zar:*** An Aramaic verb meaning to cut, to decide, to determine. The participle is used as a noun meaning soothsayer or astrologer. The verb occurs in Daniel 2:34 and 2:45 to describe a stone cut without hands—an image that symbolizes the kingdom of God. Apparently, the idea of future events being cut out led to the word being used to signify soothsayers or astrologers who could foretell the future (Dan. 2:27; 4:7[4]; 5:7, 11).

1506. גֶּזֶר ***gezer:*** A masculine noun meaning part, portion, division, half. It is found only as a plural form. It refers to the halves of animals that Abraham prepared in the covenant ceremony of Genesis 15:17 and the two halves of the Red Sea when God divided it (Ps. 136:13).

1507. גֶּזֶר ***gezer:*** A proper noun designating Gezer, a city located in the northern area of the Shephelah due east of Ashdod on the coast (Josh.

10:33; 12:12). It was given to Ephraim (Josh. 16:3) and became a Levitical city (Josh. 21:21; 1 Chr. 6:67[52]). David pursued Philistines into Gezer. According to 1 Kings 9:15–17, Pharaoh captured it and gave it to his daughter as a marriage dowry.

1508. גִּזְרָה ***gizrāh:*** A feminine noun indicating a courtyard, separate area, appearance, polishing. It depicts how something looks. It is used to describe the appearance or polishing of God's people before their corruption and judgment (Lam. 4:7). It indicates the courtyard of Ezekiel's visionary temple (41:12–15; 42:1, 10, 13), also translated as separate place (KJV), separating courtyard (NKJV), or separate area (NASB).

1509. גְּזֵרָה ***gᵉzērāh:*** A feminine noun denoting a solitary place, a solitary land. It refers to an isolated, infertile place or land to which the scapegoat was sent on the Day of Atonement (Lev. 16:22). It includes the idea of an uninhabitable land, possibly the desert.

1510. גְּזֵרָה ***gᵉzērāh:*** An Aramaic feminine noun indicating a decree, announcement, or sentence. It denotes a formal decree or sentence issued by heavenly beings (Dan. 4:17[14], 24[21]). It was later interpreted by Daniel.

1511. גִּזְרִי ***gizriy:*** A proper noun designating Gezrites, Girzites (1 Sam. 27:8).

1512. גָּחוֹן ***gāḥôn:*** A masculine noun meaning belly. Twice it refers to the belly of reptiles: (1) the belly of the serpent who deceived Eve (Gen. 3:14); and (2) to anything that crawls or moves on its belly (Lev. 11:42). In the latter case, all these creatures were detestable to the Israelites and could not be eaten.

1513. גַּחֶלֶת ***gaḥeleṯ:*** A feminine noun denoting coal, burning coal, live coals. The word literally refers to coals of fire (Lev. 16:12; 2 Sam. 22:13; Prov. 6:28) used to burn up sacrifices or provide heat (Isa. 47:14). It is often used figuratively to indicate hot coals that ignite wood as a quarrelsome person causes strife (Prov. 26:21); burning coals used to describe the living creatures in Ezekiel's vision (1:13); hot coal describes the male reproductive capacity (2 Sam. 14:7) or God's acts of judgment (Ps. 120:4). Burning coals stand for an act of kindness or warming one's enemy (Prov. 25:22; cf. Rom. 12:20).

1514. גַּחַם ***gaḥam:*** A proper noun designating Gaham (Gen. 22:24).

1515. גַּחַר ***gaḥar:*** A proper noun designating Gahar (Ezra 2:47; Neh. 7:49).

1516. גַּיְא ***gay'***, גַּי ***gay:*** A common noun meaning valley. It refers to any valley in general (2 Kgs. 2:16) but often to specify valleys, such as a valley in Moab (Num. 21:20); a valley near Beth-peor (Deut. 3:29; 4:46); or near Gedor (1 Chr. 4:39). It is used to form names of valleys, such as the Valley of Hinnom, the most often cited valley (Josh. 15:8; 18:16; Neh. 11:30) or the Valley of Ben Hinnom (2 Kgs. 23:10; 2 Chr. 28:3). Names are formed to indicate events or activities that have or will take place in a valley, e.g., the Valley of Slaughter (Jer. 7:32); Valley of Vision (Isa. 22:1); Valley of Hamon Gog (Ezek. 39:11).

1517. גִּיד *giyd:* A masculine noun indicating a sinew, tendon. It refers to the sinew or tendon of a person's hip (Gen. 32:32[33]) or body (Job 10:11). Israel's obstinacy is likened to an iron sinew (Isa. 48:4). It is used to describe the "iron" sinew of the thighs of Behemoth, possibly a hippopotamus (Job 40:17). The Lord restores sinews and tendons to Israel represented by the bones in the valley of dry bones (Ezek. 37:6, 8).

1518. גִּיחַ *giyaḥ,* גּוּחַ *gûaḥ:* A verb meaning to burst forth, to bring forth. It is used literally to depict a river gushing forth (Job 40:23) or figuratively to show the sea bursting forth as if coming from a womb (Job 38:8). A child is cast forth from its mother's womb (Ps. 22:9[10]). It depicts Jerusalem going forth after travail into captivity (Mic. 4:10). Egypt bursts forth from her rivers as a monster (Ezek. 32:2). It describes an army breaking out of ambush (Judg. 20:33).

1519. גִּיחַ *giyaḥ,* גּוּחַ *gûaḥ:* An Aramaic verb indicating a breaking forth, churning up. It is used of the four winds of heaven churning the sea, from which four beasts arise (Dan. 7:2).

1520. גִּיחַ *giyaḥ:* A proper noun designating Giah (2 Sam. 2:24).

1521. גִּיחוֹן *giyḥôn:* A proper noun designating Gihon:
A. The name of a river that flowed through Eden and on through the land of Cush (Gen. 2:13). It possibly was located in southern Mesopotamia in antiquity.
B. The name of a spring on the eastern side of Mount Zion in the Kidron Valley. As Hezekiah anticipated the Assyrian army, he directed its water into the Pool of Siloam (2 Chr. 32:30) within the city.

1522. גֵּיחֲזִי *gēyḥᵃziy,* גֵּחֲזִי *gēḥᵃziy:* A proper noun designating Gehazi, the name of Elisha's servant. He laid Elisha's staff upon the Shunnamite's dead son to restore him to life (2 Kgs. 4:12–25) but in vain. He deceitfully took gifts for himself that Elisha had refused from Naaman (2 Kgs. 5:20–25). He recounted the great things Elisha had done for the Shunnamite woman to a certain king (2 Kgs. 8:4, 5).

1523. גִּיל *giyl,* גּוּל *gûl:* A verb meaning to rejoice. It is a response of persons both religiously, as when they divide the spoils of the Lord's victories (Isa. 9:3[2]); when they rejoice in His salvation (Isa. 25:9; 65:18); or over idolatrous objects (Hos. 10:5). It describes the Lord's joyous response over His people and Jerusalem in the new heavens and earth (Isa. 65:19). The dry land, the Arabah, will even rejoice (Isa. 35:1, 2). Many things rejoice besides those just mentioned: the heart (Ps. 13:5[6]; Prov. 24:17; Zech. 10:7); the soul (Ps. 35:9; Isa. 61:10). Rejoicing in the Lord is accompanied with proper fear and trembling as well (Ps. 2:11). God's people rejoice in many things: Jerusalem (Isa. 66:10); the Lord's salvation (Ps. 9:14[15]); the Lord (Ps. 35:9; Isa. 41:16); the Lord's name (Ps. 89:16[17]); the Holy One of Israel (Isa. 29:19).

1524. גִּיל ***giyl:*** I. A masculine noun depicting rejoicing. It describes a happy state of affairs and actions compared to a previous state of suffering (Job 3:22). The Lord Himself may cause one's rejoicing (Ps. 43:4, NASB, my exceeding joy). The hills rejoice at God's bountiful favors (Ps. 65:12[13]). Rejoicing is the result of having a righteous son (Prov. 23:24). Israel's right to rejoice depended on her faithfulness to God (Hos. 9:1), and God could cut off her rejoicing with His judgments (Joel 1:16).

II. A masculine noun designating a circle, age, stage of life. It is used in a general sense of the ages(s) of Daniel and other youths (Dan. 1:10).

1525. גִּילָה ***giylāh:*** A feminine noun denoting joy, rejoicing. The dry land, the Arabah, is depicted as rejoicing (Isa. 35:2) in a picture of the future restoration of Zion. Rejoicing is the goal for which God creates His people (Isa. 65:18).

1526. גִּילֹנִי ***giylōniy:*** A proper noun designating Gilonite (2 Sam. 15:12; 23:34).

1527. גִּינַת ***giynat̲:*** A proper noun designating Ginath (1 Kgs. 16:21, 22).

1528. גִּיר ***giyr:*** An Aramaic masculine noun referring to plaster. It designates the external smooth covering of the wall on which the fingers of a man's hand wrote a puzzling riddle in Aramaic (Dan. 5:5).

1529. גֵּישָׁן ***gēyšān:*** A proper noun designating Geshan (1 Chr. 2:47).

1530. גַּל ***gal:*** I. A masculine noun designating a heap or pile of rocks. It indicates rocks piled over a person's grave to mark it (Josh. 7:26; 8:29) or a pile of rocks to which the roots of the wicked cling in vain (Job 8:17). A pile of rocks could indicate the ratification of a covenant or agreement (Gen. 31:46, 48, 51, 52). But in another context, it indicates a heap of uninhabitable ruins (2 Kgs. 19:25; Isa. 25:2; Hos. 12:11[12]).

II. A masculine noun depicting a wave, a billow, a spring. It refers to waves of the sea (Job 38:11; Isa. 51:15; Jer. 5:22; 31:35). In a figurative sense, it denotes chastisement from the Lord (Ps. 42:7[8]; Jon. 2:3[4]) or the armies of an enemy approaching (Jer. 51:42, 55). In a different context, it indicates the bride of the lover as a barred spring (Song 4:12), a spring sealed up (KJV, a spring shut up), to assert her chastity.

1531. גֹּל gōl: A masculine noun denoting a bowl, oil vessel, basin. It indicates a container for oil (Zech. 4:2) and so may indicate the bowl of a lamp positioned at the top of a lampstand.

1532. גַּלָּב gallāḇ: A masculine noun meaning barber. It is used once to depict a barber who cuts hair, normally, with a razor (Ezek. 5:1).

1533. גִּלְבֹּעַ gilbōaʻ: A proper noun designating Gilboa, the mountain range located east of the Valley of Jezreel (1 Sam. 18:4). Saul and his three sons were slain there by the Philistines (1 Sam. 31:8–10). It was in the territory of Issachar (2 Sam. 1:21).

1534. גַּלְגַּל galgal: A masculine noun meaning a wheel, a whirl, a whirlwind. This word primarily describes an object circling or rotating around and around. This can be seen in the related verb *gālal* (1556), meaning to roll. This word is often used to describe wheels, like those on a chariot (Ezek. 23:24; 26:10); an instrument used to draw water from a cistern (Eccl. 12:6); or the objects in Ezekiel's vision (Ezek. 10:2, 6, 13), which are similar to *'ôp̱ ān* (212), meaning wheels. In most passages, a sense of a whirling movement is found in swift wheels (Isa. 5:28); rumbling, noisy wheels (Jer. 47:3); swirling chaff (Isa. 17:13); thunder in the swirling storm (Ps. 77:18[19]).

1535. גַּלְגַּל galgal: An Aramaic masculine noun meaning wheel. The word occurs only in Daniel 7:9, where it describes fiery wheels on the blazing throne of the Ancient of Days. It is thought that the throne is seen as connected to a chariot. The wheeled cherubim (cf. Ezek. 10:15, 20) may be related to the wheels of this throne (cf. 1 Chr. 28:18; Ps. 99:1).

1536. גִּלְגָּל gilgāl: A masculine noun meaning a cart wheel. It is the cart wheel used in the process of threshing or crushing grain (Isa. 28:28). This word is a variation of the Hebrew word *galgal* (1534).

1537. גִּלְגָּל gilgāl: A proper noun designating Gilgal:

A. The place where Israel camped on entering Canaan (Josh. 4; 5; 9; 10; 14). The name means "circle" or "rolling" (cf. Josh. 5:9). It was an important religious center for Israel during the times of Samuel and Saul (1 Sam. 7; 10; 11; 13; 15). Twelve stones were set up there for the twelve tribes (Josh. 4:20). A great ceremony of circumcision was celebrated there, as was a great Passover feast (Josh. 5:9, 10). It is mentioned 35 times in the Old Testament. It was a place condemned by the prophets for it fostered false worship of the Lord as did Bethel (Hos. 4:15; 9:15; Amos 4:4; 5:5). Jeroboam I had built golden calves at Gilgal and Bethel. Its exact location is uncertain, but it was possibly northeast of Jericho.

B. The name of a city ruled by a king named Goyim (Josh. 12:23). Its location is uncertain.

C. Another city northeast of Judah, about 8 miles east of Jerusalem (cf. Josh. 18:7).

D. A city through which both Elijah and Elisha passed (2 Kgs. 2:1; 4:38). Its location is unknown. Elijah was shortly thereafter taken up to heaven. A famine occurred there in Elisha's day.

E. A city near to Jerusalem in the time of Nehemiah (KJV, Neh. 12:29).

1538. גֻּלְגֹּלֶת ***gulgōleṯ:*** A feminine noun meaning skull, head, and thus a person. The author of Judges used this word when he described Abimelech's skull being cracked when a woman dropped a millstone on it (Judg. 9:53). When Jezebel was killed, her skull was one of the few remnants of her body when people buried her (2 Kgs. 9:35). The Philistines hung up Saul's head in the temple of Dagon (1 Chr. 10:10). At other times, this word is used more generically to mean person, as when Moses instructed the Israelites to gather an omer of manna per person (Ex. 16:16); a beka of silver per person for the Tabernacle (Ex. 38:26); or to redeem the Levites (Num. 3:47). It is also used in passages concerning the taking of a census (Num. 1:2, 18, 20, 22; 1 Chr. 23:3, 24). This word means the same as the Aramaic word *Golgotha*—the name of the place where Jesus was crucified (Luke 23:33).

1539. גֶּלֶד ***gēleḏ:*** A masculine noun meaning skin. It is an archaic Hebrew word, since it is found only one time in the book of Job. The word is used when the text describes Job expressing his grief by sewing sackcloth over his skin (Job 16:15)—a common custom of mourning in ancient Israel.

1540. גָּלָה ***gālāh:*** A verb meaning to reveal, to be revealed, to uncover, to remove, to go into exile, to reveal oneself, to expose, to disclose. It is used with the words ear (1 Sam. 9:15; 20:2, 12, 13) and eyes (Num. 24:4), meaning to reveal. On occasion, it is used in the expression to uncover the nakedness of, which often implies sexual relations (Lev. 18:6).

1541. גְּלָה ***gᵉlāh,*** גְּלָא ***gᵉlā':*** An Aramaic verb meaning to bring over, to take away (into exile), to reveal. This word is used of those who were deported to Babylonia (Ezra 4:10; 5:12). In the book of Daniel, the meaning is to uncover or to reveal. In the story of the dreams of Nebuchadnezzar, God is shown as the One who reveals hidden things, specifically the meanings of dreams (Dan. 2:22, 28, 29, 47).

1542. גִּלֹה ***gilōh:*** A proper noun designating Giloh (Josh. 15:51; 2 Sam. 15:12).

1543. גֻּלָּה ***gullāh:*** A feminine noun used to depict a spring or a bowl. It indicates a spring of water (Josh. 15:19; Judg. 1:15). It indicates a golden bowl symbolizing life (Eccl. 12:6). It depicts two carved decorative bowls or horizontal projections on the tops of the pillar capitals in Solomon's Temple (1 Kgs. 7:41, 42). It indicates a bowl for holding lamp oil (Zech. 4:2).

1544. גִּלּוּל ***gillûl:*** A masculine noun meaning idols. The Hebrew word is always found in the plural form. The term is used thirty-eight times in Ezekiel and nine times in the rest of the Old Testament. The people are told to destroy, abandon, and remove their idols. Deuteronomy 29:17[16] implies idols can be made of wood, stone, silver, or gold. Ezekiel longs for a day when Israel will no longer worship idols (Ezek. 37:23).

1545. גְּלוֹם ***g^elôm:*** A masculine noun indicating clothes, fabric, wrapping. It refers to one of the many articles that Tyre traded among the merchants of the world (Ezek. 27:24). Combined with the word for blue (*t^ek̲ēlet̲*), it indicates a blue fabric or blue clothes.

1546. גָּלוּת ***gālût̲:*** A feminine singular noun meaning exiles, captives, captivity. This word is used with the meaning of exiles in the prophetic messages concerning the prisoners of the king of Assyria (Isa. 20:4); those exiles whom the Lord will free (Isa. 45:13); and those whom God would protect (Jer. 24:5; 28:4). It is also used to refer to Jehoiachin's captivity (2 Kgs. 25:27; Ezek. 1:2), and the exile of the Israelites as a whole (Ezek. 33:21). The word comes from the Hebrew root *gālāh* (1540).

1547. גָּלוּ ***gālû:*** An Aramaic feminine singular noun meaning captivity, exile. It is the equivalent of the Hebrew word *gālût̲* (1546). In Aramaic, it is commonly used in the phrase, sons of captivity. In the book of Ezra, the word refers to the exiles who celebrated when the temple was rebuilt after King Darius's decree (Ezra 6:16). In book of Daniel, it refers to Daniel's captivity (Dan. 2:25; 5:13; 6:13[14]).

1548. גָּלַח ***gālaḥ:*** A verb meaning to shave, shave off. It indicates the cutting or shaving of a person's head, beard, eyebrows, head, and pubic hair (Lev. 13:33; 14:9; Num. 6:19; Judg. 16:17, 22; 2 Sam. 10:4; 14:26; Isa. 7:20). In a figurative sense, it speaks of Assyria as God's razor that He will use to shave and shame His people Judah (Isa. 7:20).

1549. גִּלָּיוֹן ***gillāyôn:*** A masculine noun designating a mirror, glasses. It is found in a list of luxury items the Lord will take away from His rebellious people when He judges them (Isa. 3:23) and means mirrors. In Isaiah 8:1, it points to a tablet or scroll used for writing.

1550. גָּלִיל ***gāliyl:*** An adjective indicating something shaped like a ring; turning in a circle; pivot. It indicates a door that turns on the pivot of hinges (1 Kgs. 6:34). Also, it indicates rings or rods (Esth. 1:6) to which cords were attached. It is used by a bride to describe the groom's hands (Song 5:14), indicating their strength and beauty.

1551. גָּלִיל ***gāliyl,*** גָּלִילָה ***gāliylāh:*** A proper noun designating Galilee, a large mountainous territory or region in northern Israel. It is mentioned six times in the Old Testament and often in the New Testament. Upper and Lower Galilee were located northwest and west of the Sea of Galilee. The Plan of Acco bordered it on the Mediterranean Sea. The Jezreel Valley lay to its south. Solomon gave twenty towns in Galilee to Hiram, king of Tyre, for the cedar, pine, and gold he had supplied to Israel (1 Kgs. 9:11). The Levitical city of Kedesh was in the area (Josh. 20:7; 21:32). It came under the control of Assyria during Tiglath-pileser's reign (2 Kgs. 15:29) in Assyria and during Pekah's reign in Israel (752–732 B.C.). Many gentiles lived in the territory, giving rise to the term "Galilee of the Gentiles" (Isa. 9:1[8:23]). Jesus ministered much in this territory in and around the Sea of Galilee.

1552. גְּלִילָה ***g^eliylāh:*** A feminine noun designating a border region, district, territory. It refers to a specific district or region around Ezekiel's Temple (Ezek. 47:8) and to the region of the Philistines (Josh. 13:2; KJV, borders of the Philistines) and Philistia (Joel 3:4[4:4]).

1553. גְּלִילוֹת ***g^eliylôt:*** A proper noun designating Geliloth (Josh. 18:17; 22:10, 11).

1554. גַּלִּים ***galliym:*** A proper noun designating Gallim (1 Sam. 25:44; Isa. 10:30).

1555. גָּלְיָת ***golyāṯ,*** גָּלְיַת ***golyaṯ:*** A proper noun designating Goliath, a giant Philistine warrior around whom the Philistines rallied. He came from the city of Gath and stood over nine feet tall (1 Sam. 17:4, 32). David slew him and later acquired his sword from Ahimelech at Nob (1 Sam. 21:8–9; 22:10).

1556. גָּלַל ***gālal:*** A verb meaning to roll, to remove, to commit, to trust. The root idea of the word is to roll. The Hebrew word often refers to rolling stones (Gen. 29:8; Josh. 10:18; Prov. 26:27) as well as other concrete objects. It can also describe abstract concepts, such as reproach being rolled off (removed) from someone (Ps. 119:22) or one's ways and works rolled onto (committed, entrusted) to someone (especially God) (Ps. 37:5; Prov. 16:3). This important root word is used to form many other names and words (cf. Gilgal in Josh. 5:9).

1557. גָּלָל ***gālāl:*** A masculine noun denoting dung, dung pellets. It is something to be swept away as the Lord would sweep away the corrupt house of Jereboam (1 Kgs. 14:10). It further served as a simile for the sweeping away of Judah's flesh in the day of God's judgment (Zeph. 1:17).

1558. גָּלָל *gālāl:* A masculine noun indicating because of. It is combined with the preposition *b^e* to mean on account of, because of. It indicates why something is done. God blessed the Egyptian Potiphar because of Joseph (Gen. 39:5). Things would go well for Abraham because of his wife Sarah (Gen. 12:13), and Laban was blessed because of Jacob (Gen. 30:27). God denied Moses entrance to the Promised Land because of his reaction to Israel's behavior (Deut. 1:37).

1559. גָּלָל *gālāl:* A proper noun designating Galal:

A. A Levite (1 Chr. 9:15).

B. A Levite (1 Chr. 9:16; Neh. 11:17).

1560. גְּלָל *g^elāl:* An Aramaic adjective meaning large. It indicates, literally, stones that had to be rolled, that is, larger stones or blocks of stones (Ezra 5:8; 6:4).

1561. גֵּלֶל *gēlel:* A masculine noun denoting dung. It describes dung from a human, human dung to be used as fuel (Ezek. 4:12, 15) or to be discarded (Job 20:7). It is employed in a simile to describe human flesh poured out like dung (Zeph. 1:17).

1562. גִּלֲלַי *gil^alay:* A proper noun designating Gilalai (Neh. 12:36).

1563. גָּלַם *gālam:* A verb meaning to be rolled up, folded together. It describes the rolling or folding of the mantle of Elijah, after which he used it to part the Jordan River and walk through on dry ground (2 Kgs. 2:8).

1564. גֹּלֶם *gōlem:* A masculine noun designating a fetus or embryo. It refers to the unformed child or embryo in the womb, something that God's eyes saw before its birth (Ps. 139:16; NASB, unformed substance; KJV, substance . . . unperfect).

1565. גַּלְמוּד *galmûḏ:* An adjective meaning solitary, barren waste. It can depict a barren night, one in which a child was not born, as Job wished (Job 3:7). It describes Zion as a barren woman without children (Isa. 49:21) or the failure of the godless company to bear offspring (Job 15:34). It indicates a picture of solitary waste or desolation for the outcasts of society (Job 30:3) and the utterly despised and disdained of the community.

1566. גָּלַע *gāla':* A verb meaning to expose, burst forth, meddle with, be obstinate. It expresses quarreling and being obstinate by insists on having one's own way (Prov. 17:14; 20:3). It indicates separating oneself from others to seek one's own wishes (Prov. 18:1).

1567. גַּלְעֵד *gal'ēḏ:* A proper noun designating Galeed (Gen. 31:47, 48).

1568. גִּלְעָד *gil'āḏ:* A proper noun designating Gilead:

A. A term used generally to refer to a mountainous, rugged area east of the Jordan and south of the Yarmuk River. Its name means "heap of a witness." At times it reached as far south as the northern tip of the Dead Sea. In some cases, it is spoken of as if it extended south to the Arnon River. It reached eastward to the eastern desert area. Basham was to the north of it; the Jabbok River is in its central area. The tribe of Gad lived in its central territory; Manasseh (N) and Reuben (S) touched it on the north/south respectfully. The name Gilead could apply to all of the Transjordanian territory (Deut. 2:36; 34:1; Judg. 10:4–18; 11:5–29; 12:4–7; 20:1; Jer. 50:19). Each reference to Gilead must be studied in context to discern exactly what area is being referred to. It was a place of great abundance and prosperity (Song 4:1; 6:5; Jer. 22:6; Zech. 10:10). The term "balm of Gilead" expressed its healthy and proverbial luxury and wealth (Jer. 8:22; 46:11). It was, at times, a place where rebellions and wars were rampant (1 Kgs. 22:1–4; 2 Kgs. 8:28). In the narrowest use of the word, it refers to a city (Hos. 6:8).

B. It refers to a mountain west of the Jordan River. Some suggest the reference may be to Mount Gilboa.

C. The name of Manasseh's grandson and son of Machir (Num. 26:29, 30). He fathered the Gileadites (Josh. 17:1–6). The heads of this clan demanded a ruling about the inheritance laws for families that had daughters but no sons.

D. The father of one of Israel's infamous judges (Judg. 11:1, 2). His mother was a prostitute.

E. It refers to Gilead, a Gadite chief, who was the son of Michael.

1569. גִּלְעָדִי ***gil'āḏiy:*** A proper noun designating Gileadites:

A. A branch of the Manassites (Num. 26:29).

B. The inhabitants of Gilead (Num. 26:29; Judg. 10:3; 11:1, 40; 12:7; 2 Sam. 17:27; 19:31[32]; 1 Kgs. 2:7; 2 Kgs. 15:25; Ezra 2:61; Neh. 7:63).

1570. גָּלַשׁ ***gālaš:*** A verb meaning to appear, to descend, to leap. It refers to goats coming down from Mount Gilead (Song 4:1; 6:5) which serve as a simile for the hair of the bride.

1571. גַּם ***gam:*** An adverbial conjunction meaning also, even, moreover, indeed, yea, as well as, both, though. In different contexts, the word can be translated in various ways: it ties things together, new and old (Song 7:13[14]); includes other things or persons, such as a husband (Gen. 3:6); adds action (Gen. 3:22); intensifies, such as even a blameless nation (Gen. 20:4); indicates neither . . . nor (1 Sam. 28:20). It may stress a particular word with which it is used and mean even or else (Ex. 4:9; Num. 22:33; Prov. 14:13). It introduces a climax to a statement (Gen. 27:33) and means yes (KJV, yea). It expresses agreement in oneself with another, e.g., I also

(Gen. 20:6; Josh. 24:18; Judg. 2:21). When used in pairs *gam* . . . *gam*, it means also . . . as or as . . . as (Jer. 2:36) or as . . . so (Isa. 66:3, 4). It means though in some contexts: "They tried Me, though [*gam*] they had seen My work" (of judgment) (Ps. 95:9 NASB, cf. Ps. 129:2; Jer. 6:15; Ezek. 20:23). When used in the phrase *gam kiy* (3588), it is best rendered as yes, when, or even when (Prov. 22:6; Isa. 1:15; Lam. 3:8; Hos. 8:10).

1572. גָּמָא *gāmā':* A verb indicating to swallow, to drink. It means to let a person drink (Gen. 24:17). It is used figuratively of a galloping horse that is swallowing up the ground (Job 39:24).

1573. גֹּמֶא *gōme':* A masculine noun referring to a bulrush, a papyrus stalk, wicker. It indicates the material of the basket into which Moses was placed (Ex. 2:3). It also is the material of which sailing vessels were made (Isa. 18:2). It is grown in marshy land (Job 8:11) and is a sign of rich, fertile earth (Isa. 35:7).

1574. גֹּמֶד *gōmed* : A masculine noun denoting a cubit. It is the length attributed to a short sword (ca. 18–22 inches) that could be carried on one's thigh (Judg. 3:16).

1575. גַּמָּדִים *gammādiym:* A proper noun designating Gammadites, citizens of the city of Gammad (Ezek. 27:11).

1576. גְּמוּל *gemûl:* A masculine noun indicating recompense, benefits, something deserved, dealings, doings. It indicates the actions or dealings with others (Judg. 9:16), such as Jerubbabal. The dealing of a nation or what a person's hands return to him or her (Ps. 28:4; Prov. 12:14; Isa. 3:11; Obad. 1:15). It indicates a deserved receipt for something, whether accepted or returned (Joel 3:4[4:4], 7[4:7]), which the Lord (Ps. 28:4; Isa. 35:4; 66:6) or a person may render. God's good deeds amount to benefits received from Him (Ps. 103:2).

1577. גָּמוּל *gāmûl:* A proper noun designating Gamul (1 Chr. 24:17).

1578. גְּמוּלָה *gemûlāh:* A feminine noun indicating a recompense, that which is done. The word is used to describe God as a God of recompense who pays back fully what is deserved (Jer. 51:56) to His enemies and the enemies of His people (Isa. 59:18; Jer. 51:56). It indicates a free bestowal of benefits on someone (2 Sam. 19:36[37]).

1579. גִּמְזוֹ *gimzô:* A proper noun designating Gimzo (2 Chr. 28:18).

1580. גָּמַל *gāmal:* A verb meaning to recompense another, to bring to completion, to do good. This word has a broad spectrum of meanings. The predominant idea of this word is to recompense either with a benevolent reward (1 Sam. 24:17[18]; 2 Sam. 19:36[37]) or an evil recompense

(Deut. 32:6; 2 Chr. 20:11; Ps. 137:8). The idea of bringing to an end is demonstrated in verses that describe a child who is weaned (Gen. 21:8; 1 Sam. 1:22–24; Isa. 11:8) or plants that have ripened (Num. 17:8[23]; Isa. 18:5). At times this word is best translated to do good or to deal bountifully (Ps. 119:17; Prov. 11:17; Isa. 63:7).

1581. גָּמָל ***gāmāl:*** A common noun denoting a camel. This animal was fitted to travel in desert areas. It was a property of great value (Gen. 12:16; 24:10; Ex. 9:3; Judg. 7:12; 1 Sam. 15:3); used as a beast of burden (Gen. 24; 37:25; 1 Kgs. 10:2; Isa. 30:6); and for riding (Gen. 31:17, 34; 1 Sam. 30:17). However, it was forbidden as food (Lev. 11:4; Deut. 14:7).

1582. גְּמַלִּי ***g*^e*malliy:*** A proper noun designating Gemalli (Num. 13:12).

1583. גַּמְלִיאֵל ***gamliy'ēl:*** A proper noun designating Gamaliel, the name of an assistant to Moses who helped number the people of Israel (Num. 1:10). He came from Manasseh, a tribe from Joseph (Num. 2:20; 7:54, 59).

1584. גָּמַר ***gāmar:*** A verb meaning to complete, to perfect, to fail, to cease. The root idea of the word is to end. In three intransitive uses, the psalmist prayed for wickedness to end, cried out that the godly person fails, and asked if God's promise fails forever (Ps. 7:9[10]; 12:1[2]; 77:8[9]). In two transitive uses, God is the subject. He will perfect that which concerns the psalmist and will complete (or perform) all things for him (Ps. 57:2[3]; 138:8).

1585. גְּמַר ***g*^e*mar:*** A verb meaning to complete. This Aramaic word is used only once in the Old Testament and is equivalent to the Hebrew word *gāmar* (1584), meaning to complete. It is found only in the introductory section of Artaxerxes' decree given to Ezra (Ezra 7:12). Although the exact meaning of this word is unclear, it is best to understand this word as an introductory comment similar to Ezra 5:7, where the Hebrew word *š*^e*lām* (8001), meaning peace, is used.

1586. גֹּמֶר ***gōmer:*** A proper noun designating Gomer:

A. A son of Japheth, Noah's son (Gen. 10:2, 3).

B. It refers to the descendants, named as a people, who are among the hordes of Gog who will come against God's people (Ezek. 38:6).

C. The wife of Hosea, a daughter of Diblaim (Hos. 1:3).

1587. גְּמַרְיָה ***g*^e*maryāh,*** גְּמַרְיָהוּ ***g*^e*maryāhû:*** A proper noun designating Gemariah:

A. A son of Hilkiah (Jer. 29:3).

B. A son of Shaphan (Jer. 36:10–12, 25).

1588. גַּן ***gan:*** A common noun meaning garden, enclosure. It is used to indicate the Garden of Eden (pleasure) where the first human pair was placed (Gen. 2:8–10, 15, 16; 3:1–3, 8,

10, 23, 24; Ezek. 36:35; Joel 2:3). Hence, it refers to a place of abundant trees, water, fruits, and vegetables—where conditions for life are maximized. It could be enclosed (Lam. 2:6). It is combined with Lord to designate the garden of the LORD (Gen. 13:10) and with God to refer to the garden of God (Ezek. 28:13). A garden could feature many things, however: vegetables (Deut. 11:10; 1 Kgs. 21:2); spices, fruits, plants (Song 4:16; 5:1; 6:2). Assyria is referred to figuratively as a garden that surpassed even the garden of God (Ezek. 31:8, 9).

1589. גָּנַב ***gānab̲:*** A verb denoting to steal, rob, sweep away. It indicates wrongfully taking objects or persons (Gen. 31:19, 32; Ex. 21:16), sometimes for a good reason (2 Kgs. 11:2). It has the sense of deceiving when used with the word for heart, as when Jacob literally stole Laban's heart (Gen. 31:20, 26). With storm as its subject, the word means to carry away quickly and violently (Job 21:18), especially the wicked (Job 27:20). In its passive uses, it means to be stolen away (Gen. 40:15; Ex. 22:12[11]). Used in the reflexive sense, it means to steal away, go by stealth (2 Sam. 19:3[4]).

1590. גַּנָּב ***gannāb̲:*** A masculine noun denoting thief. A person who breaks in (Ex. 22:2[1], 7[6], 8[7]) in various ways (Jer. 49:9; Joel 2:9). One who commits the act of stealing (Ps. 50:18; Prov. 6:30; Isa. 1:23). A slave dealer (Deut. 24:7) or one who steals people.

1591. גְּנֵבָה ***g^e^nēb̲āh:*** A feminine noun referring to a thief or things stolen. The word designates the act of stealing something or theft itself (Ex. 22:3[2]), as well as the object stolen (animal) (Ex. 22:4[3]).

1592. גְּנֻבַת ***g^e^nub̲at̲:*** A proper noun designating Genubath (1 Kgs. 11:20).

1593. גַּנָּה ***gannāh:*** A feminine noun indicating a garden, orchard. The word refers to gardens in general (Amos 4:9; 9:14) that are taken away in times of judgment but restored in times of blessing. It depicts an orchard (Song 6:11) or nut garden. Gardens were places of idolatrous worship in Israel (Isa. 1:29; 66:17). They are used figuratively to indicate Israel as blessed (Num. 24:6) or cursed (Isa. 1:30). The Lord causes things to prosper and grow (Isa. 61:11). The success of the wicked, short-lived, is depicted as a garden (Job 8:16).

1594. גִּנָּה ***ginnāt̲:*** A feminine noun denoting a garden. It is combined in its construct with the king's palace to designate the garden of the king's palace (Esth. 1:5; 7:7, 8) where royal banquets were regularly held.

1595. גְּנָזִים ***g^e^nāziym:*** A masculine plural noun meaning treasury or carpets. It refers to the royal treasury (Esth. 3:9; 4:7) of King Artaxerxes. Its meaning in Ezekiel 27:24 is not certain, since it could mean wooden covers or rugs (NASB, NIV) or possibly chests (NKJV, KJV).

1596. גְּנַז ***g**^e^**naz:*** An Aramaic masculine noun indicating a treasury, archives. Used in the plural, it refers to treasure house (Ezra 5:17; 7:20). It refers to the objects or treasures themselves (Ezra 6:1).

1597. גִּנְזַךְ ***ganza<u>k</u>:*** A masculine noun denoting a treasury, storeroom, storehouse. It refers in the plural form to the storehouses of Solomon's Temple as prescribed in the building plans (1 Chr. 28:11).

1598. גָּנַן ***gānan:*** A verb meaning to defend, to shield, to protect. It indicates the Lord's defense of Jerusalem from the Assyrians (2 Kgs. 19:34; 20:6; Isa. 31:5; 37:35; Zech. 12:8) and His people Judah and Ephraim in the day of judgment (Zech. 9:15).

1599. גִּנְּתוֹי ***ginn^e<u>t</u>ôy,*** גִּנְּתוֹן ***gin-n^e<u>t</u>ôn:*** A proper noun designating Ginnethon (Neh. 10:6[7]; 12:4, 16).

1600. גָּעָה ***gā'āh:*** A verb meaning to bellow, to moo, to low (cattle). A word imitating the sound cows made when taking the ark to Beth-shemesh (1 Sam. 6:12), as well as the sound of an ox as it eats its fodder (Job 6:5).

1601. גֹּעָה ***gō'āh:*** A proper noun designating Goath, Goah (Jer. 31:39).

1602. גָּעַל ***gā'al:*** A verb meaning to detest, to abhor. It is used in Leviticus 26:15, 43 to warn Israel not to abhor God's commandments. He would otherwise abhor them (Lev. 26:30), yet not to such an extent that He would destroy them completely (Lev. 26:44). This word also describes Israel as an unfaithful wife who loathes her husband (God) and her children (Ezek. 16:45). A bull that is not able to mate with a cow or whose seed is miscarried is said, literally, to cause loathing (Job 21:10). In 2 Samuel 1:21, a shield that failed to protect its owner, Saul, was cast away as detested rather than being oiled.

1603. גַּעַל ***ga'al:*** A proper noun designating Gaal, the son of Ebed who lived in Shechem (Judg. 9:26). He incited a conspiracy against Abimelech (Judg. 9:28–29). He was, instead, driven out of Shechem (Judg. 9:41).

1604. גֹּעַל ***gō'al:*** A masculine noun indicating a loathing, a despising, an aversion, an abhorrence. It depicts a attitude of rejection or neglect toward something, in this case, Israel when she was born (Ezek. 16:5).

1605. גָּעַר ***gā'ar:*** A verb meaning to rebuke. This word depicts the sharp criticism of one person to another: Jacob rebuked Joseph for telling his dream (Gen. 37:10), and Boaz commanded his servants not to rebuke Ruth's gleaning activity (Ruth 2:16). When depicting God's actions, this word is often used to describe the result of His righteous anger (Isa. 54:9; Nah. 1:4) against those who rebel against Him, including wicked nations (Ps. 9:5[6]; Isa. 17:13); their offspring (Mal. 2:3); the proud (Ps. 119:21); and Satan (Zech. 3:2). So authoritative is the Lord's rebuke that even nature obeys His voice (Ps. 106:9; Nah. 1:4).

1606. גְּעָרָה ***geʿārāh:*** A feminine singular noun meaning rebuke. It occurs fifteen times in the Bible, always in poetic passages. Both God and humans are the subject of such rebukes (2 Sam. 22:16; Isa. 50:2).

1607. גָּעַשׁ ***gaʿaš:*** A verb meaning to shake, to quake, to move, to surge. It indicates a violent rising and falling attended sometimes with loud noises of the earth and its foundations (Ps. 18:7[8]); of waves or the sea itself (Jer. 5:22). It is used figuratively to describe drunken nations (Jer. 25:16) as they stagger (NASB) and Egypt in particular as it surges about in its pride (Jer. 46:7, 8).

1608. גַּעַשׁ ***gaʿaš:*** A proper noun designating Gaash (Josh. 24:30; Judg. 2:9; 2 Sam. 23:30; 1 Chr. 11:32).

1609. גַּעְתָּם ***gaʿtām:*** A proper noun designating Gatum (Gen. 36:11, 16; 1 Chr. 1:36).

1610. גַּף ***gap̱:*** I. A masculine noun meaning back, top, high point. It refers to the high points or tops of a city's structures or geographical features (Prov. 9:3).

II. A masculine noun meaning body, alone. It is used to indicate a person's own body, a person alone (Ex. 21:3, 4), or by himself or herself (KJV).

1611. גַּף ***gap̱:*** An Aramaic masculine noun indicating a wing. It is used to describe the wings of an eagle and in general the wings of a bird (Dan. 7:4, 6).

1612. גֶּפֶן ***gep̱en:*** A masculine noun meaning vine. It refers to any type of vine, but all except once, it refers to a grape-bearing vine: a poisonous wild vine bearing gourds (2 Kgs. 4:39); grapevine (Gen. 40:9, 10). It is often mentioned along with other fruits or the fig tree (1 Kgs. 4:25[5:5]). It often is used symbolically to refer to Israel (Ps. 80:8[9]; Ezek. 15:2, 6; 17:6–8; Hos. 10:1) and has other figurative uses: the wicked drop off like unripe grapes from a vine (Job 15:33); a fertile wife (Ps. 128:3); enemies stem from the evil vine of Sodom (Deut. 32:32); a withering vine represents the collapsing prosperity of Moab (Isa. 16:8, 9).

1613. גֹּפֶר ***gōp̱er:*** A masculine noun denoting gopher wood, cypress wood. It was a light building material for the ark (Gen. 6:14; NIV, cypress wood). The exact identity of this wood is still under investigation.

1614. גָּפְרִית ***gopriyṯ:*** A feminine noun designating sulfur, brimstone. It indicates brimstone as a part of the judgment on Sodom and Gomorrah (Gen. 19:24). In a figurative sense, it refers to God's judgment on a wicked person (Ps. 11:6; Ezek. 38:22). The breath of God is depicted as brimstone setting Topheth, a pagan place of worship, on fire (Isa. 30:33).

1615. גִּר *gir:* A masculine noun indicating chalk, lime. It is used to define certain stones, stones of chalk, which could be pulverized rather easily (Isa. 27:9). The stones were used to construct some altars.

1616. גֵּיר *gēyr,* גֵּר *gēr:* A masculine noun meaning sojourner, alien, stranger. The word indicates in general anyone who is not native to a given land or among a given people (Ex. 12:19). The word is used most often to describe strangers or sojourners in Israel who were not native-born Israelites and were temporary dwellers or newcomers. A person, family, or group might leave their homeland and people to go elsewhere because of war or immediate danger as Moses had done (Ex. 2:22; cf. 2 Sam. 4:3); Naomi and her family were forced to travel to Moab to sojourn because of a famine in Israel (Ruth 1:1). God's call to Abraham to leave his own land of Ur of the Chaldees and made him a sojourner and an alien in the land of Canaan (Gen. 12:1). Israel's divinely orchestrated descent into Egypt resulted in their becoming an alien people in a foreign land for four hundred years (Gen. 15:13). Abraham considered himself an alien, although he was in the land of Canaan, the land of promise, because he was living among the Hittites at Hebron (Gen. 23:4).

This evidence indicates that strangers or aliens were those living in a strange land among strange people. Their stay was temporary or they did not identify with the group among whom they were living, no matter how long they stayed. The transitory nature of aliens' status is indicated in passages that describe them as seeking overnight lodging or accommodations (Job 31:32; Jer. 14:8).

Sojourners or strangers in Israel were not to be oppressed but were to receive special consideration for several reasons: Israel knew about being aliens, for they had been aliens in Egypt (Ex. 23:9); aliens had a right to rest and cessation from labor just as the native Israelites did (Ex. 20:10); aliens were to be loved, for God loved them (Deut. 10:18) just as He loved widows and orphans; aliens had a right to food to satisfy their needs just as orphans and widows did (Deut. 14:29). In Ezekiel's vision of a new temple and temple area, the children of aliens and sojourners were given an allotment of land (Ezek. 47:22), for they were to be considered as native children of Israel. However, this shows that sojourners had to receive special concessions because they did not have all the rights of native Israelites. Aliens could eat the Lord's Passover only if they and their entire household submitted to circumcision (Ex. 12:48, 49).

They were then not allowed to eat anything with yeast in it during the celebration of the Passover, just like native Israelites (Ex. 12:19, 20). However, major distinctions did exist between sojourners or aliens and native Israelites. Unclean food could be given to aliens to eat, but the Israelites were prohibited from eating the same food. To have done so would violate their holiness and consecration to the Lord God. Unfortunately, David himself laid forced labor on the shoulders of aliens in Israel to prepare to build the temple (1 Chr. 22:2; cf. 2 Chr. 8:7–9).

1617. גֵּרָא *gērā':* A proper noun designating Gera (Gen. 46:21; Judg. 3:15; 2 Sam. 16:5; 19:16[17], 18[19]; 1 Kgs. 2:8; 1 Chr. 8:3, 5, 7).

1618. גָּרָב *gārāḇ:* A masculine noun indicating scabs, a festering, an eruption of skin. It designates skin disease of some kind that prohibited a priest from offering sacrifices to the Lord (Lev. 21:20) and also disqualified an animal to be used for sacrifice (Lev. 22:22). This condition was one of the curses the Lord would place on His people for breaking His covenant (Deut. 28:22).

1619. גָּרֵב *gārēḇ:* A proper noun designating Gareb:
A. An Ithrite (2 Sam. 23:38; 1 Chr. 11:40).
B. A hill (Jer. 31:39).

1620. גַּרְגַּר *gargēr:* A masculine noun indicating an olive berry. It is used once in its plural form to refer to olives left on the top boughs of an olive tree representing Damascus (Isa. 17:6).

1621. גַּרְגְּרוֹת *gargārôṯ:* A feminine plural noun meaning necks. The neck is mentioned as the place where ornaments are hung (Prov. 1:9). In a figurative sense, wisdom, discretion, kindness, and truth are to be hung around the neck (Prov. 3:3, 22). As a place of importance and prominence, the neck was where the teaching and commandments of one's parents are to be displayed (Prov. 6:21).

1622. גִּרְגָּשִׁי *girgāšiy:* A proper noun designating Girgashite, Girgasite (Gen. 10:16; 15:21; Deut. 7:1; Josh. 3:10; 24:11; 1 Chr. 1:14; Neh. 9:8).

1623. גָּרַד *gāraḏ:* A verb indicating to scrape, to scratch. A piece of potsherd served Job as a tool to scrape himself because of skin irritations (Job 2:8).

1624. גָּרָה *gārāh:* A verb meaning to meddle, to stir up strife, to provoke. It is used in Proverbs always with the object being strife (15:18; 28:25; 29:22) or those who forsake God's law (Prov. 28:4). Used reflexively, it basically means to stir up one's self against someone or something: peoples (Deut. 2:5, 19);, a king (2 Kgs. 14:10; 2 Chr. 25:19); a people or nation to provoke war (Deut. 2:9, 24; Dan. 11:10, 25).

1625. גֵּרָה gērāh: A feminine noun meaning cud. The word refers to the regurgitated food of a ruminant that is then held in the mouth and chewed (Lev. 11:3–7, 26; Deut. 14:6–8). It is used only in a legal context to help define what animals were clean and, therefore, edible for God's people.

1626. גֵּרָה gērāh: A feminine noun denoting a small unit of weight, gerah. It indicates a unit of weight used as money. The gerah was one-twentieth of a shekel (Ex. 30:13; Ezek. 45:12) as used in the sanctuary (Lev. 27:25; Num. 3:47; 18:16). It was 1/6000 of a talent and one tenth of a beka. Its modern equivalent is .5 – .6 gram or .02 ounce.

1627. גָּרוֹן gārôn: A masculine noun meaning neck, throat. It indicates the throat as a location of thirst (Jer. 2:25) or figuratively as one's voice raised like a trumpet (Isa. 58:1). The throat could be an organ of praise to God (Ps. 149:6) or an organ of pleading with Him (Ps. 69:3[4]). The throat of the wicked is a conduit of death (Ps. 5:9[10]). It was a favorite place for ornamentation (Ezek. 16:11). An outstretched neck was a sign of pride and haughtiness.

1628. גֵּרוּת gērûṯ: I. A feminine noun meaning inn, habitation, lodging place. It was a convenient place to stop on the way to Egypt (Jer. 41:17). Some translators prefer to render the word as part of the name of a location, Geruth Kimham (NIV, NASB). It was not far from Bethlehem.

II. A feminine proper noun meaning Geruth. It indicated a location to stop and rest on the way to Egypt (Jer. 41:17). Some translators prefer to render it as habitation (KJV).

1629. גָּרַז gāraz: A verb meaning to be cut off. It is used figuratively to mean separated from God (Ps. 31:22[23]) and not able to enjoy His presence or benefits.

1630. גְּרִזִּים gᵉriziym: A proper noun designating Gerizim, a mountain south, southeast of Shechem a short distance, and, south of Mount Ebal. Moses and later Joshua read out covenant blessings at a covenant renewal ceremony (Deut. 11:29; 27:12; Josh. 8:33) on this mountain. Jotham escaped to it, fleeing from Abimelech (Judg. 9:7). It became the favored place of worship for the Samaritans (John 4:20).

1631. גַּרְזֶן garzen: A masculine noun denoting an ax. It indicates an ax used to quarry stones (1 Kgs. 6:7) or to cut wood (Deut. 19:5; 20:19). Isaiah used it to refer to the king of Assyria as God's ax used to humble His people (Isa. 10:15).

1632. גָּרֹל gārōl: An adjective meaning great. It is used to describe excessive anger as great anger (Prov. 19:19, NASB, KJV, NKJV). Others prefer to translate the word as indicating a "hot-tempered" person (NIV).

1633. גָּרַם gāram: I. A verb meaning to crush, to gnaw, to break bones. It describes Israel's action of crushing the bones of her enemies as she came out of Egypt (Num. 24:8). It is used figuratively to depict Judah gnawing the cup of judgment the Lord poured out on her (Ezek. 23:34). Some translators prefer to render it as to let something be left over (Zeph. 3:3, NIV, NASB, NKJV).

II. A verb meaning to leave. It indicates letting something be left over (Zeph. 3:3). Others prefer to translate it as to gnaw (KJV).

1634. גֶּרֶם gerem: A masculine noun meaning bone or strength. It depicts animals as strong, a strong or raw-boned donkey (Gen. 49:14), used to symbolize Issachar. It depicts the strength or bones of Behemoth (Job 40:18). It is used figuratively of one's strength or bones being dried up by a despondent spirit (Prov. 17:22). A soft answer can soften a person's harsh disposition (Prov. 25:15). The word seems to refer to the bare steps or top steps of a stair, possibly referring to their hardness (2 Kgs. 9:13).

1635. גְּרַם g^e^ram: An Aramaic masculine noun meaning bone. It indicates the bones crushed of people thrown into the lion's den (Dan. 6:24[25]) before they hit the bottom of the den.

1636. גַּרְמִי garmiy: A proper noun designating Garmite (1 Chr. 4:19).

1637. גֹּרֶן gōren: A masculine noun referring to a threshing floor. It indicates the place where various grains were threshed to remove the chaff (1 Kgs. 22:10) and where they were stored (1 Sam. 23:1; 2 Kgs. 6:27; Joel 2:24). It is used to describe Israel as a threshed people because the Lord had, so to speak, put them on the threshing floor of judgment (Isa. 21:10; cf. Jer. 51:33; Hos. 13:3). The word is combined with other words to indicate names for various locations: the threshing floor of Atad (Gen. 50:10, 11); the threshing floor of Nacon (2 Sam. 6:6); the threshing floor of Chidon (1 Chr. 13:9).

1638. גָּרַס gāras: A verb meaning to be broken, crushed, to waste away. The soul wastes away or is crushed from longing after the Lord's ordinances (Ps. 119:20). It is used of teeth broken from grinding under the stress of God's judgments (Lam. 3:16) and oppression.

1639. גָּרַע gāra‘: A verb meaning to reduce, diminish, cut short, trim; withdraw, remove. It basically means to reduce or diminish something: a workload or quota (Ex. 5:8, 11, 19); marital rights (Ex. 21:10); length of a beard (Jer. 48:37); the Torah or law of God (Deut. 4:2); to remove or withdraw an inheritance (Num. 36:3, 4). It is used to indicate the taking away of worship or reverence (Job 15:4) or to ascribe wisdom only to one source (Job 15:8). With respect to God's eyes, used figuratively, it is asserted that He does not withdraw them in watchful care from the righteous (Job 36:7). In its passive use, it means to be reduced (Ex. 5:11).

1640. גָּרַף ***gārap̱:*** A verb meaning to sweep away, wash away. It is used in poetry of a strong current of water washing away the armies of Israel's enemy (Judg. 5:21).

1641. גָּרַר ***gārar:*** A verb meaning to scrape, to drag, to ruminate, to saw. The idea of a noise made in the back of the throat seems to be the root idea so that the word is onomatopoetic like the English word gargle. The word is used once to signify rumination, an essential mark of a ceremonially clean animal (Lev. 11:7). It described hostile forces dragging people away (Prov. 21:7) or catching them like fish in a net (Hab. 1:15). The word also signifies sawing, as dragging a saw over wood (1 Kgs. 7:9).

1642. גְּרָר ***g***^***e***^***rār:*** A proper noun designating Gerar, a town near the Mediterranean coast, east of Gaza. Abraham's and Isaac's encounters with two kings of the Philistines occurred in this area (Gen. 20:1, 2; 26:1, 6, 17, 20, 26). The famous "well of Isaac" was in this vicinity (Gen. 26:20, 26). It figures in a minor way in later Israelite history (2 Chr. 4).

1643. גֶּרֶשׂ ***gereś:*** A masculine noun denoting that which is beaten or crushed, grits. It designates early ripened crushed grains of wheat used as a grain offering (Lev. 2:14, 16), which the priest offered.

1644. גָּרַשׁ ***gāraš:*** A verb meaning to cast out, drive out. With God as subject, the verb depicts God driving or banishing Adam and Eve from the Garden of Eden and driving Cain from His presence (Gen. 3:24; 4:14; Jon. 2:4[5]. The Lord caused Pharaoh to literally drive out the Israelites from Egypt (Ex. 6:1; 12:39) as Pharaoh had earlier forced Moses and Aaron from his presence (Ex. 10:11). It is used of persons driving out others from a location or activity (Ex. 2:17). It is used in the general sense of banishing outcasts from society (Job 30:5). In its figurative usage, it indicates divorcing one's wife (Lev. 21:7). It describes the sea or a river as driven and tossed (Isa. 57:20; Amos 8:8).

1645. גֶּרֶשׁ ***gereš:*** A masculine noun having the sense of yield, something put forth. It is used with respect to the months' yield, their produce (Deut. 33:14, NASB, NKJV; NIV, KJV, understand the word for moon, not month, as the thing which produces the yield).

1646. גְּרֻשָׁה ***g***^***e***^***rušāh:*** A feminine noun meaning expulsion, something cast out or dispossessed, expropriation. The word refers to the injustices, specifically expulsions, committed against Israel by their leaders (Ezek. 45:9).

1647. גֵּרְשׁוֹם ***gēršôm,*** גֵּרְשֹׁם ***gēršōm:*** A proper noun designating Gershom:

A. Son of Moses (Ex. 2:22; 18:3; 1 Chr. 23:15, 16; 26:24).

B. Oldest son of Levi (1 Chr. 6:16[1], 17[2], 20[5], 43[28], 62[47], 71[56]; 15:7).

C. Son of Phinehas (Ezra 8:2).

D. The father of Jonathan (Judg 18:30).

1648. גֵּרְשׁוֹן ***gēršôn:*** A proper noun designating Gershon (Gen. 46:11; Ex. 6:16, 17; Num. 3:17, 18, 21, 25; 4:22, 38, 41; 7:7; 10:17; 26:57; Josh. 21:6, 27; 1 Chr. 6:1(5:27); 23:6). See also *gēršôm* (1647,B).

1649. גֵּרְשֻׁנִּי ***gēršunniy:*** A proper noun designating Gershonite (Num. 3:21, 23, 24; 4:24, 27, 28; 26:57; Josh. 21:33; 1 Chr. 23:7; 26:21; 29:8; 2 Chr. 29:12).

1650. גְּשׁוּר ***g***^{e}***šûr:*** A proper noun designating Geshur (Josh. 13:13; 2 Sam. 3:3; 13:37, 38; 14:23, 32; 15:8; 1 Chr. 2:23; 3:2).

1651. גְּשׁוּרִי ***g***^{e}***šûriy:*** A proper noun designating Geshurites:

A. The inhabitants of Geshur (Deut. 3:14; Josh. 12:5; 13:11, 13).

B. A tribe of people near Philistia (Josh. 13:2; 1 Sam. 27:8).

1652. גָּשַׁם ***gāšam:*** A verb meaning to cause rain. It is used in its causative sense meaning to cause rain to fall with the implied argument that only Israel's God can do so, not false idols (Jer. 14:22).

1653. גֶּשֶׁם ***gešem:*** A masculine noun meaning rain, shower. It is used literally most often to refer to rain or a rain shower (Gen. 7:12; 8:2). It is used figuratively of blessing, a shower of blessing on God's people (Ezek. 34:26) but also a shower of destruction as well (Ezek. 13:11, 13). It is combined with other words to form phrases: a (heavy) shower (Zech. 10:1); a roaring of rain (1 Kgs. 18:41), etc.

1654. גֶּשֶׁם, גַּשְׁמוּ ***gešem, gašmû:*** A proper noun designating Geshem, Gashmu (Neh. 2:19; 6:1, 2, 6).

1655. גְּשֵׁם ***g***^{e}***šēm:*** A masculine noun meaning body. This is an Aramaic term and is found only in the book of Daniel. When Shadrach, Meshach, and Abednego emerged from the fiery furnace, this word was used to describe their unscathed bodies (Dan. 3:27). This term was also used to describe the nature of Nebuchadnezzar's being when he was turned into a beast (Dan. 5:21).

1656. גֹּשֶׁם ***gōšem:*** A masculine noun designating rain, shower. It is used in a figurative passive meaning of being rained on. The Lord in His indignation had not rained on Israel (Ezek. 22:24) but had sent drought.

1657. גֹּשֶׁן ***gōšen:*** A proper noun designating Goshen:

A. It refers to territory in Egypt where Israel was enslaved by the Egyptians (Gen. 45; 46; 47; 50; Ex. 8; 9). It may have been called the "land of Rameses" in later history (Gen.

42:4–27). It was situated in the eastern part of the Nile Delta.

B. It refers to a city in Judah in the southern mountainous area. It refers to a region in this area possibly.

1658. גִּשְׁפָּא ***gišpā':*** A proper noun designating Gishpa, Gispa (Neh. 11:21).

1659. גָּשַׁשׁ ***gāšaš:*** A verb meaning to grope, to feel with the hand. It is used in a figurative sense of people groping along a wall in blindness because of their wickedness (Isa. 59:10).

1660. גַּת ***gaṯ:*** A feminine noun denoting a winepress. It refers to the upper trough or basin where grapes are pressed out, usually by treading on them (Neh. 13:15). God's harsh judgments against Jerusalem were like the city's being trodden in a winepress (Lam. 1:15) because Israel had filled the winepress with her evil deeds (Joel 3:13[4:13]). The Lord is pictured as the treader of grapes pressing out His people in judgment (Isa. 63:2). Wheat and other grains were also beaten out in this press (Judg. 6:11).

1661. גַּת ***gaṯ:*** A proper noun designating Gath, one of the five chief cities of the Philistines. Only Gath is said to have had a king (1 Sam. 21:10[11], 12[13]). Goliath, the giant, was from Gath (1 Sam. 17:4; cf. 2 Sam. 21:20). It was located nearly due east of Ashdod on the coast and lay on a major international road running north-south. The ark of God was lodged there temporarily, but the inhabitants suffered plagues, and it was moved on to Ekron (1 Sam. 5:8; 6:17). David ruled over it during his monarchy. It was captured by the Syrians (2 Kgs. 12:17[18]).

1662. גַּת־הַחֵפֶר ***gaṯ-haḥēp̱er,*** גִּתָּה־חֵפֶר ***gittāh-ḥēp̱er:*** A proper noun designating Gath Hepher, a city (Josh. 19:13; 2 Kgs. 14:25).

1663. גִּתִּי ***gittiy:*** A proper noun designating Gittite (Josh. 13:3; 2 Sam. 6:10, 11; 15:18, 19, 22; 18:2; 21:19; 1 Chr. 13:13; 20:5).

1664. גִּתַּיִם ***gittayim:*** A proper noun designating Gittaim, a region or a city (2 Sam. 4:3; Neh. 11:33).

1665. גִּתִּית ***gittiyṯ:*** A feminine noun referring to a Gittith, a musical instrument or tune. It occurs in the titles or superscriptions to three psalms (8; 81; 84). Some translations note that the word may refer to a musical tune rather than a musical instrument (NIV, notes) of some kind (cf. NKJV).

1666. גֶּתֶר ***geṯer:*** A proper noun designating Gether (Gen. 10:23; 1 Chr. 1:17).

1667. גַּת־רִמּוֹן ***gaṯ-rimmôn:*** A proper noun designating Gath Rimmon (Josh. 19:45; 21:24, 25; 1 Chr. 6:69[54]).

ד Daleth

1668. דָּא *dā'*: An Aramaic demonstrative pronoun meaning this. It is used to point out and designate something, such as a city (Dan. 4:30[27]) or horn (Dan. 7:8). With *min* (4480), than, in between, it distinguishes one thing from another, this from that, from each other (Dan. 7:3). With lamedh (ל), to, between, two appearances of the word means this to (against) that (Dan. 5:6).

1669. דָּאַב *dā'ab:* A verb indicating a state of becoming faint, sorrowful. It indicates the state of failing or wasting away. It indicates a spiritual and physical renewal, for a redeemed Israel will never faint away or languish again (Jer. 31:12). The Lord will restore those who languish (Jer. 31:25). It refers to eyesight wasting away (Ps. 88:9[10]).

1670. דְּאָבָה *de'āḇāh:* It denotes a feminine noun meaning sorrow, dismay. It depicts the hopelessness and dismay that Leviathan produces in those lying before him (Job 41:22[14]) or the fact that sorrow or dismay themselves go before his advance (cf. KJV, sorrow is turned to joy; NKJV, sorrow dances before him).

1671. דְּאָבוֹן *de'āḇôn:* A masculine noun indicating sorrow, anguish, despair. It describes a despair or anguish of soul (nephesh) or mind in God's people when He sends them into exile among the nations (Deut. 28:65).

1672. דָּאַג *dā'ag:* A verb meaning to be anxious, to fear. This word describes uneasiness of mind as a result of the circumstances of life. It denotes the anxiety of Saul's father when Saul was away from home (1 Sam. 9:5; 10:2); the anxiety of David which resulted from his sin (Ps. 38:18[19]); and the fear of famine (Jer. 42:16). On the other hand, Jeremiah described the righteous person as one who would not be anxious in drought (Jer. 17:8). This word is also used as a synonym for the Hebrew word *yārē'* (3372), meaning to fear when speaking of the anxiety of King Zedekiah (Jer. 38:19) or fear in general (Isa. 57:11).

1673. דֹּאֵג *dō'ēg,* דּוֹאֵג *dô'ēg:* A proper noun designating Doeg, one of Saul's servants who was an Edomite, Saul's chief herdsman (1 Sam. 21:7[8]). He informed on David to Saul about Ahimelech the priest at Nob (1 Sam. 22:9, 20) and subsequently slew all the priests and the inhabitants of Nob, both people and animals (1 Sam. 22:18).

1674. דְּאָגָה *de'āgāh:* A feminine noun meaning anxiety, care. This word refers to apprehension because of approaching trouble. In Joshua 22:24, it refers to a concern that Israel might forget God and prompted the building of a memorial altar. Elsewhere, it refers to anxiety over running out of food or an anxiety caused by God's judgment (Ezek. 4:16; 12:18, 19). This anxiety was sometimes roused by bad news (Jer. 49:23) and sometimes relieved by good words (Prov. 12:25).

1675. דָּאָה ***dā'āh:*** A verb indicating to fly fast, to fly swiftly, to swoop. It is used figuratively to depict a nation swooping down on another nation like a bird of prey (Deut. 28:49; Jer. 48:40) and to describe God who speeds on the wings of the wind (Ps. 18:10[11]), sometimes in judgment (Jer. 49:22).

1676. דָּאָה ***dā'āh:*** A feminine noun meaning kite, vulture. It indicates an unclean bird of prey of which no varieties were to be eaten by the Israelites (Lev. 11:14; Deut. 14:13).

1677. דֹּב ***dōḇ,*** דּוֹב ***dôḇ:*** A masculine noun referring to a bear. It refers to both male or female bears (1 Sam. 17:34; 2 Kgs. 2:24; Prov. 17:12). A female is especially dangerous when bereaved of her cubs (2 Sam. 17:8; Hos. 13:8). It was compared to the lion in savagery (Amos 5:19). Yet in the messianic reign, the bear and cow will live together in peace (Isa. 11:7).

1678. דֹּב ***dōḇ:*** An Aramaic masculine noun. It depicts the Persian Empire as a bear in Daniel's night vision (Dan. 7:5).

1679. דֹּבֶא ***dōḇe':*** A masculine noun meaning strength. It depicts the strength (NASB, leisurely walk) of Asher in Moses' blessing on the twelve tribes (Deut. 33:25).

1680. דָּבַב ***dāḇaḇ:*** A verb meaning to move slowly, to glide over. It is used in late Hebrew to mean to flow slowly or to drop. In the Old Testament, it suggests something that causes one to speak. In the discourse of the Shulamite and the beloved, this word identifies the way wine gently or slowly moves over the taster's lips and teeth (Song 7:9[10]).

1681. דִּבָּה ***dibbāh:*** A feminine noun meaning slander, bad report, calumny. It is used of the true but negative report of the ten spies to Canaan (Num. 13:32; 14:36, 37), but it also depicts an accurate report concerning evil things (Gen. 37:2). It describes a report given for an evil purpose, e.g., to defame someone (Prov. 10:18), i.e., slander, which will destroy the person who spreads the story as well. It includes whispering in the sense of spreading slander against someone (Ps. 31:13[14]; Jer. 20:10) but also in the sense of repeating an unfortunate truth about people behind their backs (Ezek. 36:3).

1682. דְּבוֹרָה ***d^eḇôrāh:*** A feminine noun denoting a bee. It refers to a swarm or colony of bees (Judg. 14:8). Bees pursuing someone is used to depict the pursuit of the Amorites after Israel (Deut. 1:44). The attack of the wicked on the psalmist is likened to bees attacking a person (Ps. 118:12). The Assyrian army is pictured as an attacking bee (Isa. 7:18).

1683. דְּבוֹרָה d^e^bôrāh: A proper noun designating Deborah:

A. A nurse to Rebekah, Isaac's wife (Gen. 35:8). She died and was buried at Bethel.

B. A prophetess and judge in Israel who led the Israelites to deliverance from the Canaanites and their king in Hazor, Jabin. Her husband was named Lapidoth (Judg. 4:4). In those days, she judged Israel (Judg. 4:5). She accompanied, at his request, Barak into battle against Sisera and his armies. She and Barak composed a victory song (Judg. 5) to celebrate the triumph.

1684. דְּבַח d^e^baḥ: An Aramaic verb meaning to sacrifice, to offer sacrifices. When King Darius issued the decree permitting the rebuilding of the Temple, he specified that it would be a place to offer sacrifices (Ezra 6:3). This word is the equivalent of the Hebrew verb *zāḇaḥ* (2076).

1685. דְּבַח d^e^baḥ: A masculine noun meaning sacrifice. This word comes from the Aramaic and is derived from the verb *d^e^ḇaḥ* (1684), meaning to sacrifice. It is the term used when King Cyrus ordered a decree for the rebuilding of the Temple, describing it as the place where the Israelites offered sacrifices (Ezra 6:3).

1686. דִּבְיוֹנִים diḇyôniym: I. A masculine plural noun referring to dove's dung. The word may be a combination of *diḇ* + *yônîm* (3123, doves) which means the waste or dung of pigeons (2 Kgs. 6:25; KJV, NASB; cf. NKJV, dove droppings; NIV, seed pods). Two quarts of this material sold at the outrageous price of five shekels during a time of siege. Such dung possibly was a substitute for salt.

II. A masculine plural noun meaning seedpods. Some translators render this as seedpods, but others translate it as dove's dung (2 Kgs. 6:25; NIV; KJV, NASB, NKJV prefer dove's dung or droppings). This material sold for the outrageous price of five shekels for two quarts in a time of heavy siege.

1687. דְּבִיר d^e^biyr: A masculine noun referring to the innermost part of Solomon's Temple, also called the Holy of Holies. This cubical room, which took up one-third of the space of the Temple, housed the ark of the covenant (1 Kgs. 6:16, 19–23). The ark contained the original tablets of the Ten Commandments, was overarched by carved cherubim covered with gold, and was especially associated with God's presence. When it was first brought into the Holy of Holies, God's glory filled the Temple (1 Kgs. 8:6; cf. 1 Kgs. 8:10). In Psalm 28:2, David spoke of lifting his hands to the *d^e^ḇiyr*. Since the Temple had not yet been built, this likely referred to the heavenly reality that was the model for the Temple and earlier

Tabernacle (cf. Ps. 18:6[7]; Heb. 8:5; 9:3–5) or perhaps to the room in the Tabernacle that housed the ark of the covenant.

1688. דְּבִיר ***dᵉḇiyr:*** A proper noun designating Debir:

A. A city in southern Judah (Josh. 10:38, 39; 11:21; 12:13; 15:15, 49; 21:15; Judg. 1:11; 1 Chr. 6:58[43]).

B. An Ammonite king (Josh. 10:3).

C. A city in Gad (Josh. 13:26).

D. A city located on the boundary of northern Judah (Josh. 15:7).

1689. דִּבְלָה ***diḇlāh:*** A proper noun designating Diblah (Ezek. 6:14).

1690. דְּבֵלָה ***dᵉḇēlāh:*** A feminine noun referring to a fig cake, a lump of pressed figs. It describes figs that were pressed into the form of a cake (2 Kgs. 20:7). They were usually round or brick-shaped. It was used for food (1 Sam. 25:18; 30:12) and as an application for skin eruptions (Isa. 38:21).

1691. דִּבְלַיִם ***diḇlayim:*** A proper noun designating Diblaim (Hos. 1:3).

1692. דָּבַק ***dāḇaq:*** A verb meaning to cling to, join with, stay with. It is used of something sticking to or clinging to something else (Ezek. 29:4); it describes Ezekiel's tongue clinging to the roof of his mouth (Ezek. 3:26). It is used figuratively or symbolically of a man cleaving or clinging to his wife (Gen. 2:24) or of evil deeds clinging to a person (Ps. 101:3). It depicts leprosy clinging to a person, not going away and persisting (2 Kgs. 5:27), as well as famine (Deut. 28:21; Jer. 13:11; 42:16). It depicts relationships created as an act of joining together, to follow (Josh. 23:12; 2 Sam. 20:2). In a spiritual sense, it describes Ruth joining and staying with Boaz's maids (Ruth 2:8, 21, 23) and Jehoram's following the sins of Jeroboam (2 Kgs. 3:3). To hold on to an inheritance or right is depicted using this verb (Num. 36:7). It depicts the scales of a crocodile tightly fastened together (Job 41:17[9]) and clods of earth stuck to each other (Job 38:38). In certain uses, it has the idea of causing things to stick or be stuck (Ps. 22:15[16]; Ezek. 29:4).

1693. דְּבַק ***dᵉḇaq:*** An Aramaic verb meaning to cling to, stay together, to adhere together. It indicates the ability to stick or adhere together. In its contextual usage, it is negated to describing iron and clay, representing diverse ethnic groups or peoples that cannot cling together (Dan. 2:43).

1694. דֶּבֶק ***deḇeq:*** A masculine noun designating a joint or place of joining, welding. It indicates the place where armor is joined and thus weak (1 Kgs. 22:34; 2 Chr. 18:33) or the spot where metal work in general is fastened in various ways (Isa. 41:7).

1695. דָּבֵק ***dāḇēq:*** An adjective indicating clinging to, holding to. The wings of the cherubs in the Holy of Holies were touching and thus joining

(2 Chr. 3:12). In a spiritual sense, it depicts faithfulness to the Lord of Israel (Deut. 4:4). It depicts the steadfast companionship of an intimate friend (Prov. 18:24).

1696. דָּבַר *dāḇar:* A verb meaning to speak, to say. God told Moses to tell Pharaoh what He said (Ex. 6:29). It can mean to promise (Deut. 1:11). When used with the word song, it can mean to sing or chant (Judg. 5:12). The word can also mean think, as when Solomon spoke in his heart (Eccl. 2:15). In Jeremiah, it means to pronounce judgment (Jer. 1:16). This verb also refers to speaking about or against someone (Mal. 3:13) or someone speaking to someone else (Mal. 3:16). It is closely related to the Hebrew noun *dāḇār* (1697).

1697. דָּבָר *dāḇār:* A masculine noun meaning word, speech, matter. This frequent word has a wide range of meanings associated with it. It signified spoken words or speech (Gen. 11:1; Isa. 36:5; Jer. 51:64); a command or royal decree (Esth. 1:12, 19); a report or tidings (Ex. 33:4); advice (Judg. 20:7); poetic writings of David (2 Chr. 29:30); business affairs (1 Chr. 26:32); a legal cause (Ex. 18:16); the custom or manner of activity (Esth. 1:13); and something indefinite (thing, Gen. 22:16). Most important was the use of this word to convey divine communication. Often the word of the Lord signified the revelation given to prophets (2 Sam. 7:4; Jer. 25:3; Hos. 1:1). Similarly, the Ten Commandments were literally called the ten words of the Lord (Ex. 34:28; Deut. 4:13).

1698. דֶּבֶר *deḇer:* A noun meaning plague or pestilence. This plague is a dreaded disease similar to the bubonic plague in the Middle Ages. It was likely carried by rat fleas and produced tumors on the infected person. First Samuel 5—6 describes the plague on the Philistines as a punishment from God. The word is also used as the most dreaded threat of the Lord against His people (Lev. 26:25; Num. 14:12). The prophets use this word frequently to predict coming judgment and destruction as in the common phrase, sword, famine, and plague (Jer. 21:9; 38:2; Ezek. 6:11, NIV).

1699. דֹּבֶר *dōḇer,* דִּבֵּר *dibbēr:* A masculine noun meaning word, pasture. It describes the word that a prophet bears (Jer. 5:13) but in a different context refers to an ideal pastureland; on the one hand, where God will collect and pasture His people (Mic. 2:12) but, on the other hand, where sheep will graze in the pasture of His devastated land (Isa. 5:17).

1700. דִּבְרָה *diḇrāh:* A feminine singular noun meaning cause, end, regard, manner. In the book of Job, Eliphaz used the word to describe how he was laying down his cause before God (Job 5:8). This word is also used in the Psalms when it describes the priest who would exercise his duties in the manner of Melchizedek (Ps. 110:4). Sometimes, it is translated much more briefly than it reads in the original language, as the literal translation in Ecclesiastes would read, "concerning the situation of mankind," while the New International Version translates it "as for men" (Eccl. 3:18). It can also mean for this reason or because (Eccl. 7:14; 8:2).

1701. דִּבְרָה ***dib̲rāh:*** An Aramaic feminine noun meaning purpose, end, cause. The word is similar to the Hebrew form of the same spelling (1700). The Aramaic form occurs in Daniel 2:30 and 4:17(14). In both places, it is used with other words to create a purpose clause which is translated in order that, for the purpose of, or for the sake of.

1702. דֹּבְרוֹת ***dob̲ᵉrôṯ:*** A feminine plural collective noun denoting a raft. It refers to logs towed by a ship (1 Kgs. 5:9[23]) or floated to their destination.

1703. דַּבֶּרֶת ***dabbereṯ:*** A feminine noun meaning word. This word is found only once in the Old Testament (Deut. 33:3), where it is best translated words. In this context, it poetically describes the words God gave Moses to deliver to the people. It comes from the verb *dāb̲ar* (1696), meaning to speak and is related to the much-used Hebrew noun *dāb̲ār* (1697).

1704. דִּבְרִי ***dib̲riy:*** A proper noun designating Dibri (Lev. 24:11).

1705. דָּבְרַת ***dāb̲ᵉraṯ:*** A proper noun designating Daberath (Josh. 19:12; 21:28; 1 Chr. 6:72[57]).

1706. דְּבַשׁ ***dᵉb̲aš:*** A masculine noun designating honey. It is combined often with milk (*ḥālāb̲*) to form the phrase milk and honey. It is used literally but also stood for the richness and fertility of a land or country such as Canaan (Ex. 3:8, 17; 13:5; Lev. 20:24; Deut. 6:3; 11:9); for honey produced by bees (Judg. 14:8, 9, 18; 1 Sam. 14:25); sometimes in nests among rocks (Deut. 32:13; Ps. 81:16[17]). It was a valuable trade article (Ezek. 27:17). It was not permitted as a burnt offering (Lev. 2:11). It is to the taste what wisdom is to life (Prov. 24:13). It is to be used only in moderation (Prov. 25:16, 27). The sweetness of God's law is like the sweetness of honey (Ps. 19:10[11]); the sweetness of a lover's lips is like that of honey (Song 4:11). It is used figuratively as a metaphor for love (Song 5:1).

1707. דַּבֶּשֶׁת ***dabbešeṯ:*** A feminine noun denoting the hump of a camel. The word depicts the hump as a place where embassaries carried their treasures for tribute or for other reasons to various nations (Isa. 30:6).

1708. דַּבֶּשֶׁת ***dabbešeṯ:*** a proper noun designating Dabbesheth (Josh. 19:11).

1709. דָּג dāg: A masculine noun meaning fish. The word is derived from *dāgāh* (1711) based on the idea that fish multiply quickly. The word is used of fish in the sea, often occurring alongside birds of the heavens and beasts of the field (Gen. 9:2; Ps. 8:7[8], 8[9]; Ezek. 38:20). The word also signifies fish as food and thus gives the name fish gate to the gate where they were brought into Jerusalem to sell (2 Chr. 33:14; Neh. 3:3; Zeph. 1:10). Further, it describes fish as an object of study (1 Kgs. 4:33[5:13]); as a symbol of defenselessness (Hab. 1:14); and as showing God's sovereign creative power (Job 12:8).

1710. דָּגָה dāgāh: A feminine noun meaning fish. This word is identical in meaning to *dāg* (1709), which can be found in the book of Jonah, where the fish was called a *dāg* (Jon. 1:17[2:1]; 2:10[11]) but was called a *dāgāh* in Jonah 2:1[2]. In all other instances, this word was used in the collective sense to refer to the fish at creation (Gen. 1:26, 28); the fish who died in the plague (Ex. 7:18, 21; Ps. 105:29); the fish eaten in Egypt (Num. 11:5); and the fish in the waters (Deut. 4:18; Ezek. 29:4, 5; 47:9, 10).

1711. דָּגָה dāgāh: A verb meaning to multiply, to grow. Its primary meaning is to cover. It is used only in Genesis 48:16 where Jacob blessed Ephraim and Manasseh, the sons of Joseph. He desired that they multiply or grow into a multitude. Jacob prophesied that Ephraim, the younger brother, would be a multitude of nations, more populous than Manasseh (cf. Gen. 48:17–19) but that both would be a model of blessedness (cf. Gen. 48:20).

1712. דָּגוֹן dāgôn: A masculine proper noun referring to a god named Dagon. It was the god of the Philistine city of Gaza (Judg. 16:23). A temple or house was dedicated to him (1 Chr. 10:10), probably in Ashdod. Other verses clearly indicate Dagon as the god of Ashdod (1 Sam. 5:2–5). The Lord set Himself against Dagon (1 Sam. 5:7).

1713. דָּגַל dāgal: A verb meaning to carry a flag, a standard, a banner; to distinguish. It indicates the display of a symbol of loyalty and commitment to the Lord for His victories (Ps. 20:5[6]). Its display showed the strength and dazzling glory of an army (Song 6:4, 10) arrayed in its orderly troops. It is used to describe the appearance of the beloved, distinguished among all others (Song 5:10).

1714. דֶּגֶל degel: A masculine noun denoting a flag, banner, standard. It depicted banners or standards to identify the various tribes of Israel (Num. 1:52; 2:2). It represented the tribe to which a group belonged (Num. 2:3, 10). It depicted the attitude and intent of the lover toward his bride (Song 2:4).

1715. דָּגָן dāgān: A masculine noun referring to corn, grain. It referred to cereal grains, one of the three blessings of the Lord on His people of wine, oil, and grain (Num. 18:12; Deut. 7:13; 11:14; 12:17; Joel 1:10; Hag. 1:11). It is used alone rarely (Neh. 5:2, 3, 10; Ezek. 36:29). It is used forty times, and it is clear that the Lord gave this grain as a blessing (Gen. 27:28, 37; Ps. 4:7[8]; Isa. 62:8; Hos. 2:9[11]). The land of Canaan is termed a land of grain and new wine (Deut. 33:28). The word indicates the firstfruits of grain and corn offered to the priests (Num. 18:12; Deut. 18:4); as a tithe (Deut. 12:17; 14:23); or for both (Neh. 10:39[40]) reasons.

1716. דָּגַר ***dāgar:*** A verb meaning to gather together, to care for. It refers to snake eggs being cared for (Isa. 34:15, NIV, NASB, after hatching; KJV, NKJV, gathered together [for care]). It refers to a partridge hatching eggs it did not lay (Jer. 17:11) (NIV, NASB; NKJV, broods; KJV, sitteth on).

1717. דַּד ***da<u>d</u>:*** A masculine noun denoting a nipple, breast. It refers to a wife's breasts (Prov. 5:19), which are to satisfy her husband alone. It is used figuratively to describe the breasts of Israel pictured as a young girl (Ezek. 23:3, 8, 21) in her early harlotry among the nations.

1718. דָּדָה ***dā<u>d</u>āh:*** A verb meaning to walk softly, to go along, to wander. It describes the happy and joyous days of the psalmist as he led his group to the temple to worship God (Ps. 42:4[5]), using steps of delight and joy. On the other hand, it describes Hezekiah's anguished walk during his life in the bitterness of his soul (Isa. 38:15).

1719. דְּדָן ***d^e<u>d</u>ān,*** דְּדָנֶה ***d^e<u>d</u>āneh,*** רֹדָן ***rō<u>d</u>ān:*** A proper noun designating Dedan:

A. A great-grandson of Ham (Gen. 10:7; 1 Chr. 1:9).

B. A grandson of Abraham (Gen. 25:3; 1 Chr. 1:32).

C. A southern Arabian tribe (Jer. 25:23; Ezek 25:13; 27:15, 20; 38:13).

D. A northern Arabian tribe, from an area near Edom (Jer. 49:8).

E. The city or island of Rhodes, after the spelling in the Septuagint (Ezek. 27:15).

1720. דְּדָנִי ***d^e<u>d</u>āniy:*** A proper noun designating Dedanite, Dedanim (Isa. 21:13).

1721. דֹּדָנִים ***dō<u>d</u>āniym,*** רֹדָנִים ***rō<u>d</u>āniym:*** A proper noun designating Dodanim:

A. Dodanim, following the spelling of the Hebrew text (Gen. 10:4, NASB, KJV; 1 Chr. 1:7, KJV).

B. Rodanim, following the spelling of the Septuagint (Gen. 10:4, NIV; 1 Chr. 1:7, NASB, NIV).

1722. דְּהַב ***d^eha<u>b</u>:*** An Aramaic masculine noun meaning gold. Gold was the most precious metal in the ancient Near East and was considered the metal of the gods. It was used in royal construction, clothing, furniture, and decorative items (Dan. 5:2–4, 7). A gold necklace was common dress for royalty and was presented as an award (Dan. 5:16, 29) for faithful or outstanding service. Nebuchadnezzar's dream involved a statue whose head was of gold (Dan. 2:32, 35, 38), and he constructed a huge image of gold possibly depicting himself (Dan. 3:1, 5, 7). Many vessels in the Lord's temple were of gold (Ezra 5:14; 6:5; 7:15; Dan. 5:2–4, 23).

1723. דְּהָוֵא ***dehāwē':*** A proper noun designating Dehavites (Ezra 4:9).

1724. דָּהַם ***dāham:*** A verb meaning to be astonished, surprised, bewildered, dismayed. It is used to describe God's seeming behavior and attitude toward Judah during a time of drought (Jer. 14:9).

1725. דָּהַר ***dāhar:*** A verb meaning to prance, to gallop, to rush, to charge. It describes the panic of military horses during the destruction and confusion of Nineveh's defeat (Nah. 3:2).

1726. דַּהֲרָה ***dah^{a}rāh:*** A feminine noun referring to the prancing, dashing, galloping of a horse. It describes the behavior of the armies' horses who defeated Sisera in the time of Deborah (Judg. 5:22).

1727. דּוּב ***dûḇ:*** A verb meaning to waste away, pine away, consume. It describes a pining away or wasting away of the souls (*nepheš*) of God's people because they rejected the statutes of the Lord (Lev. 26:16; KJV, cause sorrow of heart).

1728. דַּוָּג ***dawwāg:*** A masculine noun denoting a fisherman. It is used figuratively to depict God's searching for His people wherever they may be to bring them back to their land (Jer. 16:16). Used literally, it describes those who will catch fish, even along the Dead Sea, when God restores His people and their land (Ezek. 47:10).

1729. דּוּגָה ***dûgāh:*** A feminine noun referring to a fishhook. It was a hook usually used to snag fish but also used to hook and lead away the rebellious and corrupt rich, sophisticated but oppressive women of Bashan (Amos 4:2).

1730. דּוֹד ***dôḏ:*** A masculine noun meaning beloved, loved one, uncle. This word is used most often in the Song of Solomon and has three clear meanings: (1) the most frequent is an address to a lover, beloved (Song 5:4; 6:3; 7:9[10]); (2) love, used literally of an adulteress who seduced a naïve man (Prov. 7:18), and of Solomon and his lover (Song 1:2, 4; 4:10) (This meaning of love is also used symbolically of Jerusalem reaching the age of love [Ezek. 16:8] and Jerusalem's adultery [bed of love] with the Babylonians [Ezek. 23:17]); and finally, (3) uncle (Lev. 10:4; 1 Sam. 10:14–16; Esth. 2:15).

1731. דּוּד ***dûḏ:*** A masculine noun designating a basket, kettle. It describes a deep, two-handled cooking pot (1 Sam. 2:14). It was used as a container to carry the severed heads of Ahab's seventy sons (2 Kgs. 10:7). A basket for figs is pictured in Jeremiah's visions (24:2). It indicates Egyptian baskets that Israelites were forced to use in slavery (Ps. 81:6[7]). It refers to pots or caldrons as well (2 Chr. 35:13; Job 41:20[12]).

1732. דָּוִד ***dāwiḏ***, דָּוִיד ***dāwiyḏ:*** A proper noun designating David, the greatest and the model king of Israel, reigned 1010–970 B.C. He sired Solomon through Bathsheba, Uriah the Hittite's wife. His name may mean "beloved," coming from the root d-w-d, "to love."

The Book of Ruth records his genealogy (Ruth 4:17–22) through Ruth, the Moabitess. God chose him to reign after rejecting Saul. He "read" David's heart, thus indicating that moral and character issues were involved in God's choice of kings to reign. Samuel anointed him to be king (1 Sam. 16:13–23). David's rise was meteoric and is recorded in 1 Samuel while the place of Samuel and the demise of Saul are interwoven with David's in the author's recounting of the story. Saul unsuccessfully tried to kill David numerous times (1 Sam. 18; 19; 23; 24; 26). David is forced to live as a desperado and fugitive among the Philistines (1 Sam. 27; 29). He destroyed the Amalekites, Israel's ancient enemy (Ex. 17:8–15; 17; 1 Sam. 30). He was crowned king at Hebron and reigned over Judah for seven years and six months. He moved to Jerusalem and reigned thirty-three years, a total reign of forty years (2 Sam. 5:1–5). He captured Jerusalem and set up the ark there (2 Sam. 5:6—6:23). God established an eternal covenant with David and his house (2 Sam. 7).

David's reign saw the fulfillment of the promises and covenants with the fathers, for Israel became a mighty nation in the ancient Near East and ruled over the nations (Gen. 12:1–3; 15:12–21). But David sinned by committing murder, adultery, and deceit with respect to Bathsheba. From this time on, the house of David suffered a traumatic decline (2 Sam. 11—20). He, however, subdued the Philistines (2 Sam. 21:15–22). He became the "sweet psalmist of Israel" (2 Sam. 22:1–51). Most of the psalms are attributed to David, including some in which he confesses his guilt (Pss. 32; 51). Before his death, he made preparation for his son Solomon to succeed him (1 Kgs. 1—2) and to build the Temple (1 Chr. 23—27; 28; 29).

1733. דּוֹדָה ***dôḏāh:*** A feminine noun meaning aunt, father's sister. It designates Jochebed as Amram's father's sister whom he married (Ex. 6:20). Elsewhere, it indicates the wife of a father's brother (Lev. 18:14; 20:20).

1734. דּוֹדוֹ ***dôḏô:*** A proper noun designating Dodo:

A. Grandfather of Tola (Judg. 10:1).

B. The father of Eleazar (2 Sam. 23:9; 1 Chr. 11:12). See *dôday* (1737).

C. The father of Elhanan (2 Sam. 23:24; 1 Chr. 11:26).

1735. דֹּדָוָהוּ *dōdāwāhû:* A proper noun designating Dodavahu, Dodavah (2 Chr. 20:37).

1736. דּוּדָאִים *dûdā'iym:* A masculine plural noun meaning mandrake. A fragrant plant (Song 7:13[14]), the mandrake was considered a potent aphrodisiac. This usage can be seen in Genesis 30:14–16, where the text describes Leah using these plants to attract Jacob.

1737. דּוֹדַי *dôday:* A proper noun designating Dodai, probably the same as *dôdô* (1734,B) (1 Chr. 27:4).

1738. דָּוָה *dāwāh:* A verb designating infirmity, a reference to a woman's menstrual period. It indicates the time during a woman's menstrual period when she was considered unclean (Lev. 12:2).

1739. דָּוֶה *dāweh:* An adjective referring to a woman's menstrual state, menstrual cloth; faint, sick. The word describes the weakened state of the prophet Jeremiah because of the devastations of Jerusalem (Lam. 1:13), likewise concerning his faint heart (Lam. 5:17). It describes the menstrual flow which rendered a woman impure (Lev. 15:33). Intercourse was considered unclean during the menstrual state or period (Lev. 20:18). It refers to an impure thing or cloth to be thrown away (Isa. 30:22).

1740. דּוּחַ *dûah:* A verb meaning to rinse, to cleanse, to wash away. This word is used only four times in the Old Testament. On two occasions, it is used within the sacrificial context to describe offerings that needed to be washed (2 Chr. 4:6; Ezek. 40:38). In other contexts, the word describes the washing away of the sins of those in Jerusalem (Isa. 4:4) and Nebuchadnezzar's carrying away (or washing away) of Judah in the Babylonian exile (Jer. 51:34).

1741. דְּוַי *d^eway:* A masculine noun denoting illness, loathsomeness. It refers to odious or execrable food, intolerable for eating (Job 6:7). It describes the illness of a righteous man (Ps. 41:3[4]).

1742. דַּוָּי *dawwāy:* An adjective meaning weak, faint, sick. Used figuratively, it describes the spiritual sickness of Israel's head (Isa. 1:5). It describes the heart sorely afflicted because of the treachery of Judah (Jer. 8:18; Lam. 1:22).

1743. דּוּךְ *dûk:* A verb indicating beating, crushing, pounding. It describes the process of pounding or beating manna in a mortar (Num. 11:8).

1744. דּוּכִיפַת *dûkiypat:* A feminine noun referring to a hoopoe, lapwing; an unclean bird. It refers to one of the birds that was unclean to Israel and therefore not to be eaten (Lev. 11:19; Deut. 14:18).

1745. דּוּמָה ***dûmāh:*** A feminine noun indicating silence. It is used figuratively to refer to death, literally the land of silence (Ps. 94:17; 115:17) where the Lord is not praised.

1746. דּוּמָה ***dûmāh:*** A proper noun designating Dumah:

A. The son of Ishmael (Gen. 25:14; 1 Chr. 1:30).

B. A city in Judah (Josh. 15:52).

C. A symbolic name of Edom, indicating death and destruction (see 1745) (Isa. 21:11).

1747. דּוּמִיָּה ***dûmiyyāh,*** דֻּמִיָּה ***dumiyyāh:*** A feminine noun denoting silence, a quiet wait, in silence, rest. It indicates a time of silence in the sense of rest (Ps. 22:2[3]) or a self-imposed period of silence in the presence of evil persons (Ps. 39:2[3]). It may, on the other hand, indicate a time of reverential silence and patience as one waits for God (Ps. 62:1[2]) or a period of awesome silence in anticipation of praise to the Lord (Ps. 65:1[2]).

1748. דּוּמָם ***dûmām:*** A masculine noun indicating silence, a quiet wait, in silence. It refers to a stone of silence or mute stone that is addressed by a deluded idolater (Hab. 2:19). It is used adverbially to refer to a person's patient, silent waiting on the LORD (Lam. 3:26). It describes the silent, subdued state of a defeated Babylonian facing destruction (Isa. 47:5).

1749. דּוֹנַג ***dônag:*** A masculine noun denoting wax. It is always used figuratively to form similes symbolizing something melting or soft: mountains melt before the Lord (Ps. 97:5; Mic. 1:4); the heart is like wax in times of distress (Ps. 22:14[15]); the wicked melt away before the Lord (Ps. 68:2[3]).

1750. דּוּץ ***dûṣ:*** A verb meaning to dance, to leap. It indicates the dance of astonishment and dismay that grips those who see the beast leviathan approach (Job 41:22[14]; KJV, sorrow is turned into joy; NKJV, sorrow dances before him).

1751. דָּקוּ ***dāqû:*** An Aramaic verb meaning to break, to shatter to pieces, to crush. It is an emphatic word and describes the crushing of iron, clay, bronze, silver, and gold in the statue of Nebuchadnezzar's dream (Dan. 2:35).

1752. דּוּר ***dûr:*** A verb meaning to dwell. It is used once. It means to settle down and be at home (Ps. 84:10[11]) in the tent of wickedness, a condition the psalmist rejects compared to standing in the presence of God.

1753. דּוּר ***dûr:*** An Aramaic verb indicating to dwell, to live. It is a broad term describing the life and existence of living things in their appropriate habitats wherever they dwell: humankind, wild animals, fowl (Dan. 2:38; 4:1[3:31], 12[9], 6:25[26]).

1754. דּוּר ***dûr:*** A masculine noun indicating a heap, pile, something balled up. It is used figuratively to describe Israel's being rolled tightly like a ball and cast away (Isa. 22:18) into exile. It is used of piling wood or bones for fuel under a cooking pot (Ezek. 24:5; KJV, burn; NKJV, pile).

1755. דּוֹר ***dôr:*** A masculine noun meaning generation, period of time, posterity, age, time, setting of life. In general, the word indicates the time from birth to death; the time from one's birth to the birth of one's first child; the living adults of a certain time or place; a period as it is defined through major events, persons, behavior, and the spirit of the age. It also marks a duration of time. There is no agreed on length of time which may stretch from twenty to one hundred years, but the word is also used figuratively to mean an indefinite or unending length of time in the past or future. These basic observations can be illustrated from various passages and contexts: the generation of Noah was characterized by wickedness and violence, yet he was a righteous man in his generation (Gen. 7:1); Moses spoke of a crooked generation in his day and in the future (Deut. 32:5); however, the psalmist spoke of a generation of righteous people (Ps. 14:5) and a generation of people who seek the Lord (Ps. 24:6). These generations will be blessed by God (Ps. 112:2). Generations come and go without interruption (Eccl. 1:4).

Time can be measured by the passing of generations, as when the great deeds of the Lord are passed on from generation to generation, in effect forever (Ps. 145:4; Isa. 34:17); God's throne lasts forever, from generation to generation (Lam. 5:19). Likewise, God's judgments can endure forever (Jer. 50:39). The closing of an era can be marked by the death of all the persons belonging to that generation (Ex. 1:6; Judg. 2:10), but persons can be taken from their own proper age, dwellings, or circles of existence, as Hezekiah nearly was (Ps. 102:24[25]; Isa. 38:12), and a subgroup, such as fighting men, can pass away from an era (Deut. 2:14). On the other hand, God's length of days spans all generations without end (Ps. 102:24[25]).

The generation or generations mentioned may refer to the past, present, or future. Noah was perfect during the time of his contemporaries (Gen. 6:9); the generations extended into the future when God established His covenant with Abraham and all future generations (Gen. 17:7, 12; cf. Lev. 25:30) or when He gave His name as a memorial for all generations to come (Ex. 3:15). The word often refers to past generations, such as the generation of the fathers (Ps. 49:19[20]; Isa. 51:9). God's constancy again stands out, for His days span all past eras as well as all future generations (Ps. 102:24[25]). Israel was encouraged in Moses' song to remember the past generations of old

(Deut. 32:7) when God effected His foundational acts of deliverance for Israel and gave them the Law at Sinai. Present generations are to learn from past generations (Deut. 32:7) and can affect future generations by declaring the Lord's power (Ps. 71:18).

Certain generations were singled out for special note: the third and fourth generations of children are punished for the sins of their fathers (Ex. 20:5; 34:7); the infamous generation that wandered in the wilderness for forty years experienced God's judgments until everyone in that generation died (Ps. 95:10). Yet the love of God is not bound, for, in a figurative sense, it is passed on to thousands of generations (i.e., without limitation) forever and to every person (Ex. 20:6; 34:7).

1756. דֹּאר ***dō'r,*** דּוֹר ***dôr:*** A proper noun designating Dor (Josh. 11:2; 12:23; 17:11; Judg. 1:27; 1 Kgs. 4:11; 1 Chr. 7:29).

1757. דּוּרָא ***dûrā':*** A proper noun designating Dura (Dan. 3:1).

1758. דּוּשׁ ***dûš,*** דִּישׁ ***diyš:*** A verb indicating threshing, treading out, to trample. It means to trample grain (Deut. 25:4; Hos. 10:11) or other objects (Job 39:15). It is used figuratively of Israel's threshing the mountains (her enemies) (Isa. 41:15); of the Arameans' devastation of Israel's army and chariots under Jehoahaz, as if they were the dust left over after threshing grain (2 Kgs. 13:7); of the Lord's devastation and trampling of Moab like straw in a manure pile (Isa. 25:10; cf. Amos 1:3; Hab. 3:12).

1759. דּוּשׁ ***dûš:*** An Aramaic verb meaning to tread down, to trample. It indicates crushing or smashing something by walking on it. Daniel's fourth beast will tread down the whole earth (Dan. 7:23).

1760. דָּחָה ***dāḥāh:*** A verb meaning to push back, to lean, to drive away, to drive on or down. The psalmist cries for the Lord to defeat and frustrate his enemies (Ps. 35:5; 36:12[13]). It describes evil persons as threatening or leaning walls (Ps. 62:3[4]). Figuratively, it indicates pushing persons down, harming them (Ps. 118:13) with the intent to harm greatly (Ps. 140:4[5]). It generally describes the defeat or thrusting down of wicked persons (Prov. 14:32) and false prophets (Jer. 23:12). The Lord cares for the outcasts, the banished or dispersed of Israel (Isa. 11:12; 56:8).

1761. דַּחֲוָה ***daḥ^{a}wāh:*** An Aramaic feminine noun denoting entertainment, musical instruments. It depicts either the lack of musical instruments, entertainers, or some other diversion for rest and relaxation (Dan. 6:18[19]). The word is uncertain. Some have suggested food, perfumes, or even concubines as its meaning.

1762. דְּחִי ***d^{e}ḥiy:*** A masculine noun indicating falling, stumbling. The word denotes something to be avoided with one's feet. The Lord delivered the psalmist from this, probably stumbling or falling (Ps. 56:13[14]; 116:8).

1763. דְּחַל *dᵉḥal:* A verb meaning to fear, to slink. It comes from the Aramaic and corresponds to the Hebrew word *zāḥal* (2119). The idea is one of slinking or crawling, such as a serpent or a worm; to back away or tremble in fear. People trembled before the greatness which God gave Nebuchadnezzar (Dan. 5:19). Darius turned this and focused on the Giver of the greatness, saying that people would tremble before God's awesome being (Dan. 6:26[27]).

1764. דֹּחַן *dōḥan:* A masculine noun referring to grain, millet. It is depicted as part of a meager diet prescribed for Ezekiel to symbolize the food of a besieged city (Ezek. 4:9).

1765. דָּחַף *dāḥap̱:* A verb indicating to hurry, hasten. It indicates doing something quickly, in haste: Uzziah was quickly taken from the temple (2 y fear as he mourned (Esth. 6:12).

1766. דָּחַק *dāḥaq:* A verb meaning to oppress, to jostle, to afflict. It refers to military, economic, and political affliction (Judg. 2:18). It is used of locusts marching in disciplined array without crowding or jostling one another (Joel 2:8).

1767. דַּי *day:* A masculine noun indicating enough, as often as, sufficient. It indicates a sufficient amount of something: enough materials to build the Tabernacle (Ex. 36:7); a sufficient amount for someone, e.g., enough honey for energy (Prov. 25:16); sufficient animals for a sacrifice (Lev. 5:7; 12:8); enough money to redeem some property (Lev. 25:26, 28). Combined with other words, it can have a negative meaning: until (*'aḏ*) there is no need (NASB, until it overflows) (Mal. 3:10); nothing (Jer. 51:58); or an overabundance (*min* (4480) + day; Ex. 36:5). It is found in several idiomatic constructions: with the preposition b^e plus trumpet, it indicates as often as the trumpet sounds (Job 39:25); with the preposition k^e, it means corresponding to or fitting for (Deut. 25:2). Other idioms are: as numerous as (Judg. 6:5); according to need, e.g., yearly (1 Sam. 7:16; 2 Kgs. 4:8). With l^e plus *mâ* (*lᵉmadday*), it indicates of sufficient number (2 Chr. 30:3) or sufficiently (KJV).

1768. דִּי *diy:* An Aramaic particle meaning who, which, of which. A demonstrative and relative particle. It often means "of" after a noun (Dan. 2:15; 7:10), and sometimes indicates the material of which something is made (Dan. 2:33). It introduces a relative clause meaning who, which, what (Dan. 2:26; 4:16[19]; 5:2). Combined with *kōl,* it means everything that (Ezra 7:23). Its other uses are readily discernible if the context and words it is combined with are carefully noted: interrogative (Dan. 3:6); conjunction (Dan. 2:8; Ezra 5:14); introducing direct speech (Dan. 2:25); purpose

(Dan. 4:6[3]); result (Ezra 5:10); the reason or cause for something (Dan. 2:20).

1769. דִּיבֹן ***diybôn:*** A proper noun designating Dibon:

A. A city north of Arnon (Num. 21:30; 32:3, 34; 33:45, 46; Josh. 13:9, 17; Isa. 15:2; Jer. 48:18, 22).

B. A village in Judah (Neh. 11:25).

1770. דִּיג ***diyg:*** A verb meaning to fish, catch fish. It refers to a person who catches fish but is used figuratively of God sending fishermen to fish for His people in exile to bring them back (Jer. 16:16).

1771. דַּיָּג ***dayyāg:*** A masculine noun denoting a fisherman. It is used only in the plural of fishermen who cast fish lines or spread nets to catch fish (Isa. 19:8); fish for the exiles of Israel to bring them back to their homeland (Jer. 16:16).

1772. דַּיָּה ***dayyāh:*** A feminine noun indicating a vulture, falcon. It indicates an unclean bird of prey not edible for Israel (Deut. 14:13). It is a sinister and threatening presence predicted for the ruin of the nations God judges (Isa. 34:15).

1773. דְּיוֹ ***d***^{e}***yô:*** A masculine noun referring to ink. It was the writing material Baruch used to write down Jeremiah's prophecies (Jer. 36:18).

1774. דִּי זָהָב ***diy zāhāḇ:*** A proper noun designating Dizahab (Deut. 1:1).

1775. דִּימוֹן ***diymôn:*** A proper noun designating Dimon (Isa. 15:9).

1776. דִּימוֹנָה ***diymônāh:*** A proper noun designating Dimonah (Josh. 15:22).

1777. דִּין ***diyn:*** A verb meaning to bring justice, to go to court, to pass sentence, to contend, to act as judge, to govern, to plead a cause, to be at strife, to quarrel. The verb regularly involves bringing justice or acting as judge; the Lord Himself is the chief judge over the whole earth and especially over those who oppose Him (1 Sam. 2:10). The tribe of Dan, whose name means "He provides justice" and is followed by this verb, will indeed provide justice for His people (Gen. 30:6). The king of Israel was to deliver justice in righteousness (Ps. 72:2). Israel's many sins included failure to obtain justice in the case of the orphan (Jer. 5:28). The verb also signifies pleading a case: God's people often failed to plead the case of the orphan (Jer. 5:28); this was a heinous sin for the house of David, for Judah was to administer justice every day for all those who needed it (Jer. 21:12). Sometimes pleading a case resulted in vindication, as when God gave Rachel a son through her maidservant Bilhah, and Rachel in thanks named him Dan (Gen. 30:6). At other times, it resulted in redress for evils done, as when God judges the nations in the day of His anger (Ps. 110:6); Israel's plight because of their sin had become hopeless so they had no one to plead their cause (Jer. 30:13).

The verb also signifies governance, contention, or going to law or court. It is hopeless for individuals to contend with persons who are far more powerful and advantaged than they are (Eccl. 6:10). The high priest, Joshua, was given authority to govern, render justice, and judge the house of the Lord on the condition that he himself walked in the ways of the Lord (Zech. 3:7).

In the passive-reflexive stem, the verb signifies to be at strife or to quarrel (2 Sam. 19:10).

1778. דִּין ***diyn:*** An Aramaic verb meaning to judge. It corresponds to the Hebrew word that is spelled the same or spelled as *diyn* (1777). The word occurs only in Ezra 7:25, where Artaxerxes commanded Ezra to appoint people to judge those beyond the river who knew God's laws.

1779. דִּין ***diyn:*** A masculine noun meaning judgment, condemnation, plea, cause. This word carries a legal connotation and is found in poetic texts with most of its occurrences in the book of Job. The idea of judgment is often followed by justice (Job 36:17). Judah is called a wicked nation, one that does not plead the cause of the less fortunate (Jer. 5:28). It also occurs in relation to strife in a legal case (Prov. 22:10).

1780. דִּין ***diyn:*** An Aramaic, masculine noun meaning justice, judgment. It is used to signify punishment (Ezra 7:26) or the justice of God (Dan. 4:37[34]). It is related to the Aramaic noun *dayyān* (1782) and the Aramaic verb *diyn* (1778). It is also similar to the Hebrew verb *diyn* (1777) and the Hebrew noun *diyn* (1779).

1781. דַּיָּן ***dayyān:*** A masculine noun meaning judge, and more specifically, God as judge. David uses this word to refer to God as his judge (1 Sam. 24:15[16]). The psalmist uses this term to describe God as the defender or judge of the widows (Ps. 68:5[6]).

1782. דַּיָּן ***dayyān:*** An Aramaic masculine noun meaning judge. It corresponds to the Hebrew word of the same spelling and meaning. This word is used only in Ezra 7:25 where it refers to judges that Ezra was to appoint over those who knew God's laws. The judges were to judge diligently and had power to imprison, execute, and banish people in addition to confiscating property (cf. Ezra 7:26).

1783. דִּינָה ***diynāh:*** A proper noun designating Dinah, the daughter of Jacob. Her mother was Leah (Gen. 30:21). She was raped by Shechem, son of Hamor, a Hivite (Gen. 34:1–4). Her brothers, Simeon and Levi, avenged her and destroyed all the males of Shechem (Gen. 34:25–31).

1784. דִּינָיֵא ***diynāyē',*** דַּיָּנַיָּא ***dayyānayyā':*** I. An Aramaic masculine plural proper noun referring to the Dinaites (Ezra 4:9, KJV).

II. An Aramaic masculine plural noun meaning Judges (Ezra 4:9, NASB).

1785. דָּיֵק ***dāyēq:*** A masculine noun referring to siege works, siege mounds, siege wall, bulwarks. It describes the engines and weapons of ancient warfare. These works were built at the site of an attack and enabled Nebuchadnezzar to capture Jerusalem (2 Kgs. 25:1; Jer. 52:4; Ezek. 4:2; 17:17; 21:22[27]). Siege works were erected against the coastal city of Tyre (Ezek. 26:8) by Babylon, including a causeway out to the island city itself.

1786. דַּיִשׁ ***dayiš:*** A masculine noun designating threshing, threshing time. It refers to the process and period of time given to grape gathering and sowing (Lev. 26:5), an extended time if Israel would walk in obedience to her God.

1787. דִּישֹׁן ***diyšōn,*** דִּשׁוֹן ***dišôn,*** דִּשֹׁן ***dišōn:*** A proper noun designating Dishon:

A. The fifth son of Seir (Gen. 36:21, 26, 30; 1 Chr. 1:38).

B. Grandson of Seir (Gen. 36:25; 1 Chr. 1:41).

1788. דִּישׁוֹן ***diyšôn:*** A masculine noun referring to a gazelle, ibex, pygarg. It was an animal considered clean and suitable for eating (Deut. 14:5).

1789. דִּישָׁן ***diyšān:*** A proper noun designating Dishan, the seventh son of Seir (Gen. 36:21, 28, 30; 1 Chr. 1:38, 42).

1790. דַּךְ ***dak:*** An adjective meaning oppressed, afflicted, crushed. It indicates persons who are pressed down, oppressed (Ps. 9:9[10]; 10:18; 74:21), crushed down. The Lord cares for and is concerned for them. These persons may be the objects of verbal attacks (Prov. 26:28).

1791. דֵּךְ ***dēk,*** דָּךְ ***dāk:*** An Aramaic demonstrative pronoun (masculine, feminine), meaning this. It is used to point out something and always comes after the noun with which it is used (Ezra 4:13, 15, 16, 19, 21; 5:8, 16, 17; 6:7, 8, 12).

1792. דָּכָא ***dākā':*** A verb meaning to crush, to beat down, to bruise, to oppress. The Hebrew word is often used in a poetic or figurative sense. Eliphaz spoke of those who lived in houses of clay, whose foundations were crushed easily (Job 4:19). The psalmist prayed that the king would crush an oppressor (Ps. 72:4) and accused the wicked of crushing the Lord's people (Ps. 94:5). The wise man exhorted others not to crush the needy in court (Prov. 22:22). Isaiah said that it was the Lord's will to crush the Servant (Isa. 53:10). Metaphorically, this word can also be used in the same way the English word *crushed* is used to mean dejected or sad (Isa. 19:10).

1793. דַּכָּא dakkā': An adjective meaning destruction, a crumbled substance, an object crushed into a powder, or pulverized dust. Thus, by extension, *dakkā'* can mean humble or contrite. God is the healer and rescuer of one who is crushed in spirit (Ps. 34:18[19]). He also lives with those whose spirits are contrite and humble (Isa. 57:15). It comes from the Hebrew verb *dāḵā'* (1792), meaning to crush or to beat to pieces.

1794. דָּכָה dāḵāh: A verb meaning to crush, to break in pieces; to crouch. It is most often used figuratively of persons crushed emotionally and spiritually by the wicked (Ps. 10:10; KJV, NASB, NKJV, crouches); of persons weighed down and broken by their guilt before the Lord (Ps. 38:8[9]) or seemingly under His judgment (Ps. 44:19[20]); of bones broken by the Lord's imposition of guilt for sins (Ps. 51:8[10]); of a broken spirit as an acceptable sacrifice to God (Ps. 51:17[19]).

1795. דַּכָּה dakkāh: A feminine noun indicating a crushing of the testicles, emasculated (by crushing). It denotes the crushing of the testicles (Deut. 23:1[2]); KJV, wounded in the stones).

1796. דֳּכִי d^okiy: A masculine noun denoting a crushing or pounding of waves. It describes the mighty pounding and crashing of waves (Ps. 93:3), but the might of the Lord is far greater.

1797. דִּכֵּן dikkēn: An Aramaic demonstrative pronoun indicating this, that. It points out something: an image (Dan. 2:31); a horn (Dan. 7:20, 21).

1798. דְּכַר d^eḵar: An Aramaic masculine noun denoting a ram. It refers to rams used for sacrifice (Ezra 6:9, 17; 7:17).

1799. דִּכְרוֹן dikrôn, דָּכְרָן dokrān: I. An Aramaic masculine noun referring to minutes, a record, memorandum. It refers to a written royal decree from King Cyrus (Ezra 6:2) allowing the returned exiles to rebuild the Temple in Jerusalem.

II. An Aramaic masculine noun referring to minutes, a record, memorandum. It refers to a written record of past events concerning Jerusalem located in the archives or records of Artaxerxes (Ezra 4:15).

1800. דַּל dal: I. An adjective meaning poor, weak. It is used often as a noun to designate poor and oppressed persons for whom the Lord has a special concern (Ex. 23:3). They are on the opposite social scale from the rich (Ex. 30:15; 1 Sam. 2:8; Prov. 10:15; 22:16) and their condition often separates them from even their friends (Prov. 19:4). The poor have no power and are weak, helpless (Job 34:28; Ps. 82:3; Prov. 22:22).

It is used to describe various things or persons that are poor, weak, thin, insignificant: cattle (Gen. 41:19); people (Lev. 14:21; 2 Sam. 13:4); a clan or family line (Judg. 6:15; 2 Sam. 3:1). It depicts poor, noninfluential persons who are the opposite of great, powerful, or influential ones (Jer. 5:4).

1801. דָּלַג ***dālag:*** A verb meaning to leap, leap over, jump. It means to leap on or jump over (Zeph. 1:9); in this instance, it was part of a pagan ritual act. It is an ability restored to the lame in the time of Zion's restoration (Isa. 35:6). It is used figuratively in David's claim to leap over a wall with the Lord's help (2 Sam. 22:30; Ps. 18:29[30]). It is used of the joyous jumping and leaping of a groom coming to his bride (Song 2:8).

1802. דָּלָה ***dālāh:*** I. A verb indicating to draw up, to lift up. It describes the act of drawing water from a well (Ex. 2:16, 19), of metaphorically drawing out a wise plan from a person's heart like deep water (Prov. 20:5) or of the Lord's lifting up people beset by their enemies (Ps. 30:1[2]).

II. A verb meaning to hang down, dangle, hang limp. It describes the legs of a lame person which dangle or hang down uselessly (Prov. 26:7; KJV, are not equal).

1803. דַּלָּה ***dallāh:*** I. A feminine noun denoting sickness; the poor. It refers to poor people in the land of Israel after the nation went into exile (2 Kgs. 24:14; 25:12; Jer. 40:7; 52:15, 16). It indicates sickness which cuts a person's life (KJV, Isa. 38:12).

II. A feminine noun denoting hair, locks; loom, thrum. It indicates a loom where thread or yarn was made into cloth by weaving (NASB, NIV, NKJV, Isa. 38:12) or possibly the activity of the worker at the loom. It denotes the hair of the bridegroom (Song 7:5[6]).

1804. דָּלַח ***dālaḥ:*** A verb indicating to stir up, to churn, to muddle. It is used figuratively of troubling or stirring up the rivers of Egypt like a monster (Ezek. 32:2) or of a person's foot polluting water (Ezek. 32:13).

1805. דְּלִי ***d^e^liy:*** A masculine noun denoting a bucket. It is used of an ancient leather bucket used for scooping and pouring water (Num. 24:7; Isa. 40:15).

1806. דְּלָיָה ***d^e^lāyāh,*** דְּלָיָהוּ ***d^e^lāyāhû:*** A proper noun designating Delaiah:

A. Son of Elioenai (1 Chr. 3:24).
B. A priest (1 Chr. 24:18).
C. A royal officer (Jer. 36:12, 25).
D. A Jew (Ezra 2:60; Neh. 7:62).
E. Father of Shemaiah (Neh. 6:10).

1807. דְּלִילָה ***d^e^liylāh:*** A proper noun designating Delilah, the seductress of Samson. She was from the Valley of Sorek and may have been a Philistine. Samson loved her (Judg. 16:4). For a high price paid to her by the Philistines, she agreed to find out why Samson had his strength and relayed her knowledge to the Philistines. The Philistines then captured Samson and put his eyes out.

She showed great determination and self-control as she slowly urged Samson to tell her the secret to his great strength.

1808. דָּלִית ***dāliyṯ:*** A feminine noun indicating a branch, foliage. It refers to the branches of an olive tree (Jer. 11:16); of various vines (Ezek. 17:6, 7; 19:11); and to cedar trees (Ezek. 17:23; 31:7, 9, 12).

1809. דָּלַל ***dālal:*** I. A verb meaning to hang low, languish, become thin, to not be equal. It denotes being or becoming small, of no importance: the Midianites humbled Israel (Judg. 6:6) through military defeats; the psalmist is spiritually depleted because of the fall of Jerusalem (Ps. 79:8). The simple are brought low, but the Lord rescues them (Ps. 116:6; 142:6[7]). It depicts a lame person's legs (Prov. 26:7) or the leanness of Israel's condition (Isa. 17:4). It pictures the low water level of streams or the languishing of hope before one's eyes (Job 28:4; Isa. 38:14).

II. A verb meaning to dangle, to hang, to swing, to sway. It refers to the way men hunt for metals in far recesses of the earth (Job 28:14) or to the way the shafts they sink seem to hang or dangle in the earth.

1810. דִּלְעָן ***dil'ān:*** A proper noun designating Dilean (Josh. 15:38).

1811. דָּלַף ***dālap̱:*** A verb meaning to pour out, to leak. It refers to the roof of a house leaking (Eccl. 10:18). It describes an eye weeping before God (Job 16:20). Figuratively, it denotes a person weeping in grief (Ps. 119:28).

1812. דֶּלֶף ***delep̱:*** A masculine noun referring to dripping (Prov. 19:13; 27:15). The constant dripping of water on a rainy day (Prov. 27:15) is depicted as similar to a quarrelsome woman or contentious wife (Prov. 19:13).

1813. דַּלְפוֹן ***dalp̱ôn:*** A proper noun designating Dalphon (Esth. 9:7).

1814. דָּלַק ***dālaq:*** A verb indicating to burn, to pursue hotly. It means to set on fire (Obad. 1:18), to kindle a fire (Ezek. 24:10). It depicts fiery weapons, such as arrows (Ps. 7:13 [14]), or other kinds of dangers, such as burning lips that tell tales (Prov. 26:23). It indicates literal physical pursuit (Gen. 31:36; 1 Sam. 17:53). It is used of the wicked pursuing the righteous (Ps. 10:2), sometimes in judgment from God (Lam. 4:19). It also describes those who are addicted to wine (Isa. 5:11) pursuing it early in the morning.

1815. דְּלַק ***d***^{e}***laq:*** An Aramaic verb meaning to burn. It is used once in a participial form to describe the wheels of God's chariot throne as burning fire (Dan. 7:9).

1816. דַּלֶּקֶת ***daleqeṯ:*** A feminine noun denoting inflammation. It designates an inflammation that God may bring on a disobedient people (Deut. 28:22).

1817. דָּל **dāl,** דֶּלֶת **deleṯ:** A masculine noun designating a door. It is used figuratively in the Psalms to refer to the door of the psalmist's lips (Ps. 141:3).

1818. דָּם **dām:** A masculine singular noun meaning blood of either humans or animals. It is commonly used with the verb *šāp̱aḵ* (8210) meaning to shed. Figuratively, it signifies violence and violent individuals: man of blood (2 Sam. 16:8); house of blood (2 Sam. 21:1); in wait for blood (Prov. 1:11); shedder of blood (Ezek. 18:10). Blood also carries religious significance, having a major role in sacrificial rituals. The metaphor "blood of grapes" is used for wine (Gen. 49:11).

1819. דָּמָה **dāmāh:** A verb meaning to be like, to compare, to resemble; to use parables, to plan, to think. It can be used in the sense of to make oneself like someone or something: the king of Babylon aspired to make himself like the Most High God (Isa. 14:14). It is used to compare things or persons: to compare oneself to something (Ps. 102:6[7]); to compare God to something (Isa. 40:18, 25; 46:5) and therefore indicates the use of parables in teaching, etc. (Hos. 12:10[11]), especially in specific similes (Song 1:9; 2:9, 17; 7:7[8]; 8:14). Its meaning extends to forming an idea or planning something (Num. 33:56; Judg. 20:5; 2 Sam. 21:5; Ps. 48:9[10]; 50:21).

1820. דָּמָה **dāmāh:** A verb meaning to cease, to cause to cease, to be silent, to destroy. It is used in reference to beasts that die (Ps. 49:12[13]); a prophet who feels undone when he sees the Lord (Isa. 6:5); Zion's destruction (Jer. 6:2); eyes that weep without ceasing (Lam. 3:49); the destruction of people who have no knowledge (Hos. 4:6); the destruction of merchants (Zeph. 1:11); the destruction of the nation of Edom (Obad. 1:5).

1821. דְּמָה **d^{e}māh:** An Aramaic verb indicating to be like. It indicates that something resembles or is like something else: the fourth man in the furnace was like a son of the gods (Dan. 3:25); the second beast of Daniel's vision resembled a bear (Dan. 7:5).

1822. דֻּמָה **dumāh:** A feminine noun of debated meaning. If it derives from *dāmāh* (1820), it would mean destroyed one; if from *dāmam* (1826), it would mean silent one. It is used only in Ezekiel 27:32 where it describes the wealthy and beautiful seaport of Tyre as having sunk into the sea, a symbol of being overrun by foreign armies (cf. Ezek. 26:3–5). This judgment came on the people of Tyre because of their pride and because they rejoiced over the fall of Jerusalem (cf. Ezek. 26:2). The ruined city would be relatively silent (although fishermen would still spread their nets there), but in Ezekiel 27:32 "destroyed one" seems to fit the context better.

1823. דְּמוּת ***dᵉmûṯ:*** A feminine noun meaning likeness. This word is often used to create a simile by comparing two unlike things, such as the wickedness of people and the venom of a snake (Ps. 58:4[5]); the sound of God's gathering warriors and of many people (Isa. 13:4); or the angelic messenger and a human being (Dan. 10:16). Additionally, this word is used in describing humans being created in the image or likeness of God (Gen. 1:26; 5:1); the likeness of Seth to Adam (Gen. 5:3); the figures of oxen in the temple (2 Chr. 4:3); the pattern of the altar (2 Kgs. 16:10). But most often, Ezekiel uses it as he describes his visions by comparing what he saw to something similar on earth (Ezek. 1:5, 16; 10:1).

1824. דֳּמִי ***dᵒmiy,*** דְּמִי ***dᵉmiy:*** I. A masculine noun referring to silence or rest. It refers to the act of watchmen reporting what they see and know (Isa. 62:6) and to the Lord's resting from establishing Zion, Jerusalem (Isa. 62:7), or remaining silent towards one who prays to Him for help (Ps. 83:1[2]).

II. A masculine noun denoting half, middle, the rest, the remainder. It is used of Hezekiah's concern that he die young, deprived of half or the rest of his life span (Isa. 38:10).

1825. דִּמְיוֹן ***dimyôn:*** A masculine noun denoting likeness. It depicts an oppressor of the psalmist who is likened to a lion awaiting its prey (Ps. 17:12), secretly and stealthily planning its attack.

1826. דָּמַם ***dāmam:*** A verb meaning to be silent, to be still; to stand still. It depicts the state of being motionless (1 Sam. 14:9; Jer. 47:6). It can be used to command something to be motionless, to stand still (Josh. 10:12, 13), such as the sun. It means to refrain from speech (Lev. 10:3) at an appropriate time (Amos 5:13). It refers to persons being traumatized, rigid, or frozen from fear and fright (Ex. 15:16) like a stone or the silencing of persons through war or other means (Jer. 8:14; 48:2; 49:26; 50:30). It indicates, on the other hand, the absence of emotional distress and churning and the ability to be quiet and relax (Job 30:27; Ps. 4:4[5]; 30:12[13]; 131:2), which Job could not accomplish.

1827. דְּמָמָה ***dᵉmāmāh:*** A feminine noun indicating hushed,a whisper. It indicates a soft gentle blowing or whisper in contrast to the roar of an earthquake, fire, or a storm at sea (1 Kgs. 19:12; Ps. 107:29). It indicates the absence of any sound or voice (Job 4:16).

1828. דֹּמֶן ***dōmen:*** A masculine noun referring to dung, refuse. It is used to describe unburied corpses, lying on the ground as dung or refuse (2 Kgs. 9:37; Ps. 83:10[11]; Jer. 8:2;

9:22[21]; 16:4; 25:33), i.e., used as a simile for bodies.

1829. דִּמְנָה ***dimnāh:*** A proper noun designating Dimnah (Josh. 21:35).

1830. דָּמַע ***dāma':*** A verb meaning to weep, to shed tears. It indicates one's intense weeping (Jer. 13:17) and the shedding of tears over the threats of captivity facing Judah. It is found three times in this verse for emphasis.

1831. דֶּמַע ***dema':*** A masculine noun meaning juice, overflowing, vintage. It indicates the abundance of oil and/or wine the Lord gives to Israel in her harvests (Ex. 22:29[28]).

1832. דִּמְעָה ***dim'āh:*** A feminine noun indicating tears. The word is used in various settings to refer to the shedding of tears whether for good or deceptive reasons: in times of distress (Ps. 6:6[7]; 39:12[13]; 42:3[4]; 80:5 [6]), especially in the case of Jeremiah (Jer. 9:18[17]; 13:17; 14:17); on behalf of someone or something (Isa. 16:9); to gain God's compassion and help in time of danger or illness (2 Kgs. 20:5; Isa. 38:5); useless weeping because of one's own hypocrisy before God (Mal. 2:13). In many of these references, tears are described figuratively or metaphorically as food or drink (Ps. 42:3[4]; 80:5[6]).

1833. דְּמֶשֶׁק ***d^e^mešeq:*** I. A proper noun referring to the city of Damascus. It is paralleled with Samaria as a place of self-indulgent luxury (Amos 3:12; KJV, NIV).

II. A masculine noun referring to a piece of cloth, damask, cover. It indicates one of the things the raiders of Samaria and Israel snatched away (Amos 3:12; NASB).

1834. דּוּמֶּשֶׂק ***dûmmeśeq,*** דַּמֶּשֶׂק ***dammeśeq,*** דַּרְמֶשֶׂק ***darmeśeq:*** A proper noun designating Damascus, the name of the ancient capital of an Aram kingdom (Syria) during ca. 900–700 B.C. At times it also refers to the greater area around Damascus or to an Aramean kingdom. David and Solomon captured and controlled the city for some time (2 Sam. 8:5, 6), but in general, the city was a hotbed of resistance and hostility toward Israel (1 Kgs. 11:24; 15:18; 20:34; Isa. 7:8; 8:4). It is mentioned 43 times in the Old Testament and even 15 times in the New Testament. It is located northeast of the Sea of Galilee, east of the Anti-Lebanon Mountains. The Abana and Pharpar Rivers ran into it (2 Kgs. 5:12).

It figures in the life of Abraham (Gen. 14:15; 15:2). Elijah anointed Hazael as king over Damascus (1 Kgs. 19:15). The prophets proclaimed oracles of judgment against it (Jer. 49:23–27; cf. Ezek. 17:18; Amos 3:15; 9:1).

1835. דָּן ***dān:*** A proper noun designating Dan:

A. Dan was the fifth son of Jacob through Rachel's maidservant Bilhah (Gen. 35:25; 46:23). He went to

Egypt with his household (Ex. 1:4). Dan is pictured as a viper along the road (Gen. 49:17). The capital of the Danite territory was renamed as Dan (Josh. 19:47).

B. The city of Leshem (Laish) conquered by the Danites but renamed Dan after their ancestor (Josh. 19:47). The name is used proleptically in Genesis 14:14. It was located on the northern boundary of Israel. The phrase "Dan to Beersheba" was used to define the north-south limits of Israel (2 Sam. 3:10; 17:11; 24:2, etc.). The sound of Israel's threatening northern enemies were heard proverbially from the distant north of Dan (Jer. 4:15; 18:16). It was also the location of pagan worship in Israel where huge altars and pillars have been found (cf. Amos 8:14). Jeroboam I set up golden calves at Dan.

C. The name of the tribe of Dan or its territory. It was allotted land lying among the tribes of Ephraim, Benjamin, Judah, and Manasseh. Its western border was on the Mediterranean Sea (Josh. 19:40–48). Some of the tribe later moved to a new location because they were hard-pressed by the Philistines from the Mediterranean coast (Judg. 1:34; 18:1–30). Samson's exploits were in the older location of Dan (Judg. 13:25), as were Deborah's (Judg. 5:17). In Ezekiel's vision, the tribe of Dan is located in its northern territory (48:1–32).

1836. דְּנָה ***d^{e}nāh:*** An Aramaic demonstrative pronoun and adjective meaning this, therefore. It points out something and may come before or after the noun (Ezra 5:4; Dan. 6:3[4]). Used as a pronoun, it is translated as this is (Dan. 2:28). It is combined with *k^e* several times meaning like this or this (Ezra 5:7; Jer. 10:11; Dan. 3:29).

1837. דַּנָּה ***dannāh:*** A proper noun designating Dannah (Josh. 15:49).

1838. דִּנְהָבָה ***dinhāḇāh:*** A proper noun designating Dinhabah (Gen. 36:32; 1 Chr. 1:43).

1839. דָּנִי ***dāniy:*** A proper noun designating the Danites, the people belonging to the descendants of Dan; members of the tribe of Dan. Samson and his parents were Danites living in the original territory allotted to Dan (Judg. 13:1–2). Most of the original Danites moved north to a location near the sources of the Jordan and the city of Leshem (Laish) (Judg. 18:1–30).

1840. דָּנִאֵל ***dāni'ēl,*** דָּנִיֵּאל ***dāniyyē'l:*** A proper noun designating Daniel:

A. The second son of David, born to Abigail, former wife of Nabal from Carmel (1 Sam. 25; 1 Chr. 3:1).

B. A descendant of Ithamar who was a family head who returned from the Babylonian exile under Ezra and who sealed Nehemiah's pact to serve the Lord (Ezra 8:2; Neh. 10:6).

C. Daniel, the prophet, exiled in ca. 605 B.C. to Babylon, where he remained into the reign of Cyrus of Persia (Dan. 10:1–3; ca. 535 B.C.). His name meant "God has judged." He refused to be absorbed into Babylonian culture. He was gifted to understand and interpret dreams and visions. He was faithful to the Law of Moses even in exile. He interpreted dreams and visions of pagan kings and himself (by the help of divine intermediaries) that reported the course of world history and the divine establishment of the kingdom of God. He died and awaits the resurrection to receive his own allotment and reward (Dan. 12:1–13). His wisdom was also proverbial because of the way he handled himself in the court of Nebuchadnezzar.

D. The name may refer to the righteous Daniel mentioned in an ancient Ugaritic Epic of Aqhat (ca. 1450 B.C.). It is more likely that the prophet here refers to the biblical Daniel, since the other two persons are biblical characters and all three men were "delivered" from a crisis situation, as Daniel's name indicates.

1841. דָּנִיֵּאל ***dāniyyē'l:*** A proper noun designating Daniel, the Aramaic name for the Hebrew entry 1840.

1842. דָּן יַעַן ***dān ya'an:*** A proper noun designating Dan Jaan (2 Sam. 24:6).

1843. דֵּעַ ***dēa':*** A noun meaning knowledge. The word is possibly the masculine form of *dē'āh* (1844). It is used only by Elihu in the book of Job, where it refers to Elihu's opinion that he was about to make known to Job and his three friends (Job 32:6, 10, 17); knowledge as brought in from a distance, perhaps from heaven, since Elihu has just claimed to speak for God (Job 36:3); and God's perfect knowledge demonstrated in the clouds and lightning (37:16). The phrase "perfect in knowledge" occurs also in Job 36:4, apparently describing Elihu but using *dē'āh* (1844). It might be thought that Elihu was using a more modest word in describing his own knowledge. The word *dē'āh*, however, is also used to refer to God's knowledge (cf. 1 Sam. 2:3), and it is difficult to find any distinction of meaning between the two forms.

1844. דֵּעָה ***dē'āh:*** A feminine noun meaning knowledge. This word comes from the verb *yāḏa'* (3045), meaning to know, and is equivalent in meaning to the much more common form of this noun, *da'aṯ* (1847), meaning knowledge. This particular word refers to the knowledge within God (1 Sam. 2:3; Ps. 73:11). The word also describes the knowledge of God that was known throughout the land (Isa. 11:9) or taught either by God or by His faithful shepherds (Jer. 3:15).

1845. דְּעוּאֵל ***de'û'ēl:*** A proper noun designating Deuel (Num. 1:14; 2:14; 7:42, 47; 10:20).

1846. דָּעַךְ ***dā'aḵ:*** A verb indicating to die out, to be extinguished. It is used in a simile to depict the enemies of the psalmist and the Lord extinguishing the wicked like a wick (Ps. 118:12; Isa. 43:17) or in the natural course of their lives (Job 18:5, 6; Prov. 13:9; 20:20; 24:20). It describes watercourses drying up or vanishing (Job 6:17).

1847. דַּעַת *da'at̠:* A feminine noun meaning knowledge, knowing, learning, discernment, insight, and notion. The word occurs forty of its ninety-one times in Proverbs as one of the many words associated with the biblical concept of wisdom. The root meaning of the term is knowledge or knowing. In Proverbs 24:3, 4, it is the third word in a chain of three words describing the building of a house by wisdom, the establishment of that house by understanding, and finally, the filling of the rooms of the house by knowledge. The word describes God's gift of technical or specific knowledge along with wisdom and understanding to Bezalel so he could construct the Tabernacle (Ex. 31:3; 35:31; cf. Ps. 94:10). It also describes the Israelites when they lacked the proper knowledge to please God (Isa. 5:13; Hos. 4:6). God holds both pagan unbelievers and Israelites responsible to know Him. On the other hand, a lack of knowledge also describes the absence of premeditation or intentionality. That lack of knowledge clears a person who has accidentally killed someone (Deut. 4:42; Josh. 20:3, 5).

The word is also used in the sense of knowing by experience, relationship, or encounter. For example, Balaam received knowledge from the Most High who met him in a vision (Num. 24:16); the knowledge gained by the suffering Servant of Isaiah justified many people (Isa. 53:11); and to truly know the Holy God leads to real understanding (Prov. 9:10). This moral, experiential knowledge of good and evil was forbidden to the human race in the Garden of Eden (Gen. 2:9, 17). But the Messiah will have the Spirit of understanding in full measure as the Spirit of the Lord accompanied Him (Isa. 11:2).

The term is also used to indicate insight or discernment. God imparted discernment to the psalmist when he trusted in God's commands (Ps. 119:66). Job was guilty of speaking words without discernment (lit., words without knowledge, Job 34:35; 38:2).

God alone possesses all knowledge. No one can impart knowledge to God, for His knowledge, learning, and insight are perfect (Job 21:22); He alone has full knowledge about the guilt, innocence, or uprightness of a person (Job 10:7). God's knowledge of a human being is so profound and all-encompassing that the psalmist recognized that such knowledge is not attainable by people (Ps. 139:6).

Some knowledge is empty and useless (Job 15:2), but God's people and a wise person are marked by true knowledge of life and the divine (Prov. 2:5; 8:10; 10:14; 12:1). Knowledge affects behavior, for persons who control their speech have true knowledge (Prov. 17:27). While the preacher of Ecclesiastes admitted that knowledge may result in pain (Eccl.

1:18), he also asserted that having knowledge is, in the end, better, for it protects the life of the one who has it (Eccl. 7:12), and it is God's gift (Eccl. 2:26).

1848. דְּפִי *dᵒpiy:* A masculine noun denoting slander. It refers to harming one's own brother by verbal statements that injure his reputation (Ps. 50:20).

1849. דָּפַק *dāpaq:* A verb indicating to beat violently, to drive hard. It refers to driving small cattle (Gen. 33:13) or to knock, rap, or pound on someone's door (Judg. 19:22; Song 5:2).

1850. דָּפְקָה *dopqāh:* A proper noun designating Dophkah (Num. 33:12, 13).

1851. דַּק *daq:* An adjective meaning gaunt, fine, thin; dwarfish; low. It indicates that something is weak, undernourished, fine, small: lean cows (Gen. 41:3, 4); lean ears of corn (Gen. 41:6, 7); thin people or dwarfs (Lev. 21:20); fine manna (Ex. 16:14); or hair, incense, or dust (Lev. 13:30; 16:12; Isa. 29:5). Once it is used to describe a soft whisper (1 Kgs. 19:12). Used in a simile, the islands are described as fine dust (Isa. 40:15).

1852. דֹּק *dōq:* A masculine noun denoting a curtain, a canopy. It is used to depict the heavens stretched out like a canopy (Isa. 40:22) or curtain.

1853. דִּקְלָה *diqlāh:* A proper noun designating Diklah (Gen. 10:27; 1 Chr. 1:21).

1854. דָּקַק *dāqaq:* A verb meaning to pulverize, to beat into powder. It is used figuratively of pulverizing or crushing one's enemies (2 Sam. 22:43) or even peoples and nations (Mic. 4:13). Israel, renewed by God, will pulverize the mountains, overcoming all obstacles (Isa. 41:15). Literally, it indicates the crushing, grinding fine of various items: grain, corn (Isa. 28:28); asherahs, pagan symbols (2 Kgs. 23:6, 15); incense (Ex. 30:36); the golden calf ground up by Moses' orders (Ex. 32:20).

1855. דְּקַק *dᵉqaq:* An Aramaic verb indicating the process of breaking into pieces, crushing. It indicates the crushing of various objects in the book of Daniel: the stone crushed the feet of the statue (Dan. 2:34, 35, 45); the fourth monstrous kingdom broke all other kingdoms into pieces (Dan. 2:40); the kingdom of God will crush and destroy all other kingdoms (Dan. 2:44); the bones of Daniel's accusers (Dan. 6:24[25]); the fourth beast will trample and crush the remainder of the earth (Dan. 7:7, 19, 23).

1856. דָּקַר *dāqar:* A verb indicating to thrust through, to pierce. It is used of piercing to kill another person in vengeance (Num. 25:8); according to law (Zech. 13:3); or in an act of mercy (Judg. 9:54; 1 Sam. 31:4). It describes the killing of enemies in war (Isa. 13:15; Jer. 51:4). It is used to describe wounded men in battle, pierced (Jer. 37:10).

1857. דֶּקֶר ***deqer:*** A proper noun designating Deker (1 Kgs. 4:9, KJV).

1858. דַּר ***dar:*** A masculine noun referring to something white or mother-of-pearl. It is used once to describe one of the precious and luxurious materials in the flooring of Xerxes's or Ahasuerus's palace (Esth. 1:6).

1859. דָּר ***dār:*** An Aramaic masculine noun meaning generation. This word is used only twice in the Old Testament and is equivalent to the Hebrew word *dôr* (1755), meaning generation. In both instances, the word is used in a phrase that is literally translated "with generation and generation," the idea referring to God's kingdom enduring from generation to generation (Dan. 4:3[3:33]; 4:34[31]).

1860. דְּרָאוֹן ***d^e^rā'ôn,*** דֵּרָאוֹן ***dērā'ôn:*** A masculine noun meaning abhorrence. This word is related to an Arabic verb, which means to repel. Thus, the object of repulsion is an abhorrence. It is used only twice in the Old Testament and in both cases speaks about the eternal abhorrence of those who rebelled against the Lord. The prophet Isaiah ended his message by declaring the abhorrence of wicked men in the eternal state (Isa. 66:24). Daniel, likewise, spoke about the everlasting abhorrence of the wicked who were resurrected (Dan. 12:2).

1861. דָּרְבָן ***dorbān,*** דָּרְבֹן ***dorbōn:*** A masculine noun denoting a goad. It was an iron-tipped pole or a long stick used to drive cattle or oxen, an ox goad (1 Sam. 13:21; NASB translates as hoes). It is also used figuratively of correctly chosen words used to stir up one's audience or students (Eccl. 12:11).

1862. דַּרְדַּע ***darda':*** A proper noun designating Darda (1 Kgs. 4:31[5:11]; 1 Chr. 2:6).

1863. דַּרְדַּע ***darda':*** A masculine noun denoting thistles. It depicts weedy, prickly plants that were part of God's curse on the ground (Gen. 3:18). It was a plant that grew of itself in places abandoned by humans (Hos. 10:8).

1864. דָּרוֹם ***dārôm:*** A masculine noun used to indicate direction, south, southward. It indicates the south (Ezek. 42:18) or toward the south, southward (Job 37:17; Ezek. 40:24, 27) or gives definition to something, e.g., a south gate (lit., the gate of the south, Ezek. 40:28). It indicates the opposite of the north (Eccl. 1:6; 11:3; Ezek. 41:11; 42:13).

1865. דְּרוֹר ***d^e^rôr:*** I. A masculine noun denoting liberty, emancipation. It referred to the freedom proclaimed during the sabbatical year (Lev. 25:10; Jer. 34:8, 15, 17). In a cynical, ironical use, the prophet proclaims that Israel's liberty would be destroyed by God's judgments (Ezek. 46:17).

II. A masculine noun denoting myrrh oil. It describes literally myrrh of flowing in Exodus 30:23, liquid myrrh.

1866. דְּרוֹר ***d^e^rôr:*** A masculine noun denoting a swallow bird. It indicates one of the birds that found a nesting place in the house of the Lord (Ps. 84:3[4]). The darting and erratic flight of this bird serves as a simile for the flight patterns of a curse (Prov. 26:2).

1867. דָּרְיָוֶשׁ ***dār^e^yāweš:*** A proper noun designating Darius:

A. king of Persia and Babylon (521–486 B.C.) He supported the rebuilding of the Temple and Jerusalem. The Temple was completed in 516 B.C.

B. Darius II, named Nothus, who ruled Persia and Babylon 423–408 B.C. He is called "the Persian" in Nehemiah 12:22.

C. The name of the person in Daniel 9:1; 11:1 who became ruler over Babylon. His identification is being researched. The name may be a throne name for Cyrus or possibly someone that Cyrus placed over Babylon (e.g., Gubaru).

1868. דָּרְיָוֶשׁ ***dār^e^yāweš:*** A proper noun designating Darius:

A. The Aramaic name for Darius Hystaspes. See entry 1867,A. He ordered the Temple to be completed (Ezra 4:24; 5:5–7; 6:1–15).

B. The Aramaic name for Darius the Mede. See entry 1868,B.

1869. דָּרַךְ ***dārak:*** A verb meaning to tread, to bend. It refers to walking on, over, or along or to pressing something with one's feet, trampling. It also takes on the sense of subduing something or someone or simply going forth. Its main usages can be: a star or person may go forth, march forth (Num. 24:17; Judg. 5:21); to tread on land or one's enemy (Deut. 1:36; 11:25; Judg. 20:43; Job 28:8); a path, meaning life itself (Isa. 59:8); to defeat enemies by treading on them (Deut. 33:29); the march or assault of an enemy (1 Sam. 5:5; Ps. 11:2; 37:14; 91:13; Mic. 1:3). It is used to indicate treading wine or oil presses (Neh. 13:15; Job 24:11; Mic. 6:15) and figuratively to depict the Lord treading the winepress of judgment (Isa. 63:3). In its extended meaning, it indicates directing or bending a bow (Jer. 51:3; Zech. 9:13). It refers to the spiritual walk in high places made possible by the Lord (Hab. 3:19).

1870. דֶּרֶךְ ***Derek:*** A masculine noun meaning path, journey, way. This common word is derived from the Hebrew verb *dārak* (1869), meaning to walk or to tread, from which the basic idea of this word comes: the path that is traveled. The word may refer to a physical path or road (Gen. 3:24; Num. 22:23; 1 Kgs. 13:24) or to a journey along a road (Gen. 30:36; Ex. 5:3; 1 Sam. 15:18). However, this word is most often used metaphorically to refer to the pathways of one's life, suggesting the pattern of life (Prov. 3:6); the obedient life (Deut. 8:6); the righteous life (2 Sam. 22:22; Jer. 5:4); the wicked life (1 Kgs. 22:52[53]). The ways are described as ways of darkness (Prov. 2:13); pleasant ways (Prov. 3:17); and wise ways (Prov. 6:6).

1871. דַּרְכְּמָה ***darkᵉmāh:*** A noun meaning weight, monetary value. The word may refer to the Greek drachma that weighed 4.3 grams or to the Persian daric that weighed about twice as much. It occurs in Ezra 2:69 describing gold given toward Temple construction. In Nehemiah 7:70–72 [69–71], it also refers to gold given toward the work of revitalizing Jerusalem. This word apparently has the same meaning as *'ᵃd̲arkōn* (150) but may have a different origin.

1872. דְּרָע ***dᵉrā':*** An Aramaic feminine noun meaning arm. It designates the arms of silver on the statue of Nebuchadnezzar's dream (Dan. 2:32).

1873. דָּרַע ***dāra':*** A proper noun designating Dara, a shortened form of *darda'* (1862) (1 Chr. 2:6).

1874. דַּרְקוֹן ***darqôn:*** A proper noun designating Darkon (Ezra 2:56; Neh. 7:58).

1875. דָּרַשׁ ***dāraš:*** A verb meaning to seek, to inquire of, to examine, to require. Figuratively, it may refer to seeking out or inquiring about lovers (Jer. 30:14) or to care for Zion (Jer. 30:17). It denotes inquiring about persons (2 Sam. 11:3) or their welfare (souls)(Ps. 142:4[5]). It indicates the Lord's care for His land (Deut. 11:12). It carries the general sense of seeking out property, such as a lost ox or cattle (Deut. 22:2), or examining a matter (Deut. 13:14[15]; Judg. 6:29; 1 Kgs. 22:7) or event. It takes on the meaning of requiring or demanding someone's blood in a moral or legal sense (Gen. 9:5; 2 Chr. 24:22; Ps. 10:13) but also of seeking good itself (Amos 5:14).

Its most important theological meaning involves studying or inquiring into the Law of the Lord (Ezra 7:10) or inquiring of God (Gen. 25:22; Ex. 18:15; Deut. 12:5; 1 Kgs. 22:5; 2 Kgs. 3:11). God's people seek after their God (Deut. 4:29; Hos. 10:12; Amos 5:4). Seeking the Lord will be greatly rewarded (Ps. 34:10[11]). Seeking heathen gods or persons who deal with the dead is to be avoided (1 Sam. 28:7; Isa. 8:19; Ezek. 14:10). The works of God, however, are to be examined and studied (Ps. 111:2).

1876. דָּשָׁא ***dāšā':*** A verb meaning to produce green plants or fresh green grass. With the earth as its subject, it depicts the initial production of green vegetables or grass (Gen. 1:11). It depicts the pastures and the wilderness turning green from God's blessing and restoration after judgment (Joel 2:22).

1877. דֶּשֶׁא *dešeʼ*, דָּשָׁא *dāšāʼ*: I. A masculine noun referring to grass or tender green grass. It is the grass produced initially by the earth at God's command (Gen. 1:11), often after rain (2 Sam. 23:4). God causes it to spring forth (Job 38:27), and it is refreshed by rain (Deut. 32:2) but withers in drought (Isa. 15:6). It is food for the wild donkey (Job 6:5) and the heifer (Jer. 50:11; KJV). Its frailty and transitory nature is a picture of the wicked (Ps. 37:2), but its ability also to flourish symbolizes God's people when the Lord blesses them (Isa. 66:14).

II. A verb meaning to thresh, trample down. It is rendered to thresh, threshing grain (Jer. 50:11; NASB, NIV, NKJV), referring to Babylon's trampling of God's people.

1878. דָּשֵׁן *dāšēn*: A verb meaning to be fat, to grow fat, to fatten, or in a figurative sense, to anoint, to satisfy. In Proverbs, the word is used for one's bones growing fat (that is, one being in good health) after receiving good news (Prov. 15:30). Conversely, when Israel came to the Promised Land, she grew fat with the food of the pagan culture and turned away to other gods (Deut. 31:20). In Isaiah, the word is used to describe the ground being covered with the fat of animals (Isa. 34:7).

1879. דָּשֵׁן *dāšēn*: An adjective meaning fat, juicy, prosperous, rich. It indicates the rich and plenteous grain harvests which the Lord will grant to His people (Isa. 30:23). It describes the fruitfulness of the righteous person as full of sap, fat, being healthy spiritually from God's blessings (Ps. 92:14[15]). Finally, it denotes those who are healthy, prosperous, and who will serve the Lord (Ps. 22:29[30]).

1880. דֶּשֶׁן *dešen*: A masculine noun indicating fatness, ashes. It indicates the fat of olives (Judg. 9:9). It indicates the spiritual blessings of God as abundance (NASB), fatness (KJV), richest of food or fare (NIV) freely bestowed on His people who will respond (Ps. 36:8[9]; 63:5[6]; Isa. 55:2). It refers to food and drink (Job 36:16; Jer. 31:14). It indicates the wood ashes and fat ashes mixed together from the altar (Lev. 1:16; 4:12; 1 Kgs. 13:3, 5; Jer. 31:40).

1881. דָּת *dāṯ*: A feminine noun meaning law, edict. This word is used to describe either a permanent law that governed a nation or an edict sent out with the king's authority. The first meaning can be seen in Esther 1:13, 15, where the king counseled with those who knew the law (cf. Esth. 3:8). The second meaning appears in the several occasions where King Ahasuerus (Xerxes) sent out a decree (Esth. 2:8; 3:14, 15). At times, it is difficult to distinguish between these two meanings (Esth. 1:8), for the edict of the king became a written law among the Persians (Esth. 1:19). With several exceptions, this word occurs only in the book of Esther (Ezra 8:36; cf. Deut. 33:2).

1882. דָּת dāṯ: An Aramaic noun meaning decree, law. It corresponds to the Hebrew word of the same spelling (1881). The decrees imposed on humans may agree more or less with God's Law, but God is always presented as controlling human laws. The word describes God's changeless Law in Ezra 7:12 and Daniel 6:5(6). Elsewhere, it signifies a king's decree made in anger (Dan. 2:9, 13). In the case of the Medes and Persians, a king could make the law at his own will but could not change it even if it were wrong (Dan. 6:8[9], 12[13], 15[16]). In Ezra 7:26, God's Law and the king's law coincide. In Daniel 7:25, a ruler was prophesied to speak against the Most High God and to set up laws in opposition to Him, but the ruler could only do so for a period of time set by God.

1883. דֶּתֶא deṯe': An Aramaic masculine noun denoting grass, new grass. It refers to the grass in the field of Nebuchadnezzar's dream (Dan. 4:15[12], 23[20]) that surrounds the tree stump. It possibly serves as a symbol of fertility and hope here.

1884. דְּתָבַר d^eṯāḇar: An Aramaic masculine noun meaning a judge, a counselor. It refers to a class of officials from the Babylonian provinces (KJV, counselor; NASB, NKJV, NIV, judges) (Dan. 3:2, 3).

1885. דָּתָן dāṯān: A proper noun designating Dathan, a son of Eliab who took part in a rebellion against Moses, along with many others who challenged Moses' position "over them." They were engulfed by an earthquake (Num. 16:32; Deut. 11:6; Ps. 106:17).

1886. דֹּתָן dōṯān: A proper noun designating Dothan (Gen. 37:17; 2 Kgs. 6:13).

ה Hē

1887. הֵא ***hē':*** An interjection meaning behold, surely, there! It is used by Joseph to get people's attention as he begins to address them (Gen. 47:23). It means surely or therefore in Ezekiel 16:43 as the prophet asserts the consequences of the people's rebellion.

1888. הָא ***hā',*** הֵא ***hē':*** I. An Aramaic interjection meaning behold, look. It indicates surprise and amazement and is used to direct attention to something: the fourth man in the fiery furnace (Dan. 3:25).

II. An Aramaic interjection meaning behold, even as. It points out something evident and can make a comparison, even as (Dan. 2:43); even as iron and clay do not mix, neither do the peoples of the fourth empire of Daniel.

1889. הֶאָח ***he'āḥ:*** An interjection meaning aha! It may express joy (Isa. 44:16) or satisfaction and comfort. The same can be expressed with an evil motive toward something (Ezek. 25:3). Figuratively, it expresses the satisfied neighing and anticipation of a warhorse toward a battle (Job 39:25).

1890. הַבְהָב ***haḇhaḇ:*** A masculine noun meaning gift in the sense of sacrifice or offering. This type of sacrifice is not made by one person but always occurs with a plural subject. Israel (collectively) sacrificed animals to God as gift offerings— gifts God did not accept (Hos. 8:13). This word comes from the verb *yāhaḇ* (3051), meaning to give.

1891. הָבַל ***hāḇal:*** A verb indicating to fill with false hopes, to become vain, empty, void. It notes that those who reject God's covenants and statues become vain (2 Kgs. 17:15) in their pursuits as well (Ps. 62:10[11]; Jer. 2:5). It refers to foolish and vain talk and action (Job 27:12) and especially to futile prophecies of false prophets (Jer. 23:16).

1892. הֶבֶל ***heḇel:*** A common noun referring to vanity, emptiness, meaninglessness; idols. The word is used seventy times, thirty-five of these are in Ecclesiastes. It refers to breath because of its transitory fleeting character (Isa. 57:13) and is used as a symbol for life (Job 7:16). It refers to the vanity and ultimate emptiness and meaninglessness of all things in this life, whether they seem good or bad (Eccl. 1:2, 14; 2:11, 15, 3:19; 4:4, 7, 8; 5:7[6]; 6:2, 4, 9; 7:6, 15; 8:10; 9:9; 11:8). Combined with itself in the plural, it means absolute meaninglessness (Eccl. 1:2). Idols and the vain religious customs associated with them are all delusions (Jer. 10:3, 15). It denotes an empty, vain life (Eccl. 6:12). Used with the verb *hāḇal*, it means to carry out vain talk or action or what is empty (Job 27:12). As an adverb, it means to talk in vain, emptily (Job 35:16). To walk after *hebel* means to go after or follow vanity (2 Kgs. 17:15; Jer. 2:5). Anything obtained through evil is vain, such as wealth (Prov. 13:11).

1893. הֶבֶל ***hebel:*** A proper noun designating Abel, the second son of Adam and Eve who pleased God by his faith (Gen. 4:2, 4). He was slain by Cain his brother (Gen. 4:8, 9). Seth replaced him. Ironically, his name means "vanity, wind," depicting his ephemeral life (cf. Heb. 11:1–3).

1894. הָבְנִים ***hobniym:*** A masculine noun denoting ebony. It refers to ebony as one of the mediums of payment from India for merchandise from Tyre (Ezek. 27:15).

1895. הָבַר ***hābar:*** A verb indicating an astrologer. It denotes astrologers who prophesied by or evaluated the stars (Isa. 47:13).

1896. הֵגֶא ***hēge'***, הֵגַי ***hēgay:*** A proper noun designating Hegai, Hege (Esth. 2:3, 8, 15).

1897. הָגָה ***hāgāh:*** A verb meaning to growl, to groan, to sigh, to mutter, to speak; used figuratively: to meditate, to ponder. The Lord told Joshua to meditate on the Law day and night (Josh. 1:8), and the Psalms proclaimed people blessed if they meditate on the Law (Ps. 1:2). Job promised not to speak wickedness (Job 27:4). The Hebrew verb can also refer to the mutterings of mediums and wizards (Isa. 8:19); the moans of grief (Isa. 16:7); the growl of a lion (Isa. 31:4); the coos of a dove (Isa. 38:14).

1898. הָגָה ***hāgāh:*** A verb meaning to take away, to move, to separate. It is used of removing dross or impurities from silver (Prov. 25:4) and, in a parallel simile, of removing the wicked from a king's presence (Prov. 25:5). It refers to the Lord's driving away or taking away His rebellious people (Isa. 27:8).

1899. הֶגֶה ***hegeh:*** A masculine noun meaning a muttering, rumbling, growling, moaning, or sighing sound. It generally describes a sound that comes from deep within the body. The Lord's voice is also described as making a rumbling sound associated with thunder (Job 37:2). The idea of moaning or sighing depicts the sound uttered in mourning, lamentation, woe (Ezek. 2:10), or in deep resignation (Ps. 90:9).

1900. הָגוּת ***hāgût:*** A feminine noun denoting meditation or musing. The psalmist describes the pondering of his heart as meditation (Ps. 49:3[4]). This word is derived from the Hebrew word *hāgāh* (1897), which means to moan or to growl.

1901. הָגִיג ***hāgiyg:*** A masculine noun referring to sighing or meditation. It refers to intense meditation, musing or sighing by the psalmist in prayer as he cries out to the Lord (Ps. 5:1[2]; 39:3[4]).

1902. הִגָּיוֹן ***higgāyôn:*** A masculine noun referring to meditation, resounding music; mockery, whispering. It refers to thoughts or musing (internal) or possibly mockery or whispering (external) of persons against someone (Lam. 3:62). It denotes meditation or thinking in the heart as opposed to speech (Ps. 19:14[15]). It is best rendered as music dedicated to the Lord in Psalm 92:3[4]. It refers to a musical instrument of some kind (Ps. 9:16[17], Higgaion) or possibly instructs the reader to meditate.

1903. הָגִין ***hāgiyn:*** An adjective indicating appropriate, corresponding. It is used to indicate the way directly before the wall in Ezekiel's description of his envisioned Temple (Ezek. 42:12; NASB, the way in front of the wall; NIV, corresponding wall).

1904. הָגָר ***hāgār:*** A proper noun designating Hagar, Sarah's handmaid by whom Abraham fathered Ishmael whose descendants were numerous (Gen. 16:1–16; 25:12–18). She was driven from Abraham by Sarah (Gen. 21:9–17).

1905. הַגְרִי, הַגְרִיאִים ***hagriy, hagriy'iym:*** I. Hagrite, an officer (1 Chr. 27:31).

II. Hagri, Haggeri, the father of Mibhar (2 Sam. 23:36; 1 Chr. 11:38).

III. Hagrite, Arabian Bedouin tribes of the Transjordan region (1 Chr. 5:10, 19, 20; Ps. 83:6[7]).

1906. הֵד ***hēd:*** A masculine noun indicating a joyful shout. It indicates a happy response of joy as opposed to tumult, confusion, or panic (Ezek. 7:7) that God is bringing on His people.

1907. הַדָּבַר ***haddābar:*** An Aramaic masculine noun indicating a royal counselor, advisor. The word refers to high-ranking officials of King Nebuchadnezzar who undoubtedly served as royal advisors and counselors as well (Dan. 3:24, 27; 4:36[33]; 6:7[8]).

1908. הֲדַד ***h^a^dad:*** A. A masculine proper noun, Hadad. He was a descendant of Esau and a son of Bedad. He became king of Edom before any king reigned in Israel. His royal city was Avith, and he successfully defeated the Midianites in the territory of Moab (Gen. 36:35, 36; 1 Chr. 1:46, 47). Some translators prefer to find this name in Genesis 36:39 also, but most Masoretic manuscripts read Hadar here (NIV, Hadad; NASB, NKJV, KJV, Hadar; see B, C, below).

B. A masculine proper noun. A serious adversary of King Solomon. He was of the royal dynasty in Edom (1 Kgs. 11:14) and had fled to Egypt when a boy (1 Kgs. 11:17) from where he returned to Israel to harass Solomon (1 Kgs. 11:19, 21, 25).

C. A masculine proper noun. An Edomite king who reigned before any king reigned in Israel (Gen. 36:39, NIV; NKJV, NASB, KJV, read Hadar). His chief city was Pai (1 Chr. 1:50, 51).

1909. הֲדַדְעֶזֶר ***h^a^dad'ezer:*** A proper noun designating Hadadezer

(2 Sam. 8:3, 5, 7–10, 12; 10:16, 19; 1 Kgs. 11:23; 1 Chr. 18:3, 5, 7–10; 19:16, 19). See also h^a*ḏar'ezer* [1928].

1910. הֲדַד־רִמּוֹן **h^a*ḏaḏ-rimmôn*:** A proper noun designating Hadad Rimmon (Zech. 12:11).

1911. הָדָה **hāḏāh:** A verb meaning to put, to stretch out. Used with the word *yāḏ* (3027), hand in Hebrew, it describes the action of a child putting out his or her hand toward a viper's den (Isa. 11:8).

1912. הֹדוּ **hōddû:** A proper noun designating Hoddu, another name for India (Esth. 1:1; 8:9).

1913. הֲדוֹרָם **h^a*ḏôrām*:** A proper noun designating Hadoram:
A. Son of Joktan (Gen. 10:27; 1 Chr. 1:21).
B. Son of Tou (1 Chr. 18:10).
C. Another name for '^{a}*ḏōrām* (151) (2 Chr. 10:18).

1914. הִדַּי **hidday:** A proper noun designating Hiddai (2 Sam. 23:30).

1915. הָדַךְ **hāḏak:** A verb meaning to trample, crush, tread down. It describes the crushing or subduing of the wicked, rendering them justice (Job 40:12).

1916. הֲדֹם **h^a*ḏōm*:** A masculine noun denoting a footstool. It is always used with the word for feet and means the resting place of one's feet, indicating the place where God is pleased to dwell and to rule. Zion is depicted as His footstool (Lam. 2:1), as is the ark where worship takes place (Ps. 99:5; 132:7). The concept expands to include the entire earth as God's footstool (Isa. 66:1). But it also is used to indicate rulership or victory over one's enemies, the wicked, as when God makes His enemies a footstool (Ps. 110:1).

1917. הַדָּם **haddām:** An Aramaic masculine noun meaning pieces. It indicates the various external limbs or parts of the body which can be torn limb from limb (Dan. 2:5). It is used figuratively of the limbs of people, a nation, or a tongue (Dan. 3:29) that can be torn apart as a form of punishment.

1918. הֲדַס **h^a*ḏas*:** A masculine noun referring to a myrtle tree. God will place this tree in the desert as a part of His blessing on Israel (Isa. 41:19); it is contrasted with the nettle tree or bush (Isa. 55:13). Myrtle trees are pictured growing in a ravine (Zech. 1:8, 10, 11). Its branches were used to construct booths for the Feast of Booths or Tabernacles (Neh. 8:15).

1919. הֲדַסָּה **h^a*ḏassāh*:** A proper noun designating Hadassah (Esth. 2:7).

1920. הָדַף **hāḏap:** A verb meaning to drive out, shove away. It means to shove a person (2etimes violently (Num. 35:20, 22), to force out an enemy from Canaanite territory (Deut. 6:19). Israel sometimes does it, or God (Deut. 9:4; Josh. 23:5) does it for His people. It depicts the bullying, violent abuse of persons or groups of people by those in power (Ezek. 34:21). It is used of God's refusing the desires or cravings of the wicked (Prov. 10:3) and driving them into darkness (Job 18:18). It refers figuratively to deposing or humbling someone (Isa. 22:19; Jer. 46:15).

1921. הֲדוּרִים ***hᵃḏûriym,*** הָדַר ***hāḏar:*** A verb meaning to honor, to make glorious. The Israelites were commanded not to show unjust bias toward the poor (Ex. 23:3) and to honor older people (Lev. 19:32). This did not always happen (Lam. 5:12), but Solomon said that a person should not honor himself (Prov. 25:6). Isaiah used this word when he prophesied that the Lord would come dressed in glory (Isa. 63:1).

1922. הֲדַר ***hᵃḏar:*** An Aramaic verb meaning to glorify, to magnify. Nebuchadnezzar built up Babylon to glorify himself until God took his power away and showed him who was sovereign. Then Nebuchadnezzar glorified God (Dan. 4:34[31], 37[34]). Unfortunately, King Belshazzar did not learn from his ancestor's mistake and also decided to honor himself instead of God (Dan. 5:23).

1923. הֲדַר ***hᵃḏar:*** An Aramaic masculine noun meaning honor, majesty. In a meeting between Daniel and King Belshazzar, Daniel reminded Belshazzar that the Lord gave his father Nebuchadnezzar kingship, majesty, glory, and honor (Dan. 5:18).

1924. הֲדַר ***hᵃḏar:*** A proper noun designating Hadar, another spelling for *hᵃḏaḏ* (1908,C) (Gen. 36:39).

1925. הֶדֶר ***heḏer:*** A masculine noun meaning splendor, ornament. This word is used once in Daniel, where it speaks of the splendor of the kingdom (Dan. 11:20). This word is difficult to translate. It has been translated "the glory of the kingdom" (KJV), "royal splendor" (NIV), or a particular place, such as "the Jewel [the heart or gem] of his kingdom" (NASB).

1926. הָדָר ***hāḏār:*** A noun meaning glory, splendor, majesty. It describes the impressive character of God in 1 Chronicles 16:27 and His thunderous voice in Psalm 29:4. Isaiah describes sinners fleeing from the *hāḏār* of the Lord (Isa. 2:10, 19). Often the Psalms use this word in conjunction with others to describe God's glory, splendor, and majesty (Ps. 96:6; 145:5). It also refers to the majesty of kings (Ps. 21:5[6]; 45:3[4]). Psalm 8:5[6] expresses the splendor of God's creation of humans in comparison to the rest of creation. In Isaiah's prophetic description of the Suffering Servant, he uses *hāḏār* to say that the Servant will have no splendor to attract people to Him (Isa. 53:2).

1927. הֲדָרָה ***hᵃḏārāh:*** A feminine noun meaning adornment, glory. This word comes from the verb *hāḏar* (1921), meaning to honor or to adorn and is related to the Hebrew noun *hāḏār* (1926), meaning majesty. In four of the five occurrences of this word, it occurs in the context of worshiping the Lord, "the beauty of holiness" (KJV) (1 Chr. 16:29; 2 Chr. 20:21; Ps. 29:2; 96:9). In other instances, the word expresses the glory kings find in a multitude of people (Prov. 14:28).

1928. הֲדַרְעֶזֶר ***hᵃḏar'ezer:*** A proper noun designating Hadarezer (2 Sam. 10:16, 19; 1 Chr. 18:3, 5, 7–10; 19:16, 19): another spelling of *hᵃḏaḏ'ezer* [1909]. For the NASB, NIV, see *hᵃḏaḏ'ezer* (1909).

1929. הָהּ ***hāh:*** A strong emotional interjection, alas! It is used to announce a coming day of horrific judgment on the ancient nation of Egypt (Ezek. 30:2) and other nations of the world.

1930. הוֹ ***hô:*** A strong emotional interjection, alas! It is repeated in Amos 5:16 for even more emphasis to announce the coming of the Lord's day of judgment.

1931. הִיא ***hiy',*** הוּא ***hû':*** A pronoun appearing in masculine and feminine forms, he, she, it. Its major uses are as follows: as the third person independent pronoun meaning he, she, it, they (Gen. 3:15, 20; 13:1; 37:2; Judg. 11:1); as a demonstrative pronoun meaning that is, there is (Gen. 2:11–13; Lev. 10:3; Deut. 30:20); as an emphatic word to emphasize a subject (Gen. 2:14). Placed in front of a noun, it gives precision (Ex. 12:42); used with a pronoun, it indicates identity, *'ᵃnî hû,* it is I (Isa. 52:6). Used after a noun in agreement with the noun, it is a demonstrative adjective meaning that, e.g., that man (Job 1:1). It serves to tie two things together as the verb is, are (Lam. 1:18). It is combined with other words to form names, such as *'ᵉlîyhû(')* (453), He is my God.

1932. הוּא ***hû',*** הִיא ***hiy':*** An Aramaic pronoun in masculine and feminine forms, he, she, it. Its main uses include an independent pronoun, he, she, it (Dan. 2:21, 22; 6:4[5]; 7:7, 24); a demonstrative adjective meaning that (Dan. 2:32);0 a word indicating emphasis (Dan. 6:16[17]); translated as himself, a semiverb meaning is, are (Dan. 2:28).

1933. הָוָה ***hāwāh:*** I. A verb meaning to fall. It is used of falling snow (Job 37:6) commanded to descend by God.

II. A verb meaning to be, become, come to pass. In its imperative or command form, it regularly means to become something or someone (Gen. 27:29; Neh. 6:6; Job 37:6; Isa. 16:4); a master, a king, falling snow, a hiding place. It indicates being in a location or state (Eccl. 2:22; 11:3).

1934. הֲוָה ***hᵃwāh:*** An Aramaic verb meaning to be, to come to pass, to take place. It has the sense of to happen (Dan. 2:28), to take place, to exist, to be of a kingdom, wrath (Dan. 2:40, 43; 7:23; Ezra 7:23). It means to change or become (Dan. 2:35). It indicates the possession of something when used with the preposition *l^e*, to (Dan. 5:17, to yourself or for yourself), and it may indicate the actions or character of peoples or nations (Dan. 5:17).

1935. הוֹד ***hôḏ:*** A masculine noun meaning vigor, authority, majesty. It refers to human physical vigor (Prov. 5:9; Dan. 10:8); the fighting vigor of a horse in battle (Zech. 10:3); and the growing vigor of an olive plant (Hos. 14:6[7]). The word also implies authority, such as what Moses bestowed on Joshua (Num. 27:20); and royal majesty (1 Chr. 29:25; Jer. 22:18). Thus, it is used to describe God's majesty (Job 37:22; Ps. 145:5; Zech. 6:13). The word often describes God's glory as displayed above the heavens (Ps. 8:1[2]; 148:13; Hab. 3:3; cf. Ps. 96:6; 104:1, where the word is related to God's creation of the heavens).

1936. הוֹד ***hôḏ:*** A proper noun designating Hod (1 Chr. 7:37).

1937. הוֹדְוָה ***hôḏ^e wāh:*** A proper noun designating Hodevah (Neh. 7:43).

1938. הוֹדַוְיָה ***hôḏawyāh:*** A proper noun designating Hodaviah (1 Chr. 3:24; 5:24; 9:7; Ezra 2:40).

1939. הוֹדַיְוָהוּ ***hôḏaywāhû:*** A proper noun designating Hodaiah (1 Chr. 3:24, KJV).

1940. הוֹדִיָּה ***hôḏiyyāh:*** A proper noun designating Hodiah (1 Chr. 4:19, KJV).

1941. הוֹדִיָּה ***hôḏiyyāh:*** A proper noun designating Hodijah, Hodiah:
A. A Jew (1 Chr. 4:19, NASB, NIV).
B. A Levite (Neh. 8:7; 9:5; 10:10[11]).
C. A Levite (Neh. 10:13[14]).
D. A covenanter (Neh. 10:18[19]).

1942. הַוָּה ***hawwāh:*** A feminine noun meaning destruction, desire. This word usually describes an event associated with calamity, evil, or destruction. It can speak of the wickedness of evildoers (Ps. 5:9[10]); the devastation a foolish son could cause his father (Prov. 19:13); the destruction intended by the tongue (Ps. 38:12[13]; 52:2[4]); the calamities of life which require refuge in God for protection (Ps. 57:1[2]). In several places, this word depicts the evil desires of the wicked that resulted in destruction: God would cast away the wicked person's desire (Prov. 10:3); the evil desires of transgressors would be their downfall (Prov. 11:6); and destruction awaited the ones who trust in their own desires (Ps. 52:7[9]).

1943. הֹוָה ***hōwāh:*** A feminine noun meaning disaster. The root idea is a pit or chasm, a symbol of disaster. The word describes a disaster coming on Babylon that it will not be able to prevent with its occult practices (Isa. 47:11). The only other occurrence of this word describes a series of disasters (literally, disaster upon disaster) prophesied to come on Israel because of idolatry (Ezek. 7:26). In this passage, there will be no escape although Israel will look for a prophetic vision.

1944. הוֹהָם ***hôhām:*** A proper noun designating Hoham (Josh. 10:3).

1945. הוֹי ***hôy:*** An interjection meaning ho! woe! alas! It is used in lamenting a person's death (1 Kgs. 13:30). It is used in prophetic announcements of judgment or threats (Isa. 1:4, 24; Jer. 48:1; Ezek. 13:18; Amos 5:18). It is used to draw attention to an unexpected but momentous occasion (Isa. 18:1) or to a hope-filled and joyous expectation (Zech. 2:6[10]).

1946. הוּךְ ***hûk̠:*** An Aramaic verb indicating to go, to come. It refers to the coming or arrival of a report (Ezra 5:5); to the taking of vessels to the Temple (Ezra 6:5); and to people going to Jerusalem (Ezra 7:13).

1947. הוֹלֵלוֹת ***hôlēlôt̠:*** A feminine plural noun referring to madness, delusion. It is found only in the book of Ecclesiastes and means madness, the tendency to try anything to know its outcome. It is not a worthwhile experience to know madness but is rather vanity (Eccl. 1:17; 7:25), the opposite of wisdom. Wisdom excels madness and folly (Eccl. 2:12, 13). The desire to know madness is, unfortunately, intrinsic in the human heart (Eccl. 9:3).

1948. הוֹלֵלוּת ***hôlēlût̠:*** A feminine abstract noun denoting madness. It indicates the ultimate outcome and fruit of a fool's foolish talk (Eccl. 10:13).

1949. הוּם ***hûm:*** A verb meaning to rouse, to roar, to confuse. This verb describes a stirring or rousing, such as occurred in Bethlehem when Ruth and Naomi returned from Moab (Ruth 1:19), or would occur in the nations when God would confuse them before their destruction (Deut. 7:23). On several occasions, the audible effects of the rousing was emphasized, such as when Solomon was anointed king, the roar of the city could be heard (1 Kgs. 1:45; cf. 1 Sam. 4:5; Mic. 2:12). In the only other occurrence of this verb, David described himself as restless and roused (Ps. 55:2[3]).

1950. הוֹמָם ***hômām:*** A proper noun designating Homam (1 Chr. 1:39).

1951. הוּן ***hûn:*** A verb meaning to be ready, to consider as easy. It refers to something this is considered to be easily accomplished task. A rebellious Israel thought that taking Canaan would be an easy task for them (Deut. 1:41).

1952. הוֹן ***hôn:*** A masculine noun referring to wealth, benefit, substance, enough. It is used mainly in the Wisdom Books. It is used to refer to goods or wealth that is sufficient or enough (Prov. 30:15); to fire that consumes and wants more (Prov. 30:16). God sold His people but not for a sufficient benefit or profit (Ps. 44:12[13]) in their eyes. It regularly refers simply to wealth: wealth is a feature of the Lord's house (Ps. 112:3); it is present with true wisdom (Prov. 8:18); it is to be used to honor God (Prov. 3:9); it is the security of the rich person (Prov. 10:15); sinners pursue it (Prov. 1:13; 28:22); wealth cannot, however, purchase love (Song 8:7); wealth made a nation or city important in world trade markets (Ezek. 27:12, 18, 27, 33). Wealth will be useless in a time of God's judgment and wrath (Prov. 11:4). Virtues are of great value, however, such as diligence (Prov. 12:27). Sometimes true wealth is not visible but is a personal possession of an abundant life (Prov. 13:7). Ill-gotten wealth eventually is gone (Prov. 13:11), but wealth obtained through godly wisdom is true riches (Prov. 24:4).

1953. הוֹשָׁמָע ***hôšāmā':*** A proper noun designating Hoshama (1 Chr. 3:18).

1954. הוֹשֵׁעַ ***hôšēa':*** A proper noun designating Hoshea:

A. The name borne by Joshua before it was changed (Num. 13:8; 16). His father was Nun. Hoshea means "deliverance, salvation"; Joshua, "the Lord saves."

B. The last king of Israel. He was considered evil, as were all the kings of northern Israel (2 Kgs. 15:30). He assassinated his predecessor Pekah son of Remaliah. He was king when Israel went into exile in 722 B.C. He reigned nine years and was eventually put into prison by Shalmaneser, the Assyrian king (727–722 B.C.).

C. The prophet who prophesied in northern Israel in the central years of the eighth century B.C. He warned Israel of God's coming judgments by the Assyrians. Little is known about him. His name means "salvation, deliverance." He was from northern Israel, the son of a man named Beeri (Hos. 1:1). He prophesied under several kings (Hos. 1:1), but his message was primarily to the northern kingdom. He lived during the troublesome times of the last days of northern Israel, which was destroyed in 722 B.C.

D. The name of a leader in Ephraim. He was the son of Azaziah (1 Chr. 27:20).

E. The name of a leader of those who returned from exile (Neh. 10:23[24]). He supported Nehemiah's reforms.

1955. הוֹשַׁעְיָה ***hôša'yāh:*** A proper noun designating Hoshaiah:

A. A prince of Judah (Neh. 12:32).

B. The father of Jezaniah (Jer. 42:1; 43:2).

1956. הוֹתִיר ***hôṯiyr:*** A proper noun designating Hothir (1 Chr. 25:4, 28).

1957. הָזָה ***hāzāh:*** A verb meaning to sleep, to dream. It is used in a derisive way of useless, lazy persons who love to slumber and lounge about, mere dreamers among God's people (Isa. 56:10).

1958. הִי ***hiy:*** A masculine noun meaning woe. It refers to distress and destruction found written in Ezekiel's scroll (Ezek. 2:10), along with laments and mournings.

1959. הֵידָד ***hēydād:*** A masculine noun indicating a cheer or shout. It refers to jubilant shouting heard at harvest time (Isa. 16:10; Jer. 48:33). It refers also to Moab's shouts of mourning or the shouts of their enemies (Jer. 48:33; cf. 51:14). It indicates the Lord's shout over the nations as He treads them in judgment (Jer. 25:30).

1960. הֻיְּדוֹת ***huyy^edôt:*** A feminine plural noun referring to songs of thanksgiving. It refers to the songs of praise and thanksgiving which the Levites directed in the time of Nehemiah (Neh. 12:8).

1961. הָיָה ***hāyāh:*** A verb meaning to exist, to be, to become, to happen, to come to pass, to be done. It is used over 3, 500 times in the Old Testament. In the simple stem, the verb often means to become, to take place, to happen. It indicates that something has occurred or come about, such as events that have turned out a certain way (1 Sam. 4:16); something has happened to someone, such as Moses (Ex. 32:1, 23; 2 Kgs. 7:20); or something has occurred just as God said it would (Gen. 1:7, 9). Often a special Hebrew construction using the imperfect form of the verb asserts that something came to pass (cf. Gen. 1:7, 9). Less often, the construction is used with the perfect form of the verb to refer to something coming to pass in the future (Isa. 7:18, 21; Hos. 2:16).

The verb is used to describe something that comes into being or arises. For instance, a great cry arose in Egypt when the firstborn were killed in the tenth plague (Ex. 12:30; cf. Gen. 9:16; Mic. 7:4); and when God commanded light to appear, and it did (Gen. 1:3). It is used to join the subject and verb as in Genesis 1:2 where the earth was desolate and void, or to say Adam and Eve were naked (Gen. 2:25). With certain prepositions, it can mean to follow or to be in favor of someone (Ps. 124:1, 2). The verb is used with a variety of other words, normally prepositions, to express subtle differences in meaning, such as to be located somewhere (Ex. 1:5); to serve or function as something (e.g., gods [Ex. 20:3]); to become something or as something, as when a person becomes a living being (Gen. 2:7); to be with or by someone (Deut. 22:2); to be or come on someone or something (e.g., the fear of humans on the beasts [Gen. 9:2]); to express the idea of better than or a comparison (Ezek. 15:2), as in the idea of too small (Ex. 12:4).

1962. הַיָּה ***hayyāh:*** A feminine noun meaning destruction. This word occurs only once in the Old Testament (Job 6:2) and is a slightly different form of *hawwāh* (1942), also meaning destruction.

1963. הֵיךְ *hēyḵ:* An interrogative adverb indicating how. David used it to indicate how, in what way, he could move the ark of God to Jerusalem (1 Chr. 13:12). It asks how it was possible for a divine being to communicate with Daniel (Dan. 10:17).

1964. הֵיכָל *hēyḵāl:* A masculine noun meaning temple, palace. The word derives from the word *yāḵōl* (3201), meaning to be able and comes from the idea of capacity. It refers to a king's palace or other royal buildings (1 Kgs. 21:1; Isa. 13:22) and, likely by extension, to the dwelling of God, whether on earth (Ps. 79:1) or in heaven (Isa. 6:1). The word is used of Solomon's Temple, the second Temple (Ezra 3:6; Neh. 6:10) and also of the Tabernacle. In reference to foreign buildings, it is sometimes difficult to say whether a palace or the temple of a false god is meant (2 Chr. 36:7; Joel 3:5[4:5]). A special usage of the word designates the holy place of the Temple as opposed to the Holy of Holies (1 Kgs. 6:17; Ezek. 41:4, 15).

1965. הֵיכַל *hēyḵal:* A masculine noun meaning temple, palace. This is the Aramaic form of the Hebrew word *hēyḵāl* (1964). The word is used most often in relation to a king's palace (Ezra 4:14). When Belshazzar sees the handwriting on the wall of the palace, this is the word used (Dan. 5:5). It is also used in reference to the Temple of God in Jerusalem (Ezra 5:14, 15), as well as the temple in Babylon (Ezra 5:14).

1966. הֵילֵל *hēylēl:* A masculine noun meaning morning star, Lucifer. The word refers to the king of Babylon figuratively as the morning star (Lucifer, shining one, is from the Latin Vulgate's translation meaning shining one) (Isa. 14:12).

1967. הֵימָם *hēymām:* A proper noun designating Heman, another spelling of *hômām* (1950) (Gen. 36:22, KJV, NASB).

1968. הֵימָן *hēymān:* A proper noun designating Hemam:

A. A sage under Solomon (1 Kgs. 4:31[5:11]; 1 Chr. 2:6).

B. A chief singer (1 Chr. 6:33[18]; 15:17, 19; 16:41, 42; 25:1, 4–6; 2 Chr. 5:12; 29:14; 35:15; Ps. 88:title[1]).

1969. הִין *hiyn:* A masculine noun denoting a unit of liquid measure or hin. It indicates the amount of liquid used in a ritual (Ex. 29:40). It was used for measuring olive oil (Ex. 29:40; 30:24). The modern equivalent is about 3.8 liquid quarts or 3.3 dry quarts, although some would suggest a larger modern equivalent of over one quart liquid for a hin.

1970. הָכַר *hāḵar*, חָכַר *ḥāḵar:* I. A verb meaning to act as a stranger toward. It describes actions, words, and attitudes that indicate alienation towards another person (Job 19:3, KJV).

II. A verb meaning to injure or wrong. It indicates unduly aggressive or injurious actions toward someone (Job 19:3; NKJV, NASB, NIV).

1971. הַכָּרָה ***hakkārāh:*** A feminine noun indicating appearance, expression. The facial appearance or countenance that reveals a person's attitudes (Isa. 3:9) and character.

1972. הָלָא ***hālā':*** A verb meaning to be carried away. It is used in its passive sense to indicate those who have been carried away, gone into exile (Mic. 4:7).

1973. הָלְאָה ***hālᵉ'āh:*** An adverb indicating beyond, away; to there; from that time on. It is used mostly to indicate place or location: it means to get back, literally, to get out there (Gen. 19:9); an area beyond a certain location (Gen. 35:21; 1 Sam. 10:3; Amos 5:27); an indicator of general location (Num. 16:37[17:2]; 32:19). It indicates time beyond a certain set point: from the eighth day on (Lev. 22:27); from then on, from that day on (1 Sam. 18:9; Isa. 18:2, 7; Ezek. 39:22).

1974. הִלּוּל ***hillûl:*** A masculine noun indicating praise, rejoicing, a joyous celebration. It designates a praise offering with the fruit of the land (Lev. 19:24), holy unto the Lord. It can be translated as a joyous festival or a time of merriment to the Lord (Judg. 9:27).

1975. הַלָּז ***hallāz:*** A common demonstrative pronoun. It points out specific objects: that (other) side (1 Sam. 14:1); this Philistine (1 Sam. 17:26); this Shunamite (woman) (2 Kgs. 4:25). It is used regarding men, this one (Dan. 8:16, with *lᵉ*, to, prefixed). See 1976, 1977.

1976. הַלָּזֶה ***hallāzeh:*** A masculine demonstrative pronoun, this, that. It points out a person: that man, Isaac (Gen. 24:65); this dreamer (Joseph) (Gen. 37:19) in a disrespectful slur. See 1975, 1977.

1977. הַלֵּזוּ ***hallēzû:*** A feminine demonstrative pronoun, this, that. Used once, it points out the land of Israel, this desolate land (Ezek. 36:35).

1978. הָלִיךְ ***hāliyk̲:*** A masculine noun denoting a path, a step. It is used figuratively to refer to Job's successful life, steps, before calamity struck him (Job 29:6).

1979. הֲלִיכָה ***hᵃliyk̲ah:*** A feminine noun indicating a going, a march, procession, traveling group. It describes the confused march or scurrying about of the people of Nineveh under attack (Nah. 2:5[6]). It is used to describe those proceeding or traveling; caravans (Job 6:19). It indicates the activity and lifestyle of a family (Prov. 31:27). The psalmist uses it of God's procession or proceeding into the sanctuary (Ps. 68:24[25]), and it denotes God's ways in general (Hab. 3:6).

1980. הָלַךְ ***hālak̲:*** A verb meaning to go, to come, to walk. This common word carries with it the basic idea of movement: the flowing of a river (Gen. 2:14); the descending of floods (Gen. 8:3); the crawling of beasts (Lev. 11:27); the slithering of snakes (Lev. 11:42); the blowing of the wind (Eccl. 1:6); the tossing of the sea (Jon. 1:13). Since it is usually a person who is moving, it is frequently translated "walk" (Gen. 48:15; 2 Sam. 15:30). Like a similar verb *dārak̲* (1869), meaning to tread, this word is also used metaphorically to speak of the pathways (i.e., behavior) of one's life. A son could walk in (i.e., follow after) the ways of his father (2 Chr. 17:3) or not (1 Sam. 8:3). Israel was commanded to walk in the ways of the Lord (Deut. 28:9), but they often walked after other gods (2 Kgs. 13:11).

1981. הֲלַךְ ***hᵃlak̲:*** An Aramaic verb meaning to walk, to go, to travel, to journey. It means simply to go, to journey (Ezra 7:13). It describes things brought or delivered to a location or person (Ezra 5:5; 6:5). It depicts a person walking about (Dan. 3:25; 4:29[26], 37[34]).

1982. הֵלֶךְ ***hēlek̲:*** A masculine noun meaning to go, moving, travel, flow; traveler, visitor. It refers to flowing honey that was running from trees (1 Sam. 14:26). It indicates a person who is on the road journeying (2 Sam. 12:4).

1983. הֲלָךְ ***hᵃlāk̲:*** An Aramaic masculine noun indicating a tribute, custom tax, toll. It indicates a toll or a tax paid by cities to their rulers (Ezra 4:13, 20). The priests, Levites, singers, doorkeepers, and other Temple personnel were not subject to this toll or tax (Ezra 7:24).

1984. הָלַל ***hālal:*** A verb meaning to praise, to commend, to boast, to shine. The root meaning may be to shine but could also be to shout. The word most often means praise and is associated with the ministry of the Levites who praised God morning and evening (1 Chr. 23:30). All creation, however, is urged to join in (Ps. 148), and various instruments were used to increase the praise to God (Ps. 150). The word hallelujah is a command to praise *Yah* (the Lord), derived from the word *hālal* (Ps. 105:45; 146:1). The reflexive form of the verb is often used to signify boasting, whether in a good object (Ps. 34:2[3]) or a bad object (Ps. 49:6[7]). Other forms of the word mean to act foolishly or to be mad (1 Sam. 21:13[14]; Eccl. 7:7; Isa. 44:25).

1985. הִלֵּל ***hillēl:*** A proper noun designating Hillel (Judg. 12:13, 15).

1986. הָלַם ***hālam:*** A verb meaning to smite, to hammer, to strike down. It also carries the implication of conquering and disbanding. The author of Judges used this word to describe Jael hammering the tent peg through Sisera's head (Judg. 5:26).

Isaiah employed this word figuratively to describe nations breaking down grapevines (Isa. 16:8) and people overcome by wine (Isa. 28:1).

1987. הֶלֶם ***helem:*** A proper noun designating Helem (1 Chr. 7:35).

1988. הֲלֹם ***hᵃlōm:*** An adverb meaning here, hither. It indicates a place which one approaches (Ex. 3:5; 1 Sam. 10:22). It indicates indefinite locations as well (1 Sam. 14:16). But it can also indicate the place where a person is currently located, i.e., here (Judg. 20:7; 1 Sam. 14:36, 38), even a spot where God has revealed Himself (Gen. 16:13). It is used figuratively or metaphorically to refer to the place in a person's life that the Lord has brought them (2 Sam. 7:18), as in the case of King David. It refers to the way of the wicked as a place to which people turn to follow (Ps. 73:10).

1989. הַלְמוּת ***halmûṯ:*** A feminine noun denoting a mallet, hammer. It refers to a hammer used by Jael, wife of Heber the Kenite, to drive a tent peg through Sisera's skull, killing him (Judg. 5:26). It could have been made of metal or wood.

1990. הָם ***hām:*** A proper noun designating Ham (Gen. 14:5).

1991. הָם ***hām:*** A masculine noun designating wealth, substance. It denotes the wealth accumulated by the wicked in the land of Israel (Ezek. 7:11) but which was part of their idolatry.

1992. הֵם ***hēm,*** הֵמָּה ***hēmmāh:*** A masculine plural pronoun meaning they, these. Both forms are used alike. Its basic uses are: (1) with a verb form to serve as its subject or to emphasize its subject, meaning they or they themselves respectively (Gen. 6:4; Ex. 5:7; 18:22); (2) as a linking verb meaning is, are (Gen. 3:7; 48:5; Ex. 5:8; Job 6:7; Prov. 30:24); (3) as a demonstrative adjective coming after a noun and bearing the definite article (Gen. 6:4; Ex. 2:11) meaning those (Num. 14:38); (4) as an object of prepositions (Ex. 30:4; 36:1) meaning them, whom (Jer. 36:32) and translated as the particular preposition demands.

1993. הָמָה ***hāmāh:*** A verb meaning to murmur, growl, roar, howl. This verb takes its specific meaning from its context. Its basic renderings are: (1) to indicate a strong emotional response by birds or animals (Ps. 59:6[7]; Isa. 59:11; Ezek. 7:16), often used in a simile or comparison; (2) to indicate the murmuring of one's soul in distress (Ps. 42:5[6]; 11[12]; 55:17[18]; 77:3[4]) but also of musical instruments (Isa. 16:11; Jer. 48:36); (3) to describe the sound or roar of waves or great multitudes of people (Isa. 51:15; Jer. 5:22; 31:35); to depict the noise or uproar of a city (1 Kgs. 1:41; Isa. 22:2); (4) to describe the uproar or commotion of people in general (Ps. 39:6[7]). It indicates the restlessness of the human heart (Jer. 4:19) or of humankind itself (Ps. 77:3[4]).

1994. הִמּוֹ ***himmô,*** הִמּוֹן ***himmōn:*** An Aramaic pronoun meaning these, they, them. It is used as a linking verb meaning is or are (Ezra 5:11). It is used mostly as the accusative object of a verb meaning them (Ezra 4:23; 5:5; Dan. 2:34, 35).

1995. הָמוֹן ***hāmôn,*** הָמַן ***hāman:*** I. A masculine noun denoting a multitude, noise, tumult. It often describes the sound or tumult of a crowd of people (2 Kgs. 7:13; Ps. 65:7[8]; Isa. 13:4; 33:3; Dan. 10:6) or of a city (Isa. 5:14; 32:14; Ezek. 26:13) or of an army or troop (1 Sam. 14:19; 2 Sam. 18:29). But it also describes the roar of nature in the rain (1 Kgs. 18:41) or the rumbling of chariot wheels (Jer. 47:3). It especially is used of the tumult and roar of huge multitudes: great armies (Judg. 4:7; 1 Sam. 14:16; 1 Kgs. 20:13, 28); an entire nation (2 Sam. 6:19; Isa. 5:13). In general usage, it also indicates wealth (Ps. 37:16) and a great supply or mass of things (1 Chr. 29:16; 2 Chr. 31:10; Jer. 49:32).

II. A verb indicating to multiply. It indicates the multiplication of the people of Israel (Ezek. 5:7; KJV, NKJV) and Jerusalem.

III. A verb meaning to be in turmoil. It depicts the turmoil and tumult of Israel (Ezek. 5:7; NASB, NIV, NKJV).

1996. הֲמוֹן גּוֹג ***h^{a}môn gôg:*** A proper noun designating Hamon Gog (Ezek. 39:11, 15).

1997. הֲמוֹנָה ***h^{a}mônāh:*** A proper noun designating Hamonah (Ezek. 39:16).

1998. הֶמְיָה ***hemyāh:*** A feminine noun indicating noise, music. It depicts the noise or music of harps (Isa. 14:11) standing for the pride and joy of Babylon.

1999. הֲמֻלָּה ***h^{a}mullāh,*** הֲמוּלָּה ***h^{a}mûllāh:*** A feminine noun meaning a rushing noise. The two occurrences of this word conjure up the sound of a great wind. The first is in the prophecy of Jeremiah, where Israel was called a strong olive tree, but the Lord would set the tree on fire with a great rushing sound as a sign of judgment (Jer. 11:16). The word is also used in Ezekiel's vision, where the sound of the creatures' wings was like the roar of a rushing river (Ezek. 1:24).

2000. הָמַם ***hāmam:*** A verb meaning to make a noise, to move noisily, to confuse, to put into commotion. When it means to move noisily, it often refers to the wheels of wagons or chariots (Isa. 28:28). The idea of moving noisily or with commotion carries over into the idea of confusion: God confuses the Egyptians when they pursue Israel (Ex. 14:24); and He sends confusion to the nations before the Israelites go into Canaan (Josh. 10:10).

2001. הָמָן ***hāmān:*** A proper noun designating Haman, the name of the villain in Esther who sought to eradicate the Jews from the Persian Empire (Esth. 3:7–15). Instead, his wicked plot was ironically turned upon his own head, and he was hanged on his own gallows (Esth. 7:1–10) and his sons killed (Esth. 9:5–10, 14, 24–25). Haman was the son of Hammedatha, an Agagite, and may have been an Amalekite in ancestry. The destruction of Haman and his sons fulfilled the Lord's curse on the Amalekites (Ex. 17:8–15).

2002. הַמְנִיךְ ***hamniyk:*** An Aramaic masculine noun meaning chain, necklace. It refers to the chain Daniel would receive if he sufficiently interpreted the writing on the wall (Dan. 5:7, 29).

2003. הֲמָסִים ***hamāsiym:*** A masculine noun meaning brushwood. It was an easily kindled wood used to start a fire (Isa. 64:2[1]).

2004. הֵן ***hēn:*** A feminine pronoun meaning they, them. It is used only with prefixes *be*, in, among; *ke*, like, as; *le*, to, for; *min* (4480), from. It refers to either persons or things: in them (cities) (Gen. 19:29); for them (sons) (Ruth 1:13); like them, likewise (sins) (Ezek. 18:14); (more) than they (Israelites) (Ezek. 16:47).

2005. הֵן ***hēn:*** A particle serving as a demonstrative interjection meaning behold, since, and as a conditional conjunction meaning if. It may point out and stress a following word or clause: behold or "Since you have given no offspring to me" (Gen. 15:3, NASB); behold [since] the man . . . (Gen. 3:22). It introduces a statement that lays the basis for a following assertion or plea (Isa. 64:9[8]) or indicates a strongly felt agreement, good, behold, followed by an assertion (Gen. 30:34). It also, in some contexts, introduces conditional sentences, meaning if (Ex. 4:1; Lev. 25:20; Job 40:23; Isa. 54:15).

2006. הֵן ***hēn:*** An Aramaic particle translated as behold, if, whether. It introduces conditional sentences meaning if (Ezra 4:13, 16; Dan. 2:6). When used in sequence with intervening words, it is translated as whether . . . or . . . or (Ezra 7:26). It is found in an indirect question meaning if or whether (Dan. 4:27[24]; Ezra 5:17).

2007. הֵנָּה ***hēnnāh:*** A feminine plural noun meaning they, them. It is regularly translated as they, them. It is the long form of *hēn* and is used the same way with the same meanings (see *hēn* [2004]). But note its use with (*māh*) *hēnnāh* meaning these things (Gen. 21:29).

2008. הֵנָּה ***hēnnāh:*** An adverb indicating here, now. It is used most often of physical location or motion toward a location: It means to go to a location (Gen. 15:16; 42:15; 45:5); it indicates a specific location reached (Gen. 45:8, 13; Josh. 2:2; 2 Kgs. 8:7). Repeated, it means hither . . . hither, to and fro, back and forth (2 Kgs. 4:35). It indicates a point reached in time and location (Num. 14:19; 2 Sam. 20:16). It indicates the end or extent of Jeremiah's words (Jer. 51:64). It is used to indicate an extent or process of time: It can indicate, with a negative, that a process has not been completed (Gen. 15:16). It refers to a period of past time that touches the present (Gen. 44:28; Judg. 16:13). It indicates a point to which something has been done, e.g., the declaration of God's wonders until now (Ps. 71:17).

2009. הִנֵּה ***hinnēh:*** A interjection meaning behold, look, now; if. It is used often and expresses strong feelings, surprise, hope, expectation, certainty, thus giving vividness depending on its surrounding context. Its main meanings can only be summarized briefly here: It stresses a following word referring to persons or things (Gen. 12:19; 15:17; 18:9). It is used to answer, with the first person suffix attached, when one is called (Gen. 22:1, 7; 27:1; Ex. 3:4; 1 Sam. 3:4). It is used of God's response (Isa. 52:6; 58:9; 65:1). It indicates a call to realize something God or others have done (Gen. 1:29; 17:20). It is followed with a particle of entreaty *nā'* when a request is involved (Gen. 12:11; 16:2; 1 Kgs. 20:31). It can call attention to something about to happen, a future reference (Ex. 32:34; 34:10). It is used to announce the Lord's sending of a child as a sign (Isa. 7:14). The word adds vividness and emotional involvement for the reader: "Behold, it was very good" (NASB) (Gen. 1:31; 6:12; 8:13; 18:2; 37:7; Amos 7:1; 8:1). Finally, it is used to introduce a formula of challenge (Jer. 21:13). In a few passages, it has the sense of if (Lev. 13:5, 6, 8; Deut. 13:14[15]; 1 Sam. 20:12).

2010. הֲנָחָה ***hanāḥāh:*** A feminine noun denoting a holiday, a day of rest. It refers to a holiday declared by the Persian king Ahasueras (Xerxes) in honor of Esther's banquet (Esth. 2:18).

2011. הִנֹּם ***hinnōm:*** A proper noun designating Hinnom, the valley that lies west and south of the hill of Jerusalem. It became a place known for idolatrous practices located there (2 Kgs. 23:10; 2 Chr. 28:3; Jer. 7:31), especially the worship of the god Molech. It runs together with the Kidron Valley on the south end of the City of David.

2012. הֵנַע ***hēna':*** A proper noun designating Hena (2 Kgs. 18:34; 19:13; Isa. 37:13).

2013. הַס ***hās,*** הָסָה ***hāsāh:*** I. An interjection meaning hush! Quiet! It is a serious request or an order to keep quiet: as the order of a king to his attendants (Judg. 3:19); as a command to not mention the name of the Lord (Amos 6:10); as a command for silence in a time of pestilence and destruction (Amos 8:3); as the proper response before the Lord in His holy temple (Hab. 2:20); as the day of the Lord approaches (Zeph. 1:7) when He will act on behalf of Jerusalem (Zech. 2:13[17]). It is used to indicate the proper response to a holy day of the Lord (Neh. 8:11, but is pointed as a verb form here).

II. A verb indicating to hush, to quiet, to silence, to still. It is employed in the causal form of the verb meaning caused to be silent or stilled (Num. 13:30).

2014. הֲפוּגָה ***hapûgāh:*** A feminine noun indicating relief, stopping. It is used with a preceding negative (*mē'ên*) to indicate weeping that is continuous, without relief (Lam. 3:49) over the fall of Jerusalem.

2015. הָפַךְ ***hāpak̲:*** A verb meaning to turn around, to change, to throw down, to overturn, to pervert, to destroy, to be turned against, to turn here and there, to wander. The verb is used to describe the simple act of turning something over (2 Kgs. 21:13; Hos. 7:8) but also to indicate turning back from something (Ps. 78:9). These turnings indicate that Jerusalem would lose all its inhabitants by being turned over as a dish is turned over after wiping it; "Ephraim has become a cake not turned," that is, overdone on one side, uncooked on the other, and not edible (Hos. 7:8 NASB).

The verb becomes more figurative when it describes the act of overthrowing or destroying. Second Kings 21:13 is relevant here also, but Haggai speaks of God overthrowing the thrones of kingdoms (Persia) as well as chariots and riders (Hag. 2:22). Even more violently, the verb describes the overthrow of the enemies of God and His people; Sodom and Gomorrah were especially singled out (Gen. 19:21, 25; Deut. 29:23[22]; cf. 2 Sam. 10:3). The word also indicates a change or is used to indicate defeat in battle when an army turned in flight (Josh. 7:8) or simply the change in direction of something (1 Kgs. 22:34). Metaphorically, the word comes to mean to change (by turning). For example, the Lord changed the curse of Balaam into a blessing (Deut. 23:5[6]); He will change the mourning of His people into joy and gladness (Jer. 31:13). The simple stem is also found in a reflexive sense; the men of Israel turned themselves about in battle against the Benjamites (Judg. 20:39, 41; cf. 2 Kgs. 5:26; 2 Chr. 9:12).

The verb is used a few times in the reflexive stems to indicate turning oneself about: The Israelites are pictured as having turned themselves back against their enemies (Josh. 8:20); and Pharaoh changed his heart in himself (Ex. 14:5; Hos. 11:8), thus changing his mind. The word is used in the sense of being overwhelmed or overcome by pain (1 Sam. 4:19); the clouds rolled about (Job. 37:12); the sword placed by the Lord to guard the Garden of Eden turned itself about (Gen. 3:24); and the earth's surface was shaped and moved like clay being impressed under a seal (Job 38:14).

2016. הֵפֶךְ ***hēpek̲,*** הֶפֶךְ ***hepek̲:*** A masculine noun indicating contrary, opposite, perversity. It indicates a total reversal of what should be or what is normal (Isa. 29:16). Israel's spiritual prostitution was itself perverse for she received no pay from others (Ezek. 16:34) for her deeds.

2017. הֹפֶךְ *hōpek:* A masculine noun indicating turning things upside down. It is the same in meaning as 2016. The KJV translates Isaiah 29:16 as, "Your turning of things upside down."

2018. הֲפֵכָה *hapēkāh:* A feminine noun denoting an overthrowing, a catastrophe. It describes the overthrow of Sodom and Gomorrah (Gen. 19:29) brought about as both a natural and a divinely caused judgment.

2019. הֲפַכְפַּךְ *hapakpak:* An adjective denoting something crooked, perverted, devious. It describes the winding, crooked, serpentine path of a guilty person (Prov. 21:8).

2020. הַצָּלָה *haṣṣālāh:* A feminine noun referring to deliverance. It refers to the deliverance of the Jews from Haman and his plots through Esther (Esth. 4:14), the Jewish queen of Persia.

2021. הֹצֶן *hōṣen:* A masculine noun denoting chariots, weapons. It describes the chariots that were a part of the Babylonian army coming against Judah (Ezek. 23:24, KJV; but NIV, weapons). Its meaning is still being researched.

2022. הַר *har:* A masculine noun indicating a hill, hill country, mountain, mountain range. With a following modifying word, it may mean a mountain range, such as the mountains or hill country of Gilead (Gen. 31:21; cf. Deut. 1:7; Josh. 17:15; Judg. 12:15) or denote individual mountains or Mount Ebal (Deut. 11:29). It indicates a particular mountain from the context without naming it (Gen. 22:2). Combined with the word for God, *'elohīym,* preceding, it points out the mountain of God (Ex. 4:27; 18:5; 24:13; Ps. 68:15[16]) or mountain of the Lord used with *yhwh* (3068) (Num. 10:33). These mountains and hills were sacred places for the gods of the pagan peoples of Canaan (Deut. 12:2), also called gods of the mountains (1 Kgs. 20:23). It refers to the *har-mō'ēd* or the mountain of assembly, a dwelling place of the gods (Isa. 14:13). The word is used in a figurative sense often: the Lord weighs the mountains in His hand (Isa. 40:12) and can lay them waste as a sign of His judgments (Isa. 42:15). God causes His people to thresh the mountains as a sign of their defeating their foes (Isa. 41:15). God calls the mountains as His witnesses (Mic. 6:2) and speaks to them (Ezek. 36:1, 4, 8). They are expected to praise the Lord (Ps. 148:9), and they leap in praise (Ps. 114:4, 6). The mountains symbolize strength (Isa. 2:14); great age, antiquity, and stability (Prov. 8:25), yet the Lord's love is even more enduring (Isa. 54:10).

2023. הֹר ***hōr:*** A proper noun designating Hor:

A. A mountain near the border of Edom where Aaron was buried (Num. 20:22–29), located in the area of Kadesh (Num. 33:37–39).

B. A hill in northeastern Israel (Num. 34:7, 8). It was a key marker for the northern border of Israel. It was probably in the northern part of the Lebanon Mountains.

2024. הָרָא ***hārā':*** A proper noun designating Hara (1 Chr. 5:26).

2025. הַרְאֵל ***har'ēl:*** A masculine noun denoting an altar. It depicts the altar hearth of burnt offering in Ezekiel's Temple vision (Ezek. 43:15).

2026. הָרַג ***hārag:*** A verb meaning to kill, murder, slay. It carries a wide variety of usages. Its first use in the Bible is in the fratricide of Cain and Abel (Gen. 4:8). The word is employed for war and slaughter (Josh. 8:24; 1 Kgs. 9:16; Esth. 8:11); God's killing in judgment (Gen. 20:4; Ex. 13:15; Amos 2:3); humans killing animals (Lev. 20:15; Num. 22:29); animals killing humans (2 Kgs. 17:25; Job 20:16).

2027. הֶרֶג ***hereg:*** A masculine noun meaning slaughter. The Jews had a great victory and struck down all their enemies (Esth. 9:5), while the book of Proverbs advises that one should rescue those unwise people heading for the slaughter (Prov. 24:11). Isaiah uses the "day of the great slaughter" to refer to the time of Israel's deliverance (Isa. 30:25). In the prophecy against Tyre, Ezekiel warns of the day when a slaughter will take place there (Ezek. 26:15).

2028. הֲרֵגָה ***hᵃrēḡāh:*** A noun meaning slaughter. It is the feminine form of *hereg* (2027) and is used only five times in the Old Testament. Two of these are found in the phrase "valley of slaughter" (Jer. 7:32; 19:6). In both of these occurrences, the Lord renames the Hinnom Valley because of the slaughter He will bring on the Israelites who have done horrifying deeds by sacrificing their children to other gods. Jeremiah also uses the word when he pleads with the Lord for the wicked to be taken away for the "day of slaughter" (Jer. 12:3 NIV). Zechariah uses this word twice in a metaphor describing Israel as the "flock marked for slaughter" (Zech. 11:4 NIV).

2029. הָרָה ***hārāh:*** A verb indicating to conceive, to become pregnant. Literally, it means for a woman to become pregnant (Gen. 16:4, 5; 19:36; 25:21; 38:18). It is often followed by the verb to bear, give birth, *wattahar wattēleḏ*, she became pregnant and gave birth (Gen. 4:1, 17; 21:2; Ex. 2:2). It has several figurative or metaphorical uses: of Moses's conceiving Israel (Num. 11:12); of Israel's failed pregnancy (Isa. 26:18); of Assyria's conception of chaff (Isa. 33:11); of the godless who become pregnant with trouble and evil (Job 15:35; Ps. 7:14[15]; Isa. 59:4).

2030. הָרֶה ***hāreh:*** A feminine adjective meaning pregnant. It describes the state of being pregnant, having conceived (Gen. 16:11; 1 Sam. 4:19; 2 Sam. 11:5; Isa. 7:14) by a man legally or by prostitution (Gen. 38:24). It takes on the meaning of a noun indicating pregnant women (2 Kgs. 8:12; 15:16; Jer. 31:8; Amos 1:13). The womb of Jeremiah's mother is described as pregnant, enlarged (Jer. 20:17).

2031. הַרְהֹר ***harhōr:*** An Aramaic masculine noun indicating a fantasy, thought, image. It denotes the thoughts (KJV, NKJV) or images (NIV) which King Nebuchadnezzar had while lying on his bed (Dan. 4:5[2]).

2032. הֵרוֹן ***hērôn,*** הֵרָיוֹן ***hērāyôn:*** A masculine noun referring to childbearing, pregnancy. It refers to the pregnancy period and process of childbearing. It will be painful (Gen. 3:16). It also marks the event of conception (Ruth 4:13). It is used figuratively of Ephraim conceiving children (Hos. 9:11).

2033. הֲרוֹרִי ***h^{a}rôriy:*** A proper noun designating Harorite (1 Chr. 11:27).

2034. הֲרִיסָה ***h^{a}riysāh:*** A feminine noun indicating a ruin, ruins, a destroyed building. It is used figuratively of the line of David in ruins (Amos 9:11), which the Lord will raise up again.

2035. הֲרִיסוּת ***h^{a}riysûṯ:*** A feminine noun indicating overthrow, destruction, ruins. It denotes the land of Judah and Israel destroyed by Babylon and Assyria (Isa. 49:19) but which will again be free and full of people.

2036. הֹרָם ***hōrām:*** A proper noun designating Horam (Josh. 10:33).

2037. הָרוּם ***hārûm:*** A proper noun designating Harum (1 Chr. 4:8).

2038. הַרְמוֹן ***harmôn:*** I. A masculine noun denoting a palace. It refers to a palace, possibly a foreign palace, to which Israelite refugees will go (Amos 4:3, KJV).

II. A proper name, Harmon. It indicates the destiny of Israelite refugees (Amos 4:3; NIV, NASB) when defeated by her enemies.

2039. הָרָן ***hārān:*** A proper noun designating Haran (Gen. 11:26–29, 31; 1 Chr. 23:9).

2040. הָרַס ***hāras:*** A verb meaning to pull down, to break through, to overthrow, to destroy. In Miriam and Moses' song, God threw down His enemies (Ex. 15:7). Elijah told God that the Israelites had pulled down God's altars (1 Kgs. 19:10, 14). The psalmist wanted God to break out the teeth of the wicked (Ps. 58:6[7]) and also said that God would tear down the wicked and not build them up again (Ps. 28:5). The foolish woman tore down her own house (Prov. 14:1). On Mount Sinai, God cautioned

Moses to warn the people not to force their way through to see God and then perish (Ex. 19:21). In Exodus, this word is used in an even stronger sense when God instructs the Israelites not to worship foreign gods but to utterly demolish them (Ex. 23:24).

2041. הֶרֶס ***heres:*** A masculine noun indicating destruction. It indicates one of five cities in Egypt where the language of Canaan will be spoken, the city of destruction (Isa. 19:18; some ancient manuscripts read the city of the sun).

2042. הָרָר ***hārār:*** A masculine noun referring to a mountain, hill country. It refers to a region of hill country or mountainous terrain: of the Horites (Gen. 14:6); of the East (Num. 23:7); a place from which copper is obtained (Deut. 8:9); a region of ancient hill country or mountains (Deut. 33:15); a symbol for personal strength and stability (Ps. 30:7[8]; cf. Hab. 3:6); of righteousness as permanent as the mountains of God (Ps. 36:6[7]); a place where leopards dwell (Song 4:8); a symbol for Judah, God's mountain (Jer. 17:3).

2043. הָרָרִי ***hārāriy,*** הֲרָרִי ***h^a^rāriy:*** A proper noun designating Hararite (2 Sam. 23:11, 33; 1 Chr. 11:34, 35).

2044. הָשֵׁם ***hāšēm:*** A proper noun designating Hashem (1 Chr. 11:34).

2045. הַשְׁמָעוּת ***hašmā'ûṯ:*** A feminine noun referring to a report, a causing to hear. It refers to an oral or written report of Jerusalem's destruction (Ezek. 24:26).

2046. הִתּוּךְ ***hittûḵ:*** A masculine noun indicating a melting (of a metal). It is used as a simile or picture of the way Israel will be purified of her dross (Ezek. 22:22).

2047. הֲתָךְ ***h^a^ṯāḵ:*** A proper noun designating Hathach, Hatach (Esth. 4:5, 6, 9, 10).

2048. הָתַל ***hāṯal,*** תָּלַל ***tālal:*** I. A verb meaning to mock, deceive, deride. It is a strong word of derision and attack used by Elijah to mock the prophets of Baal (1 Kgs. 18:27).

II. A verb indicating to cheat, deceive, trifle with, tease, lead on falsely. It is used effectively to describe the deceitful ways Pharaoh dealt with Moses and Israel (Ex. 8:29[25]) and the way Laban treated Jacob (Gen. 31:7). Samson led Delilah on falsely concerning his strength (Judg. 16:10, 13, 15). It describes the deceived heart of an idolater (Isa. 44:20) or the rampant social deception that was characteristic of Zion before she fell (Jer. 9:5[4]).

2049. הֲתֻלִים ***h^a^ṯuliym:*** A masculine plural noun denoting mockers. It means to deride, to excoriate, attack with derision. Job uses the word to describe his "friends" and detractors who are crushing him with their words (Job 17:2).

2050. הָתַת *haṯaṯ*, הוּת *hûṯ*: I. A verb meaning to imagine mischief, to scheme. It indicates a scheming attitude toward persons to bring them down (Ps. 62:3[4], KJV).

II. A verb meaning to assault, assail, attack, topple. It indicates an attack mode, attitude, or actions against persons in order to injure them (Ps. 62:3[4], NASB, NIV).

ו Waw

2051. וְדָן ***wᵉḏān:*** A proper noun designating Vedan (Ezek. 27:19, NASB).

2052. וָהֵב, אֶתְוְהַב ***wāhēḇ, eṯwᵉhaḇ:*** I. Waheb, a location in Moab (Num. 21:14, NASB, NIV).

II. A masculine noun meaning that which is done, that which is accomplished (Num. 21:14, KJV).

2053. וָו ***wāw:*** A masculine noun denoting a hook. It is used only in Exodus to indicate a nail, hook, pin, or peg of some kind used to hang various hangings of the Tabernacle. Some were of gold (Ex. 26:32, 37; 36:36); some of silver (Ex. 27:10, 11, 17; 38:10, 11).

2054. וָזָר ***wāzār:*** A noun meaning guilty one. It occurs only once in the Old Testament (Prov. 21:8), where the immoral path of the guilty is contrasted to the pure behavior of the innocent. The translators for the King James Version understood the word to be a combination of the word *and* with the adjective meaning strange. Therefore, they translated this Hebrew word, "The way of man is froward and strange." But modern translators translate this word "guilty."

2055. וַיְזָתָא ***wayzāṯa':*** A proper noun designating Vaizatha, Vajezatha (Esth. 9:9).

2056. וָלָד ***wālāḏ:*** A masculine noun indicating a child. It is used to assert that Sarai had no child before Isaac; she was barren (Gen. 11:30).

2057. וַנְיָה ***wanyāh:*** A proper noun designating Vaniah (Ezra 10:36).

2058. וָפְסִי ***wopsiy:*** A proper noun designating Vophsi (Num. 13:14).

2059. וַשְׁנִי ***wašniy:*** A proper noun designating Vashni (1 Chr. 6:28[13]). See also *šēniy* (8145).

2060. וַשְׁתִּי ***waštiy:*** A proper noun designating Vashti, the queen of King Xerxes of Persia (486–465 B.C.). She was evidently removed (Esth. 1:9—2:1; 484–83 B.C.) from office for disobeying the king's command. Esther, the Jewess, was made queen in her place (Esth. 2:17). After Esther's brief reign as queen or at her death, Vashti was reinstalled as queen.

ז Zayin

2061. זְאֵב **z^e'ē<u>b</u>:** A masculine noun indicating wolf. A wild animal mentioned several ways by biblical writers: It will be tame in the time of the Messianic Age (Isa. 11:6), with even the wolf eating grass (Isa. 65:25). It was a symbol of the violent, ravenous, and fierce nature of Benjamin (Gen. 49:27) who devoured his prey. Its guile and effective actions were used to describe the cavalry of the Babylonian army (Hab. 1:8). Various classes of persons were personified as bloodthirsty wolves destroying persons: Judah's princes (Ezek. 22:27); her enemies in general (Jer. 5:6); judges who were unjust, oppressive (Zeph. 3:3).

2062. זְאֵב **z^e'ē<u>b</u>:** A proper noun designating Zeeb (Judg. 7:25; 8:3; Ps. 83:11[12]).

2063. זֹאת **zō't<u>:</u>** A feminine pronoun meaning this one, this woman, this. It is the feminine form of *zeh* (2088). It functions in various ways of which the most important are: alone it means this one, standing for a feminine noun (Gen. 2:23; 2 Sam. 13:17); it refers to any act or event itself standing alone (Gen. 3:14; 20:5, 6; 45:19); it stands next to a noun to clarify it, in apposition to it (Gen. 24:8); it can act as the verb is, are, was, were (Isa. 23:7; Ezek. 5:5); it is attached closely to other words as an adverb meaning this (Song 3:6; 6:10; 8:5), e.g., *mah-zō't<u>,</u>* means what is this? (Gen. 3:13; 12:18). It is used with prefixes attached: *b^ezō<u>t</u>,* with this (Gen. 34:15, 22; 1 Sam. 11:2; Mal. 3:10); *k^ezō't<u>,</u>* as follows, like this (Gen. 45:23; Judg. 13:23). It is used with a separate preposition, e.g., *'alzō't<u>,</u>* on this account (Amos 8:8; Mic. 1:8).

2064. זָבַד **zā<u>b</u>a<u>d</u>:** A verb indicating to endow, to give. It indicates giving or bestowing a gift on someone, as when God bestowed a child on Leah (Gen. 30:20).

2065. זֶבֶד **ze<u>b</u>e<u>d</u>,** זֵבֶד **zē<u>b</u>e<u>d</u>:** A masculine noun designating a gift. It designates a gift given or bestowed. In context it stands for the child given to Leah (Gen. 30:20).

2066. זָבָד **zā<u>b</u>ā<u>d</u>:** A proper noun designating Zabad:

A. Son of Nathan (1 Chr. 2:36, 37).

B. Son of Tahath (1 Chr. 7:21).

C. Son of Ahlai (1 Chr. 11:41).

D. Son of Shimeath (2 Chr. 24:26).

E. Son of Zattu (Ezra 10:27).

F. Son of Hashum (Ezra 10:33).

G. Son of Nebo (Ezra 10:43).

2067. זַבְדִּי **za<u>b</u>diy:** A proper noun designating Zabdi:

A. Grandfather of Achan (Josh. 7:1, 17, 18).

B. Son of Shimhi (1 Chr. 8:19).

C. A Shiphmite (1 Chr. 27:27).

D. The father of Micha (Neh. 11:17).

2068. זַבְדִּיאֵל ***zab̲diy'ēl:*** A proper noun designating Zabdiel:

A. The father of Jashobeam (1 Chr. 27:2).

B. A priestly official (Neh. 11:14).

2069. זְבַדְיָה ***zᵉb̲ad̲yāh,*** זְבַדְיָהוּ ***zᵉb̲ad̲yāhû:*** A proper noun designating Zebadiah:

A. Grandson of Elpaal (1 Chr. 8:15).

B. Son of Elpaal (1 Chr. 8:17).

C. Son of Jeroham (1 Chr. 12:7).

D. A Korahite (1 Chr. 26:2).

E. Son of Asahel (1 Chr. 27:7).

F. A Levite (2 Chr. 17:8).

G. Son of Ishmael (2 Chr. 19:11).

H. Son of Shephatiah (Ezra 8:8).

I. A priest (Ezra 10:20).

2070. זְבוּב ***zᵉb̲ûb̲:*** A masculine noun, a fly. The word literally designates a fly. It is used figuratively to refer to the most remote fly in Egypt, that is, the forces and armies of Egypt (Isa. 7:18). Its other use is with the word death or dead, flies of death, dead flies (Eccl. 10:1), which function as a concrete symbol of foolishness.

2071. זָבוּד ***zāb̲ûd̲:*** A proper noun designating Zabud (1 Kgs. 4:5).

2072. זַבּוּד ***zabbûd̲:*** A proper noun designating Zabbud (Ezra 8:14).

2073. זְבוּל ***zᵉb̲ûl,*** זְבֻל ***zᵉb̲ul:*** A masculine noun indicating magnificence; lofty habitation, exalted dwelling. It designates the exalted habitation of God (Isa. 63:15) or the lofty location of the sun and moon (Hab. 3:11). In general, it may refer to any habitation (Ps. 49:14[15]). Combined with house, it refers to the Temple of the Lord built by Solomon, the *bēyt̲* (1004) *zᵉb̲ûl,* house of loftiness (1 Kgs. 8:13; 2 Chr. 6:2; Isa. 63:15).

2074. זְבוּלוּן ***zᵉb̲ûlûn,*** זְבוּלֻן ***zᵉb̲ûlun,*** זְבֻלוּן ***zᵉb̲ulûn:*** A proper noun designating Zebulun:

A. The sixth son of Jacob. His mother was Leah (Gen. 35:23). He and his sons went to Egypt (Gen. 46:14). He lived near the shore of the Mediterranean and had some access to the sea (Gen. 49:13), evidently Galilee.

B. The name of the tribe and territory of Zebulun. The territory, in lower Galilee, was bounded on the east by Asher, on the north and south by Issachar and Naphtali, on the southeast by Issachar, and on the southwest by Manasseh. It was located near major trade routes through the Jezreel Valley to the south (Josh. 19:10–16; Judg. 1:30). The tribe failed to drive out some Canaanites from a few cities. This tribe showed itself valiant for the Lord in various battles (Judg. 4:6, 10; 5:14, 18; 6:35; 1 Chr. 12:33, 40). Its population was conquered and deported by the Assyrians (722 B.C.). Ezekiel's new Temple vision reserves a place for this tribe (48:26, 27, 33).

2075. זְבוּלֹנִי *zᵉḇûlōniy:* A proper noun designating Zebulunites (Num. 26:27; Judg. 12:11, 12).

2076. זָבַח *zāḇaḥ:* A verb meaning to slaughter, to kill, to offer, to sacrifice. The word is used in its broadest sense to indicate the slaughtering of various animals. It indicates the slaughter of animals for food (Deut. 12:21; 1 Sam. 28:24) or for sacrifice with strong political implications (1 Kgs. 1:9, 19); Elisha slaughtered his oxen to make his break with his past and establish his commitment to Elijah (1 Kgs. 19:21). The word describes a sacrifice made to create communion or to seal a covenant. Jacob made a sacrificial meal to celebrate the peace between him and Laban (Gen. 31:54); and the priests were to receive part of the bulls or sheep offered by the people (Deut. 18:3). These slaughtered sacrificial animals were presented to gods or the true God; Jacob's sacrifice was to God (Gen. 46:1) as were most of these sacrifices, but the nations sacrificed to other gods as well, such as Dagon (Judg. 16:23) or the gods of Damascus (2 Chr. 28:23).

Various kinds of sacrifices are given as the objects of this verb. For instance, sacrifices that open the womb (Ex. 13:15); offerings of well-being, peace offerings, and burnt offerings (Ex. 20:24); and animals of the flock and herd (Num. 22:40). Certain slaughtered sacrifices were prohibited, such as a sacrifice with blood and yeast in it (Ex. 23:18; cf. Ex. 12:15). In an exceptional setting, however, a prophet proclaimed the slaughter and sacrifice of the defiled priests who served at the forbidden high places (1 Kgs. 13:2). God will exercise divine judgment on the enemies of His people, Gog and Magog, slaying and providing their carcasses as a great banquet for every kind of bird and animal (Ezek. 39:17, 19); Israel, in their rebellion, offered, although forbidden, their own sons as offerings (Ezek. 16:20).

2077. זֶבַח *zeḇaḥ:* A masculine noun meaning sacrifice. This word refers to the kind of flesh sacrifice the offerer ate after it was given to God (parts of the flesh went to God and to the priests as well). This practice was ancient and did not solely apply to sacrifices to the true God of Israel (Ex. 34:15; Num. 25:2). Other sacrifices of this type included the covenant between Jacob and Laban (Gen. 31:54); the Passover Feast (Ex. 34:25); the thank offering (Lev. 22:29); the annual sacrifice (1 Sam. 1:21); the sacrifice of a covenant with God (Ps. 50:5). See the related Hebrew verb *zāḇaḥ* (2076).

2078. זֶבַח *zeḇaḥ:* A proper noun designating Zebah (Judg. 8:5–7, 10, 12, 15, 18, 21; Ps. 83:11[12]).

2079. זַבַּי *zabbay:* A proper noun designating Zabbai (Ezra 10:28; Neh. 3:20).

2080. זְבִידָה ***z^e^biydāh:*** A proper noun designating Zebidah (2 Kgs. 23:36).

2081. זְבִינָא ***z^e^biyna':*** A proper noun designating Zebina (Ezra 10:43).

2082. זָבַל ***zāḇal:*** verb meaning to honor, to dwell in an exalted fashion; to dwell with. It indicates treating someone with honor, respect. In Leah's case, she hoped her husband would treat her with honor and would dwell with her as a result of God's honoring her with her sixth son, Zebulun (Gen. 30:20).

2083. זְבֻל ***z^e^ḇul:*** A proper noun designating Zebul (Judg. 9:28, 30, 36, 38, 41).

2084. זְבַן ***z^e^ḇan:*** An Aramaic verb meaning to gain, to buy. It is used of an attempt to delay something, to gain or stall for time (Dan. 2:8).

2085. זָג ***zāg:*** A masculine noun referring to a grape skin. It was one of the least desirable parts of the grape vintage (Num. 6:4).

2086. זֵד ***zēḏ:*** An adjective meaning proud, arrogant. This word most often occurs in the Psalms where it is used in connection with sin (Ps. 19:13[14]) or to describe the ungodly (Ps. 86:14; 119:21, 85). Elsewhere in the Old Testament, *zēḏ* describes the proud who will be judged (Isa. 13:11; Mal. 4:1[3:19]) and the disobedience of the proud (Jer. 43:2).

2087. זָדוֹן ***zāḏôn:*** A noun meaning presumptuousness, pride. David's brothers accused him of being presumptuous when he wanted to challenge Goliath (1 Sam. 17:28). Obadiah 1:3 addresses the pride of the Edomites who fatally presumed that they had a safe place in the cliffs. Proverbs also describes the negative aspects of pride (Prov. 11:2; 13:10; 21:24), while Ezekiel uses this word in his description of the day of judgment (Ezek. 7:10).

2088. זֶה ***zeh:*** A masculine demonstrative pronoun meaning this, these; this is, are; this (person), they. Used alone, the word may mean this one (man) (Gen. 5:29; Ex. 10:7; 1 Sam. 10:27); an event, concept, action (Ex. 13:8; Job 15:17; Prov. 24:12; Eccl. 1:17). When repeated *zeh . . . zeh,* it means this . . . that or the one . . . the other, etc. (Ex. 14:20; 1 Kgs. 3:23; 22:20; Isa. 6:3). It points out a noun that it precedes or follows (Ex. 32:1, 23; Deut. 21:20; Josh. 2:14, 20; 9:12; Judg. 5:5). Used as a semiverb, it means this is, these are (Gen. 5:1; 20:13; 2 Kgs. 3:23). It is coupled with certain words to make idioms, etc.: *'ēy-zeh mîy zeh* meaning why, who is this, respectively (1 Sam. 17:55, 56; Job 28:12; Jer. 49:19); further one finds *mah-zeh,* how, what is this? (Gen. 27:20). With *hennēh* it means, behold, right here! (1 Kgs. 19:5; Song 2:8, 9; Isa. 21:9). It functions as the relative pronoun *'ašer,* who, which, what, etc. in poetry: which (Ps. 74:2[3]; 78:54; 104:8). It is used often with prefixes added to it: *bāzeh,* in this place (Gen. 38:21, 22; 1 Sam. 1:26); *mizzeh,* from here (Gen. 42:15); *mizzeh . . . mizzeh* means one side . . . on the other side (Ex. 17:12; 25:19). After the preposition *'al,* it means for this reason, on this account (Esth. 6:3; Lam. 5:17).

2089. זֶה zeh: A masculine noun designating a lamb, sheep. It indicates a lamb taken from David's flock (1 Sam. 17:34). See *šeh.*

2090. זֹה zōh: A feminine pronoun meaning this. It is used as the feminine form of *zeh* (2088) in a few places (2 Sam. 11:25; 2 Kgs. 6:19; Eccl. 2:24; 5:16[15]; 9:13; Ezek. 40:45).

2091. זָהָב zāhā<u>b</u>: A masculine noun denoting gold. The word is used to refer to gold in several ways: in a raw or natural state (Gen. 2:11, 12; Jer. 10:9); as wealth in general (Gen. 13:2; 24:35); or as a precious metal (Job 28:17; Ps. 19:10[11]; Prov. 22:1). It is referred to in its man-made form as bars (Josh. 7:21). Gold is referred to as booty or spoil from war (Josh. 6:19) and as merchandise (Ezek. 27:22). It was used to create money, shekels of gold (Gen. 24:22). Gold was used in jewelry (Gen. 24:22; Ex. 32:2; Judg. 8:24), and some offerings of gold were given (Ex. 35:22; Num. 31:52). It was used in weight (Num. 7:14; Judg. 8:26).

2092. זָהַם zāham: A verb meaning to abhor, loathe. It describes the loathing toward food that a critically sick person may experience (Job 33:20).

2093. זַהַם zaham: A proper noun designating Zaham (2 Chr. 11:19).

2094. זָהַר zāhar: A verb meaning to teach, to warn, to shine. Ezekiel uses this verb more than any other Old Testament writer. In chapter 3, he uses *zāhar* seven times consecutively when God commands him to warn the wicked and righteous about their sin (Ezek. 3:17–21). Similarly, Ezekiel 33 uses this word eight times to describe coming judgment for sin (Ezek. 33:3–9). Other books also use *zāhar* to mean warn (2 Kgs. 6:10; 2 Chr. 19:10) or admonish (Eccl. 4:13; 12:12). Exodus uses this word to mean teach (Ex. 18:20). Daniel is the only book which uses the future tense of the word (Dan. 12:3).

2095. זְהַר z^ehar: An Aramaic verb meaning to take heed, to be admonished, to be cautious. The word *z^ehar* is used only once in Scripture. King Artaxerxes told his secretaries and other men under his command to be careful to obey his order (Ezra 4:22).

2096. זֹהַר zōhar: A masculine noun designating brightness. It refers to the appearance of a being like a man whom Ezekiel saw in a vision. From his loins and up, he was clothed in brightness (Ezek. 8:2). It also describes figuratively the resurrected righteous who will shine like the brightness of the heavens (stars) (Dan. 12:3).

2097. זוֹ ***zô:*** A demonstrative pronoun pointing to this, which. It refers to a whole preceding sentence or thought (Hos. 7:16). It is a relative pronoun referring to the Lord's testimony (Ps. 132:12).

2098. זוּ ***zû:*** A demonstrative pronoun pointing out this, which. It is used to point something out: this strength or whose strength (Hab. 1:11); this generation (Ps. 12:7[8]); there (are) (Ps. 62:11[12]). As a relative pronoun, it refers to or is connected to something: (the people) which (Ex. 15:13; Ps. 9:15[16]); (against) whom (Isa. 42:24; 43:21).

2099. זִו ***ziw:*** A masculine proper noun denoting *Ziv, Zit*. It designates the second month in Israel's calendar year in Canaan. Equal to our April–May (1 Kgs. 6:1, 37), it was the time of barley harvest when the dry season began.

2100. זוּב ***zûb:*** A verb meaning to gush, to flow. It refers to water that (Ps. 78:20; 105:41) pours from a rock. It refers to honey and milk that flow in the land of Canaan (Ex. 3:8, 17; Num. 13:27; Deut. 6:3). It describes an active flowing discharge from a person's body (Lev. 15:2) that renders a person unclean, man (2 Sam. 3:29) or woman (Lev. 15:19). Used figuratively, it describes valleys in Ammon that were flowing, eroding away (Jer. 49:4); or to a person pining away from hunger (Lam. 4:9).

2101. זוֹב ***zôḇ:*** A masculine noun indicating a flow, issue, or discharge. It is a discharge from a man or woman's genitals (Lev. 15:33; cf. Lev. 15:3, 19). The monthly discharge of a woman's menstrual period (Lev. 15:25, 26, 28, 30).

2102. זוּד ***zûḏ,*** זִיד ***ziyḏ:*** I. A verb meaning to treat insolently, proudly, arrogantly. It describes the Egyptians's arrogant and proud treatment of the Israelites in Egypt (Ex. 18:11; Neh. 9:10). It depicts the attitude of a person acting presumptuously toward his or her neighbor or with ill will to kill him (Ex. 21:14). Israel's disrespect and presumptuous actions toward God's commands are described using the word (Deut. 1:43; 17:13; Neh. 9:16). It means to speak in God's name, receiving His command to do so (Deut. 18:20). It refers to the arrogant actions of Babylon against God and His people (Jer. 50:29).

II. A verb meaning to boil, to cook. It describes Jacob's action of boiling or preparing food (Gen. 25:29).

2103. זוּד ***zûḏ:*** An Aramaic verb meaning to act proudly, arrogantly. It describes the actions and attitude of Nebuchadnezzar which caused God to judge him harshly (Dan. 5:20).

2104. זוּזִים ***zûziym:*** A proper noun designating Zuzim, Zuzite (Gen. 14:5).

2105. **זוֹחֵת** ***zôḥēṯ:*** A proper noun designating Zoheth. It is found only in 1 Chr. 4:20.

2106. **זָוִית** ***zāwiyṯ:*** A feminine noun indicating a pillar or cornerstone. It indicates the corner of an altar (Zech. 9:15) and the corner posts of a house (Ps. 144:12) or corner pillars of a palace.

2107. **זוּל** ***zûl:*** A verb indicating to pour out, to lavish. It describes the act of providing gold to construct a useless idol (Isa. 46:6).

2108. **זוּלָה** ***zûlāh:*** A feminine noun functioning as a preposition or conjunction meaning apart from, except, besides. It regularly acts as a preposition meaning except, besides (Deut. 4:12; 1 Kgs. 3:18; preceded by a negative here, it translates as only, but (Ps. 18:31[32]; Isa. 45:21; Hos. 13:4). It functions as a conjunction, except that, in Joshua 11:13.

2109. **זוּן** ***zûn,*** **יָזַן** ***yāzan:*** I. A verb meaning to feed. It is used figuratively of well-fed, lusty horses that, in turn, stand for the Israelites who rushed after spiritual harlotry (Jer. 5:8).

II. A verb meaning to be rutting, in a state of rut; to be sexually excited. Used figuratively to symbolize the Israelites, it denotes horses well fed in the morning who eagerly displayed their sexuality (Jer. 5:8).

2110. **זוּן** ***zûn:*** An Aramaic verb indicating to feed. It is used in a reflexive sense to depict animals and creatures of the world feeding on the fruit of a huge tree in Nebuchadnezzar's dream (Dan. 4:12[9]).

2111. **זוּעַ** ***zûaʻ:*** A verb meaning to tremble, to shake. Haman was angry when Mordecai did not tremble at his sight (Esth. 5:9). This word is also used to describe an old man (Eccl. 12:3). In Habakkuk, it occurs in a causative sense, meaning to cause to tremble. This verse refers to the debtors of Israel (used figuratively for Babylon) who would make Israel tremble with fear (Hab. 2:7). See the related Aramaic verb *zûʻa* (2112).

2112. **זוּעַ** ***zûaʻ:*** An Aramaic verb meaning to tremble. This word is used only twice in the Old Testament and is equivalent to the Hebrew word *zûʻa* (2111), meaning to tremble or to shake. In Daniel 5:19, this word is used to describe the trembling fear of the people before the mighty Nebuchadnezzar. In Daniel 6:26[27], it describes the same trembling fear that people ought to have before the God of Daniel. In both instances, it is used synonymously with another Aramaic word meaning fear, *dᵉḥal* (1763).

2113. **זְוָעָה** ***zᵉwāʻāh:*** A feminine noun indicating an object of terror, horror, trembling. It refers to a scourge or pestilence that becomes an object of horror to those who experience it (Isa. 28:19). Judah becomes an object of horror because of her sins under Manasseh (Jer. 15:4). Both

Judah and Jerusalem become objects of terror, horror, and derision before the Lord and the nations because of their sins (2 Chr. 29:8).

2114. זוּר ***zûr:*** A verb meaning to be a stranger. The basic meaning of this word is to turn aside (particularly for lodging); therefore, it refers to being strange or foreign. It can mean to go astray, to be wayward (Ps. 58:3[4]). The participle is used frequently as an adjective, signifying something outside the law of God (Ex. 30:9; Lev. 10:1); a person outside the family (Deut. 25:5); the estranged way Job's guests and servants viewed him (Job 19:15); hallucinations from drunkenness (Prov. 23:33). This word is used several times in Proverbs of the adulterous woman (Prov. 2:16; 5:3, 20; 7:5; 22:14).

2115. זוּר ***zûr:*** A verb meaning to crush, squeeze. It indicates pressing or squeezing something out (Judg. 6:38) or even crushing an object, such as an egg (Isa. 59:5; Job 39:15). In a different context, it has a positive meaning of dressing a wound (Isa. 1:6).

2116. זוּרֶה ***zûreh:*** A masculine noun indicating that which is crushed. It refers to something crushed from which something else breaks forth (Isa. 59:5).

2117. זָזָא ***zāzā':*** A proper noun designating Zaza (1 Chr. 2:33).

2118. זָחַח ***zāḥaḥ:*** A verb indicating to be removed, to come loose. It indicates the loosening or falling off of an object, such as the breastpiece of the priest's garments (Ex. 28:28; 39:21) that was tightly fastened to the ephod.

2119. זָחַל ***zāḥal:*** A verb meaning to crawl, to fear, and to be afraid. It can refer to the movement of a snake on the ground (Deut. 32:24; Mic. 7:17). It can also be a metaphor for an individual who is afraid or one who creeps forward slowly and cautiously (Job 32:6).

2020. זֹחֶלֶת ***zōḥeleṯ:*** A proper noun designating Zoheleth (1 Kgs. 1:9).

2121. זֵידוֹן ***zēḏôn:*** An adjective depicting something as raging, churning. It is used figuratively of the wicked sweeping over one's soul like churning or tumultuous water (Ps. 124:5).

2122. זִיו ***ziyw:*** An Aramaic noun denoting brightness, splendor. It is used to indicate the brightness or splendor of a huge metallic statue in Daniel 2:31 as well as the glory, splendor, and impressiveness of the city of Babylon (Dan. 4:36[33]). It describes a pale or fresh-looking complexion of a person's face under terrifying circumstances (Dan. 5:6, 9, 10; 7:28).

2123. זִיז ***ziyz:*** I. A masculine collective noun indicating living creatures, moving creatures. These are small creatures that inhabit fields and belong to God's creation (Ps. 50:11). It is used figuratively of those who feed on Israel, contributing to its destruction (Ps. 80:13[14]).

II. A masculine noun indicating abundance. It is used figuratively of the abundance of Jerusalem as re-created by the Lord. It is used in conjunction with glory (*kāb̲ôd̲* [3519]) to mean, literally, the abundance of her Israel/Jerusalem's glory (Isa. 66:11).

2124. זִיזָא *ziyzā'*: A proper noun designating Ziza:

A. A Simeonite (1 Chr. 4:37).

B. A son of Rehoboam (2 Chr. 11:20).

2125. זִיזָה *ziyzāh*: A proper noun designating Zizah, same person as *ziynā'* (2126) (1 Chr. 23:11).

2126. זִינָא *ziynā'*: A proper noun designating Zina, same person as *ziyzāh* (2125) (1 Chr. 23:10).

2127. זִיעַ *ziya'*: A proper noun designating Zia (1 Chr. 5:13).

2128. זִיף *ziyp̲*: A proper noun designating Ziph:

A. A city located in southern Judah near the border of Edom (Josh. 15:24). The area around it was desert (1 Sam. 23:14). David fled there (1 Sam. 26:2).

B. A city in the hill country of Judah, possibly south of Jerusalem (Josh. 15:55).

C. A son of Jehallelel (Jehaleleel). He had three brothers and was a descendant of Judah (1 Chr. 4:16).

D. A descendant of Caleb. His father was Mesha. His son was Mareshah (1 Chr. 3:42).

2129. זִיפָה *ziyp̲āh*: A proper noun designating Ziphah (1 Chr. 4:16).

2130. זִיפִי *ziyp̲iy*: A proper noun designating Ziphite (1 Sam. 23:19; 26:1; Ps. 54:title[2]).

2131. זֵק *zēq*, זִיקָה *ziyqāh*: I. A feminine noun referring to a missile, spark, firebrand. It refers to fiery missiles of some sort (possibly flaming arrows) (Prov. 26:18). They were used as defensive weapons as well (Isa. 50:11).

II. A masculine noun indicating a fetter, chain. It refers to the trials or possibly literal chains that may confine even kings (Job 36:8; Ps. 149:8). Enemies and captives are bound by these chains (Isa. 45:14; Nah. 3:10) in order to lead them away.

2132. זַיִת *zayit̲*: I. A common noun indicating an olive, olive tree. Olive trees were a source and indication of property and wealth (Ex. 23:11). The word depicts the olives themselves as well (Deut. 28:40). Used with *šemen*, oil, it indicates olive oil (Ex. 27:20; 30:24). It is used in the phrase, mount of the ascent of the olives; that is, the Mount of Olives (Zech. 14:4). It refers to an olive tree (Judg. 9:8, 9; Job 15:33; Hos. 14:6[7]). In all these cases, it also serves as a simile or other illustration of a person (cf. Zech. 4:3, 11); beauty, a wicked man respectively. It also is a symbol of prosperity (Ps. 52:8[10]; Jer. 11:16).

II. A masculine proper noun. It is used in a phrase to indicate the Mount of Olives (2 Sam. 15:30; cf. Zech. 14:4).

2133. זֵיתָן ***zēyṯān:*** A proper noun designating Zethan (1 Chr. 7:10).

2134. זַךְ ***zaḵ:*** An adjective meaning pure, clean. It is derived from the related verbs *zāḵāh* (2135), meaning to be clear or pure, and *zāḵaḵ* (2141), meaning to be clean or pure. This word is used to describe objects used in the worship of God, such as pure oil (Ex. 27:20; Lev. 24:2) and pure frankincense (Ex. 30:34; Lev. 24:7). It also denotes the purity of the righteous, such as Job (Job 8:6; 33:9), in contrast with one living a crooked life (Prov. 21:8). This word can also speak about all aspects of one's life: one's actions in general (Prov. 16:2; 20:11); one's teaching (Job 11:4); or one's prayer (Job 16:17).

2135. זָכָה ***zāḵāh:*** A verb meaning to clean, to be clean, to cleanse. Job's friends used this word twice, questioning how one born of a woman could be clean or righteous before God (Job 15:14; 25:4). It is also used to describe the state of the heart (Ps. 73:13; Prov. 20:9). In other uses, it carries the connotation of being pure or cleansed from sin (Ps. 119:9; Isa. 1:16; Mic. 6:11).

2136. זָכוּ ***zāḵû:*** An Aramaic feminine noun indicating innocence, purity. It indicates a state of guiltlessness, freedom from guile or blame, as in the case of Daniel (6:22[23]) who was not guilty of the charges alleged against him.

2137. זְכוֹכִית ***z***^{e}***ḵôḵiyṯ:*** A feminine noun meaning fine glass, crystal, transparent glass. It refers to a luxurious and valuable glass mentioned along with gold (Job 28:17) but of less value than wisdom.

2138. זְכוּר ***z***^{e}***ḵûr:*** A masculine noun denoting man, male. It refers to the males of Israel in a collective sense (Ex. 23:17; 34:23; Deut. 16:16) and once to the males of any foreign city (Deut. 20:13).

2139. זַכּוּר ***zakkûr:*** A proper noun designating Zaccur:

A. The father of Shammuah (Num. 13:4).

B. Son of Hamuel (1 Chr. 4:26).

C. A Merarite (1 Chr. 24:27).

D. Son of Asaph (1 Chr. 25:2, 10; Neh. 12:35).

E. Son of Imri (Neh. 3:2).

F. A Levite (Neh. 10:12).

G. Ancestor of Hanan (Neh. 13:13).

H. A Simeonite (Ezra 8:14).

2140. זַכַּי ***zakkay:*** A proper noun designating Zaccai (Ezra 2:9; Neh. 7:14).

2141. זָכַךְ ***zāḵaḵ:*** A verb meaning to be clean, to be pure. This word is used only four times in the Old Testament. Job uses it to describe washing his hands to make them clean (Job 9:30). On two occasions, it speaks of the purity of the heavens (Job 15:15) and the stars (Job 25:5). The final usage of the word describes certain people as being purer than snow (Lam. 4:7) in contrast with the blackness of soot (Lam. 4:8). See the related verb, *zāḵāh* (2135), meaning to be clear or pure, and the related noun, *zaḵ* (2134), meaning pure.

2142. זָכַר *zāḵar,* מַזְכִּיר *mazkiyr:* A verb meaning to remember, to mention, to recall, to think about, to think on, to be remembered, to recall, to acknowledge, to mention, to make known. The basic meaning indicates a process of mentioning or recalling either silently, verbally, or by means of a memorial sign or symbol. The verb often means to mention, to think about. The Lord warned the people and false prophets not to verbally mention the oracle of the Lord (Jer. 23:36); the Lord thought about Ephraim in a good sense (Jer. 31:20); and the psalmist thought or meditated on the Lord in his heart and mind without words (Ps. 63:6[7]).

These meanings, of course, overlap with the primary translation of the verb, to remember. The psalmist remembered the Lord often, and 43 of the one 165 uses of the simple stem are in the Book of Psalms. Remembering in ancient Israel was a major aspect of proper worship, as it is today.

Remembering involves many things, and various connotations are possible. God or people can be the subject that remembers. For example, because God had acted so often for His people, they were to remember Him and His acts on their behalf (Deut. 5:15; 15:15; 24:18). They were to remember His covenant and commandments without fail (Ex. 20:8; Mal. 4:4[3:22]). Above all, they were to remember Him by His name. By remembering Him, they imitated the Lord, for He never forgot them (cf. Deut. 4:29–31). He faithfully remembered His people (Gen. 8:1), and they could beg Him to remember them, as Jeremiah did in his distress (Neh. 13:31; Jer. 15:15). The Lord especially remembered His covenant with the ancestors and fathers of Israel (Lev. 26:45; Deut. 9:27; Jer. 14:21) and with all humankind through Noah (Gen. 9:15, 16).

In the passive stem, the word expresses similar meanings. For example, the psalmist prayed that the sins of his accuser's parents would be remembered against his accuser (Ps. 109:14). Yet in an important passage on moral and religious responsibility before God, it was asserted that if righteous people abandoned their righteous ways and followed evil, their righteous deeds would not be remembered by the Lord. The opposite case is also true. None of the evil deeds people commit will be remembered against them if they turn to God (Ezek. 18:22), nor will the actions, good or evil, of their parents be held for or against them (Ezek. 18:22, 24). Righteous people will, in fact, be remembered throughout the ages (cf. Ps. 112:6).

The causative stem indicates the act of bringing to memory or bringing to attention. It means to recall, as when the Lord challenged His people in Isaiah to recall their past in order to state their argument for their case (Gen. 41:9; Isa. 43:26). Eli, the high priest, recalled (i.e., mentioned) the ark and then died according to God's prophetic word (1 Sam. 4:18). The verb is used to indicate urging someone to remember something, such as sin (1 Kgs. 17:18; Ezek. 21:23[28]; 29:16). It is also used to convey the idea of causing something to be acknowledged, as when the psalmist asserted that he would cause the Lord's righteousness to be acknowledged above all else (Ps. 71:16). In the infinitive form, this word sometimes means petition, as found in the superscriptions of some Psalms (Ps. 38:title[1], 70:title[1]). It may also mean performing an act of worship (Isa. 66:3).

2143. זֵכֶר ***zēker:*** A masculine noun meaning remembrance. This word comes from the verb *zākar* (2142), meaning to remember. God has given His people many things as remembrances: Himself (Ps. 102:12 [13]); His name (Ex. 3:15; Hos. 12:5[6]); His works (Ps. 111:4); His goodness (Ps. 145:7); His holiness (Ps. 30:4[5]; 97:12); His deliverance of the Jews (Esth. 9:28). God also promises the remembrance of the righteous (Prov. 10:7) but often cuts off the remembrance of the wicked (Job 18:17; Ps. 34:16[17]; 109:15; Prov. 10:7); wicked nations (Ex. 17:14; Deut. 25:19; 32:26); and the dead (Eccl. 9:5; Isa. 26:14). In several instances of this word, it is used synonymously with *šēm* (8034), meaning name, because one's name invokes the memory (Ex. 3:15; Prov. 10:7; Hos. 12:5[6]).

2144. זֶכֶר ***zeker:*** A proper noun designating Zecher, Zeker (1 Chr. 8:31).

2145. זָכָר ***zākar,*** זָכָר ***zākār:*** I. A verb meaning to be male. It indicates firstborn male animals for sacrifice (Ex. 34:19). Its form in the verse, *tizzākār*, influences some translators to render this as a verb. Others take the *Qere* form and read the word as a noun rather than a verb and understand it to refer to sacrificial animals (see II).

II. A masculine noun indicating a man, male, human. It indicates a person as male as opposed to female (Gen. 1:27; Lev. 18:22). With *kol* preceding, it indicates every male that was to be circumcised at eight days of age (Gen. 17:12). With *bēn*, son, preceding, it denotes a male child or person (Lev. 12:2; Jer. 20:15). In its collective and plural forms, it denotes men (Ex. 13:12; Judg. 21:11; 1 Kgs. 11:15). Lying with a *zākār* indicates homosexuality (Lev. 18:22) while *miškab* (4904) *zākār* refers to heterosexual intercourse (Num. 31:17; Judg.

21:12). It refers to the passover lamb (Ex. 12:5).

2146. זִכָּרוֹן *zikkārôn:* A masculine noun meaning memorial, remembrance, record, reminder. This word conveys the essential quality of remembering something in the past that has a particular significance (Eccl. 1:11). It signifies stone monuments (Josh. 4:7); the shoulder ornamentation of the ephod (Ex. 28:12; 39:7); a sacrifice calling for explicit retrospection (Num. 5:15); the securing of a progeny (Isa. 57:8); a written record (Ex. 17:14; Esth. 6:1); a memorable adage or quote (Job 13:12); some proof of an historic claim (Neh. 2:20); a festival memorializing a pivotal event (Ex. 12:14; 13:9).

2147. זִכְרִי *zik̲riy:* A proper noun designating Zichri, Zicri:

A. Son of Izhar (Ex. 6:21).

B. Son of Shimei (1 Chr. 8:19).

C. Son of Shashak (1 Chr. 8:23).

D. Son of Jeroham (1 Chr. 8:27).

E. A Levite (1 Chr. 9:15).

F. The father of Shelomith (1 Chr. 26:25).

G. The father of Eliezer (1 Chr. 27:16).

H. The father of Amasiah (2 Chr. 17:16).

I. The father of Elishaphat (2 Chr. 23:1).

J. An Ephramite (2 Chr. 28:7).

K. The father of Joel (Neh. 11:9).

L. A priest (Neh. 12:17).

2148. זְכַרְיָה ,זְכַרְיָהוּ *z^ek̲aryāh, z^ek̲aryāhû:* A proper noun designating Zechariah. Over thirty men in the Old Testament are named Zechariah. Little more than their name is known about some of them. The name means "the Lord remembers":

A. The best known is Zechariah who prophesied during the time of Ezra and Nehemiah, the postexilic period. His message encouraged the Israelites to rebuild the Temple and to dedicate themselves wholly to the Lord. Then the days of "small things" would blossom by the power of God's Spirit. His father was Berekiah, son of Iddo (Zech. 1:1, 7). He came from Babylon with the exiles to Jerusalem (538 B.C.) under Zerubbabel. His contemporary was Haggai (Ezra 5:1).

B. It refers to a descendant of Reuben (1 Chr. 5:6, 7).

C. He was son of Meshelemiah and served as the gatekeeper at the Tent of Meeting. He was a wise counselor (1 Chr. 9:21).

D. He came from the line of Saul. Jeiel was his father who came from Gibeon (1 Chr. 9:35–37).

E. The name of Levite who served in the worship at the Temple, even before the ark (1 Chr. 16:5).

F. He served as a trumpet blower before the ark of God (1 Chr. 15:24).

G. The son of Isshiah and grandson of Micah (1 Chr. 24:25).

H. A son of Horah a Merarite and a gatekeeper (1 Chr. 26:10, 11).

I. The father of Iddo, an officer over the half-tribe of Manasseh (1 Chr. 27:21).

J. An official responsible to teach the Law of the Lord in Judah (2 Chr. 17:7).

K. He was the father of a prophet, Jahaziel, who prophesied to Jehoshaphat (2 Chr. 20:14).

L. The son of Jehoshaphat and the brother of Jehoram who became king in Judah (2 Chr. 21:2).

M. A prophet, son of Jehoiada the priest who prophesied to Joash and a wicked people (2 Chr. 24:20).

N. A prophet who counseled and taught King Uzziah (2 Chr. 26:5).

O. A son of Jeroboam II who succeeded to the kingship. He reigned six months (753 B.C.). He was assassinated by Shallum who took his place (752 B.C.) (2 Kgs. 15:8–10).

P. The father of Abi (Abijah) the mother of Hezekiah (2 Chr. 29:1).

Q. A Levite, a descendant of Asaph, who helped restore the Temple under Hezekiah (2 Chr. 29:13).

R. A man asked by Isaiah to serve as one of two witnesses for him (Isa. 8:2).

S. A descendant of Kohath who directed repairs on the Temple (2 Chr. 34:12).

T. An administrator of worship at the Temple (2 Chr. 35:8).

U. One of the returnees from exile under Ezra and a family head (Ezra 5:1).

V. A descendant of Bebai and a family head (Ezra 8:11).

W. A leader who helped Ezra gather persons to serve at the Temple (Ezra 6:14).

X. A descendant of Elam who intermarried with people of the land (Ezra 10:26).

Y. A Levite present when Ezra read the Law at the Water Gate (Neh. 8:4).

Z. A new resident in Jerusalem after returning from exile and from the tribe of Judah. He was the father of Uzziah, son of Amariah, a descendant of Perez (Neh. 11:4).

AA. The father of Joiarib. He was descended from Shelah, a descendant of Perez (Neh. 11:5).

BB. A new priestly resident in Jerusalem from the returned exiles, father of Amzi and son of Phashhur (Neh. 11:12).

CC. A head of a priestly family from Iddo's family (Neh. 12:16).

DD. A priest who took part in the dedication of the wall of Jerusalem in Nehemiah's day (Neh. 12:35).

EE. Another priest who took part in the dedication of the wall of Jerusalem in Nehemiah's day (Neh. 12:41).

2149. זָלוּת ***zullûṯ:*** A feminine noun denoting vileness, worthlessness. It indicates a wicked and vile situation existing among human beings that fosters the wicked (Ps. 12:8[9]).

2150. זַלְזַל ***zalzal:*** A masculine noun denoting a twig, tender shoot, sprig. It refers to a fresh shoot of a vine just before it bears fruit (Isa. 18:5).

2151. זָלַל ***zālal:*** I. A verb meaning to be vile, frivolous, gluttonous, worthless; to despise. It describes an especially serious corruption of character in a worthless, gluttonous son (Deut. 21:20), closely akin to one who drinks too much (Prov. 23:20, 21). A good son avoids company with this vile, gluttonous person (Prov. 28:7). It is the opposite of what is useful, valuable, and precious (Jer. 15:19). It means to hold up to disdain, to despise (Lam. 1:8).

II. A verb indicating to quake, to shake, to tremble. It refers poetically to the response of the mountains to God's descent upon them (Isa. 64:1[63:19], 3[2]).

2152. זַלְעָפָה ***zal'āpāh:*** A feminine noun meaning burning heat. This word occurs only three times in the Old Testament. In two of the locations, the literal usage of this word is implied. In Lamentations 5:10, Jeremiah explains the hunger pangs as the burning heat of famine. In Psalm 11:6, David describes how God will pour out His wrath with this burning heat, along with fire and brimstone. In Psalm 119:53, the psalmist speaks figuratively about his righteous, burning zeal on account of those who forsake God's law.

2153. זִלְפָּה ***zilpāh:*** A proper noun designating Zilpah, the servant of Laban whom he gave to Leah to be her handmaid or maidservant (Gen. 29:24). She bore Jacob Gad and Asher (Gen. 35:26) who were in turn fruitful vines in Israel (Gen. 46:18).

2154. זִמָּה ***zimmāh:*** A feminine noun meaning plan, purpose, counsel, wickedness, lewdness, sin. The word refers to the plans and purposes of the mind which give rise to one's actions. Yet the word rarely pertains to good intentions (Job 17:11). It is used in reference to the evil plotting of the wicked (Isa. 32:7); the thoughts of foolish people (Prov. 24:9); and mischievous motivations (Ps. 119:150). Moreover, it relates to sexual sins that spring from lustful intentions, such as incest (Lev. 18:17); prostitution (Lev. 19:29); adultery (Job 31:11); and rape (Judg. 20:6). Figuratively, the word represents the wickedness of the people of Israel in their idolatry, calling to mind the connection with adultery (Jer. 13:27; Ezek. 16:27).

2155. זִמָּה ***zimmāh:*** A proper noun designating Zimmah:

A. Son of Janath (1 Chr. 6:20[5]).

B. A Gershomite (1 Chr. 6:42[27]).

C. The father of Joah (2 Chr. 29:12).

2156. זְמוֹרָה ***zᵉmôrāh:*** A feminine noun denoting a branch. It refers to the branch of a vine or tree (Num. 13:23; Ezek. 15:2). It was used in pagan cult practices and was placed on or near the nose (Ezek. 8:17). It indicates vine slips (Isa. 17:10) or branches (Nah. 2:2[3]).

2157. זַמְזֻמִּים ***zamzummiym:*** A proper noun designating Zamsummite, Zamzummim (Deut. 2:20).

2158. זָמִיר ***zāmiyr:*** A masculine noun indicating a song, singer; psalmist. It indicates songs (2 Sam. 23:1), and in this verse, David is called the pleasant (sweet) singer of songs of Israel. It refers to other types of songs: a hostile song of the ruthless (Isa. 25:5); a praise song to the Lord (Ps. 95:2); songs of joy even in the night given by God (Job 35:10); the statutes of the Lord as songs to God (Ps. 119:54). Preceded by *'ēṯ*, time, it defines the time as the time of songs, singing (Song 2:12), a festive time.

2159. זָמִיר ***zāmiyr:*** A masculine noun referring to branch. Preceded by *'ēṯ*, time, it describes this as the time of (pruning) branches (Song 2:12), a joyous spring event.

2160. זְמִירָה ***z^e^miyrah:*** A proper noun designating Zemirah, Zemira (1 Chr. 7:8).

2161. זָמַם ***zāmam:*** A verb meaning to consider, to purpose, to devise. This verb derives its meaning from the idea of talking to oneself in a low voice, as if arriving at some conclusion. It denotes the action of fixing thought on an object so as to acquire it (Prov. 31:16); devising a plan or an agenda (Lam. 2:17; Zech. 8:15); conceiving an idea (Gen. 11:6); and determining a course of action (Ps. 17:3). In an adverse sense, it also denotes the plotting of evil against another (Ps. 31:14; 37:12; Prov. 30:32).

2162. זָמָם ***zāmām:*** A masculine noun meaning plans. The Hebrew word occurs once in the Old Testament. David uses this word as he pleads with the Lord to intercede in the plans of the wicked (Ps. 140:8[9]).

2163. זָמַן ***zāman:*** A verb meaning to fix, to appoint a time. In the book of Ezra, so many Israelites had violated the command not to marry foreign women that leaders had to set a fixed time for people to come by towns to repent (Ezra 10:14). In Nehemiah, the Levites, priests, and people worked out a time (by casting lots) for each family to contribute wood for the altar (Neh. 10:34[35]). In the closing words of his book, Nehemiah reminded the Lord of his leadership in this matter (Neh. 13:31). See the related Aramaic verb *z^e^man* (2164).

2164. זְמַן ***z^e^man:*** An Aramaic verb meaning to agree together. Nebuchadnezzar believed that his wise men were conspiring together, which is why he insisted they tell him both his dream and its interpretation (Dan. 2:9). See the related Hebrew verb *zāman* (2163).

2165. זְמַן ***z^e^man:*** A masculine noun meaning appointed time, season. This word occurs only four times in the Old Testament. Two of these are in the book of Esther, referring to the time set for the Feast of Purim

(Esth. 9:27, 31). In the book of Nehemiah, it refers to an appointed time to return from a journey (Neh. 2:6). In Ecclesiastes, it occurs in an often-quoted verse, "To every thing there is a season" (Eccl. 3:1) to say that everything has a predestined time. The word translated time throughout Ecclesiastes 3 is *'ēṯ* (6256). Thus, *z^eman* bears a different sense, emphasizing the specificity in time.

2166. זְמָן ***z^emān:*** An Aramaic noun meaning a specific time, a time period. This word is used in Daniel indicating a duration of time or a period of time (Dan. 2:16; 7:12) and also in reference to the feast times (Dan. 7:25). See the Hebrew cognate 2165.

2167. זָמַר ***zāmar:*** A verb meaning to play an instrument, to sing with musical accompaniment. Stringed instruments are commonly specified in connection with this word, and the tambourine is also mentioned once (Ps. 33:2; 71:22, 23; 149:3). The term occurs frequently in a call to praise—usually a summons to oneself (2 Sam. 22:50; 1 Chr. 16:9; Ps. 66:4; Isa. 12:5). In the Bible, the object of this praise is always the Lord, who is lauded for both His attributes and His actions (Judg. 5:3; Ps. 101:1; 105:2). Besides the above references, this verb appears exclusively in the Book of Psalms, contributing to a note of praise in psalms of various types: hymns (Ps. 104:33); psalms of thanksgiving (Ps. 138:1); and even psalms of lament (Ps. 144:9).

2168. זָמַר ***zāmar:*** A verb meaning to trim, to prune. It indicates the pruning of vines (Lev. 25:3) or, in the case of Israel as the Lord's vine or vineyard, the lack of pruning; it will be left to perish (Isa. 5:6) without the Lord's tender care.

2169. זֶמֶר ***zemer:*** A masculine noun meaning mountain sheep, gazelle, chamois. It denotes a gazelle. It was one of the animals the Israelites could eat (Deut. 14:5), and, hence, was clean.

2170. זְמָר ***z^emār:*** An Aramaic masculine noun referring to music, instrumental music. It is a noun referring to musical sounds and instruments (Dan. 3:5, 7, 10, 15) heard at the dedication of Nebuchadnezzar's great image.

2171. זַמָּר ***zammār:*** An Aramaic masculine noun indicating a singer. It refers to singers among the temple personnel who were free from any tax, tribute, or toll (Ezra 7:24).

2172. זִמְרָה ***zimrāh:*** A feminine noun indicating music, song. It is used of the sound or playing of a musical instrument or of singing (Isa. 51:3; Amos 5:23) as one feature of a revived Zion. It is used as a metaphor for God as Israel's song (Ex. 15:2; Ps. 118:14; Isa. 12:2).

2173. זִמְרָה ***zimrāh:*** A feminine noun indicating a choice fruit. It indicates the best fruit or produce of the land of Canaan (Gen. 43:11) collected as a gift for Joseph and the Egyptians at Jacob's command.

2174. זִמְרִי ***zimriy:*** A proper noun designating Zimri:

A. A man from the tribe of Simeon who arrogantly brought a Midianite woman into his tent. His father was Salu, a Simeonite leader. Phinehas put him to death (Num. 25:14).

B. A grandson of Judah, a descendant of Hezron, son of Zerah (1 Chr. 2:6).

C. A king of Israel (1 Kgs. 16:9–20) who reigned 876 B.C. for only one week in Tirzah. He assassinated Elah, the king of Israel, and eradicated the family of Baasha (1 Kgs. 16:11, 12). He later burned himself and his palace. His name is used to indicate an "assassin" by Jezebel (2 Kgs. 9:31).

D. One of Saul's descendants whose father was Jehoaddah (1 Chr. 8:36). He was the father of Moza (1 Chr. 9:42).

E. The name of a land or nation with rulers, kings. Its location is not known (Jer. 25:25).

2175. זִמְרָן ***zimrān:*** A proper noun designating Zimran (Gen. 25:2; 1 Chr. 1:32).

2176. זִמְרָת ***zimrāṯ:*** A feminine noun meaning song. It is used as a metaphor to indicate the Lord as Israel's song (Ex. 15:2; Ps. 118:14; Isa. 12:2, but see 2172 also).

2177. זַן ***zan:*** A masculine noun meaning sort, kind, various kinds. It indicates a particular variety or group of something linked by similar traits (2 Chr. 16:14). Used in the phrase *mizzan 'el-zan,* it indicates of all sorts, of all kinds, of every kind (Ps. 144:13).

2178. זַן ***zan:*** An Aramaic masculine noun. It indicates a particular variety or group of things linked by similar traits. Preceded by *kōl* (3605), it indicates all kinds of (Dan. 3:5, 7, 10, 15).

2179. זָנַב ***zānaḇ:*** A verb indicating to attack the rear, to cut off stragglers, to destroy the rearguard. It refers to Amalek's action in cutting off or destroying the Israelites in the rear during their trek out of Egypt (Deut. 25:18). At Joshua's command, Israel used this guerrilla warfare tactic to attack the armies of five great kings (Josh. 10:19).

2180. זָנָב ***zānāḇ:*** A masculine noun indicating a tail. It refers to the posterior part or rear of an animal or reptile: of a snake or fox (Ex. 4:4; Judg. 15:4); figuratively of the lowest place of influence among nations (Deut. 28:13, 44); of the tail of Behemoth (Job 40:17); metaphorically, of the end of a burning stump (Isa. 7:4); or of a false prophet (Isa. 9:15[14]). Coupled with head, it indicates the totality of something (Isa. 9:14[13]; 19:15).

2181. זָנָה zānāh, זוֹנָה zônāh, זֹנָה zōnāh: A verb meaning to fornicate, to prostitute. It is typically used for women and only twice in reference to men (Num. 25:1). This verb occurs in connection with prostitution (Lev. 21:7; Prov. 7:10); figuratively, Israel's improper relationships with other nations (Isa. 23:17; Ezek. 23:30; Nah. 3:4); or other gods (Ex. 34:15, 16; Deut. 31:16; Ezek. 6:9; Hos. 9:1). As a metaphor, it describes Israel's breach of the Lord's covenant relationship (Ex. 34:16).

2182. זָנוֹחַ zānôaḥ: A proper noun designating Zanoah:

A. A city in Judah near En-gannim (Josh. 15:34; 1 Chr. 4:18; Neh. 3:13; 11:30).

B. A city in Judah near Juttah (Josh. 15:56).

2183. זְנוּנִים z^enûniym: A masculine noun meaning fornication, prostitution, adultery, idolatry. Judah's daughter-in-law Tamar was accused of prostitution (Gen. 38:24). This word can also be used to describe cities like Nineveh (Nah. 3:4). Most often, it is used in a religious sense to describe, for instance, the unfaithfulness of Israel. Jezebel practiced idolatry (2 Kgs. 9:22); and Jerusalem's idolatry was portrayed in a story where she was the prostitute Oho-libah (Ezek. 23:11, 29). God commanded Hosea to take an unfaithful wife (Hos. 1:2), who was also a picture of Israel (Hos. 2:2[4], 4[6]; 4:12; 5:4).

2184. זְנוּת z^enûṯ: A feminine noun meaning fornication. In the literal sense, this word refers to sexual sin that violates the marriage covenant (Hos. 4:11). Most often, however, this word is figuratively applied to God's nation Israel for their wickedness (Hos. 6:10). This fornication is usually associated with the worship of other gods (Jer. 3:2, 9; 13:27; Ezek. 23:27), but it can describe outright rebellion (Num. 14:33) or general iniquities (Ezek. 43:7, 9). This word comes from the common verb *zānāh* (2181), meaning to commit fornication.

2185. זֹנוֹת zōnôṯ: I. A feminine noun denoting armor. The word is taken to mean Ahab's armor by some translators (1 Kgs. 22:38, KJV).

II. A feminine noun referring to a prostitute. It indicates the prostitutes who bathed at the pool of Samaria where Ahab's chariot was washed after he was slain (1 Kgs. 22:38, NIV, NASB, NKJV).

2186. זָנַח zānaḥ: I. A verb meaning to reject, exclude from. It is used to note the refusal to recognize or accept various things or persons: Israel rejects what is good (Hos. 8:3); ironically, the Lord rejects Samaria's paganized calf (Hos. 8:5); often it denotes the Lord's rejection of His people or supplicants (Ps. 43:2; 60:1[3]; 77:7[8]; 88:14[15]; Zech. 10:6); individual kings rejected some holy persons and vessels (2 Chr. 11:14; 29:19).

II. A verb meaning to stink, to smell foul. It refers to the stench emitted by Egyptian canals or streams because of drought (Isa. 19:6; KJV, turn far away).

2187. זָנַק zānaq: A verb meaning to leap, to spring, to jump forth. It depicts Dan's action coming forth or leaping forth from Bashan, thus depicting a characteristic of Dan's nature (Deut. 33:22).

2188. זֵעָה zēʿāh: A feminine noun referring to sweat. It indicates a curse, the physical result of man's hard labor on the ground after God had cursed it (Gen. 3:19).

2189. זַעֲוָה za^{a}wāh: A feminine noun indicating a horror, a trembling, a terror. It depicts Israel as an example of terror and horror before the nations because of the judgments the Lord will bring on her (Deut. 28:25; Jer. 15:4; 24:9; 29:18; 34:17). It refers to the acts of war and violence to which the Lord will deliver Israel (Ezek. 23:46).

2190. זַעֲוָן za^{a}wān: A proper noun designating Zaavan (Gen. 36:27; 1 Chr. 1:42).

2191. זְעֵיר z^{e}ʿēyr: A masculine noun indicating a little of something. It refers to a small or insufficient amount of teaching or instruction from the prophet or wise men (Isa. 28:10, 13). Elihu uses the word to appeal for a little time (Job 36:2).

2192. זְעֵיר z^{e}ʿēyr: An Aramaic adjective indicating small, little. It describes the small horn that came up among the previous ten horns of Daniel's vision (Dan. 7:8), but it surprisingly made arrogant claims for itself against God and His people.

2193. זָעַךְ zāʿak̲: A verb meaning to be put out, extinguished. It refers to the conclusion or ending of Job's life, his days, because of his calamities and illnesses (Job 17:1).

2194. זָעַם zāʿam: A verb meaning to be indignant, to be enraged. The root means literally to foam at the mouth, to be enraged. It is used to describe the fury of the king of the North against the holy covenant in Daniel's vision (Dan. 11:30). Because God is a righteous judge, He shows indignation against evil every day (Ps. 7:11[12]). This theme is picked up again in Isaiah (Isa. 66:14). God was angry with the towns of Judah (Zech. 1:12), and Edom was under the wrath of the Lord (Mal. 1:4). This anger can also show in one's face (Prov. 25:23).

2195. זַעַם zaʿam: A masculine noun meaning intense anger, indignation, denunciation, curse. Although this noun can refer to a state of being or actions of a human being (Jer. 15:17; Hos. 7:16), it usually refers to those of the Lord (Isa. 26:20; 30:27; Hab. 3:12). This word is also used in parallel with other words with the connotation of anger: *'ap̄* (639) (Ps.

69:24[25]; Isa. 10:5, 25; 30:27; Zeph. 3:8); *'eḇrāh* (5678) (Ps. 78:49; Ezek. 21:31[36]; 22:31); and *qeṣeḇ* (7110) (Ps. 102:10[11]; Jer. 10:10).

2196. זָעַף *zā'ap̱:* A verb meaning to be dejected, to be enraged. The root idea of this word is to storm, which is seen in the use of the related noun *za'ap̱* (2197) to describe the raging sea in Jonah 1:15. The word describes an unsettled storm within a person that exhibits itself in either dejection or rage. The cupbearer and baker were dejected when they couldn't understand their dreams (Gen. 40:6). The guard thought that Daniel and his friends would look downcast if denied the king's food (Dan. 1:10). King Uzziah was enraged when the priests attempted to remove him from the temple (2 Chr. 26:19).

2197. זַעַף *za'ap̱:* A noun meaning wrath, rage, indignation. This word is used to refer to the rage of kings (2 ter (2 Chr. 28:9) or the stormy rage of the sea (Jon. 1:15).

2198. זָעֵף *zā'ēp̱:* An adjective meaning dejected. This particular word is only used twice in the Old Testament. In each instance, it describes the dejected attitude of King Ahab when the prophet told him bad news (1 Kgs. 20:43) and when Naboth refused to sell his vineyard to Ahab (1 Kgs. 21:4). See the related verb *zā'ap̱* (2196), meaning to be dejected and the related noun *za'ap̱* (2197), meaning raging.

2199. זָעַק *zā'aq:* A verb meaning to cry out, to exclaim, to call. The primary activity implied is that of crying out in pain or by reason of affliction (Ex. 2:23; Job 35:9; Jer. 25:34). The verb signifies the action of calling on the Lord in a time of need (Joel 1:14; Mic. 3:4); uttering sounds of sorrow, distress, or alarm (2 Sam. 13:19; Isa. 26:17; Ezek. 11:13); entreating for some favor (2 Sam. 19:28[29]); and issuing a summons for help (Judg. 12:2). By inference, it also implies assembling together as in response to a call (Judg. 6:34, 35; 1 Sam. 14:20); and the making of a proclamation by a herald (Jon. 3:7).

2200. זְעַק *z^e'aq:* An Aramaic verb indicating to call out, to cry out. It described an impassioned, urgent cry from King Darius to Daniel concerning Daniel's condition in the lion's den (Dan. 6:20[21]).

2201. זְעָקָה *z^e'āqāh:* A feminine noun indicating an outcry, crying out. It refers to a plaintive crying out for aid or help by those oppressed in Sodom and Gomorrah (Gen. 18:20); or a shouting or wailing by captains or pilots of merchant ships because of economic calamity (Ezek. 27:28). It indicates ineffective and hopeless shouting directed toward fools who will not learn (Eccl. 9:17). And in general, it indicates a cry of distress because of war, destruction, pestilence (Isa. 15:5; Jer. 18:22; 20:16); or a cry coming from the poor (Prov. 21:13).

2202. זִפְרֹן ***ziprōn:*** A proper noun designating Ziphron (Num. 34:9).

2203. זֶפֶת ***zepet:*** A feminine noun referring to tar, pitch. A bitumen, black, sticky substance used for waterproofing. The basket in which Moses was placed was waterproofed using this substance (Ex. 2:3). In figurative language, streams of Edom will be turned into pitch in a day of judgment (Isa. 34:9), indicating a hot flowing tar or pitch.

2204. זָקֵן ***zāqēn:*** A verb meaning to be old, to become old. This word is related to the adjective *zāqēn* (2205), meaning old, and the noun *zāqān* (2206), meaning beard. In Psalm 37:25, David described himself as an aged person as opposed to a youth, *na'ar* (5288), "I have been young, and now am old" (KJV). Solomon also used the same words to demonstrate the contrast between a person when young and when old (Prov. 22:6). This word is used of men (Gen. 24:1; Josh. 13:1; 1 Sam. 12:2); of women (Gen. 18:13; Prov. 23:22); or even a tree (Job 14:8). When used of older people, this word is often used to describe the last days of their lives (Gen. 27:1, 2; 1 Kgs. 1:1; 2 Chr. 24:15).

2205. זָקֵן ***zāqēn:*** An adjective meaning elder, old, aged, old man, old woman (as a noun), leader(s). The word's basic meaning is old or aged. But from this basic meaning, several different meanings arise. The word means aged persons, but the ideas of dignity, rank, and privilege also became attached to this concept. The person referred to was usually an old man (Gen. 19:4; Judg. 19:16, 17). One of the most famous was the old man in a robe (Samuel) that the witch of Endor saw (1 Sam. 28:14). Abraham and Sarah were both described as old in Genesis 18:11; the oldest servant in the master's house evidently had some prerogatives of seniority (Gen. 24:2). Old men, women, and children were often spared in war and were given special care and protection (cf. Ezek. 9:6) but not in the corrupt city of Jerusalem at its fall.

The group of men called elders in Israel were a powerfully influential group. They represented the nation from the time of the wilderness period (Ex. 19:7) and earlier (Ex. 3:16; 4:29). Of the 180 times the phrase is found, it occurs thirty-four times in Exodus when Israel was being formed into a people. There were traditionally seventy elders, and they ate and drank before the Lord with Moses and Joshua on Mount Sinai (Ex. 24:9, 11). The older priests held special respect among the priests (2 Kgs. 19:2). The elders were equal to the judges in influence and regularly took part in making decisions (Deut. 21:2, 19, 20). The elders of a city as a whole formed a major ruling group (Josh. 20:4; Ruth 4:2). For example, the elders of Jabesh tried to locate help and negotiated with the Ammonites who were besieging the city (1 Sam. 11:3). But the elders could lead in evil as well as good, for the picture Ezekiel painted of them was devastating and incriminating. The elders had become corrupt and helped lead the people astray. Their counsel would fail (Ezek. 7:26; 8:11, 12; 9:6).

2206. זָקָן zāqān: A feminine noun meaning beard. This word is usually used of the beards of men (1 Chr. 19:5; Isa. 15:2) but once refers to the mane of a lion (1 Sam. 17:35). In biblical times, to have one's beard shaved was humbling. When shaved by another, it was an act of humiliation (2 Sam. 10:4, 5; Isa. 7:20), but when pulled on (Ezra 9:3) or shaved by oneself, it was usually a sign of repentance (Jer. 41:5; 48:37). The beard is mentioned in connection with infection (Lev. 13:29, 30) and was to be trimmed properly according to ceremonial requirements (Lev. 19:27; 21:5). Ezekiel shaved and divided up his beard as a sign against Jerusalem (Ezek. 5:1).

2207. זֹקֶן zōqen: A masculine noun meaning extreme old age. The word is used only once in the Old Testament (Gen. 48:10), describing Jacob at the time he blessed Ephriam above Manasseh. By this time, he was well-advanced in years, so much so that his sight was extremely poor.

2208. זְקֻנִים z^e^quniym: A passive participle, used only in the plural as a masculine noun, meaning old age. This word is used only four times in the Old Testament, each time in the book of Genesis. It appears in reference to children born to parents late in life. Particularly, it is used of Isaac as the son of Abraham's old age (Gen. 21:2, 7); and of Joseph (Gen. 37:3) and Benjamin (Gen. 44:20) as the sons of Jacob's old age.

2209. זִקְנָה ziqnāh: A feminine noun meaning old, old age. This word is used most often to refer to people who are past their prime age. For example, it describes Sarah who is past the normal childbearing age (Gen. 24:36). Psalm 71 uses the word to ask the Lord not to turn away from the psalmist in his old age (Ps. 71:9, 18). Isaiah 46:4 describes God's care for the aged, even though their bodies grow weak.

2210. זָקַף zāqap̱: A verb indicating to lift up, raise up. It describes the Lord's raising up of people who are fallen or bowed down (Ps. 145:14), since He is their sustainer (Ps. 146:8) and helper.

2211. זְקַף z^e^qap̱: An Aramaic verb indicating to raise up, lift up; to impale on. It is used to indicate the impaling and raising up of a rebellious person on a piece of wood according to Persian law (Ezra 6:11).

2212. זָקַק zāqaq: A verb meaning to refine, to purify. The literal meaning of this word is to strain or extract. It is used in reference to gold (1 Chr. 28:18); silver (1 Chr. 29:4; Ps. 12:6[7]); water (Job 36:27); wine (Isa. 25:6). It is also used of the purification of the Levites, comparing it to refining gold and silver (Mal. 3:3).

2213. זֵר ***zēr:*** A masculine noun denoting a molding, a border. It refers to an edging or molding around the ark of the covenant (Ex. 25:11); the table of showbread (Ex. 25:24, 25); and the altar of incense (Ex. 30:3, 4).

2214. זָרָא ***zārā':*** A feminine noun indicating a loathsome thing or object. It refers to the quail meat that was given in such abundance that it became detestable as food for the Israelites (Num. 11:20).

2215. זָרַב ***zāra<u>b</u>:*** A verb meaning to be warmed, to dry up. It describes the drying up of streams, especially wadis, streams that flow only at certain times (Job 6:17).

2216. זְרֻבָּבֶל ***z^erubbā<u>b</u>el:*** A proper noun designating Zerubbabel, one of the leaders who led the exiles back from Babylonian captivity (Ezra 2:2; 12:1). He was the son of Shealtiel (Ezra 3:2). He helped organize the returned group as their civil leader, as well as helping rebuild the altar (Ezra 3:8; 4:2, 3). He received prophetic messages from Haggai the prophet (Hag. 1:1, 12) and from Zechariah (4:6–10). He was of the line of David and evidently could have become king if Israel had obeyed the Lord's instructions (Hag. 2:21–23).

2217. זְרֻבָּבֶל ***z^erubbā<u>b</u>el:*** A proper noun designating Zerubbabel, the Aramaic name corresponding to entry 2216.

2218. זֶרֶד ***zere<u>d</u>:*** A proper noun designating Zered, Zared (Num. 21:12; Deut. 2:13, 14).

2219. זָרָה ***zārāh:*** I. A verb meaning to scatter, winnow, disperse; smear, spread. It is used of the scattering or spreading out of people (Lev. 26:33; 1 Kgs. 14:15; Jer. 49:32, 36; 51:2); of objects, such as bones (Ezek. 6:5). It is used figuratively of scattering or winnowing the wicked (Prov. 20:26) as well as the Lord's dispersing His own people among the nations (Ps. 44:11; 106:27). The wicked are scattered with no place to live (Job 18:15). It is used to describe the preparation or spreading of a net for the wicked (Prov. 1:17). It describes God smearing the refuse or dung of Israel's corrupt feasts on their faces (Mal. 2:3). The word is used as an active noun to refer to winds that disperse the cold (Job 37:9).

II. A verb meaning to compass about, measure off, scrutinize, discern. It indicates keeping a careful watch on people, watching their paths closely (Ps. 139:3).

2220. זְרוֹעַ ***z^erôa',*** זְרֹעַ ***z^erōa':*** A common noun referring to arm, power, strength, might. It indicates the arm of a person (Judg. 15:14; 16:12; 2 Sam. 1:10). It is used figuratively often of the Lord's arm: the Lord's arms guided and led Ephraim (Hos. 11:3). The arm often stood for the strength or power of humans or God: of God (2 Sam. 22:35; Ps. 18:34[35]); of people (Job 26:2). Its most significant theological use is to depict the Lord's arm, His strength and power as His instruments of deliverance or even judgment; an arm stretched out (Ex. 15:16; Deut. 4:34; 5:15; 26:8; Ps. 136:12; Jer. 21:5; Ezek. 20:33, 34). But His outstretched arm and great power were forces that created the heavens and the earth (Jer. 27:5). As a good shepherd, His strong arm cares for His sheep (Isa. 40:11). The arm became a symbol of might and power of human (1 Sam. 2:31) or divine strength (Ps. 71:18). It stands for the military forces of the king of the South in Daniel 11:15 and of the king of the North (Dan. 11:31). It clearly refers to the shoulder of a sacrificial ram as well (Num. 6:19).

2221. זֵרוּעַ *zērûa'*: A masculine noun indicating what is sown, seed. It is a passive noun that indicates seed used for sowing (Lev. 11:37) or that has already been sown in the ground (Isa. 61:11). It serves as a symbol that God will make righteousness and praise to spring up in the future.

2222. זַרְזִיף *zarziyp̱, zārap̱*: I. A masculine noun indicating a downpour, a hard rain. It is used as a simile indicating heavy rain descending on the earth (Ps. 72:6; KJV).

II. A verb meaning to water, drip, pour down. It is considered a verb form with the subject being showers that water or pour down on the earth (Ps. 72:6; NIV, NASB, NKJV).

2223. זַרְזִיר *zarziyr*: A masculine noun indicating some animal, perhaps a strutting rooster, cock, or greyhound. It is specifically stated to be one of four animals which is impressive or stately in its walk (Prov. 30:31), a feature of created beings that causes the wise person to marvel at God's works.

2224. זָרַח *zāraḥ*: A verb meaning to rise up, to dawn, to shine forth; to break out. It refers to the rising or shining of the sun (Gen. 32:31[32]). It refers figuratively to the rising reputation or approval of a person who does good to the hungry and poor (Isa. 58:10) or to God dawning on Israel from Mount Seir (Deut. 33:2). Used of illnesses, it describes the breaking out of skin diseases (2 Chr. 26:19).

2225. זֶרַח *zeraḥ*: A masculine noun indicating a dawning or rising of something. It indicates sunrise or the shining forth of light (Isa. 60:3), but it is used metaphorically of the Lord rising up over Zion.

2226. זֶרַח *zeraḥ*: A proper noun designating Zerah:

A. Son of Reuel (Gen. 36:13, 17; 1 Chr. 1:37).

B. The father of Joab (Gen. 36:33; 1 Chr. 1:44).

C. Son of Judah (Gen. 38:30; 46:12; Num. 26:20; Josh. 7:1, 18, 24; 22:20; 1 Chr. 2:4, 6; 9:6; Neh. 11:24).

D. Son of Simeon, the same as *ṣōhar* (6714,B) (Num. 26:13; 1 Chr. 4:24).

E. A Gershonite (1 Chr. 6:21[6]).

F. The father of Ethni (1 Chr. 6:41[26]).

G. King of Ethiopia (2 Chr. 14:9[8]).

2227. זַרְחִי ***zarḥiy:*** A proper noun designating Zarhite:

A. Descendants of Zerah, son of Judah (2226,C) (Num. 26:20; Josh. 7:17; 1 Chr. 27:11, 13).

B. Descendants of Zerah, son of Simeon (2226,D) (Num. 26:13).

2228. זְרַחְיָה ***zᵉraḥyāh:*** A proper noun designating Zerahiah:

A. A Priest (1 Chr. 6:6[5:32], 51[36]; Ezra 7:4).

B. Head of a family (Ezra 8:4).

2229. זָרַם ***zāram:*** A verb denoting to pour out, to sweep away, to end. It refers to one of the great acts of the Lord when He caused the clouds to pour out water like a flood (Ps. 77:17[18]). It is used figuratively to indicate the death of persons, swept away by the Lord (Ps. 90:5).

2230. זֶרֶם ***zerem:*** A masculine noun indicating a storm, rain shower, cloudburst. God's remnant will be protected from the storm of their enemies seeking to destroy them (Isa. 4:6). God Himself becomes a refuge from the storm (Isa. 25:4), and His king and princes in a restored Israel will bring shelter from the storms of life (Isa. 32:2). But God also brings a storm of judgment on His enemies (Isa. 28:2; 30:30; Hab. 3:10).

2231. זִרְמָה ***zirmāh:*** A feminine noun denoting a flow or issue of liquid. It refers to a seminal discharge and is used figuratively of the excessive lustfulness of Israel's illicit lovers (Ezek. 23:20).

2232. זָרַע ***zāra':*** A verb meaning to sow, to bear seed. It indicates the act of sowing the ground or field or of planting seed (Gen. 47:23; Ex. 23:16; Deut. 22:9; Jer. 12:13). The verb can take two objects and mean to sow a city with salt (Judg. 9:45). It is used figuratively of sowing the wind (Hos. 8:7). It is the product of a plant or tree that produces its own seed in itself (Gen. 1:11, 29).

2233. זֶרַע ***zera':*** A masculine noun meaning sowing, seed, descendants, offspring, children, and posterity. The literal use of the word indicates seed of the field (i.e., seed planted in the field). When Israel entered Egypt, Joseph instructed the Israelites to keep four-fifths of the crop as seed to plant in their fields and to serve as food for them (Gen. 47:24); the season for planting seed was guaranteed by God to continue without fail (Gen. 8:22); and successful, abundant harvests were promised right up until the sowing season if Israel followed the Lord's laws and commands (Lev. 26:5). God had created the seed of the field by decreeing that plants and trees would be self-perpetuating, producing their own seed (Gen. 1:11) and that the seed-producing plants would be edible (Gen. 1:29). Manna, the heavenly food, resembled coriander seed (Ex. 16:31). Any seed could be rendered unclean and not usable if a dead body fell on it after the seed had been moistened (Lev. 11:38).

The noun is used to describe the seed (i.e., the offspring) of both people and animals. The seed of Judah and Israel would be united and planted peacefully in the land together with animals in a pleasant setting (Jer. 31:27). Seed can be translated as son (i.e., seed as when God gives Hannah a promise of a son [1 Sam. 1:11]). The seed of a woman mentioned in Genesis 3:15 is her offspring.

The offspring of humans is described many times by this word. Hannah was given additional children to replace Samuel, whom she gave to the Lord's service (1 Sam. 2:20). The most important seed that the author of Genesis describes is the seed of Abraham, the promised seed, referring to Isaac, Jacob, and his twelve sons (Gen. 12:7; 15:3). The author of Genesis uses the word twenty-one times in this setting (Ex. 32:13; Deut. 1:8). The seed of the royal line of David was crucial to Israel's existence, and the term is used nine times to refer to David's offspring or descendants (2 Sam. 7:12). In a figurative sense, seed refers to King Zedekiah and perhaps to Israelites of royal lineage, whom Nebuchadnezzar established in Jerusalem (Ezek. 17:5). Royal lines or seed were found outside Israel, such as in Edom, where Hadad belonged to the royal line (1 Kgs. 11:14), and in Judah, where the wicked Athaliah attempted to destroy the royal seed (2 Kgs. 11:1; 25:25; Jer. 41:1).

The seed or offspring of a particular nation can be characterized in moral and religious terms as well. Three verses stand out: The seed of Israel was called a holy seed (Ezra 9:2; Isa. 6:13); and, in the case of Ezra 9:2, the seed corrupted itself by mixing with the peoples around them. The seed of Israel is a seed of God or a divine seed (Mal. 2:15) through its union with God (cf. 2 Pet. 1:4). An offspring could be described as deceitful and wicked (Ps. 37:28; Isa. 57:4). It was important in Israel to prove that one's origin or seed stemmed from an Israelite ancestor, for some Israelites and Israelite priests who returned from exile could not show their origin (Ezra 2:59). The word also refers to the seed or posterity of the Messiah (Isa. 53:10).

2234. זְרַע *z^e^ra'*: An Aramaic noun meaning seed. This word is used only once in Daniel 2:43 in the idiomatic phrase "with the seed of men" (KJV). In this passage, Daniel interpreted King Nebuchadnezzar's dream about the gold, silver, bronze, iron, and clay statue. This mixing of people with the seed of men is a reference to other people groups joining a community or nation. Those who come afterward lack the national spirit to adhere to one another, just as iron does not mix with clay.

2235. זֵרֹעַ ***zērōa'***, **זֵרְעֹן** ***zēr'ōn:*** A masculine noun denoting pulse, vegetables. It describes the food Daniel and his friends ate in place of the king's rich foods and wine (Dan. 1:12, 16).

2236. זָרַק ***zāraq:*** A verb meaning to sprinkle, to scatter, to be sprinkled. This word is most often used to describe the actions of the priests performing the sacrificial rituals. They sprinkled the blood of the sacrifices (Lev. 1:5; 2 Kgs. 16:13; 2 Chr. 29:22). It is also used of water (Num. 19:13; Ezek. 36:25). In a time of grief, Job's friends sprinkled dust on their heads (Job 2:12). King Josiah destroyed the false gods and scattered their pieces (powder, NASB) over the graves of those who had worshiped them (2 Chr. 34:4).

2237. זָרַר ***zārar:*** A verb meaning to emerge. It describes the reaction of the Shunammite's son as he was being restored to life by Elisha (2 Kgs. 4:35), evidently breathing in air once again.

2238. זֶרֶשׁ ***zereš:*** A proper noun designating Zeresh (Esth. 5:10, 14; 6:13).

2239. זֶרֶת ***zereṯ:*** A feminine noun indicating a span. It indicates the width of a man's hand as a convenient means of measurement, about 25 centimeters (Ex. 28:16). It was the width of the breastpiece the high priest wore (Ex. 39:9), as well as the width of the border on the sacrificial altar of Ezekiel's vision (Ezek. 43:13). Goliath stood six cubits (ca. 9 feet) and a span (about four inches) (1 Sam. 17:4). The Lord, in great accuracy, measured the heavens to the span (Isa. 40:12).

2240. זַתּוּא ***zattû':*** A proper noun designating Zattu (Ezra 2:8; 10:27; Neh. 7:13; 10:14[15]).

2241. זֵתָם ***zēṯām:*** A proper noun designating Zetham (1 Chr. 23:8; 26:22).

2242. זֵתַר ***zēṯar:*** A proper noun designating Zethar (Esth. 1:10).

ח Heth

2243. חֹב **ḥōḇ:** A masculine noun meaning bosom, heart. It refers to Job's inner self, a place where he can hide his transgressions or guilt in his inner being or heart (Job 31:33).

2244. חָבָא **ḥāḇā':** A verb meaning to hide, be hidden. It refers to hiding oneself, such as Adam did in the Garden of Eden (Gen. 3:8, 10). It indicates being in a safe, secure location metaphorically (Job 5:21) or literally to be hidden or hide (Job 29:10; Amos 9:3). It takes on the meaning of to hide something or someone (1 Kgs. 18:4, 13). It has the unusual meaning of water being ice or hard (Job 38:30) and the meaning to hush or be silent when referring to the voices of certain persons (Job 29:10).

2245. חָבַב **ḥāḇaḇ:** A verb meaning to love. This word occurs only once in the Old Testament, in which it describes God's love for the people of Israel (Deut. 33:3). This verse is in a poetical section of Scripture, which helps to explain why this word is used only once. It is related to *ḥōḇ* (2243), meaning bosom, which is used only in Job. 31:33. Thus, the love expressed here probably signifies an embracing, motherly affection.

2246. חֹבָב **ḥōḇāḇ:** A proper noun designating Hobab (Num. 10:29; Judg. 4:11).

2247. חָבָה **ḥāḇāh:** A verb indicating to conceal, to hide, to withdraw. It refers to a persons secluding themselves for a time to escape a threat (Isa. 26:20) or danger, either literally or figuratively. It literally means to hide oneself somewhere from something or someone (Josh. 2:16; 2 Kgs. 7:12), e.g., in the hills or fields. It indicates both a literal and figurative hiding from the Lord (Jer. 49:10).

2248. חֲבוּלָה **ḥ^{a}ḇûlāh:** An Aramaic feminine noun indicating a wrong or hurtful deed. Daniel was cleared of being guilty of this kind of evil action against Darius (6:22[23]) in any way.

2249. חָבוֹר **ḥāḇôr:** A proper noun designating Habor (2 Kgs. 17:6; 18:11; 1 Chr. 5:26).

2250. חַבּוּרָה **ḥabbûrāh,** חַבֻּרָה **ḥabburāh,** חֲבֻרָה **ḥ^{a}ḇurāh:** A feminine noun denoting a bruise, a woundm or an injury. It refers to some kind of an injury received by Lamech from a young man (Gen. 4:23; NASB, striking). The Suffering Servant of Isaiah (53:5) undergoes mistreatment indicated by this word (NASB, scourging; NIV, wounds; KJV, NKJV, stripes). Certain wounds, blows, or stripes that wound or cut will purge evil from a person (Prov. 20:30). It is used figuratively of emotional or spiritual wounds (Ps. 38:5[6]); of those same wounds on a national scale in Judah (Isa. 1:6). In a legal case, a wound was to be paid back by a corresponding wound or injury (Ex. 21:25).

2251. חָבַט ***ḥabaṭ:*** A verb meaning to beat out, to thresh. It refers to the threshing or beating out of grain (Judg. 6:11); olive trees (Deut. 24:20); or cummin (Isa. 28:27). Figuratively, it indicates the Lord's gathering His people by threshing them from among the nations (Isa. 27:12).

2252. חֲבָיָה ***ḥ^a^bāyāh,*** חָבָיָּה ***ḥ^o^bāyyāh:*** A proper noun designating Habaiah (Ezra 2:61; Neh. 7:63).

2253. חֶבְיוֹן ***ḥebyôn:*** A masculine noun indicating a hiding, a concealment. It refers to the covering or hiding of the Lord's power as He comes to deliver His people (Hab. 3:4). His power is hidden evidently by the rays shining from His hand or the splendor of His presence.

2254. חבל ***ḥābal,*** חֹבְלִים ***ḥōb^e^liym:*** A verb meaning to take a pledge, to destroy. This verb is translated in a variety of ways. Most commonly, it means taking a pledge for such things as a loan (Ex. 22:26[25]; Deut. 24:6; Ezek. 18:16; Amos 2:8). The word is used in Job in reference to debts (Job 22:6; 24:3, 9). It also describes the destruction of the wicked (Prov. 13:13; Isa. 32:7) or destruction of property (Isa. 10:27; 13:5). This word can also mean to corrupt (Neh. 1:7; Job 17:1). Zechariah used it in a metaphor describing the union between Israel and Judah (Zech. 11:7, 14).

2255. חֲבַל ***ḥ^a^bal:*** An Aramaic verb meaning to ruin, to hurt, to destroy. King Darius issued a decree that ended with a plea for God to overthrow anyone who tried to destroy the Temple (Ezra 6:12). The tree in Nebuchadnezzar's dream was cut down and destroyed (Dan. 4:23[20]). Because the angel shut the lions' mouths, they did not hurt Daniel (Dan. 6:22[23]). This word also refers to a kingdom that will never be destroyed. In the interpretation of one of Nebuchadnezzar's dreams, Daniel told of a kingdom that would never be destroyed (Dan. 2:44). King Darius praised God when Daniel was not eaten by lions, saying the kingdom of God would not be destroyed (Dan. 6:26[27]). Once again, Daniel saw a kingdom like this in his dream of the four beasts (Dan. 7:14).

2256. חֶבֶל ***ḥebel,*** חֵבֶל ***ḥēbel:*** A masculine or feminine noun meaning cord, pangs, region, company. This word has many meanings, depending on the context. The most basic meaning is a rope or a cord, such as the rope the spies used to escape through Rahab's window (Josh. 2:15) or the cords used to bind Jeremiah in the dungeon (Jer. 38:11–13). Although these cords may be decorative (Esth. 1:6), they are usually used to bind and control objects, such as animals (Job 41:1[40:25]) or buildings (Isa.

33:20). This word is also used symbolically to speak of the cords of sin and death (2 Sam. 22:6; Ps. 18:4[5], 5[6]; Prov. 5:22) or the pangs of childbirth (Isa. 13:8; Jer. 13:21; Hos. 13:13). It can even be translated "destruction" (Job 21:17). This word is also used to describe a dividing line (2 Sam. 8:2; Amos 7:17); a geographical region (Deut. 3:13, 14; 1 Kgs. 4:13; Zeph. 2:5, 6); or an allotment of an inheritance (Deut. 32:9; Josh. 17:5; Ps. 105:11). In a few instances, this word describes a company of prophets (1 Sam. 10:5, 10).

2257. חֲבָל *ḥaḇāl:* An Aramaic masculine noun denoting damage, injury, harm, hurt. It refers to economic or financial damage (Ezra 4:22), specifically to King Artaxerxes. It refers to physical damage or injury by fire (Dan. 3:25) or by wild animals (Dan. 6:23[24]).

2258. חֲבֹל *ḥaḇōl,* חֲבֹלָה *ḥaḇōlāh:* A noun meaning pledge. This word is always used when speaking of those who do or do not return pledges, which were items taken to guarantee loans. These items were usually people's cloaks, and the Law stated that they were to be returned to the owners before the sun set because they were the only covering they had (cf. Ex. 22:26[25], 27[26]). Righteous persons returned the pledges (Ezek. 18:7) or did not even require them (Ezek. 18:16), whereas wicked persons kept the items used for the pledge (Ezek. 18:12). But if they repented and returned them, they would live instead of die for the evil they did (Ezek. 33:15).

2259. חֹבֵל *ḥōḇēl:* A masculine noun referring to a seaman, a sailor, a pilot. It indicates a captain of a ship (Jon. 1:6). It is used metaphorically of the wisemen of Tyre as her pilots in her maritime empire (Ezek. 27:8), but also literally it denotes pilots who transport wares in ships (Ezek. 27:27–29).

2260. חִבֵּל *ḥibbēl:* A masculine noun indicating a mast, a ship's rigging. In context, the word points out in a simile that a drunken person is like someone lying on the top of a ship's mast or upper rigging (Prov. 23:34).

2261. חֲבַצֶּלֶת *ḥaḇaṣṣeleṯ:* A feminine noun denoting a rose. It refers most likely to a plant or flower of the genus asphodel and of the lily family, lilylike flowers (Isa. 35:1: KJV, rose; NASB, NIV, crocus; NKJV, rose). The word stands parallel with lily in Song of Solomon 2:1 and is translated as rose for poetic effect (NASB, NIV, NKJV, KJV).

2262. חֲבַצִּנְיָה *ḥaḇaṣṣinyāh:* A proper noun designating Habazziniah (Jer. 35:3).

2263. חָבַק *ḥāḇaq:* A verb meaning to embrace. Its most common meaning is to embrace someone in a show of affection (Gen. 29:13; 33:4; 48:10; Prov. 5:20; Song 2:6; 8:3) and is often accompanied with the verb to kiss. There is a proper time to embrace and a proper time not to embrace (Eccl. 3:5). It means to acquire or give birth to a son (2 Kgs. 4:16); used figuratively, it refers to the oppressed who cling to or hug even rocks in search of a shelter (Job 24:8; Lam. 4:5, NASB); and to the wise person's embracing wisdom (Prov. 4:8). It indicates the folding of one's hands (Eccl. 4:5, see #2264).

2264. חִבֻּק ***ḥibbuq:*** A masculine noun indicating a folding of one's hands. An active noun built upon the verbal root *ḥāḇaq,* to embrace, and referring to the fool's folding of his or her hands as a symbol of slothfulness (Prov. 6:10; 24:33).

2265. חֲבַקּוּק ***ḥ^{a}ḇaqqûq:*** A proper noun designating Habakkuk, a prophet contemporary (ca. 620–609 B.C.) with Jeremiah who witnessed the terrible rise and power of the Babylonians against Israel. He prophesied ca. 605 B.C. He was in constant debate/dialogue with the Lord in his prophecies. His name may refer to a plant of some kind or may be from *ḥāḇaq* (2263) meaning, "to encircle, embrace." Hab. 2:4b is quoted as the chief principle of the gospel (Rom. 1:17).

2266. חָבַר ***ḥāḇar:*** I. A verb meaning to join together, to unite; to conjure, to charm; to heap up (words). It refers to simple physical proximity or touching of objects (Ex. 26:3, 6, 9, 11) or to the mental, emotional, and physical joining of forces or armies (Gen. 14:3; 2 Chr. 20:35, 36; Dan. 11:6). It is used figuratively of joining one's self in a deep religious sense to something, such as idols (Ps. 94:20; Hos. 4:17). Closely allied to this is its use to indicate the process of charming, conjuring, or casting a spell (Deut. 18:11; Ps. 58:5[6]). It is used of composing or joining words to attack someone (Job 16:4).

II. A verb meaning to adorn, to make beautiful, to be brilliant; to heap up. It refers to the joining or composing of words, a speech (Job 16:4, NASB, NIV; KJV, heap up[words]).

2267. חֶבֶר ***ḥeḇer:*** A masculine noun meaning a company, an association, a spell. It is used to refer to a band of bad priests (Hos. 6:9); a house of association, namely, a house shared with an antagonistic woman (Prov. 21:9; 25:24); or a magical spell or incantation (Deut. 18:11; Ps. 58:5[6]; Isa. 47:9, 12).

2268. חֶבֶר ***ḥeḇer:*** A proper noun designating Heber:

A. Son of Beriah (Gen. 46:17; Num. 26:45; 1 Chr. 7:31, 32).

B. Husband of Jael (Judg. 4:11, 17, 21; 5:24).

C. Son of another Beriah (1 Chr. 4:18).

D. Son of a third Beriah (1 Chr. 8:17).

2269. חֲבַר ***ḥaḇar:*** An Aramaic masculine noun indicating a companion, friend. It indicates persons joined in companionship as friends. It describes the relationship between Daniel and his fellow exiles (Dan. 2:13, 17, 18).

2270. חָבֵר ***ḥāḇēr:*** A masculine noun indicating friendship, association with, being friends with, a companion. It indicates being joined together in various ways: as a helpful friend or companion (Eccl. 4:10); with regard to a plan or campaign (Judg. 20:11); with respect to a certain group of people, good or bad in character (Ps. 45:7[8]; 119:63; Prov. 28:24; Isa. 1:23); through an association of certain groups or persons, especially the joining of Judah and Israel as companions (Ezek. 37:16, 19); with regard to religious affiliation, e.g., those who worship idols (Isa. 44:11).

2271. חַבָּר ***ḥabbār:*** A masculine noun indicating an associate, a partner, traders. It refers to a person belonging to the same business or trade (Job 41:6[40:30]).

2272. חֲבַרְבֻּרָה ***ḥ^{a}ḇarburāh:*** A feminine noun meaning spot, stripe. It refers to the spots of a leopard or panther (Jer. 13:23) that the animal cannot change. In a similar way, evil Israelites cannot change their characters to do good.

2273. חַבְרָה ***ḥaḇrāh:*** An Aramaic feminine noun indicating a companion or associate. It refers to the ten horns that arose long before the little horn of Daniel 7:20 but were still related to it in some way.

2274. חֶבְרָה ***ḥeḇrāh:*** A feminine noun meaning in company, association. It refers to the fellowship, ties, or comradeship of persons who walk together in agreement (Job 34:8), indicating like-mindedness. Elihu used it derisively of Job.

2275. חֶבְרוֹן ***ḥeḇrôn:*** A proper noun designating Hebron:

A. A city in the hill country of Judah. In Genesis 23:2 it is called Kiriath Arba. The name means "association." Abraham build an altar (Gen. 13:18) by this ancient city (Num. 13:22). The cave of Machpelah was in this field, and the patriarchs and their wives were buried in the cave. It was given to Caleb and was designated as a city of refuge and a Levitical city (Josh. 20:7; 21:11). The spies visited the area (Num. 13:22–33). David was anointed king in Hebron and ruled from there for seven and a half years (2 Sam. 5:1–13). Absalom's rebellion and conspiracy began in Hebron (2 Sam. 15:1–6).

B. A son of Kohath from the line of Moses, and a head of a family (Ex. 6:18). It was a family/clan of Kohath (Num. 3:19).

C. A descendant of Caleb, a brother of Jerahmeel (1 Chr. 2:42). He fathered many sons (1 Chr. 15:9).

2276. חֶבְרוֹנִי ***ḥeḇrôniy,*** חֶבְרֹנִי ***ḥeḇrōniy:*** A proper noun designating Hebronite (Num. 3:27; 26:58; 1 Chr. 26:23, 30, 31).

2277. חֶבְרִי ***ḥeḇriy:*** A proper noun designating Heberite (Num. 26:45).

2278. חֲבֶרֶת ***ḥ^a^ḇereṯ:*** A feminine noun indicating a female companion. It refers to a female companion by marriage covenant (Mal. 2:14).

2279. חֹבֶרֶת ***ḥōḇereṯ:*** A feminine noun referring to a junction, a connecting thing, a curtain that joins another, draperies. It indicates the outermost curtains of two sets of drapes where loops would be placed for joining (Ex. 26:4, 10; 36:17).

2280. חָבַשׁ ***ḥāḇaš:*** A verb meaning to bind. This word is used primarily to describe a binding or wrapping of one object with another. It is frequently used of saddling a donkey (Gen. 22:3; Judg. 19:10; 1 Kgs 2:40) but can be used to describe the binding of caps on the priests' heads (Ex. 29:9; Lev. 8:13); the tying of garments and carpets in a roll (Ezek. 27:24); the wrapping of weeds around Jonah's head (Jon. 2:5[6]); God stopping the floods (Job 28:11). This word is often used to describe binding wounds (both physical and spiritual) with the result that healing occurs (Isa. 61:1; Ezek. 30:21; Hos. 6:1). In a few cases, this binding may refer to one's ability to control (or rule) another (Job 34:17; 40:13).

2281. חֲבִתִּים ***ḥ^a^ḇittiym:*** A masculine plural noun referring to something flat, a flat pan, flat bread (baked in a pan). It refers to a category of food or bread that was baked in pans (1 Chr. 9:31), an important part of temple ritual.

2282. חָג ***ḥāg,*** חַג ***ḥag:*** A noun meaning a feast, a festival. This word is used numerous times throughout the Old Testament referring to the feasts of the Hebrew religious calendar. It is used of the major feasts, including the Feast of Unleavened Bread and the Passover Feast (Ex. 34:18, 25; Lev. 23:6; Deut. 16:16; Ezra 6:22); the Feast of Weeks (Deut. 16:16; 2 Chr. 8:13); and the Feast of Tabernacles (Lev. 23:34; Num. 29:12; Deut. 31:10; Zech 14:16). It was used in the Temple dedication during Solomon's reign (1 Kgs. 8:2, 65). Evil King Jeroboam held a festival described in 1 Kings 12:32, 33. The prophets often used this word to describe the negligence of the people in keeping the feasts commanded by Mosaic Law (Isa. 29:1; Amos 5:21; Mal. 2:3).

2283. חָגָּא ***ḥāggā':*** A feminine noun meaning terror. This word occurs only once in the Old Testament in Isaiah 19:17 and speaks of the reeling terror that Judah would cause in Egypt.

2284. חָגָב ***ḥāgāḇ:*** A masculine noun denoting a locust, a grasshopper. Its context influences its translation greatly. It refers most likely to grasshoppers as one of the clean insects the Israelites could eat (Lev. 11:22). It is used to indicate something very small (Num. 13:33; Isa. 40:22) compared to the Nephilim giants in Canaan. It is translated as locusts based on the context in 2 Chronicles 7:13 (NIV, NASB, KJV, NKJV) but grasshoppers in Ecclesiastes 12:5.

2285. חָגָב ***hāgāb:*** A proper noun designating Hagab (Ezra 2:46).

2286. חֲגָבָא ***ḥ***^{a}***gābā',*** חֲגָבָה ***ḥ***^{a}***gabāh:*** A proper noun designating Hagabah (Ezra 2:45; Neh. 7:48).

2287. חָגַג ***ḥāgag:*** A verb meaning to hold a feast, a pilgrim feast, to celebrate a holy day. It refers to wild and confused actions in a perilous situation (Ps. 107:27) like the behavior of a drunken person. It is usually used in the context of rejoicing and describes festive attitudes and actions, often while on the way to worship or when celebrating a feast (Ps. 42:4[5]; Nah. 1:15[2:1]). In fact, the word indicates the holding or observing of a festival (Ex. 5:1; 12:14; 23:14; Lev. 23:39; Num. 29:12; Deut. 16:15) to the Lord, such as the Passover or Feast of Booths (Zech. 14:16, 18, 19). It also is used to describe the festive dancing and celebrations of a victory over enemies in battle (1 Sam. 30:16).

2288. חָגָו ***ḥāgāw,*** חָגוּ ***ḥāgû:*** A masculine noun indicating a cleft or place of concealment, clefts in a rock or rocky area. It is a secret place away from crowds (Song 2:14) for two lovers, but also it is a strategic location for armies and one's enemies to hide and fight (Jer. 49:16; Obad. 1:3).

2289. חָגוֹר ***ḥāgôr,*** חֲגוֹר ***ḥ***^{a}***gôr:*** I. An adjective meaning girded. It was an impressive but arrogant and prideful feature of the loin section of a Babylonian officer's uniform (Ezek. 23:15) that lured Israel to adulate them.

II. A masculine noun indicating a sash, a belt, or a girdle. It was part of a military officer's uniform (1 Sam. 18:4; 2 Sam. 20:8).

2290. חֲגוֹרָה ***ḥ***^{a}***gôrāh,*** חֲגֹרָה ***ḥ***^{a}***gōrāh:*** A feminine noun referring to a sash, a belt, a girdle, a loincloth, loin coverings. It refers to a loincloth of fig leaves as the first covering of humankind (Gen. 3:7). It was a regular feature of Israelite clothing (Isa. 3:24). It was a valuable and desirable part of a soldier's military uniform (2 Sam. 18:11). To stain or to put the blood of battle on one's belt was to be guilty of violent bloodshed (1 Kgs. 2:5). To put on a military belt was to prepare for war (2 Kgs. 3:21).

2291. חַגִּי ***ḥaggiy:*** I. Haggi, son of Gad (Gen. 46:16; Num. 26:15).

II.Haggites, descendants of Haggi (2291,I) (Num. 26:15).

2292. חַגַּי ***ḥaggay:*** A proper noun designating Haggai:

A. A prophet who prophesied during the time of Ezra-Nehemiah (ca. 520 B.C.), encouraging the people and leaders to rebuild the Temple, the house of God. His name means "festive, festal." He warned the people to do the Lord's work and not put their own well-beings and economic prosperity ahead of that (Hag. 1:3–4). Postexilic Israelites had become an unholy, defiled people (2:10–14), but Haggai gave an encouraging message as well (2:20–23).

B. The Aramaic occurrence of the name Haggai. The same as entry 2292,A.

2293. חַגִּיָּה ḥaggiyyāh: A proper noun designating Haggiah (1 Chr. 6:30[15]).

2294. חַגִּית ḥaggiyṯ: A proper noun designating Haggith (2 Sam. 3:4; 1 Kgs. 1:5, 11; 2:13; 1 Chr. 3:2).

2295. חָגְלָה ḥoglāh: A proper noun designating Hoglah (Num. 26:33; 27:1; 36:11; Josh. 17:3).

2296. חָגַר ḥāgar: A verb meaning to gird oneself, to put on a belt. To gird oneself could indicate a number of things: to prepare for a journey (2 Kgs. 4:29); to prepare for war (1 Sam. 17:39) or violence (Judg. 3:16); to be capable of military service (2 Kgs. 3:21); lit., to put on a belt or to gird oneself with a belt or girdle for battle (1 Kgs. 20:11); to prepare for priestly service by girding on the priestly sash (Ex. 29:9). Other persons were girded accordingly: the priest, e.g., with an ephod (1 Sam. 2:18); or the petitioner or mourner in sackcloth (1 Kgs. 20:32; Isa. 32:11; Joel 1:8). It is used symbolically of a king girding on his sword to gain victory for his people (Ps. 45:3[4]) as he, ideally, rides forth girded in righteousness (Isa. 11:5). The divine being of Daniel's vision wears a belt of pure gold (Dan. 10:5). The wise wife of Proverbs girds herself with strength (31:17); and even the hills put on rejoicing as a belt when God blesses them (Ps. 65:12[13]).

2297. חַד ḥaḏ: A numerical adjective indicating one. It is used in the phrase *ḥaḏ 'eṯ-'aḥaḏ* meaning one to another or to one another (Ezek. 33:30).

2298. חַד ḥaḏ: An Aramaic numerical adjective indicating one. It is employed several ways: It follows *keša'āh* as a short time, indicating a rather short period of time (Dan. 4:19[16]); it was the sense of only one option (Dan. 2:9); or only one object involved (Ezra 4:8, a letter; Dan. 2:31), thus serving as an indefinite article; it indicates the first year in the phrase *bišnaṯ ḥaḏāh* (Ezra 5:13; Dan. 7:1); with a following number it means "x times," whatever that number is, e.g., seven times is *ḥaḏ-šiḇ'āh* (Dan. 3:19). With *ke* attached to the front, *ḥaḏ* takes on the meaning of as one or together (Dan. 2:35).

2299. חַד ḥaḏ: An adjective meaning sharp. It describes metaphorically the sharp tongues of those attacking the psalmist (Ps. 57:4[5]). It describes the deadly seduction of an adulteress as sharp as a two-edged sword (Prov. 5:4). The Servant's mouth is like a sharp sword (Isa. 49:2).

2300. חָדַד ḥāḏaḏ, חָדָה ḥāḏāh: I. A verb meaning to be keen; to slash, to sharpen, be quick, be fierce. It describes the horses of the Babylonian cavalry in the evening as more quick, keen, or fierce than wolves (Hab. 1:8). It depicts a sharpened sword as both literal and symbolic of the Lord's "sword" of imminent judgment on Israel (Ezek. 21:9–11[14–16], 16[21]).

II. A verb meaning to sharpen. It is used of iron sharpening iron from which comes the simile of one person sharpening another (Prov. 27:17).

2301. חֲדַד ḥᵃḏaḏ: A proper noun designating Hadad (Gen. 25:15; 1 Chr. 1:30).

2302. חָדָה ḥāḏāh, יָחַד yāḥaḏ: I. A verb meaning to rejoice, to be glad. It depicts a joyous response to something or someone: the goodness of the Lord (Ex. 18:9); figuratively of a day of birth rejoicing (Job 3:6, NASB); in certain verb forms to indicate the Lord's making someone happy (Ps. 21:6[7]).

II. A verb meaning to join. It is translated to mean joined, including an unwanted day of birth (Job 3:6, NIV, KJV).

2303. חַדּוּד ḥaddûḏ: A masculine noun meaning sharp, jagged. It describes some features of Leviathan described in Job (41:30[22]), i.e., his undersides or parts are like jagged or sharp potsherds or stones.

2304. חֶדְוָה ḥeḏwāh: A feminine noun denoting joy, gladness. The dwelling place of the Lord is the place of joy and gladness (1 Chr. 16:27). It specifically indicates the joy of the Lord which serves as the strength of the Israelites (Neh. 8:10).

2305. חֶדְוָה ḥeḏwāh: An Aramaic feminine noun indicating joy, gladness. It denotes the the Israelites' attitude and response to the completion of the new Temple in Ezra's day (Ezra 6:16).

2306. חֲדֵה ḥᵃḏēh: An Aramaic masculine noun referring to chest, breast. It describes the breast portion of the great statue in Nebuchadnezzar's dream (Dan. 2:32).

2307. חָדִיד ḥāḏiyḏ: A proper noun designating Hadid (Ezra 2:33; Neh. 7:37; 11:34).

2308. חָדַל ḥāḏal: A verb indicating to stop, to cease. It is used of the cessation or stopping of various things: worry (1 Sam. 9:5); childbearing (Gen. 18:11); natural phenomena, thunder, etc. (Ex. 9:29, 33, 34); the presence of the poor among Israel (Deut. 15:11); travel on highways; the peasantry (Judg. 5:6, 7); relationships with Job even by his family members (19:14); the Lord's judgments on Israel (Amos 7:5). The word is used to urge Israel to cease to do evil (Isa. 1:16). Jeremiah uses it to tell the Israelites to not come, to cease from coming to Babylon with him (Jer. 40:4). It can mean to leave someone alone (Ex.

14:12) or something, such as the pursuit of wealth (Prov. 23:4). In certain contexts, it means to make up one's mind and act or else (Zech. 11:12).

2309. חֶדֶל ***ḥeḏel:*** A masculine noun meaning cessation, rest. This word occurs only in Isaiah 38:11 in the lamentation of Hezekiah. Despite the fact it is translated "world," it conveys the idea of a place of termination or repose. By considering the context in the Old Testament, one comes to understand that the word refers to the grave, or more exactly, Sheol (cf. Isa. 38:10).

2310. חָדֵל ***ḥāḏēl:*** An adjective meaning transient, rejected, fleeting. It means the opposite of hearing, that is, refusing to hear or respond positively (Ezek. 3:27). It describes the Servant of Isaiah as a person rejected, refused by people (*'îšîm*). It takes on the idea of fleeting or transitoriness with respect to the impermanence of human life (Ps. 39:4[5]).

2311. חַדְלָי ***ḥaḏlay:*** A proper noun designating Hadlai (2 Chr. 28:12).

2312. חֵדֶק ***ḥēḏeq:*** A masculine noun indicating a thorn or brier. It refers to briers and the nightshade of the Jordan Valley, an unpleasant, undesirable plant. It is used in a simile to represent derisively the best leader Israel has (Mic. 7:4). In a proverb, it indicates the way of the lazy, i.e., they cannot bring themselves to traverse the road they need to in order to succeed (Prov. 15:19).

2313. חִדֶּקֶל ***ḥiddeqel:*** A proper noun designating Hiddekel, the Tigris River, running on the eastern side of Mesopotamia and a sister to the Euphrates River. It is one of the four rivers mentioned in Genesis 2:14. Daniel was given an apocalyptic vision as he stood on its shore (Dan. 10:4). Its sources begin in the southeast of southern Turkey (ancient Hittite-Harrian territory) in the Armenian Mountains. It is ca. 1, 500 miles long and empties into the Persian Gulf after it joins the Euphrates. The capital cities of Assyria, Assur, and Nineveh were on its banks.

2314. חָדַר ***ḥāḏar:*** A verb meaning to enclose, to surround; to penetrate deeply. It is used of the penetration or the enclosing of the Lord's sword of judgment on His people (Ezek. 21:14[19]).

2315. חֶדֶר ***ḥeḏer:*** A masculine noun referring to a chamber, a parlor, a room. It combines with other words to indicate various rooms, spaces, or enclosures: a room of lying down, a sleeping room (Ex. 8:3[7:28]; 2 Sam. 4:7; 2 Kgs. 6:12; Eccl. 10:20); a bedroom toilet or cool room (Judg. 3:24; 2 Kgs. 11:2); an inner chamber (1 Chr. 28:11). Repeated with b^e attached to the front of the second occurrence of the word, it means one room (in)to another (1 Kgs. 20:30). Preceded by *min* (4480), it has the meaning of indoors (Deut. 32:25). It is combined figuratively before *beṭen,* belly, womb, to refer to internal parts of the body (Prov. 18:8); and before *māšeṯ,* death, to refer to the rooms or chambers of death or Sheol (Prov. 7:27). It is used in a technical sense of the southern constellations (Job 9:9; cf. 37:9).

2316. חֲדַר ***ḥᵃḏar:*** A proper noun designating Hadar (Gen. 25:15).

2317. חַדְרָךְ ***ḥaḏrāḵ:*** A proper noun, Hadrach. It refers to a city in northern Syria against which the Lord prophesied (Zech. 9:1).

2318. חָדַשׁ ***ḥāḏaš:*** A verb meaning to renew, restore. It refers to the renovating or reconstructing of various items: an altar (1 Sam. 11:14); the altar of the Lord, i.e., rebuilding it (2 Chr. 15:8); the Temple (2 Chr. 24:4, 12); the surface of the ground or earth (Ps. 104:30). It is used figuratively in an intensive stem to indicate the restoring or revitalizing of one's spirit (Ps. 51:10[12]). In a time of restoration, ruined cities will be rebuilt (Isa. 61:4). It is used of the Lord's restoring the past blessed days of Jerusalem (Lam. 5:21).

2319. חָדָשׁ ***ḥāḏāš:*** An adjective meaning new, fresh. It is used to describe many different items as renewed or fresh: king over Egypt (Ex. 1:8); house (Deut. 20:5); covenant (Jer. 31:31); heaven and earth (Isa. 65:17); wife (Deut. 24:5); harvest of grain (Lev. 23:16); garment (1 Kgs. 11:29, 30); vessel (2 Kgs. 2:20). It is used to indicate something new in an obsolete sense, never seen or done before (Eccl. 1:9, 10). It refers to a new song of praise God's people will sing to Him (Ps. 33:3; 40:3[4]; 96:1; 98:1; 144:9; 149:1); and to a new spirit that God implants within them (Ezek. 11:19; 18:31; 36:26).

2320. חֹדֶשׁ ***ḥōḏeš:*** A masculine noun meaning new moon (first day of the lunar month), month. Its use can be put into two categories: (1) the new moon; the day when the crescent moon is once again visible (2 Kgs. 4:23). It is used in various phrases in this sense to indicate the day after the new moon (1 Sam. 20:27); second day of the new moon (1 Sam. 20:34); (2) month; a time marked by thirty days normally. A full month is a *ḥōdeš yāmîm* (Gen. 29:14). Idioms are formed that mean month by (*bᵉ*) month, that is, an entire month (Num. 28:14); the day of the month is indicated by the preposition *lᵉ*. A child who is *ben-ḥoḏeš* is one month old (Lev. 27:6). It is used to indicate the time when a wild donkey is in heat, literally, in her month (heat) (Jer. 2:24). It is used with specific names of months, such as the month of Abib (Ex. 13:4; 23:15; 34:18; Neh. 2:1; Zech. 7:1). From month to month is indicated by *min* (4480) + *ḥōḏeš* + *lᵉ* + *ḥōḏeš* (Esth. 3:7).

2321. חֹדֶשׁ ***ḥōḏeš:*** A proper noun designating Hodesh (1 Chr. 8:9).

2322. חֲדָשָׁה ***ḥ^a^dāšāh:*** A proper noun designating Hadashah (Josh. 15:37).

2323. חֲדַת ***ḥ^a^daṯ:*** An Aramaic adjective meaning new. In Ezra 6:4, it refers to a new timber (KJV, NKJV), but other translators prefer to read *ḥaḏ* here and translate as one (course, layer) of timber (NIV, NASB).

2324. חֲוָה ***ḥ^a^wāh:*** An Aramaic verb meaning to explain, to interpret. It means to declare or put forth the interpretation of a dream or written message (Dan. 2:4, 6, 7, 9–11, 16; 5:7) or to publicize or make known something, (Dan. 4:2[3:32]). Daniel 5:12 indicates that the word was used to describe the declaration or interpretation of a variety of things.

2325. חוּב ***ḥûḇ:*** A verb meaning to endanger, to bring into danger; to forfeit one's head. It means to make guilty before someone and, hence, endanger one's standing (Dan. 1:10).

2326. חוֹב ***ḥôḇ:*** A masculine noun indicating a debtor, a debt, a loan. It indicates a debt, debtor, or a loan when a pledge (*ḥ^a^ḇōlāh*) is returned as an act of a righteous man (Ezek. 18:7).

2327. חוֹבָה ***ḥôḇāh:*** A proper noun designating Hobah (Gen. 14:15).

2328. חוּג ***ḥûg:*** A verb meaning to encircle. It means to inscribe or build into or on a circle (Job 26:10), possibly as a boundary line of the earth.

2329. חוּג ***ḥûg:*** A masculine noun indicating a circle, a vault, the horizon (circular). Figuratively, it refers to the "roof" or vault of the heavens which the Lord walks on or sits on (Job 22:14; Isa. 40:22); the horizon or circular edge of the deep (*ḥûg 'al-p^e^nēy t^e^hôm*) (Prov. 8:27) that God established at the time He created the earth.

2330. חוּד ***ḥûḏ:*** A verb meaning to put forth a riddle. It means to express a problem or a puzzle in words, to present it. It is, however, used with the noun "riddle" (Judg. 14:12, 13, 16; Ezek. 17:2) each time as its object.

2331. חָוָה ***ḥāwāh:*** A verb meaning to announce, to tell, to explain; to reveal, to display. It indicates the knowledge the heavens put forth in their movements and appearance (Ps. 19:2[3]). But also the wisdom and knowledge a person puts forth in speech (Job 15:17; 32:6, 10, 17; 36:2), whether old or young.

2332. חַוָּה ***ḥawwāh:*** A proper noun designating Eve. The name of the first woman created by the Lord God. Adam gave her the name Eve, meaning "living, making alive" (Gen. 3:20). She was the wife of Adam (Gen. 4:1). In Genesis 2:23, she was designated as a woman (*'iššāh* [802]), a female being apart from the male being, Adam, both sharing common humanity. As her name indicates, she then gave birth to the human race (Gen. 4:1–2).

2333. חַוָּה ***ḥawwāh:*** A feminine noun referring to a village, a town. It refers to various villages that were taken by Jair, son of Manasseh (Num. 32:41; Josh. 13:30; 1 Kgs. 4:13; 1 Chr. 2:23) in Gilead.

2334. חַוֹּת יָאִיר *ḥawwôṯ yā'iyr:* A proper noun designating Havvoth Jair (Num. 32:41; Deut. 3:14; Judg. 10:4; 1 Chr. 2:23).

2335. חוֹזָי *ḥôzay:* A masculine proper noun for the Hozai, a professional title for a group of seers or prophets (2 Chr. 33:19). Some simply translate it as seers (KJV).

2336. חוֹחַ *ḥôaḥ:* A masculine noun referring to briars, thistles, thorns, hooks. It refers to a thorn (Prov. 26:9; Isa. 34:13) which was despised compared to a lily (Song 2:2). It indicates a thornbush in the parable of King Jehoash (2 Kgs. 14:9; 2 Chr. 25:18). It depicts thickets where persons could hide (1 Sam. 13:6). Most likely, it is best rendered as briars in some contexts (Job 31:40). It depicts a hook (thorn?) that could not penetrate Leviathan's jaw (Job 41:2[40:26]).

2337. חֲוָחִים *ḥ^{a}wāḥiym:* A masculine plural noun denoting thickets. It refers to an area heavily covered by thornbushes or similar shrubs and small trees. It could serve as a place of hiding from one's enemies (1 Sam. 13:6).

2338. חוּט *ḥûṭ:* An Aramaic verb indicating to repair, to join together. It refers to work done on the foundations of Jerusalem by the returned exiles (Ezra 4:12).

2339. חוּט *ḥûṭ:* A masculine noun referring to a thread, a cord, a ribbon, string. It was a light, fine, string-like material placed together. It can mean an insignificant piece of material of little worth (Gen. 14:23). It was used of larger and broader pieces of material of various colors (Josh. 2:18; Song 4:3) or strong cords or ropes (Judg. 16:12; Eccl. 4:12). It was used in a proper size and form as a measuring line (1 Kgs. 7:15; Jer. 52:21).

2340. חִוִּי *ḥiwwiy:* A proper noun designating Hivite, the gentilic name of a group of people descended from Canaan (Gen. 10:17; 36:2). Hamor, father of Shechem, was a Hivite. A people that inhabited Canaan (Ex. 3:8; 23:28), along with various other peoples. They evidently lived mostly in Lebanon (Judg. 3:3, 5). They worked for Solomon as builders (1 Kgs. 9:20). They are sometimes confused with the Horites (cf. Gen. 36:2, 20–30).

2341. חֲוִילָה *ḥ^{a}wiylāh:* A proper noun designating Havilah (Gen. 2:11; 10:7, 29; 25:18; 1 Sam. 15:7; 1 Chr. 1:9, 23).

2342. חוּל *ḥûl*, חִיל *ḥiyl:* A verb meaning to whirl, to shake, to fear, to dance, to writhe, to grieve. This word has many different meanings, most of which derive from two basic ideas: to whirl in motion and to writhe in pain. The first of these ideas may be seen in the shaking of the earth (Ps. 29:8);

the stirring of the waters (Ps. 77:16[17]); or the trembling of the mountains (Hab. 3:10). At times, this word is used in a context of shaking with fear (Deut. 2:25; Jer. 5:22); worshiping in trembling awe (1 Chr. 16:30; Ps. 96:9); or anxiously waiting (Gen. 8:10; Ps. 37:7). It is also used to describe dancing women (Judg. 21:21, 23). The second idea of writhing in pain can be either physical, as when Saul was wounded in battle (1 Sam. 31:3), or emotional, as when Jeremiah grieved in anguish over Jerusalem's refusal to grieve (Jer. 4:19). This word is often used to describe the labor pains of giving birth (Ps. 29:9; Isa. 26:17, 18; 51:2) but can also imply God's creating work (Deut. 32:18; Job 15:7; Ps. 90:2; Prov. 8:24, 25).

2343. חוּל ***ḥûl:*** A proper noun designating Hul (Gen. 10:23; 1 Chr. 1:17).

2344. חוֹל ***ḥôl:*** A masculine noun designating sand, mud. It is used to refer to the sand along the seashore as an example of the innumerable descendants that will belong to Abraham (Gen. 22:17; 32:12[13]) or as simply the major element of the seashore (Ex. 2:12). In the time of Solomon, Israel and Judah were said to have numbered as many as the grains of sand along the seashore (1 Kgs. 4:20). It is used regularly in this figurative sense to indicate great quantities: corn (Gen. 41:49); length of days (Job 29:18); of Solomon's wisdom (1 Kgs. 4:29[5:9]).

2345. חוּם ***ḥûm:*** An adjective meaning brown, black, dark-colored. The color indicated may be something between black and white. But translators render the word in various ways (Gen. 30:32, 33, 40, NASB, black; NIV, dark-colored; KJV, NKJV, brown).

2346. חוֹמָה ***ḥômāh:*** A feminine noun denoting a wall. It is used of the wall of a city (Lev. 25:29; 2 Kgs. 3:27). It indicates walls placed around parts of a city or temple (Deut. 28:52; Ezek. 40:5; 42:20). Nehemiah rebuilt the walls of Jerusalem (Neh. 4:1[3:33]). It is found in figurative uses where a bronze wall (Jer. 1:18) or a wall of water (Ex. 14:22, 29) is indicated. It is used as a metaphor for a beloved woman (Song 8:9) and as a symbol for Israel (Amos 7:7) as a slanted wall because of her unrighteousness. High walls around cities were signs of strong defenses (Deut. 3:5). The famous wall of Babylon became a symbol of her power (Jer. 51:58). The Lord Himself says He will be a wall of fire around Jerusalem for its protection (Zech. 2:5[9]). The wealth of a rich man is said to be his (high) wall in his mind (Prov. 18:11). To be without a wall is a sign of vulnerability (Prov. 25:28).

2347. חוּס ***ḥûs:*** A verb meaning to show pity or mercy. It is used in the sense that the subject of the verb is not to be concerned or worried about himself or herself, i.e., do not pity yourself (Gen. 45:20). It is used of pitying an object or other person (Deut. 19:21; Ezek. 16:5; Jon. 4:10,

11). The righteous person was to have pity or compassion on the poor (Ps. 72:13). It extends to sparing a person's life, even an enemy if he were the anointed of the Lord (1 Sam. 24:10[11]). The Lord is said to show no pity to His people (Jer. 13:14).

2348. חוֹף ***ḥôp̱:*** A masculine noun referring to a coast, shore, haven. It indicates a seashore (Gen. 49:13; Deut. 1:7; Josh. 9:1; Judg. 5:17; Ezek. 25:16); a harbor, port, or haven for ships (Gen. 49:13b).

2349. חוּפָם ***ḥûp̱ām:*** A proper noun designating Hupham (Num. 26:39).

2350. חוּפָמִי ***ḥûp̱amiy:*** A proper noun designating Huphamites (Num. 26:39).

2351. חוּץ ***ḥûṣ:*** A masculine noun meaning a street, the outside. It indicates a location or direction: to the outside (Judg. 19:25); in a phrase, it can modify a noun, e.g., outer gate (Ezek. 47:2). It takes on the meaning of street, lane. Used with a following word in a construct phrase, it identifies a particular street, e.g., bakers' street (*ḥûṣ hā'ōp̱îym*; Jer. 37:21). It indicates direction to the outside: from the wall outward (Num. 35:4); outside, in the street (1 Kgs. 6:6). Prepositions are added to indicate direction (*b*^{e}, *l*^{e}, *'el*, *min* (4480)) (Gen. 9:22; 2 Kgs. 4:3; Ezek. 41:9; 42:7). The phrase *ḥûṣ min*, which literally means outside from me, is rendered as more than I (Eccl. 2:25).

2352. חֻר ***ḥur:*** A masculine noun indicating a hole or pit. It is used of a hole in the ground where a cobra or asp lives (Isa. 11:8) but takes on the meaning of a large hole or possibly a cave where Israelites hide in a time of oppression and judgment (Isa. 42:22).

2353. חוּר ***ḥûr:*** A masculine noun meaning white. It is used of linen hangings in the Persian king's garden (Esth. 1:6) and of the royal robes of honor in blue and white placed on Mordecai (Esth. 8:15).

2354. חוּר ***ḥûr:*** A proper noun designating Hur:

A.Companion of Aaron (Ex. 17:10, 12; 24:14).

B. A Judaite (Ex. 31:2; 35:30; 38:22; 1 Chr. 2:19, 20, 50; 4:1, 4; 2 Chr. 1:5).

C. A Midianite king (Num. 31:8; Josh. 13:21).

D. Officer of Solomon (1 Kgs. 4:8).

E. The father of Rephaiah (Neh. 3:9).

2355. חוֹרָי ***ḥôrāy:*** A masculine noun referring to white cloth. It is used of the woven white cloth produced in Egypt, a luxurious item of international trade (Isa. 19:9).

2356. חוֹר ***ḥôr,*** חֹר ***ḥōr:*** A masculine noun designating a cave or hole. It is used of a hole in a door, in a stone wall, or in the top of a chest (2 Kgs. 12:9[10]; Song 5:4; Ezek. 8:7), created by drilling or boring. It would designate holes or short caves, as hiding places for persons in danger (1 Sam.

14:11); or for the outcasts of society (Job 30:6). It describes the lodging places of lions, and it means lairs or dens (Nah. 2:12[13]).

2357. חָוַר *ḥāwar:* A verb meaning to be pale, to become pale, to turn white. It refers to persons turning pallid or whitish because of shame or calamity (Isa. 29:22).

2358. חִוָּר *ḥiwwār:* An Aramaic adjective indicating someting is colored white. It indicates a color white like (k^e) snow as the garments of the Ancient of Days (Dan. 7:9).

2359. חוּרִי *ḥûriy:* A proper noun designating Huri (1 Chr. 5:14).

2360. חוּרַי *ḥûray:* A proper noun designating Hurai (1 Chr. 11:32).

2361. חוּרָם *ḥûrām:* A proper noun designating Hiram (Huram):

A. A king of Tyre (979–945 B.C.) with whom Solomon and also David had close ties and economic and political dealings. Hiram supplied logs and skilled workers to help build Solomon's Temple (2 Chr. 2:1–16). Hiram (Huram, a variant) also gave Solomon cities, ships, and crewmen (2 Chr. 8:18). He, with Solomon, imported gold from Ophir (9:10, 21).

B. The chief architect and skilled craftsman that Hiram sent to work for Solomon to help build the Temple (2 Chr. 2:13[12]; 4:11, 16).

C. The name of a Benjamite, a son of Bela and ancestor of Saul (1 Chr. 8:5).

2362. חַוְרָן *ḥawrān:* A proper noun designating Hauran (Ezek. 47:16, 18).

2363. חוּשׁ *ḥûš:* I. A verb meaning to hasten. Its basic sense is to hurry or do something quickly: to carry out an ambush quickly (Judg. 20:37); to hurry to a place of safety (Ps. 55:8[9]). It takes on the sense of disturbed, agitated, or unstable (1 Sam. 20:38; Job 20:2; 31:5; Isa. 28:16; Hab. 1:8).

II. A verb meaning to enjoy; to be anxious, to disturb, to dismay. Some translators see this word indicating Job's disquiet in himself (20:2) and in Isaiah 28:16. In a different context, it takes on the meaning to enjoy (Eccl. 2:25).

2364. חוּשָׁה *ḥûšāh:* A proper noun designating Hushah (1 Chr. 4:4).

2365. חוּשַׁי *ḥûšay:* A proper noun designating Hushai:

A. A faithful friend dedicated to helping and protecting King David (2 Sam. 15:32–37). He successfully confounded Ahithophel, David's deceitful earlier counselor. He was termed the "king's friend" (1 Chr. 27:33). His son was on Solomon's administrative staff (1 Kgs. 4:16). But see B below.

B. Possibly a different person than A. He had a son who served under Solomon, Baanah (1 Kgs. 4:16).

2366. חֻשִׁים *ḥušiym,* חוּשִׁים *ḥûšiym:* A proper noun designating Hushim:

A. The wife of Shaharaim (1 Chr. 8:8, 11).
B. Son of Dan (Gen. 46:23).
C. Son of Aher (1 Chr. 7:12).

2367. חֻשָׁם ḥušām, חוּשָׁם ḥûšām: A proper noun designating Husham (Gen. 36:34, 35; 1 Chr. 1:45, 46).

2368. חוֹתָם חֹתָם ḥôṯām, ḥōṯām: A masculine noun referring to a seal, a signet ring. It was usually made of baked clay, metal, or stones and was used to identify someone. It served much like an ancient identity card (Gen. 38:18) by bearing a person's distinctive mark. It also refers to a metal or other type of mold containing a person's seal that was then impressed on clay (Job 38:14) or another substance. A jeweler engraved the markings of a seal or signet ring (Ex. 28:11). It indicated a ring bearing a seal to be imposed on clay. It was a precious and intimate possession of its owner (Jer. 22:24); hence, a signet ring could be used figuratively of a person closely connected to someone (Hag. 2:23).

2369. חוֹתָם ḥôṯām: A proper noun designating Hotham:
A. An Aroerite (1 Chr. 11:44).
B. An Asherite (1 Chr. 7:32).

2370. חֲזָה ḥ^a^zāh, חֲזָא ḥ^a^zā': An Aramaic verb meaning to see, to behold, to witness, to observe. This word appears only in the books of Ezra and Daniel. It signifies the literal sense of sight (Dan. 5:23); the observation of something with the eye (Dan. 3:25; 5:5); the witnessing of a king's dishonor (Ezra 4:14); beholding something in a dream (Dan. 2:41; 4:20[17]); and having a dream (Dan. 7:1). On one occasion, the verb is used to imply the usual condition or customary state of the furnace set to receive Shadrach, Meshach, and Abednego (Dan. 3:19). This use probably stresses the difference in the appearance of the furnace, which would be obvious to the observer.

2371. חֲזָהאֵל ḥ^a^zāh'ēl: A proper noun designating Hazael, a king of Aram (Syria) (ca. 841–797? B.C.). He was a benefit to Israel in his early years. Elijah anointed him, and he helped eradicate Baalism (worship of Baal) (1 Kgs. 19:15–18). He may have killed Ben-Hadad. He succeeded him as king at any rate. Elisha prophesied of the terror and devastation Hazael and Aram would bring on Israel (2 Kgs. 8:7–15). He fought against Israel (2 Kgs. 8:28–29) successfully, but his victories were given because of the Lord's anger toward of His corrupt people (2 Kgs. 10:32; 13:3). Joash of Judah bribed him to cease his attack on Jerusalem (2 Kgs. 12:17[18], 18[19]). His son, Ben Hadad II, succeeded him (2 Kgs. 13:25). Amos announced God's judgment on Hazael and his house (1:4).

2372. חָזָה ḥāzāh: A verb meaning to see, to perceive. This term is more poetic than the common *rā'āh* (7200). It refers to seeing God (Ex. 24:11; Job 19:26, 27; Ps. 11:7; 17:15); astrological observations (Isa. 47:13);

prophetic vision and insight (Isa. 1:1; Lam. 2:14; Ezek. 12:27; Hab. 1:1; Zech. 10:2).

2373. חָזֶה ***ḥāzeh:*** A masculine noun referring to a breast, brisket. It is a technical priestly and sacrificial term denoting the breast or portion of the breast of a sacrificial animal. It was used as a wave offering and in the installation of the priests (Ex. 29:26, 27; Lev. 8:29); in the offering of peace or well-being (Lev. 7:30; 9:20, 21); as part of Hazabite or Nazirite offering (Num. 6:20). It was required of Aaron and his sons (Lev. 7:31, 34; 10:14, 15; Num. 18:18).

2374. חֹזֶה ***ḥōzeh,*** חֹזֶה ***chōzeh:*** A masculine noun meaning a seer, a prophet. It is used only seventeen times in the Old Testament, always in the present active participle. The word means one who sees or perceives; it is used in parallel with the participle of the verb that means literally to see, to perceive. In Isaiah a rebellious people sought to curb the functions of these seers (Isa. 30:10). In 1 Samuel 9:9, the author parenthetically states that the word for prophet in his day, *nāḇiy'* (5030), was formerly called a seer. However, for seer, he did not use *ḥôzeh* but a present participle of the verb *rā'āh* (7200), meaning to see, to perceive. It appears that the participles of *ḥôzeh* and of *rā'āh* function synonymously. But, terminology aside, a seer functioned the same as a prophet, who was moved by God and had divinely given insight. This Hebrew word is also used in parallel with the word prophet (2 Kgs. 17:13; Amos 7:12, 14); hence, its meaning overlaps with that term as well (cf. 2 Chr. 33:18; Isa. 29:10). Seers sometimes served a specific person: Gad served as King David's seer and did not hesitate to declare the words the Lord gave him for the king (2 Sam. 24:11). David had more than one seer (cf. 1 Chr. 25:5; 2 Chr. 29:25).

The functions of a seer as indicated by this term included, besides receiving and reporting the word of the Lord, writing about David's reign (1 Chr. 29:29); receiving and writing down visions (2 Chr. 9:29); writing genealogical records under Rehoboam's reign (2 Chr. 12:15). In general, the Lord forewarned His people through His prophets and seers (2 Kgs. 17:13; 2 Chr. 33:18). In many cases, these warnings were recorded in writing (2 Chr. 33:19).

2375. חֲזוֹ ***ḥ^{a}zô:*** A proper noun designating Hazo (Gen. 22:22).

2376. חֵזוּ ***ḥēzû:*** An Aramaic masculine noun meaning a vision, a revelation. This word appears exclusively in the book of Daniel and draws attention to the nature of revelation. It denotes the nighttime dreams of Nebuchadnezzar (Dan. 2:19, 28; 4:5[2], 13[10]) and Daniel (Dan. 7:2, 7, 13) that have prophetic significance. There appears to be some connection with the ominous or troubling nature of these revelations (Dan. 7:15; cf. 2:1). Once the word pertains to the outward appearance of an object in the vision of the fourth beast (Dan. 7:20).

2377. חָזוֹן ***ḥāzôn:*** A masculine noun meaning a revelation by means of a vision, an oracle, a divine communication. The primary essence of this word is not so much the vision or dream itself as the message conveyed. It signifies the direct, specific communication between God and people through the prophetic office (1 Sam. 3:1; 1 Chr. 17:15; Ps. 89:19[20]) or the collection of such messages (2 Chr. 32:32; Isa. 1:1; Obad. 1:1; Nah. 1:1; Hab. 2:2, 3). Also, the word is used of the messages of false prophets (Jer. 14:14; 23:16); a guiding communication from the Lord, often restricted when a people are under judgment (Lam. 2:9; Ezek. 7:26; Mic. 3:6); and the revelation of future events on a grand scale (Dan. 9:24; 10:14). People who disregard this divine communication face certain doom (Prov. 29:18).

2378. חָזוֹת ***ḥāzôṯ:*** A feminine noun meaning a vision, a revelation. This particular word is used only once in the description of a book of prophetic writings called the visions of Iddo (2 Chr. 9:29). See the related Hebrew verb *ḥāzāh* (2372).

2379. חֲזוֹת ***ḥ^azôṯ:*** An Aramaic feminine noun indicating sight, visibility. It refers to something that can be seen and is visible. In Nebuchadnezzar's dream, he saw a tree visible from anywhere on earth (Dan. 4:11[8], 20[17]).

2380. חָזוּת ***ḥāzûṯ:*** A feminine noun meaning a vision, a striking appearance. A difficult vision appeared to Isaiah (Isa. 21:2); and another vision seemed to the Israelites to be words on a scroll (Isa. 29:11). Daniel saw in his vision a goat with a visible (large) horn (Dan. 8:5). This word can also mean commitment or agreement, as in Isaiah's oracle against Ephraim (Isa. 28:18). See the related Hebrew root *ḥāzāh* (2372).

2381. חֲזִיאֵל ***ḥ^aziy'ēl:*** A proper noun designating Haziel (1 Chr. 23:9).

2382. חֲזָיָה ***ḥ^azāyāh:*** A proper noun designating Hazaiah (Neh. 11:5).

2383. חֶזְיוֹן ***ḥezyôn:*** A proper noun designating Hezion (1 Kgs. 15:18).

2384. חִזָּיוֹן ***ḥizzāyôn:*** A masculine noun meaning a dream, a vision, a revelation. The primary stress of this word lies on the means and manner of divine revelation. It is used in reference to revelations that come in the night (2 Sam. 7:17; Job 4:13; 33:15); visions imparted (Zech. 13:4); and dreams in a general sense (Job 7:14; 20:8). Metaphorically, Jerusalem is called the "valley of vision," alluding to the city as the center of prophetic activity (Isa. 22:1, 5; cf. Luke 13:33).

2385. חָזִיז ***hᵃziyz:*** A masculine noun indicating lightning, a thunderbolt; a strong, sudden wind. The Lord makes the *hᵃziyz*, the storm clouds (NASB), thunderbolt, or strong wind of a storm (Zech. 10:1), so it indicates a major feature of storms or heavy rain. It seems to refer to the lightning or thunder of a storm (Job 28:26; 38:25).

2386. חֲזִיר ***hᵃziyr:*** A masculine noun referring to a pig, a hog, a wild boar. It is among the unclean animals Israel could not eat (Lev. 11:7; Deut. 14:8; cf. Isa. 65:4; 66:17). Its blood was an abomination as an offering (Isa. 66:3). It is used metaphorically to refer to Israel's enemy that devours her (Ps. 80:13[14]). A ring in its snout is totally out of place (Prov. 11:22).

2387. חֵזִיר ***hēziyr:*** A proper noun designating Hezir:

A. A priest (1 Chr. 24:15).

B. A covenanter (Neh. 10:20[21]).

2388. חָזַק ***ḥāzaq:*** A verb meaning to be strong, to strengthen, to be courageous, to overpower. This verb is widely used to express the strength of various phenomena, such as the severity of famine (2 Kgs. 25:3; Jer. 52:6); the strength of humans to overpower each other: the condition of Pharaoh's heart (Ex. 7:13); David and Goliath (1 Sam. 17:50); Amnon and Tamar (2 Sam. 13:14); a battle situation (2 Chr. 8:3); Samson's strength for his last superhuman performance (Judg. 16:28). This word occurs in the commonly known charge, "Be strong and of good courage!" (Josh. 1:9). Moses urges Joshua (Deut. 31:6, 7) to be strong. The Lord also bids Joshua to be strong in taking the Promised Land (Deut. 31:23; Josh. 1:6, 7, 9), after which Joshua encourages the people in the same way (Josh. 10:25).

2389. חָזָק ***ḥāzāq:*** A masculine adjective meaning firmness, strength. The feminine form of this word is *hᵃzāqāh*. It can refer to human strength or power (Num. 13:18; Josh. 14:11); to human persistence or stubbornness (Ezek. 2:4; 3:8, 9); or to divine strength or power (Ex. 3:19; Isa. 40:10). In addition, it can refer to the strength of things, but it must be translated to fit the context: a *loud* trumpet blast (Ex. 19:16); a *sore* war (1 Sam. 14:52); the *hottest* battle (2 Sam. 11:15); a *sore* sickness (1 Kgs. 17:17); a *severe* famine (1 Kgs. 18:2); a *strong* wind (Ex. 10:19). This adjective can also be used as a substantive for a strong or mighty person (Job 5:15; Isa. 40:10; Ezek. 34:16).

2390. חָזֵק ***ḥāzēq:*** An adjective meaning stronger. This word is used only twice in Scripture. In Exodus 19:19, it described the trumpet blast on Mount Sinai as the Lord's presence descended around Moses. In 2 Samuel 3:1, it described the strength of David's house over the house of Saul.

2391. חֵזֶק ***ḥēzeq:*** A masculine noun meaning strength. This particular word is used only once in the Old

Testament, where God is the strength of the psalmist (Ps. 18:1[2]). See the related Hebrew root *ḥāzaq* (2388) and the feminine form of this noun, *ḥezqāh* (2393).

2392. חֹזֶק *ḥōzeq:* A masculine noun meaning strength. This word is used to describe the Lord's strength in delivering Israel out of Egyptian bondage (Ex. 13:3, 14, 16). It is also used to describe the military strength of Israel (Amos 6:13) and of other kingdoms (Hag. 2:22). Although this particular word is used only five times in the Old Testament, its related verb, *ḥāzaq* (2388), meaning to be strong, and its related adjective, *ḥāzāq* (2389), meaning strong, are used many times.

2393. חֶזְקָה *ḥezqāh:* A feminine noun meaning strength, force. This word refers to the hand of the Lord on Isaiah as the Lord spoke to him (Isa. 8:11). It is also used to describe the power of kings. When Rehoboam became strong and established his kingdom, he and his people abandoned the Law of the Lord (2 Chr. 12:1). When King Uzziah became strong, he became proud and went into the Temple to burn incense, even though that was the job of the priests (2 Chr. 26:16). In Daniel's vision, the fourth king gained power through his great wealth (Dan. 11:2). See the related Hebrew root *ḥāzaq* (2388) and the masculine form of this noun *ḥēzeq* (2391).

2394. חָזְקָה *ḥozqāh:* A feminine noun meaning strength, force. It always occurs with the preposition b^e (with or by). It can be used to modify oppression (Judg. 4:3); rebuke (Judg. 8:1); capture (1 Sam. 2:16); ruling (Ezek. 34:4); crying to God (Jon. 3:8). Only the last of these references has a positive connotation. All the others connote a harsh, cruel, and self-serving connotation of the use of one's strength and power.

2395. חִזְקִי *ḥizqiy:* A proper noun designating Hizki, Hezeki (1 Chr. 8:17).

2396. חִזְקִיָּה *ḥizqiyyāh,* חִזְקִיָּהוּ *ḥizqiyyāhû:* A proper noun designating Hezekiah:

A. The son of Ahaz who succeeded him as king in Judah (715–686 B.C.). His name means "the Lord is my strength." He began to reign at twenty-five years of age and reigned twenty-nine years. He served the Lord faithfully and was considered possibly the greatest king to rule over Judah alone (2 Kgs. 18:5); he wholly trusted the Lord. He carried out major religious reforms in his day and purified the Temple and the worship of Yahweh (2 Chr. 29:3–27), reestablishing the Passover (2 Chr. 30:26). With the help of the Lord and the prophet Isaiah, he stood against the king of Assyria (2 Kgs. 18:17—20:21). The Lord permitted him to live fifteen more years because of his trust in the Lord and total devotion to Him (2 Kgs. 20:23). At the end of his reign, he acted unwisely and arrogantly by allowing ambassadors from Babylon to examine the riches of the Temple and Jerusalem (2 Kgs. 20:12–21).

During his life, he was active in preserving Israel's written wisdom (Prov. 25:1). Micah prophesied during his reign (Jer. 26:18, 19; Hos. 1:1).

B. The name of a son of Neariah who was of the royal line of David. Most read this as Hizkiah (e.g., NASB) (1 Chr. 3:23).

C. The father of Amariah who was the son of Gedaliah. He was an ancestor of Zephaniah (Zeph. 1:1).

D. The head or father of a clan that returned from the Babylonian exile (cf. Ezra 2:16). He, with others, sealed the covenant of Nehemiah (Neh. 10:17[18]) to wholly follow the Lord. The name Ater is his Akkadian name (Neh. 7:21).

2397. חָח *ḥāḥ*: A masculine noun denoting a bracelet or brooch; a hook. It was used ironically as a hook to lead away prisoners of war (2 Kgs. 19:28; Ezek. 19:4, 9). But normally it indicates gold jewelry and was among the sources of gold for the Tabernacle (Ex. 35:22). In a figurative sense, it refers to God's sovereign activity as He leads away the king of Assyria (Isa. 37:29); Egypt (Ezek. 29:4); or Gog (Ezek. 38:4).

2398. חֵטְאָה *ḥeṭ'āh*, חָטָא *ḥāṭā'*: A verb meaning to miss the mark, to wrong, to sin, to lead into sin, to purify from sin, to free from sin. Four main Hebrew words express the idea of sin in the Hebrew Bible, with this word used most often. Its central meaning is to miss the mark or fail. It is used in a nonmoral or nonreligious sense to indicate the simple idea of missing or failing in any task or endeavor. In Judges 20:16, it indicated the idea of a slinger missing his target. The verb also indicated the situation that arose when something was missing (Job 5:24); or it described a failure to reach a certain goal or age (Prov. 19:2; Isa. 65:20). These are minor uses of the verb. The word is used the most to describe human failure and sin. It indicates failure to do what is expected; the one who fails to find God in this life destroys himself (Prov. 8:36). Many times the word indicates being at fault (Gen. 20:9; Ex. 10:16; 2 Kgs. 18:14; Neh. 6:13) as Pharaoh was toward Moses or to be guilty or responsible (Gen. 43:9; 44:32). It regularly means to sin; Pharaoh sinned against God (Ex. 10:16). People can also sin against other human beings (Gen. 42:22; 1 Sam. 19:4, 5) or against their own souls (Prov. 20:2). The verb is used to indicate sin with no object given, as when Pharaoh admitted flatly that he had sinned (Ex. 9:27; Judg. 10:15) or when Israel was described as a "sinful nation" (Isa. 1:4). Sometimes the writer used the noun from this same verbal root as the object of the verb for emphasis, such as in Exodus 32:30, 31, where Moses asserted that Israel had sinned a great sin (Lev. 4:3; Num. 12:11). Sinning, unfortunately, is a universal experience, for there is no one who does not sin (Eccl.

7:20). Persons may sin with various parts of their bodies or in certain ways or attitudes. They may sin with their tongues or lips (Job 2:10; Ps. 39:1[2]). Persons may sin innocently or in such a way as to bring guilt on others (Lev. 4:2, 3; Num. 15:27).

Three other stems of this verb are used less often. The intensive stem is used to indicate people bearing their own material losses or failures (Gen. 31:39); one freeing oneself from sin or purifying an object or person (Lev. 8:15; Ps. 51:7[9]); and one bringing a sin offering (Lev. 6:26[19]; 2 Chr. 29:24). The causative stem, besides indicating failure to miss a literal target, means to lead into sin, to lead astray. Jeroboam was an infamous king who caused all Israel to walk in sin (1 Kgs. 14:16; 15:26). The reflexive stem communicates the idea of freeing oneself from sin. The Levites purified themselves (i.e., set themselves apart from sin) so they could work at the sanctuary (Num. 8:21).

2399. חֵטְא ***ḥēṭ***^{e}***':*** A masculine noun meaning sin, an offense, a fault. The word suggests the accumulated shortcomings that lead to punishment (Gen. 41:9); errors or offenses that cause the wrath of a supervisor (Eccl. 10:4); and the charge against an individual for his or her actions contrary to the Law (Lev. 24:15; Num. 9:13; Deut. 15:9; 23:21[22]). Isaiah uses the word to reinforce the tremendous sinfulness of Judah in contrast to the Messiah's redemptive suffering (Isa. 53:12).

2400. חַטָּא ***ḥaṭṭā':*** A masculine noun meaning sinners and an adjective meaning sinful. This word comes from the common verb *ḥāṭā'* (2398), meaning to sin, and is related to the common noun *ḥaṭṭā'ṯ* (2403), meaning sin or sin offering. As a noun, it is used to describe those who, by their actions, are under the wrath and judgment of God (Ps. 1:5) and face ultimate destruction (Gen. 13:13; Ps. 104:35; Isa. 1:28). The influence of these people is to be avoided (Ps. 1:1; 26:9; Prov. 1:10), but they are to be instructed in the way of righteousness (Ps. 25:8; 51:13[15]). As an adjective, it describes the sinful people the tribes of Reuben and Gad were raising (Num. 32:14).

2401. חֲטָאָה ***ḥ***^{a}***ṭā'āh:*** A feminine noun meaning sin, a sacrifice for sin. The word generally stands as a synonym for transgression (Ps. 32:1). It is used to convey the evil committed by Abimelech in taking Sarah into his harem (Gen. 20:9); the wickedness of idolatry committed by the Israelites at Sinai (Ex. 32:21, 30, 31); and the perversion foisted on the Northern Kingdom by Jeroboam (2 Kgs. 17:21). Conversely, the psalmist uses the Hebrew word once to mean a sin offering (Ps. 40:6[7]).

2402. חַטָּאָה ***ḥaṭṭā'āh:*** A feminine noun meaning sin. This word is used only twice in the Old Testament and is equivalent to the Hebrew word *ḥaṭṭā'ṯ* (2403), meaning sin. It is used in Exodus 34:7 to speak of what God, in the greatness of His lovingkindness, will forgive. It is also used in Isaiah 5:18 to describe God's woe against those who sin greatly.

2403. חַטָּאת ***ḥaṭṭā'ṯ:*** A feminine noun meaning sin, transgression, sin offering, punishment. The word denotes youthful indiscretions (Ps. 25:7); evil committed against another (Gen. 50:17); trespasses against God (2 Chr. 33:19; Ps. 51:2[4]; Amos 5:12); a general state of sinfulness (Isa. 6:7); and the specific occasion of sin, particularly in reference to idolatry (Deut. 9:21; Hos. 10:8). It also implies an antidote to sin, including purification from ceremonial impurity (Num. 19:9, 17); the sacrificial offering for sin (Ex. 29:14; Lev. 4:3); and the punishment for sin (Lam. 4:6; Zech. 14:19). In the story of Cain and Abel, sin appears as a creature, ready to pounce, lurking "at the door" of Cain's heart (Gen. 4:7).

2404. חָטַב ***ḥāṭaḇ:*** A verb meaning to chop, to cut down. It is used to indicate the cutting of firewood (Deut. 19:5; 29:11[10]; Josh. 9:21, 23, 27; Jer. 46:22; Ezek. 39:10) or timber for construction purposes (2 Chr. 2:10[9]). It takes on the nuance of forming or chiseling corner pillars (of stone) (Ps. 144:12).

2405. חֲטֻבוֹת ***ḥᵃṭuḇôṯ:*** A feminine plural noun indicating something colored; colored embroidered fabric. It most likely refers to the famous colored linens produced in Egypt (Prov. 7:16) and considered a luxury item.

2406. חִטָּה ***ḥiṭṭāh:*** A feminine noun denoting wheat. A major food product of the land of Canaan without which Israel would not survive (Joel 1:11). It refers to grain in several stages: the wheat plant (Ex. 9:32); wheat grain and plant (Deut. 8:8); the ears or stalks beaten out (Judg. 6:11); the grain threshed, beaten out (1 Kgs. 5:11[25]). It is used in the plural following *qᵉṣîyr,* harvest, to refer to a wheat harvest (lit., harvest of wheat) (Gen. 30:14; Ex. 34:22; Judg. 15:1). Following *sōleṯ,* the phrase means fine wheat flour (Ex. 29:2).

2407. חַטּוּשׁ ***ḥaṭṭûš:*** A proper noun designating Hattush:

A. Son of Shemiah (1 Chr. 3:22).

B. A descendant of David (Ezra 8:2).

C. Son of Hashabiah (Neh. 3:10).

D. A Jew (Neh. 10:4[5]).

E. A priest (Neh. 12:2).

2408. חֲטָי ***ḥᵃṭāy:*** An Aramaic noun meaning sin. This word is used only once in the Old Testament and is equivalent to the Hebrew word *ḥaṭṭā'ṯ* (2403), meaning sin or sin offering. Daniel advised King Nebuchadnezzar to turn from his sins (Dan. 4:27[24]).

2409. חַטָּיָא ***ḥaṭṭāyā':*** A feminine noun meaning an offering for sin. This Aramaic word appears only in Ezra 6:17, where it indicates the particular sacrifice made at the dedication of the rebuilt Temple, following the return from exile. The text states that the "sin offering" consisted of twelve rams for the sins of the twelve tribes of Israel.

2410. חֲטִיטָא ḥ^{a}tiyṭā': A proper noun designating Hatita (Ezra 2:42; Neh. 7:45).

2411. חַטִּיל ḥaṭṭiyl: A proper noun designating Hattil (Ezra 2:57; Neh. 7:59).

2412. חֲטִיפָא ḥaṭiypā': A proper noun designating Hattil (Ezra 2:54; Neh. 7:56).

2413. חָטַם ḥāṭam: A verb that means to keep something back, to keep it from happening. In particular it refers to God's restraining His wrath from Israel (Isa. 48:9). Its usage in this verse parallels the word *'āraḵ*, to extend, to stretch out, to prolong.

2414. חָטַף ḥāṭap: A verb that describes seizing upon or catching a person in a physical sense (Judg. 21:21). It is used in a more figurative sense of entrapping, catching poor, weak, helpless persons (Ps. 10:9). In the immediate context, it refers to entrapping or seizing such people for oppressive purposes (Ps. 10:9).

2415. חֹטֶר ḥōṭer: A masculine noun indicating a rod or branch. In Proverbs 14:3, it describes a rod used for discipline. In Isaiah 11:1, it is nuanced by the context to mean a fresh shoot or fresh twig. It stands in parallelism with *nēṣer,* branch in this verse (Branch = Messiah, Anointed King).

2416. חַי ḥay, חַיָּה ḥayyāh: A feminine noun meaning a living thing, an animal, a beast, a living thing. The basic meaning is living things, but its most common translation is animals or beasts. The word refers to all kinds of animals and beasts of the field or earth (Gen. 1:24, 25; 1 Sam. 17:46) and sometimes stands in parallel with birds of the air (Ezek. 29:5). The nations, such as Egypt, were referred to metaphorically as beasts (Ps. 68:30[31]). Beasts were categorized in various ways: beasts of burden (Isa. 46:1); land animals (Gen. 1:28; 8:19); cattle (Num. 35:3); sea creatures (Ps. 104:25); clean, edible creatures (Lev. 11:47; 14:4); unclean, nonedible creatures (Lev. 5:2); large and small creatures (Ps. 104:25).

Two further categories of animals are noted: wild animals or animals of prey and animal or beastlike beings. God made the wild animals of the field. Sometimes the Lord used wild beasts as instruments of His judgments (Ezek. 14:15; 33:27), but on other occasions He protected His people from ravenous beasts (Gen. 37:20; Lev. 26:6). At any rate, vicious beasts will not inhabit the land of the Lord's restored people (Isa. 35:9). The bizarre living beings mentioned in Ezekiel 1:5, 13, 22; 3:13 were like birds and animals but were composite beings. They could not be described adequately by human language, for they also had the forms of humans, each with faces of a man, lion, ox, and eagle. However, they did not resemble flesh and blood in their appearance (Ezek. 1:13) and were tied to the movement of the Spirit (Ezek. 1:20).

2417. חַי *ḥay:* An Aramaic adjective meaning living, alive. In the book of Daniel, it is used of people (Dan. 2:30; 4:17[14]); and King Darius used this word in his description of God (Dan. 6:20[21], 26[27]).

2418. חֲיָה *ḥayāh*, חֲיָא *ḥayā':* An Aramaic verb meaning to live. The main usage of this word is the polite address for the king to live forever. The astrologers used this verb to address Nebuchadnezzar when they asked him to tell them his dream (Dan. 2:4) and again when they informed him that certain Jews were not bowing down to his golden image (Dan. 3:9). The queen used the verb to advise Belshazzar that Daniel could interpret the handwriting on the wall (Dan. 5:10). The king's advisors also used these words when they tricked King Darius into making a decree to worship only the king (Dan. 6:6[7]). Daniel also used this phrase when he explained to Darius that God saved him from the lions (Dan. 6:21[22]).

2419. חִיאֵל *ḥiy'ēl:* A proper noun designating Hiel (1 Kgs. 16:34).

2420. חִידָה *ḥiyḏāh:* A feminine noun possibly meaning enigma. The Greek root of this English term is used in various contexts by the Septuagint (the Greek translation of the Hebrew Old Testament) to translate the Hebrew word. Nearly half of this noun's occurrences refer to Samson's "riddle" when he tested the wits of the Philistines at his wedding feast (Judg. 14:12–19). The term is connected with several different words from the wisdom tradition, most notably the word frequently translated "proverb" (Ps. 78:2; Prov. 1:6; cf. 2 Chr. 9:1). The term is also associated with the prophetic tradition, where it was contrasted with clear speaking and compared with communication through more obscure means (Num. 12:8; Ezek. 17:2). Daniel prophesied of a future destructive king whose abilities include "understanding enigmas." A somewhat similar Aramaic expression is used of Daniel himself earlier in the book (cf. Dan. 5:12; 8:23).

2421. חָיָה *ḥāyāh:* A verb meaning to be alive, to live, to keep alive. This verb is used numerous times in Scripture. It is used in the sense of flourishing (Deut. 8:1; 1 Sam. 10:24; Ps. 22:26[27]); or to convey that an object is safe (Gen. 12:13; Num. 14:38; Josh. 6:17). It connotes reviving in Ezekiel 37:5 and 1 Kings 17:22 or healing in Joshua 5:8 and 2 Kings 8:8. Genesis often uses the word when people are kept alive in danger (Gen. 6:19, 20; 19:19; 47:25; 50:20). Also, the word is used in the genealogies of Genesis (Gen. 5:3–30; 11:11–26). Psalm 119 employs this word to say that God's Word preserves life (Ps. 119:25, 37, 40, 88). Many verses instruct hearers to obey a command (either God's or a king's) in order to live (Gen. 20:7; Prov. 4:4; Jer. 27:12).

2422. חָיֶה ḥāyeh: An adjective meaning strong, vigorous. It is found only in Exodus 1:19, where the Egyptian midwives explained to Pharaoh that the Hebrew women were so vigorous in childbirth that they delivered before the midwives arrived.

2423. חֵיוָה ḥēywāh: An Aramaic feminine noun referring to a beast, an animal. It refers in general to all beasts of the field or earth (Dan. 2:38). In Nebuchadnezzar's dream in a singular collective form, it refers to beasts of the field living under the protection of the great tree (Dan. 4:12[9], 14–16[11–13]). The hearts of beasts are differentiated from the hearts of humans (Dan. 5:21). The word is used to refer to the four beasts of Daniel's dream (7:3, 5–7, 11, 12, 17, 19, 23).

2424. חַיּוּת ḥayyûṯ: A feminine abstract noun meaning lifetime. This word occurs only in 2 Samuel 20:3, where it states that David provided for the ten concubines who were left to watch the palace in Jerusalem (2 Sam. 15:16) and were later violated by David's son, Absalom (2 Sam. 16:21, 22). Although David kept them and provided for their needs, he did not lie with them; consequently, they were like widows during the lifetime of their husband.

2425. חָיַי ḥāyay: A verb meaning to live. This verb is often used in reference to the length of a person's life (Gen 5:5; 11:12, 14; 25:7). Genesis 3:22 employs this word to describe eternal life represented by the tree of life. It is used in reference to life which is a result of seeing God (Ex. 33:20; Deut. 5:24[21]) or looking at the bronze serpent (Num. 21:8, 9). It is also used to refer to living by the Law (Lev. 18:5; Ezek. 20:11, 13, 21). Cities of refuge were established to which people could flee and live (Deut. 4:42; 19:4, 5). This verb is identical in form and meaning to the verb *ḥāyāh* (2421).

2426. חֵיל ḥēyl, חֵל ḥēl: A masculine noun meaning entrenchment, fortress, army, defense, fortified wall. The wall of Jezreel was the location where the dogs would gnaw on Jezebel's dead body (1 Kgs. 21:23). The psalmist prayed for peace within the walls of Jerusalem (Ps. 122:7). The Lord decided to tear down the wall around Israel (Lam. 2:8). A surrounding river was the defense of Thebes (Nah. 3:8). See the related noun *ḥayil* (2428).

2427. חִיל ḥiyl, חִילָה ḥiylāh: I. A masculine noun referring to fear, pain, anguish. It indicates an internal sense of fear among the nations stirred up by Israel's victory at the Red Sea (Ex. 15:14) or other great acts of God (Ps. 48:6[7]). It indicates the fear the enemies of Israel created in them (Jer. 6:24; Mic. 4:9).

II. A feminine noun indicating pain. It is used of Job's relentless agony as he wrestles with the physical and emotional torment of his plight (Job 6:10).

2428. חַיִל **ḥayil:** A masculine noun meaning strength, wealth, army. This word has the basic idea of strength and influence. It can be used to speak of the strength of people (1 Sam. 2:4; 9:1; 2 Sam. 22:40); of horses (Ps. 33:17); or of nations (Esth. 1:3). God is often seen as the supplier of this strength (2 Sam. 22:33; Hab. 3:19). When describing men, it can speak of those who are strong for war (Deut. 3:18; 2 Kgs. 24:16; Jer. 48:14); able to judge (Ex. 18:21, 25); or are righteous in behavior (1 Kgs. 1:52). When describing women, it speaks of virtuous character (Ruth 3:11; Prov. 12:4; 31:10). This idea of strength often is used to imply a financial influence (i.e., wealth) (Job 31:25; Ps. 49:6[7]; Zech. 14:14); a military influence (i.e., an army) (Ex. 14:9; 2 Chr. 14:8[7], 9[8]; Isa. 43:17); or a numerical influence (i.e., a great company) (1 Kgs. 10:2; 2 Chr. 9:1).

2429. חַיִל **ḥayil:** An Aramaic masculine noun meaning strength, power, army. In the book of Ezra, Rehum and Shimshai forced the Jews to stop rebuilding the city (Ezra 4:23). It can mean a loud or powerful voice, such as Nebuchadnezzar's herald (Dan. 3:4); a messenger from heaven (Dan. 4:14[11]); and King Belshazzar to his enchanters (Dan. 5:7). Nebuchadnezzar had the most powerful soldiers bind up Shadrach, Meshach, and Abednego (Dan. 3:20). See the related Hebrew noun *ḥayil* (2428).

2430. חֵילָה **ḥēylāh:** A feminine noun indicating a rampart, a bulwark. It indicates embankments of earth normally topped off with a defensive wall or steep banks. The defenses of the city of Zion (Ps. 48:13[14]) were pictured as exceptionally effective and impressive.

2431. חֵילָם **ḥēylām:** A proper noun designating Helam (2 Sam. 10:16, 17).

2432. חִילֵן **ḥiylēn:** A proper noun designating Hilen (1 Chr. 6:58[43]).

2433. חִין **ḥiyn:** A masculine noun depicting beauty, grace. It indicates literally the grace (*ḥiyn*) or beauty of the form (*'ereḵ*) of Leviathan (Job 41:12[4]).

2434. חַיִץ **ḥayiṣ:** A masculine noun indicating a thin, flimsy wall. It is used in a context that indicates an unstable or weak wall that will easily fall under stress (Ezek. 13:10).

2435. חִיצוֹן **ḥiyṣôn:** An adjective meaning outer, external. It describes an outer entry of the temple used by the king (2 Kgs. 16:18); to the outer court area of a palace (Esth. 6:4); or of Ezekiel's temple (Ezek. 10:5; 46:20). It refers to the external part of a wall or part of a house (Ezek. 41:17) or sanctuary (1 Kgs. 6:29, 30). It is used in general to refer to anything outside, such as work on the outside of Ezra and Nehemiah's Temple (Neh. 11:16).

2436. חֵיק ḥēyq, חֵק ḥēq: I. A masculine noun referring to bosom. It indicates the upper part of a person's body where objects and persons of love are embraced (1 Kgs. 3:20) or clasped with hands or arms: one's wife or concubine (Gen. 16:5; Deut. 28:54); one's husband, literally the man of her bosom (*h*[e]*yqāh*) (Deut. 28:56). The Lord carries His people, His flock in His bosom (Isa. 40:11). The person, animal, or object that is held in one's bosom is cherished greatly. An adulteress is not allowed into this sacred arena of personal relationship (Prov. 5:20). What is attached to one's bosom affects a person deeply (Prov. 6:27). Fools permit anger to lie in their bosoms (Eccl. 7:9). The Lord repays the sins of the fathers into the bosoms of their children (Jer. 32:18). Those who are untrustworthy should not be trusted even if they are our cherished friends or companions (Mic. 7:5). In a more literal sense, the word refers to a fold in a garment just above the belt where one's hand can be held (Ex. 4:6, 7).

II. A masculine noun meaning hollow, bottom, channel, border. It is used to indicate the hollow or bottom of a chariot (1 Kgs. 22:35); and a channel or trough running around an altar (Ezek. 43:13, 14, 17).

2437. חִירָה ḥiyrāh: A proper noun designating Hirah (Gen. 38:1, 2).

2438. חִירוֹם ḥiyrôm, חִירָם ḥiyrām: A proper noun designating Hiram:

A. The king of Tyre who befriended David and recognized him as a national power (2 Sam. 5:11). He sent both supplies and skilled workers to help him prepare to build his palace. This helpful and peaceful relationship continued under Solomon (1 Kgs. 5:1[15], 2[16]). The same person as discussed in entry 2361,A.

B. The same as Huram in entry 2361,B (1 Kgs. 7:13, 40, 45).

2439. חִישׁ ḥiyš: A verb meaning to act quickly, to make haste, to hurry. Its sense seems to be for God to hasten (or not remain distant) to the psalmist who is in need (Ps. 71:12). Some understand this as an adverb.

2440. חִישׁ ḥiyš: An adverb indicating soon, quickly. It indicates the haste with which fleeting days are gone (Ps. 90:10).

2441. חֵךְ ḥēḵ: A masculine noun indicating a palate, a mouth. It refers to the roof or upper palate of one's mouth (Ps. 137:6), used extensively to form sounds and words. Its failure to function makes one mute (Ezek. 3:26). It indicates the sensation of the sweet taste of honey (Ps. 119:103); or figuratively of the pleasant, sweet taste of love (Song 2:3; 5:16). The palate senses the taste of food (Job 12:11). It is used figuratively of one's ability to discern calamities (Job 6:30). It is used to mean speech, the place where speech is formed (Prov. 5:3; 8:7). In a case of extreme thirst, one's tongue sticks to a person's palate (Lam. 4:4).

2442. חָכָה *ḥāḵāh:* A verb indicating to wait, to tarry. It indicates delaying an action (2 Kgs. 7:9; 9:3; Job 32:4). It refers to longing or hoping for something to happen (Job 3:21), such as death or, in a good sense, for the Lord to act (Ps. 33:20; Isa. 8:17; Hab. 2:3; Zeph. 3:8); or to resurrect (Dan. 12:12). But it means to wait in order to accomplish one's purpose, good or bad (Hos. 6:9).

2443. חַכָּה *ḥakkāh:* A feminine noun denoting a fishhook, a hook. It is a curved or bent piece of metal or wood used to catch and hold or to control something or someone: Leviathan (Job 41:1[40:25]); fish (Isa. 19:8; NASB, line); prisoners of war (Hab. 1:15).

2444. חֲכִילָה *ḥ^a^ḵiylāh:* A proper noun designating Hachilah, Hakilah (1 Sam. 23:19; 26:1, 3).

2445. חַכִּים *ḥakkiym:* An Aramaic adjective meaning wise. It is used in the singular with a definite article to denote a wise man (Dan. 2:21); in the plural to refer to a group of Babylonian wise men (Dan. 2:12–14); 4:6[3], 18[15]; 5:7, 8, 15).

2446. חֲכַלְיָה *ḥ^a^ḵalyāh:* A proper noun designating Hachaliah, Hacaliah (Neh. 1:1; 10:1[2]).

2447. חַכְלִילִי *ḥaḵliyliy:* An adjective meaning dull, dark. It refers to Judah's eyes as dull, dark from drinking wine (Gen. 49:12). Perhaps the phrase should be rendered darker than wind (*ḥaḵliyliy . . . miyyāyin*), but others prefer to read sparkling.

2448. חַכְלִילוּת *ḥaḵliylûṯ:* A feminine abstract noun indicating redness, darkness. It depicts the redness or darkness of the person's eyes who had drunk too much wine (Prov. 23:29).

2449. חָכַם *ḥāḵam:* A verb meaning to be wise, to act according to wisdom, to make wise decisions, to manifest wisdom. This word is used to convey the act of instructing which if received brings wisdom (Job 35:11; Ps. 105:22); the wise activity that derives from such instruction (Prov. 6:6; 8:33); the way of conduct contrary to that of the wicked (Prov. 23:19); the wisdom manifested in the animal kingdom (Prov. 30:24). In the reflexive sense, the verb implies the tangible manifestation of wisdom (Eccl. 2:19); the exaggerated perception of one's own wisdom (Eccl. 7:16); and the cunning activities of the deceiver (Ex. 1:10). The psalmist declares that the Lord delights in dispensing wisdom to the simpleminded (Ps. 19:7[8]).

2450. חָכָם *ḥāḵām:* An adjective meaning wise. This word is used to describe one who is skilled or experienced. It was used in the physical arena to describe those men who were skilled as builders (Ex. 31:6; 36:1, 2); as craftsmen of all sorts (1 Chr. 22:15); as precious metal workers (2 Chr.

2:7[6]); those women who could spin fabrics (Ex. 35:25). This word was used in the social arena to express those who were the leaders of the day (Jer. 51:57); who could interpret dreams (Gen. 41:8; Ex. 7:11); who were able to rule (Deut. 1:13, 15); who knew the law (Esth. 1:13); who were counselors (Esth. 6:13; Jer. 18:18). In the personal arena, this word denoted skill in living, which was embodied in Solomon like no other before or since (1 Kgs. 3:12). The wise person is the one who learns (Prov. 1:5; 9:9; 13:1); who heeds a rebuke (Prov. 9:8; 15:31); and who speaks properly (Prov. 14:3; 15:2; 16:23). See the verb *ḥāḵam* (2449), meaning to be wise, and the noun *ḥoḵmāh* (2451), meaning wisdom.

2451. חָכְמָה ***ḥoḵmāh:*** A feminine noun meaning wisdom, skill, experience, shrewdness. This is one of the wisdom words that cluster in Proverbs, Ecclesiastes, Job, and other wisdom literature scattered throughout the Old Testament. The high point of this word and its concept is reached in Proverbs 8:1, 11, 12. In Proverbs 8:22–31, wisdom is personified. It is God's gracious creation and is thus inherent in the created order. God alone knows where wisdom dwells and where it originates (Job 28:12, 20); no other living being possesses this knowledge about wisdom (see Job 28:21). For humans, the beginning of wisdom and the supreme wisdom is to properly fear and reverence God (Job 28:28; Prov. 1:7; cf. Prov. 8:13); God is the master, creator, and giver of wisdom (see Job 28:27; Prov. 8:22, 23). He employed wisdom as His master craftsman to create all things (Ps. 104:24; Jer. 10:12). Rulers govern wisely by means of wisdom provided by God (1 Kgs. 3:28; cf. Prov. 8:15, 16). Wisdom keeps company with all the other virtues: prudence, knowledge, and discretion (Prov. 8:12). The portrayal of wisdom in Proverbs 8:22–24 lies behind Paul's magnificent picture of Christ in Colossians 1:15, 16, for all the treasures of wisdom are lodged in Christ (cf. Col. 2:3).

Wisdom, ordained and created by God, manifests itself in many ways in the created universe. It is expressed as a technical capability (Ex. 28:3; 31:3, 6; 1 Kgs. 7:14). It becomes evident in experience and prudence as evidenced in a wise woman (2 Sam. 20:22) who fears the Lord (see Prov. 31:30) or in a wise king (1 Kgs. 2:6). Wisdom in general, and worldly wisdom in particular, was universal to humankind created in the image of God; Babylonians, men of the East, Egyptians, and Edomites could obtain it or be found with it (Isa. 47:10; Jer. 49:7). Wrongly used, however, for self-adulation or self-aggrandizement, this wisdom could be deadly. For unbelievers, wisdom led to piety, holiness, and devotion to the Lord and His will. The psalmist asked God to give him a wise heart (Ps. 90:12). God imparted wisdom to His people by His Spirit (Ex. 31:3), but His Anointed One, the Messiah, the Branch, would have His Spirit rest upon Him, the Spirit of wisdom (Isa. 11:2), in abundance. Wisdom is also personified as a woman who seeks whoever will come and listen to her, thus receiving a blessing (Prov. 1:20; 2:2; 3:13, 19). Wisdom ends its presentation in Proverbs 8 with the striking assertion that all who hate wisdom love death.

2452. חָכְמָה *ḥoḵmāh:* An Aramaic feminine noun meaning wisdom. This word is used only nine times in the Old Testament and is equivalent to the Hebrew word *ḥoḵmāh* (2451), meaning wisdom. In these few instances, this word is used to speak of God's wisdom (Ezra 7:25; Dan. 2:20). It is God who gives this wisdom (Dan. 2:21, 23, 30) that was recognized by Belshazzar and the queen mother (Dan. 5:10, 11, 14).

2453. חַכְמוֹנִי *ḥaḵmôniy:* I. Hachmoni, father of Jehiel (1 Chr. 27:32).

II. Hachmonite, the nationality of one of David's mighty men (1 Chr. 11:11). See *taḥkᵉmōniy* (8461).

2454. חָכְמוֹת *ḥoḵmôṯ:* A feminine noun meaning wisdom or that which is wise. Found exclusively in the wisdom literature of the Old Testament, this word is a form of the Hebrew word *ḥoḵmāh* (2451). It denotes a wise woman (Prov. 14:1); the feminine personification of wisdom (Prov. 1:20; 9:1); and the wisdom that exceeds a fool's understanding (Prov. 24:7); or wisdom that reveals deep understanding (Ps. 49:3[4]).

2455. חֹל *ḥōl:* A masculine noun meaning profane or common. This word comes from the verb *ḥālal* (2490), meaning to pollute or to profane and is always used in opposition to *qōḏeš* (6944), meaning sacred or set apart. The priests were to make a distinction between the sacred and the common (Lev. 10:10). David discussed with the priest the difference between the common bread and the set–apart bread (1 Sam. 21:4[5], 5[6]). The priests would teach the difference between the sacred and the common (Ezek. 44:23)—a distinction the priests of Ezekiel's day failed to teach (Ezek. 22:26). The Temple, described by Ezekiel, had a wall separating the sacred and the common (Ezek. 42:20); there was to be a clear distinction between the land holy to the Lord and the common land (Ezek. 48:15).

2456. חָלָא *ḥālā':* A verb meaning to be sick, to be diseased. It refers to the illness that King Asa contracted in his feet during his reign (2 Chr. 16:12), crippling him.

2457. חֶלְאָה *ḥel'āh:* A feminine noun referring to rust, scum. It is used figuratively to refer to the moral and religious corruption and rebellion of Jerusalem, which the Lord would consume by fire and heat (Ezek. 24:6, 11, 12).

2458. חֶלְאָה *ḥel'āh:* A proper noun designating Helah (1 Chr. 4:5, 7).

2459. חֵלֶב *ḥēleḇ:* A masculine noun referring to fat, the best. It refers to the covering of the interior of the body, of a person's belly, of a person's face (Ex. 29:13; Judg. 3:22; Job 15:27). It indicates the best or fatty portions of an offering (Gen. 4:4; Lev. 4:26) which were pleasing to the Lord. Fat was God's portion of an offering (1 Sam. 2:15, 16). It was not to be eaten by people (Lev. 3:17; 7:23–25). The "fat of the land" refers to the best part of the land (Gen. 45:18) and also indicates the products of the land: oil, wine, corn (Num. 18:12, 29, 30, 32). But a heart grown fat symbolizes a heart that has become insensitive to God (Ps. 17:10; 119:70).

2460. חֵלֶב ***ḥēleḇ:*** A proper noun designating Heleb (2 Sam. 23:29).

2461. חָלָב ***ḥālāḇ:*** A masculine noun denoting milk, cheese. It is best known from the phrase describing Canaan as a land "flowing with milk and honey" (Ex. 3:8, 17; 13:5; Num. 13:27; Deut. 6:3; Josh. 5:6; Ezek. 20:6, 15). The hills will flow with milk in the time of God's blessings (Joel 3:18 [4:18]). Milk was a major part of the diet of Israel and her surrounding neighbors. It was served with wine as a special treat (Song 5:1; Isa. 55:1) and pictured the Lord's other blessings as well. Its whiteness served as a ready comparison (Lam. 4:7). It is found three times in the command not to boil a kid in its mother's milk (Ex. 23:19; 34:26; Deut. 14:21). The phrase *ṭelē' ḥalāḇ* refers to a sucking lamb (1 Sam. 7:9).

2462. חֶלְבָּה ***ḥelbāh:*** A proper noun designating Helbah (Judg. 1:31).

2463. חֶלְבּוֹן ***ḥelbôn:*** A proper noun designating Helbon (Ezek. 27:18).

2464. חֶלְבְּנָה ***ḥelbināh:*** A feminine noun referring to a kind of gum, galbanum. It is an unpleasant-smelling resin used in the preparation of Israel's incense (Ex. 30:34).

2465. חֶלֶד ***ḥeleḏ:*** A masculine noun meaning age, duration of life, the world. The primary sense of the word is a duration or span of time. It signifies the world, that is, this present existence (Ps. 17:14; 49:1[2]); life itself (Job 11:17); and the span of a person's life (Ps. 39:5[6]).

2466. חֶלֶד ***ḥeleḏ:*** A proper noun designating Heled (1 Chr 11:30).

2467. חֹלֶד ***ḥōleḏ:*** A masculine noun referring to a small animal, a weasel or a mole. These animals were declared unclean for Israel (Lev. 11:29).

2468. חֻלְדָּה ***ḥuldāh:*** A proper noun designating Huldah, a prophetess, the wife of Shallum, who prophesied during the reign of Josiah. She spoke a word of grace concerning the king of Judah, Josiah (2 Kgs. 22:18). Hilkiah and others sought her out and then reported her message to Josiah. She read the Book of the Law they brought to her and called forth the judgments written in it (2 Kgs. 22:14–20).

2469. חֶלְדַּי **ḥelday:** A proper noun designating Heldai:

A. One of David's mighty men (1 Chr. 27:15).

B. A Jew (Zech. 6:10, 14).

2470. חָלָה **ḥālāh,** נַחֲלָה **naḥ^a^lāh:** I. A verb indicating to be weak, sick, to be a patient. It is used to mean becoming weak or sick (Gen. 48:1; 1 Kgs. 14:1, 5; 2 Kgs. 1:2). It indicates becoming diseased in some body part (1 Kgs. 15:23). Used with *lāmûwt*, it means "sick unto death (dying)" (2 Kgs. 20:1). It takes on some nuanced meanings according to its context: to be lovesick (Song 2:5); *rā'āh ḥōlāh* meaning a great evil, a sickening evil (Eccl. 5:13[12]); to feel pain, regret, to feel sorry for (*ḥōleh . . . 'al,* 1 Sam. 22:8).

II. A feminine noun denoting disease. It describes a sickness or disease brought upon Damascus when God judged her (Isa. 17:11).

III. A verb meaning to appease, to entreat, to appeal to. It refers to a specific attempt to get the Lord to relent from judgment (Ex. 32:11; Dan. 9:13). It is used to ask for the favor of the Lord in general (Jer. 26:19; Zech. 8:21, 22) or for a specific purpose or policy (1 Sam. 13:12). It describes the nations' entreaty to the Lord for His favor (Ps. 45:12[13]). It is used to entreat the favor of persons also (Job 11:19; Prov. 19:6).

2471. חַלָּה **ḥallāh:** A feminine noun indicating a cake, a wafer, a ring-shaped bread. It refers to bread used in offerings, leavened (2 Sam. 6:19) or unleavened (Ex. 29:2; Lev. 8:26). It refers to the twelve cakes in the Holy Place made of fine wheat flour (Lev. 24:5).

2472. חֲלוֹם **ḥ^a^lôm:** A masculine noun referring to a dream. It refers to the sensations or images passing through one's mind during sleep, usually during the night (Gen. 20:3; 31:11, 24; 1 Kgs. 3:5; Job 7:14; Isa. 29:7). The Lord often caused dreams. The verb is often found with the noun (Gen. 37:5, 6). The phrase *ba'al ḥ^a^lômôṯ* means "a lord of dreams," "dreamer," or one who could interpret dreams (Gen. 37:19). Dreams were often prophetic (Gen. 37:9; 40:5; Num. 12:6; Dan. 2:1–3). The Lord will cause old men to dream dreams in the latter days (Joel 2:28[3:1]). God could give a person an understanding of dreams (Dan. 1:17). False prophets could generate dreams out of their own minds (Deut. 13:1[2], 3[4], 5[6]; Jer. 23:27; 27:9; 29:8; Zech. 10:2).

2473. חלֹן **ḥōlôn:** A proper noun designating Holon:

A. A city in Moab (Jer. 48:21).

B. A city in Judah (Josh. 15:51; 21:15).

2474. חַלּוֹן **ḥallôn:** A common noun indicating a window, an opening. It was usually a hole in the wall created for light and air (Gen. 8:6; 1 Kgs.

6:4). The window of the ark could be opened (Gen. 8:6). There were latticed windows (1 Kgs. 6:4; Ezek. 40:16); palace windows (Jer. 22:14); gate windows (Ezek. 40:16, 22, 25); temple windows (Ezek. 41:16) which were evidently covered.

2475. חֲלוֹף ***ḥ^a lôp̱:*** A masculine noun indicating destitution, unfortunate, destruction. It refers to persons in society who are unfortunate and need others to affirm and uphold their rights for them (Prov. 31:8).

2476. חֲלוּשָׁה ***ḥ^a lûšāh:*** A feminine noun referring to a defect, a weakness. It refers to the state or condition of one who has been defeated (Ex. 32:18), of one who cries out because of defeat in battle.

2477. חֲלַח ***ḥ^a laḥ:*** A proper noun designating Halah (2 Kgs. 17:6; 18:11; 1 Chr. 5:26).

2478. חַלְחוּל ***ḥalḥûl:*** A proper noun designating Halhul (Josh. 15:58).

2479. חַלְחָלָה ***ḥalḥālāh:*** A feminine noun denoting pain, anguish, trembling. It indicates a response of great distress and shaking toward God's imminent destruction of Babylon (Isa. 21:3); of Egypt (Ezek. 30:4, 9). It describes the anguish of the inhabitants of Nineveh which was about to fall (Nah. 2:10[11]).

2480. חָלַט ***ḥālaṭ:*** A verb meaning to catch, to pick up; to take as valid. It indicates an attitude and response toward something said (1 Kgs. 20:33), a catching of the significance of something.

2481. חֲלִי ***ḥ^a liy:*** A masculine noun denoting a jewel, an ornament. A piece of jewelry made of fine gold that was delightful to the eye (Prov. 25:12) and beautifully crafted (Song 7:1[2]).

2482. חֲלִי ***ḥ^a liy:*** A proper noun designating Hali (Josh. 19:25).

2483. חֳלִי ***ḥ^o liy:*** A masculine noun indicating disease, sickness. It denotes some kind of illness (1 Kgs. 17:17; 2 Kgs. 1:2, a serious illness). It is modified to indicate an illness that is strong or hangs on (Deut. 28:59). It is used of suffering brought on by the loss of one's wealth (Eccl. 6:2), "an evil disease." It is used figuratively of the ever-present evil of Jerusalem (Isa. 1:5; Jer. 6:7) that could not be healed by seeking out foreign powers for healing (Hos. 5:13). Idolatry was an especially heinous sickness of Israel before the exile (Jer. 10:19).

2484. חֶלְיָה ***ḥelyāh:*** A feminine noun referring to jewelry, an ornament. Israel's spiritual harlotry is pictured as a time when she adorned herself with jewelry or ornaments to pursue her religious and political lovers (Hos. 2:13[15]) and corrupt herself through harlotry.

2485. חָלִיל ***ḥāliyl:*** A masculine noun denoting a flute or other wind instrument. It was used in performing laments (Jer. 48:36) or during a time of joy (1 Sam. 10:5; 1 Kgs. 1:40; Isa. 5:12). It was used to create and accompany times of gladness (Isa. 30:29).

2486. חָלִילָה ***ḥāliylāh:*** An adversative interjection of strong emotion, let it never be, far be it. It strongly indicates that something should not be the case. Used by itself, it negates something stated or asserted in the context (1 Sam. 14:45); with *min* (4480), it means far be it from . . . , indicating the person who should not do such and such a thing, as slaying righteous persons along with the wicked (Gen. 18:25). It is used with an infinitive to indicate what should not be done, e.g., rebellion, etc. (Josh. 22:29); it is used to indicate that because of the Lord, something should not be done (1 Sam. 24:6[7]; 26:11).

2487. חֲלִיפָה ***ḥ^{a}liypāh:*** A feminine noun referring to a changing, a change of clothes, to renew. It gives the idea of one thing following another, change upon change (1 Kgs. 5:14[28]; Job 10:17). It indicates a new state reached, a changing (Job 14:14). God, however, does not change in His faithfulness and righteousness, His essence (Ps. 55:19[20]). It was used to indicate changes of clothing (Gen. 45:22; Judg. 14:12, 13, 19; 2 Kgs. 5:5, 22, 23).

2488. חֲלִיצָה ***ḥ^{a}liyṣāh:*** A feminine noun referring to the clothing and/or personal effects stripped off a person who has been overcome (Judg. 14:19). In a militant setting, it is used to describe the weapons taken from or stripped off a soldier or armed man (2 Sam. 2:21).

2489. חֵלְכָה ***ḥēl^{e}ḵāh:*** An adjective meaning hapless, unfortunate. It indicates a person who is the object of a wicked person's hatred and evil plans (Ps. 10:8, 10). This same helpless or unfortunate person is the object of God's help (Ps. 10:14).

2490. חָלַל ***ḥālal:*** A verb meaning to pierce, to play the pipe, to profane. This word has three distinct meanings. The first meaning is to pierce or wound, either physically unto death (Isa. 53:5; Ezek. 32:26) or figuratively unto despair (Ps. 109:22). The second meaning of this word is to play the pipe, which is used only twice in the Old Testament (1 Kgs. 1:40; Ps. 87:7). The third meaning is to profane or to defile, which is used primarily of the ceremonial objects of worship (Ex. 20:25; Ezek 44:7; Dan. 11:31); of the Sabbath (Ex. 31:14; Neh. 13:17; Ezek. 23:38); of God's name (Lev. 18:21; Jer. 34:16); of God's priests (Lev. 21:4, 6). However, it also refers to sexual defilement (Gen. 49:4; Lev. 21:9); the breaking of a covenant (Ps. 89:31[32], 34[35]; Mal. 2:10); and making a vineyard common (Deut. 20:6; 28:30). In the causative form of this verb, it means to begin (Gen. 4:26; 2 Chr. 3:2).

2491. חָלָל ***ḥālāl:*** A masculine noun or adjective meaning slain, pierced, mortally wounded, profaned. This word denotes the carnage of battle; the dead, generally as a result of warfare (Gen. 34:27; Jer. 14:18; Ezek. 21:29[34]); and those having sustained some fatal injury (Judg. 9:40; 1 Sam. 17:52). Also, by extension, the word is used twice to indicate a state of defilement or perversion. In the first instance, it denotes a woman whose virginity has been violated or, as it were, pierced (Lev. 21:7, 14). The other applies to a wicked regent of Israel destined for punishment, emphasizing that he is already, in a prophetic sense, mortally wounded (Ezek. 21:25[30]).

2492. חָלַם ***ḥālam:*** I. A verb meaning to dream. It describes the process of a person producing images or receiving images in a sleeping state. The images may be produced by God (Gen. 28:12; 37:5, 6, 9, 10; 40:5; 41:5, 11); or they may be produced by the persons' minds themselves (Deut. 13:1[2], 3[4]), a feature of false prophecy (Jer. 23:25; 27:9). Dreams could be used as a contrast to reality (Ps. 126:1; Isa. 29:8). Dreams would be a feature of God's pouring out His Spirit on persons (Joel 2:28[3:1[).

II. A verb indicating to become strong, powerful. It refers to strength gained through the natural maturation process (Job 39:4) or to restoration to health after sickness (Isa. 38:16).

2493. חֵלֶם ***ḥelem:*** An Aramaic masculine noun denoting a dream. It refers to dreams sent by God to Nebuchadnezzar (Dan. 2:4–7, 9, 26; 4:5–9[2–6]) and to Daniel (Dan. 7:1). These dreams could be interpreted (Dan. 5:12).

2494. חֵלֶם ***ḥēlem:*** A proper noun designating Heldai (Zech. 6:14). It refers to the same person as *ḥelday* (2469,B).

2495. חַלָּמוּת ***ḥallāmûṯ:*** A feminine noun referring to an egg. It is used once, and the attention is on the tasteless white of an egg (Job 6:6).

2496. חַלָּמִישׁ ***ḥallāmiyš:*** A masculine noun indicating a rock, flint. It refers to a type of rock made of flint (Deut. 8:15) from which both oil and water came (Deut. 32:13; Ps. 114:8). It is mined by men (Job 28:9). It is used in a simile indicating hardness or fairness and resolve (Isa. 50:7).

2497. חֵלֹן ***ḥēlōn:*** A proper noun designating Helon (Num. 1:9; 2:7; 7:24, 29; 10:16).

2498. חָלַף ***ḥālap̱:*** I. A verb meaning to pass on, to change, to violate, to renew. It has the meaning of passing on, to go by something (1 ; or of God Himself passing by (Job 9:11; 11:10). It takes on the nuance of something passing away, being gone (Job 9:26; Ps. 102:26[27]; Song 2:11). It describes the changing of garments or clothes (Gen. 35:2) or wages (Gen. 31:7, 41).

II. A verb indicating to pierce, to strike through. It describes the act of striking a person's head or temple (Judg. 5:26) or of an arrow piercing a person (Job 20:24).

2499. חֲלַף ḥᵃlap̱: An Aramaic verb meaning to pass over or to pass by. It is used figuratively of a period or periods of time passing by. In Daniel it refers to "seven times" or periods of time (probably seven years) passing by during which Nebuchadnezzar was judged by the Lord (Dan. 4:16[13], 23[20], 25[22], 32[29]).

2500. חֵלֶף ḥēlep̱: A masculine noun meaning in exchange for, in return for. It is used of giving something in return for services (Num. 18:21), in particular the services of the sons of Levi.

2501. חֶלֶף ḥelep̱: A proper noun designating Heleph (Josh. 19:33).

2502. חָלַץ ḥālaṣ: A verb meaning to draw out, to prepare, to deliver, to equip for war. The primary meaning of the word is that of strengthening or fortifying (Isa. 58:11). It is used to convey the activity of drawing out, such as occurs in breast-feeding (Lam. 4:3); removing a shoe (Deut. 25:9, 10; Isa. 20:2); dispatching to another location (Lev. 14:40, 43); withdrawing from a crowd (Hos. 5:6); removing or delivering from danger (2 Sam. 22:20; Ps. 6:4[5]; 50:15). Significantly, this word conveys the notion of taking up arms for battle (Num. 31:3; 32:17) or preparing for a general state of military readiness (Josh. 4:13; 2 Chr. 17:18).

2503. חֵלֶץ ḥēleṣ, חֶלֶץ ḥeleṣ: A proper noun designating Helez:
A. One of David's mighty men (2 Sam. 23:26; 1 Chr. 11:27; 27:10).
B. A Judaite (1 Chr. 2:39).

2504. חֲלָצַיִם ḥᵃlāṣayim: A Hebrew root, a feminine noun. It is used only in the dual form. It refers to loins but often has a figurative sense. In general, it is used figuratively to represent the source of strength or human virility (1 Kgs. 8:19; 2 Chr. 6:9). It represents the masculine virtue of acting like a man, being stable, strong, determined (Job 38:3); to face a rebuke (Job 40:7). To loosen or take off one's girded belt is to waver, weaken, or show fear (Isa. 5:27). It can refer to one's waist where sackcloth was worn (Isa. 32:11). It refers to a belt or sash of righteousness in a figurative sense (Isa. 11:5). It refers to the lower stomach area that is full of pangs during childbirth (Jer. 30:6).

2505. חָלַק ḥālaq: A verb indicating to share, to divide. It indicates receiving or obtaining one's share of something (1 Sam. 30:24; Jer. 37:12). It means to allot something (Deut. 4:19; 29:26[25]), to give a share to someone. Of persons it means to divide up into sections or groups or even to scatter them (Gen. 49:7; 1 Chr. 23:6; 24:3); of objects it means to divide them up (Ezek. 5:1); or distribute them (2 Chr. 23:18). It takes on the nuance of to be a sharer or partner with (Prov. 29:24).

2506. חֵלֶק ***ḥēleq:*** A masculine noun indicating a portion, a territory. It indicates a portion, a share, a piece of territory in many ways: a part of booty or spoil (Gen. 14:24; Num. 31:36); of food (Lev. 6:17[10]); a tract or portion of land (Josh. 19:9; Hos. 5:7; Mic. 2:4); of Israel as a possession of the Lord (Deut. 32:9). It is used metaphorically of a person's doing his or her part in something (Job 32:17); of one's association or part or sharing in another group or way of life (Ps. 50:18; Isa. 57:6); or of the portion or share of fortune that the Lord gives to persons (Job 31:2). The portion or proper share for the wicked is punishment or calamity (Isa. 17:14).

2507. חֵלֶק ***ḥēleq:*** A proper noun designating Helek (Num. 26:30; Josh. 17:2).

2508. חֲלָק ***ḥ*^a^*lāq:*** An Aramaic masculine noun referring to portion, possession. It is used figuratively of ownership or political right or claim (Ezra 4:16). It takes on the meaning of sharing the nature and behavior of beasts of the field (Dan. 4:15[12], 23[20]).

2509. חָלָק ***ḥālāq:*** An adjective indicating smooth, flattering. It refers to smooth stones in a riverbed or ravine (Isa. 57:6) that possibly represent idolatrous objects. Used figuratively, the word depicts slippery or dangerous conditions of life (Ps. 73:18); or a mouth that spins things deceitfully (Ps. 26:28; Ezek. 12:24; Dan. 11:32) and falsely (Ps. 12:2[3]). An adulteress uses smooth and sweet-tasting speech (Prov. 5:3).

2510. חָלָק ***ḥālāq:*** A proper noun designating Halak (Josh. 11:17; 12:7).

2511. חַלָּק ***ḥallāq:*** A masculine noun indicating smoothness. Some translate this word as *ḥālāq* (2509) in Isaiah 57:6 but with essentially the same meaning and referring to smooth stones in a ravine or dry riverbed.

2512. חַלֻּק ***ḥalluq:*** An adjective indicating smooth. It describes the five stones that David picked up from a streambed to use against Goliath (1 Sam. 17:40) and put in his sling.

2513. חֶלְקָה ***ḥelqāh:*** I. A feminine noun denoting flattery, smoothness, a smooth part. It indicates an area of skin without hair (Gen. 27:16). It indicates the smooth or flattering lips of the treacherous (Ps. 12:2[3], 3[4]); of the adulterous (Prov. 6:24); or unstable circumstances (Ps. 73:18). False prophets spoke with deceitful and slippery words (Isa. 30:10).

II. A feminine noun denoting ground, portion. It is used to indicate a plot of ground (Gen. 33:19; Josh. 24:32; Ruth 4:3; Amos 4:7); of good, productive ground (2 Kgs. 3:19). It is used of an assigned portion of a field or plot (Deut. 33:21). It designates a particular location in the phrase *ḥelqaṯ haṣṣûrîy,* the field of swords (2 Sam. 2:16).

2514. חֲלַקָּה ***ḥ^alaqqāh:*** A feminine noun indicating flattery. It indicates deceitful, smooth words employed by a deceitful king (Dan. 11:32).

2515. חֲלֻקָּה ***ḥ^aluqqāh:*** A feminine noun designating a portion, a division. It designates a particular area or section of the Holy Place (2 Chr. 35:5).

2516. חֶלְקִי ***ḥelqiy:*** A proper noun designating Helekite (Num. 26:30).

2517. חֶלְקָי ***ḥelqāy:*** A proper noun designating Helkai (Neh. 12:15).

2518. חִלְקִיָּה ***ḥilqiyyāh,*** חִלְקִיָּהוּ ***ḥilqiyyāhû:*** A proper noun designating Hilkiah, a name born by several persons. It means "my share is the Lord (Yahweh)."

A. It refers to Hilkiah, the father of Eliakim, who was the administrator of Hezekiah's palace (2 Kgs. 18:18).

B. The name of a high priest. He was in charge of the resources collected to repair the Temple (2 Chr. 35:8). He discovered the Book of the Law while renovating and cleaning out the Temple (2 Kgs. 22:8; 23:4–7) and delivered it to Shaphan the scribe or secretary. He, with others, went to Huldah the prophetess (2 Kgs. 22:14). He was an ancestor of Ezra (Ezra 7:1).

C. A descendant of Merari who helped to direct the worship and music of the Temple (1 Chr. 6:45).

D. The son of Hosah, a Merarite, who served as a gatekeeper (1 Chr. 26:11).

E. The son of Meshul, a priest who stood by Ezra as he read the Law to the people at the Water Gate (Neh. 8:4). He became a new resident of Jerusalem to populate the city (Neh. 11:11; 12:1, 7, 21). He returned from exile with Zerubbabel.

F. The father of Gemariah. He with others took Jeremiah's letter to the exiles (Jer. 29:1–23).

2519. חֲלַקְלַקּוֹת ***ḥ^alaqlaqqôṯ:*** A feminine plural noun indicating slipperiness, flattery. It describes uncertain people on treacherous paths of false prophets (Jer. 23:12) and hated enemies (Ps. 35:6). In a political sense, it refers to seizing power by intrigue, flattery, and hypocrisy (Dan. 11:21, 34).

2520. חֶלְקַת ***ḥelqaṯ:*** A proper noun designating Helkath (Josh. 19:25; 21:31).

2521. חֶלְקַת הַצֻּרִים ***ḥelqaṯ haṣṣuriym:*** A proper noun designating Helkath Hazzurim (2 Sam. 2:16).

2522. חָלַשׁ ***ḥālaš:*** A verb meaning to lie prostrate, to cause one to lie prostrate. It means to weaken or overwhelm one's enemy in battle (Ex. 17:13). It takes on the sense of to disappear, lying prostrate, dead, or totally weakened (Job 14:10) when referring to an individual. The star of morning, the king of Babylon, was known as one who weakened, incapacitated the other nations of the world (Isa. 14:12).

2523. חַלָּשׁ ḥallāš: A masculine noun referring to one who is sick. It designates a person who is powerless, weak as opposed to a mighty (*gibbôr*) person (Joel 3:10[4:10]).

2524. חָם ḥām: A masculine noun denoting a father-in-law. It refers to a husband's father, father-in-law, such as Judah (Gen. 38:13, 25; 1 Sam. 4:19, 21).

2525. חָם ḥām: An adjective meaning hot, warm. It indicates that something is giving off a moderate amount of heat: bread that is still warm from being baked (Josh. 9:12); something that is warm because it has been heated, e.g., clothes from the hot sun and south wind (Job 37:17).

2526. חָם ḥām: A proper noun designating Ham:

A. The second son of Noah (Gen. 6:10). He entered the ark along with his brothers and all their wives (Gen. 7:13). He became the father of Canaan (Gen. 9:18). Ham committed some grave sin with respect to his father after the flood, euphemistically described as "seeing his father's nakedness" (Gen. 9:24). God cursed Ham's son Canaan because of his father's behavior, illustrating God's cursing of a first through a fourth generation (Ex. 34:6–7). Ham fathered many sons, including Canaan and Cush, who was the father of Nimrod (Gen. 10:8–10). Nimrod founded Babylon, Calneh, Assyria, and Nineveh (Gen. 10:11–20). One of his sons, Mizraim, is the name for Egypt (Gen. 10:6).

B. Ham also is closely allied with the Egyptians. In poetic lines, the word Ham parallels the words Egypt or Egyptians (Ps. 78:51; 105:23, 27; 106:22).

2527. חֹם ḥōm: A masculine noun denoting warmth, heat. It functions as a predicate adjective to indicate warm bread, fresh bread (1 Sam. 21:6[7]). It refers to the heat of the day, the hottest period of the day (Gen. 18:1) or specifically to the heat of the sun (1 Sam. 11:9). In a general sense, it indicates the heat of summer as opposed to the cold of winter (Gen. 8:22). It creates certain effects: it melts snow (Job 24:19) and can threaten plants (Jer. 17:8) or trees.

2528. חֱמָא ḥ^{e}mā': An Aramaic feminine noun indicating anger, rage. It indicates the angry response of a person who has been disobeyed, especially a king (Dan. 3:13, 19).

2529. חֶמְאָה ḥem'āh, חֵמָה ḥēmāh: A feminine noun referring to butter, curds. It refers to curdled milk that is much like butter (Gen. 18:8; 2 Sam. 17:29). It was often produced by churning milk to make butter (Prov. 30:33). It was a staple of the diet of Israelites and their neighbors (Deut. 32:14), even from infancy (Isa. 7:15; 22). It could be served in high style in luxurious dishes (Judg. 5:25). It is used figuratively to describe the beauty and bounty of nature (Job 20:17) or a pleasant and unhindered state of life (Job 29:6).

2530. חָמַד ***ḥāmaḏ,*** חֲמוּדָה ***ḥ^a^mûḏāh,*** חֲמֻדָה ***ḥ^a^muḏāh:*** A verb meaning to take pleasure in, to desire, to lust, to covet, to be desirable, to desire passionately. The verb can mean to desire intensely even in its simple stem: the tenth commandment prohibits desiring to the point of coveting, such as a neighbor's house, wife, or other assets (Ex. 20:17; cf. Ex. 34:24). Israel was not to covet silver or gold (Deut. 7:25; Josh. 7:21) or the fields and lands of others (Mic. 2:2). The word can also express slight variations in its basic meaning: the mountains of Bashan, including Mt. Hermon, looked in envy on the chosen mountains of Zion (Ps. 68:16[17]); the simple fool delighted in his naïve, senseless way of life (Prov. 1:22); and a man was not to lust after the beauty of an adulterous woman (Prov. 6:25).

The word expresses the idea of finding pleasure in something as when Israel took pleasure in committing spiritual fornication among its sacred oaks (Isa. 1:29). The passive participle of the simple stem indicates someone beloved or endearing (Isa. 53:2) but has a negative meaning in Job 20:20, indicating excessive desiring or craving (cf. Ps. 39:11[12]).

The passive stem indicates something that is worthy of being desired, desirable; the fruit of the tree of the knowledge of good and evil appeared inviting to make a person wise (Gen. 2:9; 3:6; Prov. 21:20) but proved to be destructive. The plural of this verbal stem expresses satisfaction or reward for keeping God's Law (Ps. 19:10[11]).

2531. חֶמֶד ***ḥemeḏ:*** A masculine noun meaning handsome, pleasant, beautiful. It indicates what is desirable and appreciated, charming. It is used to describe a pleasant or fruitful vineyard (Isa. 27:2; 32:12, NIV; cf. KJV, NKJV, NASB; Amos 5:11) or handsome, desirable young men (Ezek. 23:6, 12, 23).

2532. חֶמְדָּה ***ḥemdāh:*** A feminine noun indicating what is desirable, pleasant. It indicates what is desirable and pleasant: a person, Saul, and his house to serve as king in Israel (1 Sam. 9:20); a goddess beloved of women (Dan. 11:37). It is used to define and describe things as excellent: beautiful craft, ships (Isa. 2:16); beautiful, pleasant houses (Ezek. 26:12); things of all nations (Hag. 2:7).

2533. חֶמְדָּן ***ḥemdān:*** A proper noun designating Hemdan (Gen. 36:26; 1 Chr. 1:41).

2534. חֵמָה ***ḥēmāh,*** חֵמָא ***ḥēmā':*** A noun meaning wrath, heat. The word is also synonymous with the feminine noun meaning heat or rage. Figuratively, it can signify anger, hot displeasure, indignation, poison, or rage. This noun describes the great fury that kings of the North executed in their utter destruction (Dan. 11:44); a person's burning anger (2 Sam.

11:20); and God's intense anger against Israel and those who practiced idolatry (2 Kgs. 22:17).

2535. חַמָּה ***ḥammāh:*** A feminine noun denoting heat, sun. It refers to the glow and heat of the sun (Ps. 19:6[7]) or to the sun itself. With God's restoration and healing of Israel, the light of the sun (*ḥammāh*) will be seven times brighter (Isa. 30:26). It takes on the sense of comfort in Job 30:28, i.e., without heat or comfort (NASB; but, NIV, KJV, NKJV, sun).

2536. חַמּוּאֵל ***ḥammû'ēl:*** A proper noun designating Hammuel (1 Chr. 4:26).

2537. חֲמוּטַל ***ḥamûṭal:*** A proper noun designating Hamutal (2 Kgs. 23:31; 24:18; Jer. 52:1).

2538. חָמוּל ***ḥāmûl:*** A proper noun designating Hamul (Gen. 46:12; Num. 26:21; 1 Chr. 2:5).

2539. חָמוּלִי ***ḥāmûliy:*** A proper noun designating Hamulite (26:21).

2540. חַמּוֹן ***ḥammôn:*** A proper noun designating Hammon:

A. A town in Asher (Josh. 19:28).

B. A town in Naphtali (1 Chr. 6:76[61]).

2541. חָמוֹץ ***ḥāmôṣ:*** A masculine noun denoting one who is oppressed, an oppressor. It refers to a ruthless or oppressive person especially regarding orphans and widows (Isa. 1:17).

2542. חַמּוּק ***ḥammûq:*** A masculine noun indicating a curve. It refers to the beautifully shaped hips of the beloved bride as viewed through the eyes of the bridegroom (Song 7:1[2]).

2543. חֲמוֹר ***ḥªmôr,*** חֲמוֹרָה ***ḥªmôrah:*** A noun, masculine, feminine, referring to a donkey. This word is used ninety-seven times in the Old Testament and refers to a donkey or a male ass, a major beast of burden in Israel (Gen. 12:16; 22:3; 42:26, 27) and considered valuable property (Gen. 24:35; Ex. 20:17; 21:33; Num. 16:15; Josh. 6:21). It was used for transportation (Ex. 4:20; 2 Sam. 16:2) and used in pairs sometimes (Judg. 19:3, 10; 2 Sam. 16:1). Issachar was said to be like a strong donkey (Gen. 49:14). An ox and donkey could not be harnessed together for plowing (Deut. 22:10), but either could be used in tilling fields (Isa. 32:20). The statement "burial of an ass" is used figuratively of a dishonorable burial of a person (Jer. 22:19), e.g., King Jehoiakim.

2544. חֲמוֹר ***ḥªmôr:*** A proper noun designating Hamor, the father of Shechem who was probably named after the city of Shechem. Hamor was a Hivite (Gen. 33:19; 34:2). He negotiated with Jacob concerning his daughter Dinah whom his son Shechem had violated (Gen. 34:5–13). The sons of Jacob dealt deceitfully with him and slew Shechem and the inhabitants of Shechem (Gen. 34:13–31). They also killed Hamor (Gen. 34:26).

2545. חֲמוֹת ***ḥamôṯ:*** A feminine noun denoting a mother-in-law. It is often used of Naomi, mother-in-law of the Moabitess, Ruth (Ruth 1:14; 2:11, 18, 19, 23; 3:1, 6, 16, 17). Hence, it refers here to one's husband's mother. Normally, there is unity and peace between mother-in-law and daughter-in-law reflecting God's will, but the presence of hostility is considered a failure among God's people (Mic. 7:6).

2546. חֹמֶט ***ḥōmeṭ:*** A masculine noun indicating a small lizard, skink. It indicates some kind of unclean reptile, not edible by Israelites (Lev. 11:30), perhaps a skink.

2547. חֻמְטָה ***ḥumṭāh:*** A proper noun designating Hamor (Gen. 33:19; 34:2, 4, 6, 8, 13, 18, 20, 24, 26; Josh. 24:32; Judg. 9:28).

2548. חָמִיץ ***ḥāmiyṣ:*** An adjective meaning seasoned, salted. It describes fodder that has been prepared with salt or seasoned by soaking (Isa. 30:24), a delicacy for animals.

2549. חֲמִישִׁי ***ḥ^amiyšiy,*** חֲמִשִּׁי ***ḥamiššiy:*** An ordinal number meaning fifth. It is used to designate the fifth in a series: a fifth son (Gen. 30:17); a fifth day (Gen. 1:23). It refers to an amount of something equaling a fifth of the whole, such as a fifth of harvested corn (Gen. 47:24; Lev. 5:16). It denotes the fifth time in a series (Neh. 6:5). It is used to indicate something that has five sides, is five-sided (1 Kgs. 6:31), a pentagon.

2550. חָמַל ***ḥāmal:*** A verb meaning to have pity, to show pity, to have compassion, to spare. It expresses pity or compassion toward something or someone, a child or other persons (Ex. 2:6; 1 Sam. 15:9, 15; 23:21; 2 Sam. 12:6; Zech. 11:5, 6; Mal. 3:17). Without pity (*lō' ḥomal*) means to do something ruthlessly (Isa. 30:14; Lam. 2:2) or without any restraint (Jer. 50:14). It can take on the nuance of holding on to something, desiring it, such as holding evil in one's mouth (Job 20:13) or being unwilling to do something right or that is costly to oneself (2 Sam. 12:4).

2551. חֶמְלָה ***ḥemlāh:*** A feminine noun meaning compassion, mercy. It describes the act of the angelic beings who led Lot and his family out of Sodom (Gen. 19:16). It is also used in Isaiah 63:9 when retelling God's deeds of the past. In light of His angel saving the people in Egypt, the text refers to God showing mercy on them. Therefore, in its two uses, it denotes God's compassion which spares one from destruction or similar dismal fates.

2552. חָמַם ***ḥāmam:*** A verb meaning to be hot, warm. It refers to bodily heat (1 Kgs. 1:1, 2; 2 Kgs. 4:34) or the use of fire to warm oneself (Isa. 44:15, 16). It indicates the act of becoming warm. It is used figuratively of anger and wrath arising within a person (Deut. 19:6); to the weather as it warms (Job 6:17); or to the sun's rays warming the day (1 Sam. 11:9).

It depicts the Babylonians as lions becoming heated in riotous banqueting or debauchery (Jer. 51:39).

2553. חַמָּן ***ḥammān:*** A masculine noun meaning sun pillar. It also means idol or pillar in general. This is a pillar used in idolatrous worship of the solar deities, similar to the images Asa and Josiah tore down as part of their religious reforms (2 Chr. 14:5[4]; 34:4). Isaiah also condemned the worship of these images (Isa. 17:8; 27:9).

2554. חָמַס ***ḥāmas:*** A verb meaning to be violent, to act violently, to act wrongly. The term can be used to describe one who treats people badly. The prophet Jeremiah condemned the wrong treatment of widows and orphans (Jer. 22:3). The word can also denote unethical behavior in a construction that takes *tôrāh* (8451) as an object (Ezek. 22:26; Zeph. 3:4) (lit., "do violence to the law"). God did violence to His dwelling when Jerusalem was sacked (Lam. 2:6). Job thought his accusers treated him wrongly (Job 21:27).

2555. חָמָס ***ḥāmās:*** A masculine noun meaning violence, wrong. It implies cruelty, damage, and injustice. Abraham's cohabiting with Hagar is described as a wrong done to Sarah (Gen. 16:5). In relation to physical violence, cruelty is implied (Judg. 9:24). When coupled with the term instrument or weapon, it becomes an attributive noun describing weapons or instruments of violence (Ps. 58:2[3]). When it describes a person, it can mean an oppressor or a violent man (Prov. 3:31).

2556. חָמֵץ ***ḥāmēṣ:*** A verb meaning to be sour, to be leavened. The verb occurs four times in the Hebrew Bible. In connection with the Exodus from Egypt, the Israelites were told not to leaven the bread before their departure (Ex. 12:34, 39). In Hosea 7:4, the prophet used the image of a baker kneading dough until it was leavened. This verb was also used metaphorically to refer to the heart being soured or embittered (Ps. 73:21).

Another root, spelled exactly the same, is listed under this entry by Strong. It occurs in Isaiah 63:1 and means to be stained red.

2557. חָמֵץ ***ḥāmēṣ,*** מַחְמֶצֶת ***maḥmeṣeṯ:*** A masculine noun meaning leaven. The Hebrew word refers particularly to yeast that causes bread to rise. Bread was made without leaven when Israel went out of Egypt because there was not enough time to leaven it. Thus, unleavened bread is known as "the bread of affliction" and is eaten the week after Passover as a celebration of the Exodus (Deut. 16:3). Leaven was later used in offerings (Lev. 7:13; 23:17) but was not allowed to be burned (Lev. 2:11). In Amos 4:5, leaven is associated with hypocrisy and insincerity, an association made more explicitly in the New Testament (Luke 12:1; 1 Cor. 5:6–8).

2558. חֹמֶץ ***ḥōmeṣ:*** A masculine noun referring to vinegar. It refers to a fermented vinegar that a Nazarite had to abstain from (Num. 6:3). Diners dipped bread in this drink (Ruth 2:14). It was administered as a drink to those who were under oppression and attack (Ps. 69:21[22]). It was injurious and bitter to the teeth (Prov. 10:26) and caused an agitated reaction when poured on soda (Prov. 25:20).

2559. חָמַק ***ḥāmaq:*** A verb indicating to wander, to withdraw. It describes the retreat or departure of one person from another (Song 5:6). In another reflexive verb form, it means to wander here and there (Jer. 31:22).

2560. חָמַר ***ḥāmar:*** I. A verb meaning to cover something with bitumen. It describes the process of waterproofing the basket which was placed in the Nile River with the infant Moses inside it (Ex. 2:3).

II. A verb meaning to ferment, burn, boil, foment, make red. It describes a person's face made red from suffering and skin disease (Job 16:16) and the troubling of a person's mind or spirit because of calamity (Lam. 1:20; 2:11). It describes the fomenting and foaming of the waters of the earth (Ps. 46:3[4]) and the agitation of wine in a cup (Ps. 75:8[9]).

2561. חֶמֶר ***ḥemer:*** A masculine noun meaning wine. It indicates fermenting wine. Figuratively, in context, Israel drank of this wine as the Lord nurtured the nation (Deut. 32:14). In the future, Israel will drink of it again (Isa. 27:2; NIV, fruitful, *ḥemed*).

2562. חֲמַר ***ḥ^a^mar:*** A masculine Aramaic noun meaning wine. It refers to wine furnished by Persian kings to the returned exiles (Ezra 6:9; 7:22) and used to excess by the Babylonians under Belshazzar (Dan. 5:1, 2, 4, 23).

2563. חֹמֶר ***ḥōmer:*** I. A masculine noun denoting mortar, mud, mire. It refers to mud in the streets (Isa. 10:6). It was a building material used with bricks (Ex. 1:14). Bitumen was used as mortar at the Tower of Babel (Gen. 11:3). Potters used a form of mud designated by this word (Isa. 29:16; Jer. 18:4, 6). It is used metaphorically to describe people as opposed to God (Job 10:9; Isa. 45:9; 64:8[7]) who is the potter that forms the clay. Seals were pressed into this malleable substance (Job 38:14). It symbolic of something weak, such as defenses (Job 13:12) or the frail human body (Job 4:19).

II. A masculine noun indicating a heap, churning, surge. Figuratively, it refers to a pile or heap of water (Hab. 3:15), a pile of dead frogs, or even a heap of dead bodies (Judg. 15:16).

III. A masculine noun indicating a homer. It was a dry measure of barley (Lev. 27:16; Ezek. 45:13; Hos. 3:2) or wheat (Ezek. 45:13). A dry homer equaled 354 dry quarts or 412 liquid quarts.

2564. חֵמָר ***ḥēmār:*** A masculine noun referring to slime, tar, pitch, bitumen, asphalt (Gen. 14:10). It was used as cement in construction work (Gen. 11:3) and used in coating the basket in which Moses was placed (Ex. 2:3, parallel to *zep̱eṯ* [2203]).

2565. חֲמֹרָתַיִם ***ḥ^amôrāṯayim:*** A feminine dual noun meaning heaps. It is found in the dual form in Judges 15:16 referring to heaps of dead Philistines where it is preceded by *ḥ^amôr* (heap).

2566. חַמְרָן ***ḥamrān:*** A masculine proper noun referring to Amram, Hamran. He is designated as the son of Dishon and had three brothers (1 Chr. 1:41).

2567. חָמַשׁ ***ḥāmaš:*** A verb meaning to take one-fifth. It is used once in a factitive or intensive form meaning to take one-fifth, or levy one-fifth as a tax (Gen. 41:34).

2568. חָמֵשׁ ***ḥāmēš,*** חֲמִשָּׁה ***ḥ^amiššāh:*** A masculine/feminine noun denoting five. It can refer to five of nearly anything: five years (Gen. 5:6); five hands, meaning five times (Gen. 43:34). It combines with other numbers: e.g., *ḥ^amiššāh ʿāśār,* fifteen (Hos. 3:2); when it is pluralized, *h^amiššîm* (2572), it means fifty.

2569. חֹמֶשׁ ***ḥōmeš:*** A masculine noun referring to one-fifth of produce. It refers to one-fifth of the produce of the land of Egypt (Gen. 47:26) that was stored up for difficult times of famine.

2570. חֹמֶשׁ ***ḥōmeš:*** A masculine noun meaning belly, stomach, a fifth rib. It refers to a person's stomach (2 Sam. 2:23; 3:27; 20:10), a vulnerable and accessible part of the body for an enemy to strike at.

2571. חֲמֻשִׁים ***ḥ^amušiym:*** A plural adjective meaning armed, arrayed for battle, in orderly array. It describes the Israelites as they went forth from Egypt (Ex. 13:18); crossed the Jordan (Josh. 1:14; 4:12); and the army of the Midianites as they encamped against Israel (Judg. 7:11).

2572. חֲמִשִּׁים ***ḥ^amiššiym:*** A pluralized numerical adjective. This is the pluralized form of five, *ḥomēš,* used to designate fifty of something. It may be used in various ways: by itself meaning fifty of something (Ex. 18:21, 25); with other numbers (Ex. 30:23); without other numbers (Num. 31:30); preceded by a word in the construct meaning of, e.g., "in the year of fifty," fiftieth year (2 Kgs. 15:23).

2573. חֵמֶת ***ḥēmeṯ:*** A masculine noun indicating a waterskin, a bottle. It is most often taken to mean a bottle or wineskin (Hab. 2:15; but NASB, venom), probably tied and stopped with pitch at both ends to hold wine, water, or oil (Gen. 21:14, 15, 19).

2574. חֲמָת ***ḥ^amāṯ,*** לְבֹא חֲמָת ***l^eḇō ḥ^amāṯ:*** A proper noun designating Hamath:

A. A city explored by the ten spies of Joshua (Num. 13:21). It is also listed as Lebo ("at the entrance" of) Hamath (the preposition l^e + *bô'* (935); see B.). It seems to refer to the larger territory of Hamath in some cases. It was located at the northern boundary of Canaan (Ezek. 47:16, 20; 48:1) and was the northernmost point of the land of Israel (Josh. 13:5; Judg. 3:3; 1 Chr. 13:5; Amos 6:14). As noted Hamath used alone may refer to a larger Hamath territory (Amos 6:2), evidently a land touched by northern Israel's territory during the monarchy (2 Sam. 8:9). The city was ca. 45 miles north of Damascus on the west side of the Orontes River.

B. Much the same as A, but each context must be carefully checked to discern whether the larger territorial kingdom of Hamath is meant or the capital city itself. See A above. Compare NIV, Lebo-Hamath; KJV, "to Hamath"; NLT, LeboHamath (Num. 13:21). Compare Amos 6:2; 6:14.

C. The name of an ancestor of the Rechabite clan, the father of the family itself (1 Chr. 2:55).

2575. חַמַּת ***ḥammaṯ:*** A proper noun designating Hammath:

A. A city in Naphtali (Josh. 19:35).

B. Ancestral head of the Rechabite clan (1 Chr. 2:55).

2576. חַמֹּת דֹּאר ***ḥammōṯ dō'r:*** A proper noun designating Hammoth Dor (Josh. 21:32).

2577. חֲמָתִי ***ḥ^{a}māṯiy:*** A proper noun designating Hamathite (Gen. 10:18; 1 Chr. 1:16).

2578. חֲמַת צוֹבָה ***ḥ^{a}maṯ ṣôḇāh:*** A proper noun designating Hamath Zobah (2 Chr. 8:3).

2579. חֲמַת רַבָּה ***ḥ^{a}maṯ rabbāh:*** A proper noun designating Hamath the great (Amos 6:2). See *ḥ^{a}māṯ* (2574,A) and *raḇ* (7227).

2580. חֵן ***ḥēn:*** A masculine noun meaning favor, grace, acceptance. Genesis 6:8 stands as the fundamental application of this word, meaning an unmerited favor or regard in God's sight. Beyond this, however, the word conveys a sense of acceptance or preference in a more general manner as well, such as the enticement of a woman (Prov. 31:30; Nah. 3:4); elegant speech (Eccl. 10:12); and some special standing or privilege with God or people (Num. 32:5; Esth. 5:2; Zech. 12:10).

2581. חֵן ***ḥēn:*** A proper noun designating Hen (Zech. 6:14).

2582. חֵנָדָד ***ḥēnāḏāḏ:*** A proper noun designating Henadad (Ezra 3:9; Neh. 3:18, 24; 10:9[10]).

2583. חָנָה ***ḥānāh:*** A verb meaning to pitch one's tent, encamp. It refers to pitching a tent or setting up camp for various reasons: to encamp in a particular location (Gen. 26:17; Ex. 14:2, 9); to encamp against an enemy (with prepositional *'al* (5921), against, 1 Sam. 11:1; with preposition b^e, against, Judg. 9:50). It is used of armies or persons (Josh. 4:19). It is used of the Lord's encamping around

His people and temple to protect them (Zech. 9:8); and in a simile of locusts "encamped" on a stone wall (NASB, settling; Nah. 3:17). Jerusalem is the city in which David set up his camp (Isa. 29:1). It takes on the idea of the day drawing to an end (Judg. 19:9).

2584. חַנָּה ***ḥannāh:*** A proper noun designating Hannah, the mother of Samuel, wife of Elkanah (1 Sam. 1:2). Her name means "grace" (1 Sam. 2:21). She consecrated her child to the Lord as a Nazarite (1 Sam. 1:9–11, 21–22) as she had promised before his birth. She named him Samuel, meaning "asked of God" (1 Sam. 1:20). Her song/prayer of praise and thanksgiving is also prophetic in both its tone and content (1 Sam. 2:1–11).

2585. חֲנוֹךְ ***ḥ***^{a}***nôḵ:*** A proper noun designating Enoch:

A. Cain's first son after whom he named the first city he built. Enoch bore Irad and was the ancestor of Lamech (Gen. 4:17–24).

B. The son of Jared in the line that led from Seth to Noah (Gen. 5:6–32).

C. The son of Midian who was a descendant of Abraham through his second wife Keturah (Gen. 25:1–6).

D. A son of Reuben, his first of three (Gen. 46:9; Ex. 6:14).

2586. חָנוּן ***ḥānûn:*** A proper noun designating Hanun:

A. The king of the Ammorites (2 Sam. 10:1–4; 1 Chr. 19:2–4, 6). He acted with hostility toward David's servants, shaming them. War resulted, and David defeated the Ammonites (see 2 Sam. 10:5–19).

B. It was also the name of an Israelite leader who returned from the exile. He helped repair the walls of Jerusalem (Neh. 3:13, 30).

2587. חַנּוּן ***ḥannûn:*** An adjective meaning gracious, merciful. This word is used solely as a descriptive term of God. The Lord used this word when He revealed Himself to Moses (Ex. 34:6), as One who is, above all else, merciful and abounding in compassion (Ps. 86:15; 103:8). Elsewhere, it expresses the Lord's response to the cry of the oppressed (Ex. 22:27[26]); His treatment of those that reverence Him (Ps. 111:4; 112:4); His attitude toward those who repent (Joel 2:13); His mercy in the face of rebellion (Neh. 9:17, 31; Jon. 4:2); and His leniency toward His people in the midst of judgment (2 Chr. 30:9).

2588. חָנוּת ***ḥānûṯ:*** A feminine noun referring to a cell, a vaulted room, a cellar. It refers to a dungeon or a vaulted cell in a house in which Jeremiah was imprisoned (Jer. 37:16).

2589. חַנּוֹת ***ḥannôṯ:*** I. A masculine noun indicating entreaty, a plea for grace. It may mean to plead, to entreat, to ask for grace (Job 19:17, KJV; cf. NASB, NIV).

II. A masculine noun meaning graciousness, mercy. It refers to God's acts of mercy or graciousness in the past (Ps. 77:9; cf. NASB, NIV).

2590. חָנַט **ḥānaṭ,** חֲנֻטִים **ḥ^a^nuṭiym:** I. A verb meaning to form, to ripen and get red. It refers to the process of the ripening of the fig tree (Song 2:13) or its production of figs.

II. A verb meaning to embalm. It refers to the Egyptian process of treating the bodies of deceased persons with various chemicals (Gen. 50:2, 26) and ceremoniously and meticulously wrapping them in material.

III. A masculine plural noun referring to embalming (Gen. 50:3). It indicates a forty-day process of the Egyptians when they treated the dead bodies of certain deceased persons.

2591. חִנְטָה **ḥinṭāh:** An Aramaic masculine noun denoting wheat. It refers to wheat provided by the Persian authorities to the returning exiles (Ezra 6:9; 7:22), a staple needed in religious worship and in a healthy diet.

2592. חַנִּיאֵל **ḥanniy'ēl:** A proper noun designating Hanniel:

A. Chief Manassite (Num. 34:23).

B. Chief Asherite (1 Chr. 7:39).

2593. חָנִיךְ **ḥāniyk̲:** An adjective meaning trained, instructed. It designates the men of Abraham's house whom he takes with him to rescue Lot (Gen. 14:14), hence, men trained by him.

2594. חֲנִינָה **ḥ^a^niynāh:** A feminine noun indicating favor, compassion, pity. It refers to a favorable and beneficial attitude of persons toward someone (Jer. 16:13), in this case, the exiles of Israel.

2595. חֲנִית **ḥ^a^niyt̲:** A feminine noun referring to javelin, spear. It refers to the spear itself (1 Sam. 13:19); the wooden spear shaft when preceded by *'ēṣ* (1 Sam. 17:7); or even the head of the spear when used with *lahebet̲* preceding it (1 Sam. 17:7). The end or butt of the spear is indicated by the phrase *'aḥ^e^rēy haḥ^a^niyt̲* (2 Sam. 2:23). It is used in a negative sense to refer to people's teeth as spears (Ps. 57:4[5]). In the phrase *hēyrîq h^a^niyt*, it means to employ one's sheath of a spear or javelin (Ps. 35:3).

2596. חָנַךְ **ḥānak̲:** A verb meaning to train, to dedicate. It is used once for training a child (Prov. 22:6). Its other use is related to the dedication of a house or temple (Deut. 20:5; 1 Kgs. 8:63; 2 Chr. 7:5).

2597. חֲנֻכָּה **ḥ^a^nukkāh:** An Aramaic feminine noun meaning dedication, consecration. The word is used in relation to the dedication of Nebuchadnezzar's image (Dan. 3:2); and the dedication of the new Temple of God (Ezra 6:16, 17).

2598. חֲנֻכָּה **ḥ^a^nukkāh:** A feminine noun meaning dedication, ceremony. It was used to show that something was officially in service. The word describes the dedication of the wall of Jerusalem after it was rebuilt under Nehemiah (Neh. 12:27). It also refers to the dedication of David's house (Ps. 30:title[1]; cf. Deut. 20:5). The word refers to an altar dedication in

2 Chronicles 7:9 and also in Numbers 7 where it appears to refer particularly to the offerings offered on the altar (Num. 7:10, 11, 84, 88). The word is best known in reference to the altar rededication described in the apocryphal books of Maccabees, which has since been celebrated as the Jewish festival, Hanukkah.

2599. חֲנֹכִי ***ḥ^a^nōḵiy:*** A proper noun designating Hanochite (Num. 26:5).

2600. חִנָּם ***ḥinnām:*** An adverb meaning freely, undeservedly, without cause, for no purpose, in vain. The primary meaning of this Hebrew word is related to the English word *gratis*. It appears in connection with goods exchanged without monetary charge (2 Sam. 24:24); services rendered without pay (Jer. 22:13); innocence, as having no offense (1 Kgs. 2:31); food without restriction or limit (Num. 11:5); faith without rational justification (Job 1:9); hostility without provocation (Ps. 69:4[5]); religious activities done in vain (Mal. 1:10).

2601. חֲנַמְאֵל ***ḥ^a^nam'ēl:*** A proper noun designating Hanamel, Hanameel (Jer. 32:7–9, 12).

2602. חֲנָמָל ***ḥ^a^nāmāl:*** A masculine noun denoting frost, sleet. It refers to a devastating cold spell that created a heavy frost or hail that destroyed Israel's sycamore trees or vines (Ps. 78:47; others suggest "devastating flood" as its meaning).

2603. חָנַן ***ḥānan:*** A verb meaning to be gracious toward, to favor, to have mercy on. In the wisdom literature, this verb is used primarily with human relations to denote gracious acts toward someone in need (Job 19:21; Prov. 19:17). Though the wicked may pretend to act graciously, they do not do so; neither should it be done so toward them (Ps. 37:21; Prov. 21:10; 26:25; Isa. 26:10). Outside of the wisdom literature, the agent of graciousness is most frequently God, including the often repeated cry, "Have mercy on me!" (Ex. 33:19; Num. 6:25; Ps. 26:11; 27:7; 119:58). A mixture of divine and human agencies occurs when God, in judgment, sends nations that will show no mercy to punish other nations through warfare (Deut. 7:2; 28:50; Isa. 27:11).

2604. חֲנַן ***ḥ^a^nan:*** An Aramaic verb meaning to show mercy, to ask for mercy. It corresponds to the Hebrew word *ḥānan* (2603). It refers to showing mercy to the poor, an action that would help Nebuchadnezzar break away from his iniquities (Dan. 4:27[24]). Daniel was discovered asking God for mercy even though it was against the new law of the Medes and Persians to do so (Dan. 6:11[12]). Here the word occurs alongside *b^e^'ā'* (1156), meaning to request.

2605. חָנָן ***ḥānān:*** A proper noun designating Hanan:

A. One of David's mighty men (1 Chr. 11:43).

B. A chief Benjamite (1 Chr. 8:23).

C. Son of Azel (1 Chr. 8:38; 9:44).

D. Head of the Nethinim (Ezra 2:46).

E. A Levite (Neh. 7:49; 8:7).

F. Son of Zaccur (Neh. 10:10[11], 22[23]; 13:13).

G. A Jewish leader (Neh. 10:26[27]).

H. Son of Igdaliah (Jer. 35:4).

2606. חֲנַנְאֵל ***ḥananʼēl:*** A proper noun designating Hananel, Hananeel (Neh. 3:1; 12:39; Jer. 31:38; Zech. 14:10).

2607. חֲנָנִי ***ḥanāniy:*** A proper noun designating Hanani:

A. Son of Heman (1 Chr. 25:4, 25).

B. A seer and the father of Jehu (1 Kgs. 16:1, 7; 2 Chr. 16:7; 19:2; 20:34).

C. Brother of Nehemiah (Neh. 1:2; 7:2).

D. A priest (Ezra 10:20).

E. A priest (Neh. 12:36).

2608. חֲנַנְיָה ,חֲנַנְיָהוּ ***ḥananyāh, ḥananyāhû:*** A proper noun designating Hananiah, the name of fourteen persons in the Old Testament. Little is known about most of them. The name means "the Lord is gracious."

A. A son of Heman who served as a singer at the Temple. Heman was the king's prophet (seer) (1 Chr. 25:4, 5).

B. A royal official who helped organize the army of Uzziah (2 Chr. 26:11).

C. The father of Zedekiah who was a royal official under Jehoiakim (Jer. 36:12).

D. The son of Azur and a false prophet who opposed Jeremiah. He proclaimed that God would destroy Babylon and not permit it to destroy Jerusalem and God would bring back Jehoiachin as king in Judah. Jeremiah correctly predicted his death because of his false prophecies and rebellion (Jer. 28:12–17).

E. His grandson Irijah accused Jeremiah of treason for leaving Jerusalem (Jer. 37:13).

F. A son of Shashak in the line of Benjamin through Saul (1 Chr. 8:24, 25).

G. The Hebrew name of Shadrach, one of the three companions of Daniel in exile (Dan. 1:6).

H. A son of Zerubbabel. He had a brother and sister and returned with his father to Jerusalem after the exile (1 Chr. 3:19).

I. A descendant of Bebai who intermarried with the people of the land (Ezra 10:28).

J. A priest under Nehemiah and a perfumer who helped repair the wall and gates of Jerusalem (Neh. 3:8).

K. A priest, son of Shele, who helped repair the walls of Jerusalem (Neh. 3:30).

L. Nehemiah's brother whom he appointed to administer the city of Jeruslem. He feared God and was honest (Neh. 7:2).

M. A leader of the Jews who affirmed the covenant of renewal set up by Nehemiah (Neh. 10:23).

N. A priest who was the head of a priestly family (Neh. 12:12).

2609. חָנֵס ***ḥānēs:*** A proper noun designating Hanes (Isa. 30:4).

2610. חָנֵף ***ḥānēp̱:*** A verb meaning to be defiled, to be profane, to pollute, to corrupt. This word most often appears in association with the defilement of the land, suggesting a tainting not by active commission but by passive contact with those committing sin. It denotes the pollution of the land through the shedding of blood (Num. 35:33); through divorce (Jer. 3:1); and through breaking God's covenant (Isa. 24:5). The prophets also used the term to define Zion's defilement by the Babylonians (Mic. 4:11) and Israel by idolatry (Jer. 3:9). Two notable exceptions to this linkage with the land further intensify the notion that the primary meaning is one of passive contamination. In Jeremiah, the Lord declared that the prophets and the priests were corrupted, seemingly by their association with the people's sin (Jer. 23:11). Likewise, Daniel uses the word in reference to the corruption that comes from association with a deceiver (Dan. 11:32).

2611. חָנֵף ***ḥānēp̱:*** An adjective meaning profane, filthy, impious, godless. It is used as a substantive to refer to a person with such qualities. The root idea is to incline away (from God). The word refers to a person whose moral uncleanness separates him or her from God (Job 13:16). It commonly describes someone without hope after this life (Job 8:13; 20:5; 27:8), who can only expect anger from God (Job 36:13; Isa. 33:14). Such people come into conflict with the righteous (Job 17:8; Prov. 11:9) and are known by their cruelty to others (Ps. 35:16; Prov. 11:9).

2612. חֹנֶף ***ḥōnep̱:*** A masculine noun meaning hypocrisy, profaneness. This word is found only once in the Hebrew Bible. Isaiah 32:6 uses the word in reference to the ungodly practices of vile or foolish persons. Such individuals have little nobility as their hearts are inclined to ruthlessness and their mouths speak nonsense and error.

2613. חֲנֻפָּה ***ḥ^a^nuppāh:*** A feminine noun meaning filthiness, profaneness, godlessness. The word occurs only in Jeremiah 23:15 where it describes the wickedness, including Baal worship, promoted by false prophets. The prophets' profaneness included substituting their own words for God's words. This led the people to hope for peace when they should have expected God's wrath.

2614. חָנַק ***ḥānaq:*** A verb meaning to strangle, to hang oneself, to kill. It is used in its reflexive stem when the subject acts upon itself to mean to hang oneself (2 Sam. 17:23). It describes a lioness killing her prey which serves figuratively as a picture of the Assyrians destroying other peoples (Nah. 2:12[13]).

2615. חַנָּתֹן *ḥannāṯōn:* A proper noun designating Hannathon (Josh. 19:4).

2616. חָסַד *ḥāsaḏ:* A verb which occurs twice in the Hebrew Bible with very different meanings. It is used reflexively as David sang to the Lord, meaning to show oneself as loyal or faithful to a covenant (2 Sam. 22:26; Ps. 18:25[26]). This verb is related to the common noun *ḥeseḏ* (2618). But in another context and in a different verbal stem, the same root carries the meaning to reproach or to bring shame upon (Prov. 25:10).

2617. חֶסֶד *ḥeseḏ:* A masculine noun indicating kindness, lovingkindness, mercy, goodness, faithfulness, love, acts of kindness. This aspect of God is one of several important features of His character: truth; faithfulness; mercy; steadfastness; justice; righteousness; goodness. The classic text for understanding the significance of this word is Psalm 136 where it is used twenty-six times to proclaim that God's kindness and love are eternal. The psalmist made it clear that God's kindness and faithfulness serves as the foundation for His actions and His character: it underlies His goodness (Ps. 136:1); it supports His unchallenged position as God and Lord (Ps. 136:2, 3); it is the basis for His great and wondrous acts in creation (Ps. 136:4–9) and delivering and redeeming His people from Pharaoh and the Red Sea (Ps. 136:10–15); the reason for His guidance in the desert (Ps. 136:16); His gift of the land to Israel and defeat of their enemies (Ps. 136:17–22); His ancient as well as His continuing deliverance of His people (Ps. 136:23–25); His rulership in heaven (Ps. 136:26). The entire span of creation to God's redemption, preservation, and permanent establishment is touched upon in this psalm. It all happened, is happening, and will continue to happen because of the Lord's covenant faithfulness and kindness.

The other more specific uses of the term develop the ideas contained in Psalm 136 in greater detail. Because of His kindness, He meets the needs of His creation by delivering them from enemies and despair (Gen. 19:19; Ex. 15:13; Ps. 109:26; Jer. 31:3); He preserves their lives and redeems them from sin (Ps. 51:1[3]; 86:13). As Psalm 136 demonstrates, God's kindness is abundant, exceedingly great, without end, and good (Ex. 34:6; Num. 14:19; Ps. 103:8; 109:21; Jer. 33:11). The plural of the noun indicates the many acts of God on behalf of His people (Gen. 32:10[11]; Isa. 63:7). He is the covenant-keeping God who maintains kindness and mercy (Deut. 7:9) to those who love Him.

People are to imitate God. They are to display kindness and faithfulness toward each other (1 Sam. 20:15; Ps. 141:5; Prov. 19:22), especially toward the poor, weak, and needy (Job 6:14; Prov. 20:28). Israel was to show kindness and faithfulness toward the Lord but often failed. In its youth, Israel showed faithfulness to God, but its devotion lagged later (Jer. 2:2). It was not constant (Hos. 6:4), appearing and leaving as the morning mist even though God desired this from His people more than sacrifices (Hos. 6:6; cf. 1 Sam 15:22). He looked for pious people (Isa. 57:1) who would perform deeds of piety, faithfulness, and kindness (2 Chr. 32:32; 35:26; Neh. 13:14); the Lord desired people who would maintain covenant loyalty and responsibility so that He could build His righteous community.

2618. חֶסֶד ***ḥeseḏ:*** A proper noun designating Hesed (1 Kgs. 4:10).

2619. חֲסַדְיָה ***ḥ^asaḏyāh:*** A proper noun designating Hasadiah (1 Chr. 3:20).

2620. חָסָה ***ḥāsāh:*** A verb meaning to seek, to take refuge. The word is used literally in reference to seeking a tree's shade (Judg. 9:15) and taking refuge in Zion (Isa. 14:32). It is commonly used figuratively in relation to deities (Deut. 32:37), particularly of Yahweh. He is a shield providing refuge (2 Sam. 22:31). Refuge is sought under His wings (Ruth 2:12; Ps. 36:7[8]; 57:1[2]; 61:4[5]; 91:4) and at the time of death (Prov. 14:32).

2621. חֹסָה ***ḥōsāh:*** A proper noun designating Hosah:

A. A Levite (1 Chr. 16:38; 26:10, 11, 16).

B. A location in Asher (Josh. 19:29).

2622. חָסוּת ***ḥāsûṯ:*** A feminine noun meaning refuge, shelter, trust. It is not used frequently in the Old Testament. Isaiah uses it to describe the false hope or trust that Israel put in Egypt (Isa. 30:3). It comes from the Hebrew word *ḥāsāh* (2620), meaning to take refuge.

2623. חָסִיד ***ḥāsiyḏ:*** An adjective meaning kind, benevolent, merciful, pious. The word carries the essential idea of the faithful kindness and piety that springs from mercy. It is used of the Lord twice: once to convey His holiness in the sense that His works are beyond reproach (Ps. 145:17); and once to declare His tender mercy (Jer. 3:12). Other occurrences of this word usually refer to those who reflect the character of God in their actions or personality. The word denotes those who share a personal relationship with the Lord (1 Sam. 2:9; Ps. 4:3[4]; 97:10; 116:15); the state of one who fully trusts in God (Ps. 86:2); and those who manifest the goodness or mercy of God in their conduct (2 Sam. 22:26; Ps. 12:1, 2; Mic. 7:2). More importantly, though, it signifies the nature of those who are specifically set apart by God to be the examples and mediators of His goodness and fidelity. Priests (Deut. 33:8); prophets (Ps. 89:19[20]); and the Messiah (Ps. 16:10) all bear this "holy" mark and function.

2624. חֲסִידָה ***ḥ^asiyḏāh:*** I. A feminine noun denoting a stork. It identifies a bird considered unclean to Israel, not to be eaten (Lev. 11:19;

Deut. 14:18). Its behavior is a witness to God's work in nature (Job 39:13; others read ostrich here: NIV, NKJV, NASB; KJV, peacock; Ps. 104:17; Jer. 8:7). Its wings are described in a simile by Zechariah as the wings of two women (Zech. 5:9).

II. A feminine noun meaning ostrich. It is a picture of a bird displaying its beauty as God's handiwork (Job 39:13; KJV, peacock).

2625. חָסִיל ***ḥāsiyl:*** A masculine noun identifying a grasshopper, a locust, a caterpillar. This seems to identify a special stage in the development of these insects. In each case, the insect is associated with God's judgment on Israel (1 Kgs. 8:37; 2 Chr. 6:28; Ps. 78:46; Isa. 33:4; Joel 1:4; 2:25).

2626. חֲסִין ***ḥ***^{a}***siyn:*** An adjective indicating strong, mighty. It describes God as mighty like no one else (Ps. 89:8[9]), the leader of His hosts.

2627. חַסִּיר ***ḥassiyr:*** An Aramaic adjective meaning lacking, deficient, of poor quality. It refers to some deficiency in a person, such as Belshazzar (Dan. 5:27).

2628. חָסַל ***ḥāsal:*** A verb indicating to devour, to consume. It is used to describe the destruction and consumption created by locusts (Deut. 28:38) as one of the covenant curses.

2629. חָסַם ***ḥāsam:*** A verb meaning to block, to muzzle. It describes muzzling an ox as it is threshing (Deut. 25:4); it takes on the idea of hindering, obstructing travel (Ezek. 39:11).

2630. חָסַן ***ḥāsan:*** A verb indicating to be laid up, hoarded. It refers to storing up something for reserve (Isa. 23:18) or to piling up excess supplies irresponsibly.

2631. חֲסַן ***ḥ***^{a}***san:*** An Aramaic verb meaning to take possession of. It refers to the passing of the kingdom to the saints of the Most High, to their taking over its administration (Dan. 7:18; 22).

2632. חֱסֵן ***ḥ***^{e}***sēn:*** An Aramaic masculine noun referring to strength, power. It refers to the authority and influences given to a king in order to rule a kingdom (Dan. 2:37; 4:30[27]), specifically a prerogative given by God.

2633. חֹסֶן ***ḥōsen:*** A masculine noun indicating a treasure, riches, wealth. It refers to individual wealth (Prov. 15:6; 27:24) taken honestly or by violence (Ezek. 22:25). Collectively, it indicates the wealth of an entire city (Jer. 20:5). The Lord is called the wealth of salvation (Isa. 33:6).

2634. חָסֹן ***ḥasōn:*** An adjective indicating strong, mighty. It describes a powerful person (Isa. 1:31) in Jerusalem. The Amorites were designated as strong as oaks (Amos 2:9), yet the Lord gave them over to Israel.

2635. חֲסַף ḥ^{a}sap̱: An Aramaic masculine noun denoting clay. It is described as mixed with iron in the feet of the statue in Nebuchadnezzar's vision, indicating weakness or instability (Dan. 2:33–35, 41–43, 45).

2636. חַסְפַּס ḥaspas: A verb meaning to be flaky, to be round; to be crisp. It is a four–letter verb. It is used to help identify the nature of manna (Ex. 16:14).

2637. חָסֵר ḥāsēr: A verb indicating to be lacking, to be needy; to decrease. In general, it refers to a failure of something to be fully complete, whole, sufficient (Ex. 16:18). It refers to a jar's being empty (of oil) (1 Kgs. 17:14). Psalm 23:1 indicates that the one whose shepherd is the Lord shall not lack. Used in a causative stem of the verb, it takes on the meaning of causing someone to lack something (Eccl. 4:8; Isa. 32:6). The psalmist used the verb with *min* (4480), thus, to indicate that a human being is less than (*min*), lower than (*min*) God (Ps. 8:5[6]). It indicates a diminution of flood waters (Gen. 8:3, 5) or a diminution of numbers (Gen. 18:28).

2638. חָסֵר ḥāsēr: An adjective indicating lacking, in need of. It can indicate a person who is lacking (1 Sam. 21:15[16]). It can refer to some benefit or goodwill that is absent or lacking (1 Kgs. 11:22). One who "lacks heart" is deficient in understanding or character (Prov. 6:32; 7:7; 9:4; Eccl. 10:3). It refers to a person who lacks nothing he or she needs to enjoy life and security (Eccl. 6:2).

2639. חֶסֶר ḥeser: A masculine noun meaning need, poverty. It indicates basically a lack of something. It describes the state of the outcasts of society (Job 30:3) and a potential need that may arise because of an improper pursuit of wealth (Prov. 28:22).

2640. חֹסֶר ḥōser: A masculine noun indicating need, lack. It describes a basic shortage or privation of the necessities of life (Deut. 28:48, 57). A lack of bread was a sign from the Lord of His displeasure with Israel (Amos 4:6).

2641. חַסְרָה ḥasrāh: A proper noun designating Hasrah (2 Chr. 34:22).

2642. חֶסְרוֹן ḥesrôn: A masculine noun indicating something that is absent, lacking. It is used to refer to basic aspects of life and the world that are not present (Eccl. 1:15).

2643. חַף ḥap̱: An adjective indicating pure, clean, innocent. It describes a state of being without iniquity (*'āwōn*) (Job 33:9).

2644. חָפָא ḥāp̱ā': A verb indicating to do something secretly, to cover; to attribute something to someone. In the stem in which it is used, it attributes Israel's doing of things, possibly secretively (2 Kgs. 17:9). It attributes to Israel certain things not approved by God.

2645. חָפָה ***ḥāp̱āh:*** A verb meaning to overlay, to cover. It indicates the covering of someone or something: with a veil (2 Sam. 15:30; Esth. 6:12; Jer. 14:3, 4), with something to hide a guilty person's face (Esth. 7:8). Figuratively, it describes the security, success, and wealth of Israel at home (Ps. 68:13[14]) with wings covered or sheathed (NIV) with silver. Used literally of metals, it means to overlay something (2 Chr. 3:5, 7–9).

2646. חֻפָּה ***ḥuppāh:*** A feminine noun referring to a chamber, a cover, a canopy. It refers figuratively to the "bridal chamber" from which the sun comes forth (Ps. 19:5[6]; cf. Joel 2:16). It indicates a mighty, protective canopy over God's people (Isa. 4:5).

2647. חֻפָּה ***ḥuppāh:*** A proper noun designating Huppah (1 Chr. 24:13).

2648. חָפַז ***ḥāp̱az:*** A verb indicating to hurry, to fear, to flee. It refers to hurrying away in haste or fear (2 Sam. 4:4) or in military flight (1 Sam. 23:26; 2 Kgs. 7:15). Leviathan does not react in haste and fear to anything (Job 40:23) nor become alarmed. It describes in figurative language how flood waters went down quickly at the Lord's command (Ps. 104:7).

2649. חִפָּזוֹן ***ḥippāzôn:*** A masculine noun indicating haste, a hurried flight. It indicates a state of watchfulness and readiness as necessary, as at the first Passover in Egypt (Ex. 12:11) when the Israelites ate their food in haste (Deut. 16:3). Or negated, the word means to do something without haste; with the Lord as comforter and guardian (Isa. 52:12).

2650. חֻפִּים ***ḥuppiym,*** חֻפִּם ***ḥuppim:*** A proper noun designating Huppim (Gen. 46:21; 1 Chr. 7:12, 15).

2651. חֹפֶן ***ḥōp̱en:*** A masculine noun meaning hand, handful. It refers to a closed hand or a hand holding all that it can. As such, it could serve as a means to measure ashes (Ex. 9:8); or ground incense (Lev. 16:12). In a metaphor, it describes the Lord's fists containing the wind (Prov. 30:4), or a fist or handful of "rest" (Eccl. 4:6). It is used of divine beings' hands filled with hot coals (Ezek. 10:2, 7).

2652. חָפְנִי ***ḥop̱niy:*** A proper noun designating Hophni. He served, with his brother Phinehas, as priest of the Lord at Shiloh, a son of Eli. They became wicked in their service at the Lord's altar and were slain as the Lord predicted (1 Sam. 2:34). They were in charge of the ark until it was captured and they were killed (1 Sam. 4:11).

2653. חָפַף ***ḥāp̱ap̱:*** A verb indicating to enclose, to cover, to shield. It means to protect and guard. The Lord protected or shielded Benjamin (Deut. 33:12).

2654. חָפֵץ ***ḥāp̱ēṣ,*** חָפַץ ***ḥāp̱aṣ:*** A verb meaning to delight in, to have pleasure, to have favor, to be pleased. Shechem took delight in Dinah (Gen. 34:19); King Ahasuerus also took delight in Esther (Esth. 2:14). This word describes Solomon's pleasure in building the Temple (1 Kgs. 9:1). The Lord is described as taking pleasure in His people Israel (Isa. 62:4). He is also pleased with those who practice justice and righteousness (Jer. 9:24[23]).

2655. חָפֵץ *ḥāp̱ēṣ:* An adjective meaning having delight in, having pleasure in. It modifies both humans and God. A good example is Psalm 35:27, which refers to people who delighted in the psalmist's vindication and the Lord who delighted in His servant's well-being. Psalm 5:4[5] notes that God does not take pleasure in wickedness. It can also mean simply to want or to desire, as in the men who wanted to be priests of the high places (1 Kgs. 13:33). See the related verb *ḥāp̱ēṣ* (2654) and noun *ḥēp̱eṣ* (2656).

2656. חֵפֶץ *ḥēp̱eṣ:* A masculine noun meaning delight, pleasure, desire, matter. The root idea is to incline toward something. The word signifies delight in or (in an unrealized sense) a desire for earthly goods, such as Solomon's desire for timber (110[22–24]); a delight in fruitful land (Mal. 3:12); or the delight of hands in their labor (Prov. 31:13). The word also refers to people's delight in God's Law (Ps. 1:2); His works (Ps. 111:2); God's own delight in His works (Isa. 46:10; 48:14); His lack of delight in foolish or disrespectful people (Eccl. 5:4[3]; Mal. 1:10). Three times the word is used to liken a person or nation to an undesirable vessel (Jer. 22:28; 48:38; Hos. 8:8). In addition, the word is used in Ecclesiastes to refer to a matter without respect to its delightfulness (Eccl. 3:1, 17).

2657. חֶפְצִי־בָהּ *ḥep̱ṣiy-ḇāh:* A proper noun designating Hephzibah (2 Kgs. 21:1; Isa. 62:4).

2658. חָפַר *ḥāp̱ar:* A verb meaning to dig, to search for. It refers to digging in the ground for various reasons: to make wells (Gen. 21:30; 26:15, 18, 19, 21, 22, 32; Num. 21:18); to find water (Ex. 7:24). In a general sense, it means to dig a hole in the ground (Deut. 23:13[14]; Jer. 13:7). It is used in the sense of to search out, spy out (Deut. 1:22; Josh. 2:2, 3; Job 3:21; 11:18). It describes digging a hole in a figurative sense (Ps. 7:15[16]; cf. Eccl. 10:8). It is rendered as a mole or rodent (digging animals) in Isaiah 2:20 (NIV, KJV).

2659. חָפֵר *ḥāp̱ēr:* A stative verb meaning to be ashamed, disgraced. It refers to a state of embarrassment, humiliation. Those who trust the Lord and look to Him will not experience shame (Ps. 34:5[6]). It is a state the righteous psalmist often calls down on his enemies (Ps. 35:4, 26; 40:14[15]; 70:2[3]; 71:24; 83:17[18]). It often parallels Hebrew *bôš,* shame; to be ashamed. Those who worship idols or who are diviners will be caught in shame (Isa. 1:29; Mic. 3:7). It is used figuratively of the moon being shamed (Isa. 24:23); or of Lebanon being abashed (Isa. 33:9). It is used of the shame of Israel that the Lord will remove (Isa. 54:4) but also of the shame and humiliation of a wicked Jerusalem (Jer. 15:9). Wicked Babylon will be abashed, shamed (Jer. 50:12). It refers to caravans being put to a shameful disappointment (Job 6:20). It depicts the customary, shameful actions of an evil person (Prov. 13:5).

2660. חֵפֶר **ḥēp̱er:** A proper noun designating Hepher:

A. Son of Gilead (Num. 26:32, 33; 27:1; Josh. 17:2, 3).

B. Son of Naarah (1 Chr. 4:6).

C. A Mecherathite (1 Chr. 11:36).

D. A city northwest of Jerusalem (Josh. 12:17; 1 Kgs. 4:10).

2661. חֲפַרְפָּרָה **ḥᵃparpārāh,** פֵּרָה חֲפֹר **ḥᵃpōr pērāh:** I. A feminine noun indicating a mole or rodent. It is used in the plural form in Isaiah 2:20 (NASB, KJV, moles; NIV, rodents). Worthless idols, in the day of judgment, are cast to these vermin.

II. A feminine noun indicating a digging mole. It is possibly developed from the Qal infinitive construct of *ḥāp̱ar* and stands in a construct relationship to the noun *pērāh* (Isa. 2:20, MT).

2662. חֶפְרִי **ḥep̱riy:** A proper noun designating Hepherite (Num. 26:32).

2663. חֲפָרַיִם **ḥᵃp̱ārayim,** חָפְרַע **ḥopra':** I. A proper noun designating Hapharaim (Josh. 19:19).

II. A proper noun designating Hophra, the pharaoh of Egypt (Jer. 44:30). See also 6548.

2664. חָפַשׂ **ḥāp̱aś:** A verb meaning to search for, to disguise oneself. It refers to searching out, looking for something with one's mind and imagination (Ps. 64:6[7]); or it denotes something sought out, such as valuable booty or spoil in war (Obad. 1:6). It means to search for spoil or booty (1 Kgs. 20:6). The Lord Himself tracks down His enemies (Amos 9:3). A person's conscience examines the inner aspects of his or her being (Prov. 20:27), as appointed by God; a person's spirit tries to understand the Lord's dealings with His people (Ps. 77:6[7]). In a reflexive of the verb, it means to disguise oneself (1 Kgs. 20:38), literally, to let oneself be searched out.

2665. חֵפֶשׂ **ḥēp̱eś:** A masculine noun denoting a plan, a plot. In context, preceding a participle of the same basic meaning, it means a plot or a plan that has been thought through thoroughly (Ps. 64:6[7]).

2666. חָפַשׁ **ḥapaš:** A verb indicating to be free. It occurs once and is negated. Its subject is a woman who has not been freed (Lev. 19:20), according to certain legal stipulations.

2667. חֹפֶשׁ **ḥōp̱eš:** A masculine noun indicating widespread; saddlecloth. It refers to an expensive item of merchandise of trade between Dedan and Tyre used to make saddlecloths for riding (Ezek. 27:20).

2668. חֻפְשָׁה ***ḥup̱šāh:*** A feminine noun meaning freedom, emancipation. It refers to a state of liberty granted to an ex-slave woman (Lev. 19:20). She had certain freedoms regarding sexual intercourse according to the Mosaic Law.

2669. חָפְשִׁית ***ḥop̱šiyt̲:*** A feminine noun denoting freedom, separateness. It refers to a special house for King Azariah because he was leprous. It was separate from other state buildings (2 Kgs. 15:5; 2 Chr. 26:21).

2670. חָפְשִׁי ***ḥop̱šiy:*** An adjective indicating something is free. It indicates freedom from slave responsibilities or duties. A person could be free (*ḥop̱šiy*) from slavery (Ex. 21:2, 5, 26, 27; Deut. 15:12, 13, 18). It indicates exemption from certain things, such as taxes (1 Sam. 17:25); or to have oppression removed from someone (Isa. 58:6), including slaves (Jer. 34:9–11, 14, 16).

2671. חֵץ ***ḥēṣ:*** A masculine noun denoting arrow. It was a hunting and military missile shot from a bow (1 horically in various ways: the Lord's arrows (Num. 24:8; Deut. 32:23, 42) which were His judgments; or even His Messianic ruler sent by Him (Ps. 45:5[6]). His arrow of deliverance for His people was like lightning (Zech. 9:14). The wickedness and harmful words of evil persons are described as arrows of violence (Ps. 11:2; 64:3[4]; 91:5; Prov. 25:18). A fool's or demented person's words are described as arrows, firebrands, and even death (Prov. 26:18). Isaiah's Servant of the Lord is His choice arrow (Isa. 49:2). Jeremiah describes himself as the target of the Lord's arrow of judgment (Lam. 3:12).

2672. חָצַב ***ḥāṣab̲,*** חָצֵב ***ḥāṣēb̲,*** חֹצֵב ***ḥōṣēb̲:*** I. A verb meaning to cut, to strike, to hew, to quarry. It is used of cutting out cisterns to hold water (Deut. 6:11; 2 Chr. 26:10; Neh. 9:25); or of digging out copper from the hills (Deut. 8:9). It describes the process of engraving a rock (Job 19:24); or of chopping or cutting wood with an ax (Isa. 10:15). Tombs were cut or hewn out of rock (Isa. 22:16). Metaphorically, it describes the Lord's voice hewing out flames of fire (Ps. 29:7); and of wisdom hewing out her seven pillars of wisdom (Prov. 9:1). Israel was the Lord's wine vat hewn out by Him (Isa. 5:2). He hewed His people from a rock (Isa. 51:1) but had been forced to hew them in pieces by the words of the prophets (Hos. 6:5).

II. A masculine noun denoting the person who cuts stones, a mason, a stonecutter. It designates those who help construct projects by preparing cut or hewn stones as building material (1 Kgs. 5:15[29]), especially in the construction of the Temple or in its repair (2 Kgs. 12:12[13]; 1 Chr. 22:2, 15; 2 Chr. 2:2[1], 18[17]; 24:12). They were used in the construction of the second Temple (Ezra 3:7).

2673. חָצָה ḥāṣāh: A verb meaning to divide, to leave out half. It is used of separating something or dividing things in half (Gen. 32:7[8]; 33:1); or distributing something among many (Num. 31:27). It describes the dividing up of a nation (Dan. 11:4). It refers to arranging an army into groups for battle (Judg. 7:16; 9:43). Combined with the preposition *'ad*, it means to reach out to something, to extend to (Isa. 30:28). It describes the parting of water before Elijah (2 Kgs. 2:8) and Elisha (2 Kgs. 2:14).

2674. חָצוֹר ḥāṣôr: A proper noun designating Hazor:

A. A large royal town in northern Canaan. It was the capital city of several kingdoms in league in the area. Joshua captured it and gave it to the tribe of Naphtali (Josh. 11:1, 10; 12:19; 19:36). Barak and Deborah had to fight strong forces from this city (Judg. 4:2–17; 1 Sam. 12:9). Solomon strengthened it as a part of his kingdom (1 Sam. 9:15). It eventually fell into the hands of the Assyrians (2 Kgs. 15:29) and Babylon (Jer. 49:28).

B. A town in southern Judah in the Negev. It was allotted to Judah (Josh. 15:23).

C. Another southern city of Judah with the alternate name of Kerioth Hegron (city of Hegron) (Josh. 15:25).

D. A town in which Benjamites settled after returning from exile (Neh. 11:33).

2675. חָצוֹר חֲדַתָּה ḥāṣôr ḥ^{a}dattāh: A proper noun designating Hazor Hadattah (Josh. 15:25).

2676. חֲצוֹת ḥ^{a}ṣôṯ: A feminine noun referring to the middle of the night. It is used with *laylāh* or *hallaylāh* following and indicates half of the night or midnight. The Lord went forth about midnight to slay the firstborn of Egypt (Ex. 11:4); persons suddenly die in the middle of the night (Job 34:20). The psalmist asserted that he would praise the Lord in the middle of the night (Ps. 119:62).

2677. חֲצִי ḥ^{a}ṣiy: A masculine noun indicating half, middle. It is used about 120 times to express half of something by placing it before the word: half of their beards (2 Sam. 10:4); with a pronoun suffix added to it, such as *nû*, us, it means half of us (2 Sam. 18:3). It is also used to indicate the middle measure of something: with *'ad* preceding, it means up to half of something (Ex. 27:5, height); with the preposition *b^{e}* followed by a time word, it means half of the days (Ps. 102:24[25]; Jer. 17:11); or half of the night, midnight (Ex. 12:29).

2678. חֵצִי ḥēṣiy: A masculine noun designating an arrow. It indicates an arrow shot from a bow as a sign to David (1 Sam. 20:36–38). It designates the slender shaft from Jehu's bow that killed Joram, king of Israel (2 Kgs. 9:24).

2679. חֲצִי הַמְּנֻחוֹת ***ḥ*ᵃ*ṣiy ham-m*ᵉ*nuḥôṯ:*** A phrase referring to half of the Manahathites, from *ḥ*ᵃ*ziy* [2677] and *mānaḥtiy* [4506,C]) (1 Chr. 2:52). See also 2680.

2680. חֲצִי הַמְּנַחְתִּי ***ḥ*ᵃ*ṣiy hamm*ᵉ*-naḥtiy:*** A phrase referring to half of the Manahathites; from *ḥ*ᵃ*ziy* [2677] and *mānaḥtiy* [4506,C] (1 Chr. 2:54). See also 2679.

2681. חָצִיר ***ḥāṣiyr:*** A masculine noun denoting a dwelling place, an abode. It is used to depict Edom as a dwelling place, destroyed by the Lord, where the ostrich will live (Isa. 34:13).

2682. חָצִיר ***ḥāṣiyr:*** I. A masculine noun referring to grass, hay, reed. It is food for animals (1 Kgs. 18:5; Job 40:15; Ps. 104:14). It is used in a simile to indicate abundant growth (Isa. 44:4). Its brief life and fragile existence is used to symbolize something that easily or quickly dies (Job 8:12), especially grass that often grew on housetops in the Middle East (2 Kgs. 19:26; Ps. 129:6; Isa. 37:27). Its frailty described the wicked (Ps. 37:2); or of human beings in general (Ps. 90:5; 103:15).

II. A masculine noun designating leeks. A large onion-like plant of the lily family (Num. 11:5), eaten by Israelites in Egypt.

2683. חֵצֶן ***ḥēṣen:*** A masculine noun meaning bosom. It refers to either the grasp of one's arms or an open space in a garment for gathering something (Ps. 129:7).

2684. חֹצֶן ***ḥōṣen:*** A masculine noun referring to bosom, lap, front folds in one's robe. It indicates the enclosing space between one's arms and breast when embracing something or someone or the part of a garment covering the bosom area of one's body (Neh. 5:13; Ps. 129:7; Isa. 49:22).

2685. חֲצַף ***ḥ*ᵃ*ṣap̱:*** An Aramaic verb asserting something to be urgent, harsh, severe. It indicates something that is either urgent or severe, such as Nebuchadnezzar's command to kill the wise men of Babylon (Dan. 2:15); or his order to heat the furnace seven times hotter than normal to kill the three Jewish young men (Dan. 3:22) when they were thrown into it.

2686. חָצַץ ***ḥāṣaṣ:*** I. A verb indicating to divide, to divide into ranks; to cut off, to come to an end, to sing. It means to divide something or separate out something for a purpose (Judg. 5:11); or to arrange something into orderly fashion (Prov. 30:27). It may have the meaning of dividing off, cutting off, or ending one's life (Job. 21:21).

II. A verb meaning to shoot an arrow. Some take this verb form in context, a masculine plural participle, to indicate those who shoot arrows (Judg. 5:11; KJV, NKJV), expert archers.

2687. חָצָץ ***ḥāṣāṣ:*** A masculine noun referring to gravel. It is used figuratively of a mouthful of bread that tastes like gravel (Prov. 20:17); and of gravel, representing God's judgments, that breaks one's teeth (Lam. 3:16).

2688. חַצְצוֹן תָּמָר ***haṣ*^e^*ṣôn tāmār*:** A proper noun referring to Hazazon-tamar. It refers to a town inhabited by Amorites and conquered in battle by Chedorlaomer, king of Elam and his allies (Gen. 14:7); and to the same town, evidently, in the reign of Jehoshaphat (2 Chr. 20:2), also named Engedi.

2689. חֲצֹצְרָה ***ḥ*^a^*ṣōṣ*^e^*rāh*:** A feminine noun indicating a trumpet. It refers to a long metal trumpet used for signaling. It was used both in sacred (Num. 10:2, 8–10; 2 Kgs. 12:13[14]; Ps. 98:6) and secular spheres (2 Kgs. 11:14; 2 Chr. 23:13; Hos. 5:8).

2690. חַצְצַר ***ḥaṣṣar*:** A verb meaning to blow a trumpet. It means to blow the trumpet (h^a^ṣōṣ^e^rāh) (1 Chr. 15:24; 2 Chr. 5:12, 13; 7:6; 13:14; 29:28) in order to announce a major event or to bring people together.

2691. חָצֵר ***ḥāṣēr*:** A masculine noun denoting a courtyard or village. It indicates a settlement without walls (Gen. 25:16; Josh. 15:46; Ps. 10:8; Isa. 42:11); or an enclosed area, a courtyard (2 Sam. 17:18); a palace area or court (1 Kgs. 7:8; Jer. 36:20). Temples often featured these "temple courts" (2 Kgs. 21:5; Ezek. 40:14). Solomon's Temple featured an inner court with cut stone and cedar beams (1 Kgs. 6:36; 7:12). It is combined with many words to indicate specific courts or aspects of courts (Jer. 32:2; 39:14, 15); the court of the Tabernacle (Ex. 27:9); the gate of the court (Ex. 35:17). It is used poetically of the courts of the Lord (Isa. 1:12; 62:9).

2692. חֲצַר אַדָּר ***ḥ*^a^*ṣar 'addār*:** A proper noun designating Hazar Addar; a city on the southern border of Canaan, possibly *'addar* [146] (Num. 34:4).

2693. חֲצַר גַּדָּה ***ḥ*^a^*ṣar gaddāh*:** A proper noun designating Hazar Gaddah (Josh. 15:27).

2694. חֲצַר הַתִּיכוֹן ***ḥ*^a^*ṣar hattiyk̲ôn*:** A proper noun designating Hazar Hatticon (Ezek. 47:16).

2695. חֶצְרוֹ ***ḥeṣrô*:** A proper noun designating Hezro (2 Sam. 23:35; 1 Chr. 11:37).

2696. חֶצְרוֹן ***ḥeṣrôn*:** A proper noun designating Hezron:

A. Son of Pharez (Gen. 46:12; Num. 26:21; Ruth 4:18, 19; 1 Chr. 2:5, 9, 18, 21, 24, 25; 4:1).

B. Son of Reuben (Gen. 46:9; Ex. 6:14; Num. 26:6; 1 Chr. 5:3).

C. A city (Josh. 15:2, 25). See also *q*^e^*riyyôt̲ ḥeṣrôn* 7152,II.

2697. חֶצְרוֹנִי ***ḥeṣrôniy*:** A proper noun designating Hezronite:

A. A descendant of Reuben through the line of his son Hezron (Num. 26:6).

B. A descendant of Pharez through the line of his son Hezron (Num. 26:21).

2698. חֲצֵרוֹת ***ḥ^aṣērôṯ:*** A proper noun designating Hazeroth (Num. 11:35; 12:16; 33:17, 18; Deut. 1:1).

2699. חֲצֵרִים ***ḥ^aṣēriym:*** A proper noun designating Hazerim (Deut. 2:23).

2700. חֲצַרְמָוֶת ***ḥ^aṣarmāweṯ:*** A proper noun designating Hazarmaveth (Gen. 10:26; 1 Chr. 1:20).

2701. חֲצַר סוּסָה ***ḥ^aṣar sûsāh:*** A proper noun designating Hazar Susah (Josh. 19:5).

2702. חֲצַר סוּסִים ***ḥ^aṣar sûsiym:*** A proper noun designating Hazar Susim (1 Chr. 4:31).

2703. חֲצַר עֵינוֹן ***ḥ^aṣar 'ēynôn:*** A proper noun designating Hazar Enan (Ezek. 47:17).

2704. חֲצַר עֵינָן ***ḥ^aṣar 'ēynān:*** A proper noun designating Hazar Enan (Num. 34:9, 10; Ezek. 48:1).

2705. חֲצַר שׁוּעָל ***ḥ^aṣar šû'āl:*** A proper noun designating Hazar Shual (Josh. 15:28; 19:3; 1 Chr. 4:28; Neh. 11:27).

2706. חֹק ***ḥōq:*** A masculine noun meaning regulation, law, ordinance, decree, custom. Primarily, this word represents an expectation or mandate prescribed by decree or custom. It is used to speak of the general decrees of God (Jer. 5:22; Amos 2:4); the statutes of God given to Moses (Ex. 15:26; Num. 30:16[17]; Mal. 4:4[3:22]); the lawful share deserved by virtue of status (Gen. 47:22; Lev. 10:13, 14); the declared boundaries or limits of something (Job 14:5; 26:10); the prevailing cultural norm (Judg. 11:39); the binding legislation made by a ruler (Gen. 47:26); and that which must be observed by strict ritual (Ex. 12:24).

2707. חָקָה ***ḥāqāh:*** A verb meaning to cut, to carve, to engrave, to portray. It is used of a process of cutting or carving on wood or stone all kinds of religious art work (1 Kgs. 6:35), especially on or in the Temple. It describes symbols and items that had been engraved on the walls of the Temple illegally as well (Ezek. 8:10), including engravings of Babylonians (Ezek. 23:14). It is used figuratively of the Lord's engraving, setting a limit, for the life of a person to follow (Job 13:27).

2708. חֻקָּה ***ḥuqqāh:*** A noun meaning a statute, an ordinance, anything prescribed. It serves as the feminine of *ḥōq*. Since its basic meaning is not specific, the word takes on different connotations in each context. Its most common meaning is decrees, statutes, or a synonym of these words. The decrees of the Lord could be oral or written; they made God's will known and gave divine directions to His people. Abraham kept them, evidently, before they were written down (Gen. 26:5). Moses and his assistants were to teach the statutes of the Lord to Israel (Ex. 18:20; Lev. 10:11) so that the Israelites could discern between the clean and the unclean. The decrees of the Lord, along with His laws, regulations, and commandments, covered all areas of life. The Israelites were to follow His decrees so they would separate themselves from the practices of the pagan nations around them (Lev. 18:3, 4). Moses admonished the Israelites to keep God's decrees and statutes (Lev. 19:37; 20:22; 25:18). Blessing was the reward for keeping them (Lev. 26:3), but curses were promised for those who didn't obey them (Lev. 26:15, 43).

Throughout the passing of Israel's history, new decrees were added (Josh. 24:25), and the people and leaders were judged with respect to their faithfulness in observing God's decrees, laws, statutes, and commandments. David was renowned for having observed them (2 Sam. 22:23). The Davidic covenant would be realized if later kings followed the Lord's decrees as David had (1 Kgs. 6:12). However, most of the kings failed, including Solomon (1 Kgs. 11:11; 2 Kgs. 17:15, 34). Josiah renewed the covenant and exerted himself to follow the Lord's decrees (2 Kgs. 23:3), but it was too late to save Judah from exile (see 2 Kgs. 23:25–27).

The psalmist found great joy in the decrees, laws, commandments, precepts, ordinances, and instructions of the Lord; they were not burdensome (Ps. 18:22[23]; 119:5). However, some leaders of Israel distorted God's decrees and established their own oppressive decrees on the people (see Isa. 10:1).

God's issuance of a decree was effective and permanent: by His decree, He established the order of creation forever, the functions of the sun and the moon (Job 28:26; Jer. 31:35). The prophets without fail condemned Israel and its leaders for not keeping the decrees of the Lord (Ezek. 11:12; 20:13; Amos 2:4) but saw a future time when a redeemed people would follow them (Ezek. 36:27; 37:24).

2709. חֲקוּפָא ***ḥ^aqûp̱ā':*** A proper noun designating Hakupha (Ezra 2:51; Neh. 7:53).

2710. חָקַק ***ḥāqaq:*** A verb meaning to cut, to inscribe, to engrave, to decree. The basic meaning, to cut, is used for cutting a tomb out of rock (Isa. 22:16), but it is used more commonly of engraving or writing (Isa. 30:8; Ezek. 4:1; 23:14). It is employed for decreeing (i.e., inscribing) a law (Isa. 10:1); and the word statute (*ḥōq*[2706]) is derived from it. Figuratively, God is said to have inscribed a boundary over the deep at creation (Prov. 8:27). It also expresses the idea of a commander of decrees (Deut. 33:21; Judg. 5:9).

2711. חֵקֶק ***ḥēqeq:*** A masculine noun meaning something prescribed, a decree, a thought. This word is the construct of *ḥôq* (2706) and is only found twice in the Old Testament.

When Deborah and Barak sang a song to commemorate the victory over the Canaanites, they sang of the "great thoughts of the heart" (KJV), referring to the thoughts and statues within a person (Judg. 5:15). In the other occurrence, Isaiah declared that the judgment of God was on those who enacted wicked statutes (Isa. 10:1).

2712. *ḥuqōq:* A proper noun designating Hukkok:

A. A location in Naphtali (Josh. 19:34).

B. Hukkok: another name for *ḥelqāṯ* [2520] (1 Chr. 6:75[60]).

2713. חָקַר *ḥāqar:* A verb meaning to explore, to search, to seek out. It means to scout or explore various things: a city (2 Sam. 10:3); land (Judg. 18:2). The foundations of the earth are said to be unsearchable (Jer. 31:37; cf. Jer. 46:23). Something can be, in general, unsearchable, unmeasured (1 Kgs. 7:47; 2 Chr. 4:18). It is used of the preacher's process of searching out or even inventing proverbs or parables to communicate with his listeners (Eccl. 12:9).

2714. חֵקֶר *ḥēqer:* A masculine noun referring to a search, an inquiry, something to be searched out. It refers to the self-examination of one's heart (Judg. 5:16); or to a general listing of things that have been examined by others (Job 8:8). The Lord's understanding is declared to be unsearchable, among other things (*'ēn ḥēqer;* Job 5:9; 9:10; Ps. 145:3; Isa. 40:28). In Job the word refers to the foundations, bases or recesses of the deep or abyss (Job 38:16). Used figuratively, it denotes the deep things or depths of God to be examined (Job 11:7).

2715. חֹר *ḥōr:* A masculine noun meaning noble. It occurs only in the plural form and apparently comes from a root, unused in the Old Testament, which means free. The nobles were a social order having power over the lower classes of people, a power which they sometimes misused, exacting usury (Neh. 5:7), even following a royal order to kill innocent Naboth (1 Kgs. 21:8, 11). In Nehemiah's time, they maintained strong family connections (Neh. 6:17). Ecclesiastes 10:17 indicates that nobility was inherited and could not be instantly attained by election or force; otherwise, all kings would be nobility by definition. Thus, nobles made the best kings (Eccl. 10:17), apparently because they came from a background of involvement in civic affairs and were not suddenly vaulted to such a high position.

2716. חֶרֶא *ḥere':* A masculine noun indicating a dove's dung, dung. The excrement of a dove. It had some food value and was eaten in extreme cases but had almost no monetary value (2 Kgs. 6:25, *ḥarēy yôniym*). It also refers to human excrement (2 Kgs. 18:27; Isa. 36:12).

2717. חָרֵב *ḥārēḇ*, חָרַב *ḥāraḇ:* A verb meaning to be desolate, to be destroyed, to be dry, to dry up, to lay waste. Two related themes constitute the cardinal meaning of this word, devastation and drying up. Although each aspect is distinct from the other, both convey the notion of wasting away. The word is used to describe the drying of the earth after the flood (Gen. 8:13); the drying of green vines (Judg. 16:7); the utter destruction of a physical structure (Ezek. 6:6); the devastation of war (Isa. 37:18); the removal of human inhabitants (Ezek. 26:19); the slaughter of animals (Jer. 50:27).

2718. חֲרַב ***ḥ*ᵃ*ra*b̲*:*** An Aramaic verb meaning to be utterly destroyed, to be laid waste. The only occurrence of this verb is preserved in a letter sent to Artaxerxes concerning the rebuilding of Jerusalem (Ezra 4:15). Certain antagonists of the Jewish people desired to hinder the rebuilding of the city and called to mind that it was due to wickedness that Jerusalem was destroyed by the Babylonians (cf. Jer. 52:12–20). The result left the city in utter desolation and without defense (cf. Neh. 2:17; Jer. 9:11).

2719. חֶרֶב ***ḥereb̲:*** A feminine noun meaning a sword, a knife, a cutting tool. The word frequently pictures the sword, along with the bow and shield, as the standard fighting equipment of the times (Gen. 48:22; Ps. 76:3[4]; Hos. 1:7). Warriors are referred to as those drawing the sword (Judg. 20; 1 Chr. 21:5). The sword may also stand for a larger unit of military power, sometimes pictured as coming on a people or land (Lev. 26:25; Lam. 1:20; Ezek. 14:17). The cutting action of a sword is likened to eating, and its edges are literally referred to as mouths. Similarly, the mouths of people are likened to swords (Ps. 59:7[8]; Prov. 30:14; Isa. 49:2). The sword is also a symbol of judgment executed by God (Gen. 3:24; Deut. 32:41; Jer. 47:6); or His people (Ps. 149:6). The word can refer to a knife (Josh. 5:2, 3); or a tool for cutting stones (Ex. 20:25).

2720. חָרֵב ***ḥārēb̲:*** An adjective meaning dry, desolate, wasted. Two connected ideas undergird the translation of this word. The first is the sense of dryness as opposed to wetness. In this line, it is used specifically of the grain offering (Lev. 7:10) or a morsel of food (Prov. 17:1). The second is the sense of desolation. In this way, it is used to describe the wasted condition of Jerusalem after the Babylonian captivity (Neh. 2:3); the emptiness of the land, which is comparable to the sparse population of the Garden of Eden (Ezek. 36:35); and the condition of the Temple in Haggai's day, as it still lay in ruins (Hag. 1:4).

2721. חֹרֶב ***ḥōreb̲:*** A masculine noun indicating heat, drought, dryness. It basically refers to heat or dryness of some kind. It refers to the heat of the day (Gen. 31:40; Isa. 4:6; Jer. 36:30). In Gideon's test with the fleece of wool, it refers to the dryness of the ground or the fleece (Judg. 6:37, 39, 40). The dryness or feverishness of Job's skin is described with this word (Job 30:30). It indicates the destruction and devastation of cities that will be renewed (Isa. 61:4); and a drought or dry spell that destroys the land (Hag. 1:11).

2722. חֹרֵב ***ḥōrē<u>b</u>:*** A proper noun designating Horeb, another name for Mount Sinai (5514) (Ex. 3:1; 17:6; 33:6; Deut. 1:2, 6, 19; 4:10, 15; 5:2; 9:8; 18:16; 29:1[28:69]; 1 Kgs. 8:9; 19:8; 2 Chr. 5:10; Ps. 106:19; Mal. 4:4[3:22]).

2723. חָרְבָּה ***ḥorbāh:*** A feminine noun meaning ruin. The word almost always refers to an area ruined by the judgment of God. The destroyed area is usually a country or city but may also be individual property (Ps. 109:10). Sometimes the ruins are referred to as being restored by God (Isa. 51:3; 52:9; 58:12). The ruins of Job 3:14 may have been rebuilt by men; if so, the context makes clear that the rebuilding was unsuccessful. In Malachi 1:4, God would not allow Edom to rebuild his ruins successfully; similarly, Psalm 9:6[7] seems to refer to an eternal state of ruin. Ezekiel 26:20 and Isaiah 58:12 refer to ancient ruins, but it is difficult to identify them definitely. The ruins of the latter passage would be restored by those who seek God sincerely with fasting.

2724. חָרָבָה ***ḥārā<u>b</u>āh:*** A feminine noun meaning dry land, dry ground. The central principle of this word is the lack of moisture. It is used to refer to the habitable ground inundated by the flood (Gen. 7:22); dry waterbeds (Ezek. 30:12); and land in general (Hag. 2:6). Three times the word describes the condition of a path made in the miraculous parting of water: for Moses and Israel (Ex. 14:21); for Joshua and Israel (Josh. 3:17); and for Elijah and Elisha (2 Kgs. 2:8).

2725. חֲרָבוֹן ***ḥ^arā<u>b</u>ôn:*** A masculine noun denoting heat, drought, dry heat. It is used of the heat of summer (*qayiṣ*) which mercilessly drained or sapped one's strength (Ps. 32:4). In the context, it is compared to David's guilt and conscience which sap his strength.

2726. חַרְבוֹנָא ***ḥar<u>b</u>ônā',*** חַרְבוֹנָה ***ḥar<u>b</u>ônāh:*** A proper noun designating Harbona (Esth. 1:10; 7:9).

2727. חָרַג ***ḥārag:*** A verb meaning to be afraid, to quake. The word occurs only in Psalm 18:45[46] where foreigners came quaking from their strongholds. The idea of foreigners coming out derives from the word *min* (4480), meaning from. However, a similar passage in Micah 7:17 (using a different verb but dependent on *min* for the idea of coming out) justifies the translation "to come quaking." The passage thus pictures foreigners surrendering their strongholds to David and coming out.

2728. חַרְגֹּל ***ḥargōl:*** A masculine noun referring to a cricket, a locust. It refers to a winged insect that was considered clean and therefore edible by God's holy people (Lev. 11:22).

John the Baptist ate locusts and wild honey.

2729. חָרַד ḥārad̲: A verb meaning to tremble, to quake, to be terrified. The term is used in reference to mountains (Ex. 19:18); islands (Isa. 41:5); birds and beasts (Jer. 7:33); and people (Ezek. 32:10). It can mark a disturbance, such as being startled from sleep (Ruth 3:8); or terror brought on by a trumpet's sound (Amos 3:6); or an act of God (1 Sam. 14:15). It is often connected with terrifying an enemy in battle. It is also used in the causative, meaning to terrify (Judg. 8:12; 2 Sam. 17:2; Zech. 1:21[2:4]). See the word *ḥ*ᵃ*rād̲āh* (2731).

2730. חָרֵד ḥārēd̲, חֲרֹד ḥᵃrōd̲: An adjective meaning trembling, reverential. God told Gideon to limit the number of warriors by telling those who were afraid or trembling to return to their camp at Gilead (Judg. 7:3). God honors and looks upon those who are contrite in spirit and tremble at His word (Isa. 66:2). Those who tremble at God's words are also accounted as obedient (Ezra 9:4).

2731. חֲרָדָה ḥᵃrād̲āh: A feminine noun meaning trembling, quaking, fear. This trembling is often brought on by acts of God. It is the terror of God that overcame the enemy (1 Sam. 14:15); and startled Daniel's friends in a vision (Dan. 10:7). Humans can also inspire fear (Prov. 29:25). See the cognate verb *ḥārad̲* (2729).

2732. חֲרָדָה ḥᵃrād̲āh: A proper noun designating Haradah (Num. 33:24, 25).

2733. חֲרֹדִי ḥᵃrōd̲iy: A proper noun designating Harodite (2 Sam. 23:25).

2734. חָרָה ḥārāh, נָחַר nāḥār: A verb meaning to burn, to be kindled, to glow, to grow warm. Figuratively, it means to get angry or to become vexed. Anger can be between two people: Potiphar's anger was kindled against Joseph when his wife accused Joseph of rape (Gen. 39:19). Anger can also be between God and a person: God's anger is against those who transgress His law (Josh. 23:16). This word can also describe a future event of one becoming angry (Isa. 41:11).

2735. חֹר הַגִּדְגָּד ḥōr haggid̲gād̲: A proper noun designating Hor Haggidgad (Num. 33:32, 33).

2736. חַרְהֲיָה ḥarhᵃyāh: A proper noun designating Harhaiah (Neh. 3:8).

2737. חָרוּז ḥārûz: A masculine noun indicating a string of beads or jewels, a necklace of shells. It was an ornament, a beautifying piece of jewelry which the writer of Song of Solomon 1:10 places on the beloved's neck.

2738. חָרוּל ***ḥārûl:*** A masculine noun referring to weeds, nettles, thistles. It depicts weeds in an orchard, vineyard, or field (Prov. 24:31) belonging to a sluggard. They provided a temporary lodging place for the outcasts of society (Job 30:7). It grew in deserted areas and fields like Gomorrah (Zeph. 2:9).

2739. חֲרוּמַף ***ḥ^arûmap̱:*** A proper noun designating Harumaph (Neh. 3:10).

2740. חָרוֹן ***ḥārôn:*** A masculine noun meaning heat, fierceness, anger. It is used metaphorically of God's anger (2 Kgs. 23:26) in the phrase *ḥ^arôn 'ap̱* or its equivalent, meaning literally, "the heat of (one's) nose." But it is used of the Lord's anger always (Ex. 32:12; Num. 25:4; Deut. 13:17 [18]; Josh. 7:26; 1 Sam. 28:18; Ps. 2:5; Jer. 4:8, 26; 25:37; Hos. 11:9; Nah. 1:6). In some cases, *'ap̱* is left out (Ex. 15:7; Neh. 13:18; Ps. 88:16[17]). The phrase *h^arôn hayyônāh* in Jeremiah 25:38 may be the only time it does not refer to the Lord's anger. Instead, it may refer to the anger of the oppressing sword or an oppressor himself. But the Lord's anger is indirectly displayed through the oppressor.

2741. חֲרוּפִי ***ḥ^arûp̱iy:*** A proper noun designating Haruphite (1 Chr. 12:5).

2742. חָרוּץ ***ḥārûṣ:*** I. An adjective meaning sharp, diligent. The word means industrious, diligent, referring to diligent or industrious persons who therefore succeed (Prov. 10:4; 13:4; 21:5); and even supervise or rule (Prov. 12:24). Diligence is considered a precious or valuable possession (Prov. 12:27). It indicates a sharp threshing sledge or cart (Isa. 28:27; 41:15; Amos 1:3). It is used in a comparison to describe aspects of Leviathan's underside (Job 41:30[22]).

II. A masculine noun indicating a decision. It is used in the phrase *'ēmeq heḥārûṣ* to refer to "the valley of decision" by the prophet Joel (3:14[4:14]), where the nations will gather for war and judgment.

III. A masculine noun indicating a moat. It refers to a channel of water around a city, especially Jerusalem (Dan. 9:25). It was dug and filled in for defensive purposes.

IV. A masculine noun denoting gold. It refers to the golden wings of a dove in a simile (Ps. 68:13[14]). Wisdom is always considered of greater value than gold (Prov. 3:14; 8:19; 16:16); as is knowledge (Prov. 8:10). The pagan city-state of Tyre piled up gold as her treasure (Zech. 9:3).

2743. חָרוּץ ***ḥārûṣ:*** A proper noun designating Haruz (2 Kgs. 21:19).

2744. חַרְחוּר ***ḥarḥûr:*** A proper noun designating Harhur (Ezra 2:51; Neh. 7:53).

2745. חַרְחַס ***ḥarḥas:*** A proper noun designating Harhas (2 Kgs. 22:14).

2746. חַרְחֻר ***ḥarḥur:*** A masculine noun indicating extreme heat, feverish heat. It refers most likely to the feverish heat of a disease rather than to the sun's heat (Deut. 28:22). It was among possible curses the Lord could bring on a disobedient nation.

2747. חֶרֶט ***ḥereṭ:*** A masculine noun designating an engraving tool, a chisel. It is an instrument used by Aaron to "fashion" or "dress down" the golden calf (Ex. 32:4). Its use implicated Aaron further into the guilt of the Israelites. The word is also used in Isaiah 8:1 as a writing utensil.

2748. חַרְטֹם ***ḥarṭōm:*** A masculine noun meaning engraver, a writer associated with the occult. These people seem to have had knowledge of astrology or divination and were commonly associated with the magicians of Egypt in Pharaoh's court. Pharaoh could not find any magicians to interpret his dream, so he called Joseph (Gen. 41:24). Moses caused plagues to come upon Egypt which the magicians could not reverse (Ex. 9:11).

2749. חַרְטֹם ***ḥarṭōm:*** An Aramaic noun meaning magician. It occurs only in the book of Daniel (Dan. 2:10, 27; 4:7[4], 9[6]; 5:11). These people, who practiced sorcery and other occult practices, were advisors and counselors of kings.

2750. חֳרִי ***ḥ°riy:*** A masculine noun meaning burning. It is used to describe anger. The word occurs with *'ap̱* (639) which primarily means nose, but in this case, it means anger as derived from the snorting of an angry person. The anger may be righteous anger, such as God's anger at Israel's unfaithfulness (Deut. 29:24[23]; Lam. 2:3); Moses' anger aroused by Pharaoh's stubbornness (Ex. 11:8); and Jonathan's anger at Saul's outburst against David (1 Sam. 20:34). It may also be unrighteous anger, such as the anger of troops dismissed with pay because of God's word (2 Chr. 25:10); and the anger of the kings of Israel and Syria against Judah (Isa. 7:4). In all cases, the heat of the anger is evident whether expressed by leaving the room or by attempting to put to death the object of anger (2 Chr. 25:10; cf. v. 13).

2751. חֹרִי ***ḥōriy:*** A masculine noun referring to white bread, white. It is used of a cake or bun of bread made of fine, white flour (Gen. 40:16), the best cooking flour available.

2752. חֹרִי ***ḥōriy:*** A proper noun designating a Horite (Gen. 14:6; 36:20, 21, 29, 30(NASB, NIV); Deut. 2:12, 22).

2753. חוֹרִי ***ḥôriy:*** A proper noun designating Hori:

A. Son of Lotan (Gen. 36:22, 30(KJV); 1 Chr. 1:39).

B. A Simeonite (Num. 13:5).

2754. חָרִיט ***ḥāriyṭ:*** A masculine noun indicating a purse, a bag. It was capable of carrying money, up to a talent of silver weighing about 75 pounds (2 Kgs. 5:23) and hence could be called a "money purse" (Isa. 3:22).

2755. חֲרֵי יוֹנִים ḥ^a^rēy yôniym: A masculine noun indicating doves' dung. It is used in the phrase *ḥ^a^rēy yôniym,* literally meaning the "excrement of doves" or "dung(s) of doves." It was eaten in times of severe famine and was normally of little monetary value. Its nutritional value was minimal (2 Kgs. 6:25).

2756. חָרִיף ḥāriyp̱: A proper noun designating Hariph:
A. A Jew (Neh. 7:24).
B. A Jew (Neh. 10:19[20]).

2757. חָרִיץ ḥāriyṣ: I. A masculine noun referring to a harrow, a wedge, a sharp instrument. It was a tool of menial, hard labor and often used by prisoners of war set to hard labor (2 Sam. 12:31; 1 Chr. 20:3).

II. A masculine noun indicating a piece (of cheese), a slice. It was a serving of cheese especially good for soldiers in combat or preparing for combat (1 Sam. 17:18).

2758. חָרִישׁ ḥāriyš: A masculine noun meaning plowing time, plowing. It refers to the tillage of the soil with a plow (1 Sam. 8:12) and the season or time of plowing the fields (Gen. 45:6; Ex. 34:21).

2759. חֲרִישִׁי ḥ^a^riyšiy: An adjective meaning hot, scorching. It describes the hot desert east wind that helped kill Jonah's shade plant (Jon. 4:8).

2760. חָרַךְ ḥārak̠: A verb meaning to roast. It refers to cooking game over the fire (Prov. 12:27), and it produced succulent-tasting food compared to boiling.

2761. חֲרַךְ ḥ^a^rak̠: An Aramaic verb indicating to be singed, to be burned. It means to be burned slightly or superficially enough to see and smell (Dan. 3:27). It was miraculous that the clothing of the three Israelites was not singed at all from the high heat of the furnace.

2762. חָרָךְ ḥārāk̠: A masculine noun indicating a lattice. It refers to a structure of open crossed strips or bars of various materials such as wood or metal, perhaps a garden trellis in Song of Solomon 2:9.

2763. חָרַם ḥāram: A verb meaning to destroy, to doom, to devote. This word is most commonly associated with the Israelites destroying the Canaanites upon their entry into the Promised Land (Deut. 7:2; Josh. 11:20). It indicates complete and utter destruction (Judg. 21:11; 1 Sam. 15:18); the severe judgment of God (Isa. 11:15); the forfeiture of property (Ezra 10:8); being "accursed" or set apart for destruction (Josh. 6:18). This latter application, being set apart, accounts for what appears to be a contradictory element in the verb. It is also used to mean devotion or consecration to the Lord (Lev. 27:28, 29; Mic. 4:13). Just as something accursed is set apart for destruction, so something devoted to God is set apart for His use.

2764. חֵרֶם ***ḥērem:*** A masculine noun meaning devoted things, devoted to destruction, devotion, things under ban, cursed. The basic meaning of the word, to be set aside or devoted, is qualified in several ways. Things, including persons, were set aside or devoted to a special function or an area of service by a declaration of God or His servants. The entire city of Jericho was a deadly threat to the formation of God's people and fell under a ban, except for Rahab and her family (Josh. 6:17, 18), and was set aside for destruction. A person could be set aside for destruction (1 Kgs. 20:42) as well as an entire people, such as Edom (Isa. 34:5). The Lord set the Israelites apart for destruction when they turned to other gods (Deut. 13:17[18]; Isa. 43:28); the Israelites could not take idols of the conquered pagans into their houses, even when acquired in battle. These items were set aside for destruction only (Deut. 7:26). This term was the last word in the text of the Prophets (Mal. 4:6[3:24]) and expressed a potential curse on the entire restored exilic community of Israel. Happily, the Lord also announced a time when the ban for destruction would be lifted from Jerusalem forever (Zech. 14:11).

Various items could become holy, that is, devoted to cultic or holy use, as in the case of a field given to the Lord (Lev. 27:21); or the spoils of war could be set aside for religious use only (Num. 18:14; Josh. 6:18; 1 Sam. 15:21), including gold, silver, items of bronze or iron, and animals. These items, set aside exclusively to holy use, could not be used for everyday purposes, for to use such items in this way was a grave sin. Achan and others died for this offense (Josh. 7:1, 12, 15; 22:20).

2765. חֳרֵם ***ḥ***^{o}***rēm:*** A proper noun designating Horem (Josh. 19:38).

2766. חָרִם ***ḥārim:*** A proper noun designating Harim:

A. A priest (1 Chr. 24:8).

B. A priest (Neh. 10:5[6]).

C. Head of a priestly course (Ezra 2:39; 10:21; Neh. 7:42; 12:15).

D. Head of a family (Ezra 2:32; 10:31; Neh. 3:11; 7:35).

E. A prince (Neh. 10:27[28]).

2767. חָרְמָה ***ḥormāh:*** A proper noun designating Hormah (Num. 14:45; 21:3; Deut. 1:44; Josh. 12:14; 15:30; 19:4; Judg. 1:17; 1 Sam. 30:30; 1 Chr. 4:30).

2768. חֶרְמוֹן ***ḥermôn:*** A proper noun designating Hermon (Deut. 3:8, 9; 4:48; Josh. 11:3, 17; 12:1, 5; 13:5, 11; 1 Chr. 5:23; Ps. 89:12(13); 133:3; Song 4:8).

2769. חֶרְמוֹנִים ***ḥermôniym:*** A proper noun designating Hermonites, peaks of Mount Hermon (Ps. 42:6[7]).

2770. חֶרְמֵשׁ ***ḥermēš:*** A masculine noun denoting a sickle. A farming or agricultural implement used to cut or harvest grain, to cut weeds and overgrowth of bushes, etc. (Deut.

23:25[26]). "To put the sickle" to standing grain means to begin harvesting it (Deut. 16:9). It is found in the Septuagint of 1 Samuel 13:20 as the last item mentioned, but the Hebrew text reads plowshare (NASB, hoe; NIV, NKJV, sickle; KJV, mattock).

2771. חָרָן ***ḥārān:*** A proper noun designating Haran:

A. The city in northern Mesopotamia to which Abraham migrated from Ur of the Chaldees. It was about seven hundred miles from Ur of the Chaldees. It was on the west side of the Balik River. The name means "road, way." Shepherding was an important agricultural pursuit there, including all kinds of livestock. Haran traded with many nations (Ezek. 27:23). It was a center for the worship of the moon god. Assyria, under Sennacherib, conquered it (2 Kgs. 19:12; Isa. 37:12). Abraham left Haran with Lot when he was seventy-five years old (Gen. 12:4, 5). Laban lived there and, of course, Jacob lived there for a long period of time with Laban. Terah lived there briefly before he died. Rebekah, Isaac's wife, came from Haran. It was the birthplace of the twelve patriarchs, except Benjamin.

B. The son of Caleb through his concubine Ephah. Haran fathered Gazez (1 Chr. 2:46).

2772. חֹרֹנִי ***ḥōrōniy:*** A proper noun designating Horonite (Neh. 2:10, 19; 13:28).

2773. חֹרֹנַיִם ***ḥōrōnayim,*** חוֹרֹנַיִם ***ḥôrōnayim:*** A proper noun designating Horonaim (Isa. 15:5; Jer. 48:3, 5, 34).

2774. חַרְנֶפֶר ***ḥarnep̱er:*** A proper noun designating Harnepher (1 Chr. 7:36).

2775. חֶרֶס ***ḥeres:*** I. A masculine noun used for sun; Heres. It refers to the sun (KJV, Judg. 8:13; 14:18; Job 9:7), but others read a proper name in Judges 8:13 (NKJV, NASB, NIV) referring to the ascent or pass of Heres.

II. A masculine noun indicating a skin disorder, an itch. It is listed among the curses as one of the skin diseases the Lord will bring on Israel if they disobey the Sinai covenant (Deut. 28:27).

2776. חֶרֶס ***ḥeres:*** A proper noun designating Heres (Judg. 1:35; 8:13).

2777. חַרְסוּת ***ḥarsûṯ:*** A feminine noun denoting a potsherd, a clay fragment. It is used with *šaʿar,* gate, to indicate the potsherd gate as literally "the gate of the potsherd" (Jer. 19:2). It is not clear whether potsherds play a part in the construction of the gate or some other activity took place there regarding potsherds, e.g., a potsherd dump.

2778. חָרַף ***ḥārap̱:*** I. A verb meaning to reproach. It means to taunt or agitate someone about something (Ps. 119:42), e.g., the psalmist was the object of taunting from his enemies. Nehemiah is the object of reproaches from his enemies (Neh. 6:13). Israel as a whole was taunted and reproached by the Philistine, Goliath. God is the object of His enemies' reproaches or revilings (2 Kgs. 19:4, 16, 22, 23; Ps. 79:12) and by the enemies of His people. To reproach one's own life (soul) is to stake one's faith or trust in something and support it (Judg. 5:18; 1 Sam. 17:10, 25, 26; Ps. 89:51[52]).

II. A verb meaning to remain to winter or to remain in harvest time. It is used in a context that refers to spending the winter at something, e.g., the wild animals spending the winter eating the remains of the Cushites (Isa. 18:6) after the Lord's judgments.

III. A verb meaning to engage, to acquire, to betroth. In context it refers to a slave woman acquired legally for a man to marry (Lev. 19:20).

2779. חֹרֶף ***ḥōrep̱:*** A masculine noun referring to the season of winter or harvesttime (Zech. 14:8). It indicates one of the four seasons; in the Middle East, it was also a time of sowing and the beginning of the land's new produce (Gen. 8:22). In the phrase "days of winter (autumn)" (*yᵉmēy ḥōrep̱*), it means the prime of one's life (Job 29:4). The rich were able to afford autumn/winter houses or palaces (Jer. 36:22; Amos 3:15). It was the time of harvesting, not plowing (Prov. 20:4).

2780. חָרֵף ***ḥārēp̱:*** A proper noun designating Hareph (1 Chr. 2:51).

2781. חֶרְפָּה ***ḥerpāh:*** A feminine noun meaning reproach, scorn, taunt. The term can be used for a taunt hurled at an enemy (1 with an individual such as barrenness (Gen. 30:23); uncircumcision (Gen. 34:14); and widowhood (Isa. 54:4).

2782. חָרַץ ***ḥāraṣ:*** A verb indicating to act promptly, sharply, to decide, to move against, to maim, to be eager for something. It indicates a cutting or maiming that an animal has that makes it unacceptable for sacrifice (Lev. 22:22). Of a dog it means to snarl or move against (Ex. 11:7); of persons it means to utter a word against, speak sharply against (Josh. 10:21). It means to determine, to define, to decide something (2 Sam. 5:24; 1 Kgs. 20:40); in its passive usage, it means something fixed, determined (Job 14:5). It refers to something set or determined or decreed (Isa. 10:23; 28:22; Dan. 9:27). The judgments of God are firmly and strictly determined (Dan. 11:36) and will come to pass.

2783. חֲרַץ ***ḥᵃraṣ:*** An Aramaic feminine noun referring to loins, hip, hip joint. It is used of the hips or hip joints of the human body. Belshazzar's loins or hips gave way at the appearance of a hand writing on the wall of his palace (Dan. 5:6).

2784. חַרְצֻבָּה ***harṣubbāh:*** A feminine noun meaning fetter, chain, bond, pain, torments. It refers to unjust, wicked bonds or chains in a figurative sense, usually indicating social, economic, or political oppression (Isa. 58:6). It indicates the pains or torments that often accompany death but which the wicked seem to be free of (Ps. 73:4).

2785. חַרְצָן *ḥarṣān:* A masculine noun referring to a seed, a kernel. It refers to the kernels or seeds of the grape (Num. 6:4). Some have suggested that its reference is to unripe grapes.

2786. חָרַק *ḥāraq:* A verb indicating to gnash, to grind the teeth at. It is used figuratively of persons grinding or striking their teeth at someone in anger (Ps. 35:16; 37:12). The wicked gnash their teeth in despair at the success of the one who fears God (Ps. 112:10). Job complains that God has gnashed His teeth at him in his suffering (Job 16:9). The enemies responsible for the fall of Jerusalem, Zion, grind their teeth in disrespect at the Lord's city (Lam. 2:16).

2787. חָרַר *ḥārar:* A verb meaning to be hot, to be scorched, to burn. Jerusalem is scorched under the figurative caldron that Ezekiel saw (Ezek. 24:11). It also describes the physical burning Job felt in his bones (Job 30:30). Figuratively, Jeremiah refers to Babylon as burning the bellows of Jerusalem (Jer. 6:29). This word can also connote an angry person kindling strife (Prov. 26:21).

2788. חָרֵר *ḥārēr:* A noun meaning parched place, a scorched place. It occurs only in Jeremiah 17:6 where it is plural and refers to places where lack of water keeps plants from prospering. This symbolizes the lives of those who trust in people rather than in God. In contrast, those who trust in God have enough water even in heat and drought (Jer. 17:7, 8).

2789. חֶרֶשׂ *ḥereś:* A masculine noun meaning earthenware, clay pottery, and potsherd. This word signifies any vessel made from clay (Lev. 15:12; Jer. 19:1); the sharp fragments of broken pottery (Job 41:30[22]); and the larger potsherd useful to scoop burning coals from a fire (Isa. 30:14); or to scrape boils (Job 2:8). Figuratively, David used the image of kiln-dried pottery to describe the depletion of his strength (Ps. 22:15[16]).

2790. חָרַשׁ *ḥāraš:* I. A verb meaning to plow, to engrave. It refers to plowing, tilling the soil (Deut. 22:10; 1 Kgs. 19:19) with animals. Hosea speaks metaphorically of Israel's "plowing wickedness" and receiving injustice as a reward (Hos. 10:13). It refers to devising or preparing evil against one's neighbor (1 Sam. 23:9; Prov. 3:29) or enemy. With the preposition *'al*, upon, it means to engrave (Jer. 17:1). Zion in judgment was plowed under as a field (Jer. 26:18; Mic. 3:12). The participial form of the verb indicates the person who does skilled work, a craftsman (*ḥōrēš*) (Gen. 4:22; 1 Kgs. 7:14).

II. A verb meaning to be deaf; silent, mute. It indicates a person's keeping still or being silent (Gen. 24:21; 2 Kgs. 18:36). It refers to keeping silent as indicating approval or consent (Num. 30:4[5]) or as indicating a lack of conviction to act about something that needs to be done (2 Sam. 19:10[11]). Keeping silent can be a way to fake being dumb (1 Sam. 10:27). To become silent is to cease speaking, to stop communicating with a person (Jer. 38:27). It can refer to a person silenced by shock, fear, or the inability to answer someone (Job 11:3). It describes God as being silent about evil (Ps. 50:21; Isa. 42:14; Hab. 1:13).

2791. חֶרֶשׁ *ḥereš:* An adverb meaning secretly. It describes doing something without giving it public exposure and keeping it from certain persons. Joshua sent out spies into Canaan secretly (Josh. 2:1).

2792. חֶרֶשׁ *ḥereš:* A proper noun designating Heresh (1 Chr. 9:15).

2793. חֹרֶשׁ *ḥōreš,* חֹרֶשׁ *ḥōres:* I. A masculine noun depicting a woods, a forest, a bough, a thicket. It refers to woodland or forest areas (2 Chr. 27:4). It describes the beauty of Assyria in her early rise to power (Ezek. 31:3). It is also sometimes described as an undesirable location as well (Isa. 17:9) and in certain contexts indicates a forested wilderness area (1 Sam. 23:15; KJV, wood; NASB, Horesh).

II. A proper noun referring to Horesh. It was a specific stand of forest and a wilderness location where David hid from Saul (1 Sam. 23:15, 16, 18, 19; KJV, wood).

2794. חֹרֵשׁ *ḥōrēš:* A masculine noun denoting a worker, craftsman. It indicates an artificer in bronze and iron (Gen. 4:22; KJV). Others understand this as referring to implements or tools (NIV, NASB).

2795. חֵרֵשׁ *ḥērēš:* An adjective indicating deaf. It indicates the inability to hear (Ps. 38:13[14]). God can make one deaf since He is the creator and ruler of life (Ex. 4:11). The deaf were not to be laughed at or cursed (Lev. 19:14). To stop one's ears is to refuse to hear instruction or change (Ps. 58:4[5]). God's future blessings include causing the deaf to hear (Isa. 29:18; 35:5). God encouraged the Israelites to hear His servant (Isa. 42:18, 19) and his message (Isa. 43:18).

2796. חָרָשׁ *ḥārāš:* A masculine noun meaning craftsman, artisan, and engraver. This Hebrew word denotes a craftsman who is skilled in a given medium. It appears in reference to one skilled in metalwork (1 Chr. 29:5; Hos. 13:2); one skilled in woodwork (1 Chr. 14:1; Isa. 40:20); and one skilled in stonework (Ex. 28:11). More broadly, the term is applied to those who make their living by fashioning idols (Isa. 45:16); or one highly skilled in his or her vocation (Ezek. 21:31[36]).

2797. חַרְשָׁא ***ḥaršā':*** A proper noun designating Harsha (Ezra 2:52; Neh. 7:54).

2798. חֲרָשִׁים ***ḥ^{a}rašiym:*** A masculine plural proper noun, Harashim. It is the name of a valley according to some translators (1 Chr. 4:14, KJV). The word literally means craftsmen and should be translated as the valley of craftsmen (1 Chr. 4:14, NASB; but NIV prefers Ge (Valley) Harashim with a note; so also NKJV).

2799. חֲרֹשֶׁת ***ḥ^{a}rōšet̲:*** A feminine noun denoting a skillful working, a cutting. Bezalel, the master architect of the Tabernacle, was given the ability to perform all kinds of craftsmanship (Ex. 31:5) and skilled work (Ex. 35:33) in order to furnish the Tabernacle with utensils and a decor of beauty and honor.

2800. חֲרֹשֶׁת הַגּוֹיִם ***ḥ^{a}rōšet̲ haggôyim,*** חֲרֹשֶׁת ***ḥ^{a}rōšet̲:*** I. Harosheth Haggoyim (NASB, NIV, Judg. 4:2, 13, 16).

II. Harosheth, used with the definite article and the plural of *gôy* [1471,I] (KJV, Judg. 4:2, 13, 16).

2801. חָרַת ***ḥārat̲:*** A verb indicting to engrave. It indicates cutting or engraving on stone tablets, the Ten Commandments (Ex. 32:16). Such engraving was a common means of communicating in the ancient world of Israel.

2802. חֶרֶת ***ḥeret̲:*** A proper noun designating Hereth (1 Sam. 22:5).

2803. חָשַׁב ***ḥāšab̲,*** חשֵׁב ***ḥōšēb̲:*** A verb meaning to think, to devise, to reckon, to regard, to invent, to consider, to be accounted, to consider, to reckon oneself. When the subject of this verb is God, the verb means to consider, to devise, to plan, to reckon. Job cried out to God and asked why God considered him His enemy (Job 13:24; 33:10); however, Job was falsely accusing his Creator. Through the evil actions of Joseph's brothers, God had intended good for all of them (Gen. 50:20; Ps. 40:17[18]). Against a wicked people, the Lord planned destruction (Jer. 18:11; Mic. 2:3). God also "reckoned" Abraham's faith as righteousness (Gen. 15:6).

When humans are the subjects of this verb, the word has similar meanings: the king of Assyria thought he would destroy many nations (Isa. 10:7); people devised or planned evil (Gen. 50:20; Ps. 35:4; Ezek. 38:10); Shimei begged David not to reckon his behavior as sin against him (2 Sam. 19:19[20]; Ps. 32:2). In addition, the word is used to mean to regard or to invent: the Medes did not esteem gold or silver as the Persians did (Isa. 13:17); and the Servant of Isaiah's passage was not highly esteemed by men (Isa. 53:3). God endowed people with the ability to invent new things, such as artistic and practical devices (Ex. 31:4; 35:32, 35; 2 Chr. 2:14[13]); and instruments for music (Amos 6:5).

When the verb is passive, the word expresses being valuable or being considered. Silver was not considered valuable in Solomon's reign (1 Kgs. 10:21). In the time of Israel's wandering, the Emites were reckoned to be Rephaites or Moabites (Deut. 2:11, 20).

This verb can also mean to plot, to think upon, to think out something. A person could think out his or her course of life (Prov. 16:9; Hos. 7:15); the evil person in Daniel 11:24 plotted the overthrow of all resistance to him; the boat that Jonah shipped out in came to the point of destruction in the storm (Jon. 1:4, lit., "it was thinking to be destroyed").

2804. חֲשַׁב ***ḥᵃšaḇ:*** An Aramaic verb meaning to regard, to account as. It refers to God's consideration or evaluation of something. He reckons the people of the earth as nothing (Dan. 4:35[32]) for His power and ability extend far beyond these things.

2805. חֵשֶׁב ***ḥēšeḇ:*** A masculine noun meaning waistband, a skillfully woven waistband. It describes the band or girdle on the ephod of the priest (Ex. 28:27, 28) used to secure it to him (Lev. 8:7) in a way that it would not come loose or fall off.

2806. חַשְׁבַּדָּנָה ***ḥašbaddānāh:*** A proper noun designating Hashbaddanah (Neh. 8:4).

2807. חֲשֻׁבָה ***ḥᵃšuḇāh:*** A proper noun designating Hashubah (1 Chr. 3:20).

2808. חֶשְׁבּוֹן ***ḥešbôn:*** A masculine noun meaning planning, a reason for things. It indicates an understanding, a grasping, or a knowledge of the scheme of things (Eccl. 7:25); the result of searching out (Eccl. 7:27). It is an activity carried out by a living person; the dead (Eccl. 9:10) do not understand nor can they plan anything.

2809. חֶשְׁבּוֹן ***ḥešbôn:*** A proper noun designating Heshbon, the city where the king of the Amorites, Sihon, lived before it was captured by Israel (Num. 21:25–28, 30, 34; Judg. 11:19, 26). Reuben inherited the city, but it eventually was given to Gad. It also functioned as a Levitical city afterwards (Josh. 21:39). Interestingly, it was retaken by the Moabites (Isa. 15:4; 16:8, 9; Jer. 49:3). It was located east of the northern end of the Dead Sea.

2810. חִשָּׁבוֹן ***ḥiššāḇôn:*** A feminine noun indicating a machine, a device. It refers to one's plans or possibly evil inventions that persons have discovered and that do not necessarily foster uprightness (Eccl. 7:29). It is used of engines of war or skillful, ingenious military devices created by King Uzziah (2 Chr. 26:15).

2811. חֲשַׁבְיָה ***ḥᵃšaḇyāh,*** חֲשַׁבְיָהוּ ***ḥᵃšaḇyāhû:*** A proper noun designating Hashabiah:

A. A Merarite Levite (1 Chr. 6:45[30]).

B. Son of Bunni (1 Chr. 9:14; Neh. 11:15).

C. Son of Jeduthun (1 Chr. 25:3, 19).

D. A Hebronite (1 Chr. 26:30).
E. Son of Kemuel (1 Chr. 27:17).
F. A Levite (2 Chr. 35:9).
G. A Levite (Ezra 8:19, 24; Neh. 3:17; 10:11(12); 12:24).
H. Son of Mattaniah (Neh. 11:22).
I. A priest (Neh. 12:21).

2812. חֲשַׁבְנָה ***ḥ***^{a}***šaḇnāh:*** A proper noun designating Hashabnah (Neh. 10:25[26]).

2813. חֲשַׁבְנְיָה ***ḥ***^{a}***šaḇn***^{e}***yāh:*** A proper noun designating Hashabneiah:

A. Father of Hattush (Neh. 3:10).
B. A Levite (Neh. 9:5).

2814. חָשָׁה ***ḥāšāh:*** A verb indicating to be silent, to be still. It describes refraining from telling some news or information (2 Kgs. 7:9; Isa. 62:1, 6) or simply to refrain from speech or even mourning (2 Kgs. 2:3, 5; Neh. 8:11). It also means to be inactive; to do nothing, to sit still and do nothing (Judg. 18:9; 1 Kgs. 22:3). It can refer to the stilling of nature (Ps. 107:29). It is used of God's not addressing or acting about iniquity (Isa. 57:11; 65:6).

2815. חַשּׁוּב ***ḥaššûḇ:*** A proper noun designating Hasshub:

A. A chief Levite (1 Chr. 9:14; Neh. 11:15).

B. A repairer of Jerusalem's wall (Neh. 3:11; 10:23[24]).

C. Another repairer of Jerusalem's wall (Neh. 3:23).

2816. חֲשׁוֹךְ ***ḥ***^{a}***šôḵ:*** An Aramaic masculine noun indicating darkness. It is used figuratively of darkness as the place of mystery or ignorance but which the God of Daniel knows fully (Dan. 2:22).

2817. חֲשׂוּפָא ***ḥ***^{a}***śûp̄ā',*** חֲשֻׂפָא ***ḥ***^{a}***śup̄ā':*** A proper noun designating Hasupha (Ezra 2:43; Neh. 7:46).

2818. חֲשַׁח ***ḥ***^{a}***šaḥ,*** חַשְׁחָה ***ḥašḥāh:*** I. An Aramaic verb meaning to need. It indicates some obligation or necessity to do or say something (Dan. 3:16), but the three Hebrew young men assert that they have no need or obligation to defend their God or themselves before Nebuchadnezzar.

II. An Aramaic feminine noun referring to necessity, something needed. In the context, it refers to what was needed for sacrifices (Ezra 6:9) and was to be supplied by the Persians or those living around the Israelites after their return from exile.

2819. חַשְׁחוּ ***ḥašḥû:*** An Aramaic feminine noun indicating something needed. It stands for the items needed to carry on proper worship at the second Temple building in Ezra's day (Ezra 7:20).

2820. חָשַׂךְ ***ḥāśaḵ:*** A verb indicating to hold back, to spare, to withhold; to keep from doing something. It means to hold something back, to retain: it is used of Abraham's not withholding Isaac from possible sacrifice (Gen. 22:12); of a parent sparing the rod in discipline (Prov. 13:24); to keep a person from something, such as God keeping Abimelech from sinning (Gen. 20:6); of the Lord's keeping David from killing Nabal (1 Sam. 25:39); of Joab holding back the people in battle pursuit (2 Sam. 18:16); of restraining one's speech and keeping one's mouth shut (Job 7:11; Prov. 10:19; 17:27); of refraining from something (Isa. 54:2; 58:1); or of sparing or holding back one's hand from a person such as Namaan (2 Kgs. 5:20). It takes on the idea of treasuring up or holding something in reserve (Job 38:23). In its passive use, it refers to something being spared (Job 16:6; 21:30). It is used in a figurative sense of not wandering into error both physically and spiritually by keeping one's feet in check (Jer. 14:10).

2821. חָשַׁךְ *ḥāšak:* A verb meaning to be dark, to grow dim, to be black, to hide, to obscure. The primary meaning of the word is to darken. It is used to describe God's bringing about nightfall (Amos 5:8); the deterioration of sight (Lam. 5:17); the covering of the earth with insects so as to obscure the ground (Ex. 10:15); the sullying of wisdom by foolishness (Job 38:2); the act of concealing from view (Ps. 139:12). Poetically, the word denotes the change in one's countenance in response to abject fear or distress (Eccl. 12:3).

2822. חֹשֶׁךְ *ḥōšek:* A masculine noun meaning darkness. As in English, the word has many symbolic uses. In its first occurrence, it is associated with disorder (Gen. 1:2) and is distinguished and separated from light (Gen. 1:4). In subsequent uses, whether used in a physical or a symbolic sense, it describes confusion and uncertainty (Job 12:25; 37:19); evil done in secret (Job 24:16; Prov. 2:13; Ezek. 8:12); obscurity, vanity, things forgotten (Job 3:4; 10:21; Eccl. 6:4); death (1 Sam. 2:9; Ps. 88:12[13]). Although God created darkness (Isa. 45:7) and uses it to judge His enemies (Ex. 10:21, 22; figuratively, Ps. 35:6), He enlightens the darkness of His people (Isa. 9:2[1]); bringing them out of desperate situations (Ps. 107:10, 14; Mic. 7:8); observing secret actions (Job 34:22; Ps. 139:11, 12); and giving insight and freedom (Isa. 29:18; 42:7).

2823. חָשֹׁךְ *ḥāšōk:* An adjective identifying something as obscure, insignificant. It is a detrimental and belittling term used of certain persons who are nobodies (Prov. 22:29) on the social scale or in political influence.

2824. חֶשְׁכַת *ḥeškat:* A feminine noun meaning dark or obscure. This Hebrew word is the construct form of the word *ḥ^ašēkāh* (2825). The psalmist alone uses this word in reference to the "dark waters" surrounding the Lord's pavilion (Ps. 18:11[12]). The vivid picture is that of the murky darkness of extremely deep water. This imagery suggests the mystical, almost ethereal, gulf between the supernatural presence of the Holy One of Israel and the natural order.

2825. חֲשֵׁיכָה *ḥ^{a}šēykāh,* חֲשֵׁכָה *ḥ^{a}šēkāh:* A feminine noun meaning darkness. The word is similar in meaning to *ḥōšeḵ* (2822). It refers to the experience of Abraham when God revealed to him the coming slavery of his descendants (Gen. 15:12); to the failure of the wicked to see God's standards and that results in disorder for them (Ps. 82:5; Isa. 8:22); to the darkness sometimes surrounding persons that requires them to trust in God (Isa. 50:10); He can see through darkness as well as light (Ps. 139:12).

2826. חָשַׁל *ḥāšal:* A verb meaning to be faint or feeble. It describes the Israelites' weakened state when Amalek attacked them from the rear in their desert wanderings (Deut. 25:18) shortly after escaping from Egypt.

2827. חֲשַׁל *ḥ*^{a}*šal:* An Aramaic verb indicating to subdue, to shatter. It refers to iron as the metal which shatters everything it is used against, a symbol of the fourth kingdom in Daniel 2:40.

2828. חָשֻׁם *ḥāšum:* A proper noun designating Hashum (Ezra 2:19; 10:33; Neh. 7:22; 8:4; 10:18[19]).

2829. חֶשְׁמוֹן *ḥešmôn:* A proper noun designating Heshmon (Josh. 15:27).

2830. חַשְׁמַל *ḥašmal,* חַשְׁמַלָה *ḥašmalāh:* A masculine noun meaning ember, a glowing substance. It is used three times in the phrase *k*^{e}*'êyn ḥ*^{a}*šmal* meaning "like the glowing or gleaming of *hašmal*" (Ezek. 1:4, 27; 8:2). The word is uncertain in meaning but may mean metal (NIV, NASB, glowing metal) or amber (KJV, NKJV).

2831. חַשְׁמַן *ḥašman:* A noun which occurs in the plural in Psalm 68:31[32]. It is translated "ambassador," but its meaning and derivation are unknown.

2832. חַשְׁמֹנָה *ḥašmōnāh:* A proper noun designating Hashmonah (Num. 33:29, 30).

2833. חֹשֶׁן *ḥōšen:* A masculine noun indicating a breastplate, a breastpiece, a breast pouch. It was a container worn by the high priest, and it was highly decorative, made by a skilled workman. It was similar to the ephod in construction and featured gold, blue, purple, scarlet material and fine twined linen. It was bound to the ephod. It also bore stones representing the tribes of Israel. It carried within it the Urim and Thummin and was worn over Aaron's heart (Ex. 28:15, 22–24, 26, 28–30; Lev. 8:8).

2834. חָשַׂף *ḥāśap̱:* A verb indicating making bare, stripping off. It is used in contexts giving the effect of locusts stripping bark off of vines and trees (Joel 1:7); figuratively, of the Lord baring His arm (Isa. 52:10); or stripping the forests bare by His voice (Ps. 29:9); of water (Isa. 30:14); or wine (Hag. 2:16). It indicates Babylon stripping off of a garment in a figurative sense (Isa. 47:2; Jer. 13:26).

2835. חָשִׂף ***ḥāśip̱:*** A masculine noun describing a small flock, a little flock. It is used as a description of Israel encamped for war against the Arameans (1 Kgs. 20:27), a small army compared to the multitude of Arameans.

2836. חָשַׁק ***ḥāšaq:*** A verb meaning to be attached to, to love, to delight in, to bind. Laws in Deuteronomy described the procedure for taking a slave woman to whom one has become attached as a wife (Deut. 21:11). Shechem's soul longed after and delighted in Dinah, who was an Israelite (Gen. 34:8). God's binding love for Israel is described as unmerited love (Deut. 7:7). Hezekiah describes the figurative way in which God's love for his soul delivered him by casting all his sins behind His back (Isa. 38:17).

2837. חֵשֶׁק ***ḥēšeq:*** A noun meaning a desired thing. Three of its uses referred to Solomon's building projects. He was able to build the Temple and the other constructions that he desired (1 Kgs. 9:1, 19; 2 Chr. 8:6). Isaiah 21:4 implied that the prophet desired Babylon's destruction, but the passage goes on to say that what he desired was so horrific that it terrified him.

2838. חָשׁוּק ***ḥāšûq:*** A masculine noun indicating a hook or band around a pillar. It refers to hooks placed on the pillars of the Tabernacle courtyard so that hangings or curtains, etc., could be fastened to them (Ex. 27:10, 11; 36:38; 38:10–12, 17, 19).

2839. חִשֻּׁק ***ḥiššuq:*** A masculine noun describing a spoke of a wheel. It is used to refer to the braces or bars that gave support between the hub and rim of a wheel holding up Solomon's great brass sea (1 Kgs. 7:33).

2840. חִשּׁוּר ***ḥiššûr:*** A masculine noun describing a wheel hub. It refers to the center part of a wheel, the part normally fastened to the end of an axle. These hubs were a part of the decorative great brass sea built by Solomon (1 Kgs. 7:33).

2841. חַשְׁרָה ***ḥašrāh:*** A feminine noun indicating a mass or collection of water. It is used in one of David's poetic psalms to depict one feature of a theophany or appearance of God. It pictures a mass of water collected around God (2 Sam. 22:12); NIV reads "dark rain clouds," following the Septuagint and Vulgate).

2842. חֲשַׁשׁ ***ḥ^{a}šaš:*** A masculine noun meaning chaff, dry grass. It is used in a figurative expression of chaff or dry grass bursting into flame to depict God's corrupted vineyard, Israel (Isa. 5:24). It is the useless part of hay, straw, or grain. It can refer to anything considered useless, worthless, and easily consumed (Isa. 33:11).

2843. חֻשָׁתִי ***ḥušāṯiy:*** A proper noun designating Hushathite (2 Sam.

21:18; 23:27; 1 Chr. 11:29; 20:4; 27:11).

2844. חַת ḥaṯ: I. A masculine noun denoting fear, filled with terror. It describes extreme dread and fear the animals have of humans after the flood (Gen. 9:2). This emotion is unknown to Job's Leviathan (Job 41:33[25]).

II. An adjective identifying something as broken, dismayed, terrified. It refers to bows of the mighty as broken (*ḥattîm*) (1 Sam. 2:4) or to warriors of Egypt who are terrified (Jer. 46:5), causing them to hesitate in fear or draw back.

2845. חֵת ḥēṯ: A proper noun designating Heth (Gen. 10:15; 23:3, 5, 7, 10, 16, 18, 20; 25:10; 27:46; 49:32; 1 Chr. 1:13).

2846. חָתָה ḥāṯāh: A verb indicating to take away, to snatch away; to get and place something. It means to take away when used with the preposition "from" (*min* [4480]). In context, it indicates taking fire or coals from a hearth (Isa. 30:14) or people from a location (Ps. 52:5[7]). Without *min*, the word can mean to get and bring into, take into, such as fire into one's bosom (Prov. 6:27). In Proverbs 25:22, it takes on the meaning of causing heaping coals, that is vengeance, to come upon the head of one's enemy.

2847. חִתָּה ḥittāh: A feminine noun meaning terror, great fear. The Lord sent terror before Jacob into the land of Canaan as he returned from Mesopotamia so he and his family could pass through without being attacked by the native population (Gen. 35:5).

2848. חִתּוּל ḥittûl: A masculine noun denoting a bandage. A cloth used to wrap up an injury. It is used figuratively of binding up the power, the "arm" of Pharaoh militarily and politically (Ezek. 30:21), especially significant since Pharaoh's arm represented his power, military, and political might.

2849. חַתְחַת ḥaṯḥaṯ: A noun meaning terror. It occurs in the plural in Ecclesiastes 12:5, referring to terrors on the road. It is part of a list of coming negative situations. The word is derived from the verbal root *ḥāṯaṯ* (2865), meaning to be dismayed or to be shattered.

2850. חִתִּי ḥittiy: A proper noun designating Hittites:

A. Descendants of Heth, some of whom lived in Palestine (Gen. 15:20). Abraham acquired Machpelah as a burial cave for the patriarchs (Gen. 23:10–20; 25:9) from the Hittites. Israelites were not to intermarry with them (Gen. 26:34–5). They were one of the peoples Israel took land from (Ex. 3:8, 17). The Hittites on the international scale made up a much larger group of people and occupied a larger area as a nation that encompassed the whole of Syria into modern day Turkey (see B). The groups of Hittites in the Old Testament in Palestine lived mainly in the area of Hebron. Israel disinherited them and took Palestine. Uriah the Hittite served in David's army (2 Sam. 23:39). Esau married a Hittite woman (Gen. 27:46) and greatly grieved his parents.

B. The greater Hittite population inhabited Anatolia (modern day areas of Turkey) and major parts of Syria. Solomon sold chariots to them and the Arameans (1 Kgs. 10:29; 2 Kgs. 7:6). Solomon even intermarried with them (1 Kgs. 11:1).

2851. חִתִּית ***ḥittiyṯ:*** A feminine noun meaning terror. This word is found exclusively in Ezekiel's writings where he described the reign of terror that powerful nations and cities brought on the Promised Land. For example, in Ezekiel's oracles to the nations, he described the terror that would come on Tyre when it was destroyed (Ezek. 26:17). When Assyria's slain army fell to the sword, they could no longer cause terror in the land (Ezek. 32:23).

2852. חָתַךְ ***ḥāṯaḵ:*** A verb indicating something decreed, determined. It is used of the seventy weeks laid out for Daniel's people, a period during which God's will for them will be accomplished (Dan. 9:24) and God's sovereignty will be demonstrated.

2853. חָתַל ***ḥāṯal:*** A verb indicating to be wrapped in cloth, to be swaddled. It describes the process of wrapping or swaddling a newborn infant at birth. It is used figuratively of Israel at her birth (Ezek. 16:4).

2854. חֲתֻלָּה ***ḥ^a^ṯullāh:*** A feminine noun referring to a girdle or swaddling band. It is used in a metaphor that describes God's placement of darkness over the earth as a swaddling band, a narrow, long piece of cloth wrapped around infants at birth (Job 38:9). Its context stresses God's sovereignty and wisdom in creation.

2855. חֶתְלֹן ***ḥeṯlōn:*** A proper noun designating Hethlon (Ezek. 47:15; 48:1).

2856. חָתַם ***ḥāṯam:*** A verb meaning to set a seal on, to seal up. It indicates the act of affixing an impression to serve as a seal on something, then sealing it up as well. It could be done to any clay object: a letter (1 Kgs. 21:8); a bill of sale, such as the one used by Jeremiah (Jer. 32:10, 11, 14, 44); a house could be sealed up (Job 24:16); something could be sealed up or stopped up (Lev. 15:3). It is used often figuratively: Daniel's vision of seventy weeks when fulfilled will seal up the prophetic vision (Dan. 9:24); Israel's testimony or law is "sealed" among his followers for future reference (Isa. 8:16). It is used in Song 4:12 to describe the bride of the bridegroom as a spring sealed up with promise of delights in marriage. It indicates sealing something so it can be opened only by the one who has the key that will open the seal (Isa. 29:11).

2857. חֲתַם ***ḥ*ᵃ*ṯam:*** An Aramaic verb referring to sealing something, to seal. Darius's lion's den was tamped, imprinted with the king's seal, his own signet ring imprint. Only he would release the royal seal (Dan. 6:17[18]).

2858. חֹתֶמֶת ***ḥōṯemeṯ:*** A feminine noun referring to a seal or signet ring. A seal that was unique to a person, imprinted on a signet ring in this case, was Judah's personal property (Gen. 38:25). It could be used to help identify a person.

2859. חָתַן ***ḥāṯan,*** חֹתֵן ***ḥōṯēn,*** חֹתֶנֶת ***ḥōṯeneṯ:*** I. A verb meaning to become related by marriage. It is used of the entire marriage process and ceremonial trappings (Gen. 34:9; Deut. 7:3; Josh. 23:12; Ezra 9:14). It naturally takes on the idea of becoming a son-in-law (1 Sam. 18:21–23, 26, 27; 1 Kgs. 3:1). It could indicate a political liaison to ally oneself with powerful and beneficial persons (2 Chr. 18:1).

II. A masculine noun indicating a father-in-law. It refers to the person who is the wife's father (Ex. 3:1; 4:18; 18:1, 2, 5–8, 12, 14, 15, 17, 24, 27; Num. 10:29; Judg. 1:16; 4:11). It usually refers to Moses' wife's father.

III. A feminine noun indicating mother-in-law. It indicates the wife's mother and is used only once in Deuteronomy 27:23 where intercourse with one's mother-in-law is forbidden as a grave sin.

2860. חָתָן ***ḥāṯān:*** A masculine noun designating a bridegroom, a son-in-law. It refers to a daughter's husband, a bridegroom. It is used to indicate a daughter's husband (Gen. 19:12, 14; Judg. 15:6; 19:5; 1 Sam. 18:18; Neh. 6:18). It is used of Ahaziah as the son-in-law of Ahab's family because his mother, Athaliah, was Ahab's daughter (2 Kgs. 8:27). In Exodus 4:25, Moses' wife addressed him with this word as her bridegroom. It is used figuratively of the Lord's gracious treatment of His oppressed people as His bridegroom (Isa. 61:10; 62:5).

2861. חֲתֻנָּה ***ḥ*ᵃ*ṯunnāh:*** A feminine noun referring to a wedding, a marriage. It refers to a person's wedding, an especially festive time (Song 3:11). In context Solomon's wedding day is literally or possibly symbolically referred to.

2862. חָתַף ***ḥāṯap̱:*** A verb indicating a snatching away, taking away. It refers to a person's sudden death brought about by the Lord (Job 9:12) who alone knows our day of birth and day of death.

2863. חֶתֶף ***ḥeṯep̱:*** A masculine noun having in mind a robber; a prey. It is used in a simile, a comparison, of an adulterous woman's behavior as a "robber," one who takes what is not hers (Prov. 23:28).

2864. חָתַר ***ḥāṯar:*** A verb depicting the act of digging or rowing. It indicates the process of scooping out dirt, of digging through a wall (Job 24:16; Ezek. 8:8; 12:7), in context into the walls of the temple or a house. It is employed figuratively of digging one's way into Sheol (Amos 9:2). It is used of the paddling motion of rowing a boat (Jon. 1:13).

2865. חָתַת *ḥāṯaṯ:* A verb meaning to be shattered, to be dismayed, to dismay, to shatter, to scare. The base meaning is probably breaking or shattering like a bow (Jer. 51:56); or of the drought-cracked ground (Jer. 14:4). Figuratively, it refers to nations shattered by God (Isa. 7:8). It is also used with a intensive and causative meaning to scare, to terrify, or to dismay (Isa. 30:31). Job said that God terrified him with dreams (Job 7:14). God's name can also cause dismay (Mal. 2:5) where it is parallel to the word *yārē'* (3372).

2866. חֲתַת *ḥ^{a}ṯaṯ:* A masculine noun referring to terror, something dreadful. It is something that inspires fear in Job's "friends," evidently his condition or other frightening things in the world (Job 6:21).

2867. חֲתַת *ḥ^{a}ṯaṯ:* A proper noun designating Hathath (1 Chr. 4:13).

ט Teth

2868. טְאֵב ***ṭeʼēḇ:*** An Aramaic verb indicating to be glad, to be pleased. It describes an appreciative and joyful response at the outcome of an event, such as Daniel's preservation from a violent death (Dan. 6:23[24]).

2869. טָב ***ṭāḇ:*** An Aramaic masculine noun denoting goodness, purity. It is used to describe pure gold, "good gold," or fine gold (Dan. 2:32), an especially high quality sample of this metal. It refers to what is pleasing to someone, such as a matter or proposal to a king (Ezra 5:17).

2870. טָבְאֵל ***ṭāḇeʼēl,*** טָבְאַל ***ṭāḇeʼal:*** A proper noun designating Tabeel, Tabeal:

A. Tabeel, a Persian official (Ezra 4:7).

B. A Syrian (Isa. 7:6).

2871. טְבוּל ***ṭeḇûl:*** A masculine noun referring to a turban. It describes a part of Chaldean dress, flowing turbans, which were on their heads (Ezek. 23:15), and hence a repulsive symbol to the prophet Ezekiel.

2872. טַבּוּר ***ṭabbûr:*** A masculine noun meaning center, the midst; the high part. It is used figuratively of the center of the land which may be thought of in Israel as the highest part of the hill country, the center of the land and earth (Judg. 9:37; Ezek. 38:12).

2873. טָבַח ***ṭāḇaḥ:*** A verb meaning to slaughter. It signifies the slaughter of livestock to prepare it for food (Gen. 43:16; Ex. 22:1[21:37]; 1 Sam. 25:11). The Hebrew word *zāḇaḥ* (2076), in contrast, signifies slaughtering livestock for sacrifice. Slaughter was used as a picture of destruction, whether attempted against righteous people (Ps. 37:14; Jer. 11:19) or brought on those being judged by God (Lam. 2:21; Ezek. 21:10[15]). The slaughter of lambs, which do not comprehend or expect slaughter, symbolized an unexpected destruction (Jer. 11:19). In Proverbs 9:2, the slaughtering of livestock symbolizes a feast prepared by wisdom.

2874. טֶבַח ***ṭeḇaḥ:*** A masculine noun meaning slaughter. Originally, the term referred to the actual slaughtering of animals for food (Gen. 43:16; Prov. 9:2); however, this term has also been used metaphorically. It describes the condition of a man seduced by an adulteress (Prov. 7:22), as well as the slaughter of the Suffering Servant (Isa. 53:7). Furthermore, it characterizes the destinies of Edom (Isa. 34:6); Moab (Jer. 48:15); Babylon (Jer. 50:27); and all those who forsake God (Isa. 34:2; 65:12). A parallel term is *zeḇaḥ* (2077), meaning slaughtering for a sacrifice.

2875. טֶבַח ***ṭeḇaḥ:*** A proper noun designating Tebah (Gen. 22:24).

2876. טַבָּח ***ṭabbāḥ:*** A masculine noun meaning guard, an imperial guard. In its plural form only, it refers to bodyguard or special elite guard of the military (Gen. 37:36; 39:1; 40:3, 4; 41:10, 12). Potiphar was the head of a group of these men. Nebuzaradan was the captain of these forces for Nebuchadnezzar (2 Kgs. 25:8, 10–12, 15, 18, 20). The connection between these meanings and the following contextual meaning seems to be that these persons were the "royal executioners." In another context, this word takes on the meaning of butcher or cook (1 Sam. 9:23, 24).

2877. טַבָּח ***ṭabbāḥ:*** An Aramaic masculine noun referring to guard, imperial guard, bodyguard; executioner. It is used in the book of Daniel to refer to Arioch who is designated as the chief or captain (*raḇ*) of this bodyguard (2:14).

2878. טִבְחָה ***ṭiḇḥāh:*** A feminine noun meaning slaughtered meat, a slaughter. In 1 Samuel, Nabal questioned why he should give his food to David and his men (1 Sam. 25:11). But in Psalm 44:22[23] and Jeremiah 12:3, it is a generic term for slaughter. In both passages, it compared the punishment of people to the slaughtering of sheep. See the cognate verb *ṭāḇaḥ* (2873).

2879. טַבָּחָה ***ṭabbāḥah:*** A feminine noun referring to a cook. It refers to a position, according to this verse, assigned to daughters of Israel in the administration of the king of Israel, along with bakers and perfumers (1 Sam. 8:13).

2880. טִבְחַת ***ṭiḇḥaṯ:*** A proper noun designating Tibnath, Tebah (1 Chr. 18:8).

2881. טָבַל ***ṭāḇal:*** A verb meaning to dip. The term is often connected with ritual behavior. The priest was to dip his fingers, a live bird, cedar wood, hyssop, and scarlet yarn into blood for various ceremonies (Lev. 4:6, 17; 9:9; 14:6, 51). The clean person was to dip hyssop in water and sprinkle it for purification on unclean persons or things (Num. 19:18). It is used intransitively with the preposition b^e when Naaman dipped himself in the Jordan to be healed of leprosy (2 Kgs. 5:14).

2882. טְבַלְיָהוּ ***ṭ^{e}ḇalyāhû:*** A proper noun designating Tebaliah (1 Chr. 26:11).

2883. טָבַע ***ṭāḇaʿ:*** A verb meaning to drown, to sink; to penetrate. It refers to death by drowning (Ex. 15:4), sunk in the waters of the Red Sea. In general, it refers to something sunk in (b^e): Jeremiah sunk into the mud of a cistern (Jer. 38:6); the gates of Jerusalem sunk into the ground (Lam. 2:9); a stone thrown by David pierced Goliath's forehead (1 Sam. 17:49). It describes a mass of something sinking together, such as mountains (Prov. 8:25). It is used metaphorically of nations sinking down (Ps. 9:15[16]) because of their rebellions; an oppressed or distressed person "sinking into the mire" (Ps. 69:2[3]), 14[15]; Jer. 38:22); the foundations of the earth sunk into their bases (Job 38:6).

2884. טַבָּעוֹת ***ṭabbāʿôṯ:*** A proper noun designating Tabbaoth (Ezra 2:43; Neh. 7:46).

2885. טַבַּעַת ***ṭabbaʿaṯ:*** A feminine noun referring to a ring, a signet ring. It designates a signet ring with a seal on it (Gen. 41:42; Esth. 3:10, 12); or to jewelry (Ex. 35:22; Isa. 3:21). It is used to refer to large rings used to hang curtains on or to put the poles into to carry the ark (Ex. 25:12; 35:22; 36:29).

2886. טַבְרִמֹּן ***ṭaḇrimmōn:*** A proper noun designating Tabrimmon (1 Kgs. 15:18).

2887. טֵבֵת ***ṭēḇēṯ:*** A proper noun indicating Tebeth. It refers to the tenth month of the seventh year of the reign of King Ahasuerus of Persia when Esther was queen (Esth. 2:16), a feature of storytelling that argues for the book's historicity.

2888. טַבָּת ***ṭabbāṯ:*** A proper noun designating Tabbath (Judg. 7:22).

2889. טָהוֹר ***ṭāhôr,*** טָהֹר ***ṭāhōr:*** An adjective meaning clean, pure, genuine. This word is used ninety times in the Old Testament, primarily to distinguish things that were culturally pure, capable of being used in, or taking part in the religious rituals of Israel. The Lord decreed that Israel must mark off the clean from the unclean (Lev. 10:10; 11:47; Job 14:4). Persons could be ceremonially clean or unclean (Deut. 12:15). A human corpse was especially defiling, and contact with it made a person unclean for seven days (Num. 19:11). When persons were clean, they could eat clean meat, but an unclean person could not (Lev. 7:19). Certain animals were considered ceremonially clean (Gen. 7:2) and needed by Noah and his family for sacrifices after the flood (Gen. 8:20). Ceremonially clean birds were used in various rituals (Lev. 14:4).

Clean things were considered normal; unclean things were considered polluted, but they could be restored to their state of purity (Lev. 11—15). Some things, however, were permanently unclean, such as unclean animals (Lev. 11:7, 26, 29–31). Other things were temporarily unclean. A woman in her period (Lev. 12:2) and a person with an infectious disease (Lev. 13:8) could be cleansed and be clean again (Lev. 12:4; 14:7); spring water could be considered as clean; even seed could be clean or unclean depending on whether a dead carcass had fallen on it while it was dry or wet (Lev. 11:36–38). Leprosy made a person unclean (Lev. 13:45, 46).

God expected His people to be morally pure and to imitate Him (Hab. 1:13). This word served to express that state. Clean hands merited God's favor (Job 17:9), and pure words were pleasing to the Lord. God judged a sacrifice's value by the quality of the offerer's heart (Ps. 51:10[12]); thus, David prayed for a pure heart.

The root meaning of the word shines through in its use to describe the quality of metals and other items. Pure gold was used in the construction of the ark of the covenant and many other items (Ex. 25:11, 17; 28:14; 30:3); pure frankincense was prepared for use on the altar of incense (Ex. 30:34, 35; 37:29). The fear of the Lord was proclaimed pure and therefore endured forever. It guided the psalmist to know God (Ps. 19:9[10]).

2890. טְהָר ***ṭᵉhār,*** טֳהָר ***ṭᵒhār:*** A masculine noun meaning cleanness. This word occurs only in Proverbs 22:11. As it is written in Hebrew, it is unpronounceable and appears to be a misspelling of the adjective *ṭāhôr* (2889). However, the noun "cleanness," fits much better than the adjective "clean," both grammatically and contextually (cf. Prov. 23:7, 8) and is the choice of the King James Version. Loving cleanness of heart (rather than "loving [the] clean of heart") results in graceful speech.

2891. טָהֵר ***ṭāhēr:*** A verb meaning to be clean, to make clean, to be pure, to make pure. The term occurs most frequently in Leviticus where it was used for ritual cleansing of either things or persons (Lev. 14:48; 16:19; 22:7). The Old Testament also speaks of ritual cleansing performed on persons within the sphere of false worship (Isa. 66:17; Ezek. 22:24). Animals were not made clean (like people), for animals were either clean or unclean by nature; the concept did not apply to plants at all. Sometimes cleanness had a moral dimension that, of course, did not exclude the spiritual. One was not to think that persons made themselves clean nor that their cleanness exceeded that of their Maker (Job 4:17; Prov. 20:9). Exilic and postexilic prophets prophesied of a future purification for God's people like the purifying of silver (Jer. 33:8; Ezek. 36:25; Mal. 3:3).

2892. טֹהַר ***ṭōhar,*** טֳהָר ***ṭᵒhār:*** A masculine noun meaning purity, pureness, clarity, luster. This word is from a verb meaning to be pure or to be clean, both physically and ceremonially. It is used to denote the lustrous quality of a clear sky (Ex. 24:10); the glory of an individual (Ps. 89:44[45]); and the purification cycle after childbirth (Lev. 12:4, 6).

2893. טָהֳרָה ***ṭāhᵒrāh:*** A feminine noun meaning cleansing, purification. The word refers to a ceremonial cleansing pronounced by a priest on one formerly unclean (Lev. 13:7). The cleansing from such things as leprosy (Lev. 14:2, 23, 32); issues relating to genital organs (Lev. 15:13); touching a dead body (Num. 6:9); and childbirth (Lev. 12:4, 5) required additional procedures such as washing clothes and bathing. The birth of a child rendered a woman unclean, remaining in the blood of her purification (i.e., extra bleeding in the days following childbirth) for a set time after which she brought a sacrifice to the priest (cf. Luke 2:24). Cleansing from leprosy involved an extensive ceremony (Lev. 14:1–32). These ceremonies promoted good hygiene, but in the days of Hezekiah, God pardoned those who were seeking Him but failed to maintain ceremonial cleanness (2 Chr. 30:19).

2894. טֵאטֵא *ṭēʼṭēʼ*: A verb indicating to sweep. It is used in a metaphor describing how the Lord will "sweep" Babylon with His broom to destroy it, removing it from the world scene forever (Isa. 14:23).

2895. טוֹב *ṭôḇ*: A verb meaning to be happy, to please, to be loved, to be favored, to seem good, to be acceptable, to endure, to be valuable, to do well, to do right. It means to be happy or glad, such as when Nabal, husband of Abigail, was joyous from drinking too much (1 Sam. 25:36; 2 Sam. 13:28; Esth. 1:10). The word naturally expresses the idea of being loved or enjoying the favor of someone. Samuel grew up in favor before the Lord and people (1 Sam. 2:26). It is used with the idiom "in the eyes of" to express the idea of seeming good or advisable; Abner informed David of everything that was good in the eyes of Israel (2 Sam. 3:19; 15:26). The word is used to express the meaning of good, as when the Israelites asserted they were better off in Egypt than in the wilderness (Num. 11:18; cf. Deut. 5:29). The idea of being better or being valuable is expressed several times using this word: Jephthah asked the Ammonites whether they were better than Balak, son of Zippor (Judg. 11:25); while the psalmist asserted that it was good for him to have been afflicted, for thereby he learned the Lord's decrees (Ps. 119:71).

The verb is used four times in the causative stem to mean to deal rightly or to deal justly. The Lord informed David that he had done well to plan to build a temple for God (2 Chr. 6:8) and informed Jehu that he had performed his assassination of Ahab's house well (2 Kgs. 10:30).

2896. טוֹב *ṭôḇ*, טוֹבָה *ṭôḇāh*, טֹבָה *ṭōḇāh*: An adjective meaning good, well-pleasing, fruitful, morally correct, proper, convenient. This word is frequently encountered in the Old Testament and is roughly equivalent to the English word *good* in terms of its function and scope of meaning. It describes that which is appealing and pleasant to the senses (Num. 14:7; Esth. 1:11; Ps. 52:9[11]); is useful and profitable (Gen. 2:18; Zech. 11:12); is abundant and plentiful (Gen. 41:22; Judg. 8:32); is kind and benevolent (1 Sam. 24:18[19]; 2 Chr. 5:13; Nah. 1:7); is good in a moral sense as opposed to evil (Gen. 2:17; Lev. 27:14; Ps. 37:27); is proper and becoming (Deut. 1:14; 1 Sam. 1:23; Ps. 92:1[2]);

bears a general state of well-being or happiness (Deut. 6:24; Eccl. 2:24); is the better of two alternatives (Gen. 29:19; Ex. 14:12; Jon. 4:3). The creation narrative of Genesis 1 best embodies all these various elements of meaning when the Lord declares each aspect of His handiwork to be "good."

2897. טוֹב ***ṭôḇ:*** A proper noun designating Tob (Judg. 11:3, 5; 2 Sam. 10:6, 8). See also *'iyš ṭôḇ* (382).

2898. טוּב ***ṭûḇ:*** A masculine noun meaning property, goods, goodness, fairness, and beauty. The root concept of this noun is that of desirability for enjoyment. It is used to identify the personal property of an individual (Gen. 24:10); the plentiful harvest of the land (Neh. 9:36; Jer. 2:7); items of superior quality and desirability (2 Kgs. 8:9); inward joy (Isa. 65:14); the manifest goodness of the Lord (Ex. 33:19; Ps. 25:7). Notably, the psalmist employs the word to describe the state of spiritual blessing (Ps. 31:19[20]; 65:4[5]).

2899. טוֹב אֲדוֹנִיָּה ***ṭôḇ 'ᵃḏôniyyāh:*** A proper noun designating Tob-Adonijah (2 Chr. 17:8).

2900. טוֹבִיָּה ***ṭôḇiyyāh,*** טוֹבִיָּהוּ ***ṭôḇiyyāhû:*** A proper noun designating Tobijah. A name meaning "the Lord is good."

A. He assisted other officials in teaching the Book of the Law throughout Judah (2 Chr. 17:8).

B. A few descendants who returned from exile in Babylon but could not demonstrate from records that they were Jews (Ezra 2:60).

C. An Ammonite leader who opposed the Jews who returned to Jerusalem from exile (Neh. 2:10). He actively tried to stop the rebuilding of walls, etc. (Neh. 2:19; 4:3[3:35]), and verbally attacked Nehemiah personally (Neh. 6:19). Nehemiah expelled him from the Temple area (Neh. 13:4–8).

D. A returned exile who possessed gold and was a leader in Israel (Zech. 6:10, 14).

2901. טָוָה ***ṭāwāh:*** A verb meaning to spin. It describes the tasks of the women of Israel as they skillfully spun goats' hair (Ex. 35:25, 26) and blue, purple, and scarlet material, as well as linen for the Tabernacle or its accessories.

2902. טוּחַ ***ṭûaḥ,*** טָחַח ***ṭāḥaḥ:*** I. A verb referring to daubing, plastering over, to overlay. It indicates covering or overlaying various things with different materials: a house with clay (Lev. 14:42); walls with gold or silver (1 Chr. 29:4). It is used metaphorically of plastering over the walls of Jerusalem to hide its sin and corruption (Ezek. 13:10–12, 15). It is a figurative expression of the soothing messages from false prophets (Ezek. 22:28).

II. A verb meaning to smear, to spread over, to daub. Isaiah uses the word in a powerful theological metaphor to describe the Lord's smearing over the eyes and hearts of the Israelites so they could not understand His message or His ways (Isa. 44:18).

2903. טוֹטָפוֹת ***ṭôṭāpôṯ:*** A feminine plural noun denoting phylacteries, headbands, symbols. They were worn around the forehead to carry select verses from Holy Scripture to remind Israel of the Lord's ways with them (Ex. 13:16; Deut. 6:8; 11:18), of His will for them. Originally, this word was probably used figuratively to indicate complete dedication to the Lord and His ways, but later it was taken literally to refer to actual physical objects, as described here.

2904. טוּל ***ṭûl:*** A verb describing hurling, throwing. It refers to a physical casting of Israel into exile (Jer. 22:28) but also figuratively of a person's being hurled headlong or violently into consternation (Ps. 37:24). It describes one's fate being cast into one's lap (Prov. 16:33); being overwhelmed or overawed emotionally from something (Job. 41:9[1]).

2905. טוּר ***ṭûr:*** A masculine noun denoting a course, a row. It indicates a number of things arranged in a straight line, such as building stones in Solomon's Temple and palace (1 Kgs. 6:36; 7:12); or in a rectangle or square to form an enclosure (Ezek. 46:23). It is used of beams or pillars as well (1 Kgs. 6:36; 7:12); or various designs (1 Kgs. 7:20, 24, 42). It is used to describe the arrangement of the jewels placed on the breastpiece of the high priest (Ex. 28:17–20; 39:10–13).

2906. טוּר ***ṭûr:*** An Aramaic masculine noun denoting a mountain. It refers to a large mountain, representing God's kingdom, that fills the whole earth (Dan. 2:35, 45) in Nebuchadnezzar's first great dream.

2907. טוּשׂ ***ṭûś:*** A verb meaning to dart, to swoop. It describes the quick flight of an eagle attacking its prey (Job 9:26). It demonstrates how quickly Job's days are flying by and the frailty of life for even a righteous man.

2908. טְוָת ***ṭᵉwāṯ:*** An Aramaic adjective indicating fasting, going without eating. It describes Darius as he refrains from eating during the night, worrying about Daniel's safety (6:18[19]).

2909. טָחָה ***ṭāḥāh:*** A verb referring to shooting a bow, or being a bowshot away. It indicates Hagar's being distant enough not to hear or witness the death of her child (Gen. 21:16). The exact distance is, of course, not certain.

2910. טֻחוֹת ***ṭuḥôṯ:*** A feminine plural noun indicating an inward part, the inner being. It refers to a person's moral consciousness (Ps. 51:6[8]); the ability to perceive right and wrong or discern wisely (Job 38:36).

2911. טְחוֹן ***ṭᵉḥôn:*** A masculine noun denoting a mill, a millstone. It indicates a place of difficult and onerous labor at a mill or grinding mill (Lam. 5:13) experienced by Israel's young men when Jerusalem fell to the Babylonians.

2912. טָחַן ***ṭaḥan,*** טֹחֲנָה ***ṭōḥᵃnāh:*** I. A verb meaning to mill, to grind, to crush. It indicates the labor of grinding at a mill (Judg. 16:21), but it is used in special cases too: the golden calf was ground up (Ex. 32:20; Deut. 9:21); the grinding or gritting of one's teeth (Eccl. 12:3); the grinding of manna (Num. 11:8). It is used figuratively and literally of Babylon's punishment and destruction as her daughters grind with millstones (Isa. 47:2); and of the "grinding" of the faces of the poor (Isa. 3:15). In a different context, it indicates serving a person (Job 31:10).

II. A feminine noun indicating a molar, a grinder. It is used to depict "grinders," that is, the teeth of older people, their molars, that are deteriorating (Eccl. 12:3). Possibly it refers, instead, to female millers or grinders.

2913. טַחֲנָה ***ṭaḥᵃnāh:*** A feminine noun meaning a grinding mill, a millstone. It refers to a mill, a grinding mill, but it may be used figuratively in this context for teeth or the chewing action of one's mouth (Eccl. 12:4).

2914. טְחוֹר ***ṭᵉḥôr:*** A masculine noun indicating a tumor, a hemorrhoid. It is used in the plural only of some pestilence or diseased growth, evidently anal hemorrhoids inflicted on the Philistines (1 Sam. 6:11, 17). Models of these tumors were presented to Israel as guilt offerings by the Philistines.

2915. טִיחַ ***ṭiyaḥ:*** A masculine noun referring to a coating, whitewash, plaster. It is used of the coating put on a wall to improve its appearance. But in context, it is symbolic of Israel's feeble attempts to cover her true condition with lies and falsities used as "plaster" (Ezek. 13:12).

2916. טִיט ***ṭiyṭ:*** A masculine noun denoting mire, mud, clay. It describes the foul clay mud at the bottom of a cistern (Jer. 38:6); the mud in which a crocodile lies (Job 41:30[22]); the muck brought up by the sea (Isa. 57:20). It is used of the more valuable clay used by a potter (Isa. 41:25); clay of bricks (Nah. 3:14) or walls. It is used in the figurative language of similes: an enemy is trampled like mire in the streets (Mic. 7:10; Zech. 10:5); enemies are poured out like mire into the streets (Ps. 18:42[43]); gold is piled up like the mud or mire in the streets; it is everywhere (Zech. 9:3); the Lord delivers His faithful follower from the mire of the streets (Ps. 69:14[15]).

2917. טִין ***ṭiyn:*** An Aramaic masculine noun indicating clay. It refers to common clay (Dan. 2:41, 43) mixed with iron in Nebuchadnezzar's vision of the feet and toes of the great image. It actually represented diverse groups of people who could not become unified among themselves.

2918. טִירָה ***ṭiyrāh:*** A feminine noun having in mind a camp, a settlement. It indicates a surrounding enclosure of some kind, such as a circular encampment or surrounding villages occupying an area: Ishmael's clans lived in such camps or villages (Gen. 25:16), probably with small stone walls. So did the Midianites and others (Num. 31:10; Ezek. 25:4). It denotes a row of stones or masonry around a court or its walls (Ezek. 46:23); or a battlement constructed around or on a wall (Song. 8:9).

2919. טַל ***ṭal:*** A masculine noun indicating dew or light rain, a mist. It is used in a literal sense often of some formation or presence of winter: night mist (Ps. 110:3; Isa. 18:4); light rain from the sky (Gen. 27:28); clouds bring it (Prov. 3:20); it collects on physical objects and the ground (Ex. 16:13, 14; Judg. 6:37–40); it can come in drops (Job 38:28); the Lord or His prophet may cause it (Gen. 27:28; 1 Kgs. 17:1). It is used often in a figurative way in a simile or a metaphor: it comes in a secretive way, quickly (2 Sam. 17:12); it describes pleasant speech that distills pleasantly (Deut. 32:2); it describes giving life (Ps. 133:3); the Lord's kindness is like dew (Isa. 18:4; Hos. 14:5, 6); the remnant of Jacob will be refreshing to the nations like dew (Mic. 5:7[6]). It depicts the faithfulness of Ephraim and Judah; it passes quickly like dew (Hos. 6:4). The faithful warriors, youth, of the Lord's chosen king are like dew to His reign (Ps. 110:3).

2920. טַל ***ṭal:*** An Aramaic masculine noun indicating dew. It refers to the early morning dew, a small collection of water on the surface of something, dew of heaven, of the fields, and of the pastures. It describes the dew which collected on Nebuchadnezzar while he lived among the animals in the fields (Dan. 4:15[12], 23[20], 25[22], 33[30]; 5:21).

2921. טָלָא ***ṭālā':*** A verb indicating to be patched, to be spotted. It is used to depict spotted sheep (Gen. 30:32, 33, 35). It indicates clothing: sandals (Josh. 9:5; Ezek. 16:16).

2922. טְלָה ***ṭ^elāh:*** A masculine plural noun denoting a lamb. It refers to the Lord's people as lambs for whom He is leader (Isa. 40:11).

2923. טְלָאִים ***ṭ^elā'iym:*** A proper noun designating Telaim (1 Sam. 15:4).

2924. טָלֶה ***ṭāleh:*** A masculine noun designating a lamb. Combined with *h^alāḇ* following, it describes a suckling lamb (1 Sam. 7:9). Elsewhere, it denotes any lamb (Isa. 40:11; 65:25) and describes God's people as lambs the Lord leads (Isa. 40:11) or as lambs in the future new heavens and new earth which the Lord will create (Isa. 65:25).

2925. טַלְטֵלָה ***ṭalṭēlāh:*** A feminine noun indicating a captivity, a hurling. It describes figuratively the casting down of a ruler, Shebna, from power and authority (Isa. 22:17).

2926. טָלַל ***ṭālal:*** A verb meaning to cover something with a roof, to supply a roof, to cover. It indicates the process of constructing a covering for the Fountain Gate in Jerusalem after the return of the exiles from Babylon (Neh. 3:15).

2927. טְלַל ***ṭ***e***lal:*** An Aramaic verb indicating to find shelter, to find shade. It describes the beasts of the field as they procure rest, shade, and shelter under the huge tree of Nebuchadnezzar's dream (Dan. 4:12[9]).

2928. טֶלֶם ***ṭelem:*** A proper noun designating Telem:

A. A town in Judah (Josh. 15:24).
B. A gatekeeper (Ezra 10:24).

2929. טַלְמוֹן ***ṭalmôn,*** טַלְמֹן ***ṭalmōn:*** A proper noun designating Talmon (1 Chr. 9:17; Ezra 2:42; Neh. 7:45; 11:19; 12:25).

2930. טָמֵא ***ṭāmē',*** טָמְאָה ***ṭām'āh:*** A verb meaning to be unclean, to desecrate, to defile, to make impure. The main idea of the action was that of contaminating or corrupting, especially in the sight of God. The Levitical Law often spoke in terms of sexual, religious, or ceremonial uncleanness. Any object or individual who was not clean could not be acceptable to the Holy God of Israel. Examples of actions that caused a state of impurity would include eating forbidden food (Hos. 9:4); worshiping idols (Ps. 106:39; Hos. 5:3); committing adultery or engaging in sexual relations outside of marriage (Gen. 34:5; Num. 5:13; Ezek. 18:6); touching unclean objects or individuals (Lev. 5:3; 18:24; 19:31); and any action that violated the sacredness of the Lord (Jer. 32:34). It was the duty of the priesthood to discern matters of impurity (Lev. 13:3; Hag. 2:13) and to see that the strict rituals of purification were followed.

2931. טָמֵא ***ṭāmē':*** An adjective meaning unclean. It can denote impurity or defilement (Isa. 6:5; Ezek. 22:5). It can also refer to ritually unclean items such as people, things, foods, and places. The land east of the Jordan (Josh. 22:19) and foreign lands (Amos 7:17) were unclean in contrast to the land of Israel.

2932. טֻמְאָה ***ṭum'āh:*** A feminine noun meaning uncleanness, filthy. It refers to the sexual impurity of a woman during the menstrual cycle (Num. 5:19; Lam. 1:9). It can also denote any unclean thing from which the temple needed to be purified (2 Chr. 29:16). Finally, both ethical and religious uncleanness were dealt with: in the laws referring to proper behavior (Lev. 16:16); and in the heart, referring to an unclean spirit that causes one to lie (Ezek. 24:13).

2933. טָמָה ṭāmāh: A verb which occurs once in the Hebrew Bible (Job 18:3). It is translated "stopped up," "stupid," or possibly "unclean."

2934. טָמַן ṭāman: A verb meaning to bury, to hide, to conceal, to keep hidden. Its basic sense is to hide something for various purposes, God or humans may be the subject: so that it would deteriorate (Jer. 13:4–7) in the crevice of a rock; so that it might ensnare others, e.g., a net (Ps. 9:15[16]) or a trap (Ps. 64:5[6]); so that it may be retrieved later, e.g., gold, silver, clothes (2 Kgs. 7:8). Moses hid an Egyptian's body in the sand (Ex. 2:12); and a miscarried child is placed in a grave (Job 3:16). It is used of person's being buried, hidden in the ground (Job 40:13) by God. Persons attempt to hide themselves "in the dust" from the Lord's judgments and majesty (Isa. 2:10). It is used of hiding spies under stalks of grain (Josh. 7:21, 22). Proverbs describes the sluggard who "buries" his hand in a dish and is too lazy to draw it out (Prov. 19:24; 26:15).

2935. טֶנֶא ṭene': A masculine noun denoting a basket. It is used to describe a container holding offerings from the ground of the Promised Land of Canaan (Deut. 26:2, 4). It is also used symbolically to represent the rich abundance of the ground (Deut. 28:5, 17).

2936. טָנַף ṭānap̱: A verb describing the act of defiling, making dirty. In context it refers to making feet that have just been washed dirty again, soiled (Song 5:3).

2937. טָעָה ṭāʿāh: A verb indicating to seduce, to lead astray. It refers to giving false information, saying the opposite of what is the case, whitewashing something (Ezek. 13:10). Deception is a part of its meaning.

2938. טָעַם ṭāʿam: A verb referring to eating, tasting, experiencing. It refers to the sense of taste, of discerning the taste of food or beverages (2 Sam. 19:35[36]). It means to eat food (parallel to *'ākal,* to eat) (1 Sam. 14:24, 29, 43) even if it were a small amount. To refrain from eating food was akin to mourning (Jon. 3:7). It is used in a figurative sense of fasting to see that the Lord is indeed good (Ps. 34:8[9]). The good wife senses ("tastes") that the food she prepares is excellent (Prov. 31:18).

2939. טְעֵם ṭᵉʿēm: An Aramaic verb meaning to feed, to cause to eat. It is used of giving grass to Nebuchadnezzar to eat like a beast (Dan. 4:25[22], 32[29]; 5:21) of the field in fulfillment of God's decreed judgment on him.

2940. טַעַם ṭaʿam: a masculine noun meaning taste, judgment, discernment, discretion. The word is used only thirteen times in the Old Testament but is a key word when considering the concept of taste, perception, or decree. It is used to describe the experience of taste: it describes the physical taste of manna as something like wafers or cakes made with honey (Ex. 16:31); or as something made with olive oil (Num. 11:8); it also refers to tasteless food needing salt in order to be eaten (Job 6:6). The word has several abstract meanings. It can mean mental or spiritual perception, discretion, or discernment. David thanked Abigail for her good discretion that kept him from killing Nabal and his men (1 Sam. 25:33). This Hebrew word is ranked along with knowledge as something the psalmist wanted from the Lord (i.e., good discernment or judgment [Ps. 119:66]); and in a famous proverb, the beautiful woman without discretion is unfavorably compared to a gold ring in a pig's snout (Prov. 11:22). The word can also mean an oral or written proclamation (i.e., a decree). It depicts the proclamation of the king of Nineveh (Jon. 3:7). Finally, its Aramaic equivalent *ṭa'am* (2941) means decree or command.

2941. טְעֵם *ṭa'am:* An Aramaic noun meaning taste, judgment, command. It is closely related to the Hebrew word of the same spelling (*ṭa'am*[2940]) and is equivalent to the Aramaic noun *ṭᵉ'ēm* (2942). In Ezra 6:14, the word refers to a command of God; and therefore some argue this vocalization is a theological scribal distinction to differentiate between it and *ṭᵉ'ēm*. The determined use of *ṭaᵉmā'* in Ezra 5:5 could be declined from either *ṭa'am* or *ṭᵉ'ēm*.

2942. טְעֵם *ṭᵉ'ēm:* An Aramaic masculine noun meaning taste, judgment, command, flavor. Belshazzar held a great feast and tasted wine from the consecrated vessels of God's Temple (Dan. 5:2). When used figuratively, the word has the meaning of judgment or discretion, such as Daniel's counsel and wisdom to Nebuchadnezzar's chief guard (Dan. 2:14). This word is also used in relaying a command of God, such as the rebuilding of the Temple (Ezra 6:14), or of a person, as in the decree to worship the golden image of Nebuchadnezzar (Dan. 3:10).

2943. טָעַן *ṭā'an:* A verb indicating to load. It means to put into or on something to be carried or transported, such as provisions or necessities for a trip (Gen. 45:17).

2944. טָעַן *ṭā'an:* A verb indicating to thrust through, to pierce. In context it refers to those persons who have been mortally stabbed, pierced with swords (Isa. 14:19), an ignominious lot.

2945. טַף *ṭap:* A masculine singular noun meaning child, little one. Though the term is sometimes used in a parallel construction with *bāniym* (plural of 1121; Deut. 1:39), elsewhere it often denotes younger children. It is distinguished from young men, virgins (Ezek. 9:6), and sons (2 Chr. 20:13, "children"). It is often used in the formulaic pattern "men, women, and children" (Deut. 2:34; 3:6; 31:12; Jer. 40:7; 43:6), meaning everyone.

2946. טָפַח ṭāpaḥ: A verb indicating to spread out. It is used in a magnificent metaphor to describe the spreading out of the heavens by the Lord's right hand (Isa. 48:13), as a person might spread out a scroll.

2947. טֶפַח ṭepaḥ, טִפְחָה ṭapḥāh: I. A masculine noun denoting a handbreadth. It was used to indicate a small lineal measurement, the breadth of a person's hand. It indicated the thickness of Solomon's great brass sea (1 Kgs. 7:26; 2 Chr. 4:5).

II. A feminine noun indicating a handbreadth; a small measure of time. It indicated a small measurement and was used by the psalmist to indicate the shortness and swiftness of the days of his life (Ps. 39:5[6]).

III. A feminine noun referring to a covering, coping, eave. Its meaning is not entirely certain, but it seems to refer to a coping or top layer of a wall or structure (1 Kgs. 7:9; NASB, KJV, coping; NKJV, NIV, eaves).

2948. טֹפַח ṭōpaḥ: A masculine noun meaning a handbreadth. This was a small measurement about the width of a man's hand. Several items bear this measurement in the Old Testament: the rim of the table of showbread (Ex. 25:25; 37:12); measuring instruments (Ezek. 40:5; 43:13); hooks for hanging (Ezek. 40:43).

2949. טִפֻּחִים ṭippuḥiym: A masculine plural noun denoting ones cared for. In Lamentations 2:20, it refers to children cared for tenderly (NIV); or possibly to children of such a quality, e.g., born healthy (NASB); or of a tiny size (KJV).

2950. טָפַל ṭāpal: A verb meaning to smear. It is used figuratively of persons covering over or smearing (Job 13:4; Ps. 119:69) over the truth or to the Lord's plastering over or sealing over one's iniquity (Job 14:17).

2951. טִפְסָר ṭipsār: A noun, probably masculine, meaning a military commander. In Jeremiah 51:27, it appears to refer to the supreme commander of an army called to oppose Babylon. In the only other occurrence, Nahum 3:17, it is plural and has a slightly different spelling. Here it refers to commanders in the army of Nineveh, the capital of Assyria. Interestingly, in both passages, comparison is made between military power and different kinds of locusts.

2952. טָפַף ṭāpap: A verb indicating to trip along with quick little steps. It refers to the proud, seductive "mincing" steps of the corrupt daughters of Zion, often highlighted with tinkling jewelry on their feet (Isa. 3:16).

2953. טְפַר ṭᵉpar: An Aramaic masculine noun indicating a claw, a fingernail. It refers to the bird-like claws which grew on Nebuchadnezzar's hands during his seven–year punishment from the Lord (Dan. 4:33[30]); and to the terrible bronze claws of the fourth beast of Daniel's dream (Dan. 7:19).

2954. טָפַשׁ ***ṭāp̱aš:*** A verb meaning to be fat, insensitive, unfeeling. It is used to depict a heart covered with fat, that is, not sensitive, not delighting in the Law of the Lord (Ps. 119:70).

2955. טָפַת ***ṭāp̱aṯ:*** A proper noun designating Taphath (1 Kgs. 4:11).

2956. טָרַד ***ṭāraḏ:*** A verb meaning to be constant, continuous, no break, no let up. It is used to describe the incessant, destructive behavior of a quarrelsome wife (Prov. 19:13). A "constant dripping of rain" is used to depict the contentious wife or woman as well (Prov. 27:15).

2957. טְרַד ***ṭ**^e**raḏ:*** An Aramaic verb referring to driving away, chasing away. It is used of the Lord's afflicting Nebuchadnezzar to remove him from human society because of his extreme pride in his great city, Babylon (Dan. 4:25[22], 32[29], 33[30]; 5:21), which he claimed to have built.

2958. טְרוֹם ***ṭ**^e**rôm:*** A conjunction indicating before. It is an adverbial conjunction of time. It indicates the time just before daylight when it was still too dark to recognize another person clearly (Ruth 3:14).

2959. טָרַח ***ṭāraḥ:*** A verb meaning to load, to place in or on. It refers to the Lord's activity of causing water to accumulate in clouds (Job 37:11), to absorb moisture, and eventually disperse as rain.

2960. טֹרַח ***ṭōraḥ:*** A masculine noun indicating a load, a burden. It indicates the responsibility of a task. Moses' load was carrying and leading Israel (Deut. 1:12). Or it indicates something that has become a burden or load that should have been otherwise, e.g., Israel's hypocritical worship of the Lord in her feasts and festivals (Isa. 1:14).

2961. טָרִי ***ṭāriy:*** An adjective indicating fresh, new. It indicates the condition of a donkey's jawbone used by Samson to slay one thousand Philistines (Judg. 15:15). Used of wounds, it indicates they are raw or bleeding, tender, but Isaiah used it of the spiritual wounds of his people (Isa. 1:6).

2962. טֶרֶם ***ṭerem:*** An adverb and adverbial preposition indicating before. Used with verbs, it often means not yet or before something else: when there was not yet a shrub in the field (Gen. 2:5). It indicates when Abraham's servant had not yet finished speaking (Gen. 24:15, 45). It means before in Genesis 27:4 and Exodus 12:34, e.g., before Isaac died. It indicates a time before morning (Isa. 17:14). It indicates the time before God created the earth (Ps. 90:2). With the preposition *min* (4480), it indicates a time before which or when certain things were happening (Gen. 27:33; Judg. 14:18; Hag. 2:15).

2963. טָרַף ṭārap̱: A verb indicating to tear in pieces. It is used especially of things torn in pieces by wild animals (Gen. 37:33; Ex. 22:13[12]; Jer. 5:6). In Proverbs 30:8, it takes a much milder sense of God's providing persons with their food. It is used figuratively often: to describe Benjamin and Gad as animals that tear their prey (Gen. 49:27; Deut. 33:20); and of Jacob's remnant in Judah (Mic. 5:8[7]). It is used of the king of Nineveh (Nah. 2:12[13]) who is depicted as a lion tearing his prey. Evil oppressors are often described as animals that tear their intended victims (Ps. 17:12). It is used of God's supposed wrath attacking and tearing Job (16:9); and of the Lord's judgment on the wicked (Hos. 5:14).

2964. טֶרֶף ṭerep̱: A masculine noun denoting a victim, prey. It indicates the prey of people or beasts: often the prey of a lion (Job 4:11; 38:39: Ps. 104:21; Amos 3:4); In a figurative way, it describes Judah conquering its prey (Gen. 49:9) or Israel (Num. 23:24) devouring its prey. The mighty empires of the ancient Near East attacked their prey: Assyrians (Isa. 5:29; Nah. 2:12[13], 13[14]). False prophets attacked their prey (Ezek. 22:25). It takes on the general meaning of food or nourishment for the poor and oppressed in Job 24:5. It is used surprisingly of human food in Psalm 111:5 provided by God and in Proverbs 31:15 by a good wife. In Ezekiel 17:9, it is used of the fruit or leaves of a tree representing Judah.

2965. טָרָף ṭārāp̱: An adjective designating something as freshly plucked, freshly picked, new. It refers to a fresh olive leaf just plucked off (Gen. 8:11). And some prefer to read this word in Ezekiel 17:9 as a fresh sprouted leaf (see 2964).

2966. טְרֵפָה ṭᵉrēp̱āh: A feminine noun indicating what is torn. It is often used of animal flesh torn by wild beasts (Gen. 31:39; Ex. 22:13[12]). Torn flesh was not to be eaten by Israel; it was unclean and forbidden (Lev. 7:24; 17:15; 22:8; Ezek. 4:14; 44:31). It is used to describe the nations that served as prey to the lion, the king of Nineveh (Nah. 2:12[13]).

2967. טַרְפְּלָי ṭarpᵉlāy: A proper noun designating Tarpelites (Ezra 4:9).

י Yodh

2968. יָאַב ***yā'aḇ:*** A verb meaning to long for, to desire. It is used metaphorically of desiring, longing for the laws and commandments of God (Ps. 119:131).

2969. יָאָה ***yā'āh:*** A verb indicating to pertain, to be fitting, to belong to. It is used to indicate what is appropriate and fitting toward a person or object. All nations should reverence and fear God, for it is appropriate because of who He is (Jer. 10:7).

2970. יַאֲזַנְיָהוּ ***ya'azanyāhû,*** יַאֲזַנְיָה ***ya'azanyāh:*** A proper noun designating Jaazaniah:

A. A Maachathite (2 Kgs. 25:23).
B. A Rechabite (Jer. 35:3).
C. Son of Shaphan (Ezek. 8:11).
D. Son of Azur (Ezek. 11:1).

2971. יָאִיר ***yā'iyr:*** A proper noun designating Jair:

A. Son of Manasseh and patronym of *hawwôṯ yā'iyr* (2334) (Num. 32:41; Deut. 3:14; Josh. 13:30; Judg. 10:4; 1 Kgs. 4:13; 1 Chr. 2:22, 23).
B. A judge in Gilead (Judg. 10:3, 5).
C. Father of Mordecai (Esth. 2:5).

2972. יָאִרִי ***yā'iriy:*** A proper noun designating Jairite (2 Sam. 20:26).

2973. יָאַל ***yā'al:*** A verb indicating to be foolish, to act foolishly; to show oneself foolish. It depicts an action, behavior, and attitude that are against what is considered wise, prudent, upright. Miriam and Aaron murmured against Moses, which was shown to be a foolish act in the circumstances (Num. 12:11). It means in some contexts to act against God's people and the Lord's plan for them (Isa. 19:13). It means to behave against the way of the Lord (Jer. 5:4). It refers to Babylonian priests being made to appear foolish by the failure and falsity of their oracles (Jer. 50:36).

2974. יָאַל ***yā'al:*** A verb meaning to choose to do something. The focus of this verb is on the decision to act. This concept is expressed on three levels. On the first level, the individual shows a willingness to act a certain way, to accept an invitation (Ex. 2:21; Josh. 7:7; Judg. 19:6). On the next level, the individual is more active and voluntarily decides to act a certain way (Gen. 18:27; Deut. 1:5). On the final level, the individual is even more active and voluntarily decides to act a certain way with determination and resolve (Josh. 17:12; Judg. 1:27, 35; Hos. 5:11). This verb provides strong support for the theological concept of human free will because humanity is permitted to decide to act a certain way. God, however, will hold humanity responsible for those decisions and actions.

2975. יְאֹר ***y^e'ōr,*** יְאוֹר ***y^e'ôr:*** A masculine noun referring to the Nile River, a river. It is used to designate the Nile River (Gen. 41:1–3; Ex. 1:22; 2 Kgs. 19:24; Amos 8:8; 9:5) often. It also refers to the branches and the canals of the Nile River (Ex. 7:19) and to various canals or streams (NASB, NIV) in general (Isa. 33:21). The word designates the Tigris River (Dan. 12:5–7). It is used of hollow shafts dug out for mining (Job 28:10). The Egyptians and their military activities of invasion are compared to a rising Nile River (Jer. 46:7, 8).

2976. יָאַשׁ ***yā'aš:*** A verb meaning to despair. The word refers to despair in the sense that one concludes that something desirable is out of reach and usually stops working toward it. In 1 Samuel 27:1, David hoped Saul would despair of finding him when he fled to the Philistines. The word may refer to loss of hope in God or a false god (Isa. 57:10; Jer. 2:25; 18:12). It may also refer, similarly, to a loss of meaning in life (Eccl. 2:20; cf. Phil. 1:21, 22). In Job 6:26, the word describes an emotional state of despair without immediately focusing on the cause of despair. In three passages, the word occurs in a passive sense as a statement or exclamation meaning "it is hopeless" (Isa. 57:10; Jer. 2:25; 18:12).

2977. יֹאשִׁיָּהוּ ***yō'šiyyāhû,*** יוֹאשִׁיָּהוּ ***yô'šiyyāhû,*** יֹאשִׁיָּה ***yō'šiyyāh:*** A proper noun designating Josiah:

A. A great reforming king in Judah. His coming was prophesied years earlier (1 Kgs. 13:2). He reigned 640–609 B.C; he began to reign when he was eight years old after his father Amon died (2 Kgs. 21:24–26; 22:1–2). He did what was right in the eyes of the Lord and walked in the Law as David had. He even removed the high places (2 Kgs. 23:15–16). His extensive reforms resulted in the finding of the Book of the Law in ca. 622 B.C., which Josiah then followed rigorously in his reign (22:1—23:30). He held a renewal ceremony for the covenant in the Book of the Law (2 Kgs. 23:1–3). He died at an early age at Megiddo in a battle against Neco, king of Egypt (2 Chr. 35:20–24). He was so esteemed that Jeremiah wrote a lament about him (2 Chr. 35:24–25).

B. An exile who returned from Babylon (Zech. 6:10).

2978. יִאתוֹן ***yi'tôn,*** אִיתוֹן ***'iyṯôn:*** I. A masculine noun denoting an entrance. It is used to describe an opening to be used as a gateway in Ezekiel's new Temple (Ezek. 40:15).

II. A masculine noun meaning entrance. Some translators prefer to read this word in the place of I (Ezek. 40:15).

2979. יְאָתְרַי ***y***^{e}***'āṯray:*** A proper noun designating Jeatherai (1 Chr. 6:21[6].

2980. יָבַב ***yāḇaḇ:*** A verb meaning to lament, to cry. It indicates a cry or expression of pain and sorrow from worry and anxiety. Sisera's mother expressed her anxiety in a lament (Judg. 5:28).

2981. יְבוּל **y**e**b̲ûl:** A masculine noun referring to a crop, produce. It indicates the fruit or produce generated by well-watered land or soil (Lev. 26:4, 20; Ezek. 34:27; Zech. 8:12), a blessing from the Lord. It also refers to the produce brought forth by people's labor (Ps. 78:46). It refers to a person's acquired goods or possessions (Job 20:28).

2982. יְבוּס **y**e**b̲ûs:** A proper noun designating Jebus, an ancient name for Jerusalem. It was formerly inhabited by Jebusites (Gen. 10:16; Judg. 1:21; 19:10; 1 Chr. 11:4).

2983. יְבוּסִי **y**e**b̲ûsiy,** יְבֻסִי **y**e**b̲usiy:** A proper noun designating Jebusite, the word is gentilic, indicating an ethnic group or nationality. The earliest inhabitants of Jerusalem (Gen. 10:16; Judg. 1:21; Josh. 15:63) were Jebusites. Jerusalem was also called Jebus in antiquity. The Jebusites were descended from Canaan, hence, were Canaanites whom Israel would displace in time (Gen. 15:17–21; Ex. 3:8, 17). They also lived in the mountain regions around Jerusalem (Num. 13:29). David gained control of the city of Jebus/Jerusalem (2 Sam. 5:6) and, hence, it was also called "the city of David."

2984. יִבְחָר **yib̲ḥār:** A proper noun designating Ibhar (2 Sam. 5:15; 1 Chr. 3:6; 14:5).

2985. יָבִין **yāb̲iyn:** A proper noun designating Jabin:

A. King of Hazor (Josh. 11:1).

B. A different king of Hazor (Judg. 4:2, 7, 17, 23, 24; Ps. 83:9[10]).

2986. יָבַל **yāb̲al:** A verb meaning to bring, to carry, to bear along. It is used of bringing or transporting items for various uses: as gifts (Ps. 68:29[30]; 76:11[12]); as booty (Hos. 10:6); as taxes or tribute (Zeph. 3:10). It indicates things brought by others: gifts (Isa. 18:7); sacrifices (Isa. 53:7); a bride in marriage (Ps. 45:14[15]). It is used of the returning exiles from Babylonian captivity led by the Lord to Jerusalem (Isa. 55:12; Jer. 31:9). In a figurative sense, it denotes being carried or led from womb to tomb (Job 10:19; 21:32) and depicts evil people being led to judgment (Job 21:30).

2987. יְבַל **y**e**b̲al:** An Aramaic verb indicating to bring, to carry. It means to transfer or transport something from one place to another, e.g., the gold and silver utensils of the Temple from Babylon to Jerusalem (Ezra 5:14; 6:5), as well as silver and gold for monetary use (Ezra 7:15).

2988. יָבָל **yāb̲āl:** A masculine noun indicating a stream, a river. It describes streams or rivulets located on the tops of mountains and high hills. In a time of God's judgments (Isa. 30:25), they will be judged. But also it describes streams of water that will feed trees in a time of God's great blessings (Isa. 44:4).

2989. יָבָל ***yāḇāl*, יַבֶּלֶת *yabbeleṯ*:** A proper noun designating Jabal (Gen. 4:20).

2990. יַבֶּלֶת ***yabbeleṯ*:** I. An adjective describing something as oozing, running, a discharging pus. It indicates a diseased condition of an animal. Animals described with running sores, and oozing pus were disqualified as sacrificial animals (Lev. 22:22; KJV, wen; NKJV, ulcer; NIV, warts; NASB, running sore).

II. A feminine noun indicating something with warts (NIV, Lev. 22:22). These ancient terms used in the Bible to describe diseases of the skin are difficult to decipher and are still being studied (see I).

2991. יִבְלְעָם ***yiḇleʿām*:** A proper noun designating Ibleam (Josh. 17:11; Judg. 1:27; 2 Kgs. 9:27).

2992. יָבַם ***yāḇam*:** A verb meaning to marry, perform one's duty in a levirate marriage; to consummate a levirate marriage. It indicates the duty of impregnating the wife of one's brother who has died so there will be offspring to him and so the family name will not die out (Gen. 38:8) in Israel (Deut. 25:5, 7).

2993. יָבָם ***yāḇām*:** A masculine noun indicating a brother-in-law, a husband's brother. It indicates the brother of a deceased husband, who was to marry the deceased brother's wife and raise up a son in his honor (Deut. 25:5, 7).

2994. יְבָמָה ***yᵉḇāmāh*:** A feminine noun indicating a sister-in-law or brother's wife. It indicates the wife of a deceased brother. The living brother is then to take this sister-in-law, the deceased brother's wife, to impregnate her so that offspring will be produced (Deut. 25:7, 9). This term is also applied to Ruth, a Moabite, who became an Israelite by choice (Ruth 1:15). Boaz raised up seed to her deceased Israelite husband and contributed to the line of David.

2995. יַבְנְאֵל ***yaḇnᵉʾēl*:** A proper noun designating Jabneel:

A. A town in Judah (Josh. 15:11).

B. A town in Naphtali (Josh. 19:33).

2996. יַבְנֶה ***yaḇneh*:** A proper noun designating Jabneh (2 Chr. 26:6).

2997. יִבְנְיָה ***yiḇnᵉyāh*:** A proper noun designating Ibneiah (1 Chr. 9:8).

2998. יִבְנִיָּה ***yiḇniyyāh*:** A proper noun designating Ibnijah (1 Chr. 9:8).

2999. יַבֹּק ***yabbōq*:** A proper noun designating the Jabbok, a Transjordanian river, swift flowing, from modern Amman, Jordan, north and west into the Jordan. Jacob wrestled with the angel of the Lord (Gen. 32:22) along its shores. Because of his effort, his name was changed to Israel. The river bounded the Amorites on the north (Num. 21:24; Deut. 2:37). It also served as a boundary to the tribes of

Manasseh and Reuben (Deut. 3:16; Josh. 12:2).

3000. יְבֶרֶכְיָהוּ ***yᵉḇereḵyāhû:*** A proper noun designating Jeberechiah (Isa. 8:2).

3001. יָבַשׁ ***yāḇaš,*** יָבֵשׁ ***yāḇēš:*** A verb meaning to be dried up, to be dry, to be withered. This common intransitive verb refers to the drying up and withering of plants, trees, grass, crops, and the earth itself after the flood (Gen. 8:14). It also occurs with a intensive and causative sense meaning to dry, to wither. *Yahweh* dried the waters, particularly the sea (Josh. 2:10; Ps. 74:15; Isa. 42:15; Jer. 51:36; Nah. 1:4). It is used figuratively to denote God destroying Babylon (Ezek. 17:24).

3002. יָבֵשׁ ***yāḇēš:*** An adjective meaning dry, dried. The Nazarite vow prohibited partaking of the fruit of the vine, including dried grapes (Num. 6:3). The Israelites complained in the desert because they had no food like they did in Egypt; all they had to eat was manna, and their souls were dried up (Num. 11:6). A second use of dry is when it refers to chaff that breaks in pieces. It is used figuratively of Job, who was weary and worn out (Job 13:25).

3003. יָבֵשׁ ***yāḇēš:*** A proper noun designating Jeberechiah:

A. A town in Gilead. It is located on the north side of the Jabbok, seven miles east of the Jordan River. The city kept aloof from the war against the Benjamites. As a result, the inhabitants were slaughtered, and the women served as wives to the Benjamites (Judg. 21:13–14). Saul rescued the city in his day (1 Sam. 11:1, 9), and the inhabitants, in turn, later rescued his body from shameful exposure (1 Sam. 31:12, 13; 2 Sam. 2). It is located at Tell-el-Maglub by archaeologists today.

B. He was the father of Shallum, a king of Israel who reigned only on month and was assassinated (2 Kgs. 15:8–14).

3004. יַבָּשָׁה ***yabbāšāh:*** A feminine noun meaning dry land. This word can be an adjective as well. In all uses, it is contrasted with water. It often describes land formerly covered with water, such as the land appearing on the third day of creation; the land on which the people of Israel crossed the Red Sea (Ex. 14:16, 22, 29; Ps. 66:6); and the land on which they crossed the Jordan (Josh. 4:22). It also describes land onto which water is poured both literally (Ex. 4:9) and as a figure of the Holy Spirit being poured on the descendants of Jacob (Isa. 44:3).

3005. יִבְשָׂם ***yiḇśām:*** A proper noun designating Ibsam, Jibsam (1 Chr. 7:2).

3006. יַבֶּשֶׁת ***yabbešeṯ:*** A feminine noun meaning dry land. It is apparently identical to *yaḇḇāšāh* (3004). This word occurs only twice. In Exodus 4:9, it refers to land upon which water had been poured and subsequently had turned to blood. In Psalm 95:5, it refers to dry land (in contrast to the sea), which the Lord's hands formed.

3007. יַבֶּשֶׁת ***yabbešeṯ:*** An Aramaic feminine noun meaning earth. This noun, appearing only in Daniel 2:10, suggests any patch of dry land on which a person can stand. Thus, the word is taken to imply the whole planet or the entire world.

3008. יִגְאָל ***yig'āl:*** A proper noun designating Igal:

A. One of the twelve spies (Num. 13:7).

B. One of David's mighty men (2 Sam. 23:36).

C. A descendant of Zerubbabel (1 Chr. 3:22).

3009. יָגַב ***yāgaḇ:*** A verb meaning to plow the earth, to be a husbandman. It is used in its participial form to refer to those who cared for the land and its produce in Israel (2 Kgs. 25:12). It was a low-class social position and included vinedressers (Jer. 52:16).

3010. יָגֵב ***yagēḇ:*** A masculine noun depicting a field. It indicates the areas of land to be plowed by the plowmen, plowed ground, or fields (Jer. 39:10).

3011. יָגְבְּהָה ***yogbᵉhāh:*** A proper noun designating Jogbehah (Num. 32:35; Judg. 8:11).

3012. יִגְדַּלְיָהוּ ***yigdalyāhû:*** A proper noun designating Igdaliah (Jer. 35:4).

3013. יָגָה ***yāgāh,*** נוּג ***nûg:*** I. A verb indicating to suffer, to afflict, to grieve. It refers to the emotion and despair brought about by some act or condition, such as Jerusalem's misfortunes (Lam. 3:33). Compassion is the cure for this state of affliction from the Lord and comes from Him as well (Lam. 1:12; 3:32). The virgins or pure daughters of Zion were in a state of despair and mourning from the Lord (Lam. 1:4, 5). It seems to refer to the sufferer tormented by his useless comforters (Job 19:2). It describes the affliction on Israel, the distress and pain from her enemies (Isa. 51:23). It indicates those who sorrow or grieve because of the failure to keep the appointed feasts of God's people (Zeph. 3:18, KJV, NASB).

II. A masculine noun indicating sorrow, grief. It indicates a response or attitude of intense emotional suffering for the failure of the appointed feasts and festivals of God's people in exile (Zeph. 3:18, NIV).

3014. יָגָה ***yāgāh:*** A verb meaning to remove, to push away, to carry off. It indicates the removal of something, e.g., the removal of a dead person from blocking the road (2 Sam. 20:13).

3015. יָגוֹן ***yāgôn:*** A masculine noun indicating grief, sorrow, torment, trouble. It indicates a state or condition of utter loss and despair (Gen. 42:38; 44:31) that seems beyond cure (Jer. 8:18). It is an emotion that is the opposite of gladness or joy (Esth. 9:22) and equal to a state of mourning. It is brought on by the oppression of an enemy and the absence of the Lord in one's life (Ps. 13:2[3]) but also by one's sin (Ps. 31:10[11]). It is related to being overcome by drunkenness (Ezek. 23:33). This condition is the bedfellow of misery and oppression (Ps. 107:39). The redeemed of the Lord experience a liberty from sorrow (Isa. 35:10).

3016. יָגוֹר ***yāgôr:*** An adjective meaning feared, fearful, dreadful. It indicates an attitude of great anxiety and apprehension towards certain persons, events, or things (Jer. 22:25), such as the dreaded Babylonians (Jer. 39:17).

3017. יָגוּר ***yāgûr:*** A proper noun designating Jagur (Josh. 15:21).

3018. יְגִיעַ ***y^egiya':*** A masculine noun denoting labor, the fruit of labor. It indicates the performance of toil, physical or mental exertion toward a task. It refers to Jacob's toil for his father-in-law Laban (Gen. 31:42). It can refer to the products produced by the land and the labor expended on it (Deut. 28:33; Ps. 78:46; 109:11; 128:2; Hag. 1:11). In Nehemiah 5:13, it indicates the possessions obtained through one's labors (Ezek. 23:29). Human beings are the products of the labor of the Lord's hands (Job 10:3). It may indicate all the tasks to be performed (Job 39:11). It is used of all the produce or production of a given nation (Isa. 45:14). It possibly indicates wages, as opposed to labor, which are spent unwisely in vain (Isa. 55:2). It has the sense of efforts put forth in Hosea 12:8[9].

3019. יָגִיעַ ***yāgiya':*** An adjective meaning weary, tired. It indicates a weariness, exhaustion, and turmoil experienced by persons, from which only the grave gives a respite (Job 3:17) or rest.

3020. יָגְלִי ***yogliy:*** A proper noun designating Jogli (Num. 34:22).

3021. יָגַע ***yāga':*** A verb indicating to work, to become weary with work. It indicates putting forth great effort and exertion to accomplish something (Josh. 7:3), especially in battle (2 Sam. 23:10), so that one becomes enervated or exhausted. It takes on the idea of putting forth effort to continue to function in the face of great obstacles (Job 9:29). It indicates the loss of energy or spirit from one's hopeless responses to illness (Ps. 6:6[7]; 69:3[4]) or adversity (Jer. 45:3). Wise persons are told not to use up their energy just to acquire wealth (Prov. 23:4). A foolish person's labor is so poorly structured that it weakens him or her excessively (Eccl. 10:15). Israel, in her rebellion, became weary of following the Lord (Isa. 43:22) and in turn "wearied" Him (Isa. 43:24; Mal. 2:17). The nations in their rebellions weary themselves against the Lord (Hab. 2:13).

3022. יָגָע ***yāgā':*** A masculine noun referring to the product of labor; earnings. It is used of the benefits, physical or immaterial, of one's toil (Job 20:18). The Lord drives the wicked person to return them.

3023. יָגֵעַ ***yāgēa':*** An adjective meaning weary, tired. It refers to a state of weakness or exhaustion from physical exertion and oppression (Deut. 25:18; 2 Sam. 17:2). It refers in general to the weariness, exhaustion, and monotony of the endless cycle of repetitiveness in the world (Eccl. 1:8).

3024. יְגִיעָה ***y^{e}giy'āh:*** A feminine noun indicating weariness. It indicates a condition of being worn out or exhausted, especially from excessive study or devotion to books (Eccl. 12:12).

3025. יָגֹר ***yāgōr:*** A verb meaning to fear, to be afraid. In comparison to the more common verb for fear, *yārē'* (3372), which often refers to a general sense of vulnerability (cf. Gen. 15:1), *yāgōr* refers to fear of specific occurrences such as catching a disease (Deut. 28:60); being reproached or scorned (Ps. 119:39); or being delivered into the power of specific people (Jer. 39:17). It describes the fear of God in Deuteronomy 9:19 but focuses on the specific possibility of God destroying Israel.

3026. יְגַר שָׂהֲדוּתָא ***y^{e}gar śāh^{a}ḏûṯā':*** A proper noun designating Jegar Sahadutha (Gen. 31:47).

3027. יָד ***yāḏ,*** יַד אַבְשָׁלוֹם ***yaḏ 'aḇšālôm:*** A feminine noun meaning hand, strength. This word frequently appears in the Old Testament with literal, figurative, and technical uses. Literally, it implies the hand of a human being (Lev. 14:28; Jer. 36:14) and occasionally the wrist (Gen. 38:28). Metaphorically, it signifies strength or power (Deut. 32:36; Isa. 37:27); authority or right of possession (Gen. 16:9; 2 Chr. 13:16); location or direction (Num. 24:24; Ps. 141:6); the side of an object (1 Sam. 4:18); a fractional portion of the whole (Gen. 47:24; Neh. 11:1). In a technical sense, the word is used to identify the upright supports for the bronze laver (1 Kgs. 7:35, 36); the tenons for the Tabernacle (Ex. 26:17); and an axle (1 Kgs. 7:32, 33).

3028. יַד ***yaḏ:*** An Aramaic noun meaning hand, power, control, possession. The word corresponds to the Hebrew noun of the same spelling (3027) and refers to a literal hand (although not a human one) as writing (Dan. 5:5). From the ability of the hand to hold and manipulate objects, the word is used figuratively to describe control, power, or possession, such as Nebuchadnezzar's power over Israel (Ezra 5:12) and other people and animals (Dan. 2:38); God's power to do whatever He wishes (Dan. 4:35[32]); the lions' power to hurt a person (Dan. 6:27[28]; cf. 1 Sam. 17:37); the Jews' control over the rebuilding of the Temple (Ezra 5:8). The stone cut out without hands (Dan. 2:34) refers to a kingdom set up by God independently of human power (Dan. 2:45). In Ezra 6:12, the word refers to an attempt to gain power to change the edict of Darius.

3029. יְדָא ***y^eḏāʼ:*** An Aramaic verb meaning to give thanks, to offer praise. Twice this word appears in the Old Testament, both times in Daniel. It is solely directed to the Lord, signifying the thanks given to God for answered prayer (Dan. 2:23) and in reference to Daniel's daily devotional practice (Dan. 6:10[11]).

3030. יִדְאֲלָה ***yiḏʼ^alāh:*** A proper noun designating Idalah (Josh. 19:15).

3031. יִדְבָּשׁ ***yiḏbāš:*** A proper noun designating Idbash (1 Chr. 4:3).

3032. יָדַד ***yāḏaḏ:*** A verb describing the casting of lots. It indicates the tossing of some object or objects to gain an answer or direction in a matter (Joel 3:3[4:3]). Even foreign nations cast lots to determine how to divide up Jerusalem (Obad. 1:11) and also concerning the great city of Nineveh (Nah. 3:10).

3033. יְדִדוּת ***y^eḏiḏûṯ:*** A feminine noun meaning beloved, highly valued, dear one. It is derived from the word *y^eḏiyḏ* (3039), which has a similar meaning. The word occurs only in Jeremiah 12:7 where it describes Israel as beloved of God's soul but forsaken by Him and delivered to their enemies because they only pretended to return His love (Jer. 12:1, 2).

3034. יָדָה ***yāḏāh:*** A verb meaning to acknowledge, to praise, to give thanks, to confess, to cast. The essential meaning is an act of acknowledging what is right about God in praise and thanksgiving (1 Chr. 16:34). It can also mean a right acknowledgment of self before God in confessing sin (Lev. 26:40) or of others in their God-given positions (Gen. 49:8). It is often linked with the word *hālal* (1984) in a hymnic liturgy of "thanking and praising" (1 Chr. 16:4; 23:30; Ezra 3:11; Neh. 12:24, 46). This rightful, heavenward acknowledgment is structured in corporate worship (Ps. 100:4; 107:1, 8, 15, 21, 31), yet is also part of personal lament and deliverance (Ps. 88:11[10]). Several uses of *yāḏāh* evidence an essence of motion or action (as something given), intensively referring twice to cast or to throw down (Lam. 3:53; Zech. 1:21 [2:4]), and once it means to shoot (as an arrow; Jer. 50:14).

3035. יִדּוֹ ***yiddô:*** A proper noun designating Iddo:

A. A Manassite (1 Chr. 27:21).

B. A Jew (Ezra 10:43, an alternate reading for Jaddai).

3036. יָדוֹן ***yāḏôn:*** A proper noun designating Jadon (Neh. 3:7).

3037. יַדּוּעַ ***yaddûaʻ:*** A proper noun designating Jaddua:

A. A Jewish leader (Neh. 10:21 [22]).

B. Son of Jonathan the high priest (Neh. 12:11, 22).

3038. יְדוּתוּן יְדֻתוּן ***y^e^dûṯûn***, ***y^e^dûṯûn:*** A proper noun designating Jeduthun (1 Chr. 9:16; 16:38, 41, 42; 25:1, 3, 6; 2 Chr. 5:12; 29:14; 35:15; Neh. 11:17; Ps. 39:title[1]; 62:title[1]; 77:title[1]).

3039. יָדִיד יְדִידוֹת ***yāḏiyḏ***, ***y^e^ḏiyḏôṯ:*** An adjective meaning beloved, well-loved. This word is often used in poetry. It is used mainly to describe a person who is beloved; for example, Moses called Benjamin the beloved of the Lord (Deut. 33:12). Another use is to describe the loveliness of the Tabernacle of the Lord (Ps. 84:1[2]). A third use is its literal meaning, love. The psalmist calls his poem (Ps. 45) a song of love.

3040. יְדִידָה ***y^e^ḏiyḏāh:*** A proper noun designating Jedidah (2 Kgs. 22:1).

3041. יְדִידְיָה ***y^e^ḏiyḏyāh:*** A proper noun designating Jedidiah (2 Sam. 12:25).

3042. יְדָיָה ***y^e^ḏāyāh:*** A proper noun designating Jedaiah:

A. Son of Shimri (1 Chr. 4:37).

B. Son of Harumaph (Neh. 3:10).

3043. יְדִיעֲאֵל ***y^e^ḏiy^a^'ēl:*** A proper noun designating Jediael:

A. Son of Benjamin (1 Chr. 7:6, 10, 11).

B. Son of Shimri (1 Chr. 11:45).

C. A Manassehite (1 Chr. 12:20).

D. A Korahite (1 Chr. 26:2).

3044. יִדְלָף ***yiḏlāp:*** A proper noun designating Jidlaph (Gen. 22:22).

3045. יָדַע ***yāḏa':*** A verb meaning to know, to learn, to perceive, to discern, to experience, to confess, to consider, to know people relationally, to know how, to be skillful, to be made known, to make oneself known, to make to know.

The simple meaning, to know, is its most common translation out of the eight hundred or more uses. One of the primary uses means to know relationally and experientially: it refers to knowing or not knowing persons (Gen. 29:5; Ex. 1:8) personally or by reputation (Job 19:13). The word also refers to knowing a person sexually (Gen. 4:1; 19:5; 1 Kgs. 1:4). It may even describe knowing or not knowing God or foreign gods (Ex. 5:2; Deut. 11:28; Hos. 2:20[22]; 8:2), but it especially signifies knowing what to do or think in general, especially with respect to God (Isa. 1:3; 56:10). One of its most important uses is depicting God's knowledge of people: The Lord knows their hearts entirely (Ex. 33:12; 2 Sam. 7:20; Ps. 139:4; Jer. 17:9; Hos. 5:3); God knows the suffering of His people (Ex. 2:25), and He cares.

The word also describes knowing various other things: when Adam and Eve sinned, knowing good and evil (Gen. 3:22); knowing nothing (1 Sam.

20:39); and knowing the way of wisdom (Job 28:23). One could know by observation (1 Sam. 23:22, 23), as when Israel and Pharaoh came to know God through the plagues He brought on Egypt (Ex. 10:2). People knew by experience (Josh. 23:14) that God kept His promises; this kind of experience could lead to knowing by confession (Jer. 3:13; 14:20). Persons could be charged to know what they were about to do (Judg. 18:14) or what the situation implied (1 Kgs. 20:7) so they would be able to discriminate between right and wrong, good and bad, what was not proper or advantageous (Deut. 1:39; 2 Sam. 19:35[36]).

The word describes different aspects of knowing in its other forms. In the passive forms, it describes making something or someone known. The most famous illustration is Exodus 6:3 when God asserted to Moses that He did not make himself known to the fathers as Yahweh.

3046. יְדַע y^ed̲aʻ: An Aramaic verb meaning to know, to communicate, to inform, to cause to know. The word primarily refers to knowledge sharing or awareness and occurs often in the books of Ezra and Daniel. In Ezra, the men opposed to the rebuilding of Jerusalem wanted to it to be known to Artaxerxes (Ezra 4:12, 13), and when opposing the Temple, they made it known to Darius (Ezra 5:8, 10). The book of Daniel presents a theological subtheme of true knowledge. In the desired and hidden meanings of life, only the God of Heaven truly knows the end from the beginning, and only He can ultimately reveal and wisely inform (Dan. 2:5, 21–23, 28–30; 4:9[6]; 5:8, 15, 16). Fearing Him is true knowing (Dan. 5:17, 21–23), a sovereign awareness that removes crippling human fear in circumstantial knowing (Dan. 3:18; 6:10[11]). *Y^ed̲aʻ* compares with the Hebrew word *yād̲aʻ* (3045), which is used with much broader variances of meaning in Scripture, ranging from cognitive to experiential to sexual relations.

3047. יָדָע yād̲āʻ: A proper noun designating Jada (1 Chr. 2:28, 32).

3048. יְדַעְיָה y^ed̲aʻyāh: A proper noun designating Jedaiah:

A. A priest under David (1 Chr. 24:7).

B. A priest under Zerubbabel (1 Chr. 9:10; Ezra 2:36; Neh. 7:39; 11:10; 12:6, 19).

C. A postexilic priest (Neh. 12:7, 21).

D. A Jew (Zech. 6:10, 14).

3049. יִדְּעֹנִי yidd^{e}ʻōniy: A masculine noun meaning a familiar spirit, a conjurer, and a wizard. In Levitical Law, this type of person was considered an abomination to the Lord (Deut. 18:11). King Saul consulted such a medium when he desired to know the outcome of his war against the Philistines (1 Sam. 28:9). King Manasseh's evil deeds included the practice of consulting mediums and wizards (2 Kgs. 21:6). Isaiah condemned the people of Israel for turning to the way of the Canaanites, who sought out mediums and wizards in order to hear from their dead (Isa. 8:19).

3050. יָהּ *yāh:* A neuter pronoun of God, a shortened form of Yahweh, often translated "LORD." This abbreviated noun for Yahweh is used in poetry, especially in the Psalms. The word is found first in Exodus 15:2 and 17:16; in both cases, the LORD is exalted after He delivered His people from possible annihilation, first by Egypt and then by the Amalekites. These two poetic passages are then quoted later (Ps. 118:14; Isa. 12:2). In a poetic prayer, Hezekiah used the endearing term also (Isa. 38:11). All other uses of the shortened name are found in Psalms (Ps. 68:18[19]; 77:11 [12]; 130:3). Many times it is found in the phrase, "Hallelujah, praise be to Yah!" (Ps. 104:35; 105:45; 106:1, 48).

3051. יָהַב *yāhab̲,* הַב *hab̲:* I. A verb indicating to give, to come; to pay attention. The basic form of this verb is given as *yāhab* or *hab̲,* but its meaning and usage are not affected by this (see II, below). It indicates the handing over or turning over of something to someone: one's wife (Gen. 29:21); a garment (Ruth 3:15); a price (Zech. 11:12). It takes on the meaning of give in its imperative form: to give lots; that is a decision from the Lord about what is to be done (1 Sam. 14:41). It means to set something or someone in a certain location (Deut. 1:13; 2 Sam. 11:15). It is used of attributing glory to the Lord (Ps. 29:1, 2) or greatness (Deut. 32:3). It has the idiomatic meaning of "Come, now!" in its imperative forms (*hab̲, hāb̲āh,* Gen. 11:3; 38:16; Ex. 1:10).

II. A verb indicating to give, to come; pay attention. The meanings and usage of this verb are the same as those given in I, above.

3052. יְהַב *y^ehab̲:* An Aramaic verb meaning to give, to pay. It is used of giving various things or of various things that are given in its possessive sense: gold and silver vessels are given to Sheshbazzar (Ezra 5:14; cf. 7:19), and materials for offerings are given (Ezra 6:9). God gave His disobedient people into the hands of Babylon (Ezra 5:12). It describes the laying of the Temple's foundation in Ezra's day (5:16) and the payment of money to cover the costs of building the Temple (Ezra 6:4, 8). The word also describes the Lord's impartations of wisdom to the wise (Dan. 2:21), especially to Daniel (2:23b). Various other items are given over: one's own body (Dan. 3:28); a change of disposition from human to beastly (Dan. 4:16[13]); rewards (Dan. 5:17); kingship and its authority (Dan. 5:18). In a political and administrative setting, it refers to giving accountability to one's superiors (Dan. 6:2[3]). In a legal sense, it is used of giving judgment (Dan. 7:22). It is used to depict the Lord's presentation of the sovereignty of the kingdom to the saints of the Most High God (Dan. 7:27). Most translators do not find this word in Numbers 21:14 but see 2052, II.

3053. יְהָב ***yᵉhāḇ:*** A masculine noun denoting a care, a burden. It indicates one's lot or portion in life which is to be cast on the Lord (Ps. 55:22[23]). The word means literally "what is given."

3054. יָהַד ***yāhaḏ:*** A verb describing becoming a Jew. It is used of many of Israel's enemies who decide to cast their lot with the Jews and join them and their God because of the great deliverance God gave to the Jews (Esth. 8:17).

3055. יְהֻד ***yᵉhuḏ:*** A proper noun designating Jehud (Josh. 19:45).

3056. יַהְדַּי ***yāhday:*** A proper noun designating Jahdai (1 Chr. 2:47).

3057. יְהֻדִיָּה ***yᵉhuḏiyyāh:*** A proper noun designating Jehudijah. It literally means the Jewess. Its only occurrence is in 1 Chronicles 4:18. See also *yᵉhûḏiy* (3064).

3058. יֵהוּא ***yēhû':*** A proper noun designating Jehu:

A. He was a king, Jehoshaphat's son, chosen by God to overthrow the dynasty of Omri. He reigned 28 years (841–814 B.C.). Elijah anointed him to be king. His divinely appointed purpose was accomplished during his evil reign (2 Kgs. 9:10). He destroyed the house of Ahab and Jezebel (2 Kgs. 9:6–10). He was an army commander and was later anointed king by his men (2 Kgs. 9:13). He killed both King Joram (Israel) and King Ahaziah (Judah) (2 Kgs. 9:21–29). Jezebel's death soon followed (2 Kgs. 9:30–37), as well as the slaughter of Baal's prophets.

B. A prophet, the son of Hanani, who prophesied the destruction of Baasha and his evil house (1 Kgs. 16:1–4, 11).

C. The name of one of David's mighty skilled warriors, a relative of Saul and a Benjamite (1 Chr. 12:3).

D. A Judahite traced to Judah's son Hezron (1 Chr. 2:9) through Jerahmeel, son of Hezron. His father was Jesse.

E. His father was Joshibiah, a Simeonite. He was the head of a clan (1 Chr. 4:35).

3059. יְהוֹאָחָז ***yᵉhô'āḥāz:*** A proper noun designating Jehoahaz:

A. The sixth king of Judah who reigned one year (841 B.C.; 2 Chr. 21:17; 25:23). Jehoahaz is another name for Ahaziah (see entry 274). The name means "the Lord has seized." He was the son of Jehoram (848–841 B.C.). His mother was the infamous Athaliah, granddaughter of Omri (see 2 Kgs. 8:25–29). He was a relative of Ahab whom he assassinated (see 2 Kgs. 9:27–29).

B. The son of Jehu who reigned 814–798 B.C. (2 Kgs. 10:35). He was an evil king; therefore the Lord oppressed Israel by the Syrians during his reign (2 Kgs. 13:3). His army was devastated by the Arameans

(2 Kgs. 13:7–9). His son Jehoash succeeded him.

C. A king of Judah who reigned (2 Kgs. 23:31–34) in Judah. He was crowned by the people. His father was Josiah, the great king. He reigned three months before the king of Egypt replaced him (2 Kgs. 23:30–34; 2 Chr. 36:1–4). Jeremiah called him Shallum (Jer. 22:11–12).

3060. יְהוֹאָשׁ *yehô'āš:* A proper noun designating Jehoash:

A. A king of Judah who was also known as Joash. The name means "the Lord has given." He was son of Ahaziah and Zibiah. He reigned forty years (835–796 B.C.). He began to reign when he was seven years old, after being shielded for six years in the Temple by Jehoiada, the high priest (2 Kgs. 11:1–21). He ironically sought to repair the Lord's house but was forced to decimate its wealth in order to buy off Hazael of Aram (2 Kgs. 12:17[18], 18[19]). He was assassinated and buried in Jerusalem.

B. Another wicked king of northern Israel (798–782 B.C.), he reigned sixteen years (2 Kgs. 13:10–25; 14:1–17). His father was Jehoahaz. He continued to pursue the sins of previous kings in Israel. He fought against Amaziah, king of Judah. Jeroboam II followed him. Jehoash sought help from Elisha (2 Kgs. 13:14–19). He successfully recovered some cities and territory from Aram (2 Kgs. 13:24–25). He captured, destroyed, and looted parts of Jerusalem (2 Kgs. 14:11–14).

3061. יְהוּד *yehûḏ:* A proper noun designating Judah, the Aramaic word corresponding to the Hebrew entry 3063 and found in the Aramaic portions of Ezra and Daniel.

3062. יְהוּדָי *yehûḏay:* An Aramaic proper noun meaning Jew (Ezra 4:12, 23; 5:1, 5; 6:7, 8, 14; Dan. 3:8, 12). The word corresponds to the Hebrew word *yehûḏiy* (3064).

3063. יְהוּדָה *yehûḏāh:* A proper noun designating Judah:

A. The fourth son of Jacob through Leah (Gen. 29:35; 35:23). He married a Canaanite woman and bore two sons by her (Er, Onan). Er died and then Onan his brother died, leaving Tamar, Er's wife, without a child. Judah, heartlessly, refused to allow his third son to have a child by Tamar. Judah then committed an unwitting, but heinous sin with his daughter-in-law by hiring her as a prostitute and unwittingly fathered twins by her (Gen. 38). His lack of compassion is evident in the story. Judah himself bore many other sons (Gen. 46:12). Jacob prophesied of the high status Judah and his descendants would have among the patriarchs (Gen. 49:8–12). He and they would be above their enemies, their own kinsmen; he was compared to a lion. He would have royal prerogatives ("scepter," "rulership"); he would be prosperous and powerful in appearance (cf. also Deut. 33:7). From Judah would come the Star out of Jacob and Israel (Gen. 24:17).

B. The territory of Judah ran north-south from north of Jerusalem and Aijalom and south to Kadesh Barnea. Its eastern border ran from Gath south to the El-Arish (River of Egypt). Its eastern border was the Dead Sea and a boundary running from the Brook Zered southwest to Kadesh Barnea. Jerusalem, Hebron, and Bethlehem, all important cities in Israel and the Old Testament, were within its boundaries.

The tribe took its territory in Canaan rather forcefully (Judg. 1:1–9) but could not totally capture Jerusalem. Judah seems gradually to have become isolated from the northern tribes (Judg. 4; 5).

Under David, Judah became powerful. David was crowned king in Judah at Hebron and then captured Jerusalem to consolidate Judah and to attract the other tribes to Jerusalem as the central capital and worship center of the nation (2 Sam. 5:1–16). Solomon attempted to consolidate the nation further, but through poor politics, poor economics, oppressive taxation, and megalomanical building projects, he forced those outside of Judah into a subordinate, almost slave-like position toward Judah and Jerusalem (2 Sam. 8—12). As a result, Israel split off from Judah after Solomon's death in 930 B.C. The nation of Israel went into exile in 722 B.C., while the nation of Judah, with the Davidic covenant and royal line intact, lingered on with a few good kings (Asa, Jehosophat, Joash, Hezekiah, Josiah) until she too was destroyed because of her religious and moral corruption (2 Kgs. 25).

Within Judah, God had chosen a king and established an eternal covenant (2 Sam. 7). The tribe of Judah went into exile in 586 B.C., as predicted by Jeremiah, but likewise returned in 538 B.C. according to the prophet's word, still bearing the promised royal seed. The tribe was a mere shadow of itself from then until the end of the Old Testament. The high priest became dominant, for no kings were permitted in Judah, now a province of Persia, then Egypt, Syria, and Rome.

C. A Levite who had intermarried with the foreign people of the land in Ezra's day (Ezra 10:23).

D. A district or sectional director in Jerusalem over its newly returned residents from exile or the surrounding region (Neh. 11:9).

E. A leading Levite who returned from exile from Babylon under Zerubbabel (Neh. 12:8).

F. A priest who took part in the procession celebrating the rebuilding of the wall of Jerusalem (Neh. 12:34).

3064. יְהוּדִי ***y^e^hûḏiy:*** A proper noun designating a Jew, a gentilic noun indicating nationality. An *iy* (ִי) ending indicated a male while *iyṯ* (ִית) indicated a female. It referred originally to those Israelites living in Judah or of the tribe of Judah after the exile (2 Kgs. 16:6; 25:25; Neh. 1:2; 2:16). The term was used by later writers to depict some inhabitants or persons of Judah who lived there earlier (1 Chr.

4:18). Foreign people used the term to describe the people of Judah in and after the eighth century B.C. (Zech. 8:23; Esth. 2:5; 3:4; 8:11). The updating or final editing of Daniel used the designation (3:8; 5:13). "Jew(s)" is a general term referring to males or females. "Jewess" refers to a female.

3065. יְהוּדִי ***yᵉhûḏiy:*** A proper noun designating Jehudi (Jer. 36:14, 21, 23).

3066. יְהוּדִית ***yᵉhûḏiyṯ:*** A feminine adjective of nationality, meaning in Hebrew or in the Jewish language. It is used as an adverb indicating that someone is speaking Hebrew, in the Hebrew language, or literally in the language of Judah (2 Kgs. 18:26, 28; 2 Chr. 32:18; Neh. 13:24; Isa. 36:11, 13).

3067. יְהוּדִית ***yᵉhûḏiyṯ:*** A proper noun designating Judith (Gen. 26:34).

3068. יְהוָֹה ***yᵉhōwāh:*** A noun meaning God. The word refers to the proper name of the God of Israel, particularly the name by which He revealed Himself to Moses (Ex. 6:2, 3). The divine name has traditionally not been pronounced, primarily out of respect for its sacredness (cf. Ex. 20:7; Deut. 28:58). Until the Renaissance, it was written without vowels in the Hebrew text of the Old Testament, being rendered as YHWH. However, since that time, the vowels of another word, *'ᵃḏōnāy* (136), have been supplied in hopes of reconstructing the pronunciation. Although the exact derivation of the name is uncertain, most scholars agree that its primary meaning should be understood in the context of God's existence, namely, that He is the "I AM THAT I AM" (Ex. 3:14), the One who was, who is, and who always will be (cf. Rev. 11:17). Older translations of the Bible and many newer ones employ the practice of rendering the divine name in capital letters, so as to distinguish it from other Hebrew words. It is most often rendered as LORD (Gen. 4:1; Deut. 6:18; Ps. 18:31[32]; Jer. 33:2; Jon. 1:9) but also as GOD (Gen. 6:5; 2 Sam. 12:22) or JEHOVAH (Ps. 83:18[19]; Isa. 26:4). The frequent appearance of this name in relation to God's redemptive work underscores its tremendous importance (Lev. 26:45; Ps. 19:14[15]). Also, it is sometimes compounded with another word to describe the character of the Lord in greater detail (see Gen. 22:14; Ex. 17:15; Judg. 6:24).

3069. יְהוִה ***yᵉhōwih:*** A masculine proper noun meaning God; Lord. Most translations render this word as GOD to distinguish it from *yᵉhōwāh,* LORD (see 3068; e.g., Gen. 15:2, 8; NASB, KJV, NKJV), but others chose to translate it as LORD (NIV, Gen. 15:2, 8; Deut. 3:24; 9:26; Josh. 7:7, etc.) based on recent studies of the word in various articles and grammars. Its exact meaning is still being researched, but it is a form of the covenant name of Israel's God revealed to Moses at Sinai (Ex. 3:14, *hāyāh* [1961]). It means "He who is or is present," "He who will be who He will be" or "He who causes to be all that is" or an organic combination of the essence of all these renderings.

3070. יְהוָה יִרְאֶה ***yᵉhōwāh yir'eh:*** A proper noun designating Jehovah Jireh, a name given to designate the Lord by Abraham for providing a sacrifice in place of Isaac (Gen. 22:14). It means "the Lord will see to it" literally but also means "the Lord will provide."

3071. יְהוָה נִסִּי ***yᵉhōwāh nissiy:*** A proper noun designating Jehovah Nissi, the name given to the altar Moses built to the Lord after defeating the Amalekites (Ex. 17:15). It means "the Lord is my banner or my standard."

3072. יְהוָה צִדְקֵנוּ ***yᵉhōwāh ṣiḏqēnû:*** A proper noun designating Jehovah Tsidkenu, a name designating the Lord. It means "the Lord is our righteousness." It occurs in a context referring to the messianic concept of "the Branch" (Jer. 23:1–6).

3073. יְהוָה שָׁלוֹם ***yᵉhōwāh šālôm:*** A proper noun designating Jehovah Shalom, a name designating an altar, "the Lord (is) peace" (Judg. 6:24). It was built by Gideon, a famous judge of Israel, because the Lord confirmed to Gideon that He was calling him to deliver Israel. It stood for many years.

3074. יְהוָה שָׁמָּה ***yᵉhōwāh šāmmāh:*** A proper noun designating Jehovah Shammah, a name given to the New Jerusalem of Ezekiel's vision meaning "the Lord is there" (Ezek. 48:35).

3075. יְהוֹזָבָד ***yᵉhôzāḇāḏ:*** A proper noun designating Jehozabad:

A. Son of Shomer (2 Kgs. 12:21[22]; 2 Chr. 24:26).

B. Son of Obededom (1 Chr. 26:4).

C. A Benjamite (2 Chr. 17:18).

3076. יְהוֹחָנָן ***yᵉhôḥānān:*** A proper noun designating Jehohanan:

A. A Levite and descendant of Korah through Meshelemiah his father. One of his sons was a leader of Ephraim (1 Chr. 26:3).

B. A commander of part of Jehoshaphat's military. He was from Judah (2 Chr. 17:15).

C. A priestly descendant of Bebai who had intermarried with people of the land (Ezra 10:28).

D. The head of a priestly family during the days of the high priest Joiakim (Neh. 12:13).

E. A priest who took part in dedicating the newly restored wall of Jerusalem with Nehemiah (Neh. 12:42).

F. Son of Eliashib, Ezra stayed in his room at the Temple and mourned the condition and sins of the returned exiles (Ezra 10:6).

G. A son of Tobiah who had married the daughter of a Jew Meshallam (cf. Neh. 6:18), a marriage not approved in Israel.

3077. יְהוֹיָדָע ***yᵉhôyāḏā‘:*** A proper noun designating Jehoiada:

A. The father of Benaiah who was in charge of the elite personal guard of David, the Kerethites and Pelethites (2 Sam. 8:18; 1 Chr. 11:22, 24). His name means "the Lord knows."

B. The son of Benaiah and grandson of Jehoiada, who counseled David and served as his wise man.

C. A high priest who notably kept Joash hidden from certain death at the hands of Athaliah (2 Kgs. 11:1–21). He led him forth and proclaimed him king (2 Kgs. 11:4–17). Jehoiada served as ruler de facto for Joash as he grew up and gave Joash important guidance (2 Kgs. 12:2–9 [3–10]; 2 Chr. 24:2–25). He was buried appropriately in a royal tomb. He was faithful to the Lord.

D. A priest in the time of Jeremiah who was over the Temple. He was replaced by Zephaniah (Jer. 29:26).

3078. יְהוֹיָכִין ***y^ehôyāḵiyn:*** A proper noun designating Jehoiachin, a king who reigned three months in Jerusalem (598–597 B.C.) but was forced to surrender to the Babylonians (2 Kgs. 24:8–20) under Nebuchadnezzar. He was taken captive to Babylon along with the royal household. Nebuchadnezzar set up Mattaniah (Zedekiah) in his place as king in Judah. He was, after some years, treated with great respect by the Babylonian king Evil-Merodach (561 B.C.). This helped maintain hope among the exiles for a return to Jerusalem.

3079. יְהוֹיָקִים ***y^ehôyāqiym:*** A proper noun designating Jehoiakim, a Judean king (609–598), son of Josiah. His mother's name was Zebidah. He was an evil king. Pharaoh Neco made him king and changed his name from Eliakim to Jehoiakim. He servilely paid tribute thereafter to Egypt by overtaxing the people of Judah. In 605 B.C. the Babylonian king Nebuchadnezzar invaded the land and made Jehoiakim his vassal. He rebelled against Babylon (2 Kgs. 24:1), but the Lord brought judgment on Judah because of its previous sins (2 Kgs. 24:1–6). He was rejected by the Lord (Jer. 22:18–19). Jeremiah prophesied during his reign (Jer. 1:3; 25:1; 35:1). In one of the most arrogant, ignominious acts recorded in Scripture, Jehoiakim cut up and burned the first draft of Jeremiah's prophecies (36:1–32). During his reign, Daniel was taken captive to Babylon (Dan. 1:1, 2). Jehoiachin, his son, reigned after him.

3080. יְהוֹיָרִיב ***y^ehôyāriyḇ:*** A proper noun designating Jehoiarib (1 Chr. 9:10; 24:7).

3081. יְהוּכַל ***y^ehûḵal:*** A proper noun designating Jehucal (Jer. 37:3).

3082. יְהוֹנָדָב ***y^ehônāḏāḇ:*** A proper noun designating Jonadab:

A. The son of Rechab who opposed Baalism and the house of Ahab as adamantly as did Jehu (2 Kgs. 10:14–17, 23). He and the Rechabites also rejected the use of wine and various other culturally developed practices in Israel. They were so faithful to their original covenant that the prophet used them and their faithfulness to shame Israel's failure for keeping the Lord's covenant steadfastly (Jer. 35:8–18).

B. A nephew of David through Shimeah. He set up Tamar for her fateful meeting with Amnon (2 Sam. 13:3–5), her half brother.

3083. יְהוֹנָתָן ***y^e^hônāṯān:*** A proper noun designating Jonathan:

A. The son of Saul who befriended David over against his father Saul. His name means "the Lord has given." He was a mighty warrior (1 Sam. 14:13–14), but his father nearly executed him for a minor incident (1 Sam. 14:44–45). He refused to kill David when Saul commanded him to do so but rather warned and shielded David (1 Sam. 19:1–7; 20:1–17). They became faithful friends and covenanted to keep faith between them (1 Sam. 20:42). David composed a powerful lament at Jonathan's death (2 Sam. 1:26–27).

B. The son of Abiathar, the high priest. He served as a liaison for David (2 Sam. 17:17–22).

C. Son of Shimeah, David's brother. He slew a huge six fingered man at Gath who taunted Israel and her God (2 Sam. 21:21).

D. Son of Shagee and one of David's top thirty mighty warriors (2 Sam. 23:32). Some translations read Shammah (NIV; NLT; cf. 1 Chr. 11:34), reflecting both Hebrew and Greek variants.

E. He was a wise counselor to David, as well as a scribe (1 Chr. 27:32).

F. A person in charge of the royal regional treasuries, a son of Uzziah (1 Chr. 27:25).

G. A scribe who served in Jeremiah's day. His house was converted into a prison (Jer. 37:15, 17).

H. A Levite who helped teach the law to Israel under the king Jehoshaphat's directions (2 Chr. 17:7–9).

I. The head of a priestly family in the time of Joiakim (Neh. 12:18).

J. The son of Gershom, son of Moses. He and his sons served idols among the Danites until northern Israel was taken into exile in 722 B.C. (Judg. 18:30).

3084. יְהוֹסֵף ***y^e^hôsēp̱:*** A proper noun designating Joseph, a spelling variant of Joseph found only in Psalm 81:5[6].

3085. יְהוֹעַדָּה ***y^e^hôʿaddāh:*** A proper noun designating Jehoadah (1 Chr. 8:36).

3086. יְהוֹעַדָּן ***y^e^hôʿaddān:*** A proper noun designating Jehoaddan (2 Kgs. 14:2; 2 Chr. 25:1).

3087. יְהוֹצָדָק ***y^e^hôṣāḏāq:*** A proper noun designating Jehozadak (1 Chr. 6:14[5:40], 15[5:41]; Hag. 1:1, 12, 14; 2:2, 4; Zech. 6:11).

3088. יְהוֹרָם ***y^e^hôrām:*** A proper noun designating Jehoram:

A. A king of Judah who ruled eight years (848–841 B.C.), son of Jehoshaphat (1 Kgs. 22:50[51]). His name means "the Lord is exalted." He became an evil king who led Judah into Baal worship and all the sins of Israel (2 Kgs. 8:16–19). He married a daughter of Ahab, king of Israel. During his reign, Edom revolted from Judah. He died unmourned by his people (1 Chr. 21:20).

B. A king of Israel, son of Ahab, who ruled 852–841 B.C. He succeeded Ahaziah as his younger brother (2 Kgs. 3:1, 6). He was an evil king but his rebellions did not equal those of his father. He even removed additional aspects of Baal worship (2 Kgs. 3:2), and the Lord granted him victory in defeating the Moabites (2 Kgs. 3:14–27). He was executed by Jehu who then reigned (2 Kgs. 9:21–26).

C. The name of a priest who helped teach the Book of the Law to Judah in the days of Jehoshaphat (2 Chr. 17:7–9).

3089. יְהוֹשֶׁבַע ***y^ehôše<u>b</u>a':*** A proper noun designating Jehosheba (2 Kgs. 11:2).

3090. יְהוֹשַׁבְעַת ***y^ehôša<u>b</u>'a<u>t</u>:*** A proper noun designating Jehoshabeath (2 Chr. 22:11).

3091. יְהוֹשׁוּעַ ***y^ehôšûa'***, יְהוֹשֻׁעַ ***y^ehôšua':*** A proper noun designating Joshua:

A. The name means "the Lord delivers." He was Moses' successor (Num. 27:12–23; Deut. 34:9–12), picked by the Lord to conquer the Promised Land (Josh. 1:1–5) that had been given to Israel. His name was previously Hoshea ("salvation"), son of Nun (Num. 13:16). He was from the tribe of Ephraim (Num. 13:8). In his first appearance, he showed himself an exceptionally capable military commander, defeating the Amalekites (Ex. 17:8–16). He became Moses' personal scribe, administrator, and intimate aide. He accompanied Moses often when others were not permitted to do so (Ex. 24:13; 32:17; 33:11). His respect and faithfulness to Moses as God's picked leader never wavered (Num. 11:28). He was one of the spies sent into Canaan and never doubted that Israel could conquer the land (Num. 14:5–9). He and Caleb lived to enter the Promised Land (Num. 26:65). He led Israel successfully, and the Lord fulfilled every promise He had made to Joshua and Israel (Josh. 21:43–45). He was buried in the land which he had conquered for God's people (Josh. 24:29–30).

B. A person of Beth Shemesh in whose field the cart carrying the ark of God back to Jerusalem came to rest beside a large stone. The Philistines were sending it back to Israel. The stone remained a memorial of this event for many years (1 Sam. 6:13, 14).

C. A postexilic high priest in the time of Haggai and Zechariah. He was the son of Jehozadak. He returned from exile in Babylon (537

B.C.). The altar and Temple were rebuilt under his direction. Zechariah called him the Branch, a powerful messianic title (Zech. 6:11–12). Under him the priesthood was to be cleansed and purified (Zech. 3:1–9), as well as the whole land.

D. A governor of Jerusalem who had a gate named after him, the Gate of Joshua (2 Kgs. 23:8–9).

3092. יְהוֹשָׁפָט ***y^e^hôšāpāṭ:*** A proper noun designating Jehoshaphat:

A. A good king of Judah, son of Asa. His name means "the Lord has judged." He ruled twenty-five years (872–852 B.C.). He tried to keep Judah and Israel united as one people (1 Kgs. 22:4, 5). He kept peace (1 Kgs. 22:44) and followed the Lord in every way (1 Kgs. 22:41–43), consulting the true prophet of God for leadership (1 Kgs. 22:7; 2 Kgs. 3:11–25). He had the Law of God taught throughout Judah (2 Chr. 17:1–9). He removed religious male prostitutes from the land (1 Kgs. 4:6). He built ships for commerce, but they were all wrecked at Ezion Geber (1 Kgs. 22:48). His son Jehoram succeeded him. The Books of 1 and 2 Chronicles consider his reign a great success as well.

B. The father of Jehu who was king in Israel (2 Kgs. 9:2). His father was Nimshi.

C. He was the recorder or secretary under David and son of Ahilud (2 Sam. 8:16).

D. He was one of Solomon's twelve area governors. He was over Issachar and was son of Paruah (1 Kgs. 4:17).

E. A valley into which the Lord will bring all nations for judgment (Joel 3:2). The name means "the Lord judges." The Lord will judge them with respect to how they treated His people Israel. It appears to be a symbolic use of the term or name or refers also to this valley near Jerusalem.

3093. יָהִיר ***yāhiyr:*** An adjective describing what is proud, arrogant. It is used to define a person who is insolent, prideful, and narcissistically self-centered. He or she acts in pride (Prov. 21:24). The use of wine by this person betrays and puts on display his or her supercilious, haughty character (Hab. 2:5), the opposite of the character of a person of faith.

3094. יְהַלֶּלְאֵל ***y^e^hallel'ēl:*** A proper noun designating Jehallelel:

A. A Judaite (1 Chr. 4:16).

B. A Levite (2 Chr. 29:12).

3095. יַהֲלֹם ***yah^a^lōm,*** יָהֲלֹם ***yāh^a^lōm:*** A masculine noun referring to a precious stone; emerald, diamond. The identification of the various precious or semiprecious stones in the Old Testament is difficult. The KJV, NASB, NKJV render this word as diamond, while the NIV translates it as emerald (Ex. 28:18; 39:11; Ezek. 28:13). Bible lexicons take a similar position on the meaning of this word.

3096. יַהַץ ***yahaṣ,*** יַהְצָה ***yahṣāh:*** A proper noun designating Jahaz (Num.

21:23; Deut. 2:32; Josh. 13:18; 21:36; Judg. 11:20; 1 Chr. 6:78[63]; Isa. 15:4; Jer. 48:21, 34).

3097. יוֹאָב ***yô'āḇ:*** A proper noun designating Joab:

A. The name of David's nephew and the commander of his army. He was the son of Zeruiah, David's half-sister. His name means "Yahweh is father." With his brothers, Asahel and Abishai, he defeated Ish-Bosheth's attempt to be king (2 Sam. 8:8–17). David made him commander of all his forces (1 Chr. 11:6). He was a great commander but also took part in David's murder of Uriah the Hittite (2 Sam. 11:6–18). He showed no mercy or hesitation about executing a person he deemed dangerous to David or the kingdom (2 Sam. 3:6–39; 18:10–17). This aspect of his character caused David to replace him for a while by Amasa (2 Sam. 19:13) whom Joab slew and replaced before long (2 Sam. 20:4[3]). He differed with David on some things and at the end of his life was executed before the altar at Gibeon because he had not supported Solomon as king but rather Adonijah (1 Kgs. 1:1—2:3–5). According to Solomon, Joab had shed innocent blood by killing Abner and Amasa.

B. He was of the line of Judah. His father was Seraiah (1 Chr. 4:14).

C. An exile who returned with Zerubbabel. He had a large posterity who returned after him (Ezra 2:6).

3098. יוֹאָח ***yô'āḥ:*** A proper noun designating Joah:

A. Son of Asaph (2 Kgs. 18:18, 26, 37; Isa. 36:3, 11, 22).

B. A Levite (1 Chr. 6:21[6]).

C. A Levite (2 Chr. 29:12).

D. Son of Joahaz (2 Chr. 34:8).

E. Son of Obed-Edom (1 Chr. 26:4).

3099. יוֹאָחָז ***yô'āḥāz:*** A proper noun designating Jehoahaz, Joahaz:

A. A king of Judah who reigned three months (609 B.C.). His name means "the Lord has seized." The king of Egypt deposed him and installed Jehoiakim in his place. Pharaoh Neco exiled him to Egypt (2 Kgs. 23:31–34).

B. A king of Israel, son of Jehu. He reigned 814–798 B.C., seventeen years. He was an evil king who was stripped of his army and buffeted by Hazael, king of Aram, most of his reign (cf. 2 Kgs. 13:1–8).

C. The recorder or chronicler for King Josiah. His son helped repair the Temple under Jehoahaz (2 Chr. 34:8).

3100. יוֹאֵל ***yô'ēl:*** A proper noun designating Joel:

A. A prophet of probably the ninth century B.C., although the date of this prophet is not certain. Some locate him in the sixth century. His name means "the Lord is God." His message was a warning to Judah of the coming Day of the Lord in which all nations, including a rebellious Israel, would be judged severely. His description of a plague of locusts, literal or figurative, was a powerful way to depict this perilous situation of the coming of God's judgment upon Israel. The nations of judgment would be real, whether the locusts were metaphorical or not.

B. The elder son of Samuel who was a priest at Beersheba. Samuel's sons became corrupt and were part of the reason Israel asked for a king who could lead them in character and behavior, as well as serve as a military conqueror (1 Sam. 8:2).

C. A prince or leader from the tribe of Simeon (1 Chr. 4:35).

D. A leading descendant of the tribe of Reuben (1 Chr. 5:4).

E. One of the heads of the descendants of the tribe of Gad. He lived in Bashan (1 Chr. 5:12).

F. A priest who served in the music and worship of the Temple (1 Chr. 6:33).

G. A head or chief of the descendants of Issachar (1 Chr. 7:3).

H. Listed among David's mighty warriors (1 Chr. 11:38).

I. A chief or leader of the descendants of Manasseh (1 Chr. 27:20).

J. A descendant of the Levites through Gershom (1 Chr. 15:7).

K. A Levite through the Kohathites. His father was Azariah (1 Chr. 29:12).

L. A descendant of Nebo who intermarried with the people of the land (Ezra 10:43).

M. The son of Zichri who served as a chief officer among the Benjamites (Neh. 11:9). All were new residents of a resettled Jerusalem.

3101. יוֹאָשׁ ***yô'āš:*** A proper noun designating Joash:

A. A king of Judah who reigned (835–796 B.C.), forty years. He was a good king who repaired the Temple of the Lord. His mother was Zibiah. He reigned during the time of the high priest Jehoiada who served as a counselor to him (2 Kgs. 12:1–2). His reforms were not thorough (2 Kgs. 12:3), but he paid the workmen fair wages (2 Kgs. 12:14). Unfortunately, he was forced to pay tribute to Hazael, king of Aram (Syria).

B. A king of Israel (798–782 B.C.) who reigned sixteen years. His reign was evil, for he followed in the footsteps of Jeroboam I, son of Nebat. He continued in the corrupt and false worship of his father. He fought with Amaziah of Judah (2 Kgs. 13:12–13). He called upon and honored Elisha the prophet (2 Kgs. 13:14–19).

C. The father of Gideon, a famous judge in Israel. He bravely defended Gideon and the Lord before the people of the city (Judg. 6:30–32).

D. A son in the house of Ahab, one of Israel's most wicked kings. He was in charge of the prison (1 Kgs. 22:26, 27).

E. One of David's mighty warriors and a Benjamite, very skilled in bow and arrow and in the use of slings (1 Chr. 12:1–3).

F. A descendant of the tribe of Judah who in ancient times exercised some rulership in Moab and Lehem (1 Chr. 4:22).

3102. יוֹב ***yôḇ:*** A proper noun designating Job (Gen. 46:13).

3103. יוֹבָב ***yôḇāḇ:*** A proper noun designating Jobab:

A. Son of Joktan (Gen. 10:29; 1 Chr. 1:23).

B. King of Edom (Gen. 36:33, 34; 1 Chr. 1:44, 45).

C. King of Madon (Josh. 11:1).

D. Son of Shaharaim (1 Chr. 8:9).

E. A Benjamite (1 Chr. 8:18).

3104. יוֹבֵל ***yôḇēl:*** A common noun referring to a ram's horn, a trumpet, the jubilee. It is used in the phrase *qeren yôḇēl,* "horn of a ram" (Josh. 6:5) or in the phrase *šôp̱ᵉrôṯ hayyôḇᵉlîym* "shophars (rams' horns) of rams" which is rendered as "trumpets of rams' horns" (e.g., NASB, Josh. 6:4). Its most famous use is in the phrase "year of the ram's horn," which means the Year of Jubilee that was announced by blowing a ram's horn (Lev. 25:13). The word is used alone with the definite article or without it to mean simply the Jubilee (Lev. 25:10–12; 25:15). Its most spectacular use was at Sinai to inaugurate God's appearance and the giving of the Law (Ex. 19:13).

3105. יוּבַל ***yûḇal:*** A masculine noun referring to a stream, water; a canal. It indicates a source of water from which a tree can draw its sustenance and thrive (Jer. 17:8).

3106. יוּבָל ***yûḇāl:*** A proper noun designating Jubal (Gen. 4:21).

3107. יוֹזָבָד ***yôzāḇāḏ:*** A proper noun designating Jozabad:

A. Soldier in David's army (1 Chr. 12:4).

B. Manassite captain (1 Chr. 12:20).

C. Another Manassite captain (1 Chr. 12:20).

D. A Levite (2 Chr. 31:13).

E. A chief Levite (2 Chr. 35:9).

F. A priest (Ezra 10:22).

G. A priest (Ezra 10:23).

H. A Levite (Ezra 8:33).

I. A Levite (Neh. 8:7).

J. A Levite (Neh. 11:16).

3108. יוֹזָכָר ***yôzāḵār:*** A proper noun designating Jozachar (2 Kgs. 12:21[22]).

3109. יוֹחָא ***yôḥā':*** A proper noun designating Joha:

A. A Benjamite (1 Chr. 8:16).

B. One of David's mighty men (1 Chr. 11:45).

3110. יוֹחָנָן ***yôḥānān:*** A proper noun designating Johanan:

A. A priest who functioned during Ezra-Nehemiah's time. He was a son of the priest Eliashib (Neh. 12:22).

B. A Jewish officer, son of Kareah, who supported Gedaliah after the fall of Jerusalem (2 Kgs. 25:23). He tried to warn and protect the appointed governor to no avail (Jer. 40:13–16). He fled to Egypt.

C. The oldest son of Josiah and of the descendants of Judah (1 Chr. 3:15).

D. The son of Elioenai of the line of Judah (1 Chr. 3:24).

E. The son of Azariah of the line of Levi (1 Chr. 6:9).

F. One of several persons from the tribe of Gad who joined David when he was fleeing from Saul (1 Chr. 12:4).

G. A capable warrior from the Benjamites who defected to David when David was fleeing Saul (1 Chr. 12:12).

H. A family head or leader who returned from exile to Jerusalem under Ezra. He was a descendant of Azgad (Ezra 8:12).

3111. יוֹיָדָע ***yôyāḏā'*:** A proper noun designating Jehoiada:

A. A son of Paseah who helped repair the Jeshanah Gate under Nehemiah (Neh. 3:6).

B. A high priest, son of Eliashib and father of Jonathan, who returned from exile to Jerusalem. His son was driven out by Nehemiah for intermarrying with a foreigner (Neh. 12:11; 13:28).

3112. יוֹיָכִין ***yôyaḵiyn*:** A proper noun designating Jehoiachin. This is a variant spelling (orthography) of *y^e^hôyāḵiyn* [3078] found in Ezek. 1:2.

3113. יוֹיָקִים ***yôyāqiym*:** A proper noun designating Joiakim (Neh. 12:10, 12, 26).

3114. יוֹיָרִיב ***yôyāriyḇ*:** A proper noun designating Joiarib:

A. Name of a priestly family (Neh. 11:10; 12:6, 19).

B. Teacher of Ezra (Ezra 8:16).

C. A Judaite (Neh. 11:5).

3115. יוֹכֶבֶד ***yôḵeḇeḏ*:** A proper noun designating Jochebed, a name that means "the Lord is glory." It is the name of Moses' mother, as well as mother of Miriam and Aaron. She was from the line of Levi. Her husband was Amram (Heb., her nephew; LXX, her cousin) (Ex. 6:20; Num. 26:59).

3116. יוּכַל ***yôḵeḇeḏ*:** A proper noun designating Jucal (Jer. 38:1).

3117. יוֹם ***yôm*:** A masculine noun meaning day, time, year. This word stands as the most basic conception of time in the Old Testament. It designates such wide-ranging elements as the daylight hours from sunrise to sunset (Gen. 1:5; 1 Kgs. 19:4); a literal twenty-four hour cycle (Deut. 16:8; 2 Kgs. 25:30); a generic span of time (Gen. 26:8; Num. 20:15); a given point in time (Gen. 2:17; 47:29; Ezek. 33:12). In the plural, the word may also mean the span of life (Ps. 102:3 [4]) or a year (Lev. 25:29; 1 Sam 27:7). The prophets often infuse the word with end–times meanings or connotations, using it in connection with a future period of consequential events, such as the "day of the LORD" (Jer. 46:10; Zech. 14:1) or simply, "that day" (Isa. 19:23; Zech. 14:20, 21).

3118. יוֹם ***yôm*:** A masculine Aramaic noun meaning day. The word corresponds to the Hebrew noun of the same spelling and meaning. It refers to a twenty-four hour period (in which Daniel prays three times) (Dan. 6:10[11], 13[14]). In the plural, it describes a time period marked by a particular state of affairs as, for example, the days of Nebuchadnezzar's madness (Dan. 4:34[31]) or the days of Belshazzar's father (Dan. 5:11). The number of days may be specified; in the book of Daniel, only King Darius could legally be worshiped for thirty days (Dan. 6:7[8], 12[13]). The word is used to refer to God as the Ancient of Days, emphasizing in human terms God's eternal existence (Dan. 7:9, 13, 22).

3119. יוֹמָם ***yômām:*** An adverb meaning in daytime, by day. It is used to mean during the day, such as the cloud of the Lord that led the Israelites by day in the wilderness (Num. 10:34; Neh. 9:19). It is often also used in parallel to something occurring by night, such as the sun by day and the moon by night (Jer. 31:35). It comes from the Hebrew word *yôm* (3117).

3120. יָוָן ***yāwān:*** A proper noun designating Javan:

A. Son of Japheth (Gen. 10:2, 4; 1 Chr. 1:5, 7).

B. The descendants of Javan or their territory (Isa. 66:19; Ezek. 27:13, 19; Dan. 8:21; 10:20; 11:2; Zech. 9:13).

3121. יָוֵן ***yāwēn:*** A masculine noun indicating something is mire, miry, mud. It describes mud or mire that is both slippery and sticky, tending to endanger anyone's life who is bogged down in it (Ps. 40:2[3]; 69:2 [3]). It is found twice and is used metaphorically each time: it represents the dangerous conditions of life the psalmist had become caught in or the clutches of his enemies and circumstances that overwhelmed him.

3122. יוֹנָדָב ***yônāḏāḇ:*** A proper noun designating Jonadab.

A. The son of Rechab and the father of the Rechabnites who were not to drink wine, build houses, raise grain or plant vineyards. Instead Jonadab commanded them to live in tents (Jer. 35:6–10).

B. David's nephew, the son of Shimeah, David's brother. He was cunning and helped arrange for Amnon to be alone with Tamar (2 Sam. 13:3–5).

3123. יוֹנָה ***yônāh:*** A feminine noun denoting a pigeon or dove. It was the bird used by Noah to test the conditions after the flood waters began to abate (Gen. 8:8–12). Its cooing sounds were compared to the moaning of a sick, suffering person (Isa. 38:14; 59:11; Ezek. 7:16). Its wings would glisten as gold or appear as gilded with silver, a symbol of a woman dwelling at home in safety (Ps. 68:13[14]). It was used as an endearing expression about one's beloved (Song 2:14; 4:1; 5:2, 12). It is used in many more figurative expressions: of Ephraim like a silly dove (Hos. 7:11); of the exiles eagerly returning as doves (Hos. 11:11); of ships with white sails (Isa. 60:8) and many more. Dove's dung was a last resort as food in a time of famine (2 Kgs. 6:25). A young dove or pigeon could be offered to the Lord (Lev. 1:14; 5:7, 11; 12:6, 8; Num. 6:10). The psalmist wished he had wings as a dove by which to escape his troubles (Ps. 55:6[7]).

3124. יוֹנָה ***yônāh:*** A proper noun designating Jonah, a prophet called to preach repentance to Nineveh. He came from Gath Hepher. His name means "dove." His father's name was Amittai. Jonah foretold the expansion of Israel under Jeroboam II (2 Kgs. 14:25). He was called by God to go to Nineveh and preach repentance to the capital of Assyria. Amazingly, it was his understanding and grasp of God's compassion and mercy toward the wicked that caused him to refuse, initially, to fulfill God's call (Jon. 4:1–2).

3125. יְוָנִי ***y^ewāniy:*** This proper noun is a reference to the Greeks, Grecians. It is used only in Joel 3:6(4:6).

3126. יֹנֵק ***yōnēq,*** יוֹנֵק ***yônēq:*** A masculine noun indicating a tender shoot of a plant; an infant, a suckling child. It is used of the Suffering Servant of the Lord (Isa. 53:2), depicting Him as a fragile young plant. It is used of a nursing infant (1 Sam. 15:3; Song 8:1) and of nursing infants who suckle the breasts (Num. 11:12; Joel 2:16). When God brings judgment, even nursing infants are included (Deut. 32:25; Jer. 44:7).

3127. יוֹנֶקֶת ***yôneqeṯ:*** A feminine noun meaning a young shoot of a plant. It is used of tender twigs from the top of a tree (Ezek. 17:22), so it indicates the fresh young growth on a tree limb or other shrubbery. It is used of the Israelites sprouting as God brings forth His renewed people (Hos. 14:6[7]). It indicates the fresh young sprouts of a garden (Job 8:16) and the green sprouts coming from the stump of a tree (Job 14:7). The growth and spread of the people of Israel in Canaan is described as shoots stretching toward water as they multiplied in the land (Ps. 80:11[12]).

3128. יוֹנַת אֵלֶם רְחֹקִים ***yônaṯ 'ēlem r^eḥōqiym:*** A proper noun, Jonath elem rehokim. The phrase occurs in the title of Psalm 56 and is transliterated into English by some translators as Jonath elem rehokim (NASB, KJV), while others translate the words (Ps. 56:title[1]): "The Silent Dove in Distant Lands" and note that this is a tune to which the psalm is set (NKJV); "A Dove on Distant Oaks" (NIV).

3129. יוֹנָתָן ***yônāṯān:*** A proper noun designating Jonathan:

A. The oldest son of Saul and became the close friend of David. His name means "the Lord has given." He deferred to David as the Lord's anointed even though he himself was next in line for the kingship when his father died. He was a successful commander and warrior against the Philistines. He made a covenant with David to be loyal to him (See 3083,A.).

B. A son of Abiathar, one of David's priests. However, Abiathar backed Adonijah, not Solomon for king against David's wishes (1 Kgs. 1:7).

C. One of David's mighty warriors, a son of Shagee who was a Hararite (1 Chr. 11:34).

D. He took part in the musical aspect of worship at the second Temple (Neh. 12:35).

E. He supported Gedaliah, the governor in Judah after Jerusalem fell. He had a brother, Johanan, and his father was Kareah (Jer. 40:8).

F. A Judahite who was son of Judah, Shammai's brother. He had sons as well (1 Chr. 2:32).

G. A descendant of Adin. His son was Ebed. They were from the family heads who returned under Ezra (Ezra 8:6).

H. He was the son of Asahel and one of the few who did not support Ezra's reforms entirely (Ezra 10:15).

I. A priest who was head of the priestly family of Malluch (Neh. 12:14).

J. A son of Jehoida who was son of Eliashib, a high priest (Neh. 12:11).

3130. יוֹסֵף ***yôsēp̱:*** A proper noun designating Joseph:

A. Jacob's eleventh son, as well as his favorite son. He was also the first son Rachel bore. His brother was Benjamin, the twelfth patriarch. The story of Joseph is a marvelous narrative of God's calling and leading in his life from the time he was young until the day he died (Gen. 34—50). God spoke to Joseph in dreams and revealed his future (Gen. 37) but also revealed, as he was dying, that his bones would be carried up from Egypt and buried in Canaan (Ex. 13:19; Josh. 24:32). The Lord used Joseph to provide for his father and family and endeared him to the Egyptians, even the Pharaoh, so that he became a powerful Egyptian vizier, second only to the Pharaoh (Gen. 41:41–45). The Lord carefully watched over his personal life and safety (Gen. 50:19–21). He demonstrated a magnanimous spirit of mercy and forgiveness toward his enemies, even his brothers. He bore two sons in Egypt who became patriarchs in Israel and provided two of the largest tribes of the nation, Ephraim and Manassah (Gen. 41:51–52). Through him the Lord fulfilled His promises and covenant to Abraham (Gen. 15:4–17). He may have been in Egypt sometime during the 1750–1550 B.C. era. Moses blessed him (Deut. 33:13, 16) as did Jacob (Gen. 49:22–26).

B. A name used in this instance for the nation of Judah since his fruitfulness of descendants includes the entire nation in a figurative sense (Ps. 80:1[2]).

C. The descendants of Joseph are referred to figuratively under the name of Joseph who represents all of his posterity (Deut. 33:13–16).

D. Joseph is used to represent all of Israel or at least northern Israel

(Ps. 77:15[16]; 78:67; Ezek. 37:16, 19; 47:13; 48:32; Amos 5:15; 6:6; Obad. 1:18). Sometimes the northern tribes are called Ephraim in honor of Joseph's son

E. A postexilic Jew who had married a foreign woman in Ezra's time (Ezra 10:42).

F. A man from Issachar with this name Joseph. He had a son Igal who was one of the twelve spies sent to Canaan (Num. 13:7).

G. A son of Asaph who was a part of the musical worship at the Temple (1 Chr. 25:2).

H. A priest who was head of the Levite family of Shecaniah (Neh. 12:14).

3131. יוֹסִפְיָה ***yôsipyāh:*** A proper noun designating Josiphiah (Ezra 8:10).

3132. יוֹעֵאלָה ***yô'ē'lāh:*** A proper noun designating Joelah (1 Chr. 12:7).

3133. יוֹעֵד ***yô'ēḏ:*** A proper noun designating Joed (Neh. 11:7).

3134. יוֹעֶזֶר ***yô'ezer:*** A proper noun designating Joezer (1 Chr. 12:6).

3135. יוֹעָשׁ ***yô'āš:*** A proper noun designating Joash:

A. Son of Becher (1 Chr. 7:8).

B. Officer under David (1 Chr. 27:28).

3136. יוֹצָדָק ***yôṣāḏāq:*** I. Jozadak, a priest (Ezra 3:2, 8; 10:18; Neh. 12:26).

II. Aramaic proper noun for Jozadak (Ezra 5:2), the same priest as in I above.

3137. יוֹקִים ***yôqiym:*** A proper noun designating Jokim (1 Chr. 4:22).

3138. יוֹרֶה ***yôreh:*** A masculine noun denoting early rain. It indicates the early rain in Palestine that fell from the end of October to the beginning of December. A regular period of early rain was considered a blessing from God (Deut. 11:14), for He was the one who gave it (Jer. 5:24). It is used in a simile to indicate the refreshing arrival of the Lord's presence (Hos. 6:3).

3139. יוֹרָה ***yôrāh:*** A proper noun designating Jorah (Ezra 2:18).

3140. יוֹרַי ***yôray:*** A proper noun designating Jorai (1 Chr. 5:13).

3141. יֹרָם ***yôrām:*** A proper noun designating Joram:

A. A king of Judah, son of the righteous king Jehoshaphat. See comments to 3088.

B. A king of Israel, son of the wicked king Ahab. See comments to 3088,B.

C. A son of Tou who was king of Hamath and sought to make friends with David (2 Sam. 8:9, 10).

D. A Levite who helped Shubael take care of the various treasuries or storehouses of the Temple (1 Chr. 26:24, 25).

3142. יוּשַׁב חֶסֶד ***yûšab ḥesed:*** A proper noun designating Jushab-Hesed (1 Chr. 3:20).

3143. יוֹשִׁבְיָה ***yôšibyāh:*** A proper noun designating Joshibiah (1 Chr. 4:35).

3144. יוֹשָׁה ***yôšāh:*** A proper noun designating Joshah (1 Chr. 4:34).

3145. יוֹשַׁוְיָה ***yôšawyāh:*** A proper noun designating Joshaviah (1 Chr. 11:46).

3146. יוֹשָׁפָט ***yôšāpāṭ:*** A proper noun designating Joshaphat:

A. One of David's mighty men (1 Chr. 11:43).

B. A priest (1 Chr. 15:24).

3147. יוֹתָם ***yôtām:*** A proper noun designating Jotham:

A. A king of Judah, son of Azariah (Uzziah). He reigned 750–732 B.C., reigning with this father, who had leprosy, for ten years (2 Kgs. 15:5–7). His mother was Jerusha, Zadok's daughter (2 Kgs. 15:32–38). He was a good king and followed the Lord, except that the high places were not removed. He also helped restore the Temple. His son Ahaz reigned after he died. Isaiah, Hosea, and Micah prophesied during his reign.

B. The youngest son of Gideon who escaped Abimelech's massacre of the seventy sons of Gideon. In a lengthy allegory, he urged the cities of Shechem and Beth Millo to rebel against Abimelich (Judg. 9:16–21), even placing a curse on them.

C. A descendant of Caleb and the son of Jahdai. He was a Judahite (1 Chr. 2:47).

3148. יוֹתֵר ***yôtēr,*** יֹתֵר ***yōtēr:*** A masculine noun indicating profit, gain; advantage. It is combined with the proposition *min* (4480) after it to express more than . . . (Esth. 6:6). The *min* can be separated from *yôtēr* (Eccl. 6:8). It can take on the meaning of an adverb meaning extremely, excessively, or so very (Eccl. 2:15; 7:16). It can have the meaning of benefit, gain, or advantage (Eccl. 6:11; 7:11). It has the sense in context sometimes of further, in addition (Eccl. 12:9), or of in addition to this, to what has just been said (Eccl. 12:12).

3149. יְזוּאֵל ***yezû'ēl:*** A proper noun designating Jeziel (1 Chr. 12:3).

3150. יִזִּיָּה ***yizziyyāh:*** A proper noun designating Izziah (Ezra 10:25).

3151. יָזִיז ***yāziyz:*** A masculine proper noun, Jaziz. It refers to a Hagrite that David put over his personal flocks (1 Chr. 27:31).

3152. יִזְלִיאָה ***yizliy'āh:*** A proper noun designating Jaziz (1 Chr. 27:31).

3153. יְזַנְיָהוּ ***yezanyāhû,*** יְזַנְיָה ***yezanyāh:*** A proper noun designating Izliah (1 Chr. 8:18).

3154. יֶזַע ***yeza':*** A masculine noun referring to sweat, perspiration. It refers to the sweat secreted by certain glands of the skin because of clothing or overheating from work (Ezek. 44:18).

3155. יִזְרָח ***yizrāḥ:*** A proper noun designating Izrahite, a descendant of Zerah. (1 Chr. 27:8).

3156. יִזְרַחְיָה ***yizraḥyāh:*** A proper noun designating Izrahiah:

A. A musical leader (Neh. 12:42).

B. Grandson of Tola (1 Chr. 7:3).

3157. יִזְרְעֶאל ***yizr^e'e'l:*** A proper noun designating Jezreel:

A. A town in Judah from which David's wife Ahinoam came. It was possibly located just south of Hebron to the west of the Dead Sea (1 Sam. 25:43).

B. A city of Issachar (Josh. 19:18). Saul used the city as did his son Ish-Bosheth later who was in charge of it (2 Sam. 2:9). One of Ahab's palaces was there (1 Kgs. 18:45). Naboth's vineyard, violently seized by Ahab, was in Jezreel and there Ahab's son, Joram, and Jezebel were executed by Jehu (2 Kgs. 8:29—10:11).

C. The name of a fertile valley in northern Israel (Hos. 2:22[24]). Its name means "God sows." Many peoples battled for control of it (Josh. 17:16; Judg. 6:33). Hosea mentioned it as a place where God will judge Israel.

D. The son of Etam, a clan head in Judah (1 Chr. 12:3).

E. A son of Hosea, so named as a symbol of the massacre and bloodshed that occurred there related to Jehu's house (Hos. 1:4).

F. Another name for Israel (see E also). The valley stands for all of Israel in the prophet's usage (Hos. 1:5).

3158. יִזְרְעֵאלִי ***yizr^e'ē'liy:*** A proper noun designating Jezreelite (1 Kgs. 21:1, 4, 6, 7, 15, 16; 2 Kgs. 9:21, 25).

3159. יִזְרְעֵאלִית ***yizr^e'ē'liyt,*** יִזְרְעֵאלת ***yizr^e'ē'liṯ:*** A proper noun designating Jezreelitess (1 Sam. 27:3; 30:5; 2 Sam. 2:2; 3:2; 1 Chr. 3:1).

3160. יְחֻבָּה ***y^{e}ḥubbāh:*** A proper noun designating Jehubbah (1 Chr. 7:34).

3161. יָחַד ***yāḥaḏ:*** A verb meaning to join, to be united. It refers to entering into the plan or thinking of a group, uniting with them (Gen. 49:6), letting one's honor be united to their cause. Job asks that the night of his birth not be joined or united to the days of the year (Job 3:6). It is used figuratively of the psalmist's desire for the Lord to unite his heart to walk in God's ways and to fear him (Ps. 86:11). It refers to persons going to the grave or Sheol upon death to "unite" with those they have known (Isa. 14:20).

3162. יַחַד ***yaḥaḏ,*** יַחְדָו ***yaḥdāw,*** יַחְדָיו ***yaḥdāyw:*** I. A masculine noun denoting unitedness, community, association. It indicates persons being put into proximity with each other. When *yaḥaḏ* is placed last, it has the meaning of together (1 Sam. 11:11);

all together (Isa. 27:4); completely. It is used of encountering an enemy and fighting against each other, together (1 Sam. 17:10). It is used with verbs of gathering, as when the Arameans gathered themselves together for battle (2 Sam. 10:15). It is used of time, as when things are done at the same time, together (Isa. 42:14). It has an inclusive sense of gathering up many things at once, leaving none out (Ps. 33:15).

II. An adverb meaning to do things all at once, together. It is used of action performed or plans and counsels made by a group together. Persons may exalt God's name together (Isa. 52:9) or gather together for counsel (Neh. 6:7; Ps. 71:10; 83:5[6]); persons may be forced to do something together, at the same time, e.g., go into exile (Amos 1:15). It is used figuratively of persons agreeing enough to be in harmony (Amos 3:3). It is used to emphasize doing something at the same time as well as together (Ex. 19:8). It may indicate something is like something else, for it is said that both the clean and the unclean "together" may eat it (Deut. 12:22; 15:22; 1 Sam. 30:24). In other words, they may share in it alike, "together."

3163. יַחְדּוֹ ***yaḥdô:*** A proper noun designating Jahdo (1 Chr. 5:14).

3164. יַחְדִּיאֵל ***yaḥdiy'ēl:*** A proper noun designating Jadiel (1 Chr. 5:24).

3165. יֶחְדְּיָהוּ ***yehdᵉyāhû:*** A proper noun designating Jehdeiah:

A. A Levite (1 Chr. 24:20).

B. A royal officer (1 Chr. 27:30).

3166. יַחֲזִיאֵל ***yaḥᵃziy'ēl:*** A proper noun designating Jahaziel:

A. A Benjamite (1 Chr. 12:4).

B. A priest (1 Chr. 16:6).

C. A Levite (1 Chr. 23:19; 24:23).

D. A Levite (2 Chr. 20:14).

E. Father of Shechaniah (Ezra 8:5).

3167. יַחְזְיָה ***yaḥzᵉyāh:*** A proper noun designating Jahzeiah (Ezra 10:15).

3168. יְחֶזְקֵאל ***yᵉḥezqē'l:*** A proper noun designating Ezekiel:

A. The exilic prophet Ezekiel. His name means "God strengthens." He was a priest and the son of Buzi (Ezek. 1:3). He was exiled in Babylon in ca. 597 B.C. He was thirty years old when God called him to prophesy (ca. 593 B.C.). He himself became a sign to the people (Ezek. 24:24). He had a vision of the corruption of God's people and the Temple (Ezek. 8) and predicted the fall of Jerusalem to Babylon. He also envisioned the final defeat of Israel's enemies (Ezek. 37—39) and the establishment of a New Jerusalem and new Temple where God would dwell permanently (Ezek. 48:35).

B. He was a head of a priestly line (1 Chr. 24:16).

3169. יְחִזְקִיָּה **y^e^ḥizqiyyāh,** יְחִזְקִיָּהוּ **y^e^ḥizqiyyāhû:** A proper noun designating Hezekiah:

A. A great king of Judah. His name means "the Lord is my strength." See comments to 2396.

B. A Jew who returned under Zerubbabel (Ezra 2:16).

C. A Jew, an Ephraimite, who disapproved of Israelites taking Judeans as prisoners of war (2 Chr. 28:12).

3170. יַחְזֵרָה **yaḥzērāh:** A proper noun designating Jahzerah (1 Chr. 9:12).

3171. יְחִיאֵל **y^e^ḥiy'ēl,** יְחוּאֵל **y^e^ḥô'ēl:** A proper noun designating Jehiel:

A. A Levite (1 Chr. 15:18, 20; 16:5).

B. A Gershonite (1 Chr. 23:8; 29:8).

C. A Jew (1 Chr. 27:32).

D. Son of Jehoshaphat (2 Chr. 21:2).

E. Son of Heman (2 Chr. 29:14).

F. A Levite (2 Chr. 31:13).

G. A ruler in the Temple (2 Chr. 35:8).

H. Father of Obadiah (Ezra 8:9).

I Father of Shechaniah (Ezra 10:2).

J. A priest (Ezra 10:21).

K. A Jew (Ezra 10:26).

3172. יְחִיאֵלִי **y^e^ḥiy'ēliy:** A proper noun designating Jehieli (1 Chr. 26:21, 22).

3173. יָחִיד **yāḥiyḏ:** An adjective meaning sole, only, solitary. This word is frequently used to refer to an only child. Isaac was Abraham's only son by Sarah (Gen. 22:2, 12, 16). Jepthah's daughter was his only child, who came running out to greet him after his vow to sacrifice the first thing to come out of his door (Judg. 11:34). The father of an only child began teaching him wisdom when he was very young (Prov. 4:3). Mourning an only child was considered an especially grievous sorrow (Jer. 6:26; Amos 8:10; Zech. 12:10). The feminine form is used parallel to life or soul, portraying the precious, only life we are given (Ps. 22:20[21]; 35:17). It is also used to mean lonely or alone (Ps. 25:16; 68:6[7]). See the related Hebrew root *yāḥaḏ* (3161).

3174. יְחִיָּה **y^e^ḥiyyāh:** A proper noun designating Jehiah (1 Chr. 15:24).

3175. יָחִיל **yāḥiyl:** This word occurs only in Lamentations 3:26, and its exact meaning is difficult to determine. It could be derived from *yāḥal* (3176) and be an adjective meaning hopeful. Or it could also be a verb derived from *ḥûl* (2342) and thus refer to waiting (cf. Ps. 37:7). In this case, the word might imply painful waiting as in childbirth, which would harmonize with the next verse. Whether hopefully or in pain (or both), the verse says it is good to wait in silence for the salvation of the Lord.

3176. יָחַל **yāḥal:** A verb meaning to wait, to hope, to tarry. It is used of

Noah (Gen. 8:12); Saul (1 Sam. 10:8; 13:8); Joab (2 Sam. 18:14); the king of Aram (2 Kgs. 6:33); Job (Job 6:11; 13:15; 14:14); Elihu (Job 32:11, 16). In the Psalms, it frequently means to wait with hope (Ps. 31:24[25]; 33:18, 22; 38:15[16]); 42:5[6], 11[12]). This meaning also occurs in Isaiah (Isa. 42:4; 51:5); Lamentations (Lam. 3:21, 24); Ezekiel (Ezek. 19:5); and Micah (Mic. 7:7).

3177. יַחְלְאֵל ***yaḥlᵉʼēl:*** A proper noun designating Jahleel (Gen. 46:14; Num. 26:26).

3178. יַחְלְאֵלִי ***yaḥlᵉʼēliy:*** A proper noun designating Jahleelites (Num. 26:26).

3179. יָחַם ***yāḥam:*** A verb meaning to be hot, to conceive. It indicates that an animal is in heat, in rut (Gen. 30:38, 39, 41; 31:10). It describes the act of conception in sexual intimacy (Ps. 51:5[7]). It refers to keeping one's body warm (1 Kgs. 1:1; Eccl. 4:11) or to heating something (Ezek. 24:11).

3180. יַחְמוּר ***yaḥmûr:*** A masculine noun referring to a roe, a deer, a member of a small species of deer, a roebuck. It refers to a roebuck (Deut. 14:5), an animal declared clean and edible for the Israelites by God. It was a choice sacrificial animal (1 Kgs. 4:23[5:3]).

3181. יַחְמַי ***yaḥmay:*** A proper noun designating Jahmai (1 Chr. 7:2).

3182. יָחֵף ***yāḥēp̄:*** An adjective describing something or someone as barefoot. It indicates the absence of shoes or footwear (2 Sam. 15:30; Jer. 2:25). In David's case, it also implied mourning and depression, as well as in the case of Isaiah whose nakedness and bare feet were a sign of the destruction about to come on Jerusalem (Isa. 20:2–4). It signifies licentiousness in Jeremiah's usage (Jer. 2:25).

3183. יַחְצְאֵל ***yaḥṣᵉʼēl:*** A proper noun designating Jahzeel (Gen. 46:24; Num. 26:48).

3184. יַחְצְאֵלִי ***yaḥṣᵉʼēliy:*** A proper noun designating Jahzeelite (Num. 26:48).

3185. יַחְצִיאֵל ***yaḥṣiyʼēl:*** A proper noun designating Jahziel (1 Chr. 7:13).

3186. יָחַר ***yāḥar:*** A verb indicating to delay, to tarry. It means to act too late based on a previous plan of action, to be tardy (2 Sam. 20:5).

3187. יָחַשׂ ***yāḥaś:*** A verb indicating the keeping of a genealogical record; to be in a genealogical record. This was especially important in Israel because the Israelites considered themselves to be God's holy people. Certain positions could be held only by proving one's ancestry. It indicates the inclusion of a person in a genealogy by establishing his or her descent (Ezra 2:62). It can be rendered "to have a genealogy" (1 Chr. 4:33, NASB;

cf. KJV, These were . . . "their genealogies") or to be enrolled in a genealogy (1 Chr. 5:1, 17; 2 Chr. 12:15; Neh. 7:5). It indicates the place where enrollment took place (Neh. 7:64).

3188. יַחַשׂ ***yaḥaś:*** A masculine noun denoting a genealogy; a genealogical record or register. It is the official listing of those included in a particular line of descent. Israel kept these records meticulously (Neh. 7:5).

3189. יַחַת ***yaḥaṯ:*** A proper noun designating Jahath:

A. Grandson of Judah (1 Chr. 4:2).

B. A Levite (1 Chr. 6:20[5]; 43[28]).

C. A Levite (1 Chr. 23:10, 11).

D. A Levite (1 Chr. 24:22).

E. A Levite (2 Chr. 34:12).

3190. יָטַב ***yāṭaḇ:*** A verb meaning to be good, to be well, to be pleasing. In the causative stem, it means to do good, to do well, to please, to make pleasing. It is often used in idiomatic expressions with heart (*lēḇ*[3820]), meaning to be pleased or to be happy (Judg. 18:20; 19:6, 9; Ruth 3:7); and with eyes, to be pleasing to someone else (i.e., pleasing or good in their eyes [Gen. 34:18; 1 Sam. 18:5]). The term does not necessarily carry a moral weight but can be translated adverbially as "well." For instance, see Micah 7:3 where their hands do evil well (cf. 1 Sam. 16:17; Prov. 30:29; Isa. 23:16). The word can also imply morality (Ps. 36:3[4]; 119:68).

3191. יְטַב ***yeṭaḇ:*** An Aramaic verb meaning to be good, to seem good. It refers to what appears or is taken to be acceptable, good, helpful from various persons' perspectives (Ezra 7:18).

3192. יָטְבָה ***yoṭḇāh:*** A proper noun designating Jotbah (2 Kgs. 21:19).

3193. יָטְבָתָה ***yoṭḇāṭāh:*** A proper noun designating Jotbathah (Num. 33:33, 34; Deut. 10:7).

3194. יוּטָּה ***yûṭṭāh,*** יֻטָּה ***yuṭṭāh:*** A proper noun designating Juttah (Josh. 15:55; 21:16).

3195. יְטוּר ***yeṭûr:*** A proper noun designating Jetur (Gen. 25:15; 1 Chr. 1:31; 5:19).

3196. יַיִן ***yayin:*** A masculine noun referring to wine. It indicates the juice of the grapevine and its fruits, a common drink for refreshment in the Old Testament (Gen. 14:18; 27:25; Judg. 19:19). It, along with grain and oil, were three great blessings to Israel in the Promised Land. It was used as a tonic (Prov. 31:6); a valuable commercial item (Neh. 13:15; Ezek. 27:18). Used properly, it made people's hearts glad (2 Sam. 13:28; Zech. 9:15) and was used figuratively to describe the fertility of the land of Israel (Isa. 40:12). In moderation, it was used in the worship of the Lord (Deut. 14:26). It was forbidden to Nazarites (Num. 6:3). Wise persons, especially kings, had no need of it for it might distort their powers of judgment (Prov. 31:4). It could intoxicate a person (Gen. 9:21, 24; 1 Sam. 1:14; Prov. 21:17). The Rechabites abstained from it (Jer. 35:2, 5). God did not approve of heavy drinkers (Prov. 23:20). Priests were not to use it while serving at the sanctuary (Lev. 10:9), but it was employed as a drink offering (Ex. 29:40; Lev. 23:13; Num. 15:5, 7, 10). In the Old Testament, different qualities of wine are noted: good wine (Song 7:9[10]); royal wine (Esth. 1:7); spiced wine (Song 8:2). Wine is used in the figurative language of metaphors: wisdom's drink (Prov. 9:2, 5); the wine of the Lord's wrath (Jer. 25:15); the wine that creates confusion, wandering (Ps. 60:3[5]). Babylon is likened to a cup of wine, causing the nations to go mad (Jer. 51:7). True love is said to surpass the intoxication of wine (Song 1:2; 4:10).

3197. יַךְ ***yak̲:*** A masculine noun meaning wayside. It is placed in front of the word *derek̲*, road, way, indicating where Eli the priest was sitting. It means side (of the road) or a more specific location along the road. Some prefer to read *yad̲* here, and they translate it as along the side of (the road) (1 Sam. 4:13).

3198. יָכַח ***yāk̲aḥ:*** A verb meaning to argue, to convince, to convict, to judge, to reprove. The word usually refers to the clarification of people's moral standing, which may involve arguments being made for them (Job 13:15; Isa. 11:4) or against them (Job 19:5; Ps. 50:21). The word may refer to the judgment of a case between people (Gen. 31:37, 42) or even (in the days before Christ) to someone desired to mediate between God and humankind (Job 9:33). The word may also refer to physical circumstances being used to reprove sin (2 Sam 7:14; Hab. 1:12). Reproving sin, whether done by God (Prov. 3:12) or persons (Lev. 19:17), was pictured as a demonstration of love, but some people were too rebellious or scornful to be reproved (Prov. 9:7; 15:12; Ezek. 3:26). In Genesis 24:14, 44, the word referred to God's appointment (or judgment) of Rebekah as the one to be married to Isaac.

3199. יָכִין ***yāk̲iyn:*** A proper noun designating Jakin:

A. The fourth son of Simeon. He fled to Egypt (Gen. 46:10; Ex. 6:15; Num. 26:12).

B. The name of the southern pillar that Solomon erected in the portico of the Temple facing east (1 Kgs. 7:21; 2 Chr. 3:17).

C. A descendant of the priests who lived in Jerusalem and had resettled in Jerusalem (1 Chr. 9:10; 24:17).

D. A priest living after the exile (538 B.C.) to whom the twenty-first lot fell. He was from Ithamar's descendants (Neh. 11:10).

3200. יָכִינִי ***yāk̲iyniy:*** A proper noun designating Jachinite (Num. 26:12).

3201. יָכֹל ***yāk̲ōl:*** A verb meaning to be able, to prevail. It indicates to be able to endure something, to be capable, to have the ability or power to do something: of God's ability (Num. 14:16; 2 Chr. 32:13, 15; Jer. 44:22) or a person's ability (Gen. 13:16); it is used of God not being able to stand Israel's false worship any longer (Isa. 1:13); not being able to endure a prideful, arrogant person (Ps. 101:5). It takes on the meaning of being incapable of maintaining an attitude or state of condition (Hos. 8:5); or indicates the ability to cause something to happen, as when Balak hoped he would be able to defeat Israel and drive them out of the land (Num. 22:6, 11). It indicates the ability to render or not to render (if negated) judgment about an issue (Gen. 24:50). It may take on the inference of daring to do something, e.g., eating in a restricted area, which, when negated, means people dare not or are not allowed to eat (Deut. 12:17). It indicates being an overcomer, a victor, to prevail over something or someone (Gen. 30:8); Rachel prevailed (*yāk̲al*) over her sister. (See also Ps. 13:4[5]; Isa. 16:12). In an intellectual discussion, it means to grasp or understand something (Job 31:23; Ps. 139:6), to attain a mastery of it.

3202. יְכִל ***yᵉk̲il:*** An Aramaic verb meaning to be able, to prevail. It means to be able and is usually followed by an infinitive to complete its meaning. It is used with God as the subject who is able to shut the lions' mouths and deliver Daniel (6:20[21]), as well as his three Hebrew companions in the furnace (Dan. 3:17); it is used of wise men who, in context negated, are not able to interpret a dream (Dan. 2:10), i.e., they do not have the needed skills and wisdom to do so (Dan. 2:27). God was able to deliver in an unparalleled way (Dan. 3:29; 4:37[34]). Daniel was able to reveal dreams and mysteries because of God's help (Dan. 2:47; 4:18[15]; 5:16). The little horn was able to overcome, overpower the saints of the Most High (Dan. 7:21).

3203. יְכָלְיָה ***yᵉk̲olyāh,*** יְכָלְיָהוּ ***yᵉk̲olyāhû:*** A proper noun designating Jecoliah (1 Kgs. 15:2; 2 Chr. 26:3).

3204. יְכוֹנְיָה ***yᵉk̲ônyāh,*** יְכָנְיָה ***yᵉk̲onyāh,*** יְכָנְיָהוּ ***yᵉk̲onyāhû:*** A proper noun designating Jeconiah (1 Chr. 3:16, 17; Esth. 2:6; Jer. 24:1; 27:20; 28:4; 29:2). This is another name for *yᵉhôyāk̲iyn* (3078); see also *konyāhû* (3659).

3205. יָלַד ***yālad̲,*** לֵדָה ***lēd̲āh:*** I. A verb meaning to give birth, to beget, to deliver. It is commonly used of women bearing children (Gen. 3:16) as well as animals who brought forth young (Gen. 30:39). In the case of birds, it may refer to the laying or production of eggs (Jer. 17:11). In a more general sense, it is used of men becoming the father of children (Gen. 4:18). It is used in figurative expressions: evil people bring forth iniquity (Job 15:35); Moses is said to beget, bear, conceive the people of Israel (Num. 11:12); God begets Israel

(Deut. 32:18); a day brings forth many things (Prov. 27:1). In a passive use of the verb, it may refer to one's birthday, literally, "the day of her birth" (Hos. 2:5).

In certain forms of the verb, it means to help bring to birth, to serve as midwife (Ex. 1:16). In other forms of the verb, it takes on a causal sense, such as causing someone to give birth, as God causes His people to come to birth (Isa. 66:9). The wicked in Israel are said to conceive, to bring forth iniquity (Isa. 59:4). In Numbers 1:18, it takes on the meaning of having one's name put into a genealogical record.

II. A feminine noun referring to childbirth, delivery. It indicates the time of or the process of childbirth (2 Kgs. 19:3); it is used of the failure of Israel to be fruitful when her time had come (Isa. 37:3). Hosea stresses Israel's failure to become that nation God was looking for on the day of her birth (Hos. 9:11). The pangs of childbirth are employed in a simile to orchestrate the pain of Israel's being thrust into exile (Jer. 13:21).

3206. יֶלֶד ***yeleḏ:*** A masculine noun referring to a child, a young man. It is commonly used to refer to a male child (Gen. 4:23) or a child (Gen. 30:26). It is used of a miscarried baby (Ex. 21:22). Followed by *z^e^qûnîm,* old age, it means a child of one's old age (Gen. 44:20). However, it refers to young men as well (1 Kgs. 12:8, 10, 14). It is also used to refer to the young of animals (Job 38:41; 39:3; Isa. 11:7).

3207. יַלְדָּה ***yaldāh:*** A feminine noun meaning girl, young woman. It is the feminine of 3206. It refers also to a marriageable young girl (Gen. 34:4) or one who becomes a slave or is sold into harlotry (Joel 3:3[4:3]). Girls playing in the streets were a sign of joy in God's restored Zion (Zech. 8:5).

3208. יַלְדוּת ***yalḏûṯ:*** A feminine noun referring to childhood, a period of youth. It designates an early period in a person's life, childhood or youth, when it is especially important to serve the Creator (Eccl. 11:9, 10). In Psalm 110:3, it refers to the period of youth of the Israelite king or to the young people of his nation (NASB) who are especially refreshing and invigorating to him.

3209. יִלּוֹד ***yillôḏ:*** An adjective designating what is born. It refers to the baby or child who has been or will be born (Ex. 1:22). The context of the word indicates: where certain persons were born (Josh. 5:5; 2 Sam. 5:14; Jer. 16:3); to whom certain persons were born (2 Sam. 12:14).

3210. יָלוֹן ***yālôn:*** A proper noun designating Jalon (1 Chr. 4:17).

3211. יָלִיד ***yāliyḏ:*** A masculine noun indicating descendants of, those born. It designates one born. It may refer to a slave born into a household (Gen. 14:14; 17:12, 13, 23, 27; Jer.

2:14) or to a slave purchased from outside a household (Lev. 22:11). It is better translated as sons or descendants of in some contexts: descendants of Anak, giants (Num. 13:22, 28; Josh. 15:14; 1 Chr. 20:4); sons or descendants of the giant Rapha (2 Sam. 21:16, 18).

3212. יָלַךְ *yālak:* A verb. For this word, see the discussion under 1980.

3213. יָלַל *yālal:* A verb meaning to wail, to howl. This is a word expressing deep mourning or distress. It is used to express dismay at the coming of the day of the Lord (Isa. 13:6). All the nations will wail at that time (Isa. 14:31; Mic. 1:8; Zeph. 1:11; Zech. 11:2), often in temples and high places (Isa. 15:2, 3; 16:7; 23:1, 6). Even palace and temple songs will turn into wailing (Amos 8:3).

3214. יְלֵל *yelēl:* A masculine noun describing a howling of beasts. It is used to depict the sounds and desolation of a wilderness or desert area (Deut. 32:10).

3215. יְלָלָה *yelālāh:* A feminine noun denoting a wailing, a howling. It describes a deep mourning of despair or distress. Because of God's judgment on Moab, a cry of distress sounds throughout the land; Babylon wails because of God's judgment on her (Jer. 25:36); as does Judah (Zeph. 1:10); and Lebanon (Zech. 11:3).

3216. יָלַע *yāla':* A verb meaning to swallow, to devour. It is translated as devour, to swallow in Proverbs 20:25 by some translators (KJV). Others find the root of *lā'a'* to say rashly, to devote rashly, and translate it accordingly (NIV, NASB, NKJV).

3217. יַלֶּפֶת *yallepet:* A feminine noun referring to a scab, a festering sore. No persons of the line of Aaron was permitted to offer sacrifices if they had this skin disease (Lev. 21:20); likewise, a sacrificial animal with this type of skin disease was not to be offered to the Lord (Lev. 22:22).

3218. יֶלֶק *yeleq:* A masculine noun referring to a young locust, a caterpillar; a creeping locust. This refers to the creeping, early stage in the life of a locust, an unwinged stage (Joel 1:4; 2:25; NASB, creeping locust; NIV, young locust; KJV, cankerworm; Ps. 105:34; Jer. 51:14, 27; Nah. 3:15, 16).

3219. יַלְקוּט *yalqûṭ:* A masculine noun indicating a pouch, a bag; a shepherd's bag. It is used only once of the pouch into which David placed five smooth stones for use in his sling. This pouch was constructed within his shepherd's bag (*kelî hārō'îym*) most likely (1 Sam. 17:40).

3220. יָם *yām:* A masculine noun denoting the sea, west. It points out significant bodies of water in general as created by God and nature at the time of God's bringing order on the earth (Gen. 1:26). It refers to all bodies of water collectively (Ex. 20:11); all the water collected into bodies of water (Dan. 11:45). The word refers often to specific bodies of water, designating them seas: the Great Sea, the Mediterranean (Josh. 1:4); the sea of the Philistines, also the Mediterranean (Ex. 23:31); the Dead Sea, literally, the Salt Sea (Gen. 14:3); the sea of the Arabah, again the Dead Sea (2 Kgs. 14:25); the sea of reeds or Red Sea (Ex. 10:19); the sea of Egypt (Isa. 11:15); the Sea of Galilee (Num. 34:11; Josh. 13:27). It was used to refer to large rivers: the Nile (Isa. 18:2); the Euphrates (Jer. 51:36).

It is used in the geographical phrase "from sea to sea" (Amos 8:12). Since it often referred to the Mediterranean Sea, the Great Sea, *yām* came to mean west (Gen. 13:14); from the west meant on the west side of (*miyyām;* Josh. 8:9). With *āh* added to the end of *yam*, the word means westward (Num. 3:23). It is used of the model bronze sea built by Solomon and used in temple worship (1 Kgs. 7:23–25). Finally, it combines in word combinations to give the shore of the sea (Josh. 11:4); sand of the sea (*ḥōl hayyām*) (Gen. 32:12[13]; 41:49).

3221. יָם *yam:* An Aramaic masculine noun meaning sea. It is used of the Great Sea, the Mediterranean Sea, from which Daniel sees four kingdoms arise (Dan. 7:2, 3).

3222. יֵם *yēm:* I. A masculine noun denoting a mule. It refers to a pack animal and work animal, some of which ran wild (Gen. 36:24, KJV) in the open fields.

II. A masculine noun indicating hot springs. It is understood as referring to hot springs by recent translators (NIV, NASB; Gen. 36:24). Some have suggested vipers as a translation.

3223. יְמוּאֵל *y^emû'ēl:* A proper noun designating Jemuel (Gen. 46:10; Ex. 6:15).

3224. יְמִימָה *y^emiymāh:* A proper noun designating Jemimah (Job 42:14).

3225. יָמִין *yāmiyn:* A feminine noun referring to a hand, a right hand, the south. It has several basic usages: It is used to indicate something on the right side: hand (Gen. 48:13). Used as an adverb, it means a direction to the right (Gen. 13:9; Ps. 45:9[10]). Something on the right is said to have special significance: God swears by His right hand (Isa. 62:8); and delivers His people by His right hand (Ex. 15:6, 12); a right-handed oath is noted (Ps. 144:8, 11); a person of honor gets to sit at the right hand (1 Kgs. 2:19; Ps. 110:1). The right side also indicates a southerly direction (Josh. 17:7; 1 Kgs. 7:39). It is used figuratively of being morally upright (Deut. 17:11; 28:14; Josh. 1:7; 2 Kgs. 22:2). The right is indicative of being morally correct or just (Eccl. 10:2).

3226. יָמִין *yāmiyn:* A proper noun designating Jamin:

A. Son of Simeon (Gen. 46:10; Ex. 6:15; Num. 26:12; 1 Chr. 4:24).

B. A Judaite (1 Chr. 2:27).

C. A Levite (Neh. 8:7).

3227. יְמִינִי ***y^emiyniy:*** An adjective indicating right, right hand. It indicates the right side or right hand of anything. In Ezekiel it comes after and modifies the noun meaning side but is used in 2 Chronicles 3:17 with the definite article added to it to mean the right (pillar).

3228. יָמִינִי ***yāmiyniy,*** יְמִינִי ***y^emiyniy:*** I. Jaminite (Num. 26:12).

II. Benjamite, a shortened form of *ben-y^emiymiy* (1145) (1 Sam. 9:1, 4; 2 Sam. 20:1; Esth. 2:5).

3229. יִמְלָא ***yimlā',*** יִמְלָה ***yimlāh:*** A proper noun designating Imlah (1 Kgs. 22:8, 9; 2 Chr. 18:7, 8).

3230. יַמְלֵךְ ***yamlēḵ:*** A proper noun designating Jamlech (1 Chr. 4:34).

3231. יָמַן ***yāman:*** A verb indicating to go to the right, to use the right hand. It is used to indicate direction, in the direction of the right side or hand (Gen. 13:9; Ezek. 21:16[21]). It is used in the phrase not to "turn to the right or to the left" to indicate steadfastness, a determination to keep on one's current path or maintain one's current attitude (Isa. 30:21). It describes the use of one's right hand to shoot a bow (1 Chr. 12:2).

3232. יִמְנָה ***yimnāh:*** A proper noun designating Imnah (Gen. 46:17; Num. 26:44; 1 Chr. 7:30; 2 Chr. 31:14).

3233. יְמָנִי ***y^emāniy:*** An adjective indicating right, right hand. It indicates Aaron's right ear, the ear on the right side of his body (Ex. 29:20; Lev. 8:23). It refers to the right pillar on the porch of Solomon's Temple (1 Kgs. 7:21) or to anything on the right (2 Kgs. 11:11). When facing the east, it indicates the south or southern direction (1 Kgs. 7:39; Ezek. 47:1, 2).

3234. יִמְנָע ***yimnā':*** A proper noun designating Imna (1 Chr. 7:35).

3235. יָמַר ***yāmar:*** I. A verb indicating to boast. It is used of glorying in something, being rightly proud in the case of enjoying the benefits and blessings on God's people (Isa. 61:6).

II. A verb meaning to change. It refers to replacing something with something else, even changing gods, a major sin of Israel (Jer. 2:11).

3236. יִמְרָה ***yimrāh:*** A proper noun designating Imrah (1 Chr. 7:36).

3237. יָמַשׁ ***yāmaš:*** A verb indicating to feel, to touch. It used once of Samson, a blind man, asking to sense, to feel, to touch with his hands the pillars of a Philistine temple (Judg. 16:26). Some derive the word used here from the verb *mûš*.

3238. יָנָה ***yānāh:*** A verb meaning to oppress, to treat violently. The term is used in Exodus 22:21[20], Leviticus 25:14, 17, and Deuteronomy 23:16 [17] to refer to improper treatment of strangers and the poor. The participle functions as a noun meaning oppressor (Jer. 25:38; 46:16; 50:16). In the Prophets, the term is typically used of foreign oppressors.

3239. יָנוֹחַ **yānôaḥ,** יָנוֹחָה **yānôḥāh:** A proper noun designating Janoah:

A. A town in Naphtali (2 Kgs. 15:29).

B. A town in Ephraim (Josh. 16:6, 7).

3240. יָנַח **yānaḥ:** The word employed here is now considered to be from *nûaḥ*. (See 5117, I).

3241. יָנִים **yāniym:** A proper noun designating Janim (Josh. 15:53).

3242. יְנִיקָה **y^eniyqāh:** A feminine noun denoting a twig, a young shoot. It refers to fresh young growth found on trees and shrubs, often in their top branches. It is used figuratively in Ezekiel 17:4.

3243. יָנַק **yānaq:** A verb meaning to care for, to nurse, to suckle. It is used to describe the nursing or feeding of children (Gen. 21:7; 1 Kgs. 3:21). It may indicate the person serving as a nurse (Gen. 24:59; Ex. 2:7) or the child nursing (Deut. 32:25; Job 3:12; Joel 2:16). It describes the nursing of young animals (Gen. 32:15 [16]). It is used figuratively in idioms, e.g., it describes the blessing the Lord bestows on Jacob, His people, making them "suck honey from a rock" (Deut. 32:13). And it is used of Zebulum describing how he will draw on the abundance of the seas and the wealth of the sand (Deut. 33:19).

3244. יַנְשׁוּף **yanšûp̱,** יַנְשׁוֹף **yanšôp̱:** A masculine noun indicating a great owl. It refers to an unclean bird of some kind, possibly a horned great owl (Lev. 11:17; Deut. 14:16; Isa. 34:11). It was not to be eaten by the Israelites.

3245. יָסַד **yāsad̲:** A verb meaning to establish, to found, to fix. In a literal sense, this term can refer to laying the foundation of a building, primarily the Temple (1 Kgs. 5:17[31]; 6:37; Ezra 3:11; Isa. 44:28); or to laying the foundation of a city like Jericho (Josh. 6:26; 1 Kgs. 16:34); or Zion (Isa. 14:32). In a metaphorical sense, it can allude to the founding of Egypt (Ex. 9:18); the earth (Isa. 48:13). This word can also connote the appointment or ordination of an individual(s) to a task or position (1 Chr. 9:22; Esth. 1:8). Probably one of the most noteworthy occurrences of this word is in Isaiah 28:16, where God declares that He will "lay in Zion for a foundation a stone, a tried stone, a precious corner stone, a sure foundation: he that believeth shall not make haste" (KJV). The New Testament writers announce that that stone is Jesus Christ (Rom. 9:33; 1 Pet. 2:6).

3246. יְסֻד **y^esud̲:** A masculine noun indicating a beginning. It is used in Ezra 7:9 to describe the beginning of Israel's journey toward Babylon. Most translators prefer to read this word as *yissad̲*, a perfect verbal form, and translate it as "he [Ezra] began" (NASB, NIV, KJV, NKJV).

3247. יְסוֹד **y^esôd̲:** A noun meaning foundation. The word refers to a base on which people build structures. It is used several times to refer to the base of the sacrificial altar, where the blood of sacrifices was poured (Ex. 29:12; Lev. 4:7, 18, 25, 30, 34). The Gate of the Foundation, mentioned in 2 Chronicles 23:5, may have been named from its proximity to the altar. In reference to larger buildings, the word is usually used to express the extent of destruction which sometimes included razing a city down to its foundation (Ps. 137:7; Mic. 1:6) and sometimes even the destruction of the foundation itself (Lam. 4:11; Ezek. 30:4). Egypt's foundations appear to symbolize its dependence on other nations (Ezek. 30:4, 5). Symbolically, the word refers to principles on which people build their lives, whether they be faulty (Job 4:19; 22:16) or sound (Prov. 10:25; cf. Matt. 7:24–27).

3248. יְסוּדָה ***y^e^sûḏāh:*** A feminine noun meaning foundation. This word occurs only in Psalm 87:1. The words in Zechariah 4:9, 8:9, and 12:1, are forms of the verb *yāsaḏ* (3245); the words in Isaiah 28:16, although difficult to analyze, also do not appear to belong under this reference. In Psalm 87:1, the word refers to Jerusalem as God's foundation or base in the holy mountain. The psalm enlarges on this, saying that Jerusalem will be the place of His particular dwelling, the home of a large number of His people, and a source of blessing.

3249. יָסוּר ***yāsûr:*** A masculine noun indicating those who depart, turn away. It indicates persons who turn away. In this case, they turn away from following the Lord, "they that depart from me" (KJV, NKJV, Jer. 17:13). Some translators edit the word to read *w^e^ṣore(y)ḵā* (NIV, NASB), with the translation then becoming "those who turn away" (NASB) or "those who turn away from you" (NIV).

3250. יִסּוֹר ***yissôr:*** A masculine singular noun meaning one who reproves. The word comes from the verb *yāsar* (3256). Its only occurrence is in Job 40:2.

3251. יָסַךְ ***yāsaḵ:*** A verb meaning to pour out. It is used of pouring out a liquid, an anointing oil (Ex. 30:32) on the skin of a person as a perfume.

3252. יִסְכָּה ***yiskāh:*** A proper noun designating Iscah (Gen. 11:29).

3253. יִסְמַכְיָהוּ ***yismaḵyāhû:*** A proper noun designating Ismakiah (2 Chr. 31:13).

3254. יָסַף ***yāsap̱:*** A verb meaning to increase, to do again, to continue. This word indicates continuing to do something, to do something repeatedly, to enhance, increase something, or to do something after a period or inactivity. Israel will revive and take root after being destroyed (Isa. 10:20); Israel continued to sin over and over, adding (*yāsap̱*) to her sins, increasing them (Judg. 13:1; 1 Sam. 12:19; Isa. 1:5); but her afflicted could increase or add to (*yāsap̱*) their joy or gladness in the Lord (Isa. 29:19). The angel of the Lord did not again (*yāsap̱*) appear to Manoah after his second appearance (cf. Num. 11:25; Judg. 13:12). It indicates an addition to the number of persons or objects (Gen. 4:2; 38:26; 2 Sam. 24:3). The Lord added sons to Jacob and Rachel (Gen. 30:24); Solomon added to the tax burden of Israel (1 Kgs. 12:11). It indicates the continuation of a plan or process (Gen. 8:10), as when Noah again (*yāsap̱*) sent out a dove. Of course, when the verb is negated, it means to do something no more, no longer. Because of Cain's sin, the ground would no longer yield its fruits abundantly to him (Gen. 4:12); it indicates something will not be done again (Ex. 11:6). It is used of human reactions and emotions. Joseph's brothers hated him still more (*yāsap̱*) (Gen. 37:5). Finally, it is found in an oath formula in which it is stated that God will do such and such "and still more" (1 Kgs. 2:23).

3255. יְסַף y^e*sap̱*: An Aramaic verb indicating to add, to increase. It means to join to something so that it is increased in quantity or quality. In Daniel 4:36(33), it is used to indicate an increase in the influence, splendor, and respect of Nebuchadnezzar's rulership.

3256. יָסַר *yāsar*, סָרַר *sārar*: A verb meaning to discipline, to chasten, to instruct, to teach, to punish. It is used with two general poles of meaning (chastening or instructing) that at times merge. Both aspects are presented in Scripture in terms of God and humans. Others can instruct and teach (Job 4:3), as can the conscience (Ps. 16:7). Still others can discipline, but God is the ultimate source of true instruction and chastening. He often chides toward an instructive end, especially for His covenant people (Lev. 26:18, 23; Jer. 46:28); wisdom presents the disciplined one as blessed, even though the process is painful (Ps. 94:12; 118:18). However, chastisement is not always presented as positive or instructive, for Rehoboam promised an evil chastening that eventually split the united kingdom (1 Kgs. 12:11, 14); and God's just, unremitted punishment would bring desolation (Jer. 6:8; 10:24).

3257. יָע *yā'*: A masculine noun meaning shovel. A hollowed-out tool or similar utensil used for cleaning the ashes and other material remains from an altar after sacrifices have been offered (Ex. 27:3; 38:3; Num. 4:14; 1 Kgs. 7:40, 45; 2 Kgs. 25:14; 2 Chr. 4:11, 16; Jer. 52:18).

3258. יַעְבֵּץ *ya'bēṣ*: A proper noun designating Jabez, a descendant of the line of Judah, a family head (1 Chr. 4:9, 10). He is called an "honorable" man. His name means "he means or causes sorrow/pain," thus the expression of his mother. Jabez prays a prayer that, playing on the meaning of Jabez ("sorrow, pain"), asks that the Lord would grant him freedom from pain by blessing him. God did so!

3259. יָעַד yā'aḏ: A verb meaning to appoint, to summon, to engage, to agree, to assemble. It also means allotted or appointed time, such as the amount of time David appointed to Amasa to assemble the men of Judah (2 Sam. 20:5). This word can also take the meaning of appointing or designating someone to be married (Ex. 21:8, 9). Another meaning is to meet someone at an appointed time. Amos asked the question, How can two walk together unless they appoint a time at which to meet (Amos 3:3)?

3260. יֶעְדוֹ ye'dô: A proper noun designating Iddo (2 Chr. 9:29).

3261. יָעָה yā'āh: A verb indicating to sweep away. It is a tool used to remove something, from context possibly with a sweeping motion (Isa. 28:17). It is used figuratively of hail "sweeping away" Jerusalem since it is a place of deceit and lies.

3262. יְעוּאֵל y^e'û'ēl: A proper noun designating Jeuel, the son of Zerah (1 Chr. 9:6).

3263. יְעוּץ y^e'ûṣ: A proper noun designating Jeuz (1 Chr. 8:10).

3264. יְעוֹרִים y^e'ôriym: A masculine plural noun referring to woods, a forest. It can indicate a thick growth of trees and accompanying shrubs and flora. It is often considered a dangerous place. God's will makes even the woods a safe place for His people to sleep (Ezek. 34:25).

3265. יָעוּר yā'ûr: A proper noun designating Jair (1 Chr. 20:5).

3266. יְעוּשׁ y^e'ûš: A proper noun designating Jeush:

A. Son of Esau (Gen. 36:5, 14, 18; 1 Chr. 1:35).

B. A Benjamite (1 Chr. 7:10).

C. A Benjamite (1 Chr. 8:39).

D. A Levite (1 Chr. 23:10, 11).

E. Son of Rehoboam (2 Chr. 11:19).

3267. יָעַז yā'az: A verb indicating to be strong, fierce, insolent. It indicates an attitude or disposition of persons, such as insolent, fierce, resistant (Isa. 33:19).

3268. יַעֲזִיאֵל ya^aziy'ēl: A proper noun designating Jaaziel (1 Chr. 15:18).

3269. יַעֲזִיָּהוּ ya^aziyyāhû: A proper noun designating Jaaziah (1 Chr. 24:26, 27).

3270. יַעֲזֵיר ya^azēyr, יַעְזֵר ya'zēr: A proper noun designating Jazer, a town east of the Jordan in Sihon's kingdom in southern Gilead. It was captured and allotted to the Gadites. It served as a Levitical city (Josh. 21:39[37]). It was later retaken by the Moabites (Isa. 16:8, 9; Jer. 48:32).

3271. יָעַט yā'at: A verb meaning to clothe, to cover. It indicates wrapping oneself with a garment (Isa. 61:10; some relate this verb to *'āṭāh* I, 5844). It is used figuratively to indicate the Lord covering a person with garments of salvation.

3272. יְעַט **y^e'aṭ:** An Aramaic verb indicating to take counsel, to deliberate. It refers to a ruse and evil plan formed in consultation by certain officials (Dan. 6:7[8]). In Ezra it refers to the seven officials who were chief advisors to the Persian king (Ezra 7:14, 15).

3273. יְעִיאֵל **y^e'iy'ēl,** יְעוּאֵל **y^e'û'ēl:** A proper noun designating Jeiel:

A. A Reubenite (1 Chr. 5:7).

B. Father of Gibeon (1 Chr. 9:35).

C. Son of Hotham (1 Chr. 11:44).

D. A Musician (1 Chr. 15:18, 21; 16:5).

E. Son of Mattaniah (2 Chr. 20:14).

F. A scribe (2 Chr. 26:11).

G. Son of Elizaphan (2 Chr. 29:13).

H. A Levite (2 Chr. 35:9).

I. Son of Adonikam (Ezra 8:13).

J. Son of Nebo (Ezra 10:43).

3274. יְעִישׁ **y^e'iyš:** A proper noun designating Jeish, alternate spelling of *y^e'ûš* (3266,A), Jeush:

A. Son of Esau (Gen. 36:5, 14). See also 3266,A.

B. A Benjamite (1 Chr. 7:10). See also 3266,B.

3275. יַעְכָּן **ya'kān:** A proper noun designating Jacan (1 Chr. 5:13).

3276. יָעַל **yā'al:** A verb meaning to gain, to profit, to benefit. It indicates something that is done beneficially, resulting in success and betterment. It is used most often figuratively of spiritual benefits from the Lord. Gods other than the Lord could not benefit His people (1 Sam. 12:21; Jer. 2:8, 11). It is possible to put forth effort to no gain or benefit (Jer. 12:13). Useless talk is of no profit (Job 15:3). Israel had come to believe that they would not gain anything (*yā'al*) by serving the Lord (Job 21:15). Wealth gotten wrongly does not ultimately result in any gain (Prov. 10:2); righteousness delivers one before the Lord but not riches (Prov. 11:4). Wrong alliances with enemies of the Lord bring no gain (Isa. 30:5, 6).

3277. יָעֵל **yā'ēl:** A masculine noun meaning wild goat. It refers to the ibex or small mountain goat (Ps. 104:18). The time and process of their calving was a wonder and mystery to people, noted by God Himself (Job 39:1).

3278. יָעֵל **yā'ēl:** A proper noun designating Jael, the wife of Heber the Kenite who killed Sisera, the commander of the army of Jabin, a great king of Canaan who reigned in Hazor (Judg. 4; 5).

3279. יַעֲלָא **ya'ala',** יַעֲלָה **ya'alāh:** A proper noun designating Jaala (Ezra 2:56; Neh. 7:58).

3280. יַעֲלָה **ya'alāh:** A feminine noun denoting a doe, a female deer, a mountain goat. Its beauty and pleasantness is used in a simile referring to the breasts of one's wife (Prov. 5:19).

3281. יַעְלָם **ya'lām:** A proper noun designating Jalam (Gen. 36:5, 14, 18; 1 Chr. 1:35).

3282. יַעַן **ya'an:** A conjunction meaning because, on account of, but also used as a preposition, because of. Used as a preposition, it is followed by either a noun (Ezek. 5:9) or infinitive (1 Kgs. 21:20; Amos 5:11). As a conjunction, it is used alone to mean because (1 Sam. 15:23; 1 Kgs. 14:13; Ezek. 34:21); with *ᵃšer* meaning because that (Deut. 1:36; Judg. 2:20); with *kî* to mean because, because that (1 Kgs. 13:21; 21:29; Isa. 3:16).

3283. יָעֵן **yā'ēn:** A masculine noun denoting an ostrich. It refers to the most powerful and swift of living birds, but it is known to try to skirt difficulties by avoiding them. It is used in a simile for Israel (Lam. 4:3).

3284. יַעֲנָה **ya'ᵃnāh:** A feminine noun meaning an unclean bird; a horned owl or ostrich. It is probably referring to the horned or great owl. In its context, it is considered unclean and detestable for Israelites, and they could not eat it (Lev. 11:16; Deut. 14:15). It was ranked on the animal social scale with jackals or wild dogs (Job 30:29; Isa. 13:21; 34:13; 43:20; Jer. 50:39; Mic. 1:8). Its forlorn howling and barking indicated mourning.

3285. יַעְנַי **ya'nay:** A proper noun designating Janai (1 Chr. 5:12).

3286. יָעֵף **yā'ēp̱:** I. A verb indicating exhaustion, fainting; fatigued, tired out. It is used in a famous assertion declaring that the Lord does not become tired or weary, while even youths do so (Isa. 40:28, 30). Yet those who look to the Lord share in His inner spiritual strength and renewal (Isa. 40:31). It is used of a strong iron worker who exhausts himself constructing a vain, useless idol (Isa. 44:12; cf. Jer. 51:58, 64; Hab. 2:13). In context it depicts the tireless lust of a female donkey in heat (Jer. 2:24). It possibly describes Gabriel's weary flight to Daniel in prayer (Dan. 9:21; but see II and 3288).

II. A verb meaning to move swiftly. It is employed in Daniel 9:21 to describe the swift flight of the angel Gabriel, according to more recent translations (see I, and Dan. 9:21). However, see 3288 also.

3287. יָעֵף **yā'ēp̱:** An adjective depicting someone as weary, faint, exhausted. It describes the state of those coming in from desert travel (2 t of an enemy (Judg. 8:15). It also describes emotional or spiritual weariness which the Lord can heal (Isa. 40:29). The Servant of the Lord spoke a word of encouragement to the weary person (Isa. 50:4).

3288. יְעָף **y^e'āp̱:** I. A masculine noun indicating weariness. It has traditionally been translated as weariness (Dan. 9:21) as a description of Daniel. It has the preposition *b^e* in the front, indicating that it is being used adverbially (*bîy'āp̱*).

II. A masculine noun indicating swift flight, swiftness. "In (swift) flight" is another way to translate this word with b^e on the front of it (Dan. 9:21), thus referring to the flight of Gabriel.

3289. יָעַץ *yāʿaṣ:* A verb meaning to advise, to consult, to counsel, to be advised, to deliberate, to conspire, to take counsel. Jethro, Moses' father-in-law, advised Moses about how to judge the people of Israel (Ex. 18:19); and wise men, such as Hushai and Ahithophel, served as counselors to kings and other important people (2 Sam. 17:15; 1 Kgs. 12:9); as did prophets (Jer. 38:15). Many counselors help ensure that plans will succeed (Prov. 15:22); God counseled His servants (Ps. 16:7); the coming ruler of Israel will be the "Wonderful Counselor" (Isa. 9:6[5]). The verb also means to decide, to make plans or decisions. These plans can be for or against someone or something with God or a human as a subject of the sentence (Isa. 7:5; 14:24; Jer. 49:20; Hab. 2:10), but God's plans will never fail (Isa. 14:24).

In the passive, this verb means to permit oneself to be counseled—wisdom is gained by a person who acts in this manner (Prov. 13:10; cf. 1:5). More often, this stem expresses a reciprocal sense: Rehoboam consulted together with the elders (1 Kgs. 12:6); and the enemies of the psalmist conspired against him (Ps. 71:10). In the reflexive stem, it means to take counsel against as when the Lord's enemies conspired against His people (Ps. 83:3[4]).

3290. יַעֲקֹב *yaʿ^{a}qōḇ:* A proper noun designating Jacob

A. Son of Isaac. He had an older twin brother, Esau (Edom). Jacob became the father of the twelve patriarchs from whom the nation of Israel was formed. He moved with his sons to Egypt because of divine providence (Gen. 41; Ex. 1:1–7), probably sometime in the eighteenth century. He lived with his sons in Egypt until his death in Egypt (Gen. 49—50). He was embalmed in Egypt, carried out of Egypt at the Exodus, and buried in Canaan (Gen. 50:1–14) in the cave located in the area of Machpelah. Abraham had purchased this burial property from the Hittites living in the land (Gen. 50:12–14). Jacob produced seventy descendants (seventy-five according to the LXX) who went down to Egypt (Ex. 1:5).

Much of Genesis is occupied with tracing the birth, growth, and development of this father of the patriarchs. His name probably means something like "he seized or he seizes." Jacob took advantage of Esau and obtained the firstborn's birthright from him, thus supplanting him (Gen. 25:29–34). Later, he deceived Isaac into giving him the firstborn's blessing (Gen. 27:1–33).

The Lord confirmed the promises and covenants to Jacob previously made to Abraham (Gen. 28:1–22), and showed His special love for him and his progeny (Mal. 1:2). Jacob himself was deceived by Laban but eventually married Leah and Rachel through whom, with their handmaids, he fathered the ancestors of the twelve tribes (Gen. 29; 30; 35; 46). He was reconciled with Esau on his return to Canaan (Gen. 33:1–20). Israel's God, the Lord, became known as the God of Abraham, Isaac, and Jacob (Ex. 2:24; 3:15, 16), and Canaan became the land sworn to Abraham, Isaac, and Jacob (Deut. 34:4).

Jacob purchased the land in Shechem as a burial place for Joseph's bones (Josh. 24:32). His name was used sometimes to refer to all of Israel (see B below; 1 Sam. 12:8). His name was changed to Israel, "(he) has striven (wrestled) with God," after he encountered the angel of the Lord (Gen. 32:22–30) at the Jabbok River.

B. The name Jacob often stands for all his descendants (Lam. 1:17; 2:3; Ezek. 20:5), in fact, for all of Israel in some cases. In other contexts, it refers to northern Israel or Judah (Amos 3:13; 6:8; Mic. 1:5; Mal. 2:12; 3:6). His name, in fact, was changed to Israel (see A above) and his descendants bore that designation and name. The seventy descendants from Jacob's "loins" became the Israelite nation in Egypt over a period of 400 years (Ex. 1:1–7). In poetry Jacob/Israel are used as parallel pairs (Ps. 14:7; 20:23[24]).

3291. יַעֲקֹבָה ***yaᵃqōḇāh:*** A proper noun designating Jaakobah (1 Chr. 4:36).

3292. יַעֲקָן ***yaᵃqān:*** A proper noun designating Jaakan, Akan (Deut. 10:6; 1 Chr. 1:42).

3293. יַעַר ***ya'ar:*** I. A masculine noun referring to a forest, woods; honeycomb. This word is used in contexts and texts where it means a forest, thicket, woods (2 Sam. 18:8; 1 Kgs. 7:2; Zech. 11:2). It depicts a man-made or humanly manicured natural park area (Eccl. 2:6).

II. A masculine noun meaning honeycomb. The word has this sense in Song of Solomon 5:1. It refers to an item the lover has eaten within his garden of delight.

III. A masculine proper noun meaning Jaar. It may refer to a city by this name, "city of forests," Kiriath Jearim, or simply the field of Jaar (NIV, Ps. 132:6).

3294. יַעְרָה ***ya'rāh:*** A proper noun designating Jarah (1 Chr. 9:42).

3295. יַעֲרָה ***yaᵃrāh:*** I. A feminine noun meaning honeycomb. It refers to honey running from its comb as well as the honeycomb itself. It is especially invigorating and gives a person quick energy (1 Sam. 14:27).

II. A feminine noun referring to a forest. It is used in a metaphor in which the Lord's voice is so powerful that it lays low the trees and foliage of a forest (Ps. 29:9).

3296. יַעֲרֵי אֹרְגִים ***yaᵃrēy 'ōrᵉgiym:*** A proper noun designating Jaare-Oregim (2 Sam. 21:19).

3297. יְעָרִים ***yeʻārîym:*** A proper noun designating Jearim (Josh. 15:10).

3298. יַעֲרֶשְׁיָה ***yaʻarešyāh:*** A proper noun designating. Jaareshiah (1 Chr. 8:27).

3299. יַעֲשָׂו ***yaʻaśāw:*** A proper noun designating Jaasu (Ezra 10:37).

3300. יַעֲשִׂיאֵל ***yaʻaśîy'ēl:*** A proper noun designating Jaasiel:

A. One of David's mighty men (1 Chr. 11:47).

B. A Benjamite (1 Chr. 27:21).

3301. יִפְדְּיָה ***yipdeyāh:*** A proper noun designating Iphdeiah (1 Chr. 8:25).

3302. יָפָה ***yāpāh:*** A verb meaning to be bright, beautiful; excellent. It is a term of approbation and of descriptive power referring to the king of Israel. It indicates excellence and splendor in both an ethical and moral sense (Ps. 45:2[3]). It is used to depict the beauty of love itself (Song 4:10); of the shoes and feet of the beloved (Song 7:1[2]). It takes on the meaning of to adorn oneself or something in some contexts and usages (Jer. 4:30; 10:4; Ezek. 16:13). It is used to describe the political, military, and royal splendor of the nation of Assyria (Ezek. 31:7).

3303. יָפֶה ***yāpeh:*** An adjective meaning lovely, beautiful. It is used in many settings to describe the beauty of various things and persons: of women (Gen. 12:11, 14; 2 Sam. 13:1; Esth. 2:7). It is used to indicate a healthy appearance (Gen. 41:2). It may be used to mean good-looking, handsome of young men or adult males (2 Sam. 14:25). It combines with the word for form (*tô'ar*) to mean beautiful of form, e.g., Joseph was "handsome of form" (Gen. 39:6). Jerusalem is said to be beautiful as to its location (*yepēh nôp*) (Ps. 48:2[3]). A singer may have a beautiful voice (Ezek. 33:32). Trees (Ezek. 31:3) and nearly everything is said to be beautiful "in its time" (Eccl. 3:11).

3304. יְפֵה־פִיָּה ***yepēypiyyah:*** An adjective indicating very pretty, handsome. It is applied in a metaphor to Egypt described as a cow. This word indicates that Egypt is a handsome or pretty cow or heifer (Jer. 46:20). She will be destroyed by a horsefly, Babylon (Jer. 46:20).

3305. יָפוֹא ***yāpô'***, יָפוֹ ***yāpô:*** A proper noun designating Joppa (Japho), a port city given to the Danites (Josh. 19:46). It was a convenient place to import building materials and other merchandise on the Mediterranean coast. Jonah tried to escape God's call by sailing from Joppa (Jon. 1:3). It was located just south of the north Yarkon River. It was still an important port in New Testament times (Acts 9:36–43, etc.).

3306. יָפַח ***yāpaḥ:*** A verb meaning to breathe hard, to gasp for breath. It is used in a metaphor to personify the last efforts of labored breathing by

Jerusalem, the daughter of Zion, before her enemies (Jer. 4:31).

3307. יָפֵחַ yāpēaḥ: An adjective indicating breathing out, exhaling. It is used figuratively to indicate the breathing out violence (*ḥmṣ*) against the psalmist by his enemies (Ps. 27:12).

3308. יְפִי yᵒpiy: A masculine noun denoting beauty. It is used to describe the pleasing and satisfying appearance of things or persons: of a woman (Esth. 1:11); a person exuding royal splendor (Isa. 33:17); of Zion (Ps. 50:2); of plants or trees (Ezek. 31:8); of Jerusalem (Ps. 45:11[12]; Ezek. 16:14). It refers to the shining attraction or sparkle of jewels or precious stones (Zech. 9:17). Some beauty is to be resisted, such as the beauty or attraction of an adulteress (Prov. 6:25).

3309. יָפִיעַ yāpiya': A proper noun designating Japhia:

A. King of Lachish (Josh. 10:3).

B. A border town of Zebulon (Josh. 19:12).

C. Son of David (2 Sam. 5:15; 1 Chr. 3:7; 14:6).

3310. יַפְלֵט yaplēṭ: A proper noun designating Japhlet (1 Chr. 7:32, 33).

3311. יַפְלֵטִי yaplēṭiy: A proper noun designating Japhletite (Josh. 16:3).

3312. יְפֻנֶּה yᵉpunneh: A proper noun designating Jephunneh:

A. Father of Caleb (Num. 13:6; 14:6, 30, 38; 26:65; 32:12; 34:19; Deut. 1:36; Josh. 14:6, 13, 14; 15:13; 21:12; 1 Chr. 4:15; 6:56[41]).

B. An Asherite (1 Chr. 7:38).

3313. יָפַע yāpa': A verb indicating to shine forth, to shine; to smile, to look favorably. It is used to indicate a bright streak of lightning (Job 37:15). It is used of the Lord's coming as if He shone forth from Mount Paran (Deut. 33:2) as well as out of Zion (Ps. 50:2). It is used of light lighting up something (Job 3:4). In an ironical statement, it depicts the deep shadow or utter gloom shining forth as darkness (Job 10:22). It is used in certain contexts to mean to look at with approval (Job 10:3). It describes God's action for His people as shining forth on their behalf (Ps. 80:1[2]; 94:1).

3314. יִפְעָה yip'āh: A feminine noun denoting brightness, splendor. It is used of the glamour and glitter of a city or nation, its splendor or reputation (Ezek. 28:7). This splendor often led to pride and corruption (Ezek. 28:17).

3315. יֶפֶת yepet: A proper noun designating Japheth, the third son of Noah. He was married and was on the ark during the great flood (Gen. 7:13). He and his descendants were blessed by Noah's prophetic words (Gen. 9:26–27) and are listed first in the author's genealogical lists (Gen. 10:1–5). They were to share in Shem's blessing. Japheth fathered 14 nations,

Ham 30, and Shem 26 for a total of seventy nations, a number indicating "all" nations (Gen. 10).

3316. יִפְתָּח ***yip̱tāḥ:*** A proper noun designating Jephthah, Iphtah:

A. Jephthah was a judge in Israel who had a Gileadite as a father and a prostitute as a mother, thus making him a rejected outcast in Israel (Judg. 11:1–40). He was ostracized but subsequently recalled because he was a competent military leader (vv. 8–11). He delivered Israel from the Ammonites. He made a foolish, rash vow concerning his only daughter that led to her death or to a life of celibacy (vv. 29–40). He delivered and judged Israel six years then died (Judg. 12:7).

B. Iphtah was a town in Judah (Josh. 15:43).

3317. יִפְתַּח־אֵל ***yip̱taḥ 'ēl:*** A proper noun designating Iphtah El (Josh. 19:14, 27).

3318. יוֹצֵאת ***yôṣē't̠,*** יָצָא ***yāṣā':*** I. A feminine noun meaning captivity. It is used of going forth from one's homeland into exile (Ps. 144:14). God's blessing on His people could prevent this from happening.

II. A verb meaning basically to go out or to come in. It is used in many settings and contexts and is nuanced by those settings. It is used of the rising or coming forth of the sun or stars (Gen. 19:23; Neh. 4:21[15]); of the birth and coming out of a child (Gen. 25:26); of the springing up of plants (1 Kgs. 4:33[5:13]). It indicates general motion or movement, stepping forth for various purposes (1 Sam. 17:4; 2 Sam. 16:5); to set out (Ex. 17:9); to set out in a military sense (Deut. 20:1; 1 Sam. 8:20; 1 Chr. 5:18; Prov. 30:27). Of birds it is used with *šûḇ*, to return, to mean to fly back and forth or here and there (Gen. 8:7).

It has many figurative uses: "to come out from" (*yāṣā'* + *min*) means to be descended from (Gen. 10:14); to die is described as one's soul, life, going out, away (Gen. 35:18; Ezek. 26:18); to lack courage, to fail occurs when one's heart goes out (Gen. 42:28). The beginning of the year is described as the (old) year going out (Ex. 23:16); it is used of the effects of something wearing off (1 Sam. 25:37). It is used of manna "coming out of one's nose," meaning becoming sick over excessive eating of a food (Num. 11:20). It describes the removal of dross from a metal (Prov. 25:4), purifying it.

It has several nuanced meanings in different settings: to escape free (1 Sam. 14:41); to leave, to go away (Dan. 10:20). The removal of a scoffer causes a quarrel to cease, to go away (Prov. 22:10). It indicates the freeing of a slave (Lev. 25:25). The context in all its uses affects its meaning and translations. In its use as a causal stem verb, it takes on the idea of causing to go out, to go forth (Gen. 15:5; Josh. 2:3); to take away (Gen. 48:12); to lead an army (2 Sam. 5:2). Or it indicates bringing forth, producing plants from the ground (Gen. 1:12); a weapon by an iron worker or smith (Isa. 54:16). Or it may, in the personal sphere, indicate bringing forth one's spirit or breath, indicating that a person makes his or her feelings known (Prov. 29:11), as is characteristic of a fool. It is used with the word justice to mean to bring forth or execute justice (Isa. 42:1, 3). In its passive uses, it indicates that someone or something is led forth (Gen. 38:25; Ezek. 14:22; cf. 38:22).

3319. יְצָא *y^e^ṣa':* An Aramaic verb meaning to complete, to finish. It is used of the conclusion of the construction of the Temple built by the returned exiles (Ezra 6:15).

3320. יָצַב *yāṣab̲:* A verb indicating to stand, to confront, to take one's stand. It is used in a reflexive stem and means to station oneself, to take a firm stand (1 Sam. 3:10). It has the sense of to present oneself at a location (Deut. 31:14) or to take a firm position on something (2 Sam. 18:13). It is used of putting oneself in a place of honor (Prov. 22:29); of a soldier taking his place in the armed forces (Jer. 46:4); or a person placing himself among the people of Israel in assembly (Judg. 20:2). To not allow someone to stand before you means to disapprove of him or her (Ps. 5:5[6]). To direct one's life in a certain way is to set oneself on a certain path of life (Ps. 36:4[5]). It is used of resisting people by taking a stand against them (Josh. 1:5; Ps. 2:2).

3321. יְצַב *y^e^ṣab̲:* An Aramaic verb meaning to take, to make a stand, to gain certainty, to know the truth. It is used only once in the entire Old Testament, in Daniel 7:19, where Daniel desired to know the truth of the fourth beast's identity. This corresponds with the Hebrew word *yāṣab̲* (3320), meaning to make one's stand, to take one's stand, or to present oneself.

3322. יָצַג *yāṣag:* A verb meaning to set, to place, to present. It is a synonym of the Hebrew *śîm,* to place, to put. It is used of placing objects or persons in a certain location or a certain way (Gen. 30:38; Judg. 8:27; 1 Sam. 5:2; 2 Sam. 6:17). It has the sense of giving persons to someone as helpers (Gen. 33:15) in certain contexts. It means to set forth someone for a purpose or with a certain result (Job 17:6), e.g., Job was set forth, made a byword, a joke of scorn. To set justice in the land means to establish justice, what is right, in the land (Amos 5:15). In Judges 7:5, it has the sense of to set out, to separate out.

3323. יִצְהָר *yiṣhār:* A masculine noun meaning fresh oil, anointing oil. It most commonly refers to fresh oil produced from the land, most likely from olive trees (2 Kgs. 18:32). This oil could be in an unprocessed state (Deut. 7:13). Concerning religious uses, people gave this oil to the Levites and priests as a means of support (2 Chr. 31:5). The Hebrew word is also used once for the purpose of anointing (Zech. 4:14).

3324. יִצְהָר ***yiṣhār:*** A proper noun designating Izhar (Ex. 6:18, 21; Num. 3:19; 16:1; 1 Chr. 6:2[5:28], 18[3], 38[23]; 23:12, 18).

3325. יִצְהָרִי ***yiṣhāriy:*** A proper noun designating Izharite (Num. 3:27; 1 Chr. 24:22; 26:23, 29).

3326. יָצוּעַ ***yāṣûa':*** I. A masculine noun referring to a bed, a couch. It refers to a place for sleeping but also figuratively means the place where husband and wife have sexual intercourse for procreation. It stands parallel with a synonym, *miškāḇ*, bed, couch, in the previous line in Genesis 49:4 (cf. 1 Chr. 5:1). Sheol is considered a place of darkness where people may make their resting places or beds (Job 17:13). It is a place of rest and sleep (Ps. 63:6[7]); 132:3). Its use in 1 Kings 6:5 seems to carry the sense of a side chamber in the temple. But see II below, for this may indicate that the word in Kings is a different root word altogether.

II. A common noun referring to a wing of a building, a side chamber, a flat surface. Its use in 1 Kings 6:5, 10 carries the sense of a side room or chamber. Its use in 1 Kings 6:6 indicates that it may refer to a flat ledge or a ledge extending out from the wall upon which things, such as timbers, could be positioned.

3327. יִצְחָק ***yiṣḥāq:*** A proper noun designating Isaac, the promised son and heir of Abraham and the Lord's promises to him (Gen. 15; 26:1–6). His name means "he laughs" (cf. Gen. 17:17). Abraham was one hundred years old when Isaac was born. Through him God would complete His goals for calling Abraham (Gen. 12:1–3). He was the son of Abraham through whom God would bless the nations and keep His covenant and promises to Abraham (Gen. 21:8–10; 25:1–6). His birth was a special act of God (Gen. 21:1–7). His preservation as the promised son was as much a miracle or more as his birth (Gen. 22). His wife Rebekah, a woman picked by God (Gen. 24), bore him Jacob, the father of the twelve patriarchs (Gen. 24; 25:21–26). He fell prey to Jacob and Rebekah's scheming and blessed Jacob instead of Esau with the birthright blessing (Gen. 27:1–33).

3328. יִצְחַר ***yiṣḥar:*** A proper noun designating Izhar (1 Chr. 4:7).

3329. יָצִיא ***yāṣiy':*** An adjective indicating the feature of coming forth, proceeding from, offspring, children. It refers to one's own children or offspring, who have come forth, in this case, the children or offspring of Sennacherib (2 Chr. 32:21).

3330. יַצִּיב ***yaṣṣiyḇ:*** An Aramaic adjective referring to something as true, reliable, certain. It is used of an interpretation of a dream or vision's being true, sure (Dan. 2:45; 7:16), or to an attitude or knowledge that is certain (Dan. 2:8; 3:24; 6:12[13]).

3331. יָצַע ***yāṣa':*** A verb indicating a spreading out, making a bed, laying.

It means to lie down for various reasons: for mourning and fasting on ashes and sackcloth (Esth. 4:3). It indicates the act of spreading out or preparing sackcloth and ashes to lie upon (Isa. 58:5). It is used figuratively of making one's bed or couch in Sheol (Ps. 139:8); God is also there. It figuratively describes maggots spread out as a bed in Sheol (Isa. 14:11).

3332. יָצַק ***yāṣaq:*** A verb indicating to pour, to pour out, to cast out; cast, set. Its exact use is determined, of course, by its context. It is used of serving up food (2 Sam. 13:9; 2 Kgs. 4:40, 41); of pouring out liquids (Gen. 28:18; 1 Kg. 18:33[34]). It is used figuratively of pouring various things: something deceitful, evil (Ps. 41:8[9]); grace (Ps. 45:2[3]); the Lord's Spirit (Isa. 44:3). It is used of pouring out molten metal to cast it (I Kg. 7:24); hence, it can be translated as to cast. The scales of Leviathan are firmly cast together (Job 41:23[15]); and his heart is described as being as hard (set, *yāṣûq*) as stone (Job 41:24[16]).

3333. יְצֻקָה ***y^eṣuqāh:*** A feminine noun indicating the casting of metal. It refers to something formed into a particular shape or form by pressing or pouring it into a mold (1 Kgs. 7:24).

3334. יָצַר ***yāṣar:*** A verb meaning to be in distress, to be frustrated. Most translators place this meaning on the root *ṣ^arar,* 6887,II. It indicates a state of anxiety, fear, and frustration in many different situations: Jacob at meeting Esau (Gen. 32:7[8]). The Lord's judgment on an unfaithful people caused them to be in great distress (Judg. 2:15). War was a time of great distress as well (Judg. 10:9). Pressure and disapproval from others may cause a person to be distressed (1 Sam. 30:6); and failure to satisfy sexual desires may lead to frustration (2 Sam. 13:2). To see one's plans thwarted may lead to a state of distress (Job 18:7). The evil person may experience frustration amid riches (Job 20:22). On the other hand, the person who follows wisdom is not ultimately distressed (Prov. 4:12).

3335. יָצַר ***yāṣar:*** A verb meaning to form, to fashion, to shape, to devise. The primary meaning of the word is derived from the idea of cutting or framing. It is used of God's fashioning man from the dust of the ground (Gen. 2:7); God's creative works in nature (Ps. 95:5; Amos 4:13); and in the womb (Ps. 139:16; Jer. 1:5; cf. Zech. 12:1); the molding of clay (Isa. 29:16; 45:9); the framing of seasons (Ps. 74:17); the forging of metal (Isa. 44:12); the crafting of weapons (Isa. 54:17); the making of plans (Ps. 94:20; Isa. 46:11; Jer. 18:11). It also signifies a potter (Ps. 2:9; Isa. 41:25); a sculptor (Isa. 44:9); or the Creator (Isa. 43:1; 44:2, 24). By extension, the word conveys the notion of predestination and election (2 Kgs. 19:25; Isa. 49:5).

3336. יֵצֶר ***yēṣer:*** A masculine noun meaning form, framing, purpose, imagination. One use of this word was to refer to a pottery vessel formed by a potter (i.e., that which was formed [Isa. 29:16]). Another example of a formed object was a graven image (Hab. 2:18). The psalmist said that man was formed from the dust (Ps. 103:14). This word also carries the connotation of something thought of in the mind, such as wickedness in people's hearts (Gen. 6:5); or something treasured or stored in the heart (1 Chr. 29:18).

3337. יֵצֶר *yēṣer:* A proper noun designating Jezer (Gen. 46:24; Num. 26:49; 1 Chr. 7:13).

3338. יְצֻרִים *y^eṣuriym:* A masculine plural noun denoting things formed, members. In its context and with reference to Job's assertion, it refers to bodily parts, members, such as one's eye (Job 17:7).

3339. יִצְרִי *yiṣriy:* A proper noun designating Izri (1 Chr. 25:11).

3340. יִצְרִי *yiṣriy:* A proper noun designating Jezerite (Num. 26:49).

3341. יָצַת *yāṣaṯ:* A verb meaning to set on fire, to burn. It means to burn up something when used "with fire" (*bā'ēš*): thorns burn in a fire (Isa. 33:12); a city burns (Jer. 49:2); the gates of Babylon burned (Jer. 51:58). It is used figuratively of evil or wickedness which burn as fire (Isa. 9:18[17]) as well as of God's own anger igniting and breaking out like fire (2 Kgs. 22:13, 17). In its passive uses, it means to be burned up as were the gates of Jerusalem (Neh. 1:3; 2:17). It takes on the meaning of to cause or set on fire in some usages and contexts (2 Sam. 14:30, 31).

3342. יֶקֶב *yeqeḇ:* A masculine noun meaning winepress, wine vat. This refers to a set up of two or more rocks, one to press the grapes, one to collect the juice. In Isaiah 5:2, it is referred to as part of the vineyard, the wine vat, representing Israel. It was a place of refreshment and energy during famine or war (2 Kgs. 6:27). A person often treads out the wine at the presses (Isa. 16:10). Wine from the press or wine vat was acceptable in sacrifices (Num. 18:27). The king often had his own wine vats (Zech. 14:10).

3343. יְקַבְצְאֵל *y^eqaḇṣ^e'ēl:* A proper noun designating Jekabzeel (Neh. 11:25).

3344. יָקַד *yāqaḏ:* A verb meaning to burn, to set fire. It is used in a powerful metaphor of God's anger; a fire is kindled, burning in His anger (Deut. 32:22; Jer. 15:14; 17:4); the Lord will burn up the glory of the Assyrian king and nation (Isa. 10:16). It describes a fire that burns in the Lord's nostrils—the offensive nature of His rebellious people (Isa. 65:5). It is used literally of fire burning on the altar of sacrifice (Lev. 6:9[2], 12[5], 13[6]); and fire in general (Isa. 30:14).

3345. יְקַד *y^eqaḏ:* An Aramaic verb meaning to burn. All the references are found in Daniel in the story of the three Hebrew men in the furnace of blazing fire (3:6, 11, 15, 17, 20, 21, 23, 26). The verb is always in an active participial form.

3346. יְקֵדָה ***y^{e}qēḏāh:*** An Aramaic active feminine noun referring to the process of burning. It refers to the burning of fire in Daniel's vision (Dan. 7:11), when the fourth beast is destroyed by burning.

3347. יָקְדְעָם ***yoqḏ^e'ām:*** A proper noun designating Jokdeam (Josh. 15:56).

3348. יָקֶה ***yāqeh:*** A proper noun designating Jakeh (Prov. 30:1).

3349. יְקָהָה ***y^{e}qāhāh:*** A feminine noun meaning obedience. In Jacob's prophecy to Judah, he said that the kingship would not depart from Judah's descendants until one came who would have the obedience of the nations (Gen. 49:10). This verse is considered by many to be prophetic of Jesus Christ. In the sayings of Agur, the disobedient child should have his eyes pecked out by ravens and vultures (Prov. 30:17).

3350. יְקוֹד ***y^{e}qôḏ,*** יְקֹד ***y^{e}qōḏ:*** An active masculine noun referring to a burning, a conflagration. In Isaiah its only use is a fire kindled like a blazing flame (10:16). It is probably being used both figuratively and literally of God's judgment on Assyria.

3351. יְקוּם ***y^{e}qûm:*** A masculine noun denoting a creature, a living thing, something that subsists. It is an all-inclusive generic term referring to all the living things God created whenever they existed (Gen. 7:4, 23). It is also inclusive of everything that was alive and tainted by the rebellion of Dathan and Abiram (Deut. 11:6).

3352. יָקוֹשׁ ***yāqôš:*** A masculine noun indicating a bird catcher, a fowler. It indicates traps or snares that are waiting to attack or hinder someone or something, e.g., the prophet of God (Hos. 9:8).

3353. יָקוּשׁ ***yaqûš:*** A masculine noun referring to a bird catcher, a fowler. It is slightly different in spelling from 3352. The basic lexical meaning is the same, but its context affects its sense in some cases. It is used figuratively of the evil plans of one's enemies (Ps. 91:3). It also refers to a bird trap in Proverbs 6:5 but is used to warn sons and daughters to avoid the subtle and dangerous snares of life by following wisdom. Evil persons lay snares to catch the unwary (Jer. 5:26). For Hosea 9:8, see 3352.

3354. יְקוּתִיאֵל ***y^{e}qûṯiy'ēl:*** A proper noun designating Jekuthiel (1 Chr. 4:18).

3355. יָקְטָן ***yoqṭān:*** A proper noun designating Joktan (Gen. 10:25, 26, 29; 1 Chr. 1:19, 20, 23).

3356. יָקִים ***yāqiym:*** A proper noun designating Jakim:

A. A Benjamite (1 Chr. 8:19).
B. A Levite (1 Chr. 24:12).

3357. יַקִּיר ***yaqqiyr:*** An adjective referring to what is dear, honored, precious. Ephraim, northern Israel, is described as God's dear, precious son. God's heart desires, yearns for what is honorable to Him (Jer. 31:20).

3358. יַקִּיר ***yaqqiyr:*** An Aramaic adjective meaning honorable, noble. It is used when referring to the king of Assyria to show great respect (Ezra 4:10). In Daniel 2:11, the word takes on the sense of astonishing, outstanding, a difficult task that the king demanded of his wise men.

3359. יְקַמְיָה ***y***^{e}***qamyāh:*** A proper noun designating Jekamiah:
A. Fifth son of Jeconiah (1 Chr. 3:18).
B. Son of Shallum (1 Chr. 2:41).

3360. יְקַמְעָם ***y***^{e}***qam'ām:*** A proper noun designating Jekameam (1 Chr. 23:19; 24:23).

3361. יָקְמְעָם ***yoqm***^{e}***'ām:*** A proper noun designating Jokmeam (1 Kgs. 4:12; 1 Chr. 6:68[53]).

3362. יָקְנְעָם ***yoqn***^{e}***'ām:*** A proper noun designating Jokneam (Josh. 12:22; 19:11; 21:34).

3363. יָקַע ***yāqa':*** A verb meaning to be dislocated, displaced. It means to turn quickly, to turn away, to be alienated (Jer. 6:8; Ezek. 23:17, 18). Used of a bodily joint, it has the meaning of dislocation (Gen. 32:25[26]). It has the sense of violent, total rejection, amounting to execution in Numbers 25:4; however, it was accomplished. A similar meaning is suggested by the context in 2 Samuel 21:6, 9, 13.

3364. יָקַץ ***yāqaṣ:*** A verb indicating to become awake, to awaken. It refers to regaining consciousness after sleeping off a drunken stupor (Gen. 9:24); or to awaken from sleep (Gen. 28:16; 41:4, 7, 21; Judg. 16:14; 1Elijah used it mockingly of the Canaanite god Baal who had perhaps been asleep (1 Kgs. 18:27). It is used in a figurative sense of the Lord as He begins to act (Ps. 78:65). It refers figuratively and literally to one's enemies or creditors beginning to attack (Hab. 2:7).

3365. יָקַר ***yāqar:*** A verb meaning to esteem, to be valuable, to be costly. It has the basic idea of being highly valuable, worthy; it indicates a high evaluation put upon someone or something (1 Sam. 18:30; Zech. 11:13). It indicates considering something worth preserving, such as human life (1 Sam. 26:21; 2 Kgs. 1:13, 14; Ps. 72:14). It can take on the idea of making something rare in certain causative usages (Isa. 13:12). The process of redeeming a person is said to cost great effort (Ps. 49:8[9]). It is used figuratively of making something scarce, rare, such as a visit to a neighbor's house (Prov. 25:17).

3366. יְקָר ***y***^{e}***qār:*** A masculine noun indicating splendor, honor, value. It indicates great value attached to something: lips that speak wisdom are more valuable than gold or jewels (Prov. 20:15). A monetary value can be called expensive or splendid (Zech. 11:13). The costly luxuries of a royal palace shows its splendor (Esth. 1:4). In a figurative sense, the word refers to deference or respect, honor given to a person (Esth. 1:20; 6:3, 6, 7, 11). An attitude of respect and appreciation can be shown to a people in general, i.e., the Jews (Esth. 8:16). It refers to the valuables of a city in a collective sense, all of them together (Jer. 20:5; Ezek. 22:25).

3367. יְקָר y^eqār: An Aramaic masculine noun referring to honor, glory. It indicates an attitude of respect and great appreciation, sometimes recognized in an official way (Dan. 2:6). God is the ultimate giver of honor or glory (Dan. 2:37; 5:18, 20). A grave sin for humans is to attribute to themselves any honor or splendor from their labor and work (Dan. 4:30[27]; 36[33]). The Son of Man in Daniel 7 is granted great glory with a kingdom and special recognition from God Himself (Dan. 7:14).

3368. יָקָר yāqār: An adjective meaning valuable, rare, precious. It carries the sense of being rare in some contexts (1 Sam. 3:1). It is used to describe precious and costly stones (2 Sam. 12:30; 1 Kgs. 10:2, 10, 11); the valuable foundation stones of buildings (1 Kgs. 5:17[31]); any expensive building stones or materials (1 Kgs. 7:9–11). It is used of the Lord's lovingkindness (*ḥesed* [2617]) to His people (Ps. 36:7[8]). Wisdom is asserted to be more valuable than jewels (Prov. 3:15). It is used as an abstract collective term for that which is valuable, noble, moral, ethical, or worthy compared to what is worthless (Jer. 15:19). In Job 31:26, it is used in a negative sense of the alluring attraction of the moon's splendor as an invitation to idolatry or astrology. The menacing figure in Daniel 11:38 casts his religious affection on the god of violence, honoring it. It may be used in Zechariah 14:6 meaning luminaries or lights, but the reading is uncertain, for it could mean cold.

3369. יָקוֹשׁ yāqōš: A verb meaning to snare. The word refers primarily to the snaring of animals, especially birds (Ps. 124:7; Eccl. 9:12). However, this word always refers figuratively to the catching of a person or people in an undesirable situation. The bait of these snares is people's desire for other gods (Deut. 7:25; Ps. 141:9, cf. Ps. 141:4). Pride makes persons susceptible to snares (Jer. 50:24[cf. Jer. 50:31, 32]) while humility (Prov. 6:2) and the help of God may deliver them. In two similar passages in Isaiah, Israel is snared by their rejection of God's word (Isa. 8:15; 28:13).

3370. יָקְשָׁן yoqšān: A proper noun designating Jokshan (Gen. 25:2, 3; 1 Chr. 1:32).

3371. יָקְתְאֵל ***yoqṯᵉʾēl:*** A proper noun designating Joktheel:

A. A location in Judah (Josh. 15:38).

B. A location in Idumea (2 Kgs. 14:7).

3372. יָרֵא ***yārēʾ:*** A verb meaning to fear, to respect, to reverence, to be afraid, to be awesome, to be feared, to make afraid, to frighten. The most common translations are to be afraid, to fear, to fear God. "The fear of the LORD is the beginning of knowledge" is a famous use of the noun (Prov. 1:7 NIV); the famous narrative of the near sacrifice of Isaac proved to God that Abraham feared Him above all (Gen. 22:12); people who feared God were considered faithful and trustworthy for such fear constrained them to believe and act morally (Ex. 18:21). The midwives of Pharaoh feared God and did not kill the newborn Hebrew males (Ex. 1:17, 21). The fear of the Lord was closely tied to keeping God's decrees and laws (Deut. 6:2); people who fear God delight in hearing of His deeds for His people (Ps. 66:16). The God of Israel was an object of respectful fear (Lev. 19:30; 26:2) for Obadiah and Hezekiah (1 Kgs. 18:3, 12; Jer. 26:19). In addition, because Israel feared and worshiped other gods, they were destroyed by Assyria (Judg. 6:10; 2 Kgs. 17:7, 35). They were to worship and fear only the Lord their God (Josh. 24:14). Israel had an unnecessary and unhealthy fear of the nations of Canaan (Deut. 7:19). The verb describes the fear of men: Jacob feared Esau, his brother (Gen. 32:7[8]); and the official in charge of Daniel feared the king (Dan. 1:10). In the sense of respectful fear, each person was to honor his mother and father (Lev. 19:3). As a stative verb, it describes a state of being or attitude, such as being afraid or fearful: a man afraid of war was to remove himself from the army of Israel (Deut. 20:3, 8; Judg. 7:3); as a result of rebellion, Adam and Eve were afraid before the Lord (Gen. 3:10).

In the passive form, the word expresses the idea of being feared, held in esteem: God was feared and awesome (Ex. 15:11; Ps. 130:4); His deeds were awe-inspiring (Deut. 10:21; 2 Sam. 7:23); the Cushites were an aggressive people feared by many (Isa. 18:2); even the threatening desert area was considered fearful or dreadful (Deut. 8:15).

The factitive or intensive form means to frighten or to impart fear: the wise woman of Tekoa was frightened by the people (2 Sam. 14:15); and the governor of Samaria, Sanballat, attempted to frighten Nehemiah so that he would not rebuild the wall of Jerusalem (Neh. 6:9).

3373. יָרֵא ***yārēʾ:*** An adjective meaning fearing, afraid. The Hebrew word is used when the author of Genesis speaks of Abraham fearing God because he did not hold back his only son (Gen. 22:12). Jacob asked God to save him from Esau, because he was afraid that Esau would attack him (Gen. 32:11[12]). Jethro told Moses to select as judges men who feared God (Ex. 18:21). Proverbs says that a woman who fears the Lord is to be praised (Prov. 31:30). Jeremiah told the Israelite army that God said not to fear the king of Babylon (Jer. 42:11). See the primary verb *yārēʼ* (3372).

3374. יִרְאָה yirʼāh: A feminine noun meaning fear. The word usually refers to the fear of God and is viewed as a positive quality. This fear acknowledges God's good intentions (Ex. 20:20). It will motivate and delight even the Messiah (Isa. 11:2, 3). This fear is produced by God's Word (Ps. 119:38; Prov. 2:5) and makes a person receptive to wisdom and knowledge (Prov. 1:7; 9:10). It is even identified with wisdom (Job 28:28; Prov. 15:33). The fear of the Lord may be lost by despair of one's own situation (Job 6:14) or envy of a sinner's (Prov. 23:17). This fear restrains people from sin (Gen. 20:11; Ex. 20:20; Neh. 5:9); gives confidence (Job 4:6; Prov. 14:26); helps rulers and causes judges to act justly (2 Sam. 23:3; 2 Chr. 19:9; Neh. 5:15); results in good sleep (Prov. 19:23); with humility, leads to riches, honor, and life (Prov. 22:4). The word also refers to the fear of briers and thorns (Isa. 7:25); and the fear of Israel that would fall on other nations (Deut. 2:25).

3375. יִרְאוֹן yirʼôn: A proper noun designating the location Iron (Josh. 19:38).

3376. יִרְאִיָּיה yirʼiyyāyh: A proper noun designating Irijah (Jer. 37:13, 14).

3377. *yārēb̲:* I. A proper noun designating the Assyrian king Jareb (KJV, NASB, Hos. 5:13; 10:6).

II. A masculine noun meaning great. It is used in the New International Version in Hosea 5:13; 10:6.

3378. יְרֻבַּעַל y^e^rubbaʻal: A proper noun designating Jerubbaal (Judg. 6:32; 7:1; 8:29, 35; 9:1, 2, 5, 16, 19, 24, 28, 57; 1 Sam. 12:11).

3379. יָרָבְעָם yārob̲ʻām: A proper noun designating Jeroboam:

A. Jeroboam I, son of Nebat, an Ephraimite, the first king of Israel. He unfortunately caused Israel to sin by building golden calves at Bethel and Dan, thus negating any possibility for true worship in northern Israel. His name possibly means "may he strive for the people [*ʻam* {5971}]." He reigned 930–910 B.C., seventeen years. He pulled the Israelites away from God's chosen Temple worship at Jerusalem and started them on the way to spiritual harlotry and corruption. He thereby became the model of rebellion and sin for all the kings of northern Israel (1 Kgs. 16:2; 22:52 [53]; 2 Kgs. 3:3). Even after a stern rebuke by a prophet, he continued to establish false priests and corrupt worship in Israel (1 Kgs. 13:33–34).

Although he had begun as one of Solomon's supporters and administrators he rebelled against the harsh policies of Solomon, but the Lord supported his move (1 Kgs. 11:29–33). Even before he was king, he had not followed the Lord in service and worship properly. The Lord gave Jeroboam the ten northern tribes to rule over, promising to prosper him if he served Him (1 Kgs. 11:34–39). Jeroboam was forced to seek asylum in Egypt with Pharaoh Shishak until Solomon died. When he returned, he tried to get Rehoboam to change Solomon's harsh policies toward Israel but to no avail (1 Kgs. 12:1–20).

B. A king of Israel, son of Jehoash. He reigned, including his coregency with Jehoash, for forty-one years (793–753 B.C.). He was a powerful political king who enlarged the borders of Israel (2 Kgs. 14:25) and brought on prosperous economic times but continued to lead Israel in the way of Jeroboam II, who made Israel sin. He ruled in his capital, Samaria, and delivered Israel from her enemies. Amos predicted his death and judgment from God (Amos 1:1; 7:9–11).

3380. יְרֻבֶּשֶׁת ***yᵉrubbešeṯ:*** A proper noun designating Jerubbesheth (2 Sam. 11:21).

3381. יָרַד ***yāraḏ:*** A verb meaning to go down, to descend. It is used of motion both literally or figuratively of someone or something coming down. It is used figuratively of the Lord's coming down to observe something or to make an announcement, e.g., the Tower of Babel or the announcement of the Exodus (Gen. 11:5, 7; Ex. 3:8; 19:11, 18). It is used of people coming down from a mountain (Ex. 19:14); of birds descending from the air (Hos. 7:12), etc. It is used to describe valleys sinking (Ps. 104:8). A crown may "come down" as a sign of humility and falling from power (Jer. 13:17, 18). It is used figuratively of going down to Sheol (Gen. 37:35); or of breaking into, going down, apart, into tears (cf. Ps. 119:136; Isa. 15:3). It depicts the falling or coming down of the pride of might (Ezek. 30:6). It describes fire from heaven or a pillar of fire coming down (Ex. 33:9; 2 Kgs. 1:10, 12, 14). It is used to depict the path of a boundary line descending down from one location to another (Josh. 16:3).

3382. יֶרֶד ***yereḏ:*** A proper noun designating Jared, Jered:

A. Father of Enoch (Gen. 5:15, 16, 18–20; 1 Chr. 1:2).

B. Son of Mered (1 Chr. 4:18).

3383. יַרְדֵּן ***yardēn:*** A proper noun designating Jordan, the most famous river in Israel. It is named over 180 times in the Old Testament and numerous times in the New Testament. Its name is appropriate (*yardēn*, "the one going down") for it becomes the lowest river on earth. After starting at an altitude of 300 feet at the foot of Mount Hermon it drops to 1, 200 feet below sea level at the Dead Sea. It runs through the Jordan Valley, a great archaeological fissure in the earth's surface averaging about ten miles in width. Its main riverbed runs 70 miles south from the Sea of Galilee to the northern part of the Dead Sea. It starts north of Hulah Lake north of the Sea of Galilee in the territory of ancient Dan and runs a meandering route to the Dead Sea. Four small tributaries join just north of Lake Hulah. Its meandering course makes it ca. 140 miles long between Galilee and the Dead Sea.

3384. יָרָה ***yārāh,*** יוֹרֶה ***yôreh,*** מוֹרֶה ***môreh,*** יָרָה ***yārah:*** A verb meaning to shoot, to throw, to pour. God hurled Pharaoh's army into the sea (Ex. 15:4); Joshua cast lots (Josh. 18:6); and God asked Job who laid the cornerstone of the earth (Job 38:6). This word is used often in reference to shooting with arrows, as Jonathan (1 Sam. 20:36); and those who killed some of David's men (2 Sam. 11:24). King Uzziah made machines that shot arrows (2 Chr. 26:15); and the wicked shot arrows at the upright of heart (Ps. 11:2; 64:4[5]). In the sense of throwing, people were overthrown (Num. 21:30); and Job said that God had thrown him in the mud (Job 30:19).

3385. יְרוּאֵל ***y^erû'ēl:*** A proper noun designating Jeruel (2 Chr. 20:16).

3386. יָרוֹחַ ***yārôah:*** A proper noun designating Jaroah (1 Chr. 5:14).

3387. יָרוֹק ***yārôq:*** A masculine noun referring to a green plant, a green thing, verdant plants. It denotes edible green plants sought out by mountain goats as food (Job 39:8).

3388. יְרוּשָׁה ***y^erûšāh,*** יְרוּשָׁא ***y^erûšā':*** A proper noun designating Jerusha (2 Kgs. 15:33; 2 Chr. 27:1).

3389. יְרוּשָׁלַםִ ***y^erûšālam,*** יְרוּשָׁלַיִם ***y^erûšālayim:*** A proper noun designating Jerusalem, the city mentioned most often in the Old Testament and Israel's capital and most important city. After Israel was split into two parts, it was the capital of Judah, both before and after the exile (Ezra 1—2). Its name appears in written texts outside the Bible and in the Bible that recall a city predating Israel or the Hebrews in Egypt, throughout the nineteenth and eighteenth centuries B.C. The name means "height or foundation of peace." An appropriate meaning for God's goal with and for His people is "shalom," "peace, well-being." The traditional meaning of the name is "city of peace." Jerusalem was the city of the Jebusites (Judg. 19:10) for many years. Even earlier, we hear of a Melchizedek, king of Salem (Jerusalem) functioning there (Gen. 14:14; Ps. 76:2[3]). It was to be a city of righteousness but became a city of oppression. It was to be a city of peace but was torn apart. It was to be "the Holy City" (Isa. 52:1), but it was corrupted (Ezek. 8). Its holiness was based on God's presence in its midst (1 Kgs. 6—8). God's presence over His ark (2 Sam. 6:1–15) sanctified the city, and His presence (Ex. 33:15–17) and made the people holy (Ezek.

48:35). Since David conquered the city, it could thereafter also be termed "the city of David" (2 Sam. 5:6–16). In 2 Samuel 5:7, it became associated with the designation "Zion," a powerful fortress or stronghold. It is called Ariel ("lion of God") several times (Isa. 29). Ezekiel saw a new purified and cleansed city and Temple in his vision and appropriately named the new city "the Lord Is There" (48:35). The Arabic name for the city is "the Holy (City," el-Quds). Mohammed visited it (by tradition). It was and is the holiest city of Jews and Christians and the third holiest of Islam. See 3390.

3390. יְרוּשְׁלֶם ***y^erûš^elem:*** A proper noun designating the Aramaic form of the name Jerusalem. See 3389. The city was rebuilt with a new Temple and walls by Ezra and Nehemiah. New residents inhabited the city, and Jerusalem again became the hoped-for "city of peace."

3391. יֶרַח ***yeraḥ:*** A masculine noun indicating month. It denotes a period of time, a month, and is probably a more recent word for month than *ḥōdeš*. It is a measure of time (Ex. 2:2; Job 39:2; Zech. 11:8). "A month of time (days)" is formed with *yāmîym* following *yeraḥ* (Deut. 21:13; 2 Kgs. 15:13).

3392. יֶרַח ***yeraḥ:*** A proper noun designating Jerah (Gen. 10:26; 1 Chr. 1:20).

3393. יְרַח ***y^eraḥ:*** An Aramaic masculine noun indicating a month. It depicts a period of time and may be used with a particular name attached to it (Ezra 6:15). There were twelve months in a normal year (Dan. 4:29[26]).

3394. יָרֵחַ ***yārēaḥ:*** A masculine noun meaning moon, the lesser light created by God (Gen. 1:16). It helped mark out the signs, seasons, festivals, days, and months of the year as well as giving light on the earth (Gen. 1:16; 37:9; Ps. 136:9; Isa. 3:10; Joel 2:10, 31[3:4]). It was often worshiped in error as a god (Job. 31:26).

3395. יְרֹחָם ***y^erōḥām:*** A proper noun designating Jeroham:

A. Father of Elkanah (1 Sam. 1:1; 1 Chr. 6:27[12], 34[19]).

B. A Benjamite (1 Chr. 8:27).

C. A Benjamite (1 Chr. 9:8).

D. A priest (1 Chr. 9:12).

E. A priest (Neh. 11:12).

F. Man from Gedor (1 Chr. 12:7).

G. A Danite (1 Chr. 27:22).

G. Father of Azariah (2 Chr. 23:1).

3396. יְרַחְמְאֵל ***y^eraḥm^e'ēl:*** A proper noun designating Jerahmeel:

A. A Judaite (1 Chr. 2:9, 25–27, 33, 42).

B. Son of Jehoiakim (Jer. 36:26).

C. A Levite (1 Chr. 24:29).

3397. יְרַחְמְאֵלִי ***y^eraḥm^e'ēliy:*** A proper noun designating Jerahmeelite (1 Sam. 27:10; 30:29).

3398. יַרְחָע ***yarḥā':*** A proper noun designating Jarha (1 Chr. 2:34, 35).

3399. יָרַט **yāraṭ:** A verb meaning to be reckless, to be contrary, to throw recklessly; steep, difficult. It carries the idea of tossing something or someone without care or concern into danger (Job 16:11). It refers to a difficult or steep road or path (Num. 22:32).

3400. יְרִיאֵל y^e**riy'ēl:** A proper noun designating Jeriel (1 Chr. 7:2).

3401. יָרִיב **yāriyḇ:** A masculine noun indicating an opponent, a contender. It refers to one's adversary in a legal way, a case, but in a more general way as well. God contends with and overcomes the adversaries of His people (Ps. 35:1; Isa. 49:25; Jer. 18:19).

3402. יָרִיב **yāriyḇ:** A proper noun designating. Jarib (1 Chr. 4:24; Ezra 8:16; 10:18).

3403. יְרִיבַי y^e**riyḇay:** A proper noun designating Jeribai (1 Chr. 11:46).

3404. יְרִיָּה y^e**riyyāh,** יְרִיָּהוּ y^e**riyyāhû:** A proper noun designating Jericho, a town northwest of the Dead Sea. It was the place Israel first conquered as they entered the land of Canaan (Josh. 4:19; 6:2).

3405. יְרֵחוֹ y^e**rēḥô,** יְרִיחוֹ y^e**riyḥô:** A proper noun designating Jericho, an important city in the Old Testament for it was the first city taken by the Israelites as they entered Canaan ca. 1250 (or 1406) B.C. Its defeat was to serve as a model of what God could and would do for His people if they were faithful to Him (Josh. 5—7). It was a great walled city that God delivered into the hands of His people by destroying its walls. Its destruction and capture stands in strong contrast to Israel's faithless failure at Ai (8:1–29). The biblical story stresses the success of capturing this great barrier to the Promised Land by Israel's failure to keep the Law. After its destruction, Joshua placed a curse on it (Josh. 6:26–27). It played a relatively subdued role in the history of Israel after Joshua's day.

The city is now reduced to an archaeological mound, Tell es-Sultan, covering about ten acres. It is located six miles west of the Jordan River, seven miles north of the Dead Sea. In antiquity it served as a major obstacle to invaders of Canaan and served as a sentinel to protect Canaan. It can be viewed from Mount Nebo (Deut. 34:1–4). It served as a well-armed, walled border city between Ephraim and Benjamin (Josh. 16:1, 7; 18:12, 21). Its fortress-like character and defenses would have been unassailable by Israel without the Lord's intervention. It is near a large spring that yields fresh water even today and in the past supported lush flora, including palm trees.

3406. יְרֵמוֹת y^e**rēmôṯ,** יְרִימוֹת y^e**riymôṯ:** A proper noun designating Jerimoth, Jeremoth:

A. Son of Bela (1 Chr. 7:7).

B. Son of Becher (1 Chr. 7:8).

C. Son of Beriah (1 Chr. 8:14).
D. A Benjamite (1 Chr. 12:5[6]).
E. Son of Mushi (1 Chr. 23:23; 24:30).
F. A Levite (1 Chr. 25:22).
G. Son of Heman (1 Chr. 25:4).
H. A Levite (2 Chr. 31:13).
I. A Naphtalite (1 Chr. 27:19).
J. Son of David (2 Chr. 11:18).
K. Descendant of Elam (Ezra 10:27).
L. Descendant of Zattu (Ezra 10:27).
M. A Jew (Ezra 10:29).
N. A covenanter in Ezra's day (also in Ezra 10:29).

3407. יְרִיעָה ***yeriy'āh:*** A feminine noun denoting a curtain, a hanging, a shelter. It is used to refer to the fabrics of goat hair used in the Tabernacle (Ex. 26:7; Num. 4:25), as well as other types of material (Ex. 26:1–10; 36:8–17). It is used of the tent that enclosed the ark of the Lord before the Temple was built (2 Sam. 7:2; 1 Chr. 17:1). Heaven is compared to a curtain stretched out by the Lord (Ps. 104:2). Many beautiful curtains or hangings adorned Solomon's palace (Song 1:5). It is used literally but with symbolic significance of wealth and riches of a nation (Jer. 4:20) or its dwellings in general (Hab. 3:7).

3408. יְרִיעוֹת ***yeriy'ôṯ:*** A proper noun designating Jerioth (1 Chr. 2:18).

3409. יָרֵךְ ***yārēḵ:*** A feminine singular noun meaning a thigh, a side, a base. The word is used of Jacob's thigh in the story of his wrestling with God (Gen. 32:25[26], 32[33]) and is most likely used euphemistically of genitals (Gen. 46:26; Ex. 1:5; Judg. 8:30). It is best translated side in the cultic language of Leviticus 1:11 and Numbers 3:29, 35. The Pentateuch also employs it with the meaning of a base (Ex. 25:31).

3410. יַרְכָה ***yarḵāh:*** An Aramaic feminine noun meaning thigh. It refers to the upper thigh, the area between the knee and the hip in humans, made of bronze in the statue envisioned by Nebuchadnezzar in his dream (Dan. 2:32).

3411. יַרְכָה ***yarḵāh,*** יְרֵכָה ***yerēḵāh:*** A feminine noun referring to a remote area, a border, the highest part, the far end. It refers to something toward the back or side, distant, far away. It refers to the part of Zebulun most distant from Jerusalem, toward the Mediterranean Sea and north (Gen. 49:13). It refers to the back or rear of a tent or building (Ex. 26:22, 23). It indicates the part of a mountain farthest away (Judg. 19:1, 18; 2 Kgs. 19:23); of the farthest part of the earth (Jer. 6:22; 25:32); of the northern territories (Isa. 14:13). It refers to the remotest parts of the pit in Sheol, its most remote areas (Isa. 14:15). It refers to the rear of an inner room, such as the Most Holy Place (1 Kgs. 6:16); the inner recesses of the hold of a ship (Jon. 1:5); a cave (1 Sam. 24:3[4]); or a house (Amos 6:10).

3412. יַרְמוּת ***yarmûṯ:*** A proper noun designating Jarmuth:

A. A Canaanite city in Judah (Josh. 10:3, 5, 23; 12:11; 15:35; Neh. 11:29).

B. A city in Issachar (Josh. 21:29).

3413. יְרֵמַי ***y^e^rēmay:*** A proper noun designating Jeremai (Ezra 10:33).

3414. יִרְמְיָה ***yirm^e^yāh,*** יִרְמְיָהוּ ***yirm^e^yāhû:*** A proper noun designating Jeremiah:

A. A great prophet of Judah who prophesied 626–586 B.C. The meaning of his name is difficult, but it seems to mean "the Lord raises up" or "the Lord loosens," which fits his task—to prophesy the rising and/or falling of nations. He was the son of Hilkiah, a priest (Jer. 1:1–6). He prophesied to Judah, warning them to submit to God's servant Nebuchadnezzar, the king of Babylon, or be taken into exile (Jer. 25:1–38). He prophesied the Lord's word under Josiah on through the debacle of Jehoiakim's reign and Zedekiah's reign, the last king of Judah. He continued to prophesy in a context in which he was harassed and threatened by both the people of Judah and their leaders and by false prophets, such as Hananiah (Jer. 26—28).

He counseled and prophesied submission to Babylon. He charged the people and nations with breaking the covenant (Jer. 11) but gave them a hope of a New Covenant (Jer. 31:31–34). He described the seventy-year exile they would undergo (Jer. 25) but also a glorious return (Jer. 25:12ff; 30–34).

He dictated a second version of his prophesies to Baruch his scribe after Jehoiakim burned an earlier draft (Jer. 36). He poured out oracles of judgment on the nations (Jer. 46—52), but he counseled Israel to circumcise their hearts (Jer. 4:4) to the Lord. His prophecies unheeded, he himself went into a forced exile in Egypt, where he uttered some concluding prophecies (Jer. 42—44).

B. The father of Hamutal, mother of Zedekiah (2 Kgs. 24:18).

C. A Gadite who joined David while he was fleeing Saul; he was an army official or commander (1 Chr. 12:10).

D. A family head of Manasseh who lived east of the Jordan River (1 Chr. 5:24).

E. A leader of a group of Benjamites who defected to David while he was fleeing Saul; they were superb warriors (1 Chr. 12:4).

F. A leader of a group of Gadites who followed David, not Saul; he was an army leader (1 Chr. 12:13).

G. A priest who returned under Zerubbabel and Jeshua. The head of a priestly family (Neh. 12:1).

H. A leader of Levites who supported Nehemiah's covenant of renewal; he helped in the dedication of the wall (Neh. 10:2).

3415. יָרַע ***yāra':*** A verb meaning to tremble. It occurs only in Isaiah 15:4. As the result of the sudden devastation of Moab, his (i.e., Moab's or possibly an individual soldier's) life (or soul) trembles. The sentence could refer to inner turmoil: his soul trembles within him; or it could refer to an objective sense that his prospects of surviving are shaky; his life trembles before him (cf. Deut. 28:66). Of course, both meanings could be true; both could even be implied.

3416. יִרְפְּאֵל ***yirpᵉ'ēl:*** A proper noun designating Irpeel (Josh. 18:27).

3417. יָרַק ***yāraq:*** A verb meaning to spit. It refers to ejecting saliva. In context it refers to spitting in someone's face as a sign of approbation or cursing (Num. 12:14; Deut. 25:9).

3418. יֶרֶק ***yereq:*** A masculine noun referring to herbs, grass, green plants, trees; something green. It refers to the greenery that sprouts from the earth and is edible by living creatures (Gen. 1:30). It defines grass as green (Ps. 37:2); or is used alone to mean grass (Num. 22:4). It was a desirable food for locusts (Ex. 10:15). Its withering was a sign of drought or scarcity (Isa. 15:6); and it was easily killed by the heat (Isa. 37:27).

3419. יָרָק ***yārāq:*** A masculine noun indicating green herbs, garden vegetables. It indicates a fresh growth of grass (Isa. 37:27) or herbs. It takes on the sense of green vegetables (Deut. 11:10; 1 Kgs. 21:2; 2 Kgs. 19:26; Isa. 37:27). It describes a meal of vegetables, considered a modest meal (Prov. 15:17).

3420. יֵרָקוֹן ***yērāqôn:*** A masculine noun referring to paleness, mildew. It was a disease attacking grains and forming rust or mildew on the grain. It was often considered a curse or pestilence from the Lord because of Israel's sin (1 Kgs. 8:37; 2 Chr. 6:28; Amos 4:9; Hag. 2:17). It was used of people's faces turning "green," that is, pale from fear of judgment (Jer. 30:6).

3421. יָרְקְעָם ***yorqᵒ'ām:*** A proper noun designating Jorkoam (1 Chr. 2:44).

3422. יְרַקְרַק ***yᵉraqraq:*** An adjective meaning greenish yellow. It indicates a sickening growth on leather or human skin, such as dry rot in a house (Lev. 13:49; 14:37). It has, however, a positive meaning in Psalm 68:13[14] where a dove's wings are gilded with a glistening or yellow-gold color.

3423. יָרַשׁ ***yāraš:*** A verb meaning to take possession, to inherit, to dispossess, to drive out. This term is sometimes used in the generic sense of inheriting possessions (Gen. 15:3, 4). But the word is used usually in connection with the idea of conquering a land. This verb is a theme of Deuteronomy in particular where God's promise of covenantal relationship is directly related to Israelite possession (and thereby foreign dispossession) of the land of Israel. This theme continued throughout Israel's history and prophetic message. Possession of the land was directly connected to a person's relationship with the Lord; breaking the covenantal relationship led to dispossession. But even in exile, Israelites awaited the day when they would repossess the land (Jer. 30:3).

3424. יְרֵשָׁה *yᵉrēšāh:* A feminine noun meaning possession, property. It refers to a nation and is used only once in the Hebrew Bible. In Numbers 24:18, Edom and Seir would become the possession of someone else (i.e., they would be defeated). This word comes from the root word *yārēš* (3423).

3425. יְרֻשָּׁה *yᵉruššāh:* A feminine noun meaning possession, inheritance. The word refers to an inheritance given, to a possession taken by force, or both. The word describes the land God gave to the Edomites, Moabites, and Ammonites (Deut. 2:5, 9, 19). The Edomites and Ammonites, however, seized land from other tribes (Deut. 2:12, 19). The Israelites, likewise, had to fight to gain their inheritance (Deut. 3:20; Josh. 12:6, 7). However, God later protected Israel's inheritance against the unjust claims of discontent Edomites, Moabites, and Ammonites (2 Chr. 20:11). The word is also used to refer to the possession of wives (Judg. 21:17) and land (Jer. 32:8), both of which still waited to be claimed (sinfully in the former passage). In Psalm 61:5[6], the word refers to God's presence as the inheritance of those who fear God.

3426. יֵשׁ *yēš:* A semiverbal expression meaning to be, to exist. This semiverb states that something exists. It should be compared to *'êyn* that asserts that something does not exist (Gen. 24:23; Ruth 3:12; Prov. 11:24). *Yēš* may be translated there is, there are. In contexts that call for a past-tense translation, it may be rendered there was, there were. Followed by the proposition *lᵉ*, to, attached to an object, the phrase shows possession (Gen. 33:9). Pronouns can be affixed to *yēš*, such as in the expression "he is" *yēšnô;* "you are" *yēšḵā* (Judg. 6:36). *Yēš* used with *lᵉ* attached to some nouns expresses possibility or ability (2 Chr. 25:9). Preceded by *'im* (518), if, the phrase translates as if . . . are, showing condition (Gen. 23:8). The interrogative *hᵃ* attached to the front of *yēš* indicates a question (Isa. 44:8). It is used with adverbs to show various locations: here is (1 Sam. 21:8[9]); under (1 Sam. 21:3[4]).

3427. יָשַׁב *yāšaḇ:* A verb meaning to sit, to dwell, to inhabit, to endure, to stay. Apparently, to sit is the root idea, and other meanings are derived from this. The subject of the verb may be God, human, animal (Jer. 50:39), or inanimate matter. The word sometimes emphasizes the location of persons, whether they were sitting under a tree (Judg. 6:11; 1 Kgs. 19:4) or in a house (2 Kgs. 6:32). It could also reflect a person's position: one sat as a judge (Prov. 20:8; Isa. 28:6); as a widow (Gen. 38:11); or on a throne as king (Ex. 12:29; 2 Kgs. 13:13). Sometimes it indicated one's companions; one sits with scoffers (Ps. 1:1); or with the elders of the land (Prov. 31:23). The word may signify "to dwell," either temporarily (Lev. 23:42) or in a permanent dwelling (Gen. 4:16; Zeph. 2:15). Sometimes the word means that an object or person stays in a limited area (Ex. 16:29); or abides for a period of time (Lev. 12:4, 5; 2 Sam. 6:11); or for eternity (Ps. 9:7[8]; 102:12[13]; 125:1). The years are even said to sit, that is, to pass (1 Kgs. 22:1).

3428. יֶשֶׁבְאָב ***yešeḇ'āḇ:*** A proper noun designating Jeshebeab (1 Chr. 24:13).

3429. יֹשֵׁב בַּשֶּׁבֶת ***yōšēḇ baššeḇeṯ:*** I. A phrase consisting of Qal active participle of *yāšaḇ* [3427] and *šeḇeṯ* [7675] with prefix preposition b^e and the definite article, it is translated who sat in the seat (NASB, NIV, 2 Sam. 23:8).

II. Josheb-Basshebeth (KJV, 2 Sam. 23:8).

3430. יִשְׁבִּי בְּנֹב ***yišbiy bᵉnōḇ:*** A proper noun designating Ishbi-Benob (2 Sam. 21:16).

3431. יִשְׁבָּח ***yišbāḥ:*** A proper noun designating Ishbah (1 Chr. 4:17).

3432. יָשׁוּבִי ***yāšûḇiy:*** A proper noun designating Jashubite (Num. 26:24).

3433. יָשֻׁבִי לָחֶם ***yāšuḇiy lāḥem:*** A proper noun designating Jashubi Lehem (1 Chr. 4:22).

3434. יָשָׁבְעָם ***yāšoḇʻām:*** A proper noun designating Jashobeam:

A. A military leader under David (1 Chr. 11:11).

B. A warrior under David, possibly the same person as in A above (1 Chr. 12:6[7]).

3435. יִשְׁבָּק ***yišbāq:*** A proper noun designating Ishbak (Gen. 25:2; 1 Chr. 1:32).

3436. יָשְׁבְּקָשָׁה ***yošbᵉqāšāh:*** A proper noun designating Joshbekashah (1 Chr. 25:4, 24).

3437. יָשׁוּב ***yāšûḇ:*** A proper noun designating Jashub:

A. Son of Issachar (Gen. 46:13; Num. 26:24; 1 Chr. 7:1).

B. Son of Bani (Ezra 10:29).

3438. יִשְׁוָה ***yišwāh:*** A proper noun designating Ishvah (Gen. 46:17; 1 Chr. 7:30).

3439. יְשׁוֹחָיָה ***yᵉšôḥāyāh:*** A proper noun designating Jeshohaiah (1 Chr. 4:36).

3440. יִשְׁוִי ***yišwiy:*** A proper noun designating Ishvi:

A. An Asherite (Gen. 46:17; Num. 26:44; 1 Chr. 7:30).

B. Son of Saul (1 Sam. 14:49).

3441. יִשְׁוִי ***yišwiy:*** A proper noun designating Ishvite, Jesuite (Num. 26:44).

3442. יֵשׁוּעַ ***yēšûaʻ:*** A proper noun designating Jeshua:

A. A priest (1 Chr. 24:11; Ezra 2:36; Neh. 7:39).

B. A Levite (2 Chr. 31:15; Ezra 2:40; Neh. 7:43).

C. A priest (Ezra 2:2; 3:2, 8, 9; 4:3; 10:18; Neh. 7:7; 12:1, 7, 10, 26). See also *yēšûaʿ* (3443).

D. Father of Jozabad (Ezra 8:33).

E. Son of Pahath-Moab (Ezra 2:6; Neh. 7:11).

F. Father of Ezer (Neh. 3:19). It may be the same as C above.

G. A Levite (Neh. 8:7; 9:4, 5; 12:8, 24).

H. Moses' successor (Neh. 8:17).

I. Son of Azaniah (Neh. 10:9[10].

J. A city in Benjamin (Neh. 11:26).

3443. יֵשׁוּעַ ***yēšûaʿ:*** An Aramaic proper noun designating Jeshua (Ezra 5:2). It corresponds to the Hebrew 3442,C.

3444. יְשׁוּעָה ***y^ešûʿāh:*** A feminine noun meaning salvation, deliverance, help, victory, prosperity. The primary meaning is to rescue from distress or danger. It is used to signify help given by other human beings (1 Sam. 14:45; 2 Sam. 10:11); help or security offered by fortified walls, delivering in the sense of preventing what would have happened if the walls were not there (Isa. 26:1); one's welfare and safety (Job 30:15); salvation by God, with reference to being rescued by Him from physical harm (Ex. 14:13; 2 Chr. 20:17); being rescued from the punishment due for sin (Ps. 70:4[5]; Isa. 33:6; 49:6; 52:7). Used in the plural, it signifies works of help (Ps. 44:4[5]; 74:12); and God's salvation (2 Sam. 22:51; Ps. 42:5[6]; 116:13).

3445. יֶשַׁח ***yešaḥ:*** A masculine noun denoting emptiness; dung (?). It is a strong word used to illustrate the corrupt, immoral condition of God's people because of their failure to be His moral, ethical, just people. Their excrement will be among them (Mic. 6:14; KJV, casting down; NASB, vileness; NIV, empty). The exact meaning is not yet clear, but its sense is evident in the context.

3446. יִשְׂחָק ***yiśḥāq:*** A proper noun designating Isaac (Ps. 105:9; Jer. 33:26; Amos 7:9, 16). It is a a variant spelling of *yiṣḥāq* (3327).

3447. יָשַׁט ***yāšaṭ:*** A verb indicating to extend, to hold out. It refers to an act of granting something to a person in a formal royal setting by handing it to the one requesting it (Esth. 4:11; 5:2; 8:4).

3448. יִשַׁי ***yišay***, אִישַׁי ***'iyšay:*** A proper noun designating Jesse, an Ephrathite from Bethlehem in Judah; the father of king David; his father was Obed (Ruth 4:21–22). He helped Samuel find David so he could anoint him (1 Sam. 16). He was an old man during Saul's reign.

3449. יִשִּׁיָּהוּ ***yiššiyyāhû***, יִשִּׁיָּה ***yiššiyyāh:*** A proper noun designating Isshiah:

A. One of David's mighty men (1 Chr. 12:6[7]).

B. A descendant of Issachar (1 Chr. 7:3).

C. A Levite (1 Chr. 23:20; 24:25).

D. A Levite (1 Chr. 24:21).

E. A postexilic Jew (Ezra 10:31).

3450. יְשִׂמִאֵל ***y^{e}śiymi'ēl:*** A proper noun designating Jesimiel (1 Chr. 4:36).

3451. יְשִׁימָה ***y^{e}šiymāh:*** A feminine noun meaning desolation. It occurs in Psalm 55:15[16] in an imprecatory sense, where desolation was to be the ultimate end of a wicked and false person. As such, it links with the developed wisdom theme of wickedness as consummating in nothingness. Here the word invoked the result of falsity and idolatry that the true believer would escape by steadfast loyalty to God (cf. Ps. 55:16, 17, 22). Ezekiel used the verb from which this word is derived (*yāšam*, 3456) several times in describing the habitation of Israel due to idolatry and unbelief (Ezek. 6:6; 12:19; 19:7). The one who would falsely break the covenant (Ps. 55:20[21], 21[22]) could expect desolation–a message Ezekiel preached to the people of the covenant.

3452. יְשִׁימוֹן, יְשִׁמוֹן ***y^{e}šiymôn, y^{e}šimôn:*** I. A masculine proper noun denoting Jeshimon. It is used in two ways. First, it may refer to a desert or wilderness (see II below), or it may refer to a location or territory called Jeshimon. Some translations render it Jeshimon (KJV, Num. 21:20; 23:28; 1 Sam. 23:19, 24; 26:1, 3).

II. A masculine common noun referring to a desert, a wilderness, a wasteland. See also I above. It is taken as referring to a desert or wasteland by some translators (NASB, NIV, Num. 21:20; 23:28). In some contexts, its use to refer to a desert or wilderness is accepted by all translators (Deut. 32:10; Ps. 68:7[8]; 78:40; 106:14; 107:4; Isa. 43:19, 20).

3453. יָשִׁישׁ ***yāšiyš:*** An adjective meaning aged. This word is found only in Job and referred to people who had gray hair; they were considered old or aged (Job 15:10; 32:6). It referred to a class of people, such as modern-day senior citizens (Job 12:12; 29:8).

3454. יְשִׁישַׁי ***y^{e}šiyšay:*** A proper noun designating Jeshishai (1 Chr. 5:14).

3455. יָשַׂם ***yāśam:*** A verb meaning to put, to place. It refers to the process of placing and arranging a person in a coffin (Gen. 50:26). Others prefer the reading from the verb with the same meaning, *siym* (7760).

3456. יָשַׁם ***yāšam:*** A verb meaning to be desolate, to lie waste. In most cases, the people affected were afraid famine would cause the land to lie waste. During the famine, the Egyptians asked Joseph to buy them and their land so they would not die and their land become desolate (Gen. 47:19). The Israelites were commanded to tell the people of Canaan that they were to soon experience the fear and trembling of the Lord that would cause them to leave their land (Ezek. 12:19).

3457. יִשְׁמָא ***yišmā':*** A proper noun designating Ishma (1 Chr. 4:3).

3458. יִשְׁמָעֵאל ***yišmā'ē'l:*** A proper noun designating Ishmael:

A. A son of Abraham by Hagar, his Egyptian concubine. His name means "God hears." He was not a city dweller but preferred the free range of the deserts (Gen. 16:11). He became an outdoors person, roamed freely in the desert wilderness, and produced a great progeny like him (Gen. 16:12). He was born when Abraham was eighty-six years old. He is considered to be the ancestor of many Arabs (Gen. 25:12–18).

B. A Judahite who was the father of Zebadiah, the leader of Judah in Jehoshaphat's day (2 Chr. 19:8–11).

C. A son of Azel, the head of a family in Jerusalem (1 Chr. 8:38).

D. The son of Jehohanan, a leader of a unit of one hundred (2 Chr. 23:1).

E. A descendant of Pashur who intermarried with the people of the land (Ezra 10:22).

F. He was of the line of David and led an uprising that assassinated Gedeliah at Mizpah. He wanted to be king himself and believed that the Jews should not submit to the Babylonians (Jer. 41:1–3).

3459. יִשְׁמְעֵאלִי ***yišm^e'ē'liy:*** A proper noun designating Ishmaelite (Gen. 37:25, 27, 28; 39:1; Judg. 8:24; 1 Chr. 2:17; 27:30; Ps. 83:6[7]).

3460. יִשְׁמַעְיָה ***yišma'yāh,*** יִשְׁמַעְיָהוּ ***yišma'yāhû:*** A proper noun designating Ishmaiah:

A. A Gibeonite (1 Chr. 12:4).

B. Man of Zebulun (1 Chr. 27:19).

3461. יִשְׁמְרַי ***yišm^{e}ray:*** A proper noun designating Ishmerai (1 Chr. 8:18).

3462. יָשֵׁן ***yāšēn:*** I. A verb meaning to fall asleep, to sleep. It indicates the process of going into a sleeping state (Gen. 2:21). It indicates the state of being asleep without fear or danger (Ezek. 34:25). It is used as a euphemism for one who is dead (Job 3:13). It is used of God's failure to act or inactivity on behalf of His people (Ps. 44:23[24]). But, in fact, the psalmist asserts that God, who watches over His people, does not sleep (Ps. 121:4). In its intensive form, it means to make someone go to sleep (Judg. 16:19), as when Delilah caused Samson to fall asleep.

II. A verb meaning to become old, to be chronic, to linger. It presents the concept of a long duration of time in general (Deut. 4:25); or for a specific situation (Lev. 26:10); or disease (Lev. 13:11).

3463. יָשֵׁן ***yāšēn:*** An adjective designating someone as sleeping. It refers to persons in a sleeping state or condition (1 Sam. 26:7, 12; 1 Kgs. 3:20); of God seemingly sleeping, being inactive (Ps. 78:65). It is used mockingly to describe the god Baal sleeping on the job (1 Kgs. 18:27). It describes those dead in the ground (Dan. 12:2). It has the sense of smoldering or active human passion that has been inordinately aroused (Hos. 7:6; others prefer to read the verb, I above, here).

3464. יָשֵׁן ***yāšēn:*** A proper noun designating Jashen (2 Sam. 23:32).

3465. יָשָׁן ***yāšān:*** An adjective meaning old, of last year's harvest. It has the basic sense of that which is seasoned or has been around for a long time, aged. It refers to crops from a previous year (Lev. 25:22; 26:10); or things that have been around a long time, e.g., an old gate or old pool (Neh. 3:6; 12:39; Isa. 22:11); old as opposed to new. Fruit and vegetables can be old as opposed to new (Song 7:13[14]).

3466. יְשָׁנָה ***y^{e}šānāh:*** A proper noun designating Jeshanah (2 Chr. 13:19).

3467. יָשַׁע ***yāša':*** A verb meaning to save, to help, to deliver, to defend. The underlying idea of this verb is bringing to a place of safety or broad pasture as opposed to a narrow strait, symbolic of distress and danger. The word conveys the notion of deliverance from tribulation (Judg. 10:13, 14); deliverance from certain death (Ps. 22:21[22]); rescue from one's enemies (Deut. 28:31; Judg. 6:14); victory in time of war (1 Sam. 14:6); the protective duty of a shepherd (Ezek. 34:22; cf. Judg. 10:1); avenging wrongs (1 Sam. 25:33); compassionate aid in a time of need (2 Kgs. 6:26, 27; Ps. 12:1[2]); the salvation that only comes from God (Isa. 33:22; Zeph. 3:17).

3468. יֵשַׁע ***yēša'***, יֶשַׁע ***yeša':*** A masculine noun meaning deliverance, rescue, liberty, welfare, salvation. David used the word salvation to describe the hope and welfare he had in the midst of strife due to his covenant with God (2 Sam. 23:5). God saves communities, as when He promised relief to Jerusalem (Isa. 62:11) as well as individuals (see Mic. 7:7).

3469. יִשְׁעִי ***yiš'iy:*** A proper noun designating Ishi:

A. A descendant of Jerahmeel (1 Chr. 2:31).

B. A Manassite (1 Chr. 5:24).

C. A Judaite (1 Chr. 4:20).

D. A Simeonite (1 Chr. 4:42).

3470. יְשַׁעְיָה ***y^{e}ša'yāh,*** יְשַׁעְיָהוּ ***y^{e}ša'yāhû:*** A proper noun designating Isaiah:

A. The prophet Isaiah who prophesied during the reigns of Uzziah, Jotham, Ahaz, and Hezekiah in Judah (ca. 792–686 B.C.) (Isa. 1:1; see also 2 Kgs. 19:2, 5, 6, 20; 20:1, 4, 7–9, 11, 14, 16, 19; 2 Chr. 26:22; 32:20, 32). He was a prophet to the kingdom of Judah. His name means "the Lord is salvation." His father was Amoz who lived in Jerusalem (Isa. 37:2). He was an astute observer of the world of his day and moved easily and boldly among the rulers of Judah, both civil and religious. Many scholars conclude that he was of the line of David, of royal descent.

His call occurred dramatically in the year of Uzziah's death (Isa. 6:1; 640 B.C.). His last historical appearance was probably in ca. 701 B.C. at the time of Sennacherib's threatened siege of Jerusalem (2 Kgs. 19–20; 37–38). He may have suffered a violent death (cf. Heb. 11:37). He was married (Isa. 7:3) and had two sons whose names served as prophetic object lessons: Shear-Jashub, "a remnant will return" and Maher-Shalal-Hash-Baz, "hasten booty, speed the loot: (Isa. 8:1–10). He warned kings, rebuked kings, and comforted kings as the Lord instructed him (Isa. 7:1–16; 36–37, 38–39). He is the prophet most cited, alluded to, or echoed in the New Testament.

B. A son of Jeduthun who took part in Temple worship, including prophecy and worship (1 Chr. 25:3).

C. A Levite, son of Rehabiah, who helped administer Temple treasuries (1 Chr. 26:25).

D. A descendant of Hananiah of the royal line of Judah (1 Chr. 3:21).

E. A descendant of Elam, a family head in Judah (Ezra 8:7).

F. A descendant of Merari of the tribe of Levi. He returned under Ezra as a Temple servant (Ezra 8:19).

G. A new Benjamite resident of Jerusalem after the exile. His son was Ithiel (Neh. 11:7).

3471. יָשְׁפֵה yāš^{e}pēh: A masculine noun denoting a jasper (stone). It was a precious stone. In context it was mounted on the breastpiece of the high priest with other stones (Ex. 28:20; 39:13). It was part of the symbolic covering of the historical king of Tyre who served also as a symbol of Lucifer (Ezek. 28:13).

3472. יִשְׁפָּה yišpāh: A proper noun designating Ishpah (1 Chr. 8:16).

3473. יִשְׁפָּן yišpān: A proper noun designating Ishpan (1 Chr. 8:22).

3474. יָשַׁר yāšar: A verb meaning to be straight, to be upright, to be smooth, to be pleasing. When it means straight, it applies in a physical and an ethical sense as in straightforward. Therefore, this word can be used to refer to a path (1 Sam. 6:12); water (2 Chr. 32:30); the commands of God (Ps. 119:128); or of a person (Hab. 2:4). This word is also used to mean pleasing, as Samson found a Philistine woman pleasing to him (Judg. 14:7); but the cities that Solomon gave to Hiram were not pleasing (1 Kgs. 9:12). It can also mean to make (or be) smooth or even, as with gold (1 Kgs. 6:35); or a level road (Isa. 40:3).

3475. יֵשֶׁר yēšer: A proper noun designating Jesher (1 Chr. 2:18).

3476. יֹשֶׁר yōšer: A masculine noun meaning straightness or uprightness, equity. The Old Testament often talks of two paths in life and warns people to stay on the straight path and not to stray onto the crooked path (Prov. 2:13). David was praised for walking in an upright manner before the Lord (1 Kgs. 9:4). Uprightness was also praised as a good quality to possess (Prov. 17:26). The word can also designate virtuous words that one speaks (Job 6:25). Another meaning less common is related to equity: one should give to another what is due to him or her (Prov. 11:24).

3477. יָשָׁר *yāšār:* An adjective meaning straight, just, right. This word can refer to something physical, such as a path (Ps. 107:7; Isa. 26:7), but it more often means right in an ethical or an emotional sense, as agreeable or pleasing. Examples of this include what is right in God's eyes (Ex. 15:26; 1 Kgs. 11:33, 38; 2 Kgs. 10:30); or in the eyes of people (Prov. 12:15; Jer. 40:5). It also means upright, such as God (Ps. 25:8); and His ways (Hos. 14:9[10]). Some people were considered upright, such as David (1 Sam. 29:6); and Job (Job 1:1). An ancient history book was called the book of Jashar or the book of the Upright (Josh. 10:13; 2 Sam. 1:18). See the Hebrew root *yāšar* (3474).

3478. יִשְׂרָאֵל *yiśrā'ēl:* A proper noun designating Israel:

A. The name given to Jacob after he successfully wrestled with the messenger of God (Gen. 32:28). The name means "he (who) struggles with God." It was used of the descendants of Jacob who went to Egypt (70 in all) but was applied to the nation that developed from those descendants (Ex. 1:1, 7). This name is explained again in Genesis 35:10. The name Jacob had been interpreted in context as well (Gen. 25:26), "he deceives."

B. The persons descended from Jacob who was renamed Israel (Gen. 35:10; see A above). His descendants became known as Israel (Ex. 1:1, 7). They were known as the "twelve tribes of Israel [Jacob]" (Gen. 49:7, 16, 28). The Lord became "the Rock of Israel (Gen. 49:24).

The land of Israel was ideally the territory first described to Abraham. It stretched from the river of Egypt (El-Arish) to the great Euphrates River and encompassed the territory of the Kenites, Kenizzites, Kadmonites, Hittites, Perizzites, Rephaites, Amorites, Canaanites, Girgashites, and Jebusites (Gen. 15:17–21; cf. also Gen. 10:15–18). The full expanse of this territory was occupied during the reign of David and Solomon and approached during the time of Israel-Judah under the respective contemporary reigns of Jeroboam II in Israel and Azariah (Uzziah) in Judah. Most often, however, the land of Israel in the Old Testament is designated as the territory from Dan (north) to Beersheba (south). After Israel divided into two kingdoms in 930 B.C., the name refers still to all of Israel but most often to northern Israel. After the return from exile in 538 B.C., the term is used of the whole restored community again regularly.

3479. יִשְׂרָאֵל yiśra'ēl: A proper noun designating the Aramaic spelling of Israel. See 3478,B. It occurs only in the Aramaic portions of Ezra.

3480. יְשַׂרְאֵלָה y^eśar'ēlāh: A proper noun designating Jesarela (1 Chr. 25:14).

3481. יִשְׂרְאֵלִי yiśr^e'ēliy: A proper noun designating Israelite (Lev. 24:10; 2 Sam 17:25).

3482. יִשְׂרְאֵלִית yiśr^e'ēliyṯ: A proper noun designating an Israelitess (Lev. 24:10, 11).

3483. יִשְׁרָה yišrāh: A feminine noun meaning uprightness. The word is derived from *yāšar* (3474). It occurs only in 1 Kings 3:6 where Solomon's prayer referred to the uprightness of David's heart that was rewarded with lovingkindness, especially the lovingkindness of having his son reign after him. David's life ruled out any meaning of sinlessness and pointed to repentance, faith, and knowledge of God as central to his uprightness (cf. Rom. 4:6–8).

3484. יְשֻׁרוּן y^ešurûn: A proper noun designating Jeshurun, Israel, and meaning "the upright one." It is found in poetry in the Song of Moses (Deut. 32:15), the blessings of Moses (Deut. 33:5, 26), and the prophecy of Isaiah (Isa. 44:2). Hence, it is often termed the "poetic" name of Israel. It is clearly parallel with Jacob in Isaiah's prophecy. It seems to be used as an ideal designation of Israel.

3485. יִשָּׂשכָר yiśśaśḵār: A proper noun designating Issachar:

A. Jacob's fifth son by Leah (Gen. 30:18; 35:23). His name means "a man of hire," i.e., "a hired man." Jacob's prophetic assertion about Issachar that he was a beast of burden between two saddle bags (NIV) or burdens (KJV) supports this view of the name. Issachar is often paired with Zebulun (Gen. 49:14; Deut. 33:18, 19) and his wealth with maritime riches. He had four sons (1 Chr. 7:1).

B. The descendants of Issachar (see A above). The growth of the tribe is indicated in 1 Chronicles 7:1–5. During David's reign, the tribe provided many soldiers and leading commanders. Deborah was from Issachar's tribe (Judg. 5:1–15). Tola, a minor judge, was from Issachar (Judg. 10:1). King Baasha in Israel was from this tribe (1 Kgs. 15:27). The tribe was located among several other tribes: Zebulon and Manasseh, west; Naphtali, north; Manasseh, south; Gad, east. The men of Issachar were noted for their understanding and action by the time of David (1 Chr. 12:32). Issachar was allotted a place in Ezekiel's vision of a new Temple and a New Jerusalem (Ezek. 48:25–33).

C. A son of Obed-Edom. He served as a gatekeeper at the Temple and city (1 Chr. 26:5).

3486. יָשֵׁשׁ yāšēš: An adjective meaning aged or decrepit. It is used only with the word *zāqēn* (2204). When King Zedekiah rebelled, the Lord caused the king of the Chaldeans to destroy Jerusalem and all the people in it. The Chaldean king showed no mercy for any of the people, including the aged or old (2 Chr. 36:17).

3487. יָת ***yāṯ:*** An Aramaic particle serving as the indicator of the accusative direct object in a sentence. It is not translated into English but helps to locate and define the direct object (Dan. 3:12). In its only use, it refers to the three Hebrews appointed by Nebuchadnezzar.

3488. יְתִב ***y***$^{\boldsymbol{e}}$***ṯiḇ:*** An Aramaic verb meaning to sit, to dwell, to cause to dwell. It is used of taking a seat, sitting down (Dan. 7:9, 10, 26). It also has the sense of dwelling or causing to dwell or settle somewhere (Ezra 4:10). It can be translated to live in an area (Ezra 4:17).

3489. יָתֵד ***yaṯēḏ:*** A feminine noun denoting a pin, a peg, a stake. It is used of a wooden peg or nail (Judg. 4:21, 22; 5:26). It could be driven into a wall for hanging something on it (Isa. 22:23). It refers to a tool used for digging a hole in the ground (Deut. 23:13[14]); or a tool for working on a loom (Judg. 16:14). Metal pegs for use in the Tabernacle are also a part of its range of meaning (Ex. 27:19). It is used metaphorically as a means of having a share in the Lord's plans (Ezra 9:8); or to symbolize a leader who will bring stability to God's people (Zech. 10:4).

3490. יָתוֹם ***yāṯôm:*** A masculine noun meaning orphan, a fatherless child. It refers to children who had no fathers or parental support group in Israel. They, along with widows, the poor, and the oppressed, were of special concern to the Lord (Ex. 22:22 [21], 24[23]; Deut. 16:11, 14; 24:17; 26:12; Ps. 10:18; 68:5[6]; 146:9; Hos. 14:3[4]). God works on their behalf (Deut. 10:18); and those who oppress them are under judgment (Deut. 27:19; Mal. 3:5). Job was concerned to care for them (Job 29:12; 31:17, 21). Israel as a whole did not care for them sufficiently (Job 24:3, 9; Ps. 94:6; Isa. 1:23; Jer. 5:28; Ezek. 22:7).

3491. יְתוּר ***y***$^{\boldsymbol{e}}$***ṯûr:*** A masculine noun indicating roaming, an area of ranging. It is used of an area where the wild donkey runs loose, searching for his pasture, as well as the act of roaming itself (Job 39:8).

3492. יַתִּיר ***yattiyr,*** יַתִּר ***yattir:*** A proper noun designating Jattir (Josh. 15:48; 21:14; 1 Sam. 30:27; 1 Chr. 6:57[42]).

3493. יַתִּיר ***yattiyr:*** An Aramaic adjective designating something as excellent, outstanding. Its basic sense is excellence, superiority. It refers to the splendor of the statue in Daniel 2:31 as extraordinary, outstanding. It has the sense of very or extremely (Dan. 3:22; 7:7, 19); surpassing, exceeding (Dan. 4:36[33]); special or excellent (Dan. 5:12, 14). Daniel had an excellent spirit (Dan. 6:3[4]) and possessed superb wisdom.

3494. יִתְלָה ***yiṯlāh:*** A proper noun designating Ithlah (Josh. 19:42).

3495. יִתְמָה ***yiṯmāh:*** A proper noun designating Ithmah (1 Chr. 11:46).

3496. יַתְנִיאֵל ***yaṯniy'ēl:*** A proper noun designating Jathniel (1 Chr. 26:2).

3497. יִתְנָן ***yiṯnān:*** A proper noun designating Ithnan (Josh. 15:23).

3498. יָתַר ***yāṯar:*** A verb meaning to be left over, to remain. Jacob was left alone after he sent his family across the river (Gen. 32:24[25]); nothing remained after the locusts came (Ex. 10:15); Absalom was thought to have killed all the king's sons with not one remaining (2 Sam. 13:30); Isaiah prophesied to Hezekiah that nothing would be left of his kingdom (2 Kgs. 20:17); God said that when He destroyed Judah, He would leave a remnant (Ezek. 6:8).

3499. יֶתֶר ***yeṯer:*** A masculine noun meaning remainder, the rest, abundance, excellence, a cord. The word refers to that which is left over: the produce of a field not used by people (and left for beasts) (Ex. 23:11); the years of a life span not yet finished (Isa. 38:10); temple vessels besides the ones specifically mentioned (Jer. 27:19). The word also signifies abundance as what was left beyond the necessities of life (Job 22:20; Ps. 17:14). In Genesis 49:3, the word means excellence, referring to the extra honor and power accorded to the firstborn. The word may refer to the cord of a tent or to a bowstring (Job 30:11; Ps. 11:2), both apparently derived from the idea of a string hanging over something, being extra. The word may be used adverbially to mean abundantly or exceedingly (Dan. 8:9).

3500. יֶתֶר ***yeṯer:*** A proper noun designating Jethro, Jether:

A. Jethro, the father of Zipporah, Moses' wife taken in Midian (Ex. 4:18). He is also called Reuel (Ex. 3:18) and functioned as a Midianite priest—but even more importantly as Moses' father-in-law (Ex. 3; 4; 18). See 3503.

B. Jether, the oldest son of the great judge Gideon. He was only a young man in the biblical text and was afraid to kill the Midianite leaders, Zebah and Zalmunna (Judg. 8:18–21).

C. Jether, the father of Amasa. Amasa served for a while as David's commander of his army. He was murdered by Joab (1 Kgs. 2:32).

D. Jether, son of Jada. He had no descendants and was in the line of Judah through Hegron (1 Chr. 2:32).

E. Jether, from Judah and the son of a clan head, Ezrah (1 Chr.4:17).

F. Jether, an Asherite and a head of a clan family (1 Chr. 7:38).

3501. יִתְרָא ***yiṯrā':*** A proper noun designating Ithra, Jether (2 Sam. 17:25).

3502. יִתְרָה ***yiṯrāh:*** A feminine noun indicating abundance, wealth. It refers to the excess or savings which have been saved up (Isa. 15:7; Jer. 48:36).

3503. יִתְרוֹ ***yiṯrô:*** A proper noun designating Jethro, the father-in-law of Moses. He was a Midianite priest. He wisely advised Moses about how to structure his administration of justice to the people (Ex. 18). See 3500,A.

3504. יִתְרוֹן ***yiṯrôn:*** A feminine noun meaning advantage, profit, gain. It is found only in Ecclesiastes. It is used of the benefit or gain that could be the result of one's labor or work (Eccl. 1:3; 5:16[15], 10:11); or knowledge (7:12). Wisdom does prove to have some benefit or advantage for attaining success (Eccl. 10:10). Under the sun, that is, in this life apart from God, there is no gain (Eccl. 2:11). All is vanity.

3505. יִתְרִי ***yiṯriy:*** A proper noun designating Ithrite (2 Sam. 23:38; 1 Chr. 2:53; 11:40).

3506. יִתְרָן ***yiṯrān:*** A proper noun designating Ithran:

A. An Edomite (Gen. 36:26; 1 Chr. 1:41).

B. An Asherite (1 Chr. 7:37).

3507. יִתְרְעָם ***yiṯrᵉʿām:*** A proper noun designating Ithream (2 Sam. 3:5; 1 Chr. 3:3).

3508. יֹתֶרֶת ***yōṯereṯ:*** A feminine noun referring to an appendage, lobes of the liver. It designates the lobes of the liver in cattle, sheep, and goats (not humans) (Ex. 29:13, 22; Lev. 3:4, 10, 15; 4:9; 7:4; 8:16, 25; 9:10, 19). All references are related to sacrifices in Israel.

3509. יְתֵת ***yᵉṯēṯ:*** A proper noun designating Jetheh (Gen. 36:40; 1 Chr. 1:51).

כ Kaph

3510. כָּאַב kāʾaḇ: A verb indicating to be sore, to be in pain, to grieve. It asserts being in physical pain (Gen. 34:25; Job 14:22) but also is used of the distress of affliction as pain (Ps. 69:29[30]). The heart suffers emotional pain (Prov. 14:13). In its causal stem, it can express acts of God or people causing pain or distress (Job 5:18; Ezek. 13:22; 28:24). In 2 Kings 3:19 in a context describing destructive acts, it describes ruining a field by scattering stones in it.

3511. כְּאֵב k^eʾēḇ: A masculine noun meaning pain, anguish, sorrow. It is used of Job's distress and pain from his calamities and disease (Job 2:13; 16:6). It has the sense of distress or perhaps despair for the psalmist (Ps. 39:2[3]); and those under God's judgment (Isa. 17:11; 65:14, "from a painful heart"; Jer. 15:18).

3512. כָּאָה kāʾāh: A verb meaning to be brokenhearted, disheartened. The word describes a feeling of depression or discouragement, a loss of hope. It describes the discouraged or depressed reaction of a person toward a superior foe who cannot be defeated (Dan. 11:30). It refers to the act of discouraging or disheartening the righteous (Ezek. 13:22); as well as those already despondent (Ps. 109:16).

3513. כָּבֵד kāḇēḏ: A verb meaning to weigh heavily, to be heavy, to be honored, to be made heavy, to get honor, to make dull, to let weigh down, to harden, to multiply.

In the simple form, the verb means to be heavy, to weigh heavily, to be honored. The hands of both humans and God were described metaphorically as heavy, that is, powerful. The heavy hand of Joseph dispossessed the Amorites of their land, and the Lord's hand was heavy against the city of Ashdod (i.e., He brought devastation upon it [1 Sam. 5:6]). The Hebrew word refers to mere physical weight as well; the description of Absalom's hair is a celebrated example of this use (2 Sam. 14:26). The labor of the Israelites in Egypt became burdensome (Ex. 5:9). The word's metaphorical use extended to the description of failing senses, such as Jacob's eyes (Israel's) in old age (Gen. 48:10; Isa. 59:1). This is one of three words describing the dulling or hardening of Pharaoh's heart in the plagues. Pharaoh's heart became dull, obstinate, heavy (Ex. 9:7) to the Lord's warnings. Yet the word also describes honor being bestowed on someone (Job 14:21; Isa. 66:5).

In the passive form, the word expresses the idea of enjoying honor or glory. It describes the smug self-glorification of Amaziah (2 Sam. 6:22; 2 Kgs. 14:10); God's honoring Himself through the defeat of Pharaoh is also expressed by this stem (Ex. 14:4, 17, 18; Isa. 26:15). In the factitive or intensive stem, the verb expresses the idea of causing or making something unfeeling (1 Sam. 6:6) but also the act of honoring people or God (Judg. 9:9; Ps. 22:23[24]). God's people also honor some things: the Sabbath (Isa. 58:13); Jerusalem; God's sanctuary (Isa. 60:13); wisdom (Prov. 4:8). The causative form carries the ideas of making something heavy (1 Kgs. 12:10; Isa. 47:6); or dull and heavy, especially Pharaoh's heart (Ex. 8:15[11], 32[28]; 9:34). In two places, the word means to make into many or multiply (Jer. 30:19); as when God's people multiplied (cf. 2 Chr. 25:19). It is used once in the reflexive form meaning to act deceptively (i.e., to pretend something [Prov. 12:9]).

3514. כֹּבֶד *kōbed:* A masculine noun indicating weight, thickness, heaviness. It basically is what is weighty, heavy, a burden: It is used figuratively of the press or load weighing on a person in battle (Isa. 21:15). It has the sense of density or thickness, e.g., clouds (Isa. 30:27); or a dense mass of corpses from battle (Nah. 3:3). It refers to the actual weight of something, e.g., a stone (Prov. 27:3).

3515. כָּבֵד *kāḇēḏ:* An adjective describing something as heavy, great, grievous. It attributes the basic feature of heavy, weighty upon things, but its sense is nuanced carefully by its context and usage: figuratively, a "yoke" of taxation can be heavy, burdensome (1 Kgs. 12:4); and heavy hands can be an expression of being tired, weary (Ex. 17:12). Various things are heavy in the sense of being oppressive or burdensome, such as famine (Gen. 12:10); hail (Ex. 9:18); an impressive or large group of officials (1 Kgs. 10:2). The word regularly means impressive, rich, noble (Gen. 13:2); large (Gen. 50:9–11). It takes on negative senses as well, for the heart can be hard, heavy (Ex. 7:14). Something can be clumsy, slow, dull. Ezekiel's tongue was *kaḇēḏ,* slow (Ezek. 3:5, 6). The phrase *kāḇēḏ ʿawôwn* has the meaning of heavy or loaded with guilt (Isa. 1:4). Used after a noun, it may mean literally heavy, a heavy rock or perhaps a huge rock (Isa. 32:2).

3516. כָּבֵד *kāḇēḏ:* A masculine noun meaning liver. A large glandular organ in humans. In some animals it has lobes, appendages (Ex. 29:13, 22; Lev. 3:4, 10, etc.). A pierced liver was a deadly wound (Prov. 7:23). In pagan religions, the liver was a religious object and was carefully inspected in the process of divination (Ezek. 21:21[26]).

3517. כְּבֵדֻת *keḇēḏuṯ:* A feminine noun indicating heaviness, difficulty. It describes the stiffness with which the chariot wheels of the Egyptians drove because of the Lord's intervention on behalf of Israel (Ex. 14:25).

3518. כָּבָה kāḇāh: A verb meaning to quench, to put out. It is used of a fire being extinguished (Lev. 6:12[5], 13[6]; 1 Sam. 3:3) as of cutting off the source of a line of descendants (2 Sam. 14:7); or of killing persons, extinguishing their lives (2 Sam. 21:17; Isa. 43:17). It is used of extinguishing, putting out the hot wrath of the Lord (2 Kgs. 22:17). It is used also of quenching or putting out the flame of love toward a person (Song 8:7). In its strong participial form, it may mean persons who quench or put out (Isa. 1:31).

3519. כָּבוֹד kāḇôḏ, כָּבֹד kāḇōḏ: A masculine singular noun meaning honor, glory, majesty, wealth. This term is commonly used of God (Ex. 33:18; Ps. 72:19; Isa. 3:8; Ezek. 1:28); humans (Gen. 45:13; Job 19:9; Ps. 8:5[6]; 21:5[6]); and objects (1 Sam. 2:8; Esth. 1:4; Isa. 10:18), particularly of the ark of the covenant (1 Sam. 4:21, 22).

3520. כָּבוֹד kāḇôḏ, כְּבוּדָּה keḇûddāh: I. An adjective meaning glorious. It is used in context to refer to the splendor of the king's daughter (Ps. 45:13[14]), including her royal attire as well as a beautiful couch (Ezek. 23:41).

II. A feminine noun indicating abundance, possessions, riches. It is used as a collective noun referring to a group of valuables (Judg. 18:21).

3521. כָּבוּל kāḇûl: A proper noun designating Cabul (Josh. 19:27; 1 Kgs. 9:13).

3522. כַּבּוֹן kabbôn: A proper noun designating Cabbon (Josh. 15:40).

3523. כָּבִיר kāḇiyr: A masculine noun referring to a garment, a pillow, a quilt. It is used of a bedspread or quilt made of goat's hair (1 Sam. 19:13, 16). Possibly the word should be translated as a cushion or pillow of goat's hair.

3524. כַּבִּיר kabbiyr: An adjective meaning mighty, great. It is found only in Job and Isaiah. It is used of mighty or influential persons (Job 34:17). It is used of God who is great and mighty but does not look down on anyone (Job 36:5). It can describe wealth as extensive and great or water as powerful (Isa. 17:12); or a population as great or renowned (Isa. 16:14). It refers to an aged or honored person (Job 15:10). The means God uses with which to work are powerful, mighty (Isa. 28:2).

3525. כֶּבֶל keḇel: A masculine noun referring to fetters, shackles. It refers to something used to restrict the freedom of a person's feet in captivity. In one context, it refers to Joseph's imprisonment in Egypt (Ps. 105:18). It is also used in a more general sense of iron fetters placed on the kings of the nations (Ps. 149:8).

3526. כָּבַס ***kāḇas:*** A verb meaning to wash. The root meaning of the verb is to trample, which was the means of washing clothes. The word most often refers to washing clothes (Gen. 49:11; 2 Sam. 19:24[25]), especially ceremonially (Ex. 19:10; Lev. 15; Num. 19). As a participle, the word means fuller, one who left clothes to dry in the fuller's field (2 Kgs. 18:17; Isa. 7:3; 36:2). An intensive form of the verb is used of the fuller in Malachi 3:2, whose soap is a symbol of Christ's demand for purity. In Jeremiah 2:22, the word may refer literally to ceremonial washings but also implies mere human effort used in an external attempt to overcome sin. In Psalm 51:2[4], 7[9], the word refers to God's internal cleansing of the heart, making it as white as snow. Jeremiah 4:14, however, showed that God's people must work to cleanse their hearts and avoid temporal destruction.

3527. כָּבַר ***kāḇar:*** A verb meaning to multiply, to increase. It is used of producing an overabundance of words (Job 35:16). Its use as a participle indicates the abundant production of something (Job 36:31).

3528. כְּבָר ***k^eḇār:*** An adverb indicating long ago, already. Its use is consistent, indicating that something existed or happened already or long ago. There is really nothing new (Eccl. 1:10; 2:12; 3:15; 4:2; 6:10; 9:6, 7). It can refer to a time in the future when "already" something will happen or be forgotten (Eccl. 2:16).

3529. כְּבָר ***k^eḇār:*** A proper noun designating the river Chebar, also spelled Kebar. Evidently a man-made canal off of the Euphrates River in Babylon where Ezekiel saw several visions and heard the sound of the presence of the Lord's throne-chariot. The river was south of Babylon near another city, Nippur, east of the city of Babylon.

3530. כִּבְרָה ***kiḇrāh:*** A feminine noun indicating a little distance, some distance. It is used to refer to the length of a journey remaining that is a relatively (Gen. 35:16; 48:7) short distance. It also refers to a relatively short distance already traversed by someone (2 Kgs. 5:19).

3531. כְּבָרָה ***k^eḇārāh:*** A feminine noun meaning sieve. It refers to tools or utensils with small openings or perforations through which chaff and other small particles could be shaken loose from various kinds of grains (Amos 9:9). It is used in a simile of the Lord shaking Israel/Jerusalem in a sieve in order to cleanse her.

3532. כֶּבֶשׂ ***keḇeś:*** A masculine noun referring to a male lamb, sheep. These animals were usually mentioned as sacrificial animals (Ex. 12:5; 29:38–41; Lev. 4:32; 9:3; Num. 6:12, 14; 7:15; 28:3; Ezra 8:35; Isa. 1:11; Ezek. 46:4–7). They are mentioned as a source of raw material for clothing (Job 31:20; Prov. 27:26). Their nature was renowned for gentleness, and the word is used to refer to Jeremiah in a simile (Jer. 11:19).

3533. כָּבַשׁ ***kāḇaš:*** A verb meaning to subdue, to bring into subjection, to enslave. It means basically to overcome, to subdue someone. It is used to describe God's mandate to humans to subdue the created order (Gen. 1:28). It describes Israel's taking of the Promised Land, Canaan (Num. 32:22, 29; Josh. 18:1). King David subjugated the land (2 Sam. 8:11). It means to put into bondage or to degrade in general (Neh. 5:5). It is used once of Haman's supposed assault on Queen Esther (Esth. 7:8). It is used in its causative stem to indicate subduing or subjugating peoples (Jer. 34:11). It is used figuratively of the Lord's subduing, removing, crushing the iniquities of His people (Mic. 7:19). It is used of the Lord's people overcoming their enemies with His help (Zech. 9:15).

3534. כֶּבֶשׁ ***keḇeš:*** A masculine noun denoting a footstool. It refers to a golden seat with no arms, a feature of Solomon's throne (2 Chr. 9:18).

3535. כִּבְשָׂה ***kiḇśāh,*** כַּבְשָׂה ***kaḇśāh:*** A feminine noun referring to a ewe lamb, a female lamb. It was valuable property and could be used as a gift to establish an oath (Gen. 21:28–30; 2 Sam. 12:3, 4, 6). It was used in certain sacrifices, such as cleansing a leper (Lev. 14:10); or in a Nazarite vow (Num. 6:14).

3536. כִּבְשָׁן ***kiḇšān:*** A masculine noun meaning a furnace, a kiln. It refers to an enclosed space where some kind of fuel is burned, producing heat and smoke. It is used in a simile to compare the smoke ascending from Sodom and Gomorrah and from Mount Sinai to that arising from a furnace (Gen. 19:28; Ex. 19:18). Moses and Aaron took handfuls of soot or ashes from a kiln or furnace and cast them into the air in the sixth plague (Ex. 9:8, 10).

3537. כַּד ***kaḏ:*** A feminine noun indicating a jar, a pitcher. It indicates a large pottery jar for water (Gen. 24:14; 1 Kgs. 18:33[34]); or for flour (1 Kgs. 17:12). Such jars were used ingeniously by Gideon in war (Judg. 7:16, 19, 20); in Ecclesiastes 12:6, a jar was a symbol of life with its breaking indicating death.

3538. כְּדַב ***kᵉḏaḇ:*** An Aramaic adjective indicating that something is misleading, lying. It is used to refer to lying or deceitful words from Nebuchadnezzar's wise men (Dan. 2:9).

3539. כַּדְכֹּד ***kaḏkōḏ:*** A masculine noun denoting a precious stone, a ruby or an agate. It indicates the Lord will use precious stones to construct Zion's military defenses (Isa. 54:12). Merchants used such stones to pay for various goods and services (Ezek. 27:16).

3540. כְּדָרְלָעֹמֶר ***kᵉḏārlā'ōmer:*** A proper noun designating Chedorlaomer (Gen. 14:1, 4, 5, 9, 17).

3541. כֹּה **kōh:** A particle meaning in this way, this; this is what. It is used as a function word in various ways. Its three main uses are as follows: 1) to indicate location or direction (Ex. 2:12; Num. 23:15); or direction to a certain place (Gen. 22:5); 2) to indicate a temporal issue, such as up to now, ʿaḏ-kōh, (Ex. 7:16; Josh. 17:14); or meanwhile in the phrase ʿaḏ-kōh wᵉʿaḏ-kōh (1 Kgs. 18:45); 3) in an adverbial expression meaning so, thus, in this way, as follows (Gen. 15:5; 24:30); to introduce a message from people (Gen. 32:4[5]); especially from God or the Lord (over 400 times; e.g., Ex. 4:22; Jer. 9:22[21]). It is found several times in idiomatic expressions: "thus may he do and thus may he do again" (kōh yaʿaśeh wᵉkōh yôsîyp, 1 Sam. 3:17); "one (said or did) this, and another person (said, did) another" (zeh (2088) bᵉkōh wᵉzeh bekōh, 1 Kgs. 22:20). It is present in the idiomatic phrase, "if he says," ʾim koh yoʾmar (Gen. 31:8; 1 Sam. 14:9, 10; 20:7; 2 Sam. 15:26).

3542. כָּה **kāh:** An Aramaic adverb meaning at this point, hitherto. It means thus, so, this point, but it is used one time only in the phrase ʿaḏ-kāh, which means "up to this point" or "at this point" (Dan. 7:28).

3543. כָּהָה **kāhāh:** I. A verb meaning to faint, to be dim, to become expressionless. It is used of something becoming weak, unable to function or respond: Jacob's eyes were dim or expressionless, while Moses' eyes did not experience this diminution (Deut. 34:7). It describes infection or disease as fading, getting better (Lev. 13:6); and of the heart becoming faint or melting (Ezek. 21:7[12]). It is used in an emphatic verbal construction to express a person's eyes being extremely weak or blind (Zech. 11:17).

II. A verb meaning to rebuke, to correct a person. It is used of the failure of Eli to rebuke or correct his sons for their wicked behavior (1 Sam. 3:13).

3544. כֵּהֶה **kēheh:** A feminine adjective meaning faint, dim, dark. It is used of the fading or healing of a skin disease causing discoloration (Lev. 13:6, 21, 26, 28, 39, 56). It describes eyes becoming dull or weak (1 Sam. 3:2); and a faintly burning wick (Isa. 42:4). Isaiah uses it to describe a person's weak or fearful spirit (61:3).

3545. כֵּהָה **kēhāh:** A feminine noun indicating healing, relief. It has the sense of let up or partial cessation. There was no let up for the city of Nineveh from God's relentless judgment upon it (Nah. 3:19).

3546. כְּהַל **kᵉhal:** An Aramaic verb indicating to be able. It refers to a skill, ability, or knowledge enabling a person to accomplish something. Daniel had the skill and the divine enablement to interpret dreams and mysteries (Dan. 2:26; 4:18[15]), while Babylonian wise men did not (Dan. 5:8, 15).

3547. כָּהַן ***kāhan:*** A verb meaning to act, to serve as a priest. This is a denominative verb from the noun *kōhēn* (3548). The verb occurs twenty-three times in the Hebrew Bible, and twelve of them occur in Exodus. The most unusual usage is Isaiah 61:10 where it seems to refer to dressing in a priestly (i.e., ornate) manner.

3548. כֹּהֵן ***kōhēn:*** A masculine noun meaning priest. The word is used to designate the various classes of priests in Israel. These people performed the function of mediators between God and His people. God called the nation of Israel to be a kingdom of priests (Ex. 19:6), but God also appointed a priesthood to function within the nation. All the priests were to come from the tribe of Levi (Deut. 17:9, 18). The Lord set up a high priest who was over all the priestly services. The high priest was literally the great priest or head priest: Jehoiada was described as a high or great priest (2 Kgs. 12:10[11]). Joshua is called the high priest over the community that returned from the Babylonian exile (Hag. 1:12; 2:2). God appointed Aaron to serve as high priest and his sons as priests when the entire priestly order was established (Lev. 21:10; Num. 35:25). The high point of the religious year was the atonement ritual the high priest performed on the Day of Atonement (Lev. 16). Aaron's family line produced the Aaronic priests or priesthood. Zadok became the ancestor of the legitimate priests from the time of Solomon's reign (1 Kgs. 1:8, 38, 44); and the prophet Ezekiel approved of this line of priests from among the Levites (Ezek. 40:46; 43:19). The priests were in charge of all the holy things in Israel: they bore the ark (Josh. 3:13, 14) and trumpets (Num. 10:8). They even counseled kings (1 Sam. 22:21; 1 Kgs. 1:38, 44). However, there arose priests who were not appointed by the Lord and who functioned illegitimately, such as Micah's priests during the time of the judges (Judg. 17:5, 10, 12) or Jeroboam's priests who did not come from the sons of Levi (1 Kgs. 12:31).

Some priests who functioned in other religions or nations are mentioned in Scripture. The most famous was Melchizedek, who was also a king in Canaan (Gen. 14:18). His priesthood became the model for Christ's eternal priesthood (Heb. 6:20). Jethro, Moses' father-in-law, was a priest among the Midianites (Ex. 2:16; 3:1). Joseph married Asenath, the daughter of an Egyptian priest (Gen. 41:45). There were priests of the Philistines (1 Sam. 6:2); and priests who served the false gods, the Baals, and the Asherim (2 Chr. 34:5) of the heathen nations.

3549. כָּהֵן ***kāhēn:*** An Aramaic masculine noun denoting a priest. It refers specifically to those able to and qualified by genealogy and their health to act as priests when Israel returned from Babylonian exile (Ezra 6:9, 16, 18; 7:12, 13, 16, 21, 24).

3550. כְּהֻנָּה kehunnāh: A feminine noun meaning priesthood, the priest's office. The priest's office belonged to Aaron and his sons and involved making sacrifices and entering the Holy of Holies (Num. 18:7), work from which the other Levites were excluded (Num. 18:1, 7). Because of the holiness of the priesthood, those without right who presumed to act in it (Num. 16:10), as well as priests who misused the office, faced severe judgments. Levites outside of Aaron's descendants were permitted to do other service in the Tabernacle; and, thus, the priesthood was referred to as their inheritance in place of land (Josh. 18:7). The ordination of priests was described in Exodus 29 and included the use of anointing oil, special clothes, and sacrifices.

3551. כַּוָּה kawwāh: An Aramaic masculine noun referring to a window, an opening through a wall or roof to look through and to let in light and air. It was through such an opening located on his roof chamber that Daniel prayed three times a day toward Jerusalem (Dan. 6:10[11]) when he was still in exile under Persia.

3552. כּוּב kûḇ: A proper noun designating Chub (Ezek. 30:5), possibly another spelling for for *lûḇ* (3864), Libya.

3553. כּוֹבַע kôḇa': A masculine noun indicating a helmet. A cover for a person's head for protection at work or in battle. Goliath, the giant, wore a bronze helmet to go into battle (1 Sam. 17:5). Helmets were a key part of an army's military dress (2 Chr. 26:14; Jer. 46:4; Ezek. 27:10; 38:5). Isaiah uses the word figuratively of the helmet of salvation (Isa. 59:17).

3554. כָּוָה kāwāh: A verb meaning to burn, to scorch. It refers to something being seared from heat or fire, such as a person's feet who walks on hot coals (Prov. 6:28). On the other hand, it is used in a metaphor to depict the people of God not being charred or singed by fire, for He would deliver them (Isa. 43:2).

3555. כְּוִיָּה kewiyyāh: A feminine noun referring to a burn, burning; a scar. It refers to skin damage or scars received from burning. In the Mosaic Law, the person who inflicted such an injury on another person could only be repaid with the same punishment; poetic justice (Ex. 21:25).

3556. כּוֹכָב kôḵāḇ: A masculine noun meaning star. Its primary referents are a star and/or the stars of heaven (Gen. 1:16) which God created. These shining heavenly bodies have several functions: to rule over the night (Gen. 1:16; Ps. 136:9); to give light; to praise God (Ps. 148:3). They were used in idioms and metaphors often: to symbolize rulership and a coming ruler (Num. 24:17). Pagans and apostate Israelites worshiped them as gods (Deut. 4:19); they were used in pagan astrology or augury to know the future (Isa. 47:13); yet the

Lord of Israel communicates with them and commands them (Job 9:7); they were used to represent Joseph's brothers (Gen. 37:9): their number is used figuratively to represent the many descendants of Abraham and the patriarchs (Gen. 15:5; 22:17; 26:4; Ex. 32:13); prideful and haughty nations are represented as stars (Obad. 1:4), especially the king of Babylon (Isa. 14:13); the Lord can use stars in battle to fight for His people (Judg. 5:20); they shout for joy in personification (Job 38:7). The Lord has numbered them (Ps. 147:4); but even these shining bodies are not pure or clean in His sight (Job 25:5).

3557. כּוּל ***kûl:*** A verb meaning to hold, to contain feed, to supply. It indicates clasping or holding in something: the heavens cannot contain God (1 Kgs. 8:27). It is used of attempting to hold in the knowledge or word of God in oneself (Jer. 20:9). It is used of maintaining a supply of food or providing it in time of famine or difficult times (Gen. 45:11; Neh. 9:21). It means to sustain or make good, to maintain a course or business in a time of judgment (Ps. 112:5). In its passive uses, it means to be provided with something (1 Kgs. 20:27). It is used to indicate the holding in or containing of something (1 Kgs. 7:26; Jer. 2:13). It is used literally of a cup containing something (Ezek. 23:32). It has the figurative sense of holding something within oneself, e.g., God's wrath held in by Jeremiah (6:11); or enduring illness (Prov. 18:14). In Ruth 4:15, the Lord is the sustainer (*kûn*) of a person in old age.

3558. כּוּמָז ***kûmāz:*** A masculine noun meaning ornament. It is an ornamental piece of jewelry for wearing around the neck or on the breast (Ex. 35:22; Num. 31:50). These items were brought as gifts and offerings to the Lord.

3559. כּוּן ***kûn:*** A verb meaning to set up, to make firm, to establish, to prepare. The primary action of this verb is to cause to stand in an upright position, and thus the word also means fixed or steadfast. It signifies the action of setting in place or erecting an object (Isa. 40:20; Mic. 4:1); establishing a royal dynasty (2 Sam. 7:13; 1 Chr. 17:12); founding a city (Hab. 2:12); creating the natural order (Deut. 32:6; Ps. 8:3[4]; Prov. 8:27); fashioning a people for oneself (2 Sam. 7:24); adjusting weapons for targets (Ps. 7:12[13]; 11:2); appointing to an office (Josh. 4:4); confirming a position (1 Kgs. 2:12); making ready or preparing for use (2 Chr. 31:11; Ps. 103:19; Zeph. 1:7); attaining certainty (Deut. 13:14[15]; 1 Sam. 23:23).

3560. כּוּן ***kûn:*** A proper noun designating Cun (1 Chr. 18:8).

3561. כַּוָּן ***kawwān:*** A masculine noun indicating a cake, a sacrificial cake. These were small wafer-like cakes baked by the women of Israel in honor of the pagan Queen of Heaven (Jer. 7:18; 44:19).

3562. כּוֹנַנְיָהוּ ***kônanyāhû:*** A proper noun designating Conaniah:

A. A Levite (2 Chr. 31:12, 13).

B. A Levite (2 Chr. 35:9).

3563. כּוֹס ***kôs:*** I. A feminine noun referring to a cup, a goblet. It is used of small drinking cups or goblets in general (Gen. 40:11; 1 Kgs. 7:26) made of ceramic, metal or wood. It is used in figurative senses: the cup in the Lord's right hand, that is, a cup of judgment (Hab. 2:16); a cup of deliverance or salvation (Ps. 116:13); a cup of drunkenness or of anger (poison?) (Isa. 51:22); a cup full of judgments for the wicked (Ps. 11:6).

II. A feminine noun denoting a pelican; a screech owl, a little owl. It is used to symbolize a forsaken, lonely, afflicted person, i.e., a pelican in the wilderness (Ps. 102:6[7]). The Israelites could not eat these birds because they were unclean and forbidden (Lev. 11:17; Deut. 14:16).

3564. כּוּר ***kûr:*** I. A masculine noun meaning a furnace, a forge, a smelting pot. It refers to a furnace or smelting pot literally but is also used in figurative language to depict human suffering in judgment or discipline: Egypt was the iron furnace (literally, furnace of iron) (Deut. 4:20; 1 Kgs. 8:51; Jer. 11:4). It is used in the phrase "furnace of affliction/oppression" (Isa. 48:10). It is compared to the Lord who tests hearts, not gold or silver (Prov. 17:3; 27:21). Israel is compared to the dross or impurities in one of these smelting furnaces (Ezek. 22:18, 20, 22).

II. A verb meaning to pierce. It is used to describe stabbing or puncturing something. The oppressed psalmist tells of his enemies piercing his hands and feet (Ps. 22:16[17]), an adumbration or foreshadowing of what would happen to the Messiah.

3565. כּוֹר עָשָׁן ***kôr 'āšān:*** A proper noun designating Chorashan, variant spelling for *bôr* (953) and *'āšān* (6227). It is only found in 1 Samuel 30:30, King James Version.

3566. כּוֹרֶשׁ ***kôreš,*** כֹּרֶשׁ ***kōreš:*** A proper noun designating the great king of Persia who destroyed Babylon, Cyrus II (559–530 B.C.). He was God's instrument both to judge Babylon and to force Israel from exile and to rebuild Jerusalem (2 Chr. 36:22, 23; Isa. 44:28; 45:1). His heart was moved by God (Ezra 1:1–8) to let Israel and other peoples return to their homelands. His decree fulfilled Jeremiah's prophecy about a return from exile. Daniel lived into his reign (Dan. 1:21; 10:1).

3567. כּוֹרֶשׁ ***kôreš:*** A proper noun designating the Aramaic name corresponding to the Hebrew name Cyrus (II). See 3566. It is found only in the Aramaic portions of Ezra-Nehemiah.

3568. כּוּשׁ ***Kûš:*** A proper noun designating Cush:

A. The first son of Ham, Noah's first son. His descendants occupied the Upper Nile territory of Egypt far to the south. Cush had five sons. Cush in Genesis 10:8 is the father of a famous mighty warrior who is mentioned in extra-biblical texts also. Hence, Cushites could also be located in southeast Mesopotamia.

B. Cush probably refers to the territory of southeast Mesopotamia, although the northern Upper Nile region is not impossible. Most often the term Cush seems to refer to the Upper Nile regions (Esth. 1:1; Job 28:19; Ps. 68:31[32]), north of Ethiopia. Tirhakah, a Cushite king of Egypt, reigned in the time of Hezekiah (2 Kgs. 19:9).

C. It refers to a person from Benjamin named Cush (Ps. 7:[title] 1).

3569. כּוּשִׁי ***kûšiy:*** A proper noun designating Cushite, Cushi:

A. Cushite, a person descended from Cush (Gen. 10:6–8) and/or from Cush, probably in the Upper Nile region. Moses took a Cushite (Ethiopian) woman as a wife (Num. 12:1), perhaps after Zipporah his first wife died (Ex. 21—22). Cushites served in David's army (2 Sam. 18:21–33). Some translations render the term "Ethiopian" (Jer. 13:23, NIV). The Cushite's skin was evidently black. A Cushite, Ebed-Melech, rescued Jeremiah from certain death (Jer. 38:7–13). The term Nubian, a southern territory in Egypt, is also used to render Cush/ite (Dan. 11:43). God considered them His people, for all peoples are His (Amos 9:7). But even the Cushites received prophetic rebuke (Zeph. 2:12).

B. Cushi, the name of a Cushite who served in David's army and whom Joab used as a messenger to David (2 Sam. 18:32).

3570. כּוּשִׁי ***kûšiy:*** A proper noun designating Cushi:

A. Great-grandfather of Jehudi (Jer. 36:14).

B. Father of Zephaniah (Zeph. 1:1).

3571. כּוּשִׁית ***kûšiyṯ:*** A feminine proper noun designating a Cushite or Ethiopian woman (Num. 12:1).

3572. כּוּשָׁן ***kûšān:*** A proper noun designating Cushan (Hab. 3:7).

3573. כּוּשַׁן רִשְׁעָתַיִם ***kûšan riš'a-ṯayim:*** A proper noun designating Cushan-Rishathaim (Judg. 3:8, 10).

3574. כּוֹשָׁרָה ***kōshārāh:*** A. A feminine noun indicating prosperity. It refers to the spiritual liberty and freedom which the Lord restores to the oppressed or lonely (Ps. 68:6[7]), a place of abundance in figurative language.

B. A feminine noun indicating singing. This is the preferred translation for this word by some. The lonely or suppressed are liberated by singing (Ps. 68:6[7]).

C. A feminine noun indicating chains. It is used of the Lord freeing those bound in chains. Again, some translators prefer this rendering, but see A and B above (Ps. 68:6[7]).

3575. כּוּת ***kûṯ***, כּוּתָה ***kûṯāh:*** A proper noun designating Iron (Josh. 19:38).

3576. כָּזַב ***kāzaḇ:*** A verb meaning to lie, to be a liar, to declare a liar, to make a liar of someone. This verb occurs sixteen times and refers to false witnesses (Prov. 14:5); worshipers (Prov. 30:6); and figuratively of water (Isa. 58:11). The book of Job, filled with courtroom rhetoric, debating the trustworthiness of the speakers' accounts, uses the verb four times (Job 6:28; 24:25; 34:6; 41:9[1]).

3577. כָּזָב ***kāzāḇ:*** A masculine noun meaning a lie, a deception, a falsehood. Indeed, the idea of non-truth is unequivocally presented as antithetical to God. He destroys liars (Ps. 5:6[7]; 62:4[5]) and calls them an abomination (Prov. 6:19). Lies and deceptions place one against God and guarantee His punishment (Prov. 19:5, 9). Isaiah graphically depicted one taking shelter in lying and falsehood as equivalent to making a covenant with death and an agreement with hell—a contract that cannot save on Judgment Day (28:15, 17). Freedom from falsehood is both the character and heritage of God's children (Ps. 40:4[5]; Zeph. 3:13). The verb *kāzaḇ* (3576) also develops the anti-God theme of lying: God cannot lie (Num. 23:19); and His word will never deceive (Ps. 89:35[36]), unlike false prophets and humans.

3578. כֹּזֵבָא ***kōzēḇa':*** A proper noun designating Cuthah (2 Kgs. 17:24, 30).

3579. כָּזְבִּי ***kozbiy:*** A proper noun designating Cozbi (Num. 25:15, 18).

3580. כְּזִיב ***k***^{e}***ziyḇ:*** A proper noun designating Chezib (Gen. 38:5).

3581. כֹּחַ ***kōaḥ***, כּוֹחַ ***kôaḥ:*** I. A masculine noun meaning power, strength. It is a general term referring to power or might in many different settings: the strength of people (Judg. 16:5; Josh. 17:17); the prophet filled with the power and Spirit of the Lord (Mic. 3:8). It is used of animals (Prov. 14:4); or even of the fertility of a field or the ground (Gen. 4:12). A son born to a father is his strength or vigor (Gen. 49:3). It is used of human labor in the fields to procure food (Lev. 26:20). Good food provides energy and strength for travel (1 Kgs. 19:8). It refers to all kinds of social, political, and economic forces (Eccl. 4:1); or general physical and intellectual capacity and determination (Eccl. 9:10). It indicates all the benefits and gains a person has accumulated (Prov. 5:10).

II. A masculine noun meaning a lizard, a reptile. It refers to a long, slender reptile considered unclean to Israel and therefore forbidden as food (Lev. 11:30).

3582. כָּחַד ***kāḥaḏ:*** A verb meaning to hide, to conceal, to cut off, to destroy. It has the basic idea of hiding or destroying by various measures: by cutting off or destroying Pharaoh and his people in plagues (Ex. 9:15); or by the Lord's destroying angel (Ex. 23:23). It has the meaning to make something disappear, to destroy or to efface it, such as the dynasty of Jeroboam (1 Kgs. 13:34). It has the sense of hiding or not revealing something in Job 20:12 (Ps. 139:15; Hos. 5:3). In other contexts, it means for something to be hidden (2 Sam. 18:13; Ps. 69:5[6]); or kept hidden (Gen. 47:18; 1 Sam. 3:17, 18; Ps. 78:4). It is used of persons being effaced, destroyed (Zech. 11:8, 9, 16) by the Lord, or even scattered.

3583. כָּחַל *kāḥal:* A verb meaning to paint something. It means to put on luxurious, alluring, and enticing cosmetics to impress and attract someone (Ezek. 23:40).

3584. כָּחַשׁ *kāḥaš:* A verb meaning to lie, to cringe, to deny. It means to deal falsely about something or with someone, the opposite of being truthful, honest. It is used of denying or disavowing something (Gen. 18:15); of deceiving or lying to a person with respect to something (Lev. 6:2[5:21], 3[5:22]; Josh. 24:27). It naturally takes on the meaning of concealing something (Josh. 7:11). False prophets were always deceiving themselves and others (1 Kgs. 13:18; Zech. 13:4). It means to deny someone wrongly (Job 31:28). It is used of wine failing, disappointing people (Hos. 9:2). It takes on the meaning of cringing or fawning before the Lord (Ps. 18:44[45]).

3585. כַּחַשׁ *kaḥaš:* A masculine noun meaning lying, leanness. It carries the meaning of deception and deceit, of Israel's lying to God (Hos. 10:13; 11:12[12:1]). Nineveh, the capital of Assyria, was full of deceit and lies (Nah. 3:1). The wicked constantly utter lies (Ps. 59:12[13]). In the context of Job 16:8, it means sickliness, leanness, or gauntness.

3586. כֶּחָשׁ *keḥāš:* An adjective meaning deceptive, false, lying. This word occurs only in Isaiah 30:9. The reference is to the deceitfulness of Israel. Their rebellious activities included urging prophets to prophesy falsely and to subvert the authority of the Lord (Isa. 30:10, 11).

3587. כִּי *kiy:* A masculine noun meaning burning, branding. It denotes a scar or mark from burning. It is used in a figurative way to mean disfigurement or scarring as opposed to beauty (Isa. 3:24).

3588. כִּי *kiy:* A demonstrative particle meaning because, for, that, when, whenever; indeed, even; if; even when, even though. It is used in various ways and must be translated accordingly. In every case, the context in which the word functions will be the key to translating correctly. Here is a listing of the major ways it is used: as a conjunction meaning because (Gen. 3:14); for (Ps. 6:2, 5); that (Gen. 1:10; 1 Kgs. 21:15); as a conjunctive time or condition indicator, when or if (Gen. 4:12); in a clause of condition, it means if, in fact, or in case (Job 7:13); as a demonstrative particle translated as yes, indeed, surely (Gen. 18:20; 1 Sam. 14:44); truly, especially found in oaths (Gen. 42:16); used with *'im* (518) . . . *kî* . . . , it means if . . . then (Isa. 7:9); in combination with *kî 'az,* it is best rendered as then; *kî 'attāh* usually means for them (Job 3:13). After a negative clause, *kî* is best rendered as rather (Gen. 3:6; 17:5; 24:4); preceded by the negative *lō'*, it is "no, but . . ." In clauses that concede something, it has the sense of even though, although, even when (Eccl. 4:14). It is used to show comparison when used in the construction *kî* . . . *kēn,* as . . . so (Isa. 55:9).

3589. כִּיד kiyḏ: A masculine noun of uncertain meaning. It comes from a primitive root word and most likely means a crushing, a calamity, or a misfortune. Job responded to Zophar and lamented about the wicked. Job wished that the wicked would see God's wrath and their own destruction (Job 21:20).

3590. כִּידוֹד kiydôḏ: A masculine noun referring to a spark. It refers to a glowing or flashing bit of something. In context it refers to a flash or sparkle of fire from Leviathan's mouth (Job 41:19[11]) and stands in parallel with torches, lamps, or firebrands in the preceding line.

3591. כִּידוֹן kiydôn: A masculine noun referring to a spear, a javelin. It refers to a weapon of some kind, traditionally a spear or javelin. It could possibly refer to a short sword for close fighting (Josh. 8:18, 26; 1 Sam. 17:6, 45). It is rendered as spear (Jer. 6:23, NIV, NASB); lance (Jer. 50:42, KJV); or javelin (Jer. 50:42, NASB).

3592. כִּידֹן kiyḏōn: A proper noun designating Chidon (1 Chr. 13:9).

3593. כִּידוֹר kiyḏôr: A masculine noun indicating an attack, a battle. It refers to a hostile, offensive action taken against someone. In the context, it denotes an attack against the wicked by a well-prepared king (Job 15:24).

3594. כִּיּוּן kiyyûn: I. A masculine proper noun, Chiun, Kiyyun. It is a name given to images in Amos 5:26, Kiyyun (KJV, NKJV, Chiun; NASB, Kiyyun); your images. See also II below.

II. A masculine noun referring to a pillar, a pedestal. It is translated as a pedestal or pillar on which to set up idols (Amos 5:26, NIV) by some recent translations.

3595. כִּיּוֹר kiyyôr: A masculine noun referring to a basin, a laver, a pot. It refers to a basin or laver for washing or cooking (Ex. 30:18; 31:9; 35:16; 38:8; Lev. 8:11; 1 Sam. 2:14; 1 Kgs. 7:30; Zech. 12:6). In 2 Chronicles 6:13, it refers to a platform on which King Solomon stood and knelt in order to pray.

3596. כִּילַי, כֵּלַי kiylay, kēlay: A masculine noun referring to a rogue, a scoundrel. It indicates a person of low, scandalous reputation, akin to a fool (Isa. 32:5). Israel's sin so blinded her that this person was held in esteem.

3597. כֵּילַף ***kēylap̱:*** A feminine noun indicating a hammer, a hatchet; a crowbar. It refers to a tool or weapon used to smash the splendid work of the temple. It is paralleled in verse 5 by the ax (Ps. 74:6).

3598. כִּימָה ***kiymāh:*** A feminine proper noun referring to the Pleiades, a constellation of seven stars. It refers to a collection of stars in the heavens. It is referred to in three places: it is the creation of God (Job 9:9; Amos 5:8); it is beyond human power or ability to control the Pleiades (Job 38:31).

3599. כִּיס ***kiys:*** A masculine noun meaning a bag, a purse. A container of leather or cloth for holding various items: stone weights (Deut. 25:13; Prov. 16:11; Mic. 6:11); gold (Isa. 46:6). It is used figuratively of fate or destiny (parallel to lot) (Prov. 1:14). For its possible use in Proverbs 23:31, see 3563. Most scholars prefer to read *kôs* as cup.

3600. כִּיר ***kiyr:*** A masculine noun meaning an oven, a range, a cooking pot; a small stove. It probably refers to a small stove for two pots (Lev. 11:35; KJV, oven or range).

3601. כִּישׁוֹר ***kiyšôr:*** A masculine noun indicating a distaff, a spindle. It is a small dish or wheel located at the bottom of a spindle to give it inertia as it spins (Prov. 31:19).

3602. כָּכָה ***kāḵāh:*** An adverbial particle meaning thus, so, in this way, as follows. It indicates how something is to be done, in this manner, thus (Ex. 12:11; Deut. 25:9); or how a person is to be treated, thus (you shall do) (Ex. 29:35; Num. 8:26). It is used to indicate the condition of something or someone (2 Sam. 13:4; Ps. 144:15). It is used in the phrase *ka'ašer* . . . *kākāh,* just as . . . so . . . (Eccl. 11:5); or to indicate that one (said) this, another that, *zeh* (2088) . . . *kākāh wezeh* . . . *kākāh* (2 Chr. 18:19). With *'al* preceding, it means upon this basis, for this reason (Esth. 9:26).

3603. כִּכָּר ***kikkār:*** A feminine noun indicating something round, such as a coin (a talent); a district; a loaf of bread. It indicates something round, dish-shaped, circular: a loaf of bread (1 Sam. 2:36; 10:3); a cover (Zech. 5:7); a unit of weight, a talent (ca. 75 lbs.) (1 Kgs. 9:14; 10:10; 20:39). It is used to refer to a district in its circuit or environs, e.g., a southern area (Gen. 13:10–12); or a surrounding mountainous area (Gen. 19:17, 25, 28, 29). It is used of the district surrounding Jerusalem (Neh. 3:22; 12:28).

3604. כַּכַּר ***kakkar:*** A feminine Aramaic noun referring to a coin or a measure of weight, a talent. It is used to refer to the talents (about 75 lbs.)

of silver given to the Jews by King Artaxerxes (Ezra 7:22).

3605. כֹּל *kōl:* A particle meaning each, every, all, everything, the whole, entire. It has an inclusive meaning of all or every one of something. Its exact meaning must be discerned from its usage in its context. Some representative samplings will help: With the definite article, it means the whole or everything of something (Eccl. 11:5); used before a definite noun, it expresses the whole of that noun, the whole earth (Gen. 9:19); whole people (Gen. 41:40). Used after a noun, it can refer to the whole or entirety of the preceding noun (2 Sam. 2:9); before a plural noun, it usually means all, all the nations (Isa. 2:2); before a collective noun, it means all or every, all people (Gen. 7:21). Before a singular noun, it means every (Esth. 3:8). Other nuances of its use can be discerned from studying its context closely.

3606. כֹּל *kōl:* An Aramaic particle that means all, every, any, entire, depending on the context: whole or all (Dan. 3:2, 3, 5); every, any (Dan. 6:7[8]). It can mean the whole, everything (Dan. 2:40). It is used figuratively in phrases like all peace, security (Ezra 5:7).

3607. כָּלָא *kālā':* I. A verb meaning to close, to hinder, to restrain. It refers to the cessation of rain (Gen. 8:2). It means to hold back something (Gen. 23:6); or to restrain one's lips or speech (Ps. 40:9[10]). It describes persons restraining themselves from something (Ex. 36:6); or being held back (Num. 11:28; 1 Sam. 25:33). It refers to penning up or keeping something in a location (1 Sam. 6:10; Jer. 32:2). It is used figuratively of God's withholding His love and compassion (Ps. 40:11[12]); and of restraining the wind (Eccl. 8:8). It describes the failure or refusal of the earth to bear its produce (Hag. 1:10).

II. A verb meaning to finish, to complete, to bring to an end. It describes the completion of God's plans for His people Israel (Dan. 9:24).

3608. כֶּלֶא *kele':* A masculine noun denoting prison. It refers to confinement, imprisonment. A *bēyṯ kele'* is a house of confinement, a prison (1 Kgs. 22:27; Isa. 42:22; Jer. 37:4; 52:33). Used in a genitive "of" form or phrase, it indicates something to do with imprisonment: *bigdēy kil'ô,* garments of imprisonment, a convict's clothing (2 Kgs. 25:29).

3609. כִּלְאָב *kil'āḇ:* A proper noun designating Chileab (2 Sam. 3:3).

3610. כִּלְאַיִם *kil'ayim:* A masculine dual noun indicating a mixing or mingling of two kinds. It refers to mixing cattle, seeds, or vines as forbidden by the Law (Lev. 19:19; Deut. 22:9).

3611. כֶּלֶב *keleḇ:* A masculine noun meaning a dog, a male prostitute. It refers to a large and varied group of canines, usually domesticated. In various contexts, it refers to a watchdog (Isa. 56:10, 11); a hunting dog (Ps. 22:16[17]); a stray dog (1 Kgs. 14:11). The concept is used in figurative expressions of contempt: of a scorned person (1 Sam. 17:43); of abasing oneself (1 Sam. 24:14[15]; 2 Sam. 3:8); of a male cult prostitute (Deut. 23:18[19]). It was used in a mocking sense of a false sacrifice as if it were the sacrifice of a dog (Isa. 66:3), a pagan practice. The manner in which a dog lapped its water is noted in Judges 7:5. Dogs ate up Jezebel's dead body as a sign of reprobation toward her (2 Kgs. 9:10, 36). Dogs were known to growl and be menacing in their demeanor (Ex. 11:7), but God protected His people from even this, figuratively, as they left Egypt.

3612. כָּלֵב *kālēb̲:* A proper noun designating Caleb, one of the twelve spies sent to check out the land of Canaan. The name means "dog." He was the son of Jephunneh, a leader in Judah. He counseled Israel to go up and take the land, as did Joshua (Num. 14:6–38). He helped conquer the Promised Land; he was from the line of Judah and fathered three sons (1 Chr. 4:15–16). Hebron was allotted to Caleb (Josh. 14:6–9). His own testimony was that he had faithfully followed the Lord (Josh. 14:8). He inherited his land at the ripe age of eighty-five but still finished driving Anakites out of the land. According to Joshua, Jephunneh's father was a Kenizzite (Josh. 14:14).

3613. כָּלֵב אֶפְרָתָה *kālēb̲ 'ep̱rāṯāh:* A proper noun designating Caleb Ephrathah (from *kālēb̲* (3612) and *'ep̱rāṯāh* (672) (1 Chr. 2:24).

3614. כָּלִבִּי *kālibbiy:* A proper noun designating Calebite (1 Sam. 25:3).

3615. כָּלָה *kālāh:* A verb meaning to complete, to accomplish, to end, to finish, to fail, to exhaust. Its primary meaning is to consummate or to bring to completion. This occasionally occurs in a positive sense as in the awesome goodness of God's perfected and finished creation (Gen. 2:1, 2). It also represents the favorable conclusion of meaningful human labor as in building the Tabernacle (Ex. 39:32); or preparing tithes (Deut. 26:12). However, *kālāh* is more often used with a negative connotation. God threatened to consume human unbelief (as in completing the life span), a promise terribly fulfilled at Korah's rebellion (Num. 16:21). Also, Israel was to be God's vehicle in consuming or finishing the heathen nations in the land (Deut. 7:22), thus completing the ban. The verb also describes the transitory reality of fallen human nature. We finish our years like a sigh (Ps. 90:9), passing away like an exhausted cloud (Job 7:9).

3616. כָּלֶה *kāleh:* An adjective meaning desiring, longing. It is used of parents' yearning for and desiring their absent children (Deut. 28:32).

3617. כָּלָה ***kālāh:*** A feminine noun meaning completion, complete destruction, annihilation. In the sense of completion, God told Moses that Pharaoh would let the Israelites go by driving them completely out of Egypt (Ex. 11:1). Complete destruction or annihilation was most often attributed to God. Isaiah prophesied that the Lord would make a determined end to Israel (Isa. 10:23); Nahum spoke of God's judgment by which He made an utter end of His enemies (Nah. 1:8). Destruction of such massive quantity is attributed to humans in Daniel's prophecy of Greece (Dan. 11:16).

3618. כַּלָּה ***kallāh:*** A feminine noun referring to a bride, a daughter-in-law. In the biblical world, it refers to a woman under the authority of her father, then of her husband and father-in-law. It indicates specifically a young daughter-in-law (Gen. 11:31; Hos. 4:13, 14); a young married woman, a bride (Isa. 49:18).

3619. כְּלוּב ***kᵉlû̲b̲:*** A masculine noun indicating a basket, a cage. It is used of a basket for fruit (Amos 8:1, 2) seen in a prophetic vision. It refers to a cage but is used figuratively of Jerusalem as full of deceit as a cage full of birds (Jer. 5:27).

3620. כְּלוּב ***kᵉlû̲b̲:*** A proper noun designating Chelub:

A. Father of Ezri (1 Chr. 27:26).
B. Father of Mehir (1 Chr. 4:11).

3621. כְּלוּבָי ***kᵉlûb̲āy:*** A proper noun designating Chelubai (1 Chr. 2:9).

3622. כְּלוּהוּ ***kᵉlûhû:*** A proper noun designating Chelluh (Ezra 10:35).

3623. כְּלוּלָה ***kᵉlûlāh:*** A feminine noun denoting betrothal, espousal. It indicates a time of engagement. It is used figuratively to refer to the time of Israel's engagement to the Lord in her youth (Jer. 2:2).

3624. כֶּלַח ***kelaḥ:*** A masculine noun indicating vigor, full strength. It indicates maturity of vigor when one is in the bloom of health (Job 5:26). If it has gone from persons, they are weak and often inactive, not good for much labor (Job 30:2).

3625. כֶּלַח ***kelaḥ:*** A proper noun designating Calah (Gen. 10:11, 12).

3626. כָּל־חֹזֶה ***kol-ḥōzeh:*** A proper noun designating Col-Hozeh:

A. Father of Shallum (Neh. 3:15).
B. A Judaite (Neh. 11:5).

3627. כְּלִי ***kᵉliy:*** A masculine noun indicating an article, a vessel, an instrument, a jewel. It has a broad inclusive sense and indicates useful objects of all kinds. The context must determine what object is indicated and for what task. It refers to vessels, receptacles of all kinds (Gen. 31:37; Lev. 6:28[21]; 11:32–34; 2 Sam. 17:28); for storing (Jer. 32:14). It indicates implements, ornaments, various kinds of equipment and utensils (Gen. 24:53; 27:3; 45:20; 49:5; 1 Sam. 8:12; 17:22; 2 Sam. 24:22; 2 Kgs. 23:4; Ezek. 40:42; Jon. 1:5). It even refers to articles of clothing or weapons (Deut. 22:5; 2 Kgs. 7:15).

3628. כְּלִיא ***k^eliy'***, כְּלוּא ***k^elû':*** A masculine noun meaning prison. A place of confinement and incarceration (Jer. 37:4; 52:31). Jeremiah spent time there. It was a good sign when Jehoiachin was freed from confinement in a Babylonian prison (Jer. 52:31).

3629. כִּלְיָה ***kilyāh:*** A feminine noun meaning a kidney; the heart as the seat of emotions. It is always used in its plural form. It is an animal's internal organ referred to often in sacrifices (Ex. 29:13; Lev. 4:9; 7:4; 9:10); it is the innermost and most private aspect of a person (Job 16:13; Ps. 139:13; Prov. 23:16; Jer. 11:20; Lam. 3:13). God created the kidneys (Ps. 139:13, "inner parts"). In a metaphor, it is used to refer to choice wheat, *kilyôṯ ḥiṭṭāh* (Deut. 32:14).

3630. כִּלְיוֹן ***kilyôn:*** A proper noun designating Chilion (Ruth 1:2, 5; 4:9).

3631. כִּלָּיוֹן ***killāyôn:*** A masculine noun meaning destruction, failing. It refers to a weakening or blurring of one's eyes. In context it was one of the Lord's curses on a disobedient people in exile (Deut. 28:65). It is used of the destruction of many Israelites in judgments from the Lord (Isa. 10:22).

3632. כָּלִיל ***kāliyl:*** An adjective meaning whole, entire, perfect, complete. This word can refer to an offering that was entirely consumed (Deut. 33:10; 1 Sam. 7:9); figuratively, it refers to burning a whole town that worshiped other gods (Deut. 13:16 [17]). The ephod had to be all purple (Ex. 28:31; 39:22); Isaiah prophesied of a day when idols would completely disappear (Isa. 2:18). This word also referred to Jerusalem's complete beauty (Lam. 2:15; Ezek. 16:14); or Tyre's (Ezek. 27:3; 28:12). See the Hebrew root *kālal* (3634).

3633. כַּלְכֹּל ***kalkōl:*** A proper noun designating Calcol (1 Kgs. 4:31[5:11]; 1 Chr. 2:6).

3634. כָּלַל ***kālal:*** A verb meaning to complete, to make perfect. Ezekiel lamented over Tyre's pride concerning her perfected beauty (Ezek. 27:4). Builders as well as war bounty came from all over the Near East to the port city of Tyre and added to the perfect beauty of the city (Ezek. 27:11).

3635. כְּלַל ***k^elal:*** An Aramaic verb meaning to complete. This word described the completed Temple (Ezra 5:11). It also carries the meaning of to restore (Ezra 4:12, 13, 16; 5:3, 9). See the related Hebrew root *kālal* (3634) and the related Hebrew adjective *kāliyl* (3632).

3636. כְּלָל ***k^elāl:*** A proper noun designating Chelal (Ezra 10:30).

3637. כָּלַם *kālam:* A verb describing to be disgraced, to be ashamed; to blush. It refers to an act that humiliates a person (2 Sam. 10:5); or an abuse or attack of words (Job 11:3). A person's own character or behavior can cause shame (2 Sam. 19:3[4]; Jer. 14:3). In some of its causative uses, it refers to disgracing or shaming someone (1 Sam. 20:34; 25:15; Prov. 28:7); or it may indicate the mistreatment of animals (1 Sam. 25:7). The Lord's help for His servant was enough to preserve him from disgrace or confusion (Isa. 50:7). The word is used of a formal sentence and a time of social disgrace (Num. 12:14). In Judges 18:7, it takes on a sense of not lacking or being in want; it was a prosperous land in every way.

3638. כִּלְמַד *kilmad:* A proper noun designating Chilmad (Ezek. 27:23).

3639. כְּלִמָּה *k^{e}limmāh:* A feminine noun referring to disgrace, shame, humiliation. It has the meaning of embarrassment, i.e., Israel would eventually be ashamed because of its attempt to gain protection from Egypt (Isa. 30:3; cf. 45:16; 61:7). It has the sense of shame or humiliation through judgment (Mic. 2:6). It is referred to figuratively as a covering, clothing (Ps. 35:26; 109:29). It is often found in Ezekiel with the verb *nāśa'*, rendering the phrase to bear, to carry, to endure ignoring or shame (Ezek. 16:52). A word or rebuke can humiliate a person (Job 20:3).

3640. כְּלִמּוּת *k^{e}limmûṯ:* A feminine noun meaning shame, humiliation. It is used of disgrace to be brought upon false prophets because of their false claims in God's name (Jer. 23:40).

3641. כַּלְנֶה *kalneh,* כַּלְנֵה *kalnēh,* כַּלְנוֹ *kalnô:* A proper noun designating Calneh, Calno (Gen. 10:10; Isa. 10:9; Amos 6:2).

3642. כָּמַהּ *kāmah:* A verb indicating to long for, to yearn for. It is used with flesh as its subject to indicate the longing of the psalmist's flesh (body?) for the Lord (Ps. 63:1[2]).

3643. כִּמְהָם *kimhām,* כִּמְהָן *kimhān:* A proper noun designating Chimham (2 Sam. 19:37[38], 38[39], 40[41]; Jer. 41:17).

3644. כְּמוֹ *k^{e}mô:* A particle meaning like, as. It is used to assert that something is like something else: the Egyptians sank like stones (Ex. 15:5). With a suffix as subject attached, it asserts a likeness of its suffix to something, e.g., *kāmōḵā k^{e}p̱ar'ôh,* "you are like Pharaoh" (Gen. 44:18). There is no one like the Lord (Ex. 9:14). Something is asserted to be as (*k^e*) it used to be (Zech. 10:8). It has the sense of time, when, in some contexts (Gen. 19:15), lit., as it was.

3645. כְּמוֹשׁ *k^{e}môš:* A masculine proper noun, Chemosh. It refers to the chief god of the Moabites (Num. 21:29: Judg. 11:24; 1 Kgs. 11:7, 33; 2 Kgs. 23:13; Jer. 48:7, 13, 46). The

Moabites are his people (Num. 21:29). Judges 11:24 claims him as the god of the Ammonites, but the text probably has a serious error.

3646. כַּמֹּן *kammōn:* A masculine noun denoting cummin. It refers to a seed that is sown by farmers and produces a herb used in seasoning, (Isa. 28:25, 27).

3647. כָּמַס *kāmas:* A verb indicating to store up, to save. It is used of preserving or saving up something. In context it is used of God saving up judgment for His people (Deut. 32:34).

3648. כָּמַר *kāmar:* A verb indicating to be aroused, to be deeply moved. It indicates something being agitated or moved with respect to something else, i.e., Joseph was moved at seeing his brother Benjamin (Gen. 43:30). A mother is gripped by feeling and emotion for her baby (1 Kgs. 3:26). It is used of skin tingling, sweating, or being feverish from lack of nourishment (Lam. 5:10). God's own being is aroused in love for His rebellious people (Hos. 11:8).

3649. כֹּמֶר *kōmer:* A masculine noun meaning a (pagan) priest. In the Old Testament, this word occurs three times. In 2 Kings 23:5, Josiah's reformation got rid of priests who burned incense in the idolatrous high places. In Hosea 10:5, Hosea prophesied that priests would mourn over the calf statue they worshiped when it was carried off to Assyrian captivity. In Zephaniah 1:4, God promised to cut off the names of unfaithful priests, along with His own priests (cf. Zeph. 1:5, 6).

3650. כִּמְרִיר *kimriyr:* A masculine noun referring to blackness, a darkening. It refers to a darkening of something to hide it or swallow it up (Job 3:5).

3651. כֵּן *kēn:* A word that is used either as an adverb or adjective, depending on the context of the sentence. The word is derived from the verb meaning to stand upright or to establish. As an adjective, it means correct, according to an established standard (Num. 27:7); upright and honest (Gen. 42:11); it is used as a statement of general agreement (Gen. 44:10; Josh. 2:21). As an adverb, it is usually translated as "thus" or "so" but conveys quality (Esth. 4:16; Job 9:35; Nah. 1:12); quantity (Judg. 21:14); cause and effect (Judg. 10:13; Isa. 5:24); or time (Neh. 2:16).

3652. כֵּן *kēn:* An Aramaic particle meaning thus, so. It is used with reference to only what follows in context, such as something written or said (Ezra 5:3; 6:2; Dan. 2:24, 25; 4:14[11]; 6:6[7]; 7:5, 23).

3653. כֵּן *kēn:* A masculine noun indicating a base, a pedestal, a stand. It is used to indicate a foundational stand for a water basin (Ex. 30:18, 28; 31:9; Lev. 8:11; 1 Kgs. 7:29, 31). It refers to the housing for a ship's mast (Isa. 33:23). Note, however, the use of words 3651, I; 3651, II, by some translators.

3654. כֵּן *kēn:* A masculine noun meaning a gnat, a louse. It is used of the gnats or lice referred to in the third plague (Ex. 8:16–18[12–14]; Ps. 105:31). Some translators find the word in Isaiah 51:6, but others prefer to read 3651, I here. A few translators render the word as flies, a less likely translation.

3655. כָּנָה *kānāh:* A verb meaning to give a surname, a title of flattery or honor. It depicts the assigning of an honorary name to someone (Job 32:21, 22); or persons calling themselves by names, e.g., Jacob (Isa. 44:5). It means to show intimate knowledge and supervision over people by calling them by name (Isa. 45:4).

3656. כַּנֶּה *kanneh:* A proper noun designating Canneh (Ezek. 27:23).

3657. כַּנָּה *kannāh:* A feminine noun indicating a root, a shoot. It is used figuratively of Israel as the root God Himself planted, indicating His son or vine (Ps. 80:15[16]).

3658. כִּנּוֹר *kinnôr:* A masculine noun referring to a lyre or harp. It indicates a stringed instrument with a built-in acoustical chest or board (Gen. 4:21; 31:27). It was used for sacred (1 Sam. 10:5; 2 Sam. 6:5) or secular (Isa. 24:8) music (1 Sam. 16:16; Isa. 5:12). It was used in a figurative way of the Lord's heart lamenting like a harp for Moab (Isa. 16:11).

3659. כָּנְיָהוּ *konyāhû:* A proper noun designating Coniah, a shortened form of *y^ekonyāh* (3204) (Jer. 22:24, 28; 37:1).

3660. כְּנֵמָא *k^enēmā':* An Aramaic adverb meaning thus, so, as follows. It refers to what follows, e.g., as something said (Ezra 4:8; 5:4, 9, 11); or to what precedes (Ezra 6:13 refers to Darius's previous decree) and may be translated as "then" if appropriate.

3661. כָּנַן *kānan:* A verb meaning to shoot up. It is probably the root for *kānāh* (3657), which see.

3662. כְּנָנִי *k^enāniy:* A proper noun designating Chenani (Neh. 9:4).

3663. כְּנַנְיָהוּ *k^enanyāhû*, כְּנַנְיָה *k^enanyāh:* A proper noun designating Chenaniah:

A. A Levite (1 Chr. 15:22, 27).
B. An Izharite (1 Chr. 26:29).

3664. כָּנַס *kānas:* A verb meaning to gather, to collect. David assembled foreigners to be stonecutters (1 Chr. 22:2). Esther instructed Mordecai to gather the Jews and fast (Esth. 4:16). The Lord gathered the waters (Ps. 33:7). The writer of Ecclesiastes collected silver and gold for himself (Eccl. 2:8); there is a time to gather stones (Eccl. 3:5). The Lord told Ezekiel that He would gather Jerusalem together for punishment (Ezek. 22:21).

3665. כָּנַע *kāna':* A verb indicating to humble, to subdue, to be humble. It has the basic sense of being lowly, meek. It is used of the Lord's humbling an uncircumcised, prideful heart (Lev. 26:41); or defeating Israel's enemies (Deut. 9:3; Judg. 3:30; 4:23; 8:28; 1 Chr. 17:10; 18:1; 20:4). It is used of humbling oneself as well (1 Kgs. 21:29), especially before the Lord. The key to the Israelites' success after failure was to repent and humble themselves before the Lord (2 Chr. 7:14). The Lord challenges Job that only He can humble and crush the wicked in due time (Job 40:12).

3666. כִּנְעָה ***kin'āh:*** A feminine noun referring to a bundle, a bag. It refers to a piece of luggage, a bag, or a bundle or the materials or wares in such a carrying bag (Jer. 10:17).

3667. כְּנַעַן ***k^ena'an:*** A proper noun designating Canaan:

A. Canaan was the son of Ham, Noah's first son. He is listed third (1 Chr. 1:8, 13) or fourth (Gen. 10:6). Noah cursed him because of his father's sin and placed him under both Shem and Japheth (Gen. 9:18, 25–27). His basic social picture was one of servitude to others.

B. See A above. The name Canaan means "land of purple" and refers to the land or people of Canaan. The Greek word Phoenicia also means the same. But this traditional explanation of the name has been strongly challenged. Canaan manufactured and exported a purple dye. The land later was called Palestine because of the Philistines who immigrated there (part of the "sea peoples"). The language of Canaan was Semitic, and Hebrew is closely tied to it. This territory was inhabited by the descendants of Ham's son Canaan (Gen. 10:6–19). The Promised Land to Israel was essentially this land and its inhabitants which God would deliver to His chosen people, Israel, according to His promises to Abraham (Gen. 11:31; 12:5; 17:8; Ex. 3:16–17). Canaan became the burial place of the patriarchs (Gen. 23:19). The Canaanites were off-limits for the Hebrews and Israelites—even in the time of the patriarchs (Gen. 28:1, 6).

The geographical and climatic features of the land were and are far ranging. It stretched from Kadesh Barnea in the south to Lebo Hamath in the north. Bordered on the west by the Great Sea, it reached to beyond the Jordan on the east, beyond the Dead Sea, and east of Damascus in the north (Gen. 15:17–21; Num. 34:2–29). Ezekiel mentions it without naming its extent in his Temple vision (Ezek. 47:13—48:29).

C. The name and even the word Canaan became synonymous with merchant, tradesman in certain historical and textual contexts. Canaan was the trade center for many nations in the Middle East. The city of Tyre was an import/export center (Isa. 23:8), but the word could in this usage refer to other nations who were merchants or tradesmen, e.g., Babylon (Ezek. 16:29; 17:4).

3668. כְּנַעֲנָה $k^e na^{a} n\bar{a}h$: A proper noun designating Chenaanah:

A. Father of the prophet Zedekiah (1 Kgs. 22:11, 24; 2 Chr. 18:10, 23).

B. A Benjamite (1 Chr. 7:10).

3669. כְּנַעֲנִי $k^e na^{a} niy$: I. A masculine proper noun, Canaanite. It refers to a person of Canaan (Gen. 12:6; 38:2). With the definite article in front, it means the Canaanite (Num. 21:1; 33:40).

II. A masculine noun meaning a merchant, a trader. The word also came to mean a tradesman as well (Prov. 31:24; Zech. 14:21), since the Canaanites were known as traders or merchants throughout the Mediterranean world.

3670. כָּנַף *kānap̱*: A verb meaning to be hidden, to be put in a corner. It is used only in a passive sense of being thrust aside, cornered, or hidden (Isa. 30:20).

3671. כָּנָף *kānāp̱*: A common noun for a wing, the skirt or corner of a garment. It has the basic sense of to cover; an attached extremity. It indicates the wings of various birds or winged creatures in general (Gen. 1:21; 7:14; Ex. 19:4; Isa. 8:8). It is used of wings of other beings as well: cherubim (1 Kgs. 6:24); seraphs (Isa. 6:2); visionary beings like women (Zech. 5:9); insects (Isa. 18:1). It took on the sense of the outer edges, corners, or extremities of something, living or inanimate, i.e., the end(s) of the world (Isa. 11:12; 24:16; Ezek. 7:2). God carried Israel to Himself on the wings of an eagle (Ex. 19:4). It indicates the edge of a garment (1 Sam. 15:27). The idiom to spread (one's) wings over means to take to wife (Ezek. 16:8). It is used in other idioms to mean an attacking king (Isa. 18:1; Jer. 48:40; 49:22; Ezek. 17:3, 7); the healing wings of God's sun of righteousness (Mal. 4:2[3:20]). God is often noted as providing a shadow of protection for His people under His wings (Ruth 2:12; Ps. 17:8; 36:7[8]; 57:1[2]; 61:4[5]; 63:7[8]; 91:4).

3672. כִּנְּרוֹת $kinn^e r\hat{o}\underline{t}$, כִּנֶּרֶת *kinnereṯ*: A proper noun designating Chinnereth:

A. A city or the region around it (Deut. 3:17; Josh. 19:35; 1 Kgs. 15:20).

B. A lake (Num. 34:11; Josh. 11:2; 12:3; 13:27).

3673. כְּנַשׁ $k^e na\check{s}$: An Aramaic verb meaning to assemble, to be assembled. It corresponds to the Hebrew word *kānas* (3664) and occurs only in Daniel 3:2, 3, and 27. It referred to the assembling of Babylonian officials, initiated by Nebuchadnezzar, to dedicate and worship an image. The assembly was apparently a formal occasion with high officials standing before the image, a herald proclaiming the purpose of the assembly, and musicians playing various instruments. Those assembled saw the Hebrews who refused to obey sentenced to the fiery furnace and subsequently delivered from it.

3674. כְּנָט kᵉnāṭ: A masculine noun referring to a colleague, an associate. It refers to a person in a group of connected individuals or companions (Ezra 4:7).

3675. כְּנָת kᵉnāṯ: An Aramaic masculine noun denoting a companion, an associate. It refers to a group of persons sharing some common ties, whether political or otherwise (Ezra 4:9, 17, 23; 5:3, 6; 6:6, 13); in context, it always refers to political ties.

3676. כֵּס kēs: A masculine noun meaning throne. It is used once to designate the throne, seat, or chair of the Lord (Ex. 17:16).

3677. כֶּסֶא kese', כֶּסֶה keseh: A masculine noun referring to a full moon. It refers, based on context, to the time when the moon is full (Ps. 81:3[4]; Prov. 7:20), the 15th day of the month (NKJV, "the appointed day"; KJV).

3678. כִּסֵּא kissē', כִּסֵּה kissēh: A masculine noun meaning throne, a place of honor. Pharaoh put Joseph over everything in his kingdom except his throne (Gen. 41:40). Other references to leaders on the throne include Pharaoh (Ex. 11:5; 12:29); Solomon and Bathsheba (1 Kgs. 2:19); King Ahasuerus (Esth. 5:1); departed kings (Isa. 14:9); the princes of the coast (Ezek. 26:16); the prophetic one who will build the temple of the Lord (Zech. 6:13). Scripture also depicts God as sitting on a throne (Isa. 6:1; Ezek. 1:26). The throne can also be a symbol of a kingdom or power (2 Sam. 7:16; 14:9; Isa. 16:5).

3679. כַּסְדָּי kasdāy: An Aramaic masculine proper noun meaning Chaldean. It is a noun with a gentilic, ethnic ending indicating nationality. It refers to Nebuchadnezzar, a Chaldean king of Babylon (Ezra 5:12).

3680. כָּסָה kāsāh: A verb meaning to cover, to clothe, to conceal. The active meaning of this verb is to cover, to cover up. It is used in a literal sense to indicate that something is covering something else, as when the waters of the Red Sea covered the Egyptians or the cloud of God's glory covered Mount Sinai or the Tabernacle (Ex. 15:5; 24:15). In a metaphorical sense, the word describes shame covering the guilty (Ps. 69:7[8]; Jer. 3:25; Hab. 2:17); the Israelites' covering the altar with tears (Mal. 2:13); and the concealing of Joseph's blood to hide his brothers' guilt and sin (Gen. 37:26). On the other hand, the psalmist found reconciliation with God by not concealing his sin but confessing it (Ps. 32:5; Prov. 10:11). The word sometimes means to cover oneself with clothing or sackcloth, to clothe oneself with something (Ezek. 16:18; Jon. 3:6).

The passive form of the verb means to be covered, such as when the mountains were covered by the waters of the great flood (Gen. 7:19; Ps. 80:10[11]). The reflexive form is used to mean to cover oneself; for example, when the people of Nineveh covered themselves in repentance at Jonah's preaching (Jon. 3:8). The word in Ecclesiastes 6:4 describes the name of a stillborn child covering itself in darkness.

3681. כָּסוּי ***kāsûy:*** A masculine noun meaning cover, covering. It is used to describe a covering of animal skins used in the transporting of articles from the Tabernacle (Num. 4:6, 14).

3682. כְּסוּת ***k^{e}sûṯ:*** A feminine active noun describing a covering or clothing. It is used figuratively of the "covering" provided by the payment of an offense against someone (Gen. 20:16). It refers literally to clothing in general or a cloak (Ex. 21:10; 22:27[26]; Deut. 22:12; Job 24:7; 31:19). It is used figuratively of God's bringing dark clouds to cover the sky (Isa. 50:3) and of His power to see destruction, since it cannot be covered from His eyes (Job 26:6).

3683. כָּסַח ***kāsaḥ:*** A verb indicating to cut up, to cut down. It describes the cutting down of vines or thorns which symbolize God's people, Israel (Ps. 80:16[17]), but also the nations that have risen against them (Isa. 33:12).

3684. כְּסִיל ***k^{e}siyl:*** A masculine noun meaning fool, foolish. It refers to one of several types of fools in Scripture, especially in Proverbs. Such persons are usually unable to deal with life in a successful, practical way (Eccl. 4:5, 13) and are lacking in religious or spiritual sympathies (Ps. 49:10[11]; Prov. 1:22, 32). Fools do not understand issues (*lō'-yāḇîn,* Ps. 92:6[7]), for they conduct their lives in a haze or darkness (Eccl. 2:14–16). Fools act rashly (Eccl. 5:1), and their laughter is senseless (Eccl. 7:6). As the proverb goes, they are always going to the left, not the right (Eccl. 10:2). Wise persons receive honor, but the *k^{e}siyl* only shame after shame (Prov. 3:35). These persons need understanding, literally *lēḇ,* hearts (Prov. 8:5). They are sources of despair to their parents (Prov. 10:1).

3685. כְּסִיל ***k^{e}siyl:*** A proper noun referring to a constellation, especially Orion. It refers to the constellation or collection of stars and heavenly bodies (Amos 5:8; Job 9:9; 38:31), always with the purpose of pointing out the Lord as their creator and orchestrator.

3686. כְּסִיל ***k^{e}siyl:*** A proper noun designating Chesil (Josh. 15:30).

3687. כְּסִילוּת ***k^{e}siylûṯ:*** A feminine noun meaning foolishness, stupidity. This abstract noun is derived from the adjective *k^{e}siyl* (3684), which means fat and, thus, (in a negative sense) stupid, foolish (or as a substantive, a foolish one). *K^{e}siylûṯ* occurs only in Proverbs 9:13, naming the woman of folly, a symbolic character who appealed to the evil desires of naive people in order to cause them to stray from right paths into paths that lead to death.

3688. כָּסַל kāsal: A verb meaning to be stupid, to become stupid. It occurs once as a verb in Jeremiah 10:8, referring to those taught by idols.

3689. כֶּסֶל kesel: A masculine noun meaning loins, confidence, stupidity. The first use can actually mean the waist area, the kidneys, etc. (Lev. 3:4, 10, 15; 4:9; 7:4; Job 15:27). The second use is more ambiguous, meaning that in which one puts trust or confidence (Job 8:14; 31:24; Ps. 78:7; Prov. 3:26). The final usage is a false self-trust or stupidity (Ps. 49:13[14]; Eccl. 7:25). See the related Hebrew verb *kāsal* (3688) and Hebrew noun *kislāh* (3690).

3690. כִּסְלָה kislāh: A feminine noun meaning foolishness, stupidity, confidence. The root idea of fatness (see *kāsal*[3688]) may have two implications. In Job 4:6, *k^esilāh* means the confidence of one who is fat and firm. Eliphaz cast doubt on Job's righteousness by asking why he was confused if he really feared God. In Psalm 85:8[9], on the other hand, God warned His restored people not to return to their former folly. In that verse, the word refers to sluggish foolishness that is no longer alive to the fear of God.

3691. כִּסְלֵו kislēw: A proper noun denoting the month Chislev or Kislev. It is the name given to the ninth month of the year, equal to our November/December (Neh. 1:1; Zech. 7:1).

3692. כִּסְלוֹן kislôn: A proper noun designating Chislon (Num. 34:21).

3693. כְּסָלוֹן k^esālôn: A proper noun designating Chesalon (Josh. 15:10).

3694. כְּסוּלּוֹת k^esûllôṯ: A proper noun designating Chesulloth (Josh. 19:18).

3695. כַּסְלֻחִים kasluḥiym: A proper noun designating Casluhites, Casluhim (Gen. 10:14; 1 Chr. 1:12).

3696. כִּסְלֹת תָּבֹר kislōṯ tāḇōr: A proper noun designating Chisloth Tabor (Josh. 19:12).

3697. כָּסַם kāsam: A verb indicating the trimming of one's hair. It refers to clipping one's hair, the requirement for priests in Ezekiel's new Temple (44:20). Long hair may have indicated a Nazarite vow during Ezekiel's day as well.

3698. כֻּסֶּמֶת kussemeṯ: A feminine noun referring to a species of wheat, spelt. It refers to a grain with split kernels which ripened later than flax and barley (Ex. 9:32; Isa. 28:25; Ezek. 4:9).

3699. כָּסַס kāsas: A verb meaning to estimate. It is used of figuring out, calculating, or determining something, e.g., the lamb needed for the Passover (Ex. 12:4).

3700. כָּסַף kāsap̱: A verb meaning to desire, to long for. It refers to a strong, affectionate desire for someone or something (Gen. 31:30), especially the presence of the Lord (Ps. 84:2[3]). It also indicates a lion's powerful hunger for food (Ps. 17:12). It takes on the sense of shameless with regard to a nation so set on its rebellion and sin that it is not ashamed (Zeph. 2:1).

3701. כֶּסֶף kesep̱: A masculine noun referring to silver, money. It refers to silver used as a metal (Job 28:1; Prov. 2:4; Zech. 13:9; Mal. 3:3); silver used in making various vessels (Gen. 24:53; Ezek. 27:12); silver as a medium of exchange (Gen. 23:9; 44:1, 2, 8). It was a sign of wealth (Gen. 13:2). Some silver was more choice, more pure (Prov. 8:19; 10:20). It was used in a system of weights and measures, especially shekels (Ex. 21:32; Lev. 5:15; Num. 18:16); and talents (ca. 75 lbs. in wt.) of silver (Ex. 38:27; 1 Kgs. 20:39). It was used as a means of atonement and ransom for the lives of individual Israelites (Ex. 30:16; Num. 3:49). It was used in idioms and figurative senses: a figure of a dove's wings (Ps. 68:13[14]); standing for a slave (Ex. 21:21); the tongue of a righteous person (Prov. 10:20). It is often found with verbs indicating refining and buying silver: to refine (Isa. 48:10; Zech. 13:9); to weigh out silver (Gen. 23:16; Ezra 8:25; Jer. 32:9); to buy something with silver (Jer. 32:25, 44; Amos 8:6. In Numbers 18:16 only, it is used with the verb to redeem. The phrase *miqnaṯ kesep̱* indicates a person purchased for money (Gen. 17:12, 13, 23, 27; Ex. 12:44; or *kesep̱ miqnaṯ* in Lev. 25:51).

3702. כְּסַף k^{e}sap̱: An Aramaic masculine noun denoting silver, money. It is used in biblical Aramaic to indicate both a metal (Ezra 5:14; Dan. 2:32, 35), second only in value to gold, or a medium of exchange, money (Ezra 7:17; 22).

3703. כָּסִפְיָא kāsipyā': A proper noun designating Casiphia (Ezra 8:17).

3704. כֶּסֶת keseṯ: A feminine noun indicating a wristband. It describes a band, some kind of wristband for religious, magical purposes (Ezek. 13:18, 20).

3705. כְּעַן k^e'an: An Aramaic adverb indicating now, now then, furthermore. The word has both a time and logical sense in its use. It occurs only at the beginning of its clause (Ezra 4:13, 14, 21; Dan. 2:23; 3:15). With *'aḏ-* preceding, the phrase means up to or until now (Ezra 5:16).

3706. כְּעֶנֶת k^e'eneṯ, כְּעֶת k^e'eṯ: An Aramaic particle meaning now, and now. It is related to what follows and serves to introduce it (Ezra 4:10, 11, 17; 7:12).

3707. כָּעַס kā'as: A verb meaning to be angry, to provoke to anger. The causative sense of the verb occurs most often and frequently signifies idolatry provoking God to anger (cf. 1 Kgs. 14:9; Ps. 106:29; Ezek. 8:17). The result of provocation may be expressed as *'ap̱*, anger (639) (Deut. 9:18; 2 Kgs. 23:26; Jer. 7:20). In a noncausative sense, the verb means to be angry; people were warned not to become angry hastily (Eccl. 7:9); God says that after He punishes, He will not be angry (Ezek. 16:42). Three times it refers to the people's anger directed toward righteousness (2 Chr. 16:10; Neh. 4:1[3:33]; Ps. 112:10).

3708. כַּעַס *ka'as*, כַּעַשׂ *ka'aś*: A masculine singular noun meaning anger, provocation, vexation. The alternate spelling of the word occurs only in Job. The majority of occurrences are in poetic literature. Human sinfulness and idolatry (1 Kgs. 15:30; Ezek. 20:28) cause God's anger, while fools, sons, wives, and rival wives can also cause vexation (1 Sam. 1:6; Prov. 27:3; 17:25; 21:19, respectively).

3709. כַּף *kap̱*: A feminine noun meaning hand, the flat of the hand, the flat of the foot, hollow, bent. The principal meaning is hollow, often used of the hollow of the physical hand or foot. It also relates to cupped or bent objects such as spoons (Num. 7:80). In metaphysical overtones, Job declared his cleanness of hand (Job 9:30); and David linked clean hands with a pure heart (Ps. 24:4). The righteous correctly lift up their hands in God's name (Ps. 63:4[5]; 141:2), but the wicked are snared by their own hands' work (Ps. 9:16). At wicked Jezebel's death, dogs devoured her but refused the palms of her hands (2 Kgs. 9:35). The Israelites inherited every place on which their soles treaded in the Promised Land (Deut. 11:24); the returning exiles were delivered from the hand of the enemy (Ezra 8:31). Ultimately, God is the skillful Shepherd, securely holding His own with a sovereign hand (Ps. 139:5).

3710. כֵּף *kēp̱*: A masculine noun designating a rock. It refers to rocks in the hills or mountains (Jer. 4:29), as well as rocks in the ground on the lowland (Job 30:6).

3711. כָּפָה *kāp̱āh*: A verb meaning to soothe, to pacify. It refers to the calming or reconciling of an attitude of anger toward someone (Prov. 21:14).

3712. כִּפָּה *kippāh*: A feminine noun referring to a palm branch, a branch; a shoot, a sprout. It is used to designate palm fronds used to celebrate at the Feast of Tabernacles (Lev. 23:40). It is used of fresh, sprouting branches (Job 15:32) as well as more developed palm branches (Isa. 9:14[13]; 19:15) but with reference to the leaders of Israel.

3713. כְּפוֹר *kᵉpôr*: I. A masculine noun indicating a bowl. It refers to a small bowl made of silver or gold for use in the Temple of Ezra's day (Ezra 1:10; 8:27) or the Solomonic Temple (1 Chr. 28:17).

II. A masculine noun meaning hoar frost. It refers to the thin flakes or wafers of manna which the Lord gave to Israel (Ex. 16:14). It was literally frost from heaven given by the Lord (Job 38:29; Ps. 147:16).

3714. כָּפִיס kāp̱iys: A masculine noun indicating a rafter, a beam. It refers to a wooden beam or support in a royal building. It is personified to speak out against the violence of the kings of Babylon toward many nations (Hab. 2:11).

3715. כְּפִיר k^{e}p̱iyr: I. A masculine noun meaning young lions; a lion. It is used to indicate the animal, a young lion (Judg. 14:5), known for its ferocity (Job 4:10; Ps. 17:12). The nature and character of a lion is understood by God alone (Job 38:39). Its roar is compared to a king's anger (Prov. 19:12). It is used often figuratively of nations or persons. Pharaoh is a young lion among the nations, a terror to others (Ezek. 32:2) as were Dedan, Tarshish (Ezek. 38:13), and Assyria (Nah. 2:11[12], 13[14]). The Lord is compared to an avenging lion (Hos. 5:14; Amos 3:4).

II. A masculine noun indicating a village, a small town. It indicates an inhabited small town often situated in the shadow of larger cities (Neh. 6:2; Ezek. 38:13).

III. A masculine proper noun referring to the village, Kephirim. It indicates a small town in Benjaminite territory, possibly located near Joppa (Neh. 6:2).

3716. כְּפִירָה k^{e}p̱iyrāh: A proper noun designating Chephirah (Josh. 9:17; 18:26; Ezra 2:25; Neh. 7:29).

3717. כָּפַל kāp̱al: A verb meaning to double something, to double, to become doable. It is used of doubling over, folding something, such as a curtain (Ex. 26:9) or other piece of cloth (Ex. 28:16; 39:9). It is used of something being done twice, doubled (Ezek. 21:14[19]).

3718. כֶּפֶל kep̱el: A masculine noun indicating something doubled, double. It refers to something doubled or divided (Job 41:13[5]). It is used to indicate the complex double side of wisdom or its real extent (Job 11:6; KJV, NIV). Israel paid double for her sins (Isa. 40:2).

3719. כָּפַן kāp̱an: A verb indicating to bend, to twist. It indicates a vine putting forth roots as it seeks nourishment for growth (Ezek. 17:7). It is used figuratively of Israel's political move toward Egyptian aid, an ill-fated move.

3720. כָּפָן kāp̱ān: A masculine noun meaning hunger, famine. It describes a time of drought and a lack of crops (Job 5:22); or a general lack of food for persons (Job 30:3) in context because of their low social standing.

3721. כָּפַף kāp̱ap̱: A verb meaning to bow down. It is used in a religious sense of humbling oneself (Isa. 58:5; Mic. 6:6) or with reference to being defeated or oppressed by one's enemies (Ps. 57:6[7]). It is used in a general sense of those who are in distress or have fallen for various reasons (Ps. 145:14; 146:8). The Lord helps them.

3722. כָּפַר kāp̱ar: A verb meaning to cover, to forgive, to expiate, to reconcile. This word is of supreme theological importance in the Old Testament as it is central to an Old Testament understanding of the remission of sin. At its most basic level, the word conveys the notion of covering but not in the sense of merely concealing. Rather, it suggests the imposing of something to change its appearance or nature. It is therefore employed to signify the cancellation or "writing over" of a contract (Isa. 28:18); the appeasing of anger (Gen. 32:20[21]; Prov. 16:14); and the overlaying of wood with pitch so as to make it waterproof (Gen. 6:14). The word also communicates God's covering of sin. Persons made reconciliation with God for their sins by imposing something that would appease the offended party (in this case the Lord) and cover the sinners with righteousness (Ex. 32:30; Ezek. 45:17; cf. Dan. 9:24). In the Old Testament, the blood of sacrifices was most notably imposed (Ex. 30:10). By this imposition, sin was purged (Ps. 79:9; Isa. 6:7) and forgiven (Ps. 78:38). The offenses were removed, leaving the sinners clothed in righteousness (cf. Zech. 3:3, 4). Of course, the imposition of the blood of bulls and of goats could never fully cover our sin (see Heb. 10:4), but with the coming of Christ and the imposition of His shed blood, a perfect atonement was made (Rom. 5:9–11).

3723. כָּפָר kāp̱ār: A masculine noun indicating a village. It refers to a small town, usually unwalled (1 Chr. 27:25). It was a pleasant place to spend time with one's beloved (Song 7:11[12]).

3724. כֹּפֶר kōp̱er: A masculine noun meaning a ransom, a bribe, a half-shekel. The most common translation of the word is ransom. It refers to the price demanded in order to redeem or rescue a person. The irresponsible owner of a bull that killed someone and was known to have gored people previously could be redeemed by the ransom that would be placed on him (Ex. 21:30). When a census of people was taken in Israel, adult males had to pay a half-shekel ransom to keep the Lord's plague from striking them (Ex. 30:12). A murderer could not be redeemed by a ransom (Num. 35:31). Yet money, without God's explicit approval, could not serve as a ransom for a human being (Ps. 49:7[8]). On the other hand, money could serve as a ransom to buy off a person's human enemies (Prov. 13:8). God sometimes used a wicked person as a ransom to redeem a righteous person (Prov. 21:18); God ransomed Israel from Babylonian captivity for the ransom price of three nations (Isa. 43:3): Egypt, Seba, and Cush.

The meaning of the word becomes a bribe when used in certain circumstances. For example, Samuel declared that he had never taken a bribe (1 Sam. 12:3); and Amos castigated the leaders of Israel for taking bribes (Amos 5:12). Proverbs 6:35 describes a jealous husband whose fury would not allow him to take a bribe to lessen his anger.

3725. כִּפֻּרִים *kippuriym:* A masculine plural noun meaning atonement, the act of reconciliation, the Day of Atonement. It is used five times to indicate the act or process of reconciliation: a young bull was sacrificed each day for seven days during the ordination ceremony of Aaron and his sons to make atonement (Ex. 29:36). Once a year, the blood of a sin offering was used to make atonement on the horns of the altar of incense located in front of the Holy of Holies (Ex. 30:10). Ransom money of a half-shekel was used to effect atonement or reconciliation for male Israelites who were at least twenty years old (Ex. 30:16). The money was then used to service the Tent of Meeting.

When a person had wronged the Lord or another person, a ram was presented to the priest, along with proper restitution (Num. 5:8); a sin offering for atonement was presented yearly on the Day of Atonement (Num. 29:11). Three times the noun is used to indicate the Day of Atonement itself (Lev. 23:27, 28; 25:9).

3726. כְּפַר הָעַמּוֹנִי *kᵉpar ha'ammôniy:* A compound proper noun designating Chephar-ammoni, which if from *kāpar* (3723) and *'ammôniy* (5984) (Josh. 18:24).

3727. כַּפֹּרֶת *kappōreṯ:* A noun meaning a lid, propitiation. This word refers to the lid that covered the ark of the testimony. It was made of gold and was decorated with two cherubim. God resided above this mercy seat (Ex. 25:17–22). Only at specific times could the high priest come before the mercy seat (Lev. 16:2). On the Day of Atonement, the high priest made atonement for himself, the Tabernacle, and the people by a sin offering, which included sprinkling blood on this lid (Lev. 16:13–15).

3728. כָּפַשׁ *kāpaš:* A verb meaning to bend, to trample down, to humiliate, to cover over. This word is a primary root, but it is used only once in the Hebrew Bible. There the writer of Lamentations felt like he was trampled in the dust (Lam. 3:16).

3729. כְּפַת *kᵉpaṯ:* An Aramaic verb meaning to tie up, to bind. It is used of the process of binding, tying up securely, the three Hebrew youth cast into a fiery furnace. It is used in its active form, to bind (Dan. 3:20); in its passive form, to be bound (Dan. 3:21); or bound (Dan. 3:23, 24).

3730. כַּפְתּוֹר *kaptôr,* כַּפְתֹּר *kaptōr:* A masculine noun indicating a bulb, a bulge, or an ornamentation on a column. A knobby decoration on a lampstand (Ex. 25:31, 33–36; 37:17, 19–22) is rendered bud(s) by some translators (NIV; KJV, knobs). It is used of the top part of a pillar or its decoration (Amos 9:1). It is a sign of desolation and desertion of a city when owls rest on the tops of its ornamental columns (Zeph. 2:14).

3731. כַּפְתּוֹר kaptôr, כַּפְתֹּר kaptōr: A proper noun designating Caphtor (Deut. 2:23; Jer. 47:4; Amos 9:7).

3732. כַּפְתֹּרִי kaptōriy: A proper noun designating Caphtorite (Gen. 10:14; Deut. 2:23; 1 Chr. 1:12).

3733. כַּר kar: A masculine noun meaning pasture, a male lamb, and a battering ram. When used to mean pasture, it describes a bountiful restoration for the Israelites. Like sheep, they would have large pastures in which to graze (Isa. 30:23). In reference to sheep, it means a male lamb as compared to ewes, lambs, or fatlings (1 Sam. 15:9). Tribute often came in the form of both ewes and rams, such as Mesha, king of Moab, paid to the king of Israel (2 Kgs. 3:4). This word also connotes a battering ram such as those used in siege warfare (Ezek. 4:2). It is also interpreted as a saddle (Gen. 31:34).

3734. כֹּר kōr: I. A masculine noun meaning a measure of grain or oil. It was a standard ancient measure of capacity, whether wet or dry (1 Kgs. 5:11[25]). It equaled one hundred gallons or about six bushels of dry measure or more.

II. An Aramaic masculine noun indicating a measure of grain. It was equal to six bushels of wheat (Ezra 7:22) and, in context, was a gift from the Persian king.

3735. כְּרָה k^erāh: An Aramaic verb meaning to be troubled, to be grieved. It indicates an agitated, worried attitude and set of emotions (Dan. 7:15). Daniel was put into this state by an overwhelming dream or vision (7:1).

3736. כִּרְבֵּל kirbēl: A verb meaning to be clothed with. It is used only to indicate the royal and Levitical regalia King David wore when he prepared to move the ark of God (1 Chr. 15:27).

3737. כַּרְבְּלָה karb^elāh: A feminine Aramaic noun indicating a cap, a turban. It was an article of clothing worn on the heads of the three Hebrew young men thrown into a fiery furnace (Dan. 3:21).

3738. כָּרָה kārāh: A verb indicating to dig. It refers to digging, cleaning out sufficient dirt and debris for various purposes: a grave (Gen. 50:5); a well (Gen. 26:25); a pit (Ex. 21:33), etc. It is used in several idioms and figures of speech: wicked persons get into a helpless situation, pits, into which they fall (Ps. 7:15[16]); persons lacking character create problems and situations that catch others (Prov. 16:27), but they themselves will fall into their own pits (Prov. 26:27). The Lord opens His servants' ears (digs their ears) so they can hear (Ps. 40:6[7]). The Lord digs a pit to receive the wicked (Ps. 94:13).

3739. כָּרָה *kārāh:* I. A verb meaning to buy, to bargain for, to barter for. It indicates getting something by barter, trade, or purchase (Deut. 2:6). Persons, friends were not to be bartered over (Job 6:27); humans did not have the power to barter or bargain over Leviathan (Job 41:6[40:30]; NIV, NASB). It is, however, used of Hosea's purchase of his wife (Hos. 3:2).

II. It indicates the giving of a feast or a banquet (2 Kgs. 6:23; Job 41:6).

3740. כֵּרָה *kērāh:* A feminine noun indicating a feast or meal. It refers to a great meal or feast and is used with its related verb for emphasis (2 Kgs. 6:23): "And he prepared a feast for them, a great feast." It describes the giving of a feast (*kērāh*) to certain persons (2 Kgs. 6:23). Some scholars find the word in Job 41:6[40:30] and translate accordingly.

3741. כָּרָה *kārāh:* A feminine noun indicating a cottage. It is used only once in Zephaniah 2:6. The ancient text of this passage is difficult to decipher. It has been traditionally rendered as cottages (KJV), but more recent translations give different interpretations, Kerethites (NIV, see 3774), pastures (NASB; NKJV).

3742. כְּרוּב *kᵉrûḇ:* A masculine noun of uncertain derivation meaning an angelic being. It is commonly translated as cherub (plural, cherubim). The Bible provides scant details concerning the likeness of these winged creatures, except for the apocalyptic visions of Ezekiel in Ezekiel 10. However, current pictures of cherubim as chubby infants with wings or as feminine creatures find no scriptural basis. The Bible portrays cherubim as the guardians of the Garden of Eden (Gen. 3:24) and seemingly the glory of the Lord (cf. Ezek. 10:3, 4, 18–20); as flanking the throne of God (Ps. 99:1; cf. Isa. 37:16; though these may be poetic references to the mercy seat in the Tabernacle [Num. 7:89]); as embroidered images on the tapestry of the Tabernacle (Ex. 26:1, 31); and as sculpted images arching above the mercy seat on the ark of the covenant (Ex. 25:18–20, 22; 1 Kgs. 6:23–28; 2 Chr. 3:10–13). Figuratively, the word is used to describe God's winged transport (2 Sam. 22:11; Ps. 18:10[11]). Interestingly, Satan is described as being the anointed cherub (Ezek. 28:14) before he was cast out of heaven.

3743. כְּרוּב *kᵉrûḇ:* A proper noun designating Cherub, Kerub (Ezra 2:59; Neh. 7:61).

3744. כָּרוֹז *kārôz:* An Aramaic masculine noun, a herald. It is used of the leader and announcer at the dedication of Nebuchadnezzar's statue (Dan. 3:4).

3745. כְּרָז ***k^{e}raz:*** An Aramaic noun announcing a proclamation. It refers to a royal report issued by a king. It refers in context to Belshazzar's official royal announcement concerning Daniel (5:29).

3746. כָּרִי ***kāriy:*** A noun meaning a military order, the Kerethites or Cherethites. Under Benaiah (2 Sam. 20:23), the Kerethites or Cherethites, along with the Pelethites, remained loyal to David and Solomon when Adonijah attempted to become king. Joab, the commander of David's army, however, supported Adonijah (cf. 1 Kgs. 1:18, 19).

The Karites or Carites again supported a king against treachery when they helped overthrow Athaliah and installed Joash as king (2 Kgs. 11:19). It is possible that the Pelethites in 2 Kings were a different group of Pelethites because the spelling of the Hebrew word is slightly different than in other references. What is clear is this term designates a special military unit.

3747. כְּרִית ***k^{e}riyṯ:*** A proper noun designating Cherith (1 Kgs. 17:3, 5).

3748. כְּרִיתוּת ***k^{e}riyṯûṯ:*** A feminine noun meaning divorce. If a man was to find that his wife was unfaithful or any uncleanness in her, he was able to write a certificate of divorce that resulted in her expulsion from his house (Deut. 24:1). Metaphorically, the Lord asked where Israel's certificate of divorce was. She should have had one to act so loosely (i.e., following other gods [Isa. 50:1; Jer. 3:8]).

3749. כַּרְכֹּב ***karkōḇ:*** A masculine noun indicating a rim, a ledge, an edge. It is used to describe a ledge or border around the edge of the bronze altar (Ex. 27:5; 38:4). The grating of the altar was located beneath the ledge.

3750. כַּרְכֹּם ***karkōm:*** A masculine noun meaning saffron. It is used in highly charged, romantic, figurative language of a bridegroom (Song 4:14) regarding the bride's garden of delights.

3751. כַּרְכְּמִישׁ ***kark^{e}miyš:*** A proper noun designating Carchemish. The name means "stronghold of Kemosh." A fortified city in Upper Mesopotamia where Babylon defeated Pharaoh Neco, king of Egypt and became the new superpower of the Middle East in 605 B.C. (2 Chr. 35:20–21) and ruled over Syro-Palestine (Jer. 46:1–2).

3752. כַּרְכַּס ***karkas:*** A proper noun designating Carcas (Esth. 1:10).

3753. כִּרְכָּרָה ***kirkārāh:*** A feminine noun denoting a camel. An animal used for swift transportation in the time of Isaiah (66:20). It will be used as one means to gather together the nations to Jerusalem to see the glory of the Lord.

3754. כֶּרֶם ***kerem:*** A common noun indicating a vineyard, an area where grapevines and their fruits are gown and cultivated intensely. Wine as well as grapes is produced from vineyards. It is referred to many times in the Old Testament (Gen. 9:20; Judg. 15:5; 1 Kgs. 21:1, 2, 6, 7, 15, 16, 18; Song 2:15). It is used as a figure of Israel with the Lord as the owner of the vineyard (Isa. 5:1, 3–5, 7, 10; Jer. 12:10). It is used of the appearance of the beloved's skin (Song 1:6) and of her in general (Song 8:12). Various verbs used with the noun indicate that a vineyard is planted (*nṭ'*) (Gen. 9:20; Amos 5:11); seeded (*zr'*) (Deut. 22:9; 20:6); pruned (*zmr*), harvested (*bṣr*), gleaned (Lev. 19:10). Locusts may, as a warning from the Lord, consume a vineyard (Amos 4:9).

3755. כֹּרֵם *kōrēm:* A masculine noun referring to a vinedresser. It refers to those people who cared for and husbanded vineyards in Israel. It is a plural participial form of the verb *kāram* (2 Kgs. 25:12; 2 Chr. 26:10; Isa. 61:5; Jer. 52:16; Joel 1:11).

3756. כַּרְמִי *karmiy:* A proper noun designating Carmi:

A. Son of Reuben (Gen. 46:9; Ex. 6:14; Num. 26:6; 1 Chr. 5:3).

B. A Judaite (Josh. 7:1, 18; 1 Chr. 2:7; 4:1).

3757. כַּרְמִי *karmiy:* A proper noun designating Carmite (Num. 26:6).

3758. כַּרְמִיל *karmiyl:* A masculine noun indicating a color, crimson, red. It refers to a dye and items colored by it, such as cloth or fabric (2 Chr. 2:7[6], 14[13]; 3:14). It was among items gathered for use in Solomon's temple.

3759. כַּרְמֶל *karmel:* I. A masculine noun meaning an orchard, a fertile field. It usually refers to an area of fertile ground set aside for growing fruit trees and vines (2 Chr. 26:10; Isa. 10:18; 16:10; 29:17; 32:15). It also denotes an area covered with a thick forest (2 Kgs. 19:23; Isa. 37:24).

II. A masculine noun indicating new grain, fresh corn. It refers to grain that is newly ripened and fresh (Lev. 2:14; 23:14; 2 Kgs. 4:42) and of new growth, often used in religious festivals.

3760. כַּרְמֶל *karmel:* A proper noun designating Carmel. The name means "fruitful land."

A. It is a high mountain protruding out from the Mediterranean coastline in northern Israel in Manasseh. By extension it refers to the range of hills in this territory as well. It was the place where Elijah defeated the prophets of Baal and restored Yahweh, the Lord, as God in Israel (1 Kgs. 18:19–42). It was known for its beauty (Song 7:5 [6]) and prominent position in the land. Its "withering" or "blossoming" tended to be used as a sign of blessing or judgment from the Lord (Amos 1:2; 9:3; Mic. 7:14, NIV, "fertile pasturelands"). In some places, it is translated as "fertile land" (esp. NIV, Isa. 16:10) or "fruitful place" (KJV, Jer. 2:7; 4:26).

B. A city near Hebron (Josh. 15:55; 1 Sam. 15:12; 25:2, 5, 7, 40).

3761. כַּרְמְלִי karmᵉliy: A proper noun designating Carmelite (1 Sam. 30:5; 2 Sam. 2:2; 3:3; 23:35; 1 Chr. 11:37).

3762. כַּרְמְלִית karmᵉliyṯ: A proper noun designating Carmelitess (1 Sam. 27:3; 1 Chr. 3:1).

3763. כְּרָן kᵉrān: A proper noun designating Cheran (Gen. 36:26; 1 Chr. 1:41).

3764. כָּרְסֵא korsē': An Aramaic masculine noun meaning throne. Daniel reminded Belshazzer that Nebuchadnezzar had been deposed from his throne because of pride (Dan. 5:20). Daniel had a dream about a throne that belonged to the Ancient of Days (Dan. 7:9). See the related Hebrew nouns *kissē'* and *kissēh* (3678).

3765. כִּרְסֵם kirsēm: A four-letter verb meaning to tear, to ravage, to tear apart. It is used to describe the ravaging of God's people by a wild boar (Ps. 80:13[14]), a symbol of their enemies.

3766. כָּרַע kāra': A verb meaning to bow. The word signifies the crouching of a lion before going to sleep (Gen. 49:9; Num. 24:9); the bowing of an animal (Job 39:3); or a woman in order to give birth (1 Sam. 4:19); the bowing down of a man over a woman in sexual intercourse (adulterous, in this case) (Job 31:10); the yielding of knees from weakness, sometimes after one has been wounded (Judg. 5:27; 2 Kgs. 9:24); the bowing of knees under a heavy burden (Isa. 10:4; 46:2); the bowing of knees in submission or subjugation (Esth. 3:2, 5; Isa. 45:23); bowing in repentance (Ezra 9:5); to worship a false god (1 Kgs. 19:18); or the true God (2 Chr. 29:29; Ps. 95:6).

3767. כְּרָע kᵉra': A masculine noun indicating a leg. It refers to the lower leg, the fibula bone of the Passover lamb (Ex. 12:9); a sacrificial ram (Ex. 29:17); and various sacrificial offerings (Lev. 1:9, 13; 4:11; 8:21; 9:14). It is used of a locust's legs (Lev. 11:21).

3768. כַּרְפַּס karpas: A masculine noun referring to linen. It is used of white and violet linen found in the palace of the Persian king, Ahasuerus (Esth. 1:6) (*hûr karpaś ûṯᵉḵēleṯ*).

3769. כָּרַר kārar: A verb meaning to dance. It is used of David's whirling, impassioned dancing before the Lord when the ark was brought to Jerusalem (2 Sam. 6:14, 16).

3770. כָּרֵשׂ kārēś: A masculine noun meaning stomach. It is used in a figure of speech referring to Nebuchadnezzar's stomach. Literally, "He has filled his stomach (*kᵉrēśôw*) from my best foods" (Jer. 51:34).

3771. כַּרְשְׁנָא karšᵉnā': A proper noun designating Carshena (Esth. 1:14).

3772. כָּרַת **kāraṯ:** A verb meaning to cut off, to cut down, to make a covenant. This word can mean literally to cut something down or off, as grapes (Num. 13:23, 24); or branches (Judg. 9:48, 49). It can also be used figuratively, as with people (Jer. 11:19; 50:16). Another important use of this word is to make a covenant (lit., to cut a covenant), perhaps deriving from the practice of cutting an animal in two in the covenant ceremony. God made a covenant with Abraham (Gen. 15:18); Abraham made one with Abimelech (Gen. 21:27). Finally, this word can also mean to destroy, as in Micah's prophecy (Mic. 5:10).

3773. כְּרֻתוֹת **kᵉruṯôṯ:** A feminine plural noun referring to trimmed beams. It describes cedar beams hewn to size, cut, and placed in the structures of Solomon's Temple and his own palace (1 Kgs. 6:36; 7:2, 12).

3774. כְּרֵתִי **kᵉrēṯiy:** A proper noun designating Cheriethite (1 Sam. 30:14; 2 Sam. 8:18; 15:18; 20:7, 23; 1 Kgs. 1:38, 44; 1 Chr. 18:17; Ezek. 25:16; Zeph. 2:5, 6).

3775. כֶּשֶׂב **keśeḇ:** A masculine noun indicating a lamb, a young sheep. It indicates lambs or young sheep used for sacrifices (Lev. 1:10; 3:7; 4:35; 22:19; Num. 18:17); in food preparation (Lev. 7:23; 17:3; Deut. 14:4). These animals constituted wealth and property (Gen. 30:32, 33, 35, 40).

3776. כִּשְׂבָּה **kiśbāh:** A feminine noun indicating a ewe lamb. It refers to a young female lamb (Lev. 5:6). It could be presented as a guilt offering.

3777. כֶּשֶׂד **keśeḏ:** A proper noun designating Chesed (Gen. 22:22).

3778. כַּשְׂדִּים **kaśdiym:** A proper noun designating Chaldean, Babylonian:

A. The gentilic name of the inhabitants of a city (Babylon) and area (Babylonia) located in southern Mesopotamia on the Euphrates River. The city's ancient ruins are located ca. 50 miles south of modern Baghdad, Iraq. The term Chaldeans is also rendered as Babylonians in various translations. (see e.g., 2 Kgs. 24:2 in NIV and textual note there). Isaiah called the people of Babylon Babylonians or Chaldeans (Isa. 13:19). The city of Babylon and the subsequent kingdom of Babylon or Babylonia were founded by Nimrod, the famous descendant of Cush and his father Ham (Gen. 10:6–10). The land of Shinar (Gen. 11:1–2) is the location where the Tower of Babel was constructed, and Daniel deftly places the exiles of Judah in the land of Shinar (Dan. 1:1–4). Abraham was called out from among the Chaldeans living in Ur (Gen. 11:31; 15:7). The neo-Babylonian Empire (626–539 B.C.) played a major role in the Old Testament, and its greatest ruler was a Chaldean king (Ezra 5:12). The nation and its people were subject to scathing invective prophecies from the Lord's messengers (e.g., Jer. 50:1—51:64).

B. A technical use of the word Chaldeans (*kaśdiym* in Hebrew) refers to a group of priestly people who were given to the study of the heavenly bodies (Dan. 2:2). They were often consulted by kings and leaders for advice. Their presence in Babylonia in the time of Nebuchadnezzar is confirmed.

C. A use of the word to refer to the nation or land of Chaldea, Babylon (Jer. 50:10; 51:24, 35).

3779. כַּשְׂדָי kaśdāy: An Aramaic proper noun designating Babylonian, Chaldean:

A. The gentilic name of the inhabitants of a city (Babylon) and area (Babylonia) located in southern Mesopotamia on the Euphrates River. It is the Aramaic word that corresponds to 3778,A.

B. A technical use of the word Chaldeans. It is the Aramaic word corresponding to 3779,B. See the comments there on Daniel 2:2.

3780. כָּשָׂה kāśāh: A verb meaning obese, filled with food; sleek. The word is difficult to translate, and its meaning is not certain. The KJV and NKJV favor the idea of fatness, obesity, filled, or covered with fullness (Deut. 32:15). The NIV and NASB render it as sleek.

3781. כַּשִּׁיל kaššiyl: A masculine noun indicating an ax, a hatchet. It was a weapon or tool used by the enemy to destroy much of the carved art work in the Solomonic Temple (Ps. 74:6).

3782. כָּשַׁל kāšal: A verb meaning to stumble, to stagger, to totter, to cause to stumble, to overthrow, to make weak. This word is used literally of individuals falling or figuratively of cities and nations falling (Isa. 3:8; Hos. 14:1[2]). People can fall by the sword (Dan. 11:33); or because of evil (Prov. 24:16); wickedness (Ezek. 33:12); and iniquity (Hos. 5:5).

3783. כִּשָּׁלוֹן kiššālôn: A masculine noun meaning a stumbling, a fall. It means literally to trip on something, to fall. It is used in context of a moral or spiritual collapse or falling from pride and inflated self-worth (Prov. 16:18).

3784. כָּשַׁף kāšap̱: A verb meaning to practice magic, to practice sorcery. It occurs with words of similar meaning in Deuteronomy 18:10 and 2 Chronicles 33:6. While the exact meaning of the word is obscure, it involved the use of supernatural powers that hardened hearts against the truth (Ex. 7:11). Those in Israel who used such powers were to be executed (Ex. 22:18[17]). King Manasseh's involvement in sorcery to the point of making his children pass through fire, helped lead Judah to the breaking point of God's patience (2 Chr. 33:6; cf. 2 Kgs. 24:3, 4). Judgment is promised against sorcerers when the Messiah returns (Mal. 3:5).

However, in a pagan country, where sorcery was practiced with greater ignorance, Daniel acted to save magicians from death while demonstrating that God's power exceeded that of the sorcerers (Dan. 2:2).

3785. כֶּשֶׁף *kešep̱:* A masculine noun meaning occult magic, sorcery. While specific practices included under this term cannot be established, the word occurs along with other similar terms such as enchantments and soothsaying, thus providing clues through association (Isa. 47:9, 12; Mic. 5:12[11]). This word always appears in a plural form, and half the time, it is modified by the word "numerous" (2 Kgs. 9:22; Isa. 47:9, 12). The plurals may indicate different manifestations, or they may represent plurals of intensification. Twice this term is linked with metaphorical harlotry (2 Kgs. 9:22; Nah. 3:4). In the Old Testament, magic was connected with several nations: Babylon, Nineveh, the Northern Kingdom and the Southern Kingdom (2 Kgs. 9:22; Isa. 47:9–12; Mic. 5:12[11]; Nah. 3:4).

3786. כַּשָּׁף *kaššāp̱:* A masculine singular noun meaning sorcerer. It occurs once in the Hebrew Bible in Jeremiah 27:9.

3787. כָּשֵׁר *kāšēr:* A verb meaning to be successful, to cause to succeed. In Ecclesiastes 10:10, the word refers to success as the result of wisdom that enables one to go through difficult situations like a sharp ax through wood. In Ecclesiastes 11:6, the word refers to the success of seeds in growing, a matter beyond complete human control. Like other human ventures, successful farming calls for diligence and diversification. In Esther 8:5, the word is used to confirm the king's opinion of Esther's proposal, whether in his view it would work smoothly.

3788. כִּשְׁרוֹן *kišrôn:* A noun meaning profit, productivity. It occurs three times and refers to increase which brings no lasting satisfaction. In Ecclesiastes 2:21, it refers to the profit from labor which, at an owner's death, is given to one who did not labor for it. In Ecclesiastes 4:4, the word refers to the profit produced by hard work which is caused by or results in competition with and is the envy of one's neighbors. In Ecclesiastes 5:11[10], the word refers to the (lack of) profit in producing more than one can use.

3789. כָּתַב *kāṯaḇ:* A verb meaning to write. It refers to communication through a system of visible signs written down. It is used to indicate the process of recording information in many ways and settings: writing in or on a stone or book (Ex. 17:14; Deut. 27:3; 2 Kgs. 23:3). The Ten Commandments or ten words were written by the finger of God on stone tablets (Ex. 31:18; 32:15; 34:1, 27, 28); covenants were written down (Ex. 24:4, 12). Descriptions of the land of Canaan were written down (Josh. 18:4). The second recording of Jeremiah's words were dictated as Baruch wrote them down again (Jer. 36:2, 4). It refers to inscribing or engraving on a crown of pure gold for the high priest to wear (Ex. 39:30). Job wished that his words would be written down (Job 19:23, 24). The Lord had a written book of remembrance that contained the names of those who feared Him (Mal. 3:16). The preacher tried to write down words of truth to teach and make the people wise (Eccl. 12:10).

3790. כְּתַב ***keṯaḇ:*** An Aramaic verb meaning to write. It refers to the recording of information of any kind through a system of visible signs. It is used of the process in many ways and settings. In Ezra it is used to describe writing letters, reports, name lists, and archives (4:8; 5:7, 10; 6:2). In Daniel it is used of writing on a wall by a mysterious hand (Dan. 5:5); in an official decree from a king (6:25[26]); in recording the summary of a vision (7:1).

3791. כְּתָב ***keṯāḇ:*** A masculine noun referring to a script, writing. It indicates the process of writing or the symbols used to write. It is used of the particular writing form or system of an area (Esth. 1:22); a written document (Esth. 3:14); an official written list (Ezra 2:62); the actual language or text in a document (Ezra 4:7). With *be*, with, in, it describes a means to gain understanding by putting something in writing (*biḵtāḇ*) (1 Chr. 28:19; 2 Chr. 35:4). It is modified to refer to a special source of truth, the writing of truth (Dan. 10:21).

3792. כְּתָב ***keṯāḇ:*** An Aramaic masculine noun indicating writing, an inscription. It refers to something that has been written down (Dan. 5:7, 8, 15–17, 24, 25). It indicates an official document and its contents (Dan. 6:8–10[9–11]). It refers to specific instructions and commands written in the Law of Moses (Ezra 6:18). The phrase *dîy-lāʾ* *keṯāḇ* means with no limit or with no written prescription (NASB, as needed) (Ezra 7:22).

3793. כְּתֹבֶת ***keṯōḇeṯ:*** A feminine noun indicating a mark, an inscription. It indicates a mark or imprintment on a person's body, possibly tattooing of some kind (Lev. 19:28).

3794. כִּתִּי ***kittiy:*** A proper noun designating Kittim (Gen. 10:4; Num. 24:24; 1 Chr. 1:7; Isa. 23:1, 12; Jer. 2:10; Ezek. 27:6; Dan. 11:30).

3795. כָּתִית ***kāṯiyṯ:*** An adjective meaning pressed, beaten. It indicates the process of beating or pounding something. It is used in combination with the Hebrew *šemen,* oil, to indicate an especially pure, beaten, costly olive oil for food preparation or for lamps (Ex. 27:20; 29:40; Lev. 24:2; Num. 28:5; 1 Kgs. 5:11[25]).

3796. כֹּתֶל ***kōṯel:*** A masculine noun meaning wall. It indicates a barrier surrounding an area or living space for protection or landscaping beauty (Song 2:9).

3797. כְּתַל k^e***tal:*** An Aramaic masculine noun indicating a wall. It indicates a barrier surrounding an area or living space for protection or beauty. It refers to the Temple walls being rebuilt in the time of Ezra (5:8); and it describes the interior wall of a banqueting room (Dan. 5:5).

3798. כִּתְלִישׁ ***kitliyš:*** A proper noun designating Kitlish (Josh. 15:40).

3799. כָּתַם ***kātam:*** A verb meaning to be marked, stained. It is used in a figurative sense in context to refer to the "remaining stain" (participle form) of iniquity after Israel's ineffective attempt to remove it (Jer. 2:22).

3800. כֶּתֶם ***ketem:*** A masculine noun indicating gold, pure gold. It serves as a poetic synonym for *zāhāb*, gold (Job 31:24; Prov. 25:12). It is described in some places as gold of *'opîyr*, gold from the East (Job 28:16; Ps. 45:9[10]; Isa. 13:12); or pure gold (Job 28:19; Song 5:11; Lam. 4:1).

3801. כֻּתֹּנֶת ***kuttōnet:*** A feminine noun indicating a coat, a garment, a tunic. It indicates a long undergarment with a collar cut out for one's head (Gen. 37:3); the main common garment worn by men or women (2 Sam. 15:32; Song 5:3). Priests wore a priestly tunic (Ex. 28:4; Lev. 16:4; Ezra 2:69; Neh. 7:70, 72). These garments could be of linen or skins (Gen. 3:21) and were sometimes embroidered (Ex. 28:4, 39). They were torn as a sign of grief and mourning (2 Sam. 15:32). Worn by kings or rulers, they indicated authority (Isa. 22:21).

3802. כָּתֵף ***kātēp:*** A feminine noun meaning a shoulder, a side. It indicates literally the upper arm and/or the shoulder of a living being: a person or animal (Ex. 28:12; Judg. 16:3; 1hoice meat (Ezek. 24:4). It is used often in figures of speech: to turn or give a stubborn shoulder is to be hostile, difficult, or rebellious (Zech. 7:11); to dwell between the shoulders of the Lord is to live in safety (Deut. 33:12). The meaning is extended to inanimate objects: the high priest's ephod had shoulder pieces (Ex. 28:7); the laver had side supports (1 Kgs. 7:30); a mountain slope is termed a shoulder, a slope (Num. 34:11; Josh. 15:8; Ezek. 25:9). As a construction term, it means a side of something, e.g., a door (Ex. 27:14, 15; 1 Kgs. 6:8; 7:39).

3803. כָּתַר ***kātar:*** A verb meaning to surround, to enclose; to crown. It has the basic meaning of encircling something. It is used figuratively of being surrounded by political or religious foes (Ps. 22:12[13]; Hab. 1:4); and literally of being pressed by an army and encircled (Judg. 20:43). To be surrounded by the righteous is to have God's blessing and protection (Ps. 142:7[8]). To surround, to enclose in the sense of to gather around and wait, seems to be the sense of the word in Job 36:2. Others would see a different root word here.

3804. כֶּתֶר *keṯer:* A masculine noun referring to a crown. An ornament worn on a king's head to symbolize his power and authority. A crown, probably a high turban, befitted a Persian king or queen (Esth. 1:11; 2:17). A decoration of some kind was placed on a royal horse to honor its rider (Esth. 6:8).

3805. כֹּתֶרֶת *kōṯereṯ:* A feminine noun indicating a capital, the crown of a pillar. It is an ancient, technical architectural term describing the decorative top or top piece of a column or pillar (1 Kgs. 7:16–20, 31, 41, 42). Sometimes it was made of bronze (2 Kgs. 25:17; Jer. 52:22).

3806. כָּתַשׁ *kāṯaš:* A verb meaning to pound, to grind. It refers to pounding or grinding something in a mortar with a pestle. It is used figuratively of grinding a fool in a mortar (Prov. 27:22), to no avail in removing his foolishness.

3807. כָּתַת *kāṯaṯ:* A verb meaning to beat, to crush, to hammer. This term is used in reference to the destruction of the golden calf (Deut. 9:21); and in the eschatological hope of hammering swords into plowshares (Isa. 2:4; Mic. 4:3). It can also be used figuratively for destroying an enemy (Deut. 1:44).

ל Lamedh

3808. לֹא *lō'*, לוֹא *lô'*, לֹה *lōh:* An adverb meaning no, not. The term is primarily utilized as an ordinary negation, as in Genesis 3:4: "You will not surely die" (NIV cf. Judg. 14:4; Ps. 16:10). Often it is used to express an unconditional prohibition, thus having the force of an imperative: "You shall not (= do not ever) steal"(Ex. 20:15 NIV; cf. Judg. 13:5). Frequently, it functions as an absolute in answer to a question (Job 23:6; Zech. 4:5). The word is also employed in questions to denote that an affirmative answer is expected (2 Kgs. 5:26; Jon. 4:11). When it is prefixed to a noun or adjective, it negates that word, making it have an opposite or contrary meaning (e.g., god becomes non-god; strong becomes weak; cf. Deut. 32:21; Prov. 30:25). When prefixed by the preposition *b^{e}*, meaning in or by, the combined term carries the temporal meaning of beyond or before (Lev. 15:25); the meaning without is also not uncommon for this combination (Job 8:11). A prefixed preposition *l^{e}*, meaning to or for, gives the term the meaning of without (2 Chr. 15:3) or as though not (Job 39:16). Occasionally, the word suggests the meaning not only, on account of the context (Deut. 5:3).

3809. לָא *lā':* An Aramaic particle indicating no, not, never. It is used to negate the assertions of clauses (Ezra 4:13; Jer. 10:11; Dan. 2:5). It is used with *'îytay* following to negate the existence of something (Ezra 4:16; Dan. 2:10). It negates particular words, e.g., with *b^{e}* attached to the noun, "not by means of any wisdom . . . ." (Dan. 2:30). Used with *dîy* preceding, it means without (Ezra 6:8; Dan. 6:8[9]). See Heb. *lô'*.

3810. לֹא דְבָר *lō' d̲^{e}ḇār*, לוֹ דְבָר *lô d̲^{e}ḇār:* A proper noun designating Lo Debar (2 Sam. 9:4, 5; 17:27).

3811. לָאָה *lā'āh:* A verb meaning to be weary, to become weary; to be frustrated. It refers to becoming weary, impatient at doing something (Gen. 19:11; Job 4:2, 5). It refers to physical exhaustion (Jer. 12:5); but it also indicates wearing oneself out even in religious efforts (Isa. 16:12; Jer. 6:11); or in seeking a multitude of advice (Isa. 47:13). The wicked frustrate themselves in their evil activities (Jer. 9:5[4]). The sluggard is weary; he is lazy (Prov. 26:15). It has the idea of worn out, impoverished (Ps. 68:9 [10]). The Egyptians wearied themselves finding drinking water; that is, they were hardly able to do so (Ex. 7:18). In its causative stem, it takes on the sense of making someone tired, weary, trying their patience (Job 16:7; Isa. 7:13; Mic. 6:3), as Israel tried the Lord's endurance with them.

3812. לֵאָה ***lē'āh:*** A proper noun designating Leah, the first wife of Jacob, given to him by Laban as an act of deception. She was Laban's daughter, an Aramaean. She bore to Jacob Reuben, Simeon, Levi, Judah, Issachar, and Zebulun. Her maidservant Zilpah bore Gad and Asher (Gen. 35:23–26).

3813. לָאַט ***lā'aṭ:*** A verb meaning to cover. It refers to shielding or hiding one's face as a gesture of sorrow and shock (2 Sam. 19:4[5]), as King David did at the death of Absalom his son.

3814. לָאט ***lā'ṭ:*** A masculine noun indicating silence, softness. It means quietness, stealth, care. Used once with b^e on the front, it functions as an adverb meaning secretly, carefully, quietly (Judg. 4:21).

3815. לָאֵל ***lā'ēl:*** A proper noun designating Lael (Num. 3:24).

3816. לְאוֹם ***l^e'ôm,*** לְאֹם ***l^e'ōm:*** A masculine singular noun meaning people. This poetic term is used often as a synonym for people (*'am* [5971]) or nation (*gôy* [1471]). It can refer to Israel or to humanity in general. A well-known passage (Gen. 25:23) uses this term in regard to the two peoples in Rebekah's womb—Israel and Edom.

3817. לְאֻמִּים ***l^e'ummiym:*** A proper noun designating Leummites (Gen. 25:3).

3818. לֹא עַמִּי ***lō' 'ammiy:*** A proper noun designating Lo-Ammi (Hos. 1:9; 2:23[25]).

3819. לֹא רֻחָמָה ***lō' ruḥāmāh:*** A proper noun designating Lo-Ruhamah (Hos. 1:6, 8; 2:23[25]).

3820. לֵב ***lēḇ:*** A masculine noun usually rendered as heart but whose range of meaning is extensive. It can denote the heart as a human physical organ (Ex. 28:29; 1 Sam. 25:37; 2 Kgs. 9:24); or an animal (Job 41:24[16]). However, it usually refers to some aspect of the immaterial inner self or being since the heart is considered to be the seat of one's inner nature as well as one of its components. It can be used in a general sense (1 Kgs. 8:23; Ps. 84:2[3]; Jer. 3:10); or it can be used of a specific aspect of personality: the mind (Gen. 6:5; Deut. 29:4[3]; Neh. 6:8); the will (Ex. 35:5; 2 Chr. 12:14; Job 11:13); the emotions (Gen. 6:6[Note that God is the subject]; 1 Sam. 24:5[6]; 25:31). In addition, the word can also allude to the inside or middle (Ex. 15:8; Deut. 4:11).

3821. לֵב ***lēḇ:*** An Aramaic masculine singular noun meaning heart. In this form, its only occurrence in the Hebrew Bible is in Daniel 7:28.

3822. לְבָאוֹת ***l^eḇā'ôṯ:*** A proper noun designating Lebaoth (Josh. 15:32).

3823. לָבַב ***lāḇaḇ:*** A verb meaning to stir the heart, to make cakes. This word is related to the common Hebrew nouns *lēḇ* (3820) and *lēḇāḇ* (3824), which both mean heart, mind, or inner being. Solomon used this word twice in the same verse to express the stirring of his heart with affection for his lover (Song 4:9); Zophar used it to describe the mind of an idiot being made intelligent (Job 11:12). In the only other instances of this word, it describes the making of bread or a cake that was kneaded and baked (2 Sam. 13:6, 8).

3824. לְבָב *lēḇāḇ:* A masculine noun meaning heart, mind, inner person. The primary usage of this word describes the entire disposition of the inner person that God can discern (1 Sam. 16:7); be devoted to the Lord (1 Kgs. 15:3); seek the Lord (2 Chr. 11:16); turn against people (Ex. 14:5); be uncircumcised (Lev. 26:41); be hardened (1 Sam. 6:6); be totally committed to the Lord (Deut. 6:5; 2 Chr. 15:15). It is also used to describe the place where the rational, thinking process occurs that allows a person to know God's blessings (Josh. 23:14); to plan for the future (1 Kgs. 8:18); to communicate (2 Chr. 9:1); and to understand God's message (Isa. 6:10). Like our English usage, it often refers to the seat of emotions, whether it refers to joy (Deut. 28:47); discouragement (Josh. 2:11); comfort (Judg. 19:8); grief (1 Sam. 1:8); sorrow (Ps. 13:2[3]); or gladness (Isa. 30:29).

3825. לְבַב *lēḇaḇ:* An Aramaic masculine noun meaning heart, mind, the inner person. This word is equivalent to the Hebrew word *lēḇāḇ* (3824). It is used to describe the entire disposition of the inner person, which God can change (Dan. 4:16[13]; 5:21; 7:4). This inner person can be lifted up in pride (Dan. 5:20) or made low in humility (Dan. 5:22). The rational, thinking process is demonstrated when Daniel described the thoughts of the king's mind (Dan. 2:30).

3826. לִבָּה *libbāh:* A feminine noun meaning heart. A variant of the word *lēḇ* (3820), it suggests the seat of emotions or the will (Ezek. 16:30).

3827. לַבָּה *labbāh:* A feminine noun meaning flame. It refers to a fire's bright light and heat. It is used with *'ēš* following to mean flame of fire (Ex. 3:2).

3828. לְבוֹנָה *leḇônah,* לְבֹנָה *leḇōnāh:* A feminine noun meaning incense, frankincense. A white resin from a tree. It was an ingredient of holy incense (Ex. 30:34; Jer. 6:20). It was put on certain offerings (Lev. 2:1, 2, 15, 16; 6:15[8]; 24:7; Neh. 13:5, 9). It was used as a perfume by burning (Song 3:6; 4:6, 14); and it was considered a valuable tribute gift (Isa. 60:6; Jer. 41:5).

3829. לְבוֹנָה *leḇônāh:* A proper noun designating Lebonah (Judg. 21:19).

3830. לְבוּשׁ *leḇûš,* לְבֻשׁ *leḇuš,* לָבוּשׁ *lāḇûš,* לָבֻשׁ *lāḇuš:* I. A masculine noun indicating clothing, garments, dress. It refers to clothing of men or women (Gen. 49:11; Ps. 45:13[14]). It is used as a collective noun of clothes or dress for women or men (2 Kgs. 10:22; Isa. 14:19). It includes clothing of various materials (Job 30:18; Ps. 35:13; Prov. 27:26); or styles (Esth. 6:8). It is used in metaphorical language: clouds like garments covering the sea (Job 38:9); or the clothing of idols (Jer. 10:9). A man was to claim and protect his wife by covering her with his garment (Mal. 2:16).

II. An adjective meaning clothed, dressed. It describes the state of a person wearing garments as opposed to being naked. The household of a wise woman may be clothed luxuriously (Prov. 31:21). It is used of a warrior outfitted in his military dress (1 Sam. 17:5; Ezek. 38:4). It is used figuratively and literally of a person attired with the clothing of those slain by a sword (Isa. 14:19). Even heavenly beings are dressed (Ezek. 9:2, 3, 11; 10:2, 6, 7; Dan. 10:5; 12:6, 7). Filthy garments may refer to a corrupt moral character (Zech. 3:3). Royal garments were often purple (Ezek. 23:6).

3831. לְבוּשׁ ***l^e^b̲ûš:*** An Aramaic masculine noun referring to clothing, a garment. It refers to a complete set of clothing worn by the three Hebrews (Dan. 3:21). The regalia of the Ancient of Days was pure white indicating holiness and purity (Dan. 7:9).

3832. לָבַט ***lāb̲aṭ:*** A verb meaning to be torn down, to be ruined. It means to become ruined from talking foolishly (Prov. 10:8, 10); or by acting wickedly and immorally from a lack of understanding (Hos. 4:14).

3833. לְבֶא ***leb̲e',*** לִבְאָה ***lib̲'āh,*** לְבִיָּא ***l^e^b̲iyyā',*** לָבִיא ***lāb̲iy':*** I. A masculine noun indicating a lion, a lioness. It is used figuratively of violent persons depicted as lions (Ps. 57:4[5]). The prophet refers to allies of or parts of Assyria's empire as lionesses to be fed (Nah. 2:12[13]) (See II.).

II. A feminine noun referring to a lioness. See I. Its feminine form is used in Nahum 2:12[13].

III. A feminine noun meaning lioness. It refers to a female lion, but in context it is used figuratively of Israel or Jerusalem (Ezek. 19:2).

IV. A masculine noun indicating a lion, a lioness. It refers to the animal itself but is used only figuratively in its contexts except once. In Job 38:39, the animal is referred to literally. Only God knows the way of the lion as it hunts its prey (Job 38:39); Judah behaves as a lion (Gen. 49:9); the people of Israel and Jacob behave as a strong lion (Num. 23:24; 24:9; Deut. 33:20). It refers to the nation God will call forth for vengeance on His people (Isa. 5:29; 30:61; Joel 1:6); and of the Lord's fury against Israel (Hos. 13:8); and her enemies (Nah. 2:11 [12]). The word is used to describe the wicked in their ways and manner of life (Job 4:11).

3834. לְבִבָה ***l^ebibāh:*** A feminine noun referring to a cake, bread. A favorite cake from kneaded dough baked for a time of celebrating (2 Sam. 13:6, 8, 10).

3835. לָבֵן ***lābēn:*** I. A verb meaning to burn or to make brick. It is used of the entire process of molding bricks for various construction projects both at Babel and in Egypt (Gen. 11:3; Ex. 5:7, 14).

II. A verb indicating to make white, spotless, pure. Its most important use is to describe the Lord's washing of persons from their sin and corruption, making them clean, white (Ps. 51:7[9]; Isa. 1:18). Persecution is a means of the Lord's purification of His people (Dan. 11:35; 12:10). It has a negative sense when used of the whitening of a vine from an attack of locusts (Joel 1:7).

3836. לָבָן ***lābān:*** An adjective meaning white. It is used of teeth (Gen. 49:12); sheep (Gen. 30:35); hair in the process of detecting a possible case of leprosy or a skin disease (Lev. 13:3, 4); skin of reddish-white, again indicating possible leprosy (Lev. 13:42, 43); or skin of a dull or faint white (Lev. 13:39); wood (Gen. 30:37); manna (Ex. 16:31); clothing (Eccl. 9:8); horses in a vision (Zech. 1:8; 6:3, 6).

3837. לָבָן ***lābān:*** A proper noun designating Laban:

A. The brother of Rebekah, daughter of Bethuel, who was the son of Nahor, Abraham's brother (Gen. 24:15–16, 28–31). He and Bethuel permitted Rebekah to return with Abraham's servant to marry Isaac, Rebekah's grandniece. He lived in northwest Mesopotamia (Aram Naha-raim) in the city of Nahor. Later, he arranged to his advantage Jacob's marriage with his sisters, first Leah and then Rachel, apparently requiring Jacob to labor fourteen years to get both wives (Gen. 29:14–30). He recognized Isaac and Jacob's God but maintained an idolatrous worship of other gods (Gen. 31:19–35) as well. He spoke at least some Aramaic (Gen. 31:47, Jegar Sahadutha, "witness pile"). Jacob and Laban were finally reconciled at Mizpah and made a covenant of respect and faith toward each other (Gen. 31:48–55).

B. A location somewhere in the Sinai Desert or on the plains of Moab. Some believe it is the same place as Libnah (Num. 33:20–21).

3838. לְבָנָה ***l^ebānāh:*** A proper noun designating Lebanah (Ezra 2:45; Neh. 7:48).

3839. לִבְנֶה ***libneh:*** A masculine noun referring to poplar, a poplar tree, or the wood from it. It is used of rods or small poles of poplar used by Jacob for some obscure breeding process (Gen. 30:37); and to the poplar trees under which pagan sacrifices were carried out by Israel (Hos. 4:13).

3840. לִבְנָה ***li<u>b</u>nāh:*** A feminine noun meaning pavement, flooring. It is used to describe the surface made of sapphire under the Lord's feet, when He appeared to Moses and the elders of Israel (Ex. 24:10; cf. Isa. 65:3).

3841. לִבְנָה ***li<u>b</u>nāh:*** A proper noun designating Libnah:

A. A city in southwest Judah (Josh. 10:29, 31, 32, 39; 12:15; 15:42; 21:13; 2 Kgs. 8:22; 19:8; 23:31; 24:18; 2 Chr. 21:10; Isa. 37:8; Jer. 52:1).

B. The site of an encampment in the Wilderness (Num. 33:20, 21).

3842. לְבָנָה ***le<u>b</u>ānāh:*** A feminine noun meaning moon, the (full) moon. It is used to refer to the moon in its full brightness. It is found in a simile describing the beloved as beautiful and fair as the full moon (*kalle<u>b</u>o<u>b</u>āh*) (Song 6:10). Its brightness is, however, eclipsed by the Lord's reigning in Jerusalem in His glory (Isa. 24:23). In that day of restoration, the moon will be as bright as the sun (Isa. 30:26).

3843. לְבֵנָה ***le<u>b</u>ēnāh:*** A feminine noun indicating a brick. It was a major man-made building material evidently dried, not fired (Gen. 11:3; Ex. 1:14; 5:7, 8, 16, 18, 19; 24:10). The Israelites used such brick in forbidden rites on which to burn incense (Isa. 65:3). It was used as material to write or draw on (Ezek. 4:1), as Ezekiel did.

3844. לְבָנוֹן ***le<u>b</u>ānôn:*** A proper noun designating Lebanon. A beautiful mountainous territory north of Israel. The name means white. Its white, snow capped peaks and the white limestone of its mountains reflect its name. It paralleled the coast of the Mediterranean from roughly the Leontes River to the Eleutherus River. The range of mountains is about one hundred miles long. Its cedars were famous for their size, beauty, and use as building materials (Judg. 9:15; 1 Kgs. 5:6; Ps. 104:1, 16; Song 5:3, 15). The great strength of the cedar became legendary as well.

3845. לִבְנִי ***li<u>b</u>niy:*** A proper noun designating Libni (Ex. 6:17; Num. 3:18; 1 Chr. 6:17[2] , 20[5] , 29[14]).

3846. לִבְנִי ***li<u>b</u>niy,*** לֵב קָמָי ***lē<u>b</u> qāmāy:*** I. Libnite, a descendant of Libni (Num. 3:21; 26:58).

II. A cryptic name for Babylon (Jer. 51:1).

3847. לָבַשׁ ***lā<u>b</u>aš,*** לָבֵשׁ ***lā<u>b</u>ēš:*** A verb meaning to wear, to dress, to put on clothing. It is used of putting on any kind of clothing or garments: clothes (Gen. 3:21; 28:20); armor (1 Sam. 17:38; Isa. 59:17); royal robes (1 Kgs. 22:10; Ezra 3:10; Esth. 6:8); clothing in general (2 Sam. 13:18; Hag. 1:6). It is used figuratively in various ways: of the Lord or people being clothed with righteousness and other qualities (Ps. 93:1; 104:1; Isa. 51:9; 59:17); of the Spirit of the Lord "clothing," coming upon a person (Judg. 6:34); of worms clothing a person (Job 7:5); terror also may clothe a person (Ezek. 7:27).

3848. לְבַשׁ ***l***^e^***ḇaš:*** An Aramaic verb meaning to be clothed. It refers to putting on clothes. In context it refers to attiring someone with a royal, purple robe (Dan. 5:7, 16, 29), indicating kingly authority.

3849. לֹג ***lōg:*** A masculine noun referring to a log, a liquid measure of oil. It is used to designate an amount of liquid equal to about two-thirds of a pint (not quite one-third of a liter) (Lev. 14:10, 12, 15, 21, 24). It was used in cleansing leprosy or a skin disease.

3850. לֹד ***lōḏ:*** A proper noun designating Lod (1 Chr. 8:12; Ezra 2:33; Neh. 7:37; 11:35).

3851. לַהַב ***lahaḇ:*** A masculine noun referring to a flame, the flashing blade of a spear or sword. It is used to indicate a flash or flame of fire (Judg. 13:20; Isa. 29:6). It is used in a figurative sense of faces of flame (*lahaḇ*), faces red and hot with fear at God's judgments (Isa. 13:8). It is used to refer to the flashing blade of a sword (Nah. 3:3) or spear (Job 39:23). The Lord's judgments are described as a flame (*lahaḇ*) of consuming fire (Isa. 29:6; 30:30; 66:15). The hot breath of Leviathan is described as a flame (Job 41:21[13]). It is used in a simile to describe the sound of a locust swarm as a flame of fire (Joel 2:5).

3852. לֶהָבָה ***lehāḇāh:*** A feminine noun meaning flame, the tip of a sword or spear. It regularly refers to a flashing flame of fire (Num. 21:28; Jer. 48:45) both literally and symbolically of destruction. It is emphasized by the following word *šalhebeṯ* in Ezekiel 20:47[21:3], a "burning flame," a metaphor of God's coming judgments. Followed or preceded by *'ēš* (fire), it indicates a flaming fire (Isa. 4:5; Lam. 2:3); or a consuming tongue of fire (Isa. 5:24). It is used to describe the flashing light and fire in a hailstorm (Ps. 105:32). The head or point of Goliath's spear is referred to by this word (1 Sam. 17:7).

3853. לְהָבִים ***l***^e^***hāḇiym:*** A proper noun designating Lehabites (Gen. 10:13; 1 Chr. 1:11).

3854. לַהַג ***lahag:*** A masculine noun referring to study, a devotion to study. In its context, it means study or examination (Eccl. 12:12). The context speaks of excessive (*harbēh*) study or searching.

3855. לָהַד ***lāhaḏ:*** A proper noun designating Lahad (1 Chr. 4:2).

3856. לָהַהּ ***lāhah,*** לָהָה ***lāhāh:*** I. A verb indicating to behave like a madman. It is used of irrational and senseless behavior and actions towards others (Prov. 26:18).

II. A verb meaning to languish. It refers to the weakening and deterioration of a people because of hardship and oppression (Gen. 47:13) brought on by famine.

3857. לָהַט ***lāhaṭ:*** I. A verb meaning to burn, to set fire on, to consume with fire. It indicates devouring or scorching something by fire or flame (Deut. 32:22); or war (Isa. 42:25). In its intensive stem, it also means to light or kindle coals (Job 41:21[13]); or to set ablaze God's enemies (Mal. 4:1[3:19]). In its participial form with *'ēš*, it depicts the Lord's minister as a burning fire (Ps. 104:4). It is used figuratively of the enemies of the righteous, those who breathe out fire (Ps. 57:4[5]). The Lord Himself may consume the enemies of His people like a fire (Ps. 83:14[15]; 106:18).

II. A verb meaning to swallow, to devour. It is used in its participial form figuratively to describe the enemies of the righteous who devour them (Ps. 57:4[5]). See I also.

3858. לַהַט ***lahaṭ***, לְהָטִים ***lᵉhāṭiym:*** A masculine noun meaning flame. This word is used only once in the Old Testament. It describes the "flaming sword" of the cherubim stationed at the east side of the Garden of Eden (Gen. 3:24). This word comes from the verb, *lāhaṭ* (3857), meaning to flame or to set on fire.

3859. לָהַם ***lāham:*** A verb meaning to swallow greedily. As a passive noun, it means something gulped. It is used to describe gossip as something that most people will swallow whole (Prov. 18:8) and be permeated by it (Prov. 26:22).

3860. לָהֵן ***lāhēn:*** An adverbial particle meaning therefore, on this account. It points out the motivation or conclusion for a previous statement or event, e.g., Naomi's encouragement for Ruth and Orpah to return to their own country (Ruth 1:13), since her sons are dead, and she will have no more.

3861. לָהֵן ***lāhēn:*** An Aramaic particle meaning therefore, on this account. It introduces the reason or cause of something (Ezra 5:12; Dan. 2:6, 9).

3862. לַהֲקָה ***lahᵃqāh:*** A feminine noun meaning company, a group. It refers to a group of persons with a common interest. In this case, it indicates a group of prophets who were prophesying (1 Sam. 19:20).

3863. לֻא ***lu'***, לוּ ***lû***, לוּא ***lû':*** A particle meaning if, oh, that. It introduces conditional statements: "Oh, if only . . ." (Gen. 17:18; Num. 14:2; Deut. 32:29); "If . . ." (Gen. 23:13; Mic. 2:11).

3864. לוּבִי ***lûḇiy:*** A proper noun designating Lubite (2 Chr. 12:3; 16:8; Dan. 11:43; Nah. 3:9).

3865. לוּד ***lûḏ:*** A proper noun designating Lud, Lydia (Gen. 10:22; 1 Chr. 1:17; Isa. 66:19; Ezek. 27:10; 30:5).

3866. לוּדִים ***lûḏiym:*** A proper noun designating Ludites, Lydians (Gen. 10:13; 1 Chr. 1:11; Jer. 46:9).

3867. לָוָה ***lāwāh:*** I. A verb meaning to join, to accompany. It has the meaning of attaching oneself to someone or something: to one's wife through affection (Gen. 29:34); to a group of fellow tribesmen who have a common purpose of serving in the work of the priesthood (Num. 18:2, 4); to the Lord as one's God, even though the persons are foreigners, strangers or eunuchs (Isa. 14:1; 56:3, 6), for the Lord will accept and prosper them. It is used of the Israelite's firm attachment to the Lord in devotion and worship (Jer. 50:5), along with many other nations in the Day of the Lord (Zech. 2:11[15]). It is used of nations aligning themselves with the enemies of God's people taking on a common cause (Ps. 83:8[9]); it is used of something that will remain with people and satisfy them during their lives, such as eating, drinking, and joy (Eccl. 8:15).

II. A verb meaning to borrow, to lend. It has the sense of to ask for something as well as to lend something according to context (Deut. 28:12), especially money that is loaned out (Ex. 22:25[24]) or borrowed (Neh. 5:4). The wicked person borrows but does not pay back (Ps. 37:21); the righteous person both gives and lends to help others (Ps. 37:26; 112:5). Lending to the poor is like giving to the Lord (Prov. 19:17). Borrowing can lead to enslavement (Prov. 22:7). God's judgments will encompass both borrower and lender (Isa. 24:2).

3868. לוּז ***lûz:*** A verb indicating to be crooked, to be perverse, to be devious. It indicates what a person or nation trusts in. In context it indicates guile, deviousness, etc. found in political alliances with Egypt rather than trust in God's word (Isa. 30:12). The wicked and perverse follow a path of perversity, crookedness, deviousness (Prov. 2:15; 3:32), and the Lord abhors them. Their way of crookedness shows that they despise and reject the Lord (Prov. 14:2). In two passages, it has the sense of losing sight of something or of something being lost sight of (Prov. 3:21; 4:21).

3869. לוּז ***lûz:*** A masculine noun meaning an almond or prunus tree bearing a small peachlike fruit. The word is used of the material (poplar?) from which Jacob made some rods in a puzzling breeding process (Gen. 30:37).

3870. לוּז ***lûz:*** A proper noun designating Luz:

A. Another name for Bethel (Gen. 28:19; 35:6; 48:3; Josh. 16:2; 18:13; Judg. 1:23).

B. A Hittite city (Judg. 1:26).

3871. לוּחַ ***lûaḥ:*** A masculine noun referring to a tablet, a slab of stone, a board or plank. It is used to indicate planks or boards of an altar or frame structure (Ex. 27:8); a ship (Ezek. 27:5); a wooden panel (1 Kgs. 7:36; Song 8:9). It indicates metal plates on slabs (1 Kgs. 7:36). Smaller tablets were often used for writing materials or for carving inscriptions (Hab. 2:2). It is used several times of stone tablets (Ex. 24:12; 31:18; 32:16; 34:1, 4; Deut.

5:22[19]; 1 Kgs. 8:9), indicating the tablets containing the Ten Commandments, the tablets of the testimony (Ex. 31:18), tablets of the covenant (Deut. 9:9). It is used in a figurative sense of the tablet of the heart (Prov. 3:3; 7:3; Jer. 17:1).

3872. לוּחִית ***lûḥiyṯ:*** A proper noun designating Luhith (Isa. 15:5; Jer. 48:5).

3873. הַלּוֹחֵשׁ ***hallôḥēš:*** A proper noun designating Hallohesh (Neh. 3:12; 10:24[25]).

3874. לוּט ***lûṭ:*** A verb indicating to wrap, to cover. It indicates the process of enveloping or folding a cover over or around something: Goliath's sword was wrapped in a cloth (1 Sam. 21:9). Elijah covered his face with his mantle (1 Kgs. 19:13). It is used figuratively of the inability of persons to perceive something clearly (Isa. 25:7, for a fuller discussion, see the noun form *ôṭ* [3875].).

3875. לוֹט ***lôṭ:*** A masculine noun indicating a shroud, a covering. It is the noun for 3874, indicating the inability of people to perceive God and His works clearly (Isa. 25:7). In this verse, Isaiah uses the noun and verb forms together meaning the covering that covers or the shroud that enfolds. This is a reference to the power of Christ's redemptive work to open the eyes of the blind.

3876. לוֹט ***lôṭ:*** A proper noun designating Lot:

A. The third son of Leah. His name means, in the biblical context, "joined" or "attached" based on the popular etymology Leah gave the word (cf. Num. 18:2, 4). Levi and Simeon avenged the rape of their sister Dinah (Gen. 34:25–30). This event influenced Jacob's blessing on Levi (Gen. 49:5–7). Moses mentioned Levi's testing of the Lord at Massah and Meribah (Deut. 33:8). Levi had three sons, Gershon (Gen. 46:11), Kohath, and Merari (Ex. 6:16–18). Moses' mother came from Levi descent (Ex. 2:1; 6:16).

B. These were the descendants of Levi (see A above) who were given the priesthood in Israel and were in charge of all of the holy things (Num. 1:47–54; 3:5–50). Within the tribe of Levi, only the sons of Aaron were to serve as high priests (Ex. 28—29). The descendants of Kohath, Gershon, and Merari were also special important family lines (Num. 2:1–31; 4:1–33; 10:11–33). In Exodus 32:26–28, the Levites showed their zeal for the Lord, not for senseless violence against other humans (cf. Gen. 54:25–30). Ezekiel had a place for the Levites in his New Temple Vision, although a reduced one (Ezek. 40:45–46); even a Gate of Levi is featured. Zadok and his sons were favored by Ezekiel's priestly scheme. Zadok was a Levite, a son of Eleazar, and hence high priest with Abiathar (2 Sam. 8:17).

3877. לוֹטָן lôṭān: A proper noun designating Lotan (Gen. 36:20, 22, 29; 1 Chr. 1:38, 39).

3878. לֵוִי lēwiy: A proper noun designating Levi:

A. Third son of Jacob by Leah (Gen. 29:34, 34:25, 35:23).

B. The tribe of Levi which was set apart for the worship of God and within which the family of Aaron possessed the right of the priesthood (Ex. 6:19; 32:26, 28; Num. 16:7, 8, 10; Deut. 10:8, 9).

3879. לֵוָי lēwāy: An Aramaic proper noun designating a Levite (Ezra 6:16, 18; 7:13, 24). It corresponds to the Hebrew 3881.

3880. לִוְיָה liwyāh: A feminine noun meaning a garland, a wreath. It indicates, probably figuratively, a decorative headpiece worn as a sign of approval and honor, gracing a person's features (Prov. 1:9) as a result of following wisdom and awarded by wisdom itself (Prov. 4:9).

3881. לֵוִי lēwiy: A proper noun designating a Levite, a descendant of Levi, a member of the tribe of Levi (see 3878) (Ex. 4:14; 6:25; 38:21; Lev. 25:32, 33; Judg. 17:7, 9–13; Isa. 66:21; Jer. 33:18, 21, 22).

3882. לִוְיָתָן liwyāṯān: I. A masculine proper noun meaning Leviathan. It describes a huge indomitable being that God created and whom only He fully comprehends and controls (Job 3:8; 41:1). Its exact meaning is complex and tied to ancient Near Eastern ideas of creatures. In Psalm 104:26, Leviathan frolics in the ocean, a harmless being made by God. In Psalm 74:14, Leviathan refers to the mighty waters of the Red Sea that the Lord subdued to rescue His people. In Isaiah 27:1, the word refers most likely to the rebellious nations whom God will slay as He slayed the monster of the sea.

II. A masculine noun meaning mourning. Its traditional meaning has been rendered as mourning regarding Job's hated day of birth (Job 3:8). Most recent translators prefer to render this as Leviathan (NASB, NIV, NKJV).

3883. לוּל lûl: A masculine noun indicating a staircase, a winding staircase. It is a technical architectural term referring traditionally to a set of spiral stairs (1 Kgs. 6:8) in Solomon's Temple. Some have suggested that it indicates a trapdoor.

3884. לוּלֵא lûlē', לוּלֵי lûlēy: An adverbial particle meaning if not, unless. It introduces conditional sentences: It may introduce a condition known to be contrary to fact (Gen. 31:42; 43:10; Deut. 32:27; Judg. 14:18; 2 Kgs. 3:14; Ps. 94:17). Sometimes the apodosis or concluding clause to the condition asserted in the *lûlē'* clause is understood but not written (Ps. 27:13). *Lûlē'* may be followed grammatically by the perfect form of a verb, the imperfect form, the participle form, or no verb at all.

3885. לִין *liyn*, לוּן *lûn*: I. A verb meaning to lodge, to tarry. It means to rest, to tarry, to stay, often overnight. Persons may spend the night or lodge somewhere (Gen. 19:2; 24:23, 25, 54; 28:11). It is used figuratively of righteousness lodging permanently in Zion (Isa. 1:21); and of evil thoughts taking residence in the city of Jerusalem (Jer. 4:14). It is used of weeping coming to "lodge" in the evening (Ps. 30:5[6]). It describes the secure, peaceful rest of one living close to the Lord (Ps. 91:1). Used with *'ayin* (5869, eye) as subject, it has the sense of to set on, to look upon (Job 17:2). Job notes that his error originates and remains in him (Job 19:4). It indicates a wise person's proper existence, abiding among the wise (Prov. 15:31). It takes on the sense of resting or sleeping when one fears the Lord (Prov. 19:23). Something may remain through the night (Ex. 23:18; Lev. 19:13; Jer. 4:14); or stay the night (Job 39:28). It is used of a dead body remaining in a tree overnight (Deut. 21:23).

II. A verb meaning to murmur, to grumble, to howl. It is found in the books of Exodus, Numbers, and Joshua and refers to the Israelites' complaining during their escape from Egypt and their wandering in the desert (Ex. 15:24; 16:2, 7, 8; 17:3; Num. 14:2, 27, 29, 36; 16:11, 41[17:6]; 17:5[20]). It is also used of the people's justified grumbling against the leaders of Israel (Josh. 9:18); and of the violent attacks of enemies on righteous persons (Ps. 59:15[16]).

3886. לָעַע *lā'a'*: I. A verb indicating to devour, to swallow, to drink. It means in context to lick up, to devour words (Job 6:3, KJV). It has the sense of the nations slurping down God's judgments (Obad. 1:16). It is used of the improper treatment of holy things (Prov. 20:25, KJV).

II. A verb meaning to act impetuously, to act rashly. Most translators render the word to indicate that Job's words were spoken rashly (6:3, NIV, NKJV, NASB). It indicates ill-timed and irrational speech (Prov. 20:25, NASB, NIV, NKJV).

3887. לוּץ *lûṣ*, לִיץ *liyṣ*, לֵץ *lēṣ*: A verb meaning to boast, to scorn, to mock, to deride, or to imitate. This Hebrew verb is frequently found in the book of Proverbs (Prov. 9:7, 8; 13:1; 20:1), and means to deride or to boast so as to express utter contempt. The activity of the scornful is condemned as an abomination to people (Prov. 24:9) and contrary to the Law of the Lord (Ps. 1:1). Both Job (Job 16:20) and the psalmist (Ps. 119:51) expressed the pain inflicted by the scornful, but in the end, the scorner will reap what he has sown (Prov. 3:34). By extension the word is used to signify ambassadors (2 Chr. 32:31);, interpreters (Gen. 42:23); and spokesmen (Isa. 43:27). These meanings arise from the sense of speaking indirectly implied in the root word. Some grammarians view the participle of this verb as a separate noun. For a list of these references, see the division in the concordance.

3888. לוּשׁ ***lûš:*** A verb indicating to knead. It is used of the preparation of dough for baking (Gen. 18:6; 1 Sam. 28:24; 2 Sam. 13:8). It is used of preparing bread to make cakes for the Queen of Heaven by apostate Israelites (Jer. 7:18). The kneading of the dough and the penetration of the leaven is a picture of the spread of corruption in Israel (Hos. 7:4).

3889. לָוִשׁ ***lāwiš:*** A proper noun designating Laish (2 Sam. 3:15).

3890. לְוָת ***lᵉwāṯ:*** An Aramaic prepositional article meaning beside, from. It is used to indicate motion away from someone or something and may take suffixes on the end of it, "from you" *lᵉwāṯāḵ* (Ezra 4:12).

3891. לָזוּת ***lāzûṯ:*** A feminine noun indicating perversity, deceitfulness. It is used in its construct form with lips (*śᵉp̱otayim*) following, which may be rendered as perverse or deceitful lips (Prov. 4:24).

3892. לַח ***laḥ:*** An adjective indicating green, fresh. It indicates that something is still green, fresh, moist, newly picked: Jacob's rod (Gen. 30:37); grapes (Num. 6:3); bowstrings, (Judg. 16:7, 8); wood (Ezek. 17:24; 20:47[21:3]).

3893. לֵחַ ***lēaḥ:*** A masculine noun indicating vigor, strength. It refers to a drive or spark of the energy of life, such as Moses still possessed at 120 years of age (Deut. 34:7).

3894. לְחוּם ***lᵉḥûm:*** A masculine noun meaning bowels, intestines. This word is of uncertain meaning, owing to its rare use in Scripture, but it is generally understood to mean the intestines or inward parts of the body. It is a derivative of the Hebrew word *lāḥam* (3898), meaning to fight. Occurring only in Job 20:23 and Zephaniah 1:17, the context is the outpouring of the Lord's wrath. In the latter text, the apocalyptic image is a most graphic picture of battle: "Their blood will be poured out like dust and their flesh [*lāḥûm*, inner parts] like dung" (NASB).

3895. לְחִי ***lᵉḥiy:*** A masculine noun meaning jaw, cheek. It refers to the jawbone of an ass used by Samson (Judg. 15:15); the jaw of any draft animal (Hos. 11:4). It is used metaphorically of the "jaws" of the nations/peoples (Isa. 30:28). It seems to stand for cheek (1 Kgs. 22:24; Lam. 1:2; 3:30; Mic. 5:1[4:14]) and in some cases refers to cheeks as an aspect of human beauty (Song 1:10; 5:13). To smite people on the cheek was to insult them (Job 16:10) and challenge them to battle (Ps. 3:7[8]). It is used figuratively of the jaws of Egypt and Gog which the Lord will pierce with hooks (Ezek. 29:4; 38:4) and lead them about. It indicates also a part of a sacrifice belonging to the priest (Deut. 18:3; jowls, NIV; cheeks, NASB, KJV, NKJV).

3896. לֶחִי ***leḥiy:*** A proper noun designating Lehi (Judg. 15:9, 14, 19).

3897. לָחַךְ *lāḥak̲:* A verb meaning to lick, to lick up. It means to lap up or scoop up something: grass like an ox (Num. 22:4); water licked up by fire (1 Kgs. 18:38). It is used of licking up dust from the ground, from someone's feet (Ps. 72:9; Isa. 49:23); or of a serpent as it seemingly licks up or eats the dust of the ground (Mic. 7:17). It is used figuratively of Israel's enemies in the last reference.

3898. לָחַם *lāḥam:* I. A verb meaning to do battle, to fight, to wage war. It is used nearly always in the niphal reciprocal stem of the verb. It means to close quarters and to engage in battle or war with the Egyptians (Ex. 1:10); against Israel (Num. 21:1, 23, 26; 22:11; Josh. 9:2); Israel against its enemies (Josh. 10:29). It is used of the Lord's fighting against Israel's enemies (Ex. 14:14, 25; 17:9, 10; Josh. 10:14) on behalf of His people. Its object is indicated with various prepositions, *'et̲, 'im, 'al.* It can be used with *yahad̲* following, to indicating fighting with each other (1 Sam. 17:10). It is used in the simple stem of the verb a few times only in Psalms to mean to do, to make battle: In the imperative form, it directs the Lord to fight against one's enemies (Ps. 35:1); in its simplest meaning, it indicates to fight (Ps. 56:1[2], 2[3]).

II. A verb meaning to eat, to taste. It indicates taking food for nourishment (Prov. 23:1). It is used figuratively of eating the food or bread of wickedness (Prov. 4:17); or the food of wisdom (Prov. 9:5). It is used symbolically of fellowshiping with a person, "eating his food" (Ps. 141:4; Prov. 23:6). It is used of famine voraciously devouring people (Deut. 32:24).

3899. לֶחֶם *leḥem:* A masculine noun meaning bread, food. It refers in a general sense to anything God has approved of for nourishment for humans or animals (Gen. 3:19; 25:34; Ps. 147:9). It often indicates grain which was used for preparing bread (Isa. 28:28). The manna was bread from the Lord, heavenly bread (Ex. 16:4, 8, 12, 15; Neh. 9:15; Ps. 105:40). Bread was set on the table of showbread in the Tabernacle and termed the "bread of the presence" (Ex. 25:30). Some bread was used as a wave offering to the Lord (Lev. 23:17). Baked from the produce of the early harvest, this word indicates the "bread of the first fruits" (2 Kgs. 4:42). It was used in figurative language to indicate the bread of affliction or adversity (Deut. 16:3; Isa. 30:20) or the bread of tears (Ps. 80:5[6]).

3900. לְחֶם *l^eḥem:* An Aramaic masculine noun used to identify a feast, a banquet. Its only usage refers to a banquet held in a royal palace (Dan. 5:1).

3901. לָחֶם *lāḥem:* A masculine noun indicating war. It is used in the song of Deborah, a poetic section, to represent war or battle (Judg. 5:8).

3902. לַחְמִי *laḥmiy:* A proper noun designating Lahmi (1 Chr. 20:5).

3903. לַחְמָס ***laḥmās:*** A proper noun designating Lahmas (Josh. 15:40).

3904. לְחֵנָה ***leḥēnāh:*** An Aramaic feminine noun meaning concubine. It refers to secondary wives, a feature of royal, ancient Near-Eastern culture (Dan. 5:2, 3, 23).

3905. לָחַץ ***lāḥaṣ:*** A verb meaning to oppress, to crush. It has the sense of pressing, crowding, or even tormenting: Hebrews as slaves in Egypt (Ex. 3:9); a stranger (Ex. 22:21[20]; 23:9); someone's foot (Num. 22:25; 2 Kgs. 6:32); to hem in and oppress in battle (2 Kgs. 13:4, 22); to confine or keep in a certain territory (Judg. 1:34).

3906. לַחַץ ***laḥaṣ:*** A masculine noun referring to oppression, affliction. It refers to various kinds of oppression or distress: the oppression of Israel (Ex. 3:9; Deut. 26:7; 2 Kgs. 13:4). The term "bread of oppression" (*lāḥaṣ*) means, in context, a prisoner's ration, a small amount (1 Kgs. 22:27). It indicates the oppression the psalmist suffered at the hands of his enemies (Ps. 42:9[10]; 43:2). It is used of a period of affliction or oppression given by the Lord (Isa. 30:20).

3907. לָחַשׁ ***lāḥaš:*** A verb meaning to whisper, to charm. This word is used only three times in the Old Testament. In two of these cases, this word is best translated as whisper to describe the quiet talk of David's servants at the death of his child (2 Sam. 12:19); and the secretive talk of David's enemies (Ps. 41:7[8]). The other instance of this word described the snake charmers (Ps. 58:5[6]). See also the related noun, *laḥaš* (3908), meaning whispering or charming.

3908. לַחַשׁ ***laḥaš:*** A masculine noun meaning whispering, enchantment, and charm. The action of whispering, with the connotations of casting a spell, is the basis for this word. It is used in the Hebrew to signify charms or amulets worn by women (Isa. 3:20); the charming of a snake (Eccl. 10:11; Jer. 8:17); one who crafts clever words so as to enchant (Isa. 3:3); a prayer whispered in a time of sudden distress (Isa. 26:16).

3909. לָט ***lāṭ:*** A masculine noun meaning secrecy, enchantment, mystery, privacy. A form of the Hebrew word *lā'ṭ* (3814), this word conveys the sense of a secret known to only a select group or to something done in secrecy. Three times the word is used in reference to the enchantments of the Egyptian sorcerers in Pharaoh's court (Ex. 7:22; 8:7[13], 18[14]). The other occurrences in the Old Testament signify an action done without another party's notice (Ruth 3:7) or in private (1 Sam. 18:22).

3910. לֹט ***lōṭ:*** A masculine noun meaning myrrh, traditionally understood to refer to the gum of a kind of cistus plant (Gen. 37:25; 43:11). Some suggest the resinous bark of the tree Pistacia mutica; mastic.

3911. לְטָאָה ***l^eṭā'āh:*** A feminine noun meaning lizard. It refers to an unclean reptile forbidden as food for the Israelites (Lev. 11:30) to set them apart from the surrounding nations.

3912. לְטוּשִׁם ***l^eṭûšiym:*** A masculine plural proper noun, Letushites. These people are mentioned in Genesis 25:3 as the sons or people descended from Abraham through Keturah. She bore Jokshan, who bore Dedan, the father of the Letushites.

3913. לָטַשׁ ***lāṭaš:*** A verb meaning to sharpen, to hammer, to instruct. It indicates the process of sharpening a tool (1 Sam. 13:20). It is used figuratively of God's sharpening a weapon, a sword (Ps. 7:12[13]); the tongue of an evil person is described as a sharpened razor (Ps. 52:2[4]). It is used of God's squinting or whetting His eyes against Job (16:9). It is used in its active participial form to indicate a smith or forger of metal tools or instruments (Gen. 4:22).

3914. לֹיָה ***lōyāh:*** A feminine noun describing a wreath, a garland; an addition. It is a technical architectural term indicating some kind of ornamental work featured on the stands for the great molten sea that Solomon built (1 Kgs. 7:29, 30, 36).

3915. לַיְלָה ***laylāh,*** לָיִל ***lāyilā,*** לֵיל ***layil:*** A masculine noun meaning night, midnight. This Hebrew word primarily describes the portion of day between sunset and sunrise (Gen. 1:5; cf. Ps. 136:9). Figuratively, it signifies the gloom or despair that sometimes engulfs the human heart from an absence of divine guidance (Mic. 3:6); calamity (Job 36:20); or affliction (Job 30:17). Nevertheless, even in the dark night of the soul, the Lord gives His people a song of joy (Job 35:10; Ps. 42:8[9]).

3916. לֵילְיָא ***lēyl^{e}yā':*** An Aramaic masculine noun meaning night. All the undisputed instances occur in the book of Daniel. Most often, the term is utilized to declare the time in which several of Daniel's visions took place (Dan. 2:19; 7:2, 7, 13). However, it functions once to indicate when the assassination of the Babylonian king, Belshazzar, transpired (Dan. 5:30). The word closely corresponds with the Hebrew noun *layil* or *lay^{e}lāh* (3915).

3917. לִילִית ***liyliyṯ:*** A feminine noun referring to a night creature; a screech owl. It refers to a creature of the night that will settle among the ruins of the nations whom God judges (Isa. 34:14; NIV, night creatures; NASB, night monster; KJV, screech owl).

3918. לַיִשׁ ***layiš:*** A masculine noun indicating a lion. It indicates a lion clearly (Job 4:11). In context, it is representative of a strong being under God's control. The lion is reckoned as majestic among all beasts (Prov. 30:30). It was present in the Negev in early Israel (Isa. 30:6).

3919. לַיִשׁ layiš, לַיְשָׁה layᵉšāh: A proper noun designating Laish:

A. A city in northern Israel (Judg. 18:6, 14, 27, 29). It was later renamed Dan (see 1835).

B. Michal's father-in-law (1 Sam. 25:44; 2 Sam. 3:15).

C. A village near Jerusalem (Isa. 10:30).

3920. לָכַד lāk̲ad̲: A verb meaning to capture, to seize. It indicates taking possession of, capturing, or catching various things: a city (Num. 21:32); a land (Josh. 10:42); captives of all social ranks in war (Judg. 7:25; 2 Sam. 8:4); foxes (Judg. 15:4); a river ford in the sense of seizing and occupying it (Judg. 3:28); as well as the waters of a river (Judg. 7:24, 25). It has the sense of the Lord choosing or picking something (Josh. 7:14–18); or seizing control of the government reins of a kingdom (1 Sam. 14:47), often by force (Dan. 11:15, 18). It is used figuratively in metaphors: of a sinner being seized in the snares of a wicked woman (Eccl. 7:26); of persons ensnared by the words of their own mouths (Prov. 6:2). It is used to indicate the "seizing" of water as it turns to ice and hardens (Job 38:30); of being seized by "cords of affliction" (Job 36:8). It is used of one thing interlocking with another (Job 41:17[9]).

3921. לֶכֶד lek̲ed̲: A masculine noun indicating a capture, a taking, a seizure. It is used figuratively of a person's being caught in the wicked's intrigues and attacks (Prov. 3:26).

3922. לֵכָה lēk̲āh: A proper noun designating Lecah (1 Chr. 4:21).

3923. לָכִישׁ lāk̲iyš: A proper noun designating Lachish. Tell Lachish today witnesses to this large important city in the Shephelah or low hills of Judah. It is only about thirty miles west from Jerusalem and a few miles south. It was first conquered by Joshua (Josh. 10:3–35; 12:11). Solomon fortified the city because it was a gateway and defense port for Jerusalem (2 Chr. 11:5–9). King Amaziah of Judah was killed in Lachish but buried in Jerusalem (2 Kgs. 14:17–20). Sennacherib, a great Assyrian king, besieged the city and conquered it (2 Kgs. 18:13–16). Nebuchadnezzar captured it again (Jer. 34:7; ca. 588 B.C.). The Jewish exiles resettled the city after 539 B.C. (Neh. 11:30).

3924. לֻלָאוֹת lulā'ôt̲: A feminine plural noun meaning loops. It indicates loops of cloth made to fasten the curtains of the Tabernacle together with clasps through them (Ex. 26:4, 5, 10, 11; 36:11, 12, 17).

3925. לָמַד lāmad̲: A verb meaning to learn, to study, to teach, to be taught, to be learned. The verb describes learning war, training for war, the lack of training (Isa. 2:4; Mic. 4:3), or the acquisition of instruction (Isa. 29:24). God's people were warned not to learn the ways of the nations, that is, to acquire their corrupt and false practices and standards (Jer. 10:2) but to learn the ways of God instead (Jer. 12:16). The verb is sometimes used with an infinitive following it suggesting the meaning to learn to do something. Israel was not to learn to do the abominations of surrounding nations (Deut. 18:9); it describes metaphorically the actions of Jehoahaz against his countrymen as he tore them as a lion would tear its prey (Ezek. 19:3).

In the intensive or factitive form, the root takes on the meaning of imparting learning (i.e., teaching). The verb simply means to teach (2 Chr. 17:7, 9) or to teach people or things; the Lord taught His people (Jer. 31:34) His decrees and laws (Deut. 4:1). The participle of this form often means teacher (Ps. 119:99).

The passive forms of this verb mean to be teachable or to be knowledgeable or well-trained by the Lord (Jer. 31:18) or people (Isa. 29:13).

3926. לְמוֹ ***l*^{e}*mô:*** A particle meaning for, at, over; in. It may be an expanded form of the preposition *l*^{e}, to. It indicates in context purpose, "for" the sword (Job 27:14); it indicates why something is done, e.g., people waited for Job's counsel (Job 29:21). It has the sense of "in," lions "in their lair" (Job 38:40 NASB). In Job 40:4 it signifies Job's purpose of covering his mouth because he is unable to reply to God.

3927. לְמוּאֵל ***l*^{e}*mû'ēl,*** לְמוֹאֵל ***l*^{e}*mô'ēl:*** A proper noun designating Lemuel (Prov. 31:1, 4).

3928. לִמּוּד ***limmûd,*** לִמֻּד ***limmud:*** A masculine adjective meaning accustomed, used to something, learned, practiced, an expert, one taught, a follower, a disciple. It was used to describe those who habitually practice evil (Jer. 13:23). It was also employed to help portray Israel as a wild donkey in heat that was accustomed to life in the rugged wilderness (Jer. 2:24). The Lord gave the Suffering Servant a "tongue of the learned," that is, the gift of inspirational and instructive speech and an ear that listens like those being taught (Isa. 50:4). Isaiah says that the children of the desolate woman or widow will be taught by the Lord Himself (Isa. 54:13). The word is also used once to denote Isaiah's disciples (Isa. 8:16). It is derived from the verb *lāmaḏ* (3925).

3929. לֶמֶךְ ***lemeḵ:*** A proper noun designating Lamech:

A. A son of Methushael who married two women, the beginning of polygamy in the human race (Gen. 4:18–24). He also displayed arrogance toward God and God's social restraints (Gen. 4:15–16, 23–24), as well as a lack of concern for harming another human being.

B. The son of Methusalah, the oldest person recorded in the Bible. He was the father of Noah. He gave his son a name with prophetic significance, "rest," asserting that his son would give humankind rest from the labor and toil of God's curse on the ground (Gen. 5:25–31).

3930. לֹעַ lōaʿ: A masculine noun meaning throat; appetite, hunger. It refers to a person's throat, but in context it is used figuratively to indicate controlling one's appetite (Prov. 23:2).

3931. לָעַב lāʿab̲: A verb meaning to mock, to make a game of somebody. It means to not take seriously, to make fun of, to despise. The Israelites mocked the prophets of God and did not listen to them (2 Chr. 36:16).

3932. לָעַג lāʿag: A verb meaning to deride, to scorn, to mock. It refers to disclaiming people, deriding them, despising them to their faces, ridiculing them as Jerusalem did to Assyria (2 Kgs. 19:21; 2 Chr. 30:10; Neh. 2:19; 4:1[3:33]). It describes the sounds of a foreign language as stammering, unintelligible (Isa. 33:19). It indicates strongly attacking and accusing people's positions and words (Job 21:3), ridiculing them. It includes sometimes the act of sneering, making faces at someone (Ps. 22:7[8]). It is used of wisdom's deriding those who despise wisdom (Prov. 1:26). Anyone mocking the poor is said to do the same to his Creator (Prov. 17:5; cf. 30:17).

3933. לַעַג laʿag: A masculine noun indicating scorn, mocking. Used with *śap̄āh*, lips, tongue, following, it indicates stammering lips. It generally means derision, scorn in a negative sense (Ezek. 23:32). Job was able to endure the scorn poured upon him (34:7). It is used of the Lord's treatment of His rebellious people, making them an object of scorn before Himself and others (Ps. 44:13[14]; 79:4; Hos. 7:16). The wicked mock the righteous (Ps. 123:4).

3934. לָעֵג lāʿēg: An adjective describing something as mocking, stammering. It is used to describe the language spoken by foreign lip(s) as (b^e) stammering (Isa. 28:11). It is also used of certain persons as jesters, mockers (Ps. 35:16, NIV, "maliciously mocked").

3935. לַעְדָּה laʿdāh: A proper noun designating Laadah (1 Chr. 4:21).

3936. לַעְדָּן laʿdān: A proper noun designating Ladan:
A. An Ephraimite (1 Chr. 7:26).
B. A Gershonite (1 Chr. 23:7–9; 26:21).

3937. לָעַז lāʿaz: A verb meaning to speak in an incomprehensible foreign language. The term is used in a participial form to describe the Egyptians among whom the Hebrews lived for 430 years, a people who spoke a much different language (Ps. 114:1). See the verb *lāʿag* (3932) that appears to semantically overlap with this word.

3938. לָעַט lāʿaṭ: A verb indicating to swallow greedily, to devour. It indicates devouring greedily, voraciously.

It is used of Esau's ill-fated eating some stew (Gen. 25:30).

3939. לַעֲנָה ***laʿanāh:*** A feminine noun indicating wormwood, bitterness. It is always used in a figurative, metaphorical sense. It describes the character of an adulteress as bitter (of wormwood) (Prov. 5:4). It is used of a rebellious or bitter root or spirit in persons (Deut. 29:18[17]) that, appropriately, results in judgments of bitterness (of wormwood), i.e., the judgments of God (Jer. 9:15[14]; 23:15; Lam. 3:15, 19). It is used to describe the opposite of justice and righteousness which should be sweet experiences (Amos 5:7; 6:12).

3940. לַפִּיד ***lappiyḏ:*** A masculine noun indicating a torch, a lamp. It is used mainly of a fiery light (Gen. 15:17; Judg. 7:16, 20; 15:4, 5) but also depicts bright flashes of lightning (Ex. 20:18; Nah. 2:4[5]). It is used figuratively of Judah's conquering clans (Zech. 12:6); and the eyes of a divine being (Dan. 10:6). Flames of fire may be called torches (Ezek. 1:13). Jerusalem's salvation will be seen like a flaming torch (Isa. 62:1). Leviathan's mouth shoots forth burning torches (Job 41:19[11]).

3941. לַפִּידוֹת ***lappiyḏôṯ:*** A proper noun designating Lappidoth (Judg. 4:4).

3942. לִפְנָי ***lipnāy:*** An adverb meaning before, in front of. It is used to indicate physical position, in front of something (1 Kgs. 6:17), i.e., the nave in front of the inner Temple sanctuary.

3943. לָפַת ***lāpaṯ:*** A verb indicating to take hold of, to turn aside. It is used of placing one's hand on something, grasping it (Judg. 16:29; Ruth 3:8). It describes the path of life as winding its way, winding along (Job 6:18).

3944. לָצוֹן ***laṣôn:*** A masculine noun indicating a scoffer, a mocker, mockery. It refers to foolish, arrogant, bragging talk (Prov. 1:22), as well as to the scoffers or babblers themselves, literally, "people of *lāṣôn,*" (Prov. 29:8; Isa. 28:14).

3945. לְצָצִים ***leṣaṣiym,*** לָצַץ ***lāṣaṣ:*** I. A masculine noun meaning a scoffer, a scorner. It is used in a masculine plural participial form to indicate those who rebel or scorn. It has the sense of scoffing that is religiously and morally wrong in context (Hos. 7:5, KJV, NASB). See II also.

II. A verb meaning to mock. It is understood to be from the word *lāṣaṣ,* not *liyṣ,* by some translators (NIV: Hos. 7:5).

3946. לַקּוּם ***laqqûm:*** A proper noun designating Lakkum (Josh. 19:33).

3947. לָקַח ***lāqaḥ:*** A verb meaning to take, to get. Its exact meaning must be discerned from its context. It is used of grasping or seizing a person or an animal (Gen. 12:5; Ex. 17:5; Ezek. 8:3; Hos. 14:2[3]). The ark was captured (1 Sam. 4:11; 17, 19). It has the sense of keeping what one has (Gen. 14:21). It may mean in context to receive or acquire, to buy (2 Kgs. 5:20; Prov. 31:16). It is used of a bird carrying or loading its young onto its wings (Deut. 32:11). It is used figuratively of obeying, "taking on" commands, instructions (Prov. 10:8). It is used of taking a wife (Gen. 25:1). With *nāqām* as its object, it means to take vengeance (Isa. 47:3). One's ear can "receive," hearken to God's Word (Jer. 9:20[19]). It is used of one's heart sweeping away, carrying away oneself (Job 15:12). In its passive usage, it means to be brought in (Gen. 12:15; Esth. 2:8, 16). It takes on the nuance of flashing, bolting here and there like fire or lightning (Ex. 9:24; Ezek. 1:4).

3948. לֶקַח *leqaḥ:* A masculine noun meaning something received, instruction. Having this basal sense, the word's usage can be divided further into three categories, each with its own distinctive variation of meaning. First, the word can signify the learning, insight, or understanding that a person receives, perceives, or learns through an instructor or some other means (Prov. 1:5; 9:9; Isa. 29:24). The second variation is similar to the first, yet only slightly different in that it arises from the perspective of the one dispensing the knowledge (i.e., a teacher or instructor), rather than that of the learner. It describes that which is being communicated to others, therefore giving the sense of teaching, instruction, or discourse (Deut. 32:2; Prov. 4:2). Finally, the term seems to have the force of persuasive speech, whether for a positive or a deceitful intent (Prov. 7:21; 16:21). This noun derives from the verb *lāqaḥ* (3947).

3949. לִקְחִי *liqḥiy:* A proper noun designating Likhi (1 Chr. 7:19).

3950. לָקַט *lāqaṭ:* A verb meaning to pick up, to gather. This word occurs with various objects such as manna, lilies, firewood, and people (Ex. 16:4, 5; Judg. 11:3; Song 6:2; Jer. 7:18); however, by far it is used most often with food, including once with grapes (Lev. 19:10; Isa. 17:5). Even animals are able to gather the food God graciously provides (Ps. 104:28). About half of the occurrences of this term relate to the provision of the Mosaic Law to take care of the needy by allowing them to glean the fields, a provision featured prominently in the story of Ruth (Lev. 19:9, 10; 23:22; Ruth 2:2, 3, 7, 8, 15–19, 23). Isaiah used this term in both a picture of judgment and of restoration for the nation of Israel (Isa. 17:5; 27:12).

3951. לֶקֶט *leqeṭ:* A masculine noun referring to gleaning. It refers to the gatherings or gleaning of a harvest, usually from a field already harvested (Lev. 19:9; 23:22).

3952. לָקַק *lāqaq:* A verb indicating to lap up, to lick. In its context in Judges, the text indicates lapping like a dog. It refers to lapping up water like a dog (Judg. 7:5; 1 Kgs. 21:19;

22:38). In the 1 Kings references, dogs lick up Ahab's blood.

3953. לָקַשׁ ***lāqaš:*** A verb of uncertain meaning, translated as to despoil, to take everything, to glean. Its only occurrence is in Job 24:6. It is most likely the denominative verb of the noun *leqeš* (3954), meaning spring crop or aftergrowth.

3954. לֶקֶשׁ ***leqeš:*** A masculine noun indicating spring crop, a second crop; late grass. It identifies a late, second spring crop, especially important for the grazing of animals (Amos 7:1).

3955. לָשָׁד ***lāšād:*** A masculine noun denoting freshness, moisture, vitality; cake(s). It refers to a cake baked with oil (Num. 11:8). Its meaning is difficult to decipher in context (NIV, something; KJV, fresh; NASB, cake; NKJV, pastry).

3956. לָשׁוֹן ***lāšôn,*** לָשֹׁן ***lāšōn:*** A common noun meaning tongue, language. It is used literally as a part of a person or animal: of a person (Ex. 4:10; Lam. 4:4); of a dog (Ex. 11:7); metaphorically of the tongue of the Lord as a consuming fire (Isa. 30:27). The tongue is the instrument of speech (2 Sam. 23:2). Being heavy of tongue meant to speak poorly (Ex. 4:10). A slanderer is a man of a tongue (Ps. 140:11[12]). The phrase *ba'al hallāšôn* referred to a charmer (Eccl. 10:11) of snakes. The same word means language (Gen. 10:5; Neh. 13:24). The tongue is a source of flattery, smooth talk (Ps. 5:9[10]); falsehood (Ps. 78:36); a lying tongue (Ps. 109:2; Prov. 6:17; 12:19; 21:6; 26:28). But the righteous use their tongues to praise the Lord (Ps. 51:14[16]). In figurative language, the tongue is pictured in various ways: a bar of gold (Josh. 7:21); a tongue of fire (Isa. 5:24); a bay along the seashore (Josh. 15:5; Isa. 11:15).

3957. לִשְׁכָּה ***liškāh:*** A feminine noun referring to a room, a chamber, a storeroom; a hall. It refers to a room whose three walls had benches for worshipers. The fourth wall was open facing the courtyard (1 Sam. 9:22; 2 Kgs. 23:11; Jer. 35:2, 4; 36:10, 12, 20, 21). It seems to refer to storerooms as well (1 Chr. 28:12; 2 Chr. 31:11). In Ezekiel's visionary Temple, it referred to cells for various temple personnel (Ezek. 40:17, 38, 44, 46; 42:1). In the Temple of Ezra and Nehemiah, the word is used of storerooms (Ezra 8:29; Neh. 10:38).

3958. לֶשֶׁם ***lešem:*** A masculine noun meaning jacinth, ligure. It refers to a precious stone. Its exact nature is not clear. In addition to jacinth, carnelian, and amber, several other identifications have been offered (Ex. 28:19; 39:12). It was placed in the high priest's breastplate.

3959. לֶשֶׁם ***lešem:*** A proper noun designating Leshem (Josh. 19:47).

3960. לָשַׁן ***lāšan:*** A verb meaning to slander. It refers to uttering false, damaging statements against a third party (Ps. 101:5). God avenges this with destruction. Even a slave was not to be slandered to his owner (Prov. 30:10).

3961. לִשָּׁן ***liššān:*** An Aramaic common noun meaning language. It refers to the tongue of a person literally but refers to a language every time it is found in Daniel (3:4, 7; 4:1[3:31]; 5:19; 6:25[26]; 7:14), except perhaps once where it has the nuance of a "tongue that speaks anything offensive" (Dan. 3:29 NASB).

3962. לֶשַׁע ***leša':*** A proper noun designating Lasha (Gen. 10:19).

3963. לֶתֶךְ ***leṯeḵ:*** A masculine noun referring to a half homer, a dry measure. This dry measure probably equaled about 110 liters or ca. 3.3 bushels. Its exact capacity is still being researched (Hos. 3:2).

מ Mem

3964. **מָא** ***mā':*** An Aramaic particle meaning what, whatever. It is an indefinite interrogative pronoun referring to what is to be done for the elders of Israel in the context of Ezra 6:8.

3965. **מַאֲבוּס** ***ma'ᵃḇûs:*** A masculine noun referring to a storehouse, a granary; barns, storehouses. It indicates a place for storing grain or other items, in this case, those of Babylon (Jer. 50:26; NIV, granaries; KJV, storehouses; NASB, barns).

3966. **מְאֹד** ***mᵉ'ōḏ:*** A substantive, adverb, or adjective in function, very, greatly, great, abundance; might, power. It is used as a noun indicating might, power, will (Deut. 6:3; 2 Kgs. 23:25). As an adverb, it usually means very, i.e., all that God created was very good (Gen. 1:31). It takes on the sense of exceedingly as an extension of very and may come at the end of a phrase (Gen. 13:13). It can precede the word it is emphasizing as in greatly exalted (Ps. 47:9[10]). Repeated, it emphasizes something greatly (Gen. 7:19); exceedingly (Gen. 17:2; Ex. 1:7). The phrase *'aḏ-mᵉ'ōḏ* adds an exceptional emphasis to a preceding assertion (Gen. 27:33; 1 Sam. 11:15; 2 Sam. 2:17; Isa. 64:9[8]).

3967. **מֵאָה** ***mē'āh:*** A feminine noun meaning a hundred. It means one hundred and may precede or follow a noun (Gen. 5:3; 17:17). In its dual form, it means two hundred, e.g., *mā'tayim 'îš,* two hundred men (1 Sam. 18:27). In its plural form *mᵉ'ôṯ*, it combines with other words to mean, e.g., three hundred, *šᵉlōš mᵉ'ôṯ* (Judg. 15:4). Military units could be made up of hundreds (1 Sam. 29:2).

3968. **מֵאָה** ***mē'āh:*** A proper noun designating Meah (Neh. 3:1; 12:39).

3969. **מְאָה** ***mᵉ'āh:*** An Aramaic feminine noun meaning one hundred. It is used to indicate a hundred of something, often with other numbers to give exact figures (Ezra 6:17; 7:22; Dan. 6:1[2]). In its dual form *mā'ṯayin,* it indicates two hundred (Ezra 6:17).

3970. **מַאֲוַי** ***ma'way:*** A masculine noun meaning desire. It is used in the plural construct form once in Psalm 140:8[9]). In context it refers to the attempts and plans of the wicked to exalt themselves by their plans.

3971. **מוּם** ***mûm,*** **מאוּם** ***m'ûm,*** **מְאוּם** ***mu'wm:*** A masculine noun meaning blemish, defect. This word usually describes a physical characteristic that is deemed to be bad. A man with any sort of blemish could not be a priest (Lev. 21:17, 18, 21, 23) nor could an animal which had a blemish be sacrificed (Lev. 22:20, 21; Num. 19:2; Deut. 17:1). The word is also used to describe an injury caused by another (Lev. 24:19, 20). On the other hand, the absence of any blemish was a sign of beauty (2 Sam. 14:25; Song 4:7) or potential (Dan. 1:4). In a figurative sense, the word is used to describe the effect of sin (Deut. 32:5; Job 11:15; 31:7) or insult (Prov. 9:7).

3972. מְאוּמָה ***mᵉ'ûmāh,*** מוּמָה ***mûmāh:*** An indefinite pronoun meaning anything. It is indefinite and may refer to anything at all (1 Kgs. 10:21) or to whatever the context demands, e.g., any evil (Jer. 39:10). Often it is negated and means "nothing at all" (Gen. 30:31; 39:6, 9; 40:15; 1 Sam. 12:4, 5). It is used adverbially at least once meaning "with respect to anything at all" (1 Sam. 21:2[3]).

3973. מָאוֹס ***mā'ôs:*** A masculine noun meaning refuse, trash. It indicates what is rejected. It refers to Israel in a figurative sense as God's rejected people (Lam. 3:45).

3974. מָאוֹר ***mā'ôr,*** מָאֹר ***mā'ōr:*** A masculine singular noun meaning luminary, a light. This noun is employed in connection with the lamp in the Tabernacle (Ex. 35:14; Lev. 24:2; Num. 4:16). It is also used to describe the heavenly lights in the creation story of Genesis 1:15, 16.

3975. מְאוּרָה ***mᵉ'ûrāh:*** A feminine noun indicating a den, hole. It refers to the hole where a viper lives. In context a child will not fear to put his or her hand on a viper's den (Isa. 11:8).

3976. מֹאזְנַיִם ***mō'zᵉnayim:*** A dual noun referring to scales, a balance scales. The word is in a dual form and refers to scales for weighing various things: money (Jer. 32:10); hair (Ezek. 5:1); figuratively, the Lord has weighed the mountains in a balance (Isa. 40:12); the nations are a speck of dust on the scales to the Lord (Isa. 40:15). Job wishes for his grief to be weighed in a balance (Job 6:2). Also, figuratively scales are used to weigh Job before the Lord as to his integrity (Job 31:6). Persons in general weigh nothing on the scales when it comes to righteousness before God (Ps. 62:9[10]). Dishonest scales were a feature of Israel's ethical corruption in their business dealings (Hos. 12:7[8]); Amos 8:5; Mic. 6:11). Such scales are an abomination to the Lord (Prov. 11:1; 20:23); He always uses just weights, as a righteous God (Prov. 16:11).

3977. מֹאזְנֵא ***mō'zᵉnē':*** An Aramaic dual noun indicating scales, a balance scales. It is used in a figurative sense once in Daniel 5:27. Belshazzar, king of Babylon, was weighed in God's scales of justice and found unfit.

3978. מַאֲכָל ***ma'ᵃkāl:*** A masculine noun meaning food, meat. It is used to depict food for humans or animals (Gen. 6:21; Deut. 28:26; Ps. 79:2; Prov. 6:8). God considered all fruit-producing trees as good (Gen. 2:9; Deut. 20:20). He created flocks of animals for food as well (Ps. 44:11[12]). Used with the adjective *ta'ᵃweh,* this word means special, best, or favorite food (Job 33:20). It is used figuratively of people as food for the Babylonians (Hab. 1:16). Its use encompasses honey (Judg. 14:14).

3979. מַאֲכֶלֶת *ma'ᵃkeleṯ:* A feminine noun meaning a knife, a butcher knife. It refers to a large knife used in sacrifices. It was used by Abraham when he was about to slay Isaac and by the Levite to carve up his concubine (Gen. 22:6, 10; Judg. 19:29). It is parallel to a sword in Proverbs 30:14, giving an especially macabre aspect to the proverb.

3980. מַאֲכֹלֶת *ma'ᵃḵōleṯ:* A feminine noun indicating fuel, food (for fire). It refers to the clothing and shoes of warriors killed in battle to be used as fuel for the fire (Isa. 9:5[4]), as well as, in a figurative and literal sense, the people of the land (Isa. 9:19[18]).

3981. מַאֲמָץ *ma'ᵃmāṣ:* A masculine noun indicating force, effort; expenditures. It refers to exertions or expenditures used to deliver a person from stress or distress but all in vain (Job 36:19).

3982. מַאֲמַר *ma'ᵃmar:* A masculine noun meaning word or command. In all three of its instances in the Old Testament, this word is best translated, command (i.e., that which is spoken with authority). It referred to the command of King Ahasuerus that Queen Vashti ignored (Esth. 1:15). It described Mordecai's instructions to Esther to keep quiet about her nationality (Esth. 2:20). Finally, it referred to Esther's edict about the establishment of the days of Purim (Esth. 9:32). This word comes from the common verb *'āmar* (559), meaning to say, which can be translated to command, depending on the context (2 Chr. 31:11; Esth. 1:10).

3983. מֵאמַר *mē'mar:* An Aramaic masculine noun meaning word, command. This word is used only twice in the Old Testament and is equivalent to the Hebrew word *ma'ᵃmar* (3982). It describes the words the priests spoke to request supplies for rebuilding the temple (Ezra 6:9); and it also refers to the words of the holy ones that issued the edict in Nebuchadnezzar's dream (Dan. 4:17[14]). This word comes from the common Aramaic verb, *'ᵃmar* (560), meaning to say.

3984. מָאן *mā'n:* An Aramaic masculine noun referring to a vessel, a utensil. It refers to a gold or silver vessel or receptacle used in the Temple (Ezra 5:14, 15; 6:5; 7:19; Dan. 5:2, 3, 23). They were taken from the temple and many were later returned under Persia.

3985. מָאַן *mā'an:* A verb meaning to refuse. The basic idea of this word is a refusal or rejection of an offer. It is used to describe the refusal to obey God (Ex. 16:28; Neh. 9:17; Isa. 1:20; Jer. 9:6[5]); His messengers, (1 Sam. 8:19); or other men (Esth. 1:12). Jacob refused comfort when he thought Joseph had died (Gen. 37:35); Joseph refused Potiphar's wife's offer to sin (Gen. 39:8); Pharaoh refused to let Israel go (Ex. 4:23; 7:14); Balaam refused Balak's offer to curse Israel (Num. 22:13, 14); both Saul and Ammon refused to eat food offered to them (1 Sam. 28:23; 2 Sam. 13:9).

3986. מָאֵן *mā'ēn:* An adjective meaning refusing, disobeying. This word is found in the context of disobedience to a command. A prime example was that of the Israelites in bondage. God said that if Pharaoh refused to let His people go, He would bring various plagues on Egypt (Ex. 8:2[7:27]; 9:2). King Zedekiah was warned that he would be captured by Babylon if he refused to surrender to the Lord (Jer. 38:21).

3987. מֵאֵן *mē'ēn:* An adjective meaning refusing. This word is used only once in the Old Testament and comes from the verb *mā'ēn* (3985), meaning to refuse. In Jeremiah 13:10, it described the people of Judah as those refusing to listen to God's words.

3988. מָאַס *mā'as:* A verb meaning to reject, to despise, to abhor, to refuse. The primary meaning of this word is to reject or treat as loathsome. It designates people's actions in refusing to heed God or accept His authority (1 Sam. 10:19; Jer. 8:9); esteeming God's commands lightly (Lev. 26:15; Isa. 30:12); and despising one's spiritual condition in an act of repentance (Job 42:6). Scripture also speaks of the Lord rejecting His people (Hos. 4:6) and their worship (Amos 5:21) because of their rejection of Him. A secondary and more rare meaning of the word is to run or flow. This use appears in Psalm 58:7[8] as David prayed for the wicked to melt away like a flowing river.

3989. מַאֲפֶה *ma'ªp̱eh:* A masculine noun indicating something baked. It refers to something that has been prepared in an oven (*tannûr*) (Lev. 2:4).

3990. מַאֲפֵל *ma'ªp̱ēl:* A masculine noun meaning darkness. It indicates the thick darkness the Lord put between Israel and the Egyptians so they could not see each other (Josh. 24:7).

3991. מַאְפֵּלְיָה *ma'pēlyāh:* A feminine noun referring to darkness, thick darkness. It refers literally to a dense darkness. It is used figuratively to refer to the judgments and "thick darkness" the Lord made the land of Israel to His people (Jer. 2:31).

3992. מָאַר *mā'ar:* A verb meaning to prick, to be painful, to be destructive. It refers to a skin disease or an eruption that is destructive, hurtful (Lev. 13:51, 52); or to some growth or malignancy found in the structure or materials of a house (Lev. 14:44). It modifies the word *ṣāra'aṯ* each time. It is used to modify brier or thorn, a figure of speech for oppressive peoples around Israel who were painful or prickly briers or thorns (Ezek. 28:24).

3993. מַאֲרָב ma'^a^rāb: A masculine noun referring to an ambush, a hiding place. It is used of accosting persons secretly, lying hidden to destroy them (Josh. 8:9; 2 Chr. 13:13); sometimes, it refers to the place of ambush more directly (Judg. 9:35). It is used of the wicked sitting in places of ambush, waiting to ambush the innocent (Ps. 10:8).

3994. מְאֵרָה m^e^'ērāh: A feminine noun designating a curse, a malediction. It refers to God's sending evil or destruction on His disobedient people (Deut. 28:20; Mal. 2:2; 3:9); or on the wicked in general (Prov. 3:33). A curse may befall those who do not help the poor (Prov. 28:27).

3995. מִבְדָּלָה mibdālāh: A feminine noun indicating a separate place; singled out. It refers to something selected, set apart, for a specific purpose, i.e., cities and villages for the sons of Ephraim (Josh. 16:9).

3996. מָבוֹא mābô': A common noun indicating entrance; the west, the going down of the sun. It indicates an entrance, a gate into a city in general (Judg. 1:24, 25); or special entrances or gates, e.g., for horses (2 Kgs. 11:16). It depicts the entrances into Ezekiel's new Temple in his vision (Ezek. 42:9; 44:5; 46:19). In a broader usage, it refers to any access to something or to somewhere, such as Tyre as an "entrance" or place of access to the Great Sea (Ezek. 27:3). It is used in a general sense of persons coming, making their entrances (Ezek. 33:31). It is used in the idiom for the "setting of the sun" (Deut. 11:30; Mal. 1:11), a way of expressing "west" as well.

3997. מְבוֹאָה m^e^bô'āh: A feminine noun meaning entrance. It is used to indicate the area of access to the Great Sea enjoyed by the city of Tyre (see also 3996) (Ezek. 27:3).

3998. מְבוּכָה m^e^bûkāh: A feminine noun indicating perplexity, confusion. It refers to the conditions in a time, a day of the God of hosts, when He will create disorder and bewilderment among the peoples of the earth (Isa. 22:5; Mic. 7:4).

3999. מַבּוּל mabbûl: A masculine noun indicating a flood. It refers to both the great flood on the earth (Gen. 6:17; Ps. 29:10) and to its sources from above and below as well (Gen. 7:6, 7, 10, 17; 9:11, 15, 28). The flood marked a turning point in history (Gen. 10:1, 32; 11:10). God was entirely in charge of it (Ps. 29:10).

4000. מְבוּנִים m^e^bûniym: A variant form of the participle from *biyn* (995). It occurs only once in 2 Chronicles 35:3 where it refers to those who instruct or teach others.

4001. מְבוּסָה m^e^bûsāh: A feminine noun meaning subjugation, downtreading. It indicates aggressiveness, subjugation, trampling. It is applied to the people of Ethiopia (Isa. 18:2, 7). It describes oppressive trampling activities creating violence and confusion on the Day of the Lord (Isa. 22:5), according to Isaiah's vision about the Valley of Vision.

4002. מַבּוּעַ *mabbûa‘*: A masculine noun indicating a spring of water. It indicates a source, a well from which water is drawn by a pitcher (Eccl. 12:6). Its abundant presence in a restored Zion is evidence of its powerful symbolism of life (Isa. 35:7) and the Lord's salvation (Isa. 49:10).

4003. מְבוּקָה *m^{e}bûqāh*: A feminine noun meaning void, emptiness. It indicates the desolation and devastation of a city in time of war (Nah. 2:10[11]), along with several other terms close in meaning.

4004. מָבְחוֹר *māḇḥôr*: A masculine noun indicating choice, major, best. It refers to the best-endowed cities, the most desirable to have (2 Kgs. 3:19) and to the most excellent cypress timber of Lebanon that the ravaging Assyrians cut down (2 Kgs. 19:23).

4005. מִבְחָר *miḇḥār*: A masculine noun meaning what is choice, choicest. It indicates what is the most desirable to have, the best (Gen. 23:6; Isa. 37:24; Jer. 22:7); elite men of rank, political, military troops, and officers (Ex. 15:4; Ezek. 23:7; Dan. 11:15); the animals of best quality for sacrifices (Deut. 12:11). The choice trees of Lebanon are personified to rejoice at the fall of Assyria (Ezek. 31:16).

4006. מִבְחָר *miḇḥār*: A proper noun designating Mibhar (1 Chr. 11:38).

4007. מַבָּט *mabbāṭ*: A masculine noun indicating expectation, an object of hope. It indicates the basis or goal of a person's hope. Israel put its hope in Cush and Egypt, not the Lord (Isa. 20:5, 6). It indicates the object of hope even if it were a false hope (Zech. 9:5).

4008. מִבְטָא *miḇṭā'*: A masculine noun meaning a rash statement, a rash promise. It refers to a promise or verbal commitment made under insufficient conditions or reasons for the vow to have been made. It may refer to a foolish vow on the spur of the moment (Num. 30:6[7], 8[9]).

4009. מִבְטָח *miḇṭāḥ*: A masculine noun referring to trust, confidence. It refers to persons or things in which one trusts or an attitude of confidence itself. People who do not trust in God have a trust like a spider's web, fragile in the extreme (Job 8:14); the wicked are torn from whatever trust or security they may have (Job 18:14). Confidence in God results in a person being blessed by Him (Ps. 40:4[5]; Jer. 17:7). Israel often trusted in Egypt or other foreign powers to help her (Jer. 2:37). The fear of God is a source of great trust for His people (Prov. 14:26). God is the ultimate trust of the entire earth, the confidence of all nations (Ps. 65:5[6]), as well as the secure dwelling of His people (Isa. 32:18).

4010. מַבְלִיגִית mabliygiyt: A feminine noun meaning cheerfulness, comforter. It indicates healing or comforting for one in great sorrow or pain. In context it is asserted to be impossible for Israel whose sorrow seems to be beyond comfort (Jer. 8:18). The text is difficult to decipher (cf. KJV, NASB, NIV for various options).

4011. מִבְנֶה mibneh: A masculine noun indicating a structure, a building. It refers to a vision of structures resembling a city; hence, the prophet saw an entire complex not just a mere building (Ezek. 40:2).

4012. מְבֻנַּי m^e^bunnay: A proper noun designating Mebunnai (2 Sam. 23:27).

4013. מִבְצָר mibṣār: I. A masculine noun meaning fortification. It is used of a building or set of structures designed for efficient military defenses: a fortified city (Num. 32:17, 36; 2 Kgs. 3:19; Isa. 25:12); a strongly fortified city (Dan. 11:15); fortresses in general (Hos. 10:14; Amos 5:9); fortifications on a wall and including the wall (Isa. 25:12); sound fortifications (Dan. 11:24, 39). It is used figuratively of Jeremiah as a fortified city to carry out his mission (Jer. 1:18; 6:27) (KJV; see II, III also).

II. A masculine noun indicating a tester of metals, an assayer. It is used figuratively of the prophet Jeremiah, the teacher of God's people (NASB; see I, III also) (Jer. 6:27).

III. A masculine noun indicating ore, metal which is tested. Some translators give the meaning ore, metal, to the word in Jeremiah 6:27 (NIV; see I, II also).

4014. מִבְצָר mibṣār: A proper noun designating Mibzar (Gen. 36:42; 1 Chr. 1:53).

4015. מִבְרָח mibrāḥ: A masculine noun meaning fugitive, a fleeing one. It refers to a person who has escaped, a survivor. In context the word refers to Israelites who have fled in every direction because of God's judgments (Ezek. 17:21).

4016. מְבוּשִׁים m^e^bûšiym: A masculine plural noun indicating private parts, male genitals. It refers to the external male reproductive organs, especially the scrotum and testicles (Deut. 25:11).

4017. מִבְשָׂם mibśām: A proper noun designating Mibsam:

A. Son of Ishmael (Gen. 25:13; 1 Chr. 1:29).

B. A descendant of Simeon (1 Chr. 4:25).

4018. מְבַשְּׁלוֹת m^e^bašš^e^lôt: A feminine plural noun meaning places for cooking. It refers to cooking or boiling places or hearths, constructed where the priests prepared sacrificial offerings in Ezekiel's vision of a new Temple (Ezek. 46:23).

4019. מַגְבִּישׁ ***magbiyš:*** A proper noun designating Magbish (Ezra 2:30).

4020. מִגְבָּלוֹת ***migbālôṯ:*** A feminine plural noun indicating something braided or twisted. It refers to hammered, twisted chains like cords to be placed on gold filigree settings (Ex. 28:14).

4021. מִגְבָּעָה ***migbā'āh:*** A feminine noun denoting a turban, a headband. It indicates special high caps that Aaron's sons wore when performing priestly duties (Ex. 28:40; 29:9; 39:28; Lev. 8:13). They were made of fine linen to project beauty and splendor in honor of God.

4022. מֶגֶד ***meḡeḏ:*** A masculine noun indicating a choice thing, the best thing: fruit and all kinds of produce from the land and heaven (Deut. 33:13–16); in a figurative sense of the choice delights of a beloved bride (Song 4:13, 16); or of the finest fruits that decorate their celebrations of love (Song 7:13[14]); it indicates precious valuables or gifts of all kinds (Gen. 24:53; 2 Chr. 21:3; 32:23; Ezra 1:6).

4023. מְגִדּוֹ ***m^e^giddô,*** מְגִדּוֹן ***m^e^giddôn:*** A proper noun designating Megiddo, a key Canaanite town located on the south side of the Jezreel Valley and situated at the meeting place of five or more major international routes. Joshua conquered it and allotted it to Manasseh who could not entirely subdue it (Josh. 12:21; 17:11; Judg. 1:27). It later became a central city of Solomon's twelve district capitals (1 Kgs. 4:12; 9:15). Several good kings of Judah were killed in it (2 Kgs. 9:27; 23:29, 30). It is depicted as a place of past mourning and a picture of future sorrow by Zechariah (12:11).

4024. מִגְדּוֹל ***migdôl,*** מִגְדֹּל ***migdōl:*** I. A masculine noun meaning tower (2 Sam. 22:51; Ezek. 29:10; 30:6).

II. A proper noun designating Migdol, a city on the northeast border of Egypt (Ex. 14:2; Num. 33:7; Jer. 44:1; 46:14; Ezek. 29:10; 30:6).

4025. מַגְדִּיאֵל ***magdiy'ēl:*** A proper noun designating Magdiel (Gen. 36:43; 1 Chr. 1:54).

4026. מִגְדָּל ***migdāl:*** A masculine noun indicating a tower. It refers to various kinds of towers: the Tower of Babel (Gen. 11:4); a watchtower in a vineyard (Isa. 5:2); a tower built into a wall (2 Chr. 14:7[6]); storage structures (1 Chr. 27:25); central defense towers in the centers of cities (Judg. 9:51, 52). In Nehemiah 8:4, the word refers to a structure for someone to stand on in order to address a crowd. It is used figuratively of God as a tower of refuge (Ps. 61:3[4]; Prov. 18:10); and of the breasts of the beloved in Song of Solomon 8:10. An ivory tower is mentioned (Song 7:4[5]); as are several towers in specific locations (Judg. 8:17; 9:46, 47, 49; Neh. 3:1, 11; Song 4:4; 7:4[5]; Jer. 31:38; Zech. 14:10).

4027. מִגְדַּל־אֵל ***migdal 'ēl:*** A proper noun designating Migdal El (Josh. 19:38).

4028. מִגְדַּל־גָּד ***migdal gāḏ:*** A proper noun designating Migdal Gad (Josh. 15:37).

4029. מִגְדַּל־עֵדֶר ***migdal-'ēḏer:*** I. Migdal Eder (KJV, NASB, Gen. 35:21). II. The tower of Edar (NIV, Gen. 35:21).

4030. מִגְדָּנָה ***migdānāh:*** A feminine noun referring to a precious thing, a costly gift. It is the same as 4022. The plural form is *migdānôṯ* and appears in Genesis 24:53; 2 Chronicles 21:3; 32:23; Ezra 1:6. It also has the expected *mᵉgāḏîym* plural.

4031. מָגוֹג ***māgôg:*** A proper noun designating Magog:

A. Son of Japheth (Gen. 10:2; 1 Chr. 1:5).

B. A mountainous region north of Israel (Ezek. 38:2; 39:6).

4032. מָגוֹר ***māgôr:*** A masculine noun meaning fear, terror. The fundamental concept underlying this word is a sense of impending doom. It is used to signify the fear that surrounds one whose life is being plotted against (Ps. 31:13[14]); the fear that causes a soldier to retreat in the face of an invincible foe (Isa. 31:9; Jer. 6:25); and the horrors that befall those facing God's judgment (Lam. 2:22). Of interest is the prophecy of Jeremiah concerning Pashur after he had Jeremiah placed in the stocks for prophesying against the idolatry of Jerusalem (cf. Jer. 20:1–6). The Lord would no longer call Pashur by his name. He gave him a new one, Magormissabib or Magor-Missabib ("fear on every side"), because the Lord would make him, as it were, afraid of his own shadow (Jer. 20:4).

4033. מָגוּר ***māgûr,*** מָגוֹר ***magôr:*** A masculine noun meaning sojourning or a dwelling place. This word comes from the verb, *gûr* (1481), meaning to sojourn. Most often, this word is used to describe Israel as a sojourning people, who will inherit the land of Canaan, where they sojourned (Gen. 17:8; 37:1; Ex. 6:4). The psalmist described the preciousness of God's statutes in his sojourning (Ps. 119:54). The wicked are described as having evil in their dwelling places (Ps. 55:15[16]), which will result with God removing them from their dwelling places (Ezek. 20:38). As a result, the wicked will have no offspring in their dwelling places (Job 18:19).

4034. מְגוֹרָה ***mᵉgôrāh:*** A feminine noun meaning fear, terror. The feminine form of *māgôr* (4032), this word occurs only once in the Bible. Proverbs 10:24 contrasts the fate of the wicked with that of the righteous. The ones serving the Lord will get their hearts' desires, but the wicked will get their worst nightmares—judgment.

4035. מְגוּרָה ***mᵉgûrāh:*** A feminine noun meaning fear, terror. The use of this word for fear tends to imply the haunting apprehensions that one holds deep within. The Lord's judgments bring people's worst fears to reality (Isa. 66:4), while His love frees us from them (Ps. 34:4[5]; cf. 1 John 4:18). Haggai, however, uses this word to signify a storage place or a barn (Hag. 2:19). The link between the divergent ideas comes from the root word *gûr* (1481), which carries the connotation of dwelling as well as fear.

4036. מָגוֹר מִסָּבִיב ***māgôr missābiyb:*** A proper noun designating Magor-Missabib (Jer. 20:3).

4037. מַגְזֵרָה ***magzērāh:*** A feminine noun meaning ax. It is used of an iron implement used by the prisoners of war which David and Joab took of the Ammonites (2 Sam. 12:31).

4038. מַגָּל ***maggāl:*** A feminine noun referring to a sickle. It refers to an instrument for harvesting grain or clearing land (Jer. 50:16; Joel 3:13 [4:13]). It is used metaphorically of God's reaping with a sickle among the nations.

4039. מְגִלָּה ***mᵉgillāh:*** A feminine noun meaning roll, volume, writing, scroll. This Hebrew word is approximately equivalent to the English word "book." In ancient Israel, instead of pages bound into a cover, "books" were written on scrolls of leather or other durable material and rolled together. All but one appearance of this word (Ps. 40:7[8]) occurs in Jeremiah 36. The importance of this word is found in its reference to the sacred volume recording God's own words (cf. Jer. 36:2).

4040. מְגִלָּה ***mᵉgillāh:*** An Aramaic noun meaning roll, scroll. The term is used to describe the object upon which was written an official record of King Cyrus' decree concerning the rebuilding of the Temple at Jerusalem (Ezra 6:2).

4041. מְגַמָּה ***mᵉgammāh:*** A feminine noun that possibly means horde; eagerness. The meaning is uncertain, but it refers to the faces or advancement of the Babylonian army coming to attack Judah (Hab. 1:9). Totality or "all of" have been offered as meanings in context.

4042. מָגַן ***māgan:*** A verb indicating to deliver up, to present. It refers to God's giving over of Abram's enemies to him (Gen. 14:20); and of wisdom's presentation of a crown (Prov. 4:9). Hosea speaks of God's inability to give up or surrender Israel to her deserved fate because of His love for her (Hos. 11:8).

4043. מָגֵן ***māgēn:*** A masculine noun meaning shield. It indicates some kind of protection, literal or figurative: a shield as a weapon (Judg. 5:8; 2 Sam. 1:21; 1 Kgs. 14:27; Job 15:26); a shield as an ornament or decorative display (1 Kgs. 10:17; 14:26); as the protective scales of a crocodile (Job 41:15[7]). Metaphorically, it refers to persons or God as sources of protection or escape, a refuge: a king (Ps. 84:9[10]; 89:18[19]). God is often referred to as a shield of refuge (Gen. 15:1; Ps. 3:3[4]; 7:10[11]; 18:2[3]; Prov. 2:7); also the rulers of the earth are referred to as shields (Ps. 47:9[10]).

4044. מְגִנָּה *meginnāh:* A feminine noun denoting sorrow, hardness. It is used only once in a difficult context. It may mean sorrow, hardness, but insolence fits the context also (Lam. 3:65).

4045. מִגְעֶרֶת *mig'ereṯ:* A feminine noun pointing to a rebuke. It means to blame, to scold sharply, to reprimand as God said He would do to His people (Deut. 28:20).

4046. מַגֵּפָה *maggēpāh:* A feminine noun describing a plague, blow. It is used of the plagues and blows God rained on Egypt, especially the seventh to the tenth plagues (Ex. 9:14); as well as other plagues brought by God on His own people (Ps. 106:29, 30). It is also used of deadly pestilences (Num. 14:37; 1 Sam. 6:4; 2 Sam. 24:21); or slaughter in war (1 Sam. 4:17; 2 Sam. 17:9; 18:7). In the final days and judgments of God, it is used of horrible calamities coming on people (Zech. 14:12, 15, 18).

4047. מַגְפִּיעָשׁ *magpiy'āš:* A proper noun designating Magpiash (Neh. 10:20[21]).

4048. מָגַר *māgar:* A verb meaning to cast before, to deliver over, to yield up. In a participial form, the term is used once to describe the people and princes of Israel who were being thrown to the sword because they stubbornly refused to heed God's discipline (Ezek. 21:12[17]). When used in its intensive form, the verb conveys the idea to cast down or to overthrow, as witnessed in Psalm 89:44[45]: "You have made his splendor to cease and cast his throne to the ground" (NASB). See the verb *nāgar* (5064).

4049. מְגַר *megar:* An Aramaic verb meaning to overthrow, to cast down. In an edict decreed by King Darius, this verb describes what Darius hoped the God of heaven would do to any king or people who altered his edict or tried to destroy the Temple in Jerusalem (Ezra 6:12). The term is closely related to the Hebrew verb *māgar* (4048).

4050. מְגֵרָה *megērāh:* A feminine noun designating a saw, an ax. It probably refers to a special saw for stoneworking (2 Sam. 12:31; 1 Kgs. 7:9; 1 Chr. 20:3).

4051. מִגְרוֹן *migrôn:* A proper noun designating Migron (1 Sam. 14:2; Isa. 10:28).

4052. מִגְרָעָה *migrā'āh:* A feminine noun meaning a recess, an offset ledge. It is a technical architectural term indicating a ledge, a rebatement of a wall, or offsets for timbers to rest on (1 Kgs. 6:6).

4053. מְגְרָפָה ***megrāp̱āh:*** A feminine noun indicating a clod of dirt. It is used of clods of dirt in a tilled garden during a time of drought (Joel 1:17). As likely meanings, spade or hoe have been suggested.

4054. מִגְרָשׁ ***migrāš:*** A masculine noun referring to open pastureland. It generally refers to a stretch of land lying outside a city and controlled by the city (Num. 35:2–5, 7; Josh. 14:4; 21:2). It also indicates land around Ezekiel's holy city (48:15, 17) or Temple (45:2).

4055. מַד ***maḏ:*** A masculine noun meaning clothes, a tunic, a robe. It refers to garments in general: an outer garment (Judg. 3:16; 1 Sam. 4:12); a military uniform or attire (1 Sam. 17:38, 39; 2 Sam. 20:8); priestly garments (Lev. 6:10[3]). It also has the meaning of apportionment or measure in some contexts (Job 11:9; Jer. 13:25). It is used figuratively of wearing cursing as a garment (Ps. 109:18).

4056. מַדְבַּח ***maḏbaḥ:*** An Aramaic masculine noun meaning altar. It refers to a place at the Temple where sacrifices of all kinds were offered (Ezra 7:17).

4057. מִדְבָּר ***miḏbār:*** I. A masculine noun meaning mouth, speech. It refers to the human instrument of talking, the mouth, but in context its beauty and pleasantness are stressed (Song 4:3). It stands in parallel usage to lips which precedes it in the previous line.

II. A masculine noun referring to a desert, a wilderness. It indicates a wilderness area, a desert, or a pasture used for animals in general (Gen. 37:22; Job 38:26; Jer. 23:10; Joel 2:22); in reference to specific areas, especially the great Sinai wilderness (Deut. 2:7). Several other specific wilderness areas are indicated: the wilderness of Shur (Ex. 15:22); of Qedesh (Ps. 29:8); of Beersheba (Gen. 21:14); of En Gedi (1 Sam. 24:1[2]) and others. It is used figuratively of the Lord making Israel like a wilderness (Hos. 2:3[5]); and of the Lord depicted as a possible wilderness to His people (Jer. 2:31). Some wilderness areas featured cities and villages (Josh. 15:61; Isa. 42:11).

4058. מָדַד ***māḏaḏ:*** A verb meaning to measure, to mete out, to stretch. It serves as a general term for various types and ways of measurement: distance or area (Num. 35:5; Deut. 21:2; Ezek. 40:5, 6, 8, 20); an amount of grain of any kind, sand, the heavens, etc. (Ruth 3:15; Isa. 40:12; Jer. 31:37; 33:22; Hos. 1:10[2:1]); counting out payment for something (Isa. 65:7). It is used to line up, measure off, and tally up prisoners of war for life or death (2 Sam. 8:2). It refers to God's actions of deliverance for His people as He measures them out for victory (Ps. 60:6[8]; 108:7[8]). It indicates Elijah's action as he "measured himself out," stretched himself over the widow's son to heal him (1 Kgs. 17:21). It is probably the preferred reading in Job 7:4, indicating the way the nights continued to drag on.

4059. מִדַּד ***middad:*** A masculine noun indicating flight. It means gone, flown away in flight (KJV, Job 7:4), but see also 4058.

4060. מִדָּה ***middāh:*** I. A feminine noun denoting measure, stature; a garment. It indicates the actual measurement or size of something: curtains for the Tabernacle (Ex. 26:2, 8); cherubim for the Temple (1 Kgs. 6:25); all kinds of measures (1 Chr. 23:29). It indicates both the process of measuring (Lev. 19:35) and the part measured or section (of a wall) (Neh. 3:11). It is used to indicate a large size, e.g., a person of great stature, literally, "a man of measure" (1 Chr. 11:23); a large house (Jer. 22:14). In certain contexts, it has an adverbial aspect translated usually as "by measure(ment)" (Ezek. 48:30).

II. A feminine noun indicating tax, tribute. It refers to a tax. In context it describes a royal tax or tribute (Neh. 5:4).

4061. מִדָּה ***middāh,*** מִנְדָּה ***mindāh:*** An Aramaic feminine noun meaning tribute, toll. It refers to revenues collected to run a nation; in context it refers to royal revenues of the kings of Persia (Ezra 4:13; 6:8) and of the kings of Israel (Ezra 4:20). The personnel of the second Temple were exempt from this imposition of taxes (Ezra 7:24).

4062. מַדְהֵבָה ***ma*d*hē*b*āh:*** I. A feminine noun meaning fury. It refers to the violent speed and fierceness of a nation's military activities, such as Babylon's (Isa. 14:4).

II. A feminine noun meaning golden city. Traditionally, it referred to Babylon as the golden city (KJV, Isa. 14:4). Various ancient manuscripts or translations suggest that the better translation is fury (see I), but this is not certain.

4063. מַדֶוֶה ***ma*d*weh:*** A masculine noun designating a garment. It is used of the garments worn by the servants of King David. Evidently, they were long garments (2 Sam. 10:4; 1 Chr. 19:4).

4064. מַדְוֶה ***ma*d*weh:*** A masculine noun referring to a sickness, a disease. It refers to the diseases the Lord placed on the Egyptians in the plagues (Deut. 7:15; 28:60), specifically defined as harmful (*Ra'*) in context.

4065. מַדּוּחַ ***maddûaḥ:*** A masculine noun indicating something misleading. It refers to oracles from prophets, describing the oracles as misleading or false in some way (Lam. 2:14). It is used with *šāw'*, vain, worthless.

4066. מָדוֹן ***mā*d*ôn:*** A masculine noun referring to strife, dissension. Its plural is *m*^{e}*dāniym, midyāniym.* It refers to a quarrel or dispute that cannot be stopped once it starts (Prov. 17:14); or to arguments and contentions that create barriers between persons (Prov. 18:19). It is preceded by *'iyš* to indicate Jeremiah as a man of strife or contention (Jer. 15:10). God can make His people an object of strife and contention (Ps. 80:6[7]). An evil heart spreads dissension and strife (Prov. 6:14, 19); as does hatred (Prov. 10:12). A person with a temper creates strife (Prov. 15:18). A contentious, quarreling wife is a curse (Prov. 25:24).

4067. מָדוֹן ***mā<u>d</u>ôn:*** A masculine noun meaning stature, size. It is used once and indicates a man of great stature or size (2 Sam. 21:20), the son of a giant.

4068. מָדוֹן ***mā<u>d</u>ôn:*** A proper noun designating Madon (Josh. 11:1; 12:19).

4069. מַדּוּעַ ***maddûa',*** מַדֻּעַ ***maddūa':*** An adverb indicating wherefore, why. It regularly means why, for what reason (Gen. 26:27; Ex. 1:18; 2:18; Ezek. 18:19). It is used in an indirect question (Ex. 3:3). Jeremiah used the word sixteen times and sometimes to ask a rhetorical question (Jer. 2:31; 8:5, 19, 22; 14:19; 22:28; 49:1). It is found after a compound or double question introduced by *h^{a}* . . . *'im* (518) . . . *maddûa'* (Jer. 2:14). It introduces a question expressing grief and pain and not expecting an answer (Job 3:12).

4070. מְדוֹר ***m^{e}<u>d</u>ôr,*** מְדָר ***m^{e}<u>d</u>ār:*** An Aramaic masculine noun meaning dwelling, place. It indicates a place where gods or people make their home, an appropriate abode (Dan. 2:11). In Nebuchadnezzar's case, he lived in the dwelling place of animals for a time (Dan. 4:25[22], 32[29]; 5:21).

4071. מְדוּרָה ***m^{e}<u>d</u>ûrāh:*** A feminine noun referring to a pile of wood or anything else for burning (Isa. 30:33). In context it is used figuratively of the woodpile on which Jerusalem would be destroyed by Babylon (Ezek. 24:9).

4072. מִדְחֶה ***mi<u>d</u>ḥeh:*** A masculine noun referring to ruin, destruction. It indicates the harm and destruction that a flattering mouth can bring about (Prov. 26:28).

4073. מַדְחֵפָה ***ma<u>d</u>ḥē<u>p</u>āh:*** A feminine noun indicating overthrow, destruction. It refers to evil pursuing the violent man and giving him thrust upon thrust, blow upon blow until he experiences destruction (Ps. 140:11[12]).

4074. מָדַי ***mā<u>d</u>ay:*** A proper noun designating Madai:

A. A descendant of Japheth (Gen. 10:2; 1 Chr. 1:5).

B. A people or land of Media (2 Kgs. 17:6; 18:11; Esth. 1:3, 14, 18, 19; 10:2; Isa. 13:17; 21:2; Jer. 25:25; 51:11, 28; Dan. 8:20; 9:1).

4075. מָדִי ***mā<u>d</u>iy:*** A proper noun designating Mede. The term Mede indicates that Darius was related to the kingdom of the Medes, a rival to the rising Persian Empire in its early stages and to the Assyrians. Darius the Mede may be a throne name for Cyrus II, who did have close connections with the Medes through a Medean father (Dan. 9:1). The country or territory was known as Media, those living there as Medes or Medians. It was rather powerful in the years ca. 600–500 B.C. but succumbed to the power of Persia under Cyrus II in ca. 550 B.C.

4076. מָדַי ***māday:*** A proper noun designating Medes, the Aramaic name corresponding to Hebrew 4074,B. It occurs in only the Aramaic portions of Ezra and Daniel.

4077. מָדָיָא ***māḏāy'ā:*** A proper noun designating Mede, the Aramaic equivalent to Hebrew 4075. It occurs in only the Aramaic portions of Daniel.

4078. מַדַּי ***madday:*** An adverb meaning enough, sufficiently. It indicates adequacy for a purpose or goal (2 Chr. 30:3), e.g., adequate numbers.

4079. מִדְיָנִים ***miḏyāniym:*** A masculine plural noun referring to disputes, contentions. It is the plural of *māḏôn* (4066). It has the same usage.

4080. מִדְיָן ***miḏyān:*** A proper noun designating Midian:

A. A son of Abraham by Keturah, his second wife. He had several sons himself (Gen. 25:2).

B. The word refers to a people or tribe (Gen. 36:25). They had priests, one of which was Jethro, Moses' father-in-law (Ex. 2:16; 3:1; 18:1), and elders as rulers (Num. 22:4, 7). They helped Balak hire Balaam to curse Israel (Num. 22:7). They were instrumental in leading Israel astray (Num. 25:16–18). The Lord called for holy war against them (Num. 31:3–9; Josh. 13:21; Ps. 83:9[10]). They continued to harass Israel in Canaan (Josh. 6; 7; 8; 9). The defeat of the Midianites, especially under Gideon, became a symbol of God's deliverance for His people (Isa. 9:4[3]; 10:26; Hab. 3:7), but its restoration was also envisioned (Isa. 60:6).

C. The land of Midian is difficult to pinpoint. Midianites were often found in northwest Arabia to the east of the Gulf of Aqaba. They, however, ranged far and wide (Judg. 6; 7). They were often close to the Moabites (Num. 22:4–7; 1 Kgs. 11:18). They were sent east by Abraham (Gen. 25:1–6) and seem to have been a people on the move, although they were largely desert dwellers (cf. Gen. 37:28–36).

4081. מִדִּין ***middiyn:*** A proper noun designating Middin (Josh. 15:61).

4082. מְדִינָה ***m***$^{\boldsymbol{e}}$***ḏiynāh:*** A feminine noun meaning a district, a province, a realm. It refers to a specific area established by the political process within national boundaries. It is used in a general sense of all provinces (1 Kgs. 20:14, 15, 17, 19; Eccl. 2:8; 5:8[7]; Ezek. 19:8); of Babylonian provinces or districts (Ezra 2:1; Neh. 7:6; Dan. 8:2); of Judah as a province (Neh. 1:3). It is used often of Persian provinces (Esth. 1:1, 3, 16, 22; Dan. 11:24) that numbered one hundred and twenty-seven.

4083. מְדִינָה m^e***d̲iynāh:*** An Aramaic feminine noun indicating a district, a province. An administrative area politically designated. It refers to the satrapies, a Persian name for provinces of the Persian Empire (Ezra 4:15; 5:8; 6:2; Dan. 3:1–3). One province encompassed all of Babylon (Ezra 7:16; Dan. 2:48, 49; 3:1, 12, 30).

4084. מִדְיָנִי ***mid̲yāniy:*** A proper noun designating Midianite (Gen. 37:36; Num. 10:29; 25:6, 14, 15, 17; 31:2).

4085. מְדֹכָה m^e***d̲ōk̲āh:*** A feminine noun meaning mortar, bowl. It was a stone bowl used to beat or grind manna (Num. 11:8).

4086. מַדְמֵן ***mad̲mēn:*** A proper noun designating Madmen (Jer. 48:2).

4087. מַדְמֵנָה ***mad̲mēnāh:*** A feminine noun indicating a dunghill, a manure pile. It is used figuratively of Moab being trodden down by the Lord like straw trodden down into a manure pile (Isa. 25:10).

4088. מַדְמֵנָה ***mad̲mēnāh:*** A proper noun designating Madmenah (Isa. 10:31).

4089. מַדְמַנָּה ***mad̲mannāh:*** A proper noun designating Madmannah:

A. A city in Judah (Josh. 15:31).

B. A descendant of Caleb (1 Chr. 2:49).

4090. מְדָנִים m^e***d̲āniym:*** A masculine plural noun designating strifes, discords. It is the plural of *mād̲ôn* and has the same meaning and usage. See 4066.

4091. מְדָן m^e***d̲an:*** A proper noun designating Medan (Gen. 25:2; 1 Chr. 1:32).

4092. מְדָנִי m^e***d̲āniy:*** A proper noun designating Midianite (Gen. 37:36).

4093. מַדָּע ***maddā':*** A masculine noun meaning knowledge, thought. It refers to the ability to gain knowledge by study (Dan. 1:4) and also to its resulting acquisition (Dan. 1:17). It is used of practical knowledge for administering a government (2 Chr. 1:10–12) and refers to something that has become known (Eccl. 10:20).

4094. מַדְקֵרָה ***mad̲qērāh:*** A feminine noun meaning thrust, piercing. It describes harmful and merciless words that are like sword thrusts to those receiving them (Prov. 12:18).

4095. מַדְרֵגָה ***mad̲rēgāh:*** A feminine noun referring to a steep place, a mountainside. It indicates a mountain pathway in widely diverse settings (Song 2:14; Ezek. 38:20).

4096. מִדְרָךְ ***miḏrāḵ:*** A masculine noun indicating a treading place, a footstep. It is used to indicate a very small portion of land or territory, e.g., on Mount Seir (Deut. 2:5).

4097. מִדְרָשׁ ***miḏrāš:*** A masculine noun designating a record, a treatise. It is used of an official writing or composition recording the official acts of a king and other events surrounding him (2 Chr. 13:22; 24:27).

4098. מְדֻשָׁה ***meḏušāh:*** A feminine noun meaning threshing, that which is threshed. It refers to something threshed or, figuratively, to someone threshed, e.g., it refers to persons God has "threshed" in judgment (Isa. 21:10).

4099. הַמְּדָתָא ***hammeḏāṯā':*** A proper noun designating Hammedatha (Esth. 3:1, 10; 8:5; 9:10, 24).

4100. מָה ***māh,*** מֶה ***meh:*** An indefinite interrogative pronoun meaning what? It is used hundreds of times and its exact function must be determined from its contextual usage. The main categories of usage are noted here: (1) as an interrogative meaning what? It is used in a direct question before verbs or nouns (Gen. 4:10; 15:2; 37:26; Ex. 3:13); with *zeh* (2088) following, it means what, now? (1 Sam. 10:11); following a word in the construct, of, state, it means of what (Num. 23:3). It is used in indirect questions after such words as see, *rā'āh* (Gen. 2:19; 37:20); it is used to indicate something of little or no value (Gen. 23:15); it is used in the idiom, "What to me and to you" (Judg. 11:12; 2 Sam. 16:10). (2) It is used as an adverb meaning how? (Gen. 44:16; Num. 23:8; Job 31:1); why? (Ex. 14:15, How! in the sense of an exclamation (Gen. 38:29). It is used as an indefinite pronoun meaning anything, whatever (Num. 23:3; 1 Sam. 19:3). (3) It combines with prepositions to express various nuances of its basic meanings: wherein, whereby, wherewith, by what means, for what reason (Gen. 15:8; Ex. 22:27[26]; 33:16; Judg. 16:5; 2 Sam. 21:3; Isa. 1:5; Mic. 6:6). *Kammeh* means how many, how much (Gen. 47:8; 2 Sam. 19:34[35]); *'aḏ-māh* (Ps. 4:2[3]) means until when?

4101. מָה ***māh:*** An Aramaic interrogative pronominal particle meaning why, what? It serves as a question marker, what (Dan. 4:35[32]); a relative pronoun (Ezra 6:9; Dan. 2:22); with *diy* following, it means whatever (Dan. 2:28). Like its Hebrew counterpart, it combines with prepositions: *kemāh,* how . . . (Dan. 4:3[3:33]); *lemāh,* for what purpose, *diy lemāh,* for what purpose (Ezra 4:22; 7:23) or lest. In context *'al-māh* for what reason, why? (Dan. 2:15).

4102. מָהָה ***māhah:*** A verb meaning to tarry, to hesitate, to linger. It means to delay doing something: Lot halted, hesitated about leaving Sodom (Gen. 19:16; 43:10). Israel could not delay leaving Egypt (Ex. 12:39). It takes on the positive sense of wait in some contexts (2 Sam. 15:28). It refers to delaying religious action (Ps. 119:60). Prophetic visions may tarry or delay but do certainly reach fulfillment (Hab. 2:3).

4103. מְהוּמָה ***meĥûmāh:*** A feminine noun meaning confusion, panic, tumult, disturbance. If the Israelites diligently observed God's covenant stipulations, He would throw the nations occupying Canaan into a great panic and give them over into the Israelites' hands (Deut. 7:23). If, however, the Israelites did not obey and thus forsook the Lord their God, this same panic would be sent upon them instead (Deut. 28:20). After the Philistines captured the ark of God and brought it to Gath (one of their five main cities), the Lord struck the people of that city with a great panic and severe tumors (1 Sam. 5:9, 11). Isaiah the prophet warned Jerusalem that a day of tumult, trampling, and confusion was at hand for it (Isa. 22:5). The term also functions to describe daily life in certain geographical locations during troubled periods of time: Jerusalem (Ezek. 22:5); Israel and the surrounding lands (2 Chr. 15:5); and the mountains of Samaria (Amos 3:9). Once the word describes the trouble wealth brings to a household that does not fear the Lord (Prov. 15:16). The term derives from the verb *hûm* (1949).

4104. מְהוּמָן ***m^ehûmān:*** A proper noun designating Mehuman (Esth. 1:10).

4105. מְהֵיטַבְאֵל ***m^ehēyṭab̲'ēl:*** A proper noun designating Mehetabel:

A. Edomite princess (Gen. 36:39; 1 Chr. 1:50).

B. An ancestor of Shemaiah (Neh. 6:10).

4106. מָהִיר ***māhiyr:*** An adjective indicating skilled, well-versed. It refers to extraordinary expertise in some area, such as the Law of Moses (Ezra 7:6; Isa. 16:5); or a fluent ability to speak glowingly of Israel's king (Ps. 45:1[2]). It extends to a person's work of any kind (Prov. 22:29).

4107. מָהַל ***māhal:*** A verb meaning to weaken, to dilute. It refers to something adulterated by water so that it loses its character and quality (Isa. 1:22).

4108. מַהְלְכִים ***mahl^ek̲iym:*** A masculine plural noun indicating access, places to walk. The plural of *mah^alak̲*. It refers figuratively to potential access before God given to the high priest Joshua if he walked in the Lord's paths (Zech. 3:7).

4109. מַהֲלָךְ ***mah^alāk̲:*** A masculine noun meaning a journey, a passageway, an access. It indicates access of some kind: a passageway or walkway by the chambers of a temple (Ezek. 42:4). It refers in general to any journey or trip (Neh. 2:6). It also takes on the sense of a "walk" as a trip or a distance covered (Jon. 3:3, 4). The plural form in Zechariah 3:7 is covered in 4108.

4110. מַהֲלָל ***mah^{a}lāl:*** A masculine noun indicating praise. It indicates strong appreciation and respect accorded to someone by others (Prov. 27:21). It serves as a way of testing for its recipient in context.

4111. מַהֲלַלְאֵל ***mah^{a}lal'ēl:*** A proper noun designating Mahalalel:

A. Great-grandson of Seth (Gen. 5:12, 13, 15–17; 1 Chr. 1:2).

B. A Judaite (Neh. 11:4).

4112. מַהֲלֻמוֹת ***mah^{a}lumōṯ:*** A feminine plural noun depicting stripes, blows. It refers to slaps or strong physical rebukes amounting to blows on the lips, mouths, or backs of fools to correct their insolent behavior (Prov. 18:6; 19:29).

4113. מַהֲמֹר ***mah^{a}mōr:*** A feminine noun meaning flood, a watery pit; deep pits. It refers to a place of confinement from which a person could never rise; a deep miry pit of some kind (Ps. 140:10[11]).

4114. מַהְפֵּכָה ***mahpēḵāh:*** A feminine noun indicating overthrow, destruction. It describes primarily the demolishing or wiping out of the city of Sodom. It never was rebuilt or used again (Deut. 29:23[22]). The word is used of various places decimated like Sodom and Gomorrah (Isa. 13:19; Jer. 49:18; 50:40; Amos 4:11); and once, with reference to the cities, of the devastation of Judah (Isa. 1:7).

4115. מַהְפֶּכֶת ***mahpeḵeṯ:*** A feminine noun referring to stocks, a prison. It is used of implements, stocks, used to confine prisoners in a stooped posture (Jer. 20:2, 3; 29:26); once combined with *bēyt,* it is used of a prison or a house of confinement (2 Chr. 16:10).

4116. מָהַר ***māhar:*** A verb meaning to hurry, to do more quickly, to hasten. It has the sense always of doing something quickly, in a hurry, hastily, or even rashly because of being in haste: to hasten to a location (Gen. 18:6); to modify any other verb adverbially in its performance (Gen. 19:22; 24:18; Ex. 2:18; 1 Sam. 23:27; 1 Kgs. 22:9); the infinitive *mahēr* is used various times as an adverb (Ex. 32:8); *l^{e}mahēr* indicates haste (Ex. 12:33; 1 Chr. 12:8). Used of counsel, it means rash, headlong advice that is quickly and easily hindered (Job 5:13). In its participial form, it indicates persons who speak hastily, too quickly (Isa. 32:4; Hab. 1:6). Used with *lēb,* heart, it refers to an agitated heart full of anxiety (Isa. 35:4).

4117. מָהַר ***māhar:*** A verb indicating the giving of a dowry. It means to get a wife by paying the *mōhar,* the marriage dowry; gifts to acquire one's wife (Ex. 22:16[15]).

4118. מַהֵר ***mahēr:*** I. An adjective indicating swift. It indicates the swiftness and, hence, nearness of something, e.g., the Day of the Lord (Zeph. 1:14; Isa. 8:1).

II. An adverb meaning quickly, speedily. It occurs right after the verb it modifies and indicates the swiftness of its performance (Ex. 32:8; Deut. 4:26; Josh. 2:5; Judg. 2:17; Ps. 69:17 [18]; 79:8; Prov. 25:8).

4119. מֹהַר ***mōhar:*** A masculine noun referring to the dowry, or purchase price of a wife. It was paid to the wife's family in order to acquire a wife (Gen. 34:12; Ex. 22:17[16]; 1 Sam. 18:25).

4120. מְהֵרָה ***m^{e}hērāh:*** A feminine noun indicating quickly, at once. It indicates adverbially how quickly, hurriedly something is done (Num. 16:46[17:11]; 2 Kgs. 1:11; Isa. 5:26; Jer. 27:16; Joel 3:4[4:4]); or something occurs quickly (Ps. 147:15; Eccl. 4:12; 8:11[negated]). God's judgments, if enacted, could cause His people to perish quickly from their land (Deut. 11:17).

4121. מַהְרַי ***mah^{a}ray:*** A proper noun designating Maharai (2 Sam. 23:28; 1 Chr. 11:30; 27:13).

4122. מַהֵר שָׁלָל חָשׁ בַּז ***mahēr šālāl ḥāš baz:*** I. A proper noun designating Maher-Shalel-Hash-Baz (NASB, Isa. 8:1).

II. A phrase meaning swift is booty speed is prey (KJV, NIV, Isa. 8:1). The phrase is made up of the words from *mahēr* (4118,I), *šālāl* (7998), *ḥûš* (2363,I) and *baz* (957).

4123. מַהֲתַלָּה ***mah^{a}ṯallāh:*** A feminine noun meaning illusion, deception. It refers to what is not true or real, such as false prophecies or false visions the people wanted to hear (Isa. 30:10).

4124. מוֹאָב ***mô'āḇ:*** A proper noun designating Moab:

A. A son of Lot who was born through an incestuous relationship with his daughter (Gen. 30—38). He became the father of the Moabites.

B. The territory of Moab was east of the Dead Sea between the Zered River and the Arnon River. It stretched eastward to the eastern desert. It was largely mountainous terrain with some plateau land toward the Arnon River and at times beyond it.

The people were, according to the writer of Genesis, descendants of Lot and his older daughter (Gen. 19:36–38). The Moabites or Moab are mentioned over 190 times in the Bible. Moab usually had a hostile relationship with the Israelites (e.g. Judg. 3:12–30; 2 Sam. 8:2–12; 2 Kgs. 4:3–27). They refused Israel passage through their land (Judg. 11:17). They were excluded from Israel (Deut. 23:3–6) because of hostilities. Balak, king of Moab, so feared Israel that he hired Balaam, a Mesopotamian soothsayer to curse them; and Balaam and Moab seduced Israel at Baal-Peor (Num. 22—26; Deut. 23:3–6). Israel crossed into the Promised Land from Moab (Josh. 3:1). On the other hand, any Moabite who would confess and follow the Lord could do so (Ruth 1:1–22), and the ancestors of David includes Ruth, a Moabitess. The Moabites conspired with the

Ammonites and Edomites more than once against Israel (2 Chr. 20:1–23). The people and country fell, as did Israel, under the power of the Assyrians, Babylonians, and Persians. They are included in many prophetic oracles of judgment (e.g., Jer. 40:11). After Israel was exiled (586 B.C.) and returned (538 B.C.), the Moabites as a nation had disappeared.

4125. מוֹאָבִי ***mô'āḇiy:*** A proper noun designating Moabite. A gentilic form of the word that indicates that a person was related to the inhabitants of Moab or a part of their descendants. The ending *iy* or *iyṯ* in Hebrew indicates this clearly. (See 4124.).

4126. מוֹבָא ***môḇā':*** A masculine noun referring to an entrance, entering. It refers to the act itself of coming in (2 Sam. 3:25). In Ezekiel 43:11, it refers to the entrances of the prophet's visionary Temple.

4127. מוּג ***mûg:*** A verb meaning to dissolve, to melt away; to faint, to become weak, to become disheartened. It is used in a powerful metaphor to describe the weakening and fearful hearts of the people of Canaan before Israel (Ex. 15:15; Josh. 2:9, 24); the weakening and falling away of warriors in battle (1 Sam. 14:16; Isa. 14:31; Jer. 49:23). It refers to the shattering and dissolution of a nation or person before God's actions (Job 30:22; Ps. 107:26; Amos 9:5). The people of the entire earth melt and cringe before the Lord (Ps. 46:6[7]; 75:3[4]). In a more literal sense, the word describes rain softening the earth (Ps. 65:10[11]).

4128. מוּד ***môḏ:*** I. A verb meaning to measure, to survey. It refers to the Lord's surveying the earth as He prepares to demolish it (Hab. 3:6, KJV, NASB).

II. A verb meaning to shake. It refers to the convulsing or shaking of the earth set in motion by the Lord as judgment (Hab. 3:6, NIV).

4129. מֹדָע ***mōḏā',*** מוֹדַע ***môḏa':*** A masculine noun meaning kinsman, relative. It indicates a person closely related to someone and having the right of the kinsman redeemer (Ruth 2:1). It has the sense of a close, intimate friend or relative (Prov. 7:4, NASB; NIV, kinsman).

4130. מוֹדַעַת ***môḏa'aṯ:*** A feminine noun referring to kindred, kinship. It indicates a relative close enough to serve as a kinsman redeemer in Israel, e.g., Boaz to Naomi and Ruth (Ruth 3:2).

4131. מוֹט ***môṭ:*** A verb indicating to be moved, removed, to fall. It is used of a wavering, wobbling action, response, or condition in various situations: it is used of the wavering or shaking of even mountains, an unheard of event (Isa. 54:10); Mount Zion was considered unshakable or unmovable (Ps. 125:1); the earth under God's fierce judgments could move violently (Isa. 24:19). It is used of the pressure or shaking of the wicked against the psalmist (Ps. 55:3[4]; 22[23]). It has the sense of fire flaming out (Ps. 140:10[11]). It describes the instability of kingdoms (Ps. 46:6[7]). It is used figuratively of a foot slipping; it indicates the failure of God's people (Deut. 32:35). It is found in the idiom, a hand wavers, that is, the person becomes weak economically (Lev. 25:35). It is used figuratively of the person who is sound, safe, secure, and will not be moved (Ps. 10:6), a claim made by the wicked but realized in the righteous (Prov. 10:30; 12:3).

4132. מוֹט ***môṭ:*** A masculine noun meaning a bar, a pole, that which shakes. It refers to a pole or rod used for carrying things (Num. 13:23); or a carrying frame or structure (Num. 4:10, 12). For Psalm 66:9 and 121:3 see 4131. It is used figuratively of a bar or yoke representing Assyria that confines Israel (Nah. 1:13).

4133. מוֹטָה ***môṭāh:*** A feminine noun meaning a bar, a yoke. It is used of a harness collar but is employed figuratively of forces that oppress God's people (Isa. 58:6, 9), especially in Egypt (Lev. 26:13). This yoke was used in prophetic messages as well (Jer. 27:2; 28:10, 12, 13), representing political subjection (Ezek. 30:18; 34:27). It describes carrying poles for the ark of God (1 Chr. 15:15).

4134. מוּךְ ***mûk̲:*** A verb meaning to become poor, to be poor. It describes the state of fellow Israelites who through various circumstances become poor (Lev. 25:25, 35, 39, 47). It has the sense of less valuable in certain contexts (Lev. 27:8).

4135. מוּל ***mûl:*** A verb meaning to cut short, to cut off, to circumcise. Abraham was commanded to circumcise both himself and his offspring as a sign of the covenant made between him and God (Gen. 17:10–14). As a result, Abraham had his son Ishmael, all the male slaves in his house, and himself circumcised that same day (Gen. 17:23–27). Later, when Isaac was born, Abraham circumcised him as well (Gen. 21:4). Moses commanded the Israelites to circumcise their hearts, that is, to remove the hardness and to love God (Deut. 10:16; cf. 30:6; Jer. 4:4). When used in its intensive form, the verb carries the meaning to cut down, as seen in Psalm 90:6: "In the morning it [the grass] flourisheth, and groweth up; in the evening it is cut down, and withereth" (KJV). Used in the causative sense, the verb gives the meaning to cut off, to destroy (Ps. 118:10–12; lit., "I will cause them to be cut off"). See also the related verbs *māhal* (4107), *mālal* (4448), and *nāmal* (5243).

4136. מוּל ***mûl,*** מוֹאל ***mô'l,*** מוֹל ***môl:*** A preposition meaning against, in front of, toward, opposite. It indicates a position in front of something (2 Sam. 11:15); or indicates toward the front of (Lev. 5:8; 1 Sam. 17:30), turning toward another person. It has a nominal (noun) sense that indicates the front or opposite (Ex. 26:9; 1 Kgs. 7:5). It is combined with prepositions on the front of it to nuance its meaning. As a geographical term, it means opposite most often (Ex. 34:3). It means in the presence of someone, especially God (Ex. 18:19). It may indicate in the direction of south, north, etc. (1 Kgs. 7:39).

4137. מוֹלָדָה ***môlāḏāh:*** A proper noun designating Moladah (Josh. 15:26; 19:2; 1 Chr. 4:28; Neh. 11:26).

4138. מוֹלֶדֶת ***môleḏeṯ:*** A feminine noun indicating birth, family background, kindred. It has the basic sense of origin, common origin, relationship by birth. It refers then to offspring, descendants (Gen. 48:6); relations (Gen. 12:1; 24:4); birthed in the same household or family (*bayit*) (Lev. 18:9). It is extended to refer to descent, parentage (Ezek. 16:3); in a figurative way of Israel, or even birth (Ezek. 16:4). Used in front of *'eres,* it indicates a land of birth, origin (Gen. 11:28; 24:7; Jer. 22:10).

4139. מוּלָה ***mûlāh:*** A feminine noun meaning circumcision. Derived from the verb *mûl* (4135), the only undisputed occurrence of the term is found at the end of Exodus 4:26.

4140. מוֹלִיד ***môliyḏ:*** A proper noun designating Molid (1 Chr. 2:29).

4141. מוּסָב ***mûsaḇ:*** A masculine noun meaning circuit. It refers to a surrounding circuitous structure as a part of the inner Temple (Ezek. 41:7).

4142. מוּסַבּוֹת ***mûsabbôṯ:*** A feminine plural adjective meaning surrounding. It is used of the surrounding filigree settings of gold encompassing two onyx stones (Ex. 28:11; 39:6, 13). It has the sense of changing around in Numbers 32:38 where names of cities are changed. It seems to mean surrounding or swinging in Ezekiel 41:24 where the doors of the Temple nave are described.

4143. מוּסָד ***mûsāḏ:*** A masculine singular noun meaning foundation, foundation laying. Its only occurrences are in Isaiah 28:16 and 2 Chronicles 8:16 that refer to the foundations of Zion and the Temple, respectively.

4144. מוֹסָד ***môsāḏ:*** A masculine noun meaning foundation. It indicates the base structure on which other things are built: the foundations or bases of the earth and mountains (Deut. 32:22; Prov. 8:29; Isa. 24:18; Jer. 31:37); it refers to the foundations of Israel's past, both symbolic and literal (Isa. 58:12); the foundations of her cities, walls, etc. It is used symbolically of the foundations of the earth (2 Sam. 22:8, 16; Ps. 18:7[8], 15[16]). Babylon's foundation stones would be removed by the Lord (Jer. 51:26). These foundations are personified by the prophets (Mic. 6:2).

4145. מוּסָדָה ***mûsāḏāh:*** A feminine noun meaning foundation or appointment. This word is used only twice in the Old Testament and comes from the verb *yāsaḏ* (3245), meaning to establish. Ezekiel used this word to describe the foundation of the Temple in his vision (Ezek. 41:8). Isaiah used it to describe the appointed rod of punishment by which the Lord would smite Assyria (Isa. 30:32).

4146. מוֹסָדָה ***môsāḏāh:*** A feminine singular noun meaning foundation. It always occurs in the plural. It often refers to the foundation of the world (2 Sam. 22:16; Ps. 18:15[16]) or to the base of a man-made construction, such as a building or wall (Jer. 51:26).

4147. מוֹסֵר ***môsēr,*** מוֹסֵרָה ***môsērāh:*** I. A masculine noun indicating a band, a chain, a fetter. It is used figuratively of the hold of death on a person (Ps. 116:16). It indicates the political and military bonds holding Jerusalem and God's people but also the chains of restraint the Lord puts on them because of their sin and rebellion (Isa. 28:22; 52:2).

II. A masculine noun indicating a band, a chain, a fetter. It is used mostly in a figurative sense: the freedom from bonds given to the wild animals (Job 39:5); of political and military oppression and control (Ps. 2:3; 107:14; Jer. 27:2) from which God can free His people (Jer. 2:20; 30:8; Nah. 1:13). But it also refers to Israel's breaking away from God's bonds on them (Jer. 5:5).

4148. מוּסָר ***mûsār:*** A masculine noun meaning instruction, discipline. It occurs almost exclusively in the poetic and prophetic literature. In Proverbs, instruction and discipline come primarily through the father (or a father figure such as a teacher) and usually are conveyed orally but may come via the rod (Prov. 1:8; 13:1, 24). Those who are wise receive instruction, but fools reject it (Prov. 1:7; 8:33; 13:1; 15:5). The reception of instruction brings life, wisdom, and the favor of the Lord (Prov. 4:13; 8:33); however, rejection brings death, poverty, and shame (Prov. 5:23; 13:18). Apart from Proverbs, this noun is always associated with God—with two exceptions (Job 20:3; Jer. 10:8). When God's instruction is rejected, it results in punishments of various kinds (Job 36:10; Jer. 7:28; 17:23; 32:33; Zeph. 3:2). The discipline of the Lord is not to be despised, for it is a demonstration of His love for His children (Job 5:17; Prov. 3:11; cf. Heb. 12:5, 6). The supreme demonstration of God's love came when Jesus Christ bore the "chastisement of our peace" (Isa. 53:5).

4149. מוֹסֵרָה ***môsērāh,*** מֹסֵרוֹת ***mōsērôṯ:*** A proper noun designating Moseroth, Moserah (Num. 33:30, 31; Deut. 10:6).

4150. מוֹעֵד ***mô'ēḏ:*** A masculine noun meaning an appointed time or place. It can signify an appointed meeting time in general (Gen. 18:14; Ex. 13:10); a specific appointed time, usually for a sacred feast or festival (Hos. 9:5; 12:9[10]); the time of the birds' migration (Jer. 8:7); the time of wine (Hos. 2:9[11]); the same time next year (Gen. 17:21). In addition to the concept of time, this word can also signify an appointed meeting place: "The mount of the congregation" identifies the meeting place of God or the gods (Isa. 14:13), and "the house appointed for all living" identifies the meeting place of the dead—that is, the netherworld (Job 30:23). Moreover, the term is used to distinguish those places where God's people were to focus on God and their relationship with Him, which would include: the tent of meeting (Ex. 33:7); the Temple (Lam. 2:6); the synagogue (Ps. 74:8).

4151. מוֹעָד ***mô'āḏ:*** A masculine noun meaning appointed place. This word is used only once in the Old Testament and comes from the verb *yā'aḏ* (3259), meaning to appoint. It describes the appointed places for soldiers, often translated as ranks (Isa. 14:31).

4152. מוּעָדָה ***mû'āḏāh:*** A feminine noun indicating something designated, appointed. It indicates something allotted to or for a specific social purpose, e.g., the six cities of refuge in Israel (Josh. 20:9). Literally, there were cities agreed upon, witnessed to as places of refuge.

4153. מוֹעַדְיָה ***mô'aḏyāh:*** A proper noun designating Moadiah (Neh. 12:17).

4154. מוּעֶדֶת ***mû'eḏeṯ:*** A feminine noun meaning unsteady, sliding out of joint. It is used of an unsteady or weak foot that cannot be counted on (Prov. 25:19; KJV, NKJV, out of joint; NIV, lame; NASB, unsteady).

4155. מוּעָף ***mû'āp̱:*** A masculine noun indicating gloom, darkness. It indicates an absence of light or brightness and pictures a condition of gloom. It is used figuratively of the dimmed understanding of peoples (Isa. 9:1[8:23]).

4156. מוֹעֵצָה ***mô'ēṣāh:*** A feminine noun referring to counsel, intrigue. It refers to advice given (Prov. 22:20) by wisdom personified (Prov. 1:30). The wicked fall from their own devices or counsel (Ps. 5:10[11]). The context determines the nature of the counsel, e.g., created by a hard, stubborn heart (Ps. 81:12[13]); or of an evil heart (Jer. 7:24).

4157. מוּעָקָה ***mû'āqāh:*** A feminine noun indicating affection, an oppressive burden. It is used of God's judgments on His people, a hardship to them at the time (Ps. 66:11).

4158. מֵיפַעַת ***mēypa'aṯ,*** מוֹפַעַת ***môpa'aṯ:*** A proper noun designating Mephaath (Josh. 13:18; 21:37; 1 Chr. 6:79[64]; Jer. 48:21).

4159. מוֹפֵת ***môpēṯ:*** A masculine noun meaning a wonder, a sign, a portent, a token. It is often a phenomenon displaying God's power, used to describe some of the plagues God placed on Egypt (Ex. 7:3; 11:9) directly or through Moses and Aaron (Ex. 4:21; 11:10); the psalmists sang of these wonders (Ps. 105:5); false prophets could work counterfeit wonders (Deut. 13:1[2], 2[3]); God worked these signs in the heavens sometimes (Joel 2:30[3:3]). Even people can become signs and tokens. Both Isaiah and his children served as signs to Israel (Isa. 8:18), as did Ezekiel (12:6, 11; Zech. 3:8). The curses that God described in the Law would be signs and wonders to cause His people to see His activity in judging them if they broke His covenant (Deut. 28:46).

4160. מֵץ ***mēṣ:*** A verb meaning to extort, to oppress. It is used in a participial form with a definite article showing a person or group of persons devastating the land of Moab (Isa. 16:4). Others read the word *ḥamûṣ* here, oppression.

4161. מוֹצָא ***môṣā':*** A masculine noun indicating an act of going forth, a proceeding; a spring. It indicates the action of going out in general (2 Sam. 3:25). It designates an exit from the Temple in Ezekiel's vision (Ezek. 42:11); also the going forth of the Lord (Hos. 6:3); or a command (Dan. 9:25). It is used in a business sense of importing something, e.g., horses (1 Kgs. 10:28). It is used in an idiom for the rising, coming out, of the sun (Ps. 19:6[7]); also indicating an easterly direction (Ps. 75:6[7]). It has the sense of spring for an outlet of water (2 Kgs. 2:21; Ps. 107:33; Isa. 58:11); in a more figurative sense, utterances that come forth from one's mouth (Num. 30:12[13]). It is used in the idiom, the east and the west, literally, the goings forth of the morning and the evening (Ps. 65:8[9]). And it indicates the sources(s) of something, e.g., silver (Job 28:1).

4162. מוֹצָא ***môṣā':*** A proper noun designating Moza:

A. A son of Caleb (1 Chr. 2:46).

B. A descendant of Saul (1 Chr. 8:36, 37; 9:42, 43).

4163. מוֹצָאָה ***môṣā'āh:*** A feminine noun indicating an origin, going out or forth; a latrine. It indicates the origin of the Messiah (Mic. 5:2[1]) from Bethlehem Ephrathah.

4164. מוּצָק ***mûṣāq,*** מוּצַק ***muṣaq:*** A masculine noun meaning constraint, restriction; frozen (water). It indicates that which hems a person in a physical or emotional way, creating compulsion or forced behavior (Job 36:16), exactly what the Lord does not place on His people. It is used to indicate the solidification of water into ice, caused metaphorically by the breath of God (Job 37:10). It has the sense of hemmed in and hence in anguish or distress (Isa. 9:1[8:23]).

4165. מוּצָק ***mûṣāq:*** A masculine noun referring to a casting, cast metal, a hard mass. It is used of artistic metal products, indicating they were cast molten bronze (1 Kgs. 7:16, 23, 33, 37; 2 Chr. 4:2; Job 37:18; 38:38).

4166. מוּצָקָה ***mûṣāqāh:*** A feminine noun referring to a casting, a pipe, a tube. It indicates metal castings (2 Chr. 4:3) for the Temple area. It indicates casting as a means of bonding or joining items together (Zech. 4:2).

4167. מוּק ***mûq:*** A verb meaning to mock, to deride. This word is used only once in the Old Testament. In Psalm 73:8, it describes the proud, mocking speech of the wicked.

4168. מוֹקֵד ***môqēḏ:*** A masculine noun referring to a burning, burning embers, a hearth. It describes something scorched or burned, like charred bones (Ps. 102:3[4]). It is used to depict God's judgment as a burning fire or embers (Isa. 33:14).

4169. מוֹקְדָה ***môq^eḏāh:*** A feminine noun indicating a hearth, the top of an altar. It is the same word as 4168 with the *āh* (Lev. 6:9[2]). It names the location where the burnt offering was to remain all night.

4170. מוֹקֵשׁ ***môqēš:*** A masculine noun meaning a snare, a trap, bait. The proper understanding of this Hebrew word is the lure or bait placed in a hunter's trap. From this sense comes the primary use of the term to mean the snare itself. It is used to signify a trap by which birds or beasts are captured (Amos 3:5); a moral pitfall (Prov. 18:7; 20:25); and anything that lures one to ruin and disaster (Judg. 2:3; Prov. 29:6).

4171. מוּר ***mûr:*** A verb meaning to change, to exchange. It indicates replacing one thing with another (Lev. 27:10, 33; Ezek. 48:14; Mic. 2:4); or an actual turning of one thing into another (Ps. 46:2[3]; Hos. 4:7). It is used of persons changing their attitudes or decisions (Ps. 15:4). The Israelites sinned gravely by replacing the Lord with an idol of an ox or calf (Ps. 106:20; Jer. 2:11). Not changing is to remain the same (Jer. 48:11).

4172. מֹרָא ***mōrā':*** A masculine noun meaning fear, terror, reverence. The primary concept underlying the meaning of this word is a sense of fear or awe that causes separation or brings respect. It is used to denote the fear animals have for humans (Gen. 9:2); terror on the Canaanites as Israel entered the Promised Land (Deut. 11:25); the reverence due those in authority (Mal. 1:6); an object of reverence, which for Israel was to be God, *y^ehōwāh* (3068), alone (Isa. 8:12, 13); a spectacle or event that inspires awe or horror (Deut. 4:34; 34:12; Jer. 32:21).

4173. מוֹרַג ***môrag:*** A masculine noun indicating a threshing sledge, an agricultural tool made of a heavy slab of wood with flint or iron points on the bottom for threshing grain (2 Sam. 24:22; 1 Chr. 21:23). It is used figuratively to illustrate Israel's power and might to subdue her enemies (Isa. 41:15).

4174. מוֹרָד ***môrāḏ:*** A masculine noun designating a descent, a steep slope, the slope or decline of a mountain or hill (Josh. 7:5; 10:11; Jer. 48:5; Mic. 1:4). In 1 Kings 7:29, it is used to describe the skilled, artistic work of part of Solomon's sea and the cast metal as a beveled (work); some kind of work with a slant to it.

4175. מוֹרֶה ***môreh:*** A masculine noun referring to early rains. It refers to the early rains in the fall of the year (Ps. 84:6[7]; Joel 2:23), as opposed to the latter rains in the spring.

4176. מוֹרֶה ***môreh:*** A proper noun designating Moreh (Gen. 12:6; Deut. 11:30; Judg. 7:1).

4177. מוֹרָה ***môrāh:*** A masculine noun meaning razor. It indicates a tool for shaving one's beard or hair (Judg. 13:5; 16:17; 1 Sam. 1:11). It was used regarding Samson and Samuel in their Nazarite vows.

4178. מוֹרָט ***môrāṭ:*** An adjective meaning smooth, polished. It describes the people of Ethiopia (Isa. 18:2, 7) who were a smooth-skinned people.

4179. מוֹרִיָּה ***môriyyāh,*** מֹרִיָּה ***mōriyyāh:*** A proper noun designating Moriah. It was the mountain on which Isaac was nearly sacrificed. According to tradition, it became the location of the Temple mount. Today the Dome of the Rock stands on top of it, with a large rock under it on which Abraham had placed Isaac after binding him.

4180. מוֹרָשׁ ***môrāš:*** I. A masculine noun indicating a possession, an inheritance. It indicates ownership of something as an inhabitant (Isa. 14:23; Obad. 1:17) of the area.

II. A masculine noun meaning a wish, a desire, a thought. It describes the wishes or longings of the heart (Job 17:11).

4181. מוֹרָשָׁה ***môrāšāh:*** A feminine noun meaning a possession, an inheritance. This word comes from the verb *yāraš* (3423), meaning to take possession of, to inherit. This word is used to refer to God giving land to Israel as an inheritance (Ex. 6:8; Ezek. 11:15; 33:24), but it also refers to God giving the land to other nations to possess (Ezek. 25:10). In one instance, the Edomites took land as a possession for themselves (Ezek. 36:5). In its other instances, God gave the Law as a possession (Deut. 33:4); God delivered the people of Israel over to other nations for a possession (Ezek. 25:4; 36:3); and the people took the high places as possessions (Ezek. 36:2).

4182. מוֹרֶשֶׁת גַּת ***môreše̱t gaṯ:*** A proper noun designating Moresheth Gath (Mic. 1:14).

4183. מוֹרַשְׁתִּי ***môraštiy***, מֹרַשְׁתִּי ***mōraštiy:*** A proper noun designating Morasthite, an inhabitant of Moreshath Gath (4182) (Jer. 26:18; Mic. 1:1).

4184. מוּשׁ ***mûš:*** A verb indicating to feel. It has the sense of touching, feeling something with one's hands to identify it (Gen. 27:21) and locate it (Judg. 16:26). This human experience is not realized by idols (Ps. 115:7), although they have hands.

4185. מוּשׁ ***mûš:*** A verb meaning to depart, to remove. It indicates failing to be present, the withdrawing of persons or things: persons (Ex. 33:11); various things (Ex. 13:22; Josh. 1:8; Prov. 17:13; Isa. 54:10); especially of God's Word, which will never depart from His people (Isa. 59:21). It is used figuratively of (not) removing one's neck from God's judgment (Mic. 2:3); of not departing from God's commands (Job 23:12). The person who trusts God will not fail to produce fruit (Jer. 17:8). It is used derisively of idols who do not leave their place and cannot move (Isa. 46:7).

4186. מוֹשָׁב ***môšāḇ:*** A masculine noun meaning a seat, a habitation, a dwelling place, inhabitants. The primary notion giving rise to this word is that of remaining or abiding in a given location. It signifies a place to be seated (1 Sam. 20:18; Job 29:7); the sitting of an assembly (Ps. 107:32); the location or situation of a city (2 Kgs. 2:19); a place of habitation (Gen. 27:39; Num. 24:21); the inhabitants of a particular residence (2 Sam. 9:12). The psalmist stated that the Lord Himself chose Zion as His dwelling place (Ps. 132:13).

4187. מוּשִׁי ***mûšiy:*** A proper noun designating Mushi (Ex. 6:19; Num. 3:20; 1 Chr. 6:19[4], 47[32]; 23:21, 23; 24:26, 30).

4188. מוּשִׁי ***mûšiy:*** A proper noun designating Mushite (Num. 3:33; 26:58).

4189. מוֹשְׁכָה ***môšᵉḵāh:*** A feminine noun indicating a cord, a band. It is used figuratively of the "cords" that bind the constellation Orion in place (Job 38:31), keeping it in its created fixed order.

4190. מוֹשָׁעָה ***môšā'āh:*** A feminine noun meaning salvation, deliverance. This word appears only once in the Bible, signifying the saving acts of the Lord (Ps. 68:20[21]).

4191. מוּת ***mûṯ:*** A verb meaning to die, to kill, to put to death, to execute. It occurs in the simple stem of the verb in 600 of its 809 occurrences, meaning to be dead or to die. It indicates a natural death in peace at an old age, as in the case of Abraham (Gen. 25:8; Judg. 8:32). Dying, however, was not intended to be a natural aspect of being human. It came about through unbelief and rebellion against God (Gen. 3:4) so that Adam and Eve died. The word describes dying because of failure to pursue a moral life (Prov. 5:23; 10:21). It describes various kinds of death: at the hand of God—the Lord smote Nabal, and he died (1 Sam. 25:37); the execution of the offender in capital offense cases (Gen. 2:17; 20:7); the sons of Job from the violence of a mighty storm (Job 1:19); a murderer could be handed over to die at the hand of the avenger of blood (Deut. 19:12). The prophets declared that many people would die by the hand of the Lord when He would bring the sword, famine, and plagues upon them (Jer. 11:22; cf. 14:12). The present participle of this form may indicate someone who is dying (Gen. 20:3); dead or a corpse (Deut. 25:5; Isa. 22:2). People could also be put to death by legal or human authority (Gen. 42:20; Ex. 10:28).

The word indicates the dying of various nonhuman, nonanimal entities. A nation could die, such as Moab, Ephraim, or Israel (Ezek. 18:31; Hos. 13:1; Amos 2:2). A more powerful use of the verb is its description of the death of wisdom (Job 12:2) or courage (1 Sam. 25:37).

4192. מוּת לַבֵּן ***mûṯ labbēn:*** A phrase found only in the superscription at the top of Psalm 9. It is part of the musical directions for the singing of this psalm, yet the meaning is ambiguous. Various renderings have been offered by interpreters, the most likely options being that the phrase is either a title of a tune to which the psalm was to be sung or that the phrase means "death to the son" or "to die for the son." Also possible is the combination of these two options, namely, that the phrase is a title of a tune called "Death to the Son"/ "To die for the Son" to which Psalm 9 was to be sung.

4193. מוֹת ***môṯ:*** An Aramaic masculine noun meaning death. In writing a letter to Ezra the scribe, King Artaxerxes of Persia used this term to designate execution as one of the viable means of punishment available to Ezra in dealing with those who refused to obey the Law of God and the law of the king in the newly resettled land of Israel (Ezra 7:26). The term is the equivalent of the Hebrew noun *māweṯ* (4194).

4194. מָוֶת ***māweṯ:*** A masculine noun meaning death. The term signifies death occurring by both natural and violent means (natural: Gen. 27:7, 10; Num. 16:29; violent: Lev. 16:1; Judg. 16:30). In other texts, it designates the place where the dead dwell known as Sheol (*šeʾôl*[7585]; Job 28:22; Ps. 9:13[14]; Prov. 7:27). Because death and disease are so intimately related and due to the context, the word suggests the intended meaning of deadly disease, plague, epidemic, or pestilence (Job 27:15; Jer. 15:2, 18:21, 43:11). Figuratively, the term expresses the idea of ruin and destruction, especially when contrasted with the desirable notions of life, prosperity, and happiness (Prov. 11:19; 12:28; cf. Ex. 10:17). This noun is derived from the verb *mûṯ* (4191).

4195. מוֹתָר ***môṯār:*** A masculine noun indicating abundance, advantage. It indicates profit or benefit, material or otherwise. In context it is what comes as result of labor (Prov. 14:23) and faithful effort (Prov. 21:5). It takes on the aspect of advantage or a more favorable position or superiority over something else (Eccl. 3:19).

4196. מִזְבֵּחַ ***mizbēaḥ:*** A masculine noun meaning the altar, the place of sacrifice. It is a noun formed from the verb *zāḇaḥ* (2076), which means to slaughter an animal, usually for a sacrifice. The sacrificial system was at the focal point of the pre-Israelite and Israelite systems of worship since the sacrifice and subsequent meal were used to solemnize a covenant or treaty and to symbolize a positive relationship between the two parties. Noah built an altar and offered sacrifices on exiting the ark (Gen. 8:20); the patriarchs built altars and sacrificed at various points along their journeys: Abram (Gen. 12:7, 8; 22:9); Isaac (Gen. 26:25); Jacob (Gen. 35:7); Moses (Ex. 24:4). At Mount Sinai, God commanded that the Israelites build the Tabernacle and include two altars: a bronze altar in the courtyard for the sacrificing of animals (Ex. 27:1–8; 38:1–7) and a golden altar inside the Tabernacle for the burning of incense (Ex. 30:1–10; 37:25–29). Solomon (1 Kgs. 6:20, 22; 8:64) and Ezekiel (Ezek. 41:22; 43:13–17) followed a similar pattern. God also commanded that the altar for burnt offerings be made of earth or undressed stones because human working of the stones would defile it. Moreover, God commanded that the altar should have no steps so that human nakedness would not be exposed on it (Ex. 20:24–26).

4197. מֶזֶג ***mezeg:*** A masculine noun referring to liquor, mixed wine. It means spiced wine, sweetened and flavored. It was considered desirable and a delightful treat (Song 7:2[3]).

4198. מָזֶה ***māzeh:*** An adjective meaning burned out, wasted. It means persons exhausted, debilitated, in this case, from famine (Deut. 32:24).

4199. מִזָּה ***mizzāh:*** A proper noun designating Mizzah (Gen. 36:13, 17; 1 Chr. 1:37).

4200. מָזוּ ***māzû:*** A masculine noun designating a granary, a barn. It was a place where grain was stored that was used in preparing all kinds of foods, a garner (Ps. 144:13).

4201. מְזוּזָה ***m^{e}zûzāh:*** A feminine noun meaning a doorpost, a gate, a post. It was a feature of houses (Ex. 12:7; 21:6; Deut. 6:9; 11:20); of temples or sacred houses (1 Sam. 1:9; 1 Kgs. 6:33; Ezek. 41:21; 43:8; 45:19); of the gates of cities (Judg. 16:3).

4202. מָזוֹן ***māzôn:*** A masculine noun denoting food, provisions. It is a general term covering a broad range of foodstuffs (Gen. 45:23; 2 Chr.

11:23). It is listed with grain (*bār*, grain; *leḥem*, bread or food).

4203. מָזוֹן ***māzôn:*** An Aramaic masculine noun meaning food, sustenance. It refers to food in a broad sense, that is, what was eaten for sustenance by all the earth (Dan. 4:12[19], 21[18]).

4204. מָזוֹר ***māzôr:*** A masculine noun depicting a trap, an ambush. It indicates some kind of ambush or ruse prepared against someone (Obad. 1:7). Some suggest a net in a figurative sense.

4205. מָזוֹר ***māzôr:*** A masculine noun meaning a sore, a wound. It indicates some kind of injury or a wound from disease; corruption in context. It is used figuratively of Israel and Judah's moral and religious corruption before God (Jer. 30:13; Hos. 5:13).

4206. מֵזַח ***mēzaḥ:*** I. A masculine noun referring to a belt, a girdle, strength. It is used of a girdle worn next to the skin. It is used figuratively of a "belt of oppression," an allusion to the inability of the mighty to contend with the Lord (Job 12:21); and the binding effects of a life of cursing and evil behavior toward others (Ps. 109:19). It has the sense of a restraining force (Isa. 23:10).

II. A masculine noun referring to a dock, a harbor. It indicates a harbor or port for ships (Isa. 23:10), something God was taking away from Tyre.

4207. מַזְלֵג ***mazlēg,*** מִזְלָגָה ***mizlāgāh:*** A common noun referring to a sacrificial utensil. It functioned as a tool to grasp a sacrificial meat offering, a meat fork, possibly of three tines (Ex. 27:3; Num. 4:14; 1 Sam. 2:13, 14; 1 Chr. 28:17; 2 Chr. 4:16).

4208. מַזָּל ***mazzāl:*** A feminine noun meaning a planet, a constellation. It refers to zodiacal signs in the heavens (2 Kgs. 23:5), often a temptation to Israel to worship them.

4209. מְזִמָּה ***meᵉzimmāh:*** A feminine noun meaning a plan, a thought. Most often the term denotes the evil plans, schemes, or plots humanity devises that are contrary to God's righteous decrees. The Lord declared to Jeremiah that in carrying out their evil, idolatrous plans, His people forfeited their right to enter His house (i.e., the Temple, Jer. 11:15). The psalmist prayed that the wicked might be ensnared by the very schemes they had planned to unleash on the poor (Ps. 10:2). The cunning plans that God's enemies intend to execute against Him never succeed (Ps. 21:11[12]; cf. Ps. 37:7). Moreover, those who plot evil are condemned and hated by Him (Prov. 12:2, 14:17). Often, the wicked are so blinded by pride that their only thought about God is that He doesn't exist (Ps. 10:4). Another significant use of this word occurs when it describes an intention of God and so conveys the idea of purpose or plan. After the Lord confronted Job in the whirlwind, Job was deeply humbled and acknowledged that no purpose of the Lord's can be thwarted (Job 42:2). The Lord's anger so burned on account of the false prophets of Jeremiah's day that it would not be turned back until He had executed and accomplished the purpose of His heart against them (Jer. 23:20; cf. Jer. 30:24). The Lord's purpose for Babylon was to utterly destroy it for all the evil they had committed against Jerusalem and the Temple (Jer. 51:11). In Proverbs, the word often conveys the sense of prudence, discretion, and wisdom. In his prologue to the book of Proverbs, Solomon expressed that one reason he was writing the work was to impart discretion to young men (Prov. 1:4; cf. Prov. 5:2). Solomon urged them to hold on to wisdom and not let it out of their sight once they acquired it (Prov. 3:21). Wisdom and prudence go hand in hand (Prov. 8:12). This noun derives from the verb *zāmam* (2161).

4210. מִזְמוֹר ***mizmôr:*** A masculine noun referring to a psalm, a melody. It is found in the titles of psalms designating them as a psalm or melody. These musical titles are still under investigation to pinpoint their exact meanings more clearly.

4211. מַזְמֵרָה ***mazmērāh:*** A feminine noun indicating a pruning hook, a pruning knife. It was a knife or short pruning tool often used to cut or prune vines, one of Israel's major agricultural products (Isa. 2:4; 18:5; Joel 3:10[4:10]; Mic. 4:3). It was often mentioned in times of judgment or restoration in Israel.

4212. מְזַמֶּרֶת ***m^ezammeret̠:*** A feminine plural noun designating snuffers, wick trimmers. It is used in the plural form only. It was used as its name indicates to put out lamps and to trim wicks (1 Kgs. 7:50; 2 Kgs. 12:13[14]; 25:14; 2 Chr. 4:22; Jer. 52:18).

4213. מִזְעָר ***miz'ār:*** A masculine noun indicating a short time, a little while, a few. It indicates that something is small, not large in size, duration, or number. It is used of the short duration in time of God's anger (Isa. 10:25); a short time before something will come to pass (Isa. 29:17); the small number of persons who will remain after God's judgments (Isa. 16:14; 24:6).

4214. מִזְרֶה ***mizreh:*** A masculine noun indicating a pitchfork, a winnowing fork. It was a farming tool used to clean out the chaff and debris from grains (Isa. 30:24). It is used figuratively of God's "winnowing fork" of judgment on His people (Jer. 15:7).

4215. מְזָרֶה ***m^ezāreh:*** I. A masculine noun indicating north. It indicates the area of north as opposed to south (Job 37:9; NASB, KJV).

II. A masculine noun indicating a driving wind. Some translations prefer this rendering of the word indicating winds that carry with them the cold of winter or a storm (Job 37:9; NIV).

4216. מַזָּרוֹת *mazzārôṯ:* A feminine plural noun, Mazzaroth: known for a constellation of stars. The word refers to constellations, possibly Venus, an evening or morning star, or Hyades in the constellation Taurus (Job 38:32). Others suggest a reference to some southern constellation of the zodiac. The Bear is mentioned in the second half of the verse.

4217. מִזְרָח *mizrāḥ:* A masculine noun showing the place of the sunrise, east, eastward. It combines with *šemeš* to indicate the direction east, *mizraḥ šemeš* (Num. 21:11; 1 Kgs. 7:25). It is used alone more often to mean east (Josh. 11:3; 1 Chr. 9:24; Neh. 12:37; Ps. 103:12). With the definite article and the preposition l^e, to, in front, it is rendered as in or toward the east (Neh. 3:26). With l^e following, it means to the east of, eastward (2 Chr. 5:12). With *min* (4480) on the front, it means from the east (Isa. 41:2; 43:5; Dan. 11:44). With a ָה, *āh*, directive attached, it means eastward (Num. 32:19).

4218. מִזְרָע *mizrā':* A masculine noun indicating that which is sown, a sown field. It depicts a fertile land sown with gracious seeds, specifically land sown in Egypt along the Nile River (Isa. 19:7).

4219. מִזְרָק *mizrāq:* A masculine noun defining a bowl, a basin. It refers to basins of bronze used in the Tabernacle and then the Temple service by priests serving in the ritual sacrifices of Israel (Ex. 27:3; 38:3; 1 Kgs. 7:40). It indicates more generally a bowl for wine (Amos 6:6). They were also used to carry flour mixed with oil for offerings (Num. 7:13, 19, 25, 31). Basins of silver and gold were also used in the temples (1 Kgs. 7:50; 2 Kgs. 12:13[14]; Neh. 7:70).

4220. מֵחַ *mēaḥ:* A masculine noun indicating the fat one, a fat beast, a wealthy one. It designates a fatling, a sheep raised for fattening (Ps. 66:15). In Isaiah 5:17, it seems to stand for wealthy or rich people, "fat ones."

4221. מֹחַ *mōaḥ:* A masculine noun referring to bone marrow. It refers to the soft fatty tissue that fills a healthy person's bones (Job 21:24), a sign of strength and health.

4222. מָחָא *māḥā':* A verb meaning to strike, to clap. It is used with *yāḏ*, hand, or *kap̱*, palm, hand, to mean strike the hands, to clap in joy (Ps. 98:8; Isa. 55:12; Ezek. 25:6); it is used figuratively of nature or nations clapping their hands.

4223. מְחָא m^e*ḥā':* An Aramaic verb meaning to smite, to strike. The term corresponds closely with the Hebrew verbs *māḵāh* (4229) and *nāḵāh* (5221). When combined with the prepositional phrase b^e*yaḏ* (3027) meaning on the hand, the term attains the idiomatic sense to restrain, to hinder, to prevent, or to stay (Dan. 4:35[32]). On one occasion, the word vividly described the penalty of impalement (on a beam) which awaited any individual who dared to alter King Darius' edict concerning the rebuilding of the Temple in Jerusalem (Ezra 6:11).

4224. מַחֲבֵא ***maḥᵃḇē'***, מַחֲבֹא ***maḥᵃḇō':*** I. A masculine noun indicating a hiding place. It indicates a place of safety or refuge from the wind (Isa. 32:2), especially a refuge under the protection of God's approved princes and rulers.

II. A masculine noun describing a hiding place. It is used of any possible hideout that one could find in the desert areas of Judah (1 Sam. 23:23).

4225. מַחְבֶּרֶת ***maḥbereṯ:*** A feminine noun meaning a place of joining; that which is joined. It is the juncture at which various parts of the priestly clothing were connected (Ex. 28:27; 39:20); a tie or connecting loop on the curtains or hangings of the Tabernacle (Ex. 26:4, 5; 36:11, 12, 17).

4226. מְחַבְּרָה ***mᵉḥabbᵉrāh:*** A feminine noun indicating a joint, a hinge, a post. It is a technical construction term for clamps or binders prepared to use on the doors of the Temple. Some of iron (1 Chr. 22:3); others of wood (2 Chr. 34:11).

4227. מַחֲבַת ***maḥᵃḇaṯ:*** A feminine noun indicating a flat pan, a griddle. It was a metal cooking utensil used for roasting or frying items prepared for sacrificial use (Lev. 2:5; 6:21[14]; 7:9; Ezek. 4:3). In 1 Chronicles 23:29, it designates that which has been cooked in one of these pans or griddles.

4228. מַחֲגֹרֶת ***maḥᵃgōreṯ:*** A feminine noun designating a wrapping, a girding. It refers to the putting on and wearing of sackcloth (Isa. 3:24), a sign of grave mourning.

4229. מָחָה ***māḥāh:*** A verb meaning to wipe, to wipe out. This term is often connected with divine judgment. It is used of God wiping out all life in the flood (Gen. 7:23); destroying Jerusalem (2 Kgs. 21:13); and threatening to wipe out Israel's name (Deut. 9:14). God also wipes out sin (Ps. 51:1[3]; Isa. 43:25); and wipes away tears (Isa. 25:8). Humans also act as the subject of this verb; the Israelites nearly wiped out the Benjamites (Judg. 21:17); and a prostitute wipes her mouth after eating (Prov. 30:20).

4230. מְחוּגָה ***mᵉḥûgāh:*** A feminine noun referring to a compass, an instrument for making circles. It refers to a craftsman's technical tool used in fine artwork (Isa. 44:13).

4231. מָחוֹז ***maḥōz:*** A masculine noun indicating a haven, an enclosure. A place of safety and peace to which God leads His people (Ps. 107:30).

4232. מְחוּיָאֵל ***mᵉḥûyā'ēl***, מְחִיָּיאֵל ***mᵉḥiyyāy'ēl:*** A proper noun designating Mehujael (Gen. 4:18).

4233. מַחֲוִים ***maḥᵃwiym:*** A proper noun designating Mahavite (1 Chr. 11:46).

4234. מָחוֹל ***māḥôl:*** A masculine noun meaning dance, dancing. It is an activity of a physical expression of joy (Ps. 30:11[12]; Jer. 31:4, 13; Lam. 5:15) and praise to the Lord (Ps. 149:3; 150:4), often accompanied by musical instruments (Ps. 149:3).

4235. מָחוֹל ***māḥôl:*** A proper noun designating Mahol (1 Kgs. 4:31 [5:11]).

4236. מַחֲזֶה ***maḥ^{a}zeh:*** A masculine noun meaning vision. This word is used only four times in the Old Testament and comes from the verb *ḥāzāh* (2372), meaning to see. God came to Abram in a vision (Gen. 15:1); Balaam could rightly prophesy because he saw a vision of the Almighty (Num. 24:4, 16). However, false prophets saw a false vision and thus prophesied falsely (Ezek. 13:7).

4237. מֶחֱזָה ***meḥ^{e}zāh:*** A feminine noun designating a window, an opening made to let in light (1 Kgs. 7:4, 5). The phrase *m^{e}ḥezāh 'el-m^{e}ḥezāh* is rendered "window toward (opposite) window."

4238. מַחֲזִיאוֹת ***maḥ^{a}ziy'ôṯ:*** A proper noun designating Mahazioth (1 Chr. 25:4, 30).

4239. מְחִי ***m^{e}ḥiy:*** A masculine noun referring to a blow delivered by a battering ram. It refers to the shock and impact of a battering ram against the walls of a city or anything else (Ezek. 26:9).

4240. מְחִידָא ***m^{e}ḥiyḏā':*** A proper noun designating Mehida (Ezra 2:52; Neh. 7:54).

4241. מִחְיָה ***miḥ^{e}yāh:*** A feminine singular noun meaning preservation of life, sustenance, raw flesh. Joseph said he was sent to Egypt for the preservation of life (Gen. 45:5). The term is also used to mean food or sustenance (Judg. 6:4; 17:10). The Levitical Law used the term to refer to raw flesh because of a skin disease (Lev. 13:10, 24).

4242. מְחִיר ***m^{e}ḥiyr:*** A masculine noun meaning price, wages, cost. It refers to the value of a transaction, a market price, or the equivalent value in goods (2 Sam. 24:24; 1 Kgs. 10:28). It means money or price (Mic. 3:11). It is used figuratively of a recompense or cost for Israel's sins (Jer. 15:13); and of the Lord's selling His people without profit from their price (Ps. 44:12[13]). It is used of the hire paid to a dog, that is a male prostitute (Deut. 23:18[19]). Wisdom has no equivalent price (Job 28:15).

4243. מְחִיר ***m^{e}ḥiyr:*** A proper noun designating Mehir (1 Chr. 4:11).

4244. מַחְלָה ***maḥlāh:*** A proper noun designating Mahlah:

A. A daughter of Zelophehad (Num. 26:33; 27:1; 36:11; Josh. 17:3).

B. A Manassite (1 Chr. 7:18).

4245. מַחֲלֶה ***maḥ^{a}leh,*** מַחֲלָה ***maḥ^{a}lāh:*** I. A masculine noun referring to sickness, a disease. It refers to any type of sickness (Prov. 18:14). God brought a sickness upon Jehoram, king of Judah (2 Chr. 21:15).

II. A feminine noun denoting a sickness, disease. It indicates sickness in general but also the sickness in particular that God put on the Egyptians (Ex. 15:26). If Israel obeyed God, He would remove illness and disease from among them (Ex. 23:25). God would heal sickness already contracted if His people would repent (1 Kgs. 8:37; 2 Chr. 6:28).

4246. מְחֹלָה ***mᵉḥōlāh:*** A feminine noun referring to dancing, a dance. It is used of a joyous celebration featuring rhythmic bodily movements by groups or individuals (Judg. 21:21; 1 Sam. 18:6; 21:11[12]; 29:5), especially in praise of the Lord (Ex. 15:20); but on any joyous occasion (Judg. 11:34; Song 6:13[7:1]).

4247. מְחִלָּה ***mᵉḥillāh:*** A feminine noun indicating a hole, a cavern. A hollow or open hole in the ground where one can reasonably seek safety (Isa. 2:19), especially during a time of God's judgment.

4248. מַחְלוֹן ***maḥlôn:*** A proper noun designating Mahlon (Ruth 1:2, 5; 4:9, 10).

4249. מַחְלִי ***maḥliy:*** A proper noun designating Mahli:

A. A Levite (Ex. 6:19; Num. 3:20; 1 Chr. 6:19[4], 29[14]; 23:21; 24:26, 28; Ezra 8:18),

B. A son of Mushi (1 Chr. 6:47 [32]; 23:23; 24:30).

4250. מַחְלִי ***maḥliy:*** A proper noun designating Mahlite (Num. 3:33; 26:58).

4251. מַחֲלוּ ***mahᵃlû:*** A masculine noun meaning sickness, a disease. It refers to some indeterminate sickness suffered by Joash, king of Judah (2 Chr. 24:25).

4252. מַחֲלָף ***mahᵃlāp:*** I. A masculine noun referring to a knife for slaughter. The meaning is not known for sure but several suggestions are (1) knives for slaughtering animals (KJV); (2) silver pans (NIV); duplicates (NASB) (Ezra 1:9). See below for these suggestions.

II. A masculine noun meaning duplicate items. Twenty-nine such items were taken back to Jerusalem from Babylon (Ezra 1:9, NASB).

III. A masculine noun referring to a silver pan. Twenty-nine of these items were taken back to Jerusalem from Babylon (Ezra 1:9, NIV).

4253. מַחְלָפָה ***maḥlāpāh:*** A feminine noun identifying a lock of hair, braid of hair. It is used of Samson's long hair as a Nazarite wherein lay his strength (Judg. 16:13, 19).

4254. מַחֲלָצָה ***mahᵃlāṣāh:*** A feminine noun meaning a festal robe, a fine garment. It indicates finely woven, white clothing; festival clothing (Isa. 3:22); festive robes. They were a sign of a time of rejoicing (Zech. 3:4).

4255. מַחְלְקָה ***maḥl^{e}qāh:*** An Aramaic feminine noun designating a group, a division. It indicates the groups into which the priests were divided (Ezra 6:18).

4256. מַחֲלֹקֶת ***maḥ^{a}lōqeṯ:*** I. A feminine noun meaning smoothness, slipperiness, an escape. It is used to define a rock where David escaped from Saul, "the rock of escape" (1 Sam. 23:28).

II. A feminine noun meaning a group, a division. It designates a part or division of people by tribes (Josh. 11:23; 12:7; 18:10); or by sons of Levi (1 Chr. 23:6); or Aaron (1 Chr. 24:1), etc. It indicates sections or portions of land as well (Neh. 11:36; Ezek. 48:29).

4257. מָחֲלַת ***māḥ^{a}laṯ:*** A feminine proper noun designating Mahalath, mahalath; part of a song title. This is probably a musical term or a designation of some musical instrument (Ps. 53:title). It may mean "according to mahalath."

4258. מָחֲלַת ***māḥ^{a}laṯ:*** A proper noun designating Mahalath:

A. A daughter of Ishmael (Gen. 28:9).

B. A granddaughter of David (2 Chr. 11:18).

4259. מְחֹלָתִי ***m^{e}ḥōlāṯiy:*** A proper noun designating a Meholathite (1 Sam. 18:19; 2 Sam. 21:8).

4260. מַחֲמָאֹת ***maḥ^{a}mā'ōṯ:*** A feminine plural noun meaning butter. It indicates butter used as a metaphor for treacherous speech that was smoother than butter or speech from a mouth smeared or smoothed with butter (Ps. 55:21[22]).

4261. מַחְמָד ***maḥmāḏ:*** A masculine noun indicating a desire, a desirable thing, a precious thing. It indicates whatever is desirable, something one wishes to have, to possess. It is used of things (1 Kgs. 20:6; 2 Chr. 36:19; Hos. 9:6; Joel 3:5[4:5]); of persons (Song 5:16). It is used especially of what is attractive to the eyes (1 Kgs. 20:6; Ezek. 24:16, 21, 25).

4262. מַחֲמֹד ***maḥ^{a}mōḏ:*** A masculine noun designating a desirable thing, a precious thing. It is used to designate things held in great esteem and considered valuable, not all of which are material (Lam. 1:7), although that is a major part of those things (Lam. 1:11).

4263. מַחְמָל ***maḥmāl:*** A masculine noun meaning an object of mercy. This word occurs only once in the Old Testament and comes from the verb *ḥāmal* (2550), meaning to spare. In Ezekiel 24:21, this word is used to describe the compassion and delight that the Temple was to the Israelites. In this section of Scripture, Ezekiel's desire and delight for his wife is compared to Israel's desire and delight for the Temple (Ezek. 24:15–27).

4264. מַחֲנֶה ***maḥ^{a}neh:*** A masculine noun meaning a camp, an army, and a company. This word comes from the verb *ḥānāh* (2583), meaning to encamp. The basic idea of this word is that of a multitude of people who have gathered together (Ezek. 1:24). This word is often used within the context of travel, like the wandering Israelites (Ex. 14:19, 20; Num. 4:5); or within the context of war (1 Sam. 17:1; 2 Kgs. 6:24; 19:35). This word is most often used of Israel but is also used to describe foreign nations (Josh. 10:5; Judg. 7:8–11, 13–15; 1 Sam. 29:1); or even God's encampment (Gen. 32:2[3]; 1 Chr. 12:22[23]).

4265. מַחֲנֵה־דָן ***maḥ^{a}nēh-ḏān:*** A proper noun designating Mahaneh Dan (Judg. 18:12).

4266. מַחֲנַיִם ***maḥ^{a}nayim:*** A proper noun designating Mahanaim. The word is in its dual form and means two or dual camps. It was used by Jacob to indicate that God had encamped in the midst of Jacob and his family (Gen. 32:1–2[3]). It is used as a boundary marker by Joshua (Josh. 13:26, 30). It became a city of the Levites (Josh. 21:38[36]). It was located in Gilead, evidently (2 Sam. 8, 12, 29) in Gad. David escaped to Mohanaim when Absalom rebelled (2 Sam. 17:24, 27). Solomon established it as the center of one of his districts in Israel (1 Kgs. 4:14).

4267. מַחֲנָק ***maḥ^{a}naq:*** A masculine noun meaning strangling, suffocation. It refers figuratively to a means of death, a way of Job's soul (life) being snuffed out (Job 7:15).

4268. מַחְסֶה ***maḥseh:*** A masculine noun designating a refuge, shelter. It indicates a place of safety and protection, security. It is used figuratively most often of God as a refuge for His people (Ps. 14:6; 46:1[2]; 61:3[4]; 62:7[8]; 71:7; 73:28; Prov. 14:26; Jer. 17:17; Joel 3:16[4:16]). It is used of various types of sheltering: from storms (Isa. 4:6; 25:4); from danger for people or animals (Ps. 104:18); a false retreat, a false haven of deceit or falsity (Isa. 28:15, 17).

4269. מַחְסוֹם ***maḥsôm:*** A masculine noun meaning muzzle, bridle. It was something used to keep a person's mouth shut, possibly a piece of thin metal over one's mouth to serve as a muzzle (Ps. 39:1[2]).

4270. מַחְסוֹר ***maḥsôr,*** מַחְסֹר ***maḥsōr:*** A masculine noun referring a lack, a need, poverty. It indicates what is needed because of a lack (Deut. 15:8); or what is required to meet a need (Judg. 19:20). Its sense becomes focused on the want or lack. There can be no lack (Judg. 18:10; 19:19). To live in a constant state of need is equivalent to poverty (Prov. 6:11; 11:24; 14:23; 21:5; 28:27).

4271. מַחְסֵיָה ***maḥsēyāh:*** A proper noun designating Mahseiah (Jer. 32:12; 51:59).

4272. מָחַץ māḥaṣ: A verb meaning to wound severely, to pierce through, and to shatter. This word describes bodily destruction and is best illustrated in Judges 5:26, where Jael pierced through Sisera's head from temple to temple with a tent peg. David used this word to describe some of his victories in which those wounded were not able to rise again (2 Sam. 22:39; Ps. 18:38[39]). In all other instances of this word, God is in complete control (Deut. 32:39; Job 5:18) and completely shatters His enemies (Ps. 68:21[22]; 110:5, 6; Hab. 3:13). This word occurs only in the poetical passages of the Old Testament, which highlights the intensity of this word.

4273. מַחַץ maḥaṣ: A masculine singular noun meaning a severe wound. It occurs only once in the Hebrew Bible (Isa. 30:26), referring to God healing His wounded people.

4274. מַחְצֵב maḥṣēḇ: A masculine noun meaning something hewed. It is used of stone that has been quarried or cut out (2 Kgs. 12:12[13]; 22:6; 2 Chr. 34:11).

4275. מֶחֱצָה meḥ^{e}ṣāh: A feminine noun indicating half. It indicates 50 percent of the whole of something: sheep, cattle, donkeys, soldiers (Num. 31:36, 43).

4276. מַחֲצִית maḥ^{a}ṣiyṯ: A feminine noun indicating half, the middle. It indicates half of something: a shekel (Ex. 30:13, 15); chariotry (1 Kgs. 16:9); flour (Lev. 6:20[13]). It is used before *hayyôm*, the day, to mean noon, midday (Neh. 8:3).

4277. מָחַק māḥaq: A verb meaning to utterly destroy. This word is used only once in the Old Testament, where it is used as a near synonym with *māḥaṣ* (4272), meaning to wound severely, to pierce through, or to shatter. It describes Jael's actions in destroying Sisera by driving a tent peg between his temples (Judg. 5:26).

4278. מֶחְקָר meḥqār: A masculine noun referring to depth, deep places. It has the sense of things to be searched out, explored. In context it is used with *'ereṣ* to mean like places of the earth to be explored, depths unknown (Ps. 95:4), too deep to know.

4279. מָחָר māḥār: A masculine noun meaning tomorrow, in the future. It refers to the immediate next day, tomorrow (Gen. 30:33; Ex. 8:10[6], 29[25]; Josh. 11:6; 1 Sam. 20:5; 1 Kgs. 19:2). It expands to have the broader sense of in time to come, the future (Ex. 13:14; Deut. 6:20; Josh. 4:6, 21).

4280. מַחֲרָאָה maḥ^{a}rā'āh: A feminine noun meaning draught house; a latrine. A place that serves as a toilet, a privy (2 Kgs. 10:27).

4281. מַחֲרֵשָׁה maḥ^{a}rēšāh: A feminine noun pointing out a mattock, a sickle, a hoe, a plowshare. A tool used in agriculture or farming (1 Sam.

13:20) for breaking up ground or plowing (NASB, NIV, NKJV).

4282. מַחֲרֶשֶׁת ***maḥ^{a}rešet̲:*** A feminine noun meaning plowshare. A plowshare used to break up tillable ground, to plow the ground (1 Sam. 13:20; KJV, share).

4283. מָחֳרָת ***moḥ^{o}rāt̲:*** A feminine noun meaning the next day, the morrow. It means the following day (Num. 11:32; 1 Chr. 29:21). In an adverbial sense, it means on the next day (Gen. 19:34; Ex. 18:13). With *min* (4480) on the front, it indicates on (from) the day after the sabbath, the new moon respectively (Lev. 23:11; 1 Sam. 20:27).

4284. מַחֲשָׁבָה ***maḥ^{a}šāb̲āh,*** מַחֲשֶׁבֶת ***maḥ^{a}šeb̲et̲:*** A feminine noun meaning a thought, a purpose, a device, an intention. Largely poetic in its use, this Hebrew word means thought or the inventions that spring from such thoughts. It denotes the thoughts of the mind, either belonging to people (1 Chr. 28:9; Ps. 94:11); or God (Jer. 29:11; Mic. 4:12); the plans or intentions that arise from these thoughts (Prov. 15:22; 19:21); the schemes of a wicked heart (Lam. 3:60); skillful inventions coming from the mind of an artist (Ex. 31:4; 2 Chr. 26:15).

4285. מַחְשָׁךְ ***maḥšāk̲:*** A masculine noun meaning a dark place, a hiding place, secrecy. The primary meaning of this word is darkness that is both blinding and confining. Poetically, it is used to draw an image of the darkness and inescapability of the grave (Ps. 88:6[7]; Lam. 3:6). The range of meaning also extends to the unknown things the Lord makes plain (Isa. 42:16); and the back alleys where deviant behavior abounds (Ps. 74:20).

4286. מַחְשֹׂף ***maḥśōp̄:*** A masculine noun indicating laying bare, peeling. It describes Jacob's carefully removing small strips of bark from fresh poplar rods or sticks (Gen. 30:37).

4287. מַחַת ***maḥat̲:*** A proper noun designating Mahath:

A. A son of Amasai (1 Chr. 6:35[20]).

B. A chief Levite (2 Chr. 29:12; 31:13).

4288. מְחִתָּה ***m^{e}ḥittāh:*** A feminine noun meaning destruction, ruin, terror. This word comes from the verb *ḥāt̲at̲* (2865), meaning to be broken or afraid. It is used most often in a figurative sense in Proverbs to describe the ruin of the foolish (Prov. 10:14; 13:3; 18:7); and the workers of iniquity (Prov. 10:29; 21:15). It also describes the result of poverty (Prov. 10:15); and the failure to support a prince (Prov. 14:28). Elsewhere, this word depicted the power of God bringing destruction (Ps. 89:40[41]), which resulted in an object lesson to all around (Jer. 48:39). It is the blessing of God that people live without this terror (Isa. 54:14; Jer. 17:17).

4289. מַחְתָּה ***maḥtāh:*** A feminine noun meaning a snuffholder, a firepan; a bucket, a pan, a small pan.

It was a gold or bronze container used to carry ashes and burned coals (1 Kgs. 7:50); or to carry coals in an offering of incense, a censer (Lev. 10:1; 16:12). It also describes a can of gold used as a lampstand accessory (Ex. 25:38) or snuffholder. It refers to bronze utensils or firepans (Ex. 27:3).

4290. מַחְתֶּרֶת ***maḥtereṯ:*** A feminine noun designating a burglary, a breaking in. It is used of the act of a burglar or thief who would attempt to gain entrance into a house to steal or loot it (Ex. 22:2[1]; Jer. 2:34).

4291. מְטָא ***meṭā'***, מְטָה ***meṭāh:*** An Aramaic verb meaning to reach, to attain, to happen. It is used to indicate that something physically or figuratively has touched or reached a certain location (Dan. 4:11[8], 20[17]; 6:24[25]; 7:13, 22); or something such as royal influence has reached a certain extent (Dan. 4:22[19]). It is used of a decree or a sentence being fulfilled (Dan. 4:28[25]).

4292. מַטְאֲטֵא ***maṭ'aṭē':*** A masculine noun meaning broom. It refers to a sweeping tool for cleaning up. It is used in an expression in which God will "sweep" away Babylon with His "broom" of destruction (Isa. 14:23).

4293. מַטְבֵּחַ ***maṭbēaḥ:*** A masculine noun referring to a slaughtering place. It defines a place where sacrificial slaughter or slaughtering in general takes place. It is used figuratively of a slaughtering place where God will judge the Babylonians (Isa. 14:21).

4294. מַטֶּה ***maṭṭeh***, מַטָּה ***maṭṭāh:*** A masculine noun meaning a rod, a staff, a branch, a tribe. This word signifies, variously, a walking stick (Ex. 4:2); a branch of a tree (Ezek. 19:11ff.); a spear used in battle (Hab. 3:14); an instrument of chastisement (Isa. 10:24); an instrument used in the threshing process (Isa. 28:27). Metaphorically, the image of a staff symbolizes the supply of food (Lev. 26:26); strength (Isa. 14:5); and authority (Ps. 110:2). Uniquely, the word also signifies a tribe, such as one of the twelve tribes of Israel (Num. 36:3, 4; Josh. 13:29). The origin of this use derives from the image of the leader of the tribe going before the company with his staff in hand (cf. Num. 17:2[17]).

4295. מַטָּה ***maṭṭāh:*** An adverb meaning beneath, downward, under. Its meaning is quite uniform. It indicates below, beneath (Ex. 26:24; Deut. 28:43; Prov. 15:24). With *le* on the front, it may mean a downward direction (2 Kgs. 19:30). It is used with *le* followed by *min* (4480) . . . to mean less than iniquity (Ezra 9:13). God's grace exceeded Israel's iniquity.

4296. מִטָּה ***miṭṭāh:*** A feminine noun meaning a bed, a couch, a funeral bier. It indicates a place for reclining, a couch, or a bed for sleep (2 Kgs. 4:10); for recovery from illness (Gen. 47:31); for the dead, a bier for carrying the dead in a funeral procession (2 Sam. 3:31); and a portable couch (1 Sam. 19:15; 2 Sam. 3:31; Esth. 1:6). It describes a couch for resting on during the day (1 Sam. 28:23; 1 Kgs. 21:4). The beds or couches mentioned in Amos 6:4 and Esther 1:6 were ornate and probably used for reclining at feasts, among high society. It is used with *ḥeder* to express bedroom (*ḥ*ᵃ*har hammiṭṭôt*) (2 Kgs. 11:2).

4297. מֻטֶּה ***muṭṭeh:*** A masculine noun meaning something perverted, twisted, warped. Occurring only in Ezekiel 9:9, this word derives its meaning from a primitive root meaning to stretch, to incline, or to bend (5186). It was used by the Lord to describe the perverseness of Judah in distorting His Law and justice.

4298. מֻטָּה ***muṭṭāh:*** A feminine noun referring to spreading out, stretching out. It describes the stretching out of a bird's wings as the picture of the flood waters of the Euphrates. This, in turn,was a picture of God's judgment on Samaria (Isa. 8:8), a mixed metaphor literary device.

4299. מַטְוֶה ***maṭweh:*** A masculine noun meaning that which is spun. The word described the things spun, clothing, cords, curtains, etc., by the skilled women of Israel for use in the Tabernacle (Ex. 35:25).

4300. מָטִיל ***māṭiyl:*** A masculine noun pointing to a metal bar, a rod. It indicates strong, powerful limbs in a figurative description of Behemoth (Job 40:18).

4301. מַטְמוֹן ***maṭmôn,*** מַטְמֻן ***maṭmun:*** A masculine noun indicating hidden treasure, riches. It refers to valuables, such as silver coins kept in a sack (Gen. 43:23); or hidden in a field (Jer. 41:8). It is used in a metaphor for death (Job 3:21). Wisdom is to be sought out even more than hidden treasure (Prov. 2:4). Cyrus was awarded hidden riches and wealth to show him that the Lord had called him (Isa. 45:3).

4302. מַטָּע ***maṭṭā':*** A masculine noun meaning a place of planting, an act of planting. It indicates a place and act of planting something (Ezek. 17:7; 31:4; Mic. 1:6). It refers to a planting by the Lord in Zion of His people, His community (Isa. 60:21; 61:3; Ezek. 34:29).

4303. מַטְעָם ***maṭ'ām:*** A masculine noun meaning tasty food, delicacy. It indicates gourmet food, special tidbits, or delicacies (Prov. 23:3, 6); a specially prepared meal of tasty food (Gen. 27:4, 7, 9, 14, 17, 31).

4304. מִטְפַּחַת ***miṭpaḥaṯ:*** A feminine noun designating a veil, a cloak. It indicates a mantle for women to wear (Ruth 3:15). It was a sign of wealthy society and an item listed with other items of fine clothing (Isa. 3:22).

4305. מָטַר ***māṭar:*** A verb meaning to rain. It indicates the falling of water droplets. Someone may be rained on (Amos 4:7). The Lord controlled the rain for His people (Isa. 5:6; Amos 4:7). It is used as a metaphor describing anything falling like rain, e.g., brimstones (Gen. 19:24; Ex. 9:18, 23; Ps. 78:24, 27; Ezek. 38:22); in a figurative sense of the Lord's raining coals of fire and brimstone upon the wicked (Ps. 11:6).

4306. מָטָר ***māṭār:*** A masculine noun indicating rain. It indicates the watering of the earth in season (Deut. 11:11); and as a blessing from God (Deut. 11:14, 17; 1 Kgs. 8:35, 36); as a time of replenishing the earth, a refreshing for God's people (Deut. 32:2; Job 29:23). It was used as a metaphor also for times of distress and hardship (Isa. 4:6). It was not fitting during harvest (Prov. 26:1). It was part of God's judgment on Egypt (Ex. 9:33, 34).

4307. מַטָּרָה ***maṭṭārāh,*** מַטָּרָא ***maṭṭārā':*** A feminine noun indicating a guard, a ward, a prison; a target. It is used of the men on guard, security forces (Neh. 3:25; 12:39). Used with *ḥaṣar,* it referred to the court of the guard; with *ša'ar* it denoted the gate of the guard (Jer. 32:2, 8, 12; 33:1; 37:21; 38:6, 13, 28; 39:14, 15).

4308. מַטְרֵד ***maṭrēḏ:*** A proper noun designating Matred (Gen. 36:39; 1 Chr. 1:50).

4309. מַטְרִי ***maṭriy:*** A proper noun designating Matri (1 Sam. 10:21).

4310. מִי ***miy:*** A pronoun meaning who, whose, whom. It is usually used interrogatively meaning who and nearly always is used of persons, not things (Gen. 24:23, 65; 2 Kgs. 10:13). Used with prepositions or as an object, it means whom (1 Sam. 12:3; 17:28). It means what in some cases (Mic. 1:5). The expression *miyyittēn* means literally who would grant and only if (Job 23:3). Repeated as in *miy wāmiy,* it means who each, who individually (Ex. 10:8).

4311. מֵידְבָא ***mēyḏ^{e}ḇā':*** A proper noun designating Medeba (Num. 21:30; Josh. 13:9, 16; 1 Chr. 19:7; Isa. 15:2).

4312. מֵידָד ***mēyḏāḏ:*** A proper noun designating Medad (Num. 11:26, 27).

4313. מֵי הַיַּרְקוֹן ***mēy hayyarqôn:*** A proper noun designating Me Jarkon (Josh. 19:46).

4314. מֵי זָהָב ***mēy zāhāḇ:*** A proper noun designating Mezahab (Gen. 36:39; 1 Chr. 1:50).

4315. מֵיטָב ***mēyṭāḇ:*** A masculine noun meaning best. It indicates what is best in quality or worth for various purposes: the best of the land of Egypt (Gen. 47:6, 11); the best part of crops at harvest time (Ex. 22:5[4]); the best of animals for sacrifice or food (1 Sam. 15:9, 15).

4316. מִיכָא ***miykā':*** A proper noun designating Mica:

A. Son of Mephibosheth (2 Sam. 9:12).

B. A Levite (1 Chr. 9:15; Neh. 10:[11]).

C. A Levite (Neh. 11:17, 22).

4317. מִיכָאֵל ***miykā'ēl:*** A proper noun designating Michael:

A. The angel who watches over Israel, Daniel's people, the holy people (Gen. 10:21).

B. The father of Sethur, a spy in Canaan (Num. 13:13).

C. A person from Gad, head of a family (1 Chr. 5:13).

D. A Gadite, of the sons of Abihail or an ancestor (1 Chr. 5:14).

E. A descendant of the Kohathites, Levites, who served in a musical capacity at the Temple (1 Cr. 6:40).

F. A son of Izrahiah from Issachar (1 Chr. 7:30).

G. From the line of Saul, from the sons of Elpaal (1 Chr. 8:16).

H. A military captain who defected to David at Ziglag (1 Chr. 27:18).

I. An officer from the tribe of Issachar (2 Chr. 21:2).

J. A son of the good king Jehoshaphat (Ezra 8:8).

K. A descendant of Shephatiah who returned from exile with Ezra.

4318. מִיכָה ***miykāh:*** A proper noun designating Micah:

A. A man from Ephraim who hired a young Levite to be his priest over his self-made shrine, ephod, and idols. His priest and religious objects were forcefully taken from him by the Danites (Judg. 17—18).

B. A prophet mentioned by some Israelites in Jeremiah's day. He had correctly prophesied war in the time of Hezekiah of Judah and was not threatened for it by the establishment (Jer. 26:18).

C. The head of a family from the tribe of Reuben, a son of Joel (1 Chr. 5:5).

D. A son of Merib-Baal who was a son of Jonathan, the friend of David and son of Saul (1 Chr. 8:34).

E. A priest from the family of Kohath (1 Chr. 23:20).

F. The son of Imlah who prophesied the defeat of Israel and death of Ahab (1 Kgs. 22:9).

G. The father of Abdon who was an official under King Josiah (2 Chr. 34:20).

4319. מִיכָהוּ ***miykāhû:*** A proper noun designating Micaiah (2 Chr. 18:8). It is the same as 4318,F.

4320. מִיכָיָה ***miykāyāh:*** A proper noun designating Micaiah:

A. The prophet Micah (Jer. 26:18), the same as 4318,B.

B. An ancestor of Zechariah who took part in the dedication of the wall of Nehemiah (Neh. 12:35).

C. A priest who took part in celebrating the dedication of Nehemiah's wall (Neh. 12:41).

D. The father of Achbor who was an official under King Josiah (2 Kgs. 22:12).

4321. מִיכָיְהוּ ***miyḵāyehû,*** מִכָיְהוּ ***miḵāyehû:*** A proper noun designating Micah:

A. Micah the Ephraimite (Judg. 17:1, 4), the same as 4318,A.

B. He always prophesied only what the Lord instructed him to say (1 Kgs. 22:14). It is the same as 4318,F.

C. A son of Gemariah who reported the words of Jeremiah's first scroll to the leading officials of King Jehoiakim (Jer. 36:13).

4322. מִיכָיָהוּ ***miyḵāyāhû:*** A proper noun designating Micaiah:

A. Mother of Abijah (2 Chr. 13:2).

B. A prince under Jehoshaphat (2 Chr. 17:7).

4323. מִיכָל ***miyḵāl:*** A masculine noun meaning brook. It refers to a small stream easily crossed and smaller than a river (2 Sam. 17:20).

4324. מִיכַל ***miyḵal:*** A proper noun designating Michal. Saul's younger daughter who married David and was severely disciplined by him when she sharply critiqued his supposed indecent behavior in front of the people (2 Sam. 6:16–23).

She had fallen in love with David, and Saul used her to gain an advantage over David (1 Sam. 18:20–30). She, in fact, helped David escape from her father several times (1 Sam. 19:9–16).

4325. מַיִם ***mayim:*** A masculine dual or plural noun meaning water. It indicates water in its various functions: as a basic element of the earth (Gen. 1:2); as water descending as rain (2 Sam. 21:10); gathered water, as seas, wells, springs, etc. (Num. 20:17; Amos 5:8; Isa. 22:9). Urine is designated as *mēymēy raglayim* (2 Kgs. 18:27). It is used in various metaphors: as a picture of justice running down like abundant waters (Amos 5:24); powers of the underworld (Ps. 18:16[17]); frailty or weakness (Josh. 7:5); distress (Isa. 43:2); sudden violence (Job 27:20; Isa. 28:2, 17; Hos. 2:5[7]); the ephemeral character of things or persons (Job 11:16); God's wrath (Hos. 5:10). Numbers 5:17 speaks of holy water. Running water is "living water" (Lev. 14:5, 6, 50–52; Num. 19:17).

4326. מִיָּמִן ***miyyāmin:*** A proper noun designating Mijamin:

A. A descendant of Aaron (1 Chr. 24:9).

B. A postexilic Jew (Ezra 10:25).

C. A priest (Neh. 10:7[8]).

D. A priest (Neh. 12:5).

4327. מִין ***miyn:*** A masculine noun indicating a kind, a species. It indicates an animal or something that shares common characteristics (Gen. 1:11, 12, 21, 24, 25; 6:20; 7:14; Lev. 11:14–16, 19, 22, 29; Deut. 14:13–15, 18; Ezek. 47:10). It does not equal the modern scientific definition of and the use of species.

4328. מְיֻסָּדָה ***meyussāḏāh:*** A feminine noun denoting a foundation. It is a construction term indicating the bases or underpinnings of a structure

(Ezek. 41:8). In this case, it refers to the foundations of some side chambers or rooms of Ezekiel's visionary temple.

4329. מוּסַךְ ***mûsak̲:*** A masculine noun meaning a covered structure, a canopy. Its exact meaning is unknown, but it is an architectural term probably referring to a covering structure. It may refer to a canopy (NIV); a covered way (NASB); a covert (KJV) (2 Kgs. 16:18).

4330. מִיץ ***miyṣ:*** A masculine noun indicating a churning, a twisting, a stirring. In context it refers to the process that produces butter from milk, i.e., churning, stirring (Prov. 30:33), but the churning of wrath or anger creates dissension and strife.

4331. מֵישָׁא ***mēyšā':*** A proper noun designating Mesha (1 Chr. 8:9).

4332. מִישָׁאֵל ***miyšā'ēl:*** A proper noun designating Mishael:

A. A cousin of Moses (Ex. 6:22; Lev. 10:4).

B. A companion of Daniel (Dan. 1:6, 7, 11, 19).

C. A postexilic Jew (Neh. 8:4).

4333. מִישָׁאֵל ***miyšā'ēl:*** An Aramaic proper noun designating Mishael (Dan. 2:17). It corresponds to the Hebrew 4332,B.

4334. מִישׁוֹר ***miyšôr:*** A masculine noun meaning plain, evenness, straightness, righteousness, equity. Evenness is the fundamental sense of this word. It denotes straight, as opposed to crooked (Isa. 40:4; 42:16); level land, such as a plain (Deut. 3:10; 1 Kgs. 20:23); and a safe, unobstructed path (Ps. 27:11). By analogy, it is likewise used to imply a righteous lifestyle (Ps. 143:10); and equitable leadership (Ps. 45:6[7]; Isa. 11:4).

4335. מֵישַׁךְ ***mēyšak̲:*** A proper noun designating Meshach, the name of one of Daniel's royal Hebrew companions in Babylonian exile (Dan. 1:6, 7). The name is Babylonian and probably means "Who is like Aku?" or "Who is it that is Aku?" Others suggest "I am of little account" (cf. Isa. 39:7).

4336. מֵישַׁךְ ***mēyšak̲:*** A proper noun designating Meshach, the Aramaic form of Hebrew 4335. The meaning is the same.

4337. מֵישָׁע ***mēyšā':*** A proper noun designating Mesha, a son of Caleb (1 Chr. 2:42).

4338. מֵישַׁע ***mēyša':*** A proper noun designating Mesha, a king of Moab (2 Kgs. 3:4).

4339. מֵישָׁר ***mēyšār:*** A masculine noun designating rightness, equity, smoothness. It is found only in the plural. It is used figuratively: a level path of righteousness means a time free of difficulties and injustice (Isa. 26:7). Used of wine, it indicates a smooth flow of wine (Prov. 23:31; Song 7:9[10]). It is used as an adverb to mean justly, rightly (Ps. 17:2; Song

1:4). It is something that wisdom leads to and encourages: it indicates just, right things (Prov. 8:6); what is correct, fair (Prov. 1:3; 2:9); just governments (Ps. 9:8[9]; 58:1[2]; 75:2[3]; 98:9); proper, fair speech or talk (Prov. 23:16; Isa. 33:15). The Lord's promises are upright (Isa. 45:19).

4340. מֵיתָר *mēyṯār:* A masculine noun meaning a cord, a string. It refers to a strong cord or rope-like string: a bowstring, used in a figurative sense (Ps. 21:12[13]); or, especially, tent cords (Ex. 35:18; 39:40; Jer. 10:20). It is used of decorative cords in the Tabernacle (Num. 3:26, 37; 4:26, 32).

4341. מַכְאוֹב *mak'ôḇ:* A masculine noun referring to pain, suffering, sorrow. It depicts pain and suffering born by the Servant of the Lord (Isa. 53:4), who was literally a "man of pain" (Isa. 53:3); of pain inflicted on him. It indicates the pain placed on the Hebrews by the Egyptians and noted by God (Ex. 3:7). Israel brought great pain on herself through her sin (Jer. 30:15; 45:3). Pain and suffering is the lot of humankind (Job 33:19; Ps. 38:17[18]; Eccl. 2:23), but the wicked are especially prone to pain and suffering (Ps. 32:10; Jer. 51:8). Even great knowledge may lead to pain in this age (Eccl. 1:18).

4342. מַכְבִּיר *makḇiyr:* A masculine noun indicating abundance. It indicates a more than adequate amount of something, e.g., food (Job 36:31), as God's gift.

4343. מַכְבֵּנָה *makḇēnāh:* A proper noun designating Machbenah (1 Chr. 2:49).

4344. מַכְבַּנַּי *makḇannay:* A proper noun designating Machbannai (1 Chr. 12:13).

4345. מִכְבָּר *mikḇār:* A masculine noun meaning a grating, a cover. It refers to a structure of interlaced or intertwined metal pieces serving as a cover or grating on the bronze altar (Ex. 27:4; 35:16; 38:4, 5, 30; 39:39).

4346. מַכְבֵּר *makḇēr:* A masculine noun meaning a thick cloth, light blanket. It refers to a blanket, a mat, or possibly netting. In its only use, it covers the face of a dying man (2 Kgs. 8:15).

4347. מַכָּה *makkāh:* A feminine noun meaning a blow, a stroke. When the word carries this literal sense, often a weapon (sword, rod, whip) functions as the instrument by which the blow is delivered. The individual judged to be in the wrong in a legal case could receive as punishment a beating of up to forty blows or lashes (Deut. 25:3). In accordance with the royal edict decreed in the name of Xerxes, King of Persia, the Jews struck down their enemies with the blow of the sword (Esth. 9:5). The Lord declared to Israel and Judah that He had dealt them their blows because their guilt was so great (Jer. 30:14).

Elsewhere, the term signifies the result of a blow: a wound. King Joram rested in Jezreel to recover from wounds incurred in battle against the Arameans (2 Kgs. 9:15). In another battle, King Ahab died of a wound, having been pierced by an arrow (1 Kgs. 22:35; cf. Isa. 1:6; Jer. 6:7; 30:17; Mic. 1:9). In other passages, the word described calamities inflicted by God: affliction, misery, and plague. The Lord solemnly warned Israel that failing to diligently obey His commands would result in His overwhelming them with severe and lasting afflictions (Deut. 28:59, 61). The Philistines remembered that the "gods" of the Hebrews struck the Egyptians with all kinds of miseries (1 Sam. 4:8; cf. Jer. 10:19, 49:17). Finally, the term can convey the sense of defeat or slaughter. Joshua and his fighting men handed the Amorites a great defeat at Gibeon (Josh. 10:10; cf. Josh. 10:20). Samson took revenge on the Philistines, killing many in a terrible slaughter because they had burned his wife and father-in-law (Judg. 15:8; cf. Judg. 11:33; 1 Sam. 4:10; 14:14). This noun is related to the verb *nāḵāh* (5221).

4348. מִכְוָה ***miḵwāh:*** A feminine noun indicating a burn, a burnt spot. It refers to a burn on a person's skin (Lev. 13:24, 25, 28) that could lead to a serious skin disease.

4349. מָכוֹן ***māḵôn:*** I. A masculine noun meaning a dwelling place. It indicates a solid support or structure that can serve as a dwelling or as a foundation for something. It is used of a dwelling place, especially the Lord's, such as Mount Zion or Mount Sinai (Ex. 15:17); the Temple of Solomon (1 Kgs. 8:13); God's heavenly dwelling place (1 Kgs. 8:39, 43, 49; Ps. 33:14). It refers to the entire area of Mount Zion (Isa. 4:5). It refers to the location of the Temple, the holy place (Dan. 8:11). Ezra 2:68 is rendered best as foundation or location (for it see 4350 too).

II. A masculine noun meaning a foundation, a basis. It stands for a support for the Lord's throne of righteousness and justice (Ps. 89:14[15]; 97:2). It is used of the foundation of the earth itself (Ps. 104:5).

4350. מְכוֹנָה ***m^e^ḵônāh,*** מְכֹנָה ***m^e^ḵōnāh:*** A feminine noun indicating a movable base, a stand. It is used of equipment used in the Temple functions; stands (1 Kgs. 7:27, 28, 30, 32, 34, 35, 37; Jer. 27:19; 52:17, 20); or basins (1 Kgs. 7:37–39). It is used to denote the foundations of a structure (Ezra 3:3). It indicates a stand or pedestal (Zech. 5:11).

4351. מְכוּרָה ***m^e^ḵûrāh,*** מְכֹרָה ***m^e^ḵōrāh:*** A feminine noun meaning birth, origin, ancestry. It is used in the singular with *'ereṣ*, land, to indicate the land of a person's or nation's origin (Ezek. 29:14; cf. 16:3; 21:30[35]).

4352. מָכִי ***māḵiy:*** A proper noun designating Machi (Num. 13:15).

4353. מָכִיר ***makiyr:*** A proper noun designating Machir:

A. A son of Ammiel (2 Sam. 9:4, 5; 17:27).

B. A son of Manasseh (Gen. 50:23; Num. 26:29; 27:1; 32:39, 40; 36:1; Deut. 3:15; Josh. 13:31; 17:1, 3; Judg. 5:14; 1 Chr. 2:21, 23; 7:14–17).

4354. מָכִירִי ***mākiyriy:*** A proper noun designating Machirite (Num. 26:29).

4355. מָכַךְ ***mākak:*** A verb meaning to be made low, to sag, to decay. It is used figuratively of sinking into wickedness and iniquity (Ps. 106:43), as Israel often did. It is used of sagging or bent rafters or roofs (Eccl. 10:18). It is used to describe in a metaphor the fall or failure of persons in life (Job 24:24).

4356. מִכְלָאָה ***miklā'āh,*** מִכְלָה ***miklāh:*** A feminine noun depicting an enclosure, a pen. It indicates a closed structure or fencing to contain animals (Ps. 50:9; Hab. 3:17); a place where the great King David labored in his youth (Ps. 78:70).

4357. מִכְלָה ***miklāh:*** A feminine noun indicating perfection, purity. It has a state of near perfection or purity. It is used in combination with *zāhāb*, gold, to indicate purest gold (2 Chr. 4:21).

4358. מִכְלוֹל ***miklôl:*** A masculine noun designating splendor, perfection. It indicates magnificence, completeness with respect to something. In context it is used in reference to splendid or magnificent clothing (Ezek. 23:12). It is used also of the splendid uniforms of an army (Ezek. 38:4).

4359. מִכְלָל ***miklāl:*** A masculine noun meaning perfection. It indicates a state or quality of the highest kind. Used with *yopîy*, beauty, it means perfect (beauty), referring to Zion (Ps. 50:2).

4360. מַכְלוּל ***maklûl:*** A masculine noun meaning perfection, beauty. It indicates fine clothes or garments, a type of merchandise desired by many peoples. It has in mind garments or clothing that was of fine quality, splendid, beautiful (Ezek. 27:24).

4361. מַכֹּלֶת ***makkōlet:*** A feminine noun indicating a food for human consumption. In context it is food made from wheat (1 Kgs. 5:11[25]).

4362. מִכְמָן ***mikmān:*** A masculine noun referring to a hidden treasure. It refers to something stored for safekeeping from common knowledge. In context it denoted a treasure of gold and silver in Egypt (Dan. 11:43).

4363. מִכְמָס ***mikmās,*** מִכְמָשׂ ***mikmāś:*** A proper noun designating Michmash, a village in Benjamin territory. It was the site of a significant battle with the Philistines. Jonathan, Saul's son, proved himself a mighty warrior on this occasion (1 Sam. 13:2—14:31), but the Philistines made a successful counter assault.

The town was resettled by Jews returning from exile in Babylon (Ezra 2:27; Neh. 7:31).

4364. מַכְמֹר **ma<u>k</u>mōr,** מִכְמָר **mi<u>k</u>mār:** A masculine noun meaning net, ensnarement. It refers to a knotted or woven string or a rope fabric for catching birds, fish, or other animals. It is used figuratively of the nets evil persons create (Ps. 141:10); and of God's people caught in the net of exile like animals (Isa. 51:20).

4365. מִכְמֶרֶת **mi<u>k</u>meret,** מִכְמֹרֶת **mi<u>k</u>mōret:** A feminine noun indicating a fishnet, a dragnet. It refers to a net spread out in the waters to catch fish (Isa. 19:8). It is used figuratively to describe the oppressive net that the Babylonians cast on Israel, a net of judgment from God on his people (Hab. 1:15, 16).

4366. מִכְמְתָת **mi<u>k</u>m^etāt:** A proper noun designating Michmethah (Josh. 16:6; 17:7).

4367. מַכְנַדְבַי **ma<u>k</u>nadbay:** A proper noun designating Machnadebai (Ezra 10:40).

4368. מְכֹנָה **m^e<u>k</u>ōnāh:** A proper noun designating Meconah (Neh. 11:28).

4369. מְכֻנָה **m^e<u>k</u>unāh:** A feminine noun meaning a pedestal, a base. It is a form of *m^e<u>k</u>ōnāh*. See 4350. It refers to a stand or platform on which to live or stand (Zech. 5:11).

4370. מִכְנָס **mi<u>k</u>nās:** A masculine noun designating breeches, underwear. These were trousers or breeches for the priests, a garment for the hips and thighs (Ex. 28:42; 39:28; Lev. 6:10[3]; 16:4; Ezek. 44:18).

4371. מֶכֶס **mekes:** A masculine noun meaning tribute, tax. It indicates a portion or levy of booty or spoil taken in war to go to the priests (Num. 31:28, 37–41).

4372. מִכְסֶה **mi<u>k</u>seh:** A masculine noun indicating a covering. It refers to something used to shelter, protect, or enclose an object, such as Noah's ark or the Tent of Meeting or Tabernacle (Gen. 8:13; Ex. 26:14; 35:11). The covering of the Tabernacle was made double of ram's skins and porpoise skins.

4373. מִכְסָה **mi<u>k</u>sāh:** A feminine noun meaning an evaluation, a number, worth. It is used as a record of the number of persons in an Israelite family (Ex. 12:4); or the actual agreed upon evaluation or worth of a piece of land (Lev. 27:23).

4374. מְכַסֶּה **m^ekasseh:** A masculine noun indicating a covering, clothes. It is used of the fatty tissue (omentum) covering the entrails of animals of sacrifice (Lev. 9:19). It is used metaphorically of worms crawling over a person in Sheol (Isa. 14:11). It indicates the clothing or covering the Lord confiscated from Tyre for His people (Isa. 23:18; Ezek. 27:7).

4375. מַכְפֵּלָה *makpēlāh:* A proper noun designating Machpelah, the cave in which the patriarchs were buried with their wives. Abraham purchased it from the Hittites, from a man named Ephron in the land of Canaan. It was located in Hebron near Mamre (Gen. 23:9–19; 25:9; 49:30; 50:13).

4376. מָכַר *mākar:* A verb meaning to sell. It is a basic verb of exchange; the selling of the right of the firstborn by Esau (Gen. 25:31); land (Gen. 47:20); cattle (Ex. 21:35); oil (2 Kgs. 4:7); even persons were sold (Gen. 31:15); sometimes persons or slaves were sold (Gen. 37:27, 28; Ex. 21:8); often persons captured in battle (Deut. 21:14). It is used in a figurative sense of selling an abstract quality like wisdom or truth (Prov. 23:23). It has the nuanced sense of handing over, surrendering something: God may give up His people (1 Sam. 12:9); or a person (Judg. 4:9). It is used of persons selling themselves (Lev. 25:47, 48); or letting oneself be sold (Deut. 28:68). Used with *le* plus *'ebed*, it indicates being sold as a slave (Ps. 105:17); with *la'aśôt*, it may mean, in its reflexive use, to sell oneself to do evil (1 Kgs. 21:20, 25; 2 Kgs. 17:17).

4377. מֶכֶר *meker:* A masculine noun referring to merchandise, a price, worth. It indicates purchase money or whatever the price for a purchase is (Num. 20:19; Prov. 31:10). Preceded by *kōl,* the phrase indicates merchandise of any kind (Neh. 13:16). The word is rendered as rubies, jewels specifically, in Proverbs 31:10 by many translators.

4378. מַכָּר *makkār:* I. A masculine noun denoting an acquaintance, a friend. It indicates a person from whom something is officially received, such as a special levy for the repair of the Temple (2 Kgs. 12:5[6], 7[8]).

II. A masculine noun meaning treasurer. It designates a person who collected a special levy of money for the repair of the Temple (2 Kgs. 12:5[6], 7[8]).

4379. מִכְרֶה *mikreh:* A masculine noun designating a pit of salt. It indicates a location where salt was mined or where it was located; in context a metaphorical feature of the land of Moab following its destruction (Zeph. 2:9).

4380. מְכֵרָה *mekērāh:* I. A feminine noun referring to a sword. In context its meaning is difficult, but it may be rendered as swords (Gen. 49:5).

II. A feminine noun designating a dwelling, a habitation. It is rendered by some translations as a dwelling, a habitation; perhaps houses, i.e., biological groups is meant (Gen. 49:5).

4381. מִכְרִי *mikriy:* A proper noun designating Michri (1 Chr. 9:8).

4382. מְכֵרָתִי *mekērātiy:* A proper noun designating Mecherathite (1 Chr. 11:36).

4383. מִכְשׁוֹל *mikšôl:* A masculine noun meaning a stumbling block, an obstacle. Sometimes the term refers to something an individual can literally stumble over. For instance, the Lord commanded the people of Israel not to put a stumbling block before the blind (Lev. 19:14). More often, however, it is used in a figurative sense. The Lord Himself will become the obstacle over which both houses of Israel will stumble (Isa. 8:14). Much later in Isaiah, it is written that the Lord will demand that the obstacle be removed from His people's way (Isa. 57:14). In other places, the word refers to that which causes people to stumble morally, that is, to sin: gold and silver (Ezek. 7:19); idols (Ezek. 14:3); the Levites (Ezek. 44:12). In other places, the term describes something that causes people to fall to their ruin. Because of Israel's persistent rejection of God's Law, He laid a stumbling block before them so they would trip and perish (Jer. 6:21; cf. Ps. 119:165; Ezek. 3:20; 18:30). This term is derived from the verb *kāšal* (3782).

4384. מַכְשֵׁלָה *makšēlāh:* A feminine noun meaning a heap of rubble, ruins. Isaiah prophesied to the people of Judah that because of their rebellion against the Lord, He was going to desolate their land so thoroughly that they would soon search for leaders to care for them and for the ruins of what remained, yet find none (Isa. 3:6). This noun stems from the verb *kāšal* (3782).

4385. מִכְתָּב *miktāb:* A masculine noun designating writing, something written. It is used of God's actual writing on the two stone tablets (Ex. 32:16); the engraving on the high priest's golden plate or crown that he wore (Ex. 39:30). With the preposition b^e, it means in writing (Deut. 10:4). It designates an entire written letter or document (2 Chr. 21:12; Isa. 38:9); a set of instructions or directives (2 Chr. 35:4); or a royal decree or proclamation (2 Chr. 36:22).

4386. מְכִתָּה *mekittāh:* A feminine noun meaning a bursting, a shattering. It is used of the shattered pieces of a smashed potter's vessel (Isa. 30:14).

4387. מִכְתָּם *miktām:* A masculine noun naming a certain kind of psalm, Michtam. It is a technical musical term whose meaning is uncertain. It is found in the titles of psalms. Words like inscription, epigrammatic (terse, witty, wisdom-like), wisdom psalm apply.

4388. מַכְתֵּשׁ *maktēš:* A masculine noun referring to a depression, a hollow in a jawbone or mortar bowl. It is used of a hollow place in a jawbone where the molar tooth was (Judg. 15:19) and indicates by extension the depression in a mortar bowl. In the case of Judges 15:19, it is probably used figuratively of a depression in the ground that resembled the molar cavity of a jawbone.

4389. מַכְתֵּשׁ ***ma<u>k</u>tēš:*** I. A proper noun designating Maktesh (KJV, Zeph. 1:11).

II. A proper noun designating Mortar (NASB, Zeph. 1:11).

III. A masculine noun meaning market district (NIV, Zeph. 1:11).

4390. מָלֵא ***mālē':*** A verb meaning to fill, to be full, to be complete, to fulfill, to finish, to satisfy. This word occurs 251 times in the Old Testament and functions both in a spatial and temporal sense. Spatially, the term pictures the act of making that which was empty of a particular content no longer so. It can also express that state of being in which a certain container is holding to capacity a particular object or objects. God commanded the water creatures to fill the seas (Gen. 1:22); and humanity to fill the earth (Gen. 1:28). Elijah directed the people to fill four water jars; the trench was also filled (1 Kgs. 18:34, 35). The word can also function in an abstract way: Judah filled the land with violence (Ezek. 8:17; cf. Lev. 19:29; Jer. 51:5). Theologically, the glory of the Lord filled the Temple (1 Kgs. 8:10, 11; cf. Isa. 6:1); and Jeremiah declared that God fills heaven and earth (Jer. 23:24). Temporally, the term refers to the completion of a specified segment of time. According to the Law, a woman who had given birth to a boy could not enter the sanctuary until the thirty-three days of her blood purification were completed (Lev. 12:4). The Lord promised to establish King David's kingdom after his days were fulfilled (i.e., he died: 2 Sam. 7:12; cf. Lam. 4:18).

A final important use of the word entails the keeping of a vow or promise. The Lord fulfilled His promise to David that his son would build a house for His name (2 Chr. 6:4, 15; cf. 2 Sam. 7:12; 1 Kgs. 2:27; 2 Chr. 36:21).

4391. מְלָא ***m^elā':*** An Aramaic verb meaning to fill, to be filled. It means to take up empty space, to make something full. In the book of Daniel, a stone fills the whole earth in a figurative sense (Dan. 2:35). It is used of a person's being full of anger (Dan. 3:19).

4392. מָלֵא ***mālē':*** An adjective meaning full, filled. It is used to qualify various items as full, ripe, grown: ears of corn (Gen. 41:7, 22); vessels (2 Kgs. 4:4); a full (shiny or powerful) wind of judgment (figurative use) (Jer. 4:12); full or complete value or price (Gen. 23:9). A full woman is a pregnant woman (Eccl. 11:5). It is used in an idiomatic sense of a family: children, husband, wife (Ruth 1:21). Used in the absolute state with accompanying words, it means full of, strewn with (2 Kgs. 7:15); full of God's anger or wrath (Jer. 6:11). It may come after its accompanying word and still mean full of, e.g., full of shoutings (Isa. 22:2). As a predicate adjective, it means full (Eccl. 1:7). It is used many more times in a figurative sense of being full of blessings (Deut. 33:23); wisdom (Deut. 34:9;

Ezek. 28:12); justice (Isa. 1:21); confusion (Isa. 22:2); lies (Nah. 3:1).

4393. מְלֹא m^elō', מְלוֹא m^elô', מְלוֹ m^elô: A masculine noun referring to what fills, makes full, fullness; abundance. It depicts in general what fills something up or out: fullness of a hand, a handful, *m^elo' kāp,* (1 Kgs. 17:12); an omer-full of manna (Ex. 16:33); a lap full or skirt full (2 Kgs. 4:39). It can be an added assertion meaning, and fullness (*ûm^{e}lō'ô*), e.g., of the seas and its fullness (Isa. 42:10); the land or earth and its fullness (Deut. 33:16). It indicates the multitude or abundance of nations (Gen. 48:19); or a (large) band or troop of shepherds (Isa. 31:4). In 1 Samuel 28:20, it has the sense of full length, full-standing height; the whole of Saul's huge bodily frame fell.

4394. מִלֻּא millu', מִלּוּא millû': A masculine noun designating a setting, a mounting; an ordination. It refers to the surrounding and enclosing metal environment in which jewels were set (Ex. 25:7; 35:9, 27). But it also extends its meaning to placing a priest in office; his ordination, consecration, installation by a special ordination, filling, offering (Ex. 29:22; Lev. 7:37; 8:22, etc.).

4395. מְלֵאָה m^elē'āh: A feminine noun meaning fall harvest, a produce of grain. It is used to indicate the fullness or best quality of the harvest in the fall (Ex. 22:29[28]; Deut. 22:9) of grain or wine (Num. 18:27).

4396. מִלֻּאָה millu'āh: A feminine noun referring to a filling, a setting (of gem stones). It describes a prepared location by a jeweler for precious stones (Ex. 25:7; 28:17, 20; 39:13), but see 4394 also.

4397. מַלְאָךְ mal'āk: A masculine noun meaning a messenger, an angel. The term often denotes one sent on business or diplomacy by another (human) personage. Jacob sent messengers on ahead to his brother Esau in the hope of finding favor in his eyes (Gen. 32:3[4], 6[7]). The elders of Jabesh sent messengers throughout Israel in a desperate attempt to locate someone who could rescue their town from the dire threat of the Ammonites (1 Sam. 11:3, 4, 9; cf. 2 Sam. 11:19; 1 Kgs. 19:2; 2 Kgs. 5:10). Very often, the term referred to messengers sent from God. Sometimes these were human messengers, whether prophets (Isa. 44:26; Hag. 1:13; Mal. 3:1); priests (Eccl. 5:6[5]; Mal. 2:7); or the whole nation of Israel (Isa. 42:19). More often, however, the term referred to heavenly beings who often assumed human form (Gen. 19:1; Judg. 13:6, 15, 16) and appeared to people as bearers of the Lord's commands and tidings (Judg. 6:11, 12; 13:3). They were often responsible for aiding, protecting, and fighting for those who trusted in the Lord (Gen. 24:7; Ex. 23:20; 33:2; 1 Kgs. 19:5; Ps. 34:7[8]; 91:11). They also acted as instruments of divine judgment, meting out punishment on the rebellious and the guilty

(2 Sam. 24:16, 17; Ps. 35:5, 6; 78:49; Isa. 37:36). Sometimes the angel of the Lord and his message are so closely identified with the Lord Himself that the text simply refers to the angel as "the Lord" or "God" (Gen. 16:7; 22:11; 31:11; Ex. 3:2; Judg. 13:18; cf. Gen. 16:13; 22:12; 31:13, 16; Ex. 3:4; Judg. 6:22; 13:22).

4398. מַלְאַךְ ***mal'ak̲:*** An Aramaic noun meaning angel (Dan. 3:28; 6:22[23]). The word is a cognate of the Hebrew noun *mal'āk̲* (4397).

4399. מְלָאכָה ***m***^{e}***lā'k̲āh:*** A feminine singular noun meaning work, occupation, business, something made, property, workmanship. This word is used for God's creative work (Gen. 2:2, 3); as well as for human labor (Ex. 20:9, 10); skilled craftsmanship (Lev. 13:48); and agricultural tasks (1 Chr. 27:26). It is used for livestock (Gen. 33:14); property (Ex. 22:8[7]); public and religious business. For instance, Ezra 10:13 employs the term in reference to the divorce of foreign wives.

4400. מַלְאֲכוּת ***mal'āk̲ûṯ:*** A feminine noun meaning message. This word is used only once in the Old Testament, where it described Haggai's message from the Lord (Hag. 1:13). This word is related to the common noun *mal'āk* (4397), meaning messenger, which is also used in Haggai 1:13.

4401. מַלְאָכִי ***mal'āk̲iy:*** A proper noun designating Malachi, the name traditionally given to the prophet of the book that bears his name. Some scholars think that the word, which means "my messenger," was not a personal name but a title.

4402. מִלֵּאת ***millē'ṯ:*** A feminine noun indicating fullness, appropriateness. It is usually rendered as a setting, a mounting location in an appropriate setting; "eyes mounted like jewels" (Song 5:12 NIV).

4403. מַלְבּוּשׁ ***malbûš:*** A masculine noun designating clothing, robes, attire. It always refers to some type of clothing: luxurious, costly garments understood figuratively of God's blessings on Jerusalem (1 Kgs. 10:5; 2 Chr. 9:4; Ezek. 16:13); foreign garments (Zeph. 1:8); working clothes as the blood-stained garments of the Lord as a warrior (Isa. 63:3). These items could also be counted as wealth (Job 27:16).

4404. מַלְבֵּן ***malbēn:*** A masculine noun meaning a brick kiln, brickwork. It designates a mold for setting bricks (2 Sam. 12:31; Nah. 3:14). It is used of the brick floor in Pharaoh's palace in Egypt (Jer. 43:9).

4405. מִלָּה ***millāh:*** A feminine singular noun meaning word, speech, utterance. It is the poetic equivalent of *dāb̲ār* (1697), carrying the same range of meaning (2 Sam. 23:2; Ps. 19:4[5]; 139:4; Prov. 23:9). Of its thirty-eight uses in the Hebrew portion of the Old Testament, Job contains thirty-four (see concordance for references).

4406. מִלָּה ***millāh:*** An Aramaic feminine noun meaning word, command, matter. This word, used only in Daniel, is equivalent to the Hebrew word *millāh* (4405), meaning word or speech, and comes from the Hebrew verb *mālal* (4448), meaning to speak or say. This word is used to describe words that were spoken (Dan. 4:31[28]; 7:11, 25), which, depending on the context, can be translated as command (Dan. 2:5; 3:22; 5:10). Often this word described an entire series of circumstances or matters (Dan. 2:9–11; 4:33[30]; 7:1).

4407. מִלּוֹא ***millô':*** I. A proper noun referring to the citadel in Jerusalem. It was a man-made construction built onto a terrace and was simply called a citadel or a fortress (2 Sam. 5:9). It was expanded in David and Solomon's reigns (1 Kgs. 9:15; 11:27; 2 Kgs. 12:20[21]; 1 Chr. 11:8; 2 Chr. 32:5).

II. A masculine noun referring to supporting terraces. Some prefer to translate the word this way. See references listed here and above in I.

III. A proper noun referring to the city of Millo, a small town near Shechem. It is preceded by the word *beyṯ;* hence, its full rendering is *beyṯ-millo,* house of Milo (Judg. 9:6, 20).

4408. מַלּוּחַ ***mallûaḥ:*** A masculine noun meaning mallow, herbs growing in salt marshes. A food eaten by the poor and destitute, it was a salty plant (Job 30:4).

4409. מַלּוּךְ ***mallûḵ,*** מַלּוּכִי ***mallûḵiy:*** A proper noun designating Malluch:

A. A son of Hashabiah (1 Chr. 6:44[29]).

B. A priest (Neh. 12:2).

C. A son of Bani (Ezra 10:29).

D. A son of Harim (Ezra 10:32).

E. A covenanter (Neh. 10:4[5]).

4410. מְלוּכָה ***m^elûḵāh:*** A feminine noun meaning a kingdom, royalty. It designates the position or authority of a king as well as kingship in general (1 Kgs. 2:15). It is found in various expressions: with *'aśāh* plus *'al* to mean to rule over, to exercise kingship (1 Kgs. 21:7); to announce or proclaim kingship, *qārā'* is found (Isa. 34:12); the justice or ruling principle of kingship is expressed by *mišpaṭ hamm^elûḵāh* (1 Sam. 10:25); *kissē' hamm^elûḵāh* means the throne of the kingship or kingdom (1 Kgs. 1:46). The Lord bestowed rulership in Israel (2 Sam. 16:8). It is used figuratively of Jerusalem attaining rulership (Ezek. 16:13). A city of rulership is a royal city (2 Sam. 12:26). Isaiah 62:3 speaks of Zion's being a royal diadem. The expression seed of royalty refers to the royal family or dynasty (2 Kgs. 25:25; Jer. 41:1; Ezek. 17:13; Dan. 1:3).

4411. מָלוֹן ***mālôn:*** A masculine noun defining an inn, a lodging. It is used of a temporary place to stay, usually for a night (Gen. 42:27; 43:21; Ex. 4:24; 2 Kgs. 19:23; Isa. 10:29; Jer. 9:2[1]). It may mean simply a place in the open to sleep overnight (Josh. 4:3, 8).

4412. מְלוּנָה ***mᵉlûnāh:*** A feminine noun indicating a cottage or a hut. It was a shack or makeshift structure for those who guarded the fields at night (Isa. 1:8; 24:20).

4413. מַלּוֹתִי ***mallôṯiy:*** A proper noun designating Mallothi (1 Chr. 25:4, 26).

4414. מָלַח ***mālaḥ:*** I. A verb meaning to salt, to season. It described the application of salt as a seasoning to various things: on a cereal or tribute offering (Lev. 2:13); on a newborn child (Ezek. 16:4). In a passive sense, it is used of something being salted, such as incense (Ex. 30:35).

II. A verb meaning to tear away, to dissipate, to vanish. It indicates the dissipation or drifting away of the sky or heavens like smoke disappearing (Isa. 51:6).

4415. מְלַח ***mᵉlaḥ:*** An Aramaic verb meaning to be in service. It means to pay with salt, to supply one's needs. Both the noun and verb occur in Ezra 4:14, literally, "We are salted [paid] by the salt of the palace."

4416. מְלַח ***mᵉlaḥ:*** An Aramaic masculine noun referring to salt. It was an important condiment and preservative in ancient times and of great value. It was used in payment (barter) for trading or services rendered (Ezra 4:14). It was used in some sacrifices (Ezra 6:9; 7:22).

4417. מֶלַח ***melaḥ:*** A masculine noun designating salt. It was an important condiment (Job 6:6) and preservative in ancient times and of great value in itself and for trading and bartering. It was used to purify water (2 Kgs. 2:20, 21) but also was scattered on the ground of a city to be destroyed (Judg. 9:45). The Dead Sea is literally, the Salt Sea, (Gen. 14:3). It occurred naturally in pits (Zeph. 2:9). Lot's wife became a pillar of salt (Gen. 19:26). It was used to season various offerings (Lev. 2:13; Ezek. 43:24). A covenant of salt was a permanent feature of some offerings (Num. 18:19; 2 Chr. 13:5). It will be a feature of a restored temple and Zion (Ezek. 47:11).

4418. מֶלַח ***melaḥ:*** A masculine noun meaning rag. It indicates a torn cloth or even scraps of clothing (Jer. 38:11, 12). In context rags were made into a rope and used to rescue Jeremiah.

4419. מַלָּח ***mallāḥ:*** A masculine noun referring to a sailor, a mariner. It is used of the seamen of the merchant vessels of the city of Tyre (Ezek. 27:9, 27, 29). They would all be judged with Tyre.

4420. מְלֵחָה ***mᵉlēḥāh:*** A feminine noun referring to saltiness, barrenness. It indicates the barren, open desert as a home for the wild donkey

(Job 39:6). It indicates that a land is not fruitful (Ps. 107:34); and harbors little, if any, life (Jer. 17:6).

4421. מִלְחָמָה ***milḥāmāh:*** A feminine noun meaning war, battle. It indicates a formal military combat declared and engaged in by peoples and nations. The Lord was a "man of war" on behalf of His people (Ex. 15:3); a mighty one of battle (Ps. 24:8); the one in charge of the battle (1 Sam. 17:47; Ps. 76:3[4]); for they were His battles (1 Sam. 18:17). It was a general term for battle, war, fighting (Gen. 14:8; Ex. 1:10; 1 Sam. 17:1; 31:3; 1 Kgs. 20:14). It refers to the place of war, a battlefield (1 Sam. 14:20). A soldier would be a man of war, a warrior (1 Sam. 16:18; Isa. 3:2). The host of the armies is indicated by the phrase *ṣᵉb̲āʾ milḥāmāh* (Num. 31:14; Isa. 13:4). Various verbs are used with the noun: *ʿārak̲,* get ready for battle (Judg. 20:22); *qārab̲,* to join into battle (1 Kgs. 20:29); *ʿāśāh,* to make war (Prov. 20:18; 24:6).

4422. מָלַט ***mālaṭ:*** A verb meaning to escape. The picture of escape is as sparks leaping out of the fire (Job 41:19[11]); or like a bird escaping the fowlers (Ps. 124:7). This word is usually used within the context of fleeing for one's life as Lot was urged to do (Gen. 19:17, 19, 20, 22); as David did from the hands of Saul (1 Sam. 19:10–12; 27:1); or as Zedekiah could not do when facing the Chaldeans (Jer. 32:4; 34:3). It is also used to describe rescue from death (Esth. 4:13; Ps. 89:48[49]; Amos 2:14, 15); calamity (Job 1:15–17, 19); or punishment (Prov. 11:21; 19:5; 28:26). In a few instances, the word is used to describe protection (Eccl. 9:15; Isa. 31:5); in one instance, it means to give birth to a child (Isa. 66:7).

4423. מֶלֶט ***meleṭ:*** A masculine noun meaning clay, mortar. A building material that could be dug up or into; hence, it refers to clay flooring or grout (Jer. 43:9).

4424. מְלַטְיָה ***mᵉlaṭyāh:*** A proper noun designating Melatiah (Neh. 3:7).

4425. מְלִילָה ***mᵉlīylāh:*** A feminine noun that designates a kernel, an ear of grain, or a head of grain. It is mentioned as a head or heads of grain in a field of standing grain (Deut. 23:25[26], NASB). The word is rendered kernels by other translators (NIV).

4426. מְלִיצָה ***mᵉlīyṣāh:*** A feminine noun referring to a literary style, literary device, or genre, a parable, a taunting song, a mocking expression, an aphorism. It is rendered as proverb often (Prov. 1:6, NASB, NIV) and stands in a close relationship to the Hebrew *māšāl* (4912), figure, parable.

4427. מָלַךְ ***mālak̲:*** A verb meaning to rule, to be king, to make king. The verb is used approximately three hundred times in its simple form to mean to rule, to be king, to have sway, power, and dominion over people and nations. God is King and will rule over the whole earth in the day when He judges the earth and establishes Mount Zion (Isa. 24:23). Israel rejected God from ruling over them during the time of Samuel (1 Sam. 8:7; cf. Ezek. 20:33); the verb is used to proclaim the rulership of a king when he is installed, as when Adonijah prematurely attempted to usurp the throne of his father David (1 Kgs. 1:11). The Lord reigns as the Lord Almighty over both earthly and divine subjects (Isa. 24:23; Mic. 4:7).

The verb also describes the rulership of human kings—the establishment of rulership and the process itself (Gen. 36:31; Judg. 9:8; Prov. 30:22). It describes the rule of Athaliah the queen over Judah for six years (2 Kgs. 11:3). In the causative form, it depicts the installation of a king. It describes God's establishment of Saul as the first king over Israel (1 Sam. 15:35). Hosea 8:4 indicates that the Israelites had set up kings without the Lord's approval.

4428. מֶלֶךְ ***melek:*** A masculine noun meaning king. The feminine form is *malkāh* (4436), meaning queen, though the concept is more of a king's consort than a monarchical ruler. The word *melek* appears over 2,500 times in the Old Testament. In many biblical contexts, this term is simply a general term, denoting an individual with power and authority. It is parallel with and conceptually related to a number of other Hebrew words that are usually translated as lord, captain, prince, chief, or ruler. It is used in reference to men and often with a genitive of people or place (Gen. 14:1; Ex. 1:15; 2 Sam. 2:4); the Lord who demonstrates His power and authority over Israel (Isa. 41:21; 44:6); and over each individual (Ps. 5:2[3]; 44:4[5]). In pagan worship, the worshipers of idols attribute this term with its connotations to their idols (Isa. 8:21; Amos 5:26).

4429. מֶלֶךְ ***melek,*** הַמֶּלֶךְ ***hammelek:*** A proper noun designating Melech, Hammelech (1 Chr. 8:35; 9:41; Jer. 36:26; 38:6).

4430. מֶלֶךְ ***melek:*** An Aramaic masculine noun meaning king. This very common word is equivalent to the Hebrew word *melek* (4428), meaning king. It is used to speak of the top government official. It is used to speak of the following kings: Artaxerxes (Ezra 4:8 ff.); Darius (Ezra 5:6ff; Dan. 6:2[3] ff.); Cyrus (Ezra 5:13 ff.); Nebuchadnezzar (Dan. 2:4 ff.); Belshazzar (Dan. 5:1 ff.); kings that will arise on the earth (Dan. 7:17, 24).

4431. מְלַךְ ***mᵉlak:*** An Aramaic masculine noun meaning counsel, advice. It is used of instructions, exhortations, or counsel given to someone (Dan. 4:27[24]).

4432. מֹלֶךְ ***mōlek:*** A proper noun designating Molech, a pagan god of the Ammorites to whom, among other things, children were sacrificed (Num. 18:21; Amos 5:26). The name means "king," and possibly the consonants were combined with the vowels of the Hebrew word *bōšeṯ* (1322) "shame" to produce Molech. Manasseh may have sacrificed his sons to this god to avert the horrors of warfare (2 Kgs. 23:10). Solomon was reduced to recognize this god (1 Kgs. 11:7).

4433. מַלְכָּה malkāh: An Aramaic feminine noun meaning queen. This word, equivalent to the Hebrew word *malkāh* (4436), is used twice in Daniel 5:10. It designated the proper title of the wife of the king. Scholars disagree as to whether she was the wife or the mother of the last king of the neo-Babylonian Empire, Belshazzar.

4434. מַלְכֹּדֶת malkōḏeṯ: A feminine noun meaning a trap, a snare, a noose. This word is found only in Job 18:10. In his disputation with Job, Bildad the Shuhite used the word to describe the pitfalls that lay before the wicked.

4435. מִלְכָּה milkāh: A proper noun designating Milcah:

A. The wife of Nahor (Gen. 11:29; 22:20, 23; 24:15, 24, 47).

B. The daughter of Zelophehad (Num. 26:33; 27:1; 36:11; Josh. 17:3).

4436. מַלְכָּה malkāh: A feminine noun meaning queen. The noun means queen exclusively, but the queen stands in several possible social positions. The queen is often merely the wife of the king; she was, for example, subordinate to the king, and was expected to do his bidding (Esth. 1:11, 12, 16, 17). She also had much court authority herself (Esth. 1:9). The only time the word is used to apply to Israelite women is in the plural, and they were part of Solomon's harem (Song 6:8, 9).

The term means queen without stressing the spousal relationship to the king, but it is not used in this way of any Israelite woman in the time of the monarchy. The queen of Sheba, from southwest Arabia, was a powerful monarch in her own right, traveled extensively (1 Kgs. 10:1, 10), and was considered a wise woman and ruler (2 Chr. 9:1). Esther became queen in Persia because of her beauty but won over the king by gaining his approval and favor (see Esth. 2:17, 18).

4437. מַלְכוּ malkû: An Aramaic feminine noun meaning royalty, reign, kingdom, kingly authority. This word, corresponding to the word *malkûṯ* (4438), distinguishes the propriety of royalty from all else (e.g., Dan. 5:20). It is used to denote the reign of a particular sovereign (Dan. 6:28[29]); the extent of a king's authority (Ezra 7:13); the territorial or administrative dominion of a monarch (Dan. 6:3[4]); the nation or kingdom in a general sense (Dan 5:31[6:1]).

4438. מַלְכוּת malkûṯ: A feminine noun meaning royalty, reign, dominion, kingdom. This term chiefly describes that which pertains to royalty or the natural outflow of power from the royal station. The book of Esther especially illustrates how this word is used to distinguish the royal from the ordinary, speaking of royal wine (Esth. 1:7); a royal command (Esth. 1:19); and royal clothing (Esth. 5:1). It is specifically used to signify the reign of a monarch (2 Chr. 15:10; Dan. 1:1); and the kingdom or territorial realm under the authority of a particular sovereign (1 Chr. 12:23 [24]; 2 Chr. 11:17; Dan. 10:13).

4439. מַלְכִּיאֵל ***malkiy'ēl:*** A proper noun designating Malchiel (Gen. 46:17; Num. 26:45; 1 Chr. 7:31).

4440. מַלְכִּיאֵלִי ***malkiy'ēliy:*** A proper noun designating Malchielites (Num. 26:45).

4441. מַלְכִּיָּה ***malkiyyāh,*** מַלְכִּיָּהוּ ***malkiyyahû:*** A proper noun designating Melchizedek (Gen. 14:18; Ps. 110:4).

4442. מַלְכִּי־צֶדֶק ***malkiy ṣeḏeq:*** A proper noun designating Melchizedek, the king and high priest of Salem (Jerusalem). The name means "king of righteousness" or "the king is righteous." Abraham paid a tithe of his spoils to this Canaanite priest of the Most High God. David and then Christ were "King-Priest" after the manner of Melchizadek. Neither his birth or death, mother or father were recorded, although he was born, died, and had parents.

4443. מַלְכִּירָם ***malkiyrām:*** A proper noun designating Malchiram (1 Chr. 3:18).

4444. מַלְכִּישׁוּעַ ***malkiyšûa',*** מַלְכִּי שׁוּעַ ***malkiy šûa':*** A proper noun designating Malchi-shua (1 Sam. 14:49; 31:2; 1 Chr. 8:33; 9:39; 10:2).

4445. מִלְכֹּם ***milkōm,*** מַלְכָּם ***malkām:*** I. A proper noun, Malcham, a Benjaminite. He is listed as a descendant of Shaharaim in the land of Moab (1 Chr. 8:9).

II. A proper noun designating Malcam, Molech, a false god. It designates Milcom as the idol of the Ammonites (1 Kgs. 11:5, 33; 2 Kgs. 23:13). It is rendered as Milcom in Zephaniah 1:5. In Jeremiah 49:1, 3, it is ambiguous. Some prefer to translate it as Molech (NIV), some as Malcam (NASB), and some as king (KJV). The preferred Hebrew text reads Malcam.

4446. מְלֶכֶת ***m^{e}leḵet:*** A feminine noun meaning queen. Rather than being just another term for a female regent, this word's significance is found in the chronicle of Judah's idolatry. It is used solely to designate a fertility goddess worshiped in Jeremiah's day, the queen of the heavens (*m^{e}leḵet haššāmayim*[8064]). Although the references are cryptic, it is believed that this queen of the heavens was either the goddess Ashtoreth, symbolized by the moon, or Astarte, symbolized by the planet Venus. Women baked cakes to offer to this goddess (Jer. 7:18) and burned incense (Jer. 44:17–19) in hopes of securing the blessings of fertility. However, the judgment of the

Lord on this practice made it counterproductive (cf. Jer. 44:25ff.).

4447. הַמֹּלֶכֶת ***hammōleḵeṯ:*** A proper noun designating Hamoleketh (1 Chr. 7:18).

4448. מָלַל ***mālal:*** A verb meaning to speak, to say, to declare, to utter. Except for an occurance found in Proverbs 6:13 (a wicked man "speaks"[that is, gives a sign] with his feet), the verb is utilized mostly with the intensive stem. Sarah said, "Who would have said to Abraham that Sarah would nurse children?" (Gen. 21:7). Elihu stated that his lips would utter upright knowledge to Job (Job 33:3; cf. Job 8:2). The psalmist exclaimed that no one can declare the mighty acts of God (Ps. 106:2). The term compares closely in meaning with the Hebrew verb *dāḇar* (1696).

4449. מְלַל ***m^elal:*** An Aramaic verb meaning to speak. All undisputed instances of this term occur in the Aramaic sections of the book of Daniel. In Daniel's vision of the four beasts, the fourth beast had a little horn upon which was a mouth speaking arrogantly (Dan. 7:8, 11, 20). This horn (symbolic of a king) spoke words against the Most High (Dan. 7:25). This term is closely related to the Hebrew verb *mālal* (4448).

4450. מִלֲלַי ***mil^alay:*** A proper noun designating Milalai (Neh. 12:36).

4451. מַלְמָד ***malmāḏ:*** A masculine noun indicating an oxgoad. It was a farming tool used to make an ox work more effectively, but Shamgar used it as a weapon (Judg. 3:31).

4452. מָלַץ ***mālaṣ:*** A verb meaning to be sweet, smooth, slippery. It means for something to be delightful, agreeable. In context God's words of Torah are satisfying (Ps. 119:103).

4453. מֶלְצַר ***melṣar:*** A masculine proper noun, Meltzar. It identifies a person as an overseer, someone in authority over designated areas or persons (Dan. 1:11, 16).

4454. מָלַק ***mālaq:*** A verb meaning to wring off. It describes the pinching off, removing of the head of a bird. The birds in context then serve as a burnt offering (Lev. 1:15) or guilt offering (Lev. 5:8). In the latter case, its head was not entirely severed. Rather, its head was nipped.

4455. מַלְקוֹחַ ***malqôaḥ:*** I. A masculine noun indicating booty, prey. It is used in context of the spoils of war or political or military intrigue (Num. 31:11, 12, 26, 27, 32; Isa. 49:24, 25).

II. A masculine noun referring to a jaw, a palate. It has in mind the inside of a person's mouth, the inner part of the cheek or palate (Ps. 22:15[16]).

4456. מַלְקוֹשׁ ***malqôš:*** A masculine noun referring to a latter or spring rain. In Israel it designates the rain that fell in the spring season in our months of March and April (Deut. 11:14; Zech. 10:1). It was a time of joy to see this refreshing rain on its way (Prov. 16:15).

4457. מֶלְקָחַיִם ***melqāḥayim,*** מַלְקָחַיִם ***malqāḥayim:*** A masculine dual noun meaning tongs, snuffers. A dual noun describing an instrument used to put out the flames of lamps and lamp wicks. Usually there was a pair of snuffers (Ex. 25:38; 37:23; Num. 4:9; 1 Kgs. 7:49; 2 Chr. 4:21). These tongs were used to remove coals from the altar as well (Isa. 6:6).

4458. מֶלְתָּחָה ***meltāḥāh:*** A feminine noun depicting a wardrobe or storeroom. It was a supply of garments or clothing (2 Kgs. 10:22). In this case, it refers to an inventory of pagan priestly garments worn by the priests of Baal.

4459. מַלְתָּעוֹת ***maltā'ôṯ:*** A feminine plural noun meaning jaws, jaw teeth, fangs; a transposed form of *m^e^ṯal'ṯô*. It refers to the location of the wicked's teeth in context, the jaw bones or in general the mouth (Ps. 58:6[7]).

4460. מַמְּגוּרָה ***mamm^e^gûrāh:*** A feminine noun meaning barn, granary. It has in mind a storage building or area; a storage barn (Joel 1:17). Some suggest grain pit as a more accurate designation.

4461. מֵמַד ***mēmaḏ:*** A masculine noun designating a measurement, a dimension. It refers specifically to the extent or size of the earth at creation (Job 38:5) which was established by God.

4462. מְמוּכָן ***m^e^mûḵān:*** A proper noun designating Memucan, a chief counselor to Ahasuerus (Esth. 1:14, 16, 21).

4463. מָמוֹת ***māmôṯ:*** A masculine noun meaning death, a deadly disease. It is used as an abstract noun meaning death. In context it is described as a group of fatal, deadly diseases brought on by the judgment of God (Jer. 16:4); or those who die in battle (Ezek. 28:8).

4464. מַמְזֵר ***mamzēr:*** A masculine noun identifying an illegitimate child, a bastard. It specifies a person who does not have a proper pedigree or genealogy and was born out of wedlock (Deut. 23:2[3]). In Zechariah 9:6, it is best rendered as a reference to foreign or mongrel persons.

4465. מִמְכָּר ***mimkār:*** A masculine noun indicating sale, that which is sold. It is used in several ways: to indicate the act of selling (Lev. 25:27, 29, 33; Deut. 18:8); the things being sold, merchandise (Lev. 25:14; Neh. 13:20); something already sold (Lev. 25:25, 28; Ezek. 7:13); or the price of a sale (Lev. 25:50).

4466. מִמְכֶּרֶת ***mimkereṯ:*** A feminine noun indicating a sale. It indicates the process or transaction of selling; the sale (Lev. 25:42). In context God's people cannot be sold as slaves.

4467. מַמְלָכָה ***mamlāḵāh:*** A feminine noun meaning kingdom. Often the term refers to the royal power an individual in sovereign authority possesses. Because Solomon did not keep the Lord's covenant and commandments, his kingdom (that is, his power to rule) was torn from his son (1 Kgs. 11:11; cf. 1 Sam. 28:17; 1 Kgs. 14:8). In many other places, however, the word is utilized concretely to denote a people under a king (that is, a realm). The kingdom (or realm) of King Sihon of the Amorites and the kingdom (realm) of King Og of Bashan were given to the Gadites, Reubenites, and the half-tribe of Manasseh (Num. 32:33; cf. Ex. 19:6; Deut. 28:25; 1 Sam. 24:20[21]). In some passages, the word functions as an adjective, meaning royal (e.g., city of the kingdom = royal city; Josh. 10:2; 1 Sam. 27:5; cf. 2 Kgs. 11:1; 2 Chr. 23:20; Amos 7:13). This noun derives from the verb *mālaḵ* (4427), as does its synonym, *malḵûṯ* (4438).

4468. מַמְלָכוּת ***mamlāḵûṯ:*** A feminine noun meaning kingdom, royal power. It is equivalent in meaning with the term *mamlāḵāh* (4467) and occurs only in the construct form. Samuel told Saul that the Lord had torn the kingdom of Israel from him and given it to another better than he (1 Sam. 15:28). The Lord declared to Hosea that He was going to put an end to the kingdom of Israel (Hos. 1:4; cf. Josh. 13:12; 2 Sam. 16:3; Jer. 26:1). This noun is derived from the verb *mālaḵ* (4427).

4469. מִמְסָךְ ***mimsāḵ:*** A masculine noun meaning mixed wine. It usually indicated wine mixed with water (Prov. 23:30; Isa. 65:11), but other things were used such as milk or spices.

4470. מֶמֶר ***memer:*** A masculine noun indicating bitterness. It indicates something difficult to process, harsh; the opposite of pleasantness. A foolish son is bitterness to his mother (Prov. 17:25), i.e., causes her grief or sharp sorrow.

4471. מַמְרֵא ***mamrē':*** A proper noun designating Mamre:

A. A location north of Hebron (Gen. 13:18; 18:1; 23:17, 19; 25:9; 35:27; 49:30; 50:13).

B. A friend of Abram (Gen. 14:13, 24).

4472. מַמְרֹר ***mamrōr:*** A masculine noun meaning bitterness, misery. It is akin to a feeling of despair, hopelessness, revulsion, revolt, something Job had because of his calamity (Job 9:18).

4473. מִמְשַׁח ***mimšaḥ:*** A masculine noun possibly meaning expansion, extension. The word occurs only in Ezekiel 28:14 and would, with this meaning, read "cherub of extension" (that is, a cherub with wings outstretched). However, this definition is now seriously questioned, largely because the term derives from the verb *māšaḥ* (4886), meaning to anoint. The term more likely expresses the sense of anointment or anointing. Taking the word this way, the phrase conveys the more satisfying expression "cherub of anointing," that is, the anointed cherub.

4474. מִמְשָׁל ***mimšāl:*** A masculine noun meaning dominion, sovereign authority, ruling power. One in human form spoke with Daniel, telling him about a warrior king and an officer who would soon rule their respective kingdoms with great authority (Dan. 11:3, 5). In 1 Chronicles 26:6, the word describes the sons of Shemaiah as those who exercised ruling authority in their ancestral homes because of their great capabilities. The term stems from the verb *māšal* (4910).

4475. מֶמְשָׁלָה ***memšālāh:*** A feminine noun meaning dominion, rule, authority, province, realm. Often this term denotes the ruling power which one in authority exercises over his domain or kingdom. God made the sun to have authority over the day and the moon to have authority over the night (Gen. 1:16; Ps. 136:8). The Lord sent the prophet Isaiah to announce to Shebna that He was going to forcibly remove him from office and give his authority to Eliakim instead (Isa. 22:21). In other places, the word refers to the territory over which one rules or governs. Hezekiah showed his whole realm to the king of Babylon's messengers (2 Kgs. 20:13; cf. Ps. 103:22; 114:2). Once it refers collectively to an envoy of powerful ambassadors, such as rulers, princes, or chief officers (2 Chr. 32:9). This term is derived from the verb *māšal* (4910; see also the related word *mimšāl* [4474]).

4476. מִמְשָׁק ***mimšāq:*** A masculine noun indicating characterized by, possessed. It means to feature, to be permeated, or to be noted for something (Zeph. 2:9). In context, it describes the destroyed, ruined locations of Moab and Ammon.

4477. מַמְתַקִּים ***mamtaqqiym:*** A masculine plural noun denoting sweetness. It is used of a drink with a taste like sugar or with an agreeable taste and smell (Neh. 8:10). In Song of Solomon 5:16, it is used figuratively of the mouth of the beloved groom.

4478. מָן ***mān:*** A masculine noun meaning manna, who, or what. This is the reaction that the Israelites had to the substance that the Lord gave them to eat (Ex. 16:15). They asked "What is it?" which translates into *mān*. This substance is described as wafers made with honey and like white coriander seeds in shape (Ex. 16:31). The manna could be ground into grain and cooked into cakes (see Num. 11:7, 8). When the Israelites entered the Promised Land, God caused the manna to cease (Josh. 5:12).

4479. מַן ***man:*** An Aramaic interrogative pronoun meaning who, whoever, what. It refers to persons, who (Ezra 5:3, 9; Dan. 3:6, 11); to things, e.g., whose names or what names (Ezra 5:4); or to gods (Dan. 3:15).

It is used in an indefinite sense, who(m)ever (Dan. 4:17[14], 25[22], 32[29]; 5:21).

4480. מִן ***min,*** מִנִּי ***minniy,*** מִנֵּי ***minnēy:*** A preposition used to indicate from, out of, away from; more than: after, since; immediately; because of, since, so that; without; direction as south*ward*, etc.). Its spelling varies according to its location and usage. Its basic meaning is from, away from, out of. Its basic meanings only can be noted here, but its exact meaning is easily discerned from its context: (1) With verbs, it expresses separation spatially or figuratively (Ex. 19:14; Deut. 22:8; Josh. 10:7). It can be used with a verb not indicating separation, e.g., to stay away from strife (Prov. 20:3; Isa. 14:19). (2) With the basic sense of out of, from (Gen. 3:22–24; 4:10; 34:26; Ex. 2:10; 8:9[5]; Judg. 15:7; Ps. 40:2[3]), it often indicates what something is made of or formed from (Gen. 2:19; Hos. 13:2). With a pronominal suffix meaning from it, it means of one piece with it (Ex. 25:19, 31). It indicates a cause for something, on account of, because (Ex. 2:23; 6:9; 1 Kgs. 14:4; Prov. 20:4; Isa. 53:5). (3) It is used to mean something is a part of something else, a part or share of it (Gen. 6:19; 7:8; 39:11; Num. 16:2). It indicates some of in an indefinite sense (Ex. 16:27; Lev. 25:49; Ps. 137:3). When repeated it means some . . . others or its equivalent expression (1 Chr. 9:28, 29). (4) It is used to mark time: from, since (Deut. 9:24), from a certain day or time (Lev. 22:27; Num. 15:23; 1 Sam. 18:9). It is used in phrases to mean from ancient times, antiquity (Hab. 1:12); from of old (Isa. 42:14). It indicates right after a certain time (Gen. 38:24; Josh. 23:1; Ezek. 38:8). (5) Paired with *'ad* (5704) it usually means from . . . even to, as far as (Gen. 10:19; 15:18; Ex. 11:7; Jer. 51:62). In a figurative sense, this same construction can mean e.g., from young . . . to old, both inclusive (Gen. 19:4; 1 Sam 5:9; Jer. 6:13). (6) It may further indicate than, in comparisons (Lev. 21:10; Judg. 14:18). (7) Prefixed to an infinitive, it is often translated as from (Gen. 16:2); a few times as on account of or because (Deut. 7:7, 8); or temporally as since or after (Num. 24:23; Isa. 44:7). (8) It is often attached to other words in compounds and is sometimes used in front of infinitives of verbs: e.g., with *'āḇaḏ* (5647) meaning from serving (Ex. 14:5); with *bāla'* (1104) meaning from destroying (Lam. 2:8). (9) It is used in front of a verb form once as a conjunction indicating a negative purpose, "that . . . not" (Deut. 33:11). Other uses almost always fall under one of the above categories.

4481. מִן ***min:*** An Aramaic preposition meaning from, out of, among, more than. It means out of something, e.g., a threshing floor (Dan. 2:35) or from a specific area, e.g., a temple as a storage area (Dan. 5:2). It is used with *yaḏ,* hand, to give the figurative idea of from the power of (Dan. 3:15). It is used to express comparison meaning different from (Dan.

7:3) or more than (Dan. 2:30). It is used to express the idea of a part of something or some group, etc. (Dan. 2:33, 41; 5:13). With *w*[e]*'ad* following it, it expresses the temporal idea of since (Dan. 2:20; Ezra 4:15; 5:16). Followed by *dî*, it functions as a conjunction expressing cause, because (Ezra 5:11). With a pronoun suffix, it means from me, from you, etc. (Dan. 2:5). It is used to express with, to point out an instrument or agent (Dan. 4:25[22]). It expresses the idea of based on or according to, e.g., the word or command of God (Ezra 6:14). The expression *min-yaṣṣib* means truly, certainly (Dan. 2:8). It is used in the idiom *min-q*[e]*šōṭ dî* indicating in fact, surely (Dan. 2:47). Judgment is rendered idiomatically as judgment upon (from, *min*) him, her, etc. (Ezra 7:26). Something may be changed from (*min*) what it was (Dan. 4:13[10]).

4482. מֵן ***mēn:*** I. A masculine noun referring to a stringed instrument, music of strings. It designates stringed instruments (Ps. 45:8[9]; 150:4; KJV, NIV, NASB).

II. A masculine noun indicating a portion, a share. It is taken to mean a portion or lot by more recent translators in Psalm 6:23 (NASB, NIV; KJV, in the same). In Psalm 45:8[9], it is taken to mean stringed instruments (see I also and 4521; NIV, NASB; KJV, "whereby").

4483. מְנָא ***m*[e]*nā',*** מְנָה ***m*[e]*nāh:*** An Aramaic verb indicating to number, to appoint. It means to set up, to install persons, to authorize them for a certain purpose (Ezra 7:25; Dan. 2:24, 49; 3:12). It has the sense of tested, tried, counted, a passive participle of the simple stem (peal stem) in Aramaic (Dan. 5:26).

4484. מְנֵא ***m*[e]*nē':*** An Aramaic noun meaning *mene*; weight of measurement. It indicates a unit of weight of gold and/or silver (Dan. 5:25, 26).

4485. מַנְגִּינָה ***mangiynāh:*** A feminine noun indicating a mocking song. It refers to a song of insult and disrespect directed at someone (Lam. 3:63).

4486. מַנְדַּע ***manda':*** An Aramaic masculine noun meaning knowledge, reason, intelligence, power of knowing. This word is found only in Daniel. When King Nebuchadnezzar was turned into an animal, he was said to have lost his reason and understanding. Upon his restoration to his human body, his mind was also restored (Dan. 4:36[33]). Daniel himself was described as a man of understanding and knowledge with an excellent spirit (Dan. 5:12).

4487. מָנָה ***mānāh:*** A verb meaning to count, to number. It means basically to count up, to tally for oneself or for someone else: to tally up the stars of heaven (Gen. 13:16); to record the bits of dust of Jacob (Num. 23:10); the number of persons in Israel and Judah (2 Sam. 24:1); or money (2 Kgs. 12:10[11]). It takes on the sense of consigning or allotting something for some reason (Job 7:3; Dan. 1:5, 10, 11). It is used figuratively of the Lord's appointing or establishing kindness and truth (Ps. 61:7[8]); and of persons numbering their days in order to be wise (Ps. 90:12). God has unlimited ability to reckon the stars and to keep track of each one (Ps. 147:4); and He appoints events and experiences for his people (Job 7:3; Jon. 1:17[2:1]; 4:6–8). In its passive sense, it means to be counted (Gen. 13:16; 1 Kgs. 3:8; 8:5; Isa. 53:12).

4488. מָנֶה ***māneh:*** A masculine noun meaning *minah,* a weight of money. It was a unit of weight of gold or silver amounting to about one pound (1/2 kilogram) (1 Kgs. 10:17; Ezra 2:69; Neh. 7:71, 72; Ezek. 45:12).

4489. מֹנֶה ***mōneh:*** A masculine noun designating time, a counted number. It refers to the act of performing something, an occurrence of something (Gen. 31:7, 41).

4490. מָנָה ***mānāh:*** A feminine noun meaning a portion or one's share. It indicates shares of something: sacrificial meat (1 Sam. 1:4, 5); of fine foods at festive times (Esth. 9:19, 22); of officially appointed portions of food (Esth. 2:9); of portions of food sent to others (Neh. 8:10, 12). It is used in a figurative sense of the Lord Himself as the portion of the psalmist's inheritance (Ps. 16:5). It also designates the judgment of the Lord on people as their portion (Jer. 13:25).

4491. מִנְהָג ***minhāg:*** A masculine noun describing the driving (of a chariot). It refers to the way one handles a chariot, the way he maneuvers it as the driver (2 Kgs. 9:20).

4492. מִנְהָרָה ***minhārāh:*** A feminine noun denoting a den, a shelter. It refers to naturally occurring holes in the mountains made suitable for living (Judg. 6:2).

4493. מָנוֹד ***mānôḏ:*** A masculine noun indicating a shaking of the head. It refers to a negative gesture of turning the head from side to side, indicating a pitiful but accusatory attitude toward someone (Ps. 44:14[15]; NASB, laughingstock).

4494. מָנוֹחַ ***mānôaḥ:*** A masculine noun designating a rest, resting place. Israel, figuratively, could find no resting place for the soles of her feet (Deut. 28:65; Lam. 1:3). A resting place was or rest was a time or place of security (Ruth 3:1). It is used of rest for the soul because of the Lord's mercies and blessings (Ps. 116:7). It points to a location where something settles down and remains there or the cessation of work in order to refresh oneself. The dove found no resting place for herself (Gen. 8:9).

4495. מָנוֹחַ ***mānôaḥ:*** A proper noun designating Manoah, the father of Samson. His name means "resting place." He and his wife carefully tried to bring up Samson as the messenger of the Lord had instructed them. They made Samson a Nazarite. Manorah conversed with the angel and was submissive to his message. He and his wife were broken and hurt when Samson married a Philistine woman (Judg. 14:3).

4496. מְנוּחָה ***mᵉnûḥāh,*** מְנֻחָה ***mᵉnuḥāh:*** A feminine noun meaning resting place, rest, quiet. It is used in several ways to denote places where peace, quiet, and trust are present (Gen. 49:15; Ruth 1:9; Ps. 23:2; Isa. 28:12). Canaan was intended to be a place where Israel could find rest (Judg. 20:43; 1 Kgs. 8:56). The rest of God is not possible when uncleanness and corruption abounds (Mic. 2:10). In Jeremiah 51:59, the word has the meaning of quartermaster, an army officer who provides soldiers with rest, fresh horses, and food. People cannot make a sufficient place of rest for the Lord (Isa. 66:1), but the Lord will supply a marvelous resting for His restored people (Isa. 11:10).

4497. מָנוֹן ***mānôn:*** I. A masculine noun meaning son. It refers to a slave who has become a son through his master's careful nurture and care (Prov. 29:21). The root meaning of the word is not known.

II. A masculine noun meaning grief. Some translators and scholars, because of the word *pampers* earlier in the proverb, prefer to render this verb as grief, sorrow, pain (Prov. 29:21). The root meaning of the word is not known.

4498. מָנוֹס ***mānôs:*** A masculine noun indicating a refuge, flight, a place of escape. It is used of a location of safety; a place to which to flee. It is used metaphorically of the Lord as one's refuge (2 Sam. 22:3; Ps. 59:16[17]; 142:4[5]); flight itself in a time when one needs refuge, safety (Jer. 46:5). The refuge or escape of the wicked perishes (Job 11:20); and the escape of God's enemies fails (Jer. 25:35; Amos 2:14).

4499. מְנוּסָה ***mᵉnûsāh,*** מְנֻסָה ***mᵉnusāh:*** A feminine noun indicating fleeing, flight. It is used of an attempted escape from an enemy by falling back in retreat or open flight (Isa. 52:12). It is brought about by the Lord Himself when His people fail to obey Him (Lev. 26:36).

4500. מָנוֹר ***mānôr:*** A masculine noun designating a beam, a rod. A rather large, wooden rod used as a weapon by attaching a spearhead by tying or winding (1 Sam. 17:7; 2 Sam. 21:19; 1 Chr. 11:23; 20:5).

4501. מְנוֹרָה ***mᵉnôrāh,*** מְנֹרָה ***mᵉnōrāh:*** A feminine noun referring to a lampstand. It refers to a stand, not the candlestick itself. These were used to hold candlesticks or wicks and were in common use in a house (2 Kgs. 4:10). Elaborate models were employed in the Tabernacle and Temple (Ex. 25:31–35; 26:35; 30:27;

31:8; 1 Kgs. 7:49). It is used figuratively of Zerubbabel (Zech. 4:2, 11).

4502. מִנְּזָר ***minnᵉzār:*** I. A masculine noun denoting a consecrated one, an anointed one. It refers to a dedicated courtier or guardsman serving the king (Nah. 3:17, KJV, crowned [ones]).

II. A masculine noun referring to a guardsman, a guard. It refers to dedicated courtiers at court serving the monarchy in some way (Nah. 3:17, NIV, NASB).

4503. מִנְחָה ***minḥāh:*** A feminine noun meaning a gift, a tribute, an offering. This word is used to signify a gift as in the peace gifts that Jacob presented to Esau (Gen. 32:13[14]). Secondly, it signifies a tribute. An example of the use of this word is Judges 3:15, where Ehud was sent from Israel to Moab on the pretense of bringing a tribute. Perhaps the most frequent use of this word is to denote a grain offering. Grain offerings were brought on pans, suggesting cakes (Lev. 2:5) and mixed with oil and other substances (Num. 6:15).

4504. מִנְחָה ***minḥāh:*** An Aramaic feminine noun meaning a gift, a sacrificial offering, an oblation, a meat offering. When Daniel was promoted to chief administrator of Babylon, the celebration included the presentation of an offering signified by this Aramaic word (Dan. 2:46). King Artaxerxes also used this Aramaic word to command Ezra to offer sacrificial gifts on the altar of God when he arrived in Jerusalem (Ezra 7:17). This word corresponds directly to *minḥāh* (4503).

4505. מְנַחֵם ***mᵉnaḥēm:*** A proper noun designating Menahem, a violent king of Israel (752–742 B.C.). He assassinated his predecessor Shallum in Samaria. He was the son of Gadi. He was evaluated as a wicked king by the biblical writer. He was cruel and merciless in war (2 Kgs. 15:16). During his reign, the king of Assyria forced him to pay a heavy tribute (2 Kgs. 15:16–22).

4506. מָנַחַת ***mānaḥaṯ,*** מָנַחְתִּי ***mānaḥtiy:*** A proper noun designating Manahath:

A. A son of Shobal (Gen. 36:23; 1 Chr. 1:40).

B. A location in Judah (1 Chr. 8:6).

C. A Manahathite (1 Chr. 2:52, 54).

4507. מְנִי ***mᵉniy:*** I. A masculine noun indicating number. It refers to the tally or reckoning of something by numbers. It refers to total persons in a group of troops (Isa. 65:11, KJV).

II. A masculine proper noun referring to a false god. It refers to the god of Fate, Meni (Isa. 65:11, NIV, NASB) and stands parallel to Fortune.

4508. מִנִּי ***minniy:*** A proper noun designating Minni (Jer. 51:27).

4509. מִנְיָמִין ***minyāmiyn:*** A proper noun designating Miniamin:

A. A priest under Nehemiah (Neh. 12:17, 41).

B. A priest under Hezekiah (2 Chr. 31:15).

4510. מִנְיָן ***minyān:*** An Aramaic masculine noun denoting number. It refers to the tally or reckoning by numbers of something. It refers to the count of the twelve tribes in Israel (Ezra 6:17).

4511. מִנִּית ***minniyṯ:*** A proper noun designating Minnith (Judg. 11:33; Ezek. 27:17).

4512. מִנְלֶה ***minleh:*** I. A masculine noun meaning perfection. Translators and scholars differ on the meaning of this word. It indicates the success for a while of an evil person (Job 15:29; KJV) in context.

II. A masculine noun referring to grain. It refers to grain or food produced by an evil person in context (Job 15:29, NASB).

III. A masculine noun meaning possession. It indicates the accumulated wealth of a wicked person in context (Job 15:29, NIV).

4513. מָנַע ***mānaʻ:*** A verb meaning to hold, to keep back. It refers to holding back, keeping, retaining, controlling something for some reason: food or grain from the market (Prov. 11:26); in a figurative sense of holding back the rivers of a fallen nation, indicating its destruction (Ezek. 31:15); of holding back something from another person, as when God withheld pregnancy from Rachel (Gen. 30:2); to restrain someone from something (Num. 24:11; 1 Sam. 25:26). It is used of something being restrained (Job 38:15; Joel 1:13); or of persons permitting themselves to be controlled (Num. 22:16). In Israel the Lord often withheld rain to warn His people (Jer. 3:3; Amos 4:7). It is used figuratively of a person holding evil in his mouth (Job 20:13). Light, understanding is withheld from the wicked person (Job 38:15). Wisdom exhorts the wise to withhold their feet from walking with the wicked (Prov. 1:15). The wise person does not keep back a good deed from those who deserve it (Prov. 3:27). Discipline is not to be withheld from a child (Prov. 23:13).

4514. מַנְעוּל ***manʻûl,*** מַנְעֻל ***manʻul:*** A masculine noun denoting a bolt, a lock on a door. It refers to an apparatus used to lock a gate (Neh. 3:3, 6, 13–15) or of a house or room (Song 5:5).

4515. מִנְעָל ***minʻāl:*** I. A masculine noun indicating a lock or bolt used to secure something. It is used figuratively of the locks of Asher to indicate the security of the tribe (Deut. 33:25, NASB, NIV).

II. A masculine noun designating a shoe. Some translators understand this to refer to a shoe or sandal, which is fitting for the context (Deut. 33:25, KJV, NKJV).

4516. מַנְעַמִּים ***manʻammiym:*** A masculine plural noun indicating morsels, delicacies. It refers to choice, luxurious portions of food but in context may refer to evil deeds of evil men as well (Ps. 141:4).

4517. מְנַעַנְעִים ***m^e na'an'iym:*** I. A masculine plural noun pointing out a musical rattle; castanets or sistrum. It indicates a small percussion instrument that rattles, a sistrum or castanets (NASB, NIV, NKJV) (2 Sam. 6:5).

II. A masculine plural noun referring to a musical horn. It is taken as a small horn, a coronet by earlier translators (2 Sam. 6:5, KJV).

4518. מְנַקִּית ***m^e naqqiyt:*** A feminine noun meaning a bowl, a cup. It refers to some of the holy vessels used around the table of showbread to pour drink offerings. It was made of gold (Ex. 25:29; 37:16; NASB, NIV, bowls).

4519. מְנַשֶּׁה ***m^e našše h:*** A proper noun designating Manasseh:

A. The firstborn son of Joseph in Egypt. His mother was Asenath, an Egyptian woman whose father was a priest in Heliopolis (On) (Gen. 41:50). The name means "cause to forget" and was given by Joseph because Manasseh's birth helped Joseph forget his family and hard times (Gen. 49:51). Jacob gave his firstborn blessing, however, to Ephraim whose descendants outstripped Manassah's (Gen. 48:19–20). Both became key tribes in northern Israel, and Jacob blessed both under Joseph's name (Gen. 49:22–26). Their fruitfulness and God's care for them are emphasized. Manasseh had a son named Machir (Gen. 50:23).

B. It refers to the descendants of Manesseh, a very fertile tribe (Josh. 17:17–18). One-half of the tribe settled east of the Jordan and as far north as Mount Hermon. Parts of the eastern half lived as far south as the Jobok River (Josh. 16:1—17:18). The other half of the tribe lived west of the Jordan. Its western border was the Mediterranean coast. Dan, Ephraim, and Benjamin touched its southern borders, and Asher, Zebulun, and Issachar touched its northern border. Key cities, such as Megiddo, Tirzah, Samaria, and Shechem were in its tribal territories. Both Mount Ebal and Gerazim were there. Gilgal and Jericho were just inside its southern tip (Josh. 13:8–13, 29–31).

C. A king in Judah, an evil king, and a son of Hezekiah. He ruled 697–686 B.C., including a coregency with his father. He began to reign when he was twelve years old and reigned 55 years (2 Kgs. 21:1). He reversed all the good that his father had done, even rebuilding pagan high places for sacrifice and worship (2 Kgs. 21:1–18) and altars for Baal. He worshiped the heavenly bodies and sacrificed his own son in fire (2 Kgs. 21:6). He set up idolatrous Asherah poles in the Temple and led Israel astray (2 Kgs. 21:9). He sinned worse than the Amorites (2 Kgs. 21:11) of Canaan had. He shed innocent blood (2 Kgs. 21:16). As a result, the Lord declared He would wipe away Jerusalem and Judah as a person wipes a dish (2 Kgs. 21:13). According to the chronicler, Manasseh repented in his old age, and God had mercy on him, but God did not relent from His judgment on Judah.

D. A man who had intermarried in the time of Ezra, son of Pahath-Moab (Ezra 10:30).

E. The son of Hashum who had intermarried during the time of Ezra or before (Ezra 10:33).

F. The father of Gershom, according to some ancient Hebrew manuscripts, but the best reading indicates that he was the son of Moses (1 Chr. 23:15).

4520. מְנַשִּׁי ***m^e naššiy:*** A proper noun designating Manassite (Deut. 4:43; 29:8[7]; 2 Kgs. 10:33; 1 Chr. 26:32).

4521. מְנָת ***m^e nāṯ:*** A feminine noun meaning portion. It indicates a part or share of something: the king's share of something (2 Chr. 31:3); a share required by law (Neh. 12:44, 47). It can indicate a share of a drink (Ps. 11:6), but in this case, used figuratively, it indicates a portion of the "cup of the wicked." It can be equivalent to one's lot in life (Jer. 13:25).

4522. מַס ***mas:*** A masculine noun designating forced labor or service, tribute. It refers to labor forced on someone or service demanded, usually by the state (Gen. 49:15; Deut. 20:11; 1 Kgs. 5:14[28]; Isa. 31:8); usually overseen by a foreman or taskmaster (Ex. 1:11; 1 Kgs. 4:6, 12:18). A person not willing to work or a lazy person may be put to forced labor (Prov. 12:24).

4523. מָס ***mās:*** An adjective describing something as afflicted, despairing. Its meaning in context is difficult but seems to describe an especially hopeless person, despondent to the point of giving up (Job 6:14).

4524. מֵסַב ***mēsaḇ,*** מְסִבָּה ***misbāh:*** A masculine noun meaning around, the surrounding area. It is used adverbially as well meaning around about an object or all over it (1 Kgs. 6:29). It designates the surrounding territory of a city (2 Kgs. 23:5); with a suffix on the end (*m^e śibbīy*), it means all around a person, surrounding him or her (Ps. 140:9[10]); or around, surrounding it, that is, a table (Song 1:12).

4525. מַסְגֵּר ***masgēr:*** I. A masculine noun referring to a smith, a locksmith. It indicates a metal worker able to work with various metals and perform many tasks (2 Kgs. 24:14, 16; Jer. 24:1; 29:2). He was highly prized by any captor.

II. A masculine noun designating a dungeon, a prison, a place of incarceration and detainment. Used figuratively, it pictured a prison of the psalmist's soul (Ps. 142:7[8]). It is used metaphorically of the place of imprisonment of the host of heaven and the dead kings of the earth, possibly Sheol (Isa. 24:22), but it was a holding place, not a final abode. It is used both literally and figuratively in Isaiah 42:7.

4526. מִסְגֶּרֶת ***misgeret:*** A feminine noun referring to a border, a rim, a fortress. It is used most often to indicate a decorative and/or functional rim or edging of a table, stand, or base (Ex. 25:25, 27; 1 Kgs. 7:28, 29, 31; 2 Kgs. 16:17). It also has the sense of a fortress erected around persons for defense or protection (2 Sam. 22:46; Ps. 18:45[46]; Mic. 7:17).

4527. מַסַּד ***massad:*** A masculine noun meaning foundation. It refers to the structural supporting base of a building (1 Kgs. 7:9).

4528. מִסְדְּרוֹן ***misd^erôn:*** A masculine noun designating a porch, a vestibule. Its meaning is uncertain. In its context, it may refer to a latrine, a toilet, or, more generally, a vestibule where toilet facilities were located (Judg. 3:23).

4529. מָסָה ***māsāh:*** A verb meaning to melt, to dissolve, to become water. It means to dissipate, to dissolve, to turn to liquid: to melt ice (Ps. 147:18). It is used figuratively most often: to lose heart, "a heart melted" (Josh. 14:8); to make something wet (Ps. 6:6[7]); to cause something to dissolve or dissipate (Ps. 39:11[12]; NASB, consume).

4530. מִסָּה ***missāh:*** A feminine noun meaning a tribute, a gift. It designates something given as a free offering during the presentation of a freewill offering to the Lord (Deut. 16:10).

4531. מַסָּה ***massāh:*** A feminine noun meaning despair, a test, a trial, proving. The Hebrew word is actually two homographs—words that are spelled the same yet have distinct origins and meanings. The first homograph is derived from the verb *māsas* (4549), meaning to dissolve or melt, and it means despair. This word occurs only in Job 9:23. The second homograph is derived from the verb *nāsāh* (5254), meaning to test or try, and denotes a test, a trial, or proving. It is used in reference to the manifestations of God's power and handiwork before the Egyptians at the Exodus (Deut. 4:34; 7:19; 29:3[2]. Furthermore, this term has become a proper noun, *massāh* (4532), to designate the place where the Israelites tested God (Ex. 17:7; Deut. 6:16; 9:22; Ps. 95:8); and where Levi was tested (Deut. 33:8).

4532. מַסָּה ***massāh:*** A proper noun designating Massah, the name of a place where the Israelites arrogantly "tested" God. The name means "testing." The event was recorded to warn Israel not to act in such a way again (Ps. 95:8).

4533. מַסְוֶה ***masweh:*** A masculine noun indicating a veil. It is used of the hanging or screen which Moses placed over his face to keep his facial skin glow from frightening the people (Ex. 34:33–35).

4534. מְסוּכָה ***m^e^sûḵāh:*** A feminine noun referring to a hedge, a thorn hedge. It was a thorny shrub bearing sharp, pointed stems (Mic. 7:4); or a detested, undesirable plant as well.

4535. מַסָּח ***massāḥ:*** A masculine noun referring to a guard, a defense. It defines the purpose of the action of watching, keeping guard over something (2 Kgs. 11:6).

4536. מִסְחָר ***mishār:*** A masculine noun depicting merchandise, the sale of merchandise. It refers to materials and goods being offered for purchase or trade (1 Kgs. 10:15).

4537. מָסַךְ ***māsak:*** A verb meaning to mix, to mingle. It means to mingle together various things: honey or various spices with wine; wisdom mixes her wine to invite persons to drink with her (Prov. 9:2, 5); mixed strong drink was a favorite of valiant, if foolish, men (Isa. 5:22). It is used twice in figurative poetry: the psalmist mixed his wine with tears (Ps. 102:9[10]); and the Lord mixed into Egypt, as a part of His judgments on her, a spirit of confusion or distortion (Isa. 19:14).

4538. מֶסֶךְ ***mesek:*** A masculine noun describing something fully mixed. It is used figuratively to describe a cup of wine, representing the judgments of the Lord, as well-mixed (Ps. 75:8[9]).

4539. מָסָךְ ***māsāḵ:*** A masculine noun meaning a curtain, a covering, a screen. It designates a screen or hanging used in the Tabernacle at the gate of entrance to the court (Ex. 27:16; 35:17; 39:40; 40:8, etc.); at the entrance into the Holy Place (Ex. 26:36, 37; 36:37; 39:38; 40:28, etc.); at the dividing point between the Holy Place and Holy of Holies (Ex. 35:12; 39:34; Num. 4:5). It refers to a covering used to cover a well where a person could hide (2 Sam. 17:19). It is used in a figurative sense to refer to a cloud used to hide the Israelites from the Egyptians (Ps. 105:39).

4540. מְסֻכָּה ***m^e^suḵāh:*** A feminine noun indicating a covering or an outward adornment. It is used figuratively of the outward splendor and dress of the king of Tyre and, according to some exegetes, Satan in the Garden of Eden in a literal sense (Ezek. 28:13).

4541. מַסֵּכָה ***massēḵāh:*** A feminine noun meaning an image, molten metal, covering, an alliance. When the word means a libation or drink offering, it is associated with sacrifices that seal a covenant relationship (Isa. 25:7; 28:20; 30:1); however, the word usually signifies an image or molten metal. In those cases, the word identifies an idol, which has been formed from molten metal and has been poured into a cast. The worship of such images is clearly prohibited by God (Ex. 34:17; Lev. 19:4; Deut. 27:15). The Israelites were commanded to destroy any idols they discovered in Canaan (Num. 33:52). The prophets proclaimed the futility of all idols, including those described as *massēḵāh* (Isa. 42:17); and God would punish those who worshiped them (Hos. 13:2, 3; Nah. 1:14; Hab. 2:18). In spite of all this, the Israelites formed and worshiped idols, including molten idols like Aaron's golden calf (Ex. 32:4, 8; Deut. 9:16; Neh. 9:18); Micah's idols (Judg. 17:3, 4; 18:17, 18); and Jeroboam's idols (1 Kgs. 14:9; cf. 1 Kgs. 12:28–30).

4542. מִסְכֵּן ***miskēn:*** An adjective referring to a poor person. It refers, in context, to a poor young lad (Eccl. 4:13) or a poor man (Eccl. 9:15, 16), both of whom were wise.

4543. מִסְכְּנוֹת ***miskᵉnôṯ:*** A feminine plural noun referring to storehouses, storage areas. It indicates a structure or even a city used for storage or supplies of various kinds, chiefly military supplies (Ex. 1:11; 1 Kgs. 9:19; 2 Chr. 8:4, 6; 17:12); grain (2 Chr. 16:4); or wine and oil (2 Chr. 32:28).

4544. מִסְכֵּנֻת ***misḵēnuṯ:*** A feminine noun indicating scarceness, scarcity. It indicates a lack or need for more of something, in this case food or anything (Deut. 8:9).

4545. מַסֶּכֶת ***masseḵeṯ:*** A feminine noun depicting a web of fabric. It was a basic pattern of cloth formed on a loom. In context it is used of weaving Samson's hair into this web-like pattern (Judg. 16:13, 14).

4546. מְסִלָּה ***mᵉsillāh:*** A feminine noun meaning a highway, a public road. It refers to key travel routes in antiquity (Num. 20:19; Judg. 20:31, 32, 45). Some were constructed of stone, gravel, or other materials; a few are named or located (2 Kgs. 18:17). The word is used in a figurative sense to describe the course of the stars (Judg. 5:20); the road of life lived by the righteous (Ps. 84:5[6]); Prov. 16:17); or locusts' manner of marching (Joel 2:8).

4547. מַסְלוּל ***maslûl:*** A masculine noun indicating a highway. It describes a major roadway. In context it is used figuratively of the Highway of Holiness that God's people will travel (Isa. 35:8).

4548. מַסְמֵר ***masmēr,*** מִסְמֵר ***mismēr,*** מַשְׂמֵר ***maśmēr:*** A masculine noun meaning nail. It is used of fasteners for doors and other items in construction work of all kinds (1 Chr. 22:3; 2 Chr. 3:9; Isa. 41:7). It is used humorously of idols being fastened together with nails (Jer. 10:4). The wise preacher sought out ways to hammer home his wise teachings with nails (Eccl. 12:11).

4549. מָסַס ***māsas:*** A verb meaning to melt, to dissolve. It indicates something is breaking up or turning to water. It is used figuratively: of persons wasting away in sickness (Isa. 10:18); of mountains breaking down (Isa. 34:3; Mic. 1:4); of persons' hearts "melting," losing courage (Deut. 1:28;

Josh. 2:11; 2 Sam. 17:10; Ps. 22:14 [15]). The unrighteous eventually are broken down (Ps. 112:10). It also refers literally to objects dissolving or melting: manna evaporated (Ex. 16:21); hot wax melts (Ps. 68:2[3]). It is used of the ropes binding Samson that came apart (Judg. 15:14).

4550. מַסַּע *massa'*: A masculine noun meaning journey, moving on. It means to travel about, to go from place to place with a purpose (Gen. 13:3; Ex. 17:1), especially with the Lord as leader (Ex. 40:36, 38). Trumpets gather Israel for setting out, journeying, breaking camp (Num. 10:2, 6). It is used in a summary sense of many travels (Num. 33:1).

4551. מַסָּע *massā'*: I. A masculine noun indicating a dart, a missile. It indicates a projectile used to kill an animal or person (Job 41:26[18]).

II. A masculine noun pointing out a stone quarry, a place where stone was located, measured, cut, dressed, and removed. It was a source of stone for building and was usually a noisy place (1 Kgs. 6:7).

4552. מִסְעָד *mis'āḏ*: A masculine noun designating a support, pillar. It refers to wooden supporting or stabilizing structures and used in various ways and for different objects (1 Kgs. 10:12).

4553. מִסְפֵּד *mispēḏ*: A masculine noun depicting wailing, mourning, lamenting. It stands for deep, despairing emotional reactions by persons and animals at some calamity: the death of a patriarch (Gen. 50:10); the prospect of being slaughtered, annihilated (Esth. 4:3); the opposite of dancing for joy (Ps. 30:11[12]); at the approach of judgment from the Lord (Isa. 22:12; Jer. 6:26; Amos 5:16, 17; Mic. 1:8); economic disaster (Ezek. 27:31). It is used of mourning for a person (Zech. 12:10, 11).

4554. מִסְפּוֹא *mispô'*: A masculine noun referring to fodder, animal food. It is used of food for animals, donkeys (Gen. 42:27; 43:24; Judg. 19:19) or camels (Gen. 24:25, 32).

4555. מִסְפָּחָה *mispāḥāh*: A feminine noun denoting a veil, a covering. It indicates an identifying covering placed on persons marked for some specific purpose (Ezek. 13:18, 21). It was probably a head covering.

4556. מִסְפַּחַת *mispaḥaṯ*: A feminine noun designating a scab, rash. It was a skin irritation or disease considered relatively harmless by the priests (Lev. 13:6–8).

4557. מִסְפָּר *mispār*: A masculine noun meaning a number, a count, an amount. In general it indicates the quantity numerically of something: years (Dan. 9:2); persons (Num. 3:22); cities (Jer. 2:28), etc. It can take on the sense of recounting something that has happened, a story or narrative (Judg. 7:15). If something is numbered, it may mean that it is fixed or few (Deut. 33:6). Something that is *'êyn mispār* is without number, innumerable (Gen. 41:49); or unlimited (Ps. 40:12[13]; 147:5). The verb *'ābar,* to cross over, plus *b^emispār* means to be counted, enrolled (2 Sam. 2:15). *'Ālāh mispar* means to go into a record, into an account (1 Chr. 27:24).

4558. מִסְפָּר ***mispār:*** A proper noun designating Mispar (Ezra 2:2).

4559. מִסְפֶּרֶת ***misperet:*** A proper noun designating Mispereth (Neh. 7:7).

4560. מָסַר ***māsar:*** A verb meaning to commit, to deliver up. It means to supply or deliver for use: to supply men for war (Num. 31:5). In Numbers 31:16, it has the meaning of committing or occasioning something, in this case, apostasy or unfaithfulness against the Lord.

4561. מֹסָר ***mōsār:*** A masculine noun indicating instruction, warnings. It indicates some communication from God that imparts warnings or teachings to persons to deliver them (Job 33:16).

4562. מָסֹרֶת ***māsōreṯ:*** A feminine noun denoting a bond. It indicates bringing persons into covenantal agreements, stipulations, making them partners in a covenant (Ezek. 20:37).

4563. מִסְתּוֹר ***mistôr:*** A masculine noun depicting a hiding place, place of protection. It refers to a shelter or place of protection from a storm, used figuratively and literally (Isa. 4:6).

4564. מַסְתֵּר ***mastēr:*** A masculine noun indicating an act of hiding. In context it indicates an act of turning away, desiring not to look at someone, because of his pathetic situation (Isa. 53:3).

4565. מִסְתָּר ***mistār:*** A masculine noun defining a hiding place, a place of ambush. It indicates a strategic secret or well-camouflaged location, literally or figuratively, from which to operate. The wicked or oppressive person lurks there to catch the innocent (Ps. 10:8, 9; 17:12; 64:4[5]; Hab. 3:14). It is used of hidden places where royal wealth was stored (Isa. 45:3). It refers figuratively to a secret place where a sorrowful person can weep (Jer. 13:17). There is no hiding place that the Lord does not see clearly (Jer. 23:24; 49:10).

4566. מַעְבָּד ***ma^abāḏ:*** A masculine noun meaning work, deed. It indicates something done, performed: the deeds of people, the conduct of their lives (Job 34:25).

4567. מַעְבָד ***ma^abāḏ:*** An Aramaic masculine noun indicating a work, deed. In context it refers to God's actions and deeds among the nations, executed in His sovereignty (Dan. 4:37[34]).

4568. מַעֲבֶה ***ma^abeh:*** A masculine noun referring to clay. A type of thick soil used to make molds for casting various metal items (1 Kgs. 7:46). Some suggest an ore foundry as a translation.

4569. מַעֲבָר ma‘ᵃḇar, מַעְבָּרָה ma‘bārāh: I. A masculine noun meaning passing. It is used to describe a spot on land or in a river where a crossing can be undertaken (Gen. 32:22[23]; 1 Sam. 13:23). In Isaiah 30:32, it has the sense of a strike or blow made with a stick or rod.

II. A feminine noun indicating a ford or passage. It refers to a suitable place for passing over or through something: over a river (Josh. 2:7; Judg. 3:28; 12:5, 6; Jer. 51:32); over land by using a ravine (1 Sam. 14:4; Isa. 10:29).

4570. מַעְגָּל ma‘gāl: I. A masculine noun meaning encampment, circle of a camp (1 Sam. 17:20; 26:5, 7).

II. A masculine noun meaning track, course, ruth, path (Ps. 17:5; 23:3; 65:11[12]; 140:5[6]; Prov. 2:9, 15, 18; 4:11, 26; 5:6, 21; Isa. 26:7; 59:8).

4571. מָעַד mā‘aḏ: A verb meaning to slip, to slide, to waver. It indicates an action of something or someone that shakes, wobbles, slips; to have one's feet (figuratively) slip, to fail (2 Sam. 22:37; Job 12:5; Ps. 18:36[37]).

In a strong figurative sense, it means to be indecisive, to be tempted to turn away, to waver (Ps. 26:1). A fool that slips is like a faithless person or nation, unstable, untrustworthy (Prov. 25:19; Ezek. 29:7).

4572. מַעֲדַי ma‘ᵃḏay: A proper noun designating Maadai (Ezra 10:34).

4573. מַעֲדְיָה ma‘aḏyāh: A proper noun designating Maadiah (Neh. 12:5).

4574. מַעֲדָן ma‘ᵃḏān, מַעֲדָנָה ma‘ᵃḏanāh, מַעֲדַנִּים ma‘ᵃḏanniym: I. A feminine noun meaning delicacy, beauty, confidence. It is used to describe the chain or bands of the Pleiades constellation (Job 38:31). It has the sense of cheerfulness or confidence in a person (1 Sam. 15:32).

II. A masculine plural noun indicating delicacies, delight. It is used of tasty food or special dishes often served at royal banquets (Gen. 49:20). It is used metaphorically of delight, making joyous, a renewal (Prov. 29:17). It refers to gourmet food or festive dishes (Lam. 4:5).

4575. מַעֲדַנּוֹת ma‘ᵃḏannôṯ: I. A feminine plural noun referring to chains, fetters. It is used to describe the chains or bands tying together the Pleiades constellation (Job 38:31).

II. A feminine plural noun denoting sweet influences. It identifies the feeling created by viewing the Pleiades (Job 38:31).

4576. מַעְדֵּר ma‘dēr: A masculine noun referring to a hoe, a mattock. It depicts an agricultural tool for loosening the ground for cultivating it (Isa. 7:25).

4577. מְעֵה ***me'ēh:*** An Aramaic masculine noun meaning belly. It refers to the abdominal area of a human figure; of a huge image with a belly of bronze (Dan. 2:32).

4578. מֵעֶה ***mē'eh:*** A masculine noun meaning internal organs, intestines, belly, womb, sexual organs, sympathy. It refers to internal organs. When Joab stabbed Amasa, his entrails fell onto the ground (2 Sam. 20:10); the digestive tract; when a woman was suspected of infidelity, she was made to take an oath cursing the water that entered her stomach (Num. 5:22); and the sexual organs; God promised Abram that he would bear a son from his own loins (Gen. 15:4). It can also be used figuratively to mean the seat of emotions or heart (Isa. 16:11).

4579. מָעָה ***mā'āh:*** A feminine noun signifying a grain of something. It identifies granules of sand in context (Isa. 48:19).

4580. מָעוֹג ***mā'ôg:*** A masculine noun meaning cake, bread. It refers to a staple food available to even a poor person (1 Kgs. 17:12). It is possibly used to stand for a whole meal, a banquet feast (Ps. 35:16), although its use in this verse is not clear.

4581. מָעוֹז ***mā'ôz,*** מָעוֹזֶן ***mā'ôzen:*** I. A masculine noun meaning a refuge, a fortress, a shelter. It signifies a stronghold or fortress (Ezek. 24:25; 30:15; Dan. 11:7, 10, 19, 39); or a protected location or place of safety (Judg. 6:26). It is used to modify sanctuary as a stronghold, indicating a temple possibly (Dan. 11:31). It also is used in the expression "god of fortresses," indicating a god of war (Dan. 11:38). It is used figuratively of God as a fortress (2 Sam. 22:33; Nah. 3:11); the joy of God as a shelter or strength (Neh. 8:10); of God as one's strength or defense (Ps. 27:1); the way of God as a stronghold or refuge (Prov. 10:29).

II. A masculine noun meaning a stronghold, a fortress. It refers to all kinds of fortified locations and structures in Canaan (Isa. 23:11).

4582. מָעוֹךְ ***mā'ô*k*:*** A proper noun designating Maoch (1 Sam. 27:2).

4583. מָעוֹן ***mā'ôn,*** מָעִין ***mā'iyn:*** A masculine noun referring to a dwelling, a habitation, a refuge. It describes a place of habitation for various reasons. It refers to God's heavenly abode (Deut. 26:15; 2 Chr. 30:27; Zech. 2:13[17]); and the sanctuary where He dwells among His people (1 Sam. 2:29; 2 Chr. 36:15). It describes in a general sense the existence and dwelling of Jerusalem as God's chosen city (Zeph. 3:7). It refers to a dwelling in general (1 Chr. 4:41; but some translate as a people called Meunites [4586], NASB, NIV). It is used of the lairs of animals (Jer. 9:11[10]; Nah. 2:11[12]).

4584. מָעוֹן ***mā'ôn:*** A proper noun designating Maon:

A. A son of Shammai (1 Chr. 2:45).

B. A city in Judah (Josh. 15:55; 1 Sam. 23:24, 25; 25:2).

C. An Arabian tribe (Judg. 10:12).

4585. מְעוֹנָה ***m^{e}'ônāh,*** מְעֹנָה ***m^{e}'ōnāh:*** A feminine noun signifying a dwelling place, a refuge. It describes a habitat for animals (Job 38:40; Ps. 104:22; Amos 3:4). It is used in a general figurative sense of God hunting for the habitations of people (Jer. 21:13); and of the Lord's dwelling place in the Temple in Zion (Ps. 76:2[3]). God is called the refuge or habitat for His own people (Deut. 33:27).

4586. מְעוּנִים ***m^{e}'ûniym:*** A proper noun designating Meunim, Meunites (1 Chr. 4:41; 2 Chr. 26:7; Ezra 2:50; Neh. 7:52).

4587. מְעוֹנֹתַי ***m^{e}'ônōṯay:*** A proper noun designating Meonothai (1 Chr. 4:14).

4588. מָעוּף ***mā'ûp̱:*** A masculine noun indicating gloom, dimness. It pictures a place of distress overhung with the gloom of anxiety and despair (Isa. 8:22).

4589. מָעוֹר ***mā'ôr:*** A masculine noun depicting a naked body. It refers to the indecent exposure of parts of the human body, especially under the influence of strong drink (Hab. 2:15).

4590. מַעַזְיָה ***ma'azyāh,*** מַעַזְיָהוּ ***ma'azyāhû:*** A proper noun designating Maaziah:

A. A priest under Nehemiah (Neh. 10:8[9]).

B. A priest under David (1 Chr. 24:18).

4591. מָעַט ***mā'aṭ:*** A verb meaning to decrease, to become small, to be small. It indicates something already relatively small, diminutive, such as a family (Ex. 12:4); a small quantity of something (Ex. 16:17); an amount less than a set standard or quantity (Ex. 30:15); the act of reducing something, such as a price or value (Lev. 25:16); or the number of things or persons (Lev. 26:22). It has the sense of getting a few or small amount of something (Num. 35:8; 2 Kgs. 4:3).

4592. מְעַט ***m^{e}'aṭ:*** A masculine noun indicating a small amount, a few, a short time. It has the basic sense of littleness, smallness, not many. It indicates a small amount of something (Gen. 18:4; 24:17; 43:11; Deut. 26:5). As a noun, it refers to a small thing, matter, issue (Gen. 30:15). It is used as an adjective to mean small, weak (Deut. 7:7; Eccl. 5:2[1]). It also functions as an adverb indicating place, time, extent, etc. (2 Sam. 16:1; Job 10:20; 2 Kgs. 10:18; Zech. 1:15). Repeated, it means little by little (Ex. 23:30; Deut. 7:22). Prefaced with h^{a}, the interrogative particle, it means, (Was) it too little? (Gen. 30:15; Num. 16:9, 13). *'Ôḏ me'at* indicates a time phrase, Yet a little . . . (Jer. 51:33). It is often used with k^e (*kim'aṭ*), almost, just about (Ps. 119:87; Prov. 5:14). At times placed before a verb form, it is best rendered as just, only, hardly (2 Sam. 19:36[37]; Ps. 2:12). Placed before r^e*ga'*, it indicates about a moment, for a little while (Ezra 9:8; Isa. 26:20).

4593. מְעֻטָּה **m^e'uṭṭāh:** An adjective meaning grasped, drawn, wrapped. It indicates something held in readiness for action, especially in battle (Ezek. 21:15[20]). See also 5844 I, II.

4594. מַעֲטֶה **ma^aṭeh:** A masculine noun pointing out a garment, a mantle. A cloak or cape, probable from the text, as an allusion to a royal or stately symbol of recognition (Isa. 61:3). It was to be granted to those who mourned for Zion.

4595. מַעֲטָפָה **ma^aṭepeṯ:** A feminine noun referring to an outer tunic, a cape. It refers to a part of the royal garments worn by officials of state or the rich (Isa. 3:22).

4596. מְעִי **m^e'iy:** A masculine noun designating a ruin, heap. It refers to the condition and status of a fallen, destroyed city (Isa. 17:1).

4597. מָעַי **mā'ay:** A proper noun designating Maai (Neh. 12:36).

4598. מְעִיל **m^e'iyl:** A masculine noun denoting a robe, a cloak. It was an important part of the clothing worn by key classes of persons in Israel and the ancient Middle East. It is used of the robe of the high priest (Ex. 28:4, 31; 29:5; 39:22). It had fringes on the bottom (Ex. 28:34; 39:24). An opening, the *pîy* (mouth), was created for a person's head (Ex. 39:23). According to 2 Samuel 13:18, David's daughter wore this garment. It was worn by other persons of rank (1 Sam. 18:4; 24:4[5]); Job (1:20); Job's friends (2:12); chief merchants (Ezek. 26:16); persons in training for high offices (1 Sam. 2:19). It is used also in a figurative sense of the character and attributes of the Lord: justice (Job 29:14); zeal for judgment (Isa. 59:17); righteousness (Isa. 61:10). It is used to describe the character of oppressors as one of shame, dishonor (Ps. 109:29).

4599. מַעְיָן **ma'yān:** A masculine noun depicting a fountain, a spring. It refers to an underground source of water coming to the surface: (Gen. 7:11; 8:2; Lev. 11:36; 1 Kgs. 18:5). It is used figuratively as a symbol of sexual pleasure (Prov. 5:16); as a vibrant carrier of God's salvation (Isa. 12:3); as a source of joy and gladness (Ps. 84:6[7]; Hos. 13:15). It describes a spring that will flow from the house of God in a restored Israel or world (Joel 3:18[4:18]).

4600. מָעַךְ **mā'aḵ:** A verb meaning to squeeze, to crush, to bruise. It means to press, crush, jab at something: to thrust an object into the ground (1 Sam. 26:7); to crush something, ruin it (Lev. 22:24, crushed testicles); to fondle or press something; used figuratively of Israel's breasts being pressed, fondled in her youth by pagan suitors (Ezek. 23:3, 21).

4601. מַעֲכָה ***maʿakāh:*** A proper noun designating Maacah:

A. A son of Nahor (Gen. 22:24).

B. A wife of Machir (1 Chr. 7:15, 16).

C. A concubine (1 Chr. 2:48).

D. The wife of Jeiel (1 Chr. 8:29; 9:35).

E. A daughter of Talmai (2 Sam. 3:3; 1 Chr. 3:2).

F. The father of Hanan (1 Chr. 11:43).

G. The father of Shephatiah (1 Chr. 27:16).

H. The father of Achish (1 Kgs. 2:39).

I. The wife of Rehoboam (1 Kgs. 15:2, 10, 13; 2 Chr. 11:20–22; 15:16).

J. A small Syrian kingdom near Mount Hermon (2 Sam. 10:6, 8; 1 Chr. 19:6, 7).

K. A descendant of Maacah, a Maacathite (Josh. 13:13). See also 4602.

4602. מַעֲכָתִי ***maʿakātiy:*** A proper noun designating Maacathite, an inhabitant of Maacah (4601,I) (Deut. 3:14; Josh. 12:5; 13:11, 13; 2 Sam. 23:34; 2 Kgs. 25:23; 1 Chr. 4:19; Jer. 40:8).

4603. מָעַל ***māʿal:*** A verb meaning to violate one's duty. The term is used often as a synonym for sin; however, this word almost always denotes a willing act (Num. 5:6; Ezek. 14:13). It occurs principally in the later books of the Old Testament and is almost exclusively a religious term. There are only two secular uses: one for a wife's unfaithfulness to her husband and the other for a king's unfaithfulness in judgment (Num. 5:12, 27; Prov. 16:10). Although the offense is usually against God Himself, three times the unfaithfulness is directed against something under divine ban and not directly against God (Josh. 22:20; 1 Chr. 10:13; Ezek. 18:24). The writer of 1 and 2 Chronicles often connected national unfaithfulness with God's sending of punitive wars; ultimately, the outcome meant deportation for the Northern Kingdom and destruction and exile for the Southern Kingdom (1 Chr. 5:25; 2 Chr. 12:2; 28:19, 22; 36:14).

4604. מַעַל ***maʿal:*** A masculine noun meaning an unfaithful act, a treacherous act. Of its twenty-nine occurrences, it appears twenty times as a cognate accusative to the verb *māʿal* (4603), meaning to act unfaithfully or treacherously. It can apply to actions against another person, such as a wife against her husband (Num. 5:12, 27); Job by his "comforters" (Job 21:34). However, it usually applies to actions against God, whether those actions be committed by an individual (Lev. 5:15; 6:2[5:21]; Josh. 7:1; 22:20); or by the nation of Israel collectively (Josh. 22:22; 1 Chr. 9:1; Ezra 9:2, 4; 10:6; Ezek. 39:26).

4605. מַעַל ***maʻal:*** An adverbial preposition meaning upward, high; above, over. It is used to mean above, often with *min* (4480) prefixed meaning from above (Ex. 20:4; Deut. 4:39; 5:8; Josh. 2:11; Job 3:4; 18:16; 1 Kgs. 7:3; 8:23; Prov. 8:28; Isa. 6:2). It expresses the idea of on top of, above by adding *l^e* to the above phrase (Gen. 22:9; Ex. 28:27; 39:20; Lev. 11:21). It indicates something above another level or room (Jer. 35:4). It is used in a figurative sense of setting one's throne above another (Jer. 52:32).

4606. מֵעָל ***meʻāl:*** An Aramaic masculine noun meaning the going down, the setting (of the sun). It is used once in Daniel to refer to sunset, "the going down of the sun" (6:14[15]), the official ending of the daylight hours.

4607. מֹעַל ***mōʻal:*** A masculine noun referring to a lifting up. It means to raise something. In context it is used of the lifting of peoples' hands to worship God (Neh. 8:6).

4608. מַעֲלֶה ***ma^aleh:*** I. A masculine noun meaning ascent. In general it refers to a gradual feature of the land, an upward grade, as well as an upward pathway or roadway (Num. 34:4; Josh. 10:10; 15:3; 18:17; Judg. 1:36; 8:13; Isa. 15:5). It indicates a man-made way of ascent or stairway (Ezek. 40:31, 34, 37). It is used for a raised platform or podium (Neh. 9:4); or of the upper levels of structures (2 Chr. 32:33).

II. A masculine proper noun meaning ascent. This represents merely a capitalization of the noun ascent or pass to include it in the proper name of the Pass of Adummin (Josh. 15:7; 18:17). Not all translators do this.

4609. מַעֲלָה ***ma^alāh:*** I. A feminine noun meaning a step, a degree, an ascent. It is used of a step or stair (Ex. 20:26; 1 Kgs. 10:19, 20; 2 Kgs. 9:13; Neh. 3:15; 12:37), especially of steps in Ezekiel's Temple vision (Ezek. 40:6, etc.). Amos 9:6 uses the word figuratively to refer to upper levels, chambers, rooms in God's habitations. The word is used in Psalms 120–134 in the titles to designate these as Songs of Ascent, indicating the pilgrimage of persons up to the city of Jerusalem. It is used of the "going up" out of Babylonian captivity (Ezra 7:9).

II. A feminine noun meaning thought. It refers to something that is rising or arising. In context with *rûh^akem,* thoughts or ideas, it means ascending spirits, ascending thoughts (Ezek. 11:5).

4610. מַעֲלֵה עַקְרַבִּים ***ma^alēh ʻaqrabbiym:*** A proper noun designating Scorpion Pass, from *ma'^aleh* (4608,I) and *ʻaqrabbiym* (6137,II):

A. A location on the southeastern section of the boundary of Canaan and Judah, so named because the mountainous region resembled the back of a scorpion (Heb. singular, *'aqrāḇ* (6137), scorpion). The name is in its plural form.

B. The transliteration of the Hebrew for "Scorpion Pass." The same as A above.

C. This is a literal translation of the Hebrew for Scorpion Pass: literally, "the ascent of Akrabbim," "the ascent of scorpions."

4611. מַעֲלָל ***ma'ªlāl:*** A masculine noun indicating action, deed, that which is done. It usually refers to an action or deed of a person. It may be good (Prov. 20:11); or evil (Deut. 28:20; Judg. 2:19; 1 Sam. 25:3; Mic. 3:4). It is used of God's marvelous deeds to save His people (Ps. 77:11[12]; 78:7) but also His works of judgment (Mic. 2:7).

4612. מַעֲמָד ***ma'ªmāḏ:*** masculine noun designating an office, a position, a place. It is used of the placement and service of a group of people, e.g., attendants or entertainers (1 Kgs. 10:5; 2 Chr. 9:4; 35:15). It is used of positions held by a group of people (1 Chr. 23:28); or a single individual (Isa. 22:19).

4613. מָעֳמָד ***mo'ºmāḏ:*** A masculine noun referring to a foothold, a place to stand. It describes a grip or firm place to stand in order to be safe or secure (Ps. 69:2[3]).

4614. מַעֲמָסָה ***ma'ªmāsāh:*** A feminine noun meaning heavy, immovable. It indicates that something is weighty, almost immovable, dangerous to handle like a weight that is too heavy to lift. It is used figuratively of Jerusalem becoming a heavy stone (Zech. 12:3).

4615. מַעֲמַקִּים ***ma'ªmaqqiym:*** A masculine plural noun describing depths (of waters). It is used of the deep waters of the sea or other bodies of water (Ps. 69:2[3], 14[15]); Ezek. 27:34). It is used figuratively and literally of the Lord's drying up the water of the Red Sea (Isa. 51:10). It stands for the psalmist's trials and entanglements of oppression (Ps. 130:1).

4616. מַעַן ***ma'an:*** A particle used with the preposition *lᵉ* prefixed meaning so that, because of, for the sake of, with respect to, in order that. Its use as a preposition is found often (Deut. 30:6; 1 Kgs. 8:41; 11:39; 2 Kgs. 19:34; Ps. 23:3; 25:11; 31:3[4]; Ezek. 20:9); with an infinitive following to express purpose, in order to, in order that (Gen. 37:22; Ex. 1:11; 9:16; 10:1; 11:9; 2 Kgs. 10:19). Followed by the imperfect form of the verb with or without *'ªšer,* it expresses either purpose or result in order that, so that (Gen. 12:13; 18:19; Deut. 27:3; Josh. 3:4; Jer. 27:15; 42:6; Hos. 8:4).

4617. מַעֲנֶה ***ma'ªneh:*** I. A masculine noun indicating an answer, a response. It refers to something said or written as a retort or reply to assertions made (Job 32:3, 5). A wise person responds with a gentle answer (Prov. 15:1); and an appropriate reply (Prov. 15:23). God is involved in the response of people (Prov. 16:1). Some cannot respond to verbal instructions alone (Prov. 29:19). It is used of God's reply or lack thereof (Mic. 3:7).

II. A masculine noun meaning end, purpose. It indicates the ultimate goal and destiny of something or someone. The wicked person is made for the purpose or time of evil (Prov. 16:4).

4618. מַעֲנָה *ma ͡ʿnāh:* A feminine noun referring to a furrow, a plowed row, a place for a furrow. It refers to the groove or path made by a plow for planting (1 Sam. 14:14). It is used figuratively of the stripes or wounds the wicked placed on the people of Zion (Ps. 129:3).

4619. מַעַץ *maʿaṣ:* A proper noun designating Maaz, a son of Ram (1 Chr. 2:27).

4620. מַעֲצֵבָה *ma ͡ʿṣēḇāh:* A feminine noun denoting torment, sorrow. It indicates a place of punishment, in context for those who attack God's servants (Isa. 50:11).

4621. מַעֲצָד *ma ͡ʿṣāḏ:* masculine noun designating an ax, tongs. It refers to an instrument for shaping a piece of wood into an idol, probably a wood-carving tool (Isa. 44:12; Jer. 10:3).

4622. מַעְצוֹר *maʿṣôr:* A masculine noun meaning a restraint, a hindrance. This noun is derived from the verb *'āṣar* (6113), meaning to restrain or to retain. It occurs only one time, where Jonathan tells his armorbearer that "there is no restraint to the LORD to save by many or by few" (1 Sam. 14:6, KJV).

4623. מַעְצָר *maʿṣār:* A masculine noun meaning a restraint, a control. This noun is derived from the verb *'āṣar* (6113), meaning to restrain or retain. Its only occurrence is to characterize a person as one who is without self-control. This person is also compared to a ruined city without walls (Prov. 25:28).

4624. מַעֲקֶה *ma ͡ʿqeh:* A masculine noun indicating a parapet, battlement. A low wall or railing put to keep anyone from falling over the edge of something (Deut. 22:8).

4625. מַעֲקַשִּׁים *ma ͡ʿqaššiym:* A masculine plural noun meaning crooked places, rough places. It describes roads, trails, or terrain in general as bumpy, hilly, uneven, difficult to traverse (Isa. 42:16). It is used figuratively in this context.

4626. מַעַר *maʿar:* A masculine noun depicting a base place, nakedness. The private aspects of the human body displayed in public in an inappropriate way. It is used figuratively of opening up the city of Nineveh to destruction (Nah. 3:5). It is used of an open space or clear space on the surface of something (1 Kgs. 7:36).

4627. מַעֲרָב *ma ͡ʿrāḇ:* A masculine noun designating merchandise, wares.

It refers to products and materials ready to be sold by bartering, money, or exchange to a seller; items for sale (Ezek. 27:9, 13, 17, 19, 25, 27, 33, 34).

4628. מַעֲרָב ***ma'ᵃrāḇ:*** A masculine noun signifying west, westward. It is used of the area and direction west (1 Chr. 7:28; 12:15; Ps. 75:6[7]; Isa. 43:5; Dan. 8:5); a westward direction sometimes with *min* (4480) prefixed, it means from the . . . (Judg. 20:33). Used with *lᵉ*, to, it means to the west of something or the west side of it (2 Chr. 32:30; 33:14).

4629. מַעֲרֵה ***ma'ᵃreh,*** מַעֲרֵה־גָבַע ***ma'ᵃrēh gāḇa':*** I. A masculine noun meaning meadow. An alternative reading for 4628. The textual reading is not clear (Judg. 20:33, KJV).

II. A proper noun meaning Maareh-geba. Another rendering (NASB) preferred by some scholars because of the uncertain reading of the Hebrew (Judg. 20:33).

4630. מַעֲרָה ***ma'ᵃrāh:*** A feminine noun pointing out an army. It refers to a group of men prepared and ready to fight for their country or people (1 Sam. 17:23). Some prefer to read this as a specific place or location.

4631. מְעָרָה ***mᵉ'ārāh:*** I. A feminine noun meaning a cave, a den. It refers to a naturally occurring place of retreat or even a place to live (Gen. 19:30; 1 Sam. 24:3[4]; 1 Kgs. 19:13). It is also a lair or den for animals (Isa. 32:14). Caves served as burial places and were valuable property (Gen. 23:9, 11, 17, 19, 20; 49:29).

II. A feminine noun indicating a wasteland, bare ground. A bare field or area of land that was deserted, uninhabited (Isa. 32:14).

4632. מְעָרָה ***mᵉ'ārāh,*** עָרָה ***'ārāh:*** I. Mearah, a location east of Sidon (KJV, NASB, Josh. 13:4).

II. Arah, a location east of Sidon (NIV, Josh. 13:4).

4633. מַעֲרָךְ ***ma'ᵃrāḵ:*** A masculine noun pointing out a plan, preparation. It refers to the aspirations and considerations that come from the heart of man according to biblical anthropology (Prov. 16:1).

4634. מַעֲרָכָה ***ma'ᵃrāḵāh:*** A feminine noun meaning rank, an orderly array, a battle line. It is used of the ordered array of an army ready to fight (1 Sam. 4:2, 12, 16; 17:22). Sometimes it refers to the orderly battle itself (1 Sam. 17:20). It indicates the ranks or sections of an army (1 Sam. 17:10, 45), especially the ranks or battalions of the living God (1 Sam. 17:26, 36). It is used of an orderly array of various objects, e.g., lamps (Ex. 39:37; Lev. 24:6).

4635. מַעֲרֶכֶת ***ma'ᵃreḵeṯ:*** A feminine noun meaning a row, a line. This word comes from the verb *'āraḵ* (6186), meaning to arrange or to line up. The first time this word appears is in Leviticus 24:6, 7, where it describes the arrangement of the showbread: two rows of bread with six pieces in a row. In the other seven instances of this word, it is best translated "showbread" (i.e., the bread that was lined up in a row) (1 Chr. 9:32; 23:29; 28:16; 2 Chr. 2:4; 13:11; 29:18; Neh. 10:33[34]).

4636. מַעֲרֹם ***maʿᵃrōm:*** A masculine noun referring to nakedness. It is used in reference to a person without clothing, someone needing to be clothed and cared for (2 Chr. 28:15).

4637. מַעֲרָצָה ***maʿᵃraṣāh:*** A feminine noun indicating great power, terror. It is used of the forcefulness and decisiveness with which the boughs of a tree are cut off. It is used figuratively of the Lord's activity against Assyria, Israel's foe (Isa. 10:33).

4638. מַעֲרָת ***maʿᵃrāṯ:*** A proper noun designating Maarath (Josh. 15:59).

4639. מַעֲשֶׂה ***maʿᵃśeh:*** A masculine noun meaning a work, a deed, workmanship. The word has an extremely broad range of meanings, but they can be deciphered by carefully examining the context of each use. Here are some main categories: the works and deeds of God, whatever they may be, especially His work of salvation and judgment (Judg. 2:7, 10; Josh. 24:31; Ps. 8:6[7]; 33:4; Eccl. 7:13; 8:17; 11:5; Isa. 26:12). The expression "the work(s) of his hands" occurs (Ps. 28:5; 92:4[5]; Isa. 5:12). God created, made Israel (Isa. 60:21); Assyria (Isa. 19:25; 64:8[7]); various things (Job 14:15; Ps. 8:6[7]; 19:1[2]; Hab. 3:17).

The word refers to various deeds or works accomplished by people: it refers to any type of deed or act performed, good or bad (Num. 16:28; Ezra 9:13; Isa. 59:6); including the worship of idols (Deut. 31:29; Jer. 25:6, 7; 32:30). People's labor such as husbandry (Gen. 5:29; Ex. 23:16; Judg. 19:16); especially Israel's enforced labor in Egypt (Ex. 5:4, 13). It refers to things produced by humans (Gen. 40:17; Ex. 26:1, 31, 36; Isa. 3:24); especially things made for the Temple (1 Kgs. 7:17); or of detestable idols (Deut. 4:28; 2 Kgs. 19:18). For things God makes, see the first paragraph above.

4640. מַעְשַׂי ***maʿśay:*** A masculine proper noun, Maasai. The name identifies a priest, a son of Adiel, who worked in Jerusalem in the Temple (1 Chr. 9:12).

4641. מַעֲשֵׂיָה ***maʿᵃśēyāh,*** מַעֲשֵׂיָהוּ ***maʿᵃśēyāhû:*** A proper noun designating Maaseiah:

A. A Levite (1 Chr. 15:18, 20).

B. A son of Adaiah (2 Chr. 23:1).

C. A ruler (2 Chr. 26:11).

D. A son of Ahaz (2 Chr. 28:7).

E. The father of Zephaniah (Jer. 21:1; 29:25; 37:3).

F. A governor of Jerusalem (2 Chr. 34:8).

G. The father of Zedekiah, a false prophet (Jer. 29:21).

H. A son of Shallum (Jer. 35:4).

I. A son of Ithiel (Neh. 11:7).

J. The father of Azariah (Neh. 3:23).

K. A descendant of Jeshua (Ezra 10:18).

L. A descendant of Harim (Ezra 10:21).

M. A descendant of Pashhur (Ezra 10:22).

N. A son of Pahath-Moab (Ezra 10:30).

O. A priest (Neh. 8:4, 7).

P. A leader under Nehemiah (Neh. 10:25[26].

Q. A son of Baruch (Neh. 11:5).

R. A priest (Neh. 12:41).

S. A priest (Neh. 12:42).

4642. מַעֲשַׁקּוֹת *ma‘ᵃšaqqôṯ:* A feminine plural noun meaning extortions, oppressions. It indicates a leader abusing his people by forcing them to pay money or contribute goods and services against their wills (Prov. 28:16). Bribes or gain through extortion (*ḇeṣa‘ ma‘ᵃšaqqôṯ*) is considered evil (Isa. 33:15).

4643. מַעֲשֵׂר *ma‘ᵃśēr:* A masculine noun meaning tithe, tenth. This word is related to *‘eśer* (6235), meaning ten, and often means tenth (Gen. 14:20; Ezek. 45:11, 14). In the Levitical system of the Old Testament, this word refers to the tenth part, which came to be known as the tithe. Israelites were to tithe from their land, herds, flocks, and other sources (Lev. 27:30–32). Such tithes were intended to support the Levites in their priestly duties (Num. 18:21, 24, 26, 28); as well as strangers, orphans, and widows (Deut. 26:12). When Israel failed to give the tithe, it was a demonstration of their disobedience (Mal. 3:8, 10); when they reinstituted the tithe, it was a sign of reform, as in Hezekiah's (2 Chr. 31:5, 6, 12) and Nehemiah's times (Neh. 10:37[38], 38[39]; 12:44).

4644. מֹף *mōp̱:* Another Hebrew name for the Egyptian city of Memphis (Hos. 9:6). See 5297.

4645. מִפְגָּע *mip̱gā‘:* A masculine noun indicating a target, a mark. It refers to the object that is aimed at by a marksman. It is used figuratively of Job being the target of God's attacks (Job 7:20).

4646. מַפָּח *mappāḥ:* A masculine noun meaning breathing out. This word comes from the verb *nāp̱aḥ* (5301), meaning to breathe or to blow, and occurs only once in the Old Testament. In Job 11:20, this word describes the soul that expires.

4647. מַפֻּחַ *mappuaḥ:* A masculine noun signifying bellows. A set of bags pressed to force air into a furnace, making it hotter (Job 7:20). It is used figuratively of God's attempts to refine and purify His people (Jer. 6:29).

4648. מְפִיבֹשֶׁת *mᵉp̱iyḇōšeṯ:* A proper noun designating Mephibosheth:

A. The son of Saul by Rizpah. He and six others were executed and left unburied by the king of Gibeah to stop a famine in the land of Israel (2 Sam. 21:8).

B. The son of Jonathan, Saul's son. He was spared from execution because of the oath between David and Jonathan (2 Sam. 21:7). He had been dropped as a baby and was lame in both feet (2 Sam. 4:4). David had spared him earlier because he was Jonathan's son (2 Sam. 9:7–8). And he had supported David faithfully (2 Sam. 19:24[25], 25[26], 30[31]).

4649. מֻפִּים *muppiym:* A proper noun designating Muppim (Gen. 46:21).

4650. מֵפִיץ *mepiyṣ:* A masculine noun meaning a club, a maul. It refers to a hammer–like tool that delivers jolting blows. The impact of a false witness on a person is compared to it (Prov. 25:18).

4651. מַפָּל *mappāl:* A masculine noun indicating fallen parts, sweepings; folds. It is used to indicate the sweepings, grains, and partial chaff left of wheat or grain (Amos 8:6). It is used of the excess skin and folds of a Leviathan, possibly a crocodile (Job 41:23[15]).

4652. מִפְלָאָה *miplā'āh:* A feminine noun designating a wonderful work. It is a description of the marvelous and awe-inspiring works of God in the atmosphere (Job 37:16).

4653. מִפְלַגָּה *miplaggāh:* A feminine noun meaning division. This word comes from the verb *pālāh* (6395), meaning to separate, and occurs only once in the Old Testament. In 2 Chronicles 35:12, this word is used to describe the household divisions among the Levites.

4654. מַפָּלָה *mappālāh:* A feminine noun referring to a ruin, a heap. It is the opposite of an inhabited city or area; an uninhabitable place (Isa. 23:13; 25:2). Damascus was reduced to a rubble, a ruin (Isa. 17:1).

4655. מִפְלָט *miplāṭ:* A masculine noun indicating an escape, a place of refuge. It depicts a location or place of safety and security (Ps. 55:8[9]). Used figuratively, it describes the psalmist's escape from the storm and tempest of suffering brought on by his enemies.

4656. מִפְלֶצֶת *mipleṣeṯ:* A feminine noun meaning horrid thing. This word comes from the verb *pālaṣ* (6426), meaning to shudder, and described something so horrible that one would shudder. It was used only to describe an image (perhaps some sort of idol) that Maacah had made as an object of worship (1 Kgs. 15:13; 2 Chr. 15:16).

4657. מִפְלָשׂ *miplaś:* A masculine noun denoting balancing, hanging. It is used to describe the floating, hanging in balance of a cloud as a wonder of God (Job 37:16). Some suggest the layering of clouds is in mind (NASB).

4658. מַפֶּלֶת *mappeleṯ:* A feminine noun meaning a carcass, a ruin, overthrow. This word comes from the verb *nāpal* (5307), meaning to fall. It described the physical carcass of a dead animal (Judg. 14:8); and the practical ruin of the wicked (Prov. 29:16). It also described the overthrow of two nations: Tyre (Ezek. 26:15, 18; 27:27); and Egypt (Ezek. 31:13, 16; 32:10).

4659. מִפְעָל *mip̱ʿāl,* מִפְעָלָה *mip̱ʿālāh:* I. A masculine noun describing a work, a deed. It refers to acts, works, deeds, and the results as well; the things produced (Prov. 8:22).

II. A feminine noun meaning a work, a deed. It is used of the destructive acts of God and their results by wars and battles in the earth (Ps. 46:8[9]); but also in context to His magnificent deeds and accomplishments of deliverance for His people (Ps. 66:5).

4660. מַפָּץ *mappāṣ:* A masculine noun meaning a smashing, a shattering. This word is used in this form only once and refers to a dangerous weapon for smashing (Ezek. 9:2). See the related Hebrew root *nāp̱aṣ* (5310), as well as the Hebrew words *nep̱eṣ* (5311) and *mapp̱ēṣ* (4661).

4661. מַפֵּץ *mappēṣ:* A masculine noun defining a war club, battle-ax. It was a weapon with a heavy blade, used in war. It is used figuratively of Babylon as God's battle-ax against His own people (Jer. 51:20).

4662. מִפְקָד *mip̱qāḏ:* A masculine noun meaning a mandate, an appointment, a counting, a census; an appointed place. Ten men became assistant overseers for the management of offerings in the house of the Lord by the appointment of King Hezekiah (2 Chr. 31:13). King David ordered Joab to take a census of the number of people under his rule (2 Sam. 24:9; 1 Chr. 21:5). Twice the word functions to designate a location. In Ezekiel 43:21, the bull of the sin offering was to be burnt in the appointed place of the Temple precincts. In Nehemiah 3:31, the word was utilized (possibly as a proper name) to identify a particular gate in the city of Jerusalem. This term stems from the verb *pāqaḏ* (6485).

4663. מִפְקָד *mip̱qāḏ:* A proper noun designating Miphkad. The word is rendered in transliteration in the KJV but translated as the "Inspection Gate" in most modern translations.

4664. מִפְרָץ *mip̱raṣ:* A masculine noun describing a cove, a landing place. It depicts a place along a seashore where boats dock, load, and unload passengers and cargo (Judg. 5:17).

4665. מַפְרֶקֶת *map̱reqeṯ:* A feminine noun meaning neck. It is the part of a human or animal that connects the head to the body and encloses portions of the backbone. Eli's neck was broken when he fell backward (1 Sam. 4:18).

4666. מִפְרָשׂ *mip̱rāś:* A masculine noun designating a spreading out. It means for something to draw out, to stretch out, to unfold, such as clouds across the sky (Job 36:29). It indicates the chief merchandising item of Tyre, fine embroidered linen. It was Tyre's "spreading out" her sail to attract merchants to her (Ezek. 27:7).

4667. מִפְשָׂעָה mipśā'āh: A feminine noun meaning hip, buttocks. It refers to the upper thighs of a person which, in the Middle East, were to be covered (1 Chr. 19:4).

4668. מַפְתֵּחַ maptēaḥ: A masculine noun designating a key. It indicates a tool used to open a lock (Judg. 3:25). To be over (*'al*) the key means to be in charge of opening a door (1 Chr. 9:27). It is used figuratively of the official right to be a part of the Davidic dynasty and its authority (Isa. 22:22).

4669. מִפְתָּח miptāḥ: A masculine noun describing the act of opening. It refers to opening, expanding something. It is used in an idiom for speaking or saying, e.g., "the opening of my lips" (Prov. 8:6).

4670. מִפְתָּן miptān: A masculine noun meaning threshold. It indicates the beginning or entrance of something, a doorsill (1 Sam. 5:4, 5), a temple, or other building (Ezek. 9:3; 10:4, 18; 46:2; 47:1; Zeph. 1:9).

4671. מֹץ mōts: A masculine noun referring to chaff. The fine pieces of grain, husks of wheat, grains in general, or fine-cut straw given to animals as fodder but figuratively indicating what is useless or worthless. The wicked are compared to chaff that is easily blown away (Job 21:18; Ps. 1:4); nations under God's judgments are like chaff (Isa. 17:13; 29:5; 41:15; Hos. 13:3). It is used to indicate the swift passage of time, as it passes away quickly like chaff (Zeph. 2:2).

4672. מָצָא māṣā': A verb meaning to find, attain. The verb is employed in both the active and passive senses (to be found). In addition, it is also used in a causative sense, to cause to find. Finally, the word is employed in several idioms that carry special meanings. The word is used to indicate finding or seeking just about anything: water (Gen. 26:32; Ex. 15:22); a place, goal, or location (Gen. 8:9); a knowledge of the Lord (Prov. 2:5); the word of the Lord (Amos 8:12); or words of wisdom (Prov. 4:22). The word indicates coming on something (Gen. 44:8); of finding something (Job 11:7; Eccl. 3:11). Additional idiomatic phrases include finding heart, meaning to be able to do something (2 Sam. 7:27); finding the vigor (life) of one's hand, renewing one's strength (Isa. 57:10); to not be found, not to exist or be dead (Job 20:8). The meanings discussed are used in passive constructions as well. Persons being sought are found (Gen. 18:29, 30; Josh. 10:17); and crime or evil can be found out (Ex. 22:4[3]; 1 Sam. 25:28); as can evildoers (Ex. 22:2[1], 7[6]). The verb means to happen to be, literally to be found, in several passages (Deut. 17:2; 18:10; Jer. 5:26). Finally, in the passive usage of the verb, it means not sufficient for someone, as in Joshua 17:16 where the hill country was not found to be sufficient for the people of Joseph. In the stem indicating cause, the verb can mean to bring on someone their just desserts, i.e., to cause proper justice to find them (Job 34:11; cf. Job 37:13). In 2 Samuel 3:8, the verb indicates the deliverance of someone into the power of another person, i.e., to make someone be found in the hand of another, in this case in the hand of David.

4673. מַצָּב *maṣṣāḇ:* A masculine noun identifying a garrison, an outpost, a place of standing. It indicates an outpost or military station (1 Sam. 13:23; 14:1, 4, 6, 11, 15) or a hideout for brigands or other bands of soldiers, etc. It has the sense of firm ground on which to stand (Josh. 4:3, 9). It is used of an established position or office a person holds (Isa. 22:19).

4674. מֻצָּב *muṣṣāḇ:* A masculine noun meaning siegework, a tower. It is used of a military engine used against cities (Isa. 29:3) but also of a specific structural location, possibly a column, pillar, or military structure (Judg. 9:6).

4675. מַצָּבָה *maṣṣāḇāh*, מִצָּבָה *miṣṣāḇāh:* A feminine noun indicating a garrison, an army. It is used of a place where armed men were gathered for battle, an outpost, a place that was defensible (1 Sam. 14:12). But, evidently, it is applied to attacking forces as well (Zech. 9:8).

4676. מַצֵּבָה *maṣṣēḇāh:* A feminine noun meaning something set upright. The word most often refers to a standing, unhewn block of stone utilized for religious and memorial purposes. After a powerful experience of the Lord in a dream, Jacob set up as a pillar the stone on which he had laid his head, in commemoration of the event (Gen. 28:18, 22; cf. Gen. 31:45; 35:20). Moses set up an altar and also twelve pillars at the base of Mount Sinai to represent the twelve tribes of Israel (Ex. 24:4). These pillars were erected as monuments to God (Hos. 3:4); or, more commonly, to pagan deities (1 Kgs. 14:23, Mic. 5:13[12]). Many times in 2 Kings, the term refers to a sacred pillar that aided people in their worship of pagan gods, especially the Canaanite god Baal. In most of these passages, the sacred columns were used by Israelites, contrary to the Lord's prohibition concerning the worship of any other god (2 Kgs. 3:2; 10:26, 27; 18:4; 23:14; cf. Hos. 10:1, 2; Mic. 5:13[12]). This noun stems from the verb *nāṣaḇ* (5324).

4677. מְצֹבָיָה *m^{e}ṣōḇyāh:* A proper noun designating Mezobaite (1 Chr. 11:47).

4678. מַצֶּבֶת *maṣṣeḇeṯ:* A feminine noun meaning a pillar, a stump, a standing stone. A monument could be set up to commemorate a divine appearance, such as the pillar of stone Jacob set up at Bethel (Gen. 35:14). The word can also refer to a pillar or monument set up to honor oneself, such as the one Absalom set up for himself in order that his name would be remembered (2 Sam. 18:18).

4679. מְצָד **m^eṣāḏ,** מְצַד **m^eṣaḏ:** A masculine noun defining a stronghold, a fortress. It refers to a place with powerful natural or man-made defenses, difficult of access, and a place for refugees, etc. Also, it refers to a place for further fortification by military engines and soldiers; strongholds (Judg. 6:2; 1 Sam. 23:14, 19, 29[24:1]; 1 Chr. 12:8, 16; Jer. 48:41; 51:30; Ezek. 33:27). Jerusalem became David's major stronghold (1 Chr. 11:7), sometimes rendered as a refuge (of the righteous) (Isa. 33:16).

4680. מָצָה **māṣāh:** A verb signifying to drain, to drain out, to wring out. It has the basic sense of removing or forcing out moisture or liquid from something: a wet fleece; a hide (Judg. 6:38); blood drained from the altar (Lev. 1:15; 5:9); water or wine consumed by people (Ps. 73:10; 75:8[9]); figuratively, of draining, drinking from the cup of the Lord's anger (Isa. 51:17; Ezek. 23:34; cf. Ps. 75:8[9]).

4681. מֹצָה **mōṣāh:** A proper noun designating Mozah (Josh. 18:26).

4682. מַצָּה **maṣṣāh:** A feminine noun meaning unleavened bread or cakes. This food was a staple in Israelite diets and could be prepared in a hurry for a meal (Gen. 19:3, 1 Sam. 28:24). One of the three Israelite national feasts was the Feast of Unleavened Bread where the people ate flat bread for seven days to commemorate their deliverance from Egypt (Ex. 23:15). Unleavened bread or cakes could also be anointed with oil and presented to the priests as a sacrifice (Ex. 29:2).

4683. מַצָּה **maṣṣāh:** A feminine noun depicting strife, contention. It refers to wrangling, quarreling, and contention (Prov. 13:10; 17:19), especially brought on by arrogant or insolent attitudes, transgressions, and trespasses. It refers to the results of false fasts that brought on fighting, quarreling, and violence (Isa. 58:4).

4684. מִצְהָלוֹת **miṣhālôṯ:** A feminine plural noun identifying the neighing of a horse. It indicates the neighing of horses getting ready for battle (Jer. 8:16); and is used figuratively of Israel's rebellious neighing for her lewd suitors (Jer. 13:27).

4685. מָצוֹד **māṣôḏ,** מְצוֹדָה **m^eṣôḏāh:** A masculine noun meaning a net, a hunting implement, a siege tower. Job claimed that God had surrounded him with a net (Job 19:6). Used figuratively, a wicked person delighted in catching other evil ones (Prov. 12:12); the seductress threw out nets to capture men (Eccl. 7:26). Siegeworks or bulwarks described the method of attack against a city (Eccl. 9:14).

4686. מְצוּדָה **m^eṣûḏāh:** I. A feminine noun identifying a net, a prey. It identifies a net used for hunting prey

(Ps. 66:11; Ezek. 12:13; 17:20). It is used figuratively of the Lord's net for His own people and their leaders. It indicates a net in which fish are caught but is used as a picture of the snares of human life (Eccl. 9:12).

II. A feminine noun meaning a stronghold. It refers to a wilderness or mountainous places for hiding, defense, and gathering supplies for battle (1 Sam. 22:4, 5; 24:22[23]); especially David's Zion (2 Sam. 5:7, 9). In nature, eagles have their safe havens, inaccessible nests, or strongholds (Job 39:28). The Lord Himself is the greatest stronghold (2 Sam. 22:2; Ps. 18:2[3]; 31:2[3], 3[4]; 71:3; 91:2; 144:2).

4687. מִצְוָה ***miṣwāh:*** A feminine noun meaning a commandment. It can apply to the edicts issued by a human being, most likely the king (1 Kgs. 2:43; Esth. 3:3; Prov. 6:20; Isa. 36:21; Jer. 35:18). It can also relate to a general corpus of human precepts (Isa. 29:13); or a body of teachings (Prov. 2:1; 3:1). On the other hand, this expression can reference God's commands. In the Pentateuch, this is its only usage. It does not refer to human commandments. In the singular, it may distinguish a certain commandment (1 Kgs. 13:21); yet it appears most frequently in the plural to designate the entire corpus of divine law and instruction (Gen. 26:5; Ex. 16:28; Deut. 6:2; 1 Kgs. 2:3). It is also important to note that, in the plural, this word often appears in synonymous parallelism with such words as *ḥuqqîm* (2706); *mišpāṭîm* (4941); *'ēḏōṯ* (5715); *tôrôṯ* (8451).

4688. מְצוֹלָה ***m^{e}ṣôlāh,*** מְצוּלָה ***m^{e}ṣûlāh,*** מְצֻלָה ***m^{e}ṣulāh:*** A feminine noun referring to a depth. It is used of the deep, the depths of the Nile (Ex. 15:5; Neh. 9:11; Ps. 107:24; Zech. 10:11); and of the sea (Jon. 2:3[4]; Mic. 7:19). In the last reference, it is used figuratively of the place where God casts the sins of His people. It is a general term for the sea itself (Job 41:31[23]); and figuratively of the place of the dead (Ps. 68:22[23]); or a perilous and dangerous set of circumstances (Ps. 69:2[3], 15[16]; 88:6[7]). It refers to a deep depression in the land, a ravine, or a hollow (Zech. 1:8).

4689. מָצוֹק ***māṣôq:*** A masculine noun meaning distress, anguish. It refers to hardships and anxiety (Deut. 28:53, 55, 57; Jer. 19:9); especially brought on from disobeying the Lord but also from general social and political conditions (1 Sam. 22:2). The psalmist suffered anguish, relieved only by following the Lord's delightful Law (Ps. 119:143).

4690. מָצוּק ***māṣûq:*** A masculine noun signifying a pillar, a foundation; standing like a pillar. It is used metaphorically of the foundations or pillars of the earth (1 Sam. 2:8). It points out the rise or structure of a natural rocky hill or crag (1 Sam. 14:5).

4691. מְצוּקָה ***m^{e}ṣûqāh:*** A feminine noun meaning distress, anguish.

It identifies a state of despair, hopelessness, and anxiety. It depicts the life of the wicked as spent in despair and distress (Job 15:24); but of the troubles of the righteous as well (Ps. 25:17; 107:6, 13, 19, 28). It is a feature of the Day of the Lord, a day of terror and distress (Zeph. 1:15).

4692. מָצוֹר ***māṣôr:*** A masculine noun indicating a siege; a besieged, fortified area. It indicates a methodical attack on people, city, or country in order to overcome and conquer it or to the period of time when this occurs (Ezek. 4:8; 5:2); siege (Mic. 5:1[4:14]; Zech. 12:2); with *bô'* it expressed the idea of coming into a state of siege (Deut. 20:19; 2 Kgs. 24:10; 25:2; Jer. 52:5); the distressful time of the siege (Deut. 28:53, 55, 57; Jer. 19:9). It indicates also the entrenchment or features of the siege itself: engines of siege (Deut. 20:20); a rampart or defense structure (Eccl. 9:14; Zech. 9:3); a besieged city (Ps. 31:21[22]; 60:9[11]).

4693. מָצוֹר ***māṣôr:*** A proper name Matsor; another name for Egypt. It indicates the land or territory of Egypt (2 Kgs. 19:24; Isa. 19:6; 37:25; Mic. 7:12).

4694. מְצוּרָה ***m^e^ṣûrāh,*** מְצֻרָה ***m^e^ṣurāh:*** A feminine noun designating a fortified place, a fortress. It indicated a fortified city or location: cities in Judah and Benjamin (2 Chr. 11:10, 11, 23; 12:4; 14:6[5]; 21:3); battle engines or fortified towers (Isa. 29:3); a fortified station or structure in a city (Nah. 2:1[2]).

4695. מַצּוּת ***maṣṣûṯ:*** A feminine noun signifying warfare, contention. It refers to that which engenders hostility, fighting, quarreling (Isa. 41:12).

4696. מֵצַח ***meṣaḥ:*** A masculine noun meaning forehead, the part of the head between the eyebrows and the front of a person's hairline. Aaron wore a holy plate on his forehead (Ex. 28:38); Goliath was killed from a stone striking his forehead (1 Sam. 17:49); Uzziah had leprosy on his forehead (2 Chr. 26:19, 20). A "bronze forehead" was symbolic of determination or obstinacy in a good or bad sense (Isa. 48:4); as is the phrase, strong, hard of forehead (Ezek. 3:7–9). A mark on the forehead served as an identifying symbol (Ezek. 9:4).

4697. מִצְחָה ***miṣḥāh:*** A feminine noun referring to leg armor, greaves. It refers to shin guards worn on a soldier's legs (1 Sam. 17:6).

4698. מְצִלָּה ***m^e^ṣillāh:*** A feminine noun defining a bell. It refers to a bell worn by horses for noise and beauty. In context the phrase Holy to the Lord will be inscribed on these bells (Zech. 14:20).

4699. מְצֻלָה ***m^e^ṣulāh:*** A feminine noun designating a ravine, bottomland; form of. It is used of a long, deep depression in the land, forming a hollow (Zech. 1:8).

4700. מְצִלְתַּיִם ***m^e^ṣiltayim:*** A dual feminine noun indicating cymbals. It describes a musical instrument, one of the cymbals used in the Levitical choir and other musical groups of Levites in worship in Israel, especially at the Temple (1 Chr. 13:8; 15:16, 19, 28; 16:5, 42; 25:1, 6; 2 Chr. 5:12, 13; 29:25; Ezra 3:10; Neh. 12:27).

4701. מִצְנֶפֶת ***miṣnep̱eṯ:*** A feminine noun depicting a turban, a miter. It was the headband, similar to a turban, worn by either the king (Ezek. 21:26[31]) or the high priest (Ex. 28:4, 37, 39; 29:6; 39:28, 31; Lev. 8:9; 16:4).

4702. מַצָּע ***maṣṣā':*** A masculine noun defining a bed. It depicts a place to rest, recline, and sleep in safety and satisfaction (Isa. 28:20).

4703. מִצְעָד ***miṣ'āḏ:*** A masculine noun meaning a step, footstep. The word is used of the way a person's life unfolds, picturesquely as one walks along a path by moving his or her feet (Ps. 37:23). The Lord orders peoples' steps (Prov. 20:24) as they go through life. To follow a persons' steps is to imitate and adopt their actions and goals (Dan. 11:43).

4704. מִצְעִירָה ***miṣ'iyrāh:*** An adjective describing something as little, small. It indicates that something is little in size, especially compared to other things of the same kind (Dan. 8:9). In this context, a horn stands for a person.

4705. מִצְעָר ***miṣ'ār:*** A masculine noun depicting a small thing, a little while. It has in mind basically a small amount or quantity or something of little importance: a number in size (Gen. 19:20); an insignificant event (Job 8:7); a small number (2 Chr. 24:24); a small period of time (Isa. 63:18).

4706. מִצְעָר ***miṣār:*** A proper noun designating Mizar (Ps. 42:6).

4707. מִצְפֶּה ***miṣpeh:*** A masculine noun depicting a watchtower. It describes a lookout in the wilderness, a watchtower (2 Chr. 20:24); a sentry post for spotting an enemy (Isa. 21:8).

4708. מִצְפֶּה ***miṣpeh:*** A proper noun designating Mizpeh, a word meaning "lookout," indicating a place where a panoramic view is possible. It refers to several places.

A. A village given to the tribe of Judah. Probably near the city of Lachish (Josh. 15:38).

B. A city in Moab, where David sent his mother and father for safety. It would be somewhere east of the Dead Sea in Moab.

C. A city in Gad (Gilead) from which the infamous judge Jephthah came. It was located south of the Jabbok River and east of the Jordan (Judg. 10:17).

D. A city allotted to the tribe of Benjamin. All Israel gathered there to decide what to do about the rape and murder of the Levite's concubine (Judg. 20:1; 21:25). Later, it became a key worship center (1 Sam. 7:2–17; 10:17). It was used briefly by Gedaliah after Jerusalem had been destroyed. It supplied workers to rebuild the wall of the city (Neh. 3:7).

E. A valley or region (Josh. 11:3, 8) where Israelites defeated Canaanites, especially the Hivites. See 4709 A also.

4709. מִצְפָּה ***miṣpāh:*** A proper noun designating Mizpah, a word meaning "lookout," indicating a place where a panoramic view is possible. It refers to several places:

A. A city located in Judah where Hivites lived. See 4708,A.

B. A city that was fortified by Asa, king of Judah (1 Kgs. 15:22).

C. A name given to the heap of stones "watchtower" Laban and Jacob set up as a witness between them (Gen. 31:49).

D. It refers to an administrative district administered by Shallun, son of Col-hozeh after the return of the exiles (Neh. 3:15).

E. A town or area that Jeshua was over (Neh. 3:19).

4710. מַצְפּוֹן ***maṣpôn:*** A masculine noun referring to a hidden treasure. It refers to the wealth and power of the kingdom of Edom (Esau) in its mountain strongholds (Obad. 1:6).

4711. מָצַץ ***māṣaṣ:*** A verb meaning to milk out, to drain out, to nurse. It describes the nursing and feeding activity of a child or small animal. It is used figuratively of God's people nursing at the bosom of a restored Jerusalem (Isa. 66:11).

4712. מֵצַר ***mēṣar:*** A masculine noun indicating a distress, an anguish, a pain. It depicts the anxieties and hope of a person in the throes of death or a serious illness (Ps. 116:3); and from threatening enemies (Ps. 118:5). It describes the tension, hopelessness, and oppression of Israel in exile in Babylon (Lam. 1:3).

4713. מִצְרִי ***miṣriy:*** A proper noun designating an Egyptian (Gen. 12:12, 14; 16:1, 3; 21:9; 25:12; 39:1, 2, 5; 43:32; Ex. 1:19; 2:11, 12, 14, 19; Lev. 24:10; Deut. 23:7[8]; 26:6; Josh. 24:7; 1 Sam. 30:11, 13; 2 Sam. 23:21; 1 Chr. 2:34; 11:23; Ezra 9:1).

4714. מִצְרַיִם ***miṣrayim:*** A proper noun designating Mizraim:

A. The son of Ham, Noah's son, and the ancestor of Egypt and its people. The name is the name of Egypt in Hebrew. Mizraim fathered several sons from whom other peoples came (1 Chr. 1:8).

B. An ancient land and nation that has a history going back beyond 3000 B.C. The word Egypt comes from the Greek term *Aiguptos*. The Hebrew name in the Old Testament is *miṣrayim*. The meaning of this word is uncertain. It is in a dual form and may hint at the Upper and Lower geographical aspects of this ancient nation. It occupied the northeastern corner of the African continent. It has been called the "gift of the Nile," referring to its central river which is the lifeblood of the nation. The Nile (or river of Egypt; Gen. 15:18) flows from the south to the northern delta where it empties into the Mediterranean. The Nile's seasonal flooding provided the land and people yearly with rich soil and abundant crops for food. To the south, past the cataracts of the Nile, lay Nubia, Cush, and Ethiopia, as well as the White Nile and Blue Nile, the highland tributaries of the Nile itself. The nation Israel and her ancestors had both friendly and hostile encounters with Egypt (Gen. 12:40, 41; Ex. 1—15).

Egypt was famed for its reception and nurture of the patriarchs (Gen. 41, 42, 43–50) but was infamous for its enslavement and oppression of the Israelites until the Lord delivered His people at the Exodus (ca. 1446 B.C. or ca. 1220 B.C.). Throughout the Old Testament after the Exodus, Egypt was a thorn in the flesh of Israel.

The patriarchs encountered Egypt during the years ca. 2134–1786 B.C., the Middle Kingdom of Egypt. The Second Intermediate Period (1786–1540 B.C.) probably saw the appearance of Joseph and the Hebrews in the land of Goshen, a northeastern area of the Nile Delta region. During the New Kingdom Era (ca. 1552–1069 B.C.), Israel was enslaved and freed (Ex. 1—15).

It is not the purpose of this article to trace the contacts of Egypt and Israel throughout the Old Testament, but in general, Egyptian power and influence on Israel declined greatly after the Exodus event. The last king of northern Israel (Hoshea) hoped futilely that Egypt would help him against Assyria (2 Kgs. 17:1–4). Assyria became dominant in the affairs of Israel until ca. 612–605 B.C. Then Babylon became the dominant superpower of the Middle East (650–538 B.C.), then Persia (538–332 B.C.). All three of these secular powers exerted their influence in Egypt as well as Canaan.

C. The designation of the inhabitants of Egypt (see A and B above) simply took on the name of the nation itself.

4715. מַצְרֵף *maṣrēp̱:* A masculine noun defining a crucible, a refining pot. It indicates a metal pot in which the impurities of precious metals were separated out (Prov. 17:3; 27:21).

4716. מַק *maq:* A masculine noun signifying stench, rottenness. It indicates a putrid, unpleasant smell or a state of decay, the opposite of sweet-smelling, healthy (Isa. 3:24; 5:24).

4717. מַקֶּבֶת *maqqeḇeṯ:* A feminine noun indicating a hammer. It refers to an iron tool used to drive nails or pegs, or to break up and shape various materials (Judg. 4:21; 1 Kgs. 6:7; Isa. 44:12; Jer. 10:4).

4718. מַקֶּבֶת *maqqeḇeṯ:* A feminine noun indicating a hole, a pit, a quarry. It refers to a place where stones were dug out, measured, cut, and shaped (Isa. 51:1).

4719. מַקֵּדָה ***maqqēḏah:*** A proper noun designating Makkedah (Josh. 10:10, 16, 17, 21, 28, 29; 12:16; 15:41).

4720. מִקְדָּשׁ ***miqdāš:*** A masculine noun meaning a holy or sacred place, a sanctuary. As a nominal form from the verb *qāḏaš* (6942), meaning to be set apart or to be consecrated, this noun designates that which has been sanctified or set apart as sacred and holy as opposed to the secular, common, or profane. It is a general term for anything sacred and holy, such as the articles of the Tabernacle that were devoted for use during worship (Num. 10:21); or the best portion of the offerings given to the Lord (Num. 18:29). Most often, it connotes a sanctuary, the physical place of worship. In this sense, the word encompasses a variety of these concepts: the old Israelite sanctuaries (Josh. 24:26); the Tabernacle (Ex. 25:8; Lev. 12:4; 21:12); the Temple (1 Chr. 22:19; 2 Chr. 29:21; Dan. 11:31); the sanctuaries dedicated to false worship (Lev. 26:31; Isa. 16:12; Amos 7:9). It can also denote a place of refuge or asylum because this status was accorded to sacred places among the Hebrews (Isa. 8:14; Ezek. 11:16; cf. 1 Kgs. 1:50; 2:28).

4721. מַקְהֵל ***maqhēl:*** A feminine noun depicting a congregation, an assembly. A group of people gathered together for a common purpose, especially for worshiping the Lord and God of Israel (Ps. 26:12; 68:26[27]).

4722. מַקְהֵלֹת ***maqhēlōṯ:*** A proper noun designating Makheloth (Num. 33:25, 26).

4723. מִקְוֵא ***miqwē',*** מִקְוֶה ***miqweh,*** קְוֵא ***qᵉwē',*** קְוֵה ***qᵉweh:*** A masculine noun meaning hope. The word is used four times and is highly significant theologically. It is used twice as a designation for the Lord. King David, shortly before he died, asserted that as for humans, their days were without any hope in this life (1 Chr. 29:15). But Jeremiah answered this challenge in the midst of drought, famine, and sword. Jeremiah cried out to the Lord, calling Him the Hope of Israel in parallel with Savior (Jer. 14:8). He also viewed the day of the Lord prophetically at a time when there was no positive outlook for Judah. Jeremiah asserted that the Lord was the only hope Judah had; to turn from Him would result in shame (Jer. 17:13).

Those who returned from exile and established the community found themselves near the brink of rejection, but one brave soul was moved to assert that there was still some hope for Israel to be spared (Ezra 10:2). The word has within its root meaning the thought of waiting for the Lord to act.

4724. מִקְוָה ***miqwāh:*** A feminine noun denoting a reservoir, a ditch. It refers to a large hole dug out of the ground for holding water for various purposes, to reserve water, to create defense, beauty, etc. (Isa. 22:11).

4725. מָקוֹם ***māqôm,*** מָקֹם ***māqōm:*** A common noun indicating a place, a spot, a space, a stand. It basically indicates a location or space, in general of any place or location specified: figuratively of the place of the wicked (Ps. 37:10); a place at a table for eating (1 Sam. 20:25); a place to live (Deut. 1:33; 2 Kgs. 6:1); a spot where one is standing (Ex. 3:5; Josh. 5:15); unspecified: in any place (Gen. 1:9; 28:16, 17; Ex. 20:24; Judg. 2:5; Amos 4:6; 8:3). It is used often to indicate a city, the place of the city (Gen. 18:24; 20:11; 22:14; 26:7; Deut. 21:19; 2 Kgs. 18:25). It refers to spots on a person's body (Lev. 13:19; 2 Kgs. 5:11). It indicates a place for a statue on a pedestal, a stand (1 Sam. 5:3). It refers often to special holy places: the place of the sanctuary (Lev. 10:13; 14:17); a holy place (*māqôm qādôš*) means a place around the Tabernacle area. Jerusalem is called this holy place (1 Kgs. 8:30). It refers to places concerning the Temple or the Temple itself; the place which God chose, where His name is (1 Kgs. 8:29, 30, 35; 2 Chr. 6:20, 21, 26; Isa. 18:7; 60:13). It is used of a holy place at any location or time (Eccl. 8:10). It has the sense of an open space or area (1 Sam. 26:13). It is found in the idiom "to yield ground" in battle (Judg. 20:36). It refers to pagan holy places (Deut. 12:2, 3; Ezek. 6:13).

4726. מָקוֹר ***māqôr:*** A masculine noun designating a fountain, a spring, a flow. It indicates a source of water (Hos. 13:15); the flow of blood during a woman's menstrual period (Lev. 12:7; 20:18). It indicates the water sources of a river literally or in a figurative sense (Jer. 51:36; Zech. 13:1). It is used often figuratively as a source of tears (Jer. 9:1[8:23]); a source of life (Ps. 36:9[10]); the Lord is pictured as the fountain or life of Israel (Ps. 68:26[27]; Jer. 2:13); a man's wife is a fountain (Prov. 5:18); the mouth of the righteous person is a spring of life (Prov. 10:11); the wise teaching of wisdom (Prov. 13:14; 18:4); the fear of the Lord is a fountain of life (Prov. 14:27); understanding is pictured as a fountain of life, a source of how to live (Prov. 16:22).

4727. מִקָּח ***miqqaḥ:*** A masculine noun meaning the act of taking, receiving. It means to accept something. In context it is used of the wrongful acceptance of bribes (2 Chr. 19:7).

4728. מַקָּחוֹת ***maqqāḥôṯ:*** A feminine noun indicating wares, merchandise. It refers to goods and products for sale (Neh. 10:31[32]).

4729. מִקְטָר ***miqṭār:*** A masculine noun meaning a place for burning. It refers to a location or spot for burning something, e.g., an altar for sacrifices (Ex. 30:1).

4730. מִקְטֶרֶת ***miqṭereṯ:*** A feminine noun referring to a censer. It was an instrument for holding and burning incense (2 Chr. 26:19; Ezek. 8:11) to create a pleasant-smelling aroma.

4731. מַקֵּל ***maqqēl:*** A masculine noun meaning a rod, a stick, a staff. It refers to a rod, a stick, a staff of wood for various uses: Jacob cut rods from poplar and peeled white stripes in them for use in a mysterious breeding process (Gen. 30:37–39, 41); a walking stick or shepherd's stick (Gen. 32:10[11]; Ex. 12:11; 1 Sam. 17:40); a prodding or riding rod (Num. 22:27); a weapon (Ezek. 39:9). It is used figuratively of covenants with Israel and Judah (Zech. 11:7, 10, 14). Hosea describes it as a kind of staff or wand used by a sorcerer or diviner (Hos. 4:12). It is used symbolically several more times (Jer. 1:11; 48:17 [of Moab]).

4732. מִקְלוֹת ***miqlôṯ:*** A proper noun designating Mikloth:

A. A Benjamite (1 Chr. 8:32; 9:37, 38).

B. An officer under David (1 Chr. 27:4).

4733. מִקְלָט ***miqlāṭ:*** A masculine noun referring to a refuge, a place of refuge. It is used to point out a city to which a person guilty of manslaughter could flee for protection (Num. 35:6, 11–15, 28, 32; 20:2, 3; 21:13, 21, 38[36]; 1 Chr. 6:57[42], 67[52]).

4734. מִקְלַעַת ***miqla'aṯ:*** A feminine noun designating something carved or engraved. It indicates something that has been cut out, whittled, such as flowers, cherubim, palm trees, etc. (1 Kgs. 6:18, 29, 32; 7:32). It could be made of wood, stone, or metal.

4735. מִקְנֶה ***miqneh:*** A masculine common noun meaning livestock, cattle, property. It refers to livestock, a major source of wealth, most often: cattle, sheep, goats, horses, donkeys (Gen. 4:20; 26:14; 47:6, 16–18; Ex. 9:3). It could also indicate collections of sheep, goats, and cows only (Gen. 13:2; 31:9; Num. 32:1). Men of cattle, *'anše miqneh,* were cattle herders or breeders (Gen. 46:32); there were herdsmen (*rō'îym*) of cattle (Gen. 13:7); foremen or guardians of cattle and livestock (Gen. 47:6).

4736. מִקְנָה ***miqnāh:*** A feminine noun referring to a purchase, a possession, a price. It refers to the purchase of something with money (*kesep̱*) (Gen. 17:12, 13, 23, 27; Ex. 12:44). It defines a document as a deed of purchase (Jer. 32:11, 12, 14, 16). It indicates the price itself of something (Lev. 25:16, 51; 27:22); or a possession acquired by purchase (Gen. 23:18).

4737. מִקְנֵיָהוּ ***miqnēyāhû:*** A proper noun designating Mikneiah (1 Chr. 15:18, 21).

4738. מִקְסָם ***miqsām:*** A masculine noun indicating divination. It refers to discerning the future or other events by a pagan process of using various devices, such as animal organs, etc. (Ezek. 12:24; 13:7). In Israel it was employed by false prophets.

4739. מָקַץ ***māqaṣ:*** A proper noun designating Makaz (1 Kgs. 4:9).

4740. מִקְצוֹעַ *miqṣôa‘*, מִקְצֹעַ *miqṣōa‘*: A masculine noun denoting a corner, an angle. It is used as an architectural term. It indicates a corner of structures such as the Tabernacle, altar, or court (Ex. 26:23, 24; 36:28, 29; Ezek. 41:22; 46:21, 22). It was used as part of certain locations in Jerusalem (2 Chr. 26:9; Neh. 3:19, 20, 24, 25).

4741. מַקְצֻעָה *maqṣu‘āh*: A feminine noun meaning a chisel, a planing tool. It was an instrument used to size and smooth wood, to shape it (Isa. 44:13); a knife or chisel tool.

4742. מְקֻצְעָת *m^equṣ‘āt*: A feminine noun indicating a corner, a bending. It describes the place where two boards come together, forming an angle (Ex. 26:23; 36:28).

4743. מָקַק *māqaq*: A verb meaning to waste away, to rot away. It means to dissipate, to decompose, to putrefy; used of Israel as a people in exile (Lev. 26:39; Ezek. 4:17; 24:23; 33:10); of parts of the body (Zech. 14:12); of injuries (Ps. 38:5[6]). It is used of anything, even in the heavens, wearing down, falling apart (Isa. 34:4).

4744. מִקְרָא *miqrā'*: A masculine noun meaning a convocation, reading, a public meeting, and an assembly. This word usually refers to an assembly for religious purposes. The Passover included a holy convocation on the first and seventh days (Ex. 12:16); other festivals also included the gathering of the people (Num. 28:18, 25, 26; 29:1, 7, 12). This word can also mean reading in the sense of a public reading or that which is read in such a meeting. For example, Ezra read the Law of God to a gathering of the Israelites, explaining so the people could understand (Neh. 8:8).

4745. מִקְרֶה *miqreh*: A masculine noun referring to a chance event, a happening, a fate. It refers to something that occurs without human planning or intervention (Ruth 2:3; 1 Sam. 20:26); or even God's intervention (1 Sam. 6:9). It is a feature of human life (Eccl. 2:14, 15; 3:19; 9:2, 3).

4746. מְקָרֶה *m^eqāreh*: A masculine noun used to signify a rafter, a building. It indicates the supporting beams in a structure or the entire structure itself (Eccl. 10:18); most likely, it means roof beams.

4747. מְקֵרָה *m^eqērāh*: A feminine noun designating a summer chamber, a cooling room. It refers to a room or special patio-like chamber where the wind cools it during the day (Judg. 3:20, 24).

4748. מִקְשֶׁה *miqšeh*: A masculine noun indicating hair. It refers to a well-groomed head of hair and scalp (Isa. 3:24).

4749. מִקְשָׁה *miqšāh*: A feminine noun indicating hammered work. It describes metal work that has been hammered out and often embossed in relief, featuring raised artwork (Ex.

25:18, 31, 36; 37:17, 22; Num. 8:4; 10:2).

4750. מִקְשָׁה *miqšāh:* A feminine noun designating a field of cucumbers or melons. It refers to an area of ground reserved for planting and harvesting cucumbers or melons (Isa. 1:8; Jer. 10:5). It plays a part in a famous metaphor of Israel and another one satirizing idolatry.

4751. מַר *mar,* מָר *mār:* A masculine adjective meaning bitter. The feminine form is *mārāh*. As is common with Hebrew adjectives, it can modify another noun (Ex. 15:23), or it can be a substantive, functioning alone as the noun bitterness (Isa. 38:15, 17). This word can also operate as an adverb, meaning bitterly (Isa. 33:7; Ezek. 27:30). Used literally, it may modify water (Ex. 15:23) and food (Prov. 27:7). The Hebrew word can also be used to describe the results of continued fighting (2 Sam. 2:26). It can be used metaphorically to modify a cry or mourning (Gen. 27:34; Esth. 4:1; Ezek. 27:30); to represent a characteristic of death (1 Sam. 15:32); or to describe a person as hot-tempered (Judg. 18:25); discontented (1 Sam. 22:2); provoked (2 Sam. 17:8); anguished (Ezek. 27:31); or ruthless (Hab. 1:6). One instance of this word that deserves special attention is the "bitter water," that determined the legal status of a woman accused of infidelity (Num. 5:18, 19, 23, 24, 27). This was holy water that was combined with dust from the Tabernacle floor and ink (see Num. 5:17, 23) and then was ingested by the accused. This water was literally "bitter" and would produce "bitterness" or punishment if the woman were guilty.

4752. מַר *mar:* A masculine noun denoting a drop or particle of water. It is used in a famous metaphor to illustrate the smallness of the nations compared to the Lord's might (Isa. 40:15).

4753. מֹר *mōr,* מוֹר *môr:* A masculine noun referring to myrrh. It refers to a fragrant resin exuded from several plants found mainly in Arabia or Africa. It is bitter in taste. It was used in the anointing oil in Israel (Ex. 30:23); and as a beauty treatment and cosmetic (Esth. 2:12; Ps. 45:8[9]; Prov. 7:17; Song 3:6; 5:1, 5). It is used figuratively of love (Song 1:13; 4:6, 14; 5:13).

4754. מָרָא *mārā':* I. A verb meaning to fly, to propel with wings. It refers to the ability to travel without touching the ground. It is used figuratively of the ostrich (Job 39:18), a wonder of God's creation.

II. A verb meaning filthy. It refers to a state of uncleanness and lack of holiness before God (Zeph. 3:1), used of a defiled Jerusalem.

4755. מָרָא *mārā':* A proper noun designating Mara (Ruth 1:20).

4756. מָרֵא *mārē':* An Aramaic noun meaning lord or king. It appears only four times, and all occurrences are found in the book of Daniel. It is applied to King Nebuchadnezzar (Dan. 4:19[16], 24[21]) and to God (Dan. 2:47; 5:23). This term appears in parallel with *melek̲* (4430), meaning king (Dan. 2:47; 4:24[21]) in two of the occurrences. It appears in reference to a human king (and in virtual parallelism with *melek̲* [4430]) in another occurrence (Dan. 4:19[16]). In the final occurrence (Dan. 5:23), it appears in the phrase, *mārē' šᵉmayyā'* (8065), "the Lord of heaven," which is a reference to the divine monarch. Therefore, it is clear that this is a term that represents an individual with much power, authority, and respect.

4757. מְרֹאדַךְ בַּלְאֲדָן ***mᵉrō'd̲ak̲ bal'ᵃd̲ān:*** A proper noun designating Merodach-Baladan (Isa. 39:1).

4758. מַרְאֶה ***mar'eh:*** A masculine noun meaning a sight, an appearance, a vision. Derived from the verb *rā'āh* (7200), meaning to see, this noun bears many of the same shades of meaning as the verb. It can represent the act of seeing (Gen. 2:9; Lev. 13:12); the appearance of the object (Lev. 13:3; Dan. 1:13); the object which is seen (Ex. 3:3); the face, being that part of the person which is visible (Song 2:14; 5:15); a supernatural vision (Ezek. 8:4; 11:24; Dan. 8:16, 27); the ability to see (Eccl. 6:9);the shining light of a fire (Num. 9:15) or of lightning (Dan. 10:6).

4759. מַרְאָה ***mar'āh:*** A feminine noun meaning a supernatural vision, a mirror. This noun is derived from the verb *rā'āh* (7200), meaning to see. As a supernatural vision, it is a means of divine revelation (Num. 12:6). This term can stand by itself (1 Sam. 3:15); or it can function as a cognate accusative (Dan. 10:7, 8). The word is sometimes used in the expression *mar'ōt̲ halaylāh* (3915), meaning visions of the night (Gen. 46:2); and *mar'ôt̲ 'ᵉlōhiym* (430), meaning visions of God (Ezek. 1:1; 8:3; 40:2). The word is only used once in the Hebrew Bible to signify a mirror or a polished metal plate (Ex. 38:8).

4760. מֻרְאָה ***mur'āh:*** A feminine noun meaning the crop or craw of a bird. It refers to a small sack-like expansion of a bird's gullet or possibly the entire stomach (Lev. 1:16).

4761. מַרְאָשׁוֹת ***mar'āšôt̲:*** A feminine plural noun meaning heads, principalities. It refers to the royal authority and splendor surrounding the office of kingship and held by the reigning king (Jer. 13:18, KJV). See 4763 also.

4762. מָרֵשָׁה ***mārēšāh,*** מָרֵאשָׁה ***mārē'šāh:*** A proper noun designating Mareshah:

A. A city in Judah (Josh. 15:44; 2 Chr. 11:8; 14:9[8], 10[9]; 20:37; Mic. 1:15).

B. The father of Hebron (1 Chr. 2:42).

C. A son of Laadah (1 Chr. 4:21).

4763. מְרַאֲשׁוֹת ***mᵉra'ᵃšôt̲:*** I. A feminine noun referring to a place at or near a head. It refers to a location at or around a person's head (Gen. 28:11, 18; 1 Sam. 26:7, 11; 1 Kgs. 19:6; Jer. 13:18).

II. A feminine noun referring to a pillow, a bolster (for the head). It refers to a head support (Gen. 28:11) or something put in place to look like a person's head (1 Sam. 19:13; 26:7, 11, 12). An exact decipherment of the use of the word and hence its meaning is difficult.

4764. מֵרַב ***mēraḇ:*** A proper noun designating Merab (1 Sam. 14:49; 18:17, 19).

4765. מַרְבַד ***marḇāḏ:*** A masculine noun meaning a covering, a spread. It refers to something similar to an afghan or a decorative blanket (Prov. 7:16) or to clothing (Prov. 31:22).

4766. מַרְבֶּה ***marbeh:*** A masculine noun referring to an abundance, an increase. It indicates prosperity, success. In context it refers to the prosperity and overflowing success to accrue to Israel's king (Isa. 9:7[6]). It is used of a huge, rich collection of booty or spoil taken from an enemy (Isa. 33:23).

4767. מִרְבָּה ***mirbāh:*** A feminine noun signifying abundance, much. It indicates a large amount of something. In context it refers to the impending judgments coming on Judah (Ezek. 23:32).

4768. מַרְבִּית ***marbiyṯ:*** A feminine noun depicting greatness, an increase, a gain. It indicates profit or gain from lending (Lev. 25:37); the increase of persons born to a family (house, *bayiṯ*) (1 Sam. 2:33). It indicates the largest part or majority (1 Chr. 12:29); the extent or breadth of something (2 Chr. 9:6). It has the sense of a large part (not necessarily a majority) of a group (2 Chr. 30:18).

4769. מַרְבֵּץ ***marbēṣ:*** A masculine noun referring to a resting place. It describes a place of safety and rest for sheep, a sheepfold (Ezek. 25:5); or a home for wild animals, a lair (Zeph. 2:15).

4770. מַרְבֵּק ***marbēq:*** A masculine noun signifying a stall; fattened, fattening. It depicts an animal that has been nourished and fattened for slaughter as food (1 Sam. 28:24). It is used figuratively of merchants grown rich through their sales and trading (Jer. 46:21). It has the sense of the place from which the fattening took place, the stalls or place of feeding and care (Amos 6:4; Mal. 4:2[3:30]).

4771. מַרְגּוֹעַ ***margôaʻ:*** A masculine noun meaning rest. It refers to a state of refreshment and life, a state of renewal for one's life and soul (Jer. 6:16).

4772. מַרְגְּלוֹת ***margᵉlôṯ:*** A masculine plural noun referring to feet, a place for the feet. It describes the place where one's feet rest or stand, the area immediately around them (Ruth 3:4, 7, 8, 14; Dan. 10:6).

4773. מַרְגֵּמָה *margēmāh:* A feminine noun signifying a sling. A weapon made of cords or ropes fastened by one end to a piece of leather broad enough to enwrap a small stone (Prov. 26:8). The cords are whirled, and the stone is released to strike its target.

4774. מַרְגֵּעָה *margē'āh:* A feminine noun referring to a place of rest. It refers to a state of relaxation and a cessation from toil, fighting, and worry (Isa. 28:12).

4775. מָרַד *mārad̲:* A verb meaning to rebel. This word usually described the activity of resisting authority, whether against the Lord (Num. 14:9; Dan. 9:9) or against human kings (Gen. 14:4; Neh. 2:19). In one instance, it is used to describe those who rebel against the light (i.e., God's truth [Job 24:13]). This word is also used to describe a general, rebellious character of a nation (Ezek. 2:3; 20:38); as well as a specific act of rebellion, such as Hezekiah's rebellion against Sennacherib (2 Kgs. 18:7, 20; Isa. 36:5); or Zedekiah's rebellion against Nebuchadnezzar (2 Kgs. 24:20; Jer. 52:3; Ezek. 17:15).

4776. מְרַד *m^e^rad̲:* An Aramaic masculine noun meaning rebellion. This word is used only once in the Old Testament and is related to the Hebrew word *mārad̲* (4775), meaning to rebel. In Ezra 4:19, this word described Jerusalem's past rebellion.

4777. מֶרֶד *mered̲:* A masculine noun meaning rebellion. This word comes from the verb *mārad̲* (4775), meaning to rebel, and occurs only once in the Old Testament. In Joshua 22:22, it was used to describe the act of building another altar on the east of the Jordan River as rebellious.

4778. מֶרֶד *mered̲:* A proper noun designating Mered (1 Chr. 4:17, 18).

4779. מָרָד *mārād̲:* An Aramaic adjective meaning rebellious. This word is used only twice in the Old Testament and is related to the Hebrew word *mārad̲* (4775), meaning to rebel. In Ezra 4:12, 15, it described the historically rebellious character of Jerusalem.

4780. מַרְדּוּת *mardûṯ:* A feminine noun meaning rebelliousness. This word comes from the verb *mārad̲* (4775), meaning to rebel, and occurs only once in the Old Testament. In 1 Samuel 20:30, Saul used it in his anger against Jonathan as a derogatory word to describe Jonathan's mother.

4781. מְרֹדָךְ *m^e^rōd̲āḵ:* A masculine proper noun. It is the name of the chief Babylonian god, Merodach. In more recent translations, it is rendered as Marduk (Jer. 50:2).

4782. מָרְדֳּכַי *mord^e^ḵay:* A proper noun designating Mordecai:

A. One of the leaders of the exiles back to Judah from Babylonian exile. He was an aide to Zerubbabel (Ezra 2:2).

B. The cousin of Esther. His name indicates a recognition or tie to the great Babylonian god Marduk. Like Daniel, he had been given or taken on a name that reflected the nation and culture where he lived. He was from the tribe of Benjamin (Esth. 2:5–6) and had gone into exile at the hands of Nebuchadnezzar.

Through divine providence, Mordecai was able to expose a plot to assassinate the Persian king Xerxes (Esth. 2:7–23). And he successfully thwarted, again through a conjunction of events by divine providence, a plan by Haman (possibly an Amalekite) to destroy all the Jews in the empire (Esth. 3—7). He encouraged Esther to use her position and power to deliver the Jews (Esth. 4:12–17). He was honored highly by the king twice (Esth. 6; 10).

4783. מֻרְדָּף ***murdāp̱:*** A masculine noun indicating persecution, aggression. It is used of Babylon's political and military aggression, pressure, and violence on other nations (Isa. 14:6).

4784. מָרָה ***mārāh:*** A verb meaning to be rebellious. In one instance, this word spoke of a son's rebellion against his parents (Deut. 21:18, 20). In all other instances, this word was used of rebellion against God, which provoked Him to action. This word is usually used as an indictment against a nation's rebellion, whether Israel's (Deut. 9:23, 24; Ps. 78:8; Jer. 5:23); Samaria's (Hos. 13:16[14:1]); or David's enemies (Ps. 5:10[11]). In a few instances, it is used to indict specific people, as Moses (Num. 20:24; 27:14), or a man of God who disobeyed (1 Kgs. 13:21, 26).

4785. מָרָה ***mārāh:*** A proper noun designating Marah (Ex. 15:23; Num. 33:8, 9).

4786. מֹרָה ***mōrāh:*** A feminine noun meaning grief, bitterness. It describes an emotional response of strong disappointment and sorrow of spirit over something (Gen. 26:35); a condition of one's soul known by one's heart (Prov. 14:10).

4787. מָרָּה ***morrah:*** A feminine noun meaning bitterness. It indicates a strong emotional response of disappointment, a feeling of being betrayed in one's soul (Prov. 14:10).

4788. מָרוּד ***mārûḏ:*** A masculine noun indicating restlessness, wandering, homelessness. It indicates a condition of being without a permanent place to live, homeless (Isa. 58:7). It refers to Jerusalem destitute of all her past inhabitants as well as to persons exiled from their native city and land (Lam. 1:7). It has the sense of aimless wandering from one place to the next (Lam. 3:19).

4789. מֵרוֹז ***mērôz:*** A proper noun designating Meroz (Judg. 5:23).

4790. מָרוֹחַ ***mārôaḥ:*** An adjective meaning crushed, broken. It indicates something pounded or crushed. It is used of testicles that have been crushed (Lev. 21:20).

4791. מָרוֹם *mārôm:* A masculine noun meaning height, a high place, exaltedness. It means something high, lifted up, literally or figuratively. It refers to something elevated, high (2 Kgs. 19:23; Job 5:11; Prov. 8:2; Isa. 37:24); especially of Zion (Jer. 17:12; 31:12); figuratively, something worthy of praise or a place of authority or safety (Eccl. 10:6; Isa. 26:5; Hab. 2:9). It has a more figurative meaning often: the high or exalted God (2 Sam. 22:17; Ps. 18:16[17]; 102:19 [20]; Mic. 6:6); exaltedness as a feature of the Lord (Ps. 92:8[9]); as a direction with *l*^{e}, to, toward, toward heaven (Isa. 38:14; 40:26); as a description of a negative attitude of pride, arrogance (Ps. 56:2[3]; 73:8).

4792. מֵרוֹם *mērôm:* A proper noun designating Merom (Josh. 11:5, 7).

4793. מֵרוֹץ *mērôṣ:* A masculine noun indicating a running race. It indicates a physical contest of speed and endurance, a race. It is used in context figuratively of life (Eccl. 9:11).

4794. מְרוּצָה *m*^{e}*rûṣāh:* A feminine noun denoting a running, a course. It means the actual visible style and characteristics of a person in the process of running (2 Sam. 18:27); or the running itself (Jer. 8:6; 23:10). In the latter case, it is used figuratively of the course of life.

4795. מָרוּק *mārûq:* A masculine noun meaning rubbing, purification. The one occurrence of this word is in the book of Esther and mentions the treatments the women underwent for a year prior to meeting King Ahasuerus. This entailed being cleansed and perfumed with various oils (Esth. 2:12). See the related Hebrew root *māraq* (4838).

4796. מָרוֹת *mārôṯ:* A proper noun designating Maroth (Mic. 1:12).

4797. מִרְזַח *mirzaḥ:* A masculine noun indicating feasting, banqueting. It refers to a meal; an extravagant festive banquet (Amos 6:7).

4798. מַרְזֵחַ *marzēaḥ:* A masculine noun referring to mourning, a funeral meal. It indicates a meal; in context a meal of mourning because of calamity and distress (Jer. 16:5; Amos 6:7). For Amos 6:7, see 4797 also.

4799. מָרַח *māraḥ:* A verb signifying to apply. It indicates the placing of something on a location or something else; a medicinal bandage on a sore or boil (Isa. 38:21).

4800. מֶרְחָב *merḥāḇ:* A masculine noun referring to a large space, a spacious place. It indicates broadness, wideness. In context it indicates the length and breadth of the earth; throughout the land (Hab. 1:6). It is used metaphorically to depict an open, free area; space; free from oppression and enemies (2 Sam. 22:20; Ps. 18:19[20]); a blessed situation in life

(Ps. 31:8[9]; 118:5). It is used of a big field (Hos. 4:16).

4801. מֶרְחָק ***merḥāq:*** A masculine noun designating a distant spot, a place, a far-away place. It indicates in context the last house, the distant house (2 Sam. 15:17). It indicates a great space; the distance between in a figurative sense (Ps. 138:6); as well as in a literal sense, i.e., a distant country (Prov. 25:25; 31:14; Isa. 10:3; 17:13). It is used in a general sense of all distant places of the earth (Isa. 8:9; Ezek. 23:40; Zech. 10:9). It is used often of the enemies God is bringing from a distant country, i.e., Assyria, Babylon (Isa. 13:5; Jer. 4:16; 5:15).

4802. מַרְחֶשֶׁת ***marḥešeṯ:*** A feminine noun signifying a pan, a frying pan. It refers to a cooking utensil for frying or possibly baking (Lev. 2:7; 7:9).

4803. מָרַט ***māraṭ:*** A verb meaning to fall off, to pluck off, to polish. It is used of pulling out a person's hair (Ezra 9:3; Neh. 13:25); as well as of a person's hair falling out, becoming bald (Lev. 13:40, 41). It indicates the plucking of a person's beard, an act of humiliation (Isa. 50:6). It is used in a passive sense of burnished, polished bronze or swords (Ezek. 21:9–11[14–16], 28[33]). Used of human skin, it means smooth, polished (Isa. 18:2, 7).

4804. מְרַט ***m^eraṭ:*** An Aramaic verb meaning to pluck off, to tear off. It means to remove something. In context it is used of plucking off, pulling out wings (Dan. 7:4).

4805. מְרִי ***m^eriy:*** A masculine noun meaning obstinacy, stubbornness, rebelliousness. The term consistently stays within this tight semantic range and most often describes the Israelites' determined refusal to obey the precepts laid down by the Lord in His Law or Torah. This characteristic attitude was a visible manifestation of their hard hearts. Moses had the Book of the Law placed beside the ark of the covenant to remain there as a witness against the Israelites' rebelliousness after he died (Deut. 31:27; Num. 17:10[25]). The Lord rejected Saul as king over Israel because of his rebellion against the command the Lord had earlier given him (1 Sam. 15:23). Continually in Ezekiel, the Lord refers to Israel as the "house of rebelliousness" (= rebellious people; Ezek. 2:5–8; 3:9, 26, 27; 12:2, 3, 9). This noun is derived from the verb *mārāh* (4784).

4806. מְרִיא ***m^eriy':*** A masculine noun referring to a fatted calf, a fattened animal. It refers to cattle raised for eating and sacrifice, the best cattle, well-nourished (2 Sam. 6:13; 1 Kgs. 1:9, 19, 25; Isa. 1:11; Ezek. 39:18; Amos 5:22). The calf will be at peace with animals of prey in the messianic kingdom (Isa. 11:6).

4807. מְרִיב בַּעַל ***m^eriy<u>b</u> ba'al:*** A proper noun designating Meri-Baal (1 Chr. 8:34; 9:40).

4808. מְרִיבָה ***m^{e}riyḇāh:*** A feminine noun indicating strife, contention. It is used of a state of quarreling or wrangling over something, a condition of hostility (Gen. 13:8; Num. 27:14). The name Meribah means striving, strife (Num. 27:14; Ps. 95:8; 106:32; Ezek. 47:19; 48:28).

4809. מְרִיבָה ***m^{e}riyḇāh,*** מְרִיבַת קָדֵשׁ ***m^{e}riyḇaṯ qāḏēš:*** A proper noun designating Meribah:

A. A word meaning "quarreling or contention" (from the Hebrew word *riyḇ* (7378), "to strive, quarrel"). It was the location of a place near Rephidim where there was no drinking water for Israel. The people verbally attacked Moses, and he struck a rock, at the Lord's command, to bring forth water (Ex. 17:7). The place is also called Massah, "testing."

B. Evidently another occasion of "contention" forty years later (see A above but C below).

C. This location is placed at Kadesh Barnea, not near Rephidim according to most authorities. But it is a clear reference to the incident in the Desert of Zin (Num. 20:13, 24). See B above.

4810. מְרִי בַעַל ***m^{e}riy ḇa'al:*** A proper noun designating Merib-Baal (1 Chr. 9:40).

4811. מְרָיָה ***m^{e}rāyāh:*** A proper noun designating Meraiah (Neh. 12:12).

4812. מְרָיוֹת ***m^{e}rāyôṯ:*** A proper noun designating Meraioth:

A. A priest (1 Chr. 6:6[5:32], 7[5:33], 52[37]; Ezra 7:3).

B. A son of Ahitub (1 Chr. 9:11; Neh. 11:11).

C. The father of Helkai (Neh. 12:15).

4813. מִרְיָם ***miryām:*** A proper noun designating Miriam:

A. The daughter of Amram and Jochebed and sister to Aaron and Moses (Num. 26:59). She was considered a leader sent by God (Mic. 6:4). She probably was the sister who watched over Moses when he was placed in the Nile River as a baby. She composed a song to celebrate the Lord's deliverance at the Red Sea (Ex. 15:20, 21) but later unwisely challenged Moses' authority and was soundly rebuked by the Lord with leprosy (Num. 12:1–15). She died and was buried at Kadesh (Num. 20:1).

B. A Judahite, a daughter of Mered (1 Chr. 4:17).

4814. מְרִירוּת ***m^{e}riyrûṯ:*** A feminine noun pointing to strife. It is used of extreme grief, a wounded spirit of disappointment and anger, especially over the coming defeat of Jerusalem (Ezek. 21:6[11]).

4815. מְרִירִי ***m^{e}riyriy:*** An adjective meaning bitter, deadly. It indicates the harsh, mortal caustic aspect of something; threatening. In context it identifies Israel's destruction as bitter, hard to swallow (Deut. 32:24).

4816. מֹרֶךְ ***mōreḵ:*** A masculine noun referring to weakness, fearfulness. It refers to a shattered state of stability, a feeling of frailty, an emotion and state experienced by those God would drive into exile (Lev. 26:36).

4817. מֶרְכָּב ***merkāḇ:*** A masculine noun describing a covering, a saddle, a place to ride, a chariot. It is used of a riding seat, a saddle, for a riding animal (Lev. 15:9). It was used to describe a two-wheeled vehicle used in battle, drawn by horses (1 Kgs. 4:26[5:6]). In Song 3:10, it is used of a seat for the king on his wedding day.

4818. מֶרְכָּבָה ***merkāḇāh:*** A feminine noun meaning chariot. It refers to something ridden, for riding and is used of a two-wheeled vehicle, drawn by horses and normally used in war. Its uses include a war chariot (Ex. 14:25; 15:4); a chariot used by the state in its processions or for travel in general (Gen. 41:43; 46:29; Isa. 22:18). It was a symbol of military might and war (Isa. 2:7). It is used figuratively of the vehicles of war used by the Lord (Isa. 66:15; Hab. 3:8). Israel constructed some idolatrous "chariots of the sun" (2 Kgs. 23:11).

4819. מַרְכֹּלֶת ***markōleṯ:*** A feminine noun referring to merchandise, a market place. It indicates the objects of trade and barter or the location where these items were offered for display and trade (Ezek. 27:24).

4820. מִרְמָה ***mirmāh:*** A feminine noun meaning fraud, deceit. The term signifies the intentional misleading of someone else through distorting or withholding the truth. Jacob stole Esau's blessing through deceit (Gen. 27:35; cf. Gen. 34:13). Deceit fills the heart of those who plan evil (Prov. 12:20; cf. Ps. 36:3[4]; Prov. 12:5, 17; 14:8). David exhorted his children to keep their tongues from evil and their lips from words of deceit (Ps. 34:13[14]). The Lord cannot tolerate deceitful weights (Mic. 6:11); and a false balance is an abomination to Him (Prov. 11:1).

4821. מִרְמָה ***mirmāh:*** A masculine proper name, Mirmah, one of the sons of Shaharaim (1 Chr. 8:10).

4822. מְרֵמוֹת ***m^e^rēmôṯ:*** A proper noun designating Meremoth:

A. A priest under Zerubbabel (Neh. 12:3).

B. A priest under Ezra (Ezra 8:33; Neh. 3:4, 21).

C. A postexilic Jew (Ezra 10:36).

D. A covenant signer (Neh. 10:5).

E. The father of Helkai (Neh. 12:15).

4823. מִרְמָס ***mirmās:*** A masculine noun identifying something trampled, trampled down. It refers to a location or something that has been trampled down, stepped on, destroyed: a vineyard (Isa. 5:5); a field (Isa. 7:25; Ezek. 34:19, used figuratively); God's people with acts of judgments on them (Isa. 10:6; 28:18; Mic. 7:10). It is used of the holy people of God and His holy place being "trodden down," trampled by pagans (Dan. 8:13).

4824. מְרֹנֹתִי ***mērōnōṯiy:*** A masculine proper noun Meronothite. It signifies the ethnicity or some other relational designation of a man named Jehdeiah, who was in charge of the donkeys as his administrative task (1 Chr. 27:30). It is also descriptive of Jadon who helped restore government quarters in Jerusalem (Neh. 3:7).

4825. מֶרֶס ***meres:*** A proper noun designating Meres (Esth. 1:14).

4826. מַרְסְנָא ***marsᵉnā':*** A proper noun designating Marsena (Esth. 1:14).

4827. מֵרַע ***mēra':*** A masculine noun meaning evil. It is used of political and military violence and intrigue (Dan. 11:27).

4828. מֵרֵעַ ***mērēa':*** A masculine noun indicating a companion, a friend. It refers to a person with a trusted relationship to another person, standing ready to help his or her companion even in an official capacity (Gen. 26:26; Job 6:14). A poor person has few loyal friends, if any at all (Prov. 19:7). It also, however, included persons newly and formally appointed as "friends" of someone to serve a social function (Judg. 14:11, 20; 15:2, 6). It refers to supports of a person, e.g., friends of Saul's house (2 Sam. 3:8).

4829. מִרְעֶה ***mir'eh:*** A masculine noun referring to a pasture. It refers to land suitable for grazing flocks of sheep or herds of other animals (Gen. 47:4; 1 Chr. 4:39–41; Lam. 1:6; Joel 1:18); including wild animals (Job 39:8; Nah. 2:11[12]). It is used as imagery for an overthrown, deserted city area (Isa. 32:14). Restored pasturelands of rich quality are a part of a renewed Israel (Ezek. 34:14, 18).

4830. מַרְעִית ***mar'iyṯ:*** A feminine noun meaning pasture, a flock feeding in it. It indicates a fertile field for feeding and raising flocks of sheep or other animals. Figuratively, it is the pasture God provides for His people (Ps. 74:1; 79:13; 95:7; 100:3; Isa. 49:9; Jer. 23:1; Ezek. 34:31). It refers to the people of Israel as the sheep of their rulers (Jer. 10:21). The Lord will destroy His pasture because of its rebellion (Jer. 25:36). Israel fed on their pasture provided by the Lord and forgot their Shepherd (Hos. 13:6).

4831. מַרְעֲלָה ***marᵃlāh:*** A proper noun designating Maralah (Josh. 19:11).

4832. מַרְפֵּא ***marpē':*** I. A masculine noun indicating health, healing, a remedy. It refers to the restoration, cure, or renewal of an illness, sickness: Jehoram had a sickness for which there was no remedy, cure (2 Chr. 21:18); Israel was spiritually sick so that there was no healing (2 Chr. 36:16; Jer. 14:19). It has the sense of health or healing with respect to the body (Prov. 4:22); a sluggard will not find a remedy for his problem (Prov. 6:15); a wise word brings healing (Prov. 12:18; 13:17; 15:4; 16:24). Healing is the opposite of experiencing dread or terror, destruction (Jer. 8:15). God provides healing for His chosen, special possession (Mal. 4:2[3:20]).

II. A masculine noun indicating peace, calmness. It refers to a state of security, stability, relaxation: a heart of peace is said to be a source of life for the body (Prov. 14:30). It has the sense of keeping calm amid tension and anger (Eccl. 10:4).

4833. מִרְפָּשׂ ***mirpaś:*** A masculine noun meaning to make muddy. It describes water made muddy, fouled by the trampling of the feet of animals (Ezek. 34:19).

4834. מָרַץ ***māraṣ:*** A verb indicating to be sick, painful. It describes a curse as hurtful, pernicious (1 Kgs. 2:8); destruction or punishment as painful (Mic. 2:10); words as unsettling, irritating (Job 6:25); an unknown motivation or cause as provoking an argument (Job 16:3).

4835. מְרוּצָה ***m^{e}rûṣāh:*** A feminine noun indicating oppression, violence. It is used of evil and hurtful activities of oppression and distress against others (Jer. 22:17).

4836. מַרְצֵעַ ***marṣēa':*** A masculine noun describing an awl, an instrument for piercing. It is used of boring a hole in a servant's ear as a mark of ownership (Ex. 21:6; Deut. 15:17).

4837. מַרְצֶפֶת ***marṣep̱eṯ:*** A feminine noun identifying a pavement, a base. It refers to a stone pavement or a stone layer serving as a base on which to set something (2 Kgs. 16:17).

4838. מָרַק ***māraq:*** A verb meaning to scour, to polish. It describes a process of cleaning a bronze vessel (Lev. 6:28[21]), as well as the process of beautifying it by polishing (2 Chr. 4:16); any metal surface (Jer. 46:4). Figuratively, it refers to scouring or removing evil (Prov. 20:30).

4839. מָרָק ***māraq:*** A masculine noun referring to broth. It describes a thin, clear soup made by boiling meat or other ingredients in water (Judg. 6:19, 20; Isa. 65:4).

4840. מֶרְקָח ***merqāḥ:*** A masculine noun referring to perfume, a sweet scent. It indicates sweet-smelling, aromatic herbs that create a pleasant aroma (Song 5:13).

4841. מֶרְקָחָה ***merqāḥāh:*** A feminine noun pointing to spices, a pot of ointment. It refers to a mixture of ointment under preparation to serve as an aromatic perfume (Job 41:31[23]); or to the condiments added as spices (Ezek. 24:10).

4842. מִרְקַחַת ***mirqaḥaṯ:*** A feminine noun indicating a mixture of ointment or perfume. It indicates Israel's anointing oil, a combination of various items (Ex. 30:25) prepared by priests (1 Chr. 9:30). It refers to the blending of spices etc., together (2 Chr. 16:14).

4843. מָרַר ***mārar:*** A verb meaning to be bitter, to make bitter, to grieve. It has the sense of harshness, embitterment, offensiveness, affliction: of a physical attack on someone (Gen. 49:23; Dan. 8:7; 11:11); of backbreaking, debilitating work (Ex. 1:14; 23:21); of the effect of calamities in life (Ruth 1:13, 20; 1 Sam. 30:6; 2 Kgs. 4:27; Job 27:2; Isa. 38:17; Lam. 1:4; Zech. 12:10); especially of the bitterness engendered by God's judgments on His people (Isa. 22:4; 24:9).

4844. מָרֹר ***mārōr:*** A masculine noun signifying a bitter herb, bitterness. It describes the sharp, biting taste of bitter herbs (Ex. 12:8; Num. 9:11); of unpleasant sour grapes (Deut. 32:32); of a bitter drink (Lam. 3:15). It is used figuratively of harsh, cutting, stinging words that create suffering in another person (Job 13:26).

4845. מְרֵרָה ***m^e^rērāh:*** A feminine noun referring to gall, bile. It indicates the liquid (Job 16:13) produced by the gallbladder (Job 20:25).

4846. מְרֹרָה ***m^e^rōrāh:*** A feminine noun referring to gall, liver, a bitter thing. It is used of the gallbladder (Job 20:25); its bile (Job 20:14; venom, NASB). It indicates words that create grief in another person (Job 13:26). It describes clusters of grapes as bitter in a figurative sense (Deut. 32:32).

4847. מְרָרִי ***m^e^rāriy:*** A proper noun designating Merari, third son of Levi (Gen. 46:11; Ex. 6:16, 19; Num. 10:17; 26:57; 2 Chr. 29:12; 34:12).

4848. מְרָרִי ***m^e^rāriy:*** A proper noun designating Merarite (Num. 26:57).

4849. מִרְשַׁעַת ***mirša'aṯ:*** A feminine noun meaning wickedness. It describes a person with evil intent. In this case, Queen Athaliah apostatized from the Lord and served the Baals (2 Chr. 24:7).

4850. מְרָתַיִם ***m^e^rāṯayim:*** A proper noun designating Merathaim (Jer. 50:21).

4851. מַשׁ ***maš:*** A proper noun designating Mash (Gen. 10:23).

4852. מֵשָׁא ***mēšā':*** A proper noun designating Mesha (Gen. 10:30).

4853. מַשָּׂא ***maśśā':*** A masculine noun meaning a burden or load; by extension, a burden in the form of a prophetic utterance or oracle. It is derived from the verb *nāśā'* (5375) meaning to lift, to bear, to carry. When used to express a burden or load, it is commonly used to describe that which is placed on the backs of pack animals, like donkeys (Ex. 23:5); mules (2 Kgs. 5:17); or camels (2 Kgs. 8:9). Another common usage is in designating what parts of the Tabernacle the sons of Kohath, Gershon, and Merari were to carry (Num. 4:15, 19, 24, 27, 31, 32, 47, 49). In Ezekiel 24:25, it is interesting that the lifting of one's soul, *maśśā' napšām* (5315), is used to mean the desires of the heart and that to which persons lift up their souls. By extension, this term is also applied to certain divine oracles that were negative proclamations. Isaiah used this formula to pronounce judgments against the nations of Babylon (Isa. 13:1); Philistia (Isa. 14:28); Moab (Isa. 15:1); Damascus (Isa. 17:1); Egypt (Isa. 19:1); the desert of the sea (Isa. 21:1); Dumah (Isa. 21:11); Arabia (Isa. 21:13); the Valley of Vision (Isa. 22:1); Tyre (Isa. 23:1). Other prophets used the same formula to pronounce judgments on Nineveh (Nah. 1:1); Judah (Hab. 1:1); Damascus (Zech. 9:1); Jerusalem (Zech. 12:1); Israel (Mal. 1:1). This formula was also employed to prophesy threats or judgments on individuals (2 Kgs. 9:25; 2 Chr. 24:27; Prov. 30:1; 31:1).

4854. מַשָּׂא ***maśśā':*** A proper noun designating Massa (Gen. 25:14; 1 Chr. 1:30).

4855. מַשָּׁא ***maššā':*** A masculine noun indicating usury. It indicates an excessive profit, often in high interest charges (Neh. 5:7, 10). It has the meaning of debt (Neh. 10:31; Prov. 22:26).

4856. מַשֹּׂא ***maśśō':*** A masculine noun meaning partiality. It means to show favor to certain people in the phrase *maśśō' pānîym,* literally, "lifting up of faces," meaning special recognition (2 Chr. 19:7).

4857. מַשְׁאָב ***maš'āḇ:*** A masculine noun referring to a watering place, a place of drawing up water. It indicates a well or spring from which water was drawn, a watering place where social conversation occurred as well (Judg. 5:11).

4858. מַשָּׂאָה ***maśśā'āh:*** I. A feminine noun referring to smoke, a cloud of smoke. It is used of the visible vaporous matter arising from something burning. It also will accompany the coming of the Lord (Isa. 30:27).

II. A feminine noun meaning burden. Some translators prefer this rendering of the noun as something lifted up, carried, a burden or message (Isa. 30:27) or a lifting up of heavy clouds.

4859. מַשָּׁאָה ***maššā'āh:*** A feminine noun depicting a debt, a loan. It indicates something given to a neighbor with the expectation that it will be paid back (Deut. 24:10; Prov. 22:26).

4860. מַשָּׁאוֹן ***maššā'ôn:*** A masculine noun indicating guile, deception. It indicates an attitude of lying, trickery, cover-up that camouflages hatred, its real cause (Prov. 26:26).

4861. מִשְׁאָל ***miš'āl:*** A proper noun designating Mishal (Josh. 19:26; 21:30). See also 4913.

4862. מִשְׁאָלָה ***miš'ālāh:*** A feminine noun indicating a petition, a request. It indicates a plea or solicitation for something. In context it denotes a plea for victory over one's evil enemies (Ps. 20:5[6]). The Lord answers the desires, petitions of those who delightfully serve Him (Ps. 37:4).

4863. מִשְׁאֶרֶת *miš'eret:* A feminine noun denoting a kneading bowl or a trough. A vessel for preparing dough for baking (Ex. 8:3[7:28]; 12:34; Deut. 28:5, 17) or clay for some use.

4864. מַשְׂאֵת *maś'ēṯ:* A feminine noun meaning an uprising, an utterance, a burden, a portion, a tribute, a reward. The main use connotes something that rises or is lifted up, such as smoke in a smoke signal (Judg. 20:38); or hands in a sacrifice of praise (Ps. 141:2). Figuratively, a reproach could be lifted up as a burden (Zeph. 3:18). This word can also depict a portion or a gift that is carried to someone, often from the table of nobility. For example, David sent a gift of food to Uriah's house (2 Sam. 11:8); as part of the feast honoring Queen Esther, the king sent gifts to his subjects (Esth. 2:18).

4865. מִשְׁבְּצוֹת *mišbᵉṣôṯ:* A feminine noun indicating filigree settings. A lace-like ornamental work of intertwined wire made of gold, silver, copper, or bronze to receive settings of precious jewels (Ex. 28:11, 13, 14, 25; 39:6, 13, 18). It can be used of any fine work like this, e.g., of clothing (Ps. 45:13[14]).

4866. מַשְׁבֵּר *mašbēr:* A masculine noun describing a birth, the opening of a womb. It is used metaphorically of giving birth to spiritual as well as physical children (Hos. 13:13). Used with *bô'* (935) and *'aḏ* (5704) meaning to come to the point of birth (2 Kgs. 19:3; Isa. 37:3).

4867. מִשְׁבָּר *mišbār:* A masculine noun referring to waves, breaking waves. It is used of breakers, incoming waves on a seashore. It is used figuratively of the waves of death (2 Sam. 22:5); or the waves of despair (Ps. 42:7[8]; 88:7[8]; Jon. 2:3[4]). They are used to compare the Lord's might with the sea's breakers (Ps. 93:4).

4868. מִשְׁבָּת *mišbāṯ:* A masculine noun indicating destruction, ruin. It indicates the destruction of a city to useless remains, used up; the ruin of Jerusalem, her reduction to nothing (Lam. 1:7).

4869. מִשְׂגָּב *miśgāḇ:* I. A masculine noun indicating a stronghold. It refers to a place naturally fortified or fortified by man: a high hill or cliff, a rock (Isa. 33:16; Jer. 48:1); walls built by men (Isa. 25:12). It is used often of God as a safe haven, a place of refuge (2 Sam. 22:3; Ps. 9:9[10]; 18:2[3]; 46:7[8], 11[12]; 48:3[4], etc.).

II. A proper noun, Misgab, in Moab. It is taken by some translators as a name for a city (Jer. 48:1, KJV). See I above also.

4870. מִשְׁגֶּה *mišgeh:* A masculine noun indicating a mistake, an oversight. It refers to an error made or an incorrect action taken by someone, e.g., the placement of money in a bag in error (Gen. 43:12).

4871. מָשָׁה ***māšāh:*** A verb meaning to draw, to pull. It indicates the action of drawing, pulling. It is used to form Moses' name and expresses the action of Pharaoh's daughter in pulling him from the Nile River (Ex. 2:10); and the action of Moses as he drew Israel out of Egypt. It is used figuratively of David being drawn from the waters of distress (2 Sam. 22:17; Ps. 18:16[17]).

4872. מֹשֶׁה ***mōšeh:*** A proper noun designating Moses, the chosen deliverer, prophet, priest, and wise man of Israel in the Old Testament. His name, based on the Hebrew word and its popular etymology, *māšāh* (4871), "to draw out," means the "one who draws out," i.e., delivers, draws out Israel from Egypt through the water of the Red Sea. He was named so by his Egyptian adoptive mother (but possibly by his own Hebrew mother) for she "drew him from the water" (Ex. 2:19).

God chose Moses to deliver His people (Ex. 3:10), to receive the "ten words" and the covenant and its accompanying laws at Sinai (Ex. 19—24), to lead Israel through the wilderness for forty years (Num. 14—Deut. 34), to perform signs and wonders before Pharaoh and his people (Deut. 34:9–12), to oversee the construction of the Tabernacle and to bless it and Israel (Ex. 39:32–43), and to install his successor, Joshua (Deut. 33; 34:9). He was the covenant human figure in the Pentateuch, but his person and work is seen and felt throughout the Old Testament. Malachi, the last prophet of the Old Testament, cried out, "Remember the law of my servant Moses, the decrees and laws I gave him at Horeb for all Israel" (4:4[3:22], NIV). Even in Egypt Moses became a great man (Ex. 11:3).

4873. מֹשֶׁה ***mōšeh:*** A proper noun designating Moses, the Aramaic name corresponding to the Hebrew word 4872.

4874. מַשֶּׁה ***maššeh:*** A masculine noun referring to a debt, a loan, something borrowed. It is found in Deuteronomy 15:2 preceded by *ba'al,* lord, possessor. It refers to a loan or a debt. The phrase translates as creditor, literally, lord of debt.

4875. מְשׁוֹאָה ***m^e^šô'āh,*** מְשֹׁאָה ***m^e^šō'āh:*** A feminine noun indicating desolation, waste. It is descriptive of land devoid of life, barren, almost useless (Job 30:3; 38:27). It is used to depict a day of judgment on Nineveh (Zeph. 1:15).

4876. מַשּׁוּאָה ***maššû'āh:*** A plural feminine noun meaning deceptions, destructions, and desolations. The psalmist took solace in the fact that God would cause the destruction of the wicked (Ps. 73:18). He also called on God to remember the righteous who had been in the depths of desolation (Ps. 74:3).

4877. מְשׁוֹבָב ***m^e^šôḇāḇ:*** A proper noun designating Meshobab (1 Chr. 4:34).

4878. מְשׁוּבָה ***m^e^šûḇāh:*** A feminine noun referring to a turning away, an apostasy, a backsliding. It indicates figuratively a way of life that is fluctuating, vacillating, insecure (Prov. 1:32). In a religious sense, it indicates apostasy, turning from truth (Jer. 2:19); a lack of constancy, a defection (Jer. 3:6; 5:6; 8:5; 14:7; Hos. 14:4[5]); or an act of turning away, a transgression (Ezek. 37:23; Hos. 11:7).

4879. מְשׁוּגָה ***m^e^šûgāh:*** A feminine noun pointing out an error. It identifies an offense, something wrongly done against another, especially against God (Job 19:4).

4880. מָשׁוֹט ***māšôṭ,*** מִשּׁוֹט ***miššôṭ:*** A masculine noun signifying an oar. It identifies an instrument for rowing a boat, moving it through water (Ezek. 27:6, 29).

4881. מְשׂוּכָה ***m^e^śûkāh,*** מְשֻׂכָה ***m^e^śukāh:*** A feminine noun referring to a hedge of thorns. It refers to a stand of thorn-bearing shrubbery used to form a hedge. The lazy person finds life as difficult as traveling through a hedge of thorns (Prov. 15:19). It is used in a more general sense of any hedge (Isa. 5:5), e.g., one of grapevines.

4882. מְשׁוּסָה ***m^e^šûsāh:*** A feminine noun meaning plunder, loot, spoil. It refers to the defeat and plunder of Israel by her enemies, in particular the spoil itself that was taken but also the devastation of the people themselves (Isa. 42:24).

4883. מַשּׂוֹר ***maśśôr:*** A masculine noun indicating a saw. It refers to a tool used for cutting wood or stones (Isa. 10:15).

4884. מְשׂוּרָה ***m^e^śûrāh:*** A feminine noun meaning a measure, a measurement. It is used of a liquid measure of capacity or weight (Lev. 19:35). It is used for volume and size as well (1 Chr. 23:29). It is used in an adverbial expression with *b^e^* attached, by measure or according to its measurement (Ezek. 4:11). It indicates the scarcity of something (Ezek. 4:16).

4885. מָשׂוֹשׂ ***māśôś:*** I. A masculine noun referring to joy, rejoicing. It indicates a response of inner happiness in the way of the Lord (Job 8:19); in anything a person chooses to rejoice in (Isa. 8:6). Jerusalem was considered to be the joy of the whole earth (Ps. 48:2[3]); especially of God's people (Isa. 66:10; Lam. 2:15); music creates joy in those hearing it (Isa. 24:8). It depicts the joy of a bridegroom (Isa. 62:5). God's people are created for joy (Isa. 65:18). It stands for the object of peoples' joy: wife, son, daughter, prophet (Ezek. 24:25). God, however, brings an end to the joy of a rebellious people and city (Hos. 2:11[13]).

II. A masculine noun describing a rotten thing, something wasted away. Some translators read Job 8:19 as a negative assertion concerning decaying roots or other rotten objects.

4886. מָשַׁח ***māšaḥ:*** A verb meaning to smear, to anoint. In its common usage, this verb can refer to the rubbing of a shield with oil (Isa. 21:5); the painting of a house (Jer. 22:14); the anointing of an individual with ointments or lotions (Amos 6:6); the spreading of oil on wafers (Ex. 29:2). If the verb is used in association with a religious ceremony, it connotes the sanctification of things or people for divine service. Once the Tabernacle was erected, it and all its furnishings were anointed with oil to consecrate them (Ex. 40:9–11). The most common usage of this verb is the ritual of divine installation of individuals into positions of leadership by the pouring oil on their heads. Most frequently, people were anointed for kingship: Saul (1 Sam. 10:1); David (1 Sam. 16:13); and Solomon (1 Kgs. 1:34). The word is also used of people anointed as priests (Ex. 28:41; Num. 35:25); and prophets (1 Kgs. 19:16; Isa. 61:1).

4887. מְשַׁח ***m***^{e}***šaḥ:*** An Aramaic noun meaning olive oil. This word appears only in two passages (Ezra 6:9; 7:22). These passages cite the provisions, including silver, livestock, wheat, salt, wine, and oil, that kings Darius and Artaxerxes supplied to the restoration priests at the Temple in Jerusalem.

4888. מִשְׁחָה ***mišḥāh,*** מָשְׁחָה ***mošḥāh:*** A feminine noun meaning anointing, a priestly portion. When used in reference to the anointing, *mišḥāh* is always used to modify *šemen* (8081), meaning olive oil (Ex. 37:29). At times, this phrase is further qualified by the addition of another modifier, like *qōḏeš* (6944), meaning holy (Ex. 30:31); *y*^{e}*hōwāh* (3068), the proper name of the God of Israel (Lev. 10:7); or *'*^{e}*lōhym* (430), meaning his God (Lev. 21:12). This "oil of anointing" was made from a combination of olive oil and spices (Ex. 30:25; 35:8, 28). It was then used to anoint someone or something and to consecrate the individual or item to God, such as the Aaronic priests (Ex. 29:7, 21; Lev. 8:2, 12, 30; 21:10); and the Tabernacle (Ex. 40:9; Lev. 8:10). It was also used in the customary ministrations of the Tabernacle (Ex. 31:11; 35:15; Num. 4:16). In addition, this term identified the portion of the sacrifices presented to God, then given to the priests (Lev. 7:35).

4889. מַשְׁחִית ***mašḥiyṯ:*** A feminine noun meaning destruction, corruption (Ex. 12:13; 2 Kgs. 23:13; 2 Chr. 20:23; 22:4; Prov. 18:9; 28:24; Isa. 54:16; Jer. 5:26; 22:7; 51:1; Ezek. 9:6; 21:31[36]; 25:15; Dan. 10:8.). See also 7843.

4890. מִשְׂחָק ***miśḥāq:*** A masculine noun indicating scorn, an object of derision. It indicates an object of laughter or of little concern or respect. In context other rulers or dignitaries were scorned by the mighty Babylonians (Hab. 1:10).

4891. מִשְׁחָר ***mišḥār:*** A masculine noun referring to the dawn, the morning. It refers to the rising sun in the phrase, from the womb of the dawn (*mišḥār*) (Ps. 110:3).

4892. מַשְׁחֵת ***mašḥēṯ:*** A feminine noun indicating destruction. It refers to the devastation, annihilation wrought by means of an instrument of destruction (*kᵉlîy mašḥēṯ*) (Ezek. 9:1).

4893. מִשְׁחַת ***mišḥaṯ,*** מָשְׁחָת ***mošḥāṯ:*** I. A masculine noun meaning disfigurement. It is used of the terrible disfigurement or distortion of a person's appearance; it describes the appearance of the Servant of the Lord (Isa. 52:14).

II. A masculine noun designating a defect. It refers to a defect or blemish in an animal, making it unacceptable for sacrifice to the Lord (Lev. 22:25).

4894. מִשְׁטוֹחַ ***mišṭôaḥ:*** A masculine noun referring to a place for spreading. It points out a location where fishing nets can be stretched out for commercial fishing (Ezek. 26:5, 14; 47:10).

4895. מַשְׂטֵמָה ***maśṭēmāh:*** A feminine noun describing hostility, hatred. In context it indicates an attitude and state of animosity and rejection, especially toward God's prophets and spokesmen (Hos. 9:7, 8).

4896. מִשְׁטָר ***mišṭār:*** A masculine noun defining rule, dominion. It indicates authoritative governance and guidance of something or someone over the earth or in general (Job 38:33).

4897. מֶשִׁי ***mešiy:*** A masculine noun referring to silk, a costly material. It refers to expensive and luxurious material made into clothing (Ezek. 16:10, 13).

4898. מְשֵׁיזַבְאֵל ***mᵉšēyzaḇ'ēl:*** A proper noun designating Meshezabel (Neh. 3:4; 10:21(22); 11:24).

4899. מָשִׁיחַ ***māšiyaḥ:*** A masculine noun meaning anointed one. Although this word is a noun, it can function both as a substantive (1 Sam. 24:6[7], 10[11]); or an adjective (Lev. 4:3, 5, 16). Since it refers to an individual who has been anointed by divine command (2 Sam. 1:14, 16), it can reference the high priest of Israel (Lev. 4:3, 5, 16; 6:22[15]); however, it is usually reserved as a marker for kingship, primarily the kings of Israel (1 Sam. 26:9, 11, 16, 23). In this way, the patriarchs were regarded as God's anointed kings (1 Chr. 16:22; Ps. 105:15). One unique instance of this term is in reference to Cyrus the Persian, a non-Israelite who was regarded as God's anointed (Isa. 45:1); therefore, one is forced to understand this characterization, not as a statement of the individual's inherent goodness and perfection, since Cyrus was a worshipper of pagan deities like Marduk. On the contrary, it is a statement of God's appointing or choosing an individual for a task. Furthermore, the concept of the *māšiyaḥ*, meaning Messiah, as a Savior is not fully developed in the Old Testament. The closest that one comes to this in the Old Testament is Daniel 9:25, 26. This concept is developed later, during the New Testament period and fits better with the parallel Greek word *christos*.

4900. מָשַׁךְ ***māšaḵ:*** A verb meaning to draw off, to drag, to pull up, to prolong. It is used of pulling someone out of a location (Gen. 37:28; Jer. 38:13); to pull an object (Deut. 21:3); to pick out and retrieve something (Ex. 12:21). It means to draw out something, such as a trumpet sound (Ex. 19:13; Josh. 6:5). Used with the word for hand, it means to extend the hand (Hos. 7:5); with reference to a bow, it means to pull the bowstring (1 Kgs. 22:34; 2 Chr. 18:33). It takes on a figurative sense when used of dragging along iniquity or evil (Ps. 10:9; Isa. 5:18). It may refer to lovingly leading, drawing someone along (Jer. 31:3); of bearing with a person or being patient (Neh. 9:30); or, conversely, of maintaining, stretching out one's anger (Ps. 85:5[6]). It has the sense of a formal procession following someone in a funeral (Job 21:33). It has an idiomatic sense of sowing seed, pulling it from a pouch and dispersing it (Amos 9:13); and of marching, proceeding somewhere (Judg. 4:6). It describes drawing out a period of time (Ps. 36:10[11]; Prov. 13:12; Isa. 13:22); or a delay of time (Ezek. 12:25, 28). It may carry the sense of titillating, drawing out the sensitivities of the flesh (Eccl. 2:3).

4901. מֶשֶׁךְ ***mešeḵ:*** I. A masculine noun indicating a price, preciousness, an acquisition. It refers to a container, a pouch for seed (Ps. 126:6); and to the acquiring of or the preciousness and unlimited value of wisdom (Job 28:18).

II. A masculine noun meaning bag. It refers to a container, a pouch, or a bag for seed used by a sower (Ps. 126:6).

III. A masculine noun referring to a trail, sowing. It refers to the trail of seeds or the path left from sowing seeds (Ps. 126:6).

4902. מֶשֶׁךְ ***mešeḵ:*** A proper noun designating Meshech (Gen. 10:2, 23; 1 Chr. 1:5, 17; Ps. 120:5; Ezek. 27:13; 32:26; 38:2, 3; 39:1).

4903. מִשְׁכַּב ***miškaḇ:*** An Aramaic masculine noun indicating a bed, a couch. It indicates a place for sleeping, resting, a place where a person can dream (Dan. 2:28, 29; 4:5[2], 10[7], 13[10]; 7:1).

4904. מִשְׁכָּב ***miškāḇ:*** A masculine noun meaning couch, bed. It refers to a place for resting, sleeping (Ex. 8:3[7:28]; 1 Kgs. 1:47). It is used figuratively to refer to the act of intercourse (approved or unapproved) (Gen. 49:4); the place of lovers (Ezek. 23:17). It is used with several verbs: to set up a bed, to make a bed (Isa.

57:7); to unroll quilts for a bed (Isa. 57:8). The phrase *ḥaḏar miškāb* refers to a bedroom (Ex. 8:3[7:28]; 2 Kgs. 6:12). It has the sense of lying, of a woman having sex with a man in the phrase *miškāb zāḵar* (Num. 31:17, 18). A noon nap or siesta is indicated in a *miškāb ṣohºrayim* (2 Sam. 4:5). It is used with the phrase *yāḏaʿ zāḵār* to indicate that one has had sexual intercourse (Judg. 21:11, 12).

4905. מַשְׂכִּיל *maśkiyl:* A masculine noun meaning a poem, a maskil. It is an unknown musical or wisdom term applied as a title or descriptive phrase to several psalms (Ps. 32; 42; 44; 45; 52—55; 74; 78; 88; 89; 142), possibly wisdom psalms indicating insight. Some translators also note this word in Psalm 47:7(8), KJV, NKJV.

4906. מַשְׂכִּית *maśkiyṯ:* A feminine noun meaning an image, the imagination. It is usually used of a carved image or sculpture, often idolatrous, whether of stone (Lev. 26:1); silver (Prov. 25:11); or of unspecified material (Num. 33:52; Ezek. 8:12). It is also utilized as a metaphor for one's imagination or conceit (Ps. 73:7 *maśkiyyôṯlēḇāḇ* [3824], meaning images of the heart; cf. Prov. 18:11).

4907. מִשְׁכַּן *miškan:* An Aramaic masculine noun indicating a habitation, a place of dwelling. It refers to the House of God, the Temple, in Jerusalem. It has the sense of a temporary habitation (Ezra 7:15).

4908. מִשְׁכָּן *miškān:* A masculine noun meaning dwelling, tabernacle, or sanctuary. The most significant meaning of the word indicates the dwelling place of the Lord, the Tabernacle. The word is often used in Exodus to indicate the temporary lodging of God and His glory among His people, the Tabernacle (Lev. 26:11; Ps. 26:8). It is used parallel to the word meaning sanctuary or holy place in the preceding verse (Ex. 25:9, cf. v. 8). The noun is formed from the verbal root *šāḵan* (7931), which indicates temporary lodging (Ex. 25:9; 26:1, 6; 2 Sam. 7:6). This noun is also often found in parallel with or described by the Hebrew word for tent (Ex. 26:35; Jer. 30:18).

The Tabernacle was called the Tent of Meeting (1 Chr. 6:32[17]; see Ex. 28:43; 30:20; 40:32), for there the Lord met with His people. It was also called the Tent of Testimony (Ex. 38:21; Num. 9:15; cf. Num. 17:22, 23; 18:2), since the covenantal documents, the Ten Commandments, were lodged in the Holy of Holies. The Hebrew noun is used with the definite article in 74 of 130 times, indicating that the author expected the reader to know what Tabernacle he meant. God gave Moses the pattern of the structure for the Tabernacle (Ex. 25:9; 26:30). The Lord had His Tabernacle set up at Shiloh in Canaan, but it was later abandoned (Ps. 78:60). The word is hardly ever used regarding the later Temple of Solomon, of Ezekiel's visionary Temple (2 Chr. 29:6; Ps. 26:8; 46:4[5]; Ezek. 37:27); or the

Lord's dwelling place in Zion (Ps. 132:5, 7). The word used most often to describe Solomon's Temple and the postexilic Temple is *bayiṯ* (1004), meaning house.

The word also indicates the dwelling places of the Israelites and other peoples; it describes Korah's dwelling place (Num. 16:24, 27); Israel's dwelling place (Num. 24:5; Isa. 32:18; Jer. 30:18). Twice the word indicates the dwelling of the dead, i.e., the grave Jerusalem made for herself, and the abode of all classes of men (Ps. 49:11[12]; Isa. 22:16).

4909. מַשְׂכֹּרֶת ***maśkōreṯ:*** A feminine noun referring to wages. It refers to payment of various kinds for services rendered to a person (Gen. 29:15; 31:7, 41); it was fixed and not to be changed arbitrarily. Wages were considered to be determined by God in Israel (Ruth 2:12).

4910. מָשַׁל ***māšal:*** A verb denoting to rule, to reign, or to have dominion over. Although its general tone communicates leadership and authority, its specific nuance and connotation are derived from the context in which it appears. In the creation narratives on the fourth day, God created the great luminaries. The greater luminary was to rule the day, and the lesser was to rule the night (Gen. 1:18). It is also applied to people who rule: a servant over his master's household (Gen. 24:2); a king over his country (Josh. 12:5); or his people (Judg. 8:22, 23); a people over another people (Judg. 14:4). God is also said to rule over His people (Judg. 8:23); not over His adversaries (Isa. 63:19); over the nations (2 Chr. 20:6; Ps. 22:28[29]); over Jacob (Ps. 59:13[14]); over all things (1 Chr. 29:12).

4911. מָשַׁל ***māšal:*** A verb meaning to compare, to be like, to quote a proverb. It is used to describe the delivery of a proverb or a comparison (Num. 21:27). It describes making something into or like something else, a proverb or byword (Job 17:6; 30:19; Ps. 28:1; 49:12[13], 20[21]; 143:7; Isa. 14:10). It compares one thing with another (Isa. 46:5). Ezekiel uses the word often to mean to speak or to use a parable (Ezek. 12:23; 17:2; 18:2, 3). Its participial form indicates a person who produces parables and speaks in proverbs (Ezek. 20:49[21:5]; 24:3).

4912. מָשָׁל ***māšāl:*** A masculine noun meaning a proverb, an oracle, a parable. It is a literary genre, device, and style in the form of short, pithy sayings, prophetic utterances, or compositions of comparison (1 Sam. 10:12; 24:13[14]; Ezek. 12:22, 23; 17:2; 20:49[21:5]). It has the sense of a byword or object spoken of in contempt or derision (Deut. 28:37; 1 Kgs. 9:7; Ps. 44:14[15]; 69:11[12]). It describes a prophetic utterance (Num. 23:7, 18; 24:3, 15, 20, 21, 23; Isa. 14:4; Mic. 2:4). Its meaning is extended to poetry, that often features comparisons, figurative language, etc. (1 Kgs. 4:32[5:12]; Ps. 49:4[5]; 78:2). This word describes short sayings or sentences of wisdom (Job 13:12; 27:1; 29:1; Prov. 10:1; 25:1, etc. in Proverbs).

4913. מָשָׁל ***māšāl:*** A proper noun designating Mashal, an abbreviated form of *miš'āl* (4861) (1 Chr. 6:74[59]).

4914. מְשֹׁל ***m^e^šōl:*** A masculine noun meaning make into a proverb, a byword. It is used of Job's designation as a byword or object of ridicule (Job 17:6).

4915. מֹשֶׁל ***mōšel:*** A masculine noun meaning likeness, dominion. This number in Strong's is associated with two words. The first comes from the verb *māšal* (4911), meaning to represent or to be like, and is found only in Job 41:33[25], where it is translated "likeness." The second comes from the verb *māšal* (4910), meaning to rule or to govern. This word is found in Daniel 11:4 and Zechariah 9:10, where it describes the dominion of Alexander and the coming Messiah.

4916. מִשְׁלוֹחַ ***mišlôaḥ,*** מִשְׁלָח ***mišlāḥ:*** I. A masculine noun referring to sending, a stretching forth. It is used to refer to land and territory that covered and belonged to a nation (Isa. 11:14). It has the meaning of sending out something, e.g., gifts (Esth. 9:19, 22).

II. A masculine noun referring to an undertaking; putting forth. It refers to that which is covered or undertaken. In its context it is used with hand, the outstretching of a person's hand, what he or she is attempting to do (Deut. 12:7, 18; 15:10; 23:20[21]; 28:8, 20). It has the sense of an area of land, a place, or a location that is covered or extended for some purpose, e.g., for pasturing (Isa. 7:25).

4917. מִשְׁלַחַת ***mišlaḥat̲:*** A feminine noun indicating a discharge, a release; a group sent out. It refers to a group sent out and the act of sending them as well (Ps. 78:49; Eccl. 8:8).

4918. מְשֻׁלָּם ***m^e^šullām:*** A proper noun designating. Meshullam:

A. A descendant of Benjamin (1 Chr. 8:17).

B. A descendant of Gad (1 Chr. 5:13).

C. Grandfather of Shaphan (2 Kgs. 22:3).

D. An overseer in the repair of the temple (2 Chr. 34:12).

E. A son of Zerubbabel (1 Chr. 3:19).

F. A son of Shephatiah (1 Chr. 9:8).

G. A son of Zadok (1 Chr. 9:11; Neh. 11:11).

H. A son of Joed (1 Chr. 9:7; Neh. 11:7).

I. A son of Ezra (Neh. 12:13, 33).

J. A son of Meshillemith (1 Chr. 9:12).

K. A Jewish leader (Ezra 8:16; 10:15; Neh. 8:4; 10:20[21]).

L. A son of Bani (Ezra 10:29).

M. A son of Berechiah (Neh. 3:4, 30; 6:18; 10:7[8]).

N. A son of Besodeiah (Neh. 3:6).

O. A descendant of Iddo (Neh. 12:16).

P. A Levite (Neh. 12:25).

4919. מְשִׁלֵּמוֹת mᵉšillēmôṯ: A proper noun designating Meshillemoth:

A. The father of Berechiah (2 Chr. 28:12).

B. A son of Immer (Neh. 11:13).

4920. מְשֶׁלֶמְיָה mᵉšelemyāh, מְשֶׁלֶמְיָהוּ mᵉšelemyāhû: A proper noun designating Meshelemiah (1 Chr. 9:21; 26:1, 2, 9).

4921. משלמית mᵉšillēmiyṯ: A proper noun designating Meshillemith (1 Chr. 9:12).

4922. מְשֻׁלֶּמֶת mᵉšullemeṯ: A proper noun designating Meshullemeth (2 Kgs. 21:19).

4923. מְשַׁמָּה mᵉšammāh: A feminine noun indicating desolation, waste. It indicates a state of isolation, desertion. It describes part of the conditions created by God's judgments on various lands and cities (Isa. 15:6; Jer. 48:34), including Jerusalem (Ezek. 5:15; 6:14; 35:3).

4924. מִשְׁמָן mišmān, מַשְׁמַנִּים mašmanniym: I. A masculine noun meaning fat, fatness. It is used of the good, abundant produce of the land (Gen. 27:28, 39). It points out strong or influential persons (Ps. 78:31); even soldiers (Isa. 10:16). It indicates a sign of an abundance of health and wealth (Isa. 17:4; Dan. 11:24).

II. A masculine plural noun describing festive food. It indicates the best portions of food at a festive meal (Neh. 8:10).

4925. מִשְׁמַנָּה mišmannāh: A proper noun designating Mishmannah (1 Chr. 12:10).

4926. מִשְׁמָע mišmāʻ: A masculine noun indicating that which is heard, a rumor. It indicates, in context, something heard but not properly confirmed or established at the time (Isa. 11:3).

4927. מִשְׁמָע mišmāʻ: A proper noun designating Mishma:

A. A son of Ishmael (Gen. 25:14; 1 Chr. 1:30).

B. A descendant of Simeon (1 Chr. 4:25, 26).

4928. מִשְׁמַעַת mišmaʻaṯ: A feminine noun meaning obedient subjects. This word comes from the verb *šāmaʻ* (8085), meaning to hear and obey, and describes a group of people who are bound to obey. In several instances of this word, it describes a king's personal guard (1 Sam. 22:14; 2 Sam. 23:23; 1 Chr. 11:25). In the only other instance, it depicts a conquered people who are bound to obey (Isa. 11:14).

4929. מִשְׁמָר mišmār: A masculine noun referring to custody, a guard, a prison. It indicates the condition of being guarded, watched, controlled (Gen. 40:3, 4, 7; 41:10; 42:17; Lev. 24:12; Num. 15:34). It describes a group of guards and their location (1 Chr. 26:16; Jer. 51:12). It is used of a group of watchmen or armed men that are established for some purpose (Neh. 4:9[3], 22[16], 23[17]; 7:3; 12:24[NASB, "division"], 25; Ezek. 38:7). It has the sense of security or safety (Neh. 13:14; NIV, NASB, services) or possibly services, indicating the objects of the guard duties performed by Nehemiah. It has the sense of to keep guard (Prov. 4:23).

4930. מַשְׂמֵרָה ***maśmērāh:*** A feminine noun indicating a nail. It refers to metal fasteners, but it is used figuratively of collected words and their authors and of the wise as firm nails which drive home instruction for life (Eccl. 12:11).

4931. מִשְׁמֶרֶת ***mišmereṯ:*** A feminine noun meaning guard, charge, duty. This word comes from the verb *šāmar* (8104), meaning to watch, to keep, to protect, or to guard, and has a multiplicity of usages. In its most basic sense, it describes a guarded place (Num. 17:10[25]; 1 Sam. 22:23); keeping for later use (Ex. 12:6; 16:32–34); or protection against enemies (2 Kgs. 11:5–7). In several instances, it is used of a guard post (Isa. 21:8; Hab. 2:1). The idea of obedience (i.e., keeping the commandments) is often depicted, which leads to a translation of charge (Gen. 26:5; Deut. 11:1; Zech. 3:7) or duty (Num. 3:7; 9:23; 2 Chr. 8:14).

4932. מִשְׁנֶה ***mišneh:*** A masculine noun meaning double, a copy, a repetition; second, next in position or rank. The word is used to indicate a doubling of something, such as money (Gen. 43:12, 15); or food (Ex. 16:5, 22). It refers to a copy of something, e.g., the Law (Deut. 17:18; Josh. 8:32). Finally, it indicates position or rank: second rank (Gen. 41:43; 2 Kgs. 23:4), second oldest (1 Sam. 8:2; 17:13). It may indicate a certain ranked part of several parts, e.g., the second district (2 Kgs. 22:14; Zeph. 1:10).

4933. מְשִׁסָּה ***m***^{e}***šissāh:*** A feminine noun identifying something as spoil, plunder. It refers to the material gains, both persons and merchandise, acquired through war. It indicates Israel (2 Kgs. 21:14; Isa. 42:22, 24; Hab. 2:7); and those who plunder Israel, God's people (Jer. 30:16; Zeph. 1:13).

4934. מִשְׁעוֹל ***miš'ôl:*** A masculine noun signifying a path. It refers to a walkway, man-made or created by nature, large enough for donkeys to travel (Num. 22:24).

4935. מִשְׁעִי ***miš'iy:*** A masculine noun referring to wash, washing. It indicates the act of cleaning up, bathing a newborn infant. Preceded by *l*^{e}, to, for, it means ready for or fit for cleansing, washing (Ezek. 16:4).

4936. מִשְׁעָם ***miš'ām:*** A proper noun designating Misham (1 Chr. 8:12).

4937. מִשְׁעָן miš'ān, מַשְׁעֵן maš'ēn: I. A masculine noun designating a staff, a support, a supply. It indicates something serving to firm, keep stable. It is used figuratively of the Lord who encourages His people and supplies their needs (2 Sam. 22:19; Ps. 18:18[19]). He can remove that protective support (Isa. 3:1).

II. A masculine noun meaning support, supply. It is used of the entire spectrum of the Lord's caring for His people (Isa. 3:1). See I.

4938. מַשְׁעֵנָה maš'ēnāh, מִשְׁעֶנֶת miš'enet̠: I. A feminine noun indicating a support, a supply. It is used of what firms up, keeps stable, furnishes needed supplies. It is a synonym to 4937, I. The Lord is able to remove the support and supply needed by Jerusalem and Judah (Isa. 3:1).

II. A feminine noun indicating a pole, a staff, a support. It refers to a physical support, such as a cane or crutch (Ex. 21:19), especially for the elderly (Zech. 8:4). It serves as a symbol of authority along with a scepter (Num. 21:18). It indicates a rod used by a divine being (Judg. 6:21); and the staff of a prophet or a man of God that represents his authority (2 Kgs. 4:29). In context it can refer to nations as feeble, frail staffs, not to be trusted (2 Kgs. 18:21; Isa. 36:6; Ezek. 29:6). The staff of the Lord, His presence and protection, comforts His people (Ps. 23:4).

4939. מִשְׂפָּח miśpāḥ: A masculine noun referring to bloodshed, oppression. It depicts social injustice or bloodshed for many in Israel, that is, the putting to death of those not deserving to die (Isa. 5:7).

4940. מִשְׁפָּחָה mišpāḥāh: A feminine noun meaning an extended family, a tribe, a clan. It is a group in which there is a close blood relationship. In a technical sense, a *mišpāḥāh* is the middle of the subdivisions of the Israelite peoples. The inhabitants of an individual household were identified as a *bayit̠* (1004), meaning house. Several households together constituted a *mišpāḥāh* (Gen. 10:31, 32; Ex. 6:14, 15, 19, 25). Several families or clans together constituted a *šēb̠et̠* (7626) or *maṭṭeh* (4294), meaning tribe. This noun is also used in a less technical sense to indicate an entire people or nation (Ezek. 20:32; Mic. 2:3); an ethnic or racial group (Gen. 10:5; 12:3); a tribe (Josh. 7:17; Judg. 13:2; 18:2, 11). It occurs in the sense of a guild of scribes in one verse (1 Chr. 2:55) because the scribal profession was originally a hereditary position. It can also represent a species or kind of animal (Gen. 8:19); or a divine plague (Jer. 15:3).

4941. מִשְׁפָּט mišpāṭ: A masculine noun meaning a judgment, a legal decision, a legal case, a claim, proper, rectitude. The word connotes several variations in meanings depending on the context. It is used to describe a legal decision or judgment rendered: it describes a legal decision given by God to be followed by the people (Isa.

58:2; Zeph. 2:3; Mal. 2:17). These decisions could come through the use of the Urim and Thummim (Num. 27:21). The high priest wore a pouch called the breastpiece of justice, containing the Urim and Thummim by which decisions were obtained from the Lord (Ex. 28:30). Doing what was right and just in the Lord's eyes was far more important than presenting sacrifices to Him (Gen. 18:19; Prov. 21:3, 15). God was declared to be the Judge of the whole earth who rendered justice faithfully (Gen. 18:25; Isa. 30:18). In the plural form, the word describes legal judgments, cases, examples, laws, and specifications.

The word describes the legal case or cause presented by someone. The Servant spoken of by Isaiah asked who brought his case of justice against him (Isa. 50:8); Job brought his case to vindicate himself (Job 13:18; 23:4). The legal claim or control in a situation is also described by the word. Samuel warned the people of the civil and legal demands a king would place on them (1 Sam. 8:9); Moses gave legislation to protect the rightful claim of daughters (Ex. 21:9). The Hebrew word also described the legal right to property (Jer. 32:8). Not surprisingly, the place where judgments were rendered was also described by this word; disputes were to be taken to the place of judgment (Deut. 25:1). Solomon built a hall of justice where he served as judge (1 Kgs. 7:7).

The word also describes plans or instructions: it describes the building plans for the Tabernacle (Ex. 35—40); and the specifications for the Temple (1 Kgs. 6:38); the instructions the angelic messenger gave to Samson's parents about how he was to be brought up (Judg. 13:12). In a more abstract sense, it depicts the manner of life a people followed, such as the Sidonians (Judg. 18:7; 1 Sam. 2:13).

The word means simple justice in some contexts, often in parallel with synonymous words, such as *ḥōq* (2706) or *ṣeḏeq* (6664), meaning ordinance or righteousness. It describes justice as one thing Jerusalem was to be filled with along with righteousness (Isa. 1:21). Justice and righteousness characterize the Lord's throne (Ps. 89:14[15]); and these were coupled with love and faithfulness (cf. Ps. 101:1; 111:7). Executing or doing justice was the central goal that Yahweh had for His people (Jer. 7:5; Ezek. 18:8), for that equaled righteousness (Ezek. 18:9).

4942. מִשְׁפְּתַיִם *mišpᵉṯayim:* I. A dual masculine noun referring to a burden, a saddlebag. The meaning is being researched. Some understand it to refer to two saddlebags on a pack animal (Gen. 49:14, NIV). Others translate it as sheepfolds (NASB). The KJV renders it as two burdens, loads carried by a baggage animal. Other less likely words have been suggested. See II.

II. A dual masculine noun referring to campfires or sheepfolds (Judg. 5:16). See comments to I above.

4943. מֶשֶׁק mešeq: A masculine noun meaning an heir, a steward. It is used of a person who has the legal and familial qualifications to inherit what is rightfully his (Gen. 15:2).

4944. מַשָּׁק maššāq: A masculine noun signifying rushing, swarming. It is used of an attack and onslaught by devouring locusts (Isa. 33:4).

4945. מַשְׁקֶה mašqeh: I. A masculine noun designating a cupbearer, a butler. It indicates someone officially appointed to, among other duties, serve wine to the king (Gen. 40:1, 2, 5, 9, 13, 20, 21, 23; 41:9) and at official banquets (1 Kgs. 10:5; 2 Chr. 9:4; Neh. 1:11).

II. A masculine noun indicating a liquid, a drinking vessel, a watering place. It is used of land that receives abundant rain and is well-watered (Gen. 13:10). It refers to liquids (Lev. 11:34; Isa. 32:6) and is used to define vessels as drinking or watering vessels (1 Kgs. 10:21; 2 Chr. 9:20). It is used of a watering place, a place where water may be drawn (Ezek. 45:15).

4946. מִשְׁקוֹל mišqôl: A masculine noun signifying weight. It signifies how much something weighs, its heaviness. Used with the preposition b^e, by, it is rendered by weight, as to weight (Ezek. 4:10).

4947. מַשְׁקוֹף mašqôp̱: A masculine noun referring to the lintel, the top of a door. It indicates the crosspiece at the top of a door. It was to be smeared with blood at the Passover (Ex. 12:7, 22, 23).

4948. מִשְׁקָל mišqāl: A masculine noun indicating weight. It refers to how much something weighs, its heaviness. Weight was expressed in various ways: shekels or part of a shekel (Gen. 24:22; Num. 7:13, 19, 25); money was valued according to its weight (Gen. 43:21, money according to its weight). To misrepresent the weight of money, food, or goods was wrong (Lev. 19:35). To serve something by weight was to use it sparingly (Lev. 26:26; Ezek. 4:16). The weight of something was determined by using scales (Ezek. 5:1). The phrase *'ên mišqāl* means something so great that it is not able to be weighed (1 Chr. 22:3; cf. 2 Kgs. 25:16; Jer. 52:20).

4949. מִשְׁקֶלֶת mišqeleṯ, מִשְׁקֹלֶת mišqōleṯ: A feminine noun referring to a plumb line, a leveling instrument. It indicates a tool able to determine if something is level, horizontal. Righteousness was God's "level" to evaluate His people (Isa. 28:17); the skewed plumb line of the house of Ahab was placed over a wicked Jerusalem to judge her (2 Kgs. 21:13).

4950. מִשְׁקָע mišqā': A masculine noun meaning clear, deep. A description of water that is clear and clean enough to drink. Sediments and impurities have settled out of it (Ezek. 34:18).

4951. מִשְׂרָה miśrāh: A feminine noun referring to government. It indicates the extent of rulership; dominion that is under authority (Isa. 9:6[5], 7[6]).

4952. מִשְׁרָה ***mišrāh:*** A feminine noun indicating juice. It refers to a flowing liquid and is used of the juice of grapes (Num. 6:3). A Nazarite could not drink this liquid.

4953. מַשְׁרוֹקִי ***mašrôqiy:*** An Aramaic feminine noun meaning flute. It refers to one of the woodwind instruments. It was among the collection of musical instruments present at Nebuchadnezzar's dedication of his golden image or obelisk (Dan. 3:5, 7, 10, 15).

4954. מִשְׁרָעִי ***mišrā'iy:*** A proper noun designating Mishraite (1 Chr. 2:53).

4955. מִשְׂרָפָה ***miśrāp̱āh:*** A feminine noun indicating a burning. It indicates the process of burning something. It refers to a burning of lime, meaning that an object was completely burned to ashes (Isa. 33:12). It is used of the burning of spices at the burial of the rebellious king Zedekiah (Jer. 34:5).

4956. מִשְׂרְפוֹת מַיִם ***miśr^e^p̱ôṯ mayim:*** A proper noun designating Misrephoth Maim (Josh. 11:8; 13:6).

4957. מַשְׂרֵקָה ***maśrēqāh:*** A proper noun designating Masrekah (Gen. 36:36; 1 Chr. 1:47).

4958. מַשְׂרֵת ***maśrēṯ:*** A feminine noun signifying a pan, a dish. It refers to a pan used for baking or frying food (2 Sam. 13:9).

4959. מָשַׁשׁ ***māšaš:*** A verb meaning to touch, to feel, to grope. It refers to feeling around, groping after something to identify it or to move around, such as Isaac did (Gen. 27:12, 22); or as the Egyptians did during the plague of darkness (Ex. 10:21). It has the sense of staggering, trying to find one's way in a figurative sense (Deut. 28:29; Job 12:25), especially of the wicked (Job 5:14).

4960. מִשְׁתֶּה ***mišteh:*** A masculine noun meaning a drink, a feast. This word comes from the verb *šāṯāh* (8354), meaning to drink. In a few instances, this word referred specifically to drinks (Ezra 3:7; Dan. 1:5, 8, 10, 16), but it usually referred to feasts prepared for special occasions: hospitality (Gen. 19:3); the weaning of a child (Gen. 21:8); making peace (Gen. 26:30; 2 Sam. 3:20); a wedding (Gen. 29:22; Judg. 14:10, 12, 17; Esth. 2:18); merriment (Esth. 1:3; 9:17–19; Job 1:4, 5; Eccl. 7:2). A feast was indicative of blessing (Prov. 15:15; Isa. 25:6).

4961. מִשְׁתֵּא ***mištē':*** An Aramaic masculine noun denoting a feast, a banquet. It refers to a large spread of food or a place of celebration with eating and drinking (Dan. 5:10).

4962. מַת ***maṯ:*** A masculine noun meaning male, man; a few in number. A word used to refer to persons: qualified by *mispār* or *m^e^'aṭ*, it refers to a few men or people (Gen. 34:30;

Deut. 4:27; 1 Chr. 16:19; Jer. 44:28); to men as opposed to women (Deut. 2:34; 3:6; Isa. 3:25); to persons in general (Job 11:3, 11; 19:19).

4963. מַתְבֵּן ***maṯbēn:*** A masculine noun referring to straw. It refers to hollow stalks or stems of grain after being threshed. It was used for fodder, for beds, or for making huts, pillows, etc. (Isa. 25:10).

4964. מֶתֶג ***meṯeg:*** A masculine noun referring to a bridle, a bit. It denotes an instrument used to control an animal, especially a horse, camel, etc. (Prov. 26:3). The phrase *meteg h^{ā}'mmāh* means to take control (2 Sam. 8:1). It is used figuratively of the Lord bridling the king of Assyria (2 Kgs. 19:28; Isa. 37:29). Persons were not made to be bridled (Ps. 32:9).

4965. מֶתֶג הָאַמָּה ***meṯeg hā'ammāh:*** I. The Philistine city Metheg Ammah (KJV, NIV, 2 Sam. 8:1).

II. A phrase meaning control of the chief city (NASB, 2 Sam. 8:1). It is made up of the words *meṯeg* (4964) and *'ammāh* (522,II).

4966. מָתוֹק ***māṯôq:*** An adjective meaning sweet. It refers to something that has a taste similar to sugar or honey (Prov. 24:13). It is the opposite of bitter or sour (Isa. 5:20). It is used to convey the idea of pleasantness, agreeableness (Judg. 14:14, 18). God's laws are sweeter than honey (Ps. 19:10[11]); pleasant words are as sweet as honey (Prov. 16:24). It is used figuratively in amorous expressions (Song 2:3).

4967. מְתוּשָׁאֵל ***m^{e}ṯûšā'ēl:*** A proper noun designating Methusael (Gen. 4:18).

4968. מְתוּשֶׁלַח ***m^{e}ṯûšelaḥ:*** A proper noun designating Methuselah, the son of Enoch. He fathered Lamech, father of Noah. He lived an astounding 969 years (Gen. 5:21, 27).

4969. מָתַח ***māṯaḥ:*** A verb referring to spreading out, stretching out. It is used of God's act of expanding the sky like spreading out a curtain (Isa. 40:22).

4970. מָתַי ***māṯay:*** An interrogative adverb of time meaning when, how long. Used alone or with *l^{e}* on the front, it means when (Gen. 30:30; Ex. 8:9[5]). With *'aḏ-* on the front, it has the sense of how long, until when (Ex. 10:3, 7; Num. 14:27; 1 Sam. 1:14; 1 Kgs. 18:21; Hos. 8:5).

4971. מַתְכֹּנֶת ***maṯkōneṯ:*** A feminine noun indicating a measure, a proportion, a quota, specifications. It indicates some kind of measurement: a quota of bricks (Ex. 5:8); a proper proportional mixing of quantities of ingredients (Ex. 30:32, 37; Ezek. 45:11). It refers to architectural and construction specifications and proportions (2 Chr. 24:13).

4972. מַתְּלָאָה ***matt^{e}lā'āh:*** A feminine noun indicating weariness. The state of being bored at something or despising it, thinking it a nuisance (Mal. 1:13).

4973. מְתַלְּעוֹת ***m^e<u>t</u>all^e'ô<u>t</u>:*** A feminine plural noun referring to a jawbone, jaw teeth, fangs. It refers to the bones or teeth of a jaw. Breaking a person's jaw or jawbone means to incapacitate him or her thoroughly (Job 29:17). It is used of the fangs, the large teeth, of young lions in a figurative sense (Ps. 58:6[7]). These jawbones were a weapon for attack (Prov. 30:14). It is used metaphorically of the teeth of the armies of Babylon (Joel 1:6).

4974. מְתֹם ***m^e<u>t</u>ōm:*** I. A masculine noun indicating wholeness, soundness. It refers to a healthy, sound spot, a sign of wholeness, health (Ps. 38:3[4]; Isa. 1:6). Some render the word as men in Judges 20:48 (KJV, NKJV). See II, below.

II. A masculine noun meaning men; entire, whole, all. It means everything, the whole, the entire (Judg. 20:48, NASB, NIV, all). See I above. It could refer to all the men.

4975. מָתְנַיִם ***mo<u>t</u>nayim:*** I. A masculine dual noun meaning loins, waist, body, side. It refers to the section of the human body which connects and supports the upper and lower parts of the body, including the buttocks lumbar region. The hips, loins, and lower back are included. In general use, it referred to the central area of the body (Ezek. 47:4). Sackcloth was placed on one's loins in times of mourning (Gen. 37:34). Clothing girded it during travel (Ex. 12:11); but a girdle was worn regularly (1 Kgs. 2:5). The righteous king is to be girded with righteousness in the messianic kingdom (Isa. 11:5). The loins were regarded as full of strength (Deut. 13:11; 1 Kgs. 12:10). In this area, various things were attached and carried such as a sword (2 Sam. 20:8; Neh. 4:18[12]). To gird up one's loins was to prepare for battle or action (1 Kgs. 18:46).

II. A masculine dual noun referring to a strutting rooster. It depicts a rooster taking long steps, crowing and stretching its neck (Prov. 30:31, NASB, NIV). It is described as a splendid thing, a stately act. See III.

III. A masculine dual noun describing a dog, a greyhound. Some translators prefer to translate this as the greyhound because of its impressive look and running style (Prov. 30:31, KJV). See II.

4976. מַתָּן ***mattān:*** A masculine noun referring to a gift. It indicates what is given and comes from the root, *nā<u>t</u>an,* to give: gifts (Gen. 34:12; Num. 18:11; Prov. 18:16; 19:6; 21:14). Gifts could be a means of attaining favor or of creating problems (Prov. 18:16; 19:6; 21:14).

4977. מַתָּן ***mattān:*** A proper noun designating Mattan:

A. A priest of Baal (2 Kgs. 11:18; 2 Chr. 23:17).

B. The father of Shephatiah (Jer. 38:1).

4978. מַתְּנָה ***mattᵉnāh:*** An Aramaic feminine noun indicating a gift. It indicates what is given, from the root *nᵉṭan,* to give (Dan. 2:6, 48; 5:17). It has the sense of a reward in context.

4979. מַתָּנָה ***mattānāh:*** A feminine noun designating a gift. It refers to what is given for various reasons: as compensation or for support (Gen. 25:6; Esth. 9:22; Ezek. 46:16, 17); as offerings, gifts, to the Lord (Ex. 28:38; Lev. 23:38; Num. 18:29; Ps. 68:18 [19]). Persons in Israel gave as they were able (Deut. 16:7). The Levites were called the Lord's gift to the priesthood (Num. 18:6, 7). This word has the sense of a bribe in the wisdom literature (Prov. 15:27; Eccl. 7:7).

4980. מַתָּנָה ***mattānāh:*** A proper noun designating Mattanah (Num. 21:18, 19).

4981. מִתְנִי ***miṯniy:*** A proper noun designating Mithnite (1 Chr. 11:43).

4982. מַתְּנַי ***mattᵉnay:*** A proper noun designating Mattenai:

A. A priest (Neh. 12:19).

B. A son of Hashum (Ezra 10:33).

C. A son of Bani (Ezra 10:37).

4983. מַתַּנְיָה ***mattanyāh,*** **מַתַּנְיָהוּ** ***mattanyāhû:*** A proper noun designating Mattaniah:

A. A descendant of Asaph (2 Chr. 20:14).

B. A Levite (1 Chr. 25:4, 16).

C. A Levite, possibly the same as A above (2 Chr. 29:13).

D. A king of Judah (2 Kgs. 24:17).

E. A son of Micah (1 Chr. 9:15; Neh. 11:17, 22; 12:8, 25, 35; 13:13).

F. A son of Elam (Ezra 10:26).

G. A son of Zattu (Ezra 10:27).

H. A son of Pahath-Moab (Ezra 10:30).

I. A son of Bani (Ezra 10:37).

4984. מִתְנַשֵּׂא ***miṯnaśē':*** A masculine noun referring to a person who exalts himself or herself. It means to show oneself as great, to lift up oneself for some purpose: Adonijah (1 Kgs. 1:5). It is used of the Lord's self-exaltation over everything (1 Chr. 29:11).

4985. מָתַק ***māṯaq:*** A verb meaning to be sweet, to be pleasant. It indicates something having a taste like sugar or honey. It is used figuratively of evil as tasting deceptively sweet (Job 20:12; Prov. 9:17). It describes a worm enjoying its food (Job 24:20); it describes, ironically, clods of earth sweetly, gently covering a person in burial (Job 21:33). It indicates the pleasantness of a friendship in the Lord (Ps. 55:14[15]).

4986. מָתֵק ***māṯēq:*** A masculine noun referring to sweetness. It describes a taste of something like sugar or honey (Prov. 16:21; 27:9). Manner of speech and good counsel give the effects of pleasantness.

4987. מֹתֶק ***mōṯeq:*** A masculine noun meaning sweetness. It refers to the sweet taste of ripe figs, a taste similar to honey (Judg. 9:11).

4988. מָתָק ***māṯāq:*** A masculine noun indicating a person who feeds on a sweet morsel. It refers to someone or something that feeds on something, in context a worm (*rimmāh,* Job 24:20) feeding on the wicked in their graves. See 4985.

4989. מִתְקָה ***miṯqāh:*** A proper noun designating Mithcah (Num. 33:28, 29).

4990. מִתְרְדָת ***miṯr***^{e}***ḏāṯ:*** A proper noun designating Mithredath:

A. A treasurer of Cyrus (Ezra 1:8).

B. A Persian governor of Samaria (Ezra 4:7).

4991. מַתַּת ***mattaṯ,*** מַתָּת ***mattāṯ:*** A feminine noun denoting a gift, a reward. It depicts what is given. In some contexts, it has the sense of a reward or a gift of thanks (1 Kgs. 13:7). Usually, it indicates a gift only (Prov. 25:14); but it can be God's gifts of food, drink, and work (Eccl. 3:13; 5:19[18]). The phrase *mattan yaḏ* means as much as is at hand or as much as a person can give (Ezek. 46:5, 11).

4992. מַתַּתָּה ***mattattāh:*** A proper noun designating Mattattah (Ezra 10:33).

4993. מַתִּתְיָה ***mattiṯyāh,*** מַתִּתְיָהוּ ***mattiṯyāhû:*** A proper noun designating Mattithiah:

A. A Levite (1 Chr. 9:31; 15:18, 21; 16:5).

B. A son of Jeduthun (1 Chr. 25:3, 21).

C. A son of Nebo (Ezra 10:43).

D. A postexilic Jew (Neh. 8:4).

נ Nun

4994. נָא *nā':* A participle meaning please, now. The most common use of this word is similar to the antiquated use of pray as in pray tell. Since it was frequently used as a polite form of asking for something, it was often left untranslated in many English versions of the Bible. Abraham used this word when he asked Sarah to say she was his sister (Gen. 12:13); Moses used the word when he asked the people to listen to him (Num. 20:10). It was often used to ask permission (Num. 20:17).

4995. נָא *nā':* An adjective describing meat as raw. It is used of meat prepared to be eaten. Israel was not to eat raw meat with blood in it (Ex. 12:9).

4996. נֹא *nō':* A proper noun designating No, a Hebrew name for Thebes in southern Egypt, an ancient capital city of Egypt. *No* represents the Egyptian *niw(t)* and means "the city." Jeremiah and Ezekiel both indicated that God was about to punish No (Thebes) and its gods, especially the god Amon. Nahum mentioned its fall in 663 B.C. to the Assyrians as a past event.

4997. נֹאד *nō'd̲,* נְאוֹד *n^{e}ôd̲:* A masculine noun pointing out a bottle, a wineskin. It was used of a container made of animal skin prepared so it would not leak. It was used to hold wine (Josh. 9:4, 13; 1 Sam. 16:20); or milk (Judg. 4:19). It is used figuratively of a container for tears (Ps. 56:8[9]); or for tears that have not yet been shed (Ps. 119:83).

4998. נָאָה *nā'āh:* A verb meaning beautiful, fitting. It indicates that something is appropriate or in order: holiness is appropriate for the Lord's house (Ps. 93:5); the cheeks of the beloved are beautiful, lovely (Song 1:10); feet that bring good news of God's grace are beautiful (Isa. 52:7).

4999. נָאָה *nā'āh:* A feminine noun meaning a dwelling, an abode, a residence, a habitation, a pasture, a meadow. This word describes a place where humans permanently settle and live; or to an area where flocks and herds graze, reside, lie down, and rest. In His fierce anger for their iniquities, the Lord vented His wrath on Israel, destroying without mercy the dwellings found within its borders (Lam. 2:2; cf. Jer. 25:37). The Lord roars from Zion, and the pastures of the shepherds wither (Amos 1:2). Painting a picture of abundant provisions, the psalmist praises God for the overflowing pastures of the wilderness (Ps. 65:12[13]; cf. the description of wilderness pastures in Jer. 9:10[9]). The most famous use of the term comes in Psalm 23, where in vivid imagery the Lord is depicted as the great Shepherd who causes His sheep to lie down in green pastures (Ps. 23:2). Once it is used in conjunction with the term used for God, forming the phrase pastures of God. In the context, the phrase refers to the land of Israel and recalls the idea of the people of Israel as God's flock (Ps. 83:12[13]). This term stems from the verb *nāʼāh* (4998).

5000. נָאוֶה *nāʼweh:* An adjective depicting something as beautiful, fitting. It depicts what is appropriate, in place: praise to the righteous person (Ps. 33:1); wise speech is not fitting for a fool (Prov. 17:7; cf. 19:10; 26:1[23]). It points out what is pleasant, lovely, beautiful: praises to God are pleasant (Ps. 147:1); a young woman is lovely (Song 1:5; 2:14; 4:3; 6:4). It can have a slightly negative sense from the context, meaning attractive, decorous (Jer. 6:2).

5001. נָאַם *nāʼam:* A verb meaning to murmur, to mutter, to whisper, to utter. The term is used once to describe the occupation which the false prophets of Jeremiah's day habitually practiced. They uttered false prophecies and claimed they were from the Lord, thus leading many people astray (Jer. 23:31).

5002. נְאֻם *n^{e}ʼum:* A masculine noun introducing an oracle, an utterance; a prophetic citing of God's speech. It is used as an introduction to various utterances and means thus says the Lord, utterance of the Lord, etc. (Isa. 14:22; 56:8; Ezek. 16:58; Hos. 2:13[15]; Joel 2:12; Amos 2:11; Obad. 1:4). It is used outside of the prophetic books in the form usually, *n^{e}ʼum-yhwh,* utterance of the Lord (Gen. 22:16; Num. 14:28; 24:3, 4, 15, 16; 1 Sam. 2:30, etc.). It is used of the utterances of people, but they were probably in a prophetic state, such as David (2 Sam. 23:1). It is used of the voice of conscience in Psalm 36:1(2) when sin is committed. The word occurs often at the end, less often in the middle, and once at the beginning of these utterances (Isa. 54:17; 56:8; Amos 3:10).

5003. נָאַף *nāʼap̱:* A verb meaning to commit adultery. It is used of the physical act (Ex. 20:14; Lev. 20:10; Prov. 6:32; Jer. 5:7; 7:9; 29:23; Hos. 4:2; Mal. 3:5); but often of spiritual adultery as well; idolatry (Isa. 57:3; Jer. 3:9; Ezek. 23:37).

5004. נִאֻף *niʼup̱:* A masculine noun referring to adultery. It is used in its plural form only. It is descriptive of spiritual, religious adulteries (Jer. 13:27; Ezek. 23:43).

5005. נַאֲפוּף *na^{a}pûp̱:* A masculine noun indicating adultery. It describes the act of adultery, the unfaithfulness of one's spouse (Hos. 2:2[4]).

5006. נָאַץ *nāʼaṣ:* A verb meaning to revile, to scorn, to reject. It is related to *nāṣaṣ* (5340), meaning to scorn or to blaspheme. This word often refers to rejecting the counsel of a wise person. This scornful attitude results in an unhappy life: people live in affliction because they reject God's counsel (Ps. 107:11). Another example of a passage that uses this word is Proverbs 1:30, where wisdom laments that people scorn her reproof. In another instance of this word, the Israelites were chastised because they had rejected God's Law (Isa. 5:24).

5007. נְאָצָה *ne'āṣāh:* I. A feminine noun indicating shame, disgrace. It describes a situation that brings embarrassment or rejection because of failure (2 Kg. 19:3; Isa. 37:3).

II. A feminine noun referring to blasphemy, aspersion. It indicates a disrespecting rejection and harmful attack by words and deeds against someone, especially God or His laws (Neh. 9:18, 26); or His holy land (Ezek. 35:12).

5008. נָאַק *nā'aq:* A verb meaning to groan. It means to moan, to make sounds of despair because of oppression; to seek help (Job 24:12; Ezek. 30:24).

5009. נְאָקָה *nᵉ'āqāh:* A feminine noun meaning groaning, a groan. To utter sounds of despair, especially because of oppression (Ex. 2:24; 6:5; Judg. 2:18; Ezek. 30:24).

5010. נָאַר *nā'ar:* A verb indicating to renounce, to spurn, to abandon. It means to reject something or someone in word and in deed: of God rejecting, spurning His covenant (Ps. 89:39[40]); and leaving, abandoning His Temple and Jerusalem (Lam. 2:7).

5011. נֹב *nōḇ:* A proper noun designating Nob (1 Sam. 21:1[2]; 22:9, 11, 19; Neh. 11:32; Isa. 10:32).

5012. נָבָא *nāḇā':* A verb meaning to prophesy, to speak by inspiration, to predict. This most commonly refers to the way in which the word of the Lord came to the people (Jer. 19:14; Ezek. 11:13). There were various means in which people came to prophesy. Eldad and Medad became ecstatic when they prophesied (Num. 11:25–27); whereas the sons of Asaph used songs and instruments when they prophesied (1 Chr. 25:1). False prophets were also known to prophesy (Zech. 13:3).

5013. נְבָא *nᵉḇā':* An Aramaic verb meaning to prophesy. This word corresponds to the Hebrew word *nāḇā'* (5012). It is possible that this word takes on the meaning of being carried away through prophecy. Only found once in the Old Testament, this word is used to describe the means by which Haggai and Zechariah prophesied to the people of Israel (Ezra 5:1).

5014. נָבַב *nāḇaḇ,* נָבוּב *nāḇûḇ:* I. A verb meaning to hollow out. The word is a verbal form of *nāḇaḇ.* It means to create an empty space inside something, a cavity. The bronze altar was to be hollowed out inside (Ex. 27:8); the pillars of the Temple were hollow (Jer. 52:21). A person described as hollow is a fool, senseless (Job 11:12).

II. A masculine noun meaning hollow. The word is considered as a set noun form meaning empty space, a place filled with air. The meanings indicate a thing or person with the feature of hollowness, empty-headed (Ex. 27:8; 38:7; Job 11:12; Jer. 52:21).

5015. נְבוֹ $n^e\underline{b}\hat{o}$, נְבוּ שַׂר־סְכִים $n^e\underline{b}\hat{u}$ *śar-s^{e}kiym*: A. A proper noun Nebo. It refers to a specific mountain or range in Moab from which a person could view the promised land of Canaan (Num. 33:47; Deut. 32:49; 34:1).

B. A proper noun Nebo. It refers to a specific town in Moab (Num. 32:3, 38; 1 Chr. 5:8; Isa. 15:2; Jer. 48:1, 22).

C. A proper noun Nebo. A city located northwest of Jerusalem. Some persons from here returned from exile to Jerusalem (Ezra 2:29; Neh. 7:33).

D. A masculine proper noun of a Jewish ancestor. Some of Nebo's sons intermarried with the people of the land after returning from exile (Ezra 10:43).

E. A masculine proper noun of a false Babylonian god, Nebo. It refers to a god of Babylon identified as an idolatrous god who would be destroyed by the Lord (Isa. 46:1).

F. A masculine proper noun Nebo-Sarsekiym. It was the name of a Babylonian official who occupied Jerusalem when it fell (Jer. 39:3). It is combined and rendered differently by translators: Samgar-nebo, NKJV, KJV; Nebo-Sarsekim, NIV; Samgar-nebu, NASB).

5016. נְבוּאָה $n^e\underline{b}\hat{u}'\bar{a}h$: A feminine noun meaning prophecy, a prophetic word. Shemaiah gave a false prophecy to Nehemiah in order to cause him to sin and to saddle him with a bad name (Neh. 6:12). The prophecy of Azariah, son of Oded, encouraged King Asa of Judah to implement religious reform in the country, bringing the people back to the Lord their God (2 Chr. 15:8). Once the word refers to a written prophecy by a prophet named Ahijah (2 Chr. 9:29). This word stems from the verb *nāḇā'* (5012).

5017. נְבוּאָה $n^e\underline{b}\hat{u}'\bar{a}h$: An Aramaic feminine noun meaning prophesying. It refers to the role and functions of a prophet and appears only once in the Old Testament, where it is recorded that the elders prospered through the prophesying of Haggai the prophet and Zechariah the son of Iddo (Ezra 6:14). It is probably closely related to the Hebrew word *n^{e}ḇû'āh* (5016).

5018. נְבוּזַרְאֲדָן $n^e\underline{b}\hat{u}zar'^a\underline{d}\bar{a}n$: A masculine proper noun Nebuzaradan. It is the name of the captain of the royal guard of Nebuchadnezzar who took many of the Israelites into exile (2 Kgs. 25:8, 11, 20; Jer. 39:9–11).

5019. נְבוּכַדְנֶאצַּר $n^e\underline{b}\hat{u}\underline{k}a\underline{d}ne'ṣṣar$, נְבוּכַדְרֶאצַּר $n^e\underline{b}\hat{u}\underline{k}a\underline{d}re'ṣṣar$: A proper noun designating Nebuchadnezzar, the great Chaldean king of the neo-

Babylonian Empire. His name means "Nabu has protected the accession right," Nabu being a Babylonian god. He ruled 605–562 B.C. and was the virtual embodiment of this empire. He defeated Assyria in 605 B.C. and became the master of the Middle East. He conquered Palestine and destroyed Jerusalem and Judah in 586 B.C. He destroyed the Temple and took its wealth to the stone house of his god Marduk in Babylon (2 Kgs. 24; 25; Dan. 1—3).

The prophet Jeremiah called him the servant of the Lord to do his bidding (Jer. 25:9; 27:6). It was the Lord's judgment that submitted Judah to this pagan king (Jer. 28:14). He listened to and promoted Daniel and his God while Daniel served as a counselor, wise man, and administrator for the king. The Lord gave him dreams, interpreted by Daniel, a Jew, that were breathtaking in their sweeping portrayals of the march of history from his time down to the rise of the kingdom of God (Dan. 2). He suffered from megalomania in his last years, but God humbled him with a humiliating disease and emotional derangement (Dan. 4:1; 23:31; 4) but later restored him to sanity.

5020. נְבוּכַדְנֶצַּר ***n******e******bûkadneṣṣar:*** A proper noun designating Nebuchadnezzar, the Aramaic form of the Hebrew name. See 5019. The meaning of the name is the same.

5021. נְבוּשַׁזְבָּן ***n^ebûšazbān:*** A proper noun designating Nebushazban (Jer. 39:13).

5022. נָבוֹת ***nāḇôṯ:*** A proper noun designating Naboth, an Israelite from Jezreel. He owned a vineyard in Jezreel near Ahab's palace. He refused to sell his property to the king because it was his sacred inheritance. Jezebel arranged to have him accused of treason and killed (1 Kgs. 21:7–10). Ahab then confiscated Naboth's vineyard. This was avenged by the Lord through Jehu (2 Kgs. 9:21–26).

5023. נְבִזְבָה ***n^eḇizbāh:*** An Aramaic feminine noun referring to a reward. Something offered to the Babylonian wise men and Daniel as a symbol of approval and appreciation for something said or done (Dan. 2:6; 5:17).

5024. נָבַח ***nāḇaḥ:*** A verb meaning to bark. It refers to a sharp, abrupt sound made by a dog; the naturally expected ability of a dog to make these sounds (Isa. 56:10).

5025. נֹבַח ***nōḇaḥ:*** A proper noun designating Nobah:

A. A Manassite (Num. 32:42).

B. A location in Gilead (Num. 32:42; Judg. 8:11).

5026. נִבְחַז ***niḇḥaz:*** A masculine proper noun Nibhaz; a false god. It refers to one of the many gods of idolatry made by pagan nations, in this case made by the Avvites (2 Kgs. 17:31).

5027. נָבַט ***na<u>b</u>aṭ:*** A verb meaning to look, to watch, to regard. It has the sense of looking somewhat intensely in a focused way at something; to gaze: to gaze at the heavens (Gen. 15:5); at Sodom and Gomorrah (Gen. 19:17, 26); at the sea (1 Kgs. 18:43). It is used in a figurative sense of looking at, considering the commands of the Lord to follow them (Ps. 74:20; 119:6, 15, 18); to look on something for help, dependence (Isa. 22:8, 11). It means to evaluate or consider by looking at something (1 Sam. 16:7; 17:42; Ps. 84:9[10]; Amos 5:22). It is used of the keen observations of an eagle from a great distance (Job 39:29); and of the Lord's gazing on the earth from His habitation (Ps. 102:19[20]).

5028. נְבָט ***n^e<u>b</u>āṭ:*** A proper noun designating Nebat, father of Jeroboam I (1 Kgs. 11:26; 12:2, 15; 15:1; 16:3, 26, 31; 2 Kgs. 3:3; 9:9; 10:29; 14:24; 23:15; 2 Chr. 9:29; 10:2, 15; 13:6).

5029. נְבִיא ***n^e<u>b</u>iy':*** An Aramaic masculine noun meaning prophet. It refers to an individual that fulfilled the role and functions of a prophet (Ezra 5:1, 2; 6:14). The word is probably closely related to the biblical Hebrew word (if not the same word), *nā<u>b</u>iy'* (5030); as such, it would share similar, if not the same, variations in meaning.

5030. נָבִיא ***nā<u>b</u>iy':*** A masculine noun meaning a prophet, a spokesman. The meaning is consistently one of prophet and inspired spokesman. Moses was the greatest prophet of the Old Testament (Deut. 34:10) and the example for all later prophets. He displayed every aspect of a true prophet, both in his call, his work, his faithfulness, and, at times, his doubts. Only Abraham is called a prophet before Moses (Gen. 20:7).

Moses received a call from God to speak His words and perform a specific task (see Ex. 3:4, 10; 4:17, 29; 5:1) with the promise that the Lord would be with him and help him accomplish it (see Ex. 3:12, 20; 4:12, 14–16). He responded, though reluctantly (see Ex. 3:11, 13; 4:1), and God did what He had said He would do (see Ex. 6:1; 14:30, 31; 40:34, 38). Moses' prophetic voice spoke to Israel of the past (see Deut. 1—3), the present (see Deut. 4:1; 26:18), and the future (see Deut. 31:20–22), as would every major prophet after him. This pattern, or much of it, is found in the case of every true prophet (see Isa. 6; Jer. 1; Ezek. 1—3; Hos. 1:2; Amos 7:14, 15; Jon. 1:1). All the true prophets stood in the counsel of God to receive their messages (see 1 Kgs. 22:19; Jer. 23:22; Amos 3:7).

This word describes one who was raised up by God and, as such, could only proclaim that which the Lord gave him to say. A prophet could not contradict the Law of the Lord or speak from his own mind or heart. To do so was to be a false prophet (Jer. 14:14; 23:16, 26, 30). What a prophet declared had to come true, or he was false (Deut. 18:22; Jer. 23:9).

The noun is found parallel to two other words meaning a seer, a prophet (*ḥōzeh*[2374], *rō'eh*[1 Sam. 9:9; 2 Sam. 24:11]), which tends to stress the visionary or perceptive aspects of a prophet's experiences. There were "sons of the prophets," a phrase indicating bands or companies of prophets, "son" in this case meaning a member (1 Kgs. 20:35; 2 Kgs. 2:3, 5; 4:1). Kings sometimes had a group of prophets around them (1 Kgs. 22:22; 2 Chr. 18:21, 22). Prophets were designated from Israel (Ezek. 13:2, 4); Samaria (Jer. 23:13); and Jerusalem (Zeph. 3:4). In an unusual development, David set aside some of the sons of Asaph, Heman, and Jeduthun to serve as prophets. Their prophesying was accompanied with musical instruments and possibly was brought on and aided by these instruments. This phenomenon is described mainly in the book of 2 Chronicles (see 2 Chr. 20:14; 29:30). Evidently, Zechariah, the priest, also prophesied in that era. But Moses himself desired that all God's people have the Spirit of God on them, as did the prophets (Num. 11:29).

5031. נְבִיאָה ***n**e**b**iy'āh:* A feminine noun meaning prophetess. It is the feminine form of the Hebrew *nā*b*î'* (5030), meaning a spokesman, a speaker, or a prophet. The ancient concept of a prophetess was a woman who had the gift of song, like Miriam (Ex. 15:20) or Deborah (Judg. 4:4; cf. 5:1). The later concept of a prophetess, being more in line with the concept of a prophet, was one who was consulted in order to receive a word from the Lord, like Huldah (2 Kgs. 22:14; 2 Chr. 34:22). It also described a false prophetess, Noadiah (Neh. 6:14). A unique usage may be its reference to the wife of Isaiah as a prophetess (Isa. 8:3). Is this because of her own position and work or because of her relationship with Isaiah, a prophet? It has been interpreted both ways.

5032. נְבָיוֹת ***n**e**bāyôt,*** נְבָיֹת ***n**e**bāyōt:*** A proper noun designating Nebaioth:

A. A son of Ishmael (Gen. 25:13; 28:9; 36:3; 1 Chr. 1:29).

B. The descendants of Nebaioth (Isa. 60:7).

5033. נֵבֶךְ ***nēbek:*** A masculine noun referring to a spring of water. It refers to water that flows of its own pressure from the ground or the floor of a sea or a lake (Job 38:16).

5034. נָבֵל ***nābēl:*** I. A verb meaning to wither, to languish, to fade. It refers to something wearing out, drying up, dying, falling off: grass (Ps. 37:2); leaves (Isa. 1:30; Jer. 8:13; Ezek. 47:12); flowers (Isa. 28:1). It is used figuratively of humans (Ex. 18:18; 2 Sam. 22:46; Ps. 18:45[46]); the land and earth (Isa. 24:4).

II. A verb meaning to be foolish, to act disdainfully. It is used of treating someone with disapproval or as unworthy (Deut. 32:15; Jer. 14:21; Mic. 7:6; Nah. 3:6); or of acting in contempt toward something or in a foolish way (Prov. 30:32).

5035. נֵבֶל nēḇel, נֶבֶל neḇel: I. A masculine noun indicating a storage jar, a skin bottle. A jug or other container for wine (1 Sam. 1:24; 10:3; 25:18; 2 Sam. 16:1); water (Job 38:37); figuratively for all kinds of purposes (Isa. 22:24; Jer. 48:12). It is used figuratively of persons (Lam. 4:2). Some vessels were made of clay (Isa. 30:14).

II. A masculine noun referring to a harp, a lyre, a stringed instrument. It refers to a stringed instrument (Amos 5:23; 6:5); a harp of ten strings (1 Sam. 10:5; 1 Kgs. 10:12; Ps. 33:2; 57:8[9]; 92:3[4]). It was used by prophets and at religious feasts, ceremonies, and in various common celebrations.

5036. נָבָל nāḇāl: An arrogant bore, dense morally, intellectually, and spiritually. As an adjective or noun, it means foolish, a fool. It is used to describe a whole nation (Deut. 32:6); or persons individually (2 Sam. 3:33). Such persons cannot speak well or civilly to anyone (Prov. 17:7) and shame their parents (Prov. 17:21). They reject God (Ps. 14:1). The person who gets unjust wealth dies a fool in God's eyes (Jer. 17:11). He dies a shameful and disrespectful death (2 Sam. 3:33). The word is used as an adjective to describe false prophets (Ezek. 13:3).

5037. נָבָל nāḇāl: A proper noun designating Nabal, the name of a rogue and boor who refused to give needed supplies to David and arrogantly insulted David and his men as they were fleeing Saul. His name means a particularly boorish type of "fool" (1 Sam. 25:25). His wife revealed his own folly to him, and he died from the shock (1 Sam. 25:36–39).

5038. נְבֵלָה n^{e}ḇēlāh: A feminine noun meaning a carcass, a corpse. It describes a body devoid of life, whether human (Josh. 8:29; Isa. 5:25) or animal (Deut. 14:8). The Law clearly stated that contact with the carcass of a dead animal (Lev. 5:2) or with the body of a dead person (cf. Num. 19:11) would render an individual unclean. Also, it was possible for the land to be defiled by the presence of an unburied corpse (Deut. 21:23). Hence, Jeremiah used the word *n^{e}ḇēlāh* for idols. Pagan idols were devoid of life just like corpses and were a source of defilement for the people, priests, and land.

5039. נְבָלָה n^{e}ḇālāh: A feminine noun meaning folly, a disgraceful act. It refers to deeds that are especially serious, grave, sinful, arrogant: rape, harlotry (Gen. 34:7; Deut. 22:21); breaking of Israel's covenantal laws (Josh. 7:15); sodomy (Judg. 19:23, 24); offering incorrect or vain advice in an arrogant way (Job 42:8); foolish talk (Isa. 9:17[16]); spiritual adultery (Jer. 29:23).

5040. נַבְלוּת nablût: A feminine noun signifying lewdness. It refers to gross sexual behavior to excite sexual desire. It is used of Israel's lewd actions to attract her forbidden lovers (Hos. 2:10[12]).

5041. נְבַלָּט nᵉballaṭ: A proper noun designating Neballat (Neh. 11:34).

5042. נָבַע nāba‘: A verb meaning to spew out, to pour out, to utter. It refers to something pouring forth, bubbling out: the language and speech of the heavens (Ps. 19:2[3]); evil persons, foolish talk (Ps. 59:7[8]; 94:4); wise speech (Ps. 78:2). It is used of the spirit of wisdom being poured out profusely on persons (Prov. 1:23; 18:4). When fools speak, they are spouting out foolishness, folly that creates dissension (Prov. 15:2, 28). It may have the sense of to cause to exude (Eccl. 10:1).

5043. נֶבְרְשָׁה nebrᵉšāh: An Aramaic feminine noun meaning lampstand. A royal lampstand used in the palace at Babylon (Dan. 5:5). It used oil and possibly wicks to create its light.

5044. נִבְשָׁן nibšān: A proper noun designating Nibshan (Josh. 15:62).

5045. נֶגֶב negeb: I. A masculine noun meaning the South, south. It refers to the area around Beersheva and south of it (Gen. 12:9; 13:1; 20:1), but see II below. It refers in general to the dry desert area in the south (Gen. 13:14; 24:62). It takes the definite article to mean the South, the southland. With *āh* added to it, the directive gives the sense of southward, to the south (Gen. 13:14). It is nuanced by the use of prepositions: *lᵉ*, from (Josh. 17:9, 10); *min-*, from or on the *negev*, south (1 Sam. 14:5). It is used to give directions, southward (Dan. 8:4, 9). Compound directions are expressed using several words: *qēdᵉmāh mimmûl negeb*, eastward toward the south, southeast (1 Kgs. 7:39); *pᵉ'at-negeb* refers to a southern area or boundary of land in a geographical context (Num. 34:3). It is used of an Egyptian king of the South often in Daniel (11:5, 6, 9, 11, etc.).

II. A proper noun, Negev, the southern district of Judah. It is used more specifically in contexts to indicate the area south of Judah (Jer. 13:19; 17:26). These areas are not always defined exactly. It may indicate land south of Babylon or southern Palestine (Isa. 21:1).

5046. נָגַד nāgad: A verb meaning to tell, to report, to make known, to explain, to be reported. The root idea of the word and the causative form in which it is used is to declare something. The manner and context in which this is done creates the various shades of meaning of the verb. Its simplest use is to announce, to report, to share. Samuel, when a child, was afraid to report the vision he had to Eli (1 Sam. 3:15, 18; 1 Kgs. 1:23). In some cases, it means to solve or explain, to make known. God asked

Adam who had made him know he was naked (Gen. 3:11; 12:18); it indicated the resolution of a riddle (Judg. 14:12, 15); or dream (Job 11:6; Dan. 2:2). Close to this is its meaning to share with or to inform someone of something, to speak out. People were responsible to speak out when they knew something relevant to a case (Lev. 5:1; Josh. 2:14; Prov. 29:24). It is used to proclaim or announce something, often proclaiming the character and attributes of the Lord. The psalmist proclaimed the great deeds of the Lord (Ps. 9:11[12]); the posterity of the righteous psalmist would declare God's righteousness (Ps. 22:31[32]); the Lord's love was regularly proclaimed (Ps. 92:2[3]). The participle of the verb may indicate a messenger (Jer. 51:31).

The passive use of the verb means to be told, to be announced. If an Israelite turned and followed false gods, this act of rebellion was to be brought to the attention of the leaders (Deut. 17:4); anything that needed to be reported could be covered by this verb (Judg. 9:25; 2 Sam. 10:17). The Queen of Sheba used this verb when she declared that not even half the splendor of Solomon's wisdom and wealth had been told her (1 Kgs. 10:7; Isa. 21:2).

5047. נְגַד ***n**^e**gaḏ:*** An Aramaic verb meaning to flow, to issue forth. It indicates the natural movement of water in a river, a stream, etc. It is used in a heavenly vision of fire flowing out from before the Ancient of Days (Dan. 7:10).

5048. נֶגֶד ***neḡeḏ:*** A preposition indicating before, in front of, opposite; corresponding to. It has a special sense to indicate Eve's likeness to Adam (Gen. 2:18, 20), with the preposition *k^e* prefixed. Its usual meanings are easily discernible from context: before (Gen. 31:32); over against, opposite (Ex. 19:2); in front of (Josh. 6:5); against (Job 10:17); in front of spatially (2 Kgs. 1:13). The phrase *'ad-neḡeḏ* means up to, as far as a certain spot (Neh. 3:16); in the presence of someone (Ps. 116:14, 18). It is used with a preposition attached often: *l^e* helps give the sense of in front of (Gen. 33:12; Num. 22:32); in the presence of (Hab. 1:3). It is used figuratively with *l^e* to point out what ought to be observed (Ps. 18:22[23]). Used with *min* (4480), it has the sense of opposite from something (Gen. 21:16; 2 Kgs. 2:7); or implies spatial distance (Num. 2:2; Deut. 32:52; 2 Kgs. 2:15).

5049. נֶגֶד ***neḡeḏ:*** An Aramaic preposition meaning toward. It indicates a directions e.g., westward, toward Jerusalem, from Babylon (Dan. 6:10[11]).

5050. נָגַהּ ***nāḡah:*** A verb meaning to shine, to illuminate. It always is used figuratively except once. It indicates the giving of light, illumination. It is used figuratively of the Lord who shines into darkness in a moral sense

(2 Sam. 22:29; Ps. 18:28[29]); and of the life of the wicked which goes out (Job 18:5). It indicates God's approval (Job 22:28). It is used of God's breaking in to enlighten His people about Himself and His gospel (Isa. 9:2[1]). It is used of the light put forth by the heavenly luminaries (Isa. 13:10).

5051. נֹגַהּ ***nōgah:*** A feminine noun referring to radiance, brightness. It indicates the blazing and bright illumination of some light source: God's brightness (2 Sam. 22:13; Ps. 18:12[13]; Isa. 60:3; Hab. 3:4, 11); the light at dawn from the sun and from the moon at night (2 Sam. 23:4; Prov. 4:18; in a simile, Isa. 60:19); light from a great blazing fire (Isa. 4:5); moral and ethical understanding in the Lord's ways (Isa. 50:10); the light and brightness of righteousness (Isa. 62:1); light from God's glory (Ezek. 1:4, 13, 27, 28; 10:4).

5052. נֹגַהּ ***nōgah:*** A proper noun designating Nogah (1 Chr. 3:7; 14:6).

5053. נֹגַהּ ***nōgah:*** An Aramaic feminine noun referring to morning, daylight. It is used of sunrise, as soon as the dawn begins (Dan. 6:19[20]).

5054. נְגֹהָה ***n^egōhāh:*** A feminine noun indicating brightness. It is used of times of blessing, prosperity, and good news; a message or event of hope amid a setting of gloom and despair (Isa. 59:9).

5055. נָגַח ***nāgaḥ:*** A verb meaning to gore, to push. It is used of the goring of a horned animal (Ex. 21:28, 31, 32); the forceful expansion of a people or nation (Deut. 33:17; 1 Kgs. 22:11; 2 Chr. 18:10; Dan. 8:4; 11:40); or the defeat of enemies (Ps. 44:5[6]). It is used of oppressing the poor, pushing them into subjection (Ezek. 34:21).

5056. נַגָּח ***naggāḥ:*** An adjective meaning in the habit of goring. It refers to an animal accustomed to behave violently by using its horns (Ex. 21:29, 36).

5057. נָגִיד ***nāgiyd̲:*** A masculine noun meaning a leader, a ruler, a prince. This term has a broad range of applications. At the top, it could allude to the king of Israel (1 Sam. 9:16; 13:14; 1 Kgs. 1:35); a ruler from a foreign land like Tyre (Ezek. 28:2); or Assyria (2 Chr. 32:21). It could also be used regarding cultic leaders and officials from the high priest down (1 Chr. 9:11, 20; 2 Chr. 31:12, 13; 35:8; Jer. 20:1). It could also be a label for various other lesser positions of leadership (1 Chr. 27:16; 2 Chr. 11:11, 22; 19:11; Job 29:10). The word is also used in an abstract sense to convey that which is princely, noble, and honorable (Prov. 8:6).

5058. נְגִינָה ***n^egiynāh,*** נְגִינַת ***n^egiynat̲:*** I. A feminine noun meaning song, music; a taunting song. It is used of a taunting song in some contexts, a song of mocking or ridicule (Job 30:9; Ps. 69:12[11]; Lam. 3:14);

of stringed instruments or music (Lam. 5:14).

II. A feminine noun denoting a stringed instrument. It describes certain psalms in their titles and is found at the end of Habakkuk 3:19 as a technical musical term, "stringed instruments."

III. A feminine proper noun indicating Neginah (singular), Neginoth (plural); proper names for stringed instruments. It is used only in the psalm titles listed below, but see I and II above also.

5059. נָגַן ***nāgan:*** A verb meaning to play a stringed instrument. It refers to the playing of stringed instruments of various kinds (1 Sam. 16:16–18, 23; 18:10; Ps. 33:3, etc.), often harps. It refers to the person playing the harp, the minstrel or musician (2 Kgs. 3:15; Ps. 68:25[26]). The prophet Ezekiel was mockingly compared to a minstrel (Ezek. 33:32).

5060. נָגַע ***nāga':*** A verb meaning to touch, to reach, to strike. The basic import of this verb is physical contact from one person to another. Since interpersonal contact can come in one (or more) of many varieties, this verb carries a range of semantic possibilities. Its use could represent mere physical contact (Gen. 3:3; 1 Kgs. 6:27; Esth. 5:2). On a deeper level, it could designate striking (Job 1:19; Isa. 53:4; Ezek. 17:10). Along these lines is the figurative use to identify God's judgment (1 Sam. 6:9; Job 1:11; 19:21). On an even deeper level, it indicates doing actual harm (Gen. 26:11; Josh. 9:19; 2 Sam. 14:10). In a metaphorical sense, this verb can also portray the concept to reach or extend (Isa. 16:8; Jer. 51:9; Jon. 3:6). In the passive form, it denotes the idea to allow oneself to be beaten in a military context (Josh. 8:15). In the intensive form, this verb means to afflict or to be afflicted (Gen. 12:17; 2 Kgs. 15:5; Ps. 73:5).

5061. נֶגַע ***nega':*** A masculine noun meaning a blemish, a mark, a stroke, a plague. This word comes from the verb *nāga'* (5060), meaning to touch or to strike, and is best understood as a blemish that has been created by touching or striking. In the majority of instances, it described a blemish inflicted by leprosy or a skin disease that the priest was to discern (used over sixty times in Lev. 13—14). It also referred to a physical injury inflicted by another person (Deut. 17:8; 21:5; Isa. 53:8); or by God Himself (Ps. 89:32[33]). When describing land or property, it is best translated plague (Gen. 12:17; Ex. 11:1; 1 Kgs. 8:37). At times, this word described a nonphysical blemish (1 Kgs. 8:38; 2 Chr. 6:29; Prov. 6:33).

5062. נָגַף ***nāgap:*** A verb meaning to strike, to smite. This word is most often used within the context of warring nations when one nation struck another (Lev. 26:17; Num. 14:42; Deut. 28:7, 25). At times, this was followed by the death of many (Judg. 20:35; 1 Sam. 4:10; 2 Sam. 18:7); at others, it merely signified defeat in war, with no mention of death (1 Kgs. 8:33; 2 Kgs. 14:12). God is often the One who smote, which led to incurable illness (2 Chr. 21:18; Zech. 14:12, 18); or even death (1 Sam. 25:38; 2 Sam. 12:15). This word is also used to describe the stumbling of the foot (Prov. 3:23; Jer. 13:16); the causing of injury to another person (Ex. 21:22); or to an animal (Ex. 21:35).

5063. נֶגֶף *negep̱:* A masculine noun meaning a plague, stumbling. This word comes from the verb *nāgap̱* (5062), meaning to strike or to smite, and described the effect of being struck or smitten. It usually described a plague that God sent on a disobedient people (Ex. 12:13; 30:12; Num. 8:19; Josh. 22:17). In one instance, it described the stone of stumbling (Isa. 8:14).

5064. נָגַר *nāgar:* A verb indicating to pour, to pour out, to spill. It has the sense of something gushing out, pouring forth. It is used of water poured out on the ground (2 Sam. 14:14); of wine poured out as a symbol of judgment (Ps. 75:8[9]); of a hand put forth (Ps. 77:2[3]); of tears flowing from weeping eyes (Lam. 3:49). It is used of the loss of possessions by the wicked (Job 20:28); and the giving over of persons to the sword (Ps. 63:10[11]; Jer. 18:21; Ezek. 35:5). It is used of the stones of cities cast down during God's judgments (Mic. 1:6).

5065. נָגַשׂ *nāgaś:* A verb meaning to oppress, to require payment. It refers to forcing someone or something to do something. It is used of forcing persons to labor (Isa. 58:3); of forcing or exacting payment of money (2 Kgs. 23:35). It refers in its participial forms to taskmasters or workers of animals (Ex. 3:7; 5:6, 10, 13, 14; Job 3:18). It is used figuratively of righteousness being a good foreman or overseer (Isa. 60:17) in a restored Jerusalem. In its passive uses, it refers to those who are oppressed by others (1 Sam. 13:6). The Suffering Servant of Isaiah is a person oppressed, ill-treated by his enemies (Isa. 53:7; cf. Isa. 3:5).

5066. נָגַשׁ *nāgaš:* A verb meaning to come near, to approach, to draw near, to bring near, to be brought near. In the simple form of the verb, it indicates coming near, as when Jacob went near to Isaac his father who reached out and touched him (Gen. 27:22); it simply describes approaching a person for whatever reason (Gen. 43:19; Ex. 19:15). It is used of priests approaching the Lord (Ezek. 44:13); or the altar to carry out their priestly duties (Ex. 28:43; 30:20); and of armies drawing near for engagement in battle (Judg. 20:23; 2 Sam. 10:13). The word asserts close proximity in all these cases and can even describe the closeness of the scales of a crocodile (Job. 41:16[8]).

In the reflexive form, it describes coming near. Deuteronomy 25:9 prescribed the action of a widow towards her brother-in-law who would not perform his Levitical duty toward her: She was to approach him, take off one of his sandals, and spit in his face (cf. Isa. 45:20).

In the causative form, the verb means to bring near: a slave who decided to remain with his master perpetually was brought to the judges and to the doorpost so his ear could be bored with an awl (Ex. 21:6; 1 Sam. 15:32); sacrifices were brought near as well (1 Sam. 13:9; 14:34). In a metaphorical sense, the word is used to call for the presentation of legal argumentation (Isa. 41:21). The passive use of this form describes what is offered or presented, once to indicate that Abner's feet were not brought near, that is, they were not placed in chains (2 Sam. 3:34); and once to describe incense and pure offerings brought in the Lord's name (Mal. 1:11).

5067. נֵד *nē<u>d</u>:* A masculine noun meaning heap. It refers to something piled up on itself. It refers to waters: the Red Sea (Ex. 15:8; Ps. 78:13); the Jordan River (Josh. 3:13, 16); the sea (Ps. 33:7). It refers to the remains of a failed harvest lying on the ground (Isa. 17:11).

5068. נָדַב *nā<u>d</u>a<u>b</u>:* A verb meaning to incite willingly. This word described the free, voluntary desire of the heart to give of oneself or of one's resources to the service of the Lord. It was used to describe the willing contributions that the people of Israel made to build the Tabernacle (Ex. 25:2; 35:21, 29); Solomon's Temple (1 Chr. 29:5, 6, 9, 14, 17); and Zerubbabel's Temple (Ezra 1:6; 2:68; 3:5). In a few other instances, it spoke of the willing sacrifice of service that Amaziah made (2 Chr. 17:16); the returning exiles made (Neh. 11:2); and Deborah commended (Judg. 5:2, 9). See the related noun *n^e<u>d</u>ā<u>b</u>āh* (5071), meaning freewill offering.

5069. נְדַב *n^e<u>d</u>a<u>b</u>:* An Aramaic verb meaning to offer willingly, to make a freewill offering. This word is used exclusively in the book of Ezra and refers to those who could leave Babylon freely (Ezra 7:13). It also indicates the gifts given freely by a king (Ezra 7:15); and the Israelites (Ezra 7:16). See the related Hebrew verbs *nā<u>d</u>a<u>b</u>* (5068) and *n^e<u>d</u>ā<u>b</u>āh* (5071).

5070. נָדָב *nā<u>d</u>ā<u>b</u>:* A proper noun designating Nadab:

A. The firstborn son of Aaron. He was slain by the Lord because of offering up improperly prepared incense offerings before the Lord (Lev. 10:1). He and Abihu served to warn the nation about the danger of not properly worshiping the Lord. He died at Sinai and had no sons (Num. 3:1–4).

B. A son of Jeroboam. He succeeded his father as king and reigned 909–908 B.C., about two years. He sinned greatly by continuing the reprehensible religious practices of his father, son of Nebat. Baasha assassinated Nadab and ruled in his place (1 Kgs. 15:25–28).

C. A son of Shammai who was the son of Onam. They were Judahites through Caleb and Hezron (1 Chr. 2:28).

D. A Gibeonite who was son of Jeiel by his wife Maacah (1 Chr. 8:29–30).

5071. נְדָבָה ***n^e^dāḇāh:*** A feminine noun meaning willingness, a freewill offering, a voluntary gift. As an adverb, it means willingly, freely, spontaneously, voluntarily. This term can denote that state of being which allows a person to offer a gift or a favor to someone else without any thought of return or payback. The favor is not given out of any obligation owed by the giver; rather, it is the result of an overflow from an abundance within the heart. The Lord declares that He loves Israel freely because His anger has turned away from them (Hos. 14:4[5]). The Hebrews were commanded to diligently perform the vows they freely uttered to the Lord (Deut. 23:23[24]). Most often, however, the term is utilized to signify an offering, a gift, or a sacrifice given voluntarily, as opposed to one offered in dutiful fulfillment of an obligation or vow (Lev. 22:23). Many from the congregation of Israel whose hearts were willing gave of their possessions as freewill offerings for the building of the Tent of Meeting and its services (Ex. 35:29; 36:3; cf. Lev. 7:16; Ezra 1:4; 3:5; 8:28; Ezek. 46:12; Amos 4:5). Once the word possibly functions to convey an abundance, that is, of rain (Ps. 68:9[10]). This term is derived from the verb *nāḏaḇ* (5068).

5072. נְדַבְיָה ***n^e^ḏaḇyāh:*** A proper noun designating Nebadiah (1 Chr. 3:18).

5073. נִדְבָּךְ ***niḏbāḵ:*** An Aramaic masculine noun indicating a row, a layer. It refers to a single thickness of something, a stratum (Ezra 6:4). Layers of timber and stones were used in constructing the Temple.

5074. נָדַד ***nāḏaḏ:*** A verb meaning to flee, to wander. It means to turn from, to take flight, to turn away from (Isa. 10:31; Jer. 4:25; 9:10[9]; Nah. 3:7, 17). It is used figuratively of sleep escaping a person (Gen. 31:40); and of persons straying from the Lord (Hos. 7:13). It has the sense of to thrust away, to drive out (2 Sam. 23:6; Job 18:18); to wander around (Job 15:23; Prov. 27:8; Hos. 9:17). It describes the movement of a bird's wings (Isa. 10:14). It is used of the disappearance or vanishing of a dream (Job 20:8). In its passive use, it means to be put out, to be banished (Job 20:8).

5075. נְדַד ***n^e^ḏaḏ:*** An Aramaic verb meaning to flee, to go away. It means to go away, to take flight. It is used figuratively of a person's sleep escaping him or her (Dan. 6:18[19]).

5076. נְדֻדִים ***n^e^ḏuḏiym:*** A masculine plural noun indicating tossing to and fro. It refers to turning back and forth in bed, turning this way and that (Job. 7:4).

5077. נָדָא *nā<u>d</u>ā'*, נָדָה *nā<u>d</u>āh*: A verb signifying to separate, to drive away, to disaffect. It means to push someone away from a course of action (2 Kgs. 17:21); or to shut out (Isa. 66:5). It is used figuratively of shoving something into the future, of keeping it at bay, e.g., the Day of the Lord (Amos 6:3).

5078. נֵדֶה *nē<u>d</u>eh*: A masculine noun designating a gift, a fee. It refers to something given for a favor or a bribe; or to attract a person to do something (Ezek. 16:33).

5079. נִדָּה *niddāh*: A feminine noun meaning impurity, a woman's menstrual cycle. It refers to a woman's flow of blood during her menstruation period. She was considered unclean and impure during this time, and the impurity had to be cleansed by water (Lev. 12:2; Num. 19:9; Ezek. 18:6; 22:10). Its meaning extended to refer to anything polluted, detestable, or unclean (Lev. 20:21; Ezra 9:11; Lam. 1:17). The phrase *hāyāh l^{e}niddāh* means to become a detestable thing (Ezek. 7:19).

5080. נָדָה *nā<u>d</u>aḥ*: I. A verb meaning to banish, to drive away, to scatter. It is used in various ways to indicate the idea of forcefully removing, impelling, or driving out: of the dispersion, the scattering of Israel into exile (Deut. 30:1, 4; Jer. 40:12; 43:5; 46:28; Mic. 4:6); of driving out something in a figurative sense (Job 6:13); Zion herself was considered an outcast, one driven out (Jer. 30:17). It is used of cattle straying off (Deut. 22:1). It means to be impelled to do something, e.g., by the lure of idolatry and false gods (Deut. 4:19; 30:17); by the seduction of a harlot (Prov. 7:21).

II. A verb meaning to wield, bring (against). It is used of wielding or swinging an ax against something, striking it (Deut. 19:5; 20:19), whether a person or a tree. It is used figuratively of bringing evil and destruction on something or someone (2 Sam. 15:14).

5081. נָדִיב *nā<u>d</u>iy<u>b</u>*: An adjective meaning willing, generous, noble; as a noun, those of noble birth. The word often denotes an attitude of heart which consents or agrees (often readily and cheerfully) to a course of action. The Hebrews who were of willing hearts gave as offerings to the Lord jewelry and gold for the construction of the Tabernacle and its accessories (Ex. 35:5, 22; cf. 2 Chr. 29:31; Ps. 51:12[14]). In many other places, the term describes an individual as one of excellent moral character. Proverbs states that to punish the noble for their integrity is wrong (Prov. 17:26; cf. Prov. 17:7; Isa. 32:5, 8). At other times, the word signifies those born into lineages of nobility. The Lord lifts the needy from the ash heap and causes them to sit with princes (1 Sam. 2:8; cf. Num. 21:18; Job 12:21; 34:18; Ps. 47:9[10]; 107:40;

113:8; 118:9; Prov. 25:7; Isa. 13:2). This term is closely related to the verb *nāḏaḇ* (5068).

5082. נְדִיבָה *neḏiyḇāh:* A feminine noun indicating dignity, honor, nobility. It indicates a positive, approving, willing spirit, a spirit of dignity (Ps. 51:12[14]). It has the sense of honor, dignity concerning a person's character (Job 30:15). It has the sense of high-class, noble, honorable aspirations of a person who is honorable (Isa. 32:8).

5083. נָדָן *nāḏān:* A masculine noun meaning gift. In context it refers to something given for sexual favors, but in a spiritual, religious sense, it is a form of bribery (Ezek. 16:33).

5084. נָדָן *nāḏān:* A masculine noun indicating a sheath. It indicates a case for holding a sword in place. It is used to hold, in context, the sword blade of a divine being (1 Chr. 21:27).

5085. נִדְנֶה *niḏneh:* An Aramaic masculine noun meaning sheath for a sword. It is used only in the book of Daniel, where it figuratively described the relationship between Daniel's spirit and body. His spirit was within his body in the same way as a sword fits into its sheath (Dan 7:15). The Hebrew counterpart of this word is *nāḏān* (5084).

5086. נָדַף *nāḏap̱:* A verb meaning to drive away, to be driven about. It means to blow something about, away or to be blown away. It is used figuratively of evil persons being blown away by the wind like chaff, having no roots or stability (Lev. 26:36; Ps. 1:4). It is used most often in a passive sense of being driven away, blown away: persons by the sound of a falling leaf (Lev. 26:36); crops by bad weather (Isa. 19:7); chaff blown in the wind, representing nations (Isa. 41:2); riches falsely gotten (Prov. 21:6); a leaf driven in the wind (Job 13:25); a person defeated and driven by God (Job 32:13).

5087. נָדַר *nāḏar:* A verb meaning to vow. The verbal concept denotes the making of an oral, voluntary promise to give or do something as an expression of consecration or devotion to the service of God. Jacob vowed to return a tenth of all that God bestowed on him if God would protect and preserve him on his journey (Gen. 28:20). Leviticus 27:8 discusses the special vow offerings to the Lord and the cost of redeeming someone or something which had been dedicated to the Lord. King David also made a vow that he would deny himself the pleasures of his house and his bed until the time came when he had established a resting place and a habitation for the Lord (Ps. 132:2). The sailors, unable to save themselves and having cast Jonah into the sea with the resulting calm, greatly feared the Lord, offered sacrifices, and made vows to Him (Jon. 1:16).

5088. נֵדֶר *nēḏer,* נֶדֶר *neḏer:* A masculine noun meaning vow. The word is found twenty-five times in the Old Testament and basically means a solemn promise to God or the thing promised. Several times, the word refers to the specific words given in a vow. Jacob vowed that the Lord would be his God and he would give Him a tenth of everything the Lord gave him (Gen. 28:20; 31:13; Num. 21:2; Judg. 11:30). The word is used to describe the object or intent of vows: a Nazirite vow (Num. 6:2, 5, 21); a vow made by a wife (Num. 30:9[10]); or by people in a difficult situation who made a promise before the Lord (Jon. 1:16). The object of the vow can be a sacrifice (Lev. 7:16; 22:21); or a person dedicated to the Lord (Lev. 27:2). Neither money earned by prostitution nor deformed animals could be used as part of a vow (Lev. 22:23; Deut. 23:18[19]). Once made, a vow had to be paid by the one who made it, for if he or she did not pay, it was considered a sin (Deut. 23:21[22]; 2 Sam. 15:7; Ps. 56:12[13]). Proverbs 20:25 warned against making a vow before carefully considering the wisdom of doing so. Jephthah made a rash vow without considering its implications and suffered greatly for it (Judg. 11:30, 39). The word also describes the vow of some of the Israelites and their wives to burn incense and give libation offerings to the Queen of Heaven in the time of Jeremiah (Jer. 44:25).

5089. נֹהַּ ***nōah:*** I. A masculine noun designating something of value, something eminent. It refers to something of significance, of a significant value. It is not further defined, and its exact meaning is difficult to determine (Ezek. 7:11).

II. A masculine noun referring to a wailing, a lament. It was a human cry mourning or bewailing calamity and judgment (Ezek. 7:11).

5090. נָהַג ***nāhag:*** I. A verb signifying to drive, to guide. It has the sense of leading, guiding something willingly or by force. It is used of driving cattle or flocks (Gen. 31:18; Ex. 3:1; 2 Kgs. 4:24; Job 24:3); taking away persons who go willingly or only with force (Gen. 31:26; Isa. 20:4); leading people or animals along (2 Sam. 6:3; 1 Chr. 20:1; Ps. 48:14[15]; Isa. 11:6; 49:10; 60:11); of God's stirring up a great wind (Ex. 10:13); charioteers driving their chariots (Ex. 14:25). It is employed figuratively of a person's mind guiding him or her (Eccl. 2:3); and the tender actions of a bride leading her bridegroom (Song 8:2).

II. A verb meaning to sob, to lament. Some translators find the sense of lamenting, sobbing in Nahum 2:7[8], perhaps as a dove's voice. Meaning I fits well here, however.

5091. נָהָה ***nāhāh:*** A verb meaning to wail, to lament. It indicates weeping, showing strong sorrow and remorse for something or a situation, e.g., for the absence of the ark of the covenant from Jerusalem (1 Sam. 7:2); for the fall of a nation (Ezek. 32:18); especially God's chosen, Israel (Mic. 2:4).

5092. נְהִי ***n^e hiy:*** A masculine noun describing wailing, a song of mourning. It depicts a formal process of expressing sorrow and distress with a show of emotions over a calamity of some kind: judgment on the hills and mountains of Israel (Jer. 9:10[9], 18–20[17–19]); the loss of the people in Israel (Jer. 31:15); the judgment of the Lord on His people (Amos 5:16; Mic. 2:4).

5093. נִהְיָה ***nihyāh:*** A feminine noun indicating dolefulness, bitterness. It refers to a formal expression of despair and hopelessness over a calamity (Mic. 2:4).

5094. נְהִיר ***n^e hiyr,*** נַהִירוּ ***nahiyrû:*** An Aramaic feminine noun meaning illumination, wisdom, or insight. This word is found only in Daniel. The story of the handwriting on the wall in Belshazzar's banquet hall established the fact that Daniel was able to discern things people found baffling. Belshazzar described Daniel's wisdom as light and understanding coming from the Spirit of God within him (Dan. 5:11, 14).

5095. נָהַל ***nāhal:*** A verb meaning to lead, to guide, to move along. It means to move at a convenient speed and manner befitting travelers and their situations (Gen. 33:14; 47:17). It has the sense of guiding people, leading them in an orderly fashion and with great care (Ex. 15:13; 2 Chr. 28:15; Ps. 23:2; 31:3[4]; Isa. 40:11; 49:10; 51:18).

5096. נַהֲלֹל ***nah^a lōl,*** נַהֲלָל ***nah^a lāl:*** A proper noun designating Nahalal, Nahalol (Josh. 19:15; 21:35; Judg. 1:30).

5097. נַהֲלֹל ***nah^a lōl:*** A masculine noun referring to bushes, watering places. It refers to a place where water was available for people, flocks, and herds. Such places were especially prized by people in the Middle East (Isa. 7:19).

5098. נָהַם ***nāham:*** A verb meaning to groan, to growl, to roar. It expresses the deep guttural, piercing growl of a lion, especially as it grasps its prey (Prov. 28:15; Isa. 5:29, 30). It expresses the despairing groan of a person who is destroyed by immoral behavior (Prov. 5:11). It is the groan of persons forced into captivity in exile (Ezek. 24:23).

5099. נַהַם ***naham:*** A masculine noun signifying a growl, a roar. It is used of the provoked threatening sound of a lion of prey. In context it is used of the roaring of a king's wrath against those who agitate it (Prov. 19:12; 20:2).

5100. נְהָמָה ***n^e hāmāh:*** A feminine noun referring to agitation, roaring. It indicates a loud, disturbing noise or emotion. It is used of a palpitating heart or a heart despairing of hope (Ps. 38:8[9]). It indicates the sound made by the breakers of the sea on the seashore (Isa. 5:30).

5101. נָהַק ***nāhaq:*** A verb expressing the braying of a donkey. It is used of a loud, shrill sound of a wild ass or a donkey (Job 6:5); and of the despairing cries of persons existing as social outcasts (Job 30:7).

5102. נָהַר ***nāhar:*** I. A verb meaning to flow, to stream. It describes the movement of something like the flow of a river or stream: a flow of people and nations (Isa. 2:2; Jer. 51:44; Mic. 4:1); of wealth, abundance (Isa. 60:5). It describes a person glowing, beaming, radiant, overjoyed about something (Jer. 31:12).

II. A verb meaning to be radiant. It means to shine, to glow, to beam over deliverance from God (Ps. 34:5[6]); the abundance of Zion (Isa. 60:5; Jer. 31:12).

5103. נְהַר ***n***^{e}***har:*** An Aramaic masculine noun identifying a river. It refers to a large, flowing body of water: the Euphrates River (Ezra 4:10, 11, 16; 5:3; 6:6; 7:21). It is used metaphorically of a flowing river of fire (Dan. 7:10).

5104. נָהָר ***nāhār:*** A masculine noun indicating a large, flowing body of water or a current within a sea: any river in general (Num. 24:6; Job 14:11); specific rivers (Gen. 2:10, 13, 14); Euphrates River (Gen. 15:18; 31:21; Num. 22:5); Tigris River (Dan. 10:4); Nile River or El Arish River (Gen. 15:18). It refers to a current of water within a sea (Jon. 2:3[4]). It is used figuratively and literally of a river flowing around the city of God (Ps. 46:4[5]); as well as to underground flows of water (Job 28:11).

5105. נְהָרָה ***n***^{e}***hārāh:*** A feminine noun referring to light, the light of day. It refers to the light of dawn, the sunlight, which illumines something and makes it known or real (Job 3:4).

5106. נוּא ***nû':*** A verb meaning to forbid, to discourage, to thwart. Negated, it means not to permit something, to stop it: the performance of a vow to the Lord (Num. 30:5[6], 8[9], 11[12]); an action that should be carried out, i.e., taking the Promised Land (Num. 32:7, 9); God thwarting the plans or designs of people (Ps. 33:10). It is used in a figurative, idiomatic expression meaning, "let it happen to me," literally, "let my head not refuse" (Ps. 141:5).

5107. נוּב ***nûḇ:*** A verb meaning to flourish, to bear fruit, to bring forth. It has the basic sense of causing something to increase, to succeed: wealth or riches to multiply, to increase (Ps. 62:10[11]). Figuratively, it speaks of the continued prosperity of a righteous person (Ps. 92:14[15]; Prov. 10:31). It indicates the prosperity and increase of the people of Judah and Ephraim when God blesses them (Zech. 9:17).

5108. נוֹב ***nôḇ,*** נִיב ***niyḇ:*** I. A masculine noun indicating fruit. It is used figuratively of good things spoken by the lips, good news (Isa. 57:19). It is used of the fruit offered on the altar, which the Israelites decried as contemptible (Mal. 1:12).

II. A masculine noun meaning fruit. It is the same as I, but its spelling is different. It is not found in Malachi 1:12 in this form. See III.

III. A masculine noun meaning praise. This is understood by some as a different word from I and II indicating praise. It is used of praise offered in response to God's offer of peace (Isa. 57:19).

5109. נֵיבָי ***nēḇāy:*** A proper noun designating Nebai (Neh. 10:19[20]).

5110. נוּד ***nûḏ:*** A verb meaning to flee, to wander, to mourn. It has the sense of aimless motion or actions. It refers to a person moving about aimlessly without a home (Gen. 4:12, 14); to birds, persons, flora, inanimate objects moving or shaking (1 Kgs. 14:15; Ps. 11:1; Isa. 24:20; Jer. 18:16). It has the meaning of to drive away, to cause to wander in a figurative sense (Ps. 36:11[12]). It takes on the sense of concern for people, sympathy, mourning for them (Job 2:11; 42:11; Ps. 69:20[21]); but also to show disdain by shaking one's head (Isa. 51:19; Jer. 48:27). It means to bemoan oneself, to grieve, in its reflexive usage (Jer. 31:18). It refers to making a person or a people wander about, homeless (2 Kgs. 21:8).

5111. נוּד ***nûḏ:*** An Aramaic verb meaning to flee. It has the sense of something going away, escaping. It is used of animals fleeing from an area (Dan. 4:14[11]).

5112. נוֹד ***nôḏ:*** I. A masculine noun indicating wandering. It refers to walking about, traveling about with no home to return to and no goal in mind. It is used of David's flight from his enemies in the wilderness (Ps. 56:8[9]).

II. A masculine noun referring to a lament. It indicates an oral and possibly a written response to calamity or oppressive situations (Ps. 56:8[9]).

5113. נוֹד ***nôḏ:*** A proper noun designating Nod (Gen. 4:16).

5114. נוֹדָב ***nôḏāḇ:*** A proper noun designating Nodab (1 Chr. 5:19).

5115. נָוָה ***nāwāh:*** I. A verb meaning to dwell, to abide, to rest. A word referring to the safety and security given to a person. It is used in a metaphor describing the Lord as this rest and security (Ex. 15:2).

II. A verb meaning to beautify; to praise. It is an expression of thanks and honor. It is used in a metaphor identifying the Lord Himself as the poet's source of praise and honor (Ex. 15:2).

5116. נָוֶה ***nāweh,*** נָוָה ***nāwāh:*** I. A masculine noun depicting a shepherd's abode, a camp; a flock. It refers to any place of habitation, natural or man-made. Its most famous reference is to the land of Canaan, Zion (Ex. 15:13; Ps. 79:7; Jer. 10:25). It refers to the pasturage used for sheep and the work of pasturing itself (2 Sam. 7:8). It refers to Jerusalem and the Temple as places of God's habitation (2 Sam. 15:25). It refers to any place of abode (Job 5:3, 24), figuratively or literally, (Prov. 3:33). It is used even of deserted areas (Isa. 27:10; Ezek. 25:5).

II. A feminine noun indicating a dwelling, a habitation, a pasturage. It has many of the same uses as I. It refers to green pasturage in the beloved psalm (23:2) and to other types of pasturage: wilderness pastures (Jer. 9:10[9]; Joel 1:19); pasturage used by shepherds (Amos 1:2). In an ironic passage, the seacoast is termed "pastures" after God's judgments (Zeph. 2:6). It refers to the land of Jacob, Canaan (Lam. 2:2).

III. An adjectival noun meaning a person dwelling, abiding. It refers to a person who remains in a location, e.g., in a home, a house, as opposed to fleeing (Ps. 68:12[13]).

5117. נוּחַ **nûaḥ,** מֻנָּח **munnāḥ:** I. A verb indicating to rest, to pause. It has many uses. Its main uses are summarized here: (1) to rest, to settle, to settle down, e.g., of the ark (Gen. 8:4); of locusts on the crops (Ex. 10:14); of a spirit on a person (2 Kgs. 2:15); of the Lord's Spirit (Num. 11:25, 26); of birds (2 Sam. 21:10); of the hand of the Lord on something (Isa. 25:10); of wisdom which rests in one's heart (Prov. 14:33). (2) It means to repose, to pause for rest after laboring (Ex. 20:11; 23:12; Deut. 5:14); freedom, respite from one's enemies (Esth. 9:16). (3) It means to leave something as it is, at rest: the nations (Num. 32:15; Judg. 2:23; 3:1; Jer. 27:11); to leave something behind (Gen. 42:33; 2 Sam. 16:21). (4) It can have the sense of departing from a position (Eccl. 10:4); or of God's abandoning a person (Ps. 119:121; Jer. 14:9). (5) It can mean to leave alone, to let be, to not bother (Ex. 32:10; Hos. 4:17). (6) It has the sense of permit, to let a person do something (Judg. 16:26). (7) It may mean, in its causative senses: (a) to cause to rest, to give rest to: to rest one's hands (Ex. 17:11); to give satisfaction to one's spirit, especially God's Spirit (Zech. 6:8); to calm someone (Prov. 29:17); it is used figuratively of letting a blessing rest, come down on a person, house, or family (Ezek. 44:30). (b) To lay something down, to deposit it somewhere, such as stones (Josh. 4:3, 8); the ark (1 Sam. 6:18); man, Adam (Gen. 2:15). In one passive usage, it is negated (*lō'*) and refers to those who are given no respite (Lam 5:5).

II. A masculine noun meaning free space, an open area. It refers to an area left open between two walls or rooms (Ezek. 41:9).

5118. נוּחַ **nûaḥ,** נוֹחַ **nôaḥ:** A masculine noun referring to a resting place, a rest. It means to free oneself from something, to get rest from, to get rid of (Esth. 9:6). It indicates the place where the Lord chose to let His name and glory dwell on earth, the Temple (2 Chr. 6:41).

5119. נֹחָה ***nôḥāh:*** A proper noun designating Nohah (1 Chr. 8:2).

5120. נוּט ***nûṭ:*** A verb meaning to move, to shake. It describes the quivering, quick, violent movements of the earth as a response to the enthronement of the Lord (Ps. 99:1).

5121. נָיוֹת ***nāyôṯ:*** A proper noun designating Naioth (1 Sam. 19:18, 19, 22, 23; 20:1).

5122. נְוָלוּ ***neẉālû,*** נְוָלִי ***neẉāliy:*** An Aramaic feminine noun indicating a refuse heap, a dunghill. It refers to a useless pile of rubble, a demolished house in this case (Ezra 6:11; Dan. 2:5; 3:29).

5123. נוּם ***nûm:*** A verb meaning to sleep, to slumber (Isa. 5:27; 56:10; Nah. 3:18). It is used figuratively of God's sending a spirit of slumber on His enemies (Ps. 76:5[6]). God Himself never sleeps or slumbers (Ps. 121:3, 4).

5124. נוּמָה ***nûmāh:*** A feminine noun referring to drowsiness. It refers to a state of sleepiness as an expression of laziness, in context; the glutton and drunkard will be overcome by drowsiness (Prov. 23:21).

5125. נוּן ***nûn:*** A verb meaning to continue, to increase. It indicates the propriety and strengthening of a person, e.g., the righteous king of God's people (Ps. 72:17).

5126. נוּן ***nun,*** נוֹן ***nôn:*** A proper noun designating Nun, Non, the father of Joshua (Ex. 33:11; Num. 11:28; Josh. 1:1; 2:1, 23; Judg. 2:8; 1 Kgs. 16:34; 1 Chr. 7:27; Neh. 8:17).

5127. נוּס ***nûs:*** A verb meaning to flee. It indicates the idea of escape, fleeing away, getting to a safe spot. It is used of warriors fleeing in battle (Gen. 14:10); of people fleeing disaster of various kinds (Gen. 19:20; Judg. 7:21; Jer. 48:44; Zech. 2:6[10]; 14:5). It is employed figuratively of seas, shadows, strength, etc., all disappearing or fleeing away (Deut. 34:7; Ps. 114:3, 5; Song 2:17). In its causative sense, it means to cause someone or something to flee, to put to flight (Ex. 9:20; Deut. 32:30; Judg. 1:6). It indicates the speedy and onrushing manner in which the Lord escorts in His Redeemer (Isa. 59:19).

5128. נוּעַ ***nûaʻ:*** A verb meaning to shake, to stagger, to wander. It refers to a displaced person, a wanderer, a vagrant (Gen. 4:12; 14). It describes a person physically shaking or trembling from fear (Ex. 20:18); and of a person's lips quivering or mumbling (1 Sam. 1:13). It depicts the wandering of Israel in the wilderness for forty years (Num. 32:13; cf. Amos 4:8). Figuratively, it describes a tree reigning, "swaying" over the other trees (Judg. 9:9, 11, 13). It is used of inanimate things moving, shaking, being shaken, tottering, etc.: (2 Kgs. 23:18; Job 28:4; Isa. 6:4; 7:2; Amos 9:9; Nah. 3:12). It is used of shaking one's head or hand

(2 Kgs. 19:21; Ps. 22:7[8]; Zeph. 2:15). It indicates the Lord's judgments that make the whole house of Israel shake in dread (Amos 9:9).

5129. נוֹעַדְיָה ***nôʿaḏyāh:*** A proper noun designating Noadiah:

A. A Levite under Ezra (Ezra 8:33).

B. A prophetess (Neh. 6:14).

5130. נוּף ***nûp̱:*** A verb meaning to move back and forth, to sprinkle. This verb only occurs in the basic verbal form once, where it refers to sprinkling a bed with myrrh (Prov. 7:17). Most often, it occurs in the causative form, where it can carry a similar semantic idea, namely making rain fall (Ps. 68:9[10]). However, it usually carries the idea of moving back and forth or waving. It could be used to represent the reciprocating motion of a tool, like a sword (Ex. 20:25); a sickle (Deut. 23:25[26]); a tool for dressing stone (Deut. 27:5); or a saw (Isa. 10:15). It could also be used of the motion of one's hand as a healing ritual (2 Kgs. 5:11); as retribution (Isa. 11:15; 19:16); or as a signal (Isa. 13:2). In a cultic context, this verb is a technical term that referenced the actions of the priest as he offered a sacrifice to God by waving it before the altar (Ex. 29:24; Lev. 23:11; Num. 5:25).

5131. נוֹף ***nôp̱:*** A masculine noun signifying height, elevation. It refers to the elevation of something. It is used both literally and figuratively of the height in elevation and splendor of Mount Zion (Ps. 48:2[3]).

5132. נוּץ ***nûṣ:*** I. A verb meaning to bud, to blossom. It refers to the flowers or blooms of a flowering plant, a feature of beauty and splendor engendering love in this context (Song 6:11; 7:12[13]).

II. A verb meaning to fly, to wander off. It refers to leaving an area or location. The inhabitants of Jerusalem were ordered to flee away, to depart from places to which they had wandered in exile (Lam 4:15).

5133. נוֹצָה ***nôṣāh,*** נֹצָה ***nōṣāh:*** I. A feminine noun indicating feathers, plumage. It refers to the tuft of feathers of a bird which were to be removed during an offering (Lev. 1:16); or to the plumage of an ostrich (Job 39:13); or eagle (Ezek. 17:3, 7).

II. A feminine noun meaning contents. It refers to the contents of a bird's crop or stomach removed when it was being offered (Lev. 1:16).

5134. נוּק ***nûq:*** A verb meaning to nurse. It means to feed a baby at its mother's breasts (Ex. 2:9), as when Moses' mother was divinely chosen to nurse him.

5135. נוּר ***nûr:*** An Aramaic masculine noun meaning fire. It refers to the flames and heat of the king's furnace into which the Hebrew young men were cast (Dan. 3:6, 11, 15, 17, 20–27); to the river of flames flowing from the throne of the Ancient of Days (Dan. 7:9, 10).

5136. נוּשׁ ***nûš:*** A verb meaning to be sick, helpless. It refers to a debilitated, weak person, depressed from the oppression of his enemies (Ps. 69:20[21]).

5137. נָזָה ***nāzāh:*** A verb meaning to spurt, to spatter, to sprinkle, to spring, to leap. This verb appears only a few times in the basic verbal form and carries the connotation of blood spurting or spattering (Lev. 6:27[20]; 2 Kgs. 9:33; Isa. 63:3). In the causative form, the verb connotes the sprinkling of a liquid as part of a ritual cleansing. The sprinkled liquid could be blood (Lev. 5:9; 14:7); oil (Lev. 8:11); water (Num. 19:18, 19); blood and oil (Ex. 29:21); or blood and water (Lev. 14:51). Also in the causative form, this verb could signify to leap or to spring, especially with the connotation of surprise or joy (Isa. 52:15).

5138. נָזִיד ***nāziyd:*** A masculine noun referring to a food, a stew. It is used to describe the boiled dish of stew Jacob prepared (Gen. 25:29, 34). The exact contents of the food are not known.

5139. נָזִיר ***nāziyr:*** A masculine noun meaning one consecrated, separated, devoted, a Nazarite. The term Nazarite means one who is consecrated to God. The Nazarite vow included abstinence from strong drink or the cutting of his hair, and no contact with dead bodies (Judg. 13:4–7). Samuel, as well as Samson, was dedicated before birth by his mother to be a Nazarite (cf. 1 Sam. 1:11). Less common is the meaning of a prince or ruler being consecrated, as was the case with Joseph, who was separated from his brothers (Gen. 49:26). A third meaning of this word depicts an untrimmed vine (Lev. 25:5).

5140. נָזַל ***nāzal,*** **נֹזֵל** ***nōzēl:*** I. A verb meaning to flow, to pour down, to drop, to melt. It refers to flowing water (Ex. 15:8; Num. 24:7); or the droplets of dew that evaporate (Deut. 32:2). It is used of rain (Job 36:28; Isa. 45:8); of running tears (Jer. 9:18[17]). In its causative usage, it means to cause water to flow (Ps. 78:16; Isa. 48:21). It is used figuratively of water from one's own cistern, one's own wife (Prov. 5:15).

II. A masculine noun referring to brooks, streams. Some translators prefer these renderings of this fixed participial form of the verb in I.

5141. נֶזֶם ***nezem:*** A masculine noun designating a ring, an earring, a nose ring. It is used to describe a circular piece of jewelry worn on the wrist, ear, or nose (Gen. 24:22, 30, 47; 35:4); sometimes associated with idolatry (Ex. 32:2; Hos. 2:13[15]). These items were considered ornaments of luxury (Isa. 3:21); and beauty (Ezek. 16:12). Earrings were characteristic of Israelites (Judg. 8:24, 26). These jewelry pieces are referred to in proverbs (Prov. 11:22) to make comparisons (Prov. 25:12).

5142. נְזַק n^e*zaq:* An Aramaic verb meaning to injure, to damage, to cause loss. It indicates, in context, a monetary loss or reduction (Ezra 4:13, 15, 22; Dan. 6:2[3]) in the royal treasuries of kings.

5143. נֵזֶק *nēzeq:* A masculine noun indicating a damage, a disturbance. It indicates an annoying disturbance, a bother, or an agitation to someone (Esth. 7:4).

5144. נָזַר *nāzar:* A verb meaning to dedicate, to consecrate. In the passive or reflexive form, it can signify a dedication to (Hos. 9:10) or a separation from a deity (Ezek. 14:7). It can also indicate considering something as sacred and consecrated (Lev. 22:2). This verb also expresses the idea of consecrating oneself by fasting (Zech. 7:3). In the causative form, it can denote to separate or to refrain from something (Lev. 15:31); or to take on the obligations of a Nazirite, a *nāziyr* (5139) (Num. 6:2, 5, 12).

5145. נֵזֶר *nēzer:* A masculine noun meaning a consecration, an ordination. This could be the consecration of the high priest (Lev. 21:12); or of a person taking a vow as a Nazirite (Num. 6:5, 7, 9, 12). This term is also used to identify a crown as the symbol of the wearer's consecration. This could be the king's crown (2 Sam. 1:10; 2 Kgs. 11:12); or the golden crown of the high priest (Ex. 29:6; 39:30). Jeremiah also used this term to refer to the hair of the personified Jerusalem (Jer. 7:29). The basis of this extension could be the connection between the Nazirite and his long, uncut hair as his symbol of consecration (Num. 6:5); or to the idea that a woman's long hair itself is her "crown of consecration." This would be similar to Paul's teaching in the New Testament (cf. 1 Cor. 11:15).

5146. נֹחַ *nōaḥ:* A proper noun designating Noah, the son of Lamech who gave rest to humankind from the curse placed on the earth (Gen. 4:28–32). He was considered a righteous man in his generation who found favor with God (Gen. 6:8–10). He followed the Lord and constructed an ark to preserve humanity from destruction (Gen. 6:14–21). God preserved him and his family. God caused the flood waters to stop and recede when He remembered Noah (Gen. 8:1). Noah offered sacrifices to God after leaving the ark (Gen. 8:21). He was sinned against by his son Ham. Noah, inspired by God, placed a curse on Ham his son and his descendants, the Canaanites (Gen. 9:1–29). The earth was repopulated by the descendants of his three sons, Ham, Shem, and Japheth (Gen. 10). The prophets remembered the time of Noah as a moral-religious message to guide (Isa. 54:9) and to warn them.

5147. נַחְבִּי *naḥbiy:* A proper noun designating Nahbi (Num. 13:14).

5148. נָחָה *nāḥāh:* A verb meaning to lead, to guide, usually in the right direction or on the proper path. The verb sometimes occurs with a human subject (Ex. 32:34; Ps. 60:9[11]; 108:10[11]); however, it usually appears with the Lord as the subject (Gen. 24:27; Ex. 13:17; 15:13). This term is also used metaphorically to represent spiritual guidance in righteousness (Ps. 5:8[9]; 27:11; 139:24). This term also carries a connotation of treating kindly (Job 31:18); blessing (Ps. 23:3); deliverance (Ps. 31:3[4]); protection (Ps. 61:2[3]); or wisdom (Ps. 73:24).

5149. נְחוּם *n^eḥûm:* A proper noun designating Nehum (Neh. 7:7).

5150. נִחוּם *niḥûm,* נִחֻם *niḥum:* A masculine noun indicating comfort, compassion. It indicates a cessation of discomfort, distress, or sorrow (Isa. 57:18). It has the sense of emotions and speaks of comfort, feelings of compassion that arise (Hos. 11:8). It indicates words that bring comfort, refreshment, or a feeling of being comforted (Zech. 1:13).

5151. נַחוּם *naḥûm:* A proper noun designating Nahum. The name means "comfort" and is the name of a prophet whose entire message announced and celebrated the Lord's destruction of the Assyrian capital, Nineveh. He came after Jonah. God's long-suffering and patience finally came to an end for Nineveh (Nah. 1:3).

5152. נָחוֹר *nāḥôr:* A proper noun designating Nahor:

A. The father of Terah, father of Abraham (Gen. 11:24–26).

B. The son of Terah and brother of Abraham. Lot was his nephew by Haran, his other brother (Gen. 11:27). He married Milcah who was Haran's daughter. He remained in Haran and did not move on to Canaan. He fathered twin sons, Uz and Buz (Gen. 22:20–21). He supplied Isaac with a wife, Rebekah, through Bethuel his son (Gen. 24:10, 15, 24, 47). Laban was Nahor's grandson (Gen. 29:5). His God was evidently the same as Abraham's God who had called them to Haran (Gen. 31:53), but he had earlier worshiped a god beyond the Euphrates River (Josh. 24:2).

5153. נָחוּשׁ *nāḥûš:* An adjective describing something of bronze. A fairly strong metal made of tin or copper and used to forge weapons, among other things (Job 6:12).

5154. נְחוּשָׁה *n^eḥûšāh:* A feminine noun referring to bronze, copper. A strong metal of copper and tin used literally to give the sense of hardness, unyieldedness, strength, firmness (Lev. 26:19; Job 40:18; Isa. 48:4, a bronze forehead;). Various things were made of bronze: bows (2 Sam. 22:35; Job 20:24; Ps. 18:34[35]); doors (Isa. 45:2). It also refers to copper, since bronze is man-made (Job 28:2). It is used in a figurative sense of bronze hoops (Mic. 4:13).

5155. נְחִילָה *n^eḥiylāh:* I. A feminine proper noun Nehiloth; a proper name in a psalm title. It is a technical musical term not fully understood.

II. A feminine proper noun. It is a technical musical term not fully understood. Some suggest that it refers to a flute (Ps. 5:title).

5156. נָחִיר nāḥiyr: A masculine noun referring to a nostril. It is used of the nostrils of Leviathan, a legendary monster or crocodile that God described (Job 41:20[12]).

5157. נָחַל nāḥal: A verb meaning to receive, to take property as a permanent possession. The verb was formed from the noun *naḥ^a^lāh* (5159) which refers to a possession or inheritance. It can refer to the actual taking of the Promised Land, whether it was the entire land of Canaan as a gift from God (Ex. 23:30; 32:13); a tribal allotment (Josh. 16:4); or a familial portion (Josh. 17:6). In addition to the taking of Canaan, God declared that Israel's remnant would possess the lands of Moab and Edom (Zeph. 2:9). It can also refer to the division and distribution of the land of Canaan to the tribal units (Josh. 14:1). This verb is further used of God acquiring possession of Israel (Ex. 34:9; Zech. 2:12[16]); and the nations as His own private property (Ps. 82:8). In the causative form, the verb denotes the giving of a possession (Deut. 1:38; 3:28); or inheritance (Deut. 21:16). This term is used figuratively to indicate the acquiring of things other than real property, like testimonies (Ps. 119:111); glory (Prov. 3:35); good things (Prov. 28:10); lies (Jer. 16:19); wind (Prov. 11:29); simplicity (Prov. 14:18); blessings (Zech. 8:12).

5158. נַחֲלָה naḥ^a^lāh, נַחַל naḥal: I. A feminine noun meaning wadi. It refers to a seasonal or semipermanent small river, often termed the River of Egypt (El-Arish?). It served as a boundary of the land of Israel in Ezekiel's vision (Ezek. 47:19; 48:28).

II. A masculine noun indicating a wadi, a stream, a torrent. A streambed or wadi with water in it permanently (a spring) or only during the rainy season (Gen. 26:19; Deut. 8:7; 1 Sam. 17:40). When it is full, it flows violently (Deut. 9:21; Judg. 5:21). It usually describes specific small streams, rivers, and brooks such as the Jabbok or Arnon (Gen. 32:23[24]; Lev. 11:9, 10; Num. 21:14; Josh. 12:2). It is used of hollows or pits dug for graves, ravines, mining, etc. (Neh. 2:15; Job 28:4). It is used figuratively of streams, veins of oil (Mic. 6:7); wadis of death (2 Sam. 22:5; Ps. 18:4[5]); a torrent of asphalt (*goprît*) describing Topheth, a stream of tears (Lam. 2:18); or a brook of wisdom (Prov. 18:4). Water breaking out from a rock is described by this term (Ps. 78:20).

5159. נַחֲלָה naḥ^a^lāh: A feminine noun meaning possession, property, inheritance. This word implied property that was given by means of a will or as a heritage. It denoted the land of Canaan given to Israel and distributed among the tribes (Num. 26:53–56; Ezek. 48:29); a portion or state of blessing assigned by God to His people (Isa. 54:17), or any possession presented by a father (Num. 27:8, 9; Job 42:15). The Lord Himself was declared to be the portion and inheritance of the Levites who served Him (Num. 18:20).

5160. נַחֲלִיאֵל ***naḥaliy'ēl:*** A proper noun designating Nahaliel (Num. 21:19).

5161. נֶחֱלָמִי ***neḥelāmiy:*** A proper noun designating Nehelamite (Jer. 29:24, 31, 32).

5162. נָחַם ***nāḥam:*** A verb meaning to be sorry, to pity, to comfort, to avenge. The verb often means to be sorry or to regret: the Lord was sorry that He had made people (Gen. 6:6); He led Israel in a direction to avoid war when they left Egypt, lest they became so sorry and grieved that they would turn back (Ex. 13:17). The Lord had compassion on His people (i.e., He became sorry for them because of the oppression their enemies placed on them [Judg. 2:18]). While the Lord could be grieved, He did not grieve or become sorry so that He changed His mind as a human does (1 Sam. 15:29). The word also means to comfort or console oneself. Isaac was comforted after Sarah, his mother, died (Gen. 24:67).

The verb always means to console or comfort. Jacob refused to be comforted when he believed that Joseph had been killed (Gen. 37:35). To console is synonymous with showing kindness to someone, as when David consoled Hanun, king of the Ammonites, over the death of his father (2 Sam. 10:2). God refused to be consoled over the destruction of His people (Isa. 22:4; 40:1); yet He comforts those who need it (Ps. 119:82; Isa. 12:1). The passive form of the word means to be comforted: the afflicted city of Zion would be comforted by the Lord (Isa. 54:11; 66:13). In the reflexive stem, it can mean to get revenge for oneself (Gen. 27:42; Ezek. 5:13); to let oneself be sorry or have compassion (Num. 23:19; Deut. 32:36); and to let oneself be comforted (Gen. 37:35; Ps. 119:52).

5163. נַחַם ***naḥam:*** A proper noun designating Nahum (1 Chr. 4:19).

5164. נֹחַם ***nōḥam:*** A masculine noun meaning sorrow, repentance, compassion. This word comes from the verb *nāḥam* (5162), meaning to be sorry or to repent, and occurs only once in the Old Testament. In Hosea 13:14, it described the compassion that God would not have toward sinful Ephraim.

5165. נֶחָמָה ***neḥāmāh:*** A feminine noun meaning compassion, consolation. This word comes from the verb *nāḥam* (5162), meaning to be sorry or to repent, and occurs twice in the Old Testament. In Job 6:10, Job was comforted that in the midst of his trials, he did not deny the Holy One; the psalmist declared that his comfort in his affliction was God's Word, which revived him (Ps. 119:50).

5166. נְחֶמְיָה ***neḥemyāh:*** A proper noun designating Nehemiah:

A. It means "the Lord comforts" (Heb. *nāḥam* [5162]) and is a fitting name for the man who was deeply distressed at the perilous and oppressive condition of his holy city Jerusalem and its Jewish inhabitants. He was cupbearer to the Persian king Artaxerxes I (465–424 B.C.), a highly prized position (Neh. 2:1–3). The king permitted Nehemiah to return to Judah and Jerusalem to aid them (Neh. 2:6–9). He led a large group of exiles back to Jerusalem and Judah (Neh. 7:4–73). When there (ca. 445 B.C.), he oversaw the rebuilding of the walls and the city in record time (Neh. 2:11—12:26). It was duly dedicated (Neh. 12:27–43). He helped repopulate the city (Neh. 11:1–36), led in a national day of prayer (Neh. 9), and helped Ezra establish the Mosaic Law again (Neh. 7:73b—8:18). He returned to Persia in 433 B.C., then went back to Jerusalem again after an indefinite period. He dealt again with the problem of Jewish intermarriage (Neh. 13:23–28) with non-Israelites as Ezra had and restored and purified the priestly services in Israel (Neh. 13:1–13). He warned them severely about not keeping the Sabbath (Neh. 13:14–22).

B. A postexilic Jew who returned from exile (Ezra 2:2).

C. The son of Azbuk who helped repair part of the wall of Jerusalem (Neh. 3:16).

5167. נַחֲמָנִי ***naḥ^a^māniy:*** A proper noun designating Nahamani (Neh. 7:7).

5168. נַחְנוּ ***naḥnû:*** A pronoun meaning we. It serves as a shortened first person plural pronoun used for both men or women (Gen. 42:11; Ex. 16:7, 8; Num. 32:32; Lam. 3:42).

5169. נָחַץ ***nāḥaṣ:*** A verb meaning to be urgent. It describes a situation or a set of circumstances as pressing, demanding attention (1 Sam. 21:8[9]).

5170. נַחַר ***naḥar,*** נַחֲרָה ***naḥ^a^rāh:***
I. A masculine noun meaning snorting. It is used of the neighing or snorting of a horse (Job 39:20).

II. A feminine noun meaning snorting. It is used of the snorting or neighing of horses (Jer. 8:16).

5171. נַחֲרַי ***naḥ^a^ray,*** נַחְרַי ***naḥray:***
I. A masculine noun meaning a snorting (Job 39:20, *naḥar*).

II. A feminine noun meaning a snorting (Jer. 8:16, *naḥ^a^rāh*).

5172. נָחַשׁ ***naḥaš:*** A verb meaning to practice divination, to observe omens. This verb described the pagan practice of seeking knowledge through divination, which was expressly forbidden in the Law of Moses (Lev. 19:26; Deut. 18:10); and was used as an indication that the kings of Israel and

Judah were wicked (2 Kgs. 17:17; 21:6; 2 Chr. 33:6). In its other usages, Laban used divination to confirm that Jacob was a blessing to him (Gen. 30:27); Joseph claimed that a cup helped him practice divination (Gen. 44:5, 15); and the Arameans took Ahab's words as an omen (1 Kgs. 20:33).

5173. נַחַשׁ *naḥaš:* A masculine noun meaning divination, omen. This word comes from the verb *nāhaš* (5172), meaning to practice divination or to observe omens, and is used only twice in the Old Testament. In both instances of this word, it is used within the context of Balaam and his prophecies. In one discourse, Balaam declared that there was no omen against Jacob (Num. 23:23); and in preparing for another discourse, he did not seek omens (Num. 24:1).

5174. נְחָשׁ *neḥāš:* An Aramaic masculine noun signifying bronze, brass. It was a highly valued metal alloy of copper and tin: In Daniel it is featured in a statue (2:32, 35, 39, 45); as part of the material of a band around a tree stump (4:15[12], 23[20]); as the material of bronze idols (5:4, 23); a bronze claw on the fourth beast of Daniel's vision (7:19).

5175. נָחָשׁ *nāḥāš:* A masculine noun meaning snake. It is used to refer to an actual serpent (Ex. 4:3; Num. 21:6; Deut. 8:15; Eccl. 10:8; Amos 5:19); or an image of one (Num. 21:9), but it is also used figuratively. Some of these symbolic uses include the tempter (Gen. 3:1, 2, 4, 13, 14); the tribe of Dan (Gen. 49:17); wicked rulers (Ps. 58:4[5]); and enemies (Isa. 14:29; Jer. 8:17; 46:22).

5176. נָחָשׁ *nāḥāš:* A proper noun designating Nahash:

A. A king of the Ammonites who was going to put out the right eye of every person in the city of Jabesh Gilead (1 Sam. 11:1–5), but Saul and the Israelites defeated the Ammonites and rescued the men of Jabesh Gilead (1 Sam. 11:9–11). He was perceived as a threat to Israel, and so the Israelites sought a human king to protect them (1 Sam. 12:12). David was able to live in peace with Nahash (2 Sam. 10:1–2). His son Hanun succeeded him. He had another son, Shobi (2 Sam. 17:27), if they are the same person.

B. The father of Abigail who was married to Nabal. Abigail was the sister of Zeruiah, David's sister (2 Sam. 17:25).

5177. נַחְשׁוֹן *naḥšôn:* A proper noun designating Nahson (Ex. 6:23; Num. 1:7; 2:3; 7:12, 17; 10:14; Ruth 4:20; 1 Chr. 2:10, 11).

5178. נְחֹשֶׁת *neḥōšeṯ:* I. A common noun referring to copper, bronze wealth. Copper is a metal occurring naturally (Deut. 8:9); bronze is a metal alloy of copper and tin. The meaning of this word depends on its use in context. It is found listed among other materials of the ancient world (Gen.

4:22; 2 Sam. 8:10). There were skilled craftsmen who worked in bronze (1 Kgs. 7:14) as a medium of construction, art, and ornamentation. Bronze made possible a better grade of all kinds of implements and tools of labor or war: weapons, pillars, columns, bases, stands, the great bronze sea of Solomon (Num. 16:39[17:14]; 1 Sam. 17:5, 6; 2 Kgs. 25:13, 14). The word describes chains of copper or bronze (Judg. 16:21). It was considered a highly prized spoil of war (2 Sam. 8:8; Jer. 52:17, 20). It is used figuratively to indicate God's refusal to respond to His people (Deut. 28:23); and in visions of bronze mountains (Zech. 6:1).

II. A common noun meaning lewdness, lust. It is used of female genitals or nakedness, shame (Ezek. 16:36) or some such obscene sense of the word.

5179. נְחֻשְׁתָּא *n^eḥuštā'*: A proper noun designating Nehushta (2 Kgs. 24:8).

5180. נְחֻשְׁתָּן *n^eḥuštān*: A proper noun designating Nehushtan, the name given to a bronze snake Moses ordered to be made in the wilderness (Num. 21:9). This was probably a model of it created in the idolatrous times of Ahaz.

5181. נָחַת *nāḥaṯ*: A verb meaning to bend, to bring down, to descend. It means to bend a strong bow for battle (2 Sam. 22:35; Ps. 18:34[35]), to pull it down. It has a general sense of to descend, to go down someplace (Job 21:13); to descend against someone in battle (Jer. 21:13; Joel 3:11 [4:11]). It depicts the penetration of something: the arrows of the Lord's rebukes penetrate (Ps. 38:2[3]; Prov. 17:10). It seems to have the sense of leveling off, smoothing something in Psalm 65:10[11].

5182. נְחֵת *n^eḥēṯ*: An Aramaic verb indicating to bring down, to descend. It means to deposit something at a location. It is used of putting down, depositing the vessels of the Temple in their proper places (Ezra 5:15; 6:5). It is used of something being permanently stored away (Ezra 6:1). In Daniel the word is used to indicate descending, coming down (Dan. 4:13[10, 23[20]); and of putting down, removing someone from the throne (Dan. 5:20).

5183. נַחַת *naḥaṯ*: I. A masculine noun referring to rest, calmness, quietness. A word referring to respite, freedom from oppression, or strife (Job 17:16, KJV; Prov. 29:9; Eccl. 4:6; 6:5; 9:17; Isa. 30:15). For Job 36:16, see 5181 also and in general.

II. A masculine noun meaning descent. It is used figuratively of the Lord's arm coming down in judgment (Isa. 30:30).

5184. נַחַת *naḥaṯ*: A proper noun designating Nahath:

A. Son of Reuel (Gen. 36:13, 17; 1 Chr. 1:37).

B. Grandson of Elkanah (1 Chr. 6:26[11]).

C. A Levite (2 Chr. 31:13).

5185. נָחֵת ***nāḥēṯ:*** An adjective indicating going down, coming down. It is used of something in the process of descending, coming down in a geographical direction, e.g., an army (2 Kgs. 6:9).

5186. נָטָה ***nāṭāh:*** A verb meaning to stretch out, to extend; to pay attention. It is used often of simply extending or stretching out something: a hand, an arm is extended or a staff or javelin is pointed (Ex. 6:6; 7:5, 19; 9:22, 23; 10:12, 13, 21, 22; Josh. 8:18). It indicates spreading sackcloth for mourning (2 Sam. 21:10). The Lord extends His arm or hand to deliver His people (Ex. 6:6; Deut. 4:34; Jer. 32:21); or to bring judgments on them and the nations (Isa. 5:25; 23:11; Ezek. 6:14). The idiom, to stretch out one's hand against someone, means to act in a hostile manner toward that person (Job 15:25). It is used of setting up a tent or tabernacle, stretching it out (Gen. 12:8; 26:25; Ex. 33:7; 2 Sam. 6:17; 16:22). The Lord has stretched out the sky, the firmament of the heavens (Jer. 10:12). It is used of God stretching out a plumb line in judgment (2 Kgs. 21:13). It describes in its passive forms something stretched out, e.g., wings (Isa. 8:8), used figuratively. It is used figuratively of establishing a people, stretching out a tent (Jer. 10:12). It has the sense of turning something, inclining to: Balaam's ass turned aside (Num. 22:23); it is used of a person turning aside (2 Sam. 2:19). It has the figurative sense of inclining one's heart and mind a certain way, of giving attention: of turning from being loyal (1 Kgs. 2:28); turning from righteousness or justice (Ex. 23:2; 1 Sam. 8:3); or preventing it (Prov. 18:5). It is used of turning one's heart (mind) in a certain direction (1 Sam. 14:7); of being loyal (Josh. 24:23); it means to turn, to show love (*ḥeseḏ*) to someone (Ezra 7:28). It describes the apostasy of Solomon's heart turning after other gods and foreign women in his old age (1 Kgs. 11:2, 4). It is used of iniquities and sin thrusting away, turning away the good benefits of God from His people (Jer. 5:25). Finally, there are those who turn aside, away, in context to twisted, crooked ways (Ps. 125:5).

5187. נָטִיל ***naṭiyl:*** An adjective indicating to weigh out, to trade in something. It is used to describe persons who weigh out silver for trading and merchandising (Zeph. 1:11).

5188. נְטִיפָה ***n^eṭiypāh,*** נְטִפָה ***n^eṭipāh:*** A feminine noun indicating a pendent, an earring. It refers to pendants or earrings. It can be rendered chains (KJV, jewelry), earrings (Isa. 3:19). The meaning is not certain in the context of Judges 8:26 ("collars," KJV; "pendants," NIV, NASB).

5189. נְטִישׁוֹת ***n^eṭiyšôṯ:*** A feminine plural noun meaning branches, tendrils. It refers to fresh branches or shoots of vines (Isa. 18:5). It is used figuratively and literally of Jerusalem (Jer. 5:10); and of Moab (Jer. 48:32) whom God will judge.

5190. נָטַל ***nāṭal:*** A verb meaning to lift up, to carry, to offer. It means to place before someone options from which to chose (2 Sam. 24:12); or, in an unusual sense, of forcing or imposing something on someone (Lam. 3:28). It takes the sense of carrying something (Isa. 40:15). It has the sense of removing afflictions or danger, of delivering from something (Isa. 63:9).

5191. נְטַל ***n^{e}ṭal:*** An Aramaic verb meaning to lift up, to raise. It is used figuratively of lifting one's eyes to heaven, recognizing God's authority (Dan. 4:34[31]). It means to set something on its feet, to set it upright (Dan. 7:4).

5192. נֵטֶל ***nēṭel:*** A masculine noun indicating a weight, a burden. It indicates that something is hard to lift, weighty compared to other things its size and volume. The word describes sand as being heavy (Prov. 27:3).

5193. נָטַע ***nāṭa':*** A verb meaning to plant, to establish. It means to start, to establish, to found something: a garden (Gen. 2:8); a vineyard (Gen. 9:20); a tree or vine (Num. 24:6); vineyards, orchards (Josh. 24:13). It is used of God's planting His people Israel (Ex. 15:17); and of Jeremiah's "planting" nations by his prophetic words (Jer. 1:10; 2:21; 12:2; cf. 2 Sam. 7:10). It has the sense of to create or to set in order, to establish the heavens by God (Isa. 51:16); or of His placement of the ear in the human body (Ps. 94:9). It describes fasteners, nails being fixed, driven in (Eccl. 12:11).

5194. נֶטַע ***neṭa':*** A noun referring to a small tree, a shrub, or an herb. It refers to a healthy well-watered plant that puts forth young shoots, green growth (Job 14:9; Isa. 17:10). It is used to describe the people of Judah as God's plants which He cares for as a gardener (Isa. 5:7). The word is a proper noun in 1 Chronicles 4:23.

5195. נָטִיעַ ***nāṭiya':*** A masculine noun referring to a plant. It refers to a small tree, a shrub, or an herb. It is used figuratively to represent strong young plants (Ps. 144:12).

5196. נְטָעִים ***n^{e}ṭā'iym:*** A proper noun Netaim, a village. It refers to a small village in Moab (1 Chr. 4:23). See 5194.

5197. נָטַף ***nāṭap:*** A verb meaning to drip, to drop, to flow. It is used to describe rain (Judg. 5:4; Ps. 68:8[9]); and words which are like rain (Job 29:22). Lips may drip with honey (Prov. 5:3); and hands may drip with myrrh (Song 5:5). This word can also be taken figuratively, meaning to prophesy (Ezek. 21:2[7]; Amos 7:16). It is sometimes used to refer to false prophets (Mic. 2:6).

5198. נָטָף nāṭāp̱, נֶטֶף neṭep̱: I. A masculine noun referring to drops of stacte, resin. It was one of the spices used by the priests to prepare the sacred incense (Ex. 30:34).

II. A masculine noun referring to a drop. It is used of the evaporation of water into the upper atmosphere that returns as drops of rain (Job 36:27).

5199. נְטֹפָה n^eṭōp̱āh: A proper noun designating Netophah (Ezra 2:22; Neh. 7:26).

5200. נְטוֹפָתִי n^eṭôp̱āṯiy: A proper noun designating Netophathite (2 Sam. 23:28, 29; 2 Kgs. 25:23; 1 Chr. 2:54; 9:16; 11:30; 27:13, 15; Neh. 12:28; Jer. 40:8).

5201. נָטַר nāṭar: A verb meaning to keep, to take care of, to be angry, to maintain a grudge. It means to hold something against another person, to disdain him or her. This attitude was forbidden in Israel (Lev. 19:18). God never maintains this disposition toward His people forever (Ps. 103:9; Jer. 3:5, 12); but He does display His wrath at times (Nah. 1:2). It is used to describe an attitude of anger toward someone (Song 1:6). It is used in its participial form to refer to those who care for vineyards (Song 8:11, 12).

5202. נְטַר n^eṭar: An Aramaic verb meaning to keep. It means to hold on to, to keep in mind. It is used of Daniel's keeping his dream and vision in his mind (Dan. 7:28).

5203. נָטַשׁ nāṭaš: A verb meaning to forsake, to leave alone. The word occurs in relation to the land that should be unused ("forsaken") in the seventh year (Ex. 23:11); the Israelites who abandoned God (Deut. 32:15); Saul's father who forgot about the donkeys and began to worry about him (1 Sam. 10:2); David who left his flock with a shepherd (1 Sam. 17:20); the psalmist who pleaded with God not to turn from him (Ps. 27:9). This word is used once to mean to not permit when Laban was not allowed to kiss his grandchildren good-bye (Gen. 31:28).

5204. נִי niy: A masculine noun referring to wailing. It describes a mournful expression of despair and lament for something. It describes formal wailing expressed by uttering a lament (Ezek. 27:32).

5205. נִיד niyḏ: I. A masculine noun depicting comfort, solace. It refers to the attempt to comfort persons, to give them assurance of hope, to comfort through words of encouragement (Job 16:5).

II. A masculine noun referring to moving. It refers to moving one's lips to speak words of encouragement (Job 16:5).

5206. נִידָה niyḏāh: I. A feminine noun referring to something unclean. It refers to something polluted, detestable. It is used of Jerusalem, a city that had become detestable because of her sins and harlotries (Lam. 1:8).

II. A feminine noun indicating something that has been removed. It describes Jerusalem as removed by God in His judgments on her (Lam. 1:8).

5207. נִיחוֹחַ ***niyḥôaḥ***, נִחֹחַ ***niyḥōaḥ:*** A masculine noun referring to something soothing, pleasing. It is used of an odor that is acceptable to God, soothing (Gen. 8:21). It is used as an adjective often to describe a pleasing odor, aroma, a feature of an acceptable sacrifice to God (Ex. 29:18, 25, 41). It is the pleasing aroma created in an offering by fire to the Lord (Lev. 1:9, 13, 17, etc.). It was offered by Israel even to idols (Ezek. 6:13; 16:19; 20:28). It describes Israel as a people approved of the Lord (Ezek. 20:41).

5208. נִיחוֹחַ ***niyḥôaḥ***, נִחֹחַ ***niyḥōaḥ:*** An Aramaic masculine noun indicating something fragrant, soothing, pleasing. It is used to describe acceptable, pleasant-smelling sacrifices to the Lord (Ezra 6:10); and to a fragrant incense offered in honor of Daniel (Dan. 2:46).

5209. נִין ***niyn:*** A masculine noun indicating an offspring, a son. It refers to the descendants of persons, their posterity (Gen. 21:23). The wicked are said to have no offspring (Job 18:19). It indicates the survivors of a group of people, e.g., Babylon (Isa. 14:22).

5210. נִינְוֵה ***niyn^e wēh:*** A proper noun designating Nineveh, the great capital city of the Assyrian Empire. It served as the last capital of the nation and was destroyed in 612 B.C. by the Babylonians. It is the sole topic of two prophetic books. In the Book of Jonah, it received mercy from God and a period of reprieve (ca. 775–750 B.C.). But Nahum celebrated the destruction of the great city that had devastated and bloodied the cities and nations around it. Zephaniah indicated the complete collapse and enduring desolation of the city (Zeph. 2:13).

Its foundation is set in the time before the call of Abraham (Gen. 10:11, 12). Nimrod had a part in its founding. In ca. 701 B.C., Sennacherib fled there after his futile attempt to destroy Jerusalem (2 Kgs. 19:35–36; Isa. 37:37).

5211. נִיס ***niys:*** A masculine noun referring to one who flees. It refers to a person trying to escape from something, e.g., danger or terror (Jer. 48:44).

5212. נִיסָן ***niysān:*** A proper noun referring to the month Nisan. It refers to Nisan, the first month of the Old Testament year. It was equal to our March/April period of time (Neh. 2:1; Esth. 3:7), a period of thirty days. It was called Abib before the Babylonian exile. The Passover, The Feast of unleavened Bread, and the Feast of Firstfruits were festivals held during this month.

5213. נִיצוֹץ niyṣôṣ: A masculine noun indicating a spark. It refers to a flash of light indicating a fire or that something has been consumed (Isa. 1:31).

5214. נִיר niyr: A verb meaning to break up something. It is used in an agricultural sense of plowing untilled ground, but in context it is used of Israel's repentance and returning to God (Jer. 4:3; Hos. 10:12).

5215. נִיר niyr: A masculine noun signifying fallow, untilled ground. It indicates farming land, property owned that lies unplowed (Prov. 13:23). In Proverbs 21:4, it is rendered as plowing (KJV) but as lamp by other translators (NIV, NASB). Used figuratively, it indicates the hardened, untilled attitudes of the people of Judah and Israel that needed to be changed and refreshed (Jer. 4:3; Hos. 10:12).

5216. נִיר niyr, נֵר nēr, נֵיר neyr: A masculine noun meaning lamp, light. This word referred to the lamps of the Tabernacle (Ex. 27:20); the lamp in the Temple with Samuel (1 Sam. 3:3); the Word of God that lights the way (Ps. 119:105); and the noble wife that does not let her lamp go out at night (Prov. 31:18). The lamp can be used figuratively, as when God promised that David would always have a lamp before Him in Jerusalem (1 Kgs. 11:36; 2 Chr. 21:7). This word corresponds to the Aramaic noun *nûr* (5135), which can be masculine or feminine and means fire or flame. See the book of Daniel, where the fire does not harm the three Hebrews (see Dan. 3:27); and where fire describes the Ancient of Days (see Dan. 7:9, 10).

5217. נָכָא nāḵā': A verb meaning to drive out. It refers to forcing someone out of society or the land in disdain (Job 30:8).

5218. נָכֵא nāḵē', נָכָא nāḵā': I. An adjective meaning broken, beaten, crushed. It describes the life, the vitality, the drive, the spirit of a person that has been oppressed, broken by a grieved heart. A spirit broken, crushed, renders a person hopeless (Prov. 15:13; 17:22; 18:14).

II. An adjective meaning stricken, broken, beaten. It is used of persons left in utter despair from judgment on Moab; they are grieved from the calamity (Isa. 16:7).

5219. נְכֹאת n^eḵō'ṯ: A feminine noun meaning spice, an aromatic gum. It refers to a highly desired spice from Gilead (Gen. 37:25) and transported by the Israelites to Egypt; but it was found in Canaan also (Gen. 43:11).

5220. נֶכֶד neḵeḏ: A masculine noun referring to descendants. It refers to the posterity and later offspring from a person or family (Gen. 21:23). The offspring of the wicked was often cut off, according to Bildad (Job 18:19). It is similar to survivors when used of a nation, e.g., Babylon (Isa. 14:22).

5221. נָכָה nāḵāh: A verb meaning to beat, to strike, to wound. There are many instances of striking physically (Ex. 21:15, 19; Job 16:10; Ps. 3:7[8]; Song 5:7). This word is also used in a different sense, as when the men of Sodom and Gomorrah were stricken blind by the two angels (Gen. 19:11); when a priest stuck a fork into the kettle (1 Sam. 2:14); when people clapped their hands (2 Kgs. 11:12); or when people verbally abused Jeremiah (Jer. 18:18). God struck the Egyptians with plagues (Ex. 3:20); and struck people down in judgment (Isa. 5:25).

5222. נֵכֶה nēḵeh: An adjective referring to smiting, attacking. It is related to the root of the verb *nāḵāh*, to smite, strike. It refers to hitting, smiting someone physically or in words (Ps. 35:15).

5223. נָכֶה nāḵeh: An adjective meaning crippled, smitten. It refers to the result of a physical accident or attack. In context Saul's son had been dropped as a child and the bones in his feet were broken as a result, and he was crippled (2 Sam. 4:4; 9:3). It is used in the phrase *nāḵeh rû(a)ḥ*, smitten of spirit, humble (Isa. 66:2).

5224. נְכוֹ n^e^ḵô: A proper noun designating Necho, an Egyptian Pharaoh who warned Josiah not to fight against him. He did not listen and was killed. It would appear that the Lord used this Pharaoh to warn the Judean king. He removed Jehoahaz as king in Judah and set up Jehoiakim (Eliakim) in his place (2 Chr. 36:2–4), taking Jehoahaz captive to Egypt.

5225. נָכוֹן nāḵôn: A proper noun designating Nacon (2 Sam. 6:6).

5226. נֵכַח nēḵaḥ: An adverb meaning before, against, opposite of. It refers to a physical location that lies opposite, in front of something. It has the sense of opposite, in front of (Ex. 14:2). In Ezekiel 46:9, it means what is opposite, directly ahead of something. See 5227 also. This word is simply a form of that word.

5227. נֹכַח nōḵaḥ: An adverb meaning before, against, opposite of. See 5226 also. It has the meaning indicated there (Num. 19:4, with preposition *'el*, toward). It is used figuratively often. The phrase *nōḵaḥ yhwh* means what reflects the Lord's will, what is acceptable to the Lord (Judg. 18:6). The preposition *l^e^* on the following word strengthens the sense of opposite (Josh. 15:7). It has the sense of, on behalf of, with regard to, when used with the verb to pray (Gen. 25:21). It means directly or straight ahead with the verbs of looking (Prov. 4:25). It is used metaphorically of something being before the eyes of the Lord (Prov. 5:21). The idiom "in front of your face" means in someone's presence (Jer. 17:16; Lam.

2:19; Ezek. 14:3), especially in the presence of the Lord.

5228. נָכֹחַ na<u>k</u>ōaḥ: An adjective meaning straightforward, honest. In 2 Samuel 15:3, it is used to describe a legal case as straightforward, obviously deserving amends. In Proverbs 8:9, it describes wisdom's words as straightforward, not perverted, to the one who has the right attitude to receive them. In Proverbs 24:26, the adjective describes words spoken honestly, without partiality (cf. Prov. 24:23–25); lips speaking this way kiss the hearer. The word occurs as a noun in Isaiah 57:2 and means straightforwardness or honesty. For the feminine form of the word, see *n*[e]*<u>k</u>ōḥāh* (5229).

5229. נְכֹחָה n[e]<u>k</u>ōḥāh: An adjective referring to something as right, upright. It is used to modify a land's social practices as upright, just (Isa. 26:10). It indicates this is correct, straight, upright dealing (Isa. 30:10; 59:14); correct practice in a situation (Amos 3:10).

5230. נָכַל nā<u>k</u>al: A verb meaning to be deceitful, to cheat. It indicates a conscious plan to deceive someone, to plan something against (Gen. 37:18); to intend to trick or deal cunningly with (Num. 25:18). It describes the plans and actions to oppress Israel in deceitful ways (Ps. 105:25). It refers to the cheat or deceptive person himself (Mal. 1:14).

5231. נֵכֶל nē<u>k</u>el: A masculine noun referring to trick, deceitfulness. A noun from the root meaning of nā<u>k</u>al describing an act of deception, trickery used to deceive a person or a people (Num. 25:18).

5232. נְכַס n[e]<u>k</u>as: An Aramaic noun indicating goods, property. It refers to resources or wealth. It indicates the royal wealth or treasury (Ezra 6:8); or the property and goods of any person (Ezra 7:26).

5233. נֶכֶס ne<u>k</u>es: A masculine noun indicating riches, wealth. It refers to all kinds of property and wealth in general. In context it refers to the riches gained as spoils of war (Josh. 22:8). It refers to wealth and material prosperity in general (2 Chr. 1:11, 12). These things are considered as gifts from God (Eccl. 5:19[18]; 6:2).

5234. נָכַר nā<u>k</u>ar: A verb meaning to pretend, to consider carefully, to investigate, to acknowledge, to recognize, to make unrecognizable. This verb is used mainly in the causative stem to indicate the process of investigation, knowing something, or knowing how to do something. Jacob told Laban to investigate to see if he could recognize his gods in any of Jacob's tents (Gen. 31:32); Tamar challenged Judah to investigate the seal and cord she had to see if he could recognize them (Gen. 38:25, 26). The Hebrew word is also used to indicate someone already known previously (1 Kgs. 18:7; 20:41). The word is found metaphorically meaning to acknowledge, to follow, or to refuse to do so: evildoers refused to acknowledge the light (God's laws) and did not walk according to God's laws (Job 24:13). When the word is used with an infinitive, it means to know how to do something or to know something so that a person acts in a certain way. Judeans, who had intermarried with foreigners, had children who did not know how to speak the language of Judah, which was Hebrew (Neh. 13:24).

Finally, in the reflexive stem, the word means to present oneself in such a way as to fool others (1 Kgs. 14:5, 6); or to hide one's identity, as Joseph hid his identity from his brothers (Gen. 42:7). In the case of children, they reflected their characters by their actions, revealing their essential dispositions (Prov. 20:11).

5235. נֶכֶר neḵer, נֹכֶר nōḵer: A masculine noun meaning disaster, calamity. The meaning derives from the idea of strangeness (cf. *nēḵār* [5236]); a calamity interrupts the normal flow of life. The word occurs in Job 31:3 where it refers to calamity as the punishment of iniquity. In Obadiah 1:12, the word occurs along with several words of similar meaning (cf. Obad. 1:13, 14), describing a time in which Judah met with calamity.

5236. נֵכָר nēḵār: A masculine noun meaning foreign. The word comes from a root meaning to scrutinize, perhaps drawing on the idea that people look closely at something foreign or strange (see *nāḵar*[5234]). The word modifies other nouns to signify a foreigner or a foreign god. Foreigners with their false gods posed a threat to Israel's service to the Lord (Deut. 32:12; Judg. 10:16; Mal. 2:11); sometimes even infiltrating the Temple service (Neh. 13:30; Ezek. 44:9). They also posed a physical threat at times (Ps. 144:7; Isa. 62:8; Jer. 5:19). However, foreigners sometimes turned to Israel's God (Isa. 56:3, 6). The word also refers (with other words) to foreign land (Ps. 137:4; Jer. 5:19); and a foreign power (Ps. 144:7).

5237. נָכְרִי nokriy: An adjective meaning strange, foreign, stranger, foreigner. It refers to someone who was not part of the family (Gen. 31:15; cf. Gen 31:14; Ps. 69:8[9]), especially the extended family of Israel (Deut. 17:15). Under the Law, strangers were not allowed to rule in Israel (Deut. 17:15); they were not released from their debts every seven years as Hebrews were (Deut. 15:3); and could be sold certain ceremonially unclean food (Deut. 14:21). Strangers were regarded as unholy (Deut. 14:21); and were often looked down on (Ruth 2:10; Job 19:15). Some hope for the conversion of foreigners was offered (Ruth 2:10; 1 Kgs. 8:41, 43); but with this word, more emphasis was placed on avoiding the defilement of foreign women (1 Kgs. 11:1; Ezra 10:2, 10, 11, 14, 17, 18, 44; Prov. 6:24); and foreign ways (Isa. 2:6; Jer. 2:21; Zeph. 1:8). The word *gēr* (1616), meaning sojourner, focuses more sympathetically on foreigners in Israel.

5238. נְכֹת ***n^{e}k̲ōt̲:*** A masculine noun referring to treasures, goods. It is used of any material wealth that a person possesses, especially a king (2 Kgs. 20:13; Isa. 39:2); a king's treasure house.

5239. נָלָה ***nālāh:*** A verb meaning to cease, to stop, to make an end. It means to stop, an activity or an attitude, to bring it to a close (Isa. 33:1).

5240. נְמִבְזָה ***n^{e}mib̲zāh:*** An adjective meaning vile. It has the sense of useless, worthless, useless booty or spoil gained in war (1 Sam. 15:9). The King James Version understands a strong sense of something corrupt or despicable.

5241. נְמוּאֵל ***n^{e}mû'ēl:*** A proper noun designating Nemuel (Num. 26:9, 12; 1 Chr. 4:24).

5242. נְמוּאֵלִי ***n^{e}mû'ēliy:*** A proper noun designating Nemuelite (Num. 26:12).

5243. נָמַל ***nāmal:*** A noun assumed to be the root for the Hebrew word *n^{e}mālāh* (5244), meaning ant (see Prov. 6:6; 30:25). The actual word does not exist in Scripture. Scholars assume that the word means cut or circumcised (Gen. 17:11; Job 14:2; 18:16; 24:24; Ps. 37:2).

5244. נְמָלָה ***n^{e}mālāh:*** A feminine noun meaning ant. It is used in Proverbs 6:6; 30:25 to set forth the ant as a model of wise living, wisdom (forethought), and industriousness.

5245. נְמַר ***n^{e}mar:*** It is an Aramaic masculine noun depicting a leopard. It is found in Daniel describing one of the beasts of his night visions (Dan. 7:6).

5246. נָמֵר ***nāmēr:*** A masculine noun meaning leopard. It refers to a panther, a large wild stalking (Hos. 13:7) animal of the cat family with spots (Jer. 13:23). It was known for its speed (Hab. 1:8). It is used in a metaphor to represent the splendor and mysterious quality of a bridegroom (Song 4:8). In the messianic kingdom, even the leopard will be tame (Isa. 11:6). It describes the Lord stalking His own rebellious people (Hos. 13:7).

5247. נִמְרָה ***nimrāh:*** A proper noun designating Nimrah (Num. 32:3).

5248. נִמְרֹד ***nimrōd̲:*** A proper noun designating Nimrod:

A. An ancient king of antiquity (possibly Sargon I of Akkad) who was celebrated both as a great warrior and as a kingdom builder in the area of ancient southern Mesopotamia and later in northern Mesopotamia near the Tigris River. Nineveh, Babylon, and Akkad are just three of the foundational cities he set up.

B. Another name for Assyria, the ancient founder of the nation. It stands in Hebrew poetry in parallelism with Assyria.

5249. נִמְרִים ***nimriym:*** A proper noun designating Nimrim (Isa. 15:6; Jer. 48:34).

5250. נִמְשִׁי ***nimšiy:*** A proper noun designating Nimshi (1 Kgs. 19:16; 2 Kgs. 9:2, 14, 20; 2 Chr. 22:7).

5251. נֵס ***nēs:*** A masculine noun indicating a banner, a standard. It refers to a symbol or sign representing a cause, a person, God: a standard, a representation of the Lord (Ex. 17:15); and the name of an altar dedicated to the Lord. It indicates a pole on which to display something (Num. 21:8, 9). It signifies a sign representing Zion (Isa. 31:9; Jer. 4:6); or a tragedy that could serve as a *nēs*, a warning or a sign (Num. 26:10). It indicates a flag or a symbol to rally around (Ex. 17:15; Isa. 18:3). The Root of Jesse will stand as an ensign, a signal for the people (Isa. 11:10).

5252. נְסִבָּה ***n*****e*****sibbāh:*** A feminine noun indicating a turn of events, a cause. It refers to the way things turn out; they change quickly, often unexpectedly or surprisingly (2 Chr. 10:15). In context God is in charge of the turn of events.

5253. נָסַג ***nāsag:*** A verb meaning to move away, to be turned. It means to change something from what it was, possibly by moving it: a boundary, a boundary marker (Deut. 19:14; 27:17; Prov. 22:28); any object (Mic. 6:14). It is used figuratively of being turned away from God, justice (Isa. 59:13, 14); changing God's standards (Hos. 5:10). It describes God's accusations and reproaches of the people being turned back (Mic. 2:6).

5254. נָסָה ***nāsāh:*** A verb meaning to test, to try, to prove. Appearing nearly forty times in the Old Testament, this term often refers to God testing the faith and faithfulness of human beings, including Abraham (Gen. 22:1); the nation of Israel (Ex. 15:25; 16:4; 20:20; Deut. 8:2, 16; 13:3[4]; Judg. 2:22; 3:1, 4); Hezekiah (2 Chr. 32:31); David (Ps. 26:2). Although people were forbidden from putting God to the test, they often did so (Ex. 17:2, 7; Num. 14:22; Deut. 6:16; 33:8; Ps. 78:18, 41, 56; 95:9; 106:14; Isa. 7:12). Testing, however, does not always suggest tempting or enticing someone to sin, as when the Queen of Sheba tested Solomon's wisdom (1 Kgs. 10:1; 2 Chr. 9:1); and Daniel's physical appearance was tested after a ten-day vegetarian diet (Dan. 1:12, 14). Finally, this term can refer to the testing of equipment, such as swords or armor (1 Sam. 17:39).

5255. נָסַח ***nāsaḥ:*** A verb meaning to tear down, to tear out. In the Hebrew Old Testament, this verb almost always occurs in poetical literature and always occurs in contexts of judgment. For example, as the result of disobedience to God's covenant,

He promised to remove Israel from the land. According to the psalmist, God would snatch the unrighteous from the comforts of their homes for putting trust in material wealth rather than in Him (Ps. 52:5[7]). Similarly, Proverbs 2:22 indicates that the righteous would remain in the land while the unrighteous would be removed from it. Finally, the Lord promised to tear down or destroy the house of the proud person (Prov. 15:25).

5256. נְסַח ***n*^e*saḥ:*** An Aramaic verb meaning to be pulled out. Found only once in the Old Testament, this word refers to the removal of a beam of wood from the house of any person who altered the decree of King Cyrus. As punishment for disregarding the decree, the offending party would be hung or impaled on the wooden beam (Ezra 6:11).

5257. נְסִיךְ ***nāsiyk̲:*** A masculine noun meaning a drink offering, a molten image. Derived from a verb meaning to pour out, this term refers to the pouring out of a drink offering or libation (Deut. 32:38). Here God mockingly inquires about the whereabouts of the gods that drank the drink offerings of wine offered by their pagan worshipers. In Daniel 11:8, this term refers to metal idols or images brought home by the Egyptian ruler Ptolemy after defeating the Syrian army.

5258. נָסַךְ ***nāsak̲:*** A verb meaning to pour out. Frequently, this term refers to pouring out drink offerings or libations. These offerings usually employed wine (Hos. 9:4); or another fermented drink (Num. 28:7). But David offered water as a drink offering to the Lord (2 Sam. 23:16; 1 Chr. 11:18). In the books of Moses (Num. 28:7), God clearly outlined instructions for making proper sacrifices. For example, He prohibited pouring a drink offering on the altar of incense (Ex. 30:9). Scripture clearly condemned the practice of making drink offerings to false gods (Jer. 19:13; 44:17–19, 25); a practice that angered God and incurred His judgment (Jer. 7:18; 32:29; Ezek. 20:28). Infrequently, this Hebrew term referred to the casting of idols from metal (Isa. 40:19; 44:10); and in one instance, to a deep sleep that the Lord poured over the inhabitants of Jerusalem (Isa. 29:10).

5259. נָסַךְ ***nāsak̲:*** A verb meaning to stretch out, to cover. It means to intertwine, to spread out something like a net or a veil. It is used figuratively of a covering that surrounds, hinders, or enshrouds the sight of the nations in a spiritual or religious sense (Isa. 25:7). It indicates pouring out a drink offering (massēk̲āh), concluding a treaty or alliance (Isa. 30:1; KJV, "cover with a covering").

5260. נְסַךְ ***n*^e*sak̲:*** An Aramaic verb indicating to pour out, to offer a liquid sacrifice. It means literally in context to pour out a drink offering, that is, to offer a sacrifice in honor of someone, in this case in honor of Daniel for reciting and interpreting the king's dream (Dan. 2:46).

5261. נְסַךְ *nᵉsak̲:* An Aramaic masculine singular noun meaning drink offering, libation. Its only occurrence in the Hebrew Bible is in Ezra 7:17 where Artaxerxes provided offerings and sacrifices to be delivered for the Temple in Jerusalem. This term is related to the verb *nᵉsak̲* (5260), meaning to pour out. For the Hebrew cognate of this noun, see *nesek̲* (5262).

5262. נֶסֶךְ *nēsek̲*, נֵסֶךְ *nēsek̲:* A masculine singular noun meaning drink offering, libation, molten image. The most common usage of the term referred to a liquid offering that was poured out (*nāsak̲*[5258]) (Gen. 35:14; Lev. 23:37; Num. 15:5, 7, 10, 24). It is employed both for offerings made to *Yahweh* as well as to foreign deities (2 Kgs. 16:13; Isa. 57:6). In four passages, the term is used for a molten image (i.e., a "poured out" thing) (Isa. 41:29; 48:5; Jer. 10:14).

5263. נָסַס *nāsas:* I. A verb meaning to be sick. It is used in its participial form to refer to a sick person, one who is sick (Isa. 10:18).

II. A verb meaning to raise as a beacon. The verb is understood to be from a root meaning to raise up a sign. In its participial form, it, therefore, refers to a standard-bearer (*nēs nōsēs*).

5264. נָסַס *nāsas:* I. A verb meaning to sparkle. It is taken by some translators to be from a verb meaning to gleam, to display, to shine. It indicates the features of the stones of a crown, that is, sparkling, shining. The sparkling stones symbolize God's people (Zech. 9:16).

II. A verb meaning to raise as a beacon. It is used to indicate the raising up of a symbol or a sign for something. It is used in a reflexive stem to indicate the raising of God's people as an ensign for the land of Israel (Zech. 9:16).

5265. נָסַע *nāsa':* A verb indicating to set out; to travel, to journey. It has the basic meaning of moving something out, pulling it out, taking it away; causing something to move out: Samson pulled out the gates (foundations included) and carried them away (Judg. 16:3); to set out on a journey (Gen. 33:12, 17; Ex. 12:37); to make or cause to set out (Ex. 15:22; Ps. 78:26, 52); of being stirred up by God (Num. 11:31). It describes pulling up a tent in order to move on (Isa. 38:12). It is used figuratively of a person's death, his or her "tent-rope" is pulled up (Job 4:21). It describes the quarrying, cutting, and carrying away of stones (1 Kgs. 5:17[31]; Eccl. 10:9). With *min* (4480) following, it means to journey or to depart from (Gen. 37:17).

5266. נָסַק *nāsaq:* A verb meaning to ascend. It means to go upward. It is used figuratively of ascending to

God in heaven to His abode (Ps. 139:8).

5267. נְסַק ***n^{e}saq:*** An Aramaic verb meaning to take up, to lift. It means to bring up an object, to carry it higher. It is used of carrying up persons (Dan. 3:22; 6:23[24]).

5268. נִסְרֹךְ ***nisrōḵ:*** A masculine proper noun Nisrock. It refers to a pagan god worshiped by Assyrians in a temple at Nineveh (2 Kgs. 19:37; Isa. 37:38).

5269. נֵעָה ***nēʿāh:*** A proper noun designating Neah (Josh. 19:13).

5270. נֹעָה ***nōʿāh:*** A proper noun designating Noah, the daughter of Zelophehad (Num. 26:33; 27:1; 36:11; Josh. 17:3).

5271. נְעוּרִים ***n^{e}ʿûriym,*** נְעוּרוֹת ***n^{e}ʿûrôṯ:*** I. A masculine plural abstract noun. It refers to the early stages and years of a person's life and the experiences and characteristics of that time: every person, all humankind experiences this time of life (Gen. 8:21). It is a time when skills are best learned (Gen. 46:34); a time of dependence on parents (Lev. 22:13; Num. 30:3[4], 16[17]). Even a nation has a time of youth (Hos. 2:15[17]). A husband is to be satisfied with the wife of his youth (Prov. 5:18; Mal. 2:14, 15).

II. A feminine plural abstract noun. It is used to refer to the early period or stage of a person's life, the early years and its experiences and characteristics. It is used of a nation's youth, its early formative years (Jer. 32:30).

5272. נְעִיאֵל ***n^{e}ʿiyʾēl:*** A proper noun designating Neiel (Josh. 19:27).

5273. נָעִים ***nāʿiym:*** I. An adjective meaning pleasant, delightful. It is used of persons who are pleasing, a joy to be around. They display attitudes that please others, such as David and Jonathan (2 Sam. 1:23). It refers to those who are delightful to enjoy (Job 36:11; Ps. 16:11); a life that has experienced good things and joy (Ps. 16:6, 11). A famous proverb illustrates the meaning of the word: brothers living together in peace, getting along with each other (Ps. 133:1). The Lord's name is called pleasant (NASB, lovely) (Ps. 135:3). Wise words and wisdom generate pleasantness (Prov. 22:18). It describes a bridegroom as delightful, pleasing (Song 1:16).

II. An adjective meaning sweet, sweet-sounding. It is used to describe David, the singer and writer of psalms, as the sweet, pleasant, pleasing psalmist of Israel (2 Sam. 23:1). It indicates pleasant-sounding music (Ps. 81:2[3]), sweet to soul and mind.

5274. נָעַל ***nāʿal:*** I. A verb meaning to bolt, to bar, to lock. It indicates the securing of a door or doors (Judg. 3:23, 24; 2 Sam. 13:17, 18). It is used in a figurative sense of a virgin whose love and attentions are locked up in her for her future husband (Song 4:12).

II. A verb meaning to shod, to furnish with footwear. It indicates furnishing sandals or some kind of footwear to persons in a general sense (2 Chr. 28:15). It is used of God's putting shoes of the highest quality on His peoples' feet (Ezek. 16:10).

5275. נַעַל na'al: A feminine noun referring to a sandal, shoe. It refers to basic footwear in the Middle East in ancient times. It may indicate a sandal secured by leather straps (1 Kgs. 2:5; Isa. 5:27). It is asserted in a figurative sense that the Israelites' sandals did not wear out during their forty years in the desert; God cared for all their needs (Deut. 29:5[4]). It is used in several idioms: A sandal was used to strike a person who would not perform his levirate marriage duties (Deut. 25:9, 10); to throw one's shoe over meant to take possession of something (Ps. 60:8[10]; 108:9[10]); wearing sandals could be a mark of beauty (Song 7:1[2]); removing one's sandals could be a sign of mourning (Isa. 20:2; Ezek. 24:17, 23). A pair of sandals indicates an insignificant price for something (Amos 2:6; 8:6).

5276. נָעֵם nā'ēm: A verb meaning to be pleasant, to be sweet, to be beautiful. It refers to what is pleasing, comfortable, delightful to enjoy: It refers to the land of Canaan (Gen. 49:15); to a person (2 Sam. 1:26); to spoken words (Ps. 141:6); to knowledge and wisdom (Prov. 2:10). It is used of an improper experience of pleasantness from doing what is not right (Prov. 9:17). More properly, it refers to the pleasantness, delightfulness of a bride (Song 7:6[7]). It depicts a nation, for even a nation has a national splendor and character (Ezek. 32:19).

5277. נַעַם na'am: A proper noun used to designate Naam, the son of Caleb (1 Chr. 4:15).

5278. נֹעַם nō'am: A masculine noun meaning pleasantness, beauty. It is used of something that can be seen or beheld, e.g., the beauty or splendor of the Lord (Ps. 27:4). It has the sense of approval of or delight in someone (Ps. 90:17). Words and wisdom both can be pleasant to a person (Prov. 3:17; 15:26; 16:24). It is used in a figurative way to name a shepherd's staff representing a people (Zech. 11:7, 10).

5279. נַעֲמָה na'amāh: A proper noun designating Naamah:

A. A sister of Tubal-Cain (Gen. 4:22).

B. The mother of Rehoboam (1 Kgs. 14:21, 31; 2 Chr. 12:13).

C. A city in Judah (Josh. 15:41).

5280. נַעֲמִי na'amiy: A proper noun distinguishing a Naamite, a descendant of Naaman (5283,A) (Num. 26:40).

5281. נָעֳמִי nā'omiy: A proper noun designating Naomi. The name means "pleasantness, delight." She traveled to Moab to live out a severe famine in Israel with her two sons and her husband. While there only she and her two daughters-in-law were left alive. Ruth, a Moabitess, was so impressed with her mother-in-law that she decided to cling to her, live with her, and adopt her God, land, and people. In the providence of God, she married Boaz and bore a son named Obed. Obed was the father of Jesse, who was the father of the great king David. Naomi was made "delightful" again after much bitterness.

5282. נַעֲמָן ***na'amān:*** A masculine abstract noun indicating pleasantness, delightfulness. It describes pretty plants, grown for pleasure, but in honor of a pagan god, exacerbating Israel's harlotry and idolatry (Isa. 17:10).

5283. נַעֲמָן ***na'amān:*** A proper noun designating Naaman:

A. A descendant of Benjamin, son of Rachel.

B. A Syrian general blessed by the Lord (2 Kgs. 5:1–2) who was willing to follow the instructions of Elisha the prophet. By dipping himself seven times in the Jordan River, he was cured of leprosy. Elisha noted that this event demonstrated that there was a God and a prophet in Israel (2 Kgs. 5:8, 15). Naman took dirt from Israel to Aram and vowed to recognize only the Lord of Israel as the true and only God (2 Kgs. 5:7–8).

5284. נַעֲמָתִי ***na'amāṯiy:*** A proper noun designating a Naamathite, an inhabitant of Naamah, an unknown site (Job 2:11; 11:1; 20:1; 42:9).

5285. נַעֲצוּץ ***na'aṣûṣ:*** A masculine noun denoting a thornbush. It refers to a small shrub featuring sharp-pointed needles sticking out from it. In context a figurative use of the word showed how extensive the attack of Judah's enemies will be (Isa. 7:19). Since it was not considered a desirable plant, in the time of God's blessings, it will, figuratively and literally, be replaced (Isa. 55:13).

5286. נָעַר ***nā'ar:*** A verb meaning to growl, to yell. It describes the sound made by lion cubs in their desire to hurt prey. It is used figuratively of the Babylonians whom God would overthrow utterly (Jer. 51:38).

5287. נָעַר ***nā'ar:*** A verb meaning to shake out, to overthrow, to sweep. It means to shake off, to defeat by casting off: the Egyptians in the midst of the Red Sea by an overwhelming power of surging waters (Ex. 14:27; Ps. 136:15); one's enemies by exercising force (Judg. 16:20). It has the idiomatic sense of disciplining, separating persons from their wealth and families, getting rid of (Neh. 5:13). It indicates shaking one's hands to show innocence (Isa. 33:15). It describes the shaking down, the judging of a nation (Isa. 33:9). It is used figuratively of Jerusalem shaking off the dust of captivity (Isa. 52:2). Its figurative use describes a person shaken off like a locust by affliction from God

(Ps. 109:23); or the wicked shaken out of the earth, swept away, removed (Job 38:13).

5288. נַעַר ***na'ar:*** A masculine noun referring to a boy, a young man, a servant. It is used of a young person, a boy (Gen. 19:4); one old enough to serve in battle or as a personal private force (Gen. 14:24; 1 Sam. 21:2[3]; 30:13, 17); or as a helper in the army (1 Sam. 14:1). It is used regularly to refer to a young male servant (Gen. 18:7; 22:3); or an attendant to the king (Esth. 2:2). It is written *na'arâ* (5291) several times but should be read as *na'ărāh,* girl, young girl (see Gen. 24:14). Its plural form *ne'ārîm* may include both male and female persons (Ruth 2:21; Job 1:19). A young man, a lad, a young boy was not capable of ruling a land (Eccl. 10:16). It figuratively describes Israel in its formative early years (Hos. 11:1).

5289. נַעַר ***na'ar:*** I. A masculine noun meaning a young one, a young person. It is the translation given to the word in Zechariah 11:16 (KJV, NIV) to indicate persons who need to be cared for, instructed, prohibited.

II. A masculine noun meaning scattered. It is understood as related to 5287 and refers, therefore, to those shaken off, scattered (Zech. 11:16, NASB).

5290. נֹעַר ***nō'ar:*** A masculine noun referring to childhood, youth. It is considered a time when life is exciting, and a person is energetic and healthy (Job 33:25); and it is not a time to die (Job 36:14; Ps. 88:15[16]). It is a time when intimate and healthy relationships can begin to be formed (Prov. 29:21).

5291. נַעֲרָה ***na'ărāh:*** A feminine noun referring to a girl, a young woman, a maidservant. It is used of a young girl (2 Kgs. 5:2); or young daughters (Job 41:5[40:29]). It indicates a young girl who is marriageable (Gen. 24:14, 16, 28, 55, 57; Ex. 2:5; Prov. 9:3); and to those attending her (Gen. 24:61). It points out a virgin (Deut. 22:15, 16, 23, 29; Judg. 21:12; 1 Kgs. 1:2). It is used figuratively of the maidservants or attendants of wisdom personified (Prov. 9:3). It describes young female gleaners in the fields (Ruth 2:5, 8, 22, 23).

5292. נַעֲרָה ***na'ărāh,*** נַעֲרָתָה ***na'ărāṯāh:*** A proper noun designating Naarah:

A. The wife of Ashur (1 Chr. 4:5, 6).

B. A town located on the border of Ephraim (Josh. 16:7).

5293. נַעֲרַי ***na'ăray:*** A proper noun designating Naarai (1 Chr. 11:37).

5294. נְעַרְיָה ***ne'aryāh:*** A proper noun designating Neariah:

A. A descendant of David (1 Chr. 3:22, 23).

B. A Simeonite (1 Chr. 4:42).

5295. נַעֲרָן ***na'ărān:*** A proper noun designating Naaran (1 Chr. 7:28).

5296. נְעֹרֶת **n^e*'ōreṯ:*** A feminine noun meaning string, tow. Tow is a weak "rope" of coarse and broken fibers from flax, hemp, or similar material. String is a weak fastener compared to a regular rope or cord and is easily snapped (Judg. 16:9). Tow or string could be used to start a fire (tinder; NASB, Judg. 16:9; Isa. 1:31).

5297. נֹף ***nōp̱:*** A proper noun designating *nōp̱*, Memphis, the name of an ancient capital of Egypt (Old Kingdom) but always a place of significance throughout Egypt's history. It was an important religious center where certain great creator gods resided (e.g., Ptah). It was usually condemned roundly and judged harshly by the prophets (Isa. 19:13; Jer. 2:16). Certain exiles from Judah settled in this area and received a prophetic word from Jeremiah (44:1, 15).

5298. נֶפֶג ***nep̱eg:*** A proper noun designating Nepheg:

A. A Levite (Ex. 6:21).

B. A son of David (2 Sam. 5:15; 1 Chr. 3:7; 14:6).

5299. נָפָה ***nāphāh,*** נָפוֹת ***nāpôṯ:*** I. A feminine noun referring to a winnow, a sieve. It was a farm instrument used to separate chaff and other impurities from certain foods, grain, etc., by letting the grain pass through a sieve or a winnow but holding back the undesirable parts (Isa. 30:28).

II. A feminine noun indicating height, elevation, a region, a border. It refers to the highlands, the tops of low-lying hills (Josh. 11:2; 12:23; 1 Kgs. 4:11).

III. A proper noun. Naphoth refers to an area just south of Mount Carmel on the Mediterranean coast (Josh. 11:2; 12:23; 17:11; 1 Kgs. 4:11).

5300. נְפוּשְׁסִים **n^e*p̱ûš*^{e}*siym:*** A proper noun designating Nephushesim, Nephussim (NASB, NIV, Ezra 2:50; Neh. 7:52). For the King James Version, see 5304.

5301. נָפַח ***nāp̱aḥ:*** A verb indicating to blow, to breathe, to boil. It is used of projecting one's breath but in a figurative sense of God blowing the breath of life into Adam (Gen. 2:7). It refers to a fire that is not blown, meaning not fanned to expand it (Job 20:26). It means to harm or to cause failure, perhaps death (Job 31:39). It is used of blowing something like smoke (Job 41:20[12]); of a blacksmith's use of something like bellows to heat up his coals (Isa. 54:16; Ezek. 22:20, 21). It depicts the rising steam of a bubbling pot (Jer. 1:13). It is used of the four winds blowing to create life (Ezek. 37:9). It is used of either blowing on an offering or sniffing it in disdain (Mal. 1:13); or of something being swept away by the Lord (Hag. 1:9).

5302. נֹפַח ***nōp̱aḥ:*** A proper noun designating Nophah (Num. 21:30).

5303. נְפִילִים **n^e*p̱iyliym:*** A masculine noun used only in the plural meaning giants. The celebrated, puzzling passage where this term is first used is Genesis 6:4 which merely transliterates the Hebrew word into English as Nephilim. These beings evidently appeared on the earth in the ancient past when divine beings cohabited with woman, and Nephilim, the mighty men or warriors of great fame, were the offspring. This huge race of Nephilim struck fear into the Israelite spies who had gone up to survey the land of Canaan (see Num. 13:31–33). The sons of Anak, a tall race of people, came from the Nephilim (Num. 13:33; cf. Deut. 2:10, 11; 9:2; Josh. 15:14). Ezekiel 32:21, 27 may have the Nephilim in mind, possibly equating them with the mighty men or mighty warriors in the passage. These beings were not divine but only at best great, powerful men.

5304. נְפִישְׁסִים ***n^e^piyš^e^siym:*** A proper noun designating Nephishesim, Nephussim (KJV, Ezra 2:50; Neh. 7:52). For the New American Standard Version and New International Version, see 5300.

5305. נָפִישׁ ***nāpiyš:*** A proper noun designating Naphish (Gen. 25:15; 1 Chr. 1:31; 5:19).

5306. נֹפֶךְ ***nōpek:*** A masculine noun indicating a precious stone, turquoise or emerald. It refers to a precious stone worn on the breastpiece of the high priest in the second row of stones. It represented one of the tribes of Israel (Ex. 28:18; 39:11). It was used to trade and barter for goods (Ezek. 27:16; 28:13).

5307. נָפַל ***nāpal:*** A verb meaning to fall, to lie, to prostrate oneself, to overthrow. This common Hebrew verb carries many possible variations in meaning, much like the English verb to fall. For instance, it can be used literally of someone or something falling down (Gen. 14:10; 1 Sam. 4:18; 17:49; 2 Kgs. 6:5); or into a pit (Ex. 21:33; Deut. 22:4). It is employed for inanimate objects like walls, towers, trees, and hailstones (1 Kgs. 20:30; Eccl. 11:3). It is used idiomatically for a violent death, especially in battle (Judg. 5:27; 1 Sam. 4:10; Amos 7:17); and for the overthrow of a city (Jer. 51:8). The word also describes those who fall prostrate before God or those in authority (Gen. 50:18; 2 Chr. 20:18). With the preposition *'al* (5921), meaning upon, it carries the meaning to attack (literally, to fall upon) (Job 1:19); to desert (to fall away) (2 Kgs. 25:11; Jer. 21:9); to be overcome by sleep or emotion (to fall into) (Gen. 4:5; 15:12; Josh. 2:9; 1 Sam. 17:32; Neh. 6:16). It is used to express the idea of being bedridden or debilitated (Ex. 21:18); to be overtaken (lit., to fall into the hands of) (Judg. 15:18; Lam. 1:7); and to be born (Isa. 26:18). In its causative usage, it also takes the meaning to cast lots (Neh. 10:34[35]; Isa. 34:17).

5308. נְפַל ***n^e^pal:*** An Aramaic verb meaning to fall, to prostrate oneself, to die. The verb is commonly used in reference to paying homage to a human being (Dan. 2:46); or to an image (Dan. 3:5–7). It is also used to denote a violent death (Dan. 7:20). It carries the meaning of responsibility in Ezra 7:20, where it referred to taking responsibility for carrying out the king's order. See the Hebrew word *nāp̱al* (5307).

5309. נֵפֶל nēp̱el, נֶפֶל nep̱el: A masculine noun meaning an untimely birth, a miscarriage. This word is taken from the Hebrew root *nāp̱al* (5307), meaning to fall. Job thought it might have been better to have been stillborn than to be born and live with his trouble (Job 3:16). The psalmist hoped the wicked would be put away like a miscarried infant (Ps. 58:8[9]). The teacher in Ecclesiastes thought it would have been better for people to never be born than not to be able to enjoy their riches and have proper burials (Eccl. 6:3).

5310. נָפַץ nāp̱aṣ: I. A verb meaning to shatter, to break, to smash. It describes the action of shattering or breaking something: pitchers (Judg. 7:19; Jer. 22:28; 48:12); ashlar stones crushed, pulverized into powder (Isa. 27:9); timber cut into logs for transport or put into rafts (1 Kgs. 5:9[23]); figuratively, of defeating the power of nations as pottery is broken (Ps. 2:9; Jer. 50:20–23); of breaking the political and military might of God's holy people (Dan. 12:7); of slaying infants by crushing their skulls (Ps. 137:9; Jer. 13:14). Used of persons, the word can indicate their dispersal, scattering (Isa. 11:12).

II. A verb meaning to spread out, to disperse, to scatter. It is used in ways similar to I: It indicates the dispersal of peoples across the earth (Gen. 9:19); of persons drifting away because of losing interest (1 Sam. 13:11); of loading logs, dividing them onto rafts or possibly cutting timber into smaller pieces (1 Kgs. 5:9[23]). See I also.

5311. נֶפֶץ nep̱eṣ: A noun indicating a cloudburst, a driving storm. It refers to a sudden falling of a heavy, pelting rain. It is used of God's making His power and presence known in this case (Isa. 30:30).

5312. נְפַק n^e^p̱aq: An Aramaic verb meaning to go out, to take out. It indicates the removal of something. The vessels of the Solomonic temple were removed (Ezra 5:14; 6:5; Dan. 5:2, 3); Shadrach, Meshach, and Abednego came out from the fiery furnace (Dan. 3:26). It also means to go out, to issue a decree, an order, to send forth fire (Dan. 2:13, 14; 7:10); and the appearance of a hand (Dan. 5:5).

5313. נִפְקָה nip̱qāh: An Aramaic feminine noun indicating cost, expense. It refers to the amount of labor and materials expended for something, its value in monetary terms (Ezra 6:4, 8).

5314. נָפַשׁ nāp̱aš: A verb meaning to refresh, to rest, to refresh oneself. It refers to a renewal of energy in mind and body and applies to persons and work animals (Ex. 23:12; 2 Sam. 16:14). It is used figuratively of the Lord resting after creation, ceasing from His labor (Ex. 31:17).

5315. נֶפֶשׁ *nepeš:* A feminine noun meaning breath, the inner being with its thoughts and emotions. It is used 753 times in the Old Testament and has a broad range of meanings. Most of its uses fall into these categories: breath, literally or figuratively (Jer. 15:9); the inner being with its thoughts and emotions (Judg. 10:16; Prov. 14:10; Ezek. 25:6); and by extension, the whole person (Gen. 12:5; Lev. 4:2; Ezek. 18:4). Moreover, the term can cover the animating force of a person or his or her dead body (Lev. 21:11; Num. 6:6; Jer. 2:34). It is even applied to animals in a number of the above senses: the breath (Job 41:21[13]); the inner being (Jer. 2:24); the whole creature (Gen. 1:20); and the animating force (Lev. 17:11). When this word is applied to a person, it doesn't refer to a specific part of a human being. The Scriptures view a person as a composite whole, fully relating to God and not divided in any way (Deut. 6:5; cf. 1 Thess. 5:23).

5316. נֶפֶת *nepet,* נָפוֹת *nāpôt:* I. A feminine proper noun meaning Naphoth, a country or region. It refers to a tribal allotment to Manasseh, possibly referring to Dor, the third name in the list (Josh. 17:11). Also Naphoth Dor south of Carmel.

II. A feminine proper noun meaning Naphoth. It is taken as a city (NASB) in Asher connected, however, to Manasseh (Josh. 17:11).

III. A feminine proper noun Naphoth. It refers to a tribal allotment to Manasseh in Asher (Josh. 17:11). See I, II. It is a short term for Naphoth Dor located on the coast south of Carmel.

5317. נֹפֶת *nōpet:* A feminine noun meaning honey, honey dripping from the comb. It is used in parallel with honey and refers to the sweetest part of honey, the drippings (Ps. 19:10 [11]). It is used metaphorically, figuratively of the allurements of an adulteress' lips that drip honey (Prov. 5:3). Honey is symbolic of wisdom (Prov. 24:13). It is used in a good sense of the lips of one's wife that drip honey (Song 4:11).

5318. נֶפְתּוֹחַ *neptôaḥ:* A proper noun designating Nephtoah (Josh. 15:9; 18:15).

5319. נַפְתּוּלִים *naptûliym:* A masculine plural noun referring to struggles, wrestlings. It describes contention and violent fighting between opponents. It refers in context to strife, competition, and jealousy between two wives competing for the affection and recognition of their husband (Gen. 30:8).

5320. נַפְתֻּחִים *naptuḥiym:* A proper noun designating Naphtuhites, Naphtuhim (Gen. 10:13; 1 Chr. 1:11).

5321. נַפְתָּלִי naptāliy: A proper noun designating Naphtali:

A. The sixth son of Jacob born by Bilhah, Rachel's servant (Gen. 30:8). His name by popular lore means "my struggle" or "my wrestling." Jacob blessed him as "a doe set free that bears beautiful fawns" (Gen. 49:21, NIV; KJV, "a hind let loose: he giveth goodly words"). Moses' blessing urged him to take possession of his territory (Deut. 33:23).

B. The descendants of Naphtali lived in the northern part of Israel, bounded on the east by the Sea of Galilee and eastern Manasseh; on the north by the Litani River and Mount Hermon; on the west by Asher and Zebulun; on the south by Issachar. Kedesh, a city of refuge, was in its northern half. The great city of Hazor was in its eastern border, below Lake Hulah.

Baruch, who helped Deborah subdue Sisera, came from Naphtali (Judg. 4:6–10). Its people were strong supporters of Gideon (Judg. 6:35; 7:23). Since it was so close to Syria, it often was battered in wars from Syrian kings and armies (1 Kgs. 15:20). The entire tribe/land was exiled by Tiglath-pileser, an Assyrian king (ca. 734 B.C.).

5322. נֵץ nēṣ: I. A masculine noun indicating flowers, blossoms. It indicates fragile buds that open into blossoms that speak of fruitfulness (Gen. 40:10). The appearance of their flowers indicates that spring has arrived (Song 2:12).

II. A masculine noun referring to a hawk. It refers to a bird of prey that was considered unclean in Israel, not edible (Lev. 11:16; Deut. 14:15). God's wisdom created the hawk and its ability to soar and fly (Job 39:26).

5323. נָצָא nāṣā': A verb meaning to flee. It means to disappear, to flee, to go away. It is used of God's destruction of Moab by His judgments (Jer. 48:9).

5324. נָצַב nāṣab̲: A verb meaning to station, to appoint, to erect, to take a stand. Abraham's servant stationed himself beside the well to find a wife for Isaac (Gen. 24:13); Jacob set up a stone pillar (Gen. 35:14, 20); the people stood up when Moses went out to the tent to meet God (Ex. 33:8); God established the boundaries for Israel (Deut. 32:8); Boaz asked the work supervisor (the one who stands over) about Ruth (Ruth 2:5, 6). See the related Hebrew noun *niṣṣāb̲* (5325) and the Aramaic noun *niṣbāh* (5326).

5325. נִצָּב niṣṣāb̲: A masculine noun indicating the handle of something. It refers to the feature of something by which it is held, grasped. In context it refers to the handle of a sword located on the end opposite the blade (Judg. 3:22).

5326. נִצְבָּה niṣbāh: An Aramaic feminine noun meaning strength, toughness. It refers to the ability of something to hold together or to perform difficult tasks. It refers to the iron in the feet of Daniel's vision (Dan. 2:41).

5327. נָצָה nāṣāh: I. A verb meaning to struggle, to quarrel. It means to contend with violently, to quarrel, to come to blows, to men fighting (Ex. 2:13; 21:22; Deut. 25:11; Lev. 24:10; 2 Sam. 14:6); to disputes, challenges, accusations among people (Num. 26:9); to battles, war (Ps. 60:title[2]).

II. A verb meaning to fall, to be devastated, to be ruined. It means to devastate, to fall, to be useless. It is used of defeated and razed cities (2 Kgs. 19:25; Isa. 37:26; Jer. 4:7).

5328. נִצָּה niṣṣāh: A feminine noun meaning a blossom, a flower. It refers to the petals that are put forth by a plant indicating fertility and displaying beauty (Isa. 18:5). It is used in a figurative sense of the wicked being cut off like the blossoms of an olive tree dropping (Job 15:33).

5329. נָצַח nāṣaḥ: A verb meaning to lead, to direct, to oversee. It is used of foremen or work supervisors (1 Chr. 23:4; 2 Chr. 2:2[1], 18[17]; 34:12, 13; Ezra 3:8, 9). It is used in a participial form to refer to the act of continuing or being a ringleader in apostasy, rebellion (Jer. 8:5). It refers to a music leader or a choir director (1 Chr. 15:21; Hab. 3:19). It is used often in Psalms to mean, probably, music director or temple worship leader (see concordance for references).

5330. נְצַח n^e^ṣaḥ: An Aramaic verb meaning to distinguish oneself. It means to show oneself a leader, to show one's skills and leadership ability (Dan. 6:3[4]).

5331. נֵצַח nēṣaḥ, נֶצַח neṣaḥ: A noun meaning ever, always, perpetual. The word is used especially in prayers to ask whether God has forgotten His people forever (Ps. 13:1[2]; 77:8[9]; Jer. 15:18); and to affirm that He has not (Ps. 9:18[19]; 103:9). With a negative, the word may be translated never (Ps. 10:11; Isa. 13:20; Amos 8:7). The word also describes as perpetual (or appearing so to the writer) such things as ruins (Ps. 74:3); and pain (Jer. 15:18). In some passages, the word points to God's eternal nature (Ps. 68:16[17]; Isa. 25:8); and in 1 Chronicles 29:11, *nēṣaḥ* is among those attributes ascribed to God, namely, the kingdom, power, and glory. God even refers to Himself as the *nēṣaḥ* of Israel (1 Sam. 15:29), a usage that may indicate His glory (see *nāṣaḥ*[5329]). It also points to His eternal, truthful nature that is contrary to lying or changing.

5332. נֵצַח nēṣaḥ: A masculine noun meaning grape juice. The word occurs only in Isaiah 63:3, 6. In this passage, God's treading of grapes is a picture of His judgment of Israel's enemies, particularly Edom (cf. Isa. 63:1). Grape juice, as elsewhere in the Old Testament (cf. Deut. 32:14) and the New Testament, is a symbol of blood. In Isaiah 63, God returned from judgment with His garments stained with blood like the garments of a grape treader are stained with juice.

5333. נְצִיב n^eṣiyḇ: A masculine noun referring to a garrison, a pillar; an officer. It is used to describe a military post, a fortified location or building (1 Sam. 10:5; 13:3, 4; 1 Kgs. 4:19). They were manned, and tribute was collected in some of them (2 Sam. 8:6, 14). It indicates a pillar of salt (Gen. 19:26).

5334. נְצִיב n^eṣiyḇ: A proper noun designating Nezib (Josh. 15:43).

5335. נְצִיחַ n^eṣiyaḥ: A proper noun designating Neziah (Ezra 2:54; Neh. 7:56).

5336. נָצִיר nāṣiyr: An adjective designating something as preserved. It indicates the Israelites whom God had kept in reserve for Himself and for restoration (Isa. 49:6).

5337. נָצַל nāṣal: A verb meaning to deliver. Deliverance often indicated the power of one entity overcoming the power of another. It was frequently expressed as deliverance from the hand (i.e., power) of another (Gen. 32:11[12]; Hos. 2:10[12]). Thus, idols (1 Sam. 12:21) and mere human might (Ps. 33:16) were belittled as unable to deliver. God was frequently honored as delivering His people, whether from earthly enemies (2 Sam. 22:1; Jer. 1:8); or from more abstract things like transgressions (Ps. 39:8[9]); and death (Ps. 33:19; 56:13[14]). The word also refers to the taking of objects from another's power and is thus translated to recover (Judg. 11:26; 1 Sam. 30:8); to strip (2 Chr. 20:25); or to spoil (Ex. 3:22; 12:36). In a special usage, the word signifies warriors delivering one's eyes, that is, escaping from sight (2 Sam. 20:6). In 2 Samuel 14:6, a participle referred to one who would separate two men fighting each other. In Psalm 119:43, the psalmist asked God not to take (or deliver) His word out of his mouth.

5338. נְצַל n^eṣal: An Aramaic verb meaning to deliver. The word corresponds to the Hebrew word *nāṣal* (5337)and occurs three times in the Old Testament. In Daniel 3:29, it referred to God's deliverance of the three Hebrews from the fiery furnace, an action Nebuchadnezzar recognized as beyond any other so-called god. In Daniel 6:14[15], the word referred to Daniel's deliverance from the lions' den, a feat that Darius unsuccessfully attempted. Daniel 6:27[28] referred to God's successful deliverance of Daniel from the hand (i.e., power) of the lions. As with the Hebrew form, this word acknowledges God as the deliverer of those who trust in Him.

5339. נִצָּן niṣṣān: A masculine noun meaning a flower, a blossom. It refers to the colorful petals put forth by a plant, indicating beauty and fertility, a sign of spring (Song. 2:12).

5340. נָצַץ nāṣaṣ: A verb signifying to gleam, to sparkle. It is used of putting forth buds, blossoms, blooms, to gleam forth in beauty (Eccl. 12:5; Song 6:11; 7:12[13]). It depicts the sparkle or shining of four strange living beings like the gleam of burnished bronze (Ezek. 1:7).

5341. נָצַר nāṣar: A verb meaning to guard, to keep, to observe, to preserve, to hide. The word refers to people's maintaining things entrusted to them, especially to keeping the truths of God in both actions and mind (Ps. 119:100, 115). God's Word is to be kept with our whole hearts (Ps. 119:69); our hearts, in turn, ought to be maintained in a right state (Prov. 4:23). The word also refers to keeping speech under control (Ps. 34:13 [14]; 141:3); the maintenance of a tree (Prov. 27:18); the work of God's character (Ps. 40:11[12]); its reflection in humans as preserving them (Ps. 25:21; Prov. 2:11). Sometimes the word refers directly to God's preservation and maintenance of His people (Prov. 24:12; Isa. 49:8). The passive participle form of the verb describes an adulteress' heart as guarded or kept secret (Prov. 7:10). It also describes a city as guarded or besieged (Isa. 1:8). The active participle is used to signify a watchman (2 Kgs. 17:9; Jer. 31:6).

5342. נֵצֶר nēṣer: A masculine noun referring to a branch. It indicates literally a shoot, a branch of a plant but is used figuratively of the Lord's servant, the Branch, who will rule in the messianic kingdom. He comes from the roots of the family of Jesse (Isa. 11:1), the chosen royal line in Israel. It refers to Israel as a whole as God's branch in a restored state (Isa. 60:21). It indicates a person as part of a family line (Isa. 14:9); as a descendant in particular (Dan. 11:7).

5343. נְקֵא n^{e}qē': An Aramaic adjective referring to what is pure, white. It refers to the color white, the quality of purity. It points out the garments of the Ancient of Days and is symbolic of holiness and purity (Dan. 7:9).

5344. נָקַב nāqab̲: A verb meaning to pierce, to designate, to curse. The word signifies the piercing of an animal's head, jaw, or nose with a spear (Job 40:24; 41:2[40:26]; Hab. 3:14). It also signifies the piercing of a person's hand by a reed, symbolic of pain. Egypt was charged with bringing such pain on its allies (2 Kgs. 18:21; Isa. 36:6). In Haggai 1:6, the passive participle described a bag as being pierced. This word can also refer to wages being paid (Gen. 30:28); and to men being singled out for some task or distinction (2 Chr. 28:15; Amos 6:1). The meaning to curse may also be derived from a different root, *qāb̲ab̲* (6895). It signified the cursing or blaspheming of God's name (Lev. 24:11, 16); the speaking of a negative spiritual sentence on people (Num. 23:8; Prov. 11:26; 24:24); or things associated with people (Job 3:8; 5:3).

5345. נֶקֶב ***neqeḇ:*** I. A masculine noun indicating a setting. It refers to a prepared location and environment for receiving precious stones, in context of settings created by God, the master craftsman (Ezek. 28:13).

II. A masculine noun denoting a pipe. It indicates a conduit, a cylinder for conducting something (Ezek. 28:13, KJV).

5346. נֶקֶב ***neqeḇ:*** A proper noun designating Nekeb:

A. A town in Naphtali (KJV, Josh. 19:33).

B. Part of the full name Adami Nekeb, see 129 and 5346,II (NASB, NIV, Josh. 19:33).

5347. נְקֵבָה ***n***^{e}***qēḇāh:*** A feminine noun meaning female. It can refer either to a female woman (Gen. 1:27; 5:2; Lev. 12:5, 7; 15:33; 27:4, 5, 6, 7; Num. 5:3; 31:15; Jer. 31:22); or a female animal (Gen. 6:19; 7:3, 9, 16; Lev. 3:1, 6; 4:28, 32; 5:6).

5348. נָקֹד ***nāqōḏ:*** An adjective indicating that something is speckled, that it has marks of contrasting colors. It refers to a certain color scheme. In context it refers to speckled cattle, sheep, or goats (Gen. 30:32, 33, 35, 39; 31:8, 10, 12).

5349. נֹקֵד ***nōqēḏ:*** A masculine noun referring to a shepherd. It refers literally to a person who grazes sheep but extends to include the total care involved in raising them. Even a king or a prophet could be a sheep breeder or grazer (2 Kgs. 3:4; Amos 1:1).

5350. נִקֻּדִים ***niqqūḏiym:*** A masculine plural noun describing something moldy, crumbling; crumbling cakes. It is a word used to describe food, bread that is dry, moldy, and crumbly (Josh. 9:5, 12); but it refers also to good, edible baked cakes as well (1 Kgs. 14:3).

5351. נְקֻדָּה ***n***^{e}***quddāh:*** A feminine noun indicating a stud or bead. It refers to small spheres of silver placed on a necklace or bracelet ornament (Song 1:11).

5352. נָקָה ***nāqāh:*** A verb meaning to be free, to be clean, to be pure. Originally, this verb meant to be emptied; therefore, its most basic sentiment is to be poured out and can have a negative or positive connotation. In the negative sense, it refers to a city which has been deserted, emptied of people (Isa. 3:26). In the positive sense, it is used to connote freedom from the obligations of an oath (Gen. 24:8, 41); from guilt (Num. 5:31; Judg. 15:3; Jer. 2:35); and from punishment (Ex. 21:19; Num. 5:28; 1 Sam. 26:9). Regardless of whether the connotation is positive or negative, most occurrences of this verb have a moral or ethical implication. Aside from the passive or stative form, this verb also has a factitive form. (The factitive concept is to make something a certain state, in this instance, to make something clean or pure.) The factitive form has two aspects: (1) acquittal, the declaration of someone as innocent (Job 9:28; 10:14; Ps. 19:12[13]); (2)

leaving someone unpunished (Ex. 20:7; 34:7; Jer. 30:11).

5353. נְקוֹדָא n^e*qôḏā'*: A proper noun designating Nekoda:

A. The head of a family of temple slaves returning from the Babylonian Exile (Ezra 2:48; Neh. 7:50).

B. The head of an exile family who could not prove their Israelite descent (Ezra 2:60; Neh. 7:62).

5354. נָקַט *nāqaṭ*: A verb meaning to be weary. It means to be tired, worn out with something. It is used of one's soul being weary of, worn out of one's self or one's suffering and complaints (KJV, Job 10:1). Others take the word from *qûṭ,* to feel a loathing for. See 6962.

5355. נָקִי *nāqiy,* נָקִיא *nāqiy'*: An adjective meaning clean, free from, exempt. This term frequently refers to innocent blood, that is, the shed blood of an innocent individual (Deut. 19:10, 13; 21:8, 9; 1 Sam. 19:5; 2 Kgs. 21:16; 24:4; Ps. 94:21; 106:38; Prov. 6:17; Isa. 59:7; Jer. 7:6; 22:3, 17). It also refers to a person who is innocent (Job 4:7; 17:8; 22:19, 30; 27:17; Ps. 10:8; 15:5; Prov. 1:11). According to Psalm 24:4, it is a necessary quality for those who will stand in the presence of the Lord. It also refers to those who are free from blame (Gen. 44:10); free from liability or punishment (Ex. 21:28; 2 Sam. 14:9); released from an oath (Gen. 24:41; Josh. 2:17, 19, 20); exempt from various obligations (Num. 32:22); or free from the obligation of military service (Deut. 24:5).

5356. נִקָּיוֹן *niqqāyôn,* נִקָּיֹן *niqqāyōn*: A masculine noun meaning cleanness, whiteness, innocence. The Hebrew word generally implies innocence or freedom from guilt applied in the realm of sexual morality (Gen. 20:5); and ritual purification or personal conduct as it relates to worship (Ps. 26:6; 73:13). Choosing to embrace idolatry rather than innocence in their worship, Israel faced God's judgment (Hos. 8:5). In Amos 4:6, this term appears in a phrase that literally means cleanness of teeth, which is an idiomatic expression implying empty stomachs or nothing to eat.

5357. נָקִיק *nāqiyq*: A masculine noun describing a cleft, crevice. It indicates a large crack creating an opening in a rock (Isa. 7:19; Jer. 13:4; 16:16); but some prefer to understand the word as referring to a rock ledge (cf. NASB, Isa. 7:19).

5358. נָקַם *nāqam*: A verb meaning to avenge, to take revenge, to be avenged, to suffer vengeance, to take one's revenge. In actual usage, the following ideas come out: in the simple, intensive, and reflexive stems, the word can mean to take vengeance, to avenge. The Lord instructed His people not to seek revenge against each other, for to do so was unworthy of them (Lev. 19:18); the Lord took vengeance on His enemies and the enemies of His people (Nah. 1:2); but He would also take vengeance on His own people if necessary (Lev. 26:25); and He would avenge the death of His servants, the prophets (2 Kgs. 9:7); and His city, Jerusalem (Jer. 51:36). The reflexive idea of taking one's vengeance is found in the Lord's avenging Himself on Judah (Jer. 5:9).

5359. נָקָם *nāqām:* A masculine noun meaning revenge or vengeance. This term is employed to signify human vengeance. For example, Samson sought revenge against the Philistines for gouging out his eyes (Judg. 16:28). According to Proverbs, a jealous husband will show no mercy when he exacts vengeance on his wife's adulterous lover (Prov. 6:34). More often, however, this Hebrew term refers to divine repayment (Lev. 26:25; Deut. 32:35, 41, 43; Ezek. 24:8; Mic. 5:15[14]). For example, the psalmist encouraged the righteous with the hope that someday they will be avenged, and God will redress the wrongs committed against them (Ps. 58:10[11]). In fact, He will judge those who have acted with vengeance toward His people (Ezek. 25:12, 15). Ultimately, the judgment of God's enemies will mean redemption for His people (Isa. 34:8; 35:4; 47:3; 59:17; 63:4).

5360. נְקָמָה *n^eqāmāh:* A feminine singular noun meaning vengeance. Jeremiah employed this word most frequently, referring to the vengeance of God (Jer. 11:20; 46:10; 50:15, 28; 51:6, 11, 36). The worship of false gods, improper sacrifices, and a plot against Jeremiah himself all stirred up the vengeance of God. But it is also used with Israel as the subject (Num. 31:2; Ps. 149:7); and object (Lam. 3:60; Ezek. 25:15). Even when Israel took vengeance on an enemy, it was God's vengeance that they delivered (Num. 31:2, 3).

5361. נָקַע *nāqa':* A verb meaning to turn away in disgust, to be alienated. It means to turn from in disdain, in disgust, and with strong disapproval (Ezek. 23:18). Those who have turned away are in a state of alienation and hostility toward someone (Ezek. 23:22, 28).

5362. נָקַף *nāqap̱:* A verb meaning to strike off, to strip away. It occurs twice in the Hebrew Bible. It is used passively in Isaiah 10:34 where it referred to the stripping away the forest thicket, describing God's destruction of Lebanon with an ax. In Job 19:26, the word is employed figuratively to describe the effects of his disease on his skin.

5363. נֹקֶף *nōqep̱:* A masculine noun denoting a shaking, a beating. In general, it means to strike, to whip, to jerk back and forth. It describes the beating of olives off olive trees in an agricultural setting (Isa. 17:6; 24:13).

5364. נִקְפָּה *niqpāh:* I. A feminine noun referring to a rope. It refers to a cord used to bind something or someone. It is found in a mocking sense of persons bound in ropes or cords, not belts of ornamentation (Isa. 3:24).

II. A feminine noun indicating a rip, a tear. It is used in opposition to a girdle. In place of a girdle, a tear will be evident (Isa. 3:24, KJV).

5365. נָקַר *nāqar:* A verb meaning to dig something; to gouge out something. It is used of putting out, gouging out the eyes of a person (Num. 16:14; 1 Sam. 11:2; Prov. 30:17); memorably of Samson's eyes blinded by the Philistines (Judg. 16:21). In a general sense, it means to dig something, e.g., a well (2 Kgs. 19:24); but in a figurative sense, it describes afflictions and pain that cut into a person (Job. 30:17). It is used in a figurative sense of God's digging wells as symbolic of His past acts of deliverance and help for His people (Isa. 37:25); with Himself as the quarry or rock pile from which Israel was created or dug (Isa. 51:1).

5366. נְקָרָה *n^eqārāh:* A feminine noun referring to a cleft, cavern. It refers to a large fissure or crevice in a rock, large enough for people to hide in or take shelter in (Ex. 33:22; Isa. 2:21).

5367. נָקַשׁ *nāqaš:* A verb meaning to strike, to strike down, to knock, to bring down. This word is associated with hunting birds, and therefore it is often translated to ensnare. It occurs four times in the Hebrew Bible and is used with the connotation of a subject attempting to destroy the object. For instance, the witch of Endor asked why Saul was entrapping her (1 Sam. 28:9). Deuteronomy 12:30 warned of being ensnared by the worship of other gods. According to Psalm 109:11, a creditor could also strike down one's estate.

5368. נְקַשׁ *n^eqaš:* An Aramaic verb meaning to knock. It occurs only once in the Hebrew Bible. Daniel 5:6 employed the idiomatic phase knocking knees to express Belshazzar's fear when he saw a finger mysteriously writing on the wall. See the Hebrew word *nāqaš* (5367).

5369. נֵר *nēr:* A proper noun designating Ner:

A. The father of Abner (1 Sam. 14:50, 51; 26:5, 14; 2 Sam. 2:8, 12; 3:23, 25, 28, 37; 1 Kgs. 2:5, 32; 1 Chr. 26:28).

B. The father of Kish (1 Chr. 8:33; 9:39).

C. The brother of Kish (1 Chr. 9:36).

5370. נֵרְגַל *nērgal:* A masculine proper noun Nergal. It is the name of a god made by the people of Cuth, a city in southern Mesopotamia (2 Kgs. 17:30).

5371. נֵרְגַל שַׂר־אֶצֶר *nērgal śar-'eṣer:* A proper noun designating Nergal-Sharezer.

A. A Babylonian official (Jer. 39:3, 13).

B. Another Babylonian official (Jer. 39:3).

5372. נִרְגָּן *nirgān:* A masculine noun indicating a gossiper, a slanderer. It depicts a person who harms others by attacking them verbally falsely (Prov. 16:28). It indicates a person who whispers things that will harm others, things that should be kept secret (Prov. 18:8; 16:22), creating tension and strife (Prov. 26:20).

5373. נֵרְדְּ *nērd:* A masculine noun indicating perfume, spikenard. It refers to a pleasant, fragrant ointment used in amorous situations (Song 1:12). It refers to the spikenard or nard plant as well (Song 4:13, 14).

5374. נֵרִיָּה *nēriyyāh,* נֵרִיָּהוּ *nēriyyāhû:* A proper noun designating Neriah, the father of Baruch (Jer. 32:12, 16; 36:4, 8, 14, 32; 43:3, 6; 45:1; 51:59).

5375. נָשָׂא *nāśā':* A verb meaning to lift, to carry, to take away. This verb is used almost six hundred times in the Hebrew Bible and covers three distinct semantic ranges. The first range is to lift, which occurs in both literal (Gen. 7:17; 29:1; Ezek. 10:16) and figurative statements: to lift the hand in taking an oath (Deut. 32:40); in combat (2 Sam. 18:28); as a sign (Isa. 49:22); in retribution (Ps. 10:12). Other figurative statements include the lifting of: the head (Gen. 40:13); the face (2 Sam. 2:22); the eyes (Gen. 13:10); the voice (1 Sam. 30:4). It is also important to note that a person can take up or induce iniquity by a number of actions (Ex. 28:43; Lev. 19:17; 22:9; Num. 18:32). The second semantic category is to bear or to carry and is used especially in reference to the bearing of guilt or punishment of sin (Gen. 4:13; Lev. 5:1). This flows easily then into the concept of the representative or substitutionary bearing of one person's guilt by another (Lev. 10:17; 16:22). The final category is to take away. It can be used in the simple sense of taking something (Gen. 27:3); to take a wife or to get married (Ruth 1:4); to take away guilt or to forgive (Gen. 50:17); to take away or to destroy (Job 32:22).

5376. נְשָׂא *n^eśā':* An Aramaic verb meaning to take, to carry away, to rise up in rebellion. It means to stand against, to resist authority or controls. It indicates a city rising up in rebellion against a foreign king ruling over it (Ezra 4:19). It refers to removing something, taking it elsewhere, e.g., vessels or chaff (Ezra 5:15; Dan. 2:35).

5377. נָשָׁא *nāšā':* A verb meaning to deceive. It means to use deceptive methods or deceit to accomplish something: to deceive a person (Gen. 3:13); to deceive people by political means or giving false hopes of deliverance (2 Kgs. 18:29; 19:10; 2 Chr. 32:15); death deceives persons, surprising them (Ps. 55:15[16]); it describes the prophecies of false prophets (Jer. 29:8). It refers to those who deceive themselves (Jer. 37:9; 49:16; Obad. 1:3, 7); or are deceived (Isa. 19:13). It describes God's deceiving His people, of His making false assertions of peace (Jer. 4:10) .

5378. נָשָׁא nāšā': A verb indicating lending or interest, serving as a creditor. It refers to a person who has made a loan (1 Sam. 22:2, "every person to whom there was a credit [*nōše'*]"). It means those who lend or charge excessive interest (Neh. 5:7; Ps. 89:22[23]; NASB reads as deceive, but see note). God's justice makes level all the financial and social classes (Isa. 24:2).

5379. נִשֵּׂאת niśśē'ṯ: A participle of *nāśā'* (5375), to carry, referring to a gift. It refers to something given to persons freely, in context in the sense of political gifts or benefits (2 Sam. 19:42[43]).

5380. נָשַׁב nāšaḇ: A verb meaning to blow, to drive away. It is used of scaring off birds of prey that have alighted on a dead animal (Gen. 15:11); of wind driving water back or making it flow again (Ps. 147:18). It is used of a dry, hot wind blowing on the grass, killing it (Isa. 40:7).

5381. נָשַׂג nāśag: A verb meaning to overtake, to reach, to get. It often means to overtake, to catch up to someone (Gen. 31:25; 44:4, 6; Ex. 14:9; 15:9; Num. 6:21). It is used figuratively of age, of years attaining a certain level (Gen. 47:9); or of joy and rejoicing arriving, becoming a reality (Isa. 35:10). It means to afford, to have at one's hand, the ability, to have sufficient (Lev. 5:11; 14:21); or to obtain, come into possession of property (Lev. 25:47).

5382. נָשָׁה nāšāh: A verb meaning to forget. It means to not call to mind or to not let something dominate one's thinking (Gen. 41:51). It is used of God's forgetting and forgiving, not choosing to count sin against a person (Job 11:6). It indicates God's causing an ostrich to forget, to not have wisdom at hand (Job 39:17). It is negated when it speaks of God's forgetting His people (Isa. 44:21); but it is affirmed when He temporarily rejects them (Jer. 23:39). It is negated to indicate that a person can no longer remember happiness because of present calamities (Lam. 3:17).

5383. נָשָׁה nāšāh, נָשָׁא nāšā': A verb meaning to lend, to borrow. See 5378. The word here is spelled with *he* (ה) instead of *aleph* (א). It means to let a person have a loan, to use the owner's money for a time (Ex. 22:25[24]; Deut. 24:10, 11). Loans were canceled, released in the sabbatical years and in the Year of Jubilee (Deut. 15:2). In its participle form, it indicates a creditor, a person who had extended a loan (2 Kgs. 4:1; Ps. 109:11). Food and other items were loaned, as well as money (Neh. 5:10, 11).

5384. נָשֶׁה nāšeh: I. A masculine noun referring to something that shrank. It refers to a portion of the sinew or tendon that was reduced in size, that shrank upon Jacob's strange encounter with a divine being (Gen. 32:32[33]).

II. A masculine noun referring to a sinew, a tendon. It is described as the tendon or sinew of the hip or thigh (Gen. 32:32[33]).

5385. נְשׂוּאָה n^eśû'āh: A feminine noun referring to what is borne or carried about. It refers, in context, satirically, to idols that were carried about by beasts of burden, idols that were stupid, immobile gods (Isa. 46:1).

5386. נְשִׁי n^ešiy: A masculine noun referring to a debt. It refers to an amount of money or other goods owed to a person (2 Kgs. 4:7). It was a problem of the poor especially, a burden that destroyed them.

5387. נָשִׂיא nāśiy': A noun meaning something that is lifted up, a prince, a mist. The Hebrew word is formed from the verb *nāśā'* (5375), meaning to lift. It refers to a leader of the people (Gen. 23:6; Ex. 16:22; 22:28[27]). Although rare, it can refer to the king (1 Kgs. 11:34); or to a non-Israelite leader (Gen. 34:2; Num. 25:18; Josh. 13:21). Some scholars have proposed that the term refers to elected officials, contending that these were common people who were elevated or lifted up. They often buttress their argument with Numbers 1:16, which talks of these leaders as the ones called, chosen, or appointed from the congregation. In a few instances, this word also indicates mist or vapors that rise from the earth to form clouds and herald the coming of rain (Ps. 135:7; Prov. 25:14; Jer. 10:13; 51:16).

5388. נְשִׁיָּה n^ešiyyāh: A feminine noun indicating forgetfulness, oblivion. It refers to a state in which nothing is remembered, there is no consciousness, memories have been blanked out. In context it is the state of being dead and in the grave (Ps. 88:12[13]).

5389. נְשִׁין n^eśiyn: A feminine plural noun referring to wives. In context the word refers to the wives of those royal officials and conspirators who tried to have Daniel killed (Dan. 6:24[25]).

5390. נְשִׁיקָה n^ešiyqāh: A feminine noun designating a kiss. It indicates an act showing an intimacy of a relationship, but in context it is used in a deceitful, false show of affection (Prov. 27:6). It describes an amorous show of love and affection (Song 1:2).

5391. נָשַׁךְ nāšak̲: I. A verb meaning to bite. It refers to a snake's bite as it strikes. It is used figuratively of the character of Dan, one of the twelve tribal ancestors of Israel (Gen. 49:17); and of serpent bites in general (Num. 21:6; Eccl. 10:8, 11; Amos 5:19; 9:3). It describes the bite of an alcoholic beverage like wine (Prov. 23:32); and of the enemies the Lord sent against His people (Jer. 8:17). False prophets are described as biting at what is available to them (Mic. 3:5).

II. A verb meaning to lend or borrow at interest. It is used to describe a loan given with the expectation of receiving back the principal plus an amount on top of that, interest. This was forbidden in Israel (Deut. 23:19[20], 20[21]). The word means creditors in its participial plural form (Hab. 2:7, see I).

5392. נֶשֶׁךְ ***nešek̲:*** A masculine noun meaning interest, usury. It refers to the amount paid back to a creditor beyond the principal (Ex. 22:25[24]; Lev. 25:36, 37), a practice forbidden in Israel with respect to other Israelites (Ps. 15:5; Prov. 28:8). A righteous man did not practice usury or charge an excessive amount of interest (Ezek. 18:8, 13, 17; 22:12).

5393. נִשְׁכָּה ***niš̲kāh:*** A feminine noun referring to a chamber, a room, living quarters. It refers to an area of a building prepared for habitation. In context an area such as this was repaired or restored (Neh. 3:30). It describes storage areas or chambers (Neh. 12:44); or an office area (Neb. 13:7).

5394. נָשַׁל ***nāšal:*** A verb meaning to remove, to drop off, to clear away. It means to take off or remove something: shoes (Ex. 3:5; Josh. 5:15); nations from a land (Deut. 7:1, 22); people (2 Kgs. 16:6); trees (Deut. 19:5); olives (Deut. 28:40).

5395. נָשַׁם ***nāšam:*** A verb meaning to breathe heavily, to pant. This particular form of the word is used only once in the Bible and describes the deep breathing and gasping of a woman in labor. God said that although He had been silent, He would cry out like a woman about to give birth (Isa. 42:14). See the related Aramaic noun *nišmāʾ* (5396) and Hebrew noun *n^e^šāmāh* (5397).

5396. נִשְׁמָה ***nišmāh:*** An Aramaic feminine noun referring to breath, life breath. It indicates the breath or spirit that animates and makes a person alive (Dan. 5:23). It is given by God.

5397. נְשָׁמָה ***n^{e}šāmāh:*** A feminine noun meaning breath, wind, spirit. Its meaning is parallel to *nep̲eš* (5315) and *rûaḥ* (7307). It refers to the breath of God as a destructive wind that kills and clears the foundations of the earth (2 Sam. 22:16; Job 4:9); a stream of brimstone that kindles a fire (Isa. 30:33); a freezing wind that produces frost (Job 37:10); the source of life that vitalizes humanity (Job 33:4). The breath of humans is recognized as the source and center of life (1 Kgs. 17:17; Job 27:3). It is also understood that such breath originates with God, and He can withhold it, thereby withholding life from humanity (Gen. 2:7; Job 34:14; Isa. 42:5). Therefore, people's breath is a symbol of their weakness and frailty (Isa. 2:22). Since breath is the source of life, by extension, this word is also used to represent life and anything that is alive (Deut. 20:16; Josh. 10:40; 11:11, 14; Isa. 57:16). Like *nep̱eš* (5315), this word also connotes the human mind or intellect (Prov. 20:27).

5398. נָשַׁף *nāšap:* A verb meaning to blow. It describes God's bringing a great wind against the waters of the Red Sea to destroy the Egyptians (Ex. 15:10). It is used figuratively of God's removal of the rulers and judges of the world by merely blowing on them to wilt them (Isa. 40:24).

5399. נֶשֶׁף *nešep̱:* A masculine noun meaning twilight, dusk, dawn. It refers to the period after the sun has set but before darkness has settled down (1ared (Job 3:9); when the adulterer made his way out (Job 24:15). It describes the early part of the day just before the sun rises or at the time of the rising of the sun (Job 7:4; Ps. 119:147; Isa. 5:11).

5400. נָשַׂק *nāśaq:* A verb meaning to kindle, to burn. It refers to starting a fire, creating a spark to get a blaze going. It indicates God's anger being fired up against His people (Ps. 78:21). It refers to wooden idols being burned, kindled, to warm its former worshipers (Isa. 44:15). It describes destroying weapons by burning them (Ezek. 39:9).

5401. נָשַׁק *nāšaq:* A verb meaning to kiss, to touch lightly. The word rarely has romantic implications (Prov. 7:13; Song. 1:2). Often, along with tears and embraces, kisses expressed the dearness of relationships between friends and family, especially at a farewell (Ruth 1:9, 14; 1 Sam. 20:41; 1 Kgs. 19:20); or a reunion (Gen. 45:15, cf. Rom. 16:16; 1 Pet. 5:14). Kisses also expressed acceptance of a person (Gen. 45:15; 2 Sam. 14:33); and even the mutual acceptance or harmony of moral qualities (Ps. 85:10[11]). They also were associated with giving blessings (Gen. 27:27; 2 Sam. 19:39[40]). Kisses sometimes expressed the worship of idols (1 Kgs. 19:18; Hos. 13:2); and the worship of the Messiah (Ps. 2:12; cf. Ps. 2:7; Heb. 1:5). Some kisses, however, were deceitful (2 Sam. 20:9). The meaning of lightly touching occurs in Ezekiel 3:13.

5402. נֵשֶׁק *nēšeq*, נֶשֶׁק *nešeq:* A noun meaning weapons, battle, armory. The word refers to a variety of weapons, both offensive (bows, arrows, spears, and clubs) and defensive (shields). Weapons were sometimes given as gifts (1 Kgs. 10:25; 2 Chr. 9:24); and were kept in the palace Solomon built (Isa. 22:8); thus, they probably involved a high level of craftsmanship and were sometimes made of precious metals (cf. 1 Kgs. 10:16, 17, shields of gold); as well as iron and bronze (Job 20:24). In Nehemiah 3:19, the word means armory, a place where weapons were kept. The word also referred to a battle (Job 39:21; Ps. 140:7[8]) as a place where horses charged, weapons flew, and one's head needed God's protection.

5403. נְשַׁר n^e^šar: An Aramaic masculine noun signifying an eagle. It refers to a large, carnivorous bird of prey known for its long feathers, power, and keen eyesight. It describes the hair of Nebuchadnezzar which had grown to look like the feathers of an eagle (Dan. 4:33[30]).

5404. נֶשֶׁר nešer: A masculine noun referring to an eagle. It refers to a large, carnivorous bird of prey known for its long feathers, wings, speed, power in flight, and keen eyesight (2 Sam. 1:23; Ps. 103:5; Isa. 40:31). It serves in the famous "eagles' wings" passage as the bird on which the Lord brought Israel to Himself (Ex. 19:4). The eagle represents the Lord as He hovers over His people to care for them (Deut. 32:11). It was forbidden as food to Israel (Lev. 11:13; Deut. 14:12). It is employed figuratively as a bird of prey to represent the attack of Israel's enemies (Deut. 28:49; Job 9:26). God is the creator of the eagle (Job 39:27).

5405. נָשַׁת našaṯ: A verb meaning to be dry, parched; to dry up, to fail. It is used of something without sufficient moisture, not wet or damp. It is used figuratively of God's drying up the seas and rivers in judgment (Isa. 19:5); and of waters going away or being removed from their natural state (Jer. 18:14). It depicts the oppressed in their abject state of need (Isa. 41:17); but also the strength and vigor of strong persons failing, and they become exhausted (Jer. 51:30).

5406. נִשְׁתְּוָן ništ^e^wān: A masculine noun indicating a letter, correspondence. It refers to a form of correspondence in writing on clay, parchment, etc. It refers to official letters sent by the government (Ezra 4:7; 7:11). Sometimes it is better understood as a document, a decree, or a report of some kind.

5407. נִשְׁתְּוָן ništ^e^wān: An Aramaic masculine noun indicating a letter, correspondence. It refers to a form of correspondence in writing on clay, parchment. It is translated according to context as a letter, a decree, a document, etc. (Ezra 4:18, 23; 5:5).

5408. נָתַח nāṯaḥ: A verb meaning to cut up, to cut into pieces. It describes the cutting a sacrifice into pieces or parts for placement on the altar (Ex. 29:17; Lev. 1:6, 12; 8:20; 1 Kgs. 18:23, 33). It indicates the chopping up of a human body into pieces (Judg. 19:29; 20:6); as well as a yoke of oxen (1 Sam. 11:7).

5409. נֵתַח nēṯaḥ: A masculine noun indicating pieces of meat. It refers to the pieces a of a sacrifice into which an animal has been cut (Ex. 29:17; Lev. 1:6, 8, 12; 8:20; 9:13); the parts into which a human body has been cut (Judg. 19:29). It is used figuratively to symbolize Judah, the city of Jerusalem, and the various classes of people in them who will be "pieces of meat" for cooking as in a pot of destruction and judgment (Ezek. 24:4, 6).

5410. נָתִיב ***naṯiyḇ,*** נְתִיבָה ***neṯiyḇāh:*** I. A masculine noun indicating a path, a pathway, a wake. It refers to a trail or navigable pass made by humans or by nature. It indicates figuratively the path, the way of life, of the wicked (Job 18:10); and the path to wisdom (Job 28:7). It is used of a wake, the foam and waves left in the water (Job 41:32[24]). God's tragic treatment of the Egyptians created a path for His people (Ps. 78:50); His commandments are a path of life (Ps. 119:35); as is the way (path) of righteousness (Prov. 12:28).

II. A feminine noun indicating a path, a pathway, a wake. It indicates well-traveled paths or roads, highways (Judg. 5:6). Figuratively, it indicates the paths of life (Job 19:8); of ethical and moral guidance (Ps. 119:105; 142:3[4]); as well as the way of the wicked (Prov. 1:15). It describes the paths of salvation and restoration which the Lord prepares for His people (Isa. 42:16). The ancient way of obedience to the Lord, the ancient paths, are the sources of guidance for God's people (Jer. 6:16). The Lord is capable of hiding, blocking the true paths of His people (Hos. 2:6[8]).

5411. נְתִינִים ***neṯiyniym:*** A proper noun designating the Nethinim, servants in the temple (1 Chr. 9:2; Ezra 2:43, 58, 70; 7:7; 8:17, 20; Neh. 3:26, 31; 7:46, 60, 73; 10:28[29]; 11:3, 21).

5412. נְתִינִין ***neṯiyniyn:*** An Aramaic plural noun designating the Nethinim, servants in the temple (Ezra 7:24). It corresponds to the Hebrew word 5411.

5413. נָתַךְ ***nāṯak:*** A verb meaning to pour out, to be poured out; to melt. It means to pour, to gush, to melt, to break out. It describes many things under these concepts: water or rain pour out (Ex. 9:33; 2 Sam. 21:10); God's anger and curse flow out or rush out on persons (Jer. 7:20; 42:18; Dan. 9:11, 27; Nah. 1:6). It describes emptying out, pouring out money (2 Kgs. 22:9; 2 Chr. 34:17). It is used of melting so that something will flow, such as metals (Ezek. 22:20–22). It is used figuratively a few times, e.g., of Job's tears being poured out (Job 3:24).

5414. נָתַן ***nāthan:*** A verb meaning to give, to place. This verb is used approximately two thousand times in the Old Testament; therefore, it is understandable that it should have a broad semantic range. However, it is possible to identify three general categories of semantic variation: (1) to give, whether it be the exchange of tangible property (Gen. 3:6; Ex. 5:18); the production of fruit (Ps. 1:3); the presentation of an offering to the Lord (Ex. 30:14); the passing on of knowledge and instruction (Prov. 9:9); the granting of permission (Gen. 20:6). Often, God provides either preservation (Lev. 26:4; Deut. 11:14, 15; Jer. 45:5); or plague (Ex. 9:23). (2) This Hebrew word also means to put, to place, or something literally placed: the luminaries in the sky (Gen. 1:17); God's bow in the clouds (Gen. 9:13);

the ark on a cart (1 Sam. 6:8); the abomination in the temple. It could also be something figuratively placed: an obstacle (Ezek. 3:20); God's Spirit (Isa. 42:1); reproach (Jer. 23:40); curses (Deut. 30:7). (3) The word can also mean to make or to constitute, such as the prohibition against making incisions in one's flesh (Lev. 19:28); God making Abraham into a father of many nations (Gen. 17:5); or Solomon making silver as stones (1 Kgs. 10:27).

5415. נְתַן *n*^{e}*<u>t</u>an*: An Aramaic verb meaning to give, to bestow. Its basic meaning, to give, is nuanced according to its context. It means to pay tribute, taxes, etc. (Ezra 4:13); to furnish, supply, provide (Ezra 7:20); to get, permit, allow (Dan. 2:16); to bestow officially (Dan. 4:17[14], 25[22], 32[29]).

5416. נָתָן *nā<u>t</u>ān*: A proper noun designating Nathan:

A. A Judahite through the line of Jerahmeel, son of Hezron. His father was Attai (1 Chr. 2:36).

B. The father of Igal, who was among David's mighty men (2 Sam. 23:36).

C. The father of Azariah who administered a district. A chief official of Solomon (1 Kgs. 4:5).

D. The prophet who charged David with adultery and murder (2 Sam. 12:1–31). His name means "(God) has given." He was also loyal to David as David followed the Lord. God revealed the covenant with David through Nathan (2 Sam. 7:4–16). He supported Solomon as king on David's death (1 Kgs. 1:1–53). Psalm 51 (title) notes his condemnation of David's adultery.

E. One of David's many sons by various wives (2 Sam. 5:14).

F. An Israelite leader summoned to help Ezra gather workers for the services of the Temple (Ezra 8:16).

G. An Israelite who had intermarried with the people of the land (Ezra 10:39).

5417. נְתַנְאֵל *n*^{e}*<u>t</u>an'ēl*: A proper noun designating Nethanel:

A. The son of Zuar (Num. 1:8; 2:5; 7:18, 23; 10:15).

B. The father of Shemaiah (1 Chr. 24:6).

C. The son of Jesse (1 Chr. 2:14).

D. A priest (1 Chr. 15:24).

E. The son of Obed-Edom (1 Chr. 26:4).

F. A prince of Judah (2 Chr. 17:7).

G. The brother of Cononiah (2 Chr. 35:9).

H. The son of Jedaiah (Neh. 12:21).

I. The son of Pashur (Ezra 10:22).

J. A priest (Neh. 12:36).

5418. נְתַנְיָה *n*^{e}*<u>t</u>anyāh*, נְתַנְיָהוּ *n*^{e}*<u>t</u>anyāhû*: A proper noun designating Nethaniah:

A. The son of Asaph (1 Chr. 25:2, 12).

B. A Levite (2 Chr. 17:8).

C. The father of Jehudi (Jer. 36:14).

D. The father of Ishmael (2 Kgs. 25:23, 25; Jer. 40:8, 14, 15; 41:1, 2, 6, 7, 9–12, 15, 16, 18).

5419. נְתַן־מֶלֶךְ ***n*****e*****ṯan-meleḵ:*** A proper noun designating Nathan-Melech (2 Kgs. 23:11).

5420. נָתַס ***nāṯas:*** A verb meaning to break up, to mar. It means to shatter, to knock apart, to destroy. It is used figuratively of breaking up, of complicating, or of destroying one's way of life (Job 30:13).

5421. נָתַע ***nāṯa':*** A verb meaning to break. It means to crush, to shatter, to crack; to defeat. It occurs in an idiomatic phrase, the teeth of young lions are shattered (Job 4:10); that is, they are defeated, rendered helpless. The reference is to the wicked depicted as young lions.

5422. נָתַץ ***nāṯaṣ:*** A verb meaning to tear down, to destroy. The idea is the breaking down of a structure so that it can no longer support its own weight. Most often the word signified the destruction of idolatrous religious structures such as the altars that Israel was commanded to tear down on entering the Promised Land (Deut. 7:5; 12:3; Judg. 2:2; 2 Chr. 31:1). The word also signified the destruction of buildings: a tower (Judg. 8:9, 17; Ezek 26:9); a leprous house (Lev. 14:45); or an entire city (Judg. 9:45). In a spiritual sense, the word signified the tearing down of an individual (Ps. 52:5[7]); or a nation (Jer. 18:7). In Psalm 58:6[7], the word signified breaking the teeth of fierce lions.

5423. נָתַק ***nāṯaq:*** A verb meaning to break, to break away, to pull away; to draw away. It means to break or snap a rope or cord (Judg. 16:9; Eccl. 4:12), the cord standing symbolically for ties of friendship in Ecclesiastes. It is used of drawing out an army from an area to deceive the soldiers (Josh. 8:6, 16; Judg. 20:32); of something that has been mutilated or damaged by tearing (Lev. 22:24). It is used of walking out of the River Jordan onto dry ground (Josh. 4:18). In a figurative sense, it describes plans or counsels being ruined, torn apart (Job 17:11); or of political or military control being broken (Ps. 2:3; Nah. 1:13). It is used of separating out impurities in a smelting process (Jer. 6:29). It is used in an allegory of pulling up the roots of a plant or tree (Ezek. 17:9).

5424. נֶתֶק ***neṯeq:*** A masculine noun referring to a scab, a skin disease, a type of leprosy. It refers to a skin disease of some kind. It has been suggested that it was leprosy, but others prefer ringworm or eczema. It probably referred to various skin eruptions under the same name (Lev. 13:30–37; 14:54).

5425. נָתַר ***nāṯar:*** I. A verb indicating to jump, to leap, to startle, to tremble. It refers to the ability of certain insects to jump, leap; insects Israel could eat (Lev. 11:21). It describes a rapid rush of the heartbeat at God's presence in nature (Job 37:1); or His actions toward the nations that startle or shock them (Hab. 3:6).

II. A verb meaning to loosen, to undo, to set free, to release, to set, to make. It means to not regard or to remove oneself from the direction of something (2 Sam. 22:33); to let something go (Job 6:9). It means to release, to set free a political prisoner or slave (Ps. 105:20); especially of the Lord freeing the oppressed (Ps. 146:7; Isa. 58:6).

5426. נְתַר ***$n^e\underline{t}ar$:*** An Aramaic verb meaning to strip off. It is used of pulling off, plucking off the fruit and greenery of a tree or large shrub (Dan. 4:14[11]).

5427. נֶתֶר ***ne̱ter:*** An masculine noun meaning niter, soda, lye. It indicates natron, a substance used in detergents, native soda (potassium nitrate, sodium nitrate) (Prov. 25:20; Jer. 2:22; KJV, nitre; NASB, lye).

5428. נָתַשׁ ***nāṯaš:*** A verb meaning to pluck up by the roots, to root out. It means to tear something out, to pull out by its roots: God pulled out pagan gods or worship symbols, Asherim (Mic. 5:14[13]); He uprooted His people from His land (Deut. 29:28[27]; 1 Kgs. 14:15; Jer. 12:14, 15, 17); Jeremiah as a prophet uprooted, plucked up nations (Jer. 1:10). In its passive sense, it means to be uprooted, to be plucked out (Ezek. 19:12; Dan. 11:4).

ס Samekh

5429. סְאָה ***s^{e}'āh:*** A feminine noun indicating a seah: a measure of flour or grain. An ancient dry measure of flour or grain that was equal to 6.6 dry quarts, 7.7 liquid quarts. It was probably used as a liquid as well as a dry measure. It equaled one-third of an ephah/bath. It was used in the Old Testament to measure fine meal (Gen. 18:6); fine grain (1 Sam. 25:18); seed (1 Kgs. 18:32); fine flour (2 Kgs. 7:1, 16, 18).

5430. סְאוֹן ***s^{e}'ôn:*** I. A masculine noun referring to a boot. In context it refers to a military boot worn by the soldiers of the mighty Assyrian army, probably made of leather (Isa. 9:5[4]). Some authorities suggest sandal as a translation.

II. A masculine noun meaning battle. It was formerly taken to mean battle by earlier translators (Isa. 9:5[4], KJV; NKJV, boot, sandal in note).

5431. סָאַן ***sā'an:*** A verb meaning to be shod, to have boots; to be a warrior. It refers to a person (*sō'ēn*) wearing boots as he marched along in military gear and in military array (Isa. 9:5[4]).

5432. סַאסְּאָה ***sa'ss^{e}'āh:*** I. A feminine noun indicating a driving away, warfare. It refers to banishing someone, especially one's enemy or advisory expelling them (Isa. 27:8).

II. A feminine noun referring to moderation, a measured response. It was formerly taken to indicate something done in a controlled, measured way (Isa. 27:8; KJV, cf. NKJV).

5433. סָבָא ***sāb̲ā':*** A verb meaning to imbibe, to carouse, to get drunk. It means to drink heavily, to drink hard: a drunkard (Deut. 21:20; Prov. 23:20, 21; Ezek. 23:42; Nah. 1:10); those who engage in drinking too much (Isa. 56:12).

5434. סְבָא ***s^{e}b̲ā':*** A proper noun designating Seba:

A. The firstborn son of Cush (Gen. 10:7; 1 Chr. 1:9).

B. The land or nation of Seba (Ps. 72:10; Isa. 43:3).

5435. סֹבֶא ***sōb̲e':*** A masculine noun referring to wine, choice wine. It refers to a drink (Isa. 1:22, NASB). Some suggest a form of beer or liquor, but it may refer to a form of wine (Hos. 4:18; Nah. 1:10).

5436. סְבָאִים ***s^{e}b̲ā'iym,*** סָבָאִים ***sāb̲ā'iym:*** A proper noun designating Sabeans (Isa. 45:14; Ezek. 23:42).

5437. סָבַב ***sāb̲ab̲:*** A verb meaning to go around, to surround; to turn around, to turn back, to change. It indicates a curving motion or an encircling motion of something, but it is used figuratively as well: to turn, to change direction (1 Sam. 15:12); to encircle or flow around about, throughout (Gen. 2:11, 13); to surround something (Gen. 19:4); to gather people around a central person or object (Gen. 37:7); to travel round about (Ex. 13:18). It indicates a surrounding setting prepared by a jeweler to receive jewels, etc. (Ex. 28:11). It refers to the motion of something that turns or moves about: a door (Prov. 26:14); the wind in its circuits (Eccl. 1:6). It is used metaphorically of a person's mind turning, its attention focusing (Eccl. 7:25); of Jerusalem opening like a door (Ezek. 26:2). It indicates the transforming of a matter, the changing of a matter (2 Sam. 14:20). It indicates the giving over, the turning over of something in its causative forms (1 Chr. 10:14); of changing a name (2 Kgs. 23:34); or of the features of a land being transformed, changed (Zech. 14:10). It describes boundaries that turn around (Num. 34:4, 5; Josh. 18:14).

5438. סִבָּה *sibbāh:* A feminine noun indicating a turn of events, a cause. It refers to a sudden change in the way things are going, a result coming about that was not expected (1 Kgs. 12:15).

5439. סָבִיב *sā<u>b</u>iy<u>b</u>:* An adverb or preposition indicating surrounding, all around, on every side. It means round about, in the vicinity or area (Gen. 23:17; Ex. 19:12; 25:11; Judg. 20:29). It indicates something scattered or present all around a certain area (Ex. 16:13). With *min* (4480) on the front, it means from all around, from round about (Jer. 4:17; Isa. 42:25; Ezek. 16:33, 37). It is repeated for emphasis (2 Chr. 4:3; Ezek. 8:10). In its plural form, it may take on the sense of the areas or parts around about (Jer. 49:5). In its singular and plural forms, it can take on the meaning of the circuit (of travel, area, etc.); the circuits (Ex. 7:24; 1 Chr. 11:8; Eccl. 1:6).

5440. סָבַךְ *sā<u>b</u>a<u>k</u>:* A verb meaning to wrap around, to intertwine, to become entangled. It describes the way the roots of a plant or tree cling to and entangle themselves to a rock pile (Job 8:17); or the way thorns become entangled (Nah. 1:10).

5441. סְבֹךְ *s^e<u>b</u>ō<u>k</u>:* A masculine noun indicating a thicket, lair. It refers to a dense growth of a forest, a thicket, brush (Ps. 74:5). It is used figuratively of the lair or home of a lion representing an attacking nation (Jer. 4:7).

5442. סְבַךְ *s^e<u>b</u>a<u>k</u>:* A masculine noun referring to a thicket. It refers to a dense growth of heavy shrubs, small trees, or underbrush (Gen. 22:13; Isa. 9:18[17]; 10:34), a major hindrance to travel.

5443. סַבְּכָא *sabb^e<u>k</u>ā',* שַׂבְּכָא *śabb^e<u>k</u>ā':* An Aramaic feminine noun indicating a musical instrument, sackbut, trigon, or harp. It refers to one of the instruments from the huge ensemble of musical instruments celebrating the dedication of Nebuchadnezzar's golden statute (Dan. 3:5, 7, 10, 15).

5444. סִבְּכַי ***sibbeḵai:*** A proper noun designating Sibbecai (2 Sam. 21:18; 1 Chr. 11:29; 20:4; 27:11).

5445. סָבַל ***sāḇal:*** A verb meaning to bear a load, to carry. It means to bear, to endure, to carry something: to carry burdens of some kind as a slave or laborer (Gen. 49:15); mockingly, it refers to bearing idols (Isa. 46:7); to the Suffering Servant's bearing of sorrows (Isa. 53:4, 11); of the Lord's carrying His people (Isa. 46:4); carrying iniquities or punishments (Lam. 5:7); to general exhaustion (Eccl. 12:5). It is used of a cow bearing or carrying its young (Ps. 144:14).

5446. סְבַל ***seḇal:*** An Aramaic verb meaning to bear a load. It refers to something bearing a load. In context it refers to older Temple foundations becoming load bearing, being restored or re-laid (Ezra 6:3).

5447. סֵבֶל ***sēḇel:*** A masculine noun indicating a burden, forced labor. It refers to labor, work, burdens borne by Israel in Egypt under taskmasters (Ps. 81:6[7]); forced state labor (1 Kgs. 11:28). It refers to the loads themselves that were carried (Neh. 4:17[11]).

5448. סֹבֶל ***sōḇel:*** A masculine noun referring to a burden. It refers to a load that a worker had to carry, his burden, often placed there by oppressors. God would remove these burdens (Isa. 9:4[3]; 10:27; 14:25).

5449. סַבָּל ***sabbāl:*** A masculine noun indicating a carrier, a burden bearer. It refers to those persons responsible for transporting or moving construction materials as needed (1 Kgs. 5:15[29]); 2 Chr. 2:2[1], 18[17]; 34:13; Neh. 4:10[4]).

5450. סְבָלָה ***seḇālāh:*** A feminine noun indicating a burden, hard labor. It refers to the forced heavy labor that Israel was subjected to in Egypt (Ex. 1:11; 2:11; 5:4, 5; 6:6, 7).

5451. סִבֹּלֶת ***sibbōleṯ:*** A feminine noun sibboleth. It describes an ear of grain, wheat. It was the way an Ephraimite pronounced *šibbōleṯ*, "s" instead of "sh" (Judg. 12:6).

5452. סְבַר ***seḇar:*** An Aramaic verb meaning to think, to do, to try. It has the sense of attempting or intending to do something, to change something from what it was (Dan. 7:25).

5453. סִבְרַיִם ***siḇrayim:*** A proper noun designating the town Sibraim (Ezek. 47:16).

5454. סַבְתָּא ***saḇtā'***, סַבְתָּה ***saḇtāh:*** A proper noun designating Sabta, Sabtah (Gen. 10:7; 1 Chr. 1:9).

5455. סַבְתְּכָא ***saḇteḵā':*** A proper noun designating Sabtecha (Gen. 10:7; 1 Chr. 1:9).

5456. סָגַד ***sāgaḏ:*** A verb meaning to fall down, to bow down, to lie down in worship. The word occurs four times, only in Isaiah (Isa. 44:15, 17, 19; 46:6). It refers to bowing or lying flat before a wooden or golden idol to worship, to pray, or to seek deliverance from it (Isa. 44:17). Isaiah satirized those who lowered themselves in this way before an idol and did not recognize that an idol is only the work of human hands.

5457. סְגִד ***s***^{e}***ghiḏ:*** An Aramaic verb meaning to worship, to bow, to lie in worship. The word corresponds to the Hebrew word *sāgaḏ* (5456). It occurs in Daniel 2:46, referring to King Nebuchadnezzar's prostration before Daniel and his command that an offering and incense be offered to Daniel for interpreting his dream. The only other occurrences are the eleven uses in Daniel 3, referring to the worship of the gold image Nebuchadnezzar made. All these occurrences are accompanied by the words to fall (5308) or to serve (6399). The three Hebrew officials appointed by Nebuchadnezzar at Daniel's recommendation refused to fall and worship this foreign gods. Instead, they yielded their own bodies to God in the fiery furnace (Dan. 3:28; cf. Rom. 12:1).

5458. סְגוֹר ***s***^{e}***gôr:*** I. A masculine noun meaning gold. It refers to high-quality, fine gold of great value (Job 28:15).

II. A masculine noun referring to an enclosure, a chest. It refers to the part of the body enclosing the heart, the chest cavity (Hos. 13:8).

5459. סְגֻלָּה ***s***^{e}***gullāh:*** A feminine noun meaning a personal possession, a special possession, property. This noun is used only six times, but it gives one of the most memorable depictions of the Lord's relationship to His people and the place established for them.

The primary meaning of the word theologically is its designation "unique possession." God has made Israel His own unique possession (Ex. 19:5). Israel holds a special position among the nations of the world, although all nations belong to the Lord. Israel's position, function, character, responsibility, and calling create its uniqueness (Deut. 7:6; 14:2; 26:18; Ps. 135:4). Israel is to be a priestly community that honors and fears the Lord, to be His alone (Mal. 3:17). In the New Testament, 1 Peter 2:9 quotes Exodus 19:5, applying it to the church.

The word is used in a secular sense to indicate personal possessions, such as when David gave his own gold and silver to the Lord (1 Chr. 29:3; Eccl. 2:8).

5460. סְגַן ***s***^{e}***gan:*** An Aramaic masculine noun meaning prefect, governor. King Nebuchadnezzar positioned Daniel to be the head of all the governors of Babylon (Dan. 2:48). Daniel 3:2 lists the various officers of the neo-Babylonian Empire, one of which was the office signified by this term. Later, King Nebuchadnezzar summoned these and other officials to the dedication of the golden image he had erected. At this dedication, all the officials were expected to fall down and worship the image. Later, Darius the Mede issued a similar edict (Dan. 6:7[8]). However, in both instances, some refused, including Daniel.

5461. סֶגֶן ***segen,*** סָגָן ***sāgān:*** A masculine noun meaning prefect or ruler. Sometimes this term refers to an official of the Assyrian or Babylonian Empire (Isa. 41:25; Jer. 51:23, 28, 57; Ezek. 23:6, 12, 23). It can also refer to the head of a Jewish community (Ezra 9:2); as well as lesser officials of Judah (Neh. 2:16; 4:14[8], 19[13]; 5:7, 17; 7:5; 12:40; 13:11).

5462. סָגַר ***sāgar:*** I. A verb meaning to close. Its meaning is uniformly to close, to shut up; to stop: to close up a hole in one's flesh (Gen. 2:21); to shut, to close a door, etc. (Gen. 7:16; 19:6, 10); to shut, enclose something, e.g., Israel in the wilderness terrain (Ex. 14:3); to close the womb from being fertile (1 Sam. 1:5). In its passive uses, it means to be shut, shut up, closed (Num. 12:14, 15; Josh. 6:1; 1 Sam. 23:7; Neh. 13:19; Eccl. 12:4). In its intensive and causative stems, it means to enclose, to deliver over to someone or something (1 Sam. 17:46; 24:18[19]); to give into another's authority or power (Deut. 23:15[16]; 1 Sam. 23:11; Amos 1:6; Obad. 1:14). It is used of things tightly fitted together, closed in on each other (Job 41:15[7]).

II. A masculine noun meaning the finest gold, pure gold. It was used for overlaying (1 Kgs. 6:20); for Temple furniture (1 Kgs. 7:49, 50); Temple vessels (1 Kgs. 10:21). It was especially valuable and used in wise comparisons (Job 28:15).

5463. סְגַר ***s^egar:*** An Aramaic verb meaning to shut. It means to close something. In context it refers to the Lord's closing the lions' mouths (Dan. 6:22[23]); an act of deliverance by the Lord on Daniel's behalf.

5464. סַגְרִיר ***sagriyr:*** A masculine noun referring to a steady rain. It refers to a moderate constant rainfall that will not let up, putting everyone in a state of agitation and aggravation (Prov. 27:15).

5465. סַד ***sad:*** A masculine noun designating stocks, shackles. It refers to a device for confining a prisoner's feet so he or she could not walk or wander away, a form of punishment or discipline (Job 13:27; 33:11). It is used figuratively in both passages.

5466. סָדִין ***sādiyn:*** A masculine noun meaning sheet, linen garment. It refers to a linen garment that was wrapped around a person. These garments were of great value (Judg. 14:12, 13; Prov. 31:24) and considered a luxury (Isa. 3:23).

5467. סְדֹם ***s^edōm:*** A proper noun designating Sodom, a city destroyed by the Lord for its egregious sins, especially "sodomy." Lot lived in it for a short while (Gen. 13) but was rescued from its destruction. It was located in the southern area of Canaan (Gen. 10:19), southeast of the Dead Sea. It engaged in war with several northern kings (Gen. 14:2–22). The story of its destruction illustrates its wickedness, for there were not enough righteous persons in it to deliver it (Gen. 18:16–26; 19:1–28). It became a symbol of wickedness (Ezek. 16:46–56).

5468. סֵדֶר ***sē<u>d</u>er:*** A masculine noun referring to orderliness. It describes a state or condition of things being in their places, not chaotic, not a state of confusion (Job 10:22).

5469. סַהַר ***sahar:*** A masculine noun indicating roundness. It refers to something shaped like a circle, a sphere, a cylinder. It describes the rounded aspect of something, a person's navel like a goblet (Song 7:2[3]).

5470. סֹהַר ***sōhar:*** A masculine noun denoting a prison, jail. It was a place for prisoners, specifically those termed prisoners of the king (Gen. 39:20–23); those persons who were formerly in the employment of the royal house in some way (Gen. 40:35).

5471. סוֹא ***sô':*** A proper noun designating So, king of Egypt (2 Kgs. 17:4).

5472. סוּג ***sûg:*** A verb meaning to turn away, to turn back, to backslide. It has the sense of deviating from or turning from an accepted or expected path or commitment: to move something, e.g., a boundary line (Deut. 19:14; Hos. 5:10); to lose heart, to fail to perform (2 Sam. 1:22[20]); to be thwarted from evil plans (Ps. 35:4; 40:14[15]); to become disloyal, to be disloyal, to apostate (Ps. 53:3[4]; 78:57); to change one's heart, to backslide (Prov. 14:14). Those who follow wrong paths will be turned back (Isa. 42:17).

5473. סוּג ***sûg:*** A verb meaning to fence in, to encircle. It refers to encircling something, surrounding it. It is used in a figurative, amorous sense of a bride's belly being fenced in or surrounded by lilies (Song 7:2[3]). It describes the fencing in of garden plants (Isa. 17:11).

5474. סוּגַר ***sûgar:*** A masculine noun referring to a cage. It describes a box-like enclosed structure for confining something, usually an animal (Ezek. 19:9). In context it describes the corpses of God's people.

5475. סוֹד ***sô<u>d</u>:*** A masculine noun meaning counsel. Confidentiality is at the heart of this term. According to Proverbs 25:9, information shared in confidence should remain confidential. Yet gossip makes it difficult to do this (Prov. 11:13; 20:19). Elsewhere, this term reflects a more general meaning of counsel, which is viewed as essential to successful planning (Prov. 15:22). When it means counsel, this term suggests the idea of intimacy. For example, Job used this term to refer to his close friendship with God (Job 29:4); and with individuals he thought of as his close friends (Job 19:19). David used this term to describe one of his close friendships (Ps. 55:14[15]). God establishes a close, intimate relationship with those who revere Him and walk uprightly (Ps. 25:14; Prov. 3:32). Sometimes, however, human relationships involve less than ideal associations (Gen. 49:6). Used in a negative sense, this term can denote evil plotting (Ps. 64:2[3]; 83:3[4]).

5476. סוֹדִי ***sôd̲iy:*** A proper noun designating Sodi (Num. 13:10).

5477. סוּחַ ***sûaḥ:*** A proper noun designating Suah (1 Chr. 7:36).

5478. סוּחָה ***sûḥāh:*** I. A feminine noun meaning refuse, rubbish. It refers to decaying garbage or other trash left to decompose (Isa. 5:25).

II. A feminine noun meaning something torn. Some earlier translators rendered this word as something killed (Isa. 5:25).

5479. סוֹטַי ***sôṭay:*** A proper noun designating Sotai (Ezra 2:55; Neh. 7:57).

5480. סוּךְ ***sûk:*** A verb meaning to anoint, to pour upon. Oil is frequently the substance used for anointing (Deut. 28:40; 2 Sam. 14:2; Ezek. 16:9; Mic. 6:15). This procedure could be performed on oneself (2 Sam. 12:20; Ruth 3:3; Dan. 10:3) as well as on another person (2 Chr. 28:15; Ezek. 16:9). In several instances, the absence of anointing oil among God's people is an indication of divine judgment (Deut. 28:40; Mic. 6:15).

5481. סוּמְפּוֹנְיָה ***sûmpônyāh:*** An Aramaic feminine noun meaning bagpipe, dulcimer. It refers to one of the ensemble of musical instruments gathered to celebrate the dedication of Nebuchadnezzar's golden statue (Dan. 3:5, 7, 10, 15). As its renderings indicate, its meaning is disputed. Recent suggestions are bagpipe, dulcimer, drum, or even "in harmony," a musical term.

5482. סְוֵנֵה ***s^{e}wēnēh:*** A proper noun designating the town of Syene (Ezek. 29:10; 30:6).

5483. סוּס ***sûs,*** סֻס ***sus:*** I. A masculine noun uniformly rendered as horse. It refers to any horse (Gen. 47:17; 49:17; Ex. 9:3). Horses were trained for special uses: chariotry and war (Ex. 14:9; 1 Kgs. 20:1; Isa. 31:1; Ezek. 27:14). They were not to be multiplied by Israel's kings, but the kings were to trust the Lord for their might, not horses (Deut. 11:4; 17:16).

II. A masculine noun referring to a swallow, a crane, a swift. It is the name of a bird. It refers to a small, swift-flying type of bird, a swift or a swallow (Isa. 38:14; Jer. 8:7). Understanding the word to refer to a crane is difficult.

5484. סוּסָה ***sûsāh:*** A feminine noun indicating a mare, a female horse. It refers to the bride in Song 1:9 as an indication of her attractiveness.

5485. סוּסִי **sûsiy:** A proper noun designating Susi (Num. 13:11).

5486. סוּף **sûp̱:** A verb meaning to come to an end, to cease, to terminate. The Old Testament describes Purim as an annual observance whose celebration should not cease (Esth. 9:28). The psalmist used the term to describe how quickly the prosperity enjoyed by the wicked is brought to an end (Ps. 73:19). Elsewhere, it is a general term that refers to the end of something as a result of God's judgment (Isa. 66:17; Jer. 8:13; Zeph. 1:2, 3).

5487. סוּף **sûp̱:** An Aramaic verb meaning to be fulfilled, to be ended, to end. The word is used in Daniel 2:44 in connection with the divinely established kingdom that will never be destroyed and will bring all other kingdoms to an end. In Daniel 4:33[30], it referred to King Nebuchadnezzar, who finished speaking as God began to address him.

5488. סוּף **sûp̱:** A masculine noun meaning a reed. It uniformly means large water plants, rushes, reeds (Ex. 2:3, 5; Isa. 19:6). The phrase *yammāh sûp̱* means unto, toward the sea of reeds, the Red Sea (Ex. 10:19). The phrase *yam-sûp̱* refers to a sea of reeds, the traditional Red Sea (Ex. 13:18; Josh. 2:10). It is extended in usage to the Gulf of Suez, the Gulf of Aqaba (1 Kgs. 9:26, Red Sea).

5489. סוּף **sûp̱:** I. A proper noun designating the place Suph, near Mount Horeb (NASB, NIV, Deut. 1:1).

II. Red [reed] from *sûp̱* (5488), a designation for the Red Sea (KJV, Deut. 1:1).

5490. סוֹף **sôp̱:** A masculine noun meaning end, conclusion, completion. It refers to the physical rear or end of something (2 nclusion to life (Eccl. 7:2); the summary or final purpose of the teachings of someone (Eccl. 12:13). It is used in the phrase *merō'š w*^{e}*'ad̲-sōp̱*, from beginning to end to mean all of it (Eccl. 3:11).

5491. סוֹף **s̱ōph:** An Aramaic masculine noun meaning end, farthest extent. It refers in context to the most extreme end of the earth (Dan. 4:11[8], 22[19]). It is used to mean unto the end *'ad̲-sōp̱ā'* with respect to the kingdom of Daniel's God: that is, on to the end, forever (Dan. 6:26[27]; 7:26). It refers to the conclusion of an event, a dream, and the recording of it (Dan. 7:28).

5492. סוּפָה **sûp̱āh:** I. A feminine noun indicating a wind, a stormy wind. It indicates a storm with strong winds that blow away chaff like nothing (Job 21:18). In general, it refers to a storm with destructive powers, a tempest, a hurricane-type storm (Job 27:20). It is used in a figurative sense of God's pursuit of the wicked (Ps. 83:15[16]; Isa. 66:15; Amos 1:14; Nah. 1:3); or of any calamity on humankind

(Prov. 1:27). God's chariots are like a tempest or a whirlwind (Jer. 4:13).

II. A proper noun, Suphah. It refers to a region in Moab near the Arnon River (Num. 21:14).

III. A proper noun referring to the Red Sea, Sea of Reeds. It is taken by some translators as a reference to the Red Sea (KJV, Num. 21:14).

5493. סוּר ***sûr,*** **סָר** ***sār:*** A verb meaning to turn away, to go away, to desert, to quit, to keep far away, to stop, to take away, to remove, to be removed, to make depart. The word is used equally in the simple and causative stems. The basic meaning of the root, to turn away, takes on various connotations in the simple stem according to context. In the simple stem, the verb means to turn aside, as Moses turned aside to see why the bush was not being consumed by the fire (Ex. 3:3, 4); it is used metaphorically to describe turning away from the Lord because of a rebellious heart (Jer. 5:23); or taking time to turn aside and seek someone's welfare (Jer. 15:5). The word describes leaving or going away literally (Ex. 8:31[27]); or figuratively, the scepter would not leave Judah (Gen. 49:10); but Samson's strength left him (Judg. 16:19). Its meaning extends further to indicate falling away, as when one is enticed to fall away from following the Lord to pursue other gods (Deut. 11:16; 1 Sam. 12:20; Ps. 14:3). It means to stop something; for example, the banqueting and carousing of Israel would cease at the time of exile (Hos. 4:18; Amos 6:7). It also indicates the act of keeping away from something, such as evil (Isa. 59:15); or when the Lord kept Himself from His people (Hos. 9:12). Wise teaching helps keep a person far from the dangers of death (Prov. 13:14, 19).

The causative stem adds the idea of making something move, go away, turn away, or simply to put aside. The priests would set aside burnt offerings to be offered up (2 Chr. 35:12); and clothing was put aside as Tamar removed her widow's clothes to deceive Judah (Gen. 38:14; 1 Sam. 17:39; 1 Kgs. 20:41). God removed Israel from His presence because He was angry with them (2 Kgs. 17:18, 23; 23:27); Jacob charged his entire clan to get rid of their strange gods (Gen. 35:2; Josh. 24:14, 23).

When the verb is passive, it means to be removed, such as when the fat of offerings was removed by the priests (Lev. 4:31, 35). In Daniel 12:11, the word expresses the idea that the daily sacrifice was removed.

5494. סוּר ***sûr:*** A masculine noun meaning degenerate. It refers to the resulting state of something that has deteriorated, become foul-smelling, rotten (Jer. 2:21).

5495. סוּר ***sûr:*** A proper noun designating the Temple gate Sur (2 Kgs. 11:6).

5496. סוּת ***sûṯ:*** A verb meaning to incite, to entice, to mislead. It has the sense of stirring up persons with the intention to get them to deviate, to act with destructive, harmful purposes or results in mind; to incite people to be evil, to lead them astray (Deut. 13:6[7]); 1 Sam. 26:19; 2 Sam. 24:1; 1 Kgs. 21:25; Isa. 36:18). It is also used of getting a person to concede or agree to something in a neutral or positive sense (Josh. 15:18; Judg. 1:14; Job 36:16).

5497. סוּת ***sûṯ:*** A masculine noun indicating a garment, clothing. It refers to garments in general, but in context it hints of the royal or kingly clothing of a ruler (Gen. 49:11).

5498. סָחַב ***sāḥaḇ:*** A verb meaning to drag, to drag off. It describes pulling down and removing the stones and other parts of a city to demolish it (2 Sam. 17:13). The activity of dogs pulling and dragging something to devour it is expressed with this word (Jer. 15:3); as well as the process of people dragging trash out to throw into a garbage heap (Jer. 22:19), a picture of the fate of Jehoiakim. It describes persons being dragged from their land (Jer. 49:20) as part of God's judgments (Jer. 50:45).

5499. סְחָבָה ***s***^{e}***ḥāḇāh:*** A feminine noun referring to an old rag, worn-out clothing. It refers to pieces of cloth good only as waste or for cleaning up (Jer. 38:11, 12).

5500. סָחָה ***sāḥāh:*** A verb meaning to scrape. It means to sweep up, to clean up something by rubbing or pulling an abrasive tool over it (Ezek. 26:4); clearing an area of debris or filth.

5501. סְחִי ***s***^{e}***ḥiy:*** A masculine noun referring to scum, offscouring. It refers to trash or what is rejected, left over, thrown away, unwanted (Lam. 3:45).

5502. סָחַף ***sāḥap̱:*** A verb meaning to sweep away, sweep off one's feet. It indicates rain water washing away crops in a field; it depicts those who have political or military power being swept away (NASB, thrust; NIV, push off; KJV, drive off) (Prov. 28:3; Jer. 46:15).

5503. סָחַר ***sāḥar:*** A verb meaning to travel as merchants, to trade. It refers to a merchant, a commercial business man, a traveling trader (Gen. 23:16; 37:28; 1 Kgs. 10:28; Isa. 23:2; Ezek. 27:12); the activity of carrying on trade, business (Gen. 34:10, 21). It has the sense of to go back and forth, to wander; to throb (of the heart) (Ps. 38:10[11]; Jer. 14:18).

5504. סַחַר ***saḥar:*** A masculine noun referring to merchandise, profit, marketplace. It figuratively indicates the benefits of wisdom (Prov. 3:14); and diligence through wisdom (Prov. 31:18). It is used in a metaphor for the merchant city of Tyre, the marketplace of the ancient world (Isa. 23:3); as well as her monetary gains (Isa. 23:18). It describes the goods or merchandise of trade (Isa. 45:14).

5505. סָחַר ***sāḥar:*** A masculine noun referring to merchandise or gain from dealing in merchandise. It refers to the goods or merchandise moved or traded or the gain and profit connected with it (Isa. 23:3, revenue, KJV, NASB, NIV). It is rendered as merchandise (Isa. 45:14, KJV, NKJV, NASB, NIV). In Proverbs 3:14, it has the sense of profit or merchandise (cf. KJV, merchandise; NKJV, NASB, profit or proceeds).

5506. סְחֹרָה ***sᵉḥōrāh:*** A feminine noun signifying market, merchandise. It depicts the various seabordering lands (isles?) as the marketplaces, the market of Tyre (Ezek. 27:15).

5507. סֹחֵרָה ***sōḥērāh:*** A feminine noun referring to a small shield, a buckler. It refers to a defensive weapon used to ward off the attacks and blows of an enemy. It is used figuratively of God's faithfulness to His people as their shield or protection (Ps. 91:4).

5508. סֹחֶרֶת ***sōḥereṯ:*** I. A feminine noun indicating a costly stone in pavement. It describes a hard, shiny, stone of luxury used in the Persian state buildings (Esth. 1:6).

II. A feminine noun referring to marble, black marble used in pavement. It is a stone used in royal palaces and houses of state in the Persian Empire (Esth. 1:6).

5509. סִיג ***siyg,*** סוּג ***sûg:*** A masculine noun referring to dross. The word is used metaphorically and euphemistically to mock the god who may be busy relieving himself. The word suggests dross or waste, excrement (1 Kgs. 18:27). It clearly means waste, dross from metals in other passages (Ps. 119:119; Prov. 25:4). It describes impurity or a false covering hiding a wicked heart (Prov. 26:23). It is symbolic of moral and religious corruption and apostasy (Isa. 1:22, 25; Ezek. 22:18).

5510. סִיוָן ***siywān:*** A proper noun indicating the month Sivan. It is used in Esther 8:9. It is the third month of the year, equaling our May-June, the time of the Feast of Weeks.

5511. סִיחוֹן ***siyḥôn:*** A proper noun designating Sihon, a king of the Amorites (ca. 1200 B.C.). Joshua conquered his kingdom. His capital was at Heshbon. He at one time ruled over Moab (Num. 21:21–36). His territory stretched from the Arnon in the south to the Jabbok River in the north. The Jordan was its western border. He refused to let Israel pass through his territory on their way to Canaan (Num. 21). For this he was conquered and slain. Reuben and Gad received much of his conquered territory (Num. 32:33). His defeat was a great victory of Israel's God, the Lord (Deut. 34:1; Josh. 9:10; Ps. 135:11; 136:19).

5512. סִין ***siyn:*** A proper noun designating the place Sin:

A. An Egyptian border town fortress (Pelusium, NIV; Sin, KJV) mentioned by Ezekiel as an object of God's wrath (Ezek. 30:15, 16). It has been located thirteen miles east of the Suez Canal and about two miles from the Mediterranean coast on a major route to Memphis. It is placed just east of Migdol.

B. A desert located west of Sinai between Elim and Rephidim. Its exact location depends on where Sinai is located.

5513. סִינַי ***siyniy:*** A proper noun designating Mount Sinai, the place where God met with the Israelites after their exodus from Egypt (Ex. 16:1; 19:1, 2, 11, 18, 20, 23; 24:16; 31:18; 34:2, 4, 29, 32; Lev. 7:38; 25:1; 26:46; 27:34). The site was revered as a special holy place (Ps. 68:8[9], 17[18]).

5514. סִינַי ***siynay:*** A proper noun designating Sinai, the "mountain of God" (Ex. 3:1; 4:27; 18:5; 24:13) where Moses received the laws of God and concluded the "Sinai Covenant" (Ex. 19:1—24:18). Many places have been suggested for its location. It has traditionally been placed at Jebel Musa ("Mountain of Moses," Arabic) in the central southern region of southern Sinai. In every instance of its use, it is tied to Moses and the giving of the Law (Ex. 19—34; Num. 1; 3; 4; 9; Deut. 33:2). The mountain was called Horeb one time (Ex. 33:6), Horeb elsewhere referring to a mountain range (Ex. 3:1; 17:6; Deut. 1:2, 6; 4:10; 29:1). Israel encamped at Sinai for ca. eleven months (Num. 10:11–12). God's giving of the Law at Sinai was celebrated in Israel's worship (Ps. 68:8[9], 17[18]), the One of Sinai (NIV), the God of Israel (Judg. 5:5).

5515. סִינִים ***siyniym:*** I. A masculine proper noun designating the Sinim people, perhaps from southern China (KJV, NASB, Isa. 49:12).

II. The people of Aswan (NIV, Isa. 49:12).

5516. סִיסְרָא ***siys^{e}rā':*** A proper noun designating Sisera:

A. The commander in charge of the Canaanite troops of Jabin, king Hazor. He was slain by Jael, wife of Heber the Kenite (Judg. 5:24–27).

B. The father of a postexilic family (Ezra 2:53; Neh. 7:55).

5517. סִיעָא ***siy'ā'***, סִיעֲהָא ***siy^{a}hā':*** A proper noun designating Siaha (Ezra 2:44; Neh. 7:47).

5518. סִיר ***siyr:*** I. A common noun meaning pot. It refers to a cooking pot for various food items (Ex. 16:3; 2 Kgs. 4:38–41; Mic. 3:3), especially those used in the Temple area (2 Kgs. 25:14; Zech. 14:20, 21). It is used in the sense of a bowl for washing one's feet (Ps. 60:8[10]; 108:9[10]).

II. A common noun meaning thorn, hook. It refers to thornbushes commonly used to fire a pot (Eccl. 7:6). They were a sign of an uncultivated area (Isa. 34:13); or a barrier (Hos. 2:6[8]). It clearly means a hook to hang something on or to use to catch something (Amos 4:2).

5519. סָךְ ***sāḵ:*** A masculine noun referring to a multitude, a throng. It refers to a group or gathering of people worshiping the Lord (Ps. 42:4[5]).

5520. סֹךְ ***sōḵ:*** A masculine noun meaning a cover, a hiding place, a tent. It describes a place where a person can be undetected. It is employed figuratively of the places from which the wicked attack the righteous (Ps. 10:9). In a positive sense, it refers to the protective, shielding hiding place of God's tent, Tabernacle, presence (Ps. 27:5). It indicates the place where God dwells (Ps. 76:2[3]; Jer. 25:38).

5521. סֻכָּה ***sukkāh:*** A feminine singular noun meaning a booth, a thicket. This term is used for temporary shelters used to cover animals (Gen. 33:17); warriors (2 Sam. 11:11); and the prophet Jonah (Jon. 4:5). It is used poetically to refer to the clouds (Job 36:29; Ps. 18:11[12]). A specialized usage is employed for booths constructed for the fall harvest festival (Lev. 23:42, 43). The festival was known as the *ḥag hassuḵḵôṯ* (2282), the Feast of Booths (Deut. 16:13, 16). This was to remind the Israelites that they lived in booths when the Lord brought them up from Egypt (Lev. 23:43).

5522. סִכּוּת ***sikkûṯ:*** An obscure masculine singular noun that occurs only in Amos 5:26 and may mean Tabernacle. This passage clearly describes the Israelites' false and improper worship. The question is how detailed the prophet's charge was. Some have translated the phrase as booth or shrine, while the Septuagint (Greek Old Testament) reads "shrine of Molech." Some have suggested that both terms represent Akkadian astral deities, Sakkut and Kaiwan.

5523. סֻכּוֹת ***sukkôṯ:*** A proper noun designating Succoth:

A. A city in Canaan (Gen. 33:17; Josh. 13:27; Judg. 8:5, 6, 8, 14–16; 1 Kgs. 7:46; 2 Chr. 4:17; Ps. 60:6[8]; 108:7[8]).

B. A campsite in Egypt (Ex. 12:37; 13:20; Num. 33:5, 6).

5524. סֻכּוֹת בְּנוֹת ***sukkôṯ b^enôṯ:*** A proper noun designating Succoth Benoth (2 Kgs. 17:30).

5525. סֻכִּיִּים ***sukkiyyiym:*** A proper noun designating Sukkites (2 Chr. 12:3).

5526. סָכַךְ ***sāḵaḵ,*** שָׂכַךְ ***śāḵaḵ:*** I. A verb meaning to cover. It means to hide something or to shield something: the mercy seat on the ark of the covenant was covered by the wings of cherubim (Ex. 25:20); God's hand covered and protected Moses (Ex. 33:22). It is used of separating off an area with a curtain or hanging (Ex. 40:3, 21). Figuratively, it shows God shielding those who trust Him (Ps. 5:11[12]; 91:4); He covers Himself in anger (Lam. 3:43) or with a cloud (Lam. 3:44).

II. A verb meaning to stir, to excite. It means to rouse up, to spur on in the context of the Lord's action (Isa. 9:11[10]; 19:2).

III. A verb meaning to weave together. It describes the Lord's activity in creating a child's fetus within the womb (Job 10:11; Ps. 139:13).

5527. סְכָכָה *s^e^k̲āk̲āh:* A proper noun designating Secacah (Josh. 15:61).

5528. סָכַל *sāk̲al:* A verb meaning to be foolish, to act foolishly. It refers to acting in an indefensible manner, without reason, in foolish haste (Gen. 31:28); especially in disobeying God's instructions (1 Sam. 13:13; 1 Chr. 21:8; 2 Chr. 16:9). In an idiom, it means to play the fool (1 Sam. 26:21).

5529. סֶכֶל *sek̲el:* A masculine noun meaning folly, foolishness. It is the opposite of wisdom. It means to act without the fear of God, without knowledge, moral integrity, or reason (Eccl. 10:6).

5530. סָכָל *sāk̲āl:* A masculine noun meaning fool. It refers to a person who acts without wisdom, moral integrity, fear of God or knowledge (Eccl. 2:19; 7:17; 10:3, 14); acting senselessly, without knowing God (Jer. 4:22; 5:21).

5531. סִכְלוּת *sik̲lût̲,* שִׂכְלוּת *śik̲lût̲:* A feminine noun meaning folly, foolishness. It is a way of life devoid of wisdom, God, self-understanding, or an understanding of others (Eccl. 1:17; 2:3, 12, 13). Wisdom exceeds folly, and evil is attached to folly (Eccl. 2:13; 7:25); foolishness and folly are corrupting (Eccl. 10:1, 13).

5532. סָכַן *sāk̲an,* סֹכֵן *sōk̲ēn:* I. A verb indicating to be useful, profitable, to attend to, to be acquainted with. It means to be accustomed to acting in a certain way (Num. 22:30); to take care of things as needed (1 Kgs. 1:2; Job 22:21). When negated, it means to do something in a useless manner, in a way that will not profit (Job 15:3). In a different context, it means to be of value, to be useful (Job 22:2); to profit (Job 34:9; 35:3). It has the sense of knowing someone intimately, closely (Ps. 139:3). It may indicate being over or in charge of something (Isa. 22:15).

II. A feminine noun meaning a steward, a nurse. It means to care for people as needed, to be a nurse to them (1 Kgs. 1:2, 4). It is understood by some as a noun in Isaiah 22:15, meaning steward or administrator.

5533. סָכַן *sāk̲an:* I. A verb meaning to be impoverished. It refers to a person who is lacking in resources or the money to get them (Isa. 40:20).

II. A verb meaning to be in danger. It refers to putting oneself in harm's way, getting into a dangerous situation (Eccl. 10:9).

5534. סָכַר *sāk̲ar:* I. A verb meaning to stop up, to shut up. It means to close up or shut off something: the deep springs of water and the heavy rain from the skies are pictured figuratively as being shut down, closed in order to stop the flood waters (Gen. 8:2). It is used of stopping a person's mouth, shutting him or her up (Ps. 63:11[12]).

II. A verb meaning to hand over, to deliver. It means to give up persons to someone or something, to deliver them for some purpose (Isa. 19:4).

5535. סָכַת sā*k*a*t*: I. A verb meaning to be silent. It means to pay attention, to listen, to stop talking in order to focus and hear an important statement (Deut. 27:9).

II. A verb meaning to take heed. It means to take care, to listen, and take seriously something that is being said (Deut. 27:9).

5536. סַל sal: A masculine noun signifying a basket. It refers to a container for holding various food or sacrificial items: loaves of bread (Gen. 40:16–18); various meal offerings of bread (Ex. 29:3); unleavened bread as an offering (Lev. 8:2; Num. 6:15); meat (Judg. 6:19).

5537. סָלָא sālā': A verb meaning to weigh, to compare. In a figurative sense, it compares Israel's lack of moral and religious value against that of the purity of fine gold (Lam. 4:2); weighed against, compared to.

5538. סִלָּא sillā': A proper noun designating Silla (2 Kgs. 12:20[21]).

5539. סָלַד sāla*d*: I. A verb meaning to rejoice. It means to take satisfaction in something, to feel good about it. It was used of Job's rejoicing in his faithfulness to God (Job 6:10).

II. A verb meaning to harden oneself. It means to stand firm, to take strength in upholding one's position or actions. God is determined to continue faithful in sorrow and oppression (Job 6:10).

5540. סֶלֶד sele*d*: A proper noun designating Seled (1 Chr. 2:30).

5541. סָלָה sālāh: I. A verb meaning to tread down, to reject, to treat as worthless. It means to put out, to exclude, to refuse to accept. It describes God's refusal to accept those who do not walk in His ways (Ps. 119:118). It means to reject anyone for various reasons (Lam. 1:15).

II. A verb meaning to value, to pay for. It refers to evaluating something, to figure its worth. Wisdom cannot be valued even in the finest gold (Job 28:16, 19).

5542. סֶלָה selāh: A verb, possibly a fixed imperative form. Its exact meaning is uncertain. It is used over seventy times in Psalms (see concordance for references). It may give musical instructions or indicate a pause for various reasons (Hab. 3:3, 9, 13).

5543. סַלּוּ sallû, סַלַּי sallay, סָלוּא sālû', סַלּוּא sallû', סַלֻּא salu': A proper noun designating Sallu, Salu:

A. A priest (Neh. 12:7, 20).

B. A Simeonite (Num. 25:14).

C. A postexilic Jew (1 Chr. 9:7; Neh. 11:7).

D. A Benjamite (Neh. 11:8).

5544. סַלּוֹן ***sallôn:*** A masculine noun referring to a briar or thorn. It is used in a figurative sense both times of persons who will prove to be troublesome "thorns" to Ezekiel and to the problems and threats of neighboring nations, such as Sidon (Ezek. 2:6; 28:24).

5545. סָלַח ***sālaḥ:*** A verb meaning to forgive, to pardon, to spare, to be forgiven. The verb's subject is always God: He forgave the people of Israel after Moses interceded for them in the desert (Num. 14:20; Isa. 55:7); Solomon prayed that the Lord would always hear and forgive His people (1 Kgs. 8:30, 39; Dan. 9:19; Amos 7:2). Some sins of Israel, however, were not forgiven. Jehoiachin had shed so much innocent blood that the Lord was not willing to forgive him (2 Kgs. 24:4; Lam. 3:42). The verb means to free from or release from something: the word describes the Lord pardoning or releasing a young woman from her vows in some instances (Num. 30:5[6], 8[9]); the Lord will not forgive an Israelite who in his heart approves of his own rebellious actions and continues in them (Deut. 29:20[19]). The Lord forgives wickedness if it is repented of (Ex. 34:9; Num. 14:19).

In the passive stem, the Hebrew word means to be forgiven; the people are forgiven (Lev. 4:20, 26; 5:10; 19:22) for their unintentional sins (Num. 15:25, 28) by turning away from them.

5546. סַלָּח ***sallāḥ:*** An adjective meaning forgiving. This particular word is used only once in the Bible in a verse that describes the love and mercy of God (Ps. 86:5). See the related Hebrew root *sālaḥ* (5545) and noun *s^eliyḥāh* (5547).

5547. סְלִיחָה ***s^eliyḥāh:*** A feminine noun meaning forgiveness. God is a forgiving God (Neh. 9:17). He does not keep a record of sin, but with Him there is forgiveness (Ps. 130:4). Daniel also proclaimed that God is forgiving, even though the Hebrews had sinned greatly against Him (Dan. 9:9). See the related Hebrew root *sālaḥ* (5545) and the related Hebrew adjective *sallāḥ* (5546).

5548. סַלְכָה ***salḵāh:*** A proper noun designating Salecah (Deut. 3:10; Josh. 12:5; 13:11; 1 Chr. 5:11).

5549. סָלַל ***sālal:*** A verb meaning to build up, to lift up; to exalt. It means to hold someone or something in a position of a high or excessively high reputation or worth: Pharaoh over God's people (Ex. 9:17). It also means to raise something up, for something to rise up: God's troops (Job 19:12); one's assailants (Job 30:12); a song of praise to God (Ps. 68:4[5]); a person exalted by wisdom (Prov. 4:8); an upward path of life, a lifting up (Prov. 15:19; Jer. 18:15); a roadway for God's people (Isa. 57:14).

5550. סֹלְלָה ***sōl^elāh,*** סוֹלְלָה ***sôl^elāh:*** A feminine noun indicating a siege mound, a siege ramp. It describes a huge amount of dirt and earthen debris, rocks, etc., piled up by an attacking army in order to put a city under siege (2 Sam. 20:15). The Lord prevented Israel from being besieged in the year 701 B.C. by the Assyrians (2 Kgs. 19:32). The related verb *šāpak̲,* to cast, to throw, is always used to describe the process of setting up, casting up a siege ramp or mound.

5551. סֻלָּם ***sullām:*** A masculine noun referring to a stairway, ladder. It refers to a series of steps constructed in order for a person to reach a location by going up or down it (Gen. 28:12).

5552. סַלְסִלָּה ***salsillāh:*** I. A feminine noun meaning branch. It refers to vine tendrils or small branches that hold grapes (Jer. 6:9). In judgment God would, figuratively, glean these tendrils.

II. A feminine noun meaning basket. It was taken by older translations to refer to a basket into which grapes were dropped (Jer. 6:9).

5553. סֶלַע ***sela':*** A masculine noun referring to a rock, a cliff. Its most memorable use is to describe God as a Rock (2 Sam. 22:2; Ps. 18:2[3]; 31:3[4]; 42:9[10]). It refers to single rocks (1 Sam. 23:25); a crag or cliff (Judg. 6:20; Isa. 2:21); a hollowed-out place in a rock for a burial spot (Isa. 22:16). It refers to the habitations of Edom in clefts of the rocks (Obad. 1:3). It is a symbol of total destruction for the city of Tyre (Ezek. 26:4, 14). It describes figuratively God's destruction of Babylon (Jer. 51:25).

5554. סֶלַע ***sela':*** A proper noun designating Sela (Judg. 1:36; 2 Kgs. 14:7; Isa. 16:1; 42:11).

5555. סֶלַע הַמַּחְלְקוֹת ***sela' hammaḥl^e^qôṯ:*** A proper noun designating Sela Hammahlekoth (1 Sam. 23:28).

5556. סָלְעָם ***sol'ām:*** A masculine noun denoting a bald locust, a devastating locust. It refers to a winged insect, a bald locust, a locust that was edible for the Israelites (Lev. 11:22).

5557. סָלַף ***sālap̲:*** A verb meaning to overthrow; to twist; to pervert. It means basically to distort, subvert, or mislead from what is normal. It is used of the effect of bribes on justice, hindering it (Ex. 23:8); and its process (Deut. 16:19); it is used of removing governmental powers as well (Job 12:19). It describes hindering or subverting the wicked and foolish in their ways (Prov. 13:6; 19:3; 21:12; 22:12).

5558. סֶלֶף ***selep̲:*** A masculine noun referring to perversion, deceitfulness. It refers to a distorted and perverse way of life or character (Prov. 11:3; 15:4).

5559. סָלַק ***sālaq,*** סְלֵק ***s^e^lēq:*** I. A verb meaning to ascend, to go up. It means to go up, to climb up, used figuratively of going up to God's abode (Ps. 139:8).

II. An Aramaic verb meaning to travel up, to go up. It is used of going up hill country, of ascending to Jerusalem from Persia, Babylon, etc., (Ezra 4:12); or to bring or carry something up (Dan. 3:22; 6:23). It describes what is coming up, growing, ascending (Dan. 7:3, 8, 20). It describes a person's thought ascending up, focusing on something (Dan. 2:29).

5560. סֹלֶת ***sōleṯ:*** A common noun meaning fine flour. It is used of a grade of flour ground fine from the best part of the wheat grain (Gen. 18:6; Ex. 29:2, 40); also translated as wheat flour. It was used in sacrifices and was considered a food to be served as a luxury item or in the king's household (1 Kgs. 4:22[5:2]; Ezek. 16:13, 19).

5561. סַם ***sam:*** A masculine noun meaning fragrant, sweet; fragrant spice. It is used of spices from which fragrant perfumes were made (Ex. 25:6; 30:7, 34, etc.). The phrase *qᵉṭoreṯ (ha)ssammîm* indicates an incense of spices.

5562. סַמְגַּר נְבוֹ ***samgar-nᵉḇô,*** סַמְגַּר ***samgar:*** I. Samgar-Nebu (KJV, NASB, Jer. 29:3).

II. Samgar (NIV, Jer. 29:3).

5563. סְמָדַר ***sᵉmāḏar:*** A masculine noun referring to young grapes, grapes in blossom. It refers to grapes as they are flowering, in blossom at various stages (Song 2:13, 15; 7:12[13]), giving off a pleasant fragrance.

5564. סָמַךְ ***sāmaḵ:*** A verb meaning to lay on, to uphold, to sustain. It indicates placing or laying something on a person or animal, often in a ritualistic or legal setting: a hand on a sacrificial animal (Ex. 29:10, 15, 19); a person to be punished (Lev. 24:14); or corrected (Num. 27:18, 23; Deut. 34:9); to lean against a wall with one's hand (Amos 5:19). It indicates figuratively God's wrath resting on someone (Ps. 88:7[8]). It has the sense of supporting or sustaining someone (Gen. 27:37). The Lord upholds, supports, and sustains someone (Ps. 3:5[6]; Isa. 59:16; 63:5). In its passive participle, it describes a heart that is supported, sustained (Ps. 112:8).

5565. סְמַכְיָהוּ ***sᵉmaḵyāhû:*** A proper noun designating Semachia (1 Chr. 26:7).

5566. סֵמֶל ***sēmel,*** סֶמֶל ***semel:*** A masculine noun meaning statue, image, idol. Moses instructed the people to keep careful watch on themselves, lest they make an idol and worship it (Deut. 4:16). Manasseh put a carved image in God's Temple but later humbled himself before God and removed it (2 Chr. 33:7, 15). In a vision, Ezekiel saw an idol of jealousy—an idol in the north gate that was standing near the glory of the God of Israel (Ezek. 8:3, 5).

5567. סָמַן ***sāman:*** I. A verb meaning to appoint. It is used in a passive sense to indicate a place picked out, determined for planting something (Isa. 28:25). Its meaning is not entirely clear.

II. A verb meaning to plot out. It is taken to mean an area of ground plotted out for something, prepared (Isa. 28:25).

5568. סָמַר ***sāmar:*** A verb meaning to bristle up, stand up; to shiver. It is used of something caused to straighten up, to bristle, to become erect. In context it is used of human hair (Job 4:15). It takes on the sense of quiver, shake, tremble before God's Word (Ps. 119:120).

5569. סָמָר ***sāmār:*** I. An adjective indicating bristly, rough. It refers to something that is standing straight up, firmly, in a threatening way, such as locusts (Jer. 51:27).

II. An adjective indicating swarming. It refers to a great number of something covering an area, coming in droves; it was used of locusts (Jer. 51:27).

5570. סְנָאָה ***s^e^nā'āh,*** הַסְּנָאָה ***has-s^e^nā'āh:*** A proper noun designating Senaah, Hassenaah (Ezra 2:35; Neh. 3:3; 7:38).

5571. סַנְבַלַּט ***sanḇallaṭ:*** A proper noun designating Sanballat, a Horonite who became an adamant enemy of the rebuilding of Jerusalem and its Temple and walls. The name is a Babylonian name meaning "the moon god gives life" (Neh. 2:10, 19). He especially fumed against the rebuilding of the city walls and Nehemiah (Neh. 4:1–2[3:33–34]). He evidently was governor of Samaria. He threatened military intervention at Jerusalem (Neh. 4:7[1]) and assassination of Nehemiah (Neh 6:1–14).

5572. סְנֶה ***s^e^neh:*** A masculine noun referring to a bush. It indicates a desert shrub, a thorny shrub. God spoke to Moses from one of these shrubs as it was ablaze with fire (Ex. 3:2–4; Deut. 33:16).

5573. סֶנֶּה ***senneh:*** A proper noun designating Seneh (1 Sam. 14:4).

5574. סְנוּאָה ***s^e^nû'āh,*** הַסְּנֻאָה ***has-s^e^u'āh:*** A proper noun designating Senuah, Hassenuah (1 Chr. 9:7; Neh. 11:9).

5575. סַנְוֵרִים ***sanwēriym:*** A masculine plural noun indicating blindness, sudden blindness. It refers to an inability to find one's way, inability to see properly (Gen. 19:11); it may be figurative as well as literal (2 Kgs. 6:18).

5576. סַנְחֵרִיב ***sanḥēriyḇ:*** A proper noun designating Sennacherib, the Assyrian king (705–681 B.C.) who steam rolled through Israel and Judah, devastating the land, its cities, and inhabitants. His name means "(the) mood god has prospered his kinsmen." He destroyed Lachish, a Judean city, after a long and horrifying siege (2 Kgs. 18:14–17; 19:8). He attempted to besiege Jerusalem and raze it in 701 B.C. when Hezekiah was king and Isaiah was prophesying (2 Kgs. 18; 19; Isa. 36; 37). The Lord destroyed his army by an act of divine providence. Sennacherib was assassinated shortly thereafter by his sons.

5577. סַנְסִנָּה ***sansinnāh:*** A masculine noun referring to a fruit stalk, a bough. It refers to a cluster of fruit, possibly a blossom cluster of dates. Figuratively, it describes the breasts of the bride (Song 7:8[9]).

5578. סַנְסַנָּה ***sansannāh:*** A proper noun designating Sansannah (Josh. 15:31).

5579. סְנַפִּיר ***s^enappiyr:*** A masculine noun referring to a fin. It is used as a feature of a fish that was clean and edible to Israel (Lev. 11:9, 10, 12; Deut. 14:9, 10).

5580. סָס ***sās:*** A masculine noun referring to a grub worm. It indicates an insect or worm that eats clothing. In context it is used symbolically of what will devour Israel's enemies (Isa. 51:8).

5581. סִסְמָי ***sismāy:*** A proper noun designating Sismai (1 Chr. 2:40).

5582. סָעַד ***sā'aḏ:*** A verb meaning to support, to sustain, to refresh. It is used of energizing people, of aiding them, refreshing them with nourishment (Gen. 18:5; Judg. 19:5); or with rest and food (1 Kgs. 13:7). It describes the strength and support of God's hand on a person (Ps. 18:35 [36]; 20:2[3]); and of righteousness supporting a king's reign (Prov. 20:28); especially with respect to the government of the messianic king (Isa. 9:7[6]).

5583. סְעַד ***s^e'aḏ:*** An Aramaic verb meaning to help, to support. It refers to lending support or giving encouragement to someone. It describes the prophetic support given to those building the second Temple (Ezra 5:2).

5584. סָעָה ***sā'āh:*** A verb indicating to blow strongly. It is used to describe a fierce wind from a gale-like storm, from which one needs to seek refuge (Ps. 55:8[9]).

5585. סָעִיף ***sa'iyp̱:*** I. A masculine noun referring to a cleft, a fissure, a crack. It refers to a large rock overhang or a crevice large enough to be used as a temporary lodging place (Judg. 15:8, 11); or as a place to seek refuge (Isa. 2:21). It was also a place used for sacred sacrificial rites of a pagan nature (Isa. 57:5).

II. A masculine noun meaning a branch, a bough. It is used of the strong, green branches of an olive tree (Isa. 17:6). Figuratively, it depicts the "branches" of a city, forsaken like the desert (Isa. 27:10).

5586. סָעַף ***sā'ap̱:*** A verb meaning to cut off, to lop off. It describes the cutting off, the pruning of tree branches. Figuratively, it describes God's cutting off the Assyrian army (Isa. 10:33).

5587. שְׂעִפִּים *s^e^'ippiym:* A noun meaning a division, an opinion, a belief. The word comes from a root meaning to divide. It occurs only in 1 Kings 18:21, where Elijah asked the Israelites how long they would halt between two opinions. In context, the word refers to belief, whether in the Lord or in Baal.

5588. סֵעֵף *sē'ēp:* A masculine noun indicating double-mindedness, vanity of thought. It indicates a person who engages in doublethink, a process of illogical thought, perverse thinking that distorts and reverses the truth (Ps. 119:113).

5589. סְעַפָּה *s^e^'appāh:* A feminine noun meaning branch, bough. It refers to the incomparable branches of a tree that are large enough for birds to nest in (Ezek. 31:6, 8). They are part of a figurative depiction of the Assyrian Empire.

5590. סָעַר *sā'ar:* A verb meaning to storm, to blow strongly; to be enraged. It is used of the violent raging and movement of a stormy sea (Jon. 1:11, 13). It indicates a stormy wind that drove Israel into exile among the nations (Zech. 7:14; cf. Hos. 13:3; Hab. 3:14), a figurative usage. In its passive forms, it means to be blown away, driven off (Isa. 54:11). It means to be agitated and angry when applied to the human heart (2 Kgs. 6:11).

5591. סַעַר *sa'ar,* סְעָרָה *s^e^'ārāh:* I. A masculine noun meaning a stormy wind, a tempest, a whirlwind. It refers to a strong gale, a windstorm. It is used figuratively of one's enemies (Ps. 55:8[9]); of God's pursuit of them (Ps. 83:15[16]); and God's wrath in judgment (Jer. 23:19; Amos 1:14). It refers to a storm at sea (Jon. 1:4, 12).

II. A feminine noun indicating a strong wind, a tempest, a whirlwind. It is similar to I. It indicates a powerful gale, high winds, a windstorm. It was such a whirlwind that took Elijah up to heaven (2 Kgs. 2:1, 11). The Lord speaks from such a windstorm (Job 38:1; 40:6); and uses it to shield His presence (Ezek. 1:4; Zech. 9:14). It was God's tool at the Exodus (Ps. 107:25, 29); and His tool in judgment (Isa. 29:6; 40:24; Jer. 30:23).

5592. סַף *sap:* I. A masculine noun referring to a basin, a bowl. It was a bowl or a large hollow dish or cup used in rituals, cultic events (Ex. 12:22; 2 Sam. 17:28; 1 Kgs. 7:50). It was among the Temple furnishings and instruments (Jer. 52:19). It is used figuratively of a cup, Jerusalem, and its contents that will cause consternation to all the nations around her (Zech. 12:2).

II. A masculine noun meaning a threshold, a doorway. The opening, sill, or entrance into a house, a building, a temple, a palace (Judg. 19:27; 1 Kgs. 14:17). The doorkeeper, the keeper of the door was an important person (2 Kgs. 25:18; Esth. 2:21; Jer. 35:4).

5593. סַף **sap:** A proper noun designating Saph (2 Sam. 21:18).

5594. סָפַד **sāpad:** A verb meaning to mourn, to lament. It means to mourn for someone, to weep, to cry (Gen. 23:2; 50:10; 1 was a sign of morning (Isa. 32:12). In its passive sense, it means to be mourned over (Jer. 16:4–6; 25:33). In its participial forms, it refers to professional wailers or mourners (Eccl. 12:5; Zech. 12:12).

5595. סָפָה **sāpāh:** A verb meaning to scrape or sweep away, to destroy, to perish, to be captured. The word refers to the destruction or sweeping away of people (Ps. 40:14[15]); or a city (Gen. 18:23, 24); especially as the judgment of God. In Deuteronomy 29:19[18], the word refers to complete destruction: the destruction of the saturated with the dry. In Isaiah 13:15, it means captured as if swept up into another's possession. It is also used of the scraping away (i.e., shaving) of a beard (Isa. 7:20).

5596. סָפַח **sāpaḥ,** שָׂפַח **śāpaḥ:** A verb meaning to join, to be gathered together, to be joined, to cleave, to join oneself, to abide in. The word refers to putting a priest into office, that is, joining him to the office (1 Sam. 2:36). It refers to David remaining in Israel's inheritance in spite of death threats from Saul (1 Sam. 26:19); similarly, it refers to the Gentiles being joined to Israel (Isa. 14:1). In Job 30:7, it refers to the gathering of foolish poor people for protection under a plant. It appears to refer to the joining of heat (that is, poison) to a drink meant to make someone drunk; but the word here may be a copyist's error for *sap* (5592), meaning goblet (Hab. 2:15). In Isaiah 3:17, the word means to smite with a scab, but here it is spelled *śippaḥ*. and may belong to another root of similar spelling.

5597. סַפַּחַת **sappaḥat:** A feminine noun referring to a scab, a rash. It refers to scaly skins, a dry rash (Lev. 13:2; 14:56). This condition had to be watched closely and tested for its seriousness by the priests.

5598. סִפַּי **sippay:** A proper noun designating Sippai (1 Chr. 20:4).

5599. סָפִיחַ **sāpiyaḥ:** I. A masculine noun referring to an aftergrowth, what grows of itself. It referred to what grew in the fields of itself, generated by nature or from spilled seeds (Lev. 25:5, 11; 2 Kgs. 19:29). God used this growth as a sign for His people (2 Kgs. 19:29; Isa. 37:30).

II. A masculine noun indicating a torrent. It refers to a powerful, fast stream of water. It is used of God's power to remove the aspirations of people (Job 14:19) if He so desires.

5600. סְפִינָה **sepiynāh:** A feminine noun referring to a ship. It refers to a floating vessel, a ship, a boat. In context it refers to a large vessel with a deck capable of carrying many persons, plus cargo (Jon. 1:5).

5601. סַפִּיר sappiyr: A masculine noun referring to a sapphire, lapis lazuli. It refers to precious stones, in one case placed in a pavement floor of God's throne room (Ex. 24:10); usually denoting separate stones for decoration, beauty, and ornamentation (Ex. 28:18; 39:11). It is used figuratively of the attractive abdomen of a bridegroom (Song 5:14). Jerusalem had been adorned by persons, figuratively, polished like sapphire or lapis lazuli stones (Lam. 4:7). These stones had been in the Garden of Eden (Ezek. 28:13). The future Zion is to have a foundation of sapphire stones (Isa. 54:11).

5602. סֵפֶל sēpel: A masculine noun indicating a bowl, a dish. It refers to a small container for milk or water (Judg. 5:25; 6:38).

5603. סָפַן sāpan: I. A verb meaning to cover with panels. It indicates covering or paneling a structure with some material (1 Kgs. 6:9; 7:3, 7), especially the Solomonic temple and palace. This was considered a sinful, social luxury by later prophets (Jer. 22:14; Hag. 1:4).

II. A verb meaning to reserve for resting. It refers to setting up or aside a section or portion of something for someone. In context it means to reserve something for a ruler (Deut. 33:21).

III. A verb meaning to cover as a treasure. It indicates covering and hiding something as a valuable possession or resource, especially resources of the Promised Land of Canaan (Deut. 33:19).

5604. סִפֻּן sippun: A masculine noun meaning ceiling. It refers to the top inside covering of the Solomonic Temple (1 Kgs. 6:15).

5605. סָפַף sāpap: A verb meaning to stand guard at the threshold, to be a doorkeeper. It indicates a relatively low-level position at the door of the Temple (Ps. 84:10[11]), as opposed to having full access to the Temple.

5606. סָפַק sāpaq, שָׂפַק śāpaq: A verb meaning to clap, to strike, to smite. It signifies the clapping of hands in derision or disrespect, sometimes accompanied by hissing (Job 27:23; 34:37; Lam. 2:15); the clapping of the hand on the thigh as a sign of grief or shame (Jer. 31:19; Ezek 21:12[17]); or the clapping of the hands in anger (Num. 24:10). The word is used to refer to God's striking of people in public rebuke for backsliding (Job 34:26); and the wallowing or splashing of Moab in its vomit (Jer. 48:26). In Isaiah 2:6, the word referred to the striking of hands, that is, making deals with foreigners. The meaning, "suffice," found in 1 Kings 20:10, appears to belong under another root, and this may also be true of Isaiah 2:6 (both passages spell the word with *ś* instead of *s*).

5607. סֶפֶק sēpeq, שֶׂפֶק śepeq, שֶׂפֶק sepeq: I. A masculine noun referring to plenty, an abundance, sufficiency.

It indicates an overabundance of goods and wealth beyond what is needed (Job 20:22).

II. A masculine noun referring to riches. It is understood as riches by some translators. Its exact meaning in context is difficult (Job 36:18). Its meaning depends on the interpretation of other difficult words in the text, as well as the difficulty of the word itself.

III. A masculine noun referring to a stroke, scoffing, chastisement. It is understood as scoffing by some (NASB, Job 36:18); as a blow or stroke by others (KJV, Job 36:18). See II.

5608. סָפַר sāp̱ar, סֹפֵר sōp̱ēr, סוֹפֵר sôp̱ēr: A verb meaning to number, to recount, to relate, to declare. It is used to signify the numbering or counting of objects (Gen. 15:5; Ps. 48:12[13]); and people, as in a census (1 Chr. 21:2; 2 Chr. 2:17[16]). It also refers to a quantity that is too great to number (Gen. 16:10; Jer. 33:22). God's numbering of one's steps is a sign of His care (Job 14:16; cf. Matt. 10:30). The word also means to relate or to recount and is used often to refer to the communication of important information and truths to those who have not heard them, especially to foreign nations (Ex. 9:16; 1 Chr. 16:24; Ps. 96:3); or to the children in Israel (Ps. 73:15; 78:4, 6; 79:13). The matter communicated included dreams (Gen. 40:9; 41:8, 12; Judg. 7:13); God's works (Ex. 18:8; Ps. 73:28; Jer. 51:10); and recounting one's own ways to God (Ps. 119:26). The word also signifies the silent witness of the creation to its Creator and His wisdom and glory (Job 12:8; 28:27; Ps. 19:1[2]).

The participle form of the word *sōp̱ēr*, means scribe and occurs about fifty times in the Old Testament. Scribes such as Ezra studied, practiced, and taught the Law (Ezra 7:11). Scribes also served kings, writing and sometimes carrying messages to and from court (2 Kgs. 18:18; 19:2; Esth. 3:12; 8:9). In 2 Kings 22:10, a scribe read the recovered scroll of the Law to King Josiah, bringing about a personal revival. Scribes, as people who could read and count, also acted militarily, gathering the troops (2 Kgs. 25:19; Jer. 52:25). The occupation of scribe could belong to a family (1 Chr. 2:55). Also, some Levites occupied the position as part of their job (2 Chr. 34:13).

5609. סְפַר s^e^p̱ar: An Aramaic masculine noun meaning a book, a scroll. The word refers to the book of Moses, the first five books of the Bible, that were used to instruct the priests and Levites in their duties (Ezra 6:18). It refers to books of national records that rulers in Babylon could check regarding Israeli-Babylonian relations (Ezra 4:15). It also refers to books that the Ancient of Days will use to judge in favor of His saints against the boastful little horn (Dan. 7:10, cf. Dan. 7:21ff.). The word is used to signify a library or archive, as a house of books in Ezra 6:1.

5610. סְפָר ***s^e^p̱ār:*** A masculine noun meaning a census, numbering. It refers to counting up, numbering something or a population of people. Solomon recorded the total number of aliens in Israel (2 Chr. 2:17[16]).

5611. סְפָר ***s^e^p̱ār:*** A proper noun designating Sephar (Gen. 10:30).

5612. סֵפֶר ***sēp̱er,*** סִפְרָה ***sip̱rāh:*** A masculine noun meaning a document, a writing, a book, a scroll. Borrowed from an Assyrian word meaning missive or message, this word can refer to a letter (2 Sam. 11:14, 15; 1 Kgs. 21:8, 9, 11; 2 Kgs. 10:1, 2, 6, 7; Jer. 29:1); a divorce decree (Deut. 24:1, 3; Isa. 50:1; Jer. 3:8); a proof of purchase deed (Jer. 32:10–12, 14, 16); a book in which things were written for a need in the future (Ex. 17:14; 1 Sam. 10:25; Isa. 30:8); a book of laws (Ex. 24:7; Deut. 30:10; Josh. 1:8; Neh. 8:1, 3; 13:1); a genealogical record (Gen. 5:1; Neh. 7:5); writing and language (Dan. 1:4, 17).

5613. סָפַר ***sāp̱ar:*** An Aramaic masculine noun meaning a clerk, a secretary, a scribe. This term can refer to someone who had the ability to read and write documents, but it can also refer to someone who held a special government office. A Persian official named Shimshai was identified as a scribe, whose duties probably included copying documents as well as translating documents from and into Aramaic (Ezra 4:8, 9, 17, 23). In the official Persian office of scribe, Ezra was especially qualified to interpret and teach the Law of God (Ezra 7:12, 21).

5614. סְפָרַד ***s^e^p̱āraḏ:*** A proper noun designating Sepharad (Obad. 1:20).

5615. סְפֹרָה ***s^e^p̱ōrāh:*** A feminine noun indicating a sum, a number, an amount. It refers to the total count or full amount of something. It is used of the totality of God's righteousness, His salvation (Ps. 71:15).

5616. סְפַרְוִי ***s^e^p̱arwiy:*** A proper noun designating a Sepharvite, an inhabitant of Sepharvaim (5617) (2 Kgs. 17:31).

5617. סְפַרְוַיִם ***s^e^p̱arwayim:*** A proper noun designating Sepharvaim, a city and/or region possibly in the territory of Aram (Syria). People were settled from Aram into northern Israel by the Assyrians (2 Kgs. 17:24–31).

5618. סֹפֶרֶת ***sōp̱ereṯ,*** הַסֹּפֶרֶת ***hassōp̱ereṯ:*** I. Sophereth (Ezra 2:55 [KJV]; Neh. 7:57).

II. Hassophereth (Ezra 2:55 [NASB, NIV]).

5619. סָקַל ***sāqal:*** A verb meaning to stone, to throw stones at, to kill by stoning. It describes a fairly common way of killing or executing persons in the Middle East (Ex. 8:26[22]; 17:4; 19:13; Josh. 7:25); or animals (Ex. 21:28). A false prophet was stoned to death (Deut. 13:10[11]). It is used in a causative way meaning to clear or remove stones (Isa. 5:2; 62:10).

5620. סַר ***sar:*** An adjective meaning sullen, sad. It refers to a state of depression, without hope, of vexation (1 Kgs. 20:43; 21); over even a minor issue (1 Kgs. 21:4, 5).

5621. סָרָב ***sārāḇ:*** A masculine noun signifying a brier, a thistle. It refers to a nettle-like shrub with prickly leaves and heads with prickly stickers (Ezek. 2:6). In context it describes bothersome, troublesome people of Israel.

5622. סַרְבָּל ***sarbāl:*** An Aramaic masculine noun referring to a coat, a robe, trousers. It refers to a piece of the extensive outfits that the three Hebrew young men wore none of which was singed by fire (Dan. 3:21, 27).

5623. סַרְגּוֹן ***sargôn:*** A proper noun designating Sargon, an Assyrian king mentioned by Isaiah who sent his troops to attack Ashdod and capture it. He reigned 721–705 B.C. Isaiah responded with a prophetic perspective on the event.

5624. סֶרֶד ***sereḏ:*** A proper noun designating Sered (Gen. 46:14; Num. 26:26).

5625. סַרְדִּי ***sardiy:*** A proper noun designating a Seredite, a descendant of Sered (5624) (Num. 26:26).

5626. סִרָה ***sirāh:*** A proper noun designating Sirah (2 Sam. 3:26).

5627. סָרָה ***sārāh:*** A feminine noun meaning a defection, a revolt, an apostasy. Derived from a verb that means to turn aside, this term refers to God's people turning away from Him to follow false gods (Deut. 13:5[6]). Frequently, it describes those who chose to rebel against God (Isa. 1:5; 31:6; 59:13; Jer. 28:16; 29:32). Although some translations of this term in Deuteronomy 19:16suggest it simply means a general offense, its use elsewhere in Deuteronomy and the rest of the Old Testament indicates that this word refers to apostasy.

5628. סָרַח ***sāraḥ:*** I. A verb meaning to spread, to hang, to sprawl. It signifies something that is lapped over, folded over, doubled over (Ex. 26:12, 13). Used of a low-growing plant, it means to spread out over the ground (Ezek. 17:6). It is used of turbans that lap around one's head and shoulders (Ezek. 23:15). Used of a person lying on a couch, it means to sprawl out, stretch out over it (Amos 6:4). It means to act riotously, carefree at a banquet hall (Amos 6:7).

II. A verb meaning to decay, to degenerate, to vanish. It means to dissipate, to thin out, to become weak (Jer. 49:7); it is used of the loss of wisdom from among people (those who understand).

5629. סֶרַח seraḥ: A masculine noun meaning excess. Derived from a verbal form that means to hang over or overrun, this noun form occurs only once in the Old Testament. In Exodus 26:12, it refers to the remaining or excess material of the curtains in the Tabernacle.

5630. סִרְיֹן siryôn: A masculine noun referring to armor, scale armor. It is part of a warrior's outfit, a heavy protective armor for defensive purposes (Jer. 46:4; 51:3).

5631. סָרִיס sariys: A masculine noun meaning a court official, a eunuch. Derived from an Assyrian phrase meaning one who is the head or chief, this word can refer to someone with a high-ranking military or political status (Gen. 40:2, 7; 1 Sam. 8:15). Potiphar held an official post called the captain of the guard while working in the court of an Egyptian pharaoh (Gen. 37:36; 39:1). The term eunuch comes from the custom of placing castrated males in certain key government positions (2 Kgs. 20:18; Esth. 2:3, 14, 15, 21; 4:4, 5; Isa. 39:7). According to Mosaic Law, males who had defective genital organs would have been excluded from the worshiping community of Israel (cf. Lev. 21:20; Deut. 23:1). In 2 Kings 18:17, the term appears in a phrase that probably does not denote a eunuch but simply means an important government official (Jer. 39:3, 13).

5632. סָרַךְ sāraḵ: An Aramaic masculine noun meaning an official, a president. A loanword from Persian for head or chief, this term appears in the Old Testament only in Daniel. It is a title given to three high-ranking government officials, one of whom was Daniel (Dan. 6:2–4[3–5], 6[7], 7[8]). Appointed by Darius the Mede, the three officials oversaw the work of 120 satraps, whose function may have been to collect taxes for the king from throughout the empire.

5633. סֶרֶן seren: A masculine singular noun meaning a lord, a tyrant. This term is a Philistine loan word and was applied only to Philistine rulers. Five rulers reigned in the five main cities of the Philistines: Ashdod, Gaza, Ashkelon, Gath, and Ekron (1 Sam. 6:16, 18). In one passage, the word is translated axle of brass, based on the Septuagint rendering (1 Kgs. 7:30), but the etymology is unknown. David and his men were sent away by the *seren* and not allowed to fight for the Philistines (1 Chr. 12:19[20]).

5634. סַרְעַפָּה sar'appāh: A feminine noun indicating a bough. It is used of the boughs, branches of a tree where birds would nest, find shelter, usually a main branch (Ezek. 31:5).

5635. סָרַף sārap̱: A verb meaning to burn. A variant spelling of 8313. It has traditionally been taken to mean to burn in context with a suffix, "he that burns him" (KJV, NIV, Amos 6:10). Some recent translations suggest reading it as to dig for, referring to a gravedigger or undertaker (NASB and others).

5636. סִרְפָּד ***sirpad:*** A masculine noun indicating a brier, a nettle. It refers to a shrub with prickly, spiny stems or leaves, possibly a prickly type of weed. Their presence indicates a forsaken, uncared for area (Isa. 55:13).

5637. סָרַר ***sārar:*** A verb meaning to be stubborn, to be rebellious. Israel was said to be stubborn for forming an alliance with Egypt against God's ordained plan (Isa. 30:1); performing improper sacrifices, eating unclean things, and worshiping ancestors (Isa. 65:2). They were even compared to a stubborn heifer (Hos. 4:16). They stubbornly turned their backs (lit., shoulders) on God and His words (Neh. 9:29; Zech. 7:11). The son who rebelled against his parents could be severely disciplined and was eventually stoned (Deut. 21:18, 21). The term is also used of an immoral woman (Prov. 7:11).

5638. סְתָו ***s^{e}ṯāw:*** A masculine noun referring to winter. It indicates the cold, rainy season, winter. Snow falls in some areas during this time (Song 2:11).

5639. סְתוּר ***s^{e}ṯûr:*** A proper noun designating Sethur (Num. 13:13).

5640. סָתַם ***sāṯam,*** שָׂתַם ***śāṯam:*** A verb meaning to stop, to stop up. It means to plug up, to stop the function of a well by filling the well cylinder with dirt and debris (Gen. 26:15, 18). It describes the filling in of springs as well (2 Kgs. 3:19, 25); or gaps in a broken wall (Neh. 4:7[1]). It is used, with b^e on the front, as an adverb to mean secretly, in secret (Ps. 51:6[8]). It means to hide or to keep something hidden, secret (Dan. 8:26; 12:4).

5641. סָתַר ***sāṯar:*** A verb meaning to hide, conceal. It has the sense of preventing someone to know or see something, to keep something from public notice or from certain persons. It has the sense of to guard and protect oneself from perceived danger (Prov. 22:3); and of trying to escape God's eyes, His presence (Gen. 4:14; Jer. 16:17). It is used of persons being hidden from each other, absent from each other's presence (Gen. 31:49). It is used in the sense of shielding and protecting a person or something from perceived danger (Ex. 3:6). It means to do something secretly, hidden, such as adultery (Num. 5:13); or to try to hide oneself physically from danger and other persons (Deut. 7:20; 1 Sam. 20:5, 24; 1 Kgs. 17:3). It is used as a noun referring to secret things known only to God (Deut. 29:29[28]). Persons are sometimes aware of hidden problems or errors in their own lives (Ps. 19:12[13]). It is used of God's not hiding His face, that is, removing His presence from a person (Ps. 22:24[25]; Mic. 3:4). God will, however, hide His people from His wrath (Zeph. 2:3).

5642. סְתַר s^e^tar: An Aramaic verb derived from two separate roots. One of these means to hide. It occurs as a passive participle in Daniel 2:22 where it refers to hidden things that God reveals to the wise. See the Hebrew word *sāṯar* (5641). The second means to destroy. Its one usage describes the actions of Nebuchadnezzar, the Chaldean, who destroyed God's Temple in Jerusalem (Ezra 5:12). It is possibly related to the Hebrew root *śāṯar* (8368).

5643. סֵתֶר sēṯer, סִתְרָה siṯrāh: I. A masculine noun meaning a covering, a hiding place, a secret. It is used as an adverb meaning secretly (Deut. 13:6[7]); literally, in secret (Deut. 27:15, 24; 28:57; Jer. 37:17; 38:16; 40:15). It modifies other words: a secret matter, a matter/word of secrecy (Judg. 3:19). It is equated with darkness as the hiding place of God (Ps. 18:11[12]); and of God as the hiding place, the refuge, of those who need help (Ps. 32:7; 61:4[5]).

II. A feminine noun indicating a hiding place, a shelter, protection. It is used mockingly of pagan gods being hiding places for their worshipers (Deut. 32:38).

5644. סִתְרִי siṯriy: A proper noun designating Sithri (Ex. 6:22).

ע Ayin

5645. עָב **'āḇ:** I. A common noun indicating thick clouds. It refers to a dense, impenetrable covering or mass of clouds. God came to Israel at Sinai in this setting (Ex. 19:9; 1 Kgs. 18:44, 45). It is used of a mist formed from dew (Isa. 18:4). It has plurals in both *-îm, ôṯ*.

II. A common noun meaning thicket. It indicates a thick growth of underbrush in a forest or a growth of thick shrubs (Jer. 4:29).

III. A common noun meaning clay. It refers to a thick clay suitable for casting metal in it (2 Chr. 4:17).

5646. עָב **'āḇ,** עֹב **'ōḇ:** I. A masculine noun indicating an overhang, thick planks. Its technical meaning is not known for sure. Suggestions are as indicated: a canopy, a threshold (1 Kgs. 7:6; Ezek. 41:25, 26).

II. A masculine noun meaning a threshold, an overhanging roof (1 Kgs. 7:6; Ezek. 41:25, 26). It was a structure in front of certain other features of the king's palace.

5647. עָבַד **'āḇaḏ:** A verb meaning to work, to serve. This labor may be focused on things, other people, or God. When it is used in reference to things, that item is usually expressed: to till the ground (Gen. 2:5; 3:23; 4:2); to work in a garden (Gen. 2:15); or to dress a vineyard (Deut. 28:39). Similarly, this term is also applied to artisans and craftsmen, like workers in fine flax (Isa. 19:9); and laborers of the city (Ezek. 48:19). When the focus of the labor is another person, that person is usually expressed: Jacob's service to Laban (Gen. 29:15); the Israelites' service for the Egyptians (Ex. 1:14); and a people's service to the king (Judg. 9:28; 1 Sam. 11:1). When the focus of the labor is the Lord, it is a religious service to worship Him. Moreover, in these cases, the word does not have connotations of toilsome labor but instead of a joyful experience of liberation (Ex. 3:12; 4:23; 7:16; Josh. 24:15, 18). Unfortunately, this worship service was often given to false gods (Deut. 7:16; 2 Kgs. 10:18, 19, 21–23).

5648. עֲבַד **'aḇaḏ:** An Aramaic verb meaning to do, to make, to carry out, to perform. It takes on the particular meaning indicated by its specific context: to revolt, to rebel (Ezra 4:19); performing, doing, carrying out something (Ezra 4:22; 6:11; Dan. 6:10[11]); it refers to the process of working, etc. (Ezra 5:8); it means to change something (Dan. 2:5); to perform signs and wonders (Dan. 6:22); to make, create the heavens and earth (Jer. 10:11). It describes God's performing of His will (Dan. 4:35[32]); to make, wage, to engage in(Dan. 7:21).

5649. עֲבַד **'aḇaḏ:** An Aramaic masculine singular noun meaning a slave, a servant. It is used for servants of God or of human beings. King Nebuchadnezzar refers to Shadrach, Meshach, and Abednego as servants of the Most High God (Dan. 3:26). Darius calls Daniel the servant of the living God (Dan. 6:20[21]). One could also be known as a servant of the king (Dan. 2:7). This noun is derived from the verb *ᵃbad* (5648), meaning to do or make. See the Hebrew cognate *'ebed* (5650).

5650. עֶבֶד ***'ebed:*** A masculine noun meaning a servant, a slave. Although the most basic concept of this term is that of a slave, slavery in the Bible was not the same as the slavery of modern times. The period of slavery was limited to six years (Ex. 21:2). Slaves had rights and protection under the Law (Ex. 21:20). It was also possible for slaves to attain positions of power and honor (Gen. 24:2; 41:12). In addition, the people under the king were called his servants (Gen. 21:25); as well as his officers (1 Sam. 19:1); officials (2 Kgs. 22:12); ambassadors (Num. 22:18); vassal kings (2 Sam. 10:19); tributary nations (1 Chr. 18:2, 6, 13). This word is also a humble way of referring to one's self when speaking with another of equal or superior rank (Gen. 33:5). The term is also applied to those who worship God (Neh. 1:10); and to those who minister or serve Him (Isa. 49:5, 6). The phrase, the servant of the Lord, is the most outstanding reference to the Messiah in the Old Testament, and its teachings are concentrated at the end of Isaiah (Isa. 42:1, 19; 43:10; 49:3, 5–7; 52:13; 53:11).

5651. עֶבֶד ***'ebed:*** A proper noun designating Ebed:

A. The father of Gaal (Judg. 9:26, 28, 30, 31, 35).

B. A companion of Ezra (Ezra 8:6).

5652. עֲבָד ***ᵃbād:*** A masculine noun meaning deed, work. It refers to anything that is performed, done, made, carried out (Eccl. 9:1).

5653. עַבְדָּא ***'abdā':*** A proper noun designating Abda:

A. The father of Adoniram (1 Kgs. 4:6).

B. A Levite (Neh. 11:17).

5654. עֹבֵד אֱדוֹם ***'ōbēd ᵉdôm:*** A proper noun designating Obed-Edom. The name means "servant of Edom/mankind(?)."

A. He evidently was a Gittite from the city of Gath. The ark of the Lord remained in his house for three months, during which time he was blessed (2 Sam. 6:10–12).

B. An ancestor of a group of doorkeepers at the Temple (1 Chr. 15:24).

5655. עַבְדְּאֵל ***'abdᵉ'ēl:*** A proper noun designating Abdeel (Jer. 36:26).

5656. עֲבוֹדָה ***ᵃbôdāh,*** עֲבֹדָה ***ᵃbōdāh:*** A feminine noun meaning service, work. This word encompasses the wide variations of meaning of the English word "work"—from delicate artistry to forced labor. The Egyptians made the Israelites do slave labor (Ex. 1:14); for certain feast days, the Israelites were not allowed to do any work (Lev. 23:7ff.); different parts of the Tabernacle were considered to be in its service (Num. 4:26, 32); the descendants of Judah included workers of linen (1 Chr. 4:21). God handed the Israelites into the hand of Shishak so they would learn the difference between serving Him and serving other kings (2 Chr. 12:8). See the related Hebrew root *'āḇaḏ* (5647).

5657. עֲבֻדָּה ***ᵃḇuddāh:*** A feminine noun meaning service, servants. This word usually refers to an entire household of servants. The Philistines were jealous of Isaac because of his wealth, including his livestock and servants (Gen. 26:14). Job was considered the wealthiest man of the East because of all his possessions, including his multitude of servants (Job 1:3). See the related Hebrew root *'āḇaḏ* (5647), Aramaic root *ᵃḇaḏ* (5648), Aramaic noun *ᵃḇēḏ* (5649), and Hebrew noun *'eḇeḏ* (5650).

5658. עַבְדּוֹן ***'aḇdôn:*** A proper noun designating Abdon:

A. A levitical city (Josh. 21:30; 1 Chr. 6:74[59]).

B. A judge (Judg. 12:13, 15).

C. A Benjamite (1 Chr. 8:23).

D. The son of Jeiel (1 Chr. 8:30; 9:36).

E. The son of Micah (2 Chr. 34:20).

5659. עַבְדֻת ***'aḇdut:*** A feminine noun meaning bondage, slavery. This word is derived from the word *'āḇaḏ* (5647), meaning to serve. It occurs three times in the Hebrew Bible. In Ezra 9:8, 9, it refers twice to the bondage of the Hebrews under Babylon, a bondage where God revived them a little by allowing them to rebuild the wall and temple. In Nehemiah 9:17, it refers to severe bondage in Egypt (see Neh. 9:9), to which some rebellious Hebrews wanted to return.

5660. עַבְדִּי ***'aḇdiy:*** A proper noun designating Abdi:

A. A Levite (1 Chr. 6:44[29]; 2 Chr. 29:12).

B. A postexilic Jew (Ezra 10:26).

5661. עַבְדִּיאֵל ***'aḇdiy'ēl:*** A proper noun designating Abdiel (1 Chr. 5:15).

5662. עֹבַדְיָה ***'ōḇaḏyāh,*** עֹבַדְיָהוּ ***'ōḇaḏyāhû:*** A proper noun designating Obadiah:

A. Son of Izrahiah. One of four sons. All, including the father were military chiefs. (1 Chr. 7:3).

B. A Gadite. The second in military command under the chief Ezar. He was a commander (1 Chr. 12:9).

C. Father of Ishmaiah. Ishamiah the son of Obadiah, was an officer of the twelve tribes of Israel (1 Chr. 27:19).

D. Governor of Ahab's house. Obadiah means "servant of the Lord." Obadiah was a faithful servant of the

Lord. He helped Ahab, his master, find Elijah. Earlier, he had hidden one hundred prophets of the Lord from Jezebel who sought to kill all the Lord's prophets. Ahab respected him and his devout faith in the Lord (Yahweh). He found Elijah and took him to Ahab (see 1 Kgs. 18).

E. Prince of Judah. One of Jehoshaphat's officials (2 Chr. 17:7).

F. Son of Azel. One of six sons. Listed in the genealogy of Saul (1 Chr. 8:38).

G. A Levite descended from Merari. The Levites were in charge of the workers under Josiah's reforms (2 Chr. 34:12).

H. Descendant of David. Listed in the genealogy of David (1 Chr. 3:21).

I. He was the son of Jehiel, and included in Ezra's list of people who returned to Jerusalem during the reign of Darius, king of Persia (Ezra 8:9).

J. Son of Shemiah. At the dedication of the wall, he was sought and brought to Jerusalem to join in the musical celebration (1 Chr. 9:16).

K. A priest, a covenanter who signed an agreement and sealed it before the Lord to uphold Nehemiah's covenant of renewal (Neh. 10:5).

L. A Levite, possibly same as J. He was also a gatekeeper and guarded the gates where supplies were kept (Neh. 12:25).

M. The prophet. The name means "servant (or worshiper)" of the Lord. Neither his place of birth nor his parents are recorded. His prophecies proclaimed the Lord's judgment on Edom because they did not mourn or help Judah in the day when Babylon destroyed Jerusalem and Judah (605–686 B.C.). Edom will be destroyed, but Jerusalem and Mount Zion will be rescued and prosper (Obad. 1:18–21). The written report of his message is twenty-one verses, the shortest book in the Old Testament.

5663. עֶבֶד מֶלֶךְ ***'ebed melek:*** A proper noun designating Ebed-Melech. The name means "servant of Melech." He was a Cushite official serving in the palace of Zedekiah. He orchestrated the release and removal of Jeremiah from a cistern where he would have died (Jer. 38:7–12). He was, henceforth, protected by the Lord (Jer. 39:15–17).

5664. עֲבֵד נְגוֹ ***'abed negô:*** A proper noun designating Abed-nego. The name means "servant of Nego," a Babylonian god. It was given to Azariah, a youth from Judah exiled in Babylon with Daniel. He showed himself faithful to his God even unto death (Dan. 3; see 5665).

5665. עֲבֵד נְגוֹא ***'abēd negô':*** A proper noun designating Abed-nego, the Aramaic name of Azariah. It corresponds to Hebrew 5664. The meaning is the same.

5666. עָבָה ***'ābāh:*** A verb meaning to be thick, fat. It indicates the state of being thick or the act of growing into this state (Deut. 32:15). It refers to something being thick, heavy, e.g., a person's thigh (1 Kgs. 12:10; 2 Chr.

10:10); it is used as a symbol of oppression.

5667. עֲבוֹט *'aḇôṭ:* A masculine noun indicating a pledge. It indicates something given, put forth to stand as collateral for something (Deut. 24:10–13), especially for a loan.

5668. עֲבוּר *'aḇûr:* A word serving as a preposition or conjunction. Its basic meanings are as a preposition, because, for the sake of, on account of (Gen. 3:17; 8:21; 12:13, 16; Ex. 9:16; Mic. 2:10); as a conjunction, so that, in order that, with a following infinitive or imperfect form of the verb (Gen. 21:30; 27:4, 10; Ex. 9:14; 19:9; 2 Sam. 10:3; 12:21; Ps. 105:45). It indicates the price for something and is placed in front of that item (Amos 2:6).

5669. עֲבוּר *'aḇûr:* A masculine noun referring to produce, food. It is used of what fields produce or generate, especially the fields of Canaan (Josh. 5:11, 12).

5670. עָבַט *'āḇaṭ:* I. A verb meaning to borrow, to lend, to take a pledge from. It refers to extending credit to someone, to a people or nations (Deut. 15:6, 8; 24:10). A pledge was usually taken as collateral for the loan.

II. A verb meaning to deviate, to swerve, to break. It means to turn aside, to get out of line, to swerve from one's course (Joel 2:7).

5671. עַבְטִיט *'aḇṭiyṭ:* I. A masculine noun referring to loans. It refers to what is borrowed from a creditor, whether goods or money (Hab. 2:6). It may have the sense of extortion (NIV) in context.

II. A masculine noun meaning thick clay. Earlier translators rendered the word as thick clay, which does not fit the context as well (Hab. 2:6).

5672. עֲבִי *'aḇiy,* עֳבִי *'oḇiy:* A masculine noun meaning thickness. It refers to the thickness of the bronze sea constructed by Solomon (1 Kgs. 7:26; 2 Chr. 4:5); and the thickness of the two pillars of the Solomonic Temple (Jer. 52:21). It describes the size or thickness of military armor (Job 15:26).

5673. עֲבִידָה *'aḇiyḏāh:* An Aramaic feminine noun indicating work, service, administration. It refers to the process of construction (Ezra 4:24; 5:8; 6:7); and the ministry of serving at the holy places (Ezra 6:18). It also is used to describe the process of administering a city or area, a portion of a governing system (Dan. 2:49; 3:12).

5674. עָבַר *'āḇar:* A verb meaning to pass through or over, to cover, to go beyond, to go along, to be crossed over, to make to cross over, to go through, to go away. This verb indicates the physical act of crossing or passing over and takes on a figurative usage that exhibits many variations in meaning. Two figurative meanings are of primary importance theologically; the verb means going beyond, overstepping a covenant or a command of God or man. Moses uses the word when charging the people with disobeying and overstepping the Lord's commands (Num. 14:41; Josh. 7:11, 15). Esther 3:3 depicts Mordecai's transgressing of the king's command. The word is used of God's passing over His people's rebellion (Mic. 7:18); but also of His decision not to pass over or spare them any longer (Amos 7:8; 8:2). The verb relates to the placement of a yoke of punishment on the neck of Ephraim, God's rebellious nation (Hos. 10:11; cf. Job 13:13).

The word indicates the literal movement of material subjects and objects in time and space in various contexts: a stream or river is passed over (Josh. 3:14); as are boundaries (Num. 20:17). An attacking army passes through its enemies' territories, conquering them like a flood (cf. Josh. 18:9; Isa. 8:8; Dan. 11:10, 40); and as the literal flood waters of Noah's day covered the earth (Ps. 42:7[8]; 88:16 [17]; Isa. 54:9). In a figurative sense, the word describes the feeling of jealousy that can come over a suspecting or jealous husband (Num. 5:14, 30); or the movement of God's Spirit (1 Kgs. 22:24; 2 Chr. 18:23; Jer. 5:28). The location of an event could move or pass on, as when the Israelites routed the Philistines, and the battle, both in location and progress, passed by Beth Aven (1 Sam. 14:23; 2 Sam. 16:1; Jer. 5:22).

The word indicates passing away or leaving (emigrating) from a certain territory (Mic. 1:11). It indicates dying or perishing, as when the Lord described the perishing of Assyria's allies (Nah. 1:12); or the disappearance of Job's safety (Job 30:15; 33:18); it describes the passing of a law's validity or its passing out of use (Esth. 1:19; 9:27).

The causative stem adds the aspect of making these things happen as described in the simple stem. Jacob caused his family to cross over the Jabbok River (Gen. 32:23[24]). The word is used of the heinous act of devoting children to pagan gods (Jer. 32:35; Ezek. 23:37). A proclamation or the sound of the shofar can pass through the land (Ex. 36:6; Lev. 25:9).

The word means to cause something to pass away. Many things could be noted: God caused Saul's kingdom to pass over to David (2 Sam. 3:10); evil could be put away, as when Asa, king of Judah, put away male prostitutes from the religions of Israel (1 Kgs. 15:12); or holy persons turned away their eyes from vain things (Ps. 119:37).

The word is used one time in the passive stem to indicate a river that cannot be crossed (Ezek. 47:5); and in the factitive or intensive stem to describe Solomon's stringing gold chains across the front area inside the Holy Place in the Temple (1 Kgs. 6:21).

5675. עֲבַר ***ᵃḇar:*** An Aramaic masculine noun indicating a region, an area beyond, across from. It is used of the area west of the Euphrates River, on the other side from Persia proper (Ezra 4:10, 11, 16, 17, 20; 7:21, 25), which was administered by the government of Persia.

5676. עֵבֶר ***'ēḇer:*** I. A masculine noun meaning side, a region beyond, a region across from. It refers to an area across from another, one of two sides situated opposite each other (1 Sam. 14:1; 26:13); an area opposite, beyond a marker, a river, etc. (Gen. 50:10, 11; Num. 21:13). It indicates what is over against, in the front of (Ex. 25:37; Ezek. 1:9). Several phrases are found: from one side and the other (1 Sam. 14:4; 40); from every side (1 Kgs. 4:24[5:4]; Jer. 49:32). It indicates the edge or side of something (Ex. 28:26); the shore of a river or sea (Deut. 30:13; Isa. 18:1). The phrase, beyond, over the Jordan means east or west depending on where the speaker is locating himself (Gen. 50:10; Deut. 3:20, 25; Josh. 12:7; 17:5). It indicates the two sides of the tablets containing the Ten Commandments, the ten words of God (Ex. 32:15). When God restores His people, they will come from beyond (*'ēḇer*) the river of Ethiopia to serve Him (Zeph. 3:10).

II. A masculine noun indicating a passage, a place of crossing over. It refers to an area located near or beside a place where a river was crossed (Josh. 22:11); as well as a passage itself (Jer. 22:20).

5677. עֵבֶר ***'ēḇer:*** A proper noun designating Eber:

A. A son of Shelah (Gen. 10:21, 24, 25; 11:14–17; Num. 24:24; 1 Chr. 1:18, 19, 25).

B. A Gadite chief (1 Chr. 5:13).

C. A Benjamite (1 Chr. 8:12).

D. A Benjamite (1 Chr. 8:22).

E. A priest (Neh. 12:20).

5678. עֶבְרָה ***'eḇrāh:*** A feminine noun meaning wrath, fury. The word is derived from the word *'āḇar* (5674) and thus implies an overflowing anger. When the word is used of people, it usually describes a fault of character, a cruel anger (Gen. 49:7; Amos 1:11); associated with pride (Prov. 21:24; Isa. 16:6). The wrath of a king toward shameful servants, however, is justifiable, representing God's anger (Prov. 14:35, cf. Prov. 14:34; Rom. 13:4). The word most often signifies God's wrath, an attribute people generally fail to properly appreciate (Ps. 90:11). God's wrath disregards a person's wealth (Prov. 11:4); and brings fiery judgment, purging the sin of His people (Ezek. 22:21, cf. Ezek. 22:22); and ultimately bringing wickedness and wicked people to an end on earth (Zeph. 1:15, 18). The instrument of wrath is sometimes pictured as a rod (Prov. 22:8; Lam. 3:1).

5679. עֲבָרָה ***ᵃḇārāh:*** A feminine noun indicating a ford, a ferry. It refers to a shallow place in a river where it can be crossed most easily (2 Sam. 15:28; 17:16; 19:18[19]).

5680. עִבְרִי ***'iḇriy:*** A proper noun designating Hebrew. The gentilic or ethnic form of the word meaning a Hebrew person, possibly a person from beyond the Euphrates River. Abraham is called a Hebrew in Genesis 14:13, where the word was first used. This is usually traced back to Eber who was a Shemite. Abraham's lineage is traced back to Shem through Eber, Shem being the ancestor of all the sons of Eber (Gen. 10:21; 11:10; 32). Eber features the root letters of "Hebrew" (*'br*), without the gentilic or ethnic ending *iy* (ִי). The term Habiru found in documents throughout the Middle East is equal to the Old Testament *Hebrew* to some extent. It also had a strong social flavor to it as well and probably was used to describe a certain social or professional class of people. The word *Hebrew* seems to have had a negative sense to it at first. It was used of Joseph, "the Hebrew or the Hebrew slave" (Gen. 39:14, 17), by Potipher's wife. In Egypt the descendants of Abraham were referred to as Hebrews and God as the God of the Hebrews (Ex. 3:18; 5:3), i.e., slaves (cf. Ex. 21:2; Deut. 15:12; Jer. 34:9, 14). The Philistines referred to the Israelites at times as Hebrews (1 Sam. 4:6, 9). Jonah asserted that he was a Hebrew (1:9). So in the Old Testament, the term is primarily an ethnic or gentilic term.

5681. עִבְרִי ***'iḇriy:*** A proper noun designating Ibri (1 Chr. 24:27).

5682. עֲבָרִים ***'aḇāriym:*** A proper noun designating Abarim (Num. 27:12; 33:47, 48; Deut. 32:49; Jer. 22:20).

5683. עֶבְרֹן ***'eḇrōn:*** A proper noun designating Hebron (Josh. 19:28).

5684. עַבְרֹנָה ***'aḇrōnāh:*** A proper noun designating Abronah, Ebronah (Num. 33:34, 35).

5685. עָבַשׁ ***'āḇaš:*** A verb meaning to shrivel, to rot. It indicates a process of decay or death. In context it describes seeds dying, shriveling instead of germinating, beginning to grow (Joel 1:17).

5686. עָבַת ***'āḇaṯ:*** A verb meaning to weave together, to conspire, to wrap up. It means to intertwine something. In context it is used figuratively of forming a plan or a conspiracy to do evil (Mic. 7:3).

5687. עָבֹת ***'āḇōṯ:*** An adjective meaning thick with leaves, dense with leaves; leafy. It refers to a tree loaded with leaves, that sends out a huge amount of foliage (Lev. 23:40; Neh. 8:15). These trees were used as places of apostate, pagan worship (Ezek. 6:13; 20:28).

5688. עֲבוֹת ***'aḇōṯ:*** I. A common noun meaning a rope, a cord, a line. It refers to twisted, finely crafted cordage (Ex. 28:14, 22, 24, 25; 39:15);

as well as ropes formed to be strong for binding prisoners (Judg. 15:13, 14; 16:11, 12; Job 39:10; Ezek. 3:25). It is used figuratively of political or military bonds or ropes (Ps. 2:3); but also of relationships of love and tender care from the Lord (Hos. 11:4).

II. A common noun indicating a branch, thick foliage, closed. The word is taken by some translators to mean boughs (NIV) or thick foliage for use in worshiping the Lord (Ps. 118:27). It is used in a figurative way to describe aspects of God's people Israel (Ezek. 19:11); or of Assyria (Ezek. 31:3). It has the meaning of clouds (NASB) or foliage (NIV) in Ezekiel 31:10, 14.

5689. עָגַב ***'āgab̲:*** A verb meaning to lust after. The word occurs in Ezekiel 23 six times where it refers to the desire of Jerusalem and Samaria for foreign ways under the figure of two sisters who lust after foreigners. Ezekiel warned that, just as Assyria, the object of Samaria's lust, had destroyed them, so sensual Babylon would destroy Jerusalem. The word also occurs as a participle in Jeremiah 4:30 and means lovers. Again, the word is used figuratively in a warning that Jerusalem's foreign lovers would despise and destroy them.

5690. עָגָב ***'āgāb̲:*** A masculine plural noun meaning love, lust. It describes words of lustfulness, words or songs of love, words that have little meaning to the hearers (Ezek. 33:31, 32).

5691. עֲגָבָה ***'agāb̲āh:*** A feminine noun meaning lust. It refers to inordinate love, sensual desire, lust. Figuratively, it indicates apostate desires and the unfaithfulness of the people of Judah (Ezek. 23:11).

5692. עֻגָה ***'ugāh:*** A feminine noun referring to a cake of bread. It indicates a cake made from bread dough and usually baked on hot stones (Gen. 18:6; 1 Kgs. 17:13; 19:6). Figuratively, it describes northern Israel (Hos. 7:8).

5693. עָגוּר ***'āgûr:*** A masculine noun referring to a kind of bird, a crane or a thrush. It is used in a simile referring to the noise this bird makes, a twittering, troubling sound (Isa. 38:14). The bird's observance of its appointed instincts are praised, compared to Israel's failure to observe her responsibilities to God (Jer. 8:7).

5694. עָגִיל ***'āgiyl:*** A masculine noun meaning earrings. It refers to jewelry or ornamentation worn by either men or women (Num. 31:50; Ezek. 16:12).

5695. עֵגֶל ***'ēgel:*** A common noun meaning calf. It refers to calves, a valuable property in ancient Israel. It was a symbol of power and fertility; Israel fell into idolatry by creating images of calves (Ex. 32:4, 8, 19; Deut. 9:16); two calf images were set up in northern Israel (1 Kgs. 12:28, 32; 2 Kgs. 10:29). It is used in figurative language of mountains leaping for joy like calves (Ps. 29:6). Fatted, grain-fed calves were eaten and used in sacrifices and rituals (1 Sam. 28:24). The word was employed in figurative speech (Jer. 46:21; Mal. 4:2[3:20]).

5696. עָגֹל ***‘āgōl,*** עָגוֹל ***‘āgôl:*** An adjective meaning round, circular. It refers to anything shaped like a circle (1 Kgs. 7:23, 35; 2 Chr. 4:2); round (1 Kgs. 7:31; 10:19).

5697. עֶגְלָה ***‘eglāh,*** עֶגְלַת שְׁלִשִׁיָּה ***‘eglaṯ šᵉlišiyyāh:*** I. A feminine noun meaning heifer. It refers to a young cow. The animals were used for milk, for certain sacrifices (Gen. 15:9); or symbolic rituals (Deut. 21:3, 4, 6). It is employed in a riddle to symbolize a woman, a wife (Judg. 14:18); and in a metaphor to refer to Egypt (Jer. 46:20); to Ephraim (Hos. 10:11). It refers to a calf, a heifer idol in Beth-aven, "house of iniquity" (Hos. 10:5).

II. A proper noun Eglath Shelishayah. It was a city in Moab east of the southern half of the Dead Sea (Isa. 15:5; Jer. 48:34).

5698. עֶגְלָה ***‘eglāh:*** A proper noun designating Eglah (2 Sam. 3:5; 1 Chr. 3:3).

5699. עֲגָלָה ***ᵃgālāh:*** A feminine noun referring to a cart, a wagon. It refers to a royal wagon or cart used for transporting people and their property (Gen. 45:19, 21, 27; 46:5). Carts or wagons in general were considered valuable gifts and offerings (Num. 7:3, 6–8); and used to carry produce (Amos 2:13). It indicates wagons or chariots used in warfare (Ps. 46:9[10]). Some carts were pulled by ropes (Isa. 5:18). The phrase *’ôpan ᵃgolāh* indicates a cartwheel (Isa. 28:27).

5700. עֶגְלוֹן ***‘eglôn:*** A proper noun designating Eglon:

A. A village in the low-lying hills of the Shephelah. Its inhabitants tried to withstand the Israelites' moving into the land. It was given to Judah as an inheritance (Josh. 15:39).

B. The name of a Moabite king who oppressed Israel for some time. Ehud, a left-handed Israelite judge, assassinated him and freed Israel.

5701. עָגַם ***‘āgam:*** A verb meaning to be grieved. It refers to a response of grief, sorrow, lamentation for something or someone, especially the poor (Job 30:25).

5702. עָגַן ***‘āgan:*** A verb meaning to shut oneself in, to remain unmarried. It means to not take a spouse, to refrain from getting married (Ruth 1:13).

5703. עַד ***‘aḏ:*** A noun meaning eternity. The word signifies God's dwelling place (Isa. 57:15). It also refers to the continuance of a king on the throne (Ex. 15:18; 1 Chr. 28:9; Ps. 132:12; Prov. 29:14). The word can indicate continual joy (Ps. 61:8[9]; Isa. 65:18); or continual anger (Mic. 7:18; Amos 1:11). The word's references to mountains that would be shattered (Hab. 3:6); the sun and the moon (Ps. 148:6) may show that the word sometimes means less than eternity or only an apparent eternity. The word occurs with the word *'ôlām* (5769) (Ps. 10:16; 45:6[7]; Dan. 12:3) and sometimes with the word *neṣaḥ* (5331) (Ps. 9:18[19]; Amos 1:11).

5704. עַד ***'aḏ:*** A preposition and adverb meaning as far as, up to, unto, until, while. It is used of time meaning until (Gen. 3:19; 8:5; 33:3; Judg. 6:31; 1 Sam. 1:14); of space indicating distance (Gen. 11:31; 12:6; 13:3); of the inclusiveness of a category of things (Gen. 6:7; 7:23). It is used adverbially to express degree: *'aḏ meᵉ'ōḏ*, greatly, quickly (Ps. 147:15); up to half of something (Esth. 5:6); the extent of something (Deut. 2:5). It may function as a conjunction as well, meaning basically until: of a past time (Ex. 32:20); of a future time (Gen. 27:44). It may indicate the time while something is being done (1 Sam. 14:9). It is found in various phases and idioms: *'aḏ merāḥôq*, unto a distant (place) (Isa. 57:9); *min* (4480) . . . (*wᵉ*) *'aḏ*, from . . . as far as, to (Gen. 10:19); *min* . . . *wᵉ'aḏ*, from . . . to (Gen. 19:4), from a boy to an old person, both.

5705. עַד ***'aḏ:*** An Aramaic particle functioning as a preposition or a conjunction meaning until, unto. It is used of spatial ideas: right up to, as far as (Dan. 7:13); up to this point (Dan. 7:28); and of temporal ideas: until evening (Dan. 6:14[15]); until right now (Ezra 5:16); until the end, finally (Dan. 4:5). As a conjunction in the phrase *'aḏ dî* (Dan. 2:9, 34; 4:23[20], 25[22], 32[29], 33[30]; 5:21), it means until. It is also used to indicate a limit in quantity (Ezra 7:22; Dan. 7:22, 25, 26, 28). Used alone, it means until (Ezra 4:21; 5:5).

5706. עַד ***'aḏ:*** A masculine noun indicating prey, booty. It refers to the victim of a ravening wolf, the wolf representing Benjamin (Gen. 49:27). It is used in an inclusive sense of all spoil or booty taken in war (Isa. 33:23). Zephaniah 3:8 is rendered as prey (KJV), but others translate it as witness (See II in concordance).

5707. עֵד ***'ēḏ:*** A masculine noun meaning witness, testimony. It refers to someone who will be accepted to bear a true testimony in various situations for various reasons. It also refers to the testimony given, written or oral, such as a covenant (Gen. 31:44; Deut. 31:19, 21); or a symbol established to confirm a covenant (Gen. 31:48). The evidence itself may be called a witness (Ex. 22:13[12]). God Himself serves as a witness (Gen. 31:50, 52; Josh. 22:27, 28, 34; Job 16:19).

5708. עֵד ***'ēḏ,*** עִדָּה ***'iddāh:*** A masculine noun referring to filthiness, menstruation. It indicates a woman's menstrual period or cloth that was considered unclean. In context it is used of God's people whose righteousness has become as a filthy rag (Isa. 64:6[5]).

5709. עֲדָה ***ᵃdāh:*** An Aramaic verb meaning to pass away, to pass on. It means to change, to disappear. It is used of times, seasons, and epochs of history coming and going, passing away (Dan. 2:21); of kingship passing from someone (Dan. 4:31[28]; 5:20; 7:26). It is used of changing a document (Dan. 6:8[9], 12[13]); or something/time being extended in other situations (Dan. 7:12). It has the sense of passing on a smell or odor (in context) to something (Dan. 3:27).

5710. עָדָה ***'āḏāh:*** I. A verb meaning to pass on, to walk; to lay aside. It refers to passing over, to walking over a place or an area of land (Job 28:8); or to removing a garment or clothing (Prov. 25:20).

II. A verb meaning to ornament, to adorn, to deck. It means to deck oneself in splendor, to dress to attract attention and respect, usually in a bad sense (Job 40:10; Isa. 61:10; Jer. 4:30; Ezek. 16:11; Hos. 2:13[15]).

5711. עָדָה ***'āḏāh:*** A proper noun designating Adah:

A. The wife of Lamech (Gen. 4:19, 20, 23).

B. The wife of Esau (Gen. 36:2, 4, 10, 12, 16).

5712. עֵדָה ***'ēḏāh:*** A feminine noun meaning a congregation, an assembly, a band, an entourage, a pack. The word is modified to indicate various kinds of groups or communities. It is used to describe a congregation of heavenly or human beings; an assembly of divine beings over which God presides (Ps. 82:1); a gathering of nations (Ps. 7:7[8]); a community of the righteous (Ps. 1:5); a group of evildoers (Num. 26:9; Ps. 22:16[17]); ruthless people (Ps. 86:14). It describes an entire circle of families and friends (Job 16:7).

Most often the word refers to Israel as a group in many settings. It describes all Israel gathered before Solomon (1 Kgs. 8:5; 12:20); or as a total community in general (Hos. 7:12); it refers to the community of Israel at the Exodus in phrases like the congregation of the Lord (Num. 27:17; 31:16; Josh. 22:16); the community of Israel (Ex. 12:3, 6; Num. 16:9); or the community of the sons of Israel (Ex. 16:1, 2; 17:1). At times leaders in Israel were described as the leaders or elders of the congregation (Ex. 16:22; Lev. 4:15; Num. 4:34).

The word is used to describe a swarm of bees (Judg. 14:8); and figuratively describes the people in Psalm 68:30[31] as bulls, evidently supporters of foreign nations.

5713. עֵדָה ***'ēḏāh:*** A feminine noun meaning a testimony, a witness. Derived from a word that denotes permanence, this term refers to the act of testifying to a fact or an event. For example, by accepting Abraham's gift of ewe lambs, Abimelech acknowledged the truth of Abraham's statement about the ownership of the well at Beersheba (Gen. 21:30). Likewise, a heap of stones became a witness to the boundary agreement reached between Jacob and Laban (Gen. 31:52). Within the context of a covenant renewal ceremony, Joshua placed a single large stone to function as a witness of the covenant established between the Lord and His people (Josh. 24:27).

5714. עִדֹּא *'iddō'*, עִדּוֹ *'iddô*, עִדּוֹא *'iddô'*, עִדֹּו *'iddō:* A proper noun designating Iddo:

A. The father of Ahinadab (1 Kgs. 4:14).

B. Grandfather of Zechariah the prophet (Neh. 12:4, 16; Zech. 1:1, 7).

C. Grandfather of Zechariah the prophet (Ezra 5:1; 6:14).

D. A Levite (1 Chr. 6:21[6]).

E. A seer (2 Chr. 12:15; 13:22).

5715. עֵדוּת *'ēḏûṯ:* A feminine noun meaning testimony, precept, warning sign. It is always used in connection with the testimony of God and most frequently in association with the Tabernacle (Ex. 38:21; Num. 1:50, 53). The stone tablets containing the Ten Commandments are identified as God's testimony (Ex. 25:16; 31:18; 32:15). Because the Ten Commandments represent the covenant that God made with Israel (see Ex. 34:27, 28), they are also called the "tables of the covenant" (see Deut. 9:9; 11:15); and they were preeminent in the Tabernacle. As a result, the Tabernacle is sometimes called the Tabernacle of the testimony (Ex. 38:21; Num. 1:50, 53); and the ark is sometimes called the ark of the testimony (Ex. 25:22; 26:33, 34; 30:6, 26). This term is also used alone to represent the ark (Ex. 16:34; 27:21; 30:36; Lev. 16:13). In time, this term came to stand for the laws or precepts that God had delivered to humanity (Ps. 19:7[8]; 119:88; 122:4).

5716. עֲדִי *ᵃḏiy:* A masculine noun referring to an ornament, jewelry. It refers to articles of gold, silver, and precious stones worn by many in Israel (Ex. 33:4–6). They were, in good times, supplied by the Lord as blessings for His people (2 Sam. 1:24). It refers to the trappings and adornments put on horses to control them (Ps. 32:9). It indicates the blessings of God to come on His people (Isa. 49:18). Its use in Psalm 103:5 is questionable. If used, its possible meanings are difficult: desires (NIV), years (NASB), mouth (KJV).

5717. עֲדִיאֵל *ᵃḏiy'ēl:* A proper noun designating Adiel:

A. A Simeonite (1 Chr. 4:36).

B. A priest (1 Chr. 9:12).

C. The father of officer under David (1 Chr. 27:25).

5718. עֲדָיָהוּ *ᵃḏāyāhû*, עֲדָיָה *ᵃḏāyāh:* A proper noun designating Adaiah:

A. The father of Maaseiah (2 Chr. 23:1).

B. Grandfather of Josiah (2 Kgs. 22:1).

C. A Levite (1 Chr. 6:41[26]).

D. A Benjamite (1 Chr. 8:21).

E. A priest (1 Chr. 9:12; Neh. 11:12).

F. A son of Bani (Ezra 10:29).

G. A son of another Bani (Ezra 10:39).

H. A Judaite (Neh. 11:5).

5719. עָדִין ***'ādiyn:*** An adjective meaning wanton, sensuous. It refers figuratively to Babylon, a wanton, sensuous people, enamored with gold, silver, royal dominion, power, and banqueting (Isa. 47:8).

5720. עָדִין ***'ādiyn:*** A proper noun designating Adin:

A. Ancestor of returning Jewish exiles (Ezra 2:15; 8:6; Neh. 7:20).

B. A covenanter in Nehemiah's day (Neh. 10:16[17]).

5721. עֲדִינָא ***'adiynā':*** A proper noun designating Adina (1 Chr. 11:42).

5722. עֲדִינוֹ הָעֶצְנִי ***'adiynô hā'eṣniy:*** A proper noun designating Adino the Eznite (2 Sam. 23:8).

5723. עֲדִיתַיִם ***'adiytayim:*** A proper noun designating Adithaim (Josh. 15:36).

5724. עַדְלַי ***'adlay:*** A proper noun designating Adlai (1 Chr. 27:29).

5725. עֲדֻלָּם ***'adullām:*** A proper noun designating Adullam, a town in the low-lying hills of the Shephelah that the Israelites conquered (Josh. 12:15) and allotted to the tribe of Judah (Josh. 15:35). Later, David fled there to hide from Saul (1 Sam. 22:1; 2 Sam. 23:13). Assyria captured it (Mic. 1:15) much later. Exiles returning from the Babylonian exile reestablished the city (Neh. 11:30).

5726. עֲדֻלָּמִי ***'adullāmiy:*** A proper noun designating Adullamite. The word is a gentilic/ethnic form that indicates an inhabitant of the city of Adullam (5725).

5727. עָדַן ***'ādan:*** A verb meaning to revel, to take pleasure in. It refers to enjoying something, using it jubilantly to the full, perhaps in an excessive or inordinate manner (Neh. 9:25).

5728. עֲדֶן ***'aden,*** עֲדֶנָה ***'adenāh:*** I. An adverb meaning still, yet. It indicates an imagined thing, a state, or a condition that has not yet occurred (Eccl. 4:3).

II. An adverb meaning still, yet. It refers to something that is currently happening, the current situation or status (Eccl. 4:2).

5729. עֶדֶן ***'eden:*** A proper noun designating the town Eden (2 Kgs. 19:12; Isa. 37:12; Ezek. 27:23).

5730. עֵדֶן ***'ēden,*** עֶדְנָה ***'ednāh:*** I. A masculine noun referring to a luxury, a pleasure, a delight. Used in the plural, it means luxury, luxurious things (2 Sam. 1:24); figuratively, of the many splendid things and enjoyments God gives (Ps. 36:8[9]). It depicts the many enjoyments and pleasurable delights Israel had enjoyed previously (Jer. 51:34).

II. A feminine noun indicating sexual delight, ecstasy. It refers to the enjoyment of intimate love with one's spouse which in context implies the ability to become pregnant (Gen. 18:12).

5731. עֵדֶן ***ʿēḏen:*** A proper noun designating Eden:

A. The place where God placed Adam and Eve to live and where they rebelled against the Lord's words. Satan was permitted in the garden and fostered the rebellion of the first human pair. They were subsequently driven from the garden by God (Gen. 3:21–24). Ezekiel takes the event seriously and notes the presence of an archetype of the King of Tyre in the Garden of Eden (Ezek. 28:11–15).

The precise location of the garden is not known, even though the Tigris and Euphrates Rivers were part of it. It became a symbol of beauty and fertility (Ezek. 31:9; Joel 2:3).

B. The name of a Levite who took part in Hezekiah's purification of the Temple and its service (2 Chr. 29:12).

5732. עִדָּן ***ʿiddān:*** An Aramaic masculine noun indicating a period of time, a moment of time. It indicates a prolongation of time or some time (Dan. 2:8); a period or length of time (Dan. 7:12). It has the sense of a time, a period when things change, changing circumstances (Dan. 2:9, 21). It refers to a proper time, a time when something should occur (Dan. 3:5, 15). From context it may refer to a year as a duration of time (Dan. 4:16[13], 23[20], 25[22], 32[29]; 7:25).

5733. עַדְנָא ***ʿaḏnāʾ:*** A proper noun designating Adna:

A. The head of a preistly family (Neh. 12:15).

B. A postexilic Jew (Ezra 10:30).

5734. עַדְנָה ***ʿaḏnāh:*** A proper noun designating Adnah:

A. A prince of Judah (2 Chr. 17:14).

B. A Manassite (1 Chr. 12:20).

5735. עַדְעָדָה ***ʿaḏʿāḏāh:*** A proper noun designating Abadah (Josh. 15:22).

5736. עָדַף ***ʿāḏap:*** A verb meaning to remain over, to be in excess. It refers to whatever is left, the remains: quails (Ex. 16:23); part of a curtain (Ex. 26:12, 13); a balance or remainder of money paid (Lev. 25:27); persons, specifically firstborn Israelites (Num. 3:46, 48, 49).

5737. עָדַר ***ʿāḏar:*** I. A verb meaning to lack, to fail; to remain. It refers to something gone or missing, absent (1 Sam. 30:19); of people (2 Sam. 17:22); of food (1 Kgs. 4:27[5:7]); of God's judgment (Isa. 34:16); of the heavens God created (Isa. 40:26); of truth (Isa. 59:15). It is used of the fact that the Lord never falls short, never fails (Zeph. 3:5).

II. A verb meaning to keep rank, to put in order. It refers to organizing a group of soldiers, of their arranging themselves in order, in battle array (KJV, 1 Chr. 12:33).

III. A verb meaning to help. It means to aid, to support, to come to the aid of (1 Chr. 12:33).

IV. A verb meaning to hoe, to weed, to cultivate. It refers to taking care of a garden or vineyard by cultivating it (Isa. 5:6; 7:25). It is used figuratively of God's cultivating, hoeing His people as a gardener (Isa. 5:6).

5738. עֶדֶר **ʻeder:** A proper noun designating Eder, Ader (1 Chr. 8:15).

5739. עֵדֶר **ʻēder:** A masculine noun referring to a flock, a herd. It is used of a group of animals, sheep, goats, cattle (Gen. 29:2, 3, 8; 30:40; 32:16[17], 19[20]; Judg. 5:16; Song 4:1; 6:5). Figuratively, it describes Israel as the flock of God (Isa. 40:11; Jer. 13:20; Zech. 10:3). It depicts the bride's hair like a flock of goats (Song 4:1).

5740. עֵדֶר **ʻēder:** A proper noun designating Eder:
A. A Levite (1 Chr. 23:23; 24:30).
B. A location in southern Judah (Josh. 15:21).

5741. עַדְרִיאֵל **ʻadriyʼēl:** A proper noun designating Adriel (1 Sam. 18:19; 2 Sam. 21:8).

5742. עֲדָשִׁים **ʻadāšiym:** A masculine plural noun referring to lentils. A vegetable-like pea with small seeds that are edible (Gen. 25:34; 2 Sam. 17:28; Ezek. 4:9). It was cultivated in Canaan (2 Sam. 23:11).

5743. עוּב **ʻûḇ:** A verb meaning to cover with a cloud. It is used of bringing a cloud over something or someone. It is employed figuratively of God's anger toward Israel (Lam. 2:1).

5744. עוֹבֵד **ʻôḇēḏ,** עֹבֵד **ʻōḇēḏ:** A proper noun designating Obed:
A. A descendant of Sheshan (1 Chr. 2:37, 38).
B. The son of Boaz (Ruth 4:17, 21, 22; 1 Chr. 2:12).
C. One of David's mighty men (1 Chr. 11:47).
D. Son of Shemaiah (1 Chr. 26:7).
E. A captain (2 Chr. 23:1).

5745. עוֹבָל **ʻôḇāl:** A proper noun designating Obal (Gen. 10:28; 1 Chr. 1:22).

5746. עוּג **ʻûḡ:** A verb meaning to bake. It refers to cooking a cake or bread on hot stones or over a fire (Ezek. 4:12).

5747. עוֹג **ʻôḡ,** עֹג **ʻōḡ:** A proper noun designating Og, a powerful king who ruled the territory of Bashan on the east side of the Jordan River. He was evidently from a race of giants (Num. 21:33; Josh. 13:12–31). His bed was an object of amazement and splendor (Deut. 3:11). He controlled a large kingdom for his time (Deut. 3:1–13), from the Jabbok River in the south to Mount Hermon in the north. Manasseh inherited Og's land (Deut. 3:1–13). It was located northeast of the Sea of Galilee (Num. 21:33). The Lord gave victory to Moses and Israel over Og (Num. 21:34–35). He was killed along with his entire army and family. His defeat was celebrated in the worship and festivals of Israel (Neh. 9:22; Ps. 135:11; 136:20).

5748. עוּגָב ʻûgāḇ, עֻגָב ʻugāḇ: A masculine noun designating a flute. It refers to a musical instrument consisting of a long, slim tube with holes in it to finger while blowing over a specially placed opening (Gen. 4:21; Job 21:12; 30:31). It was used to worship the Lord (Ps. 150:4).

5749. עוּד ʻûḏ: A verb meaning to bear witness, to testify. Specifically, it can signify either to serve as a witness or to testify against someone, albeit falsely (1 Kgs. 21:10, 13); or in favor of someone (Job 29:11). It can also mean either to admonish someone (Gen. 43:3; Neh. 9:26, 30); or to warn solemnly (Gen. 43:3; Ex. 19:21; Deut. 32:46; 1 Sam. 8:9; 1 Kgs. 2:42; 2 Chr. 24:19; Neh. 9:29; 13:15, 21; Jer. 42:19; Amos 3:13). Such warnings frequently came from the Lord (2 Kgs. 17:13, 15; Jer. 11:7); but they were also mediated through His prophets (2 Chr. 24:19; Jer. 42:19). In the causative form, it can mean to call to witness, to take as a witness (Deut. 4:26; Isa. 8:2); or to obtain witnesses, that is, authentication (Jer. 32:10, 25, 44).

5750. עוֹד ʻôḏ: An adverb meaning again, still, more, longer, also, yet. It indicates repetition and/or continuance of something. It expresses the fact that something continues to happen (Gen. 18:22; 29:7; 46:29; 1 Kgs. 22:43). It can mean not yet used with *lô'* (2 Chr. 20:33; Jer. 40:5). It is used often in the phrase, still (*ʻôḏ*) speaking (Gen. 29:9; 1 Kgs. 1:22, 42; 2 Kgs. 6:33; Esth. 6:14). It indicates repetition or repeated action (Gen. 7:4; 8:10, 12; 2 Kgs. 6:33). The construction of *lô'* . . . *ʻôḏ* means no more (Gen. 17:5; Ex. 2:3; Josh. 5:1, 12). It indicates doing something once more, again (Gen. 4:25; 9:11; 18:29). It takes on the sense of still or more in some contexts (Gen. 19:12; Josh. 14:11; Ps. 139:18; Amos 6:10). It takes prefixes: *bᵉ*, in the continuance of what is going on (Gen. 25:6; Deut. 31:27). It indicates time within which something will happen (Gen. 40:13, 19; Josh. 1:11; Isa. 7:8).

5751. עוֹד ʻôḏ: An Aramaic adverb meaning while, yet. It indicates that something is still going on (Dan. 4:31[28]), e.g., Nebuchadnezzar's words were still in his mouth.

5752. עֹדֵד ʻōḏēḏ, עוֹדֵד ōḏēḏ: A proper noun designating Obed:

A. The father of the prophet Azariah (2 Chr. 15:1, 8).

B. A prophet (2 Chr. 28:9).

5753. עָוָה ʻāwāh: A verb meaning to bend, to twist. In its various uses, the word means to do wrong, to commit iniquity (Esth. 1:16; Dan. 9:5); or to be physically or emotionally distressed (Isa. 21:3). It is used with reference to a person with a disturbed mind (Prov. 12:8). In the intensive form, it can mean to distort something, such as the face of the earth (Isa. 24:1); or the path that one walks (Lam. 3:9). In its causative form, it refers to perverting right behavior (Job 33:27; Jer. 3:21); or simply doing that which is wrong (2 Sam. 7:14; 19:19[20]; Jer. 9:5[4]); referring to behavior acknowledged as wrong by the psalmist (Ps. 106:6); by David (2 Sam. 24:17); and by Solomon (1 Kgs. 8:47; 2 Chr. 6:37).

5754. עַוָּה ***'awwāh:*** A feminine noun indicating a ruin, an overturning. It indicates the overthrow of something, turning it into rubble so that it no longer exists or functions (Ezek. 21:27[32]).

5755. עַוָּא ***'awwā'***, עִוָּה ***'iwwāh:*** A proper noun designating Ivvah, Avva (2 Kgs. 17:24; 18:34; 19:13; Isa. 37:13).

5756. עוּז ***'ûz:*** A verb meaning to seek refuge, to bring to safety. It refers to bringing something into shelter, safety, a place of protection from any kind of threat or danger (Ex. 9:19; Isa. 10:31; Jer. 4:6; 6:1).

5757. עַוִּי ***'awwiy:*** A proper noun designating Avite:

A. One of a group placed in Israel after the Assyrian deportation (2 Kgs. 17:31).

B. A member of one of the original Canaanite nations (Deut. 2:23; Josh. 13:3).

5758. עֲוָיָה ***'awāyāh:*** An Aramaic feminine noun meaning offense, iniquity. Related to a Hebrew word whose root meaning is iniquity or guilt, this Aramaic term is found only once in the Old Testament, in Daniel's interpretation of one of King Nebuchadnezzar's dreams (Dan. 4:27[24]). In his interpretation, Daniel warned the king that unless he repented of his sins and iniquities and began to act righteously and show mercy, judgment would fall on him.

5759. עֲוִיל ***'awiyl:*** A masculine noun referring to a young child, little boy. It describes little children hardly able to understand life but able to turn against someone without understanding (Job 19:18); or children in general (Job 21:11). In context it depicts the offspring of the wicked.

5760. עֲוִיל ***'awiyl:*** A masculine noun meaning an unjust one, an evil one. Derived from a verb meaning to act wrongfully, this term appears once in the Old Testament, where it has the sense of ungodly or evil people (Job 16:11). Job used the term to describe Bildad, Zophar, and Eliphaz, his accusers, whom he sarcastically referred to as his friends (cf. Job 16:20).

5761. עַוִּים ***'awwiym:*** A proper noun designating Avvim, a city in Benjamin (Josh. 18:23).

5762. עֲוִית ***'awiyṯ:*** A proper noun designating Avith (Gen. 36:35; 1 Chr. 1:46).

5763. עוּל *'ûl:* A verb meaning to nurse, to give suck. It refers to the feeding process of young animals still nursing their mothers (Gen. 33:13); to the young calves still nursing (1 Sam. 6:7, 10); or to suckling lambs (Ps. 78:71; Isa. 40:11).

5764. עוּל *'ûl:* A masculine noun referring to an infant, a nursing child. It describes a nursing baby, a child still tenderly attached to its mother (Isa. 49:15). In Isaiah 65:20, it is used of a nursing child or baby and in the immediate context indicates infant death.

5765. עָוַל *'āwal:* A verb meaning to act wrongfully, to act unjustly, to deviate from the moral standard. The word is derived from the noun meaning injustice or iniquity. It occurs in Isaiah 26:10, where the prophet bemoaned the fact that despite God's showing grace to the wicked, they continued to act wrongfully. The verb occurs as a substantive participle where the psalmist prayed for deliverance from the clutches of the unrighteous (Ps. 71:4). See the noun *'āwel* (5766).

5766. עָוֶל *'āwel,* עֶוֶל *'ewel,* עַוְלָה *'awlāh,* עֹלָתָה *'ōlāṯāh:* A masculine singular noun meaning injustice, unrighteousness. The word refers to anything that deviates from the right way of doing things. It is often the direct object of *'āśāh* (6213), meaning to do (Lev. 19:15; Deut. 25:16; Ps. 7:3[4]; Ezek. 3:20; 33:13); and is in direct contrast to words like righteous (Prov. 29:27); upright (Ps. 107:42); and justice (Deut. 32:4). God has no part with injustice (Deut. 32:4; 2 Chr. 19:7; Job 34:10; Jer. 2:5). See the verb *'āwal* (5765).

5767. עַוָּל *'awwāl:* A masculine singular noun meaning an unjust person, an unrighteous person. This word occurs five times in the Hebrew Bible with four of them occurring in the Book of Job. Job said that an *'awwāl* deserved God's punishment (Job 31:3). But he countered the implications of his friends by stating adamantly that he was not such a person (Job 29:17). Likewise, Zephaniah argued that God is righteous and not an *'awwāl*, contrary to the corrupted leaders of Jerusalem (Zeph. 3:5).

5768. עוֹלֵל *'ôlēl,* עוֹלָל *'ôlāl:* I. A masculine noun meaning a child, an infant. It refers to offspring, sons and daughters, still quite young and holding the promise of descendants. The destruction of children was especially devastating to a people (2 Kgs. 8:12; Lam. 2:11, 20; see concordance for other references).

II. A masculine noun meaning a child, an infant. See I. As noted in I, the destruction of infants was especially heinous and devastating to a people (Ps. 137:9; Jer. 6:11; 9:21[20]; Lam. 1:5; 2:19; 4:4; Joel 2:16; Mic. 2:9; Nah. 3:10).

5769. עוֹלָם *'ôlām:* A masculine noun meaning a very long time. The word usually refers to looking forward but many times expresses the idea of looking backward. It may cover a given person's lifetime (Ex. 21:6; 1 Sam. 1:22); a period of many generations (Josh. 24:2; Prov. 22:28); the time of the present created order (Deut. 33:15; Ps. 73:12); time beyond this temporal sphere, especially when used regarding God (Gen. 21:33; Ps. 90:2; Dan. 12:2, 7). The term also applies to many things associated with God, such as His decrees, His covenants, and the Messiah (Gen. 9:16; Ex. 12:14; Mic. 5:2[1]). This word describes the span of time in which God is to be obeyed and praised (1 Chr. 16:36; Ps. 89:1[2]; 119:112). In the age to come, there will be no need for sun or moon, for God Himself will be the everlasting light (Isa. 60:19, 20; cf. Rev. 22:5).

5770. עָוַן ***'āwan:*** A verb indicating to look askance, to eye with suspicion. It means to observe something with a critical and questioning attitude (1 Sam. 18:9).

5771. עָוֹן ***'āwōn:*** a masculine noun meaning iniquity, evil, guilt, punishment. This is one of the four main words indicating sin in the Old Testament. This word indicates sin that is particularly evil, since it strongly conveys the idea of twisting or perverting deliberately. The noun carries along with it the idea of guilt from conscious wrongdoing (Gen. 44:16; Jer. 2:22). The punishment that goes with this deliberate act as a consequence is indicated by the word also (Gen. 4:13; Isa. 53:11).

The Hebrew word means sin or transgression in a conscious sense, as when David kept (consciously) from transgression or sin (2 Sam. 22:24); Israel by choice returned to the sins their ancestors had committed (Jer. 11:10; 13:22).

This word for sin can also indicate the guilt that results from the act of sin: Moses prayed that the Lord would forgive the guilt and sin of rebellious Israel (Num. 14:19); the guilt of the Amorites was not yet full in the time of Abraham (Gen. 15:16); God would remove the guilt of His people when they returned from exile (Jer. 50:20); the guilt of the fathers was a recurring phrase in the Old Testament (Ex. 20:5; 34:7).

The word also indicates in some contexts the punishment that results from sin and guilt; Cain's punishment was unbearable for him (Gen. 4:13; Jer. 51:6). Edom was condemned for not helping Israel in the time of Israel's punishment (Ezek. 35:5); and the Levites had to bear their punishment because they strayed from following the Lord (Ps. 31:10[11]; Ezek. 44:10, 12).

5772. עֹנָה ***'ōnāh,*** עוֹנָה ***'ônāh:*** I. A feminine noun referring to conjugal rights, the duty of marriage. It refers to the right of a wife in a polygamous marriage to have intimacy with her husband (Ex. 21:10).

II. A feminine noun indicating sin, guilt. It refers to the burden or responsible guilt someone bears (Hos. 10:10).

5773. עִוְעִים *'iw'iym:* A masculine plural noun referring to distortion, dizziness. It is a collective plural noun indicating staggering, dizziness. In context or figurative references, it describes a deluded and misled Egyptian people (Isa. 19:14).

5774. עוּף *'ûp:* I. A verb meaning to fly, to flutter, to flicker, to glow, to shine; to grow weary. It indicates the act of flying, especially by birds (Gen. 1:20; Deut. 4:17); of a swallow in a figurative sense (Prov. 26:2). Heavenly beings fly (Isa. 6:6). It is used of the Lord flying on the cherubim (2 Sam. 22:11; Ps. 18:10[11]); arrows flying in their flight (Ps. 91:5); of a swift army swooping, flying (Isa. 11:14). The Lord is likened to hovering (flying) birds over their young (Isa. 31:5). To fly away may have the sense of to escape in certain contexts (Ps. 55:6[7]); or the sense of dying (Ps. 90:10). It is used of the to and fro motion of a drawn sword blade (Ezek. 32:10), to brandish a sword. It is used figuratively of honor or glory flying away, disappearing (Hos. 9:11).

II. A verb meaning to brandish. It pictures the to and fro threatening movements of a drawn sword (Ezek. 32:10).

5775. עוֹף *'ôp:* A collective masculine noun meaning a bird, a flying creature. It refers to winged birds or insects: birds (Gen. 1:20, 22) of all kinds, including carrion birds, birds that serve as scavengers (1 Sam. 17:44, 46); for food (Ps. 78:27); for offerings (Gen. 8:20; Lev. 1:14). It is also used of insects, clean or unclean (Lev. 11:20, 21: Deut. 14:19).

5776. עוֹף *'ôp̱:* An Aramaic masculine noun indicating a bird. It refers to a living thing with wings and feathers that normally can fly. Daniel 2:38 refers to birds of the sky, heavens. Daniel saw a vision of a leopard that had bird wings on its back (Dan. 7:6).

5777. עוֹפֶרֶת *'ôpereṯ,* עֹפֶרֶת *'ōpereṯ:* A feminine noun referring to lead. It indicates a heavy metal. It was a scarce but useful metal (Ezek. 27:12). It was used as a weight (Zech. 5:8). It is used figuratively of the way the Egyptians sank in the Red Sea, like lead (Ex. 15:10). It was used in some engraving processes (Job 19:24). It is used figuratively of the impurity of God's people (Jer. 6:29). It needed to be heated to remove its dross, as did God's people (Ezek. 22:18; 22:20).

5778. עֵיפַי *'êypay:* A proper noun designating Ephai (Jer. 40:8).

5779. עוּץ *'ûṣ:* A verb meaning to devise a plan, to take advice. It refers to the process of coming up with a response or a way to deal with a situation (Judg. 19:30). Plans that thwart God's will do not work (Isa. 8:10).

5780. עוּץ *'ûṣ:* A proper noun designating Uz:

A. One of the twins born to Nahor, the other was Buz (Gen. 22:20, 21).

B. A grandson of Seir, the Horite, and son of Dishan (Gen. 36:28).

5781. עוּק ***'ûq:*** A verb meaning to be weighed down, to be crushed. It is used of a heavy weight pressing down on something. In context it is used figuratively of the weight of Israel's rebelliousness pressing down on God (Amos 2:13).

5782. עוּר ***'ûr:*** I. A verb meaning to stir, to arouse, to awaken. It is used of raising something or someone to action, of agitating someone, of motivating him or her. It is used of stirring oneself to action (Judg. 5:12; Ps. 57:8[9]); especially of the Lord's arousing Himself or His arm (Ps. 7:6[7]; 59:4[5]; Isa. 51:9). In its passive use, it means to be stirred up (Jer. 6:22; 25:32; Zech. 4:1). It means to rouse someone to action (Zech. 9:13); to use a weapon (2 Sam. 23:18); to stir up a nest of young birds (a figure of the Lord toward His people) (Deut. 32:11).

5783. עוּר ***'ûr:*** A verb meaning to be exposed, to be uncovered. It means to be uncovered, exposed. It is used of God's bow, His weapon, being readied for battle (Hab. 3:9).

5784. עוּר ***'ûr:*** An Aramaic masculine noun referring to chaff. It refers to the husks of wheat or various grains removed in the threshing process, as well as other impurities, etc. (Dan. 2:35).

5785. עוֹר ***'ôr:*** A masculine singular noun meaning skin. It is used literally of human skin, such as Moses' shining face (Ex. 34:29); or in connection with regulations regarding leprosy or skin diseases (Lev. 13:2). It is employed figuratively in the expression, skin of my teeth (Job 19:20). It can also denote skins of animals, typically already skinned (with the exception of Job 41:7[40:31]). Skins were used for the garments that God made for Adam and Eve (Gen. 3:21); and for coverings of items like the Tabernacle (Ex. 25:5); and the ark (Num. 4:6).

5786. עָוַר ***'āwar:*** A verb meaning to make blind, to put out someone's eyes. It is used of putting out persons' eyes, blinding them (2 Kgs. 25:7; Jer. 39:7; 52:11). In a figurative sense, it indicates the blinding of officials' eyes to injustice by means of bribes (Ex. 23:8; Deut. 16:19).

5787. עִוֵּר ***'iwwēr:*** An adjective meaning blind. It refers to an inability to see, having one's eyes put out. God is the ultimate cause of blindness (Ex. 4:11). Figuratively, it describes a person who lives in a state of darkness (Deut. 28:29). Blindness was a defect in an animal, preventing it from being sacrificed (Deut. 15:21). It describes spiritual dullness, blindness (Isa. 42:18, 19; 43:8).

5788. עִוָּרוֹן ***'iwwārôn,*** עַוֶּרֶת ***'awwereṯ:*** I. An abstract masculine noun meaning blindness. It is used especially of spiritual and religious blindness (Deut. 28:28). It is used figuratively of horses being blind, that is, the power and might of the nations (Zech. 12:4).

II. A feminine noun meaning blindness. It refers to a defect in the sight of a sacrificial animal that rendered it unusable as a sacrifice (Lev. 22:22).

5789. עוּשׁ ***'ûš:*** A verb which occurs once in the Hebrew Bible (Joel 3:11[4:11]). Recent translations have abandoned the former translation, to lend aid, to come to help, for a different Arabic cognate, meaning to hurry. Joel used the word with the verb to come to summon all the nations to prepare for battle in the Valley of Jehoshaphat. At that location, God will judge them, trampling them like grapes in a winepress.

5790. עוּת ***'ûṯ:*** A verb which occurs once in the Hebrew Bible (Isa. 50:4). It is traditionally translated to help but the meaning is uncertain. In this context, Isaiah proclaimed that the Lord gave him a tongue to help the weary.

5791. עָוַת ***'āwaṯ:*** A verb meaning to be bent, to be crooked. It is always used in the intensive stems with the meaning to bend, to subvert, or to pervert. Except for Ecclesiastes 12:3, where it refers to the strong men bending themselves (that is, bowing down), it is used figuratively of bending or perverting justice and righteousness. Bildad and Elihu told Job that God does not pervert justice (Job 8:3; 34:12); but Job thought God had been crooked with him (Job 19:6).

5792. עַוָּתָה ***'awwāṯāh:*** A feminine singular noun meaning a subversion, a perversion. It is used only in Lamentations 3:59 where the poet declared that God had seen the perversion of justice done to Jerusalem (that is, its destruction). This passage is interesting because the writer saw God's judgment as severe. See the verb *'āwaṯ* (5791).

5793. עוּתַי ***'ûṯay:*** A proper noun designating Uthai:

A. A son of Ammihud (1 Chr. 9:4).
B. A son of Bigvai (Ezra 8:14).

5794. עַז ***'az:*** I. An adjective meaning strong, powerful; insolent. When referring to a person's attitude of anger or wrath, it means insolent, excessive, fierce (Gen. 49:7); used of physical strength or power, it means strong, forceful (Ex. 14:21; Judg. 14:14). The phrase *'az pānîm,* strong of faces means determined, defiant (Deut. 28:50; Dan. 8:23); in context *'az nep̱eš* indicates that persons are greedy, covetous, insatiable (Isa. 56:11). Describing bold or arrogant speech, it means arrogantly, insolently (Prov. 18:23). Ants are not considered strong but are wise (Prov. 30:25). Used as a noun, it means a strong person (Amos 5:9).

II. A masculine noun meaning power, strength. It is used as an abstract noun to refer to procreative power and the power of offspring (Gen. 49:3).

5795. עֵז *'ēz:* A female goat, kid. It refers to an animal of the flock that was milked and eaten, as well as used in many sacrificial rituals. It was valuable property, a part of a person's wealth (Gen. 15:9; 27:9, 16; Lev. 22:27). Goat's milk was a choice drink (Prov. 27:27). Goat's hair was used as a covering and for other items (Ex. 25:4; 1 Sam. 19:13, 16). The phrases *ṣᵉḇir hā'ēz* and *śᵉ'îr 'izzîm* refer to a buck or he goat (Gen. 37:31; Dan. 8:5, 8).

5796. עֵז *'ēz:* An Aramaic feminine noun meaning goat. It is used in the phrase he goats, male goats, *ṣᵉḇirê 'izzîn* (Ezra 6:17) to refer to sacrificial goats at the Temple dedication ceremonies.

5797. עֹז *'ōz,* עוֹז *'ôz:* A masculine noun referring to strength, power. It depicts the Lord as one's strength (Ps. 61:3[4]; Prov. 18:10; Isa. 12:2); and the power by which God led His people (Ex. 15:13). It is used of the power or strength of a people, a nation (Lev. 26:19); or the internal fortitude and strength of a individual (Judg. 5:21). It indicates the defense, the strength of a fortified tower (Judg. 9:51). It indicates the ability and might of God's anointed king, given by God (1 Sam. 2:10). The phrase, strength, might of the Lord, is found often as well as other combinations with *'ōz* (Job 12:16; Isa. 49:5; Hab. 3:4; Mic. 5:4[3]). The phrase *qôl 'ōz* means a strong voice (Ps. 68:35[34]). The Lord delivered by the arm of His might, His strong arm (Isa. 62:8). Political and national strength is recognized (Jer. 48:17). In Ecclesiastes 8:1, it is used in a phrase to indicate a sternness or impudence of a person. In a figurative sense, it refers to the strength or witness for God from the mouths of infants (Ps. 8:2[3]).

5798. עֻזָּא *'uzzā',* עֻזָּה *'uzzāh:* A proper noun designating Uzzah, Uzza:

A. A son of Abinadab in whose house the ark was housed briefly. He helped his brother Ahio direct the cart carrying the ark. Uzzah touched the ark to steady it and was struck dead by the Lord (2 Sam. 6:3–8). David was angry because of the event and named the place where it happened Perez Uzzah, "breaking out (against) Uzzah."

B. The son of Gera who deported certain Jews (1 Chr. 8:7).

C. A Levite descended through the line of Merari (1 Chr. 6:29).

D. A Jew in whose garden Manasseh, king of Judah, was buried (2 Kgs. 21:18).

E. He was a Levite and served at the Temple (Ezra 2:49).

5799. עֲזָאזֵל *'ᵃzā'zēl:* A masculine noun referring to a scapegoat. It is taken as a designation of the goat on which the sins of the nation were laid, hence, a scapegoat on the Day of Atonement (Lev. 16:8, 10, 26). Others suggest that this is the name of a desert demon.

5800. עָזַב ʿāza<u>b</u>: A verb derived from two separate roots. The more common in the Hebrew Bible is ʿaza<u>b</u> I, meaning to leave, to abandon, to forsake, to loose. It can be used to designate going away to a new locale (2 Kgs. 8:6); or to separate oneself from another person (Gen. 44:22; Ruth 1:16). When Zipporah's father found her without Moses, he asked, "Why did you leave him?" (Ex. 2:20). A man is to leave his parents to marry (Gen. 2:24). To leave in the hand of is an idiomatic expression meaning to entrust (Gen. 39:6). The word can also carry a much more negative connotation. Israelites abandoned their towns after the army fled (1 Sam. 31:7); the ultimate sign of defeat (and often God's judgment) were abandoned cities (Isa. 17:9; Jer. 4:29; Zeph. 2:4). The Israelites often were warned and accused of forsaking God by sacrificing to other gods (Deut. 28:20; Judg. 10:10; Jer. 1:16). The prophets called on them to forsake idols and sin instead (Isa. 55:7; Ezek. 20:8; 23:8). While the psalmist said that God would not abandon his soul (Ps. 16:10), God does on occasion abandon humans because of their sin (Deut. 31:17; Ezek. 8:12). But despite the psalmist's cry which Jesus quoted from the cross (Ps. 22:1[2]), most Biblical writers took heart because God would not abandon them (Ezra 9:9; Isa. 42:16).The word ʿaza<u>b</u> can also mean to restore or repair. It occurs only in Nehemiah 3:8 in reference to the walls of Jerusalem.

5801. עִזָּבוֹן ʿizzā<u>b</u>ôn: A masculine noun referring to waves, to merchandise. It refers to goods or merchandise available for trade and barter (Ezek. 27:12, 14, 16, 19, 22, 27, 33).

5802. עַזְבּוּק ʿaz<u>b</u>ûq: A proper noun designating Azbuk (Neh. 3:16).

5803. עַזְגָּד ʿaz<u>g</u>ā<u>d</u>: A proper noun designating Azgad (Ezra 2:12; 8:12; Neh. 7:17; 10:15[16]).

5804. עַזָּה ʿazzāh: A proper noun designating Gaza, an important city in southwest Israel. It was near the coast and at the dividing line between Canaan and the area of the Sinai Desert. The Philistines controlled it most of the time even though it was allotted to Judah (Josh. 10:41; 15:47; Judg. 1:18). It was often under the influence of Egypt or the current ruling power of Canaan since it was situated at several major trade routes.

It was initially inhabited by the Avvites, a people who preceded the Philistines (Gen. 10:19; Deut. 2:23), as well as the Anakites (Josh. 11:22). Samson visited the city and removed the doors of the city gate (Judg. 16:1–3) but was later taken there as a captive. He avenged himself on the Philistines who ruled the city (Judg. 16:21–31). The grain god Dagon was worshiped there. Later, it became part of the five-city coalition of Philistine cities (Ashdod, Gaza, Ashkelon, Gath, Ekron). It was the recognized southern extent of Philistine influence and power (2 Kgs. 18:8). The prophets spoke of God's judgment on the city often (Jer. 25:20; 47:1, 5; Amos 1:6, 7; Zeph. 2:4; Zech. 9:5).

5805. עֲזוּבָה ***ᵃzûḇāh:*** A feminine abstract noun referring to forsakenness. It refers to isolated, forsaken places after people have left them, deserted locations (Isa. 6:12); or to similar locations in a forest setting (Isa. 17:9). Others take the word to refer to a state of forsakenness, loneliness (KJV).

5806. עֲזוּבָה ***ᵃzûḇāh:*** A proper noun designating Azubah:

A. The mother of Jehoshaphat (1 Kgs. 22:42; 2 Chr. 20:31).

B. The wife of Caleb (1 Chr. 2:18, 19).

5807. עֱזוּז ***ᵉzûz:*** A masculine noun meaning strength, power, violence. It is used of God's power and strength displayed in His mighty work of salvation for His people (Ps. 78:4; 145:6). It describes the rage and violence of battle or war (Isa. 42:25).

5808. עִזּוּז ***'izzûz:*** An adjective meaning strong, mighty. It describes the Lord as one who is strong, powerful, and able to defend or fight for His people (Ps. 24:8). It refers to a mighty man or to strength, might for battle (Isa. 43:17).

5809. עַזּוּר ***'azzûr:*** A proper noun designating Azzur:

A. The father of Hananiah (Jer. 28:1).

B. The father of Jaazaniah (Ezek. 11:1).

C. A Jewish leader (Neh. 10:17[18]).

5810. עָזַז ***'āzaz:*** A verb meaning to be strong, to strengthen, to prevail. It depicts being victorious, prevailing, being victorious in battle (Judg. 3:10; 6:2; Dan. 11:12) or in various settings. It describes people triumphing instead of God (Ps. 9:19[20]). It has the sense of being fixed, determined in a course of action (Ps. 52:7[9]). It indicates a harlot's face in her arrogance, an insolent or shameless countenance (Prov. 7:13). It is used of the Lord's fixing or establishing the springs of the great deep at creation (Prov. 8:28). It describes the affect of wisdom in establishing a person (Eccl. 7:19). It has the sense of to be or to find strength when in its infinitive form (Isa. 30:2).

5811. עָזָז ***'āzāz:*** A proper noun designating Azaz (1 Chr. 5:8).

5812. עֲזַזְיָהוּ ***ᵃzazyāhû:*** A proper noun designating Azaziah:

A. A Levite (1 Chr. 15:21).

B. A Levite (2 Chr. 31:13).

C. A Benjamite (1 Chr. 27:20).

5813. עֻזִּי ***'uzziy:*** A proper noun designating Uzzi (1 Chr. 6:5[5:31], 6[5:32], 51[36]; 7:2, 3, 7; 9:8; Ezra 7:4; Neh. 11:22; 12:19, 42).

5814. עֻזִּיָּא *'uziyyā':* A proper noun designating Uzzia (1 Chr. 11:44).

5815. עֲזִיאֵל *'Aziy'ēl:* A proper noun designating Aziel (1 Chr. 15:20). It is the same as *ya'^a^ziy'ēl* (3268).

5816. עֻזִּיאֵל *'uzziy'ēl:* A proper noun designating Uzziel:

A. A son of Bela (1 Chr. 7:7).

B. A son of Kohath (Ex. 6:18, 22; Lev. 10:4; Num. 3:19, 30; 1 Chr. 6:2[5:28], 18[3]; 15:10; 23:12, 20; 24:24).

C. A son of Heman (1 Chr. 25:4; 2 Chr. 29:14).

D. A Simeonite (1 Chr. 4:42).

E. A son of Harhaiah (Neh. 3:8).

5817. עָזִּיאֵלִי *'ozziy'ēliy:* A proper noun designating Uzzielite (Num. 3:27; 1 Chr. 26:23).

5818. עֻזִּיָּהוּ *'uzziyyāhû,* עֻזִּיָּה *'uzziyyāh:* A proper noun designating Uzziah:

A. The father of Jehonathan. He was overseer of the various treasuries and storehouses of the districts set up by David (1 Chr. 27:25).

B. The son of Uriel and a priestly descendant of the family of Kohath (1 Chr. 6:24).

C. A king of Judah and son of Amaziah. He reigned the same time as Azariah (see 5838,N.). He reigned 792–767 B.C. including a coregency, a total of fifty-two years (see esp. 2 Kgs. 15:1–7; 2 Chr. 26:1–23). A great earthquake took place during his reign (Zech. 14:5).

D. A son of Zechariah who resettled in Jerusalem in the time of Nehemiah (Neh. 11:4).

E. A son of Harim who had married with a foreigner during the exile (Ezra 10:21).

5819. עֲזִיזָא *'^a^ziyzā':* A proper noun designating Aziza (Ezra 10:27).

5820. עַזְמָוֶת *'azmāwet:* A proper noun designating Azmaveth:

A. One of David's mighty men (2 Sam. 23:31; 1 Chr. 11:33; 12:3).

B. The head of a family, possibly the same as A (Ezra 2:24).

C. A village near Jerusalem (Neh. 12:29). It is the same as 1041.

D. An officer under David (1 Chr. 27:25).

E. A descendant of Micah (1 Chr. 8:36; 9:42).

5821. עַזָּן *'azzān:* A proper noun designating Azzan (Num. 34:26).

5822. עָזְנִיָּה *'ozniyyāh:* A feminine noun referring to an unclean bird: a buzzard, a black vulture. It was forbidden to Israel as food; it was unclean (Lev. 11:13; Deut. 14:12).

5823. עָזַק *'āzaq:* A verb meaning to dig around, to force in. It refers to the preparation of a plot of land for planting (Isa. 5:2).

5824. עִזְקָה *'izqāh:* An Aramaic feminine noun referring to a signet ring. It refers to a ring bearing the seal of someone and used to seal various items for identification purposes (Dan. 6:17[18]).

5825. עֲזֵקָה *ᵃzēqāh:* A proper noun designating Azekah, a town in the Shephelah area allotted to Judah (Josh. 15:35). It was west of Gath and north of Maresheth-Gath. David's combat with Goliath was in its vicinity (1 Sam. 17:1). It became a strong military outpost (2 Chr. 11:9). Some exiles who returned from Babylon resettled in it (Neh. 11:30).

5826. עָזַר *'āzar:* A verb meaning to help, to aid. It means to support, to give material or nonmaterial encouragement to a person. God was the one who helped His people (Gen. 49:25). It is used mockingly of the inability of idols or pagan gods to aid their people (Deut. 32:38). It describes people helping each other to accomplish goals (Josh. 1:14; 10:4). The name Ebenezer means literally stone of help (1 Sam. 7:12). The participial form of the verb, *'ōzer,* may mean helper (Isa. 31:3). In its passive use, it means to be helped, aided (Ps. 28:7). Zechariah 1:15 indicates that the nations helped and aided the evil, the devastation of God's people (Zech. 1:15).

5827. עֶזֶר *'ezer:* A proper noun designating Ezer:

A. An Ephraimite (1 Chr. 7:21).

B. A priest (Neh. 12:42).

5828. עֵזֶר *'ēzer:* A masculine noun meaning a helper, one who helps; help, aid. It refers to aid or assistance that is given, whether material or immaterial (Isa. 30:5; Dan. 11:34). It is often help from the Lord who helps His people (Ps. 20:2[3]; 121:1, 2; 124:8). He is called the shield or protection of Israel's help (Deut. 33:29). It indicates persons who give help: the woman created as Adam's complementary helper (Gen. 2:18, 20); the Lord as Israel's help (Hos. 13:9); the Lord as Israel's chief Helper (Ex. 18:4; Deut. 33:7; Ps. 33:20; 115:9–11). The name Eliezer means God (is) my helper (Ex. 18:4).

5829. עֵזֶר *'ēzer:* A proper noun designating Ezer:

A. A builder of the wall (Neh. 3:19).

B. A Judaite (1 Chr. 4:4).

C. One of David's mighty men (1 Chr. 12:9[10]).

D. A priest (Neh. 12:42).

5830. עֶזְרָא *'ezrā':* A proper noun designating Ezra, the name means "help, assistance." He was the scribe, mighty in the Law of Moses (Ezra 7:8–10), who returned from the exile (458 B.C.; Ezra 7:1–10) and helped establish the fledgling religious community on the basis of the Law of Moses. He cleansed the priesthood (Ezra 9; 10) and read the Law at the Water Gate (Neh. 8:2–18; ca. 444 B.C.) to the residents of Jerusalem and the surrounding areas. He also celebrated with Nehemiah the dedication of the rebuilt wall of Jerusalem (Neh. 12:26–36).

5831. עֶזְרָא **'ezrā':** A proper noun designating Ezra, the Aramaic for the Hebrew scribe's name, Ezra. It corresponds to 5830. It appears only in Aramaic portions of Ezra. The meaning is the same in both languages.

5832. עֲזַרְאֵל **ʿazar'ēl:** A proper noun designating Azarel:
A. A Benjamite warrior (1 Chr. 12:6).
B. A Levite (1 Chr. 25:18).
C. A Danite leader (1 Chr. 27:22).
D. A postexilic Jew (Ezra 10:41).
E. A priest (Neh. 11:13).
F. A priest (Neh. 12:36).

5833. עֶזְרָה **ʿezrāh,** עֶזְרָת **'ezrāth:** A feminine noun indicates help, assistance. It indicates the assistance or aid given to a person whether material or immaterial (Isa. 10:3; 20:6; 31:1; Jer. 37:7; Lam. 4:17); especially help for the Lord (Judg. 5:23); and help from the Lord (Ps. 22:19[20]; 38:22[23]; 40:13[14], 17[18]). It refers to the person who helps: persons (at the gate) who help (Job 31:21); of the Lord as Helper (Ps. 27:9; 40:17[18]; 46:1[2]; 44:26[27]).

5834. עֶזְרָה **ʿezrāh:** A proper noun designating Ezra (1 Chr. 4:17).

5835. עֲזָרָה **ʿazārāh:** A feminine noun indicating a ledge, a courtyard. It indicates some kind of enclosure, a rail or edging around an object (Ezek. 43:14, 17, 20; 45:19); or an enclosed area, a courtyard or court area (2 Chr. 4:9; 6:13).

5836. עֶזְרִי **ʿezriy:** A proper noun designating Ezri (1 Chr. 27:26).

5837. עַזְרִיאֵל **ʿazriy'ēl:** A proper noun designating Azriel:
A. A Manassite chief (1 Chr. 5:24).
B. A Naphtalite chief (1 Chr. 27:19).
C. A royal officer (Jer. 36:26).

5838. עֲזַרְיָה **ʿazaryāh,** עֲזַרְיָהוּ **ʿazaryāhû:** A proper noun designating Azariah:
A. The son of Ethan, a man from Judah (1 Chr. 2:8).
B. The son of Jehu. He was from Judah (1 Chr. 2:39).
C. The son of Zephaniah. He shared in the responsibility of the temple music (1 Chr. 6:36).
D. The son of Zadok the priest. He was one of Solomon's chief administrators (1 Chr. 9:11).
E. Son of Nathan. He was the district official in charge of the officers (1 Kgs. 4:5).
F. Son of Obed. He encouraged King Asa in his reforms (2 Chr. 15:1).
G. Son of Ahimaaz of the tribe of Levi (1 Chr. 6:9).
H. Son of Jehoshaphat, the bother of King Jehoram who was also the son of Jehoshaphat (2 Chr. 21:2).
I. A son of Jehoshaphat (2 Chr. 21:2). See H.
J. Another name for Uzziah (2 Kgs. 14:21).
K. Son of Jehoram. He was a commander of a unit of 100 men. He and others made a covenant with the king at the temple of God (2 Chr. 23:1).

L. Son of Obed. When they came to Jerusalem, the whole assembly made a covenant with the king in the temple. He commanded a 100-man unit (2 Chr. 23:1–3).

M. Son of Johanan. He was a priest in Solomon's home in Jerusalem (1 Chr. 6:10).

N. A king of Judah also called Uzziah (see 5818,C.) and son of Amaziah. He was sixteen when he began to reign and reigned fifty-two years (792–740 B.C.). His mother Jecoliah was from Jerusalem. His reign was righteous except he did not take down the competing high places of worship (2 Kgs. 15:4). At his death, Isaiah received his call from God (Isa. 6:1). He arrogantly and illegally tried to burn incense in the Temple, and the Lord smote him with leprosy. He then had to live in a separate house until his death. He reigned as coregent with Amaziah (792–767 B.C.) at the beginning of his reign; at the end of his reign, his son Jotham helped him govern.

O. Chief priest. He and eighty priests opposed Uzziah the king for burning incense in the temple. Only the priests were supposed to burn incense (2 Chr. 26:16–18).

P. Son of Johanan. He was one of the heads of the sons in Ephraim. He helped stop Israel from taking slaves in their fight against Judah (2 Chr. 28:12).

Q. A high priest of the house of God appointed by King Hezekiah (2 Chr. 31:10).

R. A Kohathite and son of Jehallelel. He was one of the priests that helped cleanse the temple under King Hezekiah during the reform (2 Chr. 29:12).

S. A Merarite. He was one of the priests that helped cleanse the temple under King Hezekiah during the reform (2 Chr. 31:13).

T. The son of Hilkiah who found the book of the Law in the Temple during the reign of Josiah. Azariah fathered Seraiah. Ezra was the son of Seraiah (Ezra 7:1). Azariah means "the Lord helps."

U. Enemy of Jeremiah. Son of Hoshaiah. Jeremiah, the prophet, advised the people not to leave Babylon to go to Egypt. Azariah was one of the arrogant men who accused Jeremiah of lying (Jer. 43:2).

V. Hebrew name of Abednego, which a commander under King Nebuchadnezzar, changed from Azariah (Dan. 1:6, 7). He was one of the three young men who were thrown into the furnace by Nebuchadnezzar.

W. Son of Maaseiah. He helped do repairs during the restoration of the walls of Jerusalem (Nah. 3:23).

X. Postexilic Jew, possibly same as W. Listed in the census of the first exiles returned to Jerusalem (Neh. 7:7).

Y. A Levite, possibly same as W. He was in the assembly of men when Ezra read the Law (Neh. 8:7).

Z. A priest, possibly same as W. His name was on the sealed document of the covenant (Neh. 10:2).

AA. Judaite prince, possibly same as W. He was in one of the celebration chairs at the dedication of the wall of Jerusalem (Neh. 12:33).

BB. Son of Meraioth. He went up to Jerusalem with Ezra from Babylon after the temple was completed (Ezra 7:3).

5839. עֲזַרְיָה *ʿazaryāh:* A proper noun designating Azariah, one of the three royal Hebrew boys taken into exile with Daniel (Dan. 2:17). His Hebrew name means "the Lord has assisted." He was also known in Babylon as Abednego ("servant of Nego") (see Dan. 1:6, 7).

5840. עַזְרִיקָם *ʿazriyqām:* A proper noun designating Azrikam:

A. A descendant of David (1 Chr. 3:23).
B. A prince of Judah (2 Chr. 28:7).
C. A Benjamite (1 Chr. 8:38; 9:44).
D. A Levite (1 Chr. 9:14; Neh. 11:15).

5841. עַזָּתִי *ʿazzāṯiy:* A proper noun designating Gazite(s), Gazathites (Josh. 13:3; Judg. 16:2).

5842. עֵט *ʿēṭ:* A masculine noun referring to an iron stylus, a pen. It indicates a writing instrument (Job 19:24). It is used in a figurative way or referred to metaphorically several times (Ps. 45:1[2]; Jer. 8:8). It is used figuratively of the recording of Judah's sins (Jer. 17:1).

5843. עֵטָה *ʿēṭāh:* An Aramaic feminine noun indicating counsel, discretion. It refers to the manner in which someone replies or acts with discernment, prudence, and wisdom (Dan. 2:14).

5844. עָטָה *ʿāṭāh:* I. A verb indicating to wrap around, to cover. It refers to shielding something, keeping it out of sight (Lev. 13:45); to put on a garment or a robe (1 Sam. 28:14). It is used to describe rain as it falls over an area (Ps. 84:6[7]). Figuratively, it describes being wrapped with or clothed in shame (Ps. 71:13). It may mean to wrap someone in or with something (Ps. 89:45[46]; cf. Isa. 61:10). To cover one's mouth is to show astonishment (Jer. 43:12).

II. A verb meaning to take hold, to grasp. It is used of seizing someone, grasping him or her (Isa. 22:17). In its immediate context, it is used figuratively. It may mean to wrap up something for use (KJV, NASB, Ezek. 21:15[20], see I) or to grasp something (NIV) for immediate deployment.

5845. עֲטִין *ʿăṭiyn:* A masculine noun designating a body. Its meaning is uncertain. It may mean a body (NIV, Job 21:24). Others suggest breasts (KJV), sides (NASB), thighs. Some suggest reading *ʿăṭāmayw* in place of *ʿăṭin* here.

5846. עֲטִישָׁה *ʿăṭiyšāh:* A feminine noun referring to sneezing, snorting. It is used to describe the sneezing, the sudden sharp coughing of Leviathan, a magnificent animal created by God (Job 41:18[10]).

5847. עֲטַלֵּף *ᵃṭallēp̱:* A masculine noun referring to a bird, a bat. It refers to a bird forbidden as food to the Israelites, a nocturnal flying animal considered unclean to Israel (Lev. 11:19; Deut. 14:18).

5848. עָטַף *'āṭap̱:* I. A verb meaning to turn, to wrap, to cover. It is used figuratively of God's mysterious, overwhelming actions with Job, turning them to the left (Job 23:9). The wicked are covered with violence (Ps. 73:6).

II. A verb meaning to be feeble, to be faint, to be weak. It refers to animals of a flock that are born unhealthy, feeble, in a weakened state (Gen. 30:42). It is used of persons becoming weary, worn out in spirit from God's dealings with them (Isa. 57:16); or from other causes so that they call on God (Ps. 61:2[3]; 77:3[4]; 142:3[4]; Jon. 2:7[8]). For Psalm 65:13[14], see I. Faint, weak persons pour out their prayers to God (Ps. 102:title[1]).

5849. עָטַר *'āṭar:* I. A verb meaning to crown. It is used figuratively of God's crowning of humankind as the kings and rulers of His creation, reflecting His image (Ps. 8:5[6]); and used figuratively of God's granting a bountiful crop for the year (Ps. 65:11 [12]); or His people with spiritual blessings (Ps. 103:4). It depicts Tyre as a powerful merchant city, granting royal favors (crowns) to the nations (Isa. 23:8). It describes the crowning of persons on their wedding day (Song 3:11).

II. A verb meaning to surround, to encompass. It means to encircle, to entrap by encircling an enemy (1 Sam. 23:26). It means to abundantly bless people, to shower them with something; in context God's approval and blessing (Ps. 5:12[13]).

5850. עֲטָרָה *ᵃṭārāh:* A feminine noun signifying a crown or a wreath. It was a circlet or headdress worn by a king to symbolize his power and authority. Crowns were often made of silver or gold with jewels set in them (2 Sam. 12:30; Esth. 8:15; Zech. 6:11, 14). It could be a garland or a wreath as well, symbolizing the same thing. It is used figuratively of honor (Job 19:9); of a wife of character (Prov. 12:4); of a crown granted by wisdom (Prov. 4:9); of a "crown" worn by the greatest drunkards of Ephraim (Isa. 28:1). In a metaphor, it pictures Jerusalem as God's crown (Isa. 62:3). In the greatest metaphor, God is described as the ultimate crown of His people (Isa. 28:5).

5851. עֲטָרָה *'ṭārāh:* A proper noun designating Atarah (1 Chr. 2:26).

5852. עֲטָרוֹת *ᵃṭārôṯ*, עֲטָרֹת *ᵃṭārōṯ:* A proper noun designating Ataroth:

A. A town east of Jordan (Num. 32:3, 34).

B. A town on the southwest border of Ephraim (Josh. 16:2).

C. A town in northeast Ephraim (Josh. 16:7).

D, A town in Judah (1 Chr. 2:54).

5853. עַטְרוֹת אַדָּר ***'aṭrôṯ 'addār:*** A proper noun designating Ataroth-addar (Josh. 16:5; 18:13).

5854. עַטְרוֹת בֵּית יוֹאָב ***'aṭrôṯ-bēṯ-yô'āḇ:*** A proper noun designating Atroth-beth-joab (1 Chr. 2:54).

5855. עַטְרוֹת שׁוֹפָן ***'aṭrôṯ šôpān:*** A proper noun designating Atroth-shophan, Atroth and Shophan (Num. 32:35).

5856. עִי ***'iy:*** A masculine noun signifying ruins, a rubbish heap. It refers to a pile of useless trash or garbage, a personal situation of helplessness and devastation (Job 30:24). It indicates a city that has been besieged and wiped out (Ps. 79:1; Jer. 26:18; Mic. 1:6; 3:12).

5857. עַי ***'ay,*** עַיָּא ***'ayya',*** עַיָּת ***'ayyāṯ:*** A proper noun designating Ai. The name means "heap, ruin."

A. It was located north, northeast of Jerusalem. There may have been at least one other Ai. See B. Abraham camped between Bethel and Ai (Gen. 12:8; 13:3). It was conquered by Joshua only after an initial failure because of Achan's sin in Israel (Josh. 7:1—8:29). Jericho and Ai became model signal victories for Israel (Josh. 9:3). Some former inhabitants of Ai returned from Babylonian exile (Ezra 2:8; Neh. 7:32).

B. A city in the Transjordian territory in Moab (Jer. 49:3). Its exact location is unclear.

5858. עֵיבָל ***'ēyḇāl:*** A proper noun designating Ebal:

A. An Edomite, a man from Edom. He was a son of Shobal who descended from Seir, the Horite (Gen. 36:23).

B. The son of Joktan, a Semite. It also indicates a son of Seir (same as A) (1 Chr. 1:20–22).

C. The mountain in the area of Shechem where, on entrance to Canaan, the Israelites proclaimed the curses written in the covenant of Sinai (Deut. 11:29; 27:4, 13; Josh. 8:30, 33). Joshua built an altar there for this ceremonial ritual.

5859. עִיּוֹן ***'iyyôn:*** A proper noun designating Ijon (1 Kgs. 15:20; 2 Kgs. 15:29; 2 Chr. 16:4).

5860. עִיט ***'iyṭ:*** A verb meaning to scorn, to insult. It is used of the people's rushing upon the spoils of battle (1 Sam. 14:32), but most read *'āśāh* here, they acted, did. This meaning fits well in 1 Samuel 15:19 and has the sense of rushing upon carelessly, scornfully. See II. It has the sense of disrespect or scorn (1 Sam. 25:14).

II. A verb meaning to pounce upon, to rush greedily. It is conjectured that this is the meaning of the original reading in 1 Samuel 14:32. The meaning fits well in 1 Samuel 15:19.

5861. עַיִט ***'ayiṭ:*** A collective masculine noun referring to a bird of prey. It is used of birds that eat carrion, previously dead animals; these birds capture and eat other animals (Gen. 15:11; Job 28:7; Isa. 18:6; 46:11; Ezek. 39:4). It is used figuratively of Judah's enemies (Jer. 12:9); or of an enemy invader (Isa. 46:11).

5862. עֵיטָם ***ʿēyṭām:*** A proper noun designating Etam:

A. A town located in Simeon's tribal territory. It was in the Shephelah area in the northwest Negev (1 Chr. 4:3, 32).

B. A town near Bethlehem in Judah and rebuilt by Rehoboam (2 Chr. 11:6). It is south, southwest of Jerusalem about six miles.

C. A rock formation or cave where Samson hid from the Philistines after he slew many of them. It was likely in Judah's western area (Judg. 15:8).

5863. עִיֵּי הָעֲבָרִים ***ʿiyyēy hāʿa-bāriym:*** A proper noun designating Iye Abarim (Num. 21:11; 33:44).

5864. עִיִּים ***ʿiyyiym:*** A proper noun designating Iyim:

A. Another name for *ʿiyyēy hāʿa-bāriym* (5863) (Gen. 10:22; 14:1, 9; 1 Chr. 1:17; Isa. 11:11; 21:2; 22:6; Jer. 25:25; 49:34–39; Ezek. 32:24; Dan. 8:2).

B. A city in Judah (Josh. 15:29).

5865. עֵילוֹם ***ʿēylôm:*** A masculine noun designating eternity. It indicates an infinite stretch of time into the future. God chose to put His name in the Temple forever (2 Chr. 33:7).

5866. עִילַי ***ʿiylay:*** A proper noun designating Ilai (1 Chr. 11:29).

5867. עֵילָם ***ʿēylām:*** A proper noun designating Elam:

A. A territory and country lying to the north and east of the modern Persian Gulf in the plain of Khuzistan. It had a king, Chedorlaomer, who tried to conquer Canaan (Gen. 14:1, 9). Their ancient ancestor was Shem (Gen. 10:22). Elam was an avenging arm of the Lord in some cases but the victim of enemies in others (Isa. 11:11; 21:2; 22:6; Jer. 25:25; 49:34–39; Ezek. 32:24; Dan. 8:2).

B. The head of a family who returned from exile under Zerubbabel (Ezra 2:7).

C. The head of a family who returned from exile under Zerubbabel (Ezra 2:31).

D. The head of a family who returned from exile under Ezra (Ezra 8:7).

E. A leader in the returned Jewish community who signed and supported Nehemiah's covenant of renewal (Neh. 10:14[15]).

F. A Benjamite, a son of Shashak (1 Chr. 8:24).

G. A Levite from the family of the Korahites who served as a gatekeeper (1 Chr. 26:3).

H. A priest who took part in the dedication of Nehemiah's wall, evidently in the musical component of the celebrations (Neh. 12:42).

5868. עֲיָם ***ʿayām:*** I. A masculine noun referring to scorching. It refers most likely to the wind that dried up the Red Sea (Isa. 11:15) or possibly to a khamsin, a hot dry wind.

II. A masculine noun referring to a mighty wind. It refers most likely to the wind that dried up the Red Sea, a mighty east wind (Isa. 11:15) or possibly a strong khamsin wind.

5869. עַיִן **'ayin,** עֵינַיִם **'ēynayim:** A feminine noun meaning an eye, a spring, a fountain. This Hebrew word is used to refer to either an aperture or a source. It is used to signify the physical organ of sight (Prov. 20:12); the providential oversight of the Lord (Ps. 33:18); and a water well (Gen. 16:7; Ex. 15:27). By extension, it refers to being in the presence of another (Jer. 32:12); the visible surface of the earth (Num. 22:5); the human face (1 Kgs. 20:38; 2 Kgs. 9:30); and the general appearance of something (1 Sam. 16:7; Ezek. 1:4). In a figurative sense, the eye was seen as the avenue of temptation (Job 31:7); the scope of personal judgment or opinion (Judg. 17:6); and the source of self-assessment (Prov. 26:5).

5870. עַיִן **'ayin:** An Aramaic masculine noun referring to an eye. It refers to the instrument of sight by which a person sees. It is used figuratively of God's eye being on His people (Ezra 5:5), that is, He watches them carefully, guarding them. To raise one's eyes heavenward toward God is to perform an act of humility and recognition of God as God (Dan. 4:34[31]). The word is used in figurative, apocalyptic language to indicate that what is not human, a horn in appearance, is indeed a symbol for a person (Dan. 7:8, 20); the little horn had human-like eyes.

5871. עַיִן **'ayin:** A proper noun designating Ain:

A. A town on the northeast border of Canaan (Num. 34:11).

B. A town in the negev of Judah (Josh. 15:32; 19:7; 21:16; 1 Chr. 4:32).

5872. עֵין גֶּדִי **'ēyn geḏiy:** A proper noun designating En Gedi, a town inherited by the tribe of Judah (Josh. 15:62) located on the west side of the Dead Sea (Ezek. 47:10). David went there for water when fleeing Saul (1 Sam. 23:29[24:1]; 24:1[2]). It produced excellent vineyards (Song 1:14).

5873. עֵין גַּנִּים **'ēyn ganniym:** A proper noun designating En Gannim:

A. A city in the foothills of Judah (Josh. 15:34).

B. A city in Issachar (Josh. 19:21; 21:29).

5874. עֵין דֹּאר **'ēyn dō'r:** A proper noun designating Endor (Josh. 17:11; 1 Sam. 28:7; Ps. 83:10[11]).

5875. עֵין הַקּוֹרֵא **'ēyn haqqôrē':** A proper noun designating En Hakkore (Judg. 15:19).

5876. עֵין חַדָּה **'ēyn ḥaddāh:** A proper noun designating En Haddah (Josh. 19:21).

5877. עֵין חָצוֹר **'ēyn ḥāṣôr:** A proper noun designating En Hazor (Josh. 19:37).

5878. עֵין חֲרֹד ***'ēyn ḥ^{a}rōḏ:*** A proper noun designating the Spring of Harod, Well of Harod (Judg. 7:1).

5879. עֵינָם ***'ēnām:*** A proper noun designating Enam, a city in Judah (Josh. 15:34).

5880. עֵין מִשְׁפָּט ***'ēyn mišpāṭ:*** A proper noun designating En Mishpat (Gen. 14:7).

5881. עֵינָן ***'ēynān:*** A proper noun designating Enan (Num. 1:15; 2:29; 7:78, 83; 10:27).

5882. עֵין עֶגְלַיִם ***'ēyn 'eglayim:*** A proper noun designating En Eglaim (Ezek. 47:10).

5883. עֵין רֹגֵל ***'ēyn rōgēl:*** A proper noun designating En Gannim, a spring located south of Jerusalem (Josh. 15:7; 18:16). Its name means "spring of (a) walker." Adonijah, trying to usurp David's throne, was crowned king there prematurely (1 Kgs. 1:9).

5884. עֵין רִמּוֹן ***'ēyn rimmôn:*** A proper noun designating En Rimmon (Neh. 11:29).

5885. עֵין שֶׁמֶשׁ ***'ēyn šemeš:*** A proper noun designating En Shemesh (Josh. 15:7; 18:17).

5886. עֵין הַתַּנִּין ***'ēyn hattanniyn:*** A proper noun designating the Jackal Well (Neh. 2:13).

5887. עֵין תַּפּוּחַ ***'ēyn tappûaḥ:*** A proper noun designating En Tappuah (Josh. 17:7).

5888. עִיף ***'iyp̱:*** A verb meaning to be faint, to be weary. It indicates physical weariness, exhaustion (Judg. 4:21; 1 Sam. 14:28; 2 Sam. 21:15); in a figurative sense, the exhaustion of Zion because of her oppressors (Jer. 4:31).

5889. עָיֵף ***'āyēp̱:*** An adjective meaning faint, weary, exhausted. It describes a person becoming weak from hard work and needing nourishment (Gen. 25:29, 30); or from exhausting travels, escapees (Deut. 25:18). It is used of a weary soul, life, needing good news (Prov. 25:25). It is used figuratively of the nations who fought against Israel being weary like a man faint from thirst (Isa. 29:8). When used of a land suffering from drought, it means parched, dried-out land (Isa. 32:2). It describes an exhausted beast or animal that must carry heavy loads (Isa. 46:1). God refreshes the weary, both physically and spiritually (Jer. 31:25).

5890. עֵיפָה ***'ēyp̱āh:*** A feminine noun meaning darkness. This word appears only twice in the Old Testament in Job 10:22 and Amos 4:13. In both instances, the word implies the darkness of night as opposed to the light of day. In Job, the word is used in parallel to the word *'ōp̱el* (652), meaning spiritual gloom or despair.

5891. עֵיפָה ***'ēyp̱āh:*** A proper noun designating Ephah:

A. Descendants of Midian (Gen. 25:4; 1 Chr. 1:33; Isa. 60:6).

B. A Judaite (1 Chr. 2:47).

C. A concubine of Caleb (1 Chr. 2:46).

5892. עִיר *'iyr:* A feminine noun meaning a city, a town. It is a place where a gathering of persons carry on life (Gen. 4:17). There are various cities: a city militarily protected, fortified (Josh. 19:29); small towns dependent on and closely connected to other cities (Josh. 13:17; Jer. 19:15); royal cities attached to the king (Josh. 10:2); country towns (1 Sam. 27:5). The Israelites built cities for storage and defense (Ex. 1:11; 1 Kgs. 9:19). The Lord had Israel set aside certain cities for refuge, asylum, and temporary safety (Num. 35:11; Josh. 20:2). The city of Jerusalem is uniquely termed the city of God (Ps. 46:4[5]; 87:3). God looked for cities that were known for righteousness (Isa. 1:26); truth (Zech. 8:3); holiness (Neh. 11:1, 18; Isa. 48:2; 52:1). Unfortunately, Jerusalem became known as a city of oppression (Zeph. 3:1); the city of blood (Ezek. 22:2; 24:6); along with Nineveh (Nah. 3:1). Cities were special to God, for there His people lived.

5893. עִיר *'iyr:* A proper noun designating Ir (1 Chr. 7:12).

5894. עִיר *'iyr:* An Aramaic masculine noun indicating a watcher. It indicates a divine being, possibly a watchful one (Dan. 4:13[10], 17[14], 23[20]) who communicated God's decrees and was responsible to God.

5895. עַיִר *'ayir,* עִיר *'iyr:* A. A masculine noun meaning a donkey, an ass. It refers to donkeys, beasts of burden (Gen. 32:15[16]; KJV, foals; Isa. 30:6, 24); and also used for human transportation (Judg. 10:4; 12:14). They were a part of a person's wealth (Job 11:12). The king of Zion would ride on a donkey (Zech. 9:9).

B. A masculine noun meaning a donkey, an ass. It is translated as foal in Genesis 49:11 (NASB, KJV); donkey (NIV, NKJV). A foal may be a young horse, a mule, or a donkey. The second line of Genesis 49:11 identifies the foal as a colt, not a filly.

5896. עִירָא *'iyrā':* A proper noun designating Ira:

A. A Jairite (2 Sam. 20:26).

B. A son of Ikkesh (2 Sam. 23:26; 1 Chr. 11:28; 27:9).

C. One of David's mighty men (2 Sam. 23:38; 1 Chr. 11:40).

5897. עִירָד *'iyrāḏ:* A proper noun designating Irad (Gen. 4:18).

5898. עִיר הַמֶּלַח *'iyr hammelaḥ:* A proper noun designating the City of Salt (Josh. 15:62).

5899. עִיר הַתְּמָרִים *'iyr hat-tᵉmāriym:* A proper noun designating City of Palms, another description and name for the city of Jericho. See appropriate entry. Hebrew *tāmār* (8558), "palm tree."

5900. עִירוּ *'iyrû:* A proper noun designating Iru (1 Chr. 4:15).

5901. עִירִי *'iyriy:* A proper noun designating Iri (1 Chr. 7:7).

5902. עִירָם *'iyrām:* A proper noun designating Iram (Gen. 36:43; 1 Chr. 1:54).

5903. עֵירֹם *'ēyrōm,* עֵרֹם *'ērōm:* An adjective indicating that something is naked. It is equivalent to being without clothing (Gen. 3:7, 10, 11). It indicates a state of penury or scarcity (Deut. 28:48; Ezek. 16:39; 23:29). It has the sense of being in a state of innocence (Ezek. 16:7); of infancy (16:22) when used figuratively of Israel.

5904. עִיר נָחָשׁ *'iyr nāḥāš:* A proper noun designating Ir Nahash (1 Chr. 4:12).

5905. עִיר שֶׁמֶשׁ *'iyr šemeš:* A proper noun designating Ir Shemesh (Josh. 19:41).

5906. עַיִשׁ *'ayiš,* עָשׁ *'āš:* I. A masculine noun referring to the constellation Arcturus, the Bear. The orderliness and splendor of this constellation is the result of God's wondrous work (Job 38:32).

II. A masculine noun referring to the constellation Arcturus, the Bear. The creation and existence of this orderly splendor in the sky is the result of God's activity (Job 9:9).

5907. עַכְבּוֹר *'akbôr:* A proper noun designating Achbor:

A. An Edomite (Gen. 36:38, 39; 1 Chr. 1:49).

B. Courier of Josiah (2 Kgs. 22:12, 14; Jer. 26:22; 36:12).

5908. עַכָּבִישׁ *'akkābiyš:* A masculine noun indicating a spider. A group of arachnids that spin out silk threads made into webs. Webs are weak and flimsy, very fragile and frail (Job 8:14). The unjust weave spider webs to catch people in evil plans (Isa. 59:5).

5909. עַכְבָּר *'akbār:* A masculine noun signifying a mouse. It is used of a rodent, often infesting dwellings. It was an unclean "swarming thing" to Israel and therefore not edible (Lev. 11:29).

5910. עַכּוֹ *'akkô:* A proper noun designating Acco (Judg. 1:31).

5911. עָכוֹר *'akôr:* A proper noun designating Achor, a valley in the Judean Desert and located between Judah and Benjamin (Josh. 15:7). It was traditionally near Jericho. Based on references in the prophets, the territory and valley were barren or wilderness (Isa. 65:10; Hos. 2:15). Achan was executed there for his treason (Josh. 7:24–26). The name means "pain" or "trouble" as does Achan's name.

5912. עָכָן *'ākān:* A proper noun designating Achan, the name of the man who coveted and took things devoted to God. His name means "pain." His sin caused God's wrath to fall on Israel, since he broke the covenant (Josh. 22:20). He was discovered, judged, and executed in the Valley of Achar. See 5911.

5913. עָכַס ***'ākas:*** A verb meaning to jingle an ornament or bracelet. It is used of the seductive, sophisticated women of Zion who tinkled or jingled foot jewelry (Isa. 3:16).

5914. עֶכֶס ***'ekes:*** I. A masculine noun describing a leg bracelet, an anklet. A showy piece of jewelry worn by the rich and vain. The Lord would remove this vanity by His judgments (Isa. 3:18).

II. A masculine noun referring to a fetter, a noose. It indicates instruments for confining persons, for controlling them to lead them to danger, execution, etc. (Prov. 7:22).

5915. עַכְסָה ***'aksāh:*** A proper noun designating Achsah (Josh. 15:16, 17; Judg. 1:12, 13; 1 Chr. 2:49).

5916. עָכַר ***'ākar:*** A verb meaning to cause trouble. It indicates stirring up resentment, to bring about hatred or danger (Gen. 34:30). It is used of bringing a curse on Israel (Judg. 11:35). It depicts a harsh law or order placed on people, troubling them, agitating them (1 Sam. 14:29). Elijah was called by the Lord to constantly harass the evil leaders and kings of Israel. He was called "the troubler of Israel" (1 Kgs. 18:17, 18). It is used of something growing worse, increasing (Ps. 39:2[3]). Persons who are cruel and violent, harm and trouble themselves (Prov. 11:17). The wicked are made for and live with trouble (Prov. 15:6, 27).

5917. עָכָר ***'ākār:*** A proper noun designating Achar (1 Chr. 2:7).

5918. עָכְרָן ***'okrān:*** A proper noun designating Ocran (Num. 1:13; 2:27; 7:72, 77; 10:26).

5919. עַכְשׁוּב ***'akšûb:*** A masculine noun referring to a viper, an adder. It refers to a snake from a family of venomous snakes, includes adders. The tongue of this reptile is long and sharp (Ps. 140:3[4]).

5920. עַל ***'al:*** I. A masculine noun meaning height, from above. It is used to point to a direction, toward a location (Gen. 27:39; 49:25); especially toward heaven, upward (Ps. 50:4). It refers to the exaltation of a person (2 Sam. 23:1); and turning upward to God (Hos. 7:16).

II. A masculine proper noun meaning Most High. It is taken as a title, an appellative for God, the Most High by some translators (2 Sam. 23:1; Hos. 7:16; 11:7).

5921. עַל ***'al:*** A preposition meaning upon, over, against, by, to, for. The various nuances of this preposition are wide-ranging, and the context determines its exact meaning and usage. Here are some basics: on, upon (Gen. 1:11, 26; Ex. 20:12; 2 Sam. 4:7); in front of (Gen. 18:8; Ex. 27:21); to, unto plus *mî,* "to whom" (Jer. 6:10); with *zô't* or *kēn* following, it means because of, therefore with respect to, concerning (Gen. 20:3; Ruth 4:7); as or according to (Ps. 110:4); besides or over against (Ex. 20:3); to come on (one's) heart, means to come to mind, to think of (Jer. 3:16); to add to, in addition to (*yāsap̱ 'al*) (Gen. 28:9; 31:50; Deut. 19:9); it has the sense of with, met with (Ex. 3:18). Other phrases include: *k^e'al-ḵōl*, according to all (Isa. 63:7); from upon, upon, e.g., a camel (Gen. 2:5; 19:24; 24:64); *'al-b^elî*, that . . . not (Gen. 31:20); *'al-'^ašer*, because (Ex. 32:35). It is used to indicate God's provincial care, His hand on (*'al*) someone (Neh. 2:8); and to indicate a burden on someone (Ex. 5:8; 21:22; Job 7:20; Ps. 42:6; Isa. 1:14). It indicates the thing one speaks about or is concerned with when used with verbs of speaking, hearing (Judg. 9:3; Jer. 16:3). It has the sense of eminence or exaltation, above (Deut. 26:19; Ps. 57:5[6], 11[12]). It indicates what one exercises authority over (Isa. 22:15). It is used in the idiom, to fall asleep, sleep falls on someone (Gen. 2:21; 15:12); and of the activity of the mind setting on (*'al*) something (2 Sam. 14:1; Jer. 22:17; Mal. 3:13). It is used of an army attacking against (*'al*) a foe (Gen. 34:25; Deut. 19:11; Amos 7:9).

5922. עַל ***'al:*** An Aramaic preposition meaning upon, to, against, for. Its basic meanings are evident in context: upon something (Dan. 2:10, 28, 46; 5:5, 7; 6:10[11]). It indicates with respect to whom emotion or appearance changes (Dan. 5:9; 7:28). Other senses of the word: on account of, because (Dan. 3:16); concerning (Dan. 2:18). With verbs of authority or rulership, it indicates what is ruled over (Dan. 2:48, 49; 3:12; 4:17[14]). It may express direction toward (Ezra 4:11, 17, 18; 5:6; Dan. 2:24; 4:34[31], 36[33]).

5923. עֹל ***'ōl:*** A masculine noun meaning a yoke. It describes a wooden frame or a bar placed on the neck of work animals to harness them for labor. Its usage includes a yoke for cattle (Deut. 21:3; 1 Sam. 6:7). It was a favorite figurative word to express servitude (1 Kgs. 12:4, 10, 11, 14). It is used of a yoke of transgressions (Lam. 1:14); or hardship (Lam. 3:27).

5924. עֵלָּא ***'ēllā':*** An Aramaic preposition meaning over. It is used figuratively of a position of power over others, above them in rank (Dan. 6:2[3]).

5925. עֻלָּא ***'ullā':*** A proper noun designating Ulla (1 Chr. 7:39).

5926. עִלֵּג ***'illēg:*** An adjective indicating stammering. It refers to the inability to speak clearly and smoothly without hesitation (Isa. 32:4).

5927. עָלָה ***'ālāh:*** A verb meaning to go up, to ascend, to take away, to lift, to offer. This Hebrew word carries with it the connotation of an upward motion. It is used generically to denote an ascension to a higher place (Num. 13:17); a departure in a northerly direction (Gen. 45:25); the flight of a bird (Isa. 40:31); the springing up of plants (Isa. 34:13); the preference of one thing above another (Ps. 137:6); and the offering of a sacrifice (Judg. 6:28; 2 Kgs. 3:20). Theologically significant is the fact that this verb is used in relationship to a person's appearance before God. One must go up to stand before the Lord (Ex. 34:24; see also Gen. 35:1).

5928. עֲלָה ***'alāh:*** An Aramaic feminine noun meaning a burnt offering, a holocaust. This word parallels the Hebrew word *'ōlāh* (5930). It is used only by Ezra in reference to the daily burnt sacrifices required under the Law (Ezra 6:9).

5929. עָלֶה ***'āleh:*** A masculine noun signifying a leaf, a branch. It refers to greenery, leaves, or foliage on trees or shrubs (Gen. 3:7; 8:11; Neh. 8:15). Ezekiel speaks of leaves of healing (Ezek. 47:12); and Isaiah of fading leaves (Isa. 1:30; 34:4). Proverbs employs a (flourishing, green) leaf as a symbol of a righteous person (Prov. 11:28).

5930. עֹלָה ***'ōlāh:*** A feminine noun meaning a whole burnt offering, that which goes up. The primary discussion of this offering is found in Leviticus 1; 6:9[2], 10[3], 12[5]). The noun is a feminine participial form of the verb meaning to go up, to ascend. The offering was voluntary. The Israelites understood the animal or fowl that was being sacrificed as a gift to God and thus ascending to God as smoke from the altar (Lev. 1:9), hence its name. The sacrifice was a pleasing odor acceptable to the Lord (Lev. 1:9). Those presenting the animal laid hands on the sacrifice—possibly to indicate ownership or to indicate that the animal was a substitute for themselves (Lev. 1:4). The blood of the sacrifice was sprinkled against the altar (Lev. 1:6). The offering and its ritual properly carried out atoned for the offerers, and they became acceptable before the Lord.

The total burning of the sacrifice indicates the total consecration of the presenter to the Lord. The animals that could be offered were bulls, sheep, rams, or male birds (Lev. 1:3, 10, 14). The ashes of the offering remained on the altar overnight. The priest removed them and deposited them in an approved location (Lev. 6:9[2], 10[3]).

The burnt offerings were presented often in conjunction with the peace and grain offerings (Josh. 8:31; Judg. 6:26; 1 Kgs. 3:4; 8:64). The burnt offerings, along with other offerings, were employed in the various feasts, festivals, and celebrations recorded in the prophetic books. Often, however, the burnt offerings were condemned as useless because the Israelites didn't have their hearts right before God (Jer. 6:20; 7:21). Ezekiel foresaw renewed burnt offerings in a new Temple (Ezek. 40:38, 39). When Israel returned from exile, burnt offerings, along with others, were once again presented to the Lord (Ezra 3:2; 8:35). David's observation was correct and to the point, for he noted that whole burnt offerings did not satisfy or delight the Lord. Only an offering of a broken spirit and humble heart could do that (Ps. 51:16[18]). Only then could acceptable sacrifices be given to the Lord (Ps. 51:19[21]; 66:13).

5931. עִלָּה ***'illāh:*** An Aramaic feminine noun indicating a basis for charges. It employs in a technical legal sense of a cause for allegation, a basis for accusing someone (Dan. 6:4[5], 5[6]).

5932. עַלְוָה ***'alwāh:*** A feminine noun meaning injustice, unrighteousness, iniquity. Hosea 10:9 is the sole occurrence of this word in the Bible. It is used to denote the supreme wickedness and depravity of Israel. The prophet relates the current situation to an episode at Gibeah during the time of the judges (cf. Judg. 19:1—20:28).

5933. עַלְוָה ***'alwāh,*** עַלְיָה ***'alyāh:*** I. Alva (Gen. 36:40; 1 Chr. 1:51).

II. Alva, different Hebrew spelling for the same as I (1 Chr. 1:51, KJV, NASB).

5934. עֲלוּמִים ***ᵃlûmiym:*** A masculine plural noun indicating youthful times, youth. It refers to the early years of a person's life, unencumbered by old age and illnesses. It is used in a positive way of youth as a time of health and vigor (Job 20:11; 33:25; Ps. 89:45[46]). But it also depicts youth as a time of indiscretions, of doing shameful things, as Israel did as a people (Isa. 54:4).

5935. עַלְוָן ***'alwān,*** עַלְיָן ***'alyān:*** I. Alvan (Gen. 36:23; 1 Chr. 1:40).

II. Alyan, another spelling for I (1 Chr. 1:40, KJV, NASB).

5936. עֲלוּקָה ***ᵃlûqāh:*** A feminine noun meaning a leech. It is a blood-sucking worm-like creature in water that, according to Proverbs, never gets enough to eat (Prov. 30:15).

5937. עָלַז ***'ālaz:*** A verb meaning to rejoice, to exult, to be jubilant. It describes a state and act of celebration, approval, support for something (2 Sam. 1:20); especially in exalting over God (Ps. 28:7; Hab. 3:18; Zeph. 3:14). God Himself exalts and is jubilant about His possession, Israel (Ps. 60:6[8]). The possession of wisdom causes a person to rejoice (Prov. 23:16). God can, however, remove the jubilation of His people (Isa. 23:12).

5938. עָלֵז ***'ālēz:*** An adjective indicating that something is exalting, rejoicing. It refers to the actions and state of people celebrating and exalting over something, a condition that Jerusalem lost (Isa. 5:14).

5939. עֲלָטָה ***ᵃlāṭāh:*** A feminine noun meaning thick darkness. It refers to a mysterious blackness and overshading brought on Abraham by God (Gen. 15:17). It is used of nighttime (Ezek. 12:6, 7); and has a symbolic significance for Israel (Ezek. 12:12).

5940. עֱלִי ***'eliy:*** A masculine noun referring to a pestle. It refers to a tool with a rounded end used to crush various substances in a mortar (Prov. 27:22).

5941. עֵלִי ***'ēliy:*** A proper noun designating Eli, the high priest in the time of Samuel's youth at Shiloh (1 Sam. 1:1–3). He did not control his sons who profaned the priesthood (2 Sam. 2:12–17). As a result, they were killed in a battle with the Philistines. Eli was warned to control his sons by a prophet, but to no avail (1 Sam. 2:27–33). Eli's house was cut off from Israel, and he died by falling backwards and breaking his neck when he heard of the fate of his sons.

Previously, he had dealt kindly with Hannah and prayed for her (1 Sam. 1:17). She dedicated her child, Samuel, to the Lord under Eli (1 Sam. 1:23–28).

5942. עִלִּי ***'illiy:*** An adjective meaning upper. It describes what is located physically higher, more elevated than something else, e.g., upper springs as opposed to lower springs (Josh. 15:19; Judg. 1:15).

5943. עִלָּי ***'illāy:*** An Aramaic masculine adjective meaning highest. This adjective always refers to God and shows the supremacy of God over humanity and other gods. It can occur as an adjective to modify *'elāh* (426), meaning God. Nebuchadnezzar used this term of God to indicate His supremacy in general (Dan. 4:2 [3:32]). Daniel also used this term of God (Dan. 5:18, 21) to reveal the difference between God and Belshazzar, who had lifted up [himself] against the Lord of heaven (see Dan. 5:23). This term can also occur as a noun to represent God, especially in His role as the supreme Ruler of the kingdoms of humanity (Dan. 4:17[14], 24[21], 25[22], 32[29], 34[31]).

5944. עֲלִיָּה ***'aliyyāh:*** A feminine noun indicating an upper room, a chamber, a parlor. It is used of a rooftop chamber or room (Judg. 3:20, 23–25; Jer. 22:13, 14); an upper room over a gate (2 Sam. 18:33[19:1]). Figuratively, it depicts God's structuring upper chambers at the time of creation (Ps. 104:3, 13).

5945. עֶלְיוֹן ***'elyôn:*** A masculine noun meaning Most High, the Highest. The word serves as an epithet for God and is used thirty-one times in the Old Testament. The most celebrated use of this word is in Genesis 14:18—20: Melchizedek was priest of God Most High (*'ēl 'elyôn*), so the term in context defines the God whom he served. But in this same passage, Abraham equated the God Most High with the Lord his God, the Creator of heaven and earth (Gen. 14:20). In Numbers 24:16, this epithet stands in parallel to the epithet God and Shaddai; it depicts the God who gave Balaam his knowledge and visions. The term also stands in parallel with other names of God, such as the LORD (Deut. 32:8; 2 Sam.

22:14; Ps. 18:13[14]); and God (Ps. 46:4[5]; 50:14).

5946. עֶלְיוֹן *'elyôn:* An Aramaic masculine adjective meaning Most High God. This term always appears in the plural of majesty, comparable to the Hebrew word *'elōhiym* (430). Furthermore, it always occurs in the construct with *qaddiyš* (6922), meaning the holy ones or saints of the Most High God, and in the context of Daniel's interpretation of Nebuchadnezzar's dream of the four beasts, where four kingdoms were represented (Dan. 7:18, 22, 25, 27).

5947. עַלִּיז *'alliyz:* An adjective meaning rejoicing, jubilant. It refers to a state of jubilation, a celebration over something. In context it is used of triumphant warriors who would destroy Babylon (Isa. 13:3); and of persons rejoicing in general (Isa. 22:2; 24:8; 32:13). It is used of Jerusalem itself (Isa. 23:7; Zeph. 3:11); and of Nineveh (Zeph. 2:15).

5948. עֲלִיל *'aliyl:* A masculine noun meaning furnace. It refers to a structure made for the production of heat or for purifying metals (Ps. 12:6[7]).

5949. עֲלִילָה *'aliylāh:* A feminine noun indicating deeds, actions; shameful actions. It refers to immoral actions or behavior (Deut. 22:14, 17); or of deeds in general of whatever kind (1 Sam. 2:3); especially those performed by the Lord (Ps. 9:11[12]; 105:1; Isa. 12:4). The prophet Ezekiel often refers to the evil deeds of people (Ezek. 14:22, 23; 20:43; 24:14; 36:17, 19); also note Zephaniah 3:11.

5950. עֲלִילִיָּה *'aliyliyyāh:* A feminine noun meaning deed, action. The Lord is said to be mighty, great (*raḇ*) in deeds on behalf of His people (Jer. 32:19).

5951. עֲלִיצֻת *'aliyṣuṯ:* A feminine noun indicating gloating, exultation. It refers to a celebration of victory over enemies, rejoicing or even gloating over their destruction (Hab. 3:14).

5952. עִלִּי *'illiy:* An Aramaic feminine noun meaning a roof, a chamber. It refers to a rooftop chamber on a house. It was used by Daniel for prayer daily (Dan. 6:10[11]). These upper chambers were cool, especially at night.

5953. עָלַל *'ālal:* I. A verb meaning to do, to deal with, to treat severely, to abuse; to glean. It basically means to treat harshly or deal severely with; to practice evil: to do evil deeds in general (Ps. 141:4); to do evil toward a person (Lam. 1:12, 22; 2:20; 3:51). It describes the Lord's dealings with Egypt to free the Israelites (Ex. 10:2; 1 Sam. 6:6). It is used of Balaam accusing his donkey of dealing treacherously with him (Num. 22:29). It describes the sexual abuse of a woman (Judg. 19:25).

II. A verb meaning to act childishly, to play the child. It means to behave foolishly as a child without maturity or strength. It is used of the enemies of Israel to depict the hopeless state of Israel who is oppressed by children (Isa. 3:12).

III. A verb meaning to defile. It means to make something unclean or unholy, to desecrate it. It is used figuratively of Job defiling and shaming his horn, a figurative expression of destroying his hope, character, strength (Job 16:15).

IV. A verb meaning to thrust in, to bury, to insert. It indicates striking an object into something. In context it refers to sticking a "horn," one's hope, character, strength, into the ground, that is, giving up (Job 16:15).

5954. עֲלַל ***'alal:*** An Aramaic verb meaning to bring in, to enter. It is used often of getting an audience with the king and entering into his presence (Dan. 2:16, 24, 25; 4:7[4]; 5:8, 10). It is used of entering into an area, a location (Dan. 6:10[11]). It is used of bringing in someone or of being brought in (Dan. 2:24, 25; 5:13, 15). It is used of an impersonal subject being brought in (Dan. 6:18[19]).

5955. עֹלֵלוֹת ***'ōlēlôṯ:*** A feminine plural noun indicating gleaning. It indicates things left over after a major harvest has taken place (Obad. 1: 5). It refers to picking the leftovers of the grape harvest as well as other harvests (Judg. 8:2). It is used figuratively of the gleanings of persons and houses left in a city after God has gone over it in judgments (Isa. 17:6). It is used of the grape pickers in Micah 7:1, fruit gatherers.

5956. עָלַם ***'ālam:*** A verb meaning to hide, to conceal, to ignore. It refers to something kept secret, not observed, not taken care of. It is used by the psalmist to point out his hidden faults, unconscious errors (Ps. 90:8). It is used in various ways: to hide oneself, conceal oneself (Deut. 22:1, 3); to hide or conceal, to cover up something (1 Sam. 12:3). In its passive sense, it means things that are hidden (1 Kgs. 10:3). With *min* (4480), it means to keep from, to hide from (2 Kgs. 4:27); to disregard, to hide eyes from (Isa. 1:15).

5957. עָלַם ***'ālam:*** An Aramaic masculine noun meaning perpetuity, antiquity. This word is related to the Hebrew word *'ôlām* (5769). It can mean a perpetual period in the future (Dan. 4:3[3:33]; 7:27); or a period of distant antiquity (Ezra 4:15, 19). It can also represent a period of time with no limits, either past or present (Dan. 4:34[31]). It can stand alone (Dan. 4:3[3:33]) or with the following prepositions, where it acts more like an adverb: *min* (4481) (Dan. 2:20); and *'aḏ* (5705) (Dan. 2:20; 7:18).

5958. עֶלֶם ***'elem:*** A masculine noun meaning a young man. Its feminine counterpart is found in the word *'almāh* (5959). The focus of this term is probably sexual maturity. It connotes an individual who has gone through puberty and is therefore sexually mature. Thus, *'elem* is the picture of an individual who has crossed (or is crossing) the threshold from boyhood or girlhood to manhood or womanhood, and, as such, is of marriageable age. Saul applied this term to David after he killed Goliath (1 Sam. 17:56); and Jonathan used it to refer to his armorbearer (1 Sam. 20:22).

5959. עַלְמָה ***'almāh:*** A feminine noun meaning a maiden, a young woman, a girl, and a virgin. The word describes young women in different categories: Rebekah was understood to be a marriageable young woman by Abraham's servant (Gen. 24:43); as was the maiden described in Proverbs 30:19, for in this case, the man was wooing her as a possible wife. Moses' sister was probably in this category (Ex. 2:8). Sometimes it is unclear how old or mature these young maidens were (Ps. 68:25[26]). The most famous passage where this term is used is Isaiah 7:14, where it asserts an *'almāh* will give birth to a son. The author of Matthew 1:23 understood this woman to be a virgin.

5960. עַלְמוֹן ***'almôn:*** A proper noun designating Almon (Josh. 21:18). See also Alemeth (5964,C).

5961. עֲלָמוֹת ***'alāmôṯ:*** A feminine plural noun transliterated as alamoth. It is a technical term used to indicate some aspect of a psalm, its tune; its formal genre, its presentation, e.g., set to a certain voice (soprano?) (Ps. 46:title[1]; 1 Chr. 15:20). It was a product of the sons of Korah.

5962. עֵלְמָי ***'ēlmāy:*** A proper noun designating Elamite (Ezra 4:9).

5963. עַלְמֹן דִּבְלָתָיְמָה ***'almon diḇlaṯāyᵉmāh:*** A proper noun designating Almon Diblathaim (Num. 33:46, 47).

5964. עָלֶמֶת ***'ālemeṯ:*** A proper noun designating Alemeth:

A. Son of Becher (1 Chr. 7:8).

B. Son of Jehoadah (1 Chr. 8:36; 9:42).

C. A town in Benjamin, the same as Almon (5960) (1 Chr. 6:60[45]).

5965. עָלַס ***'ālas,*** נֶעֱלָסָה ***neᵉlāsāh:*** I. A verb meaning to enjoy, to rejoice. It means to find delight and pleasure in something and to express it (Job 20:18). It describes the act of sexual intimacy (Prov. 7:18).

II. A verb meaning to flap joyously. It describes the appearance and manner of something acting or responding in an apparently happy manner (Job 39:13). It personifies ostrich wings in context.

III. A feminine noun indicating to be attractive, beautiful. This translation takes the form of *'ālas, neᵉlāsāh* as a noun. It is probably a passive form of the verb *'ālas.* If taken as a noun, it means beautiful (Job 39:13, KJV).

5966. עָלַע ***'āla':*** A verb meaning to suck up. It means to take something in, a liquid, by sucking it in. The young of the hawk eat blood (Job 39:30).

5967. עֲלַע *ala':* An Aramaic common noun meaning rib. It refers to one of the protective chest bones encasing the chest cavity. In context it represents a defeated nation or people (Dan. 7:5).

5968. עָלַף *'ālap:* I. A verb meaning to cover, to wrap, to overlay. It means in context to hide one's identity by wrapping oneself in something (Gen. 38:14). It is used to describe the bridegroom's abdomen in an amorous way, meaning set, decorated, inlaid (Song 5:14).

II. A verb meaning to faint. It means to grow weak, weary to the point of losing consciousness or despairing utterly (Isa. 51:20); from lack of nourishment (Amos 8:13); or sunstroke (Jon. 4:8).

5969. עֻלְפֶּה *'ulpeh:* A masculine noun referring to something withered. It describes the wilting and drying up of trees because of a lack of water (Ezek. 31:15).

5970. עָלַץ *'ālaṣ:* A verb meaning to rejoice, to be jubilant. It is used of a person (*leḇ,* heart) rejoicing, especially the Lord (1 Sam. 2:1; Ps. 5:11[12]; 9:2[3]; 68:3[4]); of nature exalting God (1round them (Prov. 11:10; 28:12). It is used of the rejoicing of one's enemies as well (Ps. 25:2).

5971. עַם *'am,* עָם *'ām:* A masculine noun meaning a people, peoples, people of the land, citizens. The word is used over nineteen hundred times to indicate groups of people that can be categorized in various ways. The largest group of people is the one comprising the whole earth (see Gen. 11:1); it constituted one people (Gen. 11:6); who shared a common language (Gen. 11:6; Ezek. 3:5); a common location (see Gen. 11:2); and a common purpose and goal (see Gen. 11:4). However, the Lord scattered the group and brought about multiple languages, thereby producing many groups who would then develop into new peoples united around common languages, including common ancestors, religious beliefs, traditions, and ongoing blood relationships.

The word is used to describe various groups that developed. The people of the sons of Israel (Ex. 1:9; Ezra 9:1), was a term referring to all Israel. The people of Judah were a subgroup of Israel (2 Sam. 19:40[41]), as was northern Israel (2 Kgs. 9:6). The people of Israel as a whole could be described in religious or moral terms as a holy, special people (Deut. 7:6; 14:2; Dan. 8:24); or the Lord's inheritance (Deut. 4:20). Above all, they were to be the Lord's people (Judg. 5:11; 1 Sam. 2:24); and the people of God (2 Sam. 14:13). They were the Lord's own people because He had rescued them from slavery to Pharaoh and his gods (Ex. 6:7). But the Lord Himself characterized His people as stiff-necked (Ex. 32:9; 33:3; 34:9; Deut. 9:13). To be a member of the Lord's people was to have the Lord as one's God (Ruth 1:16); if God's people rejected the Lord, they ceased to be His people. Therefore, it is clear that God's presence and ownership of His people gave them their identity (Ex. 33:13, 16; Hos. 1:9; cf. Deut. 32:21).

In the plural form, the word refers to many peoples or nations. Jerusalem, destroyed and lamenting, called for the people of the world to look on it and its guilt (Lam. 1:18). Israel was chosen from among all the peoples of the earth (Ex. 19:5, 7; Deut. 14:2). The Lord is in control of all the plans of the nations and peoples (Ps. 33:10). The word is used in parallel with *gôyim* (1471). Isaac prayed for Jacob's offspring to become a community of peoples that would include the twelve tribes of Israel (Gen. 28:3).

The word described people in general—that is, nonethnic or national groups. It refers to all the people as individuals in the world (Isa. 42:5). When persons died, they were gathered to their people (Gen. 25:8, 17). It also referred to people from a particular city (Ruth 4:9; 2 Chr. 32:18); or people from a specific land (e.g., Canaan [Zeph. 1:11]). Centuries earlier, Pharaoh referred to the Hebrews living in Egypt under slavery as the people of the land (Ex. 5:5). This phrase could refer to the population at large in Solomon's time and later (2 Kgs. 11:14, 18; 15:5); or to the population of Canaan in Abraham's time (Gen. 23:7).

The term also depicted foreign peoples and nations. The Moabites were the people of the god Chemosh (Num. 21:29). The word designated foreigners in general as strange or alien people (Ex. 21:8); the people of Egypt were considered the people of Pharaoh (Ex. 1:9, 22).

The word is even used to describe a gathering of ants (Prov. 30:25); or rock badgers (Prov. 30:26).

5972. עַם ***'am:*** An Aramaic masculine noun meaning people. It was not used in reference to a disparate group of individuals or to a specific ethnic group. This is seen especially in its parallel usage with *'ûmmāh* (524), meaning nation, and *liššān* (3961), meaning tongue (Dan. 3:4, 7, 29). The specific ethnic group being identified could be either the Israelites (Ezra 5:12; Dan. 7:27); or the Gentiles (Ezra 6:12; Dan. 2:44).

5973. עִם ***'im:*** A preposition meaning with, for, against, toward. With suffixes, it often appears as (-עִמָּד) *'immāḏ* (sf.). See 5978 also. It is used to indicate something done together or in common with (Gen. 3:6, 12; 13:1; 18:16); to eat with, to talk with, to travel with, to have companionship with. It ties separate things together, such as blood and flesh (Deut. 12:23); the wicked and the righteous (Gen. 18:23). It is used with the verbs *yāraš, ḥalaq,* to possess (with), to inherit along (with) (Gen. 21:10; 26:28); and words that indicate a competition or contest (with), to fight, to argue, to wrestle (with), to dispute (with), etc. (Gen. 26:20; 30:8; 32:24). It indicates an attitude taken when dealing with someone: kindness (Gen. 24:12); to be hostile toward (Ps. 94:16); be pleased with (Job 34:9; Ps. 50:18). It indicates the person or persons with whom one contends (Gen. 26:20; 30:8; 32:24). It is used sometimes to indicate the person spoken to (with) (Ex. 19:9), by God or man. It refers to the object to whom or for whom something is done, e.g., to do (show) kindness to someone (Gen. 24:12). It is used to show proximity in a physical sense, to be close by (Gen. 23:4; 25:11; Josh. 19:46); or of closeness in spirit, as God said He would be with His people, a chief defining characteristic of Israel's God (Ex. 3:12). It indicates time: how long (Ps. 72:5); time when (2 Chr. 21:19). The phrase *min* (4480) + *'im* (518), *mēʿim* means, from (being) with someone (Gen. 26:16; 1 Sam. 16:14; 2 Sam. 3:26; 2 Kgs. 2:9); the verb *nāqāh,* to be innocent, guiltless, plus *mēʿim,* means to be innocent from something, from before (2 Sam. 3:28; 1 Kgs. 2:33). It may be used to indicate possession, meaning something is with someone, belongs to them, is beside them (Deut. 17:19; Job 28:4). It has the sense of in addition to or besides in some contexts (2 Chr. 14:11[10]); or against, as to stand against, defend against (2 Chr. 20:6). It is used often with the word heart, meaning mind, to indicate a purpose or thought someone has, e.g., you will know in your heart (mind) (Deut. 8:5; 15:9; Josh. 14:7; 1 Kgs. 8:17). A person can commune with his or her own heart (Ps. 77:6[7]; Eccl. 1:16). It is used to indicate the origin of something, e.g., God, etc. (1 Sam. 20:7); especially of God as originator (Gen. 41:32; 1 Kgs. 2:33; Job 34:33; Isa. 8:18). The phrase *weʾim zeh* (2088) means yet, in spite of (Neh. 5:18). Careful attention to the usage and context will normally reveal the nuanced usage of this word.

5974. עִם ***ʿim:*** An Aramaic preposition meaning with, for. It is used to indicate connection to, action with. It indicates things that accompany something or each other (Ezra 5:2; 6:8; 7:13, 16; Dan. 2:18; 43; 7:13). It indicates relationship to, dwelling, living with (Dan. 2:11, 22; 4:15[12]; 5:21); speaking with (Dan. 6:21[22]); making war with (Dan. 7:21). It is used to indicate time during which (Dan. 7:2); or a duration of time, with (unto) all generations (Dan. 4:3[3:33], 34[31]).

5975. עָמַד ***ʿāmad:*** A verb meaning to stand, to rise up; to take one's stand. The basic uses of the word can be noted here: to stand on one's feet, not sit (Gen. 18:22; 24:30; 41:1, 3); to remain motionless or stay behind (Gen. 19:17; 24:31). It has the sense of ceasing, to stop doing something, e.g., to stop bearing children (Gen. 29:35; 30:9). It has the sense of serving before someone, as Joseph served, stood before Pharaoh (Gen. 41:46). It can mean to delay, to hold back from doing something (Gen. 45:9). It has the sense of presenting, introducing someone to someone else (Gen. 47:7). It indicates living somewhere, standing, remaining there (Ex. 8:22[18]). It is used of taking a position (physically, spatially) somewhere (Ex. 14:19). It is used of something enduring, lasting, being preserved (Jer. 32:14). Used with 'al following, it means to stand over, upon, to exercise authority over (Num. 7:2); with *lipnê,* it indicates standing before (1 Kgs. 1:28). To stand over one's life (*nepeš*) is to defend, protect one's life (Esth. 8:11). In its causative uses, it means to set up, station, appoint, restore, etc. It is used of causing persons to do something or putting them somewhere (Judg. 16:25); of setting up, standing up someone (2 Sam. 22:34; Ps. 18:33 [34]); to cause someone to endure, to continue (Ex. 9:16); to set up, to erect a structure, a temple (Ezra 2:68); to appoint, set up guards on duty (Neh. 7:3). It is used in a figurative sense of Moab standing, remaining undisturbed or unchanged (Jer. 48:11); and of a prophet standing in the presence of God, that is, receiving a message from God (Jer. 23:18, 22). In its few passive forms, it means to be presented (of a sacrifice) before the Lord (Lev. 16:10); to be set straight again or propped up (2 Chr. 18:34).

5976. עָמַד *'āmad:* A verb meaning to quake, to be at a stand. It refers to something that is trembling or violently shaken by some force, physical or spiritual. It is used of the trembling, quaking that came on those who trusted in vain in Egypt (Ezek. 29:7).

5977. עֹמֶד *'ōmed:* A masculine noun referring to a place, a standing place. It indicates an appointed position or function that a person is to fill (2 Chr. 30:16; 34:31; Neh. 8:7). It means simply where one stands (Dan. 8:18; 10:11), possibly in context meaning to stand upright in one's place. In Daniel 8:17, it functions as a participle with a suffix meaning (where) one was standing; in Daniel 11:1 it means I stood, I arose.

5978. עִמָּד *'immād:* A preposition meaning with, to. It indicates the company or presence of someone and is always used with a suffix attached, *'immādî* or *'immî.* See also 5973. Its meanings are the same as *'im* with suffixes. It means with respect to someone (Gen. 21:23; 31:7). It indicates the person one strives (with) (Ex. 17:2). It means in company with, beside someone (Deut. 5:31). It describes God's special presence with a person (Ps. 23:4; 101:6).

5979. עֶמְדָּה *'emdāh:* A feminine noun indicating support, protection. It refers to that which gives security, stability, safety and protection to someone (Mic. 1:11).

5980. עֻמָּה *'ummāh:* A preposition meaning next to, close to, against, alongside. It indicates that something is touching, alongside of, opposite, or very near something else. In the table of showbread, the rings were close up or up toward the rim (Ex. 25:27); it indicates a spot or location near a particular juncture or point (Ex. 28:27). It indicates that two people were opposite each other on opposing hillsides (2 Sam. 16:13); or in a choir (Neh. 12:24). The wings and wheels of cherubim were beside each other in Ezekiel's vision (Ezek. 11:22).

5981. עֻמָּה ***'ummāh:*** A proper noun designating Ummah (Josh. 19:30).

5982. עַמּוּד ***'ammûd:*** A masculine noun referring to a pillar, a column. It is a general term referring to a column, a pole, a pillar of various kinds: tent post (Ex. 26:32); pillars in the Tabernacle (Ex. 27:10–12, 14–17); a column in a house or a small temple (Judg. 16:25); free-standing, large bronze columns before the Temple of Solomon (1 Kgs. 7:15–22) and Ezekiel (40:49). In the Song of Solomon, it refers to a small post featured in a royal chair (Song 3:10). It is used of the pillars of cloud and fire that led Israel (Ex. 13:21, 22). Figuratively, it depicts the foundation pillars of the earth (Job 26:11; Ps. 75:3[4]). Pillars of strength are a feature of lady Wisdom's house (Prov. 9:1).

5983. עַמּוֹן ***'ammôn:*** A proper noun designating Ammon, a part of the inhabitants of Canaan whom Israel was to conquer and exterminate. They were located east of the Jordan with a capital city at Rabbah. Their territory lay between the Arnon and Jabbok Rivers. Their origin was from the incestuous relationship between Lot and his younger daughter (Gen. 19:38). They were a powerful people (Num. 21:24), and Lot's descendants continued to control the land (Deut. 2:19, 37). Their land was allotted to Gad, but through the centuries, the Ammonites largely erased the Gadites from power (Judg. 13:10–25). They became hostile toward Israel (Judg. 3:13; 10:9, 10; 11:4–36) and posed a religious threat to Israel (Judg. 10:6–18). Saul subdued them (1 Sam. 14:47–48), and David further subdued and controlled them (2 Sam. 8:12; 10; 11; 12; 17). Solomon succumbed to the lure of Molech, the god of Ammon (1 Kgs. 11:7–8). Josiah cleansed the land of Judah from Ammonite shrines (2 Kgs. 23:13). As Judah became corrupt, the Ammonites continued to help in their destruction but as part of the Lord's judgment and discipline of His people (2 Kgs. 24:1–4). The nation was condemned by the prophets and Israel's God will judge and destroy them (Isa. 11:14; Jer. 9:26[25]; 49:1; Ezek. 25:2; Amos 1:13; Zeph. 2:8, 9).

5984. עַמּוֹנִי ***'ammôniy:*** A proper noun designating Ammonite, the gentilic form or ethnic form of Ammon. It indicates a descendant of these people who accepted their culture. See 5983.

5985. עַמֹּנִית ***'ammōniyt:*** A proper noun designating Ammonitess (1 Kg. 14:21, 31; 2 Chr. 12:13; 24:29). See also 5984.

5986. עָמוֹס ***'āmôs:*** A proper noun designating Amos, the prophet from Tekoa, south of Jerusalem, sent to prophesy to northern Israel (Amos 1:1). He was a dresser of sycamore trees. He had no official or political ties to prophecy or prophets (7:1–13). He acted purely at the Lord's calling (Amos 7:14, 15). He prophesied during the reigns of Uzziah in Judah (779–740 B.C.) and Jeroboam II in Samaria, Israel (783–743 B.C.). There was a devastating earthquake in his day. The Northern Kingdom's prosperity had reached a peak under Jeroboam II, but the poor were being crushed and were enslaved to sustain the wealth of the rich (Amos 4). Amos had a universal message and passion concerning personal and social righteousness (Amos 1—3; 5:24). He was, however, given a vision of a restored house of David (9:11–13).

5987. עָמוֹק ***'āmôq:*** A proper noun designating Amok (Neh. 12:7, 20).

5988. עַמִּיאֵל ***'ammiy'el:*** A proper noun designating Ammiel (Num. 13:12; 2 Sam. 9:4, 5; 17:27; 1 Chr. 3:5; 26:5).

5989. עַמִּיהוּד ***'ammiyhûd:*** A proper noun designating Ammihud (Num. 1:10; 2:18; 7:48, 53; 10:22; 34:20, 28; 2 Sam. 13:37; 1 Chr. 7:26; 9:4).

5990. עַמִּיזָבָד ***'ammiyzabad:*** A proper noun designating Ammizabad (1 Chr. 27:6).

5991. עַמִּיחוּר ***'ammiyḥûr:*** A proper noun designating Ammichur (2 Sam. 13:37).

5992. עַמִּינָדָב ***'ammiynādab:*** A proper noun designating Amminadab (Ex. 6:23; Num. 1:7; 2:3; 7:12, 17; 10:14; Ruth 4:19, 20; 1 Chr. 2:10; 6:22(7); 15:10, 11).

5993. עַמִּי נָדִיב ***'ammiy nādiyb:*** A proper noun designating Ammi-nadib (Song 6:12).

5994. עֲמִיק ***'amiyq:*** An Aramaic adjective meaning profound, deep. It means deep in a physical sense, as a deep valley. It is used in a figurative sense of the type of things God reveals, deep things that only He knows (Dan. 2:22).

5995. עָמִיר ***'āmiyr:*** A masculine noun referring to a sheaf of grain, fallen grain. It refers to a bound bundle of newly cut stalks of grain (Jer. 9:22[21]). In English, the plural is sheaves. It is used figuratively in each context (Amos 2:13; Mic. 4:12; Zech. 12:6).

5996. עַמִּישַׁדָּי ***'ammiyšaddāy:*** A proper noun designating Ammishaddai (Num. 1:12; 2:25; 7:66, 71; 10:25).

5997. עָמִית ***'āmiyt:*** A masculine noun indicating a neighbor, an associate. It refers to a fellow friend, a comrade, a companion (Lev. 6:2 [5:21]); a neighbor (Lev. 18:20); other persons in a community in general (Lev. 19:11, 15). Every neighbor or friend was to be dealt with in truth (Lev. 25:14, 15, 17). But in times of God's judgments, things could be turned upside down against a neighbor (Zech. 13:7).

5998. עָמַל ʿāmal: A verb meaning to labor, to toil. It refers to physical labor but is also used figuratively of God's building His house, His people (Ps. 127:1). It describes hunger working as a motivating force (Prov. 16:26). It is used of every possible kind of toil and labor in this life (Eccl. 1:3; 2:11; Jon. 4:10).

5999. עָמָל ʿāmāl: A masculine singular noun meaning trouble, labor, toil. This word can be used for the general difficulties and hardships of life, which can be seen by its use in conjunction with sorrow (Jer. 20:18); affliction (Deut. 26:7; Ps. 25:18); and futility (Job 7:3). It can also refer to trouble or mischief directed at another person. The evil person talks of causing trouble (Prov. 24:2); and God cannot look at the trouble caused by sin (Hab. 1:3, 13). Its usage in Ecclesiastes and Psalm 105:44 and 107:12 is best rendered labor. The Teacher in Ecclesiastes repeatedly asked what benefit toil was (Eccl. 2:10, 11).

6000. עָמָל ʿāmāl: A proper noun designating Amal (1 Chr. 7:35).

6001. עָמֵל ʿāmēl: A verbal adjective meaning toiling. This form is used exclusively in Ecclesiastes (Eccl. 2:18, 22; 3:9; 4:8; 9:9) and always as a predicate adjective. The overall use of the word is to stress the meaninglessness of human efforts. Toiling under the sun appears to the writer to have no lasting value. One must leave the rewards to those who come afterward (Eccl. 2:18). This working results in nothing more than pain and grief (Eccl. 2:22). See the word *ʿāmāl* (5999).

6002. עֲמָלֵק ʿamālēq: A proper noun designating Amalek. Amalek was the son of Esau's son Eliphaz and his concubine Timnah. Hence, he was a grandson of Esau's wife Adah who was Canaanite and Hittite (Gen. 36:2, 10–12). His descendants became the Amalekites according to the biblical record. They were hostile toward Israel after the Exodus and threatened God's people through guerrilla warfare (Deut. 25:17–19). God placed a curse on them to exterminate them for attacking His people (Ex. 17:8–16). They ranged far and wide, but the Negev was a central location for them (Num. 13:29). God confirmed His intent to destroy them through Balaam's prophecy (24:20).

They teamed up with the Ammonites to attack Israel (Judg. 3:13) and with others (Judg. 7:12; Ps. 83:7[8]). Saul defeated them but failed to destroy them (1 Sam. 14:48; 15:1–32; 28:18). David removed them as a national threat (1 Sam. 30; 2 Sam. 8:12).

6003. עֲמָלֵקִי ʿamālēqiy: A proper noun designating Amalek (Gen. 36:12,

16; Judg. 3:13; 5:14; 6:3, 33; 7:12; 10:12; 1 Sam. 14:48; 15:2, 3, 5–8, 18, 20, 32; 28:18; 30:18; 2 Sam. 1:1; 8:12; 1 Chr. 1:36; 4:43; 18:11). It is used with *'iys* (376) to designate Amalekites (1 Sam. 30:13; 2 Sam. 1:8, 13).

6004. עָמַם ***'āmam:*** A verb meaning to grow dim, to be hidden. It refers to losing brightness, to lose the glowing shining feature of gold, etc. (Lam. 4:1). It has the sense of to be hard, difficult for someone to solve (Ezek. 28:3); and the meaning of to equal, to compare to, to match (Ezek. 31:8). Some scholars consider the word in Ezekiel to be from a different root with the same spelling.

6005. עִמָּנוּאֵל ***'immānû'ēl:*** A proper noun designating Immanuel, the name of the child who would serve as a sign to King Ahaz in his day and, in the fuller meaning of the prophecy, as a sign to the Lord's people Israel in the future. The name means "God with us" (Isa. 7:10–17). It was used as a cry to God Himself to be with Israel when the Assyrians threatened to destroy them (Isa. 8:8). It is found in Isaiah 8:10 as well as in the Hebrew text (NIV, "God is with us"; KJV also).

6006. עָמַס ***'āmas,*** עָמַשׂ ***'āmaś:*** A. A verb meaning to load, to carry a load. It indicates putting a load or burden of some kind on persons or animals—wheat, taxes, labor demands (Gen. 44:13; 1 Kgs. 12:11; 2 Chr. 10:11; Neh. 13:15). The Lord helps bear the burdens of His people (Ps. 68:19[20]); as well as carry them Himself (Isa. 46:3). It is used derisively of idols being loaded and carried in pack animals (Isa. 46:1). It is used in a figurative way of Jerusalem being carried by the nations (Zech. 12:3).

B. A verb meaning to load, to carry a load. It describes the task of carrying materials to reconstruct the wall of Jerusalem (Neh. 4:17[11]).

6007. עֲמַסְיָה ***'amasyāh:*** A proper noun designating Amasiah (2 Chr. 17:16).

6008. עַמְעָד ***'am'āḏ:*** A proper noun designating Amad (Josh. 19:26).

6009. עָמַק ***'āmaq:*** A verb signifying to be deep, profound. It describes thoughts and ideas of God which are asserted to be deep, difficult to fathom (Ps. 92:5[6]). It describes a valley of abominations (Topheth) made deep, both physically and figuratively (Isa. 30:33). It is used of apostatizing from God greatly, deeply (Isa. 31:6; Hos. 5:2; 9:9). Sin as corruption can be entered into deeply (Hos. 9:9). It refers to a sign from God which can be deep, profound, spanning the universe in its profundity (Isa. 7:11). It refers to the most distant or deeply hidden places to hide (Jer. 49:8).

6010. עֵמֶק ***'ēmeq:*** I. A masculine noun designating a valley, a plain. It refers to a vale, a valley, a lowland, the opposite of hilly or mountainous land. It is used of this kind of land in general (Isa. 22:7; Jer. 31:40). It is used of the Jordan Valley area (Josh. 13:19, 27). It was a place where chariotry would be used in battle (Josh. 17:16). Many specific places have names featuring *ʿēmeq*, valley, e.g., the Valley of Siddim, the Valley of the King, etc. (Gen. 14:17).

II. The phrase *ʿēmeq qᵉṣiys* occurs in Josh. 18:21 as the proper name Emek Keziz.

6011. עֹמֶק *ʿōmeq:* A masculine noun meaning depth. It is used of the great depth, the fathomless deeps of the earth (Prov. 25:3).

6012. עָמֵק *ʿāmēq:* An adjective meaning deep, unfathomable. Both times it is used to describe the speech of foreign peoples as unintelligible. Isaiah spoke of the return from Babylon, telling the people that they would no longer hear the unintelligible speech of foreigners (Isa. 33:19). When God called Ezekiel, He told him that he was to speak to the house of Israel, not to people of unintelligible speech (Ezek. 3:5, 6).

6013. עָמֹק *ʿāmōq:* An adjective meaning deep, mysterious. It is used of the limits of God in profundity; His limits exceed the depth of Sheol (Job 11:8); He brings the depths into light (Job 12:22). It indicates the wisdom, the words, that people speak (Prov. 18:4); or what their hearts contemplate (Prov. 20:5). The harlot is considered a dangerous and deep pit (Prov. 23:27). Even the past is depicted as extremely deep, difficult to find out (Eccl. 7:24); the word is repeated for emphasis here, *wᵉʿāmôq ʿāmôq*. It is used of a deep, wide cup of punishment from God (Ezek. 23:32).

6014. עָמַר *ʿāmar:* A verb meaning to treat as a slave, to bind. It means to treat a person harshly, without humane consideration, without compassion (Deut. 21:14); or to be brutal physically to a person (Deut. 24:7). It refers to a person who binds and ties up sheaves of grain (Ps. 129:7). Some translators find a different word, therefore, in Psalm 129:7.

6015. עֲמַר *ᵃmar:* An Aramaic masculine noun indicating white wool. It indicates the color of the hair of the Ancient of Days as well as His antiquity (Dan. 7:9).

6016. עֹמֶר *ʿōmer:* I. A masculine noun referring to a sheaf of grain. It indicates ears of grain recently cut off the stalks (Lev. 23:10–12, 15; Deut. 24:19; Ruth 2:7, 15). Sheaves were to be left for the poor and hungry (Job 24:10).

II. A masculine noun indicating an omer; a measure of grain. It is a dry measure of about two liters or two quarts (Ex. 16:16, 18, 22, 32, 33, 36).

6017. עֲמֹרָה *ᵃmōrāh:* A proper noun designating Gomorrah, the city located south, southwest of the Dead Sea that was destroyed along with Sodom for its heinous sins. There were not enough righteous persons left in the city to rescue it from God's wrath (Gen. 18: 19). It was on the border of the land occupied by Canaanites (Gen. 10:19). Its destruction resulted in a permanent change in the fertility and beauty of the land around Zoar (Gen. 13:10).

The city became a byword for wickedness and evil in the Prophets and Law (Deut. 29:23[22]; Isa. 1:9; Jer. 49:18; Amos 4:11; Zeph. 2:9).

6018. עָמְרִי *'omriy:* A proper noun designating Omri, a powerful king in northern Israel who established the "house of Omri." His son Ahab was the most wicked king of Israel. He had been the army commander before he was made king. He forced Zimri, the king in Tirzah, to commit suicide, and he reigned in his place (1 Kgs. 16:16–19). Omri reigned twelve years (885–874 B.C.), six in Tirzah. He then purchased a hill on which he built Samaria, the new capital of Samaria (1 Kgs. 16:21–24). He continued to follow the corrupt and rebellious ways of Jeroboam I, son of Nebat. He died and was buried in Samaria (1 Kgs. 16:25–28). He and his son became symbols of rebellion and evil (Mic. 6:16).

6019. עַמְרָם *'amrām:* A proper noun designating Amram (Ex. 6:18, 20; Num. 3:19; 26:58, 59; 1 Chr. 6:2[5:28], 3[5:29], 18[3]; 23:12, 13; 24:20; Ezra 10:34).

6020. עַמְרָמִי *'amrāmiy:* A proper noun designating Amramite, descendant of Amram (6019) (Num. 3:27; 1 Chr. 26:23).

6021. עֲמָשָׂא *'amāśā':* A proper noun designating Omri, a powerful king in northern Israel who established the "house of Omri." His son Ahab was the most wicked king of Israel. He had been the army commander before he was made king. He forced Zimri, the king in Tirzah, to commit suicide, and he reigned in his place (1 Kgs. 16:16–19). Omri reigned twelve years (885–874 B.C.), six in Tirzah. He then purchased a hill on which he built Samaria, the new capital of Samaria (1 Kgs. 16:21–24). He continued to follow the corrupt and rebellious ways of Jeroboam I, son of Nebat. He died and was buried in Samaria (1 Kgs. 16:25–28). He and his son became symbols of rebellion and evil (Mic. 6:16).

6022. עֲמָשַׂי *'amāśay:* A proper noun designating Amasai:

A. An ancestor of Samuel (1 Chr. 6:25[10], 35[20]).

B. One of David's warriors (1 Chr. 12:18).

C. A musician in David's day (1 Chr. 15:24).

D. A Levite in Hezekiah's day (2 Chr. 29:12).

6023. עֲמַשְׁסַי *'amašsay:* A proper noun designating Amashai (Neh. 11:13).

6024. עֲנָב *'anāb:* A proper noun designating Anab (Josh. 11:21; 15:50).

6025. עֵנָב ***ʿēnāḇ:*** A masculine noun indicating a grape, a raisin. It refers to grapes (Gen. 40:10, 11; Amos 9:13). In Numbers 13:23, the phrase *ʾeškol ᵃnāḇîm* refers to a cluster of grapes. It is used figuratively of Israel in the parable of Isaiah (5:2, 4); and in a figurative sense with *dām,* blood, in Genesis. 49:11. Grapes were used in the production of raisin cakes (Hos. 3:1), a food used in idolatrous worship as well as in a common meal.

6026. עָנַג ***ʿānag:*** A verb meaning to be delicate, to take delight. It is used of being fastidious, pampering, feminine as a woman (Deut. 28:56; Jer. 6:2); of keeping oneself clean, neat. It is, however, used of taking delight and pleasure in God (Job 22:26; Isa. 55:2). It has the sense of making merry, jesting at someone (Isa. 58:14). It is used figuratively of taking delight in a restored Jerusalem (Isa. 66:11).

6027. עֹנֶג ***ʿōneg:*** A masculine noun meaning delight, luxury. It is used to describe a palace of delight, luxury, and extravagance (Isa. 13:22). The Sabbath was to be a delight, a time of enjoyment for Israel (Isa. 58:13).

6028. עָנֹג ***ʿānōg:*** An adjective meaning delicate, sensitive. It refers to a refined, suave, fastidious, neat, clean person in formal dress and behavior (Deut. 28:54); but also of Babylon in her era of splendor and riches (Isa. 47:1).

6029. עָנַד ***ʿānaḏ:*** A verb meaning to tie, to bind. It refers to fastening something to oneself in a public and conspicuous place and manner (Job 31:36); but especially so of the binding and being aware of the guidance of one's parents (Prov. 6:21).

6030. עָנָה ***ʿānāh,*** לְעַנּוֹת ***leʿannôṯ:*** I. A verb meaning to answer, to respond, to reply, to testify. It refers to responding, answering a person: of people responding (Gen. 18:27; 23:5); of God answering, responding by word or deed (1 Sam. 7:9; 14:37; 28:6, 15; 1 Kgs. 18:37); of a lover's response (Song 2:10; 5:6). It is often coupled with *ʾāmar,* they said: he answered (*ʿānāh*) and said (*weʾāmar*) (Ex. 4:1). It has the legal sense of witness to, about, against, to testify in some contexts (Gen. 30:33; Deut. 31:21; 2 Sam. 1:16). In its passive use, it means to be given, provided with a response (Prov. 21:13; Ezek. 14:4, 7).

II. A verb meaning to sing, to shout, to howl. It is used of singing joyously to the Lord and in praise of His Law (Ex. 15:21; 1 Sam. 18:7; Ezra 3:11; Ps. 119:172); or in a riotous, uncontrolled way (Ex. 32:18). It is used of a victory song or crying out in victory (Jer. 51:14). It is used figuratively of a rested Israel singing again (Hos. 2:15). It refers to the howling or crying out of animals (Isa. 13:22).

III. A proper noun meaning Leannoth; part of a song title Mahalath Leannoth. It is found in the title of Psalm 88. The title seems to refer to affliction. The psalm is a powerful plea for deliverance from death.

6031. עָנָה *'ānāh:* A verb indicating to be afflicted, to be oppressed, to be humbled. It refers to being oppressed, in a state of oppression. It means to bow down, to humble oneself, to be humbled (Ex. 10:3; Isa. 58:10). In some senses of the verb, it means to inflict oppression, to subdue, to humble someone: of Israel's oppression in Egypt (Gen. 15:13; Ex. 1:11, 12); to deal with persons harshly, to oppress them (Gen. 16:6); to humble a woman (Deut. 21:14); to afflict, humble oneself (Gen. 16:9; Lev. 16:29; Ps. 132:1). It is used of raping a woman (Gen. 34:2). It is possible to humble oneself, to afflict oneself by fasting (Ezra 8:21; Dan. 10:12). The psalmist was often disciplined by affliction from God (Ps. 119:71); the Suffering Servant of Isaiah was afflicted by the Lord (Isa. 53:4).

6032. עֲנָה *'ănāh:* An Aramaic verb meaning to answer, to reply. Its basic translation is to answer, to reply to something said or to a situation (Dan. 2:5, 7, 8, 15, 20; 3:9, 16; 4:19[16], 30[27]). It is coupled with *'āmar,* to say: he answered and said (Dan. 2:5).

6033. עֲנָה *'ănāh:* An Aramaic verb meaning to be afflicted, to be poor, to be needy. It describes the poor and oppressed in a society; in context its reference is within the Babylonian Empire (Dan. 4:27[24]).

6034. עֲנָה *'ănāh:* A proper noun designating Anah (Gen. 36:2, 14, 18, 20, 24, 25, 29; 1 Chr. 1:38, 40, 41).

6035. עָנָו *'ānāw:* An adjective meaning poor, oppressed, afflicted, humble. It is used of persons who put themselves after others in importance; persons who are not proud, haughty, supercilious, self-assertive, low in rank or position. Moses in the Old Testament is the prototype of the humble man before God and other human beings (Num. 12:3), but he was not poor or low in rank. The word also refers to persons who are poor, afflicted, low in societal standing, oppressed (Job 24:4; Ps. 10:12, 17; 22:26[27]). God favors the humble or meek to inherit the land, to be blessed (Ps. 37:11); God gives help and grace to the afflicted (Prov. 3:34). A humble or contrite spirit is of great value (Prov. 16:19). God will finally give justice to the poor (Isa. 11:4). The poor were oppressed by the rich and the immoral (Amos 2:7).

6036. עָנוּב *'ānûḇ:* A proper noun designating Anub (1 Chr. 4:8).

6037. עַנְוָה *'anwāh:* A feminine noun identifying gentleness, meekness, humility. It refers to qualities of meekness, humility, mildness, and patience appropriate for the king over God's people, along with truth and righteousness (Ps. 45:4[5]).

6038. עֲנָוָה *'ănāwāh:* A feminine noun indicating humility. It indicates patience, mildness, tenderness, characteristics of God that foster growth in His king, David (Ps. 18:35[36]). It is found in Psalm 45:4[5], but see 6037 also. It indicates an attitude of humility that brings a person honor (Prov. 15:33; 18:12; 22:4); and possibly mercy in the day of judgment (Zeph. 2:3).

6039. עֱנוּת ***ᵉnûṯ:*** A feminine noun indicating affliction. The state of being oppressed in various ways, physically, mentally, or spiritually. God cares for this condition in His people (Ps. 22:24[25]).

6040. עֳנִי ***ᵒniy:*** A masculine noun meaning affliction, misery. It refers to a state of oppression or extreme discomfort, physically, mentally, or spiritually: Hagar was abused and afflicted by Sarah (Gen. 16:11); Leah was not loved as was Rachel (Gen. 29:32); Jacob was abused and tricked by Laban (Gen. 31:42); Israel was under affliction by the Egyptians (Ex. 3:7, 17); childlessness was an affliction in the Old Testament (1 Sam. 1:11); political, economic, and military oppression are in the range of the word (2 Kgs. 14:26). Job's illness was a burdensome affliction (Job 10:15; 30:16). The psalmist was under attack from those who hated him (Ps. 9:13[14]). Affliction is a disciplinary measure from God in some cases (Isa. 48:10).

6041. עָנִי ***'āniy:*** An adjective meaning poor, afflicted. It refers to those who are suffering, in a state of poverty, oppression, misery from various causes: from being poor, needy (Ex. 22:25[24]); unfortunate, in want (Deut. 24:15; 2 Sam. 22:28; Job 24:4). They cry out for help and for their needs (Ps. 9:12[13]; 12:5[6]; 37:14). Hope for deliverance is from the Lord (Ps. 69:29[30]) who dispenses grace (Prov. 3:34; 14:21). They are constantly abused by rich and oppressive leaders (Isa. 3:14; Amos 8:4; Hab. 3:14). God had commanded His people not to oppress the poor (Zech. 7:10); for their true King is humble Himself (Zech. 9:9).

6042. עֻנִּי ***'unniy:*** A proper noun designating Unni (1 Chr. 15:18, 20; Neh. 12:9).

6043. עֲנָיָה ***ᵃnāyāh:*** A proper noun designating Ananiah (Neh. 8:4; 10:22[23]).

6044. עָנִים ***'āniym:*** A proper noun designating Anim (Josh. 15:50).

6045. עִנְיָן ***'inyān:*** A masculine noun indicating a task, a burden. It refers to a job to be performed, a responsibility to be met, a need to be satisfied: to examine all of life, to understand it (Eccl. 1:13; 2:23); both by good and evil persons (Eccl. 2:26; 3:10); concerning what is past, present, and future (Eccl. 8:16). It indicates the effort put forth as well as the task itself (Eccl. 5:3[2]).

6046. עָנֵם ***'ānēm:*** A proper noun designating Anem (1 Chr. 6:73[58]).

6047. עֲנָמִים *ᵃnāmiym:* A proper noun designating Anamim (Gen. 10:13; 1 Chr. 1:11).

6048. עֲנַמֶּלֶךְ *ᵃnammelek̲:* A masculine proper noun designating Anammelech. It refers to a pagan god to whom the Sepharvites sacrificed their children by fire (2 Kgs. 17:31). These are said to be gods of the Sepharvites, a people otherwise unknown.

6049. עָנַן *'ānan:* A verb meaning to practice soothsaying, fortune-telling, divining, magic. While it is clear from the contexts and the versions that this term is used for some type of magic or witchcraft, its etymology is unclear. Therefore, the specifics of the practice it connotes are equally unclear. However, it is clear that it was strictly forbidden, and the one who practiced this act was detestable to God (Deut. 18:10, 12). Isaiah appears to use the term figuratively to demean the idolatrous Israelites (Isa. 57:3).

6050. עֲנַן *ᵃnan:* A masculine singular Aramaic noun meaning cloud. It occurs only in Daniel 7:13 in the phrase, clouds of heaven. In a night vision, Daniel saw the Son of Man coming with the clouds of heaven. This use of clouds in apocalyptic language is familiar to the writer of Revelation who echoes the same phrase, "Look, he is coming with the clouds" (Rev. 1:7, NIV). See the Hebrew cognate *'ānān* (6051).

6051. עָנָן *'ānān:* A masculine singular noun meaning cloud. In the ancient world, clouds were often seen as the pedestal or shroud of the divine presence. This imagery is also present in the Hebrew Bible. God preceded the Israelites through the wilderness in a pillar of cloud (Ex. 13:21, 22); and the same cloud rested over the Tabernacle (Ex. 33:10). The cloud was over Mount Sinai (Ex. 19:9); and entered the Temple in Jerusalem (1 Kgs. 8:10, 11). Clouds are typical of the apocalyptic language of the Day of God (Ezek. 30:3; Joel 2:2; Zeph. 1:15). Other poetic uses of cloud describe God's shelter (Isa. 4:5); Israel's evaporating love (Hos. 6:4); the transient nature of life (Job 7:9); and the breadth of a great army (Ezek. 38:9). See the Aramaic *ᵃnān* (6050).

6052. עָנָן *'ānān:* A proper noun designating Anan (Neh. 10:26[27]).

6053. עֲנָנָה *ᵃnānāh:* A feminine noun referring to a cloud. The context implies a thick cloud that obscures visibility, capable of hiding something (Job 3:5).

6054. עֲנָנִי *ᵃnāniy:* A proper noun designating Anani (1 Chr. 3:24).

6055. עֲנַנְיָה *ᵃnānᵉyāh:* A proper noun designating Ananiah:

A. Grandfather of Azariah (Neh. 3:23).

B. A city in Nehemiah's day (Neh. 11:32).

6056. עֲנַף *ᵃnap̱:* An Aramaic masculine noun referring to a branch of a tree. It depicts, in Nebuchadnezzar's vision, the branches of a great symbolic tree (Dan. 4:12[9], 14[11], 21[18]), the tree signifying Babylon and its king.

6057. עָנָף *'ānāp̱:* A masculine noun designating the branch of a tree. In Leviticus 23:40, it refers to palm branches; in Psalm 80:10[11], it indicates the branches or boughs of a cedar tree; various branches in Ezekiel (17:8, 23; 36:8). It is used figuratively of the Assyrian Empire (Ezek. 31:3); and of the seed of the wicked (Mal. 4:1[3:19]).

6058. עָנֵף *'ānēp̱:* An adjective meaning full of branches. It refers to an abundance of branches or boughs put forth by a well-watered tree (Ezek. 19:10).

6059. עָנַק *'ānaq:* A verb meaning to place around the neck; to supply literally. It indicates giving freely to persons to provide all their needs and more (Deut. 15:14). It refers to putting on or wearing a necklace (Ps. 73:6; the *mô* is a suffix, third masculine plural).

6060. עֲנָק *ᵃnāq:* A masculine noun indicating a necklace, a chain. It is used figuratively of wearing parents' instructions around one's neck as a necklace or chain of remembrance (Prov. 1:9). It refers to a necklace worn as an ornament or jewelry (Song 4:9). It was used of ornaments worn on animals, camels in particular (Judg. 8:26).

6061. עֲנָק *ᵃnāq:* A proper noun designating Anak (Num. 13:22, 28, 33; Deut. 9:2; Josh. 15:13, 14; 21:11; Judg. 1:20).

6062. עֲנָקִי *ᵃnaqiy:* A proper noun designating an Anakite, in the plural Anakim, the descendants of Anak (6061) (Deut. 1:28; 2:10, 11, 21; 9:2; Josh. 11:21, 22; 14:12, 15).

6063. עָנֵר *'ānēr:* A proper noun designating Aner:

A. An ally of Araham (Gen. 14:13, 24).

B. A city in Manasseh (1 Chr. 6:70[55]).

6064. עָנַשׁ *'ānaš:* A verb meaning to fine, to penalize with a fine. The primary meaning is the monetary assessment for a crime and is clearly seen in Deuteronomy 22:19 (see also Ex. 21:22). Similarly, Amos used the word to denote the condemnation that rests on those under punishment (Amos 2:8). In a practical sense, the writer of wisdom extolled the educational benefits of applying such a fine to the wicked (Prov. 21:11); but he expressly warned against punishing the righteous (Prov. 17:26).

6065. עֲנָשׁ *ᵃnāš:* An Aramaic masculine noun meaning confiscation, repossession. This word appears only once in Ezra 7:26 and simply refers to the seizure of goods as a legal penalty for crimes.

6066. עֹנֶשׁ **'ōnes̆:** A masculine noun meaning a fine, a penalty, an indemnity. The basic meaning of the word is a monetary obligation placed on one who violated the Law or was under subjugation to a higher authority. It was used to refer to the tribute forced on Jehoahaz by the Egyptian pharaoh (2 Kgs. 23:33); and the punishment facing unrestrained anger (Prov. 19:19).

6067. עֲנָת **'anāṯ:** A masculine proper noun. Anath is the name of a man who appears twice in the book of Judges. Very little is known about Anath except that he was the father of Shamgar (Judg. 3:31; 5:6).

6068. עֲנָתוֹת **'anāṯôṯ:** A proper noun designating Anathoth:

A. A city of the tribe of Benjamin which became a levitical city (Josh. 21:18). Abiathar, one of David's priests, came from there. Some exiles who returned were from this city (Ezra 2:23). Jeremiah the prophet came from Anathoth (Jer. 1:1; 11:21, 23). It was to be judged severely (Isa. 10:30).

B. A grandson of Benjamin and son of Beker (1 Chr. 7:8).

C. An Israelite who signed and supported Nehemiah's covenant of renewal (Neh. 10:19).

6069. עַנְּתוֹתִי **'anneṯôṯiy:** A proper noun designating Anathothite, an inhabitant of Anathoth (6068,A) (2 Sam. 23:27; 1 Chr. 11:28; 12:3; 27:12; Jer. 29:27).

6070. עַנְתֹתִיָּה **'anṯōṯiyyāh:** A proper noun designating Anthothijah (1 Chr. 8:24).

6071. עָסִיס **'āsiys:** A masculine noun referring to sweet wine, new wine; nectar. It refers to grape juice (Isa. 49:26; Amos 9:13); or to the nectar or juice from pomegranates (Song 8:2). It is used of sweet wine (Joel 1:5; 3:18[4:18]). Sweet wine is probably grape juice, fresh and unfermented.

6072. עָסַס **'āsas:** A verb meaning to trample, to tread down. It means to step on over and over, to flatten out, to mash into the ground. In context it is used figuratively of treading down the wicked (Mal. 4:3[3:21]).

6073. עֳפָאִים **'opa'yim:** A masculine plural noun indicating branches. It refers to extensions, boughs of a tree, as a part of God's created world (Ps. 104:12).

6074. עֳפִי **'opiy:** An Aramaic masculine noun designating branches, foliage. It is used of the foliage and branches put forth by the great symbolic tree of Nebuchadnezzar's dream (Dan. 4:12[9], 14[11], 21[18]). The foliage is described as beautiful, splendid (*s̆appîr*).

6075. עָפַל **'āpal:** A verb meaning to be proud, to presume. It describes carrying on an act of presumption, arrogance, against the best advice (Num. 14:44). It refers to a person who has become too audacious, proud (Hab. 2:4).

6076. עֹפֶל ***'ōpel:*** I. A masculine noun meaning hill, fort, citadel (2 Kgs. 5:24; Isa. 32:14; Mic. 4:8).

II. masculine noun meaning tumor (Deut. 28:27; 1 Sam. 5:6, 9, 12; 6:4, 5).

6077. עֹפֶל ***'ōpel:*** A proper noun designating Ophel, the name of a hill where Jotham did major repairs to the wall of Jerusalem (2 Chr. 27:3). Manasseh enlarged the outer wall of the City of David that went around the hill of Ophel (2 Chr. 33:14). Postexilic repairs were made to the wall of Jerusalem by Levites who served in the Temple but lived on top of the hill of Ophel (Neh. 3:26–27; 22:21).

6078. עָפְנִי ***'opniy:*** A proper noun designating Ophni (Josh. 18:24).

6079. עַפְעַף ***'ap'ap:*** I. A masculine noun meaning eyelid. It refers to the two coverings of flesh that open and close over a person's eyes. The interesting simile of Leviathan's eyelids mention the eyelids of the dawn (Job 41:18[10]). The word refers to God's sight or watchful eyes (Ps. 11:4). Sleep is the function of closed eyelids (Ps. 132:4; Prov. 6:4). Eyelids can be used for flirtation or for enticement (Prov. 4:25; 6:25). They can give forth an attitude of arrogance (Prov. 30:13); or display sorrow and weeping (Jer. 9:18[17]).

II. A masculine noun indicating the opening rays of the sun. In a metaphor, it is used of the "eyelid" of the sun beginning to open, the morning light breaking through (Job 3:9).

6080. עָפַר ***'āpar:*** A verb meaning to powder, to dust. This word literally means to sprinkle dust or dirt and conveys the image of a dusty garment whose appearance is gray. It was used to describe the scornful action of Shimei as he threw dirt on David and his procession (2 Sam. 16:13).

6081. עֵפֶר ***'ēper:*** A proper noun designating Epher:

A. Son of Midian (Gen. 25:4; 1 Chr. 1:33).

B. Son of Ezra (1 Chr. 4:17).

C. The head of a family sent into exile (1 Chr. 5:24).

6082. עֹפֶר ***'ōper:*** A masculine noun referring to a young deer, a fawn. It is used in a simile to compare one's bridegroom to a young stag, a young deer (Song 2:9, 17; 8:14); and of the breasts of the bride (Song 4:5; 7:3[4]).

6083. עָפָר ***'āpār:*** A masculine noun meaning dust, dry earth, loose dirt. The primary meaning of this word is the dry, loose dirt or dust that covers the ground (Amos 2:7; Mic. 1:10). It is used to imply earth or soil (Job 5:6; 28:2); the original material used to form the first man (Gen. 2:7); the material used to plaster walls (Lev. 14:42); the remains of a destroyed city (Ezek. 26:4); and anything pulverized into powder (Deut. 9:21). Figuratively, it signifies abundance (Gen.

13:16); utter defeat (2 Kgs. 13:7); and humiliation (Job 16:15).

6084. עָפְרָה *'oprāh:* A proper noun designating Ophrah:

A. A town in Benjamin (Josh. 18:23; 1 Sam. 13:17).

B. A town west of the Jordan River (Judg. 6:11, 24; 8:27, 32; 9:5). Ophrah was Gideon's hometown.

C. Son of Meonothai (1 Chr. 4:14).

6085. עֶפְרוֹן *'eprôn:* A proper noun designating Ephron:

A. A Hittite (Gen. 23:8, 10, 13, 14, 16, 17; 25:9; 49:29, 30; 50:13).

B. Mount Ephron (Josh. 15:9).

C. The city Ephron (2 Chr. 13:19).

6086. עֵץ *'ēṣ:* A masculine noun referring to a tree, wood, timber, a stick, a plank. It refers to trees of all kinds (Gen. 1:11; Ps. 104:16); garden trees (Gen. 2:9, 16); special trees used figuratively (Gen. 2:17; 3:22, 24; Prov. 3:18; 11:30; 13:12; 15:4); a specific kind of tree, olive tree (1 Kgs. 6:23, 31–33; Hab. 2:19). The word refers to wood, pieces of wood for various purposes (2 Kgs. 12:12[13]); concerning specific kinds of wood, gopher wood (Gen. 6:14; Ex. 25:5, 10); articles made of wood (Ex. 7:19); timbers in a building or house (1 Kgs. 15:22; Hab. 2:11; Zech. 5:4). It refers to a tree or pole on which a slain person was hanged (Gen. 40:19; Deut. 21:22, 23; Josh. 8:29; 10:26); also to a wooden gallows (Esth. 2:23). It is used of firewood (Gen. 22:3).

6087. עָצַב *'āṣab:* A verb meaning to hurt, to pain, to grieve, to shape, to fashion. This word has two separate meanings. The first meaning deals with physical pain (Eccl. 10:9); emotional pain (1 Sam. 20:34); or some combination of physical and emotional pain (1 Chr. 4:10). The word is also used of David's inaction when Adonijah attempted to usurp the throne (1 Kgs. 1:6). The second meaning generally refers to creative activity, such as the kind God exercised when He created human bodies (Job 10:8); or the creative activity of people (Jer. 44:19). In both these instances, the word occurs in parallel with the word *'āśāh* (6213), which means to make or to do.

6088. עֲצִיב *'aṣiyb:* An Aramaic verb meaning to grieve. It is similar to the Hebrew word *'āṣab* (6087). It appears only one time in the form of a passive participle and is used as an adjective to modify *qôl* (6963), meaning voice. In this instance, King Darius called into the lion's den for Daniel with a pained voice to see if God had preserved Daniel and kept him safe from harm (Dan. 6:20[21]).

6089. עֶצֶב *'eṣeb:* A masculine noun meaning pain, hurt, toil. Since, like the noun *'ōṣeb* (6090), it is derived from the verb *'āṣab* (6087), this noun carries the same variations of meaning. The word is used of physical pain, such as a woman's pain in childbirth (Gen. 3:16); or of emotional pain, such as that caused by inappropriate words (Prov. 15:1). The word can also express both meanings (cf. Prov. 10:22); and can also refer to hard work or toil (Ps. 127:2; Prov. 5:10; 14:23).

6090. עֹצֶב ***'ōṣeḇ:*** A masculine noun meaning pain, image, idol. Like the noun *'eṣeḇ* (6089), this word is derived from the verb *'āṣaḇ* (6087). It can be used to depict the physical pain of childbirth (1 Chr. 4:9); a painful way, meaning a harmful habit like idolatry (Ps. 139:24); and the sorrow and hardship of the Babylonian exile (Isa. 14:3). In the final passage, this word is in parallel with *rōgez* (7267), meaning disquiet or turmoil.

6091. עָצָב ***'āṣāḇ:*** A masculine noun used to identify an idol. This term always appears in the plural. It is derived from the second meaning of the verb *'āṣaḇ* (6087), meaning to form or fashion, and thereby highlights the fact that these idols ("gods") were formed by human hands. This term can allude to idols in general (Hos. 4:17); idols of silver (Hos. 13:2); or idols of gold and silver (Hos. 8:4). It appears in parallel with *massēḵāh* (4541), meaning a molten image (Hos. 13:2); and *gillûl* (1544), meaning idols (Jer. 50:2).

6092. עָצֵב ***'āṣēḇ:*** A masculine noun meaning a laborer, a worker. This noun is derived from the verb *'āṣaḇ* (6087), which conveys the idea of physical or emotional pain and suffering. This noun occurs only in Isaiah 58:3, where God condemned the people of Israel for not properly fasting because they sacrificed nothing personally while exploiting their laborers or workers.

6093. עִצָּבוֹן ***'iṣṣāḇôn:*** A masculine noun meaning pain, toil. This noun is derived from the verb *'āṣaḇ* (6087) and occurs three times in Genesis, relating to the curse that God placed on fallen humanity. To the woman, God stated that she would have pain and toil during childbirth (Gen. 3:16). To the man, God stated that he would have pain and toil in working the ground to produce food (Gen. 3:17; 5:29).

6094. עַצֶּבֶת ***'aṣṣeḇeṯ:*** A feminine noun meaning hurt, injury, pain. This noun is derived from the verb *'āṣaḇ* (6087). This noun is used only in Hebrew poetry and refers to the grief or sorrow that causes fear of discipline (Job 9:28); the grief caused by idolatry (Ps. 16:4); the grief that comes with being brokenhearted (Ps. 147:3); the grief caused by one who winks with the eye (Prov. 10:10); or grief that causes the spirit to be broken (Prov. 15:13). Although sometimes portrayed in physical terms (Ps. 147:3), this term clearly refers to emotional suffering and not physical pain or injury.

6095. עָצָה ***'āṣāh:*** A verb meaning to shut, to wink the eye. It refers to closing one eye, usually to indicate deception (Prov. 16:30).

6096. עָצֶה ***'āṣeh:*** A masculine noun referring to a backbone. It refers to the backbone or tailbone of an animal where the fat tail was located and had to be removed (Lev. 3:9).

6097. עֵצָה ***'ēṣāh:*** A feminine collective noun. It serves as a synonym for 6086. It refers to trees surrounding Jerusalem that were to be destroyed by a siege (Jer. 6:6).

6098. עֵצָה ***'ēṣāh:*** A feminine noun meaning advice, a plan. It sometimes may suggest the idea of a plot (Neh. 4:15[4:9]; Prov. 21:30); of a judgment or decision (Judg. 20:7; 2 Sam. 16:20; Ezra 10:3, 8). The term occurs in a positive sense in association with wisdom and understanding (Job 12:13; Prov. 8:14; 12:15). Thus, the meaning of advice came from the sages of Israel and the astrologers of Babylon who were viewed as wise in their communities (Isa. 47:13; Jer. 18:18). Kings and would-be kings sought out advice but did not always have the discernment to choose the good (2 Sam. 17:7, 14, 23; 1 Kgs. 12:8, 13, 14). This term is used quite often as a possession of God and the promised Messiah (Prov. 19:21; Isa. 5:19; 11:2; Jer. 32:19).

6099. עָצוּם ***'āṣûm:*** An adjective meaning strong, mighty. It refers to the power and influence of a person, a people, a nation, or military forces. It is used of the descendants of Abraham becoming a numerous, mighty, powerful nation (Gen. 18:18; Ex. 1:9); of a nation from Moses (Num. 14:12; Deut. 4:38). But it is used of all strong, powerful nations and peoples (Josh. 23:9; Zech. 8:22). It can stress the number in a group of people, many, a great many (Prov. 7:26). It can emphasize the influence and power of individuals (Prov. 18:18; Isa. 53:12). It is used of cattle (Num. 32:1); or indicates a large amount of water in a great river (Isa. 8:7).

6100. עֶצְיוֹן גֶּבֶר ***'eṣyôn ge<u>b</u>er:*** A proper noun designating Ezion Geber, one of the sites where Israel encamped (Num. 33:35). It was located in the northern part of the Gulf of Elath/Aquaba (1 Kgs. 9:26), and Solomon outfitted a fleet of commercial ships there. Jehosaphat did the same, but his ships were destroyed, evidently by a storm (1 Kgs. 22:48[49]).

6101. עָצַל ***'āṣal:*** A verb meaning to hesitate, to delay. It means not to act, to lay back. In context it is used of Israel's hesitation to enter the Promised Land (Judg. 18:9).

6102. עָצֵל ***'āṣēl:*** An adjective meaning sluggish, lazy. It is best known for its translation as sluggards, useless, lazy persons who always fail because of laziness that becomes moral failure (Prov. 6:6, 9); their souls want nothing, and they get nothing (Prov. 13:4). These persons take no initiative (Prov. 19:24); don't do their tasks on time (Prov. 20:4); will not work (Prov. 21:25). They create imaginary excuses (Prov. 22:13). Their wealth and health deteriorate (Prov. 24:30); but they consider themselves wise (Prov. 26:13–16).

6103. עַצְלָה ʿaṣlāh: A feminine noun referring to laziness, sluggishness. It is a state and attitude of doing nothing; it destroys persons (Prov. 19:15); and their possessions (Eccl. 10:18).

6104. עַצְלוּת ʿaṣlûṯ: A feminine noun referring to idleness, sluggishness. The description of a wise, worthy woman includes the assertion that she does not let idleness or laziness become a part of her life (Prov. 31:27).

6105. עָצַם ʿāṣam: I. A verb meaning to be numerous, mighty. It describes a person, people, or nation becoming or being powerful, strong. Israel and his family had become strong, numerous (Gen. 26:16); Israel multiplied to become a powerful people in Egypt (Ex. 1:7, 20; Ps. 105:24). It refers to the enemies of a righteous person (Ps. 38:19[20]). God's wonders are declared to be too many to number or tell about (Ps. 40:5[6]). The might and strength of horsemen is emphasized (Isa. 31:1). It is used figuratively of the might of a male goat that represents Alexander the Great (Dan. 8:8, 24).

II. A verb meaning to shut, to close. It is used of the Lord's shutting the eyes of a rebellious people (Isa. 29:10). It means to cover one's eyes or to refuse to approve or countenance what is evil in the Lord's eyes (Isa. 33:15).

6106. עֶצֶם ʿeṣem: A feminine singular noun meaning bone, substance, self. The first use of the term in the Bible is in Genesis when Adam proclaimed Eve was bone of his bones (Gen. 2:23). This phrase is echoed later as an idiom of close relationship (Judg. 9:2; 2 Sam. 19:13[14]). The word can also be employed for animal bones (Ex. 12:46; Num. 9:12; Job 40:18). Speaking figuratively, Jeremiah said that the Word of God was like fire shut in his bones (Jer. 20:9). *ʿEṣem* can also denote identity, as in the phrase *b^{e}ʿeṣem hayyôm hazzeh*, (in this very day; Ex. 12:17). A similar construction is seen in Exodus 24:10 (the sky itself).

6107. עֶצֶם ʿeṣem: A proper noun designating Ezem (Josh. 15:29; 19:3; 1 Chr. 4:29).

6108. עֹצֶם ʿōṣem: I. A masculine noun indicating strength, might. It indicates strength, might, endurance for a person as opposed to being weak, tired. It refers to the supposed power and effectiveness of magical spells or enchantments. It refers to the power and influence of a political ally (Nah. 3:9).

6109. עָצְמָה ʿoṣmāh: A feminine noun indicating might. It refers to the strength of persons, usually their social and political power as well as their physical or emotional strength (Isa. 40:29).

6110. עֲצֻמוֹת ***'aṣumôṯ:*** A feminine plural noun pointing out strong reasons, arguments. It refers to supposed proofs and arguments used in a legal case or debate (Isa. 41:21).

6111. עַצְמוֹן ***'aṣmôn:*** A proper noun designating Azmon (Num. 34:4, 5; Josh. 15:4).

6112. עֵצֶן ***'ēṣen:*** A proper noun designating Eznite (2 Sam. 23:8).

6113. עָצַר ***'āṣar:*** A verb meaning to restrain, to shut in, to keep in slavery. It means to keep from, prevent, as when the Lord kept Sarah from having children (Gen. 16:2); He closed the wombs of many women in the Old Testament (Gen. 20:18). It is used of stopping something, stopping a plague (Num. 16:48[17:13], 50[17:15]; 25:8). The Lord could check or shut up the natural processes of nature, e.g., rain (Deut. 11:17). It is used in a technical sense to refer to a person who is in bondage, not free, held in slavery (Deut. 32:36). It is used of politely detaining persons according to their wills (Judg. 13:15, 16); or of imprisoning someone (2 Kgs. 17:4). It refers to retaining strength, being strong (Dan. 10:8, 16). It is used with the sense of controlling or restraining a people, ruling over them (1 Sam. 9:17); and of driving or controlling a horse (2 Kgs. 4:24). In its passive uses, it means to be detained, to be shut up (1 Sam. 21:7[8]; 1 Kgs. 8:35).

6114. עֶצֶר ***'eṣer:*** I. A masculine noun referring to restraint. It is used of a ruler ruling over, restraining the people of Laish (Judg. 18:7). The NASB nuances the word to mean humility, humiliating (*yôrēš 'eṣer*).

II. A masculine noun meaning prosperity. It is taken by some to refer to the prosperity of the land and people of Laish (Judg. 18:7), possessing prosperity (*yôrēš 'eṣer*). The NASB nuances the word as humiliating.

6115. עֹצֶר ***'ōṣer:*** A masculine noun depicting oppression, barrenness. It refers to any kind of pressure, maltreatment, or affliction that is put on someone or a people (Ps. 107:39). It takes on the meaning of barrenness for the ultimate oppression of the womb (Prov. 30:16). It refers to military, religious, political, social rejection, and oppression in the case of the Suffering Servant (Isa. 53:8).

6116. עֲצָרָה ***'aṣārāh,*** עֲצֶרֶת ***'ᵃṣereṯ:*** A feminine singular noun meaning assembly. This use of assembly usually has some religious or cultic connection; thus, it is often translated solemn assembly. These assemblies may be according to God's Law, such as the Feast of Passover (Deut. 16:8); or the all-day gathering at the end of the Feast of Booths in Nehemiah 8:18. But other assemblies were for the worship of other gods (2 Kgs. 10:20); or were detestable to God because of Israel's wickedness (Isa. 1:13; Amos 5:21).

6117. עָקַב ***'āqaḇ:*** A verb meaning to grasp at the heel, to supplant, to deceive. This verb is derived from the noun meaning heel (*'āqēḇ*[6119]) and is connected etymologically to the name Jacob (*ya'ᵃqōḇ*). The first occurrence sets the backdrop for the other uses. After Jacob tricked his brother Esau out of Isaac's blessing, Esau says, "He is rightly called 'Jacob'—for he has tricked (*Jacobed*) me twice" (Gen. 27:36). In Jeremiah 9:4[3], reflecting on the Jacob story, the prophet said every brother deceives. Hosea used the term in its more literal meaning when he recalled that Jacob grasped the heel of his brother in the womb (Hos. 12:3[4]).

6118. עֵקֶב ***'ēqeḇ:*** A masculine noun giving an adverbial sense of consequence, because. It basically means end, the last reason for something. It is used as a conjunction meaning because (Gen. 22:18; 26:5; Num. 14:24). It refers to a good result, a reward for something done (Ps. 19:11[12]; Prov. 22:4). It refers to a goal, end, or purpose to something (Ps. 119:33); or the chronological end of a process (Ps. 119:112).

6119. עָקֵב ***'āqēḇ:*** A masculine singular noun meaning a heel, footprints, a back, a rear. The basic meaning of the word is heel and is seen in the passage where the serpent was told that he would strike at the heel of Eve's offspring (Gen. 3:15). Jacob grasped Esau's heel in the womb (Gen. 25:26). But the term can also be used to refer to the mark left by the heel (that is, a footprint) (Ps. 56:6[7]; 77:19[20]; Song 1:8). It is also used in a military context to mean rear, that is, at the heels (Gen. 49:19; Josh. 8:13).

6120. עָקֵב ***'āqēḇ:*** I. A masculine noun meaning heel. It is taken to refer to the heels of a person but also in a figurative sense of the way of life one's feet lead (Ps. 49:5[6]).

II. A masculine noun meaning a foe, a deceiver. It is used of one who attacks, withstands, accuses another person to bring him or her down (Isa. 49:5[6]).

6121. עָקֹב ***'āqōḇ:*** This form actually represents two adjectives. The first means deceitful, insidious, "footprinted." It is from the verb *'āqaḇ* (6117) and the noun *'āqēḇ* (6119). As Jeremiah proclaimed God's efforts with sinful humanity, he also declared that the heart is more deceitful than anything (Jer. 17:9). The other usage is related to the word for footprint. To describe the wickedness of Gilead, the prophet called it a town of bloody footprints (Hos. 6:8). The second adjective means steep, hilly. Isaiah spoke of making a path for the exiles to return, making the hilly places like a plain (Isa. 40:4). This famous passage is appropriated in the Gospels to describe John the Baptist's preparation for Jesus' ministry.

6122. עָקְבָה ***'oqbāh:*** A feminine noun indicating deceitfulness. It refers to trickery, acting according to a ruse, with threatening cunningness and deceit (2 Kgs. 10:19).

6123. עָקַד **'āqad:** A verb meaning to bind, to wrap. It means to tie up someone, especially for a specific purpose. Abraham bound Isaac to sacrifice him (Gen. 22:9).

6124. עָקֹד **'āqōd:** An adjective indicating streaked, striped. The word refers to male goats that were striped (NASB), speckled (NKJV), streaked (NIV), ringstraked (KJV). The various ways that the word is translated shows how difficult it is to give an exact rendering of the word (Gen. 30:35, 39, 40; 31:8, 10, 12).

6125. עָקָה **'āqāh:** I. A feminine noun meaning oppression, pressure. It is used of tension and force exerted on someone to create distress (Ps. 55:3[4]).

II. A feminine noun referring to staring. It refers to hostile gazes directed at someone intended to create fear and distress (Ps. 55:3[4]).

6126. עַקּוּב **'aqqûb:** A proper noun designating Akkub:

A. A descendant of Zerubbabel (1 Chr. 3:24).

B. A gatekeeper in Solomon's time, and the head of a family of gatekeepers (1 Chr. 9:17; Ezra 2:42; Neh. 7:45).

C. A gatekeeper in Nehemiah's time (Neh. 11:19; 12:25).

D. The head of a family of temple servants (Ezra 2:45).

E. A Levite who helped Ezra expound the Law (Neh. 8:7).

6127. עָקַל **'āqal:** A verb meaning to be perverted, to be made wrong. It refers to a twisted distortion of justice that results in injustice being done (Hab. 1:4).

6128. עֲקַלְקַל **'ᵃqalqal:** An adjective meaning roundabout, winding, crooked. It is used of a twisting, turning detour taken in order to reach one's destination (Judg. 5:6). It is used figuratively of the crooked, immoral ways of the wicked (Ps. 125:5).

6129. עֲקַלָּתוֹן **'ᵃqallāṯôn:** An adjective meaning crooked, twisted. It refers to a coiling, wiry, motion made by a serpent creature, Leviathan (Isa. 27:1).

6130. עֲקָן **'ᵃqān:** A proper noun designating Akan (Gen. 36:27).

6131. עָקַר **'āqar:** I. A verb meaning to cut tendons, to cut the hamstring. It refers to cutting the large tendons at the back of the major joint of a four-legged animal's legs (Gen. 49:6; Josh. 11:6, 9; 2 Sam. 8:4; 1 Chr. 18:4).

II. A verb signifying to pluck up, to root out. It is translated as to dig out, to tear down by some translators (KJV, Gen. 49:6). It is used of tearing out living plants and destroying, rooting out cities (Eccl. 3:2; Zeph. 2:4).

6132. עֲקַר **'ᵃqar:** An Aramaic verb referring to plucking up by the roots. It refers to tearing something out, destroying it, pulling it out by the roots. It is used figuratively of tearing out men or rulers (Dan. 7:8).

6133. עֵקֶר ***'ēqer:*** A masculine noun indicating a descendant, a member of one's family. It refers to the offspring of a person or social group living among Israel (Lev. 25:47).

6134. עֵקֶר ***'ēqer:*** A proper noun designating Eker (1 Chr. 2:27).

6135. עָקָר ***'āqār:*** An adjective meaning barren, childless. It refers to the state of not being fertile, not being able to become pregnant. God is often mentioned as the one who brought about this condition and/or the one who overcomes it. Sarah, Rebekah, Rachel, the mother of Samson, and Hannah are chief examples of this situation (Gen. 11:30; 25:21; 29:31; Judg. 13:2, 3; 1 Sam. 2:5). It is used figuratively of Zion's not having borne the spiritual children of God as the Lord had hoped (Isa. 54:1).

6136. עִקַּר ***'iqqar:*** An Aramaic masculine noun meaning a root, a stump. The word means stump primarily but seems to include the taproot or rootstock attached to it as well when used with *šaršôhî* following (Dan. 4:15[12], 23[20], 26[23]).

6137. עַקְרָב ***'aqrā<u>b</u>,*** עַקְרַבִּים ***'aqra<u>bb</u>iym:*** I. A masculine noun denoting a scorpion. An order of arachnids (spiderlike) with front pinchers, a slim body, and a poisonous stinger at the end of its body (Deut. 8:15). It is used figuratively of some kind of scourge or pestilence (1 Kgs. 12:11, 14); and of evil leaders among God's people (Ezek. 2:6).

II. A proper noun, Akrabbim. It is used of a hilly ascent at the south end of the Dead Sea that has the contours of a scorpion's body (Num. 34:4; Josh. 15:3; Judg. 1:36).

6138. עֶקְרוֹן ***'eqrôn:*** A proper noun designating Ekron. It was located on the coastal plane on the borders of Judah and Dan. It was one of five Philistine cities (Josh. 13:3) and was allotted to Judah (Josh. 15:11, 45, 46). Judah initially captured the city (Judg. 1:18). The city would not let the captured ark of God be brought into it (1 Sam. 5:10–12). Its people played a prominent part in getting the ark returned to Israel (1 Sam. 5:11—6:21). It was one of the southernmost cities of the Philistines (1 Sam. 17:52). It, with many other cities, could taste God's judgments (Jer. 25:20).

6139. עֶקְרוֹנִי ***'eqrôniy:*** A proper noun designating Ekronite (Josh. 13:3; 1 Sam. 5:10).

6140. עָקַשׁ ***'āqaš:*** A verb meaning to be twisted, to be perverse; to prove something perverted. It refers to moral, ethical, and social legal perversion. It is the opposite of *tām,* perfect, indicating that something is out of order, guilty, wrong (Job 9:20). It is the opposite of upright, straight, level, indicating that something is uneven, twisted (Prov. 10:9; Mic. 3:9). It refers to a person who leads a crooked life (Prov. 28:18; Isa. 59:8).

6141. עִקֵּשׁ ***'iqqēš:*** An adjective meaning perverse, crooked. It is used to describe the moral, religious, and social perversion and crookedness of Israel (Deut. 32:5). It is used of the perverse in general (2 Sam. 22:27; Ps. 18:26[27]; Prov. 2:15; 17:20). It is used to describe a deceitful, perverse heart, the source of evil (Ps. 101:4). The perversity of the rich destroys them (Prov. 28:6). Wisdom has no perverse or crooked way in her (Prov. 8:8); God hates the perverse (Prov. 11:20). A fool pours out perverse speech (Prov. 19:1).

6142. עִקֵּשׁ ***'iqqēš:*** A proper noun designating Ikkesh (2 Sam. 23:26; 1 Chr. 11:28; 27:9).

6143. עִקְּשׁוּת ***'iqq^{e}šûṯ:*** A feminine noun meaning perversion, deceitfulness. It is used to describe a mouth that speaks without integrity, that does not speak truth but rather deception and immorality; a mark of an evil, worthless person (Prov. 4:24; 6:12).

6144. עָר ***'ār:*** A proper noun designating Ar (Num. 21:15, 28; Deut. 2:9, 18, 29; Isa. 15:1).

6145. עָר ***'ār:*** A masculine noun meaning enemy. It refers to one who is hostile towards other persons, seeking to defeat them, to act against them (2 Sam. 28:16); in context the Lord had become Saul's adversary and accuser. In other contexts, it refers to enemies, adversaries of the Lord (Ps. 139:20).

6146. עָר ***'ār:*** An Aramaic masculine noun meaning enemy. It refers in context to those opposed to King Nebuchadnezzar, both in his kingdom and outside of it (Dan. 4:19[16]).

6147. עֵר ***'ēr:*** A proper noun designating Er:

A. Son of Judah (Gen. 38:3, 6, 7; 46:12; Num. 26:19; 1 Chr. 2:3).

B. Grandson of Judah (1 Chr. 4:21).

6148. עָרַב ***'āraḇ:*** A verb meaning to exchange, to take as a pledge, to give as a pledge. This word denotes the action of giving a pledge or a guarantee (Gen. 43:9); a pledge given in exchange for the delivery of material goods (2 Kgs. 18:23); the action of taking possession of exchanged material (Ezek. 27:9); and the mortgage of property (Neh. 5:3). By extension, it was used in reference to the scattering of the Jews among the nations (Ps. 106:35); and implied sharing or association at a meaningful level (Prov. 14:10; 20:19). In Jeremiah 30:21, it conveyed the idea of purposing or engaging to meet with the Lord.

6149. עָרֵב ***'āraḇ:*** A verb meaning to be sweet, to be pleasant. It asserts that something is acceptable, desired by someone, satisfying: David's meditation or contemplation (Ps. 104:34); sleep that is satisfying (Prov. 3:24); attaining one's goals (Prov. 13:19). It means to fit one's desires or tastes (Jer. 6:20). It is used of the pleasure Israel derived from her harlotries (Ezek. 16:37). Pleasing offerings to God were given by those with pure hearts toward Him (Mal. 3:4).

6150. עָרַב *'āraḇ:* A verb meaning to become evening; to grow dark. It refers to the close of the day, sunset, when it is becoming dark (Judg. 19:9). It has the meaning of doing something in the evening in its causative infinitive (1 Sam. 17:16). It is used figuratively of joy turning into or becoming subdued, silenced, (Isa. 24:11).

6151. עֲרַב *'araḇ:* An Aramaic verb meaning to mix, to mingle, to join together. Daniel used this word to describe the feet of the image Nebuchadnezzar saw in his dream (Dan. 2:41, 43). They were a curious mixture of clay and iron. Thus, the word implies an amalgamation of two uncomplementary materials, which is at best unstable.

6152. עֲרָב *'arāḇ*, עֲרַב *'araḇ:* A proper noun designating Arabia. This refers to traveling caravans through Israelite territory (1 Kgs. 10:15) and was a general term referring to the area from Aram (Syria) to the Arabian Desert (Ezek. 27:21). It seems to encompass the large Arabian peninsula at times. Solomon collected revenues from the people of the area. They lived and worked in a nomadic style of life, often in the desert (Isa. 21:13). Even these people would taste the judgments of the Lord (Jer. 25:24).

6153. עֶרֶב *'ereḇ:* A masculine noun referring to evening, dusk; night. It is used consistently to indicate the close of the day, evening, sunset. The phrase *lipnôt-'a\reḇ,* literally, the turning of the evening, means towards evening (Gen. 24:63; Deut. 23:11[12]). The term *bên ha\'arbayim* means between the evening, that is at dusk or at twilight (Ex. 12:6; 16:12; 30:8). *Le'eṯ 'ereḇ* means at the time of sunset, evening (Gen. 8:11). The phrase *ṣillê 'ereḇ* means shadows of evening (Jer. 6:4).

6154. עֵרֶב *'ēreḇ:* A masculine noun meaning a mixture, a mixed company, interwoven. The primary meaning is a grouping of people from various ethnic and cultural backgrounds. It was used of any heterogeneous band associated with the nation of Israel as it departed Egypt (Ex. 12:38); the tribes not aligned with any specific culture (Jer. 25:24); and the mingled people resulting from the Babylonian captivity (Jer. 50:37). By extension, the word was also used of interwoven material of varying fibers (Lev. 13:48).

6155. עֶרֶב *'ereḇ:* A masculine noun referring to a willow tree, a poplar tree. It is used to refer to particular trees: poplars (Isa. 44:4); willows (Lev. 23:40; Job 40:22; Ps. 137:2). It is given as a proper noun, brook of Arabim, by some translators

(NASB); the brook of the willows, by others (KJV) (Isa. 15:7).

6156. עָרֵב ***'ārēḇ:*** An adjective meaning sweet. It describes something tasting like sugar or honey, sweet and invigorating but is used figuratively of things obtained and enjoyed falsely (Prov. 20:17). In Song 2:14, it is used of the pleasant sound of the beloved's voice.

6157. עָרֹב ***'ārōḇ:*** A masculine noun referring to a swarm of flies (Ps. 78:45; 105:31). It is used exclusively of the insects involved in the fourth plague against Egypt (Ex. 8:29[25], 31[27]), a swarm of harmful and noxious insects (Ex. 8:21[17], 22[18], 24[20]).

6158. עֹרֵב ***'ōrēḇ:*** A masculine noun designating a raven. It refers to several species of large crows, given its name because of its cry, a harsh sound. It has a voracious appetite. It was considered unclean, not edible by Israelites (Lev. 11:15; Deut. 14:14). God feeds it (Job 38:41; Ps. 147:9); paradoxically, ravens fed Elijah, the man of God (1 Kgs. 17:4, 6), rather than eating the food themselves. It had both admirable (Song 5:11); and detestable characteristics (Prov. 30:17; Isa. 34:11).

6159. עוֹרֵב ***'ôrēḇ:*** A proper noun designating Oreb (Judg. 7:25; 8:3; Ps. 83:11[12]; Isa. 10:26).

6160. עֲרָבָה ***'arāḇāh:*** A feminine noun meaning a desert plain, a steppe, a wilderness. This word designates a prominent geographic feature of the Middle East. It is used to designate the arid plateau in south Judah (Isa. 51:3; see also 1 Sam. 23:24); various portions of the Jordan River valley and the adjacent plains (Josh. 12:1; 2 Sam. 2:29); the desert area in northern Arabia (Deut. 1:1); and any generic land formation similar to these arid plateaus (Deut. 1:7; Isa. 40:3). There is some uncertainty as to the use of this word in Psalm 68:4[5]. Most translations render the word as heavens or clouds, rather than the more literal meaning, desert.

6161. עֲרֻבָּה ***'arubbāh:*** A feminine noun meaning a pledge, a guarantee, a token. Occurring only twice in the Hebrew Bible, this word implies a tangible sign of a current or soon-expected reality. It was used specifically in reference to an assurance of well-being brought from the battlefield (1 Sam. 17:18); and a collateral exchanged at the making of a pledge (Prov. 17:18).

6162. עֵרָבוֹן ***'ērāḇôn:*** A masculine noun meaning pledge. It is a deposit given as evidence and proof that something else will be done. When the act is accomplished, the pledge is returned. Judah gave his seal and staff to Tamar, whom he believed was a temple prostitute, as a guarantee that he would return the next day so he might give her a young goat as payment for her services and then reacquire his seal and staff (Gen. 38:17,

18, 20). It is also probable that this word is what is meant in Job's reply to Eliphaz (see Job 17:3).

6163. עַרְבִי *'arḇiy*, עֲרָבִי *'ᵃrāḇiy*: A proper noun designating Arabian, an inhabitant of Arabia (2 Chr. 17:11; 21:16; 22:1; 26:7; Neh. 2:19; 4:7[1]; 6:1; Isa. 13:20; Jer. 3:2).

6164. עַרְבָתִי *'arḇāṯiy*: A proper noun designating Arbathite, an inhabitant of Beth Arabah (1026) (2 Sam. 23:31; 1 Chr. 11:32).

6165. עָרַג *'āraḡ*: A verb meaning to pant for, to long for. It is a passionate, emotional verb. It is used in emblematic poetry to depict a deer's longing for flowing brooks of water (Ps. 42:1[2]). It is used of languishing beasts of the field panting after God, their Creator (Joel 1:20).

6166. עֲרָד *'ᵃrāḏ*: A proper noun designating Arad:

A. A Canaanite king (Num. 21:1).
B. A Canaanite city (Judg. 1:16).
C. Son of Beriah (1 Chr. 8:15).

6167. עֲרָד *'ᵃrāḏ*: An Aramaic masculine noun meaning wild donkey. It refers to the wild ass that ran free in the wilderness. It is used in a passage to depict the extreme change that took place in Nebuchadnezzar's character. He then lived with the wild animals of the field (Dan. 5:21).

6168. עָרָה *'ārāh*: A verb meaning to expose, to uncover, to empty. It means to employ something, to pour something out: water from a vessel (Gen. 24:20); items from a chest or container (2 Chr. 24:11); pouring out one's soul, life (Isa. 53:12). It has the sense of something increasing, spreading out, permeating an area (Ps. 37:35); of emptying, tearing down, or razing (Ps. 137:7); of leaving someone without help, exposed to danger (Ps. 141:8). It indicates uncovering or making bare one's forehead (Isa. 3:17). It means to prepare a weapon for use, to uncover it (Isa. 22:6). It is used of not exposing a woman's menstrual flow for intercourse (Lev. 20:18, 19). It has the figurative sense of exposing oneself to destruction as a people, a nation (Lam. 4:21); as well as God's work in opening up a city to destruction (Zeph. 2:14). It indicates killing someone (Hab. 3:13).

6169. עָרוֹת *'ārôṯ*: A feminine plural noun referring to plants, bulrushes. It refers to marsh plants or to any plant growing in or around water that looks like a bulrush (Isa. 19:7). The Nile River was famous for these plants.

6170. עֲרוּגָה *'ᵃrûḡāh*: A feminine noun designating a garden bed, a plot. It refers to a cultivated bed of plants. It refers to a bed of balsam (Song 5:13; 6:2). It is used figuratively of the land, the country from which a nation would grow; here it refers to Jerusalem and Judah (Ezek. 17:7, 10).

6171. עָרוֹד *'ārôḏ*: A masculine noun meaning a wild donkey. It refers to a wild ass, a horselike animal that roamed wild in the wilderness under God's supervision alone (Job 39:5).

6172. עֶרְוָה ***'erwāh:*** A feminine noun expressing nakedness. This word can pertain to physical nakedness for either a man or a woman (Gen. 9:22, 23; Ex. 20:26); however, it is more often used in a figurative sense. When used with the verbs *gālāh* (1540), meaning to uncover or remove, and *rā'āh* (7200), meaning to see, one finds a common euphemism for sexual relations—to uncover one's nakedness (Lev. 18:6; 20:17). On the other hand, when combined with the verb *kāsāh* (3680), meaning to cover, one finds a common idiom for entering into a marriage contract (Ezek. 16:8). Nakedness is also a symbol of the shame and disgrace of Egypt (Isa. 20:4); Babylonia (Isa. 47:3); and Jerusalem (Ezek. 16:37). Furthermore, when in construct with *dāḇār* (1697), meaning a word, matter, or thing, this term forms an idiom for indecent or improper behavior (Deut. 23:14[15]; 24:1). When in construct with the word *'ereṣ* (776), it can refer to exposed or undefended areas (Gen. 42:9, 12).

6173. עַרְוָה ***'arwāh:*** An Aramaic feminine noun indicating dishonor. It refers to a show of disrespect or a loss of wealth and influence. In context it refers to the loss of revenues from the province of Judah (Ezra 4:14).

6174. עָרוֹם ***'ārôm:*** An adjective meaning naked. It can allude to physical nakedness (Gen. 2:25; 1 Sam. 19:24; Isa. 20:2–4). It can also be used figuratively to relate to one who has no possessions (Job 1:21; Eccl. 5:15 [14]). Moreover, Sheol is described as being naked before God, a statement of its openness and vulnerability to God and His power (Job 26:6).

6175. עָרוּם ***'ārûm:*** An adjective meaning crafty, shrewd, sensible. This adjective can have either a positive or negative connotation. In a positive connotation, it is understood as being prudent. As such, a prudent individual takes no offense at an insult (Prov. 12:16); does not flaunt his knowledge (Prov. 12:23); takes careful thought of his ways (Prov. 14:8); takes careful thought before action (Prov. 14:15); is crowned with knowledge (Prov. 14:18); and sees and avoids danger (Prov. 22:3; 27:12). When the word has a negative meaning, it means being crafty (Job 5:12; 15:5). This word is used when the Bible describes the serpent in the Garden of Eden. The serpent was more subtle [crafty] than any beast of the field (Gen. 3:1). This description is presented in stark contrast to the situation of Adam and Eve. They sought to be crafty like the serpent, but they only realized that they were *'ēyrōm* (5903), meaning naked.

6176. עֲרוֹעֵר ***'ᵃrô'ēr:*** A masculine noun referring to a tree, a bush; juniper. It refers to some kind of desert bush or shrub. Its isolation in the desert is used to make a point in a simile (Jer. 17:6). It possibly refers to a juniper bush in both references (Jer. 48:6).

6177. עֲרוֹעֵר *ᵃrô'ēr,* עֲרֹעֵר *ᵃrō'ēr,* עַרְעוֹר ***'ar'ôr:*** A proper noun designating Arnon

A. A city on the Arnon River in Transjordan. It was located near the Arnon Gorge (2 Kgs. 10:33). The river was the southern border of Sihon's kingdom. The city was inherited by the tribe of Reuben (Josh. 12:2; 13:9, 16; 1 Chr. 5:8). The Gadites had helped construct the city (Num. 32:34). In the time of Jephthah, Israel had owned the city for three hundred years (Judg. 11:26). Jeremiah mentions the effect of God's judgments on its inhabitants (Jer. 48:19).

B. A city near Rabbah (Josh. 13:25).

C. A city in southern Judah (1 Sam. 30:28).

6178. עָרוּץ *'ārûṣ:* I. A feminine noun indicating a cliff. It is variously translated as cliff (KJV), clefts (NKJV), dreadful (NASB), dry (NIV) (Job 30:6). Its exact meaning is not yet clear. See II, III.

II. An adjective meaning dreadful. It refers to valleys not suitable for habitation (Job 30:6). See I, III.

III. An adjective meaning dry. It refers to dry, temporary streambeds (Job 30:6; NIV). See I, II.

6179. עֵרִי *'ēriy:* A proper noun designating Eri (Gen. 46:16; Num. 26:16).

6180. עֵרִי *'ēriy:* A proper noun designating Erite, a descendant of Eri (6179) (Num. 26:16).

6181. עֶרְיָה *'eryāh:* A feminine noun meaning nakedness. This term is only used figuratively. It can function as a metaphor for shame and disgrace. In the allegory of unfaithful Jerusalem, God stated that Jerusalem was naked and bare, *'ērōm* (5903) *wᵉ'eryāh* (Ezek. 16:7). The inhabitants of Shaphir were considered to be in the nakedness of shame, *'eryāh b̲ōšet̲* (1322) (Mic. 1:11). It is also used to indicate the outpouring of God's wrath on the earth by the allusion to God's bow being naked or uncovered, meaning that it was taken from its storage place and put to use (Hab. 3:9).

6182. עֲרִיסָה *ᵃrisāh:* A feminine noun meaning dough, ground meal. It refers to some kind of dough or course meal from which cakes or bread was baked, especially as offerings (Num. 15:20, 21; Neh. 10:37[38]; Ezek. 44:30).

6183. עֲרִיפִים *ᵃriyp̱iym:* A masculine noun meaning cloud. Isaiah used this word when he pronounced God's judgments on Israel by means of foreign nations. He stated that the judgment would be so severe that there would be only darkness and distress; there would be no light, as when storm clouds block out the light (Isa. 5:30).

6184. עָרִיץ ***'āriyṣ:*** An adjective meaning ruthless, strong, violent. It refers to a ruler, a master, or anyone who behaves ruthlessly toward his subjects: tyrants (Job 6:23; 27:13; Isa. 29:20; Ezek. 31:12; 32:12); a ruthless person (Job 15:20). It indicates a person of insolence, violence (Ps. 37:35; 54:3[5]). A ruthless person is proud, haughty (Isa. 13:11). The Lord is a mighty man of violence or ruthlessness, a dreaded master (Jer. 20:11). Nations and peoples may be termed ruthless, violent (Ezek. 28:7; 30:11).

6185. עֲרִירִי ***'ăriyriy:*** An adjective meaning childless. It describes Abraham, who was childless (Gen. 15:2; Jer. 22:30); it is used for both a man or a woman (Lev. 20:20, 21).

6186. עָרַךְ ***'āraḵ:*** I. A verb meaning to arrange, to set in order, to prepare. It is used of arranging or preparing something for various reasons. As a technical military term, it means to prepare for battle, to get in battle array (Gen. 14:8); to be ready, to set up for battle (Jer. 6:23; Joel 2:5); to organize, to lay something out in order (Gen. 22:9; Lev. 24:8; Num. 23:4); to dress lamps, to care for them (Ex. 27:21); to arrange items on a table (Ex. 40:4, 23; Isa. 21:5). It is used figuratively of the terrors or words of the Lord set out, prepared against someone (Job 6:4; 32:14); of preparing an argument or legal case (Job 13:18). It describes the presentation of prayer to the Lord (Ps. 5:3[4]); of the Lord's preparation of a meal, a table for His children (Ps. 23:5; 78:19). It is used of Lady Wisdom's preparation of a table of wisdom for those who seek her (Prov. 9:2). The word is used to describe what has been prepared by God, Topheth, a place of human sacrifice (Isa. 30:33).

II. A verb meaning to set a value, to lend a tax. It describes the process of a priest setting a value on someone or something (Lev. 27:8, 12, 14); as well as the process of leveling a tax evaluation and collection on a people (2 Kgs. 23:35).

6187. עֵרֶךְ ***'ēreḵ:*** A masculine noun meaning an estimation, an evaluation, a value, an arrangement in order. It refers to a set order for something or what is to be placed into a set arrangement (Ex. 40:4, 23). It refers to the orderly construction or build of a body or its structure (Job 41:12[4]). It is used of an evaluation or price, a value placed on something (Lev. 5:15, 18; 6:6[5:25]; 27:2–8; Job 28:13). It refers to wages or keep, a maintenance for someone (Judg. 17:10); and to an assessment of money laid on someone (2 Kgs. 12:4[5]). It indicates something equal to or like something or someone else (Ps. 55:13[14]).

6188. עָרֵל ***'ārēl:*** A verb meaning to consider uncircumcised, forbidden; to be exposed. It indicates setting something aside or apart as not available for regular use, in this case, unharvested fruit (Lev. 19:23). In the context of Habakkuk, it has the sense of exposing one's nakedness, treating oneself in an uncircumcised, forbidden way (Hab. 2:16).

6189. עָרֵל ***'ārēl:*** A masculine adjective meaning uncircumcised. In the literal sense, it was used to designate a specific individual (Gen. 17:14; Ex. 12:48); a group (Josh. 5:7); or a nation, especially the Philistines (1 Sam. 14:6; Isa. 52:1). In addition to the simple statement of physical condition, the term could also convey an attitude of derision since the object was considered unclean and impure (Judg. 14:3; 15:18). Furthermore, the term could be used metaphorically to describe the corrupted nature of certain body parts: uncircumcised lips denoted an inability to speak effectively (Ex. 6:12, 30; cf. Isa. 6:5); uncircumcised in heart represented a flawed character and precluded entrance to the Temple (Ezek. 44:7, 9); and uncircumcised in the ear signified an inability to hear (Jer. 6:10). Also, the fruit of newly planted trees was considered uncircumcised (unclean) for the first three years (Lev. 19:23).

6190. עָרְלָה ***'orlāh:*** A feminine noun meaning foreskin. The word could represent just the foreskin (Gen. 17:11; 1 Sam. 18:25, 27); the state of being uncircumcised (having a foreskin [Gen. 34:14]); or the act of circumcision (cutting off the foreskin [Ex. 4:25]). Like the word *'ārēl* (6189), this term could be used figuratively to represent the impure nature of fruit trees (Lev. 19:23); or the human heart (Deut. 10:16; Jer. 4:4).

6191. עָרַם ***'āram:*** A verb meaning to be shrewd, to be subtle. This verb has a neutral tone but can assume either a negative tone: crafty and tricky (1 Sam. 23:22; Ps. 83:3[4]); or a positive tone: prudent and wise (Prov. 15:5; 19:25).

6192. עָרַם ***'āram:*** A verb meaning to be heaped up. This verb occurs once in the Hebrew Bible in Exodus 15:8. In Moses' song at the sea, he describes God's miraculous act by singing about how the waters were heaped up.

6193. עֹרֶם ***'ōrem:*** A masculine singular noun meaning craftiness. Its only use in the Hebrew Bible is in the book of Job. Eliphaz told Job that God catches the wise in their craftiness. He cannot be fooled (Job 5:13). See the verb *'āram* (6191).

6194. עֲרֵמָה ***ᵃrēmāh:*** A feminine noun meaning a heap, a pile. It refers to a pile or heap of grain, wheat, fruit, rubble (Ruth 3:7; 2 Chr. 31:6–9; Neh. 4:2[3:34]; Hag. 2:16). It describes the healthy, amorous appearance of the bride's belly (Song 7:2[3]). It is used figuratively again of overthrowing Babylon into heaps (Jer. 50:26).

6195. עָרְמָה ***'ormāh:*** A feminine singular noun meaning craftiness, prudence. Exodus 21:14 employs it adverbially (schemes craftily) as does Joshua 9:4, where the foreign kings tricked Joshua into making a treaty. In Proverbs, the word has a different connotation. Both in the instruction for a son (Prov. 1:4) and in describing Lady Wisdom who has *'ormāh* with her (Prov. 8:5, 12), the term is best translated prudence. See the verb *'āram* (6191).

6196. עַרְמוֹן ***'armôn:*** A masculine noun identifying a chestnut tree, a plane tree. It refers to a tree from the plane tree family, a broad-leafed tree with maple-like leaves (Gen. 30:37) and large branches (Ezek. 31:8).

6197. עֵרָן ***'ērān:*** A proper noun designating Eran (Num. 26:36).

6198. עֵרָנִי ***'ērāniy:*** A proper noun designating Eranite, a descendant of Eran (6197) (Num. 26:36).

6199. עַרְעָר ***'ar'ār:*** I. An adjective meaning destitute. It indicates a person who is poor, without money, house, or home (Ps. 102:17[18]). For Jeremiah 17:6, see II.

II. A masculine noun meaning bush. It refers to a bush or a shrub living in the desert or dry wilderness. It is used to compare a person who trusts only in people to this hopeless, isolated shrub (Jer. 17:6).

6200. עֲרֹעֵרִי ***^{a}rō'ēriy:*** A proper noun designating Aroerite, an inhabitant of Aroer (6177) (1 Chr. 11:44).

6201. עָרַף ***'ārap:*** A verb translated to drip, to drop. In Moses' final blessing of Israel, he says they would experience God's security and bounty where His heavens drop dew (Deut. 33:28). In Moses' final song, he prayed that his teaching would drop like rain on his listeners (Deut. 32:2). See the nominal form of this root, *^{a}rāpel* (6205), which means cloud.

6202. עָרַף ***'ārap:*** A verb meaning to break the neck. It is used of breaking the neck of an animal (Ex. 13:13; 34:20; Deut. 21:4, 6; Isa. 66:3), especially the firstborn of a donkey. It is used once of breaking down altars (Hos. 10:2).

6203. עֹרֶף ***'ōrep:*** A masculine noun meaning neck; back. It refers to the back of a person's neck or a neck in general (Gen. 49:8; Lev. 5:8). It is used in the statement to turn one's back to, to flee from (Ex. 23:27; Josh. 7:8, 12; 2 Sam. 22:41; Jer. 2:27). A stiff neck indicates an obstinate, stubborn attitude, a rebellious person or people (Ex. 32:9; 33:3; Deut. 9:6; 31:27). God's turning His back to His people indicates His displeasure (Jer. 18:17). Israel's turning their backs to God indicates their apostasy (Jer. 2:27; 32:33). To turn the back may demonstrate shame (Jer. 48:39).

6204. עָרְפָּה *'orpāh:* A proper noun designating Orpah (Ruth 1:4, 14).

6205. עֲרָפֶל *'ᵃrāpel:* A masculine singular noun meaning cloud. A cloud enshrouded God (Ex. 20:21; Job 22:13); and also served as His pedestal (2 Sam. 22:10; Ps. 18:9[10]). The term is used figuratively to depict a stormy sea that has clouds for a garment (Job 38:9). Prophetic pictures of God's judgment are filled with clouds, darkening the ominous Day of the Lord (Jer. 13:16; Ezek. 34:12; Joel 2:2; Zeph. 1:15).

6206. עָרַץ *'āraṣ:* A verb which means to tremble, to cause to tremble, to strike with awe, to strike with dread. The Lord's splendor can make the earth tremble (Isa. 2:19, 21). Job wondered why God must overwhelm humans who are nothing more than driven leaves (Job 13:25). God and His leaders continually reminded the Israelites before battle not to be terrified by the enemy because God who would fight for them (Deut. 1:29; 7:21; 20:3; 31:6; Josh. 1:9). If God is with us, we have no need to dread humans and their conspiracies and plots (Isa. 8:12).

6207. עָרַק *'āraq:* I. A verb meaning to gnaw. It means to nibble, to chew on something incessantly to get food from it (Job 30:3). It is used figuratively of pains that weaken, tear away at a person (Job 30:17).

II. A verb meaning to flee, to roam. A verb meaning to wander about aimlessly. It is used of outcasts of society wandering about searching for food (Job 30:3).

III. A masculine noun indicating that which is gnawed; sinews. It refers to tendons or muscular power, strength, or a person's strength in spirit and soul. Job's strength was continually being worn away by his suffering (Job 30:17).

6208. עַרְקִי *'arqiy:* A proper noun designating Arkite (Gen. 10:17; 1 Chr. 1:15).

6209. עָרַר *'ārar:* I. A verb meaning to strip off, to undress oneself; to raze. It indicates the complete destruction, stripping, and demolishing of a city or nation, especially its most splendid features, its palaces and walls (Isa. 23:13; Jer. 51:58). Prisoners of war were stripped of their luxurious garments (Isa. 32:11).

II. A verb meaning to raise up. It is translated as raised up since the translators understand a different contextual milieu (Isa. 23:13).

6210. עֶרֶשׂ *'ereś:* A masculine noun signifying a couch, a bed, a bedstead. It refers to a place for resting, sleeping (Deut. 3:11); a place of comfort and refreshment (Job 7:13); but at times a place of sorrow and weeping (Ps. 6:6[7]). The Lord is with those who are sick on their beds (Ps. 41:3[4]). It refers to a couch of enticement prepared by a harlot (Prov.

7:16); but a place of true love and pleasure to a bride and bridegroom (Song 1:16). Beds of ivory were enjoyed by the rich (Amos 6:4).

6211. עָשׁ ***'āš:*** A masculine noun indicating a moth. It refers to a rather fragile but destructive four-winged insect. The fragility of human life is indicated by the fact that a moth can destroy houses of earth or clay, that is people made of clay (Job 4:19). These insects were known to be destructive (Job 13:28), eating human clothing and garments. It is used in a metaphor speaking of Job's body and in other similes (Ps. 39:11[12]). Figuratively, it describes the consuming of the enemies of Isaiah (Isa. 50:9; 51:8). The Lord pictures Himself as a moth consuming Ephraim in a time of judgment (Hos. 5:12).

6212. עֵשֶׂב ***'ēśeḇ,*** עֲשַׂב ***ᵃsaḇ:*** I. A masculine noun indicating grass, plants, herbs. In a broad sense, it includes all green growth, including grass of the field (Gen. 3:18; Ex. 9:22). It is used of food for cattle (Deut. 11:15; Ps. 106:20); and, excluding grass, of food for people (Gen. 3:18). For grass, see *deše'*. The phrase *'eśeḇ zôrêᵃ' zera'* indicates seed-bearing plants (Gen. 1:29). The frailty of grass depicts a fragile, failing heart (Ps. 102:4[5]). The days of a person pass quickly like grass (Ps. 102:11[12]). It is used in an inclusive sense of all the green plants of the earth (Ps. 72:16).

II. An Aramaic masculine noun meaning grass. It is a collective noun referring to all green growth. It describes the earth (Dan. 4:15[12]). Grass is not for human consumption but for animals (Dan. 4:25[22]; 5:21).

6213. עָשָׂה ***'āśāh:*** A verb meaning to do, to make, to accomplish, to complete. This frequently used Hebrew verb conveys the central notion of performing an activity with a distinct purpose, a moral obligation, or a goal in view (cf. Gen. 11:6). Particularly, it was used in conjunction with God's commands (Deut. 16:12). It described the process of construction (Gen. 13:4; Job 9:9; Prov. 8:26); engaging in warfare (Josh. 11:18); the yielding of grain (Hos. 8:7); observing a religious ceremony (Ex. 31:16; Num. 9:4); and the completion of something (Ezra 10:3; Isa. 46:10). Provocatively, the word appears twice in Ezekiel to imply the intimate action of caressing or fondling the female breast (Ezek. 23:3, 8).

6214. עֲשָׂהאֵל ***ᵃśāh'ēl:*** A proper noun designating Asahel:

A. A son of Zeriah, David's sister. His name means "God has done/made." He was killed by Abner, son of Ner, Saul's military commander (2 Sam. 2:8, 18–23). He was the brother of Joab, David's military commander. He killed Abner because of his murder of Asahel (2 Sam. 3:27, 30). He was one of David's mighty men (2 Sam. 23:24).

B. The father of Jonathan who opposed Ezra's plans to deal with intermarriages (Ezra 10:15).

C. One of the men Jehoshaphat appointed to teach the Law of God throughout Judah (2 Chr. 17:8).

D. A Levite whom Hezekiah appointed to oversee the collection of tithes in the Temple (2 Chr. 31:13).

6215. עֵשָׂו ***'ēśāw:*** A proper noun designating Esau, the elder twin brother of Jacob (Gen. 25:25–30). The Lord revealed the general outline of Esau's life to Rebekah before the twins were born (Gen. 25:23). The elder would serve the younger. Both would father a nation. Esau foolishly sold his birthright to Jacob for food (Gen. 25:30–31). He received his secondary name, Edom, because of the "red stew" that he purchased from Jacob. Esau considered his birthright of little value (Gen. 25:34). He was the favored son of Isaac. He was a hairy man, and Jacob deceived him and received his blessing from Isaac on his deathbed (Gen. 27:1–33). But Isaac also gave Esau a secondary blessing (Gen. 27:39–40). Esau and Jacob were reconciled after Jacob's long absence from his father's house (Gen. 33). Esau's descendants were numerous (Gen. 35:1–43). He went to the mountainous territory of Seir to settle (Gen. 36:8–9). There he became the father of the Edomites after marrying Canaanite wives, Adah and Oholibamah (Gen. 36:2).

6216. עָשׁוֹק ***'āšôq:*** A masculine noun meaning oppressor. It refers to a person guilty of troubling or wearing out another person, crushing him or her (Jer. 22:3).

6217. עֲשׁוּקִים ***ᵃšûqiym:*** A masculine plural noun referring to oppressions. Oppression weighs down a person with physical or mental distress (Job 35:9); causing the oppressed to weep and mourn (Eccl. 4:1). Samaria was filled with many oppressions, physical, political, military, or economic (Amos 3:9).

6218. עָשׂוֹר ***'āśôr:*** A masculine noun meaning ten, tenth, ten-stringed instruments. It refers to a collection of ten things: days (Gen. 24:55); ten strings arranged to produce music (Ps. 33:2; 92:3[4]; 144:9). It is used as an ordinal number to designate a tenth day, a tenth month, etc. in what is called a date formula (Josh. 4:19; 2 Kgs. 25:1; Jer. 52:4, 12).

6219. עָשׁוֹת ***'āšôṯ:*** I. An adjective meaning wrought iron. It is listed as trade merchandise between Tyre and Javan (Greece) (Ezek. 27:19).

II. An adjective indicating bright. Most recent translators prefer to render this word as wrought when coupled with iron (Ezek. 27:19) but not the NIV, NKJV which render it as wrought iron. It was a valuable trade commodity between Tyre and Javan (Greece).

6220. עַשְׁוָת ***'ašwāṯ:*** A proper noun designating Ashvath (1 Chr. 7:33).

6221. עֲשִׂיאֵל ***ᵃśiy'ēl:*** A proper noun designating Asiel (1 Chr. 4:35).

6222. עֲשָׂיָה ***ʿaśāyāh:*** A proper noun designating Asaiah (2 Kgs. 22:12, 14; 1 Chr. 4:36; 6:30[15]; 9:5; 15:6, 11; 2 Chr. 34:20).

6223. עָשִׁיר ***ʿāšiyr:*** A masculine noun meaning rich. It refers to wealthy, well-to-do persons with significant power and influence socially and politically. It is the opposite of *dal,* poor, without means (2 Sam. 12:1, 2, 4). The rich were a significant social group in Israel (Ex. 30:15; Ruth 3:10). The strength of rich people lie in their wealth (Prov. 10:15; 18:11); it sustains them. The rich have many superficial friends (Prov. 14:20). The Suffering Servant of Isaiah would lie with the rich at his death (Isa. 53:9). Rich people are not to brag about their wealth, for it is given by God (Jer. 9:23[22]).

6224. עֲשִׂירִי ***ʿaśiyriy:*** A numerical adjective indicating a tenth, one-tenth. It is an ordinal number used to indicate the tenth of a series (Gen. 8:5; 1 Chr. 12:13; Zech. 8:19); or a tenth part of something (Ex. 16:36); a tenth generation (Deut. 23:3[4]).

6225. עָשַׁן ***ʿāšan:*** A verb meaning to smoke, to be angry, to be furious. The literal meaning of this Hebrew word is to smolder or smoke (Ex. 19:18; Ps. 144:5). Metaphorically, it was used by the psalmist to convey the idea of fuming anger (Ps. 74:1; 80:4[5]).

6226. עָשֵׁן ***ʿāšēn:*** An adjective meaning smoking, smoldering. It indicates that something is smoking, has smoke coming off of it or out of it. It is used of Mount Sinai when God descended on it (Ex. 20:18); and to logs that are burnt up, used up but still smoking. In the latter case, it is used figuratively of political leaders (Isa. 7:4).

6227. עָשָׁן ***ʿāšān:*** A masculine noun referring to smoke. Smoke is a vaporous matter with suspended particles of carbon in it, arising from something burning. It is a feature of a mysterious smoking oven at the time God made a covenant with Abraham (Gen. 15:17); and was a part of the theophany at Mount Sinai, created because of God's presence (Ex. 19:18). It is also used in figurative depictions of the Lord going forth in battle or in anger (2 Sam. 22:9); as well as in God's depiction of Leviathan's nostrils (Job 41:20[12]). Its quick dissipation is used in similes and metaphors (Ps. 37:20; 68:2[3]; Prov. 10:26; Hos. 13:3). Smoke is a feature of the Day of the Lord (Joel 2:30[3:3]).

6228. עָשָׁן ***ʿāšān:*** A proper noun designating Ashan (Josh. 15:42; 19:7; 1 Chr. 4:32; 6:59[44]).

6229. עָשַׂק ***ʿāśaq:*** A verb meaning to strive, to contend. It means to argue with, to fight over something, to make claims and counterclaims (Gen. 26:20).

6230. עֵשֶׂק ***ʿēśeq:*** A proper noun designating Esek (Gen. 26:20).

6231. עָשַׁק ***'āšaq:*** A verb meaning to oppress, to defraud. It refers to extorting or exploiting someone (Lev. 6:2[5:21], 4[5:23]), especially a servant. It has the sense of cheating or robbing in some contexts (Lev. 19:13); keeping what is rightfully someone else's. A righteous person does not oppress or exploit another person (1 Sam. 12:3, 4). Job thought that God was oppressing him (Job 10:3). God will curse the one who oppresses others (Ps. 72:4; 105:14). To oppress another person is to abuse, to revile one's Creator (Prov. 14:31). Even the poor may be oppressors. (Prov. 28:3). It is used to designate the guilt of blood on a person (Prov. 28:17). In its passive usage, it refers to a person who is abused or defrauded in some way (Isa. 23:12). The prophets spoke strongly against the oppressors of the poor (Amos 4:1; Mic. 2:2; Zech. 7:10; Mal. 3:5).

6232. עֵשֶׁק ***'ēšeq:*** A proper noun designating Eshek (1 Chr. 8:39).

6233. עֹשֶׁק ***'ōšeq:*** A masculine noun meaning oppression, extortion. It refers to defrauding, robbing persons of what is theirs; denying justice to the poor, the laborer, the slave, the widow, the orphan. Extortion or robbery, keeping what is another's is often in mind (Lev. 6:4[5:23]). Oppression can be personal, political, military (Eccl. 5:8[7]; Isa. 54:14). Oppression is not to be a way of life for God's people (Ps. 62:10[11]). Oppression or fraud is not the mark of a righteous person (Ezek. 18:18).

6234. עָשְׁקָה ***'ošqāh:*** A feminine noun meaning distress, oppression. It has the same meanings discussed in 6233 above. In context it is used of a person weighted down by sickness, illness (Isa. 38:14).

6235. עֶשֶׂר ***'eśer,*** עֲשָׂרָה ***^{a}śārāh:*** A feminine, masculine numerical adjective and counting number meaning ten. It indicates a number of items equaling ten (Gen. 5:14; 45:23): animals, donkeys, cities, cubits, days, etc. Its masculine form is *^{a}śarāh.* Exodus 18:21, 25 refers to captains/heads (over) tens. It may be used with other numbers either preceding or following them (Gen. 5:14; Ezra 8:12; Jer. 32:9; Ezek. 45:12). A period of time equaling ten days is possibly an idiom (Dan. 1:12, 14, 15). The phrase *'eśer yā<u>d</u>ô<u>t</u>* meaning ten times, is a hyperbolic expression indicating greatly (Dan. 1:20).

6236. עֲשַׂר ***^{a}śar,*** עַשְׂרָה ***'aśrāh:*** A feminine, masculine Aramaic numerical adjective. It indicates a collection of items numbering ten (Dan. 7:7, 20, 24). The phrase *t^{e}rê-^{a}śar* means twelve (Ezra 6:17; Dan. 4:29[26]).

6237. עָשַׂר ***'āśar:*** A verb meaning to give a tenth part, to take a tenth part, to give the tithe, to receive the tithe. This pivotal Hebrew word first appears in reference to a vow made by Jacob (Gen. 28:22). He promised to return one-tenth of his possessions to the Lord if the Lord would go with him. Under the Law given by Moses, this tithe was made mandatory on all increase (Deut. 14:22; see also Deut. 26:12). It was the duty of the priest to receive these tithes (Neh. 10:37[38], 38[39]). Samuel also used this word to describe the taxes imposed by a king (1 Sam. 8:15, 17).

6238. עָשַׁר ***'āšar:*** A verb meaning to be rich, to become rich. It means to be or to become wealthy in money, possessions, or influence. Its simple meaning is to become rich; it describes an arrogant Ephraim, a self-seeking country (Hos. 12:8[9]). It also has the sense of making someone else rich (Gen. 14:23); especially regarding the Lord who makes a person poor or rich (1 Sam. 2:7). It is used of making oneself rich, obtaining riches (Ps. 49:16[17]; Prov. 21:17; Dan. 11:2; Jer. 5:27). It is used figuratively of a city obtaining riches (Ezek. 27:33). It has the sense of persons enriching themselves (Prov. 13:7).

6239. עֹשֶׁר ***'ōšer:*** A noun referring to wealth, riches. It describes all kinds of wealth in land, possessions, cattle, and descendants (Gen. 31:16; 1 Kgs. 3:13; Esth. 1:4; Prov. 14:24; Jer. 9:23[22]). It is used with the verb *'āśāh 'ōšer,* meaning to make money, riches (Jer. 17:11).

6240. עָשָׂר ***'āśār:*** A numerical noun, an adjective, ten, used in combination with other numerals from eleven to nineteen. Used with masculine nouns, *'aḥaḏ 'aśār,* eleven (Gen. 32:22[23]). With feminine nouns, it has a companion form *'eśrēh,* e.g., *ḥᵃmēš 'eśrēh,* fifteen (years) (Gen. 5:10). It is used both as a cardinal (counting) number and an ordinal number. Hence, *'aḥaṯ 'eśrēh,* eleven (feminine) *'aḥaḏ 'āśār* (masculine); *'aštê 'āšar,* eleven (masculine) (Num. 29:20), *'aštê 'eśrēh,* eleven (feminine) (Ex. 26:7). The numbers are followed by the nouns being numbered in the singular but also in the plural. If they follow the noun, the noun is in the plural form (Josh. 15:36; Ezra 8:35).

6241. עִשָּׂרוֹן ***'iśśārôn:*** A masculine noun designating one-tenth. It refers to a tenth part of something: one-tenth of an ephah (Ex. 29:40); three-tenths of an ephah (Lev. 14:10).

6242. עֶשְׂרִים ***'eśriym:*** A plural number, adjective, noun. It designates twenty items of a group or one twentieth of something: twenty years (Gen. 6:3). It is used with other numbers to form larger numbers (Gen. 11:24). It is used as an ordinal number to represent the twentieth of something, in the twentieth year (1 Kgs. 15:9), with its noun before it in the construct form and state.

6243. עֶשְׂרִין ***'eśriyn:*** An Aramaic plural number, noun; adjective meaning twenty. It is used once in the larger number one hundred and twenty (Dan. 6:1[2]) where it is connected to one hundred (*mᵉ'āh*) with a waw, *wᵉ*.

6244. עָשֵׁשׁ *'āšēš:* A verb meaning to waste away. It is from the same root as moth, *'āś*. It refers to the deterioration or destruction of something: people's eyes, their sight (Ps. 6:7[8]; 31:9[10]); their bodies (Ps. 31:10[11]).

6245. עָשַׁת *'āšaṯ:* I. A verb meaning to shine, to excel. The word means to become slick in actions, in excelling at something (Jer. 5:28).

II. A verb meaning to think about, to be concerned about. It means to care for someone or something, especially regarding God in response to prayer (Jon. 1:6).

6246. עֲשִׁת *'ašiṯ*, עֲשִׁית *'ašiyṯ:* An Aramaic verb meaning to think about, to plan. It indicates consideration given to doing something, an intention to do something (Dan. 6:3[4]).

6247. עֶשֶׁת *'ešeṯ:* A masculine noun indicating a polishing, a carving. It refers in context to the external appearance of the bridegroom's stomach as if it were made of carved ivory (Song 5:14).

6248. עַשְׁתּוּת *'aštûṯ:* A feminine plural noun referring to plans, thoughts. Its use seems to require the meaning of thought or attitude. It refers to the attitude of those at ease, people who were not disturbed (Job 12:5).

6249. עַשְׁתֵּי *'aštēy:* A numerical form in a noun or adjective construction meaning eleven. It is the form that combines with *'āśār* to render eleven or eleventh (Ex. 26:7; 2 Kgs. 25:2).

6250. עֶשְׁתֹּנָה *'eštōnāh:* A feminine plural noun indicating a thought, a plan. It refers to the ideas, imaginations, desires produced by a person while alive (Ps. 146:4).

6251. עַשְׁתְּרוֹת *'ašt^erôṯ:* I. A feminine plural noun indicating lambs, young (sheep). It is used of young sheep or goats of a flock (Deut. 7:13; 28:4, 18, 51), no more than three years old. In context these frail animals are blessed by God, a key to Israel's success.

II. A feminine plural noun referring to flocks (of sheep). It refers to the flocks born and blessed by God (Deut. 7:13; 28:4, 18, 51).

6252. עַשְׁתָּרוֹת *'aštārôṯ:* A. A feminine proper noun Astoroth; a Canaanite false goddess. This was a pagan Canaanite goddess of love, war, and fertility, also called Astarte. Israel often apostatized from the Lord and worshiped her (Judg. 2:13; 10:6; 1 Sam. 7:3, 4; 12:10). See 6253.

B. A feminine proper noun Astaroth; a city in Manasseh, the same as *'ašt^eroṯ qarnayim* (6255). It was the capital city of Og, king of Bashan, and was given to the tribe of Manasseh (Deut. 1:4; Josh. 9:10; 12:4; 13:12, 31; 1 Chr. 6:71[56]). It was located west of the Sea of Galilee.

6253. עַשְׁתֹּרֶת *'aštōreṯ:* A feminine proper noun Ashtoreth; a Phoenician goddess. A pagan Canaanite goddess (see 6252) of love, war, fertility. She was worshiped especially by the Sidonians (1 Kgs. 11:5; 2 Kgs. 23:13).

6254. עַשְׁתְּרָתִי *'ašt^e rāṯiy:* A proper noun designating Ashterathite; inhabitant of Ashtaroth (6252,B) (1 Chr. 11:44).

6255. עַשְׁתְּרֹת קַרְנַיִם *'ašt^e rōṯ qarnayim:* A proper noun designating Ashteroth Karnaim; city in Manasseh; same as Astaroth (6252,B) (Gen. 14:5).

6256. עֵת *'ēṯ:* A masculine or feminine noun meaning time. The word basically means time. But in context, it expresses many aspects of time and kinds of time. It is used most often to express the time of the occurrence of some event. The word means at that time in a general sense, as when Abimelech and Phicol spoke to Abraham during the days when Ishmael was growing up (Gen. 21:22; 38:1). The time described can be more specific, such as when Moses refers to the time of crisis in the wilderness when the people wanted meat to eat (Deut. 1:9). It may refer to a specific date (Ex. 9:18; 1 Sam. 9:16); or a part of a day, as when the dove returned to Noah in the evening (Gen. 8:11; 24:11). The word can refer to a duration of time, as for all time (Ex. 18:22; Prov. 8:30); or for any time in general (Lev. 16:2). The time referred to may be past, present, or future (Num. 23:23; Judg. 13:23; Isa. 9:1[8:23]). The word can describe times of the Lord's anger (Ps. 21:9[10]); or times of trouble (Ps. 9:9[10]). In fact, this word can be made to refer to about any kind of time or duration of time by its modifying words and context.

It is used to describe the time when certain appropriate things took place in general. For example, kings customarily went forth to war in the spring (2 Sam. 11:1; 1 Chr. 20:1). It can depict times that are fitting or suitable for certain reasons, such as rain falling on the land in its season (Deut. 11:14; Jer. 5:24); and fruit trees bearing fruit at the proper time (Ps. 1:3). The author of Proverbs 15:23 spoke of a proper time for fitting words. Ecclesiastes 3 described all of life as a grand mosaic of times and seasons; there is a time to do everything—to be born, to die, to plant, to uproot, to kill, to heal, to love, to hate (Eccl. 3:1– 3, 8). This word occurs nineteen times in these verses (Eccl. 3:1–8), along with a synonym of this word, *z^e mān* (2165), to make twenty references to time.

The Hebrew word can be used to designate a time even more accurately. When the exiles returned, it was time for the house of the Lord to be rebuilt (Hag. 1:2). The word designated the set time of marriage (1 Sam. 18:19). It pinpointed the time of God's judgments (Isa. 13:22; Ezek. 7:7, 12); but also the many times in the past when He delivered them (Neh. 9:28). The Lord stands in readiness to judge every nation when its time comes (Jer. 27:7). There will be a time of the end for all the nations as well (Dan. 8:17;

11:35; 12:4, 9). In contrast, the word in context can be combined with chance to indicate uncertain time (Eccl. 9:11); and, appropriately, it describes life in general and its content, whether good or bad (Ps. 31:15[16]; Isa. 33:6).

6257. עָתַד ***'āṯaḏ:*** A verb meaning to be ready, to be prepared. It has the sense of something destined, prepared for a purpose or goal (Job 15:28). It is used of getting something ready beforehand to use later as needed (Prov. 24:27).

6258. עַתָּה ***'attāh:*** An adverb meaning now, already, then, therefore. It refers to a certain point in time that has been reached (Gen. 3:22; 22:12) but also has a logical function at the same time: Since we are at this time and set of circumstances, therefore. So it is also a logical connector or indicator (Ex. 3:9, 10). It may stress the current time or situation (Gen. 12:19; Num. 24:17). With *'ad-'attāh,* it means up to now, until now (Gen. 32:4[5]; Deut. 12:9). Combined with *min* (4480), *mē'attāh,* it means from now on (Isa. 48:6; Jer. 3:4). It can mean already, something has happened or is under way (Ex. 5:5).

6259. עָתוּד ***'āṯûḏ:*** An adjective meaning treasured. It is used as a noun to refer to the treasures, supplies, and goods of nations and peoples (Isa. 10:13).

6260. עַתּוּד ***'attûḏ:*** A masculine noun indicating a goat, a male goat, a leader. It refers to a strong animal of the flock, a ram, he goat (Gen. 31:10, 12). It is used figuratively, therefore, of a leader or people of strong character or position (Isa. 14:9; Jer. 50:8; Ezek. 34:17; Zech. 10:3). It was used often in sacrifices (Num. 7:17, 23, 29; Ps. 66:15; Isa. 34:6).

6261. עִתִּי ***'ittiy:*** An adjective meaning fit, ready to stand. It refers to someone prepared and waiting to perform a task, in this case, to send a goat into the wilderness on the Day of Atonement (Lev. 16:21).

6262. עַתַּי ***'attay:*** A proper noun designating Attai:

A. A descendant of Judah (1 Chr. 2:35, 36).

B. One of David's warriors (1 Chr. 12:11).

C. Son of Rehoboam (2 Chr. 11:20).

6263. עֲתִיד ***'ᵃṯiyḏ:*** An Aramaic adjective indicating ready. It means to be prepared to respond to a signal to do something, in this case, spiritually and emotionally as well as physically (Dan. 3:15).

6264. עָתִיד ***'āṯiyḏ:*** I. An adjective indicating to be ready, to be prepared. It refers to being forewarned and set to respond to a situation that will arise soon (Esth. 3:14; 8:13; Job 15:24). It means to be brave enough to do something (Job 3:8).

II. An adjective meaning impending; about to come. It is used of things about to occur, to happen, to come about, especially things to occur in Israel's future (Deut. 32:35).

III. An adjective meaning treasures. It refers to the valued things of peoples and nations, what they consider of importance to them (Isa. 10:13).

6265. עֲתָיָה ***ªṯāyāh:*** A proper noun designating Athaiah (Neh. 11:4).

6266. עָתִיק ***'āṯiyq:*** I. An adjective meaning choice, fine. It indicates clothing or garments of the finest material and craftsmanship (Isa. 23:18).

II. An adjective meaning durable. This word is taken by some translators to indicate the quality or durability of the items mentioned (Isa. 23:18).

6267. עַתִּיק ***'attiyq:*** I. An adjective indicating ancient. It is used to refer to historical, archival records, considered to be old and therefore accurate (1 Chr. 4:22). It has the sense of weaned or removed from the breast, gotten older (Isa. 28:9).

II. An adjective meaning taken, drawn from. It refers to a child just weaned from, taken from the breasts (Isa. 28:9).

6268. עַתִּיק ***'attiyq:*** An Aramaic adjective meaning ancient. It is used in the phrase ancient, old, of days, that is, old with reference to time; as old as the days that have been recorded (Dan. 7:9, 13, 22).

6269. עֲתָךְ ***ªṯāḵ:*** A proper noun designating Athach (1 Sam. 30:30).

6270. עַתְלָי ***'aṯlāy:*** A proper noun designating Athlai (Ezra 10:28).

6271. עֲתַלְיָה ***ªṯalyāh,*** עֲתַלְיָהוּ ***ªṯalyāhû:*** A proper noun designating Athaliah:

A. The daughter of King Ahab of northern Israel and granddaughter of Omri. She was the mother of Ahaziah king of Judah. She was wicked and tried to destroy the royal family of Judah (2 Kgs. 11:1–3). Joash, of the royal line was shielded from her plans and kept hidden for six years. Jehoida the priest then proclaimed Joash king. Athaliah was killed (2 Kgs. 11:9–16).

B. A Benjamite (1 Chr. 8:26).

C. A descendant of Elam (Ezra 8:7).

6272. עָתַם ***'āṯam:*** A verb meaning to scorch, to burn. It refers figuratively to Israel being ignited and consumed by fire (Isa. 9:19[18]) because of the Lord's anger.

6273. עָתְנִי ***'oṯniy:*** A proper noun designating Othniel (Josh. 15:17; Judg. 1:13; 3:9, 11; 1 Chr. 4:13; 27:15).

6274. עָתְנִיאֵל ***'oṯniy'ēl:*** A proper noun designating Othniel. Othniel was a nephew to Caleb and son to Kenaz, Caleb's younger brother. He was married to Caleb's daughter Achsah (Judg. 1:13). The Lord raised him up to "judge" Israel and to deliver them from the king of Aram Naharaim, Cushan-Rishathaim. The Spirit of God led him, and the Lord gave Israel's enemies into his hands. The land enjoyed peace for forty years (Judg. 3:8–11).

6275. עָתַק *'āṯaq:* A verb meaning to move, to proceed, to grow old. It indicates going from one place to another (Gen. 12:8); leaving a location under pressure (Gen. 26:22). It describes figuratively God's moving of mountains (Job 9:5). It describes the weakening of the eyes as the person grows old (Ps. 6:7[8]). It is used of copying literary works from one location to another, transcribing them (Prov. 25:1).

6276. עָתֵק *'āṯēq:* An adjective meaning enduring. It signifies something that lasts, is durable, does not decay, fade away (Prov. 8:18).

6277. עָתָק *'āṯāq:* An adjective meaning arrogant, insolent. It identifies an act and attitude of unwarranted or excessive pride, self-importance (1 Sam. 2:3). Or it means to speak against someone, especially a righteous person in a disrespectful or harmful way (Ps. 31:18[19]). It describes pride as especially arrogant or insolent (Ps. 75:5[6]). Especially the arrogant wicked pour out insolent speech (Ps. 94:4).

6278. עִתָּה קָצִין *'ittāh qaṣiyn,* עֵת קָצִין *'ēṯ qāṣiyn:* I. A proper noun designating Ittah Kazin (KJV, Josh. 19:13).

II. A proper noun designating Eth Kazin (NASB, NIV, Josh. 19:13).

6279. עָתַר *'āṯar:* A verb meaning to pray, to entreat, to supplicate. The fundamental meaning of this word is that of a cry to the Lord for deliverance. It was used in Isaac's prayer concerning his wife's barrenness (Gen. 25:21); and the prayers of Moses to stop the plagues in Egypt (Ex. 8:8[4]). Scripture says that the Lord is faithful to hear such prayers (Job 33:26).

6280. עָתַר *'āthar:* A verb meaning to be multiplied. It means to make larger, be more numerous, or to do often. In context it refers to enemies of God, emphasizing and increasing their words against Him (Ezek. 35:13). It has the sense of being alluring or deceitful, false like the kisses of an enemy (Prov. 27:6).

6281. עֶתֶר *'eṯer:* A proper noun designating Ether (Josh. 15:42; 19:7).

6282. עָתָר *'āṯār:* I. A masculine noun meaning worship. It is used of persons who seek, entreat, and, hence, offer worship to God, a projection of God's restored earth (Zeph. 3:10).

II. A masculine noun indicating a fragrance. It refers to the aroma, the smell that arose from burning incense (Ezek. 8:11). In this case, it took place in a forbidden pagan worship ritual.

III. A masculine noun meaning thickness. It refers to the heavy density of a cloud of incense sent up to God (Ezek. 8:11).

6283. עֲתֶרֶת *ᵃṯereṯ:* A feminine noun referring to abundance. It refers to a more than ample supply of something, more that what is sufficient (Jer. 33:6).

פ Pē

6284. פָּאָה ***pā'āh:*** A verb meaning to divide into pieces or corners. It is used in a violent manner and attitude of God's judging His people in a devastating way, visiting a covenant curse upon them (Deut. 32:26).

6285. פֵּאָה ***pē'āh:*** A feminine noun meaning side, corner. It refers to the four conjunctions at the top of the table of showbread (Ex. 25:26); or on a bed (Amos 3:12). When used of a person's head, it designates its sides (Lev. 13:41). In some passages, it refers figuratively of the forehead of a people or nation (Num. 24:17). In context it may refer to the border or boundary of a territory, its side (Josh. 15:5; Num. 24:17).

6286. פָּאַר ***pā'ar:*** A verb meaning to beautify, to glorify. In the factitive form, God brings beauty and glory to His chosen people (Ps. 149:4; Isa. 55:5; 60:9); and to His Temple (Ezra 7:27; Isa. 60:7). In the reflexive form, one beautifies and glorifies one's self and not others. Gideon is instructed to reduce the number of men in his army so the Israelites could not give themselves the glory for the victory that was to come (Judg. 7:2). In God's judgment against Assyria—a country that was merely an instrument in God's hand—Isaiah rhetorically asked whether the ax and the saw could take credit for the work accomplished through them (Isa. 10:15). Obviously, the answer is no. In the same way, people should not take glory in what God is doing through their lives. In several passages, Isaiah also states that God brings glory to Himself by His actions through His people (Isa. 44:23; 49:3; 60:21; 61:3).

6287. פְּאֵר ***p^{e}'ēr:*** A masculine noun indicating a headband, a turban. It refers to a style of headdress worn by men in the Middle East or South Asia. It is made up of lengths of cloth wound in folds around the head (Ex. 39:28). There were many styles of these, sometimes called headdresses (Isa. 3:20). The word has the sense of a garland in some contexts, a wreath or woven chain of flowers, even leaves worn on one's head (Isa. 61:3, 10).

6288. פֹּארָה, פֻּארָה ***pō'rāh, pu'rāh:*** I. A feminine noun referring to a bough, a branch. It refers to branches of a tree sent out to expand its influence. It functions in a figurative sense in a parable in Ezekiel (17:6) of Assyria's growth and expansion (Ezek. 31:5, 6, 8, 12, 13).

II. A feminine noun indicating a bough or a branch. It is used figuratively of the boughs or branches of Assyria (Isa. 10:33).

6289. פָּארוּר ***pā'rûr:*** A masculine noun whose meaning is assumed to be in dread or fear; however, the meaning of this word is uncertain. It occurs two times, each with the verb *qāḇaṣ* (6908), meaning to gather. From the context, it is clear that the term is a negative one. In Joel 2:6, the context is a warning against the Day of the Lord, when an imposing army will invade, and people will be struck with great fear. In Nahum 2:10[11], the context is a prophecy of judgment against and the impending doom of Nineveh, which was like a lion's den, a place of safety and sanctuary (yet no fear) but would soon be a place of destruction and devastation.

6290. פָּארָן *pā'rān:* A proper noun designating Paran, the desert where Ishmael settled. The Desert of Paran is hard to pinpoint. It refers to a rather large area in west central Sinai. Kadesh Barnea and lower southeast Judah are on its periphery. It lay below the Negev and touched southern Edom. Paran is a shortened form of the expression but may designate a more confined area as well. The Israelites traversed it on their wanderings to Canaan (Num. 10:12; 13:3, 26; Deut. 1:1) as did others (1 Kgs. 11:18). The Lord "came forth" shone Mount Paran in this area (Deut. 33:2).

6291. פַּג *pag:* A masculine noun signifying an early fig, a green fig. It refers to early figs put forth in spring, according to its immediate context (Song 2:13).

6292. פִּגּוּל *piggûl:* A masculine noun meaning a foul thing, refuse. It is a technical term for a part of a sacrifice that has become or been rendered unclean. This was applied to the fellowship offering that was to be eaten the same day it was offered or the next day. If it remained until the third day, it was considered unclean (Lev. 7:18; 19:7). Isaiah recorded the prophecy of God where He defined the activities of people that rendered them unclean, including contact with the deceased and eating unclean food, namely pork (Isa. 65:4). Ezekiel protested God's instruction to him because he had never eaten any unclean meat; however, he failed to define what unclean meat was (Ezek. 4:14).

6293. פָּגַע *pāga':* A verb meaning to meet, to encounter, to reach. It could simply mean to meet (Ex. 5:20; 1 Sam. 10:5). It could also signify to meet someone with hostility, where it is usually rendered to fall upon (Josh. 2:16; Judg. 8:21; Ruth 2:22). In addition, it could convey the concept of meeting with a request or entreaty and is usually rendered as intercession (Jer. 7:16). This verb is used to designate the establishment of a boundary, probably with the idea of extending the boundary to reach a certain point (Josh. 16:7; 19:11, 22, 26, 27, 34).

6294. פֶּגַע *pega':* A masculine noun pointing out a circumstantial event, a chance happening, something that takes place. In context is may mean a detrimental event or a chance happening (1 Kgs. 5:4[18]). It refers to any chance occurrence in the lives of people (Eccl. 9:11).

6295. פַּגְעִיאֵל ***pag'iy'ēl:*** A proper noun designating Pagiel (Num. 1:13; 2:27; 7:72, 77; 10:26).

6296. פָּגַר ***pāgar:*** A verb meaning to be exhausted. It describes the physical and mental exhaustion of persons, especially when pursuing soldiers (1 Sam. 30:10, 21).

6297. פֶּגֶר ***peger:*** A masculine noun meaning a corpse, a carcass. It can refer to the carcasses of animals (Gen. 15:11); however, it is usually used in connection with human corpses. Though this term can refer to a single body (Isa. 14:19), it is usually found in the plural (Isa. 34:3; Jer. 31:40; Ezek. 6:5). In several instances, the singular is used as a collective (1 Sam. 17:46; Amos 8:3; Nah. 3:3). One occurrence of this word is a metaphor for the lifelessness of idols (Lev. 26:30).

6298. פָּגַשׁ ***pāgaš:*** A verb meaning to meet, to encounter. It means to encounter, to come in contact with, to come face to face (Gen. 32:17[18]; 33:8; Ex. 4:27; 1 Sam. 25:20). It is used of God meeting Moses at a particular place for a particular purpose (Ex. 4:24). It describes figuratively the wicked encountering darkness or trouble in their lives daily (Job 5:14); or things meeting together in a positive, approving way (Ps. 85:10[11]). It denotes opposites meeting (Prov. 29:13).

6299. פָּדָה ***pāḏāh:*** A verb meaning to ransom, to redeem, and to deliver. The word is used to depict God's act of redeeming; He redeemed His people with a mighty hand from Pharaoh and the slavery they were under in Egypt (Deut. 7:8; Mic. 6:4). Egypt was literally the house of slavery and became the symbol of slavery and oppression from which Israel was delivered (Deut. 9:26; 24:18). After Israel was in exile in Babylon, the Lord redeemed them from their strong enemies (Jer. 31:11). He had longed to redeem them from their apostasy before He gave them over to judgment, but they would not respond to His call (Hos. 7:13; 13:14).

The Lord also redeemed individuals in the sense of rescuing them. He delivered David (2 Sam. 4:9; 1 Kgs. 1:29); Abraham (Isa. 29:22); Jeremiah (Jer. 15:21); and the psalmist (Ps. 26:11; 31:5[6]).

The word often describes the process of ransoming persons in the cultic setting of ancient Israel. The firstborn was ransomed or redeemed (Ex. 13:13, 15; Num. 18:15); animals were redeemed by payment of a half-shekel of ransom money (Lev. 27:27; Num. 18:15). The firstborn of an ox, sheep, or goat could not be redeemed (Num. 18:17). The word described the action of both the community and friends to redeem individuals (1 Sam. 14:45; Job 6:23).

In the passive stem, the word means to be redeemed. The word is used to describe a female slave who has not been ransomed (Lev. 19:20). A person under the ban for destruction could not be ransomed either

(Lev. 27:29). Zion would be redeemed through justice (Isa. 1:27); one person could not be redeemed by the life of another (Ps. 49:7[8]).

In the causative stem, it means to bring about deliverance or redemption; the master who did not accept his slave girl had to cause her to be redeemed (Ex. 21:8); the firstborn male of unclean animals and humans had to be redeemed as well (Num. 18:15, 16).

6300. פְּדַהְאֵל **p^e*d̲ah'ēl:*** A proper noun designating Pedahel (Num. 34:28).

6301. פְּדָהצוּר **p^e*d̲āhṣûr:*** A proper noun designating Pedahzur (Num. 1:10; 2:20; 7:54, 59; 10:23).

6302. פְּדוּיִים **p^e*d̲ûyiym:*** A masculine noun meaning ransom. Like the word *pid̲yôm* (6306), it is an abstract form of the basic passive participle derived from the verb *pād̲āh* (6299), meaning to ransom. As such, it occurs three times in the context of Israel's ransoming their firstborn males. In this context, this term is parallel with the silver that was used to redeem firstborn males and then given to Aaron and his sons (Num. 3:46, 48; 51).

6303. פָּדוֹן **pād̲ôn:** A proper noun designating Padon (Ezra 2:44; Neh. 7:47).

6304. פְּדוּת **p^e*d̲ûṯ:*** A feminine noun meaning ransom, redemption. It is used four times in the Old Testament and could refer to redemption in general (Ps. 111:9); redemption from sins (Ps. 130:7); or redemption from exile (Isa. 50:2). The meaning of the fourth occurrence of this word (Ex. 8:23[19]) is difficult to ascertain. The Septuagint renders the Hebrew with *diastole* (1293, New Testament), meaning a division or distinction, and English translations follow suit.

6305. פְּדָיָה **p^e*d̲āyāh,*** פְּדָיָהוּ **p^e*d̲āyāhû:*** A proper noun designating Pedaiah:

A. Grandfather of Jehoiakim (2 Kgs. 23:36; Neh. 3:25; 8:4; 11:7; 13:13).

B. Son of Jehoiakim (1 Chr. 3:17, 18).

C. Son of Parosh (Neh. 3:25).

D. A helper of Ezra (Neh. 8:4).

E. A descendant of Benjamin (Neh. 11:7).

F. A Levite in Nehemiah's day (Neh. 13:13).

G. The father of Joel (1 Chr. 27:20).

6306. פִּדְיוֹם **pid̲yôm,** פִּדְיוֹן **pid̲yôn:** A masculine noun meaning ransom, ransom money. Like the word *pād̲ûy* (6302), *pid̲yôm* is an abstract form of the basic passive participle derived from the verb *pād̲āh* (6299), meaning to ransom. As such, it occurs in the same context as *pād̲ûy*, referring to the ransoming of the Israelite firstborn males (Num. 3:49, 51).

Pid̲yôn is a masculine noun meaning ransom money. The word is closely related to *piḏyôm* (see above paragraph) and *pāḏûy* (6302); yet it is a substantive noun and not an abstract noun. It refers to the money exchanged as a ransom, not simply to the concept of ransoming. In addition, this term always occurs in connection with the term *nep̄eš* (5315), meaning life (Ex. 21:30; Ps. 49:8[9]).

6307. פַּדָּן *paddān*, פַּדַּן אֲרָם *paddan ʾᵃrām:* A proper noun designating Paddan, Paddan Aram:

A. Paddan, a shortened form of B (Gen. 48:7).

B. Paddan Aram (Gen. 25:20; 28:2, 5–7; 31:18; 33:18; 35:9, 26; 46:15).

6308. פָּדַע *pāḏaʿ:* A verb derived from an unknown root. It occurs only in Job 33:24, and the context requires that it carry a meaning like to deliver, to rescue. The verse talks of delivering one from going down to the pit.

6309. פֶּדֶר *peḏer:* A masculine noun meaning fat, suet. It refers to hard fat that collects around the kidneys and loins of cattle and sheep (Lev. 1:8, 12; 8:20).

6310. פֶּה *peh:* A masculine singular noun meaning mouth. Besides the literal meaning, this term is used as the instrument of speech and figuratively for speech itself. When Moses claimed to be an ineffective speaker, he was heavy of mouth (Ex. 4:10); the psalmist also uses *peh* to mean speech (Ps. 49:13[14]; Eccl. 10:13; Isa. 29:13). The word is rendered edge in the expression the mouth of the sword (Judg. 4:16; Prov. 5:4); or in some measurements from edge to edge or end to end (2 Kgs. 10:21; 21:16; Ezra 9:11). It is also used for other openings like those in caves, gates, wells, or sacks. In land and inheritance references, it is translated as share or portion (Deut. 21:17; 2 Kgs. 2:9; Zech. 13:8). With the preposition *lᵉ*, it means in proportion to or according to.

6311. פֹּא *pōʾ*, פֹּה *pōh*, פּוֹ *pô:* An adverb meaning here, hither. Its basic meaning is here (Gen. 19:12; 22:5). Combined with *min* (4480) in *mippōh*, it means on this or that side (Ezek. 40:10; 12, 21); with *ʿaḏ*, it means this far (1 Sam. 16:11; Ezra 4:2; Job 38:11). It is in the interrogative word *ʾêp̄ōh*.

6312. פּוּאָה *pûʾāh*, פֻּוָּה *puwwāh:* A proper noun designating Puah:

A. Son of Issachar (Gen. 46:13; Num. 26:23; 1 Chr. 7:1).

B. Son of Dodo (Judg. 10:1).

6313. פּוּג *pûg:* A verb meaning to be stunned, to be paralyzed, to be feeble. It indicates a response of great surprise or astonishment about something (Gen. 45:26); or a condition brought on by severe illness (Ps. 38:8[9]). It indicates weakness, frailty in an emotional or physical way (Ps. 77:2[3]). It has the sense of something being paralyzed in usage, not used, ignored (Hab. 1:4).

6314. פּוּגָה *pûḡāh:* A feminine noun referring to rest, relief. It defines a respite from some activity or thought, from an oppressive or grievous situation (Lam. 2:18).

6315. פּוּחַ *pûaḥ:* A verb translated to breathe, to blow. The word is only used in poetic contexts in the Hebrew Bible. In the Song of Songs, the expression until the day breathes refers to the early morning when shadows flee (Song 2:17; 4:6); and the north wind is told to blow on the garden (Song 4:16). But just as often, the word implies a negative connotation, such as to snort at an enemy (Ps. 10:5); to incite a city (Prov. 29:8); or the Lord to blow out His anger (Ezek. 21:31[36]). In a unique usage, Proverbs uses the verb to refer to speaking lies (Prov. 6:19; 14:5, 25; 19:5, 9); but once for speaking truth (Prov. 12:17).

6316. פּוּט *pûṭ:* A proper noun designating the nation of Put, probably Lydia (Gen. 10:6; 1 Chr. 1:8; Jer. 46:9; Ezek. 27:10; 30:5; 38:5; Nah. 3:9).

6317. פּוּטִיאֵל *pûṭiy'ēl:* A proper noun designating Putiel (Ex. 6:25).

6318. פּוֹטִיפַר *pôṭiypar:* A proper noun designating Potiphar (Gen. 37:36; 39:1).

6319. פּוֹטִי פֶרַע *pôṭiy ṗera':* A proper noun designating Potipherah (Gen. 41:45, 50; 46:20).

6320. פּוּךְ *pûḵ:* I. A masculine noun referring to glistening stones, perhaps antimony or turquoise used in decorations. It refers to the ornamental and decorative supplies David prepared for use in the Temple (1 Chr. 29:2). It is used in a figurative sense of God's adornment of a restored Zion (Isa. 54:11).

II. A masculine noun indicating glistening pigment used to paint the eyes. It describes Jezebel's adornment of her face shortly before her death (2 Kgs. 9:30). It indicates figuratively of Judah's adornment of herself (Jer. 4:30).

6321. פּוֹל *pôl:* A masculine noun referring to beans. It refers to part of a supply of victuals David had gathered together. It also probably refers to broad beans (2 Sam. 17:28; Ezek. 4:9).

6322. פּוּל *pûl:* A proper noun designating Pul:

A. A shortened form of 8407 (2 Kgs. 15:19; 1 Chr. 5:26).

B. The nation of Pul; probably Libya (Isa 66:19).

6323. פּוּן *pûn:* A verb meaning to be distracted, to be in despair. It refers to a state of great distraction or despair, hopelessness (Ps. 88:15[16]); in context it describes despair because of illness.

6324. פּוּנִי *pûniy:* A proper noun designating Punites, the descendants of Puah (6312,A) (Num. 26:23).

6325. פּוּנֹן *pûnōn:* A proper noun designating Punon (Num. 33:42, 43).

6326. פּוּעָה ***pû'āh:*** A proper noun designating Puah (Ex. 1:15).

6327. פּוּץ ***pûṣ:*** I. A verb meaning to scatter, to disperse. It describes spreading out, scattering something: of humanity on the earth (Gen. 10:18; 11:4); enemies (Num. 10:35; 1 Sam. 11:11); especially of Israel dispersed among the nations in fulfillment of God's curse (Ezek. 34:5); pictured as a scattered flock (Zech. 13:7). In its passive sense, it means to be scattered, dispersed: of an army (2 Kgs. 25:5; Jer. 52:8); peoples in general (Gen. 10:18). It has the sense of causing something to be dispersed, scattered: peoples (Gen. 11:8, 9); especially among the peoples, nations (Deut. 4:27; 28:64; Jer. 9:16[15]; Ezek. 11:16). It is used figuratively of lightning being sent forth, scattering an enemy (2 Sam. 22:15; Ps. 18:14[15]).

II. A verb meaning to shatter, to crush, to break in pieces. It points out figuratively the Lord's apparent attack on Job in sickness (Job 16:12). It describes God's word, crushing rock like a sledgehammer (Jer. 23:29); and of His look breaking, shattering mountains (Hab. 3:6).

6328. פּוּק ***pûq:*** A verb meaning to totter, to stumble. It has in mind persons who are incapacitated, unable to render judgments with integrity (Isa. 28:7). It is used derisively of idols who must be shored up so they are stable and will not totter (Jer. 10:4).

6329. פּוּק ***pûq:*** A verb meaning to obtain, to bring out. It has the sense of furthering or fostering something (Ps. 140:8[9]); or of the increase of flocks (Ps. 144:13). It indicates the acquisition of something (Prov. 3:13; 8:35). It indicates in some contexts the bringing out or giving of oneself to others who are needy (Isa. 58:10).

6330. פּוּקָה ***pûqāh:*** A feminine noun indicating grief, a burden of conscience. It refers to a feeling of grief or guilt because of something that has occurred (1 Sam. 25:31).

6331. פּוּר ***pûr:*** A verb meaning to break, to bring to naught. It refers to causing the plans or machinations of nations or peoples to come to nothing (Ps. 33:10); or to cut off or stop something (Ps. 89:33[34]; Ezek. 17:19).

6332. פּוּר ***pûr:*** A masculine noun referring to a lot cast to make decisions; in plural, Purim, a Jewish feast day. It refers to the Jewish feast day celebrating the great deliverance of the Jews under the Persian Empire (Esth. 9:24, 26, 28, 29, 31, 32). The pur was an object used in deciding a matter seemingly by chance (Esth. 3:7).

6333. פּוּרָה ***pûrāh:*** A feminine noun indicating a winepress, a wine vat. It refers to a vat constructed to hold grapes so they could be pressed to give their juice (Isa. 63:3). To tend the winepress became a reference to executing judgment or justice (Hag. 2:16).

6334. פּוֹרָתָה ***pôrāṯah:*** A proper noun designating Poratha (Esth. 9:8).

6335. פּוּשׁ ***pûš:*** I. A verb meaning to leap, to spring about, to gallop. It describes the playful, skipping, happy behavior of a heifer (Jer. 50:11; Mal. 4:2[3:20]); or the speedy gallop of warhorses (Hab. 1:8).

II. A verb meaning to scatter; to spread out, to grow fat. It refers to the scattered people of Nineveh because of God's judgment on the city (Nah. 3:18); and to the military horsemen of Babylon spreading out as they attacked (Hab. 1:8). It means to grow up, to develop as calves fed on choice grain (Mal. 4:2[3:20]).

6336. פּוּתִי ***pûṯiy:*** A proper noun designating Puthites (1 Chr. 2:53).

6337. פַּז ***paz:*** A masculine noun designating pure gold, fine gold. It refers to an especially valuable kind of gold (Job 28:17; Prov. 8:19). It is used figuratively to describe the beauty of the bridegroom (Song 5:11, 15). It was an extremely scarce commodity (Isa. 13:12).

6338. פָּזַז ***pāzaz:*** A verb meaning to refine, to be refined. It is used in a passive sense to describe gold that has had the impurities, the dross, removed from it (1 Kgs. 10:18).

6339. פָּזַז ***pāzaz:*** I. A verb meaning to be agile, limber. It is used figuratively to indicate the ability of Joseph to escape his persecutors by being agile, able to move and escape evil (Gen. 49:24).

II. A verb meaning to be strong. It is used to indicate the fortitude of Joseph in remaining firm and able before his enemies (Gen. 49:24).

III. A verb meaning to leap. It describes David's jumping and dancing before the Lord, an expression of great joy and delight before God (2 Sam. 6:16).

6340. פָּזַר ***pāzar:*** A verb meaning to scatter; to be scattered. It indicates the dispersing or distributing of something or someone: of the Jews among the Persian Empire (Esth. 3:8; Joel 3:2[4:2]); of the bones of the dead lying about wherever they fell (Ps. 53:5[6]); of one's enemies (Ps. 89:10[11]). It signifies in a good sense the sharing of things, scattering them (Prov. 11:24); but it is used of apostasy and harlotries as well (Jer. 3:13).

6341. פַּח ***paḥ:*** A masculine singular noun translated bird trap. It is used in its literal sense in Amos 3:5, Proverbs 7:23, and Ecclesiastes 9:12. But more often it is used figuratively for a human ensnarement. Jeremiah prophesied that a snare awaited Moab (Jer. 48:43); while Proverbs said that snares were set for the wicked (Prov. 22:5). Eliphaz told Job that snares surrounded him (Job 22:10). The psalmist's path was filled with the snares of his enemies (Ps. 140:5[6]; 142:3[4]). But retribution was envisioned as the enemies' tables turned into a snare (Ps. 69:22[23]).

6342. פָּחַד ***pāḥad̲:*** A verb meaning to dread, to be in dread, to be in awe. This verb occurs in poetry. Those who worship and trust God have no need to dread, but those who break the Law (Deut. 28:66); sinners in Zion (Isa. 33:14); and worshipers of idols (Isa. 44:11) have reason to fear. It often takes a cognate accusative. For a positive use, in the eschatological perspective of Isaiah 60:5, the term is best translated to be awed.

6343. פַּחַד ***paḥad̲:*** A masculine singular noun translated dread, terror. This dread was often caused by the Lord (1 Sam. 11:7; Job 13:11; Isa. 2:10, 19, 21). The dread could cause trembling (Job 13:11; Ps. 119:120). The noun often occurs in a cognate accusative construction (see *pāḥad̲* [6342]) (Deut. 28:67; Job 3:25; Ps. 14:5). A unique use of the term is found in Genesis 31:42, often translated the Dread or Fear of Isaac, parallel to the God of Abraham.

6344. פַּחַד ***paḥad̲:*** I. A noun referring to a thigh. It is used in the plural. It is used to describe Leviathan, God's masterful creation (Job 40:17). It refers to the upper front part of a person's legs.

II. A noun referring to testicle. It is rendered as stones, meaning testicles. It describes a feature of Leviathan's body (Job 40:17).

6345. פַּחְדָּה ***paḥdāh:*** A feminine noun meaning fear, religious awe. This Hebrew word appears only in Jeremiah 2:19, where it refers to the proper respect and reverence due to the Lord, which is lacking when one forsakes God and His commands.

6346. פֶּחָה ***peḥāh:*** A masculine noun meaning a governor, a captain. The primary meaning of this word is that of a lord over a given district or territory. It signified an office that is appointed and not received by virtue of birth or other right. It was generally used of the leader of the Jewish nation after the exile (Neh. 12:26; Hag. 1:14; Mal. 1:8); but in other places it was used of a deputy bureaucrat in any given location (Esth. 8:9; Jer. 51:23); or a military leader (1 Kgs. 20:24).

6347. פֶּחָה ***peḥāh:*** An Aramaic masculine noun meaning a governor, a satrap, a captain. Corresponding to the Hebrew word *peḥāh* (6346), this word means a governor or other similarly appointed authority. It was used particularly of a provincial governor in the Persian Empire (Ezra 5:6); the postexilic leader of the Jewish nation (Ezra 6:7); and various similar officers involved in the political structure (Dan. 6:7[8]).

6348. פָּחַז ***pāḥaz:*** A verb meaning to be reckless, to be arrogant. It means to be undisciplined, wild, insolent. In its plural participial form, it refers to reckless persons (Judg. 9:4). It refers to prophets who are undisciplined and unrestrained in their false prophecies (Zeph. 3:4).

6349. פַּחַז paḥaz: A masculine noun referring to recklessness, uncontrollableness. It refers to persons who are without self-control or discipline so they are unstable and cannot be counted on (Gen. 49:4).

6350. פַּחֲזוּת paḥ^a^zûṯ: A feminine noun indicating recklessness. It indicates the undisciplined, unrestrained behavior and actions of false prophets (Jer. 23:32).

6351. פָּחַח pāḥaḥ: A verb indicating to ensnare, to trap. It refers to being confined, to be held captive by circumstances. In its immediate context, Israel became ensnared as a result of her own blindness (Isa. 42:22).

6352. פֶּחָם peḥām: A masculine noun indicating pieces of coal, charcoal. It refers to a porous form of carbon that is highly flammable (Prov. 26:21). It was used to heat ovens, furnaces, etc. (Isa. 44:12; 54:16).

6353. פֶּחָר peḥār: An Aramaic masculine noun indicating a potter. It is used of a person who is skilled in and works with the craft of pottery (Dan. 2:41).

6354. פַּחַת paḥaṯ: A masculine singular noun meaning a pit, a cave. Within the prophecies of Isaiah and Jeremiah, the term is used in judgment as a trap for the wicked enemies of the Lord and Israel (Isa. 24:17, 18; Jer. 48:28, 43, 44). In Lamentations, it was a place for sinful Jerusalem (Lam. 3:47). The term is used for the cave where David and his men were hiding (2 Sam. 17:9); and for the pit in which Absalom's body was thrown (2 Sam. 18:17).

6355. פַּחַת מוֹאָב paḥaṯ mô'āḇ: A proper noun designating Pahath-Moab (Ezra 2:6; 8:4; 10:30; Neh. 3:11; 7:11; 10:14[15]).

6356. פְּחֶתֶת p^e^ḥeṯeṯ: A feminine noun meaning bored out, eaten away. This word is used once to denote the condition of a decaying leprous garment (Lev. 13:55). The image underlying the word is similar to that of a wormhole or spot eaten away by a moth.

6357. פִּטְדָה piṭḏāh: A feminine noun depicting a precious stone, a topaz. The stone indicated is a topaz, a light-colored or colorless stone used for beauty and splendor (Ex. 28:17; 39:10; Job 28:19; Ezek. 28:13). Ethiopia was famous for its topaz stones. They were found in the Garden of Eden (Ezek. 28:13).

6358. פָּטוּר pāṭûr: An adjective meaning open. It refers to something that is in a state of access, freedom of view (1 Kgs. 6:18, 29, 32, 35).

6359. פָּטִיר pāṭiyr: An adjective meaning free from, exempt from. It means to not be busy or tied up with some task or job (1 Chr. 9:33).

6360. פַּטִּישׁ paṭṭiyš: A masculine noun depicting a hammer. A tool used to hammer out or smooth out metal by pounding it (Isa. 41:7); to break up rock (Jer. 23:29). It describes figuratively God's Word (Jer. 23:29). Babylon is described as God's hammer of the whole earth, pounding it down, devastating the nations (Jer. 50:23).

6361. פַּטִּישׁ *pattiyš:* An Aramaic noun meaning trousers, hose. It refers to a garment, probably a coat or trousers, that was part of the elaborate Persian outfits worn by the Hebrew men when they were thrown into the fiery furnace (Dan. 3:21). Other translations, such as, tunics, robes, shirts, have been suggested.

6362. פָּטַר *pāṭar:* A verb meaning to open, to release, to separate. It means to make one's getaway (1 Sam. 19:10). It describes flowers with open petals or buds (1 Kgs. 6:18, 29, 32, 35, *peṭurê ṣiṣṣîm*). It indicates being free from certain duties (1 Chr. 9:33). It means to let off of a job, let off duty (2 Chr. 23:8). It is used of foolishly mocking someone with one's mouth, literally parting one's lips (Ps. 22:7[8]). It refers to letting out water, emptying one's bladder for relief (Prov. 17:14).

6363. פֶּטֶר *peṭer,* פִּטְרָה *piṭrāh:* I. A masculine noun referring to the firstborn. It indicates the first animal to part or separate from the womb (Ex. 13:2, 12, 13, 15; 34:19, 20; Num. 3:12; 18:15; Ezek. 20:26).

II. A feminine noun indicating the firstborn one. It indicates the first one to open, separate from a mother's womb (Num. 8:16).

6364. פִּי בֶסֶת *piy beset:* A proper noun designating Pi-beseth; also known as Bubastis (Ezek. 30:17).

6365. פִּיד *piyd:* A masculine noun meaning a ruin, a disaster. It is used of divine judgment (Job 30:24; 31:29), as when the father encouraged his son to avoid the wicked and focus on God because God's judgment will eventually come on the wicked (Prov. 24:22).

6366. פֵּיָה *pēyāh:* A feminine noun referring to an edge. It refers to the edge or sharpened part of a sword blade. In context it refers to the edges on a double-edged sword (Judg. 3:16).

6367. פִּי הַחִירֹת *piy haḥiyrōt:* A proper noun designating Pi Hahiroth (Ex. 14:2, 9; Num. 33:7, 8).

6368. פִּיחַ *piyaḥ:* A masculine noun referring to soot, ashes. It indicates the black carbon particles and other substances left after something has burned (Ex. 9:8, 10). Ashes include white or grayish materials left after combustion.

6369. פִּיכֹל *piykōl:* A proper noun designating Phicol (Gen. 21:22, 32; 26:26).

6370. פִּילֶגֶשׁ *piylegeš:* A feminine noun meaning a concubine. A concubine was a legitimate wife; however, she was of secondary rank. This is evident by the references to the concubine as having a husband (Judg. 19:2); and that this man and her father are considered to be son-in-law (cf. Judg. 19:5) and father-in-law (cf. Judg. 19:4), respectively. But concubines were presented opposite the wives of higher rank (1 Kgs. 11:3; Song 6:8). The ability to have and to keep concubines was a sign of wealth, status, and often of royalty (1 Kgs. 11:3; Esth. 2:14; Song 6:8). To sleep with a king's concubine would have indicated plans to usurp the throne (2 Sam. 3:7; 16:21, 22; cf. 1 Kgs. 2:21–24).

6371. פִּימָה ***piymāh:*** A feminine noun referring to bulges of fat. It refers to an excess of facial tissue creating plumpness or corpulence in context, a mark of a wicked person's face according to Eliphaz (Job 15:27).

6372. פִּינְחָס ***piyn^{e}ḥās:*** A proper noun designating Phinehas:

A. The son of Eleazar and Putiel (Ex. 6:25). He showed his zeal for the Law of the Lord and his hatred of sexual immorality at Shittim. He executed an Israelite, Zimri, who arrogantly brought a Midianite woman, Cozbi, into Israel's camp in the presence of Moses and all Israel (Num. 25:6–9). Zimri had immoral relations with her and worshiped her pagan god (Num. 25:1–9). Phinehas's zeal for the Lord and his dedication to Him was remembered as a lasting memorial by the Lord (Num. 25:10–13; Ps. 106:30). This priest was also a leader who helped avert civil war in Israel (Josh. 22:10–25). Gibeah was allotted to him in Ephraim near Shiloh (Josh. 24:33). He served with his father Eleazar at the ark of the covenant (Judg. 20:28).

B. A Phinehas was the younger son of the high priest Eli in the time of Samuel's birth (1 Sam. 1:3; 2:34). He and Hophni were killed for their wickedness (1 Sam. 4:4, 11, 17, 19). He had a son, Ahitub (1 Sam. 14:3).

C. The son of a priest in the time of Ezra (Ezra 7:5; 8:2, 33).

6373. פִּינֹן ***piynōn:*** A proper noun designating Pinon (Gen. 36:41; 1 Chr. 1:52).

6374. פִּיפִיּוֹת ***piypiyyôṯ:*** A feminine plural noun meaning double-edged. It is used to describe a sword or any blade that has been sharpened on both edges, an especially effective weapon (Ps. 149:6); even both edges on a threshing sledge could be sharpened (Isa. 41:15).

6375. פִּיק ***piyq:*** A masculine noun meaning tottering. This noun only occurs in one passage, where the devastation of Nineveh is portrayed: "She is empty, and void, and waste: and the heart melteth, and the knees smite together, and much pain is in all loins, and the faces of them all gather blackness" (Nah. 2:10[11] KJV).

6376. פִּישׁוֹן ***piyšôn:*** A proper noun designating Pishon (Gen. 2:11).

6377. פִּיתוֹן ***piyṯôn:*** A proper noun designating Pithon (1 Chr. 8:35; 9:41).

6378. פַּךְ ***pak̲:*** A masculine noun referring to a vial, a flask. It was a small bottle-shaped container for holding liquids, especially oil for anointing kings, prophets, priests, etc. (1 Sam. 10:1; 2 Kgs. 9:1, 3).

6379. פָּכָה ***pāk̲āh:*** A verb indicating to trickle, to flow. It refers to a small running stream or flow of water (Ezek. 47:2).

6380. פֹּכֶרֶת הַצְּבָיִים ***pōk̲eret̲ haṣṣ^{e}b̲āyiym:*** I. A proper noun designating Pokereth-Hazzebaim (NASB, NIV, Ezra 2:57; Neh. 7:59).

II. A proper noun designating Pokereth-Hazzebaim (KJV, Ezra 2:57; Neh. 7:59).

6381. פָּלָא ***pālā':*** A verb meaning to do something wonderful, to do something extraordinary, or difficult. It frequently signifies the wondrous works of God, especially His deliverance and judgments (Ex. 3:20; Ps. 106:22; 136:4; Mic. 7:15). Because God's extraordinary deeds inspire thanksgiving and praise, this Hebrew word occurs often in the hymnic literature of the Bible and of the Dead Sea Scrolls (Ps. 9:1[2]; 107:8; 145:5). While nothing is too extraordinary for God, various things are said to be beyond the abilities of some individuals to do or comprehend (Deut. 17:8; Prov. 30:18; Jer. 32:17); however, obeying God's commandments is not too difficult a task (Deut. 30:11). A rare use of this Hebrew word expresses the performance of a special vow beyond the ordinary commitment (Lev. 27:2; Num. 6:2; 15:3, 8).

6382. פֶּלֶא ***pele':*** A masculine noun meaning a wonder, a miracle, a marvel. This word is used to represent something unusual or extraordinary. Except for Lamentations 1:9, this term always appears in the context of God's words or deeds. It is used of God's actions among His people (Isa. 29:14); the Law of God (Psalm 119:129); God's acts of judgment and deliverance (Ex. 15:11; Ps. 78:12; Isa. 25:1); and the child to be born as the Messiah (Isa. 9:6[5]). These things then become the focus of people's worship of God (Ps. 77:11[12], 14[15]). This word is also used as an adverb to reveal how astounding, significant, and extreme was the fall of the city of Jerusalem (Lam. 1:9).

6383. פִּלְאִי ***pil'iy,*** **פֶּלִיא** ***peliy':*** A masculine adjective meaning wonderful, incomprehensible. The feminine form of this adjective is *p^{e}li'āyh* or *pil'iyyāh*. It was used as a description of the name of the angel of the Lord (Judg. 13:18); and as a description of the knowledge of the Lord (Ps. 139:6).

6384. פַּלֻּאִי ***pallu'iy:*** A proper noun designating Palluites (Num. 26:5).

6385. פָּלַג ***pālag:*** A verb meaning to split, to divide. It is used in the passive form to refer to the earth being divided (Gen. 10:25). In the factitive form, it refers to making or dividing a watercourse or cleaving a channel

(Job 38:25). The factitive form is also used metaphorically of the Lord to cause dissension, that is, dividing their tongues (Ps. 55:9[10]).

6386. פְּלַג pᵉlag: An Aramaic verb meaning to split, to divide. This word is the equivalent of the Hebrew verb *pālag* (6385). It is used only once when Daniel was interpreting Nebuchadnezzar's dream. The feet of the statue in the dream were composed partly of clay and partly of iron, representing the idea that the kingdom would be divided (Dan. 2:41).

6387. פְּלַג pᵉlag: An Aramaic masculine noun meaning half. Like the word *pᵉluggāh* (6392), this noun is derived from the verb *pᵉlag* (6386), meaning to divide, and represented the results of that action, the production of parts or divisions. Unlike the word *pᵉluggāh*, this term seems to assume a single division into two equal parts or halves. This term is used only once in the famous passage stating that the saints will be delivered for a time, times and a half time (Dan. 7:25).

6388. פֶּלֶג peleg: A masculine noun signifying a stream, a channel. It indicates any abundant flow of oil or water (Job 29:6); small or relatively large (Ps. 1:3). It refers to a channel or tributaries of a river, used figuratively of the streams of the city of God (Ps. 46:4[5]). God is the creator of the many streams (Ps. 65:9[10]) that so abundantly water the earth. It is used figuratively of a man's fertility or vigor, as well as his offspring (Prov. 5:16). It signifies the heart of the king whose streams are in God's control (Prov. 21:1). It designates man-made water channels (Isa. 30:25).

6389. פֶּלֶג peleg: A proper noun designating Peleg, a son of Eber. His name means "division." In his time the earth was divided into various languages and peoples (Gen. 11:1–9, 16–19).

6390. פְּלַגָּה pᵉlaggāh: A feminine noun meaning a stream, a division. This noun is derived from the verb *pālag* (6385), whose basic idea is to divide and which, in the extensive-factitive form, can refer to making a watercourse. It can also denote a stream (Job 20:17). See the words *nāhār* (5104), meaning river, and *naḥal* (6391), meaning a torrent or wadi.

6391. פְּלֻגָּה pᵉluggāh: A feminine noun meaning division. It can only be found in 2 Chronicles 35:5, where Josiah instructed the people of Israel to stand in the holy place by their family divisions.

6392. פְּלֻגָּה pᵉluggāh: An Aramaic feminine noun meaning division. Like the word *pᵉlag* (6387), this noun is derived from the verb *pᵉlag* (6386), meaning to divide, and represented the results of that action: the production of parts or divisions. Unlike *pᵉlag* (6387), this term seems to assume multiple divisions yielding several equal parts. It is only used once to refer to the apportionment of priests into the divisions that would share the responsibility for the restored Temple (Ezra 6:18).

6393. פְּלָדָה *p^{e}lāḏāh:* I. A feminine noun referring to metal, steel. It refers to metal of some kind; many translators prefer steel. It is used then of steel chariot frames or coverings (Nah. 2:3[4]).

II. A feminine noun meaning torch. Some translators earlier rendered the word as torch (Nah. 2:3[4]; KJV, NKJV).

6394. פִּלְדָּשׁ *pildāš:* A proper noun designating Pildash (Gen. 22:22).

6395. פָּלָה *pālāh:* A verb meaning to be distinct, separate, set apart, to be different. It describes the fact that Israel was to be a distinct or different people to God (Ex. 33:16). It can take on the sense of being wonderful or amazingly constructed (Ps. 139:14). It has a causative sense of making distinct or separate, making different (Ex. 8:22[18]; 9:4; Ps. 4:3[4]).

6396. פַּלּוּא *pallû':* A proper noun designating Pallu (Gen. 46:9; Ex. 6:14; Num. 26:5, 8; 1 Chr. 5:3).

6397. פְּלוֹנִי *p^{e}lôniy:* A proper noun designating Pelonite (1 Chr. 11:27, 36; 27:10).

6398. פָּלַח *pālaḥ:* A verb meaning to slice, to cut up, to plow, to pierce through. It refers to cutting up or splitting up something, e.g., slicing a vegetable (2 Kgs. 4:39); piercing or splitting open someone's kidney or liver (Job 16:13; Prov. 7:23). It figuratively depicts the birth process, the parting of the womb (Job 39:3); and plowing the ground, breaking it open (Ps. 141:7).

6399. פְּלַח *p^{e}laḥ:* An Aramaic verb meaning to serve, to revere, to worship. King Nebuchadnezzar was amazed when Daniel's three friends were not harmed in the furnace; he recognized their God for rescuing them because they would not serve any other (Dan. 3:28). King Darius referred to God as the One Daniel served continually (Dan. 6:16[17], 20[21]). Later, Daniel wrote of his vision of the Ancient of Days and how all nations worshiped Him (Dan. 7:14). This thought is echoed later in the same passage (Dan. 7:27). This word was also used to denote servants of the Temple (Ezra 7:24).

6400. פֶּלַח *pelaḥ:* A masculine noun indicating a piece of something. It refers to part of a millstone (Judg. 9:53; 2 Sam. 11:21; Job 41:24[16]). It describes a slice of a cake of figs (1 Sam. 30:12); or of pomegranates (Song 4:3; 6:7).

6401. פִּלְחָא *pilḥā':* A proper noun designating Pilha (Neh. 10:24[25]).

6402. פָּלְחָן *polḥan:* An Aramaic masculine abstract noun meaning service, worship. It describes the entire process involved in worshiping God (Ezra 7:19).

6403. פָּלַט pālaṯ: A verb meaning to escape, to take to safety, to bring forth. It can be used to depict a deliverer, one who helps to escape (2 Sam. 22:2). It describes deliverance or rescue from threatening situations (2 Sam. 22:44). It signifies survivors who have escaped, gotten away safely in time of danger (Ezek. 7:16). It means to give birth to a calf, to calve (Job 21:10). It means to be given a legal judgment of freedom, a clearance (Job 23:7). It describes the Lord's deliverance of the psalmist's life from oppressors (Ps. 17:13). In its causative usage, it means to take to safety, to deliver (Isa. 5:29; Mic. 6:14).

6404. פֶּלֶט peleṯ: A proper noun designating Pelet (1 Chr. 2:47; 12:3).

6405. פָּלֵט pālēṯ, פַּלֵּט pallēṯ: I. A masculine noun meaning an escaped person, a refugee; those spared. It describes persons escaped, spared from destruction (Jer. 44:14); fugitives, those who have fled (Jer. 50:28; 51:50).

II. A masculine noun meaning deliverance, escape. It modifies songs as songs of escape, deliverance (Ps. 32:7). Psalm 56:7[8] seems to employ 6403 as an imperative, cast out, separate out (KJV, escape).

6406. פַּלְטִי palṭiy: A proper noun designating Palti (Num. 13:9; 1 Sam. 25:44).

6407. פַּלְטִי palṭiy: A proper noun designating Paltite (2 Sam. 23:26).

6408. פִּלְטָי pilṭāy: A proper noun designating Piltai (Neh. 12:17).

6409. פַּלְטִיאֵל palṭiy'ēl: A proper noun designating Paltiel (Num. 34:26; 2 Sam. 3:15).

6410. פְּלַטְיָה p^elaṭyāh, פְּלַטְיָהוּ p^elaṭyāhû: A proper noun designating Pelatiah:

A. Son of Hananiah (1 Chr. 3:21).

B. Son of Ishi (1 Chr. 4:42).

C. A leader who signed Nehemiah's covenant (Neh. 10:22[23]).

D. Son of Benaiah (Ezek. 11:1, 13).

6411. פְּלָאיָה p^elā'yāh, פְּלָיָה p^elāyāh: A proper noun designating Pelaiah:

A. A descendant of David (Neh. 8:7; 10:10[11]).

B. A postexilic priest (1 Chr. 3:24).

6412. פָּלִיט pāliyṯ, פָּלֵט pālēṯ: I. A masculine noun referring to a refugee, a survivor. It indicates persons or groups who have lived through a dangerous situation; survivors or those who have escaped what might have been sure death; fugitives (Gen. 14:13; Josh. 8:22; 2 Kgs. 9:15, etc.).

II. A masculine noun indicating a refugee, a survivor. It is the same as I. In context it refers to Moabite fugitives (Num. 21:29); and to a group of survivors in the time when God will restore His people and the nations (Isa. 66:19).

6413. פְּלֵיטָה ***pᵉlēyṭāh:*** A feminine noun meaning deliverance, something delivered, a remnant. Jacob split his group into two camps so that if Esau attacked one, the other could escape (Gen. 32:8[9]). Joseph told his brothers that God used what they meant for evil to be deliverance for them (Gen. 45:7). Moses told Pharaoh that the locusts would eat whatever was left from the hail (Ex. 10:5). The Israelites looked for wives for the Benjamites who were left (Judg. 21:17). David had everyone flee, or no one would be safe from Absalom (2 Sam. 15:14).

6414. פָּלִיל ***pāliyl:*** A masculine noun meaning judge. This word is only used in the plural in the Hebrew Old Testament. The song of Moses said that even the enemies of Israel judged the Israelite God to be different from other gods (Deut. 32:31). As Job listed all the sins he had not committed, he mentioned that it would be shameful to be judged by those sins (Job 31:11). See the related Hebrew root *pālal* (6419).

6415. פְּלִילָה ***pᵉliylāh:*** A feminine noun meaning a settlement, a judgment. This form of the word is used only once in the Hebrew Old Testament in the book of Isaiah. In the oracle against Moab, the women cried out for a judgment or settlement to be made for them (Isa. 16:3). See the masculine form of this word *pāliyl* (6414) and the related Hebrew root *pālal* (6419).

6416. פְּלִילִי ***pᵉliyliy:*** An adjective indicating liable for judgment. It refers to an evil deed, adultery or idolatry, that would bring judgment, open to condemnation and punishment (Job 31:11, 28).

6417. פְּלִילִיָּה ***pᵉliyliyyah:*** A feminine noun meaning a judgment, a decision. It is a feminine abstract noun referring to the process of rendering a verdict in a case (Isa. 28:7).

6418. פֶּלֶךְ ***pelek̲:*** I. A masculine noun referring to a walking stick, a crutch; a spindle. It is a support device used by persons crippled or feeble, too weak to walk alone (2 Sam. 3:29). It refers to a share of, a part or a district in an area (Neh. 3:9, 12, 14–18). It refers to a spool or spindle holding thread or to cords for spinning (Prov. 31:19).

II. A masculine noun referring to a district, an area. It describes areas which certain men were appointed to overseer during the rebuilding of the walls of Jerusalem (Neh. 3:9, 12, 14–18).

6419. פָּלַל ***pālal:*** A verb meaning to pray, to intercede. This is the most common Hebrew word used to describe the general act of prayer (Jer. 29:7). It was often used to describe prayer offered in a time of distress, such as Hannah's prayer for a son (1 Sam. 1:10, 12); Elisha's prayer for the dead boy (2 Kgs. 4:33); Hezekiah's prayer for protection and health (2 Kgs. 19:15; 20:2); and Jonah's prayer from the fish (Jon. 2:1[2]). In some contexts, this word described a specific intercession of one person praying to the Lord for another, such as Abraham for Abimelech (Gen. 20:7, 17); Moses and Samuel for Israel (Num. 11:2; 21:7; 1 Sam. 7:5); the man of God for the king (1 Kgs. 13:6); or Ezra and Daniel for Israel's sins (Ezra 10:1; Dan. 9:4, 20). This prayer of intercession could also be made to a false god (Isa. 44:17; 45:14).

6420. פָּלָל ***pālāl:*** A proper noun designating Palal (Neh. 3:25).

6421. פְּלַלְיָה ***p^{e}lalyāh:*** A proper noun designating Pelaliah (Neh. 11:12).

6422. פַּלְמוֹנִי ***palmôniy:*** A pronoun meaning a certain one. It is used as a definite pronoun to point out a particular person or speaker (Dan. 8:13).

6423. פְּלֹנִי ***p^{e}lōniy:*** A pronoun meaning a certain one, a certain place. It is a definite pronoun used to indicate and identify a certain person (Ruth 4:1); or place (1 Sam. 21:2[3]; 2 Kgs. 6:8).

6424. פָּלַס ***pālas:*** A verb meaning to weigh out, to make level, to ponder. It means to calculate the weight of something. It is used figuratively of weighing out, pondering evil (Ps. 58:2[3]); and of the Lord's leveling or cleansing a path for His anger to pass over in judgment (Ps. 78:50). It means to guard, to watch carefully one's way of life (Prov. 4:26). It describes making one's way of life just, fair, level (Isa. 26:7).

6425. פֶּלֶס ***peles:*** A masculine noun meaning a balance, a scale. It refers to a balance or the indicator on a scale or balance (Prov. 16:11; Isa. 40:12). In context it is used to show the immensity of God and His power as He weighs even the mountains. God's scales and balances are always just and accurate.

6426. פָּלַץ ***pālaṣ:*** A verb meaning to tremble. It means to quake, to shake, to quiver, to move back and forth. It describes the shaking or trembling of the pillars or foundations of the earth (Job 9:6).

6427. פַּלָּצוּת ***pallāṣûṯ:*** A feminine noun meaning shuddering. This word describes the physical reaction of the body in response to fear. Job shuddered at the fate of the wicked (Job 21:6); David shuddered in fear of his enemy (Ps. 55:5[6]); Isaiah shuddered because of God's judgment (Isa. 21:4); and those about to be judged by God will shudder (Ezek. 7:18). See the word *mip̱leṣeṯ* (4656).

6428. פָּלַשׁ ***pālaš:*** A verb meaning to roll in, to wallow in. It means to turn over and over or to turn from side to side. Rolling in ashes or dust depicted great distress and sorrow (Jer. 6:26; 25:34; Ezek. 27:30; Mic. 1:10).

6429. פְּלֶשֶׁת ***p^elešet:*** A proper noun designating Philistia, the land where the Philistines lived. It was also called "land of the Philistines," a section of the Mediterranean coastal plain. It stretched from the Nahal Besor (a small stream or wadi) in the south to the Yarkon River in the north. It contained key Philistine cities: Gaza, Ashkelon, Ashdon, Ekron, and Gath in its northern half. It occurs only ca. seven times in the Old Testament. It is first mentioned in Moses' "song at the sea" in anticipation of Israel's march into Canaan (Ex. 15:14). The Lord would rule over it (Ps. 60:8[10]).

6430. פְּלִשְׁתִּי ***p^elištiy:*** A proper noun designating the gentilic or ethnic form of *Philistine* indicating that a person belonged to the Philistines who had settled in Philistia. Their biblical ancestors were Casluhites, sons of Mizraim (Gen. 10:14). The Philistines had been a part of the various migrations of the "sea peoples" (Amos 9:7). They were in the land in small numbers during the time of the patriarchs (Gen. 20:26). They were for many years Israel's chief enemy until David effectively disabled them (2 Sam. 15—22). Solomon ruled over them (1 Kgs. 4:20–21).

6431. פֶּלֶת ***pelet:*** A proper noun designating Peleth (Num. 16:1; 1 Chr. 2:33).

6432. פְּלֵתִי ***p^elētiy:*** A proper noun designating Pelethite (2 Sam. 8:18; 15:18; 20:7, 23; 1 Kgs. 1:38, 44; 1 Chr. 18:17).

6433. פֻּם ***pum:*** An Aramaic masculine noun meaning mouth. It is the human organ that produces words, whether righteous or evil (Dan. 4:31[28]). It is used figuratively of the front opening of a cave or den (Dan. 6:17[18]). Figuratively in literature, it personifies an object, makes it represent a person (Dan. 7:5, 8, 20).

6434. פֵּן ***pēn:*** A masculine noun indicating a corner, street corner. It is used in the plural once with the article to modify gates, the corner gate (Zech. 14:10).

6435. פֶּן ***pen:*** A conjunction meaning lest, so that, not. It indicates the prevention of a possible event: lest, so that . . . not (Gen. 3:22); or of an event that will occur unless it is stopped (Gen. 11:4; 19:19; 26:7, 9; 2 Sam. 20:6). It indicates a negative purpose or result (Gen. 3:3). It is found at the beginning of a sentence meaning in order that not, lest (Isa. 36:18). Used with the perfect form of the verb, the condition may have already been fulfilled (2 Kgs. 2:16 and above in 2 Sam. 20:6).

6436. פַּנַּג ***pannag:*** I. A masculine noun meaning a cake, a confection. It refers to one of the items in a list of goods traded among Tyre, Israel, and Judah (Ezek. 27:17). Its exact meaning is uncertain.

II. A proper noun Pannag. It is taken as a specific food item by some translators (KJV) (Ezek. 27:17; NKJV, millet).

6437. פָּנָה pānāh: A verb meaning to turn. It is used in various contexts. It has the following basic meanings: to turn toward (plus *'el*) (Judg. 6:14; Isa. 13:14; Jer. 50:16); to turn in a direction (plus *'al*) (Gen. 24:10); to turn from, away (plus *min* [4480]) (Gen. 18:22); to turn with the goal, intention of doing something (Num. 21:33; Deut. 1:7; 1 Kgs. 10:13; Eccl. 2:12); to take a specific direction, north, south, etc. (Ex. 16:10; Num. 16:42[17:7]; Josh. 15:7). In its intensive and causative stems, it may mean to turn, remove, or put something out of the way (Judg. 15:4; Jer. 48:39; Zeph. 3:15). In its passive use, it refers to being turned (Jer. 49:8). It is found in many figurative or idiomatic expressions: to turn to God in worship and time of need (Isa. 45:22); to turn and follow one's own desires (Isa. 53:6); to turn toward evening, for evening to come (Gen. 24:63); likewise for morning to come (Ex. 14:27). To turn to persons can mean to regard them compassionately, to give consideration to them (2 Sam. 9:8); it is used of inanimate things as well (Eccl. 2:11).

6438. פִּנָּה pinnāh: A feminine noun meaning corner. It refers to a location where various surfaces or lines meet to form an angle. It is used of the corners of a house (Job 1:19); a wall (Neh. 3:24); an altar (Ex. 27:2); a street (Prov. 7:8), etc. The phrase *'eben pinnāh* means cornerstone (Job 38:6). It combines with more words to indicate corner tower (Zeph. 1:16); corner gate (2 Kgs. 14:13). Figuratively, it designates a leader (Judg. 20:2; 1 Sam. 14:38; Isa. 19:13; Zech. 10:4).

6439. פְּנוּאֵל p^enû'ēl, פְּנִיאֵל p^eniy'ēl: A proper noun designating Penuel:

A. A city on the Jabbok River (Gen. 32:30[31], 31[32]; Judg. 8:8, 9, 17; 1 Kgs. 12:25).

B. A descendant of Judah (1 Chr. 4:4).

C. A descendant of Benjamin (1 Chr. 8:25).

6440. פָּנֶה pāneh, פָּנִים pāniym: A masculine plural noun meaning a face. Although the literal meaning of face is possible (Gen. 43:31; Lev. 13:41; 1 Kgs. 19:13), most of the time this word occurs in a figurative, idiomatic phrase. Face can be a substitute for the entire person (Ex. 33:14, 15); or it can be a reflection of the person's mood or attitude: defiant (Jer. 5:3); ruthless (Deut. 28:50); joyful (Job 29:24); humiliated (2 Sam. 19:5[6]); terrified (Isa. 13:8); displeased (Gen. 4:5). It is also used to indicate direction (Gen. 31:21); or purpose (Jer. 42:15, 17). This noun also designates the top or surface of something: the ground (Gen. 2:6; 4:14); a field (Isa. 28:25); or water (Gen. 1:2). It also connotes the front of something, like a pot (Jer. 1:13); or an army (Joel 2:20). With various prepositions, *pānîm* takes on the nature of a particle and expresses such concepts as upon (Ex. 23:17; Lev. 14:53); before a place (Num. 8:22); before a time (Ezek. 42:12; Amos 1:1); in the presence of (Esth. 1:10).

6441. פְּנִימָה p^eniymāh: An adverb meaning within, inside, inner. It refers to the inner recesses of a structure, what lies within, what is internal. It can mean to the inside, inward (Lev. 10:18; Ezek. 41:3); or located inside, within (1 Kgs. 6:18, 19; Ezek. 40:16). It can refer to something shared within a family or household (2 Kgs. 7:11).

6442. פְּנִימִי p^eniymiy: An adjective meaning inner, innate. It refers to something that is located inside, within another structure (1 Kgs. 6:27, 36; 7:12, 50; Esth. 4:11; 5:1). It is used often of the inner features of the Temple in Ezekiel (8:13; 46:1).

6443. פְּנִינִים p^eniyniym: A masculine plural noun indicating jewels, rubies. It refers to ornaments worn for beautification, usually made of gold, silver, and precious stones (Prov. 3:15). Jewels are known for their great value as well.

6444. פְּנִנָּה p^eninnāh: A proper noun designating Peninnah (1 Sam. 1:2, 4).

6445. פָּנַק pānaq: A verb meaning to pamper. It means to treat someone with great care and concern, to help him or her along patiently (Prov. 29:21).

6446. פַּס pas: I. An adjective meaning richly ornamented; made with many colors. It is used in its plural form *passîm.* It modifies a tunic or a robe, indicating its many colors or its length (Gen. 37:3, 23, 32; 2 Sam. 13:18, 19); a highly esteemed garment.

II. An adjective indicating something long-sleeved. It refers to a long-sleeved tunic or robe worn by the king's daughter (2 Sam. 13:18, 19); it was a highly esteemed garment.

6447. פַּס pas: An Aramaic masculine noun indicating a part. It describes the palm or back of a person's hand. In context it denotes the appearance of a strong human hand (Dan. 5:5, 24).

6448. פָּסַג pāsag: A verb meaning to go through, to view. It has the sense of walking or passing through something to view it carefully, to appreciate it (Ps. 48:13[14]).

6449. פִּסְגָּה pisgāh: A proper noun designating Pisgah, a mountain top where Israel encamped on the way to Moab (Num. 21:20). From it Balaam tried to curse Israel (Num. 23:14). Moses viewed Canaan from its heights (Deut. 34:1). It was inherited by Reuben (Josh. 13:20). Sihon, king of the Amorites, had ruled it earlier.

6450. פַּס דַּמִּים pas dammiym: A proper noun designating Pas Dammim (1 Chr. 11:13).

6451. פִּסָּה pissāh: I. A feminine noun indicating abundance. It refers to a supply or a presence of something beyond what is needed, even an excess of something (Ps. 72:16).

II. A feminine noun indicating a handful of something. In its context it refers to the presence of a handful of corn, that is, a significant presence of corn where it might least be expected, promising an abundance of God's blessings (Ps. 72:16).

6452. פָּסַח *pasaḥ:* A verb meaning to leap, to pass over, to halt, to limp, to be lame. The first occurrence of this verb is in Exodus, where God states that He will preserve the Israelites by passing over their homes when He goes through Egypt to kill the firstborn (Ex. 12:13, 23, 27). This sentiment is echoed by the prophet Isaiah (Isa. 31:5). In 2 Samuel 4:4, the word is used of Saul's grandson who became lame. Before Elijah confronted the prophets of Baal, he confronted the Israelites for their syncretism. He asked them how long they would bounce back and forth between the Lord and Baal (1 Kgs. 18:21). Then during Elijah's confrontation, the prophets of Baal began to dance on the altar that they had constructed (1 Kgs. 18:26). This was probably some sort of cultic dance performed as part of the sacrifice ritual.

6453. פֶּסַח *pesaḥ:* A masculine noun meaning Passover, a Passover animal, a sacrifice. The word is used forty-nine times, usually referring to the Passover festival or celebration. It is first used to describe the Passover ritual while Israel was still in Egypt (Ex. 12:11, 27, 43, 48; 34:25). The first Passover ideally was constituted as follows: on the human level, the Israelites killed the Passover sacrifice on the evening of the fourteenth day of the first month, Abib or Nisan (March or April). They then took some of the blood of the slain Passover animal (Deut. 16:2, 5) and smeared it on the sides and tops of the doorframes of their houses (cf. Ex. 12:7). The Passover ritual and the Passover animal were directed to and belonged to the Lord (Ex. 12:11, 48; Deut. 16:1). They then roasted the animal (lamb, kid, young ram, goat—a one-year old without any defect) and ate it with their sandals on their feet and their staffs in their hands, ready to move out in haste at any time. The angel of death passed through Egypt and passed over the Israelites' houses with the blood of the lambs on the doorposts, but the angel struck the firstborn of all the Egyptian households (cf. Ex. 12:12, 13, 29). Later Passovers were held in commemoration of the historical event of Israel's deliverance from Egyptian bondage.

The animals eaten were also called the *pesaḥ*, the Passover sacrifice (Ex. 12:21; 2 Chr. 30:15; 35:1). The Passover was celebrated throughout Israel's history before and after the exile (Num. 9:4; Josh. 5:10; 2 Kgs. 23:22; Ezra 6:19, 20).

6454. פָּסֵחַ *pāsēaḥ:* A proper noun designating Paseah (1 Chr. 4:12; Ezra 2:49; Neh. 3:6; 7:51).

6455. פִּסֵּחַ ***pissēaḥ:*** An adjective meaning lame, crippled. It denotes a person who has a physical defect, an injured leg or foot, hindering a person's walking ability. It disqualified a person for the priesthood (Lev. 21:18; 2 Sam. 9:13); or an animal for sacrifice (Deut. 15:21; Mal. 1:8, 13). Job had served as feet to the lame (Job 29:15).

6456. פָּסִיל ***pāsiyl:*** A masculine noun meaning idol. This word comes from the verb *pāsal* (6458), meaning to hew or to cut, which was done to create a carved image. In the Law of the Old Testament, it was clear that such idols should be burned (Deut. 7:5, 25); and cut down (Deut. 12:3); for they provoked God to anger (Ps. 78:58; Jer. 8:19); and incited Him to judgment (Jer. 51:47, 52; Micah 1:7; 5:13[12]). The presence of these idols were indicative of the sin and rebellion of the people (2 Chr. 33:19, 22; Hos. 11:2); while the removal of such idols was a sign of repentance (2 Chr. 34:3, 4, 7; Isa. 30:22).

6457. פָּסַךְ ***pāsak:*** A proper noun designating Pasach (1 Chr. 7:33).

6458. פָּסַל ***pāsal:*** A verb meaning to hew, to cut. This word is used most often in the context of cutting stone. Moses cut two stone tablets so God could record His words on them (Ex. 34:1, 4; Deut. 10:1, 3); the builders cut stones in building the Temple (1 Kgs. 5:18[32]); and an idol maker cut the material to create an idol (Hab. 2:18). See the related nouns *p^esiyl* (6456) and *pesel* (6459), meaning idol.

6459. פֶּסֶל ***pesel:*** A noun meaning idol, a graven image. This word comes from the verb *pāsal* (6458), meaning to hew or to cut, which was done to create an idol. In the Law of the Old Testament, the Lord forbade Israel to create such images (Ex. 20:4; Lev. 26:1; Deut. 5:8); for they were an abomination to Him (Deut. 27:15). Those who served idols would be ashamed in the judgment (Ps. 97:7; Isa. 42:17); and the Lord would cut them off from Him (Nah. 1:14). The presence of these idols were indicative of the sin and rebellion of the people (Deut. 4:16, 23, 25; 2 Chr. 33:7). The prophets often demonstrated the folly of these idols: they were profitable for nothing (Isa. 44:10; Hab. 2:18); they could easily be burned (Isa. 44:15); they had no breath (Jer. 10:14); and they could not save (Isa. 45:20). Idols could be made of metal (Judg. 17:3, 4; Isa. 40:19); wood (Isa. 40:20; 44:15, 17); or possibly stone (Hab. 2:18; cf. Hab. 2:19).

6460. פְּסַנְטֵרִין ***p^esanṭēriyn,*** פְּסַנְתֵּרִין ***p^esantēriyn:*** An Aramaic masculine plural noun designating a stringed musical instrument; a harp (psaltery). It refers to one of the many instruments present at the dedication of Nebuchadnezzar's golden statue (Dan. 3:5, 7, 10, 15). A harp and psaltery both had sounding boards to magnify the sound.

6461. פָּסַס ***pāsas:*** A verb meaning to disappear, to vanish. It means to vanish, to cease to be present. It depicts what happens to the righteous when the wicked are in control (Ps. 12:1[2]).

6462. פִּסְפָּה ***pispāh:*** A proper noun designating Pispah (1 Chr. 7:38).

6463. פָּעָה ***pāʻāh:*** A verb meaning to cry out, to groan. It describes the behavior and sounds uttered in the throes of a woman giving birth but in context is used of God's crying out as He brought judgment on His people (Isa. 42:14).

6464. פָּעוּ ***pāʻû,*** פָּעִי ***pāʻiy:*** A proper noun designating Pau (Gen. 36:39; 1 Chr. 1:50).

6465. פְּעוֹר ***pᵉʻôr:*** A proper noun designating Peor. It refers to a high point in Moab from which Balaam was to curse Israel (Num. 23:28). Israel later worshiped Baal of Peor (Num. 25:18; 31:16; Josh. 22:17). It was possibly located near Mount Nebo east of the northern end of the Dead Sea.

6466. פָּעַל ***pāʻal:*** A verb meaning to do, to make. It is used of constructing or making something (Ps. 7:13[14]); or just to make (Isa. 41:4). It takes the sense of doing or practicing something, e.g., deceit (Hos. 7:1); righteousness (Ps. 15:2). Hence, it means to accomplish, to do, to perform, to make: God made His mountain into His dwelling (Ex. 15:17); and performed His works for His people (Num. 23:23; cf. Deut. 32:27). Job refers to God, his Maker, Creator (Job 36:3), where the word has the sense of God's creative activity in it. It is used figuratively of persons acting against God (Job 7:20; 35:6). It refers to doing what God hates, evil, iniquity (Ps. 5:5[6]); Prov. 10:29; Mic. 2:1); but also of doing the Lord's ordinances, His will (Zeph. 2:3).

6467. פֹּעַל ***pōʻal:*** A masculine noun indicating a deed, an act; a work. It indicates what is performed, completed, done: God's work in all of His dealings with people (Deut. 32:4; Ps. 44:1[2]; 64:9[10]); the work and toil of people in every way (Ruth 2:12; Job 24:5; Ps. 104:23). It is used of deeds that express character (Prov. 20:11; 24:12, 29). It depicts evil acts, deeds indicated from context (Jer. 25:14; 50:29); and good actions (Prov. 21:8). It refers to the product of God's work and toil (Isa. 45:9, 11). It may have the sense of the work to acquire something (Prov. 21:6). It stands for the wages or what is due to a worker (Jer. 22:13); or it refers to one's accomplishments in life (Isa. 1:31).

6468. פְּעֻלָּה ***pᵉʻullāh:*** A feminine noun referring to wages, rewards, work. It indicates the deeds of people or God (Ps. 17:4; 28:5); whether good or bad (2 Chr. 15:7; Prov. 11:18; Isa. 65:7). It refers to rewards or wages earned (Lev. 19:13; Prov. 10:16); a reward from the Lord for doing what is right (Isa. 49:4; 61:8). It is used once of punishment earned (Ps. 109:20). It describes the divinely guided deeds and actions of a pagan king (Ezek. 29:20).

6469. פְּעֻלְּתַי ***peʿulletay:*** A proper noun designating Peullethai (1 Chr. 26:5).

6470. פָּעַם ***pāʿam:*** A verb meaning to stir, to be stirred, to be troubled. It indicates a troubling or agitation bothering persons, making them act (Gen. 41:8); especially God's Spirit stirring up persons to motivate them (Judg. 13:25). Sometimes this anxiety keeps people from being able to act (Ps. 77:4[5]); or to rest (Dan. 2:1, 3).

6471. פַּעַם ***paʿam:*** A common noun indicating time, occurrence, foot. It refers to a specific time when an occurrence takes place (Gen. 2:23; 46:30). In its dual form, it means twice (*paʿamayim*). The phrase *kepaʿam-bepaʿam* means formerly or as is usually the case (Num. 24:1). Repeated but separated, it means at one time . . . at another time (Prov. 7:12). The phrase *kap peʿāmay* means sole of one's foot (2 Kgs. 19:24).

6472. פַּעֲמֹן ***paʿamōn:*** A masculine noun indicating a bell. It refers to small bells that were fastened to the lower fringe of the High Priest's robe to indicate his presence and movement (Ex. 28:33, 34; 39:25, 26).

6473. פָּעַר ***pāʿar:*** A verb meaning to open one's mouth, to jeer. It means to mock or jeer at someone with one's mouth opened wide (Job 16:10); but in a different context, it means to open one's mouth to praise or accept someone respectfully or in positive wonderment (Job 29:23). It is used figuratively of an open mouth panting after God's commandments (Ps. 119:131). In a strong figurative illustration, Sheol, the place of the dead, is personified with a mouth open to receive its victims (Isa. 5:14).

6474. פַּעֲרַי ***paʿaray:*** A proper noun designating Paarai (2 Sam. 23:35).

6475. פָּצָה ***pāṣāh:*** I. A verb meaning to open one's mouth, to utter. It is used in a strong figure of speech depicting the earth's opening its mouth to receive the innocent blood of Abel (Gen. 4:11); or to swallow the wicked in an earthquake (Num. 16:30; Deut. 11:6). It signifies the uttering of a word, speaking (Judg. 11:35, 36; Job 35:16); especially in an accusation (Ps. 22:13[14]; Lam. 2:16; 3:46). It is used of uttering or making a vow (Ps. 66:14). It refers to a bird opening its mouth (Isa. 10:14); or the prophet Ezekiel opening his mouth to eat a scroll (Ezek. 2:8).

II. A verb meaning to rescue, to deliver. It is used in an imperative form when the psalmist implores the Lord to open up to him to rescue him from his enemies (Ps. 144:7, 10, 11).

6476. פָּצַח ***pāṣaḥ:*** I. A verb meaning to break forth in singing. It means to break out, to shout forth. It is used of the people of the earth bursting forth in jubilation (Isa. 14:7); of the mountains or nature breaking out in joy after holding in their excitement (Isa. 44:23; 49:13; 52:9; 55:12).

II. A verb meaning to break. It refers to shattering or breaking something. In context the "bones" of God's people are shattered (Mic. 3:3).

6477. פְּצִירָה p^e*ṣiyrāh:* I. A feminine noun meaning price, charge. It indicates the cost for getting various agricultural tools sharpened (1 Sam. 13:21).

II. A feminine noun indicating a file for sharpening. It indicates a file or a stone for sharpening various agricultural tools (1 Sam. 13:21).

6478. פָּצַל *pāṣal:* A verb meaning to peel or strip bark off. It indicates removing narrow, long pieces of bark from trees or wooden poles or rods (Gen. 30:37, 38).

6479. פְּצָלָה p^e*ṣālāh:* A feminine noun indicating a peeled spot, a stripe. It refers to an exposed area on fresh wooden poles or rods where the bark has been removed (Gen. 30:37).

6480. פָּצַם *pāṣam:* A verb meaning to split open, to tear open. It refers to the creation of a tear, crevass, or deep crack in something. In context it describes the effects of an earthquake on the surface of the earth (Ps. 60:2[4]).

6481. פָּצַע *pāṣa':* A verb meaning to bruise, to crush. It means to destroy or ruin something by violently inflicting blows on it. It describes the emasculating of a man's testicles by crushing (Deut. 23:1[2]). It has the sense of injuring or bruising someone (1 Kgs. 20:37; Song 5:7).

6482. פֶּצַע *peṣa':* A common noun indicating a bruise, a wound. It refers to a wound or bruise that has been inflicted, usually by striking (Gen. 4:23; Ex. 21:25). Job speaks of the wounds or injuries he has sustained from his illness (Job 9:17). Wounds, on the other hand, physical or emotional, may serve a good purpose (Prov. 20:30; 27:6). The word refers to all kinds of possible wounds (Prov. 23:29). The presence of wounds is used in a figurative sense to indicate Israel's spiritual sickness (Isa. 1:6).

6483. פִּצֵּץ *piṣṣēṣ:* I. A masculine proper noun Happizzez. A priest of Aaron's line who received an allotment when the lots were drawn to serve at the temple (1 Chr. 24:15).

II. A masculine proper noun Aphses or Happizzez. A priest, a descendant of Aaron who received the eighteenth lot as an assignment to serve at the temple.

III. A verb meaning to shatter, to break in pieces. It means to shake up people, to rattle them. It is used figuratively of God's supposed shattering of Job (16:12). It describes the Word of God breaking up a rock (Jer.

23:29); or of His look demolishing mountains (Hab. 3:6).

6484. פָּצַר *pāṣar:* A verb meaning to peck at, to press, to push. It indicates a literal physical push against someone (Gen. 19:9); figuratively, it refers to urging someone (Gen. 33:11) to do something (Judg. 19:7). In a negative sense, it refers to rebellion against someone, arrogance (1 Sam. 15:23).

6485. פָּקַד *pāqaḏ:* A verb meaning to attend, to visit, and to search out. The word refers to someone (usually God) paying attention to persons, either to do them good (Gen. 50:24, 25; Ex. 3:16; 1 Sam. 2:21; Jer. 23:2); or to bring punishment or harm (Ex. 20:5; Isa. 10:12; Jer. 23:2). The word also means, usually in a causative form, to appoint over or to commit to, that is, to cause people to attend to something placed under their care (Gen. 39:4, 5; Josh. 10:18; Isa. 62:6). The passive causative form means to deposit, that is, to cause something to be attended to (Lev. 6:4[5:23]). The word also means to number or to be numbered, which is an activity requiring attention. This meaning occurs over ninety times in the book of Numbers. The word can also mean (usually in a passive form) lacking or missing, as if a quantity was numbered less than an original amount (Judg. 21:3; 1 Sam. 20:18; 1 Kgs. 20:39).

6486. פְּקֻדָּה p^e*quddāh:* A feminine noun meaning an arrangement, an office, an officer, accounting. The root idea is something that is attended to or set in order. The word signifies the arrangement of fighting men under an officer (2 Chr. 17:14), of priests or Levites in an order (1 Chr. 23:11; 24:19); or the arrangement of the Tabernacle and its contents (Num. 4:16[2x]). It signifies the office of one in charge of something (Ps. 109:8); and the officers themselves (2 Kgs. 11:18; Isa. 60:17). Most often, the word means accounting and refers to a time of accounting when God attended to people's actions, usually to call them to account for their sins (Num. 16:29; Jer. 48:44). In Job 10:12, however, God's attention was for Job's good.

6487. פִּקָּדוֹן *piqqāḏôn:* A masculine noun meaning deposit. The root idea is that something is left under someone's care or attention. The word occurs three times in the Old Testament. In Genesis 41:36, the word referred to a store of food that Joseph advised Pharaoh to store up for the coming famine. In Leviticus 6:2[5:21], 4[5:23], the word signified any deposit left in someone's care. If the keeper of this deposit dealt dishonestly with it, he had to pay a 20 percent penalty in addition to the deposit.

6488. פְּקִדֻת p^e*qiḏuṯ:* A feminine noun meaning supervision, oversight. It occurs only in Jeremiah 37:13, where it refers with the word *ba'al* (1167), meaning master, to an official or policeman as a master of supervision. In this passage, the officer was stationed at the Gate of Benjamin where financial transactions took place (cf. Deut. 21:19; Ruth 4:1ff.); and where the king sometimes officiated (cf. Jer. 38:7). The office gave its bearer the legal power to arrest Jeremiah (Jer. 37:13).

6489. פְּקוֹד *peqôḏ:* A proper noun designating Pekod (Jer. 50:21; Ezek. 23:23).

6490. פִּקּוּד *piqqûḏ,* פִּקּוּדִים *peqûḏiym:* A masculine noun meaning precept, instruction. The root expresses the idea that God is paying attention to how He wants things ordered (see *pāqaḏ*[6485]). God's precepts strike those who love Him as right and delightful (Ps. 19:8[9]). This word is always plural and is only found in the Psalms, mostly in Psalm 119 (twenty-one times). This psalm talked of seeking (Ps. 119:40, 45, 94); keeping (Ps. 119:63, 69, 134); and not forgetting God's instructions (Ps. 119:87, 93, 141); even when opposed by the proud (Ps. 119:69, 78). The psalmist's diligence in obeying God's precepts was rewarded with understanding and the hatred of evil (Ps. 119:100, 104); liberty (Ps. 119:45); confidence in asking God's help (Ps. 119:94, 173); and spiritual life (Ps. 119:93).

6491. פָּקַח *pāqaḥ:* A verb meaning to open. It refers figuratively to one's eyes being opened to wisdom, understanding, reality (Gen. 3:5, 7); or to some physical object not noticed before (Gen. 21:19); or even of normally unseen spiritual forces (2 Kgs. 6:17, 20). Opening the eyes is a sign of life (2 Kgs. 4:35). To open one's eyes is an idiom meaning to pay attention, to be watchful, to notice what is going on (2 Kgs. 19:16; Dan. 9:18; Zech. 12:4); or to bring judgment on someone (Job 14:3). It also is used to mean to be diligent, industrious, not lazy (Prov. 20:13). It is used in a proverb to indicate the shortness of life or the possession of riches (Job 27:19). God is able to heal the blind, open their eyes (Ps. 146:8).

6492. פֶּקַח *peqaḥ:* A proper noun designating Pekah, a king of Israel who ruled twenty years (752–732 B.C.). He was son of Remaliah and ruled from Samaria. He was a typical evil Israelite king who continued to follow the evil ways of Israel's first king, Jeroboam I (2 Kgs. 15:27, 28). Assyria began to dismantle the northern kingdom in his reign (2 Kgs. 15:29). He was assassinated by Hoshea, the last king in Israel.

6493. פִּקֵּחַ *piqqēaḥ:* A masculine adjective meaning seeing, sight. This noun is derived from the verb *pāqaḥ* (6491), meaning to open the eyes and ears. In a literal sense, it occurs in Exodus 4:11 when God answered Moses' objections for leading the people out of Egypt. In a metaphorical sense, this term represented those who could see clearly but could be blinded by a gift (Ex. 23:8).

6494. פְּקַחְיָה p^eqaḥyāh: A proper noun designating Pekahiah (2 Kgs. 15:22, 23, 26).

6495. פְּקַח־קוֹחַ p^eqaḥ-qôaḥ: A masculine noun indicating an opening; a release from captivity. This phrase means literally, opening of vision as eyesight. In context it indicates the freeing of those who had been bound (Isa. 61:1).

6496. פָּקִיד pāqiyḏ: A masculine noun meaning a commissioner, a deputy, and an overseer. Depending on the context, this term has a broad range of possible meanings. It could apply to government representatives whose positions are temporary, like the officers appointed by Pharaoh to collect grain during the seven plentiful years (Gen. 41:34). It could also represent a permanent position of leadership for a king (Judg. 9:28); a high priest (2 Chr. 24:11); or a Levite (2 Chr. 31:13). It could further signify a general leader of men, such as a military officer (2 Kgs. 25:19); a tribal leader (Neh. 11:9); or a priestly leader (Neh. 11:14).

6497. פְּקָעִים p^eqā'iym: A masculine plural noun referring to gourds, knob shaped projections. It refers to decorative ornamental gourds carved from cedar wood for the Temple (1 Kgs. 6:18; 7:24).

6498. פַּקֻּעֹת paqqu'ōṯ: A feminine plural noun indicating gourds. In context it refers to poisonous gourds growing in the wild, capable of causing death to humans (2 Kgs. 4:39).

6499. פַּר par, פָּר pār: A masculine noun indicating a young bull, a bull. This refers often to young bulls (Gen. 32:15[16]), a major source of food, sacrificial animals, and wealth in the ancient Near East (Ex. 24:5; 29:1; Lev. 4:3; Num. 7:88). This term was used in peace offerings or offerings of well-being, burnt offerings (Judg. 6:25); sin offerings (Ezek. 43:19). Figuratively, it depicts leaders (Isa. 34:7; Jer. 50:27; Ezek. 39:18). It is found in a powerful figurative expression, standing for the fruit of or the offering of our lips (Hos. 14:2[3]; *pārîm ś^{e}paṯênû*).

6500. פָּרָא pārā': A verb meaning to be fruitful, to flourish. It indicates the growth and prosperity of Israel (Ephraim), economically and politically, which God would cut short (Hos. 13:15).

6501. פֶּרֶא pere': A common noun meaning wild donkey. It is generally taken to refer to a wild ass or donkey (Job 6:5). Others suggest zebra. The Lord cares for these animals (Ps. 104:11); even in their lone wanderings (Hos. 8:9). It is used in a metaphor to describe the character of Ishmael and his descendants (Gen. 16:12). Elsewhere, it serves as a depiction of Judah (Jer. 14:6) or Israel (Hos. 8:9).

6502. פִּרְאָם pir'ām: A proper noun designating Piram (Josh. 10:3).

6503. פַּרְבָּר parbār: I. A masculine noun designating a court area, a precinct. It refers, according to context, to an area located within the Temple environs or very near the Temple area (2 Kgs. 23:11). Levites were stationed in the Parbar or certain court districts (1 Chr. 26:18).

II. A masculine noun Parbar; a court area in Solomon's Temple. It is given the status of a proper name for a courtly precinct area by some translators (1 Chr. 26:18).

6504. פָּרַד pāraḏ: A verb meaning to divide, to separate, to disperse, to be separated, to be scattered. It means to split into two or more parts or pieces: a river into four streams (Gen. 2:10); the earth into various areas of habitation based on languages (Gen. 10:5). It describes the process of the nations being separated out (Gen. 10:32; 25:23). It is used of persons parting, going separate ways (Gen. 13:9; Ruth 1:17). It has the sense of being separate from, not a part of, not mixing with (Esth. 3:8). It describes the separating out of things from each other (Gen. 30:40). It describes the enemies of the Lord being dispersed, scattered (Ps. 92:9 [10]). It is used figuratively of a person's bones being out of place, separated, out of joint from distress and oppression.

6505. פֶּרֶד pereḏ: A masculine noun meaning mule. It depicts the offspring of a donkey and a horse that is nearly always sterile. It indicates a beast of burden and transportation but also a valuable piece of property (2 Sam. 13:9). It and the horse were known for their need to be contained and guided; they were without understanding (Ps. 32:9).

6506. פִּרְדָּה pirdāh: A feminine noun indicating a female mule. It is a female cross between a donkey and horse. A mule was valuable property. In context it refers to a mule belonging to King David. Riding on it gave the rider some claim to royalty and supposedly the support of the king (1 Kgs. 1:33, 38, 44).

6507. פְּרֻדֹת p^e^ruḏōṯ: A feminine noun meaning seed, grain. It refers to separated grain that has been planted in the ground after plowing (Joel 1:17).

6508. פַּרְדֵּס pardēs: A masculine noun indicating a forest, a park, an orchard. It refers to an area covered by trees and thick shrubbery (Neh. 2:8); if man-made, a place well-landscaped and manicured, a park for beauty and enjoyment (Eccl. 2:5). It describes the bride as a garden or orchard full of fruits (Song 4:13).

6509. פָּרָה pārāh: A verb meaning to be fruitful, to flourish. It indicates the multiplication and successful production of fruit, offspring, or flavors from living fruits, vegetables, animals, or human beings: human offspring (Gen. 1:22, 28; 8:17; 9:1, 7; Deut. 29:18[17]). It describes Israel as a nation (Ex. 1:7; 23:30; Ps. 105:24).

It shows the root of Jesse bearing messianic fruit, descendants (Isa. 11:1). In its causative uses, it has the sense of making fruitful (Gen. 17:6).

6510. פָּרָה ***pārāh:*** A feminine noun referring to a cow, a heifer. It refers to female cattle. Heifers are female cattle that have not yet borne a calf. Israel is likened to a stubborn heifer (Hos. 4:16). It is used derisively of the rich, narcissistic women of Bashan, "cows of Bashan" (Amos 4:1).

6511. פָּרָה ***pārāh:*** A proper noun designating Parah (Josh. 18:23).

6512. פֵּרָה ***pērāh:*** A feminine noun referring to a digging mole. It refers to digging moles (*ḥ*^{e}*p̱or pērôṯ*). It may refer to the diggings of moles in their holes and chambers underground or to the moles themselves (Isa. 2:20).

6513. פֻּרָה ***purāh:*** A proper noun designating Purah (Judg. 7:10, 11).

6514. פְּרוּדָא p^e***rûḏā',*** **פְּרִידָא** p^e***riyḏā':*** A proper noun designating Peruda, Perida (Ezra 2:55; Neh. 7:57).

6515. פָּרוּחַ ***pārûaḥ:*** A proper noun designating Paruah (1 Kgs. 4:17).

6516. פַּרְוַיִם ***parwayim:*** A proper noun designating Parvaim (2 Chr. 3:6).

6517. פָּרוּר ***pārûr:*** A masculine noun referring to a pot, a pan. It refers to a hollow vessel used for cooking and food preparation by boiling (Num. 11:8; Judg. 6:19). It refers to a pot used by the priests to boil meat offerings (1 Sam. 2:14).

6518. פָּרָז ***pārāz:*** A masculine noun meaning a warrior, a throng, a village. It refers to a throng of attacking warriors (Hab. 3:14). The Majority Text is difficult to decipher.

6519. פְּרָזָה p^e***rāzāh:*** A feminine noun referring to an unwalled village or town. It refers to rural country and the unwalled open villages in its confines (Esth. 9:19; Ezek. 38:11; Zech. 2:4[8]).

6520. פְּרָזוֹן p^e***rāzôn:*** A masculine noun referring to a village population. It refers to the inhabitants of rural areas, the peasants, small farmers, and sheepherders (Judg. 5:7, 11).

6521. פְּרָזִי p^e***rāziy:*** A masculine noun designating a village, an unwalled town. It refers to rural areas and open villages as well as the peasantry living there (Deut. 3:5; 1 Sam. 6:18; Esth. 9:19).

6522. פְּרִזִּי p^e***rizziy:*** A proper noun designating Perizzite, the name of one of the peoples who inhabited Canaan and were to be disinherited by Israel and destroyed (Gen. 13:7; 15:20). The name may mean "village dwellers." They seem to have been mixed in among the other peoples in various locations throughout the land

(Gen. 34:30; Josh. 17:15; Judg. 1:4, 5; 3:5).

6523. פַּרְזֶל *parzel:* An Aramaic noun referring to iron. It is the most common and important of all metals. Its discovery and use was a major contribution to the development of civilization. It was also symbolic of power and strength. It is used to symbolize strength, power, inhumaneness in the beast of Daniel 7, as well as and strength and power in Daniel 2 (2:33–35, 40–43, 45; 7:7, 19). It was found in various kinds of tools and equipment (Dan. 4:15[12], 23[20]); as well as in the production of idols (Dan. 5:4, 23).

6524. פָּרַח *pāraḥ:* I. A verb meaning to blossom, to flourish, to break forth, to break out. It is used of vine blossoms or other blossoming plants coming out, opening up (Gen. 40:10; Song 6:11; 7:12[13]; Hab. 3:17); or fresh green shoots or sprigs growing from a stump (Job 14:9). It is used of all kinds of sores or boils breaking out on a person's skin (Ex. 9:9, 10; Lev. 13:12, 20, 25). It is used of the divinely guarded sprouting of wooden rods (Num. 17:5[20]). Figuratively, it indicates the increase and prospering of the righteous (Ps. 72:7; Prov. 11:28; 14:11); or of evil, arrogance coming to fruition (Ezek. 7:10; Hos. 10:4).

II. A verb meaning to fly. It is used of things which fly. It refers most likely to birds in Ezekiel 13:20. The phrase *l^e^porḥôṯ* is difficult, but in context, as if birds (flying things), is a probable translation. Souls, lives were being hunted as if they were birds (flying creatures).

6525. פֶּרַח *peraḥ:* A masculine noun meaning a flower, a bud, a blossom. It refers to the petals and other parts put forth by blooming plants. It describes often the ornamental work found in the Tabernacle, Temple, or their decorative ornaments (Ex. 25:31, 33, 34; Num. 8:4; 1 Kgs. 7:26, 49). It refers figuratively to the splendor and glory of Israel (Isa. 5:24); or other nations (Isa. 18:5; Nah. 1:4). It indicates a literal blossom, a flower generated as a sign from God (Num. 17:8[23]).

6526. פִּרְחָח *pirḥāḥ:* A feminine noun referring to a brood, a tribe, a gang of young people. Its meaning is not certain. The translation brood is in line with the negative mood of the passive (NASB, Job 30:12; KJV, youth).

6527. פָּרַט *pāraṭ:* I. A verb meaning to chant, to improvise in singing. It refers to composing on the spot and possibly to performing at the same time in a rather vain, self-centered way according to context (Amos 6:5).

II. A verb meaning to strum. It means to strike the strings of a stringed instrument slowly and lightly (Amos 6:5).

6528. פֶּרֶט *pereṭ:* A masculine collective noun indicating fallen grapes. It refers to grapes fallen on the ground in a natural way (Lev. 19:10).

6529. פְּרִי ***p^e^riy:*** A masculine noun meaning fruit. It refers to what is naturally produced, the crop from trees, land (Gen. 1:11, 12, 29; 3:2, 3, 6; Ps. 107:34). It is used figuratively of one's offspring (Gen. 30:2); or the result of one's deeds or actions (Isa. 3:10). Fruit trees (*'ēṣ p^e^rî*) were a feature of the Garden of Eden and of a man-made garden of beauty and delight (Eccl. 2:5). The bride admires the fruit of her bridegroom (Song 2:3). Abundant fruit will be a mark of a restored Jerusalem (Amos 9:14; Zech. 8:12; Mal. 3:11).

6530. פָּרִיץ ***pariyṣ:*** A masculine noun meaning a violent individual. The term was usually applied to a person or people. David claimed to have refrained from the ways of the violent (Ps. 17:4). God asked if the Temple had become the dwelling place of the violent (Jer. 7:11). God proclaimed through the prophet Ezekiel that the end would come when the violent desecrate God's treasured place (Ezek. 7:22); they would be punished (Ezek. 18:10). The prophet Isaiah also applied this term to wild animals like the lion (Isa. 35:9).

6531. פֶּרֶךְ ***pereḵ:*** A masculine noun referring to ruthlessness, cruelty. It refers to a manner in which something is carried out. Israel was made to labor without mercy, cruelly by Egypt (Ex. 1:13, 14). God warned Israel not to force slaves to labor in this manner (Lev. 25:43, 46, 53; Ezek. 34:4).

6532. פָּרֹכֶת ***pārōḵeṯ:*** A feminine noun meaning a curtain, a veil. It refers to the veil hung in front of the most holy place in the Tabernacle (Ex. 26:31, 33, 35; Lev. 4:6, 17; 16:2; Num. 4:5; 18:7; 2 Chr. 3:14).

6533. פָּרַם ***pāram:*** A verb meaning to tear, to rend. It indicates ripping something apart, especially clothing or garments as a sign of mourning (Lev. 10:6; 21:10). Torn clothes were also worn to indicate that a person was a leper (Lev. 13:45).

6534. פַּרְמַשְׁתָּא ***parmaštā':*** A proper noun designating Parmashta (Esth. 9:9).

6535. פַּרְנָךְ ***parnāḵ:*** A proper noun designating Parnach (Num. 34:25).

6536. פָּרַס ***pāras:*** A verb meaning to split, to divide. It describes the split, the separated structural feature of the hoofs of certain animals; some animals were edible, some not edible by Israel (Lev. 11:3–7, 26; Deut. 14:6–8). It refers to the dividing of the hoof as well as the hoof itself (Ps. 69:31[32]). It describes the sharing, the dividing of bread with those who need it (Isa. 58:7); or to divide or solemnly break bread in the act of mourning (Jer. 16:7).

6537. פְּרַס ***pāras,*** **פְּרֵס** ***p^e^rēs,*** **וּפַרְסִין** ***ûp̱arsiyn,*** **פַּרְסִין** ***parsiyn:*** I. An Aramaic verb meaning to be divided, to be broken in two. It refers in its participial form to something divided, split up; in context Babylon (Dan. 5:28).

II. A masculine proper noun Peres. The word is set aside in quotations or put into capitals and treated in a special way by some translations since it was part of an original message that was being interpreted (Dan. 5:28).

III. A masculine plural proper noun in quotation. This is a special treatment of this word just as for Peres as noted in II.

IV. A masculine plural proper noun Parsin; a proper noun in quotations, used with the conjunction *û* (and). It refers to something divided up, such as the Babylonian kingdom (Dan. 5:25). See II also.

6538. פֶּרֶס *peres:* A masculine noun indicating a vulture, an ossifrage. It refers to a bird of prey that chiefly eats raw meats, carrion. It was forbidden as food for Israel (Lev. 11:13; Deut. 14:12).

6539. פָּרַס *pāras:* A proper noun designating Persia, the name of the Persian Empire that ruled the Middle East from ca. 539–332 B.C. It is mentioned ca. 30 times in the Old Testament. It stretched from India to Cush in Egypt. It was finally conquered by Alexander the Great in 332 B.C. when Alexander pursued its last king (Darius III) until he killed him. In the Old Testament, its history impacts Israel late but in key ways. The Jews were allowed to return from Exile under then great King Cyrus (538/39 B.C.) (2 Chr. 36:20–23; Ezra 1:1–8). Persia under several kings fostered the rebuilding of the city of Jerusalem and its Temple, which was completed in 516 B.C. (Ezra 3:4; 6; 7; 9; Isa. 44; 45). Darius the Mede was kind to Daniel and honored him (5; 6; 9). Daniel lived into the third year of Cyrus (Dan. 10:1) but foresaw the demise of the empire (Dan. 2; 7; 8). Under King Xerxes (486–405 B.C.), a great deliverance occurred on behalf of the Jews (Dan. 1; 10). Persia is mentioned in Ezekiel's vision of a huge battle of the nations against Israel when they will be defeated (Ezek. 38:15).

6540. פָּרַס *pāras:* A proper noun designating the Aramaic name Persia. See 6539. Aramaic was the lingua franca of the day when parts of Daniel and Ezra were composed (Dan. 2:4b—7:28; Ezra 4:8—6:18; 7:12–26).

6541. פַּרְסָה *parsāh:* A feminine noun meaning hoof. It refers to the horny covering on the feet of ungulate animals. It is sometimes used of the animal itself (Ex. 10:26; Lev. 11:3–7, 26; Deut. 14:6–8; Isa. 5:28; Ezek. 32:13). Bronze hoofs are mentioned as weapons to pulverize the enemy (Mic. 4:13). The sound of horses' hoofs and people trampling the streets create dread and fear (Jer. 47:3; Ezek. 26:11). Tearing off, ripping off the hoofs of animals indicates violent ruthlessness (Zech. 11:16).

6542. פַּרְסִי *parsiy:* A proper noun designating someone who is from

Persia, Persian. In Nehemiah 12:22 it is used of Darius. Compare the Aramaic entry 6543.

6543. פָּרְסָיָא *parsāyā':* An Aramaic proper noun designating something or someone that came from Persian, Persian. The word is used to describe Cyrus in Daniel 6:28(29). It corresponds to the Hebrew entry 6542.

6544. פָּרַע *pāra':* A verb meaning to let go, to let loose, to unbind. Moses saw that Aaron had let the Israelites get out of hand when Moses was up on the mountain (Ex. 32:25[2x]). This word can also apply to hair, as with those who were commanded not to let their hair down from their turbans. This warning was given to Aaron concerning mourning (Lev. 10:6); and to high priests in general (Lev. 21:10). However, lepers were to let their hair down to call attention to their condition (Lev. 13:45). A possible unfaithful wife had her hair loosened by the priest in connection with the drinking of bitter water to see if she was guilty (Num. 5:18). This word can also mean to ignore (Prov. 1:25); to avoid (Prov. 4:15); or to lead (Judg. 5:2).

6545. פֶּרַע *pera':* A masculine noun indicating hair, locks of hair. It refers to the unbraided or natural free growth of loose hair on a person's head (Num. 6:5); it could be trimmed but not shaved according to Ezekiel's directions (Ezek. 44:20).

6546. פֶּרַע *pera':* A feminine noun meaning leaders. This specific form of the word is not used in the Hebrew Bible, but the plural form is used. In the song of Moses, the Lord proclaimed that He would overcome the enemy leaders (Deut. 32:42). See the Hebrew root *pāra'* (6544).

6547. פַּרְעֹה *par'ōh:* A masculine proper noun used as a title, Pharaoh. It was a common title used of the kings of Egypt, especially in the Bible (Gen. 12:15; Ex. 1:11, 19, 22, etc.). The word builds off of the Egyptian pr-" meaning great house. At first it referred to the king's royal palace. Later (ca. 1500 B.C.), it began to refer to the king himself. Then in the Bible it is coupled with specific names of Pharaohs (2 Kgs. 23:29). The Pharaohs of the book of Exodus are symbolic of tyrants over God's people as well as historical individuals.

6548. פַּרְעֹה חָפְרַע *par'ōh ḥopra':* A proper noun designating Pharaoh Hophra, the name of an Egyptian Pharaoh (589–570 B.C.) whom the Lord, demonstrating His sovereignty over all nations, handed over to his enemies to be executed (Jer. 44:30). The Greeks called him Pharaoh Apries (Jer. 37:5).

6549. פַּרְעֹה נְכֹה *par'ōh nᵉḵōh:* A proper noun designating Pharaoh Neco, an Egyptian Pharaoh (610–595 B.C.) who attempted to aid the Assyrians against the Babylonians (2 Kgs. 23:29). Josiah, king of Judah, unwisely challenged him and was killed. Neco was wiped out by the Babylonians at the important Battle of Carchemish in 605 B.C. Jeremiah prophesied against him and Egypt (Jer. 46:1–28).

6550. פַּרְעֹשׁ ***par'ōš:*** A masculine noun designating a flea. David applies the word to himself twice in conversation with Saul (1 Sam. 24:14[15]; 26:20), indicating his insignificance before the king of Israel as well as the difficulty of finding a flea.

6551. פַּרְעֹשׁ ***Par'ōš:*** A proper noun designating Parosh (Ezra 2:3; 8:3; 10:25; Neh. 3:25; 7:8; 10:14[15]).

6552. פִּרְעָתוֹן ***pir'āṯôn:*** A proper noun designating Pirathon (Judg. 12:15).

6553. פִּרְעָתוֹנִי ***pir'āṯôniy:*** A proper noun designating Pirathonite (Judg. 12:13, 15; 2 Sam. 23:30; 1 Chr. 11:31; 27:14).

6554. פַּרְפַּר ***parpar:*** A proper noun designating Pharpar (2 Kgs. 5:12).

6555. פָּרַץ ***pāraṣ:*** A verb meaning to break out, to break down, to burst forth. It indicates the powerful multiplication and spreading of something in all directions (Gen. 28:14), especially the spread of God's people so they would be a blessing to all peoples according to the promises to Abraham. It describes the growth of the families of God's people (Gen. 30:30, 43); especially of the twelve tribes in Egypt (Ex. 1:12). It is used of making a breach, a bursting, an urging of a person to do something, of something going forth or out: a birth, breaching the womb (Gen. 38:29); of a breaking out of God's wrath against a person or people (Ex. 19:22, 24; 2 Sam. 5:20; 6:8); of breaching a wall (2 Kgs. 14:13); of broken walls that have been crumbled, breached (Neh. 2:13); of tearing down, demolishing a wall (Isa. 5:5). It refers to breaching the earth, drilling a mine shaft, a hole into it (Job 28:4). It takes on the sense of urging or pushing someone (2 Kgs. 5:23). God's plagues were a bursting forth of Him in judgment (Ps. 106:29). Wine vats or containers are described as bursting forth, breaking out (Prov. 3:10).

6556. פֶּרֶץ ***pereṣ:*** A masculine noun indicating a gap, a break. It refers to a rupture, a tear, a breaking up or shattering of something: a breach created in a wall (1of an enemy (2 Sam. 5:20); the breaking or rupture occurring in the process of childbirth (Gen. 38:29). It is used figuratively of separation created between persons or groups (Judg. 21:15). It refers to death, the ultimate breach in the fabric of life (Ps. 144:14); the death of newborn calves at birth and to an outbreaking of God's anger (2 Sam. 6:8). It is used figuratively of breaches in the walls of Israel, that is the failures of God's people to follow Him, misled by false prophets (Ezek. 13:5).

6557. פֶּרֶץ ***pereṣ:*** A proper noun designating Pharez, Perez (Gen.

38:29; 46:12; Num. 26:20, 21; Ruth 4:12, 18; 1 Chr. 2:4, 5; 4:1; 9:4; 27:3; Neh. 11:4, 6).

6558. פַּרְצִי parṣiy: A proper noun designating Pharzite, Perezite (Num. 26:20).

6559. פְּרָצִים p^e^rāṣiym: A proper noun designating Perazim (Isa. 28:21).

6560. פֶּרֶץ עֻזָּא pereṣ 'uzzā': A proper noun designating Perez Uzzah (2 Sam. 6:8; 1 Chr. 13:11).

6561. פָּרַק pāraq: A verb indicating to break off, to tear off, to rescue. It is a word that carries with it the feeling and implication of violent actions. It is used in a figurative sense of breaking a yoke of oppression (Gen. 27:40); of roughly removing gold ornaments from someone (Ex. 32:2, 3, 24). It describes tearing apart rocks violently (1 Kgs. 19:11); in a figurative sense of the wicked ripping apart the souls (lives) of the righteous (Ps. 7:2[3]). It describes the way Israel had been ripped and torn apart by her enemies (Ezek. 19:12).

6562. פְּרַק p^e^raq: An Aramaic verb meaning to break away, to renounce. It means to tear oneself away from something, to break off from it, in context from the practice of wicked oppression of certain classes of society (Dan. 4:27[24]).

6563. פֶּרֶק pereq: I. A masculine noun indicating a crossroad, a fork in the road. It refers to a place where roads meet and thus where many people will pass by (Obad. 1:14).

II. A masculine noun meaning robbery, plunder. It refers to the confiscation of goods by plundering people and to the property gained in this way (Nah. 3:1).

6564. פָּרָק pārāq: A masculine noun meaning broth. It is a thin, clear soup made by boiling meat and then removing the meat. Israel made broth from unclean meats and ate it in pagan religious rituals (Isa. 65:4).

6565. פָּרַר pārar: A verb meaning to break, to divide, to frustrate. This word is often used in conjunction with a covenant or agreement. The Lord warned the Israelites what would happen if they broke the covenant with Him (Lev. 26:15); and pledged to them that He would not break it (Lev. 26:44). Asa, king of Judah, asked the king of Aram to break a covenant Aram had made with Israel (1 Kgs. 15:19). This word is also used to refer to the frustration of plans, as the enemies of Israel did to the Israelites trying to rebuild the Temple (Ezra 4:5). However, the Lord's purposes cannot be frustrated (Isa. 14:27).

6566. פָּרַשׂ pāraś: A verb meaning to spread out, to spread. It indicated the moving out and apart of various things, of spreading something out; a garment (Judg. 8:25); a fishing net or snare (Isa. 19:8; Hos. 5:1); wings (1 Kgs. 6:27); spreading a tent out (Ex. 40:19); hands in praise and prayer (1 Kgs. 8:38); or helping someone (Prov. 31:20). It indicates covering something over (1 Sam. 17:19). Micah 3:3 used the verb figuratively to depict the violent ways of Israel's rulers over her, breaking (pulling apart, spreading out) her bones. It describes the breaking or distribution of bread, food (Lam. 4:4). In its passive use, it refers to Israel's being scattered, spread out because of God's judgment (Ezek. 17:20).

6567. פָּרַשׁ *pāraš:* I. A verb meaning to show, to make clear, to distinguish. It means to explain, to interpret something: the Lord's command about an incident (Lev. 24:12; Num. 15:34; Neh. 8:8).

II. A verb meaning to sting. It refers to a sharp, smarting pain, such as a pinprick or a bee sting, sometimes accompanied with the injection of poison into the penetrated area (Prov. 23:32).

III. A verb meaning to scatter. It means to separate in a disorderly way, creating confusion, often used of people scattered as sheep (Ezek. 34:12).

6568. פְּרַשׁ *p^eraš:* An Aramaic verb meaning to make clear. It means to translate and to explain the meaning of something, especially a foreign language spoken or written (Ezra 4:18).

6569. פֶּרֶשׁ *pereš:* A masculine noun meaning dung, refuse, offal. It refers to the feces, excrement produced in an animal or human being (Ex. 29:14; Lev. 4:11; 8:17; 16:27; Num. 19:5). It is used in a devastating figure of speech against Israel representing the refuse or excrement of their festivals (Mal. 2:3).

6570. פֶּרֶשׁ *pereš:* A proper noun designating Peresh (1 Chr. 7:16).

6571. פָּרָשׁ *pārāš:* A masculine noun referring to horsemen; cavalry. It is usually used to refer to a rider, a horseman, serving in a military capacity (Gen. 50:9; Ex. 14:9, 17, 18, 23, 26, 28). It is often listed along with chariotry (Ex. 15:9; Josh. 24:6). It is employed in a powerful metaphor in which Elijah is called "the chariots and horsemen of Israel," their true army and defense (2 Kgs. 2:12); and of Elisha (2 Kgs. 13:14). It sometimes stands for horses (Isa. 28:28; Ezek. 27:14; Joel 2:4).

6572. פַּרְשֶׁגֶן *paršegen,* פַּתְשֶׁגֶן *paṯšegen:* I. A masculine noun meaning copy. It refers to a copy of a letter or other written document, hand-copied (Ezra 7:11).

II. A masculine noun meaning copy. It refers to a duplicate reproduction of a royal edict or proclamation put into whatever language or dialect that was needed (Esth. 3:14; 4:8; 8:13).

6573. פַּרְשֶׁגֶן *paršegen:* An Aramaic masculine noun meaning copy. It refers to a duplicate of a letter or other document produced for distribution as needed (Ezra 4:11, 23; 5:6).

6574. פַּרְשְׁדֹנָה ***parš^edōnāh:*** A masculine noun referring to refuse, intestines. It refers to the bowels or other internal intestines that would protrude from a gaping hole in the skin and muscles of the lower stomach area; or to the excrement or contents of the bowels (Judg. 3:22).

6575. פָּרָשָׁה ***pārāšāh:*** A feminine noun indicating an exact amount, a sum. It indicates an accurate assessment of something in exact detail; the total sum of something; or a complete, detailed account of an incident or story (Esth. 4:7; 10:2).

6576. פַּרְשֵׁז ***paršēz:*** A verb meaning to spread. It is a verb with four letters meaning to spread. It means to cover something by spreading an opaque substance over it or in front of it (Job 26:9).

6577. פַּרְשַׁנְדָּתָא ***paršandāṯā':*** A proper noun designating Parshandatha (Esth. 9:7).

6578. פְּרָת ***p^eraṯ:*** A proper noun designating Euphrates.

I. The name refers to the Euphrates River, a major river ca. 1, 800 miles long. The Hebrew name comes from the Akkadian, *purattu*. It and the Tigris encompass the area of Mesopotamia ("between the rivers"). It has shifted its riverbed several times through the millennia. It begins in modern eastern Turkey and flows through Syria and modern Iraq to the Persian Gulf. It and the Tigris meet shortly before emptying into the gulf. It has seen the rise and fall of villages, cities (e.g. Babylon, Carchemish), and great empires (Assyria, Mitanni, Babylon, Persia, etc.) over the years. It was one of the rivers in the Garden of Eden (Gen. 2:14). It was the northernmost boundary of the land God promised to Abraham (Gen. 15:8; Deut. 1:7). It is sometimes called the "great river" or "the River" (Gen. 31:21).

II. It seems to be the name of a city or geographical area (Perath; Jer. 13:4–7, NIV). It could possibly refer to the Euphrates River (see A).

6579. פַּרְתְּמִים ***part^emiym:*** A noun meaning a prince, a noble. This word is only used in the plural form in the Hebrew Old Testament. The most important people in the kingdom were invited to King Xerxes' banquet (Esth. 1:3). Haman suggested to the king that the appropriate way to honor someone was to have a nobleman lead him around the kingdom in the king's robe and on the king's horse (Esth. 6:9). When Babylon captured Jerusalem, the young Israelite nobility were taken into Nebuchadnezzar's service (Dan. 1:3). Shadrach, Meshach, Abednego, and Daniel were part of this group.

6580. פַּשׁ ***paš:*** A masculine noun meaning folly, transgression, wickedness. It has a strong sense of rebellion. It refers to sin or rebellion against God. Many consider the word to be a misspelled form of *p^eša'*, rebellion, revolt, which is, of course, in a broader sense, transgression (Job 35:15).

6581. פָּשָׂה *pāśāh:* A verb meaning to spread. It describes the growth or permeation of an infection or various skin diseases, their spread. The condition was closely watched and diagnosed by the priests (Lev. 13:5–8, 34–36; 14:39, 44, 48).

6582. פָּשַׁח *pāšaḥ:* A verb meaning to tear in pieces, to mangle. It is used in the figurative poetry of Lamentations 3:11 to describe God's vicious actions against His people in devastating judgments.

6583. פַּשְׁחוּר *pašḥûr:* A proper noun designating Pashhur (1 Chr. 9:12; Ezra 2:38; 10:22; Neh. 7:41; 10:3[4]; 11:12; Jer. 20:1–3, 6; 21:1; 38:1).

6584. פָּשַׁט *pāšaṭ:* A verb meaning to strip off; to raid, to invade. It is used of forcefully removing clothing from a person (Gen. 37:23); and of removing the skin from a sacrificial animal (Lev. 1:6). But it also refers to persons' removal of their inner clothing, as a matter of course (Lev. 6:11[14]; 1 Sam. 18:4); or under duress (Isa. 32:11). It indicates plundering or stripping a defeated enemy (1 Sam. 31:8; 2 Sam. 23:10). It means to break forth in a raid, to rush against an enemy (Judg. 9:33; 20:37). Figuratively, it describes the ruthless way the rulers of Israel treated the people (Mic. 3:3); and of how God would strip His people because of their rebellion (Hos. 2:3[5]).

6585. פָּשַׂע *pāśaʻ:* A verb meaning to step, to march. It means to tread on something, to press on it with one's foot; in context it means to injure or destroy something (Isa. 27:4). The sense may be to pass through or over something (KJV).

6586. פָּשַׁע *pāšaʻ:* A verb meaning to rebel, to transgress, to revolt, to sin. This verb is used about forty times in the simple stem of the verb. It means to sin, but the sin involved is one of revolt or rebellion in nearly every case. It indicates rebellion against various parties; the people of Israel rebelled against their God (Isa. 1:2; 66:24; Jer. 2:29; 3:13); especially their leaders (Jer. 2:8). Nations and peoples revolted or broke with one another: Israel broke from and rebelled against Judah (1 Kgs. 12:19); Moab rebelled against Israel (2 Kgs. 1:1; 3:5); and Edom revolted against Judah (2 Kgs. 8:20). Revolt and rebellion against the Lord, Isaiah said, was a part of the character of Israel from its birth and throughout its history (Isa. 48:8; 59:13). Amos described Israel's insistence to worship at the unapproved sanctuaries at Bethel and Gilgal as revolt and rebellion (Amos 4:4). The postexilic community rebelled through intermarriages with pagans (Ezra 10:13). God asserted that He would restore His people, forgiving their sins of rebellion (Jer. 33:8). Unrestrained rebellion seems to be a mark of the end times as noted by Daniel 8:23.

6587. פֶּשַׂע ***peśa':*** A masculine noun indicating a step. It refers to the time needed to take one step or the small amount of space represented by a step (1 Sam. 20:3).

6588. פֶּשַׁע ***peša':*** A masculine noun meaning transgression, rebellion. Though it can be a transgression of one individual against another (Gen. 31:36; 50:17; Ex. 22:9[8]); or of one nation against another (Amos 1:3, 6, 9, 11, 13; 2:1); this word primarily expresses a rebellion against God and His laws (Isa. 58:1; 59:12; Amos 5:12). Since it is possible for humanity to recognize this transgression (Ps. 32:5; 51:3[5]), God's first step in dealing with it is to reveal it and call His people to accountability (Job 36:9; Mic. 3:8). He then punishes the guilty (Isa. 53:5, 8; Amos 2:4, 6) in the hope of restoring the relationship and forgiving the transgressors who repent (Ezek. 18:30, 31). In addition to the act of transgression itself, this term can also be used to convey the guilt that comes from the transgression (Job 33:9; 34:6; Ps. 59:3[4]); the punishment for the transgression (Dan. 8:12, 13; 9:24); or the offering that is presented to atone for the transgression (Mic. 6:7).

6589. פָּשַׂק ***pāśaq:*** A verb meaning to open wide, to spread. It means to open one's mouth without control, without discipline. Only evil comes from such an action (Prov. 13:3). It refers to a woman spreading her legs wide in a sensuous, seductive manner, but the action is applied figuratively to Israel who had played the harlot (Ezek. 16:25).

6590. פְּשַׁר ***p^eššar:*** An Aramaic verb meaning to interpret. It refers in a participial form (*m^eśappar*) to a person, Daniel in this case, who has the ability to interpret dreams and visions (Dan. 5:12, 16).

6591. פְּשַׁר ***p^ešar:*** An Aramaic masculine noun referring to an interpretation or interpretations of dreams, visions. It may mean to translate as well as to give the intent and meaning of something (Dan. 2:4–7; 5:7, 8, 12, 15–17, 26). It occurs in both singular and plural forms (Dan. 2:4, 7). It occurs with the definite article (Dan. 5:12); and with pronominal suffixes in the singular form (Dan. 4:18[15]; 5:8).

6592. פֵּשֶׁר ***pēšer:*** A masculine noun referring to an interpretation; an explanation. It refers to the intention and meaning of something, how it should be understood and acted on (Eccl. 8:1).

6593. פֵּשֶׁת ***pēšeṯ:*** A masculine noun meaning linen, flax. Linen was a highly valued material for certain kinds of clothing. It could be made of yarn, thread, or cloth made from flax, which consisted of threadlike fibers from various plants from the flax family. The flax was harvested (Josh. 2:6);

and used in various garments (Lev. 13:47; Prov. 31:13; Jer. 13:1; Ezek. 44:17, 18). Wool and linen could not be mixed in a garment (Deut. 22:11).

6594. פִּשְׁתָּה *pištāh:* A feminine noun referring to flax; a wick. It refers to flax in the field before harvesting, but ripe for harvest (Ex. 9:31). It indicates a lamp wick made of flax (Isa. 42:3). It is used in a simile of the destruction of Babylon (Isa. 43:17).

6595. פַּת *paṯ,* פְּתוֹת *p^e^ṯôṯ:* I. A masculine noun meaning a piece, a morsel. It refers to a piece of bread large enough to serve to guests (Gen. 18:5; *pat leḥem*). It refers to broken-off pieces of a grain or baked offering (Lev. 2:6). It represents pieces of ice or hail (Ps. 147:17). It indicates a small morsel of food or bread as symbolic of not having enough or a modest amount (Prov. 17:1). It indicates how readily a person will sin for a morsel of food (Prov. 28:21).

II. A masculine noun indicating a piece, a morsel. It designates in context a piece or morsel of bread, emphasizing its insignificant and small value (Ezek. 13:19).

6596. פֹּת *pōṯ:* I. A masculine noun referring to a door hinge. It identifies the hinges on which a door swings and is able to open and close (1 Kgs. 7:50).

II. A masculine noun referring to the private parts of a woman. It may designate such private parts of women exposed in the judgments God visited on His people because of their harlotries (Isa. 3:17).

III. A masculine noun meaning a forehead, a scalp. It may mean a forehead or scalp, since this meaning would parallel the previous line of poetry speaking of the scalp or top (crown) of the heads of women in Judah (Isa. 3:17).

6597. פִּתְאוֹם *piṯ'ôm:* An adverb meaning suddenly, unexpectedly. It refers to things occurring all at once, surprisingly, all of a sudden: death (Num. 6:9; Job 9:23); an action or word by God (Num. 12:4); at once, immediately (Job 5:3; Ps. 64:4[5]); fear that comes on unexpectedly (Prov. 3:25; Mal. 3:1); a catastrophe, calamity (Eccl. 9:12).

6598. פַּתְבַּג *paṯbag:* A masculine noun referring to food, delicacies. It refers to fine food, tasty gourmet cuisine served at the royal palace in the Middle East. To eat of it was the privilege of a few and indicated a special friendship with the king and his government (Dan. 1:5, 8, 13, 15, 16; 11:26).

6599. פִּתְגָם *piṯgām:* A masculine noun meaning an edict, a decree. This word is used only twice in the Old Testament. In Esther 1:20, it describes a king's authoritative edict (or law) that could not be repealed (cf. Esth. 1:19). In Ecclesiastes 8:11, it refers to a court sentence (or judgment) that should be executed against evil.

6600. פִּתְגָם *piṯgām:* An Aramaic masculine noun meaning a written word, an affair. This word is related to the Hebrew word *piṯgām* (6599) and was used in Ezra to describe the written communication that was used between the kings, the Israelites, and their adversaries (Ezra 4:17; 5:7, 11; 6:11). In Daniel, this word described the affair surrounding the unwillingness of Shadrach, Meshach, and Abednego to bow to the golden image (Dan. 3:16); in addition to the matters contained in Nebuchadnezzar's dream (Dan. 4:17[14]).

6601. פָּתָה *pāṯāh:* I. A verb meaning to entice, to deceive, to persuade; to be gullible. It describes persons who are simple, naïve, and overcome by vain things (Job 5:2). It depicts the seducing of persons sexually (Ex. 22:16[15]); or enticing them into sin and transgression in general (Prov. 1:10; 16:29); slander or deception with one's lips (Prov. 20:19; 24:28). It is used of strongly persuading people (Prov. 25:15). It indicates persons' deception of themselves (Deut. 11:16; Hos. 7:11); or of their being enticed or deceived into something (Job 31:9, 27; Jer. 20:10). It has the sense of being overcome or prevailed on to do something for the Lord (Ezek. 14:9).

II. A verb meaning to enlarge, to extend territory. Noah used the term to bless Japheth (Gen. 9:27).

6602. פְּתוּאֵל *peṯû'ēl:* A proper noun designating Pethuel (Joel 1:1).

6603. פִּתּוּחַ *pittûaḥ:* A masculine noun indicating an engraving, a carving, an inscription. It means to create an opening by carving or cutting a hole or channel in wood, stone, clay, etc. It refers to writing engraved on stones (Ex. 28:11, 21). It refers to the words "Holy to the Lord" engraved on a plate of pure gold (Ex. 28:36). It describes decorative engravings on the Temple walls (1 Kgs. 6:29). In a time of judgment, all of this was destroyed (Ps. 74:6). It describes a special inscription engraved on a special stone by the Lord (Zech. 3:9).

6604. פְּתוֹר *peṯôr:* A proper noun designating Pethor (Num. 22:5; Deut. 23:4[5]).

6605. פָּתַח *pāṯaḥ:* A verb meaning to open, to loosen. It is used to indicate the opening of many things: figuratively, the windows of heaven (Gen. 7:11, 8:6); storehouses opened to distribute grain (Gen. 41:56); a grave (Ezek. 37:12, 13); a cistern (Ex. 21:33); a mouth of a cave (Josh. 10:22); a letter (Neh. 6:5); one's hand (Ps. 104:28). Used of a river, it means to cause it to run, to flow with water (Isa. 41:18); it means to move, to sell commodities (Amos 8:5). In Ezekiel 21:28[33], it refers to drawing out one's sword. It has a general sense in many contexts of loosing something: saddles (Gen. 24:32); armor (1 Kgs. 20:11). Of flowers, the petals bloom, open up (Song 7:12[13]); of plowing, it means to open, loosen the ground (Isa. 28:24). It indicates unopened wine, wine still under pressure (Job 32:19).

6606. פְּתַח ***p^e^ṯaḥ:*** An Aramaic verb meaning to open. It is used to describe open windows in an upper chamber on the roof of Daniel's house (Dan. 6:10[11]); and to the books (scrolls) rolled open before the Ancient of Days (Dan. 7:10).

6607. פֶּתַח ***peṯaḥ:*** A masculine noun referring to an opening, an entrance, a door, a doorway. It refers to an unobstructed area providing entrance into an enclosure, a tent, a city, a house (Gen. 18:1; 19:6, 11; Num. 11:10; 1 Kgs. 17:10). It refers to the entrance itself in Genesis 4:7 in a figurative expression. It is used often of the door, the entrance into the sacred tent (Ex. 33:9, 10; Num. 12:5; 20:6); or Temple (1 Kgs. 6:33; Ezek. 8:16). It refers to the opening of a cave (1 Kgs. 19:13). Micah 7:5 refers to guarding the opening of one's mouth. It is used figuratively of the doorway of hope (Hos. 2:15[17]).

6608. פֵּתַח ***pēṯaḥ:*** A masculine noun indicating an entrance, an unfolding. It indicates a place of access into something. Used of God's words, it refers to the understanding and wisdom they give to a person (Ps. 119:130).

6609. פְּתִיחָה ***p^e^ṯiyḥāh:*** A feminine noun referring to a drawn sword. It is used to indicate a sword open for engagement, out of its sheath (Ps. 55:21[22]).

6610. פִּתְחוֹן ***piṯḥôn:*** A masculine noun meaning opening. In context it refers to speaking with one's mouth in a defensive or arrogant way (Ezek. 16:63); or in an expression of joy and thanksgiving for blessings (Ezek. 29:21).

6611. פְּתַחְיָה ***p^e^ṯaḥyāh:*** A proper noun designating Pethahiah:

A. A priest in David's time (1 Chr. 24:16).

B. A Levite who assisted Ezra, perhaps the same as C below (Neh. 9:5).

C. A Jew returning from exile with a foreign wife, perhaps the same as B above (Ezra 10:23).

D. A descendant of Judah and advisor to Zerubbabel (Neh. 11:24).

6612. פְּתִי ***peṯiy:*** An adjective meaning foolish, simpleminded. It refers to a person who is naïve concerning the complexities and challenges of life, inexperienced, lacking insight but made wise by God's words and laws (Ps. 19:7[8]; 119:130); but also sometimes rescued by the Lord (Ps. 116:6). The book of Proverbs is written to give insight, perception, and prudence to the simple (Prov. 1:4); wisdom can make the simple wise (Prov. 1:22); for their indecision can destroy them (Prov. 1:32). It refers to being deficient in observing or understanding the Law of God (Ezek. 45:20).

6613. פְּתָי ***p^e^ṯāy:*** An Aramaic masculine noun referring to width. It is used as an architectural term to indicate the width of a structure (Ezra 6:3) or statue (obelisk) (Dan. 3:1).

6614. פְּתִיגִיל *peṯiygiyl:* I. A masculine noun indicating a fine robe, fine clothes. It refers to fine, expensive, sartorial clothing. It is contrasted to sackcloth (Isa. 3:24).

II. A masculine noun indicating a girdle, a stomacher. Some take the word to refer to a girdle that holds in, forms, and shapes the body, especially the stomach area (Isa. 3:24).

6615. פְּתַיּוּת *peṯayyûṯ:* A feminine noun referring to simplicity; the state of being naïve. It refers to persons who are not aware of the impact their actions have nor of the complexities and disciplines of life (Prov. 9:13).

6616. פָּתִיל *pāṯiyl:* A masculine noun referring to a cord, a piece of string. It refers to a ropelike cord made of various materials (Ex. 28:28, 37; 39:3, 21, 31). Such cords were used for beauty and ornamentation depending on their color and makeup (Num. 15:38). They could be used for mundane things (Num. 19:15); or to tie up prisoners (Judg. 16:9). Certain cords were used in building and architectural work (Ezek. 40:3).

6617. פָּתַל *pāṯal:* A verb meaning to be shrewd, to be cunning, to be devious; to wrestle. It is used to describe spiritual and relational tensions that arise, difficult situations, wrestlings (Gen. 30:8). It refers to being inciteful and understanding about things (2 Sam. 22:27; Ps. 18:26[27]); but this can become a vice (Job 5:13; Prov. 8:8).

6618. פְּתַלְתֹּל *peṯaltōl:* An adjective meaning crooked, warped. It is used in a negative sense of being wickedly cunning, distorted, ingenuous, used of God's people in their rebellious ways (Deut. 32:5).

6619. פִּתֹם *piṯōm:* A proper noun designating Pithom (Ex. 1:11).

6620. פֶּתֶן *peṯen:* A masculine noun indicating a cobra, a poisonous snake. It refers to a deadly poisonous snake of Asia and Africa with loose skin around its neck close to its head (Deut. 32:33). Its venom is used to depict the character of the wicked (Job 20:14, 16; Ps. 58:4[5]). The one who trusts God need not fear the poison of the cobra (Ps. 91:13). In the Messianic Age, the cobra will be tame (Isa. 11:8).

6621. פֶּתַע *peṯa':* A masculine noun indicating suddenness. It refers to the quickness or an unexpected aspect of an event (Num. 6:9; 35:22; Hab. 2:7). A foolish and stubborn person is broken by calamity all of a sudden (Prov. 6:15; 29:1). Jerusalem's enemies would be instantly destroyed (Isa. 29:5); her own destruction would be sudden (Isa. 30:13).

6622. פָּתַר *pāṯar:* A verb meaning to interpret. It describes Joseph's God-given ability to unravel the dreams of Pharaoh, a gift from God (Gen. 40:8, 16, 22; 41:8, 12, 13, 15).

The term refers to this process in general since Pharaoh's magicians and wise men could not interpret his dreams.

6623. פִּתְרוֹן ***piṯrôn:*** A masculine noun referring to interpretation, meaning. It is the abstract noun related to 6622. It refers to the answer, solution, the result of the interpretive process (Gen. 40:5, 8, 12, 18; 41:11).

6624. פַּתְרוֹס ***paṯrôs:*** A proper noun designating Pathros (Isa. 11:11; Jer. 44:1, 15; Ezek. 29:14; 30:14).

6625. פַּתְרֻסִים ***paṯrusiym:*** A proper noun designating Pathrusites (Gen. 10:14; 1 Chr. 1:12).

6626. פָּתַת ***pāṯaṯ:*** A verb meaning to break up, to crumble. It describes the breaking up or crumbling of a fried fine-meal offering. Oil was poured on it (Lev. 2:6).

צ Tsadde

6627. צֵאָה ***tṣēʼāh:*** A feminine noun referring to excrement, dung. It refers to what is passed out of the bowel, excreted. It was unclean and to be covered with dirt immediately (Deut. 23:13[14]). Ezekiel was commanded to eat human dung to represent the uncleanness of Jerusalem and Judah; but the Lord relented from this harsh command (Ezek. 4:12).

6628. צֶאֱלִים ***ṣeʼᵉliym:*** I. A masculine plural noun referring to lotus plants. It refers to a species of thorny shrubs. It is one place where Behemoth lies down and makes his bed (Job 40:21). Most consider it to be a reference to a lotus plant, a water lily.

II. A masculine plural noun referring to shady trees. Earlier translators took this to be a reference to shade trees under which Behemoth would lie (Job 40:21).

6629. צֹאן ***ṣōʼn:*** A common noun referring to a flock, sheep. It is used literally most often to refer to small cattle, that is, goats and/or sheep (Gen. 4:2, 4; 30:31, 32; 1 Sam. 25:2). The phrase *bᵉnê ṣōʼn* refers to individual sheep or goats (Ps. 114:4). The flock was important for food (Amos 6:4); clothing materials (Gen. 31:19); drink, milk (Deut. 32:14); especially sacrificial victims (Gen. 4:4; Lev. 1:2, 10); and as a major part of a person's wealth (Gen. 12:16; 13:5). It is used figuratively often of children, of persons, multitudes of people, of Israel as sheep especially (Num. 27:17; 1 Kgs. 22:17; Job 21:11); of Israel wandering as sheep in sin (2 Sam. 24:17; Isa. 53:6; Ezek. 24:5; 34:2, 3, etc.; Zech. 9:16; 10:2; 11:4; 13:7); of Israel as sheep led by the Lord (Ps. 77:20[21]; 78:52); of a scattered, destroyed Babylon as confused sheep (Isa. 13:14; Jer. 50:45). Edom is pictured as a flock (Jer. 49:20).

6630. צַאֲנָן ***ṣaʼănan:*** A proper noun designating Zaanan (Mic. 1:11).

6631. צֶאֱצָא ***ṣeʼᵉṣāʼ:*** A masculine noun referring to a child, offspring. It refers to those who come out of the womb or from the loins of the father. It indicates offspring, descendants (Job 5:25; 21:8; 27:14; Isa. 22:24; 34:1; 44:3). In the new heavens and new earth, the term refers to the offspring of the people blessed of the Lord (Isa. 65:23).

6632. צָב ***ṣā<u>b</u>:*** I. A masculine noun indicating a cart, a covered wagon. It indicates a transportation vehicle, most probably a covered wagon or possibly a litter on which people are carried (Num. 7:3; Isa. 66:20).

II. A masculine noun meaning a litter. It refers to a basic framework built to carry a person or persons on it, a stretcher for carrying the sick (Isa. 66:20).

III. A masculine noun referring to a great lizard. It refers to a creature of the reptile family (Uromastix spinipes) (Lev. 11:29, NASB, NIV). It was unclean, not edible by Israel.

IV. A masculine noun referring to a tortoise. It refers to a turtle that lives on land. It was not edible to Israel since it was considered unclean (Lev. 11:29, KJV).

6633. צָבָא *ṣāḇā':* A verb meaning to wage war, to muster into service, to serve. This word is primarily used to describe a gathering of people waging war against another city or country (Num. 31:7, 42; Isa. 29:7, 8; Zech. 14:12). In one instance, it was used to depict the Lord waging war (Isa. 31:4). In several contexts, this word referred to the mustering of people into service (2 Kgs. 25:19; Jer. 52:25). Finally, this word described the religious service in the Tabernacle (Ex. 38:8; Num. 4:23; 8:24; 1 Sam. 2:22).

6634. צְבָא *ṣ*ᵉ*ḇā':* An Aramaic verb meaning to wish, to desire, to choose (Dan. 4:17[14], 25[22], 32[29], 35[32]; 5:19, 21; 7:19).

6635. צָבָא *ṣāḇā':* A masculine noun meaning service, servants. It may apply to military service (Num. 1:3; 1 Sam. 17:55); hard, difficult service (Job 7:1; Isa. 40:2); or divine service (Num. 4:3; 8:24, 25; Ps. 68:11[12]). The angels and the heavens alike are in divine service and therefore come under this term (Gen. 2:1; 1 Kgs. 22:19; Jer. 33:22; cf. Luke 2:13). Over half of its nearly five hundred uses come in the phrase, the Lord [or God] of hosts. The phrase is absent from the first five book of the Bible. But frequently in the Prophets, the phrase introduces a divine declaration. At least once the hosts (always plural) in this expression are identified as human armies, but elsewhere they most likely refer to angelic forces (Josh. 5:13–15; 1 Sam. 17:55; Ps. 103:21; Isa. 1:9). The title the LORD of hosts was often translated in the Septuagint as the LORD of powers or the LORD Almighty (Ps. 24:10; Zech. 4:6). On other occasions, the Hebrew word for hosts was transliterated into Greek (1 Sam. 1:3, 11). This Greek form of the Hebrew word shows up twice in the New Testament, once in a quotation from Isaiah (cf. Rom. 9:29; James 5:4).

6636. צְבֹאִים *ṣ*ᵉ*ḇō'iym,* צְבִיִּים *ṣ*ᵉ*ḇōyiym:* A proper noun designating Zeboiim, a city on the southeast edge of Canaan (Gen. 10:19) and mentioned among the five cities of the plain (Gen. 14:2, 8). Based on Hosea 11:8, it perished with Sodom and Gomorrah.

6637. צֹבֵבָה *ṣōḇēḇāh,* הַצֹּבֵבָה *haṣṣōḇēḇāh:* I. A proper noun designating Zobebah, the son of Coz, used with the definite article (KJV, NASB, 1 Chr. 4:8). See II below.

II. A proper noun designating Hazzobebah, the son of Coz (NIV, 1 Chr. 4:8). This is the same individual as I above, but the New International Version interprets the prefix as part of the name rather than as the definite article.

6638. צָבָה ṣāḇāh: A verb meaning to swell up. It means to increase in size, to puff up from disease or from stomach and intestinal gases in this context (Num. 5:22, 27).

6639. צָבֶה ṣāḇeh: An adjective meaning swollen. It describes something puffed up, extended because of a curse and trial by ordeal (Num. 5:21).

6640. צְבוּ ṣᵉḇû: An Aramaic feminine noun meaning a situation. It refers to the circumstances or conditions under which people find themselves. The NASB renders it so that nothing would be changed (Dan. 6:17 [18]); the KJV translates it as purpose.

6641. צָבוּעַ ṣāḇûaʻ: An adjective meaning speckled. It is used to describe a bird of prey as having small, contrasting dots or marks of color, specks (Jer. 12:9). It was a detestable bird in Israel, unclean and therefore not to be eaten.

6642. צָבַט ṣāḇaṭ: A verb meaning to reach out, to hand something over. It means to serve food to a guest, to serve generously (Ruth 2:14); thereby Boaz showed his respect and love toward Ruth.

6643. צְבִי ṣᵉḇiy: A masculine noun meaning beauty, glory, a gazelle. This word has essentially two meanings. The first meaning describes something that is beautiful or glorious, such as the glorious land which God gave Israel that flowed with milk and honey (Ezek. 20:6, 15); or the beautiful flower of Ephraim (Isa. 28:1). This word was normally used to depict the glory of a nation: Israel (2 Sam. 1:19); Babylon (Isa. 13:19); Tyre (Isa. 23:9); Ephraim (Isa. 28:1, 4); a city (Ezek. 25:9); a mountain (Dan. 11:45); or a land in general (Dan. 8:9; 11:16, 41). In a few instances, it speaks of the Lord Himself (Isa. 4:2; Isa. 28:5). The second meaning of this word is a gazelle, which is described in the dietary laws of the Old Testament (Deut. 12:15, 22); used to describe the speed of a runner (2 Sam. 2:18; 1 Chr. 12:8[9]; Prov. 6:5); and compared to a lover (Song 2:9, 17; 8:14).

6644. צִבְיָא ṣiḇyāʼ: A proper noun designating Zibia (1 Chr. 8:9).

6645. צִבְיָה ṣiḇyāh: A proper noun designating Zibiah (2 Kgs. 12:1[2]; 2 Chr. 24:1).

6646. צְבִיָּה ṣᵉḇiyyāh: A feminine noun referring to a female gazelle. It refers to small, graceful antelope with lustrous eyes, fragile and endearing (Song 4:5; 7:3[4]). It was used in a metaphor of love toward a bride.

6647. צְבַע ṣᵉḇaʻ: An Aramaic verb meaning to be wet, drenched. It describes a state of being covered with water; water running in droplets on something by a heavy dew from the sky. It depicts the state of a tree stump and later Nebuchadnezzar himself according to his dream (Dan. 4:15[12], 23[20], 25[22], 33[30]; 5:21).

6648. צֶבַע ṣeḇaʻ: A masculine noun referring to dyed work, a colorful garment. It is used to depict an item among the spoils of war when Deborah and Barak defeated Sisera (Judg. 5:30).

6649. צִבְעוֹן ṣiḇʻôn: A proper noun designating Zibeon (Gen. 36:2, 14, 20, 24, 29; 1 Chr. 1:38, 40).

6650. צְבֹעִים ṣᵉḇōʻiym: A proper noun designating Zeboim (1 Sam. 13:18; Neh. 11:34).

6651. צָבַר ṣāḇar: A verb meaning to heap up, to store up, to gather together. It means to pile up, to reserve an abundance of grain (Gen. 41:35, 49). It refers to piling up, heaping up anything (Ex. 8:14[10]); to hoard money, wealth (Job 27:16; Ps. 39:6[7]; Zech. 9:3); to pile up rubble to besiege a city (Hab. 1:10).

6652. צִבֻּר ṣibbur, צִבּוּר ṣibbûr: A masculine noun meaning a pile, a heap. It refers to something gathered together and left in a certain spot, a number of things randomly stashed on top of each other (2 Kgs. 10:8).

6653. צֶבֶת ṣeḇeṯ: A masculine noun indicating a handful. It refers to a small bundle of grain, wet and placed together from which some may be pulled out (Ruth 2:16).

6654. צַד ṣaḏ: A masculine noun meaning side. It refers to the left or right half of a person, an animal, or a boundary area of something in any direction, north, south, east, west. It refers to the side of any object, e.g., a window (Gen. 6:16); a lampstand (Ex. 25:32); a person (Num. 33:55; 2 Sam. 2:16). At the side of or beside something may be expressed with *min* (4480) plus *ṣaḏ, miṣṣaḏ* (1 Sam. 6:8; 20:20). It is used of Ezekiel lying on his side, side to side (Ezek. 4:4, 6, 9). On this side . . . from that side (1 Sam. 23:26).

6655. צַד ṣaḏ: An Aramaic masculine noun indicating against, regarding. It refers to a matter from whence, with respect to someone or something. In context with respect to Daniel, from the side of Daniel (Dan. 6:4[5]). It has the sense of against in an accusatory way (Dan. 7:25).

6656. צְדָא ṣᵉḏāʼ: An Aramaic masculine noun meaning purpose. The word refers to doing something with malicious intent and is found once in the Old Testament in the form of a question. Nebuchadnezzar approached Shadrach, Meshach, and Abednego, asking them if their intent was to defy him by not serving his gods or the golden image (Dan. 3:14).

6657. צְדָד ṣᵉḏāḏ: A proper noun designating Zedad (Num. 34:8; Ezek. 47:15).

6658. צָדָה ṣāḏāh: A verb meaning to hunt, to lie in wait. The word occurs only twice in the Old Testament. In Exodus 21:13, it signified deliberation and planning before a murder; those who were lying in wait were to be executed. Those, however, who committed a murder without lying in wait could flee to a city of refuge and be protected within its borders (cf. Num. 35:9–34). In 1 Samuel 24:11[12], the word signified Saul's attempt to hunt down David and kill him.

6659. צָדוֹק ***ṣāḏôq:*** A proper noun designating Zadok. The name means "righteous."

A. He was one of the priests in David's day who served along with Abiathar (2 Sam. 8:17). He was the son of Ahitub (1 Chr. 6:8[5:34], 53[38]). He helped care for the ark. He, instead of Abiathar, supported Solomon, David's choice as king before David's death (1 Kgs. 1:7–45; 2:35). His descendants, therefore, were favored to serve in the Temple until its destruction (1 Kgs. 4:2; 586 B.C.) and even after (Ezra 7:2). His line replaced the rejected priestly line of Eli (1 Sam. 2:25–36). Ezekiel placed him and his descendants in charge of the Temple in his vision (Ezek. 40:46, etc.).

B. A Levite who supported David at Hebron when David became king. (See A also) (1 Chr. 12:28).

C. A descendant of Zadok (A above). He had a son Shallum (1 Chr. 6:12).

D. The son of Meraioth and father of Meshullam. His grandfather Ahitub had been in charge of the Temple (1 Chr. 9:11).

E. The grandfather of King Jotham. His mother's name was Jerusha (2 Chr. 27:1).

F. He served as a scribe under Nehemiah and was over the treasuries in the second Temple (Neh. 13:13).

G. He supported Nehemiah and his covenant of renewal for the returned exiles (Neh. 10:21).

H. The son of Baana. He helped repair a section of the wall of Jerusalem (Neh. 3:4).

I. The son of Immer. He repaired the wall in front of his own house (Neh. 3:29).

6660. צְדִיָּה ***ṣeḏiyyāh:*** A feminine noun indicating lying in wait, ambushing. It refers to a person planning to harm someone, waiting to get a chance to do injury, to strike out in a premeditated attempt to harm someone (Num. 35:20, 22). This crime was punishable by death.

6661. צִדִּים ***ṣiddiym:*** A proper noun designating Ziddim (Josh. 19:35).

6662. צַדִּיק ***ṣaddiyq:*** An adjective meaning just, righteous. The term bears primarily a moral or ethical significance. Someone or something is considered to be just or righteous because of conformity to a given standard. It could be used to describe people or actions in a legal context, indicating they were in accordance with the legal standards (2 Kgs. 10:9); or in a religious context, that they were in accordance with God's standards (Gen. 6:9). It is used of human beings, such as the Davidic king (2 Sam. 23:3); judges and rulers (Prov. 29:2; Ezek. 23:45); and individuals (Gen. 6:9). It is also often applied to God, who is the ultimate standard used to define justice and righteousness (Ex. 9:27; Ezra 9:15; Ps. 7:11[12]). As a substantive, the righteous is used to convey the ideal concept of those who follow God's standards (Mal. 3:18). In this way, it is often in antithetic parallelism with the wicked, *rāšā'* (7563), the epitome of those who reject God and His standards (Prov. 29:7).

6663. צָדַק *ṣāḏaq*: A verb meaning to be right, to be righteous, to be just, to be innocent, to be put right, to justify, to declare right, to prove oneself innocent. The word is used twenty out of forty times in the simple stem. In this stem, it basically means to be right or just. God challenged His own people to show they were right in their claims (Isa. 43:26). The verb can also connote being innocent, for God's people, through the Lord, will be found innocent (Ps. 51:4[6]; Isa. 45:25). Job argued his case effectively, proving himself right and vindicated (Job 11:2; 40:8). The ordinances of God were declared right by the psalmist (Ps. 19:9[10]).

In the passive stem, it means to be put right. The verb refers to the altar in the second Temple being put right after its defilement (Dan. 8:14). In the intensive stem, the verb means to make or to declare righteous. Judah, because of her sin, made Samaria, her wicked sister, seem righteous (Ezek. 16:51, 52); the Lord asserted that northern Israel had been more just than Judah (Jer. 3:11; cf. Job 32:2).

In the causative stem, the verb takes on the meaning of bringing about justice: Absalom began his conspiracy against David by declaring that he would administer justice for everyone (2 Sam. 15:4). The Lord vindicates His servant (Isa. 50:8); every person of God is to declare the rights of the poor or oppressed (Ps. 82:3). In Isaiah 53:11, it has the sense of the Servant helping other persons obtain their rights. Once in the reflexive stem, it means to justify oneself, as when Judah was at a loss as to how he and his brothers could possibly justify themselves before Pharaoh (Gen. 44:16).

6664. צֶדֶק *ṣeḏeq*: A masculine noun meaning a right relation to an ethical or legal standard. The Hebrew word occurs most often in the Psalms and Isaiah. The word is frequently connected with the term justice (Ps. 119:106; Isa. 58:2). Kings, judges, and other leaders were to execute their duties based on righteous standards (Deut. 1:16; Prov. 8:15; Isa. 32:1). God Himself acts in righteousness both in judgment and deliverance (Ps. 119:75, 160; Isa. 51:5; 62:1). Furthermore, God can be credited for generating human righteousness (Ps. 4:1[2]; Jer. 23:6). The concept of righteousness was so important in the Old Testament period that the community that housed the Dead Sea scrolls called their most prominent leader the "Teacher of Righteousness," a person whom many regard as the founder of the sect.

6665. צִדְקָה *ṣiḏqāh:* An Aramaic feminine noun meaning righteousness. The word occurs only in Daniel 4:27[24] where it signifies righteousness as positive action by which a person breaks off from sin. The Hebrew word in that verse is parallel to a Hebrew word meaning to show mercy. Daniel warned Nebuchadnezzar that he would go insane because of his arrogance (see Dan. 4:25) but that righteousness might prolong his prosperous state. For the corresponding Hebrew noun, see *ṣᵉḏāqāh* (6666).

6666. צְדָקָה *ṣᵉḏāqāh:* A feminine noun meaning righteousness, blameless conduct, and integrity. The noun describes justice, right actions, and right attitudes, as expected from both God and people when they judge. God came speaking justice and righteousness as the divine Judge (Isa. 63:1; Jer. 9:24[23]; Mic. 7:9); the Lord's holiness was made known by His righteousness in judgments (Isa. 5:16; 10:22). Human judges were to imitate the divine Judge in righteousness and justice (Gen. 18:19; 2 Sam. 8:15; Ps. 72:3; Isa. 56:1).

The word describes the attitude and actions God had and expected His people to maintain. He is unequivocally righteous; righteousness is entirely His prerogative. His people are to sow righteousness, and they will receive the same in return (Hos. 10:12). He dealt with His people according to their righteousness and blamelessness (2 Sam. 22:21; Ezek. 3:20). Faith in God was counted as righteousness to Abraham (Gen. 15:6); and obedience to the Lord's Law was further evidence of faith that God considered as righteousness (Deut. 6:25). Returning a poor man's cloak was an act of obedience that was considered righteous and just before the Lord (Deut. 24:13). Jacob declared that his integrity (honesty, righteousness) would speak for him in the future to Laban (Gen. 30:33). The lives of people are to reflect righteousness and integrity (Prov. 8:20; 15:9); even old age may be attained by living a life of righteousness (Prov. 16:31).

The noun describes the justice of God or His will: persons are to act according to God's righteousness toward other persons (Deut. 33:21; Isa. 48:1). The word is also synonymous with truth or integrity. God declares His words are based on His own truthfulness (Isa. 45:23). The word depicts God's salvation or deliverance, such as when Isaiah spoke of the Lord bringing near His righteousness as equal to bringing near His salvation (Isa. 46:13; 51:6; 56:1).

The word may indicate a just claim before the king (2 Sam. 19:28[29]); or the righteous claim for vindication God gives to His people (Neh. 2:20; Isa. 54:17). A person who was denied justice but was righteous was, in fact, innocent (Isa. 5:23). In the plural, the word referred to the righteous acts that God performed for His people (1 Sam. 12:7); or, in the plural used in an abstract sense, it depicted people living righteously (Isa. 33:15). The word was used to mean legitimate and blameless, referring to the Lord's righteous Branch (Jer. 23:5; 33:15) who will act justly and righteously in the restored land.

6667. צִדְקִיָּה ***ṣiḏqiyyāh,*** צִדְקִיָּהוּ ***ṣiḏqiyyāhû:*** A proper noun designating Zedekiah:

A. One of the many false prophets under Ahab who always said what the king wanted to hear, a "state" prophet (1 Kgs. 22:11). His name means "the Lord is righteous" or "the Lord is my righteousness."

B. The last king of Judah. He reigned 597–586 B.C., eleven years. His original name was Mattaniah; Nebuchadnezzar changed it to Zedekiah (2 Kgs. 24:15–20). His nephew was the deported king, Jehoiachin. His mother's name was Hamutal, a daughter of Jeremiah. Since he followed the evil ways of Jehoiakim, the Lord destroyed him and his sons as they fled from the Babylonians at Riblah. The enemy put his eyes out and took him to Babylon in chains where he died (Jer. 52:1–11). He would not listen to the prophetic warning of Jeremiah to submit to Babylon, so he was taken into exile and executed (Jer. 34; 37:1–2). He had shown some mercy toward Jeremiah (37:21; 38:7–16; 14–26) but wavered even in that.

C. This son of Jehoiakim is not listed elsewhere.

D. A son of Maaseiah. He was a false prophet in Jeremiah's time (Jer. 29:21, 22). Jeremiah condemned him and his message as well as predicting his death.

E. A son of Hananiah (Jer. 36:12). A leader or prince in Judah who listened to the reading of Jeremiah's scroll (Jer. 36:12–21).

F. He supported and confirmed Nehemiah's covenant of renewal among the returned exiles (Neh. 10:1[2]).

6668. צָהַב ***ṣāhaḇ:*** A verb meaning to be shiny, fine. It refers to bronze of a high quality with a shiny surface (Ezra 8:27).

6669. צָהֹב ***ṣāhoḇ:*** An adjective indicating a yellowish color. Hair in an infected skin area of this color was dangerous, indicating leprosy or some serious skin disease making a person unclean (Lev. 13:30, 32, 36).

6670. צָהַל ***ṣāhal:*** I. A verb meaning to cry out, to shout; to neigh. It refers to making a loud sound, usually of great delight and joy (Esth. 8:15; Isa. 12:6; 24:14; 54:1; Jer. 31:7; 50:11). It is used of a cry of fear once (Isa. 10:30); and the lustful neighing of a stallion smelling a mare in heat (Jer. 5:8).

II. A verb meaning to shine, to glisten. It describes the healthy effect of oil on a person's skin to make it appear shiny, strong, and healthy (Ps. 104:15).

6671. צָהַר *ṣāhar:* A verb meaning to crack olives, to produce olive oil. It refers to the production of olive oil that always involved squeezing or pressing olives to obtain the oil in them (Job 24:11). Others have suggested that the usage here means to spend noon, to spend the noonday, understanding the root of the verb to be related to *ṣoh^{o}rayim,* noon, afternoon.

6672. צֹהַר *ṣōhar:* I. A masculine noun meaning noon, midday. It is used in a dual form *ṣoh^{o}rayim.* At noon is *baṣṣoh^{o}rayim* (Gen. 43:16, 25); but also without *b^{e}* (1 Kgs. 18:29). It indicates noon as a time of prayer (Ps. 55:17[18]). With *b^{e}tôḵ* preceding, it means at noonday, in broad daylight (Isa. 16:3). An afternoon nap, lying down in the afternoon, is a time of rest, a siesta (2 Sam. 4:5). It is used figuratively as a time of blessing, joy, happiness (Isa. 58:10).

II. A masculine noun meaning window space. It refers to the window Noah built into the ark (Gen. 6:16).

6673. צַו *ṣaw*, צָו *ṣāw:* A masculine noun meaning rule, command; a senseless word of mockery; unintelligible speech. In Isaiah 28:10, it refers to line on line of instruction (NASB). It describes the ineffective piling up of the Lord's words, line on line (Isa. 28:13).

II. A masculine noun referring to an idol. Some translators render this word as idol (Hos. 5:11). Its meaning is not certain (see I).

6674. צוֹא *ṣô'*, צוֹאִי *ṣô'iy:* An adjective meaning filthy. It refers to the high priest Joshua's priestly garments smeared and soiled with refuse and excrement, representing the defilement of the priesthood that occurred in Israel (Zech. 3:3, 4).

6675. צוֹאָה *ṣô'āh:* A feminine noun referring to filth, filthiness. It is used figuratively of moral, spiritual, or behavioral uncleanness (Prov. 30:12); it refers in some contexts to Israel's filth, refuse, a term standing for the corruption and rebellion of the whole nation (Isa. 4:4; 28:8).

6676. צַוַּאר *ṣawwa'r:* An Aramaic masculine noun meaning neck. It refers to the neck of a human being. It was a great honor to have a gold chain placed around one's neck by the king, especially in Babylon, an empire enamored of gold (Dan. 5:7, 16, 29).

6677. צַוָּאר *ṣawwā'r*, צַוְּרֹנִים *ṣawwārōniym:* I. A masculine noun referring to a person's neck, the part of a human or animal that fastens the head to the body, the backbone between the skull and shoulders included. It refers to a person's neck (Gen. 27:16). It is used figuratively in the expression to have a yoke on one's neck, to be enslaved (Gen. 27:40; Isa. 10:27; Jer. 27:2; 28:10–12, 14; 30:8). In the Middle East, it was a show of affection to kiss another man's neck (Gen. 33:4); while putting one's foot on an enemy's neck indicated dominance over him (Josh. 10:24). To rush into someone with one's head was to use one's neck (Job 15:26). A neck held forward while talking indicates stubbornness or insolence (Ps. 75:5 [6]). A person's neck was a place for ornamentation (Song 1:10; 4:9); and a feature of beauty and strength (Song 4:4; 7:4[5]). Swords on the neck of the wicked means to slay them (Ezek. 21:29[34]). The idiom from neck to thigh means to destroy an enemy or person utterly (Hab. 3:13).

II. A masculine plural noun indicating necklaces. It refers to a jewel, a gold chain, or other ornamentation worn around a person's neck. It was used to enhance the attraction of the wearer (Song 4:9).

6678. צוֹבָא ***ṣôḇā',*** צוֹבָה ***ṣôḇāh:*** A proper noun designating Zobah, a small city-state power with a king that Saul successfully defeated along with many others (1 Sam. 14:47). It was located north of Dan in the area of Lebanon and was evidently inhabited by Arameans. One of its later kings was named Hadedezer. David had to capture it again (2 Sam. 8:3–12; 10:6–8).

6679. צוּד ***ṣûḏ,*** צִיד ***ṣiyḏ:*** I. A verb meaning to hunt, to hunt down, to ensnare. It describes hunting animals for food (Gen. 27:3, 5, 33; Job 10:16); including birds (Lev. 17:13; Lam. 3:52). It is used figuratively of hunting people, ensnaring them (Job 10:16; Mic. 7:2); of evil pursuing violent men (Ps. 140:11[12]). An adulteress hunts down her prey (Prov. 6:26). It describes hunting down and catching, snaring souls (Ezek. 13:18, 20).

II. A verb meaning to take as provisions. It refers to taking along food provisions for a long journey, to prepare food provisions (Josh. 9:12). It is used in the reflexive form in this verse. The verb is considered to be from the basic stem *ṣûḏ.*

III. A verb meaning to pack, to take as provisions. It means to pack and prepare food for taking on a long journey (Josh. 9:12). Some consider the verb to be *ṣîḏ,* not *ṣûḏ,* its basic form.

6680. צָוָה ***ṣāwāh:*** A verb meaning to order, to direct, to appoint, to command, to charge, to be ordered, to be commanded. The word means to give an order or to command, to direct someone; it indicates commands given to people in various situations. The Lord commanded Adam and Eve to eat from certain trees but to refrain from eating from the tree of the knowledge of good and evil (Gen. 2:16; 3:17). He ordered Moses hundreds of times to do or say certain things as He established Israel's worship, feasts, festivals, and rituals (Ex. 7:2; 16:34; Num. 15:23). Israel was to keep all the directives the Lord gave them (Deut. 4:2; 1 Kgs. 11:10). The Lord commanded His prophets to speak (Amos 6:11; Nah. 1:14; Zech. 1:6). People gave orders to others as well, as when Pharaoh ordered that all newborn Hebrew males should be drowned in the Nile River (Ex. 1:22). Deborah ordered Barak to defeat Sisera (Judg. 4:6). Abraham ordered his family to follow the ways of the Lord (Gen. 18:19). Kings commanded their people (1 Kgs. 5:17[31]; Jer. 36:26). Priests in Israel gave directives to the people about what to do under certain circumstances (Lev. 9:6; cf. Lev. 13:58). A person who was chosen for a task or position was commanded concerning his responsibilities by the priestly authorities (Num. 27:19, 23). The word may mean to give directives or to set in order as when the Lord told Hezekiah to order—that is, to set things in order, in his household, for he was about to die (2 Kgs. 20:1).

God commands not only people but creation: He created all things by His command (Ps. 33:9; 148:5); He commanded the clouds not to send their rain on a disobedient vineyard (i.e., Israel [Ps. 78:23; Isa. 5:6]); He commands the entire heavenly realms (Isa. 45:12). God commands historical processes; He will ultimately set up David, His ruler, as the one who commands (Isa. 55:4).

6681. צָוַח ***ṣāwaḥ:*** A verb meaning to shout. It is used of crying out, crying aloud in joy because of what God is doing for His people (Isa. 42:11).

6682. צְוָחָה ***ṣ*^e*wāḥāh:*** A feminine noun meaning a crying out, shout. In context it refers to a cry or shout of despair because of calamities or disasters striking God's people (Ps. 144:14; Isa. 24:11; Jer. 14:2); as well as Egypt in judgment (Jer. 46:12).

6683. צוּלָה ***ṣûlāh:*** A feminine noun designating the depth of the sea. It refers to the bottom of the sea, its great depths, and the water-soaked condition of its bottom as well (Isa. 44:27).

6684. צוּם ***ṣûm:*** A verb meaning to abstain from food, to fast. It is ideally a form of worship and recognition of God. It means to refrain from eating food for various reasons: as a sign of mourning and distress, seeking God's mercy (Judg. 20:26; 1 Sam. 7:6; 31:13; 2 Sam. 12:16). It is purportedly in some cases done also to please the Lord, but evidently not with purity of motive (Zech. 7:5). Fasting was a sign of mourning before God for the dead (1 Sam. 31:13).

6685. צוֹם ***ṣôm:*** A masculine noun indicating a fast, fasting. It refers to the act or time of fasting, an act of worship in mourning, despairing while entreating God: a fast itself (2 Sam. 12:16); a public fast (1 Kgs. 21:9, 12). Some fasts were observed regularly (Esth. 9:31; Zech. 8:19). A fast could bring on weakness of body (Ps. 109:24).

6686. צוּעָר ***ṣû'ār:*** A proper noun designating Zuar (Num. 1:8; 2:5; 7:18, 23; 10:15).

6687. צוּף ***ṣûp̱:*** A verb meaning to overflow, to engulf; to float. It refers to the waters of the Red Sea overflowing and encompassing the Egyptians (Deut. 11:4); of an ax head made to float in water (2ed in a figurative sense of enemies overwhelming, overflowing people (Lam. 3:54).

6688. צוּף ṣûp̱: A masculine noun indicating a honeycomb. It refers to a wax structure built by bees to house the honey they produce. The honey from it is noted for its refreshing sweetness (Ps. 19:10[11]; Prov. 16:24).

6689. צוּף ṣûp̱, צוֹפַי ṣôp̱ay: A proper noun designating Zuph:

A. An ancestor of Samuel (1 Sam. 1:1; 1 Chr. 6:26[11], 35[20]).

B. A district in Judah (1 Sam. 9:5).

6690. צוֹפַח ṣôp̱aḥ: A proper noun designating Zophah (1 Chr. 7:35, 36).

6691. צוֹפַר ṣôp̱ar: A proper noun designating Zophar. Zophar is called a Naamathite (5284). Except for its appearance in Job, the word Naamathite is not found elsewhere. There is no connection with Naaman. He was one of Job's antagonists more than he was a true friend. He held that Job had sinned and was suffering for it. God did not approve of what he said (Job 42:9).

6692. צוּץ ṣûṣ: I. A verb meaning to blossom, to flourish. It refers to the sprouting or budding of blossoms or buds (Num. 17:8[23]; Ezek. 7:10), miraculously in the case of Aaron's rod. It often has a figurative meaning. It refers to the multiplication of people, the flourishing of God's people in the time of the Messiah (Ps. 72:16; Isa. 27:6). It indicates the temporary, fleeting flourishing of humankind in general (Ps. 90:6; 103:15); and the brief success of the wicked (Ps. 92:7[8]).

II. A verb meaning to peek, to peer. It refers to a person taking a sensitive, inquisitive look at someone or something, often through some obstacle (Song 2:9).

6693. צוּק ṣûq: A verb meaning to oppress, to distress, to constrain. It indicates forcing someone to do something under duress, often by violent means (Deut. 28:53, 55, 57; Isa. 29:7; Jer. 19:9). It refers to the Lord bringing distress on His people (Isa. 29:2). It can refer to badgering persons, nagging them, constantly urging them to do something until they give in (Judg. 14:17; 16:16). In its causative participial form, it refers to an oppressor (Isa. 51:13).

6694. צוּק ṣûq: A verb meaning to pour out, to smelt, to refine. It refers to a process of removing impurities, dross, from ores containing metals (Job 28:2). It describes God's disciplining of a people (Isa. 26:16). It is used of pure oil pouring forth like refined metal from a rock (Job 29:6).

6695. צוֹק ṣôq, צוּקָה ṣûqāh: I. A masculine noun referring to distress, anguish. It describes a condition of political, military, and religious oppression on God's people (Dan. 9:25).

II. A feminine noun indicating distress, anguish. It describes a period of personal emotional, economic, or spiritual distress or anxiety that assails a person that only wisdom can deliver from (Prov. 1:27). It refers to a time of devastating judgment on the earth (Isa. 8:22). It indicates the oppression and distress on travelers in the torrid heat and drought of the desert (Isa. 30:6).

6696. צוּר ***ṣûr:*** I. A verb meaning to besiege, to lay siege, to bind. It describes attaching a money bag to one's hand to transport it safely or to putting money into bags (Deut. 14:25; 2 Kgs. 5:23). It has the sense of gathering and agitating people to go against a city (Judg. 9:31); or of setting up siegeworks or fortress outposts against a city (Isa. 29:3); of besieging a city, attacking it (1 Sam. 23:8; 2 Sam. 11:1; 1 Kgs. 15:27; 16:17; 2 Kgs. 5:23; Dan. 1:1). It is used figuratively of constructing a protective barrier around a young girl (Song 8:9).

II. A verb meaning to attack, to harass, to be an adversary. It refers to attacking persons, putting them under duress, opposing them. God would serve as an adversary against the enemies of His people (Ex. 23:22). It refers to harassing or oppressing a people or nation (Deut. 2:9, 19); or even to attacking them (Esth. 8:11), in context with God's approval.

6697. צוּר ***ṣûr:*** A masculine noun meaning a rock. It refers to a large rock, a boulder (Judg. 6:21; 13:19; 2 Sam. 21:10); a cliff or wall of rock (Ex. 17:6). It is used in figurative expressions: honey from the rock, from rock clefts where some bees lived (Ps. 81:16[17]); of Abraham as the ancestral rock of Israel (Isa. 51:1); of a rock as a symbol of stability (Job 14:18; Nah. 1:6); of God as the Rock to look to and depend on (Ps. 31:2[3]; Isa. 17:10); of a rock personified, e.g., as Israel (2 Sam. 23:3); of God as the Rock many times (Deut. 32:4, 18; Hab. 1:12). It is used of an insufficient rock, a god of the pagan nations (Deut. 32:31).

6698. צוּר ***ṣûr:*** A proper noun designating Zur:

A. A Midianite prince (Num. 25:15; 31:8; Josh. 13:21).

B. Saul's uncle (1 Chr. 8:30; 9:36).

6699. צוּרָה ***ṣûrāh:*** A feminine noun meaning a design, a form. It refers to the planned construction patterns of a building, of Ezekiel's visionary Temple (Ezek. 43:11).

6700. צוּרִיאֵל ***ṣûriy'ēl:*** A proper noun designating Zuriel (Num. 3:35).

6701. צוּרִישַׁדָּי ***ṣûriyšadday:*** A proper noun designating Zurishaddai (Num. 1:6; 2:12; 7:36, 41; 10:19).

6702. צוּת ***ṣûṯ:*** A verb meaning to burn, to set on fire. It means to ignite, to burn up something that is in the way, an obstacle (Isa. 27:4).

6703. צַח ***ṣaḥ:*** An adjective referring to something dazzling, clear, shimmering. It refers to presenting clear and distinct ideas, without stuttering or hesitation (Isa. 32:4); to the appearance of a bright heat behaving like flashes of rising light (Isa. 18:4); probably in heat waves of a hot burning wind (Jer. 4:11). It refers to the impression of dazzling beauty radiating from a bride's face (Song 5:10).

6704. צִחֶה ***ṣiḥeh:*** An adjective meaning parched, dried up. It refers to something or someone desiccated, dried out from a serious lack of refreshing water. It is used figuratively of Israel as God's vineyard (Isa. 5:13).

6705. צָחַח ***ṣāḥaḥ:*** A verb meaning to be dazzling, white. It is used of something exceedingly pure, white, whiter than fresh milk, indicating purity and cleanness, as well as holiness (Lam. 4:7).

6706. צְחִיחַ ***ṣ^eḥiyaḥ:*** A masculine noun referring to a bare place; an exposed place. It describes totally bare places on tops of rocks (Ezek. 24:7; 26:4, 14). It indicates open, vulnerable places along a wall that has been damaged badly (Neh. 4:13[7]).

6707. צְחִיחָה ***ṣ^eḥiyḥāh:*** A feminine noun indicating a parched, sun-scorched land. It indicates something dried up and shriveled, suffering from the need for water, thirsty (Ps. 68:6[7]).

6708. צְחִיחִי ***ṣ^eḥiyḥiy:*** An adjective indicating an exposed place. It refers to something lying open, vulnerable to the elements or to danger. In context it refers to an exposed wall or an area where the wall is missing or broken down (Neh. 4:13[7]).

6709. צַחֲנָה ***ṣaḥ^anāh:*** A feminine noun meaning a stench, a foul smell. It describes the putrid smell of something rotting, decaying. It is used both literally and figuratively of the foulness of a destroyed enemy army (Joel 2:20).

6710. צַחְצָחָה ***ṣaḥṣāḥāh:*** A feminine noun used of a sun-scorched land. It refers to an area desiccated, dried up, shriveled by a burning hot sun. It is used of habitations where the conditions of life are like a parched area (Isa. 58:11).

6711. צָחַק ***ṣāḥaq:*** A verb meaning to laugh, to make jokes, to mock. It is used as an expression of joy or humor, but it also can be used to mock or make light of something serious (Judg. 16:25); sometimes in jest (Gen. 19:14). It also expresses an attitude toward something that is claimed but seems impossible to realize, e.g., Abraham's and Sarah's laughing responses to God's promises (Gen. 17:17; 18:12, 13, 15). God can create laughter, joy, where otherwise there would be none (Gen. 21:6). It may have sexual, licentious overtones (Ex. 32:6).

6712. צְחֹק ***ṣ^eḥōq:*** A masculine noun referring to laughter, scorn. It describes the act of laughing but also indicates the reason for the laughter

(Gen. 21:6); or the object at which laughter is directed, e.g., Judah (Ezek. 23:32).

6713. צַחַר ***ṣaḥar:*** I. A masculine noun meaning white; light-colored. It is used to define wool as white, white wool, one of the luxury items of trade processed by Tyre (Ezek. 27:18).

II. A proper noun, Zahar. Some translators prefer to render this word as a proper noun referring to a land, Zahar. If so, it may be the same as Sahra, northwest of Damascus (Ezek. 27:18).

6714. צֹחַר ***ṣōḥar:*** A proper noun designating Zohar:

A. The father of Ephron the Hittite (Gen. 23:8; 25:9).

B. Son of Simeon, the same as Zerah (2226,D) (Gen. 46:10; Ex. 6:15).

C. Son of Ashur (1 Chr. 4:7). See also 3328 (KJV, NASB).

6715. צָחֹר ***ṣāḥōr:*** An adjective meaning white, light-colored. It describes a white donkey ridden by the wealthy, an especially sought after animal (Judg. 5:10).

6716. צִי ***ṣiy:*** A masculine noun meaning ship. From its usage, it seems that this word refers to warships (Num. 24:24; Isa. 33:21; Ezek. 30:9; Dan. 11:30).

6717. צִיבָא ***ṣiyḇā':*** A proper noun designating Ziba. He was a servant in Saul's house. He informed David about Saul's remaining family members (2 Sam. 9:2–4). He was cared for by David and Ziba and his servants cared for Saul's grandson Mephibosheth (2 Sam. 9:9–13). He had been faithful to David, but when Ziba claimed that Mephibosheth wavered in his loyalty to David, David gave Ziba all of Mephibosheth's wealth (2 Sam. 19:15–18). Later, David discovered that Ziba had slandered Mephibosheth. David then divided the wealth between the two men (2 Sam. 19:24–30).

6718. צַיִד ***ṣayiḏ:*** I. A masculine noun referring to hunting; what is caught in hunting; game, venison. It refers to tracking down, capturing, and killing game for food. It was an ancient occupation (Gen. 10:9; 25:27). It refers to the game caught and the hunt itself (Gen. 25:28; 27:3, 5, 7, 19, 25, 30, 31, 33; Prov. 12:27).

II. A masculine noun meaning food, provisions, nourishment. In its causative stem, the verb means to take for provisions, to prepare provisions (Josh. 9:5); or to things loaded, loads, provisions (Neh. 13:15). It refers to food, nourishment for birds, animals supplied by God (Job 38:41). It is used of the provisions furnished by the Lord for His sanctuary, the Temple (Ps. 132:15).

6719. צַיָּד ***ṣayyāḏ:*** A masculine noun meaning hunter. It refers to a person who tracks down game and kills it. It is used metaphorically of the hunters the Lord would send against His people to judge them (Jer. 16:16).

6720. צֵידָה ṣēyḏāh: A feminine noun referring to food, provisions, venison. It describes the game that a hunter brings back and prepares as food. It describes various food provisions packed and taken along on a trip (Gen. 42:25; 45:21; Ex. 12:39). It is used of the miraculous provision God supplied to Israel in the desert (Ps. 78:25).

6721. צִידוֹן ṣiyḏôn, צִידֹן ṣiyḏōn: A proper noun designating Sidon, one of Phoenicia's principal walled port cities. It was on the coast of the Mediterranean north of Tyre and Carmel. It was situated on a major commercial route. Sidon was also the first son of Canaan (Gen. 10:15, 19). Sidon the city and its surrounding areas were a part of Canaan. Zebulun was to expand toward Sidon (Gen. 49:17). Asher, closest to Sidon, did not drive out its inhabitants (Judg. 1:31). Israel was enticed often to worship the Sidonian gods (Judg. 10:6). Elijah visited the widow of Zarephath in Sidonian territory (1 Kgs. 17:9). The city, like Tyre, was renounced for its trade with merchants (Isa. 23:2; Ezek. 27:8). Jeremiah and other prophets announce God's wrath to come on it (Jer. 25:22; Joel 3:4; Zech. 9:2).

6722. צִידֹנִי ṣiyḏōniy: A proper noun designating Sidonian, an inhabitant of Sidon (6721) (Deut. 3:9; Josh. 13:4, 6; Judg. 3:3; 10:12; 18:7; 1 Kgs. 5:6[20]; 11:1, 5, 33; 16:31; 2 Kgs. 23:13; 1 Chr. 22:4; Ezra 3:7; Ezek. 32:30).

6723. צִיָּה ṣiyyāh: A feminine noun indicating dryness, parched land, desert. It refers to a time of drought, a lack of rain for supplying water (Job 24:19); or to the infertile, dry ground itself (Job 30:3). The thirsting of the dry ground for water is compared to the longing of the soul for God (Ps. 63:1[2]). It refers to the desert and wilderness wanderings of Israel after the Exodus (Ps. 78:17; 105:41). The Lord is able to transform a desert into a place of flowing waters and babbling springs (Ps. 107:35), even the dry land *'ereṣ ṣiyyāh* (Isa. 41:18). But He can turn a city of splendor into a desiccated wilderness (Zeph. 2:13).

6724. צָיוֹן ṣāyôn: A masculine noun referring to a dry place, a desert. It refers to a place of extremely dry or drought conditions (Isa. 25:5; 32:2).

6725. צִיּוּן ṣiyyûn: A masculine noun indicating a roadmark, a guidepost, a sign, a tombstone. It indicates a monument or a marker set up to recall and explain past significant persons and events (2 Kgs. 23:17); or to serve as guideposts to earmark the way for travelers or to give other instructions (Jer. 31:21; Ezek. 39:15).

6726. צִיּוֹן ṣiyyôn: A proper noun designating Zion. The meaning of the word is most likely "fortress," and the word refers to (1) the city of Jerusalem, the City of David (2 Sam. 5:7); (2) the Temple Mount or Temple (Ps. 9:11[12]); or (3) to the area or cities of larger Judah (Ps. 69:35[36]). It was God's chosen location for His people. It was recognized ideally to be none other than a reference on earth to "the city of our God, His holy mountain" (Ps. 48:2[3], NASB), the city and country that God would show to Abraham and his descendants (Gen. 12:1). The word occurs most often in poetic/prophetic literature, only ca. seven times in historical prose. It occurs most often in Psalms, Isaiah, Jeremiah, Lamentations (a small book, but the word occurs 15 times in this poetic material lamenting the fall of Jerusalem in 586 B.C.), Micah, and Zechariah.

6727. צִיחָא ***ṣiyḥāʾ:*** A proper noun designating Ziha:

A. An ancestor of a family of temple slaves (Ezra 2:43; Neh. 7:46).

B. An overseer of temple slaves, possibly the same as A above (Neh. 11:21).

6728. צִיִּים ***ṣiyyiym:*** A masculine plural noun referring to desert creatures, desert people. It refers to nomadic people of the desert, possibly bedouins included, a wild bunch that could not be tamed or controlled (Ps. 72:9). It describes animals of the desert; figuratively, of God's defeating Leviathan and giving it to desert creatures to devour (Ps. 74:14). The desert animals and creatures are often mentioned as those beings that inhabit the remains of destroyed cities and the habitations of defeated peoples (Isa. 13:21; 23:13; 34:14; Jer. 50:39), especially the ruins of Babylon.

6729. צִינֹק ***ṣiynōq:*** I. A masculine noun referring to a neck iron; an iron collar. It indicates an instrument and form of punishment used to control madmen and make a public show of them (Jer. 29:26).

II. A masculine noun designating stocks. Some translators rendered this as stocks. The meaning of an iron collar is most likely correct (Jer. 29:26).

6730. צִיעֹר ***ṣiyʿōr:*** A proper noun designating Zior (Josh. 15:54).

6731. צִיץ ***ṣiyṣ:*** I. A masculine noun referring to a flower, a blossom. It refers to the flowers, petals, or blossoms put forth by an almond rod (Num. 17:8[23]); as well as carved ornamental flowers (1ob 14:2; Ps. 103:15; Isa. 40:6–8). The glory of Israel passed like a flowers (Isa. 28:1).

II. A masculine noun referring to a plate. It indicates the plate worn by the high priest in his turban bearing the inscription, "Holy unto the Lord" (Ex. 28:36).

III. A masculine noun meaning wing. It is used in a personification of Moab's flying away and being destroyed by the Lord (Jer. 48:9).

IV. A masculine noun meaning salt. It is used of putting salt on the land of Moab, which would effectively destroy its fertility forever (Jer. 48:9).

6732. צִיץ ***ṣiyṣ:*** A proper noun designating Ziz (2 Chr. 20:16).

6733. צִיצָה *ṣiyṣāh:* A feminine noun meaning flower. It is used symbolically to depict the splendor and prosperity of Ephraim, northern Israel, in her heyday, the height of her glory (Isa. 28:4).

6734. צִיצִת *ṣiyṣiṯ:* A feminine noun signifying a tassel, a lock (of something). It was an ornamental tuft of threads, cords, short strings, etc. of the same length and thickness made to hang from the edge or fringe of a garment, a knob, or some other object (Num. 15:38, 39). These tassels served as reminders. It is used of a tassel or bunch of hair (Ezek. 8:3).

6735. צִיר *ṣiyr:* I. A masculine noun meaning an ambassador, an envoy, a messenger. It describes a person appointed to represent someone else or his nation faithfully (Prov. 13:17; 25:13; Isa. 18:2; 57:9; Jer. 49:14; Obad. 1:1); a much sought after person.

II. A masculine noun meaning pain, labor pains, anguish. It refers to labor pains in giving birth (1 Sam. 4:19; Isa. 21:3); the dread and anxiety of a doomed nation (Isa. 13:8). It refers to a feeling of distress and hopelessness in the face of a divine vision (Dan. 10:16).

III. A masculine noun meaning hinge. Based upon its usage in context, the word must mean a hinge, a flexible device on which a door turns (Prov. 26:14).

6736. צִיר *ṣiyr:* A masculine noun meaning a form, an image. This noun focuses on the physical appearance of an item. That form and structure could be of the human body: the psalmist records how dead bodies decay in the grave (Ps. 49:14[15]). That form and structure could also be that of an idol: Isaiah states that those who formed idols would be ashamed and confounded (Isa. 45:16).

6737. צָיַר *ṣāyar:* A verb meaning to act as an ambassador. It describes the behavior and implies the responsibilities that a faithful representative of a person or nation fulfills (Josh. 9:4).

6738. צֵל *ṣēl:* A masculine noun meaning a shade, a shadow. This word is frequently used as a symbol for protection or refuge. This can be seen in the allegory of the trees (Judg. 9:15); and of the vine (Ps. 80:10[11]). God protects in the shadow of His wings (Ps. 17:8; 36:7[8]; 57:1[2]). The Lord is portrayed as the shade (Ps. 121:5); and hid His servant in the shadow of His hand (Isa. 49:2). The writer of Ecclesiastes taught that money and wisdom are both forms of protection, but wisdom could save one's life (Eccl. 7:12).

6739. צְלָא *ṣ*^{e}*lā':* An Aramaic verb meaning to pray. Daniel was praying to God when the royal administrators caught him after King Darius' edict petitions should only be made of the king (Dan. 6:10[11]). King Darius instructed his governors to give to the Israelites whatever they needed to rebuild the Temple so they could offer sacrifices to God and continue praying for him (Ezra 6:10).

6740. צָלָה ***ṣālāh:*** A verb meaning to roast. It means to cook something over an open fire or in hot coals or embers (1 Sam. 2:15). It describes roasting meat in a context that mocks idolatry (Isa. 44:16, 19).

6741. צִלָּה ***ṣillāh:*** A proper noun designating Zillah (Gen. 4:19, 22, 23).

6742. צְלוּל ***ṣᵉlûl,*** צְלִיל ***ṣᵉliyl:*** A masculine noun indicating a round loaf of bread. It describes in a dream a loaf of (barley?) bread. The bread was round and shaped like a dish (Judg. 7:13).

6743. צָלַח ***ṣālah,*** צָלֵחַ ***ṣālēaḥ:*** I. A verb meaning to rush, to break forth, to come mightily. It describes the Holy Spirit's affect on persons, making them powerful (Judg. 14:6, 9; 15:14; 1 Sam. 16:13); or causing persons to prophesy (1 Sam. 10:6, 10; 11:6). It indicates the effect of an evil spirit as well (1 Sam. 18:10). It has the sense of persons breaking out, rushing forward in battle (2 Sam. 19:17[18]); and of God breaking out in acts of judgment (Amos 5:6).

II. A verb meaning to prosper, to succeed, to be victorious. It is used of causing something to turn out successfully (Gen. 24:21, 40); of prospering a person (2 Chr. 26:5). It indicates a successful person (Gen. 39:2; Jer. 12:1). Some actions are not able to succeed, especially those breaking the commandments of the Lord (Num. 14:41; Deut. 28:29). It has the sense of succeeding in an endeavor (1 Kgs. 22:12, 15). It describes the success of a powerful weapon in warfare (Isa. 54:17), its successful use. What the righteous person does will eventually prosper (Ps. 1:3); but the seeming prosperousness of the wicked will fail (Ps. 37:7). Concealed sins keep one from prospering (Prov. 28:13). The will of the Lord will prosper in the hand of His Suffering Servant (Isa. 53:10). The judgment on Jerusalem renders her useless, without any hope of prospering (Ezek. 15:4). God allows the rebellious king of the end to prosper but only until a certain limit is reached (Dan. 11:36).

6744. צְלַח ***ṣᵉlaḥ:*** An Aramaic verb meaning to prosper, to succeed. It refers to the successful completion of a task or a building project (Ezra 5:8; 6:14). It describes God's prospering persons in their daily tasks and responsibilities (Dan. 3:30). It indicates the amazing success Daniel enjoyed under Persian kings (Dan. 6:28[29]).

6745. צֵלָחָה ***ṣēlāḥāh:*** A feminine noun meaning a cooking pan. It describes a cooking utensil used for boiling food and sacrifices (2 Chr. 35:13).

6746. צְלֹחִית ***ṣᵉlōḥiyṯ:*** A feminine noun referring to a jar, a bowl. It describes a dish or a deep, hollow container for holding salt or other similar substances (2 Kgs. 2:20).

6747. צַלַּחַת ṣallaḥaṯ: I. A feminine noun signifying a dish, a pan. It refers to a shallow plate or slab for eating off of. A standard set of these were used to eat from (2 Kgs. 21:13). It also refers to serving pans (2 Chr. 35:13); and serving dishes (Prov. 19:24).

II. A feminine noun referring to bosom. It indicates a person's body around the chest area (Prov. 19:24; 26:15).

6748. צָלִי ṣāliy: An adjective referring to something roasted. It indicates cooking meat over an open fire, coals, or embers (Ex. 12:8, 9; Isa. 44:16). It describes satirically the roasting of part of an idol over a fire.

6749. צָלַל ṣālal: A verb meaning to sink. It means to descend rapidly into the dark, shadowy depths of the sea (Ex. 15:10).

6750. צָלַל ṣālal: A verb meaning to tingle, to quiver. It indicates a sensitive feeling in a person's ears or lips with a corresponding quivering reaction. In context it was a result of hearing about a horrifying deed the Lord would do (1 Sam. 3:11; 2 Kgs. 21:12; Jer. 19:3).

6751. צָלַל ṣālal: A Hebrew verb meaning to be dark, to grow dim. This word is used only twice in the Hebrew Old Testament. Nehemiah spoke of the gates of Jerusalem growing dim (in other words, evening came, and it grew dark) (Neh. 13:19). Assyria was compared to a Lebanese cedar that had such long, thick branches that it darkened the forest (Ezek. 31:3).

6752. צֵלֶל ṣēlel: A masculine noun meaning shadow. This word occurs only four times in the Old Testament. In Job it described the shade of trees (Job 40:22). In the other instances, it depicted the time of day when the shadows fled (Song 2:17; 4:6) or lengthened (Jer. 6:4).

6753. צְלֶלְפּוֹנִי ṣᵉlelpôniy, הַצְלֶלְפּוֹנִי haṣṣᵉlelpôniy: A proper noun designating Hazzelelponi (1 Chr. 4:3).

6754. צֶלֶם ṣelem: A masculine noun meaning an image, a likeness, a statue, a model, a drawing, a shadow. The word means image or likeness; its most celebrated theological and anthropological use was to depict human beings as made in God's own image (Gen. 1:26, 27; 5:3). People continue to be in His image even after the fall, although the image is marred (Gen. 9:6), and still serves as the basis of the prohibition not to kill human beings.

It is used metaphorically to depict persons as shadows, phantoms, or unknowing, senseless, fleeting beings carrying out the motions of life (Ps. 39:6[7]); unless they have hope in God (see Ps. 39:7[8]). In a similar vein, the wicked before the Lord are considered as mere dreams or fantasies (Ps. 73:20).

The word is also used in a concrete sense to depict images cut out of or molded from various materials. The word describes the images or idols of foreign or strange gods (2 Kgs. 11:18; Amos 5:26). The people of Israel produced images used as idols from their own jewelry (Ezek. 7:20; 16:17). Israel was, on its entrance into Canaan, to destroy all the molten images of the heathen (Num. 33:52). In Ezekiel 23:14, this word refers to pictures of Babylonians that enticed the people of Israel into apostasy when they saw them (Ezek. 23:14).

6755. צְלֵם ***ṣelem*****, צְלֵם** ***ṣ**e**lēm:*** An Aramaic masculine noun meaning a statue, an image. This word is related to the Hebrew word *ṣelem* (6754), meaning image. It was used to describe the statue in Nebuchadnezzar's dream (Dan. 2:31, 32, 34, 35); the image that Nebuchadnezzar built (Dan. 3:1–3, 5, 7); and the distortion of Nebuchadnezzar's face in anger when he heard the response of Shadrach, Meshach, and Abednego (Dan. 3:19).

6756. צַלְמוֹן ***ṣalmôn:*** A proper noun designating Zalmon:

A. A wooded place near Shechem (Judg. 9:48; Ps. 68:14[15]).

B. One of David's warriors (2 Sam. 23:28).

6757. צַלְמָוֶת ***ṣalmāwet̲:*** A masculine noun meaning a death shadow, a deep shadow. This word is made up of two Hebrew words, *ṣēl* (6738) or *ṣēlel* (6752), meaning shadow, and *māwet̲* (4194), meaning death, which gives rise to the translation of shadow of death (Ps. 23:4). In some contexts, this word was used to describe death (Job 38:17); or those close to death (Ps. 107:10, 14). In other contexts, it was used to describe a physical darkness (Job 24:17; Amos 5:8); a spiritual darkness (Isa. 9:2[1]); a darkness of understanding (Job 12:22); a gloomy countenance (Job 16:16); or a dangerous land (Jer. 2:6). Occasionally, both elements of death and darkness are present in the context (Job 3:5; 10:21, 22).

6758. צַלְמֹנָה ***ṣalmōnāh:*** A proper noun designating Zalmonah (Num. 33:41, 42).

6759. צַלְמֻנָּע ***ṣalmunnā‘:*** A proper noun designating Zalmunna (Judg. 8:5–7, 12, 15, 18, 21; Ps. 83:11[12]).

6760. צָלַע ***ṣāla‘:*** A verb meaning to limp, to be lame. To limp means to walk unevenly, vertically or horizontally, because of an injury (Gen. 32:31[32]). To be lame means to limp badly or to be crippled, disabled.

6761. צֶלַע ***ṣela‘:*** A masculine noun indicating stumbling, a fall, a slip. It is taken by many translators to mean a fall or stumbling, used figuratively of a person falling, being overtaken (Job 18:12; Ps. 35:15; 38:17[18]; Jer. 20:10). Some prefer to translate it as side (6763) in Job 18:12.

6762. צֵלַע ***ṣēla':*** A proper noun designating Zelah (Josh. 18:28; 2 Sam. 21:14).

6763. צֵלָע ***ṣēlā':*** A feminine noun meaning side, a side room (chamber), a hillside, a wall. It refers to a side or rib from a side of a human body (Gen. 2:21, 22); or the side of an object (Ex. 25:12, 14; 26:20). It may in context be translated as hillside, the side of a hill (2 Sam. 16:13). It may have the sense of side (rooms) or side (chambers) (1 Kgs. 6:5; 7:3); or the wing or extension of a building (Ezek. 41:5). It is taken by some to mean side in Job 18:12 (cf. 6761). It refers to planks or boards, building materials (1 Kgs. 6:15, 16); or to sections or leaves of doors (1 Kgs. 6:34).

6764. צָלָף ***ṣālāp̱:*** A proper noun designating Zalaph (Neh. 3:30).

6765. צְלָפְחָד ***ṣ^e^lāp̱^e^ḥāḏ:*** A proper noun designating Zelophehad, a descendant of Manasseh, son of Hepher. He had only daughters (Num. 26:33; 27:1, 7). His daughters argued convincingly that they should receive their father's inheritance (Num. 27:3–11), but to keep the inheritance within their father's clan, they had to marry within that clan (Num. 36:2–11). Each tribe was to keep its tribal inheritances permanently (Num. 36:7–9). The daughter married cousins on their father's side. This interesting case illustrates the "living nature" of the laws God gave to Israel. They were to be interpreted in such a way to (1) preserve their original intent and (2) to treat the persons involved fairly.

6766. צֶלְצַח ***ṣelṣaḥ:*** A proper noun designating Zelzah (1 Sam. 10:2).

6767. צִלְצָל ***ṣilṣāl,*** צְלָצַל ***ṣ^e^lāṣal,*** צֶלְצְלִים ***selṣ^e^liym:*** I. A masculine noun referring to whirring. It describes the insects (locusts) of ancient Ethiopia (Nubia) or their armies. It is a word meant to imitate the sound or object it describes (Isa. 18:1), technically an onomatopoeic word.

II. A masculine noun meaning spear. A long, sharp weapon or hunting gear used to bring down wild game (Job 41:7[40:31]).

III. A masculine noun referring to a locust, a cricket. It refers to destroying insects, crickets or locusts that ravages crops, trees, all kinds of produce (Deut. 28:42).

IV. A masculine plural noun. It refers to cymbals, one or two circular, concave brass plates that create musical sound by being struck or by being struck together (2 Sam. 6:5; Ps. 150:5).

6768. צֶלֶק ***ṣeleq:*** A proper noun designating Zelek (2 Sam. 23:37; 1 Chr. 11:39).

6769. צִלְּתַי ***ṣill^e^ṯay:*** A proper noun designating Zillethai (1 Chr. 8:20; 12:20).

6770. צָמֵא ***ṣāmē':*** A verb meaning to be thirsty. It indicates a strong desire and need for water to drink. Israel thirsted in the desert and grumbled against Moses (Ex. 17:3); Samson nearly died of thirst (Judg. 15:18); and Jael used Sisera's great thirst to trick him (Judg. 4:19). It is used in beautiful metaphors of the soul thirsting for God (Ps. 42:2[3]; 63:1[2]). God met the need for water for His people (Isa. 48:21); and in the future will remove their thirst (Isa. 49:10). But rebellious people will continue to thirst (Isa. 65:13).

6771. צָמֵא *ṣāmē'*: An adjective meaning thirsty. It indicated a state of needing water, being dried out. It is used to describe a thirsty land, a dried-out land needing water (Deut. 29:19[18]; Isa. 44:3); a people suffering from lack of water in desert heat (2 Sam. 17:29). Hunger and thirst are often mentioned together (Ps. 107:5). A thirsty enemy should be given water (Prov. 25:21); but a fool withholds help from a thirsty person (Isa. 32:6). God will meet the needs of His people in a thirsty land (Isa. 44:3). In its most famous use, the word is used figuratively of those who thirst after God, for free wine and milk will be given to meet their needs (Isa. 55:1).

6772. צָמָא *ṣāmā'*: A masculine noun referring to thirst, something parched. It describes a desire for water to drink or some other liquid, milk or wine. It indicates a literal thirsting for water (Ex. 17:3). It describes the throat of a righteous man before his enemies (Ps. 69:21[22]). The Lord meets the thirsty needs of His creatures (Ps. 104:11). It is used of spiritual and emotional needs, the thirsts of God's rebellious people (Isa. 5:13); and the physical needs of the poor (Isa. 41:17). Thirst may be a feature of God's judgments (Isa. 50:2). It stands for parched places and land (Jer. 48:18). It refers to thirsting, desiring the Word of God (Amos 8:11).

6773. צִמְאָה *ṣim'āh*: A feminine noun referring to thirst, dryness. It refers to a desire and a need for water. In context it indicates a condition that Israelites can keep from if they follow the Lord, not their own desires (Jer. 2:25).

6774. צִמָּאוֹן *ṣimmā'ôn*: A feminine noun meaning thirsty ground, drought. It may stand for thirsty or parched ground, earth (Deut. 8:15; Isa. 35:7); which God can transform at his will (Ps. 107:33).

6775. צָמַד *ṣāmaḏ*: A verb meaning to join, to yoke, to harness. It indicates a joining of forces, of agreement, of becoming like each other. Israel began to take part in worshiping Baal of Peor (Num. 25:3, 5; Ps. 106:28). In a physical sense, it refers to an object being tied to or fastened to another object (2 Sam. 20:8). It is used in a figurative sense to describe a person's tongue harnessing or latching on to deceit, producing it (Ps. 50:19).

6776. צֶמֶד *ṣemeḏ*: I. A masculine noun referring to a couple, a yoke, a team of two, a pair. It refers to two of something, a team or a pair (Judg. 19:3, 10; 2 Sam. 16:1; 1 Kgs. 19:19, 21; 2 Kgs. 5:17). A yoke of oxen refers to two oxen, a pair (1 Sam. 11:7). It is used in the idiom, yoke of land, about an acre, referring to the amount of land plowed in a day by one yoke of oxen (1 Sam. 14:14). Job possessed five hundred yoke of oxen (1:3).

II. A masculine noun referring to about an acre of land; land plowed by a team of two oxen in a day. Isaiah 5:10 refers to "*ten ṣimdê-k̲erem,*" ca. ten acres. See also 1 Samuel 14:14 in I.

6777. צַמָּה *ṣammāh:* I. A feminine noun referring to a veil. It refers to a covering of cloth placed over a person's eyes (Song 4:1, 3; 6:7). It is used figuratively of the uncovering and destruction of Babylon (Isa. 47:2).

II. A feminine noun indicating a lock of hair. It refers to the beautiful, thick curls of hair on the bride (Song 4:1, 3; 6:7; Isa. 47:2). Uncovering the locks (KJV) refers to stripping bare the city and kingdom of Babylon.

6778. צִמּוּק *simmûq:* A masculine noun indicating a cluster of raisins, a cake of raisins. It refers to an especially desirable food item in the Middle East (1 Sam. 25:18); a quick energy source and delightful gift (1 Sam. 30:12; 2 Sam. 16:1; 1 Chr. 12:40).

6779. צָמַח *ṣāmaḥ:* A verb meaning to grow, to spring forth, to sprout. It refers to a plant as it breaks forth out of the ground (Gen. 2:5, 9); or to trees as they grow from the ground (Ex. 10:5). Both God and the ground cause plants, trees, etc. to sprout (Gen. 3:18). It describes human hair beginning to grow (Judg. 16:22; 2 Sam. 10:5). It is used in figurative expressions: trouble or evil sprouting from the ground (Job 5:6); of the good man's offspring (Job 8:19); of truth growing up from the earth (Ps. 85:11[12]); of the sprouting of the line of kings from David (Ps. 132:17; Jer. 33:15; Ezek. 29:21; Zech. 6:12); the springing forth of new things ordained by God (Isa. 42:9; 43:19); of Israel growing up as a child (Ezek. 16:7).

6780. צֶמַח *ṣemaḥ:* A masculine noun meaning a branch, a growth, a crop. It refers to what grows on the ground, domesticated or wild (Gen. 19:25; Ps. 65:10[11]; Isa. 61:11). It is used especially of the restored fertility of God's land and people (Isa. 4:2). It is used figuratively of a descendant, a Branch, of David (Jer. 23:5; 33:15; Zech. 3:8; 6:12); of Jerusalem (Ezek. 16:7). It refers to grain on the stalks (Hos. 8:7).

6781. צָמִיד *ṣāmiyd̲:* A masculine noun indicating a woman's bracelet. It was sometimes given as a gift (Gen. 24:22, 30, 47) to persons or to the Lord (Num. 31:50) for use in the Lord's service. It was used as an ornament of beauty (Ezek. 16:11; 23:42).

6782. צַמִּים ṣammiym: A masculine noun referring to a snare, a trap, a robber. It seems to refer to a robber or someone out to take a person's riches (Job 5:5); but in Job 18:9 it has the sense of a snare, a hindrance that traps the wicked.

6783. צְמִיתֻת ṣ^{e}miytut: A feminine noun meaning completion, finality. This word is used only twice in the Old Testament and comes from the verb *ṣāmat* (6789), meaning to put to an end. It was used in the Levitical Law to describe the duration of property ownership (Lev. 25:23, 30).

6784. צָמַק ṣāmaq: A verb meaning to dry up (of woman's breasts). It is used in a figurative expression of giving Israel dry breasts to feed from so they will starve (Hos. 9:14).

6785. צֶמֶר ṣemer: A masculine noun meaning wool. It refers to the soft, curly hair of sheep or of other animals with hair of the same or similar texture. It was used in the production of clothing (Lev. 13:47, 48, 52, 59; Deut. 22:11; Prov. 31:13). Its whiteness was used in figures of speech (Ps. 147:16; Isa. 1:18). It constituted a valuable merchandise of trade (Ezek. 27:18). Levites wore wool and linen garments (Ezek. 44:17). It is used in figurative expressions concerning Israel's harlotry (Hos. 2:5[7], 9[11]).

6786. צְמָרִי ṣ^{e}māriy: A proper noun designating Zemarite (Gen. 10:18; 1 Chr. 1:16).

6787. צְמָרַיִם ṣ^{e}mārayim: A proper noun designating Zemaraim (Josh. 18:22; 2 Chr. 13:4).

6788. צַמֶּרֶת ṣammereṯ: A feminine noun referring to a top, the highest branch. It is used in a long parable from Ezekiel to refer to various nations, e.g., Judah (Ezek. 17:3, 22) or a part of the Davidic line. It indicates the topmost branches of a tree, its top, in referring to Assyria (Ezek. 31:3, 10, 14).

6789. צָמַת ṣāmaṯ: A verb meaning to put to an end. This word appears most often in the imprecatory psalms—that is, the psalms that call down curses on one's enemies. The word occurs within the context of putting an end to the wicked (Ps. 73:27; 101:8); or to one's enemies (2 Sam. 22:41; Ps. 54:5[7]; 143:12). In both of these cases, this word alludes to the physical death of these people. But in other instances, this word describes the process of rendering powerless by putting persons in prison (Lam. 3:53); the drying up of riverbeds (Job 6:17); or the wearying of the psalmist (Ps. 119:139).

6790. צִן ṣin: A proper noun designating the Desert or Wilderness of Zin. It was the territory just north of Kadesh Barnea and south of the Negev, about one-half of the way between the coastal plains and the Arabale (the Rift Valley). Its northern boundary was part of the southern boundary of Canaan (Num. 34:3, 4) and Judah (Josh. 15:1–3). The twelve spies went out from here (Num. 13:21), and they traveled all the way to Rehob north of Israel, just beyond Dan.

6791. צֵן ṣēn: A masculine noun referring to a hook, a thorn. It refers to a sharp, prickly plant or to individual spines sticking out from its branches. It is often used figuratively of undesirable places or locations (Job 5:5; Prov. 22:5). The word is also used of sharp hooks used to lead prisoners (Amos 4:2).

6792. צֹנֵא ṣōnē', צֹנֶה ṣōneh: A common noun meaning a flock, sheep. It is another word referring to a flock, sheep, goats (Num. 32:24). God has made humankind ruler over all flocks of sheep (Ps. 8:7[8]).

6793. צִנָּה ṣinnāh: I. A feminine noun referring to a hook. It refers to a sharp instrument used to gouge and lead away prisoners (Amos 4:2).

II. A feminine noun indicating a shield, a large shield, a buckler. It refers to a large, probably rectangular shield used in battle (1 Sam. 17:7, 41; 1 Kgs. 10:16; Jer. 46:3; Ezek. 23:24). Goliath's shield was carried by someone for him. It is used figuratively often: God as a Shield (Ps. 5:12[13]); of God as a Shield or a Warrior (Ps. 35:2); of God's faithfulness or truth as a shield (Ps. 91:4).

III. A feminine noun meaning cold, coolness. It refers to the impression given through the senses of something not hot, like ice or snow (Prov. 25:13).

6794. צִנּוֹר ṣinnôr: A masculine noun referring to a water shaft, waterfalls. It refers to a water shaft hollowed out of stone, a water tunnel (2 Sam. 5:8). It describes water that drops suddenly and quickly, creating a rushing sound of turbulent water (Ps. 42:7[8]), thus conveying a certain impression and response in the hearer.

6795. צָנַח ṣānaḥ: I. A verb meaning to get off an animal. It is used of Achsah or Acsah, Caleb's daughter, getting down from her donkey (Josh. 15:10; Judg. 1:14).

II. A verb meaning to go through. It means to penetrate something and come out the other side (Judg. 4:21).

6796. צָנִין ṣāniyn: A masculine noun signifying a thorn. It is a prickly, spiny, short growth from a branch that can stick and penetrate human skin. It is used figuratively to represent the danger and trouble that the people whom Israel did not drive out of Canaan would be to Israel (Num. 33:55; Josh. 23:13).

6797. צָנִיף ṣāniyp̄: I. A masculine noun indicating a turban, a hood. It indicates a headpiece often worn by persons in authority in the ancient Near East. It was created by folding long pieces of cloth around a person's head. It was worn by the high priest of Israel (Zech. 3:5). It is used figuratively of righteousness (Job 29:14).

People considered it a valued luxury in some cases (Isa. 3:23). Zion is described as the royal turban or diadem of the Lord (Isa. 62:3).

II. A masculine noun referring to a diadem. It is translated as diadem in some cases, indicating a golden crown but used figuratively of righteousness (Job 29:14).

III. A masculine noun meaning mitre. It is translated as mitre or miter by some translators, indicating a turban, a headband of the high priest of Israel (Zech. 3:5).

6798. צָנַם *ṣānam:* A verb meaning to be withered, to be dried up. It refers to withered ears of corn seen in Pharaoh's dream and representing years of drought (Gen. 41:23).

6799. צְנָן *ṣ^e^nān:* A proper noun designating Zenan (Josh. 15:37).

6800. צָנַע *ṣāna‘*, צָנוּעַ *ṣānûa‘:* I. A verb meaning to be humble. It is used to describe those who are and act meekly. They are not arrogant, boastful (Prov. 11:2), especially before the Lord (Mic. 6:8).

II. A masculine noun indicating humility. Some translators take the forms of the word in the text as nouns, referring to a person in a state of humility, meekness (Prov. 11:2) and living accordingly (Mic. 6:8).

6801. צָנַף *ṣānap:* A verb meaning to wrap around, to roll up tightly. It describes the wrapping, folding, and fastening of a turban on a person's head (Lev. 16:4). It is used figuratively of God's rolling up, judging, and destroying a rebellious person (Isa. 22:18). In the latter reference, the verb used is in an emphatic construction.

6802. צְנֵפָה *ṣ^e^nēpāh:* I. A feminine noun indicating a tossing. It refers to the action of rolling a ball or tossing it. Used figuratively, it indicates the exiling of a person in a distant land (Isa. 22:18).

II. A feminine noun indicating a tightness. It is used figuratively to express even more emphatically the way the Lord will indeed roll Shebna into a ball tightly and cast him out (Isa. 22:18).

6803. צִנְצֶנֶת *ṣinṣeneṯ:* A feminine noun referring to a jar, a pot. It refers to a container into which a sample of manna was placed to preserve and display it (Ex. 16:33). It must have been a closed container with a lid.

6804. צַנְתָּרוֹת *ṣantārôṯ:* A feminine plural noun referring to pipes. It refers to hollow tubes through which olive oil was carried to serve as fuel for lamps (Zech. 4:12).

6805. צָעַד *ṣā‘aḏ:* A verb meaning to march, to walk, to run. It describes the process of locomotion: walking, stepping, moving forward (2 Sam. 6:13); of the growth of limbs, stems, and branches over a wall (Gen. 49:22). It depicts God figuratively marching, moving from the land of Edom (Judg. 5:4; cf. Hab. 3:12); it is used derisively of the inability of pagan gods to walk (Jer. 10:5). It depicts God's leading His people in the wilderness, walking before them (Ps. 68:7[8]). It indicates the arrogant stride of an adulterer (Prov. 7:8).

6806. צַעַד *ṣa'aḏ:* A masculine noun referring to a step taken, a stride. It refers to actual steps taken or the distance covered by a step (2 Sam. 6:13). It bears a figurative sense of success in life, prosperity (2 Sam. 22:37). The Lord numbers the steps of persons, determining their extent and their path (Job 14:16; Prov. 16:9; Jer. 10:23). Wisdom helps make life's steps successful and easier (Prov. 4:12).

6807. צְעָדָה *ṣᵉ'āḏāh:* I. A feminine noun referring to a marching. It refers to the sound created by the Lord and His armies as they go forth in battle (2 Sam. 5:24; 1 Chr. 14:15).

II. A feminine noun referring to an ankle bracelet, an ankle chain. These were items usually made of gold or silver, luxury items of jewelry for ornamentation (Isa. 3:20). The Lord would remove them as an act of judgment on His part.

6808. צָעָה *ṣā'āh:* I. A verb meaning to imprison, to take captive. It depicts a person imprisoned, kept in confinement and in chains (Isa. 51:14).

II. A verb meaning to travel, to wander. It refers figuratively to the Lord traveling, going forth, (*ṣ'h*) in might and strength (Isa. 63:1). It describes acting, behaving as a harlot (Jer. 2:20). It refers to a person who travels without purpose and wanders about (Jer. 48:12).

III. A verb meaning to march, to stride. It indicates striding forth with purpose, marching; in context it means to bring judgment (Isa. 63:1).

IV. A verb meaning to lie down. It is used with the word *zônāh,* harlot, following, so it may mean to lie down in this context for an act of harlotry (Jer. 2:20).

V. A verb meaning to tip over, to pour out. It refers to an act of destruction, destroying vessels and their contents. God will bring these events to pass on Moab (Jer. 48:12).

6809. צָעִיף *ṣa'iyp̱:* A masculine noun indicating a veil, a shawl. It refers to a piece of cloth used to cover a bride's face, a wrap (Gen. 24:65). Some prefer to understand a shawl in this context, a covering for a woman's head and shoulders (Gen. 38:14, 19).

6810. צָעִיר *ṣā'iyr:* An adjective meaning young, younger, little, small. It refers to the age of a person, someone young in years. Used with the definite article, it can be the younger or the young one of two (Gen. 19:31, 34); or even the youngest (Ps. 68:27[28]). It may indicate merely the one born first (Gen. 25:23). It indicates what is little, small, smaller, or smallest in size or number (1 Sam. 9:21; Ps. 119:141; Isa. 60:22). It refers to servants, young ones (Jer. 14:3). It has the sense of so small! or too small followed by the prepositions *lᵉ* plus the infinitive of *hāyāh,* to be (Mic. 5:2[1]).

6811. צָעִירָה ṣā'iyrāh: A proper noun designating Zair (2 Kgs. 8:21).

6812. צְעִירָה ṣ^e'iyrāh: A feminine noun meaning youth. It has the meaning of chronological age; in context it is used to rank persons (Gen. 43:33).

6813. צָעַן ṣā'an: A verb meaning to travel; to fold a tent for moving. It indicates in context either moving a tent about, traveling with it, or the folding up and, hence, taking down of a tent to move it, to journey with it (Isa. 33:20).

6814. צֹעַן ṣō'an: A proper noun designating Zoan, a city in Egypt built seven years before Hebron in Judah (Num. 13:22). Some of the ten plagues hit this area (Ps. 78:12, 43). It was probably in the northeastern delta area of Egypt and west of the Nile. It was supposed to house Egypt's wise counselors (Isa. 19:11, 13), but Isaiah called them fools. Ezekiel predicted its destruction by fire (30:14).

6815. צַעֲנַנִּים ṣa'^anannіym: A proper noun designating Zaanannim (Josh. 19:33; Judg. 4:11).

6816. צַעֲצֻעִים ṣa'^aṣu'iym: A masculine plural noun meaning sculpted. It refers to the skill of carving wood, chiseling stone; casting, cutting, or molding metal or clay into three dimensional artifacts. The cherubim in the Most Holy Place of the Temple were sculpted, probably of wood and then overlaid with gold (2 Chr. 3:10).

6817. צָעַק ṣā'aq: A verb meaning to cry out, to summon. It refers to shouting, complaining loudly, to pleading for relief or justice, calling for help. The earth, figuratively, cries out because of injustices done to it (Gen. 4:10). Cries are aimed primarily to God or His representative leaders (Ex. 5:8, 15; 8:12[8]; 14:10, 15). It indicates being called together, summoned (2 Kgs. 3:21); or indicates the act of calling people together (1 Sam. 10:17). The Lord hears the cries of His people who plead their cause with Him (Ps. 34:17[18]; 77:1[2]; Isa. 19:20).

6818. צְעָקָה ṣ^e'āqāh: A feminine noun indicating a cry, an outcry. It describes a call for help, a cry of wailing and despair. It describes the cries of outrage regarding sin that went up against Sodom and Gommorah (Gen. 18:21; 19:13); and the outcries of Israel because of her oppression in Egypt (Ex. 3:7, 9). It is used of a deep, despairing cry over calamity (Ex. 11:6). The godless also utter cries of dismay (Job 27:9). Cries of deep distress will be a feature of the Day of the Lord (Zeph. 1:10).

6819. צָעַר ṣā'ar: A verb meaning to be brought low, to be insignificant. It means for a person to be or become insignificant, trifling, small (Job 14:21; Jer. 30:19). It refers to insignificant persons or little ones without great worth or influence (Zech. 13:7).

6820. צוֹעַר ***ṣôʿar:*** A proper noun designating Zoar. Before the destruction of Sodom and Gomorrah it was located in a beautiful fertile plain of the Jordan (Gen. 13:10). It was also called Bela (Gen. 14:2, 8). The name Zoar means "little, small" (Gen. 19:22, 23, 30). Lot fled there for safety. Its territory could be seen from Mount Pisgah (Deut. 34:3).

6821. צָפַד ***ṣāp̱aḏ:*** A verb meaning to be shriveled up. It means to dry up and shrink, become wrinkled. It describes the skin of those suffering under a long siege from an attacking enemy (Lam. 4:8).

6822. צָפָה ***ṣāp̱āh:*** A verb meaning to watch, to keep guard. It means to keep an eye on something or someone, to guard someone, to watch over. It refers to God's watching over persons while they are apart (Gen. 31:49); over the nations (Ps. 66:7). A person who watches is a watchman (1 Sam. 14:16; 2 Sam. 13:34; Isa. 21:6; Mic. 7:4). The prophets were called watchmen for God (Jer. 6:17; Ezek. 3:17; 33:7; Hos. 9:8). It is used figuratively of waiting to see something, what God will do (Ps. 5:3[4]; Nah. 2:1[2]; Hab. 2:1). The wicked watch the righteous to do them harm (Ps. 37:32).

6823. צָפָה ***ṣāp̱āh:*** A verb meaning to cover, to overlay. It is used to describe glazing, plating, or overlaying something (1 Kgs. 6:20; 2 Kgs. 18:16); especially of things for the Tabernacle (Ex. 25:11, 13, 24, 28; 26:29, 32, 37). In its passive tense, it points out what has been overlaid (Ex. 26:32; Prov. 26:23).

6824. צָפָה ***ṣāp̱āh:*** I. A feminine noun indicating a flow, a discharge. It refers to the loss of blood in a time of calamity suffered by the people in Egypt (Ezek. 32:6); it is used, however, in a figurative as well as literal sense.

II. A feminine noun meaning a swimming. It indicates a profuse, large discharge of blood in battle, used figuratively as well as literally (Ezek. 32:6).

6825. צְפוֹ ***ṣᵉp̱ô***, צְפִי ***ṣᵉp̱iy:*** I. A feminine noun meaning a flow, a discharge (NASB, NIV, Ezek. 32:6).

II. A feminine noun meaning a swimming (KJV, Ezek. 32:6).

6826. צִפּוּי ***ṣippûy:*** A masculine noun meaning an overlay, a plating. Overlaying refers to the thin coating of substances placed on various objects for beauty and decorative purposes (Ex. 38:17, 19). Plating was similar but may generally involve a thicker overlay of substances (Num. 16:38[17:3], 39[17:4]; Isa. 30:22).

6827. צְפוֹן ***ṣᵉp̱ôn:*** A proper noun designating Zephon; the same as Ziphion (6837) (Num. 26:15).

6828. צָפוֹן ***ṣāp̱ôn:*** A common noun indicating north; northward. It refers to the direction north; facing east, the left hand points north (Gen. 13:14; 28:14). It combines with other directions (Gen. 13:14). With *āh* on the end, it indicates a northward direction (Ex. 40:22; Jer. 23:8); followed by *'el,* it means toward the north (Eccl. 1:6; Ezek. 42:1); or with *le* on the front (Ezek. 40:23). From the north is expressed by *min* (4480) + *ṣāp̱on* (Isa. 14:31). The north became a source of violence, evil (Jer. 1:14). It was used of the great Mount Hermon of the north (Ps. 48:2[3]; 89:12[13]; Ezek. 32:30).

6829. צָפוֹן *ṣāp̱ôn:* A proper noun designating Zaphon (Josh. 13:27; Judg. 12:1; Ps. 48:2[3]. The occurrences in Judges 12:1 and Psalm 48:2[3] are interpreted in some versions as the noun meaning north, northward (6828), which is spelled the same in Hebrew.

6830. צְפוֹנִי *ṣep̱ôniy:* An adjective meaning northern. It is an adjective form from *ṣāp̱on* meaning northern. It probably refers to an invading army (Joel 2:20).

6831. צְפוֹנִי *ṣep̱ôniy:* A proper noun designating Zephonite (Num. 26:15).

6832. צְפִיעַ *ṣep̱iya':* A masculine noun meaning dung, manure. It indicates human or animal excrement, feces (Ezek. 4:15).

6833. צִפּוֹר *ṣippôr:* A common noun meaning a fowl, a bird. Used in a collective sense, it refers to birds (Gen. 7:14; 15:10; Ps. 11:1); or it can refer to one bird (Deut. 14:11; Hos. 11:11; Amos 3:5). Ezekiel depicts birds of prey of every kind (Ezek. 39:4).

6834. צִפּוֹר *ṣippôr:* A proper noun designating Zippor (Num. 22:2, 4, 10, 16; 23:18; Josh. 24:9; Judg. 11:25).

6835. צַפַּחַת *ṣappaḥat̲:* A feminine noun indicating a jar, a jug. It refers to a container to hold water for traveling or hunting (1 Sam. 26:11, 12, 16). It also describes a household storage jar or a jug for oil or water (1 Kgs. 17:12, 14, 16; 19:6).

6836. צְפִיָּה *ṣep̱iyyāh:* A feminine noun indicating a watchtower. It refers to a lookout structure from which to spy out approaching enemies or to keep aware of what is going on in the vicinity (Lam. 4:17).

6837. צִפְיוֹן *ṣip̱yôn:* A proper noun designating Ziphion; the same as Zephon (6827) (Gen. 46:16).

6838. צַפִּיחִת *ṣap̱iyhit̲:* A feminine noun describing a wafer. It describes a thin baked cake, like a small wafer. Its appearance was used to describe manna (Ex. 16:31).

6839. צֹפִים *ṣōp̱iym:* A proper noun designating Zophim (Num. 23:14).

6840. צָפִין *ṣāp̱iyn:* An adjective indicating hidden treasure. It refers to something hidden; in context something of significant worth is in mind, satisfying those who live for this life (Ps. 17:14).

6841. צְפִיר ***ṣ***^{e}***p̱iyr:*** An Aramaic masculine noun indicating a male goat. It was a major sacrificial animal. One goat was offered for each tribe of Israel as a mass sin offering for the nation on return from exile (Ezra 6:17).

6842. צָפִיר ***ṣāp̱iyr:*** A masculine noun referring to a male goat. It was a major sacrificial animal in Israel. One was offered for each tribe of Israel as a massive sin offering for the nation (Ezra 8:35) on Judah's return from exile (cf. 2 Chr. 29:21). It is used in apocalyptic literature to stand for Alexander the Great (Dan. 8:5, 8, 21).

6843. צְפִירָה ***ṣ***^{e}***p̱iyrāh:*** I. A feminine noun meaning a diadem, a crown. It is formed and worn in a way to indicate authority; it is used figuratively of God's becoming the diadem, the crown of the returned remnant of His people (Isa. 28:5).

II. A feminine noun meaning doom. In context it has the sense of doom (crown of doom?) and destruction richly deserved by Israel (Ezek. 7:7).

III. A feminine noun indicating morning. It refers to the time of the judgment of God, the time He arrives, the morning of that day (Ezek. 7:7).

6844. צָפִית ***ṣāp̱iyṯ:*** I. A feminine noun referring to a rug, a tablecloth. It refers figuratively to a cloth spread on a tabletop in anticipation of coming disaster in Babylon (Isa. 21:5).

II. A feminine noun referring to a watchtower. It refers to a watchtower, a small elevated structure that could be fortified, where watchmen were stationed to watch for the coming attack on Babylon (Isa. 21:5).

6845. צָפַן ***ṣāp̱an:*** A verb meaning to hide, to keep secret. It is used of concealing something, often of great value, e.g., the baby Moses (Ex. 2:2, 3). Rahab concealed the Israelite spies (Josh. 2:4). It is used figuratively of keeping something hidden in a person's heart or mind (Job 10:13). It is used of God's protecting a person (Job 14:13). It is used of the storing up, the limiting of the days of the wicked and ruthless (Job 15:20). It refers to something hidden, stored up (Ps. 17:14). As a noun, it refers to God's treasured people (Ps. 83:3[4]). It means to lie in wait for, to ambush someone (Prov. 1:11). It means to hide, to constrain a person (Prov. 27:16). It refers to holding something, saving it for another person (Song 7:13[14]). The Temple or the Holy of Holies is referred to as God's hidden, secret habitation (Ezek. 7:22). It describes sin figuratively as being stored up (Hos. 13:12).

6846. צְפַנְיָה ***ṣ***^{e}***p̱anyāh,*** צְפַנְיָהוּ ***ṣ***^{e}***p̱anyāhû:*** A proper noun designating Zephaniah:

A. The prophet who zealously proclaimed the Day of the Lord. He was the son of Cushi. He prophesied in ca. 630 B.C. and was contemporary with Jeremiah, Nahum, and Habakkuk, other prophets who were equally zealous and emotional at this critical time in Israel's history. He proclaimed judgment on Judah and the nations, but he also declared that God would preserve a remnant and Israel would rise again (Zeph. 3:14–20).

B. The second-ranking priest in Jeremiah's day who was taken captive at the fall of Jerusalem, moved to Riblah, and was put to death there Kgs. 25:18). Jeremiah had warned him of this danger (Jer. 21:1; 29:24–32).

C. An ancestor of Heman. Heman was a Kohathite who served as a musician in the Temple (1 Chr. 6:33–36[21]).

D. The father of Josiah. He carried out key instructions with others as directed by the prophet Zechariah concerning the crowning of Joshua son of Jehozadak (Zech. 6:9–15).

6847. צָפְנַת פַּעְנֵחַ ***ṣāpnaṯ pa'nēaḥ:*** A proper noun designating Zaphnath-Paneah; another name for Joseph [3130,A] (Gen. 41:45).

6848. צֶפַע ***ṣepa',*** צִפְעוֹנִי ***ṣip'ôniy:*** I. A masculine noun referring to a viper; a poisonous serpent. It indicates a venomous serpent or snake but is used figuratively to refer to a dangerous, destructive people that will destroy Philista (Isa. 14:29).

II. A masculine noun referring to a viper, a poisonous serpent. It indicates a venomous serpent or snake. It illustrates the danger of drinking wine to excess (Prov. 23:32). The nature of the viper or serpent will be changed in the messianic kingdom (Isa. 11:8). It is used to represent the vile, evil character of who God's people have become in their rebellions (Isa. 59:5). Figuratively, it describes the enemies God will bring against His rebellious people (Jer. 8:17).

6849. צְפִיעָה ***ṣᵉpiy'āh:*** A feminine noun meaning an offshoot, an issue. It describes the descendants of a person, offspring; especially important will be the offspring of a messianic figure (Isa. 22:24).

6850. צָפַף ***ṣāpap:*** A verb meaning to chirp, to whisper. It refers to imitative sounds made by a group of spiritualists to consult with various gods or spirits (Isa. 8:19). The sound of birds chirping is used figuratively of peoples conquered by the Assyrians (Isa. 10:14). It is used figuratively of persons whispering from their graves (Isa. 29:4). It describes the senseless gibberish of a sick person (Isa. 38:14).

6851. צַפְצָפָה ***ṣapṣāpāh:*** A feminine noun indicating a willow tree. It refers to a large tree that flourishes where it has an ample supply of water (Ezek. 17:5).

6852. צָפַר ***ṣāpar:*** A verb meaning to leave, to depart. It refers to persons' going away from a location, taking their departure from it (Judg. 7:3).

6853. צִפַּר ṣippar: An Aramaic masculine noun referring to a bird, a fowl. In a figurative sense, it describes the people who found shelter in the kingdom of Babylon, the great tree of the king's dream (Dan. 4:12[9], 14[11], 21[18]). It is also used to describe Nebuchadnezzar's appearance when he was driven away as a madman (Dan. 33[30]).

6854. צְפַרְדֵּעַ ṣ^e^pardēa': A masculine noun meaning a frog. It is a water creature that can spread disease if it dies on land and is not buried properly. Its most notorious reference is in the second plague in Egypt (Ex. 8:2–9[7:27—8:5], 11–13[7–9]). This event was so vital to Israel's history that the recounting was repeated (Ps. 78:45; 105:30).

6855. צִפֹּרָה ṣippōrāh: A proper noun designating Zipporah. The name means "bird." The Midianite priest Jethro (Reuel) gave his daughter Zipporah to Moses as a wife. She bore Moses' two sons, Gershom and Eliezer (Ex. 18:2–4).

6856. צִפֹּרֶן ṣippōren: A masculine noun referring to a toenail or a fingernail; a pointed writing instrument. It refers to both human fingernails and toenails. A female captive in Israel who was to be taken for a wife had to have all of her nails clipped (Deut. 21:12). It indicates the diamond point of a stylus, a writing instrument in context (Jer. 17:1).

6857. צְפַת ṣ^e^paṯ: A proper noun designating Zephath (Judg. 1:17).

6858. צֶפֶת ṣepeṯ: A feminine noun referring to a capital of a pillar. It indicates the top part of a column or pilaster as opposed to the shaft and base sections (2 Chr. 3:15).

6859. צְפָתָה ṣ^e^p̄āṯāh: A proper noun designating Zephathah (2 Chr. 14:10[9]).

6860. צִיקְלַג ṣiyqlag: A proper noun designating Ziklag, a southern town in the Negev given to Judah (Josh. 15:20–31) and to Simeon (Josh. 19:5). David, as a fugitive from Saul, stayed in this town for some time (1 Sam. 27:6; 30:1–26). Some Jews returning from exile settled here (Neh. 11:28).

6861. צִקְלוֹן ṣiqlôn: I. A masculine noun meaning sack. It refers to a clothe container large enough to hold twenty loaves of barley and a supply of ears of grain (2 Kgs. 4:42).

II. A masculine noun indicating a husk of an ear of corn. It refers to the husks, the dry or green outer coverings of various fruits or seeds (2 Kgs. 4:42).

6862. צַר ṣar: I. A masculine noun indicating narrowness, tightness, distress, application, misery. It refers to a narrow space or object, not wide, with a small distance across it (Num. 22:26). It is used figuratively of a person's pain and distress; oppression, a feeling of being hemmed in (Deut.

4:30; Job 7:11; 15:24). The Lord delivers His faithful follower from affliction and distress (Ps. 4:1[2]). It describes oppressive political, economic, and military conditions suffered by a group, a people, or a nation (Judg. 11:7). It describes the threats and destruction that come on something, especially the Lord's house (1 Sam. 2:32). It indicates conditions during times of judgment on Israel (Isa. 5:30). It refers to the time, trouble, and effort given to consider an issue (Esth. 7:4). It is used figuratively to describe an adulterous woman as a narrow well with no escape (Prov. 23:27). It depicts a cry of destruction as one of great anguish (Jer. 48:5). Affliction or distress may cause a person to seek God (Hos. 5:15). It is sometimes difficult to decide whether to translate *ṣar* as I or II, for example, in Zechariah 8:10 (cf. NKJV, NASB).

II. A masculine noun indicating an enemy, a foe, an adversary, an oppressor. It refers to a personal enemy or foe rather than an impersonal situation of distress or affliction (Gen. 14:20; Num. 10:9). Nations as well as individuals may be one's adversaries (Num. 24:8; Deut. 32:27, 41, 43; 33:7; 2 Sam. 24:13; Amos 3:11). It refers to the enemies and adversaries of God's people in exile (Ezra 4:1; Neh. 4:11; 9:27; Esth. 7:4). It indicates the adversary or oppressor of Job (6:23); and the psalmist (3:1[2]; 13:4; 27:2). For Zechariah 8:10, see I.

III. A masculine noun indicating flint. It refers to a kind of chert stone that produces sparks when struck with certain metals. Used in a simile, it described the terrifying hoofs of warhorses (Isa. 5:28).

6863. צֵר *ṣēr*: A proper noun designating Zer (Josh. 19:35).

6864. צֹר *ṣōr*: A masculine noun referring to flint, a flint knife, an edge. It refers to a variety of chert, a rock that produces sparks when struck with certain metals and forms a cutting tool with sharp edges (Ex. 4:25; Josh. 5:2, 3). In fact, it has the meaning of edge in some places: of a sword (Ps. 89:43[44]). Some translators translate this word in Isaiah 5:28 as flint. It is used figuratively to refer to a forehead like flint, meaning a person with absolute determination (Ezek. 3:9).

6865. צֹר *ṣōr*, צוֹר *ṣôr*: A proper noun designating Tyre, a town located on the northern boundary of Asher (Josh. 19:29; 2 Sam. 24:7). The city was renowned as a trading and shipping center for the world's merchants. Its main center was originally on an island. It is mentioned ca. 50 times in the Old Testament. Israel never did control the city but worked closely with several of its kings. It was called to severe judgment by the prophets, especially Ezekiel (Ezek. 28). The psalmist pictured the king of Tyre bringing gifts (tribute?) to the king of Israel (45:12[13]). It is listed among the enemies of Israel's God in Psalm 83:7[8]), but Psalm 87:4 speaks of Tyre's recognition of the Lord in worship. Ezekiel could find no better ancient symbol to represent the hubris and arrogance of the king(s) of Tyre than the first Adam or Satan before his rebellion (Ezek. 28:1–10; 11–15). The city supplied David with materials for his own palace (2 Sam. 5:11). Hiram of Tyre helped Solomon with his many building projects, especially the Temple and palace (1 Kgs. 5:1[15]), even supplying chief craftsmen for him (1 Kgs. 7:13). Solomon ceded cities to Hiram as partial payment (1 Kgs. 9:11–12).

6866. צָרַב ***ṣārab̲:*** A verb meaning to burn, to scorch. It indicates igniting or kindling a fire. It is used figuratively of God's destruction of the Negev (Ezek. 20:47[21:3]).

6867. צָרָב ***ṣārāb̲,*** צָרֶבֶת ***ṣārebet̲:*** I. An adjective referring to a burning, a scorching. It indicates an area of the skin that has been burned literally or by disease; a scorched area (Lev. 13:23, 28).

II. A feminine noun indicating a scab, a scar, an inflammation. Some analyze this for a noun rather than a feminine participle of I above. The meaning is the same.

6868. צְרֵדָה ***ṣᵉrēd̲āh,*** צְרֵדָתָה ***ṣᵉrēd̲at̲ah:*** I. A proper noun designating Zereda, the place where Jeroboam was born (1 Kgs. 11:26).

II. A proper noun designating Zaredah, Zeredathah, a place in the plain of Jordan (2 Chr. 4:17).

6869. צָרָה ***ṣārāh:*** I. A feminine noun meaning trouble, distress, anguish. It refers to a situation or a time of extreme discomfort, an affliction for many different reasons. God delivers His people from this condition (Gen. 35:3; Job 5:19; Ps. 9:9). The pursuit of wisdom is also a refuge in a time of distress (Prov. 1:27). God is the author of destruction and distress in judgment on the earth (Isa. 8:22; Jer. 4:31). Daniel speaks of a final time of distress that will never be superseded (Dan. 12:1).

II. A feminine noun meaning a rival. It refers to a person who is threatening or a source of despair for various reasons (1 Sam. 1:6).

6870. צְרוּיָה ***ṣᵉrûyāh:*** A proper noun designating Zeruiah (1 Sam. 26:6; 2 Sam. 2:13, 18; 3:39; 8:16; 14:1; 16:9, 10; 17:25; 18:2; 19:21, 22; 21:17; 23:18, 37; 1 Kgs. 1:7; 2:5, 22; 1 Chr. 2:16; 11:6, 39; 18:12, 15; 26:28; 27:24).

6871. צְרוּעָה ***ṣᵉrûʿāh:*** A proper noun designating Zeruah (1 Kgs. 11:26).

6872. צְרוֹר ***ṣᵉrôr:*** I. A masculine noun indicating a bag, a bundle, a pouch, a purse. It describes a relatively large cloth bag used to carry a variety of items while traveling (Gen. 42:35; Prov. 7:20). It is used figuratively of a bundle holding persons' lives in security (1 Sam. 25:29); and of transgressors sealed in a bag by God (Job 14:17). It signifies a small leather container of cosmetics (Song 1:13) or money (Hag. 1:6).

II. A masculine noun referring to a pebble, a piece of grain. It refers to a relatively small stone left in a city, possibly a small building stone (2 Sam. 17:13). It is understood as grain in Amos 9:9 by some translators (NASB, grain; KJV, corn). A pebble or a tiny stone is also possible.

III. A masculine proper noun. Zeror is one of the ancestors of Saul, Israel's first king; he was Saul's great-grandfather (1 Sam. 9:1).

6873. צָרַח ṣāraḥ: A verb indicating a roar, war cry. It refers to a cry of despair by a warrior of Nineveh (Zeph. 1:14). It refers to the Lord's utterance of a war cry of attack as He goes forth to battle (Isa. 42:13).

6874. צְרִי ṣ^{e}riy: A proper noun designating Zeri (1 Chr. 25:3).

6875. צֳרִי ṣ^{o}riy, צְרִי ṣ^{e}riy: A masculine noun meaning balm. It indicates an aromatic gum resin from certain trees and plants. It can be used as a cosmetic or as a medicine. It was a much desired item of trade in the ancient Middle East (Gen. 37:25; 43:11; Ezek. 27:17). Its medicinal use is stressed in some passages, especially the balm available in Gilead (Jer. 8:22; 46:11; 51:8).

6876. צֹרִי ṣōriy: A proper noun designating someone from Tyre, a Tyrian (1 Kgs. 7:14; 1 Chr. 22:4; 2 Chr. 2:14[13]; Ezra 3:7; Neh. 13:16).

6877. צְרִיחַ ṣ^{e}riyaḥ: I. A masculine noun referring to a cellar, an inner chamber, a stronghold. It refers to a room located in the innermost part of a religious temple or fortress (Judg. 9:46, 49). From context it is clear that it may refer to an underground hiding place or cellar as well (1 Sam. 13:6).

II. A masculine noun referring to a high place. Some translators rendered this word as high place, a place for sacrifices to be offered (1 Sam. 13:6). In context this is understandable.

6878. צֹרֶךְ ṣōre<u>k</u>: A masculine noun referring to something that is needed. It refers to what is necessary with respect to a particular need of something (2 Chr. 2:16[15]).

6879. צָרַע ṣāra': A verb meaning to have leprosy, to be a leper. It refers to a skin disease in which the skin appears white (Ex. 4:6; Lev. 13:44, 45; 14:2, 3). It was possibly leprosy, but there were other similar diseases as well. Most translations still render the word as leprosy (2 Sam. 3:29; 2 Kgs. 5:1, 11, 27). Several people were struck with leprosy or a similar skin disease because of their rebellious attitudes (Num. 12:10; 2 Kgs. 15:5).

6880. צִרְעָה ṣir'āh: A collective feminine noun referring to hornets. The term may be literal or refer figuratively to the dread and fear that the Lord would put on the Canaanites (Ex. 23:28; Deut. 7:20; Josh. 24:12).

6881. צָרְעָה ṣor'āh: A proper noun designating Zorah (Josh. 15:33;

19:41; Judg. 13:2, 25; 16:31; 18:2, 8, 11; 2 Chr. 11:10; Neh. 11:29).

6882. צָרְעִי **ṣor'iy,** צָרְעָתִי **ṣor'āṯiy:** A proper noun designating Zorite, Zorathite (1 Chr. 2:53, 54; 4:2).

6883. צָרַעַת **ṣar'aṯ:** A feminine noun referring to a skin disease, leprosy. It refers to a skin disease on humans (Lev. 13:2, 3, 8; 2 Kgs. 5:3) but also to similarly appearing mold, mildew, or fungus in garments, walls of houses, etc. (Lev. 13:47, 49, 51, 52, 59). Most translations still render this as leprosy, but many scholars hold that it refers to leucodermia, etc.

6884. צָרַף **ṣārap̱:** A verb meaning to refine, to test. This word describes the purifying process of a refiner, who heats metal, takes away the dross, and is left with a pure substance (Prov. 25:4). As a participle, this word refers to a tradesman (i.e., a goldsmith or silversmith) who does the refining work (Judg. 17:4; Neh. 3:8; Isa. 41:7). This word is also used to speak of the Word of God that is described as pure and refined (2 Sam. 22:31; Ps. 12:6[7]; Prov. 30:5). When applied to people, this word refers to the purifying effects of external trials (Ps. 66:10; 105:19; Isa. 48:10) that God often uses to purify His people from sin (Isa. 1:25; Zech. 13:9); or to remove the wicked from His people (Jer. 6:29; Mal. 3:2, 3).

6885. צֹרְפִי **ṣōrp̱iy:** A masculine noun referring to a goldsmith. It refers to a person who is skilled in working with gold. In context it may refer to a son of a goldsmith or to a goldsmith guild (*ben-ṣōrr^e^ p̱î,* Neh. 3:31).

6886. צָרְפַת **ṣār^e^p̱aṯ:** A proper noun designating Zarephath (1 Kgs. 17:9, 10; Obad. 1:20).

6887. צָרַר **ṣārar:** I. A verb meaning to bind up, to tie up, to be distressed, to be troubled, to be oppressed, to be cramped. It refers to something being bound up, tied up physically (Ex. 12:34). It means to be hard-pressed, anxious, worried, distressed about what to do (Gen. 32:7[8]). It is used to describe the action of an enemy, a famine, or an army pressing upon a city, besieging it (Deut. 28:52). It is used figuratively of one's life (soul, *nep̱eš*) being bound in a bag (1 Sam. 25:29; cf. Hos. 4:19; 13:12); and of the law being bound for safekeeping (Isa. 8:16). It means to keep out, shut out a person (2 Sam. 20:3). It indicates something being cramped, shortened, cut back (Job 18:7).

II. A verb indicating to be an enemy, an adversary, an oppressor, a rival. It means to oppose persons, to fight against, to be hostile toward them. The Lord promised to be an adversary, an enemy to His people's enemies, if His people obeyed Him (Ex. 23:22). It is used of taking a second wife who would compete with the first wife (Lev. 18:18). The adversary of the psalmist is mentioned often (Ps. 6:7[8]; 7:4[5]; 74:4). It has the sense of those who harass someone (Isa. 11:13).

6888. צְרֵרָה ***ṣ^{e}rērāh:*** A proper noun designating Zererah (Judg. 7:22).

6889. צֶרֶת ***ṣereṯ:*** A proper noun designating Zereth (1 Chr. 4:7).

6890. צֶרֶת הַשַּׁחַר ***ṣereṯ haššaḥar:*** A proper noun designating Zereth Shahar (Josh. 13:19).

6891. צָרְתָן ***ṣār^{e}ṯān:*** A proper noun designating Zarethan, Zaretan (Josh. 3:16; 1 Kgs. 4:12; 7:46; 2 Chr. 4:17).

ק Qoph

6892. קֵא *qē'*, קֵיא *qēy'*: I. A masculine noun referring to vomit. It refers to the material, food, etc., ejected from an animal's or a person's stomach through the mouth. It is used in a proverb to parallel folly (Prov. 26:11).

II. A masculine noun referring to vomit. It refers to the ingested food, matter, etc., that is ejected from a person's or an animal's stomach. It is used in a simile to represent confusion, disarray (Isa. 19:14). It is used to describe the corrupt character of everything in Ephraim (Israel) (Isa. 28:8). It is used figuratively of Moab wallowing in the confusion and destruction it has brought upon itself (Jer. 48:26).

6893. קָאַת *qā'aṯ*: A feminine noun referring to a pelican, a desert owl, a cormorant. It refers to a bird that was considered unclean to Israel as food (Lev. 11:18; Deut. 14:17). Its exact identity is not known. Its character is used in a simile of the psalmist (Ps. 102:6[7]). It inhabited desert places and the haunts of destroyed cities (Isa. 34:11; Zeph. 2:14).

6894. קַב *qaḇ*: A masculine noun indicating a cab or kab; a dry measure of about two quarts. It is a small measure, but in a time of distress or siege, one-fourth of a kab sold for five shekels, a huge price (2 Kgs. 6:25).

6895. קָבַב *qāḇaḇ*: A verb meaning to curse. The general idea of this word is a pronouncement of bad fortune or ill favor bestowed on another. This word is used often in the story of Balaam and Balak, where Balak repeatedly requested that Balaam pronounce a curse on Israel (Num. 22:11; 23:13, 27). Rather than a curse, Balaam pronounced a blessing on them (Num. 23:8; 24:10). In other instances of this word, it describes cursing the Lord (Lev. 24:11); cursing the day of one's birth (Job 3:8); or cursing the home of the foolish (Job 5:3). It is used twice in the Proverbs in a general way (Prov. 11:26; 24:24) as an opposite to the word $b^e r\bar{a}\underline{k}āh$ (1293), meaning blessing, and similar to the much more frequent word $qālal$ (7043), meaning to curse.

6896. קֵבָה *qēḇāh*: A feminine noun meaning a stomach, a belly. It is used as a general term for the stomach or belly. It is translated body (NASB) by some but is more specific than that (Num. 25:8). It refers to the internal organ itself. In a ruminate animal, its maw was given to the priest as food in a sacrifice (Deut. 18:3).

6897. קֹבָה *qōḇāh*: A feminine noun meaning belly. Some translators render this as belly, referring to the external aspect of the body (Num. 25:8).

6898. קֻבָּה *qubbāh:* A feminine noun meaning a large tent, a domed cavity, a pavilion. This word is not found often in the Old Testament, but where it does appear, it refers to some sort of habitation. Phinehas chased a man and woman who were idolaters into one of these large tents and thrust them through with a javelin, thus ending a plague on Israel (Num. 25:8).

6899. קִבּוּץ *qibbûṣ:* A masculine noun meaning a collection, an assembly. It refers in context to a collection of some sort, probably of idols or divine objects (Isa. 57:13; KJV, companies, collections).

6900. קְבוּרָה *q*e*bûrāh*, קְבֻרָה *q*e*burāh:* A feminine noun meaning a grave, a burial place. It is the passive participle of *qāḇar* (6912), meaning to bury. The word can signify various types of graves: the dignified grave of a king (2 Kgs. 21:26; 23:30); the unknown burial place of Moses (Deut. 34:6); and the burial place of a donkey where Jehoiakim would be buried (Jer. 22:19). Burial was important to the Hebrews of the Old Testament; the lack of a grave was considered a tragedy, the sign of an unwanted life that was best forgotten (Eccl. 6:3; Isa. 14:20). The meaning is similar to the word *qeḇer* (6913).

6901. קָבַל *qāḇal:* A verb meaning to accept, to receive, to take, to undertake, to choose. As a general term, it means to accept something: a gift (Esth. 4:4); instruction (Prov. 19:20). It has the sense of willingly taking on a task (Esth. 9:23); or setting up something (Esth. 9:27). It is used of accepting what God brings on us (Job 2:10). It has the sense of compared to, to match, to be opposite and paired (Ex. 26:5; 36:12).

6902. קְבַל *qāḇal:* An Aramaic verb meaning to receive, to take over. It means to get from persons, to receive from them (Dan. 2:6); especially in the sense of taking dominion (*malkûtā'*) (Dan. 5:31[6:1]; 7:18).

6903. קֳבֵל *q*e*ḇēl:* An Aramaic conjunction meaning because, inasmuch as; before. It has the sense of, in front of, before spatially (Dan. 2:31; 3:3; 5:1); or opposite, over against (Dan. 5:5). It often means because, giving the reason for something (Dan. 5:10). It is used in combinations with *hēn, d*e*nā, dî*, to render: if . . . then; just as (Ezra 4:16; 6:13). *Kol-q*o*ḇel* means in view of, because of (Dan. 2:12, 24; 3:7, 8; 6:9[10]). The phrase *kol-q*o*ḇēl d*e*nā min-dî* can be rendered, for this reason, because, or just because (Dan. 3:22).

6904. קֹבֶל *qōḇel*, קְבֹל *q*e*ḇōl:* I. A masculine noun referring to a battering ram. It indicates an engine of war used to strike the walls and gates of cities to demolish them (Ezek. 26:9).

II. A masculine noun meaning war. It is understood to refer to the battle or to war itself by some translators. The preceding word (*m*e*ḥî*) is then taken to mean a blow, a striking (of an engine of war) (Ezek. 26:9).

III. A masculine noun meaning something in front. It refers to a physical presence in front of persons, in their presence, publicly (2 Kgs. 15:10).

6905. קָבָל ***qā<u>b</u>āl:*** A masculine noun having the sense of something in front. It seems to mean in front of, publicly (2 Kgs. 15:10).

6906. קָבַע ***qā<u>b</u>a':*** A verb meaning to rob, to plunder. It refers to taking the life and property of the oppressed and afflicted in context (Prov. 22:23). It indicates keeping back what belongs properly to God (Mal. 3:8, 9).

6907. קֻבַּעַת ***qubba'a<u>t</u>:*** A feminine noun referring to a goblet, a chalice, dregs. It is used in a figurative sense to indicate a cup holding the judgments of God (Isa. 51:17; 22).

6908. קָבַץ ***qā<u>b</u>aṣ:*** A verb meaning to gather, to collect, to assemble. The passive form is used to signify the gathering or assembling of people, especially for battle (Josh. 9:2; Neh. 4:20[14]; Jer. 49:14); and for religious and national purposes (1 1 Chr. 11:1; Ezra 10:1, 7). The word in an active form often signifies the gathering of materials: food into storehouses (Gen. 41:35); sheaves (Mic. 4:12); money and wealth (2 Chr. 24:5; Prov. 28:8); lambs by a shepherd (Isa. 13:14; 40:11; Jer. 23:3). The word also refers to God's gathering of nations for judgment in the end times (Isa. 43:9; 66:18; Joel 3:2[4:2]); and especially to the gathering of His scattered people, Israel (Ps. 106:47; Jer. 29:14; 31:10; Hos. 1:11[2:2]).

6909. קַבְצְאֵל ***qa<u>b</u>ṣ^e'ēl:*** A proper noun designating Kabzeel (Josh. 15:21; 2 Sam. 23:20; 1 Chr. 11:22).

6910. קְבֻצָה ***q^e<u>b</u>uṣāh:*** A feminine noun meaning gathering. This word is the feminine passive participle of *qā<u>b</u>aṣ* (6908), meaning to gather. It occurs only in Ezekiel 22:20 where it signifies the gathering of metals into a furnace, which is a picture of God gathering Israel to pour out His burning anger on them.

6911. קִבְצַיִם ***qi<u>b</u>ṣayim:*** A proper noun meaning Kibzaim. It is the name of a city given to the Levites and located between Geza and Beth Horon (Josh. 21:22).

6912. קָבַר ***qā<u>b</u>ar:*** A verb meaning to bury, to entomb, to be buried. The word often refers to the placing of a body in a cave or a stone sepulcher rather than directly into the ground (Gen. 23:4; 50:13; 2 Sam. 21:14; 1 Kgs. 13:31; cf. Isa. 22:16). Abraham stated that one goal of burial was to get the dead out of sight (Gen. 23:4). Dead bodies were seen as polluting the land until they were buried (Ezek. 39:11–14). It was also a reproach to the dead to be buried in a foreign place or not to be buried at all (Gen. 47:29, 30; 50:5; cf. 50:24–26; Jer. 20:6). Bones were sometimes specifically mentioned as the object of burial (Josh. 24:32; 1 Sam. 31:13; 1 Kgs. 13:31). Buried persons were said to sleep or be buried with their fathers, and they were often placed in the same tomb (Gen. 47:30; 50:13; Judg. 16:31; 2 Sam. 2:32; 17:23).

6913. קֶבֶר *qeḇer:* A masculine noun meaning a grave, a sepulchre. The grave was a place of grief (2 Sam. 3:32; Ps. 88:11[12]); the end of life in contrast to the womb (Job 10:19; Jer. 20:17). The dead were laid to rest, often with previously deceased relatives (2 Sam. 19:37[38]). In the Old Testament, graves were associated with uncleanness: one who touched a grave (or a bone, cf. 2 Chr. 34:5) had to be ceremonially cleansed (Num. 19:16–19). Josiah sprinkled the dust of crushed idolatrous paraphernalia on graves of idol worshipers to defile the idols (2 Kgs. 23:6; 2 Chr. 34:4). In a figurative sense, Isaiah prophesied against his self-righteous countrymen as living among graves and eating the flesh of swine (Isa. 65:4; cf. Matt. 23:27, 28). Ezekiel prophesied that God would revive the Israelites from their graves, that is, from their exile and defilement among idolatrous nations (Ezek. 37:12, 13).

6914. קִבְרוֹת הַתַּאֲוָה *qiḇrôṯ hatta'ᵃwāh:* A proper noun designating Kibroth Hattaavah (Num. 11:34, 35; 33:16, 17; Deut. 9:22).

6915. קָדַד *qāḏaḏ:* A verb meaning to bow down. It means to bow one's head in reverence and worship (Gen. 24:26). It is always followed by the verb to worship, *ḥāwāh*. It means to bow down, to kneel; *ḥāwāh* must be interpreted according to whom or what is being reverenced, God, a person, etc. Israel bowed (*qdd*) and worshiped (*hwh*) God for His deliverance (Ex. 4:31).

6916. קִדָּה *qiddāh:* A feminine noun indicating a spice, cassiah. It was a fine spice (cassia beds) used to make the anointing oil in the Tabernacle (Ex. 30:24). It was used in international trade in Tyre (Ezek. 27:19).

6917. קְדוּמִים *qᵉḏûmiym:* A masculine noun meaning ancient, age-old. It designates something of great age according to its usage, but its exact meaning is under investigation (Judg. 5:21).

6918. קָדוֹשׁ *qāḏôš:* An adjective meaning sacred, holy. It is used to denote someone or something that is inherently sacred or has been designated as sacred by divine rite or cultic ceremony. It designates that which is the opposite of common or profane. It could be said the *qāḏôš* is a positive term regarding the character of its referent, where common is a neutral term and profane a very negative term. This word is often used to refer to God as being inherently holy, sacred, and set apart (Ps. 22:3[4]; Isa. 6:3; 57:15); and as being free from the attributes of fallen humanity (Hos. 11:9). Therefore, in the Old Testament, God is accorded the title "The

Holy One of Israel" (2 Kgs. 19:22; Ps. 78:41; Isa. 17:7; Jer. 50:29). As such, God instructed that humanity should be holy because He is holy (Lev. 11:44, 45; 19:2). In addition to its divine references, this word can also modify places, like the court of the Tabernacle (Ex. 29:31); the camp of Israel (Deut. 23:14[15]); Jerusalem (Eccl. 8:10); heaven (Isa. 57:15); people, like the priests (Lev. 21:7, 8); a Nazirite (Num. 6:5, 8); the prophet Elisha (2 Kgs. 4:9); Levites (2 Chr. 35:3); saints [angels] (Job 5:1; 15:15; Dan. 8:13); water (Num. 5:17); time (Neh. 8:9–11; Isa. 58:13).

6919. קָדַח *qāḏaḥ*: A verb meaning to kindle, to set on fire. It describes igniting a fire, (Isa. 64:2); but is used figuratively of the kindling of the Lord's anger (Deut. 32:22; Jer. 15:14; 17:4). It indicates those persons who wrongly, wickedly try to destroy the Lord's Servant or the righteous (Isa. 50:11).

6920. קַדַּחַת *qaddaḥaṯ*: A feminine noun meaning fever. It was one of the pestilences or plagues the Lord would send on a disobedient people (Lev. 26:16; Deut. 28:22).

6921. קָדִים *qāḏiym*: A masculine noun referring to the east, an east wind. It indicates literally a wind from the east that brings evil conditions (Gen. 41:6, 23; Ex. 10:13). With *āh* on the end, it means eastward, towards the east (Ezek. 11:1; 44:1; 47:1). It indicates a structural feature of something, an east side, the east (Ezek. 40:23, 44; 42:9, 16). The phrase *dereḵ haqqādiym* means toward the east (Ez. 43:2). The word is used over fifty times in Ezekiel.

6922. קַדִּישׁ *qaddiš*: An Aramaic masculine adjective meaning holy. It is the Aramaic equivalent of the Hebrew word *qāḏôš* (6918). This term can modify the word *ʼelāh* (426), meaning God or gods (Dan. 4:8[5], 9[6], 18[15]; 5:11). As a substantive, it could stand for angel(s), the supernatural holy one(s) (Dan. 4:13[10], 17[14], 23[20]). It could also refer to God's people, human holy ones, or saints (Dan. 7:18, 21, 22, 25, 27).

6923. קָדַם *qāḏam*: A verb meaning to come before, to meet, to confront. It can mean to confront with hostility (2 Sam. 22:6, 10; Ps. 18:6, 19; Job 30:27); or as a friend (Deut. 23:4[5]; Isa. 21:14; Mic. 6:6). It means to proceed, to go before (Ps. 68:25 [26]). It carries the sense of getting in someone's face, confronting him or her (Ps. 17:13; Amos 9:10). It means to say or do something earlier, before (Jon. 4:2); something before the sun rises (Ps. 119:147); to think or meditate beforehand on something (Ps. 119:148).

6924. קֶדֶם *qeḏem*: A masculine noun meaning the east, earlier, formerly, long ago. The word is used regularly to mean east or eastern. The Lord planted the Garden of Eden in the east (Gen. 2:8; 3:24); Abraham traveled toward the eastern hills (Gen. 12:8; 13:11). The word describes the East as a place known for its wise men (Gen. 29:1; Judg. 6:3; 1 Kgs. 4:30 [5:10]); Job was the greatest among these people (Job 1:3). Isaiah, however, called the East a place of superstitions (Isa. 2:6). One of Jeremiah's oracles was directed against the people of the East (Jer. 49:28); but not, according to Ezekiel, until the Lord gave Judah to one of the peoples of the East—Babylon (Ezek 25:4, 10). The famous movement of the whole earth's population to the east to build the Tower of Babel in the plain of Shinar is toward the area of Babylon (Gen. 11:2).

The word is also used to refer to former times, times of old. It describes the works of God before the world was created (Prov. 8:22, 23). The psalmist implored the Lord to remember the people He purchased long before (Ps. 74:2; 77:11[12]; 143:5); for He was the psalmist's King from old (Ps. 74:12). The psalmist of Psalm 78:2 uttered wisdom and parables as a wise man from ancient times. God planned the fall of Assryia long before it happened (Isa. 37:26; Lam. 2:17). The word also refers to Tyre, describing it as an old, ancient city (Isa. 23:7). In an important passage, Micah 5:2[1] describes the Lord's coming Ruler from Bethlehem whose origins were from eternity or from ancient days. This word describes the mountains and the heavens as old, of long ago (Deut. 33:15; Ps. 68:33[34]; Isa. 46:10).

A few times the word means front or in front. The Lord knows His people before and behind—thus, altogether (Ps. 139:5). The Lord spurred Rezin's foes against him (i.e., from the front) to confront him (Isa. 9:12[11]).

6925. קְדָם ***q^oḏām:*** An Aramaic preposition meaning before, in the presence of. It refers to being in front of spatially or temporally; in time (Ezra 4:18, 23; Dan. 2:9; 7:7). It has the sense of in God's judgment, before Him (Dan. 6:22[23]). It means to be afraid of something from before one (*min* (4480) *q^odāmôhî;* Dan. 7:8). It is used with words meaning to pray, to answer before (Dan. 2:10, 11, 27). It describes a decree going out from (before) a king (Dan. 2:6; 6:26[27]).

6926. קִדְמָה ***qiḏmāh:*** A feminine noun meaning east. It indicates a direction to the east, eastward, toward the rising sun (Gen. 2:14; 4:16; 1 Sam. 13:5; Ezek. 39:11).

6927. קַדְמָה ***qaḏmāh:*** A feminine noun meaning a beginning, a former time. In the oracle concerning Tyre, it was called the city of old (Isa. 23:7). The Lord promised to restore Sodom, Samaria, and Jerusalem to what they were before in order to bring shame on Jerusalem (Ezek. 16:55). A prophecy to the mountains of Israel said that they would be populated as they were in the past (Ezek. 36:11). See the Hebrew noun *qeḏem* (6924) and Aramaic noun *qaḏmāh* (6928).

6928. קַדְמָה ***qaḏmāh:*** An Aramaic feminine noun meaning a former time. When the elders of Judah were questioned about rebuilding the Temple, they answered that they were restoring something built long ago (Ezra 5:11). Even after the edict from King Darius, Daniel continued to pray as he had done before (Dan. 6:10[11]). See the Hebrew noun *qaḏmāh* (6927).

6929. קֵדְמָה ***qēḏ***^{e}***māh:*** A proper noun designating Kedemah (Gen. 25:15; 1 Chr. 1:31).

6930. קַדְמוֹן ***qaḏmôn:*** An adjective meaning eastern. It indicates that something lies in the direction of the east, toward the east (Ezek. 47:8).

6931. קַדְמוֹנִי ***qaḏmôniy,*** קַדְמֹנִי ***qaḏmōniy:*** I. An adjective meaning eastern. It indicates someone or something located in the east or connected with the eastern regions of the nations. The Temple had gates north, east, west, south (Ezek. 10:19; 11:1). It refers to a place of habitation, the East (Job 18:20). The eastern sea was the Dead Sea (Joel 2:20; Zech. 14:8).

II. An adjective meaning former, previous. It is used as a noun to refer to the ancient ones, the ones who lived before (1 Sam. 24:13[14]; Job 18:20[KJV]). It refers to past days, former days (Ezek. 38:17; Mal. 3:4).

6932. קְדֵמוֹת ***q***^{e}***ḏēmôṯ:*** A proper noun designating Kedemoth (Deut. 2:26; Josh. 13:18; 21:37; 1 Chr. 6:79 [64]).

6933. קַדְמָי ***qaḏmāy:*** An Aramaic adjective meaning first, former. It refers to the initial item(s) in a sequence of things but also to previous item(s) with respect to a later item mentioned (Dan. 7:4, 8, 24).

6934. קַדְמִיאֵל ***qaḏmiy'ēl:*** A proper noun designating Kadmiel (Ezra 2:40; 3:9; Neh. 7:43; 9:4, 5; 10:9; 12:8, 24).

6935. קַדְמֹנִי ***qaḏmōniy:*** A proper noun designating Kadmonite (Gen. 15:19).

6936. קָדְקֹד ***qoḏqōḏ:*** A masculine noun referring to the top of the head, the crown of the head (Gen. 49:26; Deut. 33:16), representing the place where blessing would be most obvious and honoring. It means the entire person in the figurative expression, from the sole of one's foot to the top of one's head (Deut. 28:35; 2 Sam. 14:25; Job 2:7). It refers to a person's forehead in some contexts (Num. 24:17, NIV, NASB; corners (of Moab, KJV). But in reference to a land, it may mean its corners, chief features, or cities. God destroys His adversaries by smiting (Ps. 68:21[22]) them on the tops of their hairy heads (*qāḏqoḏ śē'ār*). It refers to the skin, scalp, or glorified hairdos of Judah's women (Isa. 3:17).

6937. קָדַר ***qāḏar:*** A verb meaning to be dark. This word can also mean to mourn in the sense of being dark with sadness or gloom (Job 5:11; Ps. 35:14; Jer. 8:21). Sometimes the sky grew dark due to an actual storm (1 Kgs. 18:45). Other times, it was not a literal darkness, as when the prophet Ezekiel prophesied against Pharaoh, saying that the heavens would be darkened when God acted against him (Ezek. 32:7, 8). Another example of symbolism was when Micah warned the false prophets that dark days were coming for them due to a lack of revelation (Mic. 3:6).

6938. קֵדָר ***qē<u>d</u>ār:*** A proper noun designating Kedar (Gen. 25:13; 1 Chr. 1:29; Ps. 120:5; Song 1:5; Isa. 21:16, 17; 42:11; 60:7; Jer. 2:10; 49:28; Ezek. 27:21).

6939. קִדְרוֹן ***qi<u>d</u>rôn:*** A proper noun designating the brook of Kidron. It is also called the Kidron Valley which is east of Jerusalem and separates it from the Mount of Olives. It runs with water only during the rainy season. David crossed it to flee Jerusalem (2 Sam. 15:23). It seemed to mark the city limits in a sense for crossing it meant leaving Jerusalem (1 Kgs. 2:37). Many foreign idols and shrines were built in this valley. The good kings of Judah always attempted to destroy and remove them (1 Kgs. 15:13). Josiah cleared the Temple of these abominations and burned or trashed them in the Kidron Valley (2 Kgs. 23:4–12). God showed Jeremiah a time, however, when even the desecrated and polluted Kidron Valley will be made holy to the Lord (Jer. 31:38–40).

6940. קַדְרוּת ***qa<u>d</u>rû<u>t</u>:*** A feminine noun meaning blackness. This word is used only once in the Old Testament and comes from the verb *qā<u>d</u>ar* (6937), meaning to be dark. In Isaiah 50:3, this word described the ability of God to clothe the heavens with blackness (that is, make them dark).

6941. קְדֹרַנִּית ***q^e<u>d</u>ōranniy<u>t</u>:*** An adverb meaning mournfully. This word is used only once in the Old Testament and comes from the verb *qā<u>d</u>ar* (6937), meaning to be dark. In Malachi 3:14, this word describes those who acted as mourners (i.e., those who were gloomy in their countenances).

6942. קָדַשׁ ***qā<u>d</u>aš:*** A verb meaning to be set apart, to be holy, to show oneself holy, to be treated as holy, to consecrate, to treat as holy, to dedicate, to be made holy, to declare holy or consecrated, to behave, to act holy, to dedicate oneself. The verb, in the simple stem, declares the act of setting apart, being holy (i.e., withdrawing someone or something from profane or ordinary use). The Lord set aside Aaron and his sons, consecrated them, and made them holy for the priesthood (Ex. 29:21). The altar was made holy, and anything coming into contact with it became holy (Ex. 29:37). The Tabernacle, the ark, the table of showbread, the altar of burnt offering, and all the smaller accessories and utensils used in the cult of Israel were anointed with a special anointing oil so they became holy.

Whatever came in contact with them became holy (Ex. 30:26–29). The men accompanying David as his military were declared holy (1 Sam. 21:5[6]).

The word is used most often in the intensive stem, meaning to pronounce or to make holy, to consecrate. The Lord pronounced the Sabbath day holy (Gen. 2:3; Ex. 20:8). Places could be dedicated as holy, such as a part of the courtyard of the Temple (1 Kgs. 8:64); or Mount Sinai itself (Ex. 19:23). The Year of Jubilee, the fiftieth year, was declared holy (Lev. 25:10). Persons could be consecrated to holy duties: Aaron and his sons were consecrated to serve as priests of the Lord (Ex. 28:3, 41; 1 Sam. 7:1); the firstborn males of people or animals were consecrated to the Lord (Ex. 13:2). Holy times were designated using this word in the factitive stem: Jehu deceitfully proclaimed a holy assembly to Baal (2 Kgs. 10:20); a holy fast could be consecrated as Joel did (Joel 1:14). With the Lord as the subject, the word describes establishing something as holy. The Lord Himself consecrated or made holy His people (Ex. 31:13; Lev. 20:8; 21:8); through His judgments on Israel and the nations, God proved the holiness of His name (Ezek. 36:23). The priests' holy garments serving in Ezekiel's restored Temple will make those who touch them holy (Ezek. 44:19; 46:20).

In the causative stem, the meanings overlap with the meanings in the intensive stem. It indicates designating something as consecrated or holy; Jeremiah was declared holy (Jer. 1:5); as was the Temple (1 Kgs. 9:3). The word means to treat as holy or dedicated. Gifts, fields, or money could be treated as holy (Lev. 27:16; 2 Sam. 8:11; 2 Kgs. 12:18[19]). God declared things holy to Himself (1 Kgs. 9:7); God Himself is to be treated as holy (Num. 20:12; 27:14; Isa. 29:23).

In the passive stems, the word means to be consecrated, to be treated as holy, or to show oneself as holy. Ezekiel described the Zadokite priests as consecrated for service at a future Temple (Ezek. 48:11); Ezra 3:5 described the established holy feasts of the Lord in the return from exile. The entrance at the Tabernacle was to be treated as consecrated and holy through the Lord's glory (Ex. 29:43). The Lord showed Himself as holy (Lev. 10:3; 22:32; Ezek. 20:41).

In the reflexive stem, the verb means to show oneself holy or consecrated: the priests had to properly consecrate themselves before coming before the Lord (Ex. 19:22; Lev. 11:44); the Lord would prove Himself holy before the nations and Israel (Ezek. 38:23). The word indicates putting oneself or another into a state of holiness to the Lord (Num. 11:18; Josh. 3:5; 1 Sam. 16:5; 2 Chr. 31:18).

6943. קֶדֶשׁ *qeḏeš*: A proper noun designating Kedesh:

A. A town in upper Galilee northwest of Lake Hulah and due north of Hazor. It was conquered by Israel and allotted to Naphtali (Josh. 19:37). It was used as a Levitical city and a city of refuge (Josh. 20:7; 21:32; 1 Chr. 7:76[61]). The Assyrians conquered it under their king Tiglath-Pileser III (2 Kgs. 15:29).

B. A town located in Judah in the southern Negev area. Current authorities do not equate the city with Kadesh Barnea.

C. A city assigned to the Levites. It was in Issachar, but its exact location is not certain (1 Chr. 6:72).

6944. קֹדֶשׁ *qōḏeš:* A masculine noun meaning a holy thing, holiness, and sacredness. The word indicates something consecrated and set aside for sacred use only; it was not to be put into common use, for if it was, it became profaned and common (*ḥôl*), not holy. This noun described holy offerings or things used in Israel's cult; it described the holy offerings which only the priest or his family could eat (Lev. 22:10). Some of the offerings of the Lord were described as Most Holy (Lev. 2:3, 10; Num. 18:9); various things could be consecrated as holy: warriors (1 Sam. 21:6); food (Ex. 29:33); and the places where the holy ark had been located (2 Chr. 8:11). Only holy priests could go into the Temple (2 Chr. 23:6). Many vessels and items used in the Tabernacle or Temple areas were holy (Ezra 8:28; Ex. 30:32, 35). The Sabbath was, of course, holy (Ex. 31:14).

This word also designates divine holiness: the Lord alone can swear by His own holiness (Ps. 89:35[36]; Amos 4:2); and His ways are holy (Ps. 77:13[14]). In fact, God is marvelous in holiness (Ex. 15:11).

Since the Lord is holy, He expected Israel to be holy. This word described the essence of the Israelites: They were His holy people (Ex. 22:31[30]; 28:36).

The word describes holiness when it relates to various things: holiness adhered to the Lord's house and beautified it (Ps. 93:5). The Lord's name is holy (Lev. 20:3; 22:2; Ezek. 39:7, 25; Amos 2:7). The Lord will establish His holy mountain when all the earth will know Him (Isa. 11:9; 56:7). Zion is God's holy hill (Dan. 9:20; Joel 3:17[4:17]).

The word is also used when referring to holy places. God's presence is what makes any place, anything, or anyone holy (Ex. 3:5). The Holy Place in the Tabernacle (Ex. 26:33; 28:29) was separated from the Most Holy Place by a curtain (Ex. 26:33); it refers to the Most Holy Place in the Temple as well (1 Kgs. 6:16). This word with the definite article refers to the entire Tabernacle (Ex. 36:1, 3, 4; 38:27) and later the Temple Solomon built (1 Kgs. 8:8); literally, the Holy Place (Ps. 60:6[8]; 63:2[3]).

6945. קָדֵשׁ *qāḏēš:* A masculine noun meaning male temple prostitute. The feminine form of this word is *qᵉḏēšāh* (6948). Although the term denotes one who was holy or sacred, the question must be asked, Holy for what?" In the context of a pagan temple cult, which was the proper context for this word, it connotes a man who was set apart for pagan temple service, namely, male prostitution (Deut. 23:17[18]; 1 Kgs. 14:24; 15:12; 22:46 [47]). This term is sometimes translated as sodomite, which is an excellent expression of the likelihood that these were homosexual or at least bisexual prostitutes.

6946. קָדֵשׁ ***qāḏēš:*** A proper noun designating a city called Kadesh ten times and used by the Israelites for several years as a base of operations while still wandering in the desert. It is also called Kadesh Barnea (10 times; see 6947). It is fifty miles southwest of Beersheba and in the southern part of the Wilderness of Zin. It is called En Mishpat, "spring of Justice" (Kadesh) in Genesis 14:7. Hazar was not too far from it (Gen. 16:14). Abraham encamped between it and Shur (Gen. 20:1); it was located in the Desert of Paran (Num. 13:26). The twelve spies returned there to report. Miriam died there (Num. 20:1–22). Mount Hor, where Aaron died, was near it.

6947. קָדֵשׁ בַּרְנֵעַ ***qāḏēš barnēaʿ:*** A proper noun designating Kadesh Barnea. The same as 6946 but here called Kadesh Barnea 14 times (e.g., Num. 32:8; Deut. 9:23; Josh. 10:41). It was allotted to Judah (Josh. 15:3).

6948. קְדֵשָׁה ***qᵉḏēšāh:*** A feminine noun meaning a female temple prostitute. The masculine form of this word is *qāḏēš* (6945). Although the term refers to a person that was holy or sacred, it is necessary to know what they were holy to. When referring to a pagan temple cult, it connotes a woman set apart for pagan temple service, namely, female prostitution (Deut. 23:17[18]; Hos. 4:14). It is also possible that this term was used as a general term for prostitution (Gen. 38:21, 22) because of its parallel usage with *zānāh* (2181) (see Gen. 38:15). However, it is at the same time possible that *zānāh* was merely the more general term for a prostitute, while *qᵉḏēšāh* was the exclusive term for a shrine prostitute.

6949. קָהָה ***qāhāh:*** I. A verb meaning to be blunt, dull. It means for a cutting tool to be unsharpened, to have a dull edge or point (Eccl. 10:10).

II. A verb meaning to be set on edge. It refers to one's teeth being sharp, ready to bite and cut. The assertion of the proverb, "and the children's teeth are set on edge" (Jer. 31:29, 30; Ezek. 18:2), refers to the wrongly supposed effect of the father's sins on the children.

6950. קָהַל ***qāhal:*** A verb meaning to gather, to assemble. The meaning of this verb is closely connected with that of *qāhāl* (6951), a Hebrew noun meaning a convocation, a congregation, or an assembly. It indicates an assembling together for a convocation or as a congregation, often for religious purposes. The word is used in reference to the act of congregating to fulfill a chiefly religious end (Josh. 18:1); of assembling for battle

(Judg. 20:1; 2 Sam. 20:14); and of summoning to an appointed religious assembly (Deut. 31:28).

6951. קָהָל *qāhāl:* A masculine noun meaning an assembly, a community, a congregation, a crowd, a company, a throng, a mob. The word describes various gatherings and assemblies called together. It can describe a gathering called for evil purposes—such as the deceitful assembly of the brothers Simeon and Levi to plan violence against the city of Shechem (Gen. 49:6; Ezek. 23:47). The man of God abhors the gathering of evildoers (Ps. 26:5); but he should proclaim the Lord's name in the worshiping congregation (Ps. 22:22[23]). An assembly for war or a group of soldiers was common in the Old Testament (Num. 22:4; Judg. 20:2; 1 Sam. 17:47); the various groups of exiles that traveled from Babylon to Jerusalem were a renewed community (Ezra 2:64; Neh. 7:66; Jer. 31:8). Many assemblies were convened for holy religious purposes: the congregation of Israel gathered at Sinai to hear the Lord's words (Deut. 9:10); many feasts and holy convocations called for worship and fasting as noted by the author of Chronicles (2 Chr. 20:5; 30:25).

The word describes Israel as a congregation, an organized community. Israel was the Lord's community (Num. 16:3; 20:4). The word also describes the gathering of Israel before King Solomon when he dedicated the Temple (1 Kgs. 8:14); the high priest atoned for the whole community of Israel on the Day of Atonement (Lev. 16:17; Deut. 31:30). The word designates the community restored in Jerusalem after the Babylonian exile (Ezra 10:8, 12, 14); the gathering of the congregation of Israel when they killed the Passover lambs (Ex. 12:6).

The word refers to gatherings of any assembled multitude: an assembly of nations (Gen. 35:11); or of peoples (Gen. 28:3), such as Abraham's descendants were to comprise. It refers to a great mass of people as mentioned by Balak, king of Moab (Num. 22:4).

6952. קְהִלָּה *qᵉhillāh:* A feminine noun meaning an assembly, a congregation. This word expresses the gathering of a collection of people, such as the congregation of Jacob referred to by Moses in his blessing of the tribes (Deut. 33:4). This word can also describe the gathering of people for legal action (Neh. 5:7).

6953. קֹהֶלֶת *qōheleṯ:* A noun meaning a collector of wisdom, a preacher. This word is the active feminine participle of the word *qāhal* (6950), meaning to gather or to assemble. Thus, the root meaning appears to indicate a person who gathered wisdom. The word has a feminine form because it referred to an office or position, but it was usually used with masculine verbs and always referred to a man. *Qōheleṯ* only occurs in Ecclesiastes: three times at the beginning and end of the book and once in the middle (Eccl. 7:27).It is also the Hebrew name of the book. The word Ecclesiastes is a translation of this Hebrew word into Greek and referred to someone who addressed a public assembly. This is another meaning of the word based on the fact that the preacher had gathered knowledge to speak about life. Solomon used the word to describe himself as one who gathered wisdom (Eccl. 12:9, 10; cf. 1 Kgs. 4:32–34[5:12–14]); and as one who spoke to people about wisdom (Eccl. 12:9; cf. 2 Chr. 9:23).

6954. קְהֵלָתָה ***qᵉhēlāṯāh:*** A proper noun designating Kehelathah (Num. 33:22, 23).

6955. קְהָת ***qᵉhāṯ:*** A proper noun designating Kohath, one of the three sons of Levi, along with Gershon and Merari (Gen. 46:11; Ex. 6:16). Among his descendants were Amram, Moses' father, and Jochebed, Moses' mother (Ex. 6:18; Num. 26:58–61). They took care of the sanctuary in the wilderness (Num. 3:28, 29; 4:1–20) and carried parts of it on their shoulders when traveling (Num. 7:9). Some of them rebelled against Moses (Num. 16:1) and were destroyed. They received Levitical cities to live in (Josh. 21:5, 20, 26).

6956. קְהָתִי ***qᵉhāṯiy:*** A proper noun designating Kohathite, the gentilic or ethnic form of the word Kohath. This is indicated by the *iy* (ִי) on the end of the word, *iyṯ* (ִית) that designates a woman. See 6955.

6957. קַו ***qaw,*** קָו ***qāw:*** A masculine noun indicating a line, a measuring line. It refers to an actual cord used in construction work as a measuring line (1 Kgs. 7:23). Figuratively, it indicates a measuring standard of justice to be applied to Jerusalem (2 Kgs. 21:13). It refers to the architectural plan, line, of the heavens that reflects God's work (Ps. 19:4). It refers to an instructive utterance of prophetic and legal speech from God (Isa. 28:10, 13). It indicates God's judgments and His sovereign distribution of His power (Isa. 34:11, 17).

6958. קוֹה ***qôh,*** קָיָה ***qāyāh:*** I. A verb meaning to vomit. It refers to the emptying of the contents of a person's stomach. It is used figuratively of the land of Canaan spewing the Israelites out of it because of their uncleanness (Lev. 18:25, 28; 20:22); of a rich man vomiting out his riches (Job 20:15). Eating in excess may result in vomiting (Prov. 25:16). Jonah was vomited by a great fish (Jon. 2:10[11]), a scene that served to humiliate the prophet for not obeying God's call.

II. A verb meaning to vomit. It is used literally and figuratively of the nations becoming drunk only to vomit, to spew out their consumed corruptions (Jer. 25:27).

6959. קוֹבַע ***qôḇa':*** A masculine noun meaning a helmet. It refers to a warrior's protective headgear to guard against serious head injuries in battle (1 Sam. 17:38; Ezek. 23:24).

6960. קָוָה *qāwāh:* A verb meaning to wait for, to look for, to hope for. The root meaning is that of twisting or winding a strand of cord or rope, but it is uncertain how that root meaning relates to the idea of hope. The word is used to signify depending on and ordering activities around a future event (Job 7:2; Mic. 5:7[6]). The hopes of someone can remain unfulfilled, especially when a person or a nation is sinning (Job 3:9; Ps. 69:20[21]; Isa. 5:2, 4, 7). Hoping, however, for what God has promised will not ultimately be disappointed, although it may not appear to succeed in the short run (Job 30:26; Isa. 59:11; cf. Isa. 59:15–21). The Lord will give strength to those who hope in Him (Ps. 27:14[2x]; Isa. 40:31). Because He is all-powerful (Jer. 14:22), He will eventually bring His promises to pass (Lam. 3:25). These promises include the establishing of His kingdom on earth (Ps. 37:9, 34; Isa. 25:9[2x]). The word also means to be gathered and refers to the gathering of waters (Gen. 1:9) and of people (Jer. 3:17).

6961. קָוֶה *qāweh:* A masculine noun referring to a cord. See 6957 and 6960.

6962. קוּט *qûṭ:* A verb meaning to loathe, to abhor. It means to despise, to feel a revulsion toward something or someone. Job loathed, despised his miserable condition (Job 10:1); God loathed, abhorred His rebellious people (Ps. 95:10). The righteous person loathes those who do not keep God's Word (Ps. 119:158; 139:21). It describes a people's feeling of disgust toward themselves (Ezek. 6:9; 20:43; 36:31).

6963. קוֹל *qôl:* A masculine noun meaning a voice, a sound, a noise, a cry. This is an all-encompassing word that is used of any kind of sound. It describes God's voice in the Garden of Eden (Gen. 3:8, 10); human voices, speech (Gen. 27:22; Josh. 6:10; 2 Kgs. 7:10); singing (Ex. 32:18); laughter (Jer. 30:19); horses hoofs (Jer. 47:3); animal sounds (1 Sam. 15:14; Jer. 8:16). It is used of noises and sounds from inanimate objects: musical instruments, e.g., a shophar (Ex. 19:16; 20:18); a clap of thunder (Isa. 30:30; Amos 1:2); feet marching (1 Kgs. 14:6); chariots (Nah. 3:2), etc. It refers to the content of speech, what is actually conveyed (Gen. 3:17; Ex. 3:18); also the contents of a written message (2 Kgs. 10:6). In a special use, it refers to the sound meaning of a divine sign (Ex. 4:8). The speech and utterances of the Lord as *qôl* are found often (Gen. 22:18; 26:5; Ex. 5:2; Zech. 6:15). The phrase *qôl gāḏôl* means a loud (great) voice (Gen. 39:14). The idiom to lift up one's voice means to cry out, to plead (Gen. 21:16); to raise up one's voice means to prepare to cry out (Gen. 39:15). The phrase *qôl qōre'* means a voice calls (Isa. 40:3, 6). It may bear the meaning of news, a report, hearsay (Gen. 45:16). The word is used as a personification of a person's blood crying out (Gen. 4:10).

6964. קוֹלָיָה ***qôlāyāh:*** A proper noun designating Kolaiah:

A. A Benjamite (Neh. 11:7).

B. The father of the false prophet Ahab (Jer. 29:21).

6965. קוּם ***qûm:*** A verb meaning to arise, to stand, to stand up. The basic meaning of this word is the physical action of rising up (Gen. 19:33, 35; Ruth 3:14); or the resultant end of that action, standing (Josh. 7:12, 13). However, a myriad of derived and figurative meanings for this term have developed. It can designate the following attributes: to show honor and respect (Gen. 27:19; Ex. 33:10; Num. 23:18); to move (Ex. 10:23); to recover (Ex. 21:19); to belong (Lev. 25:30); to cost (Lev. 27:14, 17); to be valid (Num. 30:5); to appear (Deut. 13:1[2]); to follow (Deut. 29:22[21]); to be hostile (Judg. 9:18); to endure (1 Sam. 13:14); to replace (1 Kgs. 8:20). The word can also mean to ratify (Ruth 4:7); to obligate (Esth. 9:21, 27, 31); to establish or strengthen (Ps. 119:28); to fulfill (Ezek. 13:6). In the causative form, it means to provide (Gen. 38:8; 2 Sam. 12:11); to rouse (Gen. 49:9); to perform (Deut. 9:5); to revive (Ruth 4:5, 10); to keep one's word (1 Sam. 3:12); to erect (1 Kgs. 7:21); to appoint (1 Kgs. 11:14); to be victorious (Ps. 89:43[44]); to bring to silence (Ps. 107:29).

6966. קוּם ***qûm:*** An Aramaic verb meaning to stand, to arise, to set up, to establish. It means to get up from a sitting or lying position, to stand erect (Dan. 3:24); to arise, get up from sleeping (Dan. 6:19[20]). It describes the beginning and development of nations (Dan. 7:17); or the beginning of a process, the preparation to build (Ezra 5:2). It carries the sense of something being in a standing position (Dan. 2:31; 3:3). It indicates durability of something, its continuance (Dan. 2:44). In legal language, it means to set up, to put through a legal ruling, a law (Dan. 6:8[9]). In its passive usage, it means to be set up (Dan. 7:4, 5). In its causative stem, it is used often of setting something up: a statue (Dan. 3:1, 3, 5; 6:8[9]); a kingdom (Dan. 2:44); various persons to their offices (Ezra 6:18; Dan. 5:11).

6967. קוֹמָה ***qômāh:*** A feminine noun meaning height, stature, length. It refers to the physical height of something, e.g., the ark (Gen. 6:15; Ex. 25:10, 23; 2 Kgs. 25:17); a person (1 Sam. 16:7). The use of the word in 1 Samuel 28:20 refers to Saul's full stature lying on the ground. It has the sense of tall or high in 2 Kings 19:23, referring to the legendary tall cedars of Lebanon. It is used in a figurative sense of great and powerful people (Isa. 10:33). Its use in Ezekiel 13:18 seems to refer to social stature more than physical size.

6968. קוֹמְמִיּוּת ***qôm^e^miyyûṯ:*** A feminine noun indicating uprightness, erectness. It is used of something standing straight and tall. In a figurative sense, it refers to Israel's self-worth, reasonable pride (Lev. 26:13).

6969. קוּן *qûn*, קִין *qiyn*, קוֹנֵן *qônēn*: A verb meaning to chant, to lament, to mourn. It means to present a dirge, a song, or a poem of lament and sorrow over someone or an event (2 Sam. 3:33). A lament (*qînāh*) was composed at Josiah's death by Jeremiah (2 Chr. 35:25). Ezekiel speaks of a lament sung for the fallen city of Tyre (Ezek. 27:32).

6970. קוֹעַ *qôa'*: A proper noun designating Koa (Ezek. 23:23).

6971. קוֹף *qôp̱*: A masculine noun meaning ape. It refers to an exotic animal brought to Israel by ship from Tarshish (Spain or merely large merchant ships?) (1 Kgs. 10:22; 2 Chr. 9:21). This touch of vanity added to the splendor of Solomon's kingdom.

6972. קוּץ *qûṣ*, קִיץ *qiyṣ*: A verb meaning to spend the summer. It refers to using up one's time during the summer months, to be active then (Isa. 18:6). In context it is the chronological setting for birds of prey to spend their time in the ruins remaining after God's judgment had created devastation.

6973. קוּץ *qûṣ*: A verb meaning to loathe, to be disgusted, to be sick of. The word signifies God's revulsion toward pagan practices (Lev. 20:23); by Israel toward manna (ungratefully and wrongly) after eating it for years (Num. 21:5; cf. Ps. 78:22–25); by Rebekah toward her Hittite daughters-in-law (Gen. 27:46); and by Solomon's son toward the Lord's rebuke (Prov. 3:11). It also signified the loathing felt by enemies toward Israel's prosperity (Ex. 1:12; Num. 22:3). In Isaiah 7:6, the causative sense means to vex. By taking over, the enemies planned to cause Judah to abhor them.

6974. קוּץ *qûṣ*, קִיץ *qiyṣ*: A verb meaning to wake up, to arouse. It means to arouse a person from sleep or to awake from sleep (1 Sam. 26:12; 2 Kgs. 4:31; Job 14:12). To awake and find oneself safe is considered a work of the Lord on behalf of His servants (Ps. 3:5[6]). It may have the sense of act, doing something (Ps. 35:23). It depicts resurrection and is contained in some of the key references to this reality in the Old Testament (Isa. 26:19; Dan. 12:2). It is used as an imperative call to Awake, meaning to become aware of a situation and to act accordingly (Joel 1:5). It is used mockingly of the lifeless, eternal sleep of idols (Hab. 2:19).

6975. קוֹץ *qôṣ*: A masculine noun meaning a thorn, a thornbush. It refers to an undesirable, inedible shrub that became part of God's curse on the ground (Gen. 3:18). Such shrubs were a fire hazard, easily ignited (Ex. 22:6). This word is used in similes to designate an undesirable thing (2 Sam. 23:6); and to represent enemies of the psalmist in some passages (Ps. 118:12).

6976. קוֹץ ***qôṣ***, הַקּוֹץ ***haqqôṣ:*** I. A proper noun designating Koz, a descendant of Caleb (1 Chr. 4:8).

II. A proper noun designating Hakkoz, a priest returning from Babylonian exile (1 Chr. 24:10; Ezra 2:61; Neh. 3:4, 21; 7:63).

6977. קְוֻצָּה ***qᵉwuṣṣāh:*** A feminine noun meaning hair, a lock of hair. It refers to tufts of hair hanging on a person's head. It portrays the beauty of the bridegroom (Song 5:2, 11).

6978. קַו ***qaw***, קַו־קַו ***qaw-qaw***, קָו ***qāw:*** I. A masculine noun referring to power, might. It means might, strength and was used to describe the armies of Ethiopia with their legendary fierce warriors (Isa. 18:2, 7).

II. A masculine noun indicating a measure, a meting out. The words relate to the word for a measuring cord; hence, the meaning is understood as a meting out, measured and limited (Isa. 18:2, 7).

III. A masculine noun meaning strange speech. It means speech that is gibberish, alien (Isa. 18:2, 7).

6979. קוּר ***qûr:*** I. A verb meaning to dig. It refers to removing dirt methodically for some purpose. It is used figuratively of the Lord's digging as a feature of His judgments on Egypt (2 Kgs. 19:24; Isa. 37:25).

II. A verb indicating to break down, to destroy. It means to destroy, to disable. It is used in a future sense of a royal ruler of Israel breaking down the sins of Sheth (Num. 24:17); and of a similar future action of God in the time of Isaiah (Isa. 22:5).

III. A verb meaning to cast out; to pour out. It is used of distributing, passing out, making evil available (Jer. 6:7).

6980. קוּר ***qûr:*** A masculine noun designating a spider's web. It depicts the web spun out by a spider. In context the web stands for a sinister trap or snare devised by God's corrupted people (Isa. 59:5, 6).

6981. קוֹרֵא ***qôrē'***, קֹרֵא ***qōrē':*** A proper noun designating Kore:

A. An ancestor of gatekeepers in David's day (1 Chr. 9:19; 26:1).

B. A Levite under Hezekiah (2 Chr. 31:14).

6982. קוֹרָה ***qôrāh:*** A feminine noun meaning a beam, a pole, a roof. It refers to beams used in the construction of a building that were weight-bearing (2 Kgs. 6:2, 5); they were overlaid with gold in the Temple (2 Chr. 3:7). This term may be used to refer to the entire house (Gen. 19:8). Beams of cedar or other expensive wood were highly prized for their beauty or ornamentation (Song 1:17).

6983. קוּשׁ ***qûš:*** A verb meaning to set a trap, to lay a snare. The root idea may be that of bending, as the energy stored in bent wood powers a snare. *Qôš* occurs only in Isaiah 29:21 where it figuratively refers to the laying of a snare to cause trouble and to silence the person who judges justly and thwarts the wicked.

6984. קוּשָׁיָהוּ ***qûšāyāhû:*** A proper noun designating Kushaiah (1 Chr. 15:17).

6985. קָט ***qāṭ:*** An adjective meaning little, very little, soon. It indicates something of relatively small significance. It was used specifically to state that it was an insignificant thing that Israel had not committed the abominations of Samaria and Sodom, considering the sins and rebellions they had committed (Ezek. 16:47).

6986. קֶטֶב ***qeṭeḇ:*** A masculine noun meaning destruction. It is closely associated with the word *qōṭeḇ* (6987). God is always connected with this concept of destruction. It seems ironic that in two passages, God was the source of the destruction (Deut. 32:24; Isa. 28:2), while in another passage, He was the salvation from the destruction (Ps. 91:6). On further reflection, though, it becomes evident that God is the source of this destruction, which was a means of divine retribution. The difference is that in Deuteronomy and Isaiah, God was brought His judgment on the wicked, but in Psalms, God preserved the righteous in the midst of His judgment on the wicked. The specific nature of the destruction is flexible. In each of the passages, it is set in a different context and is parallel with a different word: *rešep* (7566), meaning fire (Deut. 32:24); *deḇer* (1698), meaning plague or pestilence (Ps. 91:6); and *mayim* (4325), meaning water (Isa. 28:2).

6987. קֹטֶב ***qōṭeḇ:*** A masculine noun meaning destruction. It is closely associated with the word *qeṭeḇ* (6986). It occurs only once where it refers to the judgment that God was going to bring against Samaria for its wickedness (Hos. 13:14). See the word *deḇer* (1698), meaning plague or pestilence, as in Psalm 91:6. Even though this word appears in the context of God's impending judgment for wickedness, the specific verse in which it appears is actually a vision of hope for a coming restoration. God is going to allow judgment for a time, but then He will remove it because, without His permission, death and Sheol have no power.

6988. קְטוֹרָה ***qᵉṭôrāh:*** A masculine noun referring to incense. It refers to what goes up in a sweet-smelling, aromatic smoke to represent the prayers of God's people (Deut. 33:10).

6989. קְטוּרָה ***qᵉṭûrāh:*** A proper noun designating Keturah (Gen. 25:1, 4; 1 Chr. 1:32, 33).

6990. קָטַט ***qāṭaṭ:*** I. A verb meaning to be cut off. It refers to severing something, stopping it, removing it (Job 8:14; NASB, NIV, see II). Its subject is hope, confidence, trust that may be cut off.

II. A verb whose meaning is uncertain. It is translated to be fragile (Job 8:14; KJV, NKJV, see I).

6991. קָטַל qāṭal: A verb indicating to slay, to kill. It means to destroy persons by illness, cause them to die, to perish. It is used by Job about himself (Job 13:15). It describes the activity of a murderer (Job 24:14). It indicates God's possible slaying of the wicked.

6992. קְטַל q^eṭal: An Aramaic verb meaning to slay, to kill. It means to destroy persons, to cut off their lives. It is used in an official royal decree to kill the wise men of Babylon (Dan. 2:13, 14; cf. 5:19, 30; 7:11). It describes the death of a person by burning (Dan. 3:22).

6993. קֶטֶל qeṭel: A masculine noun meaning slaughter. It refers to a mass killing of people in battle and in pillage in Edom as part of the Lord's judgment on this rebellious nation (Obad. 1:9).

6994. קָטֹן qāṭan: A verb meaning to be a small matter, insignificant; to be small, to make small. It is used to refer to oneself as being trifling, insignificant, not worthy (Gen. 32:10); of something being considered as unimportant by God (2 Sam. 7:19; 1 Chr. 17:17). It is used in its causative sense to indicate making something smaller, but in context it describes an act of cheating (Amos 8:5).

6995. קֹטֶן qōṭen: A masculine noun meaning little. In context it refers to a person's small finger and is used in a figurative sense (1 Kgs. 12:10; 2 Chr. 10:10).

6996. קָטָן qāṭān, קָטֹן qāṭōn: I. An adjective meaning small, little, insignificant, unimportant. It describes what is not large but diminutive in size, or it describes what is small in respect to something else: animals and fish, both small and great (Ps. 104:25); vessels (2 Chr. 36:18); weights (Deut. 25:13, 14). It is used to indicate small children (Gen. 44:20; 2 Sam. 9:12); the small or smallest child, which can also mean the younger or youngest child (Gen. 9:24; 27:15; Judg. 15:2; 1 Sam. 16:11; 17:14). It can have the sense of weak or insignificant (1 Sam. 9:21; 2 Kgs. 18:24). It is used of uttering a minor prophecy (Num. 22:18). It refers to insignificant times and events in general (Zech. 4:10).

II. An adjective meaning small, little, insignificant. Its meanings are basically the same as I. It refers to: persons who are young (1 Sam. 20:35); persons young compared to others (Gen. 48:19); with the definite article, it may indicate the youngest (Gen. 42:13, 15, 20). Used in the phrase young (*Qāṯān, gāḏôl*) and old, it means everyone (Gen. 19:11; cf. Deut. 1:17; 1 Kgs. 22:31). It describes things as small: a little robe (1 Sam. 2:19); the idea of too small employs *qāṭôn + min* (4480) (1 Kgs. 8:64). It is used in a figurative sense to indicate trifling, unimportant things (Ex. 18:22, 26; 1 Sam. 20:2; Jer. 49:15; Obad. 1:2); weak things (Amos 7:2, 5).

6997. קָטָן qāṭān, הַקָּטָן haqqāṭan: A proper noun designating Hakkatan (Ezra 8:12).

6998. קָטַף ***qāṭap̱:*** A verb meaning to break off, to pluck off, to cut off. It indicates picking, removing ears of grain or small branches, etc. (Deut. 23:25[26]; Job 30:4; Ezek. 17:4, 22). In the latter reference, it is used figuratively. In its passive sense, it means to be picked or cut off (Job 8:12).

6999. קָטַר ***qāṭar:*** A verb meaning to produce smoke. Often smoke is made by burning incense, but every major offering may also be associated with this word (Ex. 30:7; Lev. 1:9; 2:2; 3:5; 4:10; 7:5). One unusual use of this term describes Solomon's carriage as perfumed with myrrh and incense (Song 3:6). Many times this verb is used of improper worship directed either to the true God or to false gods (1 Kgs. 12:33; 2 Chr. 26:16, 18, 19; Jer. 48:35). In the Old Testament, the burning of incense was restricted to the Aaronic priesthood (Num. 16:40[17:5]; 2 Chr. 26:16, 18, 19). In the New Testament, Zacharias, a priest and the father of John the Baptist, burned incense; and prayers of saints are compared to burning incense (cf. Luke 1:10, 11; Rev. 5:8; 8:3, 4).

7000. קָטַר ***qāṭar:*** A verb meaning to be joined to, to enclose. It refers to the connection or the partitioned areas to serve as courts, used only of these areas in Ezekiel's Temple (Ezek. 46:22; KJV, joined; NASB, enclosed).

7001. קְטַר ***q^e^ṭar:*** I. An Aramaic masculine noun meaning hip joint. It refers to the connecting joints of a person's hips that provide a person's major stability for standing upright (Dan. 5:6).

II. An Aramaic masculine noun referring to a difficult problem. It has the sense of a twisted connection (a knot). In a figurative sense, it refers to a complicated problem to be solved, undone (Dan. 5:12, 16).

7002. קִטֵּר ***qiṭṭēr:*** A feminine noun meaning incense. It refers to something that produces incense smoke. In context it indicates incense burned to pagan gods (Jer. 44:21).

7003. קִטְרוֹן ***qiṭrôn:*** A proper noun designating Kitron (Judg. 1:30).

7004. קְטֹרֶת ***q^e^ṭōreṯ:*** A feminine noun meaning smoke, incense, the smell of a burning sacrifice. Incense was one of the valid gifts Moses was to ask from the people (Ex. 25:6); and it played an important role in Aaron's atonement for the sin of his sons (Lev. 16:13). David's plans for the Temple included an altar for incense (1 Chr. 28:18); and David prayed that his prayers would be like incense to the Lord (Ps. 141:2). God told Judah that the smell of worthless sacrifices was detestable (Isa. 1:13). See the related Hebrew verb *qāṭar* (6999).

7005. קַטָּת ***qaṭṭāṯ:*** A proper noun designating Kattath, Kattah (Josh. 19:15).

7006. קִיא ***qiy':*** I. A verb meaning to vomit. It means to spew out the contents of one's stomach. It is used several times in a figurative sense of Canaan vomiting out its inhabitants (Lev. 18:25, 28; 20:22). It refers to a rich man spewing out his riches (Job 20:15). It represents the possible self-pollution of eating with a self-centered man (Prov. 23:8). Eating to excess, especially rich food, will result in vomiting (Prov. 25:16). It describes the action of a great fish spewing Jonah out of his mouth (Jon. 2:10[11]).

II. A masculine noun meaning vomit. It refers to what is vomited out, spewed out, filth (Isa. 19:14; 28:8). It figuratively indicates a nation wallowing in its corruption, vomit (Jer. 48:26).

7007. קַיִט *qayiṭ:* A masculine noun referring to summer. It indicates the driest and hottest time of the year when chaff would be easily wafted away by the wind (Dan. 2:35).

7008. קִיטוֹר *qiyṭôr*, קִיטֹר *qiyṭōr:* A masculine noun indicating smoke, dense smoke. It refers to the cloud of fine particles that arise from burning something (Gen. 19:28); the smoke arising from the land and cities of Sodom and Gomorrah (Gen. 19:28). It is difficult to discern something through smoke (Ps. 119:83). It indicates rising smoke, but in context it could be translated as clouds (Ps. 148:8).

7009. קִים *qiym:* I. A masculine noun referring to a foe, an adversary. It refers to those who rise up against someone, withstand someone, are hostile (Job 22:20).

II. A masculine noun meaning substance. It indicates an object, a force, or in a positive sense, an essence, the basis of something (Job 22:20).

7010. קְיָם *qᵉyām:* An Aramaic masculine noun meaning a decree, a statute. A form of this word is only used twice in the Hebrew Old Testament, both times in the book of Daniel. When King Darius' advisors wanted to get rid of Daniel, they persuaded Darius to make a law that forbade worship of anyone but himself (Dan. 6:7[8]). When Daniel broke this law, the advisors compelled Darius to enforce the punishment because the edict he issued could not be revoked (Dan. 6:15[16]).

7011. קַיָּם *qayyām:* An Aramaic adjective indicating something assured, enduring. It describes something that does not come to an end, deteriorate, or fall. It depicts God's character and actions (Dan. 6:26[27]). It indicates that a situation is certain, assured to someone (Dan. 4:26[23]).

7012. קִימָה *qiymāh:* A feminine noun indicating a rising, standing. It means to arise literally from a sitting position. In context it refers to the actions and activities of persons, their sitting and rising, all they do all the time (Lam. 3:63).

7013. קַיִן *qayin:* A masculine noun indicating a spear, a spearhead. It refers to the weapon wielded by

Ishbi-Benob, a descendant of giants. Its reference is probably to the entire weapon, including its shaft and metal end (2 Sam. 21:16).

7014. קַיִן ***qayin:*** A proper noun designating Cain, Kain:

A. The first person born of, Eve and first son of Adam. His name means "acquired" of the Lord (Gen. 4:1–3). Unfortunately, he fostered an attitude of anger toward his brother Abel which made his offering unacceptable to God (Gen. 4:5–7; Heb. 11:4). He directed this anger toward Abel and killed him (4:8). As his punishment, he became a wandering outcast, but God mercifully "marked" him in some way to protect him from would-be avengers of blood (4:10–16). The Lord somehow cursed the land for Cain and his descendants, which may have driven Cain to build a city (4:17) in the land of Nod (4:16). He had several sons, one of whom began the practice of bigamy (4:19–22). More violence and killing was spread by Lamech (4:23–24).

II. A proper noun designating Kain, a city in Judah (Num. 24:22, NASB).

III. A proper noun designating a Kenite (Num. 24:22 (KJV, NIV); Judg. 4:11).

7015. קִינָה ***qiynāh:*** A feminine noun referring to a lament, a funeral lamentation; a dirge. It was a song or poem composed to recognize and to mourn the death of a person (2 Sam. 1:17; 2 Chr. 35:25); or of the people of a nation, especially Judah (Jer. 7:29). It lamented over even the cattle and lands of Israel (Jer. 9:10[9]; Ezek. 2:10; Amos 5:1; 8:10).

7016. קִינָה ***qiynāh:*** A proper noun designating Kinah (Josh. 15:22).

7017. קֵינִי ***qēyniy:*** A proper noun designating Kenite (Gen. 15:19; Num. 24:21; Judg. 1:16; 4:11, 17; 5:24; 1 Sam. 15:6; 27:10; 30:29; 1 Chr. 2:55),

7018. קֵינָן ***qēynān:*** A proper noun designating Kenan, Cainan (Gen. 5:9, 10, 12–14; 1 Chr. 1:2).

7019. קַיִץ ***qayiṣ:*** A masculine noun meaning summer, summer fruit. It refers to the summer season, the hottest and driest time of the year (ca. May-October) as it was established by the Lord (Gen. 8:22; Amos 3:15). It also refers to summer fruits (2 Sam. 16:1, 2; Amos 8:1, 2). It refers figuratively to a time of drought, a lack of rain (Ps. 32:4), when the heat is scorching (Zech. 14:8).

7020. קִיצוֹן ***qiyṣôn:*** An adjective meaning at the end, the outermost. It refers to a border or something that lies on the outer perimeter or edge of something (Ex. 26:4, 10; 36:11, 17).

7021. קִיקָיוֹן ***qiyqāyôn:*** A masculine noun meaning a plant, a vine, a gourd. It refers to a fast-growing plant, a castor-oil plant capable of providing shade (Jon. 4:6, 7, 9, 10). It, like the fish and the worm, were all especially prepared by the Lord, according to the author.

7022. קִיקָלוֹן *qiyqālôn:* A masculine noun meaning disgrace. It is the opposite of honor; it indicates shame, having one's character impugned, a feeling of being insignificant, a recognition of one's error or sin (Hab. 2:16). This disgrace is brought by the Lord and deserved by His shameful people.

7023. קִיר *qiyr,* קִר *qir,* קִירָה *qiyrāh:* A masculine noun meaning wall. Balaam's donkey, afraid of the angel, pressed against a wall and crushed Balaam's foot (Num. 22:25). Saul wanted to pin David to a wall with his spear (1 Sam. 18:11). This word also was used to describe a place one thought was safe (Amos 5:19). Solomon lined the interior walls of the Temple with cedar (1 Kgs. 6:15); and Jezebel's blood splattered on a wall (2 Kgs. 9:33). The Hebrew phrase, walls of one's heart, means something like the depths of one's soul in Jeremiah 4:19. The King James Version translates that Hebrew phrase as, my very heart. In Ezekiel's vision of the new Temple, the walls were six cubits thick (Ezek. 41:5).

7024. קִיר *qiyr:* A proper noun designating Kir:

A. A city in Mesopotamia (2 Kgs. 16:9; Isa. 22:6; Amos 1:5; 9:7).

B. A city in Moab, possibly the same as Kir Hareseth (7025) (Isa. 15:1).

7025. קִיר חֲרֶשֶׂת *qiyr ḥᵃreśeṯ,* קִיר חֶרֶשׂ *qiyr ḥereś:* A proper noun designating Kir Hareseth, Kir Heres, a city in Moab (2 Kgs. 3:25; Isa. 16:7, 11; Jer. 48:31, 36).

7026. קֵירֹס *qēyrōs,* קֵרֹס *qērōs:* A proper noun designating Keros (Ezra 2:44; Neh. 7:47).

7027. קִישׁ *qiyš:* A proper noun designating Kish (1 Sam. 9:1, 3; 10:11, 21; 14:51; 2 Sam. 21:14; 1 Chr. 8:30, 33; 9:36, 39; 12:1; 23:21, 22; 24:29; 26:28; 2 Chr. 29:12; Esth. 2:5).

7028. קִישׁוֹן *qiyšôn:* A proper noun designating Kishon, the name of a river that played a part in the defeat of the Canaanites by the forces of Deborah and Barak. It flowed out of the Jezreel Valley east to west to the Mediterranean. Elijah killed prophets of Baal here (1 Kgs. 18:40). It overflowed and helped bog down the iron chariots of Sisera's forces (Judg. 4:7, 13; 5:21). It was a great victory for Israel at Kishon and enshrined in the memory of Israel (Ps. 83:9[10]).

7029. קִישִׁי *qiyšiy:* A proper noun designating Kishi (1 Chr. 6:44[29]).

7030. קִיתָרֹס *qiyṯārōs:* An Aramaic masculine noun referring to a zither, a lyre, a harp. It is now generally taken to refer to a lyre or a lute, a stringed instrument of the harp family (Deut. 3:5, 7, 10, 15).

7031. קַל *qal:* An adjective meaning swift, speedy. It describes something as agile, quick. It refers to a swift warrior (Amos 2:14); a fast horse (Isa. 30:16); a swift messenger from Ethiopia (Isa. 18:2); a swift-footed runner such as Asahel (2 Sam. 2:18); a fast-moving army (Isa. 5:26). The Lord is pictured as traveling on a swift-flying cloud (Isa. 19:1).

7032. קָל ***qāl:*** An Aramaic masculine noun meaning a voice, a sound. It refers often to the sound of musical instruments (Dan. 3:5, 7, 10, 15); to a voice uttering words from heaven (Dan. 4:31[28]); to a human voice crying out (Dan. 6:20[21]); to the sound of words uttered by the little horn (Dan. 7:11).

7033. קָלָה ***qālāh:*** I. A verb meaning to roast, to parch, to dry. It means to expose certain vegetables to heat, to dry them out, to parch them (Lev. 2:14; Josh. 5:11). It means to cook something or burn it in fire (Jer. 29:22).

II. A verb meaning to be burning, searing. It is used figuratively of guilt causing great inner psychological terror and pain (Ps. 38:7[8]).

III. A verb meaning to be loathsome. It refers to a person feeling abhorrent, loathsome because of guilt and the need for penitence (Ps. 38:7[8]).

7034. קָלָה ***qālāh:*** A verb meaning to be lightly esteemed, despised. It means to be of little account or value, to be belittled, shamed (Deut. 25:3). It describes dishonoring one's own parents, treating them lightly (Deut. 27:16). It indicates treating an important issue lightly (1 Sam. 18:23). It refers to a social view of someone as unimportant (Prov. 12:9); or inferior (Isa. 3:5). It describes an insignificant remnant, nation, or people (Isa. 16:14).

7035. קָלָה ***qālāh:*** A verb meaning to assemble. This word is used only once in the Old Testament. It occurs in 2 Samuel 20:14 where Joab gathered the people together.

7036. קָלוֹן ***qālôn:*** A masculine noun referring to shame, disgrace. It refers to a feeling and condition of shame, of being put on display in mockery (Job 10:15); or of being dishonored (Ps. 83:16[17]). The characters of fools make a show of dishonor; it clings to them (Prov. 3:35). It refers to losing a high social position and being ruined, shamed (Isa. 22:18). God will change the glory of His rebellious people to shame and dishonor (Hos. 4:7; Nah. 3:5).

7037. קַלַּחַת ***qallaḥaṯ:*** A feminine noun indicating a cauldron, a kettle. It refers to a large kettle or pot in which sacrificial meat was boiled (1 Sam. 2:14). It is employed in a simile in which the meat in the cauldron was the oppressed people of God (Mic. 3:3).

7038. קָלַט ***qālaṭ:*** A verb meaning to be stunted, to be deformed. It refers to an animal that has a deformed or injured member, not fully or properly developed. The animal could be used in a freewill offering but not a vow offering (Lev. 22:23).

7039. קָלִי ***qāliy,*** **קָלִיא** ***qāliy':*** A masculine noun designating parched or roasted grain. It refers to grain that has been placed in the hot sun to parch it, to dry it out, or placed over fire to roast it (Lev. 23:14). It was a most desirable food (Ruth 2:14; 1 Sam. 17:17; 2 Sam. 17:28).

7040. קַלָּי ***qāllāy:*** A proper noun designating Kallai (Neh. 12:20).

7041. קֵלָיָה ***qēlāyāh:*** A proper noun designating Kelaiah (Ezra 10:23).

7042. קְלִיטָא ***qeliyṭā':*** A proper noun designating Kelita (Ezra 10:23; Neh. 8:7; 10:10[11]).

7043. קָלַל ***qālal:*** A verb meaning to be slight, to be trivial, to be swift. This word is used in many different ways, but most uses trace back to the basic idea of this word, which is lightness. In its most simple meaning, it referred to the easing of a burden (Ex. 18:22); lightening judgment (1 Sam. 6:5); lessening labor (1 Kgs. 12:9, 10; 2 Chr. 10:9, 10); or the lightening of a ship (Jon. 1:5). This idea leads to its usage to describe people who were swifter than eagles (2 Sam. 1:23); swift animals (Hab. 1:8); or days that pass quickly (Job 7:6; 9:25). When describing an event or a circumstance, it means trivial (1 Sam. 18:23; 1 Kgs. 16:31; Isa. 49:6). In many instances, it is used to describe speaking lightly of another or cursing another: a person cursing another person (Ex. 21:17; 2 Sam. 16:9–11; Neh. 13:2); people cursing God (Lev. 24:11); or God cursing people (Gen. 12:3; 1 Sam. 2:30; Ps. 37:22).

7044. קָלָל ***qālal:*** An adjective meaning polished, burnished. It refers to a metal that has been buffed or burnished to make it gleam (Ezek. 1:7; Dan. 10:6).

7045. קְלָלָה ***qelālāh:*** A feminine noun meaning curse. This word comes from the verb *qālal* (7043), meaning to curse. This noun describes the general speaking of ill-will against another (2 Sam. 16:12; Ps. 109:17, 18); as well as the official pronouncement on a person, as Jacob feared he would receive from Isaac (Gen. 27:12, 13); or on a nation, as Balaam gave to Moab (Deut. 23:5[6]; Neh. 13:2). God's curse is on the disobedient (Deut. 11:28; 28:15; Jer. 44:8); while His blessing, *berāḵāh* (1293), is on the righteous (Deut. 11:26; 30:19). Jeremiah used several other words in close connection with this one to describe the undesirable nature of this word: reproach, proverb, taunt, curse, hissing, desolation, and imprecation (Jer. 24:9; 25:18; 42:18).

7046. קָלַס ***qālas:*** A verb meaning to mock, to deride, to scorn. It means to make fun of persons, to insult them (2 Kgs. 2:23); or to mock or insult a whole nation (Ezek. 22:5). It means to hold someone or something in disrespect; not to fear or take something seriously (Hab. 1:10). It is used figuratively to describe Israel's money gained from harlotry (Ezek. 16:31).

7047. קֶלֶס *qeles:* A masculine noun meaning derision, reproach. It refers to shame, disgrace, discredit, disrespect for someone or something (Ps. 44:13[14]). Prophets often suffered derision and reproach because of their messages and sometimes their aberrant behavior (Jer. 20:8).

7048. קַלָּסָה *qallāsāh:* A feminine noun indicating mocking; a laughingstock. It means to be the object of mockery and the brunt of jokes of humor and disrespect (Ezek. 22:4).

7049. קָלַע *qāla':* I. A verb meaning to sling or hurl something. It indicates the casting or throwing stones by using a weapon devised for this purpose (1 Sam. 17:49). It is used figuratively of destroying Israel's enemies (1 Sam. 25:29); or casting, slinging Israel out of the land of promise (Jer. 10:18).

II. A verb meaning to carve. It describes the skilled carvings and cuttings of Israel's craftsmen, especially in the Temple (1 Kgs. 6:29, 32, 35).

7050. קֶלַע *qela':* I. A masculine noun referring to a sling, a slingstone. It refers to a weapon used to throw stones with great speed and accuracy. It was made of a piece of leather to hold the stone and then fastened to two cords (1 Sam. 17:40, 50; 25:29; 2 Chr. 26:14). The term *'aḇnê-qᵉla'* refers to slingstones (Zech. 9:15).

II. A masculine noun meaning a curtain, a drape, a hanging. It describes the many hangings that were used in the Tabernacle and its court (Ex. 27:9, 11, 12, 14, 15; 38:9; 39:40; Num. 3:26; 4:26). It refers to a thin wooden leaf or door panel (1 Kgs. 6:34).

7051. קַלָּע *qallā':* A masculine noun referring to a slinger, a man armed with a sling. It refers to men armed with slings who, in context, went about slinging stones in a destructive manner as an act of war, ruining the land (2 Kgs. 3:25).

7052. קְלֹקֵל *qᵉlōqēl:* An adjective meaning worthless, miserable. It describes food that is unappetizing, unattractive, barely edible (Num. 21:5).

7053. קִלְּשׁוֹן *qillᵉšôn:* A masculine noun indicating a pitchfork. It refers to a pronged tool, possibly a three-pronged tool (trident?) for hoeing, loosening the ground (1 Sam. 13:21).

7054. קָמָה *qāmāh:* A feminine noun meaning a stalk, standing grain. It indicates grain still growing in the field, not yet cut, easily ignited and burned by fire (Ex. 22:6[5]; Deut. 16:9; Judg. 15:5; 2 Kgs. 19:26). Reapers gathered it by cutting it down with sickles (Isa. 17:5). See also 6965.

7055. קְמוּאֵל ***qᵉmû'ēl:*** A proper noun designating Kemuel:

A. A nephew of Abraham (Gen. 22:21).

B. An Ephraimite (Num. 34:24).

C. A Levite (1 Chr. 27:17).

7056. קָמוֹן ***qāmôn:*** A proper noun designating Kamon (Judg. 10:5).

7057. קִמּוֹשׂ ***qimmôś:*** A masculine collective noun meaning thistles, nettles. It refers to a large, hardy, prickly plant that grows wild and inhabits ruins (Isa. 34:13). Its presence is a sign of a lack of cultivation or care of the land (Prov. 24:31), especially after destruction (Hos. 9:6).

7058. קֶמַח ***qemaḥ:*** A masculine noun indicating flour, meal. It refers to finely ground grains of various kinds serving as flour, the basic ingredient of bread, etc. (Gen. 18:6); also translated as meal (Gen. 18:6; Num. 5:15). It was often served with a meat dish (Judg. 6:19). It could be rendered as grain (Hos. 8:7).

7059. קָמַט ***qāmaṭ:*** I. A verb meaning to cause to shrivel; to fill with wrinkles. It describes Job's pathetic, weakened condition with his devastating skin disease. It was used both literally (skin) and figuratively (Job's life, influence) (Job 16:8).

II. A verb meaning to bind. It is used in a figurative sense of Job's being hemmed in, pressed on by his friends and illness, almost to utter despair (Job 16:8).

III. A verb indicating to snatch away; to cut down. It is used as an euphemism for the death of the wicked, taking them away (Job 22:16).

7060. קָמַל ***qāmal:*** I. A verb meaning to wither, to rot away. It refers to the decaying and destruction of the reeds and rushes of the Nile River as a result of God's judgment on Egypt (Isa. 19:6). A similar fate was suffered by the cedars and forests of Lebanon that dried up, withered (Isa. 33:9a).

II. A verb meaning to wither, to rot away. It describes, as does I, the withering of the forests and cedars of Lebanon (Isa. 33:9).

7061. קָמַץ ***qāmaṣ:*** A verb meaning to take (a handful). It refers to gathering up an amount of something equal to what a person's hand can hold of flour or grain (Lev. 2:2; 5:12; Num. 5:26).

7062. קֹמֶץ ***qōmeṣ:*** A masculine noun indicating a handful, an abundance. It refers to an amount of something equal to what a person's hand can hold (Lev. 2:2; 5:12; 6:15[8]). It is used to mean a great amount of something; handfuls of grain, an abundant supply or crop (Gen. 41:47).

7063. קִמָּשׂוֹן ***qimmaśôn:*** A masculine collective noun referring to thorns. It refers to a prickly shrub bearing sharp stickers on its stems. Its presence in an area indicated a lack of care and cultivation; thorns, thorn bushes growing wild (Prov. 24:31).

7064. קֵן ***qēn:*** A masculine noun meaning a nest. The word refers to the actual constructed homes of various animals or birds (Deut. 22:6; 32:11; Job 39:27). It is used in a figurative sense to describe a safe dwelling (Num. 24:21; Hab. 2:9). The Temple is described as a nest for God's people Israel (Ps. 84:3[4]). It describes cells or units in Noah's ark (Gen. 6:14).

7065. קָנָא ***qānāʼ:*** A verb meaning to be jealous, to be envious, to be zealous. This is a verb derived from a noun, and, as such, occurs in the extensive and causative forms only. The point of the verb is to express a strong emotion in which the subject is desirous of some aspect or possession of the object. It can express jealousy, where persons are zealous for their own property or positions for fear they might lose them (Num. 5:14, 30; Isa. 11:13); or envy, where persons are zealous for the property or positions of others, hoping they might gain them (Gen. 26:14; 30:1; 37:11). Furthermore, it can indicate someone being zealous on behalf of another (Num. 11:29; 2 Sam. 21:2); on behalf of God (Num. 25:13; 1 Kgs. 19:10, 14); as well as God being zealous (Ezek. 39:25; Joel 2:18; Zech. 1:14; 8:2). It is also used to denote the arousing of one's jealousy or zeal (Deut. 32:16, 21; 1 Kgs. 14:22; Ps. 78:58).

7066. קְנָא ***q^enāʼ:*** An Aramaic verb meaning to buy, to purchase. It refers to the acquisition of something by purchase in context with money (Ezra 7:17).

7067. קַנָּא ***qannāʼ:*** An adjective meaning jealous. This word comes from the verb *qānāʼ* (7065), meaning to be jealous or zealous. In every instance of this word, it is used to describe the character of the Lord. He is a jealous God who will not tolerate the worship of other gods (Ex. 20:5; Deut. 5:9). This word is always used to describe God's attitude toward the worship of false gods, which arouses His jealousy and anger in judgment against the idol worshipers (Deut. 4:24; 6:15). So closely is this characteristic associated with God that His name is Jealous (Ex. 34:14).

7068. קִנְאָה ***qinʼāh:*** A feminine noun meaning zeal, jealousy. This word comes from the verb *qānāʼ* (7065), meaning to be jealous or zealous, and describes an intense fervor, passion, and emotion that is greater than a person's wrath and anger (Prov. 27:4). It can be either good or bad: Phinehas was commended for taking up the Lord's jealousy (Num. 25:11); but such passion can also be rottenness to the bones (Prov. 14:30). It is used to describe a spirit of jealousy, which comes on a man for his wife (Num. 5:14, 15, 29). Most often, however, this word describes God's zeal, which will accomplish His purpose (2 Kgs. 19:31; Isa. 9:7[6]; 37:32); and will be the instrument of His wrath in judgment (Ps. 79:5; Ezek. 36:5, 6; Zeph. 3:8).

7069. קָנָה *qānāh:* I. A verb meaning to buy, to purchase, to acquire, to possess. It is used with God as its subject to mean His buying back His people, redeeming them (Ex. 15:16; Ps. 74:2; Isa. 11:11); of God's creating the heavens and earth (Gen. 14:19); Israel (Deut. 32:6), but see II below also. It is used figuratively of obtaining wisdom (Prov. 4:5, 7); or good counsel (Prov. 1:5). It describes buying, acquiring various things: it describes the acquisition of a son by birth (Gen. 4:1); of land or fields (Gen. 33:19); a servant (Gen. 39:1); of persons freeing, ransoming slaves (Neh. 5:8); of various riches (Eccl. 2:7). In its participial form, it may refer to an owner (Lev. 25:30). It is used of God's possessing wisdom in the creation (Prov. 8:22).

II. A verb meaning to create, to bring forth. See also I above. It is used of acquiring a child from God (Gen. 4:1); of God acquiring, creating the heavens and earth (Gen. 14:19); of His creation of Israel (Deut. 32:6); of forming a fetus in the womb (Ps. 139:13). It can be used of God's creation of wisdom (Prov. 8:22) (see I).

7070. קָנֶה *qāneh:* A masculine noun meaning a rod, a stalk, a reed, a calamus reed; beam of scales. It is a general term that can be used of any object in the form of a long stalk or tubular shape. It refers to stalks of grain (Gen. 41:5, 22); certain tall, slim water plants, reeds (1 Kgs. 14:15; Isa. 19:6); weak supports in a figurative sense, e.g., Egypt (2 Kgs. 18:21; Isa. 36:6); aromatic, fragrant cane (Ex. 30:23; Jer. 6:20). The word was used in various ways of other items or concepts, objects: a measuring rod, a reed of about nine feet (Ezek. 40:3, 5); as a part of a scale, it is used to indicate a whole scale (Isa. 46:6). It is used often in descriptions of lamps, lampstands, and their branches extending from them (Ex. 25:31–33, 35, 36; 37:17, 18). It refers to the upper part of a person's arm (Job 31:22).

7071. קָנָה *qānāh:* A proper noun designating Kanah:

A. This seasonal stream (a *wadi* in Arabic, *nahal* in Hebrew) served as part of the boundary between west Ephraim and Manasseh. The ravine ran east.

B. A city on the border of the tribe of Asher (Josh. 19:28). It became the inheritance of Asher, located ca. eight miles southeast of Tyre.

7072. קַנּוֹא *qannô':* An adjective meaning jealous. It refers to Israel's God, a jealous God for His people; in judgment toward them or vengeance on their enemies (Josh. 24:19; Nah. 1:2). They were His own possession, His personal property.

7073. קְנַז *qᵉnaz:* A proper noun designating Kenaz:

A. Grandson of Esau (Gen. 36:11, 15, 42; 1 Chr. 1:36, 53).

B. The father of Othniel (Josh. 15:17; Judg. 1:13; 3:9, 11; 1 Chr. 4:13).

C. Grandson of Caleb (1 Chr. 4:15).

7074. קְנִזִּי *q^enizziy:* A proper noun designating Kenizzite (Gen. 15:19; Num. 32:12; Josh. 14:6, 14).

7075. קִנְיָן *qinyān:* A masculine noun meaning goods, possessions, property. It refers to all personal property acquired: sheep, goats (Gen. 31:18); capable of being moved, transferred (Gen. 34:23; 36:6; Josh. 14:4). It is used of the total work of God's creation as His possession (Ps. 104:24). It indicates a purchased slave (Zech. 13:5).

7076. קִנָּמוֹן *qinnāmôn:* A masculine noun meaning cinnamon. It refers to a pleasant- smelling, yellow-brown spice made from the dried inner bark of certain trees or shrubs (Ex. 30:23). It was used also as an aphrodisiac (Prov. 7:17; Song 4:14).

7077. קָנַן *qānan:* A verb meaning to make a nest; to build a nest. It refers to the activity of a serpent or a bird constructing its nest; in context it notes God's wisdom and sovereignty being displayed (Ps. 104:17). It is used figuratively of the people living in Lebanon, a place of hills and tall trees in certain areas (Jer. 22:23); or in the hills of Moab (Jer. 48:28). It describes the nesting of birds within the Assyrian Empire (Ezek. 31:6).

7078. קֶנֶץ *qeneṣ:* I. A masculine noun signifying a snare for hunting. It is used figuratively of catching, laying a snare for right words, seeking for right words to express one's position (Job 18:2).

II. A masculine noun referring to an ending. It is taken by some to refer to an ending, a conclusion to the speaking of many words by Job (Job 18:2).

7079. קְנָת *q^enāṯ:* A proper noun designating Kenath (Num. 32:42; 1 Chr. 2:23).

7080. קָסַם *qāsam:* A verb meaning to practice divination. It occurs most frequently in the prophetic books as God's prophets proclaimed the judgment this practice brings (Isa. 3:2; Mic. 3:6, 7). God had earlier established that He would guide His people through true prophets, not through diviners (Deut. 18:10, 14). Thus, the falsity of divination is repeatedly pointed out by the prophets (Jer. 29:8; Ezek. 13:9; 22:28; Zech. 10:2). Nevertheless, divination was a problem for Israel as well as for other nations (1 Sam. 6:2; 28:8; 2 Kgs. 17:17). This Hebrew term is broad enough to encompass necromancy, augury, and visions (1 Sam. 28:8; Ezek. 21:21–29; Mic. 3:6, 7). Divination was quite profitable for some even in New Testament times (cf. Acts 16:16–18).

7081. קֶסֶם *qesem:* A masculine noun meaning divination. This word described the cultic practice of foreign nations that was prohibited in Israel (Deut. 18:10); and considered a great sin (1 Sam. 15:23; 2 Kgs. 17:17). False prophets used divination to prophesy in God's name, but God identified them as false (Jer. 14:14; Ezek. 13:6); and pledged to remove such practices from Israel (Ezek. 13:23). Several verses give some insight into what this actual practice looked like: it was compared to a kingly sentence (Prov. 16:10); and was used to discern between two choices (Ezek. 21:21[26], 22[27]).

7082. קָסַס ***qāsas:*** A verb meaning to cut off, to strip off. It means to prune, to remove. It is used with reference to cutting off the fruit of a tree but used figuratively of peoples or a nation (Ezek. 17:9).

7083. קֶסֶת ***qeset:*** A feminine noun meaning an inkhorn; a writing kit. It refers to a set of materials needed to write, to record something (Ezek. 9:2, 3, 11).

7084. קְעִילָה ***qeʿiylāh:*** A proper noun designating Keilah, a town in the low-lying hills (Shephelah) of Judah that had been inherited by them (Josh. 15:44). David, not yet king, fought and delivered the city from attacking Philistines (1 Sam. 23:1–6) but later had to flee the city when Saul learned of his presence there (1 Sam. 23:7, 8–13). Postexilic Jews resettled the city (Neh. 3:17, 18). It was located ca. 20 miles southwest of Jerusalem and west of Hebron.

7085. קַעֲקַע ***qaʿaqaʿ:*** A masculine noun referring to a tattoo, a mark. It indicates incised marks or patterns on a person's body. The practice was forbidden in Israel (Lev. 19:28).

7086. קְעָרָה ***qeʿārāh:*** A feminine noun indicating a plate, a dish. It refers to one category of utensils prepared for use in the Tabernacle, especially on the table of sheowbread (Ex. 25:29; 37:16). It refers to silver dishes that were donated to the Lord as offerings for the altar (Num. 7:13, 19, 25, etc.).

7087. קָפָא ***qāpāʾ:*** A verb meaning to curdle, to congeal; to become settled, stagnant. It refers to something standing still or slowing down its movement, becoming thick (Ex. 15:8). It is used figuratively of a person in great suffering being curdled, tossed about like hardening cream (Job 10:10). It depicts a dead or stagnant spirit in a person (Zeph. 1:12). It means, used with reference to the heavenly bodies, to shrink, to lose brightness (Zech. 14:6).

7088. קָפַד ***qāpad:*** I. A verb meaning to roll up. It describes something being rolled up, folded into a tubular form. It is used figuratively of closing out, rolling up one's life (Isa. 38:12).

II. A verb meaning to cut off. It describes a piece of cloth being cut off. In context it refers figuratively to Hezekiah's fear of the cutting off his life, like a weaver cuts off pieces of cloth (Isa. 38:12).

7089. קְפָדָה ***q^epāḏāh:*** A feminine noun meaning horror, terror. Early Jewish interpreters translated the word as destruction; however, terror follows better from the root, which means to roll up, to contract (*qāpaḏ* [7088]). The word occurs only in Ezekiel 7:25 where it refers to the fear that would come on Israel, causing them to seek peace they would not find. Ezekiel was prophesying of the coming Babylonian invasion, which led to the fall of Jerusalem in 586 B.C.

7090. קִפּוֹד ***qippôḏ,*** קִפֹּד ***qippōḏ:*** I. A masculine noun meaning a porcupine. It indicates a hedgehog, a spinous small animal that lives in the wild or among ruins (Isa. 14:23; 34:11; Zeph. 2:14). Here and in II, III below, the exact meaning of these words is still being researched.

II. A masculine noun meaning an owl. It is taken by some translators as a reference to a short-eared owl. This translation fits the contextual references, as does the word hedgehog (Isa. 14:23; 34:11; Zeph. 2:14).

III. A masculine noun referring to a bittern, a wading marsh bird. In some contexts, translators prefer this translation, referring to a long-legged, marsh loving wading bird (Isa. 14:23; 34:11; Zeph. 2:14).

7091. קִפּוֹז ***qippôz:*** I. A masculine noun indicating an owl, a great owl. Translators are divided about whether this refers to an owl of some kind or a small tree snake. See II also. In either case, it refers to a creature that makes its home among ruins, the wild, or in places of devastation (Isa. 34:15).

II. A masculine noun referring to a tree snake (Isa. 34:15). See I.

7092. קָפַץ ***qāpaṣ:*** A verb meaning to gather up, to shut, to close. It indicates the cutting off one's feelings (hand) toward a person, ceasing to give regard to (Deut. 15:7). It is used figuratively of unrighteousness, injustice shutting its mouth (Job 5:16; Ps. 107:42). It depicts God's withholding His compassion (Ps. 77:9[10]).

7093. קֵץ ***qēṣ:*** A masculine noun indicating an end of time or space. It refers to the finish, a final point, a goal of time, a space, or a purpose: It indicates a certain point reached in time (Gen. 4:3); the finish or demise of something, e.g., the human race (Gen. 6:13); the conclusion of a set period of time, e.g. forty days with the preposition *min* (4480) (Gen. 8:6; 16:3). There is an end of things, e.g., Israel (Amos 8:2). The final end of things as foretold by the prophets will be a time of the end (Ezek. 21:25[30], 29[34]; Dan. 8:17; 11:35, 40; 12:4, 9; Hab. 2:3); of God's peace in His kingdom, there will be no end (Isa. 9:7[6]); of people's life-long labor, toil, there is no cessation (Eccl. 4:8). In a spatial sense, it refers to the most remote areas (2 Kgs. 19:23; Jer. 50:26). There is seemingly no end to the flow of people, their number or extent (Eccl. 4:16). In a figurative sense, it describes the end or limit of words (Job 16:3); the completion of perfection attained in God's commandments (Ps. 119:96). The phrase *miqqēṣ yāmim layyāmîm* means at the end time of each year (2 Sam. 14:26). The word, with *min* (4480), followed by an infinitive of *hāyāh* is used to indicate the end of a set period of time (Esth. 2:12). With the definite article attached, it combines with the two following words to mean at the end of days of two years, that is, after two years (2 Chr. 21:19). It indicates the close of Israel's long period of oppression in Egypt, 430 years (2 Chr. 21:19).

7094. קָצַב *qāṣab̲:* A verb meaning to cut down; to cut off, to shear. It means to sever something, to separate by slicing, breaking (2 Kgs. 6:6). It is used to depict the shearing of sheep, cutting off their wool (Song 4:2).

7095. קֶצֶב *qeṣeb̲:* A masculine noun referring to a shape, a form, a size. It refers to the structure or configuration of something, its basic pattern; it is used in context of supporting stands or foundations and of the cherubim (1 Kgs. 6:25; 7:37).

7096. קָצָה *qāṣāh:* A verb meaning to cut off; to scrape. It means to rub the surface of something with an edge or rough tool to clean it or to remove unwanted residue (Lev. 14:41, 43). It means to decrease something in size, to diminish it, e.g., of sections of a nation that fall to a foreign power (2 Kgs. 10:32). It is used in figurative expressions (Prov. 26:6). To cut off a nation is to destroy it; to take away its people and dominion (Hab. 2:10).

7097. קָצֶה *qāṣeh,* קֵצֶה *qēṣeh:* I. A masculine noun meaning an end, an extremity, a border, an edge. It refers to the conclusion of a period of time (Gen. 8:3; Deut. 14:28; 2 Sam. 24:8). It has the sense of a border, an extremity, an edge, an end in spatial references: the end of a shepherd's staff (Judg. 6:21); a rod (1 Sam. 14:27, 43); curtains (Ex. 26:5; 36:12); the edge of a field or valley (Gen. 23:9; Josh. 15:8); a border (Num. 20:16). It refers to the rural areas of a city (Josh. 4:19; 1 Sam. 9:27). In certain expressions, it means from (among) one's brothers, from among all of them (Gen. 47:2). The phrase *miqqāṣṣeh* has the sense of from everywhere, in its entirety (Gen. 19:4 ; cf. Jer. 51:31).

II. A masculine noun meaning an end, a limit. It is used in negative expressions of the form *'ên qēṣeh,* often with l^e following, there is no end (to) . . . (Isa. 2:7; Nah. 2:9[10]). It indicates no limit or numbering of dead people (Nah. 3:3). It refers to the unlimited resources and power of Thebes in Egypt, without end (limits) (Nah. 3:9).

7098. קָצָה *qāṣāh:* A feminine noun indicating an end, an edge, an extremity. It refers to the outer extremities or outer extend of something: the ends of the mercy seat (Ex. 25:18, 19); the outer curtain of a set (Ex. 26:4); the corners of the bronze altar (Ex. 27:4); the ends of the ephod (Ex. 28:7); and breastpiece (Ex. 28:23–26). It has the sense of the whole, the extent of a number of people or group (Judg. 18:2; 1 Kgs. 12:31; 13:33; 2 Kgs. 17:32). It refers to the end of the wings, the wing tips of the cherubim in the Temple (1 Kgs. 6:24). It describes figuratively the mere fringes or periphery of God's ways (Job 26:14); and refers to the ends of the earth, the entire world as lying within God's purview (Job 28:24). It is used to refer to one end (of heaven) to the other, the entire heavens (Ps. 19:6[7]; 65:8; Isa. 41:5; Jer. 49:36). God created the ends of the earth, the entire world (Isa. 40:28). God gathered Israel from the ends of the earth, the entire world (Isa. 41:9). Jerusalem was totally corrupt, both ends and the middle of her (Ezek. 15:4). The term has the sense of many or all peoples (Hab. 2:10).

7099. קָצוּ ***qāṣû***, קִצְוָה ***qiṣwāh:*** A masculine noun meaning an end, an extremity, a corner. It refers to the ends of the ark in the Tabernacle (Ex. 37:8); of the bronze grating (Ex. 38:5); of the corners of the shoulder pieces (Ex. 39:4). It is used figuratively of the distant corners or ends of the earth (Ps. 48:10[11]; 65:5[6]; Isa. 26:15).

7100. קֶצַח ***qeṣaḥ:*** A masculine noun referring to a plant used for seasoning; dill, caraway, fitch. It refers to a bitter herb that produces aromatic leaves and bears bitter seeds used as a seasoning to preserve and flavor various foods (Isa. 28:25, 27).

7101. קָצִין ***qāṣiyn:*** A masculine noun meaning a captain, a ruler. The root meaning is one who decides. Sometimes the word indicates military leadership (Josh. 10:24; Judg. 11:6, 11; cf. Judg. 11:9; Dan. 11:18), but it can signify a nonmilitary authority (Isa. 3:6, 7). A captain could be chosen by men (Judg. 11:6; Isa. 3:6); but he was ultimately appointed by God (Judg. 11:11; cf. Judg. 2:16, 18; 11:29). Captains were sometimes subordinate to a higher human authority (Josh. 10:24; Dan. 11:18); but not always (Judg. 11:6, 11; cf. Judg. 12:7, 8). They had responsibility before God for the moral state of their followers (Isa. 1:10; Mic. 3:1, 9); but their subordinates also had responsibility to influence their rulers positively (Prov. 25:15).

7102. קְצִיעָה ***q^eṣiy'āh:*** A feminine noun referring to cassia. It refers to a spice made from the bark of a tree of the laurel family of plants. A coarse variety of cinnamon was obtained by grinding the bark (Ps. 45:8[9]).

7103. קְצִיעָה ***q^eṣiy'āh:*** A proper noun designating Keziah (Job 42:14).

7104. קְצִיץ ***q^eṣiyṣ:*** I. A masculine noun meaning harvest, reaping (Gen. 8:22; 30:14; 45:6; Ex. 23:16; 34:21, 22; Lev. 19:9; 23:10, 22; 25:5; 1 Sam. 6:13; 8:12; 12:17; 2 Sam. 21:9, 10;

23:13; Prov. 6:8; 10:5; 20:4; 25:13; 26:1; Isa. 23:3; Jer. 5:17, 24; 8:20; 50:16; 51:33; Hos. 6:11; Joel 1:11; Amos 4:7).

II. A masculine noun meaning bough, branch (Job 14:9; 18:16; 29:19; Ps. 80:11[12]; Isa. 27:11).

7105. קָצִיר *qāṣiyr:* I. A masculine noun indicating a harvest, a reaping. It refers to the time of the year set by God when crops have ripened and are harvested (Gen. 8:22; 30:14, April-June); and to the activity of harvesting itself (2 Sam. 21:9). The failure of a harvest was devastating (Gen. 45:6). Certain feasts were centered around times of harvesting (Ex. 23:16).

II. A masculine noun meaning a bough, a branch. It refers to a fresh bough or sprig springing forth from a stump, an indication of life (Job 14:9). It is used figuratively of the wicked whose branch is dead, cut off (Job 18:16); and to the prosperity of Job in his earlier years (Job 29:19). It is used of Israel's prospering (Ps. 80:11[12), but also to her state of ruin as dry limbs (Isa. 27:11).

7106. קָצַע *qāṣa':* I. A verb meaning to scrape. It means to rub or to move a sharp-edged tool or a rough tool over a surface, such as a plastered wall, to remove unwanted features or materials (Lev. 14:41).

II. A verb meaning to form a bend or a corner. It indicates the construction of boards or frames that meet to form a jointure, corner, or point (Ex. 26:23; 36:28). It is used in a causative passive stem to refer to corners already formed (Ezek. 46:22).

7107. קָצַף *qāṣap̱:* A verb meaning to be angry, to provoke to anger. The word refers to anger that arose because people failed to perform their duties properly. Pharaoh was angry with his baker and butcher (Gen. 40:2; 41:10); while Moses was angry with the people for hoarding manna (Ex. 16:20); Aaron's sons' apparent failure to follow rules of sacrifice (Lev. 10:16); and the captains' failure to finish off the enemy (Num. 31:14). King Ahasuerus was also angry with Vashti for failing to show off her beauty when summoned (Esth. 1:12). The word often expressed an authority being angry with a subject but not always (2 Kgs. 13:19; Esth. 2:21). Sometimes the anger was not justified (2 Kgs. 5:11; Jer. 37:15). The word could also refer to God being angry or provoked (Deut. 9:7, 8, 22; Zech. 1:2; 8:14); an anger that could be aroused by a corporate failure to keep troublemakers in line (Num. 16:22; Josh. 22:18). Isaiah 8:21 contains a reflexive form of the word, as if the anger was unable to find a reasonable object and thus caused the occult practitioners to fret themselves.

7108. קְצַף *qᵉṣap̱:* An Aramaic verb meaning to be angry. It corresponds to the Hebrew word *qāṣap̱* (7107) and refers to anger aroused by someone's failure to fulfill a duty properly. It occurs only in Daniel 2:12 where Nebuchadnezzar became angry over the failure of the Babylonian wise men to tell him his dream with its interpretation.

7109. קְצַף ***q^e^ṣap̱:*** An Aramaic masculine noun meaning anger. Like the word *q^e^ṣap̱* (7108), this word refers to anger aroused by someone's failure to fulfill a duty properly. The word occurs only in Ezra 7:23 where Artaxerxes commanded that work necessary for the second Temple was to be done diligently, lest God's wrath fall on Persia. Artaxerxes understood that his responsibility was to see that his subjects did their duties.

7110. קֶצֶף ***qeṣep̱:*** A masculine noun meaning wrath. The word refers to anger aroused by someone's failure to do a duty. For example, a wife in Persia who showed contempt for her husband by not doing her duties would arouse his wrath (Esth. 1:18). This word usually refers to God's wrath aroused by people failing to do their duties (Deut. 29:28[27]; Ps. 38:1[2]; Isa. 34:2). In some cases, this wrath was directed against sinful Gentile nations (Isa. 34:2; Zech. 1:15; cf. Rom. 1:18). In Israel's case, this duty was expressed in the Law of Moses (2 Chr. 19:10; Zech. 7:12; cf. Rom. 4:15). Atonement performed by priests turned away God's wrath when laws were broken (Num. 16:46 [17:11]; 2 Chr. 29:8; 27:24; 2 Chr. 29:8).

7111. קְצָפָה ***q^e^ṣāp̱āh:*** A feminine noun referring to a splintering, a peeling of bark. It refers to wood that is cracking, breaking up into many small pieces. In Joel it is caused by a vicious attack of locusts (Joel 1:7).

7112. קָצַץ ***qāṣaṣ,*** קָצוּץ ***qāṣûṣ:*** I. A verb meaning to cut off, to cut in pieces. It refers to a process of cutting sheets of gold into thin strips to use in woven materials. It was carried out by skilled craftsmen (Ex. 39:3). The verb is used of severing or cutting off something: a human hand (Deut. 25:12); human toes, fingers (Judg. 1:6, 7); feet (2 Sam. 4:12). It is used of cutting inanimate objects (2 Kgs. 16:17).

II. A verb meaning to be at the end, the utmost. The same word is understood to refer to a spatial location: farthest places, corners (Jer. 9:26; 25:23; 49:32).

III. An adjective meaning distant. It is understood as an adjective rather than a verbal form by some scholars (Jer. 9:26; 25:23; 49:32). The form itself, however, is a simple passive participle.

7113. קְצַץ ***q^e^ṣaṣ:*** An Aramaic verb meaning to cut off, to trim off. It describes the act of cutting off or pruning branches of a tree (Dan. 4:14[11]).

7114. קָצַר ***qāṣar:*** I. A verb meaning to reap, to harvest. It describes harvesting, gathering in a crop (Lev. 19:9; 23:10; 1 Sam. 6:13; 8:12). Its participial form *qôṣēr* refers to a reaper (Jer. 9:22[21]; Amos 9:13). It is used in a figurative sense of reaping the fruits of righteousness (Hos. 10:12); of evil (Hos. 8:7). Psalm 126:5 records the famous phrase that they who sow in tears, reap in joy.

II. A verb meaning to shorten; to become impatient. It describes something not being too short, e.g., the Lord's power to deliver (Num. 11:23). It refers to a shortening of time because of wickedness (Prov. 10:27). It refers figuratively to impatience or anxiety, annoyance (Num. 21:4; Judg. 10:16; 16:16; Job 21:4; Mic. 2:7); used with *min* (4480), it expresses a comparison of too short for something (Isa. 28:20). It has the sense of the Lord's shortening Himself, of holding back (Ps. 89:45[46]).

7115. קוֹצֶר *qôṣer:* A masculine noun indicating despair, anguish, discouragement. The word means literally short. In context it refers to a shortness of spirit, depression because of oppression (Ex. 6:9).

7116. קָצָר *qāṣār:* An adjective meaning weak, few, hasty. It means literally short of something: of might, strength (2 Kgs. 19:26; Isa. 37:27); of days, short-lived (Job 14:1); of nostrils, an idiom for short-tempered, irascible (Prov. 14:17); of a short spirit, impatience (Prov. 14:29).

7117. קְצָת *qeṣāṯ:* A feminine noun meaning an end, a corner, a part. It refers to the four ends or corners of the mercy seat (Ex. 38:5); the outer top edges of the ephod (Ex. 39:4); the outer reaches of the earth (Ps. 65:8[9]). It indicates a portion or a part of some whole from among the leaders of Israel (Neh. 7:70[69]); such as the Jewish exiles(Dan. 1:2, 5, 15, 18).

7118. קְצָת *qeṣāṯ:* A feminine noun meaning an end, a part. It indicates a share or a part of a larger whole: a part or a share of a kingdom (Dan. 2:42). It indicates the conclusion of a period of time (Dan. 4:29[26], 34[31]).

7119. קַר *qar:* An adjective meaning cold, cool; even-tempered. Used in a simile, it refers to chilly or cold refreshing water that soothes the soul (Prov. 25:25; Jer. 18:14). Cold water, especially cool spring water, was highly prized in Israel, in the hot ancient Near East.

7120. קֹר *qōr:* A masculine noun referring to cold. It refers to the low temperatures of winter, to a condition that is chilly, lacking adequate heat (Gen. 8:22).

7121. קָרָא *qārā':* A verb meaning to call, to declare, to summon, to invite, to read, to be called, to be invoked, to be named. The verb means to call or to summon, but its context and surrounding grammatical setting determine the various shades of meaning given to the word. Abraham called on the name of the Lord (Gen. 4:26; 12:8); the Lord called to Adam (Gen. 3:9; Ex. 3:4). With the Hebrew preposition meaning to, the verb means to name. Adam named all the animals and birds (Gen. 2:20; 3:20); and God named the light day (Gen. 1:5). The word may introduce a long message, as in Exodus 34:6, that gives the moral and ethical definition of God. It can also mean to summon, such as when God summoned Bezalel to build the Tabernacle (Ex. 31:2).

In certain contexts, the verb has the sense of proclaiming or announcing. Jezebel urged Ahab to proclaim a holy day of fasting so Naboth could be killed (1 Kgs. 21:9); the Servant of Isaiah proclaimed freedom for the captives and prisoners (Isa. 61:1). The word may mean simply to call out or cry out, as Potiphar's wife said she did (Gen. 39:15; 1 Kgs. 18:27, 28).

The word means to read aloud from a scroll or a book: the king of Israel was to read aloud from a copy of the Law (Deut. 17:19); just as Moses read the Book of the Covenant to all Israel at Sinai (Ex. 24:7). Baruch read the scroll of Jeremiah to the people (Jer. 36:6, 8).

In the passive stem, the word means to be called or summoned: Esther was called by name (Esth. 2:14); in the book of Esther, the secretaries who were to carry out the king's orders were summoned (Esth. 3:12; Isa. 31:4). News that was delivered was called out or reported (Jer. 4:20). In Nehemiah's reform, the Book of Moses was read aloud in the audience of the people (Neh. 13:1). Also, Eve was called, that is, named, woman (Gen. 2:23). The word takes on the nuance of to be reckoned or called. Genesis 21:12 describes how Abraham's seed would be reckoned by the Lord through Isaac.

7122. קָרָא *qārā':* A verb meaning to meet, to encounter, to come across, to happen. It states that something has taken place, occurred, happened, good, bad, or neutral (Gen. 42:4, 38; Ex. 1:10). It refers to the entire sweep of events yet to happen to the sons of Jacob and their descendants (Gen. 49:1). It refers to divine encounters (Ex. 5:3). It indicates a chance happening (Deut. 22:6; 2 Sam. 1:6). It is used of divine judgments occurring (Isa. 51:19; Jer. 13:22; 32:23; 44:23).

7123. קְרָא *q^e^rā':* An Aramaic verb meaning to read; to call, to shout. It refers to the act of reading a written document, silently or orally (Ezra 4:18, 23); or to calling out or proclaiming something aloud (Dan. 3:4; 4:14[11]; 5:7, 8, 12, 15–17).

7124. קֹרֵא *qōrē':* A masculine noun meaning partridge. It refers to a relatively small bird with an orange-brown head, grayish neck, and rust-colored tail. It was difficult to spot and hunt (1 Sam. 26:20). It is used in a simile for comparison (Jer. 17:11).

7125. קִרְאָה *qir'āh:* A masculine noun referring to a meeting, an encounter. This is the *qal* infinitive construct of the verb *qārā'*, to meet, to encounter, etc. See 7122. It has the preposition *l^e^* prefixed to it. It is used most often with verbs indicating motion (Gen. 14:17; 19:1; 24:17; Judg.

4:18, 22; 7:24; 20:25, 31; 1 Sam. 4:1). It has the sense of to encounter, to experience (Josh. 11:20; Amos 4:12). It occurs several times following *hinneh,* behold, at once, thereupon (1 Sam. 10:10; 2 Sam. 15:32; 16:1).

7126. קָרַב ***qāraḇ:*** A verb meaning to come near, to approach. The basic concept is a close, spatial proximity of the subject and the object (Gen. 37:18; Deut. 4:11); although it is also possible for this word to introduce actual contact (Ezek. 37:7; cf. Ex. 14:20; Judg. 19:13). This verb is also used in a temporal context to indicate the imminence of some event (Gen. 27:41). This usage is common to communicate the impending doom of God's judgment, like Moses' day of calamity and the prophet's day of the Lord (Lam. 4:18). This term has also developed several technical meanings. It can refer to armed conflict. Sometimes it is clarified by modifiers, such as to fight or unto battle (Deut. 20:10). Other times, this word alone carries the full verbal idea of entering into battle. Some of these instances are clear by context (Deut. 25:11; Josh. 8:5); however, there are others where this meaning may be missed (Deut. 2:37; Ps. 27:2; 91:10; 119:150; cf. Deut. 2:19). Another technical meaning refers to sexual relations (Gen. 20:4; Deut. 22:14; Isa. 8:3). One other technical meaning refers to the protocol for presenting an offering to God (Ex. 29:4; Lev. 1:5, 13, 14; Num. 16:9).

7127. קְרֵב ***q^{e}rēḇ:*** An Aramaic verb meaning to approach. It is used as a technical term to describe bringing a sacrifice, offering something to God (Ezra 6:10, 17; 7:17). It means simply to step up for a purpose (Dan. 3:8; 6:12[13]); to come near to something (Dan. 3:8, 26; 6:12[13], 20[21]). It is used when formally presenting a person (Dan. 7:13); or when personally approaching a person (Dan. 7:16).

7128. קְרָב ***q^{e}rāḇ:*** A masculine noun indicating a battle, a war. It refers to a state of formally declared hostilities against a people (2 Sam. 17:11); a time for carrying out hostilities (Job 38:23).

7129. קְרָב ***q^{e}rāḇ:*** An Aramaic masculine noun meaning war. It refers to formal acts of hostility against someone, constituting a military attack, a war, a battle (Dan. 7:21). It is used figuratively of a battle carried out against someone on a personal or a spiritual level (see Ps. 55:18[19]). It describes an attitude or a state of the heart (see Ps. 55:21[22]). The Lord will fight as on a day of battle for His people to establish and defend them (see Zech. 14:3).

7130. קֶרֶב ***qereḇ:*** A masculine noun meaning midst, middle, interior, inner part, inner organs, bowels, inner being. The term occurs 222 times in the Old Testament and denotes the center or inner part of anything, e.g., the middle of a battle (1le of the streets (Isa. 5:25); but especially the inner organs of the body. In the ceremony to ordain Aaron and his sons as priests for ministry to the Lord, all the fat that covered the inner organs of the sacrifices was to be burned on the altar (Ex. 29:13, 22; see also Lev. 1:13, 9:14). On many other occasions, however, the word is utilized abstractly to describe the inner being of a person. This place was regarded as the home of the heart from which the emotions spring (Ps. 39:3[4]; 55:4[5]; Lam. 1:20). It was also viewed as the source of thoughts (Gen. 18:12; Ps. 62:4[5]; Jer. 9:8[7]), which are often deceitful, wicked, and full of cursing. Yet wisdom from God can reside there also (1 Kgs. 3:28). This inner being is also the seat of one's moral disposition and thus one's affections and desires. David, grieved over his sin with Bathsheba, pleaded with God to place a right or steadfast spirit within him (lit., in [his] inner being), so that he might always desire to stay close to God and obey His laws (Ps. 51:10[12]). The Lord promised to place His Law in the inner beings of His people Israel (Jer. 31:33; see also Ezek. 11:19, 36:26, 27).

7131. קָרֵב ***qārēḇ:*** An adjective meaning drawing near, approaching. It refers to something or someone who approaches, comes close to something or someone: those at the king's table (1 Kgs. 4:27[5:7]); an advancing soldier (1 Sam. 17:41); those approaching to engage in battle (Deut. 20:3). Some persons were forbidden to come near to certain holy things (Num. 1:51; 3:10, 38; 17:13 [28]; 18:7). Only certain people could come near and serve at Ezekiel's Temple (Ezek. 40:46; 45:4).

7132. קִרְבָה ***qirḇāh:*** A feminine noun indicating an approach; a drawing near, being near. It indicates a closeness, a proximity of someone to something; in its context, it refers to God's nearness (Ps. 73:28; Isa. 58:2).

7133. קָרְבָּן ***qorbān,*** קֻרְבָּן ***qurbān:*** A masculine noun meaning an offering, a gift. This is the most general term, used eighty times in the Old Testament, for offerings and gifts of all kinds. The word is found in Leviticus referring to animal offerings of all permissible types (Lev. 1:2, 3); grain offerings of fine flour (Lev. 2:1, 5); gifts or votive offerings of gold vessels. It is found in Numbers referring to silver vessels and rings (Num. 7:13; 31:50) and jewelry (Num. 31:50).

Ezekiel uses the word to designate an offering. Israel corrupted the land by presenting their offerings at every high hill, leafy tree, and high place (Ezek. 20:28). Happily, the second use in Ezekiel depicts the table where the flesh offering would be properly presented within the restored Temple (Ezek. 40:43).

7134. קַרְדֹּם ***qardōm:*** A masculine noun meaning ax. It refers to a tool with a sharp edge used to cut down trees and large shrubs, to chop wood, etc. (Judg. 9:48; 1 Sam. 13:20, 21; Jer. 46:22). It is used in a simile of the devastation of Israel's enemies (Ps. 74:5; Jer. 46:22).

7135. קָרָה ***qārāh:*** A feminine noun meaning cold. It refers to a condition without sufficient heat or warmth (Job 24:7; 37:9). God creates the cold (Ps. 147:17). It is used to form similes for comparison (Prov. 25:20; Nah. 3:17).

7136. קָרָה ***qārāh:*** I. A verb meaning to meet; to occur, to happen. It states that something happens, comes about, whether good or bad: Abraham's servant prayed that God would grant him success, to let it come about (Gen. 27:20); it refers to an entire episode of events (Gen. 42:29); or to a specific event (Gen. 44:29). It is used of an event in which God is involved or is behind the scenes working something out (Ex. 3:18; Ruth 2:3; Esth. 4:7). It indicates of what will happen in the future (Isa. 41:22; Dan. 10:14).

II. A verb meaning to lay beams of wood. It describes in a technical sense the putting of beams of wood into a structure, especially into the Temple (2 Chr. 34:11); into a new wall of Jerusalem (Neh. 2:8; 3:3, 6). It is used figuratively of God's laying beams in the structure of the heavens (Ps. 104:3).

7137. קָרֶה ***qāreh:*** A masculine noun indicating a temporary sickness. It refers to a man's nocturnal emission of semen during the night, which rendered him temporarily unclean (Deut. 23:10).

7138. קָרוֹב, קָרֹב ***qārôḇ, qārōḇ:*** An adjective meaning near, close by, closely related. It indicates nearness in time or space: something is about to happen, is near at hand, e.g., judgment, calamity (Deut. 32:35); (not) near at hand, a prophetic fulfillment (Num. 24:17); a fool's destruction is not far off (Prov. 10:14). It refers to the imminent coming of God's day of judgment (Zeph. 1:7, 14); to a town that is close by (Gen. 19:20). Joseph lived near the area of Pharaoh's habitation (Gen. 45:10). It is used of a neighbor's house (Ex. 12:4); or indicates a road near by (Ex. 13:17). It is used in a figurative sense of a person's coming near to listen to words of wisdom (Eccl. 5:1[4:17]). It indicates a relationship, a relative (Ex. 32:27; Num. 27:11; 2 Sam. 19:42[43]); among humans, but also a relationship to God (Lev. 10:3; 1 Kgs. 8:46, 59; Ps. 119:151). It refers to a friend (Ps. 15:3).

7139. קָרַח ***qāraḥ:*** A verb meaning to shave the head, to make bald. It refers to cutting off one's hair (Lev. 21:5; Ezek. 27:31; Mic. 1:16) as a sign of mourning; the practice was forbidden to Israelite priests for various reasons. It is a sign of great effort and of labor expended, of wearing down a person (Ezek. 29:18).

7140. קֶרַח ***qeraḥ:*** A masculine noun indicating ice, frost. It indicates extreme cold in general (Gen. 31:40; Jer. 36:30). It refers to condensed frozen water that forms small ice crystals (Job 6:16). It is described as one of God's wonderful works (Job 37:10; 38:29; Ps. 147:17). It indicates a shiny, gleaming roof or ceiling (Ezek. 1:22).

7141. קֹרַח ***qōraḥ:*** A proper noun designating Korah:

A. A son of Esau through his Canaanite wife Oholibamah, daughter of Anah and granddaughter of the Hivite, Zibeon. He was a chief or leader of Esau's descendants through Oholibamah (Gen. 36:5–18).

B. A chief or leader in Edom, the son of Eliphaz, Esau's oldest son—and grandson of Adah, his first Canaanite wife (Gen. 36:15–16).

C. A Levite of the line of Kohath who rebelled against the leadership position of Moses in the wilderness wanderings (Ex. 6:21, 24; Num. 16:1–49). He and his cohorts were "swallowed" up by an earthquake (Num. 16:28–35).

D. A descendent of Caleb through Hebron (1 Chr. 2:43).

7142. קֵרֵחַ ***qērēaḥ:*** An adjective meaning bald. It refers to a condition in which a man loses his hair (Lev. 13:40). He is still considered ritually clean. Elisha, a great prophet, was naturally bald (2 Kgs. 2:23).

7143. קָרֵחַ ***qārēaḥ:*** A proper noun designating Kareah (2 Kgs. 25:23; Jer. 40:8, 13, 15, 16; 41:11, 13, 14, 16; 42:1, 8; 43:2, 4, 5).

7144. קָרְחָה ***qorḥāh,*** קָרְחָא ***qorḥā':*** A feminine noun meaning baldness, a shaved head. It refers to baldness created by shaving one's head, a practice forbidden to priests in Israel (Lev. 21:5; Isa. 15:2). It was a practice forbidden to anyone as a sign of the dead (Deut. 14:1). It is used poetically as the opposite of hair styles that displayed the beauty of one's hair (Isa. 3:24). It could be a sign of mourning (Isa. 22:12; Mic. 1:16); or of devastation (Jer. 47:5; 48:37; Amos 8:10).

7145. קָרְחִי ***qorḥiy:*** A proper noun designating Korahites (Ex. 6:24; Num. 26:58; 1 Chr. 9:19, 31; 12:6; 26:1, 19; 2 Chr. 20:19).

7146. קָרַחַת ***qārḥaṯ:*** A feminine noun indicating a bald head, a bald spot. It refers to a bare spot or an area eaten away or deteriorating in a piece of clothing (Lev. 13:55). It refers to an area that has become bald on a person's head (Lev. 13:42, 43).

7147. קְרִי ***qeriy:*** A masculine noun indicating hostility, contrariness. It is used with the verb *halak̲* to mean to walk, to act with hostility (Lev. 26:21, 23, 24, 27, 40, 41). It is used with *ḥamāh* to mean with anger, hostility, extreme hostility (Lev. 26:28).

7148. קָרִיא ***qāriy':*** An adjective meaning appointed, called. It indicates that a person has been appointed or summoned for something (Num. 1:16; 26:9). It has the sense of important, influential (Num. 16:2).

7149. קִרְיָא qiryāʾ, קִרְיָה qiryāh: A feminine Aramaic noun meaning city. It refers to a city, e.g., Samaria, a place where groups of people had settled (Ezra 4:10, 12, 13, 15, 16, 19, 21).

7150. קְרִיאָה qᵉriyʾāh: A masculine noun meaning proclamation. It refers to a message proclaimed, literally the proclamation or oral message itself (Jonah 3:2).

7151. קִרְיָה qiryāh: A feminine noun meaning a city or town. It refers to a city or town, often Jerusalem as the central city of Judah (Num. 21:28; Deut. 2:36; 3:4). It is used also as part of the proper name of many cities: Kiriath-arba, city of Arba, Hebron (Josh. 15:13; 21:11). Jerusalem is called the city of the Great King (Ps. 48:2[3]). The word is used in its construct form (*qiryaṯ*) with a following word, e.g., the city of his strength, his fortress, a figurative expression in Proverbs 10:15 (Jer. 49:25).

7152. קְרִיּוֹת qᵉriyyôṯ, קְרִיּוֹת חֶצְרוֹן qᵉriyyôṯ ḥeṣrôn: I. A popular noun designating Kerioth (Josh. 15:25[KJV]; Jer. 48:24, 41; Amos 2:2).

II. A popular noun designating Kerioth Hezron (NASB, NIV, Josh. 15:25).

7153. קִרְיַת אַרְבַּע qiryaṯ ʾarbaʿ, קִרְיַת הָאַרְבַּע qiryaṯ hāʾarbaʿ: A proper noun designating Kiriath Arba. The name means "city of Arba," and is an older name for Hebron (Gen. 23:2; 35:27). Sarah died there. Earlier, the city had been the home of the Anakites of whom Arba was the greatest (Josh. 14:15) and an ancestor of Anak (Josh. 15:13). It was used even after the return of the exiles to Judah (Neh. 11:25).

7154. קִרְיַת בַּעַל qiryaṯ baʿal: A proper noun designating Kiriath Baal (Josh. 15:60; 18:14).

7155. קִרְיַת חֻצוֹת qiryaṯ ḥuṣôṯ: A proper noun designating Kiriath Huzoth (Num. 22:39).

7156. קִרְיָתַיִם qiryāṯayim: A proper noun designating Kiriathaim:

A. A city east of the Jordan River (Num. 32:37; Josh. 13:19; Jer. 48:1, 23; Ezek. 25:9).

B. A town in Naphtali (1 Chr. 6:76[61]).

7157. קִרְיַת יְעָרִים qiryaṯ yᵉʿāriym, קִרְיַת עָרִים qiryaṯ ʿāriym, קִרְיַת qiryaṯ: A proper noun designating Kiriath Jearim:

A. A city located about eight miles west of Jerusalem. Its name means "city of the forest." It concluded a deceitful treaty with the Israelites (along with Gibeon and Beer) so that Israel was not able to destroy its inhabitants (Josh. 9:17). The men were reduced to woodcutters and water carriers (Josh. 9:18–21). It was identified with Kiriath Baal by the biblical writer (Josh. 18:14–15; see 7154).

It was located in Judah on its northern border touching Benjamin. The ark was temporarily stored there in David's time until he transferred it to Jerusalem (1 Sam. 6:21; 7:1, 2; 1 Chr. 13:5, 6). The city produced at least one prophet (Jer. 26:20). It was resettled by returned exiles (Neh. 7:29).

B. A city given to Benjamin, possibly the same as A.

7158. קִרְיַת סֵפֶר ***qiryaṯ sēp̱er,*** קִרְיַת סַנָּה ***qiryath sannāh:*** I. A proper noun designating Kiriath Sepher (Josh. 15:15, 16; Judg. 1:11, 12).

II. A proper noun designating Kiriath Sannah (Josh. 15:49).

7159. קָרַם ***qāram:*** A verb meaning to cover. It is used figuratively of the Lord's covering the desiccated bones of a destroyed Israel with flesh (Ezek. 37:6, 8).

7160. קָרַן ***qāran:*** I. A verb meaning to radiate light; to shine. It describes the skin of Moses' face as luminous, sending out light from its surface (Ex. 34:29, 30, 35).

II. A verb meaning to have horns. It refers to a young bull with horns that made a choice sacrifice (Ps. 69:31[32]).

7161. קֶרֶן ***qeren,*** קַרְנַיִם ***qarnayim:*** I. A feminine noun meaning a horn, a hill. It refers to the bony projections that grow out of the heads of various hoofed animals (Gen. 22:13). But its meaning is expanded to refer to the horn-like protrusions on the corners or edges of altars, possibly representing strength, power (Ex. 27:2; Jer. 48:25); blood was applied to these horns during the use of the altar (Ex. 29:12). Iron horns were manufactured (1 Kgs. 22:11). Horns were used to make musical instruments, shophar, ram's horn, etc. (Josh. 6:5). The term describes strength, honor, rulership, dignity, fertility, descendants (1 Sam. 2:10); fertility, descendants (1 Sam. 2:1; Ps. 89:17[18]); the power and source of salvation (2 Sam. 22:3). To raise up one's horn meant to act arrogantly, insolently (Ps. 75:4[5]). The special anointing oil was sometimes kept in a horn, a container made of a hollowed-out horn (1 Kgs. 1:39).

II. A proper noun Karnaim. The name means two horns. This city was located about twenty miles east of the Sea of Galilee.

7162. קֶרֶן ***qeren:*** An Aramaic feminine noun meaning a horn, a cornet. It refers to a musical instrument made from a horn (Dan. 3:5, 7, 10, 15); a vision of a little horn that will arise, representing a king (Dan. 7:7, 8, 11, 20, 21, 24).

7163. קֶרֶן הַפּוּךְ ***qeren happûḵ:*** A proper noun designating Keren-Happuch, a daughter of Job (Job 42:14).

7164. קָרַס ***qāras:*** A verb meaning to stoop, to bend low. It is used mockingly of Bel, a Babylonian idol, that stoops over, wavers, for Babylon is destroyed (Isa. 46:1, 2).

7165. קֶרֶס ***qeres:*** A masculine noun referring to a clasp, a hook. It refers to the instrument used to connect curtains, tent sections, the veil, etc., to each other in the Tabernacle. They were made of gold or bronze (Ex. 26:6, 11, 33; 35:11; 36:13, 18; 39:33).

7166. קַרְסֹל *qarsōl:* A feminine noun indicating an ankle, a foot. It is used figuratively of the Lord's making His people safe and stabile of so their feet do not slide or slip (2 Sam. 22:37; Ps. 18:36[37]).

7167. קָרַע *qāra':* A verb meaning to tear, to rend. It refers to ripping apart a piece of clothing, parchment, or cloth (Gen. 37:29, 34; Ex. 28:32; Jer. 36:23, 24); sometimes it was a sign of mourning or fear (Gen. 44:13; 1 Sam. 4:12). It is used figuratively of tearing away, removing a king's authority (1 Kgs. 11:11–13); of God's tearing the heavens (Isa. 64:1[63:19]); of Israel's tearing her heart instead of her garments (Joel 2:13). It describes the process of cutting out a window in a house (Jer. 22:14). It refers figuratively to tearing apart one's eyes with cosmetics, that is, expanding them, enlarging them (Jer. 4:30). In its passive form, it means to be torn apart, torn up (Ex. 39:23; 1 Kgs. 13:3, 5). It is used of the tearing, ripping of wild beasts (Ps. 35:15; Hos. 13:8). In the latter reference, it refers to the Lord's activity.

7168. קֶרַע *qera':* A masculine noun meaning a piece. It refers to a piece of cloth or a garment that has been torn; rags, the clothing of the poor (1 Kgs. 11:30, 31; 2 Kgs. 2:12; Prov. 23:21),.

7169. קָרַץ *qāraṣ:* I. A verb meaning to wink, to compress the lips. It refers to persons' blinking or winking their eyes with mocking, malicious, or deceitful intent (Ps. 35:19). Such actions indicate worthless, useless persons (Prov. 6:13; 10:10; 16:30).

II. A verb meaning to form. In context the word means to make, to form; a man is formed from clay (Job 33:6). It would mean to compress from clay and therefore is the same word as I.

7170. קְרַץ *q^{e}raṣ:* An Aramaic verb meaning to accuse, to denounce. It refers to bringing a formal charge or accusation against a person (Dan. 3:8; 6:24[5]). Others considered this word a noun meaning piece. The word is used in the plural form and means literally pieces, their pieces, since it has a suffix in Aramaic. The word *'kl,* to eat, precedes, rendering the idiomatic, they devoured (ate) his/their pieces (bone?); that is, they maliciously accused them/Daniel.

7171. קֶרֶץ *qereṣ:* A masculine noun possibly meaning destruction. It is found only in Jeremiah 46:20. Due to the immediate context of the passage, however, the more probable meaning is biter (i.e., a biting fly, such as a gadfly, a horsefly, or a mosquito). Egypt was described as a beautiful heifer, but a biting fly from the north (i.e., Babylon) was being sent to punish her. This noun is derived from the verb *qāraṣ* (7169).

7172. קַרְקַע ***qarqa':*** A masculine noun meaning a floor, the bottom. It indicates the floor or bottom of a structure or even a dirt floor in a tent (Num. 5:17). The Temple had cypress floorboards (1 Kgs. 6:15, 16, 30). Solomon's palace featured cedar flooring (1 Kgs. 7:7). It refers to the bottom of the sea once (Amos 9:3), stressing its depth.

7173. קַרְקַע ***qarqa':*** A proper noun designating Karka (Josh. 15:3).

7174. קַרְקֹר ***qarqōr:*** A proper noun designating Karkor (Judg. 8:10).

7175. קֶרֶשׁ ***qereš:*** A masculine noun indicating a board, a frame. It refers to the boards and planks of acacia wood prepared for the Tabernacle (Ex. 26:15–23, 25–29; 35:11; 36:20–28, 30–34; 39:33; 40:18). It has the sense of an inlaid floor, a deck with boards, planks (Ezek. 27:6). Some scholars prefer to translate this word as frame or panel in some references. Its exact technical meaning still eludes us at this time.

7176. קֶרֶת ***qereṯ:*** A feminine noun meaning city. The word uniformly indicates a town, a city, a village (Job 29:7; Prov. 8:3; 9:3, 14; 11:11).

7177. קַרְתָּה ***qartāh:*** A proper noun designating Kartah (Josh. 21:34; I Chr. 6:77[62]).

7178. קַרְתָּן ***qartān:*** A proper noun designating Kartan (Josh. 21:32).

7179. קַשׁ ***qaš:*** A verb meaning stubble, chaff. It refers to the short dry stumps of grain, corn, wheat, etc., left in a field after harvesting. It burned quickly once it was ignited (Mal. 4:1[3:19]). It was of little value and not highly prized. It was a poor substitute for straw in brick making (Ex. 5:12; 15:7). Job refers to himself as died-out chaff or stubble in a metaphor (Job 13:25). God turns His enemies into stubble or chaff (Ps. 83:13[14]). God scattered His people like stubble in the wind (Jer. 13:24).

7180. קִשֻּׁאָה ***qiššu'āh:*** A feminine noun meaning a cucumber. It refers to an Egyptian family of cucumbers, succulent, full of water. They were a favorite food of the Israelites in Egypt (Num. 11:5).

7181. קָשַׁב ***qāšaḇ:*** A verb meaning to listen carefully, to pay attention, to give heed, to obey. The basic significance of the term is to denote the activity of paying close attention to something, usually another person's words or sometimes to something that can be seen (e.g., Isa. 21:7). Job pleaded for his three friends to listen to his words (Job 13:6; see also Isa. 32:3; Jer. 23:18). Often the term functioned as an appeal to God to hear and respond to an urgent prayer (Ps. 17:1; 61:1[2]; 66:19; cf. Ps. 5:2[3]). At other times, it denoted the obedience that was expected after the hearing of the Lord's requirements (1 Sam. 15:22; Neh. 9:34; Isa. 48:18). Israel's history, however, was characterized by a life of hard-heartedness and rebellion. Jeremiah declared that this was due to the fact that Israel's ears were uncircumcised; therefore, they could not listen so they were able to obey (Jer. 6:10).

7182. קֶשֶׁב *qešeḇ:* A masculine noun indicating attentiveness, response. It means to focus on something, to pay attention, to watch closely (1 Kgs. 18:29; Isa. 21:7). It can have the sense of simply any response or movement (2 Kgs. 4:31).

7183. קַשָּׁב *qaššāḇ*, קַשֻּׁב *qaššuḇ:* I. An adjective meaning attentive. It means for someone to be responsive, caring, especially of God's care and attention to His people through hearing their prayers (Neh. 1:6, 11).

II. An adjective meaning attentive. It refers to God's response figuratively to the prayers of His people (2 Chr. 6:40), through both His ears and His eyes (2 Chr. 7:15; Ps. 130:2).

7184. קַשָׂה *qaśāh*, קַשְׂוָה *qaśwāh:* I. A feminine noun referring to a jar, a cup. It refers to some of the various utensils used in the Tabernacle (Ex. 25:29; 37:16; Num. 4:7) and later the Temple (1 Chr. 28:17). They probably were used in pouring libation offerings and therefore were holy vessels.

II. A feminine noun meaning cover. In earlier translations, the word was rendered as cover or covers in certain passages (KJV; NKJV, pitchers; Ex. 25:29; 37:16; Num. 4:7).

7185. קָשָׁה *qāšāh:* A verb meaning to be hard; to be hardened, stiffnecked. It indicates that something is difficult, hard, cruel, severe, harsh, e.g., a difficult birth (Gen. 35:16, 17); harsh anger or wrath (Gen. 49:7). It is one of the words used to describe a hardened heart (Ex. 7:3; 13:15); a resentful heart or attitude (Deut. 15:18). It refers to a hardened spirit created by the Lord (Deut. 2:30). In its passive sense, it indicates a person oppressed, crushed (Isa. 8:21). It is used figuratively of making circumstances difficult for persons, making heavy yokes for them (1 Kgs. 12:4). To harden or stiffen one's neck means to become stubborn (2 Kgs. 17:14; Jer. 7:26; 17:23; 19:15).

7186. קָשֶׁה *qāšeh:* An adjective meaning hard, harsh, cruel, severe, strong, violent, fierce. This term's basic function is to describe something as hard. The word modifies a variety of different subjects and encompasses a fairly broad range of meanings. The labor the Egyptians imposed on the Hebrews was described as hard (i.e., harsh, Ex. 1:14; 6:9). Joseph spoke hard words to his brothers at first (Gen. 42:7, 30; cf. 1 Sam. 20:10). A Calebite named Nabal was labeled as being hard, i.e., cruel and evil (1 Sam. 25:3). The

Israelites were often characterized as being hard or stiff of neck, i.e., stubborn, rebellious, obstinate (Ex. 32:9, 33:3, 5; Deut. 9:6, 13; cf. Ezek. 3:7). An experience could be hard, i.e., painful (Ps. 60:3[5]); as could a vision or revelation (Isa. 21:2). Hannah was hard of spirit, that is, deeply troubled (1 Sam. 1:15). Both battles and winds could be hard, i.e., fierce (2 Sam. 2:17; Isa. 27:8). Moses chose capable men from all Israel to serve as judges; they judged minor cases while Moses himself judged the difficult ones (Ex. 18:26).

7187. קְשׁוֹט ***qāšôṭ*, קְשֹׁט *qᵉšōṭ*:** An Aramaic masculine noun meaning truth. The term is utilized twice, with both occurrences embedded within the book of Daniel. After being deeply humbled by the Lord, Nebuchadnezzar praised God and acknowledged that all His works were truth (Dan. 4:37[34]). Prior to this humbling, King Nebuchadnezzar had declared Daniel's God in truth to be the God of gods, i.e., truly (Dan. 2:47). Nevertheless, this knowledge failed to penetrate his proud heart, because in the very next section of text, Nebuchadnezzar built a monumental golden idol. This word is equivalent to the Hebrew term *qōšeṭ* (7189).

7188. קָשַׁח ***qāšah̩*:** A verb meaning to make hard, to treat roughly. Used twice in the Old Testament, this word implies a hardening similar to the formation of a callous. It signifies the hardening of a mother's heart toward her offspring (Job 39:16); and is used by Isaiah to connote the spiritual dullness of the people toward God (Isa. 63:17).

7189. קֹשֶׁט ***qōšeṭ*, קֹשְׁט *qōšᵉṭ*:** A masculine noun meaning truth, certainty. This word comes from an unused root meaning to balance, as in a scale. It appears twice in the Wisdom Literature, meaning the vindication of a true assessment by reality (Ps. 60:4[6]); and the realization of a person's truthfulness by an intimate knowledge of the individual (Prov. 22:21).

7190. קְשִׁי ***qᵉšiy*:** A masculine noun indicating stubbornness. It indicates a current condition of attitude as well as a past history of demonstrated refusal to obey the Lord's covenantal words (Deut. 9:27).

7191. קִשְׁיוֹן ***qišyôn*:** A proper noun designating Kishion (Josh. 19:20; 21:28).

7192. קְשִׂיטָה ***qᵉśiyṭāh*:** A feminine noun referring to a piece of money, silver. It refers to pieces of silver money used by Jacob to purchase a piece of land (Gen. 33:19; Josh. 24:32). It refers to money given to Job to help restore his good health and fortune (Job 42:11).

7193. קַשְׂקֶשֶׂת ***qaśqeśeṯ*:** A feminine noun indicating scales; scale armor. It refers to thin, overlapping plates for protection; the scales of a fish. Israel was permitted to eat these fish with fins and scales (Lev. 11:9, 10, 12; Deut. 14:9, 10). It refers to armor worn by a warrior made with overlapping protective materials (1 Sam. 17:5). It is used figuratively of the scales of Egypt (Ezek. 29:4).

7194. קָשַׁר ***qāšar:*** A verb meaning to conspire; to bind. It refers literally to binding or tying something up (Gen. 38:28; Josh. 2:18, 21; Jer. 51:63); figuratively attacking or fastening something on (Isa. 49:18); controlling, binding the Pleiades constellation (Job 38:31). It is used of connecting a wall together (Neh. 4:6[3:38], 8[2]). It has many figurative uses: it is used of Jacob's soul being bound up with Benjamin (Gen. 44:30); of Jonathan's soul being bound to David's soul (1 Sam. 18:1); of forming a conspiracy together, forming an alliance against someone (1 Kgs. 15:27; 16:20; 2 Kgs. 9:14). It is used to indicate the binding of religious, moral, spiritual, and eternal teachings or concepts to oneself (Deut. 6:8; 11:18; Prov. 3:3; 6:21; 7:3).

7195. קֶשֶׁר ***qešer:*** A masculine noun indicating a conspiracy, a treason. It refers to a binding together of persons for hostile reasons: Absalom against David (2 Sam. 15:12); Zimri's conspiracy (1 Kgs. 16:20), etc. Conspiracy could be good as well as bad (Isa. 8:12). There were many conspiracies among the Israelites themselves (Jer. 11:9). Even certain prophets were guilty of conspiracy against God and the people (Ezek. 22:25).

7196. קִשֻּׁרִים ***qiššuriym:*** A masculine plural noun indicating headbands, sashes, attire. It refers to the wedding dress worn at a woman's marriage ceremony (Jer. 2:32). God's coming judgments would violently remove all these luxury items from among His people (Isa. 3:20).

7197. קָשַׁשׁ ***qāšaš:*** A verb meaning to gather things; to assemble together. It describes the Israelites' gathering together stubble to make bricks (Ex. 5:7, 12); pieces of wood or sticks (Num. 15:32, 33; 1 Kgs. 17:10, 12). It indicates people gathering themselves together (Zeph. 2:1).

7198. קֶשֶׁת ***qešeṯ:*** A feminine noun indicating a bow; a rainbow. It is used figuratively of God's bow, the rainbow set for all time in the heavens (Gen. 9:13, 14, 16). Otherwise, it refers to one of the most common weapons of war in antiquity, a bow (Gen. 48:22; Josh. 24:12; Hos. 2:18 [20]). A bowshot was the distance covered by an arrow shot from a bow (Gen. 21:16). The bow and arrow was commonly used for hunting (Gen. 27:3). The phrase *ben-qešeṯ,* son of a bow referred to an arrow, a useless weapon against Leviathan (Job 41:28 [20]). Judah is described as the Lord's bow (Zech. 9:13). The phrase *rišp̱ê-qāšet* means the flaming of the bow, its arrows (Ps. 76:3[4]). Hosea speaks of a bow of deception, one that misses its goal, when referring to his people Israel (Hos. 7:16). Job speaks of a bow (20:24). Isaiah 21:17 refers to bowmen, lit., the number of the bow. Men with the bow refers to archers, bowmen (1 Sam. 31:3).

7199. קַשָּׁת ***qaššāṯ:*** A masculine noun referring to an archer. It indicates a person trained in the use of a bow; specifically it refers to Hagar's son Ishmael who learned the skill of a bowman (Gen. 21:20).

ר Resh

7200. רָאָה **rā'āh,** רֹאֶה **rō'eh:** A verb meaning to see. Its basic denotation is to see with the eyes (Gen. 27:1). It can also have the following derived meanings, all of which require the individual to see physically outside of himself or herself: to see so that one can learn to know, whether it be another person (Deut. 33:9) or God (Deut. 1:31; 11:2); to experience (Jer. 5:12; 14:13; 20:18; 42:14); to perceive (Gen. 1:4, 10, 12, 18, 21, 25, 31; Ex. 3:4); to see by volition (Gen. 9:22, 23; 42:9, 12); to look after or to visit (Gen. 37:14; 1 Sam. 20:29); to watch (1 Sam. 6:9); to find (1 Sam. 16:17); to select (2 Kgs. 10:3); to be concerned with (Gen. 39:23). It is also possible for this verb to require the individual to make a mental observation. As an imperative, it can function as an exclamation similar to *hinnēh* (2009), which means to behold (Gen. 27:27; 31:50). Further, it can denote to give attention to (Jer. 2:31); to look into or inquire (1 Sam. 24:15[16]); to take heed (Ex. 10:10); to discern (Eccl. 1:16; 3:13); to distinguish (Mal. 3:18); to consider or reflect on (Eccl. 7:14). It can also connote a spiritual observation and comprehension by means of seeing visions (Gen. 41:22; Isa. 30:10).

7201. רָאָה **rā'āh:** A feminine noun indicating a bird of prey; a red kite, a globe. It was among the unclean birds, forbidden food to the Israelites (Deut. 14:13). It is classed among accipitrine birds having long, pointed wings, possibly a forked tail. They feed on insects, reptiles, and small mammals.

7202. רָאֶה **rā'eh:** An adjective meaning seeing. This word appears in Job 10:15 in an idiomatic use, meaning to be drenched or utterly covered with affliction. The connection with the root meaning stems from the visible signs of being afflicted.

7203. רֹאֶה **rō'eh:** A masculine noun meaning a seer, prophetic vision. The word is the active participle of *rā'āh* (7200), which signifies a prophet (see 1 Chr. 9:22, Isa. 30:10). It refers to the vision or insight that the prophet receives (Isa. 28:7).

7204. רֹאֶה **rō'eh,** הָרֹאֶה **hārō'eh:** A proper noun designating Haroeh (1 Chr. 2:52).

7205. רְאוּבֵן **r^{e}'ûḇēn:** A proper noun designating Reuben, the firstborn son of Jacob. His mother was Leah (Gen. 29:32). The name means "behold (see) a son." He was more merciful toward Joseph than his other brothers (Gen. 37:21–29) and tried to save him (Gen. 42:22). During the famine, he told his father that he (Jacob) would kill his (Reuben's) sons if he did not bring Benjamin back from Egypt (Gen. 42:37). Unfortunately, Reuben slept with one of Jacob's concubines, a sin that impacted Jacob's blessing on him (Gen. 49:3–4). He became indecisive and could no longer be a leader in Israel, he or his descendants. Jacob gave a double portion of blessing to Joseph, not Reuben as firstborn (Gen. 49:22–26). Reubenites took part in the rebellion against Moses in the wilderness (Num. 16:1). The tribe inherited territory east of the Dead Sea from the Arnon River (south) to the Jabbok River (north). Mount Nebo and Heshbon were in its territory. Ezekiel alloted a place for Reuben in his vision of the new Temple and New Jerusalem (Ezek. 48:6–31).

7206. רְאוּבֵנִי ***rᵉ'ûḇēniy:*** A proper noun designating a Reubenite, a descendant of Reuben (Num. 26:7; 34:14; Deut. 3:12, 16; 4:43; 29:8[7]; Josh. 1:12; 12:6; 13:8; 22:1; 2 Kgs. 10:33; 1 Chr. 5:6, 26; 11:42; 12:37 [38]; 26:32; 27:16).

7207. רַאֲוָה ***raᵃwāh:*** A verb infinitive meaning to behold, to see. Appearing only once in the Old Testament, the word alludes to looking on the outward appearance and fondly admiring an object (Eccl. 5:11[10]).

7208. רְאוּמָה ***rᵉ'ûmāh:*** A proper noun designating Reumah (Gen. 22:24).

7209. רְאִי ***rᵉ'iy:*** A masculine noun meaning mirror . The primary meaning is that of a looking glass used to see one's own reflection. Job uses the word metaphorically to refer to the sky (Job 37:18).

7210. רֳאִי ***rᵒ'iy:*** A masculine noun meaning sight, an appearance, a spectacle. The basic force of this word is that of a visible appearance. It is used in reference to God's ability to see (Gen. 16:13); the outward look of an individual (1 Sam. 16:12); and a visual spectacle that drew attention to itself (Nah. 3:6).

7211. רְאָיָה ***rᵉ'āyāh:*** A proper noun designating Reaiah (1 Chr. 4:2; 5:5; Ezra 2:47; Neh. 7:50).

7212. רְאִית ***rᵉ'iyṯ,*** רְאוּת ***rᵉ'ûṯ:*** A feminine noun meaning look, sight. The word is derived from the verb *rā'āh* (7200) and is used to denote a looking on of goods by their owner. The author of Ecclesiastes rhetorically inquired as to the good of increasing wealth and goods, if only for the owner merely to look on them (Eccl. 5:11[10]).

7213. רָאַם ***rā'am:*** A verb meaning to rise, to be lifted up. It refers to something being raised high above other things. It refers to Jerusalem's exalted place in the era of God's Great King (Zech. 14:10).

7214. רְאֵם ***rᵉ'ēm,*** רְאֵים ***rᵉ'ēym,*** רֵים ***rēym,*** רֵם ***rēm:*** A masculine noun indicating a wild ox. It refers to a large animal with horns that are powerful offensive as well as defensive weapons (Num. 23:22; 24:8; Ps. 22:21[22]). God is its creator and provider (Job

39:9, 10). It is used figuratively of Joseph's strength and fecundity (Deut. 33:17); and of the strength God gives His people, their exalted horn indicating their success (Ps. 92:10[11]). It stands for powerful persons, influential people (Isa. 34:7).

7215. רָאמוֹת *rāʾmôṯ:* A feminine plural noun meaning coral. It refers to a precious stone or some precious substance of great value to be compared to wisdom (Job 28:18). It was used on the international scene as a medium of exchange or trading (Ezek. 27:16).

7216. רָאמוֹת *rāʾmôṯ,* רָאמֹת *rāʾmōṯ:* A proper noun designating Ramoth:

A. A city in Gilead (Deut. 4:43; Josh. 20:8; 21:38; 1 Chr. 6:80[65]). See also Ramoth Gilead (7433).

B. A city in Issachar (1 Chr. 6:73[58]).

7217. רֵאשׁ *rᵉʾēš:* An Aramaic masculine noun meaning head. The word is used to indicate the head of a man (Dan. 3:27); of an image constructed by Nebuchadnezzar (Dan. 2:32, 38); and a beast in Daniel's vision (Dan. 7:6, 20). This word is also used to denote a receptacle for dreams and visions (i.e., the head [Dan. 7:1]), and in the same verse it represents the sum total (i.e., essential matter). Ezra used this noun to indicate those people who served in the capacity of leaders (Ezra 5:10).

7218. רֹאשׁ *rōʾš:* A masculine noun meaning a head, hair, a person, a point, the top, the beginning, the best, a chief, a leader. It is clear from the multitude of legitimate translations of this word that it has many metaphorical meanings. In Scripture, the word is used to refer to a human head (Gen. 40:16); it also refers to animal heads as well, such as the serpent's head (Gen. 3:15); a dog; an ass; a living being (2 Sam. 3:8; 2 Kgs. 6:25; Ezek. 1:22). It regularly indicates the heads of animals being sacrificed (Ex. 12:9; 29:15, 19).

This word is used in several Hebrew idioms: to bring something down on someone's head is to get vengeance (Ezek. 9:10); and to sprinkle dust on one's head is to mourn and show despair (Josh. 7:6; Ezek. 27:30).

The word can designate an individual person: It refers to Joseph's head as representative of his whole tribe (Gen. 49:26; Deut. 33:16). It refers to the top or peak of things and indicates the tops of mountains (Gen. 8:5); such as the top of Mount Olives in 2 Samuel 15:32 or even the top of a bed (Gen. 47:31).

This Hebrew word commonly designates the beginning of something: It refers to the head or beginning of the year (Ezek. 40:1); or month (Ex. 12:2). Its use extends to describing the best of something. The best spices or myrrh were depicted by this word (Ex. 30:23), as were the most influential persons: commanders (Deut. 20:9; Ezek. 10:11); the heads or leaders of families and chiefs (1 Kgs. 8:1; 1 Chr.

24:31); the chief priest of Israel (1 Chr. 27:5). It is used with a superlative connotation to describe the chief cornerstone (Ps. 118:22); or the most lofty stars (Job 22:12).

In some places, the word is best translated to indicate the entire or complete amount of something: the Lord made the chief part of the dust of the earth, i.e., all of it (Prov. 8:26). It also meant to take (or lift up) the total number of people, i.e., take a census (Ex. 30:12). The psalmist asserted that the sum total of God's words are righteous forever (Ps. 119:160).

It also indicates the source of a river or branch as its head (Gen. 2:10). When combined with the noun dog, it expresses a major insult. Abner used the term of himself, a dog's head, as a term of disgust (2 Sam. 3:8).

7219. ראשׁ *rōʾš*, רוֹשׁ *rôš*: A masculine noun meaning poison, bitterness, gall. It refers to something that is a life-threatening substance. In context it refers to human hostility or bitterness (Deut. 29:18[17]). It defines grapes as poisonous, grapes that represent pagan peoples (Deut. 32:32). It describes pagan wine as like the poison of cobras (Deut. 32:33). Job described the wicked person as one who partakes of the poison of cobras (Job 20:16). It refers to water that is poisoned (Jer. 8:14; 9:15[14]; 23:15). In context it may have the sense of harshness, gall, bitterness (Lam. 3:5, 19). Justice and/or injustice is described as being poisonous, transformed into deadly corruption socially (Hos. 10:4; Amos 6:12).

7220. ראשׁ *rōʾš*: A proper noun designating Rosh:

A. Son or grandson of Benjamin (Gen. 46:21).

B. An unknown kingdom (Isa. 66:19; Ezek. 38:2, 3; 39:1). In the King James Version and New International Version, these instances are interpreted as the noun meaning chief (7218).

7221. רִאשָׁה *riʾšāh*: A feminine noun meaning a beginning. Ezekiel used the word to denote an earlier time (Ezek. 36:11). He spoke figuratively, saying that the Lord would make the mountains of Israel more prosperous than before. The Lord would also increase the number of people and animals, who would in turn be fruitful and multiply.

7222. רֹאשָׁה *rōʾšāh*: An adjective meaning head, chief. It occurs only in Zechariah 4:7 where it describes a stone. The adjective sometimes indicates that the stone is the cornerstone, the first stone laid (see *rōʾš* [7218]). However, it often refers to the top stone as being at a prominent place on the Temple structure (cf. Matt. 4:5), like the head is atop the body. The latter makes better sense in context because the foundation was already laid at the time of the prophecies that use this word (cf. Ezra 5; Zech. 1:1; 4:9). The stone may be the same stone mentioned in Zechariah

3:9 and 4:10, which is clearly a symbol of Christ (cf. Zech. 4:10; Rev. 5:6). It would make sense for Jesus, the Alpha and the Omega (Rev. 1:8), to be both the first stone (cf. Isa. 28:16; 1 Pet. 2:4–8) and the last stone laid in the Temple.

7223. רִאשׁוֹן riʾšôn, רִאשֹׁן riʾšōn: An adjective meaning first, former, foremost, earlier, head, chief. This term occurs 182 times and denotes that which comes first among given items, whether in place, rank, or order (Gen. 25:25, 32:17[18]; 2 Kgs. 1:14) or (more frequently) in time. Moses had the Tabernacle set up in the first month, just as the Lord commanded (Ex. 40:2, 17; cf. Num. 9:5; Ezra 7:9; Ezek. 45:18, 21). Zechariah warned the exiles who returned to the Promised Land from the Babylonian captivity not to be like their ancestors who refused to listen to the former prophets (Zech. 1:4, 7:7, 12). The Lord declares Himself to be the first and the last, the Eternal One (Isa. 44:6, 48:12). In later Hebrew, the word came to signify the highest in rank or authority (i.e., chief, head). The archangel Michael is portrayed as holding the rank of chief prince (Dan. 10:13; cf. 1 Chr. 18:17; Esth. 1:14). This word is derived from the noun *rōʾš* (7218).

7224. רִאשֹׁנִי riʾšôniy: An adjective meaning first. The word is derived from the noun *rōʾš* (7218) and corresponds closely in meaning to the adjective *riʾšôn* (7223). It occurs only in Jeremiah 25:1. The word of the Lord concerning all the people of Judah came to Jeremiah in the first year of King Nebuchadnezzar's reign over all Babylon.

7225. רֵאשִׁית rēʾšiyṯ: A noun meaning the beginning, the first, the chief, the best, the firstfruits. Occurring fifty-one times in the Old Testament, this term holds the honor of being the first word written in the entire Bible (Gen. 1:1). Often, the term denotes the point in time or space at which something started, except when it specifies the point when time and space themselves were started (Isa. 46:10). It conveys the beginning of strife (Prov. 17:14); of a ruler's reign (Jer. 26:1, 27:1; 28:1; 49:34); of a sin (Mic. 1:13); of a kingdom (Gen. 10:10); or of wisdom and knowledge (Ps. 111:10; Prov. 1:7). On other occasions, the term signifies the highest of anything, i.e., the best or most excellent, such as the choicest parts of offerings (1 Sam. 2:29); the best of the spoil (1 Sam. 15:21); or the finest in oils (Amos 6:6). Elsewhere, the word designates the earliest or first products or results of something. It refers many times to the first products of a harvest (Lev. 23:10; Deut. 18:4; Neh. 12:44); and sometimes to the first product, i.e., the firstborn of a father (Gen. 49:3; Deut. 21:17). Both this term and the noun *rōʾš* (7218) are derived from the same unused verbal root.

7226. רַאֲשֹׁת ra'ᵃsōṯ: A noun meaning bolster (1 Sam. 26:12). Some observe that it is not a known Hebrew form, and so assign this occurrence to the noun *mᵉra'ᵃšôṯ* (4763,II), a pillow or bolster.

7227. רַב raḇ: I. An adjective meaning many, much, great, long, mighty. The word indicates much, many, abundance, numerous; it indicates much in amount, e.g., gold (1 Kgs. 10:2); silver (2 Kgs. 12:10[11]); wine (Esth. 1:7); etc. It indicates a large number people (Gen. 50:20; Ex. 5:5; Judg. 8:30); a long time, many days (Gen. 21:34; 37:34). It indicates an abundance of some things: blessings (Prov. 28:20); straw (Gen. 24:25). It is used with *min* (4480), from, than, following to indicate more . . . than (Ex. 1:9; Num. 22:15). Used as an adverb, it indicates much, exceedingly (Ps. 123:3); greatly, seriously (Ps. 62:2[3]). It modifies and defines space at times, a long distance (1 Sam. 26:13); the depth of the sea or the deep itself (Gen. 7:11; Amos 7:4). It indicates something greater than something else (Deut. 7:1, 17; 9:14). The phrase *wayyēleḵ hālôḵ wārāḇ*, indicates in context, the sound became louder and louder, greater and greater (1 Sam. 14:19). Followed by *min* (4480), it may mean enough of . . . (Ex. 9:28). The phrase *raḇ lāḵem min-* means, too much for one to . . . (in context, to go up to Jerusalem; 1 Kgs. 12:28).

II. An adjective meaning chief, captain, high official. It indicates that someone or something is of great importance. It indicates the leader, the chief of a group (2 Kgs. 18:17; 25:8); the chief officer, head of the royal guard respectively (cf. Dan. 1:3). It indicates the captain of a ship (Jon. 1:6, *raḇ haḥoḇēl*). In the plural, it indicates the leading officers or officials (Jer. 39:13; 41:1).

7228. רַב raḇ: A masculine noun indicating an archer; an arrow. The word is uncertain. It seems to mean archers (Job 16:13) or arrows (Jer. 50:29).

7229. רַב raḇ: An Aramaic adjective meaning great, boastful, large. Used to define words, it indicates words of insolence (Dan. 7:20). It indicates that a king is great (Dan. 2:10); a statue is huge (Dan. 2:31); a magician is the head, chief musician (Dan. 4:9[6]); a nation is great (Dan. 4:30[27]).

7230. רֹב rōḇ: A masculine noun indicating a large number, a great number, an abundance. It is used to indicate that something is numerous, such as people (Gen. 16:10; 30:30); that there is an abundance of something (Gen. 27:28). Preceded by *mē* (*min*), it means because of the multitude (Gen. 32:12[13]). It is used with various words to form phrases: *roḇ dereḵ*, a long distance, road (Josh. 9:13); *roḇ yāmîm*, many days, a long time, etc. (Isa. 24:22). The idiom *lāroḇ* means in respect to a multitude, a number (Josh. 11:4).

7231. רָבַב ***rāḇaḇ:*** A verb meaning to be many; to be increased or multiplied. It refers to the multiplication of the human race on earth (Gen. 6:1). It indicates the intensity, the multiplication of the cry against the cities of Sodom and Gomorrah (Gen. 18:20). In the intensive stem it may have the sense of a ten-thousand-fold increase (Ps. 144:13). With *min* (from, than) following, it means more than . . . (Jer. 46:23).

7232. רָבַב ***rāḇaḇ:*** A verb meaning to shoot, to shoot out. It describes archers shooting arrows (Gen. 49:23). Figuratively, it describes God's sending forth His protective arrows (Ps. 18:14[15]).

7233. רְבָבָה ***r^{e}ḇāḇāh:*** A feminine noun meaning ten thousand, a myriad, countless. It indicates great multitudes of people or things, almost innumerable, thousands of ten thousands (Gen. 24:60); a number that cannot be counted (Num. 10:36). It indicates figuratively that Israel's hundred will chase ten thousands of the enemy (Lev. 26:8; Deut. 32:30; Ps. 91:7). It refers to multitudes of heavenly beings (Deut. 33:2); or to the multitudes of Israel (Deut. 33:17). It is used in proverbs and idioms to express a great multitude (Song 5:10; Mic. 6:7).

7234. רָבַד ***rāḇaḏ:*** A verb meaning to spread a covering over something. It is used of laying a blanket, a covering of some kind, over a couch; it was probably a decorative covering (Prov. 7:16).

7235. הַרְבֵּה ,רָבָה ***rāḇāh, harbēh:*** I. A verb meaning to be many or to become many; to be abundant. It means to become numerous or great: it expresses God's original mandate for humans to multiply on earth (Gen. 1:22, 28). It depicts the increase of Israelites in Egypt (Ex. 1:10, 12); it refers to an increase in volume, extent, power, or influence (Gen. 7:17, 18; Ps. 49:16[17]; Daniel 12:4). It is used for both animals and inanimate things (Ex. 11:9; Deut. 7:22; 8:13; Ezek. 31:5). It refers to an increase or multiplication of time: days (Gen. 38:12); years (Prov. 4:10). It indicates in a comprehensive sense God's greatness over humans (Job 33:12). In the intensive or causative stems of the verb, it indicates the increasing or enlarging of someone or something: (Judg. 9:29; Ps. 44:12[13]; Lam. 2:22; Ezek. 19:2). God makes His followers great (2 Sam. 22:36; Ps. 18:35[36]); the leaders of His people (1 Chr. 4:10). He increases in number persons, things (Deut. 17:16; Hos. 2:8[10]). Adverbially (especially *harbēh*), it means to do something, to perform greatly (Amos 4:4). The phrase *harbāh 'arbeh* means I will increase, multiply greatly (Gen. 3:16; 16:10; 22:17).

II. An adjective indicating to be much or many; to be abundant. It refers to a great number of something (2 Sam. 1:4; Jon. 4:11). Used with a preposition and *m^e'oḏ*, it means very much (2 Chr. 11:12; 16:8; Neh. 5:18).

As an adverb, it intensifies, usually used with m^e'*o<u>d</u>* following, much very, very much . . . (Gen. 41:49; Josh. 13:1; Neh. 2:2), but it is found alone also (2 Kgs. 10:18; Eccl. 5:20[19]). It may indicate a great amount of something, much brass (2 Sam. 8:8).

III. A verb meaning to shoot an arrow, to deliver it toward its target.

7236. רְבָה ***$r^e\underline{b}\bar{a}h$:*** An Aramaic verb meaning to become large; to become great. It refers to raising a person's official rank or position (Dan. 2:48). It describes a process of growth (Dan. 4:11[8], 20[17], 33[30]); and the process of the increase in a ruler's power and greatness (Dan. 4:22[19]).

7237. רַבָּה ***rabbāh:*** A proper noun designating Rabbah, a Transjordanian Ammonite city that housed the famous huge bed of Og, king of Bashan (Deut. 3:11). The iron bed was thirteen feet long and six feet wide. The city was in the eastern edge of Ammon toward the eastern desert, about twelve miles south of the Jabbok River. David captured the city (2 Sam. 11:1; 12:26–29). Later, its king acted kindly toward David and received him as a fugitive (2 Sam. 17:27). The prophets spoke of the city a few times in judgment, asserting that it would become a pile of ruins (Jer. 49:2, 3; Ezek. 21:20[25]; 25:5; Amos 1:14).

7238. רְבוּ ***$r^e\underline{b}\hat{u}$:*** An Aramaic feminine noun indicating greatness, majesty. It is an abstract noun referring to the splendor, grandeur, and honor surrounding a great king or ruler (Dan. 4:22[19], 36[33]); all the benefits bestowed by God (Dan. 5:18, 19). It indicates the majesty and greatness of all the kingdoms of the earth (Dan. 7:27).

7239. רִבּוֹ ***ribbô:*** A feminine noun meaning ten thousand, a myriad; a thousand. It refers to a host that cannot be numbered, usually translated as ten thousand: persons (Ezra 2:64; Neh. 7:66; Jon. 4:11). The number intended is indefinite sometimes (Dan. 11:12); of things: of numerical values: 10,000 darics, 18,000 talents of brass (1 Chr. 29:7); 61,000 drachmas (Ezra 2:69), etc. It refers to twice ten thousand charities (Ps. 68:17[18]).

7240. רִבּוֹ ***ribbô:*** An Aramaic feminine noun meaning ten thousand; a myriad. It refers to an innumerable host of persons. Ten thousand is employed figuratively (Dan. 7:10).

7241. רָבִיב ***$r\bar{a}\underline{b}iy\underline{b}$:*** A masculine noun indicating a rain shower. It refers to a refreshing, mild rain (Deut. 32:2); showers (Ps. 65:10[11]) that invigorate the grass (Ps. 72:6; Jer. 3:3). God is the giver of the rain (Jer. 14:22). It is used in similes (Mic. 5:7[6]).

7242. רָבִיד ***$r\bar{a}\underline{b}iy\underline{d}$:*** A masculine noun indicating a chain, a necklace. It indicates an ornamental necklace worn around the neck to indicate authority and honor (Gen. 41:42). It indicates in general decorative ornamental chains (2 Chr. 3:16). Figuratively, it speaks of God's magnificent care for His people (Ezek. 16:11).

7243. רְבִיעִי rᵉḇiyʻiy, רְבִעִי rᵉḇiʻiy: An adjective meaning fourth, a fourth part. It is an ordinal number indicating the fourth item in a series (Gen. 1:19; 2:14; 15:16). It indicates a fourth of something, a fraction, e.g., one-fourth of a hin (Ex. 29:40; Lev. 23:13; Num. 15:4). It can stand at the end of a construct chain to refer to the fourth in a series (2 Kgs. 10:30). It means a square, foursquare in its feminine form (Ezek. 48:20).

7244. רְבִיעִי rᵉḇiyʻiy, רְבִעִי rᵉḇiʻiy: An adjective meaning fourth, a fourth part. It serves as an ordinal number indicating the fourth in a series (Dan. 2:40; 3:25; 7:7).

7245. רַבִּית rabbiyṯ: A proper noun designating Rabbith (Josh. 19:20).

7246. רָבַךְ rāḇaḵ: I. A verb meaning to mix, to stir. It is used only in a passive form of the verb meaning something mixed, stirred. Usually olive oil is mixed with dough, cakes, etc. (Lev. 6:21[14]; 7:12; 1 Chr. 23:29).

II. A verb meaning to bake, to fry. It describes the baking, frying, preparations for dough or cakes (Lev. 6:21[14]; 7:12; 1 Chr. 23:29).

7247. רִבְלָה riḇlāh: A proper noun designating Riblah, a city located on the Orontes River in Syria. It is ca. sixty miles north and east of Damascus, capital of Syria and ca. seven miles south of Hamath. A number of destructive events for Israel occurred in this city: Pharaoh Neco of Egypt took Jehoahaz captive in chains (2 Kgs. 23:33); Zedekiah, the last king of Judah, was captured in Riblah and taken to Babylon (2 Kgs. 25:6–21; Jer. 39:5, 6; 52:9–27).

7248. רַב־מָג raḇ-māg: I. A proper noun designating Rab-mag, a position in Babylon (KJV, NASB, Jer. 39:3, 13).

II. A phrase meaning high official, from *rāḇ* (7227,II) and *māg*, official (NIV, Jer. 39:3, 13).

7249. רַב־סָרִיס raḇ-sāriys: I. A masculine proper noun Rab-saris. It refers to leading military officials for the kings of Assyria (2 Kgs. 18:17); of Babylon (Jer. 39:3, 13). *Rab* in these titular names indicates a chief, a captain, a leader.

II. A masculine noun, Rab-saris; a military title for Babylon's chief officer. A person in charge of the eunuchs or chief officials of the Babylonian king (Jer. 39:3, 13).

7250. רָבַע rāḇaʻ: A verb indicating to lie down, to mate with an animal. It is used in its biblical context of lying with someone to mate, human or beast (Lev. 18:23; 19:19; 20:16). But it is used in a neutral context of the act merely of lying down to rest (Ps. 139:3).

7251. רָבַע rāḇaʻ: A verb meaning to be square. It defines something as being square, having four equal sides, ends, tops, bottoms and is used of various items in the Tabernacle complex (Ex. 27:1; 28:16); Solomon's palace (1 Kgs. 7:5, 31); Ezekiel's court for his Temple (Ezek. 40:47); and various other items (Ezek. 41:21; 43:16; 45:2).

7252. רֶבַע ***re<u>b</u>aʻ:*** A verb meaning to lie down. The word in question is the infinitive construct of *rā<u>b</u>aʻ* used with a first person suffix, "my lying down" (Ps. 139:3).

7253. רֶבַע ***re<u>b</u>aʻ:*** A masculine noun indicating a fourth part, a quarter; four sides. It refers to a fraction or a portion of something; one-fourth of a hin of oil or wine (Ex. 29:40); one-fourth of a shekel (1 Sam. 9:8). It indicates that something has four sides (Ezek. 1:8; 43:16, 17). It indicates four options, sides, etc. (Ezek. 10:11).

7254. רֶבַע ***re<u>b</u>aʻ:*** A proper noun designating Reba (Num. 31:8; Josh. 13:21).

7255. רֹבַע ***rō<u>b</u>aʻ:*** A masculine noun meaning a quarter; a fourth part. It is used to indicate a fraction or part of something, a fourth part (Num. 23:10; 2 Kgs. 6:25).

7256. רִבֵּעַ ***ribbēaʻ:*** An adjective meaning fourth. It is employed as a noun to refer in context to the fourth generation(s) (Ex. 20:5; 34:7; Num. 14:18; Deut. 5:9).

7257. רָבַץ ***rā<u>b</u>aṣ:*** A verb meaning to lie down, to rest; to lay something down. It is used figuratively of sin lying, crouching at the door (Gen. 4:7); and it is used figuratively of a curse resting on a person (Deut. 29:20[19]). It refers to animals lying down, domestic or wild (Gen. 49:9; Ex. 23:5). It describes birds sitting on their eggs (Deut. 22:6). It describes persons lying down in rest, reposing (Job 11:19; Isa. 14:30); in security and safety (Ezek. 34:14). It means in its causative stem to lay, to set stones (Isa. 54:11); to cause one's flock to lie down to rest (Song 1:7).

7258. רֵבֶץ ***rē<u>b</u>eṣ:*** A masculine noun referring to a resting place, a dwelling place. Figuratively, it depicts a resting place, a place of security for the righteous person (Prov. 24:15). In a more literal sense, it indicates a safe resting place where danger is removed (Isa. 35:7); a pleasant place to live, a home (Isa. 65:10; Jer. 50:6).

7259. רִבְקָה ***ri<u>b</u>qāh:*** A proper noun designating Rebekah, the daughter of Bethuel and granddaughter of Nahor, Abraham's brother (Gen. 22:20–24). She became Isaac's wife and bore Esau and Jacob, twins (Gen. 25:21–26). She was an Aramean and also the sister of Laban (Gen. 25:20). Isaac gave her, deceitfully, to Abimelech for a while who quickly returned her when the Lord revealed the situation to him in a dream (Gen. 26:7–11). Esau grieved her and Isaac by marrying a Canaanite (Gen. 26:35). She helped Jacob surreptitiously get Esau's blessing (Gen. 27:1—28:9). He and Isaac happily sent Jacob to Paddan

Aram to get a wife (Gen. 28:5). She died (an event not mentioned) and was buried in the burial cave in the field of Machpelah (Gen. 49:29–30).

7260. רַבְרַב ***rab̲rab̲:*** An Aramaic adjective meaning great; great things. It refers to the value and significance of great gifts, such as rulership, authority, etc. (Dan. 2:48). It indicates the splendor and magnificence of God's signs and words as great (Dan. 4:3[3:33]). It describes the awesome and powerful aspects of the four beasts of Daniel's vision (Dan. 7:3, 7, 8, 17). It may have the sense of boastful, arrogant words uttered (Dan. 7:11, 20).

7261. רַבְרְבָן ***rab̲r***^e^***b̲ān:*** An Aramaic masculine noun meaning a noble, a lord. The term occurs only in the plural and is found only in the book of Daniel. Nebuchadnezzar and Belshazzar, both kings of Babylon at one point, were served and sought by a great host of these important officials (Dan. 4:36[33]; 5:1–3, 9, 10, 23; 6:17[18]).

7262. רַב־שָׁקֵה ***rab̲-šāqēh:*** I. A proper noun designating Rabshakeh (KJV, NASB, 2 Kgs. 18:17, 19, 26–28, 37; 19:4, 8; Isa. 36:2, 4, 11–13, 22; 37:4, 8).

II. A phrase meaning a field commander in the Assyrian army (NIV, 2 Kgs. 18:17, 19, 26–28, 37; 19:4, 8; Isa. 36:2, 4, 11–13, 22; 37:4, 8).

7263. רֶגֶב ***regeb̲:*** A masculine noun indicating a clod of soil. In Job 38:38, the phenomenon of dirt forming into clods is reckoned as a work of God. The clods of soil serve to cover the wicked dead (Job 21:33).

7264. רָגַז ***rāgaz:*** A verb meaning to shake, to tremble, to agitate, to disturb, to rouse up, to rage, to provoke. This term occurs forty-one times in the Old Testament and is utilized most often to express the idea of the physical moving or shaking of someone or something. Lands (1 Sam. 14:15; Amos 8:8); mountains (Ps. 18:7[8]; Isa. 5:25); the heavens (2 Sam. 22:8); kingdoms (Isa. 23:11); and even the whole earth (Joel 2:10) are described as being shaken in this way, with the Lord's anger often given as the basis for the quaking. Often people, whether groups or individuals, would shake, i.e., were moved or stirred by deep emotions in response to specific circumstances. They trembled in fear (Ex. 15:14; Deut. 2:25; Isa. 64:2[1]; Joel 2:1; Mic. 7:17); or shook in agitation or anger (Prov. 29:9; Ezek. 16:43); and even grief (2 Sam. 18:33[19:1]). Sometimes the word signifies the disturbing or rousing up of someone (1 Sam. 28:15; 2 Sam. 7:10; 1 Chr. 17:9). Occasionally, it conveys the act of rebelling or raging against another, literally, to shake oneself against someone (cf. 2 Kgs. 19:27, 28; Isa. 37:28, 29). This verb is related to the verbs *rāga'* and *rāgaš* (7283). The noun *rōgez* (7267) is directly derived from it.

7265. רְגַז r^egaz: An Aramaic verb meaning to provoke, to anger. The term occurs only once in the entire Old Testament. In a report written to King Darius, the elders of the Jews were quoted as conceding to the fact that the Babylonian exile and destruction of Solomon's Temple (ca. 586 B.C.) took place because their ancestors had angered the God of heaven (Ezra 5:12). This verb corresponds to the Hebrew verb *rāgaz* (7264).

7266. רְגַז r^egaz: An Aramaic masculine noun meaning violent anger, rage. The term occurs only once in the entire Old Testament. When King Nebuchadnezzar heard that three Jews—Shadrach, Meshach, and Abednego—refused to worship the image of gold that he had erected, he flew into a rage (Dan. 3:13). This term is derived from the Aramaic verb *r^egaz* (7265) and is related to the Hebrew noun *rōgez* (7267).

7267. רֹגֶז rōgez: A masculine noun meaning commotion, raging, excitement. The primary meaning of this word is a state of agitation or uproar. It denotes the tumult that comes from fear (Isa. 14:3); the fury of the Lord's judgment (Hab. 3:2); a general state of upheaval (Job 3:26); and the chaos of ordinary life in this world (Job 14:1).

7268. רַגָּז raggāz: An adjective meaning trembling, shaking. Deuteronomy 28:65 records the sole occurrence of this word. It describes a fainting heart that is full of unease.

7269. רָגְזָה rogzāh: A feminine noun meaning a trembling, a quaking. In Ezekiel 12:18, this word is used to imply a trembling or quivering hand. The suggestion is that of tremendous worry or unsteadiness even during routine activities.

7270. רָגַל rāgal: I. A verb meaning to spy out. It refers to roaming, going through a land to spy it out (Num. 21:32; Deut. 1:24; Judg. 18:2, 14, 17; 2 Sam. 10:3). Its participial form in its intensive stem indicates spies, a person who secretly scouts out a land (Gen. 42:9, 11).

II. A verb meaning to slander. It has the sense of slander (2 Sam. 19:27[28]). God's people should not slander; verbally abusing someone in spoken language (Ps. 15:3).

III. A verb meaning to walk; to teach to walk. It is used in its causative stem to describe teaching someone to walk, causing him or her to walk (Hos. 11:3).

7271. רְגַל r^egal: An Aramaic feminine noun meaning a foot. Figuratively, it describes the feet of a giant statue (Dan. 2:33, 34, 41, 42); or of terrifying animals (Dan. 7:4, 7, 19), all seen in dreams and visions by Daniel.

7272. רֶגֶל regel: A feminine noun meaning a foot. It is the common word for a literal foot, human or animal. It is used figuratively, but has acquired many other uses. It is used of a human foot (Gen. 18:4; Ex. 3:5); a foot of an animal or bird (Gen. 8:9; Ezek. 29:11); with *kap̱* preceding, it indicates the sole of a foot (Deut. 2:5; 11:24); in some places, it stands for the whole leg of a person (1 Sam. 17:6). It is used figuratively of God's foot (Ex. 24:10; 2 Sam. 22:10; Ps. 18:9[10]); or the foot or feet of other heavenly beings (2 Chr. 3:13; Isa. 6:2; Ezek. 1:7). It indicates figuratively the feet of furniture (Ex. 25:26; 37:13). With b^e attached, it means on one's feet, traveling on foot, journeying by walking (Num. 20:19; Deut. 2:28). With the verb *nāśa'*, to lift, it means to set out, to start out (Gen. 29:1). It is found once in the plural preceded by *šālōš,* three, meaning three times (Ex. 23:14). The term *mēsîḵ 'eṯ-regel* means to have a bowel movement (Judg. 3:24). The phrase *mê raglêhem* refers to urine, water of their privates (2 Kgs. 18:27).

7273. רַגְלִי ***ragliy:*** A masculine noun referring to foot soldiers; footmen. It refers simply to a person traveling on foot (Ex. 12:37); but more technically of foot soldiers (Judg. 20:2; 2 Sam. 8:4; 1 Kgs. 20:29); infantry (Jer. 12:5).

7274. רֹגְלִים ***rōgliym:*** A proper noun designating Rogelim (2 Sam. 17:27; 19:31[32]).

7275. רָגַם ***rāgam:*** A verb meaning to stone, to kill by stoning. It means to kill persons by stoning them (Lev. 20:2, 27; Num. 14:10; Deut. 21:21). The preposition b^e is usually used in the construction indicating the stone (*'eḇen*) or the person stoned (1 Kgs. 12:18). Sometimes b^e is not used at all (Josh. 7:25; Ezek. 23:47).

7276. רֶגֶם ***regem:*** A proper noun designating Regem (1 Chr. 2:47).

7277. רִגְמָה ***rigmāh:*** I. A feminine noun meaning a crowd, a throng. It refers to a large number of persons. In context it indicates a great number of rulers from Judah (Ps. 68:27[28]).

II. A feminine noun meaning council. It refers to a group of people serving as advisors and counselors for someone. In its context it indicates the leaders of Judah (Ps. 68:27[28]).

7278. רֶגֶם מֶלֶךְ ***regem meleḵ:*** A proper noun designating Regem-melech (Zech. 7:2).

7279. רָגַן ***rāgan:*** A verb meaning to gossip, to complain. It refers to Israel's complaining, murmuring in the wilderness against the Lord (Deut. 1:27; Ps. 106:25). It indicates excessive complaining in a way that evokes relational problems among persons (Prov. 16:28). It means a gossiper, a whisperer, a trouble causer (Prov. 18:8; 26:20, 22). It describes an act of criticism, complaining, fault-finding (Isa. 29:24).

7280. רָגַע ***rāga‘:*** I. A verb meaning to do something instantaneously, in a moment; to endure only for a moment. It indicates the fleeting life of something: falsity (Prov. 12:19); a passing condition (Jer. 49:19; 50:44).

II. A verb meaning to stir up, to churn up. It is rendered by the New International Version to indicate God's churning, agitating the sea (Job 26:12; Isa. 51:15; Jer. 31:35). In II and III, the context is largely responsible for the renderings chosen.

III. A verb meaning to be at rest; to cease struggles; to bring rest. The NASB prefers to render this word much differently, as the opposite of stir up, churn. It renders it in certain places meaning to quiet, to cause to rest, to cease from activity, referring to people, animals, nations, and the seas (Deut. 28:65; Job 26:12; Isa. 34:14; 51:4; Jer. 31:2; 47:6; 50:34). It has the sense of establishing in Isaiah 51:4.

IV. A verb meaning to break upon. The New International Version renders this word to describe the breaking of a person's skin (Job 7:5).

V. A verb meaning to harden; to become crusty. The New American Standard Bible translates this verb to indicate a hardening of Job's skin (Job 7:5).

7281. רֶגַע *rega‘*: A masculine noun meaning an instant, a moment. It refers to a brief, definite moment in time (Ex. 33:5; Ezra 9:8; Isa. 54:8); or to something done at once, instantly (Num. 16:21, 45[17:10]); suddenly (Ps. 6:10[11]). God's anger lasts only for a brief moment (Ps. 30:5[6]). It is combined in the plural with *l^e* to mean every moment, moment by moment (Ezek. 32:10). At one time . . . at another time is found in Jeremiah 18:7, 9 (*rega‘* . . . *w^erega‘*).

7282. רָגֵעַ *rāgēa‘*: An adjective meaning quiet. It refers to a state of rest and trust in which persons are at ease (Ps. 35:20).

7283. רָגַשׁ *rāgaš*: A verb meaning to be in commotion, to rage against. This word appears only in Psalm 2:1 where it denotes the uproar and plotting of the wicked against the righteous. The image of a gathering lynch mob conveys well the action suggested here.

7284. רְגַשׁ *r^egaš*: An Aramaic verb meaning to assemble in a throng, to be turbulent, to be in tumult. Occurring only in Daniel, this word describes the gathering of the men who conspired against the prophet (Dan. 6:6[7], 11[12], 15[16]).

7285. רֶגֶשׁ *regeš*: A noun meaning a crowd, a company, an insurrection. The basic meaning of this word is that of a thronging mass of people. The word refers to worshipers going to the Temple in a large group (Ps. 55:14 [15]); and the riotous scheming that could result from a large gathering of people whose minds were not directed toward God (Ps. 64:2[3]).

7286. רָדַד *rāḏaḏ*: A verb meaning to subdue; to beat down; to be almost gone. It indicates that something is about to pass away, is almost gone (Judg. 19:11). It is used of overlaying gold on a surface by beating it into thin sheets (1 Kgs. 6:32). It has the sense of subduing persons, a people (Ps. 144:2; Isa. 45:1).

7287. רָדָה ***rāḏāh:*** A verb meaning to rule, to have dominion, to subjugate. This Hebrew word conveys the notion of exercising domain, whether legitimate or not, over those who are powerless or otherwise under one's control. It is related as the exercise of authority by the priesthood (Jer. 5:31); by slave owners over their slaves (Lev. 25:43); by supervisors over their workers (1 Kgs. 9:23); and by a king over his kingdom (1 Kgs. 4:24[5:4]). Theologically significant is the use of this word to identify people's God-ordained relationship to the created world around them (Gen. 1:26, 28).

7288. רַדַּי ***radday:*** A proper noun designating Raddai (1 Chr. 2:14).

7289. רְדִיד ***r^{e}diyd:*** A masculine noun referring to a cloak, a shawl, a veil. It refers to a garment worn to cover someone (KJV, veil). It is a piece of fine clothing worn by the well-dressed women of Israel (Isa. 3:23; NASB, veil).

7290. רָדַם ***rāḏam:*** A verb meaning to be asleep; to fall asleep. It refers to being in a state of deep sleep from exhaustion (Judg. 4:21). It indicates a state of stupor or confusion (Ps. 76:6[7]). It describes a deep sleep or trance of a prophet (Dan. 8:18; 10:9).

7291. רָדַף ***rāḏap:*** A verb meaning to pursue, to chase, to persecute. It means to chase after, to pursue someone in a hostile manner, as when Abraham pursued Lot's captors (Gen. 14:14, 15); or Pharaoh pursued Israel (Ex. 14:4, 8, 9, 23; 15:9). It refers to a pursuit of a less hostile nature, e.g., Laban's pursuit of Jacob (Gen. 31:23). It refers to the Lord's pursuit of persons or nations to punish and judge them (Jer. 29:18; Lam. 3:43). It refers to hunting, chasing after animals (1 Sam. 26:20). It takes on the sense of persecuting persons, harassing them (Deut. 30:7); sometimes with words alone (Job 19:22). Figuratively, it describes chasing rewards (Isa. 1:23); or strong drink (Isa. 5:11). To pursue one's enemies to darkness means to utterly wipe them out (Nah. 1:8). In its passive sense, it means to be chased (Isa. 17:13). In its passive stem in Ecclesiastes 3:15, it refers to what has vanished, passed away.

7292. רָהַב ***rāhaḇ:*** A verb meaning to be bold, to be proud; to overwhelm. It indicates making a person bold, brave, strong (Ps. 138:3; KJV, strengthen). It has the sense of attempting to win back friends, pleading with them boldly (Prov. 6:3). It refers to the strong power of the bridegroom's eyes on his bride; they overwhelm her (NASB, confuse; Song 6:5). It takes on a negative sense in Isaiah 3:5, to storm against (NASB); rise against (NIV); act proudly (KJV).

7293. רַהַב ***rahaḇ:*** A masculine noun meaning pride, strength. It is treated as a common noun referring to someone arrogant, boastful, proud by some translators (Job 9:13; 26:12). It refers mockingly to the strength of Egypt, that is, their sitting still, doing nothing (Isa. 30:7).

7294. רַהַב *rahab:* A proper noun designating Rahab:

A. The word used for Egypt, sometimes with connotations of Egypt as a rebellious sea monster. The word means "arrogance, hubris."

B. A mythical sea monster but subject to the Lord God of Israel (Job 9:13; Ps. 89:10[11]). In other cultures, it was known as Tiamat (Babylon) or Leviathan (Ugarit). In Israel the "monster" became merely the forces of nature or historical evil against them, but totally subject to Israel's God, the Lord (Yahweh).

7295. רָהָב *rāhāb:* An adjective meaning proud. It is used to designate arrogant, haughty persons, having too high a view of themselves or their positions (Ps. 40:4[5]).

7296. רֹהַב *rōhab:* A masculine noun indicating strength. It refers in context to health, vigor of life, the ability to continue in life's pursuits (Ps. 90:10).

7297. רָהָה *rāhāh:* A verb meaning to be afraid, to fear. Occurring only in Isaiah 44:8, this word implies a fear that stems from uncertainty or a sense of being utterly alone. In the text, the Lord offered His assurance that He was still living and was in control of all situations.

7298. רַהַט *rahaṭ:* I. A masculine noun referring to a trough, a gutter. It refers to a hollowed, narrow open container made of wood or stone to hold water or food for animals (Gen. 30:38, 41; Ex. 2:16).

II. A masculine noun referring to a tress, a lock of hair. It describes a braid or plait of human hair, a long, thick piece of hair hanging and falling loosely (Song 7:5[6]).

III. A masculine noun referring to a gallery. It usually indicates a covered walk, a long, narrow balcony, or an area for seating. But it may have a theatric intention in the King James Version meaning to act in a way so as to please someone (Song 7:5[6]).

7299. רֵו *rēw:* An Aramaic masculine noun indicating a form, an appearance. It refers to the overall form and presentation of something, e.g., the statue in Nebuchadnezzar's vision (Dan. 2:31; 3:25).

7300. רוּד *rûd:* A verb meaning to wander restlessly, to roam. Hosea uses the verb figuratively to refer to Judah's restlessness, that is, their lack of obedience to God (Hos. 11:12[12:1]). The Lord uses the verb in Jeremiah to ask why His people felt they were free to roam (Jer. 2:31). Esau, after Jacob deceived Isaac, was doomed to live by the sword and serve his brother. However, there would come a time when he would become restless and throw off his yoke (Gen. 27:40).

7301. רָוָה rāwāh: A verb meaning to give water, to drench; to drink one's fill. It refers to giving someone a drink literally and figuratively (Ps. 36:8[9]; 65:10[11]). It means to drink all that one wants, to satisfy (Prov. 5:19; 7:18). It is used figuratively by the prophets of tears (Isa. 16:9); of a sword's being sated, satisfied (Isa. 34:5); of ground being soaked with blood (Isa. 34:7); of God's being filled with fat sacrifices (Isa. 43:24); of priests' souls being filled (Jer. 31:14).

7302. רָוֶה rāweh: An adjective meaning watered, well-watered. It refers to a condition of saturation or of having sufficient water or rain (Deut. 29:19[18]); especially a garden, a figure of a renewed people of God (Isa. 58:11; Jer. 31:12). It is used figuratively, e.g., of being satiated with dishonor, shame (Job 10:15).

7303. רוֹהֲגָה rôh^{a}gāh, רָהְגָה rohgāh: A proper noun designating Rohgah (1 Chr. 7:34).

7304. רָוַח rāwaḥ: A verb meaning to breathe freely, to be spacious, to smell. The primary meaning is to breathe freely by means of being spacious or revived. This word is used to indicate a relief that comes to a troubled mind or spirit (1 Sam. 16:23; Job 32:20). Shallem, son of Josiah, stated that he would build a great palace with spacious upper rooms (Jer. 22:14). *Rāwah* was also used to dictate the smelling of aromas of both the burnt offering and incense (see Gen. 8:21; Ex. 30:38). In Genesis, the burnt offerings had a pleasing aroma to God, which in turn prompted Him to state His covenant. In Exodus, the people were warned against making the special mixture of incense (meant only for the use of an incense offering to God) simply to enjoy its aroma. The punishment for disobeying this command was to be cut off from one's own people.

7305. רֶוַח rewaḥ: A masculine noun meaning a space, an interval, a respite, a relief, a liberation. In Genesis, the word is used in Jacob's command to keep a space between the herds that were given as gifts to his brother Esau (Gen. 32:16[17]). This space gave Jacob more time to prepare, looked more impressive to the receiver (i.e., controlled herds), and gave a better impression of the size or amount of the gift. In Esther, Mordecai indicated that if Esther kept silent, then relief for the Jews would arise from another place, and she and her father's family would die (Esth. 4:14).

7306. רוּחַ ,רִיחַ rûaḥ, riyaḥ: A verb meaning to feel relief, to be spacious, to smell. This verb is used rarely in the Hebrew Bible. In the simple stem, it occurs twice meaning to gain or feel relief. When David played the harp, Saul found relief (1 Sam. 16:23); the verbose Elihu had to speak in order to get relief from his anxiety (Job 32:20). In its single use in the passive intensive stem, it means roomy or spacious. The vain King

Shallum proposed to build himself a palace with spacious, roomy, upper chambers (Jer. 22:14).

The verb is used most often in the causative stem to mean to smell. Gods of wood cannot smell (Deut. 4:28); nor can idols of gold or silver (Ps. 115:6). Isaac smelled the clothes that Jacob wore to deceive him (Gen. 27:27). In 1 Samuel 26:19, however, the verb refers to God being pleased by the aroma of an offering (Gen. 8:21; Lev. 26:31). The verb evidently means to be burned with in Judges 16:9, for the ropes holding Samson snapped as when they sensed (i.e., were burned) with fire. The Shoot of Jesse, the Branch, will respond (i.e., be sensitive) to the fear of the Lord (Isa. 11:1, 2).

7307. רוּחַ *rûaḥ*: A feminine noun meaning spirit, wind, breath. The word is used to refer to the Spirit of God or the Lord. The Spirit of the Lord inspired prophets to utter their prophecies (Num. 11:17, 25; 1 Sam. 10:6; 19:20); the Spirit of the Lord moved the prophets in time and space, as in the case of Elijah (1 Kgs. 18:12; Ezek. 2:2). The word could be modified by an adjective to refer to an evil spirit from the Lord (1 Sam. 16:15, 16; 1 Kgs. 22:22, 23). The Spirit of God is properly referred to as the Holy Spirit (Ps. 51:11[13]; 106:33; Isa. 63:10, 11). The Spirit produced and controlled the message of the prophets, even of a Mesopotamian prophet like Balaam (Num. 24:2). David was inspired to speak as a prophet by the Spirit (2 Sam. 23:2). The Spirit was present among the returned exiles in Jerusalem (Hag. 2:5; Zech. 4:6); and will be poured out in the latter days on all flesh, imparting prophecy, dreams, and visions (Joel 2:28;[3:1]). The Spirit of God was grieved by the rebellion of God's people (Isa. 63:10).

The Lord's Spirit imparted other gifts: giving Bezalel skill and ability in all kinds of work (Ex. 31:3; 35:31); including the skill to teach others (see Ex. 35:34); the Spirit gave understanding as well (Job 32:8). The Spirit of the Lord had a part in creating the universe; the Spirit hovered over the deep and imparted life to persons (Gen. 1:2; Job 33:4); and even revived the dead (Ezek. 37:5, 10; 39:29).

The human spirit and the Spirit of God are closely linked with moral character and moral attributes. God will give His people a new spirit so they will follow His decrees and laws (Ezek. 11:19; 36:26). God's Spirit will rest on His people, transforming them (Isa. 59:21). The Lord preserves those who have heavy spirits and broken hearts (Ps. 34:18[19]; Isa. 65:14).

The human spirit is sometimes depicted as the seat of emotion, the mind, and the will. In a song of praise, Isaiah asserted that the spirit desires the Lord (Isa. 26:9; Job 7:11). The spirit imparts wisdom for understanding (Ex. 28:3; Deut. 34:9); and carrying out one's responsibilities. David prayed for a willing spirit to aid him (Ex. 35:21; Ps. 51:10[12]).

The spirit made flesh alive and is the life force of living humans and animals. The Lord makes the spirits of people that give them life (Zech. 12:1). This spirit is from God and leaves at death (Gen. 6:3; Ps. 78:39; Eccl. 3:21). The spirit is pictured as giving animation, agitation, or liveliness; the Queen of Sheba was overcome in her spirit when she saw the splendors of Solomon's world (1 Kgs. 10:5). Not to have any spirit is to lose all courage; the Amorite kings had no spirit in them when they learned how Israel had crossed the Jordan. To be short of spirit is to be despondent or impatient (Eccl. 6:9).

The word also describes the breath of a human being or the natural wind that blows. The idols of the goldsmith have no breath in them; they are inanimate (Jer. 10:14; 51:17). Human speech is sometimes only words of wind that mean nothing (Job 16:3). By the gust of his nostrils, the Lord piled up the waters of the Red Sea (Ex. 15:8). Often, the word refers to wind or a synonym of wind. The Lord sent a wind over the earth to dry up the floodwaters (Gen. 8:1; Ex. 15:10; Num. 11:31). Jeremiah spoke of the four winds, referring to the entire earth (Jer. 49:36; Ezek. 37:9). The word is also used to mean wind in the sense of nothing (Eccl. 1:14; 2:11; Isa. 26:18). The wind, like the Spirit, cannot be caught, tamed, or found (Eccl. 2:11).

7308. רוּחַ ***rûaḥ:*** An Aramaic noun meaning wind; spirit of a person, mind; spirit divine. All occurrences of the word are located in the book of Daniel. For the Hebrew mind, the term at its heart encapsulated the experience of any mysterious, invisible, awesome, living power. This included such forces as the wind (Dan. 2:35; 7:2); the active inner being of a person where attitudes, feelings, and intellect resided (Dan. 5:12, 20; 6:3[4]; 7:15); the divine Spirit that could come down from God and indwell individuals, often giving them supernatural abilities, such as Daniel's ability to interpret dreams (Dan. 4:8[5], 9[6], 18[15]; 5:11, 14). This term is identical in form and meaning to the Hebrew noun *rûah* (7307).

7309. רְוָחָה ***r^e wāḥāh:*** A feminine noun meaning breathing space, relief, respite. The term occurs only twice in the entire Old Testament and is derived from the verb *rāwah* (7304), meaning to breathe, to have breathing room, or to feel relief. In its first occurrence, the word denotes the alleviation that resulted from God's act of terminating the plague of frogs in Egypt (Ex. 8:15[11]). The second use of the term involves a desperate cry to the Lord for deliverance and rest from merciless enemies (Lam. 3:56).

7310. רְוָיָה ***r^e wāyāh:*** A feminine noun referring to abundance; a state of overflowing. It refers to an overabundance of something. It is used figuratively of the cup of life and blessing from the Lord (Ps. 23:5). It refers to the richness, safety, and blessing of God's deliverance from enemies (Ps. 66:12).

7311. רוּם ***rûm:*** A verb meaning to raise, to lift up; to be exalted. It indicates that something is literally raised up high (Gen. 7:17; Job 22:12); or indicates the act of raising, picking up something (Gen. 14:22; Ex. 14:16; Josh. 4:5; Ezek. 10:16); setting it up (Gen. 31:45; Ezra 9:9). It describes the process of something growing (Isa. 1:2; Ezek. 31:4); or of persons being promoted, raised up in their positions (1 Sam. 2:7; 1 Kgs. 14:7). It is used often of God's being exalted (Ex. 15:2; 2 Sam. 22:47; Ps. 30:1[2]; 99:2; 108:5[6]; Isa. 33:10). It describes the haughtiness and boastfulness of people: their hearts (Deut. 8:14); eyes (Ps. 18:27[28]); attitudes, with an uplifted hand, arrogant (Job 38:15). The antichrist figure exalts and lifts up himself (Dan. 11:36). It describes the presentation of a sacrifice (Lev. 2:9). It can have the sense of removing something, abolishing it (Dan. 8:11).

7312. רוּם ***rûm,*** רֻם ***rum:*** A masculine noun indicating height; haughtiness, pride. It refers to actual physical height (Prov. 25:3, the heavens). But it is used most often figuratively of the arrogance of persons, their haughtiness (Prov. 21:4; Isa. 2:11, 17), especially of the king of Assyria (Isa. 10:12) and of Moab (Jer. 48:29).

7313. רוּם ***rûm:*** An Aramaic verb meaning to lift up, to exalt. It literally means to raise up. Used of God, it means to exalt Him (Dan. 4:37[34]). It refers to honoring or promoting a person (Dan. 5:19); it indicates a person's heart being lifted up, becoming arrogant (Dan. 5:20); or persons lifting themselves up against God (Dan. 5:23).

7314. רוּם ***rûm:*** An Aramaic masculine noun indicating height. It refers to the actual measured height of a structure (Ezra 6:3; Dan. 3:1); or a natural object (Dan. 4:10[7], 11[8], 20[17]).

7315. רוֹם ***rôm:*** An adverb indicating high. It indicates how something is done. It is used figuratively of the deep sea lifting high (*rôm*) its hands (Hab. 3:10).

7316. רוּמָה ***rûmāh:*** A proper noun designating Rumah (2 Kgs. 23:36).

7317. רוֹמָה ***rômāh:*** An adverb meaning proudly, haughtily. It describes the way something is done or carried out, e.g., in a proud or haughty manner (Mic. 2:3).

7318. רוֹמַם ***rômam:*** A masculine noun referring to praise, high praise. It is used of lifting up, an exaltation of God by His holy people (Ps. 66:17; 149:6).

7319. רוֹמְמָה ***rômᵉmāh:*** A feminine noun indicating high praise. It is used of the lifting up, the exaltation of God by His holy people (Ps. 149:6).

7320. רוֹמַמְתִּי עֶזֶר ***rômamtiy 'ezer,*** רֹמַמְתִּי עֶזֶר ***rōmamtiy 'ezer:*** A proper noun designating Romamti Ezer (1 Chr. 25:4, 31).

7321. רוּעַ ***rûa':*** A verb meaning to shout, to sound a blast. The term occurs thirty-three times in the Old Testament and was utilized fundamentally to convey the action of shouting or the making of a loud noise. Shouting often took place just before a people or army rushed into battle against opposition; sometimes the war cry became the very signal used to commence engagement with the enemy (Josh. 6:10, 16, 20; Judg. 15:14; 1 Sam. 4:5; 17:20; 2 Chr. 13:15). Many times the shout was a cry of joy, often in response to the Lord's creating or delivering activity on behalf of His people (Job 38:7; Ps. 47:1[2]; 95:1, 2; Isa. 44:23; Zeph. 3:14; Zech. 9:9). In several other instances, the shout expressed triumph and victory over a foe (Ps. 41:11[12]; 60:8[10]; 108:9[10]); and occasionally mourning (Isa. 15:4; Mic. 4:9). A few times, the term denotes the shout of a trumpet (i.e., the blast), usually as a signal to begin battle (Num. 10:9; 2 Chr. 13:12; cf. Hos. 5:8; Joel 2:1).

7322. רוּף ***rûp̱,*** רָפַף ***rāp̱ap̱:*** I. A verb indicating to tremble, to quake. It describes the shaking, vibrating of the pillars of heaven, a figurative expression (Job 26:11). The root is *rûp̱*.

II. A verb meaning to tremble; to quake. Some translators understand this verbal root to be *rāp̱ap̱* (Job 26:11). It has the same meaning as I.

7323. רוּץ ***rûṣ:*** A verb meaning to run, to guard. It means to travel, to journey by moving one's legs more rapidly than in walking (Gen. 18:2). It may carry with it a sense of urgency, a need to hurry (Gen. 18:7); or a sense of intense concern, care, excitement (Gen. 24:17, 20, 28, 29). It is used of horses (Amos 6:12). It describes, figuratively, the course of the sun across the sky (Ps. 19:5[6]); or the road, way, or course of God's moral commandments (Ps. 119:32). In its intensive stem, it can indicate fright, running to and fro in battle (Nah. 2:4[5]). In its causative stem, it has the sense of to cause someone to run, to bring them (Gen. 41:14, 1 Sam. 17:17; 2 Chr. 35:13); or to cause or make someone run away (Jer. 49:19; 50:44). Followed by *liqra't̠*, it means to meet (Gen. 24:17; 29:13). It is used in a figurative sense of a prophet's activity of prophesying (Jer. 23:21; Hab. 2:2); of the swift activity of God's Word (Ps. 147:15). In its participial form, it may refer to runners (2 Sam. 15:1; 1 Kgs. 1:5).

7324. רוּק ***rûq,*** רִיק ***riyq:*** A verb meaning to empty, to pour out, to draw out. It is used of Abraham drawing out, leading forth his military men (Gen. 14:4); or, more literally, it indicates emptying out one's sacks (Gen. 42:35). It means to draw a sword, to empty its sheath (Ex. 15:9; Lev. 26:33). It describes the emptying of the heavens, pouring down rain (Eccl. 11:3; Mal. 3:10). It is used metaphorically of Moab not being emptied out (Jer. 48:11). To cause persons to be empty is to cause them to be unfed (Isa. 32:6).

7325. רוּק ***rûq,*** רִיק ***riyq:*** A verb meaning to flow. It describes the running discharge from an open sore, making a person unclean (Lev. 15:3).

7326. רוּשׁ ***rûš:*** A verb meaning to be poor. It indicates a person who has few resources and little standing or influence in a society, such as David before he was king (1 Sam. 18:23). Nathan used the concept of the poor man in a parable (2 Sam. 12:1, 3, 4). It describes a person in want (Ps. 34:10[11]). This class of people was to be especially cared for (Ps. 82:3). A poor person in this world's goods may be, in reality, rich in God's eyes (Prov. 13:7). The subject of poverty and the poor person is stressed in wisdom proverbs (Prov. 13:8, 23; 14:20; 17:5; 18:23; Eccl. 4:14; 5:8[7]).

7327. רוּת ***rûṯ:*** A proper noun designating Ruth, a Moabitess who converted to the God of Naomi and her people. God cared for her providentially, and she became the grandmother of King David (Ruth 4:5, 10–13). She married Boaz, a kinsman "redeemer" in Israel, thus rescuing her from poverty and oblivion.

7328. רָז ***raz:*** An Aramaic masculine noun referring to a secret, a mystery. It refers to the meaning of a dream or a vision that is not clear (Dan. 2:18, 19, 27–30). God is recognized as the one who reveals and gives the meaning of mysteries (Dan. 2:47); but may impart that ability to His servants (Dan. 4:9[6]).

7329. רָזָה ***rāzāh:*** A verb meaning to starve, to waste away. It indicates the wasting away of healthy flesh, fatness as a result of God's judgments (Isa. 17:4). It is used figuratively of God starving, destroying the gods of the nations (Zeph. 2:11).

7330. רָזֶה ***rāzeh:*** An adjective meaning lean, skinny. It describes land as lean; that is, without fertile soil to produce an abundance of crops, trees, shrubs (Num. 13:20). It refers figuratively to the strong in a society, the powerful, and those who oppress the weak (Ezek. 34:20).

7331. רְזוֹן ***r^{e}zôn:*** A proper noun designating Rezon (1 Kgs. 11:23).

7332. רָזוֹן ***rāzôn:*** A masculine noun referring to leanness, skimpiness. It refers to weakness, frailty, lack of strength. It is used with respect to one's soul, life (Ps. 106:15); or to the deterioration of one's fatness, health (Isa. 10:16). It indicates a reduced measure (ephah) used in business that is employed unfairly (Mic. 6:10).

7333. רָזוֹן ***rāzôn:*** A masculine noun meaning a dignitary, a ruler, a prince. The term occurs once in the entire Old Testament in Proverbs 14:28 and is synonymous with the noun *mele<u>k</u>* (4428), meaning king. The proverb states that what makes or breaks a prince is whether or not he has a multitude of subjects to rule over. The term is derived from the verb *rāzan* (7336).

7334. רָזִי ***rāziy:*** A masculine noun indicating a leanness, a wasting away. It is used only in the expression *razî-lî, razî-lî.* Its meaning is not certain in Isaiah 24:16: "leanness to me" (KJV); "woe to me, woe to me" (NASB); "I waste away" (NIV).

7335. רָזַם ***rāzam:*** A verb meaning to flash the eyes, to wink. It means to blink one's eyes in an arrogant manner. In context it implies an attitude of resistance or hostility (Job 15:12).

7336. רָזַן ***rāzan:*** A verb meaning to be heavy, to be weighty, to be honored, to be mighty. The term also occurs six times as a noun, meaning rulers. Five times the word is used in conjunction with the Hebrew word for king (*mele<u>k</u>*[4428]; Judg. 5:3; Ps. 2:2; Prov. 8:15; 31:4; Hab. 1:10); and once with judge (a participle of the verb *šā<u>p</u>aṭ*[8199]; Isa. 40:23). Rulers were summoned to listen to Deborah's victory song (Judg. 5:3); warned to not conspire against the Lord and His anointed one (Ps. 2:2); enabled by wisdom to decree just laws (Prov. 8:15); abstained from strong drink (Prov. 31:4); and were made as nothing by the Lord (Isa. 40:23). The noun *rāzôn* (7333) is derived from this verb; also see the verb *kā<u>b</u>ē<u>d</u>* (3513).

7337. רָחַב ***rāḥa<u>b</u>:*** A verb indicating to enlarge, to extend; to open wide. It means to gain living space, territory (Gen. 26:22); especially as the work of the Lord (Ex. 34:24; Deut. 12:20; 19:8). The psalmists praise God for enlarging them, giving them strength (2 Sam. 22:37). It is used of giving a person space, relief in a time of danger (Ps. 4:1). It indicates the social advancement or space from giving a gift (Prov. 18:16). Amos condemns the violent acquisition of territory (Amos 1:13).

7338. רַחַב ***rāḥa<u>b</u>:*** A proper noun designating A masculine noun meaning broad place, expanse (Job 36:16; 38:18).

7339. רְחֹב r^e***ḥō<u>b</u>,*** רְחוֹב r^e***ḥô<u>b</u>:*** A feminine noun referring to a street, a public square, an open place. It uniformly indicates an open area, a plaza, a public square of a town or village where most people met (Gen. 19:2). Nearly all cities had such an area (Deut. 13:16[17]); Judg. 19:15, 17, 20). Wisdom cries out to people in the town square, a public place (Prov. 1:20). It refers to the entire network of open areas and streets in some cases (Ps. 55:11[12]; 144:14; Prov. 5:16; Zech. 8:45). It would be a feature included in a rebuilt Jerusalem (Dan. 9:25).

7340. רְחוֹב r^e***ḥô<u>b</u>:*** A proper noun designating Rehob:

A. A town near Hamath (Num. 13:21).

B. A town in Asher (Josh. 19:28, 30; 21:31; Judg. 1:31; 1 Chr. 6:75[60]).

C. An Aramean town (2 Sam. 10:8).

D. The father of Hadadezer (2 Sam. 8:3, 12).

E. A covenanter in Nehemiah's day (Neh. 10:11[12]).

7341. רֹחַב ***rōḥaḇ:*** A masculine noun meaning breadth, width. It indicates the width of various objects: of the ark (Gen. 6:15); of land (Gen. 13:17); of the ark of the covenant (Ex. 25:10, 17, 23); of a bed (Deut. 3:11). It is used figuratively of great wisdom, breadth of mind (1 Kgs. 4:29[5:9]); the Temple (2 Chr. 3:3). It refers to a great breadth or stretch of waters (Job 37:10). It is used often to depict the breadth of various parts of Ezekiel's Temple (Ezek. 40:5–7, 11, 13, 19–21; 41:1–5, etc.). It is used to refer to the width of a reconstructed Jerusalem (Zech. 2:2[6]); and the width of a strange flying scroll (Zech. 5:2).

7342. רָחָב ***rāḥāḇ:*** An adjective meaning broad, wide, spacious, large. It indicates that something is wide, broad; land (Ex. 3:8; Isa. 22:18); a wall (Jer. 51:58). It refers to the broad freedom or openness of God's Law or to walking in it (Ps. 119:45). It indicates the size of something, e.g., land (Gen. 34:21); or to the spaciousness, extent of a land (Judg. 18:10). The inclusiveness of God's moral laws, their broadness is noted by the psalmist (Ps. 119:96). Followed by heart, the phrase refers to an arrogant heart or attitude (Ps. 101:5). An arrogant person is broad of soul (Prov. 28:25). It figuratively indicates a cup of punishment as being deep and wide (Ezek. 23:32).

7343. רָחָב ***rāḥaḇ:*** A proper noun designating Rahab, a Canaanite woman of Jericho, a harlot, who expressed fear and faith in the great acts of Israel's God and became a part of His people. She sheltered two Israelite spies and received a blessing from God for doing so (Josh. 2:1–14).

7344. רְחֹבוֹת ***r***^{e}***ḥōḇôṯ,*** רְחֹבוֹת עִיר ***r***^{e}***ḥōḇôṯ 'iyr:*** A proper noun designating Rehoboth:

A. A well dug by Isaac (Gen. 26:22).

B. A city on the Euphrates River (Gen. 36:37; 1 Chr. 1:48). See also C and D below.

C. The city of Shaul, king of Edom (KJV, Gen. 10:11), possibly the same as B above.

D. Rehoboth-Ir, from B above and *'iyr* (5892) (NASB, NIV, Gen. 10:11), possibly the same as B.

7345. רְחַבְיָה ***r***^{e}***ḥaḇyāh,*** רְחַבְיָהוּ ***r***^{e}***ḥaḇyāhû:*** A proper noun designating Rehabiah (1 Chr. 23:17; 24:21; 26:25).

7346. רְחַבְעָם ***r***^{e}***ḥaḇ'ām:*** A proper noun designating Rehoboam, the first king of the southern kingdom of Judah (930–813 B.C.). He was Solomon's son and, unfortunately, continued the oppressive administrative policies of his father (1 Kgs. 12:12–15). His mother was an Ammonite, Naamah (1 Kgs. 14:21–22). When he did so, the ten northern Israelite tribes withdrew from Judah and David (1 Kgs. 12:16). He led Israel into gross religious harlotry and immorality. King Shishak of Egypt humbled Judah (1 Kgs. 14:25–28). Rehoboam pursued hostilities of war with Jeroboam of Israel constantly (1 Kgs. 14:29–31). His son Abijah succeeded him.

7347. רֵחֶה rēḥeh, רֵחַיִם rēḥayim: A masculine noun referring to a millstone. In its dual form, it indicates the two millstones used at a hand mill where grain was ground (Ex. 11:5; Num. 11:8; Deut. 24:6). It was considered a difficult and arduous task to grind meal (Isa. 47:2); but it was a sign of a thriving town or community (Jer. 25:10).

7348. רְחוּם r^eḥûm: A proper noun designating Rehum:

A. A leader returning with Zerubbabel (Ezra 2:2; Neh. 12:3).

B. A Jewish builder of Nehemiah's wall (Neh. 3:17).

C. A covenanter in Nehemiah's day, possibly the same as B (Neh. 10:25[26]).

D. A commanding officer who opposed the rebuilding of Jerusalem (Ezra 4:8, 9, 17, 23).

7349. רַחוּם raḥûm: An adjective meaning compassionate, merciful. It indicates a merciful and forgiving character and attitude. It is an important word defining the character of God, and every use is in reference to God. It is part of the moral definition of God given in Exodus 34:6 (Deut. 4:31; Ps. 78:38; 86:15; 103:8). It is used in the phrase *ḥannûn w^eraḥûm,* gracious and compassionate (2 Chr. 30:9; Neh. 9:17, 31; Ps. 111:4; 145:8; Joel 2:13; Jon. 4:2).

7350. רָחוֹק rāḥôq, רָחֹק rāḥōq: An adjective meaning far off, far away, distant. It refers to a great spatial distance, something far away, e.g., land (Deut. 29:22[21]; Josh. 9:6, 9; 1 Kgs. 8:41); but it is used of many things (Deut. 20:15; Joel 3:8[4:8]). It indicates time far away, far off (Ezek. 12:27). It takes on the nature of a noun to mean distance (Josh. 3:4). It refers to the space between two points (Gen. 22:4). It refers to distant time, *mērāḥôq*, long ago (Isa. 22:11). *L^emerāḥôq* means long ago, used of God's distant prophecies of what was to come (2 Kgs. 19:25; Isa. 37:26). It describes figuratively God's being far from one's heart or mind (Jer. 12:2); and of a value being far above something else (Prov. 31:10). It may indicate an inability to do something; it is far from someone (Eccl. 7:24).

7351. רָהִיט rāḥiyṭ, רָהִיט rāhiyṭ: A masculine collective noun indicating rafters. It refers to the main supporting and ornamental wooden supports in a structure (Song 1:17).

7352. רַחִיק rāḥiyq: An Aramaic adjective meaning far away, distant. It serves as a predicate adjective to describe persons who are to keep themselves far away from a certain place (Ezra 6:6).

7353. רָחֵל ***rāḥēl:*** A feminine noun meaning a ewe, a female sheep. It refers to a female sheep (Gen. 31:38; 32:14[15]). It is used in a simile comparing the bride's teeth to a flock of white, clean ewes (Song 6:6). In a more famous simile, the Lord's Suffering Servant is compared to a silent sheep before its shearers (Isa. 53:7).

7354. רָחֵל ***rāḥēl:*** A proper noun designating Rachel, the second wife of Jacob. She was a shepherdess, a daughter of Laban, Nahor's grandson. Laban was Jacob's uncle. Rachel lived in Paddan Aram, Aramaic territory (Gen. 29:6–31). Through divine guidance, Jacob located and married Rachel. Jacob worked for fourteen years to acquire Rachel as a wife. Jacob favored her over Leah. She eventually bore two sons, Joseph and Benjamin (Gen. 30:22–24; 35:16–18). She died bearing Benjamin whom she had named Benoni ("son of my sorrow") but Jacob renamed him. She was buried at Bethlehem or in its vicinity (Gen. 35:19–21).

During her life, she had stolen her father's idols, household gods (Gen. 31:19–22, 33–37). She evidently continued to relate to these gods in some way. She and Leah had "built up" Israel (Ruth 4:11). She became the ancestor through Joseph of two tribes, Ephraim and Manasseh.

7355. רָחַם ***rāḥam,*** רֻחָמָה ***ruḥāmāh:*** A verb meaning to have compassion, to have mercy, to find mercy. The word pictures a deep, kindly sympathy and sorrow felt for another who has been struck with affliction or misfortune, accompanied with a desire to relieve the suffering. The word occurs forty-seven times in the Old Testament, with God being by far the most common subject and His afflicted people the object (Deut. 13:17[18]; 2 Kgs. 13:23; Isa. 14:1; 30:18; 60:10; Jer. 12:15; 31:20; Lam. 3:32). Though the Lord showed compassion, it was not because of any meritorious work the recipient had done; it was solely due to God's sovereign freedom to bestow it on whom He chose (Ex. 33:19; cf. Rom. 9:14–16). Two types of people God has sovereignly chosen to have mercy on include those who fear Him (Ps. 103:13); and those who confess and forsake their sin (Prov. 28:13).

7356. רַחַם ***raḥam:*** A feminine noun meaning womb, compassion, mercy, affection, maiden. The singular form of this word always signified the physical womb of a woman and was commonly used in this way (Gen. 49:25). Yet when the plural form was used, the author had in mind the idea of compassion, tenderness, or mercy. The Old Testament authors thought of the womb or bowels as the seat of warm and tender emotions. For example, when Joseph saw his brother Benjamin, he became overwhelmed with tender affection (lit., wombs

[Gen. 43:30]). Through the prophet Zechariah, the Lord commanded His people to show compassion to one another (Zech. 7:9; cf. Deut. 13:17 [18]; Ps. 25:6; 103:4; Isa. 47:6).

7357. רחם *raḥam:* A proper noun designating Raham (1 Chr. 2:44).

7358. רֶחֶם *reḥem:* A masculine noun referring to a womb, a matrix. It refers to the belly or womb of an animal or woman, the place where a fetus is developed and from which it exits at birth (Gen. 20:18; 29:31). The phrase *mēreḥem* means from birth (Job 3:11; Ps. 22:10[11]; 58:3; Jer. 20:17). The first births of Israel were the Lord's special possession (Ex. 13:12, 15; 34:19). The phrase *raḥam rahᵃmāṯayim* indicates a woman, two women (Judg. 5:30). A delay, a stoppage of a womb, indicates a barren womb (Prov. 30:16). A womb that miscarried could be a curse from God but not necessarily (Hos. 9:14).

7359. רַחֲמִין *rahᵃmiyn:* An Aramaic masculine noun indicating mercy, compassion. It refers to a central characteristic of God, His feeling of mercy, pity, and love toward His people (Dan. 2:18).

7360. רָחָם *rāḥām,* רָחָמָה *rāḥāmāh:* A masculine noun indicating a carrion vulture, an osprey, a great eagle. The exact identification of these birds is difficult. They are still being studied. It refers to an unclean bird that was forbidden to Israel as food. It fed upon, among other things, other animals, fish, carcasses dead or alive (Lev. 11:18; Deut. 14:17).

7361. רַחֲמָה *raḥᵃmāh:* A feminine noun meaning a maiden, a girl. It refers literally to a womb but stands for a wife taken in war, someone to carry on descendants (Judg. 5:30).

7362. רַחֲמָנִי *raḥᵃmāniy:* An adjective meaning compassionate, characterized by pity. It refers to persons who normally show great care and pity, concern for others, especially their children (Lam. 4:10).

7363. רָחַף *rāḥap̱:* A verb meaning to move, to hover, to tremble. In a participial form, it describes God's Spirit hovering over the great waters at the beginning of God's creative acts (Gen. 1:2). It describes an eagle hovering over her young. It indicates the shaking or trembling of a person's bones because of fear and anxiety (Jer. 23:9).

7364. רָחַץ *rāḥaṣ:* A verb meaning to wash off, to wash away, to bathe. This Hebrew word carries the connotation of washing with water in order to make clean. It describes the action involved in washing the hands or feet (Ex. 30:19); the face (Gen. 43:31); the body (2 Sam. 11:2); clothes (Lev. 14:9); or the parts of a sacrificial offering (Lev. 1:9). Symbolically, such a washing was declarative of innocence (Deut. 21:6); and was figurative of cleansing from sin (Prov. 30:12; Isa. 4:4).

7365. רְחַץ ***reḥaṣ:*** An Aramaic verb meaning to trust. It indicates a person's attitude of trust in the Lord, confidence in Him, commitment to Him (Dan. 3:28).

7366. רַחַץ ***raḥaṣ:*** A masculine noun meaning washing. This word appears twice where it refers to a washing pot (Ps. 60:8[10]; 108:9[10]). In both instances, it was a term of derision and was meant to convey a sense of utter contempt.

7367. רַחְצָה ***raḥṣāh:*** A feminine noun meaning washing. The primary meaning of this word is found in its two uses in the Song of Solomon. Both times it referred to the bathing of sheep in water that caused them to be clean and white (Song 4:2; 6:6).

7368. רָחַק ***rāḥaq:*** A verb meaning to be far away; to become far away. It indicates that something is or becomes a long way off, distant, or it means to wander away from. It indicates physical distance (Deut. 12:21; 14:24). Distant from is expressed by adding *min* (from) to the object. It refers to persons' distancing themselves from other persons emotionally and physically (Prov. 19:7); but especially to the Lord's distancing Himself or being distant from those who need Him (Ps. 22:11[12], 19[20]; 35:22; 38:21[22]). It also describes persons distancing themselves from God (Isa. 29:13). Israel as a nation went far from God spiritually (Jer. 2:5). God's people were to distance themselves from cases or charges against the innocent (Ex. 23:7). It has the sense of God's expanding the borders, making distant the borders of His people (Isa. 26:15; Mic. 7:11). In its intensive stem, it has a causative sense of sending someone or something away, spreading it, likewise in its causative stem itself: the Lord removes people (Job 19:13; Isa. 6:12; Ezek. 43:9). It means to be gone, to be distant, to make distance between (Gen. 44:4; Josh. 8:4; Judg. 18:22). False prophets prophesied lies to remove the people from their land (Jer. 27:10).

7369. רָחֵק ***rāḥēq:*** An adjective meaning far away. It indicates in context persons who have strayed from God, who have removed themselves from Him (Ps. 73:27).

7370. רָחַשׁ ***rāḥaš:*** I. A verb meaning to be stirred, to overflow. It refers figuratively of a person's heart, emotions being moved by something in a good sense (Ps. 45:1).

II. A verb meaning to indite; to put in words. It refers to putting something into prose or verse; in context it probably refers to writing it out (Ps. 45:1).

7371. רַחַת ***raḥaṯ:*** A feminine noun indicating a shovel, a pitchfork. It refers to a winnowing shovel or fork used to separate the chaff from grain (Isa. 30:24).

7372. רָטַב ***rāṭaḇ:*** A verb meaning to be wet, to be drenched. It refers to falling water, rain. In context it refers to mountain rains that are especially threatening to those caught in them, especially in the Middle East (Job 24:8).

7373. רָטֹב ***rāṭōb:*** An adjective meaning well-watered, thriving. It figuratively describes the prosperousness of the good person before God, his success (Job 8:16).

7374. רֶטֶט ***reṭeṭ:*** A masculine noun meaning fear, trembling, panic. From an unused root meaning to tremble, this word is found only in Jeremiah 49:24. It denoted fear or hysteria in the face of impending attack.

7375. רֻטֲפַשׁ ***ruṭᵃpaš:*** A verb meaning to become fresh, to be renewed. It indicates a renewal of health and vigor. It refers to a healthy suppleness to a young person's skin (Job 33:25).

7376. רָטַשׁ ***rāṭaš:*** A verb meaning to dash to pieces; to strike down. It is used of striking something in order to kill or destroy it; throwing it about violently (2 Kgs. 8:12; Isa. 13:16; Hos. 10:14; 13:16[14:1]; Nah. 3:10). It refers especially to infants and mothers in a time of war. It is used of arrows striking the enemy and demolishing them (Isa. 13:18).

7377. רִי ***riy:*** A masculine noun indicating moisture; watering. It describes the water taken up into as well as formed within a cloud (Job 37:11).

7378. רִיב ***riyb,*** **רוּב** ***rûb:*** A verb meaning to strive, to contend, to dispute, and to conduct a lawsuit. The verb means to conduct a lawsuit or legal case and all that it involves. The Lord conducts His case against the leaders of His people (Isa. 3:13). He relents in His case from accusing humankind, knowing how weak they are (Isa. 57:16). David pleaded with the Lord to give him vindication in his case (1 Sam. 24:15[16]); as did Israel when God contended for them (Mic. 7:9).

The word means to contend or to strive for some reason in a nonlegal setting as well. The servants of Isaac and Abimelech contended over wells they had dug or claimed to own (Gen. 26:21). Two men could quarrel and come to blows (Ex. 21:18; Judg. 11:25). Jacob and Laban disputed with one another (Gen. 31:36). The people of Israel complained bitterly against the Lord at Meribah (Num. 20:13).

The word means to raise complaints or accusations against others. The tribes of Israel complained because some of their women were taken and given as wives to the Benjamites (Judg. 21:22). An arrogant Israel would dare to bring charges against the Lord (Isa. 45:9; Jer. 2:29; 12:1). The tribe of Levi contended with the Lord at Meribah as well (Deut. 33:8; cf. Num. 20:13).

The causative stem of this verb means to bring a case against (i.e., to oppose). The Lord will judge those who oppose Him (1 Sam. 2:10).

7379. רִיב ***riyḇ,*** רִב ***riḇ,*** רִיבָה ***riyḇāh:*** A masculine noun meaning a strife, a controversy, a contention. The primary idea of this noun is that of a quarrel or dispute. It appears in reference to an argument over land-use rights (Gen. 13:7); the logical dispute the Lord has with sinners (Jer. 25:31); any general state of contention between individuals (Prov. 20:3); the clamoring of people for station or possessions (2 Sam. 22:44); and open hostilities with an enemy (Judg. 12:2). Israel is commanded not to pervert justice in a lawsuit (Ex. 23:2). Similarly, the word is used in a legal sense to refer to an argument or case made in one's defense (Deut. 21:5; Prov. 18:17; Mic. 7:9).

7380. רִיבַי ***riyḇay:*** A proper noun designating Ribai (2 Sam. 23:29; 1 Chr. 11:31).

7381. רֵיחַ ***rēyaḥ:*** A masculine noun indicating an aroma, a fragrance, an odor. It refers to the odor or scent produced by various things: clothes (Gen. 27:27); water (Job 14:9); aromatic oils (Song 1:3); sweet-smelling breath (Song 7:8[9]). It is used figuratively, not literally, of God's sensing and approving of an odor of sacrifices (Gen. 8:21), especially as described in the various sacrifices depicted in Exodus (29:18, 25, 41), Leviticus (8:21, 28), and Numbers (18:17). In Exodus 5:21, it is combined with *b'š* to indicate making someone an offensive, stinking odor. It is found often in a romantic setting describing various pleasing fragrances (Song 1:3, 12; 2:13, etc.). It is used figuratively, e.g., the smell of Moab (Jer. 48:11); and the cedar-like fragrance of a restored Israel (Hos. 14:6[7]). It is used to describe the aromas offered to pagan gods (Ezek. 6:13).

7382. רֵיחַ ***rēyaḥ:*** An Aramaic feminine noun indicating a smell, an odor. It indicates the odor produced by fire when it singes or burns clothing (Dan. 3:27).

7383. רִיפָה ***riypāh,*** רִפָה ***ripāh:*** A feminine noun referring to grain. It refers to kernels of some kind of grain (2 Sam. 17:19; some have suggested "beans"). It has the same meaning in Proverbs 27:22 where it is used in a simile.

7384. רִיפַת ***riypaṯ,*** דִּיפַת ***diypaṯ:*** I. A proper noun designating Riphath (Gen. 10:3).

II. A proper noun designating Diphath, Riphath (1 Chr. 1:6).

7385. רִיק ***riyq:*** A masculine noun meaning emptiness, vanity, a delusion. It is used with a prefixed *l^e^* to mean, in vain, uselessly (Lev. 26:16, 20; Job 39:16). It stands for an imagined plot or plan that is a delusion, vain (Ps. 2:1); or something that is worthless (Ps. 4:2[3]). It refers to professed help that is useless, vain before the Lord (Isa. 30:7; Jer. 51:58; Hab. 2:13). Figuratively, it describes Israel being treated in judgment as an empty vessel (Jer. 51:34).

7386. רֵיק *rēyq,* רֵק *rēq:* An adjective meaning empty, worthless, vain. It indicates something that has nothing in it, evacuated, e.g., a pit (Gen. 37:24); a pitcher (Judg. 7:16); vessels (2 Kgs. 4:3); a pot (Ezek. 24:11; see v. 6). It indicates that an animal is lean, skinny (Gen. 41:27). It indicates idle or trifling when describing what God's Word is not (Deut. 32:47). It describes people as worthless as to moral character (Judg. 9:4; 11:3; 2 Sam. 6:20; 2 Chr. 13:7). It is used in a parable to mean removed, taken away (Neh. 5:13). Used by itself, it means vain things (Prov. 12:11). It indicates being hungry, empty (Isa. 29:8).

7387. רֵיקָם *rēyqām:* An adverb meaning empty-handed, empty. It is used most often to indicate that a person is without something—wealth, sacrifices, gifts, money, etc. (Gen. 31:42; Ex. 3:21; 23:15; 34:20; Deut. 15:13; 16:16). It means essentially the same thing when translated empty, meaning without something (Ruth 1:21; 3:17). It indicates without a sacrifice accompanying the ark (1 Sam. 6:3). It indicates that many were slain by Saul's sword (it did not return unsatisfied) (2 Sam. 1:22; cf. Jer. 50:9). It refers to a condition of injustice (widows sent away empty-handed) (Job 22:9). It has the sense of robbing or abusing a friend (Ps. 7:4[5]). It has the sense of needlessly or without reason (Ps. 25:3). God's Word never returns empty; it accomplishes its purpose (Isa. 55:11).

7388. רִיר *riyr:* I. A masculine noun referring to saliva. It is used to describe spit, saliva. It is used when David feigned insanity and let saliva run down his beard (1 Sam. 21:13[14]).

II. A masculine noun referring to the white of an egg. It refers, evidently, to the tasteless nature of an egg white (Job 6:6). Some translators have suggested a slimy, tasteless excretion from a bugloss plant.

7389. רֵישׁ *rēyš,* רֵאשׁ *rēʾš,* רִישׁ *riyš:* A masculine noun indicating poverty. It describes a state of need, a lack of the necessary or common needs of life. In the Wisdom Literature, poverty is often a result of irresponsibility, laziness, or a lack of diligence (Prov. 6:11; 13:18); but is also looked on as a dangerous trap that ensnares some people (Prov. 10:15). Neither poverty nor riches is the ideal (Prov. 30:8).

7390. רַךְ *rak̲:* An adjective meaning gentle, tender, weak, indecisive. It describes a desirable quality of meat used for food (Gen. 18:7); but indicates frailty, weakness in a person (Gen. 33:13; 2 Sam. 3:39). Leah's eyes were weak, tender (Gen. 29:17). It describes a character, a way of life that reflects refinement (Deut. 28:54, 56). It is used to indicate a tongue that speaks with kind prudence (Prov. 25:15); that speaks softly, gently (Prov. 15:1). It indicates the way a mother sees her son as a tender, beloved child (Prov. 4:3). It indicates a soft or reconciling word (Job 41:3[40:27]). It describes the tender green growth of new branches on a tree (Ezek. 17:22).

7391. רֹךְ ***rōḵ:*** A masculine noun indicating gentleness, refinement. It is used as an abstract noun indicating a cultured, sophisticated, overly sensitive way of life (Deut. 28:56).

7392. רָכַב ***rāḵaḇ:*** A verb meaning to ride a horse; to ride in a chariot. It refers to the activity of mounting and riding an animal: a camel (Gen. 24:61); donkey (Ex. 4:20); horse (Gen. 49:17; Ex. 15:1, 21); mule (1 Kgs. 1:33). It refers to riding in general (Lev. 15:9). It includes riding in a chariot (2 Kings. 9:16; Jer. 17:25). It is used figuratively of living, enjoying the best things on earth (Deut. 32:13). God Himself rides the heavens (Deut. 33:26) on a cherub (2 Sam. 22:11; Ps. 18:10[11]). In its causative use, it can have the sense of making a person ride (Gen. 41:43; 2 Kgs. 9:28; Ps. 66:12). Used of handling a bow, it means to draw the bow (2 Kgs. 13:16). It describes harnessing, hooking up a heifer, in the context of Ephraim portrayed as a heifer (Hos. 10:11).

7393. רֶכֶב ***reḵeḇ:*** I. A masculine noun meaning a chariot. It refers to a group of chariots as a collective noun (Gen. 50:9; Ex. 14:6, 7, 9, 17, 18, 23, 26, 28); but it can refer to a single chariot (1 Kgs. 22:35). It was a major engine of war in the ancient world, but God could overthrow all of them (Ex. 15:19). It could be a symbol of royal authority (1 Kgs. 1:5); special storage cities were used to house them (1 Kgs. 9:19). It describes a caravan or a line of donkeys or camels, probably a supply van for an army (Isa. 21:7).

II. A masculine noun indicating an upper millstone. It refers to a movable stone used to crush or squeeze grapes or olives, to grind grain, etc. It was movable, usually circular in shape, with a hole in its center (Deut. 24:6; Judg. 9:53; 2 Sam. 11:21).

7394. רֵכָב ***rēḵāḇ:*** A proper noun designating Rechab:

A. He along with others assassinated Saul's son, Ishbosheth ("man of shame"), who tried to become king after Saul (2 Sam. 4:2, 5, 6, 9).

B. A person who was strongly against Baal and Baalism. He and his descendants refused to drink wine, build houses, or sow crops. God honored his faithfulness to His principles (2 Kgs. 10:15, 23; Jer. 35: 6, 8, 14, 16, 19) by making him and his followers an example of faithfulness to a covenant. He is apparently the ancestor of Malkijah who was a leader in postexilic Judah and repaired the Dung Gate (Neh. 3:14).

7395. רַכָּב ***rakkāḇ:*** A masculine noun referring to a chariot driver, a horseman. It refers to the driver of a chariot (1 Kgs. 22:34; 2 Chr. 18:33); or to a horseman, a person who rode horses for various purposes in the line of duty, often employed by the king (2 Kgs. 9:17).

7396. רִכְבָּה **riḵbāh:** I. A feminine noun meaning saddle. It refers to a seat for a rider on a horse, a donkey, a camel (Ezek. 27:20, NASB, NIV). Some suggest an abstract meaning, riding.

II. A feminine noun meaning chariot. Some translators prefer to render this as chariot (Ezek. 27:20, KJV).

7397. רֵכָה **rēḵāh,** רֵכָבִי **rēḵāḇiy:** I. A proper noun designating Recah, Rechah (1 Chr. 4:12).

II. A proper noun designating Rechabite (Jer. 35:2, 3, 5, 18).

7398. רְכוּב **rᵉḵûḇ:** A masculine noun meaning chariot. It indicates the chariotry that the clouds provide for the Lord (Ps. 104:3).

7399. רְכוּשׁ **rᵉḵûš,** רְכֶשׁ **rᵉḵuš:** A masculine noun indicating possessions; property, goods. This word describes property and possessions obtained by labor, not by purchasing them with money: possessions one has accumulated (Gen. 12:5); cattle, flocks (Gen. 13:6; 31:18; 36:7). It refers to equipment of all kinds, utensils, stored items, military baggage (Gen. 46:6; Ezra 1:4, 6; Dan. 11:13). This type of property includes the spoils and booty of war (Gen. 14:11, 12, 16, 21; Dan. 11:24, 28). It indicates the king's own property (1 Chr. 27:31).

7400. רָכִיל **rāḵiyl:** A masculine noun referring to gossip. It refers to spreading rumors or falsities about someone. It is always used in a negative manner. Such a practice was prohibited by the Mosaic Law (Lev. 19:16). Wisdom Literature condemns it. It entails revealing things that should not be made public (Prov. 11:13; 20:19). God condemns the whole people of being talebearers, especially certain leaders (Jer. 6:28; 9:4[3]; Ezek. 22:9).

7401. רָכַךְ **rāḵak:** A verb meaning to be tender, fainthearted, faint, weak, soft. It indicates that a person lacks resolve and needs to be strong in the face of danger (Deut. 20:3, 8; Isa. 7:4; Jer. 51:46). It refers, on the other hand, to a tenderness, a humility of heart, that is a strength before God (2 Kgs. 22:19; 2 Chr. 34:27). God can make a person weak of heart and frail (Job 23:16). Soft words can be deceptive, however (Ps. 55:21[22]). It refers to the healing of a bruise with oil but with reference to the healing of Israel's spiritual and moral corruption (Isa. 1:6).

7402. רָכַל **rāḵal:** A verb meaning to sell merchandise, to trade. In its participial forms, it refers to a merchant, a tradesman, or a female merchant (1 Kgs. 10:15) who sells merchandise (Ezek. 17:4; 27:3, 13; Nah. 3:16, NASB traders).

7403. רָכָל **rāḵāl:** A proper noun designating Racal, Rachal (1 Sam. 30:29).

7404. רְכֻלָּה **rᵉḵullāh:** A feminine noun referring to merchandise, trading. It refers to the material wares traded or to the process of merchandising and trading itself (Ezek. 26:12; 28:5, 18).

7405. רָכַס ***rāḵas:*** A verb meaning to bind, to tie. It refers to joining things together; in context it refers to doing so by woven cords (Ex. 28:28; 39:21).

7406. רֶכֶס ***reḵes:*** A masculine noun referring to rugged terrain. It indicates a roughness or unevenness of ground that God will turn into a habitable plain or valley (Isa. 40:4).

7407. רֹכֶס ***rōḵes:*** I. A masculine noun referring to an intrigue, a conspiracy. It refers to intrigue, ruses, and plans to act against someone (Ps. 31:20[21]).

II. A masculine noun indicating pride. Some translate the word more generally of human self-honor and self-aggrandizement (Ps. 31:20[21]).

7408. רָכַשׁ ***rāḵaš:*** A verb meaning to accumulate, to acquire. It describes the process of acquiring property, especially through God's blessing, including all kinds of possessions (Gen. 12:5; 31:18; 36:6; 46:6).

7409. רֶכֶשׁ ***reḵeš:*** I. A masculine noun meaning a horse, a steed. It refers to a pair or team of horses (1 Kgs. 4:28[5:8]; Mic. 1:13); specially bred royal horses (Esth. 8:10, 14).

II. A masculine noun referring to a camel, a dromedary. It is rendered as dromedaries, camels by some translators, that is, camels trained for speed and efficiency in transport (1 Kgs. 4:28[5:8]).

III. A masculine noun meaning a mule. It is rendered as mules, common royal possessions in the ancient Middle East (KJV, Esth. 8:10, 14).

IV. A masculine noun referring to a swift beast. It implies a chariot horse trained to pull a chariot with great speed (Mic. 1:13).

7410. רָם ***rām:*** A proper noun designating Ram:

A. Son of Hezron (Ruth 4:19; 1 Chr. 2:9).

B. Son of Jerahmeel (1 Chr. 2:25, 27).

C. Relative of Elihu (Job 32:2).

7411. רָמָה ***rāmāh:*** I. A verb meaning to throw; to shoot (an arrow). It is used of the Lord's throwing the Egyptian horsemen into the Red Sea (Ex. 15:1, 21). It indicates the shooters of bows, archers (Ps. 78:9; Jer. 4:29).

II. A verb meaning to betray; to deceive. It means to lie, to deal craftily, to betray someone in a matter (Gen. 29:25; Josh. 9:22). It refers to covering for someone, pulling a trick (1 Sam. 19:17; 28:12; 2 Sam. 19:26). A certain crass, joking deception intended as humor is condemned (Prov. 26:19). Israel and her priests strayed from God and deceived Him (Lam. 1:19).

7412. רְמָה ***r***^{e}***māh:*** An Aramaic verb meaning to cast down, to throw: to impose a tribute. It is used once in a context to indicate imposing a tax upon (*'al*). It is negated since a tribute or a tax could not be imposed on certain classes of temple workers (Ezra 7:24). It refers to the throwing down of someone or something (Dan. 3:20, 21, 24; 6:16[17], 24[25]). It is used in the sense of establishing, setting a throne in place (Dan. 7:9). In its passive reflexive use, it means to be thrown down (Dan. 3:6, 11, 15; 6:7[8], 12[13]).

7413. רָמָה ***rāmāh:*** A feminine noun indicating a height, a hill; a high place. It refers to a hill or high ground in an area (1 Sam. 22:6). It indicates literally and figuratively an artificially constructed high place created for false worship in Israel or Judah (Ezek. 16:24, 25, 31, 39).

7414. רָמָה ***rāmāh:*** A proper noun designating Ramah:

A. A town in Benjamin's territory (Josh. 18:25). Its name means "height." It was near where Deborah judged Israel (Judg. 4:5). It was located about five miles north of Jerusalem and north, northeast of Gibeah. It was also called Ramathaim. King Baasha of Israel strengthened its fortifications (1 Kgs. 15:17; 2 Chr. 16:1–6), while Asa king of Judah dismantled them (1 Kgs. 15:21, 22). Later invasions passed through it (Isa. 10:29) and brought devastation (Jer. 31:15; 40:1; Hos. 5:8). Exiles from Babylonereturned there to settle (Ezra 2:26; Neh. 7:30).

B. The town from which Israel's last great judge, Samuel, came (1Sam. 1:19, 2:11). It was his administrative center at times (1 Sam. 7:17). Here Israel demanded a king to lead them (1 Sam. 8:4). Samuel came here after anointing David (1 Sam. 16:13). David later fled here to Samuel, and Saul pursued him (1 Sam. 19:18–22; 20:1). Samuel was buried here (1 Sam. 25:1; 28:3). It is best translated "hill, height" in 1 Samuel 22:6.

C. A town on Asher's border (Josh. 19:29), near the Canaanite cities of Tyre and Sidon.

D. A town in Naphtali between upper and lower Galilee (Josh. 19:36). It is located ca. twenty-five miles west of the north end of the Sea of Galilee.

E. Located on the border of Simeon. It is probably ca. twenty miles east, southeast of Beersheba and about thirteen miles west of the southern end of the Dead Sea.

F. A town in Transjordan in the area of Gilead where Joram, king of Israel, fought with the Arameans (2 Kgs. 8:29[28]).

7415. רִמָּה ***rimmāh:*** A feminine noun referring to a worm, a maggot. It refers to wormlike insect larva. It often appears in any decaying matter (Ex. 16:24); such as decaying manna or a decomposing corpse (Job 7:5; 21:26; 24:20). It is used in various literary ways by Job: as my mother (Job 17:14); a feature of Sheol (Isa. 14:11). Humankind is figuratively compared to a maggot in its lowliness (Job 25:6).

7416. רִמּוֹן **rimmôn,** רִמֹּן ***rimmōn:*** A masculine noun meaning pomegranate. It refers to a round fruit, red in color, covered with a rind and containing many seeds. Its fleshly part is edible and juicy. It was used often in Israel as a food but also as a decorative ornamental feature on priestly clothes, carved into wood, metal, etc. (Ex. 28:33, 34; 39:24–26; Num. 13:23; 1 Kgs. 7:18, 20, 42). It was a favorite food (Num. 20:5). It is used in an amorous description of a bride (Song 4:3, 13). Its abundance in the land of Israel depended on the Lord's blessing along with Israel's faithfulness (Hag. 2:19).

7417. רִמּוֹן ***rimmôn,*** רִמּוֹנוֹ ***rimmônô,*** רִמּוֹן הַמְּתֹאָר ***rimmôn hamᵉtōʾār:*** A. A masculine proper noun referring to Rimmon: a Syrian god. It refers to the god Hadad, a storm god, under another name. He was revered in Damascus, the capital of Syria. Naaman worshiped him (2 Kgs. 5:18).

B. A masculine proper noun referring to Rimmon: a Benjaminite. He was from the city of Beeroth. He was the father of Baanah and Rechab (2 Sam. 4:2, 5, 9).

C. A proper noun, Rimmon: a rock in the wilderness of Benjamin. It refers to a cliff full of caves in the area of Gibeah (Judg. 20:45, 47; 21:13).

D. A proper noun, Rimmon: a town in an undisclosed place but in the south of Judah toward Edom (Josh. 15:32; 19:7; 1 Chr. 4:32; Zech. 14:10).

E. A proper noun, Rimmon: a town in Zebulun. It may lie about ten kilometers north of Nazareth. It was a city of the Levites (Josh. 19:13; 1 Chr. 6:77[62]).

F. A proper noun, Remmon-methoar: Rimmon. A town located on the northeast border of Zebulun, due west of the center of the Sea of Galilee (Josh. 19:13).

7418. רָמוֹת נֶגֶב ***rāmôṯ negeḇ:*** A proper noun designating Ramoth Negev, Ramoth of the south (1 Sam. 30:27). It is the same as *rāmāh* (7414,E).

7419. רָמוּת ***rāmûṯ:*** I. A feminine noun indicating remains; refuse. It refers to the remains of rotting and decaying corpses of Pharaoh and the Egyptians (Ezek. 32:5; NKJV, NIV, NASB).

II. A feminine noun meaning height. Some translators render this, less likely, as height (KJV).

7420. רֹמַח ***rōmaḥ:*** A masculine noun meaning a spear, a javelin. It refers to a weapon of war or a hunting tool with a long shaft and a pointed sharp end (Num. 25:7; Judg. 5:8). It was capable of cutting one's flesh like a knife or sword (1 Kgs. 18:28). It was a major emblem of war (Ezek. 39:9; Joel 3:10[4:10]).

7421. רַמִּי ***rammiy:*** A proper noun designating one who is from Syria, Syrian (2 Chr. 22:5).

7422. רַמְיָה ***ramyāh:*** A proper noun designating Ramaiah (Ezra 10:25).

7423. רְמִיָּה ***r^emiyyāh:*** I. A feminine noun meaning deceit, treachery, fault. It refers to what is not truth, steadfastness, or correct, e.g., of God (Job 13:7); of a person (Job 27:4). A person free of deceit is blessed (Ps. 32:2). The tongue of the wicked produces deceit (Ps. 52:2[4]; Mic. 6:12). The word indicates what is not reliable, e.g., a treacherous bow (Ps. 78:57; Hos. 7:16).

II. A feminine noun indicating laziness, negligence, sloth. It refers to loose character in the sense of slackness, laziness, lack of diligence or attention: a lazy, slothful, or negligent hand (Prov. 10:4; 12:24); a lazy person (Prov. 12:27; 19:15); negligent, inadequate action or work (Jer. 48:10).

7424. רַמָּךְ ***rammā<u>k</u>:*** I. A feminine noun referring to a royal horse. It refers to horses bred and cared for by the king and his workmen for government service (Esth. 8:10).

II. A feminine noun indicating a camel, a dromedary. Some translators render I as a camel or dromedary, a less likely translation of the word in our current understanding of it (Esth. 8:10, KJV, cf. NKJV).

7425. רְמַלְיָהוּ ***r^emalyāhû:*** A proper noun designating Remaliah (2 Kgs. 15:25, 27, 30, 32, 37; 16:1, 5; 2 Chr. 28:6; Isa. 7:1, 4, 5, 9; 8:6).

7426. רָמַם ***rāmam:*** I. A verb meaning to be exalted, to be lifted up. It can have the sense of to rise up from (*min* [4480]), to get away from (Num. 16:45[17:10]). It has the meaning in context of something literally rising up (Ezek. 10:15, 17, 19). In other contexts, it is used figuratively of a person's exaltation or high standing in society (Job 24:24). It is used figuratively of the Lord's arising, acting (Isa. 33:10).

II. A verb meaning to be full. It indicates that something is decaying, rotting. Rotting with worms (*tôlā'îm*) indicates something is full of, seething with worms (Ex. 16:20). In context it refers to manna rotting and being full of worms.

7427. רֹמֵמֻת ***rōmēmu<u>t</u>,*** רוֹמֵמֻת ***rômēmut:*** A masculine noun indicating a lifting up; a rising up. It is used in a figurative sense to refer to the Lord's raising Himself up, of His beginning to act (Isa. 33:3).

7428. רִמֹּן פֶּרֶץ ***rimmôn pereṣ:*** A proper noun designating Rimmon Perez (Num. 33:19, 20).

7429. רָמַס ***rāmas:*** A verb meaning to trample underfoot, to tread down. It indicates the trampling of clay by a potter (Isa. 41:25), of grapes. It is used figuratively of God's trampling in judgment (Isa. 63:3); of trampling God's courts in justice (Isa. 1:12); of trampling a person in time of famine (2 Kgs. 7:17, 20); of Jezebel's being trampled by horses (2 Kgs.

9:33). It is used figuratively of trampling a person's soul or life (Ps. 7:5[6]); of God's people stepping on, treading down dangerous serpents (Ps. 91:13).

7430. רָמַשׂ rāmaś: A verb meaning to creep, to move lightly. It indicates locomotion or traveling by going slowly along the ground on hands and knees for a person by wiggling or crawling for animals, insects, etc., God created all these living beings that creep, crawl, or wiggle in order to move (Gen. 1:21; 26, 28, 30; 7:8, 14, 21; 8:17, 19; 9:2; Lev. 11:44, 46). These kinds of creatures were detestable, so Israel could not eat them (Lev. 20:25). The word has the general sense of movement, whatever moves (Ps. 69:34[35]) or prowls (Ps. 104:20).

7431. רֶמֶשׂ remeś: A masculine collective noun meaning creeping things, moving things. It describes a large category of living beings that God created. It does not include large animals or birds. It includes many small animals, reptiles, beings that crawl, creep, move randomly, etc., along the earth. God created them (Gen. 1:24–26). The phrase from mankind (*'āḏām*) to animals (beasts, *behēmāh*) to creeping things (*remeś*) to fowl (*'ôp̱*) is inclusive of what God affected in the flood (Gen. 6:7; 6:20). It indicates the extent of Solomon's great knowledge of the world (1 Kgs. 4:33[5:13]). This word also describes swarming things that inhabit the seas (Ps. 104:25). Even these became idols to Israel (Ezek. 8:10). But, in the time of restoration, even these beings will be regarded as important by God (Hos. 2:18[20]). It is used in a simile comparing rebellious Israel to these creatures (Hab. 1:14).

7432. רֶמֶת remeṯ: A proper noun designating Remeth (Josh. 19:21).

7433. רָמוֹת rāmôṯ, רָמוֹת גִּלְעָד rāmôt gil'āḏ: A proper noun designating Ramoth, Ramoth Gilead:

A. A city located in Transjordan Gilead. It belonged to Gad and was also a city of refuge (Josh. 21:38) (See also 7414,F.). It was an administrative center for Solomon (1 Kgs. 4:13). Israel and Judah engaged the Arameans in battle here (1 Kgs. 22:3–29). The Lord had Jehu anointed here to destroy Ahab and Jezebel (2 Kgs. 9:1–14).

B. The name of a postexilic Jew who confirmed Nehemiah's covenant of renewal (Ezra 10:29).

7434. רָמַת הַמִּצְפֶּה rāmaṯ hammiṣpeh: A proper noun designating Ramath Mizpeh (Josh. 27:27).

7435. רָמָתִי rāmāṯiy: A proper noun designating Ramathite (1 Chr. 27:27).

7436. רָמָתַיִם צוֹפִים rāmāṯayim ṣôp̱iym, רָמָתַיִם rāmāṯayim: I. A proper noun designating Ramathaim-zophim, the same as II below and *rāmāh* (7414,B) (KJV, NASB, 1 Sam. 1:1).

II. A proper noun designating Ramathaim, used with *ṣûp̱iy* (6689), same as I above and *rāmāh* (7414,B) (NIV, 1 Sam. 1:1).

7437. רָמַת לְחִי ***rāmāṯ l^ehiy:*** A proper noun designating Ramath Lehi (Judg. 15:17).

7438. רֹן ***rōn:*** A masculine noun meaning a song. It refers to a song of jubilation, of celebration. See 7442.

7439. רָנָה ***rānāh:*** A verb meaning to rattle. It refers to the sound made by a container of arrows or darts banging against something, e.g., a war horse (Job 39:23).

7440. רִנָּה ***rinnāh:*** A feminine noun indicating glad shouting, joyful singing, crying out. It refers to the utterance and sound of a shout, a cry. It may be a sound or a cry to the Lord in supplication (1 Kgs. 8:28; Jer. 7:16); a cry of warning or of instructions (1 Kgs. 22:36); a cry of joy at the destruction of the wicked (Prov. 11:10; Isa. 14:7). The Lord Himself cries out over His people (Zeph. 3:17).

7441. רִנָּה ***rinnāh:*** A proper noun designating Rinnah (1 Chr. 4:20).

7442. רָנַן ***rānan,*** **רוּן** ***rûn:*** I. A verb meaning to shout for joy; to sing joyfully. It indicates the utterance or crying out of a person or persons. The character of the cry must be discerned by the context or actual intended use of the verb: Often it indicates crying out in joy, exaltation (Isa. 12:6; 24:14; Jer. 31:7). It is used most often of exalting or praising the Lord (Isa. 26:19; 35:2; 52:8; Jer. 31:12; 51:48); especially in Psalms (Ps. 5:11[12]; 67:4[5]; 81:1[2]; 90:14; 92:4[5]; 149:5). The absence of a cry like this is sometimes an indication of God's judgment (Isa. 16:10). God makes even a widow's heart sing for joy (Job 29:13). God causes even nature to shout for delight (Ps. 65:8[9]); and commands His just, righteous people to shout for joy (Ps. 32:11). Its opposite is a cry of distress (Isa. 65:14; Lam. 2:19). It is used in general of putting forth a cry of encouragement, exhortation, instruction (Prov. 1:20; 8:3).

II. A verb meaning to be overcome. It indicates a person who is under the influence of wine, who is making sounds, responses as a staggering person or one barely awake (Ps. 78:65, *miṯrônen*).

III. A verb meaning to awake out of stupor. It refers to a person coming from under the influence of wine, still not fully alert (Ps. 78:65).

7443. רֶנֶן ***renen:*** I. A masculine noun meaning an ostrich. It refers to the most powerful bird. It runs fast but does not fly; it has wings with which to gesture (Job 39:13).

II. A masculine noun meaning a peacock. It refers to a large bird with a crest of plumules and long, brightly colored tail coverts that can spread out like a circular fan. The bird often struts, seemingly showing off its feathers and colors (Job 39:13).

7444. רַנֵּן ***rannēn:*** An intensive verb referring to shouting, singing. It describes singing, a joyful cry. It usually describes a cry of jubilation or praise to the Lord (Isa. 35:2).

7445. רְנָנָה ***r***^{e}***nānāh:*** A feminine noun indicating a joyful shout, singing. It refers to a cry of delight over a marvelous event (Job 3:7). The joy of the godless is indicated to be brief, for a short time (Job 20:5). It is used to indicate lips of joy, lips that offer praise to God (Ps. 63:5[6]). It refers to praise and worship before God in general (Ps. 100:2).

7446. רִסָּה ***rissāh:*** A proper noun designating Rissah (Num. 33:21, 22).

7447. רָסִיס ***rāsiys:*** I. A masculine noun indicating a drop [of dew]; dampness. It refers to a light condensation of water on something or, in context, the source from which something has become wet (Song 5:2). For Amos 6:11, see II, III.

II. A masculine noun meaning a piece, a fragment. It refers to the small parts into which an object can be broken. In context, it indicates a house broken into pieces of rubble or debris (Amos 6:11).

III. A masculine noun meaning a breach, a breach in the walls. It refers to holes in the structure of a house; collapsed sections in its walls or roof (Amos 6:11).

7448. רֶסֶן ***resen:*** I. A masculine noun referring to a bridle, a restraint. It indicates control exercised over something, someone, or a behavioral pattern (Job 30:11). It may indicate the means used to restrain something (Job 41:13[5]), e.g., a bridle (Ps. 32:9). It is used figuratively of God's leading the nations with a bridle (Isa. 30:28).

II. A masculine noun meaning mail, armor. It refers to a protective covering of some kind, mail, armor, a flexible body armor. In context it refers to the natural protective covering of Leviathan (Job 41:13[5]).

7449. רֶסֶן ***resen:*** A proper noun designating Resen (Gen. 10:12).

7450. רסס ***rāsas:*** A verb meaning to moisten. It means to add water to something or to add a water substitute, such as oil, to help mix ingredients together (Ezek. 46:14).

7451. רַע ***ra',*** רָעָה ***rā'āh:*** An adjective meaning bad, evil. The basic meaning of this word displays ten or more various shades of the meaning of evil according to its contextual usage. It means bad in a moral and ethical sense and is used to describe, along with good, the entire spectrum of good and evil; hence, it depicts evil in an absolute, negative sense, as when it describes the tree of the knowledge of good and evil (Gen. 2:9; 3:5, 22). It was necessary for a wise king to be able to discern the evil or the good in the actions of his people (Eccl. 12:14); men and women are characterized as evil (1 Sam. 30:22; Esth. 7:6; Jer. 2:33). The human heart is evil all day long (Gen. 6:5) from childhood (Gen. 8:21); yet the people of God are to purge evil from among them (Deut. 17:7). The Lord is the final arbiter of whether something was good or evil; if something was evil in the eyes of the Lord, there is no further court of appeals (Deut. 9:18; 1 Kgs. 14:22). The day of the Lord's judgment is called an evil day, a day of reckoning and condemnation (Amos 6:3). Jacob would have undergone grave evil (i.e., pain, misery, and ultimate disaster) if he had lost Benjamin (Gen. 44:34). The word can refer to circumstances as evil, as when the Israelite foremen were placed in a grave situation (Ex. 5:19; 2 Kgs. 14:10).

The word takes on the aspect of something disagreeable, unwholesome, or harmful. Jacob evaluated his life as evil and destructive (Gen. 47:9; Num. 20:5); and the Israelites considered the wilderness as a threatening, terrifying place. The Canaanite women were evil in the eyes of Isaac (i.e., displeasing [Gen. 28:8]). The rabble's cry within Israel for meat was displeasing in the eyes of Moses (Num. 11:10). This word describes the vicious animal that killed Joseph, so Jacob thought (Gen. 37:33). The despondent countenances of persons can be described by this word; the baker's and the butler's faces were downcast because of their dreams (Gen. 40:7). It can also describe one who is heavy in heart (Prov. 25:20).

In a literal sense, the word depicts something that is of poor quality or even ugly in appearance. The weak, lean cows of Pharaoh's dream were decrepit, ugly-looking (Gen. 41:3, 20, 27); poisonous drinking water was described as bad (2 Kgs. 2:19; 4:41). From these observations, it is clear that the word can be used to attribute a negative aspect to nearly anything.

Used as a noun, the word indicates realities that are inherently evil, wicked, or bad; the psalmist feared no evil (Ps. 23:4). The noun also depicts people of wickedness, that is, wicked people. Aaron characterized the people of Israel as inherently wicked in order to clear himself (Ex. 32:22). Calamities, failures, and miseries are all connotations of this word when it is used as a noun.

7452. רֵעַ *rēaʻ*: A masculine noun referring to a loud shout, roar, thunder. It refers to the sound and the action of shouting. It refers to the shouts of the idolatrous Israelites as they shouted in rebellion and confusion to their gods (Ex. 32:17). It refers to the sound of thunder and lightning (Job 36:33). It refers to a cry of agony, reinforced by the use of its related verb (Mic. 4:9).

7453. רֵעַ *rēaʻ*, רֵיַע *rēyaʻ*: A masculine noun meaning another person. Most frequently, this term is used to refer to the second party in a personal interaction without indicating any particular relationship (Gen. 11:7; Judg. 7:13, 14; Ruth 3:14). It is extremely broad, covering everyone from a lover (Hos. 3:1); a close friend (Job 2:11); an acquaintance (Prov. 6:1); an adversary in court (Ex. 18:16); an enemy in combat (2 Sam. 2:16). Thus, this word is well-suited for its widely inclusive use in the Ten Commandments (see Ex. 20:16, 17; Deut. 5:20, 21; cf. Luke 10:29–37).

7454. רֵעַ *rēa‘:* A masculine noun meaning a thought, a purpose. It indicates what a persons have in mind, what their intents or purposes are (Ps. 139:2). It is used also of the thoughts of God Himself (Ps. 139:17).

7455. רֹעַ *rōa‘:* A masculine noun meaning badness, evil. This word is used to depict the quality of meat and produce (Gen. 41:19, Jer. 24:2, 3, 8). In Genesis, the word is used to describe cows, while in Jeremiah it describes figs. Eliab, David's oldest brother, describes David as conceited with a wicked heart, for he claims that David left the sheep only to come and watch the battle (1 Sam. 17:28). *Rōa'* is also used as a reason for punishment or for the wrath of God (i.e., for evil that had been done [Deut. 28:20; Isa. 1:16; Jer. 4:4; 21:12]). This word is also used to denote sadness or sorrow (Eccl. 7:3). In Ecclesiastes, the author states that sorrow is better than laughter, for a sad face is good for the heart.

7456. רָעֵב *rā‘ēḇ:* A verb meaning to be hungry, famished. It indicates that a person has a serious lack of food. It describes an entire nation during a time of famine (Gen. 41:55). Israel suffered from hunger in the wilderness (Deut. 8:3). It indicates the hunger of lions (Ps. 34:10[11]). God does not hunger as people do (Ps. 50:12). It is used of Israel, a people famished from hunger (Isa. 8:21). God, however, cares for the hunger of His servants (Isa. 65:13).

7457. רָעֵב *rā‘ēḇ:* An adjective meaning hungry, famished. It describes a state of craving, needing food. It indicates the perpetual poor of the land who are in constant hunger, lacking enough food and care (1 Sam. 2:5); often lacking rest and water as well (2 Sam. 17:29). It was a common condition in the siege of a city (2 Kgs. 7:12). The wicked will suffer from hunger (Job 18:12). The Lord delivers from hunger (Ps. 107:5, 9, 36). The famous saying in Proverbs 25:21 urges people to feed hungry enemies. Hunger can cause a person to dream (Isa. 29:8). A hungry person finds even bitter food to be enjoyable (Prov. 27:7). A righteous person helps feed the hungry (Ezek. 18:7, 16).

7458. רָעָב *rā‘āḇ:* A masculine noun referring to famine, hunger. It refers to a general and acute failure of crops, a serious shortage of food, and/or water. Canaan often experienced famines (Gen. 12:10; 26:1); but Egypt also suffered cycles of famine (Gen. 41:27, 30, 31). The word also refers to hunger itself, a strong need for certain kinds of food (Ex. 16:3;

Deut. 28:48). God can and does preserve a person in time of famine (Job 5:20; Ps. 33:19). Famine or hunger can be the punishment or discipline of God on His people (Isa. 5:13). It is one of the three judgments of God often mentioned together (Jer. 32:24), sword, famine, and pestilence. Amos mentions a famine of the Word of God, not food, that the Lord will send (Amos 8:11).

7459. רְעָבוֹן ***re'āḇôn:*** A masculine noun meaning famine, starving. It is an abstract noun referring to a famine and its conditions in general, but with reference to households (Gen. 42:19, 33). Those who trust the Lord will have an abundance, even during a time of famine (Ps. 37:19).

7460. רָעַד ***rā'aḏ:*** A verb meaning to tremble, to quake. The psalmist uses the word in a description of the holiness, majesty, and power of God, where the earth is depicted as trembling at the mere gaze of the Lord (Ps. 104:32). Daniel trembled in fear and reverence at the sight and presence of the vision before he heard the words that the messenger had been sent to deliver (Dan. 10:11).

7461. רַעַד ***ra'aḏ,*** רְעָדָה ***re'āḏāh:*** A masculine noun meaning trembling. In the song of Moses and Miriam, the leaders of Moab were described as being seized with trembling before the power of the Lord (Ex. 15:15). In a cry to God, the psalmist uses the word to state that fear and trembling had bent him (Ps. 55:5[6]). He cried out for God to come to his rescue and deliver him from his enemies.

7462. רָעָה ***rā'āh:*** I. A verb meaning to feed, to tend; to be a shepherd. It means in general to care for, to protect, to graze, to feed flocks and herds (Gen. 30:31, 36; 37:2; Ex. 3:1; 1 Sam. 17:15). In its participial form *rō'eh,* it can mean shepherd (Gen. 4:2); sheepherders (Gen. 29:9). Shepherds pasture, lead the sheep, flocks to eat (Job 24:2). It is used figuratively of God as the Shepherd of Jacob and his people (Gen. 48:15; Isa. 40:11; Hos. 4:16). The king of Israel was to shepherd the people for God (2 Sam. 5:2; 7:7; Jer. 3:15). The masculine participle refers to the leaders of God's people (Jer. 2:8; 22:22; Ezek. 34:2, 3, 8, 10). God is pictured as the one who shepherds an individual soul, a person (Ps. 49:14[15]). It is used figuratively to describe the lips of the wise as shepherding the people (Prov. 10:21). It is used figuratively of the land of Israel, the pastures of the shepherds mourn or dry up (Amos 1:2). It indicates the grazing, feeding of animals, flocks, herds, cattle (Gen. 41:2). Fools feed on folly, not wisdom (Prov. 15:14).

II. A verb meaning to associate with, to be a companion, to be a friend. It indicates a relationship of friendship between persons (Judg. 14:20); or to live in an area and develop associations with the people of the land (Ps. 37:3). It indicates a person who regularly associates with a group of persons, a companion, an associate, a friend, sharing common ideas and activities (Prov. 13:20; 22:24; 28:7; 29:3).

7463. רֵעֶה ***rē'eh:*** A masculine noun meaning a friend, a friend of the king as a personal advisor. It refers in context to a person who has a personal and official attachment to another person and promotes his or her welfare and cause (2 Sam. 15:37; 16:16). It indicates someone who has shown support for another (1 Kgs. 4:5).

7464. רֵעָה ***rē'āh:*** A feminine noun indicating a female friend. It refers to a female friend with whom strong bonds have been established (Judg. 11:37, 38). It refers to those who officially accompany and wait on the king's daughter (Ps. 45:14[15]).

7465. רֹעָה ***rō'āh:*** An adjective meaning broken. Its meaning extends beyond something being merely broken into pieces. Used of a tooth, it seems to mean a bad or infected tooth in parallel with a weak or broken, unstable foot (Prov. 25:19).

7466. רְעוּ ***r***^{e}***'û:*** A proper noun designating Reu (Gen. 11:18–21; 1 Chr. 1:25).

7467. רְעוּאֵל ***r***^{e}***'û'ēl:*** A proper noun designating Reuel:

A. Son of Esau (Gen. 36:4, 10, 13, 17; 1 Chr. 1:35, 37).

B. Moses' father-in-law (Ex. 2:18; Num. 10:29).

C. The father of Eliasaph, the same as as *d*^{e}*'û'ēl* (1845) (KJV, Num. 2:14).

D. The father of Shephatiah (1 Chr. 9:8).

7468. רְעוּת ***r***^{e}***'ûṯ:*** A feminine noun meaning a fellow woman, an associate. In Jeremiah, the women were to teach one another (i.e., their associates or companions) a lament (Jer. 19:20[19]). Isaiah used the word to denote the mates of falcons or birds of prey (Isa. 34:15, 16). In a figurative use, Zechariah used the word to denote that the people who remained would be left to eat one another's flesh (Zech. 11:9). In Esther, King Xerxes was advised to make a decree stating that Vashti was never again to enter his presence and that her position was to be given to one of her associates that was better than she was (Esth. 1:19).

7469. רְעוּת ***r***^{e}***'ûṯ:*** A masculine noun meaning striving, vexation. It refers to a person's efforts to attain something, to achieve or master something, to find out all about the world and its purposes. In Ecclesiastes, these efforts are considered vain (Eccl. 1:14; 2:11, 17, 26; 4:4, 6; 6:9). All striving ends up being a striving after nothing, the wind.

7470. רְעוּ ***r***^{e}***'û,*** רְעוּת ***r***^{e}***'ûṯ:*** An Aramaic feminine noun meaning a decision, will. It refers to making a choice in a matter, making up one's mind. It also refers to the choice or conclusion itself (Ezra 5:17). It also applies to the desires of persons or God, their desires in a matter (Ezra 7:18).

7471. רְעִי ***r**^e^**ʻiy:*** A masculine noun meaning pasture, pasture-fed. It refers to animals that have been fed and raised on good pastureland, pasture-fed cattle, oxen, etc., not raised in a stall (1 Kgs. 4:23[5:3]).

7472. רֵעִי ***rēʻiy:*** A proper noun designating Rei (1 Kgs. 1:8).

7473. רֹעִי ***rōʻiy:*** A masculine noun meaning a shepherd. It refers to one who pastures, cares for, and shepherds flocks. It may function in poetry as a simile, like the tent of a shepherd (Isa. 38:12). A useless or worthless shepherd is used to describe a corrupt leader in Israel (Zech. 11:17).

7474. רַעְיָה ***raʻyāh:*** A feminine noun meaning lover, darling. It indicates a female companion. In Song of Solomon the beloved of the bridegroom is mentioned at least nine times (Song 1:9, 15; 2:2, 10, 13; 4:1, 7; 5:2; 6:4).

7475. רַעְיוֹן ***raʻyôn:*** A masculine noun indicating striving, chasing. It indicates an effort to attain something or to gain some knowledge or wisdom about life under the sun. It is considered useless striving after the wind, nothing (Eccl. 1:17; 4:16); or simply without benefit or merit (Eccl. 2:22).

7476. רַעְיוֹן ***raʻyôn:*** An Aramaic masculine noun meaning thought. It refers to what a person is thinking about or to the process itself, what is going through a person's mind. It refers to the visionary thoughts of Babylonian kings (Dan. 2:29, 30; 4:19[16]; 5:6, 10), as well as to the thoughts of Daniel's visions that passed through his head (Dan. 7:28).

7477. רעַל ***rāʻal:*** A verb meaning to shake, to brandish. It refers to waving, shaking, exhibiting one's sword in a threatening way, a part of God's judgment upon the Assyrian capital (Nah. 2:3[4]).

7478. רַעַל ***raʻal:*** A masculine noun referring to trembling, reeling. It refers to a quaking, a shaking of fear brought on by some terrifying situation (Zech. 12:2).

7479. רְעָלָה ***r**^e^**ʻālāh:*** A feminine noun referring to a veil, a muffler. It refers to a light cloth covering worn over a woman's face or head or draped over the head and shoulders to conceal, protect, and beautify, a woman's face (Isa. 3:19). It was worn much less often by men and for different reasons.

7480. רְעֵלָיָה ***r**^e^**ʻēlāyāh:*** A proper noun designating Reelaiah, the same as *raʻamyāh* (7485) (Ezra 2:2).

7481. רָעַם ***rāʻam:*** I. A verb meaning to thunder, to roar. It means to be stirred up, agitated, noisy; confused. It describes the Lord's thundering action in judgment (1 Sam. 2:10); especially in meting out military confusion against His and Israel's enemies (1 Sam. 7:10; 2 Sam. 22:14). God's voice is heard in the thunder of a storm (Job 37:4, 5; 40:9; Ps. 18:13[14]; 29:3). It describes the roaring power of the seas (Ps. 96:11; 98:7).

II. A verb meaning to irritate, to trouble. It refers to agitating, picking on persons, possibly making fun of them or mocking them (1 Sam. 1:6). It refers to a worried or anxious countenance (face) because of a threatening situation (Ezek. 27:35).

7482. רַעַם ***ra'am:*** A masculine noun meaning thunder. It indicates the mighty works and power of God as displayed in His actions in nature (Job 26:14; Ps. 77:18[19]) but goes infinitely beyond that. It refers to the din and thunderous noise of warfare (Job 39:25). It describes a *sēṯer,* a thundercloud (Ps. 81:7[8], literally, a hiding place of thunder). His voice, thunder, awes the entire creation (Ps. 104:7). It was one feature of the Lord's great acts of punishment (Isa. 29:6).

7483. רַעְמָה ***ra'māh:*** I. A feminine noun referring to the flowing mane of a horse. It is taken by the King James Version to refer to the mane growing on the top of a horse's neck, paralleling its strength (Job 39:19).

II. A feminine noun meaning thunder, paralleling the strengths, the might of the horse on the previous poetic line (Job 39:19).

7484. רַעְמָה, רַעְמָא ***ra'māh, ra'mā':*** A proper noun designating Raamah:

A. A son of Cush (Gen. 10:7; 1 Chr. 1:9).

B. A home of traders (Ezek. 27:22).

7485. רַעַמְיָה ***ra'amyāh:*** A proper noun designating Raamiah, the same as *r^e'ēlāyāh* (7480) (Neh. 7:7).

7486. רַעַמְסֵס, רַעְמְסֵס ***ra'amsēs, ra'm^esēs:*** A proper noun designating Rameses, Raamses (Gen. 47:11; Ex. 1:11; 12:37; Num. 33:3, 5).

7487. רָעַן, רַעֲנַן ***rā'an, ra^anan:*** I. A verb indicating to grow luxurious; to be green. It indicates, with reference to a tree limb, a lively, fresh, tender green branch, flourishing and developing (Job 15:32).

II. An Aramaic adjective meaning flourishing. This adjective is used figuratively of the success of a person or a king, his prosperity (Dan. 4:4[1]).

7488. רַעֲנָן ***ra^anān:*** An adjective meaning green, flourishing. It refers to a luxuriant plant or tree, flourishing and full of vibrant life (Job 15:32); green and healthy looking, a place where fertility worship was often practiced (Deut. 12:2; 1 Kgs. 14:23; 2 Kgs. 16:4; Isa. 57:5; Jer. 2:20; Ezek. 6:13). It is used in similes for comparisons (Ps. 37:35; 52:8[10]). Used of oil, it means new, pure, fresh olive oil (Ps. 92:10[11]); of a love seat, it means luxuriant, beautiful (Song 1:16). The Lord Himself is described as the true luxuriant cypress tree for His people (Hos. 14:8[9]).

7489. רָעַע ***rā'a':*** A verb meaning to be bad, to do wrong. The root of the word indicates breaking, in contrast to the word *tāmam* (8552), which means to be whole. For example, tree branches that break are bad (Jer. 11:16). The word also refers to moral evil: an eye could be evil, that is, covetous (Deut. 15:9); or a person could do evil (Gen. 44:5; Prov. 4:16; Jer. 4:22). The word also refers to physical evil: God harmed or punished those who provoked Him (Zech. 8:14); and Laban would have hurt Jacob without God's prevention (Gen. 31:7). In addition, the word expresses sadness and describes the face or heart as being bad (1 Sam. 1:8; Neh. 2:3). The causative participle signifies an evildoer (Ps. 37:1; Isa. 9:17[16]). The idiomatic phrase, to be evil in someone's eyes, means to displease (Gen. 48:17; 2 Sam. 11:25; Jon. 4:1).

7490. רְעַע ***r**e**'a':*** An Aramaic verb meaning to break in pieces, to shatter, to crush. The term occurs only twice in the Old Testament; both are located within the same passage in the book of Daniel. In interpreting King Nebuchadnezzar's dream, Daniel declared that the fourth kingdom, represented by the legs of iron and feet of iron mixed with clay of the statue, would be as strong as iron and would break the previously mentioned kingdoms into pieces (Dan. 2:40). This term is closely related to the Hebrew verb *rā'a'* (7489).

7491. רָעַף ***rā'ap:*** A verb meaning to overflow, to drip down (of rain). It refers to rain that falls slowly and drips down on humankind (Job 36:28). It is used figuratively of the Lord's ways and paths, which, if followed, drip and are rich with an abundance of good things (Ps. 65:11[12]); even the dry pastures of the desert or wilderness (Ps. 65:12[13]); even the whole creation drips down abundance on the earth (Isa. 45:8). It is by God's wisdom that the dew of heaven is made to water, drip on the earth and humankind (Prov. 3:20).

7492. רָעַץ ***rā'aṣ:*** A verb meaning to shatter, to afflict. It refers to a violent breaking of the power of an enemy, disarming them (Ex. 15:6). It refers also to a constant oppression placed on a people or nation by force, a constant harassment of them (Judg. 10:8).

7493. רָעַשׁ ***rā'aš:*** A verb meaning to quake, to tremble, to shake, to leap, to be abundant. The word occurs thirty times in the Old Testament and most often refers to the physical, forceful (often violent), quick, back-and-forth movement of a physical body by an outside force. Frequently, the trembling or shaking takes place as nature's response to God's presence or to His activity of rendering divine judgment. Things shaken included the walls of a city (Ezek. 26:10); the thresholds of doors (Amos 9:1); the heavens (Joel 2:10, 3:16[4:16]; Hag. 2:6); the mountains (Jer. 4:24; Nah. 1:5); coastlands or islands (Ezek. 26:15); kingdoms (Isa. 14:16); the earth or lands (Judg. 5:4; 2 Sam. 22:8; Ps. 60:2[4]; 68:8[9]; 77:18[19]; Isa. 13:13; Jer. 8:16; 10:10; 49:21); Gentile nations (Ezek. 31:16; Hag. 2:7); and every living creature of creation (Ezek. 38:20). Twice the term conveys a much different action than the one related above. In the first rare usage, the verb portrays the leaping ability of a warhorse (Job 39:20). The second unique use expresses the psalmist's desire that there be an abundance of grain in the land (Ps. 72:16).

7494. רַעַשׁ ***raʿaš:*** A masculine noun referring to an earthquake, a shaking, a rumbling, a commotion. It indicates a quaking of the surface of the earth (1 Kgs. 19:11, 12); the quivering and shaking of a warhorse as it engages a battle (Job 39:24); or the brandishing, shaking of a javelin (Job 41:29[21]). It refers to the roar and commotion, the clatter of a battle itself (Isa. 9:5[4]); or the preparations for war (Jer. 10:22). It depicts the noise of a rolling chariot wheel, hastening into battle (Nah. 3:2). It is used of the sounds made by the Lord's chariot appearance and movement (Ezek. 3:12). It stands for an earthquake itself, a great shaking, trembling (Amos 1:1; Zech. 14:5).

7495. רָפָא ***rāp̱aʿ:*** A verb meaning to heal, to make fresh. It describes the process of healing, being restored to health, made healthy, usable, fertile: of Abimilech's household being restored to fertility (Gen. 20:17); of physical and spiritual healing (Isa. 53:5); of wounds being restored (Lev. 13:18; Jer. 15:18); of water being restored to a healthy state, drinkable, wholesome (2 Kgs. 2:21, 22); of the repair, restoration of an altar (1 Kgs. 18:30); of many diseases being healed (Deut. 28:27, 35). In its participial forms, it refers to a person who acts as a physician, a healer: God, the Lord, as Israel's healer (Gen. 20:17; Ex. 15:26; Job 13:4). It describes the restoring of a person's soul, life (Ps. 41:4[5]). In an emphatic construction, it indicates having a person healed, cared for (Ex. 21:19). It is used in its reflexive infinitive to note a purpose, in order to be (get) healed, from (*min*) wounds inflicted in battle (2 Kgs. 8:29; 9:15). God alone was able to heal the wounds of His broken people (Hos. 5:13; 6:1; 7:1). A true leader in Israel was to heal, care for the people of Israel (Zech. 11:16).

7496. רָפָא ***rāp̱āʿ:*** A masculine noun meaning shades, departed spirits, deceased ones, dead ones. The term always occurs in the plural form (*r^ep̱āʾiym*) and consistently denotes those who died and entered into a shadowy existence within *š^eʾôl* (7585) (Job 26:5; Prov. 9:18; Isa. 14:9). Three times the word is employed in direct parallelism with the Hebrew term for dead ones (*mēṯiym*, from *mûṯ* [4191], to die) (Ps. 88:10[11]; Isa. 26:14, 19).

"Shades" or deceased ones do not rise (Isa. 26:14). They reside in a place of darkness and oblivion (Ps. 88:10[11]). They cannot praise God (Ps. 88:10 [11]). The smooth words of the adulteress bring her victims down to death, to the place of the shades, never to return (Prov. 21:16; cf. Prov. 2:16–19; 9:13–18). Yet even in the Old Testament, a confident resurrection hope was gloriously and joyously held out to those in Sheol who obeyed God while alive (Isa. 26:19).

7497. רְפָאִים ***r**^e^**p̱ā'iym,*** רָפָא ***rāp̱a',*** רָפָה ***rāp̱ah:*** A masculine noun meaning a giant, Rephaim (an ethnic people group), Valley of Rephaim. Frequently, the term (only with the plural form) designated a Canaanite tribe that inhabited the Promised Land prior to the Hebrew conquest and who were known for their unusually large size (Gen. 14:5; 15:20; Deut. 2:11, 20; 3:11, 13; Josh. 12:4; 13:12; 17:15). In two accounts, the singular form was utilized to refer to a particular giant, perhaps an ancestor of the tribe of the Rephaim (2 Sam. 21:16, 18, 20, 22; 1 Chr. 20:6, 8). In a different vein, the word (also only in the plural form) acted as the proper name of a valley located southwest of Jerusalem (Josh. 15:8; 18:16; 2 Sam. 5:18, 22; 23:13; 1 Chr. 11:15; 14:9; Isa. 17:5).

7498. רָפָא ***rāp̱a',*** רָפָה ***rāp̱āh:*** A proper noun designating Rapha:

A. The father of several giants among David's enemies (1 Sam. 21:16, 18, 20, 22; 1 Chr. 20:6, 8). For the King James Version and New American Standard Bible see *rāp̱a'* (7497,III).

B. Son of Benjamin (1 Chr. 8:2).

C. Son of Binea, the same as Rephaiah (7509,D) (1 Chr. 8:37).

7499. רְפוּאָה ***r**^e^**p̱û'āh:*** A feminine noun indicating a remedy, healing. It refers to a process of restoration as well as the cure for a spiritual illness (Jer. 30:13); national corruption (Jer. 46:11); or a severely inflicted wound (Ezek. 30:21).

7500. רִפְאוּת ***rip̱'ûṯ:*** A feminine noun meaning health, healing. It refers to a process of restoration and refreshment to a person that brings healing. In context the fear of the Lord is the healing balm (Prov. 3:8).

7501. רְפָאֵל ***r**^e^**p̱ā'ēl:*** A proper noun designating Rephael (1 Chr. 26:7).

7502. רָפַד ***rāp̱aḏ:*** I. A verb meaning to spread out; to spread a blanket. It describes figuratively persons making themselves at home, at rest as permanent inhabitants of Sheol (Job 17:13). In another figurative expression, it describes the lying down, the spreading out of Leviathan (Job 41:30[22]).

II. A verb meaning to comfort, to refresh. It means to reinvigorate, refresh, and restore a person who is weak and faint (Song 2:5).

7503. רָפָה rāpāh: A verb meaning to become slack, to relax, to cease, to desist, to become discouraged, to become disheartened, to become weak, to become feeble, to let drop, to discourage, to leave alone, to let go, to forsake, to abandon, to be lazy. The word occurs forty-five times, often with the word *yād* (3027), meaning hand, forming an idiomatic phrase that requires careful translation within the context of a particular passage. For example, when Ish-Bosheth, Saul's son, heard that Abner had died, his hands became feeble, i.e., his courage failed him (2 Sam. 4:1; cf. 2 Chr. 15:7; Isa. 13:7; Jer. 6:24, 50:43; Ezek. 7:17; 21:7[12]). The term was also employed to signify the act of ceasing from something (Judg. 8:3; 2 Sam. 24:16; Neh. 6:9; Ps. 37:8); of leaving someone alone (Ex. 4:26; Deut. 9:14; Judg. 11:37; Job 7:19); of letting go (Job 27:6; Prov. 4:13; Song 3:4); and of abandoning or forsaking someone (Deut. 4:31; 31:6, 8; Josh. 1:5; 10:6; Ps. 138:8). On rare occasions, the term conveyed a state of laziness or complacency (Ex. 5:8, 17; Josh. 18:3; Prov. 18:9).

7504. רָפֶה rāpeh: An adjective meaning weak, feeble. It refers to the lack of vigor, strength, or power of a people, an ethnic group, especially politically and militarily (Num. 13:18). It is used with hands (*yādayim*) following or preceding to mean weak of strength, worn out, frail (2 Sam. 17:2; Job 4:3; Isa. 35:3).

7505. רָפוּא rāpû': A proper noun designating Raphu (Num. 13:9).

7506. רֶפַח repāḥ: A proper noun designating Rephah (1 Chr. 7:25).

7507. רְפִידָה r^{e}piydāh: A feminine noun referring to the bottom or back of something (a sedan chair). It refers to a part of a splendid chair for a king to sit/ride in while being carried. In context it is made of gilded gold or golden cloth (Song 3:10). Sedan comes from a Latin word meaning to sit, to recline.

7508. רְפִידִים r^{e}piydiym: A proper noun designating Rephidim (Ex. 17:1, 8; 19:2; Num. 33:14, 15).

7509. רְפָיָה r^{e}pāyāh: A proper noun designating Rephaiah:

A. Son of Jeshaiah (1 Chr. 3:21).

B. A Simeonite (1 Chr. 4:42).

C. Grandson of Issachar (1 Chr. 7:2).

D. A descendant of Saul, the same as Rapha (7498,C) (1 Chr. 9:43).

E. Son of Hur (Neh. 3:9).

7510. רִפְיוֹן ripyôn: A masculine noun referring to limpness, feebleness. It indicates a condition of weakness, weakness, a loss of strength, courage, firmness of resolve. In context it refers to the inability to act, to be strong, to be brave in action (Jer. 47:3).

7511. רָפַס rāpas: A verb meaning to submit, to humble oneself. It is translated as submit (KJV) by some translators to indicate the surrender or submission to something, in context the submission of the warring peoples. But others render this as a further picture of the enemy nations of Israel trampling down the wealth of nations (Ps. 68:30[31]). The thought of submission or humility is prominent in Proverbs 6:3.

7512. רְפַס *rāpas:* An Aramaic verb meaning to trample, to tread down. It means to stomp on something, to tread on it, to destroy it. In context it refers to political and military action (Dan. 7:7, 19).

7513. רַפְסֹדָה *rapsôdāh:* A feminine noun meaning raft. It refers to a floating wooden platform used to transport merchandise from one location to another on a river (2 Chr. 2:16). The merchandise itself may form the raft, e.g., logs.

7514. רָפַק *rāpaq:* A verb meaning to support oneself; to lean on. It means to find support from someone by leaning on him or her, especially a bridegroom or a beloved friend (Song 8:5).

7515. רָפַשׂ *rāpaś:* A verb meaning to trample down, to foul water, or to make muddy by trampling. It means to ruin something, to corrupt it by trampling on it, such as a spring of water, muddying the water (Prov. 25:26). In context it refers to muddying waters by trampling violently in them, but it refers to the confusion and turmoil spread among the nations by Egypt (Ezek. 32:2; 34:18).

7516. רֶפֶשׁ *repeś:* A masculine noun referring to mire, mud, refuse. It refers to what is not desirable, makes dirty, stinks. In context it refers to the moral, ethical, spiritual mire and refuse that wicked persons produce and throw out (Isa. 57:20).

7517. רֶפֶת *repet:* A masculine noun indicating a stall (of a stable). It refers to an area prepared to house and protect cattle, horses, etc., a place where the offspring of these animals can be safely confined and cared for (Hab. 3:17).

7518. רַץ *raṣ:* A masculine noun referring to a bar (of silver). It is used in context of tribute, bars or pieces (KJV) (of silver) to be presented to Israel and her God (Ps. 68:30[31]) by foreign nations.

7519. רָצָא *rāṣā':* A masculine noun meaning to run, to speed forth. It refers to speeding, running quickly, darting. The infinitive absolute of the verb (*râsô'*) is combined with *šôb* to give the meaning of back and forth (Ezek. 1:14).

7520. רָצַד *rāṣad:* I. A verb meaning to look with envy. It indicates looking at persons, keeping a hostile or envious eye on them. In context it is used figuratively of the mountains of Bashan (Ps. 68:16[17]).

II. A verb meaning to leap. In context this translation depicts the leaping of the high hills in expectation, yet they will not be God's chosen abode (Ps. 68:16[17]).

7521. רָצָה rāṣāh: A verb meaning to delight, to take pleasure, to treat favorably, to favor, to accept, to pay off, to pay for, to make up for. Both humans (cf. Gen. 33:10; Deut. 33:24; 1 Chr. 29:3; Ps. 50:18; Prov. 3:12); and the Lord can be found as the subjects (1 Chr. 28:4; Ps. 51:16[18]; 147:10; Mic. 6:7; Hag. 1:8). The Lord takes pleasure in uprightness (1 Chr. 29:17); in those who fear Him (Ps. 147:11); and in His Servant (Isa. 42:1). The word is also utilized within texts concerning sacrifices, offerings, and worship, denoting that which was acceptable or unacceptable to the Lord (Lev. 1:4; 7:18; Ps. 119:108; Jer. 14:12; Hos. 8:13; Amos 5:22; Mal. 1:8). Less common is the employment of the term to communicate the satisfying of a debt (e.g., when the land must pay off or make up for the Sabbath years that it owes [Lev. 26:34; cf. Lev. 26:41, 43; 2 Chr. 36:21; Isa. 40:2]).

7522. רָצוֹן rāṣôn, רָצֹן raṣōn: A masculine noun meaning pleasure, delight, desire, will, favor, acceptance. This term is ascribed both to human agents and to God. For humans, the word often described what the heart was set on having or doing, whether for good or evil (Gen. 49:6; 2 Chr. 15:15; Neh. 9:24, 37; Esth. 1:8; Ps. 145:16, 19; Dan. 8:4; 11:3). When attributed to God, the term expresses the divine goodwill which He extends to humanity as He sees fit (Deut. 33:16, 23; Ps. 5:12[13]; 69:13[14]; 106:4; Prov. 12:2; 18:22; Isa. 49:8; 60:10; 61:2). In passages pertaining to the offering of sacrifices, offerings, or fasting in worship, the word designates the favorable reception of the worshipers (and thus their worship) by the Lord (Ex. 28:38; Lev. 1:3; 19:5; 22:19–21, 29; 23:11; Isa. 56:7; 58:5; 60:7; Jer. 6:20). On a few occasions, the word denotes anything that is pleasing to God (i.e., His will [lit., His pleasure]; Ps. 40:8[9]; 103:21; 143:10). This noun is derived from the verb *rāsāh* (7521).

7523. רָצַח rāṣaḥ: A verb meaning to murder, to slay, to kill. The taking of a human life is the primary concept behind this word. It is used to indicate a premeditated murder (Deut. 5:17; 1 Kgs. 21:19; Jer. 7:9); an accidental killing (Num. 35:11; Josh. 20:3); the ultimate act of revenge (Num. 35:27); and death by means of an animal attack (Prov. 22:13). Provocatively, Hosea refers to the lewdness of the priests that led people astray as being equal to murder (Hos. 6:9).

7524. רֶצַח reṣaḥ: A masculine noun indicating slaughtering; shattering. It indicates a violent breaking, a crushing of a person's bones. In context it is used figuratively of the impact the enemies' words have on the psalmist emotionally and spiritually (Ps. 42:10, 11).

7525. רִצְיָא ***riṣyā':*** A proper noun designating Rizia (1 Chr. 7:39).

7526. רְצִין ***r^eṣiyn:*** A proper noun designating Rezin:

A. A king of Aram (Syria) who, with Pekah, king of Israel, fought against Judah (2 Kg. 15:37; 16:5–9). During his day, Isaiah uttered several famous prophecies (Isa. 7:1–8; 8:6; 9:11[10]) that called on King Ahaz of Judah to trust the Lord against these forces.

B. The head of a family who served in the second Temple after returning from exile (Ezra 2:48).

7527. רָצַע ***rāṣā':*** A verb meaning to bore, to pierce. It refers to the process of piercing a slave's ear to mark him as a permanent slave of his master, an act done with the approval of the slave and at his request (Ex. 21:6).

7528. רָצַף ***rāṣap̱:*** A verb meaning to fit out; to inlay. It indicates the décor and decorative patterns worked into the inside of a royal sedan chair for the king's wedding day (Song 3:10).

7529. רֶצֶף ***reṣep̱:*** A masculine noun indicating something baked on hot coals. It is used in its plural form to define cakes baked on hot coals (*'ugaṯ r^eṣāp̱îm*) (1 Kgs. 19:6, cf. Isa. 6:6).

7530. רֶצֶף ***reṣep̱:*** A proper noun designating Rezeph (2 Kgs. 19:12; Isa. 37:12).

7531. רִצְפָּה ***riṣpāh:*** I. A feminine noun indicating pavement. It refers to the pavement by the Temple (2 Chr. 7:3). It refers to an elaborate mosaic pavement of various stones and other materials (Esth. 1:6). It describes the pavement or covering of an outer courtyard in Ezekiel's Temple complex (Ezek. 40:17, 18; 42:3).

II. A feminine noun meaning a live coal, a hot coal. It refers to a coal that is still actively burning, live, capable of being used for cooking, heating, etc. It indicates a cooking fuel (1 Kgs. 19:6); and is used in a symbolic manner to remove uncleanness from a prophet's lips, purging Isaiah for his mission (Isa. 6:6).

7532. רִצְפָּה ***riṣpāh:*** A proper noun designating Rizpah (2 Sam. 3:7; 21:8, 10, 11).

7533. רָצַץ ***rāṣāṣ:*** A verb meaning to break; to crush; to oppress. It is used of infants tussling while still in the womb, pushing on each other (Gen. 25:22). It describes one nation crushing, oppressing another nation as part of God's judgments (Deut. 28:33; Judg. 10:8). It refers to physically crushing something, e.g., a person's head (Judg. 9:53); or other physical objects (2 Kgs. 23:12). It is used of treating another person unfairly or violently in any way, even unknowingly (1 Sam. 12:3, 4). It describes the smashing of Leviathan's head, the monster's head (Ps. 74:14). Its use in Ecclesiastes 12:6 is figurative, breaking the golden bowl of life, dying. Egypt is figuratively described as a crushed reed (Isa. 36:6). It describes the breaking or ripping open of a person's hands, again in a figurative sense of nations (Ezek. 29:7). Crushed by judgment from God describes the state of a nation receiving God's devastating blows (Hos. 5:11). The rich cows of Bashan women are described as crushing the needy to meet their luxurious needs (Amos 4:1).

7534. רַק ***raq:*** An adjective meaning lean, thin, gaunt. It refers to emaciated, skinny cows from drought conditions seen in Pharaoh's dreams (Gen. 41:19, 20, 27).

7535. רַק ***raq:*** An adverb meaning nevertheless, only, but, except. Its exact meaning must be discovered from its context. It has the sense of something being exclusive, the only thing being done, e.g., evil thoughts only (*raq*) all day long describes the fallen state of the human heart without grace (Gen. 6:5). It indicates a specific condition that must be fulfilled or maintained and means only (Gen. 14:24; 24:8; 41:40; Ex. 8:28[24]; Job 1:12). After a negative word, *raq* gives the sense of except, but for (1 Kgs. 8:9; 15:5; 22:16; 2 Kgs. 17:18). Used in front of a positive assertion, it means surely, indeed (Gen. 20:11; Deut. 4:6). With b^e following and attached to a following word, the phrase means only in, by, in the case of (Prov. 13:10). It is used to point out one from among many (Amos 3:2), e.g., Israel only (*raq*) as God's chosen instrument.

7536. רֹק ***rōq:*** A masculine noun referring to spit, saliva. It refers to the moisture or liquid present in a person's mouth. Job's condition was such that he did not have time to swallow his spittle before new calamities hit him (Job 7:19). To spit at persons was to utterly demean and detest them (Job 30:10). Even the Lord's Suffering Servant suffered this ultimate expression of rejection and disdain (Isa. 50:6).

7537. רָקַב ***rāqab̲:*** A verb meaning to rot. It means to decay, to fall apart from decomposition, infection, etc. It is used figuratively of the name of the wicked rotting (Prov. 10:7). Wood that would not decay or rot was chosen from which to make idols (Isa. 40:20).

7538. רָקָב ***rāqāb̲:*** A masculine noun referring to rottenness, decay. It indicates the process or result of decay and decomposition. Job likens himself to a rotten thing (Job 13:28). A shameful wife affects her husband as decay affects his bones and his strength (Prov. 12:4). Undue passion acts as rottenness to the heart and life (Prov. 14:30). God likens Himself to rottenness to Judah, for He will cause her to decay and fall apart because of her sin. It describes the destructive feelings a person suffers when confronted by certain dangers and fears (Hab. 3:16).

7539. רִקָּבוֹן riqqāḇôn: A masculine noun meaning rottenness, decay. It refers to a process of decay and decomposition, as well as the results. It is used in a comparison to describe wood as rotten, weak, falling apart. Leviathan treats bronze as if it were rotten wood (Job 41:27).

7540. רָקַד rāqaḏ: A verb meaning to skip, to leap, to dance. It means to make merry visibly by bodily gestures: It describes King David's dancing before the Lord (1 Chr. 15:29). It describes the happy skipping and frolicking of young calves (Job 21:11). It is used figuratively of hills and Lebanon skipping before the Lord (Ps. 29:6; 114:4, 6). It is an activity that has its time and place (Eccl. 3:4); even for animals (Isa. 13:21). It is used to describe the fast flight of chariots and of beasts (or armies?) on the mountains (Joel 2:5; Nah. 3:2).

7541. רַקָּה raqqāh: A feminine noun meaning temple (of the head). It refers to either of the flat areas alongside the forehead just in front of each ear. Jael, Heber's wife, drove a tent peg through the temple of Sisera, general of the army of Jabin, king of Canaan (Judg. 4:21, 22; 5:26). It is likened to a piece or slice of pomegranate, considered a compliment in Middle Eastern imagery (Song 4:3; 6:7).

7542. רַקּוֹן raqqôn: A proper noun designating Rakkon (Josh. 19:46).

7543. רָקַח rāqaḥ: A verb meaning to mix perfume; to mix ointment. It is used to describe an anointing oil, mixed or blended to produce a pleasant-smelling substance (Ex. 30:25). It describes the process of creating it as mixing and combining it (Ex. 30:33). It describes the process of combining ingredients to produce incense (Ex. 30:35). It describes the mixing of spices (1 Chr. 9:30; 2 Chr. 16:14). Its participial form *rōqē(a)ḥ* indicates a perfumer (Ex. 30:25; Eccl. 10:1). It describes the blending of spices in a boiling pot of food (Ezek. 24:10).

7544. רֶקַח reqaḥ: A masculine noun referring to something spicy; what is spiced. It refers to something that has powdered spice added to it, e.g., spiced wine, to improve its taste and aroma (Song 8:2).

7545. רֹקַח rōqaḥ: A masculine noun referring to an ointment, a perfume. It refers to the product, substance produced by a perfumer as he mixes various ingredients (Ex. 30:25, 35).

7546. רַקָּח raqqāḥ: A masculine noun indicating a perfume maker. It refers to a person skilled in preparing ointments and perfumes. It usually contained olive oil to hold it together (Neh. 3:8).

7547. רִקֻחַ riquaḥ, רִקּוּחַ riqûaḥ: A masculine noun meaning perfume. It refers to the product, substance prepared by a professional perfumer or ointment preparer for various purposes, such as incense, anointing oil, aromatic cosmetics, etc. (Isa. 57:9).

7548. רַקָּחָה raqqāḥāh: A feminine noun referring to a perfume maker, confectioner. It refers to a female skilled in mixing and preparing various aromatic ointments and perfumes (1 Sam. 8:13).

7549. רָקִיעַ rāqiya': A masculine noun meaning an expanse, the firmament, an extended surface. Literally, this word refers to a great expanse and, in particular, the vault of the heavens above the earth. It denotes the literal sky that stretches from horizon to horizon (Gen. 1:6–8); the heavens above that contain the sun, moon, and stars (Gen. 1:14); or any vaulted ceiling or expanse that stands above (Ezek. 10:1). By extension, the psalmist uses the word to refer to the infinite and sweeping power of the Lord (Ps. 150:1).

7550. רָקִיק rāqiyq: A masculine noun referring to a wafer, a thin cake. It denotes a thin, flat, crisp cookie or cracker like cake or bread. It is used in several situations: to consecrate priests (Ex. 29:2, 23; Lev. 8:26); in grain offerings (Lev. 2:4); peace offerings or offerings of well-being (Lev. 7:12); Nazarite offerings (Num. 6:15, 19). It was prepared by priests (1 Chr. 23:29).

7551. רָקַם rāqam: A verb meaning to embroider, to weave, to do needlework. It is used in its simple participial form to designate the person skilled in doing all kinds of embroidery work, an embroiderer (Ex. 26:36). The phrase *ma'ᵃśēh rōqēm* occurs often (Ex. 26:36; 27:16; 28:39; 36:37; 38:18; 39:29). It is used in a figurative sense of a human embryo's being woven into existence (Ps. 139:15).

7552. רֶקֶם reqem: A proper noun designating Rekem:

A. A Midianite king (Num. 31:8; Josh. 13:21).

B. A descendant of Caleb (1 Chr. 2:43, 44).

C. A descendant of Manasseh (1 Chr. 7:16).

D. City of Benjamin (Josh. 18:27).

7553. רִקְמָה riqmāh: A feminine noun referring to embroidery work; stones of various colors. It refers to colorful material embroidered on both sides (Judg. 5:30). It indicates decorative ornamental stones (1 Chr. 29:2). Embroidered garments were highly esteemed in royal circles (Ps. 45:14[15]). The Lord, in figurative language, clothed Israel in her youth in embroidered cloth (Ezek. 16:10, 13, 18). It indicates an eagle's colorful array or plumage of many colors (Ezek. 17:3).

7554. רָקַע rāqa': A verb meaning to beat, to stamp, to stretch out. The fundamental picture is that of a smith pounding a piece of metal that in turn causes the metal to spread out as it flattens. This word conveys the action of flattening metal for some specific use (Ex. 39:3); stamping one's foot on the ground as a symbol of displeasure (Ezek. 6:11); the laying out of the earth in creation (Isa. 42:5); and the flattening of an enemy (2 Sam. 22:43).

7555. רִקּוּעַ ***riqqûa‘***, רִקֻּעַ ***riqqua‘:*** A masculine noun meaning expansion, broad. Signifying the stretching effect produced when metal is beaten, this word appears only in reference to the plates covering the altar of the Tabernacle (Num. 16:38[17:3]).

7556. רָקַק ***rāqaq:*** A verb meaning to spit. It refers to a person's ejecting saliva from his or her mouth. In context, such an act is capable of making another person unclean if the saliva is ejected on them (Lev. 15:8).

7557. רַקַּת ***raqqaṯ:*** A proper noun designating Rakkath (Ezra 3:7).

7558. רִשְׁיוֹן ***rišyôn:*** A masculine noun meaning permission; authority. It refers to official legal, royal approval given to someone to do something (Ezra 3:7).

7559. רָשַׁם ***rāšam:*** A verb meaning to inscribe, to write. It refers to the process of writing with a writing instrument or engraving a message on something. In context it is used figuratively of writing or engraving in the book, writing of truth (Dan. 10:21).

7560. רְשַׁם ***r^{e}šam:*** An Aramaic verb meaning to write; to sign. It refers to something written out (*r^{e}šîm*) in a language (Dan. 5:24, 25). It refers to the act of affixing signatures to a legal document (Dan. 6:8–10[9–11], 12[13], 13[14]).

7561. רָשַׁע ***rāša‘:*** A verb meaning to be in the wrong, to be guilty, to be wicked, to do wickedly, to condemn. In the simple stem, this verb means to be or to become guilty, to act wickedly. When God's people confessed that they acted wickedly, then the Lord forgave them (1 Kgs. 8:47; Eccl. 7:17; Dan. 9:15); to depart from the Lord is an act of wickedness (2 Sam. 22:22; Ps. 18:21[22]).

In the causative stem, the word carries the idea of condemning others or doing wickedness; the people confessed that they had done wickedness (Neh. 9:33; Ps. 106:6; Dan. 12:10). The verb also means to condemn. God declares who is guilty in cases of illegal possession (Ex. 22:9[8]; Deut. 25:1); when a moral or ethical offense has occurred, the Lord will judge in order to declare the guilty (1 Kgs. 8:32; Job 9:20).

7562. רֶשַׁע ***reša‘:*** A masculine noun meaning wickedness, injustice, and unrighteousness. It embodies that character which is opposite the character of God (Job 34:10; Ps. 5:4[5]; 84:10[11]). It is also placed in opposition to justice and righteousness, *ṣeḏeq* (6664), which is often used to describe God's character (Ps. 45:7[8]). This word is presented as the bad and evil actions that are done by humanity (Job 34:8); and, as such, these actions became the object of God's judgment (see Job 34:26). It describes those actions that are violent. In Proverbs 4:17, this word is a parallel to *ḥāmās* (2555), meaning violence. In addition, the Hebrew word means violations of civil law, especially fraud and deceit (Prov. 8:7; note the word's opposition to *'emeṯ*[571], which means truth; cf. Mic. 6:10, 11). It can also denote the actions of enemy nations (Ps. 125:3; note its opposition to *ṣaddiyq* (6662), which means just or righteous; cf. Ezek. 31:11). In a general sense, it may represent wrongful deeds (Deut. 9:27; note the parallel with *ḥaṭṭā'ṯ* (2403), which means sin).

7563. רָשָׁע ***rāšāʻ:*** An adjective meaning wicked, guilty, in the wrong, criminal, transgressor. This adjective is used 264 times, many more times than the verb formed from it. It means essentially someone guilty or in the wrong and is an antonym to the Hebrew word *ṣaddiyq* (6662), meaning righteous, in the right. Moses accused the Hebrew man who was in the wrong and was fighting with another Hebrew (Ex. 2:13); no one was to aid wicked persons in their wickedness (Ex. 23:1). A murderer worthy of death could not be ransomed (Num. 35:31); guilty, wicked persons accept bribes (Prov. 17:23; 18:5). The word may describe wicked people as murderers (2 Sam. 4:11).

The word indicates people who are enemies of God and His people: the psalmist prayed to be rescued from the wicked (Ps. 17:13). Those described by this word are evil and do not learn righteousness. Instead, they pursue their wicked ways among the righteous (Isa. 26:10); but the Lord will eventually slay the wicked (Isa. 11:4). Pharaoh admitted he was in the wrong in his attitude and actions against Moses, the Lord, and His people (Ex. 9:27; Isa. 14:5).

The word indicates the guilt engendered by sinning against others, including God. The Lord moved to destroy the leaders and the wicked people who revolted against Him in the desert (Num. 16:26); the wicked are those who do not serve God and are as a result wicked and guilty before Him (Mal. 3:18). If wicked people continue in their ways toward God or others, they will die in their sins (Ezek. 3:18); but the righteous do not die with the wicked (Gen. 18:23, 25). The counsel of the wicked is avoided by the persons blessed by God (Job 10:3; 21:16; Ps. 1:1). Several phrases became idiomatic when talking about the wicked described by this word: the counsel of the wicked (Ps. 1:1); the way of the wicked (Prov. 15:9); the path of the wicked (Mic. 6:10); the tent of the wicked (Job 8:22); the life (literally, candle) of the wicked (Job 21:7). All these terms describe things, people, and locations that God's people are to avoid so He will not destroy them in the end.

7564. רִשְׁעָה ***riš'āh:*** A feminine noun meaning wickedness, guilt. This word for immorality refers to a wide range of evil. It indicates a crime worthy of punishment (Deut. 25:2); the unrestrained evil that lurks in the human heart (Isa. 9:18[17]); the vileness of surrounding enemies (Mal. 1:4); the breach of a religious expectation (Mal. 4:1[3:19]); or an unlawful act in general (Ezek. 33:19).

7565. רֶשֶׁף ***rešep̱:*** A masculine noun meaning a flame, a flash, a lightning bolt, a burning pestilence. It refers to a burning, flaming of love (Song 8:6); of flaming, burning arrows of war (Ps. 76:3[4]). It refers to lightning as a form of destruction (Ps. 78:48). It indicates a plague, one of God's curses on a disobedient Israel (Deut. 32:24); or to pestilence (Hab. 3:5), another of God's means of disciplining His people.

7566. רֶשֶׁף ***rešep̱:*** A proper noun designating Resheph (1 Chr. 7:25).

7567. רָשַׁשׁ ***rāšaš:*** A verb meaning to beat down; to demolish. It indicates the destination or ruin of something: fortified cities or towers (Jer. 5:17); or even a people or nation that has been defeated and abused (Mal. 1:4).

7568. רֶשֶׁת ***rešeṯ:*** A feminine noun meaning a net, a network. It indicates a metal network, a configuration of metal wires, strips of metal, etc., that crisscrosses at regular intervals. The large bronze altar featured this kind of network or grating (Ex. 27:4, 5; 38:4). It refers to a network of small ropes, cords, or threads for trapping animals or birds (Prov. 1:17; Ezek. 12:13). It is used figuratively of wicked persons being cast into their own traps, their own nets (Job 18:8); as well as the nations of the world (Ps. 9:15[16]). The wicked person also prepares a net to catch others in it (Ps. 10:9). Flattery or excessive praise is a net for the unwary (Prov. 29:5). In Israel corrupt priests became a net to the people to ensnare them (Hos. 5:1). The Lord can deliver a person ensnared in a net (Ps. 25:15); but He also may prepare Himself to ensnare His people (Hos. 7:12).

7569. רַתּוֹק ***rattôq:*** A masculine noun meaning a chain. It refers to a flexible connection of a series of joined links. Golden decorative chains were placed in the Temple sanctuary (1 Kgs. 6:21). It is used figuratively and literally of a chain by which the Lord will capture His own people (Ezek. 7:23).

7570. רָתַח ***rāṯaḥ:*** A verb meaning to boil; figuratively, to seethe. It refers to the great agitation and churning of the waters of the sea (Job 41:31[23]); or the bubbling motion of hot water in a pot (Ezek. 24:5). Used of a person's inner emotional turmoil, it means to seethe, to be agitated, to be upset (Job 30:27).

7571. רֶתַח ***reṯaḥ:*** A masculine noun referring to a boiling. It combines with the verb in 7570 to serve as its object. The expression becomes emphatic, to boil vigorously its boiling (Ezek. 24:5). It has a feminine suffix attached to it.

7572. רַתִּיקָה ***rattiyqāh:*** A feminine noun meaning a chain. This word has the same meaning as 7569 but is the preferred reading by some translators (1 Kgs. 6:21).

7573. רָתַם ***rāṯam:*** A verb meaning to bind, to harness. It means to hook up, to connect. Used of hooking up horses to a chariot, it means to harness (Mic. 1:13).

7574. רֶתֶם ***reṯem,*** רֹתֶם ***rōṯem:*** A masculine noun referring to a broom tree, a juniper tree. It refers to a tree or a large shrub of a genus of evergreen shrubs or trees of the cypress family (1 Kgs. 19:4, 5). It also indicates a broom tree, a flowering shrub of the pea family featuring abundant yellow flowers and long stiff fibers (Job 30:4). It could provide dried fuel for a fire (Ps. 120:4).

7575. רִתְמָה ***riṯmāh:*** A proper noun designating Rithmah (Num. 33:18, 19).

7576. רָתַק ***rāṯaq:*** A verb meaning to bind, to tie up. It means to tie up, to fasten securely. It is negated and used figuratively of the unbinding and undoing of the cord of life (silver cord) (Eccl. 12:6). It is used literally of prisoners of war being bound, fettered with chains or ropes (Nah. 3:10).

7577. רְתוּקָה ***r***^{e}***ṯûqāh:*** A feminine noun meaning a chain. It refers to decorative chains of silver made to lay over an idol (Isa. 40:19).

7578. רְתֵת ***r***^{e}***ṯēṯ:*** A masculine noun meaning trembling. It refers to an emotional response of fear or dread before a powerful person or group (Hos. 13:1).

שׂ, שׁ Sin, Shin

7579. שָׁאַב *šā'aḇ:* A verb meaning to draw (water). It means to draw out, to collect, to pull out something (Gen. 24:11). It is used often of drawing water (Gen. 24:13, 19, 20, 43–45). Drawing water was considered a low-ranking menial task (Deut. 29:11[10]; Josh. 9:21, 23, 27; Ruth 2:9). It is used figuratively of drawing water from the springs of salvation and deliverance (Isa. 12:3).

7580. שָׁאַג *šā'ag:* A verb meaning to roar (in victory or distress). It describes the sound of a lion as it is attacking (Judg. 14:5; Amos 3:4). It describes the Lord as He roars in unrelenting judgment against His people (Jer. 25:30; Hos. 11:10; Joel 3:16; Amos 1:2; 3:8). It describes the sound of thunder after lightning (Job 37:4). The enemies of the righteous roar as lions against them (Ps. 22:13; 74:4). It depicts the sound of aggressive, destroying rulers (Zeph. 3:3); or it indicates a person's crying out in distress (Ps. 38:8).

7581. שְׁאָגָה *še'āgāh:* A feminine noun depicting the roaring of a lion; roaring in distress. It describes the shouting and din of invading armies (Isa. 5:29). It is used figuratively of the cry of destroying enemies (Zech. 11:3). It has the sense of a person moaning or groaning (Job 3:24; Ps. 22:1[2]). It refers literally to the roar of a lion (Job 4:10). It is used figuratively of the Lord's action against His corrupt leaders (Ezek. 19:7).

7582. שָׁאָה *šā'āh:* I. A verb meaning to lay waste; to turn into ruins. It means to demolish, to ruin, to devastate. In context it describes making strong cities into trash heaps (2 Kgs. 19:25). It means to make cities desolate, without inhabitants (Isa. 6:11; 37:26).

II. A verb meaning to roar. It indicates figuratively the commotion and confusion, the roaring of nations in their hostile actions (Isa. 17:12, 13).

7583. שָׁאָה *šā'āh:* A verb meaning to gaze. It means to look at intently, to observe closely for some purpose (Gen. 24:21).

7584. שַׁאֲוָה *ša'awāh:* A feminine noun meaning a storm, a tempest. This type of storm is used to describe the aftermath of rejecting Lady Wisdom's advice on how to live wisely (Prov. 1:27).

7585. שְׁאוֹל *še'ôl,* שְׁאֹל *še'ōl:* A noun meaning the world of the dead, Sheol, the grave, death, the depths. The word describes the underworld but usually in the sense of the grave and is most often translated as grave. Jacob described himself as going to the grave upon Joseph's supposed death (Gen. 37:35; 42:38); Korah, Dathan, and Abiram went down into the ground, which becomes their grave, when God judges them (Num. 16:30, 33; 1 Sam. 2:6). David described his brush with death at the hands of Saul as feeling the ropes or bands of the grave clutching him (2 Sam. 22:6). The Lord declares that He will ransom His people from the grave or Sheol (Hos. 13:14). Habakkuk declared that the grave's desire for more victims is never satiated (Hab. 2:5).

The word means depths or Sheol. Job called the ways of the Almighty higher than heaven and lower than Sheol or the depths of the earth (Job 11:8). The psalmist could not escape the Lord even in the lowest depths of the earth, in contrast to the high heavens (Ps. 139:8; Amos 9:2). It means the deepest valley or depths of the earth in Isaiah 7:11.

In a few cases, Sheol seems to mean death or a similar concept; that Abaddon (destruction) lies uncovered seems to be matched with Sheol's meaning of death (Job 26:6). It means death or the grave, for neither is ever satisfied (Prov. 7:27; cf. Isa. 38:10) The word is best translated as death or the depths in Deuteronomy 32:22.

Sheol or the grave is the place of the wicked (Ps. 9:17[18]; 31:17[18]); Ezekiel pictured it as the place of the uncircumcised (Ezek. 31:15; 32:21, 27). Israel's search for more wickedness and apostasy took them to the depths of Sheol (Isa. 57:9). On the other hand, the righteous were not made for the grave or Sheol; it was not their proper abode. They were not left in the grave or Sheol (Ps. 16:10) but were rescued from that place (Ps. 49:15[16]). Adulterers and fornicators were, metaphorically, described as in the lower parts of Sheol or the grave (Prov. 9:18). Sheol and Abaddon (Destruction) are as open to the eyes of God as are the hearts and thoughts of humankind; there is nothing mysterious about them to Him (Prov. 15:11).

7586. שָׁאוּל ***šā'ûl:*** A proper noun designating Saul. The name means "asked."

A. The first king of Israel. He was from the tribe of Benjamin and the son of Kish. He was impressive in physical appearance (1 Sam. 9:1–2). He was anointed by the Lord through Samuel (1 Sam. 9:15—10:2) and was made king at Mizpah (1 Sam. 9:17–27). Saul made a good start but soon began to reject the word of the Lord through Samuel. As a result, the Lord rejected Saul as king (1 Sam. 15:1–31) over Israel and chose David as king (1 Sam. 16:11–13). Saul's kingship deteriorated as did his own personal condition. He lost a decisive battle to the Philistines and committed suicide in the field after being seriously wounded (1 Sam. 31:1–7). From being "head and shoulders" above his brethren, he was reduced to the most pitied of Israel's kings.

B. An ancient king of Edom who came from Rehoboth (Gen. 36:37).

C. A son of Simeon. His mother was a Canaanite (Gen. 46:10).

D. A Levite who descended through Kohath, Levi's son (1 Chr. 6:24).

7587. **שָׁאוּלִי** ***šā'ûliy:*** A proper noun designating Shaulite, a descendant of Simeon (7586,C) (Num. 26:13).

7588. **שָׁאוֹן** ***šā'ôn:*** A masculine noun meaning a roar, a din, a crash. This term is found mostly in the prophets and generally refers to the din of battle (Hos. 10:14; Amos 2:2); or the crash of waves (Isa. 17:12). A less frequent use of the word describes the merriment or uproar of revelers (Isa. 24:8).

7589. **שְׁאָט** ***$š^{e}$'āṭ:*** A masculine noun indicating malice, scorn, contempt. It indicates strong disrespect at the misfortune of someone (Ezek. 25:6, 15); even hatred toward a person or people (Ezek. 36:5).

7590. **שָׁאט** ***šā'ṭ,*** **שׁוּט** ***šûṭ:*** A verb meaning to despise, to scorn, to malign. It indicates a strong dislike for someone or a people, a loathing or total disrespect, a situation Israel would be free from when the Lord judges her enemies and restores her (Ezek. 16:57; 28:24, 26).

7591. **שְׁאִיָּה** ***$š^{e}$'iyyāh:*** A feminine noun meaning ruin. This word is used only once in the Old Testament and comes from the verb *šā'āh* (7582), meaning to crash into ruins. In Isaiah 24:12, it describes the destroyed gate of the city that had been battered into ruins.

7592. **שָׁאַל** ***šā'al:*** A verb meaning to ask. One could ask another person or even God for something (1 Sam. 23:2; Ps. 122:6; 137:3; Eccl. 7:10). People sometimes sought information by asking Urim and Thummim (Num. 27:21), or an occult wooden object (Ezek. 21:21[26]; Hos. 4:12). Asking could be done as a begging request or a stern demand (1 Kgs. 2:16; Job 38:3; Ps. 109:10; Mic. 7:3). The Hebrew expression of asking about someone's peace is similar to the English expression, "How are you?" (Gen. 43:27; Judg. 18:15; Jer. 15:5). Very rarely, the term could refer to borrowing or lending. But this is certainly not the meaning when the people of Israel asked goods from the Egyptians they plundered (Ex. 3:22; 22:14[13]; 1 Sam. 1:28; 2:20; 2 Kgs. 4:3; 6:5).

7593. **שְׁאֵל** ***$š^{e}$'ēl:*** An Aramaic verb meaning to ask, to demand, to require. The word is closely related to the Hebrew verb *šā'al* (7592), meaning to ask. Tattenai, the governor of the province beyond the river, asked the elders of the returned Jews for their names and for the name of the one who authorized their rebuilding of the Temple in Jerusalem (Ezra 5:9, 10). Later on, King Artaxerxes decreed that the treasurers in that same province had to provide whatever Ezra asked of them so that the priestly ministry at the newly rebuilt Temple could be maintained (Ezra 7:21; cf. Dan. 2:10, 11, 27).

7594. שְׁאָל ***šeʼāl:*** A proper noun designating Sheal (Ezra 10:29).

7595. שְׁאֵלָה ***šeʼēlāh:*** An Aramaic feminine noun meaning a decision, a verdict, a decree. The word occurs only in Daniel 4:17 (4:14) and is derived from the verbal root *šeʼēl* (7593). It is also related to the Hebrew noun *šeʼēlāh* (7596). The word denotes a question at law (i.e., a judicial decision or edict). In Nebuchadnezzar's second dream, he witnessed an angelic watchman crying out and announcing the verdict concerning the greatest tree in all the earth. Daniel later interpreted the dream, declaring that the great tree represented Nebuchadnezzar himself (cf. Dan. 4:4–27).

7596. שְׁאֵלָה ***šeʼēlāh,*** שֵׁלָה ***šēlāh:*** A feminine noun meaning a request, a petition. The term is derived from the verb *šāʼal* (7592) and signifies what a person or group asks for from another party. The request can be made of another human: Gideon, for gold earrings from the Ishmaelites (Judg. 8:24); Adonijah, for Abishag the Shunammite from Solomon with Bathsheba as intermediary (1 Kgs. 2:16, 20); Esther, for the king's presence at her banquet; also for the sparing of the Jews' and her own life (Esth. 5:6–8; 7:2, 3; 9:12); or of God: Hannah, for a son (1 Sam. 1:17, 27; 2:20); Job, for death (Job 6:8); the Israelites, for delicious food (Ps. 106:15[cf. Num. 11:4–6, 31–35]).

7597. שְׁאַלְתִּיאֵל ***šeʼaltiyʼēl,*** שַׁלְתִּיאֵל ***šaltiyʼēl:*** I. A proper noun designating Shealtiel (1 Chr. 3:17; Ezra 3:2, 8; Neh. 12:1; Hag. 1:1; 2:23). See the Aramaic entry 7598.

II. A proper noun designating Shealtiel, a slightly different name in Hebrew than I above (Hag. 1:12, 14; 2:2).

7598. שְׁאַלְתִּיאֵל ***šeʼaltiyʼēl:*** An Aramaic proper noun designating Shealtiel (Ezra 5:2). It corresponds to the entry 7597 and refers to the same individual.

7599. שָׁאַן ***šāʼan:*** A verb meaning to be at ease; to be secure. It describes a state of security, peace, rest: for individuals at death (Job 3:18); for persons who find wisdom (Prov. 1:33); and for nations who live in security and safety (Jer. 48:11). It refers to the undisturbed condition of a restored Israel cared for by God (Jer. 30:10; 46:27).

7600. שַׁאֲנָן ***šaʼanān:*** I. An adjective meaning to be at ease, to be quiet, to be complacent. It refers to a condition of relative tranquillity, undisturbed security and safety, without worries (Job 12:5; 21:23). It refers to the lack of care and worry possessed by the fortunate members of a society who dwell in security (Ps. 123:4); a condition that can be considered dangerous, evil (Isa. 32:9, 11, 18; Amos 6:1; Zech. 1:15). Jerusalem will attain this condition by the power of God (Isa. 33:20).

II. An adjective meaning arrogant, proud, insolent. It refers to a condition that can easily arise from the situation depicted in I. It refers to the arrogance of the Assyrian king and nation (2 Kgs. 19:28; Isa. 37:29). Some assign this meaning to the word in Psalm 123:4 rather than the meaning in I.

7601. שָׁאַס *šā'as:* A verb meaning to plunder spoil. It means to take the spoils or goods of oppression and war, to take violently, to seize the property or persons of another person or people, to abuse them for one's own enrichment (Jer. 30:16).

7602. שָׁאַף *šā'ap̱:* I. A verb meaning to gasp, to pant; to wait eagerly for, to hurry for. It means to desire, to long for, to seek for something. It indicates a desire to obtain the wealth of others (Job 5:5); the desire of a laborer to rest in the shade (Job 7:2). It indicates a longing for the night (Job 36:20). It depicts a donkey in heat sniffing the wind (Jer. 2:24). It describes the seeming hastening of the sun across the sky (Eccl. 1:5). It depicts the panting of a woman giving birth (Isa. 42:14). It describes an evil eagerness, a panting after the needy to oppress them further (Amos 2:7).

II. A verb meaning to pursue, to chase. It describes the psalmist's enemies pursuing him (Ps. 56:1[2], 2[3]); threatening him (Ps. 57:3[4]).

III. A verb meaning to swallow up. It is translated as to swallow up, to devour by some translators, but see I. Its use is figurative in Job 5:5. It refers to the evil enemies of the psalmist (Ps. 56:1[2], 2[3]; 57:3[4]). It describes the Lord's going forth to devour His enemies (Isa. 42:14); and also the act of Israel's enemies devouring, destroying them (Ezek. 36:3).

IV. A verb meaning to trample on; to crush. This is another alternative rendering of this word in some contexts: to trample on someone (Ps. 56:1[2], 2[3]; 57:3[4]). Israel's enemies are depicted as having crushed, trampled her (Ezek. 36:3). For Amos 2:7, see I.

7603. שְׂאֹר *śᵉ'ōr:* A masculine noun meaning leaven, yeast. It refers to a fungus that ferments sugars. It is used to cause dough to rise and in other kinds of food productions. It leavenes dough, causing it to rise. It was not used in the unleavened bread of the Passover Feast (Ex. 12:15, 19; Deut. 16:4); and it was forbidden in grain offerings (Lev. 2:11).

7604. שָׁאַר *šā'ar:* A verb meaning to remain, to be left over; to leave, to let remain, to spare. The term maintains a narrow semantic range throughout Old Testament literature. The verb and the nouns that derive from it (see *šᵉ'ār*[7605] and *šᵉ'ēriyṯ*[7611]) play a key role in the development of the remnant theme that unfolds and evolves over the course of Old Testament history. From the early beginnings of salvation history in Genesis and all the way through to the end of the Old Testament and beyond, God has sovereignly acted to preserve for Himself a remnant of people who will worship Him alone (cf. Gen. 7:23; 32:8[9]; 1 Kgs. 19:18; Ezra 9:8; Isa. 4:3; 11:11, 16; 37:31; Ezek. 9:8; Zeph. 3:12; see also Rom. 11:5). Nevertheless, though this usage became the most significant function of the term, the verb was also employed in a variety of other contexts. For instance, the Egyptians came to Joseph for help because they had no remaining money to buy food (Gen. 47:18). After the Israelites crossed the Red Sea, the waters caved in on Pharaoh's army. Not one person remained (Ex. 14:28). The blood that remained from the sin offering was to be drained out at the base of the altar (Lev. 5:9).

7605. שְׁאָר *šᵉʾār:* A masculine noun meaning a remnant, a remainder, the rest. The term plays an important role in the development of the remnant theme concerning God's people. This theme is interwoven throughout Scripture, and a variety of words were employed to convey the idea (cf. Isa. 10:20, 21, 22; 11:11, 16). However, this term is not limited to the designation of the remnant of God's people. For instance, it was also employed to denote the remnant of other nations: Assyria (Isa. 10:19); Babylon (Isa. 14:22); Moab (Isa. 16:14); Aram (Isa. 17:3); Kedar (Isa. 21:17). Moreover, the word was always utilized as a collective, never referring to a single individual (cf. 1 Chr. 16:41; Ezra 3:8; 4:3, 7; Esth. 9:16; Zeph. 1:4). See also the verb *šāʾar* (7604), from which this noun is derived, and its corresponding feminine cognate *šᵉʾēriyṯ* (7611).

7606. שְׁאָר *šᵉʾār:* An Aramaic masculine noun meaning the remainder, the rest. The word closely corresponds with the Hebrew noun *šᵉʾār* (7605). It signifies that which was left over after the removal of everything else. The fourth beast in Daniel's vision devoured, broke things in pieces, and stamped the remainder with its feet (Dan. 7:7, 19; cf. Dan. 2:18; 7:12). The people of Israel, the priests, the Levites, and the rest of the returned exiles joyfully celebrated the dedication of the newly rebuilt Temple (Ezra 6:16; cf. Ezra 4:9, 10, 17; 7:18, 20).

7607. שְׁאֵר *šᵉʾēr:* A masculine noun meaning flesh, food, meat, body, self, blood relative, blood kindred. The word is roughly synonymous with the noun *bāśār* (1320), meaning flesh. The term connotes the meaty part of an animal which can be eaten: quail (Ps. 78:20, 27; cf. Num. 11:31); or food in general (Ex. 21:10). Frequently, on account of context, the term strongly implies the idea of close (blood) relative or kindred (Lev. 18:6, 12, 13, 17; 20:19; 21:2; 25:49; Num. 27:11). In two contexts, the word suggests the notion of physical strength (Ps. 73:26; Prov. 5:11); and in Micah

3:2, 3, it refers to the actual physical flesh of a human body.

7608. שַׁאֲרָה ***ša'ᵃrāh:*** A feminine noun indicating a kinswoman. It designates a woman as a close blood relative. Intercourse was forbidden with this person (Lev. 18:17).

7609. שֶׁאֱרָה ***še'ᵉrāh:*** A proper noun designating Sheerah (1 Chr. 7:24).

7610. שְׁאָר יָשׁוּב ***šᵉ'ār yāšûḇ:*** A proper noun designating Shear-Jashub (Isa. 7:3).

7611. שְׁאֵרִית ***šᵉ'ēriyṯ:*** A feminine noun meaning a remnant, a residue, the remainder. The primary meaning conveyed by this word is that which is left over or remains. It was used with reference to scrap pieces of wood (Isa. 44:17); undesignated territory (Isa. 15:9); and any group of people that remained (Jer. 15:9; Amos 1:8). Most significant was the technical use of this word by the prophets to denote the few among Israel or Judah that remained faithful to God (Isa. 37:32; Mic. 5:7[6], 8[7]); or those who survived the calamity of the exile (Zech. 8:11). Joseph declared that the purpose of his captivity was to preserve a remnant of Jacob's lineage (Gen. 45:7).

7612. שֵׁאת ***šē'ṯ:*** A feminine noun referring to desolation, ruin. It refers to the devastation and ruin brought on Jerusalem by the exile of the people and the destruction of the entire city (Lam. 3:47).

7613. שְׂאֵת ***śᵉ'ēṯ:*** I. A feminine noun indicating honoring, elevation, dignity. It refers in general to a lifting up of someone or something: of the dignity given to the firstborn (Gen. 49:3); of a high office or place in society (Ps. 62:4); of God's unsurpassed exaltedness (Job 13:11; 31:23); of an infection, skin swelling (Lev. 13:2, 10, 19, 28, 43; 14:56); of Leviathan's stirring himself up (Job 41:25[17]); of an approving, uplifting look, recognition (Gen. 4:7).

II. A feminine noun indicating swelling. This is an expansion or enlargement of a person's flesh or skin because of an infection or irritation, a condition that was diagnosed by the priests (Lev. 13:2, 10, 19, 28, 43; 14:56).

7614. שְׁבָא ***šᵉḇā':*** A proper noun designating Sheba:

A. The son of Jokshan who was a son of Eber who was a descendant of Shem (Gen. 25:3).

B. A descendant of Ham through Cush and his son Raamah (1 Chr. 1:9).

C. A son of Abraham through Keturah. His father was Jokshan (1 Chr. 1:32).

7615. שְׁבָאִי ***šᵉḇā'iy:*** A proper noun designating a Sabean, a citizen of Sheba (7614,D) (Joel 3:8[4:8]).

7616. שְׁבָבִים ***šᵉḇaḇiym:*** A masculine plural noun referring to broken pieces. It refers to the shattered pieces or fragments of something. In context it refers to the shattered fragments of the golden calf of Samaria, an idol (Hos. 8:6).

7617. שָׁבָה šāḇāh: A verb meaning to take captive, to lead into captivity. The main idea behind this word is that of being taken prisoner as a spoil of war or other military raid. It signified the fate that befell Lot at the hands of Chedorlaomer and his compatriots (Gen. 14:14); the threat that hung over the heads of any rebellious people (1 Kgs. 8:46); and forced enslavement by a foreign military power (2 Kgs. 5:2).

7618. שְׁבוֹ šᵉḇô: A feminine noun meaning an agate, a precious stone. It refers to a precious stone set in the breastpiece of justice of the high priest (Ex. 28:19; 39:12; agate; KJV, NASB, NKJV, NIV). It was the middle stone in the third row of stones representing the twelve tribes of Israel.

7619. שְׁבוּאֵל šᵉḇû'ēl, שׁוּבָאֵל šûḇā'ēl: A proper noun designating Shebuel, Shubael:

A. A levitical official descended from Gershom (1 Chr. 23:16; 24:20; 26:24).

B. A levitical musician, son of Heman (1 Chr. 25:4, 20).

7620. שָׁבוּעַ šāḇûa': A masculine noun meaning seven; a week, a group of seven days or years. It indicates a unit of seven: a week, seven days (Lev. 12:5; Deut. 16:9); of a marriage feast (Gen. 29:27, 28); a week of days (Dan. 10:2, 3). It is used in a technical sense to name a festival, the Feast of Weeks (Ex. 34:22; Deut. 16:10). It refers to seven years, a *heptad* of years (Dan. 9:24–27).

7621. שְׁבוּעָה šᵉḇû'āh: A feminine noun meaning oath. An oath is a sacred promise attesting to what one has done or will do. God swore an oath to Abraham, Isaac, and Jacob that He would fulfill His covenant with them (Gen. 26:3; Deut. 7:8; 1 Chr. 16:16). An oath could also be sworn by a person to declare innocence (Ex. 22:11[10]; Num. 5:21); to proclaim friendship (2 Sam. 21:7); to affirm a promise (Lev. 5:4; 1 Kgs. 2:43); to ratify a peace treaty (Josh. 9:20); to pledge loyalty to God (2 Chr. 15:15); or to another person (Neh. 6:18). An oath was considered to be an un breakable contract; however, in two instances, the Bible presents well-defined possibilities in which an oath could be nullified and the obligated party could be acquitted. Abraham provided for his servant to be released from his obligation to find a bride for Isaac if the woman refused to follow (Gen. 24:8); and the spies provided for their own release from their oath to Rahab if she did not display the scarlet cord and stay in her house or if she revealed the intentions of the Israelites (Josh. 2:17, 20).

7622. שְׁבוּת šᵉḇûṯ, שְׁבִית šᵉḇiyṯ: A feminine noun meaning captivity, captives. This word conveys either a state of exile, such as being taken for a spoil of war, or the subjects of such captivity. The chief use was in declaring the liberating power of the Lord in releasing His people from such banishment (Deut. 30:3; Jer. 33:7; Hos. 6:11). Interestingly, when Job's fortunes were restored, he was said to have been freed from captivity (Job 42:10).

7623. שָׁבַח ***šāḇaḥ:*** A verb meaning to soothe, to stroke, to praise. The primary meaning of this word is to calm or still. It was used particularly in reference to the calming of the sea (Ps. 65:7[8]). A secondary current of meaning associated with this word is that of praise. In this sense, it was employed to denote either the exaltation of God (Ps. 63:3[4]); or the holding of something in higher esteem (Eccl. 4:2). The connection between the two may stem from the soothing effect of praise on the ego.

7624. שְׁבַח ***šᵉḇaḥ:*** An Aramaic verb meaning to praise, to adore. This word occurs five times in the book of Daniel. It denotes Daniel's praise of the Lord (Dan. 2:23); the praise of the Lord by a humbled Nebuchadnezzar (Dan. 4:37[34]); and the praise given to idols during Belshazzar's debaucherous feast (Dan. 5:4, 23).

7625. שְׁבַט ***šᵉḇaṭ:*** An Aramaic masculine noun meaning a clan, a tribe. This word occurs only in Ezra 6:17 and is used in reference to the tribal divisions of Israel (cf. Gen. 49:28).

7626. שֵׁבֶט ***šēḇeṭ:*** A masculine noun meaning a rod, a scepter, and a tribe. It is presented in parallel with the word *maṭṭeh* (4294) that designates a rod or a tribe (Isa. 10:15). As a rod, it represents a common tool used as a shepherd's staff (Lev. 27:32; Ezek. 20:37); a crude weapon (2 Sam. 23:21); or for beating out cumin (Isa. 28:27). It also refers to the shaft of a spear (2 Sam. 18:14). The rod was also used in meting out discipline, both literally for a slave (Ex. 21:20); a fool (Prov. 10:13; 26:3); and a son (Prov. 13:24; 22:15; 29:15); and figuratively of God against Solomon (2 Sam. 7:14); of God against Israel through Assyria (Isa. 10:24); against Philistia (Isa. 14:29); and of God against Assyria (Isa. 30:31). Because of the association between smiting and ruling, the rod became a symbol of the authority of the one bearing it; thus, this word can also mean a scepter (Gen. 49:10; Judg. 5:14; Isa. 14:5). Also, the connotation of tribe is based on the connection between this term and the concept of rulership. It can connote the tribes of Israel collectively (Gen. 49:16; Deut. 33:5); or individually (Josh. 7:16; Judg. 18:1). It can also represent a portion of one of the tribes (Num. 4:18; Judg. 20:12; 1 Sam. 9:21). Eventually, the term was used in the singular to denote Israel as a whole (Ps. 74:2; Jer. 10:16; 51:19). It is also interesting to note that this word was never used in reference to the tribes of other nations.

7627. שְׁבָט ***šᵉḇāṭ:*** A proper noun Shebat. It refers to the eleventh month of postexilic Israel, equal to a modern date of February–March. In context the exact date given refers to February 15, 519 B.C.

7628. שְׁבִי *šᵉbiy:* A masculine noun meaning captivity, captives. This word comes from the verb *šāḇāh* (7617), meaning to take captive, and was normally used to describe those captured in war and taken back to the conquering country (Num. 21:1; Ezra 3:8; Neh. 1:2). It could describe anything captured, such as booty (Num. 31:26); or horses (Amos 4:10). The word could also be used to describe prisoners in a dungeon (Ex. 12:29).

7629. שֹׁבִי *šōḇiy:* A proper noun designating Shobi (2 Sam. 17:27).

7630. שֹׁבָי *šōḇāy:* A proper noun designating Shobai (Ezra 2:42; Neh. 7:45).

7631. שְׁבִיב *šᵉḇiyḇ:* An Aramaic masculine noun meaning a flame, a fire. It refers to the visible aspect of a fire, the burning gases or vapors, the tongue of light arising from a fire (Dan. 3:22); it refers to blazing flames (of fire) (Dan. 7:9). In context it serves to emphasize the Lord as enthroned among blazing flames, expressing His purity, power, and splendor.

7632. שָׁבִיב *šāḇiyḇ:* A masculine noun referring to a spark, a flame. It indicates in a figurative sense the life and vigor of the wicked that fades away (Job 18:5).

7633. שִׁבְיָה *šiḇyāh:* A feminine noun meaning captives. This word comes from the verb *šāḇāh* (7617), meaning to take captive. It always describes those who had been defeated in war and were taken captive into a foreign land. It was also used to describe the captives taken in victory by Israel (Deut. 21:11); as well as those taken in defeat from Israel by a foreign nation (2 Chr. 28:11, 13–15; Neh. 4:4[3:36]).

7634. שָׁבְיָה *šoḇyāh:* An alternate form for *śākyāh* (7914,III), which see.

7635. שְׁבִיל *šāḇiyl*, שָׁבוּל *šāḇûl:* A masculine noun meaning a path, a way. It refers figuratively to the paths or ways of God in the many waters (Ps. 77:19[20]); and to the laws and ways of God given to Israel in ancient times (Jer. 18:15).

7636. שָׁבִיס *šaḇiys:* A masculine noun meaning a headband. It refers to a piece of luxurious clothing worn for beauty (Isa. 3:18).

7637. שְׁבִיעִי *šᵉḇiy'iy*, שְׁבִיעִת *šᵉḇiy'iṯ:* An adjective meaning seventh. This word is normally used in relation to time: the seventh day (Lev. 13:5, 6; Josh. 6:4; Esth. 1:10); the seventh week (Lev. 23:16); the seventh month (Lev. 23:27; Jer. 28:17; Hag. 2:1); and the seventh year (Lev. 25:4; 2 Kgs. 11:4; 2 Chr. 23:1). When this word refers to the seventh day, it can refer to the Sabbath (Gen. 2:2; Ex. 20:10, 11; Deut. 16:8). In other usages, this word describes the seventh of a series of events (Josh. 6:16; 1 Kgs. 18:44); the seventh lot (Josh. 19:40; 1 Chr. 24:10); the seventh son (1 Chr. 2:15; 26:3); the seventh mighty man (1 Chr. 12:11[12]); and the seventh commander (1 Chr. 27:10).

7638. שָׂבָךְ ***śāḇāḵ:*** A masculine noun meaning a net, a netting; a grating. It refers to some type of artwork made of meshed fabric, wood, or metal. It was featured in the Temple of Solomon in the form of a grating at the top of pillars (1 Kgs. 7:17).

7639. שְׂבָכָה ***śᵉḇāḵāh:*** A feminine noun indicating a net, a lattice, a grating, a screen-material. See entry 7638 for 1 Kings 7:17. In 1 Kings 7:18, 20, 41, 42; 2 Kgs. 25:17, it refers to ornamental meshed grating, most likely used to decorate and to hold other items in place by covering them (Jer. 52:22, 23). It refers to a wooden lattice structure probably used as safety fencing in the upper chambers of a house (2 Kgs. 1:2). It refers figuratively to a kind of net serving as a trap or snare that catches the wicked (Job 18:8).

7640. שֹׁבֶל ***šōḇel:*** A masculine noun meaning a skirt. It refers in context to a woven or latticed skirt or garment, a flowing train of a woman's skirt, or hem of a dress or skirt (Isa. 47:2).

7641. שִׁבֹּלֶת ***šibbōleṯ:*** I. A feminine noun referring to a head of grain. It refers to the ears of grain that grow from a stalk (Gen. 41:5, 6, 22–24, 26, 27). It contains the way the Ephraimites pronounced "Sibboleth" (Judg. 12:6). These heads or ears of grain were cut off in harvest (Job 24:24; Isa. 17:5). It refers to branches or twigs in Zechariah 4:12, representing two anointed persons.

II. A feminine noun meaning a stream, a torrent, a flood; a branch, a twig bundle. This root has the sense of a flood or a mass of water (Ps. 69:2[3]); a flood of water (Ps. 69:15[16]). It refers to the powerful waters flowing in a river (Isa. 27:12).

7642. שַׁבְלוּל ***šablûl:*** A masculine noun indicating a snail, a slug. It is used in a figure of speech to indicate the melting away of persecutors and the wicked, like a snail, a slow-moving gastropod that leaves a slimy trail behind it that soon disappears (Ps. 58:8[9]).

7643. שְׂבָם ***śᵉḇām,*** שִׂבְמָה ***śiḇmāh:*** A proper noun designating Sebam, Sibmah (Num. 32:3, 38; Josh. 13:19; Isa. 16, 8, 9; Jer. 48:32).

7644. שֶׁבְנָא ***šeḇnā',*** שֶׁבְנָה ***šeḇnāh:*** A proper noun designating Shebna, Shebnah (2 Kgs. 18:18, 26, 37; 19:2; Isa. 22:15; 36:3, 11, 22; 37:2).

7645. שְׁבַנְיָהוּ ***šᵉḇanyāhû,*** שְׁבַנְיָה ***šᵉḇanyāh:*** A proper noun designating Shebaniah:

A. A priest in David's day (1 Chr. 15:24).

B. A Levite who led worship in Nehemiah's day, possibly the same as D or E (Neh. 9:4, 5; 10:10[11]).

C. A priest in Ezra's day (Neh. 10:4[5]; 12:14[15], NIV, see 7935,C).

D. A Levite who signed Ezra's covenant, possibly the same as B (Neh. 10:10[11]).

E. Another Levite who signed Ezra's covenant, possibly the same as B (Neh. 10:12[13]).

7646. שָׂבַע *śāḇa'*, שָׂבֵעַ *śāḇēa'*: A verb meaning to be satisfied, to be filled, to be full. It basically means to be satisfied, to have had enough of something or too much: Israel had enough meat (quail) to eat in the desert, even more than enough (Ex. 16:8, 12); in Canaan Israel would be satisfied with all kinds of food and drink (Deut. 6:11). One of God's judgments was not to provide sufficient food to a disobedient people (Lev. 26:26; Hos. 4:10; Amos 4:8; Mic. 6:14). It is used figuratively of being filled with, satiated with anxiety, suffering (Job 7:4); weary of life (1 Chr. 23:1). It is used figuratively of God's having enough, being sated with burnt offerings (Isa. 1:11). It describes a positive state of being satisfied with children, having ample offspring (Ps. 17:14); but also of, in place of offspring, being satisfied, full, with seeing God, enjoying His presence (Ps. 17:15). A sick person has enough troubles (Ps. 88:3[4]); an evil person becomes satiated, sated, with their own evil deeds (Prov. 1:31). It depicts figuratively a sword in battle being satiated (Jer. 46:10). The prophet was filled with bitterness from the hand of the Lord (Lam. 3:15). Wine is depicted as causing an arrogant, proud, haughty person to become insatiable, like Sheol (Hab. 2:5). Persons who seek the Lord will become satisfied, even when they are afflicted (Ps. 22:26[27]).

7647. שָׂבָע *śāḇā'*: A masculine noun indicating an abundance, plenty, an overflow. It refers to an exact amount of something, an overflowing, e.g., grain (Gen. 41:29–31, 34, 47, 53); wine (Prov. 3:10). It is used in context with a definite article to mean a full stomach (Eccl. 5:12[11]).

7648. שֹׂבַע *śōḇa'*: A masculine noun indicating an abundance, satisfaction, fullness. It refers to a state of satiation, overfullness, being stuffed (Ex. 16:3; Lev. 25:19) but usually in a good sense. If Israel obeyed, they would enjoy God's blessing of fullness of food (Lev. 26:5; Deut. 23:24[25]). It is used in a figurative sense of the fullness of joy (Ps. 16:11); and of the fullness of food that God gave the Israelites in the wilderness (Ps. 78:25). Righteous persons will have enough and more to meet their needs (Prov. 13:25).

7649. שָׂבֵעַ *śaḇēa'*: An adjective meaning full, satisfied, abounding. It indicates fullness of life in years and in satisfaction (Gen. 25:8; 35:29; 1 Chr. 29:28; Job 42:17). It indicates a fullness or satisfaction of God's approval and favor (Deut. 33:23). It indicates a general prosperity, the possession of an abundance of wealth (1 Sam. 2:5). It refers to a satiation, an overabundance of disgrace, a consciousness of misery (Job 10:15). The general condition of humankind is a fullness of turmoil (Job 14:1). A fullness or sufficiency of sleep comes to those who fear God (Prov. 19:23).

7650. שָׁבַע ***šaḇaʿ:*** A verb meaning to swear, to take an oath, to make to swear an oath. In the passive reflexive stem, the verb means to swear, to take an oath; Abimelech and Phicol asked Abraham to swear his kindness and integrity to them and their descendants (Gen. 21:23; Judg. 21:1; 2 Sam. 21:2). The Lord swears by Himself, since there is nothing greater to swear by. God swore to multiply and bless Abraham's descendants (Gen. 22:16; Jer. 22:5). God also swore an oath to Abraham personally (Gen. 24:7; Ex. 13:11). God swore by His holiness to lead Israel into captivity (Amos 4:2).

In the causative stem, the verb means to make, to cause someone to take an oath: Abraham made his servant swear an oath to get Isaac a wife from Abraham's own people (Gen. 24:37). A wife suspected of adultery was forced to take an oath affirming the proposed curse on her if she were found guilty (Num. 5:21). Saul had ordered the people to take an oath not to eat honey or food while they were engaged in battle with the Philistines (1 Sam. 14:27; 1 Kgs. 18:10). In this stem, the word can mean to charge someone or to adjure that person. David's men adjured him not to go into battle with them again (2 Sam. 21:17; 1 Kgs. 22:16). The land of Canaan became the Promised Land the Lord gave to His people based on His oath. He brought them into the land as He had promised by oath to their fathers (Ex. 13:5; Deut. 1:8, 35; 6:10; Josh. 1:6; Judg. 2:1; Jer. 11:5).

7651. שֶׁבַע ***šeḇaʿ***, שִׁבְעָה ***šiḇʿāh:*** A masculine, feminine noun meaning seven. It is a counting number that indicates a total number of something: years (Gen. 5:7, 25), etc. It combines with other numbers, e.g., *šeḇaʿ ʿēsreh,* 17, (lit., seven and ten) (Gen. 37:2). Repeated, it means groups of seven (seven by seven) by sevens (Gen. 7:2). Its plural form in *-îm* means seventy (Gen. 50:10). The term *bešiḇʿa laḥōḏeš* indicates the seventh day of the month (Ezek. 30:20).

7652. שֶׁבַע ***šeḇaʿ:*** A proper noun designating Sheba:

A. A Benjamite (2 Sam. 20:1, 2, 6, 7, 10, 13, 21, 22).

B. A Gadite (1 Chr. 5:13).

C. A town in Simeon (Josh. 19:2).

7653. שִׂבְעָה ***śiḇʿāh:*** A feminine noun indicating abundance, fullness, satiety. It indicates an abundance of something, more than is necessary (Ezek. 16:49). This abundance is to be shared.

7654. שָׂבְעָה ***śoḇʿāh:*** A feminine noun indicating abundance, satisfaction. It refers to the satisfaction provided by an abundance of food to eat (Isa. 23:18). On the other hand, material goods do not give real satisfaction (Isa. 55:2). It indicates that a satisfaction of greed cannot be attained (Isa. 56:11). Israel had an insatiable desire for following foreign gods (Ezek. 16:28). Israel's failure to find their true satisfaction in God meant that they could not find satisfaction elsewhere (Hag. 1:6).

7655. שִׁבְעָה ***šiḇʿāh***, שְׁבַע ***šᵉbaʿ:*** An Aramaic masculine noun or feminine noun meaning seven. It is used in its masculine form (*šiḇʿāh*) with masculine nouns and in its feminine form (*š ᵉḇaʿ*) with feminine nouns. It indicates seven periods of time (Dan. 4:16[13], 23[20], 25[22], 32[29]); the seven advisors of the Persian king (Ezra 7:14). The phrase *ḥaḏ-šiḇʿāh* means seven (Dan. 3:19).

7656. שִׁבְעָה ***šiḇʿāh:*** A proper noun designating Shibah (Gen. 26:33).

7657. שִׁבְעִים ***šiḇʿiym:*** A common noun meaning seventy. It is the plural form of *šeḇaʿ*. It combines with other numbers to form larger numbers, e.g., seventy-seven (Gen. 4:24). It is used as a counting number to indicate seventy of something: seventy years (Gen. 5:12; 11:26); seventy persons (Ex. 1:5); seventy trees, seventy years (figurative?) of exile (Jer. 25:11, 12; 29:10; Zech. 1:12; 7:5); seventy weeks (or sevens) (Dan. 9:2, 24).

7658. שִׁבְעָנָה ***šiḇʿānāh:*** A masculine noun meaning seven. It is used once as a counting number indicating Job's seven restored sons (Job 42:13).

7659. שִׁבְעָתַיִם ***šiḇʿāṯayim:*** A masculine dual noun indicating sevenfold, seven times. It indicates that something is increased seven times, sevenfold (Gen. 4:15, 24). It is employed in an expression, seven times, to indicate the purity of the Lord's words (Ps. 12:6[7]); or, in a different context, the sevenfold judgment of the Lord (Ps. 79:12). Sevenfold repayment of a theft is noted (Prov. 6:31). In a restored world, a sun shining sevenfold brighter is mentioned, indicating the joyous nature of that environment (Isa. 30:26).

7660. שָׁבַץ ***šāḇaṣ:*** A verb meaning to weave in; to set (a gem). It describes the skillful work and placement of a precious stone or stones into a gold filigree or milieu (Ex. 28:20).

7661. שָׁבָץ ***šāḇaṣ:*** A masculine noun meaning anguish, agony. It refers to a state of mind and the physical state of a person in deep pain and near death (2 Sam. 1:9).

7662. שְׁבַק ***šᵉḇaq:*** An Aramaic verb indicating to leave, to let alone. It refers to not bothering or disturbing something (Dan. 4:15[12], 23[20], 26[23]), to letting something remain as it is. It means to not become involved in or interfere with persons (Ezra 6:7). In its passive use, it means to leave something to another person or people, to change hands of rulership (Dan. 2:44).

7663. שָׂבַר ***śāḇar:*** A verb meaning to scrutinize, to expect with hope and patience, to hope, to tarry, to view, to wait. Nehemiah used this word to express an examination of the broken walls of Jerusalem before the returning exiles began rebuilding (Neh. 2:13–15). In this context, the verb did not only refer to Nehemiah's viewing of simply a broken wall but also a metaphorical viewing of Israel's brokenness and need for the return of the presence of God to Jerusalem.

7664. שֵׂבֶר ***śēḇer:*** A masculine noun meaning hope. It indicates a feeling and a conviction that what one wants is going to come to pass. In context it refers to a person's hope and expectation in God (Ps. 119:116; 146:5).

7665. שָׁבַר ***šāḇar:*** A verb meaning to break, to burst, to break in pieces, to break down, to break up, to smash, to shatter, to bring to birth. The word is most often used to express bursting or breaking. Other meanings include God's actions against stubborn pride (Lev. 26:19); or a metaphor for deliverance expressed figuratively by the breaking of a yoke (Jer. 28:2). In a figurative sense, the word describes the breaking of Pharaoh's arms (Ezek. 30:21, 22). It also depicts the literal smashing or shattering of the tablets of the commandments (Ex. 32:19). Further expressions of the word can mean to bring to the moment of birth (Isa. 66:9); to break down or destroy a people (Isa. 14:25); to break objects of material quality (Gen. 19:9; Lev. 6:28[21]; Jer. 49:35).

7666. שָׁבַר ***šāḇar:*** A verb meaning to buy; to sell. It means to acquire something by an exchange of money, land, or another object (Gen. 41:57; Deut. 2:6; Isa. 55:1); it means to sell, to let someone buy something, e.g., grain (Gen. 41:56; Deut. 2:28; Prov. 11:26; Amos 8:5).

7667. שֵׁבֶר ***šēḇer:*** A masculine noun meaning destruction, ruin, affliction, fracture, solution of a dream, breach. This noun can be used to express the result from the breaking of a dream (i.e., its interpretation [Judg. 7:15]). Isaiah used this noun to express the possible result of sin by speaking metaphorically of the shattering of a wall (Isa. 30:13). In Leviticus, this noun is used to designate a fracture of the foot or hand, indicating a cripple (Lev. 21:19). The noun can also be used to indicate the primary reason for suffering due to disobedience to God.

7668. שֶׁבֶר ***šeḇer:*** A masculine noun meaning grain, i.e., that which is broken into kernels, corn, or food stuff. The word is used nine times in the Old Testament as a general term for grain, with seven being used in the Joseph narratives of Genesis. This noun can connote grain that is for sale (Gen. 42:1); especially that which is eaten during a famine (Gen. 42:19). This word is the food stuff eaten when people are less particular about what they eat. In Nehemiah, it describes the food brought in by neighboring countries to sell on the Sabbath. The remnant that had returned promised God they would not buy it (Neh. 10:31[32]). The noun is also used in reference to Israel's greed and disobedience when they were waiting impatiently for the end of the Sabbath that they might once again sell grain (Amos 8:5).

7669. שֶׁבֶר ***šeḇer:*** A proper noun designating Sheber (1 Chr. 2:48).

7670. שִׁבְרוֹן ***šiḇrôn:*** A masculine noun meaning rupture (i.e., a pang). It is used figuratively for ruin, breaking, and destruction. This noun was used figuratively in Jeremiah to describe emotional distress by way of broken loins (Jer. 17:18). It was used in reference to the coming exile, in which it would seem as if Israel had been cut off from the covenant of God, although God, being faithful and true, would provide a remnant or a branch of David. It was also used in Ezekiel as the reason for distress and sorrow (Ezek. 21:6[11]). This reference was also for the coming exile of Israel, in which God would give the Israelites over to those they hated.

7671. שְׁבָרִים ***šᵉḇāriym:*** I. A masculine proper noun designating Shebarim (KJV, NASB, Josh. 7:5).

II. A masculine plural noun meaning stone quarries (NIV, Josh. 7:5).

7672. שְׁבַשׁ ***šᵉḇaš:*** An Aramaic verb meaning to be astonished, to be perplexed. It indicates a state of astonishment accompanied by confusion and puzzlement about something, especially an unusual occurrence (Dan. 5:9).

7673. שָׁבַת ***šaḇaṯ:*** A verb meaning to repose, to rest, to rid of, to still, to put away, to leave. Most often, the word expresses the idea of resting (i.e., abstaining from labor), especially on the seventh day (see Ex. 20:8–11). It is from this root that the noun for *Sabbath* originates, a word designating the time to be set aside for rest. The verb is used of God to describe His resting after the completion of creation (Gen. 2:2). This example of rest by God at creation set the requirement of rest that He desires for His people in order that they may live lives pleasing to Him, full of worship and adoration (Ex. 31:17). In Joshua, the verb expresses a cessation of the provision of manna by God to the Israelites (Josh. 5:12). The land was also depicted as enjoying a rest from the Israelite farmers while they were in exile (Lev. 26:34, 35).

Daniel uses this verb to indicate a ceasing of ritual sacrifice and offerings (Dan. 9:27). In that passage, Daniel was speaking of the Messiah's coming and the establishment of the New Covenant, when there would be no more need for ritual sacrifices. In another context, the verb can mean to exterminate or destroy a certain object, such as in Amos 8:4 in which Amos addresses those who trampled the needy and did away with the poor. The verb means to cause, to desist from, as in God's declaration of action against the shepherds (Ezek 34:10). The word suggests a removing of people or other objects (Ex. 12:15; Ezek. 23:27, 48; Isa. 30:11). In still other contexts, the causative stem means to fail or to leave lacking. In Ruth 4:14, God was praised because He did not leave Naomi without a kinsman-redeemer.

7674. שֶׁבֶת *šeḇeṯ:* A masculine noun indicating a loss of time, a ceasing. It indicates literally a sitting or a time of recovery, inactivity (Ex. 21:19); or a refusal to become involved in something, a holding back (Prov. 20:3). It refers to a period of inactivity by a nation, an inability to act, referring to Egypt (Isa. 30:7).

7675. שֶׁבֶת *šeḇeṯ:* A feminine noun meaning a seat, a dwelling place, a site. It comes from the verb *yāšaḇ,* to sit, to dwell, to inhabit. It can indicate the site or location of a city (Num. 21:15); or the place of habitation, figuratively or literally, of the wicked (2 Sam. 23:7). It indicates the physical place where a people lives (Obad. 1:3). It is understood as part of a name by the NASB and NIV (2 Sam. 23:8); but as a common noun by the KJV (2 Sam. 23:8). It refers to a place to sit, a seat (1 Kgs. 10:19; 2 Chr. 9:18). It refers figuratively to a seat or a location of violence (Amos 6:3).

7676. שַׁבָּת *šabbāṯ:* A noun meaning Sabbath, Day of Atonement, Sabbath week or year, weeks. The word can be translated as Sabbath in practically every instance. The seventh day was set aside at creation, but the holy Sabbath was first given to Israel and first mentioned in the biblical text in Exodus 16:23 as a gift to God's people (Ex. 16:25, 26, 29). The word describes the day as it was officially established in the Ten Commandments at Sinai. It was the seventh day, and it was to be kept holy, set apart to the Lord (Ex. 20:8, 10). That day was blessed by the Lord (Ex. 20:11); and was to be observed by Israel forever (Ex. 31:13–16; Ezek. 20:12). Not even a fire could be lit in any house on the Sabbath (Ex. 35:3; Lev. 23:32; Neh. 10:31[32]; Isa. 58:13; Jer. 17:22); nor could work, even on the Tabernacle, be performed (Ex. 35:2). Special offerings were presented on the Sabbath in addition to the regular daily burnt offerings, properly termed Sabbath offerings (Num. 28:9, 10). The purpose for the Sabbath was rest for all God's people; its basis was found in God's cessation from work at Creation (Ex. 20:11; cf. Ex. 31:17); and Israel's historic experience of forced labor in Egypt (Deut. 5:15). Unfortunately, God's people chose to utterly desecrate the Lord's Sabbaths (Ezek. 20:13, 16, 20).

The high point of the religious year for Israel was the Day of Atonement which the author described as a Sabbath of Sabbaths (Lev. 16:31; 23:32), a Sabbath of rest. Every seventh year was described as a Sabbath to the Lord or, using the same term employed for the Day of Atonement, a Sabbath of Sabbaths (Lev. 25:4). During this time, the land was to remain unplowed; thus, the land itself was to enjoy its Sabbaths (Lev. 25:6; 26:34). When Israel was in exile, God remembered the land, giving it rest, so that it was refreshed by lying fallow for seventy years (Lev. 26:34, 35, 43); enjoying its Sabbaths that Israel had not observed (2 Chr. 36:21). Seven Sabbaths or seven weeks of years were equal to forty-nine years (Lev. 25:8). The produce of the land that grew of itself during the Sabbath year is described as the Sabbath (produce) of the land (Lev. 25:6).

7677. שַׁבָּתוֹן *šabbāṯôn:* A masculine noun meaning a time to rest, a special holiday, a day of rest, a Sabbath feast. The meaning most often denoted from this word is that of the day of rest (Ex. 31:15). In Leviticus, this noun is used to refer to the Day of Atonement (Lev. 16:31); the sabbatical year (Lev. 25:4); the Feast of Trumpets (Lev. 23:24); and the first and eighth days of the Feast of Tabernacles (Lev. 23:39).

During the sabbatical year, the land was not to be plowed but to be given a Sabbath rest, a time of refreshing to the Lord. This word was also used to describe the requirements of rest on the first and eighth days of the Feast of Tabernacles. In any context, however, the meaning of this noun is still one of a requirement for God's people to rest on the seventh day or any other holy day as directed.

7678. שַׁבְּתַי *šabbᵉṯay:* A proper noun designating Shabbethai, a Levite (Ezra 10:15; Neh. 8:7; 11:10).

7679. שָׂגָא *śāgā':* A verb meaning to magnify: to make great, to extol. It refers to the growth and development of a nation (Job 12:23); and to the great acts and works of God in general (Job 36:24).

7680. שְׂגָא *śᵉgā':* An Aramaic verb meaning to increase, to grow. It indicates that something grows, increases, expands, whether good or bad, such as royal finances (Ezra 4:22); or the well-being of a whole nation (Dan. 4:21[3:31]; 6:25, 26).

7681. שָׁגֵה *šāgēh:* A proper noun designating Shagee (1 Chr. 11:34).

7682. שָׂגַב *śagaḇ:* A verb indicating to be raised, to be exalted; to be high; to defend. It refers to physical size indicating great height: city walls (Deut. 2:36; Isa. 30:13). In a figurative sense, it indicates a high, impregnable city or habitation (Isa. 26:5); or God's exalted name or person (Job 36:22; Isa. 12:4). Its figurative use is developed most fully: of high inaccessible knowledge (Ps. 139:6); of the security of God's high name (Prov. 18:10, 11). Trust in the Lord results in the exaltation of a person (Prov. 29:25). It refers to persons' advancement or promotion, setting them on high (Job 5:11); or of their being placed in a place of safety (Ps. 20:1[2]; 59:1[2]; 69:29[30]). To know God's name leads to security (Ps. 91:14); and the Lord secures the poor and needy (Ps. 107:41).

7683. שָׁגַג *šāgag:* A verb meaning to stray, to be deceived, to err, to go astray, to sin ignorantly. The primary meaning of this word is to commit an error, to sin inadvertently. In Leviticus, this word referred to the unintentional sin atoned for by the sacrifice of a ram, referred to as a guilt offering (Lev. 5:18). In addition to Leviticus, Numbers 15:28 also described the priestly function in atonement for one's unintentional sin. Recognition of sin may result from a realization or awareness of covenant violations due to the work of the human consciousness. The psalmist used this word to describe an action before he was afflicted (i.e., he went astray [Ps. 119:67]). This verb was also used to designate erring mentally on the part of self or another person (i.e., being the deceived or the deceiver [Job 12:16]).

7684. שְׁגָגָה *šᵉgāgāh:* A feminine noun meaning mistake, inadvertent transgression, error, ignorance. The primary meaning is an inadvertent error performed in the daily routine of life that ranged from a slip of the tongue (Eccl. 5:6[5]); to accidental manslaughter (Num. 35:11, 15; Josh. 20:3, 9). When used with the word *ḥāṭā'* (2398), it describes a procedure or policy used by priests for the guilt offering that atones for inadvertent sin (Lev. 4:2, 22, 27; 5:15, 18). Unatoned sin breaks the order and peace between God and people, even if unintentional, and an atonement has to be made. The noun also describes acts in which the sinner is conscious, yet the sinfulness of those acts becomes known after the act takes place.

7685. שָׂגָה *śāgāh:* A verb meaning to grow, to increase; to thrive. It refers to an increase or development of something: of life's benefits in general (Job 8:7); of wealth (Ps. 73:12). The righteous person thrives, grows like a cedar in Lebanon (Ps. 92:12[13]).

7686. שָׁגָה *šagāh:* A verb meaning to stray, to go astray, to err, to deceive, to wander, to make a mistake, to reel. It is primarily used to express the idea of straying or wandering. It is used frequently to describe a wandering or aimless flock, both figuratively and literally (Ezek. 34:6). Isaiah used this verb to suggest swerving, meandering, or reeling in drunkenness (Isa. 28:7). At times, it could define intoxication, not only from wine or beer but also from love (Prov. 5:19, 20). This verb also depicts moral corruption (Prov. 5:23). Deuteronomy 27:18 describes it as a reason for being cursed (i.e., leading a blind man astray). Leviticus 4:13 indicates a sin of ignorance of which the person is still guilty and must provide an atonement when knowledge of the sin is known. The word also expresses a misleading mentally (i.e., being a deceiver or the deceived). The idea of atonement for sin, even of that which is an inadvertent or unintentional sin, is a prevalent thought found in Scripture (Ezek. 45:20).

7687. שְׂגוּב ***śᵉgûḇ:*** A proper noun designating Segub:

A. Son of Hiel (1 Kgs. 16:34).

B. Son of Hezron (1 Chr. 2:21, 22).

7688. שָׁגַח ***šāgāḥ:*** A verb meaning to gaze, to watch, to stare. It refers to a person's observing closely, looking intently at something, studying it but mainly appreciating something (Ps. 33:14; Song 2:9). It takes on a sense of looking at intently in surprise or wonder (Isa. 14:16).

7689. שַׂגִּיא ***śaggiy':*** An adjective meaning great, exalted. It refers to such greatness and magnificence as to put someone in an exalted or highly uplifted state, especially God (Job 36:26; 37:23).

7690. שַׂגִּיא ***śaggiy':*** An Aramaic adjective meaning great, abundant, many, much. It refers to the power, splendor, and influence of a king as being great (Ezra 5:11). It indicates an abundance, an extent or high degree of something, honor (Dan. 2:6); fury (Dan. 2:12); size (Dan. 2:31; 4:10[7]); quality of gifts, great gifts (Dan. 2:48); fruit, meat (Dan. 4:12[9], 21[18]; 7:5). It figuratively describes a person's emotions, e.g., great alarm, anxiety, dread (Dan. 5:9; 6:14[15]; 7:28).

7691. שְׁגִיאָה ***šᵉgiy'āh:*** A feminine noun meaning a moral mistake, an error. As written in Psalm 19:12[13], the noun signifies an error or lapse that is hidden from the sight of others. The inclusion of this noun in the verse seems to indicate that only God can see or discern this type of error or moral mistake. In its plural absolute form, this noun indicates a willful sin (Ps. 19:13).

7692. שִׁגָּיוֹן ***šiggāyôn,*** שִׁגָּיֹנָה ***šiggāyōnāh:*** A proper noun transliterated as Shiggaion, a musical term whose meaning is not certain. The NASB suggests that it is a song of passionate feeling, a dithyramb. But this term and definition is Greek in origin. The NIV notes only that it is a musical or literary term (Ps. 7:title[1]; Hab. 3:1).

7693. שָׁגַל ***šāgal:*** A verb meaning to rape; to violate sexually. It refers to violating a betrothed woman, a woman promised in marriage, as one of God's curses that He will bring on Israel (Deut. 28:30). It is used of raping or violating wives taken in war as prisoners (Isa. 13:16; Zech. 14:2). It is used figuratively of spiritual and religious harlotry of all kinds (Jer. 3:2).

7694. שֵׁגַל ***šēgal:*** A feminine noun meaning a queen, a concubine, a harem favorite, a consort. The primary meaning of this noun is queen. This noun was used by Nehemiah to describe the queen who sat beside the king (Neh. 2:6). In the book of Psalms, the psalmist used this noun to designate the queen who sat at the right hand of the king (Ps. 45:9[10]). Concubine, harem favorite, and consort are also possible definitions due to the close connection of this word with *šāgal* (7693), which can mean to sleep or to have sexual intercourse with.

7695. שֵׁגַל ***šēgal:*** An Aramaic feminine noun. It is a word referring to royal wives of the king. It may refer to the more favored wives of the royal harem (Dan. 5:2, 3, 23).

7696. שָׁגַע ***šaga':*** A verb meaning to be insane, to be demented, to be mad (Deut. 28:34; 1 Sam. 21:14[15], 15[16]; 21:15[16]; 2 Kgs. 9:11; Jer. 29:26; Hos. 9:7).

7697. שִׁגָּעוֹן ***šiggā'ôn:*** A masculine noun meaning insanity, madness. It is always used in a negative, accusatory way of persons who behave abnormally to a threatening and excessive extent (Deut. 28:28; Zech. 12:4); but it is used of especially agitated or excessive physical activity in general (2 Kgs. 9:20).

7698. שֶׁגֶר ***šeger:*** A masculine noun referring to the offspring of an animal. It may be rendered in context as offspring, increase, calves. It refers to animals born to their parents (Ex. 13:12; Deut. 28:4, 18, 51; NIV, calves). It is rendered as increase of flocks (Deut. 7:13) by the NASB (NIV, calves).

7699. שַׁד ***šaḏ,*** **שֹׁד** ***šōḏ:*** I. A masculine noun meaning breast. It is used of the breasts of both women and animals that nurture newborns (Gen. 49:25). Fertile breasts are a blessing from God. The breasts sustain a child at birth (Job 3:12; Ps. 22:9[10]; Song 8:1; Isa. 28:9). The breasts are used to depict tender loving care in an amorous setting (Song 1:13); and are depictions of beauty (Song 4:5; 7:3[4]; 8:8, 10). The beating of one's breasts, male or female, was a sign of despair (Isa. 32:12; Ezek. 23:34). For a mother to withhold her breasts from a baby, even a mother jackal does not do that, is a sign of cruelty (Lam. 4:3). The development of breasts is a sign of maturing (Ezek. 16:7). Female breasts can become a part of immorality, a sign of spiritual unfaithfulness, if their chastity is not protected (Ezek. 23:3, 21).

II. A masculine noun meaning breast. It refers to the breasts of a mother feeding her newborn child (Job 24:9). It is used figuratively of the "breasts" of royalty or kings (Isa. 60:16); and of the breasts of Jerusalem satisfying her children (Isa. 66:11).

7700. שֵׁד ***šēḏ:*** A masculine noun meaning a demon, a devil. The primary or typical translation of this noun is demon or demons. This noun was used to describe the recipient of a sacrifice (i.e., a sacrifice that was not directed or given to God [Deut. 32:17]). Certain sacrifices in which sons and daughters were sacrificed were also directed toward demons (Ps. 106:37). This word is also used to designate the recipients of forbidden sacrifices.

7701. שֹׁד ***šōḏ***, שׁוֹד ***šôḏ:*** A masculine noun meaning violence, destruction, desolation, robbery, spoil, wasting. The primary meaning of this word is violence or destruction. In Job, the noun is used to describe an object or idea of which not to fear (Job 5:21). The word is also used in Psalms to designate a reason for God's arising to protect the weak (Ps. 12:5[6]). Isaiah used the noun to depict the reason that God weeps bitterly (i.e., the destruction of His people due to their sin [Isa. 22:4]). This word was also used by Jeremiah and Amos to describe violence and havoc as social sins (Jer. 6:7; Amos 3:10). The primary meaning of destruction was used by Hosea to express God's reason for the coming destruction of a nation (Hos. 7:13).

7702. שָׂדַד ***śāḏaḏ:*** A verb indicating to harrow; to break up the ground. It refers to breaking up and leveling plowed ground, thus covering seeds and/or clearing the ground of weeds, small debris, etc. Animals had to be trained to do this by pulling a harrowing tool over the ground (Job 39:10); as the farmer guided them (Isa. 28:24). It is used figuratively of Jacob (Israel) harrowing the ground at God's command (Hos. 10:11).

7703. שָׁדַד ***šāḏaḏ:*** A verb meaning to be burly, to ravage, to destroy, to oppress, to assault, to spoil, to lay waste, to devastate. The primary meaning of the verb is to devastate or to destroy. This word is used to describe the destruction of the unfaithful, an action taken due to their duplicity (Prov. 11:3). The verb is also used in Isaiah's prophecy against Moab to describe the action that would result on its cities (Isa. 15:1). The actions of an outlaw or thief are depicted by the verb concerning a righteous person's house (Prov. 24:15). The word expresses God's judgment on Egypt and the overthrowing of its hordes (Ezek. 32:12). The verb is also used to describe the actions of subjects such as a lion, a wolf, or a leopard in the figurative sense as a response to the rebellions and backsliding of Jerusalem (Jer. 5:6). Jeremiah uses the word to describe the destruction of the Tabernacle and the barrenness when everything was taken away (Jer. 10:20).

7704. שָׂדַי ***śaḏay***, שָׂדֶה ***śāḏeh:*** A masculine noun meaning open country, a field, a domain, a plot (of land). The primary meaning of the word is a field, oftentimes defined more descriptively as an open field. The noun is used to describe pastureland in which flocks of sheep were fed (Gen. 29:2). The word is also used to describe a field or a plot of land that was normally unfrequented and in which one could meditate without being disturbed (Gen. 24:63, 65). Another meaning of the word is a field in which a slain man was found (Deut. 21:1). The word is also used as a place opposite of the Tent of Meeting in which the Israelites had made sacrifices but were to no longer (Lev. 17:5). In Numbers, the noun is used to indicate a land or territory that belonged to a nation or tribe (Num. 21:20).

7705. שִׁדָּה šiddāh: I. A feminine noun referring to a concubine; a member of a harem. It refers to secondary wives in polygamous societies (Eccl. 2:8). In Ecclesiastes, it constituted a part of the qoheleth's pursuit of total pleasure.

II. A feminine noun referring to a musical instrument. This is the rendering of the word in the KJV and NKJV. Its exact meaning is under examination (Eccl. 2:8).

7706. שַׁדַּי šadday: A masculine noun and name for God meaning Shaddai, Almighty. The word occurs only forty-eight times in the Hebrew Bible, thirty-one times in the book of Job. This is a name for the Lord—the Old Testament people of faith referring to Him as El Shaddai, God Almighty. The term is found in the passages that report God's promises of fertility, land, and abundance to them, indicating that He, the Almighty, could fulfill His promises (Gen. 17:1; 28:3; 35:11). The Lord appeared to Abraham when he was ninety-nine years old and identified himself as El Shaddai, God Almighty (Gen. 17:1). All three patriarchs knew Him by this name (Gen. 28:1–3; 35:11); as did Joseph (Gen. 48:3; cf. Ex. 6:3); Ezekiel the prophet knew the tradition of Shaddai as well (Ezek. 10:5). Balaam, Naomi, the psalmist, Joel, and Isaiah employed the term Shaddai, Almighty (Num. 24:4; Ruth 1:20; Ps. 68:14[15]; Isa. 13:6; Joel 1:15). But it is especially Job who uses the term appropriately as a non-Israelite (Job 5:17; 13:3; 24:1; 37:23), since it is a universal term for God. It is always found in poetic sections of material. The book of Job also uses the name the LORD, Yahweh, twenty-seven times, and it is found all but five times in the prose sections (Job 1—2; 42:7–17; see concordance for specific references).

7707. שְׁדֵיאוּר š^{e}ḏēy'ûr: A proper noun designating Shedeur (Num. 1:5; 2:10; 7:30, 35; 10:18).

7708. שִׂדִּים śiddiym: A proper noun designating Siddim (Gen. 14:3, 8, 10).

7709. שְׁדֵמָה š^{e}ḏēmāh: I. A feminine noun meaning a field. In general a field was a place where a variety of produce from the soil was generated (Hab. 3:17). It refers to fields transformed into vineyards, but in context it is used figuratively of the fields of Gommorah that produced evil (Deut. 32:32). It refers to open land or areas in general (2 Kgs. 23:4; Isa. 16:8; Jer. 31:40).

II. A feminine noun indicating blasted. It refers to the withering and drying up of grass or the scorching of corn by the hot sun and is used to depict the inhabitants of Egypt destroyed by the Lord's judgments (Isa. 37:27).

7710. שָׁדַף ***šāḏap:*** A verb meaning to scorch, to blight. It refers to the effect on corn. It was dried up, dehydrated, and withered by a hot east wind (Gen. 41:6, 23, 27).

7711. שְׁדֵפָה ***šᵉḏēpāh,*** שִׁדָּפוֹן ***šiddāpôn:*** I. A feminine noun indicating something scorched. It has the same meaning as 7709, II (Isa. 37:27) and is used in the same way to depict, this time in general, the withering of the people of Egypt.

II. A masculine noun indicating a blight, scorching. It is one of the curses that God may send on His disobedient people (Deut. 28:22), a disease or drying up of crops, corn, etc. It could be removed by prayer to the Lord and the repentance of His people (1 Kgs. 8:37; 2 Chr. 6:28; Amos 4:9; Hag. 2:17).

7712. שְׁדַר ***šᵉḏar:*** An Aramaic verb meaning to exert oneself, to labor. It indicates strong efforts put forth to accomplish something: Darius put forth every effort to rescue Daniel (Dan. 6:14[15]).

7713. שְׂדֵרָה ***śᵉḏērāh:*** I. A feminine noun referring to a row or rank of soldiers. It describes a configuration of soldiers standing in orderly array (NASB, 2 Kgs. 11:8, 15; 2 Chr. 23:14; KJV, ranks, ranges of soldiers), possibly to protect the king or an area.

II. A feminine noun indicating a board, a plank of wood. It refers to boards, long, flat pieces of wood sawed or cut and prepared for use in construction (1 Kgs. 6:9).

7714. שַׁדְרַךְ ***šaḏrak:*** A proper noun designating Shadrach, the Babylonian name of the Jewish royal youth named Hananiah. The name means "I am fearful (of God)." The change of name indicated (supposedly) a change of cultural views (Dan. 1:6, 7).

7715. שַׁדְרַךְ ***šaḏrak:*** A proper noun designating Shadrach, the Aramaic form of Hebrew word 7714. The meaning is the same.

7716. שֶׂה ***śeh:*** A common noun meaning sheep, lamb. It refers to a young lamb of sheep or a young kid of goats, a part of a larger unit of animals, a flock (*ṣō'n*) (Gen. 22:7). The animals were of great value for wealth in general, food, sacrifices, milk. They were a favorite subject in figures of speech indicating lost or straying persons, as well as sheep themselves (Ps. 119:176). They were used figuratively of Israel (Ezek. 34:17). The Suffering Servant was slaughtered like a sheep (Isa. 53:7). The lamb was used in the Passover ritual (Ex. 12:3–5).

7717. שָׂהֵד ***śāhēḏ:*** A masculine noun indicating an advocate, a witness. It refers to a reliable person who will argue for or support a plaintiff in a court case (Job 16:19).

7718. שֹׁהַם *šōham:* A masculine noun meaning onyx. It refers to a precious stone. It has been translated as onyx, but carnelian or lapis lazuli have been suggested as well (Gen. 2:12). It was a stone featured in the ephod and breastpiece worn by the high priests of Israel (Ex. 25:7); even bearing the names of the twelve tribes of Israel (Ex. 28:9). Wisdom, however, far exceeds it in value (Job 28:16). It was a part of the splendor of the coverings of the "king of Tyre" in the Garden of Eden (Ezek. 28:13).

7719. שֹׁהַם *šōham:* A proper noun designating Shoham (1 Chr. 24:27).

7720. שַׂהֲרוֹן *śah^a^rôn:* A masculine noun referring to an ornament. It refers to decorative ornaments used to dress and emphasize the splendor of the camels of some Midianite kings (Judg. 8:21, 26). The word also refers to ornaments worn by persons as well, luxurious items (Isa. 3:18).

7721. שׂוֹא *śô'*, שׂוֹאָה *śô'āh*, שֹׂאָה *śō'āh:* A verb meaning to arise. It is used in its infinitive construct form to indicate the rising of the waves of the sea before they turn down (Ps. 89:9[10]).

7722. *šô':* A masculine noun meaning ravage. When used in the feminine form *šō'āh*, the noun means devastation, ruin, desolation, or noise. The primary meaning of the word is devastation. Often this word carries with it a sense of something sudden or unexpected like that of a devastating storm (Ezek. 38:9). In Isaiah, the word describes a coming disaster on the day of reckoning (Isa. 10:3). The noun is used to depict a wasteland or a desert (Job 30:3; 38:27). Psalm 35:17 uses the masculine form of the word to indicate the ravages that held the psalmist down.

7723. שָׁוְא *šāw':* A masculine noun meaning emptiness, vanity, evil, ruin, uselessness, deception, worthless, without result, fraud, deceit. The primary meaning of the word is deceit, lie, or falsehood. God used the word to indicate that He punished Judah in vain. The word is used by the psalmist to state that all activities such as laboring, guarding, rising early, staying up late, and toiling for food were useless without God's assistance (Ps. 127:1, 2). In the Ten Commandments, the word is used to describe what is prohibited (Deut. 5:20). The word is used in Proverbs to indicate that which the author desires to be kept away from him: in this case, falsehood and lies (Prov. 30:8). Idols were declared worthless with the usage of the noun in Jeremiah (Jer. 18:15). These idols were those that led the people of God to forget Him.

7724. שְׁוָא *š^e^wā':* A proper noun designating Sheva:

A. A scribe (2 Sam. 20:25).

B. A descendant of Caleb (1 Chr. 2:49).

7725. שׁוּב šûḇ: A verb meaning to turn, to return, to go back, to do again, to change, to withdraw, to bring back, to reestablish, to be returned, to bring back, to take, to restore, to recompense, to answer, to hinder. The verb is used over one thousand times and has various shades of meaning in its four stems. In the simple stem, it is used to describe divine and human reactions, attitudes, and feelings. The verb describes the possibility that Israel might change (turn) their minds and return to Egypt (Ex. 13:17). Josiah the king turned back to the Lord with all his heart, soul, and strength (2 Kgs. 23:25; Jer. 34:15). Nevertheless, the Lord did not turn from the anger He held toward Judah (2 Kgs. 23:26; Jer. 4:28). Job pleaded with his miserable comforters to relent (i.e., turn away) from him (Job 6:29). God's people will return (repent) and seek Him in the last days (Deut. 30:2; Isa. 59:20; Hos. 3:5) instead of turning away from Him as they are now; to return to Egypt (Isa. 6:10; Hos. 11:5). God's call was persistently for His people to return to Him (1 Kgs. 8:33; Jer. 4:1). Any nation can repent and turn to God for forgiveness (Jer. 18:8).

The word is used metaphorically to describe things returning: God's Word will not be revoked (returned) once it has been uttered (Isa. 45:23; 55:11); Jacob stayed with Laban until Esau's anger cooled off (turned back) (Gen. 27:44, 45); blood guilt could return on one's own head (1 Kgs. 2:33; Ps. 7:16[17]). This word also describes the sword of Saul that did not return without success from the battlefield (2 Sam. 1:22).

The verb also indicates to returning to or to change into. For example, human beings return to the dust of the earth (Gen. 3:19; Eccl. 12:7); but a person cannot naturally return to life (2 Sam. 12:23); unless God's Spirit brings it about (1 Kgs. 13:6). A land of great natural fertility can be reduced (turned into) to a farmer's cropland (Isa. 29:17).

In its simplest sense, the word means to return, to restore, to go back. Abraham's descendants in their fourth generation would return to Canaan (Gen. 15:16); God returned to visit His people (Gen. 8:9; 18:10). It is also used to describe turning chariots about when needed (1 Kgs. 22:33; Mic. 2:8).

This verb is used with other verbs of motion, all in their infinitive or participial forms, to describe a back and forth motion; the ravens Noah sent out went back and forth (Gen. 8:7). Used with another verb in general, *šûḇ* is either not translated or means to do again whatever action is indicated by the other verb, such as when Isaac dug again the wells his father had previously dug (Gen. 26:18). A similar meaning is to take back or recapture when this verb is used with the Hebrew verb *lāqaḥ* (3947), meaning to take or to receive (2 Kgs. 13:25; Mic. 7:19). Finally, if this verb is used with a following infinitive of another verb, it means to do over and over or more and more; Israel angered the Lord more and more than they had already angered Him by performing pagan rituals (Ezek. 8:17).

7726. שׁוֹבָב šô*b*ā*b*: An adjective meaning faithless, backsliding. It refers to a people who are always turning away from the Lord, leaving their God, acting unfaithfully towards Him and His laws (Isa. 57:17; Jer. 3:14, 22).

7727. שׁוֹבָב šô*b*ā*b*: A proper noun designating Shobab:

A. Son of David (2 Sam. 5:14; 1 Chr. 3:5; 14:4).

B. Son of Caleb (1 Chr. 2:18).

7728. שׁוֹבֵב šô*b*ē*b*: An adjective meaning apostate, unfaithful. It refers to a person who is constantly turning aside, away from a set path, acting as an apostate, as Israel and Judah always did (Jer. 31:22; 49:4). It refers to a person of an alien faith, not of Israel's faith or possibly those in Israel who have turned from Israel's God denying their own faith (Mic. 2:4).

7729. שׁוּבָה šû*b*āh: A feminine noun indicating repentance, returning. It refers in a religious sense to an act of turning back to God, to committing oneself to Him, while turning from one's wayward ways (Isa. 30:15).

7730. שׂוֹבֶךְ śô*b*e*k*: A masculine noun referring to a thick branch (of a tree). It refers to the heavy, thick branch of a tree, in context of a great oak tree (2 Sam. 18:9). Absalom, David's son, was caught by his head and neck in such a branch.

7731. שׁוֹבָךְ šô*b*ā*k*: A proper noun designating Shobach, the same as *šôpā*k (7780) (2 Sam. 10:16, 18).

7732. שׁוֹבָל šô*b*al: A proper noun designating Shobal:

A. An Edomite leader (Gen. 36:20, 23, 29; 1 Chr. 1:38, 40).

B. Son of Caleb (1 Chr. 2:50, 52).

C. Son of Judah (1 Chr. 4:1, 2).

7733. שׁוֹבֵק šô*b*ēq: A proper noun designating Shobek (Neh. 10:24[25]).

7734. שׂוּג śûg: A verb meaning to turn. It refers to someone or something refraining from an act of some kind: Jonathan's bow did not turn back from slaying Israel's enemies (2 Sam. 1:22).

7735. שׂוּג śûg: A verb meaning to grow, to raise. It has the sense of to cause to grow (KJV, Isa. 17:11) or to nurture a plant or seed that sprouts. Others prefer to render it as fence in in order to care for a plant, something sown (NASB).

7736. שׁוּד šû*d*: A verb meaning to destroy, to lay waste. It refers to rendering something useless, devastating or destroying it. It is used in a general sense of any calamity or act of destruction (Ps. 91:6).

7737. שָׁוָה šāwāh: I. A verb meaning to be or become like or equal, to match, to suffice. It means basically to be like or equivalent (Prov. 26:4; Isa. 40:25). It also takes on the sense of being suitable or sufficient (Esth. 3:8; 7:4). In its causative stem, it means to make like (2 Sam. 22:34); or to compare or equate (Isa. 46:5; Lam. 2:13). It is used of leveling the ground (Isa. 28:25). Wisdom is not to be compared even to jewels (Prov. 3:15; 8:11). It indicates that something is fitting, sufficient or not (Job 33:27). It takes on the meaning of to set, to place, to establish (Ps. 18:33[34]. See II below).

II. A verb meaning to set, to place, to put, to lay. It means to focus on someone (Ps. 16:8); or something (Ps. 119:30); it refers to God's granting something, such as deliverance to a person (Ps. 21:5[6]; 89:19[20]). It takes on the sense of producing something. In context it is used figuratively of God causing Israel to produce fruit (Hos. 10:1).

7738. שָׁוָה ***šāwāh:*** A feminine noun meaning substance. In context it refers to a person's physical and/or spiritual essence or being (Job 30:22, KJV).

7739. שְׁוָה ***šᵉwāh:*** An Aramaic verb meaning to become like; to be made like. It is used in a reflexive verb stem indicating the making of something into something else, changing it (Dan. 3:29); and in a similar stem, it describes a human heart being made into the heart of a beast (Dan. 5:21).

7740. שָׁוֵה ***šāwēh:*** A proper noun designating Shaveh (Gen. 14:17).

7741. שָׁוֵה קִרְיָתַיִם ***šāwēh qiryāṯayim:*** A proper noun designating Shaveh Kiriathaim (Gen. 14:5).

7742. שׂוּחַ ***śûah:*** A verb meaning to meditate. It is used of Isaac's walking in a field to observe or meditate. Its translation is not certain but is traditionally given as to meditate (Gen. 24:63).

7743. שׁוּחַ ***šûaḥ,*** שִׁיחַ ***šiyaḥ:*** I. A verb meaning to sink down; to be bowed down. It is used of something descending, going down: one's soul into the dust (Ps. 44:25[26]); the house of a harlot to death (Prov. 2:18); one's soul bending down within a person, an onset of despair (Lam. 3:20).

II. A verb meaning to be bowed down; to be downcast. It refers often to the despair of one's soul, one's life that is broken within (Ps. 42:5[6], 6[7], 11[12]; 43:5); or has sunk into the ground in utter hopelessness (Ps. 44:25[26]).

7744. שׁוּחַ ***šûaḥ:*** A proper noun designating Shuah (Gen. 25:2; 1 Chr. 1:32).

7745. שׁוּחָה ***šûḥāh:*** A feminine noun meaning a ditch, a pit, a chasm. The primary meaning of the word is pit. The verb is used primarily to describe figuratively a trap that leads to ruin. Proverbs uses this word in a figurative sense to describe a prostitute as a deep pit in comparison to a wayward wife as a narrow well (Prov. 23:27). This word could also be used to describe plots against someone, as where Jeremiah stated that his accusers had dug pits for him (Jer. 18:20). The word also describes the mouth of an adulteress (i.e., a deep pit [Prov. 22:14]). Out of the six times that it is used in the Old Testament, only one is used in its literal sense, describing a rift through which God led His people (Jer. 2:6).

7746. שׁוּחָה ***šûḥāh:*** A proper noun designating Shuhah (1 Chr. 4:11).

7747. שׁוּחִי ***šûḥiy:*** A proper noun designating Shuhite (Job 2:11; 8:1; 18:1; 25:1; 42:9).

7748. שׁוּחָם ***šûḥām:*** A proper noun designating Shuham (Num. 26:42).

7749. שׁוּחָמִי ***šûḥāmiy:*** A proper noun designating Shuhamite (Num. 26:42, 43).

7750. שׂוּט ***śûṭ***, סוּט ***sûṭ:*** A verb meaning to turn aside; to fall back. It indicates an act of turning aside from the Lord to someone else; an act of unfaithfulness (Ps. 40:4[5]); to fall away or to apostatize (Ps. 101:3).

7751. שׁוּט ***šûṭ:*** I. A verb meaning to roam, to move to and fro, to wander. It has the sense of moving about here and there, to roam: hunting for something (Num. 11:8); to deliver a message throughout the land (2 Sam. 24:2, 8); or to find someone in city streets (Jer. 5:1). It is used of the scanning of an area with one's eyes, especially the Lord's eyes (2 Chr. 16:9; Zech. 4:10); of Satan's going about in the earth (Job 1:7; 2:2). It is used of sailors, mariners on a boat (Ezek. 27:8, 26); or of people going to and fro, searching out wisdom and knowledge (Dan. 12:4; Amos 8:12).

II. A verb meaning to row a boat. It is used in its participial form to indicate rowers (Ezek. 27:8, 26).

7752. שׁוֹט ***šôṭ:*** A masculine noun indicating a whip, a scourge. It refers to a lash or a whip of leather often used to make horses gallop (Nah. 3:2); or to control them (Prov. 26:3). It is used in a figurative sense of abusive political and economic oppression (1 Kgs. 12:11, 14; 2 Chr. 10:11, 14); of being scourged by an accusatory tongue (Job 5:21); or by a great calamity (Job 9:23); of a scourge of punishment brought by the Lord (Isa. 10:26; 28:15, 18).

7753. שׂוּךְ ***śûḵ:*** A verb meaning to hedge in, fence in. It refers to erecting a protective or restraining barrier of some kind (Job 1:10; Hos. 2:6[8]). It refers in a figurative sense to fencing a person about with sinews and bones (Job 10:11).

7754. שׂוֹךְ ***śôḵ***, שׂוֹכָה ***śôḵāh:*** I. A masculine noun indicating a branch, a bough. It refers to a branch or a bough of a tree. In context a bough is cut off and used to make a fire (Judg. 9:48).

II. A masculine noun referring to a branch, a bough. It has the same meaning as I, a branch or a bough cut from a tree to burn (Judg. 9:49).

7755. שׂוֹכוֹ ***šôḵô,*** שׂוֹכֹה ***šôḵōh,*** שׂוֹכֹה ***śôḵōh,*** שׂוֹכוֹ ***śôḵô:*** A proper noun designating Soco, Socoh:

A. Son of Heber (1 Chr. 4:18).

B. A city in Judah (Josh. 15:48).

C. A city in Judah-Shephelah (Josh. 15:35; 1 Sam. 17:1; 1 Kgs. 4:10; 2 Chr. 11:7; 28:18).

7756. שׂוּכָתִים ***śûḵāṯiym:*** A proper noun designating Sucathites (1 Chr. 2:55).

7757. שׁוּל ***šûl:*** A masculine noun meaning a hem, a skirt or the train of a robe. It refers to a border or edge on a garment or a piece of cloth. It indicates the decorated hem of the high priest's robe (Ex. 28:33, 34; 39:24–26). It is used figuratively of the hem of the Lord's royal garment (Isa. 6:1). It indicates more generally an entire skirt, a garment extending from a person's waist down (Jer. 13:22, 26). It figuratively indicates the skirts of Israel (Lam. 1:9; Nah. 3:5).

7758. שׁוֹלָל ***šôlāl:*** An adjective meaning barefoot, stripped. It means to be without shoes, a shameful condition for some (Job 12:17, 19). Micah, the prophet, went barefoot as he lamented the coming destruction of Israel (Mic. 1:8). The KJV renders this word as stripped (Mic. 1:8).

7759. שׁוּלַמִּית ***šûlammiyṯ:*** A proper noun designating Shulamite, the name of the beloved woman in the Song. It refers to her most likely as a Shulamite/Shunamite woman (1 Kgs. 2:21, 22).

7760. שׂוּם ***śûm,*** שִׂים ***śiym:*** A verb meaning to appoint, to bring, to call, to put, to change, to charge, to commit, to consider, to convey, to determine. The primary meaning of the verb is to put, to set, or to place. The verb indicates that which God put on the earth, as noted in Genesis where God put the man and woman that He formed in the Garden of Eden (Gen. 2:8). The usage of the verb in this sense indicates God's sovereignty over all creation, especially that of humankind. The verb is also used to describe Samuel's action concerning the stone he named Ebenezer (1 Sam. 7:12). This stone was set up between Mizpah and Shen to remember God's deliverance of the Israelites from the Philistines. The verb is used to describe a committing of one's cause before God (Job 5:8). The word is used in Exodus in response to an interaction between Moses and God, in which God gave a new decree and law to the Israelites (Ex. 15:25). In this setting, the verb again emphasizes God's sovereignty, His ability to establish the order of things, and His ability to control the elements of nature and disease. In Deuteronomy, *śûm* is used to describe God's appointing of leaders over the different tribes of Israel, for their numbers were too great for Moses alone (Deut. 1:13). The word is also used to indicate a charging of someone, as where a man charged his wife with premarital sex (Deut. 22:14).

7761. שׂוּם *śûm,* שִׂים *śiym:* An Aramaic verb meaning to issue (a decree), to appoint, to place. It is used to describe the putting forth or issuance of a formal decree (Ezra 4:19, 21; 5:3, 9, 13, 17; 6:1; Dan. 3:10); or a command (Dan. 4:6[3]). It describes the placement or laying of wooden beams in a wall (Ezra 5:8). It is used in a formal sense of appointing a person to an official position (Ezra 5:14; Dan. 3:12). It is used in a reflexive passive stem to describe something being put into a state or turned into something (Dan. 2:5). It describes a decree being issued (passive) (Ezra 4:21). It is used of placing names on persons or changing their names (Dan. 5:12). It takes on the sense of paying attention to or giving respect to someone (Dan. 6:13[14]); or focusing on something (Dan. 6:14[15]). It describes setting or imprinting a seal on something (Dan. 6:17[18]).

7762. שׁוּם *šûm:* A masculine noun referring to garlic. It is mentioned as one of the delicacies that Israel enjoyed in Egypt (Num. 11:5). It is a strong-smelling condiment of the lily family.

7763. שׁוֹמֵר *šômēr,* שֹׁמֵר *šōmēr:* A proper noun designating Shomer:

A. Mother of Jehozabad, the same as Shimrith (8116) (2 Kgs. 12:21[22]).

B. An Asherite, the same person as Shemer (8106,C) (1 Chr. 7:32, 34).

7764. שׁוּנִי *šûniy:* A proper noun designating Shuni (Gen. 46:16; Num. 26:15).

7765. שׁוּנִי *šûniy:* A proper noun designating Shunite (Num. 26:15).

7766. שׁוּנֵם *šûnēm:* A masculine proper noun, Shunem. It was a town inherited by Issachar (Josh. 19:18). It is mentioned as a city near which the Philistines encamped (1 Sam. 28:4). Abishag, a wise person, came from here, and Elisha received help from a lady of Shunem (2 Kgs. 4:8).

7767. שׁוּנַמִּית *šûnammiyṯ:* A proper noun designating Shunammite (1 Kgs. 1:3, 15; 2:17, 21, 22; 2 Kgs. 4:12, 25, 36).

7768. שָׁוַע *šāwaʻ:* A verb meaning to cry out for help, to cry out. It indicates a cry for help or of despair in general (Job 19:7; Ps. 72:12); especially a cry to God (Job 36:13; Ps. 18:41[42]; 119:147; Isa. 58:9; Hab. 1:2).

7769. שׁוּעַ *šûaʻ,* שׁוּעַ *shūaʻ:* I. A masculine noun designating a cry for help, an ejaculatory plea. It indicates a cry for help to God or people (Job 30:24), especially God (Ps. 5:2[3]).

II. A masculine noun referring to riches, wealth. It indicates one's abundant resources, excessive possessions, money, etc., so extensive that one might be tempted to rely on them for help or deliverance rather than God (Job 36:19).

7770. שׁוּעַ ***šûa‘:*** A proper noun designating Shua (Gen. 38:2, 12; 1 Chr. 2:3, for NASB, see *baṯ šûa‘* [1340,A]).

7771. שׁוֹעַ ***šôa‘:*** I. A masculine noun indicating nobility, distinguished, wealthy. It refers to wealthy, rich, and influential persons as opposed to the poor and insignificant (*dal*) (Job 34:19). It indicates a highly respected and distinguished person of means and influence (Isa. 32:5).

II. A masculine noun indicating a cry for help, an ejaculatory plea. It describes a person's plea for help in a confusing and practically hopeless situation (Isa. 22:5).

7772. שׁוֹעַ ***šôa‘:*** A proper noun designating Shoa (Ezek. 23:23).

7773. שֶׁוַע ***šewa‘:*** A masculine noun referring to a cry for help, an ejaculatory plea. It is used to describe the psalmist's cry to God for help, protection, and deliverance from the wicked (Ps. 5:2[3]).

7774. שׁוּעָא ***šû‘ā’:*** A proper noun designating Shua (1 Chr. 7:32).

7775. שַׁוְעָה ***šaw^e‘āh:*** A feminine noun describing a cry for help. It is used of Israel's cry to God for deliverance from Egyptian bondage (Ex. 2:23); and for a person's crying out to God for help in various situations (1 Sam. 5:12; Ps. 18:6[7]; 34:15[16]; 102:1[2]; Jer. 8:19; Lam. 3:56).

7776. שׁוּעָל ***šû‘āl:*** A masculine noun indicating a fox, a jackal. A small, wild canine with a bushy tail. It was abundant in ancient Palestine. Samson caught three hundred of them and chastised the Philistines with them (Judg. 15:4). They were weak, but God's judgments would make wicked people prey to foxes (Ps. 63:10[11]). They could be destructive to vineyards (Song 2:15); and they inhabited ruins (Lam. 5:18). Figuratively, Israel had driven out her prophets from God, so that they were forced to live in ruins and were ostracized like foxes (Ezek. 13:4).

7777. שׁוּעָל ***šû‘āl:*** A proper noun designating Shual:

A. An Asherite (1 Chr. 7:36).

B. A district in Benjamin (1 Sam. 13:17).

7778. שׁוֹעֵר ***šô‘ēr,*** שֹׁעֵר ***šō‘ēr:*** A masculine noun indicating a gatekeeper; a porter. It indicates a person in charge of a gate, operating it, monitoring its use and its users (2 Kgs. 7:10, 11). It is used often of gatekeepers in the Temple area (1 Chr. 9:17, 18, 24); they numbered in the thousands (1 Chr. 23:5; 26:1; Ezra 2:42, 70; 7:7; Neh. 7:1, 45, 73[72]).

7779. שׁוּף ***šûp̱:*** I. A verb meaning to crush, to bruise. A verb used twice, once referring to the attack of the serpent and once of the seed of the woman (Gen. 3:15). It may be translated as crush in Job 9:17 to describe God's supposed attack on Job. It also has the sense of to engulf, to hide, to cover (Ps. 139:11). See II.

II. A verb meaning to strike, to snap at. It is used of the attack of the serpent and the response of the seed of the woman (Gen. 3:15). The verb is rendered figuratively as follows by the various translations: KJV, bruise . . . bruise; NIV, crush . . . strike; NASB, bruise . . . bruise; NKJV, bruise . . . bruise.

III. A verb meaning to cover, to envelop, to overwhelm. It is used of darkness engulfing or hiding a person from God (Ps. 139:11).

7780. שׁוֹפַךְ ***šôpāk̲:*** A proper noun designating Shophach (1 Chr. 19:16, 18). This is another name for Shobach (7731).

7781. שׁוּפָמִי ***šûpāmiy:*** A proper noun designating Shuphamite, a descendant of Shephupham (8197,A) (Num. 26:39).

7782. שׁוֹפָר ***šôpār,*** שֹׁפָר ***šōpār:*** A masculine noun referring to a trumpet, a ram's horn. It refers to a trumpet or horn made out of a curved ram's horn. It was used to signal a time of meeting together or a significant event, especially at Sinai (Ex. 19:16, 19; Lev. 25:9; Josh. 6:4–6, 8, 9, 13. 16, 20). It was used at the time of proclaiming a new king in Israel (1 Kgs. 1:34, 39, 41; 2 Kgs. 9:13). It was sounded at the celebration of God as King over all the earth (Ps. 47:5[6]). It also warned of approaching danger (Hos. 5:8; 8:1); especially the Day of the Lord (Joel 2:1, 15).

7783. שׁוּק ***šûq:*** A verb meaning to water; to overflow. It is used figuratively of God's creating abundance, an overflowing of crops in the earth (Ps. 65:9[10]). It refers to the overflowing abundance of wine and oil both literally and figuratively (Joel 2:24; 3:13[4:13]).

7784. שׁוּק ***šûq:*** A masculine noun referring to a street. It refers to a city street that is bounded by houses (Prov. 7:8; 12:4, 5). It is used to indicate all the streets of a city (Song 3:2).

7785. שׁוֹק ***šôq:*** A masculine noun meaning a leg, a hip; a thigh (or shoulder) of a sacrificial animal. It refers to the thigh or right leg portion of a sacrificial animal (Ex. 29:22, 27; Lev. 7:32–34; 8:25, 26; 9:21; Num. 6:20; 1 Sam. 9:24). It is used to refer to the entire leg or legs of a person (Deut. 28:35; Prov. 26:7; Isa. 47:2).

7786. שׂוּר ***śûr:*** A verb meaning to vanquish, to rule, to have power. The primary meaning of this word is to rule or to have power over. In Hosea, the verb denotes what will happen to the parents of children (i.e., they will be vanquished and bereaved of their children) when God turns away from them (see Hos. 9:12).

The word is also used to describe Abimelech's ruling of Israel for three years (Judg. 9:22). God sent an evil spirit between Abimelech and the people of Shechem, and they acted treacherously against Abimelech. This was done so that the shedding of the blood of Jerub-Baal's seventy sons might be avenged on their brother Abimelech and the citizens of Shechem who helped him. The verb also denotes one of the reasons for Israel's upcoming punishment. Not only did they choose princes without Yahweh's approval, but Israel also made and worshiped idols in blatant disregard for the rulership and dominion of Yahweh over them (Hos. 8:4).

7787. שׂוּר ***śûr:*** A verb meaning to cut. It describes the process of cutting persons with saws and other tools as an act of destruction (1 Chr. 20:3).

7788. שׁוּר ***šûr:*** A verb meaning to journey; to go. It describes the descent from a mountain height (Song 4:8); it indicates to travel, to go to a location or person (Isa. 57:9). It indicates what is used to transport, to carry merchandise by ships, caravans, etc., (Ezek. 27:25).

7789. שׁוּר ***šûr:*** A verb meaning to look at, to gaze on, to regard, to see, to observe. It refers to simply looking at, observing something from the heights (Num. 23:9). It means to see a person (Job 7:8); or to regard something in one's thinking and emotions (Job 17:15). God can hide Himself so that He is not observable (Job 34:29). It means to gaze out over an area (Song 4:8, but see 7788 also). It is used of observing others to harm them (Jer. 5:26); lying in wait for them (Hos. 13:7). It describes in a prophetic figurative sense seeing something in the future (Num. 24:17); and to God's looking carefully over His people (Hos. 14:8[9]).

7790. שׁוּר ***šûr:*** A masculine noun indicating an enemy, a foe. It refers to adversaries or hostile persons who actively oppose a person (Ps. 92:11[12]).

7791. שׁוּר ***šûr,*** שׁוּרָה ***šûrāh:*** I. A masculine noun meaning a wall. It refers to a wall around a well (Gen. 49:6; but note 7794); a boundary-marking wall (2 Sam. 22:30; Ps. 18:29[30]). It indicates a wall around a field or a vineyard (Gen. 49:22).

II. A feminine noun indicating a terrace, a supporting wall. It refers to the walls of an olive vineyard, within which the poor labor oppressively to produce oil that does not benefit them (Job 24:11).

7792. שׁוּר ***šûr:*** An Aramaic masculine noun indicating a wall. It refers to the stone walls of Jerusalem needed for the protection of the city and for encouraging persons to settle in it again (Ezra 4:12, 13, 16).

7793. שׁוּר ***šûr:*** A proper noun designating Shur (Gen. 16:7; 20:1; 25:18; Ex. 15:22; 1 Sam. 15:7; 27:8).

7794. שׁוֹר ***šôr:*** A masculine noun referring to an ox, a bull, or a cow. It refers to a mature male bovine, a bull, an ox, a steer. It is used as a collective noun referring to one or more of these animals. It may be used as a common noun for cattle (Gen. 32:5[6]). They could constitute a major part of a person's wealth (Ex. 20:17). Special laws were laid out for the treatment of these animals (Ex. 21:28, 29, 32, 33, 35, 36; 22:1 [21:37], 4[3]). They were major sacrificial animals (Lev. 9:4, 18, 19; 17:3; 1 Kgs. 1:19, 25; Ps. 69:31[32]). The strange creatures in Ezekiel's' vision each included a face like an ox (Ezek. 1:10).

7795. שׂוֹרָה *šôrah:* I. A feminine noun meaning a row, order. It is taken as a reference to the furrows or rows where wheat grains were sown (Isa. 28:25).

II. A feminine noun meaning millet, chief grain, or wheat. It refers to grains of millet or wheat, principally wheat, that were sown in the ground (Isa. 28:25).

7796. שׂוֹרֵק *śôrēq,* שֹׂרֵק *śōrēq:* A proper noun designating Sorek (Judg. 16:4).

7797. שׂוּשׂ *śûś,* שִׂישׂ *śiyś:* A verb meaning to rejoice; to exalt; to be glad. It is a verb that indicates great rejoicing and jubilant celebration. It refers to the Lord's taking delight or joy over (*'al*), blessing, punishing, or disciplining His people if they need it (Deut. 28:63; 30:9; Jer. 32:41; Zeph. 3:17). It indicates finding a cause to be happy, to rejoice even over death (Job 3:22). It describes a horse enjoying his strength (Job 39:21); the sun joyfully traveling across the sky (Ps. 19:5[6]); but especially God's people rejoicing over Him (Ps. 35:9; 40:16 [17]; 68:3[4]; Isa. 61:10). It is used figuratively of the desert and the dry land rejoicing in its God-given fertility (Isa. 35:1).

7798. שַׁוְשָׁא *šawšā':* A proper noun designating Shavsha (1 Chr. 18:16).

7799. שׁוּשַׁן *šûšan,* שֹׁשָׁן *šôšān,* שׁוֹשַׁנָּה *šôšannāh,* שׁוֹשַׁנִּים *šôšanniym:* I. A masculine and feminine noun denoting a lily. It refers to a perennial plant of the lily family. It may indicate the flower of these plants, which was a major feature of their beauty (Hos. 14:5[6]). It was often used in decorative designs, e.g., the lily design on the capitals or pillars (1 Kgs. 7:19, 22); or on other objects (1 Kgs. 7:26; 2 Chr. 4:5). It is found as the name of a song or tune in psalm titles (see refs. below). Its beauty was used in similes referring to one's bride (Song 2:1, 2; 7:2[3]); or bridegroom (Song 5:13); and to the lilies of the Sharon valley area (Song 2:16). It describes part of an idyllic setting (Song 4:5; 6:2, 3).

II. A proper noun, a title of a song. It is used in several psalm titles and means literally lilies (Ps. 45:title[1]; 69:title[1]), evidently indicting the title of a recognized song or tune at the time of the author or the time of the music director.

7800. שׁוּשַׁן ***šûšan:*** A proper noun designating Shushan, Susa, one of several capitals of the Persian Empire. It was located on the upper reaches of the Karun River in southwest Persia. Esther's story begins here (Esth. 1:5, etc.). In Nehemiah 1:1, Artaxerxes is king in this city. Daniel had a vision in which he was transported to this city (Dan. 8:2).

7801. שׁוּשַׁנְכִי ***šûšanḵiy:*** A proper noun designating Susanchites, inhabitants of Susa, Shushan (7800) (Ezra 4:9).

7802. שׁוּשַׁן עֵדוּת ***šûšan ʿēḏûṯ,*** עֵדוּת שׁוֹשַׁנִּים ***šôšanniym ʿēḏûṯ:*** I. A proper noun indicating a song title, Shushan Eduth, Lily of the Covenant. It is a titular phrase; covenant refers to the covenant of the ten words or to the stone tablets where they were written (Ps. 60:title[1]). Covenant may also be rendered as Testimony.

II. A proper noun Shoshannim Eduth, a song title meaning literally Lilies of the Covenant. See I also. It is found in Psalm 80:title[1]; it may be rendered as the Lilies of the Testimony also.

7803. שׁוּתֶלַח ***šûṯelaḥ:*** A proper noun designating Shuthelah (Num. 26:35, 36; 1 Chr. 7:20, 21).

7804. שְׁזַב ***š^ezaḇ,*** שֵׁיזִב ***šēyziḇ:*** An Aramaic verb meaning to deliver, to rescue. It refers consistently to rescuing or delivering a person from an impossible situation. God or a person may be the subject who is rescuing someone (Dan. 3:15, 17, 28; 6:14[15]; 16[17], 20[21], 27[28]).

7805. שָׁזַף ***šāzap̱:*** I. A verb meaning to look at, to see. In its context it refers to seeing, regarding a person while still alive (Job 20:9). It describes the observation or sighting of a falcon's eye (Job 28:7). It has the sense of looking intently in some contexts (Song 1:6).

II. A verb meaning to burn, to darken [the result of the sun looking on one]. It refers to the effect of the sun's rays shining (looking) on persons, making them dark and swarthy (Song 1:6).

7806. שָׁזַר ***šāzar:*** A verb meaning finely twisted. It refers to finely worked threads, features of linen cloth (Ex. 26:1, 31, 36; 27:9, 16).

7807. שַׁח ***šaḥ:*** An adjective meaning humble, downcast. It refers to a person who is not overly proud, overly self-assertive, possibly low in rank but not necessarily so, a person who does not flaunt his or her abilities or achievements before others and, especially, is lowly and meek before God (Job 22:29).

7808. שֵׂחַ ***śēaḥ:*** A masculine noun meaning thought. It refers to the ideas and imaginations formed in a person's mind, consciously or unconsciously; they are all known to God (Amos 4:13).

7809. שָׁחַד ***šāḥaḏ:*** A verb meaning to give a reward, to bribe. It refers to the act of offering something unrighteously to persons to get them to act or think in a certain way (Job 6:22); usually in a way they normally would not (Ezek. 16:33).

7810. שֹׁחַד ***šōḥaḏ:*** A masculine noun referring to a bribe, a reward, a gift. It refers to what is given in a situation to influence persons to act or think in a certain way they would not normally. It was often given to pervert justice and to blind the judgment of even good persons (Ex. 23:8; Deut. 16:19). God does not take bribes (Deut. 10:17). The person who took a bribe was cursed by God (Deut. 27:25). The perversion of justice through bribes was a major downfall of Israel (1 Sam. 8:3). A bribe could consist of a major political gift or present to another king or nation, a glorified bribe (1 Kgs. 15:19).

7811. שָׂחָה ***śāḥāh:*** A verb meaning to swim, to cause to swim, to flood. It is used in a causative stem meaning to make or to cause to swim (Ps. 6:6[7]). It refers to the act of swimming, using one's hands to move through the water in a breast-stroke fashion (Isa. 25:11).

7812. שָׁחָה ***shāchāh:*** A verb meaning to bow down, to prostrate oneself, to crouch, to fall down, to humbly beseech, to do reverence, to worship. The primary meaning of the word is to bow down. This verb is used to indicate bowing before a monarch or a superior and paying homage to him or her (Gen. 43:28). In contexts such as Genesis 24:26, *šāḥāh* is used to indicate bowing down in worship to Yahweh. The psalmists used this word to describe all the earth bowing down in worship to God as a response to His great power (Ps. 66:4); or bowing down in worship and kneeling before the Lord (Ps. 95:6). This act of worship is given to God because He deserves it and because those that are speaking are people of His pasture.

The word is also used of Joseph when he described the sheaves of his brothers and parents bowing down to his sheaf after it stood upright in a dream that he had (Gen. 37:7). Gideon also interacted with a dream through which God spoke. When he overheard a man telling his friend a dream that the man had and its interpretation, he worshiped God (Judg. 7:15).

Joshua instructed the people of Israel not to associate with the nations remaining around them and not to bow down to or serve any of their gods. He instructed Israel to hold fast to the true God, Yahweh (Josh. 23:7). In Zephaniah, the word is also used for worship. When Yahweh destroys all the gods of the land, the nations on every shore will worship Him (Zeph. 2:11).

7813. שָׂחוּ ***śāḥû:*** A masculine noun referring to swimming. It is used of the action of swimming. The phrase *mê śāḥû* means literally, water of swimming, that is, water deep enough to swim in (Ezek. 47:5).

7814. שְׂחוֹק ***śᵉḥôq***, שְׂחֹק ***śᵉḥōq:*** A masculine noun indicating laughter, ridicule, derision. It refers to an expression of joy, humor, or relief usually (Job 8:21; Ps. 126:2); but laughter can be fabricated to deride and make fun of someone or something (Jer. 20:7; 48:26, 27, 39). The fool considers evil an object of laughter, humor, or even sport (Prov. 10:23; Eccl. 7:6; Lam. 3:14). Laughter can be only an outward façade with pain lying beneath it (Prov. 14:13). It does not really satisfy and may be deceptive (Eccl. 2:2); sorrow may be more beneficial (Eccl. 7:3). A meal often provides a setting for enjoyment, laughter (Eccl. 10:19).

7815. שְׁחוֹר ***šᵉḥôr:*** A masculine noun meaning dinginess, blackness. This word is used to describe a punishment of Israel, i.e., they were blacker than soot, and their skin had shriveled on their bones (Lam. 4:8). The people of different nations told the Israelites that they must leave for they were seen as unclean. This is similar to the descriptions of the results of the Day of the Lord, which will be a day of blackness (see Joel 2:2). This blackness figuratively represents an army of locusts with which Yahweh will punish those who live in the land for their sin. For this reason, the prophet declared that all who live in the land should and will tremble in fear.

7816. שְׁחוּת ***šᵉḥûṯ:*** A feminine noun meaning pit. Metaphorically speaking, it is a trap that is created as one leads the upright along the path of evil (Prov. 28:10). This trap or pit will eventually ensnare its builder. As the wicked plot and scheme against the righteous, in the end, they will only succeed in being caught in their own traps.

7817. שָׁחַח ***šāḥaḥ:*** A verb meaning to stoop, to bow down, to crouch, to sink low. It is used in a literal sense of a crouching lion (Job 38:40); knocking down a fortified wall (Isa. 25:12); defeating a powerful enemy (Isa. 26:5); as well as of God's bringing down and chastising His own people (Isa. 29:4). It depicts a crumbling hill or mountain (Hab. 3:6). It is used figuratively more often of the wicked crouching to do harm (Ps. 10:10); of bowing down in humility (Isa. 2:11, 17); or servitude (Isa. 60:14). It is used to picture the sinking of a person's soul and life (Lam. 3:20). It can have the sense of being subdued, crouched down in submission (Job 9:13). It depicts evil, wicked persons (Prov. 14:19). It signifies a sound that is low, hardly discernible (Eccl. 12:4).

7818. שָׂחַט ***śāḥaṭ:*** A verb meaning to squeeze, to press. It refers to the process of preparing wine in Pharaoh's cup by squeezing juice out of grapes into it (Gen. 40:11).

7819. שָׁחַט ***šāḥaṭ:*** A verb meaning to slaughter, to kill, to offer, to shoot out, to slay. The primary meaning of the verb is to slaughter. In Leviticus, the word is used to indicate that the one who brings the sacrifice is the person who will slaughter the animal (Lev. 1:5). After the slaughtering, the priests brought the blood and other parts of the animal to the altar. In contrast to Leviticus, 2 Chronicles indicates that the worshipers could not slaughter their sacrifices because they did not consecrate themselves and were ceremonially unclean. In this case, the Levites (i.e., priests) had to slaughter the lambs for all who were ceremonially unclean (cf. 2 Chr. 30:17). This verb is also used to indicate an ineffective sacrifice where the offerers were only going through the motions of worship (Isa. 66:3). Even though the object of their worship appears to be God, their hearts were still bent toward evil. This failure is the reason for their upcoming judgment. Another usage of the verb depicts Saul's army pouncing on the plunder, butchering sheep, cattle, and calves, and eating the meat together with the blood, which was forbidden in the Law (1 Sam. 14:32). This makes the actions of Saul's army in direct disobedience of God's Law.

The verb is also used to describe the process of a human sacrifice to Yahweh (i.e., the process used to test Abraham with his son Isaac [Gen. 22:10]). Since He does not desire human sacrifices, God stopped Abraham from sacrificing his son Isaac. When used in the context of a human sacrifice to false gods, the verb describes the actual process being carried out rather than the anticipated process such as that found with Abraham (Isa. 57:5; Ezek. 16:21; 23:39).

7820. שָׁחַט *šāḥaṭ*: A verb meaning to beat, to hammer. It is used in its passive participle to describe a shield of beaten gold, hammered into shape by skilled craftsmen (1 Kgs. 10:16, 17; 2 Chr. 9:15, 16).

7821. שְׁחִיטָה *š^{e}ḥiyṭāh*, שַׁחֲטָה *šaḥ^{a}ṭāh*: I. A feminine noun meaning slaughter, killing. It refers to the technical sacrificial slaughter and preparation of lambs for the Passover, carried out by certain Levites (2 Chr. 30:17).

II. A feminine noun denoting depravity. In context it refers to the willful rejection of God's ways and the concomitant descent into rebellious and depraved behavior as measured by God's will and laws (Hos. 5:2).

7822. שְׁחִין *š^{e}ḥiyn*: A masculine noun indicating a boil. It refers to a serious skin disease and irritation with festering sores in it (Ex. 9:9–11; Deut. 28:27, 35), as in the sixth plague on Egypt. Some skin diseases were more serious than others (Lev. 13:18–20, 23). Hezekiah's boil was healed (2 Kgs. 20:7; Isa. 38:21). Job suffered from this malady brought on by Satan (Job 2:7).

7823. שָׂחִיס *šāḥiys*, סָחִישׁ *sāḥiyš*: I. A masculine noun referring to what grows by itself, an aftergrowth. It refers to edible crops that spring up by themselves without human cultivation (Isa. 37:30).

II. A masculine noun referring to aftergrowth, that which grows by itself. It has the same meaning as I. It refers to what springs up by itself from last year's crops (2 Kgs. 19:29).

7824. שָׂחִיף ***śaḥiyp̱:*** A masculine noun meaning paneled, ceiled. It refers to a flat piece of wood or metal that forms a part of a surface of a wall, etc., usually square or rectangular in shape (Ezek. 41:16). A feature found in Ezekiel's visionary Temple.

7825. שְׁחִית ***šeḥiyṯ:*** A feminine noun meaning a pit, destruction, and pitfall. In Lamentations 4:20, the Lord's anointed, King Zedekiah, was caught in the trap of the Babylonians. In Psalms, the noun is used to indicate the crisis from which Yahweh saves those who cry out to Him in their troubles (Ps. 107:20). By simply a mere utterance and sending forth His word, God heals and rescues from destruction those who cry out to Him. The proper response of those rescued is to give thank offerings and tell of His works through songs of joy.

7826. שַׁחַל ***šaḥal:*** A masculine noun meaning a lion. It refers to a lion, possibly a fierce (KJV, NASB) lion (Job 4:10; 28:8) or a strong roaring lion (NIV). It is used to refer to God as a prowling lion (Job 10:16; Hos. 5:14; 13:7). The lion was a beast that brought great fear and dread (Prov. 26:13).

7827. שְׁחֵלֶת ***šeḥēleṯ:*** A feminine noun rendered as onycha; an ingredient in the holy incense. It is used only once, and its use indicates that it was a spice used in the preparation of holy incense (Ex. 30:34). The incense could not be used as a common perfume or cosmetic.

7828. שַׁחַף ***šaḥap̱:*** A masculine noun referring to a seagull, a cuckow. It refers to a bird that was considered unclean in Israel, and it was forbidden as an edible food to them (Lev. 11:16; Deut. 14:15).

7829. שַׁחֶפֶת ***šaḥepeṯ:*** A feminine noun indicating consumption; a wasting disease. It refers to a disease that causes a person's body to waste away (Lev. 26:16; Deut. 28:22). It could be brought about by the Lord as a curse on a disobedient people.

7830. שַׁחַץ ***šaḥaṣ:*** I. A masculine noun meaning pride. It indicates an inordinate opinion of one's self and a demeaning attitude toward others (Job 41:34[26]).

II. A masculine noun referring to a lion (as a proud beast). It stands in parallel to fierce lion (NASB) and, hence, the pride of the lion is emphasized in context (Job 28:8); both are, however, unable to find or discover where wisdom dwells.

7831. שַׁחֲצוּם ***šaḥaṣûm,*** שַׁחֲצִים ***šaḥaṣiym:*** I. A proper noun designating Shahazumah, with directional *hē* (NASB, NIV, Josh. 19:22).

II. A proper noun designating Shahazimah, with directional *hē* (KJV, Josh. 19:22).

7832. שָׂחַק śāḥaq: A verb meaning to laugh; to celebrate; to rejoice; to mock. It refers to a strong expression of joy: of celebration (Jer. 30:19); of making merry, rejoicing (2 Sam. 6:5, 21; Jer. 15:17); it means to play, to sport, to have fun (Ps. 104:26). But it is often used in a context where ridicule or mockery is directed at someone or something (Judg. 16:25). It is used in parallel with mocking (Prov. 1:26). Great kings mocked at lesser kings (Hab. 1:10). Samson was forced to serve as a tragic comedian for the Philistines (Judg. 16:27). It is used figuratively of wisdom personified, laughing, rejoicing at God's creation (Prov. 8:30, 31). The teacher taught that there is a time for genuine laughter (Eccl. 3:4). It has the sense of playing, enjoying life, in some contexts, especially in the prophet's vision of a restored people of God (Zech. 8:5). It means to sing and indicates singing women (1 Sam. 18:7). It means to play a sport, to hold a contest or a match (2 Sam. 2:14). In its causative stem, it means to cause laughter toward persons, to mock them (2 Chr. 30:10).

7833. שָׁחַק šāḥaq: A verb meaning to beat, to wear, to rub away, to beat fine, to pulverize. The primary usage of the verb is to beat fine or to rub away. In Job, the word is used to describe water wearing away stones in conjunction with torrents washing away the soil. This definition was used as a simile for Job's accusation that Yahweh was destroying a person's hope (Job 14:19). Yahweh uses the verb to dictate to Moses how a blend of incense was to be made (Ex. 30:36). This formula, which was placed in front of the Testimony in the Tent of Meeting, was to be regarded as holy and only meant for the Lord. Anyone who used it in another context would be cut off from his people. In a figurative sense, *šāḥaq* is used to describe David's victory over his enemies in which he beat them down like fine dust (2 Sam. 22:43, Ps. 18:42[Ps. 18:43]).

7834. שַׁחַק šaḥaq: A masculine noun meaning dust, a fine cloud, a thin cloud. The primary usage of the word denotes a cloud. Often this word is used to depict a cloud or clouds (in the plural) in the sky (Job 35:5, Prov. 8:28). In Psalms, this word is used to describe the heavens (Ps. 36:5[Ps. 36:6]). In a metaphorical sense, Moses described God as riding on the heavens and clouds in His majesty to help His people (Deut. 33:26). Used in this sense, it denotes Yahweh as Ruler over the heavens and all that is in them. This word is used to depict dark rain clouds which form a canopy around Him (2 Sam. 22:12). The word can also be used to denote nations as fine dust (Isa. 40:15).

7835. שָׁחַר šāḥar: A verb meaning to turn black, to be black. It refers to the darkening of a person's skin because of illness, disease, some kind of skin disease (Job 30:30).

7836. שָׁחַר ***šāḥar:*** I. A verb meaning to diligently seek; to search for. It means to inquire after something or someone diligently: a person (Job 7:21); God (Job 8:5; Ps. 63:1[2]; 78:34; Isa. 26:9; Hos. 5:15); wisdom (Prov. 1:28; 8:17). It describes a harlot seeking a man (Prov. 7:15).

II. A verb meaning to conjure away; to charm away. It describes a process or ritual of pagan religion employed to get rid of unwanted conditions or evil (Isa. 47:11). But it can be used in a proper context of Israel's properly seeking her God. For Hosea 5:15, see I above and 7837.

7837. שַׁחַר ***šaḥar:*** A masculine noun indicating morning, dawn, rising up. It is used of the coming of daylight, as the morning (dawn) came up (Gen. 19:15; 32:24[25], 26[27]). *'ālāh,* to go, to come up is used with this noun to indicate the rising or coming of dawn. The phrase *b^e'ap̱'appê-šāḥar* means at the breaking of dawn, literally, rays or blinking of dawn (Job 3:9). Psalm 22:title(1) refers to a song entitled "Hind of the Dawn." The phrase "like the dawn" is used in a simile to refer to a bride or bridegroom's beauty (Song 6:10). God is the ultimate source and cause of the dawn (Amos 4:13).

7838. שָׁחֹר ***šāḥōr:*** An adjective meaning black. It is used to describe a hair growing in an infected area of the skin that indicates that the disease may be serious and the person is quarantined (Lev. 13:31, 37). Black or dark skin and black hair locks were considered beautiful (Song 1:5; 5:11). It describes a set of horses on one of the chariots which Zechariah saw in a vision (Zech. 6:2, 6).

7839. שַׁחֲרוּת ***šaḥ^arûṯ:*** A feminine noun indicating youth, the prime of life. It refers to the most healthy and vigorous period of a person's life, which, however, is fleeting (Eccl. 11:10).

7840. שְׁחַרְחֹר ***š^eḥarḥōr:*** An adjective meaning dark, black (of a tanned skin). It refers to skin that is swarthy, darkened, in context because of the sun's rays (Song 1:6).

7841. שְׁחַרְיָה ***š^eḥaryāh:*** A proper noun designating Shehariah (1 Chr. 8:26).

7842. שַׁחֲרַיִם ***šaḥ^arayim:*** A proper noun designating Shaharaim (1 Chr. 8:8).

7843. שָׁחַת ***šāḥaṯ:*** A verb meaning to spoil, to ruin, to destroy, to pervert, to corrupt, to become corrupt, to wipe out. The verb is used to denote the action(s) of the world (i.e., it is corrupt) and ultimately the reason for God's flooding it (Gen. 6:11, 12). However, even in total destruction meant to punish the evil of humans, God was sure to save a remnant and therefore keep His part of the covenant. This idea of a saved remnant is predominant throughout the rest of the Old Testament.

Another usage of the verb depicts disobedience to God's command to be fruitful and multiply by spoiling or wasting semen on the ground (Gen. 38:9). In this case, Onan's disobedience led to his death, for what he did was wicked in the eyes of Yahweh. The verb is also used to describe violating the covenant in terms of being corrupt (Mal. 2:8). As Lot looked over the valley of the Jordan, this word was used to depict what would happen to Sodom and Gomorrah in a future time because of their wickedness (Gen. 13:10). In the context of the plagues, the smearing of blood on the lintels and doorposts protected Israel from the destruction of their firstborn (Ex. 12:23). When the destroyer came, he would pass by those who had blood on the lintels and doorposts of their houses.

Jerusalem was saved from destruction in 2 Samuel when the Lord was grieved due to the calamity of His people (2 Sam. 24:16). This verb is used to denote the destruction of a slave's eye that allowed him to go free (Ex. 21:26). In Deuteronomy, God prohibited the destruction of fruit trees, for their fruit could be eaten (Deut. 20:19–20). He commanded this, for the trees were for the benefit of humans. He also prohibited the shaving (i.e., in terms of spoiling, destroying) of one's beard (Lev. 19:27).

7844. שְׁחַת *šᵉḥaṯ:* An Aramaic verb meaning to corrupt. This word can also function as a noun, in which it designates fault. The verb is used in Daniel to depict what the astrologers did to their words in an effort to gain more time from the king (Dan. 2:9). The inability of the astrologers and other wise men to interpret Nebuchadnezzar's dream set the stage for Daniel.

In Daniel 6:5, the word is used as a noun and designated the charge against Daniel. Since no fault could be found, the administrators and satraps persuaded King Darius to issue and enforce the decree that no one could pray to anyone or anything but him for a period of thirty days or be thrown into the lions' den.

7845. שַׁחַת *šaḥaṯ:* A feminine noun denoting a pit, a ditch, a grave, a hollow place. Its prominent usage is pit. The word is used to describe the pit of destruction from which the Lord's love saves (Isa. 38:17). The psalmist uses the word figuratively to designate a type of trap that those who are seeking his life have dug for him (Ps. 35:7). The occurrence of the word in Ezekiel metaphorically denotes a pit in which lions are caught (Ezek. 19:4). The term lion is used to represent Israel's Prince Jehoahaz and is a metaphorical representation of his policies. He learned to tear prey and devour people. The noun is also used to denote Sheol (Job 33:24; Ezek. 28:8). Job uses the word in a rhetorical sense to describe a situation in which there is no hope (Job 17:14). He stated that if he allowed himself to call corruption his father and the worm his mother and sister, where would his hope lie?

7846. שֵׂט *śēṭ*, סֵט *sēṭ*: I. A masculine noun meaning a defection, a deviation, a revolt. It refers to God's people who are turning against Him and His laws, deviating from what is pleasing to Him (Hos. 5:2).

II. A masculine noun meaning a defection, a deviation, a revolt. It has the same meaning as I but is spelled differently. This time it refers to the object of the psalmist's hatred—those who turn away from God and defect from His ways (Ps. 101:3).

7847. שָׂטָה *śāṭāh*: A verb meaning to turn aside; to go astray. It means to turn aside from expected behavior or faithfulness, as when a person commits adultery, resulting in a woman's defilement (Num. 5:12, 19, 20, 29). It refers to a man's refusing to be enamored of a harlot, not going astray after her (Prov. 7:25). It is used of turning away from walking with the wicked (Prov. 4:15).

7848. שִׁטָּה *šiṭṭāh*: A feminine noun indicating acacia wood, an acacia tree; shittim wood. It may refer to several species of wood that grow in Palestine. It may refer specifically to Acacia seyal Delile, a species fairly common in the Sinai Peninsula and Jordan Valley. It was used in the construction of the Tabernacle furnishings and the ark of the covenant (Ex. 25:5, 10, 13, 23, 28; 26:15, 26, 32; 27:1, 6; 30:1, 5; 35:7, 24; 36:20, 31, 36; 37:1, 4, 10, 15, 25, 28; 38:1, 6; Deut. 10:3). God will restore this tree to a devastated Israel (Isa. 41:19). The Valley of Shittim (Joel 3:18[4:18]) refers to an area where acacia trees abounded.

7849. שָׁטַח *šāṭaḥ*: A verb meaning to spread out; to stretch out; to enlarge. It means to place something out, to spread it out over a large area rather than putting it into piles, as Israel did with an abundance of quails (Num. 11:32; Jer. 8:2). It indicates spreading out one's hands to God in prayer or worship (Ps. 88:9[10]). It refers to spreading out a blanket or some kind of covering (2 Sam. 17:19). It describes God's dispersing, leading away the nations as He pleases, demonstrating his sovereignty (Job 12:23).

7850. שֹׁטֵט *šōṭēṭ*: A masculine noun referring to a whip, a scourge. It indicates figuratively the effect the nations that Israel did not drive out of Canaan would have on them, as they acted as a punishing whip against Israel (Josh. 23:13).

7851. שִׁטִּים *šiṭṭiym*: A proper noun designating Shittim:

A. A location in the plains of Moab (Num. 25:1; Josh. 2:1; 3:1; Mic. 6:5). This is a shortened form of Abel Shittim (63).

B. A proper noun designating a valley northwest of the Dead Sea (Joel 3:18[4:18]).

7852. שָׂטַם śāṭam: A verb meaning to hate; to bear a grudge against, to harass. It means to nurse hostility and bitterness toward someone (Gen. 27:41; 50:15; Ps. 55:3[4]); or even to attack or harass a person physically (Gen. 49:23). It is rendered variously in Job 16:9 (KJV, "hateth"; NASB, "hunted"; NIV, "tears," all renderings indicating God's supposed attitude toward Job); likewise in Job 30:21.

7853. שָׂטַן śāṭan: A verb meaning to accuse, to slander, and to harbor animosity toward. The verb is used only six times and presents a negative attitude or bias against something. The psalmist complained about those who attacked or slandered him when he pursued what was good (Ps. 38:20[21]); even accusing or attacking him in spite of his positive attitude toward them (Ps. 109:4). The psalmist asked for his accusers to be destroyed by shame (Ps. 71:13; 109:20, 29). Satan stood ready to accuse or to persecute Joshua, the high priest, in the postexilic community (Zech. 3:1). Also, see the noun *śāṭān* (7854).

7854. שָׂטָן śāṭān: A masculine noun meaning an adversary, Satan, an accuser. This noun is used twenty-seven times. In Job it is found fourteen times meaning (the) Satan, the accuser. Satan presented himself among the sons of God and roundly accused Job of not loving or serving God with integrity (Job 1:6, 7; 2:1, 2, 4, 7); all of these uses are in the prologue of the book (Job 1—2). In Zechariah, this noun is used three times with the verb to accuse (*śāṭan*[7853]). Satan stood ready to accuse the high priest Joshua (Zech. 3:1, 2). In 1 Chronicles 21:1, Satan was depicted as the one who motivated David insolently to take a census of Israel's army (cf. 2 Sam. 24:1).

The noun is used in a general sense to indicate any adversary or someone who hinders or opposes. The angel of the Lord opposed Balaam and his donkey on their way to curse Israel, acting in opposition (Num. 22:22, 32); the Philistines feared that David might act in opposition to them in battle (1 Sam. 29:4; 2 Sam. 19:22[23]). In Solomon's day, the Lord had given him rest all around him (cf. 1 Kgs. 4:24[5:4]); except for Rezon who reigned in Aram (1 Kgs. 11:14, 23, 25). The psalmist's enemies appointed an accuser to attack him, a person who was wicked (Ps. 109:6).

7855. שִׂטְנָה śiṭnāh: A feminine noun meaning accusation, opposition, hostility. Its primary meaning of the word is accusation. In Ezra, the word is used to depict the accusation which those who opposed the rebuilding of the Temple in Jerusalem brought before the king (Ezra 4:6). This accusation stated that the Jews were a rebellious people and that if the completion of the Temple were allowed, they would not submit to the authority of Artaxerxes, king of Persia. This accusation resulted in stopping the building process until the second year of the reign of Darius.

7856. שִׂטְנָה *śiṭnāh:* A proper noun designating Sitnah (Gen. 26:21).

7857. שָׁטַף *šāṭap̱:* A verb meaning to gush, to cleanse, to conquer, to drown, to overflow, to overwhelm, to rinse, to run, to rush, to wash away. In its prominent meaning, the word means to wash away. *Šāṭap̱* is used to depict what the Lord will do to a hiding place, that is, He will overflow it (Isa. 28:17). This word is used to describe God's power as a flooding downpour (Isa. 28:2). It also describes a medium through which God delivers punishment (Jer. 47:2). The Lord declared that the time had come to destroy the Philistines, and He would do so, metaphorically speaking, by raising up the waters into an overflowing torrent. If a man with a discharge touched another without rinsing his hands, the person touched had to wash the infected clothing and take a bath with water; he or she would be unclean until evening (Lev. 15:11). Ezekiel used *šāṭap̱* metaphorically to describe the Lord cleansing His bride (Ezek. 16:9). The Song of Songs uses this word to depict what cannot be done to love, that is, waters cannot flood or quench it. True love withstands all tests (Song 8:7). The psalmist made use of *šāṭap̱* to indicate a weariness of life and its trials, speaking metaphorically of sinking into the miry depths in which there is no foothold (Ps. 69:2[3]). In Psalm 124:4, the psalmist used the word to indicate a physical or material tragedy that is avoided with God on his side. Isaiah used the verb to indicate divine judgment against Judah (Isa. 8:8); and Ephraim (Isa. 28:2, 15, 17, 18). The usage of this word can also indicate a flooding over or utter destruction at the hands of another nation, sometimes dictated by God and at other times simply by the nature of people (Jer. 47:2; Dan. 11:10, 22, 40).

7858. שֶׁטֶף *šeṭep̱:* A masculine noun meaning a flood, mighty waters, a torrent. Its primary usage is flood. The noun is used figuratively to indicate coming judgment (Dan. 9:26; Nah. 1:8). In Job, the Lord is depicted as being able to cut channels for torrents of rain (Job 38:25). The psalmist indicates that through prayer, one can avoid the mighty waters (Ps. 32:6). The word is also used figuratively to depict the intensity of anger (Prov. 27:4).

7859. שְׁטַר *šᵉṭar:* An Aramaic masculine noun meaning side. It refers to the side of a bear on which the bear was lying (Dan. 7:5), its side as opposed to its front or back.

7860. שֹׁטֵר *šōṭēr:* A masculine noun meaning a scribe, an official, a magistrate, a record keeper, and an officer. The word is used primarily to denote an officer or overseer. Proverbs contrasts the ant with the sluggard. While the ant has no overseer or ruler, it stores up in the summer and gathers at harvest in contrast to the sluggard who does not (Prov. 6:7). The word is also used to denote an officer in the military (2 Chr. 26:11). In Joshua, the word denoted the person that was responsible for organizing the camp for departure (Josh. 1:10; 3:2). In addition, *šōṭēr* denoted those that organized the army and appointed its officers (Deut. 20:5, 8, 9). In Exodus, the slave drivers appointed Israelite foremen over the other workers (Ex. 5:14). The word is used to denote the officials appointed over Israel (Num. 11:16); and the designation of the Levites as officials (2 Chr. 19:11).

7861. שִׁטְרַי **šiṭray:** A proper noun designating Shitrai (1 Chr. 27:29).

7862. שַׁי **šay:** A masculine noun indicating a gift, a present. It refers to something given freely to show friendship, appreciation, support, recognition, in this case because of the splendor of the Temple in Jerusalem (Ps. 68:29[30]). Gifts may be given because of reverence to a person or holy fear (Ps. 76:11[12]); or as an act of worship or homage (Isa. 18:7).

7863. שִׂיא **śiy':** A masculine noun meaning pride, loftiness. It indicates an excessive degree of pride, superciliousness, arrogance, even to the point of persons thinking they are God (Job 20:6).

7864. שְׁיָא **šᵉyā':** A proper noun designating Sheja stands in place of the name Sheva (7724,A) in 2 Samuel 20:25 in Hebrew manuscripts.

7865. שִׂיאֹן **śiy'ōn:** A proper noun designating Sion, another name for Mount Hermon (Duet. 4:48).

7866. שִׁיאֹן **šiy'ōn:** A proper noun designating Shion (Josh. 19:19).

7867. שִׂיב **śiyb̲:** A verb meaning to grow gray. In Samuel's farewell speech, he stated that it was time for him to step down, for he was old and gray (1 Sam. 12:2). Eliphaz used the word in Job to designate those that have grown gray-haired and aged, in his somewhat skewed argument to Job. These people are denoted as having wisdom above anyone else of a younger age (Job 15:10).

7868. שִׂיב **śiyb̲,** שָׂב **śāb̲:** An Aramaic verb meaning to become aged, to grow gray. The word is used in Ezra to denote those appointed as leaders over Israel (Ezra 5:5). It is again used in Ezra to depict the elders of the Jews, in whom the responsibility for rebuilding the Temple lay, according to Darius (Ezra 6:7, 8, 14).

7869. שֵׂיב **śeyb̲:** A masculine noun meaning old age. In 1 Kings, Ahijah is described as being aged, and his eyesight has failed (1 Kgs. 14:4). The usage of this word for Ahijah designates his wisdom. To have a head of gray hair is to have a crown of wisdom.

7870. שִׁבָה ***šiyḇāh:*** A feminine noun meaning captivity. It indicates a condition of confinement and subjection to others. In context captivity refers to the seventy-year exile of Israel in Babylon (Ps. 126:1).

7871. שִׁיבָה ***šiyḇāh:*** A feminine noun indicating a sojourn, a stay. It refers to a period of time, a sojourn, of King David at Mahanaim (2 Sam. 19:32[33]) during which Barzillai took care of him.

7872. שֵׂיבָה ***śeyḇāh:*** A feminine noun meaning old age or gray hair. The word is used to denote that Joseph's brothers would bring to the grave the gray head of their father (Gen. 44:31). Hosea uses the word figuratively to depict Ephraim being old before its natural time, that is, its hair was sprinkled with gray (Hos. 7:9). In Proverbs, gray hair is a crown of splendor (Prov. 16:31); while 1 Kings denotes the gray head, not as wise, but simply old (1 Kgs. 2:6, 9). The psalmist uses the word to depict a point in life in which he could not perform the same deeds as before. On account of this, the psalmist asked God not to forsake him until he was able to declare God's glory to the coming generation (Ps. 71:18). Genesis uses the word to denote the time Abraham will be buried, that is, a good old age (Gen. 15:15; 25:8). Naomi's friends predicted that her grandson Obed would renew her life and sustain her in her old age (Ruth 4:15).

7873. שִׂיג ***śiyg:*** A masculine noun meaning pursuit, a moving away. It is used in a striking and mocking way of the pagan god, Baal, who evidently had gone aside to relieve himself (1 Kgs. 18:27; NIV, NKJV, busy; NASB, gone aside; KJV, pursuing).

7874. שִׂיד ***śiyḏ:*** A verb meaning to plaster; to coat (with lime). It refers to whitewashing or putting a white coating of lime on something to serve as a writing surface (Deut. 27:2, 4).

7875. שִׂיד ***śiyḏ:*** A masculine noun referring to plaster, lime. It refers to a white substance obtained from heating limestone and grinding it. It can then be used to make mortar and cement or to coat something (Deut. 27:2, 4). Bones could be burned to lime (Isa. 33:12); completely consumed (Amos 2:1) and used to neutralize acidic soils.

7876. שָׁיָה ***šāyāh:*** A verb meaning to neglect, to desert. It means to not pay attention to something, to disregard it (Deut. 32:18), in this case Israel's Rock, God.

7877. שִׁיזָא ***šiyzā':*** A proper noun designating Shiza (1 Chr. 11:42).

7878. שִׂיחַ ***śiyaḥ:*** A verb meaning to ponder, to converse, to utter, to complain, to meditate, to pray, to speak. Its primary use is to complain. In Job, the word denotes the action that Job took against the bitterness in his soul, that is, his complaints (Job 7:11). God's people were instructed to sing praises to Him (1 Chr. 16:9; Ps. 105:2). This singing tells of all His wondrous acts. The word is used in Job to denote speaking to the earth (Job 12:8); while Isaiah used it to depict Christ's dying without children, that is, descendants (Isa. 53:8). Isaiah's rhetorical question denoted that an absence of descendants was normally a shameful thing in the culture.

7879. שִׂיחַ *śiyaḥ:* A masculine noun meaning contemplation, meditation, prayer, talk, utterance, babbling. The primary meaning of the word is a complaint. In Job's narrative, he stated that even his couch would not ease his complaint (Job 7:13); that even if he were to forget his complaint, he would still dread all of his sufferings (Job 9:27); and because he loathed his very life, he would give free reign to his complaint (Job 10:1). Elijah mocked the prophets of Baal, telling them to cry louder because their god might be deep in thought (1 Kgs. 18:27). The word is also used to denote Hannah's prayer containing words of great anguish (1 Sam. 1:16). The psalmist used the word to depict meditation that he hoped would be pleasing to the Lord (Ps. 104:34).

7880. שִׂיחַ *śiyaḥ:* A masculine noun meaning a shoot, brush, a plant, a shrub. The most common usage of this word is a shrub or brush. It is used to denote that when the Lord made the heavens and earth, no shrub of the field had yet appeared nor had any plant sprung up (Gen. 2:5). *Śiyaḥ* designates the bushes under which Hagar placed Ishmael to die (Gen. 21:15). The two were dying due to lack of water, and therefore Hagar placed Ishmael underneath bushes, walked out of sight, still in hearing distance, and sat down. She did not want to watch her son die. In his discourse, Job designated the brush as the place where fathers of the sons who mocked him gathered salt herbs (Job 30:4). The bushes were also the place in which these fathers brayed (Job 30:7).

7881. שִׂיחָה *śiyḥāh:* A feminine noun meaning meditation, reflection, concern of one's thoughts, musing, reflection. The word is primarily used to indicate meditation. The psalmist indicated the proper procedure for an individual's response to God's Law. Because of his love for God's Law, the psalmist was prompted to meditate on it all day long. Due to his practice of meditation, the psalmist received more understanding than his elders (Ps. 119:97, 99). As Job expressed his feelings and frustrations, Eliphaz responded condemningly, stating that what Job was feeling and saying was hindering devotion to God (Job 15:4). Eliphaz's response was that of an ignorant man who did not realize the true nature of devotion to God.

7882. שִׁיחָה *šiyḥāh:* A feminine noun meaning a pit. Jeremiah used a metaphorical rendering of the word to describe his enemies' actions against him, they had dug a pit to capture him (Jer. 18:22). The psalmist also used a similar rendering of the word to describe what his enemies had done. They had dug a pit for him but had fallen into it themselves (Ps. 57:6[7]). In Psalm 119:85, the word was used to indicate attempts on the part of the arrogant to cause the psalmist to act contrary to God's Law. However, the psalmist's firm grounding in the laws and precepts of *Yahweh* kept him from falling into their traps.

7883. שִׁיחוֹר ***šiyḥôr:*** A proper noun designating Shihor, a river that was a branch of the Nile (Josh. 13:3; 1 Chr. 13:5; Isa. 23:3; Jer. 2:18).

7884. שִׁיחוֹר לִבְנָת ***šiyḥôr li̱bnaṯ:*** A proper noun designating Shihor Libnath (Josh. 19:26).

7885. שַׁיִט ***šayiṭ:*** A masculine noun meaning an oar. It refers to a large oar used, possibly, to row ships of war or large cargo ships (Isa. 33:21).

7886. שִׁילֹה ***šiylōh:*** A masculine proper name meaning Shiloh. It is a noun meaning whose it is or he whose it is (Gen. 49:10). The NIV renders it to whom it belongs; the NASB uses Shiloh with a note. The KJV translates it as Shiloh.

7887. שִׁילֹה ***šiylōh,*** שִׁלֹה ***šilōh,*** שִׁילוֹ ***šiylô,*** שִׁלוֹ ***šilô:*** A proper noun designating Shiloh, the location of the ark of God and presumably the Tabernacle tent during the time of the judges in Israel (Josh. 18:1—22:12; Judg. 18:31—21:21). It was Israel's religious center located in the hills of Ephraim between Shechem and Bethel (Judg. 21:12–21). Eli and Samuel both served at Shiloh (1 Sam. 2:14; 14:3). Prophets gathered to the location (1 Kgs. 14:1–4). At some point, the Lord deserted the Tabernacle site at Shiloh, perhaps when the Philistines captured the ark of God (1 Sam. 4:3–12). This event became a religious and moral lesson for Israel (Jer. 7:12–14). The Temple of Jeremiah's day would be destroyed as the tabernacle site at Shiloh was deserted (Jer. 26:6, 9), although the town continued to be inhabited (Jer. 41:5).

7888. שִׁילֹנִי ***šiylōniy,*** שִׁילוֹנִי ***šiylôniy,*** שִׁלֹנִי ***šilōniy:*** A proper noun designating Shilonite (1 Kgs. 11:29; 12:15; 15:29; 1 Chr. 9:5; 2 Chr. 9:29; 10:15; Neh. 11:5(KJV, see *šilōniy* [8023]; NIV, see *šēlāniy* [8024]).

7889. שִׁימוֹן ***šiymôn:*** A proper noun designating Shimon (1 Chr. 4:20).

7890. שַׁיִן ***šayin:*** A masculine noun referring to urine. It refers to the waste product in liquid form secreted by the kidneys. The context refers to a desperate time of siege when persons will be reduced to drinking their own urine (2 Kgs. 18:27; Isa. 36:12).

7891. שִׁיר ***šiyr:*** A verb meaning to sing. This word occurs often in a call to praise the Lord; the call may be directed toward oneself or others (Ps. 27:6; 96:1, 2; 101:1; Jer. 20:13). This term is frequently associated with the Levitical worship established by David and emphasized by postexilic writers (1 Chr. 15:16; Ezra 2:41; Neh. 7:1). Although the Levitical singers were all men, women also were singers in ancient Israel both in religious and secular settings (Ex. 15:21; Judg. 5:1–3; Eccl. 2:8). Secular occasions for singing included celebration of victory in battle (1 Sam. 18:6); mourning over death (2 Chr. 35:25); entertainment (2 Sam. 19:35[36]); and an expression of love (Isa. 5:1). The Bible once mentions the singing of birds (Zeph. 2:14).

7892. שִׁירָה ***šiyrāh***, שִׁיר ***šiyr:*** A masculine noun meaning a song. This word is used to indicate a type of lyrical song, a religious song, or a specific song of Levitical choirs. In Amos, God uses the word to indicate that He will turn their joyful singing into mourning because of their unfaithfulness to Him (Amos 8:10). This time of mourning will be like that of mourning for an only son, and it will end in a bitter day. In a similar usage, Laban asks Jacob why he ran off secretly without telling Laban. If Jacob would have stated he wanted to leave, Laban would have sent him off with joy and singing (Gen. 31:27). Isaiah uses the word to indicate the type of songs that will no longer be sung when the Lord lays waste the earth (Isa. 24:9). The type of drunken revels associated with drinking wine and beer will no longer be heard.

This word is also used in Nehemiah to denote songs of praise (Neh. 12:46). In this particular context, Nehemiah indicates that the music directors in the days of David and Asaph led songs of praise. The noun is also used to indicate specific songs of Levitical choirs accompanied by musical instruments. When David and the Israelites brought the ark of the Lord from Baalah of Judah (Kiriath Jearim), they celebrated with songs (1 Chr. 13:8). Amos uses the word to denote complacency and apathy. Many Israelites lay on ivory couches and strummed their musical instruments while dining on fattened calves and choice lambs. These people were so caught up in themselves that they did not even give thought to the threat of destruction by the Lord.

7893. שַׁיִשׁ ***šayiš:*** A masculine noun meaning marble, alabaster. It indicates a beautiful, decorative, yet excellent grade of gypsum used in various ways in construction (1 Chr. 29:2).

7894. שִׁישָׁא ***šiyšā':*** A proper noun designating Shisha (1 Kgs. 4:3).

7895. שִׁישַׁק ***šiyšaq:*** A proper noun designating Shishak, an Egyptian king (945–924 B.C.) who fought against Rehoboam of Judah, humiliated him, and took away much wealth from Jerusalem and the Temple. He had earlier harbored Jeroboam I before he became king of Israel.

7896. שִׂית *śiyṯ:* A verb meaning to set, to put, to lay. It basically means to place or put something somewhere: hostility between the serpent and the seed of the woman (Gen. 3:15); to appoint or replace something (Gen. 4:25); to place or put sheep in a separate area (Gen. 30:40); to appoint or establish a person in an official position (Gen. 41:33; Ps. 21:6[7]; 132:11; Isa. 5:6; 26:1; Jer. 22:6). It is used of God's setting or establishing the earth on its foundations (1 Sam. 2:8). To set one's hand on a person's eyes at death means to close them (Gen. 46:4). It indicates merely placing one's hand on a person (Gen. 48:14, 17). To set one's heart on something means to pay attention to it (Ex. 7:23; 2 Sam. 13:20; Jer. 31:21). The phrase *šîṯ* *l*e*ḇaddô* means to set apart (Gen. 30:40). The phrases to set one's hand to means to help or to have a common goal (Ex. 23:1); to blame someone means to set sin upon them (Num. 12:11). It takes on the sense of to make, to constitute something as: to make someone turn the shoulder (Ps. 21:12[13]); to make something like something else, e.g., Israel like a land of hunting, a wilderness (Jer. 2:15; Hos. 2:3[5]); to make or appoint darkness (Ps. 104:20). It refers to appointing a feast (Jer. 51:39); or of setting, putting one's refuge in the Lord (Ps. 73:28). God sets, defines Israel's borders (Ex. 23:31).

7897. שִׂית *šiyṯ:* A masculine noun meaning a garment. It refers to a piece of clothing but in context describes figuratively the clothing of the wicked, which represents their characters (Ps. 73:6). It refers to the dress or clothing worn by a harlot (Prov. 7:10).

7898. שַׁיִת *šayiṯ:* A masculine noun indicating a thorn. A small tree or shrub bearing hard, leafless, prickly stems (Isa. 5:6; 7:23–25). Evil and wickedness consumes even thorns, it is so destructive (Isa. 9:18[17]). It is easily consumed by fire (Isa. 27:4).

7899. שֵׂךְ *śēḵ:* A masculine noun indicating a barb, a prick. It refers to a short needle-like stem or branch without leaves that can easily puncture a person's eye (Num. 33:55).

7900. שֹׂךְ *śōḵ:* A masculine noun indicating a tabernacle, a dwelling. A word used figuratively of Israel as the tabernacle or holy place where God would dwell (Lam. 2:6).

7901. שָׁכַב *šāḵaḇ:* A verb meaning to lie down, to sleep. It means to put oneself in a reclining position when sleeping or resting (Gen. 19:4; Lev. 14:47; Deut. 6:7; Josh. 2:1; Ps. 3:5[6]; Prov. 3:24); when ill, to recover (Lev. 15:4; 2 Kgs. 9:16). It is used of sexual intercourse, lying with a woman or man (Gen. 19:32–35; Num. 5:13, 19; Judg. 16:1; 2 Sam. 13:14); or an act of sex with an animal, bestiality (Ex. 22:19[18]) that was punishable by death. It is used of Israel's spiritual harlotries, lying with her lovers (Ezek. 23:8). To lie with one's fathers means to die and be buried (Gen. 47:30). It refers to death in general (Job 3:13). It is used figuratively of lying, being covered by shame (Jer. 3:25). It takes the sense of making or letting persons lie down, causing them to lie down (1 Kgs. 3:20; 17:19; 2 Kgs. 4:21). Figuratively, it describes the Lord's betrothing Israel to Himself (Hos. 2:18[20]). It is used of tipping or turning over a vessel, referring in a figurative sense to the clouds of the sky (Job 38:37). In a passive sense, it refers to someone or something being laid someplace (2 Kgs. 4:32; Ezek. 32:19, 32). Lying in one's bosom or lap indicates extreme intimacy (Mic. 3:5).

7902. שְׁכָבָה ***šᵉk̲āb̲āh:*** I. A feminine noun indicating a layer (as of dew). It refers to something forming a covering or a layer over something else, e.g., a thin covering of dew over the ground (Ex. 16:13, 14).

II. A feminine noun meaning to lie with (sexually); semen. It refers to semen, literally, a laying out of semen (Lev. 15:16–18, 32) which made a man unclean. It refers to sexual intercourse (Lev. 19:20; Num. 5:13).

7903. שְׁכֹבֶת ***šᵉk̲ōb̲et̲:*** A feminine noun referring to intercourse; copulation. It refers to the act of sexual intercourse (Lev. 18:20; Num. 5:20). It also refers to intercourse or copulation with an animal which was considered perversion and punishable by death (Lev. 18:23; 20:15).

7904. שָׁכָה ***šāk̲āh:*** I. A verb meaning to be full of lust. It is used to describe a sexually aroused horse, which is used figuratively to condemn and illustrate the lustfulness of the people of Jerusalem (Jer. 5:8).

II. A verb meaning to arise in the morning. It refers to well-nurtured horses rising early to neigh after their neighbors, again a figurative use (Jer. 5:8; KJV).

7905. שֻׂכָּה ***śukkāh:*** A feminine noun meaning a spear, a harpoon. It refers to a weapon used to kill huge sea creatures; in context Leviathan is in mind, the great monster God describes (Job 41:7[40:31]).

7906. שֵׂכוּ ***śēk̲û:*** A proper noun designating Secu, Sechu (1 Sam. 19:22).

7907. שֶׂכְוִי ***śek̲wiy:*** A masculine noun meaning a celestial appearance or phenomenon, the mind. This word is used in Job to denote the mind that has been given understanding (Job 38:36). In a rhetorical question, the Lord indicated His sovereignty over all, including the lives of His servants. The exact meaning of this word is unclear.

7908. שְׁכוֹל ***šᵉk̲ôl:*** A masculine noun meaning bereavement. This word primarily indicates a loss of children. In Isaiah's oracle against Babylon, he stated that the woman who thought of herself as lasting forever would become a widow and suffer the loss of her children. The Virgin Daughter of Babylon, who once thought that there was none like her, would suffer the fate of a common person (Isa. 47:8). The word is also used to denote how the soul is left after a ruthless witness repays evil for good (Ps. 35:12).

7909. שַׁכּוּל *šakkûl*, שְׁכוּלָה *š^{e}k̲ûlāh*: An adjective meaning bereaved. The word is used figuratively to describe the fierceness of David and his men by comparing them to a wild bear robbed of her cubs (2 Sam. 17:8). In another analogy, the intensity of God's punishment is described as a bear robbed of her cubs. God would attack the Israelites for their sins and rip them open (Hos. 13:8). Proverbs used the same figurative language, stating that it is better to meet a bear robbed of her cubs than a fool in his folly (Prov. 17:12). In a different sense, Jeremiah used this word to describe a punishment in which wives would be made childless and widows (Jer. 18:21).

7910. שִׁכּוֹר *šikkôr*, שִׁכֹּר *šikkor*: An adjective meaning drunk, drunken. It means to be inebriated, under the influence of wine or strong drink, out of control (1 Sam. 1:13; 25:36; 1 Kgs. 16:9; 20:16; Job 12:25; Ps. 107:27). It may indicate the drunkard, the drunken person (Prov. 26:9; Joel 1:5).

7911. שָׁכַח *šāk̲aḥ*: A verb meaning to forget. It indicates that something has been lost to memory, or a period of time has softened the memory of it: hatred (Gen. 27:45); forgetting a person or an event (Gen. 40:23); forgetting the days of much food, abundance (Gen. 41:30). It is an especially important word with respect to God and His people: God never forgets them (Isa. 49:15); they are not to forget their God, His covenant, and His deeds (Deut. 4:9, 23, 31; 6:12; 8:11; 9:7; 25:19; 32:18). But God does not pass over, wink at, or forget the wickedness of His people (Lam. 5:20; Amos 8:7). Those who forget God wither away (Job 8:13), as well as all the nations who forget Him. The helpless must not be left alone (Ps. 10:12). God's Law must not be forgotten (Ps. 119:61, 83, 93). Wisdom's teachings are not to be forgotten (Prov. 3:1; 4:5).

7912. שְׁכַח *š^{e}k̲aḥ*: An Aramaic verb meaning to find. It means to discover, to come up, to find someone or something: a person, Daniel (2:25); negated it means not to find someone or something (Dan. 2:35); to discover wisdom in a person (Dan. 5:11, 12, 14); to discover, find by weighing, evaluating (Dan. 5:27); to discover, to find a name in a registry or archives (Ezra 4:15); as well as other facts (Ezra 4:15, 19).

7913. שָׁכֵחַ *šāk̲ēaḥ*: An adjective meaning forgetting, forgetful. The nations who turn from, forget, or neglect God will be put into Sheol, along with the wicked (Ps. 9:17[18]); including God's own nation and people (Isa. 65:11).

7914. שְׂכִיָּה ***śᵉkiyyāh,*** שָׂכְיָה ***śākᵉyāh:*** I. A feminine noun indicating a vessel, a ship. It refers to seagoing vessels, further qualified in Isaiah 2:16 as pleasing, pleasant.

II. A feminine noun referring to a picture. The KJV rendered this word as pictures (Isa. 2:16), now known to be an improbable rendering.

III. A masculine proper noun Sachia. A descendant of Benjamin. Shaharaim had children in Moab by his wife Hodesh, one of which was Sachia (1 Chr. 8:10).

7915. שַׂכִּין ***śakkiyn:*** A masculine noun referring to a knife. A sharp cutting or stabbing instrument, single or double-edged (Prov. 23:2).

7916. שָׂכִיר ***śakiyr:*** A masculine adjective meaning hired. It refers to a rented or hired person, animal, or object (Ex. 12:45; 22:15[14]). Wages were to be paid promptly to hired workers (Lev. 19:13). Restrictions were laid on hired persons concerning Temple rituals and holy things (Lev. 22:10). Even a freeman's labor seems like the days of a hired man (Job 7:1). It is used figuratively of a hired razor, the Assyrians (Isa. 7:20). A hired soldier was a mercenary (Jer 46:21). It is rendered as wage earner appropriately in Malachi 3:5 (NASB).

7917. שְׂכִירָה ***śᵉkiyrāh:*** A feminine adjective meaning hired. It has the same meaning as 7916, referring to Assyria as a rented, hired razor.

7918. שָׁכַךְ ***šākak:*** A verb meaning to go down, to get lower. It refers to a lowering of the great flood waters (Gen. 8:1); to an abatement of anger (Esth. 2:1; 7:10). In its causative use, it means to lower something: personal attacks or accusations (Num. 17:5[20]). It is rendered to set a snare (KJV, Jer. 5:26); to set a trap (NASB); to set up a snare (NIV).

7919. שָׂכַל ***sākal,*** שָׂכַל ***sākhal:*** A verb meaning to act with insight, to be prudent, to give insight, to teach, to prosper, to consider, to ponder, to understand, to act prudently, to act with devotion. The primary meaning of the word is to be prudent. The word is used in Isaiah to denote what was hoped and expected of Israel, i.e., that they would consider and understand that the hand of the Lord had acted (Isa. 41:20). The word is also used in Deuteronomy to denote a lack of understanding on the part of the people. If they were wise and would understand, they would know what their end would be (Deut. 32:29). Jeremiah used this word to denote wisdom in terms of insight and comprehension (Jer. 9:24[23]). In a similar usage of the word, fools are to take heed and become wise (Ps. 94:8). The wisdom of comprehension will open their eyes to the Lord, who sees and punishes wrong actions. In a confession of sins, the Holy Spirit is remembered as having been sent to instruct (Neh. 9:20); the prudent person keeps quiet in evil times (Amos 5:13); those who meditate on the

Book of the Law day and night, being careful to do everything in it, will be prosperous and successful (Josh. 1:8). In the causative form, *śāk̲al* denoted God's actions to Solomon if he observed what the Lord required and walked in His ways. If this pattern were followed, the Lord would prosper Solomon (1 Kgs. 2:3).

7920. שְׂכַל ***ś*ᵉ*k̲al:*** An Aramaic verb meaning to consider. The reflexive form of the word is used in Daniel to depict the state of mind that Daniel was in while he was shown the vision. While Daniel was contemplating the horns that he had previously seen, a smaller horn appeared and brought his attention back to the vision itself (Dan. 7:8).

7921. שָׁכֹל ***šāk̲ōl:*** A verb meaning to be bereft of (children), deprived of (children). It means to be deprived of children (Gen. 27:45; 43:14; Lev. 26:22; 1 Sam. 15:33). It also means to miscarry (Ex. 23:26; Job 21:10). The sword and war bereaved parents of their children (Deut. 32:25). With reference to land, it can mean barren, unfruitful (2 Kgs. 2:19); with reference to vines, it refers to casting off, losing their fruit (Mal. 3:11). God Himself would bereave His people of their children as punishment for their rebellions (Jer. 15:7; Ezek. 5:17; Hos. 9:12, 14).

7922. שֶׂכֶל ***śek̲el,*** שֵׂכֶל ***śēk̲el:*** A masculine noun meaning intelligence, good sense. This intelligence is more than just mere book knowledge or learning about a particular subject. It has a greater significance and means insight or understanding. This insight is a gift from God (1 Chr. 22:12); and God holds the freedom to give it or to take it away whenever He chooses (Job 17:4). The results from having this intelligence and insight is that it gives a person patience (Prov. 19:11); and wins praise from others (Prov. 12:8). Only fools despise this intelligence (Prov. 23:9). This noun is used once with a negative connotation in Daniel 8:25 where it stands for cunning, requiring much intelligence.

7923. שִׁכֻּלִים ***šikkuliym:*** A masculine noun indicating bereavement; childlessness. It refers to the loss of living children, as well as the miscarrying of infants (Isa. 49:20).

7924. שָׂכְלְתָנוּ ***sok̲l*ᵉ*t̲ānû:*** An Aramaic feminine noun meaning wisdom, insight. It is used in Daniel 5:11, 12, and 14. In this context, it described Daniel's wisdom and insight into the interpretation of dreams. It was obvious to the people around Daniel that his wisdom was not merely human wisdom, for they said he had the spirit of the gods living in him and that he was like the gods. Thus, this wisdom cannot be gained by mere human training. It comes as a gift from God. The pagan culture did not attribute it to the one true God but to their gods.

7925. שָׁכַם šāḵam: A verb meaning to rise early. It uniformly indicates arising early to do something, often to pack and go on a journey. This procedure is especially appropriate in Israel where the afternoons are extremely hot: even angels, messengers, rose early to travel (Gen. 19:2); as well as humans (Gen. 19:27; 20:8; 21:14; 22:3, etc.). Job rose early to sacrifice and pray for his family (Job 1:5). It can be used to indicate excessive labor on the part of a person trying to get ahead, to prosper (Ps. 127:2). Some things are not appropriate at such an early hour (Prov. 27:14). The Lord had risen early and had diligently, eagerly spoken to a rebellious people (Jer. 7:13, 25). It has the sense in several contexts of eagerness (Jer. 7:25; Zeph 3:7).

7926. שְׁכֶם š^eḵem: I. A masculine noun referring to a shoulder, the upper back. It refers to the upper back and neck area (Gen. 9:23; 21:14). Often things were carried on one's shoulder (Gen. 24:15, 45; Ex. 12:34; Josh. 4:5; Judg. 9:48). To turn one's shoulder to (l^e) someone or something means to turn to leave (1 Sam. 10:9). To set one's shoulder, back is to turn away (Ps. 21:12[13]). To carry the government on one's shoulder is to bear the burden of rulership (Isa. 9:4[3], 6[5]; 22:22). A yoke is worn on the shoulders, literally or figuratively (Isa. 10:27; 14:25). In Genesis 48:22, the word refers to a geographical feature, a ridge.

II. A masculine noun used to indicate consent, shoulder to shoulder. The phrase shoulder to shoulder indicates sharing in a common effort or open consent to something, whether bad (Hos. 6:9; KJV; NASB, Shechem) or good (Zeph. 3:9).

7927. שְׁכֶם šeḵem: A proper noun designating Shechem, an important biblical and middle-eastern city located on the border of Ephraim and Manasseh (Josh. 17:2, 7). It lay between Mount Ebal on the northwest and Mount Gerazim on the southeast. It also served in Israel as a Levitical city as well as a city of refuge (Josh. 20:7; 21:21). It was the first capital city of the Northern Kingdom briefly (Tirzah and then Samaria took its place). It lies ca. thirty miles north of Jerusalem. Abraham had a vision and received promises from God in Shechem at the tree of Moreh (Gen. 12:6). Jacob purchased land in it from Hamor, father of Shechem (Gen. 33:18) and committed himself and his family to the Lord there (Gen. 35:4), as Israel and Joshua did many years later (Josh. 24:1–32). Here Dinah was raped and savagely avenged by Simon and Levi (Gen. 37). Shechem continued to be a city intertwined with Israel at various times during its history (Judg. 8:31; 9:1–57). Jeroboam I was made king at Shechem (1 Kgs. 12:1, 25).

It was God's intent to give Shechem to *his* people, for he owned it (Pss. 60:6[8]; 108:7[8]). Inhabitants of the city supported Gedaliah as governor, God's chosen vessel, after the fall of Jerusalem (Jer. 41:5).

7928. שֶׁכֶם šeḵem: A proper noun designating Shechem, the name of three individuals in the Old Testament:

A. A man of Manasseh and descendant of Gilead. Through him the family/clan of Shechem was built up (Josh. 17:2).

B. The son of Hamor, a Hivite. His father raped Dinah, daughter of Jacob, and Simeon and Levi took vengeance, killing Hamor and everyone in Shechem (Gen. 34).

C. A son of Shemediah (Shemida, NIV) from the tribe of Manasseh (1 Chr. 7:19).

7929. שִׁכְמָה šiḵmāh: A feminine noun referring to a shoulder blade, a socket. It refers to the upper part of a person's bicep, tricep, and deltoid muscle area, supported by a structural skeleton and featuring a socket where several bones come together. This is normally considered a strong feature of the human body (Job 31:22).

7930. שִׁכְמִי šiḵmiy: A proper noun designating Shechemite (Num. 26:31).

7931. שָׁכַן šāḵan: A verb meaning to settle down, to dwell. In its most simple form, three slight variations of meaning are found for this verb. First, it simply means to settle down (Ex. 24:16; Num. 24:2; Ps. 102:28[29]). Second, it can mean to lie down or rest. When used this way, it can refer to objects (Num. 9:17; Job 3:5); animals (Isa. 13:21); and people (Jer. 23:6; 33:16). When people are the object of the verb, it means that they are resting in peace and security. Third, it may mean to dwell or abide. Again, this can have several referents such as people (Ps. 37:27; Prov. 2:21); the dead (Job 26:5); God (1 Kgs. 8:12; Isa. 8:18); or objects such as the Tabernacle (Josh. 22:19). In the intensive form, it means to establish. The word is used in this way in Deuteronomy 12:11 and Psalm 78:60 to describe how God set up a dwelling place for His name, establishing Himself in Israel. Finally, the causative form means to lay, to place, to set (Gen. 3:24; Josh. 18:1); or to cause to dwell (Job 11:14; Ps. 78:55).

7932. שְׁכַן š^{e}ḵan: An Aramaic verb meaning to dwell, to lodge. It means to inhabit a certain place or location, to remain there permanently (Ezra 6:12); it is used of God's name dwelling in Jerusalem in His temple. The beasts of Nebuchadnezzar's tree vision lived in safety under the limbs of the great tree (Dan. 4:21[18]).

7933. שֶׁכֶן šēḵen: A masculine noun indicating a dwelling, a habitation. It is a noun indicating a temporary dwelling place, the Tabernacle in the wilderness (Deut. 12:5).

7934. שָׁכֵן šāḵēn: An adjective meaning inhabitant. This word usually refers to an inhabitant of a city (Isa. 33:24; Hos. 10:5). It can also have the more specific meaning of neighbor. These neighbors can either be people who are friends or enemies (Ex. 3:22; Ruth 4:17); or nations (Deut. 1:7). Neighbors can also be extremely influential (Ezek. 16:26). Israel was said to have engaged in prostitution with her neighbor Egypt, meaning that she followed the gods and religions of Egypt rather than following the one true God.

7935. שְׁכַנְיָהוּ ***šᵉḵanyāhû,*** שְׁכַנְיָה ***šᵉḵanyāh:*** A proper noun designating Shechaniah:

A. A priest (1 Chr. 24:11).

B. A Levite (2 Chr. 31:15).

C. A priest (Neh. 12:3, 14 [see also 7645,C]).

D. A descendant of Zerubbabel (1 Chr. 3:21, 22; Ezra 8:3; Neh. 3:29).

E. Son of Jahaziel (Ezra 8:5).

F. Son of Jehiel (Ezra 10:2).

G. Son of Arah (Neh. 6:18).

7936. שָׂכַר ***śāḵar,*** סָכַר ***sāḵar:*** A verb meaning to hire. It means to make an agreement with someone to do something for payment: for procreation purposes (Gen. 30:16); for the purpose of prophesying (Deut. 23:4[5]); for military use (Judg. 9:4; 2 Sam. 10:6; 2 Kgs. 7:6); for priestly services (Judg. 18:4); for political purposes (Ezra 4:5; Neh. 6:12, 13); for craftsmanship (Isa. 46:6). In the passive or causative uses, it means to be hired or to hire oneself out (1 Sam. 2:5; Hag. 1:6).

7937. שָׁכֻר ***šāḵur,*** שָׁכַר ***šāḵar:*** I. An adjective indicating drunken, made drunken. It is used to indicate a state of intoxication. In context, however, a cup of judgment and a ruling from God had intoxicated His people (Isa. 51:21).

II. A verb meaning to become drunk, intoxicated. It refers to the act and process of a person's becoming inebriated, overcome with wine or strong drink (Gen. 9:21). It indicates drinking freely when preceded by *waṯāh*, to drink (Gen. 43:34). It is used in a figure of speech describing arrows being made drunken (causative) with blood in a vicious battle (Deut. 32:42; Isa. 49:26; Jer. 48:26; 51:39, 57). It describes Hannah's condition: she appeared drunken (1 Sam. 1:14), a reflexive use of the verb. In its intensive stem, it describes making someone drunken (2 Sam. 11:13; Hab. 2:15).

7938. שֶׂכֶר ***śeḵer:*** I. A masculine noun referring to wages, a reward. The term is used figuratively of the wages of truth literally, the reward of sowing righteousness (Prov. 11:18). The phrase workers of wages means hired laborers (Isa. 19:10).

II. A masculine noun meaning sluice. It refers to an artificial channel or passage for water (Isa. 19:10, KJV). It refers to workers in a highly prosperous, luxurious society.

7939. שָׂכָר ***śāḵār:*** A masculine noun indicating wages, a reward, pay. It refers to monetary pay or pay consisting of material goods (Gen. 30:28, 32, 33; Ex. 2:9; Num. 18:31). It refers to a reward given by God to Abraham for faithfulness (Gen. 15:1). It can be rendered as hire, the amount paid to rent or hire a person or object (Ex. 22:15[14]). It is used in the sense of ordinary expenses or the costs of maintenance or travel (Jon. 1:3; Zech. 8:10). The Lord's gift of children is considered a reward to His people (Ps. 127:3). When God comes to comfort his people, His reward is with Him, just payment for what each person deserves (Isa. 40:10).

7940. שָׂכָר ***śāḵār:*** A proper noun designating Sacar:

A. The father of Ahiam, the same as Sharar (8325) (1 Chr. 11:35).

B. A Korahite gatekeeper (1 Chr. 26:4).

7941. שֵׁכָר ***šēḵār:*** A masculine noun referring to strong drink; beer. It refers to an intoxicating drink and is usually understood as some kind of beer. Priests were not to drink it when serving at the Tabernacle or Temple (Lev. 10:9). The Nazarite was not to touch it (Num. 6:3; Judg. 13:4, 7, 14). The drinkers of strong drink (*šôṯê šēḵār*) were none other than drunkards (Ps. 69:12[13]; Isa. 5:11, 22; 28:7; 29:9; 56:12). Such drinking causes violent behavior (Prov. 20:1); kings should stay away from it (Prov. 31:4); though it may be a sedative for the dying and bitter (Prov. 31:6; Isa. 24:9). It is used in a context of mockery by Micah (2:11).

7942. שִׁכְּרוֹן ***šikk***^{e}***rôn:*** A proper noun designating Shikkeron, Shicron (Josh. 15:11).

7943. שִׁכָּרוֹן ***šikkārôn:*** An abstract masculine noun indicating drunkenness. It refers to an intoxicated state brought on by strong drink or by the cup of God's wrath (Ezek. 23:33; 39:19). It refers to the state of confusion that God's judgments will bring on corrupt kings over His people (Jer. 13:13).

7944. שַׁל ***šal:*** A masculine noun meaning a sin, an error. It comes from the verb *šālāh* (7952), meaning to sin. This noun is used only once in the Old Testament in 2 Samuel 6:7, but from this usage, we can gain the insight that the error described by this word is a great one. The context is that of Uzzah, whom God struck down because he touched the ark: this error cost him his life. This word has strong connotations of a great sin or error deserving of death.

7945. שָׁ ***ša,*** שֶׁ ***še,*** שְׁ ***š***^{e}***:*** A relative pronoun meaning who, which, what. Each usage must be noted in its context carefully. It has these basic uses: (1) as a pronoun, who, which, what, whom, whomever, him who, he who, that which, etc. (Judg. 7:12; Ps. 122:3; 124:6; Eccl. 1:11; Song 1:7; 3:1); (2) as an adverbial pronoun, where, e.g., place where (Eccl. 1:7; 11:3); (3) as a conjunction meaning that (Eccl. 2:13; 3:18); or introducing a cause, a causal clause (Song 1:6; 5:2). It is used in many compounds, such as b^e + we, b^e*še,* meaning in that, since (Eccl. 2:16); k^e*še,* according as (Eccl. 5:18[17]; 12:7); *misše,* from whom, from these (Eccl. 5:5[4]). The phrase in Genesis 6:3, *bešaggam,* means, in the (fact) that they also . . . For Genesis 49:10, see 7886. It has the sense of when or until (Judg. 5:7, *šaqqamtî*).

7946. שַׁלְאֲנָן ***šal'ªnan:*** An adjective meaning secure, at ease. It refers to a time and condition of safety, health, and strength in one's life, a time seemingly safe from all dangers (Job 21:23).

7947. שָׁלַב ***šālab:*** A verb meaning to set parallel. It refers to two tenons or extensions set parallel with each other at the end of a board or panel (Ex. 26:17; 36:22).

7948. שָׁלָב ***šālāb:*** A masculine noun indicating an upright, a frame. It refers to part of the supporting structures (stands) for the great bronze sea of Solomon (1 Kgs. 7:28, 29).

7949. שָׁלַג ***šālag:*** A verb meaning to snow; to be as snow. It refers to the falling of snow at the time of the Lord's giving Israel a great victory in the wintertime (Ps. 68:14[15]). Zalmon is probably located in the area of Bashan, 60 miles southeast of Damascus.

7950. שֶׁלֶג ***šeleg:*** I. A masculine noun meaning snow. It refers to frozen falling crystals of water. Its white color was considered the example of choice for whiteness (Ex. 4:6; Num. 12:10; 2 Kgs. 5:27); leprosy was as white as snow. The coldness of snow is noted (Prov. 25:13). Snowy days were rare and memorable in Israel (2 Sam. 23:20). The Lord would make one's sins as white as snow and cleanse them away (Isa. 1:18).

II. A masculine noun meaning soap, soapwort. The NIV renders this word as soap in the text (Job 9:30). Soapwort is a genus of plants whose sap forms a lather with water for washing.

7951. שָׁלָה ***šālāh,*** שָׁלַו ***šālaw:*** I. A verb meaning to be at ease, to be safe, to prosper. It indicates being in a state of peace, quiet, and safety, at ease (Job 3:26; Job 12:6; Jer. 12:1). It refers to a time of quiet and safety, of wholeness for Jerusalem (Ps. 122:6). It can also describe a state of prosperity for the enemies of Israel and Zion (Lam. 1:5).

II. A verb meaning to deceive; to be negligent. It may indicate a kind of evil deception (2 Kgs. 4:28); or a failure to be diligent, to be neglectful in what is important (2 Chr. 29:11).

7952. שָׁלָה ***šālāh:*** A verb meaning to be careless, to be thoughtless, to sin. The sin described by this verb does not seem to be a deliberate sin but rather one that is committed by ignorance or inadvertence. The verb is used only in the passive and causative forms. In the passive form, it holds the meaning of being negligent or being careless of duties (2 Chr. 29:11). The causative form means to lead astray or to deceive. It is used in 2 Kings 4:28 when the Shunammite woman felt deceived that she had been promised a son who later died. Although the sins described by this verb were not intentional, they were still deserving of punishment in God's sight.

7953. שָׁלָה ***šālāh:*** A verb meaning to take away; to require. It refers to a demand or necessity laid on a person, in context God's demand for a person's life (Job 27:8).

7954. שְׁלֵה ***š^{e}lēh:*** An Aramaic verb indicating to be at ease. It means to be in a state of safety, contentment, and security in one's domicile, with no external threats of war or revolution according to its contextual usage (Dan. 4:4[1]).

7955. שָׁלֻה ***šālūh:*** An Aramaic feminine noun referring to anything amiss or offensive. It refers to anything spoken that is not fitting, that is derogatory toward the true God, since He is the God of great deliverance (Dan. 3:29).

7956. שֵׁלָה ***šēlāh:*** A proper noun designating Shelah, son of Judah (Gen. 38:5, 11, 14, 26; 46:12; Num. 26:20; 1 Chr. 2:3; 4:21).

7957. שַׁלְהֶבֶת ***šalhebet,*** שַׁלְהֶבֶתְיָה ***šalhebetyāh:*** I. A feminine noun indicating a flame. It refers figuratively to a flame of fire that destroys the growth of the wicked (Job 15:30). It is used figuratively of God's destruction of the area of the Negev with military might under the symbol of a flame (Ezek. 20:47[21:3]).

II. A feminine noun indicating a mighty flame. It means literally the flame of the Lord (Song 8:6), but Yah (Lord) on the end of the word could indicate a superlative flame, a vehement flame (KJV), a mighty flame (NIV), the flame of the Lord (NASB).

7958. שְׂלָו ***ś^{e}lāw:*** A masculine noun indicating quail. It refers to any of a number of small short-tailed birds (Phasianidae family). God provided these birds as food for Israel in the desert in a miraculous way (Ex. 16:13; Num. 11:31, 32; Ps. 105:40).

7959. שֶׁלֶו ***šālû:*** A masculine noun indicating security, prosperity. It indicates a state of abundance including good health that gives a false sense of total security in one's present state (Ps. 30:6[7]).

7960. שָׁלוּ ***šālû:*** An Aramaic feminine noun referring to an error, a failure, neglect, an offense. It refers to a failure to perform or to carry out one's responsibilities in a certain matter (Ezra 4:22; 6:9). It describes something hurtful or offensive in certain contexts (Dan. 3:29). It refers to neglect or failure to carry out one's responsibilities according to what is expected in a given political office (Dan. 6:4[5]).

7961. שָׁלֵו **šālēw,** שָׁלֵיו **šālēyw,** שְׁלֵיו **$š^e$lēyw:** An adjective meaning to be at ease, peaceable, prosperous, carefree. It refers to a state and attitude of being undisturbed or heedless. It describes a place to live found by some of Simeon's descendants, a place very peaceful, at ease (1 Chr. 4:40); or any nation dwelling in security (Jer. 49:31). It describes a person who is at ease, without worry or anxiety (Job 16:12). The evil person has no such state (Job 20:20). Psalm 73:12 gives a contrary view of the wicked. It refers to a luxuriously affected, carefree people (Ezek. 23:42). It takes on the sense of prosperity in a general sense (Zech. 7:7).

7962. שַׁלְוָה **šalwāh:** A feminine noun meaning security, prosperity, quietness. It indicates ease, a lack of anxiety. It describes a state of prosperity for Jerusalem (Ps. 122:7); but also a state of prosperity that contributed to her downfall (Jer. 22:21); excessive ease, security (Ezek. 16:49). It has the sense of excessive complacency or unconcern (Prov. 1:32). It depicts a state and attitude of peacefulness and enjoyment between friends or family (Prov. 17:1); and in and among nations and peoples (Dan. 8:25; 11:21, 24).

7963. שְׁלֵוָה **$š^e$lēwāh:** An Aramaic noun referring to prosperity, tranquillity. It refers to a peaceful condition and to national security, as well as prosperity in a city or nation (Dan. 4:27[24]).

7964. שִׁלּוּחִים **šillûḥiym:** A masculine noun meaning parting gifts, dowry. It refers to something given as a gift in parting (Mic. 1:14); or as a dowry to one's daughter in a marriage (1 Kgs. 9:16). For Exodus 18:2, see 7971.

7965. שָׁלוֹם **šālôm:** A masculine noun meaning peace or tranquility. This Hebrew term is used 237 times in the Old Testament and is used to greet someone (Judg. 19:20; 1 Chr. 12:18[19]; Dan. 10:19). It is common in Hebrew to ask how one's peace is (Gen. 43:27; Ex. 18:7; Judg. 18:15), which is equivalent to asking "How are you?" Moreover, this word was often used to describe someone's manner of coming or going; sometimes this took the form of a blessing: Go in peace (Judg. 8:9; 1 Sam. 1:17; Mal. 2:6). Another common expression involved dying or being buried in peace (Gen. 15:15; 2 Chr. 34:28; Jer. 34:5) Peace is present with the wise but absent from the wicked (Prov. 3:2, 17; Isa. 57:21; 59:8). It is often pictured as coming from God; Gideon built an altar and called the altar *Yahweh-shalom* (the Lord Is Peace; Num. 6:26; Judg. 6:24; Isa. 26:3).

7966. שִׁלּוּם **šillûm,** שִׁלֻּם **šillum:** A masculine noun meaning a requital, a retribution. It is derived from the verb *šālam* (7999). In context, this noun is used as God's punishment of Israel for their repeated disobedience (Isa. 34:8; Hos. 9:7). It is not something given on a whim but is deserved. This noun can also mean a reward, or more accurately, a bribe (Mic. 7:3). Only the corrupt accept these bribes, which are used to distort justice. Such people have no care for what is right or wrong but only in what they will receive. Ultimately, they will receive their retribution from God for their wrongdoings.

7967. שַׁלּוּם **šallûm,** שַׁלֻּם **šallum:** A proper noun designating Shallum:

A. King of Israel (2 Kgs. 15:10, 13–15).

B. The husband of Huldah the prophetess (2 Kgs. 22:14; 2 Chr. 34:22).

C. The father of Jekamiah (1 Chr. 2:40, 41).

D. King of Judah, fourth son of Josiah (1 Chr. 3:15; Jer. 22:11).

E. A descendant of Jacob (1 Chr. 4:25).

F. A priest (1 Chr. 6:12 [5:38], 13[5:39]; Ezra 7:2).

G. Son of Naphtali, also called Shillem (8006) (1 Chr. 7:13).

H. A Levite (1 Chr. 9:17, 19, 31; Ezra 2:42; Neh. 7:45).

I. An Ephraimite chief (2 Chr. 28:12).

J. A Levite (Ezra 10:24).

K. Son of Bani (Ezra 10:42).

L. A repairer of Jerusalem's wall, son of Halohesh (Neh. 3:12).

M. Uncle of Jeremiah the prophet (Jer. 32:7).

N. The father of Maaseiah (Jer. 35:4).

7968. שַׁלּוּן **šallûn:** A proper noun designating Shallum (Neh. 3:15).

7969. שָׁלוֹשׁ **šālôš,** שָׁלֹשׁ **šālōš,** שְׁלֹשָׁה **š^{e}lōšāh:** A masculine/feminine noun meaning three. It is a cardinal counting number indicating three of something (2 Sam. 24:12). It combines with other numbers, e.g., three hundred (Gen. 5:22, 23); three hundred fifty-six; *s^{e}lōš 'eśreh,* thirteen (1 Kgs. 7:1). The phrase *š^{e}lōšeṯ hayyāmîm* indicates within three days (Ezra 10:8, 9), literally three of days.

7970. שְׁלוֹשִׁים **š^{e}lôšiym,** שְׁלֹשִׁים **š^{e}lōšiym:** A masculine plural noun meaning thirty. It is the plural of *šālôš,* 7969, meaning thirty of something (Judg. 14:11–13, 19; Prov. 22:20, NIV; Zech. 11:12, 13). It combines with other numbers, e.g., one hundred and thirty (Gen. 5:3); thirty-five (Gen. 11:12).

7971. שָׁלַח **šālaḥ:** A verb meaning to send forth, to send away; to let go; to put. The word is used to describe God's sending forth or away in a providential manner or purpose (Gen. 45:5; 1 Sam. 15:18); even an angel or divine messenger can be sent by God (Gen. 24:7); or of commissioning someone by sending him or her, e.g., Moses (Ex. 3:12; Judg. 6:14); or Gideon to do a task (cf. Num. 21:6; Deut. 7:20; 2 Kgs. 17:13, 26). The Lord sends forth His prophets (Jer. 7:25); and His plagues on Egypt (Ex. 9:14). It is used figuratively of the Lord's sending forth arrows (2 Sam.

22:15; Ps. 18:14[15]); or is used literally of a person shooting arrows (1 Sam. 20:20, in an intensive stem). God sends forth His Word (Isa. 9:8[7]; 55:11; Zech. 7:12). It can have a strong sense of casting out someone (Lev. 18:24; 20:23; Jer. 28:16). In its intensive stem, it means to set free (Ex. 4:23; 5:2). Referring to an animal, it can mean let loose (Ex. 22:5[4]).

It can have the sense of putting forth or reaching out one's hand (Gen. 37:22; 1 Sam. 24:10[11]). It is used in a figurative sense of God's stretching out His hand, His power, against the leaders of Israel (Ex. 24:11). It may take on the idea of sending away, of letting loose (Gen. 28:5; Judg. 11:38; Ps. 50:19). In its passive sense, it refers to something being sent out (Gen. 44:3; Esth. 3:13).

It is found in contexts in which it means to put forth (branches) (Ps. 80:11[12]; Jer. 17:8; Ezek. 31:5). To put down, to let down, e.g., Jeremiah into a cistern (Jer. 38:6). The phrase to set the city on fire is literally to cast against the city with fire (Judg. 1:8; 20:48).

In its intensive passive stem, the word is used to describe a woman sent forth or divorced (Isa. 50:1), but it is used in a figurative sense. It has the sense of unrestrained, let loose, in reference to a spoiled child (Prov. 29:15). In its causative stem use, it means to send forth, to cause to go out: famine (Ezek. 14:13; Amos 8:11); wild beasts (Lev. 26:22); flies of a plague (Ex. 8:21[17]); an enemy (2 Kgs. 15:37).

7972. שְׁלַח ***šᵉlaḥ:*** An Aramaic verb meaning to send, to be sent. It describes God or a person putting forth, sending out someone or something: God sending a messenger (Dan. 3:28; 6:22[23]); a person sending a letter or report (Ezra 4:11, 18); sending to inform someone (Ezra 4:14); or sending an answer, a reply (Ezra 4:17). It describes a person being sent (Ezra 7:14); one who is sent or a word from God that is sent (Dan. 5:24). The phrase who sends forth his hand to change (it), indicates an attempt to change Darius' decree (Ezra 6:12). It is used as a technical term to indicate the sending or issuing of a royal decree (Ezra 6:13); or command (Dan. 3:2).

7973. שֶׁלַח ***šelaḥ:*** I. A masculine noun meaning a weapon, a sword, a dart. It refers to some kind of military weapon, perhaps a short sword (2 Chr. 23:10; Neh. 4:17[11], 23[17]); and further, to all kinds of weapons of war (2 Chr. 32:5). God rescues from the sword (Job 33:18; 36:12). It describes the sword as a weapon of war in Joel's vision (Joel. 2:8; but NASB, defenses).

II. A masculine noun meaning shoots, tendrils, plants. It refers to what is put forth, fresh green sprouts, shoots in an amorous expression referring to the beloved as a fertile garden (Song 4:13).

7974. שֶׁלַח ***šelaḥ:*** A proper noun designating Shelah (Gen. 10:24; 11:12–15; 1 Chr. 1:18, 24).

7975. שִׁלֹחַ ***šilōah,*** שֶׁלַח ***šelah:*** I. A proper noun designating Shiloah, a pool in southeast Jerusalem (Isa. 8:6).

II. A proper noun designating Shelah, another name for I (Neh. 3:15).

7976. שִׁלֻּחָה ***šilluḥāh:*** A feminine noun indicating a branch, a tendril, a shoot. It refers figuratively to the lively growth of Moab, represented by the vibrant clinging tendrils it puts forth (Isa. 16:8).

7977. שִׁלְחִי ***šilḥiy:*** A proper noun designating Shilhi (1 Kgs. 22:42; 2 Chr. 20:31).

7978. שִׁלְחִים ***šilḥiym:*** A proper noun designating Shilhim (Josh. 15:32).

7979. שֻׁלְחָן ***šulḥān:*** A masculine noun meaning a table. Its most significant referent is the table of showbread featured in the Tabernacle (Ex. 25:23); and then in the Temple (1 Kgs. 7:48), including Ezekiel's Temple (Ezek. 40:39–43). The idiom to eat at one's table indicated a special honor given to a person (1 Kg. 2:7). The word refers to a table where the king dined (1 Kgs. 4:27[5:7]).

7980. שָׁלַט ***šālaṭ:*** A verb meaning to domineer, to be master of. In the simple form, it takes the connotation of ruling. This can be ruling over people (Neh. 5:15; Eccl. 8:9); or possessions which one has been given control of (Eccl. 2:19). It can also mean to obtain power or to get mastery over something. Examples of this would be how sin can have power over a person (Ps. 119:133); or people can have power over each other (Esth. 9:1). This verb is also used in the causative form, meaning to give power (Eccl. 5:19[18]; 6:2). In these contexts, God gives people power over their lives, possessions, honor, and wealth. God is the only legitimate source of power, and all power flows from Him.

7981. שְׁלֵט ***š^elaṭ:*** An Aramaic verb meaning to have power, to rule over. It is found in the intensive and causative forms only. In the causative form, it means to make rule or to cause to rule, referring to someone in power who gives that power to another (Dan. 2:38, 48). In the intensive form, it may mean merely to have power in the sense of controlling other people (Dan. 3:27, 6:24[25]), or to rule or be a ruler. In this sense, it is used in the context of King Belshazzar, who promised that whoever could interpret his dream would become a ruler (Dan. 5:7, 16).

7982. שֶׁלֶט ***šeleṭ:*** A masculine noun meaning a shield. Most commonly, this word is used to refer to shields used for protection in battle. In Ezekiel 27:11, they were hung on walls; in Jeremiah 51:11, they were to be taken up as warriors prepared to defend themselves. Another context in which this word is used is in describing the gold shields that King David took from people he defeated (2 Sam. 8:7). They were then kept in the Temple and used when Jehoida presented Joash as king (2 Kgs. 11:10).

7983. שִׁלְטוֹן *šilṭôn:* A masculine noun meaning mastery. It can be used to mean powerful, as in the words of a king that are described as being supreme (Eccl. 8:4). It can also mean having power over. It is used in Ecclesiastes 8:8 to say that no one has power over the day of his or her death. This word carries the connotation of legitimate authority, not just power that persons claim they have or have taken from others. A king's words had legitimate authority, for he was the ruler of his people; and no one except God has legitimate authority over death.

7984. שִׁלְטוֹן *šilṭôn:* An Aramaic noun meaning a lord, a magistrate, an official. This noun is used only once in Daniel 3:2, where it is found at the end of a long list of officials whom King Nebuchadnezzar called together before him. This noun is the last word used and seems to be a catchall phrase to account for any official who was missed in the specific titles given before. Due to the lack of specificity, it would appear that this is a general noun used to name anyone who holds a position of authority.

7985. שָׁלְטָן *šolṭān:* An Aramaic masculine noun meaning dominion, sovereignty. Most frequently, this noun is used in conjunction with God, showing that He has dominion over everything that exists (Dan. 4:3[3:33]; 4:34[31]). His dominion is greater than that of a person's many ways, one being that it is an everlasting dominion that can never be destroyed (Dan. 7:14). This noun can also be used of kings (Dan. 4:22[19]). It was used in Daniel's dream of the four beasts to describe the dominion they have (Dan. 7:6, 12, 26). God both gives and takes away the dominion of all human rulers. Much less frequently, this word can be used in the concrete sense of a physical kingdom (Dan 6:26[27]).

7986. שַׁלֶּטֶת *šalleṭeṯ:* An adjective meaning impudent, brazen, domineering. It indicates an arrogant, insolent attitude of persons who care nothing about what others think of them (Ezek. 16:30).

7987. שְׁלִי *šeliy:* A masculine noun indicating quietness, privacy. Used in an adverbially sense, it means to do something in private, secretly, without witnesses, according to its context (2 Sam. 3:27).

7988. שִׁלְיָה *šilyāh:* I. A feminine noun indicating an afterbirth, the placenta. It refers to a temporary vascular organ developed during a mammal's gestation period to nourish the fetus and provide for the discharge of its wastes (Deut. 28:57).

II. A feminine noun meaning a young one; a child. It is taken by some translators to mean a child or newly born infant (KJV, Deut. 28:57).

7989. שַׁלִּיט ***šalliyṭ:*** An adjective meaning mastery, power. This could be used to describe power over anything, but it is used in a limited context in the Old Testament. With this meaning, it is only found in Ecclesiastes 8:8, where people are said to have no power over the wind. It can also be used as a noun meaning a ruler or one who has mastery (Gen. 42:6). Rulers can also be a cause of evil (Eccl. 10:5).

7990. שַׁלִּיט ***šalliyṭ:*** An Aramaic masculine adjective meaning mastery. It is commonly used of God and His sovereignty that gives Him mastery over everything. There is nothing that is not under His authority, including the kingdoms of people (Dan. 4:17[14]; 5:21). God's mastery covers everything that exists. This adjective can also be used in describing the power that kings have (Ezra 4:20); and the authority they can exercise (Ezra 7:24). This word can also be used as a noun meaning captain or one who has authority and mastery over others (Dan. 2:15).

7991. שָׁלִישׁ ***šāliyš:*** A masculine noun carrying many different meanings associated with the number three. First of all, it can be used to signify a measure, perhaps originally a third or an ephah. From the contexts in which it is used, it is clear the word stands for a large measure (Ps. 80:5[6]; Isa. 40:12). It is also used once as a noun for a type of musical instrument—perhaps a three-cornered one with strings, such as a lute. This instrument was played with songs of celebration (1 Sam. 18:6). Finally, this word can signify a particular type of high–ranking officer or the third man in a chariot during battle (Ex. 14:7; 2 Sam. 23:8; 2 Kgs. 9:25).

7992. שְׁלִישִׁי ***šᵉliyšiy,*** שָׁלִשִׁי ***šališiy:*** I. A masculine adjective meaning third in a series of three or more or a third part of something. It refers to any third in a series. Its feminine form is *šᵉliyšiṯ* and *šᵉlîšiyyah.* It indicates the third in any series of things (Gen. 1:13; 2:14). Its plural form means third also (1 Sam. 19:21), a third group of messengers (*mal'āḵîm šᵉlišîm*). The third day means the day after tomorrow (1 Sam. 20:5). With the definite article, it can mean a fraction or one-third of the whole (2 Sam. 18:2).

II. An adjective meaning third in a series or a third part of. With the definite article added, according to context, it refers to David's three greatest men, the three (2 Sam. 23:8, 18; NASB, captains). Its use in Ezekiel 42:3 indicates three stories or levels in the chambers of the Temple.

III. An adjective in the plural meaning thirty. The NASB reads thirty (men), a leading part of David's personal army. Not all ancient manuscripts read thirty here (2 Sam. 23:18).

IV. An adjective meaning three years old. This is combined with the word preceding it to form a proper noun of a city, Eglath-shelishiyah (Isa. 15:5; Jer. 48:34, NASB). But it is rendered as an adjective defining a heifer in other translations, a heifer three years old (Isa. 15:5; Jer. 48:34).

7993. שָׁלַךְ ***šālak̲:*** A verb meaning to throw, to cast. In the causative form, several different variations of meaning are associated with this verb. The basic meaning to cast or throw is found in Genesis 21:15 and Numbers 35:20. It can also mean to cast away in the sense of getting rid of something that hinders, such as sin (Ezek. 18:31); or fetters (Ps. 2:3). This verb is also used to describe God's rejection of someone (2 Kgs. 17:20; 24:20). In a good sense, God will sustain those who cast their cares on Him (Ps. 55:22[23]). In the passive causative form, this verb means to be cast, to be thrown or to be cast out. Usually, this is used in a negative sense, as when someone was cast out of his or her burial site (Isa. 14:19; Jer. 36:30); or when people were cast away because of their disobedience to God (Jer. 14:16). Yet it can also be used in a good sense. In Psalm 22:10[11], the writer says that from birth he had been cast on God. So this verb can have either positive or negative connotations.

7994. שָׁלָךְ ***šālak̲:*** A masculine noun meaning cormorant. It refers to a type of large, voracious, pelican-like diving bird not to be eaten by Israel, considered detestable and unclean (Lev. 11:17; Deut. 14:17).

7995. שַׁלֶּכֶת ***šalleke̲t̲:*** I. A feminine noun indicating the cutting down of a tree. It refers to the falling or cutting down of a tree (Isa. 6:13).

II. A feminine noun indicating a casting off of leaves. It refers to a tree's losing its leaves in the fall (Isa. 6:13).

7996. שַׁלֶּכֶת ***šalleke̲t̲:*** A proper noun Shallecheth. It refers to a gate on the west of the Temple (1 Chr. 26:16).

7997. שָׁלַל ***šālal:*** I. A verb meaning to pull or drain out. It is used of extracting some grain from a larger bundle of grain (Ruth 2:16).

II. A verb meaning to despoil, to plunder. It means to overcome someone or a group of persons and destroy their goods and take some of it for oneself. It is used of God's robbing or despoiling the strong (Ps. 76:5[6]). It was often an act of force and violence in war (Isa. 10:6; Jer. 50:10; Ezek. 26:12; 29:19; 38:12; Hab. 2:8; Zech. 2:8[12]). In its reflexive form, it means to turn oneself into prey, used of those who shun evil in a time when there is no justice (Isa. 59:15).

7998. שָׁלָל ***šālāl:*** A masculine noun referring to plunder, loot, spoils. It refers to what is taken by force or violence usually in war (Gen. 49:27; Ex. 15:9; Num. 31:11; Ps. 68:12[13]). Or it may be seized as an act of social and political aggression (Esth. 3:13; 8:11). Taking plunder or spoil was an act of aggression by the wicked on the weak or righteous (Prov. 1:13). It has a positive sense of prosperity or gain in certain contexts (Prov. 31:11). The Lord will make the nations plunder for His people in Zion (Zech. 2:9[13]; 14:1).

7999. שָׁלַם ***šālam:*** A verb meaning to be safe, to be completed. The primary meaning is to be safe or uninjured in mind or body (Job 8:6; 9:4). This word is normally used when God is keeping His people safe. In its simple form, this verb also means to be completed or to be finished. This could refer to something concrete such as a building (1 Kgs. 7:51); or things more abstract, such as plans (Job 23:14). Other meanings of this verb include to be at peace with another person (Ps. 7:4[5]); to make a treaty of peace (Josh. 11:19; Job 5:23); to pay, to give a reward (Ps. 62:12[13]); to restore, repay, or make retribution (Ex. 21:36; Ps. 37:21).

8000. שְׁלֵם ***šᵉlēm:*** An Aramaic verb meaning to complete, to finish. This word corresponds to the Hebrew verb *šālam* (7999). It refers to work being done, such as rebuilding the Temple in Jerusalem (Ezra 5:16). Closely related to this meaning is the secondary meaning, to make an end. In Daniel 5:26, this word is used to say that God would bring the days of Belshazzar's reign to an end. This word could also mean to restore in the sense of delivering something from captivity and returning it to the rightful owner. It was used when discussing the restoration of the temple furnishings in Jerusalem (Ezra 7:19).

8001. שְׁלָם ***šᵉlām:*** A masculine singular noun meaning peace. This word is most frequently used in the context of a greeting and may be used in both the singular and plural forms with the same meaning. As a greeting, these words signified a wish for peace, prosperity, and general good welfare to those who were being greeted. This seems to have been a common way to begin letters in ancient biblical times. In Nebuchadnezzar's letter to his subjects, he started by wishing prosperity to all his subjects (Dan. 4:1[3:31]); and in the letter which Tatnai sent to King Darius, he used this word as a greeting of well-wishing (Ezra 5:7).

8002. שֶׁלֶם ***šelem:*** A noun meaning thanksgiving offerings, also called peace offerings. These offerings were voluntary, given to God in thanks or in praise to Him. These offerings were first described in the book of Leviticus, and the word is used many times after that, especially in the remaining sections of the Law dealing with sacrifices (Lev. 3:1, 7:11; Num. 7:17). This noun is also used in the plural form, which has a wider significance (Amos 5:22). In this context, the thanksgiving offerings were offered in great distress, not out of thankful hearts. They were offered to try to gain God's favor, but God rejected them because they were not given out of love and thankfulness to Him.

8003. שָׁלֵם šālēm: An adjective meaning full, complete, safe, whole, peaceful. This adjective has several uses when it means complete, safe, unharmed, natural. Moses instructed the Israelites to build the altar on Mount Ebal of natural, unhewn or whole stones (Deut. 27:6; Josh. 8:31). Stones that were whole, finished, and from a rock quarry could be used to build the Temple (1 Kgs. 6:7). The word describes the work on the Lord's Temple as finished, complete (2 Chr. 8:16). The word describes weights that had to be solid, accurate, and fair for use in the marketplace (Deut. 25:15; Prov. 11:1); it described wages paid as full, complete, rich (Ruth 2:12). It described Jacob traveling safely to the city of Shechem (Gen. 33:18). When referring to groups of people, it means entire or whole, such as whole communities taken captive in Amos's day (Amos 1:6, 9). Something could be described as not yet complete or full; the sin of the Amorites was not yet complete (Gen. 15:16).

The word connotes the idea of whole or undivided; the hearts of the Israelites were to be wholly centered on the Lord and His decrees (1 Kgs. 8:61), but Solomon's heart was not so committed (1 Kgs. 11:4; 2 Kgs. 20:3; Isa. 38:3).

The word means peaceful or peaceable when used of persons in certain relationships; the people of Shechem believed the Israelites intended to live in a peaceful relationship with them (Gen. 34:21).

8004. שָׁלֵם šālēm: A proper noun designating Salem, a city where Melchizedek was high priest and king. The name means "peace" and is an early reference to Jerusalem. Abraham paid tithes to Melchizedek (Gen. 14:18; cf. Heb. 7:1–2), and he blessed Abraham. He served as a pattern for the priesthood of Jesus. The God of Israel, the Lord, dwelt in the city after Israel took it over and the Temple was dedicated by Solomon (Ps. 76:2[3]).

8005. שִׁלֵּם šillēm: A masculine singular noun meaning retribution, requital, recompense. It is used when speaking of a deserved punishment, in the sense of a repayment for whatever wrong was done by a person (Deut. 32:35). In addition, it can also signify rewards for good that has been done. The idea behind this word is that it is a reward or punishment that is deserved and is in conjunction with what was done beforehand. Ultimately, only God has the power of retribution. It is His right only to avenge wrongdoers and give those persons what they deserve or to reward those who have done right.

8006. שִׁלֵּם šillēm: A proper noun designating Shillem (Gen. 46:24; Num. 26:49; 1 Chr. 7:13).

8007. שַׂלְמָא śalmā’: A proper noun designating Salma (1 Chr. 2:11). It is the same as Salmon (8009) and Salmon (8012).

8008. שַׂלְמָה ***śalmāh:*** A masculine noun referring to a cloak, clothes, a robe. It refers to a major piece of clothing, a mantle, that was valuable and necessary in ancient Israel (Ex. 22:9[8]); in a pledge, it could not be retained overnight (Ex. 22:26:[25]); Deut. 24:13). It could be a long, warm garment used as a blanket at night to keep warm. These garments did not wear out during Israel's stay in the wilderness (Deut. 29:5[4]). It may refer to a covering for sheep (1 Kgs. 10:25). The Lord uses light as a cloak to cover Himself (Ps. 104:2). A cloak could be perfumed and spiced to make it smell amorous (Song 4:11).

8009. שַׂלְמָה ***śalmāh:*** A proper noun designating Salmon (Ruth 4:20). It is the same as Salma (8007) and Salmon (8012).

8010. שְׁלֹמֹה ***š^{e}lōmōh:*** A proper noun designating Solomon, the second most renowned king of all Israel during the monarchy. He was David's son through Bathsheba. He was born in Jerusalem (2 Sam. 5:14). The Lord instructed Nathan the prophet that the child was to be named Jedidiah, meaning "beloved by the Lord" (2 Sam. 12:24, 25). David named him Solomon. The Lord's special name indicated His continued love for David's descendants (2 Sam. 7). Solomon became king in 970 B.C. and ruled forty years. He was known for his wisdom, but in his old age, he was led away from serving the Lord (1 Kgs. 3:1–28). He organized Israel effectively, completed many building projects, including his own palace and the Lord's Temple (1 Kgs. 6; 7). He dedicated the Temple, and the Lord appeared to him (1 Kgs. 8; 9) for a second time (cf. 1 Kgs. 3:4–15). His first and most important request from the Lord was for wisdom to rule his people (1 Kgs. 3:4–15). His wisdom was the greatest the world had ever seen (1 Kgs. 4:29–34; 10). He built many other projects, and his wisdom attracted visitors from the ends of the earth (1 Kgs. 10) as his greatness and wealth increased (1 Kgs. 10:14–29).

After Solomon's apostasy due to his pagan wives, the Lord raised up many adversaries to harass and bring him down (1 Kgs. 11:14–40). Solomon's oppressive use of taxation, state-forced work teams, and heavy tribute, especially in northern Israel, resulted in a state of rebellion by the time he died. Solomon's name is etched on the Wisdom Literature of the Old Testament (Proverbs, Ecclesiastes, Song of Solomon).

8011. שִׁלֻּמָה ***šillumāh:*** A feminine singular noun meaning retribution, punishment, penalty. This word has negative meanings when it is used in Scripture, for example, persons were punished or repaid for whatever evil they did. The word does not seem to have anything to do with repayment in the sense of receiving rewards for doing what is right, but this could be because of its limited use in the Old Testament. The righteous remained safe in God's protection, but the wicked received their punishment before the eyes of the righteous (Ps. 91:8). God Himself is the giver of this retribution.

8012. שַׂלְמוֹן ***śalmôn:*** A proper noun designating Salmon (Ruth 4:21). It is the same as Salma (8007) and Salmon (8009).

8013. שְׁלֹמוֹת ***šᵉlōmôṯ:*** A proper noun designating Shelomoth, Shelomith:

A. A Levite, son of Izhar (1 Chr. 24:22). It is the same as Shelomith (8019,D).

B. A Gershonite Levite (1 Chr. 23:9). It is the same as Shelomith (8019,C).

C. A Levite descended from Eliezer (1 Chr. 26:25, 26, 28). It is the same as Shelomith (8019,E).

8014. שַׂלְמַי ***śalmay,*** שַׁלְמַי ***šalmay:*** A proper noun designating Shalmai (Ezra 2:46; Neh. 7:48).

8015. שְׁלֹמִי ***šᵉlōmiy:*** A proper noun designating Shelomi (Num. 34:27).

8016. שִׁלֵּמִי ***šillēmiy:*** A proper noun designating Shillemite (Num. 26:49).

8017. שְׁלֻמִיאֵל ***šᵉlumiy'ēl:*** A proper noun designating Shelumiel (Num. 1:6; 2:12; 7:36, 41; 10:19).

8018. שֶׁלֶמְיָה ***šelemyāh,*** שֶׁלֶמְיָהוּ ***šelemyāhû:*** A proper noun designating Shelemiah:

A. A gatekeeper (1 Chr. 26:14).

B. A son of Cushi (Jer. 36:14).

C. Son of Abdeel (Jer. 36:26).

D. The father of Jehucal (Jer. 37:3; 38:1).

E. The father of Irijah (Jer. 37:13).

F. Son of Bani (Ezra 10:39).

G. Another son of Bani (Ezra 10:41).

H. The father of Hananiah (Neh. 3:30).

I. A priest inNehemiah's day (Neh. 13:13).

8019. שְׁלוֹמִית ***šᵉlōmiyṯ:*** A proper noun designating Shelomith:

A. A Danite woman (Lev. 24:11).

B. Daughter of Zerubbabel (1 Chr. 3:19).

C. A Gershonite Levite (1 Chr. 23:9). It is the same as Shelomith (8013,B).

D. A Levite, son of Izhar (1 Chr. 23:18). It is the same as Shelomith (8013,A).

E. A Levite descended from Eliezer (1 Chr. 26:25; 26, 28). It is the same as Shelomith (8013,C).

F. Son of Rehoboam (2 Chr. 11:20).

G. The head of a family (Ezra 8:10).

8020. שַׁלְמַן ***šalman:*** A proper noun designating Shalman (Hos. 10:14).

8021. שַׁלְמֹן ***šalmon:*** A masculine noun meaning a gift. It is used only in its plural form of *šalmōniym*. This word is not used to describe simple gifts given out of goodwill but gifts given as bribes to try to sway persons in authority to do what the giver wants them to do (Isa. 1:23). These bribes are accepted only by corrupt people and end up corrupting people even further. Those who are totally corrupt even seek out bribes. Along with these bribes went the idea of a lack of justice and righteousness as a result of God's will not being done in those matters.

8022. שַׁלְמַנְאֶסֶר ***šalman'eser:*** A proper noun designating Shalmaneser, the Assyrian king (727–722 B.C.) usually identified as the one who destroyed northern Israel (722 B.C.) and took them into exile into various nations and cities of the Middle East (2 Kg. 17:6). Hoshea, northern Israel's last king, had stopped paying tribute to Shalmaneser. He then transported foreigners into Israel to live and till the land. He besieged Samaria for three years. Shalmaneser I's son Sargon II reigned in his place.

8023. שִׁלֹנִי ***šilōniy:*** A proper noun designating Shiloni (Neh. 11:5).

8024. שֵׁלָנִי ***šēlāniy:*** A proper noun designating a Shelanite, a descendant of Shelah (7956) (Num. 26:20; Neh. 11:5).

8025. שָׁלַף ***šālap̱:*** A verb meaning to draw out, to take off. It refers to the act of unsheathing a sword, drawing it from its sheath (Num. 22:23, 31; Josh. 5:13; 1, especially in a legal situation (Ruth 4:7, 8). It refers to the coming out or the germinating of grass (Ps. 129:6).

8026. שֶׁלֶף ***šelep̱:*** A proper noun designating Sheleph (Gen. 10:26; 1 Chr. 1:20).

8027. שָׁלַשׁ ***šālaš:*** A verb meaning to do a third time; to divide into three parts; to be three years old. It is used in its passive intensive stem to describe something that has reached three years of age (Gen. 15:9; 1 Sam. 1:24, in variant). It describes dividing land into three areas or sections (Deut. 19:3). It is used of staying three days in a location (1 Sam. 20:19); and of doing something three times or a third time (1 Kgs. 18:34). It describes something as having those features (Ezek. 42:6).

8028. שֵׁלֶשׁ ***šēleš:*** A proper noun designating Shelesh (1 Chr. 7:35).

8029. שִׁלֵּשׁ ***šillēš:*** An adjective meaning a third. In context it refers to a third generation in a family (Gen. 50:23; Ex. 20:5; 34:7; Num. 14:18; Deut. 5:9); the word generation is understood in context.

8030. שִׁלְשָׁה ***šilšāh:*** A proper noun designating Shilshah (1 Chr. 7:37).

8031. שָׁלִשָׁה ***šālišāh:*** A masculine proper noun Shalishah. It indicates a land or small area named Shalishah. Saul passed through it looking for donkeys (1 Sam. 9:4). This place is about sixteen miles northeast of Jerusalem.

8032. שִׁלְשׁוֹם **šilšôm,** שִׁלְשֹׁם **šilšōm:** An adverb indicating before, in times past, formerly. It is always found combined into an idiom with another word. It literally means three days ago, the day before yesterday, but its meaning has become generalized as well to mean formerly, in time past (Gen. 31:2, 5; Deut. 4:42: *kiṯmôl šilšom*). In Exodus 4:10, the phase *gam miṯmôl gam miššilšōm* occurs, meaning literally, neither yesterday or the day before yesterday, which as an idiom means not recently or anytime before that.

8033. שָׁם **šām:** An adverb meaning there, where, in that direction. It indicates a place or the place where: there (Gen. 2:8, 12); where (Job 39:30); where, when preceded with the relative *'ašer* (Gen. 2:11; Ex. 20:21); to where, thither after motion verbs (Deut. 1:37; Judg. 19:15). It often has a *he* (ה) on the end indicating motion there, to a place (Gen. 19:20; Deut. 1:38). With *min* (4480) on the front, it means from there (*miššām*) (Gen. 2:10; 11:8, 9; 12:8). It can express the source or origin of something, e.g., man from the ground (Gen. 3:23); Philistines from . . . (Gen. 10:14; Judg. 19:18); a goat from the flock (Gen. 27:9).

8034. שֵׁם **šēm:** A masculine noun meaning a name, fame. It is what specifically identifies a person or anything: God's name, "I am who I am" (Ex. 3:15); or the name Yahweh, LORD, which is in small capital letters in English (Ps. 5:11[12]); a person's name (Gen. 3:20); names of animals (Gen. 2:19). To make a name for oneself means to attain a renowned reputation (Gen. 11:4; 2 Sam. 8:13); as when God made Abraham's name great (Gen. 12:2). To become famous is to have one's name spread through the land (Ezek. 16:14). To have a good name is to have a good character, a good reputation (Eccl. 7:1). The expression the name (*haššem*) refers to the Lord, Yahweh. The Lord's name means to be blessed, praised (Job 1:21). A name may serve as a memorial or monument (Isa. 55:13). The phrase *yaḏ wašem* means a remembrance, a memorial (Isa. 56:5) and serves today in modern Israel as the name of a museum built to remember the victims of the Holocaust or Shoah. The names of other gods were forbidden in Israel, i.e., the recognition of them (Ex. 23:13; Josh. 23:7). Israel's God was to be called on to act according to His revealed name (Isa. 48:9; Jer. 14:7, 21; Ezek. 20:9, 14). To continue the name of a man, a family line gave him a kind of ongoing life in his sons (Deut. 25:7; 2 Sam. 8:13).

8035. שֵׁם **šēm:** A proper noun designating Shem, the first son of Noah. God established his rainbow covenant with Noah and his sons and their families (Gen. 6:18). They survived the flood (Gen. 7:13). The human race multiplied from these persons after the flood (Gen. 9:18, 19). Shem was blessed above his other brothers who were to be subordinate to him and his descendants. Shem fathered many peoples and was the ancestor of Abraham and Eber (Gen. 10:21–31; 11:10–32). The blessings of Shem were worked out most fully, in a special way in the descendants of Abraham.

8036. שֻׁם šum: An Aramaic masculine noun meaning a name. Names are important. Names indicate the specific identity of a person, a (god) God, or a thing. Prophets prophesied only in the name of the God of Israel (Ezra 5:1). The names of returning exiles were important because they helped indicate what tribe they belonged to in Israel (Ezra 5:4, 10, 14). God caused His name to dwell in Jerusalem, His holy name that stood for His presence (Ezra 6:12). The name of God is always to be blessed (Dan. 2:20). Daniel's name had been changed to Belteshazzar, a pagan name, to indicate his place in Babylonian society (Dan. 2:26; 4:8[5], 19[16]; 5:12).

8037. שַׁמָּא šammā': A proper noun designating Shamma (1 Chr. 7:37).

8038. שֶׁמְאֵבֶר šem'ēḇer: A proper noun designating Shemeber (Gen. 14:2).

8039. שִׁמְאָה šim'āh: A proper noun designating Shimeah, the same as Shimeam (8043) (1 Chr. 8:32).

8040. שְׂמֹאול śᵉmō'wl, שְׂמֹאל śᵉmō'l: A masculine noun meaning left hand, left side, north. It indicates directions to the left (Gen. 13:9; Ex. 14:22). It indicates northward in some contexts: with *'el* preceding (Josh. 19:27); by itself (Isa. 54:3); with *'el* preceding and with a suffix, it means north of (suffix) (Ezek. 16:46). With *yaḏ* preceding the phrase, it means left hand (Judg. 3:21; 7:20; Jon. 4:11). The word takes suffixes, e.g., *śᵉmō'lô* means his left hand (Gen. 48:13, 14). Traditionally, the direction left meant wrong, bad, evil (Eccl. 10:2). To raise both the left and right hand toward heaven was part of a ritual for making a vow to God (Dan. 12:7).

8041. שָׂמַאל śim'ēl: A verb meaning to go to the left; to use the left hand. It indicates movement to the left, toward the left hand (Gen. 13:9; Ezek. 21:16[21]). It is used of turning left or right, that is, deviating from a given path or set of instructions (2 Sam. 14:19; Isa. 30:21). It indicates the use of one's left hand (1 Chr. 12:2).

8042. שְׂמָאלִי śᵉmā'liy: An adjective meaning left, on the left; the north. In Israel for a person facing east, the left was literally toward the north. It defines the left palm or hand as opposed to the right (Lev. 14:15, 16, 26, 27). The left pillar, the north pillar of the temple, was named Boaz, in it is power (1 Kgs. 7:21). A house may have a left side (2 Kgs. 11:11).

The prophet was commanded to lie on his left side (Ezek. 4:4).

8043. שִׁמְאָם šim'ām: A proper noun designating Shimeam, the same as Shimeah (8039) (1 Chr. 9:38).

8044. שַׁמְגַּר šamgar: A proper noun designating Shamgar, a minor judge in Israel. He was the son of Anath. He killed six hundred Philistines with an oxgoad, a mighty deliverance for Israel (Judg. 3:31).

8045. שָׁמַד šāmad: A verb meaning to be destroyed. This verb is not used in its simple form and is only used in the passive and causative stems of the verb. The primary passive meaning is to be destroyed, to be exterminated, or to be annihilated, referring to individual people, households, or nations (Gen. 34:30; Prov. 14:11; Ezek. 32:12). It can also signify the devastation of land and places (Hos. 10:8). The causative forms have the same root meanings as the passive forms. It can mean to annihilate, to exterminate people (Deut. 1:27, 2:22); or to destroy objects such as cities, fortresses, or idols (Isa. 23:11; Mic. 5:14[13]). The difference between these two verb forms lies in who is destroying and who is being destroyed.

8046. שְׁמַד š^{e}mad: An Aramaic verb meaning to destroy. The word corresponds to the Hebrew verb *šāmad* (8045). It signifies more than simply ruining or destroying something but described a destruction that could not be reversed or fixed. Its connotations go far beyond mere destruction to mean to consume, to destroy completely without hope of restoration. In Daniel 7:26, this verb was used to signify a total destruction of a ruler's power. This verb is used only to describe a final destruction. God is the power behind this ultimate destruction.

8047. שַׁמָּה šāmmāh: A feminine singular noun meaning ruin, astonishment. The primary meaning is that of ruin and wasting. This noun can be used to refer to evil people and their households who deserved to be destroyed because of their sins (Ps. 73:19; Isa. 5:9); also of land, towns, and buildings that were destroyed as a result of the evil people who lived there (Jer. 2:15). A second meaning of astonishment, dismay, and horror is not clearly related to the primary meaning, but it is used to describe feelings toward Israel and its cities in their times of disobedience. Israel is seen as a horror, an object of scorn to all who saw her (Deut. 28:37; Jer. 19:8). It is also used to describe the extreme dismay people can feel at seeing destruction, a horror that fills persons (Jer. 8:21).

8048. שַׁמָּה šammāh: A proper noun designating Shammah:

A. An Edomite chief, son of Reuel (Gen. 36:13, 17; 1 Chr. 1:37).

B. The third son of Jesse (1 Sam. 16:9; 17:13).

C. Son of Agee the Hararite (2 Sam. 23:11, 33).

D. One of David's mighty men (2 Sam. 23:25).

8049. שַׁמְהוּת ***šamhûṯ:*** A proper noun designating Shamhuth (1 Chr. 27:8).

8050. שְׁמוּאֵל ***šᵉmû'ēl:*** A proper noun designating Samuel:

A. A man of the tribe of Simeon. He was the son of Ammihud (Num. 34:20).

B. A man from the tribe of Issachar, a head of a family (1 Chr. 7:2).

C. The last judge of Israel. He anointed Saul and David as kings (1 Sam. 9:1–27; 16:1–13) in Israel. His name means "name of God" or "head of God." He was born to Hannah who dedicated him to the Lord (1 Sam. 1:21–28). He was a special child who grew up with the favor of God and people on him (1 Sam. 2:26). He served as a prophet, priest, and judge in Israel. He served all Israel (1 Sam. 4:1) for the Lord had called him (1 Sam. 3:10). He fearlessly spoke the Lord's word to priests or kings (1 Sam. 3:15–20; 15:17–33) or people (1 Sam. 8:10–22; 12). He was the key transition figure from the time of the judges to the kingship. He, however, warned the people about clamoring for a king and the oppressive nature of kingship. When he died, he was buried in Ramah ("height"). In an unusual appearance, he spoke once more from the grave to Saul, condemning Saul sternly and prophesying his imminent death at the hands of the Philistines (1 Sam. 28:1–20).

8051. שַׁמּוּעַ ***šammûa':*** A proper noun designating Shammua:

A. Son of David (2 Sam. 5:14; 1 Chr. 14:4).

B. A Reubenite (Num. 13:4).

C. A Levite (Neh. 11:17).

D. Head of a Levite family (Neh. 12:18).

8052. שְׁמוּעָה ***šᵉmû'āh:*** A feminine noun referring to a report; news; a rumor. Literally, it means what is heard, a passive participle from *šāma'*, to hear, to understand. It refers to a report or announcement of news, a report of something, even a rumor (1 Sam. 2:24; 4:19; 2 Sam. 4:4; 13:30). Daniel uses the plural form of the word, rumors (Dan. 11:44). It indicates what is heard by a prophet, the message, the prophesy (Isa. 28:9, 19; 53:1); what is heard (Obad. 1:1).

8053. שָׁמוּר ***šāmûr:*** A proper noun designating Shamur, which stands in place of the name Shamur (8069,III) in 1 Chronicles 24:24.

8054. שַׁמּוֹת ***šammôṯ:*** A proper noun designating Shammoth (1 Chr. 11:27).

8055. שָׂמַח ***śāmaḥ:*** A verb meaning to rejoice; to be joyful, to be glad; to gloat. It describes a state and agitation of rejoicing, of being happy: of people (1 Sam. 11:9); of tribes of Israel (Deut. 33:18); of God rejoicing in His works (Ps. 104:31); of people rejoicing in the Lord Himself (Deut. 12:12; Ps. 32:11). It takes on the sense of making others rejoice, to be glad in its intensive stem (Jer. 20:15); making people rejoice the heart of others (Ps. 19:8[9]). Wine can gladden the hearts of persons (Eccl. 10:19). God gladdens His people with His presence (Isa. 56:7); but also their enemies when He judges Israel (Ps. 89:42[43]). Although the word is used of all rejoicing, it is found most often in Psalms and describes religious and spiritual rejoicing (Ps. 5:11[12]; 9:2[3]; 14:7; 16:9; 19:8[9], etc.; but also 1 Sam. 2:1; Deut. 12:7; Joel 2:23, etc.).

8056. שָׂמֵחַ *śāmēaḥ:* An adjective meaning glad, happy, many, joyful. Its feminine form is *śᵉmēḥāh;* its plural form is *śᵉmēḥîm.* It means to be filled with joy, to be exceedingly glad. The blessings of the Lord lead to great joy (Deut. 16:15, *'aḵśameaḥ*). Anointing Israel's king was cause for great joy (1 Kgs. 1:40, 45). Joy comes from having children (Ps. 113:9). God's people rejoice for what He does for them (Ps. 126:3). The wicked are perverted so that they are joyful at evil (Prov. 2:14; 17:5). A state and attitude of joy makes one's face appear healthy (Prov. 15:13). It may be rendered as pleased or happy in some contexts (Eccl. 2:10).

8057. שִׂמְחָה *śimḥāh:* A feminine noun meaning joy, rejoicing, gladness, pleasure. It refers to the reality, the experience and manifestation of joy and gladness. It refers to a celebration of something with joyful and cheerful activities (Gen. 31:27). It is practically equivalent to the Israelites' days of feasting and celebrating over their God and His blessings (Num. 10:10; Neh. 8:12; Zech. 8:19). The Israelites were expected to worship and serve their God with joy (Deut. 28:47). God's salvation consists of restoring or creating rejoicing in His people (Ps. 51:8[10]). God even gives a person a glad heart in the toils of this earthly life (Eccl. 5:20[19]). One's wedding day is a day of rejoicing (Song 3:11). It refers to great celebration and joy at conquering one's enemy (Judg. 16:23). The joy and gladness of the wicked does not last forever (Job 20:5). The Lord can remove rejoicing from His people (Isa. 16:10; Joel 1:16).

8058. שָׁמַט *šāmaṭ:* A verb meaning to throw down, to cancel, to release; to stumble; to let fall. It indicates letting the land lie free, untilled (Ex. 23:11). It is used in its absolute participial form as a command, shall release, will release (a debt) (Deut. 15:2). It means to knock something over, e.g., the ark (2 Sam. 6:6; 1 Chr. 13:9). It is used of tossing something down (2 Kgs. 9:33); in a figurative sense, it means removed from power (Ps. 141:6). It indicates letting go of something, losing it. In context Israel loses her inheritance from the Lord, gives it up under force (Jer. 17:4).

8059. שְׁמִטָּה *šᵉmiṭṭāh:* A feminine noun meaning a remission, a release, a suspension. This word signifies the cancellation of a debt that was owed to another person. This was a debt which a person would, under ordinary circumstances, be obligated to pay back. In Israel, at the end of every seven years, the people were to release and forgive their fellow people from debts owed to them. This word was used in this context of the seventh year to show that the debtor was released from any obligation to pay back what had been loaned to him before that time (Deut. 15:1, 2, 9; 31:10). In the Old Testament, this noun was used only in the context of forgiving debts at the end of every seven years.

8060. שַׁמַּי ***šammay:*** A proper noun designating Shammai:

A. Son of Onam (1 Chr. 2:28, 32).

B. Son of Rekem (1 Chr. 2:44, 45).

C. Son of Mered (1 Chr. 4:17).

8061. שְׁמִידָע ***šᵉmiydāʿ:*** A proper noun designating Shemida (Num. 26:32; Josh. 17:2; 1 Chr. 7:19).

8062. שְׁמִידָעִי ***šᵉmiydāʿiy:*** A proper noun designating Shemidaite (Num. 26:32).

8063. שְׂמִיכָה ***śᵉmiykāh:*** I. A feminine noun indicating a mantle, a covering. It describes a loose, sleeveless coat but also anything that serves to cloak, envelop, or conceal, such as a cloak, a rug, a blanket, or a covering (Judg. 4:18).

II. A feminine noun meaning a rug. It refers to a rug used to hide or cover Sisera (Judg. 4:18). The context does not fix the meaning of the word exactly nor do its root letters.

8064. שָׁמַיִם ***šāmayim:*** A masculine noun meaning sky, heaven, abode, firmament, air, stars. Although the word is plural or dual in form, it can be translated into English as singular or plural depending on the context. The word describes everything God made besides the earth: God made the heavens of the universe (Gen. 1:1; 14:19); the firmament or expanse which He created around the earth was named sky or heaven as well (Gen. 1:8). He stretched out the heavens (Isa. 40:22); creating them (Isa. 42:5; 45:18).

The heavens that humans observe with their senses are indicated by this word. The stars are part of the heavens (Gen. 15:5) and are personified in some cases (Judg. 5:20); the sun and the moon, along with the stars, make up a major part of the hosts of heaven (Deut. 4:19). Unfortunately, these things were worshiped as gods by even the Israelites (Jer. 8:2). The heavens became a source of knowing the future and life in general, for scanners of the heavens and astrologers searched the heavens for signs (Isa. 47:13). A favorite pagan deity was the Queen of Heaven whom the people worshiped (Jer. 7:18; 44:17). God created waters above and below the heavens (Gen. 1:8, 9). The clouds are a feature of the sky (Gen. 8:2; Judg. 5:4; 1 Kgs. 18:45; Job 26:13). The word indicates the total inhabited earth when it speaks of from under heaven, as when the Amalekites were to be destroyed from under heaven (Gen. 6:17; Ex. 17:14). The teacher of Ecclesiastes spoke of examining everything under heaven, i.e., everything done in the world in which humans live (Eccl. 1:13; 2:3; 3:1); birds and other fowl fly in the sky (Gen. 1:20). In God's new world, there will be a new heaven and a new earth (Isa. 65:17; 66:22).

The invisible heavens are the abode of God. Heaven is the Lord's throne, the earth is the resting place of His feet—a beautiful metaphor of God's sovereignty over the universe (Isa. 66:1). He extends the heavens as the tent roof of the universe (Isa. 40:22); He dwells in heaven (1 Kgs. 8:30, 32); yet He is not contained in even the heaven of heavens, the most exclusive part of the heavens (1 Kgs. 8:27).

Heaven describes the place from which God operates: He calls to people from heaven (Gen. 21:17; 22:11). The Ten Commandments were spoken from heaven (Ex. 20:22; Neh. 9:13). He sent down manna from heaven for His people in the desert (Ex. 16:4). He is not merely a dweller in heaven, but He is the God of heaven (Gen. 24:3; 2 Chr. 36:23; Ezra 1:2). The heavens grow old and pass away, but God is eternal (Job 14:12; Isa. 13:10; 65:17). Satan aspired to usurp God's reign in heaven and was cast out (Isa. 14:12, 13). Elijah the prophet, because he faithfully followed the Lord, was taken up into heaven in a whirlwind (2 Kgs. 2:1, 11).

8065. שְׁמַיִן ***šemayin:*** An Aramaic noun meaning sky, heavens. This word has several different connotations, but the basic meaning is that of the sky (Dan. 4:11[8]; 7:2). Reaching beyond the simple meaning of sky, this word also referred to heaven, the dwelling place of God that is much higher than any other place (Dan. 2:28; 4:34[31]). The heavens are great not because of what they are but because of who lives there. Not only does God dwell in heaven, but His messengers, the angels, also dwell there and are sent down to earth to do His work (Dan. 4:13[10]). This word also signifies the whole universe where God showed His mighty signs and made His works known to all (Dan. 6:27[28]). It is combined to form phrases such as the God of heaven (Ezra 5:11, 12; Dan. 2:18, 19, 28, 37, 44); birds of the sky (Dan. 2:38); winds of heaven (Dan. 7:2, 13). This noun corresponds to the Hebrew noun *šāmayim* (8064), that is very similar in meaning.

8066. שְׁמִינִי ***š^e^miyniy:*** An adjective meaning eighth. It is an ordinal number that points out the eighth of something in a series: the eighth day (Ex. 22:30[29]; Lev. 9:1); the eighth year (1 Kgs. 6:38); the eighth month (1 Kgs. 12:32).

8067. שְׁמִינִית ***š^e^miyniyṯ:*** A feminine noun used as a musical term; it may signify an instrument or an octave. Its meaning is not clear. The NASB has "lyres tuned to the sheminith" (1 Chr. 15:21); NIV, "according to sheminith" (probably a musical term); KJV, harps on the Sheminith. It occurs in Psalm 6:title(1); 12:title(1). Perhaps it refers to an eight-stringed lyre (NASB) or tune (KJV).

8068. שָׁמִיר ***šāmiyr:*** I. A masculine noun referring to a brier. It refers to briers or thorns, always an unwanted feature of plants growing wild (Isa. 5:6; 7:23–25; 32:13). It is said that wickedness consumes even briers and thorns in its destructive capacity (Isa. 9:18[17]).

II. A masculine noun referring to a flint stone, a diamond. It refers to a precious stone with an extremely hard point (Jer. 17:1). It seems to refer to flint, an extremely strong and hard stone; in context it is used in a simile of Ezekiel's head being hard like flint (Ezek. 3:9). It describes Israel's hearts, hardened like flint, toward God's words and laws (Zech. 7:12).

8069. שָׁמִיר ***šāmiyr:*** A proper noun designating Shamir:

A. A town in Judah (Josh. 15:48).

B. A town in Ephraim (Judg. 10:1, 2).

C. A Levite in David's day (1 Chr. 24:24).

8070. שְׁמִירָמוֹת ***šᵉmiyrāmôṯ:*** A proper noun designating Shemiramoth:

A. A Levite harpist in David's day (1 Chr. 15:18, 20; 16:5).

B. A Levite teacher in Jehoshaphat's day (2 Chr. 17:8).

8071. שִׂמְלָה ***śimlāh:*** A feminine noun meaning clothing, a garment. It refers to a relatively large garment, either an external garment heavy enough to sleep in (Ex. 22:27[26]); or a blanket large enough to cover a person lying on a bed (Gen. 9:23). A change of garments could indicate a new beginning or getting ready for travel (Gen. 35:2). It refers to clothes in general (Gen. 37:34; Deut. 22:5).

8072. שַׂמְלָה ***śamlāh:*** A proper noun designating Samlah (Gen. 36:36, 37; 1 Chr. 1:47, 48).

8073. שַׁמְלַי ***šamlay:*** A proper noun designating Shamlai stands in the place of Shalmai (8014) in Ezra 2:46.

8074. שָׁמֵם ***šāmēm:*** A verb meaning to be desolated, to be destroyed. The desolation or destruction that this verb refers to can be used of both people (2 Sam. 13:20; Lam. 1:13, 16); and places (Lev. 26:31, 32; Isa. 61:4; Ezek. 35:12) and is used in both its simple and causative forms. A second meaning of this verb, which is extremely common, is to be appalled or astonished and is used in the simple, passive, and passive causative stems (Job 18:20; Isa. 52:14; Jer. 18:16). The connection between these two meanings is not entirely clear; yet they are both used with great frequency. When this verb is used in the second meaning, it often describes a person's reaction on seeing desolation and destruction. For example, in 1 Kings 9:8, the reaction of people to a destroyed land was described with this verb. A much less common use of this verb is in the reflexive stem. Here it meant to be disheartened or dismayed (Ps. 143:4).

8075. שְׁמַם *šᵉmam:* An Aramaic verb meaning to be astonished, appalled. It means to be taken by surprise, dumbfounded at something, as well as amazed (Dan. 4:19[16]).

8076. שָׁמֵם *šāmēm:* A masculine adjective meaning ruined, wasted, desolate. This adjective corresponds to the verb *šāmēm* (8074). This adjective can be used to describe both land and objects that have been destroyed. The connotations here are of an extreme destruction that has lasting effects and causes all people to stand up and take notice of what has happened. When Jerusalem fell, the Temple was torn apart and utterly destroyed, and this adjective was used to describe the condition of the Temple (Dan. 9:17). In Jeremiah 12:11, it is also used to prophesy what the land would be like after the fall of Jerusalem. This adjective paints a picture of harsh destruction. In these contexts, this destruction is indicative of God's judgment on His people.

8077. שִׁמָמָה *šimmāh,* שְׁמָמָה *šᵉmāmāh:* A feminine singular noun meaning desolation, waste. This noun can be used to refer to many things such as land, cities, or houses (Ex. 23:29; Lev. 26:33; Isa. 1:7). Most often it is used in conjunction with a passage describing what did happen to the land of Israel after God judged His people and sent them into exile. This shows the totality of the destruction that Israel endured. Nothing was to be saved from this destruction. Fields and vineyards were turned into wastelands and desolate fields after God's judgment (Jer. 12:10). God allowed such desolation as a punishment for the sins of His people because they refused to repent. This punishment could even fall on people of other nations, such as the Edomites (Ezek. 33:28, 29; 35:3).

8078. שִׁמָּמוֹן *šimmāmôn:* A masculine noun indicating astonishment; horror, despair. It refers to a state of shock and trepidation at what is happening. In context it describes what was taking place in a besieged Jerusalem and land of Israel (Ezek. 4:16; 12:19).

8079. שְׂמָמִית *śᵉmāmiyt:* I. A feminine noun meaning a lizard. It describes a reptile with a long, slender body and tail and four short legs, often with scaly skin (Prov. 30:28). It probably refers to a gecko. It is able to inhabit unexpected places through stealth.

II. A feminine noun meaning a spider. Early translators understood this word to refer to a spider (Prov. 30:28).

8080. שָׁמַן ***šāman,*** שָׁמֵן ***šāmēn:*** A verb meaning to be fat; to become fat. It describes the process of becoming fat or being fat (Deut. 32:15; Neh. 9:25; Jer. 5:28). It means figuratively in several of these references to become surfeited, self-satisfied, lazy (Neh. 9:25); insensitive to God's will and plans (Deut. 32:15). Israel's heart became "fat," unreceptive, insensitive (Isa. 6:10).

8081. שֶׁמֶן ***šemen:*** A masculine noun meaning fat, oil. This word has a wide range of figurative meanings relating to richness and plenty. Most simply, it is used of food, relating to feasts of good, rich food (Isa. 25:6). It is also used frequently of oil. This can be oil used for food and cooking (Deut. 8:8; 32:13); for oil which was used to anoint holy objects or kings (Ex. 30:25; 1 Sam. 10:1); or for oil used as an ointment to soothe and cleanse, leading to healing (Ps. 133:2; Isa. 1:6). The figurative meanings are also important. This word can be used to signify strength, such as in Isaiah 10:27 where growing fat meant growing strong. It also frequently relates to fruitfulness and fertile places where good things grew (Isa. 5:1; 28:1). The overall picture one gets from this word is that of richness, strength, and fertility.

8082. שָׁמֵן ***šāmēn,*** שָׁמָן ***šāmān:*** I. An adjective meaning fat, rich, plentiful; robust. It refers to excellent-tasting food, gourmet food (Gen. 49:20). It indicates land that is fat, fertile, filled with an abundance of produce (Num. 13:20; Neh. 9:25, 35; Isa. 30:23; Ezek. 34:14). With reference to people, it means, strong, robust, healthy (Judg. 3:29). The King James Version renders this word as fat, meaning unresponsive, self-absorbed (Isa. 6:10). It describes captives of the nation Babylon as plentiful, many (Hab. 1:16).

II. A masculine noun indicating richness (of earth). It refers to either the rich produce that the earth generates or the fertile, nutritious state of soil (Gen. 27:28).

8083. שְׁמֹנֶה ***š^{e}mōneh,*** שְׁמֹנָה ***š^{e}mōnāh:*** A feminine noun meaning eight, eighth. As a cardinal number, it refers to eight of something and combines with other numbers to form larger numbers (Gen. 5:4; 17:12). It can be used to form an ordinal number (1 Kgs. 16:29; 2 Kgs. 15:8).

8084. שְׁמֹנִים ***š^{e}mōniym,*** שְׁמוֹנִים ***š^{e}môniym:*** A plural adjective indicating eighty, eightieth. As a cardinal number, it refers to the eightieth item of something, e.g., eighty-five years (Josh. 14:10). It combines to form other numbers (Gen. 5:25, 26, 28). It can be used as an ordinal number (1 Kgs. 6:1).

8085. שָׁמַע ***šāma':*** A verb meaning to hear, to obey, to listen, to be heard of, to be regarded, to cause to hear, to proclaim, to sound aloud. The verb basically means to hear and in context expresses various connotations of this.

The most famous use of this word is to introduce the Shema, "Hear, O, Israel," followed by the content of what the Israelites are to understand about the Lord their God and how they are to respond to Him (Deut. 6:4). In a parallel usage, the heavens are commanded to "Hear, Oh heavens!" to the prophet's message about Israel (Isa. 1:2). The word calls attention to hear various things: It means to hear another person speaking (Gen. 27:6); the Lord's voice (Gen. 3:10); or anything that can be perceived by the ear. Used with or without the preposition *'el* (413) following, the word means to listen to someone. The house of Israel was not willing to listen to Ezekiel (Ezek. 3:7); the Lord was not willing to listen to the beautiful worship services of God's people, for they were not following justice (Gen. 27:5; Amos 5:23).

The word takes on the connotation of obedience in certain contexts and with certain Hebrew constructions: It can mean to heed a request or command, such as Abraham's request concerning Ishmael (Gen. 17:20). The Lord listened to Hagar's prayer and gave her a son (Gen. 16:11; 30:6). It means to obey in certain contexts (Gen. 3:17; 22:18; Ex. 24:7; 2 Kgs. 14:11).

The word is used to connote the idea of understanding. God confused the speech of the people at the Tower of Babel so they could not understand each other (Gen. 11:7; Isa. 33:19). Solomon wanted a heart of discernment and understanding (hearing) to govern his people (Deut. 1:16; 1 Kgs. 3:9); to be able to decide between good and evil (2 Sam. 14:17).

In the passive stem, the word means to be heard. Pharaoh heard the news that Joseph's brothers had arrived in Egypt (Gen. 45:16). No sound of a tool was heard as the Temple was being built (Deut. 4:32; 1 Kgs. 6:7). It also meant to be obedient to King David (2 Sam. 22:45); or to make hear, to call, or to summon as when Saul summoned his soldiers (1 Sam. 15:4; 23:8).

The word is used often in the causative stem to mean to cause to listen, to proclaim, to announce. When Israel assembled at Mount Horeb (Sinai), the Lord caused them to hear His words (Deut. 4:10; Josh. 6:10). It also means to proclaim, to summon; Isaiah spoke of those who proclaim peace (1 Kgs. 15:22; Isa. 52:7); and the psalmist proclaimed the praise of the Lord (Ps. 26:7).

8086. שְׁמַע *šᵉma'*: An Aramaic verb meaning to hear. This verb is used only in the book of Daniel and is used when speaking of words that have been heard from another person (Dan. 5:14, 16); or when hearing sounds, such as the sounds of music from many instruments (Dan. 3:5, 7, 10). In a broader perspective, it can also mean to have a sense of hearing as opposed to being deaf (Dan. 5:23). This verb can also be used in the reflexive form and means that one shows one's obedience to what has been heard (Dan. 7:27).

8087. שֶׁמַע ***šema‘:*** A proper noun designating Shema:

A. Son of Hebron (1 Chr. 2:43, 44).

B. A Benjamite (1 Chr. 8:13).

C. A postexilic Jew (Neh. 8:4).

8088. שֵׁמַע ***šēma‘:*** A masculine noun meaning hearing. This word can mean hearing as opposed to or in addition to seeing (Job 42:5; Ps. 18:44[45]). This word can also be used to represent a rumor, a report, or an announcement, as these are things that have been announced and heard by others. These reports may be good news to be greeted joyously, such as a report of fame and good deeds (Gen. 29:13; 1 Kgs. 10:1); bad news to be concerned about (Isa. 23:5); or even lies and malicious rumors causing others to suffer (Ex. 23:1).

8089. שֹׁמַע ***šōma‘:*** A masculine noun referring to fame, a report, a reputation. It refers to a rumor or a report that indicates the fame of a person (Josh. 6:27; Esth. 9:4). It refers to the fame or reputation of the Lord, Yahweh in Canaan (Josh. 9:9). It indicates an oral message or report (Jer. 6:24).

8090. שְׁמַע ***š^{e}ma‘:*** A proper noun designating Shema (Josh. 15:26).

8091. שָׁמָע ***šāmā‘:*** A proper noun designating Shama (1 Chr. 11:44).

8092. שִׁמְעָא ***šim‘ā':*** A proper noun designating Shimea:

A. A brother of David, the third born, David being the seventh (1 Chr. 2:13).

B. A son of David, his seventh (NIV, Shammua) (1 Chr. 3:5).

C. A descendant of Levi through the family of Merari, his third born (1 Chr. 6:30).

D. A descendant of Levi through the family of Kohath (1 Chr. 6:39).

8093. שִׁמְעָה ***šim‘āh:*** A proper noun designating Shimeah, the brother of David (2 Sam. 13:3, 32; 21:21). It is the same as Shimea (8092,A).

8094. שְׁמָעָה ***š^{e}mā‘āh:*** A proper noun designating Shemaah (1 Chr. 12:3).

8095. שמעון ***šim‘ôn:*** A proper noun designating Simeon:

A. The second of Leah's sons from Jacob. His name means "hearing" (Gen. 29:33; 35:23). He and Levi savagely avenged the rape of their sister Dinah by Shechem, son of Hamor the Hivite (Gen. 34:1–4). He had many sons, one by a Canaanite woman (Gen. 46:10). Jacob noted his violent nature in his prophetic utterance (Gen. 49:5). Simeon's tribal inheritance lay within Judah. It included some strategic cities, such as Beersheba, Hormah and Ziklag in the Negev area. Ezekiel alloted Simeon's descendant a place in his vision of a new Temple and New Jerusalem (Ezek. 48:24–33).

B. The name of an Israelite who intermarried with the people of the land during or after the exile (Ezra 10:31).

8096. שִׁמְעִי ***šimʻiy:*** A proper noun designating Shimei:

A. A grandson of Levi and son of Gershon. The Gershonites were responsible to transport part of the Tabernacle when Israel journeyed in the wilderness (Num. 3:18; 4:24–28). And Shimei worked with the Temple servants in his day (1 Chr. 6:42[29]).

B. Closely related to Saul, he treated King David arrogantly and cursed him. He favored Absalom as king over David and called David a murderer of Saul and his family (2 Sam. 16:5–13). David believed that perhaps Shimei's actions and words were from the Lord. Shimei repented of these things later (2 Sam. 19:18–23). Solomon, however, confined Shimei to Jerusalem and eventually was forced to execute him (1 Kgs. 2:44–46).

C. This Shimei was the brother of David and the father of Jonathan (2 Sam. 21:21).

D. Supporter of Solomon (1 Kgs. 1:8); possibly the same as Shimei in E. He may have been the son of Ela or Elah but not the same Shimei in C above.

E. An officer for Solomon. Maybe the same Shimei as above in D. He is specifically called the son of Ala.

F. This Shimei was the brother of Zerubbabel. He was a descendant of the royal line after the exile (1 Chr. 3:19).

G. He is listed in the genealogy of Simeon. This clan settled in part of the territory of Judah. Shimei had sixteen sons and five daughters (1 Chr. 4:26–27).

H. A Reubenite. This family was descended from Reuben, the firstborn of Jacob (1 Chr. 5:4).

I. Descended from the tribe of Levi, Shimei was descended from Merari (1 Chr. 6:30).

J. Head of a family of Benjamin from whom Saul is descended (1 Chr. 8:32).

K. David set apart sons of Asaph to be ministers of prophecy. This Shimei was a part of this group. They used musical instruments to accompany their singing and prophesying (1 Chr. 25:17).

L. This Shimei was a minister of David's property and was in charge of the grape vineyards (1 Chr. 27:27).

M. A descendant of Herman, he was a Levite official during Hezekiah's reign. Maybe the same Shimei as in N below (2 Chr. 29:14).

N. Probably the same as above in M with Cananiah, his brother, they were in charge of the storerooms of Hezekiah (2 Chr. 31:12, 13).

O. He married a pagan woman and then divorced her after Ezra's condemnation. A Levite (Ezra 10:23).

P. He was not a priest—he was a layman who divorced his pagan wife in Ezra's day (Ezra 10:33).

Q. Another man who took a foreign wife and then divorced her during Ezra's day (Ezra 10:38).

R. An ancestor of Mordecai from the tribe of Benjamin. May be the same as B above (Esth. 2:5).

8097. שִׁמְעִי ***šim'iy:*** A proper noun designating Shimeites, descendants of Shimei (8096,A) (Num. 3:21; Zech. 12:13).

8098. שְׁמַעְיָה ***šᵉma'yāh,*** שְׁמַעְיָהוּ ***šᵉmāyāhû:*** A proper noun designating Shemaiah:

A. From the line of Reuben. Reuben was the firstborn of the sons of Jacob.

B. A chief from the line of Simeon (1 Chr. 4:37).

C. He was a Levite and a leader during David's reign (1 Chr. 15:8, 11).

D. This Shemaiah was a Levite scribe during David's day and son of Nathanel (1 Chr. 24:6).

E. Held the position of gatekeeper. His sons also had positions of responsibility and were leaders in their families (1 Chr. 26:4).

F. The brother of Zerubbabel and son of Pedaiah (1 Kgs. 12:22; 2 Chr. 11:2; 12:5, 7, 15).

G. A teacher who taught the Book of the Law through Judah (2 Chr. 17:8).

H. May be same as I. He was a Levite during Hezekiah's day (2 Chr. 31:15).

I. Possibly the same as H in Hezekiah's day. Kore was the keeper of the East Gate and was in charge of the freewill offering, and Shemiah was one of his assistants (2 Chr. 31:15).

J. A chief Levite under Josiah who helped provide Passover offerings (2 Chr. 35:9).

K. Father of Uriah the prophet. May be same as L or M (Jer. 26:20).

L. Father of Delaiah during time of Jeremiah the prophet. May be same as K or M (Jer. 36:12).

M. A descendant of Gershon; hence, a Gershonite. In Hezekiah's day he helped cleanse, purify, and restore the Temple (2 Chr. 29:14).

N. A priest—may be the same as O (Neh. 10:8[9]; 12:6, 18).

O. A Levite who returned to Jerusalem from exile in Babylon (Ezra 8:13).

P. Another Levite who was also among those who returned from Exile in Babylon (Neh. 12:35).

Q. A layman who returned from Babylonian exile (Neh. 10:8).

R. A priest who was guilty of intermarriage—he married a foreign woman (Ezra 10:21).

S. A priest who married a foreign woman in Ezra's day (Ezra 10:31).

T. Descended from Zerubbabel—the royal line after the Exile (1 Chr. 3:22; Neh. 3:29).

U. He was a false prophet during the time of Nehemiah (Neh. 6:10).

V. During Nehemiah's day, an official. May be same as W (Neh. 12:36).

W. Possibly same as V or X. Grandfather of the priest Zechariah (Neh. 12:35, 42).

X. Possibly same as W. He was a Levite and a musician during the time of Nehemiah (Neh. 12:42).

8099. שִׁמְעֹנִי ***šim'ōniy:*** A proper noun designating Simeonite(s), descendants of Simeon (8095,A) (Num. 25:14; 26:14; Josh. 21:4; 1 Chr. 27:16).

8100. שִׁמְעַת ***šim'aṯ:*** A proper noun designating Shimeath, the mother of Jozachar or Zabad (2 Kgs. 12:21[22]; 2 Chr. 24:26).

8101. שִׁמְעָתִים ***šim'āṯiym:*** A proper noun designating Shimeathites (1 Chr. 2:55).

8102. שֶׁמֶץ ***šēmeṣ:*** A masculine noun referring to a whisper, a faint sound. It depicts a low, almost indiscernible speech or indicates hearing a snippet or a part of an oral statement (Job 4:12). Even God's mighty deeds are said to be a mere whisper of what a full display of His wisdom and power would be (Job 26:14).

8103. שִׁמְצָה ***šimṣāh:*** A feminine noun indicating derision; a laughingstock. It refers to an object of humor and ridicule or disrespect (Ex. 32:25). Israel became such an object because of her rebellion and debauched behavior.

8104. שָׁמַר ***šāmar:*** A verb meaning to watch, to keep, to preserve, to guard, to be careful, to watch over, to watch carefully over, to be on one's guard. The verb means to watch, to guard, to care for. Adam and Eve were to watch over and care for the Garden of Eden where the Lord had placed them (Gen. 2:15); cultic and holy things were to be taken care of dutifully by priests (2 Kgs. 22:14). The word can suggest the idea of protecting: David gave orders to keep Absalom safe (1 Sam. 26:15; 2 Sam. 18:12); the Lord keeps those who look to Him (Ps. 121:7). The word can mean to simply save or to preserve certain items; objects could be delivered to another person for safekeeping (Gen. 41:35; Ex. 22:7[6]). The word also means to pay close attention to: Eli the priest continued to observe Hannah's lips closely as she prayed (1 Sam. 1:12; Isa. 42:20). Closely related to this meaning is the connotation to continue to do something, as when Joab maintained his siege of the city of Rabbah (2 Sam. 11:16). The verb also indicates caring for sheep (1 Sam. 17:20).

The Hebrew word means to maintain or to observe something for a purpose and is followed by another verb indicating the purpose or manner, as in the following examples: Israel was to observe the laws of the Lord, so as to do them (Deut. 4:6; 5:1); Balaam had to observe accurately what he had been charged with (Num. 23:12); and Israel was responsible to keep the way of the Lord and walk in it (Gen. 17:9; 18:19).

The word naturally means to watch over some physical object, to keep an eye on it. In its participial form, the word means human guards, those who watch for people or over designated objects (Judg. 1:24; Neh. 12:25). The Lord, as the moral Governor of the world, watches over the moral and spiritual behavior of people (Job 10:14).

In the passive reflexive stem, it means to be taken care of. To take care in the passive aspect, the verb was used to assert that Israel was watched over (Hos. 12:13[14]). Most often it means to take care, as when the Lord instructed Laban to take care not to harm Jacob (Gen. 31:29). Amasa did not guard himself carefully and was killed by Joab (2 Sam. 20:10). Pharaoh warned Moses to take care not to come into his presence again or he would die (Ex. 10:28; cf. Gen. 24:6; 2 Kgs. 6:10; Jer. 17:21).

The word in its intensive stem means to pay regard to or attach oneself to. In the participial form of this verb, it means those who give heed to useless vanities (Jon. 2:8[9]). In the reflexive stem, it means to keep oneself. David declared he was blameless since he had kept himself from sin (2 Sam. 22:24; Ps. 18:23[24]).

8105. שֶׁמֶר ***šemer:*** A masculine plural noun meaning dregs, aged wine. It may refer to dregs, that is, to the particles of solid matter that settle to the bottom of a liquid, such as wine (Ps. 75:8[9]). Wine in such a condition can be termed unsettled, stagnant, disturbed and is so described in a simile of Moab (Jer. 48:11). In a more positive context, it indicates fine aged wine (Isa. 25:6). Zephaniah speaks of those persons who are congealed on their dregs (Zeph. 1:12), who won't act, have no conviction, do nothing, and are "stagnant in spirit" (NASB).

8106. שֶׁמֶר ***šemer,*** שָׁמֶד ***šāmed:*** A proper noun designating Shemer, Shamer:

A. Owner of the hill where Samaria was built (1 Kgs. 16:24).

B. A Levite (1 Kgs. 16:24).

C. An Asherite (Shamer, 1 Chr. 7:34). It is the same person as Shomer (7763,B).

D. A Benjamite (Shamed, 1 Chr. 8:12).

8107. שִׁמֻּר ***šimmur:*** A masculine noun meaning a vigil, an observation. It refers to an act and a time of keen observation, vigilant watchfulness, especially on the night of the Passover (Ex. 12:42).

8108. שָׁמְרָה ***šāmrāh:*** A feminine noun indicating a guard, a watch. It refers to a state of careful observation and watchfulness over something, a protective and preventative measure (Ps. 141:3).

8109. שְׁמֻרָה ***š^{e}murāh:*** A feminine noun indicating openness, watchfulness. It refers to an alertness or awareness when used of the eyes. The Lord held and maintained the watchfulness of the psalmist's eyes (Ps. 77:4[5]).

8110. שִׁמְרוֹן ***šimrôn:*** A proper noun designating Shimron:

A. Son of Issachar (Gen. 46:13; Num. 26:24; 1 Chr. 7:1).

B. A Canaanite city (Josh. 11:1; 19:15).

8111. שֹׁמְרוֹן ***šōm^{e}rôn:*** A proper noun designating Samaria, the capital city of the Northern Kingdom (1 Kgs. 16:24, 28, 29, 32; 2 Kgs. 17:1, 5, 6, 24, 26, 28).

8112. שִׁמְרוֹן מְרֹאון ***šimrôn m^{e}rôn:*** A proper noun designating Shimron Meron (Josh. 12:20).

8113. שִׁמְרִי ***šimriy:*** A proper noun designating Shimri:

A. A Simeonite (1 Chr. 4:37).

B. The father of Jediael and Joha (1 Chr. 11:45).

C. A Levite gatekeeper in David's day (1 Chr. 26:10).

D. A Levite in Hezekiah's day (2 Chr. 29:13).

8114. שְׁמַרְיָהוּ ***š^{e}maryāhû,*** שְׁמַרְיָה ***š^{e}maryāh:*** A proper noun designating Shemariah:

A. A Benjamite warrior (1 Chr. 12:5[6]).

B. Son of King Rehoboam (2 Chr. 11:19).

C. A man who divorced a foreign wife in the time of Ezra (Ezra 10:32).

D. Another man who divorced a foreign wife in the time of Ezra (Ezra 10:41).

8115. שָׁמְרַיִן ***šām^{e}rayin:*** An Aramaic proper noun designating Samaria (Ezra 4:10, 17). It corresponds to the Hebrew entry 8111.

8116. שִׁמְרִית ***šimriyṯ:*** A proper noun designating Shimrith, the same as Shomer (7763,A) (2 Chr. 24:26).

8117. שִׁמְרֹנִי ***šimrōniy:*** A proper noun designating Shimronite, a descendant of Shimron (8110,A) (Num. 26:24).

8118. שֹׁמְרֹנִי ***šōm^{e}rōniy:*** A proper noun designating a Samaritan, an inhabitant of Samariah (8111) (2 Kgs. 17:29).

8119. שִׁמְרָת ***šimrāṯ:*** A proper noun designating Shimrath (1 Chr. 8:21).

8120. שְׁמַשׁ ***š^{e}maš:*** An Aramaic verb meaning to serve, to minister to, and to attend to. This word is used only in Daniel 7:10 in a stunning vision of God, the Ancient of Days, on His throne. Thousands attend God, serving Him only. In this limited context, we get the idea that this verb is one that signifies much more than just serving or attending someone as a paid servant or a slave would do out of necessity. The connotation here seems to be that of having absolute devotion to the person, just as all who serve God must be wholeheartedly devoted to Him. This serving is voluntary for those who love God.

8121. שֶׁמֶשׁ ***šemeš:*** A common noun meaning sun, daylight. It refers to the heavenly body, the sun: it sets, *bô'* (Gen. 15:12, 17; 28:11); rises, *yāṣa'* (Gen. 19:23). The sun becomes hot (*ḥam*) during the day (Ex. 16:21). The place of the going down or setting of the sun, sunset, indicates direction or west (Deut. 11:30); the place of its rising or shining forth indicates east (Judg. 11:18). The phrase before (*neged*) the sun means in public, in the open (2 Sam. 12:12). In a glorified Zion, the sun will not set (Isa. 60:20). Isaiah 38:8 refers to a sundial made up of steps. The Israelites time and again fell into sun worship (2 Kgs. 23:5; Jer. 8:2; Ezek. 8:16), believing the sun to be a god. The phrase under the sun (Eccl. 1:3, etc.) means on the earth in this present secular life. It refers to some shining ornamental pinnacle (Isa. 54:12). It is used metaphorically of the Lord being our Sun and Shield (Ps. 84:11[12]).

8122. שְׁמַשׁ *šemeš:* An Aramaic common noun meaning sun. It is used in the phrase *meʿālê šimšāʾ*, from the coming up of the sun, that is, until sunset (Dan. 6:14[15]).

8123. שִׁמְשׁוֹן *šimšôn:* A proper noun designating Samson, the last of the major judges or deliverers mentioned in Judges (13—16). He was called before his birth to be God's chosen vessel, a Nazarite. The Lord's special messenger announced his birth and special calling to his parents before his birth (13:1–22). The author clearly gives God's purpose in His plan for Samson: to begin to deliver Israel from the Philistines's oppression (Judg. 13:5). God's Spirit "stirred him" to do His will as he reached manhood (Judg. 13:24). Even his parents, though they know he had been chosen by the Lord, failed to understand how the Lord was using Samson to accomplish His purposes (14:4). The Philistine men and women in his life were ultimately brought in and used by the Lord to enable Samson to begin the destruction of the Philistines. Samson's great strength was a result of the Spirit's action on him (14:6, 19; 15:15; 16:28), not a result of natural powers. Because he disobeyed the Lord by letting his hair be cut, the Spirit failed to energize him until he let his hair grow again. He killed more of Israel's enemy in his death than he had in his life (16:30).

8124. שִׁמְשַׁי *šimšay:* A proper noun designating Shimshai (Ezra 4:8, 9, 17, 23).

8125. שַׁמְשְׁרַי *šamšᵉray:* A proper noun designating Shamsherai (1 Chr. 8:26).

8126. שֻׁמָתִי *šumāṯiy:* A proper noun designating Shumathite (1 Chr. 2:53).

8127. שֵׁן *šēn:* A common noun meaning a tooth, ivory, a fang, a sharp projecting rock. It refers to a person's teeth (Gen. 49:12; Ex. 21:24; Lev. 24:20); animal teeth (Deut. 32:24; Job 41:14[6]; Joel 1:6); ivory tusks (1 Kgs. 10:18; Ezek. 27:15); the prong of a metal fork (1 Sam. 2:13). It is used figuratively of a jagged cliff or rock (1 Sam. 14:4). The famous *lex talionis* law, eye for eye, tooth for tooth is

found in Exodus 21:24. This law limits the penalty in a case at law.

8128. שֵׁן ***šēn:*** An Aramaic masculine noun meaning a tooth. It describes the teeth mentioned in Daniel's vision of four great beasts (Dan. 7:5, 7, 19), especially the great iron teeth of the fourth beast.

8129. שֵׁן ***šēn:*** A proper noun designating Shen (1 Sam. 7:12).

8130. שָׂנֵא ***śānē':*** A verb meaning to hate, to be unwilling, to be hated. This verb is the antonym of the Hebrew verb *'āhab̲* (157), meaning to love. The verb means to hate God or persons; God punishes children for the sins of their fathers to the third and fourth generation of those who hate Him, but He shows kindness instead of punishment to those who love (*'āhab̲*) Him (Ex. 20:5). God hates as His enemies those who love cruelty and wickedness (Ps. 11:5); they do not keep His covenant and are not loyal to Him (Ex. 20:5). God's people were not to become allied to those who hated the Lord (2 Chr. 19:2; Ps. 139:21). God or persons can be the subject of the verb; God came to hate the palaces of Jacob (Amos 6:8; Hos. 9:15); and even the religious services of His own people because they were false (Amos 5:21). In fact, God hates all who do evil (Ps. 5:5[6]); and wickedness (Ps. 45:7[8]); thus, to fear God means to hate evil (Prov. 8:13).

God is different from all other so-called gods, so much so that He hates the corrupt things the heathen do when they worship these gods (Deut. 12:31). The word describes the haters or enemies of persons. David's enemies were those whom his soul hated (2 Sam. 5:8); the enemies of Rebekah would be those who might hate her descendants (Gen. 24:60). The lack of hatred toward a person cleared someone who accidentally killed another person without planning to do so and did not previously hate the person (Deut. 4:42). Absalom, on the other hand, hated his brother Ammon for humiliating his sister and planned his death because he hated him (2 Sam. 13:22). The negative rendition of love your neighbor as yourself asserted that you should not hate your brother in your heart (Lev. 19:17).

The word means to dislike, to be hostile to, or to loathe someone or something in some contexts: Isaac accused Abimelech of rejecting him or acting hostile toward him when he asked Isaac to move away from him (Gen. 26:27; Judg. 11:7); Joseph's brothers became bitter and hostile toward him and his dreams (Gen. 37:5); Malachi asserted that God hated Esau but loved Jacob to explain how God had dealt with their descendants (Mal. 1:3); God cared for Esau and gave him offspring. A similar use of this word is found concerning Jacob's love for Rachel and the hyperbolic statement that he hated Leah (Gen. 29:31, 33; Deut. 21:16, 17); Jethro instructed Moses to choose faithful men who despised increasing their wealth in dishonest ways (Ex.

18:21). In the passive stem of the verb, it is used once to refer to the poor who are despised by their friends or neighbors in contrast to the rich who have many friends (Prov. 14:20).

In the intensive stem, the word means one who radiates hatred (i.e., an enemy); Moses prayed for the Lord to strike the enemies of Levi (Deut. 33:11; 2 Sam. 22:41). The word described the enemies of the Lord (Num. 10:35; Deut. 32:41). The word also described the person who hates wisdom; such a person loves death (Prov. 8:36).

8131. שְׂנֵא *śᵉnē':* An Aramaic verb meaning an enemy. This word only occurs once in the Hebrew Bible and refers to those who hate a person. In Daniel 4:19[16], this word is used when Daniel is speaking to King Nebuchadnezzar about the interpretation of his dream. The interpretation is so unfavorable that Daniel says he wishes it were for the king's enemies instead of being for the king himself.

8132. שָׁנָא *šānā':* I. A verb meaning to change. It means to change something from something else: clothes (2 Kgs. 25:29). It is used of a person's complexion changing (Eccl. 8:1). It is used metaphorically of pure gold that has changed, becoming dark (Lam. 4:1).

II. A verb meaning to become dull. It is used of fine gold changing, becoming dim and dull (Lam. 4:1, KJV).

8133. שְׁנָא *šᵉnā':* An Aramaic verb meaning to change; to be different. It refers to a difference that has become evident in something or persons; they have changed (Dan. 3:27; 5:6, 9; 6:17 [18]). It is used in an extreme case of a human heart changing into the heart of a beast (Dan. 4:16[13]). It indicates that one thing is different from another (Dan. 7:3, 19, 23). God can change times and seasons (Dan. 2:21; 7:25). When used of decrees or orders, it means to alter, to violate them (Ezra 6:11; Dan. 3:28; 6:8[9], 15[16]). It indicates a change of conditions or situations (Dan. 2:9); a change in facial expression (Dan. 3:19; 5:10; 7:28).

8134. שִׁנְאָב *šin'āb:* A proper noun designating Shinab (Gen. 14:2).

8135. שִׂנְאָה *śin'āh:* A feminine noun meaning hating, hatred. The word is derived from the verb *śānē'* (8130) and signifies a strong feeling of hatred. It is most commonly used to describe hatred that one human feels towards another. This hate can be so strong that it leads to murder (Num. 35:20); or it can be a hate that causes unrest and dissension between people, yet not necessarily leading to violence (Prov. 10:12; 15:17). In one place, this noun is even used to describe sexual revulsion and is indicative of a strong hate (2 Sam. 13:15). This word can be used as a verb at times, such as in Deuteronomy 1:27 and 9:28. Here God is the subject, and the people were complaining that He

hated them, although this was not true. The connotations the people had with this word showed through because they felt that God hated them so much that He would hand them over to be killed by their enemies.

8136. שִׁנְאָן ***šin'ān:*** A masculine noun meaning repeating, repetition. This word is used only once in the Old Testament, in Psalm 68:17[18], where it is preceded by the word that means a thousand. Therefore, it means a thousand in repetition or thousands of thousands. Here it is in reference to the chariots of God, which shows how mighty and powerful God is because He is the ruler over so much. Chariots were also a sign of wealth; and since God had so many chariots, it showed that all the wealth in the world belongs to Him alone.

8137. שֶׁנְאַצַּר ***šen'aṣṣar:*** A proper noun designating Shenazzar (1 Chr. 3:18).

8138. שָׁנָה ***šānāh:*** I. A verb meaning to change; to disguise; to be different. It means to become something different or to change an attitude or character. God does not change ever (Mal. 3:6). For God's right hand to change means He would have to change His actions toward the righteous psalmist (Ps. 77:10[11]). It can have the sense of different (Esth. 1:7). In its intensive stem, it means to bring about change, to alter something: judgment (Prov. 31:5); clothes (Jer. 52:33); one's words (Ps. 89:34[35]); one's political stance (Jer. 2:36); one's face or appearance (Job 14:20). In its reflexive sense, it means to change, to disguise oneself (1 Kgs. 14:2). Even David changed and disguised himself emotionally and outwardly to save himself (1 Sam. 21:13[14]).

II. A verb meaning to repeat; to do again. It indicates doing something over a second time (1 Kgs. 18:34; Neh. 13:21; Job 29:22). God presented a dream to Joseph twice (Gen. 41:32); Abishai speaks of striking an enemy twice (1 Sam. 26:8); Amasa failed to strike a second time (2 Sam. 20:10). It can have the sense of repeating; repeating something that should be kept secret is evil (Prov. 17:9); and a fool repeats his errors (Prov. 26:11).

8139. שְׁנָה ***šᵉnāh:*** An Aramaic feminine noun referring to sleep. Darius was not able to sleep; his sleep went from him; he would not fall asleep (Dan. 6:18[19]).

8140. שְׁנָה ***šᵉnāh:*** An Aramaic feminine noun meaning a year. It refers to a cycle of the lunar year, the major division of time used in the ancient world (Ezra 4:24). In Ezra's time, Solomon's Temple had been built many years earlier (Ezra 5:11). The first year of a king was always important (Ezra 5:13; 6:3; Dan. 7:1). The second Temple was completed in the sixth year of Darius, king of Persia (Ezra 6:15). It is used in calculating ages of persons (Dan. 5:31[6:1]).

8141. שָׁנָה šānāh: A feminine noun meaning a year. It is used quite uniformly in its application, but its context must be noted carefully. It means simply a division of time, a year (Gen. 1:14). Something done yearly or year upon year is *baššānāh, šānāh* *beš*ānāh respectively (Ex. 23:14; Deut. 14:22; 15:20). It expresses a person's age, *ben šānāh,* a son of a year, means one year old (Ex. 12:5). The accession year of a king is *šenaṯ malkô,* year of his reigning (2 Kgs. 25:27). With a dual ending, *-ayim,* it means two full years (Gen. 41:1). The phrase *kešānîm qaḏmōniyyōṯ* means according to (in) former (earlier) years (Mal. 3:4).

8142. שֵׁנָא šēnā', שֵׁנָה šēnāh: A feminine noun indicating sleep. It refers to a state of rest that occurs naturally and regularly during which there is little or no conscious thought. A person dreams intermittently. In the Old Testament, God often used the time of sleep as a time to display Himself and His will to His servants and people (Gen. 28:16; Judg. 16:14, 20). God spoke in dreams to pagans during their sleep (Dan. 2:1). The loss of sleep is serious and must be regained (Gen. 31:40). It is used as a euphemism for death (Job 14:12; Ps. 76:5[6]). Sleep can be put off for a time (Ps. 132:4). Excessive sleep leads to poverty (Prov. 20:13); but the sleep of a laboring worker is sweet (Eccl. 5:12[11]).

8143. שֶׁנְהַבִּים šenhabbiym: A masculine plural noun meaning ivory. It refers to the white dentin of the tusks of elephants, walruses, etc. It was highly prized in the ancient world and very scarce (1 Kgs. 10:22; 2 Chr. 9:21). Solomon imported ivory.

8144. שָׁנִי šāniy: A masculine noun meaning scarlet. It describes a bright red color with a tinge of orange in it. It was used to color ribbons, threads, etc., in the ancient world and was easily seen (Gen. 38:28, 30; Lev. 14:4). It was a featured color of various items in the Tabernacle (Ex. 25:4; 26:1; 27:16).

8145. שֵׁנִי šēniy: An adjective meaning second. It refers to the second item in a series (Gen. 1:8; 2:13). It indicates something done for a second time (Gen. 22:15). In a conversation, it means secondly, and second, or besides (2 Sam. 16:19; Ezek. 4:6; Mal. 2:13). The plural is *šeniyyim* (Gen. 6:16).

8146. שָׂנִיא śāniy': A feminine adjective meaning one who is hated or held in aversion. It is used in Deuteronomy 21:15 contrasting a wife who is loved with a wife who is hated. There does not seem to be a connotation of extreme hate here but rather of dislike, preferring one wife to the other. The terms are used as opposites, but the strength of opposition cannot be determined accurately. In this limited context, it is difficult to tell how strong of a connotation the word really holds, but here it seems to connote more dislike or neglect than

strong hate that would lead to overtly hateful actions toward that person.

8147. שְׁנַיִם ***šᵉnayim,*** שְׁתַּיִם ***šᵉttayim:*** An adjective, dual adjective meaning two, both, a pair. It refers to two of anything, e.g., two of us (Gen. 21:27; 31:37); two brothers (Gen. 9:22); two slices of bread (1 Sam. 10:4). The phrase *šᵉnayim šᵉnayim* means two by two (Gen. 7:9). Its forms may precede *ʿāśăr* to mean twelve (Gen. 14:4; 17:20). It combines to form larger numbers, e.g., two hundred thirty-two (1 Kgs. 20:15).

8148. שְׁנִינָה ***šᵉniynāh:*** A feminine noun indicating a byword; a taunt. It refers to a scornful or jeering put-down. Israel would become a taunt before the nations because of her rebelliousness and disobedience (Deut. 28:37); especially in exile (1 Kgs. 9:7; Jer. 24:9). The Temple itself would become a byword (2 Chr. 7:20).

8149. שְׁנִיר ***šᵉniyr,*** שְׂנִיר ***śᵉniyr:*** A proper noun designating Senir, Shenir (Deut. 3:9; 1 Chr. 5:23; Song 4:8; Ezek. 27:5).

8150. שָׁנַן ***šānan:*** A verb meaning to whet, to sharpen. This word is used in three of the basic stems. In its simple meaning of sharpen, it can be used to refer to the sharpening of a sword. In context it refers to God sharpening His sword of judgment (Deut. 32:41). Also, it can be used in reference to sharp arrows (Ps. 45:5[6]; Isa. 5:28). Figuratively, this verb can be used to signify sharp words that a person says in order to hurt someone else (Ps. 64:3[4]; 140:3[4]). In the intensive form of the verb, it means to teach incisively (Deut. 6:7). The idea here is that just as words are cut into a stone tablet with a sharp object, so the Law should be impressed on the hearts of the children of every generation. Finally, in the reflexive stem, this verb means to be pierced by grief or envy or to be wounded (Ps. 73:21).

8151. שָׁנַס ***šānas:*** A verb meaning to gird up. It is used in the phrase girded up his loins figuratively of preparing to run a race, readying oneself (1 Kgs. 18:46). It would have involved, in Elijah's case, holding up or tucking in his cloak so that he could run speedily.

8152. שִׁנְעָר ***šinʿār:*** A proper noun designating Shinar, the name of the plain where the city and nation of Babylon were begun by Nimrod (Gen. 10:8–10; 11:2). Shinar lay in the area between the Tigris and Euphrates Rivers near the Persian Gulf. Amraphel is listed as an early king (Gen. 14:1, 9). It is rendered "Babylonia" by some translations (e.g., NIV, Babylonia for Shinar, Josh. 7:21; Isa. 11:11; Dan. 9:1; Zech. 5:11). Many great ancient cities were in the area: Akkad, Babylon, Calneh, Erech, Lagash, Nippur.

8153. שְׁנַת ***šᵉnaṯ:*** A feminine noun meaning sleep. It is used figuratively of closing one's eyelids for sleep in context (Ps. 132:4). In this case, it was for a worthy cause.

8154. שָׁסָה šāsāh, שָׁשָׂה šāśāh: A verb that means to spoil, to plunder. This verb is used only in the simple stem and in the participle form. It can refer to the plundering of both land and objects (Judg. 2:14; 1 Sam. 14:48; Hos. 13:15). In almost every reference where this word is found, enemies were plundering the land and the people of Israel. God allowed this in judgment on the sins of the Israelites after they had been warned and refused to repent or as a warning to call them to repentance. The participle form of this verb refers to people who do the plundering (Isa. 10:13; 42:22). Ultimately, God allowed any persons to be plunderers. But if they overstepped their boundaries, they too would be plundered as the punishment for their sins.

8155. שָׁסַס šāsas: A verb indicating to plunder, to loot. It means to rob or to take possession of the property of others, usually in a time of war (Judg. 2:14; 1 Sam. 17:53; Ps. 89:41 [42]). In its passive sense, it refers to being plundered (Isa. 13:16; Zech. 14:2). Israel was plundered because of her own sins (Ps. 89:41[42]).

8156. שָׁסַע šāsa': A verb meaning to split, to divide, to tear. It means to pull something apart, to separate it wholly or partly (Lev. 1:17). The animal that had a divided, separated hoof was edible for Israel (Lev. 11:3, 7, 26; Deut. 14:6, 7). In Samson's great might, he tore and mangled a lion (Judg. 14:6). It probably has the sense of to disperse, to separate, or to persuade (1 Sam. 24:7[8], KJV, stay; NIV, rebuke).

8157. שֶׁסַע šesa': A masculine noun indicating dividedness. It describes the separation, division in the hooves of certain animals edible in Israel (Lev. 11:3, 7, 26: Deut. 14:6).

8158. שָׁסַף šāsap̄: A verb meaning to hew into pieces; to put to death. It refers to Samuel's violent destruction of Agag, a pagan king (1 Sam. 15:33, KJV, NASB, hewed to pieces; NIV, put to death).

8159. שָׁעָה šā'āh, שָׁתַע šāṯa': I. A verb meaning to look with favor or in dismay. It means to look on something with approval, to accept it (Gen. 4:4, 5); or to look on some burdensome thing or situation in trepidation, dismay (Ex. 5:9). It can mean simply to hope for, to desire, to look for (2 Sam. 22:42). It has the sense of looking at intently (Job 7:19; Ps. 39:13). It can have the sense of looking at with high regard and appreciation (Isa. 17:7); or just the opposite according to context (Isa. 17:8; 41:10). It has the sense of seeing with understanding (Isa. 32:3).

II. A verb indicating looking at something with dismay. This is a possible nuanced meaning given to this word by some translators (Isa. 41:10, 23, NIV).

8160. שָׁעָה ***šā'āh:*** An Aramaic feminine noun meaning a short time, the same hour. It refers to a brief time span, almost immediately (Dan. 3:6, 15; 4:33[30]; 5:5); at a set moment. It can refer to a slightly longer time span (Dan. 4:19[16]).

8161. שַׁעֲטָה ***ša'aṭāh:*** A feminine noun referring to stamping, galloping. In context it refers to the noisy, powerful galloping of warhorses (Jer. 47:3).

8162. שַׁעַטְנֵז ***ša'aṭnēz:*** A masculine noun referring to mixed material; material of more than one kind. It refers to something that combines differing materials together, thus creating something forbidden in Israel because of the inequity involved (Lev. 19:19; Deut. 22:11). Others suggest a reference to a material of wide mesh (spaces).

8163. שָׂעִיר ***śā'iyr,*** שָׂעִר ***śā'ir:*** A masculine noun meaning a male goat, a buck. Occasionally, the word can be used figuratively to mean a hairy one. Under the Israelite sacrificial system, a male goat was an acceptable sin offering. This noun is used many times in conjunction with the sin offering, in which a male goat without any defects was offered by the priest to atone for the sins of himself and the people (Lev. 9:15; 2 Chr. 29:23; Ezek. 43:25). On the negative side, the Israelites worshiped the goat as an idol in times of rebellion against God; the same noun is used in these references (Lev. 17:7; 2 Chr. 11:15).

8164. שָׂעִיר ***śā'iyr:*** A masculine noun meaning a raindrop. It describes small beads of water that collect on fresh grass as dew droplets or the same effect produced by a light rain (Deut. 32:2).

8165. שֵׂעִיר ***śē'iyr:*** A proper noun designating Seir:

A. A mountain and also a mountain range in Edom usually taken to mean territory east of the Arabah Valley rift in Judah (sometimes it seemed to reach west [Deut. 1:2, 44] of the Arabah Valley). It ran from the brook Zered on the south of the Dead Sea to the Gulf of Aqaba. Genesis 32:3[4] identifies it with the country of Edom. Esau and his descendants settled in these areas. It is connected with Sinai and the Desert of Paran in the west of the Arabah (Deut. 33:2). The name designates a particular mountain in some texts (Gen. 14:6; Ezek. 35:15). Before the Edomites, the Horites lived in the territory (Gen. 36:8–30; Deut. 2:12). Some Amalekites settled in the area (1 Chr. 4:42). Ezekiel refers to the people of Seir who came to despise Israel (25:8), and he directed the Lord's judgment against it (35:1–30).

B. An ancient ancestor of the Horites who settled Edom before Esau (Gen. 36:20, 21; 1 Chr. 1:38).

C. A boundary marker on the north of Judah (Josh. 15:10). It was ca. ten miles west of Jerusalem.

8166. שְׂעִירָה s^e'iyrāh: A feminine noun indicating a female goat. It refers to a female goat of a flock designated as an offering to cover unintentional sins (Lev. 4:28; 5:6).

8167. שְׂעִירָה s^e'iyrāh: A proper noun designating Seirah (Judg. 3:26).

8168. שֹׁעַל šō'al: A masculine noun indicating the hollow of the hand; handful. In its context, it indicates figuratively a full handful of people, compared to the mere dust, the small population of Samaria (1 Kgs. 20:10; Isa. 40:12; Ezek. 13:19).

8169. שַׁעַלְבִים ša'al<u>b</u>iym, שַׁעֲלַבִּין ša^a labbiyn: A proper noun designating Shaalbim, Shaalabbin (Josh. 19:42; Judg. 1:35; 1 Kgs. 4:9).

8170. שַׁעַלְבֹנִי ša'al<u>b</u>ōniy: A proper noun designating a Shaalbonite, an inhabitant of Shaalbim (8169,A) (2 Sam. 23:32; 1 Chr. 11:33).

8171. שַׁעֲלִים ša'aliym: A proper noun designating Shaalim (1 Sam. 9:4).

8172. שָׁעַן šā'an: A verb meaning to lean, to rely, to support oneself. This verb is found only in the passive form, but it is active in meaning. In its simplest meaning, it refers to leaning on things for support, such as trees (Gen. 18:4) and pillars (Judg. 16:26). The idea conveyed here is simply that of resting one's weight against something to give it support, but not all things leaned on will actually support (Job 8:15). This verb is also used in the sense of a king leaning or relying on his closest friends and advisors. This may mean literally leaning on someone's arm or trusting in his or her counsel (2 Kgs. 5:18; 7:2, 17). Leaning on can also mean trusting in persons, whether it be God (Mic. 3:11); other people (Ezek. 29:7); or oneself (Prov. 3:5). Ultimately, God should be trusted and leaned on, for He will never fail.

8173. שָׁעַע šā'a': I. A verb indicating to close one's eyes, to be blinded. It is used of making persons' eyes dim, to blur or blind their vision in a figurative sense (Isa. 6:10; 29:9).

II. A verb meaning to take delight in; to fondle. It refers to taking joy or enjoyment from something (Ps. 94:19), especially God's laws (Ps. 119:16, 47, 40). It describes exceptional delights in the Messianic Kingdom (Isa. 11:8) in a figurative sense (Isa. 66:12).

III. A verb meaning to cry out. Some translators render this word as from a root meaning to cry out (Isa. 29:9, KJV).

8174. שַׁעַף šā'ap̱: A proper noun designating Shaaph:

A. Son of Caleb, the brother of Jerahmeel (1 Chr. 2:49).

B. Another descendant of Caleb, the brother of Jerahmeel (1 Chr. 2:47).

8175. שָׂעַר śā'ar: A verb meaning to sweep away, to whirl away. The image brought to mind when this verb is used is that of a stormy wind sweeping things away that cannot stand against its power. It appears in the simple, passive, intensive, and reflexive stems of the verb, but the meanings in each stem are all comparable. This verb is often used to describe the fate of evil persons (Job 27:21; Ps. 58:9[10]). Their punishment from God is that they will be swept away suddenly, just as a stormy wind arises suddenly to sweep things away. Another use of this word is to describe God in all His power and glory, the Ruler of the universe (Ps. 50:3); and it can also be used to describe a battle where one ruler storms out against another (Dan. 11:40).

8176. שָׁעַר ***šāʻar:*** A verb possibly meaning to cleave, to divide, but it took on the meaning of to calculate, to estimate, to set a price on. The meaning was transferred to the sense of judging something, thereby setting a price to it. There are no references to the verb meaning to cleave in the Old Testament, but in Proverbs 23:7, this verb is used to mean to calculate or to set a price on. The context here is that of misers who count the cost of everything that their guests eat or drink. They find no enjoyment in their guests but only worry about the cost of it all.

8177. שְׂעַר ***śeʻar:*** An Aramaic masculine noun referring to human hair. Hair is easily singed by fire (Dan. 3:27). God's curse on Nebuchadnezzar caused his hair to grow wild like an eagle's feathers (Dan. 4:33[30]). White hair represented antiquity, great age, and wisdom (Dan. 7:9).

8178. שַׂעַר ***śaʻar:*** A masculine noun meaning horror. The horror described by the use of this noun is what people feel when witnessing the destruction that God allows to happen to evil people of this world. In Job 18:20, it is said that people were seized with horror at the fate of an evil person. In Ezekiel 27:35 and 32:10, this word is used in the context of laments composed for the land of Tyre and Pharaoh of Egypt, who were both destroyed. When people see the destruction wrought on them, they are filled with horror at their fate. A less common use of this word holds the meaning of storm (Isa. 28:2).

8179. שַׁעַר ***šaʻar:*** A masculine noun meaning a gate, an entrance; a city, a town. It indicates the main entrance to a city or building and can be used to stand for city or town itself (Ps. 87:2; Isa. 14:31): the gate of city, which was a favorite gathering place of people for various reasons (Gen. 19:1; Ruth 4:1, 10, 11); the entrance to a court area (Ex. 27:16); the entrance to a camp (Ex. 32:26). It may mean a canal or the entrance to a river (Nah. 2:6[7]). It is used figuratively in a dream to refer to a gate of the heavens (Gen. 28:17). Sheol has an entrance gate as well (Isa. 38:10); as does death (Job 38:17). Jerusalem had many gates over its long history

(2 Kgs. 14:13; Neh. 2:13; 8:16; Jer. 37:13; Zech. 14:10). Temples and palace gates are mentioned (2 Kgs. 9:31; Jer. 7:2). The word refers to a meeting area that was often near the gate (Deut. 21:19; 2 Sam. 23:15, 16; 2 Kgs. 7:1, 18).

8180. שַׁעַר ***ša'ar:*** A masculine noun meaning a hundredfold. It indicates a huge increase in the yield of crops or produce from a field or land (Gen. 26:12).

8181. שֵׂעָר ***śē'ār:*** A masculine noun meaning hair. It refers to the hair of animals used in certain materials (Gen. 25:25). It indicates human hair (Judg. 16:22). It can be used in an inclusive sense of the whole head (Lev. 14:8, 9); or of the hair in specific body areas (Isa. 7:20). It refers to hairs involved in diagnosing leprosy (Lev. 13:3, 4, 10, etc.).

8182. שֹׁעָר ***šō'ār:*** An adjective meaning horrid, bad, disagreeable. This word is used only once in the Old Testament in Jeremiah 29:17 when describing figs that are so bad they cannot be eaten. There is absolutely no use for them but to be thrown away. This is used to explain what would become of the Israelites who remained in their land instead of going into exile. God would send the sword, famine, and plague against them so that in the end they too would be as worthless as bad figs. They would not be slightly disagreeable but would be so ruined and so horrid that they would simply be destroyed.

8183. שְׂעָרָה ***śe'ārāh:*** A feminine noun meaning a storm, a tempest. It refers figuratively and literally to the calamitous storms or illnesses suffered by Job (9:17). The Lord clothes Himself in storms and displays aspects of His character in them (Nah. 1:3).

8184. שְׂעֹרָה ***śe'ōrāh:*** A feminine noun indicating barley. It is a cereal grass with heavy, dense spikes of flowers, giving a bearded appearance. It is also used in making malt. It was a major food crop in Israel and Palestine. Egypt's barley was ruined in the seventh plague (Ex. 9:31). Barley harvest was a time of rejoicing (2 Sam. 21:9). There was barley grain and barley flour (Deut. 8:8; 1 Kgs. 4:28[5:8]; 2 Kgs. 4:42). It was also used as food for horses (1 Kgs. 4:28]5:8]).

8185. שַׂעֲרָה ***śa'arāh:*** A feminine noun meaning hair. It is used in the Old Testament to reference a single hair (Judg. 20:16; 1 Sam. 14:45; 2 Sam. 14:11; 1 Kgs. 1:52; Job 4:15; Ps. 40:12[13]; 69:4[5]). It is used often to illustrate God's care and protection of a person or to refer to the accuracy of a sling thrower who could sling a stone at a hair's breadth, etc. It indicates the relative small value of losing a single hair.

8186. שַׁעֲרוּר ***ša'arûr,*** שַׁעֲרוּרָה ***ša'arûrāh,*** שַׁעֲרוּרִי ***ša'arûriy,*** שַׁעֲרוּרִיָּה ***ša'arûriyyāh:*** A feminine noun meaning horror, a horrible thing. It is used to describe how bad the apostasy and apathy of the Israelites was. What they did in worshiping idols and prophesying falsely were truly horrible things in the eyes of God and the prophets who denounced them (Jer. 5:30; 23:14). There are two variant spellings of this word. One, *šaᵃrûriyyāh*, is found in Hosea 6:10 and another, *šaᵃrurit*, is found in Jeremiah 18:13. The uses of these variant spellings are exactly the same as the most common spelling. In every instance of the use of this word, it refers to the horror of the things that Israel was doing and the sins they were committing against the Lord.

8187. שְׁעַרְיָה ***šᵉ'aryāh:*** A proper noun designating Sheariah (1 Chr. 8:38; 9:44).

8188. שְׂעֹרִים ***śᵉ'ōriym:*** A proper noun designating Seorim (1 Chr. 24:8).

8189. שַׁעֲרַיִם ***šaᵃrayim:*** A proper noun designating Shaaraim:

A. A town in Judah (Josh. 15:36; 1 Sam. 17:52).

B. A town in Simeon (1 Chr. 4:31).

8190. שַׁעַשְׁגַז ***ša'ašgaz:*** A proper noun designating Shaashgaz (Esth. 2:14).

8191. שַׁעֲשֻׁעִים ***šaᵃšu'iym:*** A masculine plural noun meaning delight. It often describes the delight given to the one who follows God's teachings, laws, and testimonies (Ps. 119:24, 77, 92, 143, 174). Wisdom, in creation, was constantly God's delight (Prov. 8:30, 31). It is used figuratively in the phrase a delightful plant, a pleasant plant to refer to God's pleasure in the people of Judah (Isa. 5:7); likewise Ephraim was God's pleasant child (Jer. 31:20), His dear son (KJV).

8192. שָׁפָה ***šāpāh:*** A verb meaning to be bare; to stick out. It refers to something protruding out or becoming visible: the bones of a chastened person before God (Job 33:21). It is used of hoisting up a flag or a banner for all to see (Isa. 13:2).

8193. שָׂפָה ***śapāh:*** A feminine noun meaning a lip, a language, an edge, a border. The most common use of this word is that of lip. It can be used merely to describe the organ of speech (Ex. 6:12, 30; Ps. 63:5[6]); and the place from where laughter comes (Job 8:21). Yet it can also be used as a feature of beauty in descriptions of a beautiful person (Song 4:3, 11). Finally, it can refer to the place from where divine speech comes, from the lips of God (Job 23:12; Ps. 17:4). A more general meaning is that of language that originates from the lips (Gen. 11:6, 7; Ps. 81:5[6]; Isa. 33:19). When an edge or a border is the meaning of this word, it can refer to a wide variety of things such as the shore of a sea (Gen. 22:17); the edge or brim of a variety of objects (1 Kgs. 7:23; Ezek. 43:13); or the boundary between geographical sites (Judg. 7:22).

8194. שָׁפָה *šāpāh*, שְׁפוֹת *šᵉpôt*: A feminine noun indicating cheese. It refers to goat's cheese most likely. It describes the coagulated part of milk from which cheese is made. It was a food provided to David at a difficult time for him and his men (2 Sam. 17:29).

8195. שְׁפוֹ *šᵉpô*, שְׁפִי *šᵉpiy*: A proper noun designating Shepho, Shephi (Gen. 36:23; 1 Chr. 1:40).

8196. שְׁפוֹט *šᵉpôṭ*: A masculine noun meaning a judgment, a punishment. It is an abstract noun referring to both the declaration and enactment of judgment on someone (2 Chr. 20:9). It indicates, in context, the actual enactments of justice on God's people (Ezek. 23:10).

8197. שְׁפוּפָם *šᵉpûpam*, שְׁפוּפָן *šᵉpûpān*: I. A proper noun designating a Shephupham, a descendant of Benjamin (Num. 26:39).

II. A proper noun designating Shephuphan, son of Bela (1 Chr. 8:5). It is perhaps the same as I.

8198. שִׁפְחָה *šiphāh*: A feminine noun meaning a maidservant, a female slave. People of wealth and power had female servants in the ancient world to carry out tasks for their masters, from great tasks to small ones (Gen. 12:16). Hagar was Sarah's handmaid and could be permitted to bear a child to her mistress's husband (Gen. 16:1–3, 5, 6, 8). A maidservant held a humble social position (Ruth 2:13; 1 Sam. 1:18; 25:27). She was evidently marriageable (Lev. 19:20).

8199. שָׁפַט *šāpaṭ*: A verb meaning to judge, to govern. This word, though often translated as judge, is much more inclusive than the modern concept of judging and encompasses all the facets and functions of government: executive, legislative, and judicial. Consequently, this term can be understood in any one of the following ways. It could designate, in its broadest sense, to function as ruler or governor. This function could be fulfilled by individual judges (Judg. 16:31; 1 Sam. 7:16); the king (1 Kgs. 3:9); or even God Himself (Ps. 50:6; 75:7[8]); since He is the source of authority (cf. Rom. 13:1) and will eventually conduct all judgments (Ps. 96:13). In a judicial sense, the word could also indicate, because of the exalted status of the ruler, the arbitration of civil, domestic, and religious disputes (Deut. 25:1). As before, this function could be fulfilled by the congregation of Israel (Num. 35:24); individual judges (Ex. 18:16; Deut. 1:16); the king (1 Sam. 8:5, 6, 20); or even God Himself (Gen. 16:5; 1 Sam. 24:12[13], 15[16]). In the executive sense, it could denote to execute judgment, to bring about what had been decided. This could be in the form of a vindication (Ps. 10:18; Isa. 1:17, 23); or a condemnation and punishment (Ezek. 7:3, 8; 23:45).

8200. שְׁפַט ***šᵉpaṭ:*** An Aramaic verb meaning to judge, to govern. This word is used only once in the Old Testament and is related to the Hebrew word *šāpaṭ* (8199), meaning to judge or to govern. In Ezra 7:25, this word is used to describe one of the governing rulers that Ezra was to appoint. These rulers were to perform similar functions as the *dayyān* (1782) or judges that Ezra was also to appoint.

8201. שֶׁפֶט ***šepeṭ:*** A masculine noun meaning judgment. This word comes from the verb *šāpaṭ* (8199), meaning to judge, and usually describes the active role of God in punishing. In several instances, such judgment is described as the sword, famine, wild beasts, plagues, stoning, and burning (Ezek. 14:21; 16:41). The plagues that God inflicted on Egypt are described as judgments (Ex. 6:6; 7:4; 12:12; Num. 33:4). This word describes both the defeat of Israel (2 Chr. 24:24; Ezek. 5:10, 15); as well as the defeat of other nations (Ezek. 25:11; 28:22, 26). In one instance, this word speaks more generally, not of specific nations, but of unruly scoffers who will receive physical chastisement (Prov. 19:29).

8202. שָׁפָט ***šāpāṭ:*** A proper noun designating Shaphat:

A. A Simeonite (Num. 13:5).

B. The father of the prophet Elisha (1 Kgs. 19:16, 19; 2 Kgs. 3:11; 6:31).

C. A descendant of David (1 Chr. 3:22).

D. A Gadite (1 Chr. 5:12).

E. Son of Adlai (1 Chr. 27:29).

8203. שְׁפַטְיָהוּ ***šᵉpaṭyāhû,*** שְׁפַטְיָה ***šᵉpaṭyāh:*** A proper noun designating Shephatiah:

A. A Benjamite warrior (1 Chr. 12:5[6]).

B. A Simeonite official (1 Chr. 27:16).

C. A son of David (2 Sam. 3:4; 1 Chr. 3:3).

D. Son of Jehoshaphat (2 Chr. 21:2).

E. A prince who opposed Jeremiah (Jer. 38:1).

F. The head of a family returning from exile with Zerubbabel (Ezra 2:4; 8:8; Neh. 7:9).

G. Descendant of one of Solomon's servants (Ezra 2:57; Neh. 7:59).

H. Ancestor of Meshullam (1 Chr. 9:8).

I. A descendant of Perez (Neh. 11:4).

8204. שִׁפְטָן ***šipṭān:*** A proper noun designating Shiphtan, the father of Kemuel (Num. 34:24).

8205. שְׁפִי ***šᵉpiy:*** A masculine noun meaning bare. This word carries the idea of a barren or smooth place and is used to describe dry places where God will open rivers (Isa. 41:18); and infertile places where God will create pastures (Isa. 49:9). The donkeys could not find grass in such places (Jer. 14:6). The barren place was where Balaam went to meet God (Num. 23:3); and where Israel was to lament their destruction (Jer. 7:29). At times, it could describe the bare hills (Jer. 3:2, 21) from which the dry winds originated in the barren wilderness (Jer. 4:11; 12:12).

8206. שֻׁפִּים ***šuppiym:*** A proper noun designating Shuppim:

A. A Benjamite (1 Chr. 7:12, 15).

B. A Levite gatekeeper

8207. שְׁפִיפֹן ***šᵉpiypōn:*** A masculine noun referring to a snake, a viper, an adder. It represents some kind of snake, possibly a horned snake (Gen. 49:17; NASB, horned snake; KJV, adder).

8208. שָׁפִיר ***šāpiyr:*** A proper noun designating Shaphir (Mic. 1:11).

8209. שַׁפִּיר ***šapiyr:*** An Aramaic adjective meaning beautiful. It describes the splendor and attractiveness of the foliage of a great tree in its biblical context (Dan. 4:12[9], 21[18]).

8210. שָׁפַךְ ***šāpak:*** A verb meaning to pour out. In its most basic sense, this word refers to the pouring out of something, for example, fluid on the ground (Ex. 4:9; Deut. 12:16; 1 Sam. 7:6); or blood on an altar (Ex. 29:12; Lev. 4:7; Deut. 12:27). In several instances, it describes the casting up of a mound against a city to form a siege ramp for attacking it (2 Sam. 20:15; Ezek. 4:2; Dan. 11:15). This word is also used idiomatically to refer to the shedding of blood (Gen. 9:6; 1 Kgs. 2:31); especially of innocent blood (2 Kgs. 21:16; Prov. 6:17). A dependent prayer is described as the pouring out of one's soul (1 Sam. 1:15; Ps. 42:4[5]); one's heart (Ps. 62:8[9]; Lam. 2:19); or one's inner parts before the Lord (Lam. 2:11). God poured out both His wrath (Ps. 69:24[25]; Isa. 42:25; Jer. 6:11; Hos. 5:10); and His grace (Joel 2:28[3:1], 29[3:2]; Zech. 12:10) from heaven on people.

8211. שֶׁפֶךְ ***šepek:*** A masculine noun meaning a place of pouring, a place of emptying. It comes from the word *šāpak* (8210), meaning to spill forth, and is used in Leviticus to describe the place where the priest was to burn the remains of the bull sacrifice, i.e., next to the place where the ashes were poured out (Lev. 4:12).

8212. שָׁפְכָה ***šopkāh:*** A feminine noun meaning a male penis. It refers to a man's penis, literally a place of pouring out, a urinary organ (Deut. 23:1[2]).

8213. שָׁפֵל ***šāpal:*** A verb meaning to make humble, to humiliate; to bring down. It indicates that something is low, sinking down. It is used literally/figuratively of bringing down trees representing the powerful, influential people of a society (Isa. 10:33); of humbling persons (Isa. 2:9; 5:15); even a city (Isa. 32:19). It describes one's being humiliated, placed lower (Prov. 25:7; 29:23; Jer. 13:18). It describes a sound as being low (Eccl. 12:4). In its causative sense, it means to bring down (Ezek. 17:24); to lay something low (Isa. 25:12); to put lower (Prov. 25:7); to humiliate (1 Sam. 2:7). God lowers or humbles Himself to observe the things of earth (Ps. 113:6).

8214. שְׁפַל ***šᵉp̱al:*** An Aramaic verb meaning to humble, to subdue. It describes figuratively the bringing down or making humble the prideful person (Dan. 4:37[34]); of humbling anyone whom God desires to humble (Dan. 5:19). Persons can humble themselves (Dan. 5:22). In a context of war, it may mean to overcome, to defeat, to subdue (Dan. 7:24).

8215. שְׁפַל ***šᵉp̱al:*** An Aramaic adjective meaning lowliest. It means lowly, but it is placed before a masculine plural noun to indicate a superlative meaning; lowliest (Dan. 4:17[14]).

8216. שֵׁפֶל ***šēp̱el:*** A masculine noun meaning a low place, a low estate. It refers to a social position of relatively low power, influence, and esteem by the world's standards (Eccl. 10:6). It describes the people of Israel at a time when they were powerless and oppressed in the land of Canaan (Ps. 136:23).

8217. שָׁפָל ***šāp̱āl:*** An adjective meaning low, humble; lower. It refers to a tree being low (Ezek. 17:24) but often refers in a figurative way to low social positions (2 Sam. 6:22). It describes a short tree or a shrub in a parable (Ezek. 17:6). It has the sense of a humble, despondent, meek, or contrite spirit (Isa. 57:15).

8218. שִׁפְלָה ***šip̱lāh:*** A feminine noun indicating lowliness. It refers to the bringing down or lowering of a city, literally, in lowliness the city will be laid low (Isa. 32:19).

8219. שְׁפֵלָה ***šᵉp̱ēlāh:*** I. A feminine noun meaning a low country; a foothill; a valley. It refers to the lowland including not just a low-lying plain but also the low-lying foothills of western Palestine looking out over the Mediterranean (Deut. 1:7; Josh. 9:1; Judg. 1:9; 1 Kgs. 10:27). It also describes the lowland near the seacoast north of Mount Carmel (Josh. 11:2).

II. A proper noun Shephelah. The name means lowlands (KJV, low plains), an area placed under the authority of Baal-Hanan the Gederite (1 Chr. 27:28; Obad. 1:19).

8220. שִׁפְלוּת ***šip̱lûṯ:*** A feminine noun indicating idleness. It indicates an attitude and state of laziness or inactivity that in context leads to the deterioration of the roof of a house. It illustrated the result of sloth and laziness (Eccl. 10:18).

8221. שְׁפָם ***šᵉp̱ām:*** A proper noun designating Shepham (Num. 34:10, 11).

8222. שָׂפָם ***śāp̱ām:*** A masculine noun meaning a mustache, a beard. The most basic understanding of this word is evident in 2 Samuel 19:24

[25], where the text refers to the proper grooming of one's mustache or beard. By extension, this word is also used to imply the upper lip where a mustache grows (Lev. 13:45); and the mouth in general (Ezek. 24:17; Mic. 3:7).

8223. שָׁפָם *šāp̱ām:* A proper noun designating Shapham (1 Chr. 5:12).

8224. שִׂפְמוֹת *śip̱môṯ:* A proper noun designating Siphmoth (1 Sam. 30:28).

8225. שִׁפְמִי *šip̱miy:* A proper noun designating Shiphmite (1 Chr. 27:27).

8226. שָׂפַן *śāp̱an:* A verb meaning to cover as a treasure. It is used to describe valuable wealth, minerals, metals, etc., in the land of Palestine dug from the sand in the territory of Zebulun (Deut. 33:19).

8227. שָׁפָן *šāp̱ān:* I. A masculine noun meaning a coney, a badger. It refers to a kind of rabbit, a pika, a hyrax (Lev. 11:5; Deut. 14:7; Ps. 104:18; Prov. 30:26); or a rock badger (NASB, shaphan). For 2 Kings 25:22, see below, III.

II. A masculine proper name. It refers to Josiah's secretary who helped carry out Josiah's great reforms (2 Kgs. 22:3, 8–10, 12, 14), even helping to make public the Book of the Law found in the temple.

III. A masculine proper noun Shaphan; perhaps the same as II, the father of Ahikam. He was closely involved in all the issues surrounding the discovery of the Book of the Law (2 Kgs. 25:22; 2 Chr. 34:20; Jer. 26:24; 39:14). He was the grandfather of Gedeliah, governor of Judah (Jer. 40:5; 41:2; 43:6).

IV. A masculine proper noun Shaphan, the father of Elasah; perhaps the same as II. His son delivered Jeremiah's letter to the exiles (Jer. 29:3).

V. A masculine proper noun Shaphan, the father of Gemariah; perhaps the same as II. His son Gemariah had his own room or chamber in the Temple near the New Gate (Jer. 36:10–12).

VI. A masculine proper noun Shaphan, the father of Jaazeniah; perhaps the same as II. His son Jaazeniah was a participant in heinous abominations in the Lord's Temple (Ezek. 8:11).

8228. שֶׁפַע *šep̱a':* A masculine noun meaning an abundance. It refers to the huge amount of food and wealth that lies potentially in the seas near Israel (Deut. 33:19).

8229. שִׁפְעָה *šip̱'āh:* A feminine noun meaning an abundance, a multitude, a company. It is used to refer to a large number or great amount of something. It refers to a large company or group of people (2 Kgs. 9:17); a great amount of water (Job 22:11; 38:34); even a great number of camels (Isa. 60:6); or horses (Ezek. 26:10).

8230. שִׁפְעִי ***šip'iy:*** A proper noun designating Shiphi (1 Chr. 4:37).

8231. שָׁפַר ***šāpar:*** A verb meaning to be beautiful. It is used figuratively to describe the splendor and pleasantness of having the Lord as one's lot in life (Ps. 16:6).

8232. שְׁפַר ***šᵉpar:*** An Aramaic verb meaning to be good; to be pleasing. It indicates that something seems right, just, correct to a person (Dan. 4:2[3:32]; 27[24]; 6:1[2]); especially to declare the greatness of God's mighty works or to appoint certain persons or things because of their character and performance.

8233. שֶׁפֶר ***šeper:*** A masculine noun indicating goodness, beauty. It indicates the attractiveness of something, such as beautiful, fitting, appropriate words (Gen. 49:21).

8234. שֶׁפֶר ***šeper:*** A proper noun designating Shepher (Num. 33:23, 24).

8235. שִׁפְרָה ***šiprāh:*** A feminine noun indicating brightness, clearness. It refers to making something appear clean, neat, clear (of visibility). God clears the skies with His breath (Job 26:13).

8236. שִׁפְרָה ***šiprāh:*** A proper noun designating Shiphrah (Ex. 1:15).

8237. שַׁפְרִיר ***šapriyr:*** A masculine noun meaning a canopy; a pavilion. It refers to a covering structure of some kind placed in context over a specific set of stones in Egypt, indicating ownership and rulership in that spot (Jer. 43:10).

8238. שְׁפַרְפָּר ***šᵉparpār:*** An Aramaic masculine noun referring to dawn; early morning. It refers to the time of light breaking forth for a new day, dawn, early in the morning (Dan. 6:19[20]).

8239. שָׁפַת ***šāpat:*** A verb meaning to place in; to establish. It means to move something to a certain spot, to put a pot on a stove (2 Kgs. 4:38; Ezek. 24:3). God places a person in the ground in the dust of death (Ps. 22:15[16]). It is used figuratively also of God's establishing and creating peace for His people (Isa. 26:12).

8240. שְׁפַתַּיִם ***šᵉpattayim:*** I. A masculine noun indicating double-pronged hooks. It refers to special meat forks used to handle sacrifices in Ezekiel's Temple (Ezek. 40:43).

II. A masculine dual noun referring to campfires. It refers to hot cooking stones (NASB, note) or campfires (KJV, pots) used in homes in Israel (Ps. 68:13).

III. A masculine dual noun meaning pots. This translation is given to the word by the King James Version translators (Ps. 68:13).

IV. A masculine dual noun indicating sheepfolds. This translation is given by the New American Standard Bible translators (see NASB note also and I) (Ps. 68:13).

8241. שֶׁצֶף ***šeṣep̱:*** I. A masculine noun indicating a surge. It refers to the Lord's burst of angry emotion toward a disobedient nation (Isa. 54:8; NASB, outburst).

II. A masculine noun meaning a little. It is used to describe the extent of God's anger rather than its nature, a little wrath (Isa. 54:8).

8242. שַׂק ***śaq:*** A masculine noun meaning sackcloth, a sack. It refers to a material of poor quality made of goat hair (2 Sam. 21:10). It was worn traditionally to demonstrate mourning or despair; to convey the message dramatically. It might be placed only on one's loins (Gen. 37:34). Persons might tear their clothes as well, especially at the death of a son. The word is used of sacks used to transport various items of merchandise (Gen. 42:25, 27, 35).

8243. שָׁק ***šāq:*** An Aramaic masculine noun meaning a leg. It refers to the iron leg(s) of the great statue in the king's dream (Dan. 2:33).

8244. שָׂקַד ***śāqad̲:*** A verb meaning to bind. It describes figuratively persons' transgressions being tied, bound, fastened to their necks, like yokes (Lam. 1:14).

8245. שָׁקַד ***šāqad̲:*** A verb meaning to watch; to guard. It means to keep a close watch on something or someone, e.g., Temple utensils (Ezra 8:29); a tomb (Job 21:32); a city (Ps. 127:1). It describes figuratively a person's diligent pursuit of wisdom (Prov. 8:34). It indicates an intent or attitude of a person set on doing something (Isa. 29:20). It indicates a state of being vigilant, lying awake, watching (Ps. 102:7[8]); especially of God's watching over His word to do it (Jer. 1:12; 31:28; 44:27). He brings devastations and calamities to pass, carefully watching over them (Dan. 9:14).

8246. שָׁקַד ***šāqad̲:*** A verb meaning to be shaped like an almond. It indicates the almondlike forms of certain items used in the Tabernacle (Ex. 25:33, 34; 37:19, 20).

8247. שָׁקֵד ***šāqēd̲:*** A masculine noun referring to an almond, an almond tree. It refers to the nutlike kernel of the fruit of a prunus tree. It is edible and was highly desired as food in ancient Israel (Gen. 43:11). Aaron's rod produced ripe almonds as a sign of his right to the high priesthood (Num. 17:8[23]). The almond tree first bears blossoms (Eccl. 12:5). It is used in wordplay by Jeremiah, *šāqēd̲*, almond; *šōqēd̲*, to watch over (Jer. 1:11).

8248. שָׁקָה ***šāqāh:*** A verb meaning to give water; to cause one to drink. It is used often of watering camels and other animals and of giving water or other liquids to persons to drink (Gen. 19:32–35; 21:19; 24:14, 18, 19; Ex. 2:16, 17, 19). This was done sometimes as a polite social gesture, sometimes forcefully (Ex. 32:20). It is used in an impersonal sense of watering the land (Gen. 2:6, 10; Joel

3:18[4:18]). In reference to humans bones, it means to be damp, moist, wet (Job 21:24), meaning to be healthy.

8249. שִׁקּוּ ***šiqquw:*** A masculine noun referring to a drink. It refers to a liquid served up to a person to drink (Ps. 102:9[10]).

8250. שִׁקּוּי ***šiqqûy:*** A masculine noun meaning a drink, moisture. It refers to a liquid served up to drink (Ps. 102:9[10]). It takes on the meaning of vigor, renewal, health to human bones (Prov. 3:8). It indicates water, ill-gotten by harlotry (Hos. 2:5[7]).

8251. שִׁקּוּץ ***šiqqûṣ,*** שִׁקֻּץ ***šiqquṣ:*** A masculine noun meaning a detestable thing, an abomination, and an idol. This Hebrew word identifies an object that is abhorrent or blasphemous. It is used to denote filth (Nah. 3:6); forbidden food (Zech. 9:7); and a blasphemous activity (Dan. 9:27). Most often, it is used as a synonym for an idol or idolatry (Jer. 7:30; Hos. 9:10).

8252. שָׁקַט ***šāqaṭ:*** A verb meaning to be still, to be quiet, to be undisturbed. The primary meaning of this verb is the state or condition of tranquility (cf. Job 37:17). It signifies the condition during the absence of war (Judg. 3:30; 2 Chr. 20:30); a sense of safety and security (Ezek. 38:11); inactivity or passivity (Ps. 83:1[2]; Isa. 18:4); keeping silent (Ruth 3:18; Isa. 62:1); and an inner confidence or peace (Isa. 7:4). Scripture declares that righteousness brings true security and tranquility (Isa. 32:17); but also warns of the false security that comes to the unrighteous (Ezek. 16:49).

8253. שֶׁקֶט ***šeqeṭ:*** A masculine noun meaning quietness, tranquility. The only occurrence of this word is found in 1 Chronicles 22:9 and is parallel to the Hebrew word for peace (*šālôm*, 7965). It is used to describe the state of tranquility during the reign of Solomon when all enemies were defeated and the united kingdom was at its height.

8254. שָׁקַל ***šāqal:*** A verb meaning to weigh; to weigh out money, to pay. It indicates the process of calculating the actual weight of money (silver) or food items usually with the purpose of making payment for something (Gen. 23:16; Ex. 22:17[16]; 2 Sam. 18:12; Job 28:15). Absalom's hair was weighed and registered 200 shekels in weight (2 Sam. 14:26). The gold and silver vessels of the Temple were weighed out (Ezra 8:33). It is used figuratively of weighing sorrow and suffering (Job 6:2); or of weighing a person in a moral, ethical sense (Job 31:6).

8255. שֶׁקֶל ***šeqel:*** A masculine noun indicating shekel; a unit of weight for metals. It was a unit of weight for metals that was probably around twelve grams or one-half ounce. A silver shekel is expressed as *šeqel kesep̱* (Gen. 23:15); *šeqel haqqōḏeṣ* refers to a shekel of the sanctuary (Ex. 30:13). There was also a king's shekel (2 Sam. 14:26). A half shekel was *maḥᵃṣîṯ haššeqel* (Ex. 38:24–26); *reḇa'* indicated one-fourth shekel (1 Sam. 9:8).

8256. שִׁקְמָה ***šiqmāh:*** A feminine noun designating a sycamore tree; a sycamore fig. A fig tree native to Asia Minor and Egypt with edible fruit. It was abundant in Israel's territory (1 Kgs. 10:27); these trees were destroyed by the Lord in times of judgment (Ps. 78:47). It made an inferior construction material (Isa. 9:10 [9]). Amos grew and cultivated these trees (Amos 7:14).

8257. שָׁקַע ***šāqa':*** A verb meaning to sink down, to settle. It is used to describe the dying out, the going out of a fire (Num. 11:2); or of water going down, receding (Ezek. 32:14; Amos 8:8; 9:5). It is used in its causative stem in a physical sense of holding something down (Job 41:1 [40:25]). It describes figuratively the demise or fall of an empire such as Babylon (Jer. 51:64).

8258. שְׁקַעֲרוּרָה ***šᵉqaᵃrûrāh:*** A feminine noun meaning a depression; the hollow streak of a branch. It refers to a depression on the walls of a house in Israel indicating some kind of mold or fungus attack (Lev. 14:37).

8259. שָׁקַף ***šāqap̄:*** A verb meaning to look down on, to overlook. It has the sense from context of a person, of God, looking down, observing from above: It is used of people or angels (Gen. 18:16); Abraham (Gen. 19:28); God (Ex. 14:24; Ps. 14:2; 53:2[3]; 102:19[20]; Lam 3:50); evil (Jer. 6:1). It may mean simply to look over at something, to observe (Gen. 26:8; Prov. 7:6). It is used in the sense of to look forth, to shine forth (Song 6:10).

8260. שֶׁקֶף ***šeqep̄:*** I. A masculine noun referring to a squared frame. It indicates a frame with four equal sides. In context it refers to doorways and doorposts (1 Kgs. 7:5).

II. A masculine noun meaning a window. Earlier translators took this word to mean a window as a separate word (1 Kgs. 7:5).

8261. שָׁקוּף ***šāqûp̄,*** שָׁקֻף ***šāqup̄:*** I. A masculine noun referring to squared frames. It is used to indicate window frames (NASB, 1 Kgs. 6:4).

II. A masculine noun meaning windows. It is rendered as windows by many translators (KJV, 1 Kgs. 6:4); clerestory windows (windows in the upper section of walls (NIV, 1 Kgs. 6:4).

8262. שָׁקַץ ***šāqaṣ:*** A verb meaning to detest, to make abominable. The primary meaning of this word is to make or to consider something odious. It is used to describe the attitude the Israelites were to have toward a graven image or idol (Deut. 7:26); and certain nonkosher foods (Lev. 11:11, 13). If the Israelites failed to observe this command by partaking of unclean food, they would become detestable to the Lord (Lev. 20:25). On the other hand, the psalmist stated that this was never the Lord's attitude toward the cries of the afflicted (Ps. 22:24[25]).

8263. שֶׁקֶץ šeqeṣ: A masculine noun meaning a detestation, an abomination, and a detestable thing. Chiefly, this Hebrew word marks those things that were ceremonially unclean and forbidden (Lev. 7:21). It is used of certain sea creatures (Lev. 11:10); birds of prey (Lev. 11:13ff.); and various creeping things (Lev. 11:20, 23, 41, 42).

8264. שָׁקַק šāqaq, שׁוֹקֵק šôqēq: I. A verb meaning to rush about; to charge. It describes a quick, powerful motion, a movement towards someone or something (Prov. 28:15); a confused activity here and there, like swarming locusts (Isa. 33:4; Joel 2:9); or war chariots darting here and there in city streets (Nah. 2:4[5]).

II. A verb meaning to thirst; to long for. It means to experience a strong desire for liquids but is used figuratively of the desire, the longing of the soul (Ps. 107:9; 29:8).

III. An adjective meaning thirsty. It describes a thirsty soul, desiring the spiritual food it needs (Ps. 107:9; Isa. 29:8).

8265. שָׂקַר śāqar: A verb meaning to flirt. It describes the seductive eyes of the proud women of Judah, eyes painted for the purpose of flirting, looking enticing (Isa. 3:16).

8266. שָׁקַר šāqar: A verb meaning to engage in deceit, to deal falsely. The notion of a treacherous or deceptive activity forms the fundamental meaning of this word. It is used to describe an agreement entered into with deceitful intentions (Gen. 21:23); outright lying (Lev. 19:11); and the violation of a covenant (Ps. 44:17[18]). Scripture states clearly that such activity is the domain of humans, not of God (1 Sam. 15:29).

8267. שֶׁקֶר šeqer: A noun meaning a lie, vanity, without cause. This word is used of a lying witness (Deut. 19:18); of false prophets (Jer. 5:31; 20:6; 29:9); of telling lies (Lev. 19:12; Jer. 37:14); and of a liar (Prov. 17:4). In other cases, it describes something done in vain (1 Sam. 25:21; Ps. 33:17); or an action without cause (Ps. 38:19[20]; 119:78, 86).

8268. שֹׁקֶת šōqeṯ: A feminine noun indicating a water trough. It refers to a hollow structure for holding drinking water for animals, a standard piece of farming and agriculture in the ancient Near East (Gen. 24:20; 30:38).

8269. שַׂר śar: A masculine noun meaning a chieftain, a chief, a ruler, an official, a captain, a prince. The primary usage is official in the sense that this individual has immediate authority as the leader. While he was at Gath, David became the leader for those who were in distress, in debt, or were discontented (1 Sam. 22:2). The word describes the powers of a magistrate when a man posed a sarcastic question to Moses (Ex. 2:14). In Genesis, the noun refers to Phicol as the commander of Abimelech's forces (Gen. 21:22). In a similar usage of the word, Joshua was met by the commander of the Lord's army. This commander was so entrusted by God that Joshua had to take off his shoes due to the glory of God surrounding the man (Josh. 5:14).

In terms of priesthood, *śar* designates a leading priest, i.e. a priest that is above the others (Ezra 8:24, 29). In this situation with Ezra, the leading priest was entrusted with the articles of the Temple and had to guard them with his life. The noun depicts Michael as one of the chief princes who came to Daniel's aid (Dan. 10:13). In Daniel 8:11, the word is used to denote the little horn setting itself up to be as great as the Prince of the host. This horn would set itself up, take away the daily sacrifice, and desecrate the Temple of God.

8270. שֹׁר **šōr:** A masculine noun indicating a navel, a navel cord. It refers to the bride's navel, which is praised as an ornament of beauty (Song 7:2). It is used figuratively of the navel cord of the infant Israel (Ezek. 16:4). It can be read as naval (*šōr*) or body, flesh (*baśar*) (Prov. 3:8).

8271. שְׁרֵא ***šᵉrē':*** An Aramaic verb meaning to loosen, to dissolve; to solve (problems). It carries a sense of support, to aid, to help (Ezra 5:2). It has the sense of dwelling with or being dispersed when used of light in relationship to God (Dan. 2:22). It refers to someone being loosed after being bound up (Dan. 3:25). It indicates loose joints or sockets (Dan. 5:6). With reference to problems, it means to solve them, to disentangle them (Dan. 5:12, 16).

8272. שַׁרְאֶצֶר ***šar'eṣer,*** שַׂרְאֶצֶר ***śar'eṣer:*** A proper noun designating Sharezer:

A. Son of Sennacherib (2 Kgs. 19:37; Isa. 37:38).

B. An Israelite in Zechariah's day (Zech. 7:2).

8273. שָׁרָב ***šārāḇ:*** A masculine noun referring to scorched ground; scorching heat. It indicates something dried out, singed, darkened by heat from the sun (Isa. 35:7; 49:10).

8274. שֵׁרֵבְיָה ***šērēḇyāh:*** A proper noun designating Sherebiah:

A. A Levite returning from exile with Ezra (Ezra 8:18, 24), perhaps the same as B below.

B. A Levite who assisted Ezra (Neh. 8:7; 9:4, 5; 10:12[13]), perhaps the same as A or C.

C. A Levite who returned with Zerubbabel (Neh. 12:8, 24), possibly the same as B above.

8275. שַׁרְבִיט ***šarḇiyṭ:*** A masculine noun meaning a scepter. This word is only found in the book of Esther. In Esther's response to Mordecai, she stated that anyone who went to see the king without being summoned would die unless the king extended the gold scepter in a symbolic act that saved the life of the individual (Esth. 4:11). In Esther 5:2, Esther went before the king, touched the scepter that was extended to her, then stated her request that Haman come to a feast that she had provided for him and the king. Finally, Esther went again before the king and fell at his feet weeping and begging that he would stop Haman's evil plan. King Xerxes again extended the scepter to Esther, who in turn stood and restated her request (Esth. 8:4).

8276. שָׂרַג ***śārag:*** A verb meaning to be woven together. It indicates the close, orderly entwinement of the sinews of someone's tendons (Job 40:17). It is used figuratively of sins being knit together (Lam. 1:14).

8277. שָׂרַד ***śārad̲:*** A verb meaning to remain, to be left. It indicates that something remains of what was originally present. In this case, some of the defeated enemy survived (Josh. 10:20).

8278. שְׂרָד ***śᵉrād̲:*** I. A masculine noun indicating woven work. It refers to skillfully integrated and entwined materials in certain garments (Ex. 31:10); and the garment itself (Ex. 35:19; 39:1, 41).

II. A masculine noun meaning service, work. It is used of the work done by the priests and Levites in Israel (Ex. 31:10; 35:19; 39:1, 41).

8279. שֶׂרֶד ***śered̲:*** I. A masculine noun referring to a marking tool. It refers to some kind of tool used by a craftsman to mark out a design on newly dressed wood (Isa. 44:13).

II. A masculine noun indicating a line. It refers to a line drawn on newly dressed wood or a string used to mark a line (Isa. 44:13).

III. A masculine noun meaning chalk. It refers to a chalk marker used to make a pattern on newly dressed wood (Isa. 44:13).

8280. שָׂרָה ***śārāh:*** A verb meaning to persist, to exert oneself, to persevere. The primary meaning is to exert oneself. In Genesis, the word depicts Jacob, who had struggled with God and persons and prevailed. This achievement resulted in a name change to Israel (Gen. 32:28[29]). The word is used figuratively in Hosea, recollecting on the memory of Jacob's struggle with God at Peniel to describe a reason for Ephraim's punishment (Hos. 12:4[5]). This comparison relates Ephraim back to Jacob, the father of their tribe, as a call to repentance.

8281. שָׂרָה ***šārāh:*** A verb meaning to let loose. This word occurs in the Old Testament only once. In Job 37:3, it describes God's loosing of thunder and lightning.

8282. שָׂרָה ***sārāh:*** A feminine noun meaning a princess, a royal lady. This word comes from the verb *śārar* (8323), meaning to rule or to act as prince, and is the feminine form of the word *śar* (8269), meaning prince, captain, or ruler. This word always refers to women who had access to the royal court. It is used of the particular princesses who associated with Deborah, Solomon, and the nation of Persia (Judg. 5:29; 1 Kgs. 11:3; Esth. 1:18). It is also used in a general sense to describe princesses who were humbled to become nurses and servants (Isa. 49:23; Lam. 1:1).

8283. שָׂרָה *śārāh:* A proper noun designating Sarah, the wife of Abraham. Her name was changed from Sarai to Sarah (Gen. 17:15, 17). The change in name indicated the multitude of persons who would come forth from her (but was also merely an updating of the form of the word). The name means "princess" or "woman of nobility." Kings, nations, and leaders came from her.

She bore the son of the promise, Isaac, by a special act of God (Gen. 17:19–22; 18:7–15; 21:1–6). Isaiah called her the mother who gave birth to Zion, Israel (51:2). She willingly took part in Abraham's deception of her relationship to him (Gen. 20:1; 18). She died at 127 years of age in Hebron and was buried in the cave in the field in Machpelah near Mamre which Abraham purchased as a burial plot (Gen. 23:12–20).

8284. שָׁרָה *šārāh,* שׁוּרָה *šûrāh:* I. A feminine noun meaning a vineyard, a vine row. It refers to rows of grapevines in the fields around Israel, but in context it is applied figuratively to the destruction of the city of Jerusalem (Jer. 5:10).

II. It is a feminine noun designating a wall. It is understood to refer to the high protective walls surrounding Jerusalem (Jer. 5:10).

8285. שֵׁרָה *šērāh:* A feminine noun meaning bracelet. It refers to an ornamental bracelet, an item of luxury which the Lord will destroy when He brings judgment on Zion (Isa. 3:19).

8286. שְׂרוּג *śᵉrûg:* A proper noun designating Serug (Gen. 11:20–23; 1 Chr. 1:26).

8287. שָׁרוּחֶן *šārûḥen:* A proper noun designating Sharuhen (Josh. 19:6).

8288. שְׂרוֹךְ *śᵉrûḵ:* A masculine noun referring to a strap. It refers in context to straps used to keep sandals on a person's feet (Gen. 14:23; Isa. 5:27). If the straps break, it slows a person's progress.

8289. שָׁרוֹן *šārôn,* לַשָּׁרוֹן *laššārôn:* A proper noun designating Lasharon, Sharon:

A. Lasharon is the name of a Canaanite king conquered by Joshua, evidently on the west of the Jordan. The location is not known. It may be a separate town.

B. Sharon is the name given to a stretch of the coastal plain on the Mediterranean shore. It was between the Yarkon River and Mount Carmel.

Cattle pastured here. It was fertile, but God judged even this territory and its inhabitants (Isa. 33:9; 35:2). God would, however, restore its fertility (Isa. 65:10). The Philistine plain lay to its south.

C. A plain east of the Jordan in Gilead (1 Chr. 5:16).

D. A king in Lasharon. The location is not certain. (See A above.) It may have been a town. The LXX indicates a "king of Aphek" named Lasharon (Josh. 12:18).

8290. שָׁרוֹנִי ***šarôniy:*** A proper noun designating Sharonite (1 Chr. 27:29).

8291. שָׂרֹק ***śārōq:*** A masculine noun indicating a choice vine, a principal plant. It refers to the best-producing sections of a vineyard, whether they have choice vines or the best plants (Isa. 16:8).

8292. שְׁרוּקָה ***šᵉriyqāh,*** שְׁרִקָה ***šᵉriqāh:*** A feminine noun referring to flute playing, piping. It describes a shepherd's playing his flute for his flocks to keep them calm (Judg. 5:16). Its meaning in Jeremiah 18:16 must indicate scorn, possibly a mocking playing of the flute, piping in scorn, but most translators render it as a hissing or mocking.

8293. שֵׁרוּת ***šᵉrûṯ:*** A feminine noun meaning a beginning. This word is another form of the word *šārāh* (8281). In Jeremiah 15:11, this word refers to God setting Jeremiah free.

8294. שֶׂרַח ***śeraḥ:*** A proper noun designating Serah. The sister of the sons of Asher (Gen. 46:17).

8295. שָׂרַט ***śāraṭ:*** A verb meaning to cut or to injure oneself. It means to administer cuts on oneself. In context it describes a practice forbidden in Israel (Lev. 21:5). It also has the sense of injuring oneself through self-exertion, excessive straining at a task too big to handle (Zech. 12:3).

8296. שֶׂרֶט ***śereṭ,*** שָׂרֶטֶת ***śāreṭeṯ:*** A masculine/feminine noun referring to a cutting of one's body. It is an injury self-inflicted by cutting oneself, in context, for a religious reason, but this was forbidden in Israel (Lev. 19:28; 21:5).

8297. שָׂרַי ***śāray:*** A proper noun designating Sarai, the wife whom Abraham married in Ur of the Chaldees. She became the "princess" or "woman of nobility" of the covenant and promises to Abraham. This old name was changed to Sarah (Gen. 17:15). See Sarah (8283).

8298. שָׁרַי ***šāray:*** A proper noun designating Sharai (Ezra 10:40).

8299. שָׂרִיג ***śāriyg:*** A masculine noun meaning a branch. It refers to branches of a vine plant (Gen. 40:10, 12), but it is used in a figurative sense of days. It is used literally in Joel 1:7.

8300. שָׂרִיד ***śāriyḏ:*** A masculine noun meaning a survivor. This word comes from the verb *śāraḏ* (8277), meaning an escape. In one instance of this word, it is used to describe physical things that had not been devoured (Job 20:21). In all other instances, it is used to describe people who had survived the onslaught of an enemy (Num. 24:19; Josh. 10:20; Jer. 31:2). It is often used with the negative to describe total desolation, i.e., there were no survivors (Num. 21:35; Josh. 10:28; Jer. 42:17).

8301. שָׂרִיד ***śāriyḏ:*** A proper noun designating Sarid (Josh. 19:10, 12).

8302. שִׁרְיוֹן ***širyôn,*** שִׁרְיָן ***širyān,*** שִׁרְיָה ***širyāh:*** I. A masculine noun indicating body armor; a breastplate. It refers to scale armor worn as protective gear (1 Sam. 17:5, 38). It was still vulnerable at various points (1 Kgs. 22:34; 2 Chr. 18:33). It may refer to a small version of this armor, a breastplate (Neh. 4:16[10]). It is used as a figure of righteousness serving as a breastplate or scale armor (Isa. 59:17).

II. A feminine noun referring to body armor. It is rendered as javelin (NASB, NIV) or habergeon (armor) (KJV). In all cases, it refers to the protective coverings of Leviathan (Job 41:26[18]).

III. A masculine noun indicating a javelin. It is rendered as a javelin, a sharp throwing instrument or weapon (Job 41:26[18], NIV, NASB). See II.

8303. שִׂרְיֹן ***śiryōn:*** A proper noun designating Sirion (Deut. 3:9; Ps. 29:6).

8304. שְׂרָיָה ***śᵉrāyāh,*** שְׂרָיָהוּ ***śᵉrāyāhû:*** A proper noun designating Seraiah:

A. Secretary to David (2 Sam. 8:17).

B. A Judaite, father of Joab (1 Chr. 4:13, 14).

C. A Simeonite (1 Chr. 4:35).

D. An officer of King Jehoiakim (Jer. 36:26).

E. A friend and associate of Jeremiah (Jer. 51:59, 61).

F. Associate of Gedaliah (2 Kgs. 25:23; Jer. 40:8).

G. Chief priest when Jerusalem fell (2 Kgs. 25:18; 1 Chr. 6:14[5:40]; Jer. 52:24), possibly the same as H.

H. The father or ancestor of Ezra (Ezra 7:1), possibly the same as G.

I. One who returned from exile with Zerubabbel (Ezra 2:2).

J. One who signed a covenant with Nehemiah (Neh. 10:2[3]), possibly the same as K.

K. A priest in the restored temple (Neh. 11:11; 12:1, 12), possibly the same as J.

8305. שָׂרִיק ***śāriyq:*** An adjective meaning combed. It refers to a fine quality of flax made in Egypt, referred to as carded flax. It also means flax that has been combed out or brushed with a card (Isa. 19:9).

8306. שָׁרִיר ***šāriyr:*** A masculine noun indicating muscles, sinews; navel. It describes the powerful stomach muscles of Leviathan (Job 40:16; KJV, navel).

8307. שְׁרִירוּת šᵉriyrûṯ, שְׁרִרוּת šᵉrirûṯ: A feminine noun meaning hardness, stubbornness. This word has the basic idea of firmness or hardness, but in its ten usages in the Old Testament, it is always used in conjunction with the word *lēḇ* (3820), meaning heart, to describe disobedient Israel. Thus, it is best to translate this word stubbornness. It is used to describe those who did evil (Jer. 16:12); who walked after their own plans (Jer. 18:12); who refused to listen to God's words (Jer. 13:10); who did not obey God's counsel (Jer. 7:24; 9:14[13]; 11:8); and who were deluded to think they were at peace (Deut. 29:19[18]; Jer. 23:17). God gave such people over to their own devices (Ps. 81:12[13]).

8308. שָׂרַךְ śārak̲: A verb meaning to crisscross; to traverse. It refers to Israel, using the figure of a camel, entangling herself with the nations (Jer. 2:23).

8309. שְׁרֵמָה šᵉrēmāh: A feminine noun referring to a field. It refers to parts of the open country good for agriculture or grazing (Jer. 31:40).

8310. שַׂרְסְכִים śarsᵉk̲iym: A proper noun designating Sar-sekim (Jer. 39:3).

8311. שָׂרַע śāra': I. A verb meaning to stretch out. It refers to the process of extending one's body fully and comfortably on a bed; the whole context refers to Israel figuratively (Isa. 28:20).

II. A verb meaning to be superfluous, to be deformed. In context it refers most likely to a disfigured limb of a person (Lev. 21:18); or an overdeveloped or crippled member (Lev. 22:23). The King James Version renders it as an extra or superfluous member.

8312. שַׂרְעַפִּים śar'appiym: A masculine noun meaning a disquieting thought, an anxious feeling. The psalmist rejoiced that the Lord calmed his inner anxieties (Ps. 94:19). This is the same word used by the psalmist when he asked God to search him and know his anxieties (Ps. 139:23).

8313. שָׂרַף śārap̱: A verb meaning to burn. Most often, this word is used to mean to burn with intent, to destroy, or to consume. It is normally used to refer to sacrifices. Many sacrificial laws prescribed specific ways for offerings to be burnt (Ex. 29:14). Burning could also be a form of punishment, as in the story of Achan (Josh. 7:25). Buildings and cities were other common objects of burning: Men of Ephraim threatened to burn down Jephthah's house with fire (Judg. 12:1). Less frequently, this word refers to the process of firing bricks (Gen. 11:3).

8314. שָׂרָף śārāp̱: A masculine noun meaning a serpent. This word generally refers to a poisonous snake, deriving its origin from the burning sensation of the serpent's bite (see Deut. 8:15). It is used specifically of the fiery serpents that were sent as judgment. The likeness of a serpent was made of brass at the Lord's command (Num. 21:8). The word is used twice by Isaiah to apparently denote a dragon (Isa. 14:29; 30:6).

8315. שָׂרָף śārāp̱: A proper noun designating Saraph (1 Chr. 4:22).

8316. שְׂרֵפָה śᵉrēp̱āh: A feminine noun meaning burning, thoroughly burnt. The connotation of this word is that of being thoroughly consumed with fire. It is used to refer to kiln-firing brick (Gen. 11:3); a destructive flame (Amos 4:11); an inactive volcano (Jer. 51:25); divine judgment (Lev. 10:6); and the burning of the red heifer (Num. 19:6). This word vividly portrays the state of the Temple during the Babylonian captivity (Isa. 64:11[10]).

8317. שָׁרַץ šāraṣ: I. A verb meaning to swarm; to breed abundantly; to multiply. It means to teem, to swarm in numbers and rate of birth and multiplication. It is used of the land and waters swarming with swarming creatures (Gen. 1:20, 21; Ex. 8:3[7:28]; Ps. 105:30). It is used figuratively of Israel's birth rate in Egypt, her unusual multiplication (Ex. 1:7). Certain swarming things were unclean to Israel (Lev. 11:29, 41, 43, 46). But swarming creatures will be part of the new rejuvenated Israel (Ezek. 47:9).

II. A verb indicating to creep. The same verb (or its homonym, a word that sounds the same) refers to creeping things, insects, lizards, etc., on the earth (Gen. 7:21; Lev. 11:29, 41, 42, 43, 46). These things were detestable to Israel.

8318. שֶׁרֶץ šereṣ: A masculine noun indicating a creature that crawls or swarms; insects or small animals. God created them in the beginning (Gen. 1:20); they also died in the great flood (Gen. 7:21). These teeming (NASB) creatures included fish and whatever may be in the rivers and seas (Lev. 11:10; Deut. 14:19). If they had no scales, they were detestable, unclean to Israel for food.

8319. שָׁרַק šāraq: A verb meaning to hiss, to whistle, to scorn. It describes a hissing or whistling of puzzled wonderment (1 Kgs. 9:8). It is a word of rejection and mockery in some cases (Job 27:23; Jer. 19:8; 50:13; Lam. 2:15, 16). The great city of Tyre became an object of hissing at her fall (Ezek. 27:36); as did Ethiopia (Zeph. 2:15). It is used to call for, to whistle for someone or something to come (Isa. 5:26; 7:18; Zech. 10:8).

8320. שָׂרֹק śārōq: I. A masculine noun indicating sorrel or brown. It is the color of certain horses that Zechariah sees in a vision. Sorrel is a light reddish-brown color (Zech. 1:8).

II. A masculine noun indicating speckled. It is another color of certain horses seen in Zechariah's vision (Zech. 1:8). It is any color with various small specks of a different color scattered in it.

8321. שֹׂרֵק ***śōrēq,*** **שֹׂרֵקָה** ***śōrēqāh:*** A masculine/feminine noun meaning a choice wine; a choice vine. It refers to select grapes, evidently featuring a certain color (Isa. 5:2; Jer. 2:21). It seems to refer to a choice vine in Genesis 49:11, the best growth in the land.

8322. שְׁרֵקָה ***šᵉrēqāh:*** A feminine noun indicating hissing as scorn or derision. It refers to whistling or hissing at something: for instance, as an object of dread or horror (2 Chr. 29:8; Jer. 25:9); especially Jerusalem in her devastation (Jer. 19:8; 25:18). The people of Israel themselves because of their transgressions would become a hissing among the nations (Jer. 29:18; Mic. 6:16); but likewise so would Babylon (Jer. 51:37).

8323. שָׂרַר ***śārar:*** A verb meaning to reign as a prince, to be a prince, to rule. This Hebrew word means literally to rule or to govern as a prince, as is evident in Isaiah 32:1. This word also may imply an unwelcome exercise of authority over another, as the protest against Moses in Numbers 16:13 suggests.

8324. שֹׁרֵר ***šôrēr,*** **שׁוֹרֵר** ***šôrēr:*** A masculine noun referring to an enemy, a foe; a slanderer. It refers to hostile persons who want to harm or destroy righteous persons (Ps. 5:8[9]; 27:11; 54:5[7]; 56:2[3]). God gives deliverance over the psalmist's foes (Ps. 59:10[11]); but the righteous can have a victorious attitude toward their foes (Ps. 92:11[12]).

8325. שָׁרָר ***šārār:*** A proper noun designating Sharar (2 Sam. 23:33), the same as Sacar (7940,A).

8326. שֹׁרֶר ***šōrer:*** A masculine noun referring to the navel of the bridegroom as an ornament of beauty (Song 7:2[3]).

8327. שָׁרַשׁ ***šāraš:*** A verb meaning to take root, to uproot. It is used often in a figurative sense. It means to put out, to grow roots (Ps. 80:9[10]; Isa. 27:6; 40:24; Jer. 12:2). In its passive sense, it means to be uprooted (Job 31:8). Even the foolish person may take root but will not be stable (Job 5:3). The wicked person will finally be uprooted from this life (Ps. 52:5[7]).

8328. שֶׁרֶשׁ ***šereš:*** A masculine noun indicating a root, depth. It is often used figuratively. It refers to the life-generating tentacles that a plant puts out in the ground (2 Kgs. 19:30; Job 14:8; Jer. 17:8). In a figurative sense, it refers to the hostile attitudes found in persons that create strife and bitterness (Deut. 29:18[17]). It refers to an origin, a beginning (Judg. 5:14). Figuratively, good persons put their roots around rocks (Job 8:17). It may be translated as soles (NASB) of one's feet, the foundation of one's life (Job 13:27; KJV, heels). The roots of the wicked are destined to destruction (Job 18:16); the roots of the righteous stand forever (Prov. 12:3). The base or foundation of a mountain is its roots (Job 28:9). It is used of Israel herself taking root and prospering (Ps. 80:9[10]). The coming messianic king, the Branch, will spring from the roots of the Davidic line (Isa. 11:1); the root of Jesse (Isa. 11:10). The Suffering Servant's root source was fragile (Isa. 53:2). The whole picture of Ezekiel 17:6, 7, 9 utilizes the figurative use of roots to describe nations and peoples. Roots imply descendants in Daniel 11:7. Israel's roots in her future restoration will propel her to prosperity (Hos. 14:5[6]). God's final acts of judgment will destroy the roots of evildoers with fire (Mal. 4:1[3:19]).

8329. שֶׁרֶשׁ ***šereš:*** A proper noun designating Sheresh (1 Chr. 7:16).

8330. שֹׁרֶשׁ ***šōreš:*** An Aramaic masculine noun meaning a root. It is employed figuratively and refers to the roots of a huge tree in a dream which Nebuchadnezzar had (Dan. 4:15[12], 23[20], 26[23]).

8331. שַׁרְשָׁה ***šaršāh:*** A feminine noun meaning a chain. It refers to an interlocking set of metal links or intertwined pieces of rope (Ex. 28:22).

8332. שְׁרֹשׁוּ ***š^{e}rōšû:*** An Aramaic feminine noun meaning banishment. It indicates the ejection of a person from a social or political community. In context it does so because of a failure to observe the Mosaic covenant (Ezra 7:26).

8333. שַׁרְשְׁרָה ***šarš^{e}rāh:*** A feminine noun referring to a chain. It indicates a set of interlocking or intertwined metal links, in context chains of gold (Ex. 28:14); twisted chainwork (1 Kgs. 7:17); ornamental (2 Chr. 3:5, 16).

8334. שָׁרַת ***šāraṯ:*** A verb meaning to minister, to serve. This Hebrew word was utilized in a generic sense to describe various activities, including that of a domestic servant serving a ranking official (Gen. 39:4; 2 Sam. 13:17, 18); a chief assistant to an authority figure, such as Joshua was to Moses (Ex. 24:13); the angelic host to God (Ps. 103:21); and assistants to kings (Isa. 60:10). More particularly, the word is used in the context of religious service before the Lord, such as that required of the priests (Ex. 28:35; 1 Kgs. 8:11); or Levites (Num. 3:6).

8335. שָׁרֵת ***šārēṯ:*** A masculine noun meaning religious ministry, service. Service in the place of worship underlies the primary meaning of this word. It is used twice in reference to the instruments used by those ministering in the Tabernacle (Num. 4:12); and the vessels used for ritual in the Temple (2 Chr. 24:14). The stress was upon the connection to the functions of the priestly office.

8336. שֵׁשׁ ***šēš:*** I. A masculine noun referring to fine linen, linen. It refers to fine linen from Egypt, exquisitely woven. It was used in garments (Gen. 41:42); sails, priestly clothing (Ex. 28:5, 39). It was spun by women (Ex. 35:25). *Šeš mašzar* refers to fine twisted linen (Ex. 28:6, 15; 36:8).

II. A masculine noun indicating marble. A fine-grained hard limestone of great beauty and ornamental value (Esth. 1:6). It is rendered as alabaster as well, a fine-grained translucent variety of gypsum (Song 5:15).

8337. שֵׁשׁ šēš, שִׁשָּׁה šiššāh: A feminine noun meaning six. It indicates a cardinal number identifying the sixth item in counting. It combines with other numbers (Gen. 7:6, 11; 8:13; 16:16).

8338. שָׁשָׁא šāšā': I. A verb meaning to drive; to drag along. It means to urge someone, to provide impetus for moving on. It is used figuratively of God's moving Gog toward Israel and destruction (Ezek. 39:2).

II. A verb indicating to leave a sixth part. It means to take or leave behind only one-sixth of something (Ezek. 39:2, KJV).

8339. שֵׁשְׁבַּצַּר šešbaṣṣar: A proper noun designating Sheshbazzar, a prince of Judah in Babylon who was in charge of the Temple vessels returned to Babylon (Ezra 1:8, 11). The name is Babylonian. It may mean "Shamash (sun god) protect the father." He served as governor in Judah and helped rebuild the Temple. Many feel that he is none other than Zerubbabel (cf. Ezra 3:2–8; 5:14). Babylonian names were regularly given to ranking officials in Babylon (Dan. 1:7, etc.). But, Sheshbazzar could have been a non-Jew, a governor of Samaria (cf. Ezra 5:14).

8340. שֵׁשְׁבַּצַּר šēšbaṣṣār: A proper noun designating the Aramaic name for Sheshbazzar. (See 8339 above.) The facts and meaning are the same.

8341. שָׁשָׁה šāšāh: A verb meaning to give a sixth part. It refers to contributing one-sixth of an ephah from a homer of wheat or barley as an offering to the Prince in Ezekiel's' new Temple (Ezek. 45:13).

8342. שָׂשׂוֹן śāśôn: A masculine noun indicating joy, gladness. It refers to joy, exultation toward God's King (Ps. 45:7[8]); given to God's people (Ps. 51:8[10], 12[14]); in His own people at deliverance (Ps. 105:43); over the testimonies and laws of God (Ps. 119:111). God is the joy of His people (Isa. 12:3). Joy will be removed from a rebellious people (Jer. 7:34; Joel 1:12). In God's restoration of His people, joy will be abundant (Zech. 8:19).

8343. שָׁשַׁי šāšay: A proper noun designating Shashai (Ezra 10:40).

8344. שֵׁשַׁי šēšai: A proper noun designating Sheshai (Num. 13:22; Josh. 15:14; Judg. 1:10).

8345. שִׁשִּׁי šiššiy: A numerical ordinal adjective meaning sixth. It points out the sixth item in a series (Gen. 1:31; 30:19; Ex. 16:5, 22, 29; Hag. 1:1, 15).

8346. שִׁשִּׁים šiššiym: A numerical plural adjective meaning sixty. It is the plural of *šēš*. It indicates the sixtieth item in a counting series of items (Gen. 46:26). It combines with other numbers, e.g., sixty-five (Gen. 5:15, 18, 20).

8347. שֵׁשַׁךְ ***šēšak̲:*** A proper noun designating Sheshach (Jer. 25:26; 51:41).

8348. שֵׁשָׁן ***šēšān:*** A proper noun designating Sheshan (1 Chr. 2:31, 34, 35).

8349. שָׁשָׁק ***šāšāq:*** A proper noun designating Shashak (1 Chr. 8:14, 25).

8350. שָׁשֵׁר ***šāšēr:*** A masculine noun meaning red, vermilion. It is a pigment used to color paint. It was the color of red ocher or even bright red, a bright ostentatious color (Jer. 22:14; Ezek. 23:14).

8351. שֵׁת ***šēt̲:*** I. A masculine noun referring to buttocks, hip. It refers to the upper part of one's thigh or lower buttocks (2 Sam. 10:4).

II. A masculine noun meaning a foundation. It refers to the base supporting structure of something. In context it refers to the necessary moral and ethical foundations of righteousness, that is, God's will, Law, covenant, etc. (Ps. 11:3).

8352. שֵׁת ***šēt̲:*** A proper noun designating Sheshbazzar, the third son of Adam and Eve. He was named Seth, which means "placed, put, granted" in place of Abel. Abel fathered Enoch, a name meaning "mankind." He had more sons and daughters and lived to be 912 years old (Gen. 5:6–8).

8353. שֵׁת ***šēt̲,*** שִׁת ***šit̲:*** An Aramaic numerical adjective, sixth, six. It is used as an ordinal, the sixth year (Ezra 6:15, year of six, the sixth year) and as a cardinal counting number, six cubits (Dan. 3:1).

8354. שָׁתָה ***šāt̲āh:*** A verb meaning to drink. It is used of drinking any kind of liquid: people drinking wine (Gen. 9:21); people and animals drinking water (Gen. 24:14, 18, 19, 22; 25:34). God does not drink the blood of goats (Ps. 50:13). It is used of a great apocalyptic end-time banquet where animals and birds will figuratively drink blood (Ezek. 39:17). It is used figuratively of a fool drinking violence (Prov. 4:17; 26:6). It refers to drinking wine in preparation for a joyous occasion (Song 5:1). It is used of drinking the cup of the Lord's wrath (Isa. 51:17); and of Israel's successful destruction of its enemies (Num. 23:24). In its passive sense, it means to be drunk (Lev. 11:34).

8355. שְׁתָה ***šᵉt̲āh:*** An Aramaic verb meaning to drink. It refers to the imbibing of wine at a royal banquet (Dan. 5:1–4, 23).

8356. שָׁתָה ***šāt̲āh:*** I. A masculine noun indicating a pillar, a foundation. Figuratively, it indicates the supporting structures of righteousness (Ps. 11:3). It refers literally to great stone columns and pillars made in Egypt (Isa. 19:10).

II. A masculine noun indicating a purpose, a goal. It indicates the reason or rationale for doing something, why it is done (Isa. 19:10).

III. A masculine noun referring to a person who works with cloth. It refers to those who weave and spin yarns into various kinds of cloth (Isa. 19:10).

IV. A masculine noun indicating a worker in cloth. See III.

8357. שֵׁתָה ***šēṯāh:*** A masculine noun referring to buttocks, hip. It refers to the upper part of persons' hips or the lower part of their buttocks (2 Sam. 10:4). In context the exposure of the hips or buttocks brought great shame and humiliation on the king's servants. In the ancient Near East, such public exposure was a sign of humility and shame, especially to the king's messengers.

8358. שְׁתִי ***šeṯiy:*** A masculine noun indicating drunkenness (Eccl. 10:17). It indicates that a person is satiated with drinking, fully drunk with wine, beer, or strong drink (Eccl. 10:17).

8359. שְׁתִי ***šeṯiy:*** A masculine noun referring to warp, a woven material. It refers to a set of threads running lengthwise in the loom and crossed by the woof or weft, the intertwining of cloth material (Lev. 13:48, 49, 51–53, 56–59).

8360. שְׁתִיָּה ***šeṯiyyāh:*** A feminine noun referring to drinking. It refers to the process and act of drinking, in this case done at a royal banquet (Esth. 1:8).

8361. שִׁתִּין ***šittiyn:*** An Aramaic numerical plural adjective meaning sixty. It indicates the cardinal number sixty, indicating sixty items (Ezra 6:3; Dan. 3:1). It combines with other numbers, e.g., sixty-two (Dan. 5:31[6:1]).

8362. שָׁתַל ***šāṯal:*** A verb meaning to plant; to transplant. It means to plant and cultivate a seed or seedling in the ground so it may grow (Ps. 1:3). It is used figuratively of a person planted in the Temple of the Lord (Jer. 17:8); and of nations or peoples (Ezek. 17:8, 10, 22, 23); especially Israel (Ezek. 19:10, 13; Hos. 9:13).

8363. שְׁתִל ***šeṯil,*** שָׁתִיל ***šāṯiyl:*** A masculine noun referring to a plant, a shoot. It figuratively describes children as plants in a house blessed by God (Ps. 128:3).

8364. שֻׁתַלְחִי ***šuṯalḥiy:*** A proper noun designating Shuthelahite (Num. 26:35).

8365. שָׁתַם ***šāṯam:*** A verb meaning to open; to be open. It indicates that something or someone is open with respect to his eye (Num. 24:3, 15).

8366. שָׁתַן ***šaṯan:*** A verb meaning to urinate: to urinate against the wall as describing a male. It is a derogatory phrase making light of enemies who may remain (KJV, 1 Sam. 25:22, 34). It is translated politely as all who belong to him (NASB, NIV) by some translators. Likewise, compare the remaining references to see how it is translated euphemistically, except by the KJV translators. Its idiomatic sense is that every male will be cut off.

8367. שָׁתַק *šāṯaq:* A verb meaning to be calm; to be quiet. It refers to a time of quietness and safety after a storm or great danger (Ps. 107:30). It indicates the quieting down of quarreling and hostilities (Prov. 26:20). It indicates that the waters of the sea are becoming calm, quieting down, a storm is subsiding (Jon. 1:11, 12).

8368. שָׂתַר *śāṯar:* A verb meaning to break out. It refers to skin eruptions of some kind, possibly boils, tumors, etc. that burst out and appear quickly on one's skin (1 Sam. 5:9).

8369. שֵׁתָר *šēṯar:* A proper noun designating Shethar (Esth. 1:14).

8370. שְׁתַר בּוֹזְנַי *šeṯar bôzenay:* A proper noun designating Shethar-Bozenai, an associate of Tattenai, governor of the Trans-Euphrates area (west of Jordan), who opposed the building of the Temple by the Jews. He and his associates sent letters to Darius in Persepolis, Persia (Ezra 5:3–6). Darius refused their request to stop the building activity (Ezra 6:6–13).

8371. שָׁתַת *šāṯaṯ:* I. A verb meaning to set; to lay. It indicates that something is to be set or placed in a certain location (Ps. 49:14[15]). It refers to an attitude of arrogance and harangue taken toward something (Ps. 73:9).

II. A verb meaning to be appointed; to be destined. It indicates clearly that something is literally appointed or destined for something (Ps. 49:14[15]; 73:9).

III. A verb meaning to claim something. It indicates an arrogant claim of ownership or right with respect to something (Ps. 73:9).

ת Tau

8372. תָּא *tā'*: A masculine noun referring to a room, a chamber, a guardroom. It refers to a guardroom or a chamber of a palace or temple (1 Kgs. 14:28; 2 Chr. 12:11; Ezek. 40:7, 10, 12, 13, 16, 21, 29, 33, 36).

8373. תָּאַב *tā'aḇ:* A verb meaning to long for. It is used figuratively of a person's inherent desire for God's ethical and moral precepts (Ps. 119:40, 174).

8374. תָּאַב *tā'aḇ:* A verb meaning to loathe, to abhor. This unquestionably strong term of detest is used only in Amos 6:8. The Lord employed it to convey His utter contempt for the pride of the people of Jacob.

8375. תַּאֲבָה *ta'ᵃḇāh:* A feminine noun indicating a longing, a desire. It indicates an intense hunger to experience and follow God's laws and ordinances (Ps. 119:20).

8376. תָּאָה *tā'āh:* A verb indicating to mark out; to draw a line. It is used figuratively of establishing a border to mark certain boundaries of territories (Num. 34:7, 8).

8377. תְּאוֹ *tᵉ'ô:* I. A masculine noun referring to an antelope. It means a large group of swift-running and sleek herds of bovid ruminants, usually in wild herds in Africa or Asia (Deut. 14:5). It was edible in Israel and could be caught in a net (Isa. 51:20).

II. A masculine noun meaning a wild ox. A category of animal that includes cattle, buffalo, bison, yaks, and guar. It was considered edible in Israel and clean (Deut. 14:5). It would have been difficult to catch in a net (Isa. 51:20).

8378. תַּאֲוָה *ta'ᵃwāh:* A feminine noun meaning desire, delight, bounty; craving, greed. It indicates something that is attractive and delightful to the eyes, desirable (Gen. 3:6). It refers to the abundant fertility and produce of mountainous land (Gen. 49:26). It describes food that is choice (NIV, Gen. 49:26), dainty (KJV), favored (NASB). It indicates the longings of a person's heart, its cravings (Ps. 10:3; 21:2[3]); or the longings of a humble person (Ps. 10:17). It is the opposite of revulsion (Ps. 38:9[10]). The righteous will have their desires realized (Prov. 10:24; 11:23). When a desire is realized, it invigorates a person (Prov. 13:12, 19). For the prophet, the Lord's name and the remembrance of His deeds are His desires (Isa. 26:8).

8379. תַּאֲוָה *ta'ᵃwāh:* A feminine noun indicating an outer boundary. It refers to the geographical extent of an area, the farthest boundary or distance (Gen. 49:26).

8380. תְּאוֹם tā'ôm, תֹּאָם tô'ām: A masculine noun meaning a twin. It refers to two things that are alike: two boys (Gen. 25:24; 38:27); two animals (Song 4:5; 7:3[4]). See 8382.

8381. תַּאֲלָה ta'alāh: A feminine noun meaning a curse. It refers to a cause of evil, a judgment placed on someone (Lam. 3:65).

8382. תָּאַם tā'am: A verb meaning to be double, to couple, to be joined. The primary thrust of this word is that of joining in a matched pair. It is used only in two contexts: to describe the action of linking two corners of a curtain together (Ex. 26:24; 36:29); and poetically, to describe the birthing of twins (Song 4:2; 6:6).

8383. תְּאֻן te'un: I. A masculine noun indicating toil, an effort. It refers figuratively to the work, energy, and attention God has gone through for His people and Jerusalem, yet they rebel still more (Ezek. 24:12).

II. A masculine noun indicating a lie. It refers to self-deception, the employment of untruth and irreality with respect to Jerusalem, in this case (Ezek. 24:12).

8384. תְּאֵנָה te'ēnāh: A feminine noun meaning a fig, a fig tree. It describes the leaves of a fig tree, a tree bearing a hollow, pear-shaped false fruit with sweet, pulpy flesh containing numerous tiny, seedlike true fruits. The words may stand for the tree (2 Kgs. 18:31) or the fig (Num. 13. 23). The first clothing for humans was made from the leaves of a fig tree (Gen. 3:7). Figs were a prized food in the Promised Land (Num. 13:23). To have a vine and a fig tree was an ideal in Israel historically and in a restored community (Zech. 3:10).

8385. תַּאֲנָה ta'anāh: I. A feminine noun referring to heat; an occasion or a time of copulation. It refers to the time when a mare is ready to receive a male for procreation. It is used mockingly of Israel as a wild female donkey (Jer. 2:24).

II. A feminine noun meaning an occasion, an opportunity. It refers to the right time or set of situations for accomplishing something (Judg. 14:4).

8386. תַּאֲנִיָּה ta'aniyyāh: A feminine noun meaning to mourn, to lament. It describes the emotional response of feeling sorry for someone or something, grieving for some reason (Isa. 29:2); it is a response toward great loss (Lam. 2:5).

8387. תַּאֲנַת שִׁלֹה ta'anat šilōh: A proper noun designating Taanath Shiloh (Josh. 16:6).

8388. תָּאַר tā'ar: I. A verb indicating to incline; to stretch out. It describes the direction and shape of something, e.g., a borderline that curves, bends (Josh. 15:9, 11); turns, inclines in one way (Josh. 18:14, 17). It also indicates a line or a direction that continues to a certain point (Josh. 19:13).

II. A verb meaning to trace an outline. It describes the process of outlining, drawing a line, or determining a line using various tools (Isa. 44:13).

8389. תֹּאַר tō'ar: A masculine noun meaning form, appearance, beauty. It refers to the contours and outward form of something, e.g., the body of a woman or a man (Gen. 29:17; 39:6; Deut. 21:11; 1 Sam. 16:18); of an animal's body, it means healthy, strong-looking (Gen. 41:18, 19). It is used in a stereotypical way, the form of the son of a king, a royal-looking person, a person with dignity (Judg. 8:18). It also refers to the shape of trees, plants, etc. (Jer. 11:16).

8390. תַּאֲרֵעַ ta'ᵃrēa': A proper noun designating Tarea (1 Chr. 8:35).

8391. תְּאַשּׁוּר tᵉ'aššûr: A masculine noun referring to a cypress, a box tree; cypress wood. It refers to a cypress tree or its wood. It is a huge evergreen, cone-bearing tree of the cypress family. It was highly desired in the construction of buildings (Isa. 41:19). They were the glory and pride of Lebanon (Isa. 60:13).

8392. תֵּבָה tēḇāh: A feminine noun referring to an ark; a basket. It is used in two cases: to depict the ark of Noah (Gen. 6:14–16; 9:10, 18); and to depict the basket in which Moses was hidden (Ex. 2:3, 5). In both cases, persons were rescued from water.

8393. תְּבוּאָה tᵉḇû'āh: A feminine noun indicating a crop, a harvest, an increase, a revenue. It indicates the produce or yield from the ground (Ex. 23:10; Lev. 19:25; Josh. 5:12); and the fields (2 Kgs. 8:6; Ezek. 48:18). It indicates any increase or prosperity in general (Job 31:12; Prov. 10:16; 14:4). It describes the benefits or gains from wisdom (Prov. 3:14; 8:19). Even Israel's reaping of what she has sown is described as a harvest, an increase; but it is one she does not want to reap (Jer. 12:13). It means harvest in a general sense (Gen. 47:24), at the increase or at the harvest. The threshing floor and wine vats generated produce and products (Num. 18:30). It refers to increase or income (Eccl. 5:10[9]). Every increase or income is from God.

8394. תְּבוּנָה tᵉḇûnāh: A feminine noun meaning understanding, insight. It occurs primarily in the Wisdom Literature and is associated with both wisdom and knowledge (Ex. 35:31; Prov. 8:1; 21:30); and is contrasted with foolishness (Prov. 15:21; 18:2). A person of understanding is slow to wrath and walks uprightly (Prov. 14:29; 15:21). God has understanding and gives it (Job 12:13; Ps. 147:5; Prov. 2:6; Isa. 40:28). On the other hand, idolaters, who fashion idols by their own understanding, have no understanding at all (Isa. 44:19; Hos. 13:2).

8395. תְּבוּסָה tᵉḇûsāh: A feminine noun meaning ruin, downfall. The word is used in 2 Chronicles to depict God's judgment on Ahaziah and more generally the house of Ahab (2 Chr. 22:7). Jehu, God's chosen instrument, killed Ahaziah and Joram, the princes of Judah, in addition to the sons of Ahaziah's relatives.

8396. תָּבוֹר ***tābôr:*** A. A proper noun, Tabor. It was a high mountain on the northwest boundary of Issachar (Josh. 19:22; Jer. 46:18). It is noted in the Deborah-Barak cycle of stories (Judg. 4:6). God created it along with Mount Hermon (Ps. 89:12 [13]). It is used in a figure of speech (Hos. 5:1). Two hostile princes were slain near it (Judg. 8:18).

B. A proper noun meaning Tabor, a city in Zebulun. It was a Levitical city in Zebulun. Its location is not yet known.

C. A proper noun meaning Tabor. It is the name of a small area or city in which the oak of Tabor was located. It was not far from Bethel (1 Sam. 10:3). The King James Version has the plain of Tabor.

8397. תֶּבֶל ***tebel:*** A masculine noun meaning perversion; incest. It is a strong word used in condemning human-animal copulation (Lev. 18:23). Intercourse between a man and his daughter-in-law was also considered perversion and incest (Lev. 20:12).

8398. תֵּבֵל ***tēbēl:*** A feminine noun meaning world, earth. The word is used in a description of the clouds responding to the command of God, i.e., they swirled over the face of the whole earth (Job 37:12). In Proverbs, the created world was a reason for rejoicing (Prov. 8:31). This word is also used to indicate the foundations of the earth, as in 2 Samuel where the foundations of the earth were laid bare at the rebuke of the Lord (2 Sam. 22:16). *Tēbēl* is also used to denote what was firmly established, i.e., the world (Ps. 93:1; 96:10); something that would be punished for its evil (Isa. 13:11); and what will be filled by Israel upon their blossoming (Isa. 27:6). In Nahum, the world and all who live in it will tremble at the presence of the Lord (Nah. 1:5).

8399. תַּבְלִית ***tabliyt:*** A feminine noun meaning destruction. In Isaiah, the word is used to denote the end result of the direction of the wrath of the Lord, i.e., the destruction of the Assyrians (Isa. 10:25). Even though disobedient, Israel was still loved and protected by the Lord, who maintained a remnant.

8400. תְּבַלֻּל ***t^e^ballul:*** A masculine noun meaning confusion, obscurity. This word comes from the verb *bālal* (1101), meaning to mix or to confuse, and is used only once in the Old Testament. In Leviticus 21:20, it is used to describe an obscurity or some sort of defect in the eye that would prohibit a man from being a priest.

8401. תֶּבֶן ***teben:*** A masculine noun referring to straw. It was chopped stalks or stems of grain used for feed, fodder, and bedding for animals (Gen. 24:25; Judg. 19:19). It was mixed with clay to make strong bricks (Ex. 5:7). In poetry it describes the wicked blown in the wind (Job 21:18).

In the reign of the Messiah, the lion will eat straw (Isa. 11:7). It is used in a negative comparison by Jeremiah 23:28.

8402. תִּבְנִי ***tiḇniy:*** A proper noun designating Tibni (1 Kgs. 16:21, 22).

8403. תַּבְנִית ***taḇniyṯ:*** A feminine noun meaning a plan, a pattern, a form. This noun comes from the verb *bānāh* (1129), meaning to build, and refers to the plans of a building or an object, such as the pattern of the Tabernacle and its contents (Ex. 25:9, 40); an altar (Josh. 22:28; 2 Kgs. 16:10); and the Temple and its contents (1 Chr. 28:11, 12, 18, 19). However, in other contexts, it refers to an image that was patterned after something else, such as a graven image of a god (Deut. 4:16–18); the calf at Horeb (Ps. 106:20); pillars (Ps. 144:12); or a person (Isa. 44:13). In a few contexts, it refers to something in the form of an animal (Ezek. 8:10); or a hand (Ezek. 8:3; 10:8). Synonyms for this word are *temûnāh* (8544), meaning likeness or form, and *demûṯ* (1823), meaning likeness.

8404. תַּבְעֵרָה ***taḇ'ērāh:*** A proper noun designating Taberah (Num. 11:3; Deut. 9:22).

8405. תֵּבֵץ ***tēḇēṣ:*** A proper noun designating Thebez (Judg. 9:50; 2 Sam. 11:21).

8406. תְּבַר ***t***^{e}***ḇar:*** An Aramaic verb meaning to break; to be brittle. It refers to something that crumbles, comes apart easily (Dan. 2:42).

8407. תִּגְלַת פִּלְאֶסֶר ***tiglaṯ pil'eser,*** תִּלְגַת פִּלְנֶסֶר ***tilgaṯ pilneser,*** פִּלְנְאֶסֶר תִּלְגַת ***tilgaṯ piln***^{e}***'eser:*** A proper noun designating Tiglath-Pileser:

A. A great Assyrian king, Tiglath-pileser III (745–727 B.C.). He had another name, Pul (2 Kgs. 15:29; 16:7, 10; 1 Chr. 5:26). He captured many cities in Aram, including Damascus (732 B.C.). He overran Gilead, Galilee, including Naphtali in upper Galilee. He deported the Israelites into various places in Assyria. He also took tribute from Ahaz of Judah (2 Chr. 28:20–21). The name is also found rendered as Tiglath-pilneser (see B below).

B. See A above. Tiglath-pilneser is a variant of the name and may be unique to Hebrew.

8408. תַּגְמוּל ***tagmûl:*** A masculine noun indicating a benefit; goodness. It indicates things or conditions that improve the lot of persons, improving their health, spiritual validity, or their economic situations (Ps. 116:12).

8409. תִּגְרָה ***tigrāh:*** A feminine noun designating a blow, a strike; an opposition. It indicates in context God's oppression or attack on a person (Ps. 39:10[11]; possibly stirring). The King James Version renders it a blow in a figurative sense of God's hand and power.

8410. תִּדְהָר ***tiḏhār:*** A masculine noun indicating a fir tree; a pine tree.

The exact identification of the tree is uncertain: box tree (NASB, Isa. 41:19; 60:13; NIV, fir; KJV, pine).

8411. תְּדִיר ***t^e^diyr,*** תְּדִירָא ***t^e^diyrā':*** An Aramaic feminine noun meaning continuance. It is used adverbially to describe a practice or an attitude that is done or held without fail (Dan. 6:16[17], 20[21]).

8412. תַּדְמֹר ***tadmōr:*** A proper noun designating Tadmor (1 Kgs. 9:18; 2 Chr. 8:4).

8413. תִּדְעָל ***tid'āl:*** A proper noun designating Tidal, king of Goiim (nations) (Gen. 14:1, 9).

8414. תֹּהוּ ***tōhû:*** A masculine noun meaning formlessness, confusion. The exact meaning of this term is difficult at best since its study is limited to its relatively few Old Testament occurrences. It is used to describe primeval earth before the seven creative days (Gen. 1:2); a land reduced to primeval chaos and formlessness (Isa. 34:11; 45:18; Jer. 4:23); a destroyed city (Isa. 24:10); nothingness or empty space (Job 26:7); a barren wasteland (Deut. 32:10; Job 6:18; 12:24; Ps. 107:40); that which is vain and futile (1 Sam. 12:21; Isa. 45:19; 49:4); like idolatry (Isa. 41:29; 44:9); unfounded allegations (Isa. 29:21; 59:4); the nations compared to God (Isa. 40:17); or human rulers (Isa. 40:23). Although it is impossible to grasp the full import of this word, it is obvious that it has a negative and disparaging tone. It represents chaos, confusion, and disorder, all things that are opposed to the organization, direction, and order that God has demonstrated.

8415. תְּהוֹם ***t^e^hôm,*** תְּהֹם ***t^e^hōm:*** A masculine noun referring to depth, a deep place. It indicates the deep, primeval ocean on earth as created by God (Gen. 1:2). It refers to the deepest parts of the earth in a figurative sense (Ps. 71:20); and to the depths of the oceans (Gen. 7:11). It is the opposite of the heavens (Gen. 8:2). It can refer to the deep parts of a sea or a large body of water (Ex. 15:5). It refers to deep waters that can be brought up (Gen. 49:25; Deut. 8:7). It refers to sea waters (Ezek. 26:19).

8416. תְּהִלָּה ***t^e^hillāh:*** A feminine noun meaning praise, a song of praise. This word is a noun derived from the verb *hālal* (1984), which connotes genuine appreciation for the great actions or the character of its object. It is used especially of the adoration and thanksgiving that humanity renders to God (Ps. 34:1[2]). By extension, it also represents the character of God that deserves praise (Ps. 111:10); and the specific divine acts that elicit human veneration (Ex. 15:11). It can also refer to the condition of fame and renown that comes with receiving this sort of praise and, as such, was applied to God (Deut. 10:21; Hab. 3:3); Israel (Deut. 26:19; Jer. 13:11); Jerusalem (Isa. 62:7; Zeph. 3:19, 20); Damascus (Jer. 49:25); Moab (Jer. 48:2); Babylon (Jer. 51:41). In late Hebrew, this term became a technical term for a psalm of praise. In this capacity, it is used in the title of Psalm 145 to designate it as David's Psalm of Praise. It has also become the Hebrew title for the entire book of Psalms.

8417. תָּהֳלָה ***tāh^olāh:*** A feminine noun indicating an error, folly. It indicates a deviation from perfection, a flaw of any kind (Job 4:18).

8418. תַּהֲלֻכָה ***tah^aluḵāh:*** A feminine noun indicating a procession, proceeding. It refers to a festive procession, a formal march to some designated location (Neh. 12:31).

8419. תַּהְפֻּכָה ***tahpuḵāh:*** A feminine noun meaning perversity. It is used of a generation of Israelites who deviated and distorted the Lord's ways, turning from Him (Deut. 32:20), for their true life is found in Him. It describes deceptive and corrupt speech, things that are distorted (Prov. 2:12). Evil itself features perversity, a distortion of what is straight and right (Prov. 2:14). Evil persons create perversity in their hearts (Prov. 6:14). God hates a perverted mouth, perverted speech (Prov. 8:13). A slanderer is a perverted person (Prov. 16:28).

8420. תָּו ***tāw:*** A masculine noun meaning a mark, a signature. It is the name of the last letter of the Hebrew alphabet. It indicates a mark of some kind put on a person (Ezek. 9:4, 6); and also a person's identifying mark or signature (Job 31:35). In the case of Ezekiel, it was a sign of exemption from judgment.

8421. תּוּב ***tûḇ:*** A verb meaning to return; to answer. It means to respond, to give a reply to someone orally (Ezra 5:5, 11). It means literally to take something back, to return it (Ezra 6:5); or of reason returning to a person, someone recovering his or her senses (Dan. 4:34[31], 36[33]). It is used of an official reply (Dan. 2:14). The reply of the three Hebrew young men remains a classic response to a tyrant (Dan. 3:16).

8422. תּוּבַל ***tûḇal,*** תֻּבַל ***tuḇal:*** A proper noun designating Tubal (Gen. 10:2; 1 Chr. 1:5; Isa. 66:19; Ezek. 27:13; 32:26; 38:2, 3; 39:1).

8423. תּוּבַל קַיִן ***tûḇal qayin:*** A proper noun designating Tubal-Cain (Gen. 4:22).

8424. תּוּגָה ***tûgāh:*** A feminine noun indicating grief, sorrow. It refers to the emotion and process of feeling a great loss and loneliness (Ps. 119:28). A son who is a fool creates grief in his parents (Prov. 10:1; 17:21). For the wicked, even the end of joy is grief (Prov. 14:13).

8425. תּוֹגַרְמָה ***tôgarmāh,*** תֹּגַרְמָה ***tōgarmāh,*** בֵּית תּוֹגַרְמָה ***bēyṯ tôgarmāh:*** I. A proper noun designating Togarmah, son of Gomer (Gen. 10:3; 1 Chr. 1:6; Ezek. 27:14 [KJV]; 38:6[KJV]).

II. A proper noun designating Beth Togarmah (NASB, NIV, Ezek. 27:14; 38:6).

8426. תּוֹדָה *tôḏāh:* A feminine noun meaning praise, thanksgiving. The word describes an offering of thanks or a sacrifice of thanksgiving, It is a subcategory of the fellowship offering or the offering of well-being; the fellowship offering could be presented as a thank offering (Lev. 7:12, 13, 15; 22:29; 2 Chr. 29:31; Amos 4:5). The word depicts worship by the presentation of songs of thanksgiving and praise that extolled the mighty wonders of the Lord (Neh. 12:27; Ps. 26:7; Isa. 51:3). It refers to shouts of jubilation and thanksgiving (Ps. 42:4[5]; Jon. 2:9[10]). It describes the purpose of the choirs used by Nehemiah, i.e., they were choirs of praise (Neh. 12:31, 38). The goodness and praise of God were to be on the lips of even an enemy of the Lord, such as Achan, in the sense of proclaiming the glory of God while confessing and abandoning sin (Josh. 7:19).

8427. תָּוָה *tāwāh:* A verb meaning to scribble; to make a mark. It means, according to context, to write incoherently, in a confusing manner, illegibly (1 Sam. 21:13[14]). In a different context, it may have the sense of making an identifying mark, in this case, marking the righteous among God's people (Ezek. 9:4).

8428. תָּוָה *tāwāh:* I. A verb meaning to vex; to cause pain. It refers to causing another person discomfort or vexation because of one's behavior or attitude (Ps. 78:41). In this case, Israel caused God to experience wounding from her unfaithfulness.

II. A verb meaning to limit. It has the sense of restraining persons from what they can do because of one's own attitudes or actions (Ps. 78:41).

8429. תְּוַהּ *t^e^wah:* An Aramaic verb meaning to be astonished; to be amazed. It indicates a state of wonderment and amazement at something or someone or at an extraordinary event or condition (Dan. 3:24).

8430. תּוֹחַ *tôaḥ:* A proper noun designating Toah (1 Chr. 6:34[19]), the same as Tohu (8459).

8431. תּוֹחֶלֶת *tôḥeleṯ:* A feminine noun meaning hope. This word is found most often in the Wisdom Literature of Proverbs. Hope is associated with the prosperity of the righteous (Prov. 10:28; 11:7); and is seen as the spring from which the desire for life flows (Prov. 13:12). Jeremiah lamented that his soul was destitute because his hope in the Lord had perished (Lam. 3:18).

8432. תָּוֶךְ *tāweḵ:* A substantive meaning in the midst, in the middle, at the heart. The word can have the implication of something being surrounded on all sides, as when God made a firmament in the midst of the waters (Gen. 1:6). It can also refer to something in the middle of a line: Samson destroyed the Temple by pushing over two middle pillars that supported it (Judg. 16:29). In relation to people, it can mean dwelling among (1 Sam 10:10); or taken from among a group (Num. 3:12).

8433. תּוֹכֵחָה ***tôḵēḥāh,*** תּוֹכַחַת ***tôḵaḥaṯ:*** A feminine noun meaning a rebuke, a correction, a reproof, an argument. The primary thrust of this word is that of correcting some wrong. It is employed to express the concept of rebuking (Prov. 15:10); judgment (Hos. 5:9); reckoning (2 Kgs. 19:3); or the argument of a claim (Job 13:6; Hab. 2:1).

8434. תּוֹלָד ***tôlāḏ:*** A proper noun designating Tolad (1 Chr. 4:29).

8435. תּוֹלְדוֹת ***tôlēḏôṯ:*** A feminine noun meaning a generation. This key Hebrew word carries with it the notion of everything entailed in a person's life and that of his or her progeny (Gen. 5:1; 6:9). In the plural, it is used to denote the chronological procession of history as humans shape it. It refers to the successive generations in one family (Gen. 10:32); or a broader division by lineage (Num. 1:20ff.). In Genesis 2:4, the word accounts for the history of the created world.

8436. תִּילוֹן ***tiylôn:*** A proper noun designating Tilon (1 Chr. 4:20).

8437. תּוֹלָל ***tôlāl:*** A masculine noun referring to a tormentor. It refers to a person who willingly brings about pain, dread, fear in another person, psychological or physical (Ps. 137:3).

8438. תּוֹלָע ***tôlā',*** תּוֹלֵעָה ***tôlē'āh,*** תּוֹלַעַת ***tôla'aṯ:*** I. A masculine noun meaning crimson, purple, scarlet. It refers to the color of one's sins that stands out in a shocking way, drawing attention to its intensity. God can make sins white, cleanse them away (Isa. 1:18). These colors also are associated with royalty, palacial living, etc. (Lam. 4:5).

II. A masculine noun meaning a worm. It refers to some kind of soft-bodied animal that lives underground, in water, or as a parasite, which was the case of worms that fed on manna, putrefying it (Ex. 16:20).

III. A masculine noun meaning crimson (bright red), purple, scarlet. It refers to the colors attributed by scholars to expensive cloth materials or threads, ropes, chains, etc. of cloth, used in the materials found in the Tabernacle and its furnishings (Ex. 25:4; etc.; Num. 4:8). A scarlet string was involved in the ritual of cleansing a leper (Lev. 14:4, 6); a house (Lev. 14:49, 51, 52); and in the law of the red heifer (Num. 19:6).

IV. A masculine noun referring to a worm. It refers to some parasitic worm or insect larvae that destroyed manna (Ex. 16:20); vineyards (Deut. 28:39). A worm destroyed Jonah's favorite shade plant (Jon. 4:7). It is used to describe the low character and estate of a person as a worm (Job 25:6; Ps. 22:6[7]; Isa. 41:14). It is described figuratively as the bedding provided in Sheol (Isa. 14:11); a permanent tormenting feature of Sheol (Isa. 66:24).

V. A masculine noun referring to a string. It refers to a scarlet string (*šenî tôla'at*) used in several cleansing rituals (Lev. 14:4, 6, 49, 51, 52).

8439. תּוֹלָע ***tôlāʻ:*** A proper noun designating Tola.

A. The first son of Issachar and head of his clan (1 Chr. 7:1, 2).

B. The name of a judge in Israel. He was son of Puah. He was from the city of Shamir in the hill country of Ephraim. He delivered Israel twenty-three years (Judg. 10:1).

8440. תּוֹלָעִי ***tôlāʻiy:*** A proper noun designating Tolaite (Num. 26:23).

8441. תּוֹעֵבָה ***tôʻēḇāh,*** תֹּעֵבָה ***tōʻēḇāh:*** A feminine noun meaning an abomination. This word is primarily understood in the context of the Law. It identifies unclean food (Deut. 14:3); the activity of the idolater (Isa. 41:24); the practice of child sacrifice (Deut. 12:31); intermarriage by the Israelites (Mal. 2:11); the religious activities of the wicked (Prov. 21:27); and homosexual behavior (Lev. 18:22). In a broader sense, the word is used to identify anything offensive (Prov. 8:7).

8442. תּוֹעָה ***tōʻāh:*** A feminine noun meaning an error; a disturbance, trouble. It is a strongly negative term indicating confusion, perversion. It describes a confusion or disturbance raised among people by troublemakers (Neh. 4:8[2]). It refers to erroneous and wrong words, ideas, and concepts (Isa. 32:6).

8443. תּוֹעָפָה ***tôʻāp̄āh:*** I. A feminine noun referring to strength. It describes the power and strength figuratively of the mythical unicorn (Num. 23:22; 24:8); the strength and might of the hills (Ps. 95:4), all demonstrations of God's power to deliver His people.

II. A feminine noun referring to the horn (of a wild ox). It refers figuratively to the strength or horns of a wild ox as illustrative of God's power in delivering Israel (Num. 23:22; 24:8).

III. A feminine noun referring to the peak of a mountain. It is rendered as peaks by the New International Version and the New American Standard Bible, but is still illustrative of God's power and strength.

IV. A feminine noun meaning choice; abundance. It denotes a high-quality, pure silver, which is used to describe the value of the Lord (Job 22:25).

8444. תּוֹצָאָה ***tôṣā'āh,*** תֹּצָאָה ***tōṣā'āh:*** A feminine noun meaning a border, an extremity, an end point. It refers to the end point or extreme reach of a border or borders, or border extremities (Num. 34:4, 5, 8, 9, 12; Josh. 15:4, 7; 1 Chr. 5:16). It may have the sense of issues surrounding death or escapes, releases from death (Ps. 68:20[21]) that are from the Lord. From the heart go forth issues of life (Prov. 4:23). It refers literally to exits from a city (Ezek. 48:30).

8445. תּוֹקְהַת ***towq^e^hat*, תָּקְהַת *toqhat*:** A proper noun designating Tokhath (2 Chr. 34:22), the same as Tikvah (8616,A).

8446. תּוּר ***tûr*:** A verb meaning to explore; to seek out; to spy out. It refers to going into a land or country to search it out, e.g., Canaan (Num. 10:33; 13:2, 16, 17, 21, 25, 32; 14:6, 7, 34, 36, 38). It depicts persons following their own hearts or desires, seeking them out to pursue them rather than the Lord's will (Num. 15:39). It refers to merchants, those who seek out wares (1 Kgs. 10:15; 2 Chr. 9:14). It is used of the instincts and inclinations of an animal to search out its habitat (Job 39:8). It refers to a person serving as a guide who explores the way for others (Prov. 12:26). It is used figuratively of exploring and investigating wisdom and its ways (Eccl. 1:13; 2:3; 7:25). It refers to the Lord's previous exploration (NASB selection) of the land of Canaan before giving it to His people (Ezek. 20:6).

8447. תּוֹר ***tôr*, תֹּר *tōr*:** I. A masculine noun indicating a turn, an opportunity. It refers to a person's allotted time and place in a predetermined series (Esth. 2:12, 15).

II. A masculine noun referring to ornaments, earrings. It describes jewelry and decorative items of all kinds worn by a bride for beauty (Song 1:10).

III. A masculine noun indicating a row, a border. It describes an orderly set of something. In context it refers to rows of jewelry (KJV, Song 1:10).

IV. A masculine noun meaning a standard, a manner. It refers in context back to the previous manner or way in which God had dealt with David and his family (2 Sam. 7:19). In 1 Chronicles 17:17, it has a slightly different nuance, referring to the high estate or the high manner in which God regarded David in dealing with him.

8448. תּוֹר ***tôr*:** A masculine noun meaning a standard, a manner. It refers to the standard of a human against which God had measured and appointed David (1 Chr. 17:17).

8449. תּוֹר ***tôr*, תֹּר *tōr*:** A masculine noun meaning a dove, a turtledove. It refers to wild doves known for their cooing and their affectionate ways of behaving toward each other. It was a sacrificial animal in Israel, especially for the poor (Lev. 1:14; 5:7, 11; 12:6, 8; 14:22, 30; 15:14, 29). It is used charmingly of the psalmist or of Israel being the Lord's turtledove (Ps. 74:19). It was a harbinger of spring (Song 2:12); and had its built-in homing instincts (Jer. 8:7).

8450. תּוֹר ***tôr*:** An Aramaic masculine noun meaning a bull, an ox. It was a favored animal for sacrifice in Israel (Ezra 6:9, 17; 7:17). Nebuchadnezzar's disease made his mind and lifestyle like that of cattle (*tôr*) (Dan. 4:25[22]; 5:21).

8451. תּוֹרָה ***tôrāh,*** תֹּרָה ***tōrāh:*** A feminine noun meaning instruction, direction, law, Torah, the whole Law. This noun comes from the verb *yārāh* (3384), which has, as one of its major meanings, to teach, to instruct. The noun means instruction in a general way from God; for example, Eliphaz uttered truth when he encouraged Job and his readers to be willing to receive instruction from God, the Almighty (Job 22:22). In Israel, a father and mother were sources of instruction for life (Prov. 1:8; 6:20); along with wise persons (Prov. 13:14; 28:4). In contrast, rebellious people were not willing to accept God's instructions in any manner (Isa. 30:8, 9); the scribes handled the instructions of the Lord deceitfully and falsely (Jer. 8:8). Various words are found in synonyms parallel with this term: It is paralleled by the sayings of the Holy One (Isa. 5:24); the word of the Lord (Isa. 1:10); and the testimony or witness (Isa. 8:20). It is used regularly to depict priestly instructions in general or as a whole. The Lord rejected the priests of Israel for they had disregarded (lit., forgotten) the Law (Jer. 2:8; Hos. 4:6). They had been charged to carry out and teach all the instructions of the Lord (Deut. 17:11).

The term takes on the meaning of law in certain settings, although it is still currently debated about how to translate the various words that describe the laws, ordinances, commands, decrees, and requirements of the Lord. This word *tôrāh* is used as a summary term of various bodies of legal, cultic, or civil instructions. The word refers to the entire book of Deuteronomy and Moses' exposition of the Torah found in it (Deut. 1:5). By implication, the word here also refers to the laws given in Exodus, Leviticus, and Numbers. Numerous times this word refers to the whole Law of Moses, the Book of the Law of Moses, the Book of the Law of God, the Law of the Lord, and the Law of God given at Sinai (in order of titles listed, 1 Kgs. 2:3; Neh. 8:1; Josh. 24:26; Ps. 1:2; Neh. 10:28[29], 29[30]). The kings of Israel were held to the standard of the Law of Moses (1 Kgs. 2:3; 2 Kgs. 10:31; 14:6; 23:25). The word can also refer to a single law, for example, the law of the burnt offering (Lev. 6:9[2]; 7:7; Neh. 12:44).

It is used of special laws for the Feast of Unleavened Bread (Ex. 13:9); the Passover (Ex. 12:49); of decisions by Moses (Ex. 18:16, 20); for the content of the Book of the Covenant (Ex. 24:12). The Law or Torah of God is pursued diligently by the psalmist; this word is found twenty-five times in Psalm 119 in parallel with various near synonyms. The word means the usual way, custom, or manner of God as David addressed his surprise to the Lord about the way He had dealt with him (2 Sam. 7:19).

8452. תּוֹרָה ***tôrāh:*** A feminine noun meaning a custom, a manner. It is understood to refer to the way or manner in which God had dealt with David and his family concerning kingship (2 Sam. 7:19).

8453. תּוֹשָׁב ***tôšāḇ,*** תֹּשָׁב ***tōšāḇ,*** תִּשְׁבֵּי ***tišbēy:*** A masculine noun meaning a sojourner, a foreigner. This word implies temporary visitors who were dependent in some way on the nation in which they were residing. It denotes a sojourner who received shelter from a priest (Lev. 22:10); foreigners who were closely linked to the economy of the people (Lev. 25:40, 47); and a wanderer with close ties to the land occupied by another people (Gen. 23:4). David proclaimed himself to be such a sojourner with the Lord (Ps. 39:12[13]).

8454. תּוּשִׁיָּה ***tûšiyyāh:*** A feminine noun meaning sound wisdom, continuing success. The primary meaning of this Hebrew word is wisdom or ability that brings continued advancement. Used in the Wisdom Literature of the Old Testament, it describes the wisdom of the Lord that keeps a person on the right path (Prov. 3:21; Isa. 28:29); the wisdom that recognizes the things of God (Mic. 6:9); and the success that comes from heeding wise counsel (Job 5:12; 6:13).

8455. תּוֹתָח ***tôṯāḥ:*** I. A masculine noun meaning a club. It indicates a wooden, metal, or stone weapon shaped by a craftsman for use in war, hunting, or for attacking a foe (Job 41:29[21]).

II. A masculine noun meaning a dart. It refers to a piece of wood or metal sharpened to penetrate an object, used often in battle and in hunting (Job 41:29[21]).

8456. תָּזַז ***tāzaz:*** A verb meaning to cut down; to cut away. It describes the cutting off of healthy, spreading branches before harvesttime. It is used figuratively of judging Ethiopia (Isa. 18:5).

8457. תַּזְנוּת ***taznûṯ:*** A noun meaning whoredom, prostitution. This word is found only in Ezekiel 16 and 23. Chapter sixteen is an allegorical story about Jerusalem's faithlessness to the Lord (Ezek. 16:26). In this chapter, the Lord indicts Jerusalem for acting like a prostitute, throwing herself to the gods of foreign nations (Ezek. 16:15, 20, 33, 36). Chapter twenty-three is a similar story about Judah and Israel portrayed as two sisters in whoredom with the foreign nations (Ezek. 23:7, 14, 18, 35). These passages expose the vileness of the Israelites' sin.

8458. תַּחְבֻּלָה ***taḥbulāh:*** A feminine noun meaning counsel, advice. It is used of God's counsel and advice given to direct the behavior of even the clouds (Job 37:12). It refers to wise advice that a wise person seeks out (Prov. 1:5); without it, a person is at a loss to know what to do (Prov. 11:14); war was to be carried out by wise counsel (Prov. 20:18; 24:6). Counsel from a wicked person was considered destructive (Prov. 12:5).

8459. תֹּחוּ *tōḥû:* A proper noun designating Tohu (1 Sam. 1:1), the same as Toah (8430).

8460. תְּחוֹת *t^eḥôṯ:* An Aramaic preposition indicating under. It locates something under something else or below it. It is used figuratively and literally (Jer. 10:11). In the king's dream, the beasts of the field found shade under a great tree (Dan. 4:12[9], 14[11, 21[18]). God has all dominion under the heavens, and He has all rulership under Him (Dan. 7:27).

8461. תַּחְכְּמֹנִי *taḥk^emōniy:* A proper noun designating Tahkemonite (2 Sam. 23:8), the same as Hachmonite (2453,II).

8462. תְּחִלָּה *t^eḥillāh:* A feminine noun meaning a beginning, a first time. It may refer to the first time, the start, or the first place (Gen. 13:3; 41:21). It indicates the first time or start of a process (2 Kgs. 17:25). In battle it can refer to a first launched attack (2 Sam. 17:9).

8463. תַּחֲלוּא *taḥ^alû',* תַּחֲלֻא *taḥ^alu':* A masculine noun meaning a disease, a sickness, a pain. It refers to various diseases or sicknesses which God may bring on His people to curse them (Deut. 29:22[21]; Jer. 14:18; 16:4). It refers to suffering and pain from a mortal illness (2 Chr. 21:19). God, however, heals all diseases (Ps. 103:3).

8464. תַּחְמָס *taḥmās:* I. A masculine noun referring to an owl, a screech owl. It refers to a bird that Israel could not eat; it was classified as unclean (Lev. 11:16; Deut. 14:15).

II. A masculine noun referring to the night hawk. The King James Version favored this rendering of the verb (Lev. 11:16; Deut. 14:15). Its classification as inedible and unclean is the same.

8465. תַּחַן *taḥan:* A proper noun designating Tahan (Num. 26:35; 1 Chr. 7:25).

8466. תַּחֲנָה *taḥ^anāh:* A feminine noun meaning a camp. It refers to the place where a group of people set up temporary living headquarters. Usually, it refers to a military encampment that would also post sentries, etc. (2 Kgs. 6:8).

8467. תְּחִנָּה *t^eḥinnāh:* A feminine noun meaning a request for favor. The request for favor is always directed toward God—with two exceptions when the request is made to the king (Jer. 37:20; 38:26). This seldom-used term occurred predominately in connection with Solomon's dedication of the Temple (1 Kgs. 8:28, 30, 38, 45, 49, 52, 54; 2 Chr. 6:14–42). In these passages, the request was often connected with prayer and associated with a distinct relationship to God. On two occasions, the word was used to refer to favor itself (Josh. 11:20; Ezra 9:8).

8468. תְּחִנָּה ***t^eḥinnāh:*** A proper noun designating Tehinnah (1 Chr. 4:12).

8469. תַּחֲנוּן ***taḥ^anûn:*** A masculine noun meaning supplication. The word refers to asking for favor and is used in a comparison of a rich man with a poor man. The rich man answers harshly, while the poor man pleads for mercy (Prov. 18:23). Daniel used the word to indicate how he turned to the Lord in a prayer of petition, i.e., he pleaded with Him in prayers of petition with fasting and in sackcloth and ashes (Dan. 9:3). He also called to God to hear the prayers and petitions of His servant (Dan. 9:17). The noun was also used by the psalmist, who made a plea to God to hear his cry for mercy (Ps. 28:2; 31:22[23]; 86:6). In Jeremiah, a cry was heard on the barren heights, along with weeping and pleading by the people of Israel (Jer. 3:21). The word was also used to inform Daniel that as soon as he began his prayer or petition, an answer would be given to him (Dan. 9:23).

8470. תַּחֲנִי ***taḥ^aniy:*** A proper noun designating Tahanite (Num. 26:35).

8471. תַּחְפַּנְחֵס, תְּחַפְנְחֵס ***taḥpanḥēs, t^eḥapn^eḥēs:*** A proper noun designating Tahpanhes, an Egyptian city in the eastern delta. It was located south of Lake Manzaleh on the Pelusaic branch of the Nile River. It took part in the devastation of Israel. Jeremiah was taken into exile here and many Jewish refugees fleeing Nebuchadnezzar passed through it. Jeremiah prophesied here (Jer. 43:8–13). Pharaoh's palace was in the city at that time. The Babylonians conquered Egypt, passing through Tahpanhes (Jer. 46:14; Ezek. 30:18) (568–567 B.C.).

8472. תַּחְפְּנֵיס ***taḥp^enēys:*** A proper noun designating Tahpenes, the name of a Pharaoh's queen (prior to ca. 945 B.C.). The Pharaoh gave Hadad a sister of the queen for a wife (1 Kgs. 11:19–20).

8473. תַּחְרָא ***taḥrā':*** I. A feminine noun referring to a coat of mail; habergeon. The exact meaning eludes us. It refers to protective gear worn by soldiers in battle. Others suggest a leather cuirass, a tight-fitting armor to protect one's front and back (Ex. 28:32; 39:23).

II. A feminine noun meaning collar. It refers to the edging around the neck of a shirt to keep it from tearing (Ex. 28:32; 39:23).

8474. תַּחֲרָה ***taḥārāh:*** I. A verb meaning to contend; to compete; from *ḥarāh.* It means to challenge, to compete against. In context it indicates competing against swift horses (Jer. 12:5).

II. A verb meaning to close oneself in; derived from *ḥarāh.* It means to close oneself in cedar, with the connotation in order to compete with kings or to show oneself a king (Jer. 22:15).

8475. תַּחְרֵעַ taḥrēaʻ: A proper noun designating Tahrea (1 Chr. 9:41).

8476. תָּחַשׁ tāḥaš: A masculine noun referring to an unknown animal or the skin of some unknown animal. The renderings most common are: badger (KJV); dolphin (NASB); sea cow (NIV). The dugong, a large tropical sirenian mammal that inhabits the shores of the Indian Ocean, has also been suggested. Its skin was used in the construction of the covering of the Tabernacle and for making fine shoes and sandals (Ezek. 16:10).

8477. תַּחַשׁ taḥaš: A proper noun designating Tahash, Thahash (Gen. 22:24).

8478. תַּחַת taḥaṯ: A preposition meaning under, beneath; in place of. It indicates a position below or underneath some other reference point (Gen. 1:7, 9; 2:21; with suffix *taḥtennāh;* Gen. 18:4). It can mean in place of, instead of (Gen. 4:25; Ex. 21:26). *Taḥaṯ meh* means under what? why? (Jer. 5:19). Under something may be indicated by *le*, to, following this word (Ezek. 10:2). Out from under has *min*, from, attached to the front of *taḥaṯ* (Ex. 6:7), out from under the oppression of the Egyptians. It may be used as a noun (see Gen. 2:21 above) to indicate the place under someone or something, on the spot (NASB) (2 Sam. 2:23).

8479. תַּחַת taḥaṯ: An Aramaic preposition indicating under. It refers to a place or a time below something else (Dan. 4:14[11]).

8480. תַּחַת taḥaṯ: A proper noun designating Tahath:

A. A Kohathite (1 Chr. 6:24[9], 37[22]).

B. Son of Ephraim (1 Chr. 7:20).

C. Grandson of B above (1 Chr. 7:20).

D. A wilderness location (Num. 33:26, 27).

8481. תַּחְתּוֹן taḥtôn: An adjective meaning lower, lowest. It refers to the lower or the lowest of something: a territory (Josh. 16:3; 18:13; 1 Kgs. 9:17); a story or room (1 Kgs. 6:6, 8); water pool (Isa. 22:9); lower street or pavement (Ezek. 40:18); the lower of two ledges (Ezek. 43:14).

8482. תַּחְתִּי taḥtiy: An adjective meaning lower, below, lowest. It refers to the lower as opposed to upper stories (Gen. 6:16), e.g., to lower millstones (Job 41:24[16]). Used as a noun, it refers to what is in the lower parts, e.g., of the earth (Isa. 44:23; Ezek. 26:20; 31:14). It indicates the lowest areas of Sheol (Deut. 32:22). The foot of Mount Sinai is indicated by *taḥtîṯ*, a feminine form of this word.

8483. תַּחְתִּים חָדְשִׁי taḥtiym ḥoḏšiy: A proper noun designating Tahtim-Hodshi (2 Sam. 24:6).

8484. תִּיכוֹן, תִּיכֹן tiyḵôn, tiyḵōn: I. An adjective meaning middle. It indicates the place halfway between certain points, times, or other limits; in the center. In context it refers to a central stabilizing bar in a part of the Tabernacle framework (Ex. 26:28; 36:33); to the time of a middle watch (Judg. 7:19). It indicates the middle story of a building (1 Kgs. 6:8; Ezek. 41:7; 42:5, 6); and it designates a middle court area (2 Kgs. 20:4).

II. An adjective meaning lower, lowest. The word is translated as lower, lowest in some ancient versions. They are followed by the NASB (1 Kgs. 6:8).

8485. תֵּימָא *tēymā':* A proper noun designating Tema (Gen. 25:15; 1 Chr. 1:30; Job 6:19; Isa. 21:14; Jer. 25:23).

8486. תֵּימָן *tēymān:* A feminine noun meaning south. It refers to the direction lying to the right of a person facing east (Ex. 26:18, 35; 27:9; 36:23; 38:9). It can refer to a southern area of land (Josh. 15:1). With *āh* on the end, it means toward the south, southward (Ex. 26:18). It is used with reference to the entire south country (Zech. 6:6). It stands for a south wind controlled by God (Ps; 78:26; Song 4:16). It is used figuratively of the south personified (Isa. 43:6; Ezek. 20:46[21:2).

8487. תֵּימָן *tēymān:* A proper noun designating Teman:

A. The grandson of Esau (Gen. 36:11, 15, 42; 1 Chr. 1:36, 53).

B. The area in Edom occupied by the descendants of A above (Jer. 49:7, 20; Ezek. 20:46[21:2]; 25:13; Amos 1:12; Obad. 1:9; Hab. 3:3).

8488. תֵּימְנִי *tēym^{e}niy:* A proper noun designating Temeni (1 Chr. 4:6).

8489. תֵּימָנִי *tēymāniy:* A proper noun designating Temanite (Gen. 36:34[KJV, Temani]; 1 Chr. 1:45; Job 2:11; 4:1; 15:1; 22:1; 42:7, 9).

8490. תִּימָרָה *tiymārāh:* A feminine noun referring to a column, a pillar. It refers to the caravan or royal carriage of Solomon that appears like a column of smoke (Song 3:6). It refers to a display of God's wonders on the Day of the Lord, including a display of columns of smoke literally or in some figurative sense (Joel 2:30[3:3]).

8491. תִּיצִי *tiyṣiy:* A proper noun designating Tizite (1 Chr. 11:45).

8492. תִּירוֹשׁ *tiyrôš:* A masculine noun referring to new wine. It was one of the blessings God promised to His people in Canaan (Gen. 27:28, 37). The best of the new wine went to the priests (Num. 18:12). The New International Version translates this word as follows: new wine (34), grapes (1), juice (1), new (1), wine (1). The New American Standard Bible renders it: new wine (33), fresh wine (1), wine (3), grapes (1). It was intended to be a joyous blessing in Israel (Ps. 4:7[8]; Hos. 2:8[10], 9[11]); but abused, it became a curse (Hos. 4:11). God could and would therefore remove it (Hos. 9:2); but He will ultimately restore it in a renewed land (Hos. 2:22[24]).

8493. תִּירְיָא ***tiyryā':*** A proper noun designating Tiria (1 Chr. 4:16).

8494. תִּירָס ***tiyrās:*** A proper noun designating Tiras (Gen. 10:2; 1 Chr. 1:5).

8495. תַּיִשׁ ***tayiš:*** A masculine noun referring to a male goat. It was a valuable member of a person's wealth and a part of a flock (Gen. 30:35; 32:14[15]). It was considered a choice item for payment of a tribute (2 Chr. 17:11). It was among the four things impressive in their locomotion, their walk (Prov. 30:31).

8496. תֹּךְ ***tōḵ,*** תּוֹךְ ***tôḵ:*** A masculine noun meaning oppression. It refers to pressure, anxiety, feeling weighed down, something that the mouth of the evil person delights in (Ps. 10:7); it stalks those in the city (Ps. 55:11[12]). A righteous king will remove oppression (Ps. 72:14); and the Lord puts hope into the life of the oppressed person (Prov. 29:13).

8497. תָּכָה ***tāḵāh:*** I. A verb meaning to bow down; to sit down. It indicates sitting or paying homage to God as He delivered His Law at Sinai (Deut. 33:3).

II. A verb meaning to follow. It refers to God's people walking after, accepting the laws of the Lord (Deut. 33:3).

8498. תְּכוּנָה ***t^e^ḵûnāh:*** I. A feminine noun referring to a pattern, an arrangement. It refers to the layout and organization of the Temple envisioned by Ezekiel (43:11). With reference to plunder, it has the sense of a kind of merchandise or valuables (treasures) (Nah. 2:9[10]).

II. A feminine noun referring to a seat; a place of dwelling. It refers to the place or location established where someone is. In context, it depicts God's dwelling or location (Job 23:3).

8499. תְּכוּנָה ***t^e^khūnāh:*** A feminine noun meaning a seat; a place of dwelling. It refers to the place or location established where someone is, in its current context, it indicates God's dwelling or location (Job 23:3).

8500. תֻּכִּיִּים ***tukkiyyiym:*** I. A masculine plural noun meaning peacocks. It refers to a highly sought-after male bird with a crest of plumules and long, brightly colored upper tail coverts that can spread out like a colorful fan. They were imported by Solomon for displaying at court (1 Kgs. 10:22; 2 Chr. 9:21).

II. A masculine plural noun referring to baboons. The NIV translates this word as baboons. It is a type of monkey having a dog-like snout, long teeth, a large head with cheek pouches, and bare calluses on its rump (1 Kgs. 10:22; 2 Chr. 9:21). It was imported by Solomon for his court.

8501. תָּכָךְ ***tāḵaḵ:*** A masculine noun referring to deceit. It refers to what is not straightforward, true, or faithful but is rather treacherous (Prov. 29:13).

8502. תִּכְלָה ***tiḵlāh:*** A feminine noun indicating perfection. It indicates what is without fault, complete, whole, not lacking in any way. God's laws are the epitome of perfection (Ps. 119:96).

8503. תַּכְלִית ***taḵliyṯ:*** It indicates a boundary, a limit. It refers to a physical marker that delineates or sets a boundary (Neh. 3:21). It is used figuratively of the boundaries of the Almighty, which, of course, are unsearchable (Job 11:7). It figuratively points to God's setting a boundary for light and darkness (Job 26:10); and to the extreme limits of the psalmist's hatred for those who oppose God (Ps. 139:22).

8504. תְּכֵלֶת ***t^{e}ḵēleṯ:*** A feminine noun meaning blue, violet. It refers to the color of certain highly colorful wool materials used in the Tabernacle (Ex. 25:4). Some translators render it as purple. It was used in various things of the Tabernacle: hangings, an ephod (Ex. 26:1; 28:5, 6; 28:33; 35:25); Temple hangings (2 Chr. 2:7[6], 14[13]). It was employed in cords, loops, rings (Ex. 26:4; 28:28, 31, 37); palace curtains (Esth. 1:6). More generally, it refers to fabrics (Jer. 10:9; Ezek. 23:6). It was a valuable trade item (Ezek. 27:7).

8505. תָּכַן ***tāḵan:*** A verb meaning to weigh; to be equal. It describes God's weighing actions as a process of moral evaluation (1 Sam. 2:3; Prov. 16:2; 21:2; 24:12); but it is used of weighing money as well (2 Kgs. 12:11[12]). It indicates parceling out water (Job 28:25). It indicates the weighing of the pillars of the earth in the sense of establishing them (Ps. 75:3[4]). It is used figuratively of God's weighing even the mountains (Isa. 40:12). It is used in the sense of testing or perhaps informing the Spirit of God (Isa. 40:13). It means measured or weighed in the sense of being correct (Ezek. 18:25, 29; 33:17, 20; KJV, not equal).

8506. תֹּכֶן ***tōḵen:*** A masculine noun referring to quantity, quota. It refers to a set amount, a goal to be reached (Ex. 5:18; Ezek. 45:11).

8507. תֹּכֶן ***tōḵen:*** A proper noun designating Token (1 Chr. 4:32).

8508. תָּכְנִית ***toḵniyṯ:*** A feminine noun referring to perfection; a plan, a pattern. It indicates completeness in every way, wisdom, beauty, environment, blessedness, anointed of God (Ezek. 28:12). It refers appropriately to a blueprint, an arrangement laid out for the Temple, its plan (Ezek. 43:10).

8509. תַּכְרִיךְ ***taḵriyḵ:*** A masculine noun referring to a garment, a robe. It refers to a long, loose garment without sleeves, of royal stature. It was worn in the Persian palaces and awarded to Mordecai in its biblical context (Esth. 8:15).

8510. תֵּל ***tēl:*** A masculine noun meaning a mound, a heap, ruins. It refers to what signs may remain of a devastated and destroyed city, a ruin (Deut. 13:16[17]; Josh. 8:28; Jer. 49:2). The word also means mounds, small or large man-made hills on which cities were repeatedly destroyed and rebuilt. New cities could be erected on top of their ruins (Jer. 30:18).

8511. תָּלָא ***tālā':*** A verb meaning to hang; to be determined. It refers to dangling in midair with the danger of falling or dropping (Deut. 28:66). It indicates hanging objects up, not touching the ground; of hanging people or their bones (2 Sam. 21:12). It refers to having a strong opinion, one that a person will not change (Hos. 11:7).

8512. תֵּל אָבִיב ***tēl 'āḇiyḇ:*** A proper noun designating Tel Abib (Ezek. 3:15).

8513. תְּלָאָה ***teląā'āh:*** A feminine noun indicating a hardship. It refers to the bad luck, oppressions, attacks, war, famine, etc., that Israel endured in Egypt as well as in their wilderness wanderings (Ex. 18:8; Num. 20:14). In Nehemiah's prayer, it refers to the difficult circumstances Israel had to bear in exile after the fall of Jerusalem (Neh. 9:32). It refers to personal oppression and discomfort (Lam. 3:5). It is used in a derisive, mocking manner by rebellious Israelites about their worship of the Lord that had become a burden and a hardship (Mal. 1:13).

8514. תַּלְאוּבָה ***tal'ûḇāh:*** A feminine noun meaning a drought, burning heat. It refers to a time when there is no rain and a resulting scarcity of water (Hos. 13:5).

8515. תְּלַאשָּׂר ***t^ela'śśār:*** A proper noun designating Tel Assar (2 Kgs. 19:12; Isa. 37:12).

8516. תִּלְבֹּשֶׁת ***tilbōšeṯ:*** A feminine noun referring to clothing, a garment. It indicates in a figurative sense garments of revenge, clothing of revenge, clothing indicative of vengeance put on by God to effect justice and judgment on His people (Isa. 59:17).

8517. תְּלַג ***t^elag:*** An Aramaic masculine noun meaning snow. It refers to frozen crystals of water having a white color. The white color of snow is used to describe the appearance of the Ancient of Days (Dan. 7:9).

8518. תָּלָה ***tālāh:*** A verb meaning to hang. It means to suspend something or someone in the air: the king's chief baker was hanged and executed (Gen. 40:19, 22). Hanging or execution on a tree was the penalty for a crime worthy of death (Deut. 21:22, 23; Esth. 2:23). It was the fate of many in time of war (Josh. 8:29; 10:26). In the passive sense, it means to be hanged (Esth. 2:23; Lam. 5:12). Objects are hung out as well (Ezek. 27:10). It is used figuratively of hanging an abstract quality or responsibility on a person (Isa. 22:24).

8519. תְּלֻנָּה ***t^elunāh:*** A feminine noun referring to grumbling. It indicates rebellious expressions of complaint and dissatisfaction against the Lord in particular (Ex. 16:7–9, 12; Num. 14:27; 17:5[20], 10[25]).

8520. תֶּלַח ***telaḥ:*** A proper noun designating Telah (1 Chr. 7:25).

8521. תֵּל חַרְשָׁא ***tel ḥarša':*** A proper noun designating Tel Harsha (Ezra 2:59; Neh. 7:61).

8522. תְּלִי ***t^eliy:*** A masculine noun referring to a quiver. It refers to a container in which a hunter or soldier carried his arrows. It was usually made of leather and wood (Gen. 27:3).

8523. תְּלִיתָי ***t^eliyṯāy,*** תַּלְתַּי ***taltay:*** An Aramaic ordinal number meaning third. In Daniel it refers to the third kingdom to arise in a series of four, probably representing Greece (Dan. 2:39) or to the third ruler in the kingdom (Dan. 5:7).

8524. תָּלוּל ***tālûl:*** An adjective meaning lofty. It refers to anything high like the top branches of a great tree (Ezek. 17:22).

8525. תֶּלֶם ***telem:*** A masculine noun indicating a furrow. It describes the indentation in the ground left by overturned clods of earth created in a field by plowing. Job speaks figuratively of the furrows of the ground weeping (Job 31:38). The wild ox cannot be harnessed for plowing (Job 39:10, KJV, unicorn). God provides water for the plowed furrows (Ps. 65:10[11]). It is used figuratively by Hosea (10:4).

8526. תַּלְמַי ***talmay:*** A proper noun designating Talmai:

A. A descendant of the Anakim from Anak. He lived in Hebron (Num. 13:22). Joshua drove the Anakites from the area (Josh. 15:14; Judg. 1:10).

B. The grandfather of Absalom, David's son. He was the son (king?) of the king of Geshur, Ammihud (2 Sam. 13:37).

8527. תַּלְמִיד ***talmiyḏ:*** A masculine noun meaning a pupil, a student. It refers to persons who are in the process of learning, of acquiring knowledge, applying themselves diligently to study (1 Chr. 25:8).

8528. תֵּל מֶלַח ***tēl m^elaḥ:*** A proper noun designating Tel Melah (Ezra 2:59; Neh. 7:61).

8529. תָּלַע ***tāla':*** A verb meaning to dress in scarlet. It refers to the armies of Babylon being dressed in scarlet, a bright red with a tinge of orange, a dazzling sight in war (Nah. 2:3[4]).

8530. תַּלְפִּיּוֹת ***talpiyyôṯ:*** I. A feminine plural noun indicating rows of stones. It is used figuratively to describe in Middle Eastern style the attractive neck of a beloved bride (Song 4:4). The exact meaning of the word is being researched.

II. A feminine plural noun indicating armories. It describes features of the neck of a beloved bride in Middle Eastern style (Song 4:4).

III. A feminine plural noun meaning elegance. It is a word referring to the beloved bride's neck in Middle Eastern style (Song 4:4).

8531. תְּלַת ***tᵉlaṯ***, תַּלְתָּא ***taltā':*** An Aramaic ordinal number indicating third highest. It is used in a context indicating the third ranking political position in Babylon after the king and his son (Dan. 5:7).

8532. תְּלָת ***tᵉlāṯ***, תְּלָתָה ***tᵉlāṯāh:*** An Aramaic numerical noun meaning three; third. It indicates an ordinal counting number referring to the third item being counted (Ezra 6:4, 15), the third layer, the third day. It also functions as a cardinal counting number (Dan. 3:23, 24), three men. Daniel prayed three times a day (Dan. 6:10[11]; 13[14]).

8533. תְּלָתִין ***tᵉlāṯiyn:*** An Aramaic plural noun indicating thirty. It is *tᵉlaṯ* pluralized. It refers to thirty days, a special time during which Daniel was watched carefully to catch him in some error (Dan. 6:7[8], 12[13]).

8534. תַּלְתַּל ***taltal:*** I. An adjective meaning wavy, bushy. It describes the bridegroom's black, bushy locks lying in bunches (Song 5:11). Its exact nuance is not entirely clear.

II. A feminine noun meaning a cluster of dates. It refers to the hair of the bridegroom, bundled into clusters that look like bunches of dates (Song 5:11), a cluster of flowers or dates of the date palm tree.

8535. תָּם ***tām:*** An adjective meaning integrity, completeness. This is a rare, almost exclusively poetic term often translated perfect but not carrying the sense of totally free from fault, for it was used of quite flawed people. It describes the mild manner of Jacob in contrast to his brother Esau, who was characterized by shedding blood (Gen. 25:27; see also Prov. 29:10). The term often carries a rather strong moral component in certain contexts (Job 1:1; 9:20–22; Ps. 37:37; 64:4[5]). This word appears among a list of glowing terms describing the admirable qualities of the Shulamite lover (Song 5:2; 6:9).

8536. תָּם ***tām***, תַּמָּה ***tammāh:*** An Aramaic adverb meaning there. It indicates a place where, a specific location (Ezra 5:17; 6:1, 6, 12). In context a city or temple area are in mind.

8537. תֹּם ***tōm:*** A masculine noun meaning completeness, integrity. This word is used in Job to describe how a man could die, i.e., in complete security (Job 21:23). When Absalom invited two hundred men from Jerusalem to his party, the word denoted that the men did not have any idea of what was about to happen (2 Sam. 15:11). In Genesis, Abimelech acted with a clear conscience after Abraham stated that Sarah was his sister (Gen. 20:5, 6). In a statement of wisdom, Proverbs uses the word to indicate that righteousness guards the person of integrity (Prov. 13:6); while the psalmist asks that his integrity and uprightness protect him because his hope is in the Lord (Ps. 25:21).

8538. תֻּמָּה ***tummāh:*** A feminine noun meaning integrity. This comes from the verb *tāmam* (8552), meaning to be complete, and is the feminine equivalent of the word *tōm* (8537), meaning completeness or integrity. This word is used only five times in the Old Testament and is only found in the Wisdom Literature of Job and the Psalms. In four of these instances, it is used by God, Job, and Job's wife to refer to Job's integrity (Job. 2:3, 9; 27:5; 31:6). In Proverbs 11:3, integrity guides the upright person. See the related adjective *tām* (8535), meaning complete.

8539. תָּמַהּ ***tāmah:*** A verb meaning to be amazed; to be astounded. It means to be shocked, stunned at something: Joseph's brothers were astonished at the situation they found themselves in (Gen. 43:33). It is used figuratively of the pillars of heaven being amazed, shocked (Job 26:11). Kings of the nations stand amazed at the splendor of Zion (Ps. 48:5[6]). It carries the sense of being surprised at something unexpected (Eccl. 5:8[7]). God's judgments cause astonishment and disbelief among those He destroys (Isa. 13:8; Jer. 4:9; Hab. 1:5). It indicates amazement at God's vision of judgment (Isa. 29:9; NASB, wait).

8540. תְּמַהּ t^e***mah:*** An Aramaic masculine noun meaning wonder. This word is related to the Hebrew verb *tāmah* (8539), meaning to be astonished. In its only three instances, this word speaks of the wondrous and perhaps miraculous deeds of God (Dan. 4:2[3:32], 3[3:33]; 6:27[28]). In every instance, it is used in close connection with *'āṯ* (852), meaning signs.

8541. תִּמָּהוֹן ***timmāhôn:*** A masculine noun indicating bewilderment, confusion. It refers to a curse that God will bring on a disobedient people of confusion, disorientation at what is happening (Deut. 28:28); even horses will be dazed (Zech. 12:4).

8542. תַּמּוּז ***tāmmûz:*** A masculine proper noun Tammuz. It refers to a popular and widely known fertility god in the ancient Middle East (Ezek. 8:14). It had other names in different nations, Astarte, Ishtar, etc.

8543. תְּמוֹל t^e***môl,*** תְּמֹל t^e***mōl:*** An adverb meaning before; previously; yesterday. It always refers to a previous time: recent, only yesterday (Job 8:9); yesterday (Ps. 90:4, k^e*yôm 'eṯmôl*). It often used with *šilšōm*, t^e*môl šilšōm*, formerly or day before yesterday (Gen. 31:2, 5; Ex. 5:8; 1 Sam. 4:7). *Gam* t^e*môl gam hayyôm* means both yesterday and today (Ex. 5:14).

8544. תְּמוּנָה t^e*mûnāh*: A feminine noun meaning a likeness or a form. This word is related to the noun *miyn* (4327), meaning kind or species. The main idea of this word is one of likeness or similarity. It is normally used to describe God's ban on creating images of anything that would attempt to resemble (or be like) Him (Ex. 20:4; Deut. 4:15, 16; 5:8). This word can also describe the form or likeness of a visible image (Job 4:16; Ps. 17:15). Synonyms for this word are *tabniyt* (8403) meaning plan, pattern, or form, and *demût* (1823), meaning likeness.

8545. תְּמוּרָה t^e*mûrāh*: A feminine noun meaning an exchange. This word comes from the verb *mûr* (4171), meaning to change or to exchange. The word usually refers to the exchanging of one item for another. In Leviticus, it is used to give rules for the exchange of animals and land that were dedicated to the Lord (Lev. 27:10, 33). In Ruth, the word indicates the Israelite custom of exchanging items to confirm a vow (Ruth 4:7). In Job, this word describes financial transactions (Job 20:18; 28:17). This word may be translated recompense in Job 15:31, where it describes the natural result of a life trusting in vanity.

8546. תְּמוּתָה t^e*mûṯāh*: A feminine noun meaning death. This word comes from the verb *mûṯ* (4191), meaning to die. In its only two occurrences in the Old Testament, it is used to describe those who were appointed to and deserving of death. More literally, it was those who were appointed to death (Ps. 79:11; 102:20[21]).

8547. תֶּמַח *temaḥ*: A proper noun designating Temah (Ezra 2:53; Neh. 7:55).

8548. תָּמִיד *tāmiyḏ*: A masculine noun meaning continuity. This word commonly refers to actions concerning religious rituals: God commanded that the Israelites always set showbread on a table in the Tabernacle (Ex. 25:30). Similarly, special bread was to be set on the table continually every Sabbath (Lev. 24:8). Mealtime could also be seen as following a set pattern: David commanded that Mephibosheth always eat with him (2 Sam. 9:7). In another light, the psalmist referred to God as One he could continually turn to in times of need (Ps. 71:3).

8549. תָּמִים *tāmiym*: An adjective meaning blameless, complete. In over half of its occurrences, it describes an animal to be sacrificed to the Lord, whether a ram, a bull, or a lamb (Ex. 29:1; Lev. 4:3; 14:10). With respect to time, the term is used to refer to a complete day, a complete seven Sabbaths (weeks), and a complete year (Lev. 23:15; 25:30; Josh. 10:13). When used in a moral sense, this word is linked with truth, virtue, uprightness, and righteousness (Josh. 24:14; Ps. 18:23[24]; Prov. 2:21; 11:5). The term is used of one's relationship with another person (Judg. 9:19; Prov. 28:18; Amos 5:10); and of one's relationship with God (Gen. 17:1; Deut. 18:13; 2 Sam. 22:24, 26). Moreover, this word described the blamelessness of God's way, knowledge, and Law (2 Sam. 22:31; Job 37:16; Ps. 19:7[8]).

8550. תֻּמִּים ***tummiym:*** A proper noun meaning Thummin. Its meaning is not certain. It may mean perfection(s), truth, integrity. It refers to one of two small sacred lots used by the high priest to discern God's will (Ex. 28:30; Lev. 8:8; Deut. 33:8). It disappeared after the exile (Ezra 2:63; Neh. 7:65). The word begins with the last letter of the alphabet.

8551. תָּמַךְ ***tāmak:*** A verb meaning to grasp, to hold; to support. It means to grasp, seize something, to take hold of a person's hand (Gen. 48:17); a person (Isa. 41:10); a scepter or a pole (Amos 1:5, 8). It refers to grasping and supporting a person's hands and arms (Ex. 17:12). It is used figuratively of supporting someone, as God supports His people (Ps. 16:5; 41:12[13]; 63:8[9]); or of holding on firmly to God's ways (Ps. 17:5; Prov. 4:4). Those who hold to wisdom find her a tree of life (Prov. 3:18). Its passive sense refers to being held tightly, firmly, e.g., the evil person held fast by his sins (Prov. 5:22).

8552. תָּמַם ***tāmam:*** A verb meaning to be complete, to finish, to conclude. At its root, this word carries the connotation of finishing or bringing closure. It is used to signify the concluding of an oration (Deut. 31:30); the completing of a building project (1 Kgs. 6:22); the exhausting of resources (Gen. 47:15; Lev. 26:20); the utter destruction of something (Num. 14:33); and the fulfilling of an established period of time (Deut. 34:8).

8553. תִּמְנָה ***timnāh:*** A proper noun designating Timnah:

A. A city in northern Judah. Judah visited the city. It was allotted to the tribe of Dan (Josh. 15:10). Samson loved and married a Philistine woman in Timnah (Judg. 14:1–5), so it went back into Philistine control at some point. In Ahaz's day, Edomites raided it (2 Chr. 28:18). It was likely south of Hebron.

B. A city in the southern hill country of Judah (Josh. 15:57).

8554. תִּמְנִי ***timniy:*** A proper noun designating Timnite (Judg. 15:6).

8555. תִּמְנָע ***timnā':*** A proper noun designating Timna:

A. Concubine of Eliphaz (Gen. 36:12, 22; 1 Chr. 1:39).

B. A chief of Edom (Gen. 36:40; 1 Chr. 1:51).

C. Son of Eliphaz (1 Chr. 1:36).

8556. תִּמְנַת חֶרֶס ***timnat ḥeres,*** תִּמְנַת סֶרַח ***timnat seraḥ:*** I. A proper noun designating Timnath Heres (Judg. 2:9), the same as II.

II. A proper noun designating Timnath Serah (Josh. 19:50; 24:30), the same as I.

8557. תֶּמֶס ***temes:*** A masculine noun referring to a melting away. It describes a snail that seems to melt as it drags itself along in the sun (Ps. 58:8[9]).

8558. תָּמָר ***tāmār:*** A masculine noun referring to a palm tree. It refers to a water-loving date palm tree found around springs (Ex. 15:27; Num. 33:9); a desert oasis where the date palm flourishes (Ps. 92:12[13]). Its rich foliage, long leaves, and slim branches were used often in feasts and festivals to celebrate (Lev. 23:40). Jericho was known as the city of palm trees (Deut. 34:3). The righteous flourish as the date palm (Ps. 92:12[13]). The bride is likened favorably to a date palm (Song 7:7[8], 8[9]). In a time of severe judgment, Joel could envision even the date palm drying up (Joel 1:12).

8559. תָּמָר ***tāmār:*** A proper noun designating Tamar:

A. The daughter-in-law of Judah. She married Judah's son Er who died childless (Gen. 38:1–24). Onan, his second son, died at the hand of the Lord because he would not raise up seed for Israel through Tamar according to the Levirate law of marriage (Gen. 38:9–10). She then disguised herself as a prostitute, solicited Judah, and lay with him to conceive a son. She bore twins, Perez and Zerah, by Judah (Gen. 38:28–30). Perez, her son, and his fruitfulness became a model for the hoped-for offspring of Ruth and Boaz (Ruth 4:12).

B. A beautiful daughter of David with whom his son Amnon, son by his wife Ahinoam, fell in love. The name means "palm." He raped her and then viciously rejected and hated her after the affair (2 Sam. 13:1–32). She was Absalom's full sister by Maacah their mother. Absalom avenged Tamar and slew Amnon. Thus began the destruction of David's family because of his adultery and murder concerning Bathsheba.

C. The daughter of Absalom (not his sister) who also became a beautiful woman (2 Sam. 14:27).

D. A city on the border of the tribe of Gad. It was built by Solomon (1 Kgs. 9:18). Some translations give Tadmor (NIV). Ezekiel envisioned the city as part of a rebuilt Israel and located on the southeast border (Ezek. 47:18; 48:28).

8560. תֹּמֶר ***tōmer:*** I. A masculine noun meaning a palm tree. It is referred to as the place where Deborah sat to render judgment in Israel (Judg. 4:5). The KJV renders the word as palm tree in Jeremiah 10:5.

II. A masculine noun meaning a scarecrow. The word is rendered as scarecrow by most translators now (NASB, NIV; Jer. 10:5).

8561. תִּמֹרָה ***timōrāh:*** A feminine noun meaning a palm tree, a palm tree ornament. It refers to a carved palm tree ornament done by a skilled craftsman (1 Kgs. 6:29, 32, 35; 2 Chr. 3:5; Ezek. 40:16; 41:18–20). It was found in Solomon's Temple and in Ezekiel's visionary Temple.

8562. תַּמְרוּק ***tamrûq:*** A masculine noun meaning scraping, rubbing, purifying. This Hebrew word carries the connotation of scraping away that which is impure or harmful. This word appears three times in reference to ritual purification following menstruation (Esth. 2:3, 9, 12). Figuratively, it is used to imply a remedy for an illness (Prov. 20:30).

8563. תַּמְרוּר ***tamrûr:*** A masculine noun indicating bitterness. It refers to something that is difficult to endure, harsh, sharp, cutting, unpleasant: a bitter mourning for God's people (Jer. 6:26; 31:15). It refers to anger that is aggravated by bitterness and caustic hatred (Hos. 12:14[15]).

8564. תַּמְרוּר ***tamrûr:*** I. A masculine noun designating a guidepost, a road mark. It refers to an object set up to direct someone to a location. The Israelites were to set up markers, directions to the land of Israel so they could return to their homeland from exile (Jer. 31:21).

II. A masculine noun meaning a high heap. It refers to piling up stone or dirt markers to lead Israel back to her homeland after being scattered (Jer. 31:21; KJV).

8565. תַּן ***tān:*** A masculine noun meaning jackal, dragon (KJV). The word designates a jackal, wild scavenging animal or a dragon. Jackal well is the name given to a well near the wall of Jerusalem (New International Version notes Serpent or Fig as translation possibilities as well) (Neh. 2:13). A jackal is a wild dog that gains much of its food as a scavenger, an outcast of the animals (Job 30:29); dwelling in the outskirts of the desert or wilderness (Ps. 44:19[20]; Mal. 1:3). It tends to congregate in the ruins of cities (Isa. 13:22; Jer. 9:11[10]). It lets out a piercing, lonely howl like a lament (Mic. 1:8). It suckles its young on its breast, showing tenderness (Lam. 4:3).

8566. תָּנָה ***tānāh:*** A verb meaning to hire; to sell oneself. It describes a harlot hiring out her body, but in context it refers to Israel's spiritual harlotry and attempts to make forbidden liaisons with the nations (Hos. 8:9, 10).

8567. תָּנָה ***tānāh:*** A verb meaning to commemorate; to rehearse. It indicates the retelling, narrating, recounting of great events the Lord accomplished for His people (Judg. 5:11). The tragic story of Jephthah's daughter was rehearsed every year for four days in Israel (Judg. 11:40).

8568. תַּנָּה ***tānnāh:*** A feminine noun meaning dragon. It is rendered as dragon by the King James Version, referring to a lizard, a large serpent or snake, and other inhabitants of the wilderness (Mal. 1:3). This word is now understood to mean a serpent; a jackal, the old serpent (Satan), etc. See also 8565.

8569. תְּנוּאָה ***tᵉnûʼāh:*** A feminine noun meaning an opposition; a pretext. It refers to God's attitude of discipline that He took against Israel in the wilderness, His reasons for dealing with them as He did (Num. 14:34). It indicates causes, reasons for doing or acting in a certain way, e.g., God's actions against Job (Job 33:10).

8570. תְּנוּבָה ***t^enûḇāh:*** A feminine noun indicating fruit, a crop. It refers to the produce of the land, the fields, the fruit trees that God blessed (Deut. 32:13; Lam. 4:9; Ezek. 36:30). It refers to the fruit produced on a fig tree. It is employed in an interesting parable (Judg. 9:11). It is used beautifully in a figurative sense to refer to the moral, ethical, and religious fruit Israel will give to the whole earth (Isa. 27:6).

8571. תְּנוּךְ ***t^enûḵ:*** A masculine noun indicating the tip of the ear; the lobe. It refers to the thick, soft, lower part of a person's ear. It was anointed in a ritual to consecrate the priests to God and their sacred duties, indicating a demand for total commitment and obedience to the Lord's work (Ex. 29:20; Lev. 8:23, 24). The lobe of the ear was anointed with blood and oil taken from a guilt offering in a ritual that cleansed a leper (Lev. 14:14, 17, 25, 28).

8572. תְּנוּמָה ***t^enûmāh:*** A feminine noun referring to slumber. It indicates a state of sleep, rest, when persons most often dream (Job 33:15). Sleep and slumber are parallel in Psalm 132:4 and Prov. 6:4, 10. Too much sleep and slumber leads to the downfall of the fool and the sluggard (Prov. 24:33).

8573. תְּנוּפָה ***t^enûp̄āh:*** a feminine noun meaning swinging, waving, a wave offering, an offering. In a general sense, this word implies the side to side motion involved in waving. It is used specifically as a technical term for the wave offering (Ex. 29:24; Lev. 8:27). Twice the word is taken to mean an offering in general (Ex. 38:24, 29).

8574. תַּנּוּר ***tannûr:*** A masculine noun referring to an oven, a furnace. The word is used to describe a firepot (Gen. 15:17); an oven for baking bricks or food (Ex. 8:3[7:28]); a furnace for producing heat that consumes what is in it. God's enemies will be consumed by fire as in an oven (Ps. 21:9[10]). It is used as a symbol of God's avenging presence, His furnace (Isa. 31:9). It describes Israel's adulterous lust for false and forbidden liaisons among the nations (Hos. 7:4, 6, 7). The Day of the Lord is described as burning like a furnace (Mal. 4:1[3:19], NASB).

8575. תַּנְחוּם ***tanḥûm:*** A masculine/feminine noun meaning consolation, comfort, commiseration. It is used of God's words spoken to console Job in his suffering (Job 15:11). God's comforting of the psalmist delighted his soul (Ps. 94:19), that is, God's efforts at ameliorating and helping His faithful followers. It is used figuratively of the comforting breasts of Jerusalem (Isa. 66:11). In a time of God's judgments, consolations will be removed (Jer. 16:7).

8576. תַּנְחֻמֶת ***tanḥumeṯ:*** A proper noun designating Tanhumeth (2 Kgs. 25:23; Jer. 40:8).

8577. תַּנִּין ***tanniyn:*** A masculine noun meaning a serpent, a dragon, and a sea monster. It can connote a creature living in the water (Gen. 1:21; Job 7:12; Ps. 148:7). When the word is used this way, it is also used figuratively to represent the crocodile, which was the symbol of Pharaoh and Egypt (Ps. 74:13; Isa. 27:1; 51:9; Ezek. 29:3). This imagery may help us better understand the confrontation between Moses and Pharaoh, when Aaron's staff became a serpent and then swallowed the staff-serpents of Pharaoh's magicians (Ex. 7:9, 10, 12). God was providing a graphic sign of what was to come. It can also connote a creature that lives on the land (Deut. 32:33; Ps. 91:13; Jer. 51:34). There is one other occurrence of this term in the Old Testament where it is used as a descriptor or part of a proper name for a well or a spring (Neh. 2:13). In all its occurrences, this term has either a neutral (Gen. 1:21; Ps. 148:7); or a negative meaning (Isa. 27:1; 51:9; Jer. 51:34). In a few instances, the negative meaning is somewhat lessened, as when God provides a serpent to save His people (Ex. 7:9, 10, 12); or when a serpent was divinely restrained (Ps. 91:13).

8578. תִּנְיָן ***tinyān:*** An Aramaic ordinal number meaning second. It points out the second item in a series, a narrative, or a list; Daniel's vision featured a second beast (Dan. 7:5).

8579. תִּנְיָנוּת ***tinyānûṯ:*** An Aramaic adverb meaning again, a second time. It means to repeat a response, to respond again a second time, as the king's wise men did (Dan. 2:7).

8580. תִּנְשֶׁמֶת ***tinšemeṯ:*** I. A feminine noun referring to a white owl. It is classified in the Mosaic Law as a bird that was unclean, inedible for Israel (Lev. 11:18).

II. A feminine noun meaning a chameleon. The New American Standard Bible renders this as a chameleon, a kind of lizard with the ability to change color to fit its surroundings (Lev. 11:30). It was classified as a swarming thing, unclean and inedible to Israel.

III. A feminine noun meaning swan. It is rendered as a swan, a fowl unclean and inedible to Israel (KJV; Lev. 11:18; Deut. 14:16).

IV. A feminine noun meaning a mole. It is rendered as mole (KJV; Lev. 11:30), a small burrowing animal that feeds on insects and lives underground.

8581. תָּעַב ***ta'aḇ:*** A verb meaning to abhor, to be abhorrent, to do abominably. This word expresses a strongly detestable activity or the logical response to such an activity. It is associated with a severe sense of loathing (Deut. 23:7[8]; 1 Chr. 21:6); the condition of sinful people (Job 15:16); the activity of idol worship (1 Kgs. 21:26); and the Lord's opposition to sin (Ps. 5:6[7]).

8582. תָּעָה *tā'āh:* A verb meaning to err, to wander, and to go astray. The meaning of this Hebrew word primarily rests in the notion of wandering about (Ex. 23:4; Job 38:41). Figuratively, it is used in reference to one who is intoxicated (Isa. 28:7). Most often, however, it refers to erring or being misled in a moral or religious sense (Isa. 53:6; Ezek. 44:10[2x]; Hos. 4:12).

8583. תֹּעוּ *tō'û,* תֹּעִי *tō'iy:* I. A proper noun designating Tou (1 Chr. 18:9, 10), the same as II.

II. A proper noun designating Toi (2 Sam. 8:9, 10), the same as I.

8584. תְּעוּדָה *te'ûdāh:* A noun meaning a testimony, a custom. This noun is used in Isaiah 8:16, 20 in combination with the word law. In these verses, the testimony was the law of God's people that instructed them on how to live. In Ruth 4:7, this word refers to the common custom of sealing a legal agreement.

8585. תְּעָלָה *te'ālāh:* I. A feminine noun referring to a trench, a channel, an aqueduct. It indicates a conduit constructed to convey water or to hold it (1 Kgs. 18:32, 35, 38). It could deliver water into a pool (2 Kgs. 18:17; Isa. 7:3; 36:2). Hezekiah's conduit is the most famous and was hewn out of solid rock (2 Kgs. 20:20). It refers to naturally occurring channels that carry away floodwaters (Job 38:25); or channels connected to rivers (Ezek. 31:4).

II. A feminine noun meaning a remedy, a healing. It refers to an act, a medicine, or a process of healing. In its context, it refers to Judah's spiritual wounds and illnesses (Jer. 30:13). Gilead was famous for its restorative and medicinal medicines (Jer. 46:11).

8586. תַּעֲלוּלִים *ta'alûliym:* A masculine plural noun referring to punishments; capricious ones. It defines children, God's mockingly appointed rulers of His people, as indecisive or as making decisions without reason, on a whim (Isa. 3:4). In a different context, its negative connotations give it the meaning of punishments (Isa. 66:4; KJV, delusions; NIV, harsh treatment).

8587. תַּעֲלֻמָה *ta'alumāh:* A feminine noun meaning a secret; a hidden thing. It refers to that which is not evident, not public, concealed. It refers to the concealed aspects of wisdom (Job 11:6). God is able to reveal the hidden things of wisdom (Job 28:11). More importantly, God understands and knows the secrets of the heart, what a person is truly like (Ps. 44:21[22]).

8588. תַּעֲנוּג *ta'anûg:* A masculine noun meaning a delight, a pleasure. It refers to pleasure surrounding a carefree life of luxury. Such a situation is not appropriate for a fool (Prov. 19:10; KJV, delight; NIV, NASB, luxury). It refers to all possible delights and pleasures of people (Eccl. 2:8; Mic. 2:9). It describes an attractive and delightful bride (Song 7:6[7]). It describes God's children as His delight and enjoyment (Mic. 1:16).

8589. תַּעֲנִית ***taaniyṯ:*** A feminine noun meaning fasting, humiliation. It refers to a period of humbling oneself in prayer and fasting as Ezra did for the sins of himself and his people (Ezra 9:5).

8590. תַּעְנָךְ ***ta'nāḵ,*** **תַּעְנַךְ** ***ta'naḵ:*** A proper noun designating Taanach, a city southeast of Megiddo. Joshua captured it (Josh. 12:21; 17:11). Manasseh inherited it and it was a Levitical city as well (Josh. 21:25). It was near the western border of Issachar. Manasseh failed to drive out the Canaanites from it (Judg. 1:27). The battle of Deborah and Barak took place partly at Taanach and Megiddo (Judg. 5:19). It lay within Solomon's fifth administrative district of Israel (1 Kgs. 4:12).

8591. תָּעַע ***tā'a',*** **תְּעוּפָה** ***tᵉ'ûp̄āh:*** I. A verb indicating to deceive, to scoff. It means to trick someone into believing something false about oneself or something. In this case, Jacob applies the word to himself (Gen. 27:12). It may mean in context to despise, to scoff, to pay no attention to someone, e.g., a prophet (2 Chr. 36:16).

II. A feminine noun meaning darkness. It refers to the absence of light, in context the darkness of night (Job 11:17). The King James Version, however, takes the word from *'up̄*, to shine; hence, it translates it as a shining forth of light.

8592. תַּעֲצֻמָה ***taaṣumāh:*** A feminine noun meaning power, strength. It refers to the moral, ethical, and spiritual vigor and health God furnishes to His people (Ps. 68:35[36]).

8593. תַּעַר ***ta'ar:*** A masculine noun referring to a razor, a knife's sheath. It refers to a sharp-edged cutting tool used to cut one's hair or beard (Num. 6:5); a Nazarite was not to cut his hair during the time of his Nazarite vow. Ezekiel used a razor to shave his hair and beard (Ezek. 5:1). It was used to shave the Levites' entire bodies to symbolically cleanse them for their sacred service (Num. 8:7). It also describes a knife (razor?) used to cut passages from a scroll (Jer. 36:23). It refers to the sheath for a sword (1 Sam. 17:51; 2 Sam. 20:8; Ezek. 21:3[8], 4[9], 5[10], 30[35]). The tongue of an evil person is compared to a sharp razor that works deceit (Ps. 52:2[4]). It is used figuratively of the Lord shaving Judah with His razor—Assyria's army (Isa. 7:20).

8594. תַּעֲרוּבָה ***taarûḇāh:*** A feminine noun meaning a hostage. It refers to a person taken in time of war in context and kept in the power of the conquering nation (2 Kgs. 14:14; 2 Chr. 25:24).

8595. תַּעְתֻּעִים *ta'tu'iym:* A masculine plural noun meaning mockings, errors. Jeremiah used this word twice when he ridiculed the idols of the Israelites (Jer. 10:15; 51:18). These two verses are identical and are found in identical passages. Jeremiah assaulted the idols, saying how worthless they were and that they were works of mockery whose end will be judgment.

8596. תֹּף *tōp̱:* I. A masculine noun referring to a tambourine. It refers to a small, shallow, single-headed hand drum, also called a timbrel. It may have jingles around the rim, played by shaking it and/or striking it with the knuckles (Gen. 31:27). Miriam used this instrument to lead the women in a song of praise to the Lord for deliverance at the Red Sea. The King James Version renders this word as tabrets in Ezekiel 28:13.

II. A masculine noun referring to the setting for a jewel. It refers to the tiny sockets, their arrangements, and the precious jewels placed into them by a jeweler (Ezek. 28:13; KJV, tabrets).

8597. תִּפְאָרָה *tiph'ārāh:* A feminine noun meaning beauty, glory. Isaiah used the word to denote the so-called beauty of finery that would be snatched away by the Lord (Isa. 3:18). The word was used in a similar manner in Ezekiel to denote that which the people trusted in other than God, in addition to what would be stripped away (Ezek. 16:17; 23:26). The making of priestly garments and other apparel brought glory to Aaron and his sons, giving them dignity and honor (Ex. 28:2, 40). Wisdom was portrayed as giving a garland of grace and a crown of splendor in Proverbs (Prov. 4:9); Zion was told that it will be a crown of splendor in the Lord's hand (Isa. 62:3); and in the book of Jeremiah, the king and queen were told that the crowns would fall from their heads (Jer. 13:18). The word was used in Deuteronomy to describe how God would recognize His people (Deut. 26:19). In Lamentations, it was used in an opposite manner to describe the splendor of Israel that was thrown down from heaven to earth in the Lord's anger (Lam. 2:1). Deborah used the word to describe the honor or glory of a warrior which would not be Barak's because he handled the situation wrongly (Judg. 4:9).

8598. תַּפּוּחַ *tappûaḥ:* A masculine noun indicating an apple, an apple tree. It refers to a round, firm, fleshy, edible fruit grown on a tree in several colors, red, yellow, green. It is used in a famous proverb (Prov. 25:11). The bridegroom is described as an apple tree among the trees of the forest (Song 2:3, 5). The smell of apples was considered refreshing and pleasant (Song 7:8[9]). "Under the apple tree" could well have been inspired by Song 8:5.

8599. תַּפּוּחַ ***tappûaḥ:*** A proper noun designating Tappuah:

A. Descendant of Caleb (1 Chr. 2:43).

B. A city in Judah (Josh. 15:34).

C. A city on the border of Ephraim (Josh. 12:17; 16:8; 17:8).

8600. תְּפוֹצָה ***tᵉpôṣāh:*** I. A feminine noun indicating a dispersing. It indicates a spreading out or distribution of persons. In this case, the leaders of Israel, the shepherds, were dispersed among the nations (Jer. 25:34).

II. A feminine noun meaning a shattering. It refers to the destruction of and the breaking of the authority and power of the leaders, the shepherds of Israel (Jer. 25:34).

8601. תֻּפִינִים ***tuppiyniym:*** I. A masculine plural noun indicating baked pieces. It indicates portions of grain baked on a griddle and presented to the Lord at the installation of Aaron and his sons as priests (Lev. 6:21[14]).

II. A masculine plural noun referring to broken pieces. This translation emphasizes the fact that the grain offering baked on a griddle is broken up into smaller portions (Lev. 6:21[14]).

8602. תָּפֵל ***tāp̱ēl:*** I. An adjective meaning foolish, tasteless. It indicates a flat, bland taste without seasoning (Job 6:6). Used to describe oracles, it takes on the sense of useless, misleading, even foolish (Lam. 2:14).

II. A masculine noun indicating whitewash. It refers to a cheap and deceptive paintlike liquid used to whiten and cover over the outside of unsightly walls (Ezek. 13:10). In its immediate context, it indicates the whitewash representing the misleading message of peace put forth by the prophets (Ezek. 13:10, 14, 15; 22:28).

III. A masculine noun referring to untempered mortar. It refers to the lack of a process wherein mortar is both strengthened and beautified by giving it the proper hardness, smoothness, and consistency (KJV, Ezek. 13:10, 11, 14, 15; 22:28).

8603. תֹּפֶל ***tōp̱el:*** A proper noun designating Tophel (Deut. 1:1).

8604. תִּפְלָה ***tip̱lāh:*** A feminine noun indicating folly, wrongdoing. It indicates improper action, injustice, wrong, something Job refused to attribute to God (Job 1:22). According to Job, it is something God fails to pay attention to in some situations (Job 24:12). Prophecy by Israel's prophets through Baal is designated as *tip̱lāh*, a wrong thing, not right, disgusting (Jer. 23:13).

8605. תְּפִלָּה ***tᵉpillāh:*** A feminine noun meaning prayer. The word is used to describe a prayer that was similar to a plea (1 Kgs. 8:38; 2 Chr. 6:29). In Samuel, David is described as having the courage to offer his prayer to God (2 Sam. 7:27). King Hezekiah was instructed to pray for the remnant that still survived (2

Kgs. 19:4); and in Jeremiah, the word is used to denote what not to do, i.e., do not pray with any plea or petition (Jer. 7:16). The word is used by the psalmist as he cried to God to hear his prayer (Ps. 4:1[2]). He asked God not to be deaf to his weeping but to take heed to the turmoil His servant was in. In a similar manner, the psalmist again uses the word in a plea to God to hear his prayer and to know that it did not come from deceitful lips (Ps. 17:1[2]). The word is also used in Habakkuk as an introduction to the rest of the chapter, indicating that what followed was his prayer (Hab. 3:1).

8606. תִּפְלֶצֶת ***tipleṣet:*** A feminine noun meaning terror. It refers to dread, horror, fear. In context it refers to the dread that Bozrah, a city in Moab, with great arrogance, had put upon others (Jer. 49:16).

8607. תִּפְסַח ***tipsaḥ:*** A proper noun designating Tiphsah:

A. A city in northern Syria (1 Kgs. 4:24).

B. A city in northern Israel (2 Kgs. 15:16).

8608. תָּפַף ***tāpap:*** A verb meaning to play tambourines. It means to beat one's knuckles on a tambourine and shake it slightly (Ps. 68:25[26]); but in Nahum 2:7[8], the objects being struck were the breasts (lit., hearts) of the mourners.

8609. תָּפַר ***tāpar:*** A verb meaning to sew; to mend. It describes the skill of making clothes or other items by sewing materials together (Gen. 3:7; Ezek. 13:18). It is used figuratively of sewing sackcloth, a garment for mourning, over one's skin (Job 16:15); or perhaps of simply attaching sackcloth to one's body. It is used in a figurative sense of a time to sew, a time to be productive and enjoy stability (Eccl. 3:7).

8610. תָּפַשׂ ***tāpaś:*** A verb meaning to lay hold of, to seize; to capture; to wield. It basically means to seize, to get possession of, to catch in its active usages: to grab hold of something, e.g., a garment (Gen. 39:12); to catch and hold a lizard (Prov. 30:28); to capture or to seize a person (1Sam. 23:26). It has the sense figuratively of holding on to someone or something for support, e. g., Egypt (Ezek. 29:7). In a general sense, it may describe living in or occupying a hill, an area, or a location (Jer. 49:16). It takes on the sense of holding or wielding a tool or a weapon in a skillful way (Ezek. 21:11[16]; Amos 2:15). By extension, it takes on a figurative sense of handling the Law skillfully or planning strategy in warfare (Num. 31:27: Jer. 34:3). In a passive sense, it means to be seized (Jer. 38:23; 50:24).

8611. תֹּפֶת ***tōpet:*** I. A feminine noun indicating an object of spitting. It indicates an object of disgust and rejection, of no value (Job 17:6).

II. A feminine noun referring to a tabret (a drum). Job used it metaphorically to refer to himself as once in good standing with people, a drum that drew attention, was listened to, and was respected (KJV, Job 17:6).

8612. תֹּפֶת ***tōpet:*** A proper noun designating Topheth (2 Kgs. 23:10; Jer. 7:31, 32; 19:6, 11–14).

8613. תָּפְתֶּה ***topteh:*** A proper noun designating Topheth (Isa. 30:33).

8614. תִּפְתָּי ***tiptāy:*** An Aramaic masculine noun meaning a magistrate; a sheriff. It refers to a group of civil officers with delegated power to administer the law and to perform other matters of state (Dan. 3:2, 3).

8615. תִּקְוָה ***tiqwāh:*** I. A feminine noun referring to a cord, a line. It refers to a piece of rope or a cord made of bright red thread with a tinge of orange that Rahab placed in her window (Josh. 2:18, 21).

II. A feminine noun referring to hope, expectation. It refers to an attitude of anticipation with the expectation that something will happen, e.g., the hope of bearing a child (Ruth 1:12). A manner of life raises hope of certain consequences (Job 4:6). Because God cares for the oppressed and hopeless, even they have hope (Job 5:16; Ps. 9:18[19]). Hope can be equivalent to a longing or a desire (Job 6:8). The righteous person's hope is ultimately and completely in God (Ps. 62:5[6]); the same cannot be said of the wicked (Prov. 10:28). The fear of the Lord gives hope (Prov. 23:18). A self-conceited person or a person wise in his or her own thinking is more hopeless than a fool (Prov. 26:12). Even when they were in exile, God let His people know that He had a hope to give them, a positive future (Jer. 29:11). The hope for the success of Israel was lost in her captivity (Ezek. 19:5); but God gave Israel hope to return from there (Ezek. 37:11). Hosea speaks of Israel's recovery and hope of full restoration (Hos. 2:15[17]; Zech. 9:12).

8616. תִּקְוָה ***tiqwāh:*** A proper noun designating Tikvah:

A. The father-in-law of the prophetess Huldah (2 Kgs. 22:14; 2 Chr. 34:22), the same as Tokhath (8445).

B. The father of Jahaziah (Ezra 10:15).

8617. תְּקוּמָה ***t^e^qûmāh:*** A feminine noun indicating the ability to stand. It means to be strong, to stand in an erect position, to maintain one's position. In context Israel loses this ability to withstand her enemies because of breaking the covenant (Lev. 26:37).

8618. תְּקוֹמֵם ***t^e^qômēm:*** A masculine noun indicating one who rises up. It means in context to take a hostile stand against persons, to become their nemesis, to be hostile toward them (Ps. 139:21).

8619. תָּקוֹעַ ***tāqôa':*** A masculine noun referring to a trumpet. It describes an instrument with a bright, sometimes shrill, tone; it consists of a looped tube and a flared bell at the end. It was used to sound the call to battle (Ezek. 7:14).

8620. תְּקוֹעַ ***t^eqôa'*:** A proper noun designating Tekoa, the city from which the prophet Amos came (Amos 1:1). It was in the hill country of Judah. It was a city known for its wise women, for a wise woman came from here to argue a case for David's son Absalom (2 Sam. 14:2–24). She was successful. The word is used to establish an effective wordplay on "signal" in Hebrew, a favorite literary tool of the prophets (Jer. 6:1).

8621. תְּקוֹעִי, תְּקֹעִי ***t^eqô'iy, t^eqō'iy*:** A proper noun designating Tekoite, an inhabitant of Tekoah (8620) (2 Sam. 14:4, 9; 23:26; 1 Chr. 11:28; 27:9; Neh. 3:5, 27).

8622. תְּקוּפָה ***t^eqûpāh*:** A feminine noun indicating a turning around; a circuit. It indicates the completion of a yearly cycle (Ex. 34:22; 2 Chr. 24:23); the gestation period of a child (1 Sam. 1:20). It is used to describe the circuit or passage of the sun across the sky (Ps. 19:6[7]).

8623. תַּקִּיף ***taqqiyp*:** An adjective meaning strong; mighty. It indicates power and ability, especially in arguing, disputation, or in wisdom, e.g., such as God has (Eccl. 6:10).

8624. תַּקִּיף ***taqqiyp*:** An Aramaic adjective meaning mighty, strong. It describes the power and authority wielded by kings, especially the great kings over Jerusalem (Ezra 4:20); and to the massive power and influence exercised by mighty kingdoms (Dan. 2:40). It describes the unsurpassing might and wonders of God among the nations (Dan. 4:3[3:33]). It describes the terrifying power and strength of the fourth kingdom of Daniel, represented by a fourth indescribable beast (Dan. 7:7).

8625. תְּקַל, תְּקֵל ***t^eqal, t^eqēl*:** I. A verb meaning to weigh. It means literally to find the weight of something, but in context, it is used figuratively of the failure of the moral, ethical, and humanness of Belshazzar's reign to meet God's expectations (Dan. 5:27). It is used in the *peil* passive form, "You have been weighed."

II. A proper passive noun *tek^{e}l*: a unit of weight, a shekel. The significance of the word is given in Daniel 5:27 (see I). In verse 25, it was a unit of measure and weight but is understood as a passive participle meaning having been weighed, referring to Belshazzar and his kingdom.

8626. תָּקַן ***tāqan*:** A verb meaning to set straight; to set in order. It means to straighten out, to straighten what is crooked. It is used figuratively of straightening the moral, ethical, and religious ills of the world (Eccl. 1:15), the things God Himself has allowed humankind to make crooked or bent (Eccl. 7:13). It indicates putting a writing composition into proper order, especially a series of sayings or proverbs (Eccl. 12:9).

8627. תְּקַן tᵉqan: An Aramaic verb meaning to be set in order; established. It means to set up or to put something in place, to make it firm. It describes God's reestablishing, restoring, establishing (KJV) King Nebuchadnezzar in his kingship after first laying a terrifying judgment on him (Dan. 4:36[33]).

8628. תָּקַע tāqa': A verb meaning to thrust, to fasten, to clap, to blow. The basic idea of this word is a thrust or a burst, such as the wind blowing away locusts (Ex. 10:19); the thrusting of a spear through a body (2 Sam. 18:14); or the driving of a nail into the ground to secure an object, such as a tent (Gen. 31:25; Judg. 4:21; Jer. 6:3). At times, this word has the connotation of fastening as a pin fastens hair (Judg. 16:14); a nail fastens to a secure place (Isa. 22:23, 25); or the fastening of Saul's body to the wall of a pagan temple (1 Sam. 31:10; 1 Chr. 10:10). When describing hands, it can denote the clapping of hands in victory (Ps. 47:1[2]; Nah. 3:19); or the clasping of hands in an agreement (Job 17:3; Prov. 11:15; 17:18). In the majority of usages, it refers to the blowing of trumpets (Num. 10:3–8; Josh. 6:8, 9; Judg. 7:18–20; Joel 2:15).

8629. תֵּקַע tēqa': A masculine noun referring to the sound of a trumpet. It refers to the sound put forth by a shophar, a ram's horn (*bᵉṯēqa' šôp̱ār*) (Ps. 150:3), although it is normally translated as the sound of a trumpet (KJV, NIV, NASB).

8630. תָּקֵף tāqēp̱: A verb meaning to overpower; to prevail. It means to overwhelm, to overcome, to defeat. In context it refers to God's overpowering or overwhelming humankind with His sovereign acts in the world (Job 14:20). Eliphaz pictures the wicked as overcome with anxiety, despair, and anguish that crush and overwhelm them (Job 15:24). It means to gain mastery over, to defeat (Eccl. 4:12).

8631. תְּקֵף tᵉqēp̱: An Aramaic verb meaning to be strong, to grow strong. This word is related to the Hebrew verb *tāqaēp̱* (8630), meaning to prevail over. It describes the growing strength of the tree in Nebuchadnezzar's dream (Dan. 4:11[8], 20[17]) that referred to the growing strength of the king (Dan. 4:22[19]). It was also used to describe the growing arrogance of Belshazzar (Dan. 5:20). In its only other instance, it describes a strong enforcement of an edict (Dan. 6:7[8]).

8632. תְּקָף tᵉqāp̱, תְּקֹף tᵉqōp̱: I. A masculine noun meaning might, strength. It refers to the actual effective force of some power, e.g., the royal power of Nebuchadnezzar (Dan. 4:30[27]).

II. A masculine noun meaning strength, might. It refers to the strength of royal sovereignty, the strength God gives to kings when He sets them up to rule (Dan. 2:37).

8633. תֹּקֶף tōqep̱: A masculine noun referring to authority, strength, power. It indicates the legal and royal authority exercised by people in governmental positions (Esth. 9:29); especially the authority wielded by a king (Esth. 10:2; Dan. 11:17).

8634. תַּרְאֲלָה ***tar'ᵃlāh:*** A proper noun designating Taralah (Josh. 18:27).

8635. תַּרְבּוּת ***tarbûṯ:*** A feminine noun meaning offspring, a generation. It refers to a group of persons, in context a group of evil or sinful people; hence, the New American Standard Bible uses the term brood (Num. 32:14). Literally, it is a generation, a group of sinful people (*tarbûṯ 'ᵃnāšîm ḥaṭṭā'îm*) (KJV, increase, but see 3636).

8636. תַּרְבִּית ***tarbiyṯ:*** A feminine noun meaning increase, excessive interest, usury. It is used to indicate usurious interest; oppressive, unjust rates of interest (Lev. 25:36). It was a business practice condemned by the wisdom writers as well (Prov. 28:8); and the prophets (Ezek. 22:12). The righteous person does not lend money to gain benefits, increase, or interest at the expense of others (Ezek. 18:8, 13, 17).

8637. תִּרְגַּל ***tirgal:*** A verb meaning to teach to walk. It is used to describe how a person teaches or trains, with care, a child to begin walking. It was God who, in a spiritual and parental sense, taught His people, Israel, to walk (Hos. 11:3).

8638. תִּרְגַּם ***tirgam:*** A verb meaning to translate. It describes the rendering of one language into another or the giving of the sense of a written or oral communication (Ezra 4:7).

8639. תַּרְדֵּמָה ***tardēmāh:*** A feminine noun referring to deep sleep; a sound sleep. It refers to a deep unconscious state needed, usually, for rest. God may bring it on in special circumstances (Gen. 2:21; 15:12; 1 Sam. 26:12). It is a common event in the middle of the night and may be accompanied by dreams naturally or from God (Job 4:13; 33:15). Laziness, a moral problem, can result in a person falling into this state (Prov. 19:15). It is used in a figurative sense of a moral and spiritual stupor (Isa. 29:10).

8640. תִּרְהָקָה ***tirhāqāh:*** A proper noun designating Tirhakah (2 Kgs. 19:9; Isa. 37:9).

8641. תְּרוּמָה ***tᵉrûmāh:*** A feminine noun meaning offering. This word comes from the verb *rûm* (7311), meaning to be high or to lift up. The basic idea of this Hebrew noun is something being lifted up, i.e., an offering. It is normally used to describe a variety of offerings: a contribution of materials for building (Ex. 25:2; 35:5); an offering of an animal for sacrifice (Ex. 29:27; Num. 6:20); a financial offering for the priests (Num. 31:52); an allotment of land for the priests (Ezek. 45:6, 7); or even the materials for an idol (Isa. 40:20). In one instance, this word is used to describe a ruler who received bribes (Prov. 29:4).

8642. תְּרוּמִיָּה ***t^erûmiyyāh:*** A feminine noun meaning an offering, an allotment. This word occurs only once in the Old Testament and is a slightly different form of the word *t^erûmāh* (8641), meaning offering. In Ezekiel 48:12, it describes the allotment (*t^erûmiyyāh*) of the allotment of land (*t^erûmāh*) that will be given to the Levites.

8643. תְּרוּעָה ***t^erû'āh:*** A feminine noun indicating a shout of joy; a shout of alarm, a battle cry. It refers to a loud, sharp shout or cry in general, but it often indicates a shout of joy or victory (1 Sam. 4:5, 6); a great shout anticipating a coming event (Josh. 6:5, 20). It can refer to the noise or signal put out by an instrument (Lev. 23:24; 25:9). Amos used the word to refer to war cries (Amos 1:14; 2:2; cf. Job 39:25; Zeph. 1:16). The Lord puts shouts of joy into His people (Job 8:21; 33:26).

8644. תְּרוּפָה ***t^erûpāh:*** A feminine noun meaning healing, medicine. It refers in context to leaves on trees growing along the sides of Ezekiel's river of life (Ezek. 47:12). The ideas of healing, restoration, and renewal are figurative expressions for the total, wholistic healing and health of the people in God's new temple world.

8645. תִּרְזָה ***tirzāh:*** A feminine noun meaning a cypress tree. It indicates a choice, large cypress tree highly desirable for construction projects. In context it was used to construct an idol (Isa. 44:14).

8646. תֶּרַח ***teraḥ:*** A proper noun designating Terah:

A. The father of Abraham. He lived beyond the Euphrates and served pagan gods (Josh. 24:1–13) but migrated to Haran (Gen. 11:24–28, 31, 32). He fathered also Nahor and Haran and died in Haran.

B. A place in the wilderness where Israel camped on the way to Canaan. It lay between Tahath and Mithcah (Num. 33:27, 28).

8647. תִּרְחֲנָה ***tirḥ^anāh:*** A masculine proper noun, Tirhanah. It refers to one of Caleb's descendants, born to him by his concubine Maacah and, hence, a part of the genealogy of David (1 Chr. 2:48).

8648. תְּרֵין ***t^erēyn:*** An Aramaic number, two, second. Its feminine form is *tartēn*. It serves as a counting number (Ezra 4:24). It combines to form larger numbers: *t^erê-^{'a}śar*, twelve (Ezra 6:17; Dan. 4:29[26]); sixty-two (Dan. 5:31[6:1]), *šittîn w^etartên*.

8649. תָּרְמָה ***tarmāh,*** תַּרְמִית ***tarmiyṯ:*** I. A feminine noun indicating deceitfulness; under cover. It means to do something underhandedly, with evil or trickery in mind. In context messengers delivered a report and information in order to accomplish a secret plan (Judg. 9:31).

II. A feminine noun meaning deceitfulness; deception; delusion. It refers to the actions and intentions of those who turn from God's true statutes and ordinances (Ps. 119:118); a feature of even God's people who turn from Him (Jer. 8:5). False prophets suffered the deception of their own hearts and minds (Jer. 14:14; 23:26). Israel will have her deceitful tongue removed in her time of restoration in the Day of the Lord (Zeph. 3:13).

8650. תֹּרֶן ***tōren:*** A masculine noun referring to a mast; a flagstaff. It indicates a beacon, a flag, a flagstaff or pole. It is used of the people of Israel, defeated and decimated until only their lonely ensign is left to represent them (Isa. 30:17). It refers to the mast or flag representing Israel (Isa. 33:23). It refers possibly to a ship's mast for Tyre, a merchant of the seas (Ezek. 27:5).

8651. תְּרַע ***t***^{e}***ra':*** An Aramaic masculine noun meaning a door; a court. It refers to a gate or door (Dan. 2:49), but it signifies the court of the king (*biṯra' malkā'*). It indicates the opening to the great blazing furnace of Babylon (Dan. 3:26).

8652. תָּרָע ***tārā':*** An Aramaic masculine noun meaning a doorkeeper, a gatekeeper. It refers to a group of Levitical workers at the Temple area in charge of the menial tasks of keeping the gates and doors functioning and in order (Ezra 7:24). They were exempted from taxes, tribute, or any other charges.

8653. תַּרְעֵלָה ***tar'ēlāh:*** A feminine noun indicating staggering; reeling. It indicates an unsteady walk or a swagger of body and mind brought on by wine, but in context, it was brought on by God's actions against His people (Ps. 60:3[5]). In Isaiah it again refers to the dizziness and confusion brought on God's people by His cup of staggering and reeling (Isa. 51:17, 22).

8654. תִּרְעָתִים ***tir'āṯiym:*** A proper noun designating Tirahites (1 Chr. 2:55).

8655. תְּרָפִים ***t***^{e}***rāpiym:*** A masculine plural noun meaning household gods, cultic objects, teraphim. This word refers to a kind of idols or objects of worship whose ownership was possibly tied to inheritance rights. They were employed in divination. Rachel stole these objects from her father Laban for some reason not entirely clear to us now, but they were probably not tied to ancestor worship (Gen. 31:19, 34). These objects seemed to have had the shape of persons. But in one case, the word refers to something larger than the objects Rachel stole from Laban (1 Sam. 19:13, 16). Some have suggested that the teraphim used here were old pieces of cloth. The word refers to idols owned by Micah during the time of the judges (Judg. 17:5).

These objects are more strongly condemned in other passages: the wickedness of consulting teraphim is asserted in 1 Samuel 15:23 (see Ezek.

21:21[26]; Zech. 10:2). Josiah cast them out when he got rid of the mediums and spiritists, literally, the ghosts and familiar spirits (2 Kgs. 23:24).

8656. תִּרְצָה tirṣāh: A proper noun designating Tirzah:

A. A daughter of Zelophehad, evidently the youngest (Num. 26:33). She and her sisters successfully raised the issue of the inheritance laws in Israel when a man bore no sons, only daughters.

B. A city conquered by Joshua. It was the second capital of northern Israel after Shechem (1 Kgs. 14:17). Menahem, an Israelite king, was governor here (2 Kgs. 15:14–33). The Song of Solomon refers to its beauty and location (Song 6:4). It lay north, northeast from Shechem and east, northeast of Samaria. Baasha was buried there, a king of Israel (1 Kgs. 16:6). The reigns of short-lived kings in the city (Elah, Zimri, Tibni, Omri [6 years]) hastened its demise as a capital. Omri moved the capital to Samaria.

8657. תֶּרֶשׁ tereš: A proper noun designating Teresh (Esth. 2:21; 6:2).

8658. תַּרְשִׁישׁ taršiyš: I. A masculine noun referring to a gemstone: either beryl (KJV, NASB) or chrysolite (NIV). It was placed in the fourth row of the breastpiece of the high priest as one of the twelve stones representing the tribes of Israel. It is used to describe the beauty of the bridegroom (Song 5:14). The wheels in Ezekiel's vision are compared to it (Ezek. 1:16; 10:9). It was part of the covering of the king of Tyre (Satan?) in Eden (Ezek. 28:13).

II. A proper noun Tarshish: the name of the gemstone in I, perhaps referring to its origin, 8659,D. The word is given as a proper noun to indicate from where the stone came. Tarshish may refer to an area in modern Spain, a place along the shores of the Mediterranean, or perhaps North Africa or Sicily. Its location is not certain.

8659. תַּרְשִׁישׁ taršiyš: A proper noun designating Tarshish:

A. The name of a son of Javan, his second son (Gen. 10:4).

B. A descendant of Benjamin, a son of Bilhan. He was the head of a family (1 Chr. 7:10).

C. The name of a Persian advisor. He was a wise man who could interpret current events and the world situation. He had access to the Persian king and was one of the highest officials in the nation (Esth. 1:14).

8660. תִּרְשָׁתָא tiršāṯā': I. A masculine noun meaning a governor. It refers to the political office of the person placed in charge of the small province of Judah on Israel's return from exile: governor (Ezra 2:63; Neh. 7:65, 70[69]); possibly Zerubbabel or Sheshbazzar. Nehemiah is called the governor in 8:9 (Neh. 8:9).

II. A proper noun Tirshatha: title of the Persian governor of Judah. The

King James Version renders this a title (Ezra 2:63), the Tirshatha, but it is clear that it probably means governor (Neh. 7:65; 70[69]). Nehemiah is called the Tirshatha in Nehemiah 8:9 (KJV).

8661. תַּרְתָּן ***tartān:*** I. A proper noun designating Tartan, an Assyrian general (KJV, NASB, 2 Kgs. 18:17; Isa. 20:1).

II. A masculine noun meaning supreme commander (NIV, 2 Kgs. 18:17; Isa. 20:1).

8662. תַּרְתָּק ***tartāq:*** A masculine proper noun Tartak, an Avvite deity. This name of the god of the Avvites is not described fully anywhere. The Avvites made an idol of this god evidently (2 Kgs. 17:31).

8663. תְּשֻׁאָה ***tᵉshu'āh,*** תְּשׁוּאָה ***tᵉshūwāh:*** A feminine noun meaning a storm, a crashing, a noise; a substance. It is rendered as storm (NIV, NASB); God breaks Job in the storm, noise, crashing (Job 30:22; KJV, substance). It refers to the thundering of the storms from God's dwelling (KJV, Tabernacle); to His displays in nature (Job 36:29). It refers to the shouting or crying out of the drivers in the center of great cities (Job 39:7); and to the noise and bustling activity of Babylon in her prosperity (Isa. 22:2). It refers to formal shouting accompanying a religious ritual in Jerusalem (Zech. 4:7).

8664. תִּשְׁבִּי ***tišbey:*** A proper noun designating Tishbite (1 Kgs. 17:1; 21:17, 28; 2 Kgs. 1:3, 8; 9:36).

8665. תַּשְׁבֵּץ ***tašbēṣ:*** A masculine noun meaning checkered, woven, braided. It refers to the design of material used to make garments for the priests: breastpiece, ephod, robe, tunic, turban, and belt or sash (Ex. 28:4). Such beauty was worked into the clothes of the priest for splendor and dignity.

8666. תְּשׁוּבָה ***tᵉšûḇāh:*** I. A feminine noun meaning an answer; a return. It refers to a response or reply given in a conversation or debate (Job 21:34; 34:36). It also indicates a literal return to a location or destination (1 Sam. 7:17).

II. A feminine noun indicating the return (of the year); spring. It indicates the beginning of an new yearly cycle in the spring (2 Sam. 11:1; 1 Kgs. 20:22, 26; 1 Chr. 20:1; 2 Chr. 36:10). This is the rendering of the New American Standard Bible and the New International Version.

III. A feminine noun indicating the turn of the year; the end of the year. Some translators take it to refer to the expiration of a yearly cycle, the close of a year, as does the KJV (2 Sam. 11:1; 1 Kgs. 20:22, 26; 1 Chr. 20:1; 2 Chr. 36:10).

8667. תְּשׂוּמֶת ***tᵉśûmeṯ:*** A feminine noun referring to something left in security as a pledge. It refers to what is delivered to a person to keep in security; the person receiving it is responsible for it (Lev. 6:2[5:21]).

8668. תְּשׁוּעָה ***t^e^šû'āh:*** A feminine noun meaning a deliverance, a victory, safety. Typically, the term is used in the context of military conflict (Judg. 15:18; 1 Sam. 11:13; 1 Chr. 11:14). While victory was usually not obtained through human means (Ps. 33:17; 108:12[13]; 146:3; Prov. 21:31), safety came through a multitude of counselors (Prov. 11:14; 24:6). Principally, however, deliverance was to be found only in God (2 Chr. 6:41; Ps. 119:81; 144:10). The deliverance of the Lord was on the minds of both Isaiah and Jeremiah during the troubled times in which they lived (Isa. 45:17; 46:13; Jer. 3:23; Lam. 3:26).

8669. תְּשׁוּקָה ***t^e^šûqāh:*** A feminine noun meaning longing. It was used to describe the strong feelings of desire that one person had for another, but it was not always a healthy desire. As part of the judgment after Adam and Eve's sin, God said that a woman would long for her husband (Gen. 3:16). People are not the only thing that can long: God told Cain that sin was lying at his door, desiring to enter (Gen. 4:7).

8670. תְּשׁוּרָה ***t^e^šûrāh:*** A feminine noun meaning a gift, a present. It indicates something given to a person to show respect, appreciation, and honor (1 Sam. 9:7).

8671. תְּשִׁיעִי ***t^e^šiy'iy:*** An ordinal number used to indicate the ninth item in a series of nine or more: the ninth year (Lev. 25:22), the ninth day (Num. 7:60).

8672. תֵּשַׁע ***tēša':*** A masculine number meaning nine. It is a cardinal counting number, indicating the ninth item: nine bulls (Num. 29:26); nine towns (Josh. 15:44). It combines with other numbers to create larger numbers, e.g., nine hundred and thirty years (Gen. 5:5).

8673. תִּשְׁעִים ***tiš'iym:*** A masculine plural number, ninety. It is a cardinal counting number indicating the ninetieth item. It refers to any item that needs to be counted: years (Gen. 5:9). It combines with other numbers to form larger numbers (Gen. 5:17, 30), e.g., eight hundred and ninety-five years.

8674. תַּתְּנַי ***tatt^e^nay:*** A proper noun designating Tattenai, Tatnai (Ezra 5:3, 6; 6:6, 13).

The Complete Word Study Old Testament Concordance

This concordance contains a catalog of every Hebrew word used in the Old Testament with its corresponding number from Strong's Hebrew and Chaldee Dictionary as well as a complete list of verses where it occurs.

Several unique and helpful features have been included in this concordance of which the user should be aware. The division of a single entry into A, B, C, etc., represents different uses of the same word. For example, see *b^e^rāḵāh* (1294). Roman numerals under a single entry number indicate entirely distinct words. For example, see *'āval* (56). In addition, as this example shows, we have endeavored to account for important differences between the KJV and the NASB and NIV. Whenever a cross-reference is made to an entry with a multiple listing, the note specifies which letter or Roman number is to be consulted.

In determining the division of proper nouns we utilized, along with Hebrew lexicons, chiefly the following works: Geoffrey Bromiley, gen. ed., *The International Standard Bible Encyclopedia,* 4 vols. (Grand Rapids: Eerdman's, 1979–1988); Charles F. Pfeiffer, Howard F. Vos, John Rea, eds., *Wycliffe Bible Encyclopedia,* 2 vols. (Chicago: Moody Press, 1975); Alfred Jones, Jones' Dictionary of Old Testament Proper Names (1856; reprint, Grand Rapids: Kregel, 1990).

The reader will also notice references to [Q^{e}] and [K^{e}]. These two abbreviations stand for the Qeri (oral tradition) and Kethiv (written tradition). The difference is often simply a matter of spelling (e.g., see 1213). However, many times the two readings represent two different words. This may occur even in the same entry (e.g., see 5094).

The spelling of each word is based upon a comparative study of several standard lexical works. Among these are the following: William Holladay, *A Concise Hebrew and Aramaic Lexicon of the Old Testament* (Grand Rapids: Eerdman's, 1971); F. Brown, S. R. Driver, and Charles A. Briggs, *Hebrew and English Lexicon of the Old Testament,* (BDB) (1907; reprint, Peabody, Mass.: Hendrickson, 1979); Georg Fohrer, ed., *Hebrew and Aramaic Dictionary of the Old Testament,* trans. Walter de Gruyter (London: SCM Press, 1973); Alexander Harkavy, *Student's Hebrew and Chaldee Dictionary to the Old Testament* (New York: Hebrew Publishing Co., 1914); Karl Feyerabend, *A Complete Hebrew-English Pocket-Dictionary to the Old Testament,* 5th ed. (New York: International News

Comp., 1931). Since the late 19th Century, the knowledge of Semitic languages has increased exponentially. Hence, it was necessary to update and correct the spellings given in Strong's Hebrew and Chaldee Dictionary. However, even with the most recent scholarship available disagreement still exists regarding the exact spelling of certain words as well as their meanings or referents. This was particularly troublesome in deciding the division of some proper nouns. Our research, like all work of its kind, is provisional and, therefore, not final.

The primary source for concordance data was George Wigram's *The Englishman's Hebrew and Chaldee Concordance of the Old Testament* (Grand Rapids: Baker, 1980). We further consulted *Konkordanz Zum Hebräischen Alten Testament* (Stuttgart: Deutsche Bibelgesellschaft, n.d.) by Gerhard Lisowsky. Again, this latter work was essential in updating Wigram's material which appeared originally in 1843.

Next to some verse references will be others in parentheses. These identify the position of the passage according to the text of the Hebrew Old Testament. If a word occurs more than once in a verse, that verse has been entered only once. The exception to this is when one of the occurrences involves some kind of textual variant or an important difference between English versions.

א Aleph

1. אָב *'āḇ* **masc. noun**
(father, forefather)
Gen. 2:24; 4:20,21; 9:18,22,23; 10:21; 11:28,29; 12:1; 15:15; 17:4,5; 19:31–38; 20:12,13; 22:7,21; 24:7,23,38,40; 26:3, 15,18,24; 27:6,9,10,12,14,18,19,22,26, 30–32,34,38,39,41; 28:2,7,8,13,21; 29:9,12; 31:1,3,5–7,9,14,16,18,19,29,30, 35,42,53; 32:9(10); 33:19; 34:4,6,11,13, 19; 35:18,22,27; 36:9,24,43; 37:1,2,4, 10–12,22,32,35; 38:11; 41:51; 42:13,29, 32,35–37; 43:2,7,8,11,23,27,28; 44:17, 19,20,22,24,25,27,30–32,34; 45:3,8,9, 13,18,19,23,25,27; 46:1,3,5,29,31,34; 47:1,3,5–7,9,11,12,30; 48:1,9,15–19,21; 49:2,4,8,25,26,28,29; 50:1,2,5–8,10, 14–17,22; **Ex.** 2:16,18; 3:6,13,15,16; 4:5; 6:14,25; 10:6; 12:3; 13:5,11; 15:2; 18:4; 20:5,12; 21:15,17; 22:17(16); 34:7; 40:15; **Lev.** 16:32; 18:7–9,11,12,14; 19:3; 20:9,11,17,19; 21:2,9,11; 22:13; 25:41; 26:39,40; **Num.** 1:2,4,16,18,20,22,24,26, 28,30,32,34,36,38,40,42,44,45,47; 2:2, 32,34; 3:4,15,20,24,30,35; 4:2,22,29,34, 38,40,42,46; 6:7; 7:2; 11:12; 12:14; 13:2; 14:18,23; 17:2(17),3(18),6(21); 18:1,2; 20:15; 25:14,15; 26:2,55; 27:3,4,7,10,11; 30:3–5(4–6),16(17); 31:26; 32:8,14,28; 33:54; 34:14; 36:1,3,4,6–8,12; **Deut.** 1:8,11,21,35; 4:1,31,37; 5:3,9,16; 6:3, 10,18,23; 7:8,12,13; 8:1,3,16,18; 9:5; 10:11,15,22; 11:9,21; 12:1; 13:6(7), 17(18); 18:8; 19:8; 21:13,18,19; 22:15,16, 19,21,29,30; 24:16; 26:3,5,7,15; 27:3,16, 20,22; 28:11,36,64; 29:13(12),25(24); 30:5,9,20; 31:7,16,20; 32:6,7,17; 33:9; **Josh.** 1:6; 2:12,13,18; 4:21; 5:6; 6:23,25; 14:1; 15:13,18; 17:1,4; 18:3; 19:47,51; 21:1,11,43(41),44(42); 22:14,28; 24:2,3, 6,14,15,17,32; **Judg.** 1:14; 2:1,10,12,17, 19,20,22; 3:4; 6:13,15,25,27; 8:32; 9:1,5, 17,18,28,56; 11:2,7,36,37,39; 14:2–6,9, 10,15,16,19; 15:1,2,6; 16:31; 17:10; 18:19,29; 19:2–6,8,9; 21:22; **Ruth** 2:11; 4:17; **1 Sam.** 2:25,27,28,30,31; 9:3,5,20; 10:2,12; 12:6–8,15; 14:1,27–29,51; 17:15,25,34; 18:2,18; 19:2–4; 20:1–3,6, 8–10,12,13,32–34; 22:1,3,11,15,16,22; 23:17; 24:11(12),21(22); **2 Sam.** 2:32; 3:7,8,29; 6:21; 7:12,14; 9:7; 10:2,3; 13:5; 14:9; 15:34; 16:3,19,21,22; 17:8,10,23; 19:28(29),37(38); 21:14; 24:17; **1 Kgs.** 1:6,21; 2:10,12,24,26,31,32,44; 3:3,6, 7,14; 5:1(15),3(17),5(19); 6:12; 7:14,51; 8:1,15,17,18,20,21,24–26,34,40,48,53,57 ,58; 9:4,5,9; 11:4,6,12,17,21,27,33,43; 12:4,6,9–11,14; 13:11,12,22; 14:15, 20,22,31; 15:3,8,11,12,15,19,24,26; 16:6,28; 18:18; 19:4,20; 20:34; 21:3,4; 22:40,43,46(47),50(51),52(53),53(54); **2 Kgs.** 2:12; 3:2,13; 4:18,19; 5:13; 6:21; 8:24; 9:25,28; 10:3,35; 12:18(19),21(22); 13:9,13,14,25; 14:3,5,6,16,20–22,29; 15:3,7,9,22,34,38; 16:2,20; 17:13–15,41; 18:3; 19:12; 20:5,17,21; 21:3,8,15,18, 20–22; 22:2,13,20; 23:30,32,34,37; 24:6,9; **1 Chr.** 2:17,21,23,24,42,44,45, 49–52,55; 4:3–5,11,12,14,17–19,21,38; 5:1,13,15,24,25; 6:19(4); 7:2,4,7,9,11, 14,22,31,40; 8:6,10,13,28,29(see *'ăbiy giḇ'ôn* [25]); 9:9,13,19,33,34,35(see *'ăbiy gib'ôn* [25]); 12:17,28,30; 15:12; 17:11,13; 19:2,3; 21:17; 22:10; 23:9, 11,24; 24:2,4,6,19,30,31; 25:3,6; 26:6,10,13,21,26,31,32; 27:1; 28:4,6,9; 29:6,10,15,18,20,23; **2 Chr.** 1:2,8,9; 2:3(2),7(6),13(12),14(13),17(16); 3:1; 4:16; 5:1,2; 6:4,7,8,10,15,16,25,31,38; 7:17,18,22; 8:14; 9:31; 10:4,6,9–11,14; 11:16; 12:16; 13:12,18; 14:1(13:23),4(3); 15:12,18; 16:3,13; 17:2–4,14; 19:4,8; 20:6,32,33; 21:1,3,4,10,12,13,19; 22:4;

23:2; 24:18,22,24; 25:3–5,28; 26:1,2, 4,12,23; 27:2,9; 28:1,6,9,25,27; 29:2,5, 6,9; 30:7,8,19,22; 31:17; 32:13–15,33; 33:3,8,12,20,22,23; 34:2,3,21,28,32,33; 35:4,5,12,24; 36:1,15; **Ezra** 1:5; 2:59,68; 3:12; 4:2,3; 7:27; 8:1,28,29; 9:7; 10:11,16; **Neh.** 1:6; 2:3,5; 7:61,70,71; 8:13; 9:2, 9,16,23,32,34,36; 10:34(35); 11:13; 12:12,22,23; 13:18; **Esth.** 2:7; 4:14; **Job** 8:8; 15:10,18; 17:14; 29:16; 30:1; 31:18; 34:36; 38:28; 42:15; **Ps.** 22:4(5); 27:10; 39:12(13); 44:1(2); 45:10(11),16(17); 49:19(20); 68:5(6); 78:3,5,8,12,57; 89:26(27); 95:9; 103:13; 106:6,7; 109:14; **Prov.** 1:8; 3:12; 4:1,3; 6:20; 10:1; 13:1; 15:5,20; 17:6,21,25; 19:13,14,26; 20:20; 22:28; 23:22,24,25; 27:10; 28:7,24; 29:3; 30:11,17; **Isa.** 3:6; 7:17; 8:4; 9:6(5); 14:21; 22:21,23,24; 37:12; 38:5,19; 39:6; 43:27; 45:10; 51:2; 58:14; 63:16; 64:8(7), 11(10); 65:7; **Jer.** 2:5,27; 3:4,18,19,24,25; 6:21; 7:7,14,18,22,25,26; 9:14(13),16(15); 11:4,5,7,10; 12:6; 13:14; 14:20; 16:3, 7,11–13,15,19; 17:22; 19:4; 20:15; 22:11,15; 23:27,39; 24:10; 25:5; 30:3; 31:9,29,32; 32:18,22; 34:5,13,14; 35:6, 8,10,14–16,18; 44:3,9,10,17,21; 47:3; 50:7; **Lam.** 5:3,7; **Ezek.** 2:3; 5:10; 16:3,45; 18:2,4,14,17–20; 20:4,18, 24,27,30,36,42; 22:7,10,11; 36:28; 37:25; 44:25; 47:14; **Dan.** 9:6,8,16; 11:24,37,38; **Hos.** 9:10; **Joel** 1:2; **Amos** 2:4,7; **Mic.** 7:6,20; **Zech.** 1:2,4–6; 8:14; 13:3; **Mal.** 1:6; 2:10; 3:7; 4:6(3:24).

2. אַב *'aḇ* **Aram. masc. noun**
(father, forefather; corr. to Hebr. 1)
Ezra 4:15; 5:12; **Dan.** 2:23; 5:2,11, 13,18.

3. אֵב *'ēḇ* **masc. noun**
(greenness, new growth)
Job 8:12; **Song** 6:11.

4. אֵב *'ēḇ* **Aram. masc. noun**
(fruit; corr. to Hebr. 3)
Dan. 4:12(9),14(11),21(18).

5. אֲבַגְתָא *'aḇagtā'* **masc. proper noun**
(Abagtha)
Esth. 1:10.

6. אָבַד *'aḇaḏ* **verb**
(to perish, be destroyed)
Ex. 10:7; **Lev.** 23:30; 26:38; **Num.** 16:33; 17:12(27); 21:29,30; 24:19; 33:52; **Deut.** 4:26; 7:10,20,24; 8:19,20; 9:3; 11:4,17; 12:2,3; 22:3; 26:5; 28:20,22, 51,63; 30:18; 32:28; **Josh.** 7:7; 23:13,16; **Judg.** 5:31; **1 Sam.** 9:3,20; **2 Sam.** 1:27; **2 Kgs.** 9:8; 10:19; 11:1; 13:7; 19:18; 21:3; 24:2; **Esth.** 3:9,13; 4:7,14,16; 7:4; 8:5,11; 9:6,12,24; **Job** 3:3; 4:7,9,11,20; 6:18; 8:13; 11:20; 12:23; 14:19; 18:17; 20:7; 29:13; 30:2; 31:19; **Ps.** 1:6; 2:12; 5:6(7); 9:3(4),5(6),6(7),18(19); 10:16; 21:10(11); 31:12(13); 37:20; 41:5(6); 49:10(11); 68:2(3); 73:27; 80:16(17); 83:17(18); 92:9(10); 102:26(27); 112:10; 119:92,95,176; 142:4(5); 143:12; 146:4; **Prov.** 1:32; 10:28; 11:7,10; 19:9; 21:28; 28:28; 29:3; 31:6; **Eccl.** 3:6; 5:14(13); 7:7,15; 9:6,18; **Isa.** 26:14; 27:13; 29:14; 37:19; 41:11; 57:1; 60:12; **Jer.** 1:10; 4:9; 6:21; 7:28; 9:12(11); 10:15; 12:17; 15:7; 18:7,18; 23:1; 25:10,35; 27:10,15; 31:28; 40:15; 46:8; 48:8,36,46; 49:7,38; 50:6; 51:18,55; 56:8; **Lam.** 2:9; 3:18; **Ezek.** 6:3; 7:26; 12:22; 19:5; 22:27; 25:7,16; 26:17; 28:16; 30:13; 32:13; 34:4,16; 37:11; **Joel** 1:11; **Amos** 1:8; 2:14; 3:15; **Obad.** 1:8,12; **Jon.** 1:6,14; 3:9; 4:10; **Mic.** 4:9; 5:10(9); 7:2; **Zeph.** 2:5,13; **Zech.** 9:5.

7. אֲבַד *'aḇaḏ* **Aram. verb**
(to perish, cause to perish; corr. to Hebr. 6)
Jer. 10:11; **Dan.** 2:12,18,24; 7:11,26.

8. אֹבֵד *'ōḇēḏ* **masc. noun**
(ruin, destruction)
Num. 24:20,24.

9. אֲבֵדָה *'a<u>b</u>ē<u>d</u>āh* **fem. noun**
(something lost, destruction)
Ex. 22:9(8); **Lev.** 6:3(5:22),4(5:23); **Deut.** 22:3.

10. אֲבַדֹּה *'a<u>b</u>addōh* **fem. noun**
(destruction)
Prov. 27:20(NASB, [Q[e]] *'a<u>b</u>addôn* [11]).

11. אֲבַדּוֹן *'a<u>b</u>addôn* **masc. noun**
(destruction, place of destruction)
Job 26:6; 28:22; 31:12; **Ps.** 88:11(12); **Prov.** 15:11; 27:20(KJV, NIV, [K[e]] *'abaddôh* [10]).

12. אַבְדָן *'ab<u>d</u>ān* **masc. noun**
(destruction)
Esth. 9:5.

13. אָבְדָן *'ob<u>d</u>ān* **masc. noun**
(destruction)
Esth. 8:6.

14. אָבָה *'ā<u>b</u>āh* **verb**
(to be willing, to consent)
Gen. 24:5,8; **Ex.** 10:27; **Lev.** 26:21; **Deut.** 1:26; 2:30; 10:10; 13:8(9); 23:5(6); 25:7; 29:20(19); **Josh.** 24:10; **Judg.** 11:17; 19:10,25; 20:13; **1 Sam.** 15:9; 22:17; 26:23; 31:4; **2 Sam.** 2:21; 6:10; 12:17; 13:14,16,25; 14:29; 23:16,17; **1 Kgs.** 20:8; 22:49(50); **2 Kgs.** 8:19; 13:23; 24:4; **1 Chr.** 10:4; 11:18,19; 19:19; **2 Chr.** 21:7; **Job** 39:9; **Ps.** 81:11(12); **Prov.** 1:10,25,30; 6:35; **Isa.** 1:19; 28:12; 30:9,15; 42:24; **Ezek.** 3:7; 20:8.

15. אָבֶה *'ā<u>b</u>eh* **fem. noun**
(that which is desired, which ought to be)
Job 34:36.

16. אֵבֶה *'ē<u>b</u>eh* **masc. noun**
(reed, papyrus)
Job 9:26.

17. אֲבוֹי *'a<u>b</u>ôy* **interj.**
(sorrow! woe!)
Prov. 23:29.

18. אֵבוּס *'ē<u>b</u>ûs* **masc. noun**
(crib, manger)
Job 39:9; **Prov.** 14:4; **Isa.** 1:3.

19. אִבְחָה *'i<u>b</u><u>h</u>āh* **fem. noun**
(slaughter)
Ezek. 21:15(20).

20. אֲבַטִּיחַ *'a<u>b</u>aṭṭiyaḥ* **masc. noun**
(melon, watermelon)
Num. 11:5.

21. אֲבִי *'a<u>b</u>iy* **fem. proper noun**
(Abi: form of *'a<u>b</u>iyyāh* [29,G])
2 Kgs. 18:2.

22. A. אֲבִיאֵל *'a<u>b</u>iy'ēl* **masc. proper noun**
(Abiel: father of Kish and Ner)
1 Sam. 9:1; 14:51.
B. אֲבִיאֵל *'a<u>b</u>iy'ēl* **masc. proper noun**
(Abiel: one of David's mighty men)
1 Chr. 11:32.

23. אֲבִיאָסָף *'a<u>b</u>iy'āsā<u>p</u>* **masc. proper noun**
(Abiasaph, see also *'a<u>b</u>yāsa<u>p</u>* [43])
Ex. 6:24.

24. I. אָבִיב *'ā<u>b</u>iy<u>b</u>* **proper noun**
(the month Abib)
Ex. 13:4; 23:15; 34:18; **Deut.** 16:1.
II. אָבִיב *'ā<u>b</u>iy<u>b</u>* **masc. noun**
(ear of barley)
Ex. 9:31; **Lev.** 2:14.

25. אֲבִי גִּבְעוֹן *'a<u>b</u>iy gi<u>b</u>'ôn* **masc. proper noun**
(Abi Gibeon [KJV, NASB, NIV, *ā<u>b</u>* {1} and *gi<u>b</u>'ôn* {1391}])
1 Chr. 8:29; 9:35.

26. A. אֲבִיגַיִל *'aḇiygayil* fem. proper noun
(Abigail: wife of David)
1 Sam. 25:3,14,18,23,32,36,39,40,42; 27:3; 30:5; 2 Sam. 2:2; 3:3; 1 Chr. 3:1.
B. אֲבִיגַיִל *'aḇiygayil* fem. proper noun
(Abigail: sister of David)
2 Sam. 17:25; 1 Chr. 2:16,17.

27. אֲבִידָן *'aḇiyḏān* masc. proper noun
(Abidan)
Num. 1:11; 2:22; 7:60,65; 10:24.

28. אֲבִידָע *'aḇiyḏā'* masc. proper noun
(Abida)
Gen. 25:4; 1 Chr. 1:33.

29. A. אֲבִיָּה *'aḇiyyāh* fem. proper noun
(Abijah: wife of Hezron)
1 Chr. 2:24.
B. אֲבִיָּה *'aḇiyyāh* masc. proper noun
(Abijah: descendant of Aaron)
1 Chr. 24:10.
C. אֲבִיָּה *'aḇiyyāh* masc. proper noun
(Abijah: descendant of Benjamin)
1 Chr. 7:8.
D. אֲבִיָּה *'aḇiyyāh* masc. proper noun
(Abijah: younger son of Samuel)
1 Sam. 8:2; 1 Chr. 6:28.
E. אֲבִיָּה *'aḇiyyāh* masc. proper noun
(Abijah: son of Jeroboam)
1 Kgs. 14:1.
F. אֲבִיָּה, אֲבִיָּהוּ *'aḇiyyāh, 'aḇiyāhû* masc. proper noun
(Abijah: successor to Rehoboam [see also *'aḇiyyām* {38}])
1 Chr. 3:10; 2 Chr. 11:20,22; 12:16; 13:1–4,15,17,19–22; 14:1.
G. אֲבִיָּה *'aḇiyyāh* fem. proper noun
(Abijah: mother of Hezekiah; same as *'aḇiy* [21])
2 Chr. 29:1.
H. אֲבִיָּה *'aḇiyyāh* masc. proper noun
(Abijah: a priest)
Neh. 10:7; 12:4,17.

30. אֲבִיהוּא *'aḇiyhû'* masc. proper noun
(Abihu)
Ex. 6:23; 24:1,9; 28:1; Lev. 10:1; Num. 3:2,4; 26:60,61; 1 Chr. 6:3(5:29); 24:1,2.

31. אֲבִיהוּד *'aḇiyhûḏ* masc. proper noun
(Abihud)
1 Chr. 8:3.

32. A. אֲבִיחַיִל *'aḇiyhayil* masc. proper noun
(Abihail: father of Zuriel)
Num. 3:35.
B. אֲבִיחַיִל *'aḇiyhayil* fem. proper noun
(Abihail: wife of Abishur)
1 Chr. 2:29.
C. אֲבִיחַיִל *'aḇiyhayil* masc. proper noun
(Abihail: son of Huri)
1 Chr. 5:14.
D. אֲבִיחַיִל *'aḇiyhayil* fem. proper noun
(Abihail: mother-in-law of Rehoboam)
2 Chr. 11:18.
E. אֲבִיחַיִל *'aḇiyhayil* masc. proper noun
(Abihail: father of Esther)
Esth. 2:15; 9:29.

33. אֲבִי הָעֶזְרִי *'aḇiy hā'ezriy* masc. proper noun
(Abiezrite)
Judg. 6:11,24; 8:32.

34. אֶבְיוֹן *'eb̲yôn* **adj.**
(needy, poor)
Ex. 23:6,11; **Deut.** 15:4,7,9,11; 24:14; **1 Sam.** 2:8; **Esth.** 9:22; **Job** 5:15; 24:4,14; 29:16; 30:25; 31:19; **Ps.** 9:18(19); 12:5(6); 35:10; 37:14; 40:17(18); 49:2(3); 69:33(34); 70:5(6); 72:4,12,13; 74:21; 82:4; 86:1; 107:41; 109:16,22,31; 112:9; 113:7; 132:15; 140:12(13); **Prov.** 14:31; 30:14; 31:9,20; **Isa.** 14:30; 25:4; 29:19; 32:7; 41:17; **Jer.** 2:34; 5:28; 20:13; 22:16; **Ezek.** 16:49; 18:12; 22:29; **Amos** 2:6; 4:1; 5:12; 8:4,6.

35. אֲבִיּוֹנָה *'a̲b̲iyyônāh* **fem. noun**
(desire, caperberry)
Eccl. 12:5.

36. אֲבִיטוּב *'a̲b̲iyṭûb̲* **masc. proper noun**
(Abitub)
1 Chr. 8:11.

37. אֲבִיטַל *'a̲b̲iyṭal* **fem. proper noun**
(Abital)
2 Sam. 3:4; **1 Chr.** 3:3.

38. אֲבִיָּם *'a̲b̲iyyām* **masc. proper noun**
(Abijam: successor to Rehoboam [another name for *'a̲b̲iyyāh* {29,F}])
1 Kgs. 14:31; 15:1,7,8.

39. אֲבִימָאֵל *'a̲b̲iymā'ēl* **masc. proper noun**
(Abimael)
Gen. 10:28; **1 Chr.** 1:22.

40. A. אֲבִימֶלֶךְ *'a̲b̲iymelek̲* **masc. proper noun**
(Abimelech: king of Gerar during Abraham's life)
Gen. 20:2–4,8–10,14,15,17,18; 21:22,25–27,29,32.
B. אֲבִימֶלֶךְ *'a̲b̲iymelek̲* **masc. proper noun**
(Abimelech: king of Gerar during Isaac's life)
Gen. 26:1,8–11,16,26.
C. אֲבִימֶלֶךְ *'a̲b̲iymelek̲* **masc. proper noun**
(Abimelech: son of Gideon)
Judg. 8:31; 9:1,3,4,6,16,18–25,27–29,31,34,35,38–42,44,45,47–50,52,53,55,56; 10:1; **2 Sam.** 11:21.
D. אֲבִימֶלֶךְ *'a̲b̲iymelek̲* **masc. proper noun**
(Abimelech: son of Abiathar)
1 Chr. 18:16.
E. אֲבִימֶלֶךְ *'a̲b̲iymelek̲* **masc. proper noun**
(Abimelech: king of Philistia)
Ps. 34:[title](1).

41. A. אֲבִינָדָב *'a̲b̲iynād̲āb̲* **masc. proper noun**
(Abinadab: a Levite)
1 Sam. 7:1; **2 Sam.** 6:3,4; **1 Chr.** 13:7.
B. אֲבִינָדָב *'a̲b̲iynād̲āb̲* **masc. proper noun**
(Abinadab: second son of Jesse)
1 Sam. 16:8; 17:13; **1 Kgs.** 4:11; **1 Chr.** 2:13.
C. אֲבִינָדָב *'a̲b̲iynād̲āb̲* **masc. proper noun**
(Abinadab: son of Saul)
1 Sam. 31:2; **1 Chr.** 8:33; 9:39; 10:2.

42. אֲבִינֹעַם *'a̲b̲iynō'ām* **masc. proper noun**
(Abinoam)
Judg. 4:6,12; 5:1,12.

43. אֶבְיָסָף *'eb̲yāsāp̲* **masc. proper noun**
(Ebiasaph [a form of *'a̲b̲iy'āsāp̲* {23}])
1 Chr. 6:23(8),37(22); 9:19.

44. A. אֲבִיעֶזֶר *'a̲b̲iy'ezer* **masc. proper noun**
(Abiezer: a Manassite)

Josh. 17:2; **Judg.** 6:34; 8:2; **1 Chr.** 7:18.
B. אֲבִיעֶזֶר *'aḇiy'ezer* **masc. proper noun**
(Abiezer: a Benjamite)
2 Sam. 23:27; **1 Chr.** 11:28; 27:12.

45. אֲבִי עַלְבוֹן *'aḇiy 'alḇôn* **masc. proper noun**
(Abi-Albon)
2 Sam. 23:31.

46. אָבִיר *'āḇiyr* **masc. adj.**
(mighty, strong)
Gen. 49:24; **Ps.** 132:2,5; **Isa.** 1:24; 49:26; 60:16.

47. אַבִּיר *'abbiyr* **adj.**
(mighty ones; mighty horses or angels)
Judg. 5:22; **1 Sam.** 21:7(8); **Job** 24:22; 34:20; **Ps.** 22:12(13); 50:13; 68:30(31); 76:5(6); 78:25; **Isa.** 10:13(KJV, NASB, *kabbiyr* [3524]); 34:7; 46:12; **Jer.** 8:16; 46:15; 47:3; 50:11; **Lam.** 1:15.

48. A. אֲבִירָם *'aḇiyrām* **masc. proper noun**
(Abiram: son of Eliab)
Num. 16:1,12,24,25,27; 26:9; **Deut.** 11:6; **Ps.** 106:17.
B. אֲבִירָם *'aḇiyrām* **masc. proper noun**
(Abiram: son of Hiel)
1 Kgs. 16:34.

49. אֲבִישַׁג *'aḇiyšag* **fem. proper noun**
(Abishag)
1 Kgs. 1:3,15; 2:17,21,22.

50. A. אֲבִישׁוּעַ *'aḇiyšûa'* **masc. proper noun**
(Abishua: son of Phinehas)
1 Chr. 6:4(5:30),5(5:31),50(35); **Ezra** 7:5.
B. אֲבִישׁוּעַ *'aḇiyšûa'* **masc. proper noun**
(Abishua: son of Bela)
1 Chr. 8:4.

51. אֲבִישׁוּר *'aḇiyšûr* **masc. proper noun**
(Abishur)
1 Chr. 2:28,29.

52. אֲבִישַׁי *'aḇiyšay* **masc. proper noun**
(Abishai)
1 Sam. 26:6–9; **2 Sam.** 2:18,24; 3:30; 10:10,14; 16:9,11; 18:2,5,12; 19:21(22); 20:6,10; 21:17; 23:18; **1 Chr.** 2:16; 11:20; 18:12; 19:11,15.

53. A. אַבְשָׁלוֹם *'aḇšālôm* **masc. proper noun**
(Absalom: third son of David)
2 Sam. 3:3; 13:1,4,20,22–30,32,34, 37–39; 14:1,21,23–25,27–33; 15:1–4, 6,7,10–14,31,34,37; 16:8,15–18,20–23; 17:1,4–7,9,14,15,18,20,24–26; 18:5, 9,10,12,14,15,17,18(see *yaḏ 'aḇšālôm* [3027]),29,32,33(19:1); 19:1(2),4(5),6(7), 9(10),10(11); 20:6; **1 Kgs.** 1:6; 2:7,28; **1 Chr.** 3:2; **Ps.** 3:[title](1).
B. אֲבִישָׁלוֹם *'abiysālôm,* אַבְשָׁלוֹם *'aḇšālôm* **masc. proper noun**
(Abishalom, Absalom: father of Maacah)
1 Kgs. 15:2,10; **2 Chr.** 11:20,21.

54. אֶבְיָתָר *'eḇyāṯār* **masc. proper noun**
(Abiathar)
1 Sam. 22:20–22; 23:6,9; 30:7; **2 Sam.** 8:17; 15:24,27,29,35,36; 17:15; 19:11(12); 20:25; **1 Kgs.** 1:7,19,25,42; 2:22,26,27,35; 4:4; **1 Chr.** 15:11; 18:16; 24:6; 27:34.

55. אָבַךְ *'āḇaḵ* **verb**
(to roll upward)
Isa. 9:18(17).

56. אָבַל **'aḇal verb**
(to mourn, to dry up, to wither)
Gen. 37:34; Ex. 33:4; Num. 14:39;
1 Sam. 6:19; 15:35; 16:1; 2 Sam. 13:37;
14:2; 19:1(2); 1 Chr. 7:22; 2 Chr. 35:24;
Ezra 10:6; Neh. 1:4; 8:9; Job 14:22;
Isa. 3:26; 19:8; 24:4,7; 33:9; 66:10;
Jer. 4:28; 12:4,11; 14:2; 23:10; Lam.
2:8; Ezek. 7:12,27; 31:15; Dan. 10:2;
Hos. 4:3; 10:5; Joel 1:9,10; Amos 1:2;
8:8; 9:5.

57. אָבֵל **'āḇēl adj.**
(mourning, sorrowing)
Gen. 37:35; Esth. 6:12; Job 29:25;
Ps. 35:14; Isa. 57:18; 61:2,3; Lam. 1:4.

58. אָבֵל **'āḇēl fem. noun**
(plain)
Judg. 11:33(see 'āḇēl k^{e}rāmiym
[64,I]).

59. A. אָבֵל **'āḇēl proper noun**
(Abel: a great stone)
1 Sam. 6:18(NASB, NIV, 'eḇen [68]).
B. אָבֵל **'āḇēl proper noun**
(Abel: shortened form of 'āḇēl
bēyt-m^a'akāh [62])
2 Sam. 20:14(KJV, NASB, 'āḇēl [59] and
bēyt-m^a'akāh [1004 and 4601]); NIV,
'āḇēl bēyt-m^a'akāh [62],15(KJV, 'āḇēl
[59] and bēyt-m^a'akāh [1004 and 4601];
NASB, NIV, 'āḇēl hēyt-m^a'akāh [62]),18.

60. אֵבֶל **'ēḇel masc. noun**
(mourning, period of mourning)
Gen. 27:41; 50:10,11(NIV, 'āḇēl
miṣrayim [67]); Deut. 34:8; 2 Sam.
11:27; 14:2; 19:2(3); Esth. 4:3; 9:22;
Job 30:31; Eccl. 7:2,4; Isa. 60:20; 61:3;
Jer. 6:26; 16:7; 31:13; Lam. 5:15; Ezek.
24:17; Amos 5:16; 8:10; Mic. 1:8.

61. אֲבָל **'aḇāl adv.**
(surely, indeed, however)
Gen. 17:19; 42:21; 2 Sam. 14:5; 1 Kgs.
1:43; 2 Kgs. 4:14; 2 Chr. 1:4; 19:3;
33:17; Ezra 10:13; Dan. 10:7,21.

62. אָבֵל בֵּית־מַעֲכָה **'āḇēl bēyt-
m^a'akāh proper noun**
(Abel Beth Maacah; see also 'āḇēl
[59])
2 Sam. 20:14(KJV, NASB, 'āḇēl [59], bēyt
ma'akāh [1038]); 15(KJV, 'āḇēl [59], bēyt
ma'akāh [1038]).

63. אָבֵל הַשִּׁטִּים **'āḇēl haššiṭṭiym
proper noun**
(Abel Shittim: long form of šiṭṭiym
[7851,A])
Num. 33:49.

64. אָבֵל כְּרָמִים **'āḇēl
k^{e}rāmiym proper noun**
(Abel Keramim)
Judg. 11:33(KJV, 'āḇēl [58] kerem
[3754]).

65. אָבֵל מְחוֹלָה **'āḇēl
m^{e}ḥôlāh proper noun**
(Abel Meholah)
Judg. 7:22; 1 Kgs. 4:12; 19:16.

66. אָבֵל מַיִם **'āḇēl mayim proper
noun**
(Abel Maim)
2 Chr. 16:4.

67. אָבֵל מִצְרַיִם **'āḇēl
miṣrayim proper noun**
(Abel Mizraim)
Gen. 50:11(KJV, NASB, see 'ēḇel [60] and
miṣrayim [4714,C]).

68. אֶבֶן **'eḇen fem. noun**
(stone)
Gen. 2:12; 11:3; 28:11,18,22;
29:2,3,8,10; 31:45,46; 35:14; 49:24; Ex.
7:19; 15:5,16; 17:12; 20:25; 21:18; 24:12;
25:7; 28:9–12,17,21; 31:5,18; 34:1,4;
35:9,27,33; 39:6,7,10,14; Lev. 14:40,

42,43,45; 19:36; 20:2,27; 24:23; 26:1; **Num.** 14:10; 15:35,36; 35:17,23; **Deut.** 4:13,28; 5:22(19); 8:9; 9:9–11; 10:1,3; 13:10(11); 17:5; 21:21; 22:21,24; 25:13, 15; 27:2,4–6,8; 28:36,64; 29:17(16); **Josh.** 4:3,5–9,20,21; 7:25,26; 8:29,31,32; 10:11,18,27; 15:6; 18:17; 24:26,27; **Judg.** 9:5,18; 20:16; **1 Sam.** 4:1(see *'eḇen hā'ēzer* [72]); 5:1(see *'eḇen hā'ēzer* [72]); 6:14,15,18(KJV, *'āḇēl* [59]); 7:12 (see *'eḇen hā'ēzer* [72]); 14:33; 17:40,49, 50; 20:19; 25:37; **2 Sam.** 5:11; 12:30; 14:26; 16:6,13; 18:17; 20:8; **1 Kgs.** 1:9; 5:17(31),18(32); 6:7,18; 7:9–11; 8:9; 10:2,10,11,27; 12:18; 15:22; 18:31, 32,38; 21:13; **2 Kgs.** 3:19,25; 12:12(13); 16:17; 19:18; 22:6; **1 Chr.** 12:2; 20:2; 22:2,14,15; 29:2,8; **2 Chr.** 1:15; 2:14(13); 3:6; 9:1,9,10,27; 10:18; 16:6; 24:21; 26:14,15; 32:27; 34:11; **Neh.** 4:2(3:34),3(3:35); 9:11; **Job** 5:23; 6:12; 8:17; 14:19; 28:2,3,6; 38:6,30; 41:24(16), 28(20); **Ps.** 91:12; 102:14(15); 118:22; **Prov.** 11:1; 16:11; 17:8; 20:10,23; 24:31; 26:8,27; 27:3; **Eccl.** 3:5; 10:9; **Isa.** 8:14; 14:19; 27:9; 28:16; 30:30; 34:11; 37:19; 54:11,12; 60:17; 62:10; **Jer.** 2:27; 3:9; 43:9,10; 51:26,63; **Lam.** 3:53; 4:1; **Ezek.** 1:26; 10:1,9; 11:19; 13:11,13; 16:40; 20:32; 23:47; 26:12; 27:22; 28:13,14,16; 36:26; 38:22; 40:42; **Dan.** 11:38; **Mic.** 1:6; 6:11; **Hab.** 2:11,19; **Hag.** 2:15; **Zech.** 3:9; 4:7,10; 5:4,8; 9:15,16; 12:3.

69. אֶבֶן *'eḇen* **Aram. fem. noun**
(stone; corr. to Hebr. 68)
Ezra 5:8; 6:4; **Dan.** 2:34,35,45; 5:4,23; 6:17(18).

70. אֹבֶן *'ōḇen* **fem. noun**
(delivery stool, potter's wheel)
Ex. 1:16; **Jer.** 18:3.

71. אֲבָנָה *'aḇānāh* **proper noun**
(Abana)
2 Kgs. 5:12([Ke] *'amānāh* [549]).

72. A. אֶבֶן הָעֵזֶר *'eḇen hā'ēzer* proper noun
(Ebenezer: an unknown city; *'eḇen* [68] and *'ēzer* [5828])
1 Sam. 4:1; 5:1.
B. אֶבֶן הָעֵזֶר *'eḇen hā'ēzer* proper noun
(Ebenezer: a stone erected by Samuel; from *'eḇen* [68] and *'ēzer* [5828])
1 Sam. 7:12.

73. אַבְנֵט *'aḇnēṭ* **masc. noun**
(girdle, sash)
Ex. 28:4,39,40; 29:9; 39:29; **Lev.** 8:7,13; 16:4; **Isa.** 22:21.

74. אֲבִינֵר ,אַבְנֵר *'aḇnēr, 'aḇiynēr* **masc. proper noun**
(Abner)
1 Sam. 14:50,51; 17:55,57; 20:25; 26:5,7,14,15; **2 Sam.** 2:8,12,14,17, 19–26,29–31; 3:6–9,11,12,16,17, 19–28,30–33,37; 4:1,12; **1 Kgs.** 2:5,32; **1 Chr.** 26:28; 27:21.

75. אָבַס *'āḇas* **verb**
(to fatten)
1 Kgs. 4:23(5:3); **Prov.** 15:17.

76. אֲבַעְבֻּעֹת *'aḇa'bu'ōt* **fem. noun**
(festering boil)
Ex. 9:9,10.

77. אֶבֶץ *'eḇeṣ* **proper noun**
(Ebez, Abez [KJV])
Josh. 19:20.

78. אִבְצָן *'iḇṣān* **masc. noun**
(Ibzan)
Judg. 12:8,10.

79. אָבַק *'āḇaq* **verb**
(to wrestle)
Gen. 32:24(25),25(26).

80. אָבָק *'āḇāq* **masc. noun**
(dust, powder)

Ex. 9:9; **Deut.** 28:24; **Isa.** 5:24; 29:5; **Ezek.** 26:10; **Nah.** 1:3.

81. אֲבָקָה *'ᵃḇāqāh* **fem. noun**
(powder, spice)
Song 3:6.

82. אָבַר *'āḇar* **verb**
(to fly)
Job 39:26.

83. אֵבֶר *'ēḇer* **masc. noun**
(wing)
Ps. 55:6(7); **Isa.** 40:31; **Ezek.** 17:3.

84. אֶבְרָה *'eḇrāh* **fem. noun**
(wings, feathers)
Deut. 32:11; **Job** 39:13; **Ps.** 68:13(14); 91:4.

85. אַבְרָהָם *'aḇrāhām* **masc. proper noun**
(Abraham, see also *'aḇrām* [87])
Gen. 17:5,9,15,17,18,22–24,26; 18:6,7, 11,13,16–19,22,23,27,33; 19:27,29; 20:1,2,9–11,14,17,18; 21:2–5,7–12,14, 22,24,25,27–29,34; 22:1,3–11,13–15, 19,20,23; 23:2,3,5,7,10,12,14,16,18–20; 24:1,2,6,9,12,15,27,34,42,48,52,59; 25:1,5–8,10–12,19; 26:1,3,5,15,18,24; 28:4,9,13; 31:42,53; 32:9(10); 35:12,27; 48:15,16; 49:30,31; 50:13,24; **Ex.** 2:24; 3:6,15,16; 4:5; 6:3,8; 32:13; 33:1; **Lev.** 26:42; **Num.** 32:11; **Deut.** 1:8; 6:10; 9:5,27; 29:13(12); 30:20; 34:4; **Josh.** 24:2,3; **1 Kgs.** 18:36; **2 Kgs.** 13:23; **1 Chr.** 1:27,28,32,34; 16:16; 29:18; **2 Chr.** 20:7; 30:6; **Neh.** 9:7; **Ps.** 47:9(10); 105:6,9,42; **Isa.** 29:22; 41:8; 51:2; 63:16; **Jer.** 33:26; **Ezek.** 33:24; **Mic.** 7:20.

86. אַבְרֵךְ *'aḇrēḵ* **verb**
(make way, bow the knee)
Gen. 41:43.

87. אַבְרָם *'aḇrām* **masc. proper noun**
(Abram, early name of Abraham [85])
Gen. 11:26,27,29,31; 12:1,4–7,9,10,14, 16–18; 13:1,2,4,5,7,8,12,14,18; 14:12–14, 19,21–23; 15:1–3,11–13,18; 16:1–3,5, 6,15,16; 17:1,3,5; **1 Chr.** 1:27; **Neh.** 9:7.

88. אֹבֹת *'ōḇōṯ* **proper noun**
(Oboth)
Num. 21:10,11; 33:43,44.

89. אָגֵא *'āgē'* **masc. proper noun**
(Agee)
2 Sam. 23:11.

90. A. אֲגַג *'ᵃgag* **masc. proper noun**
(Agag: earlier Amalekite king)
Num. 24:7.
B. אֲגַג *'ᵃgag* **masc. proper noun**
(Agag: later Amalekite king)
1 Sam. 15:8,9,20,32,33.

91. אֲגָגִי *'ᵃgāgiy* **masc. proper noun**
(Agagite)
Esth. 3:1,10; 8:3,5; 9:24.

92. אֲגֻדָּה *'ᵃguddāh* **fem. noun**
(a bunch, a group, a bundle)
Ex. 12:22; **2 Sam.** 2:25; **Isa.** 58:6; **Amos** 9:6.

93. אֱגוֹז *'ᵉgôz* **masc. noun**
(nuts, nut trees)
Song 6:11.

94. אָגוּר *'āgûr* **masc. proper noun**
(Agur)
Prov. 30:1.

95. אֲגוֹרָה *'ᵃgôrāh* **fem. noun**
(piece)
1 Sam. 2:36.

96. אֶגֶל *'egel* **masc. noun**
(a drop)
Job 38:28.

97. אֶגְלַיִם *'eglayim* **proper noun**
(Eglaim)
Isa. 15:8.

98. אֲגַם *'ᵃgam* **masc. noun**
(pond, pool)
Ex. 7:19; 8:5(1); **Ps.** 107:35; 114:8; **Isa.** 14:23; 35:7; 41:18; 42:15; **Jer.** 51:32.

99. I. אָגֵם *'āgēm* **adj.**
(stagnant, sick)
Isa. 19:10(KJV, see II).
II. אָגֵם *'āgēm* **masc. noun**
(grieved, troubled)
Isa. 19:10(NASB, NIV, see I).

100. אַגְמוֹן *'agmôn* **masc. noun**
(reed, cord of reeds)
Job 41:2(40:26),20(12); **Isa.** 9:14(13); 19:15; 58:5.

101. אַגָּן *'aggān* **masc. noun**
(basin, bowl)
Ex. 24:6; **Song** 7:2(3); **Isa.** 22:24.

102. אֲגַף *'ᵃgap̲* **masc. noun**
(band of soldiers, troops)
Ezek. 12:14; 17:21; 38:6,9,22; 39:4.

103. אָגַר *'āgar* **verb**
(to gather crops)
Deut. 28:39; **Prov.** 6:8; 10:5.

104. אִגְּרָא *'iggᵉrā'* **Aram. fem. noun**
(letter, correspondence)
Ezra 4:8,11; 5:6.

105. אֲגַרְטָל *'ᵃgarṭāl* **masc. noun**
(bowl, basin)
Ezra 1:9.

106. אֶגְרֹף *'egrōp̲* **masc. noun**
(fist)
Ex. 21:18; **Isa.** 58:4.

107. אִגֶּרֶת *'iggeret̲* **fem. noun**
(letter, correspondence)
2 Chr. 30:1,6; **Neh.** 2:7–9; 6:5,17,19; **Esth.** 9:26,29.

108. אֵד *'ēd̲* **masc. noun**
(mist)
Gen. 2:6; **Job** 36:27.

109. אָדַב *'ād̲ab̲* **verb**
(to grieve, to cause grief)
1 Sam. 2:33.

110. אַדְבְּאֵל *'ad̲bᵉ'ēl* **masc. proper noun**
(Adbeel)
Gen. 25:13; **1 Chr.** 1:29.

111. אֲדַד *'ᵃd̲ad̲* **masc.n proper noun**
(Hadad: another form of *hᵃd̲ad̲* [1908,B])
1 Kgs. 11:17.

112. אִדּוֹ *'iddô* **masc. proper noun**
(Iddo)
Ezra 8:17.

113. אָדוֹן *'ādôn* **masc. noun**
(lord, master, owner)
Gen. 18:12; 19:2,18(NASB, *'ᵃd̲ōnāy* [136]); 23:6,11,15; 24:9,10,12,14,18, 27,35–37,39,42,44,48,49,51,54,56,65; 31:35; 32:4(5),5(6),18(19); 33:8,13–15; 39:2,3,7,8,16,19,20; 40:1,7; 42:10,30,33; 43:20; 44:5,7–9,16,18–20,22,24,33; 45:8,9; 47:18,25; **Ex.** 21:4–6,8,32; 23:17; 32:22; 34:23; **Num.** 11:28; 12:11; 32:24, 27; 36:2; **Deut.** 10:17; 23:15(16); **Josh.** 3:11,13; 5:14; **Judg.** 3:25; 4:18; 6:13; 19:11,12,26,27; **Ruth** 2:13; **1 Sam.** 1:15,26; 16:16; 20:38; 22:12; 24:6(7), 8(9),10(11); 25:10,14,17,24–31,41; 26:15–19; 29:4,8,10; 30:13,15; **2 Sam.** 1:10; 2:5,7; 3:21; 4:8; 9:9–11; 10:3; 11:9,11,13; 12:8; 13:32,33; 14:9,12,15, 17–20,22; 15:15,21; 16:3,4,9; 18:28, 31,32; 19:19(20),20(21),26–28(27–29), 30(31),35(36),37(38); 20:6; 24:3,21,22;

1 Kgs. 1:2,11,13,17,18,20,21,24,27,31, 33,36,37,43,47; 2:38; 3:17,26; 11:23; 12:27; 16:24; 18:7,8,10,11,13,14; 20:4,9; 22:17; **2 Kgs.** 2:3,5,16,19; 4:16,28; 5:1,3,4,18,20,22,25; 6:5,12,15,22,23,26, 32; 8:5,12,14; 9:7,11,31; 10:2,3,6,9; 18:23,24,27; 19:4,6; **1 Chr.** 12:19; 21:3,23; **2 Chr.** 2:14(13),15(14); 13:6; 18:16; **Neh.** 3:5; 8:10; 10:29(30); **Job** 3:19; **Ps.** 8:1(2),9(10); 12:4(5); 45:11(12); 97:5; 105:21; 110:1; 114:7; 123:2; 135:5; 136:3; 147:5; **Prov.** 25:13; 27:18; 30:10; **Isa.** 1:24; 3:1; 10:16,33; 19:4; 21:8; 22:18; 24:2; 26:13; 36:8,9,12; 37:4,6; 51:22; **Jer.** 22:18; 27:4; 34:5; 37:20; 38:9; **Dan.** 1:10; 10:16,17,19; 12:8; **Hos.** 12:14(15); **Amos** 4:1; **Mic.** 4:13; **Zeph.** 1:9; **Zech.** 1:9; 4:4,5,13,14; 6:4,5; **Mal.** 1:6; 3:1.

114. אַדּוֹן *'addôn* **masc. proper noun**
(Addon)
Neh. 7:61.

115. אֲדוֹרַיִם *'aḏôrayim* **proper noun**
(Adoraim)
2 Chr. 11:9.

116. אֱדַיִן *'eḏayin* **Aram. adv.**
(then)
Ezra 4:9,23,24; 5:2,4,5,9,16; 6:1,13; **Dan.** 2:14,15,17,19,25,35,46,48; 3:3,13,19,21,24,26,30; 4:7(4),19(16); 5:3,6,8,9,13,17,24,29; 6:3–6(4–7),11–16 (12–17),18(19),19(20),21(22),23(24), 25(26); 7:1,11,19.

117. אַדִּיר *'addiyr* **adj.**
(noble, mighty, glorious)
Ex. 15:10; **Judg.** 5:13,25; **1 Sam.** 4:8; **2 Chr.** 23:20; **Neh.** 3:5; 10:29(30); **Ps.** 8:1(2),9(10); 16:3; 76:4(5); 93:4; 136:18; **Isa.** 10:34; 33:21; **Jer.** 14:3; 25:34–36; 30:21; **Ezek.** 17:23; 32:18; **Nah.** 2:5(6); 3:18; **Zech.** 11:2.

118. אֲדַלְיָא *'aḏalyā'* **masc. proper noun**
(Adalia)
Esth. 9:8.

119. אָדַם *'āḏam* **verb**
(to be red, dyed red)
Ex. 25:5; 26:14; 35:7,23; 36:19; 39:34; **Prov.** 23:31; **Isa.** 1:18; **Lam.** 4:7; **Nah.** 2:3(4).

120. אָדָם *'āḏām* **masc. noun**
(man, mankind)
Gen. 1:26,27; 2:5,7,8,15,16,18,20(KJV, *'āḏām* [121,A]),22,25; 3:12,22,24; 5:1; 6:1–7; 7:21,23; 8:21; 9:5,6; 11:5; 16:12; **Ex.** 4:11; 8:17(13),18(14); 9:9,10,19,22, 25; 12:12; 13:2,13,15; 30:32; 33:20; **Lev.** 1:2; 5:3,4; 6:3(5:22); 7:21; 13:2,9; 16:17; 18:5; 22:5; 24:17,20,21; 27:28,29; **Num.** 3:13; 5:6; 8:17; 9:6,7; 12:3; 16:29,32; 18:15; 19:11,13,14,16; 23:19; 31:11,26, 28,30,35,40,46,47; **Deut.** 4:28,32; 5:24(21); 8:3; 20:19; 32:8; **Josh.** 11:14; 14:15; **Judg.** 16:7,11,17; 18:7,28; **1 Sam.** 15:29; 16:7; 17:32; 24:9(10); 25:29; 26:19; **2 Sam.** 7:14,19; 23:3; 24:14; **1 Kgs.** 4:31(5:11); 8:38,39,46; 13:2; **2 Kgs.** 7:10; 19:18; 23:14,20; **1 Chr.** 5:21; 17:17; 21:13; 29:1; **2 Chr.** 6:18,29,30,36; 19:6; 32:19; **Neh.** 2:10, 12; 9:29; **Job** 5:7; 7:20; 11:12; 14:1,10; 15:7; 16:21; 20:4,29; 21:4,33; 25:6; 27:13; 28:28; 31:33(KJV, NASB, *'āḏām* [121,A]); 32:21; 33:17,23; 34:11,15, 29,30; 35:8; 36:25,28; 37:7; 38:26; **Ps.** 8:4(5); 11:4; 12:1(2),8(9); 14:2; 17:4; 21:10(11); 22:6(7); 31:19(20); 32:2; 33:13; 36:6(7),7(8); 39:5(6),11(12); 45:2(3); 49:2(3),12(13),20(21); 53:2(3); 56:11(12); 57:4(5); 58:1(2),11(12); 60:11(13); 62:9(10); 64:9(10); 66:5; 68:18(19); 73:5; 76:10(11); 78:60; 80:17(18); 82:7; 84:5(6),12(13); 89:47(48); 90:3; 94:10,11; 104:14,23; 105:14; 107:8,15,21,31; 108:12(13); 115:4,16; 116:11; 118:6,8; 119:134;

124:2; 135:8,15; 140:1(2); 144:3,4; 145:12; 146:3; **Prov.** 3:4,13,30; 6:12; 8:4,31,34; 11:7; 12:3,14,23,27; 15:11,20; 16:1,9; 17:18; 18:16; 19:3,11,22; 20:6,24, 25,27; 21:16,20; 23:28; 24:9,12,30; 27:19,20; 28:2,12,14,17,23,28; 29:23,25; 30:2,14; **Eccl.** 1:3,13; 2:3,8,12,18,21, 22,24,26; 3:10,11,13,18,19,21,22; 5:19(18); 6:1,7,10–12; 7:2,14,20,28,29; 8:1,6,8,9,11,15,17; 9:1,3,12,15; 10:14; 11:8; 12:5,13; **Isa.** 2:9,11,17,20,22; 5:15; 6:11,12; 13:12; 17:7; 22:6; 29:19,21; 31:3,8; 37:19; 38:11; 43:4; 44:11,13,15; 45:12; 47:3; 51:12; 52:14; 56:2; 58:5; **Jer.** 2:6; 4:25; 7:20; 9:22(21); 10:14,23; 16:20; 17:5; 21:6; 27:5; 31:27,30; 32:19, 20,43; 33:5,10,12; 36:29; 47:2; 49:15, 18,33; 50:3,40; 51:14,17,43,62; **Lam.** 3:36,39; **Ezek.** 1:5,8,10,26; 2:1,3,6,8; 3:1,3,4,10,17,25; 4:1,12,15,16; 5:1; 6:2; 7:2; 8:5,6,8,12,15,17; 10:8,14,21; 11:2, 4,15; 12:2,3,9,18,22,27; 13:2,17; 14:3, 13,17,19,21; 15:2; 16:2; 17:2; 19:3,6; 20:3,4,11,13,21,27,46(21:2); 21:2(7), 6(11),9(14),12(17),14(19),19(24),28(33); 22:2,18,24; 23:2,36,42; 24:2,16,25; 25:2, 13; 26:2; 27:2,13; 28:2,9,12,21; 29:2,8, 11,18; 30:2,21; 31:2,14; 32:2,13,18; 33:2, 7,10,12,24,30; 34:2,31; 35:2; 36:1,10–14, 17,37,38; 37:3,9,11,16; 38:2,14,20; 39:1, 15,17; 40:4; 41:19; 43:7,10,18; 44:5,25; 47:6; **Dan.** 8:16,17; 10:16,18; **Hos.** 6:7(NASB, NIV, *'ā<u>d</u>am* [121,A]); 9:12; 11:4; 13:2; **Joel** 1:12; **Amos** 4:13; **Jon.** 3:7,8; 4:11; **Mic.** 2:12; 5:5(4),7(6); 6:8; 7:2; **Hab.** 1:14; 2:8,17; **Zeph.** 1:3,17; **Hag.** 1:11; **Zech.** 2:4(8); 8:10; 9:1; 11:6; 12:1; 13:5; **Mal.** 3:8.

121. A. אָדָם *'ā<u>d</u>ām* **masc. proper noun**
(Adam: the first man)
Gen. 2:19,20(NASB, NIV, *'ā<u>d</u>ām* [120]),21,23; 3:8,9,17,20,21; 4:1,25; 5:1–5; **1 Chr.** 1:1; **Job** 31:33(NIV, *'ā<u>d</u>ām* [120]); **Hos.** 6:7(KJV, *'ā<u>d</u>ām* [120]).

B. אָדָם *'ā<u>d</u>ām* **masc. proper noun**
(Adam: city near Zaretan)
Josh. 3:16.

122. אָדֹם *'ā<u>d</u>ōm* **adj.**
(red, reddish)
Gen. 25:30; **Num.** 19:2; **2 Kgs.** 3:22; **Song** 5:10; **Isa.** 63:2; **Zech.** 1:8; 6:2.

123. A. אֱדוֹם *'e<u>d</u>ôm,* אֱדֹם *'e<u>d</u>ōm* **masc. proper noun**
(Edom: son of Isaac)
Gen. 25:30; 36:1,8,19.

B. אֱדוֹם *'e<u>d</u>ôm,* אֱדֹם *'e<u>d</u>ōm* **masc. proper noun**
(Edom: people or country of Edom)
Gen. 32:3(4); 36:9,16,17,21,31,32,43; **Ex.** 15:15; **Num.** 20:14,18,20,21,23; 21:4; 24:18; 33:37; 34:3; **Josh.** 15:1,21; **Judg.** 5:4; 11:17,18; **1 Sam.** 14:47; **2 Sam.** 8:14; **1 Kgs.** 9:26; 11:14–16; 22:47(48); **2 Kgs.** 3:8,9,12,20,26; 8:20–22; 14:7,10; **1 Chr.** 1:43,51,54; 18:11–13; **2 Chr.** 8:17; 21:8–10; 25:19,20; **Ps.** 60:8(10),9(11); 83:6(7); 108:9(10),10(11); 137:7; **Isa.** 11:14; 34:5,6; 63:1; **Jer.** 9:26(25); 25:21; 27:3; 40:11; 49:7,17,20,22; **Lam.** 4:21,22; **Ezek.** 25:12–14; 32:29; 35:15; 36:5; **Dan.** 11:41; **Joel** 3:19(4:19); **Amos** 1:6,9,11; 2:1; 9:12; **Obad.** 1:1,8; **Mal.** 1:4.

124. אֹדֶם *'ō<u>d</u>em* **fem. noun**
(ruby, sardius)
Ex. 28:17; 39:10; **Ezek.** 28:13.

125. אֲדַמְדָּם *'a<u>d</u>amdām* **adj.**
(reddish)
Lev. 13:19,24,42,43,49; 14:37.

126. אַדְמָה *'a<u>d</u>māh* **proper noun**
(Admah)
Gen. 10:19; 14:2,8; **Deut.** 29:23(22); **Hos.** 11:8.

127. אֲדָמָה *'a<u>d</u>āmāh* **fem. noun**
(land, ground, earth)

Gen. 1:25; 2:5–7,9,19; 3:17,19,23;
4:2,3,10–12,14; 5:29; 6:1,7,20; 7:4,8,23;
8:8,13,21; 9:2,20; 12:3; 19:25; 28:14,15;
47:18–20,22,23,26; **Ex.** 3:5; 8:21(17);
10:6; 20:12,24; 23:19; 32:12; 33:16;
34:26; **Lev.** 20:24,25; **Num.** 11:12; 12:3;
16:30,31; 32:11; **Deut.** 4:10,18,40; 5:16;
6:15; 7:6,13; 11:9,17,21; 12:1,19; 14:2;
21:1,23; 25:15; 26:2,10,15; 28:4,11,18,
21,33,42,51,63; 29:28(27); 30:9,18,20;
31:13,20; 32:43,47; **Josh.** 23:13,15;
1 Sam. 4:12; 20:15,31; **2 Sam.** 1:2; 9:10;
14:7; 15:32; 17:12; **1 Kgs.** 7:46; 8:34,40;
9:7; 13:34; 14:15; 17:14; 18:1; **2 Kgs.**
5:17; 17:23; 21:8; 25:21; **1 Chr.** 27:26;
2 Chr. 4:17; 6:25,31; 7:20; 26:10; 33:8;
Neh. 9:1,25; 10:35(36),37(38); **Job** 5:6;
31:38; **Ps.** 49:11(12); 83:10(11); 104:30;
105:35; 137:4; 146:4; **Prov.** 12:11; 28:19;
Isa. 1:7; 6:11; 7:16; 14:1,2; 15:9; 19:17;
23:17; 24:21; 28:24; 30:23,24; 32:13;
45:9; **Jer.** 7:20; 8:2; 12:14; 14:4; 16:4,15;
23:8; 24:10; 25:5,26,33; 27:10,11; 28:16;
35:7,15; 42:12; 52:27; **Ezek.** 7:2; 11:17;
12:19,22; 13:9; 18:2; 20:38,42; 21:2(7),
3(8); 25:3,6; 28:25; 33:24; 34:13,27;
36:6,17,24; 37:12,14,21; 38:18–20;
39:26,28; **Dan.** 11:9,39; 12:2; **Hos.**
2:18(20); **Joel** 1:10; 2:21; **Amos** 3:2,5;
5:2; 7:11,17; 9:8,15; **Jon.** 4:2; **Zeph.**
1:2,3; **Hag.** 1:11; **Zech.** 2:12(16); 9:16;
13:5; **Mal.** 3:11.

128. אֲדָמָה *'a̱dāmāh* **proper noun**
(Adamah)
Josh. 19:36.

129. אֲדָמִי *'a̱dāmiy* **proper noun**
(Adami)
Josh. 19:33(NASB, NIV, *'a̱dāmiy neqeḇ*
[5346,II]).

130. אֲדֹמִי *'e̱dōmiy* **masc. proper noun**
(Edomite)
Deut. 23:7(8); **1 Sam.** 21:7(8);
22:9,18,22; **1 Kgs.** 11:1,14,17; **2 Kgs.**
16:6(KJV, NASB, [Kᵉ] *'a̱rômiym* [726]);
2 Chr. 25:14; 28:17; **Ps.** 52:[title](2).

131. אֲדֻמִּים *'a̱dummiym* **proper noun**
(Adummim)
Josh. 15:7; 18:17.

132. אַדְמֹנִי *'a̱dmōniy,* אַדְמוֹנִי
'a̱dmôniy **adj.**
(red; reddish)
Gen. 25:25; **1 Sam.** 16:12; 17:42.

133. אַדְמָתָא *'a̱dmāṯā'* **masc. proper noun**
(Admatha)
Esth. 1:14.

134. אֶדֶן *'eḏen* **masc. noun**
(base, pedestal, socket)
Ex. 26:19,21,25,32,37; 27:10–12,14–18;
35:11,17; 36:24,26,30,36,38; 38:10–12,
14,15,17,19,27,30,31; 39:33,40; 40:18;
Num. 3:36,37; 4:31,32; **Job** 38:6;
Song 5:15.

135. אַדָּן *'addān* **masc. proper noun**
(Addan)
Ezra 2:59.

136. אֲדֹנָי *'a̱ḏōnāy* **masc. [proper] noun**
(Lord, my Lord, spoken primarily of God)
Gen. 15:2,8; 18:3,27,30–32; 19:18(NASB, NIV, *'ā̱ḏôn* [113]); 20:4; **Ex.** 4:10,13;
5:22; 15:17; 34:9; **Num.** 14:17; **Deut.**
3:24; 9:26; **Josh.** 7:7,8; **Judg.** 6:15,22;
13:8; 16:28; **2 Sam.** 7:18–20,22(KJV,
'elōhiym [430],28,29; **1 Kgs.** 2:26;
3:10,15; 8:53; 22:6; **2 Kgs.** 7:6; 19:23;
Ezra 10:3; **Neh.** 1:11; 4:14(8); **Job**
28:28; **Ps.** 2:4; 16:2; 22:30(31); 30:8(9);
35:17,22,23; 37:13; 38:9(10),15(16);
22(23); 39:7(8); 40:17(18); 44:23(24);
51:15(17); 54:4(6); 55:9(10); 57:9(10);

59:11(12); 62:12(13); 66:18; 68:11(12), 17(18),19(20),20(21),22(23),32(33); 69:6(7); 71:5,16; 73:20,28; 77:2(3),7(8); 78:65; 79:12; 86:3–5,8,9,12,15; 89:49(50), 50(51); 90:1,17; 109:21; 110:5; 130:2,3,6; 140:7(8); 141:8; **Isa.** 3:15,17,18; 4:4; 6:1,8,11; 7:7,14,20; 8:7; 9:8(7),17(16); 10:12,23,24; 11:11; 21:6,8(KJV, NIV, *'ādôn* [113],16; 22:5,12,14,15; 25:8; 28:2,16,22; 29:13; 30:15,20; 37:24; 38:14,16; 40:10; 48:16; 49:14,22; 50:4,5,7,9; 52:4; 56:8; 61:1,11; 65:13,15; **Jer.** 1:6; 2:19,22; 4:10; 7:20; 14:13; 32:17,25; 44:26; 46:10; 49:5; 50:25,31; **Lam.** 1:14,15; 2:1,2,5,7,18–20; 3:31,36,37,58; **Ezek.** 2:4; 3:11,27; 4:14; 5:5,7,8,11; 6:3,11; 7:2,5; 8:1; 9:8; 11:7,8, 13,16,17,21; 12:10,19,23,25,28; 13:3,8,9, 13,16,18,20; 14:4,6,11,14,16,18,20,21,23; 15:6,8; 16:3,8,14,19,23,30,36,43,48, 59,63; 17:3,9,16,19,22; 18:3,9,23,25,29, 30,32; 20:3,5,27,30,31,33,36,39,40,44, 47(21:3),49(21:5); 21:7(12),9(14),13(18), 24(29),26(31),28(33); 22:3,12,19,28,31; 23:22,28,32,34,35,46,49; 24:3,6,9,14,21, 24; 25:3,6,8,12–16; 26:3,5,7,14,15,19,21; 27:3; 28:2,6,10,12,22,24,25; 29:3,8,13, 16,19,20; 30:2,6,10,13,22; 31:10,15,18; 32:3,8,11,14,16,31,32; 33:11,17,20, 25,27; 34:2,8,10,11,15,17,20,30,31; 35:3,6,11,14; 36:2–7,13–15,22,23,32, 33,37; 37:3,5,9,12,19,21; 38:3,10,14, 17,18,21; 39:1,5,8,10,13,17,20,25,29; 43:18,19,27; 44:6,9,12,15,27; 45:9,15, 18; 46:1,16; 47:13,23; 48:29; **Dan.** 1:2; 9:3,4,7,9,15–17,19; **Amos** 1:8; 3:7, 8,11,13; 4:2,5; 5:3,16; 6:8; 7:1,2,4–8; 8:1,3,9,11; 9:1,5,8; **Obad.** 1:1; **Mic.** 1:2; **Hab.** 3:19; **Zeph.** 1:7; **Zech.** 9:4,14; **Mal.** 1:12,14.

137. אֲדֹנִי בֶזֶק *'adōniy bezeq* **masc. proper noun**
(Adoni-Bezek)
Judg. 1:5–7.

138. A. אֲדֹנִיָּה *'adōniyyah*, אֲדֹנִיָּהוּ *'adōniyyāhû* **masc. proper noun**
(Adonijah: son of David)
2 Sam. 3:4; **1 Kgs.** 1:5,7–9,11,13,18,24,25,41–43,49–51; 2:13,19,21–24,28; **1 Chr.** 3:2.
B. אֲדֹנִיָּהוּ *'adōniyyāhû* **masc. proper noun**
(Adonijah: Levite in Jehoshaphat's time)
2 Chr. 17:8.
C. אֲדֹנִיָּה *'adōniyyah* **masc. proper noun**
(Adonijah: head of a family of priests)
Neh. 10:16.

139. אֲדֹנִי צֶדֶק *'adōniy ṣedeq* **masc. proper noun**
(Adoni-Zedek)
Josh. 10:1,3.

140. אֲדֹנִיקָם *'adōniyqām* **masc. proper noun**
(Adonikam)
Ezra 2:13; 8:13; **Neh.** 7:18.

141. אֲדֹנִירָם *'adōniyrām* **masc. proper noun**
(Adoniram)
1 Kgs. 4:6; 5:14(28).

142. אָדַר *'ādar* **verb**
(to be glorious, majestic)
Ex. 15:6,11; **Isa.** 42:21.

143. אֲדָר *'adār* **proper noun**
(the twelfth month, Adar)
Esth. 3:7,13; 8:12; 9:1,15,17,19,21.

144. אֲדָר *'adār* **Aram. proper noun**
(the twelfth month, Adar; corr. to Hebr. 143)
Ezra 6:15.

145. אֶדֶר *'eder* **masc. noun**
(something great, handsome, a rich robe)
Mic. 2:8; **Zech.** 11:13.

146. A. אַדָּר *'addār* **masc. proper noun**
(Addar: grandson of Benjamin)
1 Chr. 8:3.
B. אַדָּר *'addār* **proper noun**
(Addar: city in Judah possibly *ḥaṣar 'addar* [2692])
Josh. 15:3.

147. אִדַּר *'iddar* **Aram. fem. noun**
(threshing floor)
Dan. 2:35.

148. אֲדַרְגָּזֵר *'ad̲argāzēr* **Aram. masc. noun**
(judge, adviser)
Dan. 3:2,3.

149. אַדְרַזְדָּא *'ad̲razdā'* **Aram. adv.**
(diligently)
Ezra 7:23.

150. אֲדַרְכֹּן *'ad̲arkōn* **masc. noun**
(dram: small unit of weight)
1 Chr. 29:7; **Ezra** 8:27.

151. אֲדֹרָם *'ad̲ōrām* **masc. proper noun**
(Adoram [NIV, *'ad̲ōniyrām* {141}])
2 Sam. 20:24; **1 Kgs.** 12:18.

152. A. אַדְרַמֶּלֶךְ *'ad̲rammelek* **masc. proper noun**
(Adrammelech: an idol)
2 Kgs. 17:31.
B. אַדְרַמֶּלֶךְ *'ad̲rammelek* **masc. proper noun**
(Adrammelech: son of Sennacherib)
2 Kgs. 19:37; **Isa.** 37:38.

153. אֶדְרָע *'ed̲rā'* **Aram. noun**
(strength, force)
Ezra 4:23.

154. אֶדְרֶעִי *'ed̲re'iy* **proper noun**
(Edrei)
Num. 21:33; **Deut.** 1:4; 3:1,10; **Josh.** 12:4; 13:12,31; 19:37.

155. אַדֶּרֶת *'adderet̲* **fem. noun**
(cloak, robe, glory)
Gen. 25:25; **Josh.** 7:21,24; **1 Kgs.** 19:13,19; **2 Kgs.** 2:8,13,14; **Ezek.** 17:8; **Jon.** 3:6; **Zech.** 11:3; 13:4.

156. אָדוֹשׁ *'ād̲ôš* **verb**
(to thresh; NASB, NIV, inf. of *dûš* [1758])
Isa. 28:28.

157. אָהַב *'āhab̲* **verb**
(to love)
Gen. 22:2; 24:67; 25:28; 27:4,9,14; 29:18,30,32; 34:3; 37:3,4; 44:20; **Ex.** 20:6; 21:5; **Lev.** 19:18,34; **Deut.** 4:37; 5:10; 6:5; 7:9,13; 10:12,15,18,19; 11:1,13,22; 13:3(4); 15:16; 19:9; 21:15,16; 23:5(6); 30:6,16,20; **Josh.** 22:5; 23:11; **Judg.** 5:31; 14:16; 16:4,15; **Ruth** 4:15; **1 Sam.** 1:5; 16:21; 18:1, 16,20,22,28; 20:17; **2 Sam.** 1:23; 12:24; 13:1,4,15; 19:6(7); **1 Kgs.** 3:3; 5:1(15); 10:9(NIV, *'ahab̲āh* [160]); 11:1,2; **2 Chr.** 11:21; 19:2; 20:7; 26:10; **Neh.** 1:5; 13:26; **Esth.** 2:17; 5:10,14; 6:13; **Job** 19:19; **Ps.** 4:2(3); 5:11(12); 11:5,7; 26:8; 31:23(24); 33:5; 34:12(13); 37:28; 38:11(12); 40:16(17); 45:7(8); 47:4(5); 52:3(5),4(6); 69:36(37); 70:4(5); 78:68; 87:2; 88:18(19); 97:10; 99:4; 109:17; 116:1; 119:47,48,97,113,119,127,132, 140,159,163,165,167; 122:6; 145:20; 146:8; **Prov.** 1:22; 3:12; 4:6; 8:17,21,36; 9:8; 12:1; 13:24; 14:20; 15:9,12; 16:13; 17:17,19; 18:21,24; 19:8; 20:13; 21:17; 22:11; 27:6; 29:3; **Eccl.** 3:8; 5:10(9); 9:9; **Song** 1:3,4,7; 3:1–4; **Isa.** 1:23; 41:8; 43:4; 48:14; 56:6,10; 57:8; 61:8; 66:10; **Jer.** 2:25; 5:31; 8:2; 14:10; 20:4,6; 22:20,22; 30:14; 31:3; **Lam.** 1:2,19; **Ezek.** 16:33,36,37; 23:5,9,22; **Dan.** 9:4; **Hos.** 2:5(7),7(9),10(12),12(14), 13(15); 3:1; 4:18; 9:1,10,15; 10:11; 11:1; 12:7(8); 14:4(5); **Amos** 4:5; 5:15; **Mic.** 3:2; 6:8; **Zech.** 8:17,19; 13:6; **Mal.** 1:2; 2:11.

158. אַהַב *'ahab̲* **masc. noun**
(lover)
Prov. 5:19; **Hos.** 8:9.

159. אֹהַב *'ōhab̲* **masc. noun**
(loving actions)
Prov. 7:18.

160. אַהֲבָה *'ah^a^b̲āh* **fem. noun**
(love)
Gen. 29:20; **Deut.** 7:8; **1 Sam.** 18:3; 20:17; **2 Sam.** 1:26; 13:15; **1 Kgs.** 10:9(KJV, NASB, *'āhab̲* [157]); **2 Chr.** 2:11(10); 9:8; **Ps.** 109:4,5; **Prov.** 5:19; 10:12; 15:17; 17:9; 27:5; **Eccl.** 9:1,6; **Song** 2:4,5,7; 3:5,10; 5:8; 7:6(7); 8:4,6,7; **Isa.** 63:9; **Jer.** 2:2,33; 31:3; **Hos.** 3:1; 11:4; **Zeph.** 3:17.

161. אֹהַד *'ōhad̲* **masc. proper noun**
(Ohad)
Gen. 46:10; **Ex.** 6:15.

162. אֲהָהּ *'^a^hāh* **interj.**
(oh! alas!)
Josh. 7:7; **Judg.** 6:22; 11:35; **2 Kgs.** 3:10; 6:5,15; **Jer.** 1:6; 4:10; 14:13; 32:17; **Ezek.** 4:14; 9:8; 11:13; 20:49(21:5); **Joel** 1:15.

163. אַהֲוָא *'ah^a^wā'* **proper noun**
(Ahava)
Ezra 8:15,21,31.

164. A. אֵהוּד *'ēhûd̲* **masc. proper noun**
(Ehud: son of Gera)
Judg. 3:15,16,20,21,23,26; 4:1.
B. אֵהוּד *'ēhûd̲* **masc. proper noun**
(Ehud: another Benjamite)
1 Chr. 7:10.

165. I. אֱהִי *'^e^hiy* **verb**
(I will be: Qal imperf. 1st sing. of *hāyāh* **[1961]**)
Hos. 13:10(NASB, NIV, see II),14(NASB, NIV, see II).

II. אֱהִי *'^e^hiy* **interrog. pron.**
(where?)
Hos. 13:10(KJV, see I),14(KJV, see I).

166. אָהַל *'āhal* **verb**
(to be bright, shine)
Job 25:5.

167. אָהַל *'āhal* **verb**
(to pitch a tent)
Gen. 13:12,18; **Isa.** 13:20.

168. אֹהֶל *'ōhel* **masc. noun**
(tent, tabernacle as God's tent)
Gen. 4:20; 9:21,27; 12:8; 13:3,5; 18:1,2,6,9,10; 24:67; 25:27; 26:25; 31:25,33,34; 33:19; 35:21; **Ex.** 16:16; 18:7; 26:7,9,11–14,36; 27:21; 28:43; 29:4,10,11,30,32,42,44; 30:16,18,20, 26,36; 31:7; 33:7–11; 35:11,21; 36:14, 18,19,37; 38:8,30; 39:32,33,38,40; 40:2,6,7,12,19,22,24,26,29,30,32,34,35; **Lev.** 1:1,3,5; 3:2,8,13; 4:4,5,7,14,16,18; 6:16(9),26(19),30(23); 8:3,4,31,33,35; 9:5,23; 10:7,9; 12:6; 14:8,11,23; 15:14,29; 16:7,16,17,20,23,33; 17:4–6,9; 19:21; 24:3; **Num.** 1:1; 2:2,17; 3:7,8,25,38; 4:3,4,15,23,25,28,30,31,33,35,37,39,41,4 3,47; 6:10,13,18; 7:5,89; 8:9,15,19,22, 24,26; 9:15,17; 10:3; 11:10,16,24,26; 12:4,5,10; 14:10; 16:18,19,26,27,42(17:7), 43(17:8),50(17:15); 17:4(19),7(22),8(23); 18:2–4,6,21–23,31; 19:4,14,18; 20:6; 24:5; 25:6; 27:2; 31:54; **Deut.** 1:27; 5:30(27); 11:6; 16:7; 31:14,15; 33:18; **Josh.** 3:14; 7:21–24; 18:1; 19:51; 22:4,6–8; **Judg.** 4:11,17,18,20,21; 5:24; 6:5; 7:8,13; 8:11; 19:9; 20:8; **1 Sam.** 2:22; 4:10; 13:2; 17:54; **2 Sam.** 6:17; 7:6; 16:22; 18:17; 19:8(9); 20:1,22; **1 Kgs.** 1:39; 2:28–30; 8:4,66; 12:16; **2 Kgs.** 7:7,8,10; 8:21; 13:5; 14:12; **1 Chr.** 4:41; 5:10; 6:32(17); 9:19,21,23; 15:1; 16:1; 17:5; 23:32; **2 Chr.** 1:3,4,6,13; 5:5; 7:10; 10:16; 14:15(14); 24:6; 25:22; **Job** 5:24; 8:22; 11:14; 12:6; 15:34; 18:6,14,15; 19:12; 20:26; 21:28; 22:23; 29:4; 31:31;

Ps. 15:1; 19:4(5); 27:5,6; 52:5(7); 61:4(5); 69:25(26); 78:51,55,60,67; 83:6(7); 84:10(11); 91:10; 106:25; 118:15; 120:5; 132:3; **Prov.** 14:11; **Song** 1:5; **Isa.** 16:5; 33:20; 38:12; 40:22; 54:2; **Jer.** 4:20; 6:3; 10:20; 30:18; 35:7,10; 37:10; 49:29; **Lam.** 2:4; **Ezek.** 41:1; **Dan.** 11:45; **Hos.** 9:6; 12:9(10); **Hab.** 3:7; **Zech.** 12:7; **Mal.** 2:12.

169. אֹהֶל *'ōhel* **masc. proper noun**
(Ohel)
1 Chr. 3:20.

170. אָהֳלָה *'oh^olah* **fem. proper noun**
(Oholah)
Ezek. 23:4,5,36,44.

171. אָהֳלִיאָב *'oh^oliyāb* **masc. proper noun**
(Oholiab)
Ex. 31:6; 35:34; 36:1,2; 38:23.

172. אָהֳלִיבָה *'oh^oliybāh* **fem. proper noun**
(Oholibah)
Ezek. 23:4,11,22,36,44.

173. A. אָהֳלִיבָמָה *'oh^oliybāmāh* **fem. proper noun**
(Oholibamah: wife of Esau)
Gen. 36:2,5,14,18,25.
B. אָהֳלִיבָמָה *'oh^oliybāmāh* **fem. proper noun**
(Oholibamah: Edomite chief)
Gen. 36:41; **1 Chr.** 1:52.

174. אֲהָל *'ahāl* **masc. noun**
(aloe: only pl. *'^ahāliym, ^ahālôt*)
Num. 24:6; **Ps.** 45:8(9); **Prov.** 7:17; **Song** 4:14.

175. אַהֲרוֹן *'ah^arôn* **masc. proper noun**
(Aaron)
Ex. 4:14,27–30; 5:1,4,20; 6:13,20,23,25–27; 7:1,2,6–10,12,19,20; 8:5(1),6(2),8(4),12(8),16(12),17(13), 25(21); 9:8,27; 10:3,8,16; 11:10; 12:1,28,31,43,50; 15:20; 16:2,6,9,10, 33,34; 17:10,12; 18:12; 19:24; 24:1,9,14; 27:21; 28:1–4,12,29,30,35,38,40,41,43; 29:4,5,9,10,15,19–21,24,26–29,32,35,44; 30:7,8,10,19,30; 31:10; 32:1–3,5,21,22, 25,35; 34:30,31; 35:19; 38:21; 39:1, 27,41; 40:12,13,31; **Lev.** 1:5,7,8,11; 2:2,3,10; 3:2,5,8,13; 6:9(2),14(7),16(9), 18(11),20(13),25(18); 7:10,31,33–35; 8:2,6,12–14,18,22–24,27,30,31,36; 9:1,2,7–9,12,18,21–23; 10:1,3,4,6,8, 12,16,19; 11:1; 13:1,2; 14:33; 15:1; 16:1–3,6,8,9,11,21,23; 17:2; 21:1,17,21, 24; 22:2,4,18; 24:3,9; **Num.** 1:3,17,44; 2:1; 3:1–4,6,9,10,32,38,39,48,51; 4:1, 5,15–17,19,27,28,33,34,37,41,45,46; 6:23; 7:8; 8:2,3,11,13,19–22; 9:6; 10:8; 12:1,4,5,10,11; 13:26; 14:2,5,26; 15:33; 16:3,11,16–18,20,37(17:2),40–43(17:5–8), 46(17:11),47(17:12),50(17:15); 17:3(18), 6(21),8(23),10(25); 18:1,8,20,28; 19:1; 20:2,6,8,10,12,23–26,28,29; 25:7,11; 26:1,9,59,60,64; 27:13; 33:1,38,39; **Deut.** 9:20; 10:6; 32:50; **Josh.** 21:4,10, 13,19; 24:5,33; **Judg.** 20:28; **1 Sam.** 12:6,8; **1 Chr.** 6:3(5:29),49(34),50(35), 54(39),57(42); 12:27; 15:4; 23:13,28,32; 24:1,19,31; 27:17; **2 Chr.** 13:9,10; 26:18; 29:21; 31:19; 35:14; **Ezra** 7:5; **Neh.** 10:38(39); 12:47; **Ps.** 77:20(21); 99:6; 105:26; 106:16; 115:10,12; 118:3; 133:2; 135:19; **Mic.** 6:4.

176. I. אַו *'aw* **fem. noun**
(desire; only const. *'ō*)
Prov. 31:4(KJV, [Q^e] *'ey* [335]).
II. אוֹ *'ô* **conj.**
(or, rather, except)
Gen. 24:49,50,55; 31:43; 44:8,19; **Ex.** 4:11; 5:3; 19:13; 21:4,6,18,20,21, 26–29,31–33,36; 22:1(21:37),5(4),6(5), 7(6),10(9),14(13); 23:4; 28:43; 30:20; **Lev.** 1:10,14; 3:6; 4:23,28; 5:1–4,6,7,11; 6:2–5 (5:21–24); 7:16,21; 11:32; 12:6–8; 13:2, 16,19,24,29,30,38,42,43,47–49,51–53,

55–59; 14:22,30,37; 15:3,14,23,25,29; 17:3,8,13; 18:9,10; 19:20; 20:17,27; 21:18–20; 22:4,5,21,22,27,28; 25:14,47, 49; 26:41; 27:10; **Num.** 5:6,14,30; 6:2,10; 9:10,21,22; 11:8; 14:2; 15:3,5,6,8,11,14; 18:17; 19:16,18; 22:18; 24:13; 30:2(3), 6(7),10(11),14(15); 35:18,20–23; **Deut.** 4:16,32,34; 13:1(2),3(4),5(6),6(7),7(8); 14:21; 15:12,21; 17:2,3,5,6,12; 19:15; 22:1,4,6; 24:3,14; 27:22; 29:18(17); **Josh.** 7:3; **Judg.** 11:34; 18:19; 19:13; 21:22; **1 Sam.** 2:14; 13:19; 14:6; 20:2,10; 21:3(4),8(9); 22:15; 26:10; 29:3; **2 Sam.** 2:21; 3:35; 17:9; 18:13; **1 Kgs.** 8:46; 20:39; 21:6; **2 Kgs.** 2:16; 4:13; 6:27; 13:19; **2 Chr.** 6:36; **Job** 3:15,16; 12:8; 13:22; 16:3; 22:11; 35:7; 38:5,6,28,31,36; **Prov.** 30:31; 31:4([Q[e]] *'ey* [335]; NASB, NIV, see I); **Eccl.** 2:19; 11:6; **Song** 2:7,9,17; 3:5; 8:14; **Isa.** 7:11; 27:5; 41:22; 50:1; **Jer.** 23:33; 40:5; **Ezek.** 14:17,19; 21:10 (15); 46:12; **Amos** 3:12; **Mal.** 1:8; 2:17.

177. אוּאֵל *'ûēl* **masc. proper noun**
(Uel)
Ezra 10:34.

178. I. אוֹב *'ôḇ* **masc. noun**
(wineskin)
Job 32:19.
II. אוֹב *'ôḇ* **masc. noun**
(necromancer, prophesying spirit of the dead)
Lev. 19:31; 20:6,27; **Deut.** 18:11; **1 Sam.** 28:3,7–9; **2 Kgs.** 21:6; 23:24; **1 Chr.** 10:13; **2 Chr.** 33:6; **Isa.** 8:19; 19:3; 29:4.

179. אוֹבִיל *'ôḇiyl* **masc. proper noun**
(Obil)
1 Chr. 27:30.

180. אוּבָל *'ûḇāl,* אֻבָל *'uḇāl* **masc. noun**
(river, canal)
Dan. 8:2,3,6.

181. אוּד *'ûḏ* **masc. noun**
(firebrand, piece of firewood)
Isa. 7:4; **Amos** 4:11; **Zech.** 3:2.

182. אוֹדוֹת *'ôḏôt,* אֹדוֹת *'ōḏôt* **fem. noun**
(cause, reason: only pl. *'ōḏôṯ*)
Gen. 21:11,25; 26:32; **Ex.** 18:8; **Num.** 12:1; 13:24; **Josh.** 14:6; **Judg.** 6:7; **2 Sam.** 13:16; **Jer.** 3:8.

183. אָוָה *'āwāh* **verb**
(to crave, to desire)
Num. 11:4,34; **Deut.** 5:21(18); 12:20; 14:26; **1 Sam.** 2:16; **2 Sam.** 3:21; 23:15; **1 Kgs.** 11:37; **1 Chr.** 11:17; **Job** 23:13; **Ps.** 45:11(12); 106:14; 132:13,14; **Prov.** 13:4; 21:10,26; 23:3,6; 24:1; **Eccl.** 6:2; **Isa.** 26:9; **Jer.** 17:16; **Amos** 5:18; **Mic.** 7:1.

184. אָוָה *'āwāh* **verb**
(to mark out, to draw)
Num. 34:10.

185. אַוָּה *'awwāh* **fem. noun**
(a desire, something one lusts after)
Deut. 12:15,20,21; 18:6; **1 Sam.** 23:20; **Jer.** 2:24; **Hos.** 10:10.

186. אוּזַי *'ûzay* **masc. proper noun**
(Uzai)
Neh. 3:25.

187. אוּזָל *'ûzāl* **masc. proper noun**
(Uzal)
Gen. 10:27; **1 Chr.** 1:21.

188. אוֹי *'ôy* **interj.**
(woe! alas!)
Num. 21:29; 24:23; **1 Sam.** 4:7,8; **Ps.** 120:5(see *'ôyāh* [190]); **Prov.** 23:29; **Isa.** 3:9,11; 6:5; 24:16; **Jer.** 4:13,31; 6:4; 10:19; 13:27; 15:10; 45:3; 48:46; **Lam.** 5:16; **Ezek.** 16:23; 24:6,9; **Hos.** 7:13; 9:12.

189. אֱוִי *'ᵉwiy* **masc. proper noun**
(Evi)
Num. 31:8; **Josh.** 13:21.

190. אוֹיָה *'ôyāh* **interj.**
(woe! alas!: poetic form of *'ôy* [188])
Ps. 120:5.

191. אֱוִיל *'ᵉwiyl* **adj.**
(foolish, one who despises wisdom and morality)
Job 5:2,3; **Ps.** 107:17; **Prov.** 1:7; 7:22; 10:8,10,14,21; 11:29; 12:15,16; 14:3,9; 15:5; 16:22; 17:28; 20:3; 24:7; 27:3,22; 29:9; **Isa.** 19:11; 35:8; **Jer.** 4:22; **Hos.** 9:7.

192. אֱוִיל מְרֹדַךְ *'ᵉwiyl mᵉrōdak̲* **masc. proper noun**
(Evil-Merodach)
2 Kgs. 25:27; **Jer.** 52:31.

193. I. אוּל *'ûl* **masc. noun**
(belly, body, strength)
Ps. 73:4.
II. אוּל *'ûl* **masc. noun**
(leader, noble)
2 Kgs. 24:15(NIV, [Qᵉ] *'ayil* [352,III]).

194. אוּלַי *'ûlay*, אֻלַי *'ulay* **adv.**
(perhaps, peradventure)
Gen. 16:2; 18:24,28–32; 24:5,39; 27:12; 32:20(21); 43:12; **Ex.** 32:30; **Num.** 22:6,11,33; 23:3,27; **Josh.** 9:7; 14:12; **1 Sam.** 6:5; 9:6; 14:6; **2 Sam.** 14:15; 16:12; **1 Kgs.** 18:5,27; 20:31; **2 Kgs.** 19:4; **Job** 1:5; **Isa.** 37:4; 47:12; **Jer.** 20:10; 21:2; 26:3; 36:3,7; 51:8; **Lam.** 3:29; **Ezek.** 12:3; **Hos.** 8:7; **Amos** 5:15; **Jon.** 1:6; **Zeph.** 2:3.

195. אוּלַי *'ûlay* **proper noun**
(Ulai)
Dan. 8:2,16.

196. אֱוִלִי *'ᵉwiliy* **adj.**
(foolish)
Zech. 11:15.

197. אוּלָם *'ûlām* **masc. noun**
(porch, portico)
1 Kgs. 6:3; 7:6–8,12,19,21; **1 Chr.** 28:11; **2 Chr.** 3:4; 8:12; 15:8; 29:7,17; **Ezek.** 8:16; 40:7–9,15,39,40,48,49; 41:15,25,26; 44:3; 46:2,8; **Joel** 2:17.

198. A. אוּלָם *'ûlām* **masc. proper noun**
(Ulam: son of Sheresh)
1 Chr. 7:16,17.
B. אוּלָם *'ûlām* **masc. proper noun**
(Ulam: son of Eshek)
1 Chr. 8:39,40.

199. אוּלָם *'ûlām* **conj.**
(but, however)
Gen. 28:19; 48:19; **Ex.** 9:16; **Num.** 14:21; **Judg.** 18:29; **1 Sam.** 20:3; 25:34; **1 Kgs.** 20:23; **Job** 1:11; 2:5; 5:8; 11:5; 12:7; 13:3,4; 14:18; 17:10; 33:1; **Mic.** 3:8.

200. אִוֶּלֶת *'iwwelet̲* **fem. noun**
(foolishness, folly)
Ps. 38:5(6); 69:5(6); **Prov.** 5:23; 12:23; 13:16; 14:1,8,17,18,24,29; 15:2,14,21; 16:22; 17:12; 18:13; 19:3; 22:15; 24:9; 26:4,5,11; 27:22.

201. אוֹמָר *'ômār* **masc. proper noun**
(Omar)
Gen. 36:11,15; **1 Chr.** 1:36.

202. אוֹן *'ôn* **masc. noun**
(strength, manhood)
Gen. 49:3; **Deut.** 21:17; **Job** 18:7,12; 20:10; 40:16; **Ps.** 78:51; 105:36; **Isa.** 40:26,29; **Hos.** 12:3(4),8(9).

203. אוֹן *'ôn* **masc. proper noun**
(On: son of Peleth)
Num. 16:1.

204. אוֹן *'ôn* **proper noun**
(On: a city in Egypt)
Gen. 41:45,50; 46:20; **Ezek.** 30:17 (see *'āwen* [206,A]).

205. אָוֶן *'āwen* **masc. noun**
(wickedness, evil, misfortune)
Num. 23:21; **Deut.** 26:14; **1 Sam.** 15:23; **Job** 4:8; 5:6; 11:11,14; 15:35; 21:19; 22:15; 31:3; 34:8,22,36; 36:10,21; **Ps.** 5:5(6); 6:8(9); 7:14(15); 10:7; 14:4; 28:3; 36:3(4),4(5),12(13); 41:6(7); 53:4(5); 55:3(4),10(11); 56:7(8); 59:2(3),5(6); 64:2(3); 66:18; 90:10; 92:7(8),9(10); 94:4,16,23; 101:8; 119:133; 125:5; 141:4,9; **Prov.** 6:12,18; 10:29; 11:7; 12:21; 17:4; 19:28; 21:15; 22:8; 30:20; **Isa.** 1:13; 10:1; 29:20; 31:2; 32:6; 41:29; 55:7; 58:9; 59:4,6,7; 66:3; **Jer.** 4:14,15; **Ezek.** 11:2; **Hos.** 6:8; 9:4; 10:8(KJV, NASB, *'āwen* [206,B]); 12:11(12); **Amos** 5:5; **Mic.** 2:1; **Hab.** 1:3; 3:7; **Zech.** 10:2.

206. A. אָוֶן *'āwen* **proper noun**
(Aven: another form of *'ôn* [204])
Ezek. 30:17.
B. אָוֶן *'āwen* **proper noun**
(Aven: shortened form of *bēyṯ 'āwen* [1007])
Hos. 10:8(NIV, *'āwen* [205]).
C. אָוֶן *'āwen* **proper noun**
(Aven: town in the kingdom of Damascus)
Amos 1:5.

207. אוֹנוֹ *'ônô* **proper noun**
(Ono)
1 Chr. 8:12; **Ezra** 2:33; **Neh.** 6:2; 7:37; 11:35.

208. A. אוֹנָם *'ônām* **masc. proper noun**
(Onam: son of Shobal)
Gen. 36:23; **1 Chr.** 1:40.
B. אוֹנָם *'ônām* **masc. proper noun**
(Onam: son of Jerahmeel)
1 Chr. 2:26,28.

209. אוֹנָן *'ônān* **masc. proper noun**
(Onan)
Gen. 38:4,8,9; 46:12; **Num.** 26:19; **1 Chr.** 2:3.

210. אוּפָז *'ûp̱āz* **proper noun**
(Uphaz)
Jer. 10:9; **Dan.** 10:5.

211. A. אוֹפִיר *'ôp̱iyr* **proper noun**
(Ophir: territory in S. Arabia)
1 Kgs. 9:28; 10:11; 22:48(49); **1 Chr.** 29:4; **2 Chr.** 8:18; 9:10; **Job** 22:24; 28:16; **Ps.** 45:9(10); **Isa.** 13:12.
B. אוֹפִיר *'ôp̱iyr* **masc. proper noun**
(Ophir: son of Joktan)
Gen. 10:29; **1 Chr.** 1:23.

212. אוֹפָן *'ôp̱ān* **masc. noun**
(wheel)
Ex. 14:25; **1 Kgs.** 7:30,32,33; **Prov.** 20:26; **Isa.** 28:27; **Ezek.** 1:15,16,19–21; 3:13; 10:6,9,10,12,13,16,19; 11:22; **Nah.** 3:2.

213. אוּץ *'ûṣ* **verb**
(to hasten, to urge)
Gen. 19:15; **Ex.** 5:13; **Josh.** 10:13; 17:15; **Prov.** 19:2; 21:5; 28:20; 29:20; **Isa.** 22:4; **Jer.** 17:16.

214. אוֹצָר *'ôṣār* **masc. noun**
(treasure, storehouse)
Deut. 28:12; 32:34; **Josh.** 6:19,24; **1 Kgs.** 7:51; 14:26; 15:18; **2 Kgs.** 12:18(19); 14:14; 16:8; 18:15; 20:13,15; 24:13; **1 Chr.** 9:26; 26:20,22,24,26; 27:25,27,28; 28:12; 29:8; **2 Chr.** 5:1; 8:15; 11:11; 12:9; 16:2; 25:24; 32:27; 36:18; **Ezra** 2:69; **Neh.** 7:70,71; 10:38(39); 12:44; 13:12,13; **Job** 38:22; **Ps.** 33:7; 135:7; **Prov.** 8:21; 10:2; 15:16; 21:6,20; **Isa.** 2:7; 30:6; 33:6; 39:2,4; 45:3; **Jer.** 10:13; 15:13; 17:3; 20:5; 38:11; 48:7; 49:4; 50:25,37; 51:13,16; **Ezek.** 28:4; **Dan.** 1:2; **Hos.** 13:15; **Joel** 1:17; **Mic.** 6:10; **Mal.** 3:10.

215. אוֹר *'ôr* **verb**
(to give light, to shine)
Gen. 1:15,17; 44:3; **Ex.** 13:21; 14:20; 25:37; **Num.** 6:25; 8:2; **1 Sam.**

14:27([K^{e}] *rā'āh* [7200]),29; 29:10(KJV, NASB, *'ôr* [216]); **2 Sam.** 2:32; **Ezra** 9:8; **Neh.** 9:12,19; **Job** 33:30; 41:32(24); **Ps.** 13:3(4); 18:28(29); 19:8(9); 31:16(17); 67:1(2); 76:4(5); 77:18(19); 80:3(4),7(8),19(20); 97:4; 105:39; 118:27; 119:130,135; 139:12; **Prov.** 4:18; 29:13; **Eccl.** 8:1; **Isa.** 27:11; 60:1,19; **Ezek.** 32:7; 43:2; **Dan.** 9:17; **Mal.** 1:10.

216. אוֹר *'ôr* **masc. noun**
(light, daylight)
Gen. 1:3–5,18; **Ex.** 10:23; **Judg.** 16:2; 19:26; **1 Sam.** 14:36; 19:10(NIV, *'ôr* [215]); 25:34,36; **2 Sam.** 17:22; 23:4; **2 Kgs.** 7:9; **Neh.** 8:3; **Job** 3:9,16,20; 12:22,25; 17:12; 18:5,6,18; 22:28; 24:13,14,16; 25:3; 26:10; 28:11; 29:3,24; 30:26; 31:26; 33:28,30; 36:30,32; 37:3, 11,15,21; 38:15,19,24; 41:18(10); **Ps.** 4:6(7); 27:1; 36:9(10); 37:6; 38:10(11); 43:3; 44:3(4); 49:19(20); 56:13(14); 78:14; 89:15(16); 97:11; 104:2; 112:4; 119:105; 136:7; 139:11; 148:3; **Prov.** 4:18; 6:23; 13:9; 16:15; **Eccl.** 2:13; 11:7; 12:2; **Isa.** 2:5; 5:20,30; 9:2(1); 10:17; 13:10; 18:4; 30:26; 42:6,16; 45:7; 49:6; 51:4; 58:8,10; 59:9; 60:1,3,19,20; **Jer.** 4:23; 13:16; 25:10; 31:35; **Lam.** 3:2; **Ezek.** 32:7,8; **Hos.** 6:5; **Amos** 5:18,20; 8:9; **Mic.** 2:1; 7:8,9; **Hab.** 3:4,11; **Zeph.** 3:5; **Zech.** 14:6,7.

217. אוּר *'ûr* **masc. noun**
(fire, flame, firelight)
Isa. 24:15; 31:9; 44:16; 47:14; 50:11; **Ezek.** 5:2.

218. A. אוּר *'ûr* **proper noun**
(Ur of the Chaldees)
Gen. 11:28,31; 15:7; **Neh.** 9:7.
B. אוּר *'ûr* **masc. proper noun**
(Ur: father of one of David's mighty men)
1 Chr. 11:35.

219. I. אוֹרָה *'ôrāh* **fem. noun**
(light, dawn, radiant joy)
Esth. 8:16; **Ps.** 139:12; **Isa.** 26:19 (KJV, see II).
II. אוֹרָה *'ôrāh* **fem. noun**
(herb, mallow)
2 Kgs. 4:39; **Isa.** 26:19(NASB, NIV, see I).

220. אֲוֵרוֹת *'ᵃwērôṯ* **fem. pl. noun**
(stalls, pens; NASB, NIV, spelling variant of *'urwāh* [723])
2 Chr. 32:28(NASB, NIV, *'urwāh* [723]).

221. A. אוּרִי *'ûriy* **masc. proper noun**
(Uri: father of Bezaleel)
Ex. 31:2; 35:30; 38:22; **1 Chr.** 2:20; **2 Chr.** 1:5.
B. אוּרִי *'ûriy* **masc. proper noun**
(Uri: father of Geber)
1 Kgs. 4:19.
C. אוּרִי *'ûriy* **masc. proper noun**
(Uri: a gatekeeper)
Ezra 10:24.

222. A. אוּרִיאֵל *'ûriyēl* **masc. proper noun**
(Uriel: Levite under David)
1 Chr. 15:5,11.
B. אוּרִיאֵל *'ûriyēl* **masc. proper noun**
(Uriel: a Levite)
1 Chr. 6:24(9).
C. אוּרִיאֵל *'ûriyēl* **masc. proper noun**
(Uriel: grandfather of Abijah)
2 Chr. 13:2.

223. A. אוּרִיָּה *'ûriyyah* **masc. proper noun**
(Uriah: husband of Bathsheba)
2 Sam. 11:3,6–12,14–17,21,24,26; 12:9,10,15; 23:39; **1 Kgs.** 15:5; **1 Chr.** 11:41.
B. אוּרִיָּה *'ûriyyah* **masc. proper noun**
(Uriah: high priest in Ahaz's reign)
2 Kgs. 16:10,11,15,16; **Isa.** 8:2.
C. אוּרִיָּה *'ûriyyah* **masc. proper noun**

(Uriah: a prophet)
Jer. 26:20,21,23.
D. אוּרִיָּה *'ûriyyah* **masc. proper noun**
(Uriah: a priest, father of Meremoth)
Ezra 8:33; **Neh.** 3:4,21.
E. אוּרִיָּה *'ûriyyah* **masc. proper noun**
(Uriah: Jewish leader; possibly same as D)
Neh. 8:4.

224. אוּרִים *'ûriym* **masc. noun**
(Urim [lit. "lights," pl. of 217]; part of the high priest's breastplate)
Ex. 28:30; **Lev.** 8:8; **Num.** 27:21; **Deut.** 33:8; **1 Sam.** 28:6; **Ezra** 2:63; **Neh.** 7:65.

225. אוּת *'ût* **verb**
(to consent, to agree)
Gen. 34:15,22,23; **2 Kgs.** 12:8(9).

226. אוֹת *'ôt* **masc./fem. noun**
(sign, token)
Gen. 1:14; 4:15; 9:12,13,17; 17:11; **Ex.** 3:12; 4:8,9,17,28,30; 7:3; 8:23(19); 10:1,2; 12:13; 13:9,16; 31:13,17; **Num.** 2:2; 14:11,22; 16:38(17:3); 17:10(25); **Deut.** 4:34; 6:8,22; 7:19; 11:3,18; 13:1(2),2(3); 26:8; 28:46; 29:3(2); 34:11; **Josh.** 2:12; 4:6; 24:17; **Judg.** 6:17; **1 Sam.** 2:34; 10:7,9; 14:10; **2 Kgs.** 19:29; 20:8,9; **Neh.** 9:10; **Job** 21:29; **Ps.** 65:8(9); 74:4,9; 78:43; 86:17; 105:27; 135:9; **Isa.** 7:11,14; 8:18; 19:20; 20:3; 37:30; 38:7,22; 44:25; 55:13; 66:19; **Jer.** 10:2; 32:20,21; 44:29; **Ezek.** 4:3; 14:8; 20:12,20.

227. A. אָז *'āz* **adv.**
(then)
Gen. 4:26; 12:6; 13:7; 24:41; 49:4; **Ex.** 4:26; 12:44,48; 15:1,15; **Lev.** 26:34,41; **Num.** 21:17; **Deut.** 4:41; 29:20(19); **Josh.** 1:8; 8:30; 10:12,33; 14:11; 20:6; 22:1,31; **Judg.** 5:8,11,13,19,22; 8:3; 13:21; **1 Sam.** 6:3; 20:12; **2 Sam.** 2:27; 5:24; 19:6(7); 21:17,18; 23:14; **1 Kgs.** 3:16; 8:1,12; 9:11,24; 11:7; 16:21; 22:49(50); **2 Kgs.** 5:3; 8:22; 12:17(18); 13:19; 14:8; 15:16; 16:5; **1 Chr.** 11:16; 14:15; 15:2; 16:7,33; 20:4; 22:13; **2 Chr.** 5:2; 6:1; 8:12,17; 21:10; 24:17; **Job** 3:13; 9:31; 11:15; 13:20; 22:26; 28:27; 33:16; 38:21; **Ps.** 2:5; 19:13(14); 40:7(8); 51:19(21); 56:9(10); 69:4(5); 89:19(20); 96:12; 119:6,92; 126:2; **Prov.** 1:28; 2:5,9; 3:23; 20:14; **Eccl.** 2:15; **Song** 8:10; **Isa.** 33:23; 35:5,6; 41:1; 58:8,9,14; 60:5; **Jer.** 11:15,18; 22:15,16,22; 31:13; 32:2; 44:18; **Ezek.** 32:14; **Hos.** 2:7(9); **Mic.** 3:4; **Hab.** 1:11; **Zeph.** 3:9,11; **Mal.** 3:16.
B. מֵאָז *mē'āz* **adv.**
(then, since: with the prefix *min* [4480])
Gen. 39:5; **Ex.** 4:10; 5:23; 9:24; **Josh.** 14:10; **Ruth** 2:7; **2 Sam.** 15:34; **Ps.** 76:7(8); 93:2; **Prov.** 8:22; **Isa.** 14:8; 16:13; 44:8; 45:21; 48:3,5,7,8.

228. אֲזָא *'azā'*, אֲזָה *'azāh* **Aram. verb**
(to make hot, to heat)
Dan. 3:19,22.

229. אֶזְבַּי *'ezbay* **masc. proper noun**
(Ezbai)
1 Chr. 11:37.

230. אֲזַד *'azād* **Aram. verb**
(to be gone)
Dan. 2:5,8.

231. אֵזוֹב *'ēzôb* **masc. noun**
(hyssop)
Ex. 12:22; **Lev.** 14:4,6,49,51,52; **Num.** 19:6,18; **1 Kgs.** 4:33(5:13); **Ps.** 51:7(9).

232. אֵזוֹר *'ēzôr* **masc. noun**
(girdle, belt)

2 Kgs. 1:8; **Job** 12:18; **Isa.** 5:27; 11:5; **Jer.** 13:1,2,4,6,7,10,11; **Ezek.** 23:15.

233. אֲזַי *'ᵃzay* **adv.**
(then, in that case)
Ps. 124:3–5.

234. אַזְכָּרָה *'azkārāh* **fem. noun**
(memorial portion, offering)
Lev. 2:2,9,16; 5:12; 6:15(8); 24:7; **Num.** 5:26.

235. אָזַל *'āzal* **verb**
(to go away, to fail)
Deut. 32:36; **1 Sam.** 9:7; **Job** 14:11; **Prov.** 20:14; **Jer.** 2:36; **Ezek.** 27:19.

236. אֲזַל *'ᵃzal* **Aram. verb**
(to go up, to go away; corr. to Hebr. 235)
Ezra 4:23; 5:8,15; **Dan.** 2:17,24; 6:18(19),19(20).

237. אֶזֶל *'ezel* **proper noun**
(Ezel)
1 Sam. 20:19.

238. אָזַן *'āzan* **verb**
(to hear, to listen)
Gen. 4:23; **Ex.** 15:26; **Num.** 23:18; **Deut.** 1:45; 32:1; **Judg.** 5:3; **2 Chr.** 24:19; **Neh.** 9:30; **Job** 9:16; 32:11; 33:1; 34:2,16; 37:14; **Ps.** 5:1(2); 17:1; 39:12(13); 49:1(2); 54:2(4); 55:1(2); 77:1(2); 78:1; 80:1(2); 84:8(9); 86:6; 135:17; 140:6(7); 141:1; 143:1; **Prov.** 17:4; **Isa.** 1:2,10; 8:9; 28:23; 32:9; 42:23; 51:4; 64:4(3); **Eccl.** 12:9(NASB, NIV, *'āzan* [239]); **Jer.** 13:15; **Hos.** 5:1; **Joel** 1:2.

239. אָזַן *'āzan* **verb**
(to ponder, to consider)
Eccl. 12:9(KJV, *'āzan* [238]).

240. אָזֵן *'āzēn* **masc. noun**
(tool, weapon)
Deut. 23:13(14).

241. אֹזֶן *'ōzen* **masc. fem. noun**
(ear)
Gen. 20:8; 23:10,13,16; 35:4; 44:18; 50:4; **Ex.** 10:2; 11:2; 17:14; 21:6; 24:7; 29:20; 32:2,3; **Lev.** 8:23,24; 14:14,17, 25,28; **Num.** 11:1,18; 14:28; **Deut.** 5:1; 15:17; 29:4(3); 31:11,28,30; 32:44; **Josh.** 20:4; **Judg.** 7:3; 9:2,3; 17:2; **Ruth** 4:4; **1 Sam.** 3:11; 8:21; 9:15; 11:4; 15:14; 18:23; 20:2,12,13; 22:8,17; 25:24; **2 Sam.** 3:19; 7:22,27; 18:12; 22:7,45; **2 Kgs.** 18:26; 19:16,28; 21:12; 23:2; **1 Chr.** 17:20,25; 28:8; **2 Chr.** 6:40; 7:15; 34:30; **Neh.** 1:6,11; 8:3; 13:1; **Job** 4:12; 12:11; 13:1,17; 15:21; 28:22; 29:11; 33:8,16; 34:3; 36:10,15; 42:5; **Ps.** 10:17; 17:6; 18:6(7),44(45); 31:2(3); 34:15(16); 40:6(7); 44:1(2); 45:10(11); 49:4(5); 58:4(5); 71:2; 78:1; 86:1; 88:2(3); 92:11(12); 94:9; 102:2(3); 115:6; 116:2; 130:2; 135:17; **Prov.** 2:2; 4:20; 5:1,13; 15:31; 18:15; 20:12; 21:13; 22:17; 23:9,12; 25:12; 26:17; 28:9; **Eccl.** 1:8; **Isa.** 5:9; 6:10; 11:3; 22:14; 30:21; 32:3; 33:15; 35:5; 36:11; 37:17,29; 42:20; 43:8; 48:8; 49:20; 50:4,5; 55:3; 59:1; **Jer.** 2:2; 5:21; 6:10; 7:24,26; 9:20(19); 11:8; 17:23; 19:3; 25:4; 26:11,15; 28:7; 29:29; 34:14; 35:15; 36:6,10,13–15,20,21; 44:5; **Lam.** 3:56; **Ezek.** 3:10; 8:18; 9:1,5; 10:13; 12:2; 16:12; 23:25; 24:26; 40:4; 44:5; **Dan.** 9:18; **Amos** 3:12; **Mic.** 7:16; **Zech.** 7:11.

242. אֻזֵּן שֶׁאֱרָה *'uzzēn šeʾᵉrāh* **proper noun**
(Uzzen Sheerah)
1 Chr. 7:24.

243. אַזְנוֹת תָּבוֹר *'aznôṯ tāḇôr* **proper noun**
(Aznoth Tabor)
Josh. 19:34.

244. אָזְנִי *'ozniy* **masc. proper noun**
(Ozni, descendent of Ozni)
Num. 26:16.

245. אֲזַנְיָה *'azanyāh* **masc. proper noun**
(Azaniah)
Neh. 10:9(10).

246. אֲזֵק *'azēq* **masc. noun**
(chain)
Jer. 40:1,4.

247. אָזַר *'āzar* **verb**
(to gird up, to arm)
1 Sam. 2:4; **2 Sam.** 22:40; **2 Kgs.** 1:8; **Job** 30:18; 38:3; 40:7; **Ps.** 18:32(33), 39(40); 30:11(12); 65:6(7); 93:1; **Isa.** 8:9; 45:5; 50:11; **Jer.** 1:17.

248. אֶזְרוֹעַ *'ezrôa'* **fem. noun**
(arm)
Job 31:22; **Jer.** 32:21.

249. אֶזְרָח *'ezrāḥ* **masc. noun**
(to be born as a native of a land)
Ex. 12:19,48,49; **Lev.** 16:29; 17:15; 18:26; 19:34; 23:42; 24:16,22; **Num.** 9:14; 15:13,29,30; **Josh.** 8:33; **Ps.** 37:35; **Ezek.** 47:22.

250. אֶזְרָחִי *'ezrāḥiy* **masc. proper noun**
(Ezrahite)
1 Kgs. 4:31(5:11); **Ps.** 88:[title](1); 89:[title](1).

251. אָח *'āḥ* **masc. noun**
(brother)
Gen. 4:2,8–11,21; 9:5,22,25; 10:21,25; 12:5; 13:8,11; 14:12–14,16; 16:12; 19:7; 20:5,13,16; 22:20,21,23; 24:15,27,29,48, 53,55; 25:18,26; 26:31; 27:6,11,23,29, 30,35,37,40–45; 28:2,5; 29:4,10,12,15; 31:23,25,32,37,46,54; 32:3(4),6(7), 11(12),13(14),17(18); 33:3,9; 34:11,25; 35:1,7; 36:6; 37:2,4,5,8–14,16,17,19, 23,26,27,30; 38:1,8,9,11,29,30; 42:3,4, 6–8,13,15,16,19–21,28,32–34,38; 43:3–7,13,14,29,30; 44:14,19,20,23, 26,33; 45:1,3,4,12,14–17,24; 46:31; 47:1–3,5,6,11,12; 48:6,19,22; 49:5,8,26; 50:8,14,15,17,18,24; **Ex.** 1:6; 2:11; 4:14, 18; 7:1,2; 10:23; 16:15; 25:20; 28:1,2, 4,41; 32:27,29; 37:9; **Lev.** 7:10; 10:4,6; 16:2; 18:14,16; 19:17; 20:21; 21:2,10; 25:14,25,35,36,39,46–48; 26:37; **Num.** 6:7; 8:26; 14:4; 16:10; 18:2,6; 20:3,8,14; 25:6; 27:4,7,9–11,13; 32:6; 36:2; **Deut.** 1:16,28; 2:4,8; 3:18,20; 10:9; 13:6(7); 15:2,3,7,9,11,12; 17:15,20; 18:2,7,15,18; 19:18,19; 20:8; 22:1–4; 23:7(8),19(20), 20(21); 24:7,14; 25:3,5–7,9,11; 28:54; 32:50; 33:9,16,24; **Josh.** 1:14,15; 2:13,18; 6:23; 14:8; 15:17; 17:4; 22:3,4,7,8; **Judg.** 1:3,13,17; 3:9; 8:19; 9:1,3,5,18,21,24,26,31,41,56; 11:3; 14:3; 16:31; 18:8,14; 19:23; 20:13,23,28; 21:6,22; **Ruth** 4:3,10; **1 Sam.** 14:3; 16:13; 17:17,18,22,28; 20:29; 22:1; 26:6; 30:23; **2 Sam.** 1:26; 2:22,26,27; 3:8,27,30; 4:6,9; 10:10; 13:3,4,7,8,10,12,20,26,32; 14:7; 15:20; 18:2; 19:12(13),41(42); 20:9,10; 21:21; 23:18,24; **1 Kgs.** 1:9,10; 2:7,15,21,22; 9:13; 12:24; 13:30; 20:32,33; **2 Kgs.** 7:6; 9:2; 10:13; 23:9; **1 Chr.** 1:19; 2:32,42; 4:9,11,27; 5:2,7,13; 6:39(24),44(29),48(33); 7:5,16,22,35; 8:32,39; 9:6,9,13,17,19,25,32,38; 11:20, 26,38,45; 12:2,29,32,39; 13:2; 15:5–10, 12,16–18; 16:7,37–39; 19:11,15; 20:5,7; 23:22,32; 24:25,31; 25:7,9–31; 26:7–9, 11,12,22,25,26,28,30,32; 27:7,18; 28:2; **2 Chr.** 5:12; 11:4,22; 19:10; 21:2,4,13; 22:8; 28:8,11,15; 29:15,34; 30:7,9; 31:12, 13,15; 35:5,6,9,15; 36:4,10; **Ezra** 3:2,8,9; 6:20; 8:17–19,24; 10:18; **Neh.** 1:2; 3:1, 18; 4:2(3:34),14(8),19(13),23(17); 5:1, 5,7,8,10,14; 7:2; 10:10(11),29(30); 11:12–14,17,19; 12:7–9,24,36; 13:13; **Esth.** 10:3; **Job** 1:13,18; 6:15; 19:13; 22:6; 30:29; 41:17(9); 42:11,15; **Ps.** 22:22(23); 35:14; 49:7(8); 50:20; 69:8(9); 122:8; 133:1; **Prov.** 6:19; 17:2,17; 18:9, 19,24; 19:7; 27:10; **Eccl.** 4:8; **Song** 8:1; **Isa.** 3:6; 9:19(18); 19:2; 41:6; 66:5,20; **Jer.** 7:15; 9:4(3); 12:6; 13:14; 22:18; 23:35; 25:26; 29:16; 31:34; 34:9,14,17;

35:3; 41:8; 49:10; **Ezek.** 4:17; 11:15; 18:10,18; 24:23; 33:30; 38:21; 44:25; 47:14; **Hos.** 2:1(3); 12:3(4); 13:15; **Joel** 2:8; **Amos** 1:9,11; **Obad.** 1:10,12; **Mic.** 5:3(2); 7:2; **Hag.** 2:22; **Zech.** 7:9,10; **Mal.** 1:2; 2:10.

252. אַח *'aḥ* **Aram. masc. noun**
(brother; corr. to Hebr. 251)
Ezra 7:18.

253. אָהּ *'āh* **interj.**
(alas! oh!)
Ezek. 6:11; 21:15(20).

254. אָח *'aḥ* **fem. noun**
(firepot, brazier)
Jer. 36:22,23.

255. אֹחַ *'ōaḥ* **masc. noun**
(jackal, owl)
Isa. 13:21.

256. A. אַחְאָב *'aḥ'āḇ* **masc. proper noun**
(Ahab: son of Omri)
1 Kgs. 16:28–30,33; 17:1; 18:1–3,5,6,9,12,16,17,20,41,42,44–46; 19:1; 20:2,13,14; 21:1–4,8,15,16,18,20, 21,24,25,27,29; 22:20,39–41,49(50), 51(52); **2 Kgs.** 1:1; 3:1,5; 8:16,18,25, 27–29; 9:7–9,25,29; 10:1,10,11,17,18,30; 21:3,13; **2 Chr.** 18:1–3,19; 21:6,13; 22:3–8; **Mic.** 6:16.
B. אַחְאָב *'aḥ'āḇ* **masc. proper noun**
(Ahab: a false prophet)
Jer. 29:21,22.

257. אַחְבָּן *'aḥbān* **masc. proper noun**
(Ahban)
1 Chr. 2:29.

258. אָחַד *'āḥad* **verb**
(to go one way or another)
Ezek. 21:16(21)(NASB, NIV, *ḥāḏaḏ* [2300,I]).

259. אֶחָד *'eḥāḏ* **adj.**
(one, first)
Gen. 1:5,9; 2:11,21,24; 3:22; 4:19; 8:5,13; 10:25; 11:1,6; 19:9; 21:15; 22:2; 26:10; 27:38,44,45; 29:20; 32:8(9),22(23); 33:13; 34:16,22; 37:9,20; 40:5; 41:5,11, 22,25,26; 42:11,13,16,19,27,32,33; 44:28; 48:22; 49:16; **Ex.** 1:15; 8:31(27); 9:6,7; 10:19; 11:1; 12:18,46,49; 14:28; 16:22,33; 17:12; 18:3,4; 23:29; 24:3; 25:12,19,32,33,36; 26:2,4–6,8,10,11, 16,17,19,21,24–26; 27:9; 28:10,17; 29:1,3,15,23,39,40; 30:10; 33:5; 36:9–13, 15,18,21,22,24,26,29–31; 37:3,8,18, 19,22; 39:10; 40:2,17; **Lev.** 4:2,13,22,27; 5:4,5,7,13,17; 6:3(5:22),7(5:26); 7:7,14; 8:26; 12:8; 13:2; 14:5,10,12,21,22,30, 31,50; 15:15,30; 16:5,8,34; 22:28; 23:18,19,24; 24:5,22; 25:48; 26:26; **Num.** 1:1,18,41,44; 2:16,28; 6:11,14,19; 7:3,11,13–16,19–22,25–28,31–34,37–40, 43–46,49–52,55–58,61–64,67–70,73–76, 79–82,85; 8:12; 9:14; 10:4; 11:19,26; 13:2,23; 14:15; 15:5,11,12,15,16,24, 27,29; 16:15,22; 17:3(18),6(21); 28:4,7, 11–13,15,19,21,22,27–30; 29:1,2,4,5, 8–11,14–16,19,22,25,28,31,34,36,38; 31:28,30,34,39,47; 33:38; 34:18; 35:30; 36:3,8; **Deut.** 1:2,3,23; 4:42; 6:4; 12:14; 13:12(13); 15:7; 16:5; 17:2,6; 18:6; 19:5, 11,15; 21:15; 23:16(17); 24:5; 25:5,11; 28:7,25,55; 32:30; **Josh.** 3:12,13,16; 4:2,4,5; 6:3,11,14; 7:21; 9:2; 10:2,42; 12:9–24; 15:51; 17:14,17; 20:4; 22:14,20; 23:10,14; **Judg.** 4:16; 6:16; 8:18; 9:2,5, 18,37,53; 13:2; 15:4; 16:7,11,28,29; 17:5,11; 18:19; 19:13; 20:1,8,11,31; 21:3, 6,8; **Ruth** 1:4; 2:13; **1 Sam.** 1:1,2,5,24; 2:34,36; 6:4,7,12,17; 7:9,12; 9:3,15; 10:3; 11:7; 13:17,18; 14:4,5,40; 16:18,20; 17:36; 22:20; 24:14(15); 25:14; 26:8,15,20,22; 27:1,5; **2 Sam.** 1:15; 2:1,18,21,25; 3:13; 4:2; 6:19,20; 7:7,23; 9:11; 12:1,3; 13:13,30; 14:6,27; 15:2; 17:9,12,22; 18:10,11; 19:14(15); 23:8; 24:12; **1 Kgs.** 2:16,20; 3:17,25; 4:7,19,22(5:2); 6:24–27,34,38; 7:15–18,27,30,32,34,

37,38,42,44; 8:56; 10:14,16,17,22; 11:13,32,36; 12:29,30; 13:11; 14:21; 15:10; 16:23; 18:6,23,25; 19:2,4,5; 20:13,29,35; 22:8,9,13; **2 Kgs.** 2:16; 3:11; 4:1,22,35,39; 6:2,3,5,10,12; 7:8,13; 8:6,26; 9:1,29; 12:9(10); 14:23; 15:20; 17:27,28; 18:24; 22:1; 23:36; 24:18; 25:16,17,19; **1 Chr.** 1:19; 11:11; 12:14,38; 17:6,21; 21:10; 23:11; 24:6,17; 25:28; 27:1; 29:1; **2 Chr.** 3:11,12,17; 4:13,15; 5:13; 9:13,15,16,21; 12:13; 16:13; 18:7,8,12; 22:2; 24:8; 28:6; 29:17; 30:12; 32:12; 34:1; 36:5,11,22; **Ezra** 1:1; 2:26,64; 3:1,6,9; 6:20; 7:9; 10:13, 16,17; **Neh.** 1:2; 4:17(11); 5:18; 7:30, 37,66; 8:1,2; 11:1; **Esth.** 3:8,13; 4:11; 7:9; 8:12; **Job** 2:10; 9:3,22; 14:4; 23:13; 31:15; 33:14,23; 40:5; 41:16(8); 42:11, 14; **Ps.** 14:3; 27:4; 34:20(21); 53:3(4); 62:11(12); 82:7; 89:35(36); 106:11; 139:16; **Prov.** 1:14; 28:18; **Eccl.** 2:14; 3:19,20; 4:8–12; 6:6; 7:27,28; 9:2,3,18; 11:6; 12:11; **Song** 4:9; 6:9; **Isa.** 4:1; 5:10; 6:2,6; 9:14(13); 10:17; 19:18; 23:15; 27:12; 30:17; 34:16; 36:9; 47:9; 51:2; 65:25; 66:8,17; **Jer.** 3:14; 10:8; 24:2; 32:39; 35:2; 51:60; 52:1,20–22,25; **Ezek.** 1:6,15,16; 4:9; 7:5; 8:7,8; 9:2; 10:9,10,14,21; 11:19; 16:5; 17:7; 18:10; 19:3,5; 21:19(24); 23:2,13; 26:1; 29:17; 30:20; 31:1; 33:2,24,30; 34:23; 37:16,17,19,22,24; 40:5–8,10,12, 26,42–44,49; 41:11,24; 42:4; 43:13,14; 45:7,11,15,18; 46:17,22; 48:1–8, 23–27,31–34; **Dan.** 1:21; 8:3,9,13; 9:1,2,27; 10:5,13,21; 11:1,20,27; 12:5; **Hos.** 1:11(2:2); **Amos** 4:7,8; 6:9; **Obad.** 1:11; **Jon.** 3:4; **Zeph.** 3:9; **Hag.** 1:1; 2:1,6; **Zech.** 3:9; 4:3; 5:7; 8:21; 11:7,8; 14:7,9; **Mal.** 2:10,15.

260. אָחוּ *'āḥû* **masc. noun**
(reed, marsh plant)
Gen. 41:2,18; **Job** 8:11.

261. אֵהוּד *'ēhûḏ* **masc. proper noun**
(Ehud)
1 Chr. 8:6.

262. אַחְוָה *'aḥwāh* **fem. noun**
(declaration, speech)
Job 13:17.

263. אַחֲוָיָה *'aḥ^a^wāyah* **Aram. fem. noun**
(explanation; corr. to Hebr. 262)
Dan. 5:12(NIV, *ḥ^a^wāh* [2324]).

264. אַחֲוָה *'aḥ^a^wāh* **fem. masc. noun**
(brotherhood)
Zech. 11:14.

265. אֲחוֹחַ *'^a^ḥôaḥ* **masc. proper noun**
(Ahoah)
1 Chr. 8:4.

266. אֲחוֹחִי *'aḥôḥiy* **masc. proper noun**
(Ahohite)
2 Sam. 23:9,28; **1 Chr.** 11:12,29; 27:4.

267. אֲחוּמַי *'^a^ḥûmay* **masc. proper noun**
(Ahumai)
1 Chr. 4:2.

268. אָחוֹר *'āḥôr* **masc. noun**
(back)
Gen. 49:17; **Ex.** 26:12; 33:23; **2 Sam.** 1:22; 10:9; **1 Kgs.** 7:25; **1 Chr.** 19:10; **2 Chr.** 4:4; 13:14; **Job** 23:8; **Ps.** 9:3(4); 35:4; 40:14(15); 44:10(11),18(19); 56:9(10); 70:2(3); 78:66; 114:3,5; 129:5; 139:5; **Prov.** 29:11; **Isa.** 1:4; 9:12(11); 28:13; 41:23; 42:17,23; 44:25; 50:5; 59:14; **Jer.** 7:24; 15:6; 38:22; 46:5; **Lam.** 1:8,13; 2:3; **Ezek.** 2:10; 8:16.

269. אָחוֹת *'āḥôṯ* **fem. noun**
(sister)
Gen. 4:22; 12:13,19; 20:2,5,12; 24:30,59,60; 25:20; 26:7,9; 28:9; 29:13;

30:1,8; 34:13,14,27,31; 36:3,22; 46:17; **Ex.** 2:4,7; 6:23; 15:20; 26:3,5,6,17; **Lev.** 18:9,11–13,18; 20:17,19; 21:3; **Num.** 6:7; 25:18; 26:59; **Deut.** 27:22; **Josh.** 2:13; **Judg.** 15:2; **2 Sam.** 13:1,2, 4–6,11,20,22,32; 17:25; **1 Kgs.** 11:19,20; **2 Kgs.** 11:2; **1 Chr.** 1:39; 2:16; 3:9,19; 4:3,19; 7:15,18,30,32; **2 Chr.** 22:11; **Job** 1:4; 17:14; 42:11; **Prov.** 7:4; **Song** 4:9,10,12; 5:1,2; 8:8; **Jer.** 3:7,8,10; 22:18; **Ezek.** 1:9,23; 3:13; 16:45,46,48,49,51, 52,55,56,61; 22:11; 23:4,11,18,31–33; 44:25; **Hos.** 2:1(3).

270. אָחַז *'aḥaz* **verb**
(to seize, to grasp, to take hold)
Gen. 22:13; 25:26; 34:10; 47:27; **Ex.** 4:4; 15:14,15; **Num.** 31:30,47; 32:30; **Deut.** 32:41; **Josh.** 22:9,19; **Judg.** 1:6; 12:6; 16:3,21; 20:6; **Ruth** 3:15; **2 Sam.** 1:9; 2:21; 4:10; 6:6; 20:9; **1 Kgs.** 1:51; 6:6,10; **1 Chr.** 13:9; 24:6; **2 Chr.** 9:18; 25:5; **Neh.** 7:3; **Esth.** 1:6; **Job** 16:12; 17:9; 18:9,20; 21:6; 23:11; 26:9; 30:16; 38:13; **Ps.** 48:6(7); 73:23; 77:4(5); 119:53; 137:9; 139:10; **Eccl.** 2:3; 7:18; 9:12; **Song** 2:15; 3:4,8; 7:8(9); **Isa.** 5:29; 13:8; 21:3; 33:14; **Jer.** 13:21; 49:24; **Ezek.** 41:6.

271. A. אָחָז *'āḥāz* **masc. proper noun**
(Ahaz: king of Judah)
2 Kgs. 15:38; 16:1,2,5,7,8,10,11,15–17,19,20; 17:1; 18:1; 20:11; 23:12; **1 Chr.** 3:13; **2 Chr.** 27:9; 28:1,16,19,21,22,24,27; 29:19; **Isa.** 1:1; 7:1,3,10,12; 14:28; 38:8; **Hos.** 1:1; **Mic.** 1:1.
B. אָחָז *'āḥāz* **masc. proper noun**
(Ahaz: a Benjamite)
1 Chr. 8:35,36; 9:42.

272. אֲחֻזָּה *'ᵃḥuzzāh* **fem. noun**
(possession, property)
Gen. 17:8; 23:4,9,20; 36:43; 47:11; 48:4; 49:30; 50:13; **Lev.** 14:34; 25:10,13,24, 25,27,28,32–34,41,45,46; 27:16,21,22, 24,28; **Num.** 27:4,7; 32:5,22,29,32; 35:2,8,28; **Deut.** 32:49; **Josh.** 21:12,41; 22:4,9,19; **1 Chr.** 7:28; 9:2; **2 Chr.** 11:14; 31:1; **Neh.** 11:3; **Ps.** 2:8; **Ezek.** 44:28; 45:5–8; 46:16,18; 48:20–22.

273. אַחְזַי *'aḥzay* **masc. proper noun**
(Ahzai)
Neh. 11:13.

274. A. אֲחַזְיָהוּ *'ᵃḥazyāhû,* אֲחַזְיָה *'ᵃḥazyāh* **masc. proper noun**
(Ahaziah: king of Israel)
1 Kgs. 22:40,49(50),51(52); **2 Kgs.** 1:2,18; **2 Chr.** 20:35,37.
B. אֲחַזְיָהוּ *'ᵃḥazyāhû,* אֲחַזְיָה *'ᵃḥazyāh* **masc. proper noun**
(Ahaziah: king of Judah; see also *'ᵃzaryāh* [5838,J] and *yᵉhô'āḥāz* [3059,A])
2 Kgs. 8:24–26,29; 9:16,21,23,27,29; 10:13; 11:1,2; 12:18(19); 13:1; 14:13; **1 Chr.** 3:11; **2 Chr.** 22:1,2,7–11.

275. אֲחֻזָּם *'ᵃḥuzzām* **masc. proper noun**
(Ahuzzam)
1 Chr. 4:6.

276. אֲחֻזַּת *'ᵃḥuzzaṯ* **masc. proper noun**
(Ahuzzath)
Gen. 26:26.

277. A. אֲחִי *'ᵃḥiy* **masc. proper noun**
(Ahi: a Gadite)
1 Chr. 5:15.
B. אֲחִי *'ᵃḥiy* **masc. proper noun**
(Ahi: an Asherite)
1 Chr. 7:34.

278. אֵחִי *'ēḥiy* **masc. proper noun**
(Ehi)
Gen. 46:21.

279. אֲחִיאָם 'aḥiy'ām masc. proper noun
(Ahiam)
2 Sam. 23:33; 1 Chr. 11:35.

280. אֲחִידָה 'aḥidāh Aram. fem. noun
(puzzle, riddle)
Dan. 5:12.

281. A. אֲחִיָּה 'aḥiyyāh masc. proper noun
(Ahijah: high priest at Gibeah under Saul)
1 Sam. 14:3,18.
B. אֲחִיָּה 'aḥiyyāh masc. proper noun
(Ahijah: scribe in Solomon's time)
1 Kgs. 4:3.
C. אֲחִיָּה 'aḥiyyāh masc. proper noun
(Ahijah: a prophet)
1 Kgs. 11:29,30; 12:15; 14:2,4–6,18; 2 Chr. 9:29; 10:15.
D. אֲחִיָּה 'aḥiyyāh masc. proper noun
(Ahijah: father of Baasha)
1 Kgs. 15:27,29,33; 21:22; 2 Kgs. 9:9.
E. אֲחִיָּה 'aḥiyyāh masc. proper noun
(Ahijah: grandson of Hezron)
1 Chr. 2:25.
F. אֲחִיָּה 'aḥiyyāh masc. proper noun
(Ahijah: a Benjamite)
1 Chr. 8:7.
G. אֲחִיָּה 'aḥiyyāh masc. proper noun
(Ahijah: one of David's mighty men)
1 Chr. 11:36.
H. אֲחִיָּה 'aḥiyyāh masc. proper noun
(Ahijah: Levite in David's time)
1 Chr. 26:20.
I. אֲחִיָּה 'aḥiyyāh masc. proper noun
(Ahijah, Ahiah: chief of the people under Nehemiah)
Neh. 10:26(27).

282. אֲחִיהוּד 'aḥiyhûd masc. proper noun
(Ahihud)
Num. 34:27.

283. A. אַחְיוֹ 'aḥyô masc. proper noun
(Ahio: son of Abinadab)
2 Sam. 6:3,4; 1 Chr. 13:7.
B. אַחְיוֹ 'aḥyô masc. proper noun
(Ahio: a Benjamite)
1 Chr. 8:14.
C. אַחְיוֹ 'aḥyô masc. proper noun
(Ahio: a Gibeonite)
1 Chr. 8:31; 9:37.

284. אֲחִיחֻד 'aḥiyḥud masc. proper noun
(Ahihud)
1 Chr. 8:7.

285. A. אֲחִיטוּב 'aḥiyṭûḇ masc. proper noun
(Ahitub: son of Phinehas)
1 Sam. 14:3; 22:9,11,12,20.
B. אֲחִיטוּב 'aḥiyṭûḇ masc. proper noun
(Ahitub: father of Zadok)
2 Sam. 8:17; 1 Chr. 6:7(5:33),8(5:34),52(37); 18:16.
C. אֲחִיטוּב 'aḥiyṭûḇ masc. proper noun
(Ahitub: a priest)
1 Chr. 6:11(5:37),12(5:38); Ezra 7:2.
D. אֲחִיטוּב 'aḥiyṭûḇ masc. proper noun
(Ahitub: a priest)
1 Chr. 9:11; Neh. 11:11.

286. A. אֲחִילוּד 'aḥiylûḏ masc. proper noun
(Ahilud: father of Jehoshaphat)

2 Sam. 8:16; 20:24; **1 Kgs.** 4:3; **1 Chr.** 18:15.
B. אֲחִילוּד *'aḥiylûd̲* **masc. proper noun**
(Ahilud: father of Baana)
1 Kgs. 4:12.

287. אֲחִימוֹת *'aḥiymôt̲* **masc. proper noun**
(Ahimoth)
1 Chr. 6:25(10).

288. A. אֲחִימֶלֶךְ *'aḥiymelek̲* **masc. proper noun**
(Ahimelech: a priest)
1 Sam. 21:1(2),2(3),8(9); 22:9,11,14,16; **1 Chr.** 24:3,6,31; **Ps.** 52:[title](2).
B. אֲחִימֶלֶךְ *'aḥiymelek̲* **masc. proper noun**
(Ahimelech: a Hittite)
1 Sam. 26:6.
C. אֲחִימֶלֶךְ *'aḥiymelek̲* **masc. proper noun**
(Ahimelech: father of Abiathar)
1 Sam. 22:20; 23:6; 30:7; **2 Sam.** 8:17.

289. A. אֲחִימַן *'aḥiyman*, אֲחִימָן *'aḥiymān* **masc. proper noun**
(Ahiman: son of Anak)
Num. 13:22; **Josh.** 15:14; **Judg.** 1:10.
B. אֲחִימַן *'aḥiyman* **masc. proper noun**
(Ahiman: a Levite)
1 Chr. 9:17.

290. A. אֲחִימַעַץ *'aḥiyma'aṣ* **masc. proper noun**
(Ahimaaz: son of Zadok)
2 Sam. 15:27,36; 17:17,20; 18:19,22,23,27–29; **1 Chr.** 6:8(5:34),9(5:35),53(38).
B. אֲחִימַעַץ *'aḥiyma'aṣ* **masc. proper noun**
(Ahimaaz: father of Ahinoam)
1 Sam. 14:50.
C. אֲחִימַעַץ *'aḥiyma'aṣ* **masc. proper noun**
(Ahimaaz: officer under Solomon)
1 Kgs. 4:15.

291. אַחְיָן *'aḥyān* **masc. proper noun**
(Ahian)
1 Chr. 7:19.

292. אֲחִינָדָב *'aḥiynād̲āb̲* **masc. proper noun**
(Ahinadab)
1 Kgs. 4:14.

293. A. אֲחִינֹעַם *'aḥiynō'am* **fem. proper noun**
(Ahinoam: wife of Saul)
1 Sam. 14:50.
B. אֲחִינֹעַם *'aḥiynō'am* **fem. proper noun**
(Ahinoam: wife of David)
1 Sam. 25:43; 27:3; 30:5; **2 Sam.** 2:2; 3:2; **1 Chr.** 3:1.

294. אֲחִיסָמָךְ *'aḥiysāmāk̲* **masc. proper noun**
(Ahisamach)
Ex. 31:6; 35:34; 38:23.

295. A. אֲחִיעֶזֶר *'aḥiy'ezer* **masc. proper noun**
(Ahiezer: Danite chief)
Num. 1:12; 2:25; 7:66,71; 10:25.
B. אֲחִיעֶזֶר *'aḥiy'ezer* **masc. proper noun**
(Ahiezer: one of David's mighty men)
1 Chr. 12:3.

296. אֲחִיקָם *'aḥiyqām* **masc. proper noun**
(Ahikam)
2 Kgs. 22:12,14; 25:22; **2 Chr.** 34:20; **Jer.** 26:24; 39:14; 40:5–7,9,11,14,16; 41:1,2,6,10,16,18; 43:6.

297. אֲחִירָם *'ᵃḥiyrām* **masc. proper noun**
(Ahiram)
Num. 26:38.

298. אֲחִירָמִי *'ᵃḥirāmiy* **masc. proper noun**
(Ahiramite)
Num. 26:38.

299. אֲחִירַע *'ᵃḥiyra'* **masc. proper noun**
(Ahira)
Num. 1:15; 2:29; 7:78,83; 10:27.

300. אֲחִישַׁחַר *'ᵃḥiyšaḥar* **masc. proper noun**
(Ahishahar)
1 Chr. 7:10.

301. אֲחִישָׁר *'ᵃḥiyšār* **masc. proper noun**
(Ahishar)
1 Kgs. 4:6.

302. אֲחִיתֹפֶל *'ᵃḥiytōp̱el* **masc. proper noun**
(Ahithophel)
2 Sam. 15:12,31,34; 16:15,20,21,23; 17:1,6,7,14,15,21,23; 23:34; **1 Chr.** 27:33,34.

303. אַחְלָב *'aḥlāḇ* **proper noun**
(Ahlab)
Judg. 1:31.

304. A. אַחְלַי *'aḥlay* **masc. proper noun**
(Ahlai: son of Sheshan)
1 Chr. 2:31.
B. אַחְלַי *'aḥlay* **masc. proper noun**
(Ahlai: father of one of David's mighty men)
1 Chr. 11:41.

305. אַחֲלֵי *aḥᵃlēy*, אַחֲלַי, *'aḥᵃlay* **interj.**
(would that! if only!)
2 Kgs. 5:3; **Ps.** 119:5.

306. אַחְלָמָה *'aḥlāmāh* **fem. noun**
(amethyst)
Ex. 28:19; 39:12.

307. אַחְמְתָא *'aḥmᵉṯa'* **Aram. proper noun**
(Achmetha, Ecbatana)
Ezra 6:2.

308. אֲחַסְבַּי *'ᵃḥasbay* **masc. proper noun**
(Ahasbai)
2 Sam. 23:34.

309. אָחַר *'āḥar* **verb**
(to delay, hold back)
Gen. 24:56; 32:4(5); 34:19; **Ex.** 22:29(28); **Deut.** 7:10; 23:21(22); **Judg.** 5:28; **2 Sam.** 20:5(KJV, [Qᵉ] *yāḥar* [3186]); **Ps.** 40:17(18); 70:5(6); 127:2; **Prov.** 23:30; **Eccl.** 5:4(3); **Isa.** 5:11; 46:13; **Dan.** 9:19; **Hab.** 2:3.

310. אַחַר *'aḥar* **prep.**
(after, behind)
Gen. 5:4,7,10,13,16,19,22,26,30; 6:4; 9:9,28; 10:1,18,32; 11:10,11,13,15, 17,19,21,23,25; 13:14; 14:17; 15:1,14; 16:13; 17:7–10,19; 18:5,10,12,19; 19:6, 17,26; 22:1,13,20; 23:19; 24:5,8,36,39, 55,61,67; 25:11,26; 26:18; 30:21; 31:23,36; 32:18–20(19–21); 33:7; 35:5,12; 37:17; 38:30; 39:7; 40:1; 41:3,6,19,23,27,30,31,39; 44:4; 45:15; 46:30; 48:1,4,6; 50:14; **Ex.** 3:1,20; 5:1; 7:25; 10:14; 11:1,5,8; 14:4,8–10,17, 19,23,28; 15:20; 18:2; 23:2; 28:43; 29:29; 33:8; 34:15,16,32; **Lev.** 13:7,35,55,56; 14:8,19,36,43,48; 15:28; 16:1,26,28; 17:7; 20:5,6; 22:7; 25:15,46,48; 26:33; 27:18; **Num.** 3:23; 4:15; 5:26; 6:19,20; 7:88; 8:15,22; 9:17; 12:14,16; 14:24,43; 15:39; 16:25; 19:7; 25:8,13; 26:1(25:19); 30:15(16); 31:2,24; 32:11,12,15,22;

35:28; **Deut.** 1:4,8,36; 4:3,37,40; 6:14; 7:4; 8:19; 10:15; 11:4,28,30; 12:25,28,30; 13:2(3),4(5); 19:6; 21:13; 23:14(15); 24:4,20,21; 25:18; 28:14; 29:22(21); 31:16,27,29; **Josh.** 1:1; 2:5,7,16; 3:3; 6:8,9,13; 7:8; 8:2,4,6,14,16,17,20,34; 9:16; 10:14,19,26; 14:8,9,14; 20:5; 22:16, 18,23,27,29; 23:1; 24:5,6,20,29,31; **Judg.** 1:1,6,9; 2:7,10,12,17,19; 3:22,28, 31; 4:14,16; 5:14; 6:34,35; 7:11,23; 8:5,12,27,33; 9:3,4,49; 10:1,3; 11:36; 12:8,11,13; 13:11; 15:7; 16:4; 18:12; 19:3,5,23; 20:40,45; **Ruth** 1:15,16; 2:2,3,7,9,11; 3:10; 4:4; **1 Sam.** 1:9; 5:9; 6:7,12; 7:2; 8:3; 9:13; 10:5; 11:5,7; 12:14,20,21; 13:4,7; 14:12,13,22,36, 37,46; 15:11,31; 17:13,14,35,53; 20:37,38; 21:9(10); 22:20; 23:25,28; 24:1(2),5(6),8(9),14(15),21(22); 25:13,19,42; 26:3,18; 30:8,21; **2 Sam.** 1:1,7,10; 2:1,10,19–28,30; 3:16,26,28,31; 5:13,23; 7:8,12; 8:1; 10:1; 11:8,15; 13:1, 17,18,34; 15:1,13; 17:1,9,21; 18:16,22; 19:30(31); 20:2,6,7,10,11,13,14; 21:1, 14,18; 23:9–11; 24:10; **1 Kgs.** 1:6,7,13, 14,17,20,24,27,30,35,40; 2:28; 3:12; 9:6,21; 10:19; 11:2,4–6,10; 12:20; 13:14, 23,31,33; 14:8–10; 15:4; 16:3,21,22; 17:17; 18:18,21; 19:11,12,20,21; 20:15, 19; 21:1,21,26; 22:33; **2 Kgs.** 1:1; 2:24; 4:30; 5:20,21; 6:19,24,32; 7:14,15; 9:18, 19,25,27; 10:29; 11:6,15; 13:2; 14:17, 19,22; 17:15,21; 18:5,6; 19:21; 23:3,25; 25:5; **1 Chr.** 2:21,24; 5:25; 10:2; 11:12; 14:14; 17:7,11; 18:1; 19:1; 20:4; 27:7,34; 28:8; **2 Chr.** 1:12; 2:17(16); 8:8; 11:16,20; 13:13,19; 18:32; 20:1,35; 21:18; 22:4; 23:14; 24:4,17; 25:14,25,27; 26:2,17; 32:1,9,23; 33:14; 34:31,33; 35:14,20; **Ezra** 3:5; 7:1; 9:10,13; **Neh.** 3:16–18, 20–25,27,29–31; 4:13(7),16(10),23(17); 5:15; 9:26; 11:8; 12:32,38; 13:19; **Esth.** 2:1; 3:1; **Job** 3:1; 18:2; 19:26; 21:3,21,33; 29:22; 31:7; 34:27; 37:4; 39:8,10; 41:32(24); 42:7,16; **Ps.** 45:14(15); 49:13(14),17(18); 50:17; 63:8(9); 68:25(26); 73:24; 78:71; 94:15; **Prov.** 7:22; 20:7,17,25; 24:27; 28:23; **Eccl.** 2:12,18; 3:22; 6:12; 7:14; 9:3; 10:14; 12:2; **Song** 1:4; 2:9; **Isa.** 1:26; 30:21; 37:22; 38:17; 43:10; 45:14; 57:8; 59:13; 65:2; 66:17; **Jer.** 2:2,5,8,23,25; 3:7,17,19; 7:6,9; 8:2; 9:14(13),16(15),22(21); 11:10; 12:6,15; 13:10,27; 16:11,12,16; 17:16; 18:12; 21:7; 24:1; 25:6,26; 28:12; 29:2, 18; 31:19,33; 32:16,18,39,40; 34:8,11; 35:15; 36:27; 39:5; 40:1; 41:16; 42:16; 46:26; 48:2; 49:6,37; 50:21; 51:46; 52:8; **Ezek.** 3:12; 5:2,12; 6:9; 9:5; 10:11; 12:14; 13:3; 14:7,11; 16:23,34; 20:16,24,30,39; 23:30,35; 29:16; 33:31; 40:1; 41:15; 44:10,26; 46:12; **Dan.** 8:1; 9:26; **Hos.** 1:2; 2:5(7),13(15); 3:5; 5:8,11; 11:10; **Joel** 2:2,3,14,28(3:1); **Amos** 2:4; 7:1,15; **Zeph.** 1:6; **Zech.** 1:8; 2:8(12); 6:6; 7:14.

311. אַחֲרֵי *'aḥ^{a}rēy* **Aram. prep.**
(after, afterward; corr. to Hebr. 310)
Dan. 2:29,45; 7:24.

312. אַחֵר *'aḥēr* **adj.**
(other, another)
Gen. 4:25; 8:10,12; 17:21; 26:21,22; 29:19,27,30; 30:24; 37:9; 41:3,19; 43:14,22; **Ex.** 20:3; 21:10; 22:5(4); 23:13; 34:14; **Lev.** 6:11(4); 14:42; 27:20; **Num.** 14:24; 23:13,27; 36:9; **Deut.** 5:7; 6:14; 7:4; 8:19; 11:16,28; 13:2(3),6(7),13(14); 17:3; 18:20; 20:5–7; 24:2; 28:14,30,32, 36,64; 29:26(25),28(27); 30:17; 31:18,20; **Josh.** 23:16; 24:2,16; **Judg.** 2:10,12, 17,19; 10:13; 11:2; **Ruth** 2:8,22; **1 Sam.** 8:8; 10:6,9; 17:30; 19:21; 21:9(10); 26:19; 28:8; **2 Sam.** 13:16; 18:20,26; **1 Kgs.** 3:22; 7:8; 9:6,9; 11:4,10; 13:10; 14:9; 20:37; **2 Kgs.** 1:11; 5:17; 6:29; 7:8; 17:7, 35,37,38; 22:17; **1 Chr.** 2:26; 16:20; 23:17; **2 Chr.** 3:11,12; 7:19,22; 28:25; 30:23; 32:5; 34:25; **Ezra** 1:10; 2:31; **Neh.** 5:5; 7:33,34; **Esth.** 4:14; **Job** 8:19; 31:8,10; 34:24; **Ps.** 16:4; 49:10(11); 105:13; 109:8,13; **Prov.** 5:9; 25:9; **Eccl.** 7:22; **Isa.** 28:11; 42:8; 48:11; 65:15,22; **Jer.** 1:16; 3:1; 6:12; 7:6,9,18; 8:10; 11:10;

13:10; 16:11,13; 18:4; 19:4,13; 22:9,26; 25:6; 32:29; 35:15; 36:28,32; 44:3,5,8,15; **Ezek.** 12:3; 40:40; 41:24; 42:14; 44:19; **Dan.** 11:4; 12:5; **Hos.** 3:1; **Joel** 1:3; **Zech.** 2:3(7).

313. אַחֵר *'aḥēr* **masc. proper noun**
(Aher)
1 Chr. 7:12.

314. אַחֲרוֹן *'aḥarôn*, אַחֲרֹן *'aḥarōn* **adj.**
(last, afterwards, next)
Gen. 33:2; **Ex.** 4:8; **Num.** 2:31; **Deut.** 11:24; 13:9(10); 17:7; 24:3; 29:22(21); 34:2; **Ruth** 3:10; **1 Sam.** 29:2; **2 Sam.** 2:26; 19:11(12),12(13); 23:1; **1 Kgs.** 17:13; **1 Chr.** 23:27; 29:29; **2 Chr.** 9:29; 12:15; 16:11; 20:34; 25:26; 26:22; 28:26; 35:27; **Ezra** 8:13; **Neh.** 8:18; **Job** 18:20; 19:25; **Ps.** 48:13(14); 78:4,6; 102:18(19); **Prov.** 31:25; **Eccl.** 1:11; 4:16; **Isa.** 9:1(8:23); 30:8; 41:4; 44:6; 48:12; **Jer.** 50:17; **Dan.** 8:3; 11:29; **Joel** 2:20; **Hag.** 2:9; **Zech.** 14:8.

315. אַחְרַח *'aḥraḥ* **masc. proper noun**
(Aharah)
1 Chr. 8:1.

316. אֲחַרְחֵל *'aḥarḥēl* **masc. proper noun**
(Aharhel)
1 Chr. 4:8.

317. אָחֳרִי *'oḥoriy* **Aram. adj.**
(another, other)
Dan. 2:39; 7:5,6,8,20.

318. אָחֳרֵין *'oḥorēyn* **Aram. adv.**
(last, end, finally)
Dan. 4:8(5).

319. אַחֲרִית *'aḥariyṯ* **fem. noun**
(the end, last time, latter time)
Gen. 49:1; **Num.** 23:10; 24:14,20; **Deut.** 4:30; 8:16; 11:12; 31:29; 32:20,29; **Job** 8:7; 42:12; **Ps.** 37:37,38; 73:17; 109:13; 139:9; **Prov.** 5:4,11; 14:12,13; 16:25; 19:20; 20:21; 23:18,32; 24:14,20; 25:8; 29:21; **Eccl.** 7:8; 10:13; **Isa.** 2:2; 41:22; 46:10; 47:7; **Jer.** 5:31; 12:4; 17:11; 23:20; 29:11; 30:24; 31:17; 48:47; 49:39; 50:12; **Lam.** 1:9; **Ezek.** 23:25; 38:8,16; **Dan.** 8:19,23; 10:14; 11:4; 12:8; **Hos.** 3:5; **Amos** 4:2; 8:10; 9:1; **Mic.** 4:1.

320. אַחֲרִית *'aḥariyṯ* **Aram. fem. noun**
(end time, latter time; corr. to Hebr. 319)
Dan. 2:28.

321. אָחֳרָן *'oḥorān* **Aram. adj.**
(other, another)
Dan. 2:11,44; 3:29; 5:17; 7:24.

322. אֲחֹרַנִּית *'aḥōranniyṯ* **adv.**
(backward)
Gen. 9:23; **1 Sam.** 4:18; **1 Kgs.** 18:37; **2 Kgs.** 20:10,11; **Isa.** 38:8.

323. אֲחַשְׁדַּרְפַּן *'aḥašdarpan* **masc. noun**
(satrap, governor of a Persian province)
Ezra 8:36; **Esth.** 3:12; 8:9; 9:3.

324. אֲחַשְׁדַּרְפַּן *'aḥašdarpan* **Aram. masc. noun**
(satrap, governor of a Persian province; corr. to Hebr. 323)
Dan. 3:2,3,27; 6:1–4(2–5),6(7),7(8).

325. אֲחַשְׁוֵרוֹשׁ *'aḥašwērôš* **masc. proper noun**
(Ahasuerus, king of Persia; perhaps Xerxes)
Ezra 4:6; **Esth.** 1:1,2,9,10,15–17,19; 2:1,12,16,21; 3:1,6–8,12; 6:2; 7:5; 8:1,7,10,12; 9:2,20,30; 10:1,3; **Dan.** 9:1.

326. אֲחַשְׁתָּרִי *'ᵃḥaštāriy* **masc. proper noun**
(Haahashtari)
1 Chr. 4:6.

327. אֲחַשְׁתְּרָן *'ᵃḥaštᵉrān* **masc. noun**
(royal, speedy)
Esth. 8:10,14.

328. I. אַט *'aṭ* **adv.**
(gently, softly)
Gen. 33:14; **2 Sam.** 18:5; **1 Kgs.** 21:27; **Job** 15:11; **Isa.** 8:6.
II. אִטִּים *'iṭṭiym* **masc. pl. noun**
(mutterers, ghosts)
Isa. 19:3.

329. I. אָטָד *'āṭāḏ* **masc. noun**
(bramble, thorn)
Judg. 9:14,15; **Ps.** 58:9(10).
II. אָטָד *'āṭāḏ* **masc. proper noun**
(Atad: threshing floor in Transjordan; another name for *'āḇēl miṣrayim* [67])
Gen. 50:10,11.

330. אֵטוּן *'ēṭûn* **masc. noun**
(fine linen)
Prov. 7:16.

331. אָטַם *'āṭam* **verb**
(to stop up, to be narrow)
1 Kgs. 6:4; **Ps.** 58:4(5); **Prov.** 17:28; 21:13; **Isa.** 33:15; **Ezek.** 40:16; 41:16,26.

332. אָטַר *'āṭar* **verb**
(to shut, to close)
Ps. 69:15(16).

333. אָטֵר *'āṭēr* **masc. proper noun**
(Ater)
Ezra 2:16,42; **Neh.** 7:21,45; 10:17(18).

334. אִטֵּר *'iṭṭēr* **adj.**
(left-handed)
Judg. 3:15; 20:16.

335. אֵי *'ēy* **adv.**
(where, whence)
Gen. 3:9; 4:9; 16:8; **Deut.** 32:37; **Judg.** 13:6; **1 Sam.** 9:18; 25:11; 26:16; 30:13; **2 Sam.** 1:3,13; 15:2; **1 Kgs.** 13:12; 22:24; **2 Kgs.** 3:8; **2 Chr.** 18:23; **Esth.** 7:5; **Job** 2:2; 20:7; 28:12,20; 38:19,24; **Eccl.** 2:3; 11:6; **Isa.** 19:12; 50:1; 66:1; **Jer.** 5:7; 6:16; **Jon.** 1:8; **Nah.** 3:17.

336. אִי *'iy* **masc. noun**
(not)
Job 22:30(KJV, *'iy* [239]).

337. אִי *'iy* **interj.**
(woe!)
Eccl. 4:10; 10:16.

338. אִי *'iy* **masc. noun**
(hyena, jackal)
Isa. 13:22; 34:14; **Jer.** 50:39.

339. אִי *'iy* **masc. noun**
(island, coastland)
Gen. 10:5; **Esth.** 10:1; **Ps.** 72:10; 97:1; **Isa.** 11:11; 20:6; 23:2,6; 24:15; 40:15; 41:1,5; 42:4,10,12,15; 49:1; 51:5; 59:18; 60:9; 66:19; **Jer.** 2:10; 25:22; 31:10; 47:4; **Ezek.** 26:15,18; 27:3,6,7,15,35; 39:6; **Dan.** 11:18; **Zeph.** 2:11.

340. אָיַב *'āyaḇ* **verb**
(to be an enemy; NASB, see also *'ōyēḇ* [341])
Ex. 23:22.

341. אֹיֵב *'ōyēḇ* **masc. noun**
(enemy; NASB, part. of *'āyaḇ* [340])
Gen. 22:17; 49:8; **Ex.** 15:6,9; 23:4,22,27; **Lev.** 26:7,8,16,17,25,32,34,36–39,41,44; **Num.** 10:9,35; 14:42; 23:11; 24:10,18; 32:21; 35:23; **Deut.** 1:42; 6:19; 12:10; 20:1,3,4,14; 21:10; 23:9(10),14(15);

25:19; 28:7,25,31,48,53,55,57,68; 30:7; 32:27,31,42; 33:27,29; **Josh.** 7:8,12,13; 10:13,19,25; 21:44(42); 22:8; 23:1; **Judg.** 2:14,18; 3:28; 5:31; 8:34; 11:36; 16:23,24; **1 Sam.** 2:1; 4:3; 12:10,11; 14:24,30,47; 18:25,29; 19:17; 20:15,16; 24:4(5),19(20); 25:22,26,29; 26:8; 29:8; 30:26; **2 Sam.** 3:18; 4:8; 5:20; 7:1,9,11; 12:14; 18:19,32; 19:9(10); 22:1,4,18,38, 41,49; **1 Kgs.** 3:11; 8:33,37,44,46,48; 21:20; **2 Kgs.** 17:39; 21:14; **1 Chr.** 14:11; 17:8,10; 21:12; 22:9; **2 Chr.** 6:24,28,34,36; 20:27,29; 25:8; 26:13; **Ezra** 8:22,31; **Neh.** 4:15(9); 5:9; 6:1,16; 9:28; **Esth.** 7:6; 8:13; 9:1,5,16,22; **Job** 13:24; 27:7; 33:10; **Ps.** 3:7(8); 6:10(11); 7:5(6); 8:2(3); 9:3(4),6(7); 13:2(3),4(5); 17:9; 18:3(4),17(18),37(38),40(41), 48(49); 21:8(9); 25:2,19; 27:2,6; 30:1(2); 31:8(9),15(16); 35:19; 37:20; 38:19(20); 41:2(3),5(6),11(12); 42:9(10); 43:2; 44:16(17); 45:5(6); 54:7(9); 55:3(4), 12(13); 56:9(10); 59:1(2); 61:3(4); 64:1(2); 66:3; 68:1(2),21(22),23(24); 69:4(5),18(19); 71:10; 72:9; 74:3,10,18; 78:53; 80:6(7); 81:14(15); 83:2(3); 89:10(11),22(23),42(43),51(52); 92:9(10); 102:8(9); 106:10,42; 110:1,2; 119:98; 127:5; 132:18; 138:7; 139:22; 143:3,9,12; **Prov.** 16:7; 24:17; **Isa.** 1:24; 9:11(10); 42:13; 59:18; 62:8; 63:10; 66:6,14; **Jer.** 6:25; 12:7; 15:9,11,14; 17:4; 18:17; 19:7,9; 20:4,5; 21:7; 30:14; 31:16; 34:20,21; 44:30; 49:37; **Lam.** 1:2,5,9, 16,21; 2:3–5,7,16,17,22; 3:46,52; 4:12; **Ezek.** 36:2; 39:27; **Hos.** 8:3; **Amos** 9:4; **Mic.** 2:8; 4:10; 5:9(8); 7:6,8,10; **Nah.** 1:2,8; 3:11,13; **Zeph.** 3:15.

342. אֵיבָה *'ēyḇāh* **fem. noun**
(enmity, hatred)
Gen. 3:15; **Num.** 35:21,22; **Ezek.** 25:15; 35:5.

343. אֵיד *'ēyḏ* **masc. noun**
(disaster, calamity)
Deut. 32:35; **2 Sam.** 22:19; **Job** 18:12; 21:17,30; 30:12; 31:3,23; **Ps.** 18:18(19); **Prov.** 1:26,27; 6:15; 17:5; 24:22; 27:10; **Jer.** 18:17; 46:21; 48:16; 49:8,32; **Ezek.** 35:5; **Obad.** 1:13.

344. אַיָּה *'ayyāh* **fem. noun**
(falcon, black kite)
Lev. 11:14; **Deut.** 14:13; **Job** 28:7.

345. A. אַיָּה *'ayyāh* **masc. proper noun**
(Aiah: son of Zibeon)
Gen. 36:24; **1 Chr.** 1:40.
B. אַיָּה *'ayyāh* **masc. proper noun**
(Aiah: father of Rizpah)
2 Sam. 3:7; 21:8,10,11.

346. אַיֵּה *'ayyēh* **adv.**
(where?)
Gen. 18:9; 19:5; 22:7; 38:21; **Ex.** 2:20; **Judg.** 6:13; 9:38; **2 Sam.** 16:3; 17:20; **2 Kgs.** 2:14; 18:34; 19:13; **Job** 14:10; 15:23; 17:15; 21:28; 35:10; **Ps.** 42:3(4), 10(11); 79:10; 89:49(50); 115:2; **Isa.** 33:18; 36:19; 37:13; 51:13; 63:11,15; **Jer.** 2:6,8,28; 13:20; 17:15; 37:19; **Lam.** 2:12; **Ezek.** 13:12; **Joel** 2:17; **Mic.** 7:10; **Nah.** 2:11(12); **Zech.** 1:5; **Mal.** 1:6; 2:17.

347. אִיּוֹב *'iyyôḇ* **masc. proper noun**
(Job)
Job 1:1,5,8,9,14,20,22; 2:3,7,10,11; 3:1,2; 6:1; 9:1; 12:1; 16:1; 19:1; 21:1; 23:1; 26:1; 27:1; 29:1; 31:40; 32:1–4,12; 33:1,31; 34:5,7,35,36; 35:16; 37:14; 38:1; 40:1,3,6; 42:1,7–10,12,15–17; **Ezek.** 14:14,20.

348. אִיזֶבֶל *'iyzeḇel* **fem. proper noun**
(Jezebel)
1 Kgs. 16:31; 18:4,13,19; 19:1,2; 21:5,7,11,14,15,23,25; **2 Kgs.** 9:7,10,22, 30,36,37.

349. I. אֵיךְ *'ēyk̲* **adv.**
(how? how!)
Gen. 26:9; 39:9; 44:8,34; **Ex.** 6:12,30; **Josh.** 9:7; **Judg.** 16:15; **Ruth** 3:18; **1 Sam.** 16:2; **2 Sam.** 1:5,14,19,25,27; 2:22; 6:9; 12:18; **1 Kgs.** 12:6; **2 Kgs.** 10:4; 17:28; 18:24; **2 Chr.** 10:6; **Job** 21:34; **Ps.** 11:1; 73:19; 137:4; **Prov.** 5:12; **Isa.** 14:4,12; 19:11; 20:6; 36:9; 48:11; **Eccl.** 2:16; 4:11; **Jer.** 2:21,23; 3:19; 9:7(6),19(18); 12:5; 36:17; 47:7; 48:14,39; 49:25; 50:23; 51:41; **Ezek.** 26:17; 33:10; **Hos.** 11:8; **Obad.** 1:5,6; **Mic.** 2:4; **Zeph.** 2:15.
II. אֵיכָה *'ēyk̲āh* **adv.**
(how? how!)
Deut. 1:12; 7:17; 12:30; 18:21; 32:30; **Judg.** 20:3; **2 Kgs.** 6:15; **Ps.** 73:11; **Song** 1:7; **Isa.** 1:21; **Jer.** 8:8; 48:17; **Lam.** 1:1; 2:1; 4:1,2.
III. אֵיכָכָה *'ēyk̲āk̲āh* **adv.**
(how?)
Esth. 8:6; **Song** 5:3.

350. אִי־כָבוֹד *'iy-k̲āb̲ôd̲* **masc. proper noun**
(Ichabod)
1 Sam. 4:21; 14:3.

351. אֵיכֹה *'ēyk̲ōh* **adv.**
(where)
2 Kgs. 6:13.

352. I. אַיִל *'ayil* **masc. noun**
(ram)
Gen. 15:9; 22:13; 31:38; 32:14(15); **Ex.** 25:5; 26:14; 29:1,3,15–20,22,26,27, 31,32; 35:7,23; 36:19; 39:34; **Lev.** 5:15,16,18; 6:6(5:25); 8:2,18,20–22,29; 9:2,4,18,19; 16:3,5; 19:21,22; 23:18; **Num.** 5:8; 6:14,17,19; 7:15,17,21,23,27, 29,33,35,39,41,45,47,51,53,57,59,63,65, 69,71,75,77,81,83,87,88; 15:6,11; 23:1,2, 4,14,29,30; 28:11,12,14,19,20,27,28; 29:2,3,8,9,13,14,17,18,20,21,23,24,26, 27,29,30,32,33,36,37; **Deut.** 32:14; **1 Sam.** 15:22; **2 Kgs.** 3:4; **1 Chr.** 15:26; 29:21; **2 Chr.** 13:9; 17:11; 29:21,22,32; **Ezra** 8:35; 10:19; **Job** 42:8; **Ps.** 66:15; 114:4,6; **Isa.** 1:11; 34:6; 60:7; **Jer.** 51:40; **Ezek.** 27:21; 34:17; 39:18; 43:23,25; 45:23,24; 46:4–7,11; **Dan.** 8:3,4,6,7,20; **Mic.** 6:7.
II. אַיִל *'ayil* **masc. noun**
(post or lintel)
1 Kgs. 6:31; **Ezek.** 40:9,10,14,16,21,24, 26,29,31,33,34,36–38,48,49; 41:1,3.
III. אַיִל *'ayil* **masc. noun**
(leader, mighty man)
Ex. 15:15; **2 Kgs.** 24:15(KJV, NASB, [K[e]] *'ûl* [193,II]); **Ps.** 58:1(2)(KJV, *'ēlem* [482,II]; NASB, *'ēl* [410]); **Ezek.** 17:13; 31:11(KJV, *'ēl* [410]).
IV. אַיִל *'ayil* **masc. noun**
(terebinth, oak tree)
Isa. 1:29; 57:5(KJV, *'ēl* [410]); 61:3; **Ezek.** 31:14.

353. אֱיָל *'eyāl* **masc. noun**
(strength)
Ps. 88:4(5).

354. אַיָּל *'ayyāl* **masc. noun**
(deer, hart)
Deut. 12:15,22; 14:5; 15:22; **1 Kgs.** 4:23(5:3); **Ps.** 42:1(2); **Song** 2:9,17; 8:14; **Isa.** 35:6; **Lam.** 1:6.

355. אַיָּלָה *'ayyālāh* **fem. noun**
(doe, female deer)
Gen. 49:21; **2 Sam.** 22:34; **Job** 39:1; **Ps.** 18:33(34); 29:9; **Prov.** 5:19(see *'ayyelet̲* [365]); **Song** 2:7; 3:5; **Jer.** 14:5 (see *'ayyelet̲* [365]); **Hab.** 3:19.

356. A. אֵלֹון *'ēlôn* **masc. proper noun**
(Elon: son of Zebulun)
Gen. 46:14; **Num.** 26:26.
B. אֵילֹון *'ēylôn* **masc. proper noun**
(Elon: Esau's father-in-law)
Gen. 26:34; 36:2.

357. A. אַיָּלוֹן 'ayyālôn

C. אֵלוֹן **'ēlôn masc. proper noun**
(Elon: judge of Israel)
Judg. 12:11,12.

D. אֵילוֹן **'ēylôn masc. proper noun**
(Elon: town in Dan)
Josh. 19:43; **1 Kgs.** 4:9(see *'ēylôn bēyt ḥānān* [358]).

357. A. אַיָּלוֹן **'ayyālôn proper noun**
(Aijalon: city in Dan)
Josh. 10:12; 19:42; 21:24; **Judg.** 1:35;
1 Sam. 14:31; **1 Chr.** 6:69(54); 8:13;
2 Chr. 11:10; 28:18.

B. אַיָּלוֹן **'ayālôn proper noun**
(Aijalon: city in Zebulon)
Judg. 12:12.

358. אֵילוֹן בֵּית חָנָן **'ēylôn bēyt ḥānān proper noun**
(Elon Bethhanan: full name for *'ēylôn* [356,D])
1 Kgs. 4:9.

359. אֵילַת **'ēylaṯ,** אֵילוֹת **'ēylôṯ proper noun**
(Elath)
Deut. 2:8; **1 Kgs.** 9:26; **2 Kgs.** 14:22; 16:6; **2 Chr.** 8:17; 26:2.

360. אֱיָלוּת **'eyālûṯ fem. noun**
(strength)
Ps. 22:19(20).

361. אֵילָם **'ēylām masc. noun**
(portico, porch)
Ezek. 40:16,21,22,24–26,29,30,31,33,34,36.

362. אֵילִם **'ēylim proper noun**
(Elim)
Ex. 15:27; 16:1; **Num.** 33:9,10.

363. אִילָן **'iylān Aram. masc. noun**
(tree)
Dan. 4:10(7),11(8),14(11),20(17),23(20), 26(23).

364. אֵיל פָּארָן **'ēyl pā'rān proper noun**
(El Paran)
Gen. 14:6.

365. I. אַיֶּלֶת **'ayyeleṯ fem. noun**
(doe: const. of *'ayyālāh* [355])
Ps. 22:[title](1)(KJV, NASB, see II);
Prov. 5:19; **Jer.** 14:5 .

II. אַיֶּלֶת **'ayyeleṯ fem. proper noun**
(Aijeleth)
Ps. 22:[title](1)(NIV, see I).

366. אָיֹם **'āyōm adj.**
(terrible, awesome)
Song 6:4,10; **Hab.** 1:7.

367. אֵימָה **'ēymāh fem. noun**
(terror, dread)
Gen. 15:12; **Ex.** 15:16; 23:27; **Deut.** 32:25; **Josh.** 2:9; **Ezra** 3:3; **Job** 9:34; 13:21; 20:25; 33:7; 39:20; 41:14(6);
Ps. 55:4(5); 88:15(16); **Prov.** 20:2;
Isa. 33:18; **Jer.** 50:38; **Ezek.** 42:16([K^e] *'ammāh* [520]).

368. אֵימִים **'ēymiym masc. proper noun**
(Emim, Emites)
Gen. 14:5; **Deut.** 2:10,11.

369. אַיִן **'ayin particle**
(no, none, nothing)
Gen. 2:5; 5:24; 7:8; 11:30; 19:31;
20:7,11; 28:17; 30:1,33; 31:2,5,50;
37:24,29,30; 39:9,11,23; 40:8; 41:8,
15,24,39,49; 42:13,32,36; 43:5; 44:26,
30,31,34; 45:6; 47:4,13; **Ex.** 2:12; 3:2;
5:10,11,16; 8:10(6),21(17); 9:14; 12:30;
14:11; 17:1,7; 21:11; 22:2(1),3(2),10(9),
14(13); 32:18,32; 33:15; **Lev.** 11:4,10,
12,26; 13:4,21,26,31,32,34; 14:21; 22:13;
25:31; 26:6,17,36,37; **Num.** 5:8,13; 11:6;
13:20; 14:42; 19:2,15; 20:5,19; 21:5;
22:26; 27:4,8–11,17; 35:27; **Deut.**
1:32,42; 4:12,22,35,39; 8:15; 12:12;
14:10,27,29; 19:6; 21:18,20; 22:26,27;

25:5; 28:26,29,31,32,68; 29:15(14); 31:17; 32:4,12,28,39; 33:26; **Josh.** 6:1; 18:7; 22:25,27; **Judg.** 3:25; 4:20; 6:5; 7:12,14; 9:15,20; 11:34; 12:3; 13:9; 14:3,6; 16:15; 17:6; 18:1,7,10,28; 19:1,15,18, 19,28; 21:9,25; **Ruth** 4:4; **1 Sam.** 1:2; 2:2; 3:1; 9:2,4,7; 10:14,24; 11:3,7; 14:6, 17,26,39; 17:50; 18:25; 19:11; 20:2,21; 21:1(2),4(5),8(9),9(10); 22:8; 24:11(12); 26:12; 27:1; 30:4; **2 Sam.** 3:22; 7:22; 12:3; 14:6; 15:3; 17:6; 18:18,22; 19:6(7), 7(8); 20:1; 21:4; 22:42; **1 Kgs.** 3:18; 5:4(18),6(20); 6:18; 8:9,23,46,60; 10:21; 15:22; 18:10,26,29,43; 20:40; 21:5,15; 22:1,7,17,47; **2 Kgs.** 1:3,6,16; 2:10; 3:11; 4:2,6,14,31; 5:15; 7:5,10; 9:10; 12:7(8); 14:26; 17:26,34; 19:3; **1 Chr.** 4:27; 17:20; 22:3,4,14,16; 23:26; 29:15; **2 Chr.** 5:10,11; 6:14,36; 9:20; 12:3; 14:6(5), 11(10),13(12); 15:5; 18:6,7,16; 19:7; 20:6,12,24,25; 21:18; 22:9; 25:7; 35:3,15; 36:16; **Ezra** 3:13; 9:14,15; 10:13; **Neh.** 2:2,12,14,20; 4:23; 5:5; 7:4; 8:10; 13:24; **Esth.** 1:8; 2:7,20; 3:5,8; 4:2; 5:13; 7:4; 8:8; **Job** 1:8; 2:3,13; 3:9,21; 5:4,9; 6:13; 7:8,21; 8:22; 9:10; 10:7; 11:3,19; 12:3; 18:19; 19:7; 20:21; 21:33; 22:5; 23:8; 24:7,24; 26:6; 27:19; 28:14; 31:19(20); 32:5,12; 33:33; 34:22(23); 35:15; 41:33; **Ps.** 3:2(3); 5:9; 6:5; 7:2; 10:4; 14:1,3; 18:41; 19:3,6; 22:11; 32:2,9; 33:16; 34:9; 36:1; 37:10,36; 38:3,7,10,14; 39:5,13; 40:5(6),12; 50:22; 53:1,3; 55:19; 59:13; 69:2,20; 71:11; 72:12; 73:2,4,5; 74:9; 79:3; 86:8; 88:4; 103:16; 104:25,35; 105:34,37; 107:12; 119:165; 135:17; 139:4; 142:4; 144:14; 145:3; 146:3; 147:5; **Prov.** 1:24; 5:17,23; 6:7,15; 7:19; 8:8,24; 10:25; 11:14; 12:7; 13:4,7; 14:4,6; 15:22; 17:16; 20:4; 21:30; 22:27; 23:5; 25:3,14,28; 26:20; 28:1,3,24,27; 29:1,9, 18,19; 30:27; **Eccl.** 1:7,9,11; 2:11,16,24; 3:12,14,19,22; 4:1,8,10,16; 5:1(4:17), 4(3),12(11),14(13); 6:2; 7:20; 8:7,8,11, 13,15,16; 9:1,2,5,6,10,16; 10:11; 11:5,6; 12:1,12; **Song** 4:2,7; 6:6,8; 8:8; **Isa.** 1:6,15,30,31; 2:7; 3:7; 5:9,27,29; 6:11; 8:20; 9:7; 13:14; 14:31; 17:2,14; 19:7; 22:22; 23:10; 27:4; 33:19; 34:10,12; 37:3; 40:16,17,23,28,29; 41:11,12,17,24,26,28; 42:22; 43:11–13; 44:6,8,12; 45:5,6,9,14, 18,21,22; 46:9; 47:1,10,14,15; 48:22; 50:2,10; 51:18; 55:1; 57:1,21; 59:4,8,10, 11,15,16; 60:15; 63:3,5; 64:7(6); 66:4; **Jer.** 2:32; 4:4,7,23,25,29; 5:13,21; 6:14; 7:16,17,32,33; 8:6,11,13,15,17,19,22; 9:22(21); 10:5–7,20; 11:14; 12:11,12; 13:19; 14:6,12,16,19; 15:1; 16:19; 19:11; 21:12; 22:17,28; 26:9,16; 30:5,7,10, 13,17; 31:15; 32:33,43; 33:10,12; 34:22; 37:14; 38:4–6,9; 39:10; 44:2,16,22; 46:11, 19,23,27; 48:2,9,38; 49:1,5,7,10,12; 50:20, 32; 51:29,37; **Lam.** 1:2,7,9,17,21; 2:9; 3:49; 4:4; 5:3,7,8; **Ezek.** 3:7; 7:14,25; 8:12; 9:9; 13:10,15,16; 20:39; 26:21; 27:36; 28:19; 33:28,32; 34:6,8,28; 37:8; 38:11; 39:26; 42:6; **Dan.** 1:4; 8:4,5,27; 9:26; 10:21; 11:15,16,45; **Hos.** 3:4; 4:1; 5:14; 7:7,11; 8:7,8; 10:3; 13:4; **Joel** 1:6,18; 2:27; **Amos** 2:11; 3:4,5; 5:2,6; **Obad.** 1:7; **Mic.** 3:7; 4:4,9; 5:8(7); 7:1,2; **Nah.** 2:8(9),9(10), 11(12); 3:3,9,18,19; **Hab.** 2:19; 3:17; **Zeph.** 2:5; 3:6,13; **Hag.** 1:6; 2:3; **Zech.** 8:10; 9:11; 10:2; **Mal.** 1:8,10; 2:2,9,13.

370. אַיִן *'ayin* **adv.**
(whence, from where)
Gen. 29:4; 42:7; **Num.** 11:13; **Josh.** 2:4; 9:8; **Judg.** 17:9; 19:17; **2 Kgs.** 5:25; 6:27; 20:14; **Job** 1:7; 28:12,20; **Ps.** 121:1; **Isa.** 39:3; **Jon.** 1:8; **Nah.** 3:7.

371. אִין *'iyn* **interrog. adv.**
(Is there not? Have you not?)
1 Sam. 21:8(9).

372. אִיעֶזֶר *'iy'ezer* **masc. proper noun**
(Iezer: form of *'abiy'ezer* [44,A])
Num. 26:30.

373. אִיעֶזְרִי *'iy'ezriy* **masc. proper noun**
(Iezerite)
Num. 26:30.

374. אֵיפָה *'ēypāh*, אֵפָה *'ēpāh* **fem. noun**
(ephah [unit of dry measure], basket that could hold an ephah)
Ex. 16:36; **Lev.** 5:11; 6:20(13); 19:36; **Num.** 5:15; 28:5; **Deut.** 25:14,15; **Judg.** 6:19; **Ruth** 2:17; **1 Sam.** 1:24; 17:17; **Prov.** 20:10; **Isa.** 5:10; **Ezek.** 45:10,11, 13,24; 46:5,7,11,14; **Amos** 8:5; **Mic.** 6:10; **Zech.** 5:6–10.

375. אֵיפֹה *'eypōh* **interrog. adv.**
(where? what kind?)
Gen. 37:16; **Judg.** 8:18; **Ruth** 2:19; **1 Sam.** 19:22; **2 Sam.** 9:4; **Job** 4:7; 38:4; **Isa.** 49:21; **Jer.** 3:2; 36:19.

376. אִישׁ *'iyš* **masc. noun**
(man, male)
Gen. 2:23,24; 3:6,16; 4:1,23; 6:4,9; 7:2; 9:5,20; 10:5; 11:3,7; 12:20; 13:8,11, 13,16; 14:24; 15:10; 16:3; 17:23,27; 18:2, 16,22; 19:4,5,8–12,16,31; 20:7,8; 23:6; 24:13,16,21,22,26,29,30,32,54,58,59,61, 65; 25:27; 26:7,11,13,31; 27:11; 29:19, 22,32,34; 30:15,18,20,43; 31:49,50; 32:6(7),24(25),28(29); 33:1; 34:7,14, 20–22,25; 37:15,17,19,28; 38:1,2,21, 22,25; 39:1,2,11,14; 40:5; 41:11,12,33, 38,44; 42:11,13,21,25,28,30,33,35; 43:3,5–7,11,13–19,21,24,33; 44:1,3, 4,11,13,15,17,26; 45:1,22; 46:32,34; 47:2,6,20; 49:6,28; **Ex.** 1:1; 2:1,11–14, 19–21; 4:10,19; 5:9; 7:12; 10:7,23; 11:2,3,7; 12:3,4,22,44; 15:3; 16:15,16, 18–21,29; 17:9; 18:7,16,21,25; 19:13; 21:7,12,14,16,18,20,22,26,28,29,33,35; 22:1(21:37),5(4),7(6),10(9),14(13), 16(15),31(30); 25:2,20; 28:21; 30:12, 33,38; 32:1,23,27–29; 33:4,8,10,11; 34:3,24; 35:21–23,29; 36:1,2,4,6; 37:9; 39:14; **Lev.** 7:8–10; 10:1; 13:29,38,40, 44; 14:11; 15:2,5,16,18,24,33; 16:21; 17:3,4,8–10,13; 18:6,27; 19:3,11,20; 20:2–5,9–15,17,18,20,21,27; 21:3,7,9, 17–19,21; 22:3–5,12,14,18,21; 24:10, 15,17,19; 25:10,13,14,17,26,27,29,46; 26:37; 27:2,14,16,20,26,28,31; **Num.** 1:4,5,17,44,52; 2:2,17,34; 4:19,49; 5:6,8,10,12,13,15,19,20,27,29–31; 6:2; 7:5; 9:6,7,10,13; 11:10,16,24–26; 12:3; 13:2,3,16,31,32; 14:4,15,22,36–38; 15:32,35; 16:2,7,14,17,18,22,26,30,35, 40(17:5); 17:2(17),5(20),9(24); 19:9, 18,20; 21:9; 22:9,20,35; 23:19; 25:5,6, 8,14; 26:10,54,64,65; 27:8,16,18; 30:2(3), 6–8(7–9),10–14(11–15),16(17); 31:3,17, 21,28,42,49,50,53; 32:11,14,18; 34:17,19; 35:8; 36:7–9; **Deut.** 1:13,15–17,22, 23,31,35,41; 2:14,16; 3:11,20; 4:3; 7:24; 8:5; 11:25; 12:8; 13:13; 16:17; 17:2,5, 12,15; 18:19; 19:11,15–17; 20:5–8; 21:15,18,21,22; 22:13,16,18,21–26, 28–30(23:1); 23:10(11); 24:1–3,5,7,11, 12,16; 25:1,5,7,9,11; 27:14,15; 28:30, 54,56; 29:10(9),18(17),20(19); 31:12; 32:25,26; 33:1,8; 34:6; **Josh.** 1:5,18; 2:1–5,7,9,11,14,17,23; 3:12; 4:2,4,5; 5:4,6,13; 6:3,5,20–22,26; 7:2–5; 8:3,12, 14,17,20,21,25; 9:6,7,14; 10:2,6,8,14, 18,21,24; 14:6; 17:1; 18:4,8,9; 21:44(42); 22:14,20; 23:9,10; 24:28; **Judg.** 1:4, 24–26; 2:6,21; 3:15,17,28,29,31; 4:6,10, 14,20,22; 6:8,16,27–30; 7:6–8,13,14,16, 19,21–24; 8:1,4,5,8–10,14–18,21,22, 24,25; 9:2,4,5,9,13,18,28,36,49,51,55,57; 10:1,18; 11:3,39; 12:1,2,4,5; 13:2,6,8–11; 14:15,18,19; 15:10,11,15,16; 16:5,19,27; 17:1,5,6,8,11; 18:2,7,11,14,16,17,19, 22,25; 19:1,3,6,7,9,10,15–18,20, 22–26,28; 20:1,2,4,8,10–13,15–17, 20–22,25,31,33–36,38,39,41,42,44–48; 21:1,8–10,12,21,22,24,25; **Ruth** 1:1–3, 5,9,11–13; 2:1,11,19,20; 3:3,8,14,16,18; 4:2,7; **1 Sam.** 1:1,3,8,11,21–23; 2:9,13, 15–17,19,25–27,33; 4:2,9,10,12–14,16, 18,19,21; 5:7,9,12; 6:10,15,19,20; 7:1,11; 8:22; 9:1,2,6–10,16,17,22; 10:2,3,6,11, 12,22,25; 11:1,5,7–10,12,13,15; 12:4; 13:2,6,14,15,20; 14:2,8,12,14,20,22, 24,28,34,36,52; 15:3,4; 16:16–18; 17:2, 4,8,10,12,19,23–28,33,41,52; 18:5,23,27; 20:15,41; 21:1(2),2(3),7(8),14(15); 22:2, 6,18,19; 23:3,5,8,12,13,24–26; 24:2–4

(3–5),6(7),7(8),19(20),22(23); 25:2,3,10, 11,13,15,19,20,25; 26:2,15,23; 27:2,3,8, 9,11; 28:1,8,14; 29:2,4,11; 30:1–3,6, 9–11,13,17,21,22,31; 31:1,3,6,7,12; **2 Sam.** 1:2,11,13; 2:3–5,16,17,27,29–32; 3:15,16,20,39; 4:2,11; 6:19; 7:14; 8:4,5,10; 9:3; 10:5,6(KJV, *'iyš-ṭôḇ* [382]),8(KJV, *'iyš-ṭôḇ* [382]); 11:16,17,23,26; 12:1,4, 5,7; 13:3,9,29; 14:5,7,16,19,25; 15:1,2, 4–6,11,13,18,22,30; 16:5,7,8,13,15, 18,23; 17:1,3,8,12,14,18,24,25; 18:10–12, 17,20,24,26–28; 19:7(8),8(9),14(15), 16(17),17(18),22(23),28(29),32(33),41–4 3(42–44); 20:1,2,4,7,11–13,21,22; 21:4–6,17,20; 22:49; 23:7,9,17,20,21; 24:9,15; **1 Kgs.** 1:5,9,42,49; 2:2,4,9, 26,32; 3:13; 4:25(5:5),27(5:7),28(5:8); 5:6(20),13(27); 7:14,30,36; 8:2,25,31, 38,39; 9:5,22,27; 10:8,15,25; 11:17,18, 24,28; 12:22,24; 13:1,4–8,11,12,14,21, 25,26,29,31; 17:18,24; 18:4,13,22,40,44; 20:17,20,24,28,30,33,35,37,39,42; 21:10,11,13; 22:6,8,10,17,34,36; **2 Kgs.** 1:6–13; 2:7,16,17,19; 3:23,25,26; 4:1,7, 9,14,16,21,22,25–27,29,40,42,43; 5:1,7, 8,14,15,20,24,26; 6:2,6,9,10,15,19,32; 7:2,3,5,6,9,10,17–19; 8:2,4,7,8,11; 9:11, 13,21; 10:5–7,14,19,21,24,25; 11:8,9,11; 12:4(5),5(6),9(10),15(16); 13:19,21; 14:6, 12; 15:20,25; 17:30; 18:21,27,31,33; 20:14; 22:15; 23:2,8,10,16–18,35; 24:16; 25:4,19,23–25; **1 Chr.** 4:12,22,42; 5:18,24; 7:21,40; 8:40; 9:9; 10:1,7,12; 11:19,22,23; 12:8(9),30(31),38(39); 16:3,21,43; 18:4,5,10; 19:5,18; 20:6; 21:5,14; 22:9; 23:14; 25:1; 26:8; 27:32; 28:3; **2 Chr.** 2:2(1),7(6),13(12),14(13), 17(16); 5:3; 6:5,16,22,29,30; 7:18; 8:9,14; 9:7,14,24; 10:16; 11:2,4; 13:3,7,15,17; 15:13; 17:13; 18:5,7,9,16,33; 20:23,27; 23:7,8,10; 24:24; 25:4,7,9,22; 28:12,15; 30:11,16; 31:1,2,19; 34:12,23,30; **Ezra** 1:4; 2:1,2,22,23,27,28; 3:1,2; 8:18; 10:1, 9,16,17; **Neh.** 1:2,11; 2:12; 3:2,7,22,28; 4:15(9),18(12),19(13),22(16),23(17); 5:7,13,17; 6:11; 7:2,3,6,7,26–33; 8:1–3, 16; 11:2,3,6,20; 12:24,36,44; 13:10, 25,30; **Esth.** 1:8,22; 2:5; 4:11; 6:6,7,9,11; 7:6; 9:2,4,6,12,15,19,22; **Job** 1:1,3,4,8; 2:3,4,11,12; 4:13; 9:32; 11:2,12; 12:10,14; 14:12; 15:16; 22:8; 31:35; 32:1,5,13,21; 33:15,16,27; 34:8,10,11,21,23,34,36; 35:8; 36:24; 37:7,20,24; 38:26; 41:17(9); 42:11; **Ps.** 1:1; 4:2(3); 5:6(7); 12:2(3); 18:48(49); 22:6(7); 25:12; 26:9; 31:20(21); 34:12(13); 37:7,37; 38:14(15); 39:6(7), 11(12); 41:9(10); 43:1; 49:2(3),7(8), 16(17); 55:23(24); 59:2(3); 62:3(4),9(10), 12(13); 64:6(7); 76:5(6); 78:25; 80:17(18); 87:5; 92:6(7); 105:17; 109:16; 112:1,5; 119:24; 139:19; 140:1(2),4(5),11(12); 141:4; 147:10; **Prov.** 2:12; 3:31; 5:21; 6:11,12,26–28; 7:19; 8:4; 10:23; 11:12,17; 12:2,8,14,25; 13:2,8; 14:7,12,14,17; 15:18,21,23; 16:2,7,14,25,27–29; 17:12,27; 18:4,12,14,20,24; 19:6,21,22; 20:3,5,6,17; 21:2,8,17,28,29; 22:7,24,29; 24:1,5,29,30,34; 25:1,14,18,28; 26:12, 19,21; 27:8,17,21; 28:5,11,20,22,24; 29:1,3,4,6,8–10,13,20,22,26,27; 30:2; **Eccl.** 1:8; 4:4; 6:2,3; 7:5; 9:14,15; 12:3; **Song** 3:8; 8:7,11; **Isa.** 2:9,11,17; 3:2,5,6; 4:1; 5:3,7,15,22; 6:5; 7:13,21; 9:19(18), 20(19); 13:8,14; 14:16,18; 19:2; 21:9; 28:14; 29:13; 31:7,8; 32:2; 36:6,12,16,18; 39:3; 40:13,26; 41:6,11,12,28; 42:13; 44:13; 45:14; 46:11; 47:15; 50:2; 52:14; 53:3,6; 55:7; 56:11; 57:1; 59:16; 63:3; 66:3,13,24; **Jer.** 1:15; 2:6; 3:1; 4:3,4,29; 5:1,8,26; 6:3,11,23; 7:5; 8:6; 9:4(3),5(4), 10(9),12(11); 10:23; 11:2,3,8,9,21,23; 12:11,15; 13:11,14; 14:9; 15:10; 16:12; 17:10,25; 18:11,12,21; 19:9,10; 20:15,16; 22:7,8,28,30; 23:9,14,24,27,30,34–36; 25:5,26; 26:3,11,16,17,20,22; 29:6,26,32; 31:30,34; 32:19,32; 33:17,18; 34:9,10, 14–18; 35:4,13,15,19; 36:3,7,16,19,31; 37:10; 38:4,7,9–11,16,22,24; 39:4,17; 40:7–9,15; 41:1–5,7–9,12,15,16; 42:17; 43:2,9; 44:7,15,19,26,27; 46:16; 48:14, 31,36; 49:5,18,26,33; 50:16,30,40,42; 51:6,9,22,32,43,45; 52:7,25; **Lam.** 3:33; **Ezek.** 1:9,11,12,23; 3:26; 4:17; 7:13,16; 8:11,12,16; 9:1–4,6,11; 10:2,3,6,22;

11:1,2,15; 12:16; 14:1,3,4,7,8,14,16,18; 16:32,45; 18:5,7,8,16,30; 20:1,7,8,39; 21:31; 22:6,9,11,30; 23:14,40,42,45; 24:17,22,23; 27:10,27; 32:10; 33:2, 20,26,30; 38:21; 39:14,20; 40:3–5; 43:6; 44:2,25; 45:20; 46:16,18; 47:3,14; **Dan.** 9:7,21; 10:5,7,11,19; 12:6,7; **Hos.** 2:2(4),7(9),10(12),16(18); 3:3; 4:4; 6:9; 9:7; 11:9; **Joel** 2:7,8; 3:9(4:9); **Amos** 2:7; 5:19; 6:9; **Obad.** 1:7,9; **Jon.** 1:5,7,10,13,14,16; 3:5,8; **Mic.** 2:2,11; 4:4,5; 5:7(6); 6:10; 7:2,6; **Nah.** 2:3(4); **Zeph.** 1:12; 2:11; 3:4,6; **Hag.** 1:9; 2:12,22; **Zech.** 1:8,10,21(2:4); 2:1(5); 3:8,10; 4:1; 6:12; 7:2,9,10; 8:4,10,16, 17,23; 10:1; 11:6; 13:3–5; 14:13; **Mal.** 2:10,12; 3:16,17.

377. I. אִישׁ *'iyš* **verb**
(show oneself to be a man)
Isa. 46:8(NASB, NIV, see II).
II. אָשַׁשׁ *'āšaš* **verb**
(to fix in mind)
Isa. 46:8(KJV, see I).

378. אִישׁ בֹּשֶׁת *'iyš bōšet̲* **masc. proper noun**
(Ish-Bosheth)
2 Sam. 2:8,10,12,15; 3:8,14,15; 4:5, 8,12.

379. אִישְׁהוֹד *'iyšhôd̲* **masc. proper noun**
(Ishhod)
1 Chr. 7:18.

380. I. אִישׁוֹן *'iyšôn* **masc. noun**
(pupil, apple of the eye)
Deut. 32:10; **Ps.** 17:8; **Prov.** 7:2; 20:20.
II. אֱשׁוּן *'ešûn* **masc. noun**
(time, approach of darkness)
Prov. 7:9.

381. אִישׁ־חַיִל *'iyš-ḥayil* **masc. noun**
(valiant man, from *iyš* [376] and *ḥayil* [2428])
1 Sam. 31:12; **2 Sam.** 23:20([K^e] *iyš* [376] and *ḥay* [2416,I]); 24:9; **1 Kgs.** 1:42.

382. I. אִישׁ־טוֹב *'iyš-ṭôb̲* **proper noun**
(Ish-tob)
2 Sam. 10:6(NASB, NIV, see II),8(NASB, NIV, see II).
II. אִישׁ טוֹב *'iyš ṭôb̲* **masc. noun**
(men of Tob; from *'iyš* [376] and *ṭôb̲* [2897])
2 Sam. 10:6(KJV, see I),8(KJV, see I).

383. אִיתַי *'it̲ay* **Aram. particle**
(there is, there are)
Ezra 4:16; 5:17; **Dan.** 2:10,11,26,28,30; 3:12,14,15,17,18,25,29; 4:35(32); 5:11.

384. A. אִיתִיאֵל *'iyt̲iy'ēl* **masc. proper noun**
(Ithiel: a person instructed by Agur)
Prov. 30:1.
B. אִיתִיאֵל *'iyt̲iy'ēl* **masc. proper noun**
(Ithiel: a Benjamite)
Neh. 11:7.

385. אִיתָמָר *'iyt̲āmār* **masc. proper noun**
(Ithamar)
Ex. 6:23; 28:1; 38:21; **Lev.** 10:6,12,16; **Num.** 3:2,4; 4:28,33; 7:8; 26:60; **1 Chr.** 6:3(5:29); 24:1–6; **Ezra** 8:2.

386. אֵיתָן *'ēytān* **masc. noun**
(strength, permanence)
Gen. 49:24; **Ex.** 14:27; **Num.** 24:21; **Deut.** 21:4; **Job** 12:19; 33:19; **Ps.** 74:15; **Prov.** 13:15; **Jer.** 5:15; 49:19; 50:44; **Amos** 5:24; **Mic.** 6:2.

387. אֵיתָן *'ēyt̲ān* **masc. proper noun**
(Ethan)

1 Kgs. 4:31(5:11); 1 Chr. 2:6,8;
6:42(27),44(29); 15:17,19; Ps.
89:[title](1).

388. אֵיתָנִים 'eṯāniym proper
noun
(Ethanim; the seventh month)
1 Kgs. 8:2.

389. אַךְ 'aḵ particle
(surely, only, but)
Gen. 7:23; 9:4,5; 18:32; 20:12; 23:13;
26:9; 27:13,30; 29:14; 34:15,22,23;
44:28; Ex. 10:17; 12:15,16; 21:21; 31:13;
Lev. 11:4,21,36; 21:23; 23:27,39;
27:26,28; Num. 1:49; 12:2; 14:9; 18:3,
15,17; 22:20; 26:55; 31:22,23; 36:6;
Deut. 12:22; 14:7; 16:15; 18:20; 28:29;
Josh. 3:4; 22:19; Judg. 3:24; 6:39; 7:19;
10:15; 16:28; 20:39; 1 Sam. 1:23; 2:10;
3:13; 8:9; 12:20,24; 16:6; 18:8,17; 20:39;
21:4(5); 25:21; 29:9; 2 Sam. 23:10;
1 Kgs. 9:24; 11:12,39; 17:13; 22:32,43;
2 Kgs. 5:7; 12:13(14); 13:6; 18:20; 22:7;
23:9,26,35; 24:3; 1 Chr. 22:12; 2 Chr.
20:33; 30:11; Ezra 10:15; Job 2:6;
13:15,20; 14:22; 16:7; 18:21; 19:13; 23:6;
30:24; 33:8; 35:13; 36:16; Ps. 23:6; 37:8;
39:5(6),6(7),11(12); 49:15(16); 58:11(12);
62:1(2),2(3),4–6(5–7),9(10); 68:6(7),
21(22); 73:1,13,18; 75:8; 85:9(10);
139:11; 140:13(14); Prov. 11:23,24;
14:23; 17:11; 21:5; 22:16; Isa. 14:15;
16:7; 19:11; 34:14,15; 36:5; 43:24;
45:14,24; 63:8; Jer. 2:35; 3:13; 5:4,5;
10:19,24; 12:1; 16:19; 26:15,24; 28:7;
30:11; 32:30; 34:4; Lam. 2:16; 3:3;
Ezek. 46:17; Hos. 4:4; 12:8(9),11(12);
Jon. 2:4(5); Zeph. 1:8; 3:7; Zech. 1:6.

390. אַכַּד 'akkaḏ proper noun
(Akkad)
Gen. 10:10.

391. אַכְזָב 'aḵzāḇ adj.
(lying, deceptive)
Jer. 15:18; Mic. 1:14.

392. A. אַכְזִיב 'aḵziyḇ proper noun
(Achzib: a lowland in Judah)
Josh. 15:44; Mic. 1:14.
B. אַכְזִיב 'aḵziyḇ proper noun
(Achzib: a lowland in Asher)
Josh. 19:29; Judg. 1:31.

393. אַכְזָר 'aḵzār adj.
(cruel, deadly)
Deut. 32:33; Job 30:21; 41:10(2);
Lam. 4:3.

394. אַכְזָרִי 'aḵzāriy adj.
(cruel)
Prov. 5:9; 11:17; 12:10; 17:11; Isa. 13:9;
Jer. 6:23; 30:14; 50:42.

395. אַכְזְרִיּוּת 'aḵzᵉriyyûṯ fem. noun
(cruelty, fierceness)
Prov. 27:4.

396. אֲכִילָה 'aḵiylāh fem. noun
(food, meal)
1 Kgs. 19:8.

397. אָכִישׁ 'āḵiyš masc. proper
noun
(Achish)
1 Sam. 21:10–12(11–13),14(15);
27:2,3,5,6,9,10,12; 28:1,2; 29:2,3,6,8,9;
1 Kgs. 2:39,40.

398. אָכַל 'āḵal verb
(to eat, to consume, to devour)
Gen. 2:16,17;
3:1–3,5,6,11–14,17–19,22; 6:21; 9:4;
14:24; 18:8; 19:3; 24:33,54; 25:34; 26:30;
27:4,7,10,19,25,31,33; 28:20; 31:15,38;
40,46,54; 32:32(33); 37:20,25,33; 39:6;
40:17,19; 41:4,20; 43:2,16,25,32; 45:18;
47:22,24; 49:27; Ex. 2:20; 3:2; 10:5,
12,15; 12:7–9,11,15,16,18–20,43–46,48;
13:3,6,7; 15:7; 16:3,8,12,25,32,35; 18:12;
21:28; 22:6(5),31(30); 23:11,15; 24:11,
17; 29:32–34; 32:6; 34:15,18,28; Lev.
3:17; 6:10(3),16(9),18(11),23(16),
26(19),29(22),30(23); 7:6,15,16,

18–21,23–27; 8:31; 9:24; 10:2,12–14, 17–19; 11:2–4,8,9,11,13,21,22,34, 40–42,47; 14:47; 17:10,12–15; 19:6–8, 23,25,26; 21:22; 22:4,6–8,10–14,16,30; 23:6,14; 24:9; 25:7,12,19,20,22; 26:5, 10,16,26,29,38; **Num.** 6:3,4; 9:11; 11:1, 4,5,13,18,19,21; 12:12; 13:32; 15:19; 16:35; 18:10,11,13,31; 21:28; 23:24; 24:8; 25:2; 26:10; 28:17; **Deut.** 2:6,28; 4:24,28; 5:25(22); 6:11; 7:16; 8:3,9,10, 12,16; 9:3,9,18; 11:15; 12:7,15–18, 20–25,27; 14:3,4,6–12,19–21,23,26,29; 15:20,22,23; 16:3,7,8; 18:1,8; 20:14,19; 23:24(25); 26:12,14; 27:7; 28:31,33, 39,51,53,55,57; 29:6(5); 31:17,20; 32:13,22,38,42; **Josh.** 5:11,12; 24:13; **Judg.** 6:21; 9:15,20,27; 13:4,7,14,16; 14:9,14; 19:4,6,8,21; **Ruth** 2:14; 3:3,7; **1 Sam.** 1:7–9,18; 2:36; 9:13,19,24; 14:24,28,30,32–34; 20:5,24,34; 28:20,22,23,25; 30:11,12,16; **2 Sam.** 2:26; 9:7,10,11,13; 11:11,13,25; 12:3, 20,21; 13:5,9,11; 16:2; 17:29; 18:8; 19:28(29),35(36),42(43); 22:9; **1 Kgs.** 1:25,41; 2:7; 4:20; 13:8,9,15,17–19, 22,23,28; 14:11; 16:4; 17:12,15; 18:19, 38,41,42; 19:5–8,21; 21:4,5,7,23,24; 22:27; **2 Kgs.** 1:10,12,14; 4:8,40–44; 6:22,23,28,29; 7:2,8,19; 9:10,34,36; 18:27,31; 19:29; 23:9; 25:29; **1 Chr.** 12:39; 29:22; **2 Chr.** 7:1,13; 18:26; 28:15; 30:18,22; 31:10; **Ezra** 2:63; 6:21; 9:12; 10:6; **Neh.** 2:3,13; 5:2,14; 7:65; 8:10,12; 9:25,36; **Esth.** 4:16; **Job** 1:4,13, 16,18; 5:5; 6:6; 13:28; 15:34; 18:13; 20:26; 21:25; 22:20; 31:8,12,17,39; 34:3; 40:15; 42:11; **Ps.** 14:4; 18:8(9); 21:9(10); 22:26(27),29(30); 27:2; 41:9(10); 50:3,13; 53:4(5); 59:15(16); 69:9(10); 78:24,25, 29,45,63; 79:7; 80:5(6); 81:16(17); 102:4(5),9(10); 105:35; 106:20,28; 127:2; 128:2; **Prov.** 1:31; 13:2,25; 18:21; 23:7,8; 24:13; 25:16,21,27; 27:18; 30:14,17,20; 31:27; **Eccl.** 2:24,25; 3:13; 4:5; 5:11(10), 12(11),17–19(16–18); 6:2; 8:15; 9:7; 10:16,17; **Song** 4:16; 5:1; **Isa.** 1:7,19,20; 3:10; 4:1; 5:17,24; 7:15,22; 9:12(11), 18(17),20(19); 10:17; 11:7; 21:5; 22:13; 23:18; 24:6; 26:11; 29:6,8; 30:24,27,30; 31:8; 33:11,14; 36:12,16; 37:30; 44:16, 19; 49:26; 50:9; 51:8; 55:1,2,10; 56:9; 58:14; 59:5; 61:6; 62:9; 65:4,13,21,22,25; 66:17; **Jer.** 2:3,7,30; 3:24; 5:14,17; 7:21; 8:16; 9:15(14); 10:25; 12:12; 15:3,16; 16:8; 17:27; 19:9; 21:14; 22:15; 23:15; 24:2,3,8; 29:5,17,28; 30:16; 31:29,30; 41:1; 46:10,14; 48:45; 49:27; 50:7,17,32; 51:34; 52:33; **Lam.** 2:3,20; 4:5,11; **Ezek.** 2:8; 3:1–3; 4:9,10,12–14,16; 5:10; 7:15; 12:18,19; 15:4,5,7; 16:13,19,20; 18:2,6,11,15; 19:3,6,12,14; 20:47(21:3); 21:28(33); 22:9,25; 23:25; 24:17,22; 25:4; 28:18; 33:25,27; 34:3,28; 36:13,14; 39:17–19; 42:5(KJV, *yākal* [3201]),13; 43:8(KJV, NASB, see *kālāh* [3615]); 44:3,29,31; 45:21; **Dan.** 1:12,13,15; 10:3; 11:26; **Hos.** 2:12(14); 4:8,10; 5:7; 7:7,9; 8:13,14; 9:3,4; 10:13; 11:4,6; 13:8; **Joel** 1:4,19,20; 2:3,5,25,26; **Amos** 1:4,7,10,12,14; 2:2,5; 4:9; 5:6; 6:4; 7:2,4,12; 9:14; **Obad.** 1:18; **Mic.** 3:3; 6:14; 7:1; **Nah.** 1:10; 2:13(14); 3:12, 13,15; **Hab.** 1:8; 3:14; **Zeph.** 1:18; 3:8; **Hag.** 1:6; **Zech.** 7:6; 9:4,15; 11:1,9,16; 12:6; **Mal.** 3:11.

399. I. אֲכַל *'akal* **Aram. verb**
(to eat, to consume, to devour; corr. to Hebr. 398)
Dan. 4:33(30); 7:5,7,19,23.
II. אֲכַל *'akal* **Aram. verb**
(to slander [with *qeraṣ* {7170}])
Dan. 3:8; 6:24(25).

400. אֹכֶל *'ōkel* **masc. noun**
(food)
Gen. 14:11; 41:35,36,48; 42:7,10; 43:2,4,20,22; 44:1,25; 47:24; **Ex.** 12:4; 16:16,18,21; **Lev.** 11:34; 25:37; **Deut.** 2:6,28; 23:19(20); **Ruth** 2:14; **Job** 9:26; 12:11; 20:21; 36:31; 38:41; 39:29; **Ps.** 78:18,30; 104:21,27; 107:18; 145:15; **Prov.** 13:23; **Lam.** 1:11,19; **Joel** 1:16; **Hab.** 3:17; **Mal.** 1:12.

401. אֻכָּל *'ukkāl* **masc. proper noun**
(Ucal)
Prov. 30:1.

402. אָכְלָה *'oklāh* **fem. noun**
(food, that which is eaten)
Gen. 1:29,30; 6:21; 9:3; **Ex.** 16:15; **Lev.** 11:39; 25:6; **Jer.** 12:9; **Ezek.** 15:4,6; 21:32 (37); 23:37; 29:5; 34:5,8,10; 35:12; 39:4.

403. אָכֵן *'ākēn* **adv.**
(surely, truly, yet)
Gen. 28:16; **Ex.** 2:14; **1 Sam.** 15:32; **1 Kgs.** 11:2; **Job** 32:8; **Ps.** 31:22(23); 66:19; 82:7; **Isa.** 40:7; 45:15; 49:4; 53:4; **Jer.** 3:20,23; 4:10; 8:8; **Zeph.** 3:7.

404. אָכַף *'ākap* **verb**
(to crave, to urge)
Prov. 16:26.

405. אֶכֶף *'ekep* **masc. noun**
(hand, pressure)
Job 33:7.

406. אִכָּר *'ikār* **masc. noun**
(plowmen, farm workers)
2 Chr. 26:10; **Isa.** 61:5; **Jer.** 14:4; 31:24; 51:23; **Joel** 1:11; **Amos** 5:16.

407. אַכְשָׁף *'akšāp* **proper noun**
(Achshaph)
Josh. 11:1; 12:20; 19:25.

408. אַל *'al* **adv.**
(no, not, without)
Gen. 13:8; 15:1; 18:3,30,32; 19:7,8,17,18; 21:12,16,17; 22:12; 24:56; 26:2,24; 31:34; 33:10; 35:17; 37:22,27; 42:22; 43:23; 44:18; 45:5,9,20,24; 46:3; 47:29; 49:4,6; 50:19,21; **Ex.** 3:5; 5:9; 8:29(25); 10:48; 12:9; 14:13; 16:19,29; 19:15,24; 20:19,20; 23:1,7,21; 32:22; 33:15; 34:3; 36:6; **Lev.** 10:6,9; 11:43; 16:2; 18:24; 19:4,29,31; 25:14,36; **Num.** 4:18; 10:31; 11:15; 12:11,12; 14:9,42; 16:15,26; 21:34; 22:16; 32:5; **Deut.** 1:21; 2:5,9,19; 3:2,26; 9:4,7,26,27; 20:3; 21:8; 31:6; 33:6; **Josh.** 1:7,9; 3:4; 7:3,19; 8:1,4; 10:6,8,19,25; 11:6; 13:13; 22:19,22; **Judg.** 4:18; 6:18,23,39; 13:4,7,14; 18:9,25; 19:20,23; **Ruth** 1:13,16,20; 2:8; 3:3,11,14,17; **1 Sam.** 1:16; 2:3,24; 3:17; 4:20; 6:3; 7:8; 9:20; 12:19,20; 16:7; 17:32; 18:17; 19:4; 20:3,38; 21:2(3); 22:15,23; 23:17; 25:25; 26:9,20; 27:10; 28:13; **2 Sam.** 1:20,21; 3:29; 9:7; 11:25; 13:12,16,20,25,28,32,33; 14:2,18; 17:16; 19:19(20); 24:14; **1 Kgs.** 2:16,19,20,36; 3:26; 8:57; 13:22; 17:13; 18:40; 20:8,11; 22:8; **2 Kgs.** 1:15; 2:18; 3:13; 4:3,16,24; 6:16,27; 9:15; 10:19,25; 11:15; 12:7(8); 18:26,29–32; 19:6,10; 23:18; 25:24; **1 Chr.** 16:22; 21:13; 22:13; 28:20; **2 Chr.** 6:42; 13:12; 14:11(10); 15:7; 18:7; 20:15,17; 23:6; 25:7; 29:11; 30:7,8; 32:7,15; 35:21; **Ezra** 9:12; **Neh.** 4:5 (3:37),14(8); 8:9–11; 9:32; 13:14; **Esth.** 4:13,16; 6:10; **Job** 1:12; 3:4,6,7,9; 5:17,22; 6:29; 9:34; 10:2; 11:14; 13:20,21; 15:31; 16:18; 20:17; 24:25; 32:21; 36:18,20,21; 41:8(40:32); **Ps.** 4:4; 6:1(2); 9:19(20); 10:12; 19:13(14); 22:11(12),19; 25:2,7,20; 26:9; 27:9,12; 28:1,3; 31:1(2),17(18); 32:9; 34:5(6); 35:19,22,24,25; 36:11(12); 37:1,7,8; 38:1(2),21(22); 39:8(9),12(13); 40:17(18); 41:2; 44:23(24); 49:16(17); 50:3; 51:11(12); 57:[title](1)(KJV, NASB, *'al tašḥēṯ* [516]); 58:[title](1)(KJV, NASB, *'al tašḥēṯ* [516]); 59:[title](1)(KJV, NASB, *'al tašḥēṯ* [516]),5(6),11(12); 62:10(11); 66:7; 69:6(7),14–17(15–18),25(26), 27(28),29; 70:5(6); 71:1,9,12,18; 74:19,21,23; 75:[title](1)(KJV, NASB, *'al tašḥēṯ* [516]),4,5; 79:8; 83:1(2); 85:8; 95:8; 102:2(3),24(25); 103:2; 105:15; 109:1,12,14; 119:8,10,19,31,36,43, 116,122,133; 121:3; 132:10; 138:8; 140:8(9); 141:4,5,8; 143:2,7; 146:3; **Prov.** 1:8,10,15; 3:1,3,5,7,11,21,25, 27–31; 4:2,5,6,13–15,21,27; 5:7,8; 6:4,20,25; 7:25; 8:10,33; 9:8; 12:28;

17:12; 19:18; 20:13,22; 22:22,24,26,28; 23:3,4,6,9,10,13,17,20,22,23,31; 24:1,15, 17,19,21,28,29; 25:6,8,9; 26:4,25; 27:1, 2,10; 28:17; 30:6,8,10,31(NASB, NIV, *'alqûm* [510]); 31:3,4; **Eccl.** 5:2(1),4(3), 6(5),8(7); 7:9,10,16–18; 8:3; 9:8; 10:4,20; 11:6; **Song** 1:6; 7:2(3); **Isa.** 2:9; 6:9; 7:4; 10:24; 14:29; 16:3; 22:4; 28:22; 35:4; 36:11,14–16; 37:6,10; 40:9; 41:10,13,14; 43:1,5,6,18; 44:2,8; 51:7; 52:11; 54:2,4; 56:3; 58:1; 62:6,7; 64:9(8); 65:5,8; **Jer.** 1:7,8,17; 4:3,6; 5:10; 6:25; 7:4,6,16; 9:4(3),23(22); 10:2,5,24; 11:14; 12:6; 13:15; 14:9,11,17,21; 15:15; 16:5; 17:17,18,21; 18:18,23; 20:14; 22:3,10; 23:16; 25:6; 26:2; 27:9,14,16,17; 29:6,8; 30:10; 35:15; 36:19; 37:9,20; 38:14, 24,25; 39:12; 40:9,16; 41:8; 42:11,19; 44:4; 45:5; 46:6,27,28; 50:2,14,26,29; 51:3,6,50; **Lam.** 2:18; 3:56,57; 4:15; **Ezek.** 2:6,8; 7:12; 9:5,6; 20:7,18; **Dan.** 9:19; 10:12,19; **Hos.** 4:4,15; 9:1; **Joel** 2:13,17,21,22; **Amos** 5:5,14; **Obad.** 1:12–14; **Jon.** 1:14; 3:7; **Mic.** 1:10; 2:6; 7:5,8; **Zeph.** 3:16; **Hag.** 2:5; **Zech.** 1:4; 7:10; 8:13,15,17; **Mal.** 2:15.

409. אַל *'al* **Aram. adv.**
(no, not; corr. to Hebr. 408)
Dan. 2:24; 4:19(16); 5:10.

410. אֵל *'ēl* **masc. noun**
(God, god, mighty one, hero)
Gen. 14:18–20,22; 16:13; 17:1; 21:33; 28:3; 31:13,29; 33:20; 35:1,3,7,11; 43:14; 46:3; 48:3; 49:25; **Ex.** 6:3; 15:2,11; 20:5; 34:6,14; **Num.** 12:13; 16:22; 23:8,19, 22,23; 24:4,8,16,23; **Deut.** 3:24; 4:24,31; 5:9; 6:15; 7:9,21; 10:17; 28:32; 32:4,12, 18,21; 33:26; **Josh.** 3:10; 22:22; 24:19; **Judg.** 9:46; **1 Sam.** 2:3; **2 Sam.** 22:31–33,48; 23:5; **Neh.** 1:5; 5:5; 9:31,32; **Job** 5:8; 8:3,5,13,20; 9:2; 12:6; 13:3,7,8; 15:4,11,13,25; 16:11; 18:21; 19:22; 20:15,29; 21:14,22; 22:2,13,17; 23:16; 25:4; 27:2,9,11,13; 31:14,23,28; 32:13; 33:4,6,14,29; 34:5,10,12,23,31,37; 35:2,13; 36:5,22,26; 37:5,10,14; 38:41; 40:9,19; 41:25(17); **Ps.** 5:4(5); 7:11(12); 10:11,12; 16:1; 17:6; 18:2(3),30(31), 32(33),47(48); 19:1(2); 22:1(2),10(11); 29:1,3; 31:5(6); 36:6(7); 42:2(3),8(9), 9(10); 43:4; 44:20(21); 50:1; 52:1(3),5(7); 55:19(20); 57:2(3); 58:1(2)(KJV, *'ēlem* [482,II]; NIV, *'ayil* [352,III]); 63:1(2); 68:19(20),20(21),24(25),35(36); 73:11, 17; 74:8; 77:9(10),13(14),14(15); 78:7, 8,18,19,34,35,41; 80:10(11); 81:9(10); 82:1; 83:1(2); 84:2(3); 85:8(9); 86:15; 89:6(7),7(8),26(27); 90:2; 94:1; 95:3; 99:8; 102:24(25); 104:21; 106:14,21; 107:11; 118:27,28; 136:26; 139:17,23; 140:6(7); 146:5; 149:6; 150:1; **Prov.** 3:27; **Isa.** 5:16; 8:10; 9:6(5); 10:21; 12:2; 14:13; 31:3; 40:18; 42:5; 43:10,12; 44:10,15,17; 45:14,15,20–22; 46:6,9; 57:5(NASB, NIV, *'ayil* [352,IV]); **Jer.** 32:18; 51:56; **Lam.** 3:41; **Ezek.** 10:5; 28:2,9; 31:11(NASB, NIV, *'ayil* [352]); 32:21; **Dan.** 9:4; 11:36; **Hos.** 1:10(2:1); 11:9,12(12:1); **Jon.** 4:2; **Mic.** 2:1; 7:18; **Nah.** 1:2; **Zech.** 7:2(NASB, NIV, *bēyṯ-ēl* [1008]); **Mal.** 1:9; 2:10,11.

411. אֵל *'ēl* **demons. pl. pron.**
(these, those)
Gen. 19:8,25; 26:3,4; **Lev.** 18:27; **Deut.** 4:42; 7:22; 19:11; **1 Chr.** 20:8.

412. אֵל *'ēl* **Aram. demons. pl. pron.**
(these: another form of *'ēlleh* [429])
Ezra 5:15([K^e] *'ēlleh* [429]).

413. אֵל *'ēl*, אֶל *'el* **prep.**
(to, into, concerning)
Gen. 1:9; 2:19,22; 3:1,2,4,9,14,16,19; 4:4–10,13; 6:4,6,16,18–21; 7:1,7,9,13,15; 8:9,11,12,15,21; 9:8,17; 11:3; 12:1,4,7, 11,15; 13:4,8,14; 14:3,7,17,21,22; 15:1,4,7,9,15; 16:2,4–6,9,11,13; 17:1, 9,15,18; 18:1,6,7,9,10,13,14,21,27, 29,31,33; 19:2,3,5,6,8,10,12,14,18, 21,27,31,34; 20:2–4,6,10,13,17; 21:12,

14,17,22,29,32; 22:1–3,5,7,9,11,12, 15,19; 23:3,13,16,19; 24:2,4–6,10,11, 14,20,24,25,29,30,38–45,50,56,58,65; 25:6,8,9,17,30; 26:1,2,9,16,24,26,27; 27:1,5,6,9,11,18–22,26,38,39,42,43,46; 28:1,5,7,9,15,21; 29:13,21,23,25,30,34; 30:1,3,4,14,16,17,22,25,27,29,39,40; 31:3–5,11,13,16,18,24,29,35,39,43,52; 32:3,6,8,9,16,19,27,30; 33:13,14; 34:4,6,11,12,14,17,20,24,30; 35:1, 2,4,7,9,27,29; 36:6; 37:2,6,10,13,18, 19,22,23,26,29,30,32,35,36; 38:2,8,9,16, 18,22,25; 39:7,8,10,14,16,17,19–21; 40:3,6,8,11,14,16; 41:14,15,17,21,24,25, 28,32,38,39,41,44,55,57; 42:7,9,10,12, 14,17,18,20–22,24,25,28,29,31,33,34,36, 37; 43:2,3,5,8,9,11,13,19,21,23,29,30, 33,34; 44:4,6–8,17,18,20–24,27,30, 32,34; 45:1,3,4,9,10,12,17,18,24,25,27; 46:28–31; 47:3–5,8,9,15,17,18,23; 48:2–5,9–11,13,18,21; 49:1,2,29,33; 50:4,16,17,19,24; **Ex.** 1:9,17,19; 2:7, 11,18,20,23; 3:1,2,4,6,8–11,13–18; 4:1,2,4,5,7,10,11,15,16,18,19,21–23,27,30; 5:1,4,10,15,21–23; 6:1–3,8–13,27–30; 7:1,2,4,7–10,13–16,19,22,23; 8:1,5,8, 12,15,16,19,20,25,27,29,30; 9:1,8,12–14, 20–22,27–29,33; 10:1,3,7,8,10,12,18,21, 24; 11:1,8,9; 12:1,3,4,21–23,25,26,43; 13:1,3,5,11,14; 14:1,2,5,10–13,15,20, 23,24,26; 15:13,22,25; 16:1,3,4,6,9–12, 15,19,20,23,28,33–35; 17:4,5,9,14; 18:5, 6,15–17,19,22,26,27; 19:3,4,6,8–10,14, 15,20–25; 20:19–22,24; 21:6; 22:7,8, 10,23,27; 23:13,17,20,23,27; 24:1,2, 11–16,18; 25:1,2,16,20–22; 26:3,5,6,9, 17,24,28; 27:20; 28:1,3,7,24–26,28–30, 35,37,43; 29:4,12,30,42; 30:11,17,20,22, 31,34; 31:1,12,13,18; 32:1–3,7,9,13,17, 19,21,26,30,31,33,34; 33:1,3,5,7,8,11, 12,15,17; 34:1–4,27,30,31,34; 35:1,4,30; 36:2,3,5,10,12,13,22,29,33; 37:9; 38:14; 39:18,19,21,33; 40:1,12,20,21,32,35; **Lev.** 1:1–3,15,16; 2:2,8,12; 4:1,2,4,5, 7,12,16,18,21,23,25,28,30,34; 5:8,9,12, 14,18; 6:1,6,8,11,14,19,24,25,30; 7:22, 23,28,29; 8:1,3–5,8,9,15,31; 9:2–9,12, 13,18,22,23; 10:3–6,8,9,11,12,18,19; 11:1,2,33; 12:1,2,4,6; 13:1,2,7,9,16,19; 14:1–3,5,8,23,33,34,38,40–42,45,46,50,51,53; 15:1,2,14,29; 16:1–3,15,18,22,23, 26–28; 17:1,2,4,5,8,9; 18:1,2,6,14,18–20; 19:1,2,4,21,23,31; 20:1,2,6,16; 21:1–3, 16,17,23,24; 22:1–3,13,17,18,26; 23:1,2, 9,10,23,24,26,33,34,44; 24:1,2,11,13–15, 23; 25:1,2,10,13,25,41; 26:9,25; 27:1, 2,34; **Num.** 1:1,48; 2:1; 3:5,11,14,40,44; 4:1,10,12,15,17,19,21; 5:1,3–6,8,11,12, 15,17,19,23,25; 6:1,2,10,13,22,23,25,26; 7:4–6,11,89; 8:1–3,5,19,23; 9:1,4,7–10; 10:1,3,4,29,30; 11:2,6,11,12,16,18, 23–25,30; 12:4,6,8,10,11,13,14; 13:1,17, 26,27,30–32; 14:2–4,7,8,10,11,13,14,16, 24,26,28,30,39,40,44; 15:1,2,17,18,22, 23,33,35–38; 16:3,5,8,9,14–16,18–20, 23–26,36,37,42–44,46,47,50; 17:1,2, 6,8–10,12,13; 18:1,3,4,8,20,22,25,26,30; 19:1–4,6,7,14,17; 20:4–8,10,12,14,16, 18,19,23,24,27; 21:7–9,21,34; 22:4,5, 7–10,12–14,16–18,20,25,30,32,34–38; 23:1,4–6,11,13–17,25–27,29; 24:1, 10–12; 25:1,4–6,8,10,16; 26:1,52; 27:6, 8,11–13,15,18; 28:1,2; 29:40; 30:1,14; 31:1–3,12,13,15,21,24,25,48,49,54; 32:2,7,9,14,16–20,25,29,31; 33:38,50, 51,54; 34:1,2,16; 35:1,9,10,25,28,32; 36:7,13; **Deut.** 1:1,3,6,7,9,17,20,22, 25,29,41–43,45; 2:1,2,9,17,26,29,31,37; 3:2,23,26; 4:1,7,10,12,15,21,39,42,45; 5:1,22,23,27,28,31; 6:10; 7:1,10,26; 8:7; 9:10–13,19,21,26–28; 10:1,4,10,11; 11:13,27–29; 12:5,9,26; 13:1–3,7,8,16; 14:25; 15:9,16; 16:6; 17:5,8,9,12,14; 18:6,9,11,14,15,17–19; 19:5,11; 20:2, 3,5,8–10,19; 21:2–4,6,12,13,18–20; 22:2,13–16,21,24; 23:5,10,11,15,24; 24:10,11,15; 25:1,7–9; 26:1–3,7,9; 27:2,3,9,14; 28:7,13,25,32,36; 29:2,7,28; 30:1,5,10,13,14; 31:1,2,7,9,14,16,18, 20,21,23,28; 32:40,45,46,48–50,52; 33:7,28; 34:1,4,9,10; **Josh.** 1:1–3,16,17; 2:3,4,9,17,18,23,24; 3:4–7,9; 4:1,4,5,8, 10,12,13,15,18,21; 5:2,3,9,13–15; 6:2, 6–8,16; 7:2,3,10,19,23; 8:1,5,9,18,20,

23,29,33; 9:1,6–9,11,12,16,17,19,21, 22,27; 10:3,4,6,8,9,15,18–25,27,43; 11:1, 2,5,6,19,23; 13:1,22; 14:6,10; 15:1,3, 7–11,13,15,21; 16:2,3; 17:4,7,8,15,17; 18:3,4,6,8,9,12–19; 19:11,12,27; 20:1,2, 4,6; 21:1–3,45; 22:2,4,6–11,13,15,18, 19,28,31,32; 23:2,15; 24:2,7,8,11,19, 21–24,27; **Judg.** 1:1,11; 2:1,4,10,17; 3:9,13,15,20,28; 4:3,5–8,13,14,17–22; 6:6–8,12–20,22,27,29,30,36,39,40; 7:2,4–7,9–11,15,17,25; 8:1,2,8,14,15, 18,22–24; 9:1,7,14,15,31,33,36,38,46, 48,50,54,57; 10:10,12,14,15,18; 11:3, 7–10,12–14,17,19,28,32,34–37,39; 12:2,3,6; 13:3,6,8–11,13,15–17,21,22; 14:3,9,10; 15:1,4,11,18; 16:1,3,5–7, 9–15,18,26,28; 17:9; 18:2,4,8,10,14,15, 18,23–26; 19:2,5,6,11,12,18,22,23,25, 28,29; 20:1,11,16,20,23,24,29,30,32, 36,37,42,45,47,48; 21:5,6,8,12,13,22,23; **Ruth** 1:7,15,16,18,20; 2:2,8–11,21,22; 3:5,16,17; 4:11,13,14; **1 Sam.** 1:14,19, 25–27; 2:16,27,34,36; 3:4–9,11,12,15, 17,21; 4:3,5–7,16,19,21; 5:4,6,8,10; 6:8,11,14,15,20,21; 7:1,3,5,7–9; 8:4–7,10,22; 9:3,10,16,17,21,23,26,27; 10:2,3,8,11,14,16–18,22,24,25; 11:1–3,10,12,14; 12:1,5,6,8,10,17–20; 13:9,12,13,17,23; 14:1,6,8,9,11,12,19, 26,27,32–34,36,40,41,43,45,52; 15:1, 6,10,11,13,16,19,20,24,26,28,32,34,35; 16:1,3,7,8,10,11,13,15,17,19–23; 17:3, 8,20,26,28,30,32–34,37,39–41,43–45,49, 51,55,58; 18:1,10,17,18,21,22; 19:1,3,4, 7,9,11,13,15–18,23; 20:4,5,10–13,19, 25,27,29,31,32,34,38,40; 21:1,2,4,10, 11,13–15; 22:1–3,5,9,11,13,14; 23:2,3,6,8–10,16,17,19,22–24,26,27; 24:3,4,7,16,17,22; 25:1,5,9,17,25,26, 36,40; 26:1,2,4–9,14,15,25; 27:1,2,5, 8–10; 28:1,2,7–9,12,13,15,21,23; 29:3, 4,6,8,9,11; 30:1,3,7,11,12,15,21,26; 31:3,11; **2 Sam.** 1:2–5,7–10,13,14,16,24; 2:1,5,9,14,22,23,26; 3:7,8,12,14,16,18, 20,21,23,24,27,29,31–33,38; 4:5,6,8; 5:1,3,6,8,11,17,19,23; 6:3,6,9,10,21; 7:2–5,17,19,20,27,28; 8:7,10; 9:2–4,6, 8,9,11; 10:2,3,9; 11:4,6,7,9–16,19–21, 23–25,27; 12:1,4,5,7,13,15,18–21,23, 24,27; 13:5–7,10,11,13,20,24,25,28, 30,33,35,37,39; 14:2–4,8–10,12,15,18, 21,22,24,29–33; 15:2,3,6,7,13,15,19, 22,27,36; 16:2,3,9,11,16–18,20–22; 17:1,3,6,7,12–15,18,20,21,23,25; 18:2–4, 12,17,22,24,26,28,32; 19:5,11,14,19,23, 27,28,30,33–35,41,42; 20:3,4,6,10, 15–17,21–23; 21:1–3,5,10; 22:7,42; 23:10,13,16,21,23; 24:2–7,9–14, 16–18,21–24; **1 Kgs.** 1:11,13,15,33; 2:7,13,14,16,18,19,28–30,39,40,42,44; 3:1,5,11,16,21,26; 4:27,28; 5:1,2,5,8,9; 6:8,11,12,18,27; 7:4,5,14,34; 8:1,2,6,7, 18,28–30,33–35,38,41–44,46–48,52,54,5 8,59; 9:2,3,24,28; 10:2,6,7,19; 11:2,9,10, 18,21,22,40; 12:3,5,7,9,10,12,14–16, 20,22,23,27,28; 13:1,4,6–8,10–15, 17,18,20–22,27,29,31; 14:3,5,6,10,13,28; 15:18,20; 16:1,7,12,13,18; 17:1,2,8,10, 11,13,18–21,24; 18:1–3,5,15,17,19–22, 30,31,40,42–44,46; 19:2,3,9,13,15,19; 20:2,5–10,12,13,22,23,28,30–35,39,40, 42; 21:2–8,11,14–17,19–22,28; 22:2–6, 8,9,13–18,22,26,30,35,36,49; **2 Kgs.** 1:2,3,5–13,15,16; 2:2,3,5,9,16,18–21,25; 3:7,12–14,24,26; 4:1,2,5,6,8–13,17–20, 22–25,27,33,36,39,41; 5:3,5–8,10,11, 13,15,22–26; 6:1,5,8–11,15,18,19,21–23, 26,28,29,32,33; 7:3–10,12,17,18; 8:1, 3–5,8–10,14,21; 9:3,5,6,11–14,18–20, 23,25,27,32,33; 10:1,2,5–7,9,14, 15,17–19,30; 11:4,7–9,13–15; 12:4,7; 13:4,14,15,23; 14:8,9; 15:12; 16:7,9,10; 17:4,13; 18:14,17–19,22,25–27, 30–32,37; 19:2,3,5,6,9,10,20,27,28, 32–34; 20:1,2,4,5,8,11,12,14,16,19; 21:7; 22:4,8,9,14–16,18,20; 23:1,6,9,11,12, 17,25; 25:6,23; **1 Chr.** 2:21; 7:23; 8:6; 9:25; 10:4; 11:1,3,15,18,23,25; 12:1,8, 17,19,20,23,40; 13:2,3,6,12,13; 14:1; 15:3,12; 16:20,23; 17:1–5,15,18; 18:10; 19:2,3,10,17; 21:2,5,8–11,13,17,18,22, 23,26,27; 28:1; 29:18,23; **2 Chr.** 2:3,11; 4:2; 5:2,3,7; 6:8,19–21,25–27,29, 32–34,36–38; 7:2,12; 8:11,17,18;

9:1,5,12; 10:3,5,7,9,10,12,14,15; 11:2–4; 12:5,7,11; 14:9,11; 16:2,4,7,9,10; 18:2–5, 7,8,12,14,15,17,20,25,28,29; 19:1,2,4,6; 20:9,21,24,27,28,37; 21:9,12; 22:7,9; 23:2,7,12,14,15; 24:11,12,17,19,23; 25:7,10,15–18; 26:16,20; 27:2; 29:18; 30:6,9,20; 31:10; 32:1,6,19,24; 33:7, 10,13,18; 34:9,15,16,22,23,26,28; 35:21,22; 36:13,20; **Ezra** 3:1,7,8; 4:2; 6:21; 7:7,9; 8:15,17,28; 9:1,4–6,11; 10:1,6,10; **Neh.** 1:6,9,11; 2:4,5,7–9, 11–14,17; 4:4,9,11,14,15,19,20; 5:1,17; 6:2–5,8,10,11,17; 7:5; 8:1,3,13; 9:4,16, 23,26,27,29,34; 10:28,37–39; 11:25; 13:6,21; **Esth.** 1:14,22; 2:3,8,12–16; 3:4,9,12,13; 4:2,6,8,10,11,13,15,16; 5:4,5,8,10,12,14; 6:5,7,12,14; 7:7,8; 8:9; 9:20,23,26,30; **Job** 1:7,8,12,14; 2:2,3, 5,6,10,13; 3:22; 4:2,5,12; 5:1,5,8,26; 7:17; 8:5; 9:4,12; 10:2,9,21; 11:13; 13:3,15; 15:8,13,22,25,26; 16:11,20; 18:18; 21:5,19; 22:26,27; 29:19,24; 30:20,22; 31:23; 32:14,21; 33:13,26; 34:14,18,23,31; 36:21; 38:20,22,41; 39:11; 40:23; 41:3,9; 42:7–9,11; **Ps.** 2:5,7; 3:4; 4:3,5,8; 5:2,7; 7:6; 18:6; 22:5,8,24,27; 25:1,15,16; 27:14; 28:1,2,5; 30:2,8,9; 31:2,6,22; 32:6,9; 33:14,15,18; 34:5,15; 36:2; 37:34; 39:12; 40:1,4,5; 41:1; 42:1,3,7,10; 43:3,4; 50:4,23; 51:13,19; 55:16; 56:3; 59:9,17; 61:2; 62:1; 66:17; 69:16,18,26,33; 71:2; 73:17; 77:1; 78:54; 79:6,12,13; 80:11; 84:2,7; 85:8; 86:2–4,16; 88:9,13; 90:16; 91:7,10; 95:11; 99:6,7; 101:2; 102:1,2,17,19; 104:8,22,27,29; 105:13; 107:6,7,13, 19,28,30; 109:14; 119:6,20,36,48,59,132; 120:1; 121:1; 123:1,2; 129:8; 130:7; 131:3; 137:9; 138:2; 141:8; 142:1,5,6; 143:1,6,8,9; 144:13; 145:15; **Prov.** 2:18; 3:5; 5:8; 6:6,29; 7:22,23,25,27; 8:4; 15:12; 16:3; 17:8; 19:18,24; 26:15,27; 30:10; 31:8; **Eccl.** 1:5–7; 3:20; 5:1; 6:6; 7:2; 8:14; 9:1,3,4,13,14; 10:15; 12:5–7; **Song** 2:4; 3:4; 4:6; 6:11; 8:2; **Isa.** 1:23; 2:2–4; 3:8; 6:3,6; 7:3,4,6,10; 8:1,3, 5,11,19,22; 9:19; 10:21; 11:10; 13:8,14; 14:2,10,15,16,19; 16:1,12,13; 17:7,8; 18:2,4,7; 19:3,11,17,20; 21:6,11,16; 22:5,8,11,15,18; 23:11; 24:18; 28:11,12; 29:11,22; 30:29; 31:4; 32:6; 36:2–4,7, 10–12,15–17,22; 37:2,3,5–7,9,10,15, 21,23,28,29,33,34; 38:1,2,4,5,18,19; 39:1,3,5,8; 40:2,18,25; 41:1; 44:17,19,22; 45:14,20,22; 46:3,7,12; 48:12,13,16; 49:1,5,22; 50:8; 51:1,2,4–7; 54:14; 55:2,3,5,7,11; 56:3,7; 60:8,11,13,14; 62:11; 63:15; 65:1,2,5,7; 66:2,5,12,17,19; **Jer.** 1:4,7,9,11–14,17,19; 2:1,3,7,19,27, 29,31; 3:1,6–8,10,11,17; 4:1,3,5,23; 5:5, 8,19; 6:3,19,21; 7:1,4,12,13,20,25–28; 8:4,14; 9:3,12,17; 10:2; 11:1–3,6,9,11, 12,14,20,23; 12:1,6; 13:1,3,6,8,11–14; 14:1,11,12,14,17,18; 15:1,2,19,20; 16:1, 10–12,19; 17:15,19,20,24,27; 18:1,5,11, 18,19; 19:2,11,14,15; 20:3,12; 21:1,3,4, 8,13; 22:8,11,18,21; 23:21,33,35,37,38; 24:3,4,7; 25:2–4,7,9,15,17,26–28,30,32; 26:2–5,8,9,11–13,15–19,22,23; 27:1–4,9, 12–14,16,17,19,22; 28:1,3–6,8,12,13, 15,16; 29:1,3,7,8,10,12,14,16,19,21, 24–26,28,30,31; 30:1–4,21; 31:6,9,12,21; 32:1,6–8,12,16,18,25,26,33,36,37,42; 33:1,3,4,14,19,23,26; 34:1,2,6–8,12,14, 17,22; 35:1,2,4,5,11–17; 36:1,2,4,7, 14–16,18–20,23,25,27,31,32; 37:2,3,6,7, 13,14,16,18; 38:1,2,4,6–9,11,12,14–20, 22–27; 39:1,5,12,14–16; 40:1,2,4–6,8, 10,12–16; 41:1,6–8,10,12,14,15; 42:2,4,5,7–10,12,20,21; 43:1,2,8,10; 44:1,4,7,16,20,24; 45:1,4; 46:1,10,13, 16,25; 47:1,3,5–7; 48:1,8,11,19,21,31, 36,40,44; 49:2,4,19,20,28,31,34,36; 50:1,5,6,14,16,18,19,21,29,31,35–38,44, 45; 51:1,3,9,12,25,35,44,60–63; 52:9, 15,26; **Lam.** 1:12; 2:12,18,19; 3:21,41; 4:4,17; 5:21; **Ezek.** 1:3,9,10,12,23; 2:1–4,6–10; 3:1,3–7,10,11,13,15,16, 22–24,26,27; 4:3,7,8,15,16; 5:4; 6:1,2, 9–11,13; 7:1,6,7,12–14,16,18,26; 8:3, 5–9,12–17; 9:3,4,7,9; 10:1,2,7,11,22; 11:1,2,5,11,14,21,24,25; 12:1,3,8–10, 12,17,19,21,23,26,28; 13:1,2,8,9,11,12, 14,16,17,19,20; 14:1,2,4,6,7,12,19,21,22;

15:1; 16:1,5,25,26,28,29,33,37,61; 17:1–4, 6,8,11,12; 18:1,6,11,12,15; 19:1,4,9,11; 20:2,3,5–10,15,18,27–30,35,38,39,42,45, 46; 21:1–4,7,8,12,14,17,18,21,28–30; 22:1,9,13,17,19,20,23; 23:1,5,12,14,16, 17,27,36,39,40,42,44; 24:1–4,15,18–20, 23,26; 25:1–3,6; 26:1,2,7,20; 27:1,3,29, 31,32; 28:1,11,20,21; 29:1,10,17,18; 30:1,20,22,25; 31:1,2,4,7,8,10,12–14, 17,18; 32:1,2,6,17,18,24; 33:1,2,10–12, 21–23,25,27,31; 34:1,2,10,13,14,20,21; 35:1,3; 36:1,9,15,16,20,24,29; 37:3,4,7,9, 11,12,15,17–19,21; 38:1–3,8,12; 39:1, 15,28; 40:2,4,6,14,16–18,23,26–28,31, 32,34,35,37,39–46,48,49; 41:1,4,6,9, 12,15,17,19,22,25,26; 42:1–4,7,10,13, 14,19; 43:1,3–7,13,16–20; 44:2,4–7, 9,11,13,15–17,19,21,25,27,30; 45:2,7, 11,16,19; 46:19–21,24; 47:1,2,6–9,16,19; 48:1,12,20,21,28,32; **Dan.** 1:11; 8:1,6,7, 9,14,17; 9:2,3,6,17,21; 10:3,11,12,16,20; 11:6,7,9,16,23; 12:7; **Hos.** 1:1,2,4; 2:7; 3:1,3,5; 4:8; 5:4,13,15; 6:1; 7:7,10,14,15; 8:1; 9:1,13; 11:4,5,7; 12:4,6; 14:2; **Joel** 1:1,14,19,20; 2:13,20; 3:2,3,8,12; **Amos** 2:7; 3:7; 4:8; 5:16; 7:8,10,12, 14,15; 8:2; **Jon.** 1:1,2,4–15; 2:1,2,4,7,10; 3:1–3,6,8; 4:1,2,9; **Mic.** 1:1; 3:4; 4:2,3; 7:10,17; **Nah.** 1:9; 2:13; 3:5; **Hab.** 1:2,13; 2:5; **Zeph.** 1:1; 3:2,9; **Hag.** 1:1,6,9; 2:2,10,12,15–17,20,21; **Zech.** 1:1,3,4,7,9,14,19,21; 2:2,4,8,11; 3:2,4,10; 4:2,4–6,8,9,11–13; 5:2–5,8,10,11; 6:4–6, 8,9,12,15; 7:1,3–5,8; 8:3,18,21; 10:10; 11:12,13,15; 12:10; 13:3,6; 14:2,5,8,17; **Mal.** 1:1.

414. אֵלָא *'ēlā'* **masc. proper noun**
(Ela)
1 Kgs. 4:18.

415. אֵל אֱלֹהֵי יִשְׂרָאֵל *'ēl 'elōhey yisrā'ēl* **masc. proper noun**
(El Elohe Israel [the Mighty God of Israel])
Gen. 33:20.

416. אֵל בֵּית אֵל *'ēl bēyṯ 'ēl* **proper noun**
(El Bethel)
Gen. 35:7.

417. אֶלְגָּבִישׁ *'elgāḇiyš* **masc. noun**
(hailstone)
Ezek. 13:11,13; 38:22.

418. אַלְגּוּמִּים *'algûmmiym* **masc. pl. noun**
(algum trees, algum logs)
2 Chr. 2:8(7); 9:10,11.

419. אֶלְדָּד *'eldāḏ* **masc. proper noun**
(Eldad)
Num. 11:26,27.

420. אֶלְדָּעָה *'eldā'āh* **masc. proper noun**
(Eldaah)
Gen. 25:4; **1 Chr.** 1:33.

421. אָלָה *'ālāh* **verb**
(to lament, to wail)
Joel 1:8.

422. אָלָה *'ālāh* **verb**
(to swear, to take an oath, to curse)
Judg. 17:2; **1 Sam.** 14:24; **1 Kgs.** 8:31; **2 Chr.** 6:22; **Hos.** 4:2; 10:4.

423. אָלָה *'ālāh* **fem. noun**
(oath, curse)
Gen. 24:41; 26:28; **Lev.** 5:1; **Num.** 5:21, 23,27; **Deut.** 29:12(11),14(13),19–21 (18–20); 30:7; **1 Kgs.** 8:31; **2 Chr.** 6:22; 34:24; **Neh.** 10:29(30); **Job** 31:30; **Ps.** 10:7; 59:12(13); **Prov.** 29:24; **Isa.** 24:6; **Jer.** 23:10; 29:18; 42:18; 44:12; **Ezek.** 16:59; 17:13,16,18,19; **Dan.** 9:11; **Zech.** 5:3.

424. אֵלָה *'ēlāh* **fem. noun**
(oak tree, terebinth tree)
Gen. 35:4; **Judg.** 6:11,19; **2 Sam.** 18:9,10,14; **1 Kgs.** 13:14; **1 Chr.**

10:12; **Isa.** 1:30; 6:13; **Ezek.** 6:13; **Hos.** 4:13.

425. A. אֵלָה *'ēlāh* **masc. proper noun**
(Elah: prince or duke of Edom)
Gen. 36:41; **1 Chr.** 1:52.
B. אֵלָה *'ēlāh* **masc. proper noun**
(Elah: valley in Judah)
1 Sam. 17:2,19; 21:9(10).
C. אֵלָה *'ēlāh* **masc. proper noun**
(Elah: son of Baasha)
1 Kgs. 16:6,8,13,14.
D. אֵלָה *'ēlāh* **masc. proper noun**
(Elah: father of Hoshea)
2 Kgs. 15:30; 17:1; 18:1,9.
E. אֵלָה *'ēlāh* **masc. proper noun**
(Elah: son of Caleb)
1 Chr. 4:15.
F. אֵלָה *'ēlāh* **masc. proper noun**
(Elah: son of Uzzi)
1 Chr. 9:8.

426. אֱלָהּ *'elāh* **Aram. masc. noun**
(God, god)
Ezra 4:24; 5:1,2,5,8,11–17; 6:3,5,7–10, 12,14,16–18; 7:12,14–21,23–26; **Jer.** 10:11; **Dan.** 2:11,18–20,23,28,37, 44,45,47; 3:12,14,15,17,18,25,26,28,29; 4:2(3:32),8(5),9(6),18(15); 5:3,4,11,14, 18,21,23,26; 6:5(6),7(8),10–12(11–13), 16(17),20(21),22(23),23(24),26(27).

427. אַלָּה *'allāh* **fem. noun**
(oak tree, terebinth tree)
Josh. 24:26.

428. אֵלֶּה *'ēlleh* **demons. pl. pron.**
(these, those)
Gen. 2:4; 6:9; 9:19; 10:1,5,20,29,31,32; 11:10,27; 14:3; 15:1,10,17; 20:8; 21:29; 22:1,20,23; 24:28; 25:4,7,12,13,16,17,19; 27:46; 29:13; 31:43; 32:17(18); 33:5; 34:21; 35:26; 36:1,5,9,10,12–21,23–31, 40,43; 37:2; 38:25; 39:7,17,19; 40:1; 41:35; 43:7; 44:6,7; 46:8,15,18,22,25; 48:1,8; 49:28; **Ex.** 1:1; 4:9; 6:14–16,19, 24,25; 10:1; 11:8,10; 19:6,7; 20:1; 21:1,11; 24:8; 25:39; 28:4; 32:4,8; 34:27; 35:1; 38:21; **Lev.** 2:8; 5:4,5,13; 10:19; 11:13,22,24,31; 18:24,26,29; 20:23; 21:14; 22:22,25; 23:2,4,37; 25:54; 26:14, 18,23,46; 27:34; **Num.** 1:5,16,17,44; 2:32; 3:1–3,17,18,20,21,27,33; 4:15,37, 41,45; 5:19,22,23; 10:28; 13:4,16; 14:39; 15:13,22; 16:26,28–31,38(17:3); 21:25; 22:9,15; 26:7,14,18,22,25,27,30,34–37, 41,42,47,50,51,53,57,58,63,64; 27:1; 28:23,24; 29:39; 30:16(17); 33:1,2; 34:17,19,29; 35:15,24,29; 36:13; **Deut.** 1:1,35; 3:5,21; 4:6,30,45; 5:3,22(19–20); 6:6,24; 7:12,17; 9:4,5; 10:21; 11:18,23; 12:1,28,30; 16:12; 17:19; 18:12,14; 19:5, 9; 20:15,16; 22:5,17; 25:3,16; 26:16; 27:4,12,13; 28:2,15,45; 29:1; 30:1,7; 31:1,3,17,28; 32:45; **Josh.** 4:6,7,20,21; 8:22; 9:13; 10:16,22–24,42; 11:5,10,12, 14,18; 12:1,7; 13:32; 14:1; 17:2,3,9,12; 19:8,16,31,48,51; 20:4,9; 21:3,8,9,16, 42(40); 23:3,4,7,12,13; 24:17,26,29; **Judg.** 2:4,23; 3:1; 9:3; 13:23; 18:14,18; 20:25,35,44,46; **Ruth** 3:17; 4:18; **1 Sam.** 2:23; 4:8; 6:17; 7:16; 10:7,9; 11:6; 14:6; 16:10; 17:11,18,23,39; 18:23,24,26; 19:7; 21:12(13); 23:2; 24:16(17); 25:9,12,37; 29:3; 31:4; **2 Sam.** 2:13; 3:5,39; 5:14; 7:17; 13:21; 14:19; 16:2; 21:22; 23:1,8, 17,22; 24:17; **1 Kgs.** 4:2,8,27; 7:9,45; 8:59; 9:13,23; 10:8; 17:1,17; 18:36; 20:19,29; 21:1,27; 22:11,17,23; **2 Kgs.** 1:7,13; 2:21; 3:10,13; 4:4; 6:20; 7:8; 10:9; 17:41; 18:27; 20:14; 21:11; 23:16,17; 25:16,17; **1 Chr.** 1:23,29,31,33,43,54; 2:1,18,23,33,50,53; 3:1,5; 4:2–4,6,12, 18,31,33,38,41; 5:14,24; 6:17(2),19(4), 31(16),33(18),50(35),54(39),65(50); 7:8,11,17,29,33,40; 8:6,10,28,38,40; 9:9,25,33,34,44; 10:4; 11:10,11,19,24; 12:1,14,15,23,38; 14:4; 17:15; 21:17; 23:4,9,10,24; 24:5,19,30; 25:5,6; 26:8, 12,19; 27:22,31; 29:17; **2 Chr.** 3:3,13; 4:18; 8:10; 9:7; 14:6–8(5–7); 15:8; 17:14,19; 18:10,16,22; 21:2; 24:26; 29:32; 32:1,14; 35:7; **Ezra** 1:9; 2:1,59,

62,65; 7:1; 8:1,13; 9:1,14; 10:44; **Neh.** 1:4; 5:6; 6:6–8,14; 7:6,61,64,67; 10:8(9); 11:3,7; 12:1,7,26; 13:26; **Esth.** 1:5; 2:1; 3:1; 9:20,26–28,31,32; **Job** 8:2; 10:13; 12:3,9; 16:2; 18:21; 26:14; 32:1; 33:29; 42:7; **Ps.** 15:5; 20:7(8); 42:4(5); 50:21; 73:12; 107:43; 126:2; **Prov.** 24:23; 25:1; **Eccl.** 7:10,28; 11:9; **Isa.** 7:4; 28:7; 36:12,20; 39:3; 40:26; 41:28; 42:16; 44:21; 45:7; 47:7,9; 48:14; 49:12,15,21; 57:6; 60:8; 64:12(11); 65:5; 66:2,8; **Jer.** 2:34; 3:7,12; 4:12,18; 5:9,19,25,29; 7:2,10,13,27; 9:9(8),24(23); 10:16; 11:6; 13:22; 14:22; 16:10; 17:20; 18:13; 20:1; 22:2,5; 24:5; 25:9,11,30; 26:7,10,15; 27:6,12; 28:14; 29:1; 30:4,15; 31:21,36; 32:14; 34:6; 36:16–18,24; 38:4,9,16, 24,27; 43:1,10; 45:1; 49:36; 51:19,60, 61; 52:20,22; **Lam.** 1:16; 5:17; **Ezek.** 4:6; 8:15; 9:5; 11:2; 14:3,14,16,18; 16:5,30,43; 17:12,15,18; 18:10,11,13; 23:30; 24:19; 33:24; 36:20; 37:3–5,9,11; 40:24,25,28,29,32,33,35; 42:9; 43:13, 18; 45:25; 46:24; 47:8,9; 48:1,10,16, 29,30; **Dan.** 1:17; 10:15,21; 11:4,41; 12:2,7,8; **Hos.** 14:19; **Amos** 6:2; **Mic.** 2:6,7; **Hab.** 2:6; **Hag.** 2:13; **Zech.** 1:9,10,19,21; 3:7; 4:4,5,10,11,13,14; 6:4,5; 8:9,12,15–17; 13:6.

429. אֵלֶּה *'ēlleh* **Aram. demons. pl. pron.**
(these; corr. to Hebr. 428)
Ezra 5:15([Qe] *'ēl* [412]); **Jer.** 10:11.

430. אֱלֹהִים *'elōhiym* **masc. pl. noun**
(God, gods, angels)
Gen. 1:1–12,14,16–18,20–22,24–29,31; 2:2–5,7–9,15,16,18,19,21,22; 3:1,3,5,8, 9,13,14,21–23; 4:25; 5:1,22,24; 6:2,4,9, 11–13,22; 7:9,16; 8:1,15; 9:1,6,8,12, 16,17,26,27; 17:3,7–9,15,18,19,22,23; 19:29; 20:3,6,11,13,17; 21:2,4,6,12,17, 19,20,22,23; 22:1,3,8,9,12; 23:6; 24:3,7, 12,27,42,48; 25:11; 26:24; 27:20,28; 28:4,12,13,17,20–22; 30:2,6,8,17,18,20, 22,23; 31:5,7,9,11,16,24,29,30,32,42, 50,53; 32:1(2),2(3),9(10),28(29),30(31); 33:5,10,11,20; 35:1,2,4,5,7,9–11,13,15; 39:9; 40:8; 41:16,25,28,32,38,39,51,52; 42:18,28; 43:23,29; 44:16; 45:5,7–9; 46:1–3; 48:9,11,15,20,21; 50:17,19,20, 24,25; **Ex.** 1:17,20,21; 2:23–25; 3:1,4, 6,11–16,18; 4:5,16,20,27; 5:1,3,8; 6:2,7; 7:1,16; 8:10(6),19(15),25–28(21–24); 9:1,13,28,30; 10:3,7,8,16,17,25,26; 12:12; 13:17–19; 14:19; 15:2,26; 16:12; 17:9; 18:1,4,5,11,12,15,16,19,21,23; 19:3,17,19; 20:1–3,5,7,10,12,19–21,23; 21:6,13; 22:8(7),9(8),20(19),28(27); 23:13,19,24,25,32,33; 24:10,11,13; 29:45,46; 31:3,18; 32:1,4,8,11,16,23, 27,31; 34:15–17,23,24,26; 35:31; **Lev.** 2:13; 4:22; 11:44,45; 18:2,4,21,30; 19:2–4,10,12,14,25,31,32,34,36; 20:7,24; 21:6–8,12,17,21,22; 22:25,33; 23:14,22, 28,40,43; 24:15,22; 25:17,36,38,43,55; 26:1,12,13,44,45; **Num.** 6:7; 10:9,10; 15:40,41; 16:9,22; 21:5; 22:9,10,12,18, 20,22,38; 23:4,21,27; 24:2; 25:2,13; 27:16; 33:4; **Deut.** 1:6,10,11,17,19–21, 25,26,30–32,41; 2:7,29,30,33,36,37; 3:3,18,20–22; 4:1–5,7,10,19,21,23–25, 28–35,39,40; 5:2,6,7,9,11,12,14–16, 24–27(21–24),32(29),33(30); 6:1–5,10, 13–17,20,24,25; 7:1,2,4,6,9,12,16, 18–23,25; 8:2,5–7,10,11,14,18–20; 9:3–7,10,16,23; 10:9,12,14,17,20–22; 11:1,2,12,13,16,22,25,27–29,31; 12:1–5,7,9–12,15,18,20,21,27–31; 13:2–7(3–8),10(11),12(13),13(14),16(17, 18(19); 14:1,2,21,23–26,29; 15:4–7,10, 14,15,18–21; 16:1,2,5–8,10,11,15–18, 20–22; 17:1–3,8,12,14,15,19; 18:5,7,9, 12–16,20; 19:1–3,8–10,14; 20:1,4,13, 14,16–18; 21:1,5,10,23; 22:5; 23:5(6), 14(15),18(19),20(21),21(22),23(24); 24:4,9,13,18,19; 25:15,16,18,19; 26:1–5, 7,10,11,13,14,16,17,19; 27:2,3,5–7,9,10; 28:1,2,8,9,13–15,36,45,47,52,53,58,62,6 4; 29:6(5),10(9),12(11),13(12),15(14), 18(17),25(24),26(25),29(28); 30:1–7,9, 10,16,17,20; 31:3,6,11–13,16–18,20,26;

32:3,17,37,39; 33:1,27; **Josh.** 1:9,11,13, 15,17; 2:11; 3:3,9; 4:5,23,24; 7:13,19,20; 8:7,30; 9:9,18,19,23,24; 10:19,40,42; 13:14,33; 14:6,8,9,14; 18:3,6; 22:3–5,16, 19,22,24,29,33,34; 23:3,5,7,8,10,11, 13–16; 24:1,2,14–20,23,24,26,27; **Judg.** 1:7; 2:3,12,17,19; 3:6,7,20; 4:6,23; 5:3, 5,8; 6:8,10,20,26,31,36,39,40; 7:14; 8:3, 33,34; 9:7,9,13,23,27,56,57; 10:6,10,13, 14,16; 11:21,23,24; 13:5–9,22; 15:19; 16:17,23,24,28; 17:5; 18:5,10,24,31; 20:2,18,27; 21:2,3; **Ruth** 1:15,16; 2:12; **1 Sam.** 1:17; 2:2,25,27,30; 3:3,17; 4:4,7, 8,11,13,17–19,21,22; 5:1,2,7,8,10,11; 6:3,5,20; 7:3,8; 8:8; 9:6–10,27; 10:3,5, 7,9,10,18,19,26; 11:6; 12:9,12,14,19; 13:13; 14:15,18,36,37,41,44,45; 15:15, 21,30; 16:15,16,23; 17:26,36,43,45,46; 18:10; 19:20,23; 20:12; 22:3,13,15; 23:7, 10,11,14,16; 25:22,29,32,34; 26:8,19; 28:13,15; 29:9; 30:6,15; **2 Sam.** 2:27; 3:9,35; 5:10; 6:2–4,6,7,12; 7:2,22–28; 9:3; 10:12; 12:7,16; 14:11,13,14,16, 17,20; 15:24,25,29,32; 16:23; 18:28; 19:13(14),27(28); 21:14; 22:3,7,22,30, 32,47; 23:1,3; 24:3,23,24; **1 Kgs.** 1:17,30,36,47,48; 2:3,23; 3:5,7,11,28; 4:29(5:9); 5:3–5(17–19); 8:15,17,20,23, 25–28,57,59–61,65; 9:6,9; 10:9,24; 11:2,4,5,8–10,23,31,33; 12:22,28; 13:1, 4–8,11,12,14,21,26,29,31; 14:7,9,13; 15:3,4,30; 16:13,26,33; 17:1,12,14, 18,20,21,24; 18:10,21,24,25,27,36,37,39; 19:2,8,10,14; 20:10,23,28; 21:10,13; 22:53(54); **2 Kgs.** 1:2,3,6,9–13,16; 2:14; 4:7,9,16,21,22,25,27,40,42; 5:7,8,11,14, 15,17,20; 6:6,9,10,15,31; 7:2,17–19; 8:2,4,7,8,11; 9:6; 10:31; 13:19; 14:25; 16:2; 17:7,9,14,16,19,26,27,29,31,33,35, 37–39; 18:5,12,22,33–35; 19:4,10, 12,15,16,18–20,37; 20:5; 21:12,22; 22:15,17,18; 23:16,17,21; **1 Chr.** 4:10; 5:20,22,25,26; 6:48(33),49(34); 9:11, 13,26,27; 10:10; 11:2,19; 12:17,18,22; 13:2,3,5–8,10,12,14; 14:10–12,14–16; 15:1,2,12–15,24,26; 16:1,4,6,14,25, 26,35,36,42; 17:2,3,16,17,20–22,24–26; 19:13; 21:7,8,15,17,30; 22:1,2,6,7,11, 12,18,19; 23:14,25,28; 24:5,19; 25:5,6; 26:5,20,32; 28:2–4,8,9,12,20,21; 29:1–3, 7,10,13,16–18,20; **2 Chr.** 1:1,3,4,7–9,11; 2:4(3),5(4),12(11); 3:3; 4:11,19; 5:1,14; 6:4,7,10,14,16–19,40–42; 7:5,19,22; 8:14; 9:8,23; 10:15; 11:2,16; 13:5,8–12, 15,16,18; 14:2(1),4(3),7(6),11(10); 15:1, 3,4,6,9,12,13,18; 16:7; 17:4; 18:5,13,31; 19:3,4,7; 20:6,7,12,15,19,20,29,30,33; 21:10,12; 22:7,12; 23:3,9; 24:5,7,9,13, 16,18,20,24,27; 25:7–9,14–16,20,24; 26:5,7,16,18; 27:6; 28:5,6,9,10,23–25; 29:5–7,10,36; 30:1,5–9,12,16,19,22; 31:6,13,14,20,21; 32:8,11,13–17,19, 21,29,31; 33:7,12,13,15–18; 34:3,8,9, 23,25–27,32,33; 35:3,8,21,22; 36:5,12, 13,15,16,18,19,23; **Ezra** 1:2–5,7; 2:68; 3:2,8,9; 4:1–3; 6:21,22; 7:6,9,27,28; 8:17,18,21–23,25,28,30,31,33,35,36; 9:4–6,8–10,13,15; 10:1–3,6,9,11,14; **Neh.** 1:4,5; 2:4,8,12,18,20; 4:4(3:36), 9(3),15(9),20(14); 5:9,13,15,19; 6:10, 12,14,16; 7:2,5; 8:6,8,9,16,18; 9:3–5,7, 18,32; 10:28(29),29(30),32–34(33–35), 36–39(37–40); 11:11,16,22; 12:24,36, 40,43,45,46; 13:1,2,4,7,9,11,14,18,22, 25–27,29,31; **Job** 1:1,5,6,8,9,16,22; 2:1,3,9,10; 5:8; 20:29; 28:23; 32:2; 34:9; 38:7; **Ps.** 3:2(3),7(8); 4:1(2); 5:2(3), 10(11); 7:1(2),3(4),9–11(10–12); 8:5(6); 9:17(18); 10:4,13; 13:3(4); 14:1,2,5; 18:6(7),21(22),28(29),29(30),31(32), 46(47); 20:1(2),5(6),7(8); 22:2(3); 24:5; 25:2,5,22; 27:9; 30:2(3),12(13); 31:14(15); 33:12; 35:23,24; 36:1(2),7(8); 37:31; 38:15(16),21(22); 40:3(4),5(6),8(9), 17(18); 41:13(14); 42:1–6(2–7),10(11), 11(12); 43:1,2,4,5; 44:1(2),4(5),8(9), 20(21),21(22); 45:2(3),6(7),7(8); 46:1(2),4(5),5(6),7(8),10(11),11(12); 47:1(2),5–9(6–10); 48:1(2),3(4),8–10 (9–11),14(15); 49:7(8),15(16); 50:1–3,6, 7,14,16,23; 51:1(3),10(12),14(16),17(19); 52:7(9),8(10); 53:1(2),2(3),4–6(5–7); 54:1–4(3–6); 55:1(2),14(15),16(17), 19(20),23(24); 56:1(2),4(5),7(8),9–13

(10–14); 57:1–3(2–4),5(6),7(8),11(12); 58:6(7),11(12); 59:1(2),5(6),9(10), 10(11),13(14),17(18); 60:1(3),6(8), 10(12),12(14); 61:1(2),5(6),7(8); 62:1(2),5(6),7(8),8(9),11(12); 63:1(2), 11(12); 64:1(2),7(8),9(10); 65:1(2),5(6), 9(10); 66:1,3,5,8,10,16,19,20; 67:1(2), 3(4),5–7(6–8); 68:1–10(2–11),15–18 (16–19),21(22),24(25),26(27),28(29), 31(32),32(33),34(35),35(36); 69:1(2), 3(4),5(6),6(7),13(14),29(30),30(31), 32(33),35(36); 70:1(2),4(5),5(6); 71:4,11, 12,17–19,22; 72:1,18; 73:1,26,28; 74:1, 10,12,22; 75:1(2),7(8),9(10); 76:1(2), 6(7),9(10),11(12); 77:1(2),3(4),13(14), 16(17); 78:7,10,19,22,31,35,56,59; 79:1,9,10; 80:3(4),4(5),7(8),14(15), 19(20); 81:1(2),4(5),10(11); 82:1,6,8; 83:1(2),12(13),13(14); 84:3(4),7–11 (8–12); 85:4(5); 86:2,8,10,12,14; 87:3; 88:1(2); 89:8(9); 90:[title](1),17; 91:2; 92:13(14); 94:7,22,23; 95:3,7; 96:4,5; 97:7,9; 98:3; 99:5,8,9; 100:3; 104:1,33; 105:7; 106:47,48; 108:1(2),5(6),7(8), 11(12),13(14); 109:1,26; 113:5; 115:2,3; 116:5; 118:28; 119:115; 122:9; 123:2; 135:2,5; 136:2; 138:1; 143:10; 144:9,15; 145:1; 146:2,5,10; 147:1,7,12; **Prov.** 2:5, 17; 3:4; 25:2; 30:9; **Eccl.** 1:13; 2:24,26; 3:10,11,13–15,17,18; 5:1(4:17),2(1),4(3), 6(5),7(6),18–20(17–19); 6:2; 7:13,14,18, 26,29; 8:2,12,13,15,17; 9:1,7; 11:5,9; 12:7,13,14; **Isa.** 1:10; 2:3; 7:11,13; 8:19,21; 13:19; 17:6,10; 21:9,10,17; 24:15; 25:1,9; 26:13; 28:26; 29:23; 30:18; 35:2,4; 36:7,18–20; 37:4,10,12,16,17, 19–21,38; 38:5; 40:1,3,8,9,27,28; 41:10, 13,17,23; 42:17; 43:3; 44:6; 45:3,5,14, 15,18,21; 46:9; 48:1,2,17; 49:4,5; 50:10; 51:15,20,22; 52:7,10,12; 53:4; 54:5,6; 55:5,7; 57:21; 58:2; 59:2,13; 60:9,19; 61:2,6,10; 62:3,5; 64:4(3); 65:16; 66:9; **Jer.** 1:16; 2:11,17,19,28; 3:13,21–23,25; 5:4,5,7,14,19,24; 7:3,6,9,18,21,23,28; 8:14; 9:15(14); 10:10; 11:3,4,10,12,13; 13:10,12,16; 14:22; 15:16; 16:9–11, 13,20; 19:3,4,13,15; 21:4; 22:9; 23:2, 23,36; 24:5,7; 25:6,15,27; 26:13,16; 27:4,21; 28:2,14; 29:4,8,21,25; 30:2,9,22; 31:1,6,18,23,33; 32:14,15,27,29,36,38; 33:4; 34:2,13; 35:4,13,15,17–19; 37:3,7; 38:17; 39:16; 40:2; 42:2–6,9,13,15,18, 20,21; 43:1,2,10,12,13; 44:2,3,5,7,8, 11,15,25; 45:2; 46:25; 48:1,35; 50:4, 18,28,40; 51:5,10,33; **Ezek.** 1:1; 8:3,4; 9:3; 10:19,20; 11:20,22,24; 14:11; 20:5,7,19,20; 28:2,6,9,13,14,16,26; 31:8,9; 34:24,30,31; 36:28; 37:23,27; 39:22,28; 40:2; 43:2; 44:2; **Dan.** 1:2,9,17; 9:3,4,9–11,13–15,17–20; 10:12; 11:8,32,37; **Hos.** 1:7; 2:23(25); 3:1,5; 4:1,6,12; 5:4; 6:6; 7:10; 8:2,6; 9:1,8,17; 12:3(4),5(6),6(7),9(10); 13:4,16(14:1); 14:1(2),3(4); **Joel** 1:13,14,16; 2:13,14,17,23,26,27; 3:17(4:17); **Amos** 2:8; 3:13; 4:11–13; 5:14–16,26,27; 6:8,14; 8:14; 9:15; **Jon.** 1:5,6,9; 2:1(2),6(7); 3:3,5,8–10; 4:6–9; **Mic.** 3:7; 4:2,5; 5:4(3); 6:6,8; 7:7,10,17; **Nah.** 1:14; **Hab.** 1:12; 3:18; **Zeph.** 2:7,9,11; 3:2,17; **Hag.** 1:12,14; **Zech.** 6:15; 8:8,23; 9:7,16; 10:6; 11:4; 12:5,8; 13:9; 14:5; **Mal.** 2:15–17; 3:8,14,15,18.

431. אֲלוּ *'alû* **Aram. interj.**
(behold, lo)
Dan. 2:31; 4:10(7),13(10); 7:8.

432. אִלּוּ *'illû* **interj.**
(but if, yea though)
Esth. 7:4; **Eccl.** 6:6.

433. אֱלוֹהַּ *'elôah* **masc. noun**
(God, god)
Deut. 32:15,17; **2 Chr.** 32:15; **Neh.** 9:17; **Job** 3:4,23; 4:9,17; 5:17; 6:4,8,9; 9:13; 10:2; 11:5–7; 12:4,6; 15:8; 16:20,21; 19:6,21,26; 21:9,19; 22:12,26; 24:12; 27:3,8,10; 29:2,4; 31:2,6; 33:12,26; 35:10; 36:2; 37:15,22; 39:17; 40:2; **Ps.** 18:31(32); 50:22; 114:7; 139:19; **Prov.** 30:5; **Isa.** 44:8; **Dan.** 11:37–39; **Hab.** 1:11; 3:3.

434. אֱלוּל *'elûl* **masc. noun**
(worthless thing, futility)
Jer. 14:14(NASB, NIV, [Qe] *'eliyl* [457]).

435. אֱלוּל *'elûl* **proper noun**
(the month Elul)
Neh. 6:15.

436. אֵלוֹן *'ēlôn* **masc. noun**
(oak, great tree [NASB, NIV]; plain [KJV])
Gen. 12:6; 13:18; 14:13; 18:1; **Deut.** 11:30; **Judg.** 4:11; 9:6,37; **1 Sam.** 10:3.

437. אַלּוֹן *'allôn* **masc. noun**
(oak tree)
Gen. 35:8; **Josh.** 19:33(KJV, *'allôn* [438,A]); **Isa.** 2:13; 6:13; 44:14; **Ezek.** 27:6; **Hos.** 4:13; **Amos** 2:9; **Zech.** 11:2.

438. A. אַלּוֹן *'allôn* **proper noun**
(Allon: city near Kadesh Naphtali)
Josh. 19:33(NASB, NIV, *'allôn* [437]).
B. אַלּוֹן *'allôn* **masc. proper noun**
(Allon: father of Shiphi)
1 Chr. 4:37.

439. אַלּוֹן בָּכוּת *'allôn bāḵûṯ* **proper noun**
(Allon Bacuth)
Gen. 35:8.

440. אֵלֹנִי *'ēlôniy* **masc. proper noun**
(Elonite)
Num. 26:26.

441. I. אַלּוּף, אַלֻּף *'allûp̱*, *'allup̱* **masc. noun**
(chief)
Gen. 36:15–19,21,29,30,40–43; **Ex.** 15:15; **1 Chr.** 1:51–54; **Jer.** 13:21(KJV, see II); **Zech.** 9:7; 12:5,6.
II. אַלּוּף *'allûp̱* **adj., noun**
(tame, familiar; subst., friend, ally)
Ps. 55:13(14); 144:14; **Prov.** 2:17; 16:28; 17:9; **Jer.** 3:4; 11:19; 13:21(NASB, NIV, see I); **Mic.** 7:5.

442. אָלוּשׁ *'ālûš* **proper noun**
(Alush)
Num. 33:13,14.

443. A. אֶלְזָבָד *'elzāḇāḏ* **masc. proper noun**
(Elzabad: a Gadite)
1 Chr. 12:12.
B. אֶלְזָבָד *'elzāḇāḏ* **masc. proper noun**
(Elzabad: a Korahite)
1 Chr. 26:7.

444. אָלַח *'ālaḥ* **verb**
(to be corrupt, to be filthy)
Job 15:16; **Ps.** 14:3; 53:3.

445. A. אֶלְחָנָן *'elḥānān* **masc. proper noun**
(Elhanan: son of Jair)
2 Sam. 21:19; **1 Chr.** 20:5.
B. אֶלְחָנָן *'elḥānān* **masc. proper noun**
(Elhanan: son of Dodo)
2 Sam. 23:24; **1 Chr.** 11:26.

446. A. אֱלִיאָב *'eliy'āḇ* **masc. proper noun**
(Eliab: prince of Zebulon)
Num. 1:9; 2:7; 7:24,29; 10:16.
B. אֱלִיאָב *'eliy'āḇ* **masc. proper noun**
(Eliab: prince of Reuben)
Num. 16:1,12; 26:8,9; **Deut.** 11:6.
C. אֱלִיאָב *'eliy'āḇ* **masc. proper noun**
(Eliab: brother of David)
1 Sam. 16:6; 17:13,28; **1 Chr.** 2:13; **2 Chr.** 11:18.
D. אֱלִיאָב *'eliy'āḇ* **masc. proper noun**
(Eliab: a Kohathite)
1 Chr. 6:27(12).
E. אֱלִיאָב *'eliy'āḇ* **masc. proper noun**
(Eliab: a Gadite)
1 Chr. 12:9.

F. אֱלִיאָב *'eliy'āḇ* **masc. proper noun**
(Eliab: a Levite singer)
1 Chr. 15:18,20; 16:5.

447. A. אֱלִיאֵל *'eliy'ēl* **masc. proper noun**
(Eliel: chief Kohathite)
1 Chr. 6:34(19).
B. אֱלִיאֵל *'eliy'ēl* **masc. proper noun**
(Eliel: chief of Manasseh)
1 Chr. 5:24.
C. אֱלִיאֵל *'eliy'ēl* **masc. proper noun**
(Eliel: son of Shimei)
1 Chr. 8:20.
D. אֱלִיאֵל *'eliy'ēl* **masc. proper noun**
(Eliel: son of Shashak)
1 Chr. 8:22.
E. אֱלִיאֵל *'eliy'ēl* **masc. proper noun**
(Eliel: captain of David's army)
1 Chr. 11:46.
F. אֱלִיאֵל *'eliy'ēl* **masc. proper noun**
(Eliel: one of David's mighty men)
1 Chr. 11:47.
G. אֱלִיאֵל *'eliy'ēl* **masc. proper noun**
(Eliel: a Gadite; possibly same as F)
1 Chr. 12:11.
H. אֱלִיאֵל *'eliy'ēl* **masc. proper noun**
(Eliel: chief of the Hebronites)
1 Chr. 15:9,11.
I. אֱלִיאֵל *'eliy'ēl* **masc. proper noun**
(Eliel: a Levite)
2 Chr. 31:13.

448. אֱלִיָּתָה *'eliyyāṯah*, אֱלִיאָתָה *'eliy'āṯah* **masc. proper noun**
(Eliathah)
1 Chr. 25:4,27.

449. אֶלְדָּד *'elidāḏ* **masc. proper noun**
(Elidad)
Num. 34:21.

450. A. אֶלְיָדָע *'elyāḏā'* **masc. proper noun**
(Eliada: son of David)
2 Sam. 5:16; **1 Chr.** 3:8.
B. אֶלְיָדָע *'elyāḏā'* **masc. proper noun**
(Eliada: Benjamite chief)
2 Chr. 17:17.
C. אֶלְיָדָע *'elyāḏā'* **masc. proper noun**
(Eliada: an Aramite)
1 Kgs. 11:23.

451. אַלְיָה *'alyāh* **fem. noun**
(fat tail, rump [of sheep])
Ex. 29:22; **Lev.** 3:9; 7:3; 8:25; 9:19.

452. A. אֵלִיָּה *'ēliyyāh*, אֵלִיָּהוּ *'ēliyyāhû* **masc. proper noun**
(Elijah: the Tishbite)
1 Kgs. 17:1,13,15,16,18,22–24; 18:1,2,7,8,11,14–17,21,22,25,27,30, 31,36,40–42,46; 19:1,2,9,13,19–21; 21:17,20,28; **2 Kgs.** 1:3,4,8,10,12, 13,15,17; 2:1,2,4,6,8,9,11,13–15; 3:11; 9:36; 10:10,17; **2 Chr.** 21:12; **Mal.** 4:5(3:23).
B. אֵלִיָּה *'ēliyyāh* **masc. proper noun**
(Elijah: a Benjamite)
1 Chr. 8:27.
C. אֵלִיָּה *'ēliyyāh* **masc. proper noun**
(Elijah: a priest)
Ezra 10:21.
D. אֵלִיָּה *'ēliyyāh* **masc. proper noun**
(Elijah: son of Elam)
Ezra 10:26.

453. A. אֱלִיהוּ *'eliyhû*, אֱלִיהוּא *'eliyhû'* **masc. proper noun**

(Elihu: great-grandfather of Samuel)
1 Sam. 1:1.
B. אֱלִיהוּ *'eliyhû,* אֱלִיהוּא *'eliyhû'* **masc. proper noun**
(Elihu: a Manassite)
1 Chr. 12:20.
C. אֱלִיהוּ *'eliyhû,* אֱלִיהוּא *'eliyhû'* **masc. proper noun**
(Elihu: friend of Job)
Job 32:2,4–6; 34:1; 35:1; 36:1.
D. אֱלִיהוּ *'eliyhû* **masc. proper noun**
(Elihu: a Kohathite)
1 Chr. 26:7.
E. אֱלִיהוּ *'eliyhû* **masc. proper noun**
(Elihu: brother of David)
1 Chr. 27:18.

454. A. אֶלְיְהוֹעֵינַי *'elyehô'ēynay,* אֶלְיוֹעֵינַי *'elyô'ēynay* **masc. proper noun**
(Eliehoenai, Elioenai: son of Meshelemiah)
1 Chr. 26:3.
B. אֶלְיְהוֹעֵינַי *'elyehô'ēynay* **masc. proper noun**
(Eliehoenai: son of Zerahiah)
Ezra 8:4.
C. אֶלְיוֹעֵינַי *'elyô'ēynay* **masc. proper noun**
(Elioenai: son of Neariah)
1 Chr. 3:23,24.
D. אֶלְיוֹעֵינַי *'elyô'ēynay* **masc. proper noun**
(Elioenai: son of Becher)
1 Chr. 7:8.
E. אֶלְיוֹעֵינַי *'elyô'ēynay* **masc. proper noun**
(Elioenai: Simeonite leader)
1 Chr. 4:36.
F. אֶלְיוֹעֵינַי *'elyô'ēynay* **masc. proper noun**
(Elioenai: son of Pashhur)
Ezra 10:22.
G. אֶלְיוֹעֵינַי *'elyô'ēynay* **masc. proper noun**
(Elioenai: a priest, son of Zattu)
Ezra 10:27.
H. אֶלְיוֹעֵינַי *'elyô'ēynay* **masc. proper noun**
(Elioenai: a priest)
Neh. 12:41.

455. אֶלְיַחְבָּא *'elyaḥbā'* **masc. proper noun**
(Eliahba)
2 Sam. 23:32; **1 Chr.** 11:33.

456. אֱלִיחֹרֶף *'eliyḥōrep̱* **masc. proper noun**
(Elihoreph)
1 Kgs. 4:3.

457. אֱלִיל *'eliyl* **masc. noun**
(idol, a worthless thing)
Lev. 19:4; 26:1; **1 Chr.** 16:26; **Job** 13:4; **Ps.** 96:5; 97:7; **Isa.** 2:8,18,20; 10:10,11; 19:1,3; 31:7; **Jer.** 14:14(KJV, [Ke] *'elûl* [434]); **Ezek.** 30:13; **Hab.** 2:18; **Zech.** 11:17.

458. אֱלִימֶלֶךְ *'eliymelek̲* **masc. proper noun**
(Elimelech)
Ruth 1:2,3; 2:1,3; 4:3,9.

459. אִלֵּין *'illēyn* **Aram. demons. pl. pron.**
(these, those)
Dan. 2:40,44; 6:2(3),6(7); 7:17.

460. A. אֶלְיָסָף *'elyāsāp̱* **masc. proper noun**
(Eliasaph: chief of Gad)
Num. 1:14; 2:14; 3:24; 7:42,47; 10:20.
B. אֶלְיָסָף *'elyāsāp̱* **masc. proper noun**
(Eliasaph: chief of Gershon)
Num. 3:24.

461. A. אֱלִיעֶזֶר *'eliy'ezer* **masc. proper noun**
(Eliezer: Abraham's steward)
Gen. 15:2.

B. אֱלִיעֶזֶר *'eliy'ezer* **masc. proper noun**
(Eliezer: son of Moses)
Ex. 18:4; **1 Chr.** 23:15,17; 26:25.
C. אֱלִיעֶזֶר *'eliy'ezer* **masc. proper noun**
(Eliezer: a Benjamite)
1 Chr. 7:8.
D. אֱלִיעֶזֶר *'eliy'ezer* **masc. proper noun**
(Eliezer: a Reubenite)
1 Chr. 27:16.
E. אֱלִיעֶזֶר *'eliy'ezer* **masc. proper noun**
(Eliezer: a prophet)
2 Chr. 20:37.
F. אֱלִיעֶזֶר *'eliy'ezer* **masc. proper noun**
(Eliezer: a priest)
1 Chr. 15:24.
G. אֱלִיעֶזֶר *'eliy'ezer* **masc. proper noun**
(Eliezer: chief under Ezra)
Ezra 8:16.
H. אֱלִיעֶזֶר *'eliy'ezer* **masc. proper noun**
(Eliezer: a priest)
Ezra 10:18.
I. אֱלִיעֶזֶר *'eliy'ezer* **masc. proper noun**
(Eliezer: a Levite)
Ezra 10:23.
J. אֱלִיעֶזֶר *'eliy'ezer* **masc. proper noun**
(Eliezer: son of Harim)
Ezra 10:31.

462. אֱלִיעֵינַי *'eliy'ēynay* **masc. proper noun**
(Elienai)
1 Chr. 8:20.

463. A. אֱלִיעָם *'eliy'ām* **masc. proper noun**
(Eliam: father of Bathsheba)
2 Sam. 11:3.
B. אֱלִיעָם *'eliy'ām* **masc. proper noun**
(Eliam: one of David's mighty men)
2 Sam. 23:34.

464. A. אֱלִיפַז *'eliypaz* **masc. proper noun**
(Eliphaz: son of Esau)
Gen. 36:4,10–12,15,16; **1 Chr.** 1:35,36.
B. אֱלִיפַז *'eliypaz* **masc. proper noun**
(Eliphaz: friend of Job)
Job 2:11; 4:1; 15:1; 22:1; 42:7,9.

465. אֱלִיפָל *'eliypāl* **masc. proper noun**
(Eliphal)
1 Chr. 11:35.

466. אֱלִיפְלֵהוּ *'eliyp^e^lēhû* **masc. proper noun**
(Elipheleh)
1 Chr. 15:18,21.

467. A. אֱלִיפֶלֶט *'eliypeleṭ* **masc. proper noun**
(Eliphelet: son of David)
1 Chr. 3:6.
B. אֱלִיפֶלֶט *'eliypeleṭ*, אֶלְפֶּלֶט *'elpeleṭ* **masc. proper noun**
(Eliphelet: another son of David)
2 Sam. 5:16; **1 Chr.** 3:8; 14:5,7.
C. אֱלִיפֶלֶט *'eliypeleṭ* **masc. proper noun**
(Eliphelet: son of Ahasbai)
2 Sam. 23:34.
D. אֱלִיפֶלֶט *'eliypeleṭ* **masc. proper noun**
(Eliphelet: a Benjamite)
1 Chr. 8:39.
E. אֱלִיפֶלֶט *'eliypeleṭ* **masc. proper noun**
(Eliphelet: son of Adonikam)
Ezra 8:13.

F. אֱלִיפֶלֶט 'eliypeleṭ masc. proper noun
(Eliphelet: son of Hashum)
Ezra 10:33.

468. אֱלִיצוּר 'eliyṣûr masc. proper noun
(Elizur)
Num. 1:5; 2:10; 7:30,35; 10:18.

469. A. אֱלִיצָפָן 'eliyṣāpān, אֶלְצָפָן 'elṣāpān masc. proper noun
(Elizaphan: chief of the Kohathites)
Ex. 6:22; Lev. 10:4; Num. 3:30; 1 Chr. 15:8; 2 Chr. 29:13.

B. אֶלְצָפָן 'eliyṣāpān masc. proper noun
(Elizaphan: chief of Zebulon)
Num. 34:25.

470. אֱלִיקָא 'eliyqā' masc. proper noun
(Elika)
2 Sam. 23:25.

471. A. אֶלְיָקִים 'elyāqiym masc. proper noun
(Eliakim: son of Hilkiah)
2 Kgs. 18:18,26,37; 19:2; Isa. 22:20; 36:3,11,22; 37:2.

B. אֶלְיָקִים 'elyāqiym masc. proper noun
(Eliakim: son of Josiah)
2 Kgs. 23:34; 2 Chr. 36:4.

C. אֶלְיָקִים 'elyāqiym masc. proper noun
(Eliakim: a priest)
Neh. 12:41.

472. אֱלִישֶׁבַע 'eliyšeba' fem. proper noun
(Elisheba)
Ex. 6:23.

473. אֱלִישָׁה 'eliyšāh masc. proper noun
(Elishah)
Gen. 10:4; 1 Chr. 1:7; Ezek. 27:7.

474. אֱלִישׁוּעַ 'eliyšûa' masc. proper noun
(Elishua)
2 Sam. 5:15; 1 Chr. 14:5.

475. A. אֶלְיָשִׁיב 'elyāšiyḇ masc. proper noun
(Eliashib: son of Elioenai)
1 Chr. 3:24.

B. אֶלְיָשִׁיב 'elyāšiyḇ masc. proper noun
(Eliashib: a priest)
1 Chr. 24:12.

C. אֶלְיָשִׁיב 'elyāšiyḇ masc. proper noun
(Eliashib: high priest)
Ezra 10:6; Neh. 3:1,20,21; 12:10,22,23; 13:4,7,28.

D. אֶלְיָשִׁיב 'elyāšiyḇ masc. proper noun
(Eliashib: a singer)
Ezra 10:24.

E. אֶלְיָשִׁיב 'elyāšiyḇ masc. proper noun
(Eliashib: son of Bani)
Ezra 10:36.

F. אֶלְיָשִׁיב 'elyāšiyḇ masc. proper noun
(Eliashib: son of Zattu)
Ezra 10:27.

476. A. אֱלִישָׁמָע 'eliyšāmā' masc. proper noun
(Elishama: chief of Ephraim)
Num. 1:10; 2:18; 7:48,53; 10:22; 1 Chr. 7:26.

B. אֱלִישָׁמָע 'eliyšāmā' masc. proper noun
(Elishama: son of David)
2 Sam. 5:16; 1 Chr. 3:8; 14:7.

C. אֱלִישָׁמָע 'eliyšāmā' masc. proper noun
(Elishama: son of David)
1 Chr. 3:6.

D. אֱלִישָׁמָע *'eliyšāmā'* **masc. proper noun**
(Elishama: scribe of Jehoiakim)
Jer. 36:12,20,21.
E. אֱלִישָׁמָע *'eliyšāmā'* **masc. proper noun**
(Elishama: one of the royal descendants)
2 Kgs. 25:25; **Jer.** 41:1.
F. אֱלִישָׁמָע *'eliyšāmā'* **masc. proper noun**
(Elishama: a Judaite)
1 Chr. 2:41.
G. אֱלִישָׁמָע *'eliyšāmā'* **masc. proper noun**
(Elishama: a priest)
2 Chr. 17:8.

477. אֱלִישָׁע *'eliyšā'* **masc. proper noun**
(the prophet Elisha)
1 Kgs. 19:16,17,19; **2 Kgs.** 2:1–5,9,12,14,15,19,22; 3:11,13,14; 4:1, 2,8,17,32,38; 5:8–10,20,25; 6:1,12, 17–21,31,32; 7:1; 8:1,4,5,7,10,13,14; 9:1; 13:14–17,20,21.

478. אֱלִישָׁפָט *'eliyšāp̄āṭ* **masc. proper noun**
(Elishaphat)
2 Chr. 23:1.

479. אִלֵּךְ *'illēḵ* **Aram. demons. pl. pron.**
(these, those)
Ezra 4:21; 5:9; 6:8; **Dan.** 3:12,13, 21–23,27; 6:5(6),11(12),15(16), 24(25).

480. אַלְלַי *'allay* **interj.**
(woe! alas!)
Job 10:15; **Mic.** 7:1.

481. I. אָלַם *'ālam* **verb**
(to bind)
Gen. 37:7.

II. אָלַם *'ālam* **verb**
(to be bound, speechless)
Ps. 31:18(19); 39:2(3),9(10); **Isa.** 53:7; **Ezek.** 3:26; 24:27; 33:22; **Dan.** 10:15.

482. I. אֵלֶם *'ēlem* **masc. noun**
(oak trees; same as *'ayil* [354,IV])
Ps. 56:[title](1)(KJV, NASB, see II).
II. אֵלֶם *'ēlem* **masc. noun**
(part of Jonath elem rehokim; see *yônaṯ 'ēlem rᵉḥōqiym* [3128])
Ps. 56:[title](1)(NIV, see I).
III. אֵלֶם *'ēlem* **masc. noun**
(congregation, company)
Ps. 58:1(2)(NASB, *'ēl* [410]; NIV, *'ayil* [352,III]).

483. אִלֵּם *'illēm* **adj.**
(mute, unable to speak, dumb)
Ex. 4:11; **Ps.** 38:13(14); **Prov.** 31:8; **Isa.** 35:6; 56:10; **Hab.** 2:18.

484. אַלְמֻגִּים *'almuggiym* **masc. pl. noun**
(almug [trees])
1 Kgs. 10:11,12.

485. אֲלֻמָּה *'ᵃlummah* **fem. noun**
(sheaf, bundle of stalks)
Gen. 37:7; **Ps.** 126:6.

486. אַלְמוֹדָד *'almôḏāḏ* **masc. proper noun**
(Almodad)
Gen. 10:26; **1 Chr.** 1:20.

487. אַלַּמֶּלֶךְ *'allammeleḵ* **proper noun**
(Allammelech)
Josh. 19:26.

488. אַלְמָן *'almān* **adj.**
(widowed, forsaken)
Jer. 51:5.

489. אַלְמֹן *'almōn* **masc. noun**
(widowhood)
Isa. 47:9.

490. אַלְמָנָה *'almānāh* **fem. noun**
(widow)
Gen. 38:11; **Ex.** 22:22(21),24(23); **Lev.** 21:14; 22:13; **Num.** 30:9(10); **Deut.** 10:18; 14:29; 16:11,14; 24:17,19–21; 26:12,13; 27:19; **2 Sam.** 14:5; **1 Kgs.** 7:14; 11:26; 17:9,10,20; **Job** 22:9; 24:3, 21; 27:15; 29:13; 31:16; **Ps.** 68:5(6); 78:64; 94:6; 109:9; 146:9; **Prov.** 15:25; **Isa.** 1:17,23; 9:17(16); 10:2; 13:22; 47:8; **Jer.** 7:6; 15:8; 18:21; 22:3; 49:11; **Lam.** 1:1; 5:3; **Ezek.** 19:7(NASB, NIV, *'armôn* [759]); 22:7,25; 44:22; **Zech.** 7:10; **Mal.** 3:5.

491. אַלְמָנוּת *'almānûṯ* **fem. noun**
(widowhood)
Gen. 38:14,19; **2 Sam.** 20:3; **Isa.** 54:4.

492. אַלְמֹנִי *'almōniy* **masc. noun**
(a certain one, such a one)
Ruth 4:1; **1 Sam.** 21:2(3); **2 Kgs.** 6:8.

493. אֶלְנַעַם *'elna'am* **masc. proper noun**
(Elnaam)
1 Chr. 11:46.

494. A. אֶלְנָתָן *'elnāṯān* **masc. proper noun**
(Elnathan: grandfather of Jehoiachin)
2 Kgs. 24:8; **Jer.** 26:22; 36:12,25.
B. אֶלְנָתָן *'elnāṯān* **masc. proper noun**
(Elnathan: a Levite)
Ezra 8:16.
C. אֶלְנָתָן *'elnāṯān* **masc. proper noun**
(Elnathan: a Levite)
Ezra 8:16.
D. אֶלְנָתָן *'elnāṯān* **masc. proper noun**
(Elnathan: a Levite)
Ezra 8:16.

495. אֶלָּסָר *'ellāsār* **proper noun**
(Ellasar)
Gen. 14:1,9.

496. אֶלְעָד *'el'āḏ* **masc. proper noun**
(Elead)
1 Chr. 7:21.

497. אֶלְעָדָה *'el'āḏāh* **masc. proper noun**
(Eladah [Eleadah])
1 Chr. 7:20.

498. אֶלְעוּזַי *'el'ûzay* **masc. proper noun**
(Eluzai)
1 Chr. 12:5.

499. A. אֶלְעָזָר *'el'āzār* **masc. proper noun**
(Eleazar: third son of Aaron)
Ex. 6:23,25; 28:1; **Lev.** 10:6,12,16; **Num.** 3:2,4,32; 4:16; 16:37(17:2),39(17:4); 19:3,4; 20:25, 26,28; 25:7,11; 26:1,3,60,63; 27:2,19, 21,22; 31:6,12,13,21,26,29,31,41, 51,54; 32:2,28; 34:17; **Deut.** 10:6; **Josh.** 14:1; 17:4; 19:51; 21:1; 22:13, 31,32; 24:33; **Judg.** 20:28; **1 Chr.** 6:3(5:29),4(5:30),50(35); 9:20; 24:1–6; **Ezra** 7:5; 10:25.
B. אֶלְעָזָר *'el'āzār* **masc. proper noun**
(Eleazar: son of Abinadab)
1 Sam. 7:1.
C. אֶלְעָזָר *'el'āzār* **masc. proper noun**
(Eleazar: son of Dodo)
2 Sam. 23:9; **1 Chr.** 11:12.
D. אֶלְעָזָר *'el'āzār* **masc. proper noun**
(Eleazar: a Merarite)
1 Chr. 23:21,22; 24:28.
E. אֶלְעָזָר *'el'āzār* **masc. proper noun**
(Eleazar: a priest)
Neh. 12:42.

F. אֶלְעָזָר *'el'āzār* **masc. proper noun**
(Eleazar: son of Phinehas)
Ezra 8:33.
G. אֶלְעָזָר *'el'āzār* **masc. proper noun**
(Eleazar: son of Parosh)
Ezra 10:25.

500. אֶלְעָלֵא *'el'ālē'* **proper noun**
(Elealeh)
Num. 32:3,37; **Isa.** 15:4; 16:9; **Jer.** 48:34.

501. A. אֶלְעָשָׂה *'el'āśāh* **masc. proper noun**
(Eleasah: son of Helez)
1 Chr. 2:39,40.
B. אֶלְעָשָׂה *'el'āśāh* **masc. proper noun**
(Eleasah: son of Rapha)
1 Chr. 8:37; 9:43.
C. אֶלְעָשָׂה *'el'āśāh* **masc. proper noun**
(Elasah: descendant of Pashhur)
Ezra 10:22.
D. אֶלְעָשָׂה *'el'āśāh* **masc. proper noun**
(Elasah: son of Shaphan)
Jer. 29:3.

502. אָלַף *'ālap̱* **verb**
(to learn, to teach)
Job 15:5; 33:33; 35:11; **Prov.** 22:25.

503. אָלַף *'ālap̱* **verb**
(to make thousandfold, to bring forth thousands)
Ps. 144:13.

504. אֶלֶף *'elep̱* **masc. noun**
(cattle, oxen)
Deut. 7:13; 28:4,18,51; **Ps.** 8:7(8); **Prov.** 14:4; **Isa.** 30:24.

505. אֶלֶף *'elep̱* **masc. noun**
(thousand, groups of a thousand)
Gen. 20:16; 24:60; **Ex.** 12:37; 18:21,25; 20:6; 32:28; 34:7; 38:25,26,28,29; **Num.** 1:16,21,23,25,27,29,31,33,35,37,39,41,43,46; 2:4,6,8,9,11,13,15,16,19,21,23,24,26,28,30–32; 3:22,28,34,39,43,50; 4:36,40,44,48; 7:85; 10:4,36; 11:21; 16:49(17:14); 25:9; 26:7,14,18,22,25,27,34,37,41,43,47,50,51,62; 31:4–6,14,32–36,38–40,43–46,48,52,54; 35:4,5; **Deut.** 1:11,15; 5:10; 7:9; 32:30; 33:17; **Josh.** 3:4; 4:13; 7:3,4; 8:3,12,25; 22:14,21,30; 23:10; **Judg.** 1:4; 3:29; 4:6,10,14; 5:8; 6:15; 7:3; 8:10,26; 9:49; 12:6; 15:11,15,16; 16:5,27; 17:2,3; 20:2,10,15,17,21,25,34,35,44–46; 21:10; **1 Sam.** 4:2,10; 6:19; 8:12; 10:19; 11:8; 13:2,5; 15:4; 17:5,18; 18:7,8,13; 21:11(12); 22:7; 23:23; 24:2(3); 25:2; 26:2; 29:2,5; **2 Sam.** 6:1; 8:4,5,13; 10:6,18; 17:1; 18:1,3,4,7,12; 19:17(18); 24:9,15; **1 Kgs.** 3:4; 4:26(5:6),32(5:12); 5:11(25),13–16(27–30); 7:26; 8:63; 10:26; 12:21; 19:18; 20:15,29,30; **2 Kgs.** 3:4; 5:5; 13:7; 14:7; 15:19; 18:23; 19:35; 24:14,16; **1 Chr.** 5:18,21; 7:2,4,5,7,9,11,40; 9:13; 12:14,20,24–27,29–31,33–37; 13:1; 15:25; 16:15; 18:4,5,12; 19:6,7,18; 21:5,14; 22:14; 23:3–5; 26:26,30,32; 27:1,2,4,5,7–15; 28:1; 29:4,6,7,21; **2 Chr.** 1:2,6,14; 2:2(1),10(9),17(16),18(17); 4:5; 7:5; 9:25; 11:1; 12:3; 13:3,17; 14:8(7),9(8); 15:11; 17:11,14–18; 25:5,6,11–13; 26:12,13; 27:5; 28:6,8; 29:33; 30:24; 35:7–9; **Ezra** 1:9–11; 2:3,6,7,12,14,31,35,37–39,64,65,67,69; 8:27; **Neh.** 3:13; 7:8,11,12,17,19,34,38,40–42,66,67,69–72; **Esth.** 3:9; 9:16; **Job** 1:3; 9:3; 33:23; 42:12; **Ps.** 50:10; 60:1:[title](1); 68:17(18); 84:10(11); 90:4; 91:7; 105:8; 119:72; **Eccl.** 6:6; 7:28; **Song** 4:4; 8:11,12; **Isa.** 7:23; 30:17; 36:8; 37:36; 60:22; **Jer.** 32:18; 52:28,30; **Ezek.** 45:1,3,5,6; 47:3–5; 48:8–10,13,15,16,18,20,21,30,32–35; **Dan.** 8:14; 12:11,12; **Amos** 5:3; **Mic.** 5:2(1); 6:7.

506. אֲלַף *'ᵃlap̱* **Aram. masc. noun**
(thousand; corr. to Hebr. 505)
Dan. 5:1; 7:10.

507. אֶלֶף *'elep̱* **proper noun**
(Eleph)
Josh. 18:28(NASB, NIV, *hā'elep̱*).

508. אֶלְפַּעַל *'elpa'al* **masc. proper noun**
(Elpaal)
1 Chr. 8:11,12,18.

509. אָלַץ *'ālaṣ* **verb**
(to urge, to prod)
Judg. 16:16.

510. I. אַלְקוּם *'alqûm* **masc. noun**
(band of soldiers, army)
Prov. 30:31(KJV, see II).
II. אַלְקוּם *'alqûm* **masc. noun**
(no uprising; from *'al* [408] and *qûm* [6965])
Prov. 30:31(NASB, NIV, see I).

511. A. אֶלְקָנָה *'elqānāh* **masc. proper noun**
(Elkanah: grandson of Korah)
Ex. 6:24; **1 Chr.** 6:23(8).
B. אֶלְקָנָה *'elqānāh* **masc. proper noun**
(Elkanah: father of Samuel)
1 Sam. 1:1,4,8,19,21,23; 2:11,20;
1 Chr. 6:27(12),34(19).
C. אֶלְקָנָה *'elqānāh* **masc. proper noun**
(Elkanah: descendant of Levi)
1 Chr. 6:25(10),36(21).
D. אֶלְקָנָה *'elqānāh* **masc. proper noun**
(Elkanah: father of Zuph)
1 Chr. 6:26(11),35(20).
E. אֶלְקָנָה *'elqānāh* **masc. proper noun**
(Elkanah: a Levite)
1 Chr. 9:16.
F. אֶלְקָנָה *'elqānāh* **masc. proper noun**
(Elkanah: a Korhite)
1 Chr. 12:6.
G. אֶלְקָנָה *'elqānāh* **masc. proper noun**
(Elkanah: a Levite)
1 Chr. 15:23.
H. אֶלְקָנָה *'elqānāh* **masc. proper noun**
(Elkanah: officer of Ahaz)
2 Chr. 28:7.

512. אֶלְקֹשִׁי *'elqōšiy* **masc. proper noun**
(Elkoshite)
Nah. 1:1.

513. אֶלְתּוֹלַד *'eltôlaḏ* **proper noun**
(Eltolad)
Josh. 15:30; 19:4.

514. אֶלְתְּקֵא *'elt^e^qē'* **proper noun**
(Eltekeh)
Josh. 19:44; 21:23.

515. אֶלְתְּקֹן *'elt^e^qōn* **proper noun**
(Eltekon)
Josh. 15:59.

516. I. אַל תַּשְׁחֵת *'al tašḥēṯ* **masc. proper noun**
(Al-taschcheth; tune title)
Ps. 57:[title](1)(NIV, see II);
58:[title](1)(NIV, see II);
59:[title](1)(NIV, see II);
75:[title](1)(NIV, see II).
II. אַל תַּשְׁחֵת *'al tašḥēṯ* **masc. proper noun**
("Do Not Destroy"; tune title or directions to preserve)
Ps. 57:[title](1)(KJV, NASB, see I);
58:[title](1)(KJV, NASB, see I);
59:[title](1)(KJV, NASB, see I);
75:[title](1)(KJV, NASB, see I).

517. אֵם *'ēm* **fem. noun**
(mother)
Gen. 2:24; 3:20; 20:12; 21:21; 24:28,53, 55,67; 27:11,13,14,29; 28:2,5,7; 29:10;

30:14; 32:11(12); 37:10; 43:29; 44:20; **Ex.** 2:8; 20:12; 21:15,17; 22:30(29); 23:19; 34:26; **Lev.** 18:7,9,13; 19:3; 20:9,14,17,19; 21:2,11; 22:27; 24:11; **Num.** 6:7; 12:12; **Deut.** 5:16; 13:6(7); 14:21; 21:13,18,19; 22:6,7,15; 27:16,22; 33:9; **Josh.** 2:13,18; 6:23; **Judg.** 5:7,28; 8:19; 9:1,3; 14:2–6,9,16; 16:17; 17:2–4; **Ruth** 1:8; 2:11; **1 Sam.** 2:19; 15:33; 20:30; 22:3; **2 Sam.** 17:25; 19:37(38); 20:19; **1 Kgs.** 1:11; 2:13,19,20,22; 3:27; 11:26; 14:21,31; 15:2,10,13; 17:23; 19:20; 22:42,52(53); **2 Kgs.** 3:2,13; 4:19,20,30; 8:26; 9:22; 11:1; 12:1(2); 14:2; 15:2,33; 18:2; 21:1,19; 22:1; 23:31,36; 24:8,12,15,18; **1 Chr.** 2:26; 4:9; **2 Chr.** 12:13; 13:2; 15:16; 20:31; 22:2,3,10; 24:1; 25:1; 26:3; 27:1; 29:1; **Esth.** 2:7; **Job** 1:21; 17:14; 31:18; **Ps.** 22:9(10),10(11); 27:10; 35:14; 50:20; 51:5(7); 69:8(9); 71:6; 109:14; 113:9; 131:2; 139:13; **Prov.** 1:8; 4:3; 6:20; 10:1; 15:20; 19:26; 20:20; 23:22,25; 28:24; 29:15; 30:11,17; 31:1; **Eccl.** 5:15(14); **Song** 1:6; 3:4,11; 6:9; 8:1,2,5; **Isa.** 8:4; 49:1; 50:1; 66:13; **Jer.** 15:8,10; 16:3,7; 20:14,17; 22:26; 50:12; 52:1; **Lam.** 2:12; 5:3; **Ezek.** 16:3,44,45; 19:2,10; 21:21(20); 22:7; 23:2; 44:25; **Hos.** 2:2(4),5(7); 4:5; 10:14; **Mic.** 7:6; **Zech.** 13:3.

518. אִם *'im* particle

(if, when)

Gen. 4:7; 13:9,16; 14:23; 15:4,5; 17:17; 18:3,21,26,28,30; 20:7; 21:23; 23:8,13; 24:8,19,21,33,38,41,42,49; 25:22; 26:29; 27:21,46; 28:15,17,20; 30:1,27,31; 31:8, 50,52; 32:8(9),26(27),28(29); 33:10; 34:15,17; 35:10; 37:8,32; 38:9,17; 39:6,9; 40:14; 42:15,16,19,37; 43:4,5,9,11; 44:23,26,32; 47:6,16,18,29; 50:4; **Ex.** 1:16; 4:8,9; 8:2(7:27),21(17); 9:2; 10:4; 12:4,9; 13:13; 15:26; 16:4; 17:7; 18:23; 19:5,13; 20:25; 21:3–5,8–11,19,21,23, 27,29,30,32; 22:2–4(1–3),7(6),8(7), 11–13(10–12),15(14),17(16),23(22), 25(24),26(25); 23:22; 29:34; 32:32; 33:13,15; 34:9,20; 40:37; **Lev.** 1:3,10,14; 2:5,7,14; 3:1,6,7,12; 4:3,13,27,32; 5:1,7, 11,17; 6:28(21); 7:12,16,18; 12:5,8; 13:4, 7,12,21–23,26–28,35,37,41,53,56,57; 14:21,43,48; 15:23,24,28; 17:16; 19:7; 20:4; 21:2,14; 22:6; 25:28,30,51,52,54; 26:3,14,15,18,21,23,27; 27:4–11,13, 15–20,22,26,27,31,33; **Num.** 5:8,19, 27,28; 10:4,30; 11:12,15,22,23; 12:6; 13:18,19,20; 14:8,23,28,30,35; 15:24,27; 16:29,30; 17:13(28); 19:12; 20:19; 21:2,9; 22:18,20,34; 24:13,22; 26:33,65; 27:9–11; 30:5(6),6(7),8(9),10(11),12(13),14(15),1 5(16); 32:5,11,17,20,23,29,30; 33:55; 35:16,17,20,22,26,33; 36:4; **Deut.** 1:35; 5:25(22); 7:5; 8:2,19; 10:12; 11:13,22, 28; 12:5,14,18; 15:5; 16:6; 18:3; 19:8; 20:11,12; 15:5; 16:6; 18:3; 19:8; 20:11, 12; 21:14; 22:2,20,25; 24:1,12; 25:2,7; 28:1,15,58; 30:4,17; 32:30,41; **Josh.** 2:14,19,20; 5:13; 7:12; 14:4,9; 17:3,15; 22:19,22–24; 23:8,12; 24:15; **Judg.** 2:22; 4:8,20; 5:8; 6:3,17,31,34,37; 7:10,14; 9:2,15,16,19,20; 11:9,10,25,30; 13:16; 14:12,13; 15:7; 16:7,11,13,17; 20:28; 21:21; **Ruth** 2:21; 3:10,12,13,18; 4:4; **1 Sam.** 1:11; 2:15,16,25; 3:9,14,17; 6:3,9; 7:3; 8:19; 11:3; 12:14,15,25; 13:2; 14:9,10,39,45; 15:17; 17:9,55; 19:6,11; 20:6–9,14,21,22,29; 21:4–6(5–7),9(10); 23:23; 24:6(7),21(22); 25:22,34; 26:10, 19; 27:5; 28:10; 30:15,17,22; **2 Sam.** 3:13,35; 5:6; 10:11; 11:20; 12:3,8; 13:33; 14:11,19,32; 15:8,21,25,26,33,34; 17:6,13; 18:3,25; 19:7(8),13(14),28(29),35(36), 42(43); 20:20; 21:2; 24:13; **1 Kgs.** 1:27,51,52; 2:4,8; 3:14; 6:12; 8:19,25; 9:4,6; 11:38; 12:7,27; 13:8; 17:1,12; 18:10,18,21; 20:6,10,18,23,25,39; 21:2,6; 22:6,8,15,18,28,31; **2 Kgs.** 1:2,10,12; 2:2,4,6,10; 3:14; 4:2,24,30; 5:15–17,20; 6:31; 7:4,10; 9:15,26,35; 10:6,23; 13:7; 14:6; 17:36,39,40; 18:23; 19:18; 20:9,19; 21:8; 23:9,23; **1 Chr.** 2:34; 4:10; 12:17; 13:2; 15:2; 19:12; 21:12; 22:13; 23:22; 28:7,9; **2 Chr.** 2:6(5); 6:16,22,24; 7:13, 17,19; 10:7; 15:2; 18:5,14,19,27,30; 20:9;

21:17; 23:6; 25:8; 30:9; 33:8; **Ezra** 2:59; **Neh.** 1:9; 2:2,5,7,12; 4:3(3:35); 7:61; 13:21,25; **Esth.** 1:19; 2:14,15; 3:9; 4:14; 5:4,8,12; 6:13; 7:3; 8:5; 9:13; **Job** 1:11; 2:5; 4:17; 6:5,12,13,28,30; 7:12; 8:3–6,18; 9:2,3,15,16,18,19,20,23,24,26,27,30; 10:4,5,14,15; 11:2,7,10,13,14; 13:8–10; 14:5,7,8,14; 16:6; 17:2,13,16; 19:5; 20:6, 12; 21:4,6; 22:3,20,23; 24:25; 25:4; 26:10; 27:4,5,10,14,16; 30:24; 31:5,7, 9,13,16,19,20,21,24–26,29,31,33,36,38,3 9; 33:5,23,32,33; 34:14,16,17,32; 35:6,7; 36:8,11,12; 37:13,20; 38:4,18,33; 39:9, 10,13,27; 40:9; 41:3(40:27); 42:8; **Ps.** 1:2,4; 7:3(4),4(5),12(13); 27:3; 41:6(7); 44:20(21); 50:12,18; 59:15(16); 63:6(7); 66:18; 68:13(14); 73:15; 77:9(10); 78:20, 34; 81:8(9); 88:10(11); 89:30(31),31(32), 35(36); 90:10; 94:9,18; 95:7,11; 127:1; 130:3; 132:3,4,12; 137:5,6; 138:7; 139:8, 19,24; **Prov.** 1:10,11; 2:1,3,4; 3:24,30,34; 4:12,16; 6:1,28; 9:12; 18:2; 19:19; 20:11; 22:27; 23:2,15,17,18; 24:11,14,21; 25:21; 27:22,24; 29:9; 30:32; **Eccl.** 4:10,11,12; 5:8(7),11(10),12(11); 6:3; 8:15,17; 10:4, 10,11; 11:3,6,8; 12:14; **Song** 1:8; 2:7; 3:5; 5:8; 7:12(13); 8:7,9; **Isa.** 1:18–20; 4:4; 5:9; 6:11; 7:9; 8:20; 10:9,15,22; 14:24; 21:12; 22:14; 24:13; 27:7; 28:25; 29:16; 30:17; 33:21; 36:8; 37:19; 40:28; 42:19; 49:24; 50:2; 53:10; 55:10,11; 58:9,13; 59:2; 62:8; 65:6,18; 66:8,9; **Jer.** 2:14,22,28,31; 3:5,10; 4:1; 5:1,2,9,22,29; 7:5,23,32; 8:4,19,22; 9:9(8),24(23); 12:16,17; 13:17; 14:7,18,19,22; 15:1,11, 19; 16:15; 17:24,27; 18:14; 19:6; 20:3; 22:4–6,17,24,28; 23:8,22,24,38; 26:4,15; 27:18; 30:6; 31:20,30,36,37; 33:20,25; 37:10; 38:4,6,16,17,18,21; 39:12; 40:4; 42:5,6,10,13,15; 44:14:26; 48:27; 49:1, 9,20; 50:45; 51:14; **Lam.** 1:12; 2:20; 3:32; 5:22; **Ezek.** 2:5,7; 3:6,11; 5:11; 12:23; 14:16,20; 15:3; 16:48; 17:16,19; 18:3; 20:3,31,33,39; 21:13(18); 22:14; 33:11,27; 34:8; 35:6; 36:5,7,22; 38:19; 43:11; 44:10,22,25; **Dan.** 10:21; **Hos.** 4:15; 9:12; 12:11(12); **Joel** 1:2; 3:4(4:4); **Amos** 3:3,4,6,7; 4:22; 6:2,9,12; 7:2; 8:7,11; 9:2–4; **Obad.** 1:4,5; **Mic.** 2:7; 4:9; 5:8(7); 6:8; **Nah.** 1:12; 3:12; **Hab.** 2:3; 3:8; **Hag.** 2:13; **Zech.** 3:7; 4:6; 6:15; 11:12; **Mal.** 1:6; 2:2; 3:10.

519. אָמָה *'āmāh* **fem. noun**
(maidservant, slave girl)
Gen. 20:17; 21:10,12,13; 30:3; 31:33; **Ex.** 2:5; 20:10,17; 21:7,20,26,27,32; 23:12; **Lev.** 25:6,44; **Deut.** 5:14,21(18); 12:12,18; 15:17; 16:11,14; **Judg.** 9:18; 19:19; **Ruth** 3:9; **1 Sam.** 1:11,16; 25:24,25,28,31,41; **2 Sam.** 6:20,22; 14:15,16; 20:17; **1 Kgs.** 1:13,17; 3:20; **Ezra** 2:65; **Neh.** 7:67; **Job** 19:15; 31:13; **Ps.** 86:16; 116:16; **Nah.** 2:7(8).

520. אַמָּה *'ammāh* **fem. noun.**
(cubit)
Gen. 6:15,16; 7:20; **Ex.** 25:10,17,23; 26:2,8,13,16; 27:1,9,12–14,16,18; 30:2; 36:9,15,21; 37:1,6,10,25; 38:1,9, 11–15,18; **Num.** 11:31; 35:4,5; **Deut.** 3:11; **Josh.** 3:4; **1 Sam.** 17:4; **1 Kgs.** 6:2,3,6,10,16,17,20,23–26; 7:2,6,10,15, 16,19,23,24,27,31,32,35,38; **2 Kgs.** 14:13; 25:17; **1 Chr.** 11:23; **2 Chr.** 3:3,4,8,11–13,15; 4:1–3; 6:13; 25:23; **Neh.** 3:13; **Esth.** 5:14; 7:9; **Isa.** 6:4; **Jer.** 51:13; 52:21,22; **Ezek.** 40:5,7,9, 11–15,19,21,23,25,27,29,30,33,36,42,47 –49; 41:1–5,8–15,22; 42:2,4,7,8,16(NASB, NIV, [Q^{e}] *mē'āh* [367]); 43:13–15,17; 45:2; 47:3; **Zech.** 5:2.

521. אַמָּה *'ammāh* **Aram. fem. noun**
(cubit; corr. to Hebr. 520)
Ezra 6:3; **Dan.** 3:1.

522. I. אַמָּה *'ammāh* **proper noun**
(Ammah: hill near the Jordan Valley)
2 Sam. 2:24.
II. אַמָּה *'ammāh* **fem. noun**
(mother city)

2 Sam. 8:1(KJV, NIV, see III).
III. אַמָּה *'ammāh* **proper noun**
(Part of Metheg Ammah [4965,I])
2 Sam. 8:1(NASB, see II).

523. אֻמָּה *'ummāh* **fem. noun**
(people, nation, tribe)
Gen. 25:16; **Num.** 25:15; **Ps.** 117:1.

524. אֻמָּה *'ummāh* **Aram. fem. noun**
(people, nation, tribe; corr. to Hebr. 523)
Ezra 4:10; **Dan.** 3:4,7,29; 4:1(3:31); 5:19; 6:25(26); 7:14.

525. I. אָמוֹן *'āmôn* **masc. noun**
(artisan, craftsman)
Prov. 8:30(KJV, see II); **Jer.** 52:15(KJV, *'āmôn* [527]).
II. אָמוֹן *'āmôn* **masc. noun**
(one brought up)
Prov. 8:30(NASB, NIV, see I).

526. A. אָמוֹן *'āmôn* **masc. proper noun**
(Amon: governor of Samaria)
1 Kgs. 22:26; **2 Chr.** 18:25.
B. אָמוֹן *'āmôn* **masc. proper noun.**
(Amon: son of Manasseh)
2 Kgs. 21:18,19,23–25; **1 Chr.** 3:14; **2 Chr.** 33:20–23,25; **Jer.** 1:2; 25:3; **Zeph.** 1:1.
C. אָמוֹן *'āmôn* **masc. proper noun.**
(Amon: a Jew)
Neh. 7:59.

527. אָמוֹן *'āmôn* **masc. noun**
(multitude)
Jer. 46:25(NASB, NIV, *'āmôn* [528]; 51:15(NASB, NIV, *'āmôn* [525,I]); **Nah.** 3:8(NASB, *'āmôn* [528,II]; NIV, *nō' 'āmôn* [528,III]).

528. I. אָמוֹן *'āmôn* **masc. proper noun**
(Amon: god of Egypt)
Jer. 46:25(KJV, *'āmôn* [527]).
II. אָמוֹן *'āmôn* **proper noun**
(Part of the full name No-amon [4996] and [528,I])
Nah. 3:8(KJV, *'āmôn* [527]; NIV, see III).
III. נֹא אָמוֹן *nō' 'āmôn* **masc. proper noun**
(Thebes; city that worshiped Amon [528,I])
Nah. 3:8(KJV, *'āmôn* [527]; NASB, see II).

529. אֵמוּן *'ēmûn* **masc. noun**
(faithfulness, trustworthiness)
Deut. 32:20; **Prov.** 13:17; 14:5; 20:6; **Isa.** 26:2.

530. אֱמוּנָה *'ᵉmûnāh* **fem. noun.**
(faithfulness, steadfastness)
Ex. 17:12; **Deut.** 32:4; **1 Sam.** 26:23; **2 Kgs.** 12:15(16); 22:7; **1 Chr.** 9:22, 26,31; **2 Chr.** 19:9; 31:12,15,18; 34:12; **Ps.** 33:4; 36:5(6); 37:3; 40:10(11); 88:11(12); 89:1(2),2(3),5(6),8(9),24(25), 33(34),49(50); 92:2(3); 96:13; 98:3; 100:5; 119:30,75,86,90,138; 143:1; **Prov.** 12:17,22; 28:20; **Isa.** 11:5; 25:1; 33:6; 59:4; **Jer.** 5:1,3; 7:28; 9:3(2); **Lam.** 3:23; **Hos.** 2:20(22); **Hab.** 2:4.

531. אָמוֹץ *'āmôṣ* **masc. proper noun**
(Amoz)
2 Kgs. 19:2,20; 20:1; **2 Chr.** 26:22; 32:20,32; **Isa.** 1:1; 2:1; 13:1; 20:2; 37:2,21; 38:1.

532. אָמִי *'āmiy* **masc. proper noun**
(Ami)
Ezra 2:57.

533. אמִּיץ *'ammiyṣ*, אַמִּץ *'ammiṣ* **adj.**
(mighty, strong, brave)
2 Sam. 15:12; **Job** 9:4,19; **Isa.** 28:2; 40:26; **Amos** 2:16.

534. אָמִיר *'āmiyr* **masc. noun**
(topmost, upper branch)
Isa. 17:6,9.

535. אָמַל *'āmal* **verb**
(to languish, to pine away, to be feeble)
1 Sam. 2:5; **Isa.** 16:8; 19:8; 24:4,7; 33:9; **Jer.** 14:2; 15:9; **Lam.** 2:8; **Ezek.** 16:30; **Hos.** 4:3; **Joel** 1:10,12; **Nah.** 1:4.

536. אֻמְלַל *'umlal* **adj.**
(weak, faint)
Ps. 6:2(3).

537. אֲמֵלָל *'^{a}mēlāl* **adj.**
(weak, feeble)
Neh. 4:2(3:34).

538. אֲמָם *'^{a}mām* **proper noun**
(Amam)
Josh. 15:26.

539. אָמַן *'āman* **verb**
(to believe, to trust, to be faithful)
Gen. 15:6; 42:20; 45:26; **Ex.** 4:1,5,8, 9,31; 14:31; 19:9; **Num.** 11:12; 12:7; 14:11; 20:12; **Deut.** 1:32; 7:9; 9:23; 28:59,66; **Judg.** 11:20; **Ruth** 4:16; **1 Sam.** 2:35; 3:20; 22:14; 25:28; 27:12; **2 Sam.** 4:4; 7:16; 20:19; **1 Kgs.** 8:26; 10:7; 11:38; **2 Kgs.** 10:1,5; 17:14; 18:16(see *'ōm^{e}nāh* [547]); **1 Chr.** 17:23,24; **2 Chr.** 1:9; 6:17; 9:6; 20:20; 32:15; **Neh.** 9:8; 13:13; **Esth.** 2:7; **Job** 4:18; 9:16; 12:20; 15:15,22,31; 24:22; 29:24; 39:12,24; **Ps.** 12:1(2); 19:7(8); 27:13; 31:23(24); 78:8,22,32,37;89: 28(29),37(38); 93:5; 101:6; 106:12,24; 111:7; 116:10; 119:66; **Prov.** 11:13; 14:15; 25:13; 26:25; 27:6; **Isa.** 1:21,26; 7:9; 8:2; 22:23,25; 28:16; 33:16; 43:10; 49:7,23; 53:1; 55:3; 60:4; **Jer.** 12:6; 15:18; 40:14; 42:5; **Lam.** 4:5,12; **Hos.** 5:9; 11:12(12:1); **Jon.** 3:5; **Mic.** 7:5; **Hab.** 1:5.

540. אֲמַן *'^{a}man* **Aram. verb**
(to believe, to be faithful; corr. to Hebr. 539)
Dan. 2:45; 6:4(5),23(24).

541. אָמַן *'āman* **verb**
(turn to the right)
Isa. 30:21(NASB, NIV, *yāman* [3231]).

542. אָמָּן *'ommān* **masc. noun**
(craftsman, artist)
Song 7:1(2).

543. אָמֵן *'āmēn* **adv.**
(amen, truly)
Num. 5:22; **Deut.** 27:15–26; **1 Kgs.** 1:36; **1 Chr.** 16:36; **Neh.** 5:13; 8:6; **Ps.** 41:13(14); 72:19; 89:52(53); 106:48; **Isa.** 65:16; **Jer.** 11:5; 28:6.

544. אֹמֶן *'ōmen* **masc. noun**
(truth, faithfulness)
Isa. 25:1.

545. אָמְנָה *'omnāh* **fem. noun**
(bringing up, rearing)
Esth. 2:20.

546. אָמְנָה *'omnāh* **particle**
(indeed, truly)
Gen. 20:12; **Josh.** 7:20.

547. אֹמְנָה *'ōm^{e}nāh* **fem. noun**
(pillar, doorpost; Qal act. part. of *'āman* [539])
2 Kgs. 18:16.

548. אֲמָנָה *'^{a}mānāh* **fem. noun**
(certainty, regulation)
Neh. 9:38(10:1); 11:23.

549. אֲמָנָה *'^{a}mānāh* **fem. proper noun**
(Amana: region in Anti-Lebanon)
Song 4:8.

550. A. אַמְנוֹן *'amnôn,* אֲמִינוֹן *'amiynôn* **masc. proper noun**
(Amnon: son of David)
2 Sam. 3:2; 13:1–4,6–10,15,20,22, 26–29,32,33,39; **1 Chr.** 3:1.

B. אַמְנוֹן *ʼamnôn* **masc. proper noun**
(Amnon: son of Shimon)
1 Chr. 4:20.

551. אָמְנָם *ʼomnām* **particle**
(truly, undoubtedly)
Ruth 3:12; **2 Kgs.** 19:17; **Job** 9:2; 12:2; 19:4,5; 34:12; 36:4; **Isa.** 37:18.

552. אֻמְנָם *ʼumnām* **particle**
(indeed, really)
Gen. 18:13; **Num.** 22:37; **1 Kgs.** 8:27; **2 Chr.** 6:18; **Ps.** 58:1(2).

553. אָמַץ *ʼāmaṣ* **verb**
(to be strong, to be courageous, to persist)
Gen. 25:23; **Deut.** 2:30; 3:28; 15:7; 31:6,7,23; **Josh.** 1:6,7,9,18; 10:25; **Ruth** 1:18; **2 Sam.** 22:18; **1 Kgs.** 12:18; **1 Chr.** 22:13; 28:20; **2 Chr.** 10:18; 11:17; 13:7,18; 24:13; 32:7; 36:13; **Job** 4:4; 16:5; **Ps.** 18:17(18); 27:14; 31:24(25); 80:15(16),17(18); 89:21(22); 142:6(7); **Prov.** 8:28; 24:5; 31:17; **Isa.** 35:3; 41:10; 44:14; **Amos** 2:14; **Nah.** 2:1(2).

554. אָמֹץ *ʼāmōṣ* **adj.**
(strong, powerful)
Zech. 6:3,7.

555. אֹמֶץ *ʼōmeṣ* **masc. noun**
(strength)
Job 17:9.

556. אַמְצָה *ʼamṣāh* **fem. noun**
(strength)
Zech. 12:5.

557. A. אַמְצִי *ʼamṣiy* **masc. proper noun**
(Amzi: son of Bani)
1 Chr. 6:46(31).
B. אַמְצִי *ʼamṣiy* **masc. proper noun.**
(Amzi: son of Zechariah)
Neh. 11:12.

558. A. אֲמַצְיָה *ʼamaṣyāh*, אֲמַצְיָהוּ *ʼamaṣyāhû* **masc. proper noun**
(Amaziah: son of Joash)
2 Kgs. 12:21(22); 13:12; 14:1,8,9,11,13,15,17,18,21,23; 15:1,3; **1 Chr.** 3:12; **2 Chr.** 24:27; 25:1,5,9–11, 13–15,17,18,20,21,23,25–27; 26:1,4.
B. אֲמַצְיָה *ʼamaṣyāh* **masc. proper noun**
(Amaziah: son of Elkanah)
1 Chr. 4:34.
C. אֲמַצְיָה *ʼamaṣyāh* **masc. proper noun**
(Amaziah: son of Hilkiah)
1 Chr. 6:45(30).
D. אֲמַצְיָה *ʼamaṣyāh* **masc. proper noun**
(Amaziah: priest of Bethel)
Amos 7:10,12,14.

559. I. אָמַר *ʼāmar* **verb**
(to say)
Gen. 1:3,6,9,11,14,20,22,24,26,28,29; 2:16,18,23; 3:1–4,9–14,16,17,22; 4:1, 6,8–10,13,15,23; 5:29; 6:3,7,13; 7:1; 8:15,21; 9:1,8,12,17,25,26; 10:9; 11:3, 4,6; 12:1,7,11–13,18,19; 13:8,14; 14:19, 21–23; 15:1–5,7–9,13,18; 16:2,5,6, 8–11,13; 17:1,3,9,15,17–19; 18:3,5,6, 9,10,12,13,15,17,20,23,26–32; 19:2,5,7, 9,12,14,15,17,18,21,31,34; 20:2–6,9–11, 13,15,16; 21:1,6,7,10,12,16,17,22,24, 26,29,30; 22:1–3,5,7–9,11,12,14,16,20; 23:3,5,8,10,13,14; 24:2,5–7,12,14,17–19, 23–25,27,30,31,33,34,37,39,40,42–47,50 ,54–58,60,65; 25:22,23,30–33; 26:2,7, 9–11,16,20,22,24,27,28,32; 27:1,2,6,11, 13,18–22,24–27,31–39,41,42,46; 28:1,6, 13,16,17,20; 29:4–8,14,15,18,19,21,25, 26,32–35; 30:1–3,6,8,11,13–16,18,20, 23–25,27–29,31,34; 31:1,3,5,8,11,12,14, 16,24,26,29,31,35,36,43,46,48,49,51; 32:2,4,6,8,9,12,16–20,26–29; 33:5, 8–10,12,13,15; 34:4,8,11,12,14,20,30,31; 35:1,2,10,11,17; 37:6,8–10,13–17,19–22, 26,30,32,33,35; 38:8,11,13,16–18, 21–26,28,29; 39:7,8,12,14,17,19;

40:7–9,12,16,18; 41:9,15,16,24,25,38, 39,41,44,54,55; 42:1,2,4,7,9,10,12–14, 18,21,22,28,29,31,33,36–38; 43:2,3,5–8, 11,16–18,20,23,27–29,31; 44:1,4,7,10, 15–23,25–28,32; 45:3,4,9,16,17,24, 26,28; 46:2,3,30,31,33,34; 47:1,3–5,8, 9,15,16,18,23,25,29–31; 48:1–4,8,9,11, 15,18–21; 49:1,29; 50:4–6,11,15–19, 24,25; **Ex.** 1:9,15,16,18,19,22; 2:6–10, 13,14,18–20,22; 3:3–7,11–18; 4:1–4, 6,7,10,11,13,14,18,19,21–23,25–27; 5:1–6,8,10,13–17,19,21,22; 6:1,2,6,10, 12,26,29,30; 7:1,8,9,14,16,17,19; 8:1,5, 8–10,16,19,20,25–29; 9:1,5,8,13,22, 27,29; 10:1,3,7–10,12,16,21,24,25,28,29; 11:1,4,8,9; 12:1,3,21,26,27,31,33,43; 13:1,3,8,14,17,19; 14:1,3,5,11–13,15, 25,26; 15:1,9,24,26; 16:3,4,6,8,9,11,12, 15,19,23,25,28,32,33; 17:2–5,7,9,10, 14,16; 18:3,6,10,14,15,17,24; 19:3, 8–10,12,15,21,23–25; 20:1,19,20,22; 21:5; 22:9; 23:13; 24:1,3,7,8,12,14; 25:1; 30:11,17,22,31,34; 31:1,12,13; 32:1,2, 4,5,8,9,11–13,17,18,21–24,26,27,29–31, 33; 33:1,5,12,14,15,17–21; 34:1,9,10,27; 35:1,4,30; 36:5,6; 40:1; **Lev.** 1:1,2; 4:1,2; 5:14; 6:1,8,9,19,24,25; 7:22,23,28,29; 8:1,5,31; 9:2,3,6,7; 10:3,4,6,8,16; 11:1,2; 12:1,2; 13:1; 14:1,33,35; 15:1,2; 16:2; 17:1,2,8,12,14; 18:1,2; 19:1,2; 20:1,2,24; 21:1,16,17; 22:1,3,17,18,26; 23:1,2,9, 10,23,24,26,33,34; 24:1,13,15; 25:1,2,20; 27:1,2; **Num.** 1:1,48; 2:1; 3:5,11,14, 40,44; 4:1,17,21; 5:1,5,11,12,19,21,22; 6:1,2,22,23; 7:4,11; 8:1,2,5,23; 9:1,7–10; 10:1,29–31,35,36; 11:4,11–13,16,18, 20,21,23,27–29; 12:2,4,6,11,13,14; 13:1,17,27,30–32; 14:2,4,7,10,11,13–15, 17,20,26,28,31,40,41; 15:1,2,17,18,35, 37,38; 16:3,5,8,12,15,16,20,22–24,26, 28,34,36,37,41,44,46; 17:1,10,12; 18:1, 20,24–26,30; 19:1,2; 20:3,7,10,12,14, 18–20,23; 21:2,7,8,14,16,21,27,34; 22:4,5,8–10,12–14,16–18,20,28–30,32,3 4,35,37,38; 23:1,3–5,7,11–13,15–19,23, 25–27,29,30; 24:3,10–12,15,20,21,23; 25:4,5,10,12,16; 26:1,3,52,65; 27:2,6,8, 12,15,18; 28:1–3; 29:40; 30:1; 31:1,3,15, 21,25,49; 32:2,5,6,10,16,20,25,29,31; 33:50,51; 34:1,2,13,16; 35:1,9,10; 36:2, 5,6; **Deut.** 1:5,6,9,14,16,20,22,25,27–29, 34,37,39,41,42; 2:2,4,9,17,26,31; 3:2,18, 21,23,26; 4:6,10; 5:1,5,24,27,28,30; 6:20,21; 7:17; 8:17; 9:4,12,13,23,25, 26,28; 10:1,11; 12:20,30; 13:2,6,12,13; 15:9,11,16; 17:11,14,16; 18:16,17,21; 19:7; 20:3,5,8; 21:7,20; 22:14,16,17; 25:7–9; 26:3,5,13,17,18; 27:1,9,11, 14–26; 28:67,68; 29:2,19,22,24,25; 30:12,13; 31:2,7,10,14,16,17,23,25; 32:7,20,26,27,37,40,46,48; 33:2,7–9, 12,13,18,20,22–24,27; 34:4; **Josh.** 1:1,10–13,16; 2:1–4,9,14,16,17,21,24; 3:3,5–10; 4:1,3,5–7,15,17,21,22; 5:2, 9,13–15; 6:2,6–8,10,16,22,26; 7:2,3, 7,8,10,13,19,20,25; 8:1,4,6,18; 9:6–9,11,19,21,22,24; 10:3,6,8,12, 17,18,22,24,25; 11:6,9; 13:1; 14:6,9; 15:16,18,19; 17:4,14–17; 18:3,8; 20:1,2; 21:2; 22:2,8,11,15,16,24,26–28,31,33; 23:2; 24:2,16,19,21,22,24,27; **Judg.** 1:1–3,7,12,14,15,24; 2:1,3,20; 3:19,20, 24,28; 4:6,8,9,14,18–20,22; 5:1,23; 6:8,10,12–18,20,22,23,25,29–32,36,39; 7:2–5,7,9,13–15,17,18,24; 8:1,2,5–7,9, 15,18–25; 9:1,3,7–15,28,29,31,36–38, 48,54; 10:10,11,15,18; 11:2,6–10,12, 13,15,17,19,30,35–38; 12:1,2,4–6; 13:3,6–8,10–13,15–18,22,23; 14:2,3, 12–16,18; 15:1–3,6,7,10–13,16,18; 16:2,5–7,9–15,17,18,20,23–26,28,30; 17:2,3,9,10,13; 18:2–6,8,9,14,18,19, 23–25; 19:5,6,8,9,11–13,17,18,20, 22,23,28,30; 20:3,4,8,12,18,23,28,32,39; 21:1,3,5,6,8,10,16–20,22; **Ruth** 1:8, 10–12,15,16,19,20; 2:2,4–8,10,11,13–15, 19–22; 3:1,5,9–11,14–18; 4:1–6,8,9,11, 14,17; **1 Sam.** 1:8,11,14,15,17,18,22, 23,26; 2:1,15,16,20,23,27,30,36; 3:4–6, 8–11,16–18; 4:3,6,7,14,16,17,21,22; 5:7,8,10,11; 6:2–4,20,21; 7:3,5,6,8,12; 8:5–7,10,11,19,22; 9:3,5–12,15,17–19, 21,23,24,26,27; 10:1,2,11,12,14–16, 18,19,22,24,27; 11:1–3,5,7,9,10,12–14;

12:1,4–6,10,12,19,20; 13:3,4,9,11–13,19; 14:1,6–12,17–19,24,28,29,33,34,36,38, 40–45; 15:1,2,6,10,12–18,20,22,24,26, 28,30,32,33; 16:1–12,15–19,22; 17:8, 10,17,25–30,32–34,37,39,43–45,55,56,5 8; 18:7,8,11,17,18,21–25; 19:2,4,11,14, 15,17,19,22,24; 20:1–7,9–12,18,21,22, 26,27,29,30,32,36,37,40,42; 21:1,2,4, 5,8,9,11,14; 22:3,5,7,9,12–14,16–18,22; 23:1–4,7,9–12,17,19,21,22,27; 24:1,4,6, 8–10,13,16,17; 25:5,6,10,13,14,19,21,24, 32,35,39–41; 26:1,6,8–10,14,15,17–19, 21,22,25; 27:1,5,10–12; 28:1,2,7–16, 21,23; 29:3–6,8,9; 30:6–8,13,15,20,22, 23,26; 31:4; **2 Sam.** 1:3–9,13–16,18; 2:1,4,5,14,20–22,26,27; 3:7,8,12–14, 16–18,21,23,24,28,31,33,35,38; 4:8–10; 5:1,2,6,8,19,20,23; 6:9,12,20–22; 7:2–5, 7,8,18,26,27; 9:1–4,6–9,11; 10:2,3,5,11; 11:3,5,8,10–12,15,19–21,23,25; 12:1,5, 7,11,13,18,19,21,22,27; 13:4–7,9–12, 15–17,20,24–26,28,30,32,33,35; 14:2,4, 5,7–13,15,17–19,21,22,24,30–32; 15:2–4,7–10,13–15,19,21,22,25–27,31, 33,34; 16:2–4,7,9–11,16–18,20,21; 17:1, 5–9,14–16,20,21,29; 18:2–5,10–12,14, 18–23,25–33; 19:2,5,8,9,11,13,19,21–23, 25,26,29,30,33,34,38,41,43; 20:1,4,6,9, 11,16–18,20,21; 21:1–6,16,17; 22:2; 23:3,15,17; 24:1–3,10–14,16–18,21–24; **1 Kgs.** 1:2,5,6,11,13,16,17,23–25,28–34, 36,39,41–43,47,48,51–53; 2:1,4,8,13–18, 20–23,26,29–31,36,38,39,42,44; 3:5,6, 11,17,22–27; 5:2,5–8; 6:11; 8:12,15,18, 23,25,29,47,55; 9:3,5,8,9,13; 10:6; 11:2, 11,18,21,22,31; 12:3,5–7,9,10,12,14,16, 22–24,26,28; 13:2–4,6,8,9,13–16,18,21, 26,27,31; 14:2,5–7; 15:18; 16:1,16; 17:1, 2,8,10–14,18–21,23,24; 18:1,5,7–11,14, 15,17,18,21,22,24–27,30,31,33,34,36,39 –41,43,44; 19:2,4,5,7,9–11,13–15,20; 20:2,4,5,7–14,17,18,22,23,28,31–37,39, 40,42; 21:2–4,6,7,9,10,13–15,17,19,20, 23,28; 22:3–9,11–22,24–28,30–32,34, 36,49; **2 Kgs.** 1:2,4–6,8,11,16; 2:2–6,9, 10,14–21,23; 3:7,8,10–14,16,17,23; 4:1–3,6,7,9,12–16,19,22–31,36,38,

40–43; 5:3–8,10,11,13,15–17,19–23, 25,26; 6:1–3,5–13,15–22,26–29,31–33; 7:1–4,6,9,10,12–14,18,19; 8:1,4–10, 12–14,19; 9:1,3,5,6,11–13,15,17–23,25, 27,31–34,36,37; 10:1,4–6,8,9,13–16,18, 20,22–25,30; 11:5,12,15; 12:4,7; 13:14–19; 14:6,8,9; 15:12; 16:7,15; 17:12,13,26,27,35; 18:14,19,20,22, 25–32,36; 19:3,6,9,10,15,20,23,32; 20:1, 2,4,5,7–10,14–17,19; 21:4,7,10,12; 22:3, 8–10,12,15,16,18; 23:17,18,21,27; 25:24; **1 Chr.** 4:9,10; 10:4; 11:1,2,5,6,17,19; 12:17,19; 13:2,4,12; 14:10–12,14; 15:2, 12,16; 16:18,31,35,36; 17:1–4,6,7,16,24; 19:2,3,5,12; 21:2,3,8–11,13,15,17,18, 22–24,27; 22:1,2,5,7,8; 23:25; 27:23; 28:2,3,6,20; 29:1,10,20; **2 Chr.** 1:2,7, 8,11; 2:1,3,11,12,15; 6:1,4,8,14,16,20,37; 7:12,18,21,22; 8:11; 9:5; 10:3,5–7,9,10, 12,14,16; 11:2–4; 12:5–7; 13:4,8; 14:4, 7,11; 15:2; 16:2,7; 18:3–8,10–21,23–27, 29–31,33; 19:2,6,9; 20:2,6,8,15,20,21,37; 21:7,12; 22:9; 23:3,11,13,14; 24:5,6,8, 20,22; 25:4,7,9,15–19; 26:18,23; 28:9, 10,13,23; 29:5,18,21,24,27,30,31; 30:6, 18; 31:4,10,11; 32:1,4,6,9–12,17,24; 33:4,7,16; 34:15,16,18,20,23,24,26; 35:3,21,23,25; 36:22,23; **Ezra** 1:1,2; 2:63; 4:2,3; 8:22,28; 9:1,6,10,11; 10:2, 10,12; **Neh.** 1:3,5,8; 2:2–7,17–20; 4:2, 3,10–12,14,19,22; 5:2–4,7–9,12,13; 6:2, 3,6–11,19; 7:3,65; 8:1,9–11,15; 9:5,15, 18,23; 13:9,11,17,19,21,22; **Esth.** 1:10, 13,16–18; 2:2,13,15,22; 3:3,4,8,11; 4:7, 10,13,15; 5:3–7,12,14; 6:1,3–7,10,13; 7:2,3,5,6,8,9; 8:5,7; 9:12–14,25; **Job** 1:5,7–9,12,14,16–18,21; 2:2–4,6,9,10; 3:2,3; 4:1; 6:1,22; 7:4,13; 8:1,10; 9:1, 7,12,22,27; 10:2; 11:1,4; 12:1; 15:1; 16:1; 18:1; 19:1,28; 20:1,7; 21:1,14,28; 22:1, 13,17,29; 23:1,5; 24:15; 25:1; 26:1; 27:1; 28:14,22,28; 29:1,18; 31:24,31; 32:6,7, 10,13; 33:8,24,27; 34:1,5,9,18,31,34; 35:1–3,10,14; 36:1,10,23; 37:6,19,20; 38:1,11,35; 39:25; 40:1,3,6; 42:1,7; **Ps.** 2:7; 3:2; 4:4,6; 10:6,11,13; 11:1; 12:4,5; 13:4; 14:1; 16:2; 17:15; 27:8; 29:9; 30:6;

31:14,22; 32:5; 33:9; 35:3,10,21,25,27; 38:16; 39:1; 40:7,10,15,16; 41:4,5; 42:3, 9,10; 45:1; 50:12,16; 51:19; 53:1,6; 55:6; 58:11; 64:5; 66:3; 68:22; 70:3,4; 71:10,11; 73:11,15; 74:8; 75:4; 77:10; 78:19; 79:10; 82:6; 83:4,12; 87:5; 89:2, 19; 90:3; 91:2; 94:4,7,18; 95:10; 96:10; 102:24; 105:11,31,34; 106:23,34,48; 107:2,25; 115:2; 116:11; 118:2–4; 119:57,82; 122:1; 124:1; 126:2; 129:1,8; 137:7; 139:11,20; 140:6; 142:5; 145:6,11; **Prov.** 1:11,21; 3:28; 4:4; 5:12; 7:4,13; 9:4,16; 20:9,14,22; 22:13; 23:7; 24:12, 24,29; 25:7; 26:13,19; 28:24; 30:9,15, 16,20; **Eccl.** 1:2,10,16; 2:1,2,15; 3:17,18; 5:6; 6:3; 7:10,23,27; 8:4,14,17; 9:16; 10:3; 12:1,8; **Song** 2:10; 7:8; **Isa.** 1:11, 18; 2:3; 3:7,10,16; 4:1,3; 5:19,20; 6:3, 5,7–9,11; 7:2–5,7,10,12,13; 8:1,3,5, 11,12,19,20; 9:9; 10:8,13,24; 12:1,4; 14:4,10,13,24; 16:14; 18:4; 19:11,18,25; 20:2,3,6; 21:6,9,12,16; 22:4,14,15; 23:4,12; 24:16; 25:9; 28:12,15,16; 29:11–13,15,16,22; 30:10,12,15,16,21, 22; 31:4; 32:5; 33:10,24; 35:4; 36:4,5,7, 10–16,18,21; 37:3,6,9,10,15,21,24,33; 38:1,3–5,10,11,15,21,22; 39:3–6,8; 40:1,6,9,25,27; 41:6,7,9,13,21,26; 42:5,17,22; 43:1,6,9,14,16; 44:2,5,6, 16,17,19,20,24,26–28; 45:1,9–11,13, 14,18,19,24; 46:10; 47:7,8,10; 48:5,7,17, 20,22; 49:3–9,14,20–22,25; 50:1; 51:16, 22,23; 52:3,4,7; 54:1,6,8,10; 56:1,3,4; 57:10,14,15,19,21; 58:9; 59:21; 61:6; 62:4,11; 63:8; 65:1,5,7,8,13,25; 66:1,5,9, 12,20,21,23; **Jer.** 1:4,6,7,9,11–14; 2:1,2, 5,6,8,20,23,25,27,31,35; 3:1,6,7,11,12, 16,19; 4:3,5,10,11,27; 5:2,4,12,14,19, 20,24; 6:6,9,14–17,21,22; 7:1–4,10,20, 21,23,28,32; 8:4,6,8,11,12; 9:7,13,15, 17,23; 10:2,18,19; 11:1,3–7,9,11,21,22; 12:4,14; 13:1,3,6,8,9,12,13,18,21,22; 14:10,11,13–15,17; 15:1,2,11,19; 16:1, 3,5,9–11,14,19; 17:5,15,19–21; 18:1,5, 10–13,18; 19:1,3,11,14,15; 20:3,4,9,15; 21:1,3,4,8,12,13; 22:1–3,6,8,9,11,14,18, 21,30; 23:2,7,15–17,25,33–35,37,38; 24:3–5,8; 25:2,5,8,15,27,28,30,32; 26:1, 2,4,8,9,11,12,16–18; 27:1,2,4,9,12,14, 16,19,21; 28:1,2,5,6,11–16; 29:3,4,8,10, 15–17,21,22,24,25,28,30–32; 30:1–3,5,1 2,18; 31:2,7,10,15,16,23,29,34,35,37; 32:3,6–8,13–16,25,26,28,36,42,43; 33:1, 2,4,10–13,17,19,20,23–25; 34:1,2,4,12, 13,17; 35:1,5,6,11–13,15,17–19; 36:1,5, 14–19,27,29,30; 37:3,6,7,9,13,14,17–19; 38:1–5,8,10,12,14–17,19,20,22,24–26; 39:11,15,16; 40:2,9,14–16; 41:6,8; 42:2, 4,5,9,13–15,18,20; 43:2,8,10; 44:1,2,4, 7,11,15,20,24–26,30; 45:1–4; 46:8,14, 16,25; 47:2; 48:1,8,14,17,19,40; 49:1,2, 7,12,18,28,34,35; 50:2,7,18,33; 51:1, 33,35,36,58,61,62,64; **Lam.** 2:12,15,16; 3:18,24,37,54,57; 4:15,20; **Ezek.** 2:1,3,4; 3:1,3,4,10,11,16,18,22,24,27; 4:13–16; 5:5,7,8; 6:1,3,11; 7:1,2,5; 8:5,6,8,9,12, 13,15,17; 9:1,4,5,7–9,11; 10:2,6; 11:2,3, 5,7,13–17; 12:1,8–11,17,19,21–23, 26–28; 13:1–3,6–8,10–13,15,18,20; 14:2,4,6,12,17,21; 15:1,6; 16:1,3,6,36, 44,59; 17:1,3,9,11,12,19,22; 18:1,2,19, 25,29; 19:2; 20:2,3,5,7,8,13,18,21,27, 29,30,32,39,45,47,49; 21:1,3,7–9,18,24, 26,28; 22:1,3,17,19,23,24,28; 23:1,22,28, 32,35,36,43,46; 24:1,3,6,9,15,19–21; 25:1,3,6,8,12,13,15,16; 26:1–3,7,15,17, 19; 27:1,3; 28:1,2,6,9,11,12,20,22,25; 29:1,3,8,9,13,17,19; 30:1,2,6,10,13, 20,22; 31:1,2,10,15; 32:1–3,11,17; 33:1,2,8,10–14,17,20,21,23–25,27,30; 34:1,2,10,11,17,20; 35:1,3,10,12,14; 36:1–7,13,16,20,22,33,35,37; 37:3–5, 9,11,12,15,18,19,21; 38:1,3,10,11,13, 14,17; 39:1,17,25; 41:4; 42:13; 43:7,18; 44:2,5,6,9; 45:9,18; 46:1,16,20,24; 47:6, 8,13; **Dan.** 1:3,10,11,18; 2:2,3; 8:13,14, 16,17,19,26; 9:4,22; 10:11,12,16,19,20; 12:6,8,9; **Hos.** 1:2,4,6,9,10; 2:1,5,7, 12,23; 3:1,3; 7:2; 10:3,8; 12:8; 13:2,10; 14:2,3; **Joel** 2:17,19,32; 3:10; **Amos** 1:2,3,5,6,8,9,11,13,15; 2:1,3,4,6,12; 3:1,9,11,12; 4:1; 5:3,4,14,16,17,27; 6:10,13; 7:2,3,5,6,8,10–12,14–17; 8:2,5,14; 9:1,10,15; **Obad.** 1:1,3;

Jon. 1:1,6–12,14; 2:2,4,10; 3:1,4,7; 4:2, 4,8–10; **Mic.** 2:3,4,7; 3:1,5,11; 4:2,11; 6:1; 7:10; **Nah.** 1:12; 3:7; **Hab.** 2:2,6,19; **Zeph.** 1:12; 2:15; 3:7,16,20; **Hag.** 1:1–3,5,7,8,13; 2:1,2,6,7,9–14,20,21; **Zech.** 1:1,3,4,6,7,9–12,14,16,17,19,21; 2:2,4,8; 3:2,4–7; 4:2,4–6,8,11–14; 5:2,3, 5,6,8,10,11; 6:4,5,7–9,12; 7:3–5,8,9,13; 8:1–4,6,7,9,14,18–21,23; 11:4,5,9,12, 13,15; 12:5; 13:3,5,6,9; **Mal.** 1:2,4–14; 2:2,4,8,14,16,17; 3:1,5,7,8,10–14,17; 4:1,3.

II. אָמַר *'āmar* **verb**
(to boast)
Ps. 94:4; **Isa.** 61:6(KJV, NASB, *yāmar* [3235,I]).

560. אֲמַר *'amar* **Aram. verb**
(to say; corr. to Hebr. 559)
Ezra 5:3,4,9,11,15; **Jer.** 10:11; **Dan.** 2:4,5,7–10,12,15,20,24–27,36,46,47; 3:4,9,13,14,16,19,20,24–26,28,29; 4:7–9(4–6),14(11),18(15),19(16),23(20), 26(23),30(27),31(28),35(32); 5:2,7,10, 13,17,29; 6:5(6),6(7),12(13),13(14), 15(16),16(17),20(21),23(24),24(25); 7:1,2,5,16,23.

561. I. אֵמֶר *'ēmer* **masc. noun**
(word, saying)
Gen. 49:21(NIV, see II); **Num.** 24:4,16; **Deut.** 32:1; **Josh.** 24:27; **Judg.** 5:29; **Job** 6:10,25,26; 8:2; 20:29; 22:22; 23:12; 32:12,14; 33:3; 34:37; **Ps.** 5:1(2); 19:14(15); 54:2(4); 78:1; 107:11; 138:4; 141:6; **Prov.** 1:2,21; 2:1,16; 4:5,10,20; 5:7; 6:2; 7:1,5,24; 8:8; 15:26; 16:24; 17:27; 19:7,27; 22:21; 23:12; **Isa.** 32:7; 41:26; **Hos.** 6:5.

II. אֵמֶר *'ēmer* **masc. noun**
(fawn)
Gen. 49:21(KJV, NASB, see I).

562. אֹמֶר *'ōmer* **masc. noun**
(word, speech, promise)
Job 22:28; **Ps.** 19:2(3),3(4); 68:11(12); 77:8(9); **Hab.** 3:9.

563. אִמַּר *'immar* **Aram. masc. noun**
(lamb)
Ezra 6:9,17; 7:17.

564. A. אִמֵּר *'immēr* **masc. proper noun**
(Immer: priest under Zerubbabel)
1 Chr. 9:12; **Ezra** 2:37; 10:20; **Neh.** 3:29; 7:40; 11:13.

B. אִמֵּר *'immēr* **masc. proper noun**
(Immer: a priest)
1 Chr. 24:14.

C. אִמֵּר *'immēr* **masc. proper noun**
(Immer: village in Babylon)
Ezra 2:59; **Neh.** 7:61.

D. אִמֵּר *'immēr* **masc. proper noun**
(Immer: a priest)
Jer. 20:1.

565. אֶמְרָה *'emrāh*, אִמְרָה *'imrāh* **fem. noun**
(word, speech)
Gen. 4:23; **Deut.** 32:2; 33:9; **2 Sam.** 22:31; **Ps.** 12:6(7); 17:6; 18:30(31); 105:19; 119:11,38,41,50,58,67,76, 82,103,116,123,133,140,148,154,158,16 2,170,172; 138:2; 147:15; **Prov.** 30:5; **Isa.** 5:24; 28:23; 29:4; 32:9; **Lam.** 2:17.

566. A. אִמְרִי *'imriy* **masc. proper noun**
(Imri: a Judaite)
1 Chr. 9:4.

B. אִמְרִי *'imriy* **masc. proper noun**
(Imri: assistant to Nehemiah)
Neh. 3:2.

567. אֱמֹרִי *'ĕmōriy* **masc. proper noun**
(Amorite)
Gen. 10:16; 14:7,13; 15:16,21; 48:22; **Ex.** 3:8,17; 13:5; 23:23; 33:2; 34:11; **Num.** 13:29; 21:13,21,25,26,29,31, 32,34; 22:2; 32:33,39; **Deut.** 1:4,7,19,

20,27,44; 2:24; 3:2,8,9; 4:46,47; 7:1; 20:17; 31:4; **Josh.** 2:10; 3:10; 5:1; 7:7; 9:1,10; 10:5,6,12; 11:3; 12:2,8; 13:4, 10,21; 24:8,11,12,15,18; **Judg.** 1:34–36; 3:5; 6:10; 10:8,11; 11:19,21–23; **1 Sam.** 7:14; **2 Sam.** 21:2; **1 Kgs.** 4:19; 9:20; 21:26; **2 Kgs.** 21:11; **1 Chr.** 1:14; **2 Chr.** 8:7; **Ezra** 9:1; **Neh.** 9:8; **Ps.** 135:11; 136:19; **Ezek.** 16:3,45; **Amos** 2:9,10.

568. A. אֲמַרְיָה *ʾamaryāh* **masc. proper noun**
(Amariah: grandfather of Zadok)
1 Chr. 6:7(5:33),52(37); **Ezra** 7:3.
B. אֲמַרְיָה *ʾamaryāh* **masc. proper noun**
(Amariah: son of Azariah)
1 Chr. 6:11(5:37).
C. אֲמַרְיָה *ʾamaryāh*, אֲמַרְיָהוּ *ʾamaryāhû* **masc. proper noun**
(Amariah: son of Hebron)
1 Chr. 23:19; 24:23.
D. אֲמַרְיָה *ʾamaryāh*, אֲמַרְיָהוּ *ʾamaryāhû* **masc. proper noun**
(Amariah: chief priest)
2 Chr. 19:11.
E. אֲמַרְיָה *ʾamaryāh*, אמַרְיָהוּ *ʾamaryāhû* **masc. proper noun**
(Amariah: a Levite)
2 Chr. 31:15.
F. אֲמַרְיָה *ʾamaryāh* **masc. proper noun**
(Amariah: son of Bani)
Ezra 10:42.
G. אֲמַרְיָה *ʾamaryāh* **masc. proper noun**
(Amariah: a priest)
Neh. 10:3(4); 12:2,13.
H. אֲמַרְיָה *ʾamaryāh* **masc. proper noun**
(Amariah: son of Shephatiah)
Neh. 11:4.
I. אֲמַרְיָה *ʾamaryāh* **masc. proper noun**
(Amariah: son of Hizkiah)
Zeph. 1:1.

569. אַמְרָפֶל *ʾamrāpel* **masc. proper noun**
(Amraphel)
Gen. 14:1,9.

570. אֶמֶשׁ *ʾemeš* **adv.**
(yesterday, last night)
Gen. 19:34; 31:29,42; **2 Kgs.** 9:26; **Job** 30:3.

571. אֱמֶת *ʾemet* **fem. noun.**
(truth, faithfulness)
Gen. 24:27,48,49; 32:10(11); 42:16; 47:29; **Ex.** 18:21; 34:6; **Deut.** 13:14(15); 17:4; 22:20; **Josh.** 2:12,14; 24:14; **Judg.** 9:15,16,19; **1 Sam.** 12:24; **2 Sam.** 2:6; 7:28; 15:20; **1 Kgs.** 2:4; 3:6; 10:6; 17:24; 22:16; **2 Kgs.** 20:3,19; **2 Chr.** 9:5; 15:3; 18:15; 31:20; 32:1; **Neh.** 7:2; 9:13,33; **Esth.** 9:30; **Ps.** 15:2; 19:9(10); 25:5,10; 26:3; 30:9(10); 31:5(6); 40:10(11),11(12); 43:3; 45:4(5); 51:6(8); 54:5(7); 57:3(4),10(11); 61:7(8); 69:13(14); 71:22; 85:10(11), 11(12); 86:11,15; 89:14(15); 91:4; 108:4(5); 111:7,8; 115:1; 117:2; 119:43,142,151,160; 132:11; 138:2; 145:18; 146:6; **Prov.** 3:3; 8:7; 11:18; 12:19; 14:22,25; 16:6; 20:28; 22:21; 23:23; 29:14; **Eccl.** 12:10; **Isa.** 10:20; 16:5; 38:3,18,19; 39:8; 42:3; 43:9; 48:1; 59:14,15; 61:8; **Jer.** 2:21; 4:2; 9:5(4); 10:10; 14:13; 23:28; 26:15; 28:9; 32:41; 33:6; 42:5; **Ezek.** 18:8,9; **Dan.** 8:12,26; 9:13; 10:1,21; 11:2; **Hos.** 4:1; **Mic.** 7:20; **Zech.** 7:9; 8:3, 8,16,19; **Mal.** 2:6.

572. אַמְתַּחַת *ʾamtaḥat* **fem. noun**
(sack, bag)
Gen. 42:27,28; 43:12,18,21–23; 44:1,2,8,11,12.

573. אֲמִתַּי *ʾamittay* **masc. proper noun**
(Amittai)
2 Kgs. 14:25; **Jon.** 1:1.

574. אֵימְתָן *'ēmtān* **Aram. adj.**
(terrifying)
Dan. 7:7.

575. אָן *'ān* **adv.**
(whither, where)
Gen. 16:8; 32:17(18); 37:30; **Ex.** 16:28; **Num.** 14:11; **Deut.** 1:28; **Josh.** 2:5; **Judg.** 19:17; **1 Sam.** 10:14; **2 Sam.** 2:1; 13:13; **1 Kgs.** 2:36,42; **2 Kgs.** 5:25; 6:6; **Neh.** 2:16; **Job** 8:2; 18:2; 19:2; **Ps.** 13:1,2; 62:3(4); 139:7; **Song** 6:1; **Isa.** 10:3; **Jer.** 15:2; **Ezek.** 21:16(11); **Hab.** 1:2; **Zech.** 2:2(6); 5:10.

576. אֲנָא *'anā'*, אֲנָה, *'anāh* **Aram. 1st person sing. pron.**
(I, me; corr. to Hebr. 589)
Ezra 6:12; 7:21; **Dan.** 2:8,23,30; 3:25; 4:4(1),7(4),9(6),18(15),30(27),34(31), 37(34); 5:16; 7:15,28.

577. אָנָּא *'ānnā'*, אָנָּה *'ānnāh* **interj.**
(O, I beseech thee)
Gen. 50:17; **Ex.** 32:31; **2 Kgs.** 20:3; **Neh.** 1:5,11; **Ps.** 116:4,16; 118:25; **Isa.** 38:3; **Dan.** 9:4; **Jon.** 1:14; 4:2.

578. אָנָה *'ānāh* **verb**
(to mourn, to lament)
Isa. 3:26; 19:8.

579. אָנָה *'ānāh* **verb**
(to meet, to allow to meet, to seek occasion)
Ex. 21:13; **2 Kgs.** 5:7; **Ps.** 91:10; **Prov.** 12:21.

580. אֲנוּ *'anû* **1st. person pl. pron.**
(we)
Jer. 42:6([Q^{e}] *'anaḥnû* [587]).

581. אִנּוּן *'innûn*, אִנִּין, *'inniyn* **Aram. demons. pl. pron.**
(these, they)
Ezra 5:4; **Dan.** 2:44; 6:24(25); 7:17.

582. אֱנוֹשׁ *'enôš* **masc. noun**
(man, humanity [Irregular plural forms of *'iyš* [376] are sometimes confused as plurals of this noun; references are listed under 376.])
2 Chr. 14:11(10); **Job** 4:17; 5:17; 7:1,17; 9:2; 10:4,5; 13:9; 14:19; 15:14; 25:4,6; 28:4,13; 32:8; 33:12,26; 36:25; **Ps.** 8:4(5); 9:19(20),20(21); 10:18; 55:13(14); 56:1(2); 59:2(3); 66:12; 73:5; 90:3; 103:15; 104:15; 144:3; **Isa.** 8:1; 13:7,12; 24:6; 33:8; 51:7,12; 56:2.

583. אֱנוֹשׁ *'enôš* **masc. proper noun**
(Enosh)
Gen. 4:26; 5:6,7,9–11; **1 Chr.** 1:1.

584. אָנַח *'ānaḥ* **verb**
(to groan, to moan)
Ex. 2:23; **Prov.** 29:2; **Isa.** 24:7; **Jer.** 22:23(KJV, NASB, *ḥānan* [2603]); **Lam.** 1:4,8,11,21; **Ezek.** 9:4; 21:6(11),7(12); **Joel** 1:18.

585. אֲנָחָה *'anāḥāh* **fem. noun**
(groaning, sighing)
Job 3:24; 23:2; **Ps.** 6:6(7); 31:10(11); 38:9(10); 102:5(6); **Isa.** 21:2; 35:10; 51:11; **Jer.** 45:3; **Lam.** 1:22.

586. אֲנַחְנָא *'anaḥnā'*, אֲנַחְנָה *'anaḥnāh* **Aram. 1st person pl. pron.**
(we; corr. to Hebr. 587)
Ezra 4:16; 5:11; **Dan.** 3:16,17.

587. אֲנַחְנוּ *'anaḥnû* **1st person pl. pron.**
(we, us)
Gen. 13:8; 19:13; 29:4; 37:7; 42:11,13,21,31,32; 43:8,18; 44:9,16; 46:34; 47:3,19; **Ex.** 10:26; **Num.** 9:7; 10:29; 20:4,16; 32:17; **Deut.** 1:28,41; 5:3,25(22); 12:8; **Josh.** 2:17–19; 9:8, 11,19,22; 24:18; **Judg.** 9:28; 16:5; 18:5; 19:18; 21:7,18; **1 Sam.** 8:20; 14:8; 20:42

(21:1); 23:3; 30:14; **2 Sam.** 5:1; **1 Kgs.** 3:18; 22:3; **2 Kgs.** 6:1; 7:3,9,12; 10:4, 5,13; **1 Chr.** 11:1; 29:13,15; **2 Chr.** 2:16(15); 13:10,11; 20:12; **Ezra** 4:2,3; 9:7,9; 10:2,4; **Neh.** 2:17,20; 4:1(3:33), 10(4),19(13),21(15),23(17); 5:2,3,5,8; 9:33,36,37,38(10:1); **Job** 8:9; **Ps.** 20:7(8), 8(9); 79:13; 95:7; 100:3; 103:14; 115:18; 124:7; **Isa.** 20:6; 36:11; 53:4; 64:8(7); **Jer.** 3:25; 8:8,14,20; 26:19; 35:8; 42:6([Kᵉ] *'ªnû* [580]); 44:17,19; 48:14; **Lam.** 5:7; **Ezek.** 11:3; 33:10,24; **Dan.** 9:18; **Mic.** 4:5; **Mal.** 3:15.

588. אֲנָחֲרַת *'ªnāḥªrāṯ* **proper noun**
(Anaharath)
Josh. 19:19.

589. אֲנִי *'ªniy* **1st person sing. pron.**
(I, me)
Gen. 6:17; 9:9,12; 14:23; 15:7; 17:1,4; 18:13,17; 22:5; 24:45; 27:8,24,32,34,38; 28:13; 31:44,52; 33:14; 34:30; 35:11; 37:10,30; 40:16; 41:9,11,15,44; 42:18,37; 43:14; 45:3,4; 48:7,22; 49:29; 50:19; **Ex.** 2:9; 3:19; 4:21; 6:2,5–8,12,29,30; 7:3,5, 17; 8:22(18); 9:14,27; 10:1,2; 11:4; 12:12; 13:15; 14:4,17,18; 15:26; 16:12; 18:6; 22:27(26); 25:9; 29:46; 31:6,13; 33:16,19; 34:10; **Lev.** 11:44,45; 14:34; 17:11; 18:2–6,21,24,30; 19:2–4,10,12, 14,16,18,25,26,28,30–32,34,36,37; 20:3,5,7,8,22–24; 21:8,12,15,23; 22:2, 3,8,9,16,30,31–33; 23:10,22,43; 24:22; 25:2,17,38,55; 26:1,2,13,16, 24,28,32,41,44,45; **Num.** 3:12,13,41,45; 5:3; 6:27; 10:10; 13:2; 14:21,28,35; 15:2, 18,41; 18:6,8,20; 20:19; 35:34; **Deut.** 12:30; 29:6(5); 32:21,39,49,52; **Josh.** 17:14; 23:2; **Judg.** 1:3; 2:21; 6:10; 8:23; 9:2; 12:2; 13:11; 15:3; 16:17; 17:2; 19:18; 20:4; **Ruth** 1:21; 4:4; **1 Sam.** 1:26; 3:13; 4:16; 12:2; 14:40; 16:1; 17:9,10,28; 19:3; 20:20,23; 21:15(16); 23:4; 24:17(18); 25:24,25; 26:6; **2 Sam.** 3:13; 7:8,14; 11:11; 12:12,23,28; 13:4,131; 14:5,8,32; 15:20,34; 16:19; 17:15; 18:2,22,27, 33(19:1); 19:20(21),22(23),38(39), 43(44); 20:17; 21:6; **1 Kgs.** 1:5,14,21,26; 3:17; 5:8(22),9(23); 12:11,14; 13:14,18; 17:20; 18:8,12,22–24,36; 19:10,14; 20:4,13,28,34; 21:7; 22:8,16,21; **2 Kgs.** 1:10,12; 2:3,5; 3:14; 5:7; 6:3; 9:17,25; 10:9,24; 16:7; 19:23,24; 22:20; 23:17; **1 Chr.** 17:7,13,16; 21:10,17; 22:7,10; 28:2,6; 29:14,17; **2 Chr.** 2:4–6(3–5), 8(7),9(8); 6:2; 7:14; 10:11,14; 12:5; 18:7,15,20; 32:13; 34:27,28; **Ezra** 7:28; 9:4; **Neh.** 1:1,6,8,11; 2:2,12,16; 4:23(17); 5:10,14,15; 6:3,10; 12:38,40; **Esth.** 4:11,16; 5:12,13; 7:4; 8:5; **Job** 1:15–17,19; 5:3,8; 6:24; 7:11,12; 9:20,21; 13:2,3, 13,18; 15:6; 19:25,27; 29:15; 32:6,10,73; 33:6,9; 34:33; 35:4; 40:14; **Ps.** 2:6,7; 3:5(6); 5:7(8); 6:2(3); 13:5(6); 17:4,6, 15,16; 25:16; 26:1,11; 27:3; 30:6(7); 31:6(7),14(15),22(23); 35:3,13; 38:13(14),17(18); 39:4(5),10(11); 40:17(18); 41:4(5),12(13); 45:1(2); 51:3(4); 52:8; 55:16(17),23(24); 56:3(4); 59:16(17); 69:13(14),29(30); 70:5(6); 71:14,22; 73:2,22,23,28; 75:2(3),9(10); 82:6; 86:1,2; 88:13(14),15(16); 89:27(28), 47(48); 102:11(12); 109:4,25; 116:10, 11,16; 118:7; 119:63,67,69,70,78,87, 94,125; 120:7; 135:5; 143:12; **Prov.** 1:26; 8:12,14,17,27; 23:15; 26:19; **Eccl.** 1:12, 16; 2:1,11–15,18,20,24; 3:17,18; 4:1,2, 4,7,8; 5:18(17); 7:25,26; 8:2,12,15; 9:16; **Song** 1:5,6; 2:1,5,16; 5:2,5,6,8; 6:3; 7:10(11); 8:10; **Isa.** 5:5; 6:5; 10:14; 13:3; 19:11; 27:3; 37:24,25; 38:10; 41:4,10,13, 14,17; 42:6,8,9; 43:2–5,10,12,13,15; 44:5,6; 45:2,3,5–8,12,18,19,21,22; 46:4; 47:8,10; 48:12,13,15–17; 49:4,19,21, 23,26; 52:6; 56:3; 57:11,12,16; 59:21; 60:16,22; 61:8; 63:1; 65:18,24; 66:4,9,22; **Jer.** 1:8,11–13,18,19; 3:12; 4:12; 5:4; 9:24(23); 10:19; 11:14,19; 13:26; 14:15; 15:20; 17:10,16,18; 21:5; 22:24; 23:3, 23,24; 24:7; 25:29; 26:14; 28:3,4; 29:31,32; 30:11; 31:37; 32:27,38; 34:5; 36:5,18; 38:14,19,20,26; 40:10; 42:11,17;

44:29; 45:4; 46:18,28; 48:30; 49:10,11; **Lam.** 1:16,21; 3:1,63; **Ezek.** 1:1; 2:3,4, 8; 3:3; 4:5; 5:8,11,13,15,17; 6:3,7,10, 13,14; 7:4,9,27; 8:1,18; 9:8,10; 11:5,10, 12,20; 12:11,15,16,20,25; 13:7,9,14, 21–23; 14:4,7–9,11,16,18,20; 15:7; 16:43,48,60,62; 17:16,19,21,22,24; 18:3; 20:3,5,7,12,15,19,20,23,25,26,31,33,38,4 2,44,48(21:4); 21:5(10),17(22),32(37); 22:14,16,22; 23:34,49; 24:9,14,24,27; 25:5,7,11,17; 26:5,6,14; 27:3; 28:2,9, 10,22–24,26; 29:3,6,9,16,21; 30:8,12, 19,25,26; 32:15; 33:11,27,29; 34:8,11, 15,20,24,27,30,31; 35:4,6,9,11–13,15; 36:7,11,22,23,32,36,38; 37:5,6,12–14, 19,21,23,28; 38:23; 39:5–7,17,22,28; 40:4; 44:5,28; **Dan.** 1:10; 8:1,2,5,15,27; 9:2,20,21,23; 10:2,4,7–9,12,13,20; 11:1; 12:5,8; **Hos.** 3:3; 4:6; 5:2,3,12,14; 7:15; 10:11; 13:5; 14:8(9); **Joel** 2:27; 3:10 (4:10),17(4:17); **Amos** 4:6; **Jon.** 1:9,12; 2:4(5),9(10); 4:11; **Mic.** 6:13; 7:7; **Hab.** 3:18; **Zeph.** 2:9,15; **Hag.** 1:13; 2:4,6,21; **Zech.** 1:9,15; 2:5(9); 5:2; 7:5; 8:8,11,21; 10:6; 13:9; **Mal.** 1:4,6,14; 2:9; 3:6,17; 4:3(3:21).

590. אֳנִי *'oniy* **masc. noun**
(fleet of ships)
1 Kgs. 9:26,27; 10:11,22; **Isa.** 33:21.

591. אֳנִיָּה *'oniyyāh* **fem. noun.**
(ship, boat)
Gen. 49:13; **Deut.** 28:68; **Judg.** 5:17; **1 Kgs.** 9:27; 22:48(49),49(50); **2 Chr.** 8:18; 9:21; 20:36,37; **Job** 9:26; **Ps.** 48:7(8); 104:26; 107:23; **Prov.** 30:19; 31:14; **Isa.** 2:16; 23:1,14; 43:14; 60:9; **Ezek.** 27:9, 25,29; **Dan.** 11:40; **Jon.** 1:3–5.

592. אֲנִיָּה *'aniyyāh* **fem. noun**
(mourning, sorrow)
Isa. 29:2; **Lam.** 2:5.

593. אֲנִיעָם *'aniy'ām* **masc. proper noun**
(Aniam)
1 Chr. 7:19.

594. אֲנָךְ *'anāḵ* **masc. noun**
(plumbline, plumb)
Amos 7:7,8.

595. אָנֹכִי *'ānōḵiy* **1st person sing. pron.**
(I, me)
Gen. 3:10; 4:9; 7:4; 15:1,2,14; 16:5,8; 18:27; 19:19; 20:6; 21:24,26; 23:4; 24:3, 13,24,27,31,34,37,42,43; 25:22,30,32; 26:24; 27:11,19; 28:15,16,20; 29:33; 30:1–3,30; 31:5,13,38,39; 32:11(12); 37:16; 38:17,25; 43:9; 46:3,4; 47:30; 48:21; 50:5,21,24; **Ex.** 3:6,11–13; 4:10–12,15,23; 7:17; 8:2(7:27),28(24), 29(25); 17:9; 19:9; 20:2,5; 23:20; 32:18; 34:10,11; **Num.** 11:12,14,21; 22:30,32; 23:15; **Deut.** 4:1,2,8,22,40; 5:1,5,6,9, 31(28); 6:2,6; 7:11; 8:1,11; 10:10,13; 11:8,13,22,26–28,32; 12:11,28,32; 13:18(19); 15:5,11,15; 18:19; 19:7,9; 24:18,22; 27:1,4,10; 28:1,13–15; 29:14(13); 30:2,8,11,16; 31:2,18,23,27; 32:39,40,46; **Josh.** 1:2; 7:20; 11:6; 14:7,8,10; 23:14; 24:15; **Judg.** 5:3; 6:8,15,18,37; 7:17,18; 8:5; 11:9,27,35,37; 17:9,10; 19:18; **Ruth** 2:10,13; 3:9,12,13; 4:4; **1 Sam.** 1:8,15,28; 2:23,24; 3:11; 4:16; 9:19,21; 10:8,18; 12:23; 15:14; 16:3; 17:8,43,45; 18:18,23; 20:5,36; 21:2(3); 22:22; 23:17; 24:4(5); 30:13; **2 Sam.** 1:8,13,16; 2:6,20; 3:8,13,28,39; 7:2,18; 11:5; 12:7; 13:28; 14:18; 15:28; 18:12; 19:35(36); 20:17,19; 24:12,17; **1 Kgs.** 2:2,16,18,20; 3:7; 14:6; 19:4; **2 Kgs.** 4:13; 22:19; **1 Chr.** 17:1; **Neh.** 1:6; **Job** 9:14,29,35; 12:3; 13:2,22; 14:15; 16:4; 21:3,4; 29:16; 33:9,31; 42:4; **Ps.** 22:6(7); 39:12(13); 46:10(11); 50:7; 75:3(4); 81:10(11); 91:15; 104:34; 109:22; 119:19,141,162; 141:10; **Prov.** 24:32; 30:2; **Isa.** 21:8; 43:11,12,25; 44:24; 45:12,13; 46:9; 49:15,25; 50:5; 51:12,15; 54:11,16; 66:13,18; **Jer.** 1:6,7,17; 2:21; 3:14,19; 4:6; 6:19; 7:11; 11:4; 14:12; 18:11; 23:32; 24:7; 25:27,29; 26:5; 27:5,6; 28:7; 29:11,23; 30:22;

31:32; 32:42; 33:9; 34:13; 35:14; 36:3; 50:9; 51:64; **Ezek.** 36:28; **Dan.** 10:11; **Hos.** 1:9; 2:2[4],8[10],14[16]; 5:14; 7:13; 11:3,9; 12:9,10; 13:4; **Amos** 2:9,10,13; 4:7; 5:1; 6:8; 7:14; 9:9; **Jon.** 1:9; 3:2; **Mic.** 3:8; **Zech.** 11:6,16; 12:2; 13:5; **Mal.** 4:5.

596. אָנַן *'ānan* **verb**
(to complain)
Num. 11:1; **Lam.** 3:39.

597. אָנַס *'ānas* **verb**
(to compel)
Esth. 1:8.

598. אֲנַס *'anas* **Aram. verb**
(to be too difficult, to baffle)
Dan. 4:9(6).

599. אָנַף *'ānap̱* **verb**
(to be angry, to be displeased)
Deut. 1:37; 4:21; 9:8,20; **1 Kgs.** 8:46; 11:9; **2 Kgs.** 17:18; **2 Chr.** 6:36; **Ezra** 9:14; **Ps.** 2:12; 60:1(3); 79:5; 85:5(6); **Isa.** 12:1.

600. אֲנַף *'anap̱* **Aram. masc. noun**
(face, facial expression)
Dan. 2:46; 3:19.

601. אֲנָפָה *'anāp̱āh* **fem. noun**
(heron)
Lev. 11:19; **Deut.** 14:18.

602. אָנַק *'ānaq* **verb**
(to cry, to groan)
Jer. 51:52; **Ezek.** 9:4; 24:17; 26:15.

603. אֲנָקָה *'anāqāh* **fem. noun**
(crying, groaning)
Ps. 12:5(6); 79:11; 102:20(21); **Mal.** 2:13.

604. אֲנָקָה *'anāqāh* **fem. noun**
(ferret, gecko)
Lev. 11:30.

605. אָנַשׁ *'ānaš* **verb**
(to be sick, to be incurable)
2 Sam. 12:15; **Job** 34:6; **Isa.** 17:11; **Jer.** 15:18; 17:9,16; 30:12,15; **Mic.** 1:9.

606. אֱנָשׁ *'enāš* **Aram. masc. noun**
(man, mankind; corr. to Hebr. 582)
Ezra 4:11; 6:11; **Dan.** 2:10,38,43; 3:10; 4:16(13),17(14),25(22),32(29),33(30); 5:5,7,21; 6:7(8),12(13); 7:4,8,13.

607. אַנְתָּה *'antah,* אַנְתְּ *'anet* **Aram. 2nd person sing. pron.**
(you, thou; corr. to Hebr. 859)
Ezra 7:25; **Dan.** 2:29,31,37,38; 3:10; 4:18(15),22(19); 5:13,18,22,23; 6:16(17),20(21).

608. אַנְתּוּן *'antûn* **Aram. 2nd person pl. pron.**
(ye)
Dan. 2:8.

609. A. אָסָא *'āsā'* **masc. proper noun**
(Asa: king of Judah)
1 Kgs. 15:8,9,11,13,14,16–18,20,22–25,28,32,33; 16:8,10,15,23,29; 22:41,43,46(47); **1 Chr.** 3:10; **2 Chr.** 14:1(13:23),2(1), 8(7),10–13(9–12); 15:2,8,10,16,17,19; 16:1,2,4,6,7,10–13; 17:2; 20:32; 21:12; **Jer.** 41:9.
B. אָסָא *'āsā'* **masc. proper noun**
(Asa: a Levite)
1 Chr. 9:16.

610. אָסוּךְ *'āsûḵ* **masc. noun**
(pot, jar)
2 Kgs. 4:2.

611. אָסוֹן *'āsôn* **masc. noun**
(injury, harm)
Gen. 42:4,38; 44:29; **Ex.** 21:22,23.

612. אֵסוּר *'ēsûr* **masc. noun**
(bond, binding, prison)
Judg. 15:14; **Eccl.** 7:26; **Jer.** 37:15.

613. אֱסוּר *'esûr* **Aram. masc. noun**
(band, imprisonment; corr. to Hebr. 612)
Ezra 7:26; Dan. 4:15(12),23(20).

614. אָסִיף *'āsiyp̱*, אָסִף *'āsip̱* **masc. noun**
(ingathering, harvest)
Ex. 23:16; 34:22.

615. אָסִיר *'āsiyr* **masc. noun**
(prisoner, captive)
Gen. 39:20([K^e] *'āsar* [631]),22;
Judg. 16:21(NASB, NIV, [Q^e] *'āsar* [631]),25(NASB, NIV, [Q^e] *'āsar* [631]);
Job 3:18; Ps. 68:6(7); 69:33(34); 79:11; 102:20(21); 107:10; Isa. 14:17; Lam. 3:34; Zech. 9:11,12.

616. אַסִּיר *'assiyr* **masc. noun**
(prisoners, captives [collective])
Isa. 10:4; 24:22; 42:7.

617. A. אַסִּיר *'assiyr* **masc. proper noun**
(Assir: son of Korah)
Ex. 6:24.
B. אַסִּיר *'assiyr* **masc. proper noun**
(Assir: son of Ebiasaph)
1 Chr. 6:22(7),23(8),37(22).
C. אַסִּיר *'assiyr* **masc. proper noun**
(Assir: son of Jeconiah)
1 Chr. 3:17.

618. אָסָם *'āsām* **masc. noun**
(storehouse, barn)
Deut. 28:8; Prov. 3:10.

619. אַסְנָה *'asnāh* **masc. proper noun**
(Asnah)
Ezra 2:50.

620. אָסְנַפַּר *'osnappar* **Aram. masc. proper noun**
(Osnappar [prob. Ashurbanipal])
Ezra 4:10.

621. אָסְנַת *'ās^{e}nat̠* **fem. proper noun**
(Asenath)
Gen. 41:45,50; 46:20.

622. אָסַף *'āsap̱* **verb**
(to gather, to assemble, to lose, to take away, to be a rear guard)
Gen. 6:21; 25:8,17; 29:3,7,8,22; 30:23; 34:30; 35:29; 42:17; 49:1,29,33; Ex. 3:16; 4:29; 9:19; 23:10,16; 32:26; Lev. 23:39; 25:3,20; 26:25; Num. 10:25; 11:16,22,24,30,32; 12:14,15; 19:9,10; 20:24,26; 21:16,23; 27:13; 31:2; Deut. 11:14; 16:13; 22:2; 28:38; 32:50; 33:5; Josh. 2:18; 6:9,13; 10:5; 20:4; 24:1; Judg. 2:10; 3:13; 6:33; 9:6; 10:17; 11:20; 16:23; 18:25; 19:15,18; 20:11,14; Ruth 2:7; 1 Sam. 5:8,11; 13:5,11; 14:19,52; 15:6; 17:1,2; 2 Sam. 6:1; 10:15,17; 11:27; 12:28,29; 14:14; 17:11,13; 21:13; 23:9,11; 1 Kgs. 10:26; 2 Kgs. 5:3,6,7,11; 22:4,20; 23:1; 1 Chr. 11:13; 15:4; 19:7,17; 23:2; 2 Chr. 1:14; 12:5; 24:11; 28:24; 29:4,15,20; 30:3,13; 34:9,28,29; Ezra 3:1; 9:4; Neh. 8:1,13; 9:1; 12:28; Job 27:19; 34:14; 39:12; Ps. 26:9; 27:10; 35:15; 39:6(7); 47:9(10); 50:5; 85:3(4); 104:22,29; Prov. 27:25; 30:4; Eccl. 2:26; Isa. 4:1; 10:14; 11:12; 13:4; 16:10; 17:5; 24:22; 33:4; 43:9; 49:5; 52:12; 57:1; 58:8; 60:20; 62:9; Jer. 4:5; 8:2,13,14; 9:22(21); 10:17; 12:9; 16:5; 21:4; 25:33; 40:10,12; 47:6; 48:33; Ezek. 11:17; 24:4; 29:5; 34:29; 38:12; 39:17; Dan. 11:10; Hos. 4:3; 10:10; Joel 1:14; 2:10,16; 3:15 (4:15); Amos 3:9; Mic. 2:12; 4:6,11; Hab. 1:9,15; 2:5; Zeph. 1:2; 3:8,18; Zech. 12:3; 14:2,14.

623. A. אָסָף *'āsāp̱* **masc. proper noun**
(Asaph: chief musician)
1 Chr. 6:39(24); 15:17,19; 16:5,7,37; 25:1,2,6,9; 2 Chr. 5:12; 20:14; 29:13,30; 35:15; Ezra 2:41; 3:10; Neh. 7:44; 11:17,22; 12:35,46; Ps. 50:[title](1); 73:[title](1); 74:[title](1); 75:[title](1);

76:[title](1); 77:[title](1); 78:[title](1); 79:[title](1); 80:[title](1); 81:[title](1); 82:[title](1); 83:[title](1).
B. אָסָף *ʼāsāp̱* **masc. proper noun**
(Asaph: father of Hezekiah's recorder)
2 Kgs. 18:18,37; **Isa.** 36:3,22.
C. אָסָף *ʼāsāp̱* **masc. proper noun**
(Asaph: a Korahite)
1 Chr. 26:1.
D. אָסָף *ʼāsāp̱* **masc. proper noun**
(Asaph: a royal steward)
Neh. 2:8.
E. אָסָף *ʼāsāp̱* **masc. proper noun**
(Asaph: a Levite; possibly same as A)
1 Chr. 9:15.

624. I. אָסֹף *ʼāsōp̱* **masc. noun**
(storehouse)
1 Chr. 26:15(KJV, see II),17(KJV, see II); **Neh.** 12:25(KJV, see III).
II. אֲסֻפִּים *ʼasuppiym* **masc. proper noun**
(Asuppim)
1 Chr. 26:15(NASB, NIV, see I),17(NASB, NIV, see I).
III. אֲסֻפִּים *ʼasuppiym* **masc. noun**
(threshold)
Neh. 12:25(NASB, NIV, see I).

625. אֹסֶף *ʼōsep̱* **masc. noun**
(gathering, harvest)
Isa. 32:10; 33:4; **Mic.** 7:1.

626. אֲסֵפָה *ʼasēp̱āh* **fem. noun**
(together)
Isa. 24:22.

627. אֲסֻפָּה *ʼasuppah* **fem. noun**
(collection, assembly)
Eccl. 12:11.

628. אֲסַפְסֻף *ʼasapsup̱* **masc. noun**
(collected multitude, rabble)
Num. 11:4.

629. אָסְפַּרְנָא *ʼosparnāʼ* **Aram. adv.**
(diligently, speedily)
Ezra 5:8; 6:8,12,13; 7:17,21,26.

630. אַסְפָּתָא *ʼaspāṯāʼ* **masc. proper noun**
(Aspatha)
Esth. 9:7.

631. אָסַר *ʼāsar* **verb**
(to bind, to imprison)
Gen. 39:20(KJV, NASB, NIV, [Qe] *ʼāsiyr* [615]); 40:3,5; 42:16,19,24; 46:29; 49:11; **Ex.** 14:6; **Num.** 30:2–11(3–12); **Judg.** 15:10,12,13; 16:5–8,10–13,21(KJV, [Ke] *ʼāsiyr* [615]),25(KJV, [Ke] *ʼāsiyr* [615]); **1 Sam.** 6:7,10; **2 Sam.** 3:34; **1 Kgs.** 18:44; 20:14; **2 Kgs.** 7:10; 9:21; 17:4; 23:33; 25:7; **2 Chr.** 13:3; 33:11; 36:6; **Neh.** 4:18(12); **Job** 12:18; 36:8,13; **Ps.** 105:22; 118:27; 146:7; 149:8; **Eccl.** 4:14; **Song** 7:5(6); **Isa.** 22:3; 49:9; 61:1; **Jer.** 39:7; 40:1; 46:4; 52:11; **Ezek.** 3:25; **Hos.** 10:10.

632. אֱסָר *ʼesār,* אִסָּר *ʼissār* **masc. noun**
(bond, obligation)
Num. 30:2–5(3–6),7(8),10–14(11–15).

633. אֱסָר *ʼesār* **Aram. masc. noun**
(decree, injunction; corr. to Hebr. 622)
Dan. 6:7–9(8–10),12(13),13(14),15(16).

634. אֵסַרְחַדּוֹן *ʼēsarḥaddôn* **masc. proper noun**
(Esarhaddon)
2 Kgs. 19:37; **Ezra** 4:2; **Isa.** 37:38.

635. אֶסְתֵּר *ʼestēr* **fem. proper noun**
(Esther)
Esth. 2:7,8,10,11,15–18,20,22; 4:4,5, 8–10,12,13,15,17; 5:1–7,12; 6:14; 7:1–3,5–8; 8:1–4,7; 9:12,13,29,31,32.

636. אָע *ʼāʻ* **Aram. masc. noun**
(wood beam, timber)
Ezra 5:8; 6:4,11; **Dan.** 5:4,23.

637. אַף *'ap̱* **particle**
(also, yea)
Gen. 3:1; 18:13,23,24; 40:16; **Lev.** 26:16,24,28,39–42,44; **Num.** 16:14; **Deut.** 2:11,20; 15:17; 31:27; 33:3,20,28; **Judg.** 5:29; **1 Sam.** 2:7; 14:30; 21:5; 23:3; **2 Sam.** 4:11; 16:11; 20:14; **1 Kgs.** 8:27; **2 Kgs.** 5:13; **1 Chr.** 8:32; 9:38; 16:30; **2 Chr.** 6:18; 12:5; 32:15; **Neh.** 2:18; 9:18; 13:15; **Esth.** 5:12; **Job** 4:19; 6:27; 9:14; 14:3; 15:4,6; 19:4; 25:6; 32:10,17; 34:12,17; 35:14; 36:16,29,33; 37:1,11; 40:8; **Ps.** 16:6,7,9; 18:48(49); 44:9(10); 58:2(3); 65:13(14); 68:8(9), 16(17),18(19); 74:16; 77:16(17),17(18); 89:5(6),11(12),21(22),27(28),43(44); 93:1; 96:10; 108:1(2); 119:3; 135:17; **Prov.** 9:2; 11:31; 15:11; 17:7; 19:7,10; 21:27; 22:19; 23:28; **Eccl.** 2:9; **Song** 1:16; **Isa.** 26:8,9,11; 33:2; 35:2; 40:24; 41:10,23,26; 42:13; 43:7,19; 44:15,16,19; 45:21; 46:6,7,11; 48:12,13,15; **Ezek.** 14:21; 15:5; 23:40; **Amos** 2:11; **Hab.** 2:5,15.

638. אַף *'ap̱* **Aram. conj.**
(also, even; corr. to Hebr. 637)
Ezra 5:10,14; 6:5; **Dan.** 6:22(23).

639. אַף *'ap̱* **masc. noun**
(nostrils, anger, face)
Gen. 2:7; 3:19; 7:22; 19:1; 24:47; 27:45; 30:2; 39:19; 42:6; 44:18; 48:12; 49:6,7; **Ex.** 4:14; 11:8; 15:8; 22:24(23); 32:10–12,19,22; 34:6; **Num.** 11:1,10, 20,33; 12:9; 14:18; 22:22,27,31; 24:10; 25:3,4; 32:10,13,14; **Deut.** 6:15; 7:4; 9:19; 11:17; 13:17(18); 29:20(19), 23(22),24(23),27(26),28(27); 31:17; 32:22; 33:10; **Josh.** 7:1,26; 23:16; **Judg.** 2:14,20; 3:8; 6:39; 9:30; 10:7; 14:19; **1 Sam.** 1:5; 11:6; 17:28; 20:30,34,41; 24:8(9); 25:23,41; 28:14,18; **2 Sam.** 6:7; 12:5; 14:4,33; 18:28; 22:9,16; 24:1,20; **1 Kgs.** 1:23,31; **2 Kgs.** 13:3; 19:28; 23:26; 24:20; **1 Chr.** 13:10; 21:21; **2 Chr.** 7:3; 12:12; 20:18; 25:10,15; 28:11,13; 29:10; 30:8; **Ezra** 8:22; 10:14; **Neh.** 8:6; 9:17; **Job** 4:9; 9:5,13; 14:13; 16:9; 18:4; 19:11; 20:23,28; 21:17; 27:3; 32:2,3,5; 35:15; 36:13; 40:11,24; 41:2 (40:26); 42:7; **Ps.** 2:5,12; 6:1(2); 7:6(7); 10:4; 18:8(9),15(16); 21:9(10); 27:9; 30:5(6); 37:8; 55:3(4); 56:7(8); 69:24(25); 74:1; 76:7(8); 77:9(10); 78:21,31,38, 49,50; 85:3(4),5(6); 86:15; 90:7,11; 95:11; 103:8; 106:40; 110:5; 115:6; 124:3; 138:7; 145:8; **Prov.** 11:22; 14:17,29; 15:1,18; 16:32; 19:11; 21:14; 22:24; 24:18; 25:15; 27:4; 29:8,22; 30:33; **Song** 7:4(5),8(9); **Isa.** 2:22; 3:21; 5:25; 7:4; 9:12(11),17(16),21(20); 10:4,5,25; 12:1; 13:3,9,13; 14:6; 30:27,30; 37:29; 42:25; 48:9; 49:23; 63:3,6; 65:5; 66:15; **Jer.** 2:35; 4:8,26; 7:20; 10:24; 12:13; 15:14,15; 17:4; 18:23; 21:5; 23:20; 25:37,38; 30:24; 32:31,37; 33:5; 36:7; 42:18; 44:6; 49:37; 51:45; 52:3; **Lam.** 1:12; 2:1,3,6,21,22; 3:43,66; 4:11,20; **Ezek.** 5:13,15; 7:3,8; 8:17; 13:13; 16:12; 20:8,21; 22:20; 23:25; 25:14; 35:11; 38:18; 43:8; **Dan.** 9:16; 11:20; **Hos.** 8:5; 11:9; 13:11; 14:4(5); **Joel** 2:13; **Amos** 1:11; 4:10; **Jon.** 3:9; 4:2; **Mic.** 5:15(14); 7:18; **Nah.** 1:3,6; **Hab.** 3:8,12; **Zeph.** 2:2,3; 3:8; **Zech.** 10:3.

640. אָפַד *'āp̱aḏ* **verb**
(to gird, to bind)
Ex. 29:5; **Lev.** 8:7.

641. אֵפֹד *'ēp̱ōḏ* **masc. proper noun**
(Ephod)
Num. 34:23.

642. אֲפֻדָּה *'ᵃp̱uddāh* **fem. noun**
(ephod, a garment of the priest)
Ex. 28:8; 39:5; **Isa.** 30:22.

643. אַפֶּדֶן *'appeḏen* **masc. noun**
(palace, pavilion)
Dan. 11:45.

644. אָפָה *'āp̱āh* **verb**
(to bake)

Gen. 19:3; 40:1,2,5,16,17,20,22; 41:10; **Ex.** 12:39; 16:23; **Lev.** 6:17(10); 7:9; 23:17; 24:5; 26:26; **1 Sam.** 8:13; 28:24; **Isa.** 44:15,19; **Jer.** 37:21; **Ezek.** 46:20; **Hos.** 7:4,6.

645. אֵפוֹ *'ēpô*, אֵפוֹא *'ēpô'* **particle**
(then, now)
Gen. 27:33,37; 43:11; **Ex.** 33:16; **Judg.** 9:38; **2 Kgs.** 10:10; **Job** 9:24; 17:15; 19:6,23; 24:25; **Prov.** 6:3; **Isa.** 19:12; 22:1; **Hos.** 13:10.

646. אֵפוֹד *'ēpôd*, אֵפֹד *'ēpōd* **masc. noun**
(ephod, a garment of the priest)
Ex. 25:7; 28:4,6,12,15,25–28,31; 29:5; 35:9,27; 39:2,7,8,18–22; **Lev.** 8:7; **Judg.** 8:27; 17:5; 18:14,17,18,20; **1 Sam.** 2:18,28; 14:3; 21:9(10); 22:18; 23:6,9; 30:7; **2 Sam.** 6:14; **1 Chr.** 15:27; **Hos.** 3:4.

647. אֲפִיחַ *'apiyah* **masc. proper noun**
(Aphiah)
1 Sam. 9:1.

648. אָפִיל *'āpiyl* **adj.**
(ripening late)
Ex. 9:32.

649. אַפַּיִם *'appayim* **masc. proper noun**
(Appaim)
1 Chr. 2:30,31.

650. I. אָפִיק *'āpiyq* **masc. noun**
(stream channel, ravine, tube)
2 Sam. 22:16; **Job** 6:15; 40:18(KJV, see II); 41:15(7); **Ps.** 18:15(16); 42:1(2); 126:4; **Song** 5:12; **Isa.** 8:7; **Ezek.** 6:3; 31:12; 32:6; 34:13; 35:8; 36:4,6; **Joel** 1:20; 3:18(4:18).
II. אָפִיק *'āpiyq* **adj.**
(strong, mighty)
Job 12:21; 40:18(NASB, NIV, see I).

651. אָפֵל *'āpēl* **adj.**
(gloomy, dark)
Amos 5:20.

652. אֹפֶל *'ōpel* **masc. noun**
(thick darkness, gloom)
Job 3:6; 10:22; 23:17; 28:3; 30:26; **Ps.** 11:2; 91:6; **Isa.** 29:18.

653. אֲפֵלָה *'apēlāh* **fem. noun**
(gloom, darkness)
Ex. 10:22; **Deut.** 28:29; **Prov.** 4:19; 7:9; **Isa.** 8:22; 58:10; 59:9; **Jer.** 23:12; **Joel** 2:2; **Zeph.** 1:15.

654. אֶפְלָל *'eplāl* **masc. proper noun**
(Ephlal)
1 Chr. 2:37.

655. אֹפֶן *'ōpen* **masc. noun**
(right time, right circumstance)
Prov. 25:11.

656. אָפֵס *'āpēs* **verb**
(to come to an end, to be used up, to cease)
Gen. 47:15,16; **Ps.** 77:8(9); **Isa.** 16:4; 29:20.

657. I. אֶפֶס *'epes* **masc. noun**
(ceasing)
Num. 13:28; 22:35; 23:13; **Deut.** 15:4; 32:36; 33:17; **Judg.** 4:9; **1 Sam.** 2:10; 17:1; **2 Sam.** 9:3; 12:14; **2 Kgs.** 14:26; **Job** 7:6; **Ps.** 2:8; 22:27(28); 59:13(14); 67:7(8); 72:8; 98:3; **Prov.** 14:28; 26:20; 30:4; **Isa.** 5:8; 34:12; 40:17; 41:12,29; 45:6,14,22; 46:9; 47:8,10; 52:4,10; 54:15; **Jer.** 16:19; **Dan.** 8:25; **Amos** 6:10; 9:8; **Mic.** 5:4(3); **Zeph.** 2:15; **Zech.** 9:10.
II. אֹפֶס *'ōphes* **masc. noun**
(extremeties, ankles, soles of the feet)
Ezek. 47:3.

658. אֶפֶס דַּמִּים *'epes dammiym* **proper noun**
(Ephes-dammim)
1 Sam. 17:1.

659. אֶפַע *'epa'* **masc. noun**
(worthlessness, nothing)
Isa. 41:24.

660. אֶפְעֶה *'ep̲'eh* **masc. noun**
(viper, snake)
Job 20:16; **Isa.** 30:6; 59:5.

661. אָפַף *'āpap̲* **verb**
(to encompass, to entangle, to engulf)
2 Sam. 22:5; **Ps.** 18:4(5); 40:12(13); 116:3; **Jon.** 2:5(6).

662. אָפַק *'āp̲aq* **verb**
(to hold back, to restrain oneself, to be compelled)
Gen. 43:31; 45:1; **1 Sam.** 13:12; **Esth.** 5:10; **Isa.** 42:14; 63:15; 64:12(11).

663. A. אֲפִיק *'ap̲iyq*, אֲפֵק *'ap̲ēq* **proper noun**
(Aphek: city in Asher)
Josh. 19:30; **Judg.** 1:31.
B. אֲפֵק *'ap̲ēq* **proper noun**
(Aphek: city N. of Sidon)
Josh. 13:4.
C. אֲפֵק *'ap̲ēq* **proper noun**
(Aphek: city in Issachar)
Josh. 12:18; **1 Sam.** 4:1; 29:1.
D. אֲפֵק *'ap̲ēq* **proper noun**
(Aphek: city E. of the Jordan)
1 Kgs. 20:26,30; **2 Kgs.** 13:17.

664. אֲפֵקָה *'ap̲ēqāh* **proper noun**
(Aphekah)
Josh. 15:53.

665. אֵפֶר *'ēp̲er* **masc. noun**
(ashes, dust)
Gen. 18:27; **Num.** 19:9,10; **2 Sam.** 13:19; **Esth.** 4:1,3; **Job** 2:8; 13:12; 30:19; 42:6; **Ps.** 102:9(10); 147:16; **Isa.** 44:20; 58:5; 61:3; **Jer.** 6:26; **Lam.** 3:16; **Ezek.** 27:30; 28:18; **Dan.** 9:3; **Jon.** 3:6; **Mal.** 4:3(3:21).

666. A. אֲפֵר *'ap̲ēr* **masc. noun**
(headband, bandage)
1 Kgs. 20:38(KJV, see B),41(KJV, see B).
B. אֲפֵר *'ap̲ēr* **masc. noun**
(ashes, dust)
1 Kgs. 20:38(NASB, NIV, see A),41(NASB, NIV, see A).

667. אֶפְרֹחַ *'ep̲rōaḥ* **masc. noun**
(young one [of birds])
Deut. 22:6; **Job** 39:30; **Ps.** 84:3(4).

668. אַפִּרְיוֹן *'appiryôn* **masc. noun**
(chariot, carriage)
Song 3:9.

669. A. אֶפְרַיִם *'ep̲rayim* **masc. proper noun**
(Ephraim: second son of Joseph)
Gen. 41:52; 46:20; 48:1,5,13,14,17,20; 50:23; **Num.** 26:28; **1 Chr.** 7:20,22.
B. אֶפְרַיִם *'ep̲rayim* **masc. proper noun**
(Ephraim: name, tribe, or territory of Ephraim)
Num. 1:10,32,33; 2:18,24; 7:48; 10:22; 13:8; 26:35,37; 34:24; **Deut.** 33:17; 34:2; **Josh.** 14:4; 16:4,5,8–10; 17:8–10,15,17; 19:50; 20:7; 21:5,20,21; 24:30,33; **Judg.** 1:29; 2:9; 3:27; 4:5; 5:14; 7:24; 8:1,2; 10:1,9; 12:1,4–6,15; 17:1,8; 18:2,13; 19:1,16,18; **1 Sam.** 1:1; 9:4; 14:22; **2 Sam.** 2:9; 18:6; 20:21; **1 Kgs.** 4:8; 12:25; **2 Kgs.** 5:22; **1 Chr.** 6:66(51), 67(52); 9:3; 12:30; 27:10,14,20; **2 Chr.** 13:4; 15:8,9; 17:2; 19:4; 25:7,10; 28:7,12; 30:1,10,18; 31:1; 34:6,9; **Ps.** 60:7(9); 78:9,67; 80:2(3); 108:8(9); **Isa.** 7:2,5,8, 9,17; 9:9(8),21(20); 11:13; 17:3; 28:1,3; **Jer.** 4:15; 7:15; 31:6,9,18,20; 50:19; **Ezek.** 37:16,19; 48:5,6; **Hos.** 4:17; 5:3,5,9,11–14; 6:4,10; 7:1,8,11; 8:9,11; 9:3,8,11,13,16; 10:6,11; 11:3,8,9, 12(12:1); 12:1(2),8(9),14(15); 13:1,12; 14:8(9); **Obad.** 1:19; **Zech.** 9:10,13; 10:7.

C. אֶפְרַיִם *'eprayim* **masc. proper noun**
(Ephraim: a town)
2 Sam. 13:23.
D. אֶפְרַיִם *'eprayim* **proper noun**
(Ephraim: a gate in Jerusalem)
2 Kgs. 14:13; **2 Chr.** 25:23; **Neh.** 8:16; 12:39.

670. I. אֲפָרְסָי *'apārᵉsāy* **Aram. proper noun**
(Apharsites)
Ezra 4:9(NASB, see III; NIV, see II).
II. אֲפָרְסָי *'apārᵉsāy* **Aram. proper noun**
(men of Persia)
Ezra 4:9(KJV, see I; NASB, see III).
III. אֲפָרְסָי *'apārᵉsāy* **Aram. masc. noun**
(secretaries)
Ezra 4:9(KJV, see I; NIV, see II).

671. I. אֲפַרְסְכָי *'aparsᵉkāy*, אפרסתכי *'aparsatkāy* **Aram. masc. pl. proper noun**
(Apharsathchites: a people settled in Samaria; NASB, NIV, see II)
Ezra 4:9; 5:6; 6:6.
II. אֲפַרְסְכָי *'aparsᵉkāy*, אפרסתכי *'aparsatkāy* **Aram. masc. pl. proper noun**
(officials, lesser governors; KJV, see I)
Ezra 4:9; 5:6; 6:6.

672. A. אֶפְרָת *'eprāt*, אֶפְרָתָה *'eprātāh* **proper noun**
(Ephrath: old name for Bethlehem)
Gen. 35:16,19; 48:7; **Ruth** 4:11; **1 Chr.** 2:24; **Ps.** 132:6; **Mic.** 5:2(1).
B. אֶפְרָת *'eprāt*, אֶפְרָתָה *'eprātāh* **fem. proper noun**
(Ephrath: second wife of Caleb)
1 Chr. 2:19,50; 4:4.

673. A. אֶפְרָתִי *'eprātiy* **masc. proper noun**
(Ephraimite: descendant of Ephraim)
Judg. 12:5; **1 Sam.** 1:1; **1 Kgs.** 11:26.
B. אֶפְרָתִי *'eprātiy* **masc. proper noun**
(Ephrathite: inhabitant of Ephratah)
Ruth 1:2; **1 Sam.** 17:12.

674. אַפְּתֹם *'appᵉtōm* **Aram. masc. noun**
(revenue)
Ezra 4:13.

675. A. אֶצְבּוֹן *'eṣbôn* **masc. proper noun**
(Ezbon: son of Gad)
Gen. 46:16.
B. אֶצְבּוֹן *'eṣbôn* **masc. proper noun**
(Ezbon: grandson of Benjamin)
1 Chr. 7:7.

676. אֶצְבַּע *'eṣba'* **fem. noun**
(finger, toe)
Ex. 8:19(15); 29:12; 31:18; **Lev.** 4:6,17,25,30,34; 8:15; 9:9; 14:16,27; 16:14,19; **Num.** 19:4; **Deut.** 9:10; **2 Sam.** 21:20; **1 Chr.** 20:6; **Ps.** 8:3(4); 144:1; **Prov.** 6:13; 7:3; **Song** 5:5; **Isa.** 2:8; 17:8; 58:9; 59:3; **Jer.** 52:21.

677. אֶצְבַּע *'eṣba'* **Aram. fem. noun**
(finger, toe; corr. to Hebr. 676)
Dan. 2:41,42; 5:5.

678. I. אָצִיל *'āṣiyl* **masc. noun**
(eminent; noble)
Ex. 24:11; **Isa.** 41:9(KJV, see II).
II. אָצִיל *'āṣiyl* **masc. noun**
(extremity, most distant parts)
Isa. 41:9(NASB, NIV, see I).

679. A. אַצִּיל *'aṣṣiyl* **fem. noun**
(joint, armpit, wrist)
Jer. 38:12; **Ezek.** 13:18.
B. אַצִּיל *'aṣṣiyl* **fem. noun**
(great, long [of different measures for a cubit])
Ezek. 41:8.

680. אָצַל *'āṣal* **verb**
(to reserve, to hold back, to take part of)
Gen. 27:36; **Num.** 11:17,25; **Eccl.** 2:10; **Ezek.** 42:6.

681. אֵצֶל *'ēṣel* **masc. noun**
(nearness; position beside, next to)
Gen. 39:10,15,16,18; 41:3; **Lev.** 1:16; 6:10(3); 10:12; **Deut.** 11:30; 16:21; **Judg.** 19:14; **1 Sam.** 5:2; 17:30; 20:19,41; **1 Kgs.** 1:9; 2:29; 3:20; 4:12; 10:19; 13:24,25,28,31; 20:36; 21:1,2; **2 Kgs.** 12:9(10); **2 Chr.** 9:18; 28:15; **Neh.** 2:6; 3:23; 4:3(3:35),12(6),18(12); 8:4; **Prov.** 7:8,12; 8:30; **Isa.** 19:19; **Jer.** 35:4; 41:17; **Ezek.** 1:15,19; 9:2; 10:6,9,16; 33:30; 39:15; 40:7; 43:6,8; **Dan.** 8:7,17; 10:13; **Amos** 2:8.

682. I. אָצֵל *'āṣēl* **masc. proper noun**
(Azel: a Benjamite)
1 Chr. 8:37,38; 9:43,44.
II. אָצַל *'āṣal* **proper noun**
(Azel: a city)
Zech. 14:5.

683. אֲצַלְיָהוּ *'ᵃṣalyāhû* **masc. proper noun**
(Azaliah)
2 Kgs. 22:3; **2 Chr.** 34:8.

684. A. אֹצֶם *'ōṣem* **masc. proper noun**
(Ozem: brother of David)
1 Chr. 2:15.
B. אֹצֶם *'ōṣem* **masc. proper noun**
(Ozem: descendant of Judah)
1 Chr. 2:25.

685. אֶצְעָדָה *'eṣ'āḏāh* **fem. noun**
(armlet, bracelet)
Num. 31:50; **2 Sam.** 1:10.

686. אָצַר *'āṣar* **verb**
(to store up, to put in charge of that which is stored up)
2 Kgs. 20:17; **Neh.** 13:13; **Isa.** 23:18; 39:6; **Amos** 3:10.

687. אֵצֶר *'ēṣer* **masc. proper noun**
(Ezer)
Gen. 36:21,27,30; **1 Chr.** 1:38,42.

688. אֶקְדָּח *'eqḏāḥ* **masc. noun**
(crystal, sparkling jewel)
Isa. 54:12.

689. אַקּוֹ *'aqqô* **masc. noun**
(wild goat)
Deut. 14:5.

690. אֲרָא *'ᵃrā'* **masc. proper noun**
(Ara)
1 Chr. 7:38.

691. אֶרְאֵל *'er'ēl* **masc. noun**
(brave one)
Isa. 33:7.

692. A. אַרְאֵלִי *'ar'ēliy* **masc. proper noun**
(Areli: son of Gad)
Gen. 46:16; **Num.** 26:17.
B. אַרְאֵלִי *'ar'ēliy* **masc. pl. proper noun**
(Arelites: descendants of Areli)
Num. 26:17.

693. אָרַב *'āraḇ* **verb**
(to lie in wait, to ambush)
Deut. 19:11; **Josh.** 8:2,4,7,12,14,19,21; **Judg.** 9:25,32,34,43; 16:2,9,12; 20:29, 33,36–38; 21:20; **1 Sam.** 15:5; 22:8,13; **2 Chr.** 20:22; **Ezra** 8:31; **Job** 31:9; **Ps.** 10:9; 59:3(4); **Prov.** 1:11,18; 7:12; 12:6; 23:28; 24:15; **Jer.** 51:12; **Lam.** 3:10; 4:19; **Hos.** 7:6(NIV, *'ōreḇ* [696]); **Mic.** 7:2.

694. אֲרָב *'ᵃrāḇ* **proper noun**
(Arab)
Josh. 15:52.

695. אֶרֶב **'ereḇ** **masc. noun**
(a den, lying in wait)
Job 37:8; 38:40.

696. אֹרֶב **'ōreḇ** **masc. noun**
(ambush, trap)
Jer. 9:8(7); **Hos.** 7:6(KJV, NASB, *'ārab* [693]).

697. אַרְבֶּה **'arbeh** **masc. noun**
(locust, grasshopper)
Ex. 10:4,12–14,19; **Lev.** 11:22; **Deut.** 28:38; **Judg.** 6:5; 7:12; **1 Kgs.** 8:37; **2 Chr.** 6:28; **Job** 39:20; **Ps.** 78:46; 105:34; 109:23; **Prov.** 30:27; **Jer.** 46:23; **Joel** 1:4; 2:25; **Nah.** 3:15,17.

698. אָרְבָּה **'orbāh** **fem. noun**
(trickery, deceit)
Isa. 25:11.

699. אֲרֻבָּה **'ᵃrubbāh** **fem. noun**
(window, floodgate)
Gen. 7:11; 8:2; **2 Kgs.** 7:2,19; **Eccl.** 12:3; **Isa.** 24:18; 60:8; **Hos.** 13:3; **Mal.** 3:10.

700. אֲרֻבּוֹת **'ᵃrubbôṯ** **proper noun**
(Arubboth)
1 Kgs. 4:10.

701. אַרְבִּי **'arbiy** **masc. proper noun**
(Arbite)
2 Sam. 23:35.

702. אַרְבַּע **'arba'**, אַרְבָּעָה **'arbā'āh** **masc. noun**
(four, fourth)
Gen. 2:10; 11:13,15–17; 14:5,9; 15:13; 23:15,16; 31:41; 32:6(7); 33:1; 46:22; 47:24; **Ex.** 12:6,18,40,41; 22:1(21:37); 25:12,26,34; 26:2,8,32; 27:2,4,16; 28:17; 36:9,15,36; 37:3,13,20; 38:2,5,19,29; 39:10; **Lev.** 11:20,21,23,27,42; 23:5; **Num.** 1:27,29,31,37,43; 2:4,6,8, 9,16,23,30; 7:7,8,85,88; 9:3,5,11; 16:49(17:14); 25:9; 26:25,43,47,50; 28:16; 29:13,15,17,20,23,26,29,32; **Deut.** 3:11; 22:12; **Josh.** 5:10; 15:36; 18:28; 19:7; 21:18,22,24,29,31,35,37,39; **Judg.** 9:34; 11:40; 19:2; 20:2,17,47; 21:12; **1 Sam.** 4:2; 22:2; 25:13; 27:7; 30:10,17; **2 Sam.** 12:6(see *'arba'tayim* [706]); 21:20,22; **1 Kgs.** 6:1; 7:2,19, 27,30,32,34,38,42; 8:65; 9:28; 10:26; 15:33; 18:19,22,33(34); 22:6,41; **2 Kgs.** 7:3; 14:13; 18:13; **1 Chr.** 3:5; 5:18; 7:1,7; 9:24,26; 12:26; 20:6; 21:5,20; 23:4,5, 10,12; 24:13,18; 25:5,21,31; 26:17,18; 27:1,2,4,5,7–15; **2 Chr.** 1:14; 3:2; 4:13; 8:18; 9:25; 13:3,21; 18:5; 25:23; 30:15; 35:1; **Ezra** 1:10,11; 2:7,15,31,40,64,67; 6:19; **Neh.** 6:4; 7:12,23,34,43,66,69; 9:1; 11:6,18; **Esth.** 9:15,17–19,21; **Job** 1:19; 42:12,16; **Prov.** 30:15,18,21,24,29; **Isa.** 11:12; 17:6; 36:1; **Jer.** 15:3; 36:23; 49:36; 52:21,30; **Ezek.** 1:5,6,8,10,15–18; 7:2; 10:9–12,14,21; 14:21; 37:9; 40:1,41,42; 41:5; 42:20; 43:14–17,20; 45:19,21; 46:21–23; 48:16,30,32–34; **Dan.** 1:17; 8:8,22; 10:4; 11:4; **Amos** 1:3,6,9,11,13; 2:1,4,6; **Hag.** 1:15; 2:10,18,20; **Zech.** 1:7,18(2:1),20(2:3); 2:6(10); 6:1,5; 7:1.

703. אַרְבַּע **'arba'** **Aram. com. noun**
(four; corr. to Hebr. 702)
Ezra 6:17; **Dan.** 3:25; 7:2,3,6,17.

704. אַרְבַּע **'arba'** **proper noun**
(Arba; see also *qiryaṯ 'arba'* [7153])
Josh. 15:13(NASB, NIV, *qiryaṯ 'arḇa'* [7153]); 21:11(NASB, NIV, *qiryaṯ 'arḇa'* [7153]).

705. אַרְבָּעִים **'arbā'iym** **masc. noun**
(forty, fortieth)
Gen. 5:13; 7:4,12,17; 8:6; 18:28,29; 25:20; 26:34; 32:15(16); 47:28; 50:3; **Ex.** 16:35; 24:18; 26:19,21; 34:28; 36:24,26; **Lev.** 25:8; **Num.** 1:21,25,33,41; 2:11,15, 19,28; 13:25; 14:33,34; 26:7,18,41,50;

32:13; 33:38; 35:6,7; **Deut.** 1:3; 2:7; 8:2,4; 9:9,11,18,25; 10:10; 25:3; 29:5(4); **Josh.** 4:13; 5:6; 14:7,10; 21:41(39); **Judg.** 3:11; 5:8,31; 8:28; 12:6,14; 13:1; **1 Sam.** 4:18; 17:16; **2 Sam.** 2:10; 5:4; 10:18; 15:7; **1 Kgs.** 2:11; 4:26(5:6); 6:17; 7:3,38; 11:42; 14:21; 15:10; 19:8; **2 Kgs.** 2:24; 8:9; 10:14; 12:1(2); 14:23; **1 Chr.** 5:18; 12:36; 19:18; 26:31; 29:27; **2 Chr.** 9:30; 12:13; 16:13; 22:2; 24:1; **Ezra** 2:8,10,24,25,34,38,66; **Neh.** 5:15; 7:13,15,28,29,36,41,44,62,67,68; 9:21; 11:13; **Job** 42:16; **Ps.** 95:10; **Jer.** 52:30; **Ezek.** 4:6; 29:11–13; 41:2; 46:22; **Amos** 2:10; 5:25; **Jon.** 3:4.

706. אַרְבַּעְתַּיִם *’arba‘tayim* **masc. noun**
(fourfold; dual of *’arba‘* [702])
2 Sam. 12:6.

707. אָרַג *’ārag* **verb**
(to weave, to braid)
Ex. 28:32; 35:35; 39:22,27; **Judg.** 16:13; **1 Sam.** 17:7; **2 Sam.** 21:19; **2 Kgs.** 23:7; **1 Chr.** 11:23; 20:5; **Isa.** 19:9; 38:12; 59:5.

708. אֶרֶג *’ereg* **masc. noun**
(weaver's shuttle, loom)
Judg. 16:14; **Job** 7:6.

709. A. אַרְגֹּב *’argōḇ* **proper noun**
(Argob: territory in Bashan)
Deut. 3:4,13,14; **1 Kgs.** 4:13.
B. אַרְגֹּב *’argōḇ* **proper noun**
(Argob: officer under Pekah)
2 Kgs. 15:25.

710. אַרְגְּוָן *’arg^ewān* **masc. noun**
(purple: shortened form of *’argāmān* [713])
2 Chr. 2:7(6).

711. אַרְגְּוָן *’arg^ewān* **Aram. masc. noun**
(purple, scarlet; corr. to Hebr. 710)
Dan. 5:7,16,29.

712. אַרְגָּז *’argāz* **masc. noun**
(box, chest)
1 Sam. 6:8,11,15.

713. אַרְגָּמָן *’argāmān* **masc. noun**
(purple)
Ex. 25:4; 26:1,31,36; 27:16; 28:5,6,8, 15,33; 35:6,23,25,35; 36:8,35,37; 38:18, 23; 39:1–3,5,8,24,29; **Num.** 4:13; **Judg.** 8:26; **2 Chr.** 2:14(13); 3:14; **Esth.** 1:6; 8:15; **Prov.** 31:22; **Song** 3:10; 7:5(6); **Jer.** 10:9; **Ezek.** 27:7,16.

714. אַרְדְּ *’ard* **masc. proper noun**
(Ard)
Gen. 46:21; **Num.** 26:40.

715. אַרְדּוֹן *’ardôn* **masc. proper noun**
(Ardon)
1 Chr. 2:18.

716. אַרְדִּי *’ardiy* **masc. proper noun**
(Ardite)
Num. 26:40.

717. אָרָה *’ārāh* **verb**
(to gather, to pluck)
Ps. 80:12(13); **Song** 5:1.

718. אֲרוּ *’^arû* **Aram. interj.**
(lo, behold)
Dan. 7:2,5–7,13.

719. אַרְוַד *’arwaḏ* **proper noun**
(Arvad)
Ezek. 27:8,11.

720. אֲרוֹד *’^arôḏ* **masc. proper noun**
(Arod)
Num. 26:17.

721. אַרְוָדִי *’arwāḏiy* **masc. proper noun**
(Arvadite)
Gen. 10:18; **1 Chr.** 1:16.

722. A. אֲרוֹדִי *'ᵃrôḏiy* **masc. proper noun**
(Arodi: son of Gad)
Gen. 46:16.
B. אֲרוֹדִי *'ᵃrôḏiy* **masc. proper noun**
(Arodi: son of Arod)
Num. 26:17.

723. אֻרְוָה *'urwāh* **fem. noun**
(stall, pen)
1 Kgs. 4:26(5:6); **2 Chr.** 9:25; 32:28 (see *'ᵃwērôṯ* [220]).

724. אֲרוּכָה *'ᵃrûḵāh,* אֲרֻכָה *'ᵃruḵāh* **fem. noun**
(healing, health, restoration)
2 Chr. 24:13; **Neh.** 4:7(1); **Isa.** 58:8; **Jer.** 8:22; 30:17; 33:6.

725. אֲרוּמָה *'ᵃrûmāh* **proper noun**
(Arumah)
Judg. 9:41.

726. אֲרוֹמִים *'ᵃrômiym* **masc. proper noun**
(Aramean, Syrian)
2 Kgs. 16:6(NIV, [Qᵉ] *'ᵃḏômiym* [130]).

727. אָרוֹן *'ārôn,* אָרֹן *'ārōn* **masc. noun**
(ark, chest, coffin)
Gen. 50:26; **Ex.** 25:10,14–16,21,22; 26:33,34; 30:6,26; 31:7; 35:12; 37:1,5; 39:35; 40:3,5,20,21; **Lev.** 16:2; **Num.** 3:31; 4:5; 7:89; 10:33,35; 14:44; **Deut.** 10:1–3,5,8; 31:9,25,26; **Josh.** 3:3,6,8,11,13–15,17; 4:5,7,9–11,16,18; 6:4,6–9,11–13; 7:6; 8:33; **Judg.** 20:27; **1 Sam.** 3:3; 4:3–6,11,13,17–19,21,22; 5:1–4,7,8,10,11; 6:1–3,8,11,13,15,18, 19,21; 7:1,2; 14:18; **2 Sam.** 6:2–4,6, 7,9–13,15–17; 7:2; 11:11; 15:24,25,29; **1 Kgs.** 2:26; 3:15; 6:19; 8:1,3–7,9,21; **2 Kgs.** 12:9(10),10(11); **1 Chr.** 6:31(16); 13:3,5–7,9,10,12–14; 15:1–3,12,14, 15,23–29; 16:1,4,6,37; 17:1; 22:19; 28:2,18; **2 Chr.** 1:4; 5:2,4–10; 6:11,41; 8:11; 24:8,10,11; 35:3; **Ps.** 132:8; **Jer.** 3:16.

728. אֲרַוְנָה *'ᵃrawnāh* **masc. proper noun**
(Araunah)
2 Sam. 24:16,18,20–24.

729. A. אָרוּז *'ārûz* **adj.**
(made of cedar)
Ezek. 27:24(NASB, NIV, see II).
B. אָרוּז *'ārûz* **adj.**
(made firm, tightly wound or knotted)
Ezek. 27:24(KJV, see I).

730. אֶרֶז *'erez* **masc. noun**
(cedar, cedar tree)
Lev. 14:4,6,49,51,52; **Num.** 19:6; 24:6; **Judg.** 9:15; **2 Sam.** 5:11; 7:2,7; **1 Kgs.** 4:33(5:13); 5:6(20),8(22),10(24); 6:9, 10,15,16,18,20,36; 7:2,3,7,11,12; 9:11; 10:27; **2 Kgs.** 14:9; 19:23; **1 Chr.** 14:1; 17:1,6; 22:4; **2 Chr.** 1:15; 2:3(2),8(7); 9:27; 25:18; **Ezra** 3:7; **Job** 40:17; **Ps.** 29:5; 80:10(11); 92:12(13); 104:16; 148:9; **Song** 1:17; 5:15; 8:9; **Isa.** 2:13; 9:10(9); 14:8; 37:24; 41:19; 44:14; **Jer.** 22:7,14,15,23; **Ezek.** 17:3,22,23; 27:5; 31:3,8; **Amos** 2:9; **Zech.** 11:1,2.

731. אַרְזָה *'arzāh* **fem. noun**
(beams of cedar, cedar work)
Zeph. 2:14.

732. אָרַח *'ārah* **verb**
(to travel, to wander)
Judg. 19:17; **2 Sam.** 12:4; **Job** 34:8; **Jer.** 9:2(1); 14:8.

733. A. אָרַח *'ārah* **masc. proper noun**
(Arah: an Asherite)
1 Chr. 7:39.
B. אָרַח *'ārah* **masc. proper noun**
(Arah: head of a family)
Ezra 2:5; **Neh.** 6:18; 7:10.

734. ארח *'ōraḥ* **masc. noun**
(path, way)
Gen. 18:11; 49:17; **Judg.** 5:6; **Job** 6:18,19; 8:13; 13:27; 16:22; 19:8; 22:15; 30:12; 31:32; 33:11; 34:11; **Ps.** 8:8(9); 16:11; 17:4; 19:5(6); 25:4,10; 27:11; 44:18(19); 119:9,15,101,104,128; 139:3; 142:3(4); **Prov.** 1:19; 2:8,13,15,19,20; 3:6; 4:14,18; 5:6; 8:20; 9:15; 10:17; 12:28; 15:10,19,24; 17:23; 22:25; **Isa.** 2:3; 3:12; 26:7,8; 30:11; 33:8; 40:14; 41:3; **Joel** 2:7; **Mic.** 4:2.

735. אֲרַח *'ᵃraḥ'* **Aram. fem. noun**
(way, manner of life; corr. to Hebr. 734)
Dan. 4:37(34); 5:23.

736. אֹרְחָה *'ōrᵉḥāh* **fem. noun**
(caravan, traveling group)
Gen. 37:25; **Isa.** 21:13.

737. אֲרֻחָה *'ᵃruḥāh* **fem. noun**
(allowance, portion)
2 Kgs. 25:30; **Prov.** 15:17; **Jer.** 40:5; 52:34.

738. I. אֲרִי *'ᵃriy* **masc. noun**
(lion)
Num. 23:24; 24:9; **Judg.** 14:5,18; **1 Sam.** 17:34,36,37; **2 Sam.** 1:23; 23:20([Kᵉ] see II); **1 Kgs.** 7:29,36; 10:19,20; **2 Kgs.** 17:25,26; **1 Chr.** 11:22; **2 Chr.** 9:18,19; **Prov.** 22:13; 26:13; 28:15; **Song** 4:8; **Isa.** 38:13; **Jer.** 50:17; 51:38; **Lam.** 3:10; **Ezek.** 19:2,6; 22:25; **Amos** 3:12; 5:19; **Nah.** 2:11(12); **Zeph.** 3:3.
II. אַרְיֵה *'aryēh* **fem. noun**
(lion)
Gen. 49:9; **Deut.** 33:22; **Judg.** 14:8,9; **2 Sam.** 17:10; 23:20([Qᵉ] see I); **1 Kgs.** 13:24–26,28; 20:36; **1 Chr.** 12:8(9); **Job** 4:10; **Ps.** 7:2(3); 10:9; 17:12; 22:13(14),21(22); **Eccl.** 9:4; **Isa.** 11:7; 15:9; 21:8; 31:4; 35:9; 65:25; **Jer.** 2:30; 4:7; 5:6; 12:8; 49:19; 50:44; **Ezek.** 1:10; 10:14; **Hos.** 11:10; **Joel** 1:6; **Amos** 3:4,8; **Mic.** 5:8(7); **Nah.** 2:11(12),12(13).
III. אֲרִי *'ᵃriy* **masc. noun**
(one pierced)
Ps. 22:16(17)(NASB, *kûr* [3564,II]; NIV, *kārāh* [7378]).

739. A. אֲרִיאֵל *'ᵃriy'ēl* **masc. proper noun**
(Ariel: a Moabite)
2 Sam. 23:20(KJV, NIV, see B); **1 Chr.** 11:22(KJV, NIV, see B).
B. אֲרִיאֵל *'ᵃriy'ēl* **masc. noun**
(hero, warrior, man of courage [lit., "lion of God" from *'ᵃriy* {738,I} and *'ēl* {410}])
2 Sam. 23:20(Sept., NASB, see A); **1 Chr.** 11:22(Sept., NASB, see A).

740. A. אֲרִיאֵל *'ᵃriy'ēl* **masc. proper noun**
(Ariel: a Jew)
Ezra 8:16.
B. אֲרִיאֵל *'ᵃriy'ēl* **masc. proper noun**
(Ariel: symbolic name for Jerusalem; same as *'ᵃriy'ēl* [741])
Isa. 29:1,2,7.

741. אֲרִיאֵל *'ᵃriy'ēl,* אֲרִאֵל *'ᵃri'ēl* **masc. noun**
(altar, hearth)
Ezek. 43:15(1st occurrence NIV, *har'ēl* [2025]),16.

742. אֲרִידַי *'ᵃriyḏay* **masc. proper noun**
(Aridai)
Esth. 9:9.

743. אֲרִידָתָא *'ᵃriyḏāṯā'* **masc. proper noun**
(Aridatha)
Esth. 9:8.

744. אַרְיֵה *'aryēh* **Aram. masc. noun**
(lion; corr. to Hebr. 738)
Dan.
6:7(8),12(13),16(17),19(20),20(21), 22(23),24(25),27(28); 7:4.

745. אַרְיֵה *'aryēh* **masc. proper noun**
(Arieh)
2 Kgs. 15:25.

746. A. אַרְיוֹךְ *'aryôk̲* **masc. proper noun**
(Arioch: king of Ellasar)
Gen. 14:1,9.
B. אַרְיוֹךְ *'aryôk̲* **Aram. masc. proper noun**
(Arioch: Babylonian officer)
Dan. 2:14,15,24,25.

747. אֲרִיסַי *'ᵃriysay* **masc. proper noun**
(Arisai)
Esth. 9:9.

748. אָרַךְ *'ārak̲* **verb**
(to be long, to live long, to lengthen)
Gen. 26:8; **Ex.** 20:12; **Num.** 9:19,22; **Deut.** 4:26,40; 5:16,33(30); 6:2; 11:9; 17:20; 22:7; 25:15; 30:18; 32:47; **Josh.** 24:31; **Judg.** 2:7; **1 Kgs.** 3:14; 8:8; **2 Chr.** 5:9; **Job** 6:11; **Ps.** 129:3; **Prov.** 19:11; 28:2,16; **Eccl.** 7:15; 8:12,13; **Isa.** 48:9; 53:10; 54:2; 57:4; **Ezek.** 12:22; 31:5.

749. אֲרִיךְ *'ariyk̲* **Aram. adj.**
(fitting, proper)
Ezra 4:14.

750. אָרֵךְ *'ārēk̲* **adj.**
(long-suffering, slow [to get angry], long [of a bird's wing])
Ex. 34:6; **Num.** 14:18; **Neh.** 9:17; **Ps.** 86:15; 103:8; 145:8; **Prov.** 14:29; 15:18; 16:32; **Eccl.** 7:8; **Jer.** 15:15; **Ezek.** 17:3; **Joel** 2:13; **Jon.** 4:2; **Nah.** 1:3.

751. אֶרֶךְ *'erek̲* **proper noun**
(Erech)
Gen. 10:10.

752. אָרֹךְ *'ārōk̲* **adj.**
(long-lasting, long in measure)
2 Sam. 3:1; **Job** 11:9; **Jer.** 29:28.

753. אֹרֶךְ *'ōrek̲* **masc. noun**
(length)
Gen. 6:15; 13:17; **Ex.** 25:10,17,23; 26:2,8,13,16; 27:1,9,11,18; 28:16; 30:2; 36:9,15,21; 37:1,6,10,25; 38:1,18; 39:9; **Deut.** 3:11; 30:20; **Judg.** 3:16; **1 Kgs.** 6:2,3,20; 7:2,6,27; **2 Chr.** 3:3,4,8,11,15; 4:1; 6:13; **Job** 12:12; **Ps.** 21:4(5); 23:6; 91:16; 93:5; **Prov.** 3:2,16; 25:15; **Lam.** 5:20; **Ezek.** 31:7; 40:7,11,18,20,21,25, 29,30,33,36,42,47,49; 41:2,4,12,13, 15,22; 42:2,7,8,11,20; 43:16,17; 45:1, 3,5–7; 46:22; 48:8–10,13,18; **Zech.** 2:2(6); 5:2.

754. אַרְכָה *'ark̲āh* **Aram. fem. noun**
(a prolonging, lengthening)
Dan. 4:27(24); 7:12.

755. אַרְכֻבָּה *'ark̲ubbāh* **Aram. fem. noun**
(knee)
Dan. 5:6.

756. אַרְכְּוָי *'arkᵉwāy* **Aram. masc. proper noun**
(Archevite, native of Erech)
Ezra 4:9.

757. אַרְכִּי *'arkiy* **masc. proper noun**
(Archite)
Josh. 16:2; **2 Sam.** 15:32; 16:16; 17:5,14; **1 Chr.** 27:33.

758. A. אֲרָם *'ᵃrām* **proper noun**
(Aram, another name for Syria)
Num. 23:7; **Judg.** 3:10(KJV, NASB, *'ᵃram nahᵃrayim* [763]); 10:6; **2 Sam.** 8:5,6,12,13; 10:6,8,9,11,13–19; 15:8; **1 Kgs.** 10:29; 11:25; 15:18; 19:15; 20:1,20–23,26–29; 22:1,3,11,31,35; **2 Kgs.** 5:1,2,5; 6:8,9,11,23,24; 7:4–6, 10,12,14–16; 8:7,9,13,28,29; 9:14,15; 12:17(18),18(19); 13:3–5,7,17,19,22,24; 15:37; 16:5–7; 24:2; **1 Chr.** 18:5,6; 19:6,10,12,14–19; **2 Chr.** 1:17; 16:2,7; 18:10,30,34; 20:2; 22:5,6; 24:23,24; 28:5,23; **Isa.** 7:1,2,4,5,8; 9:12(11); 17:3; **Jer.** 35:11; **Ezek.** 16:57; 27:16; **Hos.** 12:12(13); **Amos** 1:5; 9:7.
B. אֲרָם *'ᵃrām* **masc. proper noun**
(Aram: son of Shem)
Gen. 10:22,23; **1 Chr.** 1:17.
C. אֲרָם *'ᵃrām* **masc. proper noun**
(Aram: son of Kemuel)
Gen. 22:21.
D. אֲרָם *'ᵃrām* **masc. proper noun**
(Aram: region north of Canaan)
1 Chr. 2:23.
E. אֲרָם *'ᵃrām* **masc. proper noun**
(Aram: son of Shamer)
1 Chr. 7:34.

759. אַרְמוֹן *'armôn* **masc. noun**
(fortress, citadel, palace)
1 Kgs. 16:18; **2 Kgs.** 15:25; **2 Chr.** 36:19; **Ps.** 48:3(4),13(14); 122:7; **Prov.** 18:19; **Isa.** 23:13; 25:2; 32:14; 34:13; **Jer.** 6:5; 9:21(20); 17:27; 30:18; 49:27; **Lam.** 2:5,7; **Ezek.** 19:7(KJV, *'almānāh* [490]); **Hos.** 8:14; **Amos** 1:4,7,10,12,14; 2:2,5; 3:9–11; 6:8; **Mic.** 5:5(4).

760. אֲרַם צוֹבָה *'ᵃram ṣôḇāh* **proper noun**
(Aram-zobah)
Ps. 60:[title](1).

761. אֲרַמִּי *'ᵃrammiy* **masc. proper noun**
(Aramean, Syrian)
Gen. 25:20; 28:5; 31:20,24; **Deut.** 26:5; **2 Kgs.** 5:20; 8:28,29; 9:15; **1 Chr.** 7:14.

762. אֲרָמִית *'ᵃrāmiyṯ* **proper noun**
(Aramaic, the Syrian language)
2 Kgs. 18:26; **Ezra** 4:7; **Isa.** 36:11; **Dan.** 2:4.

763. אֲרַם נַהֲרַיִם *'ᵃram nahᵃrayim* **proper noun**
(Aram-naharaim, another name for Mesopotamia)
Gen. 24:10; **Deut.** 23:4(5); **Judg.** 3:8,10(NIV, *'ᵃrām* [758,A]); **1 Chr.** 19:6; **Ps.** 60:[title](1).

764. אַרְמֹנִי *'armōniy* **masc. proper noun**
(Armoni)
2 Sam. 21:8.

765. אֲרָן *'ᵃrān* **masc. proper noun**
(Aran)
Gen. 36:28; **1 Chr.** 1:42.

766. אֹרֶן *'ōren* **masc. noun**
(fir tree, ash tree)
Isa. 44:14.

767. אֹרֶן *'ōren* **masc. proper noun**
(Oren)
1 Chr. 2:25.

768. אַרְנֶבֶת *'arneḇeṯ* **fem. noun**
(arnebeth, rabbit, unknown species of animal)
Lev. 11:6; **Deut.** 14:7.

769. אַרְנוֹן *'arnôn* **proper noun**
(Arnon)
Num. 21:13,14,24,26,28; 22:36; **Deut.** 2:24,36; 3:8,12,16; 4:48; **Josh.** 12:1,2; 13:9,16; **Judg.** 11:13,18,22,26; **2 Kgs.** 10:33; **Isa.** 16:2; **Jer.** 48:20.

770. אַרְנָן *'arnān* **masc. proper noun**
(Arnan)
1 Chr. 3:21.

771. אָרְנָן *'ornān* or *'ārnān* **masc. proper noun**
(Ornan)
1 Chr. 21:15,18,20–25,28; **2 Chr.** 3:1.

772. אֲרַע *'ara'* **Aram. fem. noun**
(earth, ground; corr. to Hebr. 776)
Ezra 5:11; **Jer.** 10:11; **Dan.** 2:35,39; 4:1(3:31),10(7),11(8),15(12),20(17), 22(19),23(20),35(32); 6:25(26),27(28); 7:4,17,23.

773. אַרְעִי *'ar'iy* **Aram. fem. noun**
(bottom, floor)
Dan. 6:24(25).

774. אַרְפָּד *'arpāḏ* **proper noun**
(Arpad)
2 Kgs. 18:34; 19:13; **Isa.** 10:9; 36:19; 37:13; **Jer.** 49:23.

775. אַרְפַּכְשַׁד *'arpakšad* **masc. proper noun**
(Arphaxad)
Gen. 10:22,24; 11:10–13; **1 Chr.** 1:17,18,24.

776. אֶרֶץ *'ereṣ* **fem. noun**
(earth, ground, land, country)
Gen. 1:1,2,10–12,15,17,20,22,24–26,28–30; 2:1,4–6,11–13; 4:12,14,16; 6:4–6, 11–13,17; 7:3,4,6,10,12,14,17–19, 21,23,24; 8:1,3,7,9,11,13,14,17,19,22; 9:1,2,7,10,11,13,14,16,17,19; 10:5,8, 10,11,20,25,31,32; 11:1,2,4,8,9,28,31; 12:1,5–7,10; 13:6,7,9,10,12,15–17; 14:19,22; 15:7,13,18; 16:3; 17:8; 18:2, 18,25; 19:1,23,28,31; 20:1,15; 21:21, 23,32,34; 22:2,18; 23:2,7,12,13,15,19; 24:3–5,7,37,52,62; 25:6; 26:1–4,12,22; 27:28,39,46; 28:4,12–14; 29:1; 30:25; 31:3,13,18; 32:3(4),9(10); 33:3,18; 34:1, 2,10,21,30; 35:6,12,16,22; 36:5–7,16,17, 20,21,30,31,34,43; 37:1,10; 38:9; 40:15; 41:19,29–31,33,34,36,41,43–48,52–57; 42:5–7,9,12,13,29,30,32–34; 43:1,11,26; 44:8,11,14; 45:6–8,10,17–20,25,26; 46:6, 12,20,28,31,34; 47:1,4,6,11,13–15,20, 27,28; 48:3–5,7,12,16,21; 49:15,30; 50:5,7,8,11,13,24; **Ex.** 1:7,10; 2:15,22; 3:8,17; 4:3,20; 5:5,12; 6:1,4,8,11,13,26, 28; 7:2–4,19,21; 8:5–7(1–3),14(10), 16(12),17(13),22(18),24(20),25(21); 9:5,9,14–16,22–26,29,33; 10:5, 12–15,21,22; 11:3,5,6,9,10; 12:1,12, 13,17,19,25,33,41,42,48,51; 13:5,11, 15,17,18; 14:3; 15:12; 16:1,3,6,14,32,35; 18:3,27; 19:1,5; 20:2,4,11; 22:21(20); 23:9,10,26,29–31,33; 29:46; 31:17; 32:1, 4,7,8,11,13,23; 33:1,3; 34:8,10,12,15,24; **Lev.** 4:27; 11:2,21,29,41,42,44–46; 14:34; 16:22; 18:3,25,27,28; 19:9,23,29, 33,34,36; 20:2,4,22,24; 22:24,33; 23:10, 22,39,43; 25:2,4–7,9,10,18,19,23,24,31, 38,42,45,55; 26:1,4–6,13,19,20,32–34, 36,38,39,41–45; 27:24,30; **Num.** 1:1; 3:13; 8:17; 9:1,14; 10:9,30; 11:31; 13:2, 16–21,25–29,32; 14:2,3,6–9,14,16,21,23, 24,30,31,34,36–38; 15:2,18,19,41; 16:13,14,32–34; 18:13,20; 20:12,17, 23,24; 21:4,22,24,26,31,34,35; 22:5, 6,11,13; 26:4,10,19,53,55; 27:12; 32:1, 4,5,7–9,17,22,29,30,32,33; 33:1,37,38, 40,51–55; 34:2,12,13,17,18,29; 35:10, 14,28,32–34; 36:2; **Deut.** 1:5,7,8,21,22, 25,27,35,36; 2:5,9,12,19,20,24,27,29, 31,37; 3:2,8,12,13,18,20,24,25,28; 4:1, 5,14,17,18,21,22,25,26,32,36,38,39,43,4 6,47; 5:6,8,15,31(28),33(30); 6:1,3,10,12, 18,23; 7:1; 8:1,7–10,14; 9:4–7,23,28; 10:7,11,14,19; 11:3,6,8–12,14,17,21,25, 29–31; 12:1,10,16,24,29; 13:5(6),7(8), 10(11); 15:4,7,11,15,23; 16:3,20; 17:14; 18:9; 19:1–3,8,10,14; 20:1; 22:6; 23:7(8), 20(21); 24:4,14,22; 25:19; 26:1–3,9,15; 27:2,3; 28:1,8,10,12,23–26,49,52,56,64; 29:1(28:69),2(1),8(7),16(15),22–25(21–2 4),27(26),28(27); 30:5,16,19; 31:4,7, 16,21,23,28; 32:1,10,13,22,49,52; 33:13, 16,17,28; 34:1,2,4–6,11; **Josh.** 1:2,4,6,

11,13–15; 2:1–3,9,11,14,18,24; 3:11,13; 4:24; 5:6,11,12,14; 6:22,27; 7:2,6,9,21; 8:1; 9:6,9,11,24; 10:40–42; 11:3,16, 22,23; 12:1,7; 13:1,2,4,5,7,21,25; 14:1,4, 5,7,9,15; 15:19; 17:5,6,8,12,15,16; 18:1, 3,4,6,8–10; 19:49,51; 21:2,43(41); 22:4, 9–11,13,15,19,32,33; 23:5,14,16; 24:3,8, 13,15,17,18; **Judg.** 1:2,15,26,27,32,33; 2:1,2,6,12; 3:11,25,30; 4:21; 5:4,31; 6:4, 5,9,10,37,39,40; 8:28; 9:37; 10:4,8; 11:3, 5,12,13,15,17–19,21; 12:12,15; 13:20; 16:24; 18:2,7,9,10,14,17,30; 19:30; 20:1, 21,25; 21:12,21; **Ruth** 1:1,7; 2:10,11; **1 Sam.** 2:8,10; 3:19; 4:5; 5:3,4; 6:5; 9:4, 5,16; 12:6; 13:3,7,17,19; 14:15,25,29, 32,45; 17:46,49; 20:41; 21:11(12); 22:5; 23:23,27; 24:8(9); 25:23,41; 26:7,8,20; 27:1,8,9; 28:3,9,13,14,20,23; 29:11; 30:16; 31:9; **2 Sam.** 1:2; 2:22; 3:12; 4:11; 5:6; 7:9,23; 8:2; 10:2; 12:16,17,20; 13:31; 14:4,11,14,20,22,33; 15:4,23; 17:26; 18:8,9,11,28; 19:9(10); 20:10; 21:14; 22:8,43; 23:4; 24:6,8,13,20,25; **1 Kgs.** 1:23,31,40,52; 2:2; 4:10,19,21(5:1), 34(5:14); 6:1; 8:9,21,23,27,36,37,41,43, 46–48,53,60; 9:8,9,11,13,18,19,21,26; 10:6,13,15,23,24; 11:18,21,22; 12:28; 14:24; 15:12,20; 17:7; 18:5,6,42; 20:7,27; 22:36,46(47); **2 Kgs.** 2:15,19; 3:20,27; 4:37,38; 5:2,4,15,19; 6:23; 8:1–3,6; 10:10,33; 11:3,14,18–20; 13:18,20; 15:5,19,20,29; 16:15; 17:5,7,26,27,36; 18:25,32,33,35; 19:7,11,15,17,19,37; 20:14; 21:24; 23:24,30,33,35; 24:7,14,15; 25:3,12,19,21,22,24; **1 Chr.** 1:10,19, 43,45; 2:22; 4:40; 5:9,11,23,25; 6:55(40); 7:21; 10:9; 11:4; 13:2; 14:17; 16:14,18, 23,30,31,33; 17:8,21; 19:2,3; 20:1; 21:12, 16,21; 22:2,5,8,18; 28:8; 29:11,15,30; **2 Chr.** 1:9; 2:12(11),17(16); 6:5,14,18, 27,28,32,33,36–38; 7:3,13,14,21,22; 8:6,8,17; 9:5,11,12,14,22,23,26,28; 11:23; 12:8; 13:9; 14:1(13:23),6(5),7(6); 15:5,8; 16:9; 17:2,10; 19:3,5; 20:7,10,18,24,29; 22:12; 23:13,20,21; 26:21; 30:9,10,25; 32:4,13,17,19,21,31; 33:25; 34:7,8,33; 36:1,3,21,23; **Ezra** 1:2; 3:3; 4:4; 6:21; 9:1,2,7,11,12; 10:2,11; **Neh.** 4:4(3:36); 5:14; 8:6; 9:6,8,10,15, 22–24,30,35,36; 10:28(29),30(31), 31(32); **Esth.** 8:17; 10:1; **Job** 1:1,7,8, 10,20; 2:2,3,13; 3:14; 5:10,22,25; 7:1; 8:9; 9:6,24; 10:21,22; 11:9; 12:8,15,24; 14:8,19; 15:19,29; 16:13,18; 18:4,10,17; 20:4,27; 22:8; 24:4,18; 26:7; 28:5,13,24; 30:8; 34:13; 35:11; 37:3,6,12,13,17; 38:4,13,18,24,26,33; 39:14,24; 42:15; **Ps.** 2:2,8,10; 7:5(6); 8:1(2),9(10); 10:16,18; 12:6(7); 16:3; 17:11; 18:7(8); 19:4(5); 21:10(11); 22:27(28),29(30); 24:1; 25:13; 27:13; 33:5,8,14; 34:16(17); 35:20; 37:3,9,11,22,29,34; 41:2(3); 42:6(7); 44:3(4),25(26); 45:16(17); 46:2(3),6(7),8–10(9–11); 47:2(3),7(8), 9(10); 48:2(3),10(11); 50:1,4; 52:5(7); 57:5(6),11(12); 58:2(3),11(12); 59:13(14); 60:2(4); 61:2(3); 63:1(2), 9(10); 65:5(6),9(10); 66:1,4; 67:2(3), 4(5),6(7),7(8); 68:8(9),32(33); 69:34(35); 71:20; 72:6,8,16,19; 73:9,25; 74:7,8,12, 17,20; 75:3(4),8(9); 76:8(9),9(10),12(13); 77:18(19); 78:12,69; 79:2; 80:9(10); 81:5(6),10(11); 82:5,8; 83:18(19); 85:1(2),9(10),11(12),12(13); 88:12(13); 89:11(12),27(28),39(40),44(45); 90:2; 94:2; 95:4; 96:1,9,11,13; 97:1,4,5,9; 98:3,4,9; 99:1; 100:1; 101:6,8; 102:15(16),19(20),25(26); 103:11; 104:5,9,13,14,24,32,35; 105:7,11,16, 23,27,30,32,35,36,44; 106:17,22,24, 27,38; 107:3,34,35; 108:5(6); 109:15; 110:6; 112:2; 113:6; 114:7; 115:15,16; 116:9; 119:19,64,87,90,119; 121:2; 124:8; 134:3; 135:6,7,12; 136:6,21; 138:4; 139:15; 140:11(12); 141:7; 142:5(6); 143:3,6,10; 146:6; 147:6,8,15; 148:7,11,13; **Prov.** 2:21,22; 3:19; 8:16, 23,26,29,31; 10:30; 11:31; 17:24; 21:19; 25:3,25; 28:2; 29:4; 30:4,14,16,21,24; 31:23; **Eccl.** 1:4; 3:21; 5:2(1),9(8); 7:20; 8:14,16; 10:7,16,17; 11:2,3; 12:7; **Song** 2:12; **Isa.** 1:2,7,19; 2:7,8,19,21; 3:26; 4:2; 5:8,26,30; 6:3,12; 7:18,22,24; 8:8,9,22; 9:1(8:23),2(1),19(18); 10:14,23; 11:4,9,

12,16; 12:5; 13:5,9,13,14; 14:7,9,12, 16,20,21,25,26; 16:1,4; 18:1–3,6,7; 19:18–20,24; 21:1,9,14; 22:18; 23:1, 8–10,13,17; 24:1,3–6,11,13,16–20; 25:8,12; 26:1,5,9,10,15,18,19,21; 27:13; 28:2,22; 29:4; 30:6; 32:2; 33:9,17; 34:1, 6,7,9; 36:10,17,18,20; 37:7,11,16, 18,20,38; 38:11; 39:3; 40:12,21–24,28; 41:5,9,18; 42:4,5,10; 43:6; 44:23,24; 45:8,12,18,19,22; 46:11; 47:1; 48:13,20; 49:6,8,12,13,19,23; 51:6,13,16,23; 52:10; 53:2,8; 54:5,9; 55:9,10; 57:13; 58:14; 60:2,18,21; 61:7,11; 62:4,7,11; 63:6; 65:16,17; 66:1,8,22; **Jer.** 1:1,14,18; 2:2,6, 7,15,31; 3:1,2,9,16,18,19; 4:5,7,16,20, 23,27,28; 5:19,30; 6:8,12,19,20,22; 7:7,22,25,33,34; 8:16,19; 9:3(2),12(11), 19(18),24(23); 10:10,12,13,17,18,22; 11:4,5,7,19; 12:4,5,11,12,15; 13:13; 14:2,4,8,15,18; 15:3,4,7,10,14; 16:3,4, 6,13–15,18,19; 17:4,6,13,26; 18:16; 19:7; 22:10,12,26–29; 23:3,5,7,8,10,15,24; 24:5,6,8,9; 25:9,11–13,20,26,29–33,38; 26:6,17,20; 27:5–7; 28:8; 29:18; 30:3,10; 31:8,16,22,23,32,37; 32:8,15,17,20–22, 37,41,43,44; 33:9,11,13,15,25; 34:1,13, 17,19,20; 35:11; 36:29; 37:1,2,7,12,19; 39:5,10; 40:4,6,7,9,11,12; 41:2,18; 42:10, 13,14,16; 43:4,5,7,11–13; 44:1,8,9,12–15, 21,22,24,26–28; 45:4; 46:8,10,12,13,16, 27; 47:2; 48:21,24,33; 49:21; 50:1,3,8,9, 16,18,21–23,25,28,34,38,41,45,46; 51:2, 4,5,7,9,15,16,25,27–29,41,43,46–49,52,5 4; 52:6,9,16,25,27; **Lam.** 2:1,2,9–11, 15,21; 3:34; 4:12,21; **Ezek.** 1:3,15,19,21; 5:5,6; 6:8,14; 7:2,7,21,23,27; 8:3,12,17; 9:9; 10:16,19; 11:15–17; 12:6,12,13, 15,19,20; 13:14; 14:13,15–17,19; 15:8; 16:3,29; 17:4,5,13; 19:4,7,12,13; 20:5, 6,8–10,15,23,28,32,34,36,38,40–42; 21:19(24),30(35),32(37); 22:4,15,24, 29,30; 23:15,19,27,48; 24:7; 25:7,9; 26:11,16,20; 27:17,29,33; 28:17,18; 29:5,9,10,12,14,19,20; 30:5,7,11–13, 23,25,26; 31:12,14,16,18; 32:4,6,8,9,15, 18,23–27,32; 33:2,3,24–26,28,29; 34:6, 13,25,27–29; 35:10,14; 36:5,18–20,24, 28,34,35; 37:22,25; 38:2,8,9,11,12,16,20; 39:12–16,18,27; 40:2; 41:16,20; 42:6; 43:2,14; 45:1,4,8,16,22; 46:3,9; 47:13–15, 18,21; 48:12,14,29; **Dan.** 1:2; 8:5,7,10, 12,18; 9:6,7,15; 10:9,15; 11:16,19,28, 40–42; **Hos.** 1:2,11(2:2); 2:3(5),15(17), 18(20),21–23(23–25); 4:1,3; 6:3; 7:16; 9:3; 10:1; 11:5,11; 12:9(10); 13:4,5; **Joel** 1:2,6,14; 2:1,3,10,18,20,30(3:3); 3:2(4:2), 16(4:16),19(4:19); **Amos** 2:7,10; 3:1,5,9, 11,14; 4:13; 5:7,8; 7:2,10,12; 8:4,8,9,11; 9:5–7,9; **Obad.** 1:3; **Jon.** 1:8; 2:6(7); **Mic.** 1:2,3; 4:13; 5:4–6(3–5),11(10); 6:2,4; 7:2,13,15,17; **Nah.** 1:5; 2:13(14); 3:13; **Hab.** 1:6; 2:8,14,17,20; 3:3,6,7, 9,12; **Zeph.** 1:18; 2:3,5,11; 3:8,19,20; **Hag.** 1:10,11; 2:4,6,21; **Zech.** 1:10,11, 21(2:4); 2:6(10); 3:9; 4:10,14; 5:3,6,9,11; 6:5–8; 7:5,14; 8:7,12; 9:1,10; 10:10; 11:6,16; 12:1,3,12; 13:2,8; 14:9,10,17; **Mal.** 3:12; 4:6(3:24).

777. אַרְצָא *'arṣā'* **masc. proper noun**
(Arza)
1 Kgs. 16:9.

778. אֲרַק *'araq* **Aram. fem. noun**
(earth)
Jer. 10:11.

779. אָרַר *'ārar* **verb**
(to curse, to be cursed)
Gen. 3:14,17; 4:11; 5:29; 9:25; 12:3; 27:29; 49:7; **Ex.** 22:28; **Num.** 5:18,19, 22,24,27; 22:6,12; 23:7; 24:9; **Deut.** 27:15–26; 28:16–19; **Josh.** 6:26; 9:23; **Judg.** 5:23; 21:18; **1 Sam.** 14:24,28; 26:19; **2 Kgs.** 9:34; **Job** 3:8; **Ps.** 119:21; **Jer.** 11:3; 17:5; 20:14,15; 48:10; **Mal.** 1:14; 2:2; 3:9.

780. אֲרָרַט *'arāraṭ* **proper noun**
(Ararat)
Gen. 8:4; **2 Kgs.** 19:37; **Isa.** 37:38; **Jer.** 51:27.

781. אָרַשׂ *'āraś* **verb**
(to betroth, to pledge to marry)
Ex. 22:16(15); **Deut.** 20:7; 22:23,25, 27,28; 28:30; **2 Sam.** 3:14; **Hos.** 2:19(21),20(22).

782. אֲרֶשֶׁת *'ᵃrešet̲* **fem. noun**
(request)
Ps. 21:2(3).

783. אַרְתַּחְשַׁסְתְּא *'artaḥšast'*, אַרְתַּחְשַׁשְׂתָּא *'artaḥšastā'* **masc. proper noun**
(Artaxerxes)
Ezra 4:7,8,11,23; 6:14; 7:1,7,11,12,21; 8:1; **Neh.** 2:1; 5:14; 13:6.

784. אֵשׁ *'ēš* **fem. noun**
(fire)
Gen. 15:17; 19:24; 22:6,7; **Ex.** 3:2; 9:23,24; 12:8–10; 13:21,22; 14:24; 19:18; 22:6(5); 24:17; 29:14,34; 32:20,24; 35:3; 40:38; **Lev.** 1:7,8,12,17; 2:14; 3:5; 4:12; 6:9(2),10(3),12(5),13(6),30(23); 7:17,19; 8:17,32; 9:11,24; 10:1,2; 13:24,52,55,57; 16:12,13,27; 19:6; 20:14; 21:9; **Num.** 3:4; 6:18; 9:15,16; 11:1–3; 14:14; 16:7, 18,35,37(17:2),46(17:11); 18:9; 21:28; 26:10,61; 31:10,23; **Deut.** 1:33; 4:11, 12,15,24,33,36; 5:4,5,22–26(19–23); 7:5,25; 9:3,10,15,21; 10:4; 12:3,31; 13:16(17); 18:10,16; 32:22; **Josh.** 6:24; 7:15,25; 8:8,19; 11:6,9,11; **Judg.** 1:8; 6:21; 9:15,20,49,52; 12:1; 14:15; 15:5, 6,14; 16:9; 18:27; 20:48; **1 Sam.** 30:1, 3,14; **2 Sam.** 14:30,31; 22:9,13; 23:7; **1 Kgs.** 9:16; 16:18; 18:23–25,38; 19:12; **2 Kgs.** 1:10,12,14; 2:11; 6:17; 8:12; 16:3; 17:17,31; 19:18; 21:6; 23:10,11; 25:9; **1 Chr.** 14:12; 21:26; **2 Chr.** 7:1,3; 28:3; 33:6; 35:13; 36:19; **Neh.** 1:3; 2:3,13,17; 9:12,19; **Job** 1:16; 15:34; 18:5; 20:26; 22:20; 28:5; 31:12; 41:19(11); **Ps.** 11:6; 18:8(9),12(13),13(14); 21:9(10); 29:7; 39:3(4); 46:9(10); 50:3; 66:12; 68:2(3); 74:7; 78:14,21,63; 79:5; 80:16(17); 83:14(15); 89:46(47); 97:3; 104:4; 105:32,39; 106:18; 118:12; 140:10(11); 148:8; **Prov.** 6:27; 16:27; 26:20,21; 30:16; **Song** 8:6; **Isa.** 1:7; 4:5; 5:24; 9:5(4),18(17),19(18); 10:16,17; 26:11; 29:6; 30:14,27,30,33; 33:11,12,14; 37:19; 43:2; 44:16,19; 47:14; 50:11; 54:16; 64:2(1),11(10); 65:5; 66:15,16,24; **Jer.** 4:4; 5:14; 6:29([Kᵉ] אֶשָּׁה [800]); 7:18,31; 11:16; 15:14; 17:4,27; 19:5; 20:9; 21:10, 12,14; 22:7; 23:29; 29:22; 32:29; 34:2,22; 36:23,32; 37:8,10; 38:17,18,23; 39:8; 43:12,13; 48:45; 49:2,27; 50:32; 51:32,58; 52:13; **Lam.** 1:13; 2:3,4; 4:11; **Ezek.** 1:4,13,27; 5:4; 8:2; 10:2,6,7; 15:4–7; 16:41; 19:12,14; 20:31,47(21:3); 21:31(36),32(37); 22:20,21,31; 23:25,47; 24:10,12; 28:14,16,18; 30:8,14,16; 36:5; 38:19,22; 39:6,9,10; **Dan.** 10:6; **Hos.** 7:6; 8:14; **Joel** 1:19,20; 2:3,5,30(3:3); **Amos** 1:4,7,10,12,14; 2:2,5; 5:6; 7:4; **Obad.** 1:18; **Mic.** 1:4,7; **Nah.** 1:6; 2:3(4); 3:13,15; **Hab.** 2:13; **Zeph.** 1:18; 3:8; **Zech.** 2:5(9); 3:2; 9:4; 11:1; 12:6; 13:9; **Mal.** 3:2.

785. אֶשָּׁא *'eššā'* **Aram. fem. noun**
(fire, flame; corr. to Hebr. 784)
Dan. 7:11.

786. אִשׁ *'iš* **adv.**
(there is one, is there one?; NASB, *yēš* [3426])
2 Sam. 14:19; **Mic.** 6:10.

787. אֹשׁ *'ōš* **Aram. masc. noun**
(foundation)
Ezra 4:12; 5:16; 6:3.

788. אַשְׁבֵּל *'ašbēl* **masc. proper noun**
(Ashbel)
Gen. 46:21; **Num.** 26:38; **1 Chr.** 8:1.

789. אַשְׁבֵּלִי *'ašbēliy* **masc. proper noun**
(Ashbelite)
Num. 26:38.

790. אֶשְׁבָּן *'ešbān* **masc. proper noun**
(Eshban)
Gen. 36:26; **1 Chr.** 1:41.

791. אַשְׁבֵּעַ *'ašbēa'* **masc. proper noun**
(Ashbea)
1 Chr. 4:21(NASB, NIV, *beyt 'ašbēa'* [1004] and [791]).

792. אֶשְׁבַּעַל *'ešba'al* **masc. proper noun**
(Esh-baal)
1 Chr. 8:33; 9:39.

793. אֶשֶׁד *'āšēḏ* **masc. noun**
(slope)
Num. 21:15.

794. אֲשֵׁדָה *'ašēḏāh* **fem. noun**
(slope)
Deut. 3:17(KJV, *'ašdôt happisgāh* [798]); 4:49; 33:2(see *'ēšdāṯ* [799]); **Josh.** 10:40; 12:3(KJV, *'ašdôt happisgāh* [798]),8; 13:20(KJV, *'ašdôt happisgāh* [798]).

795. אַשְׁדּוֹד *'ašdôḏ* **proper noun**
(Ashdod)
Josh. 11:22; 15:46,47; **1 Sam.** 5:1,5–7; 6:17; **2 Chr.** 26:6; **Isa.** 20:1; **Jer.** 25:20; **Amos** 1:8; 3:9; **Zeph.** 2:4; **Zech.** 9:6.

796. אַשְׁדּוֹדִי *'ašdôḏiy* **masc. proper noun**
(Ashdodite)
Josh. 13:3; **1 Sam.** 5:3,6; **Neh.** 4:7(1); 13:23.

797. אַשְׁדּוֹדִית *'ašdôḏiyṯ* **proper noun**
(language of Ashdod)
Neh. 13:24.

798. אַשְׁדּוֹת הַפִּסְגָּה *'ašdôṯ happisgāh* **proper noun**
(Ashdothpisgah; NASB, NIV, *'ašēdāh* [794] and *pisgāh* [6449])
Deut. 3:17; **Josh.** 12:3; 13:20.

799. I. אֵשְׁדָּת *'ēšdāṯ* **fem. noun**
(fiery law; [Q^e] *'ēš* [784] and *dāṯ* [1881])
Deut. 33:2(NASB, see II; NIV, see III).
II. אֵשְׁדָּת *'ēšdāṯ* **fem. noun**
(flashing lightning)
Deut. 33:2(KJV, see I; NASB, see III).
III. אֵשְׁדָּת *'ēšdāṯ* **fem. noun**
(mountain slope; const. of *'ašēḏāh* [794])
Deut. 33:2(KJV, see I; NASB, see II).

800. אֶשָּׁה *'eššāh* **fem. noun**
(fire)
Jer. 6:29([Q^e] *'ēš* [784] and *tāmam* [8552]).

801. אִשֶּׁה *'iššeh* **fem. noun**
(burnt offering, offering made by fire)
Ex. 29:18,25,41; 30:20; **Lev.** 1:9,13,17; 2:2,3,9–11,16; 3:3,5,9,11,14,16; 4:35; 5:12; 6:17(10),18(11); 7:5,25,30,35; 8:21,28; 10:12,13,15; 21:6,21; 22:22,27; 23:8,13,18,25,27,36,37; 24:7,9; **Num.** 15:3,10,13,14,25; 18:17; 28:2,3,6,8,13, 19,24; 29:6,13,36; **Deut.** 18:1; **Josh.** 13:14; **1 Sam.** 2:28.

802. אִשָּׁה *'iššāh* **fem. noun**
(woman, female)
Gen. 2:22–25; 3:1,2,4,6,8,12,13,15–17,20,21; 4:1,17,19, 23,25; 6:2,18; 7:2,7,13; 8:16,18; 11:29,31; 12:5,11,12,14,15,17–20; 13:1; 14:16; 16:1,3; 17:15,19; 18:9–11; 19:15,16,26; 20:2,3,7,11,12,14,17,18; 21:21; 23:19; 24:3–5,7,8,15,36–40,44,51,67; 25:1,10, 20,21; 26:7–11,34; 27:46; 28:1,2,6,9; 29:21,28; 30:4,9,26; 31:17,35,50; 32:22(23); 33:5; 34:4,8,12,21,29; 36:2, 6,10,12–14,17,18,39; 37:2; 38:6,8,9,12, 14,20; 39:7–9,19; 41:45; 44:27; 45:19; 46:5,19,26; 49:31; **Ex.** 1:19; 2:2,7,9;

3:22; 4:20; 6:20,23,25; 11:2; 15:20; 18:2, 5,6; 19:15; 20:17; 21:3–5,22,28,29; 22:16(15),24(23); 26:3,5,6,17; 32:2; 35:22,25,26,29; 36:6; **Lev.** 12:2; 13:29,38; 15:18,19,25; 18:8,11,14–20, 22,23; 19:20; 20:10,11,13,14,16,18, 21,27; 21:7,13,14; 24:10,11; 26:26; **Num.** 5:6,12,14,15,18,19,21,22,24–31; 6:2; 12:1; 14:3; 16:27; 25:8,15; 26:59; 30:3(4),16(17); 31:9,17,18,35; 32:26; 36:3,6,8,11,12; **Deut.** 2:34; 3:6,19; 5:21(18); 13:6(7); 17:2,5,17; 20:7,14; 21:11,13,15; 22:5,13,14,16,19,22,24, 29,30(23:1); 24:1,3–5; 25:5,11; 27:20; 28:30,54; 29:11(10),18(17); 31:12; **Josh.** 1:14; 2:1,4; 6:21,22; 8:25,35; 15:16,17; **Judg.** 1:12,13; 3:6; 4:4,9,17,21; 5:24; 8:30; 9:49,51,53,54; 11:1,2; 13:2,3,6, 9–11,13,19–24; 14:1–3,7,10,15,16,20; 15:1,6; 16:1,4,27; 19:1,26,27; 20:4; 21:1,7,10,11,14,16,18,21–23; **Ruth** 1:1,2,4,5,8,9; 3:8,11,14; 4:5,10,11,13,14; **1 Sam.** 1:2,4,15,18,19,23,26; 2:20,22; 4:19; 14:50; 15:3,33; 18:6,7,17,19,27; 19:11; 21:4(5),5(6); 22:19; 25:3,14,37, 39,40,42–44; 27:3,9,11; 28:7–9,11–13, 21,23,24; 30:2,3,5,18,22; **2 Sam.** 1:26; 2:2; 3:3,5,8,14; 5:13; 6:19; 11:2,3,5,11, 21,26,27; 12:8–11,15,24; 14:2,4,5,8,9,12, 13,18,19,27; 15:16; 17:19,20; 19:5(6); 20:3,16,17,21,22; **1 Kgs.** 2:17,21; 3:16–19,22,26; 4:11,15; 7:14; 9:16; 11:1, 3,4,8,19,26; 14:2,4–6,17; 16:31; 17:9, 10,17,24; 20:3,5,7; 21:5,7,25; **2 Kgs.** 4:1,8,17; 5:2; 6:26,28,30; 8:1–3,5,6,18; 14:9; 22:14; 23:7; 24:15; **1 Chr.** 1:50; 2:18,24,26,29,35; 3:3; 4:5,18,19; 7:4,15, 16,23; 8:8,9,29; 9:35; 14:3; 16:3; **2 Chr.** 2:14(13); 8:11; 11:18,21,23; 13:21; 15:13; 20:13; 21:6,14,17; 22:11; 24:3; 25:18; 28:8; 29:9; 31:18; 34:22; **Ezra** 2:61; 10:1–3,10,11,14,17–19,44; **Neh.** 4:14(8); 5:1; 7:63; 8:2,3; 10:28(29); 12:43; 13:23, 26,27; **Esth.** 1:9,17,20; 2:3,8,9,11–15,17; 3:13; 4:11; 5:10,14; 6:13; 8:11; **Job** 2:9; 14:1; 15:14; 19:17; 25:4; 31:9,10; 42:15; **Ps.** 58:8(9); 109:9; 128:3; **Prov.** 2:16; 5:18; 6:24,26,29,32; 7:5,10; 9:13; 11:16,22; 12:4; 14:1; 18:22; 19:13,14; 21:9,19; 25:24; 27:15; 30:20; 31:3,10,30; **Eccl.** 7:26,28; 9:9; **Song** 1:8; 5:9; 6:1; **Isa.** 3:12; 4:1; 13:16; 19:16; 27:11; 32:9; 34:15,16; 45:10; 49:15; 54:6; **Jer.** 3:1, 3,20; 5:8; 6:11,12; 7:18; 8:10; 9:20(19); 13:21; 14:16; 16:2; 18:21; 29:6,23; 35:8; 38:22,23; 40:7; 41:16; 43:6; 44:7,9,15, 20,24,25; 48:41; 49:22; 50:37; 51:22,30; **Lam.** 2:20; 4:10; 5:11; **Ezek.** 1:9,23; 3:13; 8:14; 9:6; 16:30,32,34,41; 18:6,11, 15; 22:11; 23:2,10,44,48; 24:18; 33:26; 44:22; **Dan.** 11:17,37; **Hos.** 1:2; 2:2(4); 3:1; 12:12(13); **Amos** 4:3; 7:17; **Mic.** 2:9; **Nah.** 3:13; **Zech.** 5:7,9; 11:9; 12:12–14; 14:2; **Mal.** 2:14,15.

803. אָשְׁיָה *'āšyāh* **fem. noun**
(support, pillar)
Jer. 50:15.

804. A. אַשּׁוּר *'aššûr* **masc. proper noun**
(Asshur: second son of Shem)
Gen. 10:22; **1 Chr.** 1:17.

B. אַשּׁוּר *'aššûr* **masc. proper noun**
(Asshur: also known as Assyria)
Gen. 2:14; 10:11; 25:18; **Num.** 24:22, 24; **2 Kgs.** 15:19,20,29; 16:7–10,18; 17:3–6,23,24,26,27; 18:7,9,11,13,14,16, 17,19,23,28,30,31,33; 19:4,6,8,10,11,17, 20,32,35,36; 20:6; 23:29; **1 Chr.** 5:6,26; **2 Chr.** 28:16,20,21; 30:6; 32:1,4,7,9–11, 21,22; 33:11; **Ezra** 4:2; 6:22; **Neh.** 9:32; **Ps.** 83:8(9); **Isa.** 7:17,18,20; 8:4,7; 10:5,12,24; 11:11,16; 14:25; 19:23–25; 20:1,4,6; 23:13; 27:13; 30:31; 31:8; 36:1,2,4,8,13,15,16,18; 37:4,6,8,10,11, 18,21,33,36,37; 38:6; 52:4; **Jer.** 2:18,36; 50:17,18; **Lam.** 5:6; **Ezek.** 16:28; 23:5,7,9,12,23; 27:23; 31:3; 32:22; **Hos.** 5:13; 7:11; 8:9; 9:3; 10:6; 11:5,11; 12:1(2); 14:3(4); **Mic.** 5:5(4),6(5); 7:12; **Nah.** 3:18; **Zeph.** 2:13; **Zech.** 10:10,11.

805. אַשּׁוּרִי *'aššûriy* **masc. proper noun**
(Asshurite)
Gen. 25:3; **2 Sam.** 2:9.

806. אַשְׁחוּר *'ašḥûr* **masc. proper noun**
(Ashhur)
1 Chr. 2:24; 4:5.

807. אֲשִׁימָא *'ašiymā'* **masc. proper noun**
(Ashima)
2 Kgs. 17:30.

808. A. אָשִׁישׁ *'āšiyš* **masc. noun**
(foundation; similar to *'ošyāh* [803])
Isa. 16:7(NASB, see B; NIV, see C).
B. אָשִׁישׁ *'āšiyš* **masc. noun**
(sacrificial raisin cake; same as *'ašiyšāh* [809])
Isa. 16:7(KJV, see A; NIV, see C).
C. אָשִׁישׁ *'āšiyš* **masc. noun**
(men; related to *'iyš* [376])
Isa. 16:7(KJV, see A; NASB, see B).

809. אֲשִׁישָׁה *'ašiyšāh* **fem. noun**
(raisin cake)
2 Sam. 6:19; **1 Chr.** 16:3; **Song** 2:5; **Hos.** 3:1.

810. אֶשֶׁךְ *'ešek̲* **masc. noun**
(testicle)
Lev. 21:20.

811. אֶשְׁכּוֹל *'eškôl*, אֶשְׁכֹּל *'eškōl* **masc. noun**
(cluster [as of grapes])
Gen. 40:10; **Num.** 13:23,24; **Deut.** 32:32; **Song** 1:14; 7:7(8),8(9); **Isa.** 65:8; **Mic.** 7:1.

812. A. אֶשְׁכֹּל *'eškōl* **masc. proper noun**
(Eshcol: an Amorite)
Gen. 14:13,24.
B. אֶשְׁכּוֹל *'eškôl* **masc. proper noun**
(Eshcol: a valley)
Num. 13:23,24; 32:9; **Deut.** 1:24.

813. A. אַשְׁכְּנַז *'aškᵉnaz* **masc. proper noun**
(Ashkenaz: descendant of Japheth)
Gen. 10:3; **1 Chr.** 1:6.
B. אַשְׁכְּנַז *'aškᵉnaz* **masc. proper noun**
(Ashkenaz: people from the north)
Jer. 51:27.

814. אֶשְׁכָּר *'eškār* **masc. noun**
(gift)
Ps. 72:10; **Ezek.** 27:15.

815. אֶשֶׁל *'ēšel* **masc. noun**
(tamarisk tree)
Gen. 21:33; **1 Sam.** 22:6; 31:13.

816. אָשַׁם *'āšam*, אָשֵׁם *āšēm* **verb**
(to do wrong, to be guilty)
Lev. 4:13,22,27; 5:2–5,17,19; 6:4(5:23); **Num.** 5:6,7; **Judg.** 21:22; **2 Chr.** 19:10; **Ps.** 5:10(11); 34:21(22),22(23); **Prov.** 30:10; **Isa.** 24:6; **Jer.** 2:3; 50:7; **Ezek.** 6:6; 22:4; 25:12; **Hos.** 4:15; 5:15; 10:2; 13:1,16(14:1); **Joel** 1:18; **Hab.** 1:11; **Zech.** 11:5.

817. אָשָׁם *'āšām* **masc. noun**
(guilt offering, trespass offering, guiltiness)
Gen. 26:10; **Lev.** 5:6,7,15,16,18,19; 6:6(5:25),17(10); 7:1,2,5,7,37; 14:12–14,17,21,24,25,28; 19:21,22; **Num.** 5:7,8; 6:12; 18:9; **1 Sam.** 6:3,4,8,17; **2 Kgs.** 12:16(17); **Ps.** 68:21(22); **Prov.** 14:9; **Isa.** 53:10; **Jer.** 51:5; **Ezek.** 40:39; 42:13; 44:29; 46:20.

818. אָשֵׁם *'āšēm* **adj.**
(guilty, at fault)
Gen. 42:21; **2 Sam.** 14:13; **Ezra** 10:19.

819. אַשְׁמָה *'ašmāh* **fem. noun**
(guilt, shame)

Lev. 4:3; 6:5(5:24),7(5:26); 22:16; **1 Chr.** 21:3; **2 Chr.** 24:18; 28:10,13; 33:23; **Ezra** 9:6,7,13,15; 10:10,19; **Ps.** 69:5(6); **Amos** 8:14.

820. A. אַשְׁמָן *'ašmān* **masc. noun**
(desolate)
Isa. 59:10(NASB, NIV, see B).
B. אַשְׁמָן *'ašmān* **masc. noun**
(strong, vigorous; prob. related to *šemen* [8081])
Isa. 59:10(KJV, see A).

821. אַשְׁמוּרָה *'ašmûrāh,* אַשְׁמֹרֶת *'ašmōreṯ* **fem. noun**
(watch [as a period of time], night watch)
Ex. 14:24; **Judg.** 7:19; **1 Sam.** 11:11; **Ps.** 63:6(7); 90:4; 119:148; **Lam.** 2:19.

822. אֶשְׁנָב *'ešnāḇ* **masc. noun**
(window lattice)
Judg. 5:28; **Prov.** 7:6.

823. A. אַשְׁנָה *'ašnāh* **proper noun**
(Ashnah: city in Judah)
Josh. 15:33.
B. אַשְׁנָה *'ašnāh* **proper noun**
(Ashnah: another city in Judah)
Josh. 15:43.

824. אֶשְׁעָן *'eš'ān* **proper noun**
(Eshan)
Josh. 15:52.

825. אַשָּׁף *'aššāp̱* **masc. noun**
(astrologer, conjurer)
Dan. 1:20; 2:2.

826. אָשַׁף *'āšap̱* **Aram. masc. noun**
(astrologer, conjurer; corr. to Hebr. 825)
Dan. 2:10,27; 4:7(4); 5:7,11,15.

827. אַשְׁפָּה *'ašpāh* **fem. noun**
(quiver, container for arrows)
Job 39:23; **Ps.** 127:5; **Isa.** 22:6; 49:2; **Jer.** 5:16; **Lam.** 3:13.

828. אַשְׁפְּנַז *'ašp^{e}naz* **masc. proper noun**
(Ashpenaz)
Dan. 1:3.

829. אֶשְׁפָּר *'ešpār* **masc. noun**
(a piece or portion [of meat, dates, etc.])
2 Sam. 6:19; **1 Chr.** 16:3.

830. אַשְׁפֹּת *'ašpōṯ,* אַשְׁפּוֹת *'ašpôṯ* **masc. noun**
(ash heap, refuse heap, dunghill)
1 Sam. 2:8; **Neh.** 2:13; 3:13,14; 12:31; **Ps.** 113:7; **Lam.** 4:5.

831. אַשְׁקְלוֹן *'ašq^{e}lôn* **proper noun**
(Ashkelon)
Judg. 1:18; 14:19; **1 Sam.** 6:17; **2 Sam.** 1:20; **Jer.** 25:20; 47:5,7; **Amos** 1:8; **Zeph.** 2:4,7; **Zech.** 9:5.

832. אֶשְׁקְלוֹנִי *'ešq^{e}lôniy* **masc. proper noun**
(Ashkelonite)
Josh. 13:3.

833. אָשַׁר *'āšar* **verb**
(to be blessed, to be happy, to be called blessed)
Gen. 30:13; **Job** 29:11; **Ps.** 41:2(3); 72:17; **Prov.** 3:18; 4:14; 9:6; 23:19; 31:28; **Song** 6:9; **Isa.** 1:17; 3:12; 9:16(15); **Mal.** 3:12,15.

834. אֲשֶׁר *'ašer* **rel. pron.**
(which, who, that)
Gen. 1:7,11,12,21,29–31; 2:2,3,8,11,19,22; 3:1,3,11,12,17,23; 4:11; 5:5,29; 6:2,4,7,15,17,21,22; 7:2,4,5,8,9, 15,16,19,22,23; 8:1,6,17,21; 9:2,3,10, 12,15–17,24; 10:14; 11:5–7; 12:1,4,5, 11,20; 13:1,3,4,14–16,18; 14:5,6,15,17, 20,23,24; 15:4,7,14,17; 16:15; 17:10, 12,14,21,23; 18:5,8,17,19,24,33; 19:5, 8,11,12,19,21,27,29; 20:3,7,9,13,16; 21:1–4,9,12,17,22,23,25,29; 22:2,3,9,

14,16–18; 23:9,11,16,17,20; 24:2,3,5,7,14,15,22,24,27,32,36,37,40,42,44,47,48,51,52,54,66; 25:5–7,9,10,12,18; 26:1–3,5,15,18,29,32; 27:4,8–10,14,15,17,19,27,30,40,41,44,45; 28:4,13,15,18,20,22; 29:9,10,27; 30:2,18,25,26,29,30,33,35,37,38; 31:1,12,13,16,18,19,21,32,43,49,51; 32:2,7,10,12,23,31,32; 33:5,8,9,11,14,15,18,19; 34:1,11–14,22,27–29; 35:2–6,12–15,26,27; 36:5,6,24,31; 37:6,10,22,23; 38:10,14,18,25,30; 39:1,3,5,6,8,9,17,19,20,22,23; 40:3,5,7,13,14,22; 41:13,21,25,28,36,38,43,48,50,53–56; 42:9,14,21,38; 43:2,14,16,17,19,26,27,29; 44:1,2,4,5,8–10,15–17,34; 45:4,6,10,11,13,27; 46:1,5,6,15,18,20,22,25,27,31,32; 47:1,4,6,11,14,22,24; 48:6,9,15,22; 49:1,28–30,32; 50:5,6,10–13,15,24; **Ex.** 1:8,12,14,15,17; 2:14; 3:5,7,9,14,20; 4:9,12,15,17,18,21,28,30; 5:2,8,11,13,14,21; 6:1,4,5,8,26,29; 7:2,6,10,13,15,17,18,20–22; 8:12,15,19,21,22,27; 9:3,12,18,19,21,24–26,35; 10:2,6,10,12,15; 11:5–8; 12:7,13,16,22,25,27–30,32,39,40,50; 13:3,5,11,12; 14:12,13,31; 15:26; 16:1,5,8,15,16,23,24,32,34; 17:5,10,11; 18:1,3,5,8–11,14,17,18,20,24; 19:4,6–8,16,18; 20:2,4,7,10–12,17,21,24,26; 21:1,8,13,22,30; 22:9,16; 23:13,15,16,20,22,27,30; 24:3,7,8,12,14; 25:2,3,9,16,21,22,26,29,40; 26:5,30; 27:8,21; 28:3,4,8,26,38; 29:1,13,21–23,26,27,29,30,32,33,35,38,42,46; 30:6,33,36–38; 31:6,7,11; 32:1–4,7,8,11,13,14,19,20,23,32–35; 33:1,7,11,12,16,17,19; 34:1,4,10–12,18,32,34; 35:1,4,10,16,21–24,26,29; 36:1–5,12; 37:13,16; 38:8,21,22,30; 39:1,5,7,19,21,29,31,32,39,42,43; 40:9,15,16,19,21,23,25,27,29,32; **Lev.** 1:5,8,12,17; 2:8,11; 3:3–5,9,10,14,15; 4:2,3,7–10,13,14,18,20–24,27,28,31,33,35; 5:2–8,10,11,13,16–18; 6:3–5,7,10,15,18,20,25,27,28,30; 7:2,4,7–9,11,19–21,25,27,36,38; 8:4,5,9,10,13,16,17,21,25,26,29–31,34,36; 9:5–8,10,15,18,21; 10:1,3,5,6,11,15,18; 11:2,9,10,12,21,23,26,32–35,37,39,47; 13:45,46,51,52,54,57,58; 14:13,16–18,22,27–32,34–36,40,41; 15:4–6,9–12,17,18,20,22–24,26,31–33; 16:2,6,9–11,13,15,18,23,27,32,34; 17:2,3,5,7,8,10,13,15; 18:3,5,24,27–30; 19:22,36; 20:2,6,9–18,20–25; 21:3,10,17–19,21; 22:2–6,15,18,20; 23:2,4,10,29,30,37,38; 24:19,20,23; 25:2,7,27,30,31,33,38,42,44,45,55; 26:13,35,40,45,46; 27:8,9,11,14,22,24,26,28,29,32,34; **Num.** 1:5,17,19,44,50,54; 2:17,33,34; 3:3,16,26,31,39,42,51; 4:9,12,14,16,25,26,37,41,45,46,49; 5:3,4,7–10,17,29,30; 6:4,5,11,18,21; 7:89; 8:3,4,20,22,24; 9:5,6,13,17,18,20,21; 10:29,32; 11:4,5,12,16,17,20,21,25; 12:1,3,11,12; 13:2,16,19,24,27,31,32; 14:7,8,11,14–17,19,22–24,27–31,34,36,40; 15:2,12,14,18,22,23,30,36,39,41; 16:5,7,26,30–34,39,40,47; 17:4,5,11; 18:9,12,13,15,19,21,24,26,28; 19:2,13–16,18,20,22; 20:9,12–14,17,24,27; 21:11,13,15,16,20,22,30,32,34; 22:2,5,6,8,17,20,26,30,35,36,38,40; 23:2,12,13,26,30; 24:4,12–14; 25:13,14,18; 26:4,9,59,63,64; 27:11–14,17,18,22,23; 28:3,23; 29:40; 30:1,4–9,11,14,16; 31:7,12,18,21,23,31,32,35,41,42,47–50,52; 32:4,7,9,11,17,23,25,27,31,38,39; 33:1,4,6,7,54–56; 34:2,13,17,29; 35:4,6–8,13,17,18,23,25,26,31,33,34; 36:3,4,6,10,13; **Deut.** 1:1,3,4,8,11,14,17–22,25,30,31,33,35,36,39,41,44,46; 2:1,12,14,16,22,25,29,35–37; 3:2,4,6,8,12,19–21,24,25,28; 4:1–3,5–10,13,14,17–19,21,23,26–28,31–34,40,42,44–48; 5:1,6,8,11,12,14,16,21,26–28,31–33; 6:1–3,6,10–12,14,16–20,23,25; 7:1,6,8,11–13,15,16,18,19; 8:1–3,5,9–11,13,15,16,18,20; 9:2,3,5,7,9,10,12,16,18,19,21,23,25,26,28,29; 10:2,4,5,9,11,13,14,17,21; 11:2–13,17,21,22,24,25,27–29,31,32; 12:1,2,5,7–15,17,18,20–22,26,28,29,31,32; 13:2,5–7,12,13,15,17,18; 14:2,4,9,10,12,21,23–27,29; 15:2–8,14,18–20; 16:2,4–7,10,11,14–18,20–22; 17:1–3,5,8–12,14,15; 18:2,6,9,14,16–22; 19:1–5,8–10,14,15,17,19; 20:5–7,14–18,20; 21:1–4,

8,14,16,17,23; 22:3,9,12,24–26,28,29; 23:4,8,10,15,16,19,20,23; 24:3–5,8,9, 11,14; 25:6,9,15,17–19; 26:1–3,10,11, 13–15,18,19; 27:1–4,10,15,26; 28:1,8,9, 11,13–15,20,21,23,27,29,33–37,43,45,47 –57,60–64,67,68; 29:1–3,9,11–13,15–18, 22,23,25,26; 30:1–3,5,7–9,11,16,18,20; 31:3–5,7,11–13,16,18,20,21,23,29; 32:38,46,47,49–52; 33:1,8,29; 34:1,4, 9–12; **Josh.** 1:2,3,5–7,9,11,13–18; 2:3, 7,10,13,17–20; 3:4,7,16,17; 4:1,3,4,7,8, 10–12,14,20,21,23; 5:1,4,6,8,15; 6:17, 21–26; 7:2,8,11,14,15,24; 8:2,5,6,11,13, 16–18,24,26,27,31–33,35; 9:1,3,9,10,13, 16,20,21,24,27; 10:1,11,25,27,28,30,32, 35,37,39,40; 11:2,4,9,11,12,15,19,20,23; 12:1,2,7,9; 13:3,4,6,8–10,12,14,16,17,21, 25,30,32,33; 14:1,2,5–12,14; 15:7,8, 16,46; 17:5,7,14,16; 18:2,3,7,13,14,16, 17; 19:8,11,50,51; 20:2,6; 21:8,9,43–45; 22:2,4,5,9,10,16,17,19,28–31,33; 23:1, 3–5,8,10,13–16; 24:5,7,13–15,17,20,23, 26,27,30–33; **Judg.** 1:7,12,16,20; 2:1,7, 10,12,15,17,20–22; 3:1,2,4,18–20; 4:2, 9,11,13,14,22,24; 5:27; 6:2,10,11,13,21, 25–28,30,31,36,37; 7:1,2,4,5,11,17–19; 8:4,5,8,15,18,21,26,31,33,35; 9:6,9,17, 24,25,32–35,38,44,45,48,56; 10:4,8,14, 18; 11:5,7,24,26,28,31,36,39; 13:8,10,11, 13,14; 14:6,17,20; 15:10,11,14,19; 16:3, 7–9,11,22,24,26,29,30; 17:2,8,9; 18:5–7, 10,16,22,24,27–29,31; 19:12,14,22, 23,26; 20:4,9,10,12,13,22,31,36,42; 21:5,8,11–14,19,23; **Ruth** 1:7,8,13,16, 17; 2:2,3,9,11,12,17–21; 3:1,2,4–6, 11,15,16,18; 4:1,3,9,11,12,14,15; **1 Sam.** 1:17,24,27,28; 2:14,16,20,22–24,29, 32,34,35; 3:3,11–13,17; 4:9; 5:12; 6:4,6–8,15,17,18; 7:14; 8:1,6–9,11,18; 9:5,6,10,17,19,23; 10:2,5,7,8,16,19,24, 26; 11:7; 12:1,6–8,13,14,16,17,21,24; 13:3,5,8,13,14,22; 14:1,2,4,7,11,14,17, 19–21,24,27,28,30,43,45,47; 15:2,3, 7,14–16,20,33; 16:3,4,7,19; 17:1,13,20, 25–27,31,37,40,45; 18:4,5,15; 19:3, 18,22; 20:13,19,23,31,36,37,40,42; 21:2,7,9; 22:2,3,6,11,23; 23:11,13,19, 22,23; 24:1,4,5,10,13,18,19; 25:6–8,11, 21,22,25–27,30,32–35,39,44; 26:3,5,11, 16,20,21,23,24; 27:2,7,8,11; 28:2,8,9, 17,18,21; 29:1,3–5,8,10; 30:2,4,9,10, 14,16–19,21–23,27–31; 31:7,11; **2 Sam.** 1:4,10,11; 2:3–6,8,11,16,18,23,24,32; 3:8,9,14,19–21,23,25,30,31,36; 4:8–10; 5:25; 6:2–4,8,12,17,20–22; 7:3,7,9–12, 14,15,22,23,25; 8:6,7,10,11,14; 9:1,8, 9,11; 10:2,13,16; 11:16,20,22,27; 12:3,6, 15,21,31; 13:5,10,15,16,19,22,23,29; 14:7,14,15,18–20,22,26,31; 15:2,4,6,7, 14,15,18,20–22,26,30,32,35,36; 16:4,8, 11,14,16,18,19,21,23; 17:2,3,7,9–13, 16,22,25,29; 18:1,4,9,18,21,28,32; 19:3, 7,10,16,19,24,30,35,37,38; 20:3,5,8, 10–13,15; 21:1,5,7,8,11,12,14,16,18; 23:8,15,16; 24:2,5,10,19,24; **1 Kgs.** 1:8,9,29,30,33,37,41,45,48,49; 2:3–5, 9,11,24,26,27,31,32,38,43,44; 3:6,8, 11–14,19,21,26,28; 4:2,12,13,19,20, 28,29,33,34; 5:3,5–9,12,16; 6:2,12,22; 7:3,7,8,17–20,29,40–42,45,48,51; 8:4, 5,9,15,16,18,20,21,24–31,33,34,36,38–4 1,43,44,46–48,50,51,53,56–59,63,64,66; 9:1–7,9,10,12,13,15,19–21,23–26; 10:2–7, 9–11,13,14,24,27,28; 11:2,7,10,11,13, 23,25,27,30,32–34,36–38,41,42; 12:2,4 ,6,8–10,12,13,15,18,28,31–33; 13:3–5, 9–12,14,17,20–23,25,26,31,32; 14:7–10, 14–16,18–22,24,26,29; 15:3,5,7,12,13, 20,22,23,26,27,29–31,34; 16:2,5,7,9, 12–15,19,20,22,24–27,30,32–34; 17:1,3, 5,9,16,17,19,20; 18:3,10,12,13,15,24,26, 31,38; 19:1,3,18; 20:4,9,10,19,22,28, 34,36; 21:1,4,8,11,15,18,19,22,25,26; 22:13,14,16,17,25,31,38,39,45,46,52,53; **2 Kgs.** 1:2,4,6,7,16–18; 2:3,5,13–15, 19,22; 3:2,3,9,11,14,27; 4:17; 5:3,4,16, 20,26; 6:1,10,12,16,19,22; 7:2,7,10,12, 13,15,17; 8:1,4–6,12,18,19,23,29; 9:15, 27,36,37; 10:5,10,15,17,19,21,22,24, 29–31,33,34,36; 11:5,9,10; 12:2,4,5,12, 15,18,19; 13:2,6,8,11,12,14,25; 14:3,5, 6,9,11,15,24,25,28; 15:3,6,9,12,15,16,18, 21,24,26,28,31,34,36; 16:3,10,11,13,14, 16–19; 17:2,4,8,9,11–15,19,20,22,23,

26–29,33,34,36–38,41; 18:3–7,12,14, 16–19,21,22,26,35,37; 19:2,4,6,10–12, 16,20,21,28,33; 20:3,9,11,13,15,17–20; 21:2–4,7–9,11–13,15–17,20,21,25; 22:4, 5,13,15–20; 23:5,7,8,10–13,15–20,22, 24–28,32,37; 24:2–5,7,9,13,19; 25:4, 10,11,13–16,19,22,25,28; **1 Chr.** 1:12, 43; 2:7,9; 3:1; 4:10,18,22,33,41; 5:6,25; 6:10,31,49,65; 7:14; 9:2; 10:7,11,13; 11:10,11,17,18; 12:15,20,31; 13:6,10,14; 14:4,16; 15:3,15; 16:1,12,16,32,39–41; 17:1,2,5,6,8–11,13,20,21,23; 18:6,7,10, 11,13; 19:5,9,14,16; 20:3; 21:8,17,19, 24,29; 22:2,11,13; 23:5; 24:19; 26:26; 27:28,31; 28:12; 29:16,19,25,27,30; **2 Chr.** 1:3,5,6,11–13,15; 2:3,5–9,12, 14,15,17; 3:1,4,15; 4:11–13,19; 5:1,5, 6,10; 6:4,5,8,10,11,15–21,25,27, 29–34,36–39; 7:6,7,10,14,17–22; 8:1,2,4,6–12; 9:1–6,8–10,12,13,23,27; 10:2,4,6,8–10,12,15,18; 11:10,13,15; 12:3–5,9,13; 13:4,8; 14:13; 15:8,13,16; 16:4,6,14; 17:2,10,19; 18:2,12,13,15, 16,24,30; 19:10; 20:10,11,34; 21:6,7, 12,16; 22:6,7,9; 23:3,4,8,9,18; 24:22; 25:3,4,9,10,13,15,18,21,27; 26:4,23; 27:2; 28:3,11,15; 29:2,8,16,19,32; 30:7,8, 14,17; 31:19,21; 32:3,7,9,14,17,18,31; 33:2–4,7–9,11,15,19,22; 34:4,9–11,16, 21–26,28,33; 35:3,18,20,21,24; 36:8,13, 14,23; **Ezra** 1:2–5,7; 2:1,2,61,63,68; 3:12; 4:3; 7:6,11,27; 9:11; 10:8,14,18; **Neh.** 1:2,3,6–10; 2:3,5,7,8,10,12,13, 17–19; 3:25; 4:1,3,7,11,12,15,20,23; 5:2–4,6,9,11–15,17–19; 6:1,3,8,11,14,16, 17; 7:1,6,63,65,72; 8:1,3,4,12,14,15; 9:6,7,12,15,17–19,23,26,29,32,34–37; 10:29,30; 11:3; 12:1; 13:1,7,14,17,19,22; **Esth.** 1:2,9,12,15,16,18–20; 2:1,4,6,10, 13,15,20; 3:1–4,6,12; 4:1,3,5–8,11,16,17; 5:2,4,5,8,11–13; 6:2,4,6–11,13,14; 7:5, 8–10; 8:2,3,5–9,11,17; 9:1,3,13,15,16,18, 20,22,23,25,31; 10:2; **Job** 1:10–12; 2:4; 3:23,25; 4:8,19; 5:5; 6:4; 8:14; 9:5,15,17; 10:19; 12:6,10; 15:18,28; 19:27; 22:15,16; 27:11; 29:4,25; 30:1; 32:3; 34:19,27; 36:24,28; 37:12,17; 38:23; 39:6,30; 40:15; 42:9–11; **Ps.** 1:1,3,4; 3:6; 6:10; 8:1,3; 10:6; 12:4; 16:3,7; 17:15; 24:4; 26:10; 31:7,19; 33:12,22; 35:8,11; 38:14; 40:4; 41:8,9; 46:8; 47:4; 48:8; 50:23; 55:14,19; 56:6; 58:5; 64:3; 66:14, 16,20; 69:4,26; 71:19,20,23; 78:3–5,11, 42,43,68; 79:6,12; 80:15; 83:12; 84:3; 86:9; 88:5; 89:21,51; 94:12; 95:4,5,9,11; 96:12; 104:16,17; 105:5,9,26; 106:34,38; 107:2; 109:11,16; 112:8; 115:3,8; 119:38, 39,47–49,63,85,158; 127:5; 132:2; 135:6,18; 139:15,20; 140:2,4; 144:8, 11,12; 145:18; 146:6; 147:9; 148:4; **Prov.** 2:15; 3:12; 6:7; 17:8; 21:1; 22:28; 23:1; 24:29; 25:1,7,28; 31:1; **Eccl.** 1:10,13,16; 2:3,10,12; 3:9–11,14,15,22; 4:1–3,9, 13,15,16; 5:1,4,5,15,18,19; 6:1,2,10,12; 7:2,13,18–22,26,28,29; 8:3,4,7,9–17; 9:1–4,6,9,10; 10:14,15; 11:5; 12:1,2,6,7; **Song** 1:1; **Isa.** 1:1,29,30; 2:1,8,20,22; 5:5,28; 6:11,13; 7:16–18,25; 8:12,18,20; 9:1,3; 10:10,11; 11:10,11,16; 13:1,17; 14:3,24; 16:13; 17:8,9; 18:1,2,7; 19:15–17,25; 20:3,6; 21:6,10; 22:15,25; 23:5,8; 24:2; 25:11; 26:9; 27:1; 28:1,4,12, 14; 29:8,11,12,22; 30:10,13,23,24,32; 31:4,6,7,9; 33:13; 36:3,4,6,7,11,20,22; 37:2,4,6,10–12,17,21,22,29,34; 38:3,7,8; 39:2,4,6–8; 41:8,9,22; 43:4,10; 44:7; 45:1; 46:10; 47:12,13,15; 49:3,7,9,23; 50:1,10; 51:13,17,23; 52:14,15; 53:12; 54:9; 55:1,10,11; 56:4,5; 58:2,11; 59:21; 60:12; 62:2,8; 63:7; 64:11; 65:7,8,10, 12,16,18,20; 66:1,4,13,19,20,22; **Jer.** 1:1,2,7,16,17; 2:13,28,36; 3:6,8,18; 5:9,17,19,22,29; 6:18; 7:1,7,9–12,14, 15,23,25,28,30,31; 8:2,3,17; 9:9,12–14, 16; 10:1,25; 11:1,3–5,8,10–12,17; 12:14, 16; 13:4–7,10,11,25; 14:1,16; 15:2,4; 16:10,11,13–15; 17:4,5,7,19,22; 18:1,4, 8,10; 19:2–5,9,11,13–15; 20:2,6,14–17; 21:1,4; 22:9,11,12,25–28; 23:3,6–8,25, 27,28,34,39,40; 24:2,3,5,8–10; 25:1,2, 5,8,13,15–17,22,26,27,29; 26:2–5,8, 11–13,19; 27:5,8,9,11,13,20; 28:1,3,6–9; 29:1,3,4,7,8,11,14,16–20,22,23,25,31,32; 30:1–4,9,11; 31:28,32,33,37; 32:1–3,7–9,

19,20,22–24,29,31,32,34–37,40,42,43; 33:5,8–10,14,16,22,24; 34:1,5,8,10, 11,14–16,18; 35:1,4,7,8,10,14–18; 36:2–4,6–8,13,14,23,27,28,31,32; 37:1,2,19; 38:1,6,9,14,16,19–22,27,28; 39:4,9,10,12,17; 40:1,3–5,7,10–13; 41:2,3,7,9–14,16–18; 42:2–6,8–11, 14,16–18,20–22; 43:1,5,6,9–13; 44:1–4, 8–10,12–14,16,17,21–25,27,30; 45:1,4,5; 46:1,2,13,28; 47:1; 48:8,13; 49:12,19,20, 28,34,36; 50:1,7,15,18,20,21,29,37, 44,45; 51:12,24,48,59,60,64; 52:2,7,14, 15,17–20,25,28,32; **Lam.** 1:7,10,12,22; 2:17,22; 4:20; **Ezek.** 1:12,16,20,25,26, 28; 2:2,3,8; 3:1,3,6,10,20,23; 4:4,9,10,13; 5:6,7,9,14–16; 6:9,11,13; 7:15; 8:3,4,6,9, 12–14,17; 9:2,3,6,11; 10:1,7,10,11,15, 20,22; 11:7,12,15–17,23–25; 12:2,7, 10–12,14,16,25,27,28; 13:3,12,14,19,20; 14:4,5,7,22,23; 15:2,6; 16:14,17,19,20, 36,37,43,45,48,50–52,54,59,63; 17:3,16, 19,20; 18:14,18,21,22,24,26–28,31; 20:6, 9,11,13–15,21,22,26,28,29,32,34,36, 41–43; 21:4,25,27,29,30; 22:4,13,14; 23:7,9,18–20,22,28,30,37,40; 24:6,18, 21,22,24; 26:2,6,17–19; 27:27; 28:25; 29:3,13,18,20; 31:9,10,14; 32:9,23,24 ,27,29,30; 33:13,16,27,29; 34:2,12,21; 35:11,12,15; 36:4,5,7,18,20–23,27,28, 30,31,34,36; 37:7,10,18–21,23,25; 38:8,17,20,22; 39:4,8,17,19,21,23,26,29; 40:1,4,6,20,22,40,42,44–46,49; 41:6, 9,12,15,22,25; 42:1,3,7,8,11–15; 43:1, 3,4,7,8,11,19,22; 44:5,9,10,12–15, 19,22,25; 45:13; 46:4,7,9,12,18–20,24; 47:5,9,13,14,16,22,23; 48:8,9,11,22,29; **Dan.** 1:4,8,10,11,13,18,20; 8:2,6, 19–21,26; 9:1,2,6–8,10–15,18,21; 10:1,7,11,12,14; 11:4,24,38,39; 12:1,6,7; **Hos.** 1:1,10; 2:12,13; 5:15; 7:12; 9:13; 12:8; 13:10; 14:3; **Joel** 1:1; 2:25,26,32; 3:1,2,5,7,19; **Amos** 1:1; 2:4,9,13; 3:1,12; 4:1,7; 5:1,14,19,26; 6:10; 9:9,12,15; **Obad.** 1:15,16,20; **Jon.** 1:5,8,9,14; 2:9; 3:2,8,10; 4:5,10,11; **Mic.** 1:1; 2:3; 3:3–5; 4:6; 5:7,8,15; 6:1,12,14; 7:9,20; **Nah.** 2:11; 3:8; **Hab.** 1:1; 2:5; 3:16; **Zeph.** 1:1,6; 2:3,8; 3:7,11; **Hag.** 1:9,11,12; 2:3,5,14,18; **Zech.** 1:4,6,8,10,12,15, 19,21; 3:9; 4:1,2,12; 6:6,10; 7:3,7,12–14; 8:9,13,14,16,17,20,23; 10:6; 11:2,5, 10,13; 12:10; 13:6; 14:4,5,12,15,17–19; **Mal.** 1:4; 2:9,11,12,14; 3:1,17,18; 4:1,3,4.

835. אֶשֶׁר *'ešer* **masc. noun**
(happy ones; only pl. const. *'ašrēy*)
Deut. 33:29; **1 Kgs.** 10:8; **2 Chr.** 9:7; **Job** 5:17; **Ps.** 1:1; 2:12; 32:1,2; 33:12; 34:8(9); 40:4(5); 41:1(2); 65:4(5); 84:4(5),5(6),12(13); 89:15(16); 94:12; 106:3; 112:1; 119:1,2; 127:5; 128:1,2; 137:8,9; 144:15; 146:5; **Prov.** 3:13; 8:32,34; 14:21; 16:20; 20:7; 28:14; 29:18; **Eccl.** 10:17; **Isa.** 30:18; 32:20; 56:2; **Dan.** 12:12.

836. A. אָשֵׁר *'āšēr* **masc. proper noun**
(Asher: son of Jacob)
Gen. 30:13; 35:26; 46:17; **Ex.** 1:4; **Num.** 26:46; **1 Chr.** 2:2.
B. אָשֵׁר *'āšēr* **masc. proper noun**
(Asher: tribe of Israel)
Gen. 49:20; **Num.** 1:13,40,41; 2:27; 7:72; 10:26; 13:13; 26:44,47; 34:27; **Deut.** 27:13; 33:24; **Josh.** 17:7,10,11; 19:24,31,34; 21:6,30; **Judg.** 1:31; 5:17; 6:35; 7:23; **1 Kgs.** 4:16; **1 Chr.** 6:62(47), 74(59); 7:30,40; 12:36; **2 Chr.** 30:11; **Ezek.** 48:2,3,34.

837. אֹשֶׁר *'ōšer* **masc. noun**
(happiness)
Gen. 30:13.

838. אָשֻׁר *'ošsur,* אַשֻּׁר *'aššur* **fem. noun**
(step, path)
Job 23:11; 31:7; **Ps.** 17:5,11; 37:31; 40:2(3); 44:18(19); 73:2; **Prov.** 14:15.

839. אֲשֻׁרִים *'ᵃšuriym* **masc. pl. proper noun**
(Ashurites)
Ezek. 27:6(NASB, NIV, *te'aššûr* [8391]).

840. אֲשַׂרְאֵל *'ᵃśar'ēl* **masc. proper noun**
(Asarel)
1 Chr. 4:16.

841. אֲשַׂרְאֵלָה *'ᵃśar'ēlāh* **masc. proper noun**
(Asarelah)
1 Chr. 25:2.

842. אֲשֵׁרָה *'ᵃšērāh,* אֲשֵׁירָה *'ᵃšēyrāh* **fem. noun**
(Asherah pole in Canaanite idolatry [KJV, groves])
Ex. 34:13; **Deut.** 7:5; 12:3; 16:21; **Judg.** 3:7; 6:25,26,28,30; **1 Kgs.** 14:15,23; 15:13; 16:33; 18:19; **2 Kgs.** 13:6; 17:10,16; 18:4; 21:3,7; 23:4,6,7,14,15; **2 Chr.** 14:3(2); 15:16; 17:6; 19:3; 24:18; 31:1; 33:3,19; 34:3,4,7; **Isa.** 17:8; 27:9; **Jer.** 17:2; **Mic.** 5:14(13).

843. אָשֵׁרִי *'āšēriy* **masc. proper noun**
(Asherite)
Judg. 1:32.

844. אַשְׂרִיאֵל *'aśriy'ēl* **masc. proper noun**
(Asriel)
Num. 26:31; **Josh.** 17:2; **1 Chr.** 7:14.

845. אַשְׂרִאֵלִי *'aśri'ēliy* **masc. proper noun**
(Asrielite)
Num. 26:31.

846. אֻשַּׁרְנָא *'uššarnā'* **Aram. masc. noun**
(wall, structure)
Ezra 5:3,9.

847. אֶשְׁתָּאוֹל *'eštā'ôl* **proper noun**
(Eshtaol)
Josh. 15:33; 19:41; **Judg.** 13:25; 16:31; 18:2,8,11.

848. אֶשְׁתָּאֻלִי *'eštā'uliy* **masc. proper noun**
(Eshtaolite)
1 Chr. 2:53.

849. אֶשְׁתַּדּוּר *'eštaddûr* **Aram. masc. noun**
(revolt, rebellion)
Ezra 4:15,19.

850. אֶשְׁתּוֹן *'eštôn* **masc. proper noun**
(Eshton)
1 Chr. 4:11,12.

851. I. אֶשְׁתְּמוֹעַ *'eštᵉmôa',* אֶשְׁתְּמֹה *'eštᵉmōh* **proper noun**
(Eshtemoa: city in Judah)
Josh. 15:50; 21:14; **1 Sam.** 30:28; **1 Chr.** 6:57(42).
II. אֶשְׁתְּמוֹעַ *'eštᵉmôa'* **masc. proper noun**
(Eshtemoa: a Judaite)
1 Chr. 4:17,19.

852. אָת *'āṯ* **Aram. masc. noun**
(sign, miraculous sign; corr. to Hebr. 226)
Dan. 4:2(3:32),3(3:33); 6:27(28).

853. אֵת *'ēṯ* **particle**
(untranslated sign of the direct object)
Gen. 1:1,4,7,16,17,21,22,25,27–31; 2:3, 5–8,10,11,13,15,19,22,24; 3:8,10,18, 23,24; 4:1,2,11,12,14,15,17,18,20,22, 25,26; 5:1–4,6,7,9,10,12,13,15,16,18, 19,21,22,24–26,29,30,32; 6:2,6,7,10, 12,14,15,17,18,22; 7:1,4,9,16,17,23; 8:1,6–10,12,13,21; 9:1,3,5,6,9,11,13, 15,22–24; 10:8,11–18,24,26–29; 11:5, 8,10–27,31; 12:5,7,12,14,15,17,19,20;

13:6,10,11,15,16; 14:4–7,11,12,14,16, 17,23; 15:3,5,7,10,11,13,14,18–21; 16:3,10,16; 17:2,5–9,11,14–16,19–21, 23,25; 18:7,19,28; 19:5,8,10,11,13–15,17, 19,21,25,27,29,32,33,35; 20:2,6,8,10,13, 14,17; 21:1–5,8–10,13–19,25,26,28,30; 22:1–4,6,9,10,12,13,16,17,21–24; 23:5,6, 8–10,13–16,19; 24:1,5–9,14,30,35,36,47, 48,52,56,57,59–61,64,66,67; 25:2,3,5,9, 11,19,20,22,26,28,31,33,34; 26:3,4,8,11, 14,18,24,27,33,34; 27:1,6,8,9,15–17,27, 30,34,36,37,40–42,45; 28:1,3–6,9,15, 18,19; 29:3,5,8,10,11,13,18–24,27–31, 33,35; 30:4,9,11,13–15,20–26,29,30,35, 36,38,41; 31:1,2,5–7,9,12,15,17–21,23, 25–27,30–32,34,35,37,41,42,50,52,55; 32:4,7,10–12,17,19,22,23,29,31,32; 33:1,2,5,11,18,19; 34:2–5,7–9,12–14,16, 17,21,26,28–31; 35:2–4,9,10,12,15, 22,29; 36:2–7,12,14,24,35; 37:2–5,8, 9,11,12,14,16,18,22–24,26,28,29,31,32,3 5,36; 38:3–5,8,10,20,21; 39:4,5,7,9,19, 20,22,23; 40:3,4,6–9,11,13,15,17,19–23; 41:4,7–10,12–16,20,24,25,28,30,34,35, 39,41–45,48,51,52,56; 42:4,7–9,16–18, 20,22,24–27,29,30,33–38; 43:2,4,7, 12–18,21,23–26,29; 44:1,2,4,6,11,16, 19,22,24,29,31,32,34; 45:2–5,8,11,13, 17–19,24,27; 46:5,6,18,20,25,28,30; 47:6,7,9–12,14,17,19–23,26; 48:1,3, 4,8,10–17,20,21; 49:1,15,25,28,29,31,33; 50:2,3,5–7,11,13–15,21,24–26; **Ex.** 1:8,11–14,16–18,21; 2:1–3,5–9,12, 14–17,19–22,24,25; 3:1,3,7,9–12,16, 17,19–22; 4:15,17,19–21,23,25,28–31; 5:1,2,4–6,8,19–21,23; 6:4–8,11,13,20, 23,25–27,29; 7:2–6,9,10,12,16,20,25; 8:1,2,5–8,14–18,21,22,26,28,29,32; 9:1,6,7,10,12–16,19–23,25,28,29,33,35; 10:1,2,4,5,7,8,10–13,15,17,19,20,22–24, 26,27; 11:1,3,10; 12:6–8,11,13,14,17, 23–25,27,28,31,32,34,36,39,44,47,50,51; 13:3,5,7,10,17–19; 14:4–6,8–10,12,13, 16,17,20,21,24–28,30,31; 15:1,19,20,22; 16:3,5–9,12,13,21,23,24,31–33,35; 17:2,3,5,7,13,14; 18:1–3,8,10,13,14,16, 19,20,22,23,25–27; 19:4,5,7–9,12, 14,17,23; 20:1,7,8,11,12,18,20,24,25; 21:5–7,18,20,26,28,35; 22:5,6,23–25,31; 23:9,10,15,16,22,25–28,30,31,33; 24:3–5,8,10–12,15; 25:2,9,11,13,14, 16,18,19,21,22,24,26–29,37,39; 26:1,6,7, 9,11,15,18,29–35,37; 27:1,2,5–9,20,21; 28:1,3,5,6,9–12,14,15,23–31,37,38,41; 29:1–20,22,24–27,29,31–37,39,41,44,46; 30:1,3–8,12,15,16,18,19,25–30,35; 31:3, 6–11,13,14,16,17; 32:3,4,9–13,17,19,20, 22,25,27,34,35; 33:2,4,6,7,10,12,13, 17–20,23; 34:1,4,10,11,13,16,18,23,24, 27,28,30,32,34,35; 35:1,5,10–19,21, 24–29,31,35; 36:1–5,7,8,10,13,14,16,18, 20,23,33–35,38; 37:1,4,5,7,8,10,11, 13–17,23–29; 38:1–3,6–9,22,27,28, 30,31; 39:1–3,5–9,16,18,21,22,25–43; 40:2–16,18–35; **Lev.** 1:2,3,5,6,8,9, 11–17; 2:2,6,8,9,12,14,16; 3:2–5,7–10, 13–15; 4:4–9,11,12,14,15,17–19, 21,23–26,29–31,33–35; 5:6–8,10–12, 15,16; 6:2,4–6,9–11,14,15,17,20,22,26; 7:2–5,8,9,14,16,18,29–36,38; 8:2–4, 6–22,24,25,27–31,33,35,36; 9:5,7–24; 10:1,2,4,6,11–14,16–19; 11:3–7,9, 11,13–19,21,22,28,33,40,43–45; 13:3, 4,6,12,13,15,17,22,25,27,30–34,43,49–5 2,54–57; 14:5–9,11–13,16,19,20,23–25, 30,31,36–38,40–43,45–53; 15:10,15,16, 18,24,29–31,33; 16:4,6,7,9–11,13,15, 20–34; 17:5–7,9,10,13; 18:3–5,17,21, 25–28,30; 19:3,8–10,12,13,17–19,21,23, 25,27,29,30,33,36,37; 20:3–6,8,9,14–19, 21–27; 21:6,8–10,12,14,21,23; 22:2,9, 14–16,23,25,28,31–33; 23:2,4,10–12, 14,15,20,22,27,30,32,37,39,41,43,44; 24:2–6,11,14,23; 25:3,5,10–12,14,17, 18,20–22,25,27,28,30,37,38,42,46,52,55; 26:2,3,5,7,9,11,13–20,22,24,28,30–36,38 ,40–43,45; 27:8,10–12,14,15,18–20,22, 23,26,34; **Num.** 1:2,3,17–19,49–51, 53,54; 2:33,34; 3:6–10,12,15,16,26, 40–42,45,46,49–51; 4:2,5,7–15,18–20, 22,23,25–27,29,30,32,34,46,49; 5:2–4,7,10,14–16,18–21,23–27,30,31; 6:11–14,16–20,23,27; 7:1,3,5–8,10–12, 19,84,88,89; 8:2–4,6,9–22; 9:2,3,5,7,11,

12,15,19,23; 10:2,7,9,21,29,31; 11:5,8, 10–12,14,16,20,22,24,29,32,34; 13:2,3,16–18,21,26,30,32,33; 14:1, 3,6–10,12,13,15,16,21–23,27,30,31,33, 34,36,38,39,41; 15:13,18,20,22,23,25, 30,31,33–36,39–41; 16:5,9,10,15,19,21, 28,30–32,35,37–39,41,45–47; 17:2,3,5, 7,9–11; 18:1,2,4–8,10,11,15,17,21,23, 24,26,28–32; 19:3,5,8–10,13,20; 20:4, 5,8–12,14,21,24–26,28,29; 21:2–4, 6–9,14,16,17,23–26,32,34,35; 22:2, 4–6,8,11,12,17,18,20,21,23,25,27,28, 31–33,35,38,41; 23:4,10,12,26,28; 24:1, 2,10,13,20,21; 25:4,6,8,11,12,17; 26:2, 4,10,29,55,58–60,63,64; 27:5,7–13,18, 19,22,23; 28:2,4,8,23; 29:7,40; 30:4,5,8, 11,12,14–16; 31:6–12,21,22,26,27,30, 31,41,47,49–51,54; 32:1,5,7–9,11,20,21, 23,28,29,31,33–42; 33:2,4,51–55; 34:2, 13,17,18,29; 35:2,5–7,10,14,19,21, 25–27,30,33,34; 36:2,5,10; **Deut.** 1:3–5,8–11,14–16,18,19,21,22,24–28,31, 34–36,38,41,43,44; 2:1,3–5,7,9,13,14, 18,22,24,29–31,33,34,36; 3:2–4,6,8, 12,14,15,18,20,21,24,25,27,28; 4:1–3, 5,6,9,10,13,14,19–23,26,27,29,31,36–38, 40,42,43,47; 5:1,3,5,11,12,15,16,22–25, 27–29,31–33; 6:1,2,5,12,13,16–20, 23–25; 7:2,4,8,11,12,16,18,20,22,24; 8:1,2,5,6,10,11,14,17–19; 9:1,4–8,10, 11,13,14,16,19,21–25,28; 10:2,4,5,8, 11–13,15,16,19–21; 11:1–4,6–8,10,12, 13,17–19,22,23,27–29,31,32; 12:2,3,5,6, 10,11,19,20,22,28–32; 13:3–5,13,15, 16,18; 14:6–9,13–17,22,23,28; 15:2,3,5, 7,8,11,15–18,23; 16:1,3,5,6,12,16,18,20; 17:2,5,9,16,18,19; 18:12,14,16,18,20,21; 19:1,3–5,8,9,12; 20:4,8,13,14,18–20; 21:4,6,7,12,13,16–19,22,23; 22:1,2,4, 7,14–16,18,19,21,24,25,30; 23:4,5,13; 24:4,5,8,9,11,13,15,18,22; 25:1,7,9,11, 12,17,19; 26:6,7,9,10,12,15–17; 27:1–4, 6,8,10–12,26; 28:1,7–9,12,14,15,20,21, 24,29,36,47,48,51,58–60,63; 29:1,2, 5,8,9,13,14,16–20,22,25,27,29; 30:3, 6–8,12,13,15,16,18–20; 31:1–5,7, 9–14,16,19–30; 32:44–47,49,51,52; 33:1,9; 34:1–3,6,8,9; **Josh.** 1:2,6,8,10, 11,13–16,18; 2:1–4,9,10,13,14,18, 20,21,23,24; 3:3,4,6,8–10,14,17; 4:1,3, 10,14,16,17,20–24; 5:1–3,6,7,9,10; 6:2–7, 10–12,14–18,20–23,25,26; 7:2,3,7,9,11, 13,15–18,20,24,25; 8:1,4,6–8,10,12,13, 17,19,21–24,26–29,31–34; 9:3,9,10,12, 14,20,22,24,26; 10:1,4,12,19,21–25,28, 30,32,33,35,37,39–42; 11:6,9–17, 19–21,23; 12:1; 13:7,13,21,22; 14:1, 5–8,10–13; 15:13,14,16,17,19,63; 16:6,10; 17:4,11–14,18; 18:1–6,8,10,20; 19:14,47,49–51; 20:2,4,5,7,8; 21:3,8, 9,11–18,21–25,27–32,34–39,43,44; 22:2,3,5,11,13,17,19,21,24–28,30–33; 23:3–6,11,13,15,16; 24:1,3–12,14–24, 26–28,30–33; **Judg.** 1:2,4–6,8,10,12,13, 15,17–21,24,25,27–31,33,34; 2:1,3,4,6, 7,9–14,20,22,23; 3:1,4,6–10,12–18,21, 24–26,28,29,31; 4:3,4,7,9,10,13–15,19, 21–24; 6:2,4,8–10,14–16,18,20,21, 25–28,30–32,34,36–38; 7:2,4,5,7,8, 14–16,19,22,24,25; 8:3,7–9,11,12,14–17, 19–21,25,27,31,34; 9:3,5,6,9,11,13, 15–18,20,24,25,27–31,36,41,43,45,48,49 ,53,56,57; 10:1–3,6,8–10,12,13,16; 11:1, 2,5,7,9,11,13,15,18,20–24,27,29,30,35,3 6,38,39; 12:2,4–9,11,13,14; 13:5,6,15,19, 23,24; 14:2,3,6,8,11,12,15,19; 15:1,6,8, 10,18–20; 16:5,9,13,14,17–19,21,23–26, 29,31; 17:3–5,12; 18:2,3,7,9,14,17,18, 20–22,24,27,28,30,31; 19:15,17,18, 22–25,29; 20:5,13,35,37,42–44,46; 21:10,12,20,22,23; **Ruth** 1:6; 2:9,11, 15,17–19,21; 3:2,4,14,16; 4:6,9–11, 13,15,16,18–22; **1 Sam.** 1:5,11,12, 14–17,19–23,25,27; 2:11,12,15,17–23, 28,29,31–33; 3:1,7,12,13,15,16,18; 4:3,4,6,8,14,18,19; 5:1–3,6,8–11; 6:3, 5–11,13–15,18,21; 7:1,3–6,11,12,14–17; 8:1,7,8,11,13,14,16,18,20,21; 9:3,6,8,12, 13,15–20,22–24,27; 10:1,2,8,14,16–21, 25; 11:3–6,11,15; 12:3,6–11,14–16,18, 20,22–24; 13:3,4,7,13–15,20; 14:12,23, 24,26–29,35,39,45,48; 15:1–4,7–9,11,13, 15,16,18,20,23–26,28,32,33,35; 16:3–6, 13,19,23; 17:1,9–11,15,18,20,22,24–26,

28,34,36,38–40,42–44,46,47,49–55,57; 18:3,4,6,9,11,16,17,19,20,22,23,25–27,29; 19:1,5,7,10–15,17,18,20; 20:1,2,8,9, 12,13,15,17,21,28,29,31–33,36,38–41; 21:2,4,5,9,12–15; 22:4,8–11,14,17,19, 21,23; 23:1,2,4,5,7,8,12,15,16,22,23; 24:2–7,9–11,15,16,18,19,21; 25:2,4,8, 10,11,13,14,20,21,23–25,29–31,34,35, 37–39,43,44; 26:2,5,8,11,12,15–17,19, 20,23; 27:6,9; 28:1–5,8,9,11,12,15,17, 19,21; 29:1,4; 30:1,2,4,7,10,11,14,18, 20–23; 31:2,4,7–13; **2 Sam.** 1:1,14, 16,17; 2:4–8,21,29,30,32; 3:10–14, 17–19,21,25,26,30,32,35; 4:5,7–9,11,12; 5:2,3,7,8,17,19–21,24,25; 6:1–3,9–12, 15–18,20,21; 7:6,7,9,12,13,20,21,24, 27–29; 8:1–4,6,7,9,10,13,14; 9:7,10,11; 10:3,4,6,7,10,16–19; 11:1,6,11,15,16,18, 19,21,22,25; 12:1,4,6,8–12,14–16,24–31; 13:4,5,8–10,12–14,17,18,20–22,27,28, 30–32,34; 14:3,6,7,11,13,15,16,18–23, 26,29–32; 15:5–8,10,12,14,16,20,21, 23–25,29,31,34; 16:3,6,8–11,17; 17:2,6, 8,13–15,18,19,21–25; 18:1,2,5,10,12, 15–19,23,24,27–29; 19:4–6,10–12,14, 15,18,19,21,24,28–33,35–41,43; 20:3–6,12,21,22; 21:1,3,8,10–19,21,22; 22:1,20,28; 23:12,16,18,20,21; 24:1,2, 4,5,9,10,17,20,21,24; **1 Kgs.** 1:3,6,9, 10,12,14,15,27,29,33–39,41,43–45,47, 51; 2:1,3–5,9,16,17,20–23,26,27,29,30, 32,35,37,40,43,44,46; 3:1,3,6,7,9–11, 14,20,21,25–28; 4:7,15,21,27,34; 5:1, 3,7–9; 6:5,9,10,12–16,19,21,22, 27–32, 36; 7:1,2,6,13–15,18,21,23,24,27,37, 39–45,47–49,51; 8:1,3,4,6,10,11,14,16, 20,21,24,25,31–33,35,36,39,42,43,45,48, 49,53–55,58,63–66; 9:1,3,5,7,9–12, 15–19,24,25,27; 10:1–4,8,9,12,13,24,27; 11:2–4,10,11,13–15,19,20,23,24,27–29,31,34,35,37–40; 12:1,4,6,8–11,13–16,18, 20,21,24,25,29,31,32; 13:2,4,6,8,9,11,12, 21,25–31,33; 14:6,8,9,13–16,18,21,22, 26; 15:4,5,8,12,13,15,17–23,26,29,30,34; 16:2,3,7,11–13,16,18,19,22,24,26,31,33, 34; 17:4,18–20,23; 18:3,4,6,9,10,12,13, 17–21,23,26,30,33,35–38,40; 19:1–4,10, 14–16,19–21; 20:1,6,12,13,15,16,21,22, 24–29,31,36,39,41,42; 21:2–4,6,7,9,12, 13,15,19,22,23,25,27; 22:3,5,6,8,11,14, 17,19,20,24,26,27,31,32,34,37,38,52,53; **2 Kgs.** 1:6,7,10,12,14; 2:1,3,5,8,10,13, 14,16; 3:2,3,6,10,11,13,18,22–24,27; 4:1, 7,25,28,31,35,37; 5:3,6–8,20,24,26; 6:5, 6,12,15,17–21,24,28–30,32; 7:2,6,7,12, 16,17,19,20; 8:1,4–6,8,11–13,19,21, 28,29; 9:2,7,9–11,16,17,22,24–28,30, 34,36; 10:6–11,13,15–19,26–29,31, 33,35; 11:1,2,4,6,7,9,10,12–15,17–20; 12:5–12,14,15,18,20,21; 13:2,4,6,11,17, 19,21–23,25; 14:5–7,9,10,13,14,20–22, 24–28; 15:5,7,9,14,16,18,20,24,28,29, 35,37; 16:3,6,8–15,17,18; 17:6,7,11–17, 19,21,23–28,30–34,36,37,39,41; 18:4,6, 8,11,12,14–17,22,24,27,29,30,32–36; 19:1,2,4,6,8,11,12,14–18,22,25,27; 20:2, 3,5,6,9,11,13,15,20; 21:3,4,6–9,11,13–16, 21–24,26; 22:3–6,8,9,11–13,15,16,18–20; 23:2–8,10–17,19–22,24,27,29,30,34,35; 24:2,4,12–17,20; 25:5–7,9–11,13–15, 18–25,27–29; **1 Chr.** 1:10–16,18,20–23, 32,34,46; 2:4,9–13,17,19–24,29,35–41, 44,46,48,49; 4:2,6,8,10–12,14,17,18,41, 43; 5:26; 6:4–15,32,55–60,64,65,67–81; 7:14,18,21,23,24,32; 8:1,7–13,32–34,36, 37; 9:38–40,42,43; 10:2,4,8–12,14; 11:2, 3,5,8,11,14,18,20,22,23; 12:15,18,31,38; 13:3,5–7,9,12–14; 14:8,11,12,15–17; 15:2–4,12,14–17,25–29; 16:1,2,24,33, 39,43; 17:5,6,8,10–12,18,19,22,25,27; 18:1–4,7–13; 19:3,4,7,8,11,16–19; 20:1–5,7; 21:1,2,5,7,8,12,16,20,21; 22:2,12,13,18,19; 23:1,2,26,32; 27:1,23; 28:1,7–9,11,16; 29:10,20,25; **2 Chr.** 1:10,11,15; 2:11,12,16,18; 3:1,3,5–8, 10,14,17; 4:2,3,6,7,10–16,19,20; 5:1,2,4,5,7,14; 6:3,5,10,11,15,16,23,24, 26,30,33,35,38,39; 7:1,2,5,7,8,10–12,14, 16,18,20,22; 8:1,2,4–6,11,14; 9:1–3,7,8, 11,12,23,27; 10:1,4,8–11,13–16,18; 11:1,4,6–11,14,16–22; 12:1,4,5,9,13,14; 13:3,9,11,13,15,19; 14:1,3–5,7,12,14; 15:2,8,9,12,16,18; 16:1,4–6,12; 17:5, 6,19; 18:4,5,7,10,13,16,18,19,23,25,30,

31,33; 19:10; 20:3,4,7,16,17,25,26,37; 21:3,4,7,9–11,13,16,17; 22:1,5–11; 23:1,2,7–14,17,20,21; 24:4–7,11–14,18, 20,22–25; 25:3–5,11,14,15,18–20,23, 24,28; 26:1,2,5,6,21,23; 27:3,9; 28:3, 6–8,13,14,18,19,21,23–25; 29:3–5,7, 15–20,22,23,25,34; 30:8,13,14,16,18,20, 21,27; 31:1,2,8,10,12; 32:3–5,11–15,18, 22,30; 33:3,6–9,11,12,15,16,25; 34:3–5, 7–11,14–17,19–21,23,24,26–33; 35:3, 17,20; 36:1,3,4,10,13,14,17,19,21,22; **Ezra** 1:1,3,5,7; 3:2,4,8,10,12; 4:2,4; 6:19; 7:10,27; 8:17,19,25,36; 9:3,9,12; 10:5; **Neh.** 1:4,7–9,11; 2:1,8,9,17,18,20; 3:1,3,6,11,13–15; 4:1,2,6,11,13–15,20; 5:5–8,10,12–14; 6:1,4,5,9,14,18; 7:2,5; 8:1,2,6,7,9; 9:5,6,8,9,11,12,14–17,19, 22,24,26,32,34,36; 10:29–31,35–39; 12:10,11,27,30,31; 13:2,3,5,8,17,18,22, 23,26,27; **Esth.** 1:4,10,11,15,17,18; 2:1,3,7,9–11,13,15,17,18,20; 3:1,3,6, 8,10,13; 4:1,4,7–9,11,12,16; 5:2,5,8–14; 6:1,4,9–11,13,14; 7:8,10; 8:1–7,11; 9:3, 7–10,12–23,25,27,29,31; **Job** 1:7,9,15, 17,20; 2:2,4,6,7,10–12; 3:1; 7:21; 13:9–11,25; 14:3; 27:5,11; 28:23; 32:1,3,4,6; 35:4; 38:1; 40:1,3,6; 41:34; 42:1,7,9–12,16; **Ps.** 2:3,11; 3:7; 9:12; 12:4; 13:1; 14:2; 15:4; 16:4,7; 17:15; 25:5,22; 26:6; 27:2,4,8; 28:9; 29:5,11; 31:5,7,23; 33:13,22; 34:1,4,9,18; 35:1; 37:28; 47:4; 51:18; 53:2; 55:23; 58:11; 59:17; 60:[title](2); 67:7; 69:33; 72:19; 78:5,42,53,56,68; 79:1,2,7; 80:2; 83:12; 84:3; 92:6; 94:23; 98:3; 100:2; 101:5; 102:14,15,17,22; 103:1,2,12,22; 104:1,35; 105:11,24,28,29,42,43; 106:7,8,20,26,33,34,36,37,40,44,46; 112:1; 113:1; 115:12; 116:1,8; 117:1; 119:8,9,135; 121:7; 123:1; 126:1,4; 127:5; 129:8; 130:8; 132:1; 133:3; 134:1,2; 135:1,19,20; 136:8,9; 137:1,4,6,9; 138:2; 140:13; 142:7; 144:10; 145:15,16,19,20; 146:1,6,9; 147:11,12; 148:1,5,7,13; **Prov.** 1:19,23; 2:17; 3:7,9,12; 5:22; 6:22,31; 16:33; 22:23; 23:1,6,11; 24:21; 25:8; 26:19; 27:22; 30:11; **Eccl.** 1:13,14; 2:3,10, 17,18,20,24; 3:10,11,15,17; 4:1–5,8, 10,15; 5:4,6,7,19,20; 7:7,13–15,18,21, 26,29; 8:8,9,15–17; 9:1,7,11,12,14,15; 10:19,20; 11:5–8; 12:1,9,13,14; **Song** 1:6,8; 2:7,14; 3:1,3–5; 5:3,7,8; 7:12; 8:4,7,11,12; **Isa.** 1:4,7; 2:20; 3:18; 4:4; 5:5,12,24; 6:1,5,8,12; 7:6,12,13,17,20; 8:2,4,6,7,12,13; 9:4,7,11–13,17,21; 10:2,12,15; 11:9,11,13–15; 13:17,19; 14:1; 15:8; 18:5; 19:4,13,14,17,21,22; 20:1,4; 21:4; 22:8–10; 23:17; 24:3; 26:21; 27:1,11; 28:4,9,19; 29:10,11,22,23; 30:11,20,22,23,26,30; 31:1,2; 33:18,19; 36:2,7,9,12–15,17–22; 37:1,2,4,6,8,12, 14,16–19,23,26,28; 38:3,5–8; 39:2,4; 40:13,14; 41:6,7,16,22; 42:9; 43:22; 44:20; 45:20; 47:14; 48:14; 49:6,21,25, 26; 50:1,4; 51:17,22; 52:10; 53:6,8; 55:10,11; 56:4,6; 57:11–13; 58:2; 59:19; 61:1; 62:6–9; 63:10,11; 64:5; 65:3,11,12, 18,20; 66:2,8,18–20; **Jer.** 1:7,9,16,17; 2:6,7,13,17,19,30,33,35,36; 3:1,7–9, 12–15,18,21,24; 4:12,17,22,23; 5:3,5,7, 14,19,22,24; 6:12,14,18,24,27; 7:2,3,5, 7,10,12,13,15,16,18,19,22–27,29,31; 8:1,7,10,11,17; 9:2,3,6,11–13,15,16,24; 10:1,18,21–23,25; 11:2–8,10,17,20,21; 12:4,7,10,14–17; 13:2,4–7,9–13,21,25; 14:12,16,17,19,22; 15:3,6,7,11; 16:3,5,7, 10,11,13–15,18,21; 17:4,13,22–24,27; 18:2,10,20,21,23; 19:2,4,5,7–9,11,12,15; 20:1–5,12,13,15; 21:1,2,4,6–8; 22:1,4,5, 9,10,12,16,26,27,30; 23:1–3,7,8,13,15, 16,18,21,22,24,25,27,32,33,36,38,39; 24:1,5,7,8,10; 25:4,6,8,9,11,13,15, 17–26,30,36; 26:6–8,10,15,19,21–24; 27:4–15,17,20,22; 28:2–4,6,10–12,14,15; 29:5–7,10–14,17,19,21,26,28,29,31; 30:2,3,9–11,14,21; 31:7,8,11,14,23,27, 32–34; 32:3–5,7–9,11–14,16,17,21–23, 28–31,33,35,39–42,44; 33:2,7,9,11,14, 20,22,24,26; 34:2,3,6,9–11,13–18,20–22; 35:2–4,14–18; 36:2–6,10,11,13,14, 16–18,20,21,24–29,31,32; 37:3–5,7,10, 13,15,18,21; 38:1,4–7,9–11,13,14,16, 19,23,27; 39:5–9,14,16; 40:1,2,4,7,9,11,

14–16; 41:2–4,6,9–13,16,18; 42:2–4, 6,9–12,16–18,20; 43:1,3,5,6,10–13; 44:2,4,5,9,11,12,14,15,17,20,21,23,25,30 ; 45:1,4,5; 46:13,27,28; 47:1,4; 48:38; 49:1,2,6,10,16,28,32,35,37,39; 50:3,4, 19,20,25,28,34,40,43; 51:2,9–12,24,25, 28,29,32,36,39,44,45,50,55,59–61,63; 52:3,8–11,13–15,17–19,24–27,31–33; **Lam.** 1:9,19; 2:1,2; 3:2; 4:11; 5:1; **Ezek.** 1:11,23,24; 2:1–4,7,8,10; 3:1,2,8–10, 17,19,21,27; 4:1,3–6,9,13,15; 5:2–4, 6,7,9–11,16; 6:5,9,14; 7:3,8,18,22,24,27; 8:3,7,9,12,14,16–18; 9:7–9; 10:3,6,7,16, 17,19,22; 11:1,7,9–11,13,17,18,20,22,25; 12:6,12,13,15,16,23,25; 13:10,14,15, 19–21,23; 14:4,5,9,22,23; 15:4,6–8; 16:2,4,5,15,18,20–22,25,26,29,30,32,33, 37,39,40,43,50,51,53,54,57,58,60–62; 17:3,4,7,9,12–14,16,17,21; 18:2,6,11, 13–15,19,21,27,30,31; 20:1,3,4,8,11–13, 15–24,26–28,34,35,37–43; 21:11,29,30; 22:2,8,11,12,14,15,19–21,29; 23:8,10, 11,17–19,21,22,27,34–39,45–47; 24:2, 8,13,16,21,25,27; 25:5,7,9,14,16,17; 26:4,11,16,19; 27:5,26; 28:6,24–26; 29:4,5,10,12–14,18–20; 30:9–12,14, 15,18,21–26; 31:4,14–16; 32:3,5,7,12, 13,15,16,18,20,27,31,32; 33:2–7,20,22, 24,26,28,29,31,32; 34:2–4,7,8,10–12, 14,16,18,21,23,26,27; 35:5,7,8,10,12; 36:3,5,7,11,12,17,19,20,23–27,29–31,33, 37; 37:12–14,17,19,21–24,26,28; 38:4,6, 16,17; 39:7,10–12,14,15,21,24–29; 40:1,3–6,8,9,11,13,14,28,32,38,42,47; 41:1,4,13; 42:15,18; 43:3,7–11,17, 20–22,24,26,27; 44:1,3–5,7,11,12,14–16, 19,20,23,24; 45:1,4,8,17,18,20; 46:2, 12–15,18,20,24; 47:13,14,17–19,21,22; 48:20; **Dan.** 1:2,9,10,12,13,15,16; 2:3; 8:4,7,15,16,19,27; 9:3,11–13,15; 10:1,5,7–9,11,12,14,21; 12:7; **Hos.** 1:3–8; 2:4,6,7,9,10,13,15,17,20–23; 3:1,5; 4:10,19; 5:4,6,13; 6:3; 7:7; 8:14; 9:12; 10:3,6,12; 12:3,13; **Joel** 2:19, 20,23,25,26,28,29; 3:1,2,7,8,12,18; **Amos** 1:3,13; 2:4,7,9,10,12; 3:1,2; 4:2,7,9,11; 5:1,6,11,18,26,27; 6:8,14; 7:2,4,10; 8:11,12; 9:1,3,4,7–9,11,12,14; **Obad.** 1:14,17,19–21; **Jon.** 1:5,9,15–17; 2:7,10; 3:2,10; 4:3,7; **Mic.** 3:1,3–5,9; 4:7; 5:1,6; 6:1,2,4,5,16; 7:2; **Nah.** 2:2; **Hab.** 1:4,6; 2:14; **Zeph.** 1:3–6,12,13; 2:3,8, 11,13; 3:7,19,20; **Hag.** 1:14; 2:3,5–7, 11,17,21; **Zech.** 1:6,11–13,17–19,21; 2:2,6,8,9,12; 3:1,4,7–9; 4:7,10; 5:4,8–10; 6:8,12,13; 7:2,7,12; 8:7–10,12–15,17, 21,22; 10:3,6; 11:4,6–14; 12:2–4,6,7, 9,10; 13:2,7,9; 14:2,12,16,18,19; **Mal.** 1:2,3,6,12,13; 2:2–4,9,13; 3:2,3,8–12,17; 4:1,4–6.

854. אֵת *'ēṯ* **prep.**
(with, against, near, among)
Gen. 4:1; 5:22,24; 6:9,13,18,19; 7:7,13,23; 8:1,8,16–18; 9:8–12; 11:31; 12:4; 13:5; 14:2,5,8,9,17,24; 15:18; 17:3,4,19,21–23,27; 19:24,33; 20:16; 21:18,20; 22:3; 23:8,20; 24:32,40,49,55; 25:10; 26:10,24,27,31; 27:15,30; 28:4; 30:29,33; 31:25; 32:7(8); 33:15; 34:5,6, 8–10,16,21–23; 35:13–15; 37:2; 38:1; 39:2,3,6,8,21,23; 40:4,7,14; 41:12; 42:4, 7,13,16,24,30,32,33; 43:3–5,8,16,32,34; 44:9,10,23,26,28,30,34; 45:1,15; 46:6, 7,15; 47:22; 49:30; 50:7,13,14; **Ex.** 1:1,7; 2:21,24; 5:20; 6:4; 10:11; 11:2; 12:38,48; 13:19; 17:5; 18:22; 20:23; 25:2,3,22,39; 27:21; 28:1,41; 29:21,28; 30:16; 31:6,18; 33:21; 34:27,29,32–35; 35:5,23,24; 38:23; 40:3; **Lev.** 1:12; 6:4(5:23),10(3); 7:34,36; 8:2,7,30; 10:4,9,14,15; 15:3; 16:5,15,16; 18:22; 19:13,20,33,34; 20:10–13,18,20; 24:8; 25:15,36,44; 26:9,39,44; 27:24; **Num.** 1:4,5; 3:1,9, 49,50; 5:13,19; 7:5,84,89; 8:11,26; 9:14; 10:29; 11:17,31; 13:17; 14:9; 15:14,16; 16:10,35; 17:2(17); 18:1,2,7,11,19,26,28; 20:13; 22:20,40; 23:13,17; 25:11,14; 26:3,10; 27:21; 31:2,3,28,51,52,54; 32:19,29,30,32; 35:6,8; **Deut.** 1:22,30; 2:6,8; 3:4; 5:3,24(21); 8:3; 10:21; 11:2; 12:12; 15:3; 17:12; 18:3; 19:5; 28:8; 29:1(28:69),14(13),15(14),19(18); 31:7,16; **Josh.** 2:19; 3:3; 6:10,17,27;

8:5,11; 10:1,4,24; 11:18; 14:12; 15:18; 17:14; 22:9,15,30,32; 23:12; 24:8,32; **Judg.** 1:3,14,16,17,19,21; 2:1; 3:19; 4:11,13; 7:1,2,4,18,19; 8:1,4,7; 9:32, 33,35,48; 12:4; 13:19; 14:11; 16:15; 17:2,11; 19:2,4; 20:20; **Ruth** 1:10,18; 2:11,20,23; 3:2; 4:5; **1 Sam.** 2:13, 19,22,23; 6:11,15; 7:14,16; 8:10; 9:3,7; 12:2,7; 13:22; 14:17,20; 16:5,14; 17:9; 20:41; 21:1; 22:3,6,23; 23:23; 24:18(19); 25:15,29; 26:2,6; 28:1; 29:3,6,10; 30:4,9, 21,23; 31:9; **2 Sam.** 1:11; 3:12,13,16,20, 21,23,27,31; 6:2; 7:7,12; 10:19; 11:9,17; 12:17; 13:26,27; 14:19; 15:11,12,14,19, 22,24,27,30,33; 16:14,15,17,18,21; 17:2, 8,10,12,16,22,29; 18:1; 19:7(8),17(18), 26(27),31(32),33(34); 20:15; 21:12,15; 24:2,24; **1 Kgs.** 1:27,41,44; 2:16; 3:1,18; 4:34(5:14); 6:12,33; 7:14; 8:5,15; 9:25,26; 11:1,17,23,25; 12:6,8,10,21,24; 13:7,15, 16,18,19; 15:19; 16:24; 18:12,32; 20:1, 23; 21:8; 22:4,7,8,24,31; **2 Kgs.** 1:15; 2:10,16; 3:7,11,12,20,26; 4:3,5,13,28; 5:15,19,20; 6:3,4,16,32,33; 8:8,14,28,29; 9:15,27,32; 10:2,6,16; 11:3,8; 12:5(6), 7(8),8(9),15(16); 13:14,23; 15:19,25; 16:14; 17:15,26,35,38; 18:23,31; 19:9; 20:9; 22:4,7; 23:2,18; 25:6,25,28,30; **1 Chr.** 2:18,23; 16:16; 17:6,18; 20:5; 21:6; 29:8; **2 Chr.** 6:4,18; 10:6,8,10; 11:4; 16:3; 18:6,7,23,30; 22:5,12; 23:7; 24:24; 29:24,29; 30:22; 31:17; **Ezra** 8:19; 9:8; **Neh.** 6:16; 13:9,11,17; **Esth.** 2:9,20; 3:1; 7:7; 9:29; **Job** 2:7,10,13; 12:3; 14:5; 19:4; 26:4; 36:7; **Ps.** 12:2(3); 16:11; 21:6(7); 22:25(26); 24:5; 27:4; 34:3(4); 35:1; 38:10(11); 47:4(5); 66:20; 67:1; 74:9(10); 78:8; 105:9; 109:2,20,21; 118:23; 125:5; 127:5; 132:1; 137:7,8; 141:4; 143:2; **Prov.** 1:11,15; 2:1; 3:28, 29,32; 5:17; 7:1; 8:18,31; 11:2; 13:10, 20,21; 16:7,19; 17:24; 22:24; 23:1,11; 24:1; 25:9; 29:9; 30:7; **Eccl.** 2:12,14; **Song** 4:8; **Isa.** 14:20; 19:23; 21:10; 23:17; 28:15,18,22; 29:13,14; 30:8; 34:14; 36:8,16; 37:9; 38:7; 40:10,14; 41:4; 43:2,5; 44:24; 45:9; 49:4,25,26; 50:8; 51:4; 53:9,12; 54:10,15,17; 57:8,15; 59:12,21; 60:9; 62:11; 63:3,11; 65:23; 66:10,14,16; **Jer.** 1:8,19; 2:9,35; 3:1,9; 5:18; 6:3,11; 8:8; 9:2(1),8(9); 10:5; 11:1,10; 12:1,3,5; 13:25; 14:21; 15:14,20; 16:5,8; 18:1; 19:10; 20:11; 21:1,2,5; 23:15,28,30; 24:1; 25:12; 26:1,22,24; 27:1,18; 29:16,23; 30:1,11; 31:14,31–33; 32:1,5,9; 33:5,21; 34:1,3,8,12,13; 35:1; 36:1,22; 37:10,17; 38:25; 39:5; 40:1, 4–6,7; 41:1–3,7,11,13,16; 42:8,11; 43:6,12; 46:28; 49:14; 50:39; 51:53,59; 52:9,14,32,34; **Ezek.** 2:6; 3:3,22,24,27; 6:9; 8:14; 10:4; 14:22; 16:8,59,60,62; 17:13,16,20; 20:35,36,44; 21:12(17), 20(25); 22:11; 23:8,22,23,25,26,29,37; 26:20; 30:5,11; 31:4,16–18; 32:18,19, 21,24,25,27–30,32; 33:30; 34:3,30; 36:27; 37:26; 38:5,6,9,15,22; 39:4; 43:8; 47:22, 23; **Dan.** 1:19; 11:2; **Hos.** 1:7; 2:4(6), 23(25); 5:7; 7:5; 12:3; **Joel** 2:19,20; **Amos** 5:14; **Obad.** 1:1; **Jon.** 4:8; **Mic.** 1:12; 3:8; 5:7(6),15(14); 6:1; **Hab.** 2:13; 3:13; **Zeph.** 1:3,18; **Hag.** 1:13; 2:4,5,17; **Zech.** 1:6; 6:10; 7:9,12; 8:16; 10:9; 11:10; 14:17; **Mal.** 2:4–6; 3:16.

855. אֵת *'ēṯ* **masc. noun**
(plowshare, mattock)
1 Sam. 13:20,21; **Isa.** 2:4; **Joel** 3:10(4:10); **Mic.** 4:3.

856. אֶתְבַּעַל *'eṯba'al* **masc. proper noun**
(Ethbaal)
1 Kgs. 16:31.

857. אָתָה *'āṯāh,* אָתָא *'āṯā'* **verb**
(to come, to arrive)
Deut. 33:2,21; **Job** 3:25; 16:22; 30:14; 37:22; **Ps.** 68:31(32); **Prov.** 1:27; **Isa.** 21:12,14; 41:5,23,25; 44:7; 45:11; 56:9,12; **Jer.** 3:22; 12:9; **Mic.** 4:8.

858. אֲתָה *'aṯāh,* אֲתָא *'aṯā'* **Aram. verb**
(to come, to arrive, to bring; corr. to Hebr. 857)

Ezra 4:12; 5:3,16; **Dan.** 3:2,13,26; 5:2,3,13,23; 6:16(17),17(18),24(25); 7:13,22.

859. אַתָּה *'attāh* **2nd person sing. pron.**
(you [sing.])
Gen. 3:11,14,15,19; 4:7,11; 6:18,21; 7:1; 8:16; 9:7; 12:11,13; 13:14,15; 15:15; 16:13; 17:9; 20:7; 21:22,26; 22:12; 23:6,13; 24:23,44,47,60; 26:27,29; 27:18,21,24,32; 28:13; 29:4,14,15; 30:26,29; 31:6,43,44,52; 32:12(13), 17(18); 38:23; 39:9; 41:40; 42:9,14,16, 19,33,34; 43:8; 44:10,17,27; 45:8,10, 11,19; 49:3,8; 50:20; **Ex.** 2:14; 3:5,18; 4:16,25; 5:11,17; 7:2; 8:2(7:27); 9:2,30; 10:4,11,25; 11:8; 12:13,22,31; 13:4; 14:14,16; 16:8; 18:14,17–19,21; 19:4, 6,23,24; 20:10,19,22; 23:9; 24:1; 25:40; 27:20; 28:1,3; 30:23; 31:13; 32:22(23), 30(31); 33:1,3,5,12; 34:10,12 ; **Lev.** 10:9,14; 18:26; 20:24; 25:23; 26:12,34; **Num.** 1:3,50; 5:20; 11:15,17,21,29; 14:9,14,30,32,41; 15:39; 16:11,16,17, 41(17:6); 18:1–3,7,28,31; 20:8,14; 22:19,34; 27:13; 31:19,26; 32:6; 33:51, 55; 34:2; 35:10,33,34; **Deut.** 1:37,40; 2:4,18; 3:21,24; 4:4,5,12,14,22,26,33,35; 5:14,27(24),31(28); 6:1,2; 7:1,6,7,19; 9:1,2,5,6; 11:8,10,11,29,31; 12:1,2,7, 12,18,29; 13:6(7); 14:1,2,21,26; 15:6,20; 16:11,14; 18:9,14; 20:3; 21:9; 23:20(21); 24:11; 25:18; 26:11; 28:3,6,12,16,19, 21,36,43,44,52,63,64; 29:2,10,16; 30:2, 8,16,18,19; 31:7,13,23; 32:47,50; 33:29; **Josh.** 1:2,6,11,14; 2:12; 3:3,8; 5:13,15; 6:18; 7:10; 8:4,7; 9:7,8,22,23; 10:19,25; 13:1; 14:6,12; 17:15,17; 18:3,6; 22:2,18; 23:3,9; 24:13,15,22; **Judg.** 2:2; 4:9,22; 6:10,17,31; 7:10,18; 8:21,22; 9:10,12,14, 15,18,32,36; 10:13,15; 11:2,7,9,23,25, 27,35; 12:4,5; 13:3,11; 14:3,13; 15:12,18; 18:3,8,9,18; 21:22; **Ruth** 3:9,10,16; 4:6, 9,10; **1 Sam.** 7:3; 8:5,17; 9:27; 10:19; 12:14,20,25; 13:11; 14:40; 15:6,13,17; 16:1; 17:8,33,43,45,56,58; 19:3,11; 20:8,23,31; 21:1(2); 22:13,16,18,23; 23:17,21; 24:11(12),14(15),17(18), 18(19); 25:6,33; 26:14–16,25; 28:1,2,9, 12,19,22; 29:6,9; 30:13; **2 Sam.** 1:8,13; 2:5,20; 3:25; 5:2; 7:5,20,24,27–29; 9:2, 7,10; 11:10; 12:7,12; 13:4,13; 15:2,19,27; 16:8; 17:3,6,8; 18:13,20,22; 19:10(11), 12–14(13–15),29(30),33(34); 20:4,6,9, 17,19; 21:4; 22:29; **1 Kgs.** 1:13,17,20, 24,42; 2:5,9,15,22,26,44; 3:6,7; 5:3(17), 6(20),9(23); 6:12; 8:19,30,32,34,36, 39,43,53; 9:4,6; 11:22; 12:4,6,9,10; 13:14; 14:2,6,12; 17:24; 18:7,9,11, 14,17,18,21,25,36,37; 20:14,25,40; 21:6,7,19; 22:30; **2 Kgs.** 1:3,6; 3:17; 4:1,7,16,23; 6:22; 8:1; 9:11,25; 10:6,9,13; 14:10; 19:10,11,15,19; 20:1; **1 Chr.** 11:2; 15:12,13; 17:4,18,22,25–27; 28:3,9; 29:10,12,17; **2 Chr.** 1:8,9; 2:16(15); 6:9,21,23,25,27,30,33,41; 7:17,19; 10:6,9,10; 12:5; 13:8,11; 14:11(10); 15:7; 18:29; 19:6; 20:6,7,15; 21:15; 24:5,20; 25:8,19; 28:10,13; 29:8; 30:7; 32:10; 35:21; **Ezra** 8:28; 9:11,13,15; 10:10; **Neh.** 1:8; 2:2,4,17,19; 5:7–9,11,12; 6:6,8; 9:6–8,17,19,27,28,31,33; 13:17,18,21; **Esth.** 3:3; 4:14; 8:8; **Job** 1:10; 5:27; 8:5,6; 11:13,16; 12:2; 13:4; 15:4; 17:14; 19:21; 27:12; 32:6; 33:33; 34:32,33; **Ps.** 2:7; 3:3(4); 4:8(9); 5:4(5),12(13); 6:3(4); 10:14; 12:7(8); 16:2,5; 18:27(28),28(29); 22:3(4), 9(10),10(11),19(20); 23:4; 25:5,7; 31:3(4),4(5),14(15); 32:5,7; 38:15(16); 39:9(10); 40:5(6),9(10),11(12),17(18); 41:10(11); 43:2; 44:2(3),4(5); 50:17; 55:13(14),23(24); 56:8(9); 59:5(6),8(9); 60:10(12); 61:5(6); 63:1(2); 65:3(4); 68:9(10); 69:5(6),19(20),26(27); 70:5(6); 71:3,5–7; 74:13–17; 76:4(5),7(8); 77:14(15); 82:6,8; 83:18(19); 85:6(7); 86:2,5,10,15,17; 89:9–12(10–13), 17(18),26(27),38(39); 90:1,2; 91:9; 92:8(9); 93:2; 97:9; 99:4,8; 102:12(13) ,13(14),26(27),27(28); 109:21,27,28;

110:4; 115:15; 118:28; 119:4,12,68, 102,114,137,151; 132:8; 139:2,8,13; 140:6(7); 142:3(4),5(6); 143:10; 145:15; **Prov.** 22:19; 23:2,14,19; 24:24; 25:22; 26:4; 31:29; **Eccl.** 5:2(1); 7:22; 9:9,10; **Song** 6:4; **Isa.** 3:14; 7:3,16; 14:10,13,19; 25:1; 27:12; 33:1; 36:14; 37:10,11,16,20; 38:1,17; 41:8,9,16,23,24; 42:17; 43:1,10, 12,26; 44:8,17,21; 45:15; 48:4,6; 49:3; 51:9,10,12,16; 54:10,17; 57:3,4; 61:6; 63:16; 64:5(4),8(7); 65:11,13,14; **Jer.** 1:11,13,17; 2:20,27,31; 3:1,4,22; 4:30; 5:17; 7:8,14,16,23; 10:6; 11:14; 12:1–3,5; 13:21,23; 14:9,22; 15:6,15,19; 16:12,13; 17:14,16,17; 18:6,23; 20:6; 21:4; 22:2,6, 15,25; 23:2; 24:3; 25:29,30; 26:15; 27:9, 13,15; 28:15,16; 29:8,20,25; 30:10; 31:18; 32:3,17,25,36,43; 33:10; 34:3, 15,17; 35:6,7; 36:6,19,29; 37:13; 38:17, 18,21,23; 39:17; 40:10,16; 42:11,13,15, 16,20; 43:2; 44:2,3,7,8,21,25; 45:5; 46:27,28; 48:7; 49:12; 50:24; 51:20,62; **Lam.** 1:21; 3:42; 5:19; **Ezek.** 2:6,8; 3:5,19,21,25; 4:1,3,4,9; 5:1; 7:2; 8:6; 9:8; 11:11,13; 12:2–4,9; 13:11,17,20; 16:7, 33,45,48,52,55,58; 18:2; 19:1; 20:3, 29–32; 39; 21:6(11),7(12),14(19),19(24), 25(30),28(33); 22:2,24; 23:35; 24:19,25; 27:2,3; 28:2,3,9,12,14,15; 32:2,28; 33:7,9,10,12,30; 34:17,31; 35:4; 36:1,8,13; 37:3,16; 38:7,9,13,15,17; 39:1,4,17; 40:4; 43:10; **Dan.** 8:26; 9:23; 12:4,13; **Hos.** 1:9,10(2:1); 2:23(25); 4:6,15; 12:6(7); **Joel** 3:4(4:4); **Amos** 7:8,16,17; 8:2; 9:7; **Obad.** 1:2, 11,13; **Jon.** 1:8,14; 4:2,10; **Mic.** 4:8; 5:2(1); 6:14,15; **Nah.** 3:11; **Hab.** 1:12; 2:8,16; **Zeph.** 2:12(16); **Hag.** 1:4,9; 2:3; **Zech.** 1:12; 2:2(6); 3:7,8; 4:2,7; 5:2; 6:10; 7:6; 9:11; **Mal.** 1:5,12; 2:8,14; 3:1,6,8,9,12.

860. אָתוֹן *ʼāṯôn* **fem. noun**
(donkey)
Gen. 12:16; 32:15(16); 45:23; 49:11; **Num.** 22:21–23,25,27–30,32,33; **Judg.** 5:10; **1 Sam.** 9:3,5,20; 10:2,14,16; **2 Kgs.** 4:22,24; **1 Chr.** 27:30; **Job** 1:3,14; 42:12; **Zech.** 9:9.

861. אַתּוּן *ʼattûn* **Aram. masc. noun**
(furnace)
Dan. 3:6,11,15,17,19–23,26.

862. אַתּוּק *ʼattûq*, אַתִּיק *ʼattiyq* **masc. noun**
(gallery, porch)
Ezek. 41:15,16; 42:3,5.

863. A. אִתַּי *ʼittay* **masc. proper noun**
(Ittai: one of David's captains)
2 Sam. 15:19,21,22; 18:2,5,12.
B. אִתַּי *ʼittay* **masc. proper noun**
(Ittai: one of David's mighty men)
2 Sam. 23:29; **1 Chr.** 11:31.

864. אֵתָם *ʼēṯām* **proper noun**
(Etham)
Ex. 13:20; **Num.** 33:6–8.

865. אֶתְמוֹל *ʼeṯmôl*, אֶתְמוּל *ʼeṯmûl* **adv.**
(yesterday, formerly, recently)
1 Sam. 4:7(NASB, *t^emôl* [8543]); 10:11; 14:21; 19:7; **2 Sam.** 5:2; **Ps.** 90:4(NASB, *t^emôl* [8543]); **Isa.** 30:33; **Mic.** 2:8.

866. אֶתְנָה *ʼeṯnāh* **fem. noun**
(reward, hire [of a prostitute])
Hos. 2:12(14).

867. אֶתְנִי *ʼeṯniy* **masc. proper noun**
(Ethni)
1 Chr. 6:41(26).

868. אֶתְנַן *ʼeṯnan* **masc. noun**
(hire of a prostitute)
Deut. 23:18(19); **Isa.** 23:17,18; **Ezek.** 16:31,34,41; **Hos.** 9:1; **Mic.** 1:7.

869. אֶתְנָן *'eṯnān* **masc. proper noun**
(Ethnan)
1 Chr. 4:7.

870. אֲתַר *'aṯar* **Aram. masc. noun**
(place, site, in place of)
Ezra 5:15; 6:3,5,7; **Dan.** 2:35; 7:6,7.

871. I. אֲתָרִים *'aṯāriym* **masc. pl. noun**
(spies)
Num. 21:1(NASB, NIV, see II).
II. אֲתָרִים *'aṯāriym* **masc. proper noun**
(Atharim)
Num. 21:1(KJV, see I).

ב Beth

872. בִּאָה *bi'āh* **fem. noun**
(entranceway)
Ezek. 8:5.

873. בִּאִישׁ *bi'ysh* **Aram. adj.**
(wicked, evil)
Ezra 4:12.

874. בָּאַר *bā'ar* **verb**
(to declare, to expound)
Deut. 1:5; 27:8; **Hab.** 2:2.

875. בְּאֵר *b*^{e}*'ēr* **fem. noun**
(well, pit)
Gen. 14:10; 16:14; 21:19,25,30; 24:11,20; 25:11(NASB, NIV, *be'ēr lahay rō'iy* [883]); 26:15,18–22,25,32; 29:2,3,8,10; **Ex.** 2:15; **Num.** 20:17; 21:16–18,22; **2 Sam.** 17:18,19,21; **Ps.** 55:23(24); 69:15(16); **Prov.** 5:15; 23:27; **Song** 4:15; **Jer.** 6:7(KJV, NASB, [K^{e}] *bôr* [953]).

876. בְּאֵר *b*^{e}*'ēr* **proper noun**
(Beer)
Num. 21:16; **Judg.** 9:21.

877. בֹּאר *bō'r* **masc. noun**
(cistern, well)
2 Sam. 23:15(KJV, NIV, *bôr* [953]),16(KJV, NIV, *bôr* [953]),20(KJV, NIV, *bôr* [953]); **Jer.** 2:13(NIV, *bôr* [953]).

878. בְּאֵרָא *b*^{e}*'ērā'* **masc. proper noun**
(Beera)
1 Chr. 7:37.

879. בְּאֵר אֵלִים *b*^{e}*'ēr 'ēliym* **proper noun**
(Beer-elim)
Isa. 15:8.

880. בְּאֵרָה *b*^{e}*'ērāh* **masc. proper noun**
(Beerah)
1 Chr. 5:6.

881. בְּאֵרוֹת *'b*^{e}*'ērôṯ* **proper noun**
(Beeroth)
Deut. 10:6(KJV, NASB, *b*^{e}*'ērōt b*^{e}*nēy-ya'*^{a}*qān* [885]); **Josh.** 9:17; 18:25; **2 Sam.** 4:2; **Ezra** 2:25; **Neh.** 7:29.

882. A. בְּאֵרִי *b*^{e}*'ēriy* **masc. proper noun**
(Beeri: a Hittite)
Gen. 26:34.
B. בְּאֵרִי *b*^{e}*'ēriy* **masc. proper noun**
(Beeri: Hosea's father)
Hos. 1:1.

883. בְּאֵר לַחַי רֹאִי *b*^{e}*'ēr laḥay rō'iy* **proper noun**
(Beer-lahai-roi)
Gen. 16:14; 24:62; 25:11.

884. בְּאֵר שֶׁבַע *b*^{e}*'ēr šeḇa'* **proper noun**
(Beersheba)
Gen. 21:14,31–33; 22:19; 26:23,33; 28:10; 46:1,5; **Josh.** 15:28; 19:2; **Judg.** 20:1; **1 Sam.** 3:20; 8:2; **2 Sam.** 3:10; 17:11; 24:2,7,15; **1 Kgs.** 4:25(5:5); 19:3; **2 Kgs.** 12:1(2); 23:8; **1 Chr.** 4:28; 21:2; **2 Chr.** 19:4; 24:1; 30:5; **Neh.** 11:27,30; **Amos** 5:5; 8:14.

885. I. בְּאֵרֹת בְּנֵי־יַעֲקָן *b*^{e}*'ērōṯ b*^{e}*nēy ya'*^{a}*qān* **proper noun**
(Beeroth Bene-jaakan)
Deut. 10:6(KJV, see II; NIV, see III).
II. בְּאֵרֹת בְּנֵי־יַעֲקָן *b*^{e}*'ērōṯ b*^{e}*nēy ya'*^{a}*qān* **proper noun**

(Beeroth of the children of Jaakan; const. of b^e'ērōt [881]; pl. construct of *bēn* [1121]; *ya'aqān* [3292])
Deut. 10:6(NASB, see I; NIV, see III).

III. בְּאֵרֹת בְּנֵי־יַעֲקָן *b^e'ērōṯ b^enēy ya'aqān* **fem. noun**
(wells of the Jaakanites: pl. of b^e'ēr [875]; pl. const. of *bēn* [1121]; *ya'aqān* [3292])
Deut. 10:6(KJV, see I; NASB, see II).

886. בְּאֵרֹתִי *b^e'ērōṯiy* **masc. proper noun**
(Beerothite)
2 Sam. 4:2,3,5,9; 23:37.

887. בָּאַשׁ *bā'ash* **verb**
(to stink, to smell bad)
Gen. 34:30; **Ex.** 5:21; 7:18,21; 8:14(10); 16:20,24; **1 Sam.** 13:4; 27:12; **2 Sam.** 10:6; 16:21; **1 Chr.** 19:6; **Ps.** 38:5(6); **Prov.** 13:5; **Eccl.** 10:1; **Isa.** 50:2.

888. בְּאֵשׁ *b^e'ēš* **Aram. verb**
(to be displeased, to be distressed)
Dan. 6:14(15).

889. בְּאֹשׁ *b^e'ōš* **masc. noun**
(stench, foul odor)
Isa. 34:3; **Joel** 2:20; **Amos** 4:10.

890. בָּאְשָׁה *bo'šāh* **fem. noun**
(weeds, stinkweed)
Job 31:40.

891. בְּאֻשׁ *bā'uš* **masc. noun**
(worthless thing)
Isa. 5:2,4.

892. בָּבָה *bāḇāh* **fem. noun**
(the apple [pupil] of the eye)
Zech. 2:8(12).

893. בֵּבַי *bēḇay* **masc. proper noun**
(Bebai)
Ezra 2:11; 8:11; 10:28; **Neh.** 7:16; 10:15(16).

894. בָּבֶל *bāḇel* **proper noun**
(Babel or Babylon)
Gen. 10:10; 11:9; **2 Kgs.** 17:24,30; 20:12,14,17,18; 24:1,7,10–12,15–17,20; 25:1,6–8,11,13,20–24,27,28; **1 Chr.** 9:1; **2 Chr.** 32:31; 33:11; 36:6,7,10,18,20; **Ezra** 1:11; 2:1; 7:6,9; 8:1; **Neh.** 7:6; 13:6; **Esth.** 2:6; **Ps.** 87:4; 137:1,8; **Isa.** 13:1,19; 14:4,22; 21:9; 39:1,3,6,7; 43:14; 47:1; 48:14,20; **Jer.** 20:4–6; 21:2,4,7,10; 22:25; 24:1; 25:1,9,11,12; 27:6,8,9, 11–14,16–18,20,22; 28:2–4,6,11,14; 29:1,3,4,10,15,20–22,28; 32:2–5,28,36; 34:1–3,7,21; 35:11; 36:29; 37:1,17,19; 38:3,17,18,22,23; 39:1,3,5–7,9,11,13; 40:1,4,5,7,9,11; 41:2,18; 42:11; 43:3,10; 44:30; 46:2,13,26; 49:28,30; 50:1,2,8,9, 13,14,16–18,23,24,28,29,34,35,42,43,45, 46; 51:1,2,6–9,11,12,24,29–31,33–35, 37,41,42,44,47–49,53–56,58–61,64; 52:3,4,9–12,15,17,26,27,31,32,34; **Ezek.** 12:13; 17:12,16,20; 19:9; 21:19(24), 21(26); 23:15,17,23; 24:2; 26:7; 29:18,19; 30:10,24,25; 32:11; **Dan.** 1:1; **Mic.** 4:10; **Zech.** 2:7(11); 6:10.

895. בָּבֶל *bāḇel* **Aram. proper noun**
(Babel or Babylon; corr. to Hebr. 894)
Ezra 5:12–14,17; 6:1,5; 7:16; **Dan.** 2:12,14,18,24,48,49; 3:1,12,30; 4:6(3),29(26),30(27); 5:7; 7:1.

896. בָּבְלָי *bāḇ^{e}lāy* **Aram. masc. proper noun**
(Babylonian)
Ezra 4:9.

897. בַּג *bag* **masc. noun**
(spoil, booty)
Ezek. 25:7([Q^e] *baz* [957]).

898. בָּגַד *bāgaḏ* **verb**
(to act treacherously, to act deceitfully)
Ex. 21:8; **Judg.** 9:23; **1 Sam.** 14:33; **Job** 6:15; **Ps.** 25:3; 59:5(6); 73:15; 78:57;

119:158; **Prov.** 2:22; 11:3,6; 13:2,15; 21:18; 22:12; 23:28; 25:19; **Isa.** 21:2; 24:16; 33:1; 48:8; **Jer.** 3:8,11,20; 5:11; 9:2(1); 12:1,6; **Lam.** 1:2; **Hos.** 5:7; 6:7; **Hab.** 1:13; 2:5; **Mal.** 2:10,11,14–16.

899. I. בֶּגֶד *beged̲* **masc. noun**
(garment, clothes)
Gen. 24:53; 27:15,27; 28:20; 37:29; 38:14,19; 39:12,13,15,16,18; 41:42; **Ex.** 28:2–4; 29:5,21,29; 31:10; 35:19,21; 39:1,41; 40:13; **Lev.** 6:11(4),27(20); 8:2,30; 10:6; 11:25,28,32,40; 13:6,34, 45,47,49,51–53,56–59; 14:8,9,47,55; 15:5–8,10,11,13,17,21,22,27; 16:4,23,24, 26,28,32; 17:15; 19:19; 21:10; **Num.** 4:6–9,11–13; 8:7,21; 14:6; 15:38; 19:7,8, 10,19,21; 20:26,28; 31:20,24; **Deut.** 24:17; **Judg.** 8:26; 11:35; 14:12,13; 17:10; **1 Sam.** 19:13,24; 27:9; 28:8; **2 Sam.** 1:2,11; 3:31; 13:31; 14:2; 19:24(25); 20:12; **1 Kgs.** 1:1; 21:27; 22:10,30; **2 Kgs.** 2:12; 4:39; 5:5,7,8,22,23,26; 6:30; 7:8,15; 9:13; 11:14; 18:37; 19:1; 22:11,14,19; 25:29; **2 Chr.** 18:9,29; 23:13; 34:19,22,27; **Ezra** 9:3,5; **Neh.** 4:23(17); **Esth.** 4:1,4; **Job** 13:28; 22:6; 37:17; **Ps.** 22:18(19); 45:8(9); 102:26(27); 109:19; **Prov.** 6:27; 20:16; 25:20; 27:13; **Eccl.** 9:8; **Isa.** 36:22; 37:1; 50:9; 51:6,8; 52:1; 59:6,17; 61:10; 63:1–3; 64:6(5); **Jer.** 36:24; 41:5; 43:12; 52:33; **Ezek.** 16:16,18,39; 18:7,16; 23:26; 26:16; 27:20; 42:14; 44:17,19; **Joel** 2:13; **Amos** 2:8; **Hag.** 2:12; **Zech.** 3:3–5; 14:14.
II. בֶּגֶד *beged̲* **masc. noun**
(treachery, fraud)
Isa. 24:16; **Jer.** 12:1.

900. בֹּגְדוֹת *bōgᵉd̲ôt̲* **fem. pl. noun**
(treacherousness)
Zeph. 3:4.

901. בָּגוֹד *bāgôd̲* **adj.**
(treacherous, unfaithful)
Jer. 3:7,10.

902. A. בִּגְוַי *bigway* **proper noun**
(Bigvai: leader under Zerubbabel)
Ezra 2:2,14; 8:14; **Neh.** 7:7,19.
B. בִּגְוַי *bigway* **proper noun**
(Bigvai: a Jew)
Neh. 10:16(17).

903. בִּגְתָא *big̲tā'* **masc. proper noun**
(Bigtha)
Esth. 1:10.

904. בִּגְתָן *big̲tān,* בִּגְתָנָא *big̲tānā'* **masc. proper noun**
(Bigthan, Bigthana)
Esth. 2:21; 6:2.

905. I. בַּד *bad̲* **adj.; masc. noun**
(alone, by itself, piece, part)
Gen. 2:18; 21:28,29; 26:1; 30:40; 32:16(17),24(25); 42:38; 43:32; 44:20; 46:26; 47:26; **Ex.** 12:16,37; 18:14,18; 22:20,27; 24:2; 26:9; 30:34; 36:16; **Lev.** 9:17; 23:38; **Num.** 5:8; 6:21; 11:14,17; 16:49(17:14); 28:23,31; 29:6,11,16,19, 22,25,28,31,34,38,39; **Deut.** 1:9,12; 3:5; 4:35; 8:3; 18:8; 22:25; 29:1(28:69), 14(13); **Josh.** 11:13; 17:5; 22:29; **Judg.** 3:20; 6:37,39,40; 7:5; 8:26; 20:15,17; **1 Sam.** 7:3,4; 21:1(2); **2 Sam.** 10:8; 13:32,33; 17:2; 18:24–26; 20:21; **1 Kgs.** 4:23(5:13); 5:16(30); 8:39; 10:13,15; 11:29; 12:20; 14:13; 18:6,22; 19:10,14; 22:31; **2 Kgs.** 10:23; 17:18; 19:15,19; 21:16; **1 Chr.** 3:9; 19:9; **2 Chr.** 6:30; 9:12,14; 17:19; 18:30; 31:6; **Ezra** 1:6; 2:65; **Neh.** 7:67; 9:6; **Esth.** 1:16; 3:6; 4:11; **Job** 1:15–17,19; 9:8; 15:19; 18:13; 31:17; 41:12(4); **Ps.** 51:4(6); 71:16; 72:18; 83:18(19); 86:10; 136:4; 148:13; **Prov.** 5:17; 9:12; **Eccl.** 7:29; **Isa.** 2:11, 17; 5:8; 26:13; 37:16,20; 44:24; 49:21; 63:3; **Lam.** 3:28; **Ezek.** 14:16,18; **Dan.** 10:7,8; 11:4; **Zech.** 12:12–14.
II. בַּד *bad̲* **masc. noun**
(pole, plant stalk)
Ex. 25:13–15,27,28; 27:6,7; 30:4,5; 35:12,13,15,16; 37:4,5,14,15,27,28; 38:5–7; 39:35,39; 40:20; **Num.** 4:6,8,

11,14; **1 Kgs.** 8:7,8; **2 Chr.** 5:8,9; **Job** 17:16; **Ezek.** 17:6; 19:14; **Hos.** 11:6.

906. בַּד *bad̲* **masc. noun**
(linen)
Ex. 28:42; 39:28; **Lev.** 6:10(3); 16:4,23,32; **1 Sam.** 2:18; 22:18; **2 Sam.** 6:14; **1 Chr.** 15:27; **Ezek.** 9:2,3,11; 10:2,6,7; **Dan.** 10:5; 12:6,7.

907. בַּד *bad̲* **masc. noun**
(idle talk, boasting, lying)
Job 11:3; 41:12(4); **Isa.** 16:6; 44:25; **Jer.** 48:30; 50:36.

908. בָּדָא *bād̲ā'* **verb**
(to make something up, to devise)
1 Kgs. 12:33; **Neh.** 6:8.

909. בָּדַד *bād̲ad̲* **verb**
(to be isolated, to be alone, to be lonely)
Ps. 102:7(8); **Isa.** 14:31; **Hos.** 8:9.

910. בָּדָד *bād̲ād̲* **masc. noun**
(isolation, separation, aloneness)
Lev. 13:46; **Num.** 23:9; **Deut.** 32:12; 33:28; **Ps.** 4:8(9); **Isa.** 27:10; **Jer.** 15:17; 49:31; **Lam.** 1:1; 3:28; **Mic.** 7:14.

911. בְּדַד *b^e^d̲ad̲* **masc. proper noun**
(Bedad)
Gen. 36:35; **1 Chr.** 1:46.

912. בֵּדְיָה *bēd̲^e^yāh* **masc. proper noun**
(Bedeiah)
Ezra 10:35.

913. בְּדִיל *b^e^d̲iyl* **masc. noun**
(tin)
Num. 31:22; **Isa.** 1:25; **Ezek.** 22:18,20; 27:12; **Zech.** 4:10.

914. בָּדַל *bād̲al* **verb**
(to divide, to separate, to set apart)
Gen. 1:4,6,7,14,18; **Ex.** 26:33; **Lev.** 1:17; 5:8; 10:10; 11:47; 20:24–26; **Num.** 8:14; 16:9,21; **Deut.** 4:41; 10:8; 19:2,7; 29:21(20); **1 Kgs.** 8:53; **1 Chr.** 12:8; 23:13; 25:1; **2 Chr.** 25:10; **Ezra** 6:21; 8:24; 9:1; 10:8,11,16; **Neh.** 9:2; 10:28(29); 13:3; **Isa.** 56:3; 59:2; **Ezek.** 22:26; 39:14; 42:20.

915. בָּדָל *bād̲āl* **masc. noun**
(a piece)
Amos 3:12.

916. בְּדֹלַח *b^e^d̲ōlaḥ* **masc. noun**
(bdellium, aromatic resin)
Gen. 2:12; **Num.** 11:7.

917. A. בְּדָן *b^e^d̲ān* **masc. proper noun**
(Bedan: a judge)
1 Sam. 12:11(NIV, *bārāq* [1301]).
B. בְּדָן *b^e^d̲ān* **masc. proper noun**
(Bedan: a Manassite)
1 Chr. 7:17.

918. בָּדַק *bād̲aq* **verb**
(to restore, to repair)
2 Chr. 34:10.

919. בֶּדֶק *bed̲eq* **masc. noun**
(damage, breach)
2 Kgs. 12:5–8(6–9),12(13); 22:5; **Ezek.** 27:9,27.

920. בִּדְקַר *bid̲qar* **masc. proper noun**
(Bidkar)
2 Kgs. 9:25.

921. בְּדַר *b^e^d̲ar* **Aram. verb**
(to scatter)
Dan. 4:14(11).

922. בֹּהוּ *bōhû* **masc. noun**
(void, emptiness)
Gen. 1:2; **Isa.** 34:11; **Jer.** 4:23.

923. בַּהַט *bahaṭ* **masc. noun**
(porphyry stone, red stone)
Esth. 1:6.

924. בְּהִילוּ *b^{e}hiylû* **Aram. fem. noun**
(haste)
Ezra 4:23.

925. בָּהִיר *bāhiyr* **adj.**
(bright)
Job 37:21.

926. בָּהַל *bāhal* **verb**
(to tremble, to alarm, to terrify)
Gen. 45:3; **Ex.** 15:15; **Judg.** 20:41; **1 Sam.** 28:21; **2 Sam.** 4:1; **2 Chr.** 26:20; 32:18; 35:21; **Ezra** 4:4(KJV, NASB, [K^{e}] *bālah* [1089]); **Esth.** 2:9; 6:14; 8:14; **Job** 4:5; 21:6; 22:10; 23:15,16; **Ps.** 2:5; 6:2(3),3(4),10(11); 30:7(8); 48:5(6); 83:15(16),17(18); 90:7; 104:29; **Prov.** 20:21(NASB, [K^{e}] *bāḥal* [973]); 28:22; **Eccl.** 5:2(1); 7:9; 8:3; **Isa.** 13:8; 21:3; **Jer.** 51:32; **Ezek.** 7:27; 26:18; **Dan.** 11:44; **Zeph.** 1:18.

927. בְּהַל *b^{e}hal* **Aram. verb**
(to frighten, to terrify, to move in haste; corr. to Hebr. 926)
Dan. 2:25; 3:24; 4:5(2),19(16); 5:6,9,10; 6:19(20); 7:15,28.

928. בֶּהָלָה *behālāh* **fem. noun**
(terror, trouble)
Lev. 26:16; **Ps.** 78:33; **Isa.** 65:23; **Jer.** 15:8.

929. בְּהֵמָה *b^{e}hēmāh* **fem. noun, usually collective**
(animals, cattle)
Gen. 1:24–26; 2:20; 3:14; 6:7,20; 7:2,8,14,21,23; 8:1,17,20; 9:10; 34:23; 36:6; 47:18; **Ex.** 8:17(13),18(14); 9:9,10, 19,22,25; 11:5,7; 12:12,29; 13:2,12,15; 19:13; 20:10; 22:10(9),19(18); **Lev.** 1:2; 5:2; 7:21,25,26; 11:2,3,26,39,46; 18:23; 19:19; 20:15,16,25; 24:18,21; 25:7; 26:22; 27:9–11,26–28; **Num.** 3:13,41,45; 8:17; 18:15; 31:9,11,26,30,47; 32:26; 35:3; **Deut.** 2:35; 3:7; 4:17; 5:14; 7:14; 11:15; 13:15(16); 14:4,6; 20:14; 27:21; 28:4,11,26,51; 30:9; 32:24; **Josh.** 8:2,27; 11:14; 21:2; **Judg.** 20:48; **1 Sam.** 17:44; **1 Kgs.** 4:33(5:13); 18:5; **2 Kgs.** 3:9,17; **2 Chr.** 32:28; **Ezra** 1:4,6; **Neh.** 2:12,14; 9:37; 10:36(37); **Job** 12:7; 18:3; 35:11; **Ps.** 8:7(8); 36:6(7); 49:12(13),20(21); 50:10; 73:22; 104:14; 107:38; 135:8; 147:9; 148:10; **Prov.** 12:10; 30:30; **Eccl.** 3:18,19,21; **Isa.** 18:6; 30:6; 46:1; 63:14; **Jer.** 7:20,33; 9:10(9); 12:4; 15:3; 16:4; 19:7; 21:6; 27:5; 31:27; 32:43; 33:10,12; 34:20; 36:29; 50:3; 51:62; **Ezek.** 8:10; 14:13,17,19,21; 25:13; 29:8,11; 32:13; 36:11; 44:31; **Joel** 1:18,20; 2:22; **Jon.** 3:7,8; 4:11; **Mic.** 5:8(7); **Hab.** 2:17; **Zeph.** 1:3; **Hag.** 1:11; **Zech.** 2:4(8); 8:10; 14:15.

930. בְּהֵמוֹת *b^{e}hēmôṯ* **masc. noun**
(behemoth, very large animal)
Job 40:15.

931. בֹּהֶן *bōhen* **masc. noun**
(thumb, big toe)
Ex. 29:20; **Lev.** 8:23,24; 14:14,17,25,28; **Judg.** 1:6,7.

932. בֹּהַן *bōhan* **masc. proper noun**
(Bohan)
Josh. 15:6; 18:17.

933. בֹּהַק *bōhaq* **masc. noun**
(skin spot, freckle, harmless rash)
Lev. 13:39.

934. בַּהֶרֶת *bahereṯ* **fem. noun**
(bright spot [on the skin])
Lev. 13:2,4,19,23–26,28,38,39; 14:56.

935. בּוֹא *bô'* **verb**
(to come, to go, to bring)
Gen. 2:19,22; 4:3,4; 6:4,13,17–20; 7:1,7,9,13,15,16; 8:9,11; 10:19,30; 11:31;

12:5,11,14; 13:10,18; 14:5,7,13; 15:12, 15,17; 16:2,4,8; 18:11,19,21; 19:1,3,5, 8–10,22,23,31,33,34; 20:3,9,13; 22:9; 23:2,10,18; 24:1,30–32,41,42,62,63,67; 25:18,29; 26:10,27,32; 27:4,5,7,10,12, 14,18,25,30,31,33,35; 28:11; 29:6,9,13, 21,23,30; 30:3,4,11(NASB, NIV, [K^e] *b* [prep] and *gāḏ* [1409,A]),14,16,33,38; 31:18,24,33,39; 32:6(7),8(9),11(12), 13(14); 33:1,11,14,18; 34:5,7,20,25,27; 35:6,9,16,27; 37:2,10,14,19,23,25,28, 30,32; 38:2,8,9,16,18; 39:11,14,16,17; 40:6; 41:14,21,29,35,50,54,57; 42:5–7, 9,10,12,15,19–21,29,34,37; 43:2,9, 16–18,21,23–26,30; 44:14,30,32; 45:16–19,25; 46:1,6–8,26–28,31,32; 47:1,4,5,7,14,15,17,18; 48:2,5,7; 49:6,10; 50:10; **Ex.** 1:1,19; 2:10,16–18; 3:1,9,13, 18; 4:6; 5:1,15,23; 6:8,11; 7:10,23; 8:1(7:26),3(7:28),24(20); 9:1; 10:1,3, 4,26; 11:1; 12:23,25; 13:5,11; 14:16,17, 20,22,23,28; 15:17,19,23,27; 16:1,5, 22,35; 17:8,12; 18:5–7,12,15,16,19, 22,23,26; 19:1,2,4,7,9; 20:20,24; 21:3; 22:9(8),13(12),15(14),26(25); 23:19, 20,23,27; 24:3,18; 25:14; 26:11,33; 27:7; 28:29,30,35,43; 29:30; 30:20; 32:2,3,21; 33:8,9; 34:12,26,34,35; 35:5,10,21–25, 27,29; 36:3–6; 37:5; 38:7; 39:33; 40:4, 21,32,35; **Lev.** 2:2,8; 4:4,5,14,16,23,28, 32; 5:6–8,11,12,15,18; 6:6(5:25),21(14), 30(23); 7:29,30; 9:23; 10:9,15,18; 11:32, 34; 12:4,6; 13:2,9,16; 14:2,8,23,34–36, 42,44,46,48; 15:14,29; 16:2,3,12,15,17, 23,26–28; 17:4,5,9; 18:3; 19:21,23; 20:22; 21:11,23; 22:7; 23:10,14,15,17; 24:11; 25:2,22,25; 26:25,36,41; **Num.** 4:3,5,15,19,20,23,30,35,39,43,47; 5:15,22,24,27; 6:6,10,12,13; 7:3,89; 8:15,22,24; 10:9,21; 13:21–23,26,27; 14:3,8,16,24,30,31; 15:2,18,25; 16:14, 43(17:8); 17:8(23); 18:13; 19:7,14; 20:1,4–6,12,22,24; 21:1,7,23,27; 22:7, 9,14,16,20,36,38,39; 23:17; 25:6,8; 27:17,21; 31:12,14,21,23,24,54; 32:2, 6,9,17,19; 33:9,40; 34:2,8; **Deut.** 1:7,8, 19,20,22,24,31,37–39; 4:1,5,21,34,38; 6:10,18,23; 7:1,26; 8:1,7; 9:1,4,5,7,28; 10:11; 11:5,8,10,29,31; 12:5,6,9,11, 26,29; 13:2(3); 14:29; 16:6; 17:9,14; 18:6,9,22; 19:5; 20:19; 21:12,13; 22:13; 23:1–3(2–4),8(9),10(11),11(12),18(19),2 0(21),24(25),25(26); 24:10,13,15; 25:5; 26:1–3,9,10; 27:3; 28:2,6,15,19,21,45,63; 29:7(6),22(21),27(26); 30:1,5,16,18; 31:2,7,11,16,20,21,23; 32:17,44,52; 33:2,7,16; **Josh.** 1:11; 2:1–4,18,22,23; 3:1,8,15; 5:14; 6:1,11,19,22,23; 7:23; 8:11,19,29; 9:6,8,9,17; 10:9,13,19,20,27; 11:5,7,21; 13:1,5; 14:11; 15:18; 18:3,4, 6,9; 20:6; 21:45(43); 22:10,15; 23:1,2,7, 12,14,15; 24:6–8,11; **Judg.** 1:7,14; 2:1; 3:3,20,22,24,27; 4:20–22; 5:19,23,28; 6:4,5,11,18,19; 7:13,17,19,25; 8:4,15; 9:5,15,24,26,27,31,37,46,52,57; 11:7,12, 16,18,33,34; 12:9; 13:6,8–12,17; 14:5,18; 15:1,14; 16:1,2; 17:8,9; 18:2,3,7–10,13, 15,17,18,20,27; 19:3,10,14–17,21–23, 26,29; 20:4,10,26,34; 21:2,8,12,22; **Ruth** 1:2,19,22; 2:3,4,7,12,18; 3:4,7,14–17; 4:11,13; **1 Sam.** 1:19,22,24,25; 2:13–15, 27,31,34,36; 3:10; 4:3,5–7,12–14,16; 5:1,2,5,10; 6:14; 7:1,13; 8:4; 9:5–7, 12–16,22; 10:3,5,7–10,13,14,22,27; 11:4, 5,9,11; 12:8,12; 13:8,10,11; 14:20,25,26; 15:5,7,12,13,15,20; 16:2,4–6,11,12, 17,21; 17:12,18,20,22,34,43,45,52,54,57; 18:6,13,16,27; 19:7,16,18,22,23; 20:1,8, 9,19,21,27,29,37,38,40,41,42(21:1); 21:1(2),10(11),14(15),15(16); 22:5,9,11; 23:7,10,27; 24:3(4); 25:5,8,9,12,19,26, 27,33–36,40; 26:1,3–5,7,10,15; 27:8,9, 11; 28:4,8,21; 29:6,8,10; 30:1,3,9, 21,23,26; 31:4,7,8,12; **2 Sam.** 1:2,3,10; 2:4,23,24,29; 3:7,13,20,22–25,35; 4:4–8; 5:1–3,6,8,13,18,20,23,25; 6:6,9,16,17; 7:18; 8:5,7; 9:6,10; 10:2,14,16,17; 11:4,7, 10,11,22; 12:1,4,16,20,24; 13:5,6,10, 11,24,30,35,36; 14:3,10,15,23,29,31–33; 15:2,4,6,13,18,20,28,32,37; 16:5,14–16, 21,22; 17:2,6,12,14,17,18,20,24,25,27; 18:9,27,31; 19:3(4),5(6),7(8),8(9), 11(12),15(16),20(21),24(25),25(26), 30(31),41(42); 20:3,8,12,14,15,22;

23:13,16,19,23; 24:6–8,13,18,21; **1 Kgs.** 1:1,3,13–15,22,23,28,32,35,42,47,53; 2:13,19,28,30,40; 3:1,7,15,16,24; 4:28(5:8),34(5:14); 7:14,51; 8:3,6,31,41 ,42,65; 9:9,28; 10:1,2,7,10–12,14,22,25; 11:2,17,18; 12:1,3,12,21; 13:1,7,8,10–12, 14,16,21,22,25,29; 14:3–6,10,12,13, 17,28; 15:15,17; 16:10,18; 17:6,10,12,13, 18; 18:12,46; 19:3,4,9,15; 20:30,32,33, 39,43; 21:4,5,13,21,29; 22:15,25,27,30, 36,37; **2 Kgs.** 1:13; 2:4,15; 3:20,24; 4:1,4,7,10,11,20,25,27,32,33,36,37,39,42 ; 5:4–6,8,9,15,18,20,22,24,25; 6:4,14, 20,23,32; 7:4–6,8–10,12; 8:1,7,9,14; 9:2,5,6,11,17–20,30,31,34; 10:2,6–8, 12,17,21,23–25; 11:4,5,8,9,13,15,16, 18,19; 12:4(5),9(10),13(14),16(17); 13:20; 14:13,25; 15:14,19,29; 16:6,11,12; 17:24,28; 18:17,21,32,37; 19:1,3,5,23, 25,27,28,32,33; 20:1,14,17,20; 21:12; 22:4,9,16,20; 23:8,11,17,18,30,34; 24:10,11,16; 25:1,2,7,8,23,25,26; **1 Chr.** 2:21,55; 4:10,38,41; 5:9,26; 7:22,23; 9:25,28; 10:4,7,8,12; 11:2,3,5,18,19, 21,25; 12:1,16,17,19,22,23,31,38,40; 13:5,9,12; 14:9,14; 15:29; 16:1,29,33; 17:16; 18:5,7; 19:2,3,7,9,15,17; 20:1; 21:2,4,11,21; 22:4,19; 24:19; 27:1; **2 Chr.** 1:10,13; 2:16(15); 5:1,4,7; 6:22, 32; 7:2,8,11,22; 8:11,18; 9:1,6,10,12–14, 21,24; 10:1,3,12; 11:1,16; 12:3–5,11; 13:9,13; 14:9(8),11(10); 15:5,11,12,18; 16:1,7; 17:11; 18:14,24,29,34; 19:10; 20:1,2,4,9–12,22,24,25,28; 21:12; 22:1,7,9; 23:2,4,6–8,12,14,15,17,19,20; 24:6,9–11,14,17,23,24; 25:7,8,10,12, 14,23; 26:8,16,17; 27:2; 28:5,8,9,12, 13,15,17,20,27; 29:4,15–18,21,31,32; 30:1,5,8,11,15,25,27; 31:5,6,8,10,12,16; 32:1,2,4,21,23,26; 33:11,14; 34:9,14,16, 24,28; 35:22; 36:4,7,10,18; **Ezra** 2:2,68; 3:7,8; 7:8,9; 8:15,17,18,30,32,35; 9:11, 13; 10:8,14; **Neh.** 1:2,9; 2:7–11,15; 3:5; 4:8(2),11(5),12(6); 5:17; 6:10,11,17; 7:7; 8:1,2,15,16; 9:15,23,24,33; 10:29(30), 31(32),34–37(35–38),39(40); 11:1; 12:27; 13:1,6,7,12,15,16,18,19,21,22; **Esth.** 1:11,12,17,19; 2:12–15; 3:9; 4:2,4,8,9,11,16; 5:4,5,8,10,12,14; 6:1,4–6,8,14; 7:1; 8:1; 9:11,25; **Job** 1:6,7,14,16–19; 2:1,2,11; 3:6,7,24–26; 4:5; 5:21,26; 6:8,20; 9:32; 12:6; 13:16; 14:3,14; 15:21; 17:10; 19:12; 20:22; 21:17; 22:4,21; 23:3; 27:9; 28:20; 29:13; 30:26; 34:28; 37:8,9; 38:11,16,22; 41:13(5),16(8); 42:11; **Ps.** 5:7(8); 18:6(7); 22:31(32); 24:7,9; 26:4; 35:8; 36:11(12); 37:13,15; 40:7(8); 41:6(7); 42:2(3); 43:3,4; 44:17(18); 45:14(15), 15(16); 49:19(20); 50:3; 51:[title](1); 52:[title](1); 54:[title](1); 55:5(6); 63:9(10); 65:2(3); 66:11–13; 69:1(2), 2(3),27(28); 71:3,16,18; 73:17; 74:5; 78:29,54,71; 79:1,11; 86:9; 88:2(3); 90:12; 95:6,11; 96:8,13; 98:9; 100:2,4; 101:2; 102:1(2),13(14); 105:18,19, 23,31,34,40; 109:17,18; 118:19,20,26; 119:41,77,170; 121:1,8; 126:6; 132:3,7; 143:2; **Prov.** 1:26,27; 2:10,19; 3:25; 4:14; 6:3,11,15,29; 7:20,22; 10:24; 11:2,8,27; 13:12; 18:3,6,17; 21:27; 22:24; 23:10, 12,30; 24:25,34; 26:2; 27:10; 28:22; 31:14; **Eccl.** 1:4,5; 2:12,16; 3:22; 5:3(2),15(14),16(15); 6:4; 8:10; 9:14; 11:8,9; 12:1,14; **Song** 1:4; 2:4,8; 3:4; 4:8,16; 5:1; 8:2,11; **Isa.** 1:12,13,23; 2:10,19,21; 3:14; 5:19,26; 7:17,19,24,25; 10:3,28; 13:2,5,6,9,22; 14:2,9,31; 16:3, 12; 19:1,23; 20:1; 21:1,9; 22:15; 23:1; 24:10; 26:2,20; 27:6,11,13; 28:15; 30:8,13,27,29; 31:2; 32:10; 35:4,10; 36:6,17,22; 37:1,3,5,24,26,28,29,33,34; 38:1; 39:3,6; 40:10; 41:3,22,25; 42:9; 43:5,6,23; 44:7; 45:20,24; 46:11; 47:5, 9,11,13; 48:3,5,15; 49:12,18,22; 50:2; 51:11; 52:1; 56:1,7; 57:2; 58:7; 59:14,19,20; 60:1,4–6,9,11,13,17,20; 62:11; 63:1,4; 66:4,7,15,18,20,23; **Jer.** 1:15; 2:3,7,31; 3:14,18; 4:5,6,12,16,29; 5:12,15; 6:3,19,20,22,26; 7:2,10,32; 8:7, 14,16; 9:17(16),21(20),25(24); 10:9,22; 11:8,11,23; 12:12; 13:1,20; 14:3,18; 15:8,9; 16:5,8,14,19; 17:6,8,15,18–21, 24–27; 18:22; 19:3,6,14,15; 20:5,6;

21:13; 22:2,4,23; 23:5,7,8,12,17; 24:1; 25:9,13,31; 26:2,21,23; 27:3,7,11,12, 18,22; 28:3,4,9; 30:3; 31:8,9,12,27,31,38; 32:7,8,23,24,29,42; 33:5,11,14; 34:3,10; 35:2,4,11,17; 36:5,6,9,14,20,29,31; 37:4,14,16,19; 38:11,25,27; 39:1,3,7,16; 40:3,4,6,8,10,12,13; 41:1,5–7,17; 42:14, 15,17–19,22; 43:2,7,11; 44:2,8,12,14,28; 45:5; 46:13,18,20–22; 47:4,5; 48:8,12,16, 21,44; 49:2,4,5,8,9,14,32,36,37; 50:4,5, 26,27,31,41; 51:10,13,33,46–48,51–53, 56,60,61,64; 52:4,5,11,12; **Lam.** 1:4, 10,21,22; 3:13; 4:12,18; 5:4,9; **Ezek.** 1:4; 2:2; 3:4,11,15,24; 4:14; 5:17; 6:3; 7:2, 5–7,10,12,22,24–26; 8:3,7,9,10,14,16; 9:2; 10:2,3,6; 11:1,8,16,18,24; 12:13,16; 13:9; 14:1,4,7,17,22; 16:7,8,16,33; 17:3, 4,12,13,20; 19:4,9; 20:1,3,10,15,28,29, 35,37,38,42; 21:7(12),19(24),20(25), 25(30),27(32),29(34); 22:3,4; 23:17, 22,24,39,40,42,44; 24:14,16,24,26; 26:7,10; 27:26; 28:7; 29:8; 30:4,9,11; 32:9,11; 33:2–4,6,21,22,30,31,33; 34:13; 36:8,20–22,24; 37:5,9,10,12,21; 38:8,9, 11,13,15–18; 39:2,8,17; 40:1–4,6,17, 28,32,35,48; 41:1,3,6; 42:1,9,12,14; 43:2–5; 44:2–4,7,9,16,17,21,25,27; 46:2,8–10,19; 47:8,9,15,20; 48:1; **Dan.** 1:1–3,18; 2:2; 8:5,6,17; 9:12–14,23, 24,26; 10:3,12–14,20; 11:6–10,13,15–17, 21,24,29,30,40,41,45; **Hos.** 4:15; 6:3; 7:1; 9:4,7,10; 10:12; 11:9; 13:13,15; **Joel** 1:13,15; 2:1,9,31; 3:5(4:5),11(4:11), 13(4:13); **Amos** 4:1,2,4; 5:5,9,19; 6:1,14; 8:2,9,11; 9:13; **Obad.** 1:5,11,13; **Jon.** 1:3,8; 2:7(8); 3:4; **Mic.** 1:9,15; 3:6,11; 4:8,10; 5:5(4),6(5); 7:4,12; **Nah.** 3:14; **Hab.** 1:8,9; 2:3; 3:3,16; **Zeph.** 2:2; 3:20; **Hag.** 1:2,6,8,9,14; 2:7,16; **Zech.** 1:21(2:4); 2:10(14); 3:8; 5:4; 6:10,15; 8:8,10,20,22; 9:9; 10:10; 12:9; 13:9; 14:1,5,16,18,21; **Mal.** 1:13; 3:1,2,10; 4:1(3:19),5(3:23),6(3:24).

936. בּוּז *bûz* **verb**
(to despise, to hold in contempt)
Prov. 1:7; 6:30; 11:12; 13:13; 14:21; 23:9,22; 30:17; **Song** 8:1,7; **Isa.** 37:22 (KJV, NASB, *bāzāh* [959]); **Zech.** 4:10.

937. בּוּז *bûz* **masc. noun**
(contempt, shame)
Gen. 38:23; **Job** 12:5,21; 31:34; **Ps.** 31:18(19); 107:40; 119:22; 123:3,4; **Prov.** 12:8; 18:3.

938. A. בּוּז *bûz* **masc. proper noun**
(Buz: second son of Nahor)
Gen. 22:21; **Jer.** 25:23.
B. בּוּז *bûz* **masc. proper noun**
(Buz: a Gadite)
1 Chr. 5:14.

939. בּוּזָה *bûzāh* **fem. noun**
(contempt)
Neh. 4:4(3:36).

940. בּוּזִי *bûziy* **masc. proper noun**
(Buzite)
Job 32:2,6.

941. בּוּזִי *bûziy* **masc. proper noun**
(Buzi)
Ezek. 1:3.

942. בַּוַּי *bawway* **masc. proper noun**
(Bavvai)
Neh. 3:18(NIV, *binnûy* [1131]).

943. בּוּךְ *bûḵ* **verb**
(to be confused, to wander aimlessly)
Ex. 14:3; **Esth.** 3:15; **Joel** 1:18.

944. בּוּל *bûl* **masc. noun**
(food, produce; trunk of a tree)
Job 40:20; **Isa.** 44:19.

945. בּוּל *bûl* **masc. proper noun**
(Bul)
1 Kgs. 6:38(37).

946. בּוּנָה *bûnāh* **masc. proper noun**
(Bunah)
1 Chr. 2:25.

947. בּוּס *bûs* **verb**
(to trample down)
Ps. 44:5(6); 60:12(14); 108:13(14); **Prov.** 27:7; **Isa.** 14:19,25; 63:6,18; **Jer.** 12:10; **Ezek.** 16:6,22; **Zech.** 10:5.

948. בּוּץ *bûṣ* **masc. noun**
(fine linen)
1 Chr. 4:21; 15:27; **2 Chr.** 2:14(13); 3:14; 5:12; **Esth.** 1:6; 8:15; **Ezek.** 27:16.

949. בּוֹצֵץ *bôṣēṣ* **proper noun**
(Bozez)
1 Sam. 14:4.

950. בּוּקָה *bûqāh* **fem. noun**
(emptiness)
Nah. 2:10(11).

951. בּוֹקֵר *bôqēr* **masc. noun**
(herdsman, shepherd)
Amos 7:14.

952. בּוּר *bûr* **verb**
(to declare, to explain)
Eccl. 9:1.

953. בּוֹר *bôr* **masc. noun**
(pit, cistern, well)
Gen. 37:20,22,24,28,29; 40:15; 41:14; **Ex.** 12:29; 21:33,34; **Lev.** 11:36; **Deut.** 6:11; **1 Sam.** 13:6; 19:22; **2 Sam.** 3:26; 23:15(NASB, [K[e]] *bo'r* [877]),16(NASB, [K[e]] *bo'r* [877]),20(NASB, [K[e]] *bo'r* [877]); **2 Kgs.** 10:14; 18:31; **1 Chr.** 11:17,18,22; **2 Chr.** 26:10; **Neh.** 9:25; **Ps.** 7:15(16); 28:1; 30:3(4); 40:2(3); 88:4(5),6(7); 143:7; **Prov.** 1:12; 5:15; 28:17; **Eccl.** 12:6; **Isa.** 14:15,19; 24:22; 36:16; 38:18; 51:1; **Jer.** 2:13(KJV, NASB, *bō'r* [877]); 6:7(NIV, [Q[e]] *be'ēr* [875]); 37:16; 38:6,7,9–11,13; 41:7,9; **Lam.** 3:53,55; **Ezek.** 26:20; 31:14,16; 32:18,23–25,29,30; **Zech.** 9:11.

954. בּוֹשׁ *bôš* **verb**
(to put to shame, to be ashamed; KJV, see also *yāḇuš* [3001,I])
Gen. 2:25; **Ex.** 32:1; **Judg.** 3:25; 5:28; **2 Kgs.** 2:17; 8:11; 19:26; **Ezra** 8:22; 9:6; **Job** 6:20; 19:3; **Ps.** 6:10(11); 14:6; 22:5(6); 25:2,3,20; 31:1(2),17(18); 35:4,26; 37:19; 40:14(15); 44:7(8); 53:5(6); 69:6(7); 70:2(3); 71:1,13,24; 83:17(18); 86:17; 97:7; 109:28; 119:6,31,46,78,80,116; 127:5; 129:5; **Prov.** 10:5; 12:4; 14:35; 17:2; 19:26; 29:15; **Isa.** 1:29; 19:9; 20:5; 23:4; 24:23; 26:11; 29:22; 30:5; 37:27; 41:11; 42:17; 44:9,11; 45:16,17,24; 49:23; 50:7; 54:4; 65:13; 66:5; **Jer.** 2:36; 6:15; 8:9,12; 9:19(18); 12:13; 14:3,4; 15:9; 17:13,18; 20:11; 22:22; 31:19; 48:13,39; 49:23; 50:12; 51:47,51; **Ezek.** 16:52,63; 32:30; 36:32; **Hos.** 4:19; 10:6; 13:15; **Joel** 1:11; 2:26,27; **Mic.** 3:7; 7:16; **Zeph.** 3:11; **Zech.** 9:5; 10:5; 13:4.

955. בּוּשָׁה *bûšāh* **fem. noun**
(shame)
Ps. 89:45(46); **Ezek.** 7:18; **Obad.** 1:10; **Mic.** 7:10.

956. בִּית *biyt* **Aram. verb**
(to pass the night)
Dan. 6:18(19).

957. בַּז *baz* **masc. noun**
(that which is plundered, booty)
Num. 14:3,31; 31:32; **Deut.** 1:39; **2 Kgs.** 21:14; **Isa.** 8:1(KJV, NIV, *māhēr šālāl ḥāš baz* [4122,I]); 10:6; 33:23; 42:22; **Jer.** 2:14; 15:13; 17:3; 30:16; 49:32; **Ezek.** 7:21; 23:46; 25:7([K[e]] *bāg* [897]); 26:5; 29:19; 34:8,22,28; 36:4,5; 38:12,13.

958. בָּזָא *bāzā'* **verb**
(to divide, to cut through)
Isa. 18:2,7.

959. בָּזָה *bāzāh* **verb**
(to despise, to hold in contempt)
Gen. 25:34; **Num.** 15:31; **1 Sam.** 2:30; 10:27; 15:9(KJV, *n^emibzāh* [5240]); 17:42; **2 Sam.** 6:16; 12:9,10; **2 Kgs.** 19:21; **1 Chr.** 15:29; **2 Chr.** 36:16; **Neh.** 2:19; **Esth.** 1:17; 3:6; **Ps.** 15:4; 22:6(7),24(25); 51:17(19); 69:33(34); 73:20; 102:17(18); 119:141; **Prov.** 14:2; 15:20; 19:16; **Eccl.** 9:16; **Isa.** 37:22(NIV, *bûz* [936]); 49:7(KJV, NASB, *bāzōh* [960]); 53:3; **Jer.** 22:28; 49:15; **Ezek.** 16:59; 17:16,18,19; 22:8; **Dan.** 11:21; **Obad.** 1:2; **Mal.** 1:6,7,12; 2:9.

960. בָּזֹה *bāzōh* **adj.**
(despised)
Isa. 49:7(NIV, *bāzāh* [959]).

961. בִּזָּה *bizzāh* **fem. noun**
(plunder, loot)
2 Chr. 14:14(13); 25:13; 28:14; **Ezra** 9:7; **Neh.** 4:4(3:36); **Esth.** 9:10,15,16; **Dan.** 11:24,33.

962. בָּזַז *bāzaz* **verb**
(to plunder, to loot)
Gen. 34:27,29; **Num.** 31:9,32,53; **Deut.** 2:35; 3:7; 20:14; **Josh.** 8:2,27; 11:14; **1 Sam.** 14:36; **2 Kgs.** 7:16; **2 Chr.** 14:14(13); 20:25; 25:13; 28:8; **Esth.** 3:13; 8:11; **Ps.** 109:11; **Isa.** 10:2,6; 11:14; 17:14; 24:3; 33:23; 42:22,24; **Jer.** 20:5; 30:16; 50:37; **Ezek.** 26:12; 29:19; 38:12,13; 39:10; **Amos** 3:11; **Nah.** 2:9(10); **Zeph.** 2:9.

963. בִּזָּיוֹן *bizzāyôn* **masc. noun**
(contempt, disrespect)
Esth. 1:18.

964. בִּזְיוֹתְיָה *bizyôṯyāh* **proper noun**
(Biziothiah)
Josh. 15:28.

965. בָּזָק *bāzāq* **masc. noun**
(lightning, flash of lightning)
Ezek. 1:14.

966. בֶּזֶק *bezeq* **proper noun**
(Bezek)
Judg. 1:4,5; **1 Sam.** 11:8.

967. בָּזַר *bāzar* **verb**
(to scatter)
Ps. 68:30(31); **Dan.** 11:24.

968. בִּזְּתָא *bizz^eṯā'* **masc. proper noun**
(Biztha)
Esth. 1:10.

969. I. בָּחוֹן *bāḥôn* **masc. noun**
(assayer, tester)
Jer. 6:27(KJV, see II).
II. בָּחוֹן *bāḥôn* **masc. noun**
(fortification, tower)
Jer. 6:27(NASB, NIV, see I).

970. בָּחוּר *baḥûr* **masc. noun**
(young man)
Deut. 32:25; **Judg.** 14:10; 20:15(NASB, NIV, *bāḥar* [977]); **Ruth** 3:10; **1 Sam.** 8:16; 9:2; **2 Kgs.** 8:12; **2 Chr.** 36:17; **Ps.** 78:31,63; 89:19(NASB, *bāḥar* [977]); 148:12; **Prov.** 20:29; **Eccl.** 11:9; **Isa.** 9:17(16); 23:4; 31:8; 40:30; 62:5; **Jer.** 6:11; 9:21(20); 11:22; 15:8; 18:21; 31:13; 48:15; 49:26; 50:30; 51:3,22; **Lam.** 1:15, 18; 2:21; 5:13,14; **Ezek.** 9:6; 23:6,12,23; 30:17; **Joel** 2:28(3:1); **Amos** 2:11; 4:10; 8:13; **Zech.** 9:17.

971. בַּחוּן *baḥûn,* בַּחִין *baḥiyn* **masc. noun**
(seige tower)
Isa. 23:13.

972. בָּחִיר *bāḥiyr* **adj.**
(chosen)
2 Sam. 21:6; **1 Chr.** 16:13; **Ps.** 89:3(4); 105:6,43; 106:5,23; **Isa.** 42:1; 43:20; 45:4; 65:9,15,22.

973. בָּהַל *bāhal* **verb**
(to loathe, to despise, to gain by greed)
Prov. 20:21(KJV, NIV, [Q^{e}] *bāhal* [926]); **Zech.** 11:8.

974. בָּחַן *bāḥan* **verb**
(to be tested, to be examined)
Gen. 42:15,16; **1 Chr.** 29:17; **Job** 7:18; 12:11; 23:10; 34:3,36; **Ps.** 7:9(10); 11:4,5; 17:3; 26:2; 66:10; 81:7(8); 95:9; 139:23; **Prov.** 17:3; **Jer.** 6:27; 9:7(6); 11:20; 12:3; 17:10; 20:12; **Ezek.** 21:13(18); **Zech.** 13:9; **Mal.** 3:10,15.

975. בַּחַן *baḥan* **masc. noun**
(watchtower)
Isa. 32:14.

976. בֹּחַן *bōḥan* **masc. noun**
(a testing, an approving)
Isa. 28:16.

977. בָּחַר *bāḥar* **verb**
(to choose, to select, to be chosen)
Gen. 6:2; 13:11; **Ex.** 14:7; 17:9; 18:25; **Num.** 16:5,7; 17:5(20); **Deut.** 4:37; 7:6,7; 10:15; 12:5,11,14,18,21,26; 14:2, 23–25; 15:20; 16:2,6,7,11,15,16; 17:8, 10,15; 18:5,6; 21:5; 23:16(17); 26:2; 30:19; 31:11; **Josh.** 8:3; 9:27; 24:15,22; **Judg.** 5:8; 10:14; 20:15(KJV, *bāḥûr* [970]),16,34; **1 Sam.** 2:28; 8:18; 10:24; 12:13; 13:2; 16:8–10; 17:40; 20:30; 24:2(3); 26:2; **2 Sam.** 6:1,21; 10:9; 15:15; 16:18; 17:1; 19:38(39); 24:12; **1 Kgs.** 3:8; 8:16,44,48; 11:13,32,34,36; 12:21; 14:21; 18:23,25; **2 Kgs.** 21:7; 23:27; **1 Chr.** 15:2; 19:10; 21:10; 28:4–6,10; 29:1; **2 Chr.** 6:5,6,34,38; 7:12,16; 11:1; 12:13; 13:3,17; 25:5; 29:11; 33:7; **Neh.** 1:9; 9:7; **Job** 7:15; 9:14; 15:5; 29:25; 34:4,33; 36:21; **Ps.** 25:12; 33:12; 47:4(5); 65:4(5); 78:67,68,70; 84:10(11); 89:19(20)(KJV, NIV, *bāḥûr* [970]); 105:26; 119:30,173; 132:13; 135:4; **Prov.** 1:29; 3:31; 8:10,19; 10:20; 16:16; 21:3; 22:1; **Eccl.** 9:4(NASB, NIV, [Q^{e}] *ḥābar* [2266,I]); **Song** 5:15; **Isa.** 1:29; 7:15,16; 14:1; 40:20; 41:8,9,24; 43:10; 44:1,2; 48:10; 49:7; 56:4; 58:5,6; 65:12; 66:3,4; **Jer.** 8:3; 33:24; 49:19; 50:44; **Ezek.** 20:5; **Hag.** 2:23; **Zech.** 1:17; 2:12(16); 3:2.

978. בַּחֲרוּמִי *baḥ^{a}rûmiy* **masc. proper noun**
(Baharumite; see also *barḥumiy* [1273])
1 Chr. 11:33.

979. בְּחוּרוֹת *b^{e}ḥûrôṯ*, בְּחוּרִים *b^{e}ḥûriym* **fem. pl. or masc. pl. noun**
(youth, age of youth)
Eccl. 11:9; 12:1; **Num.** 11:28.

980. בַּחוּרִים *baḥûriym*, בַּחֻרִים *baḥuriym* **proper noun**
(Bahurim)
2 Sam. 3:16; 16:5; 17:18; 19:16(17); **1 Kgs.** 2:8.

981. בָּטָה *bāṭāh*, בָּטָא *bāṭā'* **verb**
(to speak thoughtlessly or rashly)
Lev. 5:4; **Ps.** 106:33; **Prov.** 12:18.

982. בָּטַח *bāṭaḥ* **verb**
(to trust, to have confidence in)
Deut. 28:52; **Judg.** 9:26; 18:7,10,27; 20:36; **2 Kgs.** 18:5,19–22,24,30; 19:10; **1 Chr.** 5:20; **2 Chr.** 32:10; **Job** 6:20; 11:18; 39:11; 40:23; **Ps.** 4:5(6); 9:10(11); 13:5(6); 21:7(8); 22:4(5),5(6),9(10); 25:2; 26:1; 27:3; 28:7; 31:6(7),14(15); 32:10; 33:21; 37:3,5; 40:3(4); 41:9(10); 44:6(7); 49:6(7); 52:7(9),8(10); 55:23(24); 56:3(4),4(5),11(12); 62:8(9),10(11); 78:22; 84:12(13); 86:2; 91:2; 112:7; 115:8–11; 118:8,9; 119:42; 125:1; 135:18; 143:8; 146:3; **Prov.** 3:5; 11:15, 28; 14:16; 16:20; 28:1,25,26; 29:25; 31:11; **Isa.** 12:2; 26:3,4; 30:12; 31:1; 32:9–11; 36:4–7,9,15; 37:10; 42:17;

47:10; 50:10; 59:4; **Jer.** 5:17; 7:4,8,14; 9:4(3); 12:5; 13:25; 17:5,7; 28:15; 29:31; 39:18; 46:25; 48:7; 49:4,11; **Ezek.** 16:15; 33:13; **Hos.** 10:13; **Amos** 6:1; **Mic.** 7:5; **Hab.** 2:18; **Zeph.** 3:2.

983. בֶּטַח *beṭaḥ* **masc. noun**
(safety, boldness, confidence)
Gen. 34:25; **Lev.** 25:18,19; 26:5; **Deut.** 12:10; 33:12,28; **Judg.** 8:11; 18:7; **1 Sam.** 12:11; **1 Kgs.** 4:25(5:5); **Job** 11:18; 24:23; **Ps.** 4:8(9); 16:9; 78:53; **Prov.** 1:33; 3:23,29; 10:9; **Isa.** 14:30; 32:17; 47:8; **Jer.** 23:6; 32:37; 33:16; 49:31; **Ezek.** 28:26; 30:9; 34:25,27,28; 38:8,11,14; 39:6,26; **Hos.** 2:18(20); **Mic.** 2:8; **Zeph.** 2:15; **Zech.** 14:11.

984. בֶּטַח *beṭaḥ* **proper noun**
(Betah)
2 Sam. 8:8(NIV, *ṭeḇaḥ*).

985. בִּטְחָה *biṭḥāh* **fem. noun**
(trust, confidence)
Isa. 30:15.

986. בִּטָּחוֹן *biṭṭāḥôn* **masc. noun**
(confidence, hope)
2 Kgs. 18:19; **Eccl.** 9:4; **Isa.** 36:4.

987. בַּטֻּחוֹת *baṭṭuḥôṯ* **fem. pl. noun**
(security, safety)
Job 12:6.

988. בָּטַל *bāṭal* **verb**
(to cease)
Eccl. 12:3.

989. בְּטֵל *b^e^ṭēl* **Aram. verb**
(to cease, to cause to cease; corr. to Hebr. 988)
Ezra 4:21,23,24; 5:5; 6:8.

990. בֶּטֶן *beṭen* **fem. noun**
(belly, womb, body)
Gen. 25:23,24; 30:2; 38:27; **Num.** 5:21,22,27; **Deut.** 7:13; 28:4,11,18,53; 30:9; **Judg.** 3:21,22; 13:5,7; 16:17; **1 Kgs.** 7:20; **Job** 1:21; 3:10,11; 10:19; 15:2,35; 19:17; 20:15,20,23; 31:15,18; 32:18,19; 38:29; 40:16; **Ps.** 17:14; 22:9(10),10(11); 31:9(10); 44:25(26); 58:3(4); 71:6; 127:3; 132:11; 139:13; **Prov.** 13:25; 18:8,20; 20:27,30; 22:18; 26:22; 31:2; **Eccl.** 5:15(14); 11:5; **Song** 7:2(3); **Isa.** 13:18; 44:2,24; 46:3; 48:8; 49:1,5,15; **Jer.** 1:5; **Ezek.** 3:3; **Hos.** 9:11,16; 12:3(4); **Jon.** 2:2(3); **Mic.** 6:7; **Hab.** 3:16.

991. בֶּטֶן *beṭen* **proper noun**
(Beten)
Josh. 19:25.

992. בָּטְנָה *boṭnāh* **masc. noun**
(pistachio nut)
Gen. 43:11.

993. בְּטֹנִים *b^e^ṭōniym* **proper noun**
(Betonim)
Josh. 13:26.

994. בִּי *biy* **particle interj.**
(excuse me, please)
Gen. 43:20; 44:18; **Ex.** 4:10,13; **Num.** 12:11; **Josh.** 7:8; **Judg.** 6:13,15; 13:8; **1 Sam.** 1:26; **1 Kgs.** 3:17,26.

995. בִּין *biyn* **verb**
(to understand, to have understanding, to be discerning)
Gen. 41:33,39; **Deut.** 1:13; 4:6; 32:7,10,29; **1 Sam.** 3:8; 16:18; **2 Sam.** 12:19; **1 Kgs.** 3:9,11,12,21; **1 Chr.** 15:22; 25:7,8; 27:32; 28:9; **2 Chr.** 11:23; 26:5; 34:12; 35:3(KJV, *m^e^ḇûniym* [4000]); **Ezra** 8:15,16; **Neh.** 8:2, 3,7–9,12; 10:28(29); 13:7; **Job** 6:24,30; 9:11; 11:11; 13:1; 14:21; 15:9; 18:2; 23:5,8,15; 26:14; 28:23; 30:20; 31:1; 32:8,9,12; 36:29; 37:14; 38:18,20; 42:3; **Ps.** 5:1(2); 19:12(13); 28:5; 32:9; 33:15; 37:10; 49:20(21); 50:22; 58:9(10); 73:17; 82:5; 92:6(7); 94:7,8; 107:43; 119:27,34, 73,95,100,104,125,130,144,169; 139:2;

Prov. 1:2,5,6; 2:5,9; 7:7; 8:5,9; 10:13; 14:6,8,15,33; 15:14; 16:21; 17:10,24,28; 18:15; 19:25; 20:24; 21:29(KJV, NASB, [Qe] *kûn* [3559]); 23:1; 24:12; 28:2,5,7, 11; 29:7,19; **Eccl.** 9:11; **Isa.** 1:3; 3:3; 5:21; 6:9,10; 10:13; 14:16; 28:9,19; 29:14,16; 32:4; 40:14,21; 43:10,18; 44:18; 52:15; 56:11; 57:1; **Jer.** 2:10; 4:22; 9:12(11),17(16); 23:20; 30:24; 49:7; **Dan.** 1:4,17; 8:5,16,17,23,27; 9:2,22,23; 10:1,11,12,14; 11:30,33,37; 12:8,10; **Hos.** 4:14; 14:9(10); **Mic.** 4:12.

996. בַּיִן *bayin* **subst. used as prep.**
(between, among, in the midst)
Gen. 1:4,6,7,14,18; 3:15; 9:12,13,15–17; 10:12; 13:3,7,8; 15:17; 16:5,14; 17:2,7, 10,11; 20:1; 23:15; 26:28; 30:36; 31:37, 44,48–51,53; 32:16(17); 42:23; 49:10,14; **Ex.** 8:23(19); 9:4; 11:7; 12:6; 13:9,16; 14:2,20; 16:1,12; 18:16; 22:11(10); 25:22; 26:33; 29:39,41; 30:8,18; 31:13,17; 40:7,30; **Lev.** 10:10; 11:47; 20:25; 23:5; 26:46; 27:12,14,33; **Num.** 7:89; 9:3,5,11; 11:33; 16:37(17:2),48(17:13); 21:13; 26:56; 28:4,8; 30:16(17); 31:27; 35:24; **Deut.** 1:1,16; 5:5; 6:8; 11:18; 14:1; 17:8; 25:1; 28:57; 33:12; **Josh.** 3:4; 8:9,11,12; 18:11; 22:25,27,28,34; 24:7; **Judg.** 4:5,17; 5:11,16,27; 9:23; 11:10,27; 13:25; 15:4; 16:25,31; **Ruth** 1:17; 2:15; **1 Sam.** 7:12,14; 14:4,42; 17:1,3,6; 20:3,23,42; 24:12(13),15(16); 26:13; **2 Sam.** 3:1,6; 14:6; 18:9,24; 19:35; 21:7; **1 Kgs.** 3:9; 5:12(26); 7:28,29,46; 14:30; 15:6,7,16, 19,32; 18:42; 22:1,34; **2 Kgs.** 2:11; 9:24; 11:17; 16:14; 25:4; **1 Chr.** 21:16; **2 Chr.** 4:17; 13:2; 14:11(10); 16:3; 18:33; 19:10; 23:16; **Neh.** 3:32; 5:18; **Esth.** 3:8; **Job** 9:33; 24:11; 30:7; 34:4,37; 41:6(40:30), 16(8); **Ps.** 68:13(14); 104:10,12; **Prov.** 6:19; 14:9; 18:18; 26:13; **Song** 1:13; 2:2,3; **Isa.** 2:4; 5:3; 22:11; 44:4; 59:2; **Jer.** 7:5; 25:16,27; 34:18,19; 39:4; 48:45; 52:7; **Lam.** 1:3,17; **Ezek.** 1:13; 4:3; 8:3,16; 10:2,6,7; 18:8; 19:2,11; 20:12,20; 22:26; 31:3,10,14; 34:17,20,22; 37:21; 40:7; 41:10,18; 42:20; 43:8; 44:23; 47:16,18; 48:22; **Dan.** 8:5,16,21; 11:45; **Hos.** 2:2(4); 13:15; **Joel** 2:17; **Obad.** 1:4; **Jon.** 4:11; **Mic.** 4:3; **Zech.** 1:8, 10,11; 3:7; 5:9; 6:1,13; 9:7; 11:14; 13:6; **Mal.** 2:14; 3:18.

997. בֵּין *bēyn* **Aram. prep.**
(between, among; corr. to Hebr. 996)
Dan. 7:5,8.

998. בִּינָה *biynāh* **fem. noun**
(understanding, insight)
Deut. 4:6; **1 Chr.** 12:32; 22:12; **2 Chr.** 2:12(11),13(12); **Job** 20:3; 28:12,20,28; 34:16; 38:4,36; 39:17,26; **Prov.** 1:2; 2:3; 3:5; 4:1,5,7; 7:4; 8:14; 9:6,10; 16:16; 23:4,23; 30:2; **Isa.** 11:2; 27:11; 29:14, 24; 33:19; **Jer.** 23:20; **Dan.** 1:20; 8:15; 9:22; 10:1.

999. בִּינָה *biynāh* **Aram. fem. noun**
(understanding, discerning; corr. to Hebr. 998)
Dan. 2:21.

1000. בֵּיצָה *bēyṣāh* **fem. noun**
(egg)
Deut. 22:6; **Job** 39:14; **Isa.** 10:14; 59:5.

1001. בִּירָה *biyrāh* **Aram. fem. noun**
(palace, citadel; corr. to Hebr. 1002)
Ezra 6:2.

1002. בִּירָה *biyrāh* **fem. noun**
(citadel, palace)
1 Chr. 29:1,19; **Neh.** 1:1; 2:8; 7:2; **Esth.** 1:2,5; 2:3,5,8; 3:15; 8:14; 9:6,11,12; **Dan.** 8:2.

1003. בִּירָנִיּוֹת *biyrāniyyôṯ* **fem. noun**
(fortress)
2 Chr. 17:12; 27:4.

1004. בַּיִת *bayiṯ* **masc. noun** (house, household, temple, palace) **Gen.** 6:14; 7:1; 12:1,15,17; 14:14; 15:2,3; 17:12,13,23,27; 18:19; 19:2–4, 10,11; 20:13,18; 24:2,7,23,27,28,31, 32,38,40; 27:15; 28:2,17,21,22; 29:13; 30:30; 31:14,30,37,41; 33:17; 34:19,26, 29,30; 35:2; 36:6; 38:11; 39:2,4,5,8,9,11, 14,16,20–23; 40:3,5,7,14; 41:10,40,51; 42:19,33; 43:16–19,24,26; 44:1,4,8,14; 45:2,8,11,16,18; 46:27,31; 47:12,14,24; 50:4,7,8,22; **Ex.** 1:1,21; 2:1; 3:22; 6:14; 7:23; 8:3(7:28),9(5),11(7),13(9),21(17), 24(20); 9:19,20; 10:6; 12:3,4,7,13,15,19, 22,23,27,29,30,46; 13:3,14; 16:31; 19:3; 20:2,17; 22:7(6),8(7); 23:19; 25:11,27; 26:29,33; 28:26; 30:4; 34:26; 36:34; 37:2,14,27; 38:5; 39:19; 40:38; **Lev.** 10:6; 14:34–39,41–49,51–53,55; 16:2, 6,11,12,15,17; 17:3,8,10; 18:9; 22:11,13, 18; 25:29–33; 27:14,15; **Num.** 1:2,4,18, 20,22,24,26,28,30,32,34,36,38,40,42,44, 45; 2:2,32,34; 3:15,20,24,30,35; 4:2,22, 29,34,38,40,42,46; 7:2; 12:7; 16:32; 17:2(17),3(18),6(21),8(23); 18:1,7,11, 13,31; 20:29; 22:18; 24:13; 25:14,15; 26:2; 30:3(4),10(11),16(17); 32:18; 34:14; **Deut.** 5:6,21(18); 6:7,9,11,12,22; 7:8,26; 8:12,14; 11:6,19,20; 12:7; 13:5(6), 10(11); 14:26; 15:16,20; 19:1; 20:5–8; 21:12,13; 22:2,8,21; 23:18(19); 24:1–3, 5,10; 25:9,10,14; 26:11,13; 28:30; **Josh.** 2:1,3,12,15,18,19; 6:17,22,24,25; 7:14, 18; 9:12,23; 17:17; 18:5; 20:6; 21:45(43); 22:14; 24:15,17; **Judg.** 1:22,23,35; 4:17; 6:8,15,27; 8:27,29,35; 9:1,4,5,6(NASB, NIV, *bēyṯ millô'* [1037,I]),16,18,19, 20(NASB, NIV, *bēyṯ millô'* [1037,I]),27,46; 10:9; 11:2,7,31,34; 12:1; 14:15,19; 16:21, 25–27,29–31; 17:4,5,8,12; 18:2,3,13–15, 18,19,22,25,26,31; 19:2,3,15,18,21–23, 26,27,29; 20:5,8; **Ruth** 1:8,9; 2:7; 4:11,12; **1 Sam.** 1:7,19,21,24; 2:11,27,28,30–33,35,36; 3:12–15; 5:2,5; 6:7,10; 7:1–3,17; 9:18,20; 10:25,26; 15:34; 17:25; 18:2,10; 19:9,11; 20:15,16; 21:15(16); 22:1,11,14–16,22; 23:18; 24:21(22),22(23); 25:1,6,17,28,35,36; 27:3; 28:24; 31:9,10; **2 Sam.** 1:12; 2:3,4, 7,10,11; 3:1,6,8,10,19,29; 4:5–7,11; 5:8, 9,11; 6:3–5,10–12,15,19–21; 7:1,2,5–7, 11,13,16,18,19,25–27,29; 9:1–5,9,12; 11:2,4,8–11,13,27; 12:8,10,11,15,17,20; 13:7,8,20; 14:8,9,24,31; 15:16,17,35; 16:2,3,5,8,21; 17:18,20,23; 19:5(6), 11(12),17(18),18(19),20(21),28(29),30(31),41(42); 20:3; 21:1,4; 23:5; 24:17; **1 Kgs.** 1:53; 2:24,27,31,33,34,36; 3:1,2, 17,18; 4:6,7; 5:3(17),5(19),9(23),11(25), 14(28),17(31),18(32); 6:1–10,12, 14–19,21,22,27,29,30,37,38; 7:1,2,8,9, 12,25,31,39,40,45,48,50,51; 8:6,10,11, 13,16–20,27,29,31,33,38,42–44,48,63,64; 9:1,3,7,8,10,15,24,25; 10:4,5,12,17,21; 11:18,20,28,38; 12:16,19–21,23,24,26, 27,31; 13:2,7,8,15,18,19,32,34; 14:4,8, 10,12–14,17,26–28; 15:15,18,27,29; 16:3,7,9,11,12,18,32; 17:15,17,23; 18:3,18,32; 20:6,31,43; 21:2,4,22,29; 22:17,27,39; **2 Kgs.** 4:2,32,35; 5:9,18,24; 6:30,32; 7:9,11; 8:1–3,5,18,27; 9:6–9,27; 10:3,5,10,11,12(NASB, NIV, *bēyṯ 'ēqeḏ* [1044]),14(NASB, NIV, *bēyṯ 'ēqeḏ* [1044]), 21,23,25–27,30; 11:3–7,10,11,13,15,16, 18–20; 12:4–14(5–15),16(17),18(19), 20(21)(NIV, *bēyṯ millō'* [1037,III]); 13:6; 14:10,14; 15:5,25,35; 16:8,14,18; 17:4, 21,29,32; 18:15,18,37; 19:1,2,14,30,37; 20:1,5,8,13,15,17; 21:4,5,7,13,18,23; 22:3–6,8,9; 23:2,6,7,11,12,19,24,27; 24:13; 25:9,13,16,27; **1 Chr.** 2:54(NASB, NIV, *'aṭrôṯ bēyṯ yô'āḇ* [5854]),55; 4:21, 38; 5:13,15,24; 6:10(5:36),31(16), 32(17),48(33); 7:2,4,7,9,23,40; 9:9,11, 13,19,23,26,27; 10:6,10; 12:28–30; 13:7, 13,14; 14:1; 15:1,25; 16:43; 17:1,4–6, 10,12,14,16,17,23–25,27; 21:17; 22:1,2, 5–8,10,11,14,19; 23:4,11,24,28,32; 24:4,6,19,30; 25:6; 26:6,12,13,15,20, 22,27; 28:2–4,6,10–13,20,21; 29:2–4,7, 8,16; **2 Chr.** 2:1(1:18),3–6(2–5),9(8), 12(11); 3:1,3–8,10–13,15; 4:4,11,16, 19,22; 5:1,7,13,14; 6:2,5,7–10,18,20,22, 24,29,32–34,38; 7:1–3,5,7,11,12,16,

20,21; 8:1,11,16; 9:3,4,11,16,20; 10:16, 19; 11:1,4; 12:9–11; 15:18; 16:2,10; 17:14; 18:16,26; 19:1,11; 20:5,9,28; 21:6, 7,13,17; 22:3,4,7–10,12; 23:3,5–7,9,10, 12,14,15,17–20; 24:4,5,7,8,12–14, 16,18,21,27; 25:5,19,24; 26:19,21; 27:3; 28:7,21,24; 29:3,5,15–18,20,25,31,35; 30:1,15; 31:10,11,13,16,17,21; 32:21; 33:4,5,7,15,20,24; 34:8–11,14,15,17,30; 35:2–5,8,12,20,21; 36:7,10,14,17–19,23; **Ezra** 1:2–5,7; 2:36,59,68; 3:8,9,11,12; 4:3; 6:22; 7:27; 8:17,25,29,30,33,36; 9:9; 10:1,6,9,16; **Neh.** 1:6; 2:3,8; 3:10,16,20, 21,23–25,28,29,31; 4:14(8),16(10); 5:3, 11,13; 6:10; 7:3,4,39,61; 8:16; 9:25; 10:32–39(33–40); 11:11,12,16,22; 12:29(NASB, NIV, *bēyṯ haggilgāh* [1019]), 37,40; 13:4,7–9,11,14; **Esth.** 1:8,9,22; 2:3,8,9,11,13,14,16; 4:13,14; 5:1,10; 6:4, 12; 7:8,9; 8:1,2,7; 9:4; **Job** 1:4,10,13,18, 19; 3:15; 4:19; 7:10; 8:14,15,17; 15:28; 17:13; 19:15; 20:19,28; 21:9,21,28; 22:18; 24:16; 27:18; 30:23; 38:20; 39:6; 42:11; **Ps.** 5:7(8); 23:6; 26:8; 27:4; 30:[title](1); 31:2(3); 36:8(9); 42:4(5); 45:10(11); 49:11(12),16(17); 50:9; 52:[title](1),8(10); 55:14(15); 59:[title] (1); 65:4(5); 66:13; 68:6(7),12(13); 69:9(10); 84:3(4),4(5),10(11); 92:13(14); 93:5; 98:3; 101:2,7; 104:17; 105:21; 112:3; 113:9; 114:1; 115:10,12; 116:19; 118:3,26; 119:54; 122:1,5,9; 127:1; 128:3; 132:3; 134:1; 135:2,19,20; **Prov.** 1:13; 2:18; 3:33; 5:8,10; 6:31; 7:6,8,11, 19,20,27; 8:2; 9:1,14; 11:29; 12:7; 14:1,11; 15:6,25,27; 17:1,13; 19:14; 21:9,12; 24:3,27; 25:17,24; 27:10,27; 30:26; 31:15,21,27; **Eccl.** 2:4,7; 4:14; 5:1(4:17); 7:2,4; 10:18; 12:3,5; **Song** 1:17; 2:4; 3:4; 8:2,7; **Isa.** 2:2,3,5,6; 3:6,7,14,20; 5:7–9; 6:4,11; 7:2,13,17; 8:14,17; 10:20,32; 13:16,21; 14:1,2,17, 18; 22:8,10,15,18,21–24; 23:1; 24:10; 29:22; 31:2; 32:13; 36:3,22; 37:1,2,14, 31,38; 38:1,20,22; 39:2,4,6; 42:7,22; 44:13; 46:3; 48:1; 56:5,7; 58:1,7; 60:7; 63:7; 64:11(10); 65:21; 66:1,20; **Jer.** 2:4,14,26; 3:18,20; 5:7,11,15,20,27; 6:12; 7:2,10,11,14,30; 9:26(25); 10:1; 11:10,15, 17; 12:6,7,14; 13:11; 16:5,8; 17:22,26; 18:2,3,6,22; 19:13,14; 20:1,2,6; 21:11,12; 22:1,4–6,13,14; 23:8,11,34; 26:2,6,7,9, 10,12,18; 27:16,18,21; 28:1,3,5,6; 29:5, 26,28; 31:27,31,33; 32:2,15,29,34; 33:4, 11,14,17; 34:13,15; 35:2–5,7,9,18; 36:3, 5,6,8,10,12,22; 37:4,15–18,20; 38:7,8, 11,14,17,22,26; 39:8,14; 41:5; 43:9, 12,13; 48:13; 51:51; 52:11,13,17,20,31; **Lam.** 1:20; 2:7; 5:2; **Ezek.** 1:27; 2:5,6,8; 3:1,4,5,7,9,17,24,26,27; 4:3–6; 5:4; 6:11; 7:15,24; 8:1,6,10–12,14,16,17; 9:3,6,7,9; 10:3,4,18,19; 11:1,3,5,15; 12:2,3,6,9,10, 24,25,27; 13:5,9; 14:4–7,11; 16:41; 17:2,12; 18:6,15,25,29–31; 20:5,13,27, 30,31,39,40,44; 22:18; 23:39,47; 24:3,21; 25:3,8,12; 26:12; 27:14; 28:24–26; 29:6, 16,21; 33:7,10,11,20,30; 34:30; 35:15; 36:10,17,21,22,32,37; 37:11,16; 38:6; 39:12,22,23,25,29; 40:4,5,7–9,43,45, 47,48; 41:5–10,13,14,17,19,26; 42:15; 43:4–7,10–12,21; 44:4–7,11,12,14,17, 22,30; 45:4–6,8,17,19,20; 46:24; 47:1; 48:21; **Dan.** 1:2; **Hos.** 1:4,6,7; 5:1,12,14; 6:10; 8:1; 9:4,8,15; 11:11,12(12:1); **Joel** 1:9,13,14,16; 2:9; 3:18(4:18); **Amos** 1:4,5(NASB, NIV, *bēyṯ ʿeḏen* [1040]); 2:8; 3:13,15; 5:1,3,4,6,11,19,25; 6:1,9–11,14; 7:9,10,13,16; 9:8,9; **Obad.** 1:17,18; **Mic.** 1:5,10,14; 2:2,7,9; 3:1,9,12; 4:1,2; 6:4,10,16; 7:6; **Nah.** 1:14; **Hab.** 2:9,10; 3:13; **Zeph.** 1:9,13; 2:7; **Hag.** 1:2,4,8, 9,14; 2:3,7,9; **Zech.** 1:16; 3:7; 4:9; 5:4, 11; 6:10; 7:2(NASB, NIV, *bēyṯ-ʾēl* [1008]), 3; 8:9,13,15,19; 9:8; 10:3,6; 11:13; 12:4,7,8,10,12,13; 13:1,6; 14:2,20,21; **Mal.** 3:10.

1005. בַּיִת *bayiṯ* **Aram. masc. noun**

(house, temple; corr. to Hebr. 1004)
Ezra 4:24; 5:2,3,8,9,11–17; 6:1,3–5,7,8, 11,12,15–17; 7:16,17,19,20,23,24; **Dan.** 2:5,17; 3:29; 4:4(1),30(27); 5:3,10,23; 6:10(11).

1006. בַּיִת *bayiṯ* **proper noun**
(Bajith)
Isa. 15:2(NASB, NIV, *bayiṯ* [1004]).

1007. בֵּית אָוֶן *bēyṯ 'āwen* **proper noun**
(Beth Aven; see also *'āwen* [206,B])
Josh. 7:2; 18:12; **1 Sam.** 13:5; 14:23; **Hos.** 4:15; 5:8; 10:5,8.

1008. A. בֵּית־אֵל *bēyṯ–'ēl* **proper noun**
(Bethel: a town in Ephraim)
Gen. 12:8; 13:3; 28:19; 31:13; 35:1,3,6, 8,15,16; **Josh.** 7:2; 8:9,12,17; 12:9,16; 16:1,2; 18:13,22; **Judg.** 1:22,23; 4:5; 20:18,26,31; 21:2,19; **1 Sam.** 7:16; 10:3; 13:2; **1 Kgs.** 12:29,32,33; 13:1,4,10, 11,32; **2 Kgs.** 2:2,3,23; 10:29; 17:28; 23:4,15,17,19; **1 Chr.** 7:28; **2 Chr.** 13:19; **Ezra** 2:28; **Neh.** 7:32; 11:31; **Jer.** 48:13; **Hos.** 10:15; 12:4(5); **Amos** 3:14; 4:4; 5:5,6; 7:10,13.
B. בֵּית־אֵל *bēyṯ–'ēl* **proper noun**
(Bethel: a town of Simeon)
1 Sam. 30:27.

1009. בֵּית אַרְבֵּאל *bēyṯ 'arbē'l* **proper noun**
(Beth Arbel)
Hos. 10:14.

1010. בֵּית בַּעַל מְעוֹן *bēyṯ ba'al m^e'ôn*, בֵּית מְעוֹן *bēyṯ m^e'ôn* **proper noun**
(Beth Baal Meon, Beth Meon)
Josh. 13:17; **Jer.** 48:23.

1011. בֵּית בִּרְאִי *bēyṯ bir'iy* **proper noun**
(Beth Biri)
1 Chr. 4:31.

1012. בֵּית בָּרָה *bēyṯ bārāh* **proper noun**
(Beth Barah)
Judg. 7:24.

1013. בֵּית־גָּדֵר *bēyṯ-gāḏēr* **proper noun**
(Beth Gader)
1 Chr. 2:51.

1014. בֵּית גָּמוּל *bēyṯ gāmûl* **proper noun**
(Beth Gamul)
Jer. 48:23.

1015. בֵּית דִּבְלָתַיִם *bēyṯ diḇlāṯayim* **proper noun**
(Beth Diblathaim)
Jer. 48:22.

1016. A. בֵּית־דָּגוֹן *bēyṯ-dāgôn* **proper noun**
(Beth Dagon: town of Judah)
Josh. 15:41.
B. בֵּית־דָּגוֹן *bēyṯ-dāgôn* **proper noun**
(Beth Dagon: town of Asher)
Josh. 19:27.

1017. בֵּית הָאֱלִי *bēyṯ hā'^eliy* **masc. proper noun**
(Bethelite)
1 Kgs. 16:34.

1018. בֵּית הָאֵצֶל *bēyṯ hā'ēṣel* **proper noun**
(Beth Ezel)
Mic. 1:11.

1019. בֵּית הַגִּלְגָּל *bēyṯ haggilgāl* **proper noun**
(Beth Gilgal)
Neh. 12:29(KJV, *bēyṯ* [1004] and *gilgāl* [1537,E]).

1020. בֵּית הַיְשִׁימוֹת *bēyṯ hay^ešiymôṯ* **proper noun**
(Beth Jeshimoth)
Num. 33:49; **Josh.** 12:3; 13:20; **Ezek.** 25:9.

1021. בֵּית הַכֶּרֶם *bēyṯ hakkerem* **proper noun**
(Beth Hakkerem)
Neh. 3:14; **Jer.** 6:1.

1022. בֵּית הַלַּחְמִי *bēyṯ hallaḥmiy* **masc. proper noun**
(Bethlehemite)
1 Sam. 16:1,18; 17:58; **2 Sam.** 21:19.

1023. בֵּית הַמֶּרְחָק *bēyṯ hammerḥāq* **phrase**
(outskirts, last house, place that is far off; see *bēyṯ* [1004] and *merḥāq* [4801])
2 Sam. 15:17.

1024. בֵּית מַרְכָּבוֹת *beyṯ markāḇôṯ*, בֵּית הַמַּרְכָּבוֹת *beyṯ hammarkāḇôṯ* **proper noun**
(Beth Marcaboth)
Josh. 19:5; **1 Chr.** 4:31.

1025. בֵּית הָעֵמֶק *bēyṯ hā'ēmeq* **proper noun**
(Beth Emek)
Josh. 19:27.

1026. בֵּית הָעֲרָבָה *bēyṯ hā'ᵃrāḇāh* **proper noun**
(Beth Arabah)
Josh. 15:6,61; 18:18(Sept.; KJV, NASB, [Hebr.] *'ᵃrāḇāh* [6160,II]),22.

1027. בֵּית הָרָם *bēyṯ hārām* **proper noun**
(Beth Haram)
Josh. 13:27.

1028. בֵּית הָרָן *bēyṯ hārān* **proper noun**
(Beth Haran)
Num. 32:36.

1029. בֵּית הַשִּׁטָּה *bēyṯ haššiṭṭah* **proper noun**
(Beth Shittah)
Judg. 7:22.

1030. בֵּית הַשִּׁמְשִׁי *bēyṯ haššimšiy* **masc. proper noun**
(Beth-shemite)
1 Sam. 6:14,18.

1031. בֵּית חָגְלָה *bēyṯ ḥoglāh* **proper noun**
(Beth Hoglah)
Josh. 15:6; 18:19,21.

1032. בֵּית חוֹרוֹן *bēyṯ ḥôrôn* **proper noun**
(Beth Horon)
Josh. 10:10,11; 16:3,5; 18:13,14; 21:22; **1 Sam.** 13:18; **1 Kgs.** 9:17; **1 Chr.** 6:68(53); 7:24; **2 Chr.** 8:5; 25:13.

1033. בֵּית כָּר *bēyṯ kār* **proper noun**
(Beth Car)
1 Sam. 7:11.

1034. בֵּית לְבָאוֹת *bēyṯ leḇā'ôṯ* **proper noun**
(Beth Lebaoth)
Josh. 19:6.

1035. A. בֵּית לֶחֶם *beyṯ leḥem* **proper noun**
(Bethlehem: village in Judea)
Gen. 35:19; 48:7; **Judg.** 17:7–9; 19:1, 2,18; **Ruth** 1:1,2,19,22; 2:4; 4:11; **1 Sam.** 16:4; 17:12,15; 20:6,28; **2 Sam.** 2:32; 23:14–16,24; **1 Chr.** 2:51,54; 4:4; 11:16–18,26; **2 Chr.** 11:6; **Ezra** 2:21; **Neh.** 7:26; **Jer.** 41:17; **Mic.** 5:2(1).
B. בֵּית לֶחֶם *beyṯ leḥem* **proper noun**
(Bethlehem: city in Zebulon)
Josh. 19:15; **Judg.** 12:8,10.

1036. I. בֵּית לְעַפְרָה *beyṯ le'ap̱rāh* **proper noun**
(Beth Ophrah)
Mic. 1:10(KJV, see II).
II. בֵּית לְעַפְרָה *beyṯ le'ap̱rāh* **masc. noun**
(house of Aphrah; *bēyṯ* [1004] with prep. and fem. of *'āp̱ār* [6083])
Mic. 1:10(NASB, NIV, see I).

1037. I. בֵּית מִלּוֹא *bêyṯ millô'* **proper noun**
(Beth Millo; loc. near Shechem)
Judg. 9:6(KJV, see III),20(KJV, see III).
II. בֵּית מִלּוֹא *bêyṯ millô'* **proper noun**
(Beth Millo; citadel in Jerusalem)
2 Kgs. 12:20(21)(KJV, NASB, see IV).
III. בֵּית מִלּוֹא *bêyṯ millô'* **proper noun**
(house of Millo, loc. near Shechem; from *bêyṯ* [1004] and *millô'* [4407])
Judg. 9:6(NASB, NIV, see I),20(NASB, NIV, see I).
IV. בֵּית מִלּוֹא *bêyṯ millô'* **proper noun**
(house of Millo; citadel in Jerusalem; from *bêyṯ* [1004] and *millô'* [4407,III])
2 Kgs. 12:20(21)(NIV, see II).

1038. בֵּית מַעֲכָה *bêyṯ ma'ᵃḵāh* **proper noun**
(Beth Maachah; shortened form of *'āḇēl beyṯ-ma'ᵃḵāh* [62])
2 Sam. 20:14(NIV, *'āḇēl bêyṯ-ma'ᵃḵāh* [62]),15(NASB, NIV, *'āḇēl bêyṯ-ma'ᵃḵāh* [62]).

1039. בֵּית נִמְרָה *bêyṯ nimrāh* **proper noun**
(Beth Nimrah)
Num. 32:36; **Josh.** 13:27.

1040. בֵּית עֶדֶן *bêyṯ 'eḏen* **proper noun**
(Beth Eden)
Amos 1:5(KJV, *bêyṯ* [1004] and *'ēḏen* [5729]).

1041. בֵּית עַזְמָוֶת *bêyṯ 'azmāweṯ* **proper noun**
(Beth Azmaveth: see also *'azmāweṯ* [5820,C])
Neh. 7:28.

1042. בֵּית עֲנוֹת *bêyṯ 'ᵃnôṯ* **proper noun**
(Beth Anoth)
Josh. 15:59.

1043. בֵּית עֲנָת *bêyṯ 'ᵃnāṯ* **proper noun**
(Beth Anath)
Josh. 19:38; **Judg.** 1:33.

1044. בֵּית עֵקֶד *bêyṯ 'ēqeḏ* **proper noun**
(Beth Eked)
2 Kgs. 10:12(KJV, *bêyṯ* [1004] and *'āqaḏ* [6123]),14(KJV, *bêyṯ* [1004] and *'āqaḏ* [6123]).

1045. בֵּית עַשְׁתָּרוֹת *bêyṯ 'aštārôṯ* **proper noun**
(temple of Ashtaroth; see *bêyṯ* [1004] and *'aštārôṯ* [6252])
1 Sam. 31:10.

1046. בֵּית פֶּלֶט *bêyṯ peleṭ* **proper noun**
(Beth Pelet)
Josh. 15:27; **Neh.** 11:26.

1047. בֵּית פְּעוֹר *bêyṯ pᵉ'ôr* **??er noun**
(Beth Peor)
Deut. 3:29; 4:46; 34:6; **Josh.** 13:20.

1048. בֵּית פַּצֵּץ *bêyṯ paṣṣēṣ* **proper noun**
(Beth Pazzez)
Josh. 19:21.

1049. בֵּית צוּר *bêyṯ ṣûr* **proper noun**
(Beth Zur)
Josh. 15:58; **1 Chr.** 2:45; **2 Chr.** 11:7; **Neh.** 3:16.

1050. בֵּית רְחוֹב *bêyṯ rᵉḥôḇ* **proper noun**
(Beth Rehob)
Judg. 18:28; **2 Sam.** 10:6.

1051. בֵּית רָפָא *bêyṯ rāpā'* **masc. proper noun**
(Beth Rapha)
1 Chr. 4:12.

1052. בֵּית שְׁאָן *bēyt s^e^'ān*, בֵּית שָׁן *bēyt šān* **proper noun**
(Beth Shean)
Josh. 17:11,16; **Judg.** 1:27; **1 Sam.** 31:10,12; **2 Sam.** 21:12; **1 Kgs.** 4:12; **1 Chr.** 7:29.

1053. A. בֵּית שֶׁמֶשׁ *bēyt šemeš* **proper noun**
(Beth Shemesh: city in N.W. Judah)
Josh. 15:10; 21:16; **1 Sam.** 6:9,12,13,15,19,20; **1 Kgs.** 4:9; **2 Kgs.** 14:11,13; **1 Chr.** 6:59(44); **2 Chr.** 25:21, 23; 28:18.
B. בֵּית שֶׁמֶשׁ *bēyt šemeš* **proper noun**
(Beth Shemesh: city in Naphtali)
Josh. 19:38; **Judg.** 1:33.
C. בֵּית שֶׁמֶשׁ *bēyt šemeš* **proper noun**
(Beth Shemesh: city in Issachar)
Josh. 19:22.
D. בֵּית שֶׁמֶשׁ *bēyt šemeš* **proper noun**
(Beth Shemesh: Egyptian sacred city of On, also known as Heliopolis)
Jer. 43:13.

1054. בֵּית תַּפּוּחַ *bēyt tappûaḥ* **proper noun**
(Beth Tappuah)
Josh. 15:53.

1055. בִּיתָן *biytān* **masc. noun**
(palace)
Esth. 1:5; 7:7,8.

1056. בָּכָא *bākā'* **proper noun**
(Baca)
Ps. 84:6(7).

1057. בָּכָא *bākā'* **masc. noun**
(balsam tree)
2 Sam. 5:23,24; **1 Chr.** 14:14,15.

1058. בָּכָה *bākāh* **verb**
(to weep, to wail)
Gen. 21:16; 23:2; 27:38; 29:11; 33:4; 37:35; 42:24; 43:30; 45:14,15; 46:29; 50:1,3,17; **Ex.** 2:6; **Lev.** 10:6; **Num.** 11:4,10,13,18,20; 14:1; 20:29; 25:6; **Deut.** 1:45; 21:13; 34:8; **Judg.** 2:4; 11:37,38; 14:16,17; 20:23,26; 21:2; **Ruth** 1:9,14; **1 Sam.** 1:7,8,10; 11:4,5; 20:41; 24:16(17); 30:4; **2 Sam.** 1:12,24; 3:16,32,34; 12:21,22; 13:36; 15:23,30; 18:33(19:1); 19:1(2); **2 Kgs.** 8:11,12; 13:14; 20:3; 22:19; **2 Chr.** 34:27; **Ezra** 3:12; 10:1; **Neh.** 1:4; 8:9; **Esth.** 8:3; **Job** 2:12; 27:15; 30:25,31; 31:38; **Ps.** 69:10 (11); 78:64; 126:6; 137:1; **Eccl.** 3:4; **Isa.** 16:9; 30:19; 33:7; 38:3; **Jer.** 9:1(8:23); 13:17; 22:10; 31:15; 41:6; 48:32; 50:4; **Lam.** 1:2,16; **Ezek.** 8:14; 24:16,23; 27:31; **Hos.** 12:4(5); **Joel** 1:5; 2:17; **Mic.** 1:10; **Zech.** 7:3.

1059. בֶּכֶה *bekeh* **masc. noun**
(a weeping)
Ezra 10:1.

1060. בְּכוֹר *b^e^kôr*, בְּכֹר *b^e^kōr* **masc. noun**
(firstborn)
Gen. 4:4(KJV, *b^e^kôrāh* [1062]); 10:15; 22:21; 25:13; 27:19,32; 35:23; 36:15; 38:6,7; 41:51; 43:33; 46:8; 48:14,18; 49:3; **Ex.** 4:22,23; 6:14; 11:5; 12:12,29; 13:2,13,15; 22:29(28); 34:20; **Lev.** 27:26; **Num.** 1:20; 3:2,12,13,40–43,45,46,50; 8:16–18; 18:15,17; 26:5; 33:4; **Deut.** 12:6(KJV, *b^e^kôrāh* [1062]),17(KJV, *b^e^kôrāh* [1062]); 14:23(KJV, *b^e^kôrāh* [1062]); 15:19; 21:15–17; 25:6; 33:17; **Josh.** 6:26; 17:1; **Judg.** 8:20; **1 Sam.** 8:2; 17:13; **2 Sam.** 3:2; **1 Kgs.** 16:34; **2 Kgs.** 3:27; **1 Chr.** 1:13,29; 2:3,13, 25,27,42,50; 3:1,15; 4:4; 5:1,3; 6:28(13); 8:1,30,39; 9:5,31,36; 26:2,4,10; **2 Chr.** 21:3; **Neh.** 10:36(37)(2nd occurrence KJV, *b^e^kôrāh* [1062]); **Job** 1:13,18; 18:13; **Ps.** 78:51; 89:27(28); 105:36; 135:8;

136:10; **Isa.** 14:30; **Jer.** 31:9; **Mic.** 6:7; **Zech.** 12:10.

1061. בִּכּוּרִים *bikkûriym* **masc. pl. noun**
(firstfruits)
Ex. 23:16,19; 34:22,26; **Lev.** 2:14; 23:17,20; **Num.** 13:20; 18:13; 28:26; **2 Kgs.** 4:42; **Neh.** 10:35(36); 13:31; **Isa.** 28:4(NASB, NIV, *bikkûrāh* [1063]); **Ezek.** 44:30; **Nah.** 3:12.

1062. בְּכוֹרָה *bekōrāh,* בְּכֹרָה *bekōrāh* **fem. noun**
(birthright, firstborn)
Gen. 4:4(NASB, NIV, *bekôr* [1060]); 25:31–34; 27:36; 43:33; **Deut.** 12:6(NASB, NIV, *bekôr* [1060]),17(NASB, NIV, *bekôr* [1060]); 14:23(NASB, NIV, *bekôr* [1060]); 21:17; **1 Chr.** 5:1,2; **Neh.** 10:36(37)(NASB, NIV, *bekôr* [1060]).

1063. בִּכּוּרָה *bikkûrāh* **fem. noun**
(firstfruit, early fruit)
Isa. 28:4(KJV, *bikkûriym* [1061]); **Jer.** 24:2(see *bakkurôt* [1073]); **Hos.** 9:10; **Mic.** 7:1.

1064. בְּכוֹרַת *bekôrat* **masc. proper noun**
(Becorath)
1 Sam. 9:1.

1065. בְּכִי *bekiy* **masc. noun**
(weeping, tears)
Gen. 45:2; **Deut.** 34:8; **Judg.** 21:2; **2 Sam.** 13:36; **2 Kgs.** 20:3; **Ezra** 3:13; **Esth.** 4:3; **Job** 16:16; 28:11; **Ps.** 6:8(9); 30:5(6); 102:9(10); **Isa.** 15:2,3,5; 16:9; 22:4,12; 38:3; 65:19; **Jer.** 3:21; 9:10(9); 31:9,15,16; 48:5,32; **Joel** 2:12; **Mal.** 2:13.

1066. בֹּכִים *bōkiym* **proper noun**
(Bochim)
Judg. 2:1,5.

1067. בְּכִירָה *bekiyrāh* **fem. noun**
(firstborn daughter)
Gen. 19:31,33,34,37; 29:26; **1 Sam.** 14:49.

1068. בְּכִית *bekiyt* **fem. noun**
(mourning)
Gen. 50:4.

1069. בָּכַר *bākar* **verb**
(to be born first, to have the birthright)
Lev. 27:26; **Deut.** 21:16; **Jer.** 4:31; **Ezek.** 47:12.

1070. בֵּכֶר *bēker* **fem. noun**
(young camel)
Isa. 60:6.

1071. A. בֶּכֶר *beker* **masc. proper noun**
(Becher: son of Ephraim)
Num. 26:35.
B. בֶּכֶר *beker* **masc. proper noun**
(Becher: son of Benjamin)
Gen. 46:21; **1 Chr.** 7:6,8.

1072. בִּכְרָה *bikrāh* **fem. noun**
(young female camel)
Jer. 2:23.

1073. בַּכֻּרוֹת *bakkûrôt* **fem. noun**
(first ripe: pl. of *bikkûrāh* [1063])
Jer. 24:2.

1074. בֹּכְרוּ *bōkerû* **masc. proper noun**
(Bocheru)
1 Chr. 8:38; 9:44.

1075. בִּכְרִי *bikriy* **masc. proper noun**
(Bichri)
2 Sam. 20:1,2,6,7,10,13,21,22.

1076. בַּכְרִי *bakriy* **masc. proper noun**
(Becherite)
Num. 26:35.

1077. בַּל *bal* **particle**
(not, cannot)
1 Chr. 16:30; **Job** 41:23(15); **Ps.** 10:4,6,11,15,18; 16:2,4,8; 17:3,5; 21:2(3),7(8),11(12); 30:6(7); 32:9; 46:5(6); 49:12(13); 58:8(9); 78:44; 93:1; 96:10; 104:5,9; 119:121; 140:10(11), 11(12); 141:4; 147:20; **Prov.** 9:13; 10:30; 12:3; 14:7; 19:23; 22:29; 23:7,35; 24:23; **Isa.** 14:21; 26:10,11,14,18; 33:20,21, 23,24; 35:9; 40:24; 43:17; 44:8,9; **Hos.** 7:2; 9:16.

1078. בֵּל *bēl* **masc. proper noun**
(Bel)
Isa. 46:1; **Jer.** 50:2; 51:44.

1079. בָּל *bāl* **Aram. masc. noun**
(mind, heart)
Dan. 6:14(15).

1080. בְּלָא b^e*lā'* **Aram. verb**
(to wear down, to oppress; corr. to Hebr. 1086)
Dan. 7:25.

1081. בַּלְאֲדָן *bal'*^{a}*dān* **masc. proper noun**
(Baladan)
2 Kgs. 20:12; **Isa.** 39:1.

1082. בָּלַג *bālag* **verb**
(to flash forth, to be happy, to smile)
Job 9:27; 10:20; **Ps.** 39:13(14); **Amos** 5:9.

1083. A. בִּלְגָּה *bilgāh* **masc. proper noun**
(Bilgah: a priest)
1 Chr. 24:14.
B. בִּלְגָּה *bilgāh* **masc. proper noun**
(Bilgah: a priest)
Neh. 12:5,18.

1084. בִּלְגַּי *bilgay* **masc. proper noun**
(Bilgai)
Neh. 10:8(9).

1085. בִּלְדַּד *bildad* **masc. proper noun**
(Bildad)
Job 2:11; 8:1; 18:1; 25:1; 42:9.

1086. בָּלָה *bālāh* **verb**
(to wear out, to grow old)
Gen. 18:12; **Deut.** 8:4; 29:5(4); **Josh.** 9:13; **1 Chr.** 17:9; **Neh.** 9:21; **Job** 13:28; 21:13(KJV, NIV, [Q^e] *kālāh* [3615]); **Ps.** 32:3; 49:14(15); 102:26(27); **Isa.** 50:9; 51:6; 65:22; **Lam.** 3:4.

1087. בָּלֶה *bāleh* **adj.**
(worn out, old)
Josh. 9:4,5; **Ezek.** 23:43.

1088. בָּלָה *bālāh* **proper noun**
(Balah; see also *bilhāh* [1090,C])
Josh. 19:3.

1089. בָּלַהּ *bālah* **verb**
(to terrify, to frighten)
Ezra 4:4(NIV, [Q^e] *bāhal* [926]).

1090. A. בִּלְהָה *bilhāh* **fem. proper noun**
(Bilhah: handmaid of Rachel)
Gen. 29:29; 30:3–5,7; 35:22,25; 37:2; 46:25; **1 Chr.** 7:13.
B. בִּלְהָה *bilhāh* **proper noun**
(Bilhah: another name for *bālāh* [1088])
1 Chr. 4:29.

1091. בַּלָּהָה *ballāhāh* **fem. noun**
(terror, calamity)
Job 18:11,14; 24:17; 27:20; 30:15; **Ps.** 73:19; **Isa.** 17:14; **Ezek.** 26:21; 27:36; 28:19.

1092. A. בִּלְהָן *bilhān* **masc. proper noun**
(Bilhan: son of Ezer)
Gen. 36:27; **1 Chr.** 1:42.

B. בִּלְהָן *bilhān* **masc. proper noun**
(Bilhan: a Benjamite)
1 Chr. 7:10.

1093. בְּלוֹ *b^elô* **Aram. masc. noun**
(tribute)
Ezra 4:13,20; 7:24.

1094. בְּלוֹי *b^elôy* **masc. noun**
(old, worn-out)
Jer. 38:11,12.

1095. בֵּלְטְשַׁאצַּר *bēlṭ^{e}ša'ṣṣar* **masc. proper noun**
(Belteshazzar)
Dan. 1:7; 10:1.

1096. בֵּלְטְשַׁאצַּר *bēlṭ^{e}ša'ṣṣar* **Aram. masc. proper noun**
(Belteshazzar; corr. to Hebr. 1095)
Dan. 2:26; 4:8(5),9(6),18(15),19(16); 5:12.

1097. בְּלִי *b^eliy* **particle**
(not, without)
Gen. 31:20; **Deut.** 4:42; 9:28; 28:55; **Josh.** 20:3,5; **2 Sam.** 1:21; **2 Kgs.** 1:3,6,16; **Job** 4:11,20; 6:6; 8:11; 18:15; 24:7,8,10; 30:8; 31:19,39; 33:9; 34:6; 35:16; 36:12; 38:2,41; 39:16; 41:26(18), 33(25); 42:3; **Ps.** 19:3(4); 59:4(5); 63:1(2); 72:7; **Prov.** 19:2; **Eccl.** 3:11; **Isa.** 5:13,14; 14:6; 28:8; 32:10; 38:17; **Jer.** 2:15; 9:10(9),11(10),12(11); **Lam.** 1:4; **Ezek.** 14:15; 34:5; **Hos.** 4:6; 7:8; 8:7; **Zeph.** 3:6; **Mal.** 3:10.

1098. בְּלִיל *b^eliyl* **masc. noun**
(fodder)
Job 6:5; 24:6; **Isa.** 30:24.

1099. בְּלִימָה *b^eliymāh* **fem. noun**
(nothingness)
Job 26:7.

1100. I. בְּלִיַּעַל *b^eliyya'al* **masc. proper noun**
(Belial [NASB, NIV, see II])
Deut. 13:13(14); **Judg.** 19:22; 20:13; **1 Sam.** 1:16; 2:12; 10:27; 25:17,25; 30:22; **2 Sam.** 16:7; 20:1; 23:6; **1 Kgs.** 21:10,13; **2 Chr.** 13:7.
II. בְּלִיַּעַל *b^eliyya'al* **masc. noun**
(worthlessness, wickedness)
Deut. 13:13(14)(KJV, see I); 15:9; **Judg.** 19:22(KJV, see I); 20:13(KJV, see I); **1 Sam.** 1:16(KJV, see I); 2:12(KJV, see I); 10:27(KJV, see I); 25:17(KJV, see I),25(KJV, see I); 30:22(KJV, see I); **2 Sam.** 16:7(KJV, see I); 20:1(KJV, see I); 22:5; 23:6(KJV, see I); **1 Kgs.** 21:10(KJV, see I),13(KJV, see I); **2 Chr.** 13:7(KJV, see I); **Job** 34:18; **Ps.** 18:4(5); 41:8(9); 101:3; **Prov.** 6:12; 16:27; 19:28; **Nah.** 1:11,15(2:1).

1101. בָּלַל *bālal* **verb**
(to mix, to mingle, to confuse)
Gen. 11:7,9; **Ex.** 29:2,40; **Lev.** 2:4,5; 7:10,12; 9:4; 14:10,21; 23:13; **Num.** 6:15; 7:13,19,25,31,37,43,49,55,61,67, 73,79; 8:8; 15:4,6,9; 28:5,9,12,13,20,28; 29:3,9,14; **Judg.** 19:21; **Ps.** 92:10(11); **Hos.** 7:8.

1102. בָּלַם *bālam* **verb**
(to hold in, to restrain)
Ps. 32:9.

1103. בָּלַס *bālas* **verb**
(to gather)
Amos 7:14.

1104. I. בָּלַע *bāla'* **verb**
(to swallow up, to consume, to destroy)
Gen. 41:7,24; **Ex.** 7:12; 15:12; **Num.** 4:20; 16:30,32,34; 26:10; **Deut.** 11:6; **2 Sam.** 17:16; 20:19,20; **Job** 2:3; 7:19; 8:18; 10:8; 20:15,18; 37:20; **Ps.** 21:9(10); 35:25; 55:9(10)(NASB, NIV, see III); 69:15(16); 106:17; 124:3; **Prov.** 1:12; 19:28(NASB, see II); 21:20; **Eccl.** 10:12; **Isa.** 3:12(NASB, NIV, see III); 9:16(15)

(NASB, NIV, see III); 19:3(NASB, NIV, see III); 25:7,8; 28:4,7(NASB, NIV, see III); 49:19; **Jer.** 51:34; **Lam.** 2:2,5,8,16; **Hos.** 8:7,8; **Jon.** 1:17(2:1); **Hab.** 1:13.

II. בָּלַע *bāla'* **verb**
(to communicate, to spread abroad)
Prov. 19:28(KJV, NIV, see I).

III. בָּלַע *bāla'* **verb**
(to confuse)
Ps. 55:9(10)(KJV, see I); 107:27; **Isa.** 3:12(KJV, see I); 9:16(15)(KJV, see I); 19:3(KJV, see I); 28:7(KJV, see I).

1105. בֶּלַע *bela'* **masc. noun**
(a swallowing, devouring)
Ps. 52:4(6); **Jer.** 51:44.

1106. A. בֶּלַע *bela'* **proper noun**
(Bela: another name for *ṣō'ar* [6820])
Gen. 14:2,8.

B. בֶּלַע *bela'* **masc. proper noun**
(Bela: Edomite king)
Gen. 36:32,33; 46:21; **1 Chr.** 1:43,44.

C. בֶּלַע *bela'* **masc. proper noun**
(Bela: son of Benjamin)
Num. 26:38,40; **1 Chr.** 7:6,7; 8:1,3.

D. בֶּלַע *bela'* **masc. proper noun**
(Bela: son of Azaz)
1 Chr. 5:8.

1107. בַּלְעֲדֵי *bal'ᵃḏēy*, בִּלְעֲדֵי *bil'ᵃḏēy* **particle**
(apart from, except)
Gen. 14:24; 41:16,44; **Num.** 5:20; **Josh.** 22:19; **2 Sam.** 22:32; **2 Kgs.** 18:25; **Job** 34:32; **Ps.** 18:31(32); **Isa.** 36:10; 43:11; 44:6,8; 45:6,21; **Jer.** 44:19.

1108. בַּלְעִי *bal'iy* **masc. proper noun**
(Belaite)
Num. 26:38.

1109. A. בִּלְעָם *bil'ām* **masc. proper noun**
(Bileam: the false prophet Balaam)
Num. 22:5,7–10,12–14,16,18,20,21, 23,25,27–31,34–41; 23:1–5,11,16,25–30; 24:1–3,10,12,15,25; 31:8,16; **Deut.** 23:4(5),5(6); **Josh.** 13:22; 24:9,10; **Neh.** 13:2; **Mic.** 6:5.

B. בִּלְעָם *bil'ām* **masc. proper noun**
(Bileam: a city)
1 Chr. 6:70(55).

1110. בָּלַק *bālaq* **verb**
(to lay waste, to destroy)
Isa. 24:1; **Nah.** 2:10(11).

1111. בָּלָק *bālāq* **masc. proper noun**
(Balak)
Num. 22:2,4,7,10,13–16,18,35–41; 23:1–3,5,7,11,13,15–18,25–30; 24:10,12,13,25; **Josh.** 24:9; **Judg.** 11:25; **Mic.** 6:5.

1112. בֵּלְשַׁאצַּר *bēlša'ṣṣar* **masc. proper noun**
(Belshazzar)
Dan. 8:1.

1113. בֵּלְשַׁאצַּר *bēlša'ṣṣar* **Aram. masc. proper noun**
(Belshazzar; corr. to Hebr. 1112)
Dan. 5:1,2,9,22,29,30; 7:1.

1114. בִּלְשָׁן *bilšān* **masc. proper noun**
(Bilshan)
Ezra 2:2; **Neh.** 7:7.

1115. בִּלְתִּי *biltiy* **particle**
(not, except)
Gen. 3:11; 4:15; 19:21; 21:26; 38:9; 43:3,5; 47:18; **Ex.** 8:22(18),29(25); 9:17; 14:11; 20:20; 22:20(19); **Lev.** 18:30; 20:4; 26:15; **Num.** 9:7; 11:6; 14:16; 21:35; 32:9,12; **Deut.** 3:3; 4:21; 8:11; 12:23; 17:12,20; **Josh.** 5:6; 8:22; 10:33; 11:8,19,20; 22:25; 23:6,7; **Judg.** 2:23; 7:14; 8:1; 21:7; **Ruth** 1:13; 2:9; 3:10;

1 Sam. 2:2; 20:26; **2 Sam.** 14:7,13; **1 Kgs.** 6:6; 11:10; 15:17; **2 Kgs.** 10:11; 12:8(9); 17:15; 23:10; **1 Chr.** 4:10; **2 Chr.** 16:1; **Job** 14:12; 42:8; **Isa.** 10:4; 14:6; 44:10; 48:9; 65:8; **Jer.** 7:8; 17:23, 24,27; 18:10; 19:15; 23:14; 26:24; 27:18; 32:40; 33:20; 34:9,10; 35:8,9,14; 36:25; 38:26; 42:13; 44:5,7; 51:62; **Ezek.** 3:21; 13:3,22; 16:28; 17:14; 20:9,14,15,22; 22:30; 24:8; 29:15; 33:15; 46:20; **Dan.** 9:11; 11:18; **Hos.** 13:4; **Amos** 3:3,4.

1116. בָּמָה *bāmāh* **fem. noun**
(high place, mound)
Lev. 26:30; **Num.** 21:28; 22:41(NIV, *bāmôṯ ba'al* [1181]); 33:52; **Deut.** 32:13; 33:29; **1 Sam.** 9:12–14,19,25; 10:5,13; **2 Sam.** 1:19,25; 22:34; **1 Kgs.** 3:2–4; 11:7; 12:31,32; 13:2,32,33; 14:23; 15:14; 22:43(44); **2 Kgs.** 12:3(4); 14:4; 15:4,35; 16:4; 17:9,11,29,32; 18:4,22; 21:3; 23:5,8,9,13,15,19,20; **1 Chr.** 16:39; 21:29; **2 Chr.** 1:3,13; 11:15; 14:3(2),5(4); 15:17; 17:6; 20:33; 21:11; 28:4,25; 31:1; 32:12; 33:3,17,19; 34:3; **Job** 9:8; **Ps.** 18:33(34); 78:58; **Isa.** 14:14; 15:2; 16:12; 36:7; 58:14; **Jer.** 7:31; 17:3; 19:5; 26:18; 32:35; 48:35; **Ezek.** 6:3,6; 16:16; 20:29; 36:2; 43:7; **Hos.** 10:8; **Amos** 4:13; 7:9; **Mic.** 1:3,5; 3:12; **Hab.** 3:19.

1117. בָּמָה *bāmāh* **proper noun**
(Bamah)
Ezek. 20:29.

1118. בִּמְהָל *bimhāl* **masc. proper noun**
(Bimhal)
1 Chr. 7:33.

1119. בְּמוֹ *b^e^mô* **prep.**
(in, from, with)
Job 9:30([Q^e^] *mayim* [4325]); 16:4,5; 19:16; 37:8; **Ps.** 11:2; **Isa.** 25:10(NASB, [K^e^] *mayim* [4325]); 43:2; 44:16,19.

1120. I. בָּמוֹת *bāmôṯ* **proper noun**
(Bamoth)
Num. 21:19,20.

II. בָּמוֹת בַּעַל *bāmôṯ ba'al* **proper noun**
(Bamoth Baal)
Num. 22:41(KJV, NASB, *bāmôt* [pl. of 1116]; and *ba'al* [1168,A]); **Josh.** 13:17.

1121. בֵּן *bēn* **masc. noun**
(son, descendant, child [of])
Gen. 3:16; 4:17,25,26; 5:4,7,10,13,16,19,22,26,28,30,32; 6:2,4, 10,18; 7:6,7,13; 8:16,18; 9:1,8,18,19,24; 10:1–4,6,7,20–23,25,29,31,32; 11:5,10, 11,13,15,17,19,21,23,25,31; 12:4,5; 14:12; 15:2,3; 16:11,15,16; 17:1,12,16, 17,19,23–27; 18:7,8,10,14,19; 19:12, 37,38; 21:2–5,7,9–11,13; 22:2,3,6–10, 12,13,16,20; 23:3,5,7,8,10,11,16,18,20; 24:3–8,15,24,36–38,40,44,47,48,51; 25:3,4,6,9–13,16,19,20,22,26; 26:34; 27:1,5,6,8,13,15,17,18,20,21,24–27,29,3 1,32,37,42,43; 28:5,9; 29:1,5,12,13, 32–35; 30:1,5–7,10,12,14–17,19,20, 23,24,35; 31:1,16,17,28,43,55(32:1); 32:11(12),15(16),32(33); 33:19; 34:2,5, 7,8,13,18,20,24–27; 35:5,17,22–26,29; 36:5,6,10–28,31–33,35,38,39; 37:2,3, 32–35; 38:3–5,11,26; 41:46,50; 42:1,5, 11,13,32,37,38; 43:29; 45:9,10,21,28; 46:5,7–19,21–27; 47:29; 48:1,2,5,8,9,19; 49:1,2,8,9,11,22,32,33; 50:12,13,23, 25,26; **Ex.** 1:1,7,9,12,13,16,22; 2:2,10, 22,23,25; 3:9–11,13–15,22; 4:20,22,23, 25,29,31; 5:14,15,19; 6:5,6,9,11–19,21, 22,24–27; 7:2,4,5,7; 9:4,6,26,35; 10:2, 9,20,23; 11:7,10; 12:5,24,26–28,31,35, 37,40,42,43,50,51; 13:2,8,13–15,18,19; 14:2,3,8,10,15,16,22,29; 15:1,19; 16:1–3, 6,9,10,12,15,17,35; 17:1,3,7; 18:3,5,6; 19:1,3,6; 20:5,10,22; 21:4,5,9,31; 22:24 (23),29(28); 23:12; 24:5,11,17; 25:2,22; 27:20,21; 28:1,4,9,11,12,21,29,30,38, 40,41,43; 29:1,4,8–10,15,19–21,24, 27–30,32,35,38,43–45; 30:12,14,16,19, 30,31; 31:2,6,10,13,16,17; 32:2,20,26, 28,29; 33:5,6,11; 34:7,16,20,30,32,34,35; 35:1,4,19,20,29,30,34; 36:3; 38:21–23,26;

39:6,7,14,27,32,41,42; 40:12,14,31,36; **Lev.** 1:2,5,7,8,11,14; 2:2,3,10; 3:2,5, 8,13; 4:2,3,14; 5:7,11; 6:9(2),14(7),16(9), 18(11),20(13),22(15),25(18); 7:10,23,29, 31,33–36,38; 8:2,6,13,14,18,22,24,27, 30,31,36; 9:1–3,9,12,18; 10:1,4,6,9, 11–16; 11:2; 12:2,6,8; 13:2; 14:22,30; 15:2,14,29,31; 16:1,3,5,16,19,21,34; 17:2,5,12–14; 18:2,10,15,17; 19:2,18; 20:2,17; 21:1,2,24; 22:2,3,15,18,25, 28,32; 23:2,10,12,18,19,24,34,43,44; 24:2,8–11,15,23; 25:2,33,41,45,46,49, 54,55; 26:29,46; 27:2,3,5–7,34; **Num.** 1:2,3,5–15,18,20,22,24,26,28,30,32,34, 36,38,40,42,45,49,52–54; 2:2,3,5,7,10, 12,14,18,20,22,25,27,29,32–34; 3:2–4, 8–10,12,15,17–20,22,24,25,28–30,32,34 –36,38–43,45,46,48,50,51; 4:2–5,15,16, 19,22,23,27–30,33–35,38,39,41–43,45, 47; 5:2,4,6,9,12; 6:2,10,12,14,23,27; 7:7–9, 12,15,17,18,21,23,24,27,29,30,33,35,36, 39,41,42,45,47,48,51,53,54,57,59,60,63, 65,66,69,71,72,75,77,78,81,83,87,88; 8:6,8–11,13,14,16–20,22,24,25; 9:2,4,5, 7,10,17–19,22; 10:8,12,14–20,22–29; 11:4,28; 13:2–16,24,26,32,33; 14:2,5–7, 10,18,27,29,30,33,38,39; 15:2,8,9,18, 24–26,29,32,38; 16:1,2,7,8,10,12,27, 37(17:2),38(17:3),40(17:5),41(17:6); 17:2(17),5(20),6(21),9(24),10(25),12(27) ; 18:1,2,5–9,11,16,19–24,26,28,32; 19:2,9,10; 20:1,12,13,19,22,24–26,28; 21:10,24,29,35; 22:1–5,10,16; 23:18,19; 24:3,15,17; 25:6–8,11,13,14; 26:1,2,4, 5,8,9,11,12,15,18–21,23,26,28–30,33,35 –38,40–42,44,45,47,48,51,62–65; 27:1,3, 4,8,11,12,18,20,21; 28:2,3,9,11,19,27; 29:2,8,13,17,20,23,26,29,32,36,40(30:1); 30:1(2); 31:2,6,8,9,12,16,30,42,47,54; 32:1,2,6,7,9,11,12,17,18,25,28,29,31,33, 34,37,39–41; 33:1,3,5,38–40,51; 34:2,13, 14,17,19–29; 35:2,8,10,15,34; 36:1–5,7–9, 11–13; **Deut.** 1:3,28,31,36,38,39; 2:4,8, 9,12,19,22,29,33,37; 3:11,14,16,18; 4:9, 10,25,40,44–46; 5:9,14,29(26); 6:2,7,20, 21; 7:3,4; 8:5; 9:2; 10:6(see *bᵉʾērōt bᵉnēy-yaᵃqān* [885]); 11:2,6,19,21; 12:12,18,25,28,31; 13:6(7),13(14); 14:1; 16:11,14; 17:20; 18:5,10; 21:5,15–18,20; 22:6,7; 23:4(5),8(9),17(18); 24:7,16; 25:2,5; 28:32,41,53–57; 29:1(28:69), 22(21),29(28); 30:2; 31:2,9,13,19,22,23; 32:5,8,14,19,20,44,46,49,51,52; 33:1,9, 24; 34:7–9; **Josh.** 1:1,2; 2:1,2,23; 3:1,9; 4:4–8,12,21,22; 5:1–3,6,7,10,12; 6:1,6; 7:1,12,18,19,23,24; 8:31,32; 9:17,18,26; 10:4,11,12,20,21; 11:14,19,22; 12:1,2, 6,7; 13:6,10,13,15,22–25,28,29,31; 14:1, 4–7,9,10,13,14; 15:1,6,8,12–14,17,20, 21,63; 16:1,4,5,8,9; 17:2–4,6,8,12–14,16; 18:1–3,10,11,14,16,17,20,21,28; 19:1, 8–10,16,17,23,24,31,32,39,40,47–49,51; 20:2,9; 21:1,3–10,12,13,19,20,26,27,34, 40(38),41(39); 22:9–13,15,20,21,24,25, 27,30–34; 24:4,9,29,32,33; **Judg.** 1:1,8, 9,13,16,20,21,34; 2:4,6,8,11; 3:2,5–9, 11–15,27,31; 4:1,3,5,6,11,12,23,24; 5:1, 6,12; 6:1–3,6–8,11,29,30,33; 7:12,14; 8:10,13,18,19,22,23,28–34; 9:1,2,5,18, 24,26,28,30,31,35,57; 10:1,4,6–11,15, 17,18; 11:1,2,4–6,8,9,12–15,25,27–34,36; 12:1–3,9,13–15; 13:1,3,5,7,24; 14:16,17; 17:2,3,5,11; 18:2,16,22,23,25,26,30; 19:12,22,30; 20:1,3,7,13–15,18,19,21, 23–28,30–32,35,36,48; 21:5,6,10,13, 18,20,23,24; **Ruth** 1:1–3,11,12; 4:13,15,17; **1 Sam.** 1:1,3,4,8,20,23; 2:5,12,21,22,24,28,29,34; 3:6,13,16; 4:4,11,15–17,20; 6:7,10; 7:1,4,6–8; 8:1–3,5,11; 9:1–3; 10:2,11,18,21,27; 11:8; 12:2,12; 13:1,16,22; 14:1,3,18,32, 39,40,42,47,49–52; 15:6; 16:1,5,10, 18–20; 17:12,13,17,53,55,56,58; 18:17; 19:1,2(1); 20:27,30,31; 22:7–9,11–13,20; 23:6,16; 24:16(17); 25:8,10,17,44; 26:5,6,14,16,17,19,21,25; 27:2; 28:19; 30:3,6,7,19,22; 31:2,6–8,12; **2 Sam.** 1:4,5,12,13,17,18; 2:7,8,10,12,13,15, 18,25; 3:2–4,14,15,23,25,28,34,37,39; 4:1,2,4,5,8,9; 5:4,13; 6:3; 7:6,7,10,14; 8:3,10,12,16–18; 9:3–6,9–12; 10:1–3, 6,8,10,11,14,19; 11:1,21,27; 12:3,5,9,14, 24,26,31; 13:1,3,4,23,25,27–30,32,33, 35–37; 14:1,6,11,16,27; 15:27,36; 16:3,

5,8–11,19; 17:10,25,27; 18:2,12,18–20, 22,27,33(19:1); 19:2(3),4(5),5(6),16–18 (17–19),21(22),22(23),24(25),32(33), 35(36); 20:1,2,6,7,10,13,21–24; 21:2, 6–8,12–14,17,19,21; 22:45,46; 23:1,9,11, 18,20,22,24,26,29,32–34,36,37; **1 Kgs.** 1:5,7–9,11–13,17,19,21,25,26,30,32,33, 36,38,42,44,52; 2:1,4,5,7,8,13,22,25,29, 32,34,35,39,46; 3:6,19–23,26; 4:2–6, 12–14,16–19,30(5:10),31(5:11); 5:5(19), 7(21); 6:1,13; 7:14; 8:1,9,19,25,39,63; 9:6,20–22; 11:2,7,12,13,20,23,26,33,35, 36,43; 12:2,15–17,21,23,24,31,33; 13:2, 11–13,27,31; 14:1,5,20,21,24,31; 15:1,4, 8,18,24,25,27,33; 16:1,3,6–8,13,21,22, 26,28–31,34; 17:12,13,17–20,23; 18:20,31; 19:10,14,16,19; 20:3,5,7,15,27,29,35; 21:10,13,22,26,29; 22:8,9,11,24,26, 40–42,49–52(50–53); **2 Kgs.** 1:17; 2:3,5,7,15,16; 3:1,3,11,27; 4:1,4–7,14, 16,17,28,36–38; 5:22; 6:1,28,29,31,32; 8:1,5,9,12,16,17,19,24–26,28,29; 9:1,2, 9,14,20,26,29; 10:1–3,6–8,13,15,23,29, 30,35; 11:1,2,4,12,21(12:1); 12:21(22); 13:1–3,5,9–11,24,25; 14:1,2,6,8,9,13,14, 16,17,21,23–25,27,29; 15:1,2,5,7–10, 12–14,18,22–25,27,28,30,32,33,37,38; 16:1–3,5,7,20; 17:1,7–9,17,21,22,24,31, 34,41; 18:1,2,4,9,18,26,37; 19:2,3,12, 20,37; 20:1,12,18,21; 21:1,2,6,7,9,18,19, 24,26; 22:1,3,12,14; 23:6,10,13,15,30,31, 34,36; 24:2,6,8,18; 25:7,22,23,25; **1 Chr.** 1:5–9,17,19,23,28,31–44,46,49; 2:1, 3–10,16,18,21,23,25,27,28,30–34,42,43, 45,47,50,52,54; 3:1,2,9–17,19,21–24; 4:1,2,4,6–8,13,15–21,24–27,34,35,37,42; 5:1,3–6,8,11,14,15,18,23; 6:1–3(5:27–29), 16–30(1–15),33–47(18–32),49–54(34–39), 56(41),57(42),61–66(46–51),70(55), 71(56),77(62); 7:1–4,7,8,10–14,16,17, 19–21,23,25–27,29–31,33–36,38–40; 8:3,6,10,12,16,18,21,25,27,30,34,35, 37–40; 9:3–8,11,12,14–16,18–21,23,30, 32,36,40,41,43,44; 10:2,6–8,12,14; 11:6,11,12,22,24,26,28,30,31,34,35, 37–39,41–46; 12:1,3,7,14,16,18,24–26, 29,30,32; 14:3; 15:4–10,15,17; 16:13,38, 42; 17:9,11,13; 18:10–12,15–17; 19:1–3, 6,7,9,11,12,15,19; 20:1,3,5,7; 21:20; 22:5–7,9–11,17; 23:1,3,6,8–24,27,28,32; 24:1–6,20–31; 25:1–5,9–31; 26:1,2,4, 6–11,14,15,19,21,22,24,25,28–30,32; 27:1–3,5–7,9,10,14,16–26,29,32,34; 28:1,4–6,8,9,11,20; 29:1,19,22,24,26,28; **2 Chr.** 1:1,5; 2:12(11),14(13); 5:2,10,12; 6:9,11,16,30; 7:3; 8:2,8,9; 9:29,31; 10:2, 15–18; 11:3,14,17–19,21–23; 12:13,16; 13:5–10,12,16,18,21; 14:1(13:23); 15:1; 17:1,16; 18:7,8,10,23,25; 19:2,11; 20:1, 10,13,14,19,22,23,31,34,37; 21:1,2,5,7, 14,17,20; 22:1,2,5–11; 23:1,3,11; 24:1,3, 7,15,20,22,25–27; 25:1,4,5,7,11–14, 17,18,23–25; 26:1,3,17,18,21–23; 27:1,5, 8,9; 28:1,3,6–8,10,12,27; 29:1,9,11–14, 21; 30:6,9,21,26; 31:1,5,6,14,16–19; 32:20,32,33; 33:1,2,6,7,9,20,21,25; 34:1, 8,12,20,22,33; 35:3–5,7,12–15,17; 36:1, 2,5,8,9,11,20; **Ezra** 2:1,3–21,24–26, 29–58,60,61; 3:1,2,8–10; 4:1; 6:19–21; 7:1–5,7; 8:2–15,18,19,33,35; 9:2,12; 10:2,6,7,15,16,18,20–22,25–31,33,34,43, 44; **Neh.** 1:1,6; 2:10; 3:2–4,6,8–12,14–21, 23–25,29–31; 4:14(8); 5:2,5; 6:10,18; 7:6,8–25,34–60,62,63,73; 8:14,17; 9:1,2, 23,24; 10:1(2),9(10),28(29),30(31), 36(37),38(39),39(40); 11:3–7,9–15,17, 22,24,25,31; 12:1,23,24,26,28,35,45,47; 13:2,13,16,24,25,28; **Esth.** 2:5; 3:1,10; 5:11; 8:5,10; 9:10,12–14,24,25; **Job** 1:2–6,13,18; 2:1; 4:11; 5:4,7; 8:4; 14:21; 16:21; 17:5; 19:17; 20:10; 21:19; 25:6; 27:14; 28:8; 30:8; 32:2,6; 35:8; 38:7,32; 39:4,16; 41:28(20),34(26); 42:13,16; **Ps.** 2:7; 3:[title](1); 4:2(3); 8:4(5); 11:4; 12:1(2),8(9); 14:2; 17:14; 18:44(45),45(46); 21:10(11); 29:1,6; 31:19(20); 33:13; 34:11(12); 36:7(8); 42:[title](1); 43:[title](1); 45:[title](1), 2(3),16(17); 46:[title](1); 47:[title](1); 48:[title](1); 49:[title](1),2(3); 50:20; 53:2(3); 57:4(5); 58:1(2); 62:9(10); 66:5; 69:8(9); 72:1,4,20; 73:15; 77:15(16); 78:4–6,9; 79:11; 80:15(16),17(18); 82:6; 83:8(9); 84:[title](1); 85:[title](1); 86:16;

87:[title](1); 88:[title](1); 89:6(7),22(23), 30(31),47(48); 90:3,16; 102:20(21), 28(29); 103:7,13,17; 105:6; 106:37,38; 107:8,15,21,31; 109:9,10; 113:9; 114:4,6; 115:14,16; 116:16; 127:3,4; 128:3,6; 132:12; 137:7; 144:3,7,11,12; 145:12; 146:3; 147:9,13; 148:14; 149:2; **Prov.** 1:1,8,10,15; 2:1; 3:1,11,12,21; 4:1,3, 10,20; 5:1,7,20; 6:1,3,20; 7:1,7,24; 8:4,31,32; 10:1,5; 13:1,22,24; 14:26; 15:11,20; 17:2,6,25; 19:13,18,26,27; 20:7; 23:15,19,26; 24:13,21; 27:11; 28:7; 29:17; 30:1,4,17; 31:5,8,28; **Eccl.** 1:1,13; 2:3,7,8; 3:10,18,19,21; 4:8; 5:14(13); 8:11; 9:3,12; 10:17; 12:12; **Song** 1:6; 2:3; **Isa.** 1:1,2,4; 2:1; 5:1; 7:1,3–6,9,14; 8:2,3,6; 9:6(5); 11:14; 13:1,18; 14:12,21; 17:3,9; 19:11; 20:2; 21:10,17; 22:20; 27:12; 30:1,9; 31:6; 36:3,22; 37:2,3, 12,21,38; 38:1,19; 39:1,7; 43:6; 45:11; 49:15,17,20,22,25; 51:12,18,20; 52:14; 54:1,13; 56:2,3,5,6; 57:3; 60:4,9,10,14; 61:5; 62:5,8; 63:8; 65:20; 66:8,20; **Jer.** 1:1–3; 2:9,16,30; 3:14,19,21,22,24; 4:22; 5:7,17; 6:1,21; 7:18,30–32; 9:26(25); 10:20; 11:22; 13:14; 14:16; 15:4; 16:2, 3,14,15; 17:2,19; 18:21; 19:2,5,6,9; 20:1, 15; 21:1; 22:11,18,24; 23:7; 24:1; 25:1,3,21; 26:1,20,22–24; 27:1,3,7,20; 28:1,4; 29:3,6,21,25; 30:20; 31:12,15,17, 20,29; 32:7–9,12,16,18,19,30,32,35,39; 33:21; 35:1,3–6,8,14,16,19; 36:1,4, 8–12,14,26,32; 37:1,3,13; 38:1,6,23; 39:6,14; 40:5–9,11,13–16; 41:1,2,6,7, 9–16,18; 42:1,8; 43:2–6; 45:1; 46:2; 47:3; 48:45,46; 49:1,2,6,18,28,33; 50:4,33,40; 51:43,59; 52:1,10; **Lam.** 1:16; 3:13,33; 4:2; **Ezek.** 1:3; 2:1,3,4,6,8; 3:1,3,4,10,11, 17,25; 4:1,13,16; 5:1,10; 6:2,5; 7:2; 8:5,6, 8,11,12,15,17; 11:1,2,4,13,15; 12:2,3, 9,18,22,27; 13:2,17; 14:3,13,16,18,20,22; 15:2; 16:2,20,21,26,28,36,45; 17:2; 18:2, 4,10,14,19,20; 20:3,4,18,21,27,31, 46(21:2); 21:2(7),6(11),9(14),10(15), 12(17),14(19),19(24),20(25),28(33); 22:2,18,24; 23:2,4,7,9,10,12,15,17,23,25, 36,37,39,47; 24:2,16,21,25; 25:2–5,10; 26:2; 27:2,11,15; 28:2,12,21; 29:2,18; 30:2,5,21; 31:2,14; 32:2,18; 33:2,7,10, 12,17,24,30; 34:2; 35:2,5; 36:1,17; 37:3, 9,11,16,18,21,25; 38:2,14; 39:1,17; 40:4,46; 43:7,10,18,19,23,25; 44:5,7,9, 15,25; 45:18; 46:6,13,16–18; 47:6,22; 48:11; **Dan.** 1:3,6; 8:17; 9:1; 10:16; 11:10,14,41; 12:1; **Hos.** 1:1,3,8,10(2:1), 11(2:2); 2:4(6); 3:1,4,5; 4:1,6; 5:7; 9:12, 13; 10:9,14; 11:1,10; 13:13; **Joel** 1:1,3, 12; 2:23,28(3:1); 3:6(4:6),8(4:8),16(4:16), 19(4:19); **Amos** 1:1,13; 2:11; 3:1,12; 4:5; 7:14,17; 9:7; **Obad.** 1:12,20; **Jon.** 1:1; 4:10; **Mic.** 1:16; 5:3(2),7(6); 6:5,6; 7:6; **Zeph.** 1:1,8; 2:8,9; **Hag.** 1:1,12,14; 2:2,4,23; **Zech.** 1:1,7; 4:14; 6:10,11,14; 9:9,13; 10:7,9; **Mal.** 1:6; 3:3,6,17; 4:6(3:24).

1122. בֵּן *bēn* **masc. proper noun**
(Ben)
1 Chr. 15:18.

1123. בְּנֵי *b^e^nēy* **Aram. masc. noun**
(children, sons, young: pl. const. of *bar* [1247]; corr. to Hebr. 1121)
Ezra 6:9,10,16; 7:23; **Dan.** 2:25,38; 5:13,21; 6:13(14),24(25).

1124. בְּנָה *b^e^nāh*, בְּנָא *b^e^nā'* **Aram. verb**
(to build, to rebuild; corr. to Hebr. 1129)
Ezra 4:12,13,16,21; 5:2–4,8,9,11, 13,15–17; 6:3,7,8,14; **Dan.** 4:30(27).

1125. בֶּן־אֲבִינָדָב *ben 'a̲biynādā̲b* **masc. proper noun**
(Ben Abinadab; KJV, *bēn* [1121] and *'a̲biynādā̲b* [41])
1 Kgs. 4:11.

1126. בֶּן־אוֹנִי *ben 'ôniy* **masc. proper noun**
(Ben-Oni)
Gen. 35:18.

1127. בֶּן־גֶּבֶר *ben-geber* **masc. proper noun**
(Ben-Geber; KJV, *bēn* [1121] and *geber* [1398])
1 Kgs. 4:13.

1128. בֶּן־דֶּקֶר *ben-deqer* **masc. proper noun**
(Ben-Deker; KJV, *bēn* [1121] and *deqer* [1857])
1 Kgs. 4:9.

1129. בָּנָה *bānāh* **verb**
(to build, to build up, to rebuild)
Gen. 2:22; 4:17; 8:20; 10:11; 11:4,5,8; 12:7,8; 13:18; 16:2; 22:9; 26:25; 30:3; 33:17; 35:7; **Ex.** 1:11; 17:15; 20:25; 24:4; 32:5; **Num.** 13:22; 21:27; 23:1,14,29; 32:16,24,34,37,38; **Deut.** 6:10; 8:12; 13:16(17); 20:5,20; 22:8; 25:9; 27:5,6; 28:30; **Josh.** 6:26; 8:30; 19:50; 22:10, 11,16,19,23,26,29; 24:13; **Judg.** 1:26; 6:24,26,28; 18:28; 21:4,23; **Ruth** 4:11; **1 Sam.** 2:35; 7:17; 14:35; **2 Sam.** 5:9,11; 7:5,7,13,27; 24:21,25; **1 Kgs.** 2:36; 3:1,2; 5:3(17),5(19),18(32); 6:1,2,5,7,9,10,12, 14–16,36,38; 7:1,2; 8:13,16–20,27,43, 44,48; 9:1,3,10,15,17,19,24,25; 10:4; 11:7,27,38; 12:25; 14:23; 15:17,21–23; 16:24,32,34; 18:32; 22:39; **2 Kgs.** 12:11 (12); 14:22; 15:35; 16:11,18; 17:9; 21:3–5; 22:6; 23:13; 25:1; **1 Chr.** 6:10(5:36), 32(17); 7:24; 8:12; 11:8; 14:1; 17:4,6,10, 12,25; 21:22,26; 22:2,5–8,10,11,19; 28:2, 3,6,10; 29:16,19; **2 Chr.** 2:1(1:18),3–6 (2–5),9(8),12(11); 3:1–3; 6:2,5,7–10,18, 33,34,38; 8:1,2,4–6,11,12; 9:3; 11:5,6; 14:6(5),7(6); 16:1,5,6; 17:12; 20:8; 26:2, 6,9,10; 27:3,4; 32:5; 33:3–5,14–16,19; 34:11; 35:3; 36:23; **Ezra** 1:2,3,5; 3:2,10; 4:1–4; **Neh.** 2:5,17,18,20; 3:1–3,13–15; 4:1(3:33),3(3:35),5(3:37),6(3:38),10(4), 17(11),18(12); 6:1,6; 7:1,4; 12:29; **Job** 3:14; 12:14; 20:19; 22:23; 27:18; **Ps.** 28:5; 51:18(20); 69:35(36); 78:69; 89:2(3),4(5); 102:16(17); 118:22; 122:3; 127:1; 147:2; **Prov.** 9:1; 14:1; 24:3,27; **Eccl.** 2:4; 3:3; 9:14; **Song** 4:4; 8:9; **Isa.** 5:2; 9:10(9); 25:2; 44:26,28; 45:13; 58:12; 60:10; 61:4; 65:21,22; 66:1; **Jer.** 1:10; 7:31; 12:16; 18:9; 19:5; 22:13,14; 24:6; 29:5,28; 30:18; 31:4,28,38; 32:31,35; 33:7; 35:7,9; 42:10; 45:4; 52:4; **Lam.** 3:5; **Ezek.** 4:2; 11:3; 13:10; 16:24,25,31; 17:17; 21:22(27); 26:14; 27:4,5; 28:26; 36:10,33,36; 39:15; **Dan.** 9:25; **Hos.** 8:14; **Amos** 5:11; 9:6,11,14; **Mic.** 3:10; 7:11; **Hab.** 2:12; **Zeph.** 1:13; **Hag.** 1:2,8; **Zech.** 1:16; 5:11; 6:12,13,15; 8:9; 9:3; **Mal.** 1:4; 3:15.

1130. A. בֶּן־הֲדַד *ben hadad* **masc. proper noun**
(Ben-Hadad: king of Syria)
1 Kgs. 15:18,20; 20:1,2(3),5,9,10,16, 17,20,26,30,32,33; **2 Kgs.** 6:24; 8:7,9; **2 Chr.** 16:2,4; **Jer.** 49:27.
B. בֶּן־הֲדַד *ben hadad* **masc. proper noun**
(Ben-Hadad: son of Hazael)
2 Kgs. 13:3,24,25; **Amos** 1:4.

1131. A. בִּנּוּי *binnûy* **masc. proper noun**
(Binnui: father of Noadiah)
Ezra 8:33.
B. בִּנּוּי *binnûy* **masc. proper noun**
(Binnui: son of Pahath-moab)
Ezra 10:30.
C. בִּנּוּי *binnûy* **masc. proper noun**
(Binnui: son of Bani)
Ezra 10:38.
D. בִּנּוּי *binnûy* **masc. proper noun**
(Binnui: son of Henadad)
Neh. 3:24; 10:9(10); 12:8.
E. בִּנּוּי *binnûy* **masc. proper noun**
(Binnui: head of a family)
Neh. 7:15.

1132. בֶּן־זוֹחֵת *ben zôḥēt* **masc. proper noun**
(Ben-Zoheth)
1 Chr. 4:20.

1133. בֶּן־חוּר *ben ḥûr* **masc. proper noun**
(Ben-Hur: officer under Solomon)
1 Kgs. 4:8(KJV, *bēn* [1121] and *ḥûr* [2354]).

1134. בֶּן חַיִל *ben ḥayil* **masc. proper noun**
(Ben-Hail)
2 Chr. 17:7.

1135. בֶּן־חָנָן *ben-ḥānān* **masc. proper noun**
(Ben-Hanan)
1 Chr. 4:20.

1136. בֶּן־חֶסֶד *ben-ḥeseḏ* **masc. proper noun**
(Ben-Hesed)
1 Kgs. 4:10(KJV, *bēyn* [1121] and *ḥeseḏ* [2618]).

1137. A. בָּנִי *bāniy* **masc. proper noun**
(Bani: one of David's mighty men)
2 Sam. 23:36.
B. בָּנִי *bāniy* **masc. proper noun**
(Bani: an Aaronite)
1 Chr. 6:46(31).
C. בָּנִי *bāniy* **masc. proper noun**
(Bani: descendant of Pharez)
1 Chr. 9:4; **Ezra** 2:10; 10:29,34.
D. בָּנִי *bāniy* **masc. proper noun**
(Bani: son of Bani)
Ezra 10:38.
E. בָּנִי *bāniy* **masc. proper noun**
(Bani: a Levite)
Neh. 3:17; 8:7; 9:4,5; 10:13(14),14(15); 11:22.

1138. A. בּוּנִּי *bûnniy* **masc. proper noun**
(Bunni: a Levite)
Neh. 11:15.
B. בּוּנִּי *bûnniy* **masc. proper noun**
(Bunni: a Levite)
Neh. 9:4.
C. בּוּנִּי *bûnniy* **masc. proper noun**
(Bunni: Jewish man or family)
Neh. 10:15(16).

1139. בְּנֵי־בְרַק *b^{e}nēy ḇ^{e}raq* **proper noun**
(Bene Berak)
Josh. 19:45.

1140. בִּנְיָה *binyāh* **fem. noun**
(building, structure)
Ezek. 41:13.

1141. A. בְּנָיָה *b^{e}nāyāh*, בְּנָיָהוּ *b^{e}nāyāhû* **masc. proper noun**
(Benaiah: officer of David)
2 Sam. 8:18; 20:23; 23:20,22; **1 Kgs.** 1:8, 10,26,32,36,38,44; 2:25,29,30,34,35,46; 4:4; **1 Chr.** 4:36; 11:22,24; 18:17; 27:5,6.
B. בְּנָיָה *b^{e}nāyāh*, בְּנָיָהוּ *b^{e}nāyāhû* **masc. proper noun**
(Benaiah: a soldier)
2 Sam. 23:30; **1 Chr.** 11:31; 27:14.
C. בְּנָיָה *b^{e}nāyāh*, בְּנָיָהוּ *b^{e}nāyāhû* **masc. proper noun**
(Benaiah: a Simeonite)
1 Chr. 4:36.
D. בְּנָיָה *b^{e}nāyāh*, בְּנָיָהוּ *b^{e}nāyāhû* **masc. proper noun**
(Benaiah: a priest)
1 Chr. 15:18,20,24; 16:5,6.
E. בְּנָיָה *b^{e}nāyāh*, בְּנָיָהוּ *b^{e}nāyāhû* **masc. proper noun**
(Benaiah: father of Jehoiada)
1 Chr. 27:34.
F. בְּנָיָה *b^{e}nāyāh*, בְּנָיָהוּ *b^{e}nāyāhû* **masc. proper noun**
(Benaiah: grandfather of Jahaziel)
2 Chr. 20:14.
G. בְּנָיָה *b^{e}nāyāh*, בְּנָיָהוּ *b^{e}nāyāhû* **masc. proper noun**
(Benaiah: a Levite)
2 Chr. 31:13.
H. בְּנָיָה *b^{e}nāyāh*, בְּנָיָהוּ *b^{e}nāyāhû* **masc. proper noun**
(Benaiah: son of Parosh)
Ezra 10:25.

I. בְּנָיָה b^e*nāyāh*, בְּנָיָהוּ b^e*nāyāhû* **masc. proper noun**
(Benaiah: son of Pahath-moab)
Ezra 10:30.
J. בְּנָיָה b^e*nāyāh*, בְּנָיָהוּ b^e*nāyāhû* **masc. proper noun**
(Benaiah: son of Bani)
Ezra 10:35.
K. בְּנָיָה b^e*nāyāh*, בְּנָיָהוּ b^e*nāyāhû* **masc. proper noun**
(Benaiah: son of Nebo)
Ezra 10:43.
L. בְּנָיָה b^e*nāyāh*, בְּנָיָהוּ b^e*nāyāhû* **masc. proper noun**
(Benaiah: father of Pelatiah)
Ezek. 11:1,13.

1142. בְּנֵי יַעֲקָן b^e*nēy ya'aqān* **proper noun**
(Bene-jaakan)
Num. 33:31,32.

1143. בֵּנַיִם *bēnayim* **masc. dual noun**
(champion)
1 Sam. 17:4,23.

1144. A. בִּנְיָמִין *binyāmiyn* **masc. proper noun**
(Benjamin: son of Jacob)
Gen. 35:18,24; 42:4,36; 43:14–16,29,34; 44:12; 45:12,14,22; 46:19,21; 49:27; **Ex.** 1:3; **Deut.** 33:12; **1 Chr.** 2:2; 7:6.
B. בִּנְיָמִין *binyāmiyn* **masc. proper noun**
(Benjamin: tribe or territory of Benjamin)
Num. 1:11,36,37; 2:22; 7:60; 10:24; 13:9; 26:38,41; 34:21; **Deut.** 27:12; **Josh.** 18:11,20,21,28; 21:4,17; **Judg.** 1:21; 5:14; 10:9; 19:14; 20:3,4,10,12–15, 17,18,20,21,23–25,28,30–32,35,36,39–41,43,44,46,48; 21:1,6,13–18,20,21,23; **1 Sam.** 4:12; 9:1,16,21; 10:2,20,21; 13:2,15,16; 14:16; **2 Sam.** 2:9,15,25,31; 3:19; 4:2; 19:17(18); 21:14; 23:29; **1 Kgs.** 4:18; 12:21,23; 15:22; **1 Chr.** 6:60(45),65(50); 8:1,40; 9:3,4,7; 11:31; 12:2,16,29; 21:6; 27:21; **2 Chr.** 11:1,3, 10,12,23; 14:8(7); 15:2,8,9; 17:17; 25:5; 31:1; 34:9,32; **Ezra** 1:5; 4:1; 10:9; **Ps.** 68:27(28); 80:2(3); **Jer.** 1:1; 6:1; 17:26; 32:8,44; 33:13; 37:12; **Ezek.** 48:22–24, 32; **Hos.** 5:8; **Obad.** 1:19.
C. בִּנְיָמִין *binyāmiyn* **masc. proper noun**
(Benjamin: son of Bilhan)
1 Chr. 7:10.
D. בִּנְיָמִין *binyāmiyn* **masc. proper noun**
(Benjamin: son of Harim)
Ezra 10:32; **Neh.** 3:23; 11:4,7,31,36; 12:34.
E. בִּנְיָמִין *binyāmiyn* **masc. proper noun**
(Benjamin: one of the gates of Jerusalem)
Jer. 20:2; 37:13; 38:7; **Zech.** 14:10.

1145. בֶּן־יְמִינִי *ben-y*^{e}*miyniy* **masc. proper noun**
(Benjamite: see also y^e*miyniy* [3228,II])
Judg. 3:15; 19:16; **1 Sam.** 9:21; 22:7; **2 Sam.** 16:11; 19:16,17; 20:1(see y^e*miyniy* [3228,II]); **1 Kgs.** 2:8; **1 Chr.** 27:12; **Ps.** 7:[title](1).

1146. בִּנְיָן *binyān* **masc. noun**
(building, structure)
Ezek. 40:5; 41:12,15; 42:1,5,10.

1147. בִּנְיָן *binyān* **Aram. masc. noun**
(building, structure; corr. to Hebr. 1146)
Ezra 5:4.

1148. בְּנִינוּ b^e*niynû* **masc. proper noun**
(Beninu)
Neh. 10:13(14).

1149. בְּנַס b^e*nas* **Aram. verb**
(to be angry)
Dan. 2:12.

1150. בִּנְעָא *bin'ā'* **masc. proper noun**
(Binea)
1 Chr. 8:37; 9:43.

1151. בֶּן־עַמִּי *ben-'ammiy* **masc. proper noun**
(Ben-Ammi)
Gen. 19:38.

1152. בְּסוֹדְיָה *b^esôd^eyāh* **masc. proper noun**
(Besodeiah)
Neh. 3:6.

1153. בֵּסַי *bēsay* **masc. proper noun**
(Besai)
Ezra 2:49; **Neh.** 7:52.

1154. בֶּסֶר *beser* **masc. noun**
(sour grape[s])
Job 15:33(NASB, NIV, *bōser* [1155]).

1155. בֹּסֶר *bōser* **masc. noun**
(sour grape[s])
Job 15:33(KJV, *beser* [1154]); **Isa.** 18:5; **Jer.** 31:29,30; **Ezek.** 18:2.

1156. בְּעָא *b^e'ā'* **Aram. verb**
(to ask for, to request, to seek; corr. to Hebr. 1158)
Dan. 2:13,16,18,23,49; 4:36(33); 6:4(5),7(8),11–13(12–14); 7:16.

1157. בַּעַד *ba'ad* **particle**
(for, through, behind)
Gen. 7:16; 20:7,18; 26:8; **Ex.** 8:28(24); 32:30; **Lev.** 9:7; 16:6,11,17,24; **Num.** 21:7; **Deut.** 9:20; **Josh.** 2:15; **Judg.** 3:22,23; 5:28; 9:51; **1 Sam.** 1:6; 4:18; 7:5,9; 12:19,23; 19:12; **2 Sam.** 6:16; 10:12; 12:16; 20:21; **1 Kgs.** 13:6; **2 Kgs.** 1:2; 4:4,5,21,33; 9:30; 19:4; 22:13; **1 Chr.** 15:29; 19:13; **2 Chr.** 30:18; 34:21; **Job** 1:10; 2:4; 3:23; 6:22; 9:7; 22:13; 42:8,10; **Ps.** 3:3(4); 72:15; 138:8; 139:11; **Prov.** 6:26; 7:6; 20:16; 27:13; **Song** 4:1,3; 6:7; **Isa.** 8:19; 26:20; 32:14; 37:4; **Jer.** 7:16; 11:14; 14:11; 21:2; 29:7; 37:3; 42:2,20; **Lam.** 3:7; **Ezek.** 22:30; 45:17,22; **Joel** 2:8,9; **Amos** 9:10; **Jon.** 2:6(7); **Zech.** 12:8.

1158. I. בָּעָה *bā'āh* **verb**
(to ask; search out)
Isa. 21:12; **Obad.** 1:6.
II. בָּעָה *bā'āh* **verb**
(to bring to a boil; to protrude)
Isa. 30:13; 64:2(1).

1159. בָּעוּ *ba'û* **Aram. fem. noun**
(petition, prayer)
Dan. 6:7(8),13(14).

1160. A. בְּעוֹר *b^e'ôr* **masc. proper noun**
(Beor: father of Balaam)
Num. 22:5; 24:3,15; 31:8; **Deut.** 23:4(5); **Josh.** 13:22; 24:9; **Mic.** 6:5.
B. בְּעוֹר *b^e'ôr* **masc. proper noun**
(Beor: father of a king of Edom)
Gen. 36:32; **1 Chr.** 1:43.

1161. בִּעוּתִים *bi'ûṯiym* **masc. pl. noun**
(terrors)
Job 6:4; **Ps.** 88:16(17).

1162. A. בֹּעַז *bō'az* **masc. proper noun**
(Boaz: second husband of Ruth)
Ruth 2:1,3–5,8,11,14,15,19,23; 3:2,7; 4:1,5,8,9,13,21; **1 Chr.** 2:11,12.
B. בֹּעַז *bō'az* **masc. proper noun**
(Boaz: name of a temple pillar)
1 Kgs. 7:21; **2 Chr.** 3:17.

1163. בָּעַט *bā'aṭ* **verb**
(to kick out, to kick at)
Deut. 32:15; **1 Sam.** 2:29.

1164. בְּעִי *b^e'iy* **masc. noun**
(grave)
Job 30:24(NASB, NIV, *'iy* [5856]).

1165. בְּעִיר *b^e'iyr* **masc. noun**
(livestock, cattle)
Gen. 45:17; **Ex.** 22:5(4); **Num.** 20:4,8,11; **Ps.** 78:48.

1166. בָּעַל *bā'al* **verb**
(to marry, to be married, to be a husband or wife)
Gen. 20:3; **Deut.** 21:13; 22:22; 24:1; **1 Chr.** 4:22; **Prov.** 30:23; **Isa.** 26:13; 54:1,5; 62:4,5; **Jer.** 3:14; 31:32; **Mal.** 2:11.

1167. בַּעַל *ba'al* **masc. noun**
(owner, master, husband)
Gen. 14:13; 20:3; 37:19; 49:23; **Ex.** 21:3, 22,28,29,34,36; 22:8(7),11(10),12(11), 14(13),15(14); 24:14; **Lev.** 21:4; **Num.** 21:28; **Deut.** 15:2; 22:22; 24:4; **Josh.** 24:11; **Judg.** 9:2,3,6,7,18,20,23–26, 39,46,47,51; 19:22,23; 20:5; **1 Sam.** 23:11,12; **2 Sam.** 1:6; 11:26; 21:12; **2 Kgs.** 1:8; **Neh.** 6:18; **Esth.** 1:17,20; **Job** 31:39; **Prov.** 1:17,19; 3:27; 12:4; 16:22; 17:8; 18:9; 22:24; 23:2; 24:8; 29:22; 31:11,23,28; **Eccl.** 5:11(10), 13(12); 7:12; 8:8; 10:11,20; 12:11; **Isa.** 1:3; 16:8; 41:15; 50:8; **Jer.** 37:13; **Dan.** 8:6,20; **Hos.** 2:16(18); **Joel** 1:8; **Nah.** 1:2.

1168. A. בַּעַל *ba'al* **masc. proper noun**
(Baal: the Canaanite god)
Num. 22:41(NIV, see *bāmôt ba'al* [1120,II]); **Judg.** 2:11,13; 3:7; 6:25,28,30–32; 8:33; 10:6,10; **1 Sam.** 7:4; 12:10; **1 Kgs.** 16:31,32; 18:18, 19,21,22,25,26,40; 19:18; 22:53(54); **2 Kgs.** 3:2; 10:18–23,25–28; 11:18; 17:16; 21:3; 23:4,5; **2 Chr.** 17:3; 23:17; 24:7; 28:2; 33:3; 34:4; **Jer.** 2:8,23; 7:9; 9:14(13); 11:13,17; 12:16; 19:5; 23:13,27; 32:29,35; **Hos.** 2:8(10),13(15),17(19); 11:2; 13:1; **Zeph.** 1:4.
B. בַּעַל *ba'al* **proper noun**
(Baal: city in Simeon)
1 Chr. 4:33(NIV, *b^e'ālôṯ* [1175]).
C. בַּעַל *ba'al* **masc. proper noun**
(Baal: a Reubenite)
1 Chr. 5:5.
D. בַּעַל *ba'al* **masc. proper noun**
(Baal: a Gibeonite)
1 Chr. 8:30; 9:36.

1169. בְּעֵל *b^e'ēl* **Aram. masc. noun**
(commanding officer; corr. to Hebr. 1167)
Ezra 4:8,9,17.

1170. בַּעַל בְּרִית *ba'al b^eriyṯ* **masc. proper noun**
(the false god Baal-Berith)
Judg. 8:33; 9:4.

1171. בַּעַל גָּד *ba'al gāḏ* **proper noun**
(Baal Gad)
Josh. 11:17; 12:7; 13:5.

1172. בַּעֲלָה *ba^alāh* **fem. noun**
(mistress, owner)
1 Sam. 28:7; **1 Kgs.** 17:17; **Nah.** 3:4.

1173. בַּעֲלָה *ba^alāh* **proper noun**
(Baalah)
Josh. 15:9–11,29; **2 Sam.** 6:2(see *ba^alēy y^ehûḏāh* [1184]); **1 Chr.** 13:6.

1174. בַּעַל הָמוֹן *ba'al hāmôn* **proper noun**
(Baal Hamon)
Song 8:11.

1175. בְּעָלוֹת *b^e'ālôṯ* **proper noun**
(Bealoth)
Josh. 15:24; **1 Chr.** 4:33(KJV, NASB, *ba'al* [1168,B]); **1 Kgs.** 4:16.

1176. בַּעַל זְבוּב *ba'al z^eḇûḇ* **masc. proper noun**
(Baal-Zebub)
2 Kgs. 1:2,3,6,16.

1177. A. בַּעַל חָנָן *ba'al ḥānān* **masc. proper noun**
(Baal-Hanan: king of Edom)
Gen. 36:38,39; **1 Chr.** 1:49,50.
B. בַּעַל חָנָן *ba'al ḥānān* **masc. proper noun**
(Baal-Hanan: a Gederite)
1 Chr. 27:28.

1178. בַּעַל חָצוֹר *ba'al ḥāṣôr* **proper noun**
(Baal Hazor)
2 Sam. 13:23.

1179. בַּעַל חֶרְמוֹן *ba'al ḥermôn* **proper noun**
(Baal Hermon)
Judg. 3:3; **1 Chr.** 5:23.

1180. I. בַּעֲלִי *ba'^{a}liy* **masc. noun**
(my master; *ba'al* [1167] with pronom. suff.)
Hos. 2:16(18)(KJV, NASB, see II).
II. בַּעֲלִי *ba'^{a}liy* **masc. proper noun**
(Baali)
Hos. 2:16(18)(NIV, see I).

1181. בַּעֲלֵי בָמוֹת *ba'^{a}lēy bāmôṯ* **masc. noun**
(dominant heights; lit., lords of the high places)
Num. 22:41(NIV, *bāmôṯ ba'al* [1120,B]).

1182. בְּעֶלְיָדָע *b^{e}'elyāḏā'* **proper noun**
(Beeliada)
1 Chr. 14:7.

1183. בְּעַלְיָה *b^{e}'alyāh* **masc. proper noun**
(Bealiah)
1 Chr. 12:5.

1184. בַּעֲלֵי יְהוּדָה *ba'^{a}lēy y^{e}hûḏāh* **proper noun**
(Baale Judah: another name for *ba'^{a}lāh* [1173])
2 Sam. 6:2.

1185. בַּעֲלִיס *ba'^{a}liys* **masc. proper noun**
(Baalis)
Jer. 40:14.

1186. בַּעַל מְעוֹן *ba'al m^{e}'ôn* **proper noun**
(Baal Meon)
Num. 32:38; **1 Chr.** 5:8; **Ezek.** 25:9.

1187. בַּעַל פְּעוֹר *ba'al p^{e}'ôr* **masc. proper noun**
(Baal Peor)
Num. 25:3(NASB, NIV, *ba'al* [1168] and *p^{e}'ôr* [6465]),5(NASB, NIV, *ba'al* [1168] and *p^{e}'ôr* [6465]); **Deut.** 4:3; **Ps.** 106:28 (NASB, NIV, *ba'al* [1168] and *p^{e}'ôr* [6465]); **Hos.** 9:10.

1188. בַּעַל פְּרָצִים *ba'al p^{e}rāṣiym* **proper noun**
(Baal Perazim)
2 Sam. 5:20; **1 Chr.** 14:11.

1189. בַּעַל צְפוֹן *ba'al ṣ^{e}p̱ôn*, בַּעַל צְפֹן *ba'al ṣ^{e}p̱ōn* **proper noun**
(Baal Zephon)
Ex. 14:2,9; **Num.** 33:7.

1190. בַּעַל שָׁלִשָׁה *ba'al šālišāh* **proper noun**
(Baal Shalishah)
2 Kgs. 4:42.

1191. בַּעֲלָת *ba'^{a}lāṯ* **proper noun**
(Baalath)
Josh. 19:44; **1 Kgs.** 9:18; **2 Chr.** 8:6.

1192. בַּעֲלַת בְּאֵר *ba'^{a}laṯ b^{e}'ēr* **proper noun**
(Baalath Beer)
Josh. 19:8.

1193. בַּעַל תָּמָר *ba'al tāmār* **proper noun**
(Baal Tamar)
Judg. 20:33.

1194. בְּעֹן *bᵉʿōn* **proper noun**
(Beon)
Num. 32:3.

1195. A. בַּעֲנָא *baʿᵃnāʾ* **masc. proper noun**
(Baana: son of Ahilud)
1 Kgs. 4:12.
B. בַּעֲנָא *baʿᵃnāʾ* **masc. proper noun**
(Baana: son of Hushai)
1 Kgs. 4:16.
C. בַּעֲנָא *baʿᵃnāʾ* **masc. proper noun**
(Baana: father of Zadok)
Neh. 3:4.

1196. A. בַּעֲנָה *baʿᵃnāh* **masc. proper noun**
(Baanah: captain of Ishbosheth's army)
2 Sam. 4:2,5,6,9.
B. בַּעֲנָה *baʿᵃnāh* **masc. proper noun**
(Baanah: father of Heleb)
2 Sam. 23:29; **1 Chr.** 11:30.
C. בַּעֲנָה *baʿᵃnāh* **masc. proper noun**
(Baanah: a Jew)
Ezra 2:2; **Neh.** 7:7.
D. בַּעֲנָה *baʿᵃnāh* **masc. proper noun**
(Baanah: a leader)
Neh. 10:27(28).

1197. I. בָּעַר *bāʿar* **verb**
(to burn, to consume)
Ex. 3:2,3; 22:6(5); 35:3; **Lev.** 6:12(5); **Num.** 11:1,3; **Deut.** 4:11; 5:23(20); 9:15; **Judg.** 15:5,14; **2 Sam.** 22:9,13; **2 Chr.** 4:20; 13:11; 28:3; **Neh.** 10:34 (35); **Esth.** 1:12; **Job** 1:16; **Ps.** 2:12; 18:8(9); 39:3(4); 79:5; 83:14(15); 89:46 (47); 106:18; **Isa.** 1:31; 3:14; 4:4; 5:5; 6:13; 9:18(17); 10:17; 30:27,33; 34:9; 40:16; 42:25; 43:2; 44:15; 50:11; 62:1; **Jer.** 4:4; 7:18,20; 20:9; 21:12; 36:22; 44:6; **Lam.** 2:3; **Ezek.** 1:13; 5:2; 20:48 (21:4); 39:9,10; **Hos.** 7:4,6; **Nah.** 2:13 (14); **Mal.** 4:1(3:19).
II. בָּעַר *bāʿar* **verb**
(to remove, to graze)
Ex. 22:5(4); **Num.** 24:22; **Deut.** 13:5(6); 17:7,12; 19:13,19; 21:9,21; 22:21,22,24; 24:7; 26:13,14; **Judg.** 20:13; **2 Sam.** 4:11; **1 Kgs.** 14:10; 16:3; 21:21; 22:46(47); **2 Kgs.** 23:24; **2 Chr.** 19:3; **Isa.** 3:14(KJV, NASB, see I).
III. בָּעַר *bāʿar* **verb**
(to be stupid, to be brutish)
Ps. 94:8; **Isa.** 19:11; **Jer.** 10:8,14,21; 51:17; **Ezek.** 21:31(36).

1198. בַּעַר *baʿar* **adj.**
(senseless, foolish)
Ps. 49:10(11); 73:22; 92:6(7); **Prov.** 12:1; 30:2.

1199. בַּעֲרָא *baʿᵃrāʾ* **fem. proper noun**
(Baara)
1 Chr. 8:8.

1200. בְּעֵרָה *bᵉʿērāh* **fem. noun**
(fire)
Ex. 22:6(5).

1201. בַּעְשָׁא *baʿšāʾ* **masc. proper noun**
(Baasha)
1 Kgs. 15:16,17,19,21,22,27,28,32,33; 16:1,3–8,11–13; 21:22; **2 Kgs.** 9:9; **2 Chr.** 16:1,3,5,6; **Jer.** 41:9.

1202. בַּעֲשֵׂיָה *baʿᵃśēyāh* **masc. proper noun**
(Baaseiah)
1 Chr. 6:40(25).

1203. בְּעֶשְׁתְּרָה *bᵉʿeštᵉrāh* **proper noun**
(Be-eshterah)
Josh. 21:27.

1204. בָּעַת *bāʿaṯ* **verb**
(to terrify, to overwhelm)
1 Sam. 16:14,15; **2 Sam.** 22:5; **1 Chr.** 21:30; **Esth.** 7:6; **Job** 3:5; 7:14; 9:34; 13:11,21; 15:24; 18:11; 33:7; **Ps.** 18:4(5); **Isa.** 21:4; **Dan.** 8:17.

1205. בְּעָתָה *bᵉʿāṯāh* **fem. noun**
(terror, trouble)
Jer. 8:15; 14:19.

1206. בֹּץ *bōṣ* **masc. noun**
(mire, mud)
Jer. 38:22.

1207. בִּצָּה *biṣṣāh* **fem. noun**
(mire, marsh)
Job 8:11; 40:21; **Ezek.** 47:11.

1208. I. בָּצוּר *bāṣûr* **adj.**
(thick, inaccessible; [Kᵉ] from *bāṣar* [1219,III])
Zech. 11:2(KJV, see II).
II. בָּצִיר *bāṣiyr* **adj.**
(vintage, time of grape harvest; [Qᵉ] same as *bāṣiyr* [1210])
Zech. 11:2(NASB, NIV, see I).

1209. בֵּצַי *bēṣay* **masc. proper noun**
(Bezai)
Ezra 2:17; **Neh.** 7:23; 10:18(19).

1210. בָּצִיר *bāṣiyr* **masc. noun**
(vintage, time of grape harvest)
Lev. 26:5; **Judg.** 8:2; **Isa.** 24:13; 32:10; **Jer.** 48:32; **Mic.** 7:1; **Zech.** 11:2([Kᵉ] NASB, NIV, [Kᵉ] *bāṣûr* [1208,I]).

1211. בָּצָל *bāṣāl* **masc. noun**
(onion)
Num. 11:5.

1212. A. בְּצַלְאֵל *bᵉṣalʾēl* **masc. proper noun**
(Bezalel: an artisan)
Ex. 31:2; 35:30; 36:1,2; 37:1; 38:22; **1 Chr.** 2:20; **2 Chr.** 1:5.
B. בְּצַלְאֵל *bᵉṣalʾēl* **masc. proper noun**
(Bezalel: an Israelite)
Ezra 10:30.

1213. בַּצְלוּת *baṣlûṯ* **masc. proper noun**
(Bazluth)
Ezra 2:52; **Neh.** 7:54(KJV, NASB, [Qᵉ] *bazliyṯ*).

1214. בָּצַע *bāṣaʿ* **verb**
(to cut off, to break off, to gain wrongfully)
Job 6:9; 27:8; **Ps.** 10:3; **Prov.** 1:19; 15:27; **Isa.** 10:12; 38:12; **Jer.** 6:13; 8:10; **Lam.** 2:17; **Ezek.** 22:12,27; **Joel** 2:8; **Amos** 9:1; **Hab.** 2:9; **Zech.** 4:9.

1215. בֶּצַע *beṣaʿ* **masc. noun**
(profit, gain, dishonest gain)
Gen. 37:26; **Ex.** 18:21; **Judg.** 5:19; **1 Sam.** 8:3; **Job** 22:3; **Ps.** 30:9(10); 119:36; **Prov.** 1:19; 15:27; 28:16; **Isa.** 33:15; 56:11; 57:17; **Jer.** 6:13; 8:10; 22:17; 51:13; **Ezek.** 22:13,27; 33:31; **Mic.** 4:13; **Hab.** 2:9; **Mal.** 3:14.

1216. בָּצַק *bāṣaq* **verb**
(to become swollen)
Deut. 8:4; **Neh.** 9:21.

1217. בָּצֵק *bāṣēq* **masc. noun**
(dough)
Ex. 12:34,39; **2 Sam.** 13:8; **Jer.** 7:18; **Hos.** 7:4.

1218. בָּצְקַת *boṣqaṯ* **proper noun**
(Bozkath)
Josh. 15:39; **2 Kgs.** 22:1.

1219. I. בָּצַר *bāṣar* **verb**
(to gather, to harvest)
Lev. 25:5,11; **Deut.** 24:21; **Judg.** 9:27; **Jer.** 6:9; 49:9; **Obad.** 1:5.
II. בָּצַר *bāṣar* **verb**
(to humble)

Ps. 76:12(13).
III. בָּצַר *bāṣar* **verb**
(to be or make inaccessible, to strengthen)
Gen. 11:6; **Num.** 13:28; **Deut.** 1:28; 3:5; 9:1; 28:52; **Josh.** 14:12; **2 Sam.** 20:6; **2 Kgs.** 18:13; 19:25; **2 Chr.** 17:2; 19:5; 32:1; 33:14; **Neh.** 9:25; **Job** 42:2; **Isa.** 2:15; 22:10; 25:2; 27:10; 36:1; 37:26; **Jer.** 15:20; 33:3; 51:53; **Ezek.** 21:20(25); 36:35; **Hos.** 8:14; **Zeph.** 1:16; **Zech.** 11:2([Q^{e}] *bāṣiyr* [1210]; KJV, [K^{e}] *bāṣôr* [1208,II]; NIV, [K^{e}] *bāṣûr* [1208,I]).
IV. בָּצַר *bāṣar* **verb**
(gold tester [participle form])
Jer. 6:27(KJV, *mibṣār* [4013,I]; NIV, *mibṣār* [4013,II]).

1220. I. בֶּצֶר *beṣer* **masc. noun**
(gold)
Job 22:24,25(KJV, see II).
II. בֶּצֶר *beṣer* **masc. noun**
(defense)
Job 22:25(NASB, NIV, see I).

1221. A. בֶּצֶר *beṣer* **proper noun**
(Bezer: city in Reuben)
Deut. 4:43; **Josh.** 20:8; 21:36; **1 Chr.** 6:78(63).
B. בֶּצֶר *beṣer* **proper noun**
(Bezer: descendant of Asher)
1 Chr. 7:37.

1222. בְּצַר *b^{e}ṣar* **masc. noun**
(gold)
Job 36:19(NASB, NIV, *ṣar* [6862,I]).

1223. בָּצְרָה *boṣrāh* **fem. noun**
(pen, sheepfold)
Mic. 2:12(KJV, *boṣrāh* [1224,A]).

1224. A. בָּצְרָה *boṣrāh* **proper noun**
(Bozrah: city in and sometime capital of Edom)
Gen. 36:33; **1 Chr.** 1:44; **Isa.** 34:6; 63:1; **Jer.** 49:13,22; **Amos** 1:12; **Mic.** 2:12(NASB, NIV, *boṣrāh* [1223]).
B. בָּצְרָה *boṣrāh* **proper noun**
(Bozrah: city in Moab)
Jer. 48:24.

1225. בִּצָּרוֹן *biṣṣārôn* **masc. noun**
(stronghold, fortress)
Zech. 9:12.

1226. בַּצֹּרֶת *baṣṣōreṯ* **fem. noun**
(drought, dearth)
Jer. 14:1; 17:8.

1227. בַּקְבּוּק *baqbûq* **masc. proper noun**
(Bakbuk)
Ezra 2:51; **Neh.** 7:53.

1228. בַּקְבֻּק *baqbuq* **masc. noun**
(bottle, jar)
1 Kgs. 14:3; **Jer.** 19:1,10.

1229. בַּקְבֻּקְיָה *baqbuqyāh* **masc. proper noun**
(Bakbukiah)
Neh. 11:17; 12:9,25.

1230. בַּקְבַּקַּר *baqbaqqar* **masc. proper noun**
(Bakbakkar)
1 Chr. 9:15.

1231. A. בֻּקִּי *buqqiy* **masc. proper noun**
(Bukki: a Danite)
Num. 34:22.
B. בֻּקִּי *buqqiy* **masc. proper noun**
(Bukki: descendant of Aaron)
1 Chr. 6:5(5:31),51(36); **Ezra** 7:4.

1232. בֻּקִּיָּהוּ *buqqiyyāhû* **masc. proper noun**
(Bukkiah)
1 Chr. 25:4,13.

1233. בָּקִיעַ *bāqiya'* **masc. noun**
(breach, small fragment)
Isa. 22:9; **Amos** 6:11.

1234. בָּקַע *bāqa'* **verb**
(to split, to divide, to break open)
Gen. 7:11; 22:3; **Ex.** 14:16,21; **Num.** 16:31; **Josh.** 9:4,13; **Judg.** 15:19; **1 Sam.** 6:14; **2 Sam.** 23:16; **1 Kgs.** 1:40; **2 Kgs.** 2:24; 3:26; 8:12; 15:16; 25:4; **1 Chr.** 11:18; **2 Chr.** 21:17; 25:12; 32:1; **Neh.** 9:11; **Job** 26:8; 28:10; 32:19; **Ps.** 74:15; 78:13,15; 141:7; **Prov.** 3:20; **Eccl.** 10:9; **Isa.** 7:6; 34:15; 35:6; 48:21; 58:8; 59:5; 63:12; **Jer.** 39:2; 52:7; **Ezek.** 13:11,13; 26:10; 29:7; 30:16; **Hos.** 13:8, 16(14:1); **Amos** 1:13; **Mic.** 1:4; **Hab.** 3:9; **Zech.** 14:4.

1235. בֶּקַע *beqa'* **masc. noun**
(beka, half a shekel)
Gen. 24:22; **Ex.** 38:26.

1236. בִּקְעָה *biq'āh* **Aram. fem. noun**
(plain; corr. to Hebr. 1237)
Dan. 3:1.

1237. בִּקְעָה *biq'āh* **fem. noun**
(plain)
Gen. 11:2; **Deut.** 8:7; 11:11; 34:3; **Josh.** 11:8,17; 12:7; **2 Chr.** 35:22; **Neh.** 6:2; **Ps.** 104:8; **Isa.** 40:4; 41:18; 63:14; **Ezek.** 3:22,23; 8:4; 37:1,2; **Amos** 1:5; **Zech.** 12:11.

1238. I. בָּקַק *bāqaq* **verb**
(to empty)
Isa. 19:3; 24:1,3; **Jer.** 19:7; 51:2; **Hos.** 10:1(NASB, NIV, see II); **Nah.** 2:2(3).
II. בָּקַק *bāqaq* **verb**
(to be or grow luxuriant)
Hos. 10:1(KJV, see I).

1239. בָּקַר *bāqar* **verb**
(to seek, to look for, to consider)
Lev. 13:36; 27:33; **2 Kgs.** 16:15; **Ps.** 27:4; **Prov.** 20:25; **Ezek.** 34:11,12.

1240. בְּקַר *b^eqar* **Aram. verb**
(to seek, to search; corr. to Hebr. 1239)
Ezra 4:15,19; 5:17; 6:1; 7:14.

1241. בָּקָר *bāqār* **masc. noun**
(ox, oxen, herd, cattle)
Gen. 12:16; 13:5; 18:7,8; 20:14; 21:27; 24:35; 26:14; 32:7(8); 33:13; 34:28; 45:10; 46:32; 47:1,17; 50:8; **Ex.** 9:3; 10:9,24; 12:32,38; 20:24; 22:1(21:37); 29:1; 34:3; **Lev.** 1:2,3,5; 3:1; 4:3,14; 9:2; 16:3; 22:19,21; 23:18; 27:32; **Num.** 7:3,6–8,15,17,21,23,27,29,33,35,39,41,45,47,51,53,57,59,63,65,69,71,75,77,81,83,87,88; 8:8; 11:22; 15:3,8,9,24; 22:40; 28:11,19,27; 29:2,8,13,17; 31:28,30,33, 38,44; **Deut.** 8:13; 12:6,17,21; 14:23,26; 15:19; 16:2; 21:3; 32:14; **Judg.** 3:31; **1 Sam.** 11:5,7; 14:32; 15:9,14,15,21; 16:2; 27:9; 30:20; **2 Sam.** 6:6; 12:2,4; 17:29; 24:22,24; **1 Kgs.** 1:9; 4:23(5:3); 7:25,29,44; 8:5,63; 19:20,21; **2 Kgs.** 5:26; 16:17; **1 Chr.** 12:40; 13:9; 21:23; 27:29; **2 Chr.** 4:3,4,15; 5:6; 7:5; 13:9; 15:11; 18:2; 29:22,32,33; 31:6; 32:29; 35:7–9,12; **Neh.** 10:36(37); **Job** 1:3,14; 40:15; 42:12; **Ps.** 66:15; **Eccl.** 2:7; **Isa.** 7:21; 11:7; 22:13; 65:10,25; **Jer.** 3:24; 5:17; 31:12; 52:20; **Ezek.** 4:15; 43:19, 23,25; 45:18; 46:6; **Hos.** 5:6; **Joel** 1:18; **Amos** 6:12; **Jon.** 3:7; **Hab.** 3:17.

1242. בֹּקֶר *bōqer* **masc. noun**
(morning, daybreak)
Gen. 1:5,8,13,19,23,31; 19:27; 20:8; 21:14; 22:3; 24:54; 26:31; 28:18; 29:25; 31:55(32:1); 40:6; 41:8; 44:3; 49:27; **Ex.** 7:15; 8:20(16); 9:13; 10:13; 12:10,22; 14:24,27; 16:7,8,12,13,19–21,23,24; 18:13,14; 19:16; 23:18; 24:4; 27:21; 29:34,39,41; 30:7; 34:2,4,25; 36:3; **Lev.** 6:9(2),12(5),20(13); 7:15; 9:17; 19:13; 22:30; 24:3; **Num.** 9:12,15,21; 14:40; 16:5; 22:13,21,41; 28:4,8,23; **Deut.** 16:4,7; 28:67; **Josh.** 3:1; 6:12; 7:14,16; 8:10; **Judg.** 6:28,31; 9:33; 16:2; 19:5,8, 25–27; 20:19; **Ruth** 2:7; 3:13,14; **1 Sam.** 1:19; 3:15; 5:4; 9:19; 11:11; 14:36; 15:12; 17:20; 19:2,11; 20:35; 25:22,34,36,37; 29:10,11; **2 Sam.** 2:27; 11:14; 13:4; 17:22; 23:4; 24:11,15; **1 Kgs.** 3:21; 17:6;

18:26; **2 Kgs.** 3:20,22; 7:9; 10:8,9; 16:15; 19:35; **1 Chr.** 9:27; 16:40; 23:30; **2 Chr.** 2:4(3); 13:11; 20:20; 31:3; **Ezra** 3:3; **Esth.** 2:14; 5:14; **Job** 1:5; 4:20; 7:18; 11:17; 24:17; 38:7,12; **Ps.** 5:3(4); 30:5(6); 46:5(6); 49:14(15); 55:17(18); 59:16(17); 65:8(9); 73:14; 88:13(14); 90:5,6,14; 92:2(3); 101:8; 130:6; 143:8; **Prov.** 7:18; 27:14; **Eccl.** 10:16; 11:6; **Isa.** 5:11; 17:11,14; 21:12; 28:19; 33:2; 37:36; 38:13; 50:4; **Jer.** 20:16; 21:12; **Lam.** 3:23; **Ezek.** 12:8; 24:18; 33:22; 46:13–15; **Dan.** 8:14,26; **Hos.** 6:4; 7:6; 13:3; **Amos** 4:4; 5:8; **Mic.** 2:1; **Zeph.** 3:3,5.

1243. בַּקָּרָה *baqqārāh* **fem. noun**
(a seeking, a caring)
Ezek. 34:12.

1244. בִּקֹּרֶת *biqqōreṯ* **fem. noun**
(punishment)
Lev. 19:20.

1245. בָּקַשׁ *bāqaš* **verb**
(to seek, to require)
Gen. 31:39; 37:15,16; 43:9,30; **Ex.** 2:15; 4:19,24; 10:11; 33:7; **Lev.** 19:31; **Num.** 16:10; 35:23; **Deut.** 4:29; 13:10(11); **Josh.** 2:22; 22:23; **Judg.** 4:22; 6:29; 14:4; 18:1; **Ruth** 3:1; **1 Sam.** 9:3; 10:2, 14,21; 13:14; 14:4; 16:16; 19:2,10; 20:1, 16; 22:23; 23:10,14,15,25; 24:2(3),9(10); 25:26,29; 26:2,20; 27:1,4; 28:7; **2 Sam.** 3:17; 4:8,11; 5:17; 12:16; 16:11; 17:3,20; 20:19; 21:1,2; **1 Kgs.** 1:2,3; 2:40; 10:24; 11:22,40; 18:10; 19:10,14; 20:7; **2 Kgs.** 2:16,17; 6:19; **1 Chr.** 4:39; 14:8; 16:10, 11; 21:3; **2 Chr.** 7:14; 9:23; 11:16; 15:4, 15; 20:4; 22:9; **Ezra** 2:62; 8:21–23; **Neh.** 2:4,10; 5:12,18; 7:64; 12:27; **Esth.** 2:2, 15,21,23; 3:6; 4:8; 6:2; 7:7; 9:2; **Job** 10:6; **Ps.** 4:2(3); 24:6; 27:4,8; 34:14(15); 35:4; 37:25,32,36; 38:12(13); 40:14(15), 16(17); 54:3(5); 63:9(10); 69:6(7); 70:2(3),4(5); 71:13,24; 83:16(17); 86:14; 104:21; 105:3,4; 119:176; 122:9; **Prov.** 2:4; 11:27; 14:6; 15:14; 17:9,11,19; 18:1,15; 21:6; 23:35; 28:5; 29:10,26; **Eccl.** 3:6,15; 7:25,28,29; 8:17; 12:10; **Song** 3:1,2; 5:6; 6:1; **Isa.** 1:12; 40:20; 41:12,17; 45:19; 51:1; 65:1; **Jer.** 2:24,33; 4:30; 5:1; 11:21; 19:7,9; 21:7; 22:25; 26:21; 29:13; 34:2,20,21; 38:16; 44:30; 45:5; 46:26; 49:37; 50:4,20; 69:13; **Lam.** 1:11,19; **Ezek.** 3:18,20; 7:25,26; 22:30; 26:21; 33:8; 34:4,6,16; **Dan.** 1:8,20; 8:15; 9:3; **Hos.** 2:7(9); 3:5; 5:6,15; 7:10; **Amos** 8:12; **Nah.** 3:7,11; **Zeph.** 1:6; 2:3; **Zech.** 6:7; 8:21,22; 11:16; 12:9; **Mal.** 2:7,15; 3:1.

1246. בַּקָּשָׁה *baqqāšāh* **fem. noun**
(a request)
Ezra 7:6; **Esth.** 5:3,6–8; 7:2,3; 9:12.

1247. בַּר *bar* **Aram. masc. noun**
(son)
Ezra 5:1,2; 6:9(see *bᵉnēy* [1123]),10(see *bᵉnēy* [1123]),14,16(see *bᵉnēy* [1123]); 7:23(see *bᵉnēy* [1123]); **Dan.** 2:25(see *bᵉnēy* [1123]),38(see *bᵉnēy* [1123]); 3:25; 5:13(see *bᵉnēy* [1123]),21(see *bᵉnēy* [1123]),22,31(6:1); 6:13(14)(see *bᵉnēy* [1123]),24(25)(see *bᵉnēy* [1123]); 7:13.

1248. בַּר *bar* **masc. noun**
(son)
Ps. 2:12; **Prov.** 31:2.

1249. בַּר *bar* **adj.**
(clean, pure, bright)
Job 11:4; **Ps.** 19:8(9); 24:4; 73:1; **Prov.** 14:4; **Song** 6:9,10.

1250. בַּר *bar,* בָּר *bār* **masc. noun**
(corn, grain)
Gen. 41:35,49; 42:3,25; 45:23; **Job** 39:4; **Ps.** 65:13(14); 72:16; **Prov.** 11:26; **Jer.** 23:28; **Joel** 2:24; **Amos** 5:11; 8:5,6.

1251. בַּר *bar* **Aram. masc. noun**
(field; corr. to Hebr. 1250)
Dan. 2:38; 4:12(9),15(12),21(18),23(20), 25(22),32(29).

1252. בֹּר *bōr* **masc. noun**
(cleanness, pureness)
2 Sam. 22:21,25; **Job** 22:30; **Ps.** 18:20(21),24(25); **Isa.** 1:25(NASB, *bōr* [1253]).

1253. בֹּר *bōr* **masc. noun**
(lye, washing soda)
Job 9:30; **Isa.** 1:25(KJV, NIV, *bōr* [1252]).

1254. I. בָּרָא *bārā'* **verb**
(to create, to make)
Gen. 1:1,21,27; 2:3,4; 5:1,2; 6:7; **Ex.** 34:10; **Num.** 16:30; **Deut.** 4:32; **Ps.** 51:10(12); 89:12(13),47(48); 102:18(19); 104:30; 148:5; **Eccl.** 12:1; **Isa.** 4:5; 40:26,28; 41:20; 42:5; 43:1,7,15; 45:7,8,12,18; 48:7; 54:16; 57:19; 65:17,18; **Jer.** 31:22; **Ezek.** 21:30(35); 28:13,15; **Amos** 4:13; **Mal.** 2:10.
II. בָּרָא *bārā'* **verb**
(to make fat)
1 Sam. 2:29.
III. בָּרָא *bārā'* **verb**
(to hew, to clear timber, to cut out, to make)
Josh. 17:15,18; **Ezek.** 21:19(24)(KJV, see IV); 23:47.
IV. בָּרָא *bārā'* **verb**
(to choose)
Ezek. 21:19(24)(NASB, NIV, see III).

1255. בְּרֹאדַךְ בַּלְאֲדָן *b^e^rō'da<u>k</u> bal'^a^<u>d</u>ān* **masc. proper noun**
(Berodach-baladan)
2 Kgs. 20:12(NIV, *m^e^rō<u>d</u>a<u>k</u> bal'^a^<u>d</u>ān* [4757]).

1256. בְּרָאיָה *b^e^rā'yāh* **masc. proper noun**
(Beraiah)
1 Chr. 8:21.

1257. בַּרְבֻּר *barbur* **masc. noun**
(fowl, bird)
1 Kgs. 4:23(5:3).

1258. בָּרַד *bāra<u>d</u>* **verb**
(to hail)
Isa. 32:19.

1259. בָּרָד *bārā<u>d</u>* **masc. noun**
(hail, hailstone)
Ex. 9:18,19,22–26,28,29,33,34; 10:5,12,15; **Josh.** 10:11; **Job** 38:22; **Ps.** 18:12(13),13(14); 78:47,48; 105:32; 148:8; **Isa.** 28:2,17; 30:30; **Hag.** 2:17.

1260. A. בֶּרֶד *bere<u>d</u>* **masc. proper noun**
(Bered: a town)
Gen. 16:14.
B. בֶּרֶד *bere<u>d</u>* **masc. proper noun**
(Bered: an Ephraimite)
1 Chr. 7:20.

1261. בָּרֹד *bārō<u>d</u>* **adj.**
(mottled, spotted)
Gen. 31:10,12; **Zech.** 6:3,6.

1262. I. בָּרָה *bārāh* **verb**
(to eat, to feed)
2 Sam. 3:35; 12:17; 13:5,6,10; **Lam.** 4:10.
II. בָּרָה *bārāh* **verb**
(to select, to make a covenant with)
1 Sam. 17:8.

1263. A. בָּרוּךְ *bārû<u>k</u>* **masc. proper noun**
(Baruch: son of Zabbai)
Neh. 3:20; 10:6(7).
B. בָּרוּךְ *bārû<u>k</u>* **masc. proper noun**
(Baruch: a Judaite)
Neh. 11:5.
C. בָּרוּךְ *bārû<u>k</u>* **masc. proper noun**
(Baruch: a scribe)
Jer. 32:12,13,16; 36:4,5,8,10,13–19,26, 27,32; 43:3,6; 45:1,2.

1264. בְּרֹמִים *b^e^rōmiym* **masc. pl. noun**
(multicolored)
Ezek. 27:24.

1265. בְּרוֹשׁ *b^erôš* **masc. noun**
(fir wood, pinewood, fir tree)
2 Sam. 6:5(NIV, *šiyr* [7891]); **1 Kgs.** 5:8(22),10(24); 6:15,34; 9:11; **2 Kgs.** 19:23; **2 Chr.** 2:8(7); 3:5; **Ps.** 104:17; **Isa.** 14:8; 37:24; 41:19; 55:13; 60:13; **Ezek.** 27:5; 31:8; **Hos.** 14:8(9); **Nah.** 2:3(4); **Zech.** 11:2.

1266. בְּרוֹת *b^erôṯ* **masc. noun**
(fir, pine)
Song 1:17.

1267. בָּרוּת *bārûṯ* **fem. noun**
(food)
Ps. 69:21(22).

1268. בֵּרוֹתָה *bērôṯāh*, בֵּרֹתַי *bērōṯay* **proper noun**
(Berothai, Berothah)
2 Sam. 8:8; **Ezek.** 47:16.

1269. בִּרְזָוִת *birzāwiṯ* **masc. proper noun**
(Birzaith)
1 Chr. 7:31.

1270. בַּרְזֶל *barzel* **masc. noun**
(iron, iron ax head)
Gen. 4:22; **Lev.** 26:19; **Num.** 31:22; 35:16; **Deut.** 3:11; 4:20; 8:9; 19:5; 27:5; 28:23,48; 33:25; **Josh.** 6:19,24; 8:31; 17:16,18; 22:8; **Judg.** 1:19; 4:3,13; **1 Sam.** 17:7; **2 Sam.** 12:31; 23:7; **1 Kgs.** 6:7; 8:51; 22:11; **2 Kgs.** 6:5,6; **1 Chr.** 20:3; 22:3,14,16; 29:2,7; **2 Chr.** 2:7(6),14(13); 18:10; 24:12; **Job** 19:24; 20:24; 28:2; 40:18; 41:27(19); **Ps.** 2:9; 105:18; 107:10,16; 149:8; **Prov.** 27:17; **Eccl.** 10:10; **Isa.** 10:34; 44:12; 45:2; 48:4; 60:17; **Jer.** 1:18; 6:28; 11:4; 15:12; 17:1; 28:13,14; **Ezek.** 4:3; 22:18,20; 27:12,19; **Amos** 1:3; **Mic.** 4:13.

1271. A. בַּרְזִלַּי *barzillay* **masc. proper noun**
(Barzillai: a Gileadite)
2 Sam. 17:27; 19:31–34(32–35),39(40); **1 Kgs.** 2:7.
B. בַּרְזִלַּי *barzillay* **masc. proper noun**
(Barzillai: a Meholathite)
2 Sam. 21:8.
C. בַּרְזִלַּי *barzillay* **masc. proper noun**
(Barzillai: a priest)
Ezra 2:61; **Neh.** 7:63.

1272. בָּרַח *bāraḥ* **verb**
(to flee, to run away)
Gen. 16:6,8; 27:43; 31:20–22,27; 35:1,7; **Ex.** 2:15; 14:5; 26:28; 36:33; **Num.** 24:11; **Judg.** 9:21; 11:3; **1 Sam.** 19:12,18; 20:1; 21:10(11); 22:17,20; 23:6; 27:4; **2 Sam.** 4:3; 13:34,37,38; 15:14; 19:9(10); **1 Kgs.** 2:7,39; 11:17,23,40; 12:2; **1 Chr.** 8:13; 12:15; **2 Chr.** 10:2; **Neh.** 6:11; 13:10,28; **Job** 9:25; 14:2; 20:24; 27:22; 41:28(20); **Ps.** 3:[title](1); 57:[title](1); 139:7; **Prov.** 19:26; **Song** 8:14; **Isa.** 22:3; 48:20; **Jer.** 4:29; 26:21; 39:4; 52:7; **Dan.** 10:7; **Hos.** 12:12(13); **Amos** 7:12; **Jon.** 1:3,10; 4:2.

1273. בַּרְחֻמִי *barḥumiy* **masc. proper noun**
(Barhumite: transposed form of *baḥ^{a}rûmiy* [978])
2 Sam. 23:31.

1274. בְּרִי *b^eriy* **adj.**
(fat)
Ezek. 34:20(NASB, NIV, *bāriy'* [1277]).

1275. בֵּרִי *bēriy* **masc. proper noun**
(Beri)
1 Chr. 7:36.

1276. בֵּרִי *bēriy* **masc. proper noun**
(Berite)
2 Sam. 20:14.

1277. בָּרִיא *bāriy'* **adj.**
(fat, healthy)

Gen. 41:2,4,5,7,18,20; **Judg.** 3:17; **1 Kgs.** 4:23(5:3); **Ps.** 73:4; **Ezek.** 34:3,20(KJV, $b^{e}riy$ [1274]); **Dan.** 1:15; **Hab.** 1:16; **Zech.** 11:16.

1278. בְּרִיאָה $b^{e}riy'\bar{a}h$ **fem. noun**
(something new)
Num. 16:30.

1279. בִּרְיָה *biryāh* **fem. noun**
(food)
2 Sam. 13:5,7,10.

1280. בְּרִיחַ $b^{e}riya\d{h}$ **masc. noun**
(bar, bolt, gate; noble)
Ex. 26:26–29; 35:11; 36:31–34; 39:33; 40:18; **Num.** 3:36; 4:31; **Deut.** 3:5; **Judg.** 16:3; **1 Sam.** 23:7; **1 Kgs.** 4:13; **2 Chr.** 8:5; 14:7(6); **Neh.** 3:3,6,13–15; **Job** 38:10; **Ps.** 107:16; 147:13; **Prov.** 18:19; **Isa.** 43:14(NASB, NIV, *bāriyaḥ* [1281]); 45:2; **Jer.** 49:31; 51:30; **Lam.** 2:9; **Ezek.** 38:11; **Amos** 1:5; **Jon.** 2:6(7); **Nah.** 3:13.

1281. בָּרִחַ *bāriaḥ*, בָּרִיחַ *bāriyaḥ* **masc. noun**
(one fleeing, fugitive, crooked)
Job 26:13; **Isa.** 15:5; 27:1; 43:14(KJV, $b^{e}riya\d{h}$ [1280]).

1282. בָּרִיחַ *bāriyaḥ* **masc. proper noun**
(Bariah)
1 Chr. 3:22.

1283. A. בְּרִיעָה $b^{e}riy'\bar{a}h$ **masc. proper noun**
(Beriah: son of Asher)
Gen. 46:17; **Num.** 26:44,45; **1 Chr.** 7:30,31; 23:10,11.
B. בְּרִיעָה $b^{e}riy'\bar{a}h$, בְּרִעָה $b^{e}ri'\bar{a}h$ **masc. proper noun**
(Beriah: son of Ephraim)
1 Chr. 7:23.
C. בְּרִיעָה $b^{e}riy'\bar{a}h$ **masc. proper noun**
(Beriah: a Benjamite)
1 Chr. 8:13,16.
D. בְּרִיעָה $b^{e}riy'\bar{a}h$ **masc. proper noun**
(Beriah: a Levite)
1 Chr. 23:10,11.

1284. בְּרִיעִי $b^{e}riy'iy$ **masc. proper noun**
(Beriite)
Num. 26:44.

1285. בְּרִית $b^{e}riy\underline{t}$ **fem. noun**
(covenant, treaty, alliance)
Gen. 6:18; 9:9,11–13,15–17; 14:13; 15:18; 17:2,4,7,9–11,13,14,19,21; 21:27, 32; 26:28; 31:44; **Ex.** 2:24; 6:4,5; 19:5; 23:32; 24:7,8; 31:16; 34:10,12,15,27,28; **Lev.** 2:13; 24:8; 26:9,15,25,42,44,45; **Num.** 10:33; 14:44; 18:19; 25:12,13; **Deut.** 4:13,23,31; 5:2,3; 7:2,9,12; 8:18; 9:9,11,15; 10:8; 17:2; 29:1(28:69),9(8), 12(11),14(13),21(20),25(24); 31:9,16,20, 25,26; 33:9; **Josh.** 3:3,6,8,11,14,17; 4:7, 9,18; 6:6,8; 7:11,15; 8:33; 9:6,7,11,15,16; 23:16; 24:25; **Judg.** 2:1,2,20; 20:27; **1 Sam.** 4:3–5; 11:1; 18:3; 20:8; 23:18; **2 Sam.** 3:12,13,21; 5:3; 15:24; 23:5; **1 Kgs.** 3:15; 5:12(26); 6:19; 8:1,6,21,23; 11:11; 15:19; 19:10,14; 20:34; **2 Kgs.** 11:4,17; 13:23; 17:15,35,38; 18:12; 23:2,3,21; **1 Chr.** 11:3; 15:25,26,28,29; 16:6,15,17,37; 17:1; 22:19; 28:2,18; **2 Chr.** 5:2,7; 6:11,14; 13:5; 15:12; 16:3; 21:7; 23:1,3,16; 29:10; 34:30–32; **Ezra** 10:3; **Neh.** 1:5; 9:8,32; 13:29; **Job** 5:23; 31:1; 41:4(40:28); **Ps.** 25:10,14; 44:17 (18); 50:5,16; 55:20(21); 74:20; 78:10,37; 83:5(6); 89:3(4),28(29),34(35),39(40); 103:18; 105:8,10; 106:45; 111:5,9; 132:12; **Prov.** 2:17; **Isa.** 24:5; 28:15,18; 33:8; 42:6; 49:8; 54:10; 55:3; 56:4,6; 59:21; 61:8; **Jer.** 3:16; 11:2,3,6,8,10; 14:21; 22:9; 31:31–33; 32:40; 33:20, 21,25; 34:8,10,13,15,18; 50:5; **Ezek.** 16:8,59–62; 17:13–16,18,19; 20:37; 30:5; 34:25; 37:26; 44:7; **Dan.** 9:4,27; 11:22,

28,30,32; **Hos.** 2:18(20); 6:7; 8:1; 10:4; 12:1(2); **Amos** 1:9; **Obad.** 1:7; **Zech.** 9:11; 11:10; **Mal.** 2:4,5,8,10,14; 3:1.

1286. בְּרִית b^e*riyṯ* **masc. proper noun**
(Berith)
Judg. 9:46.

1287. בֹּרִית *bōriyṯ* **fem. noun**
(soap)
Jer. 2:22; **Mal.** 3:2.

1288. I. בָּרַךְ *bāraḵ* **verb**
(to kneel)
Gen. 24:11; **2 Chr.** 6:13; **Ps.** 95:6.
II. בָּרַךְ *bāraḵ* **verb**
(to bless)
Gen. 1:22,28; 2:3; 5:2; 9:1,26; 12:2,3; 14:19,20; 17:16,20; 18:18; 22:17,18; 24:1,27,31,35,48,60; 25:11; 26:3,4,12, 24,29; 27:4,7,10,19,23,25,27,29–31,33, 34,38,41; 28:1,3,6,14; 30:27,30; 31:55 (32:1); 32:26(27),29(30); 35:9; 39:5; 47:7,10; 48:3,9,15,16,20; 49:25,28; **Ex.** 12:32; 18:10; 20:11,24; 23:25; 39:43; **Lev.** 9:22,23; **Num.** 6:23,24,27; 22:6,12; 23:11,20,25; 24:1,9,10; **Deut.** 1:11; 2:7; 7:13,14; 8:10; 10:8; 12:7; 14:24,29; 15:4, 6,10,14,18; 16:10,15; 21:5; 23:20(21); 24:13,19; 26:15; 27:12; 28:3–6,8,12; 29:19(18); 30:16; 33:1,11,13,20,24; **Josh.** 8:33; 14:13; 17:14; 22:6,7,33; 24:10; **Judg.** 5:2,9,24; 13:24; 17:2; **Ruth** 2:4,19,20; 3:10; 4:14; **1 Sam.** 2:20; 9:13; 13:10; 15:13; 23:21; 25:14,32,33,39; 26:25; **2 Sam.** 2:5; 6:11,12,18,20; 7:29; 8:10; 13:25; 14:22; 18:28; 19:39(40); 21:3; 22:47; **1 Kgs.** 1:47,48; 2:45; 5:7(21); 8:14, 15,55,56,66; 10:9; **2 Kgs.** 4:29; 10:15; **1 Chr.** 4:10; 13:14; 16:2,36,43; 17:27; 18:10; 23:13; 26:5; 29:10,20; **2 Chr.** 2:12(11); 6:3,4; 9:8; 20:26; 30:27; 31:8, 10; **Ezra** 7:27; **Neh.** 8:6; 9:5; 11:2; **Job** 1:10,21; 31:20; 42:12; **Ps.** 5:12(13); 10:3 (NASB, see III); 16:7; 18:46(47); 26:12; 28:6,9; 29:11; 31:21(22); 34:1(2); 37:22; 41:13(14); 45:2(3); 49:18(19); 62:4(5); 63:4(5); 65:10(11); 66:8,20; 67:1(2),6(7), 7(8); 68:19(20),26(27),35(36); 72:15, 17–19; 89:52(53); 96:2; 100:4; 103:1,2, 20–22; 104:1,35; 106:48; 107:38; 109:28; 112:2; 113:2; 115:12,13,15,18; 118:26; 119:12; 124:6; 128:4,5; 129:8; 132:15; 134:1–3; 135:19–21; 144:1; 145:1,2,10, 21; 147:13; **Prov.** 3:33; 5:18; 20:21; 22:9; 27:14; 30:11; **Isa.** 19:25; 51:2; 61:9; 65:16, 23; 66:3; **Jer.** 4:2; 17:7; 20:14; 31:23; **Ezek.** 3:12; **Hag.** 2:19; **Zech.** 11:5.
III. בָּרַךְ *bāraḵ* **verb**
(to curse)
1 Kgs. 21:10,13; **Job** 1:5,11; 2:5,9; **Ps.** 10:3(KJV, NIV, see II).

1289. I. בְּרַךְ b^e*raḵ* **Aram. verb**
(to kneel; corr. to Hebr. 1288,I)
Dan. 6:10(11).
II. בְּרַךְ b^e*raḵ* **Aram. verb**
(to bless; corr. to Hebr. 1288,II)
Dan. 2:19,20; 3:28; 4:34(31).

1290. בֶּרֶךְ *bereḵ* **fem. noun**
(knee)
Gen. 30:3; 48:12; 50:23; **Deut.** 28:35; **Judg.** 7:5,6; 16:19; **1 Kgs.** 8:54; 18:42; 19:18; **2 Kgs.** 1:13; 4:20; **2 Chr.** 6:13; **Ezra** 9:5; **Job** 3:12; 4:4; **Ps.** 109:24; **Isa.** 35:3; 45:23; 66:12; **Ezek.** 7:17; 21:7(12); 47:4; **Dan.** 10:10; **Nah.** 2:10(11).

1291. בְּרֵךְ b^e*rēḵ* **Aram. fem. noun**
(knee; corr. to Hebr. 1290)
Dan. 6:10(11).

1292. בַּרַכְאֵל *baraḵ'ēl* **masc. proper noun**
(Barachel)
Job 32:2,6.

1293. בְּרָכָה b^e*rāḵāh* **fem. noun**
(blessing)
Gen. 12:2; 27:12,35,36,38,41; 28:4; 33:11; 39:5; 49:25,26,28; **Ex.** 32:29; **Lev.** 25:21; **Deut.** 11:26,27,29; 12:15;

16:17; 23:5(6); 28:2,8; 30:1,19; 33:1,23; **Josh.** 8:34; 15:19; **Judg.** 1:15; **1 Sam.** 25:27; 30:26; **2 Sam.** 7:29; **2 Kgs.** 5:15; 18:31; **Neh.** 9:5; 13:2; **Job** 29:13; **Ps.** 3:8(9); 21:3(4),6(7); 24:5; 37:26; 84:6(7); 109:17; 129:8; 133:3; **Prov.** 10:6,7,22; 11:11,25,26; 24:25; 28:20; **Isa.** 19:24; 36:16; 44:3; 65:8; **Ezek.** 34:26; 44:30; **Joel** 2:14; **Zech.** 8:13; **Mal.** 2:2; 3:10.

1294. A. בְּרָכָה *b^{e}rāḵāh* **masc. proper noun**
(Beracah: a Benjamite)
1 Chr. 12:3.
B. בְּרָכָה *b^{e}rāḵāh* **proper noun**
(Beracah: a valley)
2 Chr. 20:26.

1295. בְּרֵכָה *b^{e}rēḵāh* **fem. noun**
(pool)
2 Sam. 2:13; 4:12; **1 Kgs.** 22:38; **2 Kgs.** 18:17; 20:20; **Neh.** 2:14; 3:15,16; **Eccl.** 2:6; **Song** 7:4(5); **Isa.** 7:3; 22:9,11; 36:2; **Nah.** 2:8(9).

1296. A. בֶּרֶכְיָה *bereḵyah,* בֶּרֶכְיָהוּ *bereḵyāhû* **masc. proper noun**
(Berechiah, Berekiah: father of Zechariah)
Zech. 1:1,7.
B. בֶּרֶכְיָה *bereḵyah,* בֶּרֶכְיָהוּ *bereḵyāhû* **masc. proper noun**
(Berechiah, Berekiah: an Ephraimite)
2 Chr. 28:12.
C. בֶּרֶכְיָה *bereḵyah,* בֶּרֶכְיָהוּ *bereḵyāhû* **masc. proper noun**
(Berechiah, Berekiah: father of Asaph)
1 Chr. 6:39(24); 15:17.
D. בֶּרֶכְיָה *bereḵyah* **masc. proper noun**
(Berechiah, Berekiah: son of Zerubbabel)
1 Chr. 3:20.
E. בֶּרֶכְיָה *bereḵyah* **masc. proper noun**
(Berechiah, Berekiah: a Levite)
1 Chr. 9:16; 15:23.
F. בֶּרֶכְיָה *bereḵyah* **masc. proper noun**
(Berechiah, Berekiah: father of Meshullam)
Neh. 3:4,30; 6:18.

1297. בְּרַם *b^{e}ram* **Aram. adv.**
(but, nevertheless)
Ezra 5:13; **Dan.** 2:28; 4:15(12),23(20); 5:17.

1298. בֶּרַע *bera'* **masc. proper noun**
(Bera)
Gen. 14:2.

1299. בָּרַק *bāraq* **verb**
(to cast forth, to send forth)
Ps. 144:6.

1300. בָּרָק *bārāq* **masc. noun**
(lightning)
Ex. 19:16; **Deut.** 32:41; **2 Sam.** 22:15; **Job** 20:25; 38:35; **Ps.** 18:14(15); 77:18(19); 97:4; 135:7; 144:6; **Jer.** 10:13; 51:16; **Ezek.** 1:13; 21:10(15),15(20), 28(33); **Dan.** 10:6; **Nah.** 2:4(5); 3:3; **Hab.** 3:11; **Zech.** 9:14.

1301. בָּרָק *bārāq* **masc. proper noun**
(Barak)
Judg. 4:6,8–10,12,14–16,22; 5:1,12,15.

1302. בַּרְקוֹס *barqôs* **masc. proper noun**
(Barkos)
Ezra 2:53; **Neh.** 7:55.

1303. בַּרְקֳנִים *barq^{o}niym* **masc. pl. noun**
(briers)
Judg. 8:7,16.

1304. בָּרֶקֶת *bāreqeṯ,* בָּרְקַת *bār^{e}qath* **fem. noun**

(emerald, beryl)
Ex. 28:17; 39:10; **Ezek.** 28:13.

1305. I. בָּרַר *bārar* **verb**
(to purify, to cleanse, to polish, to select)
2 Sam. 22:27; **1 Chr.** 7:40; 9:22; 16:41; **Neh.** 5:18; **Job** 33:3(NIV, see III); **Ps.** 18:26(27); **Eccl.** 3:18; **Isa.** 49:2; 52:11; **Jer.** 4:11; 51:11(NASB, NIV, see II); **Ezek.** 20:38; **Dan.** 11:35; 12:10; **Zeph.** 3:9(NIV, see III).
II. בָּרַר *bārar* **verb**
(to sharpen)
Jer. 51:11(KJV, see I).
III. בָּרוּר *bārûr* **adj.**
(pure)
Job 33:3(KJV, NASB, see I); **Zeph.** 3:9(KJV, NASB, see I).

1306. בִּרְשַׁע *birša'* **masc. proper noun**
(Birsha)
Gen. 14:2.

1307. בֵּרֹתִי *bērōṯiy* **masc. proper noun**
(Berothite)
1 Chr. 11:39.

1308. בְּשׂוֹר *b^e^sôr* **proper noun**
(Besor)
1 Sam. 30:9,10,21.

1309. בְּשׂוֹרָה *b^e^śôrāh*, בְּשֹׂרָה *b^e^śōrāh* **fem. noun**
(news, tidings)
2 Sam. 4:10; 18:20,22,25,27; **2 Kgs.** 7:9.

1310. בָּשַׁל *bāšal* **verb**
(to boil, to cook)
Gen. 40:10; **Ex.** 12:9; 16:23; 23:19; 29:31; 34:26; **Lev.** 6:28(21); 8:31; **Num.** 11:8; **Deut.** 14:21; 16:7; **1 Sam.** 2:13,15; **2 Sam.** 13:8; **1 Kgs.** 19:21; **2 Kgs.** 4:38; 6:29; **2 Chr.** 35:13; **Lam.** 4:10; **Ezek.** 24:5; 46:20,24; **Joel** 3:13(4:13); **Zech.** 14:21.

1311. בָּשֵׁל *bāšēl* **adj.**
(boiled, cooked)
Ex. 12:9; **Num.** 6:19.

1312. בִּשְׁלָם *bišlām* **masc. proper noun**
(Bishlam)
Ezra 4:7.

1313. בָּשָׂם *bāśām* **masc. noun**
(spice, balsam)
Song 5:1(NASB, NIV, *bōśem* [1314]).

1314. בֶּשֶׂם *beśem*, בֹּשֶׂם *bōśem* **masc. noun**
(spice, balsam)
Ex. 25:6; 30:23; 35:8,28; **1 Kgs.** 10:2,10,25; **2 Kgs.** 20:13; **1 Chr.** 9:29,30; **2 Chr.** 9:1,9,24; 16:14; 32:27; **Esth.** 2:12; **Song** 4:10,14,16; 5:1(see *bāśām* [1313]),13; 6:2; 8:14; **Isa.** 3:24; 39:2; **Ezek.** 27:22.

1315. A. בָּשְׂמַת *bāś^e^maṯ* **fem. proper noun**
(Bashemath, Basemath: wife of Esau, a daughter of a Hittite)
Gen. 26:34.
B. בָּשְׂמַת *bāś^e^maṯ* **fem. proper noun**
(Bashemath, Basemath: wife of Esau, daughter of Ishmael)
Gen. 36:3,4,10,13,17.
C. בָּשְׂמַת *bāś^e^maṯ* **fem. proper noun**
(Bashemath, Basemath: daughter of Solomon)
1 Kgs. 4:15.

1316. בָּשָׁן *bāšān* **proper noun**
(Bashan)
Num. 21:33; 32:33; **Deut.** 1:4; 3:1,3,4,10,11,13,14(KJV, *bāšān ḥûṯ yā'iyr* [see *ḥawwōṯ yā'iyr* {2334}]); 4:43,47; 29:7(6); 32:14; 33:22; **Josh.** 9:10; 12:4,5;

13:11,12,30,31; 17:1,5; 20:8; 21:6,27; 22:7; **1 Kgs.** 4:13,19; **2 Kgs.** 10:33; **1 Chr.** 5:11,12,16,23; 6:62(47),71(56); **Neh.** 9:22; **Ps.** 22:12(13); 68:15(16), 22(23); 135:11; 136:20; **Isa.** 2:13; 33:9; **Jer.** 22:20; 50:19; **Ezek.** 27:6; 39:18; **Amos** 4:1; **Mic.** 7:14; **Nah.** 1:4; **Zech.** 11:2.

1317. בָּשְׁנָה *bošnāh* **fem. noun**
(shame)
Hos. 10:6.

1318. בָּשַׁס *bāšas* **verb**
(to tread, to trample)
Amos 5:11.

1319. בָּשַׂר *bāśar* **verb**
(to bear news, to proclaim)
1 Sam. 4:17; 31:9; **2 Sam.** 1:20; 4:10; 18:19,20,26,31; **1 Kgs.** 1:42; **1 Chr.** 10:9; 16:23; **Ps.** 40:9(10); 68:11(12); 96:2; **Isa.** 40:9; 41:27; 52:7; 60:6; 61:1; **Jer.** 20:15; **Nah.** 1:15(2:1).

1320. בָּשָׂר *bāśār* **masc. noun**
(flesh)
Gen. 2:21,23,24; 6:3,12,13,17,19; 7:15,16,21; 8:17; 9:4,11,15–17; 17:11, 13,14,23–25; 29:14; 37:27; 40:19; 41:2–4,18,19; **Ex.** 4:7; 12:8,46; 16:3,8,12; 21:28; 22:31(30); 28:42; 29:14,31,32,34; 30:32; **Lev.** 4:11; 6:10(3),27(20); 7:15,17–21; 8:17,31,32; 9:11; 11:8,11; 12:3; 13:2–4,10,11, 13–16,18,24,38,39,43; 14:9; 15:2,3,7, 13,16,19; 16:4,24,26–28; 17:11,14,16; 18:6; 19:28; 21:5; 22:6; 25:49; 26:29; **Num.** 8:7; 11:4,13,18,21,33; 12:12; 16:22; 18:15,18; 19:5,7,8; 27:16; **Deut.** 5:26(23); 12:15,20,23,27; 14:8; 16:4; 28:53,55; 32:42; **Judg.** 6:19–21; 8:7; 9:2; **1 Sam.** 2:13,15; 17:44; **2 Sam.** 5:1; 19:12(13),13(14); **1 Kgs.** 17:6; 19:21; 21:27; **2 Kgs.** 4:34; 5:10,14; 6:30; 9:36; **1 Chr.** 11:1; **2 Chr.** 32:8; **Neh.** 5:5; **Job** 2:5; 4:15; 6:12; 7:5; 10:4,11; 12:10; 13:14; 14:22; 19:20,22,26; 21:6; 31:31; 33:21,25; 34:15; 41:23(15); **Ps.** 16:9; 27:2; 38:3(4),7(8); 50:13; 56:4(5); 63:1(2); 65:2(3); 78:39; 79:2; 84:2(3); 102:5(6); 109:24; 119:120; 136:25; 145:21; **Prov.** 4:22; 5:11; 14:30; 23:20; **Eccl.** 2:3; 4:5; 5:6(5); 11:10; 12:12; **Isa.** 9:20(19); 10:18; 17:4; 22:13; 31:3; 40:5,6; 44:16,19; 49:26; 58:7; 65:4; 66:16,17, 23,24; **Jer.** 7:21; 11:15; 12:12; 17:5; 19:9; 25:31; 32:27; 45:5; **Lam.** 3:4; **Ezek.** 4:14; 10:12; 11:3,7,11,19; 16:26; 20:48(21:4); 21:4(9),5(10); 23:20; 24:10; 32:5; 36:26; 37:6,8; 39:17,18; 40:43; 44:7,9; **Dan.** 1:15; 10:3; **Hos.** 8:13; **Joel** 2:28(3:1); **Mic.** 3:3; **Hag.** 2:12; **Zech.** 2:13(17); 11:9,16; 14:12.

1321. בְּשַׂר *b^{e}śar* **Aram. masc. noun**
(flesh; corr. to Hebr. 1320)
Dan. 2:11; 4:12(9); 7:5.

1322. בֹּשֶׁת *bōšeṯ* **fem. noun**
(shame)
1 Sam. 20:30; **2 Chr.** 32:21; **Ezra** 9:7; **Job** 8:22; **Ps.** 35:26; 40:15(16); 44:15(16); 69:19(20); 70:3(4); 109:29; 132:18; **Isa.** 30:3,5; 42:17; 54:4; 61:7; **Jer.** 2:26; 3:24,25; 7:19; 11:13; 20:18; **Dan.** 9:7,8; **Hos.** 9:10; **Mic.** 1:11; **Hab.** 2:10; **Zeph.** 3:5,19.

1323. בַּת *baṯ* **fem. noun**
(daughter)
Gen. 5:4,7,10,13,16,19,22,26,30; 6:1,2, 4; 11:11,13,15,17,19,21,23,25,29; 17:17; 19:8,12,14–16,30,36; 20:12; 24:3,13,23, 24,37,47,48; 25:20; 26:34; 27:46; 28:1,2, 6,8,9; 29:6,10,16,18,23,24,28,29; 30:13,21; 31:26,28,31,41,43,50,55(32:1); 34:1,3,5, 7–9,16,17,19,21; 36:2,3,6,14,18,25,39; 37:35; 38:2,12; 41:45,50; 46:7,15,18,20, 25; 49:22; **Ex.** 1:16,22; 2:1,5,7–10,16, 20,21; 3:22; 6:23,25; 10:9; 20:10; 21:4,7,9,31; 32:2; 34:16; **Lev.** 10:14; 11:16; 12:6; 14:10; 18:9–11,17; 19:29;

20:17; 21:2,9; 22:12,13; 24:11; 26:29; **Num.** 6:14; 15:27; 18:11,19; 21:25, 29,32; 25:1,15,18; 26:33,46,59; 27:1,7–9; 30:16(17); 32:42; 36:2,6,8,10,11; **Deut.** 5:14; 7:3; 12:12,18,31; 13:6(7); 14:15; 16:11,14; 18:10; 22:16,17; 23:17(18); 27:22; 28:32,41,53,56; 32:19; **Josh.** 7:24; 15:16,17,45,47; 17:3,6,11,16; **Judg.** 1:12,13,27; 3:6; 11:26,34,35,40; 12:9; 14:1–3; 19:24; 21:1,7,18,21; **Ruth** 1:11–13; 2:2,8,22; 3:1,10,11,16,18; **1 Sam.** 1:4,16; 2:21; 8:13; 14:49,50; 17:25; 18:17,19,20,27,28; 25:44; 30:3,6,19; **2 Sam.** 1:20,24; 3:3,7,13; 5:13; 6:16,20,23; 11:3; 12:3; 13:18; 14:27; 17:25; 19:5(6); 21:8,10,11; **1 Kgs.** 3:1; 4:11,15; 7:8; 9:16,24; 11:1; 15:2,10; 16:31; 22:42; **2 Kgs.** 8:18,26; 9:34; 11:2; 14:9; 15:33; 17:17; 18:2; 19:21; 21:19; 22:1; 23:10,31,36; 24:8,18; **1 Chr.** 1:50; 2:3,21,23,34,35,49; 3:2,5; 4:18,27; 5:16; 7:15,24,28,29; 8:12; 14:3; 15:29; 18:1; 23:22; 25:5; **2 Chr.** 2:14(13); 8:11; 11:18,20,21; 13:2,19,21; 20:31; 21:6; 22:2,11; 24:3; 25:18; 27:1; 28:8,18; 29:1,9; 31:18; **Ezra** 2:61; 9:2,12; **Neh.** 3:12; 4:14(8); 5:2,5; 6:18; 7:63; 10:28(29), 30(31); 11:25,27,28,30,31; 13:25; **Esth.** 2:7,15; 9:29; **Job** 1:2,13,18; 30:29; 42:13,15; **Ps.** 9:14(15); 17:8; 45:9(10), 10(11),12(13),13(14); 48:11(12); 97:8; 106:37,38; 137:8; 144:12; **Prov.** 30:15; 31:29; **Eccl.** 12:4; **Song** 1:5; 2:2,7; 3:5,10,11; 5:8,16; 6:9; 7:1(2); 8:4; **Isa.** 1:8; 3:16,17; 4:4; 10:30,32([K^e] *bayit̲* [1004]); 13:21; 16:1,2; 22:4; 23:10,12; 32:9; 34:13; 37:22; 43:6,20; 47:1,5; 49:22; 52:2; 56:5; 60:4; 62:11; **Jer.** 3:24; 4:11,31; 5:17; 6:2,23,26; 7:31; 8:11,19, 21,22; 9:1(8:23),7(6),20(19); 11:22; 14:16,17; 16:2,3; 19:9; 29:6; 31:22; 32:35; 35:8; 41:10; 43:6; 46:11,19,24; 48:18,46; 49:2–4; 50:39,42; 51:33; 52:1; **Lam.** 1:6,15; 2:1,2,4,5,8,10,11,13,15,18; 3:48,51; 4:3,6,10,21,22; **Ezek.** 13:17; 14:16,18,20,22; 16:20,27,44–46,48,49, 53,55,57,61; 22:11; 23:2,4,10,25,47; 24:21,25; 26:6,8; 27:6(NASB, NIV, prep. *b^e* and *t^e'aššûr* [8391]); 30:18; 32:16,18; 44:25; **Dan.** 11:6,17; **Hos.** 1:3,6; 4:13,14; **Joel** 2:28(3:1); 3:8(4:8); **Amos** 7:17; **Mic.** 1:8,13; 4:8,10,13; 5:1(4:14); 7:6; **Zeph.** 3:10,14; **Zech.** 2:7(11),10(14); 9:9; **Mal.** 2:11.

1324. בַּת *bat̲* **masc./fem. noun**
(bath, a unit of liquid measure)
1 Kgs. 7:26,38; **2 Chr.** 2:10(9); 4:5; **Isa.** 5:10; **Ezek.** 45:10,11,14.

1325. בַּת *bat̲* **Aram. masc. noun**
(bath, corr. to Hebr. 1324)
Ezra 7:22.

1326. בָּתָה *bāt̲āh* **fem. noun**
(wasteland)
Isa. 5:6.

1327. בַּתָּה *battāh* **fem. noun**
(desolate, steep)
Isa. 7:19.

1328. A. בְּתוּאֵל *b^{e}t̲û'ēl* **masc. proper noun**
(Bethuel: son of Nahor)
Gen. 22:22,23; 24:15,24,47,50; 25:20; 28:2,5.
B. בְּתוּאֵל *b^{e}t̲û'ēl* **proper noun**
(Bethuel: a town)
1 Chr. 4:30.

1329. בְּתוּל *b^{e}t̲ûl* **proper noun**
(Bethul)
Josh. 19:4.

1330. בְּתוּלָה *b^{e}t̲ûlāh* **fem. noun**
(virgin, maiden)
Gen. 24:16; **Ex.** 22:16(15),17(16); **Lev.** 21:3,14; **Deut.** 22:19,23,28; 32:25; **Judg.** 19:24; 21:12; **2 Sam.** 13:2,18; **1 Kgs.** 1:2; **2 Kgs.** 19:21; **2 Chr.** 36:17; **Esth.** 2:2,3,17,19; **Job** 31:1; **Ps.** 45:14(15); 78:63; 148:12; **Isa.** 23:4,12; 37:22; 47:1; 62:5; **Jer.** 2:32; 14:17;

18:13; 31:4,13,21; 46:11; 51:22; **Lam.** 1:4,15,18; 2:10,13,21; 5:11; **Ezek.** 9:6; 44:22; **Joel** 1:8; **Amos** 5:2; 8:13; **Zech.** 9:17.

1331. בְּתוּלִים *b^e^ṯûliym* **fem. pl. noun**
(virginity)
Lev. 21:13; **Deut.** 22:14,15,17,20; **Judg.** 11:37,38; **Ezek.** 23:3,8.

1332. בִּתְיָה *biṯyāh* **fem. proper noun**
(Bithiah)
1 Chr. 4:18.

1333. בָּתַק *bāṯaq* **verb**
(to thrust through, to cut up)
Ezek. 16:40.

1334. בָּתַר *bāṯar* **verb**
(to cut in half)
Gen. 15:10.

1335. בֶּתֶר *beṯer* **masc. noun**
(piece, half)
Gen. 15:10; **Jer.** 34:18,19.

1336. I. בֶּתֶר *beṯer* **masc. proper noun**
(Bether)
Song 2:17(NIV, see II).
II. בֶּתֶר *beṯer* **masc. noun**
(rugged)
Song 2:17(KJV, NASB, see I).

1337. בַּת רַבִּים *baṯ rabbiym* **proper noun**
(Bath Rabbim)
Song 7:4(5).

1338. בִּתְרוֹן *biṯrôn* **proper noun**
(Bithron; NASB, morning)
2 Sam. 2:29.

1339. בַּת־שֶׁבַע *baṯ-šeḇaʿ* **fem. proper noun**
(Bathsheba)
2 Sam. 11:3; 12:24; **1 Kgs.** 1:11,15,16,28,31; 2:13,18,19; **Ps.** 51:[title](1).

1340. A. בַּת שׁוּעַ *baṯ šûaʿ* **fem. proper noun**
(Bath-shua: wife of Judah)
1 Chr. 2:3(KJV, NIV, *baṯ* [1323] and *šûaʿ* [7770]).
B. בַּת שׁוּעַ *baṯ šûaʿ* **fem. proper noun**
(Bath-shua [alternate spelling for Bathsheba]: wife of David)
1 Chr. 3:5.

ג Gimel

1341. גֵּא *gē'* **adj.**
(pride)
Isa. 16:6.

1342. גָּאָה *gā'āh* **verb**
(to rise up, to be lifted up)
Ex. 15:1,21; **Job** 8:11; 10:16; **Ezek.** 47:5.

1343. גֵּאֶה *gē'eh* **adj.**
(proud)
Job 40:11,12; **Ps.** 94:2; 140:5(6); **Prov.** 15:25; 16:19; **Isa.** 2:12; **Jer.** 48:29.

1344. גֵּאָה *gē'āh* **fem. noun**
(pride)
Prov. 8:13.

1345. גְּאוּאֵל *g^e'û'ēl* **masc. proper noun**
(Geuel)
Num. 13:15.

1346. גַּאֲוָה *ga'^awāh* **fem. noun**
(pride, arrogance)
Deut. 33:26,29; **Job** 41:15(7); **Ps.** 10:2; 31:18(19),23(24); 36:11(12); 46:3(4); 68:34(35); 73:6; **Prov.** 14:3; 29:23; **Isa.** 9:9(8); 13:3,11; 16:6; 25:11; **Jer.** 48:29; **Zeph.** 3:11.

1347. גָּאוֹן *gā'ôn* **masc. noun**
(pride, majesty, arrogance)
Ex. 15:7; **Lev.** 26:19; **Job** 35:12; 37:4; 38:11; 40:10; **Ps.** 47:4(5); 59:12(13); **Prov.** 8:13; 16:18; **Isa.** 2:10,19,21; 4:2; 13:11,19; 14:11; 16:6; 23:9; 24:14; 60:15; **Jer.** 12:5; 13:9; 48:29; 49:19; 50:44; **Ezek.** 7:20,24; 16:49,56; 24:21; 30:6,18; 32:12; 33:28; **Hos.** 5:5; 7:10; **Amos** 6:8; 8:7; **Mic.** 5:4(3); **Nah.** 2:2(3); **Zeph.** 2:10; **Zech.** 9:6; 10:11; 11:3.

1348. גֵּאוּת *gē'ûṯ* **fem. noun**
(majesty, pride)
Ps. 17:10; 89:9(10); 93:1; **Isa.** 9:18(17); 12:5; 26:10; 28:1,3.

1349. גַּאֲיוֹן *ga'^ayôn* **adj.**
(proud)
Ps. 123:4(KJV, [Q^e] *gē'eh* [1343]).

1350. I. גְּאוּלִים *g^e'ûliym* **masc. pl. noun**
(redemption)
Isa. 63:4(KJV, NASB, see II).
II. גָּאַל *gā'al* **verb**
(to redeem, to act as a kinsman)
Gen. 48:16; **Ex.** 6:6; 15:13; **Lev.** 25:25,26,30,33,48,49,54; 27:13,15,19, 20,27,28,31,33; **Num.** 5:8; 35:12,19,21, 24,25,27; **Deut.** 19:6,12; **Josh.** 20:3,5,9; **Ruth** 2:20; 3:9,12,13; 4:1,3,4,6,8,14; **2 Sam.** 14:11; **1 Kgs.** 16:11; **Job** 3:5; 19:25; **Ps.** 19:14(15); 69:18(19); 72:14; 74:2; 77:15(16); 78:35; 103:4; 106:10; 107:2; 119:154; **Prov.** 23:11; **Isa.** 35:9; 41:14; 43:1,14; 44:6,22–24; 47:4; 48:17, 20; 49:7,26; 51:10; 52:3,9; 54:5,8; 59:20; 60:16; 62:12; 63:4(NIV, see I),9,16; **Jer.** 31:11; 50:34; **Lam.** 3:58; **Hos.** 13:14; **Mic.** 4:10.

1351. גָּאַל *gā'al* **verb**
(to defile, to pollute)
Ezra 2:62; **Neh.** 7:64; **Isa.** 59:3; 63:3; **Lam.** 4:14; **Dan.** 1:8; **Zeph.** 3:1; **Mal.** 1:7,12.

1352. גֹּאַל *gō'al* **masc. noun**
(defilement)
Neh. 13:29.

1353. גְּאֻלָּה *g^e'ullāh* **fem. noun**
(redemption)

Lev. 25:24,26,29,31,32,48,51,52; Ruth 4:6,7; Jer. 32:7,8; Ezek. 11:15.

1354. גַּב *gab̲* **masc. noun**
(convex surface, mound, back)
Lev. 14:9; **1 Kgs.** 7:33; **Job** 13:12; 15:26; **Ps.** 129:3; **Ezek.** 1:18; 10:12; 16:24,31,39; 43:13(NASB, NIV, *gōb̲ah* [1363]).

1355. גַּב *gab̲* **Aram. masc. noun**
(back; corr. to Hebr. 1354)
Dan. 7:6.

1356. I. גֵּב *gēb̲* **masc. noun**
(pit, ditch, well, cistern)
2 Kgs. 3:16; **Jer.** 14:3.
II. גֵּב *gēb̲* **masc. noun**
(beam)
1 Kgs. 6:9.

1357. גֵּב *gēb̲* **masc. noun**
(locust)
Isa. 33:4.

1358. גֹּב *gōb̲* **Aram. masc. noun**
(den)
Dan. 6:7(8),12(13),16(17),17(18), 19(20),20(21),23(24),24(25).

1359. גֹּב *gōb̲*, גּוֹב *gôb̲* **proper noun**
(Gob)
2 Sam. 21:18,19.

1360. גֶּבֶא *geb̲e'* **masc. noun**
(cistern, marsh)
Isa. 30:14; **Ezek.** 47:11.

1361. גָּבַהּ *gāb̲ah* **verb**
(to be high, to be exalted, to be arrogant)
1 Sam. 10:23; **2 Chr.** 17:6; 26:16; 32:25; 33:14; **Job** 5:7; 35:5; 36:7; 39:27; **Ps.** 103:11; 113:5; 131:1; **Prov.** 17:19; 18:12; **Isa.** 3:16; 5:16; 7:11; 52:13; 55:9; **Jer.** 13:15; 49:16; **Ezek.** 16:50; 17:24; 19:11; 21:26(31); 28:2,5,17; 31:5,10,14; **Obad.** 1:4; **Zeph.** 3:11.

1362. גָּבֹהַּ *gāb̲ōah* **adj.**
(high, lofty, proud)
Ps. 101:5; **Prov.** 16:5; **Eccl.** 7:8; **Ezek.** 31:3.

1363. גֹּבַהּ *gōb̲ah* **masc. noun**
(height, grandeur)
1 Sam. 17:4; **2 Chr.** 3:4; 32:26; **Job** 11:8; 22:12; 40:10; **Ps.** 10:4; **Prov.** 16:18; **Jer.** 48:29; **Ezek.** 1:18; 19:11; 31:10,14; 40:42; 41:8; 43:13(KJV, *gab̲* [1354]); **Amos** 2:9.

1364. גָּבוֹהַּ *gāb̲ôah*, גָּבֹהַּ *gāb̲ōah* **adj.**
(high, exalted)
Gen. 7:19; **Deut.** 3:5; 28:52; **1 Sam.** 2:3; 9:2; 16:7; **1 Kgs.** 14:23; **2 Kgs.** 17:10; **Esth.** 5:14; 7:9; **Job** 41:34(26); **Ps.** 104:18; 138:6; **Eccl.** 5:8(7); 12:5; **Isa.** 2:15; 5:15; 10:33; 30:25; 40:9; 57:7; **Jer.** 2:20; 3:6; 17:2; 51:58; **Ezek.** 17:22,24; 21:26(31); 40:2; 41:22; **Dan.** 8:3; **Zeph.** 1:16.

1365. גַּבְהוּת *gab̲hût̲* **fem. noun**
(lofty, arrogant)
Isa. 2:11,17.

1366. גְּבוּל *g^e^b̲ûl* **masc. noun**
(border, boundary, territory)
Gen. 10:19; 23:17; 47:21; **Ex.** 8:2(7:27); 10:4,14,19; 13:7; 23:31; 34:24; **Num.** 20:16,17,21,23; 21:13,15,22–24; 22:36; 33:44; 34:3–12; 35:26,27; **Deut.** 2:4,18; 3:14,16,17; 11:24; 12:20; 16:4; 19:3,8,14; 27:17; 28:40; **Josh.** 1:4; 12:2,4,5; 13:3,4, 10,11,16,23,25–27,30; 15:1,2,4–12,21,47 ([Q^e^] *gādôl* [1419,I]); 16:2,3,5,6,8; 17:7–10; 18:5,11–16,19; 19:10–12,14, 18,22,25,29,33,34,41,46,47; 22:25; 24:30; **Judg.** 1:18,36; 2:9; 11:18,20,22; 19:29; **1 Sam.** 5:6; 6:9,12; 7:13,14; 10:2; 11:3,7; 13:18; 27:1; **2 Sam.** 21:5; **1 Kgs.** 1:3; 4:21(5:1); **2 Kgs.** 3:21; 10:32; 14:25; 15:16; 18:8; **1 Chr.** 4:10; 6:54(39),

66(51); 21:12; **2 Chr.** 9:26; 11:13; **Job** 38:20; **Ps.** 78:54; 104:9; 105:31,33; 147:14; **Prov.** 15:25; 22:28; 23:10; **Isa.** 15:8; 19:19; 54:12; 60:18; **Jer.** 5:22; 15:13; 17:3; 31:17; **Ezek.** 11:10,11; 27:4; 29:10; 40:12; 43:12,13,17,20; 45:1,7; 47:13,15–18,20; 48:1–8,12,13,21,22, 24–28; **Hos.** 5:10; **Joel** 3:6(4:6); **Amos** 1:13; 6:2; **Obad.** 1:7; **Mic.** 5:6(5); **Zeph.** 2:8; **Mal.** 1:4,5.

1367. גְּבוּלָה $g^e\underline{b}\hat{u}l\bar{a}h$ **fem. noun**
(boundary, territory)
Num. 32:33; 34:2,12; **Deut.** 32:8; **Josh.** 18:20; 19:49; **Job** 24:2; **Ps.** 74:17; **Isa.** 10:13; 28:25.

1368. גִּבּוֹר *gibbôr,* גִּבֹּר *gibbōr* **adj.**
(mighty, strong, brave)
Gen. 6:4; 10:8,9; **Deut.** 10:17; **Josh.** 1:14; 6:2; 8:3; 10:2,7; **Judg.** 5:13,23; 6:12; 11:1; **Ruth** 2:1; **1 Sam.** 2:4; 9:1; 14:52; 16:18; 17:51; **2 Sam.** 1:19,21,22, 25,27; 10:7; 16:6; 17:8,10; 20:7; 22:26; 23:8,9,16,17,22; **1 Kgs.** 1:8,10; 11:28; **2 Kgs.** 5:1; 15:20; 24:14,16; **1 Chr.** 1:10; 5:24; 7:2,5,7,9,11,40; 8:40; 9:13,26; 11:10–12,19,24,26; 12:1,4,8,21,25,28,30; 19:8; 26:6,31; 27:6; 28:1; 29:24; **2 Chr.** 13:3; 14:8(7); 17:13,14,16,17; 25:6; 26:12; 28:7; 32:3,21; **Ezra** 7:28; **Neh.** 3:16; 9:32; 11:14; **Job** 16:14; **Ps.** 19:5(6); 24:8; 33:16; 45:3(4); 52:1(3); 78:65; 89:19(20); 103:20; 112:2; 120:4; 127:4; **Prov.** 16:32; 21:22; 30:30; **Eccl.** 9:11; **Song** 3:7; 4:4; **Isa.** 3:2; 5:22; 9:6(5); 10:21; 13:3; 21:17; 42:13; 49:24,25; **Jer.** 5:16; 9:23(22); 14:9; 20:11; 26:21; 32:18; 46:5,6,9,12; 48:14,41; 49:22; 50:9,36; 51:30,56,57; **Ezek.** 32:12,21,27; 39:18,20; **Dan.** 11:3; **Hos.** 10:13; **Joel** 2:7; 3:9–11(4:9–11); **Amos** 2:14,16; **Obad.** 1:9; **Nah.** 2:3(4); **Zeph.** 1:14; 3:17; **Zech.** 9:13; 10:5,7.

1369. גְּבוּרָה $g^e\underline{b}\hat{u}r\bar{a}h$ **fem. noun**
(power, strength, might)
Ex. 32:18; **Deut.** 3:24; **Judg.** 5:31; 8:21; **1 Kgs.** 15:23; 16:5,27; 22:45(46); **2 Kgs.** 10:34; 13:8,12; 14:15,28; 18:20; 20:20; **1 Chr.** 29:11,12,30; **2 Chr.** 20:6; **Esth.** 10:2; **Job** 12:13; 26:14; 39:19; 41:12(4); **Ps.** 20:6(7); 21:13(14); 54:1:(3); 65:6(7); 66:7; 71:16,18; 80:2(3); 89:13(14); 90:10; 106:2,8; 145:4,11,12; 147:10; 150:2; **Prov.** 8:14; **Eccl.** 9:16; 10:17; **Isa.** 3:25; 11:2; 28:6; 30:15; 33:13; 36:5; 63:15; **Jer.** 9:23(22); 10:6; 16:21; 23:10; 49:35; 51:30; **Ezek.** 32:29,30; **Mic.** 3:8; 7:16.

1370. גְּבוּרָה $g^e\underline{b}\hat{u}r\bar{a}h$ **Aram. fem. noun**
(might, power; corr. to Hebr. 1369)
Dan. 2:20,23.

1371. גִּבֵּחַ *gibbēaḥ* **adj.**
(bald)
Lev. 13:41.

1372. גַּבַּחַת *gabbahat̲* **fem. noun**
(bald forehead, forehead)
Lev. 13:42,43,55.

1373. גַּבַּי *gabbay* **masc. proper noun**
(Gabbai)
Neh. 11:8.

1374. גֵּבִים $g\bar{e}\underline{b}iym$ **proper noun**
(Gebim)
Isa. 10:31.

1375. גָּבִיעַ $g\bar{a}\underline{b}iya$ʻ **masc. noun**
(cup, bowl)
Gen. 44:2,12,16,17; **Ex.** 25:31,33,34; 37:17,19,20; **Jer.** 35:5.

1376. גְּבִיר $g^e\underline{b}iyr$ **masc. noun**
(lord, ruler)
Gen. 27:29,37.

1377. גְּבִירָה $g^e\underline{b}iyr\bar{a}h$ **fem. noun**
(queen, lady)
Gen. 16:4(KJV, NASB, $g^e\underline{b}ere\underline{t}$ [1404]),

8(KJV, NASB, g^eḇereṯ [1404]),9(KJV, NASB, g^eḇereṯ [1404]); **1 Kgs.** 11:19; 15:13; **2 Kgs.** 5:3(KJV, NASB, g^eḇereṯ [1404]); 10:13; **2 Chr.** 15:16; **Ps.** 123:2(KJV, NASB, g^eḇereṯ [1404]); **Prov.** 30:23(KJV, NASB, g^eḇereṯ [1404]); **Isa.** 24:2(KJV, NASB, g^eḇereṯ [1404]); **Jer.** 13:18; 29:2.

1378. גָּבִישׁ *gāḇiyš* **masc. noun**
(pearl, crystal, jasper)
Job 28:18.

1379. גָּבַל *gāḇal* **verb**
(to set bounds, to set limits)
Ex. 19:12,23; **Deut.** 19:14; **Josh.** 18:20; **Zech.** 9:2.

1380. גְּבַל *g^eḇal* **proper noun**
(Gebal; a city in Phoenicia)
Ezek. 27:9.

1381. גְּבָל *g^eḇāl* **proper noun**
(Gebal; area south of the Dead Sea)
Ps. 83:7(8).

1382. I. גִּבְלִי *giḇliy* **masc. proper noun**
(Inhabitants of the city of Gebal [*g^eḇal* {1380}])
Josh. 13:5; **1 Kgs.** 5:18(32)(KJV, see II).
II. גִּבְלִי *giḇliy* **masc. noun**
(craftsmen in stone)
1 Kgs. 5:18(32)(NASB, NIV, see I).

1383. גַּבְלֻת *gaḇluṯ* **fem. noun**
(a twisting, braiding)
Ex. 28:22; 39:15.

1384. גִּבֵּן *gibbēn* **adj.**
(hunchbacked)
Lev. 21:20.

1385. גְּבִינָה *g^eḇiynāh* **fem. noun**
(cheese)
Job 10:10.

1386. גַּבְנֹן *gaḇnôn* **masc. noun**
(high, rugged)
Ps. 68:15(16),16(17).

1387. גֶּבַע *geḇa'* **proper noun**
(Geba, Gaba)
Josh. 18:24; 21:17; **Judg.** 20:10,33(NASB, see *ma'^{a}rēh gāḇa'* [4626], KJV, NIV, *giḇ'āh* [1390,C]); **1 Sam.** 13:3,16; 14:5; **2 Sam.** 5:25; **1 Kgs.** 15:22; **2 Kgs.** 23:8; **1 Chr.** 6:60(45); 8:6; **2 Chr.** 16:6; **Ezra** 2:26; **Neh.** 7:30; 11:31; 12:29; **Isa.** 10:29; **Zech.** 14:10.

1388. גִּבְעָא *giḇ'ā'* **masc. proper noun**
(Gibea)
1 Chr. 2:49.

1389. גִּבְעָה *giḇ'āh* **fem. noun**
(hill)
Gen. 49:26; **Ex.** 17:9,10; **Num.** 23:9; **Deut.** 12:2; 33:15; **Josh.** 5:3; 24:33(NASB, NIV, see 1390,B); **Judg.** 7:1; **1 Sam.** 7:1; 10:5,10(NIV, *giḇ'āh* [1390,C]); 23:19; 26:1,3; **2 Sam.** 2:24,25; 6:3(KJV, *giḇ'āh* [1390,C]),4(KJV, *giḇ'āh* [1390,C]; not translated in NIV); **1 Kgs.** 14:23; **2 Kgs.** 16:4; 17:10; **2 Chr.** 28:4; **Job** 15:7; **Ps.** 65:12(13); 72:3; 114:4,6; 148:9; **Prov.** 8:25; **Song** 2:8; 4:6; **Isa.** 2:2,14; 10:32; 30:17,25; 31:4; 40:4,12; 41:15; 42:15; 54:10; 55:12; 65:7; **Jer.** 2:20; 3:23; 4:24; 13:27; 16:16; 17:2; 31:39; 49:16; 50:6; **Ezek.** 6:3,13; 20:28; 34:6,26; 35:8; 36:4,6; **Hos.** 4:13; 10:8; **Joel** 3:18(4:18); **Amos** 9:13; **Mic.** 4:1; 6:1; **Nah.** 1:5; **Hab.** 3:6; **Zeph.** 1:10.

1390. A. גִּבְעָה *giḇ'āh* **proper noun**
(Gibeah: a city in Judah)
Josh. 15:57.
B. גִּבְעָה *giḇ'āh* **proper noun**
(Gibeah: a city in Ephraim)
Josh. 24:33(KJV, see 1389).

C. גִּבְעָה *gib̲'āh* **proper noun**
(Gibeah: a city in Benjamin)
Josh. 18:28(KJV, *gib̲'at̲* [1394]); **Judg.** 19:12–16; 20:4,5,9,13–15,19–21,25, 29–31,34,36,37,43; **1 Sam.** 10:10(KJV, NASB, see *gib̲'āh* [1389]),26; 11:4; 13:2,15; 14:2,16; 15:34; 22:6; 23:19; 26:1; **2 Sam.** 6:3(NASB, NIV, *gib̲'āh* [1389]),4(NASB, *gib̲'āh* [1389]; not translated in NIV); 21:6; 23:29; **1 Chr.** 11:31; **2 Chr.** 13:2; **Isa.** 10:29; **Hos.** 5:8; 9:9; 10:9.

1391. גִּבְעוֹן *gib̲'ôn* **proper noun**
(Gibeon)
Josh. 9:3,17; 10:1,2,4–6,10,12,41; 11:19; 18:25; 21:17; **2 Sam.** 2:12,13,16,24; 3:30; 20:8; **1 Kgs.** 3:4,5; 9:2; **1 Chr.** 8:29(see *'ab̲iy gib̲'ôn* [25]); 9:35(see *'ab̲iy gib̲'ôn* [25]); 14:16; 16:39; 21:29; **2 Chr.** 1:3,13; **Neh.** 3:7; 7:25; **Isa.** 28:21; **Jer.** 28:1; 41:12,16.

1392. גִּבְעֹל *gib̲'ōl* **masc. noun**
(bolled, in bud)
Ex. 9:31.

1393. גִּבְעוֹנִי *gib̲'ôniy* **masc. proper noun**
(Gibeonites)
2 Sam. 21:1–4,9; **1 Chr.** 12:4; **Neh.** 3:7.

1394. גִּבְעַת *gib̲'at̲* **proper noun**
(Gibeath)
Josh. 18:28(NASB, NIV, *gib'āh* [1390,C]).

1395. גִּבְעָתִי *gib̲'āt̲iy* **masc. proper noun**
(Gibeathite)
1 Chr. 12:3.

1396. גָּבַר *gāb̲ar* **verb**
(to prevail, to be strong)
Gen. 7:18–20,24; 49:26; **Ex.** 17:11; **1 Sam.** 2:9; **2 Sam.** 1:23; 11:23; **1 Chr.** 5:2; **Job** 15:25; 21:7; 36:9; **Ps.** 12:4(5); 65:3(4); 103:11; 117:2; **Eccl.** 10:10; **Isa.** 42:13; **Jer.** 9:3(2); **Lam.** 1:16; **Dan.** 9:27; **Zech.** 10:6,12.

1397. גֶּבֶר *geb̲er* **masc. noun**
(man, strong man)
Ex. 10:11; 12:37; **Num.** 24:3,15; **Deut.** 22:5; **Josh.** 7:14,17,18; **Judg.** 5:30; **2 Sam.** 23:1; **1 Chr.** 23:3; 24:4; 26:12; **Job** 3:3,23; 4:17; 10:5; 14:10,14; 16:21; 22:2; 33:17,29; 34:7,9,34; 38:3; 40:7; **Ps.** 18:25(26)(KJV, *g^e^b̲ar* [1399]); 34:8(9); 37:23; 40:4(5); 52:7(9); 88:4(5); 89:48(49); 94:12; 127:5; 128:4; **Prov.** 6:34; 20:24; 24:5; 28:3,21; 29:5; 30:1,19; **Isa.** 22:17; **Jer.** 17:5,7; 22:30; 23:9; 30:6; 31:22; 41:16; 43:6; 44:20; **Lam.** 3:1,27,35,39; **Dan.** 8:15; **Joel** 2:8; **Mic.** 2:2; **Hab.** 2:5; **Zech.** 13:7.

1398. גֶּבֶר *geb̲er* **masc. proper noun**
(Geber)
1 Kgs. 4:19.

1399. גְּבַר *g^e^b̲ar* **masc. noun**
(man)
Ps. 18:25(26)(NASB, NIV, *geb̲er* [1397]).

1400. גְּבַר *g^e^b̲ar* **Aram. masc. noun**
(man; corr. to Hebr. 1397 and 1399)
Ezra 4:21; 5:4,10; 6:8; **Dan.** 2:25; 3:8,12,13,20–25,27; 5:11; 6:5(6),11(12), 15(16),24(25).

1401. גִּבָּר *gibbar* **Aram. masc. noun**
(mighty)
Dan. 3:20.

1402. גִּבָּר *gibbār* **masc. proper noun**
(Gibbar)
Ezra 2:20.

1403. גַּבְרִיאֵל *gab̲riy'ēl* **masc. proper noun**
(Gabriel)
Dan. 8:16; 9:21.

1404. גְּבֶרֶת *g^e^b̲eret̲* **fem. noun**
(mistress, female owner)
Gen. 16:4,8,9(NIV, *g^e^b̲iyrāh* [1377]); **2 Kgs.** 5:3(NIV, *g^e^b̲iyrāh* [1377]); **Ps.** 123:2(NIV, *g^e^b̲iyrāh* [1377]); **Prov.** 30:23(NIV, *g^e^b̲iyrāh* [1377]); **Isa.** 24:2; 47:5,7.

1405. גִּבְּתוֹן *gibb^e^t̲ôn* **proper noun**
(Gibbethon)
Josh. 19:44; 21:23; **1 Kgs.** 15:27; 16:15,17.

1406. גָּג *gāg* **masc. noun**
(roof, top)
Ex. 30:3; 37:26; **Deut.** 22:8; **Josh.** 2:6,8; **Judg.** 9:51; 16:27; **1 Sam.** 9:25,26; **2 Sam.** 11:2; 16:22; 18:24; **2 Kgs.** 19:26; 23:12; **Neh.** 8:16; **Ps.** 102:7(8); 129:6; **Prov.** 21:9; 25:24; **Isa.** 15:3; 22:1; 37:27; **Jer.** 19:13; 32:29; 48:38; **Ezek.** 40:13; **Zeph.** 1:5.

1407. גַּד *gad̲* **masc. noun**
(corriander)
Ex. 16:31; **Num.** 11:7.

1408. גַּד *gad̲* **masc. proper noun**
(Fortune, a false god)
Isa. 65:11(KJV, *gad̲* [1409,B]).

1409. A. גַּד *gad̲* **masc. noun**
(good fortune)
Gen. 30:11(KJV, [Q^e^] *bô'* [935] and *gad̲* [1409,B]).
B. גַּד *gad̲* **masc. noun**
(troop)
Gen. 30:11(NASB, NIV, [K^e^] *b^e^* prep. and *gad̲* [1409,A]); **Isa.** 65:11(NASB, NIV, *gad̲* [1408]).

1410. A. גָּד *gād̲* **masc. proper noun**
(Gad: a son of Jacob)
Gen. 30:11; 35:26; 46:16; 49:19; **Ex.** 1:4; **1 Chr.** 2:2.
B. גָּד *gād̲* **masc. proper noun**
(Gad: the tribe of Gad)
Num. 1:14,24,25; 2:14; 7:42; 10:20; 13:15; 26:15,18; 32:1,2,6,25,29,31,33,34; **Deut.** 27:13; 33:20; **Josh.** 4:12; 13:24, 28; 18:7; 20:8; 21:7,38(36); 22:9–11,13, 15,21,25,30–34; **1 Sam.** 13:7; **2 Sam.** 24:5; **1 Chr.** 5:11; 6:63(48),80(65); 12:14; **Jer.** 49:1; **Ezek.** 48:27,28,34.
C. גָּד *gād̲* **masc. proper noun**
(Gad: a prophet)
1 Sam. 22:5; **2 Sam.** 24:11,13,14,18,19; **1 Chr.** 21:9,11,13,18,19; 29:29; **2 Chr.** 29:25.

1411. גְּדָבַר *g^e^d̲āb̲ar* **Aram. masc. noun**
(treasurer)
Dan. 3:2,3.

1412. גֻּדְגֹּדָה *gud̲gōd̲ah* **proper noun**
(Gudgodah)
Deut. 10:7.

1413. I. גָּדַד *gād̲ad̲* **verb**
(to make incisions)
Deut. 14:1; **1 Kgs.** 18:28; **Jer.** 16:6; 41:5; 47:5.
II. גָּדַד *gād̲ad̲* **verb**
(to band together)
Ps. 94:21(22)(NASB, *gûr* [1481,II]); **Jer.** 5:7; **Mic.** 5:1(4:14).

1414. גְּדַד *g^e^d̲ad̲* **Aram. verb**
(to cut down; corr. to Hebr. 1413,I)
Dan. 4:14(11),23(20).

1415. גָּדָה *gād̲āh* **fem. noun**
(riverbank)
Josh. 3:15; 4:18; **1 Chr.** 12:15(16)(KJV, NIV, [K^e^] *gid̲yāh* [1428]); **Isa.** 8:7(NIV, *gid̲yāh* [1428]).

1416. גְּדוּד *g^e^d̲ûd̲* **masc. noun**
(a band of soldiers, troops)
Gen. 49:19; **1 Sam.** 30:8,15,23; **2 Sam.**

3:22; 4:2; 22:30; **1 Kgs.** 11:24; **2 Kgs.** 5:2; 6:23; 13:20,21; 24:2; **1 Chr.** 7:4; 12:18,21; **2 Chr.** 22:1; 25:9,10,13; 26:11; **Job** 19:12; 25:3; 29:25; **Ps.** 18:29(30); **Jer.** 18:22; **Hos.** 6:9; 7:1; **Mic.** 5:1(4:14).

1417. גְּדוּד *g^e^d̲ûd̲* **masc. noun**
(furrow, ridge)
Ps. 65:10(11).

1418. גְּדוּדָה *g^e^d̲ûd̲āh* **fem. noun**
(a cutting, slashing, only pl. *g^e^d̲ud̲ōt̲*)
Jer. 48:37.

1419. I. גָּדוֹל *gād̲ôl,* גָּדֹל *gād̲ōl* **adj.**
(great)
Gen. 1:16,21; 4:13; 10:12,21; 12:2,17; 15:12,14,18; 17:20; 18:18; 19:11; 20:9; 21:8,18; 27:1,15,33,34,42; 29:2,7,16; 39:9,14; 41:29; 44:12; 45:7; 46:3; 50:10; **Ex.** 3:3; 6:6; 7:4; 11:3,6; 12:30; 14:31; 15:16; 18:11,22; 32:10,11,21,30,31; **Lev.** 19:15; 21:10; **Num.** 13:28; 14:12; 22:18; 34:6,7; 35:25,28; **Deut.** 1:7,17,19,28; 2:7,10,21; 4:6–8,32,34,36–38; 5:22(19), 25(22); 6:10,22; 7:19,21,23; 8:15; 9:1, 2,29; 10:17,21; 11:7,23; 18:16; 25:13,14; 26:5,8; 27:2; 28:59; 29:3(2),24(23), 28(27); 34:12; **Josh.** 1:4; 6:5,20; 7:9,26; 8:29; 9:1; 10:2,10,11,18,20,27; 14:12,15; 15:12,47([K^e^] *g^e^b̲ûl* [1366]); 17:17; 20:6; 22:10; 23:4,9; 24:17,26; **Judg.** 2:7; 5:15,16; 11:33; 15:8,18; 16:5,6,15,23; 21:2,5; **1 Sam.** 2:17; 4:5,6,10,17; 5:9; 6:9,14,15,18,19; 7:10; 12:16,22; 14:20,33,45; 17:13,14,25,28; 18:17; 19:5,8,22; 20:2; 22:15; 23:5; 25:2,36; 28:12; 30:2,16,19; **2 Sam.** 3:38; 5:10; 7:9; 13:15,16,36; 15:23; 18:7,9,17,29; 19:4(5),32(33); 20:8; 23:10,12; **1 Kgs.** 1:40; 2:22; 3:4,6; 4:13; 5:17(31); 7:9,10, 12; 8:42,55,65; 10:18; 18:27,28,45; 19:11; 20:13,21,28; 22:31; **2 Kgs.** 3:27; 4:8,38; 5:1,13; 6:23,25; 7:6; 8:4,13; 10:6,11,19; 12:10(11); 16:15; 17:21,36; 18:19,28; 20:3; 22:4,8,13; 23:2,4,26; 25:9,26; **1 Chr.** 11:14; 12:14,22; 16:25; 17:8; 22:8; 25:8; 26:13; 29:1,9,22; **2 Chr.** 1:8,10; 2:5(4),9(8); 3:5; 4:9; 6:32; 7:8; 9:17; 15:13,14; 16:14; 18:30; 20:19; 21:14; 26:15; 28:5; 30:21,26; 31:15; 32:18; 34:9,21,30; 36:18; **Ezra** 3:11–13; 9:7,13; 10:12; **Neh.** 1:3,5,10; 2:10; 3:1,20,27; 4:14(8); 5:1,7; 6:3; 7:4; 8:6,12,17; 9:4,18,25,26,32,37; 11:14 (NASB, NIV, see II); 12:31,43; 13:5,27,28; **Esth.** 1:5,20; 2:18; 4:1,3; 8:15; 9:4; 10:3; **Job** 1:3,19; 3:19; 5:9; 9:10; 37:5; **Ps.** 12:3(4); 21:5(6); 47:2(3); 48:1(2); 57:10(11); 71:19; 76:1(2); 77:13(14); 86:10,13; 95:3; 96:4; 99:2,3; 104:25; 106:21; 108:4(5); 111:2; 115:13; 131:1; 135:5; 136:4,7,17; 138:5; 145:3,8; 147:5; **Prov.** 18:16; 19:19(KJV, [K^e^] *gārōl* [1632]); 25:6; 27:14; **Eccl.** 9:13,14; 10:4; **Isa.** 5:9; 8:1; 9:2(1); 12:6; 27:1,13; 29:6; 34:6; 36:4,13; 38:3; 54:7; 56:12; **Jer.** 4:6; 5:5; 6:1,13,22; 8:10; 10:6,22; 11:16; 14:17; 16:6,10; 21:5,6; 22:8; 25:14,32; 26:19; 27:5,7; 28:8; 30:7; 31:8,34; 32:17–19,21,37,42; 33:3; 36:7; 42:1,8; 43:9; 44:7,12,15,26; 45:5; 48:3; 50:9, 22,41; 51:54,55; 52:13; **Lam.** 2:13; **Ezek.** 1:4; 3:12,13; 8:6,13,15,18; 9:1,9; 11:13; 16:46,61; 17:3,7,9,17; 21:14(19); 23:4; 25:17; 29:3,18; 36:23; 37:10; 38:13, 15,19; 39:17; 43:14; 47:10,15,19,20; 48:28; **Dan.** 8:8,21; 9:4,12; 10:1,4,7,8; 11:2,13,25,28,44; 12:1; **Hos.** 1:11(2:2); **Joel** 2:11,25,31(3:4); **Amos** 6:11; **Jon.** 1:2,4,10,12,16,17(2:1); 3:2,3,5,7; 4:1, 6,11; **Mic.** 7:3; **Nah.** 1:3; 3:10; **Zeph.** 1:10,14; **Hag.** 1:1,12,14; 2:2,4,9; **Zech.** 1:14,15; 3:1,8; 4:7; 6:11; 7:12; 8:2; 14:4; **Mal.** 1:11,14; 4:5(3:23).

II. הַגְּדוֹלִים *hagg^e^d̲ôliym* **masc. proper noun**
(Haggedolim: father of Zabdiel)
Neh. 11:14(KJV, see I).

1420. גְּדוּלָּה *g^e^d̲ûllāh,* גְּדֻלָּה *g^e^d̲ullāh* **fem. noun**
(greatness)

2 Sam. 7:21,23; **1 Chr.** 17:19,21; 29:11; **Esth.** 1:4; 6:3; 10:2; **Ps.** 71:21; 145:3,6.

1421. גִּדּוּף *giddûp̱* **masc. noun**
(scorn, insult)
Isa. 43:28; 51:7; **Zeph.** 2:8.

1422. גְּדוּפָה *g^e^ḏûp̱āh* **fem. noun**
(taunt)
Ezek. 5:15.

1423. גְּדִי *g^e^ḏiy* **masc. noun**
(kid, young goat)
Gen. 27:9,16; 38:17,20,23; **Ex.** 23:19; 34:26; **Deut.** 14:21; **Judg.** 6:19; 13:15, 19; 14:6; 15:1; **1 Sam.** 10:3; 16:20; **Isa.** 11:6.

1424. גָּדִי *gāḏiy* **masc. proper noun**
(Gadi)
2 Kgs. 15:14,17.

1425. גָּדִי *gāḏiy* **proper noun**
(a Gadite, of Gad)
Num. 34:14; **Deut.** 3:12,16; 4:43; 29:8(7); **Josh.** 1:12; 12:6; 13:8; 22:1; **2 Sam.** 23:36(NIV, *hāgriy* [1905,II]); **2 Kgs.** 10:33; **1 Chr.** 5:18,26; 12:8,37; 26:32.

1426. גַּדִּי *gaddiy* **masc. proper noun**
(Gaddi)
Num. 13:11.

1427. גַּדִּיאֵל *gaddiy'ēl* **masc. proper noun**
(Gaddiel)
Num. 13:10.

1428. גִּדְיָה *giḏyāh* **fem. noun**
(riverbank)
1 Chr. 12:15(16)(NASB, [Q^e^] *gāḏāh* [1415]; **Isa.** 8:7(KJV, NASB, *gāḏāh* [1415]).

1429. גְּדִיָּה *g^e^ḏiyyāh* **fem. noun**
(kid, young goat)
Song 1:8.

1430. I. גָּדִישׁ *gāḏiyš* **masc. noun**
(heap, grainstack)
Ex. 22:6(5); **Judg.** 15:5; **Job** 5:26.
II. גָּדִישׁ *gāḏiyš* **masc. noun**
(tomb, gravemound)
Job 21:32.

1431. גָּדַל *gāḏal* **verb**
(to become great, to make great, to magnify)
Gen. 12:2; 19:13,19; 21:8,20; 24:35; 25:27; 26:13; 38:11,14; 41:40; 48:19; **Ex.** 2:10,11; **Num.** 6:5; 14:17; **Josh.** 3:7; 4:14; **Judg.** 11:2; 13:24; **Ruth** 1:13; **1 Sam.** 2:21; 3:19; 12:24; 20:41; 26:24; **2 Sam.** 7:22,26; 12:3; 22:51(NASB, [Q^e^] *migdôl* [4024,A] KJV); **1 Kgs.** 1:37,47; 10:23; 12:8,10; **2 Kgs.** 4:18; 10:6; **1 Chr.** 17:24; 22:5; 29:12,25; **2 Chr.** 1:1; 9:22; 10:8,10; **Ezra** 9:6; **Esth.** 3:1; 5:11; 10:2; **Job** 2:13; 7:17; 19:5; 31:18; **Ps.** 18:50(51); 34:3(4); 35:26,27; 38:16(17); 40:16(17); 41:9(10); 55:12(13); 69:30(31); 70:4(5); 92:5(6); 104:1; 126:2,3; 138:2; 144:12; **Eccl.** 1:16; 2:4,9; **Isa.** 1:2; 9:3(2); 10:15; 23:4; 28:29; 42:21; 44:14; 49:21; 51:18; **Jer.** 5:27; 48:26,42; **Lam.** 1:9; 4:6; **Ezek.** 16:7; 24:9; 31:4; 35:13; 38:23; **Dan.** 1:5; 8:4,8–11,25; 11:36,37; **Hos.** 9:12; **Joel** 2:20,21; **Amos** 8:5; **Obad.** 1:12; **Jon.** 4:10; **Mic.** 5:4(3); **Zeph.** 2:8,10; **Zech.** 12:7,11; **Mal.** 1:5.

1432. גָּדֵל *gāḏēl* **adj.**
(growing up, becoming great)
Gen. 26:13; **1 Sam.** 2:26; **2 Chr.** 17:12; **Ezek.** 16:26.

1433. גֹּדֶל *gōḏel* **masc. noun**
(greatness, majesty)
Num. 14:19; **Deut.** 3:24; 5:24(21); 9:26; 11:2; 32:3; **Ps.** 79:11; 150:2; **Isa.** 9:9(8); 10:12; **Ezek.** 31:2,7,18.

1434. גָּדִל *gād̲il* **masc. noun**
(a tassel, a festoon)
Deut. 22:12; **1 Kgs.** 7:17.

1435. A. גִּדֵּל *giddēl* **masc. proper noun**
(Giddel: head of a family)
Ezra 2:47; **Neh.** 7:49.
B. גִּדֵּל *giddēl* **masc. proper noun**
(Giddel: servant of Solomon)
Ezra 2:56; **Neh.** 7:58.

1436. A. גְּדַלְיָה *g^e^d̲alyāh*, גְּדַלְיָהוּ *g^e^d̲alyāhû* **masc. proper noun**
(Gedaliah: son of Ahikam)
2 Kgs. 25:22–25; **Jer.** 39:14; 40:5–9,11–16; 41:1–4,6,9,10,16,18; 43:6.
B. גְּדַלְיָה *g^e^d̲alyāh* **masc. proper noun**
(Gedaliah: a Levite)
1 Chr. 25:3,9.
C. גְּדַלְיָה *g^e^d̲alyāh* **masc. proper noun**
(Gedaliah: a priest)
Ezra 10:18.
D. גְּדַלְיָה *g^e^d̲alyāh*, גְּדַלְיָהוּ *g^e^d̲alyāhû* **masc. proper noun**
(Gedaliah: grandfather of Zephaniah)
Zeph. 1:1.
E. גְּדַלְיָה *g^e^d̲alyāh* **masc. proper noun**
(Gedaliah: a prince)
Jer. 38:1.

1437. גִּדַּלְתִּי *giddaltiy* **masc. proper noun**
(Giddalti)
1 Chr. 25:4,29.

1438. גָּדַע *gād̲a'* **verb**
(to cut down)
Deut. 7:5; 12:3; **Judg.** 21:6; **1 Sam.** 2:31; **2 Chr.** 14:3(2); 31:1; 34:4,7; **Ps.** 75:10(11); 107:16; **Isa.** 9:10(9); 10:33; 14:12; 15:2; 22:25; 45:2; **Jer.** 48:25; 50:23; **Lam.** 2:3; **Ezek.** 6:6; 19:7(KJV, *yād̲a'* [3045]; NASB, *rā'a'* [7489,II]); **Amos** 3:14; **Zech.** 11:10,14.

1439. גִּדְעוֹן *gid̲'ôn* **masc. proper noun**
(Gideon)
Judg. 6:11,13,19,22,24,27,29,34,36,39; 7:1,2,4,5,7,13–15,18–20,24,25; 8:4,7, 11,13,21–24,27,28,30,32,33,35.

1440. גִּדְעֹם *gid̲'ōm* **proper noun**
(Gidom)
Judg. 20:45.

1441. גִּדְעֹנִי *gid̲'ōniy* **masc. proper noun**
(Gideoni)
Num. 1:11; 2:22; 7:60,65; 10:24.

1442. גָּדַף *gād̲ap̲* **verb**
(to blaspheme, to revile)
Num. 15:30; **2 Kgs.** 19:6,22; **Ps.** 44:16(17); **Isa.** 37:6,23; **Ezek.** 20:27.

1443. גָּדַר *gād̲ar* **verb**
(to wall up, to close off)
2 Kgs. 12:12(13); 22:6; **Job** 19:8; **Isa.** 58:12; **Lam.** 3:7,9; **Ezek.** 13:5; 22:30; **Hos.** 2:6(8); **Amos** 9:11.

1444. גֶּדֶר *ged̲er* **masc. noun**
(wall, fence)
Prov. 24:31; **Ezek.** 42:10(NASB, NIV, *gād̲ar* [1447]).

1445. גֶּדֶר *ged̲er* **proper noun**
(Geder)
Josh. 12:13.

1446. A. גְּדוֹר *g^e^d̲ôr* **masc. proper noun**
(Gedor: son of Jehiel)
1 Chr. 8:31; 9:37.
B. גְּדוֹר *g^e^d̲ôr* **masc. proper noun**
(Gedor: a city)
Josh. 15:58; **1 Chr.** 12:7.

C. גְּדוֹר *g^eḏôr* **masc. proper noun**
(Gedor: a city)
1 Chr. 4:39.
D. גְּדוֹר *g^eḏôr* **masc. proper noun**
(Gedor: son of Penuel)
1 Chr. 4:4.
E. גְּדוֹר *g^eḏôr* **masc. proper noun**
(Gedor: son of Jered)
1 Chr. 4:18.

1447. גָּדֵר *gāḏēr* **masc. noun**
(wall, fence)
Num. 22:24; **Ezra** 9:9; **Ps.** 62:3(4)(Sept. *g^eḏērah* [1448]); 80:12(13); **Prov.** 24:31(KJV, *geḏer* [1444]); **Eccl.** 10:8; **Isa.** 5:5; **Ezek.** 13:5; 22:30; 42:7,10(KJV, *geḏer* [1444]); **Hos.** 2:6(8); **Mic.** 7:11.

1448. גְּדֵרָה *g^eḏērāh* **fem. noun**
(wall, hedge, sheepfold)
Num. 32:16,24,36; **1 Sam.** 24:3(4); **1 Chr.** 4:23; **Ps.** 89:40(41); **Jer.** 49:3; **Ezek.** 42:12; **Nah.** 3:17; **Zeph.** 2:6.

1449. גְּדֵרָה *g^eḏērāh* **proper noun**
(Gederah)
Josh. 15:36.

1450. גְּדֵרוֹת *g^eḏērôṯ* **proper noun**
(Gederoth)
Josh. 15:41; **2 Chr.** 28:18.

1451. גְּדֵרִי *g^eḏēriy* **masc. proper noun**
(Gederite)
1 Chr. 27:28.

1452. גְּדֵרָתִי *g^eḏērāṯiy* **masc. proper noun**
(Gederathite)
1 Chr. 12:4.

1453. גְּדֵרֹתַיִם *g^eḏērōṯayim* **proper noun**
(Gederothaim)
Josh. 15:36.

1454. גֵּה *gēh* **pron.**
(this is a scribal error for *zeh* [2088])
Ezek. 47:13.

1455. גָּהָה *gāhāh* **verb**
(to cure)
Hos. 5:13.

1456. גֵּהָה *gēhāh* **fem. noun**
(medicine, a cure)
Prov. 17:22.

1457. גָּהַר *gāhar* **verb**
(to crouch down, to bend)
1 Kgs. 18:42; **2 Kgs.** 4:34,35.

1458. גַּו *gaw* **masc. noun**
(back)
1 Kgs. 14:9; **Neh.** 9:26; **Ezek.** 23:35.

1459. גַּו *gaw* **Aram. masc. noun**
(midst, middle; corr. to Hebr. 1460,II)
Ezra 4:15; 5:7; 6:2; **Dan.** 3:6,11,15,21,23–26; 4:10(7); 7:15.

1460. I. גֵּו *gēw* **masc. noun**
(back)
Prov. 10:13; 19:29; 26:3; **Isa.** 38:17; 50:6; 51:23.
II. גֵּו *gēw* **masc. noun**
(community, midst)
Job 30:5.

1461. גּוּב *gûḇ* **verb**
(digger, plowman [participle form])
2 Kgs. 25:12(NASB, NIV, [K^e] *yāgaḇ* [3009]).

1462. גּוֹב *gôḇ*, גּוֹבַי *gôḇay* **masc. noun**
(locusts)
Amos 7:1; **Nah.** 3:17.

1463. A. גּוֹג *gôg* **masc. proper noun**
(Gog: son of Joel)

1 Chr. 5:4.
B. גּוֹג *gôg* **masc. proper noun**
(Gog: enemy of God's people)
Ezek. 38:2,3,14,16,18; 39:1,11,15.

1464. גּוּד *gûḏ* **verb**
(to attack, to overcome)
Gen. 49:19; **Hab.** 3:16.

1465. גֵּוָה *gēwāh* **fem. noun**
(back, body)
Job 20:25.

1466. גֵּוָה *gēwāh* **fem. noun**
(pride, a lifting up)
Job 22:29; 33:17; **Jer.** 13:17.

1467. גֵּוָה *gēwāh* **Aram. fem. noun**
(pride; corr. to Hebr. 1466)
Dan. 4:37(34).

1468. גּוּז *gûz* **verb**
(to bring in, to pass away)
Num. 11:31; **Ps.** 90:10.

1469. גּוֹזָל *gôzzāl* **fem. noun**
(young bird, young pigeon)
Gen. 15:9; **Deut.** 32:11.

1470. גּוֹזָן *gôzān* **proper noun**
(Gozan)
2 Kgs. 17:6; 18:11; 19:12; **1 Chr.** 5:26; **Isa.** 37:12.

1471. I. גּוֹי *gôy* **masc. noun**
(gentile, nation; pl. nations, Gentiles)
Gen. 10:5,20,31,32; 12:2; 14:1(NASB, NIV, see II),9(NASB, NIV, see II); 15:14; 17:4–6,16,20; 18:18; 20:4; 21:13,18; 22:18; 25:23; 26:4; 35:11; 46:3; 48:19; **Ex.** 9:24; 19:6; 32:10; 33:13; 34:10,24; **Lev.** 18:24,28; 20:23; 25:44; 26:33, 38,45; **Num.** 14:12,15; 23:9; 24:8,20; **Deut.** 4:6–8,27,34,38; 7:1,17,22; 8:20; 9:1,4,5,14; 11:23; 12:2,29,30; 15:6; 17:14; 18:9,14; 19:1; 20:15; 26:5,19; 28:1,12,36,49,50,65; 29:16(15),18(17), 24(23); 30:1; 31:3; 32:8,21,28,43; **Josh.** 3:17; 4:1; 5:6,8; 10:13; 12:23(NASB, NIV, see II); 23:3,4,7,9,12,13; **Judg.** 2:20,21, 23; 3:1; 4:2(NASB, NIV, see III),13(NASB, NIV, see III),16(NASB, NIV, see III); **1 Sam.** 8:5,20; **2 Sam.** 7:23; 8:11; 22:44,50; **1 Kgs.** 4:31(5:11); 11:2; 14:24; 18:10; **2 Kgs.** 6:18; 16:3; 17:8,11,15,26, 29,33,41; 18:33; 19:12,17; 21:2,9; **1 Chr.** 14:17; 16:20,24,31,35; 17:21; 18:11; **2 Chr.** 15:6; 20:6; 28:3; 32:13–15,17,23; 33:2,9; 36:14; **Ezra** 6:21; **Neh.** 5:8, 9,17; 6:6,16; 13:26; **Job** 12:23; 34:29; **Ps.** 2:1,8; 9:5(6),15(16),17(18),19(20), 20(21); 10:16; 18:43(44),49(50); 22:27(28),28(29); 33:10,12; 43:1; 44:2(3),11(12),14(15); 46:6(7),10(11); 47:8(9); 59:5(6),8(9); 66:7; 67:2(3); 72:11,17; 78:55; 79:1,6,10; 80:8(9); 82:8; 83:4(5); 86:9; 94:10; 96:3,10; 98:2; 102:15(16); 105:13,44; 106:5,27,35,41, 47; 110:6; 111:6; 113:4; 115:2; 117:1; 118:10; 126:2; 135:10,15; 147:20; 149:7; **Prov.** 14:34; **Isa.** 1:4; 2:2,4; 5:26; 9:1(8:23),3(2); 10:6,7; 11:10,12; 13:4; 14:6,9,12,18,26,32; 16:8; 18:2,7; 23:3; 25:3,7; 26:2,15; 29:7,8; 30:28; 33:3; 34:1,2; 36:18; 37:12; 40:15,17; 41:2; 42:1,6; 43:9; 45:1,20; 49:6,7,22; 52:10, 15; 54:3; 55:5; 58:2; 60:3,5,11,12,16,22; 61:6,9,11; 62:2; 64:2(1); 65:1; 66:8,12, 18–20; **Jer.** 1:5,10; 2:11; 3:17,19; 4:2,7, 16; 5:9,15,29; 6:18,22; 7:28; 9:9(8),16(15), 26(25); 10:2,7,10,25; 12:17; 14:22; 16:19; 18:7–9,13; 22:8; 25:9,11–15,17,31,32; 26:6; 27:7,8,11,13; 28:11,14; 29:14,18; 30:11; 31:7,10,36; 33:9,24; 36:2; 43:5; 44:8; 46:1,12,28; 48:2; 49:14,15,31,36; 50:2,3,9,12,23,41,46; 51:7,20,27,28, 41,44; **Lam.** 1:1,3,10; 2:9; 4:15,17,20; **Ezek.** 2:3; 4:13; 5:5–8,14,15; 6:8,9; 7:24; 11:12,16; 12:15,16; 16:14; 19:4,8; 20:9, 14,22,23,32,41; 22:4,15,16; 23:30; 25:7, 8,10; 26:3,5; 28:7,25; 29:12,15; 30:3,11, 23,26; 31:6,11,12,16,17; 32:2,9,12,16,18; 34:28,29; 35:10; 36:3–7,13–15,19–24,30, 36; 37:21,22,28; 38:12,16,23; 39:7,21,23,

27,28; **Dan.** 8:22; 11:23; 12:1; **Hos.** 8:8, 10; 9:17; **Joel** 1:6; 2:17,19; 3:2(4:2), 8(4:8),9(4:9),11(4:11),12(4:12); **Amos** 6:1,14; 9:9,12; **Obad.** 1:1,2,15,16; **Mic.** 4:2,3,7,11; 5:8(7),15(14); 7:16; **Nah.** 3:4,5; **Hab.** 1:5,6,17; 2:5,8; 3:6,12; **Zeph.** 2:1,5,9,11,14; 3:6,8; **Hag.** 2:7, 14,22; **Zech.** 1:15,21(2:4); 2:8(12), 11(15); 7:14; 8:13,22,23; 9:10; 12:3,9; 14:2,3,14,16,18,19; **Mal.** 1:11,14; 3:9,12.

II. גּוֹיִם *gôyim* **masc. pl. noun**
(Goiim: a Mesopotamian nation or tribe)
Gen. 14:1(KJV, see I),9(KJV, see I); **Josh.** 12:23(KJV, see I).

III. הַגּוֹיִם *hāggôyim* **masc. pl. proper noun**
(Haggoyim: part of the name of the city of Harosheth Haggoyim [see 2800])
Judg. 4:2(KJV, see I),13(KJV, see I), 16(KJV, see I).

1472. גְּוִיָּה *g^ewiyyāh* **fem. noun**
(body, corpse)
Gen. 47:18; **Judg.** 14:8,9; **1 Sam.** 31:10,12; **Neh.** 9:37; **Ps.** 110:6; **Ezek.** 1:11,23; **Dan.** 10:6; **Nah.** 3:3.

1473. גּוֹלָה *gôlāh,* גֹּלָה *gōlāh* **fem. noun**
(captivity, exile)
2 Kgs. 24:15,16; **1 Chr.** 5:22; **Ezra** 1:11; 2:1; 4:1; 6:19–21; 8:35; 9:4; 10:6–8,16; **Neh.** 7:6; **Esth.** 2:6; **Jer.** 28:6; 29:1,4,16,20,31; 46:19; 48:7,11; 49:3; **Ezek.** 1:1; 3:11,15; 11:24,25; 12:3,4,7,11; 25:3; **Amos** 1:15; **Nah.** 3:10; **Zech.** 6:10; 14:2.

1474. גּוֹלָן *gôlān* **proper noun**
(Golan)
Deut. 4:43; **Josh.** 20:8([K^e] *gōlāwn*); 21:27; **1 Chr.** 6:71(56).

1475. גּוּמָּץ *gûmmāṣ* **masc. noun**
(pit)
Eccl. 10:8.

1476. A. גּוּנִי *gûniy* **masc. proper noun**
(Guni: a Naphtalite)
Gen. 46:24; **Num.** 26:48; **1 Chr.** 7:13.

B. גּוּנִי *gûniy* **masc. proper noun**
(Guni: a Gadite)
1 Chr. 5:15.

1477. גּוּנִי *gûniy* **masc. proper noun**
(Gunites)
Num. 26:48.

1478. גָּוַע *gāwa'* **verb**
(to die)
Gen. 6:17; 7:21; 25:8,17; 35:29; 49:33; **Num.** 17:12(27),13(28); 20:3,29; **Josh.** 22:20; **Job** 3:11; 10:18; 13:19; 14:10; 27:5; 29:18; 34:15; 36:12; **Ps.** 88:15(16); 104:29; **Lam.** 1:19; **Zech.** 13:8.

1479. גּוּף *gûp̱* **verb**
(to shut)
Neh. 7:3.

1480. גּוּפָה *gûp̱āh* **fem. noun**
(body, corpse)
1 Chr. 10:12.

1481. I. גּוּר *gûr* **verb**
(to sojourn)
Gen. 12:10; 19:9; 20:1; 21:23,34; 26:3; 32:4(5); 35:27; 47:4; **Ex.** 3:22; 6:4; 12:48,49; **Lev.** 16:29; 17:8,10,12,13; 18:26; 19:33,34; 20:2; 25:6,45; **Num.** 9:14; 15:14–16,26,29; 19:10; **Deut.** 18:6; 26:5; **Josh.** 20:9; **Judg.** 5:17; 17:7–9; 19:1,16; **Ruth** 1:1; **2 Sam.** 4:3; **1 Kgs.** 17:20; **2 Kgs.** 8:1,2; **1 Chr.** 16:19; **2 Chr.** 15:9; **Ezra** 1:4; **Job** 19:15; 28:4; **Ps.** 5:4(5); 15:1; 61:4(5); 105:12,23; 120:5; **Isa.** 5:17; 11:6; 16:4; 23:7; 33:14; 52:4; **Jer.** 35:7; 42:15,17,22; 43:2,5; 44:8,12,14,28; 49:18,33; 50:40; **Lam.** 4:15; **Ezek.** 14:7; 47:22,23; **Hos.** 7:14.

II. גּוּר *gûr* **verb**
(to quarrel, to attack, to cause strife)

Ps. 56:6(7); 59:3(4); 94:21(KJV, NIV, *gādad* [1413]); 140:2(3); **Isa.** 54:15.

III. גּוּר *gûr* **verb**
(to dread, to be afraid)
Num. 22:3; **Deut.** 1:17; 18:22; 32:27; **1 Sam.** 18:15; **Job** 19:29; 41:25(17); **Ps.** 22:23(24); 33:8; **Hos.** 10:5.

1482. גּוּר *gûr* **masc. noun**
(lion's cub)
Gen. 49:9; **Deut.** 33:22; **Lam.** 4:3; **Ezek.** 19:2,3,5; **Nah.** 2:11(12).

1483. גּוּר *gûr* **proper noun**
(Gur)
2 Kgs. 9:27.

1484. גּוֹר *gôr* **masc. noun**
(cub)
Jer. 51:38; **Nah.** 2:12(13).

1485. גּוּר־בַּעַל *gûr-ba'al* **proper noun**
(Gur Baal)
2 Chr. 26:7.

1486. גּוֹרָל *gôrāl* **masc. noun**
(lot, portion, share)
Lev. 16:8–10; **Num.** 26:55,56; 33:54; 34:13; 36:2,3; **Josh.** 14:2; 15:1; 16:1; 17:1,14,17; 18:6,8,10,11; 19:1,10,17,24, 32,40,51; 21:4–6,8,10,20,40(38); **Judg.** 1:3; 20:9; **1 Chr.** 6:54(39),61(46),63(48), 65(50); 24:5,7,31; 25:8,9; 26:13,14; **Neh.** 10:34(35); 11:1; **Esth.** 3:7; 9:24; **Ps.** 16:5; 22:18(19); 125:3; **Prov.** 1:14; 16:33; 18:18; **Isa.** 17:14; 34:17; 57:6; **Jer.** 13:25; **Ezek.** 24:6; **Dan.** 12:13; **Joel** 3:3(4:3); **Obad.** 1:11; **Jon.** 1:7; **Mic.** 2:5; **Nah.** 3:10.

1487. גּוּשׁ *gûš* **masc. noun**
(clod, scab)
Job 7:5([K[e]] גִּישׁ).

1488. גֵּז *gēz* **masc. noun**
(fleece, mown field)
Deut. 18:4; **Job** 31:20; **Ps.** 72:6; **Amos** 7:1.

1489. גִּזְבָּר *gizbār* **masc. noun**
(treasurer)
Ezra 1:8.

1490. גִּזְבַּר *gizbar* **Aram. masc. noun**
(treasurer; corr. to Hebr. 1489)
Ezra 7:21.

1491. גָּזָה *gāzāh* **verb**
(to take)
Ps. 71:6.

1492. גִּזָּה *gizzāh* **fem. noun**
(fleece)
Judg. 6:37–40.

1493. גִּזוֹנִי *gizôniy* **masc. proper noun**
(Gizonite)
1 Chr. 11:34.

1494. גָּזַז *gāzaz* **verb**
(to shear, to cut off)
Gen. 31:19; 38:12,13; **Deut.** 15:19; **1 Sam.** 25:2,4,7,11; **2 Sam.** 13:23,24; **Job** 1:20; **Isa.** 53:7; **Jer.** 7:29; **Mic.** 1:16; **Nah.** 1:12.

1495. גָּזֵז *gāzēz* **masc. proper noun**
(Gazez)
1 Chr. 2:46.

1496. גָּזִית *gāziyṯ* **fem. noun**
(dressed or cut stone)
Ex. 20:25; **1 Kgs.** 5:17(31); 6:36; 7:9,11,12; **1 Chr.** 22:2; **Isa.** 9:10(9); **Lam.** 3:9; **Ezek.** 40:42; **Amos** 5:11.

1497. גָּזַל *gāzal* **verb**
(to rob, to take away by force)
Gen. 21:25; 31:31; **Lev.** 6:4(5:23); 19:13; **Deut.** 28:29,31; **Judg.** 9:25;

21:23; **2 Sam.** 23:21; **1 Chr.** 11:23; **Job** 20:19; 24:2,9,19; **Ps.** 35:10; 69:4(5); **Prov.** 4:16; 22:22; 28:24; **Isa.** 10:2; **Jer.** 21:12; 22:3; **Ezek.** 18:7,12,16,18; 22:29; **Mic.** 2:2; 3:2; **Mal.** 1:13.

1498. גָּזֵל *gāzēl* **masc. noun**
(robbery, something stolen)
Lev. 6:2(5:21); **Ps.** 62:10(11); **Isa.** 61:8; **Ezek.** 22:29.

1499. גֵּזֶל *gēzel* **masc. noun**
(robbery, stealing)
Eccl. 5:8(7); **Ezek.** 18:18.

1500. גְּזֵלָה *g^e^zēlāh* **fem. noun**
(robbery, something stolen)
Lev. 6:4(5:23); **Isa.** 3:14; **Ezek.** 18:7,12,16; 33:15.

1501. גָּזָם *gāzām* **masc. noun**
(palmerworm, growing locust)
Joel 1:4; 2:25; **Amos** 4:9.

1502. גַּזָּם *gazzām* **masc. proper noun**
(Gazzam)
Ezra 2:48; **Neh.** 7:51.

1503. גֶּזַע *geza'* **masc. noun**
(stem, trunk)
Job 14:8; **Isa.** 11:1; 40:24.

1504. I. גָּזַר *gāzar* **verb**
(to cut off; to divide)
1 Kgs. 3:25,26; **2 Kgs.** 6:4; **2 Chr.** 26:21; **Esth.** 2:1; **Job** 22:28; **Ps.** 88:5(6); 136:13; **Isa.** 9:20(19)(KJV, NIV, see II); 53:8; **Lam.** 3:54; **Ezek.** 37:11; **Hab.** 3:17.
II. גָּזַר *gāzar* **verb**
(to devour, to eat)
Isa. 9:20(19)(NASB, see I).

1505. גְּזַר *g^e^zar* **Aram. verb**
(to cut, to divide; corr. to Hebr. 1504,I)
Dan. 2:27,34,45; 4:7(4); 5:7,11.

1506. גֶּזֶר *gezer* **masc. noun**
(a piece, a part)
Gen. 15:17; **Ps.** 136:13.

1507. גֶּזֶר *gezer* **proper noun**
(Gezer)
Josh. 10:33; 12:12; 16:3,10; 21:21; **Judg.** 1:29; **2 Sam.** 5:25; **1 Kgs.** 9:15–17; **1 Chr.** 6:67(52); 7:28; 14:16; 20:4.

1508. גִּזְרָה *gizrāh* **fem. noun**
(courtyard, appearance)
Lam. 4:7; **Ezek.** 41:12–15; 42:1, 10,13.

1509. גְּזֵרָה *g^e^zērāh* **fem. noun**
(solitary place)
Lev. 16:22.

1510. גְּזֵרָה *g^e^zērāh* **Aram. fem. noun**
(decree, announcement)
Dan. 4:17(14),24(21).

1511. גִּזְרִי *gizriy* **masc. proper noun**
(Gezrites, Girzites)
1 Sam. 27:8([K^e^] *girziy*).

1512. גָּחוֹן *gāḥôn* **masc. noun**
(belly)
Gen. 3:14; **Lev.** 11:42.

1513. גַּחֶלֶת *gaḥeleṯ* **fem. noun**
(coal, burning coal)
Lev. 16:12; **2 Sam.** 14:7; 22:9,13; **Job** 41:21(13); **Ps.** 18:8(9),12(13),13(14); 120:4; 140:10(11); **Prov.** 6:28; 25:22; 26:21; **Isa.** 44:19; 47:14; **Ezek.** 1:13; 10:2; 24:11.

1514. גַּחַם *gaḥam* **masc. proper noun**
(Gaham)
Gen. 22:24.

1515. גַּחַר *gaḥar* **masc. proper noun**
(Gahar)
Ezra 2:47; **Neh.** 7:49.

1516. גַּיְא *gay'*, גַּי *gay* **masc./fem. noun**
(valley)
Num. 21:20; **Deut.** 3:29; 4:46; 34:6; **Josh.** 8:11; 15:8; 18:16; 19:14,27; **1 Sam.** 13:18; 17:3,52; **2 Sam.** 8:13; **2 Kgs.** 2:16; 14:7; 23:10; **1 Chr.** 4:14,39; 18:12; **2 Chr.** 14:10(9); 25:11; 26:9; 28:3; 33:6; **Neh.** 2:13,15; 3:13; 11:30,35; **Ps.** 23:4; 60:[title](1); **Isa.** 22:1,5; 28:1,4; 40:4; **Jer.** 2:23; 7:31,32; 19:2,6; 32:35; **Ezek.** 6:3; 7:16; 31:12; 32:5; 35:8; 36:4,6; 39:11,15; **Mic.** 1:6; **Zech.** 14:4,5.

1517. גִּיד *giyḏ* **masc. noun**
(sinew, tendon)
Gen. 32:32(33); **Job** 10:11; 40:17; **Isa.** 48:4; **Ezek.** 37:6,8.

1518. גִּיחַ *giyaḥ*, גּוּחַ *gûaḥ* **verb**
(to burst forth, to bring forth)
Judg. 20:33; **Job** 38:8; 40:23; **Ps.** 22:9(10); **Ezek.** 32:2; **Mic.** 4:10.

1519. גִּיחַ *giyaḥ*, גּוּחַ *gûaḥ* **Aram. verb**
(to break forth, to churn up; corr. to Hebr. 1618)
Dan. 7:2.

1520. גִּיחַ *giyaḥ* **proper noun**
(Giah)
2 Sam. 2:24.

1521. A. גִּיחוֹן *giyḥôn* **proper noun**
(Gihon: river in Eden)
Gen. 2:13.
B. גִּיחוֹן *giyḥôn* **proper noun**
(Gihon: a spring)
1 Kgs. 1:33,38,45; **2 Chr.** 32:30; 33:14.

1522. גֵּיחֲזִי *gēyḥᵃziy*, גֵּחֲזִי *gēḥᵃziy* **masc. proper noun**
(Gehazi)
2 Kgs. 4:12,14,25,27,29,31,36; 5:20,21,25; 8:4,5.

1523. גִּיל *giyl*, גּוּל *gûl* **verb**
(to rejoice)
1 Chr. 16:31; **Ps.** 2:11; 9:14(15); 13:4(5),5(6); 14:7; 16:9; 21:1(2); 31:7(8); 32:11; 35:9; 48:11(12); 51:8(10); 53:6(7); 89:16(17); 96:11; 97:1,8; 118:24; 149:2; **Prov.** 2:14; 23:24(NIV, *giyl* [1524]),25; 24:17; **Song** 1:4; **Isa.** 9:3(2); 25:9; 29:19; 35:1,2; 41:16; 49:13; 61:10; 65:18,19; 66:10; **Hos.** 10:5; **Joel** 2:21,23; **Hab.** 1:15; 3:18; **Zeph.** 3:17; **Zech.** 9:9; 10:7.

1524. I. גִּיל *giyl* **masc. noun**
(rejoicing)
Job 3:22; **Ps.** 43:4; 45:15(16); 65:12(13); **Prov.** 23:24(KJV, NASB, *giyl* [1523]); **Isa.** 16:10; **Jer.** 48:33; **Hos.** 9:1; **Joel** 1:16.
II. גִּיל *giyl* **masc. noun**
(circle, age, stage of life)
Dan. 1:10.

1525. גִּילָה *giylāh* **fem. noun**
(rejoicing, joy)
Isa. 35:2; 65:18.

1526. גִּילֹנִי *giylōniy* **masc. proper noun**
(Gilonite)
2 Sam. 15:12; 23:34.

1527. גִּינַת *giynaṯ* **masc. proper noun**
(Ginath)
1 Kgs. 16:21,22.

1528. גִּיר *giyr* **Aram. masc. noun**
(plaster; corr. to Hebr. 1615)
Dan. 5:5.

1529. גֵּישָׁן *gēyšān* **masc. proper noun**
(Geshan)
1 Chr. 2:47.

1530. I. גַּל *gal* **masc. noun**
(heap, pile of rocks)
Gen. 31:46,48,51,52; **Josh.** 7:26; 8:29; **2 Sam.** 18:17; **2 Kgs.** 19:25; **Job** 8:17; 15:28; **Song** 4:12(KJV, NIV, see II); **Isa.** 25:2; 37:26; **Jer.** 9:11(10); 51:37; **Hos.** 12:11(12).
II. גַּל *gal* **masc. noun**
(wave, billow, spring)
Job 38:11; **Ps.** 42:7(8); 65:7(8); 89:9(10); 107:25,29; **Song** 4:12(NASB, see I); **Isa.** 48:18; 51:15; **Jer.** 5:22; 31:35; 51:42,55; **Ezek.** 26:3; **Jon.** 2:3(4); **Zech.** 10:11.

1531. גֹּל *gōl* **masc. noun**
(bowl, oil container for a lamp, basin)
Zech. 4:2(NASB, NIV, *gullāh* [1543]).

1532. גַּלָּב *gallāḇ* **masc. noun**
(barber)
Ezek. 5:1.

1533. גִּלְבֹּעַ *gilbōa'* **proper noun**
(Gilboa)
1 Sam. 28:4; 31:1,8; **2 Sam.** 1:6,21; 21:12; **1 Chr.** 10:1,8.

1534. I. גַּלְגַּל *galgal* **masc. noun**
(wheel, whirl, whirlwind)
Ps. 77:18(19); **Eccl.** 12:6; **Isa.** 5:28; **Jer.** 47:3; **Ezek.** 10:2,6,13; 23:24; 26:10.
II. גַּלְגַּל *galgal* **masc. noun**
(tumbleweed, rolling chaff)
Ps. 83:13(14); **Isa.** 17:13.

1535. גַּלְגַּל *galgal* **Aram. masc. noun**
(wheel; corr. to Hebr. 1534,I)
Dan. 7:9.

1536. גִּלְגָּל *gilgāl* **masc. noun**
(wheel)
Isa. 28:28.

1537. A. גִּלְגָּל *gilgāl* **proper noun**
(Gilgal: a city loc. east of Jericho)
Deut. 11:30; **Josh.** 4:19,20; 5:9,10; 9:6; 10:6,7,9,15,43; 14:6; **Judg.** 2:1; 3:19; **1 Sam.** 7:16; 10:8; 11:14,15; 13:4, 7,8,12,15; 15:12,21,33; **2 Sam.** 19:15(16),40(41); **Hos.** 4:15; 9:15; 12:11(12); **Amos** 4:4; 5:5; **Mic.** 6:5.
B. גִּלְגָּל *gilgāl* **proper noun**
(Gilgal: a city)
Josh. 12:23.
C. גִּלְגָּל *gilgāl* **proper noun**
(Gilgal: a city)
Josh. 15:7.
D. גִּלְגָּל *gilgāl* **proper noun**
(Gilgal: loc. in N. Israel)
2 Kgs. 2:1; 4:38.
E. גִּלְגָּל *gilgāl* **proper noun**
(Gilgal: a city loc. near Jerusalem)
Neh. 12:29(NASB, NIV, *bēyṯ hāgilgal* [1019]).

1538. גֻּלְגֹּלֶת *gulgōleṯ* **fem. noun**
(skull; metaph. one by one [head for head])
Ex. 16:16; 38:26; **Num.** 1:2,18,20,22; 3:47; **Judg.** 9:53; **2 Kgs.** 9:35; **1 Chr.** 10:10; 23:3,24.

1539. גֶּלֶד *gēleḏ* **masc. noun**
(skin)
Job 16:15.

1540. גָּלָה *gālāh* **verb**
(to uncover, to carry into exile)
Gen. 9:21; 35:7; **Ex.** 20:26; **Lev.** 18:6–19; 20:11,17–21; **Num.** 22:31; 24:4,16; **Deut.** 22:30(23:1); 27:20; 29:29(28); **Judg.** 18:30; **Ruth** 3:4,7; 4:4; **1 Sam.** 2:27; 3:7,21; 4:21,22; 9:15; 14:8,11; 20:2,12,13; 22:8,17; **2 Sam.** 6:20; 7:27; 15:19; 22:16; **2 Kgs.** 15:29; 16:9; 17:6,11,23,26–28,33; 18:11; 24:14,15; 25:11,21; **1 Chr.** 5:6,26; 6:15(5:41); 8:6,7; 9:1; 17:25; **2 Chr.** 36:20; **Ezra** 2:1; **Neh.** 7:6; **Esth.** 2:6; 3:14; 8:13; **Job** 12:22; 20:27,28; 33:16; 36:10,15; 38:17; 41:13(5); **Ps.** 18:15(16); 98:2; 119:18; **Prov.** 11:13; 18:2; 20:19; 25:9; 26:26; 27:5,25; **Isa.** 5:13; 16:3;

22:8,14; 23:1; 24:11; 26:21; 38:12; 40:5; 47:2,3; 49:9,21; 53:1; 56:1; 57:8; **Jer.** 1:3; 11:20; 13:19,22; 20:4,12; 22:12; 24:1; 27:20; 29:1,4,7,14; 32:11,14; 33:6; 39:9; 40:1,7; 43:3; 49:10; 52:15,27–30; **Lam.** 1:3; 2:14; 4:22; **Ezek.** 12:3; 13:14; 16:36, 37,57; 21:24(29); 22:10; 23:10, 18,29; 39:23,28; **Dan.** 10:1; **Hos.** 2:10(12); 7:1; 10:5; **Amos** 1:5,6; 3:7; 5:5,27; 6:7; 7:11,17; **Mic.** 1:6,16; **Nah.** 2:7(8); 3:5.

1541. גְּלָה *g^elāh*, גְּלָא *g^elā'* **Aram. verb**
(to uncover, to carry into exile; corr. to Hebr. 1540)
Ezra 4:10; 5:12; **Dan.** 2:19,22,28–30,47.

1542. גִּלֹה *gilōh* **proper noun**
(Giloh)
Josh. 15:51; **2 Sam.** 15:12.

1543. גֻּלָּה *gullāh* **fem. noun**
(spring, bowl)
Josh. 15:19; **Judg.** 1:15; **1 Kgs.** 7:41,42; **2 Chr.** 4:12,13; **Eccl.** 12:6; **Zech.** 4:2 (KJV, *gōl* [1531]).

1544. גִּלּוּל *gillûl* **masc. noun**
(idol)
Lev. 26:30; **Deut.** 29:17(16); **1 Kgs.** 15:12; 21:26; **2 Kgs.** 17:12; 21:11,21; 23:24; **Jer.** 50:2; **Ezek.** 6:4–6,9,13; 8:10; 14:3–7; 16:36; 18:6,12,15; 20:7,8,16,18, 24,31,39; 22:3,4; 23:7,30,37,39,49; 30:13; 33:25; 36:18,25; 37:23; 44:10,12.

1545. גְּלוֹם *g^elôm* **masc. noun**
(clothes, fabric)
Ezek. 27:24.

1546. גָּלוּת *gālûṯ* **fem. noun**
(captivity, exile)
2 Kgs. 25:27; **Isa.** 20:4; 45:13; **Jer.** 24:5; 28:4; 29:22; 40:1; 52:31; **Ezek.** 1:2; 33:21; 40:1; **Amos** 1:6,9; **Obad.** 1:20.

1547. גָּלוּ *gālû* **Aram. fem. noun**
(captivity, exile; corr. to Hebr. 1546)
Ezra 6:16; **Dan.** 2:25; 5:13; 6:13(14).

1548. גָּלַח *gālaḥ* **verb**
(to shave, to shave off)
Gen. 41:14; **Lev.** 13:33; 14:8,9; 21:5; **Num.** 6:9,18,19; **Deut.** 21:12; **Judg.** 16:17,19,22; **2 Sam.** 10:4; 14:26; **1 Chr.** 19:4; **Isa.** 7:20; **Jer.** 41:5; **Ezek.** 44:20.

1549. גִּלָּיוֹן *gillāyôn* **masc. noun**
(glasses, mirror)
Isa. 3:23; 8:1.

1550. גָּלִיל *gāliyl* **adj.**
(shaped like a ring, turning in a circle)
1 Kgs. 6:34; **Esth.** 1:6; **Song** 5:14.

1551. גָּלִיל *gāliyl*, גָּלִילָה *gāliylāh* **proper noun**
(Galilee)
Josh. 20:7; 21:32; **1 Kgs.** 9:11; **2 Kgs.** 15:29; **1 Chr.** 6:76(61); **Isa.** 9:1(8:23).

1552. גְּלִילָה *g^eliylāh* **fem. noun**
(border, region)
Josh. 13:2; 22:10(NIV, *g^eliylôt* [1553]), 11(NIV, *g^eliylôt* [1553]); **Ezek.** 47:8; **Joel** 3:4(4:4).

1553. גְּלִילוֹת *g^eliylôt* **proper noun**
(Geliloth)
Josh. 18:17; 22:10(KJV, NASB, *g^eliylāh* [1552]),11(KJV, NASB, *g^eliylāh* [1552]).

1554. גַּלִּים *galliym* **proper noun**
(Gallim)
1 Sam. 25:44; **Isa.** 10:30.

1555. גָּלְיָת *golyāṯ*, גָּלְיַת *golyaṯ* **masc. proper noun**
(Goliath)
1 Sam. 17:4,23; 21:9(10); 22:10; **2 Sam.** 21:19; **1 Chr.** 20:5.

1556. גָּלַל *gālal* **verb**
(to roll)
Gen. 29:3,8,10; 43:18; **Josh.** 5:9; 10:18; **1 Sam.** 14:33; **2 Sam.** 20:12; **Job** 30:14; **Ps.** 22:8(9); 37:5; 119:22; **Prov.** 16:3; 26:27; **Isa.** 9:5(4); 34:4; **Jer.** 51:25; **Amos** 5:24.

1557. גָּלָל *gālāl* **masc. noun**
(dung)
1 Kgs. 14:10; **Zeph.** 1:17(KJV, *gēlel* [1561]).

1558. גָּלָל *gālāl* **masc. noun**
(because of)
Gen. 12:13; 30:27; 39:5; **Deut.** 1:37; 15:10; 18:12; **1 Kgs.** 14:16; **Jer.** 11:17; 15:4; **Mic.** 3:12.

1559. A. גָּלָל *gālāl* **masc. proper noun**
(Galal: a Levite)
1 Chr. 9:15.
B. גָּלָל *gālāl* **masc. proper noun**
(Galal: a Levite)
1 Chr. 9:16; **Neh.** 11:17.

1560. גְּלָל *g^e^lāl* **Aram. adj.**
(large)
Ezra 5:8; 6:4.

1561. גֵּלֶל *gēlel* **masc. noun**
(dung)
Job 20:7; **Ezek.** 4:12,15; **Zeph.** 1:17(NASB, NIV, *gālāl'* [1557]).

1562. גִּלֲלַי *gil^a^lay* **masc. proper noun**
(Gilalai)
Neh. 12:36.

1563. גָּלַם *gālam* **verb**
(to roll up, to fold together)
2 Kgs. 2:8.

1564. גֹּלֶם *gōlem* **masc. noun**
(embryo, fetus)
Ps. 139:16.

1565. גַּלְמוּד *galmûd̲* **adj.**
(solitary, barren)
Job 3:7; 15:34; 30:3; **Isa.** 49:21.

1566. גָּלַע *gāla'* **verb**
(to expose, to burst out)
Prov. 17:14; 18:1; 20:3.

1567. גַּלְעֵד *gal'ēd̲* **proper noun**
(Galeed)
Gen. 31:47,48.

1568. A. גִּלְעָד *gil'ād̲* **proper noun**
(Gilead: a district and city E. of Jordan)
Gen. 31:21,23,25; 37:25; **Num.** 32:1,26, 29,39,40; **Deut.** 2:36; 3:10,12,13,15,16; 4:43; 34:1; **Josh.** 12:2,5; 13:11,25,31; 17:5,6; 20:8; 21:38(36); 22:9,13,15,32; **Judg.** 5:17; 10:4,8,17,18; 11:5,7–11,29; 12:4,5,7; 20:1; 21:8–10,12,14; **1 Sam.** 11:1,9; 13:7; 31:11; **2 Sam.** 2:4,5,9; 17:26; 21:12; 24:6; **1 Kgs.** 4:13,19; 17:1; 22:3(NASB, NIV, see 7433); **2 Kgs.** 8:28; 9:1,4,14; 10:33; 15:29; **1 Chr.** 5:9,10,16; 6:80(65); 10:11; 26:31; 27:21; **Ps.** 60:7(9); 108:8(9); **Song** 4:1; 6:5; **Jer.** 8:22; 22:6; 46:11; 50:19; **Ezek.** 47:18; **Hos.** 6:8; 12:11(12); **Amos** 1:3,13; **Obad.** 1:19; **Mic.** 7:14; **Zech.** 10:10.
B. גִּלְעָד *gil'ād̲* **proper noun**
(Gilead: mountain W. of Jordan)
Judg. 7:3.
C. גִּלְעָד *gil'ād̲* **proper noun**
(Gilead: son of Machir)
Num. 26:29,30; 27:1; 36:1; **Josh.** 17:1,3; **1 Chr.** 2:21–23; 7:14,17.
D. גִּלְעָד *gil'ād̲* **proper noun**
(Gilead: father of Jephthah)
Judg. 11:1,2.
E. גִּלְעָד *gil'ād̲* **proper noun**
(Gilead: Gadite chief)
1 Chr. 5:14.

1569. A. גִּלְעָדִי *gil'ād̲iy* **masc. proper noun**
(Gileadites: branch of Manassites)

Num. 26:29.
B. גִּלְעָדִי *gil'ādiy* **masc. proper noun**
(Gileadites: inhabitants of Gilead [*gil'ād*{1568,A}])
Num. 26:29; **Judg.** 10:3; 11:1,40; 12:7; **2 Sam.** 17:27; 19:31(32); **1 Kgs.** 2:7; **2 Kgs.** 15:25; **Ezra** 2:61; **Neh.** 7:63.

1570. גָּלַשׁ *gālaš* **verb**
(to appear, to descend)
Song 4:1; 6:5.

1571. גַּם *gam* **conj.**
(also, even)
Gen. 3:6,22; 4:4,22,26; 6:3(KJV, NASB, *šāgag* [7683,II]),4; 7:3; 10:21; 13:5,16; 14:7,16; 15:14; 16:13; 17:16; 19:21,34, 35,38; 20:4–6,12; 21:13,26; 22:20,24; 24:14,19,25,44,46; 26:21; 27:31,33,34, 38,45; 29:27,30,33; 30:3,6,8,15,30; 31:15; 32:6(7),18–20(19–21); 33:7; 35:17; 37:7; 38:10,11,22,24; 40:15; 42:22,28; 43:8; 44:9,10,16,29; 46:4,34; 47:3,19; 48:11,19; 50:9,18,23; **Ex.** 1:10; 2:19; 3:9; 4:9,10,14; 5:2,14; 6:4,5; 7:11,23; 8:21(17),32(28); 10:24–26; 11:3; 12:31,32,38,39; 18:18,23; 19:9,22; 21:29,35; 33:12,17; 34:3; **Lev.** 25:45; 26:24,44; **Num.** 4:22; 11:4; 12:2; 13:27,28; 16:10,13; 18:2,3,28; 22:19,33; 23:25; 24:12,24,25; 27:13; **Deut.** 1:28,37; 2:6,15; 3:3,20; 7:20; 9:19,20; 10:10; 12:30,31; 22:22; 23:2(3),3(4), 18(19); 26:13; 28:61; 32:25; **Josh.** 1:15; 2:12,24; 7:11; 9:4; 10:30; 22:7; 24:18; **Judg.** 1:3,22; 2:3,10,17,21; 3:22,31; 5:4; 6:35; 7:18; 8:9,22,31; 9:19,49; 10:9; 11:17; 17:2; 19:19; 20:48; **Ruth** 1:5,12; 2:8,15,16,21; 3:12; 4:10; **1 Sam.** 1:6,28; 2:15,26; 4:17; 8:8,20; 10:11,12,26; 12:14, 16,23,25; 13:4; 14:15,21,22; 15:29; 16:8,9; 17:36; 18:5; 19:20–24; 20:27; 21:8(9); 22:7,17; 23:17; 24:11(12); 25:13,16; 26:25; 28:6,15,19,20,22,23; 31:5,6; **2 Sam.** 1:4,11; 2:2,6,7; 3:17,19; 4:2; 5:2; 7:19; 8:11; 11:12,17,21,24; 12:13,14,27; 13:36; 14:7; 15:19,24; 16:23; 17:5,10,12,13,16; 18:2,22,26; 19:30(31),40(41),43(44); 20:26; 21:20; **1 Kgs.** 1:6,46–48; 2:5; 3:13,18,26; 4:15; 7:20,31; 8:41; 10:11; 13:18; 14:14,23,24; 15:13; 16:7,16; 17:20; 18:35; 21:19,23; 22:22; **2 Kgs.** 2:3,5; 8:1; 9:27; 13:6; 16:3; 17:19,41; 21:11,16; 22:19; 23:15,19, 24,27; 24:4; **1 Chr.** 10:5,13; 11:2; 12:38,40; 18:11; 19:15; 20:6; 23:26; 24:31; 29:9,24; **2 Chr.** 1:11; 6:32; 9:10; 12:12; 14:15(14); 15:16; 16:12; 17:11; 18:21; 19:8; 20:4,13; 21:4,11,13,17; 22:3,5; 24:7,12; 26:20; 28:2,5,8; 29:7,35; 30:1,12; 31:6; 34:27; 36:13,14,22; **Ezra** 1:1; **Neh.** 4:3(3:35),22(16); 5:8,10,13–16; 6:1,7,14,17,19; 12:43; 13:22,23,26; **Esth.** 1:9; 4:16; 5:12; 7:2,8,9; 9:13,15; **Job** 1:6; 2:1,10; 7:11; 12:3; 13:2,16; 15:10; 16:4,19; 18:5; 19:18; 21:7; 23:2; 24:19; 28:27; 30:2,8; 31:28; 33:6; 40:14; 41:9(1); **Ps.** 8:7(8); 14:3; 19:11(12),13(14); 23:4; 25:3; 37:25; 38:10(11); 41:9(10); 49:2(3); 52:5(7); 53:3(4); 71:18,22,24; 78:20,21; 83:8(9); 84:2(3),3(4),6(7); 85:12(13); 95:9; 107:5; 118:11; 119:23,24; 129:2; 132:12; 133:1; 137:1; 139:10,12; 148:12; **Prov.** 1:26; 11:25; 14:13,20; 16:4,7; 17:15,26,28; 18:3,9; 19:2,24; 20:10–12; 21:13; 22:6; 23:15; 24:23; 25:1; 26:4; 28:9; **Eccl.** 1:11,17; 2:1,7,8,14,15,19,21,23,24,26; 3:11,13; 4:4,8,11,14,16;5:10(9),16(15),17(16), 19(18); 6:3,5,7,9; 7:6,14,18,21,22; 8:10,12,14,16,17; 9:1,3,6,11–13; 10:3,20; 11:2; 12:5; **Song** 7:13(14); 8:1; **Isa.** 1:15; 5:2; 7:13,20; 13:3; 14:8,10; 21:12; 23:12; 26:12; 28:7,29; 30:5,33; 31:2; 40:24; 43:13; 44:12; 45:16; 47:3; 48:8; 49:15,25; 57:6,7; 66:3,4,8,21; **Jer.** 2:16,33,34, 36,37; 3:8,10; 4:12; 5:18,28; 6:11,15; 7:11; 8:7,12; 10:5; 12:2,6; 13:23,26; 14:5,18; 23:11; 25:14; 26:20; 27:6,7; 28:14; 31:19,36,37; 33:21,26; 36:6,25; 40:11; 46:16,21; 48:2,7,26,34; 50:24; 51:12,44,49; 52:10; **Lam.** 1:8; 2:9; 3:8;

4:3,15,21; **Ezek.** 5:8,11; 8:18; 9:10; 10:16; 16:28,29,41,43,52; 18:11; 20:12, 15,23,25; 21:9(14),13(18),17(22),27(32); 23:35,37; 24:3,5,9; 31:17; 39:16; **Dan.** 11:8,22; **Hos.** 3:3; 4:3,5,6; 5:5; 6:11; 7:9; 8:10; 9:12,16; 10:6; 12:11(12); **Joel** 1:12,18,20; 2:3,12,29(3:2); 3:4(4:4); **Amos** 4:6,7; **Obad.** 1:11,13; **Mic.** 6:13; **Nah.** 3:10,11; **Hab.** 2:16; **Zeph.** 1:18; 2:12,14; **Zech.** 3:7; 8:6,21; 9:2,7,11,12; 11:8; 12:2; 13:2; 14:14; **Mal.** 1:10; 2:2,9; 3:15.

1572. גָּמָא *gāmā'* **verb**
(to swallow, to drink)
Gen. 24:17; **Job** 39:24.

1573. גֹּמֶא *gōme'* **masc. noun**
(bullrush, papyrus stalk)
Ex. 2:3; **Job** 8:11; **Isa.** 18:2; 35:7.

1574. גֹּמֶד *gōme<u>d</u>* **masc. noun**
(cubit)
Judg. 3:16.

1575. גַּמָּדִים *gammā<u>d</u>iym* **masc. pl. proper noun** (Gammadites: citizens of the city of Gammad)
Ezek. 27:11.

1576. גְּמוּל *g^e^mûl* **masc. noun**
(recompense, that which is deserved)
Judg. 9:16; **2 Chr.** 32:25; **Ps.** 28:4; 94:2; 103:2; 137:8; **Prov.** 12:14; 19:17; **Isa.** 3:11; 35:4; 59:18; 66:6; **Jer.** 51:6; **Lam.** 3:64; **Joel** 3:4(4:4),7(4:7); **Obad.** 1:15.

1577. גָּמוּל *gāmûl* **masc. proper noun**
(Gamul)
1 Chr. 24:17.

1578. גְּמוּלָה *g^e^mûlāh* **fem. noun**
(recompense, that which is due)
2 Sam. 19:36(37); **Isa.** 59:18; **Jer.** 51:56.

1579. גִּמְזוֹ *gimzô* **proper noun**
(Gimzo)
2 Chr. 28:18.

1580. גָּמַל *gāmal* **verb**
(to wean, to reward, to recompense)
Gen. 21:8; 50:15,17; **Num.** 17:8(23); **Deut.** 32:6; **1 Sam.** 1:22–24; 24:17(18); **2 Sam.** 19:36(37); 22:21; **1 Kgs.** 11:20; **2 Chr.** 20:11; **Ps.** 7:4(5); 13:6; 18:20(21); 103:10; 116:7; 119:17; 131:2; 137:8; 142:7(8); **Prov.** 3:30; 11:17; 31:12; **Isa.** 3:9; 11:8; 18:5; 28:9; 63:7; **Hos.** 1:8; **Joel** 3:4(4:4).

1581. גָּמָל *gāmāl* **masc. noun**
(camel)
Gen. 12:16; 24:10,11,14,19,20,22, 30–32,35,44,46,61,63,64; 30:43; 31:17,34; 32:7(8),15(16); 37:25; **Ex.** 9:3; **Lev.** 11:4; **Deut.** 14:7; **Judg.** 6:5; 7:12; 8:21,26; **1 Sam.** 15:3; 27:9; 30:17; **1 Kgs.** 10:2; **2 Kgs.** 8:9; **1 Chr.** 5:21; 12:40; 27:30; **2 Chr.** 9:1; 14:15(14); **Ezra** 2:67; **Neh.** 7:69; **Job** 1:3,17; 42:12; **Isa.** 21:7; 30:6; 60:6; **Jer.** 49:29,32; **Ezek.** 25:5; **Zech.** 14:15.

1582. גְּמַלִּי *g^e^malliy* **masc. proper noun**
(Gemalli)
Num. 13:12.

1583. גַּמְלִיאֵל *gamliy'ēl* **masc. proper noun**
(Gamaliel)
Num. 1:10; 2:20; 7:54,59; 10:23.

1584. גָּמַר *gāmar* **verb**
(to cease, to come to an end)
Ps. 7:9(10); 12:1(2); 57:2(3); 77:8(9); 138:8.

1585. גְּמַר *g^e^mar* **Aram. verb**
(to perfect peace; to offer greetings; corr. to Hebr. 1584)
Ezra 7:12.

1586. A. גֹּמֶר *gōmer* **masc. proper noun**
(Gomer: son of Japheth)
Gen. 10:2,3; **1 Chr.** 1:5,6.
B. גֹּמֶר *gōmer* **masc. proper noun**
(Gomer: descendants of Gomer)
Ezek. 38:6.
C. גֹּמֶר *gōmer* **masc. proper noun**
(Gomer: wife of Hosea)
Hos. 1:3.

1587. A. גְּמַרְיָה *g^e^maryāh* **masc. proper noun**
(Gemariah: son of Hilkiah)
Jer. 29:3.
B. גְּמַרְיָהוּ *g^e^maryāhû* **masc. proper noun**
(Gemariah: son of Shaphan)
Jer. 36:10–12,25.

1588. גַּן *gan* **masc. noun**
(garden)
Gen. 2:8–10,15,16; 3:1–3,8,10,23,24; 13:10; **Deut.** 11:10; **1 Kgs.** 21:2; **2 Kgs.** 9:27; 21:18,26; 25:4; **Neh.** 3:15; **Song** 4:12,15,16; 5:1; 6:2; 8:13; **Isa.** 51:3; 58:11; **Jer.** 31:12; 39:4; 52:7; **Lam.** 2:6; **Ezek.** 28:13; 31:8,9; 36:35; **Joel** 2:3.

1589. גָּנַב *gānab̲* **verb**
(to steal)
Gen. 30:33; 31:19,20,26,27,30,32,39; 40:15; 44:8; **Ex.** 20:15; 21:16; 22:1(21:37),7(6),12(11); **Lev.** 19:11; **Deut.** 5:19(17); 24:7; **Josh.** 7:11; **2 Sam.** 15:6; 19:3(4),41(42); 21:12; **2 Kgs.** 11:2; **2 Chr.** 22:11; **Job** 4:12; 21:18; 27:20; **Prov.** 6:30; 9:17; 30:9; **Jer.** 7:9; 23:30; **Hos.** 4:2; **Obad.** 1:5; **Zech.** 5:3.

1590. גַּנָּב *gannāb̲* **masc. noun**
(thief)
Ex. 22:2(1),7(6),8(7); **Deut.** 24:7; **Job** 24:14; 30:5; **Ps.** 50:18; **Prov.** 6:30; 29:24; **Isa.** 1:23; **Jer.** 2:26; 48:27; 49:9; **Hos.** 7:1; **Joel** 2:9; **Obad.** 1:5; **Zech.** 5:4.

1591. גְּנֵבָה *g^e^nēb̲āh* **fem. noun**
(theft, thing stolen)
Ex. 22:3(2),4(3).

1592. גְּנֻבַת *g^e^nub̲at̲* **masc. proper noun**
(Genubath)
1 Kgs. 11:20.

1593. גַּנָּה *gannāh* **fem. noun**
(garden)
Num. 24:6; **Esth.** 1:5(see *ginnah* [1594]); 7:7(see *ginnah* [1594]),8(see *ginnah* [1594]); **Job** 8:16; **Eccl.** 2:5; **Song** 6:11(see *ginnah* [1594]); **Isa.** 1:29,30; 61:11; 65:3; 66:17; **Jer.** 29:5,28; **Amos** 4:9; 9:14.

1594. גִּנַּת *ginnāt̲* **fem. noun**
(garden; const. of *gannah* [1593])
Esth. 1:5; 7:7,8; **Song** 6:11.

1595. גְּנָזִים *g^e^nāziym* **masc. pl. noun**
(treasury)
Esth. 3:9; 4:7; **Ezek.** 27:24.

1596. גְּנַז *g^e^naz* **Aram. masc. noun**
(treasury, archives; corr. to Hebr. 1595)
Ezra 5:17; 6:1; 7:20.

1597. גַּנְזַךְ *ganzak̲* **masc. noun**
(treasury, storeroom)
1 Chr. 28:11.

1598. גָּנַן *gānan* **verb**
(to defend, to shield)
2 Kgs. 19:34; 20:6; **Isa.** 31:5; 37:35; 38:6; **Zech.** 9:15; 12:8.

1599. גִּנְּתוֹי *ginn^e^t̲ôy,* גִּנְּתוֹן *ginn^e^t̲ôn* **masc. proper noun**
(Ginnethon)
Neh. 10:6(7); 12:4,16.

1600. גָּעָה *gāʿāh* **verb**
(to bellow, to moo [of cattle])
1 Sam. 6:12; **Job** 6:5.

1601. גֹּעָה *gōʻāh* **proper noun**
(Goath, Goah)
Jer. 31:39.

1602. גָּעַל *gāʻal* **verb**
(to abhor, to despise)
Lev. 26:11,15,30,43,44; **2 Sam.** 1:21; **Job** 21:10; **Jer.** 14:19; **Ezek.** 16:45.

1603. גַּעַל *gaʻal* **masc. proper noun**
(Gaal)
Judg. 9:26,28,30,31,35–37,39,41.

1604. גֹּעַל *gōʻal* **masc. noun**
(a loathing, a despising)
Ezek. 16:5.

1605. גָּעַר *gāʻar* **verb**
(to rebuke, to reprove)
Gen. 37:10; **Ruth** 2:16; **Ps.** 9:5(6); 68:30(31); 106:9; 119:21; **Isa.** 17:13; 54:9; **Jer.** 29:27; **Nah.** 1:4; **Zech.** 3:2; **Mal.** 2:3; 3:11.

1606. גְּעָרָה *g^eʻārāh* **fem. noun**
(rebuke, reproof)
2 Sam. 22:16; **Job** 26:11; **Ps.** 18:15(16); 76:6(7); 80:16(17); 104:7; **Prov.** 13:1,8; 17:10; **Eccl.** 7:5; **Isa.** 30:17; 50:2; 51:20; 66:15.

1607. גָּעַשׁ *gaʻaš* **verb**
(to shake, to quake)
2 Sam. 22:8; **Job** 34:20; **Ps.** 18:7(8); **Jer.** 5:22; 25:16; 46:7,8.

1608. גַּעַשׁ *gaʻaš* **proper noun**
(Gaash)
Josh. 24:30; **Judg.** 2:9; **2 Sam.** 23:30; **1 Chr.** 11:32.

1609. גַּעְתָּם *gaʻtām* **masc. proper noun**
(Gatam)
Gen. 36:11,16; **1 Chr.** 1:36.

1610. I. גַּף *gap̱* **masc. noun**
(back, top, high point)
Prov. 9:3.
II. גַּף *gap̱* **masc. noun**
(body)
Ex. 21:3,4.

1611. גַּף *gap̱* **Aram. masc. noun**
(wing [of a bird])
Dan. 7:4,6.

1612. גֶּפֶן *gep̱en* **masc. noun**
(vine)
Gen. 40:9,10; 49:11; **Num.** 6:4; 20:5; **Deut.** 8:8; 32:32; **Judg.** 9:12,13; 13:14; **1 Kgs.** 4:25(5:5); **2 Kgs.** 4:39; 18:31; **Job** 15:33; **Ps.** 78:47; 80:8(9),14(15); 105:33; 128:3; **Song** 2:13; 6:11; 7:8(9), 12(13); **Isa.** 7:23; 16:8,9; 24:7; 32:12; 34:4; 36:16; **Jer.** 2:21; 5:17; 6:9; 8:13; 48:32; **Ezek.** 15:2,6; 17:6–8; 19:10; **Hos.** 2:12(14); 10:1; 14:7(8); **Joel** 1:7,12; 2:22; **Mic.** 4:4; **Hab.** 3:17; **Hag.** 2:19; **Zech.** 3:10; 8:12; **Mal.** 3:11.

1613. גֹּפֶר *gōp̱er* **masc. noun**
(gopher wood, cypress wood)
Gen. 6:14.

1614. גָּפְרִית *gop̱riyṯ* **fem. noun**
(brimstone, sulfur)
Gen. 19:24; **Deut.** 29:23(22); **Job** 18:15; **Ps.** 11:6; **Isa.** 30:33; 34:9; **Ezek.** 38:22.

1615. גִּר *gir* **masc. noun**
(chalk)
Isa. 27:9.

1616. גֵּיר *gēyr,* גֵּר *gēr* **masc. noun**
(stranger, alien)
Gen. 15:13; 23:4; **Ex.** 2:22; 12:19,48,49; 18:3; 20:10; 22:21(20); 23:9,12; **Lev.** 16:29; 17:8,10,12,13,15; 18:26; 19:10, 33,34; 20:2; 22:18; 23:22; 24:16,22; 25:23,35,47; **Num.** 9:14; 15:14–16,26, 29,30; 19:10; 35:15; **Deut.** 1:16; 5:14; 10:18,19; 14:21,29; 16:11,14; 23:7(8); 24:14,17,19–21; 26:11–13; 27:19; 28:43; 29:11(10); 31:12; **Josh.** 8:33,35; 20:9;

2 Sam. 1:13; **1 Chr.** 22:2; 29:15; **2 Chr.** 2:17(16); 30:25; **Job** 31:32; **Ps.** 39:12(13); 94:6; 119:19; 146:9; **Isa.** 14:1; **Jer.** 7:6; 14:8; 22:3; **Ezek.** 14:7; 22:7,29; 47:22,23; **Zech.** 7:10; **Mal.** 3:5.

1617. גֵּרָא *gērā'* **masc. proper noun**
(Gera)
Gen. 46:21; **Judg.** 3:15; **2 Sam.** 16:5; 19:16(17),18(19); **1 Kgs.** 2:8; **1 Chr.** 8:3,5,7.

1618. גָּרָב *gārāḇ* **masc. noun**
(scab, festering sore)
Lev. 21:20; 22:22; **Deut.** 28:27.

1619. A. גָּרֵב *gārēḇ* **masc. proper noun**
(Gareb: an Ithrite)
2 Sam. 23:38; **1 Chr.** 11:40.
B. גָּרֵב *gārēḇ* **proper noun**
(Gareb: a hill)
Jer. 31:39.

1620. גַּרְגֵּר *gargēr* **masc. noun**
(olive berry)
Isa. 17:6.

1621. גַּרְגָּרוֹת *gargārôṯ* **fem. pl. noun**
(neck)
Prov. 1:9; 3:3,22; 6:21.

1622. גִּרְגָּשִׁי *girgāšiy* **masc. proper noun**
(Girgashite, Girgasite)
Gen. 10:16; 15:21; **Deut.** 7:1; **Josh.** 3:10; 24:11; **1 Chr.** 1:14; **Neh.** 9:8.

1623. גָּרַד *gāraḏ* **verb**
(to scrape, to scratch)
Job 2:8.

1624. גָּרָה *gārāh* **verb**
(to stir up strife, to meddle)
Deut. 2:5,9,19,24; **2 Kgs.** 14:10; **2 Chr.** 25:19; **Prov.** 15:18; 28:4,25; 29:22; **Jer.** 50:24; **Dan.** 11:10,25.

1625. גֵּרָה *gērāh* **fem. noun**
(cud)
Lev. 11:3–7,26; **Deut.** 14:6–8.

1626. גֵּרָה *gērāh* **fem. noun**
(gerah: a small unit of weight)
Ex. 30:13; **Lev.** 27:25; **Num.** 3:47; 18:16; **Ezek.** 45:12.

1627. גָּרוֹן *gārôn* **masc. noun**
(throat, neck)
Ps. 5:9(10); 69:3(4); 115:7; 149:6; **Isa.** 3:16; 58:1; **Jer.** 2:25; **Ezek.** 16:11.

1628. I. גֵּרוּת *gērûṯ* **fem. noun**
(inn, habitation)
Jer. 41:17(NASB, NIV, see II).
II. גֵּרוּת *gērûṯ* **fem. proper noun**
(Geruth: a city near Bethlehem)
Jer. 41:17(KJV, see I).

1629. גָּרַז *gāraz* **verb**
(to be cut off)
Ps. 31:22(23).

1630. גְּרִזִים *g^e^riziym* **proper noun**
(Gerizim: a mountain)
Deut. 11:29; 27:12; **Josh.** 8:33; **Judg.** 9:7.

1631. גַּרְזֶן *garzen* **masc. noun**
(ax)
Deut. 19:5; 20:19; **1 Kgs.** 6:7; **Isa.** 10:15.

1632. גָּרֹל *gārōl* **adj.**
(great)
Prov. 19:19(NASB, NIV, [Q^e^] *gāḏôl* [1419,I]).

1633. I. גָּרַם *gāram* **verb**
(to break bones, to crush, to gnaw)
Num. 24:8; **Ezek.** 23:34; **Zeph.** 3:3(NASB, NIV, see II).
II. גָּרַם *gāram* **verb**
(to leave)
Zeph. 3:3(KJV, see I).

1634. גֶּרֶם *gerem* **masc. noun**
(bone, strength [as of the bones of the arm])
Gen. 49:14; **2 Kgs.** 9:13; **Job** 40:18; **Prov.** 17:22; 25:15.

1635. גְּרַם *g^e^ram* **Aram. masc. noun**
(bone; corr. to Hebr. 1634])
Dan. 6:24(25).

1636. גַּרְמִי *garmiy* **masc. proper noun**
(Garmite)
1 Chr. 4:19.

1637. גֹּרֶן *gōren* **masc. noun**
(threshing floor)
Gen. 50:10,11; **Num.** 15:20; 18:27,30; **Deut.** 15:14; 16:13; **Judg.** 6:37; **Ruth** 3:2,3,6,14; **1 Sam.** 23:1; **2 Sam.** 6:6; 24:16,18,21,24; **1 Kgs.** 22:10; **2 Kgs.** 6:27; **1 Chr.** 13:9; 21:15,18,21,22,28; **2 Chr.** 3:1; 18:9; **Job** 39:12; **Isa.** 21:10; **Jer.** 51:33; **Hos.** 9:1,2; 13:3; **Joel** 2:24; **Mic.** 4:12.

1638. גָּרַס *gāras* **verb**
(to be broken, to be crushed)
Ps. 119:20; **Lam.** 3:16.

1639. גָּרַע *gāra'* **verb**
(to reduce, to diminish)
Ex. 5:8,11,19; 21:10; **Lev.** 27:18; **Num.** 9:7; 27:4; 36:3,4; **Deut.** 4:2; 12:32(13:1); **Job** 15:4,8; 36:7,27; **Eccl.** 3:14; **Jer.** 26:2; 48:37; **Ezek.** 5:11; 16:27.

1640. גָּרַף *gārap̱* **verb**
(to sweep away)
Judg. 5:21.

1641. גָּרַר *gārar* **verb**
(to drag, to saw, to chew)
Lev. 11:7; **1 Kgs.** 7:9; **Prov.** 21:7; **Jer.** 30:23; **Hab.** 1:15.

1642. גְּרָר *g^e^rār* **proper noun**
(Gerar)
Gen. 10:19; 20:1,2; 26:1,6,17,20,26; **2 Chr.** 14:13(12),14(13).

1643. גֶּרֶשׂ *gereś* **masc. noun**
(that which is beaten, crushed)
Lev. 2:14,16.

1644. גָּרַשׁ *gāraš* **verb**
(to drive out, to cast out)
Gen. 3:24; 4:14; 21:10; **Ex.** 2:17; 6:1; 10:11; 11:1; 12:39; 23:28–31; 33:2; 34:11; **Lev.** 21:7,14; 22:13; **Num.** 22:6,11; 30:9(10); **Deut.** 33:27; **Josh.** 24:12,18; **Judg.** 2:3; 6:9; 9:41; 11:2,7; **1 Sam.** 26:19; **1 Kgs.** 2:27; **1 Chr.** 17:21; **2 Chr.** 20:11; **Job** 30:5; **Ps.** 34:[title](1); 78:55; 80:8(9); 109:10(KJV, NASB, *dāraš* [1875]); **Prov.** 22:10; **Isa.** 57:20; **Ezek.** 31:11; 36:5(NIV, *migrāš* [4054]); 44:22; **Hos.** 9:15; **Amos** 8:8; **Jon.** 2:4(5); **Mic.** 2:9; **Zeph.** 2:4.

1645. גֶּרֶשׁ *gereš* **masc. noun**
(to put forth, yield)
Deut. 33:14.

1646. גְּרֻשָׁה *g^e^rušāh* **fem. noun**
(a casting out, expulsion)
Ezek. 45:9.

1647. A. גֵּרְשׁוֹם *gēršôm*, גֵּרְשֹׁם *gēršōm* **masc. proper noun**
(Gershom: son of Moses)
Ex. 2:22; 18:3; **1 Chr.** 23:15,16; 26:24.
B. גֵּרְשׁוֹם *gēršôm*, גֵּרְשֹׁם *gēršōm* **masc. proper noun**
(Gershom: oldest son of Levi [the same as *geršōn* {1648}])
1 Chr. 6:16(1),17(2),20(5),43(28), 62(47),71(56); 15:7.
C. גֵּרְשׁוֹם *gēršôm* **masc. proper noun**
(Gershom: son of Phinehas)
Ezra 8:2.

D. גֵּרְשֹׁם *gēršōm* **masc. proper noun**
(Gershom: father of Jonathan)
Judg. 18:30.

1648. גֵּרְשׁוֹן *gēršōn* **masc. proper noun**
(Gershon; see also *gēršōm* [1647,B])
Gen. 46:11; **Ex.** 6:16,17; **Num.** 3:17, 18,21,25; 4:22,38,41; 7:7; 10:17; 26:57; **Josh.** 21:6,27; **1 Chr.** 6:1(5:27); 23:6.

1649. גֵּרְשֻׁנִּי *gēršunniy* **masc. proper noun**
(Gershonite)
Num. 3:21,23,24; 4:24,27,28; 26:57; **Josh.** 21:33; **1 Chr.** 23:7; 26:21; 29:8; **2 Chr.** 29:12.

1650. גְּשׁוּר *g^e^šûr* **proper noun**
(Geshur)
Josh. 13:13; **2 Sam.** 3:3; 13:37,38; 14:23,32; 15:8; **1 Chr.** 2:23; 3:2.

1651. A. גְּשׁוּרִי *g^e^šûriy* **masc. proper noun**
(Geshurites: inhabitants of Geshur)
Deut. 3:14; **Josh.** 12:5; 13:11,13.
B. גְּשׁוּרִי *g^e^šûriy* **masc. proper noun**
(Geshurites: a tribe of people near Philistia)
Josh. 13:2; **1 Sam.** 27:8.

1652. גָּשַׁם *gāšam* **verb**
(to cause rain)
Jer. 14:22.

1653. גֶּשֶׁם *gešem* **masc. noun**
(rain, shower)
Gen. 7:12; 8:2; **Lev.** 26:4; **1 Kgs.** 17:7,14; 18:41,44,45; **2 Kgs.** 3:17; **Ezra** 10:9,13; **Job** 37:6; **Ps.** 68:9(10); 105:32; **Prov.** 25:14,23; **Eccl.** 11:3; 12:2; **Song** 2:11; **Isa.** 44:14; 55:10; **Jer.** 5:24; 14:4; **Ezek.** 1:28; 13:11,13; 34:26; 38:22; **Hos.** 6:3; **Joel** 2:23; **Amos** 4:7; **Zech.** 10:1; 14:17.

1654. גֶּשֶׁם *gešem,* גַּשְׁמוּ *gašmû* **masc. proper noun**
(Geshem, Gashmu)
Neh. 2:19; 6:1,2,6.

1655. גְּשֵׁם *g^e^šēm* **Aram. masc. noun**
(body)
Dan. 3:27,28; 4:33(30); 5:21; 7:11.

1656. גֹּשֶׁם *gōšem* **masc. noun**
(rain, shower)
Ezek. 22:24.

1657. A. גֹּשֶׁן *gōšen* **proper noun**
(Goshen: a region in Egypt)
Gen. 45:10; 46:28,29,34; 47:1,4,6,27; 50:8; **Ex.** 8:22(18); 9:26.
B. גֹּשֶׁן *gōšen* **proper noun**
(Goshen: a city in Judah)
Josh. 10:41; 11:16; 15:51.

1658. גִּשְׁפָּא *gišpā'* **masc. proper noun**
(Gishpa, Gispa)
Neh. 11:21.

1659. גָּשַׁשׁ *gāšaš* **verb**
(to grope, to feel with the hand)
Isa. 59:10.

1660. גַּת *gaṯ* **fem. noun**
(winepress)
Judg. 6:11; **Neh.** 13:15; **Isa.** 63:2; **Lam.** 1:15; **Joel** 3:13(4:13).

1661. גַּת *gaṯ* **proper noun**
(Gath)
Josh. 11:22; **1 Sam.** 5:8; 6:17; 7:14; 17:4,23,52; 21:10(11),12(13); 27:2–4,11; **2 Sam.** 1:20; 15:18; 21:20,22; **1 Kgs.** 2:39–41; **2 Kgs.** 12:17(18); **1 Chr.** 7:21; 8:13; 18:1; 20:6,8; **2 Chr.** 11:8; 26:6; **Ps.** 56:[title](1); **Amos** 6:2; **Mic.** 1:10.

1662. גַּת־הַחֵפֶר *gaṯ-haḥēp̱er,* גִּתָּה־חֵפֶר *gittāh-ḥēp̱er* **proper noun**

(Gath Hepher: a city)
Josh. 19:13; **2 Kgs.** 14:25.

1663. גִּתִּי *gittiy* **masc. proper noun**
(Gittite)
Josh. 13:3; **2 Sam.** 6:10,11; 15:18,19,22; 18:2; 21:19; **1 Chr.** 13:13; 20:5.

1664. גִּתַּיִם *gittayim* **proper noun**
(Gittaim: a region or city)
2 Sam. 4:3; **Neh.** 11:33.

1665. גִּתִּית *gittiyṯ* **fem. noun**
(Gittith: a musical instrument or musical tune)
Ps. 8:[title](1); 81:[title](1); 84:[title](1).

1666. גֶּתֶר *geṯer* **masc. proper noun**
(Gether)
Gen. 10:23; **1 Chr.** 1:17.

1667. גַּת־רִמּוֹן *gaṯ-rimmôn* **proper noun**
(Gath Rimmon)
Josh. 19:45; 21:24,25; **1 Chr.** 6:69(54).

ד Daleth

1668. דָּא *dā'* **Aram. pron.**
(this)
Dan. 4:30(27); 5:6; 7:3,8.

1669. דָּאַב *dā'aḇ* **verb**
(to become faint, to sorrow)
Ps. 88:9(10); **Jer.** 31:12,25.

1670. דְּאָבָה *de'āḇāh* **fem. noun**
(sorrow, dismay)
Job 41:22(14).

1671. דְּאָבוֹן *de'āḇôn* **masc. noun**
(sorrow, despair)
Deut. 28:65.

1672. דָּאַג *dā'ag* **verb**
(to be afraid, to be anxious)
1 Sam. 9:5; 10:2; **Ps.** 38:18(19); **Isa.** 57:11; **Jer.** 17:8; 38:19; 42:16.

1673. דֹּאֵג *dō'ēg,* דּוֹאֵג *dô'ēg* **masc. proper noun**
(Doeg)
1 Sam. 21:7(8); 22:9,18,22.

1674. דְּאָגָה *de'āgāh* **fem. noun**
(anxiety, fear)
Josh. 22:24; **Prov.** 12:25; **Jer.** 49:23; **Ezek.** 4:16; 12:18,19.

1675. דָּאָה *dā'āh* **verb**
(to fly fast, to fly swiftly)
Deut. 28:49; **Ps.** 18:10(11); **Jer.** 48:40; 49:22.

1676. דָּאָה *dā'āh* **fem. noun**
(vulture, kite)
Lev. 11:14; **Deut.** 14:13(KJV, NIV, *rā'āh* [7201]).

1677. דֹּב *dōḇ,* דּוֹב *dôḇ* **masc. noun**
(bear)
1 Sam. 17:34,36,37; **2 Sam.** 17:8; **2 Kgs.** 2:24; **Prov.** 17:12; 28:15; **Isa.** 11:7; 59:11; **Lam.** 3:10; **Hos.** 13:8; **Amos** 5:19.

1678. דֹּב *dōḇ* **Aram. masc. noun**
(bear)
Dan. 7:5.

1679. דֹּבֶא *dōḇe'* **masc. noun**
(strength)
Deut. 33:25.

1680. דָּבַב *dāḇaḇ* **verb**
(to speak, to flow gently)
Song 7:9(10).

1681. דִּבָּה *dibbāh* **fem. noun**
(slander, bad report)
Gen. 37:2; **Num.** 13:32; 14:36,37; **Ps.** 31:13(14); **Prov.** 10:18; 25:10; **Jer.** 20:10; **Ezek.** 36:3.

1682. דְּבוֹרָה *deḇôrāh* **fem. noun**
(bee)
Deut. 1:44; **Judg.** 14:8; **Ps.** 118:12; **Isa.** 7:18.

1683. A. דְּבוֹרָה *deḇôrāh* **fem. proper noun**
(Deborah: nurse of Rebekah)
Gen. 35:8.
B. דְּבוֹרָה *deḇôrāh* **fem. proper noun**
(Deborah: a prophetess)
Judg. 4:4,5,9,10,14; 5:1,7,12,15.

1684. דְּבַח *deḇah* **Aram. verb**
(to offer [sacrifices])
Ezra 6:3.

1685. דְּבַח *deḇah* **Aram. masc. noun**
(a sacrifice)
Ezra 6:3.

1686. I. דִּבְיוֹנִים *dibyôniym* masc. pl. noun
(dove's dung)
2 Kgs. 6:25(KJV, [K^e] h^a riy [2755]; NIV, see II).

II. דִּבְיוֹנִים *dibyôniym* masc. pl. noun
(seed pods)
2 Kgs. 6:25(KJV, [K^e] h^a riy [2755]; NASB, see I).

1687. דְּבִיר *d^e biyr* masc. noun
(the inner sanctuary, the Holy of Holies)
1 Kgs. 6:5,16,19–23,31; 7:49; 8:6,8;
2 Chr. 3:16(NIV, *rāḇiyd* [7242]); 4:20; 5:7,9; **Ps.** 28:2.

1688. A. דְּבִיר *d^e biyr* proper noun
(Debir: a city in S. Judah)
Josh. 10:38,39; 11:21; 12:13; 15:15,49; 21:15; **Judg.** 1:11; **1 Chr.** 6:58(43).
B. דְּבִיר *d^e biyr* proper noun
(Debir: an Ammonite king)
Josh. 10:3.
C. דְּבִיר *d^e biyr* proper noun
(Debir: a city in Gad)
Josh. 13:26.
D. דְּבִיר *d^e biyr* proper noun
(Debir: a city loc. on the boundary of N. Judah)
Josh. 15:7.

1689. דִּבְלָה *diblāh* proper noun
(Diblah)
Ezek. 6:14.

1690. דְּבֵלָה *d^e bēlāh* fem. noun
(a fig cake, a lump of pressed figs)
1 Sam. 25:18; 30:12; **2 Kgs.** 20:7;
1 Chr. 12:40; **Isa.** 38:21.

1691. דִּבְלַיִם *diblayim* masc. proper noun
(Diblaim)
Hos. 1:3.

1692. דָּבַק *dāḇaq* verb
(to cling to, to join with, to stay with)
Gen. 2:24; 19:19; 31:23; 34:3; **Num.** 36:7,9; **Deut.** 10:20; 11:22; 13:4(5), 17(18); 28:21,60; 30:20; **Josh.** 22:5; 23:8,12; **Judg.** 18:22; 20:42,45; **Ruth** 1:14; 2:8,21,23; **1 Sam.** 14:22; 31:2; **2 Sam.** 1:6; 20:2; 23:10; **1 Kgs.** 11:2; **2 Kgs.** 3:3; 5:27; 18:6; **1 Chr.** 10:2; **Job** 19:20; 29:10; 31:7; 38:38; 41:17(9), 23(15); **Ps.** 22:15(16); 44:25(26); 63:8(9); 101:3; 102:5(6); 119:25,31; 137:6; **Jer.** 13:11; 42:16; **Lam.** 4:4; **Ezek.** 3:26; 29:4.

1693. דְּבַק *d^e ḇaq* Aram. verb
(to cling to, to stay together; corr. to Hebr. 1692)
Dan. 2:43.

1694. דֶּבֶק *deḇeq* masc. noun
(place of joining, joint)
1 Kgs. 22:34; **2 Chr.** 18:33; **Isa.** 41:7.

1695. דָּבֵק *dāḇēq* adj.
(holding to, clinging to)
Deut. 4:4; **2 Chr.** 3:12; **Prov.** 18:24.

1696. I. דָּבַר *dāḇar* verb
(to speak, to utter, to pronounce)
Gen. 8:15; 12:4; 16:13; 17:3,22,23; 18:5,19,27,29–33; 19:14,21; 20:8; 21:1,2; 23:3,8,13,16; 24:7,15,30,33,45,50,51; 27:5,6,19; 28:15; 29:9; 31:24,29; 32:19(20); 34:3,6,8,13,20; 35:13–15; 37:4; 39:10,17,19; 41:9,17,28; 42:7,14, 24,30; 43:19; 44:2,6,7,16,18; 45:12, 15,27; 49:28; 50:4,17,21; **Ex.** 1:17; 4:10, 12,14–16,30; 5:23; 6:2,9–13,27–29; 7:2, 7,9,13,22; 8:15(11),19(15); 9:1,12,35; 10:29; 11:2; 12:3,25,31,32; 13:1; 14:1,2, 12,15; 16:10–12,23; 19:6,8,9,19; 20:1, 19,22; 23:22; 24:3,7; 25:1,2,22; 28:3;

29:42; 30:11,17,22,31; 31:1,13,18; 32:7, 13,14,34; 33:1,9,11,17; 34:29,31–35; 40:1; **Lev.** 1:1,2; 4:1,2; 5:14; 6:1(5:20), 8(1),19(12),24(17),25(18); 7:22,23,28,29; 8:1; 9:3; 10:3,5,8,11,12,19; 11:1,2; 12:1,2; 13:1; 14:1,33; 15:1,2; 16:1,2; 17:1,2; 18:1,2; 19:1,2; 20:1; 21:16,17,24; 22:1,2, 17,18,26; 23:1,2,9,10,23,24,26,33, 34,44; 24:1,13,15,23; 25:1,2; 27:1,2; **Num.** 1:1,48; 2:1; 3:1,5,11,14,44; 4:1, 17,21; 5:1,4–6,11,12; 6:1,2,22,23; 7:89; 8:1,2,5,23; 9:1,4,9,10; 10:1,29; 11:17, 24,25; 12:1,2,6,8; 13:1; 14:17,26,28, 35,39; 15:1,2,17,18,22,38; 16:5,20,23,24, 26,31,36(17:1),40(17:5),44(17:9),47(17:1 2); 17:1(16),2(17),6(21); 18:8,25,26; 19:1,2; 20:7,8; 21:5,7; 22:7,8,19,20, 35,38; 23:2,5,12,16,17,19,26; 24:12,13; 25:10,16; 26:3,52; 27:7,8,15,23; 28:1; 30:1(2); 31:1,3; 32:27,31; 33:50,51; 34:1,16; 35:1,9,10; 36:1,5; **Deut.** 1:1,3, 6,11,14,21,43; 2:1,17; 3:26; 4:12,15, 33,45; 5:1,4,22(19),24(21),26–28 (23–25),31(28); 6:3,7,19; 9:3,10,28; 10:4, 9; 11:19,25; 12:20; 13:2(3),5(6); 15:6; 18:2,17–22; 19:8; 20:2,5,8,9; 23:23(24); 25:8; 26:18,19; 27:3,9; 29:13(12); 31:1,3, 28,30; 32:1,44,45,48; **Josh.** 1:3; 4:8, 10,12; 5:14; 9:21,22; 10:12; 11:23; 13:14,33; 14:6,10,12; 17:14; 20:1,2,4; 21:2,45(43); 22:4,15,21,30; 23:5,10, 14,15; 24:27; **Judg.** 1:20; 2:4,15; 5:12; 6:17,27,36,37,39; 7:11; 8:3,8; 9:1–3,37; 11:11; 12:6; 13:11; 14:7; 15:17; 16:10,13; 19:3,30; 20:3; 21:13; **Ruth** 1:18; 2:13; 4:1; **1 Sam.** 1:13,16; 2:3; 3:9,10,12,17; 4:20; 8:21; 9:6,21,25; 10:25; 11:4; 14:19; 15:16; 16:4; 17:23,28,31; 18:1,22–24; 19:1,3,4; 20:23,26; 24:16(17); 25:9,17,24, 30,39,40; 28:17,21; **2 Sam.** 2:27; 3:19,27; 7:7,17,19,20,25,28,29; 11:19; 12:18; 13:13,22,36; 14:3,10,12,13,15,18,19; 17:6; 19:7(8),11(12),29(30); 20:16,18; 22:1; 23:2,3; 24:12; **1 Kgs.** 1:14,22,42; 2:4,14,16,18,19,23,24,27,30,31,38; 3:22; 4:32(5:12),33(5:13); 5:5(19),12(26); 6:12; 8:15,20,24–26,53,56; 9:5; 10:2; 12:3, 7,9,10,12,14,15; 13:3,7,11,12,18,22, 25–27; 14:2,5,11,18; 15:29; 16:12,34; 17:16; 20:11; 21:2,4–6,19,23; 22:13,14, 16,23,24,28,38; **2 Kgs.** 1:3,6,7,9–13, 15–17; 2:11,22; 4:13,17; 5:4,13; 6:12,33; 7:17,18; 8:1,4; 9:36; 10:10,17; 14:25,27; 15:12; 17:23; 18:26–28; 19:21; 20:9,19; 21:10; 22:14,19; 24:2,13; 25:6,28; **1 Chr.** 17:6,15,17,23,26; 21:9,10,19; 22:11; **2 Chr.** 6:4,10,15–17; 9:1; 10:3,7,9,10, 12,14,15; 18:12,13,15,22,23,27; 23:3; 25:16; 30:22; 32:6,16,19; 33:10,18; 34:22; **Ezra** 8:17; **Neh.** 6:12; 9:13; 13:24; **Esth.** 1:22; 6:10,14; 7:9; 8:3; 10:3; **Job** 1:16–18; 2:10,13; 7:11; 9:35; 10:1; 11:5; 13:3,7,13,22; 16:4,6; 18:2; 19:18; 21:3; 27:4; 32:7,16,20; 33:2,14,31,32; 34:33,35; 37:20; 40:5; 41:3(40:27); 42:4, 7–9; **Ps.** 2:5; 5:6(7); 12:2(3),3(4); 15:2; 17:10; 18:[title](1); 28:3; 31:18(19); 34:13(14); 35:20; 37:30; 38:12(13); 39:3(4); 40:5(6); 41:6(7); 49:3(4); 50:1, 7,20; 51:4(6); 52:3(5); 58:1(2),3(4); 60:6(8); 62:11(12); 63:11(12); 66:14; 73:8; 75:5(6); 77:4(5); 78:19; 85:8(9); 87:3; 89:19(20); 94:4; 99:7; 101:7; 108:7(8); 109:2,20; 115:5; 116:10; 119:23,46; 120:7; 122:8; 127:5; 135:16; 144:8,11; 145:11,21; **Prov.** 2:12; 8:6; 16:13; 18:23; 21:28(NIV, see II); 23:9, 16,33; 24:2; 25:11; **Eccl.** 1:8,16; 2:15; 3:7; 7:21; **Song** 5:6(NIV, see II); 8:8; **Isa.** 1:2,20; 7:10; 8:5,10; 9:17(16); 16:13,14; 19:18; 20:2; 21:17; 22:25; 24:3; 25:8; 28:11; 29:4; 30:10; 32:4,6,7; 33:15; 36:11,12; 37:22; 38:7,15; 39:8; 40:2,5,27; 41:1; 45:19; 46:11; 48:15,16; 52:6; 58:9,13,14; 59:3,4,13; 63:1; 65:12,24; 66:4; **Jer.** 1:6,7,16,17; 3:5; 4:12,28; 5:5, 14,15; 6:10; 7:13,22,27; 8:6; 9:5(4),8(7), 12(11),22(21); 10:1,5; 11:2,17; 12:1,6; 13:15; 14:14; 16:10; 18:7–9,20; 19:2, 5,15; 20:8,9; 22:1,21; 23:16,17,21,28, 35,37; 25:2,3,13; 26:2,7,8,13,15,16,19; 27:12,13,16; 28:7,16; 29:23,32; 30:2,4; 31:20; 32:4,24,42; 33:14,24; 34:3,5,6; 35:2,14,17; 36:2,4,7,31; 37:2; 38:1,4,8,

20,25; 39:5,12; 40:2,3,16; 42:19; 43:1,2; 44:16,25; 45:1; 46:13; 50:1; 51:12,62; 52:9,32; **Ezek.** 1:28; 2:1,2,7,8; 3:1,4, 10,11,18,22,24,27; 5:13,15,17; 6:10; 10:5; 11:25; 12:23,25,28; 13:7,8; 14:4,9; 17:21,24; 20:3,27; 21:17(22),32(37); 22:14,28; 23:34; 24:14,18,27; 26:5,14; 28:10; 29:3; 30:12; 32:21; 33:2,8,30; 34:24; 36:5,6,36; 37:14,19,21; 38:17,19; 39:5,8; 40:4,45; 41:22; 43:6; 44:5; **Dan.** 1:19; 2:4; 8:13,18; 9:6,12,20–22; 10:11, 15–17,19; 11:27,36; **Hos.** 1:2; 2:14(16); 7:13; 10:4; 12:4(5),10(11); 13:1; **Joel** 3:8(4:8); **Amos** 3:1,8; 5:10; **Obad.** 1:18; **Jon.** 3:2,10; **Mic.** 4:4; 6:12; 7:3; **Hab.** 2:1; **Zeph.** 3:13; **Zech.** 1:9,13,14, 19(2:2); 2:3(7),4(8); 4:1,4,5; 5:5,10; 6:4,8; 8:16; 9:10; 10:2; 13:3; **Mal.** 3:13,16.

II. דָּבַר *dāḇar* **verb**
(to detest, to subdue, to destroy)
2 Chr. 22:10; **Ps.** 18:47(48); 47:3(4); **Prov.** 21:28(KJV, NASB, see I); **Song** 5:6(KJV, NASB, see I).

1697. דָּבָר *dāḇār* **masc. noun**
(word, speech, matter, thing)
Gen. 11:1; 12:17; 15:1,4; 18:14,25; 19:8,21,22; 20:8,10,11,18; 21:11,26; 22:1,16,20; 24:9,28,30,33,50,52,66; 27:34,42; 29:13; 30:31,34; 31:1; 32:19(20); 34:14,18,19; 37:8,11,14; 39:7,17,19; 40:1; 41:28,32,37; 42:16,20; 43:7,18; 44:2,6,7,10,18,24; 45:27; 47:30; 48:1; **Ex.** 1:18; 2:14,15; 4:10,15,28,30; 5:9,11,13,19; 8:10(6),12(8),13(9),31(27); 9:4–6,20,21; 12:24,35; 14:12; 16:4,16,32; 18:11,14,16–19,22,23,26; 19:6–9; 20:1; 22:9(8); 23:7,8; 24:3,4,8,14; 29:1; 32:28; 33:4,17; 34:1,27,28; 35:1,4; **Lev.** 4:13; 5:2; 8:5,36; 9:6; 10:7; 17:2; 23:37; **Num.** 11:23,24; 12:6; 13:26; 14:20,39; 15:31; 16:31,49(17:14); 18:7; 20:19; 22:7,8,20,35,38; 23:3,5,16; 25:18; 30:1(2),2(3); 31:16,23; 32:20; 36:6; **Deut.** 1:1,14,17,18,22,23,25,32,34; 2:7,26; 3:26; 4:2,9,10,12,13,21,30,32,36; 5:5,22(19),28(25); 6:6; 9:5,10; 10:2,4; 11:18; 12:28,32(13:1); 13:3(4),11(12), 14(15); 15:2,9,10,15; 16:19; 17:1,4,5, 8–11,19; 18:18–22; 19:4,15,20; 22:14, 17,20,24,26; 23:4(5),9(10),14(15),19(20); 24:1,5,18,22; 27:3,8,26; 28:14,58; 29:1 (28:69),9(8),19(18),29(28); 30:1,14; 31:1,12,24,28,30; 32:44–47; **Josh.** 1:13,18; 2:14,20,21; 3:9; 4:10; 5:4; 6:10; 8:8,27,34,35; 9:24; 11:15; 14:6,7,10; 20:4; 21:45(43); 22:24,30,32,33; 23:14, 15; 24:26,29; **Judg.** 2:4; 3:19,20; 6:29; 8:1,3; 9:3,30; 11:10,11,28,37; 13:12,17; 16:16; 18:7,10,28; 19:19,24; 20:7,9; 21:11; **Ruth** 3:18; 4:7; **1 Sam.** 1:23; 2:23; 3:1,7,11,17–19,21; 4:1,16; 8:6,10, 21; 9:10,21,27; 10:2,16; 11:4–6; 12:16; 14:12; 15:1,10,11,13,23,24,26; 16:18; 17:11,23,27,29–31; 18:8,20,23,24,26; 19:7; 20:2,21,23,39; 21:2(3),8(9),12(13); 22:15; 24:6(7),7(8),9(10),16(17); 25:9,12, 24,36,37; 26:16,19; 28:10,18,20,21; 30:24; **2 Sam.** 1:4; 2:6; 3:8,11,13,17; 7:4, 7,17,21,25,28; 11:11,18,19,25,27; 12:6,9,12,14,21; 13:20–22,33,35; 14:3, 12,13,15,17–22; 15:3,6,11,28,35,36; 16:23; 17:4,6,19; 18:5,13; 19:11(12), 29(30),42(43),43(44); 20:17,21; 22:1; 23:1; 24:3,4,11,13,19; **1 Kgs.** 1:7,14,27; 2:4,14,23,27,30,38,42; 3:10–12; 4:27 (5:7); 5:7(21); 6:11,12,38; 8:20,26,56,59; 9:15; 10:3,6,7,25; 11:10,27,41; 12:6,7,9, 15,16,22,24,30; 13:1,2,4,5,9,11,17,18, 20,26,32–34; 14:5,13,18,19,29; 15:5,7, 23,29,31; 16:1,5,7,12,14,20,27,34; 17:1, 2,5,8,13,15–17,24; 18:1,21,24,31,36; 19:9; 20:4,9,12,24,35; 21:1,4,17,27,28; 22:5,13,19,38,39,45(46); **2 Kgs.** 1:7, 16–18; 2:22; 3:12; 4:41,44; 5:13,14,18; 6:11,12,18,30; 7:1,2,16,19; 8:2,13,23; 9:5,26,36; 10:10,17,34; 11:5; 12:19(20); 13:8,12; 14:15,18,25,28; 15:6,11,12,15, 21,26,31,36; 16:19; 17:9,11,12; 18:20,27, 28,36,37; 19:4,6,16,21; 20:4,9,13,15–17, 19,20; 21:17,25; 22:9,11,13,16,18,20; 23:2,3,16,17,24,28; 24:2,5; 25:30; **1 Chr.** 4:22; 10:13; 11:3,10; 13:4; 15:15; 16:15,37; 17:3,6,15,23; 21:4,6–8,12,19;

22:8; 23:27; 25:5; 26:32; 27:1,24; 28:21; 29:29; **2 Chr.** 1:9; 6:10,17; 8:13–15; 9:2, 5,6,24,29; 10:6,7,9,15; 11:2,4; 12:7, 12,15; 13:22; 15:8; 16:11; 18:4,12,18; 19:3,6,11; 20:34; 23:4,19; 24:5; 25:26; 26:22; 27:7; 28:26; 29:15,30,36; 30:4,5, 12; 31:5,16; 32:1,8,32; 33:18,19; 34:16, 19,21,26–28,30,31; 35:6,22,26,27; 36:8,16,21,22; **Ezra** 1:1; 3:4; 7:1,11; 8:17; 9:3,4; 10:4,5,9,12–14,16; **Neh.** 1:1,4,8; 2:18–20; 5:6,8,9,12,13; 6:4–8,19; 8:4,9,12,13; 9:8; 11:23,24; 12:23,47; 13:17; **Esth.** 1:12,13,17–19,21; 2:1,4, 8,15,22,23; 3:1,4,15; 4:3,9,12; 5:5,8,14; 6:1,3,10; 7:8; 8:5,14,17; 9:1,20,26,30–32; 10:2; **Job** 2:13; 4:2,12; 6:3; 9:14; 11:2; 15:3,11; 16:3; 19:28; 26:14; 29:22; 31:40; 32:4,11; 33:1,13; 34:35; 41:12(4); 42:7; **Ps.** 7:[title](1); 17:4; 18:[title](1); 19:3(4); 22:1(2); 33:4,6; 35:20; 36:3(4); 41:8(9); 45:1(2),4(5); 50:17; 52:4(6); 55:21(22); 56:4(5),5(6),10(11); 59:12(13); 64:3(4), 5(6); 65:3(4); 79:9; 101:3; 103:20; 105:8, 19,27,28,42; 106:12,24; 107:20; 109:3; 112:5; 119:9,16,17,25,28,42,43,49,57, 65,74,81,89,101,105,107,114,130,139, 147,160,161,169; 130:5; 137:3; 141:4; 145:5; 147:15,18,19; 148:8; **Prov.** 1:6,23; 4:4,20; 10:19; 11:13; 12:6,25; 13:5,13; 14:15,23; 15:1,23; 16:20; 17:9; 18:4,8,13; 22:12,17; 23:8; 24:26; 25:2,11; 26:6,22; 27:11; 29:12,19,20; 30:1,6,8; 31:1; **Eccl.** 1:1,8,10; 5:2(1),3(2),7(6); 6:11; 7:8,21; 8:1,3–5; 9:16,17; 10:12–14,20; 12:10, 11,13; **Isa.** 1:10; 2:1,3; 8:10,20; 9:8(7); 16:13; 24:3; 28:13,14; 29:11,18,21; 30:12,21; 31:2; 36:5,12,13,21,22; 37:4, 6,17,22; 38:4,7; 39:2,4–6,8; 40:8; 41:28; 42:16; 44:26; 45:23; 50:4; 51:16; 55:11; 58:13; 59:13,21; 66:2,5; **Jer.** 1:1,2,4,9, 11–13; 2:1,4,31; 3:12; 5:14,28; 6:10,19; 7:1,2,4,8,22,23,27; 8:9; 9:20(19); 10:1; 11:1–3,6,8,10; 13:2,3,8,10,12; 14:1,17; 15:16; 16:1,10; 17:15,20; 18:1,2,5,18; 19:2,3,15; 20:1,8; 21:1,11; 22:1,2,4,5,29; 23:9,16,18,22,28–30,36,38; 24:4; 25:1,3, 8,13,30; 26:1,2,5,7,10,12,15,20,21; 27:1, 12,14,16,18; 28:6,7,9,12; 29:1,10,19,20, 23,30; 30:1,2,4; 31:10,23; 32:1,6,8,17, 26,27; 33:1,14,19,23; 34:1,4–6,8,12,18; 35:1,12–14; 36:1,2,4,6,8,10,11,13, 16–18,20,24,27,28,32; 37:2,6,17; 38:1, 4,5,14,21,24,27; 39:15,16; 40:1,3,16; 42:3–5,7,15; 43:1,8; 44:1,4,16,17,20,24, 26,28,29; 45:1; 46:1,13; 47:1; 48:27; 49:34; 50:1; 51:59–61,64; 52:34; **Ezek.** 1:3; 2:6,7; 3:4,6,10,16,17; 6:1,3; 7:1; 9:11; 11:14,25; 12:1,8,17,21,23,25,26,28; 13:1,2,6; 14:2,9,12; 15:1; 16:1,35; 17:1,11; 18:1; 20:2,45(21:1),47(21:3); 21:1(6),8(13),18(23); 22:1,17,23; 23:1; 24:1,15,20; 25:1,3; 26:1; 27:1; 28:1, 11,20; 29:1,17; 30:1,20; 31:1; 32:1,17; 33:1,7,23,30–32; 34:1,7,9; 35:1,13; 36:1,4,16; 37:4,15; 38:1,10; **Dan.** 1:5, 14,20; 9:2,12,23,25; 10:1,6,9,11,12,15; 12:4,9; **Hos.** 1:1; 4:1; 10:4; 14:2(3); **Joel** 1:1; 2:11; **Amos** 1:1; 3:1,7; 4:1; 5:1; 6:13; 7:10,16; 8:11,12; **Jon.** 1:1; 3:1,3,6; 4:2; **Mic.** 1:1; 2:7; 4:2; **Zeph.** 1:1; 2:5; **Hag.** 1:1,3,12; 2:1,5,10,20; **Zech.** 1:1,6,7,13; 4:6,8; 6:9; 7:1,4,7,8,12; 8:1,9,16,18; 9:1; 11:11; 12:1; **Mal.** 1:1; 2:17; 3:13.

1698. I. דֶּבֶר *deḇer* **masc. noun**
(plague, pestilence)
Ex. 5:3; 9:3,15; **Lev.** 26:25; **Num.** 14:12; **Deut.** 28:21; **2 Sam.** 24:13,15; **1 Kgs.** 8:37; **1 Chr.** 21:12,14; **2 Chr.** 6:28; 7:13; 20:9; **Ps.** 78:50; 91:3,6; **Jer.** 14:12; 21:6, 7,9; 24:10; 27:8,13; 28:8; 29:17,18; 32:24,36; 34:17; 38:2; 42:17,22; 44:13; **Ezek.** 5:12,17; 6:11,12; 7:15; 12:16; 14:19,21; 28:23; 33:27; 38:22; **Hos.** 13:14(NASB, see II); **Amos** 4:10; **Hab.** 3:5.

II. דֶּבֶר *deḇer* **masc. noun**
(thorn)
Hos. 13:14(KJV, NIV, see I).

1699. דֹּבֶר *dōḇer,* דִּבֵּר *dibbēr*
masc. noun
(pasture, word)
Isa. 5:17; **Jer.** 5:13; **Mic.** 2:12.

1700. דִּבְרָה *dibrāh* **fem. noun**
(cause, reason)
Job 5:8; **Ps.** 110:4; **Eccl.** 3:18; 7:14; 8:2.

1701. דִּבְרָה *dibrāh* **Aram. fem. noun**
(cause, reason; corr. to Hebr. 1700)
Dan. 2:30; 4:17(14).

1702. דֹּבְרוֹת *dob^e^rôt* **fem. pl. noun**
(rafts)
1 Kgs. 5:9(23).

1703. דַּבֶּרֶת *dabberet* **fem. noun**
(word, instruction, only pl. *dabrôt*)
Deut. 33:3.

1704. דִּבְרִי *dibriy* **masc. proper noun**
(Dibri)
Lev. 24:11.

1705. דָּבְרַת *dāb^e^rat* **proper noun**
(Daberath)
Josh. 19:12; 21:28; **1 Chr.** 6:72(57).

1706. דְּבַשׁ *d^e^baš* **masc. noun**
(honey)
Gen. 43:11; **Ex.** 3:8,17; 13:5; 16:31; 33:3; **Lev.** 2:11; 20:24; **Num.** 13:27; 14:8; 16:13,14; **Deut.** 6:3; 8:8; 11:9; 26:9,15; 27:3; 31:20; 32:13; **Josh.** 5:6; **Judg.** 14:8,9,18; **1 Sam.** 14:25–27, 29,43; **2 Sam.** 17:29; **1 Kgs.** 14:3; **2 Kgs.** 18:32; **2 Chr.** 31:5; **Job** 20:17; **Ps.** 19:10(11); 81:16(17); 119:103; **Prov.** 16:24; 24:13; 25:16,27; **Song** 4:11; 5:1; **Isa.** 7:15,22; **Jer.** 11:5; 32:22; 41:8; **Ezek.** 3:3; 16:13,19; 20:6,15; 27:17.

1707. דַּבֶּשֶׁת *dabbešet* **fem. noun**
(hump [of a camel])
Isa. 30:6.

1708. דַּבֶּשֶׁת *dabbešet* **proper noun**
(Dabbesheth)
Josh. 19:11.

1709. דָּג *dāg* **masc. noun**
(a fish)
Gen. 9:2; **Num.** 11:22; **1 Kgs.** 4:33(5:13); **2 Chr.** 33:14; **Neh.** 3:3; 12:39; 13:16; **Job** 12:8; 41:7(40:31); **Ps.** 8:8(9); **Eccl.** 9:12; **Ezek.** 38:20; **Hos.** 4:3; **Jon.** 1:17(2:1); 2:10(11); **Hab.** 1:14; **Zeph.** 1:3,10.

1710. דָּגָה *dāgāh* **fem. noun**
(a fish)
Gen. 1:26,28; **Ex.** 7:18,21; **Num.** 11:5; **Deut.** 4:18; **Ps.** 105:29; **Isa.** 50:2; **Ezek.** 29:4,5; 47:9,10; **Jon.** 2:1(2).

1711. דָּגָה *dāgāh* **verb**
(to grow, to increase)
Gen. 48:16.

1712. דָּגוֹן *dāgôn* **masc. proper noun**
(Dagon: a Philistine god)
Judg. 16:23; **1 Sam.** 5:2–5,7; **1 Chr.** 10:10.

1713. דָּגַל *dāgal* **verb**
(to carry a banner, standard, flag)
Ps. 20:5(6); **Song** 5:10; 6:4,10.

1714. דֶּגֶל *degel* **masc. noun**
(standard, banner, flag)
Num. 1:52; 2:2,3,10,17,18,25,31,34; 10:14,18,22,25; **Song** 2:4.

1715. דָּגָן *dāgān* **masc. noun**
(corn, grain)
Gen. 27:28,37; **Num.** 18:12,27; **Deut.** 7:13; 11:14; 12:17; 14:23; 18:4; 28:51; 33:28; **2 Kgs.** 18:32; **2 Chr.** 31:5; 32:28; **Neh.** 5:2,3,10,11; 10:39(40); 13:5,12; **Ps.** 4:7(8); 65:9(10); 78:24; **Isa.** 36:17; 62:8; **Jer.** 31:12; **Lam.** 2:12; **Ezek.** 36:29; **Hos.** 2:8(10),9(11),22(24); 7:14; 9:1; 14:7(8); **Joel** 1:10,17; 2:19; **Hag.** 1:11; **Zech.** 9:17.

1716. דָּגַר *dāgar* **verb**

(to gather together)
Isa. 34:15; **Jer.** 17:11.

1717. דַּד *daḏ* **masc. noun**
(breast, nipple)
Prov. 5:19; **Ezek.** 23:3,8,21.

1718. דָּדָה *dāḏāh* **verb**
(to walk softly)
Ps. 42:4(5); **Isa.** 38:15.

1719. A. דְּדָן *d^e^ḏān* **masc. proper noun**
(Dedan: great-grandson of Ham)
Gen. 10:7; **1 Chr.** 1:9.
B. דְּדָן *d^e^ḏān* **masc. proper noun**
(Dedan: grandson of Abraham)
Gen. 25:3; **1 Chr.** 1:32.
C. דְּדָן *d^e^ḏān,* דְּדָנֶה *d^e^ḏāneh* **masc. proper noun**
(Dedan: southern Arabian tribe)
Jer. 25:23; **Ezek.** 25:13; 27:15(NIV, see E),20; 38:13.
D. דְּדָן *d^e^ḏān* **masc. proper noun**
(Dedan: northern Arabian tribe near Edom)
Jer. 49:8.
E. רֹדָן *rōḏān* **proper noun**
(city or island of Rhodes; following Sept. spelling)
Ezek. 27:15(KJV, NASB, see C).

1720. דְּדָנִי *d^e^ḏāniy* **masc. proper noun**
(Dedanite, Dedanim)
Isa. 21:13.

1721. A. דֹּדָנִים *dōḏāniym* **masc. pl. proper noun**
(Dodanim)
Gen. 10:4(NIV, see B); **1 Chr.** 1:7(NASB, NIV, see B).
B. רֹדָנִים *rōḏāniym* **masc. pl. proper noun**
(Rodanim; following Sept. spelling)
Gen. 10:4(KJV, NASB, see A); **1 Chr.** 1:7(KJV, see A).

1722. דְּהַב *d^e^haḇ* **Aram. masc. noun**
(gold)
Ezra 5:14; 6:5; 7:15,16,18; **Dan.** 2:32,35,38,45; 3:1,5,7,10,12,14,18; 5:2–4,7,16,23,29.

1723. דֶּהָוֵא *dehāwēʾ* **Aram. masc. proper noun**
(Dehavites)
Ezra 4:9(NASB, NIV, [Q^e^] *diy* [1768]).

1724. דָּהַם *dāham* **verb**
(to be astonished, to be surprised)
Jer. 14:9.

1725. דָּהַר *dāhar* **verb**
(to prance [of a horse], to gallop)
Nah. 3:2.

1726. דַּהֲרָה *dah^a^rāh* **fem. noun**
(a prancing [of a horse], a galloping)
Judg. 5:22.

1727. דּוּב *dûḇ* **verb**
(to cause one to pine away, to waste away)
Lev. 26:16.

1728. דַּוָּג *dawwāg* **masc. noun**
(fisherman)
Jer. 16:16(NIV, [Q^e^] *dayyāg* [1771]); **Ezek.** 47:10.

1729. דּוּגָה *dûgāh* **fem. noun**
(fishhook)
Amos 4:2.

1730. דּוֹד *dôḏ* **masc. noun**
(lover, uncle)
Lev. 10:4; 20:20; 25:49; **Num.** 36:11; **1 Sam.** 10:14–16; 14:50; **2 Kgs.** 24:17; **1 Chr.** 27:32; **Esth.** 2:7,15; **Prov.** 7:18; **Song** 1:2,4,13,14,16; 2:3,8–10,16,17; 4:10,16; 5:1,2,4–6,8–10,16; 6:1–3; 7:9–13(10–14); 8:5,14; **Isa.** 5:1;

Jer. 32:7–9,12; **Ezek.** 16:8; 23:17; **Amos** 6:10.

1731. דּוּד *dûḏ* **masc. noun** (basket, kettle)
1 Sam. 2:14; **2 Kgs.** 10:7; **2 Chr.** 35:13; **Job** 41:20(12); **Ps.** 81:6(7); **Jer.** 24:2.

1732. דָּוִד *dāwiḏ,* דָּוִיד *dāwiyḏ* **masc. proper noun** (David)
Ruth 4:17,22; **1 Sam.** 16:13,19–23; 17:12,14,15,17,20,22,23,26,28,29,31–34, 37–39,41–45,48–51,54,55,57,58; 18:1, 3–12,14,16–30; 19:1,2,4,5,7–12,14,15, 18–20,22; 20:1,3–6,10–12,15–17,24,25, 27,28,33–35,39,41,42; 21:1(2),2(3),4(5), 5(6),8–12(9–13); 22:1,3–6,14,17,20–22; 23:1–10,12–16,18,19,24–26,28,29(24:1); 24:1–5(2–6),7–9(8–10),16(17),17(18),22 (23); 25:1,4,5,8–10,12–14,20–23,32,35, 39,40,42–44; 26:1–10,12–15,17,21, 22,25; 27:1–5,7–12; 28:1,2,17; 29:2,3,5, 6,8,9,11; 30:1,3–11,13,15,17–23,26,31; **2 Sam.** 1:1–5,11,13–17; 2:1–5,10,11,13, 15,17,30,31; 3:1,2,5,6,8–10,12,14,17–22, 26,28,31,35; 4:8,9,12; 5:1,3,4,6–13,17, 19–21,23,25; 6:1,2,5,8–10,12,14–18, 20,21; 7:5,8,17,18,20,26; 8:1–11,13–15, 18; 9:1,2,5–7; 10:2–7,17,18; 11:1–8, 10–14,17,18,22,23,25,27; 12:1,5,7,13, 15,16,18–20,24,27,29–31; 13:1,3,7,21, 30,32,39; 15:12–14,22,30–33,37; 16:1,5, 6,10,11,13,16,23; 17:1,16,17,21,22,24, 27,29; 18:1,2,7,9,24; 19:11(12),16(17), 22(23),41(42),43(44); 20:1–3,6,11,21,26; 21:1,3,7,11,12,15–17,21,22; 22:1,51; 23:1,8,9,13–16,23; 24:1,10–14,17–19, 21,22,24,25; **1 Kgs.** 1:1,8,11,13,28,31, 32,37,38,43,47; 2:1,10–12,24,26,32,33, 44,45; 3:1,3,6,7,14; 5:1(15),3(17),5(19), 7(21); 6:12; 7:51; 8:1,15–18,20,24–26,66; 9:4,5,24; 11:4,6,12,13,15,21,24,27, 32–34,36,38,39,43; 12:16,19,20,26; 13:2; 14:8,31; 15:3–5,8,11,24; 22:50(51); **2 Kgs.** 8:19,24; 9:28; 11:10; 12:21(22); 14:3,20; 15:7,38; 16:2,20; 17:21; 18:3; 19:34; 20:5,6; 21:7; 22:2; **1 Chr.** 2:15; 3:1,9; 4:31; 6:31(16); 7:2; 9:22; 10:14; 11:1,3–7,9–11,13,15–18,25; 12:1,8, 16–19,21–23,31,38,39; 13:1,2,5,6,8, 11–13; 14:1–3,8,10–12,14,16,17; 15:1–4,11,16,25,27,29; 16:1,2,7,43; 17:1, 2,4,7,15,16,18,24; 18:1–11,13,14,17; 19:2–6,8,17–19; 20:1–3,7,8; 21:1,2,5, 8–11,13,16–19,21–26,28,30; 22:1–5, 7,17; 23:1,6,25,27; 24:3,31; 25:1; 26:26, 31,32; 27:18,23,24,31,32; 28:1,2,11,20; 29:1,9,10,20,22–24,26,29; **2 Chr.** 1:1,4,8,9; 2:3(2),7(6),12(11),14(13), 17(16); 3:1; 5:1,2; 6:4,6–8,10,15–17,42; 7:6,10,17,18; 8:11,14; 9:31; 10:16,19; 11:17,18; 12:16; 13:5,6,8; 14:1(13:23); 16:14; 17:3; 21:1,7,12,20; 23:3,9,18; 24:16,25; 27:9; 28:1; 29:2,25–27,30; 30:26; 32:5,30,33; 33:7,14; 34:2,3; 35:3,4,15; **Ezra** 3:10; 8:2,20; **Neh.** 3:15,16; 12:24,36,37,45,46; **Ps.** 3:[title](1); 4:[title](1); 5:[title](1); 6:[title](1); 7:[title](1); 8:[title](1); 9:[title](1); 11:[title](1); 12:[title](1); 13:[title](1); 14:[title](1); 15:[title](1); 16:[title](1); 17:[title](1); 18:[title](1), 50(51); 19:[title](1); 20:[title](1); 21:[title](1); 22:[title](1); 23:[title](1); 24:[title](1); 25:[title](1); 26:[title](1); 27:[title](1); 28:[title](1); 29:[title](1); 30:[title](1); 31:[title](1); 32:[title](1); 34:[title](1); 35:[title](1); 36:[title](1); 37:[title](1); 38:[title](1); 39:[title](1); 40:[title](1); 41:[title](1); 51:[title](1); 52:[title](1); 53:[title](1); 54:[title](1); 55:[title](1); 56:[title](1); 57:[title](1); 58:[title](1); 59:[title](1); 60:[title](1); 61:[title](1); 62:[title](1); 63:[title](1); 64:[title](1); 65:[title](1); 68:[title](1); 69:[title](1); 70:[title](1); 72:20; 78:70; 86:[title](1); 89:3(4),20(21),35(36), 49(50); 101:[title](1); 103:[title](1); 108:[title](1); 109:[title](1); 110:[title] (1); 122:[title](1),5; 124:[title](1); 131: [title](1); 132:1,10,11,17; 133:[title](1); 138:[title](1); 139:[title](1); 140:[title] (1); 141:[title](1); 142:[title](1);

143:[title](1); 144:[title](1),10; 145:[title](1); **Prov.** 1:1; **Eccl.** 1:1; **Song** 4:4; **Isa.** 7:2,13; 9:7(6); 16:5; 22:9,22; 29:1; 37:35; 38:5; 55:3; **Jer.** 13:13; 17:25; 21:12; 22:2,4,30; 23:5; 29:16; 30:9; 33:15,17,21,22,26; 36:30; **Ezek.** 34:23,24; 37:24,25; **Hos.** 3:5; **Amos** 6:5; 9:11; **Zech.** 12:7,8,10,12; 13:1.

1733. דּוֹדָה *dôḏāh* **fem. noun**
(father's sister, aunt)
Ex. 6:20; **Lev.** 18:14; 20:20.

1734. A. דּוֹדוֹ *dôḏô* **masc. proper noun**
(Dodo: grandfather of Tola)
Judg. 10:1.
B. דּוֹדוֹ *dôḏô* **masc. proper noun**
(Dodo: father of Eleazar; see *dôḏay* [1737])
2 Sam. 23:9; **1 Chr.** 11:12.
C. דּוֹדוֹ *dôḏô* **masc. proper noun**
(Dodo: father of Elhanan)
2 Sam. 23:24; **1 Chr.** 11:26.

1735. דֹּדָוָהוּ *dōḏāwāhû* **masc. proper noun**
(Dodavahu, Dodavah)
2 Chr. 20:37.

1736. דּוּדָאִים *dûḏā'iym* **masc. pl. noun**
(mandrakes; as an aphrodisiac)
Gen. 30:14–16; **Song** 7:13(14); **Jer.** 24:1.

1737. דּוֹדַי *dôḏay* **masc. proper noun**
(Dodai: probably the same as *dôḏô* [1734,B])
1 Chr. 27:4.

1738. דָּוָה *dāwāh* **verb**
(to be infirm, unclean: a reference to a woman's menstrual period)
Lev. 12:2.

1739. דָּוֶה *dāweh* **adj.**
(having to do with a woman's menstrual period, menstrual cloth; faint)
Lev. 15:33; 20:18; **Isa.** 30:22; **Lam.** 1:13; 5:17.

1740. דּוּחַ *dûah* **verb**
(to wash, to rinse, to cleanse)
2 Chr. 4:6; **Isa.** 4:4; **Jer.** 51:34; **Ezek.** 40:38.

1741. דְּוַי *d^e^way* **masc. noun**
(illness, loathsomeness)
Job 6:7; **Ps.** 41:3(4).

1742. דַּוָּי *dawwāy* **adj.**
(faint, weak)
Isa. 1:5; **Jer.** 8:18; **Lam.** 1:22.

1743. דּוּךְ *dûḵ* **verb**
(to beat, to crush)
Num. 11:8.

1744. דּוּכִיפַת *dûḵiypaṯ* **fem. noun**
(hoopoe, lapwing; an unclean bird)
Lev. 11:19; **Deut.** 14:18.

1745. דּוּמָה *dûmāh* **fem. noun**
(silence)
Ps. 94:17; 115:17.

1746. A. דּוּמָה *dûmāh* **masc. proper noun**
(Dumah: son of Ishmael)
Gen. 25:14; **1 Chr.** 1:30.
B. דּוּמָה *dûmāh* **masc. proper noun**
(Dumah: a city in Judah)
Josh. 15:52.
C. דּוּמָה *dûmāh* **masc. proper noun**
(Dumah: a symbolic name of Edom, indicating death and destruction [see 1745])
Isa. 21:11.

1747. דּוּמִיָּה *dûmiyyāh*, דֻּמִיָּה *dumiyyāh* **fem. noun**
(silence, a quiet wait)
Ps. 22:2(3); 39:2(3); 62:1(2); 65:1(2).

1748. דּוּמָם *dûmām* **masc. noun**
(silence, a quiet wait)
Isa. 47:5; **Lam.** 3:26; **Hab.** 2:19.

1749. דּוֹנַג *dônag* **masc. noun**
(wax)
Ps. 22:14(15); 68:2(3); 97:5; **Mic.** 1:4.

1750. דּוּץ *dûṣ* **verb**
(to leap, to dance)
Job 41:22(14).

1751. דָּקוּ *dāqû* **Aram. verb**
(to break, to shatter to pieces; the same as *deqaq* [1855])
Dan. 2:35.

1752. דּוּר *dûr* **verb**
(to dwell)
Ps. 84:10(11).

1753. דּוּר *dûr* **Aram. verb**
(to dwell, to live; corr. to Hebr. 1752)
Dan. 2:38; 4:1(3:31),12(9),21(18),35(32); 6:25(26).

1754. I. דּוּר *dûr* **masc. noun**
(heap, pile, ball)
Isa. 22:18; 29:3; **Ezek.** 24:5(KJV, see II).
II. דּוּר *dûr* **verb**
(to burn)
Ezek. 24:5(NASB, NIV, see I).

1755. I. דּוֹר *dôr* **masc. noun**
(dwelling place, house)
Isa. 38:12(KJV, see II).
II. דּוֹר *dôr* **masc. noun**
(generation, life)
Gen. 6:9; 7:1; 9:12; 15:16; 17:7,9,12; **Ex.** 1:6; 3:15; 12:14,17,42; 16:32,33; 17:16; 27:21; 29:42; 30:8,10,21,31; 31:13,16; 40:15; **Lev.** 3:17; 6:18(11); 7:36; 10:9; 17:7; 21:17; 22:3; 23:14,21,31,41,43; 24:3; 25:30; **Num.** 9:10; 10:8; 15:14, 15,21,23,38; 18:23; 32:13; 35:29; **Deut.** 1:35; 2:14; 7:9; 23:2(3),3(4),8(9); 29:22(21); 32:5,7,20; **Josh.** 22:27,28; **Judg.** 2:10; 3:2; **1 Chr.** 16:15; **Esth.** 9:28; **Job** 8:8; 42:16; **Ps.** 10:6; 12:7(8); 14:5; 22:30(31); 24:6; 33:11; 45:17(18); 48:13(14); 49:11(12),19(20); 61:6(7); 71:18; 72:5; 73:15; 77:8(9); 78:4,6,8; 79:13; 85:5(6); 89:1(2),4(5); 90:1; 95:10; 100:5; 102:12(13),18(19),24(25); 105:8; 106:31; 109:13; 112:2; 119:90; 135:13; 145:4,13; 146:10; **Prov.** 27:24; 30:11–14; **Eccl.** 1:4; **Isa.** 13:20; 34:10,17; 38:12 (NASB, NIV, see I); 41:4; 51:8,9; 53:8; 58:12; 60:15; 61:4; **Jer.** 2:31; 7:29; 50:39; **Lam.** 5:19; **Joel** 1:3; 2:2; 3:20(4:20).

1756. דֹּאר *dō'r*, דּוֹר *dôr* **proper noun**
(Dor)
Josh. 11:2; 12:23; 17:11; **Judg.** 1:27; **1 Kgs.** 4:11; **1 Chr.** 7:29.

1757. דּוּרָא *dûrā'* **Aram. proper noun**
(Dura)
Dan. 3:1.

1758. דּוּשׁ *dûš*, דִּישׁ *diyš* **verb**
(to thresh, to tread out)
Deut. 25:4; **Judg.** 8:7; **2 Kgs.** 13:7; **1 Chr.** 21:20; **Job** 39:15; **Isa.** 25:10; 28:27,28(KJV, *'adaš* [156]); 41:15; **Jer.** 50:11(see *dāšā'* [1877,II]; KJV, *deše'* [1877,I]); **Hos.** 10:11; **Amos** 1:3; **Mic.** 4:13; **Hab.** 3:12.

1759. דּוּשׁ *dûš* **Aram. verb**
(to tread down, to trample; corr. to Hebr. 1758)
Dan. 7:23.

1760. דָּחָה *dāḥāh* **verb**
(to push back, to drive away)

Ps. 35:5; 36:12(13); 62:3(4); 118:13; 140:4(5); 147:2; **Prov.** 14:32; **Isa.** 11:12(NASB, NIV, *nāḏaḥ* [5080]); 56:8; **Jer.** 23:12.

1761. דַּחֲוָה *daḥᵃwāh* **Aram. fem. noun**
(entertainment, instruments of music)
Dan. 6:18(19).

1762. דְּחִי *dᵉḥiy* **masc. noun**
(stumbling, falling)
Ps. 56:13(14); 116:8.

1763. דְּחַל *dᵉḥal* **Aram. verb**
(to fear, to be terrifying)
Dan. 2:31; 4:5(2); 5:19; 6:26(27); 7:7,19.

1764. דֹּחַן *dōḥan* **masc. noun**
(millet, grain)
Ezek. 4:9.

1765. דָּחַף *dāḥap̱* **verb**
(to hasten, to hurry)
2 Chr. 26:20; **Esth.** 3:15; 6:12; 8:14.

1766. דָּחַק *dāḥaq* **verb**
(to jostle, to oppress)
Judg. 2:18; **Joel** 2:8.

1767. דַּי *day* **masc. noun**
(enough, as often as, sufficient)
Ex. 36:5,7; **Lev.** 5:7; 12:8; 25:26,28; **Deut.** 15:8; 25:2; **Judg.** 6:5; **1 Sam.** 1:7; 7:16; 18:30; **1 Kgs.** 14:28; **2 Kgs.** 4:8; **2 Chr.** 12:11; 24:5; 30:3(KJV, NASB, *madday* [4078]); **Neh.** 5:8; **Esth.** 1:18; **Job** 39:25; **Prov.** 25:16; 27:27; **Isa.** 28:19; 40:16; 66:23; **Jer.** 20:8; 31:20; 48:27; 49:9; 51:58; **Obad.** 1:5; **Nah.** 2:12(13); **Hab.** 2:13; **Zech.** 14:16; **Mal.** 3:10.

1768. דִּי *diy* **Aram. particle**
(who, which, of which)
Ezra 4:9(KJV, see [Kᵉ] *dahᵃwāh* [1723]),10–19,23,24; 5:1,2,4,6,8,10–17; 6:1–6,8–13,15,18; 7:12–26; **Jer.** 10:11; **Dan.** 2:8–11,14–16,18–20,23–30, 32–35,37–41,43–45,47,49; 3:1–3,5–8, 10–12,14,15,17–20,22,25–29; 4:1(3:31), 2(3:32),6(3),8(5),9(6),15(12),17–20 (14–17),22–26(19–23),29(26),30(27), 32–35(29–32),37(34); 5:2,3,5,7,11–16, 19–25,29; 6:1–5(2–6),7(8),8(9),10(11), 12–17(13–18),19(20),20(21),22–27 (23–28); 7:4,6,7,9–11,14,17,19,20,22, 23,27,28.

1769. A. דִּיבוֹן *diyḇôn* **proper noun**
(Dibon: a city N. of Arnon)
Num. 21:30; 32:3,34; 33:45,46; **Josh.** 13:9,17; **Isa.** 15:2; **Jer.** 48:18,22.
B. דִּיבֹן *diyḇôn* **proper noun**
(Dibon: a village in Judah)
Neh. 11:25.

1770. דִּיג *diyg* **verb**
(to fish, to catch fish)
Jer. 16:16.

1771. דַּיָּג *dayyāg* **masc. noun**
(fisherman)
Isa. 19:8; **Jer.** 16:16(KJV, NASB, [Kᵉ] *dawwāg* [1728]).

1772. דַּיָּה *dayyāh* **fem. noun**
(vulture, falcon)
Deut. 14:13; **Isa.** 34:15.

1773. דְּיוֹ *dᵉyô* **masc. noun**
(ink)
Jer. 36:18.

1774. דִּי זָהָב *diy zāhāḇ* **proper noun**
(Dizahab)
Deut. 1:1.

1775. דִּימוֹן *diymôn* **proper noun**
(Dimon)
Isa. 15:9.

1776. דִּימוֹנָה *diymônāh* **proper noun**
(Dimonah)
Josh. 15:22.

1777. דִּין *diyn* **verb**
(to judge, to contend)
Gen. 6:3; 15:14; 30:6; 49:16; **Deut.** 32:36; **1 Sam.** 2:10; **2 Sam.** 19:9(10); **Job** 36:31; **Ps.** 7:8(9); 9:8(9); 50:4; 54:1(3); 72:2; 96:10; 110:6; 135:14; **Prov.** 31:9; **Eccl.** 6:10; **Isa.** 3:13; **Jer.** 5:28; 21:12; 22:16; 30:13; **Zech.** 3:7.

1778. דִּין *diyn* **Aram. verb**
(to judge; corr. to Hebr. 1777)
Ezra 7:25.

1779. דִּין *diyn* **masc. noun**
(judgment, cause)
Deut. 17:8; **Esth.** 1:13; **Job** 19:29; 35:14; 36:17; **Ps.** 9:4(5); 76:8(9); 140:12(13); **Prov.** 20:8; 22:10; 29:7; 31:5,8; **Isa.** 10:2; **Jer.** 5:28; 22:16; 30:13.

1780. דִּין *diyn* **Aram. masc. noun**
(judgment, court; corr. to Hebr. 1779)
Ezra 7:26; **Dan.** 4:37(34); 7:10,22,26.

1781. דַּיָּן *dayyān* **masc. noun**
(a judge)
1 Sam. 24:15(16); **Ps.** 68:5(6).

1782. דַּיָּן *dayyān* **Aram. masc. noun**
(a judge; corr. to Hebr. 1781)
Ezra 4:9(KJV, *diynāyē'* [1784,I]; NASB, *dayyānayyā'* [1784,II]); 7:25.

1783. דִּינָה *diynāh* **fem. proper noun**
(Dinah: daughter of Jacob)
Gen. 30:21; 34:1,3,5,13,25,26; 46:15.

1784. I. דִּינָיֵא *diynāyē'* **Aram. masc. pl. proper noun**
(Dinaites)
Ezra 4:9(NASB, see II; NIV, *dayyān* [1782]).
II. דַּיָּנַיָּא *dayyānayyā'* **Aram. masc. pl. noun**
(judges)
Ezra 4:9(KJV, see I; NIV, *dayyān* [1782]).

1785. דָּיֵק *dāyēq* **masc. noun**
(siege works, bulwarks)
2 Kgs. 25:1; **Jer.** 52:4; **Ezek.** 4:2; 17:17; 21:22(27); 26:8.

1786. דַּיִשׁ *dayiš* **masc. noun**
(threshing)
Lev. 26:5.

1787. A. דִּישֹׁן *diyšōn,* דִּשׁוֹן *dišôn* **masc. proper noun**
(Dishon: fifth son of Seir)
Gen. 36:21,26,30; **1 Chr.** 1:38.
B. דִּשֹׁן *dišōn,* דִּשׁוֹן *dišôn* **masc. proper noun**
(Dishon: grandson of Seir)
Gen. 36:25; **1 Chr.** 1:41.

1788. דִּישֹׁן *diyšôn* **masc. noun**
(gazelle, ibex, pygarg)
Deut. 14:5.

1789. דִּישָׁן *diyšān* **masc. proper noun**
(Dishan: seventh son of Seir)
Gen. 36:21,28,30; **1 Chr.** 1:38,42.

1790. דַּךְ *dak̲* **adj.**
(oppressed, afflicted)
Ps. 9:9(10); 10:18; 74:21; **Prov.** 26:28.

1791. דֵּךְ *dēk̲,* דָּךְ *dāk̲* **Aram. masc., fem. pron.**
(this)
Ezra 4:13,15,16,19,21; 5:8,16,17; 6:7,8,12.

1792. דָּכָא *dāk̲ā'* **verb**
(to crush, to break in pieces)
Job 4:19; 5:4; 6:9; 19:2; 22:9; 34:25;

Ps. 72:4; 89:10(11); 94:5; 143:3; **Prov.** 22:22; **Isa.** 3:15; 19:10; 53:5,10; 57:15; **Jer.** 44:10; **Lam.** 3:34.

1793. דַּכָּא *dakkā'* **masc. noun**
(contrition, dust)
Ps. 34:18(19); 90:3; **Isa.** 57:15.

1794. דָּכָה *dākāh* **verb**
(to crush)
Ps. 10:10; 38:8(9); 44:19(20); 51:8(10),17(19).

1795. דַּכָּה *dakkāh* **fem. noun**
(a crushing of the testicles)
Deut. 23:1(2).

1796. דֳּכִי *d^okiy* **masc. noun**
(a crashing, pounding of waves)
Ps. 93:3.

1797. דִּכֵּן *dikkēn* **Aram. pron.**
(this, that)
Dan. 2:31; 7:20,21.

1798. דְּכַר *d^ekar* **Aram. masc. noun**
(a ram)
Ezra 6:9,17; 7:17.

1799. I. דִּכְרוֹן *dikrôn* **Aram. masc. noun**
(minutes, record, memorandum)
Ezra 6:2.
II. דָּכְרָן *dokrān* **Aram. masc. noun**
(minutes, record, memorandum)
Ezra 4:15.

1800. I. דַּל *dal* **adj.**
(poor, weak)
Gen. 41:19; **Ex.** 23:3; 30:15; **Lev.** 14:21; 19:15; **Judg.** 6:15; **Ruth** 3:10; **1 Sam.** 2:8; **2 Sam.** 3:1; 13:4; **Job** 5:16; 20:10, 19; 31:16; 34:19,28; **Ps.** 41:1(2); 72:13; 82:3,4; 113:7; **Prov.** 10:15; 14:31; 19:4,17; 21:13; 22:9,16,22; 28:3,8,11,15; 29:7,14; **Isa.** 10:2; 11:4; 14:30; 25:4; 26:6; **Jer.** 5:4; 39:10; **Amos** 2:7; 4:1; 5:11; 8:6; **Zeph.** 3:12.
II. דַּל *dal* **masc. noun**
(door)
Ps. 141:3(KJV, *dāl* [1817,I]).

1801. דָּלַג *dālag* **verb**
(to leap, to leap over)
2 Sam. 22:30; **Ps.** 18:29(30); **Song** 2:8; **Isa.** 35:6; **Zeph.** 1:9.

1802. I. דָּלָה *dālāh* **verb**
(to draw up, to lift up)
Ex. 2:16,19; **Ps.** 30:1(2); **Prov.** 20:5.
II. דָּלָה *dālāh* **verb**
(to hang down)
Prov. 26:7(KJV, *dālal* [1809,I]).

1803. I. דַּלָּה *dallāh* **fem. noun**
(sickness, the poor)
2 Kgs. 24:14; 25:12; **Isa.** 38:12(NASB, NIV, see II); **Jer.** 40:7; 52:15,16.
II. דַּלָּה *dallāh* **fem. noun**
(hair; loom, thrum)
Song 7:5(6); **Isa.** 38:12(KJV, see I).

1804. דָּלַח *dālah* **verb**
(to stir up, to churn)
Ezek. 32:2,13.

1805. דְּלִי *d^eliy* **masc. noun**
(bucket)
Num. 24:7; **Isa.** 40:15.

1806. A. דְּלָיָה *d^elāyāh* **masc. proper noun**
(Delaiah: son of Elioenai)
1 Chr. 3:24.
B. דְּלָיָהוּ *d^elāyāhû* **masc. proper noun**
(Delaiah: a priest)
1 Chr. 24:18.
C. דְּלָיָהוּ *d^elāyāhû* **masc. proper noun**
(Delaiah: a royal officer)
Jer. 36:12,25.
D. דְּלָיָהוּ *d^elāyāhû* **masc. proper noun**

(Delaiah: a Jew)
Ezra 2:60; **Neh.** 7:62.
E. דְּלָיָהוּ *d^e^lāyāhû* **masc. proper noun**
(Delaiah: father of Shemaiah)
Neh. 6:10.

1807. דְּלִילָה *d^e^liylāh* **fem. proper noun**
(Delilah)
Judg. 16:4,6,10,12,13,18.

1808. דָּלִית *dāliyt̲* **fem. noun**
(branch)
Jer. 11:16; **Ezek.** 17:6,7,23; 19:11; 31:7,9,12.

1809. I. דָּלַל *dālal* **verb**
(to hang low, to languish, to become thin, to not be equal)
Judg. 6:6; **Job** 28:4(NASB, NIV, see II); **Ps.** 79:8; 116:6; 142:6(7); **Prov.** 26:7 (NASB, NIV, *dālāh*[1802,II]); **Isa.** 17:4; 19:6; 38:14.
II. דָּלַל *dālal* **verb**
(to dangle, to hang)
Job 28:4(KJV, see I).

1810. דִּלְעָן *dil'ān* **proper noun**
(Dilean)
Josh. 15:38.

1811. דָּלַף *dālap̲* **verb**
(to pour out, to leak)
Job 16:20; **Ps.** 119:28; **Eccl.** 10:18.

1812. דֶּלֶף *delep̲* **masc. noun**
(dripping)
Prov. 19:13; 27:15.

1813. דַּלְפוֹן *dalp̲ôn* **masc. proper noun**
(Dalphon)
Esth. 9:7.

1814. דָּלַק *dālaq* **verb**
(to burn, to hotly pursue)
Gen. 31:36; **1 Sam.** 17:53; **Ps.** 7:13(14); 10:2; **Prov.** 26:23; **Isa.** 5:11; **Lam.** 4:19; **Ezek.** 24:10; **Obad.** 1:18.

1815. דְּלַק *d^e^laq* **Aram. verb**
(to burn; corr. to Hebr. 1814)
Dan. 7:9.

1816. דַּלֶּקֶת *daleqet̲* **fem. noun**
(inflammation)
Deut. 28:22.

1817. I. דַּל *dāl* **masc. noun**
(door)
Ps. 141:3(NASB, NIV, *dāl* [1800,II]).
II. דֶּלֶת *delet̲* **fem. noun**
(door)
Gen. 19:6,9,10; **Ex.** 21:6; **Deut.** 3:5; 15:17; **Josh.** 2:19; 6:26; **Judg.** 3:23–25; 11:31; 16:3; 19:22,27; **1 Sam.** 3:15; 21:13(14); 23:7; **2 Sam.** 13:17,18; **1 Kgs.** 6:31,32,34; 7:50; 16:34; **2 Kgs.** 4:4,5,33; 6:32; 9:3,10; 12:9(10); 18:16; **1 Chr.** 22:3; **2 Chr.** 3:7; 4:9,22; 8:5; 14:7(6); 28:24; 29:3,7; **Neh.** 3:1,3, 6,13–15; 6:1,10; 7:1,3; 13:19; **Job** 3:10; 31:32; 38:8,10; 41:14(6); **Ps.** 78:23; 107:16; **Prov.** 8:34; 26:14; **Eccl.** 12:4; **Song** 8:9; **Isa.** 26:20; 45:1,2; 57:8; **Jer.** 36:23; 49:31; **Ezek.** 26:2; 38:11; 41:23–25; **Zech.** 11:1; **Mal.** 1:10.

1818. דָּם *dām* **masc. noun**
(blood)
Gen. 4:10,11; 9:4–6; 37:22,26,31; 42:22; 49:11; **Ex.** 4:9,25,26; 7:17,19,20,24; 12:7,13,22,23; 22:2(1),3(2); 23:18; 24:6,8; 29:12,16,20,21; 30:10; 34:25; **Lev.** 1:5, 11,15; 3:2,8,13,17; 4:5–7,16–18,25,30, 34; 5:9; 6:27(20),30(23); 7:2,14,26,27,33; 8:15,19,23,24,30; 9:9,12,18; 10:18; 12:4, 5,7; 14:6,14,17,25,28,51,52; 15:19,25; 16:14,15,18,19,27; 17:4,6,10–14; 19:16,26; 20:9,11–13,16,18,27; **Num.** 18:17; 19:4,5; 23:24; 35:19,21,24,25, 27,33; **Deut.** 12:16,23,27; 15:23; 17:8; 19:6,10,12,13; 21:7–9; 22:8; 27:25; 32:14,42,43; **Josh.** 2:19; 20:3,5,9; **Judg.**

9:24; **1 Sam.** 14:32–34; 19:5; 25:26,31, 33; 26:20; **2 Sam.** 1:16,22; 3:27,28; 4:11; 14:11; 16:7,8; 20:12; 21:1; 23:17; **1 Kgs.** 2:5,9,31–33,37; 18:28; 21:19; 22:35,38; **2 Kgs.** 3:22,23; 9:7,26,33; 16:13,15; 21:16; 24:4; **1 Chr.** 11:19; 22:8; 28:3; **2 Chr.** 19:10; 24:25; 29:22,24; 30:16; **Job** 16:18; 39:30; **Ps.** 5:6(7); 9:12(13); 16:4; 26:9; 30:9(10); 50:13; 51:14(16); 55:23(24); 58:10(11); 59:2(3); 68:23(24); 72:14; 78:44; 79:3,10; 94:21; 105:29; 106:38; 139:19; **Prov.** 1:11,16,18; 6:17; 12:6; 28:17; 29:10; 30:33; **Isa.** 1:11,15; 4:4; 9:5(4); 15:9; 26:21; 33:15; 34:3,6,7; 49:26; 59:3,7; 66:3; **Jer.** 2:34; 7:6; 19:4; 22:3,17; 26:15; 46:10; 48:10; 51:35; **Lam.** 4:13,14; **Ezek.** 3:18,20; 5:17; 7:23; 9:9; 14:19; 16:6,9,22,36,38; 18:10,13; 19:10 (NASB, NIV, *kerem* [3754]); 21:32(37); 22:2–4,6,9,12,13,27; 23:37,45; 24:6–9; 28:23; 32:6; 33:4–6,8,25; 35:6; 36:18; 38:22; 39:17–19; 43:18,20; 44:7,15; 45:19; **Hos.** 1:4; 4:2; 6:8; 12:14(15); **Joel** 2:30(3:3),31(3:4); 3:19(4:19),21(4:21); **Jon.** 1:14; **Mic.** 3:10; 7:2; **Nah.** 3:1; **Hab.** 2:8,12,17; **Zeph.** 1:17; **Zech.** 9:7,11.

1819. דָּמָה *dāmāh* **verb**
(to be like, to compare)
Num. 33:56; **Judg.** 20:5; **2 Sam.** 21:5; **Esth.** 4:13; **Ps.** 48:9(10); 50:21; 89:6(7); 102:6(7); 144:4; **Song** 1:9; 2:9,17; 7:7(8); 8:14; **Isa.** 1:9; 10:7; 14:14,24; 40:18,25; 46:5; **Jer.** 6:2(NASB, NIV, *dāmāh* [1820]); **Lam.** 2:13; **Ezek.** 31:2,8,18; 32:2; **Hos.** 12:10(11).

1820. דָּמָה *dāmāh* **verb**
(to cut off)
Ps. 49:12(13),20(21); **Isa.** 6:5; 15:1; **Jer.** 6:2(KJV, *dāmāh* [1819]); 14:17; 47:5; **Lam.** 3:49; **Hos.** 4:5,6; 10:7,15; **Obad.** 1:5; **Zeph.** 1:11.

1821. דְּמָה *d*e*māh* **Aram. verb**
(to be like; corr. to Hebr. 1819)
Dan. 3:25; 7:5.

1822. דֻּמָה *dumāh* **fem. noun**
(to be silenced)
Ezek. 27:32.

1823. דְּמוּת *d*e*mûṯ* **fem. noun**
(likeness)
Gen. 1:26; 5:1,3; **2 Kgs.** 16:10; **2 Chr.** 4:3; **Ps.** 58:4(5); **Isa.** 13:4; 40:18; **Ezek.** 1:5,10,13,16,22,26,28; 8:2; 10:1,10,21,22; 23:15; **Dan.** 10:16.

1824. I. דֳּמִי *d*o*miy* **masc. noun**
(rest, silence)
Ps. 83:1(2); **Isa.** 62:6,7.
II. דְּמִי *d*e*miy* **masc. noun**
(middle, half)
Isa. 38:10.

1825. דִּמְיוֹן *dimyôn* **masc. noun**
(likeness)
Ps. 17:12.

1826. דָּמַם *dāmam* **verb**
(to be still, to be silent)
Ex. 15:16; **Lev.** 10:3; **Josh.** 10:12,13; **1 Sam.** 2:9; 14:9; **Job** 29:21; 30:27; 31:34; **Ps.** 4:4(5); 30:12(13); 31:17(18); 35:15; 37:7; 62:5(6); 131:2; **Isa.** 23:2; **Jer.** 8:14; 25:37; 47:6; 48:2; 49:26; 50:30; 51:6; **Lam.** 2:10,18; 3:28; **Ezek.** 24:17; **Amos** 5:13.

1827. דְּמָמָה *d*e*māmāh* **fem. noun**
(hushed, whispering)
1 Kgs. 19:12; **Job** 4:16; **Ps.** 107:29.

1828. דֹּמֶן *dōmen* **masc. noun**
(dung, refuse)
2 Kgs. 9:37; **Ps.** 83:10(11); **Jer.** 8:2; 9:22(21); 16:4; 25:33.

1829. דִּמְנָה *dimnāh* **proper noun**
(Dimnah)
Josh. 21:35.

1830. דָּמַע *dāma'* **verb**
(to weep)
Jer. 13:17.

1831. דֶּמַע *dema'* **masc. noun**
(juice)
Ex. 22:29(28).

1832. דִּמְעָה *dim'āh* **fem. noun**
(tears)
2 Kgs. 20:5; **Ps.** 6:6(7); 39:12(13); 42:3(4); 56:8(9); 80:5(6); 116:8; 126:5; **Eccl.** 4:1; **Isa.** 16:9; 25:8; 38:5; **Jer.** 9:1(8:23),18(17); 13:17; 14:17; 31:16; **Lam.** 1:2; 2:11,18; **Ezek.** 24:16; **Mal.** 2:13.

1833. I. דְּמֶשֶׁק *d^e^mešeq* **proper noun**
(Damascus: another form of *dammeśeq* [1834])
Amos 3:12(NASB, see II).
II. דְּמֶשֶׁק *d^e^mešeq* **masc. noun**
(damask, cloth)
Amos 3:12(KJV, NIV, see I).

1834. דַּמֶּשֶׂק *dûmmeśeq,* דַּמֶּשֶׂק *dammeśeq,* דַּרְמֶשֶׂק *darmeśeq* **proper noun**
(Damascus)
Gen. 14:15; 15:2; **2 Sam.** 8:5,6; **1 Kgs.** 11:24; 15:18; 19:15; 20:34; **2 Kgs.** 5:12; 8:7,9; 14:28; 16:9–12; **1 Chr.** 18:5,6; **2 Chr.** 16:2; 24:23; 28:5,23; **Song** 7:4(5); **Isa.** 7:8; 8:4; 10:9; 17:1,3; **Jer.** 49:23,24,27; **Ezek.** 27:18; 47:16–18; 48:1; **Amos** 1:3,5; 3:12(see *d^e^mešeq* [1833,I]); 5:27; **Zech.** 9:1.

1835. A. דָּן *dān* **masc. proper noun**
(Dan: fifth son of Jacob)
Gen. 30:6; 35:25; 46:23; 49:10,17; **Ex.** 1:4; **Num.** 26:42; **Josh.** 19:47; **1 Chr.** 2:2.
B. דָּן *dān* **proper noun**
(Dan: a city)
Gen. 14:14; **Deut.** 34:1; **Josh.** 19:47; **Judg.** 18:29; 20:1; **1 Sam.** 3:20; **2 Sam.** 3:10; 17:11; 24:2,15; **1 Kgs.** 4:25(5:5); 12:29,30; 15:20; **2 Kgs.** 10:29; **1 Chr.** 21:2; **2 Chr.** 16:4; 30:5; **Jer.** 4:15; 8:16; **Ezek.** 27:19(NASB, *w^e^dān* [2051]; NIV, see C); **Amos** 8:14.
C. דָּן *dān* **masc. proper noun**
(Dan: the tribe or territory of Dan)
Ex. 31:6; 35:34; 38:23; **Lev.** 24:11; **Num.** 1:12,38,39; 2:25,31; 7:66; 10:25; 13:12; 26:42; 34:22; **Deut.** 27:13; 33:22; **Josh.** 19:40,47,48; 21:5,23; **Judg.** 1:34; 5:17; 13:25; 18:2,16,22,23,25,26,30; **1 Chr.** 27:22; **2 Chr.** 2:14(13); **Ezek.** 27:19(NASB, *w^e^dān* [2051]; KJV, see B); 48:1,2,32.

1836. דְּנָה *d^e^nāh* **Aram. pron.**
(this, therefore)
Ezra 4:11,14–16,22; 5:3–5,7,9,11–13,17; 6:11,15–17; 7:17,24; **Jer.** 10:11; **Dan.** 2:10,12,18,24,28–30,36,43,45,47; 3:7,8, 16,22,29; 4:18(15),24(21); 5:7,15,22, 24–26; 6:3(4),5(6),9(10),10(11),28(29); 7:6,7,16.

1837. דַּנָּה *dannāh* **proper noun**
(Dannah)
Josh. 15:49.

1838. דִּנְהָבָה *dinhābāh* **proper noun**
(Dinhabah)
Gen. 36:32; **1 Chr.** 1:43.

1839. דָּנִי *dāniy* **masc. proper noun**
(Danites)
Judg. 13:2; 18:1,11,30; **1 Chr.** 12:35.

1840. A. דָּנִיֵּאל *dāniyyē'l* **masc. proper noun**
(Daniel: second son of David)
1 Chr. 3:1.
B. דָּנִיֵּאל *dāniyyē'l* **masc. proper noun**
(Daniel: descendant of Ithmar)
Ezra 8:2; **Neh.** 10:6(7).
C. דָּנִאֵל *dāni'ēl,* דָּנִיֵּאל *dāniyyē'l* **masc. proper noun**

(Daniel: the prophet)
Ezek. 14:14(see D),20(see D); 28:3(see D); **Dan.** 1:6–11,17,19,21; 8:1,15,27; 9:2,22; 10:1,2,7,11,12; 12:4,5,9.

D. דָּנִאֵל *dāni'ēl* **masc. proper noun**
(Daniel: possibly a legendary ruler in Ugaritic Epic of Aqhat; see C)
Ezek. 14:14,20; 28:3.

1841. דָּנִיֵּאל *dāniyyē'l* **Aram. masc. proper noun**
(Daniel; corr. to Hebr. 1840)
Dan. 2:13–20,24–27,46–49; 4:8(5), 19(16); 5:12,13,17,29; 6:2–5(3–6), 10(11),11(12),13(14),14(15),16(17), 17(18),20(21),21(22),23(24),24(25), 26–28(27–29); 7:1,2,15,28.

1842. דָּן יַעַן *dān ya'an* **proper noun**
(Dan Jaan)
2 Sam. 24:6.

1843. דֵּעַ *dēa'* **masc. noun**
(knowledge, opinion)
Job 32:6,10,17; 36:3; 37:16.

1844. דֵּעָה *dē'āh* **fem. noun**
(knowledge)
1 Sam. 2:3; **Job** 36:4; **Ps.** 73:11; **Isa.** 11:9; 28:9; **Jer.** 3:15.

1845. דְּעוּאֵל *d^e'û'ēl* **masc. proper noun**
(Deuel)
Num. 1:14; 2:14(KJV, *r^e'û'ēl* [7467,C]); 7:42,47; 10:20.

1846. דָּעַךְ *dā'aḵ* **verb**
(to be extinguished, to die out)
Job 6:17; 18:5,6; 21:17; **Ps.** 118:12; **Prov.** 13:9; 20:20; 24:20; **Isa.** 43:17.

1847. דַּעַת *da'aṯ* **fem. noun**
(knowledge)
Gen. 2:9,17; **Ex.** 31:3; 35:31; **Num.** 24:16; **Deut.** 4:42; 19:4; **Josh.** 20:3,5; **1 Kgs.** 7:14; **Job** 10:7; 13:2; 15:2; 21:14,22; 33:3; 34:35; 35:16; 36:12; 38:2; 42:3; **Ps.** 19:2(3); 94:10; 119:66; 139:6; **Prov.** 1:4,7,22,29; 2:5,6,10; 3:20; 5:2; 8:9,10,12; 9:10; 10:14; 11:9; 12:1,23; 13:16; 14:6,7,18; 15:2,7,14; 17:27; 18:15; 19:2,25,27; 20:15; 21:11; 22:12,17,20; 23:12; 24:4,5; 29:7; 30:3; **Eccl.** 1:16,18; 2:21,26; 7:12; 9:10; 12:9; **Isa.** 5:13; 11:2; 32:4(NIV, *yāda'* [3045]); 33:6; 40:14; 44:19,25; 47:10; 48:4(NASB, NIV, *yāda'* [3045]); 53:11; 58:2; **Jer.** 10:14; 22:16; 51:17; **Dan.** 1:4; 12:4; **Hos.** 4:1,6; 6:6; **Mal.** 2:7.

1848. דֳּפִי *d^opiy* **masc. noun**
(slander)
Ps. 50:20.

1849. דָּפַק *dāpaq* **verb**
(to beat violently, to drive hard)
Gen. 33:13; **Judg.** 19:22; **Song** 5:2.

1850. דָּפְקָה *dopqāh* **proper noun**
(Dophkah)
Num. 33:12,13.

1851. דַּק *daq* **adj.**
(thin, gaunt)
Gen. 41:3,4,6,7,23,24; **Ex.** 16:14; **Lev.** 13:30; 16:12; 21:20; **1 Kgs.** 19:12; **Isa.** 29:5; 40:15.

1852. דֹּק *dōq* **masc. noun**
(curtain, canopy)
Isa. 40:22.

1853. דִּקְלָה *diqlāh* **masc. proper noun**
(Diklah)
Gen. 10:27; **1 Chr.** 1:21.

1854. דָּקַק *dāqaq* **verb**
(to beat into powder, to pulverize)
Ex. 30:36; 32:20; **Deut.** 9:21; **2 Sam.** 22:43; **2 Kgs.** 23:6,15; **2 Chr.** 15:16; 34:4,7; **Isa.** 28:28; 41:15; **Mic.** 4:13.

1855. דְּקַק $d^e qaq$ **Aram. verb**
(to break into pieces, to crush; corr. to Hebr. 1854)
Dan. 2:34,35,40,44,45; 6:24(25); 7:7,19,23.

1856. דָּקַר *dāqar* **verb**
(to thrust through, to pierce)
Num. 25:8; **Judg.** 9:54; **1 Sam.** 31:4; **1 Chr.** 10:4; **Isa.** 13:15; **Jer.** 37:10; 51:4; **Lam.** 4:9; **Zech.** 12:10; 13:3.

1857. דֶּקֶר *deqer* **proper noun**
(Deker)
1 Kgs. 4:9(NASB, NIV, see 1128).

1858. דַּר *dar* **masc. noun**
(white, mother-of-pearl)
Esth. 1:6.

1859. דָּר *dār* **Aram. masc. noun**
(generation; corr. to Hebr. 1755)
Dan. 4:3(3:33),34(31).

1860. דְּרָאוֹן $d^e r\bar{a}'\hat{o}n$, דֵּרָאוֹן *dērāʾôn* **masc. noun**
(contempt, abhorring)
Isa. 66:24; **Dan.** 12:2.

1861. דָּרְבָן *dorbān*, דָּרְבֹן *dorbōn* **masc. noun**
(goad)
1 Sam. 13:21; **Eccl.** 12:11.

1862. דַּרְדַּע *darda'* **masc. proper noun**
(Darda)
1 Kgs. 4:31(5:11); **1 Chr.** 2:6(see *dāra'* [1873]).

1863. דַּרְדַּר *dardar* **masc. noun**
(thistles)
Gen. 3:18; **Hos.** 10:8.

1864. דָּרוֹם *dārôm* **masc. noun**
(south, southward)
Deut. 33:23; **Job** 37:17; **Eccl.** 1:6; 11:3; **Ezek.** 20:46(21:2); 40:24,27,28,44,45; 41:11; 42:12,13,18.

1865. I. דְּרוֹר $d^e r\hat{o}r$ **masc. noun**
(liberty, emancipation)
Lev. 25:10; **Isa.** 61:1; **Jer.** 34:8,15,17; **Ezek.** 46:17.
II. דְּרוֹר $d^e r\hat{o}r$ **masc. noun**
(myrrh oil)
Ex. 30:23.

1866. דְּרוֹר $d^e r\hat{o}r$ **masc. noun**
(a swallow [bird])
Ps. 84:3(4); **Prov.** 26:2.

1867. A. דָּרְיָוֶשׁ $d\bar{a}r^e y\bar{a}we\check{s}$ **masc. proper noun**
(Darius: Darius Hystaspes)
Ezra 4:5; **Hag.** 1:1,15; 2:10; **Zech.** 1:1,7; 7:1.
B. דָּרְיָוֶשׁ $d\bar{a}r^e y\bar{a}we\check{s}$ **masc. proper noun**
(Darius: Darius Nothus)
Neh. 12:22.
C. דָּרְיָוֶשׁ $d\bar{a}r^e y\bar{a}we\check{s}$ **masc. proper noun**
(Darius: Darius the Mede)
Dan. 9:1; 11:1.

1868. A. דָּרְיָוֶשׁ $d\bar{a}r^e y\bar{a}we\check{s}$ **Aram. masc. proper noun**
(Darius: Darius Hystaspes; corr. to Hebr. 1867,A)
Ezra 4:24; 5:5–7; 6:1,12–15.
B. דָּרְיָוֶשׁ $d\bar{a}r^e y\bar{a}we\check{s}$ **Aram. masc. proper noun**
(Darius: Darius the Mede; corr. to Hebr. 1867,C)
Dan. 5:31(6:1); 6:1(2),6(7),9(10),25(26),28(29).

1869. דָּרַךְ *dārak̠* **verb**
(to tread, to bend)
Num. 24:17; **Deut.** 1:36; 11:24,25; 33:29; **Josh.** 1:3; 14:9; **Judg.** 5:21; 9:27;

20:43; **1 Sam.** 5:5; **1 Chr.** 5:18; 8:40; **2 Chr.** 14:8(7); **Neh.** 13:15; **Job** 9:8; 22:15; 24:11; 28:8; **Ps.** 7:12(13); 11:2; 25:5,9; 37:14; 58:7(8); 64:3(4); 91:13; 107:7; 119:35; **Prov.** 4:11; **Isa.** 5:28; 11:15; 16:10; 21:15; 42:16; 48:17; 59:8; 63:2,3; **Jer.** 9:3(2); 25:30; 46:9; 48:33; 50:14,29; 51:3,33; **Lam.** 1:15; 2:4; 3:12; **Amos** 4:13; 9:13; **Mic.** 1:3; 5:5(4),6(5); 6:15; **Hab.** 3:15,19; **Zech.** 9:13.

1870. דֶּרֶךְ *derek* **masc. noun**
(way, road, journey)
Gen. 3:24; 6:12; 16:7; 18:19; 19:2,31; 24:21,27,40,42,48,56; 28:20; 30:36; 31:23,35; 32:1(2); 33:16; 35:3,19; 38:14,16,21; 42:25,38; 45:21,23,24; 48:7; 49:17; **Ex.** 3:18; 4:24; 5:3; 8:27(23); 13:17,18,21; 18:8,20; 23:20; 32:8; 33:3,13; **Lev.** 26:22; **Num.** 9:10,13; 10:33; 11:31; 14:25; 20:17; 21:1,4,22,33; 22:22,23,26,31,32,34; 24:25; 33:8; **Deut.** 1:2,19,22,31,33,40; 2:1,8,27; 3:1; 5:33(30); 6:7; 8:2,6; 9:12,16; 10:12; 11:19,22,28,30; 13:5(6); 14:24; 17:16; 19:3,6,9; 22:4,6; 23:4(5); 24:9; 25:17,18; 26:17; 27:18; 28:7,9,25,29,68; 30:16; 31:29; 32:4; **Josh.** 1:8; 2:7,16,22; 3:4; 5:4,5,7; 8:15; 9:11,13; 10:10; 12:3; 22:5; 23:14; 24:17; **Judg.** 2:17,19,22; 4:9; 5:10; 8:11; 9:25,37; 17:8; 18:5,6,26; 19:9,27; 20:42; **Ruth** 1:7; **1 Sam.** 1:18; 4:13; 6:9,12; 8:3,5; 9:6,8; 12:23; 13:17,18; 15:2,18,20; 17:52; 18:14; 21:5(6); 24:3(4),7(8),19(20); 25:12; 26:3,25; 28:22; 30:2; **2 Sam.** 2:24; 4:7; 11:10; 13:30,34; 15:2,23; 16:13; 18:23; 22:22,31,33; **1 Kgs.** 1:49; 2:2–4; 3:14; 8:25,32,36,39,44,48,58; 11:29,33,38; 13:9,10,12,17,24–26,28,33; 15:26,34; 16:2,19,26; 18:6,7,27,43; 19:4,7,15; 20:38; 22:43,52(53); **2 Kgs.** 2:23; 3:8,9, 20; 6:19; 7:15; 8:18,27; 9:27; 10:12; 11:16,19; 16:3; 17:13; 19:28,33; 21:21,22; 22:2; 25:4; **2 Chr.** 6:16,23,27, 30,31,34,38; 7:14; 11:17; 13:22; 17:3,6; 18:23; 20:32; 21:6,12,13; 22:3; 27:6,7; 28:2,26; 34:2; **Ezra** 8:21,22,31; **Neh.** 9:12,19; **Job** 3:23; 4:6; 6:18; 8:19; 12:24; 13:15; 17:9; 19:12; 21:14,29,31; 22:3,28; 23:10,11; 24:4,13,18,23; 26:14; 28:23,26; 29:25; 31:4,7; 34:21,27; 36:23; 38:19,24, 25; 40:19; **Ps.** 1:1,6; 2:12; 5:8(9); 10:5; 18:21(22),30(31),32(33); 25:4,8,9,12; 27:11; 32:8; 35:6; 36:4(5); 37:5,7,14, 23,34; 39:1(2); 49:13(14); 50:23; 51:13(15); 67:2(3); 77:13(14),19(20); 80:12(13); 81:13(14); 85:13(14); 86:11; 89:41(42); 91:11; 95:10; 101:2,6; 102:23(24); 103:7; 107:4,7,17,40; 110:7; 119:1,3,5,14,26,27,29,30,32,33,37,59,16 8; 128:1; 138:5; 139:3,24; 143:8; 145:17; 146:9; **Prov.** 1:15,31; 2:8,12,13,20; 3:6,17,23,31; 4:11,14,19,26; 5:8,21; 6:6,23; 7:8,19,25,27; 8:2,13,22,32; 9:6,15; 10:9,29; 11:5,20; 12:15,26,28; 13:6,15; 14:2,8,12,14; 15:9,19; 16:2,7, 9,17,25,29,31; 19:3,16; 20:24; 21:2,8, 16,29; 22:5,6; 23:19,26; 26:13; 28:6, 10,18; 29:27; 30:19,20; 31:3; **Eccl.** 10:3; 11:5,9; 12:5; **Isa.** 2:3; 3:12; 8:11; 9:1(8:23); 10:24,26; 15:5; 30:11,21; 35:8; 37:29,34; 40:3,14,27; 42:16,24; 43:16,19; 45:13; 48:15,17; 49:9,11; 51:10; 53:6; 55:7–9; 56:11; 57:10,14,17,18; 58:2,13; 59:8; 62:10; 63:17; 64:5(4); 65:2; 66:3; **Jer.** 2:17,18,23,33,36; 3:2,13,21; 4:11,18; 5:4,5; 6:16,25,27; 7:3,5,23; 10:2,23; 12:1,16; 15:7; 16:17; 17:10; 18:11,15; 21:8; 22:21; 23:12,22; 25:5; 26:3,13; 28:11; 31:9,21; 32:19,39; 35:15; 36:3,7; 39:4; 42:3; 48:19; 50:5; 52:7; **Lam.** 1:4,12; 2:15; 3:9,11,40; **Ezek.** 3:18,19; 7:3,4,8,9,27; 8:5; 9:2,10; 11:21; 13:22; 14:22,23; 16:25,27,31,43,47,61; 18:23, 25,29,30; 20:30,43,44,46(21:2); 21:19–21 (24–26); 22:31; 23:13,31; 24:14; 28:15; 33:8,9,11,17,20; 36:17,19,31,32; 40:6,10, 20,22,24,27,32,44–46; 41:11,12; 42:1,4, 7,10–12,15; 43:1,2,4; 44:1,3,4; 46:2,8,9; 47:2,15; 48:1; **Hos.** 2:6(8); 4:9; 6:9; 9:8; 10:13; 12:2(3); 13:7; 14:9(10); **Joel** 2:7;

Amos 2:7; 4:10; 8:14; **Jon.** 3:8,10; **Mic.** 4:2; **Nah.** 1:3; 2:1(2); **Hag.** 1:5,7; **Zech.** 1:4,6; 3:7; **Mal.** 2:8,9; 3:1.

1871. דַּרְכְּמָה *darkemāh* **masc. noun**
(dram, drachma; a coin and unit of weight)
Ezra 2:69; **Neh.** 7:70–72.

1872. דְּרָע *d^e^rā'* **Aram. fem. noun**
(arm)
Dan. 2:32.

1873. דָּרַע *dāra'* **masc. proper noun**
(Dara: shortened form of *darda'* [1862])
1 Chr. 2:6(NIV, *darda'* [1862]).

1874. דַּרְקוֹן *darqôn* **proper noun**
(Darkon)
Ezra 2:56; **Neh.** 7:58.

1875. דָּרַשׁ *dāraš* **verb**
(to seek, to inquire of, to require)
Gen. 9:5; 25:22; 42:22; **Ex.** 18:15; **Lev.** 10:16; **Deut.** 4:29; 11:12; 12:5,30; 13:14(15); 17:4,9; 18:11,19; 19:18; 22:2; 23:6(7),21(22); **Judg.** 6:29; **1 Sam.** 9:9; 28:7; **2 Sam.** 11:3; **1 Kgs.** 14:5; 22:5,7,8; **2 Kgs.** 1:2,3,6,16; 3:11; 8:8; 22:13,18; **1 Chr.** 10:13,14; 13:3; 15:13; 16:11; 21:30; 22:19; 26:31; 28:8,9; **2 Chr.** 1:5; 12:14; 14:4(3),7(6); 15:2,12,13; 16:12; 17:3,4; 18:4,6,7; 19:3; 20:3; 22:9; 24:6,22; 25:15,20; 26:5; 30:19; 31:9,21; 32:31; 34:3,21,26; **Ezra** 4:2; 6:21; 7:10; 9:12; 10:16; **Esth.** 10:3; **Job** 3:4; 5:8; 10:6; 39:8; **Ps.** 9:10(11),12(13); 10:4,13,15; 14:2; 22:26(27); 24:6; 34:4(5),10(11); 38:12(13); 53:2(3); 69:32(33); 77:2(3); 78:34; 105:4; 109:10(NIV, *gāraš* [1644]); 111:2; 119:2,10,45,94,155; 142:4(5); **Prov.** 11:27; 31:13; **Eccl.** 1:13; **Isa.** 1:17; 8:19; 9:13(12); 11:10; 16:5; 19:3; 31:1; 34:16; 55:6; 58:2; 62:12; 65:1,10; **Jer.** 8:2; 10:21; 21:2; 29:7,13; 30:14,17; 37:7; 38:4; **Lam.** 3:25; **Ezek.** 14:3,7,10; 20:1,3,31,40; 33:6; 34:6,8,10,11; 36:37; **Hos.** 10:12; **Amos** 5:4–6,14; **Mic.** 6:8; **Zeph.** 1:6.

1876. דָּשָׁא *dāšā'* **verb**
(to produce green plants)
Gen. 1:11; **Joel** 2:22.

1877. I. דֶּשֶׁא *deše'* **masc. noun**
(grass, tender grass)
Gen. 1:11,12; **Deut.** 32:2; **2 Sam.** 23:4; **2 Kgs.** 19:26; **Job** 6:5; 38:27; **Ps.** 23:2; 37:2; **Prov.** 27:25; **Isa.** 15:6; 37:27; 66:14; **Jer.** 14:5; 50:11(NASB, NIV, see II).

II. דָּשָׁא *dāšā'* **verb**
(to trample on, to thresh: qal act. part. of *dûš* [1758])
Jer. 50:11(KJV, see I).

1878. דָּשֵׁן *dāšēn* **verb**
(to prosper, to become fat, to remove ashes)
Ex. 27:3; **Num.** 4:13; **Deut.** 31:20; **Ps.** 20:3(4); 23:5; **Prov.** 11:25; 13:4; 15:30; 28:25; **Isa.** 34:6,7.

1879. דָּשֵׁן *dāšēn* **adj.**
(fat, prosperous, rich)
Ps. 22:29(30); 92:14(15); **Isa.** 30:23.

1880. דֶּשֶׁן *dešen* **masc. noun**
(ashes, fatness)
Lev. 1:16; 4:12; 6:10(3),11(4); **Judg.** 9:9; **1 Kgs.** 13:3,5; **Job** 36:16; **Ps.** 36:8(9); 63:5(6); 65:11(12); **Isa.** 55:2; **Jer.** 31:14,40.

1881. דָּת *dāṯ* **fem. noun**
(law, decree)
Ezra 8:36; **Esth.** 1:8,13,15,19; 2:8,12; 3:8,14,15; 4:3,8,11,16; 8:13,14,17; 9:1,13,14.

1882. דָּת *dāṯ* **Aram. fem. noun**
(law, decree; corr. to Hebr. 1881)
Ezra 7:12,14,21,25,26; **Dan.** 2:9,13,15; 6:5(6),8(9),12(13),15(16); 7:25.

1883. דֶּתֶא *deṯe'* **Aram. masc. noun**
(grass)
Dan. 4:15(12),23(20).

1884. דְּתָבַר *d^eṯāḇar* **Aram. masc. noun**
(counselor, judge)
Dan. 3:2,3.

1885. דָּתָן *dāṯān* **masc. proper noun**
(Dathan)
Num. 16:1,12,24,25,27; 26:9; **Deut.** 11:6; **Ps.** 106:17.

1886. דֹּתָן *dōṯān* **proper noun**
(Dothan)
Gen. 37:17; **2 Kgs.** 6:13.

ה Hē

1887. הֵא *hē'* **interj.**
(behold, surely)
Gen. 47:23; **Ezek.** 16:43.

1888. I. הָא *hā'* **Aram. interj.**
(behold!; corr. to Hebr. 1887)
Dan. 3:25.
II. הֵא *hē'* **Aram. interj.**
(behold! even as; corr. to Hebr. 1887)
Dan. 2:43.

1889. הֶאָח *he'āḥ* **interj.**
(aha!)
Job 39:25; **Ps.** 35:21,25; 40:15(16); 70:3(4); **Isa.** 44:16; **Ezek.** 25:3; 26:2; 36:2.

1890. הַבְהַב *hab̲hab̲* **masc. noun**
(gift, offering)
Hos. 8:13.

1891. הָבַל *hāb̲al* **verb**
(to become vain, to fill with false hopes)
2 Kgs. 17:15; **Job** 27:12; **Ps.** 62:10(11); **Jer.** 2:5; 23:16.

1892. הֶבֶל *heb̲el* **masc. noun**
(vanity, emptiness, idols)
Deut. 32:21; **1 Kgs.** 16:13,26; **2 Kgs.** 17:15; **Job** 7:16; 9:29; 21:34; 27:12; 35:16; **Ps.** 31:6(7); 39:5(6),6(7),11(12); 62:9(10); 78:33; 94:11; 144:4; **Prov.** 13:11; 21:6; 31:30; **Eccl.** 1:2,14; 2:1,11, 15,17,19,21,23,26; 3:19; 4:4,7,8,16; 5:7(6),10(9); 6:2,4,9,11,12; 7:6,15; 8:10,14; 9:9; 11:8,10; 12:8; **Isa.** 30:7; 49:4; 57:13; **Jer.** 2:5; 8:19; 10:3,8,15; 14:22; 16:19; 51:18; **Lam.** 4:17; **Jon.** 2:8(9); **Zech.** 10:2.

1893. הֶבֶל *heb̲el* **masc. proper noun**
(Abel)
Gen. 4:2,4,8,9,25.

1894. הָבְנִים *hob̲niym* **masc. noun**
(ebony)
Ezek. 27:15.

1895. הָבַר *hāb̲ar* **verb**
(to practice astrology)
Isa. 47:13.

1896. הֵגֶא *hēge'*, הֵגַי *hēgay* **masc. proper noun**
(Hegai, Hege)
Esth. 2:3,8,15.

1897. הָגָה *hāgāh* **verb**
(to meditate, to ponder)
Josh. 1:8; **Job** 27:4; **Ps.** 1:2; 2:1; 35:28; 37:30; 38:12(13); 63:6(7); 71:24; 77:12(13); 115:7; 143:5; **Prov.** 8:7; 15:28; 24:2; **Isa.** 8:19; 16:7; 31:4; 33:18; 38:14; 59:3,11,13; **Jer.** 48:31.

1898. הָגָה *hāgāh* **verb**
(to take away, to remove)
Prov. 25:4,5; **Isa.** 27:8.

1899. הֶגֶה *hegeh* **masc. noun**
(a moaning, rumbling)
Job 37:2; **Ps.** 90:9; **Ezek.** 2:10.

1900. הָגוּת *hāgûṯ* **fem. noun**
(meditation, utterance)
Ps. 49:3(4).

1901. הָגִיג *hāgiyg* **masc. noun**
(meditation, sighing)
Ps. 5:1(2); 39:3(4).

1902. הִגָּיוֹן *higgāyôn* **masc. noun**
(meditation, resounding music)
Ps. 9:16(17); 19:14(15); 92:3(4); **Lam.** 3:62.

1903. הָגִין *hāgiyn* **adj.**
(appropriate, corresponding)
Ezek. 42:12.

1904. הָגָר *hāgār* **fem. proper noun**
(Hagar)
Gen. 16:1,3,4,8,15,16; 21:9,14,17; 25:12.

1905. I. הַגְרִי *hagriy* **masc. proper noun**
(Hagrite: an officer)
1 Chr. 27:31.
II. הַגְרִי *hagriy* **masc. proper noun**
(Hagri, Haggeri: father of Mibhar)
2 Sam. 23:36(KJV, NASB, *gādiy* [1425]);
1 Chr. 11:38.
III. הַגְרִיאִים *hagriy'iym* **masc. pl. proper noun**
(Hagrite: Arabian Bedouin tribes of Transjordan)
1 Chr. 5:10,19,20; **Ps.** 83:6(7).

1906. הֵד *hēd* **masc. noun**
(joyful shout)
Ezek. 7:7.

1907. הַדָּבָר *haddābar* **Aram. masc. noun**
(royal counselor, adviser)
Dan. 3:24,27; 4:36(33); 6:7(8).

1908. A. הֲדַד *hadad* **masc. proper noun**
(Hadad: son of Bedad)
Gen. 36:35,36,39(KJV, NASB, *hadar* [1924]); **1 Chr.** 1:46,47.
B. הֲדַד *hadad* **masc. proper noun**
(Hadad: an Edomite; see also *'adad* [111])
1 Kgs. 11:14,17,19,21,25.
C. הֲדַד *hadad* **masc. proper noun**
(Hadad: Edomite King)
Gen. 36:39(KJV, NASB *hadar* [1924]);
1 Chr. 1:50,51.

1909. הֲדַדְעֶזֶר *hadad'ezer* **masc. proper noun**
(Hadadezer; see also *hadar'ezer* [1928])
2 Sam. 8:3,5,7–10,12; 10:16(KJV, NASB, *hadar'ezer* [1928]),19(KJV, NASB, *hadar'ezer* [1928]); **1 Kgs.** 11:23;
1 Chr. 18:3,5(KJV, NASB, *hadar'ezer* [1928]),7–10(KJV, NASB, *hadar'ezer* [1928]); 19:16(KJV, NASB, *hadar'ezer* [1928]),19(KJV, NASB, *hadar'ezer* [1928]).

1910. הֲדַד-רִמּוֹן *hadad-rimmôn* **proper noun**
(Hadad Rimmon)
Zech. 12:11.

1911. הָדָה *hādāh* **verb**
(to stretch out, to put)
Isa. 11:8.

1912. הֹדּוּ *hōddû* **proper noun**
(Hoddu [India])
Esth. 1:1; 8:9.

1913. A. הֲדוֹרָם *hadōrām* **masc. proper noun**
(Hadoram: son of Joktan)
Gen. 10:27; **1 Chr.** 1:21.
B. הֲדוֹרָם *hadôrām* **masc. proper noun**
(Hadoram: son of Tou)
1 Chr. 18:10.
C. הֲדוֹרָם *hadôrām* **masc. proper noun**
(Hadoram: another name for *'adōrām* [151])
2 Chr. 10:18.

1914. הִדַּי *hidday* **masc. proper noun**
(Hiddai)
2 Sam. 23:30.

1915. הָדַךְ *hādak* **verb**
(to trample, to crush)
Job 40:12.

1916. הֲדֹם *h^{a}d̲ôm* **masc. noun**
(footstool)
1 Chr. 28:2; **Ps.** 99:5; 110:1; 132:7; **Isa.** 66:1; **Lam.** 2:1.

1917. הַדָּם *haddām* **Aram. masc. noun**
(piece, limb)
Dan. 2:5; 3:29.

1918. הֲדַס *h^{a}das* **masc. noun**
(myrtle tree)
Neh. 8:15; **Isa.** 41:19; 55:13; **Zech.** 1:8,10,11.

1919. הֲדַסָּה *h^{a}d̲assāh* **fem. proper noun**
(Hadassah)
Esth. 2:7.

1920. הָדַף *hād̲ap̱* **verb**
(to shove away, to drive out)
Num. 35:20,22; **Deut.** 6:19; 9:4; **Josh.** 23:5; **2 Kgs.** 4:27; **Job** 18:18; **Prov.** 10:3; **Isa.** 22:19; **Jer.** 46:15; **Ezek.** 34:21.

1921. I. הֲדוּרִים *h^{a}d̲ûriym* **masc. pl. noun**
(mountains, mountainous land)
Isa. 45:2(KJV, NASB, see II).
II. הָדַר *hād̲ar* **verb**
(to swell, to lift up, to exalt, to honor, to respect, to treat with distinction)
Ex. 23:3; **Lev.** 19:15,32; **Prov.** 25:6; **Isa.** 45:2(NIV, see I); 63:1; **Lam.** 5:12.

1922. הֲדַר *h^{a}d̲ar* **Aram. verb**
(to honor, to glorify; corr. to Hebr. 1921,II)
Dan. 4:34(31),37(34); 5:23.

1923. הֲדַר *h^{a}d̲ar* **Aram. noun**
(majesty, honor)
Dan. 4:30(27),36(33); 5:18.

1924. הֲדַר *h^{a}d̲ar* **masc. proper noun**
(Hadar: another spelling for *h^{a}d̲ad̲* [1908,C])
Gen. 36:39(NIV, *h^{a}d̲ad̲* [1908,C]).

1925. הֶדֶר *hed̲er* **masc. noun**
(glory, majesty; const. of *hādār* [1926])
Dan. 11:20.

1926. הָדָר *hād̲ār* **masc. noun**
(glory, majesty)
Lev. 23:40; **Deut.** 33:17; **1 Chr.** 16:27; **Job** 40:10; **Ps.** 8:5(6); 21:5(6); 29:4; 45:3(4),4(5); 90:16; 96:6; 104:1; 110:3; 111:3; 145:5,12; 149:9; **Prov.** 20:29; 31:25; **Isa.** 2:10,19,21; 5:14; 35:2; 53:2; **Lam.** 1:6; **Ezek.** 16:14; 27:10; **Dan.** 11:20(see *hed̲er* [1925]); **Mic.** 2:9.

1927. הֲדָרָה *h^{a}d̲ārāh* **fem. noun**
(glory, majesty)
1 Chr. 16:29; **2 Chr.** 20:21; **Ps.** 29:2; 96:9; **Prov.** 14:28.

1928. הֲדַרְעֶזֶר *h^{a}d̲ar'ezer* **masc. proper noun**
(Hadarezer: another spelling of *h^{a}d̲ad̲'ezer* [1909]; NASB, NIV, *h^{a}d̲ad̲'ezer* [1909])
2 Sam. 10:16,19; **1 Chr.** 18:3,5,7–10; 19:16,19.

1929. הָהּ *hāh* **interj.**
(alas!)
Ezek. 30:2.

1930. הוֹ *hô* **interj.**
(alas)
Amos 5:16.

1931. הִיא *hiy'*, הוּא *hû'* **masc., fem. pron.**
(he, she, it)
Gen. 2:11–14,19; 3:6,12,15,16,20; 4:4, 20–22,26; 6:3; 7:2; 9:3,18; 10:8,9,11,

12,21; 12:14,18,19; 13:1; 14:2,3,7,8,12, 13,15,17,18; 15:2,4,18; 16:12; 17:12,14; 18:1,8,10; 19:20,30,33,35,37,38; 20:2,3, 5,7,12,13,16; 21:13,17,22,31; 22:14, 20,24; 23:2,15,19; 24:7,15,44,54,62,65; 25:21,29; 26:7,9,12,24,32; 27:31,33,38; 28:11,19; 29:2,9,12,25; 30:16,33,35; 31:16,20,21,43; 32:2,13,18,21,22,31; 33:3,16; 34:14,19; 35:6,19,20,22,27; 36:1,8,19,24,43; 37:2,3,27,32; 38:1,11, 12,14,16,21,25; 39:3,6,22,23; 40:10; 41:11,25,26,28,31; 42:6,14,27,38; 43:12,32; 44:5,10,14,17,20; 45:20,26; 47:6,17,18; 48:7,14,19,20; 49:13,19,20; 50:14,22; **Ex.** 1:6,10,16; 2:2; 3:5,8; 4:14,16; 5:6; 6:26,27; 8:19,22; 9:34; 10:13; 12:2,4,11,15,16,19,27,30,42; 13:2,8,17; 14:30; 16:15,23,29,31,36; 18:5,14; 21:3,4,21,29,36; 22:9,15,27; 29:14,18,21,22,25,28,34; 30:10,32; 31:13,14,17; 32:9,16,22,25,28; 34:3,9, 10,14; 35:34; 39:5; **Lev.** 1:13,17; 2:6,15; 3:1,7; 4:21,24; 5:1–4,9,11,12,18,19; 6:5,9,17,25,29; 7:1,5,6,20,21,27; 8:21,28; 10:3,12,13,17; 11:4–7,12,20,23,26, 37–39,41; 13:3,4,6,8,10,11,13,15,17, 20–23,25–28,30,36,37,39–42,44,46,49, 51,52,55,57; 14:13,21,44; 15:2,3,23,25; 16:31; 17:4,9,11,14; 18:7,8,11–17,22,23; 19:7,8,20; 20:3–6,14,17,18,21; 21:7–9,13; 22:3,4,7,11,12,30; 23:3,27,28,30,32,36; 24:9,10; 25:10–12,16,33,34,41,54; 27:4,8,10,23,26,28,30,33; **Num.** 1:4; 5:6,13–15,18,28,31; 6:8,11,20; 8:4; 9:6,13; 10:32; 11:3,7,30,32,34; 12:7; 13:18–20,24,27,31,32; 14:1,8,41,45; 15:25,30,31; 16:7,11,40; 18:9,16,19 ,23,31; 19:9,12,13,15,20; 21:16,26,33; 22:3–6,12,22; 23:6,19; 24:24; 25:15; 26:9; 27:3,21; 32:4,10; 33:36,40; 35:16–19,21,23,31,33; **Deut.** 1:9,16–19, 30,36,38,44; 2:20,32,34; 3:1,4,8,11–13, 18,21–23,28; 4:6,14,24,35,39,42,48; 5:5; 7:9,16,25,26; 8:18; 9:3,13,19,20; 10:1, 8–10,17,21; 11:10; 12:3,23; 13:3,5,15; 14:8,10,19,28; 17:1,5,10,12,15,20; 18:2 ,5,6,20,22; 19:4–6; 20:20; 21:3,4,6,17,23; 22:17,18,24; 23:7; 24:4,6,7,12,15; 27:11; 28:44; 29:13,20,22,27; 30:11–13,20; 31:3,6,8,16–18,21,22; 32:4,6,34,39, 44,47; **Josh.** 2:6,8,11,15,21; 3:1; 4:14,24; 5:2,9,12,15; 6:17,19,26; 7:6,26; 8:9,10, 13,14,25,27; 9:27; 10:2,7,13,14,28,35; 11:10,21; 13:12,14,33; 14:9,12,15; 15:8–11,13,25,49,54,60; 17:1,18; 18:13,14,28; 20:4,6,7; 21:11; 22:20,22, 23,27,28,34; 23:3,5,10; 24:17–19,25,27; **Judg.** 1:26; 2:5,10; 3:19,20,24,26,27, 29–31; 4:2–5,21,23; 5:1,29; 6:22,25,31, 32,35,40; 7:1,4,9,11; 8:4,31; 9:3,18,19, 33,45,48; 10:1,8; 11:1,21,26,34,38,39; 12:6; 13:5,6,9,16,18,21; 14:3,4; 15:14,17; 16:20,31; 17:7; 18:1,12,28,30; 19:9, 10,16; 20:15,21,26,35,39,46; 21:14,24; **Ruth** 1:1,3,6,18; 2:6,20; 3:2,4; 4:15,17; **1 Sam.** 1:3,10,13,28; 3:2,12,18; 4:12,18; 6:9,15,16; 7:6,10; 8:18; 9:13,24,26; 10:9,19,22; 12:18; 14:18,23,24,31,37; 15:29; 16:12,13; 17:5,14,23,29,33,37; 18:2,9,15,16,19,27; 19:9,10,14,17,18, 22–24; 20:26,29,31,33,36; 21:5,7,9,10; 22:9,17,18,22; 23:22,28; 24:6,10; 25:3, 17,20,25,36,37; 27:2,3,6; 28:8,14,25; 29:11; 30:9,10,20,25,31; 31:5,6; **2 Sam.** 2:16,17,29; 3:37; 4:5,7,10; 5:7,8,20; 6:8,9; 7:4,13,14,28; 9:4,13; 11:4,12; 12:23; 13:2,8,20; 14:19,27; 15:30; 17:2,5,9,10,13,24; 18:7,8; 19:2,3,9,32; 20:8; 21:16,20; 22:31; 23:8,10,18,20,21; 24:13,18; **1 Kgs.** 1:6,13,17,24,30,35,45; 2:8,22; 3:3,4,27; 4:15,24; 5:5; 6:1,17,38; 7:14; 8:1,2,19,41,60,64,65; 10:10,13; 11:14,17,28,29; 12:2; 13:3,26; 14:1–3, 5,17; 16:9,16; 17:15,19; 18:24,27,39; 19:4,8,19; 20:3,12,16,28,32,39–41; 21:2; 22:25,32,33,35; **2 Kgs.** 1:8; 2:12,14, 18,23; 3:6,17; 4:5,9; 5:7,15,18,25; 6:5,13,30,32; 7:7,9; 8:2,5,21,22,27,29; 9:14,34,36; 10:12; 14:7,11,21,22,25; 15:12,35; 16:6; 17:39; 18:4,8–10,16, 22,36; 19:15,35,37; 20:12; 22:13,14; 23:15; 24:10,12; 25:1,8,19; **1 Chr.** 1:10,27; 2:21,26,42; 4:11; 5:1,6,8; 6:10; 7:31; 8:7,12; 9:31; 10:5; 11:4,5,11–13,

20,22,23,25; 12:15; 13:11,12; 14:11; 15:22; 16:7,14,25; 17:3,12,13,26; 20:6; 21:17,28,29; 22:1,9,10; 23:13; 25:9; 26:26; 27:6,32; 28:6; 29:16,21,22; **2 Chr.** 1:7; 4:21; 5:2,3; 6:9,32; 7:8; 9:9,12; 10:2; 13:18; 15:11; 16:7,10; 18:7,24,31,34; 20:2,6,25,26,35; 21:3,10,11; 22:3,6,9,11; 25:20,21; 26:1,2,20,23; 27:3,5; 28:3, 16,22; 29:3; 30:3; 32:9,12,26,30; 33:6, 13,23; 34:3,22; 35:16,17; 36:23; **Ezra** 1:2–4; 7:6,8,9; 8:34; 9:11; 10:8,9,23; **Neh.** 1:2; 2:18,20; 3:12,14,15; 4:16,22; 6:1,10,13,18; 7:2; 8:9,10,17; 9:6,7; 12:8, 43,44; 13:1,21; **Esth.** 1:1,11,20; 2:7, 14,16; 3:4,7,13; 5:9; 6:1; 7:5; 8:1,9,12; 9:1,11,24; **Job** 1:1,3; 2:8; 3:4,6,7,19; 4:7; 5:18,27; 8:16,19; 9:22,24; 11:11; 13:16, 19,28; 15:9,20,22,23; 17:3; 21:22,31,32; 22:18; 23:6,13; 24:18; 28:3,14,23,24,28; 31:4,11,12,28; 32:1,8; 34:29; 37:12,21; 39:30; 40:19; 41:10,11,34; **Ps.** 9:8; 18:30; 19:5; 24:2,10; 25:11,15; 28:8; 33:9,20; 37:5; 39:4,7; 44:4,21; 45:11; 48:14; 50:6; 55:22; 60:12; 62:2,6; 68:35; 73:16; 77:10; 78:38; 81:4; 87:5; 89:26; 91:3; 95:5,7; 96:4; 99:2,3,5,6; 100:3; 101:6; 102:27; 103:14; 105:7; 108:13; 115:9–11; 118:23; 119:97,98; 130:8; 146:4; 148:5; 149:9; **Prov.** 3:6,15,18,29,34; 4:13; 5:23; 6:22,32; 7:11,23; 10:18,22,24; 11:25,28; 13:13; 18:9,13; 19:1,21; 21:13,29; 22:9,22; 23:3,7,11,28; 24:12; 28:6,10, 24,26; 30:5,28; 31:30; **Eccl.** 1:5,9,10, 13,17; 2:1,22–24; 3:9,13–15,21,22; 4:4,8; 5:6,9,14,18,19; 6:1,2,10; 7:2,23,26; 8:15; 9:4,9,13,15; 10:3,10; **Song** 6:9; 8:9; **Isa.** 1:13; 2:11,17,20,22; 3:7,18; 4:1,2; 5:30; 7:14,18,20,21,23; 8:13; 9:15; 10:5,7, 20,27; 11:10,11; 12:1,4; 14:24; 17:4,7,9; 18:2,7; 19:16–19,21,23,24; 20:2,6; 22:8,12,20,25; 23:15; 24:21; 25:9; 26:1; 27:1,2,11–13; 28:5; 29:11,18; 30:9,23,33; 31:2,7; 32:7; 33:6,16,22; 34:16,17; 35:4,8; 36:7,21; 37:16,38; 38:15,19; 39:1; 41:4,7; 42:8,22; 43:10,13,25; 45:13,18; 46:4; 47:10; 48:12; 50:9; 51:9,10,12; 52:6; 53:4,5,7,11,12; 59:16; 63:5,9,10; **Jer.** 2:14; 3:1,6,17; 4:9,11; 5:12,15; 6:6,23; 8:1; 10:3,8,10,16; 12:17; 14:22; 17:9; 18:4,8; 20:1,16; 22:4,16,28; 23:34; 25:1,12,13,31,33; 27:7,8; 28:1,17; 29:28; 30:7,8,17,21; 31:1,9; 32:1,8,43; 33:1,10, 15; 37:2,13; 38:4,5,7; 39:10,16,17; 40:1; 41:7,9; 45:4; 46:10; 48:11,26,41; 49:12, 22,26; 50:3,4,15,20,25,30,38; 51:6,11,19; 52:4,12; **Lam.** 1:3,4,8,18; 3:10; **Ezek.** 1:2,13,28; 2:10; 3:18–21; 4:3,12; 10:15,20; 11:3,7,11,15; 12:12,27; 13:10; 14:8,9,17,19; 16:14,46,48; 17:8; 18:4,9, 11,17,20,27; 19:14; 20:6,15,49; 21:11, 12,14,23; 22:24; 23:38,39,43; 24:26,27; 26:17; 28:18; 29:21; 30:9,11,18; 31:18; 32:16; 33:5,6,8,9,13,19; 34:23; 37:1; 38:8,10,14,17–19; 39:8,11,22; 40:3; 44:1,3; 45:1,4,17,22; 46:3,16; 48:15; **Dan.** 8:21,26; 10:4; 11:6,8; 12:1; **Hos.** 1:5; 2:2,8,16,18,21,23; 5:13; 6:1; 7:6,8,9; 8:6; 10:2; 11:5,10; 13:1,13,15; **Joel** 2:13; 3:1,18; **Amos** 1:15; 2:9,16; 5:13,18; 7:2,5,6,13; 8:3,9,13; 9:11; **Obad.** 1:8; **Jon.** 1:10; **Mic.** 1:13; 2:3,4; 3:4; 4:1,6; 5:10; 7:3,11,12,18; **Nah.** 1:2,9; 2:8,11; 3:10; **Hab.** 1:7,10; 2:5,19; **Zeph.** 1:9, 10,12,15; 3:11,16,19,20; **Hag.** 1:9; 2:6,14,23; **Zech.** 1:7,8; 2:11; 3:9,10; 5:6; 6:10,13; 9:4,7,9,16; 11:11; 12:3,4,6,8, 9,11; 13:1,2,4,9; 14:4,6–9,12,13,20,21; **Mal.** 1:7,12; 2:5,7,14,17; 3:2.

1932. הוּא ***hû'***, הִיא ***hiy'*** **Aram. masc., fem. pron.**
(he, she, it; corr. to Hebr. 1931)
Ezra 5:8; 6:15; **Dan.** 2:9,20,21,22,28,32,38,44,47; 3:15; 4:22(19),24(21),30(27); 5:13; 6:4(5),10(11),16(17),26(27); 7:7,24.

1933. I. הָוָה ***hāwāh*** **verb**
(to fall)
Job 37:6(KJV, see II).
II. הָוָה ***hāwāh*** **verb**
(to be, to become, to come to pass)
Gen. 27:29; **Neh.** 6:6; **Job** 37:6(NASB, NIV, see I); **Eccl.** 2:22; 11:3; **Isa.** 16:4.

1934. הֲוָה *hawāh* **Aram. verb**
(to be, to come to pass; corr. to Hebr. 1933,II)
Ezra 4:12,13,20,22,24; 5:5,8,11; 6:6, 8–10; 7:23,25,26; **Dan.** 2:20,28,29,31, 34,35,40–43,45; 3:18; 4:4(1),10(7), 13(10),25(22),27(24),29(26); 5:17,19,29; 6:1–4(2–5),10(11),14(15),26(27); 7:2,4, 6–9,11,13,19,21,23.

1935. הוֹד *hôḏ* **masc. noun**
(splendor, majesty)
Num. 27:20; **1 Chr.** 16:27; 29:11,25; **Job** 37:22; 39:20; 40:10; **Ps.** 8:1(2); 21:5(6); 45:3(4); 96:6; 104:1; 111:3; 145:5; 148:13; **Prov.** 5:9; **Isa.** 30:30; **Jer.** 22:18; **Dan.** 10:8; 11:21; **Hos.** 14:6(7); **Hab.** 3:3; **Zech.** 6:13; 10:3.

1936. הוֹד *hôḏ* **masc. proper noun**
(Hod)
1 Chr. 7:37.

1937. הוֹדְוָה *hôdᵉwāh* **masc. proper noun**
(Hodevah)
Neh. 7:43 (NIV, *hôḏawyāh* [1938]).

1938. הוֹדַוְיָה *hôḏawyāh* **masc. proper noun**
(Hodaviah)
1 Chr. 3:24(KJV, *hôḏaywāhû* [1939]); 5:24; 9:7; **Ezra** 2:40.

1939. הוֹדַיְוָהוּ *hôḏaywāhû* **masc. proper noun**
(Hodaiah)
1 Chr. 3:24(NASB, NIV, *hôḏawyāh* [1938]).

1940. הוֹדִיָּה *hôḏiyyāh* **fem. proper noun**
(Hodiah)
1 Chr. 4:19(NASB, NIV, *hôḏiyyāh* [1941,A]).

1941. A. הוֹדִיָּה *hôḏiyyāh* **masc. proper noun**
(Hodiah: a Jew)
1 Chr. 4:19(KJV, *hôḏiyyah* [1940]).
B. הוֹדִיָּה *hôḏiyyāh* **masc. proper noun**
(Hodijah, Hodiah: a Levite)
Neh. 8:7; 9:5; 10:10(11).
C. הוֹדִיָּה *hôḏiyyāh* **masc. proper noun**
(Hodijah, Hodiah: a Levite)
Neh. 10:13(14).
D. הוֹדִיָּה *hôḏiyyāh* **masc. proper noun**
(Hodijah, Hodiah: a covenanter)
Neh. 10:18(19).

1942. I. הַוָּה *hawwāh* **fem. noun**
(mischief, destruction, calamity)
Job 6:2([Kᵉ] *hayyāh* [1962]),30; 30:13([Kᵉ] *hayyāh* [1962]); **Ps.** 5:9(10); 38:12(13); 52:2(4),7(9)(NASB, see II); 55:11(12); 57:1(2); 91:3; 94:20; **Prov.** 11:6(NASB, NIV, see II); 17:4; 19:13; **Mic.** 7:3(NASB, NIV, see II).
II. הַוָּה *hawwāh* **fem. noun**
(a craving, desire, thing desired)
Ps. 52:7(9)(KJV, NIV, see I); **Prov.** 10:3; 11:6(KJV, see I); **Mic.** 7:3(KJV, see I).

1943. הֹוָה *hōwāh* **fem. noun**
(calamity, ruin)
Isa. 47:11; **Ezek.** 7:26.

1944. הוֹהָם *hôhām* **masc. proper noun**
(Hoham)
Josh. 10:3.

1945. הוֹי *hôy* **interj.**
(ho, woe, alas)
1 Kgs. 13:30; **Isa.** 1:4,24; 5:8,11,18,20–22; 10:1,5; 17:12; 18:1; 28:1; 29:1,15; 30:1; 31:1; 33:1; 45:9,10; 55:1; **Jer.** 22:13,18; 23:1; 30:7; 34:5; 47:6; 48:1; 50:27; **Ezek.** 13:3,18; 34:2; **Amos** 5:18; 6:1; **Mic.** 2:1; **Nah.** 3:1; **Hab.** 2:6,9,12,15,19; **Zeph.** 2:5; 3:1; **Zech.** 2:6(10),7(11); 11:17.

1946. הוּךְ *hûḵ* **Aram. verb**
(to go, to come; NASB, NIV, *halaḵ* [1981])
Ezra 5:5; 6:5; 7:13.

1947. הוֹלֵלוֹת *hôlēlôṯ* **fem. pl. noun**
(madness)
Eccl. 1:17; 2:12; 7:25; 9:3.

1948. הוֹלֵלוּת *hôlēlûṯ* **fem. noun**
(madness)
Eccl. 10:13.

1949. הוּם *hûm* **verb**
(to make a great noise, to stir up, to confuse)
Deut. 7:23(NIV, *hāmam* [2000]); **Ruth** 1:19; **1 Sam.** 4:5; **1 Kgs.** 1:45(NIV, *hāmam* [2000]); **Ps.** 55:2(3); **Mic.** 2:12.

1950. הוֹמָם *hômām* **masc. proper noun**
(Homam)
1 Chr. 1:39.

1951. הוּן *hûn* **verb**
(to be ready, to consider as easy)
Deut. 1:41.

1952. הוֹן *hôn* **masc. noun**
(wealth, substance)
Ps. 44:12(13); 112:3; 119:14; **Prov.** 1:13; 3:9; 6:31; 8:18; 10:15; 11:4; 12:27; 13:7,11; 18:11; 19:4,14; 24:4; 28:8,22; 29:3; 30:15,16; **Song** 8:7; **Ezek.** 27:12, 18,27,33.

1953. הוֹשָׁמָע *hôšāmā'* **masc. proper noun**
(Hoshama)
1 Chr. 3:18.

1954. A. הוֹשֵׁעַ *hôšēa'* **masc. proper noun**
(Hoshea: another name of Joshua)
Num. 13:8,16; **Deut.** 32:44.
B. הוֹשֵׁעַ *hôšēa'* **masc. proper noun**
(Hoshea: king in Israel)
2 Kgs. 15:30; 17:1,3,4,6; 18:1,9,10.
C. הוֹשֵׁעַ *hôšēa'* **masc. proper noun**
(Hoshea: the prophet Hosea)
Hos. 1:1,2.
D. הוֹשֵׁעַ *hôšēa'* **masc. proper noun**
(Hoshea: an Ephramite chief)
1 Chr. 27:20.
E. הוֹשֵׁעַ *hôšēa'* **masc. proper noun**
(Hoshea: a Jewish leader)
Neh. 10:23(24).

1955. A. הוֹשַׁעְיָה *hôša'yāh* **masc. proper noun**
(Hoshaiah: a prince of Judah)
Neh. 12:32.
B. הוֹשַׁעְיָה *hôša'yāh* **masc. proper noun**
(Hoshaiah: father of Jezaniah)
Jer. 42:1; 43:2.

1956. הוֹתִיר *hôṯiyr* **masc. proper noun**
(Hothir)
1 Chr. 25:4,28.

1957. הָזָה *hāzāh* **verb**
(to sleep, to dream)
Isa. 56:10.

1958. הִי *hiy* **masc. noun**
(woe)
Ezek. 2:10.

1959. הֵידָד *hēyḏāḏ* **masc. noun**
(a shout, cheer)
Isa. 16:9,10; **Jer.** 25:30; 48:33; 51:14.

1960. הֻיְּדוֹת *huyyeḏôṯ* **fem. pl. noun**
(songs of thanksgiving)
Neh. 12:8.

1961. הָיָה *hāyāh* **verb**
(to be, to become)

Gen. 1:2,3,5–9,11,13–15,19,23,24,29–31; 2:5,7,10,18,24,25; 3:1,5,20,22; 4:2,3,8,12, 14,17,20,21; 5:4,5,8,11,14,17,20,23,27, 31,32; 6:1,3,4,9,19,21; 7:6,10,12,17; 8:5,6,13; 9:2,3,11,13–16,18,25–27,29; 10:8–10,19,30; 11:1–3,30,32; 12:2,10–12, 14,16; 13:3,5–8; 14:1; 15:1,5,12,13,17; 16:12; 17:1,4,5,7,8,11,13,16; 18:11,12, 18,25; 19:14,17,26,29,34; 20:12,13; 21:20,22,30; 22:1,20; 23:1; 24:14,15,22, 30,41,43,51,52,60,67; 25:3,11,20,27; 26:1,3,8,14,28,32,34,35; 27:1,12,23,30, 33,39,40; 28:3,14,20–22; 29:10,13,17, 20,23,25; 30:25,29,30,32,34,41–43; 31:3,5,8,10,40,42,44; 32:5,8,10; 33:9; 34:5,10,15,16,22,25; 35:3,5,10,11, 16–18,22,28; 36:7,11–14,22; 37:2,20, 23,27; 38:1,5,7,9,21–24,27–29; 39:2,5–7, 10,11,13,15,18–22; 40:1,4,13,20; 41:1,8, 13,27,36,40,48,53,54,56; 42:5,11,31, 35,36; 43:2,21; 44:9,10,17,24,31; 45:10; 46:12,32–34; 47:9,19,20,24–26,28; 48:1,5,6,19,21; 49:15,17,26; 50:9; **Ex.** 1:5,10,21; 2:10,11,22,23; 3:1,12,14,21; 4:3,4,8,9,12,15,16,24; 5:13; 6:7,28; 7:1,9, 10,12,19,21; 8:15–18,22,23; 9:3,9–11,18, 22,24,26,28,29; 10:6,7,10,13,14,21–23; 11:6; 12:4–6,13,14,16,25,26,29,30,41, 48,49,51; 13:5,9,11,12,14–17; 14:20,24; 15:2; 16:5,10,13,22,24,26,27; 17:11,12; 18:3,13,16,19,22; 19:5,6,11,15,16,19; 20:3,20; 21:4,22,23,34,36; 22:11,21,24, 25,27,30,31; 23:1,2,9,26,29,33; 24:12,18; 25:15,20,27,31,36; 26:3,6,11,13,24,25; 27:1,2,5,7; 28:7,8,16,20,21,28,30,32,35, 37,38,42,43; 29:9,26,28,29,37,45; 30:2,4,12,16,21,25,29,31,32,34,36,37; 32:1,19,23,30; 33:7–9,22; 34:1,2,12,28,29; 35:2; 36:7,13,18,29,30; 37:9,14,17,22,25; 38:2,24,27; 39:9,21; 40:9,10,15,17,38; **Lev.** 2:1,5; 5:5,13; 6:4,23; 7:7–10,14,18, 31,33; 8:29; 9:1; 10:15; 11:11,35,36, 44,45; 13:2,9,18,19,24,29,32,38,42,45, 47,49,52; 14:2,9,22; 15:2,3,10,17,19, 24–26; 16:4,17,29,34; 17:7; 19:2,20,23, 24,34,36; 20:7,14,21,26,27; 21:3,6,8, 17,19; 22:12,13,20,21,27,33; 23:7,15, 17,18,20,21,24,27,36; 24:5,7,9,22; 25:4–8,10–12,26,28,29,31,32,38,40,44, 45,48,50,53; 26:12,13,33,37,44,45; 27:3–7,9,10,12,15,16,21,25,32,33; **Num.** 1:4,20,44–46,53; 3:4,12,13,17,43,45; 4:7,27,36,40,44,48; 5:9,10,17,18,27; 6:5; 7:1,5,12; 8:11,14,19; 9:6,10,13–16,20,21; 10:2,8,10,11,31,32,35; 11:1,8,20,25,35; 12:6,12; 13:33; 14:3,24,31,33,43; 15:15, 16,19,24,29,32,39–41; 16:7,16,31,38,40, 42,49; 17:5,8; 18:5,9,10,13–15,18,20; 19:9,10,13,18,21; 20:2; 21:8,9; 22:41; 23:10; 24:2,18,22; 25:9,13; 26:1,7,10,20, 21,33,40,62,64; 27:3,11,17; 28:14,19,25, 26,31; 29:1,7,8,12,13,35; 30:6; 31:3,16, 32,36,37,43,52; 32:1,22,26; 33:14,54–56; 34:3–9,12; 35:3,5,11–15,29; 36:3,4,6,8, 11,12; **Deut.** 1:3,39; 2:15,16,36; 3:4; 4:20,32; 5:7,15,23,29; 6:6,8,10,21,25; 7:6,12,14,26; 8:19; 9:7,11,22,24; 10:2,5, 9,19; 11:13,17,18,24,29; 12:11,26; 13:9,16; 14:2; 15:3,4,7,9,15–17,21; 16:12,15; 17:1,7,9,18,19; 18:1–3,13, 19,22; 19:3,10,11,17; 20:2,9,11,14; 21:3,5,13–16,18,22; 22:2,5,19,20,23,29; 23:7,10–14,17,21,22; 24:1,2,4,5,13,15, 18–22; 25:1,2,5,6,13–15,19; 26:1,3,5, 17–19; 27:2,4,9; 28:1,13,15,23,25,26,29, 33,34,37,40,41,44,46,62,63,65,66; 29:13,19; 30:1,4; 31:8,17,19,21,23, 24,26,27; 32:38; 33:5–7,24; **Josh.** 1:1,4,5,17; 2:5,14,19,20; 3:2,4,7,13,14; 4:1,6,7,9,11,18; 5:1,5,7,8,12,13; 6:5,8, 15–17,20,27; 7:5,12,14,15; 8:4,5,8,14, 20,22,24,25,35; 9:1,5,12,16,20,21; 10:1, 11,14,20,24,26,27; 11:1,19,20; 13:16, 23,25,29,30; 14:4,9,14; 15:1,2,4,7,18,21; 16:3,5,8,10; 17:1–3,6–11,13,17,18; 18:12,14,
19,21; 19:1,2,9,10,14,18,22,25,29,33,41; 20:3,6,9; 21:4,10,20,40,42; 22:17,18, 20,28; 23:1,13,15; 24:27,29,32; **Judg.** 1:1,7,14,19,28,30,33,35; 2:3,4,15,18,19; 3:4,10,18,27,31; 4:9,20; 6:3,7,16,25,27, 37–40; 7:1,4,6,8,9,15,17; 8:11,26,27, 30,33; 9:33,42,51; 10:4,18; 11:1,4–6,8–10, 29,31,35,39; 12:2,5,9,14; 13:2,5,7,12,20;

14:11,15,17,20; 15:1,2,14,17; 16:4,7,11, 16,17,21,25,30; 17:1,4,5,7,10–13; 18:4,19,27,30,31; 19:1,2,5,30; 20:3,12, 38,46; 21:3–5,22; **Ruth** 1:1,2,7,11–13, 19; 2:12,13,17,19; 3:2,4,8,13; 4:12,13, 15,16; **1 Sam.** 1:1,2,4,12,18,20,28; 2:11, 17,27,31,32,36; 3:1,2,9,19; 4:1,5,7,9,10, 13,16–18; 5:9–11; 6:1,9; 7:2,10,13,14; 8:1,2,11,17,19,20; 9:1,2,26; 10:5,7,9,11, 12,27; 11:8,9,11; 12:14,15; 13:2,10,21,22; 14:1,14,15,18–21,25,38,40,49,52; 15:10,26; 16:6,16,21,23; 17:9,25,34,36, 37,42,48; 18:1,6,9,10,12,14,17–19, 21,29,30; 19:7–9,20,23; 20:13,24,27, 35,42; 21:6,8; 22:2,4; 23:6,17,22,23,26; 24:1,5,12,13,15,16; 25:2,7,15,16,20,26, 29–31,37,38,42,43; 27:6,7,12; 28:1,16, 20,22; 29:3,4,8; 30:1,25; 31:8; **2 Sam.** 1:1,2,4; 2:1,7,10,11,17,18,23,25,26; 3:1, 2,6,17,37; 4:2–4,10; 5:2,24; 6:13,16,22,23; 7:1,4,6,8,9,14,16,24,26,28,29; 8:1,2,6,7, 10,14,15,18; 9:9,10; 10:1,5,9,11; 11:1,2, 14,16,20,23,27; 12:1–3,10,18,30; 13:1, 13,20,23,28,30,32,35,36,38; 14:2,17, 25–27; 15:1,2,4,5,7,12–14,21,32–35; 16:16,18,19; 17:3,9,21,27; 18:3,6–8, 22,23,32; 19:2,9,11–13,22,25,28,35,43; 20:3,26; 21:1,15,18–20; 22:19,24; 23:11, 19; 24:9,11,13,16,17; **1 Kgs.** 1:2,4,7,8, 21,27,35,37,52; 2:2,7,15,27,33,37,39,45; 3:12,13,18,21,26; 4:1,7,11,21,22,24,26, 28,31,32; 5:1,6,7,10,12–15; 6:1,11,17; 7:8; 8:8,10,16–18,29,35,37,38,52,54,57, 59,61; 9:1,3,7,8,10,19; 10:2,3,5,6,9,14,26; 11:3,4,11,15,20,24,25,29,32,36–38,40; 12:2,6,7,15,20,22,24,30,31; 13:4,6,20,23, 24,31–34; 14:3,5,6,8,9,24,25,28,30; 15:3,6,7,14,16,21,29,32; 16:1,7,11,18, 21,31,33; 17:1,2,4,7,8,17; 18:1,3,4,7,12, 17,24,27,29,31,36,44–46; 19:13,17; 20:6, 12,15,26,29,39,40,42; 21:1,2,15–17, 25,27,28; 22:2,13,22,32,33,35; **2 Kgs.** 1:17; 2:1,9–11,21; 3:4,5,9,15,20,27; 4:1,6,8,10,11,18,25,40,41; 5:1,2,7,8; 6:5,8,20,24–26,30; 7:2,3,16,18–20; 8:3,5,15,17,18,21; 9:14,22,37; 10:7,9,25; 11:3,8,17; 12:6,10,16; 13:21; 14:2,5; 15:2,5,12,19,33; 16:15; 17:2,3,7,25,28, 29,32,33,41; 18:1,2,4,5,7,9; 19:1,25, 26,35,37; 20:4,13,15,18,19; 21:14,15; 22:3,11,19; 23:25,27; 24:1,3,7,20; 25:1,3,16,25,27; **1 Chr.** 1:10,51; 2:3,22,25–28,33,34,50,52; 3:1; 4:5,9, 10,14; 6:32,54,66; 7:15,19,23; 8:3,40; 9:20,24,26; 10:8; 11:2,6,13,20,21; 12:17,21,39; 14:4,15; 15:25,26,29; 16:19; 17:1,3,5,7,8,11,13,14,22,27; 18:1,2, 6,7,10,13,14; 19:1,5,10,12; 20:1,2,4–6; 21:3,5,17; 22:7–11,14,16; 23:3,11,17,22; 24:2,5,28; 25:1,7; 26:10; 27:24; 28:4,6, 12; 29:25; **2 Chr.** 1:3,11,12,14; 5:8,9, 11,13; 6:5–8,20,26,28,29,40; 7:13, 15,16,21; 8:1,6; 9:1,4,8,9,13,25,26; 10:2,6,7,15; 11:2,4,12; 12:1,2,7,8,11,12; 13:2,7,9,13,15; 14:8,14; 15:1,2,17,19; 16:5,8; 17:3,5,10,12,13; 18:1,12, 21,31,32,34; 19:7,10,11; 20:1,14,25,29; 21:6,9,19,20; 22:3,4,7,8,11,12; 23:7,16; 24:4,11,12,14,18,23; 25:3,14,16; 26:5,10,11,15,21; 27:8; 28:9,23; 29:8,11,32,34,36; 30:7,10,12,26; 32:25,27,31; 33:4; 34:19; 36:16,20; **Ezra** 1:3; 4:4; 8:31; 9:2,8; **Neh.** 1:1,4,6,9,11; 2:1,6,11,13,15,17; 3:26; 4:1,4,6,7,12,15, 16,22; 5:1,13,14,18; 6:1,8,13,14,16,19; 7:1; 8:5,17; 10:38; 12:12; 13:3,5,6,19, 22,26; **Esth.** 1:1,22; 2:5,7,8,12,15,20; 3:4,14; 5:1,2; 6:1; 8:13,16; 9:21,27; **Job** 1:1,3,5,6,13,14,21; 2:1; 3:4,7,16; 5:16; 6:10,21,29; 8:7; 10:19; 11:4,15,17; 12:4; 13:5; 15:31; 16:8,12,18; 17:6; 18:12; 19:15; 20:23; 21:2,18; 22:25; 24:13,14; 27:7; 29:4,15; 30:9,29,31; 38:4; 42:7, 12,13; **Ps.** 1:3; 9:9; 10:14; 18:18,23; 19:14; 22:14; 27:9; 30:7,10; 31:2,11,12; 32:9; 33:9,22; 35:5,6; 37:18,25; 38:14; 42:3; 45:16; 50:21; 53:5; 55:18; 59:16; 61:3; 62:12; 63:7,10; 64:7; 69:8,10,11, 22,25; 71:3,7; 72:16,17; 73:14,19,22; 76:2; 78:8; 79:4; 80:17; 81:9,15; 83:8,10; 88:4; 89:36,41; 90:1,5,17; 92:14; 94:22; 99:8; 102:6,7; 104:20,31; 105:12; 106:36; 109:7–9,12,13,15,19,25; 112:2,6; 113:2; 114:2; 115:8; 118:14,21–23; 119:54,56,

76,80,83,173; 122:2,7; 124:1,2; 126:1,3; 129:6; 130:2; 135:18; 139:22; 141:10; **Prov.** 1:14; 3:7,8,22,26,27; 4:3; 5:14, 17,18; 8:30; 12:8,24; 13:19; 14:23,26,35; 22:19,26; 23:20,34; 24:1,20,28; 26:5; 29:21; 31:14; **Eccl.** 1:9–12,16; 2:7,9,10, 18,19; 3:14,15,20,22; 4:3,16; 5:2; 6:3, 10,12; 7:10,14,16,17,19,24; 8:7,12,13; 9:8; 10:14; 11:2,8; 12:7,9; **Song** 1:7; 7:8; 8:10,11; **Isa.** 1:9,14,18,21,22,30,31; 2:2; 3:6,7,24; 4:2,3,6; 5:1,5,9,12,24,25; 6:13; 7:1,7,18,21–25; 8:8,14,21; 9:5,6,16,19; 10:2,12,14,17–20,22,27; 11:5,10,11,16; 12:2; 13:14,19; 14:2,3,24,28; 15:6; 16:2,12; 17:1–5,9; 18:5; 19:10,15–20, 23,24; 22:7,20,21,23; 23:3,13,15,17,18; 24:2,13,18,21; 25:4; 26:17; 27:12,13; 28:4,5,13,18,19; 29:2,4,5,7,8,11,13,15; 30:3,4,8,13,15,20,23,25,26,29,32; 31:8; 32:2,14,15,17; 33:2,6,9,12; 34:9,12,13; 35:7–9; 36:1; 37:1,26,27,38; 38:4; 39:2, 4,7,8; 40:4; 41:11,12; 42:22; 43:10; 44:15; 45:14; 46:1; 47:7,14,15; 48:16, 18,19; 49:5,6,23; 50:11; 51:6,8; 55:6, 11,13; 56:6,12; 58:5,11; 59:2,6,15; 60:15,19,20,22; 61:7; 62:3; 63:8,19; 64:6,10,11; 65:10,20,24; 66:2,23,24; **Jer.** 1:2–4,11,13; 2:1,10,14,28,31; 3:1,3,9,16; 4:9,10,17,27; 5:8,13,19,23,30; 6:10; 7:1, 11,23,24,33,34; 8:2; 11:1,4,13,23; 12:8, 15,16; 13:3,6,8,10,11; 14:1,4,5,8,9,13, 15,16; 15:2,16,18,19; 16:1,2,4,10; 17:6–8,11,16,17,24; 18:1,5,21,23; 19:13; 20:3,7–9,14,16,17; 21:1,9; 22:5,24; 23:9, 10,12,14,17,36; 24:4,7; 25:1,3,11,12,28, 33,38; 26:1,8,9,18,20,24; 27:1,8,17,22; 28:1,8,12; 29:7,26,30,32; 30:1,8,16, 20–22; 31:1,9,12,28,33,36; 32:1,2,5,6,24, 26,30,31,38; 33:1,9,12,19–21,23,24; 34:1,5,8,12,16,20; 35:1,7,9,11,12; 36:1, 9,16,23,27,28,30; 37:6,11,13; 38:2,28; 39:4,15,16,18; 40:1,3; 41:1–4,6,7,13; 42:4,5,7,16–18; 43:1,8; 44:1,6,8,12,14, 17,22,26; 46:1,2,19; 47:1,2; 48:6,9,19, 26–28,34,39,41; 49:2,13,17,22,32–34, 36,39; 50:3,6,8,10,13,23,26,29,37; 51:2, 26,30,37,41,43,62,63; 52:3,4,6,20,23, 25,31; **Lam.** 1:1,2,5–8,11,16,17,21; 2:5,22; 3:14,37,47; 4:8–10,19; 5:1,3,17; **Ezek.** 1:1,3,12,16,20,25,28; 2:5,8; 3:3,16,22,26; 4:3; 5:15,16; 6:1,8,13; 7:1,4,9,16,19,26; 8:1; 9:3,8; 10:6,10; 11:11,13,14,16,20; 12:1,8,17,20,21, 24,26; 13:1,4,9,11,13,21; 14:2,10–12, 14–16; 15:1,2,5; 16:1,8,15,16,19,22, 23,31,34,49,56,63; 17:1,6–8,11,14,23; 18:1,3,5,13,20,30; 19:3,6,10,11,14; 20:1,2,12,20,24,32,45; 21:1,7,8,10,12, 13,18,22,23,27,32; 22:1,6,9,13,17–19,23; 23:1,2,4,10,32; 24:1,7,15,20,24,27; 25:1; 26:1,5,14,17; 27:1,7–11,19,36; 28:1,11, 13,14,19,20,24; 29:1,6,9,12,14–19; 30:1,3,4,7,9,13,16,20; 31:1,3,7,8,13; 32:1,17,23,27; 33:1,4,5,21–24,33; 34:1,2,5,8,10,12,14,22–24,26–29; 35:1,4,5,10,15; 36:2–4,12,13,16,17, 28,34,35,38; 37:1,7,15,17,19,20, 22–24,26–28; 38:1,7–10,16,18,19,21; 39:8,11,13; 40:1,21; 41:6; 43:6,27; 44:2,7,11,12,17,18,22,25,28–30; 45:2–6,8,10–12,16,17,21; 46:1,6,11, 16,17; 47:9,10,12,17,22,23; 48:1,8, 10,12,15,17,18,21,22,28; **Dan.** 1:6,16,21; 2:1; 8:2,5,7,15,19,27; 9:2; 10:2,4,7,9; 11:17,29,42; 12:1; **Hos.** 1:1,5,9,10; 2:16,21; 3:3; 4:9; 5:1,9,10; 7:2,8,11,16; 8:6,8,11; 9:10,17; 11:4; 12:11; 13:3,7,10,14; 14:5,6; **Joel** 1:1,2; 2:2,3,28,32; 3:17–19; **Amos** 1:1; 3:6; 4:11; 5:5,14; 6:9; 7:2,3,6; 8:9; **Obad.** 1:16–18,21; **Jon.** 1:1,4,17; 3:1,3; 4:2,5,6,8,10; **Mic.** 1:1,2; 2:4,5,11; 3:12; 4:1; 5:2,5,7,8,10,12; 7:1,4,10,13; **Nah.** 3:7,9,11; **Hab.** 1:3; 2:7; 3:4; **Zeph.** 1:1,8,10,12,13; 2:4,6,7,9,15; 3:18; **Hag.** 1:1,3; 2:1,9,10,16,20; **Zech.** 1:1,4,7; 2:5,9,11; 3:3; 4:8; 6:9,13–15; 7:1,4,7,8, 12,13; 8:1,8,10,13,18,19; 9:7; 10:5–7; 12:2,3,8,9; 13:1–4,8; 14:6–9,11–13, 15–21; **Mal.** 1:9; 2:4–6; 3:3,5,10,12,17; 4:1,3.

1962. הַיָּה *hayyāh* **fem. noun** (calamity, destruction)

Job 6:2(KJV, NASB, NIV, [Q[e]] *hawwāh* [1942]).

1963. הֵיךְ *hēyk̲* **adv.**
(how)
1 Chr. 13:12; **Dan.** 10:17.

1964. הֵיכָל *hēyk̲āl* **masc. noun**
(temple, palace)
1 Sam. 1:9; 3:3; **2 Sam.** 22:7; **1 Kgs.** 6:3,5,17,33; 7:21,50; 21:1; **2 Kgs.** 18:16; 20:18; 23:4; 24:13; **2 Chr.** 3:17; 4:7,8,22; 26:16; 27:2; 29:16; 36:7; **Ezra** 3:6,10; 4:1; **Neh.** 6:10,11; **Ps.** 5:7(8); 11:4; 18:6(7); 27:4; 29:9; 45:8(9),15(16); 48:9(10); 65:4(5); 68:29(30); 79:1; 138:2; 144:12; **Prov.** 30:28; **Isa.** 6:1; 13:22; 39:7; 44:28; 66:6; **Jer.** 7:4; 24:1; 50:28; 51:11; **Ezek.** 8:16; 41:1,4,15,20,21, 23,25; 42:8; **Dan.** 1:4; **Hos.** 8:14; **Joel** 3:5(4:5); **Amos** 8:3; **Jon.** 2:4(5),7(8); **Mic.** 1:2; **Nah.** 2:6(7); **Hab.** 2:20; **Hag.** 2:15,18; **Zech.** 6:12–15; 8:9; **Mal.** 3:1.

1965. הֵיכַל *hēyk̲al* **Aram. masc. noun**
(temple, palace; corr. to Hebr. 1964)
Ezra 4:14; 5:14,15; 6:5; **Dan.** 4:4(1),29(26); 5:2,3,5; 6:18(19).

1966. הֵילֵל *hēylēl* **masc. noun**
(morning star, Lucifer)
Isa. 14:12.

1967. הֵימָם *hēymām* **masc. proper noun**
(Hemam: another spelling of *hômām* [1950])
Gen. 36:22(NIV, *hômām* [1950]).

1968. A. הֵימָן *hēymān* **masc. proper noun**
(Heman: a sage under Solomon)
1 Kgs. 4:31(5:11); **1 Chr.** 2:6.
B. הֵימָן *hēymān* **masc. proper noun**
(Heman: a chief singer)
1 Chr. 6:33(18); 15:17,19; 16:41,42; 25:1,4–6; **2 Chr.** 5:12; 29:14; 35:15; **Ps.** 88:[title](1).

1969. הִין *hiyn* **masc. noun**
(hin: a unit of liquid measure)
Ex. 29:40; 30:24; **Lev.** 19:36; 23:13; **Num.** 15:4–7,9,10; 28:5,7,14; **Ezek.** 4:11; 45:24; 46:5,7,11,14.

1970. I. הָכַר *hāk̲ar* **verb**
(to act as a stranger)
Job 19:3(NASB, NIV, see II).
II. הָכַר *hāk̲ar*, חָכַר *hāk̲ar* **verb**
(to injure, to wrong, to attack)
Job 19:3(KJV, see I).

1971. הַכָּרָה *hakkārāh* **fem. noun**
(appearance, expression)
Isa. 3:9.

1972. הָלָא *hālā'* **verb**
(to be carried away)
Mic. 4:7.

1973. הָלְאָה *hāl[e]'āh* **adv.**
(beyond, away)
Gen. 19:9; 35:21; **Lev.** 22:27; **Num.** 15:23; 16:37(17:2); 32:19; **1 Sam.** 10:3; 18:9; 20:22,37; **Isa.** 18:2,7; **Jer.** 22:19; **Ezek.** 39:22; 43:27; **Amos** 5:27.

1974. הִלּוּל *hillûl* **masc. noun**
(praise, a rejoicing)
Lev. 19:24; **Judg.** 9:27.

1975. הַלָּז *hallāz* **demons. pron.**
(this, that)
Judg. 6:20; **1 Sam.** 14:1; 17:26; **2 Kgs.** 4:25; 23:17; **Dan.** 8:16; **Zech.** 2:4(8).

1976. הַלָּזֶה *hallāzeh* **masc. pron.**
(this, that)
Gen. 24:65; 37:19.

1977. הַלֵּזוּ *hallēzû* **fem. pron.**
(this)
Ezek. 36:35.

1978. הָלִיךְ *hāliyk̲* **masc. noun**
(a step, path)
Job 29:6.

1979. הֲלִיכָה *h^aliyk̲ah* **fem. noun**
(a going, procession, traveling group)
Job 6:19; **Ps.** 68:24(25); **Prov.** 31:27; **Nah.** 2:5(6); **Hab.** 3:6.

1980. הָלַךְ *hālak̲* **verb**
(to go, to walk, to proceed, to follow)
Gen. 2:14; 3:8,14; 5:22,24; 6:9; 7:18; 8:3,5; 9:23; 11:31; 12:1,4,5,9,19; 13:3, 5,17; 14:11,12,24; 15:2; 16:8; 17:1; 18:16,22,33; 19:2,32; 21:14,16,19; 22:2,3,5,6,8,13,19; 24:4,5,8,10,38–40, 42,51,55,56,58,61,65; 25:22,32,34; 26:1,13,16,17,26,31; 27:5,9,13,14; 28:2,5,7,9,10,15,20; 29:1,7; 30:14,25,26; 31:19,30,44,55; 32:1,6,17,19,20; 33:12; 34:17; 35:3,22; 36:6; 37:12–14,17,20, 25,27; 38:11,19; 41:55; 42:19,26,33,38; 43:8; 45:17,24,28; 48:15; 50:18; **Ex.** 2:1,5,7–9; 3:10,11,16,18,19,21; 4:12,18, 19,21,27,29; 5:3,4,7,8,11,17,18; 7:15; 8:25,27,28; 9:23; 10:8,9,11,24,26,28; 12:28,31,32; 13:21; 14:19,21,29; 15:19,22; 16:4; 17:5; 18:20,27; 19:10,19, 24; 21:19; 23:23; 32:1,7,23,34; 33:1, 14–16; 34:9; **Lev.** 11:20,21,27,42; 18:3,4; 19:16; 20:23; 26:3,12,13,21,23, 24,27,28,40,41; **Num.** 10:29,30,32; 12:9; 13:26; 14:14,38; 16:25,46; 20:17; 21:22; 22:6,7,11–14,16,17,20–23,35,37,39; 23:3,7,13,27; 24:1,14,25; 32:39,41,42; 33:8; **Deut.** 1:19,30,31,33; 2:7,14,27; 4:3; 5:30,33; 6:7,14; 8:2,6,15,19; 10:11,12; 11:19,22,28; 13:2,4–6,13; 14:25; 16:7; 17:3; 19:9; 20:4–8; 23:14; 24:2; 26:2,17; 28:9,14,36,41; 29:5, 18,19,26; 30:16; 31:1,6,8,14; **Josh.** 1:7,9,16; 2:1,5,16,21,22; 3:3,4,6; 4:18; 5:6,13; 6:8,9,13; 8:9,13,35; 9:4,6,11,12; 10:24; 14:10; 16:8; 17:7; 18:4,8,9; 22:4–6,9; 23:14,16; 24:3,17; **Judg.** 1:3,10,11,16,17,26; 2:6,12,17,19,22; 3:13; 4:6,8,9,22,24; 5:6,10; 6:14,21; 7:4,7; 8:1,29; 9:1,4,6–14,21,49,50,55; 10:14; 11:5,6,8,11,16,18,37,38,40; 12:1; 13:11; 14:3,9; 15:4; 16:1; 17:8–10; 18:2,5–7,9,14,19,21,24,26; 19:2,3,5, 7–11,13,14,17,18,27,28; 20:8; 21:10,20, 21,23,24; **Ruth** 1:1,7,8,11,12,16,18, 19,21; 2:2,3,8,9,11; 3:10; **1 Sam.** 1:17,18; 2:11,20,26,30,35; 3:5,6,8,9; 6:6,8,12; 7:16; 8:3,5,22; 9:3,5–7,9,10; 10:2,9,14,26; 11:14,15; 12:2; 14:1,3,6, 16,17,19,46; 15:3,6,18,20,27,32,34; 16:1,2,13; 17:7,13–15,20,32,33,37, 39,41,44,48; 18:27; 19:12,18,22,23; 20:11,13,21,22,40,42; 22:1,3,5; 23:2,3,5,13,16,18,22–28; 24:2,7,22; 25:15,27,42; 26:11,12,19,25; 28:7,8, 22,25; 29:7,8,10,11; 30:2,9,21,22,31; 31:12; **2 Sam.** 2:19,29,32; 3:1,16, 19,21–24; 4:5,7; 5:6,10; 6:2,4,12,19; 7:3,5–7,9,23; 8:3,6,14; 10:11; 11:2,22; 12:15,23,29; 13:7,8,13,15,19,24–26, 34,37,38; 14:8,21,23,30; 15:7,9,11,12, 14,19,20,22,30; 16:13,17; 17:11,17,18, 21,23; 18:21,24,25,33; 19:15,24–26; 20:5,21; 21:12; 23:17; 24:1,12; **1 Kgs.** 1:12,13,38,49,50,53; 2:2–4,8,26,29, 40–42; 3:3,4,6,14; 6:12; 8:23,25,36,58, 61,66; 9:4,6; 10:13; 11:5,10,21,22,24, 33,38; 12:1,5,16,24,30; 13:9,10,12,14, 15,17,24,28; 14:2,4,7–9,12,17; 15:3, 19,26,34; 16:2,19,26,31; 17:3,5,9–11,15; 18:1,2,5,6,8,11,12,14,16,18,21,35,45; 19:3,4,8,15,19–21; 20:9,22,27,36,38,43; 21:26,27; 22:4,6,13,15,43,48,49,52; **2 Kgs.** 1:2–4,6; 2:1,6,7,11,16,18,25; 3:7,9,13; 4:3,5,7,23–25,29,30,35; 5:5,10–12,19,24–26; 6:2–4,13,19,22,23; 7:4,8,9,14,15; 8:1,2,8–10,14,18,27,28; 9:1,4,15,16,18,35; 10:12,15,16,25,31; 13:2,6,11,21; 14:8; 16:3,10; 17:8,15, 19,22,27; 19:36; 20:3,9; 21:21,22; 22:2,13,14; 23:3,29; 24:15; 25:4,20; **1 Chr.** 4:39,42; 6:15; 11:4,9; 12:20; 15:25; 16:20,43; 17:4,6,8,11,21; 18:3, 6,13; 19:5; 21:2,4,10,30; **2 Chr.** 1:3; 6:14,16,27,31; 7:17,19; 8:3,17; 9:12,21;

10:1,5,16; 11:4,14,17; 16:3; 17:3,4,12; 18:3,5,12,14; 20:32,36,37; 21:6,12,13,20; 22:3,5; 24:25; 25:10,11,13,17; 26:8; 28:2; 30:6; 33:11; 34:2,21,22,31; 35:24; 36:6; **Ezra** 8:31; 10:6; **Neh.** 2:16,17; 5:9; 6:2,7,17; 8:10,12; 9:12,19; 10:29; 12:31(KJV, NASB, *tah^a^lukāh* [8418]), 32,38; **Esth.** 2:11; 4:16; 9:4; **Job** 1:4,7; 2:2; 7:9; 10:21; 12:17,19; 14:20; 16:6,22; 18:8; 19:10; 20:25; 22:14; 23:8; 24:10; 27:21; 29:3; 30:28; 31:5,7,26; 34:8,23; 38:16,35; 41:19; 42:8,9; **Ps.** 1:1; 12:8; 15:2; 23:4; 26:1,3,11; 32:8; 33:22; 34:11; 35:14; 38:6; 39:6,13; 42:9; 43:2; 46:8; 55:14; 56:13; 58:7,8; 66:5,16; 68:21; 73:9; 77:17; 78:10,39; 80:2; 81:12,13; 82:5; 83:4; 84:7,11; 85:13; 86:11; 89:15,30; 91:6; 95:1; 97:3; 101:2,6; 104:3,10,26; 105:13,41; 106:9; 107:7; 109:23; 115:7; 116:9; 119:1,3,45; 122:1; 125:5; 126:6; 128:1; 131:1; 136:16; 138:7; 139:7; 142:3; 143:8; **Prov.** 1:11,15; 2:7,13,20; 3:23,28; 4:12,18; 6:3,6,11,12,22,28; 7:18,19,22; 8:20; 9:5; 10:9; 11:13; 13:20; 14:2,7; 15:12,21; 16:29; 19:1; 20:7,19; 23:31; 24:34; 28:6,18,26; 30:29; **Eccl.** 1:4,6,7; 2:1,14; 3:20; 4:15; 5:1,15,16; 6:4,6,8,9; 7:2; 8:3,10; 9:7,10; 10:3,7,15,20; 11:9; 12:5; **Song** 2:10,11,13; 4:6; 6:1; 7:9,11; **Isa.** 1:18; 2:3,5; 3:16; 6:8,9; 8:6,7,11; 9:2; 18:2; 20:2,3; 21:6; 22:15; 26:20; 28:13; 30:2,21,29; 33:15,21; 35:8,9; 37:37; 38:3,5,10; 40:31; 42:5,16,24; 43:2; 45:2,14,16; 46:2; 48:17,21; 50:10,11; 52:12; 55:1,3; 57:2,17; 58:8; 59:9; 60:3,14; 63:12,13; 65:2; **Jer.** 1:7; 2:2,5,6,8,17,23,25; 3:1,6,8,12,17,18; 5:5,23; 6:16,25,28; 7:6,9,12,23,24; 8:2; 9:2,4,10,13,14; 10:23; 11:8,10,12; 12:2,9; 13:1,4–7,10; 15:6; 16:5,11,12; 17:19; 18:12,15,18; 19:1,10; 20:6; 22:10,22; 23:14,17; 25:6; 26:4; 28:11,13; 29:12; 30:16; 31:2,9,21; 32:5,23; 34:2; 35:2, 13,15; 36:14,19; 37:9,12; 39:16; 40:4, 5,15; 41:6,10,12,14,15,17; 42:3; 44:3, 10,23; 45:5; 46:22; 48:2,11; 49:3; 50:3, 4,6; 51:9,50,59; 52:7,26; **Lam.** 1:5,6,18; 3:2; 4:18; 5:18; **Ezek.** 1:9,12,13,17, 19–21,24; 3:1,4,11,14; 5:6,7; 7:14,17; 10:11,16,22; 11:12,20,21; 12:11; 13:3; 16:47; 18:9,17; 19:6; 20:13,16,18,19,21, 39; 21:7; 23:31; 25:3; 28:14; 30:17,18; 31:4; 32:14; 33:15,31; 36:12,27; 37:21, 24; 40:24; 43:1; 47:6; **Dan.** 9:10; 12:9,13; **Hos.** 1:2,3; 2:5,7,13,14; 3:1; 5:6,11,13–15; 6:1,4; 7:11,12; 9:6; 11:2,10; 13:3; 14:6,9; **Joel** 2:7,8; 3:18; **Amos** 1:15; 2:4,7,10; 3:3; 6:2; 7:12,15; 9:4; **Jon.** 1:2,7,11,13; 3:2,3; **Mic.** 1:8; 2:3,7,10,11; 4:2,5; 6:8,16; **Nah.** 2:11; 3:10; **Hab.** 1:6; 3:5,11; **Zeph.** 1:17; **Zech.** 1:10,11; 2:2; 3:7; 5:10; 6:7; 8:21,23; 9:14; 10:12; **Mal.** 2:6; 3:14.

1981. הֲלַךְ ***h^a^lak*** **Aram. verb**
(to walk; corr. to Hebr. 1980)
Ezra 5:5(KJV, *hûk* [1946]); 6:5(KJV, *hûk* [1946]); 7:13(KJV, *hûk* [1946]); **Dan.** 3:25; 4:29(26),37(34).

1982. הֵלֶךְ ***hēlek*** **masc. noun**
(a going, a moving)
1 Sam. 14:26; **2 Sam.** 12:4.

1983. הֲלָךְ ***h^a^lāk*** **Aram. masc. noun**
(a custom tax, tribute)
Ezra 4:13,20; 7:24.

1984. I. הָלַל ***hālal*** **verb**
(to boast, to praise)
Gen. 12:15; **Judg.** 16:24; **1 Sam.** 21:13(14); **2 Sam.** 14:25; 22:4; **1 Kgs.** 20:11; **1 Chr.** 16:4,10,25,36; 23:5,30; 25:3; 29:13; **2 Chr.** 5:13; 7:6; 8:14; 20:19,21; 23:12,13; 29:30; 30:21; 31:2; **Ezra** 3:10,11; **Neh.** 5:13; 12:24; **Ps.** 10:3; 18:3(4); 22:22(23),23(24),26(27); 34:2(3); 35:18; 44:8(9); 48:1(2); 49:6(7); 52:1(3); 56:4(5),10(11); 63:5(6),11(12); 64:10(11); 69:30(31),34(35); 74:21; 78:63; 84:4(5); 96:4; 97:7; 102:18(19); 104:35; 105:3,45; 106:1,5,48; 107:32;

109:30; 111:1; 112:1; 113:1,3,9; 115:17,18; 116:19; 117:1,2; 119:164,175; 135:1, 3,21; 145:2,3; 146:1,2,10; 147:1,12,20; 148:1–5,7,13,14; 149:1,3,9; 150:1–6; **Prov.** 12:8; 20:14; 25:14; 27:1,2; 28:4; 31:28,30,31; **Eccl.** 7:7; **Song** 6:9; **Isa.** 38:18; 41:16; 44:25; 62:9; 64:11(10); **Jer.** 4:2; 9:23(22),24(23); 20:13; 31:7; 49:4; **Ezek.** 26:17; **Joel** 2:26.

II. הָלַל *hālal* **verb**
(to be foolish, to be mad, to be deluded)
1 Sam. 21:13(14); **Job** 12:17; **Ps.** 5:5(6)(NASB, NIV, see I); 73:3(NASB, NIV, see I); 75:4(5)(NASB, NIV, see I); 102:8(9)(NASB, NIV, see I); **Eccl.** 2:2; 7:7; **Isa.** 44:25; **Jer.** 25:16; 46:9; 50:38; 51:7; **Nah.** 2:4(5).

III. הָלַל *hālal* **verb**
(to shine)
Job 29:3; 31:26; 41:18(10); **Isa.** 13:10.

1985. הִלֵּל *hillēl* **masc. proper noun**
(Hillel)
Judg. 12:13,15.

1986. הָלַם *hālam* **verb**
(to strike, to beat)
Judg. 5:22,26; **1 Sam.** 14:16(NASB, NIV, *h^a^lōm* [1988]); **Ps.** 74:6; 141:5; **Prov.** 23:35; **Isa.** 16:8; 28:1; 41:7.

1987. הֶלֶם *helem* **masc. proper noun**
(Helem)
1 Chr. 7:35.

1988. הֲלֹם *h^a^lōm* **adv.**
(here, hither)
Gen. 16:13; **Ex.** 3:5; **Judg.** 18:3; 20:7; **Ruth** 2:14; **1 Sam.** 10:22; 14:16(KJV, *hālam* [1986]),36,38; **2 Sam.** 7:18; **1 Chr.** 17:16; **Ps.** 73:10.

1989. הַלְמוּת *halmûṯ* **fem. noun**
(hammer, mallet)
Judg. 5:26.

1990. הָם *hām* **proper noun**
(Ham)
Gen. 14:5.

1991. הָם *hām* **masc. noun**
(substance, wealth)
Ezek. 7:11.

1992. הֵם *hēm,* הֵמָּה *hēmmāh* **masc. pl. pron.**
(these, they)
Gen. 3:7; 6:4; 7:14; 14:13,24; 25:16; 34:21–23; 37:16; 40:12,18; 42:8,23,35; 44:3,4; 47:14; 48:5,9; **Ex.** 2:11,23; 5:7,8; 6:27; 7:11; 8:21; 14:3; 15:23; 18:22,26; 19:13; 24:2; 28:5; 29:33; 30:4; 32:15,16; 36:1,3,4; 38:17; **Lev.** 8:28; 11:8,10,13, 26–28,35,42; 16:4; 17:5,7; 21:6; 22:2,11; 23:2; 25:42,55; 26:43; **Num.** 1:16,50; 3:9,20,21,27,33; 4:22; 7:2; 8:16; 9:7; 11:16,26; 13:3; 14:9,27,38; 15:25; 16:14, 16,33; 17:5; 18:3,17,21,23; 20:13; 25:6,18; 27:14; **Deut.** 1:39; 2:11; 3:20; 4:10; 9:29; 11:30; 14:7; 17:9; 18:9; 19:17; 26:3; 28:65; 29:3(2),18(17); 32:20,21,28; 33:3,17; **Josh.** 1:15; 2:4,8; 7:3,16,11; 9:4,16; 10:5,11; 11:4; 20:6; 23:12; **Judg.** 1:22; 2:22; 6:5; 8:5,19,24; 10:14; 17:6; 18:1,3,7,22,26,27; 19:1,11,22; 20:27, 28,32,34; 21:25; **Ruth** 1:22; **1 Sam.** 3:1; 4:8; 8:8; 9:5,11,14,22,27; 10:5; 12:21; 14:15,21,22; 17:19; 19:20,21; 23:1; 25:11; 26:19; 28:1; 29:4; **2 Sam.** 2:24; 13:30; 16:23; 17:8,17; 20:8; 21:2,9; 24:3; **1 Kgs.** 1:41; 3:2; 8:40,51; 9:20,22; 10:25; 11:2,41; 13:20; 14:23,29; 15:7,23,31; 16:5,14,20,27; 20:3,31; 22:32,39,45; **2 Kgs.** 1:18; 2:11; 4:5,40; 7:10; 8:23; 9:18; 10:32,34; 12:5(6),15(16),19(20); 13:8, 12,21; 14:15,18,28; 15:6,21,36,37; 16:19; 17:29,34,40,41; 18:4; 19:18,37; 20:1,20; 21:17,25; 22:7; 23:28; 24:5; 25:23; **1 Chr.** 1:31; 2:55; 4:23; 5:23; 8:6,13,32; 9:18,22,23,26,27,38; 12:1,15(16),21(22); 19:15; 21:3; 23:27; 24:31; 26:6,8; **2 Chr.** 3:13; 6:31; 8:7,9,11; 9:11,24,29; 12:15; 15:5; 18:31; 20:11; 22:4; 23:6; 28:23;

31:6; 34:16; **Ezra** 2:59; **Neh.** 1:10; 3:1,3,6,13; 4:2(3:34),3(3:35); 6:2,17; 7:3,61; 9:16,29,35; 10:37(38); 13:15,23; **Esth.** 1:2; 2:21; 9:1; 10:2; **Job** 6:7; 8:10; 24:13; 32:4; **Ps.** 9:6(7),20(21); 16:3; 20:8; 22:17(18); 23:4; 25:6; 27:2; 37:9; 38:10(11); 43:3; 48:5(6); 55:21(22); 56:6(7); 59:15(16); 62:9(10); 63:9(10); 78:39; 88:5(6); 94:11; 95:10; 102:26(27); 106:43; 107:24; 109:28; 119:111; 120:7; **Prov.** 1:9,18; 4:22; 18:8; 19:7; 26:22; 30:18,24,29; **Eccl.** 1:7; 3:18; 4:2; 7:29; 12:12; **Song** 6:5,8; **Isa.** 1:2; 9:21(20); 24:14; 30:7; 35:2; 37:19,38; 38:1; 44:9,11; 49:21; 56:11; 57:6; 61:9; 63:8,10; 65:23,24; 66:3,5; **Jer.** 2:11,26; 3:16,18; 4:22; 5:4,5,10,18; 6:28; 7:4, 17,19; 9:16; 10:2,5,15; 11:10,12; 12:6; 14:14–16; 15:19; 16:20; 17:15,18,25; 19:4; 22:27; 23:16,21; 25:14; 27:9,10, 14–16,18; 29:9; 31:1,29,33; 32:32; 33:15,16; 36:32; 40:7,8; 42:5; 44:3,14; 46:5,21; 50:4,20,42; 51:18; **Lam.** 1:19; 4:9; **Ezek.** 2:3,5–7; 3:6,7,9,15,26,27; 8:6,9,13,16; 10:16,20,22; 11:7; 12:2, 3,10; 14:14,16,18,20; 20:9,49(21:5); 23:8,10,25,45; 25:4; 27:8,10,11,13, 17,21,22,24; 31:17; 32:29; 33:17,21; 34:30; 36:7; 37:11,25,27; 38:17; 40:46; 43:7,19; 44:11,15,16,19,24,29; 47:12; **Dan.** 10:2; 11:14; **Hos.** 2:4(6),12(14), 21(23),22(24); 4:14; 6:7; 7:13; 8:4, 9,13; 9:10; 13:2; **Joel** 2:29; 3:1(4:1); **Mic.** 4:12; **Nah.** 2:8(9); **Hab.** 1:16; **Zeph.** 2:12; 3:13; **Zech.** 1:5,9,15; 3:8; 4:5,10; 5:10; 8:6,10,23; 14:3,15; **Mal.** 1:4.

1993. הָמָה *hāmāh* **verb**
(to murmer, to growl, to roar)
1 Kgs. 1:41; **Ps.** 39:6(7); 42:5(6),11(12); 43:5; 46:3(4),6(7); 55:17(18); 59:6(7), 14(15); 77:3(4); 83:2(3); **Prov.** 1:21; 7:11; 9:13; 20:1; **Song** 5:4; **Isa.** 16:11; 17:12; 22:2; 51:15; 59:11; **Jer.** 4:19; 5:22; 6:23; 31:20,35; 48:36; 50:42; 51:55; **Ezek.** 7:16; **Zech.** 9:15.

1994. הִמּוֹ *himmô,* הִמּוֹן *himmōn* **Aram. pron.**
(they, these; corr. to Hebr. 1992)
Ezra 4:10,23; 5:5,11,12,14,15; 7:17; **Dan.** 2:34,35; 3:22.

1995. I. הָמוֹן *hāmôn* **masc. noun**
(multitude, noise, tumult)
Gen. 17:4,5; **Judg.** 4:7; **1 Sam.** 4:14; 14:16,19; **2 Sam.** 6:19; 18:29; **1 Kgs.** 18:41; 20:13,28; **2 Kgs.** 7:13; 25:11; **1 Chr.** 29:16; **2 Chr.** 11:23; 13:8; 14:11(10); 20:2,12,15,24; 31:10; 32:7; **Job** 31:34; 39:7; **Ps.** 37:16; 42:4(5); 65:7(8); **Eccl.** 5:10(9); **Isa.** 5:13,14; 13:4; 16:14; 17:12; 29:5,7,8; 31:4; 32:14; 33:3; 60:5; 63:15; **Jer.** 3:23; 10:13; 47:3; 49:32; 51:16,42; **Ezek.** 7:11–14; 23:42; 26:13; 29:19; 30:4,10,15; 31:2,18; 32:12, 16,18,20,24–26,31,32; 39:11,15; **Dan.** 10:6; 11:10–13; **Joel** 3:14(4:14); **Amos** 5:23.
II. הָמַן *hāman* **verb**
(to multiply)
Ezek. 5:7(NASB, NIV, see III).
III. הָמַן *hāman* **verb**
(to rage, to be in turmoil)
Ezek. 5:7(KJV, see II).

1996. הֲמוֹן גּוֹג *h^a^môn gôg* **proper noun**
(Hamon Gog)
Ezek. 39:11,15.

1997. הֲמוֹנָה *h^a^mônāh* **proper noun**
(Hamonah)
Ezek. 39:16.

1998. הֶמְיָה *hemyāh* **fem. noun**
(noise, music)
Isa. 14:11.

1999. הֲמֻלָּה *h^a^mullāh,* הֲמוּלָּה *h^a^mûllāh* **fem. noun**
(tumult, storm)
Jer. 11:16; **Ezek.** 1:24.

2000. הָמַם *hāmam* **verb**
(to trouble, to confuse)
Ex. 14:24; 23:27; **Deut.** 2:15; 7:23(KJV, NASB, *hûm* [1949]); **Josh.** 10:10; **Judg.** 4:15; **1 Sam.** 7:10; **2 Sam.** 22:15; **1 Kgs.** 1:45(KJV, NASB, *hûm* [1949]); **2 Chr.** 15:6; **Esth.** 9:24; **Ps.** 18:14(15); 144:6; **Isa.** 28:28; **Jer.** 51:34.

2001. הָמָן *hāmān* **masc. proper noun**
(Haman)
Esth. 3:1,2,4–8,10–12,15; 4:7; 5:4,5,8–12,14; 6:4–7,10–14; 7:1,6–10; 8:1–3,5,7; 9:10,12–14,24.

2002. הַמְנִיךְ *hamniyk̲* **Aram. masc. noun**
(chain)
Dan. 5:7,16,29.

2003. הֲמָסִים *hamāsiym* **masc. noun**
(brushwood)
Isa. 64:2(1).

2004. הֵן *hēn* **fem. pron.**
(they, them: shortened form of *hēnnāh* [2007]; only with prefix prep. *b, k, l* and *min* [4480])
Gen. 19:29; 30:26,37; **Ex.** 25:29; 37:16; **Lev.** 10:1; 11:21; 14:40; **Num.** 10:3; 16:7; **Deut.** 28:52; **Ruth** 1:13(NASB, *lāhēn* [3860]); **1 Sam.** 31:7; **Isa.** 38:16; **Jer.** 4:29; 48:9; 51:43; **Ezek.** 16:47,52; 18:14.

2005. הֵן *hēn* **particle**
(behold, if)
Gen. 3:22; 4:14; 11:6; 15:3; 19:34; 27:11,37; 29:7; 30:34; 39:8; 44:8; 47:23; **Ex.** 4:1; 5:5; 6:12,30; 8:26(22); **Lev.** 10:18,19; 25:20; **Num.** 17:12(27); 23:9,24; 31:16; **Deut.** 5:24(27); 10:14; 31:14,27; **Job** 4:18; 8:19,20; 9:11,12; 12:14,15; 13:1,15; 15:5; 19:7; 21:16,27; 23:8; 24:5; 25:5; 26:14; 27:12; 28:28; 31:35; 32:11; 33:6,10,12,29; 36:5,22, 26,30; 40:4,23; 41:9(1); **Ps.** 51:5(6),6(7); 68:33(34); 78:20; 139:4; **Prov.** 11:31; 24:12; **Isa.** 23:13; 32:1; 33:7; 40:15; 41:11,24,29; 42:1; 44:11; 49:16,21; 50:1,2,9,11; 54:15,16(NIV, [Qe] *hinneh* [2009]); 55:4,5; 56:3; 58:3,4; 59:1; 64:5(4),9(8); **Ezek.** 18:4; **Hag.** 2:12.

2006. הֵן *hēn* **Aram. particle**
(if, behold; corr. to Hebr. 2005)
Ezra 4:13,16; 5:17; 7:26; **Dan.** 2:5,6,9; 3:15,17,18; 4:27(24); 5:16.

2007. הֵנָּה *hēnnāh* **fem. pl. pron.**
(they, them; see also *hōn* [2004])
Gen. 6:2; 21:29; 33:6; 41:19,26,27; **Ex.** 1:19; 9:32; 39:14; **Lev.** 4:2; 6:3(5:25); 18:10,17; **Num.** 13:19; 31:16; **Judg.** 19:12; **1 Sam.** 7:12; 17:28; 27:8; **2 Sam.** 12:8; **1 Chr.** 21:10; **Job** 23:14; **Ps.** 34:20; 71:17(KJV, *hēnnāh* [2008]); **Prov.** 6:16; 30:15; **Isa.** 34:16; 41:25; 51:19; **Jer.** 5:6; 34:7; 38:22; **Ezek.** 1:5,23; 18:4,14; 23:45; 30:17; 42:5,6,9,13,14; **Zech.** 5:9.

2008. הֵנָּה *hēnnāh* **adv.**
(here, now)
Gen. 15:16; 21:23; 42:15; 44:28; 45:5,8,13; **Num.** 14:19; **Deut.** 20:15; **Josh.** 2:2; 3:9; 8:20; 18:6; **Judg.** 16:2,13; **2 Sam.** 1:10; 4:6; 5:6; 14:32; 20:16; **1 Kgs.** 20:40; **2 Kgs.** 2:8,14; 4:35; 8:7; **1 Chr.** 9:18; 11:5; 12:29; **2 Chr.** 28:13; **Ps.** 71:17(NASB, NIV, *hēnnāh* [2007]); **Prov.** 9:4,16; 25:7; **Isa.** 57:3; **Jer.** 27:22; 28:3,4,6,7,15; 31:8; 48:47; 50:5; 51:64; **Ezek.** 40:4; **Dan.** 12:5.

2009. הִנֵּה *hinnēh* **interj.**
(behold, look)
Gen. 1:29; 31; 6:12,13,17; 8:11,13; 9:9; 12:11,19; 15:3,4,12,17; 16:2,6,11,14; 17:4,20; 18:2,9,10,27,31; 19:2,8, 19–21,28; 20:3,15,16; 22:1,7,11,13,20; 24:13,15,30,43,45,51,63; 25:24,32;

26:8,9; 27:1,2,6,18,36,39,42; 28:12, 13,15; 29:2,6,25; 30:3; 31:2,10,11,51; 32:18(19),20(21); 33:1; 34:21; 37:7,9, 13,15,19,25,29; 38:13,23,24,27,29; 40:6,9,16; 41:1–3,5–7,17–19,22,23,29; 42:2,13,22,27,28,35; 43:21; 44:16; 45:12; 46:2; 47:1; 48:1,2,4,11,21; 50:5,18; **Ex.** 1:9; 2:6,13; 3:2,4,9,13; 4:6,7,14,23; 5:16; 7:15–17; 8:2,20,21,29; 9:3,7,18; 10:4; 14:10,17; 16:4,10,14; 17:6; 19:9; 23:20; 24:8,14; 31:6; 32:9,34; 33:21; 34:10, 11,30; 39:43; **Lev.** 10:16; 13:5,6,8,10, 13,17,20,21,25,26,30–32,34,36,39,43,53, 55,56; 14:3,37,39,44,48; **Num.** 3:12; 12:10; 14:40; 16:42(17:7),47(17:12); 17:8(23); 18:6,8,21; 20:16; 22:5,11,32,38; 23:6,11,17,20; 24:10,11,14; 25:6,12; 32:1,14,23; **Deut.** 1:10; 3:11; 9:13,16; 13:14(15); 17:4; 19:18; 22:17; 26:10; 31:16; **Josh.** 2:2,18; 3:11; 5:13; 7:21,22; 8:20; 9:12,13,25; 14:10; 22:11; 23:14; 24:27; **Judg.** 1:2; 3:24,25; 4:22; 6:15, 28,37; 7:13,17; 8:15; 9:31,33,36,37,43; 11:34; 13:3,5,7,10; 14:5,8,16; 16:10; 17:2; 18:9,12; 19:9,16,22,24,27; 20:7,40; 21:8,9,19,21; **Ruth** 1:15; 2:4; 3:2,8; 4:1; **1 Sam.** 2:31; 3:4,5,6,8,11,16; 4:13; 5:3,4; 8:5; 9:6–8,12,14,17,24; 10:2,8,10,11,22; 11:5; 12:1–3,13; 13:10; 14:7,8,11,16,17, 20,26,33,43; 15:12,22; 16:11,15,18; 17:23; 18:17,22; 19:16,19,22; 20:2,5, 12,21–23; 21:9(10),14(15); 22:12; 23:1,3; 24:1,4,9,10,20; 25:14,19,20,36,41; 26:7, 21,22,24; 28:7,9,21; 30:3,16,26; **2 Sam.** 1:2,6,7,18; 3:12,22,24; 4:8,10; 5:1; 9:4,6; 12:11,18; 13:24,34–36; 14:7,21,32; 15:15,24,26,32,36; 16:1,3–5,8,11; 17:9; 18:10,11,24,26,31; 19:1(2),8(9),20(21), 37(38),41(42); 20:21; 24:17; **1 Kgs.** 1:14,18,22,23,25,42,51; 2:8,29,39; 3:12,15,21; 5:5(19); 8:27; 10:7; 11:22,31; 12:28; 13:1–3,25; 14:2,5,10,19; 15:19; 16:3; 17:9,10,12; 18:7,8,11,14,44; 19:5, 6,9,11,13; 20:13,31,36,39; 21:18,21; 22:13,23,25; **2 Kgs.** 1:9,14; 2:11,16,19; 3:20; 4:9,13,25,32; 5:6,11,15,20,22; 6:1,13,15,17,20,25,30,33; 7:2,5,6, 10,13,15,19; 8:5; 9:5; 10:4,9; 11:14; 13:21; 15:11,15,26,31; 17:26; 18:21; 19:7,9,11,35; 20:5,17; 21:12; 22:16,20; **1 Chr.** 9:1; 11:1,25; 17:1; 22:9,14; 28:21; 29:29; **2 Chr.** 2:4(3),8(7),10(9); 6:18; 9:6; 13:12,14; 16:3,11; 18:12,22,24; 19:11; 20:2,10,11,16,24,34; 21:14; 23:3,13; 24:27; 25:19,26; 26:20; 27:7; 28:9,26; 29:9,19; 32:32; 33:18,19; 34:24,28; 35:25,27; 36:8; **Ezra** 9:15; **Neh.** 5:5; 6:12; 9:36; **Esth.** 6:5; 7:9; 8:7; **Job** 1:12,19; 2:6; 3:7; 4:3; 5:17,27; 9:19; 13:18; 16:19; 32:12,19; 33:2,7; 38:35; 40:15,16; **Ps.** 7:14(15); 11:2; 33:18; 37:36; 39:5(6); 40:7(8),9(10); 48:4(5); 52:7(8); 54:4(6); 55:7(8); 59:3(4),7(8); 73:12,15,27; 83:2(3); 87:4; 92:9(10); 119:40; 121:4; 123:2; 127:3; 128:4; 132:6; 133:1; 134:1; 139:8; **Prov.** 1:23; 7:10; 24:31; **Eccl.** 1:14,16; 2:1,11; 4:1; 5:18(17); **Song** 1:15,16; 2:8,9,11; 3:7; 4:1; **Isa.** 3:1; 5:7,26,30; 6:7,8; 7:14; 8:7,18,22; 10:33; 12:2; 13:9,17; 17:1,14; 19:1; 20:6; 21:9; 22:13,17; 24:1; 25:9; 26:21; 28:2,16; 29:8,14; 30:27; 34:5; 35:4; 36:6; 37:7,11,36; 38:5,8,17; 39:6; 40:9,10; 41:15,27; 42:9; 43:19; 47:14; 48:7,10; 49:12,22; 51:22; 52:6,13; 54:11,16(KJV, NASB, [K^{e}] *hēn* [2005]); 58:9; 59:9; 60:2; 62:11; 65:1,6,13,14, 17,18; 66:12,15; **Jer.** 1:6,9,15,18; 2:35; 3:5,22; 4:13,16,23–26; 5:14,15; 6:10,19, 21,22; 7:8,11,20,32; 8:8,9,15,17,19; 9:7(6),15(14),25(24); 10:18,22; 11:11,22; 12:14; 13:7,13; 14:13,18,19; 16:9,12,14, 16,21; 17:15; 18:3,6,11; 19:3,6,15; 20:4; 21:4,8,13; 22:2,5,7,15,19,30–32; 23:5,7, 19; 24:1; 25:9,29,32; 26:14; 27:16; 28:16; 29:17,21,32; 30:3,10,18,23; 31:8,27, 31,38; 32:3,7,17,24,27,28,37; 33:6,14; 34:2,17,22; 35:17; 36:12; 37:7; 38:5,22; 39:16; 40:4,10; 42:4; 43:10; 44:2,11,26, 27,30; 45:4,5; 46:25,27; 47:2; 48:12,40; 49:2,5,12,15,19,22,35; 50:9,12,18,31, 41,44; 51:1,25,36,47,52; **Ezek.** 1:4,15; 2:9; 3:8,23,25; 4:8,14,16; 5:8; 6:3; 7:5,6,10; 8:2,4,5,7,8,10,14,16,17; 9:2,11;

2010. הֲנָחָה hᵃnāḥāh

10:1,9; 11:1; 12:27; 13:8,10,12,20; 14:22; 15:4,5; 16:8,27,37,44,49; 17:7,10,12,18; 18:14,18; 20:47(21:3); 21:3(8),7(12); 22:6,13,19; 23:22,28,39,40; 24:16,21; 25:4,7–9,16; 26:3,7; 28:3,7,22; 29:3,8,19; 30:9,21,22; 31:3; 33:32,33; 34:10,11, 17,20; 35:3; 36:6,9; 37:2,5,7,8,11,12, 19,21; 38:3; 39:1,8; 40:3,5,17,24; 42:8; 43:2,5,12; 44:4; 46:19,21; 47:1,2,7; **Dan.** 8:3,5,15,19; 10:5,10,13,16,20; 11:2; 12:5; **Hos.** 2:6(8),14(16); 9:6; **Joel** 2:19; 3:1(4:1),7(4:7); **Amos** 2:13; 4:2,13; 6:11,14; 7:1,4,7,8; 8:1,11; 9:8,9,13; **Obad.** 1:2; **Mic.** 1:3; 2:3; **Nah.** 1:15 (2:1); 2:13(14); 3:5,13; **Hab.** 1:6; 2:4, 13,19; **Zeph.** 3:19; **Hag.** 1:9; **Zech.** 1:8,11,18(2:1–4); 2:1(5),3(8),9(13), 10(14); 3:8,9; 4:2; 5:1,7,9; 6:1,12; 8:7; 9:4,9; 11:6,16; 12:2; 14:1; **Mal.** 1:13; 2:3; 3:1; 4:1(3:19),5(3:23).

2010. הֲנָחָה hᵃnāḥāh **fem. noun**
(holiday, day of rest)
Esth. 2:18.

2011. הִנֹּם hinnōm **masc. proper noun**
(Hinnom)
Josh. 15:8; 18:16; **2 Kgs.** 23:10; **2 Chr.** 28:3; 33:6; **Neh.** 11:30; **Jer.** 7:31,32; 19:2,6; 32:35.

2012. הֵנַע hēnaʿ **proper noun**
(Hena)
2 Kgs. 18:34; 19:13; **Isa.** 37:13.

2013. I. הָס hās **interj.**
(hush! quiet!)
Judg. 3:19; **Neh.** 8:11; **Amos** 6:10; 8:3; **Hab.** 2:20; **Zeph.** 1:7; **Zech.** 2:13(17).
II. הָסָה hāsāh **verb**
(to hush, to quiet, to silence, to make still)
Num. 13:30.

2014. הֲפוּגָה hᵃpûgāh **fem. noun**
(stopping, relief)
Lam. 3:49.

2015. הָפַךְ hāp̱aḵ **verb**
(to turn, to overthrow, to change)
Gen. 3:24; 19:21,25,29; **Ex.** 7:15,17,20; 10:19; 14:5; **Lev.** 13:3,4,10,13,16,17, 20,25,55; **Deut.** 23:5(6); 29:23(22); **Josh.** 7:8; 8:20; **Judg.** 7:13; 20:39,41; **1 Sam.** 4:19; 10:6,9; 25:12; **2 Sam.** 10:3; **1 Kgs.** 22:34; **2 Kgs.** 5:26; 9:23; 21:13; **1 Chr.** 19:3; **2 Chr.** 9:12; 18:33; **Neh.** 13:2; **Esth.** 9:1,22; **Job** 9:5; 12:15; 19:19; 20:14; 28:5,9; 30:15,21; 34:25; 37:12; 38:14; 41:28(20); **Ps.** 30:11(12); 32:4; 41:3(4); 66:6; 78:9,44,57; 105:25,29; 114:8; **Prov.** 12:7; 17:20; **Isa.** 29:16(see hᵃp̱ōḵ [2017,II]); 34:9; 60:5; 63:10; **Jer.** 2:21; 13:23; 20:16; 23:36; 30:6; 31:13; **Lam.** 1:20; 3:3; 4:6; 5:2,15; **Ezek.** 4:8; **Dan.** 10:8,16; **Hos.** 7:8; 11:8; **Joel** 2:31(3:4); **Amos** 4:11; 5:7,8; 6:12; 8:10; **Jon.** 3:4; **Zeph.** 3:9; **Hag.** 2:22.

2016. הֵפֶךְ hēp̱eḵ, הֶפֶךְ hep̱eḵ **masc. noun**
(contrary, opposite)
Isa. 29:16(KJV, hop̱eḵ [2017]); **Ezek.** 16:34.

2017. הֹפֶךְ hōp̱eḵ **masc. noun**
(turning things upside down)
Isa. 29:16(NASB, NIV, hēp̱eḵ [2016]).

2018. הֲפֵכָה hᵃp̱ēḵāh **fem. noun**
(an overthrowing)
Gen. 19:29.

2019. הֲפַכְפַּךְ hᵃp̱aḵp̱aḵ **adj.**
(crooked, perverted)
Prov. 21:8.

2020. הַצָּלָה haṣṣālāh **fem. noun**
(deliverance)
Esth. 4:14.

2021. הֹצֶן hōṣen **masc. noun**
(weapons, chariots)
Ezek. 23:24.

2022. הַר *har* **masc. noun**
(mountain, hill)
Gen. 7:19,20; 8:4,5; 10:30; 12:8; 14:10; 19:17,19,30; 22:2,14; 31:21,23,25,54; 36:8,9; **Ex.** 3:1,12; 4:27; 15:17; 18:5; 19:2,3,11–14,16–18,20,23; 20:18; 24:4,12,13,15–18; 25:40; 26:30; 27:8; 31:18; 32:1,12,15,19; 33:6; 34:2–4,29,32; **Lev.** 7:38; 25:1; 26:46; 27:34; **Num.** 3:1; 10:33; 13:17,29; 14:40,44,45; 20:22,23, 25,27,28; 21:4; 23:7(see *hārār* [2042]); 27:12; 28:6; 33:23,24,37–39,41,47,48; 34:7,8; **Deut.** 1:2,6,7,19,20,24,41,43,44; 2:1,3,5,37; 3:8,12,25; 4:11,48; 5:4,5, 22(19),23(20); 8:7,9(see *hārār* [2042]); 9:9,10,15,21; 10:1,3–5,10; 11:11,29; 12:2; 27:4,12,13; 32:22,49,50; 33:2,19; 33:15(see *hārār* [2042]); 34:1; **Josh.** 2:16,22,23; 8:30,33; 9:1; 10:6,40; 11:2, 3,16,17,21; 12:1,5,7,8; 13:5,6,11,19; 14:12; 15:8–11,48; 16:1; 17:15,16,18; 18:12–14,16; 19:50; 20:7; 21:11,21; 24:4,30,33; **Judg.** 1:9,19,34,35; 2:9; 3:3,27; 4:5,6,12,14; 5:5; 6:2; 7:3,24; 9:7,25,36,48; 10:1; 11:37,38; 12:15; 16:3; 17:1,8; 18:2,13; 19:1,16,18; **1 Sam.** 1:1; 9:4; 13:2; 14:22; 17:3; 23:14,26; 25:20; 26:13,20; 31:1,8; **2 Sam.** 1:6,21; 13:34; 16:13; 20:21; 21:9; **1 Kgs.** 4:8; 5:15(29); 11:7; 12:25; 16:24; 18:19,20; 19:8,11; 20:23,28; 22:17; **2 Kgs.** 1:9; 2:16,25; 4:25,27; 5:22; 6:17; 19:23,31; 23:13,16; **1 Chr.** 4:42; 5:23; 6:67(52); 10:1,8; 12:8; **2 Chr.** 2:2(1),18(17); 3:1; 13:4; 15:8; 18:16; 19:4; 20:10,22,23; 21:11; 26:10; 27:4; 33:15; **Neh.** 8:15; 9:13; **Job** 9:5; 14:18; 24:8; 28:9; 39:8; 40:20; **Ps.** 2:6; 3:4(5); 11:1; 15:1; 18:7(8); 24:3; 30:7(8) (see *hārār* [2042]); 36:6(7)(see *hārār* [2042]); 42:6(7); 43:3; 46:2(3),3(4); 48:1(2),2(3),11(12); 50:10(see *hārār* [2042]),11; 65:6(7); 68:15(16),16(17); 72:3,16; 74:2; 75:6(7); 76:4(5)(see *hārār* [2042]); 78:54,68; 80:10(11); 83:14(15); 87:1(see *hārār* [2042]); 90:2; 95:4; 97:5; 98:8; 99:9; 104:6,8,10,13,18,32; 114:4,6; 121:1; 125:1,2; 133:3(see *hārār* [2042]); 144:5; 147:8; 148:9; **Prov.** 8:25; 27:25; **Song** 2:8,17; 4:1,6,8(see *hārār* [2042]); 8:14; **Isa.** 2:2,3,14; 4:5; 5:25; 7:25; 8:18; 10:12,32; 11:9; 13:2,4; 14:13,25; 16:1; 17:13; 18:3,6,7; 22:5; 24:23; 25:6,7,10; 27:13; 28:21; 29:8; 30:17,25,29; 31:4; 34:3; 37:24,32; 40:4,9,12; 41:15; 42:11,15; 44:23; 49:11,13; 52:7; 54:10; 55:12; 56:7; 57:7,13; 64:1(63:19),3(2); 65:7,9,11,25; 66:20; **Jer.** 3:6,23; 4:15,24; 9:10(9); 13:16; 16:16; 17:3(see *hārār* [2042]),26; 26:18; 31:5,6,23; 32:44; 33:13; 46:18; 50:6,19; 51:25; **Lam.** 4:19; 5:18; **Ezek.** 6:2,3,13; 7:7,16; 11:23; 17:22,23; 18:6,11,15; 19:9; 20:40; 22:9; 28:14,16; 31:12; 32:5,6; 33:28; 34:6, 13,14; 35:2,3,7,8,12,15; 36:1,4,6,8; 37:22; 38:8,20,21; 39:2,4,17; 40:2; 43:12; **Dan.** 9:16,20; 11:45; **Hos.** 4:13; 10:8; **Joel** 2:1,2,5,32(3:5); 3:17(4:17),18(4:18); **Amos** 3:9; 4:1,13; 6:1; 9:13; **Obad.** 1:8,9,16,17,19,21; **Jon.** 2:6(7); **Mic.** 1:4; 3:12; 4:1,2,7; 6:1,2; 7:12; **Nah.** 1:5,15 (2:1); 3:18; **Hab.** 3:3,6(see *hārār* [2042]),10; **Zeph.** 3:11; **Hag.** 1:8,11; **Zech.** 4:7; 6:1; 8:3; 14:4,5; **Mal.** 1:3.

2023. A. הֹר *hōr* **proper noun**
(Mt. Hor)
Num. 20:22,23,25,27; 21:4; 33:37–39,41; **Deut.** 32:50.
B. הֹר *hōr* **proper noun**
(Hor: a hill in N.E. Israel)
Num. 34:7,8.

2024. הָרָא *hārā'* **proper noun**
(Hara)
1 Chr. 5:26.

2025. הַרְאֵל *har'ēl* **masc. noun**
(altar)
Ezek. 43:15(NASB, *'ari'ēyl* [741]).

2026. הָרַג *hārag* **verb**
(to kill, to slay)
Gen. 4:8,14,15,23,25; 12:12; 20:4,11; 26:7; 27:41,42; 34:25,26; 37:20,26; 49:6;

Ex. 2:14,15; 4:23; 5:21; 13:15; 21:14; 22:24(23); 23:7; 32:12,27; **Lev.** 20:15,16; **Num.** 11:15; 22:29,33; 25:5; 31:7,8, 17,19; **Deut.** 13:9(10); **Josh.** 8:24; 9:26; 10:11; 13:22; **Judg.** 7:25; 8:17–21; 9:5, 18,24,45,54,56; 16:2; 20:5; **1 Sam.** 16:2; 22:21; 24:10(11),11(12),18(19); **2 Sam.** 3:30; 4:10–12; 10:18; 12:9; 14:7; 23:21; **1 Kgs.** 2:5,32; 9:16; 11:24; 12:27; 18:12–14; 19:1,10,14; **2 Kgs.** 8:12; 9:31; 10:9; 11:18; 17:25; **1 Chr.** 7:21; 11:23; 19:18; **2 Chr.** 21:4,13; 22:1,8; 23:17; 24:22,25; 25:3; 28:6,7,9; 36:17; **Neh.** 4:11(5); 6:10; 9:26; **Esth.** 3:13; 7:4; 8:11; 9:6,10–12,15,16; **Job** 5:2; 20:16; **Ps.** 10:8; 44:22(23); 59:11(12); 78:31,34,47; 94:6; 135:10; 136:18; **Prov.** 1:32; 7:26; **Eccl.** 3:3; **Isa.** 10:4; 14:19,20,30; 22:13; 26:21; 27:1,7; **Jer.** 4:31; 15:3; 18:21; **Lam.** 2:4,20,21; 3:43; **Ezek.** 9:6; 21:11; 23:10,47; 26:6,8,11,15; 28:9; 37:9; **Hos.** 6:5; 9:13; **Amos** 2:3; 4:10; 9:1,4; **Hab.** 1:17; **Zech.** 11:5.

2027. הֶרֶג *hereg* **masc. noun**
(a slaughter, a killing)
Esth. 9:5; **Prov.** 24:11; **Isa.** 27:7; 30:25; **Ezek.** 26:15(Sept. *ḥereḇ* [2719]).

2028. הֲרֵגָה *h^arēgāh* **fem. noun**
(a slaughter, a killing)
Jer. 7:32; 12:3; 19:6; **Zech.** 11:4,7.

2029. הָרָה *hārāh* **verb**
(to conceive, to become pregnant)
Gen. 4:1,17; 16:4,5; 19:36; 21:2; 25:21; 29:32–35; 30:5,7,17,19,23; 38:3,4,18; 49:26; **Ex.** 2:2; **Num.** 11:12; **Judg.** 13:3,5(KJV, NASB, *hāreh* [2030]),7(KJV, NASB, *hāreh* [2030]); **1 Sam.** 1:20; 2:21; **2 Sam.** 11:5; **2 Kgs.** 4:17; **1 Chr.** 4:17; 7:23; **Job** 3:3; 15:35; **Ps.** 7:14(15); **Song** 3:4; **Isa.** 8:3; 26:18; 33:11; 59:4,13; **Hos.** 1:3,6,8; 2:5(7).

2030. הָרֶה *hāreh* **fem. adj.**
(pregnant)
Gen. 16:11; 38:24,25; **Ex.** 21:22; **Judg.** 13:5(KJV, NASB, *hārāh* [2029]),7(KJV, NASB, *hārāh* [2029]); **1 Sam.** 4:19; **2 Sam.** 11:5; **2 Kgs.** 8:12; 15:16; **Isa.** 7:14; 26:17; **Jer.** 20:17; 31:8; **Hos.** 13:16(14:1); **Amos** 1:13.

2031. הַרְהֹר *harhōr* **Aram. masc. noun**
(a thought, fantasy)
Dan. 4:5(2).

2032. הֵרוֹן *hērôn,* הֵרָיוֹן *hērāyôn* **masc. noun**
(pregnancy; childbearing)
Gen. 3:16; **Ruth** 4:13; **Hos.** 9:11.

2033. הֲרוֹרִי *h^arôriy* **masc. proper noun**
(Harorite)
1 Chr. 11:27.

2034. הֲרִיסָה *h^ariysāh* **fem. noun**
(a ruin, destroyed building)
Amos 9:11.

2035. הֲרִיסוּת *h^ariysûṯ* **fem. noun**
(destruction, overthrow)
Isa. 49:19.

2036. הֹרָם *hōrām* **masc. proper noun**
(Horam)
Josh. 10:33.

2037. הָרוּם *hārûm* **masc. proper noun**
(Harum)
1 Chr. 4:8.

2038.
I. הַרְמוֹן *harmôn* **masc. noun**
(palace)
Amos 4:3(NASB, NIV, see II).
II. הַרְמוֹן *harmôn* **proper noun**
(Harmon)
Amos 4:3(KJV, see I).

2039. הָרָן *hārān* **masc. proper noun**
(Haran)
Gen. 11:26–29,31; **1 Chr.** 23:9.

2040. הָרַס *hāras* **verb**
(to tear down, to overthrow)
Ex. 15:7; 19:21,24; 23:24; **Judg.** 6:25; **2 Sam.** 11:25; **1 Kgs.** 18:30; 19:10,14; **2 Kgs.** 3:25; **1 Chr.** 20:1; **Job** 12:14; **Ps.** 11:3; 28:5; 58:6(7); **Prov.** 11:11; 14:1; 24:31; 29:4; **Isa.** 14:17; 22:19; 49:17; **Jer.** 1:10; 24:6; 31:28,40; 42:10; 45:4; 50:15; **Lam.** 2:2,17; **Ezek.** 13:14; 16:39; 26:4,12; 30:4; 36:35,36; 38:20; **Joel** 1:17; **Mic.** 5:11(10); **Mal.** 1:4.

2041. הֶרֶס *heres* **masc. noun**
(destruction)
Isa. 19:18.

2042. הָרָר *hārār* **masc. noun**
(mountain, hill country)
Gen. 14:6; **Num.** 23:7; **Deut.** 8:9; 33:15; **Ps.** 30:7(8); 36:6(7); 50:10; 76:4(5); 87:1; 133:3; **Song** 4:8; **Jer.** 17:3; **Hab.** 3:6.

2043. הָרָרִי *hārāriy*, הֲרָרִי *h^arāriy* **masc. proper noun**
(Hararite)
2 Sam. 23:11,33; **1 Chr.** 11:34,35.

2044. הָשֵׁם *hāšēm* **masc. proper noun**
(Hashem)
1 Chr. 11:34.

2045. הַשְׁמָעוּת *hašmā'ûṯ* **fem. noun**
(a causing to hear, a report)
Ezek. 24:26.

2046. הִתּוּךְ *hittûḵ* **masc. noun**
(a melting [of a metal])
Ezek. 22:22.

2047. הֲתָךְ *haṯāḵ* **masc. proper noun**
(Hathach, Hatach)
Esth. 4:5,6,9,10.

2048. I. הָתַל *hāṯal* **verb**
(to mock, to deride, to deceive)
1 Kgs. 18:27.
II. תָּלַל *tālal* **verb**
(to cheat, to deceive, to trifle with, to tease, to lead on falsely)
Gen. 31:7; **Ex.** 8:29(25); **Judg.** 16:10,13,15; **Job** 13:9; **Isa.** 44:20; **Jer.** 9:5(4).

2049. הֲתֻלִים *haṯuliym* **masc. pl. noun**
(mockers)
Job 17:2.

2050. I. הָתַת *hataṯ* **verb**
(to imagine mischief, to scheme)
Ps. 62:3(4)(NASB, NIV, see II).
II. הוּת *hûṯ* **verb**
(to assault, to assail, to attack violently)
Ps. 62:3(4)(KJV, see I).

ו Waw

2051. וְדָן *w^e^d̲ān* **proper noun**
(Vedan)
Ezek. 27:19(KJV, *dān* [1835,B], NIV, *dān* [1835,C]).

2052. I. וָהֵב *wāhēb̲* **proper noun**
(Waheb: loc. in Moab)
Num. 21:14(KJV, see II).
II. אֶתְוְהַב *et̲w^e^hab̲* **masc. noun**
(that which is done, accomplished)
Num. 21:14(NASB, NIV, see I).

2053. וָו *wāw* **masc. noun**
(a hook)
Ex. 26:32,37; 27:10,11,17; 36:36,38; 38:10–12,17,19,28.

2054. וָזָר *wāzār* **masc. noun**
(crooked, devious)
Prov. 21:8.

2055. וַיְזָתָא *wayzāt̲a'* **masc. proper noun**
(Vaizatha, Vajezatha)
Esth. 9:9.

2056. וָלָד *wālād̲* **masc. noun**
(child)
Gen. 11:30.

2057. וַנְיָה *wanyāh* **masc. proper noun**
(Vaniah)
Ezra 10:36.

2058. וָפְסִי *wop̲siy* **masc. proper noun**
(Vophsi)
Num. 13:14.

2059. וַשְׁנִי *wašniy* **masc. proper noun**
(Vashni)
1 Chr. 6:28(13)(NASB, NIV, *šēniy* [8145]).

2060. וַשְׁתִּי *waštiy* **fem. proper noun**
(Vashti)
Esth. 1:9,11,12,15–17,19; 2:1,4,17.

ז Zayin

2061. זְאֵב *zᵉʾēḇ* **masc. noun**
(wolf)
Gen. 49:27; **Isa.** 11:6; 65:25; **Jer.** 5:6; **Ezek.** 22:27; **Hab.** 1:8; **Zeph.** 3:3.

2062. זְאֵב *zᵉʾēḇ* **masc. proper noun**
(Zeeb)
Judg. 7:25; 8:3; **Ps.** 83:11(12).

2063. זֹאת *zōʾṯ* **fem. pron.**
(this one; fem. of *zeh* [2088]; NASB, NIV, *zeh* [2088])
Gen. 2:23; 3:13,14; 9:12,17; 12:7,12,18; 15:7,18; 17:10; 19:20; 20:5,6; 21:10; 24:5,7,8; 26:3,10; 28:15,22; 29:25,27,28; 31:13,52; 34:4,15,22; 37:32; 39:9; 41:39; 42:15,18,21,28,33; 42:11,15; 44:17; 45:17,19,23; 48:4; 49:28; 50:24; **Ex.** 7:17,23; 8:32; 9:14,16; 12:25,26,43; 13:5,10,14; 14:5,11; 15:1; 17:14; 25:3; 32:13; **Lev.** 6:9(2),14(12),25(23); 7:1,11,35,37; 11:2,46; 12:7; 13:59; 14:2,32,54,57; 15:3,32; 16:3,34; 17:7; 25:13; 26:16,27,44; **Num.** 4:4,19,24, 28,31,33; 5:29,30; 6:13,21; 7:84,88; 8:24; 14:3,8,14,27,35; 16:6,21,28,45(17:10); 19:2,14; 21:17; 28:14; 31:21; 32:5,22; 34:2,12,13; **Deut.** 1:5; 3:12,18; 4:8, 22,44; 5:3,25(28); 6:1,25; 9:4,6; 11:22; 13:14(15); 14:4; 15:5; 17:4,18,19; 18:16; 19:9; 22:14; 26:9; 27:3,8,26; 28:58,61; 29:9(8),14(13),19(18),24(23),29(28); 30:11; 31:9,11,12,19,21,22,24,30; 32:6, 27,29,44,46; 33:1,7; 34:4; **Josh.** 1:13; 3:10; 4:6; 6:26; 7:20; 9:20; 11:6,16; 13:2,7,23,28; 15:20; 16:8; 18:14,20,28; 19:8,16,23,31,39,48; 22:24; 23:13,15; 24:27; **Judg.** 1:27; 2:2; 6:13; 7:14; 8:8; 13:23; 15:6,7,11,18; 19:11,23,24,30; 20:3,12; 21:3; **Ruth** 1:19; 2:5; 4:7,12; **1 Sam.** 2:20; 4:6,7; 6:9; 9:6; 11:2; 12:20; 14:38,45; 20:2,3; 22:15; 25:27,31; **2 Sam.** 1:17; 2:6; 6:22; 7:19,21,27,28; 11:3; 12:5,11; 13:12,16,17; 14:13,19; 17:7,15; 19:7(8),21(22),36(37); 22:1; 23:17; **1 Kgs.** 3:17–19,22,23,26; 7:37; 8:54; 9:8,9; 11:11,39; 14:15; **2 Kgs.** 3:18; 4:12,13,36; 5:4; 6:28,33; 8:5; 9:12,26, 34,37; 18:25,30; 19:31–34; 20:6; 23:3,27; **1 Chr.** 4:33; 11:19; 17:17,19,26; 21:3; 27:24; 29:14,18; **2 Chr.** 1:11; 2:4(3); 6:34; 7:21,22; 16:9,10; 19:2; 20:7,17; 21:18; 24:18; 25:16; 27:5; 30:9,26; 31:1, 20; 32:15,20; 34:22; 35:20; **Ezra** 7:27; 8:23; 9:10,13,15; 10:2,15; **Neh.** 5:16; 6:16; 9:38(10:1); 13:14,18,22,27; **Esth.** 4:14; 9:26,29; **Job** 1:22; 2:10,11; 5:27; 10:13; 12:9; 17:8; 19:26; 20:4; 21:2; 33:12; 34:16; 35:2; 37:1,14; 42:16; **Ps.** 7:3(4); 18:[title](1); 27:3; 32:6; 41:11(12); 44:17(18),21(22); 49:1(2); 50:22; 73:16; 74:18(19); 78:32; 80:14(15); 92:6(7); 102:18(19); 109:20,27; 118:23; 119:50,56; 132:14; **Prov.** 6:3; **Song** 3:6; 6:10; 7:7(8); 8:5; **Isa.** 1:12; 3:6; 5:25; 9:7(6),12(11), 17(16),21(20); 10:4; 12:5; 14:26; 23:7,8; 27:9; 28:12,29; 30:7; 36:10,15; 37:32–35; 38:6; 41:20; 42:23; 43:9; 45:21; 46:8; 47:8; 48:1,16,20; 50:11; 51:21; 54:9,17; 56:2; 59:21; 66:8; **Jer.** 2:10,12,17; 3:10; 4:8,18,28; 5:7,20,21; 8:3; 9:12(11), 24(23); 10:18; 11:2,3,6,8; 13:13; 14:15; 16:6,10,13,21; 17:24,25; 19:8,11,12,15; 20:5; 21:4,6,7,9,10; 22:8,12; 24:6,8; 25:9,11,15; 26:6,9,11,12,15,20; 27:17,19; 29:16; 31:26,33; 32:3,15,22,23,28,29, 31,35,36,41–43; 33:4,5; 34:2,22; 36:29; 37:8,10,19; 38:2–4,16–18,23; 39:16; 40:2; 42:2,10,13; 44:4,23; **Lam.** 2:15; 3:21; **Ezek.** 3:1–3; 5:5; 6:10; 11:2,6; 16:29; 17:7; 20:27; 21:26,27; 23:38; 36:37; 43:12; 45:3,13,16; 47:14,20,21; 48:29; **Dan.** 9:13; 10:8; **Hos.** 5:1; 7:10;

Joel 1:2; 3:9(4:9); **Amos** 2:11; 4:12; 7:3,6; 8:4,8; 9:12; **Jon.** 1:7,8,10; **Mic.** 1:5,8; 2:3,10; 3:9; **Zech.** 5:3,5–8; 14:12, 15,19; **Zeph.** 2:10,15; **Mal.** 1:9; 2:1,4, 13; 3:10.

2064. זָבַד *zāḇaḏ* **verb**
(to endow, to give)
Gen. 30:20.

2065. זֶבֶד *zeḇeḏ,* זֵבֶד *zēḇeḏ* **masc. noun**
(endowment, gift)
Gen. 30:20.

2066. A. זָבָד *zāḇāḏ* **masc. proper noun**
(Zabad: son of Nathan)
1 Chr. 2:36,37.
B. זָבָד *zāḇāḏ* **masc. proper noun**
(Zabad: son of Tahath)
1 Chr. 7:21.
C. זָבָד *zāḇāḏ* **masc. proper noun**
(Zabad: son of Ahlai)
1 Chr. 11:41.
D. זָבָד *zāḇāḏ* **masc. proper noun**
(Zabad: son of Shimeath)
2 Chr. 24:26.
E. זָבָד *zāḇāḏ* **masc. proper noun**
(Zabad: son of Zattu)
Ezra 10:27.
F. זָבָד *zāḇāḏ* **masc. proper noun**
(Zabad: son of Hashum)
Ezra 10:33.
G. זָבָד *zāḇāḏ* **masc. proper noun**
(Zabad: son of Nebo)
Ezra 10:43.

2067. A. זַבְדִּי *zaḇdiy* **masc. proper noun**
(Zabdi: grandfather of Achan)
Josh. 7:1,17,18.
B. זַבְדִּי *zaḇdiy* **masc. proper noun**
(Zabdi: son of Shimhi)
1 Chr. 8:19.
C. זַבְדִּי *zaḇdiy* **masc. proper noun**
(Zabdi: a Shiphmite)
1 Chr. 27:27.
D. זַבְדִּי *zaḇdiy* **masc. proper noun**
(Zabdi: father of Micha)
Neh. 11:17.

2068. A. זַבְדִּיאֵל *zaḇdiy'ēl* **masc. proper noun**
(Zabdiel: father of Jashobeam)
1 Chr. 27:2.
B. זַבְדִּיאֵל *zaḇdiy'ēl* **masc. proper noun**
(Zabdiel: a priestly official)
Neh. 11:14.

2069. A. זְבַדְיָה *z^{e}ḇaḏyāh,* זְבַדְיָהוּ *z^{e}ḇaḏyāhû* **masc. proper noun**
(Zebadiah: grandson of Elpaal)
1 Chr. 8:15.
B. זְבַדְיָה *z^{e}ḇaḏyāh,* זְבַדְיָהוּ *z^{e}ḇaḏyāhû* **masc. proper noun**
(Zebadiah: son of Elpaal)
1 Chr. 8:17.
C. זְבַדְיָה *z^{e}ḇaḏyāh,* זְבַדְיָהוּ *z^{e}ḇaḏyāhû* **masc. proper noun**
(Zebadiah: son of Jeroham)
1 Chr. 12:7.
D. זְבַדְיָה *z^{e}ḇaḏyāh* **masc. proper noun**
(Zebadiah: a Korahite)
1 Chr. 26:2.
E. זְבַדְיָה *z^{e}ḇaḏyāh,* זְבַדְיָהוּ *z^{e}ḇaḏyāhû* **masc. proper noun**
(Zebadiah: son of Asahel)
1 Chr. 27:7.
F. זְבַדְיָה *z^{e}ḇaḏyāh* **masc. proper noun**
(Zebadiah: a Levite)
2 Chr. 17:8.
G. זְבַדְיָה *z^{e}ḇaḏyāh* **masc. proper noun**
(Zebadiah: son of Ishmael)
2 Chr. 19:11.
H. זְבַדְיָה *z^{e}ḇaḏyāh,* זְבַדְיָהוּ *z^{e}ḇaḏyāhû* **masc. proper noun**
(Zebadiah: son of Shephatiah)
Ezra 8:8.
I. זְבַדְיָה *z^{e}ḇaḏyāh,* זְבַדְיָהוּ

z^e^baḏyāhû **masc. proper noun**
(Zebadiah: a priest)
Ezra 10:20.

2070. זְבוּב *z^e^ḇûḇ* **masc. noun**
(a fly)
Eccl. 10:1; **Isa.** 7:18.

2071. זָבוּד *zāḇûḏ* **masc. proper noun**
(Zabud)
1 Kgs. 4:5.

2072. זַבּוּד *zabbûḏ* **masc. proper noun**
(Zabbud)
Ezra 8:14(NIV, [Q^e^] *zakkûr* [2139]).

2073. זְבוּל *z^e^ḇûl*, זְבֻל *z^e^ḇul* **masc. noun**
(magnificence, lofty habitation)
1 Kgs. 8:13; **2 Chr.** 6:2; **Ps.** 49:14(15); **Isa.** 63:15; **Hab.** 3:11.

2074. A. זְבוּלֻן *z^e^ḇûlûn*, זְבוּלֻן *z^e^ḇûlun*, זְבֻלוּן *z^e^ḇulûn* **masc. proper noun**
(Zebulun: sixth son of Jacob)
Gen. 30:20; 35:23; 46:14; 49:13; **Ex.** 1:3; **1 Chr.** 2:1.
B. זְבוּלוּן *z^e^ḇûlûn*, זְבוּלֻן *z^e^ḇûlun*, זְבֻלוּן *z^e^ḇulûn* **masc. proper noun**
(Zebulun: tribe or territory of Zebulun)
Num. 1:9,30,31; 2:7; 7:24; 10:16; 13:10; 26:26; 34:25; **Deut.** 27:13; 33:18; **Josh.** 19:10,16,27,34; 21:7,34; **Judg.** 1:30; 4:6,10; 5:14,18; 6:35; 12:12; **1 Chr.** 6:63(48),77(62); 12:33,40; 27:19; **2 Chr.** 30:10,11,18; **Ps.** 68:27(28); **Isa.** 9:1(8:23); **Ezek.** 48:26,27,33.

2075. זְבוּלֹנִי *z^e^ḇûlōniy* **masc. proper noun**
(Zebulunites)
Num. 26:27; **Judg.** 12:11,12.

2076. זָבַח *zāḇaḥ* **verb**
(to sacrifice, to offer)
Gen. 31:54; 46:1; **Ex.** 3:18; 5:3,8,17; 8:8(4),25–29(21–25); 13:15; 20:24; 22:20(19); 23:18; 24:5; 32:8; 34:15; **Lev.** 9:4; 17:5,7; 19:5; 22:29; **Num.** 22:40; **Deut.** 12:15,21; 15:21; 16:2,4–6; 17:1; 18:3; 27:7; 32:17; 33:19; **Josh.** 8:31; **Judg.** 2:5; 16:23; **1 Sam.** 1:3,4,21; 2:13,15,19; 6:15; 10:8; 11:15; 15:15,21; 16:2,5; 28:24; **2 Sam.** 6:13; 15:12; **1 Kgs.** 1:9,19,25; 3:2–4; 8:5,62,63; 11:8; 12:32; 13:2; 19:21; 22:43(44); **2 Kgs.** 12:3(4); 14:4; 15:4,35; 16:4; 17:35,36; 23:20; **1 Chr.** 15:26; 21:28; 29:21; **2 Chr.** 5:6; 7:4,5; 11:16; 15:11; 18:2; 28:4,23; 30:22; 33:16,17,22; 34:4; **Ezra** 4:2; **Neh.** 4:2(3:34); 12:43; **Ps.** 4:5(6); 27:6; 50:14,23; 54:6(8); 106:37,38; 107:22; 116:17; **Eccl.** 9:2; **Isa.** 57:7; 65:3; 66:3; **Ezek.** 16:20; 20:28; 34:3; 39:17,19; **Hos.** 4:13,14; 8:13; 11:2; 12:11(12); 13:2; **Jon.** 1:16; 2:9(10); **Hab.** 1:16; **Zech.** 14:21; **Mal.** 1:8,14.

2077. זֶבַח *zeḇaḥ* **masc. noun**
(a sacrifice, offering)
Gen. 31:54; 46:1; **Ex.** 10:25; 12:27; 18:12; 23:18; 24:5; 29:28; 34:15,25; **Lev.** 3:1,3,6,9; 4:10,26,31,35; 7:11–13,15–18, 20,21,29,32,34,37; 9:18; 10:14; 17:5,7,8; 19:5,6; 22:21,29; 23:19,37; **Num.** 6:17,18; 7:17,23,29,35,41,47,53,59,65, 71,77,83,88; 10:10; 15:3,5,8; 25:2; **Deut.** 12:6,11,27; 18:3; 32:38; 33:19; **Josh.** 22:23,26–29; **Judg.** 16:23; **1 Sam.** 1:21; 2:13,19,29; 3:14; 6:15; 9:12,13; 10:8; 11:15; 15:22; 16:3,5; 20:6,29; **2 Sam.** 15:12; **1 Kgs.** 8:62,63; 12:27; **2 Kgs.** 5:17; 10:19,24; 16:15; **1 Chr.** 29:21; **2 Chr.** 7:1,4,5,12; 29:31; 30:22; 33:16; **Neh.** 12:43; **Ps.** 4:5(6); 27:6; 40:6(7); 50:5,8; 51:16(18),17(19),19(21); 106:28; 107:22; 116:17; **Prov.** 7:14; 15:8; 17:1; 21:3,27; **Eccl.** 5:1(4:17); **Isa.** 1:11; 19:21; 34:6; 43:23,24; 56:7; 57:7; **Jer.** 6:20; 7:21,22; 17:26; 33:18; 46:10; **Ezek.**

20:28; 39:17,19; 40:42; 44:11; 46:24; **Dan.** 9:27; **Hos.** 3:4; 4:19; 6:6; 8:13; 9:4; **Amos** 4:4; 5:25; **Jon.** 1:16; **Zeph.** 1:7,8.

2078. זֶבַח *ze<u>b</u>aḥ* **masc. proper noun**
(Zebah)
Judg. 8:5–7,10,12,15,18,21; **Ps.** 83:11(12).

2079. זַבַּי *zabbay* **masc. proper noun**
(Zabbai)
Ezra 10:28; **Neh.** 3:20([Q^e] *zakkay* [2140]).

2080. זְבִידָה *z^e<u>b</u>iy<u>d</u>āh* **fem. proper noun**
(Zebidah)
2 Kgs. 23:36(KJV, [Q^e] *ze<u>b</u>û<u>d</u>āh*).

2081. זְבִינָא *z^e<u>b</u>iyna'* **masc. proper noun**
(Zebina)
Ezra 10:43.

2082. זָבַל *zā<u>b</u>al* **verb**
(to honor, to dwell exaltedly)
Gen. 30:20.

2083. זְבֻל *z^e<u>b</u>ul* **masc. proper noun**
(Zebul)
Judg. 9:28,30,36,38,41.

2084. זְבַן *z^e<u>b</u>an* **Aram. verb**
(to gain)
Dan. 2:8.

2085. זָג *zāg* **masc. noun**
(skin [of a grape])
Num. 6:4.

2086. זֵד *zē<u>d</u>* **adj.**
(presumptuous, willful)
Ps. 19:13(14); 86:14; 119:21,51,69,78,85,122; **Prov.** 21:24; **Isa.** 13:11; **Jer.** 43:2; **Mal.** 3:15; 4:1(3:19).

2087. זָדוֹן *zā<u>d</u>ôn* **masc. noun**
(presumptuousness, arrogance)
Deut. 17:12; 18:22; **1 Sam.** 17:28; **Prov.** 11:2; 13:10; 21:24; **Jer.** 49:16; 50:31,32; **Ezek.** 7:10; **Obad.** 1:3.

2088. זֶה *zeh* **demons. masc. pron.**
(this, these)
Gen. 5:1,29; 6:15; 7:1,7,13; 11:6; 15:4; 16:8; 17:21,23,26; 18:13,25; 19:13,14,21; 20:10,11,13; 21:26,30; 22:16; 24:9,58; 25:22,30,32; 26:11,33; 27:20,21,24,36; 28:16,17,20; 29:33; 30:31; 31:1,38,41,48, 51,52; 32:2(3),10(11),19(20),29(30), 32(33); 33:8,15; 34:14; 35:17; 37:6,10, 17,22; 38:21–23,28; 39:9,11; 40:12, 14,18; 41:38; 42:15; 43:10,29; 44:5,7, 15,29; 45:6; 47:26; 48:9,15,18; 50:11, 20,25; **Ex.** 1:18; 2:6,9,15,20; 3:3,12, 15,21; 4:2,17; 5:22,23; 8:23(19); 9:5,6; 10:6,7,17; 11:1; 12:2,3,6,8,12,14,17, 24,41,42,51; 13:3,5,8,19; 14:12,20; 15:2; 16:3,16,32; 17:3,4,12; 18:14,18,23; 19:1; 21:31; 22:9(8); 24:14; 25:19; 26:13; 29:1,38; 30:13,31; 32:1,9,15,21,23,24,31; 33:1,4,12,13,15,17; 35:4; 37:8; 38:15; **Lev.** 6:20(13); 8:5,34; 9:6; 11:4,9,21,29; 16:30; 17:2; 23:6,14,21,27–30,34; **Num.** 7:17,23,29,35,41,47,53,59,65,71,77,83; 8:4; 9:3; 11:11–14,20; 13:17,27; 14:2,11, 13–16,19,22,29,32,35,41; 18:9,11; 20:4, 5,10,12; 21:2; 22:6,17,19,24,28,30,32,33; 23:1,29; 24:10,14; 27:12; 28:3,17; 29:7; 30:1(2); 32:15,20; 34:6,7,9; 35:5; 36:6; **Deut.** 1:6,31,32,35; 2:3,7,22,25,30; 3:14, 25–28; 4:6,20,22,32,38; 5:24,28,29; 6:24; 8:2,4,17,18; 9:4,7,12,13,27; 10:8,15; 11:4,5; 13:11(12); 14:7,9,12; 15:2,10,15; 17:5,16; 18:3; 19:4,20; 21:7,20; 22:16, 20,26; 24:18,22; 26:9,16; 27:9; 28:58; 29:4(3),7(6),20(19),21(20),24(23),27(26), 28(27); 30:10; 31:2,7,16,26; 32:47–49; 34:6; **Josh.** 1:2,4,6,8,11; 2:14,17,18,20;

3:7; 4:3,9,22; 5:4,9,11; 6:15,25,26; 7:7, 10,25,26; 8:22,28,29,33; 9:12,24,27; 10:27; 13:13; 14:10,12,14; 15:4,12,63; 16:10; 17:12; 18:19; 22:3,16,17,22,31; 23:8,9; **Judg.** 1:21,26; 2:20; 4:14; 5:5; 6:14,18,24,26,29; 7:4; 8:1,3,4; 9:19, 29,38; 10:4,15; 11:37; 12:3; 13:6,18; 15:19; 16:15,28; 18:3,4,12,24; 19:23, 24,30; 20:9,16,17; 21:11; **Ruth** 2:8; **1 Sam.** 1:26,27; 2:34; 4:14; 5:5; 6:18,20; 8:8,11; 9:11,17,18,21; 10:11,27; 11:13; 12:2,5,8,16; 14:4,10,29,34,45; 15:14; 16:8,9,12; 17:3,10,12,17,25–27,30,32,33, 36,37,46,47,55,56; 18:8; 20:2; 21:9(10), 11(12),15(16); 22:8,13; 23:26; 24:6(7), 10(11),16(17),19(20); 25:11,21,25,32,33; 26:16–18,21,24; 27:6; 28:10,18; 29:3–6,8; 30:8,13,15,20,24,25; **2 Sam.** 1:3; 2:5, 6,13; 3:38; 4:3,8; 6:8; 7:6,17; 11:11, 12,25; 12:6,12,14,21,23; 13:20; 14:2,3, 13,15,20,21; 15:2,6; 16:9,12,17,18; 17:6; 18:18,20,22,26,27; 19:42(43); 24:3; **1 Kgs.** 1:27,30; 2:23,26; 3:6,9–11,23; 5:7(21); 6:12; 7:8,28; 8:8,24,27,29–31, 33,35,38,42,43,61; 9:3,8,13,15,21; 10:12, 19,20; 11:10,27; 12:6,7,9,10,19,24,27,30; 13:3,8,12,16,33,34; 14:2,5,6,13,14; 17:3, 21,24; 18:7,17,37; 19:5; 20:7,9,12,13,24, 28,39; 21:2,5; 22:20,24,27; **2 Kgs.** 1:2,5; 2:22; 3:8,16,23; 4:16,17,43; 5:6,7,18, 20,22; 6:9,11,18,19,32; 7:2,9,19; 8:5,8,9, 13,22; 9:1,11,25; 10:2; 11:5; 14:7; 16:6; 17:12,23,34,41; 18:19,21,22,25; 19:3, 21,29; 20:9,17; 21:7,15; 22:13,16,17, 19,20; 23:3,21–23; **1 Chr.** 4:41,43; 5:26; 13:11; 17:5,15; 21:7,8; 22:1; 28:7; 29:16; **2 Chr.** 1:10; 5:9; 6:15,18,20–22,24,26, 29,32,33,40; 7:12,15,16,20,21; 8:8; 9:18,19; 10:6,7,9,19; 11:4; 14:11(10); 18:19,23,26; 20:9,12,15; 21:10; 23:4; 25:9; 31:10; 32:9; 33:7; 34:21,24,25,27, 28,31; 35:19; **Ezra** 3:12; 7:11; 9:2,3, 7,15; 10:5,13,14; **Neh.** 1:11; 2:2,4,19; 5:10,12,13,18,19; 6:4,5; 9:1,10,18,32; 13:4,6,17; **Esth.** 1:18; 2:13; 3:14; 4:5,11; 5:13; 6:3; 7:5,6; 8:13; **Job** 1:16–18; 2:2; 9:29; 14:3; 15:17; 18:21; 19:3,19; 20:29; 21:23,25; 27:12,13; 28:12,20; 36:21; 38:2,19,24; 42:3; **Ps.** 24:6,8,10; 25:12; 34:6(7); 48:14(15); 49:13(14); 56:9(10); 68:8(9); 74:2(3); 75:7,8; 78:54; 87:4,6; 104:8,25,26; 118:20,24; 132:12(MT *zô* [2097]); **Prov.** 17:16; 23:22; 24:12; **Eccl.** 1:10,17; 2:3,10,15,19,21,23,26; 3:19; 4:4,8,16; 5:10(9); 6:2,5,9; 7:6,10,14,18, 27,29; 8:9,10,14; 9:1,3; 11:6; 12:13; **Song** 2:8,9; 5:16; **Isa.** 6:3,7,9,10; 8:6, 11,12,20; 9:16(15); 14:4,16,28; 16:13; 17:14; 20:6; 21:9; 22:14,15; 23:13; 24:3; 25:6,7,9,10; 26:1; 27:9; 28:11,14; 29:11–14; 30:12,13,21; 36:4,6,7; 37:3,22,30; 38:7; 39:6; 44:5; 50:1; 56:12; 58:5,6; 63:1; 66:1,2; **Jer.** 1:10; 2:37; 3:25; 4:10,11; 5:9,14,23,29; 6:16,19–21; 7:2,3, 6,7,10,11,16,20,23,25,28,33; 8:5; 9:9(8), 15(14); 10:19; 11:14; 13:10,12,25; 14:10, 11,13,17; 15:1,20; 16:2,3,5,9,10; 18:6; 19:3,4,6,7,11,12; 20:18; 21:8; 22:1,3–5, 11,21,28,30; 23:6,32,33,38; 24:5; 25:3, 13,18; 26:1,6,9,11,12,16; 27:1,16; 29:10, 29,32; 30:21; 31:23; 32:14,20,31,37,42; 33:10,12,16,24; 35:14,16; 36:1,2,7; 37:18; 38:4,10,21; 40:2,3,16; 42:18; 44:2,6,10,22,23,29; 46:7; 49:19; 50:17, 44; 51:62,63; 52:28; **Lam.** 2:16; 3:37; 5:17; **Ezek.** 1:5; 2:3; 8:5; 12:10,22,23; 16:49; 18:2,3; 20:29; 24:2; 40:1; 41:4,22; 43:13; 44:2; 45:2,7; 46:20; 47:7,12,15; 48:21; **Dan.** 1:14; 9:7,15; 10:11,17; **Amos** 3:1; 4:1; 5:1,18; **Obad.** 1:20; **Jon.** 1:8, 12,14; 4:2; **Mic.** 2:11; 5:5(4); **Zeph.** 1:4; **Hag.** 1:2,4; 2:3,7,9,14,15,18,19; **Zech.** 1:12; 3:2; 4:6,9; 5:3; 7:3,5; 8:6,11,12.

2089. זֶה *zeh* **masc. noun** (lamb, sheep; variant spelling of *śeh* [7716])

1 Sam. 17:34(NASB, NIV, *śeh* [7716]).

2090. זֹה *zōh* **fem. demons. pron.** (this)

Judg. 18:4; **2 Sam.** 11:25; **1 Kgs.** 14:5; **2 Kgs.** 6:19; **Eccl.** 2:2,24; 5:16(15), 19(18); 7:23; 9:13; **Ezek.** 40:45.

2091. זָהָב *zāhāḇ* **masc. noun**
(gold)
Gen. 2:11,12; 13:2; 24:22,35,53; 41:42; 44:8; **Ex.** 3:22; 11:2; 12:35; 20:23; 25:3, 11–13,17,18,24–26,28,29,31,36,38,39; 26:6,29,32,37; 28:5,6,8,11,13–15,20, 22–24,26,27,33,34,36; 30:3–5; 31:4; 32:2,3,24,31; 35:5,22,32; 36:13,34,36,38; 37:2–4,6,7,11–13,15–17,22–24,26–28; 38:24; 39:2,3,5,6,8,13,15–17,19,20,25, 30,38; 40:5,26; **Lev.** 8:9; **Num.** 4:11; 7:14,20,26,32,38,44,50,56,62,68,74,80,8 4,86; 8:4; 22:18; 24:13; 31:22,50–52,54; **Deut.** 7:25; 8:13; 17:17; 29:17(16); **Josh.** 6:19,24; 7:21,24; 22:8; **Judg.** 8:24,26; **1 Sam.** 6:4,8,11,15,17,18; **2 Sam.** 1:24; 8:7,10,11; 12:30; 21:4; **1 Kgs.** 6:20–22,28,30,32,35; 7:48–51; 9:11,14,28; 10:2,10,11,14,16–18,21, 22,25; 12:28; 14:26; 15:15,18,19; 20:3,5,7; 22:48(49); **2 Kgs.** 5:5; 7:8; 10:29; 12:13(14),18(19); 14:14; 16:8; 18:14; 20:13; 23:33,35; 24:13; 25:15; **1 Chr.** 18:7,10,11; 20:2; 21:25; 22:14,16; 28:14–18; 29:2–5,7; **2 Chr.** 1:15; 2:7(6), 14(13); 3:4–10; 4:7,8,19–22; 5:1; 8:18; 9:1,9,10,13–18,20,21,24; 12:9; 13:8,11; 15:18; 16:2,3; 21:3; 24:14; 25:24; 32:27; 36:3; **Ezra** 1:4,6,9–11; 2:69; 8:25–28, 30,33; **Neh.** 7:70–72; **Esth.** 1:6,7; 4:11; 5:2; 8:4,15; **Job** 3:15; 23:10; 28:1,6,17; 31:24; 37:22; 42:11; **Ps.** 19:10(11); 45:13 (14); 72:15; 105:37; 115:4; 119:72,127; 135:15; **Prov.** 11:22; 17:3; 20:15; 22:1; 25:11,12; 27:21; **Eccl.** 2:8; 12:6; **Song** 1:11; 3:10; 5:14; **Isa.** 2:7,20; 13:17; 30:22; 31:7; 39:2; 40:19; 46:6; 60:6,9,17; **Jer.** 4:30; 10:4,9; 51:7; 52:19; **Lam.** 4:1; **Ezek.** 7:19; 16:13,17; 27:22; 28:4,13; 38:13; **Dan.** 11:8,38,43; **Hos.** 2:8(10); 8:4; **Joel** 3:5(4:5); **Nah.** 2:9(10); **Hab.** 2:19; **Zeph.** 1:18; **Hag.** 2:8; **Zech.** 4:2,12; 6:11; 13:9; 14:14; **Mal.** 3:3.

2092. זָהַם *zāham* **verb**
(to loathe, to abhor)
Job 33:20.

2093. זַהַם *zaham* **masc. proper noun**
(Zaham)
2 Chr. 11:19.

2094. I. זָהַר *zāhar* **verb**
(to enlighten, to warn)
Ex. 18:20; **2 Kgs.** 6:10; **2 Chr.** 19:10; **Ps.** 19:11(12); **Eccl.** 4:13; 12:12; **Ezek.** 3:17–21; 33:3–9.
II. זָהַר *zāhar* **verb**
(to be bright, to be shining)
Dan. 12:3.

2095. זְהַר *z^ehar* **Aram. verb**
(to take heed, to be careful; corr. to 2094,I)
Ezra 4:22.

2096. זֹהַר *zōhar* **masc. noun**
(brightness)
Ezek. 8:2; **Dan.** 12:3.

2097. זוֹ *zô* **demons. pron.**
(this, which)
Ps. 132:12; **Hos.** 7:16.

2098. זוּ *zû* **demons. pron.**
(this, which)
Ex. 15:13,16; **Ps.** 9:15(16); 10:2; 12:7(8); 17:9; 31:4(5); 32:8; 62:11(12); 68:28(29); 142:3(4); 143:8; **Isa.** 42:24; 43:21; **Hab.** 1:11.

2099. זִו *ziw* **masc. proper noun**
(Ziv, Zif)
1 Kgs. 6:1,37.

2100. זוּב *zûb* **verb**
(to flow, to gush)
Ex. 3:8,17; 13:5; 33:3; **Lev.** 15:2,4,6–9,11–13,19,25,32,33; 20:24; 22:4; **Num.** 5:2; 13:27; 14:8; 16:13,14; **Deut.** 6:3; 11:9; 26:9,15; 27:3; 31:20; **Josh.** 5:6; **2 Sam.** 3:29; **Ps.** 78:20; 105:41; **Isa.** 48:21; **Jer.** 11:5; 32:22; 49:4; **Lam.** 4:9; **Ezek.** 20:6,15.

2101. זוֹב *zô<u>b</u>* **masc. noun**
(a flow, issue, discharge)
Lev. 15:2,3,13,15,19,25,26,28,30,33.

2102. I. זוּד *zû<u>d</u>,* זִיד *ziy<u>d</u>* **verb**
(to act presumptuously, to be arrogant)
Ex. 18:11; 21:14; **Deut.** 1:43; 17:13; 18:20; **Neh.** 9:10,16,29; **Jer.** 50:29.
II. זוּד *zû<u>d</u>,* זִיד *ziy<u>d</u>* **verb**
(to boil, to cook)
Gen. 25:29.

2103. זוּד *zû<u>d</u>* **Aram. verb**
(to act proudly, to act arrogantly; corr. to Hebr. 2102,I)
Dan. 5:20.

2104. זוּזִים *zûziym* **masc. pl. proper noun**
(Zuzim, Zuzite)
Gen. 14:5.

2105. זוֹחֵת *zôḥē<u>t</u>* **masc. proper noun**
(Zoheth)
1 Chr. 4:20.

2106. זָוִית *zāwiy<u>t</u>* **fem. noun**
(cornerstone, pillar)
Ps. 144:12; **Zech.** 9:15.

2107. זוּל *zûl* **verb**
(to lavish, to pour out)
Isa. 46:6; **Lam.** 1:8(NASB, NIV, *zālal* [2151,I]).

2108. זוּלָה *zûlāh* **fem. noun**
(except, apart from)
Deut. 1:36; 4:12; **Josh.** 11:13; **Ruth** 4:4; **1 Sam.** 21:9(10); **2 Sam.** 7:22; **1 Kgs.** 3:18; 12:20; **2 Kgs.** 24:14; **1 Chr.** 17:20; **Ps.** 18:31(32); **Isa.** 26:13; 45:5,21; 64:4(3); **Hos.** 13:4.

2109. I. זוּן *zûn* **verb**
(to feed)
Jer. 5:8(NASB, NIV, [Q^e] see II).
II. יָזַן *yāzan* **verb**
(to be in a state of rut, to be rutting)
Jer. 5:8(KJV, [K^e] see I).

2110. זוּן *zûn* **Aram. verb**
(to feed; corr. to Hebr. 2109,I)
Dan. 4:12(9).

2111. זוּעַ *zûaʿ* **verb**
(to tremble, to cause to tremble)
Esth. 5:9; **Eccl.** 12:3; **Hab.** 2:7.

2112. זוּעַ *zûaʿ* **Aram. verb**
(to tremble; corr. to Hebr. 2111)
Dan. 5:19; 6:26(27).

2113. זְוָעָה *z^ewāʿāh* **fem. noun**
(horror, object of terror; see also *za^aweh* [2189])
2 Chr. 29:8(KJV, [Q^e] *za^awāh* [2189]); **Isa.** 28:19; **Jer.** 15:4(KJV, [Q^e] *za^awāh* [2189]); 24:9(KJV, [Q^e] *za^awāh* [2189]); 29:18(KJV, [Q^e] *za^awāh* [2189]); 34:17(KJV, [Q^e] *za^awāh* [2189]).

2114. I. זוּר *zûr* **verb**
(to be strange, to be alienated; to turn away, to desert, to become estranged; NIV, class. as adj.)
Ex. 29:33; 30:9,33; **Lev.** 10:1; 22:10,12,13; **Num.** 1:51; 3:4,10,38; 16:40(17:5); 18:4,7; 26:61; **Deut.** 25:5; 32:16; **1 Kgs.** 3:18; **2 Kgs.** 19:24; **Job** 15:19; 19:13(NIV, see II),15,17(NASB, NIV, see III),27; **Ps.** 44:20(21); 54:3(5); 58:3(4)(NIV, see II); 69:8(9)(NIV, see II); 78:30(NIV, see II); 81:9(10); 109:11; **Prov.** 2:16; 5:3,10,17,20; 6:1; 7:5; 11:15; 14:10; 20:16; 22:14; 23:33; 27:2,13; **Isa.** 1:4(NIV, see II),7; 17:10; 25:2,5; 28:21; 29:5; 43:12; 61:5; **Jer.** 2:25; 3:13; 5:19; 18:14; 30:8; 51:2,51; **Lam.** 5:2; **Ezek.** 7:21; 11:9; 14:5(NIV, see II); 16:32; 28:7,10; 30:12; 31:12; **Hos.** 5:7; 7:9; 8:7,12; **Joel** 3:17(4:17); **Obad.** 1:11.

II. זוּר *zûr* **verb**
(to turn aside, to turn away from, to alienate; KJV, NASB, see I)
Job 19:13; **Ps.** 58:3(4); 69:8(9); 78:30; **Isa.** 1:4; **Ezek.** 14:5.
III. זוּר *zûr* **verb**
(to be loathsome, to be offensive)
Job 19:17(KJV, see I).

2115. זוּר *zûr* **verb**
(to squeeze, to crush)
Judg. 6:38; **Job** 39:15; **Isa.** 1:6; 59:5(KJV, *zûreh* [2116]).

2116. זוּרֶה *zûreh* **masc. noun**
(that which is crushed)
Isa. 59:5(NASB, NIV, *zûr* [2115]).

2117. זָזָא *zāzā'* **masc. proper noun**
(Zaza)
1 Chr. 2:33.

2118. זָחַח *zāḥah* **verb**
(to be removed, to come loose)
Ex. 28:28; 39:21.

2119. I. זָחַל *zāḥal* **verb**
(to crawl, to creep away)
Deut. 32:24; **Mic.** 7:17.
II. זָחַל *zāḥal* **verb**
(to fear, to be afraid of)
Job 32:6.

2120. זֹחֶלֶת *zōḥelet* **proper noun**
(Zoheleth)
1 Kgs. 1:9.

2121. זֵידוֹן *zēḏôn* **adj.**
(churning, raging)
Ps. 124:5.

2122. זִיו *ziyw* **Aram. masc. noun**
(brightness, splendor)
Dan. 2:31; 4:36(33); 5:6,9,10; 7:28.

2123. I. זִיז *ziyz* **masc. coll. noun**
(living creatures, moving creatures)
Ps. 50:11; 80:13(14).
II. זִיז *ziyz* **masc. noun**
(abundance)
Isa. 66:11.

2124. A. זִיזָא *ziyzā'* **masc. proper noun**
(Ziza: a Simeonite)
1 Chr. 4:37.
B. זִיזָא *ziyzā'* **masc. proper noun**
(Ziza: son of Rehoboam)
2 Chr. 11:20.

2125. זִיזָה *ziyzāh* **masc. proper noun**
(Zizah: same person as *ziynā'* [2126])
1 Chr. 23:11.

2126. זִינָא *ziynā'* **masc. proper noun**
(Zina: same person as *ziyzāh* [2125])
1 Chr. 23:10(NIV, *ziyza'*).

2127. זִיעַ *ziya'* **masc. proper noun**
(Zia)
1 Chr. 5:13.

2128. A. זִיף *ziyp̱* **proper noun**
(Ziph: a city)
Josh. 15:24; **1 Sam.** 23:14,15,24; 26:2; **2 Chr.** 11:8.
B. זִיף *ziyp̱* **proper noun**
(Ziph: a city)
Josh. 15:55.
C. זִיף *ziyp̱* **masc. proper noun**
(Ziph: son of Jehaleleel)
1 Chr. 4:16.
D. זִיף *ziyp̱* **masc. proper noun**
(Ziph: a descendant of Caleb)
1 Chr. 2:42.

2129. זִיפָה *ziyp̱āh* **masc. proper noun**
(Ziphah)
1 Chr. 4:16.

2130. זִיפִי *ziyp̱iy* **masc. proper noun**
(Ziphite)
1 Sam. 23:19; 26:1; **Ps.** 54:[title](2).

2131. I. זֵק *zēq*, זִיקָה *ziyqāh* **fem. noun**
(missile, spark, firebrand)
Prov. 26:18; **Isa.** 50:11.
II. זֵק *zēq* **masc. noun**
(fetter, chain)
Job 36:8; **Ps.** 149:8; **Isa.** 45:14; **Nah.** 3:10.

2132. I. זַיִת *zayiṯ* **masc. noun**
(olive, olive tree)
Gen. 8:11; **Ex.** 23:11; 27:20; 30:24; **Lev.** 24:2; **Deut.** 6:11; 8:8; 24:20; 28:40; **Josh.** 24:13; **Judg.** 9:8,9; 15:5; **1 Sam.** 8:14; **2 Kgs.** 5:26; 18:32; **1 Chr.** 27:28; **Neh.** 5:11; 8:15; 9:25; **Job** 15:33; **Ps.** 52:8(10); 128:3; **Isa.** 17:6; 24:13; **Jer.** 11:16; **Hos.** 14:6(7); **Amos** 4:9; **Mic.** 6:15; **Hab.** 3:17; **Hag.** 2:19; **Zech.** 4:3,11,12; 14:4.
II. זַיִת *zayiṯ* **masc. proper noun**
(Olives, Olivet)
2 Sam. 15:30.

2133. זֵיתָן *zēyṯān* **masc. proper noun**
(Zethan)
1 Chr. 7:10.

2134. זַךְ *zaḵ* **adj.**
(pure, clean)
Ex. 27:20; 30:34; **Lev.** 24:2,7; **Job** 8:6; 11:4; 16:17; 33:9; **Prov.** 16:2; 20:11; 21:8.

2135. זָכָה *zāḵāh* **verb**
(to be pure, to be clean)
Job 15:14; 25:4; **Ps.** 51:4(6); 73:13; 119:9; **Prov.** 20:9; **Isa.** 1:16; **Mic.** 6:11.

2136. זָכוּ *zāḵû* **Aram. fem. noun**
(purity, innocence)
Dan. 6:22(23).

2137. זְכוֹכִית *z^eḵôḵiyṯ* **fem. noun**
(crystal, fine glass)
Job 28:17.

2138. זְכוּר *z^eḵûr* **masc. noun**
(a male, man)
Ex. 23:17; 34:23; **Deut.** 16:16; 20:13.

2139. A. זַכּוּר *zakkûr* **masc. proper noun**
(Zaccur: father of Shammuah)
Num. 13:4.
B. זַכּוּר *zakkûr* **masc. proper noun**
(Zaccur: son of Hamuel)
1 Chr. 4:26.
C. זַכּוּר *zakkûr* **masc. proper noun**
(Zaccur: a Merarite)
1 Chr. 24:27.
D. זַכּוּר *zakkûr* **masc. proper noun**
(Zaccur: son of Asaph)
1 Chr. 25:2,10; **Neh.** 12:35.
E. זַכּוּר *zakkûr* **masc. proper noun**
(Zaccur: son of Imri)
Neh. 3:2.
F. זַכּוּר *zakkûr* **masc. proper noun**
(Zaccur: a Levite)
Neh. 10:12.
G. זַכּוּר *zakkûr* **masc. proper noun**
(Zaccur: ancestor of Hanan)
Neh. 13:13.
H. זַכּוּר *zakkûr* **masc. proper noun**
(Zaccur: a Simeonite)
Ezra 8:14(KJV, NASB, [K^e] *zabbûd* [2072]).

2140. זַכַּי *zakkay* **masc. proper noun**
(Zaccai)
Ezra 2:9; **Neh.** 7:14.

2141. זָכַךְ *zāḵaḵ* **verb**
(to be clean, to be pure)
Job 9:30; 15:15; 25:5; **Lam.** 4:7.

2142. I. זָכַר *zāḵar* **verb**
(to remember, to recall)
Gen. 8:1; 9:15,16; 19:29; 30:22; 40:14,23; 41:9; 42:9; **Ex.** 2:24; 6:5; 13:3; 20:8,24; 23:13; 32:13; 34:19; **Lev.** 26:42,45; **Num.** 5:15; 10:9; 11:5; 15:39,40; **Deut.** 5:15; 7:18; 8:2,18; 9:7,27; 15:15; 16:3,12; 24:9,18,22; 25:17; 32:7; **Josh.** 1:13; 23:7; **Judg.** 8:34; 9:2; 16:28; **1 Sam.** 1:11,19; 4:18; 25:31; **2 Sam.** 14:11; 18:18; 19:19 (20); **1 Kgs.** 17:18; **2 Kgs.** 9:25; 20:3; **1 Chr.** 16:4,12,15; **2 Chr.** 6:42; 24:22; **Neh.** 1:8; 4:14(8); 5:19; 6:14; 9:17; 13:14,22,29,31; **Esth.** 2:1; 9:28; **Job** 4:7; 7:7; 10:9; 11:16; 14:13; 21:6; 24:20; 28:18; 36:24; 41:8(40:32); **Ps.** 8:4(5); 9:12(13); 20:3(4),7(8); 22:27(28); 25:6,7; 38:[title](1); 42:4(5),6(7); 45:17(18); 63:6(7); 70:[title](1); 71:16; 74:2,18,22; 77:3(4),6(7),11(12); 78:35,39,42; 79:8; 83:4(5); 87:4; 88:5(6); 89:47(48),50(51); 98:3; 103:14,18; 105:5,8,42; 106:4,7,45; 109:14,16; 111:5; 112:6; 115:12; 119:49, 52,55; 132:1; 136:23; 137:1,6,7; 143:5; **Prov.** 31:7; **Eccl.** 5:20(19); 9:15; 11:8; 12:1; **Song** 1:4; **Isa.** 12:4; 17:10; 19:17; 23:16; 26:13; 38:3; 43:18,25,26; 44:21; 46:8,9; 47:7; 48:1; 49:1; 54:4; 57:11; 62:6; 63:7,11; 64:5(4),9(8); 65:17; 66:3; **Jer.** 2:2; 3:16; 4:16; 11:19; 14:10,21; 15:15; 17:2; 18:20; 20:9; 23:36; 31:20,34; 44:21; 51:50; **Lam.** 1:7,9; 2:1; 3:19,20; 5:1; **Ezek.** 3:20; 6:9; 16:22,43,60,61,63; 18:22,24; 20:43; 21:23(28),24(29), 32(37); 23:19,27; 25:10; 29:16; 33:13,16; 36:31; **Hos.** 2:17(19); 7:2; 8:13; 9:9; **Amos** 1:9; 6:10; **Jon.** 2:7(8); **Mic.** 6:5; **Nah.** 2:5(6); **Hab.** 3:2; **Zech.** 10:9; 13:2; **Mal.** 4:4(3:22).

II. מַזְכִּיר *mazkiyr* **masc. noun**
(recorder)
2 Sam. 8:16; 20:24; **1 Kgs.** 4:3; **2 Kgs.** 18:18,37; **1 Chr.** 18:15; **2 Chr.** 34:8; **Isa.** 36:3,22.

2143. זֵכֶר *zēḵer* **masc. noun**
(memorial, remembrance)
Ex. 3:15; 17:14; **Deut.** 25:19; 32:26; **Esth.** 9:28; **Job** 18:17; **Ps.** 6:5(6); 9:6(7); 30:4(5); 34:16(17); 97:12; 102:12(13); 109:15; 111:4; 112:6; 135:13; 145:7; **Prov.** 10:7; **Eccl.** 9:5; **Isa.** 26:8,14; **Hos.** 12:5(6); 14:7(8).

2144. זֶכֶר *zeḵer* **masc. proper noun**
(Zecher, Zeker)
1 Chr. 8:31.

2145. I. זָכַר *zāḵar* **verb**
(to be male)
Ex. 34:19.

II. זָכָר *zāḵār* **masc. noun**
(man, male, human; male)
Gen. 1:27; 5:2; 6:19; 7:3,9,16; 17:10, 12,14,23; 34:15,22,24,25; **Ex.** 12:5,48; 13:12,15; **Lev.** 1:3,10; 3:1,6; 4:23; 6:18(11),29(22); 7:6; 12:2,7; 15:33; 18:22; 20:13; 22:19; 27:3,5–7; **Num.** 1:2,20,22; 3:15,22,28,34,39,40,43; 5:3; 18:10; 26:62; 31:7,17,18,35; **Deut.** 4:16; 15:19; **Josh.** 5:4; 17:2; **Judg.** 21:11,12; **1 Kgs.** 11:15,16; **2 Chr.** 31:16,19; **Ezra** 8:3–14; **Isa.** 66:7; **Jer.** 20:15; 30:6; **Ezek.** 16:17; **Mal.** 1:14.

2146. זִכָּרוֹן *zikkārôn* **masc. noun**
(memorial)
Ex. 12:14; 13:9; 17:14; 28:12,29; 30:16; 39:7; **Lev.** 23:24; **Num.** 5:15,18; 10:10; 16:40(17:5); 31:54; **Josh.** 4:7; **Neh.** 2:20; **Esth.** 6:1; **Job** 13:12; **Eccl.** 1:11; 2:16; **Isa.** 57:8; **Zech.** 6:14; **Mal.** 3:16.

2147. A. זִכְרִי *ziḵriy* **masc. proper noun**
(Zichri, Zicri: son of Izhar)
Ex. 6:21.

B. זִכְרִי *ziḵriy* **masc. proper noun**
(Zichri, Zicri: son of Shimei)
1 Chr. 8:19.

C. זִכְרִי *ziḵriy* **masc. proper noun**
(Zichri, Zicri: son of Shashak)
1 Chr. 8:23.

D. זִכְרִי *zikriy* **masc. proper noun**
(Zichri, Zicri: son of Jeroham)
1 Chr. 8:27.
E. זִכְרִי *zikriy* **masc. proper noun**
(Zichri, Zicri: a Levite)
1 Chr. 9:15.
F. זִכְרִי *zikriy* **masc. proper noun**
(Zichri, Zicri: father of Shelomith)
1 Chr. 26:25.
G. זִכְרִי *zikriy* **masc. proper noun**
(Zichri, Zicri: father of Eliezer)
1 Chr. 27:16.
H. זִכְרִי *zikriy* **masc. proper noun**
(Zichri, Zicri: father of Amasiah)
2 Chr. 17:16.
I. זִכְרִי *zikriy* **masc. proper noun**
(Zichri, Zicri: father of Elishaphat)
2 Chr. 23:1.
J. זִכְרִי *zikriy* **masc. proper noun**
(Zichri, Zicri: an Ephramite)
2 Chr. 28:7.
K. זִכְרִי *zikriy* **masc. proper noun**
(Zichri, Zicri: father of Joel)
Neh. 11:9.
L. זִכְרִי *zikriy* **masc. proper noun**
(Zichri, Zicri: a priest)
Neh. 12:17.

2148. A. זְכַרְיָה *z^e^karyāh* **masc. proper noun**
(Zechariah: the prophet)
Ezra 5:1; 6:14; **Zech.** 1:1,7; 7:1,8.
B. זְכַרְיָה *z^e^karyāh,* זְכַרְיָהוּ *z^e^karyāhû* **masc. proper noun**
(Zechariah: a Reubenite)
1 Chr. 5:6,7.
C. זְכַרְיָה *z^e^karyāh* **masc. proper noun**
(Zechariah: son of Meshelemiah)
1 Chr. 9:21; 26:2,14.
D. זְכַרְיָה *z^e^karyāh* **masc. proper noun**
(Zechariah: son of Jehiel)
1 Chr. 9:37.
E. זְכַרְיָה *z^e^karyāh,* זְכַרְיָהוּ *z^e^karyāhû* **masc. proper noun**
(Zechariah: a Levite)
1 Chr. 15:18,20; 16:5.
F. זְכַרְיָה *z^e^karyāh,* זְכַרְיָהוּ *z^e^karyāhû* **masc. proper noun**
(Zechariah: a priest)
1 Chr. 15:24.
G. זְכַרְיָה *z^e^karyāh,* זְכַרְיָהוּ *z^e^karyāhû* **masc. proper noun**
(Zechariah: son of Isshiah)
1 Chr. 24:25.
H. זְכַרְיָה *z^e^karyāh,* זְכַרְיָהוּ *z^e^karyāhû* **masc. proper noun**
(Zechariah: fourth son of Hosah)
1 Chr. 26:11.
I. זְכַרְיָה *z^e^karyāh,* זְכַרְיָהוּ *z^e^karyāhû* **masc. proper noun**
(Zechariah: father of Iddo)
1 Chr. 27:21.
J. זְכַרְיָה *z^e^karyāh* **masc. proper noun**
(Zechariah: prince of Judah)
2 Chr. 17:7.
K. זְכַרְיָה *z^e^karyāh,* זְכַרְיָהוּ *z^e^karyāhû* **masc. proper noun**
(Zechariah: father of Jahaziel)
2 Chr. 20:14.
L. זְכַרְיָה *z^e^karyāh,* זְכַרְיָהוּ *z^e^karyāhû* **masc. proper noun**
(Zechariah: son of Jehoshaphat)
2 Chr. 21:2.
M. זְכַרְיָה *z^e^karyāh* **masc. proper noun**
(Zechariah: son of Jehoiada)
2 Chr. 24:20.
N. זְכַרְיָה *z^e^karyāh,* זְכַרְיָהוּ *z^e^karyāhû* **masc. proper noun**
(Zechariah: a prophet)
2 Chr. 26:5.
O. זְכַרְיָה *z^e^karyāh,* זְכַרְיָהוּ *z^e^karyāhû* **masc. proper noun**
(Zechariah: son of Jeroboam II)
2 Kgs. 14:29; 15:8,11.
P. זְכַרְיָה *z^e^karyāh,* זְכַרְיָהוּ *z^e^karyāhû* **masc. proper noun**
(Zechariah: father of Abi)
2 Kgs. 18:2; **2 Chr.** 29:1.
Q. זְכַרְיָה *z^e^karyāh,* זְכַרְיָהוּ

z^e*karyāhû* **masc. proper noun**
(Zechariah: son of Asaph)
2 Chr. 29:13.
R. זְכַרְיָה z^e*karyāh,* זְכַרְיָהוּ z^e*karyāhû* **masc. proper noun**
(Zechariah: son of Jeberechiah)
Isa. 8:2.
S. זְכַרְיָה z^e*karyāh* **masc. proper noun**
(Zechariah: a Kohathite)
2 Chr. 34:12.
T. זְכַרְיָה z^e*karyāh,* זְכַרְיָהוּ z^e*karyāhû* **masc. proper noun**
(Zechariah: temple officer)
2 Chr. 35:8.
U. זְכַרְיָה z^e*karyāh* **masc. proper noun**
(Zechariah: descendant of Pharosh)
Ezra 8:3.
V. זְכַרְיָה z^e*karyāh* **masc. proper noun**
(Zechariah: son of Bebai)
Ezra 8:11.
W. זְכַרְיָה z^e*karyāh* **masc. proper noun**
(Zechariah: leader summoned by Ezra)
Ezra 8:16.
X. זְכַרְיָה z^e*karyāh* **masc. proper noun**
(Zechariah: son of Elam)
Ezra 10:26.
Y. זְכַרְיָה z^e*karyāh* **masc. proper noun**
(Zechariah: a Levite)
Neh. 8:4.
Z. זְכַרְיָה z^e*karyāh* **masc. proper noun**
(Zechariah: descendant of Perez or Pharez)
Neh. 11:4.
AA. זְכַרְיָה z^e*karyāh* **masc. proper noun**
(Zechariah: son of Shiloni)
Neh. 11:5.
BB. זְכַרְיָה z^e*karyāh* **masc. proper noun**
(Zechariah: a priest)
Neh. 11:12.
CC. זְכַרְיָה z^e*karyāh* **masc. proper noun**
(Zechariah: a priest)
Neh. 12:16.
DD. זְכַרְיָה z^e*karyāh* **masc. proper noun**
(Zechariah: son of Jonathan)
Neh. 12:35.
EE. זְכַרְיָה z^e*karyāh* **masc. proper noun**
(Zechariah: a priest)
Neh. 12:41.

2149. זְלוּת *zullûṯ* **fem. noun**
(vileness, worthlessness)
Ps. 12:8(9).

2150. זַלְזַל *zalzal* **masc. noun**
(twig, tender shoot)
Isa. 18:5.

2151. I. זָלַל *zālal* **verb**
(to be vile, to be gluttonous, to be worthless)
Deut. 21:20; **Prov.** 23:20,21; 28:7; **Jer.** 15:19; **Lam.** 1:8(KJV, *zûl* [2107]),11.
II. זָלַל *zālal* **verb**
(to quake, to shake, to tremble)
Isa. 64:1(63:19),3(2).

2152. זַלְעָפָה *zal'āpāh* **fem. noun**
(a horror, burning)
Ps. 11:6; 119:53; **Lam.** 5:10.

2153. זִלְפָּה *zilpāh* **fem. proper noun**
(Zilpah)
Gen. 29:24; 30:9,10,12; 35:26; 37:2; 46:18.

2154. זִמָּה *zimmāh* **fem. noun**
(wickedness, lewdness)
Lev. 18:17; 19:29; 20:14; **Judg.** 20:6; **Job** 17:11; 31:11; **Ps.** 26:10; 119:150; **Prov.** 10:23; 21:27; 24:9; **Isa.** 32:7;

Jer. 13:27; **Ezek.** 16:27,43,58; 22:9,11; 23:21,27,29,35,44,48,49; 24:13; **Hos.** 6:9.

2155. A. זִמָּה *zimmāh* **masc. proper noun**
(Zimmah: son of Jahath)
1 Chr. 6:20(5).
B. זִמָּה *zimmāh* **masc. proper noun**
(Zimmah: a Gershomite)
1 Chr. 6:42(27).
C. זִמָּה *zimmāh* **masc. proper noun**
(Zimmah: father of Joah)
2 Chr. 29:12.

2156. זְמוֹרָה *z^emôrāh* **fem. noun**
(a branch)
Num. 13:23; **Isa.** 17:10; **Ezek.** 8:17; 15:2; **Nah.** 2:2(3).

2157. זַמְזֻמִּים *zamzummiym* **masc. pl. proper noun**
(Zamzummite, Zamzummim)
Deut. 2:20.

2158. זָמִיר *zāmiyr* **masc. noun**
(song, singer, psalmist)
2 Sam. 23:1; **Job** 35:10; **Ps.** 95:2; 119:54; **Song** 2:12(NASB, *zāmiyr* [2159]); **Isa.** 24:16; 25:5(KJV, *zāmiyr* [2159]).

2159. זָמִיר *zāmiyr* **masc. noun**
(branch)
Song 2:12(KJV, NIV, *zāmiyr* [2158]); **Isa.** 25:5(NASB, NIV, *zāmiyr* [2158]).

2160. זְמִירָה *z^emiyrah* **masc. proper noun**
(Zemirah, Zemira)
1 Chr. 7:8.

2161. זָמַם *zāmam* **verb**
(to devise, to purpose, to plan)
Gen. 11:6; **Deut.** 19:19; **Ps.** 17:3; 31:13(14); 37:12; **Prov.** 30:32; 31:16; **Jer.** 4:28; 51:12; **Lam.** 2:17; **Zech.** 1:6; 8:14,15.

2162. זָמָם *zāmām* **masc. noun**
(a wicked plan, device)
Ps. 140:8(9).

2163. זָמַן *zāman* **verb**
(to set a time, to appoint a time)
Ezra 10:14; **Neh.** 10:34(35); 13:31.

2164. זְמַן *z^eman* **Aram. verb**
(to appoint a time, to agree together; corr. to Hebr. 2163)
Dan. 2:9.

2165. זְמַן *z^eman* **masc. noun**
(an appointed time)
Neh. 2:6; **Esth.** 9:27,31; **Eccl.** 3:1.

2166. זְמָן *z^emān* **Aram. masc. noun**
(a time, season; corr. to Hebr. 2165)
Ezra 5:3; **Dan.** 2:16,21; 3:7,8; 4:36(33); 6:10(11),13(14); 7:12,22,25.

2167. זָמַר *zāmar* **verb**
(to sing, to sing praise)
Judg. 5:3; **2 Sam.** 22:50; **1 Chr.** 16:9; **Ps.** 7:17(18); 9:2(3),11(12); 18:49(50); 21:13(14); 27:6; 30:4(5),12(13); 33:2; 47:6(7),7(8); 57:7(8),9(10); 59:17(18); 61:8(9); 66:2,4; 68:4(5),32(33); 71:22,23; 75:9(10); 92:1(2); 98:4,5; 101:1; 104:33; 105:2; 108:1(2),3(4); 135:3; 138:1; 144:9; 146:2; 147:1,7; 149:3; **Isa.** 12:5.

2168. זָמַר *zāmar* **verb**
(to trim, to prune)
Lev. 25:3,4; **Isa.** 5:6.

2169. זֶמֶר *zemer* **masc. noun**
(mountain sheep, chamois)
Deut. 14:5.

2170. זְמָר *z^emār* **Aram. masc. noun**
(music, instrumental music)
Dan. 3:5,7,10,15.

2171. זַמָּר *zammār* **Aram. masc. noun**
(a singer)
Ezra 7:24.

2172. זִמְרָה *zimrāh* **fem. noun**
(song, music)
Ex. 15:2(KJV, *zimrāt* [2176]); **Ps.** 81:2(3); 98:5; 118:14(KJV, *zimrāt* [2176]); **Isa.** 12:2(KJV, *zimrāt* [2176]); 51:3; **Amos** 5:23.

2173. זִמְרָה *zimrāh* **fem. noun**
(choice fruit)
Gen. 43:11.

2174. A. זִמְרִי *zimriy* **masc. proper noun**
(Zimri: a Simeonite)
Num. 25:14.
B. זִמְרִי *zimriy* **masc. proper noun**
(Zimri: grandson of Judah)
1 Chr. 2:6.
C. זִמְרִי *zimriy* **masc. proper noun**
(Zimri: king of Israel)
1 Kgs. 16:9,10,12,15,16,18,20; **2 Kgs.** 9:31.
D. זִמְרִי *zimriy* **masc. proper noun**
(Zimri: descendant of Saul)
1 Chr. 8:36; 9:42.
E. זִמְרִי *zimriy* **masc. proper noun**
(Zimri: Arabian people)
Jer. 25:25.

2175. זִמְרָן *zimrān* **masc. proper noun**
(Zimran)
Gen. 25:2; **1 Chr.** 1:32.

2176. זִמְרָת *zimrāṯ* **fem. noun**
(song)
Ex. 15:2(NASB, NIV, *zimrāh* [2172]); **Ps.** 118:14(NASB, NIV, *zimrāh* [2172]); **Isa.** 12:2(NASB, NIV, *zimrāh* [2172]).

2177. זַן *zan* **masc. noun**
(kind, sort)
2 Chr. 16:14; **Ps.** 144:13.

2178. זַן *zan* **Aram. masc. noun**
(kind, sort; corr. to Hebr. 2177)
Dan. 3:5,7,10,15.

2179. זָנַב *zānaḇ* **verb**
(to attack the rear, to cut off the straggler)
Deut. 25:18; **Josh.** 10:19.

2180. זָנָב *zānāḇ* **masc. noun**
(a tail)
Ex. 4:4; **Deut.** 28:13,44; **Judg.** 15:4; **Job** 40:17; **Isa.** 7:4; 9:14(13),15(14); 19:15.

2181. I. זָנָה *zānāh* **verb**
(to fornicate, to commit adultery, to engage in prostitution, to be unfaithful)
Gen. 34:31(NIV, see II); 38:15(NIV, see II),24; **Ex.** 34:15,16; **Lev.** 17:7; 19:29; 20:5,6; 21:7(NIV, see II),9,14(NIV, see II); **Num.** 15:39; 25:1; **Deut.** 22:21; 23:18(19)(NIV, see II); 31:16; **Josh.** 2:1(NIV, see II); 6:17(NIV, see II),22(NIV, see II),25(NIV, see II); **Judg.** 2:17; 8:27,33; 11:1(NIV, see II); 16:1(NIV, see II); 19:2; **1 Kgs.** 3:16(NIV, see II); **1 Chr.** 5:25; **2 Chr.** 21:11,13; **Ps.** 73:27; 106:39; **Prov.** 6:26(NIV, see II); 7:10(NIV, see II); 23:27(NIV, see II); 29:3(NIV, see II); **Isa.** 1:21(NIV, see II); 23:15(NIV, see II),16(NIV, see II),17; 57:3; **Jer.** 2:20(NIV, see II); 3:1,3(NIV, see II),6,8; 5:7(NIV, see II); **Ezek.** 6:9; 16:15–17,26, 28,30(NIV, see II),31(NIV, see II),33(NIV, see II),34,35(NIV, see II),41; 20:30; 23:3,5,19,30,43,44(NIV, see II); **Hos.** 1:2; 2:5(7); 3:3; 4:10,12,13,14(NIV, see II),15,18; 5:3; 9:1; **Joel** 3:3(4:3)(NIV, see II); **Amos** 7:17; **Mic.** 1:7; **Nah.** 3:4(NIV, see II).

II. זוֹנָה *zônāh,* זֹנָה *zōnāh* **fem. noun**
(prostitute, whore, fornicator; KJV, NASB, see I)
Gen. 34:31; 38:15; **Lev.** 21:7,9,14; **Deut.** 23:18(19); **Josh.** 2:1; 6:17,22,25; **Judg.** 11:1; 16:1; **1 Kgs.** 3:16; 22:38(see *zōnôṯ* [2185]); **Prov.** 6:26; 7:10; 23:27; 29:3; **Isa.** 1:21; 23:15,16; **Jer.** 2:20; 3:3; 5:7; **Ezek.** 16:30,31,33,35; 23:44; **Hos.** 4:14; **Joel** 3:3(4:3); **Nah.** 3:4.

2182. A. זָנוֹחַ *zānôaḥ* **proper noun**
(Zanoah: a city in Judah near En-gannim)
Josh. 15:34; **1 Chr.** 4:18; **Neh.** 3:13; 11:30.
B. זָנוֹחַ *zānôaḥ* **proper noun**
(Zanoah: a city in Judah near Juttah)
Josh. 15:56.

2183. זְנוּנִים *z^enûniym* **masc. pl. noun**
(prostitution, adultery)
Gen. 38:24; **2 Kgs.** 9:22; **Ezek.** 23:11,29; **Hos.** 1:2; 2:2(4),4(6); 4:12; 5:4; **Nah.** 3:4.

2184. זְנוּת *z^enûṯ* **fem. noun**
(prostitution, unfaithfulness)
Num. 14:33; **Jer.** 3:2,9; 13:27; **Ezek.** 23:27; 43:7,9; **Hos.** 4:11; 6:10.

2185.
I. זֹנוֹת *zōnôṯ* **fem. noun**
(armor)
1 Kgs. 22:38(NASB, NIV, see II).
II. זֹנוֹת *zōnôṯ* **fem. noun**
(prostitute: Qal part. of *zānāh* [2181])
1 Kgs. 22:38(KJV, see I).

2186. I. זָנַח *zānaḥ* **verb**
(to reject)
1 Chr. 28:9; **2 Chr.** 11:14; 29:19; **Ps.** 43:2; 44:9(10),23(24); 60:1(3),10(12); 74:1; 77:7(8); 88:14(15); 89:38(39); 108:11(12); **Isa.** 19:6(NASB, NIV, see II); **Lam.** 2:7; 3:17,31; **Hos.** 8:3,5; **Zech.** 10:6.

II. זָנַח *zānaḥ* **verb**
(to stink)
Isa. 19:6(KJV, see I).

2187. זָנַק *zānaq* **verb**
(to leap, to spring)
Deut. 33:22.

2188. זֵעָה *zē'āh* **fem. noun**
(sweat)
Gen. 3:19.

2189. זַעֲוָה *za'^awāh* **fem. noun**
(a horror; see also *z^ewā'āh* [2113])
Deut. 28:25; **2 Chr.** 29:8([K^e] *z^ewā'āh* [2113]); **Jer.** 15:4([K^e] *z^ewā'āh* [2113]); 24:9([K^e] *z^ewā'āh* [2113]); 29:18([K^e] *z^ewā'āh* [2113]); 34:17([K^e] *z^ewā'āh* [2113]); **Ezek.** 23:46.

2190. זַעֲוָן *za'^awān* **masc. proper noun**
(Zaavan)
Gen. 36:27; **1 Chr.** 1:42.

2191. זְעֵיר *z^e'ēyr* **masc. noun**
(a little [of quantity or of time])
Job 36:2; **Isa.** 28:10,13.

2192. זְעֵיר *z^e'ēyr* **Aram. adj.**
(little, small; corr. to Hebr. 2191)
Dan. 7:8.

2193. זָעַךְ *zā'aḵ* **verb**
(to be extinguished)
Job 17:1.

2194. זָעַם *zā'am* **verb**
(to denounce, to defy)
Num. 23:7,8; **Ps.** 7:11(12); **Prov.** 22:14; 24:24; 25:23; **Isa.** 66:14; **Dan.** 11:30; **Mic.** 6:10; **Zech.** 1:12; **Mal.** 1:4.

2195. זַעַם *za'am* **masc. noun**
(wrath, indignation, anger)
Ps. 38:3(4); 69:24(25); 78:49; 102:10(11); **Isa.** 10:5,25; 13:5; 26:20;

30:27; **Jer.** 10:10; 15:17; 50:25; **Lam.** 2:6; **Ezek.** 21:31(36); 22:24,31; **Dan.** 8:19; 11:36; **Hos.** 7:16; **Nah.** 1:6; **Hab.** 3:12; **Zeph.** 3:8.

2196. זָעַף *zāʿap̱* **verb**
(to be sad, to be enraged)
Gen. 40:6; **2 Chr.** 26:19; **Prov.** 19:3; **Dan.** 1:10.

2197. זַעַף *zaʿap̱* **masc. noun**
(rage, anger)
2 Chr. 16:10; 28:9; **Prov.** 19:12; **Isa.** 30:30; **Jon.** 1:15; **Mic.** 7:9.

2198. זָעֵף *zāʿēp̱* **adj.**
(displeased, angry)
1 Kgs. 20:43; 21:4.

2199. זָעַק *zāʿaq* **verb**
(to cry out)
Ex. 2:23; **Josh.** 8:16; **Judg.** 3:9,15; 4:10,13; 6:6,7,34,35; 10:10,14; 12:2; 18:22,23; **1 Sam.** 4:13; 5:10; 7:8,9; 8:18; 12:8,10; 14:20; 15:11; 28:12; **2 Sam.** 13:19; 19:4(5),28(29); 20:4,5; **1 Kgs.** 22:32; **1 Chr.** 5:20; **2 Chr.** 18:31; 20:9; 32:20; **Neh.** 9:4,28; **Esth.** 4:1; **Job** 31:38; 35:9; **Ps.** 22:5(6); 107:13,19; 142:1(2),5(6); **Isa.** 14:31; 15:4,5; 26:17; 30:19; 57:13; **Jer.** 11:11,12; 20:8; 25:34; 30:15; 47:2; 48:20,31; **Lam.** 3:8; **Ezek.** 9:8; 11:13; 21:12(17); 27:30; **Hos.** 7:14; 8:2; **Joel** 1:14; **Jon.** 1:5; 3:7; **Mic.** 3:4; **Hab.** 1:2; 2:11; **Zech.** 6:8.

2200. זְעַק *zᵉʿaq* **Aram. verb**
(to cry out, to call out; corr. to Hebr. 2199)
Dan. 6:20(21).

2201. זְעָקָה *zᵉʿāqāh* **fem. noun**
(an outcry)
Gen. 18:20; **Neh.** 5:6; 9:9; **Esth.** 4:1; 9:31; **Job** 16:18; **Prov.** 21:13; **Eccl.** 9:17; **Isa.** 15:5,8; 65:19; **Jer.** 18:22; 20:16; 48:4,34; 50:46; 51:54; **Ezek.** 27:28.

2202. זִפְרֹן *zip̱rōn* **proper noun**
(Ziphron)
Num. 34:9.

2203. זֶפֶת *zep̱eṯ* **fem. noun**
(pitch, tar)
Ex. 2:3; **Isa.** 34:9.

2204. זָקֵן *zāqēn* **verb**
(to be old, to grow old)
Gen. 18:12,13; 19:31; 24:1; 27:1,2; **Josh.** 13:1; 23:1,2; **Ruth** 1:12; **1 Sam.** 2:22; 4:18; 8:1,5; 12:2; 17:12; **2 Sam.** 19:32(33); **1 Kgs.** 1:1,15; **2 Kgs.** 4:14; **1 Chr.** 23:1; **2 Chr.** 24:15; **Job** 14:8; **Ps.** 37:25; **Prov.** 22:6; 23:22.

2205. זָקֵן *zāqēn* **adj.**
(old, elder in the sense of having authority)
Gen. 18:11; 19:4; 24:2; 25:8; 35:29; 43:27; 44:20; 50:7; **Ex.** 3:16,18; 4:29; 10:9; 12:21; 17:5,6; 18:12; 19:7; 24:1, 9,14; **Lev.** 4:15; 9:1; 19:32; **Num.** 11:16,24,25,30; 16:25; 22:4,7; **Deut.** 5:23(20); 19:12; 21:2–4,6,19,20; 22:15–18; 25:7–9; 27:1; 28:50; 29:10(9); 31:9,28; 32:7; **Josh.** 6:21; 7:6; 8:10,33; 9:11; 20:4; 23:2; 24:1,31; **Judg.** 2:7; 8:14,16; 11:5,7–11; 19:16,17,20,22; 21:16; **Ruth** 4:2,4,9,11; **1 Sam.** 2:31,32; 4:3; 8:4; 11:3; 15:30; 16:4; 28:14; 30:26; **2 Sam.** 3:17; 5:3; 12:17; 17:4,15; 19:11(12); **1 Kgs.** 8:1,3; 12:6,8,13; 13:11,25,29; 20:7,8; 21:8,11; **2 Kgs.** 6:32; 10:1,5; 19:2; 23:1; **1 Chr.** 11:3; 15:25; 21:16; **2 Chr.** 5:2,4; 10:6,8,13; 34:29; 36:17; **Ezra** 3:12; 10:8,14; **Esth.** 3:13; **Job** 12:20; 32:4,9; 42:17; **Ps.** 105:22; 107:32; 119:100; 148:12; **Prov.** 17:6; 20:29; 31:23; **Eccl.** 4:13; **Isa.** 3:2,5,14; 9:15(14); 20:4; 24:23; 37:2; 47:6; 65:20; **Jer.** 6:11; 19:1; 26:17; 29:1; 31:13; 51:22; **Lam.** 1:19; 2:10,21; 4:16; 5:12,14; **Ezek.** 7:26; 8:1,11,12; 9:6; 14:1; 20:1,3; 27:9; **Joel** 1:2,14; 2:16,28(3:1); **Zech.** 8:4.

2206. זָקָן *zāqān* **masc. noun**
(beard, chin)
Lev. 13:29,30; 14:9; 19:27; 21:5; **1 Sam.** 17:35; 21:13(14); **2 Sam.** 10:4,5; 20:9; **1 Chr.** 19:5; **Ezra** 9:3; **Ps.** 133:2; **Isa.** 7:20; 15:2; **Jer.** 41:5; 48:37; **Ezek.** 5:1.

2207. זֹקֶן *zōqen* **masc. noun**
(old age)
Gen. 48:10.

2208. זְקֻנִים *z^e^quniym* **masc. pl. noun**
(old age)
Gen. 21:2,7; 37:3; 44:20.

2209. זִקְנָה *ziqnāh* **fem. noun**
(old age)
Gen. 24:36; **1 Kgs.** 11:4; 15:23; **Ps.** 71:9,18; **Isa.** 46:4.

2210. זָקַף *zāqap̱* **verb**
(to raise up, to lift up)
Ps. 145:14; 146:8.

2211. זְקַף *z^e^qap̱* **Aram. verb**
(to raise up, to lift up; corr. to Hebr. 2210)
Ezra 6:11.

2212. זָקַק *zāqaq* **verb**
(to refine, to purify)
1 Chr. 28:18; 29:4; **Job** 28:1; 36:27; **Ps.** 12:6(7); **Isa.** 25:6; **Mal.** 3:3.

2213. זֵר *zēr* **masc. noun**
(molding, border)
Ex. 25:11,24,25; 30:3,4; 37:2,11,12,26,27.

2214. זָרָא *zārā'* **fem. noun**
(a loathsome thing)
Num. 11:20.

2215. זָרַב *zāraḇ* **verb**
(to dry up, to be warmed)
Job 6:17.

2216. זְרֻבָּבֶל *z^e^rubbāḇel* **masc. proper noun**
(Zerubbabel)
1 Chr. 3:19; **Ezra** 2:2; 3:2,8; 4:2,3; **Neh.** 7:7; 12:1,47; **Hag.** 1:1,12,14; 2:2,4,21,23; **Zech.** 4:6,7,9,10.

2217. זְרֻבָּבֶל *z^e^rubbāḇel* **Aram. masc. proper noun**
(Zerubbabel; corr. to Hebr. 2216)
Ezra 5:2.

2218. זֶרֶד *zereḏ* **proper noun**
(Zered, Zared)
Num. 21:12; **Deut.** 2:13,14.

2219. I. זָרָה *zārāh* **verb**
(to scatter, to winnow; to disperse)
Ex. 32:20; **Lev.** 26:33; **Num.** 16:37 (17:2); **Ruth** 3:2; **1 Kgs.** 14:15; **Job** 18:15; 37:9(KJV, *m^e^zāreh* [4215,I]; NIV, *m^e^zāreh* [4215,II]); **Ps.** 44:11(12); 106:27; **Prov.** 1:17; 15:7; 20:8,26; **Isa.** 30:22,24; 41:16; **Jer.** 4:11; 15:7; 31:10; 49:32,36; 51:2; **Ezek.** 5:2,10,12; 6:5,8; 12:14,15; 20:23; 22:15; 29:12; 30:23,26; 36:19; **Zech.** 1:19(2:2),21(2:4); **Mal.** 2:3.
II. זָרָה *zārāh* **verb**
(to compass about, to measure off; to scrutinize, to discern)
Ps. 139:3.

2220. זְרוֹעַ *z^e^rôa'*, זְרֹעַ *z^e^rōa'* **fem. noun**
(arm, power)
Gen. 49:24; **Ex.** 6:6; 15:16; **Num.** 6:19; **Deut.** 4:34; 5:15; 7:19; 9:29; 11:2; 18:3; 26:8; 33:20,27; **Judg.** 15:14; 16:12; **1 Sam.** 2:31; **2 Sam.** 1:10; 22:35; **1 Kgs.** 8:42; **2 Kgs.** 9:24; 17:36; **2 Chr.** 6:32; 32:8; **Job** 22:8,9; 26:2; 35:9; 38:15; 40:9; **Ps.** 10:15; 18:34(35); 37:17; 44:3(4); 71:18; 77:15(16); 79:11; 83:8(9); 89:10(11), 13(14),21(22); 98:1; 136:12; **Prov.** 31:17; **Song** 8:6; **Isa.** 9:20(19); 17:5; 30:30; 33:2; 40:10,11; 44:12; 48:14; 51:5,9; 52:10; 53:1; 59:16; 62:8; 63:5,12; **Jer.** 17:5; 21:5;

27:5; 32:17; 48:25; **Ezek.** 4:7; 13:20; 17:9; 20:33,34; 22:6; 30:21,22,24,25; 31:17; **Dan.** 10:6; 11:6,15,22,31; **Hos.** 7:15; 11:3; **Zech.** 11:17.

2221. זֵרוּעַ *zērûa‘* **masc. noun**
(that which is sown, seed)
Lev. 11:37; **Isa.** 61:11.

2222. I. זַרְזִיף *zarziyp̱* **masc. noun**
(downpour, hard rain)
Ps. 72:6(NIV, see II).
II. זָרַף *zārap̱* **verb**
(to water, to drip, to pour down)
Ps. 72:6(KJV, NASB, see I).

2223. זַרְזִיר *zarziyr* **masc. noun**
(a strutting rooster, greyhound; exact meaning unknown)
Prov. 30:31.

2224. זָרַח *zāraḥ* **verb**
(to rise up)
Gen. 32:31(32); **Ex.** 22:3(2); **Deut.** 33:2; **Judg.** 9:33; **2 Sam.** 23:4; **2 Kgs.** 3:22; **2 Chr.** 26:19; **Job** 9:7; **Ps.** 104:22; 112:4; **Eccl.** 1:5; **Isa.** 58:10; 60:1,2; **Jon.** 4:8; **Nah.** 3:17; **Mal.** 4:2(3:20).

2225. זֶרַח *zeraḥ* **masc. noun**
(a dawning, rising [as of the sun])
Isa. 60:3.

2226. A. זֶרַח *zeraḥ* **masc. proper noun**
(Zerah: son of Reuel)
Gen. 36:13,17; **1 Chr.** 1:37.
B. זֶרַח *zeraḥ* **masc. proper noun**
(Zerah: father of Jobab)
Gen. 36:33; **1 Chr.** 1:44.
C. זֶרַח *zeraḥ* **masc. proper noun**
(Zerah: son of Judah)
Gen. 38:30; 46:12; **Num.** 26:20; **Josh.** 7:1,18,24; 22:20; **1 Chr.** 2:4,6; 9:6; **Neh.** 11:24.
D. זֶרַח *zeraḥ* **masc. proper noun**
(Zerah: son of Simeon; the same as *ṣōhar* [6714,B])
Num. 26:13; **1 Chr.** 4:24.
E. זֶרַח *zeraḥ* **masc. proper noun**
(Zerah: a Gershonite)
1 Chr. 6:21(6).
F. זֶרַח *zeraḥ* **masc. proper noun**
(Zerah: father of Ethni)
1 Chr. 6:41(26).
G. זֶרַח *zeraḥ* **masc. proper noun**
(Zerah: king of Ethiopia)
2 Chr. 14:9(8).

2227. A. זַרְחִי *zarḥiy* **masc. proper noun**
(Zarhite: descendants of Zerah, son of Judah [2226,C])
Num. 26:20; **Josh.** 7:17; **1 Chr.** 27:11,13.
B. זַרְחִי *zarḥiy* **masc. proper noun**
(Zarhite: descendants of Zerah, son of Simeon [2226,D])
Num. 26:13.

2228. A. זְרַחְיָה *zᵉraḥyāh* **masc. proper noun**
(Zerahiah: a priest)
1 Chr. 6:6(5:32),51(36); **Ezra** 7:4.
B. זְרַחְיָה *zᵉraḥyāh* **masc. proper noun**
(Zerahiah: head of a family)
Ezra 8:4.

2229. זָרַם *zāram* **verb**
(to pour out, to sweep away [as with a flood])
Ps. 77:17(18); 90:5.

2230. זֶרֶם *zerem* **masc. noun**
(a rain shower, storm)
Job 24:8; **Isa.** 4:6; 25:4; 28:2; 30:30; 32:2; **Hab.** 3:10.

2231. זִרְמָה *zirmāh* **fem. noun**
(a flow, issue [of seminal discharge])
Ezek. 23:20.

2232. זָרַע *zāra'* **verb**
(to sow, to bear seed)
Gen. 1:11,29; 26:12; 47:23; **Ex.** 23:10,16; **Lev.** 11:37; 12:2; 19:19; 25:3,4,11,20,22; 26:16; **Num.** 5:28; **Deut.** 11:10; 21:4; 22:9; 29:23(22); **Judg.** 6:3; 9:45; **2 Kgs.** 19:29; **Job** 4:8; 31:8; **Ps.** 97:11; 107:37; 126:5; **Prov.** 11:18; 22:8; **Eccl.** 11:4,6; **Isa.** 17:10; 28:24; 30:23; 32:20; 37:30; 40:24; 55:10; **Jer.** 2:2; 4:3; 12:13; 31:27; 35:7; 50:16; **Ezek.** 36:9; **Hos.** 2:23(25); 8:7; 10:12; **Mic.** 6:15; **Nah.** 1:14; **Hag.** 1:6; **Zech.** 10:9.

2233. זֶרַע *zera'* **masc. noun**
(seed, descendants)
Gen. 1:11,12,29; 3:15; 4:25; 7:3; 8:22; 9:9; 12:7; 13:15,16; 15:3,5,13,18; 16:10; 17:7–10,12,19; 19:32,34; 21:12,13; 22:17,18; 24:7,60; 26:3,4,24; 28:4,13,14; 32:12(13); 35:12; 38:8,9; 46:6,7; 47:19, 23,24; 48:4,11,19; **Ex.** 16:31; 28:43; 30:21; 32:13; 33:1; **Lev.** 11:37,38; 15:16–18,32; 18:20,21; 19:20; 20:2–4; 21:15,17,21; 22:3,4,13; 26:5,16; 27:16,30; **Num.** 5:13,28; 11:7; 14:24; 16:40(17:5); 18:19; 20:5; 24:7; 25:13; **Deut.** 1:8; 4:37; 10:15; 11:9,10; 14:22; 22:9; 28:38,46,59; 30:6,19; 31:21; 34:4; **Josh.** 24:3; **Ruth** 4:12; **1 Sam.** 1:11; 2:20; 8:15; 20:42; 24:21(22); **2 Sam.** 4:8; 7:12; 22:51; **1 Kgs.** 2:33; 11:14,39; 18:32; **2 Kgs.** 5:27; 11:1; 17:20; 25:25; **1 Chr.** 16:13; 17:11; **2 Chr.** 20:7; 22:10; **Ezra** 2:59; 9:2; **Neh.** 7:61; 9:2,8; **Esth.** 6:13; 9:27, 28,31; 10:3; **Job** 5:25; 21:8; 39:12; **Ps.** 18:50(51); 21:10(11); 22:23(24),30(31); 25:13; 37:25,26,28; 69:36(37); 89:4(5), 29(30),36(37); 102:28(29); 105:6; 106:27; 112:2; 126:6; **Prov.** 11:21; **Eccl.** 11:6; **Isa.** 1:4; 5:10; 6:13; 14:20; 17:11; 23:3; 30:23; 41:8; 43:5; 44:3; 45:19,25; 48:19; 53:10; 54:3; 55:10; 57:3,4; 59:21; 61:9; 65:9,23; 66:22; **Jer.** 2:21; 7:15; 22:28,30; 23:8; 29:32; 30:10; 31:27,36,37; 33:22,26; 35:7,9; 36:31; 41:1; 46:27; 49:10; **Ezek.** 17:5,13; 20:5; 43:19; 44:22; **Dan.** 1:3; 9:1; **Amos** 9:13; **Hag.** 2:19; **Zech.** 8:12; **Mal.** 2:3,15.

2234. זְרַע *z^{e}ra'* **Aram. masc. noun**
(seed, descendants; corr. to Hebr. 2233)
Dan. 2:43.

2235. זֵרֹעַ *zērōa'*, זֵרְעֹן *zēr'ōn* **masc. noun**
(vegetable, pulse)
Dan. 1:12,16.

2236. זָרַק *zāraq* **verb**
(to sprinkle, to scatter)
Ex. 9:8,10; 24:6,8; 29:16,20; **Lev.** 1:5,11; 3:2,8,13; 7:2,14; 8:19,24; 9:12,18; 17:6; **Num.** 18:17; 19:13,20; **2 Kgs.** 16:13,15; **2 Chr.** 29:22; 30:16; 34:4; 35:11; **Job** 2:12; **Isa.** 28:25; **Ezek.** 10:2; 36:25; 43:18; **Hos.** 7:9.

2237. זָרַר *zārar* **verb**
(to sneeze, to press or squeeze out)
2 Kgs. 4:35.

2238. זֶרֶשׁ *zereš* **fem. proper noun**
(Zeresh)
Esth. 5:10,14; 6:13.

2239. זֶרֶת *zereṯ* **fem. noun**
(a span)
Ex. 28:16; 39:9; **1 Sam.** 17:4; **Isa.** 40:12; **Ezek.** 43:13.

2240. זַתּוּא *zattû'* **masc. proper noun**
(Zattu)
Ezra 2:8; 10:27; **Neh.** 7:13; 10:14(15).

2241. זֵתָם *zēṯām* **masc. proper noun**
(Zetham)
1 Chr. 23:8; 26:22.

2242. זֵתַר *zēṯar* **masc. proper noun**
(Zethar)
Esth. 1:10.

ח Heth

2243. חֹב *ḥōḇ* **masc. noun**
(bosom, heart)
Job 31:33.

2244. חָבָא *ḥāḇā'* **verb**
(to hide, to be hidden)
Gen. 3:8,10; 31:27; **Josh.** 2:16(KJV, NASB, *ḥāḇāh* [2247]); 6:17,25; 10:16, 17,27; **Judg.** 9:5; **1 Sam.** 10:22; 13:6; 14:11,22; 19:2; 23:23; **2 Sam.** 17:9; **1 Kgs.** 18:4,13; 22:25(KJV, NASB, *ḥāḇāh* [2247]); **2 Kgs.** 6:29; 7:12(KJV, NASB, *ḥāḇāh* [2247]); 11:3; **1 Chr.** 21:20; **2 Chr.** 18:24; 22:9,12; **Job** 5:21; 24:4; 29:8,10; 38:30; **Isa.** 42:22; 49:2; **Dan.** 10:7; **Amos** 9:3.

2245. חָבַב *ḥāḇaḇ* **verb**
(to love)
Deut. 33:3.

2246. חֹבָב *ḥōḇāḇ* **masc. proper noun**
(Hobab)
Num. 10:29; **Judg.** 4:11.

2247. חָבָה *ḥāḇāh* **verb**
(to hide, to conceal)
Josh. 2:16(NIV, *ḥāḇā'* [2244]); **1 Kgs.** 22:25(NIV, *ḥāḇā'* [2244]); **2 Kgs.** 7:12 (NIV, *ḥāḇā'* [2244]); **Isa.** 26:20; **Jer.** 49:10.

2248. חֲבוּלָה *ḥaḇûlāh* **Aram. fem. noun**
(a hurtful deed, wrong deed)
Dan. 6:22(23).

2249. חָבוֹר *ḥāḇôr* **proper noun**
(Habor)
2 Kgs. 17:6; 18:11; **1 Chr.** 5:26.

2250. חַבּוּרָה *ḥabbûrāh*, חַבֻּרָה *ḥabburāh*, חֲבֻרָה *ḥaḇurāh* **fem. noun**
(a bruise, wound, injury)
Gen. 4:23; **Ex.** 21:25; **Ps.** 38:5(6); **Prov.** 20:30; **Isa.** 1:6; 53:5.

2251. חָבַט *ḥaḇaṭ* **verb**
(to beat out, to thresh)
Deut. 24:20; **Judg.** 6:11; **Ruth** 2:17; **Isa.** 27:12; 28:27.

2252. חֲבָיָה *ḥaḇāyāh*, חֳבַיָּה *ḥoḇāyyāh* **masc. proper noun**
(Habaiah)
Ezra 2:61; **Neh.** 7:63.

2253. חֶבְיוֹן *ḥeḇyôn* **masc. noun**
(a hiding, concealment)
Hab. 3:4.

2254. I. חָבַל *ḥāḇal* **verb**
(to bind, to hold by a pledge)
Ex. 22:26(25); **Deut.** 24:6,17; **Job** 22:6; 24:3,9; **Prov.** 13:13(KJV, see II); 20:16; 27:13; **Ezek.** 18:16; **Amos** 2:8.
II. חָבַל *ḥāḇal* **verb**
(to act corruptly, to destroy, to spoil, to injure)
Neh. 1:7; **Job** 17:1; 34:31; **Prov.** 13:13(NASB, NIV, see I); **Eccl.** 5:6(5); **Song** 2:15; **Isa.** 10:27; 13:5; 32:7; 54:16; **Mic.** 2:10.
III. חבל *ḥāḇal* **verb**
(to be pregnant, to be in labor, to travail)
Ps. 7:14(15); **Song** 8:5.
IV. חֹבְלִים *ḥōḇeliym* **verb**
(union, band; participle form)
Zech. 11:7,14.

2255. חֲבַל *ḥaḇal* **Aram. verb**
(to destroy; corr. to Hebr. 2254,II)
Ezra 6:12; **Dan.** 2:44; 4:23(20); 6:22(23),26(27); 7:14.

2256. I. חֶבֶל *ḥeḇel* **masc. noun**
(cord, rope; lot, inheritence)
Deut. 3:4,13,14; 32:9; **Josh.** 2:15; 17:5,14; 19:9,29; **2 Sam.** 8:2; 17:13; 22:6(KJV, see II); **1 Kgs.** 4:13; 20:31,32; **1 Chr.** 16:18; **Esth.** 1:6; **Job** 18:10; 36:8; 41:1(40:25); **Ps.** 16:6; 18:4(5)(KJV, see II),5(6)(KJV, see II); 78:55; 105:11; 116:3; 119:61; 140:5(6); **Prov.** 5:22; **Eccl.** 12:6; **Isa.** 5:18; 33:20,23; **Jer.** 38:6,11–13; **Ezek.** 27:24; 47:13; **Hos.** 11:4; **Amos** 7:17; **Mic.** 2:5; **Zeph.** 2:5–7; **Zech.** 2:1(5).
II. חֵבֶל *ḥēḇel* **masc. noun**
(pain, pang, sorrow)
2 Sam. 22:6(NASB, NIV, see I); **Job** 21:17(NASB, see IV); 39:3; **Ps.** 18:4(5) (NASB, NIV, see I),5(6)(NASB, NIV, see I); **Isa.** 13:8; 26:17; 66:7; **Jer.** 13:21; 22:23; 49:24; **Hos.** 13:13.
III. חֶבֶל *ḥeḇel* **masc. noun**
(destruction)
Job 21:17(KJV, NIV, see II); **Mic.** 2:10.
IV. חֶבֶל *ḥeḇel* **masc. noun**
(band, group, procession, troop)
1 Sam. 10:5,10.

2257. חֲבָל *ḥᵃḇāl* **Aram. masc. noun**
(harm, damage, injury; corr. to Hebr. 2256,IV)
Ezra 4:22; **Dan.** 3:25; 6:23(24).

2258. חֲבֹל *ḥᵃḇōl*, חֲבֹלָה *ḥᵃḇōlāh* **masc. noun**
(a pledge; a guarantee for a loan)
Ezek. 18:7,12,16; 33:15.

2259. חֹבֵל *ḥōḇēl* **masc. noun**
(a seaman, a sailor)
Ezek. 27:8,27–29; **Jon.** 1:6.

2260. חִבֵּל *ḥibbēl* **masc. noun**
(a mast, ship's rigging)
Prov. 23:34.

2261. חֲבַצֶּלֶת *ḥᵃḇaṣṣeleṯ* **fem. noun**
(a rose)
Song 2:1; **Isa.** 35:1.

2262. חֲבַצִּנְיָה *ḥᵃḇaṣṣinyāh* **masc. proper noun**
(Habazziniah)
Jer. 35:3.

2263. חָבַק *ḥāḇaq* **verb**
(to embrace)
Gen. 29:13; 33:4; 48:10; **2 Kgs.** 4:16; **Job** 24:8; **Prov.** 4:8; 5:20; **Eccl.** 3:5; 4:5; **Song** 2:6; 8:3; **Lam.** 4:5.

2264. חִבֻּק *ḥibbuq* **masc. proper noun**
(a folding [of the hands])
Prov. 6:10; 24:33.

2265. חֲבַקּוּק *ḥᵃḇaqqûq* **masc. proper noun**
(Habakkuk)
Hab. 1:1; 3:1.

2266. I. חָבַר *ḥāḇar* **verb**
(to join together, to unite; to conjure, to charm)
Gen. 14:3; **Ex.** 26:3,6,9,11; 28:7; 36:10,13,16,18; 39:4; **Deut.** 18:11; **2 Chr.** 20:35–37; **Job** 16:4(NIV, see II); **Ps.** 58:5(6); 94:20; 122:3; **Eccl.** 9:4(KJV, [Kᵉ] *bāḥar* [977]); **Ezek.** 1:9,11; **Dan.** 11:6,23; **Hos.** 4:17.
II. חָבַר *ḥāḇar* **verb**
(to adorn, to make beautiful, to be brilliant)
Job 16:4(KJV, NASB, see I).

2267. חֶבֶר *ḥeḇer* **masc. noun**
(a spell, enchantment; a magician; something shared)
Deut. 18:11; **Ps.** 58:5(6); **Prov.** 21:9; 25:24; **Isa.** 47:9,12; **Hos.** 6:9.

2268. A. חֶבֶר *ḥeḇer* **masc. proper noun**
(Heber: son of Beriah)
Gen. 46:17; **Num.** 26:45; **1 Chr.** 7:31,32.
B. חֶבֶר *ḥeḇer* **masc. proper noun**
(Heber: husband of Jael)

Judg. 4:11,17,21; 5:24.
C. חֶבֶר *ḥeber* masc. proper noun
(Heber: son of another Beriah)
1 Chr. 4:18.

D. חֶבֶר *ḥeber* masc. proper noun
(Heber: son of a third Beriah)
1 Chr. 8:17.

2269. חֲבַר *ḥabar* Aram. masc. noun
(a companion, friend; corr. to Hebr. 2270)
Dan. 2:13,17,18.

2270. חָבֵר *ḥāḇēr* masc. noun
(associate, friend)
Judg. 20:11; **Ps.** 45:7(8); 119:63; **Prov.** 28:24; **Eccl.** 4:10; **Song** 1:7; 8:13; **Isa.** 1:23; 44:11; **Ezek.** 37:16,19.

2271. חַבָּר *ḥabbār* masc. noun
(an associate, partner [in trade])
Job 41:6(40:30).

2272. חֲבַרְבֻּרָה *ḥªḇarburāh* fem. noun
(a spot)
Jer. 13:23.

2273. חַבְרָה *ḥaḇrāh* Aram. fem. noun
(an associate, companion; corr. to Hebr. 2274)
Dan. 7:20.

2274. חֶבְרָה *ḥeḇrāh* fem. noun
(company)
Job 34:8.

2275. A. חֶבְרוֹן *ḥeḇrôn* proper noun
(Hebron: city in Judah)
Gen. 13:18; 23:2,19; 35:27; 37:14; **Num.** 13:22; **Josh.** 10:3,5,23,36,39; 11:21; 12:10; 14:13–15; 15:13,54; 20:7; 21:11,13; **Judg.** 1:10,20; 16:3; **1 Sam.** 30:31; **2 Sam.** 2:1,3,11,32; 3:2,5,19,20, 22,27,32; 4:1,8,12; 5:1,3,5,13; 15:7,9,10;

1 Kgs. 2:11; **1 Chr.** 3:1,4; 6:55(40), 57(42); 11:1,3; 12:23,38; 29:27; **2 Chr.** 11:10.

B. חֶבְרוֹן *ḥeḇrôn* masc. proper noun
(Hebron: son of Kohath)
Ex. 6:18; **Num.** 3:19; **1 Chr.** 6:2(5:28), 18(3); 23:12,19.

C. חֶבְרוֹן *ḥeḇrôn* masc. proper noun
(Hebron: descendant of Caleb)
1 Chr. 2:42,43; 15:9.

2276. חֶבְרוֹנִי *ḥeḇrônîy*, חֶבְרֹנִי *ḥeḇrōnîy* masc. proper noun
(Hebronite)
Num. 3:27; 26:58; **1 Chr.** 26:23,30,31.

2277. חֶבְרִי *ḥeḇrîy* masc. proper noun
(Heberite)
Num. 26:45.

2278. חֲבֶרֶת *ḥªḇereṯ* fem. noun
(companion)
Mal. 2:14.

2279. חֹבֶרֶת *ḥōḇereṯ* fem. noun
(a junction, thing [as a curtain] that joins to another)
Ex. 26:4,10; 36:17.

2280. חָבַשׁ *ḥāḇaš* verb
(to tie, to bind, to saddle)
Gen. 22:3; **Ex.** 29:9; **Lev.** 8:13; **Num.** 22:21; **Judg.** 19:10; **2 Sam.** 16:1; 17:23; 19:26(27); **1 Kgs.** 2:40; 13:13,23,27; **2 Kgs.** 4:24; **Job** 5:18; 28:11; 34:17; 40:13; **Ps.** 147:3; **Isa.** 1:6; 3:7; 30:26; 61:1; **Ezek.** 16:10; 24:17; 27:24; 30:21; 34:4,16; **Hos.** 6:1; **Jon.** 2:5(6).

2281. חֲבִתִּים *ḥªḇittîym* masc. pl. noun
(something flat, either flat pans or flat bread)
1 Chr. 9:31.

2282. חָג *ḥāg*, חַג *ḥag* **masc. noun**
(festival, feast)
Ex. 10:9; 12:14; 13:6; 23:15,16,18; 32:5; 34:18,22,25; **Lev.** 23:6,34,39,41; **Num.** 28:17; 29:12; **Deut.** 16:10,13,14,16; 31:10; **Judg.** 21:19; **1 Kgs.** 8:2,65; 12:32,33; **2 Chr.** 5:3; 7:8,9; 8:13; 30:13,21; 35:17; **Ezra** 3:4; 6:22; **Neh.** 8:14,18; **Ps.** 81:3(4); 118:27; **Isa.** 29:1; 30:29; **Ezek.** 45:17,21,23,25; 46:11; **Hos.** 2:11(13); 9:5; **Amos** 5:21; 8:10; **Nah.** 1:15(2:1); **Zech.** 14:16,18,19; **Mal.** 2:3.

2283. חָגָּא *ḥāggā'* **fem. noun**
(a terror)
Isa. 19:17.

2284. חָגָב *ḥāgāḇ* **masc. noun**
(grasshopper, locust)
Lev. 11:22; **Num.** 13:33; **2 Chr.** 7:13; **Eccl.** 12:5; **Isa.** 40:22.

2285. חָגָב *ḥāgāḇ* **masc. proper noun**
(Hagab)
Ezra 2:46.

2286. חֲגָבָא *ḥagāḇā'*, חֲגָבָה *ḥagaḇāh* **masc. proper noun**
(Hagabah)
Ezra 2:45; **Neh.** 7:48.

2287. חָגַג *ḥāgag* **verb**
(to hold a feast, to celebrate a holy day)
Ex. 5:1; 12:14; 23:14; **Lev.** 23:39,41; **Num.** 29:12; **Deut.** 16:15; **1 Sam.** 30:16; **Ps.** 42:4(5); 107:27; **Nah.** 1:15(2:1); **Zech.** 14:16,18,19.

2288. חָגָו *ḥāgāw*, חָגוּ *ḥāgû* **masc. noun**
(a cleft, place of concealment)
Song 2:14; **Jer.** 49:16; **Obad.** 1:3.

2289. I. חָגוֹר *ḥāgôr* **adj.**
(girded)
Ezek. 23:15.
II. חֲגוֹר *ḥagôr* **masc. noun**
(sash, belt, girdle)
1 Sam. 18:4; **2 Sam.** 20:8; **Prov.** 31:24.

2290. חֲגוֹרָה *ḥagôrāh*, חֲגֹרָה *ḥagōrāh* **fem. noun**
(sash, belt, girdle, loincloth)
Gen. 3:7; **2 Sam.** 18:11; **1 Kgs.** 2:5; **2 Kgs.** 3:21; **Isa.** 3:24.

2291. I. חַגִּי *ḥaggiy* **masc. proper noun**
(Haggi: son of Gad)
Gen. 46:16; **Num.** 26:15.
II. חַגִּי *ḥaggiy* **masc. proper noun**
(Haggites: descendants of Haggi [2291,I])
Num. 26:15.

2292. I. חַגַּי *ḥaggay* **masc. proper noun**
(the prophet Haggai)
Hag. 1:1,3,12,13; 2:1,10,13,14,20.
II. חַגַּי *ḥaggay* **Aram. masc. proper noun**
(the prophet Haggai)
Ezra 5:1; 6:14.

2293. חַגִּיָּה *ḥaggiyyāh* **masc. proper noun**
(Haggiah)
1 Chr. 6:30(15).

2294. חַגִּית *ḥaggiyṯ* **fem. proper noun**
(Haggith)
2 Sam. 3:4; **1 Kgs.** 1:5,11; 2:13; **1 Chr.** 3:2.

2295. חָגְלָה *ḥoglāh* **fem. proper noun**
(Hoglah)
Num. 26:33; 27:1; 36:11; **Josh.** 17:3.

2296. חָגַר *ḥāgar* **verb**
(to gird oneself, to put on a belt)

Ex. 12:11; 29:9; **Lev.** 8:7,13; 16:4; **Deut.** 1:41; **Judg.** 3:16; 18:11,16,17; **1 Sam.** 2:18; 17:39; 25:13; **2 Sam.** 3:31; 6:14; 20:8; 21:16; 22:46; **1 Kgs.** 20:11,32; **2 Kgs.** 3:21; 4:29; 9:1; **Ps.** 45:3(4); 65:12(13); 76:10(11); 109:19; **Prov.** 31:17; **Isa.** 15:3; 22:12; 32:11; **Jer.** 4:8; 6:26; 49:3; **Lam.** 2:10; **Ezek.** 7:18; 27:31; 44:18; **Dan.** 10:5; **Joel** 1:8,13.

2297. חַד *ḥaḏ* **num. adj.**
(one, each)
Ezek. 33:30.

2298. חַד *ḥaḏ* **Aram. num. adj.**
(one, the indefinite article: a; corr. to Hebr. 2297)
Ezra 4:8; 5:13; 6:2,3; **Dan.** 2:9,31,35; 3:19; 4:19(16); 6:2(3),17(18); 7:1,5,16.

2299. חַד *ḥaḏ* **adj.**
(sharp)
Ps. 57:4(5); **Prov.** 5:4; **Isa.** 49:2; **Ezek.** 5:1.

2300. I. חָדַד *ḥāḏaḏ* **verb**
(to sharpen, to slash, to be keen)
Ezek. 21:9–11(14–16),16(21)(KJV, *'āḥad* [258]); **Hab.** 1:8.
II. חָדָה *ḥāḏāh* **verb**
(to sharpen)
Prov. 27:17.

2301. חֲדַד *ḥᵃḏaḏ* **masc. proper noun**
(Hadad)
Gen. 25:15(KJV, *ḥᵃḏar* [2316]); **1 Chr.** 1:30.

2302. I. חָדָה *ḥāḏāh* **verb**
(to rejoice, to be glad)
Ex. 18:9; **Job** 3:6(KJV, NIV, see II); **Ps.** 21:6(7).
II. יָחַד *yāḥaḏ* **verb**
(to join)
Job 3:6(NASB, see I).

2303. חַדּוּד *ḥaddûḏ* **masc. noun**
(sharp, jagged)
Job 41:30(22).

2304. חֶדְוָה *ḥeḏwāh* **fem. noun**
(gladness, joy)
1 Chr. 16:27; **Neh.** 8:10.

2305. חֶדְוָה *ḥeḏwāh* **Aram. fem. noun**
(joy, gladness; corr. to Hebr. 2304)
Ezra 6:16.

2306. חֲדֵה *ḥᵃḏēh* **Aram. masc. noun**
(breast, chest)
Dan. 2:32.

2307. חָדִיד *ḥāḏiyḏ* **masc. proper noun**
(Hadid)
Ezra 2:33; **Neh.** 7:37; 11:34.

2308. חָדַל *ḥāḏal* **verb**
(to cease, to stop)
Gen. 11:8; 18:11; 41:49; **Ex.** 9:29,33,34; 14:12; 23:5; **Num.** 9:13; **Deut.** 15:11; 23:22(23); **Judg.** 5:6,7; 9:9,11,13; 15:7; 20:28; **Ruth** 1:18; **1 Sam.** 2:5; 9:5; 12:23; 23:13; **1 Kgs.** 15:21; 22:6,15; **2 Chr.** 16:5; 18:5,14; 25:16; 35:21; **Job** 3:17; 7:16; 10:20; 14:6,7; 16:6; 19:14; **Ps.** 36:3(4); 49:8(9); **Prov.** 10:19; 19:27; 23:4; **Isa.** 1:16; 2:22; 24:8; **Jer.** 40:4; 41:8; 44:18; 51:30; **Ezek.** 2:5,7; 3:11,27; **Amos** 7:5; **Zech.** 11:12.

2309. חֶדֶל *ḥeḏel* **masc. noun**
(world, a place of rest; NASB, spelling variation of *ḥeled* [2465])
Isa. 38:11.

2310. חָדֵל *ḥāḏēl* **adj.**
(transcient, rejected, fleeting)
Ps. 39:4(5); **Isa.** 53:3; **Ezek.** 3:27.

2311. חַדְלַי *ḥaḏlay* **masc. proper noun**
(Hadlai)
2 Chr. 28:12.

2312. חֵדֶק *ḥēḏeq* **masc. noun**
(thorn, brier)
Prov. 15:19; **Mic.** 7:4.

2313. חִדֶּקֶל *ḥiddeqel* **proper noun**
(Hiddekel, a river in Assyria referred to in the LXX as the Tigris River)
Gen. 2:14; **Dan.** 10:4.

2314. חָדַר *ḥāḏar* **verb**
(to surround, to enclose)
Ezek. 21:14(19).

2315. חֶדֶר *ḥeḏer* **masc. noun**
(a chamber, room, parlor)
Gen. 43:30; **Ex.** 8:3(7:28); **Deut.** 32:25; **Judg.** 3:24; 15:1; 16:9,12; **2 Sam.** 4:7; 13:10; **1 Kgs.** 1:15; 20:30; 22:25; **2 Kgs.** 6:12; 9:2; 11:2; **1 Chr.** 28:11; **2 Chr.** 18:24; 22:11; **Job** 9:9; 37:9; **Ps.** 105:30; **Prov.** 7:27; 18:8; 20:27,30; 24:4; 26:22; **Eccl.** 10:20; **Song** 1:4; 3:4; **Isa.** 26:20; **Ezek.** 8:12; **Joel** 2:16.

2316. חֲדַר *ḥaḏar* **masc. proper noun**
(Hadar)
Gen. 25:15(NASB, NIV, *ḥaḏaḏ* [2301]).

2317. חַדְרָךְ *ḥaḏrāḵ* **proper noun**
(Hadrach)
Zech. 9:1.

2318. חָדַשׁ *ḥāḏaš* **verb**
(to renew, to restore)
1 Sam. 11:14; **2 Chr.** 15:8; 24:4,12; **Job** 10:17; **Ps.** 51:10(12); 103:5; 104:30; **Isa.** 61:4; **Lam.** 5:21.

2319. חָדָשׁ *ḥāḏāš* **adj.**
(new, fresh)
Ex. 1:8; **Lev.** 23:16; 26:10; **Num.** 28:26; **Deut.** 20:5; 22:8; 24:5; 32:17; **Josh.** 9:13; **Judg.** 5:8; 15:13; 16:11,12; **1 Sam.** 6:7; **2 Sam.** 6:3; 21:16; **1 Kgs.** 11:29,30; **2 Kgs.** 2:20; **1 Chr.** 13:7; **2 Chr.** 20:5; **Job** 29:20; 32:19; **Ps.** 33:3; 40:3(4); 96:1; 98:1; 144:9; 149:1; **Eccl.** 1:9,10; **Song** 7:13(14); **Isa.** 41:15; 42:9,10; 43:19; 48:6; 62:2; 65:17; 66:22; **Jer.** 26:10; 31:22,31; 36:10; **Lam.** 3:23; **Ezek.** 11:19; 18:31; 36:26.

2320. חֹדֶשׁ *ḥōḏeš* **masc. noun**
(month, new moon [the first day of the lunar month])
Gen. 7:11; 8:4,5,13,14; 29:14; 38:24; **Ex.** 12:2,3,6,18; 13:4,5; 16:1; 19:1; 23:15; 34:18; 40:2,17; **Lev.** 16:29; 23:5,6,24,27, 32,34,39,41; 25:9; 27:6; **Num.** 1:1,18; 3:15,22,28,34,39,40,43; 9:1,3,5,11,22; 10:10,11; 11:20,21; 18:16; 20:1; 26:62; 28:11,14,16,17; 29:1,6,7,12; 33:3,38; **Deut.** 1:3; 16:1; **Josh.** 4:19; 5:10; **Judg.** 11:37–39; 19:2; 20:47; **1 Sam.** 6:1; 20:5, 18,24,27,34; 27:7; **2 Sam.** 2:11; 5:5; 6:11; 24:8,13; **1 Kgs.** 4:7,27(5:7); 5:14(28); 6:1,38; 8:2; 11:16; 12:32,33; **2 Kgs.** 4:23; 15:8; 23:31; 24:8; 25:1,3,8,25,27; **1 Chr.** 3:4; 12:15; 13:14; 21:12; 23:31; 27:1–5, 7–15; **2 Chr.** 2:4(3); 3:2; 5:3; 7:10; 8:13; 15:10; 29:3,17; 30:2,13,15; 31:3,7; 35:1; 36:2,9; **Ezra** 3:1,5,6,8; 6:19; 7:8,9; 8:31; 10:9,16,17; **Neh.** 1:1; 2:1; 7:73; 8:2,14; 9:1; 10:33(34); **Esth.** 2:12,16; 3:7,12,13; 8:9,12; 9:1,15,17,19,21,22; **Job** 14:5; 21:21; **Ps.** 81:3(4); **Isa.** 1:13,14; 47:13; 66:23; **Jer.** 1:3; 2:24; 28:1,17; 36:9,22; 39:1,2; 41:1; 52:4,6,12,31; **Ezek.** 1:1,2; 8:1; 20:1; 24:1; 26:1; 29:1,17; 30:20; 31:1; 32:1,17; 33:21; 39:12,14; 40:1; 45:17,18,20,21,25; 46:1,3,6; 47:12; **Dan.** 10:4; **Hos.** 2:11(13); 5:7; **Amos** 4:7; 8:5; **Hag.** 1:1,15; 2:1,20; **Zech.** 1:1,7; 7:1,3.

2321. חֹדֶשׁ *ḥōḏeš* **fem. proper noun**
(Hodesh)
1 Chr. 8:9.

2322. חֲדָשָׁה ḥ^aḏāšāh **proper noun**
(Hadashah)
Josh. 15:37.

2323. חֲדַת ḥ^aḏaṯ **Aram. adj.**
(new)
Ezra 6:4.

2324. חֲוָה ḥ^awāh **Aram. verb**
(to interpret, to explain; corr. to Hebr. 2331)
Dan. 2:4,6,7,9–11,16,24,27; 4:2(3:32); 5:7,12(KJV, NASB, 'aḥ^awāyaṯ [263]),12,15.

2325. חוּב ḥûḇ **verb**
(to endanger)
Dan. 1:10.

2326. חוֹב ḥôḇ **masc. noun**
(a debt, debtor)
Ezek. 18:7.

2327. חוֹבָה ḥôḇāh **proper noun**
(Hobah)
Gen. 14:15.

2328. חוּג ḥûḡ **verb**
(to encircle)
Job 26:10.

2329. חוּג ḥûḡ **masc. noun**
(circle, vault [of the heavens])
Job 22:14; Prov. 8:27; Isa. 40:22.

2330. חוּד ḥûḏ **verb**
(to put forth [a riddle])
Judg. 14:12,13,16; Ezek. 17:2.

2331. חָוָה ḥāwāh **verb**
(to tell, to explain)
Job 15:17; 32:6,10,17; 36:2; Ps. 19:2(3).

2332. חַוָּה ḥawwāh **fem. proper noun**
(Eve)
Gen. 3:20; 4:1.

2333. חַוָּה ḥawwāh **fem. noun**
(village, town: only pl. ḥawwōṯ)
Num. 32:41; Josh. 13:30; 1 Kgs. 4:13; 1 Chr. 2:23(NIV, ḥawwōṯ yā'îr [2334]).

2334. חַוֹּת יָאִיר ḥawwōṯ yā'îr **proper noun**
(Havvoth Jair)
Num. 32:41; Deut. 3:14(KJV, bāšān-ḥawwōṯ-yā'îr [see bāšān {1316}]); Judg. 10:4; 1 Chr. 2:23(KJV, NASB, ḥawwāh [2333] and yā'îr [2971,A]).

2335. I. חוֹזַי ḥôzay **masc. pl. noun**
(seers)
2 Chr. 33:19(NASB, see II, NIV, ḥōzeh [2374,I]).

II. חוֹזַי ḥôzay **masc. proper noun**
(Hozai; professional title for a group of seers or prophets)
2 Chr. 33:19(KJV, see I; NIV, ḥōzeh [2374,I]).

2336. חוֹחַ ḥôaḥ **masc. noun**
(thistle, thorn, hook)
1 Sam. 13:6(see ḥāwāḥ [2337]); 2 Kgs. 14:9; 2 Chr. 25:18; 33:11; Job 31:40; 41:2(40:26); Prov. 26:9; Song 2:2; Isa. 34:13; Hos. 9:6.

2337. חֲוָחִים ḥ^awāḥiym **masc. pl. noun**
(thickets: pl. of ḥôaḥ [2336])
1 Sam. 13:6.

2338. חוּט ḥûṭ **Aram. verb**
(to repair, to join together)
Ezra 4:12.

2339. חוּט ḥûṭ **masc. noun**
(thread, ribbon, cord)
Gen. 14:23; Josh. 2:18; Judg. 16:12; 1 Kgs. 7:15; Eccl. 4:12; Song 4:3; Jer. 52:21.

2340. חִוִּי *ḥiwwiy* **masc. proper noun**
(Hivite)
Gen. 10:17; 34:2; 36:2; **Ex.** 3:8,17; 13:5; 23:23,28; 33:2; 34:11; **Deut.** 7:1; 20:17; **Josh.** 3:10; 9:1,7; 11:3,19; 12:8; 24:11; **Judg.** 3:3,5; **2 Sam.** 24:7; **1 Kgs.** 9:20; **1 Chr.** 1:15; **2 Chr.** 8:7.

2341. חֲוִילָה *ḥawiylāh* **proper noun**
(Havilah)
Gen. 2:11; 10:7,29; 25:18; **1 Sam.** 15:7; **1 Chr.** 1:9,23.

2342. I. חוּל *ḥûl,* חִיל *ḥiyl* **verb**
(to dance, to whirl; to tremble, to writhe; to wait, to look or hope for; to be in labor, to bring to birth, to form; to wound)
Gen. 8:10; **Deut.** 2:25; 32:18; **Judg.** 3:25; 21:21,23; **1 Sam.** 31:3; **2 Sam.** 3:29; **1 Chr.** 10:3; 16:30; **Esth.** 4:4; **Job** 15:7,20; 20:21(NASB, NIV, see II); 26:5,13 (NASB, NIV, *ḥālal* [2490,II]); 35:14; 39:1; **Ps.** 10:5(NASB, NIV, see II); 29:8,9; 37:7; 51:5(7); 55:4(5); 77:16(17); 90:2; 96:9; 97:4; 114:7; **Prov.** 8:24,25; 25:23; 26:10 (NIV, *ḥālal* [2490,II]); **Isa.** 13:8; 23:4,5; 26:17,18; 45:10; 51:2; 54:1; 66:7,8; **Jer.** 4:19(KJV, [Qe] *yāḥal* [3176]); 5:3,22; 23:19; 30:23; 51:29; **Lam.** 1:12(KJV, NASB, *ḥālāh* [2470,I]); 4:6; **Ezek.** 30:16; **Hos.** 11:6; **Joel** 2:6; **Mic.** 4:10; **Hab.** 3:10; **Zech.** 9:5.
II. חוּל *ḥûl,* חִיל *ḥiyl* **verb**
(to be firm, to be strong, to prosper, to endure)
Job 20:21(KJV, see I); **Ps.** 10:5(KJV, see I).

2343. חוּל *ḥûl* **masc. proper noun**
(Hul)
Gen. 10:23; **1 Chr.** 1:17.

2344. חוֹל *ḥôl* **masc. noun**
(sand)
Gen. 22:17; 32:12(13); 41:49; **Ex.** 2:12; **Deut.** 33:19; **Josh.** 11:4; **Judg.** 7:12; **1 Sam.** 13:5; **2 Sam.** 17:11; **1 Kgs.** 4:20,29(5:9); **Job** 6:3; 29:18; **Ps.** 78:27; 139:18; **Prov.** 27:3; **Isa.** 10:22; 48:19; **Jer.** 5:22; 15:8; 33:22; **Hos.** 1:10(2:1); **Hab.** 1:9.

2345. חוּם *ḥûm* **adj.**
(dark-colored, brown, black)
Gen. 30:32,33,35,40.

2346. חוֹמָה *ḥômāh* **fem. noun**
(a wall)
Ex. 14:22,29; **Lev.** 25:29–31; **Deut.** 3:5; 28:52; **Josh.** 2:15; 6:5,20; **1 Sam.** 25:16; 31:10,12; **2 Sam.** 11:20,21,24; 18:24; 20:15,21; **1 Kgs.** 3:1; 4:13; 9:15; 20:30; **2 Kgs.** 3:27; 6:26,30; 14:13; 18:26,27; 25:4,10; **2 Chr.** 8:5; 14:7(6); 25:23; 26:6; 27:3; 32:5,18; 33:14; 36:19; **Neh.** 1:3; 2:8,13,15,17; 3:8,13,15,27; 4:1(3:33), 3(3:35),6(3:38),7(1),10(4),13(7),15(9), 17(11),19(13); 5:16; 6:1,6,15; 7:1; 12:27, 30,31,37,38; 13:21; **Ps.** 51:18(20); 55:10(11); **Prov.** 18:11; 25:28; **Song** 5:7; 8:9,10; **Isa.** 2:15; 22:10,11; 25:12; 26:1; 30:13; 36:11,12; 49:16; 56:5; 60:10,18; 62:6; **Jer.** 1:15,18; 15:20; 21:4; 39:4,8; 49:27; 50:15; 51:12,44,58; 52:7,14; **Lam.** 2:7,8,18; **Ezek.** 26:4,9,10,12; 27:11; 38:11, 20; 40:5; 42:20; **Joel** 2:7,9; **Amos** 1:7, 10,14; 7:7; **Nah.** 2:5(6); 3:8; **Zech.** 2:5(9).

2347. חוּס *ḥûs* **verb**
(to pity, to show mercy)
Gen. 45:20; **Deut.** 7:16; 13:8(9); 19:13,21; 25:12; **1 Sam.** 24:10(11); **Neh.** 13:22; **Ps.** 72:13; **Isa.** 13:18; **Jer.** 13:14; 21:7; **Ezek.** 5:11; 7:4,9; 8:18; 9:5,10; 16:5; 20:17; 24:14; **Joel** 2:17; **Jon.** 4:10,11.

2348. חוֹף *ḥôp̱* **masc. noun**
(coast, shore, haven)
Gen. 49:13; **Deut.** 1:7; **Josh.** 9:1; **Judg.** 5:17; **Jer.** 47:7; **Ezek.** 25:16.

2349. חוּפָם *ḥûp̱ām* **masc. proper noun**
(Hupham)
Num. 26:39.

2350. חוּפָמִי *ḥûp̱amiy* **masc. proper noun**
(Huphamites)
Num. 26:39.

2351. חוּץ *ḥûṣ* **masc. noun**
(outside, street)
Gen. 6:14; 9:22; 15:5; 19:16,17; 24:11, 29,31; 39:12,13,15,18; **Ex.** 12:46; 21:19; 25:11; 26:35; 27:21; 29:14; 33:7; 37:2; 40:22; **Lev.** 4:12,21; 6:11(4); 8:17; 9:11; 10:4,5; 13:46; 14:3,8,40,41,45,53; 16:27; 17:3; 18:9; 24:3,14,23; **Num.** 5:3,4; 12:14,15; 15:35,36; 19:3,9; 31:13,19; 35:4,5,27; **Deut.** 23:10(11),12(13), 13(14); 24:11; 25:5; 32:25; **Josh.** 2:19; 6:23; **Judg.** 12:9; 19:25; **1 Sam.** 9:26; **2 Sam.** 1:20; 13:17,18; 22:43; **1 Kgs.** 6:6; 7:9; 8:8; 20:34; 21:13; **2 Kgs.** 4:3; 10:24; 23:4,6; **2 Chr.** 5:9; 24:8; 29:16; 32:3,5; 33:15; **Ezra** 10:13; **Neh.** 13:8,20; **Job** 5:10; 18:17; 31:32; **Ps.** 18:42(43); 31:11(12); 41:6(7); 144:13; **Prov.** 1:20; 5:16; 7:12; 8:26; 22:13; 24:27; **Eccl.** 2:25; **Song** 8:1; **Isa.** 5:25; 10:6; 15:3; 24:11; 33:7; 42:2; 51:20,23; **Jer.** 5:1; 6:11; 7:17,34; 9:21(20); 11:6,13; 14:16; 21:4; 33:10; 37:21; 44:6,9,17,21; 51:4; **Lam.** 1:20; 2:19,21; 4:1,5,8,14; **Ezek.** 7:15,19; 11:6; 26:11; 28:23; 34:21; 40:5, 19,40,44; 41:9,17,25; 42:7; 43:21; 46:2; 47:2; **Hos.** 7:1; **Amos** 5:16; **Mic.** 7:10; **Nah.** 2:4(5); 3:10; **Zeph.** 3:6; **Zech.** 9:3; 10:5.

2352. חֻר *ḥur* **masc. noun**
(hole, pit)
Isa. 11:8; 42:22.

2353. חוּר *ḥûr* **masc. noun**
(white)
Esth. 1:6; 8:15.

2354. A. חוּר *ḥûr* **masc. proper noun**
(Hur: companion of Aaron)
Ex. 17:10,12; 24:14.
B. חוּר *ḥûr* **masc. proper noun**
(Hur: a Judaite)
Ex. 31:2; 35:30; 38:22; **1 Chr.** 2:19,20,50; 4:1,4; **2 Chr.** 1:5.
C. חוּר *ḥûr* **masc. proper noun**
(Hur: Midianite king)
Num. 31:8; **Josh.** 13:21.
D. חוּר *ḥûr* **masc. proper noun**
(Hur: officer of Solomon)
1 Kgs. 4:8(NASB, NIV, see *bēn-ḥûr* [1133]).
E. חוּר *ḥûr* **masc. proper noun**
(Hur: father of Rephaiah)
Neh. 3:9.

2355. חוֹרָי *ḥôrāy* **masc. noun**
(white cloth)
Isa. 19:9.

2356. חוֹר *ḥôr*, חֹר *ḥōr* **masc. noun**
(hole, cave)
1 Sam. 14:11; **2 Kgs.** 12:9(10); **Job** 30:6; **Song** 5:4; **Ezek.** 8:7; **Nah.** 2:12(13); **Zech.** 14:12.

2357. חָוַר *ḥāwar* **verb**
(to be or become pale, to be or become white)
Isa. 29:22.

2358. חִוָּר *ḥiwwār* **Aram. adj.**
(white)
Dan. 7:9.

2359. חוּרִי *ḥûriy* **masc. proper noun**
(Huri)
1 Chr. 5:14.

2360. חוּרַי *ḥûray* **masc. proper noun**
(Hurai)
1 Chr. 11:32.

2361. A. חוּרָם *ḥûrām* **masc. proper noun**
(Huram, Hiram: king of Tyre; see also *ḥiyrôm* [2438,A])
2 Chr. 2:3(2),11(10),12(11); 4:11; 8:2,18; 9:10,21.
B. חוּרָם *ḥûrām* **masc. proper noun**
(Huram, Hiram: an architect; see also *ḥiyrām* [2438,B])
2 Chr. 2:13(12); 4:11,16.
C. חוּרָם *ḥûrām* **masc. proper noun**
(Huram, Hiram: a Benjamite)
1 Chr. 8:5.

2362. חַוְרָן *ḥawrān* **proper noun**
(Hauran)
Ezek. 47:16,18.

2363. I חוּשׁ *ḥûš* **verb**
(to hasten)
Num. 32:17; **Deut.** 32:35; **Judg.** 20:37; **1 Sam.** 20:38; **Job** 20:2(NIV, see II); 31:5; **Ps.** 22:19(20); 38:22(23); 40:13(14); 55:8(9); 70:1(2),5(6); 71:12(KJV, [Ke] *ḥiyš* [2439]); 119:60; 141:1; **Eccl.** 2:25(NASB, NIV, see II); **Isa.** 5:19; 8:1(KJV, NIV, see *mahēr šālāl ḥāš baz* [4122,I]); 28:16(NIV, see II); 60:22; **Hab.** 1:8.
II. חוּשׁ *ḥûš* **verb**
(to enjoy; to be anxious, to disturb, to dismay)
Job 20:2(KJV, NASB, see I); **Eccl.** 2:25 (KJV, see I); **Isa.** 28:16(KJV, NASB, see I).

2364. חוּשָׁה *ḥûšāh* **masc. proper noun**
(Hushah)
1 Chr. 4:4.

2365. A. חוּשַׁי *ḥûšay* **masc. proper noun**
(Hushai: friend of David)
2 Sam. 15:32,37; 16:16–18; 17:5–8, 14,15; **1 Chr.** 27:33.
B. *ḥûšay* **masc. proper noun**
(Hushai: father of Baanah)
1 Kgs. 4:16.

2366. A. חֻשִׁים *ḥušiym,* חוּשִׁים *ḥûšiym* **fem. proper noun**
(Hushim: wife of Shaharaim)
1 Chr. 8:8,11.
B. חֻשִׁים *ḥušiym* **masc. proper noun**
(Hushim: son of Dan)
Gen. 46:23.
C. חֻשִׁים *ḥušiym* **masc. proper noun**
(Hushim: son of Aher)
1 Chr. 7:12.

2367. חֻשָׁם *ḥušām,* חוּשָׁם *ḥûšām* **masc. proper noun**
(Husham)
Gen. 36:34,35; **1 Chr.** 1:45,46.

2368. חוֹתָם *ḥôṯām,* חֹתָם *ḥōṯām* **masc. noun**
(seal, signet ring)
Gen. 38:18; **Ex.** 28:11,21,36; 39:6,14,30; **1 Kgs.** 21:8; **Job** 38:14; 41:15(7); **Song** 8:6; **Jer.** 22:24; **Hag.** 2:23.

2369. A. חוֹתָם *ḥôṯām* **masc. proper noun**
(Hotham: an Aroerite)
1 Chr. 11:44.
B. חוֹתָם *ḥôṯām* **masc. proper noun**
(Hotham: an Asherite)
1 Chr. 7:32.

2370. חֲזָה *ḥazāh,* חֲזָא *ḥazā'* **Aram. verb**
(to see, to observe; corr. to Hebr. 2372)
Ezra 4:14; **Dan.** 2:8,26,31,34,41,43,45; 3:19,25,27; 4:5(2),9(6),10(7),13(10), 18(15),20(17),23(20); 5:5,23; 7:1,2,4,6, 7,9,11,13,21.

2371. חֲזָהאֵל *ḥazāh'ēl* **masc. proper noun**
(Hazael)

1 Kgs. 19:15,17; **2 Kgs.** 8:8,9,12,13,15,28,29; 9:14,15; 10:32; 12:17(18),18(19); 13:3,22,24,25; **2 Chr.** 22:5,6; **Amos** 1:4.

2372. חָזָה *ḥāzāh* **verb**
(to see, to observe, to select)
Ex. 18:21; 24:11; **Num.** 24:4,16; **Job** 8:17; 15:17; 19:26,27; 23:9; 24:1; 27:12; 34:32; 36:25; **Ps.** 11:4,7; 17:2,15; 27:4; 46:8(9); 58:8(9),10(11); 63:2(3); **Prov.** 22:29; 24:32; 29:20; **Song** 6:13(7:1); **Isa.** 1:1; 2:1; 13:1; 26:11; 30:10; 33:17,20; 47:13; 48:6; 57:8; **Lam.** 2:14; **Ezek.** 12:27; 13:6–9,16,23; 21:29; **Amos** 1:1; **Mic.** 1:1; 4:11; **Hab.** 1:1; **Zech.** 10:2.

2373. חָזֶה *ḥāzeh* **masc. noun**
(breast [of animals])
Ex. 29:26,27; **Lev.** 7:30,31,34; 8:29; 9:20,21; 10:14,15; **Num.** 6:20; 18:18.

2374. I. חֹזֶה *ḥōzeh* **masc. noun**
(seer, prophet)
2 Sam. 24:11; **2 Kgs.** 17:13; **1 Chr.** 21:9; 25:5; 29:29; **2 Chr.** 9:29; 12:15; 19:2; 29:25,30; 33:18,19(KJV, *ḥôzay* [2335,I]; NASB, *ḥôzay* [2335,II]); 35:15; **Isa.** 29:10; 30:10; **Ezek.** 22:28; **Amos** 7:12; **Mic.** 3:7.
II. חֹזֶה *chōzeh* **masc. noun**
(agreement, pact)
Isa. 28:15.

2375. חֲזוֹ *ḥazô* **masc. proper noun**
(Hazo)
Gen. 22:22.

2376. חֵזוּ *ḥēzû* **Aram. masc. noun**
(vision, dream)
Dan. 2:19,28; 4:5(2),9(6),10(7),13(10); 7:1,2,7,13,15,20.

2377. חָזוֹן *ḥāzôn* **masc. noun**
(vision, revelation)
1 Sam. 3:1; **1 Chr.** 17:15; **2 Chr.** 32:32; **Ps.** 89:19(20); **Prov.** 29:18; **Isa.** 1:1; 29:7; **Jer.** 14:14; 23:16; **Lam.** 2:9; **Ezek.** 7:13,26; 12:22–24,27; 13:16; **Dan.** 1:17; 8:1,2,13,15,17,26; 9:21,24; 10:14; 11:14; **Hos.** 12:10(11); **Obad.** 1:1; **Mic.** 3:6; **Nah.** 1:1; **Hab.** 2:2,3.

2378. חָזוֹת *ḥāzôṯ* **fem. noun**
(vision, revelation)
2 Chr. 9:29.

2379. חֲזוֹת *ḥazôṯ* **Aram. fem. noun**
(sight, visability)
Dan. 4:11(8),20(17).

2380. חָזוּת *ḥāzûṯ* **fem. noun**
(a vision, agreement, prominence)
Isa. 21:2; 28:18; 29:11; **Dan.** 8:5,8.

2381. חֲזִיאֵל *ḥaziy'ēl* **masc. proper noun**
(Haziel)
1 Chr. 23:9.

2382. חֲזָיָה *ḥazāyāh* **masc. proper noun**
(Hazaiah)
Neh. 11:5.

2383. חֶזְיוֹן *hezyôn* **masc. proper noun**
(Hezion)
1 Kgs. 15:18.

2384. חִזָּיוֹן *ḥizzāyôn* **masc. noun**
(vision, revelation)
2 Sam. 7:17; **Job** 4:13; 7:14; 20:8; 33:15; **Isa.** 22:1,5; **Joel** 2:28(3:1); **Zech.** 13:4.

2385. חֲזִיז *ḥaziyz* **masc. noun**
(lightning, thunderbolt)
Job 28:26; 38:25; **Zech.** 10:1.

2386. חֲזִיר *ḥaziyr* **masc. noun**
(hog, pig)
Lev. 11:7; **Deut.** 14:8; **Ps.** 80:13(14); **Prov.** 11:22; **Isa.** 65:4; 66:3,17.

2387. A. חֵזִיר *ḥēziyr* **masc. proper noun**
(Hezir: a priest)
1 Chr. 24:15.
B. חֵזִיר *ḥēziyr* **masc. proper noun**
(Hezir: a covenanter)
Neh. 10:20(21).

2388. חָזַק *ḥāzaq* **verb**
(to make strong, to be strong; to make hard, to make firm, to seize)
Gen. 19:16; 21:18; 41:56,57; 47:20; 48:2; **Ex.** 4:4,21; 7:13,22; 8:19(15); 9:2,12,35; 10:20,27; 11:10; 12:33; 14:4,8,17; 19:19 (KJV, NIV, *ḥāzeq* [2390]); **Lev.** 25:35; **Num.** 13:20; **Deut.** 1:38; 3:28; 11:8; 12:23; 22:25; 25:11; 31:6,7,23; **Josh.** 1:6,7,9,18; 10:25; 11:20; 17:13; 23:6; **Judg.** 1:28; 3:12; 7:8,11,20; 9:24; 16:26,28; 19:4,25,29; 20:22; **1 Sam.** 4:9; 15:27; 17:35,50; 23:16; 30:6; **2 Sam.** 1:11; 2:7,16; 3:1(KJV, NIV, *ḥāzeq* [2390]), 6,29; 10:11,12; 11:25; 13:11,14,28; 15:5; 16:21; 18:9; 24:4; **1 Kgs.** 1:50; 2:2,28; 9:9; 16:22; 20:22,23,25; **2 Kgs.** 2:12(13) (KJV, *ḥozqāh* [2394,II]); 3:26; 4:8,27; 12:5–8(6–9),12(13),14(15); 14:5; 15:19; 22:5,6; 25:3; **1 Chr.** 11:10; 19:12,13; 21:4; 22:13; 26:27; 28:7,10,20; 29:12; **2 Chr.** 1:1; 4:5; 7:22; 8:3; 11:11,12,17; 12:13; 13:7,8,21; 15:7,8; 16:9; 17:1; 19:11; 21:4; 23:1; 24:5,12; 25:3,8,11; 26:8,9,15; 27:5,6; 28:15,20; 29:3,34; 31:4; 32:5,7; 34:8,10; 35:2; **Ezra** 1:6; 6:22; 7:28; 9:12; 10:4; **Neh.** 2:18; 3:4–24,27–32; 4:16(10),17(11),21(15); 5:16; 6:9; 10:29(30); **Job** 2:3,9; 4:3; 8:15,20; 18:9; 27:6; **Ps.** 27:14; 31:24(25); 35:2; 64:5(6); 147:13; **Prov.** 3:18; 4:13; 7:13; 26:17; **Isa.** 4:1; 22:21; 27:5; 28:22; 33:23; 35:3,4; 39:1; 41:6,7,9,13; 42:6; 45:1; 51:18; 54:2; 56:2,4,6; 64:7(6); **Jer.** 5:3; 6:23,24; 8:5,21; 10:4; 20:7; 23:14; 31:32; 49:24; 50:33,42,43; 51:12; 52:6; **Ezek.** 7:13; 13:22; 16:49; 22:14; 27:9,27; 30:21,24,25; 34:4,16; **Dan.** 10:18,19,21; 11:1,5–7,21,32; **Hos.** 7:15; **Mic.** 4:9; 7:18; **Nah.** 2:1(2); 3:14; **Hag.** 2:4; **Zech.** 8:9,13,23; 14:13; **Mal.** 3:13.

2389. חָזָק *ḥāzāq* **adj.**
(strong, mighty)
Ex. 3:19; 6:1; 10:19; 13:9; 19:16; 32:11; **Num.** 13:18,31; 20:20; **Deut.** 3:24; 4:34; 5:15; 6:21; 7:8,19; 9:26; 11:2; 26:8; 34:12; **Josh.** 4:24; 14:11; 17:18; **Judg.** 18:26; **1 Sam.** 14:52; **2 Sam.** 11:15; **1 Kgs.** 8:42; 17:17; 18:2; 19:11; **2 Chr.** 6:32; **Neh.** 1:10; **Job** 5:15; 37:18; **Ps.** 35:10; 136:12; **Prov.** 23:11; **Isa.** 27:1; 28:2; 40:10; **Jer.** 21:5; 31:11; 32:21; 50:34; **Ezek.** 2:4; 3:7–9,14; 20:33,34; 26:17; 30:22; 34:16; **Dan.** 9:15; **Amos** 2:14.

2390. חָזֵק *ḥāzēq* **verbal adj.**
(stronger)
Ex. 19:19(NASB, *ḥāzaq* [2388]); **2 Sam.** 3:1(NASB, *ḥāzaq* [2388]).

2391. חֵזֶק *ḥēzeq* **masc. noun**
(strength)
Ps. 18:1(2).

2392. חֹזֶק *ḥōzeq* **masc. noun**
(strength)
Ex. 13:3,14,16; **Amos** 6:13; **Hag.** 2:22.

2393. חֶזְקָה *ḥezqāh* **fem. noun**
(strength)
2 Chr. 12:1(KJV, *ḥozqāh* [2394,I]); 26:16(KJV, *ḥozqāh* [2394,I]); **Isa.** 8:11; **Dan.** 11:2.

2394. I. חָזְקָה *ḥozqāh* **fem. noun**
(strength, violence)
Judg. 4:3; 8:1; **1 Sam.** 2:16; **2 Chr.** 12:1(NASB, NIV, *ḥezqāh* [2393]); 26:16(NASB, NIV, *ḥezqāh* [2393]); **Ezek.** 34:4; **Jon.** 3:8.
II. חָזְקָה *ḥozqāh* **verb**
(strengthening in the sense of repairing)
2 Kgs. 12:12(13)(NASB, NIV, *ḥāzaq* [2388]).

2395. חִזְקִי *ḥizqiy* **masc. proper noun**
(Hizki, Hezeki)
1 Chr. 8:17.

2396. A. חִזְקִיָּה *ḥizqiyyāh,* חִזְקִיָּהוּ *ḥizqiyyāhû* **masc. proper noun**
(Hezekiah: king of Judah)
2 Kgs. 16:20; 18:1,9,10,13–17,19,22,29–32,37; 19:1,3, 5,9,10,14,15,20; 20:1,3,5,8,12–16,19–21; 21:3; **1 Chr.** 3:13; **2 Chr.** 29:18,27; 30:24; 32:15; **Prov.** 25:1; **Isa.** 36:1,2,4,7,14–16, 18,22; 37:1,3,5,9,10,14,15,21; 38:1–3,5, 9,22; 39:1–5,8; **Jer.** 26:18,19.
B. חִזְקִיָּה *ḥizqiyyāh* **masc. proper noun**
(Hezekiah: son of Neariah)
1 Chr. 3:23.
C. חִזְקִיָּה *ḥizqiyyāh* **masc. proper noun**
(Hezekiah: father of Amariah)
Zeph. 1:1.
D. חִזְקִיָּה *ḥizqiyyāh* **masc. proper noun**
(Hezekiah: a Jew)
Neh. 7:21; 10:17(18).

2397. חָח *ḥāḥ* **masc. noun**
(a hook, brooch, bracelet)
Ex. 35:22; **2 Kgs.** 19:28; **Isa.** 37:29; **Ezek.** 19:4,9; 29:4; 38:4.

2398. I. חֶטְאָה *ḥeṭʾāh* **fem. noun**
(sinning, lapse, fault)
Num. 15:28(KJV, NASB, see II).
II. חָטָא *ḥāṭāʾ* **verb**
(to sin, to miss, to be at fault)
Gen. 20:6,9; 31:39; 39:9; 40:1; 42:22; 43:9; 44:32; **Ex.** 5:16; 9:27,34; 10:16; 20:20; 23:33; 29:36; 32:30,31,33; **Lev.** 4:2,3,14,22,23,27,28,35; 5:1,5–7,10,11, 13,15–17; 6:2–4(5:21–23),26(19); 8:15; 9:15; 14:49,52; 19:22; **Num.** 6:11; 8:21; 12:11; 14:40; 15:27,28(NIV, see I); 16:22; 19:12,13,19,20; 21:7; 22:34; 31:19,20,23; 32:23; **Deut.** 1:41; 9:16,18; 19:15; 20:18; 24:4; **Josh.** 7:11,20; **Judg.** 10:10,15; 11:27; 20:16; **1 Sam.** 2:25; 7:6; 12:10,23; 14:33,34; 15:24,30; 19:4,5; 24:11(12); 26:21; **2 Sam.** 12:13; 19:20(21); 24:10,17; **1 Kgs.** 8:31,33,35,46,47,50; 14:16,22; 15:26,30,34; 16:2,13,19,26; 18:9; 21:22; 22:52(53); **2 Kgs.** 3:3; 10:29,31; 13:2, 6,11; 14:24; 15:9,18,24,28; 17:7,21; 18:14; 21:11,16,17; 23:15; **1 Chr.** 21:8,17; **2 Chr.** 6:22,24,26,36,37,39; 29:24; **Neh.** 1:6; 6:13; 9:29; 13:26; **Job** 1:5,22; 2:10; 5:24; 7:20; 8:4; 10:14; 24:19; 31:30; 33:27; 35:6; 41:25(17); **Ps.** 4:4(5); 39:1(2); 41:4(5); 51:4(6),7(9); 78:17,32; 106:6; 119:11; **Prov.** 8:36; 11:31; 13:22; 14:21; 19:2; 20:2; **Eccl.** 2:26; 5:6(5); 7:20,26; 8:12; 9:2,18; **Isa.** 1:4; 29:21; 42:24; 43:27; 64:5(4); 65:20; **Jer.** 2:35; 3:25; 8:14; 14:7,20; 16:10; 32:35; 33:8; 37:18; 40:3; 44:23; 50:7,14; **Lam.** 1:8; 5:7,16; **Ezek.** 3:21; 14:13; 16:51; 18:4,20,24; 28:16; 33:12,16; 37:23; 43:20,22,23; 45:18; **Dan.** 9:5,8,11,15; **Hos.** 4:7; 8:11; 10:9; 13:2; **Mic.** 7:9; **Hab.** 2:10; **Zeph.** 1:17.

2399. חֵטְא *ḥēṭ^{e}ʾ* **masc. noun**
(a sin, offense)
Gen. 41:9; **Lev.** 19:17; 20:20; 22:9; 24:15; **Num.** 9:13; 18:22,32; 27:3; **Deut.** 15:9; 19:15; 21:22; 22:26; 23:21(22),22(23); 24:15,16; **2 Kgs.** 10:29; 14:6; **2 Chr.** 25:4; **Ps.** 51:5(7),9(11); 103:10; **Eccl.** 10:4; **Isa.** 1:18; 31:7; 38:17; 53:12; **Lam.** 1:8; 3:39; **Ezek.** 23:49; **Dan.** 9:16; **Hos.** 12:8(9).

2400. חַטָּא *ḥaṭṭāʾ* **masc. noun**
(sinner)
Gen. 13:13; **Num.** 16:38(17:3); 32:14; **1 Sam.** 15:18; **1 Kgs.** 1:21; **Ps.** 1:1,5; 25:8; 26:9; 51:13(15); 104:35; **Prov.** 1:10; 13:21; 23:17; **Isa.** 1:28; 13:9; 33:14; **Amos** 9:8,10.

2401. חֲטָאָה *ḥ^{a}ṭāʾāh* **fem. noun**
(a sin, sin offering)
Gen. 20:9; **Ex.** 32:21,30,31; **2 Kgs.** 17:21; **Ps.** 32:1; 40:6(7); 109:7.

2402. חַטָּאָה *ḥaṭṭā'āh* **fem. noun**
(a sin offering)
Isa. 5:18.

2403. חַטָּאת *ḥaṭṭā't* **fem. noun**
(sin, sin offering)
Gen. 4:7; 18:20; 31:36; 50:17; **Ex.** 10:17; 29:14,36; 30:10; 32:30,32,34; 34:7,9; **Lev.** 4:3,8,14,20,21,23–26,28,29,32–35; 5:6–13; 6:17(10),25(18),30(23); 7:7,37; 8:2,14; 9:2,3,7,8,10,15,22; 10:16,17,19; 12:6,8; 14:13,19,22,31; 15:15,30; 16:3,5, 6,9,11,15,16,21,25,27,30,34; 19:22; 23:19; 26:18,21,24,28; **Num.** 5:6,7; 6:11,14,16; 7:16,22,28,34,40,46,52,58,64,70,76,82, 87; 8:7,8,12; 12:11; 15:24,25,27; 16:26; 18:9; 19:9,17; 28:15,22; 29:5,11,16,19, 22,25,28,31,34,38; 32:23; **Deut.** 9:18, 21,27; 19:15; **Josh.** 24:19; **1 Sam.** 2:17; 12:19; 14:38; 15:23,25; 20:1; **2 Sam.** 12:13; **1 Kgs.** 8:34–36; 12:30; 13:34; 14:16,22; 15:3,26,30,34; 16:2,13,19, 26,31; **2 Kgs.** 3:3; 10:31; 12:16(17); 13:2,6,11; 14:24; 15:9,18,24,28; 17:22; 21:16,17; 24:3; **2 Chr.** 6:25–27; 7:14; 28:13; 29:21,23,24; 33:19; **Ezra** 8:35; **Neh.** 1:6; 4:5(3:37); 9:2,37; 10:33(34); **Job** 10:6; 13:23; 14:16; 34:37; 35:3; **Ps.** 25:7,18; 32:5; 38:3(4),18(19); 51:2(4), 3(5); 59:3(4),12(13); 79:9; 85:2(3); 109:14; **Prov.** 5:22; 10:16; 13:6; 14:34; 20:9; 21:4; 24:9; **Isa.** 3:9; 6:7; 27:9; 30:1; 40:2; 43:24,25; 44:22; 58:1; 59:2,12; **Jer.** 5:25; 14:10; 15:13; 16:10,18; 17:1,3; 18:23; 30:14,15; 31:34; 36:3; 50:20; **Lam.** 4:6, 13,22; **Ezek.** 3:20; 16:51,52; 18:14,21,24; 21:24(29); 33:10,14,16; 40:39; 42:13; 43:19,21,22,25; 44:27,29; 45:17,19,22,23, 25; 46:20; **Dan.** 9:20,24; **Hos.** 4:8; 8:13; 9:9; 10:8; 13:12; **Amos** 5:12; **Mic.** 1:5,13; 3:8; 6:7,13; 7:19; **Zech.** 13:1; 14:19.

2404. חָטַב *ḥāṭab̲* **verb**
(to chop, to cut down)
Deut. 19:5; 29:11(10); **Josh.** 9:21,23,27; **2 Chr.** 2:10(9); **Ps.** 144:12; **Jer.** 46:22; **Ezek.** 39:10.

2405. חֲטֻבוֹת *ḥᵃṭub̲ôt̲* **fem. pl. noun**
(something colored)
Prov. 7:16.

2406. חִטָּה *ḥiṭṭāh* **fem. noun**
(wheat)
Gen. 30:14; **Ex.** 9:32; 29:2; 34:22; **Deut.** 8:8; 32:14; **Judg.** 6:11; 15:1; **Ruth** 2:23; **1 Sam.** 6:13; 12:17; **2 Sam.** 4:6; 17:28; **1 Kgs.** 5:11(25); **1 Chr.** 21:20,23; **2 Chr.** 2:10(9),15(14); 27:5; **Job** 31:40; **Ps.** 81:16(17); 147:14; **Song** 7:2(3); **Isa.** 28:25; **Jer.** 12:13; 41:8; **Ezek.** 4:9; 27:17; 45:13; **Joel** 1:11.

2407. A. חַטּוּשׁ *ḥaṭṭûš* **masc. proper noun**
(Hattush: son of Shemiah)
1 Chr. 3:22.
B. חַטּוּשׁ *ḥaṭṭûš* **masc. proper noun**
(Hattush: descendant of David)
Ezra 8:2.
C. חַטּוּשׁ *ḥaṭṭûš* **masc. proper noun**
(Hattush: son of Hashabniah)
Neh. 3:10.
D. חַטּוּשׁ *ḥaṭṭûš* **masc. proper noun**
(Hattush: a Jew)
Neh. 10:4(5).
E. חַטּוּשׁ *ḥaṭṭûš* **masc. proper noun**
(Hattush: a priest)
Neh. 12:2.

2408. חֲטָי *ḥᵃṭāy* **Aram. masc. noun**
(sin)
Dan. 4:27(24).

2409. חַטָּיָא *ḥaṭṭāyā'* **Aram. fem. noun**
(sin offering)
Ezra 6:17.

2410. חֲטִיטָא *ḥᵃṭiyṭā'* **masc. proper noun**
(Hatita)
Ezra 2:42; **Neh.** 7:45.

2411. חַטִּיל *ḥaṭṭiyl* masc. proper noun
(Hattil)
Ezra 2:57; **Neh.** 7:59.

2412. חֲטִיפָא *ḥaṭiypā'* masc. proper noun
(Hatipha)
Ezra 2:54; **Neh.** 7:56.

2413. חָטַם *ḥāṭam* verb
(to hold back, to restrain)
Isa. 48:9.

2414. חָטַף *ḥāṭap̱* verb
(to catch, to seize)
Judg. 21:21; **Ps.** 10:9.

2415. חֹטֶר *ḥōṭer* masc. noun
(a rod, branch)
Prov. 14:3; **Isa.** 11:1.

2416. I. חַי *ḥay* adj.
(alive, living)
Gen. 1:20,21,24,30; 2:7,19; 3:20; 6:19; 7:11; 8:21; 9:3,12,15,16; 18:10,14; 25:6; 26:19; 42:15,16; 43:7,27,28; 45:3,26,28; 46:30; **Ex.** 4:18; 21:35; 22:4(3); **Lev.** 11:10,46; 13:10,14–16; 14:4–7,50–53; 15:13; 16:10,20,21; **Num.** 14:21,28; 16:30,33,48(17:13); 19:17; **Deut.** 4:4,10; 5:3,26(23); 12:1; 31:13,27; 32:40; **Josh.** 3:10; 8:23; **Judg.** 8:19; **Ruth** 2:20; 3:13; **1 Sam.** 1:26; 2:15; 14:39,45; 15:8; 17:26,36,55; 18:18(NIV, see VI); 19:6; 20:3,14,21; 25:6,26,29,34; 26:10,16; 28:10; 29:6; **2 Sam.** 2:27; 4:9; 11:11; 12:5,18,21,22; 14:11,19; 15:21; 18:14; 19:6(7); 22:47; 23:11,13,20(KJV, NASB, NIV, [Qe] *ḥayil* [2428]); **1 Kgs.** 1:29; 2:24; 3:22,23,25–27; 4:21(5:1); 8:40; 12:6; 17:1,12,23; 18:10,15; 20:18,32; 21:15; 22:14; **2 Kgs.** 2:2,4,6; 3:14; 4:16,17,30; 5:16,20; 7:12; 10:14; 19:4,16; **2 Chr.** 6:31; 10:6; 18:13; 25:12; **Job** 12:10; 19:25; 27:2; 28:13,21; 30:23; 33:22; **Ps.** 18:46(47); 27:13; 30:5(6); 38:19(20); 42:2(3); 52:5(7); 55:15(16); 58:9(10); 68:10(11)(KJV, NIV, see V); 84:2(3); 116:9; 124:3; 133:3; 142:5(6); 143:2,3; 145:16; **Prov.** 1:12; **Eccl.** 4:2,15; 5:18(17)([Qe] see II); 6:8; 7:2; 9:4,5; **Song** 4:15; **Isa.** 4:3; 8:19; 37:4, 17; 38:11,19,20; 40:16; 49:18; 53:8; **Jer.** 2:13; 4:2; 5:2; 8:3; 10:10; 11:19; 12:16; 16:14,15; 17:13; 21:8; 22:24; 23:7,8,36; 38:16; 44:26; 46:18; 52:33, 34; **Lam.** 3:39; **Ezek.** 5:11; 14:16, 18,20; 16:48; 17:16,19; 18:3; 20:3, 31,33; 26:20; 32:23–27,32; 33:11, 15,27; 34:8; 35:6,11; 47:9; **Dan.** 12:7; **Hos.** 1:10(2:1); 4:15; **Amos** 8:14; **Jon.** 4:3,8; **Zeph.** 2:9; **Zech.** 14:8; **Mal.** 2:5.

II. חַי *ḥay* masc. noun
(life)
Gen. 2:7,9; 3:14,17,22,24; 6:17; 7:15,22; 23:1; 25:7,17; 27:46; 47:8,9,28; **Ex.** 1:14; 6:16,18,20; **Lev.** 18:18; **Deut.** 4:4,9,10; 6:2; 16:3; 17:19; 28:66; 30:6,15,19,20; 32:47; **Josh.** 1:5; 4:14; **Judg.** 16:30; **1 Sam.** 1:11; 7:15; **2 Sam.** 1:23; 15:21; 18:18; 19:34(35); **1 Kgs.** 4:21(5:1); 11:34; 15:5,6; **2 Kgs.** 25:29,30; **Job** 3:20; 7:7; 9:21; 10:1,12; 24:22; 33:30; **Ps.** 7:5(6); 16:11; 17:14; 21:4(5); 23:6; 26:9; 27:1,4; 30:5(6); 31:10(11); 34:12(13); 36:9(10); 42:8(9); 49:18(19); 56:13(14); 63:3(4),4(5); 64:1(2); 66:9; 69:28(29); 88:3(4); 103:4; 104:33; 128:5; 146:2; **Prov.** 2:19; 3:2,18,22; 4:10,13,22,23; 5:6; 6:23; 8:35; 9:11; 10:11,16,17; 11:19,30; 12:28; 13:12,14; 14:27,30; 15:4,24,31; 16:15,22; 18:21; 19:23; 21:21; 22:4; 27:27; 31:12; **Eccl.** 2:3,17; 3:12; 5:18 (17)([Ke] see I),20(19); 6:12; 8:15; 9:3,9; 10:19; **Isa.** 38:12,16; **Lam.** 3:53,58; **Dan.** 12:2; **Jon.** 2:6(7).

III. חַיָּה *ḥayyāh* fem. noun
(living creature, animal, life)
Gen. 1:24,25,28,30; 2:19,20; 3:1,14; 7:14,21; 8:1,17,19; 9:2,5,10; 37:20,33; **Ex.** 23:11,29; **Lev.** 5:2; 11:2,27,47;

17:13; 25:7; 26:6,22; **Num.** 35:3; **Deut.** 7:22; **1 Sam.** 17:46; **2 Sam.** 21:10; **2 Kgs.** 14:9; **2 Chr.** 25:18; **Job** 5:22,23; 37:8; 39:15; 40:20; **Ps.** 50:10; 68:30(31); 79:2; 104:11,20,25; 148:10; **Isa.** 35:9; 43:20; 46:1; 56:9; **Jer.** 12:9; 27:6; 28:14; **Ezek.** 1:5,13–15,19–22; 3:13; 5:17; 10:15,17,20; 14:15,21; 29:5; 31:6,13; 32:4; 33:27; 34:5,8,25,28; 35:6,11; 38:20; 39:4,17; **Dan.** 8:4; **Hos.** 2:12(14),18(20); 4:3; 13:8; **Zeph.** 2:14,15.

IV. חַיָּה *ḥayyāh* **fem. noun**
(life, soul)
Job 33:18,20,22,28; 36:14; 38:39; **Ps.** 74:19(KJV, see V); 78:50; **Isa.** 57:10; **Ezek.** 7:13.

V. חַיָּה *ḥayyāh* **fem. noun**
(community, host, multitude, troop, band)
2 Sam. 23:11,13; **Ps.** 68:10(11)(NASB, see I); 74:19(NASB, NIV, see IV).

VI. חַי *ḥay* **masc. noun**
(kinsmen, family)
1 Sam. 18:18(KJV, NASB, see I).

2417. חַי *ḥay* **Aram. adj.**
(living)
Ezra 6:10; **Dan.** 2:30; 4:17(14),34(31); 6:20(21),26(27); 7:12.

2418. חֲיָה *ḥ^a^yāh*, חֲיָא *ḥ^a^yā'* **Aram. verb**
(to live; corr. to Hebr. 2421)
Dan. 2:4; 3:9; 5:10,19; 6:6(7),21(22).

2419. חִיאֵל *ḥiy'ēl* **masc. proper noun**
(Hiel)
1 Kgs. 16:34.

2420. חִידָה *ḥiydāh* **fem. noun**
(a riddle, hard question)
Num. 12:8; **Judg.** 14:12–19; **1 Kgs.** 10:1; **2 Chr.** 9:1; **Ps.** 49:4(5); 78:2; **Prov.** 1:6; **Ezek.** 17:2; **Dan.** 8:23; **Hab.** 2:6.

2421. חָיָה *ḥāyāh* **verb**
(to live; see also *ḥāyay* [2425])
Gen. 5:3,6,7,9,10,12,13,15,16,18,19,21, 25,26,28,30; 6:19,20; 7:3; 9:28; 11:11–26; 12:12,13; 17:18; 19:19,20,32,34; 20:7; 27:40; 31:32; 42:2,18; 43:8; 45:7,27; 47:19,25,28; 50:20,22; **Ex.** 1:17,18,22; 19:13; 22:18(17); **Num.** 4:19; 14:38; 22:33; 24:23; 31:15,18; **Deut.** 4:1,33; 5:26(23),33(30); 6:24; 8:1,3; 16:20; 20:16; 30:16,19; 32:39; 33:6; **Josh.** 2:13; 5:8; 6:17,25; 9:15,20,21; 14:10; **Judg.** 8:19; 15:19; 21:14; **1 Sam.** 2:6; 10:24; 27:9,11; **2 Sam.** 1:10; 8:2; 12:3; 16:16; **1 Kgs.** 1:25,31,34,39; 17:22; 18:5; 20:31,32; **2 Kgs.** 1:2; 4:7; 5:7; 7:4; 8:1,5,8–10,14; 10:19; 11:12; 13:21; 14:17; 18:32; 20:1,7; **1 Chr.** 11:8; **2 Chr.** 23:11; 25:25; **Neh.** 2:3; 4:2(3:34); 5:2; 9:6,29; **Esth.** 4:11; **Job** 7:16; 14:14; 21:7; 33:4; 36:6; 42:16; **Ps.** 22:26(27), 29(30); 30:3(4); 33:19; 41:2(3); 49:9(10); 69:32(33); 71:20; 72:15; 80:18(19); 85:6(7); 89:48(49); 118:17; 119:17,25,37, 40,50,77,88,93,107,116,144,149,154,156 ,159,175; 138:7; 143:11; **Prov.** 4:4; 7:2; 9:6; 15:27; **Eccl.** 6:3,6; 7:12; 11:8; **Isa.** 7:21; 26:14,19; 38:1,9,16,21; 55:3; 57:15; **Jer.** 21:9; 27:12,17; 35:7; 38:2,17,20; 49:11; **Lam.** 4:20; **Ezek.** 3:18,21; 13:18, 19,22; 16:6; 18:9,13,17,19,21–23,27, 28,32; 20:25; 33:10–13,15,16,19; 37:3, 5,6,9,10,14; 47:9; **Hos.** 6:2; 14:7(8); **Amos** 5:4,6,14; **Hab.** 2:4; 3:2; **Zech.** 1:5; 10:9; 13:3.

2422. חָיֶה *ḥāyeh* **adj.**
(vigorous, lively)
Ex. 1:19.

2423. חֵיוָה *ḥēywāh* **Aram. fem. noun**
(beast, animal)
Dan. 2:38; 4:12(9),14–16(11–13),21(18),23(20), 25(22),32(29); 5:21; 7:3,5–7,11,12,17, 19,23.

2424. חַיּוּת *ḥayyûṯ* **fem. noun**
(the act of living)
2 Sam. 20:3.

2425. חָיַי *ḥāyay* **verb**
(to live; NASB, NIV, *ḥāyāh* [2421])
Gen. 3:22; 5:5; 11:12,14; 25:7; **Ex.** 1:16; 33:20; **Lev.** 18:5; 25:35,36; **Num.** 21:8,9; **Deut.** 4:42; 5:24(21); 19:4,5; **1 Sam.** 20:31; **Neh.** 6:11; **Jer.** 38:2; **Ezek.** 18:13,24; 20:11,13,21; 47:9.

2426. חֵיל *ḥēyl,* חֵל *ḥēl* **masc. noun**
(rampart, fortification)
2 Sam. 20:15; **1 Kgs.** 21:23; **2 Kgs.** 18:17; **Ps.** 10:10(see *ḥēl kā'eh* [2489,II]); 48:13(14)(KJV, *ḥēylā*h [2430]); 122:7; **Isa.** 26:1; **Lam.** 2:8; **Obad.** 1:20; **Nah.** 3:8.

2427. I. חִיל *ḥiyl* **masc. noun**
(anguish, pain)
Ex. 15:14; **Ps.** 48:6(7); **Jer.** 6:24; 22:23; 50:43; **Mic.** 4:9.
II. חִילָה *ḥiylāh* **fem. noun**
(pain)
Job 6:10.

2428. חַיִל *ḥayil* **masc. noun**
(army, strength, wealth)
Gen. 34:29; 47:6; **Ex.** 14:4,9,17,28; 15:4; 18:21,25; **Num.** 24:18; 31:9,14; **Deut.** 3:18; 8:17,18; 11:4; 33:11; **Josh.** 1:14; 6:2; 8:3; 10:7; **Judg.** 3:29; 6:12; 11:1; 18:2; 20:44,46; 21:10; **Ruth** 2:1; 3:11; 4:11; **1 Sam.** 2:4; 9:1; 10:26; 14:48,52; 16:18; 17:20; 18:17; 31:12; **2 Sam.** 2:7; 8:9; 11:16; 13:28; 17:10; 22:33,40; 23:20([K^{e}] חַי [2416,I]); 24:2,4,9; **1 Kgs.** 1:42,52; 10:2; 11:28; 15:20; 20:1,19,25; **2 Kgs.** 2:16; 5:1; 6:14,15; 7:6; 9:5; 11:15; 15:20; 24:14,16; 25:1,5,10,23,26; **1 Chr.** 5:18,24; 7:2,5,7,9,11,40; 8:40; 9:13; 10:12; 11:22,26; 12:8,21,25,28,30; 18:9; 20:1; 26:6–9,30–32; 28:1; **2 Chr.** 9:1; 13:3; 14:8(7),9(8); 16:4,7,8; 17:2,13,14,16,17; 23:14; 24:23,24; 25:6; 26:11–13,17; 28:6; 32:21; 33:14; **Ezra** 8:22; **Neh.** 2:9; 4:2 (3:34); 11:6,14; **Esth.** 1:3; 8:11; **Job** 5:5; 15:29; 20:15,18; 21:7; 31:25; **Ps.** 18:32(33),39(40); 33:16,17; 49:6(7), 10(11); 59:11(12); 60:12(14); 62:10(11); 73:12; 76:5(6); 84:7(8); 108:13(14); 110:3; 118:15,16; 136:15; **Prov.** 12:4; 13:22; 31:3,10,29; **Eccl.** 10:10; 12:3; **Isa.** 5:22; 8:4; 10:14; 30:6; 36:2; 43:17; 60:5,11; 61:6; **Jer.** 15:13; 17:3; 32:2; 34:1,7,21; 35:11; 37:5,7,10,11; 38:3; 39:1,5; 40:7,13; 41:11,13,16; 42:1,8; 43:4,5; 46:2,22; 48:14; 52:4,8,14; **Ezek.** 17:17; 26:12; 27:10,11; 28:4,5; 29:18,19; 32:31; 37:10; 38:4,15; **Dan.** 11:7,10,13,25,26; **Joel** 2:11,22,25; **Obad.** 1:11,13; **Mic.** 4:13; **Nah.** 2:3(4); **Hab.** 3:19; **Zeph.** 1:13; **Zech.** 4:6; 9:4; 14:14.

2429. חַיִל *ḥayil* **Aram. masc. noun**
(strength, power, force, army; corr. to Hebr. 2428)
Ezra 4:23; **Dan.** 3:4,20; 4:14(11),35(32); 5:7.

2430. חֵילָה *ḥēylāh* **fem. noun**
(rampart, bulwark)
Ps. 48:13(14)(NASB, NIV, *heyl* [2426]).

2431. חֵילָם *ḥēylām* **masc. proper noun**
(Helam)
2 Sam. 10:16,17.

2432. חִילֵן *ḥiylēn* **?roper noun**
(Hilen)
1 Chr. 6:58(43).

2433. חִין *ḥiyn* **masc. noun**
(grace, beauty)
Job 41:12(4).

2434. חַיִץ *ḥayiṣ* **masc. noun**
(a thin, flimsy wall)
Ezek. 13:10.

2435. חִיצוֹן *ḥiyṣôn* **adj.**
(outer, external)
1 Kgs. 6:29,30; **2 Kgs.** 16:18; **1 Chr.** 26:29; **2 Chr.** 33:14; **Neh.** 11:16; **Esth.** 6:4; **Ezek.** 10:5; 40:17,20,31,34,37; 41:17; 42:1,3,7–9,14; 44:1,19; 46:20,21.

2436. I. חֵיק *ḥēyq*, חֵק *ḥēq* **masc. noun**
(bosom)
Gen. 16:5; **Ex.** 4:6,7; **Num.** 11:12; **Deut.** 13:6(7); 28:54,56; **Ruth** 4:16; **2 Sam.** 12:3,8; **1 Kgs.** 1:2; 3:20; 17:19; **Job** 19:27; **Ps.** 35:13; 74:11; 79:12; 89:50(51); **Prov.** 5:20; 6:27; 16:33; 17:23; 21:14; **Eccl.** 7:9; **Isa.** 40:11; 65:6,7; **Jer.** 32:18; **Lam.** 2:12; **Ezek.** 43:13,14,17; **Mic.** 7:5.
II. חֵיק *ḥēyq*, חֵק *ḥēq* **masc. noun**
(channel, trough)
1 Kgs. 22:35; **Ezek.** 43:13,14,17.

2437. חִירָה *ḥiyrāh* **masc. proper noun**
(Hirah)
Gen. 38:1,12.

2438. A. חִירוֹם *ḥiyrôm*, חִירָם *ḥiyrām* **masc. proper noun**
(Hiram: king of Tyre)
2 Sam. 5:11; **1 Kgs.** 5:1(15),2(16),7(21),8(22),10–12(24–26), 18(32); 9:11,12,14,27; 10:11,22; **1 Chr.** 14:1.
B. חִירוֹם *ḥiyrôm*, חִירָם *ḥiyrām* **masc. proper noun**
(Hiram: an architect; see also *ḥûrām* [2361,B])
1 Kgs. 7:13,40,45; **2 Chr.** 4:11.

2439. חִישׁ *ḥiyš* **verb**
(to make haste, to act quickly)
Ps. 71:12(NASB, NIV, [Qe] *ḥûš* [2363,I]).

2440. חִישׁ *ḥiyš* **adv.**
(quickly, soon)
Ps. 90:10.

2441. חֵךְ *ḥēḵ* **masc. noun**
(mouth, palate)
Job 6:30; 12:11; 20:13; 29:10; 31:30; 33:2; 34:3; **Ps.** 119:103; 137:6; **Prov.** 5:3; 8:7; 24:13; **Song** 2:3; 5:16; 7:9(10); **Lam.** 4:4; **Ezek.** 3:26; **Hos.** 8:1.

2442. חָכָה *ḥāḵāh* **verb**
(to wait, to tarry)
2 Kgs. 7:9; 9:3; **Job** 3:21; 32:4; **Ps.** 33:20; 106:13; **Isa.** 8:17; 30:18; 64:4(3); **Dan.** 12:12; **Hos.** 6:9; **Hab.** 2:3; **Zeph.** 3:8.

2443. חַכָּה *ḥakkāh* **fem. noun**
(a hook, fishhook)
Job 41:1(40:25); **Isa.** 19:8; **Hab.** 1:15.

2444. חֲכִילָה *ḥaḵiylāh* **proper noun**
(Hachilah, Hakilah)
1 Sam. 23:19; 26:1,3.

2445. חַכִּים *ḥakkiym* **Aram. adj.**
(wise)
Dan. 2:12–14,18,21,24,27,48; 4:6(3),18(15); 5:7,8,15.

2446. חֲכַלְיָה *ḥaḵalyāh* **masc. proper noun**
(Hachaliah, Hacaliah)
Neh. 1:1; 10:1(2).

2447. חַכְלִילִי *ḥaḵliyliy* **adj.**
(dull, dark)
Gen. 49:12.

2448. חַכְלִילוּת *ḥaḵliylûṯ* **fem. noun**
(redness, darkness)
Prov. 23:29.

2449. חָכַם *ḥāḵam* **verb**
(to be wise, to be skillful)
Ex. 1:10; **Deut.** 32:29; **1 Kgs.** 4:31(5:11); **Job** 32:9; 35:11; **Ps.** 19:7(8); 58:5(6); 105:22; 119:98; **Prov.** 6:6; 8:33; 9:9,12; 13:20; 19:20; 20:1; 21:11;

23:15,19; 27:11; 30:24; **Eccl.** 2:15,19; 7:16,23; **Zech.** 9:2.

2450. חָכָם ḥāḵām adj.
(wise, skilled)
Gen. 41:8,33,39; **Ex.** 7:11; 28:3; 31:6; 35:10,25; 36:1,2,4,8; **Deut.** 1:13,15; 4:6; 16:19; 32:6; **Judg.** 5:29; **2 Sam.** 13:3; 14:2,20; 20:16; **1 Kgs.** 2:9; 3:12; 5:7(21); **1 Chr.** 22:15; **2 Chr.** 2:7(6),12–14 (11–13); **Esth.** 1:13; 6:13; **Job** 5:13; 9:4; 15:2,18; 17:10; 34:2,34; 37:24; **Ps.** 49:10(11); 107:43; **Prov.** 1:5,6; 3:7,35; 9:8,9; 10:1,8,14; 11:29,30; 12:15,18; 13:1,14,20; 14:1(KJV, *ḥoḵmôṯ* [2454]),3,16,24; 15:2,7,12,20,31; 16:14, 21,23; 17:28; 18:15; 20:26; 21:11,20,22; 22:17; 23:24; 24:5,23; 25:12; 26:5,12,16; 28:11; 29:8,9,11; 30:24; **Eccl.** 2:14,16,1 9; 4:13; 6:8; 7:4,5,7,19; 8:1,5,17; 9:1, 11,15,17; 10:2,12; 12:9,11; **Isa.** 3:3; 5:21; 19:11,12; 29:14; 31:2; 40:20; 44:25; **Jer.** 4:22; 8:8,9; 9:12(11),17(16),23(22); 10:7,9; 18:18; 50:35; 51:57; **Ezek.** 27:8, 9; 28:3; **Hos.** 13:13; 14:9(10); **Obad.** 1:8.

2451. חָכְמָה ḥoḵmāh fem. noun
(wisdom, skill)
Ex. 28:3; 31:3,6; 35:26,31,35; 36:1,2; **Deut.** 4:6; 34:9; **2 Sam.** 14:20; 20:22; **1 Kgs.** 2:6; 3:28; 4:29(5:9),30(5:10); 34(5:14); 5:12(26); 7:14; 10:4,6–8,23,24; 11:41; **1 Chr.** 28:21; **2 Chr.** 1:10–12; 9:3,5–7,22,23; **Job** 4:21; 11:6; 12:2, 12,13; 13:5; 15:8; 26:3; 28:12,18,20,28; 32:7,13; 33:33; 38:36,37; 39:17; **Ps.** 37:30; 49:3(4)(KJV, NIV, *ḥoḵmôṯ* [2454]); 51:6(8); 90:12; 104:24; 107:27; 111:10; **Prov.** 1:2,7,20(KJV, NIV, *ḥoḵmôṯ* [2454]); 2:2,6,10; 3:13,19; 4:5,7,11; 5:1; 7:4; 8:1,11,12; 9:1(KJV, NIV, *ḥoḵmôṯ* [2454]), 10; 10:13,23,31; 11:2; 13:10; 14:1(KJV, NIV, *ḥoḵmôṯ* [2454]),6,8,33; 15:33; 16:16; 17:16,24; 18:4; 21:30; 23:23; 24:3,7(KJV, NIV, *ḥoḵmôṯ* [2454]),14; 28:26; 29:3,15; 30:3; 31:26; **Eccl.** 1:13,16–18; 2:3,9, 12,13,21,26; 7:10–12,19,23,25; 8:1,16; 9:10,13,15,16,18; 10:1,10; **Isa.** 10:13; 11:2; 29:14; 33:6; 47:10; **Jer.** 8:9; 9:23(22); 10:12; 49:7; 51:15; **Ezek.** 28:4,5,7,12,17; **Dan.** 1:4,17,20.

2452. חָכְמָה ḥoḵmāh Aram. fem. noun
(wisdom, understanding; corr. to Hebr. 2451)
Ezra 7:25; **Dan.** 2:20,21,23,30; 5:11,14.

2453. I. חַכְמוֹנִי ḥaḵmôniy masc. proper noun
(Hachmoni: father of Jehiel)
1 Chr. 27:32.
II. חַכְמוֹנִי ḥaḵmôniy masc. proper noun
(Hachmonite: nationality of one of David's mighty men; the same as *taḥkᵉmōniy* [8461])
1 Chr. 11:11.

2454. חָכְמוֹת ḥoḵmôṯ fem. noun
(wisdom)
Ps. 49:3(4)(NASB, *ḥoḵmāh* [2451]); **Prov.** 1:20(NASB, *ḥoḵmāh* [2451]); 9:1(NASB, *ḥoḵmāh* [2451]); 14:1(NASB, NIV, *ḥāḵām* [2450]); 24:7(NASB, *ḥoḵmāh* [2451]).

2455. חֹל ḥōl adj.
(unclean, unholy)
Lev. 10:10; **1 Sam.** 21:4(5),5(6); **Ezek.** 22:26; 42:20; 44:23; 48:15.

2456. חָלָא ḥālā' verb
(to be diseased, to be sick)
2 Chr. 16:12.

2457. חֶלְאָה ḥel'āh fem. noun
(rust, scum)
Ezek. 24:6,11,12.

2458. חֶלְאָה ḥel'āh fem. proper noun
(Helah)
1 Chr. 4:5,7.

2459. חֵלֶב *ḥēleḇ* **masc. noun**
(fat, best)
Gen. 4:4; 45:18; **Ex.** 23:18; 29:13,22; **Lev.** 3:3,4,9,10,14–17; 4:8,9,19,26, 31,35; 6:12(5); 7:3,4,23–25,30,31,33; 8:16,25,26; 9:10,19,20,24; 10:15; 16:25; 17:6; **Num.** 18:12,17,29,30,32; **Deut.** 32:14,38; **Judg.** 3:22; **1 Sam.** 2:15,16; 15:22; **2 Sam.** 1:22; **1 Kgs.** 8:64; **2 Chr.** 7:7; 29:35; 35:14; **Job** 15:27; **Ps.** 17:10; 63:5(6); 73:7; 81:16(17); 119:70; 147:14; **Isa.** 1:11; 34:6,7; 43:24; **Ezek.** 34:3; 39:19; 44:7,15.

2460. חֵלֶב *ḥēleḇ* **masc. proper noun**
(Heleb)
2 Sam. 23:29.

2461. חָלָב *ḥālāḇ* **masc. noun**
(milk, cheese)
Gen. 18:8; 49:12; **Ex.** 3:8,17; 13:5; 23:19; 33:3; 34:26; **Lev.** 20:24; **Num.** 13:27; 14:8; 16:13,14; **Deut.** 6:3; 11:9; 14:21; 26:9,15; 27:3; 31:20; 32:14; **Josh.** 5:6; **Judg.** 4:19; 5:25; **1 Sam.** 7:9; 17:18; **Job** 10:10; 21:24; **Prov.** 27:27; 30:33; **Song** 4:11; 5:1,12; **Isa.** 7:22; 28:9; 55:1; 60:16; **Jer.** 11:5; 32:22; **Lam.** 4:7; **Ezek.** 20:6,15; 25:4; **Joel** 3:18(4:18).

2462. חֶלְבָּה *ḥelbāh* **proper noun**
(Helbah)
Judg. 1:31.

2463. חֶלְבּוֹן *ḥelbôn* **proper noun**
(Helbon)
Ezek. 27:18.

2464. חֶלְבְּנָה *ḥelbinâh* **fem. noun**
(galbanum, a kind of gum)
Ex. 30:34.

2465. חֶלֶד *ḥeleḏ* **masc. noun**
(defect, weakness)
Job 11:17; **Ps.** 17:14; 39:5(6); 49:1(2); 89:47(48); **Isa.** 38:11(see *ḥeḏel* [2309]).

2466. חֵלֶד *ḥeleḏ* **masc. proper noun**
(Heled)
1 Chr. 11:30.

2467. חֹלֶד *ḥōleḏ* **masc. noun**
(weasel, mole)
Lev. 11:29.

2468. חֻלְדָּה *ḥuldāh* **fem. proper noun**
(Huldah)
2 Kgs. 22:14; **2 Chr.** 34:22.

2469. A. חֶלְדַּי *ḥelday* **masc. proper noun**
(Heldai: one of David's mighty men)
1 Chr. 27:15.
B. חֶלְדַּי *ḥelday* **masc. proper noun**
(Heldai: a Jew)
Zech. 6:10,14(see *ḥēlēm* [2494]; KJV, NASB, *ḥēlēm* [2494]).

2470. I. חָלָה *ḥālāh* **verb**
(to be weak, to be sick, to be patient)
Gen. 48:1; **Deut.** 29:22(21); **Judg.** 16:7,11,17; **1 Sam.** 19:14; 22:8; 30:13; **2 Sam.** 13:2,5,6; **1 Kgs.** 14:1,5; 15:23; 17:17; 22:34; **2 Kgs.** 1:2; 8:7,29; 20:1,12; **2 Chr.** 18:33; 22:6; 32:24; 35:23; **Neh.** 2:2; **Ps.** 35:13; 77:10(11); **Prov.** 13:12; 23:35; **Eccl.** 5:13(12),16(15); **Song** 2:5; 5:8; **Isa.** 14:10; 17:11(NIV, see II); 33:24; 38:1,9; 39:1; 53:10; 57:10; **Jer.** 4:31; 10:19; 12:13; 14:17; 30:12; **Ezek.** 34:4,16,21; **Dan.** 8:27; **Hos.** 7:5; **Amos** 6:6; **Mic.** 1:12(NIV, *ḥiyl* [2342]); 6:13; **Nah.** 3:19; **Zech.** 7:2; **Mal.** 1:8,13.
II. נַחֲלָה *naḥ*ᵃ*lāh* **fem. noun**
(disease)
Isa. 17:11(KJV, NASB, see I).
III. חָלָה *ḥālāh* **verb**
(to appease, to appeal to, to entreat)
Ex. 32:11; **1 Sam.** 13:12; **1 Kgs.** 13:6; **2 Kgs.** 13:4,14; **2 Chr.** 33:12; **Job**

11:19; **Ps.** 45:12(13); 119:58; **Prov.** 19:6; **Jer.** 26:19; **Dan.** 9:13; **Zech.** 8:21,22; **Mal.** 1:9.

2471. חַלָּה *ḥallāh* **fem. noun**
(cake, wafer)
Ex. 29:2,23; **Lev.** 2:4; 7:12,13; 8:26; 24:5; **Num.** 6:15,19; 15:20; **2 Sam.** 6:19.

2472. חֲלוֹם *ḥalôm* **masc. noun**
(dream)
Gen. 20:3,6; 31:10,11,24; 37:5,6,8–10,19,20; 40:5,8,9,16; 41:7,8,11,12,15,17,22,25,26,32; 42:9; **Num.** 12:6; **Deut.** 13:1(2),3(4),5(6); **Judg.** 7:13,15; **1 Sam.** 28:6,15; **1 Kgs.** 3:5,15; **Job** 7:14; 20:8; 33:15; **Ps.** 73:20; **Eccl.** 5:3(2),7(6); **Isa.** 29:7; **Jer.** 23:27, 28,32; 27:9(KJV, *ḥālam* [2492,I]); 29:8; **Dan.** 1:17; 2:1–3; **Joel** 2:28(3:1); **Zech.** 10:2.

2473. A. חלון *ḥōlôn* **proper noun**
(Holon: city in Moab)
Jer. 48:21.
B. חלון *ḥōlôn* **proper noun**
(Holon: city in Judah)
Josh. 15:51; 21:15.

2474. חַלּוֹן *ḥallôn* **masc./fem. noun**
(window, opening)
Gen. 8:6; 26:8; **Josh.** 2:15,18,21; **Judg.** 5:28; **1 Sam.** 19:12; **2 Sam.** 6:16; **1 Kgs.** 6:4; **2 Kgs.** 9:30,32; 13:17; **1 Chr.** 15:29; **Prov.** 7:6; **Song** 2:9; **Jer.** 9:21(20); 22:14; **Ezek.** 40:16,22,25,29, 33,36; 41:16,26; **Joel** 2:9; **Zeph.** 2:14.

2475. חֲלוֹף *ḥalôp̱* **masc. noun**
(destruction, destitution)
Prov. 31:8.

2476. חֲלוּשָׁה *ḥalûšāh* **fem. noun**
(weakness, defect)
Ex. 32:18.

2477. חֲלַח *ḥalaḥ* **proper noun**
(Halah)
2 Kgs. 17:6; 18:11; **1 Chr.** 5:26.

2478. חַלְחוּל *ḥalḥûl* **proper noun**
(Halhul)
Josh. 15:58.

2479. חַלְחָלָה *ḥalḥālāh* **fem. noun**
(pain, anguish)
Isa. 21:3; **Ezek.** 30:4,9; **Nah.** 2:10(11).

2480. חָלַט *ḥālaṭ* **verb**
(to catch, to pick up [a word])
1 Kgs. 20:33.

2481. חֲלִי *ḥaliy* **masc. noun**
(ornament, jewel)
Prov. 25:12; **Song** 7:1(2).

2482. חֲלִי *ḥaliy* **proper noun**
(Hali)
Josh. 19:25.

2483. חֳלִי *ḥoliy* **masc. noun**
(sickness, disease)
Deut. 7:15; 28:59,61; **1 Kgs.** 17:17; **2 Kgs.** 1:2; 8:8,9; 13:14; **2 Chr.** 16:12; 21:15,18,19; **Ps.** 41:3(4); **Eccl.** 5:17(16); 6:2; **Isa.** 1:5; 38:9; 53:3,4; **Jer.** 6:7; 10:19; **Hos.** 5:13.

2484. חֶלְיָה *ḥelyāh* **fem. noun**
(jewelry)
Hos. 2:13(15).

2485. חָלִיל *ḥāliyl* **masc. noun**
(flute)
1 Sam. 10:5; **1 Kgs.** 1:40; **Isa.** 5:12; 30:29; **Jer.** 48:36.

2486. חָלִילָה *ḥāliylāh* **interj.**
(far be it, let it never be)
Gen. 18:25; 44:7,17; **Josh.** 22:29; 24:16; **1 Sam.** 2:30; 12:23; 14:45; 20:2,9; 22:15; 24:6(7); 26:11; **2 Sam.** 20:20; 23:17; **1 Kgs.** 21:3; **1 Chr.** 11:19; **Job** 27:5; 34:10.

2487. חֲלִיפָה *ḥaliypāh* **fem. noun.**
(a changing, change of clothes)
Gen. 45:22; **Judg.** 14:12,13,19; **1 Kgs.** 5:14(28); **2 Kgs.** 5:5,22,23; **Job** 10:17; 14:14; **Ps.** 55:19(20).

2488. חֲלִיצָה *ḥaliyṣāh* **fem. noun**
(what is stripped off a person [in war])
Judg. 14:19; **2 Sam.** 2:21.

2489. חֵלְכָה *ḥēlekāh* **adj.**
(hapless, unfortunate)
Ps. 10:8,10,14.

2490. I. חָלַל *ḥālal* **verb**
(to profane, to defile)
Gen. 4:26; 6:1; 9:20; 10:8; 11:6; 41:54; 44:12; 49:4; **Ex.** 20:25; 31:14; **Lev.** 18:21; 19:8,12,29; 20:3; 21:4,6,9,12, 15,23; 22:2,9,15,32; **Num.** 16:46(17:11), 47(17:12); 18:32; 25:1; 30:2(3); **Deut.** 2:24,25,31; 3:24; 16:9; 20:6; 28:30; **Josh.** 3:7; **Judg.** 10:18; 13:5,25; 16:19,22; 20:31,39,40; **1 Sam.** 3:2,12; 14:35; 22:15; **2 Kgs.** 10:32; 15:37; **1 Chr.** 1:10; 5:1; 27:24; **2 Chr.** 3:1,2; 20:22; 29:17,27; 31:7,10,21; 34:3; **Ezra** 3:6,8; **Neh.** 4:7(1); 13:17,18; **Esth.** 6:13; 9:23; **Ps.** 55:20(21); 74:7; 89:31(32),34(35),39(40); **Isa.** 23:9; 43:28; 47:6; 48:11; 56:2,6; **Jer.** 16:18; 25:29; 31:5; 34:16; **Lam.** 2:2; **Ezek.** 7:21,22,24; 9:6; 13:19; 20:9,13, 14,16,21,22,24,39; 22:8,16(KJV, *nāḥal* [5157]),26; 23:38,39; 24:21; 25:3; 28:7 (NIV, see II),16,18; 36:20–23; 39:7; 44:7; **Dan.** 11:31; **Hos.** 8:10; **Amos** 2:7; **Jon.** 3:4; **Zeph.** 3:4; **Mal.** 1:12; 2:10,11.
II. חָלַל *ḥālal* **verb**
(to bore, to wound, to pierce)
Job 26:13(KJV, *ḥûl* [2342,I]); **Ps.** 109:22; **Prov.** 26:10(KJV, NASB, *ḥûl* [2342,I]); **Isa.** 51:9; 53:5; **Ezek.** 28:7(KJV, NASB, see I),9; 32:26.
III. חָלַל *ḥālal* **verb**
(to play the flute)
1 Kgs. 1:40; **Ps.** 87:7.

2491. חָלָל *ḥālāl* **masc. noun**
(pierced, wounded, slain)
Gen. 34:27; **Lev.** 21:7,14; **Num.** 19:16,18; 23:24; 31:8,19; **Deut.** 21:1–3,6; 32:42; **Josh.** 11:6; 13:22; **Judg.** 9:40; 16:24; 20:31,39; **1 Sam.** 17:52; 31:1,8; **2 Sam.** 1:19,22,25; 23:8,18; **1 Kgs.** 11:15; **1 Chr.** 5:22; 10:1,8; 11:11,20; **2 Chr.** 13:17; **Job** 24:12; 39:30; **Ps.** 69:26(27); 88:5(6); 89:10(11); **Prov.** 7:26; **Isa.** 22:2; 34:3; 66:16; **Jer.** 9:1(8:23); 14:18; 25:33; 41:9; 51:4,47,49,52; **Lam.** 2:12; 4:9; **Ezek.** 6:4,7,13; 9:7; 11:6,7; 12:24(KJV, NASB, *ḥālāq* [2509]); 21:14(19),25(30),29(34); 26:15; 28:8,23; 30:4,11,24; 31:17,18; 32:20–25,28–32; 35:8; **Dan.** 11:26; **Nah.** 3:3; **Zeph.** 2:12.

2492. I. חָלַם *ḥālam* **verb**
(to dream)
Gen. 28:12; 37:5,6,9,10; 40:5,8; 41:5,11, 15; 42:9; **Deut.** 13:1(2),3(4),5(6); **Judg.** 7:13; **Ps.** 126:1; **Isa.** 29:8; **Jer.** 23:25; 27:9(NASB, NIV, *ḥalôm* [2472]); 29:8; **Dan.** 2:1,3; **Joel** 2:28(3:1).
II. חָלַם *ḥālam* **verb**
(to be healthy, to become powerful)
Job 39:4; **Isa.** 38:16.

2493. חֵלֶם *ḥēlem* **Aram. masc. noun**
(dream)
Dan. 2:4–7,9,26,28,36,45; 4:5–9(2–6), 18(15),19(16); 5:12; 7:1.

2494. חֵלֶם *ḥēlem* **masc. proper noun**
(Heldai: same person as *ḥelday* [2469,B])
Zech. 6:14(NIV, *ḥelday* [2469,B]).

2495. חַלָּמוּת *ḥallāmûṯ* **fem. noun**
(egg)
Job 6:6.

2496. חַלָּמִישׁ *ḥallāmiyš* **masc. noun**
(flint, rock)
Deut. 8:15; 32:13; **Job** 28:9; **Ps.** 114:8; **Isa.** 50:7.

2497. חֵלֹן *ḥēlōn* **masc. proper noun**
(Helon)
Num. 1:9; 2:7; 7:24,29; 10:16.

2498. I. חָלַף *ḥālap̱* **verb**
(to pass on, to change, to renew, to violate)
Gen. 31:7,41; 35:2; 41:14; **Lev.** 27:10; **1 Sam.** 10:3; **2 Sam.** 12:20; **Job** 4:15; 9:11,26; 11:10; 14:7; 29:20; **Ps.** 90:5,6; 102:26(27); **Song** 2:11; **Isa.** 2:18; 8:8; 9:10(9); 21:1; 24:5; 40:31; 41:1; **Hab.** 1:11.
II. חָלַף *ḥālap̱* **verb**
(to pierce, to strike through)
Judg. 5:26; **Job** 20:24.

2499. חֲלַף *ḥᵃlap̱* **Aram. verb**
(to pass over, to pass by; corr. to Hebr. 2498,I)
Dan. 4:16(13),23(20),25(22),32(29).

2500. חֵלֶף *ḥēlep̱* **masc. noun**
(in return for, in exchange for)
Num. 18:21,31.

2501. חֵלֶף *ḥēlep̱* **proper noun**
(Heleph)
Josh. 19:33.

2502. I. חָלַץ *ḥālaṣ* **verb**
(to withdraw, to deliver)
Lev. 14:40,43; **Deut.** 25:9,10; **Josh.** 4:13; 6:7,9,13; **2 Sam.** 22:20; **Job** 36:15; **Ps.** 6:4(5); 7:4(5); 18:19(20); 34:7(8); 50:15; 60:5(7); 81:7(8); 91:15; 108:6(7); 116:8; 119:153; 140:1(2); **Prov.** 11:8,9; **Isa.** 20:2; 58:11; **Lam.** 4:3; **Hos.** 5:6.
II. חָלַץ *ḥālaṣ* **verb**
(to ready, to arm for war)
Num. 31:3,5; 32:17,20,21,27,29,30,32; **Deut.** 3:18; **Josh.** 4:13; 6:7,9,13; **1 Chr.** 12:23(24),24(25); **2 Chr.** 17:18; 20:21; 28:14; **Isa.** 15:4.

2503. A. חֵלֶץ *ḥēleṣ,* חֶלֶץ *ḥeleṣ* **masc. proper noun**
(Helez: one of David's mighty men)
2 Sam. 23:26; **1 Chr.** 11:27; 27:10.
B. חֶלֶץ *ḥeleṣ* **masc. proper noun**
(Helez: a Judaite)
1 Chr. 2:39.

2504. חֲלָצַיִם *ḥᵃlāṣayim* **fem. dual noun**
(loins [as girded or as the place of origin of a man's seed or offspring])
Gen. 35:11; **1 Kgs.** 8:19; **2 Chr.** 6:9; **Job** 31:20; 38:3; 40:7; **Isa.** 5:27; 11:5; 32:11; **Jer.** 30:6.

2505. I. חָלַק *ḥālaq* **verb**
(to divide, to share)
Gen. 14:15; 49:7,27; **Ex.** 15:9; **Num.** 26:53,55,56; **Deut.** 4:19; 29:26(25); **Josh.** 13:7; 14:5; 18:2,5,10; 19:51; 22:8; **Judg.** 5:30; **1 Sam.** 30:24; **2 Sam.** 6:19; 19:29(30); **1 Kgs.** 16:21; 18:6; **1 Chr.** 16:3; 23:6; 24:3–5; **2 Chr.** 23:18; 28:21; **Neh.** 9:22; 13:13; **Job** 21:17; 27:17; 38:24; 39:17; **Ps.** 22:18(19); 60:6(8); 68:12(13); 108:7(8); **Prov.** 16:19; 17:2; 29:24; **Isa.** 9:3(2); 33:23; 34:17; 53:12; **Jer.** 37:12; **Lam.** 4:16; **Ezek.** 5:1; 47:21; **Dan.** 11:39; **Hos.** 10:2(NASB, NIV, see II); **Joel** 3:2(4:2); **Amos** 7:17; **Mic.** 2:4; **Zech.** 14:1.
II. חָלַק *ḥālaq* **verb**
(to be smooth, to be flattering)
Ps. 5:9(10); 36:2(3); 55:21(22); **Prov.** 2:16; 7:5; 28:23; 29:5; **Isa.** 41:7; **Hos.** 10:2(KJV, see I).

2506. I. חֵלֶק *ḥēleq* **masc. noun**
(portion, territory)
Gen. 14:24; 31:14; **Lev.** 6:17(10); **Num.** 18:20; 31:36; **Deut.** 10:9; 12:12; 14:27,29; 18:1,8; 32:9; **Josh.** 14:4; 15:13; 18:5–7,9;

19:9; 22:25,27; **1 Sam.** 30:24; **2 Sam.** 20:1; **1 Kgs.** 12:16; **2 Kgs.** 9:10,36,37; **2 Chr.** 10:16; **Neh.** 2:20; **Job** 17:5(KJV, see II); 20:29; 27:13; 31:2; 32:17; **Ps.** 16:5; 17:14; 50:18; 73:26; 119:57; 142:5(6); **Eccl.** 2:10,21; 3:22; 5:18(17), 19(18); 9:6,9; 11:2; **Isa.** 17:14; 57:6; 61:7; **Jer.** 10:16; 51:19; **Lam.** 3:24; **Ezek.** 45:7; 48:8,21; **Hos.** 5:7; **Amos** 7:4; **Mic.** 2:4; **Hab.** 1:16; **Zech.** 2:12(16).
II. חֵלֶק *ḥēleq* **masc. noun**
(smoothness, seductiveness)
Job 17:5(NASB, NIV, see I); **Prov.** 7:21.

2507. חֵלֶק *ḥēleq* **masc. proper noun**
(Helek)
Num. 26:30; **Josh.** 17:2.

2508. חֲלָק *ḥ^a^lāq* **Aram. masc. noun**
(portion, possession)
Ezra 4:16; **Dan.** 4:15(12),23(20).

2509. חָלָק *ḥālāq* **adj.**
(flattering, smooth)
Gen. 27:11; **Ps.** 12:2(3)(KJV, NASB, *ḥelqāh* [2513,I]),3(4)(KJV, NASB, *ḥelqāh* [2513,I]); 73:18(KJV, NASB, *ḥelqāh* [2513,I]); **Prov.** 5:3; 26:28; **Isa.** 57:6(KJV, *ḥallāk* [2511]); 30:10(KJV, NASB, *ḥelqāh* [2513,I]); **Ezek.** 12:24(NIV, *ḥālāl* [2491,I]); **Dan.** 11:32(KJV, NASB, *ḥ^a^laqqāh* [2514]).

2510. חָלָק *ḥālāq* **proper noun**
(Halak)
Josh. 11:17; 12:7.

2511. חַלָּק *ḥallāq* **masc. noun**
(smooth)
Isa. 57:6(NASB, NIV, *ḥālāk* [2509]).

2512. חַלֻּק *ḥalluq* **adj.**
(smooth)
1 Sam. 17:40.

2513. I. חֶלְקָה *ḥelqāh* **fem. noun**
(smooth part, smoothness, flattery)
Gen. 27:16; **Ps.** 12:2(3)(NIV, *ḥālāq* [2509]),3(4)(NIV, *ḥālāq* [2509]); 73:18 (NIV, *ḥālāq* [2509]); **Prov.** 6:24; **Isa.** 30:10(NIV, *ḥālāq* [2509]).
II. חֶלְקָה *ḥelqāh* **fem. noun**
(portion, ground)
Gen. 33:19; **Deut.** 33:21; **Josh.** 24:32; **Ruth** 2:3; 4:3; **2 Sam.** 2:16; 14:30,31; 23:11,12; **2 Kgs.** 3:19,25; 9:21,25,26; **1 Chr.** 11:13,14; **Job** 24:18; **Jer.** 12:10; **Amos** 4:7.

2514. חֲלַקָּה *ḥ^a^laqqāh* **fem. noun**
(flattery)
Dan. 11:32(NIV, *ḥālaq* [2509]).

2515. חֲלֻקָּה *ḥ^a^luqqāh* **fem. noun**
(division, portion)
2 Chr. 35:5.

2516. חֶלְקִי *ḥelqiy* **masc. proper noun**
(Helekite)
Num. 26:30.

2517. חֶלְקַי *ḥelqāy* **masc. proper noun**
(Helkai)
Neh. 12:15.

2518. A. חִלְקִיָּה *ḥilqiyyāh,* חִלְקִיָּהוּ *ḥilqiyyāhû* **masc. proper noun**
(Hilkiah: father of Eliakim)
2 Kgs. 18:18,26,37; **Isa.** 22:20; 36:3,22.
B. חִלְקִיָּה *ḥilqiyyāh,* חִלְקִיָּהוּ *ḥilqiyyāhû* **masc. proper noun**
(Hilkiah: high priest)
2 Kgs. 22:4,8,10,12,14; 23:4,24; **1 Chr.** 6:13(5:39); 9:11; **2 Chr.** 34:9,14,15,18,20,22; 35:8; **Ezra** 7:1.
C. חִלְקִיָּה *ḥilqiyyāh* **masc. proper noun**
(Hilkiah: descendant of Merari)
1 Chr. 6:45(30).

D. חִלְקִיָּה *ḥilqiyyāh* **masc. proper noun**
(Hilkiah: son of Hosah)
1 Chr. 26:11.
E. חִלְקִיָּה *ḥilqiyyāh* **masc. proper noun**
(Hilkiah: son of Meshullam)
Neh. 8:4; 11:11; 12:7,21.
F. חִלְקִיָּהוּ *ḥilqiyyāhû* **masc. proper noun**
(Hilkiah: father of Jeremiah)
Jer. 1:1.
G. חִלְקִיָּה *ḥilqiyyāh* **masc. proper noun**
(Hilkiah: father of Gemariah)
Jer. 29:3.

2519. חֲלַקְלַקּוֹת *ḥ*[a]*laqlaqqôṯ* **fem. pl. noun**
(flattery, slipperiness)
Ps. 35:6; **Jer.** 23:12; **Dan.** 11:21,34.

2520. חֶלְקַת *ḥelqaṯ* **proper noun**
(Helkath)
Josh. 19:25; 21:31.

2521. חֶלְקַת הַצֻּרִים *ḥelqaṯ haṣṣuriym* **proper noun**
(Helkath Hazzurim)
2 Sam. 2:16.

2522. חָלַשׁ *ḥālaš* **verb**
(to lie prostrate, to cause one to lie prostrate)
Ex. 17:13; **Job** 14:10; **Isa.** 14:12.

2523. חַלָּשׁ *ḥallāš* **masc. noun**
(one who is weak)
Joel 3:10(4:10).

2524. חָם *ḥām* **masc. noun**
(father-in-law)
Gen. 38:13,25; **1 Sam.** 4:19,21.

2525. חָם *ḥām* **adj.**
(hot, warm)
Josh. 9:12; **Job** 37:17.

2526. A. חָם *ḥām* **masc. proper noun**
(Ham: son of Noah)
Gen. 5:32; 6:10; 7:13; 9:18,22; 10:1,6,20; **1 Chr.** 1:4,8; 4:40.
B. חָם *ḥām* **masc. proper noun**
(Ham: another name for Egyptians)
Ps. 78:51; 105:23,27; 106:22.

2527. חֹם *ḥōm* **masc. noun**
(heat, warmth)
Gen. 8:22; 18:1; **1 Sam.** 11:9(NASB, NIV, *ḥāmam* [2552]),11; 21:6(7); **2 Sam.** 4:5; **Neh.** 7:3(NASB, NIV, *ḥāmam* [2552]); **Job** 6:17(NASB, NIV, *ḥāmam* [2552]); 24:19; **Isa.** 18:4; **Jer.** 17:8; 51:39(NASB, NIV, *ḥāmam* [2552]); **Hag.** 1:6(NASB, NIV, *ḥāmam* [2552]).

2528. חֱמָא *ḥ*[e]*mā'* **Aram. fem. noun**
(anger, rage; corr. to Hebr. 2534)
Dan. 3:13,19.

2529. חֶמְאָה *ḥem'āh*, חֵמָה *ḥēmāh* **fem. noun**
(curds, butter)
Gen. 18:8; **Deut.** 32:14; **Judg.** 5:25; **2 Sam.** 17:29; **Job** 20:17; 29:6; **Prov.** 30:33; **Isa.** 7:15,22.

2530. I. חָמַד *ḥāmaḏ* **verb**
(to desire, to take pleasure in)
Gen. 2:9; 3:6; **Ex.** 20:17; 34:24; **Deut.** 5:21(18); 7:25; **Josh.** 7:21; **Job** 20:20; **Ps.** 19:10(11); 39:11(12); 68:16(17); **Prov.** 1:22; 6:25; 12:12; 21:20; **Song** 2:3; **Isa.** 1:29; 44:9; 53:2; **Mic.** 2:2.
II. חֲמוּדָה *ḥ*[a]*mûḏāh*, חֲמֻדָה *ḥ*[a]*muḏāh* **fem. noun**
(preciousness, valuables)
Gen. 27:15; **2 Chr.** 20:25; **Ezra** 8:27; **Dan.** 9:23; 10:3,11,19; 11:38,43.

2531. חֶמֶד *ḥemeḏ* **masc. noun**
(handsome, pleasant, beautiful)
Isa. 27:2(KJV, NASB, *ḥemer* [2561]); 32:12; **Ezek.** 23:6,12,23; **Amos** 5:11.

2532. חֶמְדָּה *ḥemdāh* **fem. noun**
(that which is desirable, pleasant)
1 Sam. 9:20; **2 Chr.** 21:20; 32:27; 36:10; **Ps.** 106:24; **Isa.** 2:16; **Jer.** 3:19; 12:10; 25:34; **Ezek.** 26:12; **Dan.** 11:8,37; **Hos.** 13:15; **Nah.** 2:9(10); **Hag.** 2:7; **Zech.** 7:14.

2533. חֶמְדָּן *ḥemdān* **masc. proper noun**
(Hemdan)
Gen. 36:26; **1 Chr.** 1:41(KJV, NASB, *ḥamrān* [2566]).

2534. חֵמָה *ḥēmāh,* חֵמָא *ḥēmā'* **fem. noun**
(wrath, fury, rage)
Gen. 27:44; **Lev.** 26:28; **Num.** 25:11; **Deut.** 9:19; 29:23(22),28(27); 32:24,33; **2 Sam.** 11:20; **2 Kgs.** 5:12; 22:13,17; **2 Chr.** 12:7; 28:9; 34:21,25; 36:16; **Esth.** 1:12; 2:1; 3:5; 5:9; 7:7,10; **Job** 6:4; 19:29; 21:20; 36:18; **Ps.** 6:1(2); 37:8; 38:1(2); 58:4(5); 59:13(14); 76:10(11); 78:38; 79:6; 88:7(8); 89:46(47); 90:7; 106:23; 140:3(4); **Prov.** 6:34; 15:1,18; 16:14; 19:19; 21:14; 22:24; 27:4; 29:22; **Isa.** 27:4; 34:2; 42:25; 51:13,17,20,22; 59:18; 63:3,5,6; 66:15; **Jer.** 4:4; 6:11; 7:20; 10:25; 18:20; 21:5,12; 23:19; 25:15; 30:23; 32:31,37; 33:5; 36:7; 42:18; 44:6; **Lam.** 2:4; 4:11; **Ezek.** 3:14; 5:13,15; 6:12; 7:8; 8:18; 9:8; 13:13,15; 14:19; 16:38,42; 19:12; 20:8,13,21,33,34; 21:17(22); 22:20,22; 23:25; 24:8,13; 25:14,17; 30:15; 36:6,18; 38:18; **Dan.** 8:6; 9:16; 11:44; **Hos.** 7:5; **Mic.** 5:15(14); **Nah.** 1:2,6; **Zech.** 8:2.

2535. חַמָּה *ḥammāh* **fem. noun**
(the sun, heat)
Job 30:28; **Ps.** 19:6(7); **Song** 6:10; **Isa.** 24:23; 30:26.

2536. חַמּוּאֵל *ḥammû'ēl* **masc. proper noun**
(Hammuel)
1 Chr. 4:26.

2537. חֲמוּטַל *ḥamûṭal* **fem. proper noun**
(Hamutal)
2 Kgs. 23:31; 24:18; **Jer.** 52:1.

2538. חָמוּל *ḥāmûl* **masc. proper noun**
(Hamul)
Gen. 46:12; **Num.** 26:21; **1 Chr.** 2:5.

2539. חָמוּלִי *ḥāmûliy* **masc. proper noun**
(Hamulite)
Num. 26:21.

2540. A. חַמּוֹן *ḥammôn* **proper noun**
(Hammon: town in Asher)
Josh. 19:28.
B. חַמּוֹן *ḥammôn* **proper noun**
(Hammon: town in Naphtali)
1 Chr. 6:76(61).

2541. חָמוֹץ *ḥāmôṣ* **masc. noun**
(one who is oppressed, an oppressor)
Isa. 1:17.

2542. חַמּוּק *ḥammûq* **masc. noun**
(a curve)
Song 7:1(2).

2543. חֲמוֹר *ḥ^a^môr,* חֲמוֹרָה *ḥ^a^môrah* **masc., fem. noun**
(**donkey**)
Gen. 12:16; 22:3,5; 24:35; 30:43; 32:5(6); 34:28; 36:24; 42:26,27; 43:18,24; 44:3,13; 45:23; 47:17; 49:14; **Ex.** 4:20; 9:3; 13:13; 20:17; 21:33; 22:4(3),9(8),10(9); 23:4, 5,12; 34:20; **Num.** 16:15; 31:28,30,34, 39,45; **Deut.** 5:14,21(18); 22:3,4,10; 28:31; **Josh.** 6:21; 7:24; 9:4; 15:18; **Judg.** 1:14; 6:4; 15:15,16,16(KJV, NASB, *ḥōmer* [2563,II]),16(KJV, NASB, *ḥ^a^môrāṯayim* [2565]); 19:3,10,19,21,28; **1 Sam.** 8:16; 12:3; 15:3; 16:20; 22:19; 25:18,20,23,42; 27:9; **2 Sam.** 16:1,2;

17:23; 19:26(27); **1 Kgs.** 2:40; 13:13,23, 24,27–29; **2 Kgs.** 6:25; 7:7,10; **1 Chr.** 5:21; 12:40; **2 Chr.** 28:15; **Ezra** 2:67; **Neh.** 7:69; 13:15; **Job** 24:3; **Prov.** 26:3; **Isa.** 1:3; 21:7; 32:20; **Jer.** 22:19; **Ezek.** 23:20; **Zech.** 9:9; 14:15.

2544. חֲמוֹר *ḥ*^{a}*môr* **masc. proper noun**
(Hamor)
Gen. 33:19; 34:2,4,6,8,13,18,20,24,26; **Josh.** 24:32; **Judg.** 9:28.

2545. חֲמוֹת *ḥamôṯ* **fem. noun**
(mother-in-law)
Ruth 1:14; 2:11,18,19,23; 3:1,6,16,17; **Mic.** 7:6.

2546. חֹמֶט *ḥōmeṭ* **masc. noun**
(a skink, a small lizard)
Lev. 11:30.

2547. חֻמְטָה *ḥumṭāh* **proper noun**
(Humtah)
Josh. 15:54.

2548. חָמִיץ *ḥāmiyṣ* **adj.**
(seasoned)
Isa. 30:24.

2549. חֲמִישִׁי *ḥ*^{a}*miyšiy*, חֲמִשִּׁי *ḥamiššiy* **ordinal num.**
(fifth)
Gen. 1:23; 30:17; 47:24; **Lev.** 5:16; 6:5(5:24); 19:25; 22:14; 27:13,15,19, 27,31; **Num.** 5:7; 7:36; 29:26; 33:38; **Josh.** 19:24; **Judg.** 19:8; **2 Sam.** 3:4; **1 Kgs.** 6:31; 14:25; **2 Kgs.** 25:8; **1 Chr.** 2:14; 3:3; 8:2; 12:10; 24:9; 25:12; 26:3,4; 27:8; **2 Chr.** 12:2; **Ezra** 7:8,9; **Neh.** 6:5; **Jer.** 1:3; 28:1; 36:9; 52:12; **Ezek.** 1:2; 20:1; **Zech.** 7:3,5; 8:19.

2550. חָמַל *ḥāmal* **verb**
(to pity, to have compassion)
Ex. 2:6; **Deut.** 13:8(9); **1 Sam.** 15:3,9,15; 23:21; **2 Sam.** 12:4,6; 21:7; **2 Chr.** 36:15,17; **Job** 6:10; 16:13; 20:13; 27:22; **Prov.** 6:34; **Isa.** 9:19(18); 30:14; **Jer.** 13:14; 15:5; 21:7; 50:14; 51:3; **Lam.** 2:2,17,21; 3:43; **Ezek.** 5:11; 7:4,9; 8:18; 9:5,10; 16:5; 36:21; **Joel** 2:18; **Hab.** 1:17; **Zech.** 11:5,6; **Mal.** 3:17.

2551. חֶמְלָה *ḥemlāh* **fem. noun**
(mercy, compassion)
Gen. 19:16; **Isa.** 63:9.

2552. חָמַם *ḥāmam* **verb**
(to be hot, to be warm)
Ex. 16:21; **Deut.** 19:6(KJV, *yāḥam* [3179]); **1 Sam.** 11:9(KJV, *ḥōm* [2527]); **1 Kgs.** 1:1(KJV, *yāḥam* [3179]),2; **2 Kgs.** 4:34; **Neh.** 7:3(KJV, *ḥōm* [2527]); **Job** 6:17(KJV, *ḥōm* [2527]); 31:20; 39:14; **Ps.** 39:3(4); **Eccl.** 4:11; **Isa.** 44:15,16; 47:14; 57:5; **Jer.** 51:39(KJV, *ḥōm* [2527]); **Ezek.** 24:11(KJV, *yāḥam* [3179]); **Hos.** 7:7; **Hag.** 1:6(KJV, *ḥōm* [2527]).

2553. חַמָּן *ḥammān* **masc. noun**
(idol, incense altar; only in the plural)
Lev. 26:30; **2 Chr.** 14:5(4); 34:4,7; **Isa.** 17:8; 27:9; **Ezek.** 6:4,6.

2554. חָמַס *ḥāmas* **verb**
(to do wrong, to do violence, to strip violently)
Job 15:33; 21:27; **Prov.** 8:36; **Jer.** 13:22; 22:3; **Lam.** 2:6; **Ezek.** 22:26; **Zeph.** 3:4.

2555. חָמָס *ḥāmās* **masc. noun**
(violence)
Gen. 6:11,13; 16:5; 49:5; **Ex.** 23:1; **Deut.** 19:16; **Judg.** 9:24; **2 Sam.** 22:3,49; **1 Chr.** 12:17; **Job** 16:17; 19:7; **Ps.** 7:16(17); 11:5; 18:48(49); 25:19; 27:12; 35:11; 55:9(10); 58:2(3); 72:14; 73:6; 74:20; 140:1(2),4(5),11(12); **Prov.** 3:31; 4:17; 10:6,11; 13:2; 16:29; 26:6; **Isa.** 53:9; 59:6; 60:18; **Jer.** 6:7; 20:8; 51:35,46; **Ezek.** 7:11,23; 8:17; 12:19; 28:16; 45:9; **Joel** 3:19(4:19); **Amos** 3:10;

6:3; **Obad.** 1:10; **Jon.** 3:8; **Mic.** 6:12; **Hab.** 1:2,3,9; 2:8,17; **Zeph.** 1:9; **Mal.** 2:16.

2556. I. חָמֵץ *ḥāmēṣ* **verb**
(to be leavened)
Ex. 12:34,39; **Hos.** 7:4.
II. חָמֵץ *ḥāmēṣ* **verb**
(to oppress, to be cruel)
Ps. 71:4.
III. חָמֵץ *ḥāmēṣ* **verb**
(to embitter, to grieve)
Ps. 73:21.
IV. חָמֵץ *ḥāmēṣ* **verb**
(to be red)
Isa. 63:1.

2557. I. חָמֵץ *ḥāmēṣ* **masc. noun**
(that which is leavened)
Ex. 12:15; 13:3,7; 23:18; 34:25; **Lev.** 2:11; 6:17(10); 7:13; 23:17; **Deut.** 16:3; **Amos** 4:5.
II. מַחְמֶצֶת *maḥmeṣeṯ* **masc. noun**
(something sour or leavened)
Ex. 12:19,20.

2558. חֹמֶץ *ḥōmeṣ* **masc. noun**
(vinegar)
Num. 6:3; **Ruth** 2:14; **Ps.** 69:21(22); **Prov.** 10:26; 25:20.

2559. חָמַק *ḥāmaq* **verb**
(to withdraw, to wander)
Song 5:6; **Jer.** 31:22.

2560. I. חָמַר *ḥāmar* **verb**
(to cover with bitumen)
Ex. 2:3.
II. חָמַר *ḥāmar* **verb**
(to ferment, to burn, to boil, to foment, to make red)
Job 16:16; **Ps.** 46:3(4); 75:8(9); **Lam.** 1:20; 2:11.

2561. חֶמֶר *ḥemer* **masc. noun**
(wine)
Deut. 32:14; **Isa.** 27:2(NIV, *ḥemeḏ* [2531]).

2562. חֲמַר *ḥ^a^mar* **Aram. masc. noun**
(wine; corr. to Hebr. 2561)
Ezra 6:9; 7:22; **Dan.** 5:1,2,4,23.

2563. I. חֹמֶר *ḥōmer* **masc. noun**
(mortar, mud, mire)
Gen. 11:3; **Ex.** 1:14; **Job** 4:19; 10:9; 13:12; 27:16; 30:19; 33:6; 38:14; **Isa.** 10:6; 29:16; 41:25; 45:9; 64:8(7); **Jer.** 18:4,6; **Nah.** 3:14.
II. חֹמֶר *ḥōmer* **masc. noun**
(a heap, surge, churning)
Ex. 8:14(10); **Judg.** 15:16(NIV, *ḥ^a^môr* [2543]); **Hab.** 3:15.
III. חֹמֶר *ḥōmer* **masc. noun**
(an homer)
Lev. 27:16; **Num.** 11:32; **Isa.** 5:10; **Ezek.** 45:11,13,14; **Hos.** 3:2.

2564. חֵמָר *ḥēmār* **masc. noun**
(slime, pitch, tar)
Gen. 11:3; 14:10; **Ex.** 2:3.

2565. חֲמֹרָתַיִם *ḥ^a^môrāṯayim* **fem. dual noun**
(heaps)
Judg. 15:16(NIV, *ḥ^a^môr* [2543]).

2566. חַמְרָן *ḥamrān* **masc. proper noun**
(Hamran, Amram)
1 Chr. 1:41(NIV, *ḥemdān* [2533]).

2567. חָמַשׁ *ḥāmaš* **verb**
(to take one-fifth)
Gen. 41:34.

2568. חָמֵשׁ *ḥāmēš*, חֲמִשָּׁה *ḥ^a^miššāh* **masc., fem. noun**
(five [NIV, see also *ḥ^a^mišiym* [2572])
Gen. 5:6,10,11,15,17,21,23,30,32; 7:20; 11:11,12,32; 12:4; 14:9; 18:28; 25:7; 43:34; 45:6,11,22; 47:2; **Ex.** 16:1; 22:1(21:37); 26:3,9,26,27,37; 27:1,14,15,18; 30:23,24; 36:10,16,31,32,38; 38:1,14,15,18,25,26,28; **Lev.** 23:6,34,39; 26:8;

27:5–7; **Num.** 1:21,25,33,37,41,46; 2:11,15,19,23,28,32; 3:22,47,50; 4:48; 7:17,23,29,35,41,47,53,59,65,71,77,83; 8:24; 11:19; 18:16; 26:18,22,27,37,41,50; 28:17; 29:12; 31:8,28,32,36,37,39,43,45; 33:3; **Josh.** 8:12; 10:5,16,17,22,23,26; 13:3; 14:10; **Judg.** 3:3; 8:10; 18:2,7, 14,17; 20:35,45,46; **1 Sam.** 6:4,16,18; 17:5,40; 21:3(4); 22:18; 25:18,42; **2 Sam.** 4:4; 9:10; 19:17(18); 21:8; 24:9; **1 Kgs.** 4:32(5:12); 6:6,10,24; 7:3,16,23, 39,49; 9:23; 12:32,33; 22:42; **2 Kgs.** 6:25; 7:13; 8:16; 13:19; 14:2,17,23; 15:33; 18:2; 19:35; 20:6; 21:1; 23:36; 25:19; **1 Chr.** 2:4,6; 3:20; 4:32,42; 7:3,7; 11:23; 24:14; 25:22; 29:7; **2 Chr.** 3:11,12,15; 4:2,6–8; 6:13; 13:17; 15:10,19; 20:31; 25:1,25; 26:13; 27:1,8; 29:1; 33:1; 35:9; 36:5; **Ezra** 1:11; 2:5,8,20,33,34,66,67,69; **Neh.** 6:15; 7:13,20,25,36,67–70; **Esth.** 9:6,12,16,18,21; **Job** 1:3; **Isa.** 7:8; 17:6; 19:18; 30:17; 37:36; 38:5; **Jer.** 52:22, 30,31; **Ezek.** 1:1,2; 8:1,16; 11:1; 32:17; 33:21; 40:1,7,13,21,25,29,30,33,36,48; 41:2,9,11,12; 42:16–20; 45:1–3,5,6, 12,25; 48:8–10,13,15,16,20,21,30,32–34; **Dan.** 12:12; **Hos.** 3:2.

2569. חֹמֶשׁ *ḥōmeš* **masc. noun**
(one-fifth [of produce])
Gen. 47:26.

2570. חֹמֶשׁ *ḥōmeš* **masc. noun**
(fifth rib, belly, stomach)
2 Sam. 2:23; 3:27; 4:6; 20:10.

2571. חֲמֻשִׁים *ḥamušiym* **pl. adj.**
(armed, arrayed for battle)
Ex. 13:18; **Josh.** 1:14; 4:12; **Judg.** 7:11.

2572. חֲמִשִּׁים *ḥamiššiym* **pl. num. adj.**
(fifty; NIV, *ḥāmēš* [2568])
Gen. 6:15; 7:24; 8:3; 9:28,29; 18:24, 26,28; **Ex.** 18:21,25; 26:5,6,10,11; 27:12,13,18; 30:23; 36:12,13,17,18; 38:12,13,26; **Lev.** 23:16; 25:10,11; 27:3,16; **Num.** 1:23,25,29,31,43,46; 2:6,8,13,15,16,30–32; 4:3,23,30,35, 36,39,43,47; 8:25; 16:2,17,35; 26:10, 34,47; 31:30,47,52; **Deut.** 1:15; 22:29; **Josh.** 7:21; **1 Sam.** 6:19; 8:12; **2 Sam.** 15:1; 24:24; **1 Kgs.** 1:5; 7:2,6; 9:23; 10:29; 18:4,13,19,22; **2 Kgs.** 1:9–14; 2:7,16,17; 13:7; 15:2,20,23,25,27; 21:1; **1 Chr.** 5:21; 8:40; 9:9; 12:33; **2 Chr.** 1:17; 2:17(16); 3:9; 8:10,18; 26:3; 33:1; **Ezra** 2:7,14,15,22,29–31,37,60; 8:3,6,26; **Neh.** 5:17; 6:15; 7:10,12,20,33,34,40,70; **Esth.** 5:14; 7:9; **Isa.** 3:3; **Ezek.** 40:15, 21,25,29,33,36; 42:2,7,8; 45:2; 48:17; **Hag.** 2:16.

2573. חֵמֶת *ḥēmeṯ* **masc. noun**
(waterskin, bottle)
Gen. 21:14,15,19; **Hab.** 2:15.

2574. A. חֲמָת *ḥamāṯ* **proper noun**
(Hamath: a Syrian city)
Num. 13:21(NASB, NIV, see B); 34:8 (NASB, NIV, see B); **Josh.** 13:5(NASB, NIV, see B); **Judg.** 3:3(NASB, NIV, see B); **2 Sam.** 8:9; **1 Kgs.** 8:65(NASB, NIV, see B); **2 Kgs.** 14:25(NASB, NIV, see B),28; 17:24,30; 18:34; 19:13; 23:33; 25:21; **1 Chr.** 13:5(NASB, NIV, see B); 18:3,9; **2 Chr.** 7:8(NASB, NIV, see B); 8:3(see *ḥamaṯ ṣôḇāh* [2578]),4; **Isa.** 10:9; 11:11; 36:19; 37:13; **Jer.** 39:5; 49:23; 52:9,27; **Ezek.** 47:16,17,20(NASB, NIV, see B); 48:1(NASB, NIV, see B); **Amos** 6:2(NASB, NIV, see B),14; **Zech.** 9:2.

B. לְבֹא חֲמָת *leḇō ḥamāṯ* **proper noun**
(Lebo Hamath: a Syrian city, KJV, sometimes NASB, the entrance of Hamath [prep. *l*, *bô'* [935], and *ḥamāṯ* [2574,A])
Num. 13:21(KJV, see A); 34:8(KJV, see A); **Josh.** 13:5(KJV, see A); **Judg.** 3:3(KJV, see A); **1 Kgs.** 8:65(KJV, NASB, see A); **2 Kgs.** 14:25(KJV, NASB, see A); **1 Chr.** 13:5(KJV, NASB, see A); **2 Chr.** 7:8(KJV, NASB, see A); **Ezek.** 47:15(KJV,

NASB, prep. *l* and *bô'* [935]),20(KJV, see A); 48:1(KJV, see A); **Amos** 6:14 (KJV, NASB, see A).

C. חֲמָת *ḥ^a^māṯ* **masc. proper noun**
(Hamath: anscestral head of Rechabite clan)
1 Chr. 2:55(NASB, NIV, *ḥammaṯ* [2575,B]).

2575. A. חַמַּת *ḥammaṯ* **proper noun**
(Hammath: a city in Naphtali)
Josh. 19:35.

B. חַמַּת *ḥammaṯ* **masc. proper noun**
(Hammath: Ancestral head of Rechabite clan)
1 Chr. 2:55(KJV, *ḥ^a^māṯ* [2574,C]).

2576. חַמֹּת דֹּאר *ḥammōṯ dō'r* **proper noun**
(Hammoth Dor [*hammôṯ* [2575] and *dôr* [1756])
Josh. 21:32.

2577. חֲמָתִי *ḥ^a^māṯiy* **masc. proper noun**
(Hamathite)
Gen. 10:18; **1 Chr.** 1:16.

2578. חֲמַת צוֹבָה *ḥ^a^maṯ ṣôḇāh* **proper noun**
(Hamath Zobah [*ḥ^a^māṯ* {2574,A} and *ṣôḇāh* {6678}])
2 Chr. 8:3.

2579. חֲמַת רַבָּה *ḥ^a^maṯ rabbāh* **proper noun**
(Hamath the great [see *ḥ^a^māṯ* {2574,A} and *raḇ* {7227}])
Amos 6:2.

2580. חֵן *ḥēn* **masc. noun**
(favor, grace)
Gen. 6:8; 18:3; 19:19; 30:27; 32:5(6); 33:8,10,15; 34:11; 39:4,21; 47:25,29; 50:4; **Ex.** 3:21; 11:3; 12:36; 33:12,13, 16,17; 34:9; **Num.** 11:11,15; 32:5; **Deut.** 24:1; **Judg.** 6:17; **Ruth** 2:2,10,13; **1 Sam.** 1:18; 16:22; 20:3,29; 25:8; 27:5; **2 Sam.** 14:22; 15:25; 16:4; **1 Kgs.** 11:19; **Esth.** 2:15,17; 5:2,8; 7:3; 8:5; **Ps.** 45:2(3); 84:11(12); **Prov.** 1:9; 3:4,22,34; 4:9; 5:19; 11:16; 13:15; 17:8; 22:1,11; 28:23; 31:30; **Eccl.** 9:11; 10:12; **Jer.** 31:2; **Nah.** 3:4; **Zech.** 4:7; 12:10.

2581. חֵן *ḥēn* **masc. proper noun**
(Hen)
Zech. 6:14.

2582. חֵנָדָד *ḥēnāḏāḏ* **masc. proper noun**
(Henadad)
Ezra 3:9; **Neh.** 3:18,24; 10:9(10).

2583. חָנָה *ḥānāh* **verb**
(to pitch one's tent, to encamp)
Gen. 26:17; 33:18; **Ex.** 13:20; 14:2,9; 15:27; 17:1; 18:5; 19:2; **Num.** 1:50–53; 2:2,3,5,12,17,27,34; 3:23,29,35,38; 9:17, 18,20,22,23; 10:5,6,31; 12:16; 21:10–13; 22:1; 31:19; 33:5–37,41–49; **Deut.** 1:33; **Josh.** 4:19; 5:10; 8:11; 10:5,31,34; 11:5; **Judg.** 6:4,33; 7:1; 9:50; 10:17; 11:18,20; 15:9; 18:12; 19:9; 20:19; **1 Sam.** 4:1; 11:1; 13:5,16; 17:1,2; 26:3,5; 28:4; 29:1; **2 Sam.** 11:11; 12:28; 17:26; 23:13; 24:5; **1 Kgs.** 16:15,16; 20:27,29; **2 Kgs.** 25:1; **1 Chr.** 11:15; 19:7; **2 Chr.** 32:1; **Ezra** 8:15; **Neh.** 11:30; **Job** 19:12; **Ps.** 27:3; 34:7(8); 53:5(6); **Isa.** 29:1,3; **Jer.** 50:29; 52:4; **Nah.** 3:17; **Zech.** 9:8.

2584. חַנָּה *ḥannāh* **fem. proper noun**
(Hannah)
1 Sam. 1:2,5,8,9,13,15,19,20,22; 2:1,21.

2585. A. חֲנוֹךְ *ḥ^a^nôḵ* **masc. proper noun**
(Enoch: son of Cain)
Gen. 4:17,18.

B. חֲנוֹךְ *ḥ^a^nôḵ* **masc. proper noun**
(Enoch: son of Jared)
Gen. 5:18,19,21–24; **1 Chr.** 1:3.

C. חֲנוֹךְ *ḥ^anôḵ* **masc. proper noun**
(Hanoch, Enoch: son of Midian)
Gen. 25:4; **1 Chr.** 1:33.
D. חנוֹךְ *ḥ^anôḵ* **masc. proper noun**
(Hanoch, Enoch: son of Reuben)
Gen. 46:9; **Ex.** 6:14; **Num.** 26:5; **1 Chr.** 1:3,33; 5:3.

2586. A. חָנוּן *ḥānûn* **masc. proper noun**
(Hanun)
2 Sam. 10:1–4; **1 Chr.** 19:2–4,6.
B. חָנוּן *ḥānûn* **masc. proper noun**
(Hanun)
Neh. 3:13,30.

2587. חַנּוּן *ḥannûn* **adj.**
(gracious, compassionate)
Ex. 22:27(26); 34:6; **2 Chr.** 30:9; **Neh.** 9:17,31; **Ps.** 86:15; 103:8; 111:4; 112:4; 116:5; 145:8; **Joel** 2:13; **Jon.** 4:2.

2588. חָנוּת *ḥānûṯ* **fem. noun**
(a cell, vaulted room)
Jer. 37:16.

2589. I. חַנּוֹת *ḥannôṯ* **masc. noun**
(entreaty)
Job 19:17(NASB, NIV, *ḥānan* II).
II. חַנּוֹת *ḥannôṯ* **masc. noun**
(graciousness)
Ps. 77:9(NASB, NIV, *ḥānan* I).

2590. I. חָנַט *ḥānaṭ* **verb**
(to ripen, to form)
Song 2:13.
II. חָנַט *ḥānaṭ* **verb**
(to embalm)
Gen. 50:2,26.
III. חֲנֻטִים *ḥ^anuṭiym* **masc. pl. noun**
(embalming)
Gen. 50:3.

2591. חִנְטָה *ḥinṭāh* **Aram. masc. noun**
(wheat; corr. to Hebr. 2406)
Ezra 6:9; 7:22.

2592. A. חַנִּיאֵל *ḥanniy'ēl* **masc. proper noun**
(Hanniel: chief Manassite)
Num. 34:23.
B. חַנִּיאֵל *ḥanniy'ēl* **masc. proper noun**
(Hanniel: chief Asherite)
1 Chr. 7:39.

2593. חָנִיךְ *ḥāniyḵ* **adj.**
(trained, instructed)
Gen. 14:14.

2594. חֲנִינָה *ḥ^aniynāh* **fem. noun**
(favor, compassion)
Jer. 16:13.

2595. חֲנִית *ḥ^aniyṯ* **fem. noun**
(spear, javelin)
1 Sam. 13:19,22; 17:7,45,47; 18:10,11; 19:9,10; 20:33; 21:8(9); 22:6; 26:7,8,11, 12,16,22; **2 Sam.** 1:6; 2:23; 21:19; 23:7, 18,21; **2 Kgs.** 11:10; **1 Chr.** 11:11,20,23; 12:34; 20:5; **2 Chr.** 23:9; **Job** 39:23; 41:26(18); **Ps.** 35:3; 46:9(10); 57:4(5); **Isa.** 2:4; **Mic.** 4:3; **Nah.** 3:3; **Hab.** 3:11.

2596. חָנַךְ *ḥānaḵ* **verb**
(to dedicate, to train up)
Deut. 20:5; **1 Kgs.** 8:63; **2 Chr.** 7:5; **Prov.** 22:6.

2597. חֲנֻכָּה *ḥ^anukkāh* **Aram. fem. noun**
(dedication; corr. to Hebr. 2598)
Ezra 6:16,17; **Dan.** 3:2,3.

2598. חֲנֻכָּה *ḥ^anukkāh* **fem. noun**
(dedication, consecration)
Num. 7:10,11,84,88; **2 Chr.** 7:9; **Neh.** 12:27; **Ps.** 30:[title](1).

2599. חֲנֹכִי *ḥ^anōḵiy* **masc. proper noun**
(Hanochite)
Num. 26:5.

2600. חִנָּם *ḥinnām* **adv.**
(freely, without cause)
Gen. 29:15; **Ex.** 21:2,11; **Num.** 11:5; **1 Sam.** 19:5; 25:31; **2 Sam.** 24:24; **1 Kgs.** 2:31; **1 Chr.** 21:24; **Job** 1:9; 2:3; 9:17; 22:6; **Ps.** 35:7,19; 69:4(5); 109:3; 119:161; **Prov.** 1:11,17; 3:30; 23:29; 24:28; 26:2; **Isa.** 52:3,5; **Jer.** 22:13; **Lam.** 3:52; **Ezek.** 6:10; 14:23; **Mal.** 1:10.

2601. חֲנַמְאֵל *ḥanam'ēl* **masc. proper noun**
(Hanamel, Hanameel)
Jer. 32:7–9,12.

2602. חֲנָמָל *ḥanāmāl* **masc. noun**
(frost, sleet)
Ps. 78:47.

2603. I. חָנַן *ḥānan* **verb**
(to be merciful, to be gracious)
Gen. 33:5,11; 42:21; 43:29; **Ex.** 33:19; **Num.** 6:25; **Deut.** 3:23; 7:2; 28:50; **Judg.** 21:22; **2 Sam.** 12:22; **1 Kgs.** 8:33,47,59; 9:3; **2 Kgs.** 1:13; 13:23; **2 Chr.** 6:24,37; **Esth.** 4:8; 8:3; **Job** 8:5; 9:15; 19:16,17(NASB, NIV, *ḥānan* [2589,II]),21; 33:24; **Ps.** 4:1(2); 6:2(3); 9:13(14); 25:16; 26:11; 27:7; 30:8(9), 10(11); 31:9(10); 37:21,26; 41:4(5), 10(11); 51:1(3); 56:1(2); 57:1(2); 59:5(6); 67:1(2); 77:9(10)(see *ḥannôṯ* [2589,I]); 86:3,16; 102:13(14),14(15); 109:12; 112:5; 119:29,58,132; 123:2,3; 142:1(2); **Prov.** 14:21,31; 19:17; 21:10; 26:25; 28:8; **Isa.** 26:10; 27:11; 30:18,19; 33:2; **Jer.** 22:23(NIV, *'ānaḥ*[584]); **Lam.** 4:16; **Hos.** 12:4(5); **Amos** 5:15; **Mal.** 1:9.
II. חָנַן *ḥānan* **verb**
(to be loathsome)
Ps. 77:9(10)(KJV, *ḥānnôṯ* [2589,I]).

2604. חֲנַן *ḥanan* **Aram. verb**
(to show mercy, pray for mercy)
Dan. 4:27(24); 6:11(12).

2605. A. חָנָן *ḥānān* **masc. proper noun**
(Hanan: one of David's mighty men)
1 Chr. 11:43.
B. חָנָן *ḥānān* **masc. proper noun**
(Hanan: chief Benjamite)
1 Chr. 8:23.
C. חָנָן *ḥānān* **masc. proper noun**
(Hanan: son of Azel)
1 Chr. 8:38; 9:44.
D. חָנָן *ḥānān* **masc. proper noun**
(Hanan: head of the Nethinim)
Ezra 2:46.
E. חָנָן *ḥānān* **masc. proper noun**
(Hanan: a Levite)
Neh. 7:49; 8:7.
F. חָנָן *ḥānān* **masc. proper noun**
(Hanan: son of Zaccur)
Neh. 10:10(11),22(23); 13:13.
G. חָנָן *ḥānān* **masc. proper noun**
(Hanan: Jewish leader)
Neh. 10:26(27).
H. חָנָן *ḥānān* **masc. proper noun**
(Hanan: son of Igdaliah)
Jer. 35:4.

2606. חֲנַנְאֵל *ḥanan'ēl* **masc. proper noun**
(Hananel, Hananeel)
Neh. 3:1; 12:39; **Jer.** 31:38; **Zech.** 14:10.

2607. A. חֲנָנִי *ḥanāniy* **masc. proper noun**
(Hanani: son of Heman)
1 Chr. 25:4,25.
B. חֲנָנִי *ḥanāniy* **masc. proper noun**
(Hanani: a seer and father of Jehu)
1 Kgs. 16:1,7; **2 Chr.** 16:7; 19:2; 20:34.
C. חֲנָנִי *ḥanāniy* **masc. proper noun**
(Hanani: brother of Nehemiah)
Neh. 1:2; 7:2.
D. חֲנָנִי *ḥanāniy* **masc. proper noun**
(Hanani: a priest)
Ezra 10:20.

E. חֲנָנִי *ḥanāniy* **masc. proper noun**
(Hanani: a priest)
Neh. 12:36.

2608. A. חֲנַנְיָה *ḥananyāh* **masc. proper noun**
(Hananiah: son of Heman)
1 Chr. 25:4,23.
B. חֲנַנְיָה *ḥananyāh* **masc. proper noun**
(Hananiah: military officer)
2 Chr. 26:11.
C. חֲנַנְיָהוּ *ḥananyāhû* **masc. proper noun**
(Hananiah: father of Zedekiah)
Jer. 36:12.
D. חֲנַנְיָה *ḥananyāh* **masc. proper noun**
(Hananiah: son of Azur)
Jer. 28:1,5,10–13,15,17.
E. חֲנַנְיָה *ḥananyāh* **masc. proper noun**
(Hananiah: father of Shelemiah)
Jer. 37:13.
F. חֲנַנְיָה *ḥananyāh* **masc. proper noun**
(Hananiah: son of Shashak)
1 Chr. 8:24.
G. חֲנַנְיָה *ḥananyāh* **masc. proper noun**
(Hananiah: Hebrew name of Shadrach)
Dan. 1:6,7,11,19; 2:17.
H. חֲנַנְיָה *ḥananyāh* **masc. proper noun**
(Hananiah: son of Zerubbabel)
1 Chr. 3:19,21.
I. חֲנַנְיָה *ḥananyāh* **masc. proper noun**
(Hananiah: son of Bebai)
Ezra 10:28.
J. חֲנַנְיָה *ḥananyāh* **masc. proper noun**
(Hananiah: a priest)
Neh. 3:8.
K. חֲנַנְיָה *ḥananyāh* **masc. proper noun**
(Hananiah: son of Shele)
Neh. 3:30.
L. חֲנַנְיָה *ḥananyāh* **masc. proper noun**
(Hananiah: a ruler)
Neh. 7:2.
M. חֲנַנְיָה *ḥananyāh* **masc. proper noun**
(Hananiah: a Jew)
Neh. 10:23(24).
N. חֲנַנְיָה *ḥananyāh* **masc. proper noun**
(Hananiah: a priest)
Neh. 12:12,41.

2609. חָנֵס *ḥānēs* **proper noun**
(Hanes)
Isa. 30:4.

2610. חָנֵף *ḥānēp̱* **verb**
(to pollute, to defile)
Num. 35:33; **Ps.** 106:38; **Isa.** 24:5; **Jer.** 3:1,2,9; 23:11; **Dan.** 11:32; **Mic.** 4:11.

2611. חָנֵף *ḥānēp̱* **adj.**
(profane, godless)
Job 8:13; 13:16; 15:34; 17:8; 20:5; 27:8; 34:30; 36:13; **Ps.** 35:16; **Prov.** 11:9; **Isa.** 9:17(16); 10:6; 33:14.

2612. חֹנֶף *ḥōnep̱* **masc. noun**
(ungodliness, hypocrisy)
Isa. 32:6.

2613. חֲנֻפָּה *ḥanuppāh* **fem. noun**
(ungodliness, pollution)
Jer. 23:15.

2614. חָנַק *ḥānaq* **verb**
(to strangle, to hang oneself)
2 Sam. 17:23; **Nah.** 2:12(13).

2615. חַנָּתֹן *ḥannāṯōn* **proper noun**
(Hannathon)
Josh. 19:14.

2616. I. חָסַד *ḥāsaḏ* **verb**
(to be good, to be kind)
2 Sam. 22:26; **Ps.** 18:25(26).
II. חָסַד *ḥāsaḏ* **verb**
(to insult, to shame, to disgrace)
Prov. 25:10.

2617. I. חֶסֶד *ḥeseḏ* **masc. noun**
(grace, lovingkindness)
Gen. 19:19; 20:13; 21:23; 24:12,14,27,49; 32:10(11); 39:21; 40:14; 47:29; **Ex.** 15:13; 20:6; 34:6,7; **Num.** 14:18,19; **Deut.** 5:10; 7:9,12; **Josh.** 2:12,14; **Judg.** 1:24; 8:35; **Ruth** 1:8; 2:20; 3:10; **1 Sam.** 15:6; 20:8,14,15; **2 Sam.** 2:5,6; 3:8; 7:15; 9:1,3,7; 10:2; 15:20; 16:17; 22:51; **1 Kgs.** 2:7; 3:6; 8:23; 20:31; **1 Chr.** 16:34,41; 17:13; 19:2; **2 Chr.** 1:8; 5:13; 6:14,42; 7:3,6; 20:21; 24:22; 32:32; 35:26; **Ezra** 3:11; 7:28; 9:9; **Neh.** 1:5; 9:17,32; 13:14,22; **Esth.** 2:9,17; **Job** 6:14; 10:12; 37:13; **Ps.** 5:7(8); 6:4(5); 13:5(6); 17:7; 18:50(51); 21:7(8); 23:6; 25:6,7,10; 26:3; 31:7(8), 16(17),21(22); 32:10; 33:5,18,22; 36:5(6), 7(8),10(11); 40:10(11),11(12); 42:8(9); 44:26(27); 48:9(10); 51:1(3); 52:1(3), 8(10); 57:3(4),10(11); 59:10(11),16(17), 17(18); 61:7(8); 62:12(13); 63:3(4); 66:20; 69:13(14),16(17); 77:8(9); 85:7(8),10(11); 86:5,13,15; 88:11(12); 89:1(2),2(3),14(15),24(25),28(29),33(34) ,49(50); 90:14; 92:2(3); 94:18; 98:3; 100:5; 101:1; 103:4,8,11,17; 106:1,7,45; 107:1,8,15,21,31,43; 108:4(5); 109:12, 16,21,26; 115:1; 117:2; 118:1–4,29; 119:41,64,76,88,124,149,159; 130:7; 136:1–26; 138:2,8; 141:5; 143:8,12; 144:2; 145:8; 147:11; **Prov.** 3:3; 11:17; 14:22; 16:6; 19:22; 20:6,28; 21:21; 31:26; **Isa.** 16:5; 40:6; 54:8,10; 55:3; 57:1; 63:7; **Jer.** 2:2; 9:24(23); 16:5; 31:3; 32:18; 33:11; **Lam.** 3:22,32; **Dan.** 1:9; 9:4; **Hos.** 2:19(21); 4:1; 6:4,6; 10:12; 12:6(7); **Joel** 2:13; **Jon.** 2:8(9); 4:2; **Mic.** 6:8; 7:18,20; **Zech.** 7:9.
II. חֶסֶד *ḥeseḏ* **masc. noun**
(shame, reproach, disgrace)
Lev. 20:17; **Prov.** 14:34.

2618. חֶסֶד *ḥeseḏ* **masc. proper noun**
(Hesed)
1 Kgs. 4:10.

2619. חֲסַדְיָה *ḥ^a^saḏyāh* **masc. proper noun**
(Hasadiah)
1 Chr. 3:20.

2620. חָסָה *ḥāsāh* **verb**
(to take refuge, to trust)
Deut. 32:37; **Judg.** 9:15; **Ruth** 2:12; **2 Sam.** 22:3,31; **Ps.** 2:12; 5:11(12); 7:1(2); 11:1; 16:1; 17:7; 18:2(3),30(31); 25:20; 31:1(2),19(20); 34:8(9),22(23); 36:7(8); 37:40; 57:1(2); 61:4(5); 64:10(11); 71:1; 91:4; 118:8,9; 141:8; 144:2; **Prov.** 14:32; 30:5; **Isa.** 14:32; 30:2; 57:13; **Nah.** 1:7; **Zeph.** 3:12.

2621. A. חֹסָה *ḥōsāh* **masc. proper noun**
(Hosah: a Levite)
1 Chr. 16:38; 26:10,11,16.
B. חֹסָה *ḥōsāh* **masc. proper noun**
(Hosah: loc. in Asher)
Josh. 19:29.

2622. חָסוּת *ḥāsûṯ* **fem. noun**
(shelter, refuge, shadow)
Isa. 30:3.

2623. חָסִיד *ḥāsiyḏ* **adj.**
(holy, faithful, saintly)
Deut. 33:8; **1 Sam.** 2:9; **2 Sam.** 22:26; **2 Chr.** 6:41; **Job** 39:13(KJV, *ḥ^a^siyḏāh* [2624,II], NIV, *ḥ^a^siyḏāh* [2624,I]); **Ps.** 4:3(4); 12:1(2); 16:10; 18:25(26); 30:4(5); 31:23(24); 32:6; 37:28; 43:1; 50:5; 52:9(11); 79:2; 85:8(9); 86:2; 89:19(20); 97:10; 116:15; 132:9,16; 145:10,17; 148:14; 149:1,5,9; **Prov.** 2:8; **Jer.** 3:12; **Mic.** 7:2.

2624. I. חֲסִידָה *ḥ^asiyd̲āh* **fem. noun**
(stork)
Lev. 11:19; **Deut.** 14:18; **Job** 39:13(KJV, see II, NASB, *ḥāsiyd̲* [2623]); **Ps.** 104:17; **Jer.** 8:7; **Zech.** 5:9.
II. חֲסִידָה *ḥ^asiyd̲āh* **fem. noun**
(ostrich)
Job 39:13(NASB, *ḥāsiyd̲* [2623]; KJV, NIV, see I).

2625. חָסִיל *ḥāsiyl* **masc. noun**
(grasshopper, locust, caterpillar)
1 Kgs. 8:37; **2 Chr.** 6:28; **Ps.** 78:46; **Isa.** 33:4; **Joel** 1:4; 2:25.

2626. חֲסִין *ḥ^asiyn* **adj.**
(strong, mighty)
Ps. 89:8(9).

2627. חַסִּיר *ḥassiyr* **Aram. adj.**
(lacking, deficient)
Dan. 5:27.

2628. חָסַל *ḥāsal* **verb**
(to consume, to devour)
Deut. 28:38.

2629. חָסַם *ḥāsam* **verb**
(to muzzle, to block)
Deut. 25:4; **Ezek.** 39:11.

2630. חָסַן *ḥāsan* **verb**
(to be laid up, to be hoarded)
Isa. 23:18.

2631. חֲסַן *ḥ^asan* **Aram. verb**
(to take possession of; corr. to Hebr. 2630)
Dan. 7:18,22.

2632. חֱסֵן *ḥ^esēn* **Aram. masc. noun**
(power, strength)
Dan. 2:37; 4:30(27).

2633. חֹסֶן *ḥōsen* **masc. noun**
(treasure, wealth, riches)
Prov. 15:6; 27:24; **Isa.** 33:6; **Jer.** 20:5; **Ezek.** 22:25.

2634. חָסֹן *ḥasōn* **adj.**
(strong, mighty)
Isa. 1:31; **Amos** 2:9.

2635. חֲסַף *ḥ^asap̱* **Aram. masc. noun**
(clay)
Dan. 2:33–35,41–43,45.

2636. חַסְפַּס *ḥaspas* **verb**
(to be round, to be flaky)
Ex. 16:14.

2637. חָסֵר *ḥāsēr* **verb**
(to be lacking, to be needy, to decrease)
Gen. 8:3,5; 18:28; **Ex.** 16:18; **Deut.** 2:7; 8:9; 15:8; **1 Kgs.** 17:14,16; **Neh.** 9:21; **Ps.** 8:5(6); 23:1; 34:10(11); **Prov.** 13:25; 31:11; **Eccl.** 4:8; 9:8; **Song** 7:2(3); **Isa.** 32:6; 51:14; **Jer.** 44:18; **Ezek.** 4:17.

2638. חָסֵר *ḥāsēr* **adj.**
(lacking, in need of)
1 Sam. 21:15(16); **2 Sam.** 3:29; **1 Kgs.** 11:22; **Prov.** 6:32; 7:7; 9:4,16; 10:13,21; 11:12; 12:9,11; 15:21; 17:18; 24:30; 28:16; **Eccl.** 6:2; 10:3.

2639. חֶסֶר *ḥeser* **masc. noun**
(poverty, need)
Job 30:3; **Prov.** 28:22.

2640. חֹסֶר *ḥōser* **masc. noun**
(lack, need)
Deut. 28:48,57; **Amos** 4:6.

2641. חַסְרָה *ḥasrāh* **masc. proper noun**
(Hasrah)
2 Chr. 34:22.

2642. חֶסְרוֹן *ḥesrôn* **masc. noun**
(that which is lacking)
Eccl. 1:15.

2643. חַף *ḥap̱* **adj.**
(innocent, pure, clean)
Job 33:9.

2644. חָפָא *ḥāp̱āʾ* **verb**
(to cover, to do secretly)
2 Kgs. 17:9.

2645. חָפָה *ḥāp̱āh* **verb**
(to cover, to overlay)
2 Sam. 15:30; **2 Chr.** 3:5,7–9; **Esth.** 6:12; 7:8; **Ps.** 68:13(14); **Jer.** 14:3,4.

2646. חֻפָּה *ḥuppāh* **fem. noun**
(chamber, cover, canopy)
Ps. 19:5(6); **Isa.** 4:5; **Joel** 2:16.

2647. חֻפָּה *ḥuppāh* **masc. proper noun**
(Huppah)
1 Chr. 24:13.

2648. חָפַז *ḥāp̱az* **verb**
(to hurry, to flee, to fear)
Deut. 20:3; **1 Sam.** 23:26; **2 Sam.** 4:4; **2 Kgs.** 7:15; **Job** 40:23; **Ps.** 31:22(23); 48:5(6); 104:7; 116:11.

2649. חִפָּזוֹן *ḥippāzôn* **masc. noun**
(haste, hurried flight)
Ex. 12:11; **Deut.** 16:3; **Isa.** 52:12.

2650. חֻפִּים *ḥuppiym*, חֻפִּם *ḥuppim* **masc. proper noun**
(Huppim)
Gen. 46:21; **1 Chr.** 7:12,15.

2651. חֹפֶן *ḥōp̱en* **masc. noun**
(hand, handful)
Ex. 9:8; **Lev.** 16:12; **Prov.** 30:4; **Eccl.** 4:6; **Ezek.** 10:2,7.

2652. חָפְנִי *ḥop̱niy* **masc. proper noun**
(Hophni)
1 Sam. 1:3; 2:34; 4:4,11,17.

2653. חָפַף *ḥāp̱ap̱* **verb**
(to cover, to enclose)
Deut. 33:12.

2654. I. חָפֵץ *ḥāp̱ēs* **verb**
(to desire, to delight in)
Gen. 34:19; **Num.** 14:8; **Deut.** 21:14; 25:7,8; **Judg.** 13:23; **Ruth** 3:13; **1 Sam.** 2:25; 18:22; 19:2(1); **2 Sam.** 15:26; 20:11; 22:20; 24:3; **1 Kgs.** 9:1; 10:9; **2 Chr.** 9:8; **Esth.** 2:14; 6:6,7,9,11; **Job** 9:3; 13:3; 21:14; 33:32; **Ps.** 18:19(20); 22:8(9); 37:23; 40:6(7),8(9); 41:11(12); 51:6(8),16(18),19(21); 68:30(31); 73:25; 109:17; 112:1; 115:3; 119:35; 135:6; 147:10; **Prov.** 18:2; 21:1; **Eccl.** 8:3; **Song** 2:7; 3:5; 8:4; **Isa.** 1:11; 13:17; 42:21; 53:10; 55:11; 56:4; 58:2; 62:4; 65:12; 66:3,4; **Jer.** 6:10; 9:24(23); 42:22; **Ezek.** 18:23,32; 33:11; **Hos.** 6:6; **Jon.** 1:14; **Mic.** 7:18; **Mal.** 2:17.
II. חָפֵץ *ḥāp̱aṣ* **verb**
(to bend, to hang down, to sway, to move)
Job 40:17.

2655. חָפֵץ *ḥāp̱ēṣ* **adj.**
(desiring, having pleasure in)
1 Kgs. 13:33; 21:6; **1 Chr.** 28:9; **Neh.** 1:11; **Ps.** 5:4(5); 34:12(13); 35:27; 40:14(15); 70:2(3); **Mal.** 3:1.

2656. חֵפֶץ *ḥēp̱eṣ* **masc. noun**
(pleasure, delight)
1 Sam. 15:22; 18:25; **2 Sam.** 23:5; **1 Kgs.** 5:8–10(22–24); 9:11; 10:13; **2 Chr.** 9:12; **Job** 21:21; 22:3; 31:16; **Ps.** 1:2; 16:3; 107:30; 111:2; **Prov.** 3:15; 8:11; 31:13; **Eccl.** 3:1,17; 5:4(3),8(7); 8:6; 12:1,10; **Isa.** 44:28; 46:10; 48:14; 53:10; 54:12; 58:3,13; 62:4; **Jer.** 22:28; 48:38; **Hos.** 8:8; **Mal.** 1:10; 3:12.

2657. חֶפְצִי־בָהּ *ḥep̱siy-ḇāh* **fem. proper noun**
(Hephzibah)
2 Kgs. 21:1; **Isa.** 62:4.

2658. חָפַר *ḥāp̱ar* **verb**
(to dig, to search for)
Gen. 21:30; 26:15,18,19,21,22,32; **Ex.** 7:24; **Num.** 21:18; **Deut.** 1:22; 23:13 (14); **Josh.** 2:2,3; **Job** 3:21; 11:18; 39:21,29; **Ps.** 7:15(16); 35:7; **Eccl.** 10:8; **Isa.** 2:20(see *ḥ^a^p̱ōr pērôṯ* [2661,II]; KJV, NASB, NIV, *ḥ^a^p̱arpārāh* [2661,I]); **Jer.** 13:7.

2659. חָפֵר *ḥāp̱ēr* **verb**
(to be ashamed, to be disgraced)
Job 6:20; **Ps.** 34:5(6); 35:4,26; 40:14(15); 70:2(3); 71:24; 83:17(18); **Prov.** 13:5; 19:26; **Isa.** 1:29; 24:23; 33:9; 54:4; **Jer.** 15:9; 50:12; **Mic.** 3:7.

2660. A. חֵפֶר *ḥēp̱er* **masc. proper noun**
(Hepher: son of Gilead)
Num. 26:32,33; 27:1; **Josh.** 17:2,3.
B. חֵפֶר *ḥēp̱er* **masc. proper noun**
(Hepher: son of Naarah)
1 Chr. 4:6.
C. חֵפֶר *ḥēp̱er* **masc. proper noun**
(Hepher: a Mecherathite)
1 Chr. 11:36.
D. חֵפֶר *ḥēp̱er* **masc. proper noun**
(Hepher: city N. W. of Jerusalem)
Josh. 12:17; **1 Kgs.** 4:10.

2661. I. חֲפַרְפָּרָה *ḥ^a^p̱arpārāh* **fem. noun**
(mole, rodent; only pl. *ḥ^a^p̱arpārôṯ*)
Isa. 2:20(MT, see II).
II. חֲפֹר פֵּרָה *ḥ^a^p̱ōr pērāh* **fem. noun**
(a digging mole: Qal inf. const. of *ḥāp̱ar* [2658] and the noun *pērāh* [6512])
Isa. 2:20(KJV, NASB, NIV, see I).

2662. חֶפְרִי *ḥep̱riy* **masc. proper noun**
(Hepherite)
Num. 26:32.

2663. I. חֲפָרַיִם *ḥ^a^p̱ārayim* **proper noun**
(Hapharaim)
Josh. 19:19.
II. חָפְרַע *ḥop̱ra‘* **masc. proper noun**
(Hophra: pharaoh of Egypt)
Jer. 44:30(KJV, NASB, see *par‘ōh ḥop̱ra‘* [6548]).

2664. חָפַשׂ *ḥāp̱aś* **verb**
(to search for, to disguise oneself)
Gen. 31:35; 44:12; **1 Sam.** 23:23; 28:8; **1 Kgs.** 20:6,38; 22:30; **2 Kgs.** 10:23; **2 Chr.** 18:29; 35:22; **Job** 30:18; **Ps.** 64:6(7); 77:6(7); **Prov.** 2:4; 20:27; 28:12; **Lam.** 3:40; **Amos** 9:3; **Obad.** 1:6; **Zeph.** 1:12.

2665. חֵפֶשׂ *ḥēp̱eś* **masc. noun**
(a plot, a plan)
Ps. 64:6(7).

2666. חָפַשׁ *ḥap̱aš* **verb**
(to be free)
Lev. 19:20.

2667. חֹפֶשׁ *ḥōp̱eš* **masc. noun**
(a wide spread; saddlecloth)
Ezek. 27:20.

2668. חֻפְשָׁה *ḥup̱šāh* **fem. noun**
(freedom)
Lev. 19:20.

2669. חָפְשִׁית *ḥop̱šiyṯ* **fem. noun**
(separateness, freedom)
2 Kgs. 15:5; **2 Chr.** 26:21.

2670. חָפְשִׁי *ḥop̱šiy* **adj.**
(free)
Ex. 21:2,5,26,27; **Deut.** 15:12,13,18; **1 Sam.** 17:25; **Job** 3:19; 39:5; **Ps.** 88:5(6); **Isa.** 58:6; **Jer.** 34:9–11,14,16.

2671. חֵץ *ḥēṣ* **masc. noun**
(arrow)

Gen. 49:23; **Num.** 24:8; **Deut.** 32:23,42; **1 Sam.** 17:7(NIV, [Q[e]] *'ēṣ* [6086]); 20:20–22,36; **2 Sam.** 22:15; **2 Kgs.** 13:15,17,18; 19:32; **1 Chr.** 12:2; **2 Chr.** 26:15; **Job** 6:4; 34:6; **Ps.** 7:13(14); 11:2; 18:14(15); 38:2(3); 45:5(6); 57:4(5); 58:7(8); 64:3(4),7(8); 77:17(18); 91:5; 120:4; 127:4; 144:6; **Prov.** 7:23; 25:18; 26:18; **Isa.** 5:28; 7:24; 37:33; 49:2; **Jer.** 9:8(7); 50:9,14; 51:11; **Lam.** 3:12; **Ezek.** 5:16; 21:21(26); 39:3,9; **Hab.** 3:11; **Zech.** 9:14.

2672. I. חָצַב *ḥāṣaḇ*, חָצֵב *ḥāṣēḇ* **verb**
(to cut, to strike, to hew, to quarry)
Deut. 6:11; 8:9; **2 Chr.** 26:10; **Neh.** 9:25; **Job** 19:24; **Ps.** 29:7; **Prov.** 9:1; **Isa.** 5:2; 10:15; 22:16; 51:1,9; **Jer.** 2:13; **Hos.** 6:5.
II. חֹצֵב *ḥōṣēḇ* **masc. noun**
(stonecutter, mason)
1 Kgs. 5:15(29); **2 Kgs.** 12:12(13); **1 Chr.** 22:2,15; **2 Chr.** 2:2(1),18(17); 24:12; **Ezra** 3:7.

2673. חָצָה *ḥāṣāh* **verb**
(to divide; to leave out half)
Gen. 32:7(8); 33:1; **Ex.** 21:35; **Num.** 31:27,42; **Judg.** 7:16; 9:43; **2 Kgs.** 2:8,14; **Job** 41:6(40:30); **Ps.** 55:23(24); **Isa.** 30:28; **Ezek.** 37:22; **Dan.** 11:4.

2674. A. חָצוֹר *ḥāṣôr* **proper noun**
(Hazor: royal town in N. Canaan)
Josh. 11:1,10,11,13; 12:19; 19:36; **Judg.** 4:2,17; **1 Sam.** 12:9; **1 Kgs.** 9:15; **2 Kgs.** 15:29; **Jer.** 49:28,30,33.
B. חָצוֹר *ḥāṣôr* **proper noun**
(Hazor: town in S. Judah)
Josh. 15:23.
C. חָצוֹר *ḥāṣôr* **proper noun**
(Hazor: another town in S. Judah)
Josh. 15:25.
D. חָצוֹר *ḥāṣôr* **proper noun**
(Hazor: town N. of Jerusalem)
Neh. 11:33.

2675. חָצוֹר חֲדַתָּה *ḥāṣôr ḥaḏattāh* **proper noun**
(Hazor Hadattah)
Josh. 15:25(KJV, as two towns; Hazor [2674] and Hadattah [from 2323]).

2676. חֲצוֹת *ḥaṣôṯ* **fem. noun**
(middle [of the night])
Ex. 11:4; **Job** 34:20; **Ps.** 119:62.

2677. חֲצִי *ḥaṣiy* **masc. noun**
(half, middle)
Ex. 12:29; 24:6; 25:10,17,23; 26:12,16; 27:5; 36:21; 37:1,6,10; 38:4; **Num.** 12:12; 15:9,10; 28:14; 32:33; 34:13–15; **Deut.** 3:12,13; 29:8(7); **Josh.** 1:12; 4:12; 8:33; 10:13; 12:2,5,6; 13:7,25,29,31; 14:2,3; 18:7; 21:5,6,27; 22:1,7,9–11,13, 15,21; **Judg.** 16:3; **Ruth** 3:8; **1 Sam.** 14:14; **2 Sam.** 10:4; 18:3; 19:40(41); **1 Kgs.** 3:25; 7:31,32,35; 10:7; 13:8; 16:21; **1 Chr.** 2:52(see *ḥaṣiy hammenuḥôṯ* [2679]),54(see *ḥaṣiy hammenaḥtiy* [2680]); 5:18,23,26; 6:61(46),71(56); 12:31,37; 19:4; 26:32; 27:20,21; **2 Chr.** 9:6; **Neh.** 3:9,12,16–18; 4:6(3:38), 16(10),21(15); 12:32,38,40; 13:24; **Esth.** 5:3,6; 7:2; **Ps.** 102:24(25); **Isa.** 44:16,19; **Jer.** 17:11; **Ezek.** 16:51; 40:42; 43:17; **Dan.** 9:27; 12:7; **Zech.** 14:2,4,8.

2678. חֵצִי *ḥēṣiy* **masc. noun**
(arrow)
1 Sam. 20:36–38([Q[e]] חֵץ [2671]); **2 Kgs.** 9:24.

2679. חֲצִי הַמְּנֻחוֹת *ḥaṣiy hammenuḥôṯ* **proper noun**
(half of the Manahathites; from *ḥaziy* [2677] and *mānaḥtiy* [4506,C])
1 Chr. 2:52(NASB, NIV, see *ḥaziy* [2677] and *mānaḥtiy* [4506,C]).

2680. חֲצִי הַמְּנַחְתִּי *ḥaṣiy hammenaḥtiy* **proper noun**
(half of the Manahathites; from

ḥ^a ziy [2677] and *mānaḥtiy* [4506,C])
1 Chr. 2:54(NASB, NIV, see *ḥ^a ziy* [2677] and *mānaḥtiy* [4506,C]).

2681. חָצִיר *ḥāṣiyr* **masc. noun**
(dwelling place, abode)
Isa. 34:13.

2682. I. חָצִיר *ḥāṣiyr* **masc. noun**
(grass, hay, reed)
1 Kgs. 18:5; **2 Kgs.** 19:26; **Job** 8:12; 40:15; **Ps.** 37:2; 90:5; 103:15; 104:14; 129:6; 147:8; **Prov.** 27:25; **Isa.** 15:6; 35:7; 37:27; 40:6–8; 44:4; 51:12.
II. חָצִיר *ḥāṣiyr* **masc. noun**
(leeks)
Num. 11:5.

2683. חֵצֶן *ḥēṣen* **masc. noun**
(bosom)
Ps. 129:7(NIV, *ḥōṣen* [2684]).

2684. חֹצֶן *ḥōṣen* **masc. noun**
(bosom, lap, folds in the front of one's robe)
Neh. 5:13; **Ps.** 129:7(KJV, NASB, *ḥēṣen* [2683]); **Isa.** 49:22.

2685. חֲצַף *ḥ^a ṣap̱* **Aram. verb**
(to be urgent)
Dan. 2:15; 3:22.

2686. I. חָצַץ *ḥāṣaṣ* **verb**
(to divide, to divide into ranks; to cut off, to come to an end, to sing)
Judg. 5:11(KJV, see II); **Job** 21:21; **Prov.** 30:27.
II. חָצַץ *ḥāṣaṣ* **verb**
(to shoot an arrow)
Judg. 5:11(NASB, NIV, see I).

2687. חָצָץ *ḥāṣāṣ* **masc. noun**
(gravel)
Prov. 20:17; **Lam.** 3:16.

2688. חַצְצוֹן תָּמָר *ḥaṣ^e ṣôn tāmār* **proper noun**
(Hazazon Tamar)
Gen. 14:7; **2 Chr.** 20:2.

2689. חֲצֹצְרָה *ḥ^a ṣōṣ^e rāh* **fem. noun**
(trumpet)
Num. 10:2,8–10; 31:6; **2 Kgs.** 11:14; 12:13(14); **1 Chr.** 13:8; 15:24,28; 16:6,42; **2 Chr.** 5:12,13; 13:12,14; 15:14; 20:28; 23:13; 29:26–28; **Ezra** 3:10; **Neh.** 12:35,41; **Ps.** 98:6; **Hos.** 5:8.

2690. חִצְצַר *ḥaṣṣar* **verb**
(to blow a trumpet)
1 Chr. 15:24; **2 Chr.** 5:12,13; 7:6; 13:14; 29:28.

2691. חָצֵר *ḥāṣēr* **masc. noun**
(courtyard, village)
Gen. 25:16; **Ex.** 8:13(9); 27:9,12,13,16–19; 35:17,18; 38:9,15–18, 20,31; 39:40; 40:8,33; **Lev.** 6:16(9), 26(19); 25:31; **Num.** 3:26,37; 4:26,32; **Deut.** 2:23(KJV, *ḥ^a ṣēriym* [2699]); **Josh.** 13:23,28; 15:32,36,41,44–47,51,54,57, 59,60,62; 16:9; 18:24,28; 19:6–8,15,16, 22,23,30,31,38,39,48; 21:12; **2 Sam.** 17:18; **1 Kgs.** 6:36; 7:8,9,12; 8:64; **2 Kgs.** 20:4; 21:5; 23:12; **1 Chr.** 4:32,33; 6:56(41); 9:16,22,25; 23:28; 28:6,12; **2 Chr.** 4:9; 7:7; 20:5; 23:5; 24:21; 29:16; 33:5; **Neh.** 3:25; 8:16; 11:25,30; 12:28,29; 13:7; **Esth.** 1:5; 2:11; 4:11; 5:1,2; 6:4,5; **Ps.** 10:8; 65:4(5); 84:2(3), 10(11); 92:13(14); 96:8; 100:4; 116:19; 135:2; **Isa.** 1:12; 42:11; 62:9; **Jer.** 19:14; 26:2; 32:2,8,12; 33:1; 36:10,20; 37:21; 38:6,13,28; 39:14,15; **Ezek.** 8:7,16; 9:7; 10:3–5; 40:14,17,19,20,23,27,28,31, 32,34,37,44,47; 41:15; 42:1,3,6–10,14; 43:5; 44:17,19,21,27; 45:19; 46:1,20–22; 47:16; **Zech.** 3:7.

2692. חֲצַר אַדָּר *ḥ^a ṣar 'addār*
proper noun
(Hazar Addar; a city on the southern border of Canaan, possibly *'addar* [146])
Num. 34:4.

2693. חֲצַר גַּדָּה *ḥaṣar gaddāh* **proper noun**
(Hazar Gaddah)
Josh. 15:27.

2694. חֲצַר הַתִּיכוֹן *ḥaṣar hattiyk̲ôn* **proper noun**
(Hazar Hatticon)
Ezek. 47:16.

2695. חֶצְרוֹ *ḥeṣrô* **masc. proper noun**
(Hezro)
2 Sam. 23:35; **1 Chr.** 11:37.

2696. A. חֶצְרוֹן *ḥeṣrôn* **masc. proper noun**
(Hezron: son of Pharez)
Gen. 46:12; **Num.** 26:21; **Ruth** 4:18,19; **1 Chr.** 2:5,9,18,21,24,25; 4:1.
B. חֶצְרוֹן *ḥeṣrôn* **masc. proper noun**
(Hezron: son of Reuben)
Gen. 46:9; **Ex.** 6:14; **Num.** 26:6; **1 Chr.** 5:3.
C. חֶצְרוֹן *ḥeṣrôn* **masc. proper noun**
(Hezron: a city)
Josh. 15:3,25(NASB, NIV, *qᵉriyyôt̲ ḥeṣrôn* [7152,II]).

2697. A. חֶצְרוֹנִי *ḥeṣrôniy* **masc. proper noun**
(Hezronite: descendant of Reuben)
Num. 26:6.
B. חֶצְרוֹנִי *ḥeṣrôniy* **masc. proper noun**
(Hezronites: descendants of Pharez)
Num. 26:21.

2698. חֲצֵרוֹת *ḥaṣērôt̲* **proper noun**
(Hazeroth)
Num. 11:35; 12:16; 33:17,18; **Deut.** 1:1.

2699. חֲצֵרִים *ḥaṣēriym* **proper noun**
(Hazerim)
Deut. 2:23(NASB, NIV, *ḥāṣēr* [2691]).

2700. חֲצַרְמָוֶת *ḥaṣarmāwet̲* **proper noun**
(Hazarmaveth)
Gen. 10:26; **1 Chr.** 1:20.

2701. חֲצַר סוּסָה *ḥaṣar sûsāh* **proper noun**
(Hazar Susah)
Josh. 19:5.

2702. חֲצַר סוּסִים *ḥaṣar sûsiym* **proper noun**
(Hazar Susim)
1 Chr. 4:31.

2703. חֲצַר עֵינוֹן *ḥaṣar ʿēynôn* **proper noun**
(Hazar Enan)
Ezek. 47:17.

2704. חֲצַר עֵינָן *ḥaṣar ʿēynān* **proper noun**
(Hazar Enan)
Num. 34:9,10; **Ezek.** 48:1.

2705. חֲצַר שׁוּעָל *ḥaṣar šûʿāl* **proper noun**
(Hazar Shual)
Josh. 15:28; 19:3; **1 Chr.** 4:28; **Neh.** 11:27.

2706. חֹק *ḥōq* **masc. noun**
(decree, statute, portion)
Gen. 47:22,26; **Ex.** 5:14; 12:24; 15:25,26; 18:16,20; 29:28; 30:21; **Lev.** 6:18(11), 22(15); 7:34; 10:11,13–15; 24:9; 26:46; **Num.** 18:8,11,19; 30:16(17); **Deut.** 4:1, 5,6,8,14,40,45; 5:1,31(28); 6:1,17,20,24; 7:11; 11:32; 12:1; 16:12; 17:19; 26:16,17; 27:10; **Josh.** 24:25; **Judg.** 5:15(see KJV, [Kᵉ] *ḥēqeq* [2711]; NIV, [Qᵉ] *ḥāqar* [2713]); 11:39; **1 Sam.** 30:25; **1 Kgs.** 3:14; 8:58,61; 9:4; **2 Kgs.** 17:15,37; **1 Chr.** 16:17; 22:13; 29:19; **2 Chr.** 7:17; 19:10; 33:8; 34:31; 35:25; **Ezra** 7:10,11; **Neh.** 1:7; 9:13,14; 10:29(30); **Job** 14:5, 13; 23:12,14; 26:10; 28:26; 38:10; **Ps.** 2:7;

50:16; 81:4(5); 94:20; 99:7; 105:10,45; 119:5,8,12,23,26,33,48,54,64,68,71,80,83,112,117,118,124,135,145,155,171; 147:19; 148:6; **Prov.** 8:29; 30:8; 31:15; **Isa.** 5:14; 10:1(KJV, *ḥēqeq* [2711]; KJV, *ḥēqeq* [2711,I]); 24:5; **Jer.** 5:22; 31:36; 32:11; **Ezek.** 11:12; 16:27; 20:18,25; 36:27; 45:14; **Amos** 2:4; **Mic.** 7:11; **Zeph.** 2:2; **Zech.** 1:6; **Mal.** 3:7; 4:4(3:22).

2707. חָקָה *ḥāqāh* **verb**
(to cut, to carve, to engrave, to portray)
1 Kgs. 6:35; **Job** 13:27; **Ezek.** 8:10; 23:14.

2708. חֻקָּה *ḥuqqāh* **fem. noun**
(statute, ordinance)
Gen. 26:5; **Ex.** 12:14,17,43; 13:10; 27:21; 28:43; 29:9; **Lev.** 3:17; 7:36; 10:9; 16:29, 31,34; 17:7; 18:3–5,26,30; 19:19,37; 20:8,22,23; 23:14,21,31,41; 24:3; 25:18; 26:3,15,43; **Num.** 9:3,12,14; 10:8; 15:15; 18:23; 19:2,10,21; 27:11; 31:21; 35:29; **Deut.** 6:2; 8:11; 10:13; 11:1; 28:15,45; 30:10,16; **2 Sam.** 22:23; **1 Kgs.** 2:3; 3:3; 6:12; 9:6; 11:11,33,34,38; **2 Kgs.** 17:8, 13,19,34; 23:3; **2 Chr.** 7:19; **Job** 38:33; **Ps.** 18:22(23); 89:31(32); 119:16; **Jer.** 5:24; 10:3; 31:35; 33:25; 44:10,23; **Ezek.** 5:6,7; 11:20; 18:9,17,19,21; 20:11,13,16, 19,21,24; 33:15; 37:24; 43:11,18; 44:5,24; 46:14; **Mic.** 6:16.

2709. חֲקוּפָא *ḥᵃqûp̄ā'* **masc. proper noun**
(Hakupha)
Ezra 2:51; **Neh.** 7:53.

2710. חָקַק *ḥāqaq* **verb**
(to cut out, to engrave, to decree law, to govern)
Gen. 49:10; **Num.** 21:18; **Deut.** 33:21; **Judg.** 5:9,14; **Job** 19:23; **Ps.** 60:7(9); 108:8(9); **Prov.** 8:15,27,29; 31:5; **Isa.** 10:1; 22:16; 30:8; 33:22; 49:16; **Ezek.** 4:1; 23:14.

2711. חֵקֶק *ḥēqeq* **masc. noun**
(thought, decree)
Judg. 5:15(NASB, [Kᵉ] *ḥōq* [2706]; NIV, [Qᵉ] *ḥāqar* [2713]); **Isa.** 10:1(NASB, NIV, *ḥōq* [2706]).

2712. A. חֻקֹּק *ḥuqōq* **proper noun**
(Hukkok: loc. in Naphtali)
Josh. 19:34.
B. *ḥuqōq* **proper noun**
(Hukkok: another name for *ḥelqāṯ* [2520])
1 Chr. 6:75(60).

2713. חָקַר *ḥāqar* **verb**
(to explore, to search, to seek out)
Deut. 13:14(15); **Judg.** 5:15(KJV, [Kᵉ] *ḥēqeq* [2711]; NASB, [Kᵉ] *ḥōq* [2706]); 18:2; **1 Sam.** 20:12; **2 Sam.** 10:3; **1 Kgs.** 7:47; **1 Chr.** 19:3; **2 Chr.** 4:18; **Job** 5:27; 13:9; 28:3,27; 29:16; 32:11; **Ps.** 44:21(22); 139:1,23; **Prov.** 18:17; 23:30; 25:2; 28:11; **Eccl.** 12:9; **Jer.** 17:10; 31:37; 46:23; **Lam.** 3:40; **Ezek.** 39:14.

2714. חֵקֶר *ḥēqer* **masc. noun**
(a search, inquiry, thing to be searched out)
Judg. 5:16; **Job** 5:9; 8:8; 9:10; 11:7; 34:24; 36:26; 38:16; **Ps.** 145:3; **Prov.** 25:3,27; **Isa.** 40:28.

2715. חֹר *ḥōr* **masc. noun**
(a noble, freeborn one)
1 Kgs. 21:8,11; **Neh.** 2:16; 4:14(8), 19(13); 5:7; 6:17; 7:5; 13:17; **Eccl.** 10:17; **Isa.** 34:12; **Jer.** 27:20; 39:6.

2716. חֶרֶא *ḥere'* **masc. noun**
(dung, dove's dung)
2 Kgs. 6:25(see *ḥᵃrēy yôniym* [2755]; NASB, [Qᵉ] *diḇyôniym* [1686,I]); 18:27; **Isa.** 36:12.

2717. I. חָרֵב *ḥārēḇ* **verb**
(to be dry, to be desolate)
Gen. 8:13; **Judg.** 16:7,8,24; **2 Kgs.**

3:23; 19:17,24; **Job** 14:11; **Ps.** 106:9; **Isa.** 19:5,6; 34:10; 37:18,25; 42:15; 44:27; 49:17; 50:2; 51:10; 60:12; **Jer.** 2:12; 26:9; 51:36; **Ezek.** 6:6; 12:20; 19:7; 26:2,19; 29:12; 30:7; **Hos.** 13:15; **Amos** 7:9; **Nah.** 1:4; **Zeph.** 3:6.

II. חָרַב *ḥāraḇ* **verb**
(to slay, to attack)
2 Kgs. 3:23; **Jer.** 50:21,27.

2718. חֲרַב *ḥ^a^raḇ* **Aram. verb**
(to be laid waste, to be destroyed; corr. to Hebr. 2717,II)
Ezra 4:15.

2719. חֶרֶב *ḥereḇ* **fem. noun**
(sword, knife)
Gen. 3:24; 27:40; 31:26; 34:25,26; 48:22; **Ex.** 5:3,21; 15:9; 17:13; 18:4; 20:25; 22:24(23); 32:27; **Lev.** 26:6–8, 25,33,36,37; **Num.** 14:3,43; 19:16; 20:18; 21:24; 22:23,29,31; 31:8; **Deut.** 13:15(16); 20:13; 28:22; 32:25,41,42; 33:29; **Josh.** 5:2,3,13; 6:21; 8:24; 10:11, 28,30,32,35,37,39; 11:10–12,14; 13:22; 19:47; 24:12; **Judg.** 1:8,25; 3:16,21,22; 4:15,16; 7:14,20,22; 8:10,20; 9:54; 18:27; 20:2,15,17,25,35,37,46,48; 21:10; **1 Sam.** 13:19,22; 14:20; 15:8,33; 17:39,45,47, 50,51; 18:4; 21:8(9),9(10); 22:10,13,19; 25:13; 31:4,5; **2 Sam.** 1:12,22; 2:16,26; 3:29; 11:25; 12:9,10; 15:14; 18:8; 20:8,10; 23:10; 24:9; **1 Kgs.** 1:51; 2:8,32; 3:24; 18:28; 19:1,10,14,17; **2 Kgs.** 3:26; 6:22; 8:12; 10:25; 11:15,20; 19:7,37; **1 Chr.** 5:18; 10:4,5; 21:5,12,16,27,30; **2 Chr.** 20:9; 21:4; 23:14,21; 29:9; 32:21; 34:6; 36:17,20; **Ezra** 9:7; **Neh.** 4:13(7),18(12); **Esth.** 9:5; **Job** 1:15,17; 5:15,20; 15:22; 19:29; 27:14; 39:22; 40:19; 41:26(18); **Ps.** 7:12(13); 17:13; 22:20(21); 37:14,15; 44:3(4),6(7); 45:3(4); 57:4(5); 59:7(8); 63:10(11); 64:3(4); 76:3(4); 78:62,64; 89:43(44); 144:10; 149:6; **Prov.** 5:4; 12:18; 25:18; 30:14; **Song** 3:8; **Isa.** 1:20; 2:4; 3:25; 13:15; 14:19; 21:15; 22:2; 27:1; 31:8; 34:5,6; 37:7,38; 41:2; 49:2; 51:19; 65:12; 66:16; **Jer.** 2:30; 4:10; 5:12,17; 6:25; 9:16(15); 11:22; 12:12; 14:12, 13,15,16,18; 15:2,3,9; 16:4; 18:21; 19:7; 20:4; 21:7,9; 24:10; 25:16,27,29,31; 26:23; 27:8,13; 29:17,18; 31:2; 32:24,36; 33:4; 34:4,17; 38:2; 39:18; 41:2; 42:16, 17,22; 43:11; 44:12,13,18,27,28; 46:10, 14,16; 47:6; 48:2,10; 49:37; 50:16,35–37; 51:50; **Lam.** 1:20; 2:21; 4:9; 5:9; **Ezek.** 5:1,2,12,17; 6:3,8,11,12; 7:15; 11:8,10; 12:14,16; 14:17,21; 16:40; 17:21; 21:3–5 (8–10),9(14),11(16),12(17),14(19),15(20), 19(24),20(25),28(33); 23:10,25,47; 24:21; 25:13; 26:6,8,9,11; 28:7,23; 29:8; 30:4–6,11,17,21,22,24,25; 31:17,18; 32:10–12,20–32; 33:2–4,6,26,27; 35:5,8; 38:4,8,21; 39:23; **Dan.** 11:33; **Hos.** 1:7; 2:18(20); 7:16; 11:6; 13:16(14:1); **Joel** 3:10(4:10); **Amos** 1:11; 4:10; 7:9,11,17; 9:1,4,10; **Mic.** 4:3; 5:6(5); 6:14; **Nah.** 2:13(14); 3:3,15; **Zeph.** 2:12; **Hag.** 2:22; **Zech.** 9:13; 11:17; 13:7.

2720. חָרֵב *ḥārēḇ* **adj.**
(waste, desolate, dry)
Lev. 7:10; **Neh.** 2:3,17; **Prov.** 17:1; **Jer.** 33:10,12; **Ezek.** 36:35,38; **Hag.** 1:4,9.

2721. חֹרֶב *ḥōreḇ* **masc. noun**
(heat, dryness, drought)
Gen. 31:40; **Judg.** 6:37,39,40; **Job** 30:30; **Isa.** 4:6; 25:4,5; 61:4; **Jer.** 36:30; 49:13; 50:38; **Ezek.** 29:10; **Zeph.** 2:14; **Hag.** 1:11.

2722. חֹרֵב *ḥōrēḇ* **proper noun**
(Horeb)
Ex. 3:1; 17:6; 33:6; **Deut.** 1:2,6,19; 4:10,15; 5:2; 9:8; 18:16; 29:1(28:69); **1 Kgs.** 8:9; 19:8; **2 Chr.** 5:10; **Ps.** 106:19; **Mal.** 4:4(3:22).

2723. חָרְבָּה *ḥorbāh* **fem. noun**
(ruins, a desolate place)
Lev. 26:31,33; **Ezra** 9:9; **Job** 3:14; **Ps.** 9:6(7); 102:6(7); 109:10; **Isa.** 5:17; 44:26; 48:21; 49:19; 51:3; 52:9; 58:12;

61:4; 64:11(10); **Jer.** 7:34; 22:5; 25:9, 11,18; 27:17; 44:2,6,22; 49:13; **Ezek.** 5:14; 13:4; 25:13; 26:20; 29:9,10; 33:24, 27; 35:4; 36:4,10,33; 38:8,12; **Dan.** 9:2; **Mal.** 1:4.

2724. חָרָבָה *ḥārāḇāh* **fem. noun**
(dry land, dry ground)
Gen. 7:22; **Ex.** 14:21; **Josh.** 3:17; 4:18; **2 Kgs.** 2:8; **Ezek.** 30:12; **Hag.** 2:6.

2725. חֲרָבוֹן *ḥarāḇôn* **masc. noun**
(drought, heat)
Ps. 32:4.

2726. חַרְבוֹנָא *ḥarḇônā'*, חַרְבוֹנָה *ḥarḇônāh* **masc. proper noun**
(Harbona)
Esth. 1:10; 7:9.

2727. חָרַג *ḥārag* **verb**
(to tremble with fear)
Ps. 18:45(46).

2728. חַרְגֹּל *ḥargōl* **masc. noun**
(a cricket, locust)
Lev. 11:22.

2729. חָרַד *ḥāraḏ* **verb**
(to tremble, to be afraid)
Gen. 27:33; 42:28; **Ex.** 19:16,18; **Lev.** 26:6; **Deut.** 28:26; **Judg.** 8:12; **Ruth** 3:8; **1 Sam.** 13:7; 14:15; 16:4; 21:1(2); 28:5; **2 Sam.** 17:2; **1 Kgs.** 1:49; **2 Kgs.** 4:13; **Job** 11:19; 37:1; **Isa.** 10:29; 17:2; 19:16; 32:11; 41:5; **Jer.** 7:33; 30:10; 46:27; **Ezek.** 26:16,18; 30:9; 32:10; 34:28; 39:26; **Hos.** 11:10,11; **Amos** 3:6; **Mic.** 4:4; **Nah.** 2:11(12); **Zeph.** 3:13; **Zech.** 1:21(2:4).

2730. I. חָרֵד *ḥārēḏ* **adj.**
(trembling, afraid)
Judg. 7:3; **1 Sam.** 4:13; **Ezra** 9:4; 10:3; **Isa.** 66:2,5.
II. חֲרֹד *ḥarōḏ* **proper noun**
(Harod; part of the proper noun *ēyn ḥarōd* [5878])
Judg. 7:1.

2731. חֲרָדָה *ḥarāḏāh* **fem. noun**
(trembling, terror, fear)
Gen. 27:33; **1 Sam.** 14:15; **2 Kgs.** 4:13; **Prov.** 29:25; **Isa.** 21:4; **Jer.** 30:5; **Ezek.** 26:16; **Dan.** 10:7.

2732. חֲרָדָה *ḥarāḏāh* **proper noun**
(Haradah)
Num. 33:24,25.

2733. חֲרֹדִי *ḥarōḏiy* **masc. proper noun**
(Harodite)
2 Sam. 23:25.

2734. I. חָרָה *ḥārāh* **verb**
(to be angry)
Gen. 4:5,6; 18:30,32; 30:2; 31:35,36; 34:7; 39:19; 44:18; 45:5; **Ex.** 4:14; 22:24; 32:10,11,19,22; **Num.** 11:1,10,33; 12:9; 16:15; 22:22,27; 24:10; 25:3; 32:10,13; **Deut.** 6:15; 7:4; 11:17; 29:27(26); 31:17; **Josh.** 7:1; 23:16; **Judg.** 2:14,20; 3:8; 6:39; 9:30; 10:7; 14:19; **1 Sam.** 11:6; 15:11; 17:28; 18:8; 20:7,30; **2 Sam.** 3:8; 6:7,8; 12:5; 13:21; 19:42(43); 22:8; 24:1; **2 Kgs.** 13:3; 23:26; **1 Chr.** 13:10,11; **2 Chr.** 25:10,15; **Neh.** 3:20; 4:1(3:33), 7(1); 5:6; **Job** 19:11; 32:2,3,5; 42:7; **Ps.** 18:7(8); 37:1,7,8; 106:40; 124:3; **Prov.** 24:19; **Song** 1:6(NIV, see II); **Isa.** 5:25; 41:11; 45:24; **Jer.** 12:5(see *miṯḥareh* [8474,I]); 22:15; **Hos.** 8:5; **Jon.** 4:1,4,9; **Hab.** 3:8; **Zech.** 10:3.
II. נָחַר *nāḥār* **verb**
(to be angry)
Song 1:6(KJV, NASB, see I); **Jer.** 6:29(KJV, NASB, *ḥārar* [2787]).

2735. חֹר הַגִּדְגָּד *ḥōr haggiḏgāḏ* **proper noun**
(Hor Haggidgad)
Num. 33:32,33.

2736. חַרְהֲיָה *ḥarhayāh* **masc. proper noun**
(Harhaiah)
Neh. 3:8.

2737. חָרוּז *ḥārûz* **masc. noun**
(string of beads or jewels)
Song 1:10.

2738. חָרוּל *ḥārûl* **masc. noun**
(nettles, weeds)
Job 30:7; **Prov.** 24:31; **Zeph.** 2:9.

2739. חֲרוּמַף *ḥarûmap̱* **masc. proper noun**
(Harumaph)
Neh. 3:10.

2740. חָרוֹן *ḥārôn* **masc. noun**
(anger, heat, fierceness)
Ex. 15:7; 32:12; **Num.** 25:4; 32:14; **Deut.** 13:17(18); **Josh.** 7:26; **1 Sam.** 28:18; **2 Kgs.** 23:26; **2 Chr.** 28:11,13; 29:10; 30:8; **Ezra** 10:14; **Neh.** 13:18; **Job** 20:23; **Ps.** 2:5; 58:9(10); 69:24(25); 78:49; 85:3(4); 88:16(17); **Isa.** 13:9,13; **Jer.** 4:8,26; 12:13; 25:37,38; 30:24; 49:37; 51:45; **Lam.** 1:12; 4:11; **Ezek.** 7:12,14; **Hos.** 11:9; **Jon.** 3:9; **Nah.** 1:6; **Zeph.** 2:2; 3:8.

2741. חֲרוּפִי *ḥarûp̱iy* **masc. proper noun**
(Haruphite)
1 Chr. 12:5.

2742. I. חָרוּץ *ḥārûṣ* **adj.**
(sharp, diligent)
Job 41:30(22); **Prov.** 10:4; 12:24,27; 13:4; 21:5; **Isa.** 28:27; 41:15; **Amos** 1:3.
II. חָרוּץ *ḥārûṣ* **masc. noun**
(decision)
Joel 3:14(4:14).
III. חָרוּץ *ḥārûṣ* **masc. noun**
(moat)
Dan. 9:25.
IV. חָרוּץ *ḥārûṣ* **masc. noun**
(gold)
Ps. 68:13(14); **Prov.** 3:14; 8:10,19; 16:16; **Zech.** 9:3.

2743. חָרוּץ *ḥārûṣ* **masc. proper noun**
(Haruz)
2 Kgs. 21:19.

2744. חַרְחוּר *ḥarḥûr* **masc. proper noun**
(Harhur)
Ezra 2:51; **Neh.** 7:53.

2745. חַרְחַס *ḥarḥas* **masc. proper noun**
(Harhas)
2 Kgs. 22:14.

2746. חַרְחֻר *ḥarḥur* **masc. noun**
(extreme heat)
Deut. 28:22.

2747. חֶרֶט *ḥereṭ* **masc. noun**
(engraving tool, chisel)
Ex. 32:4; **Isa.** 8:1.

2748. חַרְטֹם *ḥarṭōm* **masc. noun**
(magician [only in the plural])
Gen. 41:8,24; **Ex.** 7:11,22; 8:7(3),18(14),19(15); 9:11; **Dan.** 1:20; 2:2.

2749. חַרְטֹם *ḥarṭōm* **Aram. masc. noun**
(magician; corr. to Hebr. 2748)
Dan. 2:10,27; 4:7(4),9(6); 5:11.

2750. חֳרִי *ḥoriy* **masc. noun**
(fierce, burning)
Ex. 11:8; **Deut.** 29:24(23); **1 Sam.** 20:34; **2 Chr.** 25:10; **Isa.** 7:4; **Lam.** 2:3.

2751. חֹרִי *ḥōriy* **masc. noun**
(white, white bread)
Gen. 40:16.

2752. חֹרִי *ḥōriy* **masc. proper noun**
(Horite)
Gen. 14:6; 36:20,21,29,30(KJV, *ḥôriy* [2753,A]); **Deut.** 2:12,22.

2753. A. חוֹרִי *ḥôriy* **masc. proper noun**
(Hori: son of Lotan)
Gen. 36:22,30(NASB, NIV, *ḥōriy* [2752]); **1 Chr.** 1:39.
B. חוֹרִי *ḥôriy* **masc. proper noun**
(Hori: a Simeonite)
Num. 13:5.

2754. חָרִיט *ḥāriyṭ* **masc. noun**
(bag, purse)
2 Kgs. 5:23; **Isa.** 3:22.

2755. חֲרֵי יוֹנִים *ḥ^arēy yôniym* **masc. noun**
(doves' dung; from the pl. of *ḥere'* [2716] and the pl. of *yônāh* [3123])
2 Kgs. 6:25(NASB, [Q^e] *diḇyôniym* [1686,I]; NIV, [Q^e] *diḇyôniym* [1686,II]).

2756. A. חָרִיף *ḥāriyp̱* **masc. proper noun**
(Hariph: a Jew)
Neh. 7:24.
B. חָרִיף *ḥāriyp̱* **masc. proper noun**
(Hariph: a Jew)
Neh. 10:19(20).

2757. I. חָרִיץ *ḥāriyṣ* **masc. noun**
(harrow, wedge, sharp instrument)
2 Sam. 12:31; **1 Chr.** 20:3.
II. חָרִיץ *ḥāriyṣ* **masc. noun**
(slice, piece [of cheese])
1 Sam. 17:18.

2758. חָרִישׁ *ḥāriyš* **masc. noun**
(plowing, plowing time)
Gen. 45:6; **Ex.** 34:21; **1 Sam.** 8:12.

2759. חֲרִישִׁי *ḥ^ariyšiy* **adj.**
(very hot, scorching)
Jon. 4:8.

2760. חָרַךְ *ḥārak̲* **verb**
(to roast)
Prov. 12:27.

2761. חֲרַךְ *ḥ^arak̲* **Aram. verb**
(to be singed, to be burned; corr. to Hebr. 2760)
Dan. 3:27.

2762. חָרָךְ *ḥārāk̲* **masc. noun**
(lattice)
Song 2:9.

2763. I. חָרַם *ḥāram* **verb**
(to ban, to exterminate, to destroy; to devote, to utterly set apart)
Ex. 22:20(19); **Lev.** 27:28,29; **Num.** 21:2,3; **Deut.** 2:34; 3:6; 7:2; 13:15(16); 20:17; **Josh.** 2:10; 6:18,21; 8:26; 10:1, 28,35,37,39,40; 11:11,12,20,21; **Judg.** 1:17; 21:11; **1 Sam.** 15:3,8,9,15,18,20; **1 Kgs.** 9:21; **2 Kgs.** 19:11; **1 Chr.** 4:41; **2 Chr.** 20:23; 32:14; **Ezra** 10:8; **Isa.** 11:15; 34:2; 37:11; **Jer.** 25:9; 50:21,26; 51:3; **Dan.** 11:44; **Mic.** 4:13.
II. חָרַם *ḥāram* **verb**
(to mutilate, to slit, to disfigure)
Lev. 21:18.

2764. I. חֵרֶם *ḥērem* **masc. noun**
(something banned, accursed; destruction; something utterly devoted)
Lev. 27:21,28,29; **Num.** 18:14; **Deut.** 7:26; 13:17(18); **Josh.** 6:17,18; 7:1, 11–13,15; 22:20; **1 Sam.** 15:21; **1 Kgs.** 20:42; **1 Chr.** 2:7; **Isa.** 34:5; 43:28; **Ezek.** 44:29; **Zech.** 14:11; **Mal.** 4:6(3:24).
II. חֵרֶם *ḥērem* **masc. noun**
(net, fishnet, trap, snare)
Eccl. 7:26; **Ezek.** 26:5,14; 32:3; 47:10; **Mic.** 7:2; **Hab.** 1:15–17.

2765. חֹרֵם *ḥ^o^rēm* **proper noun**
(Horem)
Josh. 19:38.

2766. A. חָרִם *ḥārim* **masc. proper noun**
(Harim: a priest)
1 Chr. 24:8.
B. חָרִם *ḥārim* **masc. proper noun**
(Harim: a priest)
Neh. 10:5(6).
C. חָרִם *ḥārim* **masc. proper noun**
(Harim: head of a priestly course)
Ezra 2:39; 10:21; **Neh.** 7:42; 12:15.
D. חָרִם *ḥārim* **masc. proper noun**
(Harim: head of a family)
Ezra 2:32; 10:31; **Neh.** 3:11; 7:35.
E. חָרִם *ḥārim* **masc. proper noun**
(Harim: a prince)
Neh. 10:27(28).

2767. חָרְמָה *ḥormāh* **proper noun**
(Hormah)
Num. 14:45; 21:3; **Deut.** 1:44; **Josh.** 12:14; 15:30; 19:4; **Judg.** 1:17; **1 Sam.** 30:30; **1 Chr.** 4:30.

2768. חֶרְמוֹן *ḥermôn* **proper noun**
(Hermon)
Deut. 3:8,9; 4:48; **Josh.** 11:3,17; 12:1,5; 13:5,11; **1 Chr.** 5:23; **Ps.** 89:12(13); 133:3; **Song** 4:8.

2769. חֶרְמוֹנִים *ḥermôniym* **masc. pl. proper noun**
(Hermonites, peaks of Mount Hermon)
Ps. 42:6(7).

2770. חֶרְמֵשׁ *ḥermēš* **masc. noun**
(sickle)
Deut. 16:9; 23:25(26); **1 Sam.** 13:20 (Sept.; KJV, NASB, [Hebr] *maḥ^a^rēšāh* [4281]).

2771. A. חָרָן *ḥārān* **proper noun**
(Haran: city in N. Mesopotamia)
Gen. 11:31,32; 12:4,5; 27:43; 28:10; 29:4; **2 Kgs.** 19:12; **Isa.** 37:12; **Ezek.** 27:23.
B. חָרָן *ḥārān* **proper noun**
(Haran: son of Caleb)
1 Chr. 2:46.

2772. חֹרֹנִי *ḥōrōniy* **masc. proper noun**
(Horonite)
Neh. 2:10,19; 13:28.

2773. חֹרֹנַיִם *ḥōrōnayim*, חוֹרֹנַיִם *ḥōrônayim* **proper noun**
(Horonaim)
Isa. 15:5; **Jer.** 48:3,5,34.

2774. חַרְנֶפֶר *ḥarnep̱er* **masc. proper noun**
(Harnepher)
1 Chr. 7:36.

2775. I. חֶרֶס *ḥeres* **masc. noun**
(sun)
Judg. 8:13(NASB, NIV, *ḥeres* [2776]); 14:18; **Job** 9:7.
II. חֶרֶס *ḥeres* **masc. noun**
(a skin disorder, an itch)
Deut. 28:27.

2776. חֶרֶס *ḥeres* **proper noun**
(Heres)
Judg. 1:35; 8:13(KJV, *ḥeres* [2775,I]).

2777. חַרְסוּת *ḥarsûṯ* **fem.** noun
(potsherd, clay fragment)
Jer. 19:2.

2778. I. חָרַף *ḥārap̱* **verb**
(to reproach)
Judg. 5:18; 8:15; **1 Sam.** 17:10,25,26,36,45; **2 Sam.** 21:21; 23:9; **2 Kgs.** 19:4,16,22,23; **1 Chr.** 20:7; **2 Chr.** 32:17; **Neh.** 6:13; **Job** 27:6; **Ps.** 42:10(11); 44:16(17); 55:12(13); 57:3(4); 69:9(10); 74:10,18; 79:12; 89:51(52); 102:8(9); 119:42; **Prov.** 14:31;

17:5; 27:11; **Isa.** 37:4,17,23,24; 65:7; **Zeph.** 2:8,10.
II. חָרַף *ḥārap̱* verb
(to remain in harvesttime, to winter)
Isa. 18:6.
III. חָרַף *ḥārap̱* verb
(to engage, to betroth, to acquire)
Lev. 19:20.

2779. חֹרֶף *ḥōrep̱* masc. noun
(winter)
Gen. 8:22; **Job** 29:4; **Ps.** 74:17; **Prov.** 20:4; **Jer.** 36:22; **Amos** 3:15; **Zech.** 14:8.

2780. חָרֵף *ḥārēp̱* masc. proper noun
(Hareph)
1 Chr. 2:51.

2781. חֶרְפָּה *ḥerpāh* fem. noun
(reproach, scorn, disgrace)
Gen. 30:23; 34:14; **Josh.** 5:9; **1 Sam.** 11:2; 17:26; 25:39; **2 Sam.** 13:13; **Neh.** 1:3; 2:17; 4:4(3:36); 5:9; **Job** 16:10; 19:5; **Ps.** 15:3; 22:6(7); 31:11(12); 39:8(9); 44:13(14); 69:7(8),9(10),10(11),19(20), 20(21); 71:13; 74:22; 78:66; 79:4,12; 89:41(42),50(51); 109:25; 119:22,39; **Prov.** 6:33; 18:3; **Isa.** 4:1; 25:8; 30:5; 47:3; 51:7; 54:4; **Jer.** 6:10; 15:15; 20:8; 23:40; 24:9; 29:18; 31:19; 42:18; 44:8,12; 49:13; 51:51; **Lam.** 3:30,61; 5:1; **Ezek.** 5:14,15; 16:57; 21:28(33); 22:4; 36:15, 30; **Dan.** 9:16; 11:18; 12:2; **Hos.** 12:14(15); **Joel** 2:17,19; **Mic.** 6:16; **Zeph.** 2:8; 3:18.

2782. חָרַץ *ḥāraṣ* verb
(to act promptly, to act sharply, to decide, to move against, to maim)
Ex. 11:7; **Lev.** 22:22; **Josh.** 10:21; **2 Sam.** 5:24; **1 Kgs.** 20:40; **Job** 14:5; **Isa.** 10:22,23; 28:22; **Dan.** 9:26,27; 11:36.

2783. חֲרַץ *ḥaraṣ* Aram. fem. noun
(loins)
Dan. 5:6.

2784. חַרְצֻבָּה *ḥarṣubbāh* fem. noun
(fetter, chain, pain)
Ps. 73:4; **Isa.** 58:6.

2785. חַרְצָן *ḥarṣān* masc. noun
(kernel, seed)
Num. 6:4.

2786. חָרַק *ḥāraq* verb
(to gnash, to grind [the teeth at])
Job 16:9; **Ps.** 35:16; 37:12; 112:10; **Lam.** 2:16.

2787. חָרַר *ḥārar* verb
(to burn, to be charred)
Job 30:30; **Ps.** 69:3(4); 102:3(4); **Prov.** 26:21; **Isa.** 24:6; **Jer.** 6:29(NIV, *nāḥar* [2734,II]); **Ezek.** 15:4,5; 24:10,11.

2788. חָרֵר *ḥārēr* masc. noun
(parched place; scorched place)
Jer. 17:6.

2789. חֶרֶשׂ *ḥereś* masc. noun
(clay pottery, clay fragment)
Lev. 6:28(21); 11:33; 14:5,50; 15:12; **Num.** 5:17; **Job** 2:8; 41:30(22); **Ps.** 22:15(16); **Prov.** 26:23; **Isa.** 30:14; 45:9; **Jer.** 19:1; 32:14; **Lam.** 4:2; **Ezek.** 23:34.

2790. I. חָרַשׁ *ḥāraš* verb
(to plow, to cut, to engrave)
Gen. 4:22(KJV, *ḥōrēš* [2794]); **Num.** 30:11(12); **Deut.** 22:10; **Judg.** 14:18; **1 Sam.** 8:12; 23:9; **1 Kgs.** 7:14; 19:19; **Job** 1:14; 4:8; **Ps.** 129:3; **Prov.** 3:29; 6:14,18; 12:20; 14:22; 20:4; **Isa.** 28:24; **Jer.** 17:1; 26:18; **Hos.** 10:11,13; **Amos** 6:12; 9:13; **Mic.** 3:12.
II. חָרַשׁ *ḥāraš* verb
(to be silent, to be mute; to be deaf)
Gen. 24:21; 34:5; **Ex.** 14:14; **Num.** 30:4(5),7(8),14(15); **Judg.** 16:2; 18:19; **1 Sam.** 7:8; 10:27; **2 Sam.** 13:20; 19:10(11); **2 Kgs.** 18:36; **Neh.** 5:8; **Esth.** 4:14; 7:4; **Job** 6:24; 11:3; 13:5, 13,19; 33:31,33; 41:12(4); **Ps.** 28:1; 32:3;

35:22; 39:12(13); 50:3,21; 83:1(2); 109:1; **Prov.** 11:12; 17:28; **Isa.** 36:21; 41:1; 42:14; **Jer.** 4:19; 38:27; **Mic.** 7:16; **Hab.** 1:13; **Zeph.** 3:17.

2791. חֶרֶשׁ *ḥereš* **adv.**
(secretly)
Josh. 2:1.

2792. חֶרֶשׁ *ḥereš* **masc. proper noun**
(Heresh)
1 Chr. 9:15.

2793. I. חֹרֶשׁ *ḥōreš* **masc. noun**
(woods, forest, bough, thicket)
1 Sam. 23:15(NASB, NIV, see II),16(NASB, NIV, see II),18(NASB, NIV, see II),19(NASB, NIV, see II); **2 Chr.** 27:4; **Isa.** 17:9; **Ezek.** 31:3.
II. חֹרֶשׁ *ḥores* **proper noun**
(Horesh: loc. in the Wilderness of Ziph)
1 Sam. 23:15(KJV, see I),16(KJV, see I),18(KJV, see I),19(KJV, see I).

2794. חֹרֵשׁ *ḥōrēš* **masc. noun**
(worker)
Gen. 4:22(NASB, NIV, *ḥāraš* [2790,I]).

2795. חֵרֵשׁ *ḥērēš* **adj.**
(deaf)
Ex. 4:11; **Lev.** 19:14; **Ps.** 38:13(14); 58:4(5); **Isa.** 29:18; 35:5; 42:18,19; 43:8.

2796. חָרָשׁ *ḥārāš* **masc. noun**
(craftsman)
Ex. 28:11; 35:35; 38:23; **Deut.** 27:15; **1 Sam.** 13:19; **2 Sam.** 5:11; **2 Kgs.** 12:11(12); 22:6; 24:14,16; **1 Chr.** 4:14; 14:1; 22:15; 29:5; **2 Chr.** 24:12; 34:11; **Ezra** 3:7; **Neh.** 11:35; **Isa.** 3:3; 40:19,20; 41:7; 44:11–13; 45:16; 54:16; **Jer.** 10:3,9; 24:1; 29:2; **Ezek.** 21:31(36); **Hos.** 8:6; 13:2; **Zech.** 1:20(2:3).

2797. חַרְשָׁא *ḥaršā'* **masc. proper noun**
(Harsha)
Ezra 2:52; **Neh.** 7:54.

2798. חֲרָשִׁים *ḥ^a^rašiym* **masc. pl. proper noun**
(Harashim)
1 Chr. 4:14.

2799. חֲרֹשֶׁת *ḥ^a^rōšet̲* **fem. noun**
(a cutting, skillful working)
Ex. 31:5; 35:33.

2800. I. חֲרֹשֶׁת הַגּוֹיִם *ḥ^a^rōšet̲ haggôyim* **proper noun**
(Harosheth Haggoyim)
Judg. 4:2(KJV, see II),13(KJV, see II),16(KJV, see II).
II. חֲרֹשֶׁת *ḥ^a^rōšet̲* **proper noun**
(Harosheth, used with article and pl. of *gôy* [1471,I])
Judg. 4:2(NASB, NIV, see I),13(NASB, NIV, see I),16(NASB, NIV, see I).

2801. חָרַת *ḥārat̲* **verb**
(to engrave)
Ex. 32:16.

2802. חֶרֶת *ḥeret̲* **proper noun**
(Hereth)
1 Sam. 22:5.

2803. I. חָשַׁב *ḥāšab̲* **verb**
(to account, to plan, to consider, to reckon, to invent)
Gen. 15:6; 31:15; 38:15; 50:20; **Ex.** 26:1(NIV, see II),31(NIV, see II); 28:6(NIV, see II),15(NIV, see II); 31:4; 35:32,35(NIV, see II); 36:8(NIV, see II),35(NIV, see II); 38:23(NIV, see II); 39:3(NIV, see II),8(NIV, see II); **Lev.** 7:18; 17:4; 25:27,31,50,52; 27:18,23; **Num.** 18:27,30; 23:9; **Deut.** 2:11,20; **Josh.** 13:3; **1 Sam.** 1:13; 18:25; **2 Sam.** 4:2; 14:13,14; 19:19(20); **1 Kgs.** 10:21; **2 Kgs.** 12:15(16); 22:7; **2 Chr.** 2:14(13); 9:20; 26:15(NIV, see II); **Neh.** 6:2,6;

13:13; **Esth.** 8:3; 9:24,25; **Job** 6:26; 13:24; 18:3; 19:11,15; 33:10; 35:2; 41:27(19),29(21),32(24); **Ps.** 10:2; 21:11(12); 32:2; 35:4,20; 36:4(5); 40:17(18); 41:7(8); 44:22(23); 52:2(4); 73:16; 77:5(6); 88:4(5); 106:31; 119:59; 140:2(3),4(5); 144:3; **Prov.** 16:9,30; 17:28; 24:8; 27:14; **Isa.** 2:22; 5:28; 10:7; 13:17; 29:16,17; 32:15; 33:8; 40:15,17; 53:3,4; **Jer.** 11:19; 18:8,11,18; 23:27; 26:3; 29:11; 36:3; 48:2; 49:20,30; 50:45; **Lam.** 2:8; 4:2; **Ezek.** 11:2; 38:10; **Dan.** 11:24,25; **Hos.** 7:15; 8:12; **Amos** 6:5; **Jon.** 1:4; **Mic.** 2:1,3; **Nah.** 1:9,11; **Zech.** 7:10; 8:17; **Mal.** 3:16.

II. חֹשֵׁב *ḥōšēḇ* **masc. noun**
(inventor, weaver, designer, craftsman)
Ex. 26:1(KJV, NASB, see I),31(KJV, NASB, see I); 28:6(KJV, NASB, see I),15(KJV, NASB, see I); 35:35(KJV, NASB, see I); 36:8(KJV, NASB, see I),35(KJV, NASB, see I); 38:23(KJV, NASB, see I); 39:3(KJV, NASB, see I),8(KJV, NASB, see I); **2 Chr.** 26:15(KJV, NASB, see I).

2804. חֲשַׁב *ḥᵃšaḇ* **Aram. verb**
(to regard, to account as; corr. to Hebr. 2803,I)
Dan. 4:35(32).

2805. חֵשֶׁב *ḥēšeḇ* **masc. noun**
(waistband, skillfully woven waistband)
Ex. 28:8,27,28; 29:5; 39:5,20,21; **Lev.** 8:7.

2806. חַשְׁבַּדָּנָה *ḥašbaddānāh* **masc. proper noun**
(Hashbaddanah)
Neh. 8:4.

2807. חֲשֻׁבָה *ḥᵃšuḇāh* **masc. proper noun**
(Hashubah)
1 Chr. 3:20.

2808. חֶשְׁבּוֹן *ḥešbôn* **masc. noun**
(reason for things, planning)
Eccl. 7:25,27; 9:10.

2809. חֶשְׁבּוֹן *ḥešbôn* **proper noun**
(Heshbon)
Num. 21:25–28,30,34; 32:3,37; **Deut.** 1:4; 2:24,26,30; 3:2,6; 4:46; 29:7(6); **Josh.** 9:10; 12:2,5; 13:10,17,21,26,27; 21:39(37); **Judg.** 11:19,26; **1 Chr.** 6:81(66); **Neh.** 9:22; **Song** 7:4(5); **Isa.** 15:4; 16:8,9; **Jer.** 48:2,34,45; 49:3.

2810. חִשָּׁבוֹן *ḥiššāḇôn* **fem. noun**
(machine, device)
2 Chr. 26:15; **Eccl.** 7:29.

2811. A. חֲשַׁבְיָה *ḥᵃšaḇyāh* **masc. proper noun**
(Hashabiah: Merarite Levite)
1 Chr. 6:45(30).
B. חֲשַׁבְיָה *ḥᵃšaḇyāh* **masc. proper noun**
(Hashabiah: son of Bunni)
1 Chr. 9:14; **Neh.** 11:15.
C. חֲשַׁבְיָה *ḥᵃšaḇyāh*, חֲשַׁבְיָהוּ *ḥᵃšaḇyāhû* **masc. proper noun**
(Hashabiah: son of Jeduthun)
1 Chr. 25:3,19.
D. חֲשַׁבְיָהוּ *ḥᵃšaḇyāhû* **masc. proper noun**
(Hashabiah: a Hebronite)
1 Chr. 26:30.
E. חֲשַׁבְיָה *ḥᵃšaḇyāh* **masc. proper noun**
(Hashabiah: son of Kemuel)
1 Chr. 27:17.
F. חֲשַׁבְיָהוּ *ḥᵃšaḇyāhû* **masc. proper noun**
(Hashabiah: a Levite)
2 Chr. 35:9.
G. חֲשַׁבְיָה *ḥᵃšaḇyāh* **masc. proper noun**
(Hashabiah: a Levite)
Ezra 8:19,24; **Neh.** 3:17; 10:11(12); 12:24.

H. חֲשַׁבְיָה *ḥᵃšaḇyāh* **masc. proper noun**
(Hashabiah: son of Mattaniah)
Neh. 11:22.
I. חֲשַׁבְיָה *ḥᵃšaḇyāh* **masc. proper noun**
(Hashabiah: a priest)
Neh. 12:21.

2812. חֲשַׁבְנָה *ḥᵃšaḇnāh* **masc. proper noun**
(Hashabnah)
Neh. 10:25(26).

2813. A. חֲשַׁבְנְיָה *ḥᵃšaḇnᵉyāh* **masc. proper noun**
(Hashabneiah: father of Hattush)
Neh. 3:10.
B. חֲשַׁבְנְיָה *ḥᵃšaḇnᵉyāh* **masc. proper noun**
(Hashabneiah: a Levite)
Neh. 9:5.

2814. חָשָׁה *ḥāšāh* **verb**
(to be silent, to be still)
Judg. 18:9; **1 Kgs.** 22:3; **2 Kgs.** 2:3,5; 7:9; **Neh.** 8:11; **Ps.** 28:1; 39:2(3); 107:29; **Eccl.** 3:7; **Isa.** 42:14; 57:11; 62:1,6; 64:12(11); 65:6.

2815. A. חַשּׁוּב *ḥaššûḇ* **masc. proper noun**
(Hasshub: chief Levite)
1 Chr. 9:14; **Neh.** 11:15.
B. חַשּׁוּב *ḥaššûḇ* **masc. proper noun**
(Hasshub: repairer of Jerusalem's wall)
Neh. 3:11; 10:23(24).
C. חַשּׁוּב *ḥaššûḇ* **masc. proper noun**
(Hasshub: another repairer of Jerusalem's wall)
Neh. 3:23.

2816. חֲשׁוֹךְ *ḥᵃšôḵ* **Aram. masc. noun**
(darkness)
Dan. 2:22.

2817. חֲשׂוּפָא *ḥᵃśûpā'*, חֲשֻׂפָא *ḥᵃśupā'* **masc. proper noun**
(Hasupha)
Ezra 2:43; **Neh.** 7:46.

2818. I. חֲשַׁח *ḥᵃšaḥ* **Aram. verb**
(to need)
Dan. 3:16.
II. חַשְׁחָה *ḥašḥāh* **Aram. fem. noun**
(something needed, necessity)
Ezra 6:9.

2819. חַשְׁחוּ *ḥašḥû* **Aram. fem. noun**
(something needed)
Ezra 7:20.

2820. חָשַׂךְ *ḥāśaḵ* **verb**
(to hold back, to withhold, to spare)
Gen. 20:6; 22:12,16; 39:9; **1 Sam.** 25:39; **2 Sam.** 18:16; **2 Kgs.** 5:20; **Ezra** 9:13; **Job** 7:11; 16:5,6; 21:30; 30:10; 33:18; 38:23; **Ps.** 19:13(14); 78:50; **Prov.** 10:19; 11:24; 13:24; 17:27; 21:26; 24:11; **Isa.** 14:6; 54:2; 58:1; **Jer.** 14:10.

2821. חָשַׁךְ *ḥāšaḵ* **verb**
(to be dark, to be darkened, to be black)
Ex. 10:15; **Job** 3:9; 18:6; 38:2; **Ps.** 69:23(24); 105:28; 139:12; **Eccl.** 12:2,3; **Isa.** 5:30; 13:10; **Jer.** 13:16; **Lam.** 4:8; 5:17; **Ezek.** 30:18; **Amos** 5:8; 8:9; **Mic.** 3:6.

2822. חֹשֶׁךְ *ḥōšeḵ* **masc. noun**
(darkness)
Gen. 1:2,4,5,18; **Ex.** 10:21,22; 14:20; **Deut.** 4:11; 5:23(20); **Josh.** 2:5; **1 Sam.** 2:9; **2 Sam.** 22:12(NIV, *ḥᵃšēḵāh* [2825]), 29; **Job** 3:4,5; 5:14; 10:21; 12:22,25; 15:22,23,30; 17:12,13; 18:18; 19:8; 20:26; 22:11; 23:17; 24:16; 26:10; 28:3; 29:3; 34:22; 37:19; 38:19; **Ps.** 18:11(12), 28(29); 35:6; 88:12(13); 104:20; 105:28;

107:10,14; 112:4; 139:11,12; **Prov.** 2:13; 20:20; **Eccl.** 2:13,14; 5:17(16); 6:4; 11:8; **Isa.** 5:20,30; 9:2(1); 29:18; 42:7; 45:3,7, 19; 47:5; 49:9; 58:10; 59:9; 60:2; **Lam.** 3:2; **Ezek.** 8:12; 32:8; **Joel** 2:2,31(3:4); **Amos** 5:18,20; **Mic.** 7:8; **Nah.** 1:8; **Zeph.** 1:15.

2823. חָשֹׁךְ *ḥāšōḵ* **adj.**
(obscure, insignificant)
Prov. 22:29.

2824. חֶשְׁכַת *ḥeškaṯ* **fem. noun**
(darkness: const. of *ḥ*ᵃ*šēyḵāh* [2825])
Ps. 18:11(12).

2825. חֲשֵׁיכָה *ḥ*ᵃ*šēyḵāh*, חֲשֵׁכָה *ḥ*ᵃ*šēḵāh* **fem. noun**
(darkness)
Gen. 15:12; **2 Sam.** 22:12(KJV, NASB, *ḥōšeḵ* [2822]); **Ps.** 18:11(12)(see *heškaṯ* [2824]); 82:5; 139:12; **Isa.** 8:22; 50:10.

2826. חָשַׁל *ḥāšal* **verb**
(to be feeble, to be faint)
Deut. 25:18.

2827. חֲשַׁל *ḥ*ᵃ*šal* **Aram. verb**
(to subdue, shatter)
Dan. 2:40.

2828. חָשֻׁם *ḥāšum* **masc. proper noun**
(Hashum)
Ezra 2:19; 10:33; **Neh.** 7:22; 8:4; 10:18(19).

2829. חֶשְׁמוֹן *ḥešmôn* **proper noun**
(Heshmon)
Josh. 15:27.

2830. חַשְׁמַל *ḥašmal*, חַשְׁמַלָה *ḥašmalāh* **masc. noun**
(a glowing substance, ember)
Ezek. 1:4,27; 8:2.

2831. חַשְׁמַן *ḥašman* **masc. noun**
(an ambassader, envoy, prince)
Ps. 68:31(32).

2832. חַשְׁמֹנָה *ḥašmōnāh* **proper noun**
(Hashmonah)
Num. 33:29,30.

2833. חֹשֶׁן *ḥōšen* **masc. noun**
(breastplate, breastpiece)
Ex. 25:7; 28:4,15,22–24,26,28–30; 29:5; 35:9,27; 39:8,9,15–17,19,21; **Lev.** 8:8.

2834. חָשַׂף *ḥāśap̱* **verb**
(to strip off, to make bare)
Ps. 29:9; **Isa.** 20:4; 30:14; 47:2; 52:10; **Jer.** 13:26; 49:10; **Ezek.** 4:7; **Joel** 1:7; **Hag.** 2:16.

2835. חָשִׂף *ḥāśip̱* **masc. noun**
(a small flock, little flock)
1 Kgs. 20:27.

2836. I. חָשַׁק *ḥāšaq* **verb**
(to love, to be attached to)
Gen. 34:8; **Deut.** 7:7; 10:15; 21:11; **1 Kgs.** 9:19; **2 Chr.** 8:6; **Ps.** 91:14; **Isa.** 38:17.
II. חָשַׁק *ḥāšaq* **verb**
(to fasten together)
Ex. 27:17; 38:17,28.

2837. חֵשֶׁק *ḥēšeq* **masc. noun**
(desire, thing desired)
1 Kgs. 9:1,19; **2 Chr.** 8:6; **Isa.** 21:4.

2838. חָשׁוּק *ḥāšûq* **masc. noun**
(a hook or band around a pillar)
Ex. 27:10,11; 36:38; 38:10–12,17,19.

2839. חִשֻּׁק *ḥiššuq* **masc. noun**
(a spoke of a wheel)
1 Kgs. 7:33.

2840. חִשּׁוּר *ḥiššûr* **masc. noun**
(the hub of a wheel)
1 Kgs. 7:33.

2841. חַשְׁרָה *ḥašrāh* **fem. noun**
(a collection or mass of water)
2 Sam. 22:12.

2842. חֲשַׁשׁ *ḥ*^{a}*šaš* **masc. noun**
(chaff, dry grass)
Isa. 5:24; 33:11.

2843. חֻשָׁתִי *ḥušāṯiy* **masc. proper noun**
(Hushathite)
2 Sam. 21:18; 23:27; **1 Chr.** 11:29; 20:4; 27:11.

2844. I. חַת *ḥaṯ* **masc. noun**
(terror, fear)
Gen. 9:2; **Job** 41:33(25).
II. חַת *ḥaṯ* **adj.**
(broken, dismayed, terrified)
1 Sam. 2:4; **Jer.** 46:5.

2845. חֵת *ḥēṯ* **masc. proper noun**
(Heth)
Gen. 10:15; 23:3,5,7,10,16,18,20; 25:10; 27:46; 49:32; **1 Chr.** 1:13.

2846. חָתָה *ḥāṯāh* **verb**
(to snatch up, to take away)
Ps. 52:5(7); **Prov.** 6:27; 25:22; **Isa.** 30:14.

2847. חִתָּה *ḥittāh* **fem. noun**
(terror)
Gen. 35:5.

2848. חִתּוּל *ḥittûl* **masc. noun**
(bandage)
Ezek. 30:21.

2849. חַתְחַת *ḥaṯḥaṯ* **masc. noun**
(danger, fear)
Eccl. 12:5.

2850. A. חִתִּי *ḥittiy* **masc. proper noun**
(Hittites: descendants of Heth in Palestine)
Gen. 15:20; 23:10; 25:9; 26:34; 36:2; 49:29,30; 50:13; **Ex.** 3:8,17; 13:5; 23:23,28; 33:2; 34:11; **Num.** 13:29; **Deut.** 7:1; 20:17; **Josh.** 1:4; 3:10; 9:1; 11:3; 12:8; 24:11; **Judg.** 1:26; 3:5; **1 Sam.** 26:6; **2 Sam.** 11:3,6,17,21,24; 12:9,10; 23:39; **1 Kgs.** 9:20; 15:5; **1 Chr.** 11:41; **2 Chr.** 8:7; **Ezra** 9:1; **Neh.** 9:8; **Ezek.** 16:3,45.
B. חִתִּי *ḥittiy* **masc. proper noun**
(Hittites: Hittites in Anatolia)
1 Kgs. 10:29; 11:1; **2 Kgs.** 7:6; **2 Chr.** 1:17.

2851. חִתִּית *ḥittiyṯ* **fem. noun**
(terror)
Ezek. 26:17; 32:23–27,30,32.

2852. חָתַךְ *ḥāṯaḵ* **verb**
(to be decreed, to be determined)
Dan. 9:24.

2853. חָתַל *ḥāṯal* **verb**
(to be wrapped in cloth, to be swaddled)
Ezek. 16:4.

2854. חֲתֻלָּה *ḥ*^{a}*ṯullāh* **fem. noun**
(swaddlingband, girdle)
Job 38:9.

2855. חֶתְלֹן *heṯlōn* **proper noun**
(Hethlon)
Ezek. 47:15; 48:1.

2856. חָתַם *ḥāṯam* **verb**
(to seal up, to set a seal on)
Lev. 15:3; **Deut.** 32:34; **1 Kgs.** 21:8; **Neh.** 9:38(10:1); 10:1(2); **Esth.** 3:12; 8:8,10; **Job** 9:7; 14:17; 24:16; 33:16; 37:7; **Song** 4:12; **Isa.** 8:16; 29:11; **Jer.** 32:10,11,14,44; **Ezek.** 28:12; **Dan.** 9:24(NASB, NIV, [Q^e] *tāmam* [8592]); 12:4,9.

2857. חֲתַם *ḥaṯam* **Aram. verb**
(to seal; corr. to Hebr. 2856)
Dan. 6:17(18).

2858. חֹתֶמֶת *ḥōṯemeṯ* **fem. noun**
(a signet ring, seal)
Gen. 38:25.

2859. I. חָתַן *ḥāṯan* **verb**
(to become related by marriage)
Gen. 34:9; **Deut.** 7:3; **Josh.** 23:12; **Judg.** 19:4,7,9; **1 Sam.** 18:21–23,26,27; **1 Kgs.** 3:1; **2 Chr.** 18:1; **Ezra** 9:14.
II. חֹתֵן *ḥōṯēn* **masc. noun**
(father-in-law)
Ex. 3:1; 4:18; 18:1,2,5–8,12,14,15,17,24,27; **Num.** 10:29; **Judg.** 1:16; 4:11.
III. חֹתֶנֶת *ḥōṯeneṯ* **fem. noun**
(mother-in-law)
Deut. 27:23.

2860. חָתָן *ḥāṯān* **masc. noun**
(son-in-law, bridegroom)
Gen. 19:12,14; **Ex.** 4:25,26; **Judg.** 15:6; 19:5; **1 Sam.** 18:18; 22:14; **2 Kgs.** 8:27; **Neh.** 6:18; 13:28; **Ps.** 19:5(6); **Isa.** 61:10; 62:5; **Jer.** 7:34; 16:9; 25:10; 33:11; **Joel** 2:16.

2861. חֲתֻנָּה *ḥaṯunnāh* **fem. noun**
(wedding, marriage)
Song 3:11.

2862. חָתַף *ḥāṯap̱* **verb**
(to snatch away, to take away)
Job 9:12.

2863. חֶתֶף *ḥeṯep̱* **masc. noun**
(a robber, prey)
Prov. 23:28.

2864. חָתַר *ḥāṯar* **verb**
(to dig [into a house], to row [in water])
Job 24:16; **Ezek.** 8:8; 12:5,7,12; **Amos** 9:2; **Jon.** 1:13.

2865. חָתַת *ḥāṯaṯ* **verb**
(to be dismayed, to be discouraged)
Deut. 1:21; 31:8; **Josh.** 1:9; 8:1; 10:25; **1 Sam.** 2:10; 17:11; **2 Kgs.** 19:26; **1 Chr.** 22:13; 28:20; **2 Chr.** 20:15,17; 32:7; **Job** 7:14; 21:13; 31:34; 32:15; 39:22; **Isa.** 7:8; 8:9; 9:4(3); 20:5; 30:31; 31:4,9; 37:27; 51:6,7; **Jer.** 1:17; 8:9; 10:2; 14:4; 17:18; 23:4; 30:10; 46:27; 48:1, 20,39; 49:37; 50:2,36; 51:56; **Ezek.** 2:6; 3:9; **Obad.** 1:9; **Hab.** 2:17; **Mal.** 2:5.

2866. חֲתַת *ḥaṯaṯ* **masc. noun**
(a terror, something dreadful)
Job 6:21.

2867. חֲתַת *ḥaṯaṯ* **masc. proper noun**
(Hathath)
1 Chr. 4:13.

ט Teth

2868. טְאֵב *ṭ^{e}'ēḇ* **Aram. verb**
(to be glad, to be pleased; corr. to Hebr. 2895)
Dan. 6:23(24).

2869. טָב *ṭāḇ* **Aram. masc. noun**
(goodness, purity)
Ezra 5:17; **Dan.** 2:32.

2870. A. טָבְאֵל *ṭāḇ^{e}'ēl* **masc. proper noun**
(Tabeel: a Persian official)
Ezra 4:7.
B. טָבְאַל *ṭāḇ^{e}'al* **masc. proper noun**
(Tabeal: a Syrian)
Isa. 7:6.

2871. טְבוּל *ṭ^{e}ḇûl* **masc. noun**
(turban)
Ezek. 23:15.

2872. טַבּוּר *ṭabbûr* **masc. noun**
(center, midst)
Judg. 9:37; **Ezek.** 38:12.

2873. טָבַח *ṭāḇaḥ* **verb**
(to slaughter, to kill)
Gen. 43:16; **Ex.** 22:1(21:37); **Deut.** 28:31; **1 Sam.** 25:11; **Ps.** 37:14; **Prov.** 9:2; **Jer.** 11:19; 25:34; 51:40; **Lam.** 2:21; **Ezek.** 21:10(15).

2874. טֶבַח *ṭeḇaḥ* **masc. noun**
(a slaughtering, killing)
Gen. 43:16; **Prov.** 7:22; 9:2; **Isa.** 34:2,6; 53:7; 65:12; **Jer.** 48:15; 50:27; **Ezek.** 21:10(15),15(20),28(33).

2875. טֶבַח *ṭeḇaḥ* **masc. proper noun**
(Tebah)
Gen. 22:24.

2876. טַבָּח *ṭabbāḥ* **masc. noun**
(guard, imperial guard)
Gen. 37:36; 39:1; 40:3,4; 41:10,12; **1 Sam.** 9:23,24; **2 Kgs.** 25:8,10–12, 15,18,20; **Jer.** 39:9–11,13; 40:1,2,5; 41:10; 43:6; 52:12,14–16,19,24,26,30.

2877. טַבָּח *ṭabbāḥ* **Aram. masc. noun**
(guard, imperial guard; corr. to Hebr. 2876)
Dan. 2:14.

2878. טִבְחָה *ṭiḇḥāh* **fem. noun**
(a thing slaughtered, meat)
1 Sam. 25:11; **Ps.** 44:22(23); **Jer.** 12:3.

2879. טַבָּחָה *ṭabbāḥah* **fem. noun**
(a cook)
1 Sam. 8:13.

2880. טִבְחַת *ṭiḇḥaṯ* **proper noun**
(Tibhath, Tebah)
1 Chr. 18:8.

2881. טָבַל *ṭāḇal* **verb**
(to dip, to plunge)
Gen. 37:31; **Ex.** 12:22; **Lev.** 4:6,17; 9:9; 14:6,16,51; **Num.** 19:18; **Deut.** 33:24; **Josh.** 3:15; **Ruth** 2:14; **1 Sam.** 14:27; **2 Kgs.** 5:14; 8:15; **Job** 9:31.

2882. טְבַלְיָהוּ *ṭ^{e}ḇalyāhû* **masc. proper noun**
(Tebaliah)
1 Chr. 26:11.

2883. טָבַע *ṭāḇaʿ* **verb**
(to sink, to drown)
Ex. 15:4; **1 Sam.** 17:49; **Job** 38:6; **Ps.** 9:15(16); 69:2(3),14(15); **Prov.** 8:25; **Jer.** 38:6,22; **Lam.** 2:9.

2884. טַבָּעוֹת *ṭabbā'ōṯ* **masc. proper noun**
(Tabbaoth)
Ezra 2:43; **Neh.** 7:46.

2885. טַבַּעַת *ṭabba'aṯ* **fem. noun**
(ring, signet ring)
Gen. 41:42; **Ex.** 25:12,14,15,26,27; 26:24,29; 27:4,7; 28:23,24,26–28; 30:4; 35:22; 36:29,34; 37:3,5,13,14,27; 38:5,7; 39:16,17,19–21; **Num.** 31:50; **Esth.** 3:10,12; 8:2,8,10; **Isa.** 3:21.

2886. טַבְרִמֹּן *ṭaḇrimmōn* **masc. proper noun**
(Tabrimmon)
1 Kgs. 15:18.

2887. טֵבֵת *ṭēḇēṯ* **proper noun**
(Tebeth)
Esth. 2:16.

2888. טַבַּת *ṭabbāṯ* **proper noun**
(Tabbath)
Judg. 7:22.

2889. טָהוֹר *ṭāhôr,* טָהֹר *ṭāhōr* **adj.**
(clean, pure)
Gen. 7:2,8; 8:20; **Ex.** 25:11,17,24,29,31,36,38,39; 28:14,22,36; 30:3,35; 31:8; 37:2,6,11,16,17,22–24, 26,29; 39:15,25,30,37; **Lev.** 4:12; 6:11(4); 7:19; 10:10,14; 11:36,37,47; 13:13,17, 37,39–41; 14:4,57; 15:8; 20:25; 24:4,6; **Num.** 5:28; 9:13; 18:11,13; 19:9,18,19; **Deut.** 12:15,22; 14:11,20; 15:22; 23:10(11); **1 Sam.** 20:26; **1 Chr.** 28:17; **2 Chr.** 3:4; 9:17; 13:11; 30:17; **Ezra** 6:20; **Job** 14:4; 17:9(KJV, *ṭᵉhār* [2890]; NIV, *ṭōhar* [2892,I]); 28:19; **Ps.** 12:6(7); 19:9(10); 51:10(12); **Prov.** 15:26; 22:11(KJV, *ṭᵉhōr* [2890]); 30:12; **Eccl.** 9:2; **Isa.** 66:20; **Ezek.** 22:26; 36:25; 44:23; **Hab.** 1:13; **Zech.** 3:5; **Mal.** 1:11.

2890. טְהָר *ṭᵉhār,* טֳהָר *ṭᵒhār* **masc. noun**
(cleanness, pureness)
Job 17:9(NASB, *ṭāhôr* [2889]; NIV, *ṭōhar* [2892,I]); **Prov.** 22:11(NASB, NIV, *ṭāhôr* [2889]).

2891. טָהֵר *ṭāhēr* **verb**
(to be clean, to make clean)
Gen. 35:2; **Lev.** 11:32; 12:7,8; 13:6,13, 17,23,28,34,37,58,59; 14:4,7–9,11,14, 17–20,25,28,29,31,48,53; 15:13,28; 16:19,30; 17:15; 22:4,7; **Num.** 8:6,7, 15,21; 19:12,19; 31:23,24; **Josh.** 22:17; **2 Kgs.** 5:10,12–14; **2 Chr.** 29:15,16,18; 30:18; 34:3,5,8; **Ezra** 6:20; **Neh.** 12:30; 13:9,22,30; **Job** 4:17; 37:21; **Ps.** 51:2(4), 7(9); **Prov.** 20:9; **Isa.** 66:17; **Jer.** 13:27; 33:8; **Ezek.** 22:24; 24:13; 36:25,33; 37:23; 39:12,14,16; 43:26; **Mal.** 3:3.

2892. I. טֹהַר *ṭōhar* **masc. noun**
(purity)
Ex. 24:10; **Lev.** 12:4,6; **Job** 17:9(KJV, NASB, *ṭᵉhār* [2890]).
II. טֳהָר *ṭᵒhār* **masc. noun**
(clearness)
Ps. 89:44(45).

2893. טָהֳרָה *ṭāhᵒrāh* **fem. noun**
(purifying, cleansing)
Lev. 12:4,5; 13:7,35; 14:2,23,32; 15:13; **Num.** 6:9; **1 Chr.** 23:28; **2 Chr.** 30:19; **Neh.** 12:45; **Ezek.** 44:26.

2894. טֵאטֵא *ṭē'ṭē'* **verb**
(to sweep)
Isa. 14:23.

2895. טוֹב *ṭôḇ* **verb**
(to be good, to be pleasing)
Num. 10:29,32(NASB, NIV, *yāṭaḇ* [3190]); 11:18; 24:1,5; **Deut.** 5:33(30); 15:16; 19:13; **Judg.** 11:25; **1 Sam.** 16:16,23; 20:12; **2 Sam.** 3:36(see טוֹב [2896,II]); 13:28; **1 Kgs.** 8:18; **2 Kgs.** 10:30; 21:2; **1 Chr.** 13:2; **2 Chr.** 6:8; **Neh.** 2:5,7; **Esth.** 1:10,19; 3:9; 5:4,8; 7:3; 8:9; 9:13; **Ps.** 119:68; **Song** 4:10;

Isa. 3:10; **Jer.** 32:41; **Ezek.** 36:11(NASB, *yāṭab* [3190]); **Hos.** 14:2(3)(see טוֹב [2896]); **Zech.** 11:12.

2896. I. טוֹב *ṭôḇ* **adj.**
(sweet)
Jer. 6:20.
II. טוֹב *ṭôḇ* **masc. adj.**
(good)
Gen. 1:4,10,12,18,21,25,31; 2:9,12, 17,18; 3:5,6,22; 6:2; 15:15; 16:6; 18:7; 19:8; 20:15; 24:16,50; 25:8; 26:7,29; 27:9; 29:19; 30:20; 31:24,29; 40:16; 41:5,22,24,26,35; 49:15; **Ex.** 2:2; 3:8; 14:12; 18:17; **Lev.** 27:10,12,14,33; **Num.** 10:29,32; 13:19; 14:3,7; 36:6; **Deut.** 1:14,25,35,39; 3:25; 4:21,22; 6:10,18,24; 8:7,10,12; 9:6; 10:13; 11:17; 12:28; 23:16(17); 26:11; 28:12; 30:15; **Josh.** 7:21; 9:25; 21:45(43); 23:13–16; **Judg.** 8:2,32; 9:2,11; 10:15; 11:25; 15:2; 16:25; 18:9,19; 19:24; **Ruth** 2:22; 3:13; 4:15; **1 Sam.** 1:8,23; 2:24,26; 3:18; 8:14,16; 9:2,10; 11:10; 12:23; 14:36,40; 15:9,22,28; 16:12; 19:4; 20:7; 24:18(19); 25:3,8,15,36; 26:16; 27:1; 29:6,9; **2 Sam.** 3:13,19,36; 10:12; 11:2; 13:22; 14:17,32; 15:3,26; 17:7,14; 18:3,27; 19:18(19), 27(28),35(36),37(38),38(39); 24:22; **1 Kgs.** 1:6,42; 2:18,32,38,42; 3:9; 8:36, 56,66; 10:7; 12:7; 14:13,15; 18:24; 19:4; 20:3; 21:2; 22:8,13,18; **2 Kgs.** 2:19; 3:19,25; 5:12; 10:3,5; 20:3,13,19; **1 Chr.** 4:40; 16:34; 19:13; 21:23; 28:8; 29:28; **2 Chr.** 3:5,8; 5:13; 6:27,41; 7:3; 10:7; 12:12; 14:2(1); 18:7,12,17; 19:3,11; 21:13; 30:18,22; 31:20; **Ezra** 3:11; 7:9; 8:18,27; **Neh.** 2:8; 5:9; 9:13,20; **Esth.** 1:11,19; 2:2,3,7,9; 3:11; 5:9; 7:9; 8:8,17; 9:19,22; 10:3; **Job** 2:10; 7:7; 10:3; 13:9; 21:13; 22:18,21; 30:26; 34:4; 36:11; **Ps.** 4:6(7); 14:1,3; 21:3(4); 23:6; 25:8,13; 34:8(9),10(11),12(13),14(15); 36:4(5); 37:3,16,27; 39:2(3); 45:1(2); 52:3(5), 9(11); 53:1(2),3(4); 54:6(8); 63:3(4); 69:16(17); 73:1,28; 84:10(11),11(12); 85:12(13); 86:5,17; 92:1(2); 100:5; 103:5; 104:28; 106:1; 107:1,9; 109:21; 111:10; 112:5; 118:1,8,9,29; 119:39,65,68,71, 72,122; 122:9; 125:4; 128:2; 133:1,2; 135:3; 136:1; 143:10; 145:9; 147:1; **Prov.** 2:9,20; 3:4,14,27; 4:2; 8:11,19; 11:23,27; 12:2,9,14,25; 13:2,15,21,22; 14:14,19,22; 15:3,15–17,23,30; 16:8,16,19,20,29,32; 17:1,20,26; 18:5,22; 19:1,2,8,22; 20:23; 21:9,19; 22:1,9; 24:13,23,25; 25:7,24, 25,27; 27:5,10; 28:6,10,21; 31:12,18; **Eccl.** 2:1,3,24,26; 3:12,13,22; 4:3,6,8, 9,13; 5:5(4); 6:3,6,9,12; 7:1–3,5,8,10, 11,18,20,26; 8:12,13,15; 9:2,4,7,16; 11:6,7; 12:14; **Song** 1:2,3; 7:9(10); **Isa.** 5:9,20; 7:15,16; 38:3; 39:2,8; 41:7; 52:7; 55:2; 56:5; 65:2; **Jer.** 5:25; 6:16; 8:15; 14:19; 15:11; 17:6; 22:15,16; 24:2,3; 26:14; 29:10,32; 32:39; 33:11,14; 40:4; 42:6; 44:17; **Lam.** 3:25–27,38; 4:1,9; **Ezek.** 17:8; 18:18; 20:25; 24:4; 31:16; 34:14,18; 36:31; **Dan.** 1:4,15; **Hos.** 2:7(9); 4:13; 8:3; 10:1; 14:2(3); **Joel** 3:5(4:5); **Amos** 5:14,15; 6:2; 9:4; **Jon.** 4:3,8; **Mic.** 1:12; 3:2; 6:8; 7:4; **Nah.** 1:7; 3:4; **Zech.** 1:13,17; 8:19; **Mal.** 2:17.
III. טוֹבָה *ṭôḇāh,* טֹבָה *ṭōḇāh* **fem. adj.**
(good)
Gen. 44:4; 50:20; **Ex.** 18:9; **Num.** 24:13; **Deut.** 23:6(7); 28:11; 30:9; **Judg.** 8:35; 9:16; **1 Sam.** 24:17, 19(18,20); 25:21,30; **2 Sam.** 2:6; 7:28; 16:12; **2 Kgs.** 25:28; **1 Chr.** 17:26; **2 Chr.** 7:10; 24:16; **Ezra** 8:22; 9:12; **Neh.** 2:10,18; 5:19; 6:19; 13:31; **Job** 9:25; 21:25; 22:21; **Ps.** 16:2; 35:12; 38:20(21); 65:11(12); 68:10(11); 106:5; 109:5; **Prov.** 17:13; **Eccl.** 4:8; 5:11(10), 18(17); 6:3,6; 7:14; 9:18; **Jer.** 6:20; 12:6; 14:11; 18:10,20; 21:10; 24:5,6; 32:42; 33:9; 39:16; 44:27; 52:32; **Lam.** 3:17; **Amos** 9:4.

2897. טוֹב *ṭôḇ* **proper noun**
(Tob)
Judg. 11:3,5; **2 Sam.** 10:6(KJV, *'iyš ṭôḇ* [382]),8(KJV, *'iyš ṭôḇ* [382]).

2898. טוּב *ṭûḇ* **masc. noun**
(goodness, good things)
Gen. 24:10; 45:18,20,23; **Ex.** 33:19; **Deut.** 6:11; 28:47; **2 Kgs.** 8:9; **Ezra** 9:12; **Neh.** 9:25,35,36; **Job** 20:21; 21:16; **Ps.** 25:7; 27:13; 31:19(20); 65:4(5); 119:66; 128:5; 145:7; **Prov.** 11:10; **Isa.** 1:19; 63:7; 65:14; **Jer.** 2:7; 31:12,14; **Hos.** 3:5; 10:11; **Zech.** 9:17.

2899. טוֹב אֲדוֹנִיָּה *ṭôḇ 'aḏôniyyāh* **masc. proper noun**
(Tob-Adonijah)
2 Chr. 17:8.

2900. A. טוֹבִיָּה *ṭôḇiyyāh,* טוֹבִיָּהוּ *ṭôḇiyyāhû* **masc. proper noun**
(Tobijah: a Levite)
2 Chr. 17:8.
B. טוֹבִיָּה *ṭôḇiyyāh* **masc. proper noun**
(Tobiah: a Jew)
Ezra 2:60; **Neh.** 7:62.
C. טוֹבִיָּה *ṭôḇiyyāh* **masc. proper noun**
(Tobiah: an Ammonite)
Neh. 2:10,19; 4:3(3:35),7(1); 6:1,12,14, 17,19; 13:4,7,8.
D. טוֹבִיָּה *ṭôḇiyyāh,* טוֹבִיָּהוּ *ṭôḇiyyāhû* **masc. proper noun**
(Tobijah: Jewish leader)
Zech. 6:10,14.

2901. טָוָה *ṭāwāh* **verb**
(to spin [yarn])
Ex. 35:25,26.

2902. I. טוּחַ *ṭûaḥ* **verb**
(to daub, to plaster over)
Lev. 14:42,43,48; **1 Chr.** 29:4; **Isa.** 44:18 (NASB, NIV, see II); **Ezek.** 13:10–12,14,15; 22:28.
II. טָחַח *ṭāḥaḥ* **verb**
(to smear or spread over, to daub)
Isa. 44:18(KJV, see I).

2903. טוֹטָפוֹת *ṭôṭāp̄ôṯ* **fem. pl. noun**
(phylacteries, headbands, symbols)
Ex. 13:16; **Deut.** 6:8; 11:18.

2904. טוּל *ṭûl* **verb**
(to throw, to hurl)
1 Sam. 18:11; 20:33; **Job** 41:9(1); **Ps.** 37:24; **Prov.** 16:33; **Isa.** 22:17; **Jer.** 16:13; 22:26,28; **Ezek.** 32:4; **Jon.** 1:4,5,12,15.

2905. טוּר *ṭûr* **masc. noun**
(a row, course)
Ex. 28:17–20; 39:10–13; **1 Kgs.** 6:36; 7:2–4,12,18,20,24,42; **2 Chr.** 4:3,13; **Ezek.** 46:23.

2906. טוּר *ṭûr* **Aram. masc. noun**
(mountain; corr. to Hebr. 2905)
Dan. 2:35,45.

2907. טוּשׂ *ṭûś* **verb**
(to swoop, to dart)
Job 9:26.

2908. טְוָת *ṭ^ewāṯ* **Aram. adj.**
(fasting, going without eating)
Dan. 6:18(19).

2909. טָחָה *ṭāḥāh* **verb**
(to shoot with a bow, to be a bow-shot away)
Gen. 21:16.

2910. טֻחוֹת *ṭuḥôṯ* **fem. pl. noun**
(inward part, inner being)
Job 38:36; **Ps.** 51:6(8).

2911. טְחוֹן *ṭ^eḥôn* **masc. noun**
(mill, millstone)
Lam. 5:13.

2912. I. טָחַן *ṭaḥan* **verb**
(to crush, to grind, to mill)
Ex. 32:20; **Num.** 11:8; **Deut.** 9:21; **Judg.** 16:21; **Job** 31:10; **Eccl.** 12:3(NIV, see II); **Isa.** 3:15; 47:2.

II. טְחֳנָה *ṭōḥ*^a^*nāh* **fem. noun**
(molar, grinder)
Eccl. 12:3(KJV, NASB, see I).

2913. טַחֲנָה *ṭaḥ*^a^*nāh* **fem. noun**
(grinding mill, millstone)
Eccl. 12:4.

2914. טְחוֹר *ṭ*^e^*ḥôr* **masc. noun**
(tumor, hemorrhoid)
1 Sam. 6:11,17.

2915. טִיחַ *ṭiyaḥ* **masc. noun**
(coating, whitewash, plaster)
Ezek. 13:12.

2916. טִיט *ṭiyṭ* **masc. noun**
(mud, mire, clay)
2 Sam. 22:43; **Job** 41:30(22); **Ps.** 18:42(43); 40:2(3); 69:14(15); **Isa.** 41:25; 57:20; **Jer.** 38:6; **Mic.** 7:10; **Nah.** 3:14; **Zech.** 9:3; 10:5.

2917. טִין *ṭiyn* **Aram. masc. noun**
(clay)
Dan. 2:41,43.

2918. טִירָה *ṭiyrāh* **fem. noun**
(a camp, settlement)
Gen. 25:16; **Num.** 31:10; **1 Chr.** 6:54(39); **Ps.** 69:25(26); **Song** 8:9; **Ezek.** 25:4; 46:23.

2919. טַל *ṭal* **masc. noun**
(dew)
Gen. 27:28,39; **Ex.** 16:13,14; **Num.** 11:9; **Deut.** 32:2; 33:13,28; **Judg.** 6:37–40; **2 Sam.** 1:21; 17:12; **1 Kgs.** 17:1; **Job** 29:19; 38:28; **Ps.** 110:3; 133:3; **Prov.** 3:20; 19:12; **Song** 5:2; **Isa.** 18:4; 26:19; **Hos.** 6:4; 13:3; 14:5(6); **Mic.** 5:7(6); **Hag.** 1:10; **Zech.** 8:12.

2920. טַל *ṭal* **Aram. masc. noun**
(dew; corr. to Hebr. 2919)
Dan. 4:15(12),23(20),25(22),33(30); 5:21.

2921. טָלָא *ṭālāʾ* **verb**
(to be spotted, to be patched)
Gen. 30:32,33,35,39; **Josh.** 9:5; **Ezek.** 16:16.

2922. טְלָה *ṭ*^e^*lāh* **masc. pl. noun**
(lamb)
Isa. 40:11(NASB, *ṭāleh* [2924]).

2923. טְלָאִים *ṭ*^e^*lāʾiym* **proper noun**
(Telaim)
1 Sam. 15:4.

2924. טָלֶה *ṭāleh* **masc. noun**
(lamb)
1 Sam. 7:9; **Isa.** 40:11(KJV, NIV, *ṭ*^e^*lāh* [2922]); 65:25.

2925. טַלְטֵלָה *ṭalṭēlāh* **fem. noun**
(a hurling, captivity)
Isa. 22:17.

2926. טָלַל *ṭālal* **verb**
(to cover with a roof)
Neh. 3:15.

2927. טְלַל *ṭ*^e^*lal* **Aram. verb**
(to find shade, to find shelter; corr. to Hebr. 2926)
Dan. 4:12(9).

2928. A. טֶלֶם *ṭelem* **proper noun**
(Telem: a town in Judah)
Josh. 15:24.
B. טֶלֶם *ṭelem* **masc. proper noun**
(Telem: a gatekeeper)
Ezra 10:24.

2929. טַלְמוֹן *ṭalmôn*, טַלְמֹן *ṭalmōn* **masc. proper noun**
(Talmon)
1 Chr. 9:17; **Ezra** 2:42; **Neh.** 7:45; 11:19; 12:25.

2930. I. טָמֵא *ṭāmēʾ* **verb**
(to become unclean)
Gen. 34:5,13,27; **Lev.** 5:3; 11:24–28,

31–36,39,40,43,43,44; 12:2,5; 13:3,8,11, 14,15,20,22,25,27,30,44,46,59; 14:36,46; 15:4–11,16–24,27,31,32; 17:15; 18:20, 23–25,27,28,30; 19:31; 20:3,25; 21:1,3, 4,11; 22:5,6,8; **Num.** 5:3,13,14,20, 27–29; 6:7,9,12; 19:7,8,10,11,13,14, 16,20–22; 35:34; **Deut.** 21:23; 24:4; **2 Kgs.** 23:8,10,13,16; **2 Chr.** 36:14; **Ps.** 79:1; 106:39; **Isa.** 30:22; **Jer.** 2:7,23; 7:30; 32:34; **Ezek.** 4:14; 5:11; 9:7; 14:11; 18:6,11,15; 20:7,18,26,30,31,43; 22:3,4,11; 23:7,13,17,30,38; 33:26; 36:17,18; 37:23; 43:7,8; 44:25; **Hos.** 5:3; 6:10; 9:4; **Mic.** 2:10(NASB, see II); **Hag.** 2:13.
II. טָמְאָה *ṭām'āh* **fem. noun**
(uncleanness)
Mic. 2:10(KJV, NIV, see I).

2931. טָמֵא *ṭāmē'* **adj.**
(unclean, defiled)
Lev. 5:2; 7:19,21; 10:10; 11:4–8,26–29, 31,35,38,47; 13:11,15,36,44–46,51,55; 14:40,41,44,45,57; 15:2,25,26,33; 20:25; 22:4; 27:11,27; **Num.** 5:2; 9:6,7,10; 18:15; 19:13,15,17,19,20,22; **Deut.** 12:15,22; 14:7,8,10,19; 15:22; 26:14; **Josh.** 22:19; **Judg.** 13:4; **2 Chr.** 23:19; **Job** 14:4; **Eccl.** 9:2; **Isa.** 6:5; 35:8; 52:1,11; 64:6(5); **Jer.** 19:13; **Lam.** 4:15; **Ezek.** 4:13; 22:5,10,26; 44:23; **Hos.** 9:3; **Amos** 7:17; **Hag.** 2:13,14.

2932. טֻמְאָה *ṭum'āh* **fem. noun**
(uncleanness, filthiness)
Lev. 5:3; 7:20,21; 14:19; 15:3,25,26, 30,31; 16:16,19; 18:19; 22:3,5; **Num.** 5:19; 19:13; **Judg.** 13:7,14; **2 Sam.** 11:4; **2 Chr.** 29:16; **Ezra** 6:21; 9:11; **Lam.** 1:9; **Ezek.** 22:15; 24:11,13; 36:17,25,29; 39:24; **Zech.** 13:2.

2933. I. טָמָה *ṭāmāh* **verb**
(to be unclean)
Job 18:3(NASB, NIV, see II).
II. טָמָה *ṭāmāh* **verb**
(to be stupid)
Job 18:3(KJV, see I).

2934. טָמַן *ṭāman* **verb**
(to hide, to conceal, to bury)
Gen. 35:4; **Ex.** 2:12; **Deut.** 33:19; **Josh.** 2:6; 7:21,22; **2 Kgs.** 7:8; **Job** 3:16; 18:10; 20:26; 31:33; 40:13; **Ps.** 9:15(16); 31:4(5); 35:7,8; 64:5(6); 140:5(6); 142:3(4); **Prov.** 19:24; 26:15; **Isa.** 2:10; **Jer.** 13:4–7; 18:22; 43:9,10.

2935. טֶנֶא *ṭene'* **masc. noun**
(basket)
Deut. 26:2,4; 28:5,17.

2936. טָנַף *ṭānap̱* **verb**
(to defile, to make dirty)
Song 5:3.

2937. טָעָה *ṭā'āh* **verb**
(to lead astray, to seduce)
Ezek. 13:10.

2938. טָעַם *ṭā'am* **verb**
(to taste, to eat)
1 Sam. 14:24,29,43; **2 Sam.** 3:35; 19:35(36); **Job** 12:11; 34:3; **Ps.** 34:8(9); **Prov.** 31:18; **Jon.** 3:7.

2939. טְעֵם *ṭe'ēm* **Aram. verb**
(to feed, to cause to eat; corr. to Hebr. 2938)
Dan. 4:25(22),32(29); 5:21.

2940. טַעַם *ṭa'am* **masc. noun**
(one's taste, judgment)
Ex. 16:31; **Num.** 11:8; **1 Sam.** 21:13(14); 25:33; **Job** 6:6; 12:20; **Ps.** 34:[title](1); 119:66; **Prov.** 11:22; 26:16; **Jer.** 48:11; **Jon.** 3:7.

2941. טַעַם *ṭa'am* **Aram. masc. noun**
(a decree, command; NASB, NIV, *ṭe'ēm* [2942])
Ezra 4:21; 5:5; 6:14; 7:23; **Dan.** 6:2(3).

2942. טְעֵם *ṭe'ēm* **Aram. masc. noun**

(a decree, commandment)
Ezra 4:8,9,17,19,21(KJV, *ṭa'am* [2941]); 5:3,5(see *ṭa'am* [2941]),9,13,17; 6:1,3, 8,11,12,14(see *ṭa'am* [2941]); 7:13,21, 23(see *ṭa'am* [2941]); **Dan.** 2:14; 3:10, 12,29; 4:6(3); 5:2; 6:2(3)(see *ṭa'am* [2941]),13(14),26(27).

2943. טָעַן *ṭā'an* **verb**
(to load)
Gen. 45:17.

2944. טָעַן *ṭā'an* **verb**
(to pierce, to thrust through)
Isa. 14:19.

2945. טַף *ṭap̱* **masc. noun**
(child, little one)
Gen. 34:29; 43:8; 45:19; 46:5; 47:12,24; 50:8,21; **Ex.** 10:10,24; 12:37; **Num.** 14:3,31; 16:27; 31:9,17,18; 32:16,17, 24,26; **Deut.** 1:39; 2:34; 3:6,19; 20:14; 29:11(10); 31:12; **Josh.** 1:14; 8:35; **Judg.** 18:21; 21:10; **2 Sam.** 15:22; **2 Chr.** 20:13; 31:18; **Ezra** 8:21; **Esth.** 3:13; 8:11; **Jer.** 40:7; 41:16; 43:6; **Ezek.** 9:6.

2946. I. טָפַח *ṭāp̱aḥ* **verb**
(to spread out)
Isa. 48:13.
II. טָפַח *ṭāp̱aḥ* **verb**
(to care for, to nurse, to mother)
Lam. 2:22.

2947. I. טֶפַח *ṭep̱aḥ* **masc. noun**
(handbreadth)
1 Kgs. 7:26; **2 Chr.** 4:5.
II. טִפְחָה *ṭap̱ḥāh* **fem. noun**
(handbreadth)
Ps. 39:5(6).
III. טְפָחָה *ṭap̱ḥāh* **fem. noun**
(covering, coping, eave)
1 Kgs. 7:9.

2948. טֹפַח *ṭōp̱aḥ* **masc. noun**
(handbreadth)
Ex. 25:25; 37:12; **Ezek.** 40:5,43; 43:13.

2949. טִפֻּחִים *ṭippuḥiym* **masc. pl. noun**
(ones cared for)
Lam. 2:20.

2950. טָפַל *ṭāp̱al* **verb**
(to smear)
Job 13:4; 14:17; **Ps.** 119:69.

2951. טִפְסָר *ṭip̱sār* **masc. noun**
(commander, captain)
Jer. 51:27; **Nah.** 3:17.

2952. טָפַף *ṭāp̱ap̱* **verb**
(to trip along with quick little steps)
Isa. 3:16.

2953. טְפַר *ṭ^e^p̱ar* **Aram. masc. noun**
(fingernail, claw)
Dan. 4:33(30); 7:19.

2954. טָפַשׁ *ṭāp̱aš* **verb**
(to be fat, to be insensitive)
Ps. 119:70.

2955. טָפַת *ṭāp̱aṯ* **fem. proper noun**
(Taphath)
1 Kgs. 4:11.

2956. טָרַד *ṭāraḏ* **verb**
(to be continuous, to be constant)
Prov. 19:13; 27:15.

2957. טְרַד *ṭ^e^raḏ* **Aram. verb**
(to drive away, to chase away)
Dan. 4:25(22),32(29),33(30); 5:21.

2958. טְרוֹם *ṭ^e^rôm* **conj.**
(before)
Ruth 3:14(NASB, NIV, [Q^e^] *terem* [2962]).

2959. טָרַח *ṭāraḥ* **verb**
(to place a load)
Job 37:11.

2960. טֹרַח *ṭōraḥ* **masc. noun**
(a burden, load)
Deut. 1:12; **Isa.** 1:14.

2961. טָרִי *ṭāriy* **adj.**
(new, fresh)
Judg. 15:15; **Isa.** 1:6.

2962. טֶרֶם *ṭerem* **adv.**
(before)
Gen. 2:5; 19:4; 24:15,45; 27:4,33; 37:18; 41:50; 45:28; **Ex.** 1:19; 9:30; 10:7; 12:34; **Lev.** 14:36; **Num.** 11:33; **Deut.** 31:21; **Josh.** 2:8; 3:1; **Judg.** 14:18; **Ruth** 3:14(KJV, [Ke] *ṭerôm* [2958]); **1 Sam.** 2:15; 3:3,7; 9:13; **2 Kgs.** 2:9; 6:32; **Job** 10:21; **Ps.** 39:13; 58:9; 90:2; 119:67; **Prov.** 8:25; 18:13; 30:7; **Isa.** 7:16; 8:4; 17:14; 28:4; 42:9; 48:5; 65:24; 66:7; **Jer.** 1:5; 13:16; 38:10; 47:1; **Ezek.** 16:57; **Zeph.** 2:2; **Hag.** 2:15.

2963. טָרַף *ṭārap̱* **verb**
(to tear in pieces)
Gen. 37:33; 44:28; 49:27; **Ex.** 22:13(12); **Deut.** 33:20; **Job** 16:9; 18:4; **Ps.** 7:2(3); 17:12; 22:13(14); 50:22; **Prov.** 30:8; **Jer.** 5:6; **Ezek.** 19:3,6; 22:25,27; **Hos.** 5:14; 6:1; **Amos** 1:11; **Mic.** 5:8(7); **Nah.** 2:12(13).

2964. טֶרֶף *ṭerep̱* **masc. noun**
(prey, victim)
Gen. 49:9; **Num.** 23:24; **Job** 4:11; 24:5; 29:17; 38:39; **Ps.** 76:4(5); 104:21; 111:5; 124:6; **Prov.** 31:15; **Isa.** 5:29; 31:4; **Ezek.** 17:9(NIV, *ṭārāp̱* [2965]); 19:3,6; 22:25,27; **Amos** 3:4; **Nah.** 2:12(13), 13(14); 3:1; **Mal.** 3:10.

2965. טָרָף *ṭārāp̱* **adj.**
(freshly plucked, freshly picked, new)
Gen. 8:11; **Ezek.** 17:9(KJV, NASB, *ṭerep̱* [2964]).

2966. טְרֵפָה *ṭerēp̱āh* **fem. noun**
(that which is torn)
Gen. 31:39; **Ex.** 22:13(12),31(30); **Lev.** 7:24; 17:15; 22:8; **Ezek.** 4:14; 44:31; **Nah.** 2:12(13).

2967. טַרְפְּלָי *ṭarpelāy* **Aram. masc. proper noun**
(Tarpelites)
Ezra 4:9.

י Yodh

2968. יָאַב *yāʾab̲* **verb**
(to long for, to desire)
Ps. 119:131.

2969. יָאָה *yāʾāh* **verb**
(to pertain, to be fitting, to belong to)
Jer. 10:7.

2970. A. יַאֲזַנְיָהוּ *yaʾ^{a}zanyāhû* **masc. proper noun**
(Jaazaniah: a Maachathite)
2 Kgs. 25:23.
B. יַאֲזַנְיָה *yaʾ^{a}zanyāh* **masc. proper noun**
(Jaazaniah: a Rechabite)
Jer. 35:3.
C. יַאֲזַנְיָהוּ *yaʾ^{a}zanyāhû* **masc. proper noun**
(Jaazaniah: son of Shaphan)
Ezek. 8:11.
D. יַאֲזַנְיָה *yaʾ^{a}zanyāh* **masc. proper noun**
(Jaazaniah: son of Azur)
Ezek. 11:1.

2971. A. יָאִיר *yāʾiyr* **masc. proper noun**
(Jair: son of Manasseh and patronym of *hawwōt̲ yāʾiyr* [2334])
Num. 32:41(NIV, *hawwōt̲ yāʾiyr* [2334]); **Deut.** 3:14(NIV, *hawwōt̲ yāʾiyr* [2334]); **Josh.** 13:30(NIV, *hawwōt̲ yāʾiyr* [2334]); **Judg.** 10:4(NIV, *hawwōt̲ yāʾiyr* [2334]); **1 Kgs.** 4:13(NIV, *hawwōt̲ yāʾiyr* [2334]); **1 Chr.** 2:22,23(NIV, *hawwōt̲ yāʾiyr* [2334]).
B. יָאִיר *yāʾiyr* **masc. proper noun**
(Jair: judge in Gilead)
Judg. 10:3,5.
C. יָאִיר *yāʾiyr* **masc. proper noun**
(Jair: father of Mordecai)
Esth. 2:5.

2972. יָאִרִי *yāʾiriy* **masc. proper noun**
(Jairite)
2 Sam. 20:26.

2973. יָאַל *yāʾal* **verb**
(to be foolish, to act foolishly)
Num. 12:11; **Isa.** 19:13; **Jer.** 5:4; 50:36.

2974. יָאַל *yāʾal* **verb**
(to be willing, to be pleased, to undertake)
Gen. 18:27,31; **Ex.** 2:21; **Deut.** 1:5; **Josh.** 7:7; 17:12; **Judg.** 1:27,35; 17:11; 19:6; **1 Sam.** 12:22; 17:39; **2 Sam.** 7:29; **2 Kgs.** 5:23; 6:3; **1 Chr.** 17:27; **Job** 6:9,28; **Hos.** 5:11.

2975. יְאֹר *y^{e}ʾōr*, יְאוֹר *y^{e}ʾôr* **masc. noun**
(river, esp. the Nile River)
Gen. 41:1–3,17,18; **Ex.** 1:22; 2:3,5; 4:9; 7:15,17–21,24,25; 8:3(7:28),5(1),9(5), 11(7); 17:5; **2 Kgs.** 19:24; **Job** 28:10; **Ps.** 78:44; **Isa.** 7:18; 19:6–8; 23:3,10; 33:21; 37:25; **Jer.** 46:7,8; **Ezek.** 29:3–5,9,10; 30:12; **Dan.** 12:5–7; **Amos** 8:8; 9:5; **Nah.** 3:8; **Zech.** 10:11.

2976. יָאַשׁ *yāʾaš* **verb**
(to despair, to be hopeless)
1 Sam. 27:1; **Job** 6:26; **Eccl.** 2:20; **Isa.** 57:10; **Jer.** 2:25; 18:12.

2977. A. יֹאשִׁיָּהוּ *yōʾšiyyāhû*, יוֹאשִׁיָּהוּ *yôʾšiyyāhû* **masc. proper noun**
(Josiah: son of Amon)
1 Kgs. 13:2; **2 Kgs.** 21:24,26; 22:1,3; 23:16,19,23,24,28–30,34; **1 Chr.** 3:14,15; **2 Chr.** 33:25; 34:1,33; 35:1,7,16,18–20, 22–26; 36:1; **Jer.** 1:2,3; 3:6; 22:11,18; 25:1,3; 26:1; 27:1; 35:1; 36:1,2,9; 37:1; 45:1; 46:2; **Zeph.** 1:1.

B. יֹאשִׁיָּה *yō'šiyyāh* **masc. proper noun**
(Josiah: an exile)
Zech. 6:10.

2978. I. יִאתוֹן *yi'tôn* **masc. noun**
(entrance)
Ezek. 40:15(NASB, NIV, [Q[e]] see II).
II. אִיתוֹן *'iyṯôn* **masc. noun**
(entrance)
Ezek. 40:15(KJV, [K[e]] see I).

2979. יְאָתְרַי *y[e]'āṯray* **masc. proper noun**
(Jeatherai)
1 Chr. 6:21(6).

2980. יָבַב *yāḇaḇ* **verb**
(to cry, to lament)
Judg. 5:28.

2981. יְבוּל *y[e]ḇûl* **masc. noun**
(crop, produce)
Lev. 26:4,20; **Deut.** 11:17; 32:22; **Judg.** 6:4; **Job** 20:28; **Ps.** 67:6(7); 78:46; 85:12(13); **Ezek.** 34:27; **Hab.** 3:17; **Hag.** 1:10; **Zech.** 8:12.

2982. יְבוּס *y[e]ḇûs* **proper noun**
(Jebus)
Judg. 19:10,11; **1 Chr.** 11:4,5.

2983. יְבוּסִי *y[e]ḇûsiy,* יְבֻסִי *y[e]ḇusiy* **masc. proper noun**
(Jebusite)
Gen. 10:16; 15:21; **Ex.** 3:8,17; 13:5; 23:23; 33:2; 34:11; **Num.** 13:29; **Deut.** 7:1; 20:17; **Josh.** 3:10; 9:1; 11:3; 12:8; 15:8,63; 18:16,28; 24:11; **Judg.** 1:21; 3:5; 19:11; **2 Sam.** 5:6,8; 24:16,18; **1 Kgs.** 9:20; **1 Chr.** 1:14; 11:4,6; 21:15,18,28; **2 Chr.** 3:1; 8:7; **Ezra** 9:1; **Neh.** 9:8; **Zech.** 9:7.

2984. יִבְחָר *yiḇḥār* **masc. proper noun**
(Ibhar)
2 Sam. 5:15; **1 Chr.** 3:6; 14:5.

2985. A. יָבִין *yāḇiyn* **masc. proper noun**
(Jabin: king of Hazor)
Josh. 11:1.
B. יָבִין *yāḇiyn* **masc. proper noun**
(Jabin: king of Hazor)
Judg. 4:2,7,17,23,24; **Ps.** 83:9(10).

2986. יָבַל *yāḇal* **verb**
(to bring, to carry, to bear along)
Job 10:19; 21:30,32; **Ps.** 45:14(15), 15(16); 60:9(11); 68:29(30); 76:11(12); 108:10(11); **Isa.** 18:7; 23:7; 53:7; 55:12; **Jer.** 11:19; 31:9; **Hos.** 10:6; 12:1(2); **Zeph.** 3:10.

2987. יְבַל *y[e]ḇal* **Aram. verb**
(to bring, to carry; corr. to Hebr. 2986)
Ezra 5:14; 6:5; 7:15.

2988. יָבָל *yāḇāl* **masc. noun**
(stream, river)
Isa. 30:25; 44:4.

2989. יָבָל *yāḇāl* **masc. proper noun**
(Jabal)
Gen. 4:20.

2990. I. יַבֶּלֶת *yabbeleṯ* **adj.**
(running, discharging pus)
Lev. 22:22(NIV, see II).
II. יַבֶּלֶת *yabbeleṯ* **fem. noun**
(something with warts)
Lev. 22:22(KJV, NASB, see I).

2991. יִבְלְעָם *yiḇl[e]'ām* **proper noun**
(Ibleam)
Josh. 17:11; **Judg.** 1:27; **2 Kgs.** 9:27.

2992. יָבַם *yāḇam* **verb**
(to marry, to perform one's duty in a levirate marriage)
Gen. 38:8; **Deut.** 25:5,7.

2993. יָבָם *yāḇām* **masc. noun**
(brother-in-law, husband's brother)
Deut. 25:5,7.

2994. יְבָמָה *y^eḇāmāh* **fem. noun**
(sister-in-law, brother's wife)
Deut. 25:7,9; **Ruth** 1:15.

2995. A. יַבְנְאֵל *yaḇn^e'ēl* **proper noun**
(Jabneel: a town in Judah)
Josh. 15:11.
B. יַבְנְאֵל *yaḇn^e'ēl* **proper noun**
(Jabneel: a town in Naphtali)
Josh. 19:33.

2996. יַבְנֶה *yaḇneh* **proper noun**
(Jabneh)
2 Chr. 26:6.

2997. יִבְנְיָה *yiḇn^eyāh* **masc. proper noun**
(Ibneiah)
1 Chr. 9:8.

2998. יִבְנִיָּה *yiḇniyyāh* **masc. proper noun**
(Ibnijah)
1 Chr. 9:8.

2999. יַבֹּק *yabbōq* **proper noun**
(Jabbok)
Gen. 32:22(23); **Num.** 21:24; **Deut.** 2:37; 3:16; **Josh.** 12:2; **Judg.** 11:13,22.

3000. יְבֶרֶכְיָהוּ *y^eḇereḵyāhû* **masc. proper noun**
(Jeberechiah)
Isa. 8:2.

3001. I. יָבַשׁ *yāḇaš* **verb**
(to be confounded, to put to shame; NASB, NIV, hiph. of *bôš* [954])
2 Sam. 19:5(6); **Jer.** 2:26; 6:15; 8:9,12; 10:14; 46:24; 48:1,20; 50:2; 51:17; **Hos.** 2:5(7); **Joel** 1:11; **Zech.** 9:5; 10:5.

II. יָבֵשׁ *yāḇēš* **verb**
(to wither)
Gen. 8:7,14; **Josh.** 2:10; 4:23; 5:1; 9:5,12; **1 Kgs.** 13:4; 17:7; **Job** 8:12; 12:15; 14:11; 15:30; 18:16; **Ps.** 22:15(16); 74:15; 90:6; 102:4(5),11(12); 129:6; **Prov.** 17:22; **Isa.** 15:6; 19:5,7; 27:11; 40:7,8,24; 42:15; 44:27; **Jer.** 12:4; 23:10; 50:38; 51:36; **Lam.** 4:8; **Ezek.** 17:9, 10,24; 19:12; 37:11; **Hos.** 9:16; **Joel** 1:10,12,17,20; **Amos** 1:2; 4:7; **Jon.** 4:7; **Nah.** 1:4; **Zech.** 10:11; 11:17.

3002. יָבֵשׁ *yāḇēš* **adj.**
(dry, dried)
Num. 6:3; 11:6; **Job** 13:25; **Isa.** 56:3; **Ezek.** 17:24; 20:47(21:3); 37:2,4; **Nah.** 1:10.

3003. A. יָבֵשׁ *yāḇēš* **proper noun**
(Jabesh: city in Gilead)
Judg. 21:8–10,12,14; **1 Sam.** 11:1,3,5,9,10; 31:11–13; **1 Chr.** 10:11,12.
B. יָבֵשׁ *yāḇēš* **masc. proper noun**
(Jabesh: father of Shallum)
2 Kgs. 15:10,13,14.

3004. יַבָּשָׁה *yabbāšāh* **fem. noun**
(dry ground, dry land)
Gen. 1:9,10; **Ex.** 4:9; 14:16,22,29; 15:19; **Josh.** 4:22; **Neh.** 9:11; **Ps.** 66:6; **Isa.** 44:3; **Jon.** 1:9,13; 2:10(11).

3005. יִבְשָׂם *yiḇśām* **masc. proper noun**
(Ibsam, Jibsam)
1 Chr. 7:2.

3006. יַבֶּשֶׁת *yabbešeṯ* **fem. noun**
(dry land)
Ex. 4:9; **Ps.** 95:5.

3007. יַבֶּשֶׁת *yabbešeṯ* **Aram. fem. noun**
(earth [as a planet]; corr. to Hebr. 3006)
Dan. 2:10.

3008. A. יִגְאָל *yig'āl* **masc. proper noun**
(Igal: one of the twelve spies)
Num. 13:7.
B. יִגְאָל *yig'āl* **masc. proper noun**
(Igal: one of David's mighty men)
2 Sam. 23:36.
C. יִגְאָל *yig'āl* **masc. proper noun**
(Igal: descendant of Zerubbabel)
1 Chr. 3:22.

3009. יָגַב *yāgab̲* **verb**
(to plow the earth, to be a husbandman)
2 Kgs. 25:12(KJV, [Qe] *gûb̲* [1461]); **Jer.** 52:16.

3010. יָגֵב *yagēb̲* **masc. noun**
(field)
Jer. 39:10.

3011. יָגְבְּהָה *yogbᵉhāh* **proper noun**
(Jogbehah)
Num. 32:35; **Judg.** 8:11.

3012. יִגְדַּלְיָהוּ *yigdalyāhû* **masc. proper noun**
(Igdaliah)
Jer. 35:4.

3013. I. יָגָה *yāgāh* **verb**
(to afflict; to suffer)
Job 19:2; **Isa.** 51:23; **Lam.** 1:4,5,12; 3:32,33; **Zeph.** 3:18(NIV, see II).
II. נוּג *nûg* **masc. noun**
(sorrow, grief)
Zeph. 3:18(KJV, NASB, see I).

3014. יָגָה *yāgāh* **verb**
(to push away, to remove)
2 Sam. 20:13.

3015. יָגוֹן *yāgôn* **masc. noun**
(sorrow, grief)
Gen. 42:38; 44:31; **Esth.** 9:22; **Ps.** 13:2(3); 31:10(11); 107:39; 116:3; **Isa.** 35:10; 51:11; **Jer.** 8:18; 20:18; 31:13; 45:3; **Ezek.** 23:33.

3016. יָגוֹר *yāgôr* **adj.**
(fearful, feared)
Jer. 22:25; 39:17.

3017. יָגוּר *yāgûr* **proper noun**
(Jagur)
Josh. 15:21.

3018. יְגִיעַ *yᵉgiya'* **masc. noun**
(labor, fruit of labor)
Gen. 31:42; **Deut.** 28:33; **Neh.** 5:13; **Job** 10:3; 39:11,16; **Ps.** 78:46; 109:11; 128:2; **Isa.** 45:14; 55:2; **Jer.** 3:24; 20:5; **Ezek.** 23:29; **Hos.** 12:8(9); **Hag.** 1:11.

3019. יָגִיעַ *yāgiya'* **adj.**
(weary, tired)
Job 3:17.

3020. יָגְלִי *yogliy* **masc. proper noun**
(Jogli)
Num. 34:22.

3021. יָגַע *yāga'* **verb**
(to work, to become weary with work)
Josh. 7:3; 24:13; **2 Sam.** 23:10; **Job** 9:29; **Ps.** 6:6(7); 69:3(4); **Prov.** 23:4; **Eccl.** 10:15; **Isa.** 40:28,30,31; 43:22–24; 47:12,15; 49:4; 57:10; 62:8; 65:23; **Jer.** 45:3; 51:58; **Lam.** 5:5; **Hab.** 2:13; **Mal.** 2:17.

3022. יָגָע *yāgā'* **masc. noun**
(earnings, product of labor)
Job 20:18.

3023. יָגֵעַ *yāgēa'* **adj.**
(weary, tired)
Deut. 25:18; **2 Sam.** 17:2; **Eccl.** 1:8.

3024. יְגִיעָה *yᵉgiy'āh* **fem. noun**
(weariness)
Eccl. 12:12.

3025. יָגֹר *yāḡōr* **verb**
(to fear, to be afraid)
Deut. 9:19; 28:60; **Job** 3:25; 9:28; **Ps.** 119:39.

3026. יְגַר שָׂהֲדוּתָא *y^{e}gar śāh^{a}ḏûṯā'* **Aram. proper noun**
(Jegar Sahadutha)
Gen. 31:47.

3027. A. יָד *yāḏ* **masc./fem. noun**
(hand)
Gen. 3:22; 4:11; 5:29; 8:9; 9:2,5; 14:20,22; 16:6,9,12; 19:10,16; 21:18,30; 22:6,10,12; 24:2,9,10,18,22,30,47; 25:26; 27:16,17, 22,23; 30:35; 31:29,39; 32:11(12),13(14), 16(17); 33:10,19; 34:21; 35:4; 37:21,22,27; 38:18,20,28–30; 39:1,3,4,6,8,12,13,22,23; 40:11,13; 41:35,42,44; 42:37; 43:9,12,15, 21,22,26,34; 44:16,17; 46:4; 47:24,29; 48:14,17,22; 49:8,24; **Ex.** 2:5,19; 3:8, 19,20; 4:2,4,6,7,13,17,20,21; 5:21; 6:1,8; 7:4,5,15,17,19; 8:5(1),6(2),17(13); 9:3, 15,22,35; 10:12,21,22,25; 12:11; 13:3,9, 14,16; 14:8,16,21,26,27,30,31; 15:9, 17,20; 16:3; 17:5,9,11,12,16; 18:9,10; 19:13; 21:13,16,20,24; 22:4(3),8(7), 11(10); 23:1,31; 24:11; 26:17,19; 28:41; 29:9,10,15,19,20,25,29,33,35; 30:19,21; 32:4,11,15,19,29; 34:4,29; 35:25,29; 36:22,24; 38:21; 40:31; **Lev.** 1:4; 3:2, 8,13; 4:4,15,24,29,33; 5:7,11; 6:2(5:21); 7:30; 8:14,18,22–24,33,36; 9:22; 10:11; 12:8; 14:14,17,21,22,25,28,30–32; 15:11; 16:21,32; 21:10,19; 22:25; 24:14; 25:14, 26,28,35,47,49; 26:25,46; 27:8; **Num.** 2:17; 3:3; 4:28,33,37,45,49; 5:18,25; 6:21; 7:8; 8:10,12; 9:23; 10:13; 11:23; 13:29; 14:30; 15:23,30; 16:40(17:5); 20:11,20; 21:2,26,34; 22:7,23,29,31; 24:24; 25:7; 27:18,23; 31:6,49; 33:1,3; 34:3; 35:17,18,21,25; 36:13; **Deut.** 1:25,27; 2:7,15,24,30,37; 3:2,3,8,24; 4:28,34; 5:15; 6:8,21; 7:8,19,24; 8:17; 9:15,17,26; 10:3; 11:2,18; 12:6,7,11, 17,18; 13:9(10),17(18); 14:25,29; 15:2,3, 7,8,10,11; 16:10,15,17; 17:7; 19:5,12,21; 20:13; 21:6,7,10; 23:12(13),20(21),25(26); 24:1,3,19; 25:11; 26:4,8; 27:15; 28:8,12, 20,32; 30:9; 31:29; 32:27,36,39–41; 33:3, 7,11; 34:9,12; **Josh.** 2:19,24; 4:24; 5:13; 6:2; 7:7; 8:1,7,18–20,26; 9:11,25,26; 10:6,8,19,30,32; 11:8; 14:2; 15:46; 20:2, 5,9; 21:2,8,44(42); 22:9,31; 24:8,10,11; **Judg.** 1:2,4,6,7,35; 2:14–16,18,23; 3:4, 8,10,15,21,28,30; 4:2,7,9,14,21,24; 5:26; 6:1,2,9,21,36,37; 7:2,6–9,11,14–16,19,20; 8:3,6,7,15,22,34; 9:16,17,24,29,33,48; 10:7,12; 11:21,26,30,32; 12:2,3; 13:1, 5,23; 14:6; 15:12–15,17,18; 16:18,23, 24,26; 17:3,5,12; 18:10,19; 19:27; 20:16,28; **Ruth** 1:13; 4:5,9; **1 Sam.** 2:13; 4:8,13(KJV, [K^{e}] *yaḵ* [3197]),18; 5:4,6,7, 9,11; 6:3,5,9; 7:3,8,13,14; 9:8,16; 10:4, 7,18; 11:7; 12:3–5,9–11,15; 13:22; 14:10, 12,13,19,26,27,34,37,43,48; 15:12; 16:2, 16,20,23; 17:22,37,40,46,47,49,50,57; 18:10,17,21,25; 19:3,9; 20:16; 21:3(4), 4(5),8(9),13(14); 22:6,17; 23:4,6,7,11,12, 14,16,17,20; 24:4(5),6(7),10–13(11–14), 15(16),18(19),20(21); 25:8,26,33,35,39; 26:8,9,11,18,23; 27:1; 28:15,17,19; 30:15,23; **2 Sam.** 1:14; 2:7; 3:8,12,18,34; 4:1,11,12; 5:19; 8:1,3,10; 10:2,10; 11:14; 12:7,25; 13:5,6,10,19; 14:19,30; 15:2,5, 18,36; 16:8,21; 17:2; 18:2,4,12,18(see B),19,28,31; 19:43(44); 20:9,10,21; 21:9, 20,22; 22:21,35; 23:6,10,21; 24:14,16,17; **1 Kgs.** 2:25,46; 7:32,33,35,36; 8:15,24, 42,53,56; 10:13,19,29; 11:12,26,27,31, 34,35; 12:15; 13:4,6,33; 14:3,18,27; 15:18,29; 16:7,12,34; 17:11,16; 18:9,46; 20:6,13,28,42; 22:3,6,12,15,34; **2 Kgs.** 3:10,11,13,15,18; 4:29; 5:5,11,18,20,24; 6:7; 7:2,17; 8:8,9,20,22; 9:1,7,23,24, 35,36; 10:10,15,24; 11:7,8,11,16; 12:11(12),15(16); 13:3,5,16,25; 14:5, 25,27; 15:19; 17:7,13,20,23,39; 18:29, 30,33–35; 19:10,14,18,19,23,26; 21:10, 14; 22:5,7,9,17; 24:2; **1 Chr.** 4:10,40; 5:10,20; 6:15(5:41),31(16); 7:29; 11:3,23; 13:9,10; 14:10,11; 16:7; 18:1,3,17; 19:11; 20:8; 21:13,15–17; 22:18; 23:28; 24:19; 25:2,3,6; 26:28; 28:19; 29:5,8,12,14,

16,24; **2 Chr.** 1:17; 6:4,15,32; 7:6; 8:18; 9:18; 10:15; 12:5,7,10; 13:8,9,16; 15:7; 16:7,8; 17:5,15,16,18; 18:5,11,14,33; 20:6; 21:8,10,16; 23:7,10,15,18; 24:11, 13,24; 25:15,20; 26:11,13,19; 28:5,9; 29:23,25,27,31; 30:6,8,12,16; 31:13,15; 32:13–15,17,19,22; 33:8; 34:9,10,14,16, 17,25; 35:6,11; 36:15,17; **Ezra** 1:6,8; 3:10; 4:4; 6:22; 7:6,9,28; 8:18,22,26,31, 33; 9:2,7,11; 10:19; **Neh.** 1:10; 2:8,18; 3:2,4,5,7–10,12,17,19; 4:17(11); 5:5; 6:5,9; 7:4; 8:6,14; 9:14,15,24,27,28,30; 10:29(30),31(32); 11:1,24; 13:13,21; **Esth.** 1:7,12,15; 2:3,8,14,18,21; 3:6,9, 10,13; 5:2; 6:2,9; 8:7,10; 9:2,10,15,16; **Job** 1:10–12,14; 2:5,6; 4:3; 5:12,15, 18,20; 6:9,23; 8:4,20; 9:24,33; 10:7,8; 11:14; 12:6,9,10; 14:15; 15:23,25; 16:11; 17:3,9; 19:21; 20:10,22; 21:5,16; 23:2; 26:13; 27:11,22; 28:9; 29:20; 30:2,21,24; 31:21,25,27; 34:19,20; 35:7; 37:7; 40:4; **Ps.** 8:6(7); 10:12,14; 17:14; 18:[title](1), 20(21),24(25),34(35); 19:1(2); 21:8(9); 22:16(17),20(21); 26:10; 28:2,4,5; 31:5(6),8(9),15(16); 32:4; 36:11(12); 37:24,33; 38:2(3); 39:10(11); 44:2(3); 49:15(16); 55:20(21); 58:2(3); 63:10(11); 68:31(32); 71:4; 73:23; 74:11; 75:8(9); 76:5(6); 77:2(3),20(21); 78:42,61; 80:17(18); 81:14(15); 82:4; 88:5(6); 89:13(14),21(22),25(26),48(49); 90:17; 92:4(5); 95:4,5,7; 97:10; 102:25(26); 104:25,28; 106:10,26,41,42; 107:2; 109:27; 111:7; 115:4,7; 119:73,173; 121:5; 123:2; 125:3; 127:4; 134:2; 135:15; 136:12; 138:7,8; 139:10; 140:4(5), 5(6); 141:6,9; 143:5,6; 144:1,7,11; 145:16; 149:6; **Prov.** 1:24; 3:27; 6:5,10,17; 7:20; 8:3; 10:4; 11:21; 12:14,24; 13:11; 14:1; 16:5; 17:16; 18:21; 19:24; 21:1,25; 24:33; 26:6,9,15; 30:28,32; 31:19,20,31; **Eccl.** 2:11,24; 4:1,5; 5:6(5),14(13),15(14); 7:18,26; 9:1,10; 10:18; 11:6; **Song** 5:4,5,14; 7:1(2); **Isa.** 1:12,15,25; 2:8; 3:6,11; 5:12,25; 6:6; 8:11; 9:12(11), 17(16),21(20); 10:4,5,10,13,14,32; 11:8,11,14,15; 13:2,7; 14:26,27; 17:8; 19:4,16,25; 20:2; 22:18,21; 23:11; 25:10,11; 26:11; 28:2; 29:23; 31:3,7; 33:21; 34:17; 35:3; 36:15,18–20; 37:10, 14,19,20,24,27; 40:2; 41:20; 42:6; 43:13; 44:5; 45:9,11,12; 47:6,14; 48:13; 49:2,22; 50:2,11; 51:16–18,22,23; 53:10; 56:2,5; 57:8,10; 59:1; 60:21; 62:3; 64:7(6),8(7); 65:2,22; 66:2,14; **Jer.** 1:9,16; 2:37; 5:31; 6:3,9,12,24; 10:3,9; 11:21; 15:6,17,21; 16:21; 18:4,6,21; 19:7; 20:4,5,13; 21:4, 5,7,10,12; 22:3,24,25; 23:14; 25:6,7,14, 15,17,28; 26:14,24; 27:3,6,8; 29:3,21; 30:6; 31:11,32; 32:3,4,21,24,25,28,30, 36,43; 33:13; 34:1–3,20,21; 36:14; 37:2, 17; 38:3–5,10–12,16,18,19,23; 39:11,17; 40:4; 41:5,9; 42:11; 43:3,9; 44:8,25,30; 46:6,24,26; 47:3; 48:37; 50:1,15,43; 51:7,25; **Lam.** 1:7,10,14,17; 2:7,8; 3:3,64; 4:2,6,10; 5:6,8,12; **Ezek.** 1:3,8; 2:9; 3:14,18,20,22; 6:14; 7:17,21,27; 8:1,3,11; 9:1,2; 10:7,8,12,21; 11:9; 12:7; 13:9,18,21–23; 14:9,13; 16:11,27,39,49; 17:18; 18:8,17; 20:5,6,15,22,23,28,33, 34,42; 21:7(12),11(16),19(24),31(36); 22:14; 23:9,28,31,37,42,45; 25:6,7,13, 14,16; 27:15,21; 28:9,10; 30:10,12,22, 24,25; 31:11; 33:6,8,22; 34:10,27; 35:3,5; 36:7; 37:1,17,19,20; 38:12,17; 39:3,9,21, 23; 40:1,3,5; 43:26; 44:12; 46:5,7,11; 47:3,14; 48:1; **Dan.** 1:2,20; 8:4,7,25; 9:10,15; 10:4,10; 11:11,16,41,42; 12:7; **Hos.** 2:10(12); 7:5; 12:7(8),10(11); 13:14; 14:3(4); **Joel** 3:8(4:8); **Amos** 1:8; 5:19; 7:7; 9:2; **Mic.** 2:1; 5:9(8),12(11), 13(12); 7:16; **Hab.** 3:4,10; **Zeph.** 1:4; 2:13,15; 3:16; **Hag.** 1:1,3; 2:1,14,17; **Zech.** 2:1(5),9(13); 4:9,10,12; 7:7,12; 8:4,9,13; 11:6; 13:6,7; 14:13; **Mal.** 1:1,9,10,13; 2:13.

B. יַד אַבְשָׁלוֹם *yaḏ 'aḇšālôm* **masc. proper noun**
(Monument of Absalom: name of a pillar combining *yaḏ* [3027] and *'aḇšālôm* [53])
2 Sam. 18:18.

3028. יַד *yaḏ* **Aram. com. noun**
(hand, power; corr. to Hebr. 3027)
Ezra 5:8,12; 6:12; 7:14,25; **Dan.** 2:34, 38,45; 3:15,17; 4:35(32); 5:5,23,24; 6:27(28); 7:25.

3029. יְדָא *y*^{e}*ḏā'* **Aram. verb**
(to give thanks; corr. to Hebr. 3034,II)
Dan. 2:23; 6:10(11).

3030. יִדְאֲלָה *yiḏ'*^{a}*lāh* **proper noun**
(Idalah)
Josh. 19:15.

3031. יִדְבָּשׁ *yiḏbāš* **masc. proper noun**
(Idbash)
1 Chr. 4:3.

3032. יָדַד *yāḏaḏ* **verb**
(to cast lots)
Joel 3:3(4:3); **Obad.** 1:11; **Nah.** 3:10.

3033. יְדִדוּת *y*^{e}*ḏiḏûṯ* **fem. noun**
(one dearly loved, object of love)
Jer. 12:7.

3034. I. יָדָה *yāḏāh* **verb**
(to shoot, to throw)
Jer. 50:14; **Lam.** 3:53; **Zech.** 1:21(2:4).
II. יָדָה *yāḏāh* **verb**
(to praise, to confess)
Gen. 29:35; 49:8; **Lev.** 5:5; 16:21; 26:40; **Num.** 5:7; **2 Sam.** 22:50; **1 Kgs.** 8:33,35; **1 Chr.** 16:4,7,8,34,35,41; 23:30; 25:3; 29:13; **2 Chr.** 5:13; 6:24,26; 7:3,6; 20:21; 30:22; 31:2; **Ezra** 3:11; 10:1; **Neh.** 1:6; 9:2,3; 11:17; 12:24,46; **Job** 40:14; **Ps.** 6:5(6); 7:17(18); 9:1(2); 18:49(50); 28:7; 30:4(5),9(10),12(13); 32:5; 33:2; 35:18; 42:5(6),11(12); 43:4,5; 44:8(9); 45:17(18); 49:18(19); 52:9(11); 54:6(8); 57:9(10); 67:3(4),5(6); 71:22; 75:1(2); 76:10(11); 79:13; 86:12; 88:10(11); 89:5(6); 92:1(2); 97:12; 99:3; 100:4; 105:1; 106:1,47; 107:1,8,15,21,31; 108:3(4); 109:30; 111:1; 118:1,19,21,28,29; 119:7,62; 122:4; 136:1–3,26; 138:1,2,4; 139:14; 140:13(14); 142:7(8); 145:10; **Prov.** 28:13; **Isa.** 12:1,4; 25:1; 38:18,19; **Jer.** 33:11; **Dan.** 9:4,20.

3035. A. יִדּוֹ *yiddô* **masc. proper noun**
(Iddo: a Manassite)
1 Chr. 27:21.
B. יִדּוֹ *yiddô* **masc. proper noun**
(Iddo: a Jew; alternate reading for Jaddai)
Ezra 10:43.

3036. יָדוֹן *yāḏôn* **masc. proper noun**
(Jadon)
Neh. 3:7.

3037. A. יַדּוּעַ *yaddûa'* **masc. proper noun**
(Jaddua: Jewish leader)
Neh. 10:21(22).
B. יַדּוּעַ *yaddûa'* **masc. proper noun**
(Jaddua: son of Jonathan the high priest)
Neh. 12:11,22.

3038. יְדוּתוּן *y*^{e}*ḏûṯûn*, יְדֻתוּן *y*^{e}*ḏûṯûn* **masc. proper noun**
(Jeduthun)
1 Chr. 9:16; 16:38,41,42; 25:1,3,6; **2 Chr.** 5:12; 29:14; 35:15; **Neh.** 11:17; **Ps.** 39:[title](1); 62:[title](1); 77:[title](1).

3039. I. יָדִיד *yāḏiyḏ* **adj.**
(beloved, lovely)
Deut. 33:12; **Ps.** 45:[title](1)(NIV, see II); 60:5(7); 84:1(2); 108:6(7); 127:2; **Isa.** 5:1; **Jer.** 11:15.
II. יְדִידוֹת *y*^{e}*ḏiyḏôṯ* **fem. pl. noun**
(marriage, loves)
Ps. 45:[title](1)(KJV, NASB, see I).

3040. יְדִידָה y^e*<u>d</u>iy<u>d</u>āh* **fem. proper noun**
(Jedidah)
2 Kgs. 22:1.

3041. יְדִידְיָהּ y^e*<u>d</u>iy<u>d</u>yāh* **masc. proper noun**
(Jedidiah)
2 Sam. 12:25.

3042. A. יְדָיָה y^e*<u>d</u>āyāh* **masc. proper noun**
(Jedaiah: son of Shimri)
1 Chr. 4:37.
B. יְדָיָה y^e*<u>d</u>āyāh* **masc. proper noun**
(Jedaiah: son of Harumaph)
Neh. 3:10.

3043. A. יְדִיעֲאֵל y^e*<u>d</u>iy'a'ēl* **masc. proper noun**
(Jediael: son of Benjamin)
1 Chr. 7:6,10,11.
B. יְדִיעֲאֵל y^e*<u>d</u>iy'a'ēl* **masc. proper noun**
(Jediael: son of Shimri)
1 Chr. 11:45.
C. יְדִיעֲאֵל y^e*<u>d</u>iy'a'ēl* **masc. proper noun**
(Jediael: a Manassehite)
1 Chr. 12:20.
D. יְדִיעֲאֵל y^e*<u>d</u>iy'a'ēl* **masc. proper noun**
(Jediael: a Korahite)
1 Chr. 26:2.

3044. יִדְלָף *yi<u>d</u>lā<u>p</u>* **masc. proper noun**
(Jidlaph)
Gen. 22:22.

3045. יָדַע *yā<u>d</u>a'* **verb**
(to know, to perceive, to understand)
Gen. 3:5,7,22; 4:1,9,17,25; 8:11; 9:24; 12:11; 15:8,13; 18:19,21; 19:5,8,33,35; 20:6,7; 21:26; 22:12; 24:14,16,21; 25:27; 27:2; 28:16; 29:5; 30:26,29; 31:6,32; 33:13; 38:9,16,26; 39:6,8; 41:21,31,39; 42:23,33,34; 43:7,22; 44:15,27; 45:1; 47:6; 48:19; **Ex.** 1:8; 2:4,14,25; 3:7,19; 4:14; 5:2; 6:3,7; 7:5,17; 8:10(6),22(18); 9:14,29,30; 10:2,7,26; 11:7; 14:4,18; 16:6,12,15; 18:11,16,20; 21:36; 23:9; 29:46; 31:13; 32:1,22,23; 33:5,12,13, 16,17; 34:29; 36:1; **Lev.** 4:14,23,28; 5:1,3,4,17,18; 23:43; **Num.** 10:31; 11:16; 12:6; 14:31,34; 16:5,28,30; 20:14; 22:6, 19,34; 24:16; 31:17,18,35; 32:23; **Deut.** 1:13,15,39; 2:7; 3:19; 4:9,35,39; 7:9,15; 8:2,3,5,16; 9:2,3,6,24; 11:2,28; 13:2(3), 3(4),6(7),13(14); 18:21; 20:20; 21:1; 22:2; 28:33,36,64; 29:4(3),6(5),16(15), 26(25); 31:13,21,27,29; 32:17; 33:9; 34:6,10; **Josh.** 2:4,5,9; 3:4,7,10; 4:22,24; 8:14; 14:6; 22:22,31; 23:13,14; 24:31; **Judg.** 2:10; 3:1,2,4; 6:37; 8:16; 11:39; 13:16,21; 14:4; 15:11; 16:9,20; 17:13; 18:5,14; 19:22,25; 20:34; 21:11,12; **Ruth** 2:1(NASB, NIV, [Q^e] *mô<u>d</u>a'* [4129]),11; 3:3,4,11,14,18; 4:4; **1 Sam.** 1:19; 2:12; 3:7,13,20; 4:6; 6:2,3,9; 10:8,11; 12:17; 14:3,12,38; 16:3,16,18; 17:28,46,47,55; 18:28; 20:3,7,9,30,33,39; 21:2(3); 22:3, 6,15,17,22; 23:9,17,22,23; 24:11(12), 20(21); 25:11,17; 26:4,12; 28:1,2,9,14,15; 29:9; **2 Sam.** 1:5,10; 2:26; 3:25,26,37,38; 5:12; 7:20,21; 11:16,20; 12:22; 14:1,20,22; 15:11; 17:8,10,19; 18:29; 19:6(7),20(21), 22(23),35(36); 22:44; 24:2,13; **1 Kgs.** 1:4,11,18,27; 2:5,9,15,32,37,42,44; 3:7; 5:3(17),6(20); 8:38,39,43,60; 9:27; 14:2; 17:24; 18:12,36,37; 20:7,13,22,28; 22:3; **2 Kgs.** 2:3,5; 4:1,9,39; 5:7,8,15; 7:12; 8:12; 9:11; 10:10,11; 17:26; 19:19,27; **1 Chr.** 12:32; 14:2; 16:8; 17:18,19; 21:2; 28:9; 29:17; **2 Chr.** 2:7(6),8(7),12–14 (11–13); 6:29,30,33; 8:18; 12:8; 13:5; 20:12; 23:13; 25:16; 32:13,31; 33:13; **Neh.** 2:16; 4:11(5),15(9); 6:16; 8:12; 9:10,14; 10:28(29); 13:10; **Esth.** 1:13; 2:11,22; 4:1,5,11,14; **Job** 5:24,25,27; 8:9; 9:2,5,21,28; 10:2,13; 11:6,8,11; 12:9; 13:2,18,23; 14:21; 15:9,23; 18:21; 19:6,

13,14,25,29; 20:4,20; 21:19,27; 22:13; 23:3,5,10; 24:1,16; 26:3; 28:7,13,23; 29:16; 30:23; 31:6; 32:7,22; 34:2,4,33; 35:15; 36:26; 37:5,7,15,16,19; 38:3–5, 12,18,21,33; 39:1,2; 40:7; 42:2–4,11; **Ps.** 1:6; 4:3(4); 9:10(11),16(17),20(21); 14:4; 16:11; 18:43(44); 20:6(7); 25:4,14; 31:7(8),11(12); 32:5; 35:8,11,15; 36:10(11); 37:18; 39:4(5),6(7); 40:9(10); 41:11(12); 44:21(22); 46:10(11); 48:3(4); 50:11; 51:3(5),6(8); 53:4(5); 55:13(14); 56:9(10); 59:13(14); 67:2(3); 69:5(6), 19(20); 71:15; 73:11,16,22; 74:5,9; 76:1(2); 77:14(15),19(20); 78:3,5,6; 79:6,10; 81:5(6); 82:5; 83:18(19); 87:4; 88:8(9),12(13),18(19); 89:1(2),15(16); 90:11,12; 91:14; 92:6(7); 94:11; 95:10; 98:2; 100:3; 101:4; 103:7,14; 104:19; 105:1; 106:8; 109:27; 119:75,79,125,152; 135:5; 138:6; 139:1,2,4,14,23; 140:12(13); 142:3(4); 143:8; 144:3; 145:12; 147:20; **Prov.** 1:2,23; 3:6; 4:1,19; 5:6; 7:23; 9:9,13,18; 10:9,32; 12:10,16; 14:7,10,33; 17:27; 22:19,21; 23:35; 24:12,14,22; 27:1,23; 28:2,22; 29:7; 30:3,4,18; 31:23; **Eccl.** 1:17; 2:14,19; 3:12,14,21; 4:13; 5:1(4:17); 6:5,8,10,12; 7:22,25; 8:1,5, 7,12,16,17; 9:1,5,11,12; 10:14,15; 11:2, 5,6,9; **Song** 1:8; 6:12; **Isa.** 1:3; 5:5,19; 6:9; 7:15,16; 8:4; 9:9(8); 12:4,5; 19:12,21; 29:11,12,15,24; 32:4(KJV, NASB, *da'aṯ* [1847]); 33:13; 37:20,28; 38:19; 40:13, 14,21,28; 41:20,22,23,26; 42:16,25; 43:10,19; 44:8,9,18; 45:3–6,20; 47:8, 11,13; 48:4(KJV, *da'aṯ* [1847]),6–8; 49:23,26; 50:4,7; 51:7; 52:6; 53:3; 55:5; 56:10,11; 58:3; 59:8,12; 60:16; 61:9; 63:16; 64:2(1); 66:14; **Jer.** 1:5,6; 2:8, 19,23; 3:13; 4:22; 5:1,4,5,15; 6:15,18,27; 7:9; 8:7,12; 9:3(2),6(5),16(15),24(23); 10:23,25; 11:18,19; 12:3; 13:12; 14:18,20; 15:14,15; 16:13,21; 17:4,9,16; 18:23; 19:4; 22:28; 24:7; 26:15; 28:9; 29:11,23; 31:19,34; 32:8; 33:3; 36:19; 38:24; 40:14,15; 41:4; 42:19,22; 44:3, 15,28,29; 48:17,30; 50:24; **Ezek.** 2:5; 5:13; 6:7,10,13,14; 7:4,9,27; 10:20; 11:5,10,12; 12:15,16,20; 13:9,14,21,23; 14:8,23; 15:7; 16:2,62; 17:12,21,24; 19:7(NASB, *rā'a'* [7489,II]; NIV, *gāḏa'* [1438]); 20:4,5,9,11,12,20,26,38,42,44; 21:5(10); 22:2,16,22,26; 23:49; 24:24,27; 25:5,7,11,14,17; 26:6; 28:19,22–24,26; 29:6,9,16,21; 30:8,19,25,26; 32:9,15; 33:29,33; 34:27,30; 35:4,9,11,12,15; 36:11,23,32,36,38; 37:3,6,13,14,28; 38:14,16,23; 39:6,7,22,23,28; 43:11; 44:23; **Dan.** 1:4; 2:3; 8:19; 9:25; 10:20; 11:32,38; **Hos.** 2:8(10),20(22); 5:3,4,9; 6:3; 7:9; 8:2,4; 9:7; 11:3; 13:4,5; 14:9(10); **Joel** 2:14,27; 3:17(4:17); **Amos** 3:2,10; 5:12,16; **Jon.** 1:7,10,12; 3:9; 4:2,11; **Mic.** 3:1; 4:12; 6:5; **Nah.** 1:7; 3:2; **Hab.** 2:14; 3:2; **Zeph.** 3:5; **Zech.** 2:9(13), 11(15); 4:5,9,13; 6:15; 7:14; 11:11; 14:7; **Mal.** 2:4.

3046. יְדַע $y^e\underline{d}a$' **Aram. verb**
(to know, to be known; corr. to Hebr. 3045)
Ezra 4:12–16; 5:8,10; 7:24,25; **Dan.** 2:5,8,9,15,17,21–23,25,26,28–30,45; 3:18; 4:6(3),7(4),9(6),17(14),18(15), 25(22),26(23),32(29); 5:8,15–17,21–23; 6:10(11),15(16); 7:16.

3047. יָדָע *yāḏā'* **masc. proper noun**
(Jada)
1 Chr. 2:28,32.

3048. A. יְדַעְיָה $y^e\underline{d}a$'yāh **masc. proper noun**
(Jedaiah: a priest under David)
1 Chr. 24:7.
B. יְדַעְיָה $y^e\underline{d}a$'yāh **masc. proper noun**
(Jedaiah: a priest under Zerubbabel)
1 Chr. 9:10; **Ezra** 2:36; **Neh.** 7:39; 11:10; 12:6,19.
C. יְדַעְיָה $y^e\underline{d}a$'yāh **masc. proper noun**
(Jedaiah: postexilic priest)
Neh. 12:7,21.

D. יְדַעְיָה *ye̱da'yāh* **masc. proper noun**
(Jedaiah: a Jew)
Zech. 6:10,14.

3049. יִדְּעֹנִי *yidde'ōniy* **masc. noun**
(a spiritist, medium)
Lev. 19:31; 20:6,27; **Deut.** 18:11; **1 Sam.** 28:3,9; **2 Kgs.** 21:6; 23:24; **2 Chr.** 33:6; **Isa.** 8:19; 19:3.

3050. יָהּ *yāh* **masc. proper noun**
(LORD, JAH; a shortened form of *yehōwāh* [3068])
Ex. 15:2; 17:16; **Ps.** 68:4(5),18(19); 77:11(12); 89:8(9); 94:7,12; 102:18(19); 104:35; 105:45; 106:1,48; 111:1; 112:1; 113:1,9; 115:17,18; 116:19; 117:2; 118:5, 14,17–19; 122:4; 130:3; 135:1,3,4,21; 146:1,10; 147:1,20; 148:1,14; 149:1,9; 150:1,6; **Song** 8:6(KJV, NIV, *šalhebetyāh* [7957,II]); **Isa.** 12:2; 26:4; 38:11.

3051. I. יָהַב *yāhab̲* **verb**
(to give; to come; NIV, see II)
Gen. 11:3,4,7; 29:21; 30:1; 38:16; 47:15,16; **Ex.** 1:10; **Deut.** 1:13; 32:3; **Josh.** 18:4; **Judg.** 1:15; 20:7; **Ruth** 3:15; **1 Sam.** 14:41; **2 Sam.** 11:15; 16:20; **1 Chr.** 16:28,29; **Job** 6:22; **Ps.** 29:1,2; 60:11(13); 96:7,8; 108:12; **Prov.** 30:15; **Hos.** 4:18; **Zech.** 11:12.
II. הַב *hab̲* **verb**
(to give; to come; KJV, NASB, see I)
Gen. 11:3,4,7; 29:21; 30:1; 38:16; 47:15,16; **Ex.** 1:10; **Deut.** 1:13; 32:3; **Josh.** 18:4; **Judg.** 1:15; 20:7; **Ruth** 3:15; **1 Sam.** 14:41; **2 Sam.** 11:15; 16:20; **1 Chr.** 16:28,29; **Job** 6:22; **Ps.** 29:1,2; 60:11(13); 96:7,8; 108:12; **Prov.** 30:15; **Hos.** 4:18; **Zech.** 11:12.

3052. יְהַב *yehab̲* **Aram. verb**
(to give, to pay; corr. to Hebr. 3051)
Num. 21:14(see *'etwehab̲* [2052,II]; NASB, NIV, *wāhēb̲* [2052,I]).; **Ezra** 4:20; 5:12,14,16; 6:4,8,9; 7:19; **Dan.** 2:21,23, 37,38,48; 3:28; 4:16(13); 5:17–19,28; 6:2(3); 7:4,6,11,12,14,22,25,27.

3053. יְהָב *yehāb̲* **masc. noun**
(burden, care)
Ps. 55:22(23).

3054. יָהַד *yāhad̲* **verb**
(to become a Jew)
Esth. 8:17.

3055. יְהֻד *yehud̲* **proper noun**
(Jehud)
Josh. 19:45.

3056. יָהְדַי *yāhday* **masc. proper noun**
(Jahdai)
1 Chr. 2:47.

3057. יְהֻדִיָּה *yehud̲iyyāh* **fem. proper noun**
(Jehudijah [lit., the Jewess])
1 Chr. 4:18(NASB, NIV, *yehûd̲iy* [3064]).

3058. A. יֵהוּא *yēhû'* **masc. proper noun**
(Jehu, king of Israel)
1 Kgs. 19:16,17; **2 Kgs.** 9:2,5,11,13–22, 24,27,30,31; 10:1,5,11,13,18–21,23–25, 28–31,34–36; 12:1(2); 13:1; 14:8; 15:12; **2 Chr.** 22:7–9; 25:17; **Hos.** 1:4.
B. יֵהוּא *yēhû'* **masc. proper noun**
(Jehu: a prophet)
1 Kgs. 16:1,7,12; **2 Chr.** 19:2; 20:34.
C. יֵהוּא *yēhû'* **masc. proper noun**
(Jehu: one of David's mighty men)
1 Chr. 12:3.
D. יֵהוּא *yēhû'* **masc. proper noun**
(Jehu: a Judaite)
1 Chr. 2:38.
E. יֵהוּא *yēhû'* **masc. proper noun**
(Jehu: a Simeonite)
1 Chr. 4:35.

3059. A. יְהוֹאָחָז *yehô'āḥāz* **masc. proper noun**

(Jehoahaz: king of Judah, son of Jehoram; see also *'ᵃḥazyāhû* [274])
2 Chr. 21:17; 25:23.

B. יְהוֹאָחָז y^e*hô'āḥāz* masc. proper noun
(Jehoahaz: king of Israel, son of Jehu; see also *yô'āḥāz* [3099,B])
2 Kgs. 10:35; 13:1,4,7–10,22,25; 14:8,17; **2 Chr.** 25:17,25.

C. יְהוֹאָחָז y^e*hô'āḥāz* masc. proper noun
(Jehoahaz: king of Judah, son of Josiah; see also *yô'āḥaz* [3099,A])
2 Kgs. 23:30,31,34; **2 Chr.** 36:1.

3060. A. יְהוֹאָשׁ y^e*hô'āš* masc. proper noun
(Jehoash: king of Judah, son of Ahaziah; see also *yô'āš* [3101,A])
2 Kgs. 11:21(12:1); 12:1(2),2(3),4(5),6(7),7(8),18(19).

B. יְהוֹאָשׁ y^e*hô'āš* masc. proper noun
(Jehoash: king of Israel, son of Jehoahaz; see also *yô'āš* [3101,B])
2 Kgs. 13:10,25; 14:8,9,11,13,15–17.

3061. יְהוּד y^e*hûḏ* Aram. proper noun
(Judah; corr. to Hebr 3063,B)
Ezra 5:1,8; 7:14; **Dan.** 2:25; 5:13; 6:13(14).

3062. יְהוּדַי y^e*hûḏay* Aram. masc. proper noun
(Jew; corr. to Hebr. 3064)
Ezra 4:12,23; 5:1,5; 6:7,8,14; **Dan.** 3:8,12.

3063. A. יְהוּדָה y^e*hûḏāh* masc. proper noun
(Judah: son of Jacob)
Gen. 29:35; 35:23; 37:26; 38:1,2,6–8,11,12,15,20,22–24,26; 43:3,8; 44:14,16,18; 46:12,28; 49:8–10; **Num.** 26:19; **1 Chr.** 2:3,4; 4:1.

B. יְהוּדָה y^e*hûḏāh* masc. proper noun
(Judah: tribe, territory, or kingdom of Judah)
Ex. 1:2; 31:2; 35:30; 38:22; **Num.** 1:7,26,27; 2:3,9; 7:12; 10:14; 13:6; 26:20,22; 34:19; **Deut.** 27:12; 33:7; 34:2; **Josh.** 7:1,16–18; 11:21; 14:6; 15:1,12,13, 20,21,63; 18:5,11,14; 19:1,9,34; 20:7; 21:4,9,11; **Judg.** 1:2–4,8–10,16–19; 10:9; 15:9–11; 17:7–9; 18:12; 19:1,2,18; 20:18; **Ruth** 1:1,2,7; 4:12; **1 Sam.** 11:8; 15:4; 17:1,12,52; 18:16; 22:5; 23:3,23; 27:6,10; 30:14,16,26; **2 Sam.** 1:18; 2:1,4,7,10,11; 3:8,10; 5:5; 6:2; 11:11; 12:8; 19:11(12),14–16(15–17),40–43 (41–44); 20:2,4,5; 21:2; 24:1,7,9; **1 Kgs.** 1:9,35; 2:32; 4:20,25(5:5); 12:17,20,21, 23,27,32; 13:1,12,14,21; 14:21,22,29; 15:1,7,9,17,22,23,25,28,33; 16:8,10,15, 23,29; 19:3; 22:2,10,29,41,45(46),51(52); **2 Kgs.** 1:17; 3:1,7,9,14; 8:16,19,20,22, 23,25,29; 9:16,21,27,29; 10:13; 12:18(19), 19(20); 13:1,10,12; 14:1,9–13,15,17,18, 21–23,28; 15:1,6,8,13,17,23,27,32,36,37; 16:1,19; 17:1,13,18,19; 18:1,5,13,14, 16,22; 19:10,30; 20:20; 21:11,12,16, 17,25; 22:13,16,18; 23:1,2,5,8,11,12,17, 22,24,26–28; 24:2,3,5,12,20; 25:21, 22,27; **1 Chr.** 2:1,10; 4:21,27,41; 5:2,17; 6:15(5:41),55(40),65(50); 9:1,3,4; 12:16,24; 13:6; 21:5; 27:18; 28:4; **2 Chr.** 2:7(6); 9:11; 10:17; 11:1,3,5,10,12,14, 17,23; 12:4,5,12; 13:1,13–16,18; 14:4–8(3–7),12(11); 15:2,8,9,15; 16:1,6,7,11; 17:2,5–7,9,10,12–14,19; 18:3,9,28; 19:1,5,11; 20:3–5,13,15,17,18, 20,22,24,27,31,35; 21:3,8,10–13,17; 22:1,6,8,10; 23:2,8; 24:5,6,9,17,18,23; 25:5,10,12,13,17–19,21–23,25,26,28; 26:1,2; 27:4,7; 28:6,9,10,17–19,25,26; 29:8,21; 30:1,6,12,24,25; 31:1,6,20; 32:1,8,9,12,23,25,32,33; 33:9,14,16; 34:3,5,9,11,21,24,26,29,30; 35:18,21, 24,27; 36:4,8,10,23; **Ezra** 1:2,3,5,8; 2:1; 3:9; 4:1,4,6; 9:9; 10:7,9; **Neh.** 1:2; 2:5,7; 4:10(4),16(10); 5:14; 6:7,17,18; 7:6;

11:3,4,20,24,25,36; 12:31,32,34,44; 13:12,15–17; **Esth.** 2:6; **Ps.** 48:11(12); 60:7(9); 63:[title](1); 68:27(28); 69:35(36); 76:1(2); 78:68; 97:8; 108:8(9); 114:2; **Prov.** 25:1; **Isa.** 1:1; 2:1; 3:1,8; 5:3,7; 7:1,6,17; 8:8; 9:21(20); 11:12,13; 19:17; 22:8,21; 26:1; 36:1,7; 37:10,31; 38:9; 40:9; 44:26; 48:1; 65:9; **Jer.** 1:2,3, 15,18; 2:28; 3:7,8,10,11,18; 4:3–5,16; 5:11,20; 7:2,17,30,34; 8:1; 9:11(10), 26(25); 10:22; 11:2,6,9,10,12,13,17; 12:14; 13:9,11,19; 14:2,19; 15:4; 17:1, 19,20,25,26; 18:11; 19:3,4,7,13; 20:4,5; 21:7,11; 22:1,2,6,11,18,24,30; 23:6; 24:1,5,8; 25:1–3,18; 26:1,2,10,18,19; 27:1,3,12,18,20,21; 28:1,4; 29:2,3,22; 30:3,4; 31:23,24,27,31; 32:1–4,30,32, 35,44; 33:4,7,10,13,14,16; 34:2,4,6,7,19, 21,22; 35:1,13,17; 36:1–3,6,9,28–32; 37:1,7; 38:22; 39:1,4,6,10; 40:1,5,11, 12,15; 42:15,19; 43:4,5; 44:2,6,7,9,11,12, 14,17,21,24,26–28,30; 45:1; 46:2; 49:34; 50:4,20,33; 51:5,59; 52:3,10,27,31; **Lam.** 1:3,15; 2:2,5; 5:11; **Ezek.** 4:6; 8:1,17; 9:9; 21:20(25); 25:3,8,12; 27:17; 37:16,19; 48:7,8,22,31; **Dan.** 1:1,2,6; 9:7; **Hos.** 1:1,7,11(2:2); 4:15; 5:5,10, 12–14; 6:4,11; 8:14; 10:11; 11:12(12:1); 12:2(3); **Joel** 3:1(4:1),6(4:6),8(4:8), 18–20(4:18–20); **Amos** 1:1; 2:4,5; 7:12; **Obad.** 1:12; **Mic.** 1:1,5,9; 5:2(1); **Nah.** 1:15(2:1); **Zeph.** 1:1,4; 2:7; **Hag.** 1:1,14; 2:2,21; **Zech.** 1:12,19(2:2),21(2:4); 2:12(16); 8:13,15,19; 9:7,13; 10:3,6; 11:14; 12:2,4–7; 14:5,14,21; **Mal.** 2:11; 3:4.

C. יְהוּדָה y^e*hûḏāh* **masc. proper noun**
(Judah: a Levite)
Ezra 10:23.

D. יְהוּדָה y^e*hûḏāh* **masc. proper noun**
(Judah: an overseer)
Neh. 11:9.

E. יְהוּדָה y^e*hûḏāh* **masc. proper noun**
(Judah: a Levite)
Neh. 12:8.

F. יְהוּדָה y^e*hûḏāh* **masc. proper noun**
(Judah: a priest)
Neh. 12:36.

3064. יְהוּדִי y^e*hûḏiy* **masc. proper noun**
(Jew)
2 Kgs. 16:6; 25:25; **1 Chr.** 4:18(KJV, y^e*huḏiyyāh* [3057]); **Neh.** 1:2; 2:16; 4:1(3:33),2(3:34),12(6); 5:1,8,17; 6:6; 13:23; **Esth.** 2:5; 3:4,6,10,13; 4:3,7,13, 14,16; 5:13; 6:10,13; 8:1,3,5,7–9,11,13, 16,17; 9:1–3,5,6,10,12,13,15,16,18–20, 22–25,27–31; 10:3; **Jer.** 32:12; 34:9; 38:19; 40:11,12; 41:3; 43:9; 44:1; 52:28,30; **Zech.** 8:23.

3065. יְהוּדִי y^e*hûḏiy* **masc. proper noun**
(Jehudi)
Jer. 36:14,21,23.

3066. יְהוּדִית y^e*hûḏiyṯ* **fem. proper adj.**
(in the Jewish language, in Hebrew)
2 Kgs. 18:26,28; **2 Chr.** 32:18; **Neh.** 13:24; **Isa.** 36:11,13.

3067. יְהוּדִית y^e*hûḏiyṯ* **fem. proper noun**
(Judith)
Gen. 26:34.

3068. יְהוָה y^e*hōwāh* **masc. proper noun**
(Jehovah [LORD]: [Q^e] *'aḏōnāy* [136])
Gen. 2:4,5,7–9,15,16,18,19,21,22; 3:1,8, 9,13,14,21–23; 4:1,3,4,6,9,13,15,16,26; 5:29; 6:3,5–8; 7:1,5,16; 8:20,21; 9:26; 10:9; 11:5,6,8,9; 12:1,4,7,8,17; 13:4,10, 13,14,18; 14:22; 15:1,4,6,7,18; 16:2,5, 7,9–11,13; 17:1; 18:13,14,17,19,20,22, 26,33; 19:13,14,16,24,27; 20:18; 21:1,33; 22:11,14–16; 24:1,3,7,12,21,26,27,31, 35,40,42,44,48,50–52,56; 25:21–23;

26:2,12,22,24,25,28,29; 27:7,20,27; 28:13,16,21; 29:31–33,35; 30:24,27,30; 31:3,49; 32:9(10); 38:7,10; 39:2,3,5, 21,23; 49:18; **Ex.** 3:2,4,7,15,16,18; 4:1,2,4–6,10,11,14,19,21,22,24,27,28,30, 31; 5:1–3,17,21,22; 6:1–3,6–8,10,12,13, 26,28–30; 7:1,5,6,8,10,13,14,16,17,19, 20,22,25; 8:1(7:26),5(1),8(4),10(6),12(8), 13(9),15(11),16(12),19(15),20(16),22(18), 24(20),26–31(22–27); 9:1,3–6,8,12,13, 20–23,27–30,33,35; 10:1–3,7–13,16–21, 24–27; 11:1,3,4,7,9,10; 12:1,11,12,14,23, 25,27–29,31,36,41–43,48,50,51; 13:1,3, 5,6,8,9,11,12,14–16,21; 14:1,4,8,10, 13–15,18,21,24–27,30,31; 15:1,3,6,11, 16–19,21,25,26; 16:3,4,6–12,15,16,23, 25,28,29,32–34; 17:1,2,4,5,7,14,16; 18:1, 8–11; 19:3,7–11,18,20–24; 20:2,5,7, 10–12,22; 22:11(10),20(19); 23:17,19,25; 24:1–5,7,8,12,16,17; 25:1; 27:21; 28:12, 29,30,35,36,38; 29:11,18,23–26,28,41, 42,46; 30:8,10–17,20,22,34,37; 31:1,12, 13,15,17; 32:5,7,9,11,14,26,27,29–31, 33,35; 33:1,5,7,11,12,17,19,21; 34:1,4–6, 10,14,23,24,26–28,32,34; 35:1,2,4,5,10, 21,22,24,29,30; 36:1,2,5; 38:22; 39:1,5, 7,21,26,29–32,42,43; 40:1,16,19,21,23, 25,27,29,32,34,35,38; **Lev.** 1:1–3,5,9,11, 13,14,17; 2:1–3,8–12,14,16; 3:1,3,5–7,9, 11,12,14,16; 4:1–4,6,7,13,15,17,18,22, 24,27,31,35; 5:6,7,12,14,15,17,19; 6:1 (5:20),2(5:21),6(5:25),7(5:26),8(1), 14(17),15(8),18–22(11–15),24(17), 25(18); 7:5,11,14,20–22,25,28–30,35, 36,38; 8:1,4,5,9,13,17,21,26–29,34–36; 9:2,4–7,10,21,23,24; 10:1–3,6–8,11–13, 15,17,19; 11:1,44,45; 12:1,7; 13:1; 14:1, 11,12,16,18,23,24,27,29,31,33; 15:1,14, 15,30; 16:1,2,7–10,12,13,18,30,34; 17:1, 2,4–6,9; 18:1,2,4–6,21,30; 19:1–5,8,10, 12,14,16,18,21,22,24,25,28,30–32,34,36, 37; 20:1,7,8,24,26; 21:1,6,8,12,15,16, 21,23; 22:1–3,8,9,15–18,21,22,24,26, 27,29–33; 23:1–6,8,9,11–13,16–18, 20,22,23,25–28,33,34,36–41,43,44; 24:1, 3,4,6–9,12,13,16,22,23; 25:1,2,4,17, 38,55; 26:1,2,13,44–46; 27:1,2,9,11,14, 16,21–23,26,28,30,32,34; **Num.** 1:1,19, 48,54; 2:1,33,34; 3:1,4,5,11,13,14,16, 39–42,44,45,51; 4:1,17,21,37,41,45,49; 5:1,4–6,8,11,16,18,21,25,30; 6:1,2,5,6,8, 12,14,16,17,20–22,24–26; 7:3,4,11; 8:1, 3–5,10–13,20–23; 9:1,5,7–10,13,14, 18–20,23; 10:1,9,10,13,29,32–36; 11:1–3,10,11,16,18,20,23–25,29,31,33; 12:2,4–6,8,9,13,14; 13:1,3; 14:3,8–11,13, 14,16,18,20,21,26,28,35,37,40–44; 15:1, 3,4,7,8,10,13–15,17,19,21–25,28,30,31,3 5–37,39,41; 16:3,5,7,9,11,15–17,19,20, 23,28–30,35,36(17:1),38(17:3),40–42 (17:5–7),44(17:9),46(17:11); 17:1(16), 7(22),9–11(24–26),13(28); 18:1,6,8,12, 13,15,17,19,20,24–26,28,29; 19:1,2, 13,20; 20:3,4,6,7,9,12,13,16,23,27; 21:2, 3,6–8,14,16,34; 22:8,13,18,19,22–28,31, 32,34,35; 23:3,5,8,12,16,17,21,26; 24:1, 6,11,13; 25:3,4,10,16; 26:1,4,9,52,61,65; 27:3,5,6,11,12,15–18,21–23; 28:1,3, 6–8,11,13,15,16,19,24,26,27; 29:2,6,8, 12,13,36,39,40(30:1); 30:1–3(2–4),5(6), 8(9),12(13),16(17); 31:1,3,7,16,21,25, 28–31,37–41,47,50,52,54; 32:4,7,9,10, 12–14,20–23,27,29,31,32; 33:2,4,38,50; 34:1,13,16,29; 35:1,9,34; 36:2,5,6,10,13; **Deut.** 1:3,6,8,10,11,19–21,25–27,30–32, 34,36,37,41–43,45; 2:1,2,7,9,12,14,15, 17,21,29–31,33,36,37; 3:2,3,18,20–23,26; 4:1–5,7,10,12,14,15,19–21,23–25,27, 29–31,34,35,39,40; 5:2–6,9,11,12,14–16, 22(19),24(21),25(22),27(24),28(25), 32(29),33(30); 6:1–5,10,12,13,15–22, 24,25; 7:1,2,4,6–9,12,15,16,18–23,25; 8:1–3,5–7,10,11,14,18–20; 9:3–13,16, 18–20,22–26,28; 10:1,4,5,8–15,17,20,22; 11:1,2,4,7,9,12,13,17,21–23,25,27–29, 31; 12:1,4,5,7,9–12,14,15,18,20,21, 25–29,31; 13:3–5(4–6),10(11),12(13), 16–18(17–19); 14:1,2,21,23–26,29; 15:2, 4–7,9,10,14,15,18–21; 16:1,2,5–8,10,11, 15–18,20–22; 17:1,2,8,10,12,14–16,19; 18:1,2,5–7,9,12–17,21,22; 19:1–3,8–10, 14,17; 20:1,4,13,14,16–18; 21:1,5, 8–10,23; 22:5; 23:1–3(2–4),5(6),8(9), 14(15),18(19),20(21),21(22),23(24);

24:4,9,13,15,18,19; 25:15,16,19; 26:1–5, 7,8,10,11,13,14,16–19; 27:2,3,5–7,9, 10,15; 28:1,2,7–13,15,20–22,24,25,27, 28,35–37,45,47–49,52,53,58,59,61–65, 68; 29:1(28:69),2(1),4(3),6(5),10(9), 12(11),15(14),18(17),20–25(19–24), 27–29(26–28); 30:1–10,16,20; 31:2–9, 11–16,25–27,29; 32:3,6,9,12,19,27,30, 36,48; 33:2,7,11–13,21,23,29; 34:1,4,5, 9–11; **Josh.** 1:1,9,11,13,15,17; 2:9–12, 14,24; 3:3,5,7,9,13,17; 4:1,5,7,8,10,11, 13–15,18,23,24; 5:1,2,6,9,14,15; 6:2, 6–8,11–13,16,17,19,24,26,27; 7:1,6,10, 13–15,19,20,23,25,26; 8:1,7,8,18,27,30, 31,33; 9:9,14,18,19,24,27; 10:8,10–12, 14,19,25,30,32,40,42; 11:6,8,9,12,15, 20,23; 12:6; 13:1,8,14,33; 14:2,5–10, 12,14; 15:13; 17:4,14; 18:3,6–8,10; 19:50,51; 20:1; 21:2,3,8,43–45(41–43); 22:2–5,9,16–19,22–25,27–29,31,34; 23:1,3,5,8–11,13–16; 24:2,7,14–24,26, 27,29,31; **Judg.** 1:1,2,4,19,22; 2:1,4,5, 7,8,10–18,20,22,23; 3:1,4,7–10,12,15,28; 4:1–3,6,9,14,15; 5:2–5,9,11,13,23,31; 6:1,6–8,10–14,16,21–27,34; 7:2,4,5,7,9, 15,18,20,22; 8:7,19,23,34; 10:6,7,10,11, 15,16; 11:9–11,21,23,24,27,29–32,35,36; 12:3; 13:1,3,8,13,15–21,23–25; 14:4, 6,19; 15:14,18; 16:20,28; 17:2,3,13; 18:6; 19:18; 20:1,18,23,26–28,35; 21:3,5,7,8, 15,19; **Ruth** 1:6,8,9,13,17,21; 2:4,12,20; 3:10,13; 4:11–14; **1 Sam.** 1:3,5–7,9–12, 15,19–24,26–28; 2:1–3,6–8,10–12,17, 18,20,21,24–27,30; 3:1,3,4,6–11,15, 18–21; 4:3–6; 5:3,4,6,9; 6:1,2,8,11,14,15, 17–21; 7:1–6,8–10,12,13,17; 8:6,7,10,18, 21,22; 9:15,17; 10:1,6,17–19,22,24,25; 11:7,13,15; 12:3,5–20,22–24; 13:12–14; 14:3,6,10,12,23,33–35,39,41,45; 15:1,2, 10,11,13,15–26,28,30,31,33,35; 16:1,2, 4–10,12–14,18; 17:37,45–47; 18:12,14, 17,28; 19:5,6,9; 20:3,8,12–16,21–23,42; 21:6(7),7(8); 22:10,17,21; 23:2,4,10–12, 18,21; 24:4(5),6(7),10(11),12(13),15(16), 18(19),19(20),21(22); 25:26,28–32,34, 38,39; 26:9–12,16,19,20,23,24; 28:6,10, 16–19; 29:6; 30:6,8,23,26; **2 Sam.** 1:12, 14,16; 2:1,5,6; 3:9,18,28,39; 4:8,9; 5:2, 3,10,12,19,20,23–25; 6:2,5,7–18,21; 7:1, 3–5,8,11,18,22,24–27; 8:6,11,14; 10:12; 11:27; 12:1,5,7,9,11,13–15,20,22,24,25; 14:11,17; 15:7,8,21,25,31; 16:8,10–12,18; 17:14; 18:19,28,31; 19:7(8),21(22); 20:19; 21:1,3,6,7,9; 22:1,2,4,7,14,16,19,21,22, 25,29,31,32,42,47,50; 23:2,10,12,16,17; 24:1,3,10–12,14–19,21,23–25; **1 Kgs.** 1:17,29,30,36,37,48; 2:3,4,8,15,23,24, 27–30,32,33,42–45; 3:1–3,5,7; 5:3–5 (17–19),7(21),12(26); 6:1,2,11,19,37; 7:12,40,45,48,51; 8:1,4,6,9–12,15,17, 18,20–23,25,28,44,54,56,57,59–66; 9:1–3,8–10,15,25; 10:1,5,9,12; 11:2,4, 6,9–11,14,31; 12:15,24,27; 13:1–3,5, 6,9,17,18,20,21,26,32; 14:5,7,11,13–15, 18,21,22,24,26,28; 15:3–5,11,14,15,18, 26,29,30,34; 16:1,7,12,13,19,25,26,30, 33,34; 17:1,2,5,8,12,14,16,20–22,24; 18:1,3,4,10,12,13,15,18,21,22,24,30–32, 36–39,46; 19:4,7,9–12,14,15; 20:13,14, 28,35,36,42; 21:3,17,19,20,23,25,26,28; 22:5,7,8,11,12,14–17,19–21,22(21),23,24 ,28,38,43,52(53),53(54); **2 Kgs.** 1:3,4,6, 15–17; 2:1–6,14,16,21,24; 3:2,10–18; 4:1,27,30,33,43,44; 5:1,11,16–18,20; 6:17,18,20,27,33; 7:1,2,16,19; 8:1,8,10, 13,18,19,27; 9:3,6,7,12,25,26,36; 10:10, 16,17,23,30–32; 11:3,4,7,10,13,15, 17–19; 12:2(3),4(5),9–14(10–15),16(17), 18(19); 13:2–5,11,17,23; 14:3,6,14, 24–27; 15:3,5,9,12,18,24,28,34,35,37; 16:2,3,8,14,18; 17:2,7–9,11–21,23,25, 28,32–36,39,41; 18:3,5–7,12,15,16,22, 25,30,32,35; 19:1,4,6,14–17,19–21, 31–33,35; 20:1–5,8,9,11,16,17,19; 21:2,4–7,9,10,12,16,20,22; 22:2–5, 8,9,13,15,16,18,19; 23:2–4,6,7,9,11, 12,16,21,23–27,32,37; 24:2–4,9,13, 19,20; 25:9,13,16; **1 Chr.** 2:3; 6:15 (5:41),31(16),32(17); 9:19,20,23; 10:13, 14; 11:2,3,9,10,14,18; 12:23; 13:2,6,10, 11,14; 14:2,10,17; 15:2,3,12–15,25,26, 28,29; 16:2,4,7,8,10,11,14,23,25,26,28, 29,31,33,34,36,37,39–41; 17:1,4,7,10,16, 17,19,20,22–24,26,27; 18:6,11,13; 19:13;

21:3,9–19,22,24,26–30; 22:1,5–8,11–14, 16,18,19; 23:4,5,13,24,25,28,30–32; 24:19; 25:3,6,7; 26:12,22,27,30; 27:23; 28:2,4,5,8–10,12,13,18–20; 29:1,5,8–11, 16,18,20–23,25; **2 Chr.** 1:1,3,5,6,9; 2:1(1:18),4(3),11(10),12(11); 3:1; 4:16; 5:1,2,7,10,13,14; 6:1,4,7,8,10–12,14, 16,17,19,41,42; 7:1–4,6,7,10–12,21,22; 8:1,11,12,16; 9:4,8,11; 10:15; 11:2,4, 14,16; 12:1,2,5–7,9,11–14; 13:5,8–12,14, 18,20; 14:2(1),4(3),6(5),7(6),11–14 (10–13); 15:2,4,8,9,11–15; 16:2,7–9,12; 17:3,5,6,9,10,16; 18:4,6,7,10,11,13,15, 16,18–20,22,23,27,31; 19:2,4,6–11; 20:3–6,13–15,17–22,26–29,32,37; 21:6, 7,10,12,14,16,18; 22:4,7,9; 23:3,5,6,12, 14,16,18–20; 24:2,4,6–9,12,14,18–22,24; 25:2,4,7,9,15,27; 26:4,5,16–21; 27:2,3,6; 28:1,3,5,6,9–11,13,19,21,22,24,25; 29:2, 3,5,6,8,10,11,15–21,25,27,30–32,35; 30:1,5–9,12,15,17–22; 31:2–4,6,8,10,11, 14,16,20; 32:8,11,16,17,21–24,26; 33:2, 4–6,9–13,15–18,22,23; 34:2,8,10,14,15, 17,21,23,24,26,27,30,31,33; 35:1–3,6,12, 16,26; 36:5,7,9,10,12–16,18,21–23; **Ezra** 1:1–3,5,7; 2:68; 3:3,5,6,8,10,11; 4:1,3; 6:21,22; 7:6,10,11,27,28; 8:28,29,35; 9:5, 8,15; 10:11; **Neh.** 1:5; 5:13; 8:1,6,9,10, 14; 9:3–7; 10:29(30),34(35),35(36); **Job** 1:6–9,12,21; 2:1–4,6,7; 12:9; 38:1; 40:1, 3,6; 42:1,7,9–12; **Ps.** 1:2,6; 2:2,7,11; 3:1(2),3–5(4–6),7(8),8(9); 4:3(4),5(6), 6(7),8(9); 5:1(2),3(4),6(7),8(9),12(13); 6:1–4(2–5),8(9),9(10); 7:[title](1),1(2), 3(4),6(7),8(9),17(18); 8:1(2),9(10); 9:1(2),7(8),9–11(10–12),13(14),16(17), 19(20),20(21); 10:1,3,12,16,17; 11:1,4, 5,7; 12:1(2),3(4),5–7(6–8); 13:1(2), 3(4),6; 14:2,4,6,7; 15:1,4; 16:2,5,7,8; 17:1,13,14; 18:[title](1),1–3(2–4), 6(7),13(14),15(16),18(19),20(21),21(22), 24(25),28(29),30(31),31(32),41(42), 46(47),49(50); 19:7–9(8–10),14(15); 20:1(2),5–7(6–8),9(10); 21:1(2),7(8), 9(10),13(14);22:8(9),19(20),23(24), 26–28(27–29); 23:1,6; 24:1,3,5,8,10; 25:1,4,6–8,10–12,14,15; 26:1,2,6,8,12; 27:1,4,6–8,10,11,13,14; 28:1,5–8; 29:1–5,7–11; 30:1–4(2–5),7(8),8(9), 10(11),12(13); 31:1(2),5(6),6(7),9(10), 14(15),17(18),21(22),23(24),24(25); 32:2,5,10,11; 33:1,2,4–6,8,10–13,18, 20,22; 34:1–4(2–5),6–11(7–12),15–19 (16–20),22(23); 35:1,5,6,9,10,22,24,27; 36:[title](1),5(6),6(7); 37:3–5,7,9,17,18, 20,23,24,28,33,34,39,40; 38:1(2),15(16), 21(22); 39:4(5),12(13); 40:1(2),3–5(4–6), 9(10),11(12),13(14),16(17); 41:1–4(2–5), 10(11),13(14); 42:8(9); 46:7(8),8(9), 11(12); 47:2(3),5(6); 48:1(2),8(9); 50:1; 54:6(8); 55:16(17),22(23); 56:10(11); 58:6(7); 59:3(4),5(6),8(9); 64:10(11); 68:16(17),26(27); 69:13(14),16(17), 31(32),33(34); 70:1(2),5(6); 71:1; 72:18; 74:18; 75:8(9); 76:11(12); 78:4,21; 79:5; 80:4(5),19(20); 81:10(11),15(16); 83:16(17),18(19); 84:1–3(2–4),8(9), 11(12),12(13); 85:1(2),7(8),8(9),12(13); 86:1,6,11,17; 87:2,6; 88:1(2),9(10), 13(14),14(15); 89:1(2),5(6),6(7),8(9), 15(16),18(19),46(47),51(52),52(53); 90:13; 91:2,9; 92:1(2),4(5),5(6),8(9), 9(10),13(14),15(16); 93:1,3–5; 94:1, 3,5,11,14,17,18,22,23; 95:1,3,6; 96:1, 2,4,5,7–10,13; 97:1,5,8–10,12; 98:1,2, 4–6,9; 99:1,2,5,6,8,9; 100:1–3,5; 101:1,8; 102:1(2),12(13),15(16),16(17),19(20), 21(22),22(23); 103:1,2,6,8,13,17,19–22; 104:1,16,24,31,33–35; 105:1,3,4,7,19; 106:1,2,4,16,25,34,40,47,48; 107:1,2,6, 8,13,15,19,21,24,28,31,43; 108:3(4); 109:14,15,20,26,27,30; 110:1,2,4; 111:1,2,4,10; 112:1,7; 113:1–5; 115:1,9–16; 116:1,4–7,9,12–19; 117:1,2; 118:1,4,6–13,15,16,20,23–27,29; 119:1, 12,31,33,41,52,55,57,64,65,75,89,107,10 8,126,137,145,149,151,156,159,166,169, 174; 120:1,2; 121:2,5,7,8; 122:1,4,9; 123:2,3; 124:1,2,6,8; 125:1,2,4,5; 126:1–4; 127:1,3; 128:1,4,5; 129:4,8; 130:1,5,7; 131:1,3; 132:1,2,5,8,11,13; 133:3; 134:1–3; 135:1–3,5,6,13,14, 19–21; 136:1; 137:4,7; 138:4–6,8; 139:1,4,21; 140:1(2),4(5),6(7),8(9),

12(13); 141:1,3; 142:1(2),5(6); 143:1,7, 9,11; 144:1,3,5,15; 145:3,8–10,14,17, 18,20,21; 146:1,2,5,7–10; 147:2,6,7, 11,12; 148:1,5,7,13; 149:1,4; **Prov.** 1:7,29; 2:5,6; 3:5,7,9,11,12,19,26,32,33; 5:21; 6:16; 8:13,22,35; 9:10; 10:3,22, 27,29; 11:1,20; 12:2,22; 14:2,26,27; 15:3, 8,9,11,16,25,26,29,33; 16:1–7,9,11,20,33; 17:3,15; 18:10,22; 19:3,14,17,21,23; 20:10,12,22,23,24,27; 21:1–3,30,31; 22:2,4,12,14,19,23; 23:17; 24:18,21; 25:22; 28:5,25; 29:13,25,26; 30:9; 31:30; **Isa.** 1:2,4,9–11,18,20,24,28; 2:2,3,5, 10–12,17,19,21; 3:1,8,13,14,16,17; 4:2,5; 5:7,9,12,16,24,25; 6:3,5,12; 7:3,10–12, 17,18; 8:1,3,5,11,13,17,18; 9:7(6), 11(10),13(12),14(13),19(18); 10:16,20, 26,33; 11:2,3,9,15; 12:1,2,4,5; 13:4–6, 9,13; 14:1–3,5,22–24,27,32; 16:13,14; 17:3,6; 18:4,7; 19:1,4,12,14,16–22,25; 20:2,3; 21:10,17; 22:14,17,25; 23:9,11, 17,18; 24:1,3,14,15,21,23; 25:1,6,8–10; 26:4,8,10–13,15–17,21; 27:1,3,12,13; 28:5,13,14,21,29; 29:6,10,15,19,22; 30:1,9,18,26,27,29–33; 31:1,3–5,9; 32:6; 33:2,5,6,10,21,22; 34:2,6,8,16; 35:2,10; 36:7,10,15,18,20; 37:1,4,6,14–18,20–22, 32–34,36; 38:1–5,7,20,22; 39:5,6,8; 40:2, 3,5,7,13,27,28,31; 41:4,13,14,16,17, 20,21; 42:5,6,8,10,12,13,19,21,24; 43:1, 3,10–12,14–16; 44:2,5,6,23,24; 45:1,3, 5–8,11,13,14,17–19,21,24,25; 47:4; 48:1, 2,14,17,20,22; 49:1,4,5,7,8,13,14,18,23, 25,26; 50:1,10; 51:1,3,9,11,13,15,17, 20,22; 52:3,5,8–12; 53:1,6,10; 54:1,5,6, 8,10,13,17; 55:5–8,13; 56:1,3,4,6; 57:19; 58:5,8,9,11,13,14; 59:1,13,15,19–21; 60:1,2,6,9,14,16,19,20,22; 61:1–3,6, 8–10; 62:2–4,6,8,9,11,12; 63:7,14,16,17; 64:8(7),9(8),12(11); 65:7,8,11,23,25; 66:1,2,5,6,9,12,14–17,20–23; **Jer.** 1:2,4, 7–9,11–15,19; 2:1–6,8,9,12,17,19,29, 31,37; 3:1,6,10–14,16,17,20–23,25; 4:1–4,8,9,17,26,27; 5:2–5,9–12,14,15,18, 19,22,24,29; 6:6,9–12,15,16,21,22,30; 7:1–4,11,13,19,21,28–30,32; 8:1,3,4, 7–9,12–14,17,19; 9:3(2),6(5),7(6),9(8), 12(11),13(12),15(14),17(16),20(19), 22–25(21–24); 10:1,2,6,10,16,18,21, 23,24; 11:1,3,5,6,9,11,16–18,20–22; 12:1,3,12–14,16,17; 13:1–3,5,6,8,9, 11–17,25; 14:1,7,9–11,14,15,20,22; 15:1–3,6,9,11,15,16,19,20; 16:1,3,5, 9–11,14–16,19,21; 17:5,7,10,13–15, 19–21,24,26; 18:1,5,6,11,13,19,23; 19:1,3,6,11,12,14,15; 20:1–4,7,8,11–13, 16; 21:1,2,4,7,8,10–14; 22:1–3,5,6,8,9, 11,16,18,24,29,30; 23:1,2,4–9,11,12, 15–20,23,24,28–38; 24:1,3–5,7,8; 25:3–5,7–9,12,15,17,27–33,36,37; 26:1,2,4,7–10,12,13,15,16,18–20; 27:1,2,4,8,11,13,15,16,18,19,21,22; 28:1–6,9,11–16; 29:4,7–11,14–17, 19–23,25,26,30–32; 30:1–5,8–12,17, 18,21,23,24; 31:1–3,6,7,10–12,14–18,20, 22,23,27,28,31–38,40; 32:1,3,5,6,8, 14–16,18,26–28,30,36,42,44; 33:1,2, 4,10–14,16,17,19,20,23–25; 34:1,2 ,4,5,8,12,13,17,22; 35:1,2,4,12,13,17–19; 36:1,4–11,26,27,29,30; 37:2,3,6,7,9,17; 38:2,3,14,16,17,20,21; 39:15–18; 40:1–3; 41:5; 42:2–7,9,11,13,15,18–21; 43:1,2, 4,7,8,10; 44:2,7,11,16,21–26,29,30; 45:2–5; 46:1,5,13,15,18,23,25,26,28; 47:1,2,4,6,7; 48:1,8,10,12,15,25,26,30, 35,38,40,42–44,47; 49:1,2,6,7,12–14,16, 18,20,26,28,30–32,34,35,37–39; 50:1,4, 5,7,10,13–15,18,20,21,24,25,28–30, 33–35,40,45; 51:1,5–7,10–12,14,19, 24–26,29,33,36,39,45,48,50–53,55–58,6 2; 52:2,3,13,17,20; **Lam.** 1:5,9,11,12,17, 18,20; 2:6–9,17,20,22; 3:18,22,24–26,40, 50,55,59,61,64,66; 4:11,16,20; 5:1,19,21; **Ezek.** 1:3,28; 3:12,14,16,22,23; 4:13; 5:13,15,17; 6:1,7,10,13,14; 7:1,4,9,19,27; 8:12,14,16; 9:4,9; 10:4,18,19; 11:1,5,10, 12,14,15,23,25; 12:1,8,15–17,20,21, 25,26; 13:1,2,5–7,14,21,23; 14:2,4, 7–9,12; 15:1,7; 16:1,35,58,62; 17:1,11, 21,24; 18:1; 20:1,2,5,7,12,19,20,26,38, 42,44,45(21:1),47(21:3),48(21:4); 21:1(6),3(8),5(10),8(13),17(22),18(23), 32(37); 22:1,14,16,17,22,23,28; 23:1,36; 24:1,14,15,20,27; 25:1,5,7,11,17; 26:1,6,

14; 27:1; 28:1,11,20,22,23,26; 29:1,6, 9,17,21; 30:1,3,6,8,12,19,20,25,26; 31:1; 32:1,15,17; 33:1,22,23,29,30; 34:1,7,9, 24,27,30; 35:1,4,9,10,12,15; 36:1,11,16, 20,23,36,38; 37:1,4,6,13–15,28; 38:1,23; 39:6,7,22,28; 40:1,46; 41:22; 42:13; 43:4, 5,24; 44:2–5; 45:1,4,23; 46:3,4,9,12–14; 48:9,10,14,35; **Dan.** 9:2,4,10,13,14,20; **Hos.** 1:1,2,4,7; 2:13(15),16(18),20(22), 21(23); 3:1,5; 4:1,10,15,16; 5:4,6,7; 6:1,3; 7:10; 8:1,13; 9:3–5,14; 10:3,12; 11:10,11; 12:2(3),5(6),9(10),13(14); 13:4,15; 14:1(2),2(3),9(10); **Joel** 1:1,9,14,15,19; 2:1,11–14,17–19,21,23,26,27,31(3:4), 32(3:5); 3:8(4:8),11(4:11),14(4:14),16–18 (4:16–18),21(4:21); **Amos** 1:2,3,5,6,9,11, 13,15; 2:1,3,4,6,11,16; 3:1,6,10,12,15; 4:3,6,8–11,13; 5:4,6,8,14–18,20,27; 6:8,10,11,14; 7:3,6,8,15–17; 8:2,7,11,12; 9:6–8,12,13,15; **Obad.** 1:1,4,8,15,18,21; **Jon.** 1:1,3,4,9,10,14,16,17(2:1); 2:1(2), 2(3),6(7),7(8),9(10),10(11); 3:1,3; 4:2–4 ,6,10; **Mic.** 1:1,3,12; 2:3,5,7,13; 3:4,5, 8,11; 4:1,2,4–7,10,12,13; 5:4(3),7(6), 10(9); 6:1,2,5–9; 7:7–10,17; **Nah.** 1:2,3,7,9,11,12,14; 2:2(3),13(14); 3:5; **Hab.** 1:2,12; 2:2,13,14,16,20; 3:2,8,18; **Zeph.** 1:1–3,5–8,10,12,14,17,18; 2:2, 3,5,7,9–11; 3:2,5,8,9,12,15,17,20; **Hag.** 1:1–3,5,7–9,12–14; 2:1,4,6–11,14,15,17, 18,20,23; **Zech.** 1:1–4,6,7,10–14,16,17, 20(2:3); 2:5(9),6(10),8–13(12–17); 3:1, 2,5–7,9,10; 4:6,8–10; 5:4; 6:9,12–15; 7:1–4,7–9,12,13; 8:1–4,6,7,9,11,14, 17–23; 9:1,14–16; 10:1,3,5–7,12; 11:4–6, 11,13,15; 12:1,4,5,7,8; 13:2,3,7–9; 14:1, 3,5,7,9,12,13,16–18,20,21; **Mal.** 1:1,2, 4–11,13–14; 2:2,4,7,8,11–14,16,17; 3:1, 3–7,10–14,16,17; 4:1(3:19),3(3:21),5(3:23).

3069. יֱהוִה *y^{e}hōwih* **masc. proper noun**
(GOD: const. form of 3068 with the vowels of [Q^e] *'elōhiym* [430] used in reading)
Gen. 15:2,8; **Deut.** 3:24; 9:26; **Josh.** 7:7; **Judg.** 6:22; 16:28; **2 Sam.** 7:18–20, 28,29; **1 Kgs.** 2:26; 8:53; **Ps.** 68:20(21); 69:6(7); 71:5,16; 73:28; 109:21; 140:7(8); 141:8; **Isa.** 3:15; 7:7; 10:23,24; 22:5,12, 14,15; 25:8; 28:16,22; 30:15; 40:10; 48:16; 49:22; 50:4,5,7,9; 52:4; 56:8; 61:1,11; 65:13,15; **Jer.** 1:6; 2:19,22; 4:10; 7:20; 14:13; 32:17,25; 44:26; 46:10; 49:5; 50:25,31; **Ezek.** 2:4; 3:11,27; 4:14; 5:5, 7,8,11; 6:3,11; 7:2,5; 8:1; 9:8; 11:7,8, 13,16,17,21; 12:10,19,23,25,28; 13:3,8, 9,13,16,18,20; 14:4,6,11,14,16,18,20, 21,23; 15:6,8; 16:3,8,14,19,23,30,36, 43,48,59,63; 17:3,9,16,19,22; 18:3,9,23, 30,32; 20:3,5,27,30,31,33,36,39,40,44, 47(21:3),49(21:5); 21:7(12),13(18), 24(29),26(31),28(33); 22:3,12,19,28,31; 23:22,28,32,34,35,46,49; 24:3,6,9,14, 21,24; 25:3,6,8,12–16; 26:3,5,7,14,15, 19,21; 27:3; 28:2,6,10,12,22,24,25; 29:3,8,13,16,19,20; 30:2,6,10,13,22; 31:10,15,18; 32:3,8,11,14,16,31,32; 33:11,25,27; 34:2,8,10,11,15,17,20, 30,31; 35:3,6,11,14; 36:2–7,13–15,22, 23,32,33,37; 37:3,5,9,12,19,21; 38:3, 10,14,17,18,21; 39:1,5,8,10,13,17,20, 25,29; 43:18,19,27; 44:6,9,12,15,27; 45:9,15,18; 46:1,16; 47:13,23; 48:29; **Amos** 1:8; 3:7,8,11,13; 4:2,5; 5:3; 6:8; 7:1,2,4–6; 8:1,3,9,11; 9:5,8; **Obad.** 1:1; **Mic.** 1:2; **Hab.** 3:19; **Zeph.** 1:7; **Zech.** 9:14.

3070. יְהוָה יִרְאֶה *y^{e}hōwāh yir'eh* **proper noun**
(Jehovah jireh)
Gen. 22:14(NASB, NIV, see *y^{e}hōwāh* [3068] and *rā'āh* [7200]).

3071. יְהוָה נִסִּי *y^{e}hōwāh nissiy* **proper noun**
(Jehovah nissi)
Ex. 17:15(NASB, NIV, see *y^{e}hōwāh* [3068] and *nēs* [5251]).

3072. יְהוָה צִדְקֵנוּ *y^{e}hōwāh ṣiḏqēnû* **masc. proper noun**
(Jehovah Tsidkenu)

Jer. 23:6(KJV, NASB, NIV, see *y^e^hōwāh* [3068] and *ṣeḏeq* [6664]); 33:16(KJV, NASB, NIV, see *y^e^hōwāh* [3068] and *ṣeḏeq* [6664]).

3073. שָׁלוֹם יְהוָֹה *y^e^hōwāh šālôm* **proper noun**
(Jehovah shalom)
Judg. 6:24(NASB, NIV, see *y^e^hōwāh* [3068] and *šālôm* [7965]).

3074. שָׁמָּה יְהוָֹה *y^e^hōwāh šāmmāh* **proper noun**
(Jehovah shammah)
Ezek. 48:35(KJV, NASB, NIV, see *y^e^hōwāh* [3068] and *šām* [8033]).

3075. A. יְהוֹזָבָד *y^e^hôzāḇāḏ* **masc. proper noun**
(Jehozabad: son of Shomer)
2 Kgs. 12:21(22); **2 Chr.** 24:26.
B. יְהוֹזָבָד *y^e^hôzāḇāḏ* **masc. proper noun**
(Jehozabad: son of Obed-Edom)
1 Chr. 26:4.
C. יְהוֹזָבָד *y^e^hôzāḇāḏ* **masc. proper noun**
(Jehozabad: a Benjamite)
2 Chr. 17:18.

3076. A. יְהוֹחָנָן *y^e^hôḥānān* **masc. proper noun**
(Jehohanan: a Levite)
1 Chr. 26:3; **2 Chr.** 28:12.
B. יְהוֹחָנָן *y^e^hôḥānān* **masc. proper noun**
(Jehohanan: a general under Jehoshaphat)
2 Chr. 17:15; 23:1.
C. יְהוֹחָנָן *y^e^hôḥānān* **masc. proper noun**
(Jehohanan: an Israelite)
Ezra 10:28.
D. יְהוֹחָנָן *y^e^hôḥānān* **masc. proper noun**
(Jehohanan: a priest)
Neh. 12:13.
E. יְהוֹחָנָן *y^e^hôḥānān* **masc. proper noun**
(Jehohanan: a priest)
Neh. 12:42.
F. יְהוֹחָנָן *y^e^hôḥānān* **masc. proper noun**
(Jehohanan: high priest)
Ezra 10:6.
G. יְהוֹחָנָן *y^e^hôḥānān* **masc. proper noun**
(Jehohanan: son of Tobiah)
Neh. 6:18.

3077. A. יְהוֹיָדָע *y^e^hôyāḏā'* **masc. proper noun**
(Jehoiada: father of Benaiah)
2 Sam. 8:18; 20:23; 23:20,22; **1 Kgs.** 1:8,26,32,36,38,44; 2:25,29,34,35,46; 4:4; **1 Chr.** 11:22,24; 12:27; 18:17; 27:5.
B. יְהוֹיָדָע *y^e^hôyāḏā'* **masc. proper noun**
(Jehoiada: son of Benaiah)
1 Chr. 27:34.
C. יְהוֹיָדָע *y^e^hôyāḏā'* **masc. proper noun**
(Jehoiada: high priest who coronated King Joash)
2 Kgs. 11:4,9,15,17; 12:2(3),7(8),9(10); **2 Chr.** 22:11; 23:1,8,9,11,14,16,18; 24:2, 3,6,12,14,15,17,20,22,25.
D. יְהוֹיָדָע *y^e^hôyāḏā'* **masc. proper noun**
(Jehoiada: a priest)
Jer. 29:26.

3078. יְהוֹיָכִין *y^e^hôyāḵiyn* **masc. proper noun**
(Jehoiachin; see also *yôyāḵiyn* [3112], NIV, see also *y^e^ḵônyāh* [3204])
2 Kgs. 24:6,8,12,15; 25:27; **2 Chr.** 36:8,9; **Jer.** 52:31.

3079. יְהוֹיָקִים *y^e^hôyāqiym* **masc. proper noun**
(Jehoiakim)
2 Kgs. 23:34–36; 24:1,5,6,19; **1 Chr.**

3:15,16; **2 Chr.** 36:4,5,8; **Jer.** 1:3; 22:18,24; 24:1; 25:1; 26:1,21–23; 27:1,20; 28:4; 35:1; 36:1,9,28–30,32; 37:1; 45:1; 46:2; 52:2; **Dan.** 1:1,2.

3080. יְהוֹיָרִיב y^e*hôyāriyḇ* **masc. proper noun**
(Jehoiarib)
1 Chr. 9:10; 24:7.

3081. יְהוּכַל y^e*hûḵal* **masc. proper noun**
(Jehucal)
Jer. 37:3.

3082. A. יְהוֹנָדָב y^e*hônāḏāḇ* **masc. proper noun**
(Jonadab: son of Rechab [see also *yônāḏaḇ* [3122,A])
2 Kgs. 10:15,23; **Jer.** 35:8,14,16,18.
B. יְהוֹנָדָב y^e*hônāḏāḇ* **masc. proper noun**
(Jonadab: nephew of David; see also *yônāḏaḇ* [3122,B])
2 Sam. 13:5.

3083. A. יְהוֹנָתָן y^e*hônāṯān* **masc. proper noun**
(Jonathan: son of Saul; see also *yônāṯān* [3129,A])
1 Sam. 14:6,8; 18:1,3,4; 19:1,2,4,6,7; 20:1,3–5,9–13,16–18,25,27,28,30 ,32–35,37–40,42(21:1); 23:16,18; 31:2; **2 Sam.** 1:4,5,12,17,22,23,25,26; 4:4; 9:1,3,6,7; 21:7,12–14; **1 Chr.** 8:33,34; 9:39,40.
B. יְהוֹנָתָן y^e*hônāṯān* **masc. proper noun**
(Jonathan: son of Abiathar; see also *yōnāṯān* [3129,B])
2 Sam. 15:27,36; 17:17,20.
C. יְהוֹנָתָן y^e*hônāṯān* **masc. proper noun**
(Jonathan: son of Shimeah)
2 Sam. 21:21; **1 Chr.** 20:7.
D. יְהוֹנָתָן y^e*hônāṯān* **masc. proper noun**
(Jonathan: one of David's mighty men and son of Shagee)
2 Sam. 23:32; **1 Chr.** 11:34.
E. יְהוֹנָתָן y^e*hônāṯān* **masc. proper noun**
(Jonathan: David's uncle)
1 Chr. 27:32.
F. יְהוֹנָתָן y^e*hônāṯān* **masc. proper noun**
(Jonathan: son of Uzziah)
1 Chr. 27:25.
G. יְהוֹנָתָן y^e*hônāṯān* **masc. proper noun**
(Jonathan: a scribe)
Jer. 37:15,20; 38:26.
H. יְהוֹנָתָן y^e*hônāṯān* **masc. proper noun**
(Jonathan: a Levite)
2 Chr. 17:8.
I. יְהוֹנָתָן y^e*hônāṯān* **masc. proper noun**
(Jonathan: a priest)
Neh. 12:18.
J. יְהוֹנָתָן y^e*hônāṯān* **masc. proper noun**
(Jonathan: a priest)
Judg. 18:30.

3084. יְהוֹסֵף y^e*hôsēp̱* **masc. proper noun**
(Joseph: var. of *yôsēp̱* [3130,B])
Ps. 81:5(6).

3085. יְהוֹעַדָּה y^e*hôʿaddāh* **masc. proper noun**
(Jehoadah)
1 Chr. 8:36.

3086. יְהוֹעַדָּן y^e*hôʿaddān* **fem. proper noun**
(Jehoaddan)
2 Kgs. 14:2; **2 Chr.** 25:1.

3087. יְהוֹצָדָק y^e*hôṣāḏāq* **masc. proper noun**
(Jehozadak)
1 Chr. 6:14(5:40),15(5:41); **Hag.** 1:1,12,14; 2:2,4; **Zech.** 6:11.

3088. A. יְהוֹרָם *y^ehôrām* **masc. proper noun**
(Jehoram: king of Judah, son of Jehoshaphat; see also *yôrām* [3141,A])
1 Kgs. 22:50(51); **2 Kgs.** 8:16,25,29; 12:18(19); **2 Chr.** 21:1,3–5,9,16; 22:1, 6,11.
B. יְהוֹרָם *y^ehôrām* **masc. proper noun**
(Jehoram: king of Israel, son of Ahab; see also *yôrām* [3141,B])
2 Kgs. 1:17; 3:1,6; 9:15,17,21–24; **2 Chr.** 22:5,7.
C. יְהוֹרָם *y^ehôrām* **masc. proper noun**
(Jehoram: a priest)
2 Chr. 17:8.

3089. יְהוֹשֶׁבַע *y^ehôšeḇa'* **fem. proper noun**
(Jehosheba)
2 Kgs. 11:2.

3090. יְהוֹשַׁבְעַת *y^ehôšaḇ'aṯ* **fem. proper noun**
(Jehoshabeath)
2 Chr. 22:11.

3091. A. יְהוֹשׁוּעַ *y^ehôšûa'*, יְהוֹשֻׁעַ *y^ehôšua'* **masc. proper noun**
(Joshua: the son of Nun)
Ex. 17:9,10,13,14; 24:13; 32:17; 33:11; **Num.** 11:28; 13:16; 14:6,30,38; 26:65; 27:18,22; 32:12,28; 34:17; **Deut.** 1:38; 3:21,28; 31:3,7,14,23; 34:9; **Josh.** 1:1, 10,12,16; 2:1,23,24; 3:1,5–7,9,10; 4:1,4, 5,8–10,14,15,17,20; 5:2–4,7,9,13–15; 6:2,6,8,10,12,16,22,25–27; 7:2,3,6,7,10, 16,19,20,22–25; 8:1,3,9,10,13,15,16,18, 21,23,26–30,35; 9:2,3,6,8,15,22,24,27; 10:1,4,6–9,12,15,17,18,20–22,24–29,31, 33,34,36,38,40–43; 11:6,7,9,10,12,13, 15,16,18,21,23; 12:7; 13:1; 14:1,6,13; 15:13; 17:4,14,15,17; 18:3,8–10; 19:49,51; 20:1; 21:1; 22:1,6,7; 23:1,2; 24:1,2,19,21,22,24–29,31; **Judg.** 1:1; 2:6–8,21,23; **1 Kgs.** 16:34; **1 Chr.** 7:27.
B. יְהוֹשֻׁעַ *y^ehôšua'* **masc. proper noun**
(Joshua: citizen of Beth Shemesh)
1 Sam. 6:14,18.
C. יְהוֹשֻׁעַ *y^ehôšua'* **masc. proper noun**
(Joshua: high priest)
Hag. 1:1,12,14; 2:2,4; **Zech.** 3:1,3,6,8,9; 6:11.
D. יְהוֹשֻׁעַ *y^ehôšua'* **masc. proper noun**
(Joshua: governor of Jerusalem)
2 Kgs. 23:8.

3092. A. יְהוֹשָׁפָט *y^ehôšāp̱āṭ* **masc. proper noun**
(Jehoshaphat: king of Judah, son of Asa)
1 Kgs. 15:24; 22:2,4,5,7,8,10,18,29,30,32,41,42,44(45), 45(46),48–51(49–52); **2 Kgs.** 1:17; 3:1, 7,11,12,14; 8:16; 12:18(19); **1 Chr.** 3:10; **2 Chr.** 17:1,3,5,10–12; 18:1,3,4,6,7,9,17, 28,29,31; 19:1,2,4,8; 20:1–3,5,15,18,20, 25,27,30,31,34,35,37; 21:1,2,12; 22:9.
B. יְהוֹשָׁפָט *y^ehôšāp̱āṭ* **masc. proper noun**
(Jehoshaphat: father of Jehu)
2 Kgs. 9:2,14.
C. יְהוֹשָׁפָט *y^ehôšāp̱āṭ* **masc. proper noun**
(Jehoshaphat: son of Ahilud)
2 Sam. 8:16; 20:24; **1 Kgs.** 4:3; **1 Chr.** 18:15.
D. יְהוֹשָׁפָט *y^ehôšāp̱āṭ* **masc. proper noun**
(Jehoshaphat: a royal officer)
1 Kgs. 4:17.
E. יְהוֹשָׁפָט *y^ehôšāp̱āṭ* **proper noun**
(Jehoshaphat: a valley)
Joel 3:2(4:2),12(4:12).

3093. יָהִיר *yāhiyr* **adj.**
(proud, arrogant)
Prov. 21:24; **Hab.** 2:5.

3094. A. יְהַלֶּלְאֵל *y^e^hallel'ēl* **masc. proper noun**
(Jehallelel: a Judaite)
1 Chr. 4:16.
B. יְהַלֶּלְאֵל *y^e^hallel'ēl* **masc. proper noun**
(Jehallelel: a Levite)
2 Chr. 29:12.

3095. יַהֲלֹם *yah^a^lōm,* יָהֲלֹם *yāh^a^lōm* **masc. noun**
(diamond, emerald)
Ex. 28:18; 39:11; **Ezek.** 28:13.

3096. יַהַץ *yahaṣ,* יַהְצָה *yahṣāh* **proper noun**
(Jahaz)
Num. 21:23; **Deut.** 2:32; **Josh.** 13:18; 21:36; **Judg.** 11:20; **1 Chr.** 6:78(63); **Isa.** 15:4; **Jer.** 48:21,34.

3097. A. יוֹאָב *yô'āḇ* **masc. proper noun**
(Joab: David's nephew)
1 Sam. 26:6; **2 Sam.** 2:13,14,18,22,24,26–28,30,32; 3:22–24, 26,27,29–31; 8:16; 10:7,9,13,14; 11:1,6, 7,11,14,16–18,22,25; 12:26,27; 14:1–3, 19–23,29–33; 17:25; 18:2,5,10–12, 14–16,20–22,29; 19:1(2),5(6),13(14); 20:7–11,13,15–17,20–23; 23:18,24,37; 24:2–4,9; **1 Kgs.** 1:7,19,41; 2:5,22, 28–31,33; 11:15,16,21; **1 Chr.** 2:16,54 (NASB, NIV, *'aṭrôṯ bēṯ yô'aḇ* [5854]); 11:6,8,20,26,39; 18:15; 19:8,10,14,15; 20:1; 21:2–6; 26:28; 27:7,24,34; **Ps.** 60:[title](1).
B. יוֹאָב *yô'āḇ* **masc. proper noun**
(Joab: son of Seraiah)
1 Chr. 4:14.
C. יוֹאָב *yô'āḇ* **masc. proper noun**
(Joab: head of a family)
Ezra 2:6; 8:9; **Neh.** 7:11.

3098. A. יוֹאָח *yô'āḥ* **masc. proper noun**
(Joah: son of Asaph)
2 Kgs. 18:18,26,37; **Isa.** 36:3,11,22.
B. יוֹאָח *yô'āḥ* **masc. proper noun**
(Joah: a Levite)
1 Chr. 6:21(6).
C. יוֹאָח *yô'āḥ* **masc. proper noun**
(Joah: a Levite)
2 Chr. 29:12.
D. יוֹאָח *yô'āḥ* **masc. proper noun**
(Joah: son of Joahaz)
2 Chr. 34:8.
E. יוֹאָח *yô'āḥ* **masc. proper noun**
(Joah: son of Obed-Edom)
1 Chr. 26:4.

3099. A. יוֹאָחָז *yô'āḥāz* **masc. proper noun**
(Joahaz, Jehoahaz: king of Judah, son of Josiah; var. of *y^e^hô'āḥāz* [3059,C])
2 Chr. 36:2,4.
B. יוֹאָחָז *yô'āḥāz* **masc. proper noun**
(Joahaz, Jehoahaz: king of Israel, son of Jehu; var. of *y^e^hô'āḥāz* [3059,B])
2 Kgs. 14:1.
C. יוֹאָחָז *yô'āḥāz* **masc. proper noun**
(Joahaz: Josiah's chronicler)
2 Chr. 34:8.

3100. A. יוֹאֵל *yô'ēl* **masc. proper noun**
(the prophet Joel)
Joel 1:1.
B. יוֹאֵל *yô'ēl* **masc. proper noun**
(Joel: Samuel's elder son)
1 Sam. 8:2; **1 Chr.** 6:28(13)(KJV, [K^e^] omits),33(18); 15:17.
C. יוֹאֵל *yô'ēl* **masc. proper noun**
(Joel: Simeonite prince)
1 Chr. 4:35.
D. יוֹאֵל *yô'ēl* **masc. proper noun**
(Joel: a Reubenite)
1 Chr. 5:4,8.

E. יוֹאֵל *yôʾēl* **masc. proper noun**
(Joel: a Gadite chief)
1 Chr. 5:12.
F. יוֹאֵל *yôʾēl* **masc. proper noun**
(Joel: a Levite)
1 Chr. 6:36(21).
G. יוֹאֵל *yôʾēl* **masc. proper noun**
(Joel: chief of Issachar)
1 Chr. 7:3.
H. יוֹאֵל *yôʾēl* **masc. proper noun**
(Joel: one of David's mighty men)
1 Chr. 11:38.
I. יוֹאֵל *yôʾēl* **masc. proper noun**
(Joel: Manassite chief)
1 Chr. 27:20.
J. יוֹאֵל *yôʾēl* **masc. proper noun**
(Joel: a Levite)
1 Chr. 15:7,11,17; 23:8; 26:22.
K. יוֹאֵל *yôʾēl* **masc. proper noun**
(Joel: Kohathite Levite)
2 Chr. 29:12.
L. יוֹאֵל *yôʾēl* **masc. proper noun**
(Joel: son of Nebo)
Ezra 10:43.
M. יוֹאֵל *yôʾēl* **masc. proper noun**
(Joel: son of Zichri)
Neh. 11:9.

3101. A. יוֹאָשׁ *yôʾāš* **masc. proper noun**
(Joash: king of Judah, son of Ahaziah; var. of *y^{e}hôʾaš* [3060,A])
2 Kgs. 11:2; 12:19(20),20(21); 13:1,10; 14:3,17; **1 Chr.** 3:11; **2 Chr.** 22:11; 24:1,2,4,22,24.
B. יוֹאָשׁ *yôʾāš* **masc. proper noun**
(Joash: king of Israel, son of Jehoahaz; var. of *y^{e}hôʾaš* [3060,B])
2 Kgs. 13:9,12–14,25; 14:1,23,27; **2 Chr.** 25:17,18,21,23,25; **Hos.** 1:1; **Amos** 1:1.
C. יוֹאָשׁ *yôʾāš* **masc. proper noun**
(Joash: father of Gideon)
Judg. 6:11,29–31; 7:14; 8:13,29,32.
D. יוֹאָשׁ *yôʾāš* **masc. proper noun**
(Joash: prince of Ahab's house)
1 Kgs. 22:26; **2 Chr.** 18:25.
E. יוֹאָשׁ *yôʾāš* **masc. proper noun**
(Joash: one of David's mighty men)
1 Chr. 12:3.
F. יוֹאָשׁ *yôʾāš* **masc. proper noun**
(Joash: Judaite prince)
1 Chr. 4:22.

3102. יוֹב *yôḇ* **masc. proper noun**
(Job)
Gen. 46:13(NIV, *yāšûḇ* [3437,A]).

3103. A. יוֹבָב *yôḇāḇ* **masc. proper noun**
(Jobab: son of Joktan)
Gen. 10:29; **1 Chr.** 1:23.
B. יוֹבָב *yôḇāḇ* **masc. proper noun**
(Jobab: king of Edom)
Gen. 36:33,34; **1 Chr.** 1:44,45.
C. יוֹבָב *yôḇāḇ* **masc. proper noun**
(Jobab: king of Madon)
Josh. 11:1.
D. יוֹבָב *yôḇāḇ* **masc. proper noun**
(Jobab: son of Shaharaim)
1 Chr. 8:9.
E. יוֹבָב *yôḇāḇ* **masc. proper noun**
(Jobab: a Benjamite)
1 Chr. 8:18.

3104. יוֹבֵל *yôḇēl* **masc. noun**
(ram's horn, trumpet, jubilee)
Ex. 19:13; **Lev.** 25:10–13,15,28,30,31,33,40,50,52,54; 27:17,18,21,23,24; **Num.** 36:4; **Josh.** 6:4–6,8,13.

3105. יוּבַל *yûḇal* **masc. noun**
(stream, water)
Jer. 17:8.

3106. יוּבָל *yûḇāl* **masc. proper noun**
(Jubal)
Gen. 4:21.

3107. A. יוֹזָבָד *yôzāḇāḏ* **masc. proper noun**
(Jozabad: soldier in David's army)
1 Chr. 12:4.

B. יוֹזָבָד *yôzā<u>b</u>ā<u>d</u>* **masc. proper noun**
(Jozabad: Manassite captain)
1 Chr. 12:20.
C. יוֹזָבָד *yôzā<u>b</u>ā<u>d</u>* **masc. proper noun**
(Jozabad: another Manassite captain)
1 Chr. 12:20.
D. יוֹזָבָד *yôzā<u>b</u>ā<u>d</u>* **masc. proper noun**
(Jozabad: a Levite)
2 Chr. 31:13.
E. יוֹזָבָד *yôzā<u>b</u>ā<u>d</u>* **masc. proper noun**
(Jozabad: a chief Levite)
2 Chr. 35:9.
F. יוֹזָבָד *yôzā<u>b</u>ā<u>d</u>* **masc. proper noun**
(Jozabad: a priest)
Ezra 10:22.
G. יוֹזָבָד *yôzā<u>b</u>ā<u>d</u>* **masc. proper noun**
(Jozabad: a priest)
Ezra 10:23.
H. יוֹזָבָד *yôzā<u>b</u>ā<u>d</u>* **masc. proper noun**
(Jozabad: a Levite)
Ezra 8:33.
I. יוֹזָבָד *yôzā<u>b</u>ā<u>d</u>* **masc. proper noun**
(Jozabad: a Levite)
Neh. 8:7.
J. יוֹזָבָד *yôzā<u>b</u>ā<u>d</u>* **masc. proper noun**
(Jozabad: a Levite)
Neh. 11:16.

3108. יוֹזָכָר *yôzā<u>k</u>ār* **masc. proper noun**
(Jozachar)
2 Kgs. 12:21(22).

3109. A. יוֹחָא *yôḥā'* **masc. proper noun**
(Joha: a Benjamite)
1 Chr. 8:16.
B. יוֹחָא *yôḥā'* **masc. proper noun**
(Joha: one of David's mighty men)
1 Chr. 11:45.

3110. A. יוֹחָנָן *yôḥānān* **masc. proper noun**
(Johanan: a priest)
Neh. 12:22,23.
B. יוֹחָנָן *yôḥānān* **masc. proper noun**
(Johanan: Jewish captain)
2 Kgs. 25:23; **Jer.** 40:8,13,15,16; 41:11, 13–16; 42:1,8; 43:2,4,5.
C. יוֹחָנָן *yôḥānān* **masc. proper noun**
(Johanan: oldest son of Josiah)
1 Chr. 3:15.
D. יוֹחָנָן *yôḥānān* **masc. proper noun**
(Johanan: son of Elioenai)
1 Chr. 3:24.
E. יוֹחָנָן *yôḥānān* **masc. proper noun**
(Johanan: son of Azariah)
1 Chr. 6:9(5:35),10(5:36).
F. יוֹחָנָן *yôḥānān* **masc. proper noun**
(Johanan: a Gadite)
1 Chr. 12:12(13).
G. יוֹחָנָן *yôḥānān* **masc. proper noun**
(Johanan: a Benjamite)
1 Chr. 12:4(5).
H. יוֹחָנָן *yôḥānān* **masc. proper noun**
(Johanan: a Jew)
Ezra 8:12.

3111. A. יוֹיָדָע *yôyāḏāʿ* **masc. proper noun**
(Jehoiada: son of Paseah)
Neh. 3:6.
B. יוֹיָדָע *yôyāḏāʿ* **masc. proper noun**
(Jehoiada: high priest)
Neh. 12:10,11,22; 13:28.

3112. יוֹיָכִין *yôyakiyn* **masc. proper noun**
(Jehoiachin: var. of *yehôyākiyn* [3078])
Ezek. 1:2.

3113. יוֹיָקִים *yôyāqiym* **masc. proper noun**
(Joiakim)
Neh. 12:10,12,26.

3114. A. יוֹיָרִיב *yôyāriyb* **masc. proper noun**
(Joiarib: name of a priestly family)
Neh. 11:10; 12:6,19.
B. יוֹיָרִיב *yôyāriyb* **masc. proper noun**
(Joiarib: teacher of Ezra)
Ezra 8:16.
C. יוֹיָרִיב *yôyāriyb* **masc. proper noun**
(Joiarib: a Judaite)
Neh. 11:5.

3115. יוֹכֶבֶד *yôkebed* **fem. proper noun**
(Jochebed)
Ex. 6:20; **Num.** 26:59.

3116. יוּכַל *yûkal* **masc. proper noun**
(Jucal)
Jer. 38:1.

3117. יוֹם *yôm* **masc. noun**
(day, time, period, daily)
Gen. 1:5,8,13,14,16,18,19,23,31; 2:2–4,17; 3:5,8,14,17; 4:3,14; 5:1,2,4,5, 8,11,14,17,20,23,27,31; 6:3–5; 7:4, 10–13,17,24; 8:3,4,6,10,12,14,22; 9:29; 10:25; 11:32; 14:1; 15:18; 17:12,23,26; 18:1,11; 19:37,38; 21:4,8,26,34; 22:4,14; 24:1,12,42,55; 25:7,24,31,33; 26:1,8,15, 18,32,33; 27:2,41,44,45; 29:7,14,20,21; 30:14,32,33,35,36; 31:22,23,39,40,43,48; 32:32(33); 33:13,16; 34:25; 35:3,20, 28,29; 37:34; 38:12; 39:10,11; 40:4,7,12, 13,18–20; 41:1,9; 42:13,17,18,32; 43:9; 44:32; 47:8,9,23,26,28,29; 48:15,20; 49:1; 50:3,4,10,20; **Ex.** 2:11,13,18,23; 3:18; 5:3,6,13,14,19; 6:28; 7:25; 8:22(18), 27(23); 9:18; 10:6,13,22,23,28; 12:6, 14–19,41,51; 13:3,4,6–8,10; 14:13,30; 15:22; 16:1,4,5,22,25–27,29,30; 19:1, 10,11,15,16; 20:8–12; 21:21; 22:30(29); 23:12,15,26; 24:16,18; 29:30,35–38; 31:15,17; 32:28,29,34; 34:11,18,21,28; 35:2,3; 40:2,37; **Lev.** 6:5(5:24),20(13); 7:15–18,35,36,38; 8:33–35; 9:1,4; 10:19; 12:2–6; 13:4–6,14,21,26,27,31–34,46, 50,51,54; 14:2,8–10,23,38,39,46,57; 15:13,14,19,24–26,28,29; 16:30; 19:6,7; 22:27,28,30; 23:3,6–8,12,14–16,21, 27–30,34–37,39–42; 24:8; 25:8,9,29,50; 26:34,35; 27:23; **Num.** 3:1,13; 6:4–6, 8–13; 7:1,10–12,18,24,30,36,42,48,54, 60,66,72,78,84; 8:17; 9:3,5,6,11,15, 18–20,22; 10:10,33; 11:19–21,31,32; 12:14,15; 13:20,25; 14:34; 15:23,32; 19:11,12,14,16,19; 20:15,29; 22:30; 24:14; 25:18; 28:3,9,16–18,24–26; 29:1, 12,17,20,23,26,29,32,35; 30:5(6),7(8), 8(9)12(13),14(15); 31:19,24; 32:10; 33:3,8; **Deut.** 1:2,10,39,46; 2:1,14,18,22, 25,30; 3:14; 4:4,8–10,15,20,26,30,32, 38–40; 5:1,3,12–16,24(21),29(26), 33(30); 6:2,6,24; 7:11; 8:1,11,18,19; 9:1,3,7,9–11,18,24,25; 10:4,8,10,13,15; 11:1,2,4,8,9,13,21,26–28,32; 12:1,8,19; 13:18(19); 14:23; 15:5,15; 16:3,4,8,13,15; 17:9,19,20; 18:5,16; 19:9,17; 20:3,19; 21:13,16,23; 22:7,19,29; 23:6(7); 24:15; 25:15; 26:3,16–18; 27:1,2,4,9–11; 28:1, 13–15,29,32,33; 29:4(3),10(9),12(11), 13(12),15(14),18(17),28(27); 30:2,8,11, 15,16,18–20; 31:2,13,14,17,18,21,22, 27,29; 32:7,35,46–48; 33:12,25; 34:6,8; **Josh.** 1:5,11; 2:16,22; 3:2,7,15; 4:9, 14,24; 5:9–11; 6:3,4,10,14,15,25; 7:25,26; 8:25,28,29; 9:12,16,17,27; 10:12–14,27,28,32,35; 11:18; 13:1,13; 14:9–12,14; 15:63; 16:10; 20:6; 22:3, 16–18,22,29,31; 23:1,2,8,9,14; 24:7,15, 25,31; **Judg.** 1:21,26; 2:7,18; 3:30;

4:14,23; 5:1,6; 6:24,32; 8:28; 9:18,19,45; 10:4,15; 11:4,27,40; 12:3; 13:7,10; 14:8, 12,14,15,17,18; 15:1,19,20; 16:16; 17:6,10; 18:1,12,30,31; 19:1,2,4,5,8,9,11,30; 20:15,21,22,24–28,30,35,46; 21:3,6, 19,25; **Ruth** 1:1; 2:19; 3:18; 4:5,9,10,14; **1 Sam.** 1:3,4,11,20,21,28; 2:16,19,31,32, 34,35; 3:1,2,12; 4:3,12,16; 5:5; 6:15,16,18; 7:2,6,10,13,15; 8:8,18; 9:9,12,13,15,19, 20,24,27; 10:2,8,9,19; 11:3,11,13; 12:2, 5,17,18; 13:8,11,22; 14:1,18,23,24,28,30, 31,33,37,38,45,52; 15:28,35; 16:13; 17:10,12,16,46; 18:2,9,10,21,26,29; 19:24; 20:6,19,26,27,31,34; 21:5–7(6–8), 10(11); 22:4,8,13,15,18,22; 23:14; 24:4(5), 10(11),18(19),19(20); 25:7,8,10,15,16, 28,32,33,38; 26:8,10,19,21,23,24; 27:1,6, 7,10,11; 28:1,2,18,20; 29:3,6,8; 30:1,12, 13,25; 31:6,13; **2 Sam.** 1:1,2; 2:11,17; 3:8,35,37–39; 4:3,5,8; 5:8; 6:8,9,20,23; 7:6,11,12; 11:12; 12:18; 13:23,32,37; 14:2,22,26,28; 15:20; 16:3,12,23; 18:7,8, 18,20,31; 19:2(3),3(4),5(6),6(7),13(14), 19(20),20(21),22(23),24(25),34(35), 35(36); 20:3,4; 21:1,9,12; 22:1,19; 23:10,20; 24:8,13,18; **1 Kgs.** 1:1,6,25,30, 48,51; 2:1,8,11,24,26,37,38,42; 3:2,6,11, 13,14,18; 4:21(5:1),22(5:2),25(5:5); 5:1(15),7(21); 8:8,16,24,28,29,40,59,61, 64–66; 9:3,13,21; 10:12,21; 11:12,25,34, 36,39,42; 12:5,7,12,19,32,33; 13:3,11; 14:14,19,20,29,30; 15:5–7,14,16,23, 31,32; 16:5,14–16,20,27,34; 17:7,14,15; 18:1,15,36; 19:4,8; 20:13,29; 21:29; 22:5, 25,35,39,45(46),46(47); **2 Kgs.** 1:18; 2:3, 5,17,22; 3:6,9; 4:8,11,18,23; 6:28,29,31; 7:9; 8:6,19,20,22,23; 10:27,32,34,36; 12:2(3),19(20); 13:3,8,12,22; 14:7,15,18,28; 15:5,6,11,13,15,18,21,26, 29,31,36,37; 16:6,19; 17:23,34,37,41; 18:4; 19:3,25; 20:1,5,6,8,17,19,20; 21:15, 17,25; 23:22,28,29; 24:1,5; 25:29,30; **1 Chr.** 1:19; 4:41,43; 5:10,17,26; 7:2,22; 9:25; 10:12; 11:22; 12:22,39; 13:3,11,12; 16:7,23,37; 17:5,10,11; 21:12; 22:9; 23:1; 26:17; 27:24; 28:7; 29:5,15,21,22,27,28; **2 Chr.** 1:11; 5:9; 6:5,15,31; 7:8–10,16; 8:8,13,14,16; 9:20; 10:5,7,12,19; 12:15; 13:20; 14:1(13:23); 15:3,11,17; 18:4,7, 24,34; 20:25,26; 21:7,8,10,15,19; 24:2, 11,14,15; 26:5,21; 28:6; 29:17; 30:21–23,26; 31:16; 32:24,26; 34:33; 35:16–18,21,25; 36:9,21; **Ezra** 3:4,6; 4:2,5,7; 6:22; 8:15,32,33; 9:7,15; 10:8, 9,13,16,17; **Neh.** 1:4,6,11; 2:11; 4:2(3:34),16(10),22(16); 5:11,14,18; 6:15,17; 8:2,3,9–11,13,17,18; 9:1,3, 10,32,36; 10:31(32); 11:23; 12:7,12, 22,23,26,43,44,46,47; 13:1,6,15,17, 19,22,23; **Esth.** 1:1,2,4,5,10,18; 2:11, 12,21,23; 3:4,7,12–14; 4:11,16; 5:1,4,9; 6:1; 7:2; 8:1,12,13,17; 9:1,11,13,15, 17–19,21,22,26–28,31; 10:2; **Job** 1:4–6,13; 2:1,13; 3:1,3–6,8; 7:1,6,16; 8:9; 9:25; 10:5,20; 12:12; 14:1,5,6,14; 15:10, 20,23,32; 17:1,11,12; 18:20; 20:28; 21:13,30; 23:2; 24:1; 27:6; 29:2,4,18; 30:1,16,25,27; 32:4,6,7; 33:25; 36:11; 38:12,21,23; 42:17; **Ps.** 2:7; 7:11(12); 18:[title](1),18(19); 19:2(3); 20:1(2), 9(10); 21:4(5); 23:6; 25:5; 27:4,5; 32:3; 34:12(13); 35:28; 37:13,18,19,26; 38:6(7),12(13); 39:4(5),5(6); 41:1(2); 42:3(4),10(11); 44:1(2),8(9),15(16), 22(23); 49:5(6); 50:15; 52:1(3); 55:23(24); 56:1–3(2–4),5(6),9(10); 59:16(17); 61:6(7),8(9); 68:19(20); 71:8,15,24; 72:7,15; 73:14; 74:16,22; 77:2(3),5(6); 78:9,33,42; 81:3(4); 84:10(11); 86:3,7; 88:1(2),9(10),17(18); 89:16(17),29(30),45(46); 90:4,9,10,12, 14,15; 91:16; 93:5; 94:13; 95:7,8; 96:2; 102:2(3),3(4),8(9),11(12),23(24),24(25); 103:15; 109:8; 110:3,5; 116:2; 118:24; 119:84,91,97,164; 128:5; 136:8; 137:7; 138:3; 139:12,16; 140:2(3),7(8); 143:5; 144:4; 145:2; 146:4; **Prov.** 3:2,16; 4:18; 6:34; 7:9,14,20; 8:30,34; 9:11; 10:27; 11:4; 12:16; 15:15; 16:4; 21:26,31; 22:19; 23:17; 24:10; 25:13,19,20; 27:1,10,15; 28:16; 31:12,25; **Eccl.** 2:3,16,23; 5:17(16),18(17),20(19); 6:3,12; 7:1,10, 14,15; 8:8,13,15,16; 9:9; 11:1,8,9; 12:1,3; **Song** 2:17; 3:11; 4:6; 8:8; **Isa.** 1:1; 2:2,

11,12,17,20; 3:7,18; 4:1,2; 5:30; 7:1,17, 18,20,21,23; 9:4(3),14(13); 10:3,17,20, 27,32; 11:10,11,16; 12:1,4; 13:6,9,13,22; 14:3; 17:4,7,9,11; 19:16,18,19,21,23,24; 20:6; 22:5,8,12,20,25; 23:7,15; 24:21,22; 25:9; 26:1; 27:1–3,8,12,13; 28:5,19,24; 29:18; 30:8,23,25,26; 31:7; 32:10; 34:8; 37:3,26; 38:1,5,10,12,13,19,20; 39:6,8; 43:13; 47:9; 48:7; 49:8; 51:9,13; 52:5,6; 53:10; 56:12; 58:2–5,13; 60:20; 61:2; 62:6; 63:4,9,11; 65:2,5,20,22; 66:8; **Jer.** 1:2,3,10,18; 2:32; 3:6,16,18,25; 4:9; 5:18; 6:4,11; 7:22,25,32; 9:25(24); 11:4,5,7; 12:3; 13:6; 16:9,14,19; 17:11,16–18,21, 22,24,27; 18:17; 19:6; 20:7,8,14,18; 22:30; 23:5–7,20; 25:3,18,33,34; 26:18; 27:22; 28:3,11; 30:3,7,8,24; 31:6,27,29, 31–33,36,38; 32:14,20,31,39; 33:14–16, 18,20; 34:13,15; 35:1,7,8,14,19; 36:2, 6,30; 37:16,21; 38:28; 39:10,16,17; 40:4; 41:4; 42:7,19,21; 44:2,6,10,22,23; 46:10, 21,26; 47:4; 48:12,41,47; 49:2,22,26,39; 50:4,20,27,30,31; 51:2,47,52; 52:11,33,34; **Lam.** 1:7,12,13,21; 2:1,7,16,17,21,22; 3:3,14,57,62; 4:18; 5:20,21; **Ezek.** 1:28; 2:3; 3:15,16; 4:4–6,8–10; 5:2; 7:7,10, 12,19; 12:22,23,25,27; 13:5; 16:4,5,22, 43,56,60; 20:5,6,29,31; 21:25(30),29(34); 22:4,14,24; 23:19,38,39; 24:2,25–27; 26:18; 27:27; 28:13,15; 29:21; 30:2,3, 9,18; 31:15; 32:10; 33:12; 34:12; 36:33; 38:8,10,14,16–19; 39:8,11,13,22; 40:1; 43:18,22,25–27; 44:26,27; 45:21–23,25; 46:1,4,6,12,13; 48:35; **Dan.** 1:5,12,14, 15,18; 8:26,27; 9:7,15; 10:2–4,12–14; 11:20,33; 12:11–13; **Hos.** 1:1,5,11(2:2); 2:3(5),13(15),15(17),16(18),18(20), 21(23); 3:3–5; 4:5; 5:9; 6:2; 7:5; 9:5,7,9; 10:9,14; 12:1(2),9(10); **Joel** 1:2,15; 2:1,2, 11,29(3:2),31(3:4); 3:1(4:1),14(4:14), 18(4:18); **Amos** 1:1,14; 2:16; 3:14; 4:2,4; 5:8,18,20; 6:3; 8:3,9–11,13; 9:11,13; **Obad.** 1:8,11–15; **Jon.** 1:17(2:1); 3:3,4; **Mic.** 1:1; 2:4; 3:6; 4:1,6; 5:2(1),10(9); 7:4,11,12,14,15,20; **Nah.** 1:7; 2:3(4), 8(9); 3:17; **Hab.** 1:5; 3:16; **Zeph.** 1:1, 7–10,14–16,18; 2:2,3; 3:8,11,16; **Hag.** 1:1,15; 2:15,18,19,23; **Zech.** 1:7; 2:11(15); 3:9,10; 4:10; 6:10; 8:4,6,9–11, 15,23; 9:12,16; 11:11; 12:3,4,6,8,9,11; 13:1,2,4; 14:1,3–9,13,20,21; **Mal.** 3:2,4,7,17; 4:1(3:19),3(3:21),5(3:23).

3118. יוֹם *yôm* **Aram. masc. noun**
(day, time; corr. to Hebr. 3117)
Ezra 4:15,19; 6:9,15; **Dan.** 2:28,44; 4:34(31); 5:11; 6:7(8),10(11),12(13), 13(14); 7:9,13,22.

3119. יוֹמָם *yômām* **subst.; adv.**
(by day, in the daytime)
Ex. 13:21,22; 40:38; **Lev.** 8:35; **Num.** 9:21; 10:34; 14:14; **Deut.** 1:33; 28:66; **Josh.** 1:8; **Judg.** 6:27; **1 Sam.** 25:16; **2 Sam.** 21:10; **1 Kgs.** 8:59; **1 Chr.** 9:33; **2 Chr.** 6:20; **Neh.** 1:6; 4:9(3); 9:12,19; **Job** 5:14; 24:16; **Ps.** 1:2; 13:2(3); 22:2(3); 32:4; 42:3(4),8(9); 55:10(11); 78:14; 91:5; 121:6; **Isa.** 4:5,6; 21:8; 34:10; 60:11,19; **Jer.** 9:1(8:23); 14:17; 15:9; 16:13; 31:35; 33:20,25; **Lam.** 2:18; **Ezek.** 12:3,4,7; 30:16.

3120. A. יָוָן *yāwān* **masc. proper noun**
(Javan: son of Japheth)
Gen. 10:2,4; **1 Chr.** 1:5,7.
B. יָוָן *yāwān* **masc. proper noun**
(Javan: descendants of Javan or their territory)
Isa. 66:19; **Ezek.** 27:13,19; **Dan.** 8:21; 10:20; 11:2; **Zech.** 9:13.

3121. יָוֵן *yāwēn* **masc. noun**
(mire, miry)
Ps. 40:2(3); 69:2(3).

3122. A. יוֹנָדָב *yônāḏāḇ* **masc. proper noun**
(Jonadab: son of Rechab; var. of y^e*hônāḏāḇ* [3082,A])
Jer. 35:6,10,19.
B. יוֹנָדָב *yônāḏāḇ* **masc. proper noun**

(Jonadab: David's nephew; var. of *y*e*hônāḏāḇ* [3082,B])
2 Sam. 13:3,32,35.

3123. יוֹנָה *yônāh* **fem. noun**
(dove, pigeon)
Gen. 8:8–12; **Lev.** 1:14; 5:7,11; 12:6,8; 14:22,30; 15:14,29; **Num.** 6:10; **2 Kgs.** 6:25(NASB, [Qe] *diḇyôniym* [1686,I]; NIV, [Qe] *diḇyôniym* [1686,II]); **Ps.** 55:6(7); 56:[title](1)(KJV, NASB, see *yônaṯ 'ēlem r*e*ḥōqiym* [3128]); 68:13(14); **Song** 1:15; 2:14; 4:1; 5:2,12; 6:9; **Isa.** 38:14; 59:11; 60:8; **Jer.** 48:28; **Ezek.** 7:16; **Hos.** 7:11; 11:11; **Nah.** 2:7(8).

3124. יוֹנָה *yônāh* **masc. proper noun**
(the prophet Jonah)
2 Kgs. 14:25; **Jon.** 1:1,3,5,7,15,17(2:1); 2:1(2),10(11); 3:1,3,4; 4:1,5,6,8,9.

3125. יְוָנִי *y*e*wāniy* **masc. proper noun**
(Grecians)
Joel 3:6(4:6).

3126. יֹנֵק *yōnēq*, יוֹנֵק *yônēq* **masc. noun**
(a tender shoot of a plant, infant, suckling child)
Num. 11:12(KJV, NASB, *yānaq* [3243]); **Deut.** 32:25(KJV, NASB, *yānaq* [3243]); **1 Sam.** 15:3(KJV, NASB, *yānaq* [3243]); 22:19(KJV, NASB, *yānaq* [3243]); **Ps.** 8:2(KJV, NASB, *yānaq* [3243]); **Song** 8:1(KJV, NASB, *yānaq* [3243]); **Isa.** 53:2; **Jer.** 44:7(KJV, NASB, *yānaq* [3243]); **Lam.** 2:11(KJV, NASB, *yānaq* [3243]); 4:4(KJV, NASB, *yānaq* [3243]); **Joel** 2:16(KJV, NASB, *yānaq* [3243]).

3127. יוֹנֶקֶת *yôneqeṯ* **fem. noun**
(young shoot of a plant)
Job 8:16; 14:7; 15:30; **Ps.** 80:11(12); **Ezek.** 17:22; **Hos.** 14:6(7).

3128. יוֹנַת אֵלֶם רְחֹקִים *yônaṯ 'ēlem r*e*ḥōqiym* **proper noun**
(Jonath elem rehokim)
Ps. 56:[title](1)(NIV, see *yônāh* [3123], *'ēlāh* [424], and *rāḥôq* [7350]).

3129. A. יוֹנָתָן *yônāṯān* **masc. proper noun**
(Jonathan: son of Saul)
1 Sam. 13:2,3,16,22; 14:1,3,4,12–14,17,21,27,29,39–45,49; 19:1; **1 Chr.** 10:2.
B. יוֹנָתָן *yônāṯān* **masc. proper noun**
(Jonathan: son of Abiathar)
1 Kgs. 1:42,43.
C. יוֹנָתָן *yônāṯān* **masc. proper noun**
(Jonathan: one of David's mighty men)
1 Chr. 11:34.
D. יוֹנָתָן *yônāṯān* **masc. proper noun**
(Jonathan: a Levite)
Neh. 12:35.
E. יוֹנָתָן *yônāṯān* **masc. proper noun**
(Jonathan: a Judaite captain)
Jer. 40:8.
F. יוֹנָתָן *yônāṯān* **masc. proper noun**
(Jonathan: a Judaite)
1 Chr. 2:32,33.
G. יוֹנָתָן *yônāṯān* **masc. proper noun**
(Jonathan: father of Ebed)
Ezra 8:6.
H. יוֹנָתָן *yônāṯān* **masc. proper noun**
(Jonathan: son of Asahel)
Ezra 10:15.
I. יוֹנָתָן *yônāṯān* **masc. proper noun**
(Jonathan: a priest)
Neh. 12:14.
J. יוֹנָתָן *yônāṯān* **masc. proper noun**

(Jonathan: son of Joiada)
Neh. 12:11.

3130. A. יוֹסֵף *yôsēp̱* **masc. proper noun**
(Joseph: son of Jacob)
Gen. 30:24,25; 33:2,7; 35:24; 37:2,3,5, 13,17,23,28,29,31,33; 39:1,2,4–7,10, 20–22; 40:3,4,6,8,9,12,16,18,22,23; 41:14–17,25,39,41,42,44–46,49–51,54–57; 42:3,4,6–9,14,18,23,25,36; 43:15–19, 24–26,30; 44:2,4,14,15; 45:1,3,4,9,16, 17,21,26–28; 46:4,19,20,27–31; 47:1, 5,7,11,12,14–17,20,23,26,29; 48:1–3, 8,9,11–13,15,17,18,21; 49:22,26; 50:1, 2,4,7,8,14–17,19,22–26; **Ex.** 1:5,6,8; 13:19; **Num.** 1:10,32; 13:7,11; 26:28,37; 27:1; 32:33; 34:23; 36:1,5,12; **Josh.** 14:4; 16:1,4; 17:1,2,14,16,17; 18:5,11; 24:32; **Judg.** 1:22,23,35; **2 Sam.** 19:20(21); **1 Kgs.** 11:28; **1 Chr.** 2:2; 5:1,2; 7:29; **Ps.** 105:17; **Amos** 5:6; **Zech.** 10:6.
B. יוֹסֵף *yôsēp̱* **masc. proper noun**
(Joseph: another name for the entire nation of Judah; see also *y^e^hôsēp̱* [3084])
Ps. 80:1(2).
C. יוֹסֵף *yôsēp̱* **masc. proper noun**
(Joseph: tribe of Joseph)
Deut. 27:12; 33:13,16.
D. יוֹסֵף *yôsēp̱* **masc. proper noun**
(Joseph: another name for the Northern Kingdom)
Ps. 77:15(16); 78:67; **Ezek.** 37:16,19; 47:13; 48:32; **Amos** 5:15; 6:6; **Obad.** 1:18.
E. יוֹסֵף *yôsēp̱* **masc. proper noun**
(Joseph: postexilic Jew)
Ezra 10:42.
F. יוֹסֵף *yôsēp̱* **masc. proper noun**
(Joseph: an Issacharite)
Num. 13:7.
G. יוֹסֵף *yôsēp̱* **masc. proper noun**
(Joseph: son of Asaph)
1 Chr. 25:2,9.
H. יוֹסֵף *yôsēp̱* **masc. proper noun**
(Joseph: a priest)
Neh. 12:14.

3131. יוֹסִפְיָה *yôsip̱yāh* **masc. proper noun**
(Josiphiah)
Ezra 8:10.

3132. יוֹעֵאלָה *yôʿēʾlāh* **masc. proper noun**
(Joelah)
1 Chr. 12:7.

3133. יוֹעֵד *yôʿēḏ* **masc. proper noun**
(Joed)
Neh. 11:7.

3134. יוֹעֶזֶר *yôʿezer* **masc. proper noun**
(Joezer)
1 Chr. 12:6.

3135. A. יוֹעָשׁ *yôʿāš* **masc. proper noun**
(Joash: son of Becher)
1 Chr. 7:8.
B. יוֹעָשׁ *yôʿāš* **masc. proper noun**
(Joash: officer under David)
1 Chr. 27:28.

3136. I. יוֹצָדָק *yôṣāḏāq* **masc. proper noun**
(Jozadak: a priest)
Ezra 3:2,8; 10:18; **Neh.** 12:26.
II. יוֹצָדָק *yôṣāḏāq* **Aram. masc. proper noun**
(Jozadak: the same priest)
Ezra 5:2.

3137. יוֹקִים *yôqiym* **masc. proper noun**
(Jokim)
1 Chr. 4:22.

3138. יוֹרֶה *yôreh* **masc. noun**
(early rain)
Deut. 11:14; **Jer.** 5:24; **Hos.** 6:3(NASB, NIV, *yārāh* [3384,III]).

3139. יוֹרָה *yôrāh* **masc. proper noun**
(Jorah)
Ezra 2:18.

3140. יוֹרַי *yôray* **masc. proper noun**
(Jorai)
1 Chr. 5:13.

3141. A. יוֹרָם *yôrām* **masc. proper noun**
(Joram: king of Judah, son of Jehoshaphat; var. of *y^ehôrām* [3088,A])
2 Kgs. 8:21,23,24; 11:2; **1 Chr.** 3:11.
B. וֹרָם *yôrām* **masc. proper noun**
(Joram: king of Israel, son of Ahab; var. of *y^ehôrām* [3088,B])
2 Kgs. 8:16,25,28,29; 9:14,16,29; **2 Chr.** 22:5,7.
C. יוֹרָם *yôrām* **masc. proper noun**
(Joram: son of Tou)
2 Sam. 8:10.
D. יֹרָם *yôrām* **masc. proper noun**
(Joram: a Levite)
1 Chr. 26:25.

3142. יוּשַׁב חֶסֶד *yûšab ḥeseḏ* **masc. proper noun**
(Jushab-Hesed)
1 Chr. 3:20.

3143. יוֹשִׁבְיָה *yôšiḇyāh* **masc. proper noun**
(Joshibiah)
1 Chr. 4:35.

3144. יוֹשָׁה *yôšāh* **masc. proper noun**
(Joshah)
1 Chr. 4:34.

3145. יוֹשַׁוְיָה *yôšawyāh* **masc. proper noun**
(Joshaviah)
1 Chr. 11:46.

3146. A. יוֹשָׁפָט *yôšāp̄āṭ* **masc. proper noun**
(Joshaphat: one of David's mighty men)
1 Chr. 11:43.
B. יוֹשָׁפָט *yôšāp̄āṭ* **masc. proper noun**
(Joshaphat: a priest)
1 Chr. 15:24.

3147. A. יוֹתָם *yôṯām* **masc. proper noun**
(Jotham: king of Judah, son of Azariah)
2 Kgs. 15:5,7,30,32,36,38; 16:1; **1 Chr.** 3:12; 5:17; **2 Chr.** 26:21,23; 27:1,6,7,9; **Isa.** 1:1; 7:1; **Hos.** 1:1; **Mic.** 1:1.
B. יוֹתָם *yôṯām* **masc. proper noun**
(Jotham: youngest son of Gideon)
Judg. 9:5,7,21,57.
C. יוֹתָם *yôṯām* **masc. proper noun**
(Jotham: descendant of Caleb)
1 Chr. 2:47.

3148. יוֹתֵר *yôṯēr,* יֹתֵר *yōṯēr* **masc. noun**
(advantage, gain, profit)
Esth. 6:6; **Eccl.** 2:15; 6:8,11; 7:11,16; 12:9,12.

3149. יְזוּאֵל *y^ezû'ēl* **masc. proper noun**
(Jeziel)
1 Chr. 12:3.

3150. יִזִּיָּה *yizziyyāh* **masc. proper noun**
(Izziah)
Ezra 10:25.

3151. יָזִיז *yāziyz* **masc. proper noun**
(Jaziz)
1 Chr. 27:31.

3152. יִזְלִיאָה *yizliy'āh* **masc. proper noun**
(Izliah)
1 Chr. 8:18.

3153. A. יְזַנְיָהוּ *y^e^zanyāhû* **masc. proper noun**
(Jezaniah: a Judean)
Jer. 40:8.
B. יְזַנְיָה *y^e^zanyāh* **masc. proper noun**
(Jezaniah: Judean leader)
Jer. 42:1.

3154. יֶזַע *yeza'* **masc. noun**
(sweat, perspiration)
Ezek. 44:18.

3155. יִזְרָח *yizrāḥ* **masc. proper noun**
(Izrahite: descendant of Zerah)
1 Chr. 27:8.

3156. A. יִזְרַחְיָה *Yizraḥyāh* **masc. proper noun**
(Izrahiah: musical leader)
Neh. 12:42.
B. יִזְרַחְיָה *Yizraḥyāh* **masc. proper noun**
(Izrahiah: grandson of Tola)
1 Chr. 7:3.

3157. A. יִזְרְעֶאל *yizr^e^'e'l* **proper noun**
(Jezreel: a city)
Josh. 15:56; **1 Sam.** 25:43; 29:1,11.
B. יִזְרְעֶאל *yizr^e^'e'l* **proper noun**
(Jezreel: a city)
Josh. 19:18; **2 Sam.** 2:9; 4:4; **1 Kgs.** 4:12; 18:45,46; 21:1,23; **2 Kgs.** 8:29; 9:10,15–17,30,36,37; 10:1,6,7,11; **2 Chr.** 22:6.
C. יִזְרְעֶאל *yizr^e^'e'l* **proper noun**
(Jezreel: a valley)
Josh. 17:16; **Judg.** 6:33; **Hos.** 1:5; 2:22(24).
D. יִזְרְעֶאל *yizr^e^'e'l* **proper noun**
(Jezreel: son of Etam)
1 Chr. 4:3.
E. יִזְרְעֶאל *yizr^e^'e'l* **proper noun**
(Jezreel: son of Hosea)
Hos. 1:4.
F. יִזְרְעֶאל *yizr^e^'e'l* **proper noun**
(Jezreel: another name for Israel)
Hos. 1:4,11(2:2).

3158. יִזְרְעֵאלִי *yizr^e^'ēliy* **masc. proper noun**
(Jezreelite)
1 Kgs. 21:1,4,6,7,15,16; **2 Kgs.** 9:21,25.

3159. יִזְרְעֵאלִית *yizr^e^'ēliyṯ*, יִזְרְעֵאלִת *yizr^e^'ēliṯ* **fem. proper noun**
(Jezreelitess)
1 Sam. 27:3; 30:5; **2 Sam.** 2:2; 3:2; **1 Chr.** 3:1.

3160. יְחֻבָּה *y^e^ḥubbāh* **masc. proper noun**
(Jehubbah)
1 Chr. 7:34(NIV, [Q^e^] *ḥubbah*).

3161. יָחַד *yāḥaḏ* **verb**
(to join, to be united)
Gen. 49:6; **Job** 3:6(see *yēḥad* [2302,II]; NASB, *ḥādāh* [2302,I]); **Ps.** 86:11; **Isa.** 14:20.

3162. I. יַחַד *yaḥaḏ* **masc. noun**
(unitedness)
Deut. 33:5; **1 Sam.** 11:11; 17:10; **2 Sam.** 10:15; 14:16; 21:9; **1 Chr.** 12:17; **Ezra** 4:3; **Job** 3:18; 6:2; 10:8; 16:10; 17:16; 19:12; 21:26; 24:4; 31:38; 34:15,29; 38:7; 40:13; **Ps.** 2:2; 31:13(14); 33:15; 40:14(15); 41:7(8); 49:2(3),10(11); 62:9(10); 74:6,8; 88:17(18); 98:8; 133:1; 141:10; **Isa.** 22:3; 27:4; 42:14; 43:26; 44:11; 45:8; 50:8; **Jer.** 48:7([Q^e^] see II); **Hos.** 11:7,8.
II. יַחְדָּו *yaḥdāw*, יַחְדָּיו *yaḥdāyw* **adv.**
(together)
Gen. 13:6; 22:6,8,19; 36:7; **Ex.** 19:8; 26:24; 36:29; **Deut.** 12:22; 15:22; 22:10,11; 25:5,11; 33:17; **Josh.** 9:2; 11:5; **Judg.** 6:33; 19:6; **1 Sam.** 30:24; 31:6; **2 Sam.** 2:13,16; 12:3; **1 Kgs.** 3:18; **1 Chr.** 10:6; **Neh.** 4:8(2); 6:2,7; **Job**

2:11; 9:32; 24:17; **Ps.** 4:8(9); 14:3; 19:9(10); 34:3(4); 35:26; 37:38; 48:4(5); 53:3(4); 55:14(15); 71:10; 83:5(6); 102:22(23); 122:3; **Prov.** 22:18; **Isa.** 1:28,31; 9:21(20); 10:8; 11:6,7,14; 18:6; 31:3; 40:5; 41:1,19,20,23; 43:9,17; 45:16, 20,21; 46:2; 48:13; 52:8,9; 60:13; 65:7; 66:17; **Jer.** 3:18; 5:5; 6:11,12,21; 13:14; 31:8,13,24; 41:1; 46:12,21; 48:7([K^{e}] see I); 49:3; 50:4,33; 51:38; **Lam.** 2:8; **Hos.** 1:11(2:2); **Amos** 1:15; 3:3; **Mic.** 2:12; **Zech.** 10:4.

3163. יַחְדּוֹ *yaḥdô* **masc. proper noun**
(Jahdo)
1 Chr. 5:14.

3164. יַחְדִּיאֵל *yaḥdiy'ēl* **masc. proper noun**
(Jadiel)
1 Chr. 5:24.

3165. A. יֶחְדְּיָהוּ *yeḥd^{e}yāhû* **masc. proper noun**
(Jehdeiah: a Levite)
1 Chr. 24:20.
B. יֶחְדְּיָהוּ *yeḥd^{e}yāhû* **masc. proper noun**
(Jehdeiah: a royal officer)
1 Chr. 27:30.

3166. A. יַחֲזִיאֵל *yaḥ^{a}ziy'ēl* **masc. proper noun**
(Jahaziel: a Benjamite)
1 Chr. 12:4.
B. יַחֲזִיאֵל *yaḥ^{a}ziy'ēl* **masc. proper noun**
(Jahaziel: a priest)
1 Chr. 16:6.
C. יַחֲזִיאֵל *yaḥ^{a}ziy'ēl* **masc. proper noun**
(Jahaziel: a Levite)
1 Chr. 23:19; 24:23.
D. יַחֲזִיאֵל *yaḥ^{a}ziy'ēl* **masc. proper noun**
(Jahaziel: a Levite)
2 Chr. 20:14.
E. יַחֲזִיאֵל *yaḥ^{a}ziy'ēl* **masc. proper noun**
(Jahaziel: father of Shechaniah)
Ezra 8:5.

3167. יַחְזְיָה *yaḥz^{e}yāh* **masc. proper noun**
(Jahzeiah)
Ezra 10:15.

3168. A. יְחֶזְקֵאל *y^{e}ḥezqē'l* **masc. proper noun**
(the prophet Ezekiel)
Ezek. 1:3; 24:24.
B. יְחֶזְקֵאל *y^{e}ḥezqē'l* **masc. proper noun**
(Jehezekel, Jehezkel: a priest)
1 Chr. 24:16.

3169. A. יְחִזְקִיָּה *y^{e}ḥizqiyyāh*, יְחִזְקִיָּהוּ *y^{e}ḥizqiyyāhû* **masc. proper noun**
(Hezekiah: king of Judah)
2 Kgs. 20:10; **1 Chr.** 4:41; **2 Chr.** 28:27; 29:1,20,30,31,36; 30:1,18,20,22; 31:2,8,9,11,13,20; 32:2,8,9,11,12,16,17, 20,22–27,30,32,33; 33:3; **Isa.** 1:1; **Jer.** 15:4; **Hos.** 1:1; **Mic.** 1:1.
B. יְחִזְקִיָּהוּ *y^{e}ḥizqiyyāhû* **masc. proper noun**
(Hezekiah: a Jew)
Ezra 2:16.
C. יְחִזְקִיָּהוּ *y^{e}ḥizqiyyāhû* **masc. proper noun**
(Hezekiah: an Ephraimite)
2 Chr. 28:12.

3170. יַחְזֵרָה *yaḥzērāh* **masc. proper noun**
(Jahzerah)
1 Chr. 9:12.

3171. A. יְחִיאֵל *y^{e}ḥiy'ēl* **masc. proper noun**
(Jehiel: a Levite)
1 Chr. 15:18,20; 16:5.

B. יְחִיאֵל y^e*ḥiy'ēl*, יְחוּאֵל y^e*ḥô'ēl* **masc. proper noun**
(Jehiel: a Gershonite)
1 Chr. 23:8; 29:8.
C. יְחִיאֵל y^e*ḥiy'ēl* **masc. proper noun**
(Jehiel: a Jew)
1 Chr. 27:32.
D. יְחִיאֵל y^e*ḥiy'ēl* **masc. proper noun**
(Jehiel: son of Jehoshaphat)
2 Chr. 21:2.
E. יְחִיאֵל y^e*ḥiy'ēl* **masc. proper noun**
(Jehiel: son of Heman)
2 Chr. 29:14.
F. יְחִיאֵל y^e*ḥiy'ēl* **masc. proper noun**
(Jehiel: a Levite)
2 Chr. 31:13.
G. יְחִיאֵל y^e*ḥiy'ēl* **masc. proper noun**
(Jehiel: ruler in the Temple)
2 Chr. 35:8.
H. יְחִיאֵל y^e*ḥiy'ēl* **masc. proper noun**
(Jehiel: father of Obadiah)
Ezra 8:9.
I. יְחִיאֵל y^e*ḥiy'ēl* **masc. proper noun**
(Jehiel: father of Shechaniah)
Ezra 10:2.
J. יְחִיאֵל y^e*ḥiy'ēl* **masc. proper noun**
(Jehiel: a priest)
Ezra 10:21.
K. יְחִיאֵל y^e*ḥiy'ēl* **masc. proper noun**
(Jehiel: a Jew)
Ezra 10:26.

3172. יְחִיאֵלִי y^e*ḥiy'ēliy* **masc. proper noun**
(Jehieli)
1 Chr. 26:21,22.

3173. יָחִיד *yāḥiyd̲* **adj.; subst.**
(only, unique)
Gen. 22:2,12,16; **Judg.** 11:34; **Ps.** 22:20(21); 25:16; 35:17; 68:6(7); **Prov.** 4:3; **Jer.** 6:26; **Amos** 8:10; **Zech.** 12:10.

3174. יְחִיָּה y^e*ḥiyyāh* **masc. proper noun**
(Jehiah)
1 Chr. 15:24.

3175. יָחִיל *yāḥiyl* **adj.**
(hoping, waiting)
Lam. 3:26.

3176. יָחַל *yāḥal* **verb**
(to wait, to hope, to expect)
Gen. 8:12; **1 Sam.** 10:8; 13:8; **2 Sam.** 18:14; **2 Kgs.** 6:33; **Job** 6:11; 13:15; 14:14; 29:21,23; 30:26; 32:11,16; **Ps.** 31:24(25); 33:18,22; 38:15(16); 42:5(6), 11(12); 43:5; 69:3(4); 71:14; 119:43,49, 74,81,114,147; 130:5,7; 131:3; 147:11; **Isa.** 42:4; 51:5; **Jer.** 4:19(NASB, NIV, [K^e] *ḥûl* [2342,I]); **Lam.** 3:21,24; **Ezek.** 13:6; 19:5; **Mic.** 5:7(6); 7:7.

3177. יַחְלְאֵל *yaḥl^e'ēl* **masc. proper noun**
(Jahleel)
Gen. 46:14; **Num.** 26:26.

3178. יַחְלְאֵלִי *yaḥl^e'ēliy* **masc. proper noun**
(Jahleelites)
Num. 26:26.

3179. יָחַם *yāḥam* **verb**
(to conceive, to be hot)
Gen. 30:38,39,41; 31:10; **Deut.** 19:6(NASB, NIV, *ḥāmam* [2552]); **1 Kgs.** 1:1(NASB, NIV, *ḥāmam* [2552]); **Ps.** 51:5(7); **Eccl.** 4:11; **Ezek.** 24:11(NASB, NIV, *ḥāmam* [2552]).

3180. יַחְמוּר *yaḥmûr* **masc. noun**
(roe, deer, member of a small species of deer)
Deut. 14:5; **1 Kgs.** 4:23(5:3).

3181. יַחְמַי *yaḥmay* **masc. proper noun**
(Jahmai)
1 Chr. 7:2.

3182. יָחֵף *yāḥēp̱* **adj.**
(barefoot)
2 Sam. 15:30; **Isa.** 20:2–4; **Jer.** 2:25.

3183. יַחְצְאֵל *yaḥṣᵉʼēl* **masc. proper noun**
(Jahzeel)
Gen. 46:24; **Num.** 26:48.

3184. יַחְצְאֵלִי *yaḥṣᵉʼēliy* **masc. proper noun**
(Jahzeelite)
Num. 26:48.

3185. יַחְצִיאֵל *yaḥṣiyʼēl* **masc. proper noun**
(Jahziel)
1 Chr. 7:13.

3186. יָחַר *yāḥar* **verb**
(to delay, to tarry)
2 Sam. 20:5(NASB, NIV, [Kᵉ] *ʼāḥar* [309]).

3187. יָחַשׂ *yāḥaś* **verb**
(to keep a genealogical record, to be in a genealogical record)
1 Chr. 4:33; 5:1,7,17; 7:5,7,9,40; 9:1,22; **2 Chr.** 12:15; 31:16–19; **Ezra** 2:62; 8:1,3; **Neh.** 7:5,64.

3188. יַחַשׂ *yaḥaś* **masc. noun**
(genealogy)
Neh. 7:5.

3189. A. יַחַת *yaḥaṯ* **masc. proper noun**
(Jahath: grandson of Judah)
1 Chr. 4:2.
B. יַחַת *yaḥaṯ* **masc. proper noun**
(Jahath: a Levite)
1 Chr. 6:20(5),43(28).
C. יַחַת *yaḥaṯ* **masc. proper noun**
(Jahath: a Levite)
1 Chr. 23:10,11.
D. יַחַת *yaḥaṯ* **masc. proper noun**
(Jahath: a Levite)
1 Chr. 24:22.
E. יַחַת *yaḥaṯ* **masc. proper noun**
(Jahath: a Levite)
2 Chr. 34:12.

3190. יָטַב *yāṭaḇ* **verb**
(to be good, to go well)
Gen. 4:7; 12:13,16; 32:9(10),12(13); 34:18; 40:14; 41:37; 45:16; **Ex.** 1:20; 30:7; **Lev.** 5:4; 10:19,20; **Num.** 10:32(KJV, *ṭôḇ* [2895]); **Deut.** 1:23; 4:40; 5:16,28(25), 29(26); 6:3,18; 8:16; 9:21; 12:25,28; 13:14(15); 17:4; 18:17; 19:18; 22:7; 27:8; 28:63; 30:5; **Josh.** 22:30,33; 24:20; **Judg.** 17:13; 18:20; 19:6,9,22; **Ruth** 3:1,7,10; **1 Sam.** 2:32; 16:17; 18:5; 20:13; 24:4(5); 25:31; **2 Sam.** 3:36; 18:4; **1 Kgs.** 1:47; 3:10; 21:7; **2 Kgs.** 9:30; 11:18; 25:24; **Neh.** 2:5,6; **Esth.** 1:21; 2:4,9; 5:14; **Job** 24:21; **Ps.** 33:3; 36:3(4); 49:18(19); 51:18(20); 69:31(32); 125:4; **Prov.** 15:2,13; 17:22; 30:29; **Eccl.** 7:3; 11:9; **Isa.** 1:17; 23:16; 41:23; **Jer.** 1:12; 2:33; 4:22; 7:3,5,23; 10:5; 13:23; 18:10,11; 26:13; 32:40; 35:15; 38:20; 40:9; 42:6; **Ezek.** 33:22; 36:11(KJV, NIV, *ṭôḇ* [2895]); **Hos.** 10:1; **Jon.** 4:4,9; **Mic.** 2:7; 7:3; **Nah.** 3:8; **Zeph.** 1:12; **Zech.** 8:15.

3191. יְטַב *yᵉṭaḇ* **Aram. verb**
(to be good, to seem good; corr. to Hebr. 3190)
Ezra 7:18.

3192. יָטְבָה *yoṭḇāh* **proper noun**
(Jotbah)
2 Kgs. 21:19.

3193. יָטְבָתָה *yoṭḇāṯāh* **proper noun**
(Jotbathah)
Num. 33:33,34; **Deut.** 10:7.

3194. יוּטָּה *yûṭṭāh*, יֻטָּה *yuṭṭāh* **proper noun**
(Juttah)
Josh. 15:55; 21:16.

3195. יְטוּר *y^e^ṭûr* **masc. proper noun**
(Jetur)
Gen. 25:15; **1 Chr.** 1:31; 5:19.

3196. יַיִן *yayin* **masc. noun**
(wine)
Gen. 9:21,24; 14:18; 19:32–35; 27:25; 49:11,12; **Ex.** 29:40; **Lev.** 10:9; 23:13; **Num.** 6:3,4,20; 15:5,7,10; 28:14; **Deut.** 14:26; 28:39; 29:6(5); 32:33,38; **Josh.** 9:4,13; **Judg.** 13:4,7,14; 19:19; **1 Sam.** 1:14,15,24; 10:3; 16:20; 25:18,37; **2 Sam.** 13:28; 16:1,2; **1 Chr.** 9:29; 12:40; 27:27; **2 Chr.** 2:10(9),15(14); 11:11; **Neh.** 2:1; 5:15,18; 13:15; **Esth.** 1:7,10; 5:6; 7:2,7,8; **Job** 1:13,18; 32:19; **Ps.** 60:3(5); 75:8(9); 78:65; 104:15; **Prov.** 4:17; 9:2,5; 20:1; 21:17; 23:20, 30,31; 31:4,6; **Eccl.** 2:3; 9:7; 10:19; **Song** 1:2,4; 2:4; 4:10; 5:1; 7:9(10); 8:2; **Isa.** 5:11,12,22; 16:10; 22:13; 24:9,11; 28:1,7; 29:9; 51:21; 55:1; 56:12; **Jer.** 13:12; 23:9; 25:15; 35:2,5,6,8,14; 40:10,12; 48:33; 51:7; **Lam.** 2:12; **Ezek.** 27:18; 44:21; **Dan.** 1:5,8,16; 10:3; **Hos.** 4:11; 7:5; 9:4; 14:7(8); **Joel** 1:5; 3:3(4:3); **Amos** 2:8,12; 5:11; 6:6; 9:14; **Mic.** 2:11; 6:15; **Hab.** 2:5; **Zeph.** 1:13; **Hag.** 2:12; **Zech.** 9:15; 10:7.

3197. יַךְ *yaḵ* **masc. noun**
(wayside)
1 Sam. 4:13(NASB, NIV, [Q^e^] *yaḏ* [3027,A]).

3198. יָכַח *yāḵaḥ* **verb**
(to rebuke, to judge, to correct)
Gen. 20:16; 21:25; 24:14,44; 31:37,42; **Lev.** 19:17; **2 Sam.** 7:14; **2 Kgs.** 19:4; **1 Chr.** 12:17; 16:21; **Job** 5:17; 6:25,26; 9:33; 13:3,10,15; 15:3; 16:21; 19:5; 22:4; 23:7; 32:12; 33:19; 40:2; **Ps.** 6:1(2); 38:1(2); 50:8,21; 94:10; 105:14; 141:5; **Prov.** 3:12; 9:7,8; 15:12; 19:25; 24:25; 25:12; 28:23; 30:6; **Isa.** 1:18; 2:4; 11:3,4; 29:21; 37:4; **Jer.** 2:19; **Ezek.** 3:26; **Hos.** 4:4; **Amos** 5:10; **Mic.** 4:3; 6:2; **Hab.** 1:12.

3199. A. יָכִין *yāḵiyn* **masc. proper noun**
(Jakin: a Simeonite)
Gen. 46:10; **Ex.** 6:15; **Num.** 26:12.
B. יָכִין *yāḵiyn* **masc. proper noun**
(Jakin: pillar in Solomon's temple)
1 Kgs. 7:21; **2 Chr.** 3:17.
C. יָכִין *yāḵiyn* **masc. proper noun**
(Jakin: a priest)
1 Chr. 9:10; 24:17.
D. יָכִין *yāḵiyn* **masc. proper noun**
(Jakin: postexilic priest)
Neh. 11:10.

3200. יָכִינִי *yāḵiyniy* **masc. proper noun**
(Jachinite)
Num. 26:12.

3201. יָכֹל *yāḵōl* **verb**
(to be able, to prevail)
Gen. 13:6,16; 15:5; 19:19,22; 24:50; 29:8; 30:8; 31:35; 32:25(26),28(29); 34:14; 36:7; 37:4; 43:32; 44:1,22,26; 45:1,3; 48:10; **Ex.** 2:3; 7:21,24; 8:18(14); 9:11; 10:5; 12:39; 15:23; 18:18,23; 19:23; 33:20; 40:35; **Num.** 9:6; 11:14; 13:30,31; 14:16; 22:6,11,18,37,38; 24:13; **Deut.** 1:9; 7:17,22; 9:28; 12:17; 14:24; 16:5; 17:15; 21:16; 22:3,19,29; 24:4; 28:27,35; 31:2; **Josh.** 7:12,13; 9:19; 15:63; 17:12; 24:19; **Judg.** 2:14; 8:3; 11:35; 14:13,14; 16:5; 21:18; **Ruth** 4:6; **1 Sam.** 3:2; 4:15; 6:20; 17:9,33,39; 26:25; **2 Sam.** 3:11; 12:23; 17:17; **1 Kgs.** 3:9; 5:3(17); 8:11; 9:21; 13:4,16; 14:4; 20:9; 22:22; **2 Kgs.**

3:26; 4:40; 16:5; 18:23,29; **1 Chr.** 21:30; **2 Chr.** 5:14; 7:2,7; 18:21; 29:34; 30:3; 32:13–15; **Ezra** 2:59; **Neh.** 4:10(4); 6:3; 7:61; **Esth.** 6:13; 8:6; **Job** 4:2; 31:23; 33:5; 42:2; **Ps.** 13:4(5); 18:38(39); 21:11(12); 36:12(13); 40:12(13); 78:19,20; 101:5; 129:2; 139:6; **Prov.** 30:21; **Eccl.** 1:8,15; 6:10; 7:13; 8:17; **Song** 8:7; **Isa.** 1:13; 7:1; 16:12; 29:11; 36:8,14; 46:2; 47:11,12; 56:10; 57:20; 59:14; **Jer.** 1:19; 3:5; 5:22; 6:10; 11:11; 13:23; 14:9; 15:20; 18:6; 19:11; 20:7,9–11; 36:5; 38:5,22; 44:22; 49:10,23; **Lam.** 1:14; 4:14; **Ezek.** 7:19; 33:12; 47:5; **Dan.** 10:17; **Hos.** 5:13; 8:5; 12:4(5); **Amos** 7:10; **Obad.** 1:7; **Jon.** 1:13; **Hab.** 1:13; **Zeph.** 1:18.

3202. יְכִל *y^e^kil* **Aram. verb**
(to be able, to prevail; corr. to Hebr. 3201)
Dan. 2:10,27,47; 3:17,29; 4:18(15),37(34); 5:16; 6:4(5),20(21); 7:21.

3203. יְכָלְיָה *y^e^kolyāh,* יְכָלְיָהוּ *y^e^kolyāhû* **fem. proper noun**
(Jecoliah)
1 Kgs. 15:2; **2 Chr.** 26:3.

3204. יְכוֹנְיָה *y^e^kônyāh,* יְכָנְיָה *y^e^konyāh,* יְכָנְיָהוּ *y^e^konyāhû* **masc. proper noun**
(Jeconiah: NIV, another name for *y^e^hôyākiyn* [3078]; see also *konyāhû* [3659])
1 Chr. 3:16,17; **Esth.** 2:6; **Jer.** 24:1; 27:20; 28:4; 29:2.

3205. I. יָלַד *yālad* **verb**
(to give birth, to beget, to deliver)
Gen. 3:16; 4:1,2,17,18,20,22,25,26; 5:3, 4,6,7,9,10,12,13,15,16,18,19,21,22,25,26 ,28,30,32; 6:1,4,10; 10:1,8,13,15,21, 24–26; 11:10–27; 16:1,2,11,15,16; 17:17, 19–21; 18:13; 19:37,38; 20:17; 21:2,3,5, 7,9; 22:20,23,24; 24:15,24,36,47; 25:2,3, 12,19,24,26; 29:32–35; 30:1,3,5,7,9,10, 12,17,19–21,23,25,39; 31:8,43; 34:1; 35:16,17,26; 36:4,5,12,14; 38:3–5,27,28; 40:20; 41:50; 44:27; 46:15,18,20,22, 25,27; 48:5,6; 50:23; **Ex.** 1:15–21; 2:2,22; 6:20,23,25; 21:4; **Lev.** 12:2,5,7; 22:27; 25:45; **Num.** 1:18; 11:12; 26:29, 58–60; **Deut.** 4:25; 15:19; 21:15; 23:8(9); 25:6; 28:41,57; 32:18; **Judg.** 8:31; 11:1,2; 13:2,3,5,7,8,24; 18:29; **Ruth** 1:12; 4:12,13,15,17–22; **1 Sam.** 1:20; 2:5,21; 4:19,20; **2 Sam.** 3:2,5; 5:13; 11:27; 12:15,24; 14:27; 21:8,20,22; **1 Kgs.** 1:6; 3:17,18,21,26,27; 11:20; 13:2; **2 Kgs.** 4:17; 19:3(NIV, see II); 20:18; **1 Chr.** 1:10,11,13,18–20,32,34; 2:3,4,9–13,17–22,24,29,35–41,44,46,48, 49; 3:1,4,5; 4:2,6,8,9,11,12,14,18; 6:4–14 (5:30–40); 7:14,16,18,21,23,32; 8:1,7–9, 11,32–34,36,37; 9:38–40,42,43; 14:3,4; 20:6,8; 22:9; 26:6; **2 Chr.** 11:19–21; 13:21; 24:3; **Ezra** 10:3; **Neh.** 12:10,11; **Job** 1:2; 3:3; 5:7; 11:12; 14:1; 15:7,14,35; 24:21; 25:4; 38:21,28,29; 39:1,2; **Ps.** 2:7; 7:14(15); 22:31(32); 48:6(7); 78:6; 87:4–6; 90:2; **Prov.** 17:17,21,25; 23:22,24,25; 27:1; **Eccl.** 3:2; 4:14; 5:14(13); 6:3; 7:1; **Song** 6:9; 8:5; **Isa.** 7:14; 8:3; 9:6(5); 13:8; 21:3; 23:4; 26:17,18; 33:11; 37:3 (NIV, see II); 39:7; 42:14; 45:10; 49:21; 51:18; 54:1; 55:10; 59:4; 65:23; 66:7–9; **Jer.** 2:27; 6:24; 13:21(NIV, see II); 14:5; 15:9,10; 16:3; 17:11; 20:14,15; 22:23,26; 29:6; 30:6; 31:8; 49:24; 50:12,43; **Ezek.** 16:4,5,20; 18:10,14; 23:4,37; 31:6; 47:22; **Dan.** 11:6; **Hos.** 1:3,6,8; 2:3(5); 5:7; 9:11(NIV, see II),16; 13:13; **Mic.** 4:9,10; 5:3(2); **Zeph.** 2:2; **Zech.** 13:3.
II. לֵדָה *lēdāh* **fem. noun**
(childbirth, delivery)
2 Kgs. 19:3(KJV, NASB, see I); **Isa.** 37:3(KJV, NASB, see I); **Jer.** 13:21(KJV, NASB, see I); **Hos.** 9:11(KJV, NASB, see I).

3206. יֶלֶד *yeled* **masc. noun**
(child, young man)
Gen. 4:23; 21:8,14–16; 30:26; 32:22(23); 33:1,2,5–7,13,14; 37:30; 42:22; 44:20;

Ex. 1:17,18; 2:3,6–10; 21:4,22; **Ruth** 1:5; 4:16; **1 Sam.** 1:2; **2 Sam.** 6:23; 12:15,18,19,21,22; **1 Kgs.** 3:25; 12:8, 10,14; 14:12; 17:21–23; **2 Kgs.** 2:24; 4:1,18,26,34; **2 Chr.** 10:8,10,14; **Ezra** 10:1; **Neh.** 12:43; **Job** 21:11; 38:41; 39:3; **Eccl.** 4:13,15; **Isa.** 2:6; 8:18; 9:6(5); 11:7; 29:23; 57:4,5; **Jer.** 31:20; **Lam.** 4:10; **Dan.** 1:4,10,13,15,17; **Hos.** 1:2; **Joel** 3:3(4:3); **Zech.** 8:5.

3207. יַלְדָּה *yaldāh* **fem. noun**
(girl, young woman)
Gen. 34:4; **Joel** 3:3(4:3); **Zech.** 8:5.

3208. יַלְדוּת *yaldûṯ* **fem. noun**
(childhood, period of youth)
Ps. 110:3; **Eccl.** 11:9,10.

3209. יִלּוֹד *yillôḏ* **adj.**
(born)
Ex. 1:22; **Josh.** 5:5; **2 Sam.** 5:14; 12:14; **Jer.** 16:3.

3210. יָלוֹן *yālôn* **masc. proper noun**
(Jalon)
1 Chr. 4:17.

3211. יָלִיד *yāliyḏ* **masc. noun**
(those born, descendants of)
Gen. 14:14; 17:12,13,23,27; **Lev.** 22:11; **Num.** 13:22,28; **Josh.** 15:14; **2 Sam.** 21:16,18; **1 Chr.** 20:4; **Jer.** 2:14.

3212. יָלַךְ *yālaḵ* **verb**
(classified as a separate root by Strong; all forms classified under *hālaḵ* [1980] by NASB, and NIV, which see).

3213. יָלַל *yālal* **verb**
(to howl, to wail)
Isa. 13:6; 14:31; 15:2,3; 16:7; 23:1,6,14; 52:5(NIV, *hālal* [1984,II]); 65:14; **Jer.** 4:8; 25:34; 47:2; 48:20,31,39; 49:3; 51:8; **Ezek.** 21:12(17); 30:2; **Hos.** 7:14; **Joel** 1:5,11,13; **Amos** 8:3; **Mic.** 1:8; **Zeph.** 1:11; **Zech.** 11:2.

3214. יְלֵל *y^elēl* **masc. noun**
(a howling [of beasts])
Deut. 32:10.

3215. יְלָלָה *y^elālāh* **fem. noun**
(a howling, wailing)
Isa. 15:8; **Jer.** 25:36; **Zeph.** 1:10; **Zech.** 11:3.

3216. יָלַע *yāla'* **verb**
(to devour, to swallow)
Prov. 20:25(NASB, NIV, *lā'a'* [3886,II]).

3217. יַלֶּפֶת *yallepeṯ* **fem. noun**
(a scab or festering sore)
Lev. 21:20; 22:22.

3218. יֶלֶק *yeleq* **masc. noun**
(young locust, caterpillar)
Ps. 105:34; **Jer.** 51:14,27; **Joel** 1:4; 2:25; **Nah.** 3:15,16.

3219. יַלְקוּט *yalqûṭ* **masc. noun**
(a pouch, bag)
1 Sam. 17:40.

3220. יָם *yām* **masc. noun**
(sea, west)
Gen. 1:10,22,26,28; 9:2; 12:8; 13:14; 14:3; 22:17; 28:14; 32:12(13); 41:49; 49:13; **Ex.** 10:19; 13:18; 14:2,9,16, 21–23,26–30; 15:1,4,8,10,19,21,22; 20:11; 23:31; 26:22,27; 27:12; 36:27,32; 38:12; **Lev.** 11:9,10; **Num.** 2:18; 3:23; 11:22,31; 13:29; 14:25; 21:4,14(see *yam-sûp̱* [5492,III]; NASB, NIV, *sûp̱āh* [5492,II]); 33:8,10,11; 34:3,5–7,11,12; 35:5; **Deut.** 1:7,40; 2:1; 3:17,27; 4:49; 11:4,24; 30:13; 33:19,23; 34:2; **Josh.** 1:4; 2:10; 3:16; 4:23; 5:1; 8:9,12,13; 9:1; 11:2–4; 12:3,7; 13:27; 15:2,4,5,8,10–12, 46,47; 16:3,6,8; 17:9,10; 18:12,14,15,19; 19:11,26,29,34; 22:7; 23:4; 24:6,7; **Judg.** 5:17; 7:12; 11:16; **1 Sam.** 13:5; **2 Sam.** 17:11; 22:16; **1 Kgs.** 4:20,29(5:9);

5:9(23); 7:23–25,39,44; 9:26,27; 10:22; 18:43,44; **2 Kgs.** 14:25; 16:17; 25:13,16; **1 Chr.** 9:24; 16:32; 18:8; **2 Chr.** 2:16(15); 4:2–4,6,10,15; 8:17,18; 20:2; **Ezra** 3:7; **Neh.** 9:6,9,11; **Esth.** 10:1; **Job** 6:3; 7:12; 9:8; 11:9; 12:8; 14:11; 26:12; 28:14; 36:30; 38:8,16; 41:31(23); **Ps.** 8:8(9); 24:2; 33:7; 46:2(3); 65:5(6),7(8); 66:6; 68:22(23); 69:34(35); 72:8; 74:13; 77:19(20); 78:13,27,53; 80:11(12); 89:9(10),25(26); 93:4; 95:5; 96:11; 98:7; 104:25; 106:7,9,22; 107:3,23; 114:3,5; 135:6; 136:13,15; 139:9; 146:6; **Prov.** 8:29; 23:34; 30:19; **Eccl.** 1:7; **Isa.** 5:30; 9:1(8:23); 10:22,26; 11:9,11,14,15; 16:8; 17:12; 18:2; 19:5; 21:1; 23:2,4,11; 24:14,15; 27:1; 42:10; 43:16; 48:18; 49:12; 50:2; 51:10,15; 57:20; 60:5; 63:11; **Jer.** 5:22; 6:23; 15:8; 25:22; 27:19; 31:35; 33:22; 46:18; 47:7; 48:32; 49:21,23; 50:42; 51:36,42; 52:17,20; **Lam.** 2:13; **Ezek.** 25:16; 26:3,5,16–18; 27:3,4,9, 25–27,29,32–34; 28:2,8; 32:2; 38:20; 39:11; 41:12; 42:19; 45:7; 46:19; 47:8,10, 15,17–20; 48:1–8,10,16–18,21,23–28,34; **Dan.** 8:4; 11:45; **Hos.** 1:10(2:1); 4:3; 11:10; **Joel** 2:20; **Amos** 5:8; 8:12; 9:3,6; **Jon.** 1:4,5,9,11–13,15; 2:3(4); **Mic.** 7:12,19; **Nah.** 1:4; 3:8; **Hab.** 1:14; 2:14; 3:8,15; **Zeph.** 1:3; 2:5,6; **Hag.** 2:6; **Zech.** 9:4,10; 10:11; 14:4,8.

3221. יַם *yam* **Aram. masc. noun**
(sea; corr. to Hebr. 3220)
Dan. 7:2,3.

3222. I. יֵם *yēm* **masc. noun**
(mule)
Gen. 36:24(NASB, NIV, see II).
II. יֵם *yēm* **masc. noun**
(hot springs)
Gen. 36:24(KJV, see I).

3223. יְמוּאֵל *y^e^mû'ēl* **masc. proper noun**
(Jemuel)
Gen. 46:10; **Ex.** 6:15.

3224. יְמִימָה *y^e^miymāh* **fem. proper noun**
(Jemimah)
Job 42:14.

3225. יָמִין *yāmiyn* **fem. noun**
(hand, right hand, south)
Gen. 13:9; 24:49; 48:13,14,17,18; **Ex.** 14:22,29; 15:6,12; 29:22; **Lev.** 7:32,33; 8:25,26; 9:21; **Num.** 18:18; 20:17; 22:26; **Deut.** 2:27; 5:32(29); 17:11,20; 28:14; 33:2; **Josh.** 1:7; 17:7; 23:6; **Judg.** 3:15,16,21; 5:26; 7:20; 16:29; 20:16; **1 Sam.** 6:12; 11:2; 23:19,24; **2 Sam.** 2:19,21; 16:6; 20:9; 24:5; **1 Kgs.** 2:19; 7:39,49; 22:19; **2 Kgs.** 12:9(10); 22:2; 23:13; **1 Chr.** 6:39(24); **2 Chr.** 3:17; 4:6–8; 18:18; 34:2; **Neh.** 8:4; 12:31; **Job** 23:9; 30:12; 40:14; **Ps.** 16:8,11; 17:7; 18:35(36); 20:6(7); 21:8(9); 26:10; 44:3(4); 45:4(5),9(10); 48:10(11); 60:5(7); 63:8(9); 73:23; 74:11; 77:10(11); 78:54; 80:15(16),17(18); 89:12(13), 13(14),25(26),42(43); 91:7; 98:1; 108:6(7); 109:6,31; 110:1,5; 118:15,16; 121:5; 137:5; 138:7; 139:10; 142:4(5); 144:8,11; **Prov.** 3:16; 4:27; 27:16; **Eccl.** 10:2; **Song** 2:6; 8:3; **Isa.** 9:20(19); 41:10,13; 44:20; 45:1; 48:13; 54:3; 62:8; 63:12; **Jer.** 22:24; **Lam.** 2:3,4; **Ezek.** 1:10; 10:3; 16:46; 21:22(27); 39:3; **Dan.** 12:7; **Jon.** 4:11; **Hab.** 2:16; **Zech.** 3:1; 4:3,11; 11:17; 12:6.

3226. A. יָמִין *yāmiyn* **masc. proper noun**
(Jamin: son of Simeon)
Gen. 46:10; **Ex.** 6:15; **Num.** 26:12; **1 Chr.** 4:24.
B. יָמִין *yāmiyn* **masc. proper noun**
(Jamin: a Judaite)
1 Chr. 2:27.
C. יָמִין *yāmiyn* **masc. proper noun**
(Jamin: a Levite)
Neh. 8:7.

3227. יְמִינִי *y^{e}miyniy* **adj.**
(right, right hand)
2 Chr. 3:17(NASB, NIV, [Q^{e}] *y^{e}māniy* [3233]); **Ezek.** 4:6(NASB, NIV, [Q^{e}] *y^{e}māniy* [3233]).

3228. I. יָמִינִי *yāmiyniy* **masc. proper noun**
(Jaminite)
Num. 26:12.
II. יְמִינִי *y^{e}miyniy* **masc. proper noun**
(Benjamite: shortened form of *ben-y^{e}miymiy* [1145])
1 Sam. 9:1,4; **2 Sam.** 20:1; **Esth.** 2:5.

3229. יִמְלָא *yimlā'*, יִמְלָה *yimlāh* **masc. proper noun**
(Imlah)
1 Kgs. 22:8,9; **2 Chr.** 18:7,8.

3230. יַמְלֵךְ *yamlēḵ* **masc. proper noun**
(Jamlech)
1 Chr. 4:34.

3231. יָמַן *yāman* **verb**
(to go to the right, to use the right hand)
Gen. 13:9; **2 Sam.** 14:19; **1 Chr.** 12:2; **Isa.** 30:21(KJV, *'āman* [541]); **Ezek.** 21:16(21).

3232. יִמְנָה *yimnāh* **masc. proper noun**
(Imnah)
Gen. 46:17; **Num.** 26:44; **1 Chr.** 7:30; **2 Chr.** 31:14.

3233. יְמָנִי *y^{e}māniy* **adj.**
(right, right hand)
Ex. 29:20; **Lev.** 8:23,24; 14:14,16,17,25,27,28; **1 Kgs.** 6:8; 7:21,39; **2 Kgs.** 11:11; **2 Chr.** 3:17(KJV, [K^{e}] *y^{e}miyniy* [3227]); 4:10; 23:10; **Ezek.** 4:6(KJV, [K^{e}] *y^{e}miyniy* [3227]); 47:1,2.

3234. יִמְנָע *yimnā'* **masc. proper noun**
(Imna)
1 Chr. 7:35.

3235. I. יָמַר *yāmar* **verb**
(to boast)
Isa. 61:6(NIV, *'āmar* [559,II]).
II. יָמַר *yāmar* **verb**
(to change)
Jer. 2:11(KJV, NASB, *mûr* [4171]).

3236. יִמְרָה *yimrāh* **masc. proper noun**
(Imrah)
1 Chr. 7:36.

3237. יָמַשׁ *yāmaš* **verb**
(to touch, to feel)
Judg. 16:26(KJV, NASB, NIV, [Q^{e}] *mûš* [4185]).

3238. יָנָה *yānāh* **verb**
(to oppress, to vex)
Ex. 22:21(20); **Lev.** 19:33; 25:14,17; **Deut.** 23:16(17); **Ps.** 74:8; **Isa.** 49:26; **Jer.** 22:3; 25:38; 46:16; 50:16; **Ezek.** 18:7,12,16; 22:7,29; 45:8; 46:18; **Zeph.** 3:1.

3239. A. יָנוֹחַ *yānôaḥ* **proper noun**
(Janoah: town in Naphtali)
2 Kgs. 15:29.
B. יָנוֹחָה *yānôḥāh* **proper noun**
(Janoah: town in Ephraim)
Josh. 16:6,7.

3240. יָנַח *yānaḥ* **verb**
(classified as a separate root by Strong; all forms classified by NASB, and NIV, under *nûaḥ* [5117,I], which see).

3241. יָנִים *yāniym* **masc. proper noun**
(Janim)
Josh. 15:53(KJV, NASB, [Q^{e}] *yānûm*).

3242. יְנִיקָה y^e*niyqāh* **fem. noun**
(young shoot, twig)
Ezek. 17:4.

3243. יָנַק *yānaq* **verb**
(to nurse, to care for)
Gen. 21:7; 24:59; 32:15(16); 35:8; **Ex.** 2:7,9,9(KJV, NASB, *nûq* [5134]); **Num.** 11:12(KJV, NASB, *nûq* [3126]); **Deut.** 32:13,25(KJV, NASB, *yōnēq* [3126]); 33:19; **1 Sam.** 1:23; 15:3(KJV, NASB, *yōnēq* [3126]); 22:19(KJV, NASB, *yōnēq* [3126]); **1 Kgs.** 3:21; **2 Kgs.** 11:2; **2 Chr.** 22:11; **Job** 3:12; 20:16; **Ps.** 8:2(3)(KJV, NASB, *yōnēq* [3126]); **Song** 8:1(KJV, NASB, *yōnēq* [3126]); **Isa.** 11:8; 49:23; 60:16; 66:11,12; **Jer.** 44:7(KJV, NASB, *yōnēq* [3126]); **Lam.** 2:11(KJV, NASB, *yōnēq* [3126]); 4:3,4(KJV, NASB, *yōnēq* [3126]); **Joel** 2:16(KJV, NASB, *yōnēq* [3126]).

3244. יַנְשׁוּף *yanšûp̱*, יַנְשׁוֹף *yanšôp̱* **masc. noun**
(great owl)
Lev. 11:17; **Deut.** 14:16; **Isa.** 34:11.

3245. I. יָסַד *yāsad̠* **verb**
(to lay a foundation)
Ex. 9:18; **Josh.** 6:26; **1 Kgs.** 5:17(31); 6:37; 7:10(see m^e*yussād̠* [4328]); 16:34; **1 Chr.** 9:22; **2 Chr.** 3:3; 31:7; **Ezra** 3:6,10–12; **Esth.** 1:8; **Job** 38:4; **Ps.** 8:2(3); 24:2; 78:69; 89:11(12); 102:25(26); 104:5,8; 119:152; **Prov.** 3:19; **Song** 5:15(see m^e*yussād̠* [4328]); **Isa.** 14:32; 23:13; 28:16; 44:28; 48:13; 51:13,16; 54:11; **Ezek.** 41:8(see m^e*yussād̠ah* [4328]; NIV, [Q^e] *mûssād̠ah* [4145]); **Amos** 9:6; **Hab.** 1:12; **Hag.** 2:18; **Zech.** 4:9; 8:9; 12:1.
II. יָסַד *yāsad̠* **verb**
(to gather, to conspire together)
Ps. 2:2; 31:13(14).

3246. יְסֻד y^e*sud̠* **masc. noun**
(a beginning)
Ezra 7:9.

3247. יְסוֹד y^e*sôd̠* **masc. noun**
(foundation, bottom)
Ex. 29:12; **Lev.** 4:7,18,25,30,34; 5:9; 8:15; 9:9; **2 Chr.** 23:5; 24:27; **Job** 4:19; 22:16; **Ps.** 137:7; **Prov.** 10:25; **Lam.** 4:11; **Ezek.** 13:14; 30:4; **Mic.** 1:6; **Hab.** 3:13.

3248. יְסוּדָה y^e*sûd̠āh* **fem. noun**
(foundation)
Ps. 87:1.

3249. יָסוּר *yāsûr* **masc. noun**
(those who depart, turn away)
Jer. 17:13(NASB, NIV, [Q^e] *sûr* [5493,I]).

3250. יִסּוֹר *yissôr* **masc. noun**
(one who contends, instructs)
Job 40:2.

3251. יָסַךְ *yāsak̠* **verb**
(to pour)
Ex. 30:32(NASB, NIV, *sûk̠* [5480]).

3252. יִסְכָּה *yiskāh* **fem. proper noun**
(Iscah)
Gen. 11:29.

3253. יִסְמַכְיָהוּ *yismak̠yāhû* **masc. proper noun**
(Ismakiah)
2 Chr. 31:13.

3254. יָסַף *yāsap̱* **verb**
(to increase, to do again, to continue)
Gen. 4:2,12; 8:10,12,21; 18:29; 25:1; 30:24; 37:5,8; 38:5,26; 44:23; **Ex.** 1:10; 5:7; 8:29(25); 9:28,34; 10:28,29; 11:6; 14:13; **Lev.** 5:16; 6:5(5:24); 19:25; 22:14; 26:18,21; 27:13,15,19,27,31; **Num.** 5:7; 11:25; 22:15,19,25,26; 32:15; 36:3,4;

Deut. 1:11; 3:26; 4:2; 5:22(19),25(22); 12:32(13:1); 13:11(12); 17:16; 18:16; 19:9,20; 20:8; 25:3; 28:68; 32:23(KJV, NASB, *sāpāh* [5595,II]); **Josh.** 7:12; 23:13; **Judg.** 2:21; 3:12; 4:1; 8:28; 9:37; 10:6,13; 11:14; 13:1,21; 20:22,23,28; **Ruth** 1:17; **1 Sam.** 3:6,8,17,21; 7:13; 9:8; 12:19; 14:44; 15:35; 18:29; 19:8,21; 20:13,17; 23:4; 25:22; 27:4; **2 Sam.** 2:22,28; 3:9,34,35; 5:22; 6:1; 7:10,20; 12:8; 14:10; 18:22; 19:13(14); 24:1,3; **1 Kgs.** 2:23; 10:7; 12:11,14; 16:33; 19:2; 20:10; **2 Kgs.** 6:23,31; 19:30; 20:6; 21:8; 24:7; **1 Chr.** 14:13; 17:9,18; 21:3; 22:14; **2 Chr.** 9:6; 10:11,14; 28:13,22; 33:8; **Ezra** 10:10; **Neh.** 13:18; **Esth.** 8:3; **Job** 17:9; 20:9; 27:1; 29:1; 34:32,37; 36:1; 38:11; 40:5; 41:8(40:32); 42:10; **Ps.** 10:18; 41:8(9); 61:6(7); 71:14; 77:7(8); 78:17; 115:14; 120:3; **Prov.** 1:5; 3:2; 9:9,11; 10:22,27; 11:24; 16:21,23; 19:4,19; 23:28,35; 30:6; **Eccl.** 1:16,18; 2:9; 3:14; **Isa.** 1:5,13; 7:10; 8:5; 10:20; 11:11; 15:9; 23:12; 24:20; 26:15; 29:1(KJV, *sāpāh* [5595,II]),14,19; 30:1(KJV, NASB, *sāpāh* [5595,II]); 37:31; 38:5; 47:1,5; 51:22; 52:1; **Jer.** 7:21(KJV, *sāpāh* [5595,II]); 31:12; 36:32; 45:3; **Lam.** 4:15,16,22; **Ezek.** 5:16; 23:14; 36:12; **Dan.** 10:18; **Hos.** 1:6; 9:15; 13:2; **Joel** 2:2; **Amos** 5:2; 7:8,13; 8:2; **Jon.** 2:4(5); **Nah.** 1:15(2:1); **Zeph.** 3:11.

3255. יְסַף *y^esap* **Aram. verb**
(to add, to increase; corr. to Hebr. 3254)
Dan. 4:36(33).

3256. I. יָסַר *yāsar* **verb**
(to admonish, to chastise, to discipline, to instruct)
Lev. 26:18,23,28; **Deut.** 4:36; 8:5; 21:18; 22:18; **1 Kgs.** 12:11,14; **1 Chr.** 15:22(NIV, see II); **2 Chr.** 10:11,14; **Job** 4:3; **Ps.** 2:10; 6:1(2); 16:7; 38:1(2); 39:11(12); 94:10,12; 118:18; **Prov.** 9:7; 19:18; 29:17,19; 31:1; **Isa.** 8:11; 28:26; **Jer.** 2:19; 6:8; 10:24; 30:11; 31:18; 46:28; **Ezek.** 23:48; **Hos.** 7:12,15; 10:10.
II. סָרַר *sārar* **verb**
(to superintend, to be in charge)
1 Chr. 15:22(KJV, NASB, see I).

3257. יָע *yāʿ* **masc. noun**
(shovel)
Ex. 27:3; 38:3; **Num.** 4:14; **1 Kgs.** 7:40,45; **2 Kgs.** 25:14; **2 Chr.** 4:11,16; **Jer.** 52:18.

3258. A. יַעְבֵּץ *yaʿbēṣ* **masc. proper noun**
(Jabez: descendant of Judah)
1 Chr. 4:9,10.
B. יַעְבֵּץ *yaʿbēṣ* **proper noun**
(Jabez: loc. in Judah)
1 Chr. 2:55.

3259. יָעַד *yāʿad* **verb**
(to meet, to appoint, to gather)
Ex. 21:8,9; 25:22; 29:42,43; 30:6,36; **Num.** 10:3,4; 14:35; 16:11; 17:4(19); 27:3; **Josh.** 11:5; **2 Sam.** 20:5; **1 Kgs.** 8:5; **2 Chr.** 5:6; **Neh.** 6:2,10; **Job** 2:11; 9:19; **Ps.** 48:4(5); **Jer.** 24:1; 47:7; 49:19; 50:44; **Ezek.** 21:16(21); **Amos** 3:3; **Mic.** 6:9.

3260. יֶעְדוֹ *yeʿdô* **masc. proper noun**
(Iddo)
2 Chr. 9:29.

3261. יָעָה *yāʿāh* **verb**
(to sweep away)
Isa. 28:17.

3262. יְעוּאֵל *y^eʿûʾēl* **masc. proper noun**
(Jeuel: son of Zerah)
1 Chr. 9:6.

3263. יְעוּץ *y^eʿûṣ* **masc. proper noun**
(Jeuz)
1 Chr. 8:10.

3264. יְעוֹרִים *y*ᵉ*ʿôriym* **masc. pl. noun**
(woods, forest)
Ezek. 34:25(NASB, NIV, *yaʿar* [3293,I]).

3265. יָעוּר *yāʿûr* **masc. proper noun**
(Jair)
1 Chr. 20:5.

3266. A. יְעוּשׁ *y*ᵉ*ʿûš* **masc. proper noun**
(Jeush: son of Esau)
Gen. 36:5([Kᵉ] *y*ᵉ*ʿiyš* [3274,A]),14([Kᵉ] *y*ᵉ*ʿiyš* [3274,A]),18; **1 Chr.** 1:35.
B. יְעוּשׁ *y*ᵉ*ʿûš* **masc. proper noun**
(Jeush: a Benjamite)
1 Chr. 7:10([Kᵉ] *y*ᵉ*ʿiyš* [3274,B]).
C. יְעוּשׁ *y*ᵉ*ʿûš* **masc. proper noun**
(Jeush: a Benjamite)
1 Chr. 8:39.
D. יְעוּשׁ *y*ᵉ*ʿûš* **masc. proper noun**
(Jeush: a Levite)
1 Chr. 23:10,11.
E. יְעוּשׁ *y*ᵉ*ʿûš* **masc. proper noun**
(Jeush: son of Rehoboam)
2 Chr. 11:19.

3267. יָעַז *yāʿaz* **verb**
(to be strong, to be fierce)
Isa. 33:19.

3268. יַעֲזִיאֵל *yaʿᵃziyʾēl* **masc. proper noun**
(Jaaziel)
1 Chr. 15:18.

3269. יַעֲזִיָּהוּ *yaʿᵃziyyāhû* **masc. proper noun**
(Jaaziah)
1 Chr. 24:26,27.

3270. יַעֲזֵיר *yaʿᵃzēyr*, יַעְזֵר *yaʿzēr* **proper noun**
(Jazer)
Num. 21:32; 32:1,3,35; **Josh.** 13:25; 21:39(37); **2 Sam.** 24:5; **1 Chr.** 6:81(66); 26:31; **Isa.** 16:8,9; **Jer.** 48:32.

3271. יָעַט *yāʿaṭ* **verb**
(to cover, to clothe)
Isa. 61:10.

3272. יְעַט *y*ᵉ*ʿaṭ* **Aram. verb**
(to advise, to give counsel)
Ezra 7:14,15; **Dan.** 6:7(8).

3273. A. יְעִיאֵל *y*ᵉ*ʿiyʾēl* **masc. proper noun**
(Jeiel: a Reubenite)
1 Chr. 5:7.
B. יְעוּאֵל *y*ᵉ*ʿûʾēl* **masc. proper noun**
(Jeiel: father of Gibeon)
1 Chr. 9:35([Qᵉ] *y*ᵉ*ʿûʾēl* [3262,B]).
C. יְעוּאֵל *y*ᵉ*ʿûʾēl* **masc. proper noun**
(Jeiel: son of Hotham)
1 Chr. 11:44.
D. יְעִיאֵל *y*ᵉ*ʿiyʾēl* **masc. proper noun**
(Jeiel: a musician)
1 Chr. 15:18,21; 16:5.
E. יְעִיאֵל *y*ᵉ*ʿiyʾēl* **masc. proper noun**
(Jeiel: son of Mattaniah)
2 Chr. 20:14.
F. יְעוּאֵל *y*ᵉ*ʿûʾēl* **masc. proper noun**
(Jeiel: a scribe)
2 Chr. 26:11.
G. יְעוּאֵל *y*ᵉ*ʿûʾēl* **masc. proper noun**
(Jeiel: son of Elizaphan)
2 Chr. 29:13.
H. יְעִיאֵל *y*ᵉ*ʿiyʾēl* **masc. proper noun**
(Jeiel: a Levite)
2 Chr. 35:9.
I. יְעִיאֵל *y*ᵉ*ʿiyʾēl* **masc. proper noun**
(Jeiel: son of Adonikam)
Ezra 8:13.
J. יְעִיאֵל *y*ᵉ*ʿiyʾēl* **masc. proper noun**
(Jeiel: son of Nebo)
Ezra 10:43.

3274. A. יְעִישׁ *y^e'iyš* **masc. proper noun**
(Jeish, alternate spelling in the [K^e] for *y^e'ûš* [3266,A], Jeush: son of Esau; KJV, NASB, NIV, [Q^e] *y^e'ûš* [3266,A])
Gen. 36:5,14.
B. יְעִישׁ *y^e'iyš* **masc. proper noun**
(Jeish, alternate spelling in the [K^e] for *y^e'ûš* [3266,B], Jeush: a Benjamite; KJV, NASB, NIV, [Q^e] *y^e'ûš* [3266,B])
1 Chr. 7:10.

3275. יַעְכָּן *ya'kān* **masc. proper noun**
(Jacan)
1 Chr. 5:13.

3276. יָעַל *yā'al* **verb**
(to gain, to profit, to benefit)
1 Sam. 12:21; **Job** 15:3; 21:15; 30:13; 35:3; **Prov.** 10:2; 11:4; **Isa.** 30:5,6; 44:9,10; 47:12; 48:17; 57:12; **Jer.** 2:8,11; 7:8; 12:13; 16:19; 23:32; **Hab.** 2:18.

3277. יָעֵל *yā'ēl* **masc. noun**
(wild goat)
1 Sam. 24:2(3); **Job** 39:1; **Ps.** 104:18.

3278. יָעֵל *yā'ēl* **fem. proper noun**
(Jael)
Judg. 4:17,18,21,22; 5:6,24.

3279. יַעֲלָא *ya'ala'*, יַעֲלָה *ya'alāh* **masc. proper noun**
(Jaala)
Ezra 2:56; **Neh.** 7:58.

3280. יַעֲלָה *ya'alāh* **fem. noun**
(doe, female deer or mountain goat)
Prov. 5:19.

3281. יַעְלָם *ya'lām* **masc. proper noun**
(Jalam)
Gen. 36:5,14,18; **1 Chr.** 1:35.

3282. יַעַן *ya'an* **conj.**
(because)
Gen. 22:16; **Lev.** 26:43; **Num.** 11:20; 20:12; **Deut.** 1:36; **Josh.** 14:14; **Judg.** 2:20; **1 Sam.** 15:23; 30:22; **1 Kgs.** 3:11; 8:18; 11:11,33; 13:21; 14:9,13,15; 16:2; 20:28,36,42; 21:20,29; **2 Kgs.** 19:28; 21:11,15; 22:19; **2 Chr.** 1:11; 34:27; **Ps.** 109:16; **Prov.** 1:24; **Isa.** 3:16; 7:5; 8:6; 29:13; 30:12; 37:29; 61:1; 65:12; 66:4; **Jer.** 5:14; 7:13; 19:4; 23:38; 25:8; 29:23, 25,31; 35:17,18; 48:7; **Ezek.** 5:7,9,11; 12:12; 13:8,10,22; 15:8; 16:36,43; 20:16, 24; 21:4(9),24(29); 22:19; 23:35; 24:13; 25:3,6,8,12,15; 26:2; 28:2,6; 29:6,9; 31:10; 34:8,21; 35:5,10; 36:2,3,6,13; 44:12; **Hos.** 8:1; **Amos** 5:11; **Hag.** 1:9.

3283. יָעֵן *yā'ēn* **masc. noun**
(ostrich)
Lam. 4:3.

3284. יַעֲנָה *ya'anāh* **fem. noun**
(an unclean bird, perhaps the horned owl or the ostrich)
Lev. 11:16; **Deut.** 14:15; **Job** 30:29; **Isa.** 13:21; 34:13; 43:20; **Jer.** 50:39; **Mic.** 1:8.

3285. יַעְנַי *ya'nay* **masc. proper noun**
(Janai)
1 Chr. 5:12.

3286. I. יָעֵף *yā'ēp̱* **verb**
(to faint, to be exhausted)
Isa. 40:28,30,31; 44:12; **Jer.** 2:24; 51:58,64; **Dan.** 9:21(KJV, NIV, see II); **Hab.** 2:13.
II. יָעֵף *yā'ēp̱* **verb**
(to move swiftly)
Isa. 40:28,30,31; 44:12; **Jer.** 2:24; 51:58,64; **Dan.** 9:21(NASB, see I); **Hab.** 2:13.

3287. יָעֵף *yā'ēp̱* **adj.**
(weary, faint, exhausted)

Judg. 8:15(NIV, *'ayēp̱* [5889]); **2 Sam.** 16:2; **Isa.** 40:29; 50:4.

3288. I. יְעָף *y^e'āp̱* **masc. noun**
(weariness)
Dan. 9:21(KJV, NIV, see II).
II. יְעָף *y^e'āp̱* **masc. noun**
(swiftness, swift flight)
Dan. 9:21(NASB, see I).

3289. יָעַץ *yā'aṣ* **verb**
(to advise, to give counsel)
Ex. 18:19; **Num.** 24:14; **2 Sam.** 15:12; 16:23; 17:7,11,15,21; **1 Kgs.** 1:12; 12:6, 8,9,13,28; **2 Kgs.** 6:8; **1 Chr.** 13:1; 26:14; 27:32,33; **2 Chr.** 10:6,8,9; 20:21; 22:3,4; 25:16,17; 30:2,23; 32:3; **Ezra** 4:5; 7:28; 8:25; **Neh.** 6:7; **Job** 3:14; 12:17; 26:3; **Ps.** 16:7; 32:8; 62:4(5); 71:10; 83:3(4),5(6); **Prov.** 11:14; 12:20; 13:10; 15:22; 24:6; **Isa.** 1:26; 3:3; 7:5; 9:6(5); 14:24,26,27; 19:11,12,17; 23:8,9; 32:7,8; 40:14; 41:28; 45:21; **Jer.** 38:15; 49:20,30; 50:45; **Ezek.** 11:2; **Mic.** 4:9; 6:5; **Nah.** 1:11; **Hab.** 2:10.

3290. A. יַעֲקֹב *ya'^aqōḇ* **masc. proper noun**
(Jacob: son of Isaac)
Gen. 25:26–31,33,34; 27:6,11,15,17,19, 21,22,30,36,41,42,46; 28:1,5–7,10,16, 18,20; 29:1,4,10–13,15,18,20,21,28; 30:1,2,4,5,7,9,10,12,16,17,19,25,31,36, 37,40–42; 31:1–4,11,17,20,22,24–26,29, 31–33,36,43,45–47,51,53,54; 32:1–4(2–5), 6(7),7(8),9(10),18(19),20(21),24(25), 25(26),27–30(28–31),32(33); 33:1,10, 17,18; 34:1,3,5–7,13,19,25,27,30; 35:1,2, 4–6,9,10,14,15,20,22,23,26,27,29; 36:6; 37:1,2,34; 42:1,4,29,36; 45:25,27; 46:2, 5,6,8,15,18,19,22,25–27; 47:7–10,28; 48:2,3; 49:1,2,7,24,33; 50:24; **Ex.** 1:1,5; 2:24; 3:6,15,16; 4:5; 6:3,8; 19:3; 33:1; **Lev.** 26:42; **Num.** 32:11; **Deut.** 1:8; 6:10; 9:5,27; 29:13(12); 30:20; 34:4; **Josh.** 24:4,32; **1 Sam.** 12:8; **2 Kgs.** 13:23; **Mal.** 1:2.

B. יַעֲקֹב *ya'^aqōḇ* **masc. proper noun**
(Jacob: descendants of Jacob)
Num. 23:7,10,21,23; 24:5,17,19; **Deut.** 32:9; 33:4,10,28; **2 Sam.** 23:1; **1 Kgs.** 18:31; **2 Kgs.** 17:34; **1 Chr.** 16:13,17; **Ps.** 14:7; 20:1(2); 22:23(24); 24:6; 44:4(5); 46:7(8),11(12); 47:4(5); 53:6(7); 59:13(14); 75:9(10); 76:6(7); 77:15(16); 78:5,21,71; 79:7; 81:1(2),4(5); 84:8(9); 85:1(2); 87:2; 94:7; 99:4; 105:6,10,23; 114:1,7; 132:2,5; 135:4; 146:5; 147:19; **Isa.** 2:3,5,6; 8:17; 9:8(7); 10:20,21; 14:1; 17:4; 27:6,9; 29:22,23; 40:27; 41:8,14,21; 42:24; 43:1,22,28; 44:1,2,5,21,23; 45:4,19; 46:3; 48:1,12,20; 49:5,6,26; 58:1,14; 59:20; 60:16; 65:9; **Jer.** 2:4; 5:20; 10:16,25; 30:7,10,18; 31:7,11; 33:26; 46:27,28; 51:19; **Lam.** 1:17; 2:2,3; **Ezek.** 20:5; 28:25; 37:25; 39:25; **Hos.** 10:11; 12:2(3),12(13); **Amos** 3:13; 6:8; 7:2,5; 8:7; 9:8; **Obad.** 1:10,17,18; **Mic.** 1:5; 2:7,12; 3:1,8,9; 4:2; 5:7(6),8(7); 7:20; **Nah.** 2:2(3); **Mal.** 2:12; 3:6.

3291. יַעֲקֹבָה *ya'^aqōḇāh* **masc. proper noun**
(Jaakobah)
1 Chr. 4:36.

3292. יַעֲקָן *ya'^aqān* **masc. proper noun**
(Jaakan, Akan)
Deut. 10:6(see *b^e'ērōt b^enēy-ya'^aqān* [885]); **1 Chr.** 1:42.

3293. I. יַעַר *ya'ar* **masc. noun**
(honeycomb; forest, wood)
Deut. 19:5; **Josh.** 17:15,18; **1 Sam.** 14:25,26; 22:5; **2 Sam.** 18:6,8,17; **1 Kgs.** 7:2; 10:17,21; **2 Kgs.** 2:24; 19:23; **1 Chr.** 16:33; **2 Chr.** 9:16,20; **Ps.** 29:9(KJV, *ya^e rāh* [3295,II]); 50:10; 80:13(14); 83:14(15); 96:12; 104:20; 132:6(NASB, NIV, see III); **Eccl.** 2:6; **Song** 2:3; **Isa.** 7:2; 9:18(17); 10:18,19,34; 21:13; 22:8; 29:17; 32:15,19; 37:24; 44:14,23; 56:9;

Jer. 5:6; 10:3; 12:8; 21:14; 26:18; 46:23; **Ezek.** 15:2,6; 20:46(21:2),47(21:3); 34:25(KJV, *y^e'ôriym* [3264]); 39:10; **Hos.** 2:12(14); **Amos** 3:4; **Mic.** 3:12; 5:8(7); 7:14; **Zech.** 11:2.
II. יַעַר *ya'ar* **masc. noun**
(honeycomb)
Song 5:1.
III. יַעַר *ya'ar* **masc. proper noun**
(Jaar: perhaps another name for *qiryat y^e'āriym* [7157])
Ps. 132:6(KJV, see I).

3294. יַעְרָה *ya'rāh* **masc. proper noun**
(Jarah)
1 Chr. 9:42(NIV, [Q^e] *ya'ar*).

3295. I. יַעֲרָה *ya'^arāh* **fem. noun**
(honeycomb)
1 Sam. 14:27.
II. יַעֲרָה *ya'^arāh* **fem. noun**
(forest)
Ps. 29:9(NASB, NIV, *ya'ar* [3293,I]).

3296. יַעְרֵי אֹרְגִים *ya'^arēy 'ōr^egiym* **masc. proper noun**
(Jaare-Oregim)
2 Sam. 21:19.

3297. יְעָרִים *y^e'āriym* **proper noun**
(Jearim)
Josh. 15:10.

3298. יַעֲרֶשְׁיָה *ya'^arešyāh* **masc. proper noun**
(Jaareshiah)
1 Chr. 8:27.

3299. יַעֲשָׂו *ya'^aśāw* **masc. proper noun**
(Jaasu)
Ezra 10:37.

3300. A. יַעֲשִׂיאֵל *ya'^aśiy'ēl* **masc. proper noun**
(Jaasiel: one of David's mighty men)
1 Chr. 11:47.

B. יַעֲשִׂיאֵל *ya'^aśiy'ēl* **masc. proper noun**
(Jaasiel: a Benjamite)
1 Chr. 27:21.

3301. יִפְדְיָה *yipd^eyāh* **masc. proper noun**
(Iphdeiah)
1 Chr. 8:25.

3302. יָפָה *yāpāh* **verb**
(to be beautiful, to be bright)
Ps. 45:2(3); **Song** 4:10; 7:1(2),6(7); **Jer.** 4:30; 10:4; **Ezek.** 16:13; 31:7.

3303. יָפֶה *yāpeh* **adj.**
(beautiful, lovely)
Gen. 12:11,14; 29:17; 39:6; 41:2,4,18; **Deut.** 21:11; **1 Sam.** 16:12; 17:42; 25:3; **2 Sam.** 13:1; 14:25,27; **1 Kgs.** 1:3,4; **Esth.** 2:7; **Job** 42:15; **Ps.** 48:2(3); **Prov.** 11:22; **Eccl.** 3:11; 5:18(17); **Song** 1:8, 15,16; 2:10,13; 4:1,7; 5:9; 6:1,4,10; **Jer.** 11:16; **Ezek.** 31:3,9; 33:32; **Amos** 8:13.

3304. יְפֵיפִיָּה *y^epēypiyyah* **adj.**
(very pretty)
Jer. 46:20.

3305. יָפוֹא *yāpô'*, יָפוֹ *yāpô* **proper noun**
(Japho, Joppa)
Josh. 19:46; **2 Chr.** 2:16(15); **Ezra** 3:7; **Jon.** 1:3.

3306. יָפַח *yāpaḥ* **verb**
(to breathe hard, to gasp for breath)
Jer. 4:31.

3307. יָפֵחַ *yāpēaḥ* **adj.**
(breathing out)
Ps. 27:12.

3308. יֳפִי *y^opiy* **masc. noun**
(beauty)
Esth. 1:11; **Ps.** 45:11(12); 50:2; **Prov.** 6:25; 31:30; **Isa.** 3:24; 33:17; **Lam.** 2:15;

Ezek. 16:14,15,25; 27:3,4,11; 28:7,12, 17; 31:8; **Zech.** 9:17.

3309. A. יָפִיעַ *yāp̱iyaʻ* **masc. proper noun**
(Japhia: king of Lachish)
Josh. 10:3.
B. יָפִיעַ *yāp̱iyaʻ* **masc. proper noun**
(Japhia: border town of Zebulon)
Josh. 19:12.
C. יָפִיעַ *yāp̱iyaʻ* **masc. proper noun**
(Japhia: son of David)
2 Sam. 5:15; **1 Chr.** 3:7; 14:6.

3310. יַפְלֵט *yap̱lēṭ* **masc. proper noun**
(Japhlet)
1 Chr. 7:32,33.

3311. יַפְלֵטִי *yap̱lēṭiy* **proper noun**
(Japhletite)
Josh. 16:3.

3312. A. יְפֻנֶּה *y^e^p̱unneh* **masc. proper noun**
(Jephunneh: father of Caleb)
Num. 13:6; 14:6,30,38; 26:65; 32:12; 34:19; **Deut.** 1:36; **Josh.** 14:6,13,14; 15:13; 21:12; **1 Chr.** 4:15; 6:56(41).
B. יְפֻנֶּה *y^e^p̱unneh* **masc. proper noun**
(Jephunneh: an Asherite)
1 Chr. 7:38.

3313. יָפַע *yāp̱aʻ* **verb**
(to shine, to shine forth)
Deut. 33:2; **Job** 3:4; 10:3,22; 37:15; **Ps.** 50:2; 80:1(2); 94:1.

3314. יִפְעָה *yip̱ʻāh* **fem. noun**
(brightness, splendor)
Ezek. 28:7,17.

3315. יֶפֶת *yep̱eṯ* **masc. proper noun**
(Japheth)
Gen. 5:32; 6:10; 7:13; 9:18,23,27; 10:1,2,21; **1 Chr.** 1:4,5.

3316. A. יִפְתָּח *yip̱tāḥ* **masc. proper noun**
(Jephthah: a judge)
Judg. 11:1–3,5–15,28–30,32,34,40; 12:1,2,4,7; **1 Sam.** 12:11.
B. יִפְתָּח *yip̱tāḥ* **masc. proper noun**
(Iphtah: town in Judah)
Josh. 15:43.

3317. יִפְתַּח־אֵל *yip̱taḥ ʼēl* **proper noun**
(Iphtah El)
Josh. 19:14,27.

3318. I. יוֹצֵאת *yôṣēʼṯ* **fem. noun**
(captivity)
Ps. 144:14(KJV, NASB, see II).
II. יָצָא *yāṣāʼ* **verb**
(to come out, to go out)
Gen. 1:12,24; 2:10; 4:16; 8:7,16–19; 9:10,18; 10:11,14; 11:31; 12:4,5; 14:8, 17,18; 15:4,5,7,14; 17:6; 19:5,6,8,12,14, 16,17,23; 24:5,11,13,15,43,45,50,53,63; 25:25,26; 27:3,30; 28:10; 30:16; 31:13,33; 34:1,6,24,26; 35:11,18; 38:24,25,28–30; 39:12,15; 40:14; 41:45,46; 42:15,28; 43:23,31; 44:4,28; 45:1; 46:26; 47:10; 48:12; **Ex.** 1:5; 2:11,13; 3:10–12; 4:6, 7,14; 5:10,20; 6:6,7,13,26,27; 7:4,5,15; 8:12(8),18(14),20(16),29(25),30(26); 9:29,33; 10:6,18; 11:4,8; 12:17,22,31,39, 41,42,46,51; 13:3,4,8,9,14,16; 14:8,11; 15:20,22; 16:1,3,4,6,27,29,32; 17:6,9; 18:1,7; 19:1,17; 20:2; 21:2–5,7,11,22; 22:6(5); 23:15,16; 25:32,33,35; 28:35; 29:46; 32:11,12,24; 33:7,8; 34:18,34; 35:20; 37:18,19,21; **Lev.** 4:12,21; 6:11(4); 8:33; 9:23,24; 10:2,7; 14:3,38,45; 15:16,32; 16:17,18,24,27; 19:36; 21:12; 22:4,33; 23:43; 24:10,14,23; 25:28,30,31, 33,38,41,42,54,55; 26:10,13,45; 27:21; **Num.** 1:1,3,20,22,24,26,28,30,32,34,36, 38,40,42,45; 9:1; 11:20,24,26; 12:4,5,12;

13:32; 14:36,37; 15:36,41; 16:27,35, 46(17:11); 17:8(23),9(24); 19:3; 20:8,10, 11,16,18,20; 21:13,23,28,33; 22:5,11 ,32,36; 23:22; 24:8; 26:2,4; 27:17,21; 30:2(3); 31:13,27,28,36; 32:24; 33:1,3, 38,54; 34:4,9; 35:26; **Deut.** 1:27,44; 2:23,32; 3:1; 4:20,37,45,46; 5:6,15; 6:12,21,23; 7:8,19; 8:7,14,15; 9:7,12,26, 28,29; 11:10; 13:5(6),10(11),13(14); 14:22,28; 15:16; 16:1,3,6; 17:5; 20:1; 21:2,10,19; 22:14,15,19,21,24; 23:4(5), 9(10),10(11),12(13); 24:2,5,9,11; 25:17; 26:8; 28:6,7,19,25,38,57; 29:7(6),25(24); 31:2; 33:18; **Josh.** 2:3,5,7,10,19; 5:4–6; 6:1,10,22,23; 8:5,6,14,17,22; 9:12; 10:22–24; 11:4; 14:11; 15:3,4,9,11; 16:1,2,6,7; 18:11,15,17; 19:1,12,13,17, 24,27,32,34,40,47; 21:4; 24:5,6; **Judg.** 1:24; 2:12,15; 3:10,19,22–24; 4:14,18,22; 5:4,31; 6:8,18,19,30; 8:30; 9:15,20,27,29, 33,35,38,39,42,43; 11:3,31,34,36; 13:14; 14:14; 15:19; 16:20; 19:22–25,27; 20:1, 14,20,21,25,28,31; 21:21,24; **Ruth** 1:7,13; 2:18,22; **1 Sam.** 2:3; 4:1; 7:11; 8:20; 9:11,14,26; 11:3,7,10; 12:8; 13:10, 17,23; 14:11,41; 17:4,8,20,35,55; 18:5,6, 13,16,30; 19:3,8; 20:11,35; 21:5(6); 22:3; 23:13,15; 24:8(9),13(14),14(15); 25:37; 26:20; 28:1; 29:6; 30:21; **2 Sam.** 2:12, 13,23; 3:26; 5:2,24; 6:20; 7:12; 10:8,16; 11:1,8,13,17,23; 12:30,31; 13:9,18,39; 15:16,17; 16:5,7,11; 18:2–4,6; 19:7(8), 19(20); 20:7,8; 21:17; 22:20,49; 24:4, 7,20; **1 Kgs.** 2:30,36,37,42,46; 3:7; 4:33 (5:13); 6:1; 8:9,10,16,19,21,44,51,53; 9:9,12; 10:29; 11:29; 12:25; 15:17; 17:13; 19:11,13; 20:16–19,21,31,33,39; 21:10,13; 22:21,22,34; **2 Kgs.** 2:3,21,23,24; 3:6; 4:18,21,37,39; 5:2,11,27; 6:15; 7:12,16; 8:3; 9:11,15,21,24; 10:9,22,25,26; 11:7–9, 12,15; 12:11(12),12(13); 13:5; 15:20; 18:7,18,31; 19:9,27,31,35; 20:4,18; 21:15; 23:4,6; 24:7,12,13; **1 Chr.** 1:12; 2:53; 5:18; 7:11; 9:28; 11:2; 12:17,33,36; 14:8,15,17; 19:9,16; 20:1–3; 21:4,21; 24:7; 25:9; 26:14; 27:1; **2 Chr.** 1:10,17; 5:10,11; 6:5,9,34; 7:22; 9:28; 14:9(8), 10(9); 15:2,5; 16:1,2; 18:20,21,33; 19:2,4; 20:17,20,21; 21:15,19; 22:7; 23:7,8, 11,14; 24:5; 25:5; 26:6,11,15,18,20; 28:9; 29:5,16; 31:1; 34:14; 35:20; **Ezra** 1:7,8; 8:17(KJV, NIV, [Q^{e}] *ṣāwāh* [6680]); 10:3,19; **Neh.** 2:13; 3:25–27; 4:21(15); 6:19; 8:15,16; 9:7,15; **Esth.** 1:17,19; 3:15; 4:1,6; 5:9; 7:8; 8:14,15; **Job** 1:12,21; 2:7; 3:11; 5:6; 8:10,16; 10:18; 12:22; 14:2; 15:13; 20:25; 23:10; 24:5; 26:4; 28:5,11; 29:7; 31:34,40; 37:2; 38:8,29,32; 39:4,21; 41:20(12),21(13); **Ps.** 17:2; 18:19(20); 19:4(5),5(6); 25:15,17; 31:4(5); 37:6; 41:6(7); 44:9(10); 60:10(12); 66:12; 68:6(7),7(8); 73:7; 78:16; 81:5(6); 88:8(9); 104:14,23; 105:37,38,43; 107:14,28; 108:11(12); 109:7; 114:1; 121:8; 135:7; 136:11; 142:7(8); 143:11; 144:14(NIV, see I); 146:4; **Prov.** 7:15; 10:18; 12:13; 22:10; 25:4,8; 29:11; 30:27,33; **Eccl.** 4:14; 5:2(1),15(14); 7:18; 10:5; **Song** 1:8; 3:11; 5:6; 7:11(12); **Isa.** 2:3; 7:3; 11:1; 13:10; 14:29; 26:21; 28:29; 30:22; 36:3,16; 37:9,28,32,36; 39:7; 40:26; 42:1,3,7,13; 43:8,17; 45:23; 48:1,3,20; 49:9,17; 51:4,5; 52:11,12; 54:16; 55:11,12; 61:11; 62:1; 65:9; 66:24; **Jer.** 1:5; 2:37; 4:4,7; 5:6; 6:25; 7:22,25; 8:1; 9:3(2); 10:13,20; 11:4,11; 14:18; 15:1,2,19; 17:19,22; 19:2; 20:3,18; 21:9,12; 22:11; 23:15,19; 25:32; 26:23; 29:2,16; 30:19,21,23; 31:4,32,39; 32:21; 34:13; 37:4,5,7,12; 38:2,8,17,18, 21–23; 39:4,14; 41:6; 43:12; 44:17; 46:9; 48:7,9,45; 50:8,25; 51:10,16,44,45; 52:7,31; **Lam.** 1:6; 3:7,38; **Ezek.** 1:13; 3:22,23,25; 5:4; 7:10; 9:7; 10:7,18,19; 11:7,9; 12:4–7,12; 14:22; 15:7; 16:14; 19:14; 20:6,9,10,14,22,34,38,41; 21:3–5 (8–10),19(24); 24:6,12; 26:18; 27:33; 28:18; 30:9; 33:30; 34:13; 36:20; 37:1; 38:4,8; 39:9; 42:1,14,15; 44:3,19; 46:2, 8–10,12,20,21; 47:1–3,8,12; **Dan.** 8:9; 9:15,22,23; 10:20; 11:11,44; **Hos.** 6:5; 9:13; **Joel** 2:16; 3:18(4:18); **Amos** 4:3; 5:3; 6:10; **Jon.** 4:5; **Mic.** 1:3,11; 2:13; 4:2,10; 5:2(1); 7:9,15; **Nah.** 1:11; **Hab.**

1:4,7; 3:5,13; **Hag.** 1:11; 2:5; **Zech.** 2:3(7); 4:7; 5:3–6,9; 6:1,5–8; 8:10; 9:14; 10:4; 14:2,3,8; **Mal.** 4:2(3:20).

3319. יְצָא *y^eṣa'* **Aram. verb**
(to finish, to complete)
Ezra 6:15.

3320. יָצַב *yāṣaḇ* **verb**
(to stand, to take one's stand, to confront)
Ex. 2:4; 8:20(16); 9:13; 14:13; 19:17; 34:5; **Num.** 11:16; 22:22; 23:3,15; **Deut.** 7:24; 9:2; 11:25; 31:14; **Josh.** 1:5; 24:1; **Judg.** 20:2; **1 Sam.** 3:10; 10:19,23; 12:7,16; 17:16; **2 Sam.** 18:13,30; 21:5; 23:12; **1 Chr.** 11:14; **2 Chr.** 11:13; 20:6,17; **Job** 1:6; 2:1; 33:5; 38:14; 41:10(2); **Ps.** 2:2; 5:5(6); 36:4(5); 94:16; **Prov.** 22:29; **Jer.** 46:4,14; **Hab.** 2:1; **Zech.** 6:5.

3321. יְצַב *y^eṣaḇ* **Aram. verb**
(to find out the truth, to learn the true meaning)
Dan. 7:19.

3322. יָצַג *yāṣag* **verb**
(to place, to set, to present)
Gen. 30:38; 33:15; 43:9; 47:2; **Ex.** 10:24; **Deut.** 28:56; **Judg.** 6:37; 7:5; 8:27; **1 Sam.** 5:2; **2 Sam.** 6:17; **1 Chr.** 16:1; **Job** 17:6; **Jer.** 51:34; **Hos.** 2:3(5); **Amos** 5:15.

3323. יִצְהָר *yiṣhār* **masc. noun**
(fresh oil)
Num. 18:12; **Deut.** 7:13; 11:14; 12:17; 14:23; 18:4; 28:51; **2 Kgs.** 18:32; **2 Chr.** 31:5; 32:28; **Neh.** 5:11; 10:37(38),39(40); 13:5,12; **Jer.** 31:12; **Hos.** 2:8(10),22(24); **Joel** 1:10; 2:19,24; **Hag.** 1:11; **Zech.** 4:14.

3324. יִצְהָר *yiṣhār* **masc. proper noun**
(Izhar)
Ex. 6:18,21; **Num.** 3:19; 16:1; **1 Chr.** 6:2(5:28),18(3),38(23); 23:12,18.

3325. יִצְהָרִי *yiṣhāriy* **masc. proper noun**
(Izharite)
Num. 3:27; **1 Chr.** 24:22; 26:23,29.

3326. I. יָצוּעַ *yāṣûa'* **masc. noun**
(couch, bed)
Gen. 49:4; **1 Kgs.** 6:5([Q^e] see II), 6([Q^e] see II),10([Q^e] see II); **1 Chr.** 5:1; **Job** 17:13; **Ps.** 63:6(7); 132:3.
II. יָצוּעַ *yāṣûa'* **masc. noun**
(flat surface, wing of a building, side chamber)
1 Kgs. 6:5,6,10.

3327. יִצְחָק *yiṣḥāq* **masc. proper noun**
(Isaac: see also *yiśḥāq* [3446])
Gen. 17:19,21; 21:3–5,8,10,12; 22:2,3 ,6,7,9; 24:4,14,62–64,66,67; 25:5,6,9,11, 19–21,26,28; 26:1,6,8,9,12,16–20,25,27, 31,32,35; 27:1,5,20–22,26,30,32,33,37, 39,46; 28:1,5,6,8,13; 31:18,42,53; 32:9(10); 35:12,27–29; 46:1; 48:15,16; 49:31; 50:24; **Ex.** 2:24; 3:6,15,16; 4:5; 6:3,8; 32:13; 33:1; **Lev.** 26:42; **Num.** 32:11; **Deut.** 1:8; 6:10; 9:5,27; 29:13(12); 30:20; 34:4; **Josh.** 24:3,4; **1 Kgs.** 18:36; **2 Kgs.** 13:23; **1 Chr.** 1:28,34; 16:16; 29:18; **2 Chr.** 30:6.

3328. יִצְחַר *yiṣḥar* **masc. proper noun**
(Izhar)
1 Chr. 4:7(NIV, [Q^e] *ṣōḥar* [6714,C]).

3329. יָצִיא *yāṣiy'* **adj.**
(coming forth, proceding from)
2 Chr. 32:21.

3330. יַצִּיב *yaṣṣiyḇ* **Aram. adj.**
(true, reliable, certain)
Dan. 2:8,45; 3:24; 6:12(13); 7:16.

3331. יָצַע *yāṣa‘* **verb**
(to spread out, to make a bed, to lay)
Esth. 4:3; **Ps.** 139:8; **Isa.** 14:11; 58:5.

3332. יָצַק *yāṣaq* **verb**
(to pour, to pour out, to cast)
Gen. 28:18; 35:14; **Ex.** 25:12; 26:37; 29:7; 36:36; 37:3,13; 38:5,27; **Lev.** 2:1,6; 8:12,15; 9:9; 14:15,26; 21:10; **Num.** 5:15; **Josh.** 7:23; **1 Sam.** 10:1; **2 Sam.** 13:9; 15:24; **1 Kgs.** 7:16(NIV, *mûṣāq* [4165]),23(NIV, *mûṣāq* [4165]),24,30,33 (NIV, *mûṣāq* [4165]),46; 18:33(34); 22:35; **2 Kgs.** 3:11; 4:4,5,40,41; 9:3,6; **2 Chr.** 4:2(NIV, *mûṣāq* [4165]),3,17; **Job** 11:15; 22:16; 37:10(KJV, NASB, *mûṣāq* [4164]),18(NIV, *mûṣāq* [4165]); 38:38; 41:23(15),24(16); **Ps.** 41:8(9); 45:2(3); **Isa.** 44:3; **Ezek.** 24:3.

3333. יְצֻקָה *y^e^ṣuqāh* **fem. noun**
(a casting [of metal])
1 Kgs. 7:24.

3334. יָצַר *yāṣar* **verb**
(to be in distress, to be frustrated; NASB, NIV, *ṣārar* [6887,I])
Gen. 32:7(8); **Judg.** 2:15; 10:9; **1 Sam.** 30:6; **2 Sam.** 13:2; **Job** 18:7; 20:22; **Prov.** 4:12; **Isa.** 49:19.

3335. יָצַר *yāṣar* **verb**
(to form, to fashion)
Gen. 2:7,8,19; **2 Sam.** 17:28; **2 Kgs.** 19:25; **1 Chr.** 4:23; **Ps.** 2:9; 33:15; 74:17; 94:9,20; 95:5; 104:26; 139:16; **Isa.** 22:11; 27:11; 29:16; 30:14; 37:26; 41:25; 43:1,7, 10,21; 44:2,9,10,12,21,24; 45:7,9,11,18; 46:11; 49:5; 54:17; 64:8(7); **Jer.** 1:5; 10:16; 18:2–4,6,11; 19:1,11; 33:2; 51:19; **Lam.** 4:2; **Amos** 4:13; 7:1; **Hab.** 2:18; **Zech.** 11:13; 12:1.

3336. יֵצֶר *yēṣer* **masc. noun**
(a forming, intention, plan)
Gen. 6:5; 8:21; **Deut.** 31:21; **1 Chr.** 28:9; 29:18; **Ps.** 103:14; **Isa.** 26:3; 29:16; **Hab.** 2:18.

3337. יֵצֶר *yēṣer* **masc. proper noun**
(Jezer)
Gen. 46:24; **Num.** 26:49; **1 Chr.** 7:13.

3338. יְצֻרִים *y^e^ṣuriym* **masc. pl. noun**
(things formed, members)
Job 17:7.

3339. יִצְרִי *yiṣriy* **masc. proper noun**
(Izri)
1 Chr. 25:11.

3340. יִצְרִי *yiṣriy* **masc. proper noun**
(Jezerite)
Num. 26:49.

3341. יָצַת *yāṣaṯ* **verb**
(to set on fire, to burn)
Josh. 8:8,19; **Judg.** 9:49; **2 Sam.** 14:30,31; **2 Kgs.** 22:13,17; **Neh.** 1:3; 2:17; **Isa.** 9:18(17); 27:4(KJV, NIV, *ṣûṯ* [6702]); 33:12; **Jer.** 2:15; 9:10(9),12(11); 11:16; 17:27; 21:14; 32:29; 43:12; 46:19; 49:2,27; 50:32; 51:30,58; **Lam.** 4:11; **Ezek.** 20:47(21:3); **Amos** 1:14.

3342. יֶקֶב *yeqeḇ* **masc. noun**
(winepress, wine vat)
Num. 18:27,30; **Deut.** 15:14; 16:13; **Judg.** 7:25; **2 Kgs.** 6:27; **Job** 24:11; **Prov.** 3:10; **Isa.** 5:2; 16:10; **Jer.** 48:33; **Hos.** 9:2; **Joel** 2:24; 3:13(4:13); **Hag.** 2:16; **Zech.** 14:10.

3343. יְקַבְצְאֵל *y^e^qaḇṣ^e^'ēl* **proper noun**
(Jekabzeel)
Neh. 11:25.

3344. יָקַד *yāqaḏ* **verb**
(to burn, to set on fire)

Lev. 6:9(2),12(5),13(6); **Deut.** 32:22; **Isa.** 10:16; 30:14; 65:5; **Jer.** 15:14; 17:4.

3345. יְקַד *y^{e}qad* **Aram. verb**
(to burn; corr. to Hebr. 3344)
Dan. 3:6,11,15,17,20,21,23,26.

3346. יְקֵדָה *y^{e}qēdāh* **Aram. fem. noun**
(a burning)
Dan. 7:11.

3347. יָקְדְעָם *yoqd^{e}ʿām* **proper noun**
(Jokdeam)
Josh. 15:56.

3348. יָקֶה *yāqeh* **masc. proper noun**
(Jakeh)
Prov. 30:1.

3349. יְקָהָה *y^{e}qāhāh* **fem. noun**
(obedience)
Gen. 49:10; **Prov.** 30:17.

3350. יְקוֹד *y^{e}qôd,* יְקֹד *y^{e}qōd* **masc. noun**
(a burning)
Isa. 10:16.

3351. יְקוּם *y^{e}qûm* **masc. noun**
(a living thing, creature)
Gen. 7:4,23; **Deut.** 11:6.

3352. יָקוֹשׁ *yāqôš* **masc. noun**
(a fowler, bird catcher)
Hos. 9:8(NIV, *yāqûš* [3353]).

3353. יָקוּשׁ *yaqûš* **masc. noun**
(a fowler, bird catcher)
Ps. 91:3; **Prov.** 6:5; **Jer.** 5:26; **Hos.** 9:8 (KJV, NASB, *yāqôš* [3352]).

3354. יְקוּתִיאֵל *y^{e}qûtiy'ēl* **masc. proper noun**
(Jekuthiel)
1 Chr. 4:18.

3355. יָקְטָן *yoqṭān* **masc. proper noun**
(Joktan)
Gen. 10:25,26,29; **1 Chr.** 1:19,20,23.

3356. A. יָקִים *yāqiym* **masc. proper noun**
(Jakim: a Benjamite)
1 Chr. 8:19.
B. יָקִים *yāqiym* **masc. proper noun**
(Jakim: a Levite)
1 Chr. 24:12.

3357. יַקִּיר *yaqqiyr* **adj.**
(dear, honored, precious)
Jer. 31:20.

3358. יַקִּיר *yaqqiyr* **Aram. adj.**
(noble, honorable; corr. to Hebr. 3357)
Ezra 4:10; **Dan.** 2:11.

3359. A. יְקַמְיָה *y^{e}qamyāh* **masc. proper noun**
(Jekamiah: fifth son of Jeconiah)
1 Chr. 3:18.
B. יְקַמְיָה *y^{e}qamyāh* **masc. proper noun**
(Jekamiah: son of Shallum)
1 Chr. 2:41.

3360. יְקַמְעָם *y^{e}qamʿām* **masc. proper noun**
(Jekameam)
1 Chr. 23:19; 24:23.

3361. יָקְמְעָם *yoqm^{e}ʿām* **proper noun**
(Jokmeam)
1 Kgs. 4:12; **1 Chr.** 6:68(53).

3362. יָקְנְעָם *yoqn^{e}ʿām* **proper noun**
(Jokneam)
Josh. 12:22; 19:11; 21:34.

3363. יָקַע *yāqaʿ* **verb**
(to be dislocated)
Gen. 32:25(26); **Num.** 25:4; **2 Sam.** 21:6,9,13; **Jer.** 6:8; **Ezek.** 23:17,18.

3364. יָקַץ *yāqaṣ* **verb**
(to awaken, to become awake)
Gen. 9:24; 28:16; 41:4,7,21; **Judg.** 16:14,20; **1 Kgs.** 3:15; 18:27; **Ps.** 78:65; **Hab.** 2:7.

3365. יָקַר *yāqar* **verb**
(to esteem, to be valuable, to be costly)
1 Sam. 18:30; 26:21; **2 Kgs.** 1:13,14; **Ps.** 49:8(9); 72:14; 139:17; **Prov.** 25:17; **Isa.** 13:12; 43:4; **Zech.** 11:13.

3366. יְקָר *y*^{e}*qār* **masc. noun**
(honor, splendor, value)
Esth. 1:4,20; 6:3,6,7,9,11; 8:16; **Job** 28:10; **Ps.** 49:12(13),20(21); **Prov.** 20:15; **Jer.** 20:5; **Ezek.** 22:25; **Zech.** 11:13.

3367. יְקָר *y*^{e}*qār* **Aram. masc. noun**
(honor, glory; corr. to Hebr. 3366)
Dan. 2:6,37; 4:30(27),36(33); 5:18,20; 7:14.

3368. יָקָר *yāqār* **adj.**
(precious, valuable, rare)
1 Sam. 3:1; **2 Sam.** 12:30; **1 Kgs.** 5:17(31); 7:9–11; 10:2,10,11; **1 Chr.** 20:2; 29:2; **2 Chr.** 3:6; 9:1,9,10; 32:27; **Job** 28:16; 31:26; **Ps.** 36:7(8); 37:20; 45:9(10); 116:15; **Prov.** 1:13; 3:15; 6:26; 12:27; 17:27; 24:4; **Eccl.** 10:1; **Isa.** 28:16; **Jer.** 15:19; **Lam.** 4:2; **Ezek.** 27:22; 28:13; **Dan.** 11:38; **Zech.** 14:6 (NIV, [following some versions], *gārāh* [7135]).

3369. יָקֹשׁ *yāqōš* **verb**
(to be lured by a bait and trapped, to be ensnared)
Deut. 7:25; **Ps.** 9:16(17)(KJV, NASB, *nāqaš* [5367]); 124:7; 141:9; **Prov.** 6:2; **Eccl.** 9:12; **Isa.** 8:15; 28:13; **Jer.** 50:24.

3370. יָקְשָׁן *yoqšān* **masc. proper noun**
(Jokshan)
Gen. 25:2,3; **1 Chr.** 1:32.

3371. A. יָקְתְאֵל *yoqṯ*^{e}*'ēl* **proper noun**
(Joktheel: loc. in Judah)
Josh. 15:38.
B. יָקְתְאֵל *yoqṯ*^{e}*'ēl* **proper noun**
(Joktheel: loc. in Idumea)
2 Kgs. 14:7.

3372. יָרֵא *yārē'* **verb**
(to fear, to be afraid, see also *yārē'* [3373])
Gen. 3:10; 15:1; 18:15; 19:30; 20:8; 21:17; 26:7,24; 28:17; 31:31; 32:7(8); 35:17; 42:35; 43:18,23; 46:3; 50:19,21; **Ex.** 1:17,21; 2:14; 3:6; 9:30; 14:10,13,31; 15:11; 20:20; 34:10,30; **Lev.** 19:3,14,30, 32; 25:17,36,43; 26:2; **Num.** 12:8; 14:9; 21:34; **Deut.** 1:19,21,29; 2:4; 3:2,22; 4:10; 5:5,29(26); 6:2,13,24; 7:18,21; 8:6,15; 10:12,17,20,21; 13:4(5),11(12); 14:23; 17:13,19; 19:20; 20:1,3; 21:21; 25:18; 28:10,58; 31:6,8,12,13; **Josh.** 4:14,24; 8:1; 9:24; 10:2,8,25; 11:6; 22:25; 24:14; **Judg.** 4:18; 6:10,23,27; 8:20; 13:6; **Ruth** 3:11; **1 Sam.** 3:15; 4:7,20; 7:7; 12:14,18,20,24; 14:26; 15:24; 17:11,24; 18:12,29; 21:12(13); 22:23; 23:17; 28:5,13,20; 31:4; **2 Sam.** 1:14; 3:11; 6:9; 7:23; 9:7; 10:19; 12:18; 13:28; 14:15; **1 Kgs.** 1:50,51; 3:28; 8:40,43; 17:13; 18:12; **2 Kgs.** 1:15; 6:16; 10:4; 17:7,25,28,35–39; 19:6; 25:24,26; **1 Chr.** 10:4; 13:12; 16:25; 17:21; 22:13; 28:20; **2 Chr.** 6:31,33; 20:3,15,17; 32:7,18; **Neh.** 1:5,11; 2:2; 4:14(8); 6:9,13,14,19; 7:2; 9:32; **Job** 1:9; 5:21,22; 6:21; 9:35; 11:15; 32:6; 37:22,24; **Ps.** 3:6(7); 23:4; 27:1,3; 33:8; 34:9(10); 40:3(4); 45:4(5);

46:2(3); 47:2(3); 49:5(6),16(17); 52:6(8); 55:19(20); 56:3(4),4(5),11(12); 64:4(5), 9(10); 65:5(6),8(9); 66:3,5; 67:7(8); 68:35(36); 72:5; 76:7(8),8(9),12(13); 86:11; 89:7(8); 91:5; 96:4; 99:3; 102:15(16); 106:22; 111:9; 112:1,7,8; 118:6; 119:63,120; 130:4; 139:14; 145:6; **Prov.** 3:7,25; 24:21; 31:21; **Eccl.** 3:14; 5:7(6); 8:12; 12:5,13; **Isa.** 7:4; 8:12; 10:24; 18:2,7; 21:1; 25:3; 35:4; 37:6; 40:9; 41:5,10,13,14; 43:1,5; 44:2; 51:7,12; 54:4,14; 57:11; 59:19; 64:3(2); **Jer.** 1:8; 3:8; 5:22,24; 10:5,7; 23:4; 26:19,21; 30:10; 32:39; 40:9; 41:18; 42:11; 44:10; 46:27,28; 51:46; **Lam.** 3:57; **Ezek.** 1:22; 2:6; 3:9; 11:8; **Dan.** 9:4; 10:12,19; **Hos.** 10:3; **Joel** 2:11,21, 22,31(3:4); **Amos** 3:8; **Jon.** 1:5,10,16; **Mic.** 7:17; **Hab.** 1:7; 3:2; **Zeph.** 2:11; 3:7,16; **Hag.** 1:12; 2:5; **Zech.** 8:13,15; 9:5; **Mal.** 1:14; 2:5; 3:5; 4:5(3:23).

3373. יָרֵא *yārēʾ* **adj.**
(fearing; Qal. Participle of *yārēʾ* [3372])
Gen. 22:12; 32:11(12); 42:18; **Ex.** 9:20; 18:21; **Deut.** 7:19; 20:8; **Judg.** 7:3,10; **1 Sam.** 23:3; **1 Kgs.** 18:3; **2 Kgs.** 4:1; 17:32–34,41; **Job** 1:1,8; 2:3; **Ps.** 15:4; 22:23(24),25(26); 25:12,14; 31:19(20); 33:18; 34:7(8),9(10); 60:4(6); 61:5(6); 66:16; 85:9(10); 103:11,13,17; 111:5; 115:11,13; 118:4; 119:74,79; 128:1,4; 135:20; 145:19; 147:11; **Prov.** 13:13; 14:2,16; 31:30; **Eccl.** 7:18; 8:12,13; 9:2; **Isa.** 50:10; **Jer.** 42:11,16; **Dan.** 1:10; **Jon.** 1:9; **Mal.** 3:16; 4:2(3:20).

3374. יִרְאָה *yirʾāh* **fem. noun**
(fear, reverence)
Gen. 20:11; **Ex.** 20:20; **Deut.** 2:25; **2 Sam.** 23:3; **2 Chr.** 19:9; **Neh.** 5:9,15; **Job** 4:6; 6:14; 15:4; 22:4; 28:28; **Ps.** 2:11; 5:7(8); 19:9(10); 34:11(12); 55:5(6); 90:11; 111:10; 119:38; **Prov.** 1:7,29; 2:5; 8:13; 9:10; 10:27; 14:26,27; 15:16,33; 16:6; 19:23; 22:4; 23:17; **Isa.** 7:25; 11:2,3; 29:13; 33:6; 63:17; **Jer.** 32:40; **Ezek.** 1:18; 30:13; **Jon.** 1:10,16.

3375. יִרְאוֹן *yirʾôn* **proper noun**
(Iron)
Josh. 19:38.

3376. יִרְאִיָּיה *yirʾiyyāyh* **masc. proper noun**
(Irijah)
Jer. 37:13,14.

3377. I. יָרֵב *yārēb̲* **masc. proper noun**
(Jareb: Assyrian king)
Hos. 5:13(NIV, see II); 10:6(NIV, see II).
II. יָרֵב *yārēb̲* **masc. noun**
(great)
Hos. 5:13(KJV, NASB, see I); 10:6(KJV, NASB, see I).

3378. יְרֻבַּעַל *y^e^rubbaʿal* **masc. proper noun**
(Jerubbaal)
Judg. 6:32; 7:1; 8:29,35; 9:1,2,5,16,19,24,28,57; **1 Sam.** 12:11.

3379. A. יָרָבְעָם *yārob̲ʿām* **masc. proper noun**
(Jeroboam: first king of the Northern Kingdom)
1 Kgs. 11:26,28,29,31,40; 12:2,3,12,15, 20,25,26,32; 13:1,4,33,34; 14:1,2,4–7,10, 11,13,14,16,17,19,20,30; 15:1,6,7,9,25, 29,30,34; 16:2,3,7,19,26,31; 21:22; 22:52(53); **2 Kgs.** 3:3; 9:9; 10:29,31; 13:2,6,11; 15:9,18,24,28; 17:21,22; 23:15; **2 Chr.** 9:29; 10:2,3,12,15; 11:4,14; 12:15; 13:1–4,6,8,13,15,19,20.
B. יָרָבְעָם *yārob̲ʿām* **masc. proper noun**
(Jeroboam: king of Israel, son of Jehoash)
2 Kgs. 13:13; 14:16,23,24,27–29; 15:1,8; **1 Chr.** 5:17; **Hos.** 1:1; **Amos** 1:1; 7:9–11.

3380. יְרֻבֶּשֶׁת *yᵉrubbešet* **masc. proper noun**
(Jerubbesheth)
2 Sam. 11:21.

3381. יָרַד *yārad* **verb**
(to go down, to descend)
Gen. 11:5,7; 12:10; 15:11; 18:21; 24:16,18,45,46; 26:2; 28:12; 37:25,35; 38:1; 39:1; 42:2,3,38; 43:4,5,7,11,15, 20,22; 44:11,21,23,26,29,31; 45:9,13; 46:3,4; **Ex.** 2:5; 3:8; 9:19; 11:8; 15:5; 19:11,14,18,20,21,24,25; 32:1,7,15; 33:5,9; 34:5,29; **Lev.** 9:22; **Num.** 1:51; 4:5; 10:17; 11:9,17,25; 12:5; 14:45; 16:30,33; 20:15,28; 34:11,12; **Deut.** 1:25; 9:12,15,21; 10:5,22; 20:20; 21:4; 26:5; 28:24,43,52; **Josh.** 2:15,18,23; 3:13,16; 8:29; 10:27; 15:10; 16:3,7; 17:9; 18:13,16–18; 24:4; **Judg.** 1:9,34; 3:27, 28; 4:14,15; 5:11,13(KJV, *rāḏāh* [7287,I]),14; 7:4,5,9–11,24; 9:36,37; 11:37; 14:1,5,7,10,19; 15:8,11,12; 16:21,31; 19:11(KJV, NASB, *rāḏaḏ* [7286]); **Ruth** 3:3,6; **1 Sam.** 2:6; 6:15,21; 9:25,27; 10:5,8; 13:12,20; 14:36,37; 15:6,12; 17:8,28; 19:12; 20:19; 21:13(14); 22:1; 23:4,6,8,11,20,25; 25:1, 20,23; 26:2,6,10; 29:4; 30:15,16,24; **2 Sam.** 5:17; 11:8–10,13; 17:18; 19:16(17),20(21),24(25),31(32); 21:15; 22:10,48; 23:13,20,21; **1 Kgs.** 1:25,33, 38,53; 2:6,8,9; 5:9(23); 17:23; 18:40,44; 21:16,18; 22:2; **2 Kgs.** 1:4,6,9–12,14–16; 2:2; 3:12; 5:14; 6:18,33; 7:17; 8:29; 9:16; 10:13; 11:19; 12:20(21); 13:14; 16:17; 20:11; **1 Chr.** 7:21; 11:15,22,23; **2 Chr.** 7:1,3; 18:2; 20:16; 22:6; 23:20; **Neh.** 3:15; 6:3; 9:13; **Job** 7:9; 17:16; 33:24; **Ps.** 7:16(17); 18:9(10); 22:29(30); 28:1; 30:3(4),9(10); 49:17(18); 55:15(16), 23(24); 56:7(8); 59:11(12); 72:6; 78:16; 88:4(5); 104:8; 107:23,26; 115:17; 119:136; 133:2,3; 143:7; 144:5; **Prov.** 1:12; 5:5; 7:27; 18:8; 21:22; 26:22; 30:4; **Eccl.** 3:21; **Song** 6:2,11; **Isa.** 5:14; 10:13; 14:11,15,19; 15:3; 30:2; 31:1,4; 32:19; 34:5,7; 38:8,18; 42:10; 43:14; 45:1(KJV, NASB, *rāḏaḏ* [7286]); 47:1; 52:4; 55:10; 63:6,14; 64:1(63:19),3(2); **Jer.** 9:18(17); 13:17,18; 14:17; 18:2,3; 22:1; 36:12; 48:15,18; 49:16; 50:27; 51:40; **Lam.** 1:9,16; 2:10,18; 3:48; **Ezek.** 26:11,16,20; 27:29; 28:8; 30:6; 31:12,14–18; 32:18,19,21,24,25,27, 29,30; 34:26; 47:1,8; **Hos.** 7:12; **Joel** 2:23; 3:2(4:2),13(4:13); **Amos** 3:11; 6:2; 9:2; **Obad.** 1:3,4; **Jon.** 1:3,5; 2:6(7); **Mic.** 1:3,12; **Hag.** 2:22; **Zech.** 10:11; 11:2.

3382. A. יֶרֶד *yereḏ* **masc. proper noun**
(Jared: father of Enoch)
Gen. 5:15,16,18–20; **1 Chr.** 1:2.
B. יֶרֶד *yereḏ* **masc. proper noun**
(Jered: son of Mered)
1 Chr. 4:18.

3383. יַרְדֵּן *yardēn* **proper noun**
(Jordan)
Gen. 13:10,11; 32:10(11); 50:10,11; **Num.** 13:29; 22:1; 26:3,63; 31:12; 32:5,19,21,29,32; 33:48–51; 34:12,15; 35:1,10,14; 36:13; **Deut.** 1:1,5; 2:29; 3:8,17,20,25,27; 4:21,22,26,41,46,47,49; 9:1; 11:30,31; 12:10; 27:2,4,12; 30:18; 31:2,13; 32:47; **Josh.** 1:2,11,14,15; 2:7,10; 3:1,8,11,13–15,17; 4:1,3,5,7–10, 16–20,22,23; 5:1; 7:7; 9:1,10; 12:1,7; 13:8,23,27,32; 14:3; 15:5; 16:1,7; 17:5; 18:7,12,19,20; 19:22,33,34; 20:8; 22:4, 7,10,11,25; 23:4; 24:8,11; **Judg.** 3:28; 5:17; 7:24,25; 8:4; 10:8,9; 11:13,22; 12:5,6; **1 Sam.** 13:7; 31:7; **2 Sam.** 2:29; 10:17; 17:22,24; 19:15(16),17(18),18(19),31(32),36(37),39(40),41(42); 20:2; 24:5; **1 Kgs.** 2:8; 7:46; 17:3,5; **2 Kgs.** 2:6,7,13; 5:10,14; 6:2,4; 7:15; 10:33; **1 Chr.** 6:78(63); 12:15,37; 19:17; 26:30; **2 Chr.** 4:17; **Job** 40:23; **Ps.** 42:6(7); 114:3,5; **Isa.** 9:1(8:23); **Jer.** 12:5; 49:19; 50:44; **Ezek.** 47:18; **Zech.** 11:3.

3384. I. יָרָה *yārāh* **verb**
(to cast, to shoot, to hurl, to throw)
Gen. 31:51; **Ex.** 15:4; 19:13; **Num.** 21:30; **Josh.** 18:6; **1 Sam.** 20:20,36,37; 31:3; **2 Sam.** 11:20,24; **2 Kgs.** 13:17; 19:32; **1 Chr.** 10:3; **2 Chr.** 26:15; 35:23; **Job** 30:19; 38:6; **Ps.** 11:2; 64:4(5),7(8); **Prov.** 26:18; **Isa.** 37:33.
II. יָרָה *yārāh* **verb**
(to teach, to instruct, to direct)
Gen. 46:28; **Ex.** 4:12,15; 15:25; 24:12; 35:34; **Lev.** 10:11; 14:57; **Deut.** 17:10,11; 24:8; 33:10; **Judg.** 13:8; **1 Sam.** 12:23; **1 Kgs.** 8:36; **2 Kgs.** 12:2(3); 17:27,28; **2 Chr.** 6:27; 15:3; **Job** 6:24; 8:10; 12:7,8; 27:11; 34:32; 36:22; **Ps.** 25:8,12; 27:11; 32:8; 45:4(5); 86:11; 119:33,102; **Prov.** 4:4,11; 5:13; 6:13; **Isa.** 2:3; 9:15(14); 28:9,26; 30:20; **Ezek.** 44:23; **Mic.** 3:11; 4:2; **Hab.** 2:18,19.
III. יָרָה *yārāh* **verb**
(to water, to refesh)
Prov. 11:25; **Hos.** 6:3(KJV, *yôreh* [3138]); 10:12.
IV. יוֹרֶה *yôreh* **noun**
(archer)
2 Chr. 35:23.
V. מוֹרֶה *môreh* **noun**
(archer)
1 Sam. 31:3; **2 Sam.** 11:24; **1 Chr.** 10:3.
VI. יָרֵה *yārah* **verb**
(to be afraid)
Isa. 44:8(KJV, *rāhāh* [7297]).

3385. יְרוּאֵל *y^e^rû'ēl* **proper noun**
(Jeruel)
2 Chr. 20:16.

3386. יָרוֹחַ *yārôaḥ* **masc. proper noun**
(Jaroah)
1 Chr. 5:14.

3387. יָרוֹק *yārôq* **masc. noun**
(a green thing, green plant)
Job 39:8.

3388. יְרוּשָׁה *y^e^rûšāh,* יְרוּשָׁא *y^e^rûšā'* **fem. proper noun**
(Jerusha)
2 Kgs. 15:33; **2 Chr.** 27:1.

3389. יְרוּשָׁלַםִ *y^e^rûšālam,* יְרוּשָׁלַיִם *y^e^rûšālayim* **proper noun**
(Jerusalem)
Josh. 10:1,3,5,23; 12:10; 15:8,63; 18:28; **Judg.** 1:7,8,21; 19:10; **1 Sam.** 17:54; **2 Sam.** 5:5,6,13,14; 8:7; 9:13; 10:14; 11:1,12; 12:31; 14:23,28; 15:8,11,14, 29,37; 16:3,15; 17:20; 19:19(20),25(26), 33(34),34(35); 20:2,3,7,22; 24:8,16; **1 Kgs.** 2:11,36,38,41; 3:1,15; 8:1; 9:15,19; 10:2,26,27; 11:7,13,29,32,36,42; 12:18,21,27,28; 14:21,25; 15:2,4,10; 22:42; **2 Kgs.** 8:17,26; 9:28; 12:1(2), 17(18),18(19); 14:2,13,19,20; 15:2,33; 16:2,5; 18:2,17,22,35; 19:10,21,31; 21:1,4,7,12,13,16,19; 22:1,14; 23:1,2, 4–6,9,13,20,23,24,27,30,31,33,36; 24:4, 8,10,14,15,18,20; 25:1,8–10; **1 Chr.** 3:4,5; 6:10(5:36),15(5:41),32(17); 8:28, 32; 9:3,34,38; 11:4; 14:3,4; 15:3; 18:7; 19:15; 20:1,3; 21:4,15,16; 23:25; 28:1; 29:27; **2 Chr.** 1:4,13–15; 2:7(6),16(15); 3:1; 5:2; 6:6; 8:6; 9:1,25,27,30; 10:18; 11:1,5,14,16; 12:2,4,5,7,9,13; 13:2; 14:15(14); 15:10; 17:13; 19:1,4,8; 20:5, 15,17,18,20,27,28,31; 21:5,11,13,20; 22:1,2; 23:2; 24:1,6,9,18,23; 25:1,23,27; 26:3,9,15; 27:1,8; 28:1,10,24,27; 29:1,8; 30:1–3,5,11,13,14,21,26; 31:4; 32:2,9,10, 12,18,19,22,23,25,26,33; 33:1,4,7,9,13, 15,21; 34:1,3,5,7,9,22,29,30,32; 35:1, 18,24; 36:1–5,9–11,14,19,23; **Ezra** 1:2–5,7,11; 2:1,68; 3:1,8; 4:6; 7:7–9,27; 8:29–32; 9:9; 10:7,9; **Neh.** 1:2,3; 2:11–13, 17,20; 3:8,9,12; 4:7(1),8(2),22(16); 6:7; 7:2,3,6; 8:15; 11:1–4,6,22; 12:27–29,43; 13:6,7,15,16,19,20; **Esth.** 2:6; **Ps.** 51:18(20); 68:29(30); 79:1,3; 102:21(22); 116:19; 122:2,3,6; 125:2; 128:5; 135:21; 137:5–7; 147:2,12; **Eccl.** 1:1,12,16; 2:7,9; **Song** 1:5; 2:7; 3:5,10; 5:8,16; 6:4; 8:4; **Isa.** 1:1; 2:1,3; 3:1,8; 4:3,4; 5:3; 7:1;

8:14; 10:10–12,32; 22:10,21; 24:23; 27:13; 28:14; 30:19; 31:5,9; 33:20; 36:2,7,20; 37:10,22,32; 40:2,9; 41:27; 44:26,28; 51:17; 52:1,2,9; 62:1,6,7; 64:10(9); 65:18,19; 66:10,13,20; **Jer.** 1:3,15; 2:2; 3:17; 4:3–5,10,11,14,16; 5:1; 6:1,6,8; 7:17,34; 8:1,5; 9:11(10); 11:2,6, 9,12,13; 13:9,13,27; 14:2,16; 15:4,5; 17:19–21,25–27; 18:11; 19:3,7,13; 22:19; 23:14,15; 24:1,8; 25:2,18; 26:18; 27:3,18, 20,21; 29:1,2,4,20,25; 32:2,32,44; 33:10, 13,16; 34:1,6–8,19; 35:11,13,17; 36:9,31; 37:5,11,12; 38:28; 39:1,8; 40:1; 42:18; 44:2,6,9,13,17,21; 51:35,50; 52:1,3,4, 12–14,29; **Lam.** 1:7,8,17; 2:10,13,15; 4:12; **Ezek.** 4:1,7,16; 5:5; 8:3; 9:4,8; 11:15; 12:10,19; 13:16; 14:21,22; 15:6; 16:2,3; 17:12; 21:2(7),20(25),22(27); 22:19; 23:4; 24:2; 26:2; 33:21; 36:38; **Dan.** 1:1; 9:2,7,12,16,25; **Joel** 2:32(3:5); 3:1(4:1),6(4:6),16(4:16),17(4:17), 20(4:20); **Amos** 1:2; 2:5; **Obad.** 1:11,20; **Mic.** 1:1,5,9,12; 3:10,12; 4:2,8; **Zeph.** 1:4,12; 3:14,16; **Zech.** 1:12,14,16,17, 19(2:2); 2:2(6),4(8),12(16); 3:2; 7:7; 8:3, 4,8,15,22; 9:9,10; 12:2,3,5–11; 13:1; 14:2, 4,8,10–12,14,16,17,21; **Mal.** 2:11; 3:4.

3390. יְרוּשְׁלֶם *y^erûš^{e}lem* **Aram. proper noun**
(Jerusalem; corr. to Hebr. 3389)
Ezra 4:8,12,20,23,24; 5:1,2,14–17; 6:3,5, 9,12,18; 7:13–17,19; **Dan.** 5:2,3; 6:10(11).

3391. יֶרַח *yeraḥ* **masc. noun**
(month)
Ex. 2:2; **Deut.** 21:13; 33:14; **1 Kgs.** 6:37,38; 8:2; **2 Kgs.** 15:13; **Job** 3:6; 7:3; 29:2; 39:2; **Isa.** 60:20; **Zech.** 11:8.

3392. יֶרַח *yeraḥ* **masc. proper noun**
(Jerah)
Gen. 10:26; **1 Chr.** 1:20.

3393. יְרַח *y^eraḥ* **Aram. masc. noun**
(month; corr. to Hebr. 3391)
Ezra 6:15; **Dan.** 4:29(26).

3394. יָרֵחַ *yārēaḥ* **masc. noun**
(moon)
Gen. 37:9; **Deut.** 4:19; 17:3; **Josh.** 10:12,13; **2 Kgs.** 23:5; **Job** 25:5; 31:26; **Ps.** 8:3(4); 72:5,7; 89:37(38); 104:19; 121:6; 136:9; 148:3; **Eccl.** 12:2; **Isa.** 13:10; 60:19; **Jer.** 8:2; 31:35; **Ezek.** 32:7; **Joel** 2:10,31(3:4); 3:15(4:15); **Hab.** 3:11.

3395. A. יְרֹחָם *y^erōḥām* **masc. proper noun**
(Jeroham: father of Elkanah)
1 Sam. 1:1; **1 Chr.** 6:27(12),34(19).
B. יְרֹחָם *y^erōḥām* **masc. proper noun**
(Jeroham: a Benjamite)
1 Chr. 8:27.
C. יְרֹחָם *y^erōḥām* **masc. proper noun**
(Jeroham: a Benjamite)
1 Chr. 9:8.
D. יְרֹחָם *y^erōḥām* **masc. proper noun**
(Jeroham: a priest)
1 Chr. 9:12.
E. יְרֹחָם *y^erōḥām* **masc. proper noun**
(Jeroham: a priest)
Neh. 11:12.
F. יְרֹחָם *y^erōḥām* **masc. proper noun**
(Jeroham: man of Gedor)
1 Chr. 12:7.
G. יְרֹחָם *y^erōḥām* **masc. proper noun**
(Jeroham: a Danite)
1 Chr. 27:22.
H. יְרֹחָם *y^erōḥām* **masc. proper noun**
(Jeroham: father of Azariah)
2 Chr. 23:1.

3396. A. יְרַחְמְאֵל *y^eraḥm^e'ēl* **masc. proper noun**

(Jerahmeel: a Judaite)
1 Chr. 2:9,25–27,33,42.
B. יְרַחְמְאֵל *y^e^raḥm^e^'ēl* **masc. proper noun**
(Jerahmeel: son of Jehoiakim)
Jer. 36:26.
C. יְרַחְמְאֵל *y^e^raḥm^e^'ēl* **masc. proper noun**
(Jerahmeel: a Levite)
1 Chr. 24:29.

3397. יְרַחְמְאֵלִי *y^e^raḥm^e^'ēliy* **masc. proper noun**
(Jerahmeelite)
1 Sam. 27:10; 30:29.

3398. יַרְחָע *yarḥā'* **masc. proper noun**
(Jarha)
1 Chr. 2:34,35.

3399. יָרַט *yāraṭ* **verb**
(to be reckless, to be contrary; to throw recklessly)
Num. 22:32; **Job** 16:11.

3400. יְרִיאֵל *y^e^riy'ēl* **masc. proper noun**
(Jeriel)
1 Chr. 7:2.

3401. יָרִיב *yāriyḇ* **masc. noun**
(opponent, contender)
Ps. 35:1; **Isa.** 49:25; **Jer.** 18:19.

3402. יָרִיב *yāriyḇ* **masc. proper noun**
(Jarib)
1 Chr. 4:24; **Ezra** 8:16; 10:18.

3403. יְרִיבַי *y^e^riyḇay* **masc. proper noun**
(Jeribai)
1 Chr. 11:46.

3404. יְרִיָּה *y^e^riyyāh*, יְרִיָּהוּ *y^e^riyyāhû* **masc. proper noun**
(Jeriah)
1 Chr. 23:19; 24:23; 26:31.

3405. יְרֵחוֹ *y^e^rēḥô*, יְרִיחוֹ *y^e^riyḥô* **proper noun**
(Jericho)
Num. 22:1; 26:3,63; 31:12; 33:48,50; 34:15; 35:1; 36:13; **Deut.** 32:49; 34:1,3; **Josh.** 2:1–3; 3:16; 4:13,19; 5:10,13; 6:1,2,25,26; 7:2; 8:2; 9:3; 10:1,28,30; 12:9; 13:32; 16:1,7; 18:12,21; 20:8; 24:11; **2 Sam.** 10:5; **1 Kgs.** 16:34; **2 Kgs.** 2:4,5,15,18; 25:5; **1 Chr.** 6:78(63); 19:5; **2 Chr.** 28:15; **Ezra** 2:34; **Neh.** 3:2; 7:36; **Jer.** 39:5; 52:8.

3406. A. יְרִימוֹת *y^e^riymôṯ* **masc. proper noun**
(Jerimoth: son of Bela)
1 Chr. 7:7.
B. יְרֵימוֹת *y^e^rēymôṯ* **masc. proper noun**
(Jerimoth: son of Becher)
1 Chr. 7:8.
C. יְרֵמוֹת *y^e^rēmôṯ* **masc. proper noun**
(Jeremoth: son of Beriah)
1 Chr. 8:14.
D. יְרִימוֹת *y^e^riymôṯ* **masc. proper noun**
(Jerimoth: a Benjamite)
1 Chr. 12:5(6).
E. יְרֵמוֹת *y^e^rēmôṯ*, יְרִימוֹת *y^e^riymôṯ* **masc. proper noun**
(Jeremoth, Jerimoth: son of Mushi)
1 Chr. 23:23; 24:30.
F. יְרֵימוֹת *y^e^rēymôṯ* **masc. proper noun**
(Jeremoth, Jerimoth: a Levite)
1 Chr. 25:22.
G. יְרִימוֹת *y^e^riymôṯ* **masc. proper noun**
(Jerimoth: son of Heman)
1 Chr. 25:4.
H. יְרֵימוֹת *y^e^rēymôṯ* **masc. proper noun**
(Jerimoth: a Levite)

2 **Chr.** 31:13.
I. יְרִימוֹת *yᵉriymôṯ* **masc. proper noun**
(Jerimoth: a Naphtalite)
1 Chr. 27:19.
J. יְרִימוֹת *yᵉriymôṯ* **masc. proper noun**
(Jerimoth: son of David)
2 Chr. 11:18.
K. יְרֵמוֹת *yᵉrēmôṯ* **masc. proper noun**
(Jeremoth: descendant of Elam)
Ezra 10:26.
L. יְרֵמוֹת *yᵉrēmôṯ* **masc. proper noun**
(Jeremoth: descendant of Zattu)
Ezra 10:27.
M. יְרֵמוֹת *yᵉrēmôṯ* **masc. proper noun**
(Jeremoth: a Jew)
Ezra 10:29(KJV, [Qᵉ] *rāmoṯ* [7433]).
N. יְרֵמוֹת *yᵉrēmôṯ* **proper noun**
(Jeremoth: covenanter in Ezra's day)
Ezra 10:29(KJV, [Qᵉ] *rāmoṯ* [7433,B]).

3407. יְרִיעָה *yᵉriyʻāh* **fem. noun**
(curtain, shelter)
Ex. 26:1–10,12,13; 36:8–17; **Num.** 4:25; **2 Sam.** 7:2; **1 Chr.** 17:1; **Ps.** 104:2; **Song** 1:5; **Isa.** 54:2; **Jer.** 4:20; 10:20; 49:29; **Hab.** 3:7.

3408. יְרִיעוֹת *yᵉriyʻôṯ* **fem. proper noun**
(Jerioth)
1 Chr. 2:18.

3409. יָרֵךְ *yārēḵ* **fem. noun**
(thigh, loin, side)
Gen. 24:2,9; 32:25(26),31(32),32(33); 46:26; 47:29; **Ex.** 1:5; 25:31; 28:42; 32:27; 37:17; 40:22,24; **Lev.** 1:11; **Num.** 3:29,35; 5:21,22,27; 8:4; **Judg.** 3:16,21; 8:30; 15:8; **2 Kgs.** 16:14; **Ps.** 45:3(4); **Song** 3:8; 7:1(2); **Jer.** 31:19; **Ezek.** 21:12(17); 24:4.

3410. יַרְכָה *yarḵāh* **Aram. fem. noun**
(thigh)
Dan. 2:32.

3411. יַרְכָה *yarḵāh*, יְרֵכָה *yᵉrēḵāh* **fem. noun**
(far end, remote area, border, utmost height)
Gen. 49:13; **Ex.** 26:22,23,27; 36:27, 28,32; **Judg.** 19:1,18; **1 Sam.** 24:3(4); **1 Kgs.** 6:16; **2 Kgs.** 19:23; **Ps.** 48:2(3); 128:3; **Isa.** 14:13,15; 37:24; **Jer.** 6:22; 25:32; 31:8; 50:41; **Ezek.** 32:23; 38:6,15; 39:2; 46:19; **Amos** 6:10; **Jon.** 1:5.

3412. A. יַרְמוּת *yarmûṯ* **proper noun**
(Jarmuth: Canaanite city in Judah)
Josh. 10:3,5,23; 12:11; 15:35; **Neh.** 11:29.
B. יַרְמוּת *yarmûṯ* **proper noun**
(Jarmuth: city in Issachar)
Josh. 21:29.

3413. יְרֵמַי *yᵉrēmay* **masc. proper noun**
(Jeremai)
Ezra 10:33.

3414. A. יִרְמְיָה *yirmᵉyāh*, יִרְמְיָהוּ *yirmᵉyāhû* **masc. proper noun**
(Jeremiah: son of Hilkiah)
2 Chr. 35:25; 36:12,21,22; **Ezra** 1:1; **Jer.** 1:1,11; 7:1; 11:1; 14:1; 18:1,18; 19:14; 20:1–3; 21:1,3; 24:3; 25:1,2,13; 26:7–9,12,20,24; 27:1; 28:5,6,10–12,15; 29:1,27,29,30; 30:1; 32:1,2,6,26; 33:1, 19,23; 34:1,6,8,12; 35:1,3,12,18; 36:1,4, 5,8,10,19,26,27,32; 37:2–4,6,12–18,21; 38:1,6,7,9–17,19,20,24,27,28; 39:11, 14,15; 40:1,2,6; 42:2,4,5,7; 43:1,2,6,8; 44:1,15,20,24; 45:1; 46:1,13; 47:1; 49:34; 50:1; 51:59–61,64; 52:1; **Dan.** 9:2.
B. יִרְמְיָהוּ *yirmᵉyāhû* **masc. proper noun**
(Jeremiah: grandfather of Zedekiah)

2 Kgs. 23:31; 24:18.
C. יִרְמְיָהוּ *yirm*^{e}*yāhû* **masc. proper noun**
(Jeremiah: a Gadite)
1 Chr. 12:13.
D. יִרְמְיָה *yirm*^{e}*yāh* **masc. proper noun**
(Jeremiah: a Manassite)
1 Chr. 5:24.
E. יִרְמְיָה *yirm*^{e}*yāh* **masc. proper noun**
(Jeremiah: a Benjamite)
1 Chr. 12:4.
F. יִרְמְיָה *yirm*^{e}*yāh* **masc. proper noun**
(Jeremiah: a Gadite)
1 Chr. 12:10.
G. יִרְמְיָה *yirm*^{e}*yāh* **masc. proper noun**
(Jeremiah: head of a priestly family)
Neh. 12:1,12.
H. יִרְמְיָה *yirm*^{e}*yāh* **masc. proper noun**
(Jeremiah: a covenanter)
Neh. 10:2(3); 12:34.

3415. יָרַע *yāra'* **verb**
(to tremble, to faint, to be displeased, to be evil)
Isa. 15:4.

3416. יִרְפְּאֵל *yirp*^{e}*'ēl* **proper noun**
(Irpeel)
Josh. 18:27.

3417. יָרַק *yāraq* **verb**
(to spit)
Num. 12:14; **Deut.** 25:9.

3418. יֶרֶק *yereq* **masc. noun**
(something green; herbs, grass, or trees)
Gen. 1:30; 9:3; **Ex.** 10:15; **Num.** 22:4; **2 Kgs.** 19:26(KJV, NASB, *yārāq* [3419]); **Ps.** 37:2; **Isa.** 15:6; 37:27(KJV, NASB, *yārāq* [3419]).

3419. יָרָק *yārāq* **masc. noun**
(green herbs, garden vegetables)
Deut. 11:10; **1 Kgs.** 21:2; **2 Kgs.** 19:26(NIV, *yereq* [3418]); **Prov.** 15:17; **Isa.** 37:27(NIV, *yereq* [3418]).

3420. יֵרָקוֹן *yērāqôn* **masc. noun**
(mildew, paleness)
Deut. 28:22; **1 Kgs.** 8:37; **2 Chr.** 6:28; **Jer.** 30:6; **Amos** 4:9; **Hag.** 2:17.

3421. יָרְקְעָם *yorq*^{o}*'ām* **masc. proper noun**
(Jorkoam)
1 Chr. 2:44.

3422. יְרַקְרַק *y*^{e}*raqraq* **adj.**
(greenish, yellow)
Lev. 13:49; 14:37; **Ps.** 68:13(14).

3423. יָרַשׁ *yāraš* **verb**
(to possess, to be heir)
Gen. 15:3,4,7,8; 21:10; 22:17; 24:60; 28:4; 45:11; **Ex.** 15:9; 34:24; **Lev.** 20:24; 25:46; **Num.** 13:30; 14:12,24; 21:24, 32,35; 27:11; 32:21,39; 33:52,53,55; 36:8; **Deut.** 1:8,21,39; 2:12,21,22,24,31; 3:12,18,20; 4:1,5,14,22,26,38,47; 5:31(28),33(30); 6:1,18; 7:1,17; 8:1; 9:1,3–6,23; 10:11; 11:8,10,11,23,29,31; 12:1,2,29; 15:4; 16:20; 17:14; 18:12,14; 19:1,2,14; 21:1; 23:20(21); 25:19; 26:1; 28:21,42,63; 30:5,16,18; 31:3,13; 32:47; 33:23; **Josh.** 1:11,15; 3:10; 8:7; 12:1; 13:1,6,12,13; 14:12; 15:14,63; 16:10; 17:12,13,18; 18:3; 19:47; 21:43(41); 23:5,9,13; 24:4,8; **Judg.** 1:19–21,27–33; 2:6,21,23; 3:13; 11:21–24; 14:15; 18:7,9; **1 Sam.** 2:7; **2 Sam.** 14:7; **1 Kgs.** 14:24; 21:15,16,18,19,26; **2 Kgs.** 16:3; 17:8,24; 21:2; **1 Chr.** 28:8; **2 Chr.** 20:7,11; 28:3; 33:2; **Ezra** 9:11,12; **Neh.** 9:15,22–25; **Job** 13:26; 20:15; **Ps.** 25:13; 37:9,11,22, 29,34; 44:2(3),3(4); 69:35(36); 83:12(13); 105:44; **Prov.** 20:13; 23:21; 30:9,23; **Isa.** 14:21; 34:11,17; 54:3; 57:13; 60:21; 61:7; 63:18; 65:9; **Jer.** 8:10; 30:3; 32:23; 49:1,2;

Ezek. 7:24; 33:24–26; 35:10; 36:12; **Hos.** 9:6; **Amos** 2:10; 9:12; **Obad.** 1:17,19,20; **Mic.** 1:15; **Hab.** 1:6; **Zech.** 9:4.

3424. יְרֵשָׁה *yerēšāh* **fem. noun**
(possession)
Num. 24:18.

3425. יְרֻשָּׁה *yeruššāh* **fem. noun**
(possession, inheritance)
Deut. 2:5,9,12,19; 3:20; **Josh.** 1:15; 12:6,7; **Judg.** 21:17; **2 Chr.** 20:11; **Ps.** 61:5(6); **Jer.** 32:8.

3426. יֵשׁ *yēš* **verb**
(to be, to exist)
Gen. 18:24; 23:8; 24:23,42,49; 28:16; 31:29; 33:9,11; 39:4,5,8; 42:1,2; 43:4,7; 44:19,20,26; 47:6; **Ex.** 17:7; **Num.** 9:20,21; 13:20; 22:29; **Deut.** 13:3(4); 29:15(14),18(17); **Judg.** 4:20; 6:13,36; 18:14; 19:19; **Ruth** 1:12; 3:12; **1 Sam.** 9:11,12; 14:39; 17:46; 20:8; 21:3(4),4(5),8(9); 23:23; **2 Sam.** 9:1; 14:19(KJV, NIV, *'iš* [786]),32; 19:28(29); **1 Kgs.** 17:12; 18:10; **2 Kgs.** 2:16; 3:12; 4:2,13; 5:8; 9:15; 10:15,23; **1 Chr.** 29:3; **2 Chr.** 15:7; 16:9; 25:8,9; **Ezra** 10:2,44; **Neh.** 5:2–5; **Esth.** 3:8; **Job** 5:1; 6:6,30; 9:33; 11:18; 14:7; 16:4; 25:3; 28:1; 33:23,32; 38:28; **Ps.** 7:3(4); 14:2; 53:2(3); 58:11(12); 73:11; 135:17; **Prov.** 3:28; 8:21; 11:24; 12:18; 13:7,23; 14:12; 16:25; 18:24; 19:18; 20:15; 23:18; 24:14; **Eccl.** 1:10; 2:13,21; 4:8,9; 5:13(12); 6:1,11; 7:15; 8:6,14; 9:4; 10:5; **Isa.** 43:8; 44:8; **Jer.** 5:1; 14:22; 23:26; 27:18; 31:6,16,17; 37:17; 41:8; **Lam.** 1:12; 3:29; **Jon.** 4:11; **Mic.** 2:1; 6:10(KJV, NIV, *'iš* [786]); **Mal.** 1:14.

3427. יָשַׁב *yāšab̲* **verb**
(to dwell, to abide, to inhabit, to remain)
Gen. 4:16,20; 11:2,31; 13:6,7,12,18; 14:7,12; 16:3; 18:1; 19:1,25,29,30; 20:1,15; 21:16,20,21; 22:5,19; 23:10; 24:3,37,55,62; 25:11,27; 26:6,17; 27:19,44; 29:14,19; 31:34; 34:10,16, 21–23,30; 35:1; 36:7,8,20; 37:1,25; 38:11,14; 43:33; 44:33; 45:10; 46:34; 47:4,6,11,27; 48:2; 49:24; 50:11,22; **Ex.** 2:15,21; 11:5; 12:29,40; 15:14,15,17; 16:3,29,35; 17:12; 18:13,14; 23:31,33; 24:14; 32:6; 34:12,15; **Lev.** 8:35; 12:4,5; 13:46; 14:8; 15:4,6,20,22,23,26; 18:3,25; 20:22; 23:42,43; 25:10,18,19; 26:5,32,35; **Num.** 13:18,19,28,29,32; 14:14,25,45; 20:1,15; 21:1,15(NASB, NIV, *šeb̲eṯ* [7675]),25,31,34; 22:5,8,19; 25:1; 32:6,17,40; 33:40,52,53,55; 35:2,3,25, 28,32,34; **Deut.** 1:4,6,44,46; 2:4,8,10, 12,20–23,29; 3:2,19,29; 4:46; 6:7; 8:12; 9:9; 11:19,30,31; 12:10,29; 13:12(13), 13(14),15(16); 17:14,18; 19:1; 21:13; 23:13(14),16(17); 25:5; 26:1; 28:30; 29:16(15); 30:20; **Josh.** 1:14; 2:9,15 ,22,24; 5:8; 6:25; 7:7,9; 8:9,24,26; 9:3, 7,11,16,22,24; 10:1,6; 11:19; 12:2,4; 13:6,13,21; 14:4; 15:15,63; 16:10; 17:7, 11,12,16; 19:47,50; 20:4,6; 21:2,43(41); 22:33; 24:2,7,8,13,15,18; **Judg.** 1:9–11, 16,17,19,21,27,29–33,35; 2:2; 3:3,5,20; 4:2,5; 5:10,16,17,23; 6:10,11,18; 8:29; 9:21,41; 10:1,18; 11:3,8,17,21,26; 13:9; 15:8; 16:9,12; 17:10,11; 18:1,7,28; 19:4, 6,15; 20:15,26,47; 21:2,9,10,12,23; **Ruth** 1:4; 2:7,14,23; 3:18; 4:1,2,4; **1 Sam.** 1:9, 22,23; 2:8; 4:4,13; 5:7; 6:21; 7:2; 12:8,11; 13:16; 14:2; 19:2,9,18; 20:5,19,24,25; 22:4–6,23; 23:5,14,18,25,29(24:1); 24:3(4); 25:13; 26:3; 27:3,5,7,8,11; 28:23; 30:21,24; 31:7,11; **2 Sam.** 1:1; 2:3,13; 5:6,9; 6:2,11; 7:1,2,5,6,18; 9:13; 10:5; 11:1,11,12; 13:20; 14:28; 15:8,19,29; 16:3,18; 18:24; 19:8(9); 23:8(see *yōšēb̲ baššeb̲eṯ* [3429]); **1 Kgs.** 1:13,17,20,24, 27,30,35,46,48; 2:12,19,24,36,38; 3:6,17; 4:25(5:5); 7:8; 8:13,20,25,27,30,39,43,49; 9:16; 11:16,24; 12:2,17,25; 13:11,14, 20,25; 15:18,21; 16:11; 17:5,9,19; 19:4; 21:8–13; 22:1,10,19; **2 Kgs.** 1:9; 2:2,4, 6,18; 4:13,20,38; 6:1,2,32; 7:3,4; 9:5;

10:30; 11:19; 13:5,13; 14:10; 15:5,12; 16:6; 17:6,24–29; 18:27; 19:15,26,27,36; 22:14,16,19; 23:2; 25:24; **1 Chr.** 2:55; 4:23,28,40,41,43; 5:8–11,16,22,23; 7:29; 8:6,13,28,29,32; 9:2,3,16,34,35,38; 10:7; 11:4,5,7; 13:6,14; 17:1,4,5,16; 19:5; 20:1; 22:18; 28:5; 29:23; **2 Chr.** 2:3(2); 6:2,10, 16,18,21,30,33,39; 8:2,11; 9:18(NASB, NIV, *šeḇeṯ* [7675]); 10:17; 11:5; 15:5; 16:2; 18:9,18; 19:4,10; 20:7,8,15,18,20, 23; 21:11,13; 22:1; 23:20; 25:19; 26:7,21; 28:18; 30:25; 31:4,6; 32:10,22,26,33; 33:9; 34:9,22,24,27,28,30,32; 35:18; **Ezra** 2:70; 4:6; 8:32; 9:3,4; 10:2,9,10, 14,16–18; **Neh.** 1:4; 2:6; 3:13,26; 4:12(6); 7:3,73; 8:14,17; 9:24; 11:1–4,6, 21,25; 13:16,23,27; **Esth.** 1:2,14; 2:19, 21; 3:15; 5:1,13; 6:10; 9:19; **Job** 2:8,13; 15:28; 22:8; 24:13; 29:25; 36:7; 38:40; **Ps.** 1:1; 2:4; 4:8(9); 9:4(5),7(8),11(12); 10:8; 17:12; 22:3(4); 23:6; 24:1; 26:4,5; 27:4; 29:10; 33:8,14; 47:8(9); 49:1(2); 50:20; 55:19(20); 61:7(8); 65:8(9); 68:6(7),10(11),16(17); 69:12(13),25(26), 35(36); 75:3(4); 80:1(2); 83:7(8); 84:4(5); 91:1; 98:7; 99:1; 101:6,7; 102:12(13); 107:10,34,36; 110:1; 113:5,8,9; 119:23; 122:5; 123:1; 125:1; 127:2; 132:12,14; 133:1; 137:1; 139:2; 140:13(14); 143:3; **Prov.** 3:29; 9:14; 20:3(KJV, NASB, *šeḇeṯ* [7674]),8; 21:9,19; 23:1; 25:24; 31:23; **Eccl.** 10:6; **Song** 2:3; 5:12; 8:13; **Isa.** 3:26; 5:3,8,9; 6:1,5,11; 8:14; 9:2(1),9(8); 10:13,24,31; 12:6; 13:20; 14:13; 16:5; 18:3; 20:6; 21:14; 22:21; 23:2,6,18; 24:1,5,6,17; 26:5,9,18,21; 28:6; 30:19; 32:16,18; 33:24; 36:12; 37:16,27,28,37; 38:11; 40:22; 42:7,10,11; 44:13,26; 45:18; 47:1,5,8,14; 49:19,20; 51:6; 52:2; 54:3; 58:12; 65:4,21,22; **Jer.** 1:14; 2:6,15; 3:2; 4:4,7,29; 6:8,12; 8:1,14,16; 9:6(5), 11(10),26(25); 10:17,18; 11:2,9,12; 12:4; 13:13,18; 15:17; 16:8; 17:6,20,25; 18:11; 19:3,12; 20:6; 21:6,9,13; 22:2,4,6,23,30; 23:8,14; 24:8; 25:2,5,9,29,30; 26:9,10,15; 27:11; 29:5,16,28,32; 30:18; 31:24; 32:12,32,37; 33:10,17; 34:22; 35:7,9–11, 13,15,17; 36:12,15,22,30,31; 37:16,21; 38:2,7,13,28; 39:3,14; 40:5,6,9,10; 41:17; 42:10,13,14,18; 43:4; 44:1,2,13–15, 22,26; 46:8,19; 47:2; 48:9,18,19,28,43; 49:1,8,18,20,30,31,33; 50:3,13,21,34, 35,39,40; 51:1,12,24,29,30,35,37,43,62; **Lam.** 1:1,3; 2:10; 3:6,28,63; 4:12,21; 5:19; **Ezek.** 2:6; 3:15; 7:7; 8:1,14; 11:15; 12:2,19,20; 14:1; 15:6; 16:46; 20:1; 23:41; 25:4; 26:16,17,19,20; 27:3,8,35; 28:2,25,26; 29:6,11; 31:6,17; 32:15; 33:24,31; 34:25,28; 35:9; 36:10,11,17, 28,33,35; 37:25; 38:8,11,12,14; 39:6, 9,26; 44:3; **Dan.** 9:7; **Hos.** 3:3,4; 4:1,3; 9:3; 11:11; 12:9(10); 14:7(8); **Joel** 1:2,14; 2:1; 3:12(4:12),20(4:20); **Amos** 1:5,8; 3:12; 5:11; 8:8; 9:5,14; **Obad.** 1:3(NASB, NIV, *šeḇeṯ* [7675]); **Jon.** 3:6; 4:5; **Mic.** 1:11–13,15; 4:4; 5:4(3); 6:12,16; 7:8,13; **Nah.** 1:5; 3:8; **Hab.** 2:8,17; **Zeph.** 1:4,11,13,18; 2:5,15; 3:6; **Hag.** 1:4; **Zech.** 1:11; 2:4(8),7(11); 3:8; 5:7; 6:13; 7:7; 8:4,20,21; 9:5,6; 11:6; 12:5–8,10; 13:1; 14:10,11; **Mal.** 3:3.

3428. יֶשֶׁבְאָב *yešeḇ'āḇ* **masc. proper noun**
(Jeshebeab)
1 Chr. 24:13.

3429. I. יֹשֵׁב בַּשֶּׁבֶת *yōšēḇ baššeḇeṯ* **masc. noun**
(who sat in the seat: Qal act. part. of *yāšaḇ* [3427] and *šeḇeṯ* [7675] with prefix prep. *ḇ* and def. art.)
2 Sam. 23:8(NASB, NIV, see II).
II. יֹשֵׁב בַּשֶּׁבֶת *yōšēḇ baššeḇeṯ* **masc. proper noun**
(Josheb-Basshebeth)
2 Sam. 23:8(KJV, see I).

3430. יִשְׁבִּי בְּנֹב *yišbiy bᵉnōḇ* **masc. proper noun**
(Ishbi-Benob)
2 Sam. 21:16.

3431. יִשְׁבָּח *yišbāḥ* **masc. proper noun**
(Ishbah)
1 Chr. 4:17.

3432. יָשׁוּבִי *yāšûḇiy* **masc. proper noun**
(Jashubite)
Num. 26:24.

3433. יָשֻׁבִי לָחֶם *yāšuḇiy lāḥem* **masc. proper noun**
(Jashubi Lehem)
1 Chr. 4:22.

3434. A. יָשָׁבְעָם *yāšoḇʿām* **masc. proper noun**
(Jashobeam: military leader under David)
1 Chr. 11:11(Sept. יִשְׁבַּעַל); 27:2.
B. יָשָׁבְעָם *yāšoḇʿām* **masc. proper noun**
(Jashobeam: warrior under David; possibly same as A)
1 Chr. 12:6(7).

3435. יִשְׁבָּק *yišbāq* **masc. proper noun**
(Ishbak)
Gen. 25:2; **1 Chr.** 1:32.

3436. יָשְׁבְּקָשָׁה *yošb^{e}qāšāh* **masc. proper noun**
(Joshbekashah)
1 Chr. 25:4,24.

3437. A. יָשׁוּב *yāšûḇ* **masc. proper noun**
(Jashub: son of Issachar)
Gen. 46:13(KJV, NASB, *yôḇ* [3102]); **Num.** 26:24; **1 Chr.** 7:1.
B. יָשׁוּב *yāšûḇ* **masc. proper noun**
(Jashub: son of Bani)
Ezra 10:29.

3438. יִשְׁוָה *yišwāh* **masc. proper noun**
(Ishvah)
Gen. 46:17; **1 Chr.** 7:30.

3439. יְשׁוֹחָיָה *y^{e}šôḥāyāh* **masc. proper noun**
(Jeshohaiah)
1 Chr. 4:36.

3440. A. יִשְׁוִי *yišwiy* **masc. proper noun**
(Ishvi: an Asherite)
Gen. 46:17; **Num.** 26:44; **1 Chr.** 7:30.
B. יִשְׁוִי *yišwiy* **masc. proper noun**
(Ishvi: son of Saul)
1 Sam. 14:49.

3441. יִשְׁוִי *yišwiy* **masc. proper noun**
(Ishvite, Jesuite)
Num. 26:44.

3442. A. יֵשׁוּעַ *yēšûaʿ* **masc. proper noun**
(Jeshua: a priest)
1 Chr. 24:11; **Ezra** 2:36; **Neh.** 7:39.
B. יֵשׁוּעַ *yēšûaʿ* **masc. proper noun**
(Jeshua: a Levite)
2 Chr. 31:15; **Ezra** 2:40; **Neh.** 7:43.
C. יֵשׁוּעַ *yēšûaʿ* **masc. proper noun**
(Jeshua: a priest; see also *yēšûaʿ* [3443])
Ezra 2:2; 3:2,8,9; 4:3; 10:18; **Neh.** 7:7; 12:1,7,10,26.
D. יֵשׁוּעַ *yēšûaʿ* **masc. proper noun**
(Jeshua: father of Jozabad)
Ezra 8:33.
E. יֵשׁוּעַ *yēšûaʿ* **masc. proper noun**
(Jeshua: son of Pahath-Moab)
Ezra 2:6; **Neh.** 7:11.
F. יֵשׁוּעַ *yēšûaʿ* **masc. proper noun**
(Jeshua: father of Ezer; possibly the same as C)
Neh. 3:19.
G. יֵשׁוּעַ *yēšûaʿ* **masc. proper noun**
(Jeshua: a Levite)
Neh. 8:7; 9:4,5; 12:8,24.
H. יֵשׁוּעַ *yēšûaʿ* **masc. proper noun**
(Joshua: Moses' successor)
Neh. 8:17.

I. יֵשׁוּעַ *yēšûa'* **masc. proper noun**
(Jeshua: son of Azaniah)
Neh. 10:9(10).
J. יֵשׁוּעַ *yēšûa'* **masc. proper noun**
(Jeshua: city in Benjamin)
Neh. 11:26.

3443. יֵשׁוּעַ *yēšûa'* **Aram. masc. proper noun**
(Jeshua; corr. to Hebr. 3442,C)
Ezra 5:2.

3444. יְשׁוּעָה y^e*šû'āh* **fem. noun**
(salvation, deliverance)
Gen. 49:18; **Ex.** 14:13; 15:2; **Deut.** 32:15; **1 Sam.** 2:1; 14:45; **2 Sam.** 10:11; 22:51; **1 Chr.** 16:23; **2 Chr.** 20:17; **Job** 13:16; 30:15; **Ps.** 3:2(3),8(9); 9:14(15); 13:5(6); 14:7; 18:50(51); 20:5(6); 21:1(2), 5(6); 22:1(2); 28:8; 35:3,9; 42:5(6),11(12); 43:5; 44:4(5); 53:6(7); 62:1(2),2(3),6(7); 67:2(3); 68:19(20); 69:29(30); 70:4(5); 74:12; 78:22; 80:2(3); 88:1(2); 89:26(27); 91:16; 96:2; 98:2,3; 106:4; 116:13; 118:14,15,21; 119:123,155,166,174; 140:7(8); 149:4; **Isa.** 12:2,3; 25:9; 26:1, 18; 33:2,6; 49:6,8; 51:6,8; 52:7,10; 56:1; 59:11,17; 60:18; 62:1; **Jon.** 2:9(10); **Hab.** 3:8.

3445. יֶשַׁח *yešaḥ* **masc. noun**
(emptiness)
Mic. 6:14.

3446. יִשְׂחָק *yiśḥāq* **masc. proper noun**
(Isaac; a variant spelling of *yiṣḥāq* [3327])
Ps. 105:9; **Jer.** 33:26; **Amos** 7:9,16.

3447. יָשַׁט *yāšaṭ* **verb**
(to hold out, to extend)
Esth. 4:11; 5:2; 8:4.

3448. יִשַׁי *yišay,* אִישַׁי *'iyšay* **masc. proper noun**
(Jesse)
Ruth 4:17,22; **1 Sam.** 16:1,3,5,8–11,18–20,22; 17:12,13,17, 20,58; 20:27,30,31; 22:7–9,13; 25:10; **2 Sam.** 20:1; 23:1; **1 Kgs.** 12:16; **1 Chr.** 2:12,13; 10:14; 12:18; 29:26; **2 Chr.** 10:16; 11:18; **Ps.** 72:20; **Isa.** 11:1,10.

3449. A. יִשִּׁיָּהוּ *yiššiyyāhû* **masc. proper noun**
(Isshiah: one of David's mighty men)
1 Chr. 12:6(7).
B. יִשִּׁיָּה *yiššiyyāh* **masc. proper noun**
(Isshiah: descendant of Issachar)
1 Chr. 7:3.
C. יִשִּׁיָּה *yiššiyyāh* **masc. proper noun**
(Isshiah: a Levite)
1 Chr. 23:20; 24:25.
D. יִשִּׁיָּה *yiššiyyāh* **masc. proper noun**
(Isshiah: a Levite)
1 Chr. 24:21.
E. יִשִּׁיָּה *yiššiyyāh* **masc. proper noun**
(Ishijah: postexilic Jew)
Ezra 10:31.

3450. יְשִׂמִאֵל y^e*śiymi'ēl* **masc. proper noun**
(Jesimiel)
1 Chr. 4:36.

3451. יְשִׁימָה y^e*šiymāh* **fem. noun**
(desolation, death)
Ps. 55:15(16)(KJV, NASB, NIV, [Q^e] *māweṯ* [4194] and *nāšā* [5377]).

3452. I. יְשִׁימוֹן y^e*šiymôn* **masc. proper noun**
(Jeshimon)
Num. 21:20(NASB, NIV, see II); 23:28(NASB, NIV, see II); **1 Sam.** 23:19,24; 26:1,3.
II. יְשִׁימוֹן y^e*šiymôn,* יְשִׁמוֹן y^e*šimôn* **masc. noun**
(wasteland, wilderness, desert)

Num. 21:20(KJV, see I); 23:28(KJV, see I); **Deut.** 32:10; **Ps.** 68:7(8); 78:40; 106:14; 107:4; **Isa.** 43:19,20.

3453. יָשִׁישׁ *yāšiyš* **adj.**
(old, aged)
Job 12:12; 15:10; 29:8; 32:6.

3454. יְשִׁישַׁי *y^ešiyšay* **masc. proper noun**
(Jeshishai)
1 Chr. 5:14.

3455. יָשַׂם *yāśam* **verb**
(to put, to place)
Gen. 50:26(NASB, NIV, [Q^e] *siym* [7760]).

3456. יָשַׁם *yāšam* **verb**
(to be desolate)
Gen. 47:19(NIV, *šāmēm* [8074]); **Ezek.** 6:6(NASB, NIV, *šāmēm* [8074]); 12:19(NIV, *šāmēm* [8074]); 19:7(NIV, *šāmēm* [8074]).

3457. יִשְׁמָא *yišmā'* **masc. proper noun**
(Ishma)
1 Chr. 4:3.

3458. A. יִשְׁמָעֵאל *yišmā'ē'l* **masc. proper noun**
(Ishmael: son of Abraham)
Gen. 16:11,15,16; 17:18,20,23,25,26; 25:9,12,13,16,17; 28:9; 36:3; **1 Chr.** 1:28,29,31.
B. יִשְׁמָעֵאל *yišmā'ē'l* **masc. proper noun**
(Ishmael: a Judaite)
2 Chr. 19:11.
C. יִשְׁמָעֵאל *yišmā'ē'l* **masc. proper noun**
(Ishmael: son of Azel)
1 Chr. 8:38; 9:44.
D. יִשְׁמָעֵאל *yišmā'ē'l* **masc. proper noun**
(Ishmael: son of Jehohanan)
2 Chr. 23:1.
E. יִשְׁמָעֵאל *yišmā'ē'l* **masc. proper noun**
(Ishmael: a priest)
Ezra 10:22.
F. יִשְׁמָעֵאל *yišmā'ē'l* **masc. proper noun**
(Ishmael: son of Nethaniah)
2 Kgs. 25:23,25; **Jer.** 40:8,14–16; 41:1–3,6–16,18.

3459. יִשְׁמְעֵאלִי *yišm^e'ē'liy* **masc. proper noun**
(Ishmaelite)
Gen. 37:25,27,28; 39:1; **Judg.** 8:24; **1 Chr.** 2:17; 27:30; **Ps.** 83:6(7).

3460. A. יִשְׁמַעְיָה *yišma'yāh* **masc. proper noun**
(Ishmaiah: a Gibeonite)
1 Chr. 12:4.
B. יִשְׁמַעְיָהוּ *yišma'yāhû* **masc. proper noun**
(Ishmaiah: man of Zebulun)
1 Chr. 27:19.

3461. יִשְׁמְרַי *yišm^eray* **masc. proper noun**
(Ishmerai)
1 Chr. 8:18.

3462. I. יָשֵׁן *yāšēn* **verb**
(to sleep, to fall asleep)
Gen. 2:21; 41:5; **Judg.** 16:19; **1 Kgs.** 19:5; **Job** 3:13; **Ps.** 3:5(6); 4:8(9); 13:3(4); 44:23(24); 121:4; **Prov.** 4:16; **Eccl.** 5:12(11); **Isa.** 5:27; **Jer.** 51:39,57; **Ezek.** 34:25; **Hos.** 7:6(KJV, NASB, *yāšēn* [3463]).
II. יָשֵׁן *yāšēn* **verb**
(to become old, to be chronic, to linger)
Lev. 13:11; 26:10; **Deut.** 4:25.

3463. יָשֵׁן *yāšēn* **adj.**
(sleeping)
1 Sam. 26:7,12; **1 Kgs.** 3:20; 18:27; **Ps.** 78:65; **Song** 5:2; 7:9(10)(NIV, omits);

Dan. 12:2; **Hos.** 7:6(NIV, *yāšēn* [3462,I]).

3464. יָשֵׁן *yāšēn* **masc. proper noun**
(Jashen)
2 Sam. 23:32.

3465. יָשָׁן *yāšān* **adj.**
(old, of last year's harvest)
Lev. 25:22; 26:10; **Neh.** 3:6; 12:39; **Song** 7:13(14); **Isa.** 22:11.

3466. יְשָׁנָה y^e*šānāh* **proper noun**
(Jeshanah)
2 Chr. 13:19.

3467. יָשַׁע *yāšaʿ* **verb**
(to save, to deliver)
Ex. 2:17; 14:30; **Num.** 10:9; **Deut.** 20:4; 22:27; 28:29,31; 33:29; **Josh.** 10:6; 22:22; **Judg.** 2:16,18; 3:9,15,31; 6:14,15, 31,36,37; 7:2,7; 8:22; 10:1,12–14; 12:2,3; 13:5; **1 Sam.** 4:3; 7:8; 9:16; 10:19,27; 11:3; 14:6,23,39; 17:47; 23:2,5; 25:26, 31,33; **2 Sam.** 3:18; 8:6,14; 10:11,19; 14:4; 22:3,4,28,42; **2 Kgs.** 6:26,27; 13:5; 14:27; 16:7; 19:19,34; **1 Chr.** 11:14; 16:35; 18:6,13; 19:12,19; **2 Chr.** 20:9; 32:22; **Neh.** 9:27; **Job** 5:15; 22:29; 26:2; 40:14; **Ps.** 3:7(8); 6:4(5); 7:1(2),10(11); 12:1(2); 17:7; 18:3(4),27(28),41(42); 20:6(7),9(10); 22:21(22); 28:9; 31:2(3), 16(17); 33:16; 34:6(7),18(19); 36:6(7); 37:40; 44:3(4),6(7),7(8); 54:1(3); 55:16(17); 57:3(4); 59:2(3); 60:5(7); 69:1(2),35(36); 71:2,3; 72:4,13; 76:9(10); 80:3(4),7(8),19(20); 86:2,16; 98:1; 106:8,10,21,47; 107:13,19; 108:6(7); 109:26,31; 116:6; 118:25; 119:94, 117,146; 138:7; 145:19; **Prov.** 20:22; 28:18; **Isa.** 19:20; 25:9; 30:15; 33:22; 35:4; 37:20,35; 38:20; 43:3,11,12; 45:15,17,20–22; 46:7; 47:13,15; 49:25,26; 59:1,16; 60:16; 63:1,5,8,9; 64:5(4); **Jer.** 2:27,28; 4:14; 8:20; 11:12; 14:8,9; 15:20; 17:14; 23:6; 30:7,10,11; 31:7; 33:16; 42:11; 46:27; **Lam.** 4:17; **Ezek.** 34:22; 36:29; 37:23; **Hos.** 1:7; 13:4,10; 14:3(4); **Obad.** 1:21; **Hab.** 1:2; **Zeph.** 3:17,19; **Zech.** 8:7,13; 9:9,16; 10:6; 12:7.

3468. יֵשַׁע *yēšaʿ*, יֶשַׁע *yešaʿ* **masc. noun**
(salvation, deliverance)
2 Sam. 22:3,36,47; 23:5; **1 Chr.** 16:35; **Job** 5:4,11; **Ps.** 12:5(6); 18:2(3),35(36), 46(47); 20:6(7); 24:5; 25:5; 27:1,9; 50:23; 51:12(14); 62:7(8); 65:5(6); 69:13(14); 79:9; 85:4(5),7(8),9(10); 95:1; 132:16; **Isa.** 17:10; 45:8; 51:5; 61:10; 62:11; **Mic.** 7:7; **Hab.** 3:13,18.

3469. A. יִשְׁעִי *yišʿiy* **masc. proper noun**
(Ishi: descendant of Jerahmeel)
1 Chr. 2:31.
B. יִשְׁעִי *yišʿiy* **masc. proper noun**
(Ishi: a Manassite)
1 Chr. 5:24.
C. יִשְׁעִי *yišʿiy* **masc. proper noun**
(Ishi: a Judaite)
1 Chr. 4:20.
D. יִשְׁעִי *yišʿiy* **masc. proper noun**
(Ishi: a Simeonite)
1 Chr. 4:42.

3470. A. יְשַׁעְיָה y^e*šaʿyāh* **masc. proper noun**
(the prophet Isaiah)
2 Kgs. 19:2,5,6,20; 20:1,4,7–9,11,14,16,19; **2 Chr.** 26:22; 32:20,32; **Isa.** 1:1; 2:1; 7:3; 13:1; 20:2,3; 37:2,5,6,21; 38:1,4,21; 39:3,5,8.
B. יְשַׁעְיָהוּ y^e*šaʿyāhû* **masc. proper noun**
(Jeshaiah: son of Jeduthun)
1 Chr. 25:3,15.
C. יְשַׁעְיָהוּ y^e*šaʿyāhû* **masc. proper noun**
(Jeshaiah: a Levite)
1 Chr. 26:25.

D. יְשַׁעְיָה *yᵉšaʿyāh* **masc. proper noun**
(Jeshaiah: grandson of Zerubbabel)
1 Chr. 3:21.
E. יְשַׁעְיָה *yᵉšaʿyāh* **masc. proper noun**
(Jeshaiah: son of Athaliah)
Ezra 8:7.
F. יְשַׁעְיָה *yᵉšaʿyāh* **masc. proper noun**
(Jeshaiah: son of Merari)
Ezra 8:19.
G. יְשַׁעְיָה *yᵉšaʿyāh* **masc. proper noun**
(Jeshaiah: a Benjamite)
Neh. 11:7.

3471. יָשְׁפֵה *yāšᵉp̄ēh* **masc. noun**
(jasper)
Ex. 28:20; 39:13; **Ezek.** 28:13.

3472. יִשְׁפָּה *yišpāh* **masc. proper noun**
(Ishpah)
1 Chr. 8:16.

3473. יִשְׁפָּן *yišpān* **masc. proper noun**
(Ishpan)
1 Chr. 8:22.

3474. יָשַׁר *yāšar* **verb**
(to be right, to be straight, to be pleasing, to lead, to direct)
Num. 23:27; **Judg.** 14:3,7; **1 Sam.** 6:12; 18:20,26; **2 Sam.** 17:4; **1 Kgs.** 6:35; 9:12; **1 Chr.** 13:4; **2 Chr.** 30:4; 32:30; **Job** 37:3(NASB, NIV, *šārāh* [8281]); **Ps.** 5:8(9); 119:128; **Prov.** 3:6; 4:25; 9:15; 11:5; 15:21; **Isa.** 40:3; 45:2,13; **Jer.** 18:4; 27:5; **Hab.** 2:4.

3475. יֵשֶׁר *yēšer* **masc. proper noun**
(Jesher)
1 Chr. 2:18.

3476. יֹשֶׁר *yōšer* **masc. noun**
(uprightness, straightness, integrity)
Deut. 9:5; **1 Kgs.** 9:4; **1 Chr.** 29:17; **Job** 6:25; 33:3,23; **Ps.** 25:21; 119:7; **Prov.** 2:13; 4:11; 11:24; 14:2; 17:26; **Eccl.** 12:10.

3477. יָשָׁר *yāšār* **adj.**
(upright, right)
Ex. 15:26; **Num.** 23:10; **Deut.** 6:18; 12:8,25,28; 13:18(19); 21:9; 32:4; **Josh.** 9:25; 10:13; **Judg.** 17:6; 21:25; **1 Sam.** 12:23; 29:6; **2 Sam.** 1:18; 19:6(7); **1 Kgs.** 11:33,38; 14:8; 15:5,11; 22:43; **2 Kgs.** 10:3,15,30; 12:2(3); 14:3; 15:3,34; 16:2; 18:3; 22:2; **2 Chr.** 14:2(1); 20:32; 24:2; 25:2; 26:4; 27:2; 28:1; 29:2,34; 31:20; 34:2; **Ezra** 8:21; **Neh.** 9:13; **Job** 1:1,8; 2:3; 4:7; 8:6; 17:8; 23:7; 33:27; **Ps.** 7:10(11); 11:2,7; 19:8(9); 25:8; 32:11; 33:1,4; 36:10(11); 37:14,37; 49:14(15); 64:10(11); 92:15(16); 94:15; 97:11; 107:7,42; 111:1,8; 112:2,4; 119:137; 125:4; 140:13(14); **Prov.** 2:7,21; 3:32; 8:9; 11:3,6,11; 12:6,15; 14:9,11,12; 15:8,19; 16:13,17,25; 20:11; 21:2,8, 18,29; 28:10; 29:10,27; **Eccl.** 7:29; **Isa.** 26:7; **Jer.** 26:14; 31:9; 34:15; 40:4,5; **Ezek.** 1:7,23; **Dan.** 11:17; **Hos.** 14:9(10); **Mic.** 2:7; 3:9; 7:2,4.

3478. A. יִשְׂרָאֵל *yiśrāʾēl* **masc. proper noun**
(Israel: another name for Jacob)
Gen. 32:28(29); 35:10,21,22; 36:31; 37:3,13; 42:5; 43:6,8,11; 45:21,28; 46:1,2,5,8,29,30; 47:27,29,31; 48:2,8, 10,11,13,14,21; 49:2; 50:2; **Ex.** 1:1,7; 6:14; 32:13; **Num.** 1:20; 26:5; **Judg.** 18:29; **1 Kgs.** 18:31,36; **2 Kgs.** 17:34; **1 Chr.** 1:34; 2:1; 5:1,3; 6:38(23); 7:29; 29:10,18; **2 Chr.** 30:6; **Ezra** 8:18.
B. יִשְׂרָאֵל *yiśrāʾēl* **masc. proper noun**
(People or territory of Israel)
Gen. 32:32(33); 34:7; 48:20; 49:7,16,24,28; 50:25; **Ex.** 1:9,12,13;

2:23,25; 3:9–11,13–16,18; 4:22,29,31; 5:1,2,14,15,19; 6:5,6,9,11–13,26,27; 7:2, 4,5; 9:4,6,7,26,35; 10:20,23; 11:7,10; 12:3,6,15,19,21,27,28,31,35,37,40,42,47, 50,51; 13:2,18,19; 14:2,3,5,8,10,15,16, 19,20,22,25,29–31; 15:1,19,22; 16:1–3,6, 9,10,12,15,17,31,35; 17:1,5–8,11; 18:1,8, 9,12,25; 19:1–3,6; 20:22; 24:1,4,5,9–11, 17; 25:2,22; 27:20,21; 28:1,9,11,12,21, 29,30,38; 29:28,43,45; 30:12,16,31; 31:13,16,17; 32:4,8,13,20,27; 33:5,6; 34:23,27,30,32,34,35; 35:1,4,20,29,30; 36:3; 39:6,7,14,32,42; 40:36,38; **Lev.** 1:2; 4:2,13; 7:23,29,34,36,38; 9:1,3; 10:6, 11,14; 11:2; 12:2; 15:2,31; 16:5,16,17,19, 21,34; 17:2,3,5,8,10,12–14; 18:2; 19:2; 20:2; 21:24; 22:2,3,15,18,32; 23:2,10, 24,34,42–44; 24:2,8,10,15,23; 25:2,33, 46,55; 26:46; 27:2,34; **Num.** 1:2,3,16,44, 45,49,52–54; 2:2,32–34; 3:8,9,12,13,38, 40–42,45,46,50; 4:46; 5:2,4,6,9,12; 6:2, 23,27; 7:2,84; 8:6,9–11,14,16–20; 9:2, 4,5,7,10,17–19,22; 10:4,12,28,29,36; 11:4,16,30; 13:2,3,24,26,32; 14:2,5,7,10, 27,39; 15:2,18,25,26,29,32,38; 16:2,9, 25,34,38(17:3),40(17:5),41(17:6); 17:2(17),5(20),6(21),9(24),12(27); 18:5, 6,8,11,14,19–24,26,28,32; 19:2,9,10,13; 20:1,12–14,19,21,22,24,29; 21:1–3,6,10, 17,21,23–25,31; 22:1–3; 23:7,10,21,23; 24:1,2,5,17,18; 25:1,3–6,8,11,13,14; 26:2,4,51,62–64; 27:8,11,12,20,21; 28:2; 29:40(30:1); 30:1(2); 31:2,4,5,9,12,16, 30,42,47,54; 32:4,7,9,13,14,17,18,22,28; 33:1,3,5,38,40,51; 34:2,13,29; 35:2,8,10, 15,34; 36:1–5,7–9,13; **Deut.** 1:1,3,38; 2:12; 3:18; 4:1,44–46; 5:1; 6:3,4; 9:1; 10:6,12; 11:6; 13:11(12); 17:4,12,20; 18:1,6; 19:13; 20:3; 21:8,21; 22:19,21,22; 23:17(18); 24:7; 25:6,7,10; 26:15; 27:1,9, 14; 29:1(28:69),2(1),10(9),21(20); 31:1,7, 9,11,19,22,23,30; 32:8,45,49,51,52; 33:1,5,10,21,28,29; 34:8–10,12; **Josh.** 1:2; 2:2; 3:1,7,9,12,17; 4:4,5,7,8,12,14, 21,22; 5:1–3,6,10,12; 6:1,18,23,25; 7:1,6,8,11–13,15,16,19,20,23–25; 8:10,14,15,17,21,22,24,27,30–33,35;

9:2,6,7,17–19,26; 10:1,4,10–12,14,15, 20,21,24,29–32,34,36,38,40,42,43; 11:5,6,8,13,14,16,19–23; 12:1,6,7; 13:6,13,14,22,33; 14:1,5,10,14; 17:13; 18:1–3,10; 19:49,51; 20:2,9; 21:1,3,8,41, 43,45; 22:9,11–14,16,18,20–22,24, 30–33; 23:1,2; 24:1,2,9,23,31,32; **Judg.** 1:1,28; 2:4,6,7,10,11,14,20,22; 3:1,2,4, 5,7–10,12–15,27,30,31; 4:1,3–6,23,24; 5:2,3,5,7–9,11; 6:1–4,6–8,14,15,36,37; 7:2,8,14,15,23; 8:22,27,28,33–35; 9:22,55; 10:1–3,6–11,15–17; 11:4,5,13, 15–17,19–21,23,25–27,33,39,40; 12:7–9, 11,13,14; 13:1,5; 14:4; 15:20; 16:31; 17:6; 18:1,19; 19:1,12,29,30; 20:1–3,6,7, 10–14,17–27,29–36,38,39,41,42,48; 21:1,3,5,6,8,15,17,18,24,25; **Ruth** 2:12; 4:7,11,14; **1 Sam.** 1:17; 2:14,22,28–30,32; 3:11,20; 4:1–3,5,10,17,18,21,22; 5:7,8, 10,11; 6:3,5; 7:2–11,13–17; 8:1,4,22; 9:2,9,16,20,21; 10:18,20; 11:2,3,7,8, 13,15; 12:1; 13:1,2,4–6,13,19,20; 14:12, 18,21–24,37,39–41,45,47,48; 15:1,2,6, 17,26,28–30,35; 16:1; 17:2,3,8,10,11, 19,21,24–26,45,46,52,53; 18:6,16,18; 19:5; 20:12; 23:10,11,17; 24:2(3),14(15), 20(21); 25:1,30,32,34; 26:2,15,20; 27:1, 12; 28:1,3,4,19; 29:1,3; 30:25; 31:1,7; **2 Sam.** 1:3,12,19,24; 2:9,10,17,28; 3:10, 12,17–19,21,37,38; 4:1; 5:1–3,5,12,17; 6:1,5,15,19–21; 7:6–8,10,11,23,24,26,27; 8:15; 10:9,15,17–19; 11:1,11; 12:7,8,12; 13:12,13; 14:25; 15:2,6,10,13; 16:3,15, 18,21,22; 17:4,10,11,13–15,24,26; 18:6, 7,16,17; 19:8(9),9(10),11(12),22(23), 40–43(41–44); 20:1,2,14,19,23; 21:2,4, 5,15,17,21; 23:1,3,9; 24:1,2,4,9,15,25; **1 Kgs.** 1:3,20,30,34,35,48; 2:4,5,11, 15,32; 3:28; 4:1,7,20,25(5:5); 5:13(27); 6:1,13; 8:1–3,5,9,14–17,20,22,23,25, 26,30,33,34,36,38,41,43,52,55,56,59,62, 63,65,66; 9:5,7,20–22; 10:9; 11:2,9,16, 25,31,32,37,38,42; 12:1,3,16–21,24, 28,33; 14:7,10,13–16,18,19,21,24; 15:9,16,17,19,20,25–27,30–34; 16:2,5, 8,13,14,16,17,19–21,23,26,27,29,33; 17:1,14; 18:17–20; 19:10,14,16,18;

20:2,4,7,11,13,15,20–22,26–29,31,32,40, 41,43; 21:7,18,21,22,26; 2:1–6,8–10,17, 18,26,29–34,39,41,44(45),51–53(52–54); **2 Kgs.** 1:1,3,6,16,18; 2:12; 3:1,3–6,9–13, 24,27; 5:2,4–8,12,15; 6:8–12,21,23,26; 7:6,13; 8:12,16,18,25,26; 9:3,6,8,12, 14,21; 10:21,28–32,34,36; 13:1–6,8, 10–14,16,18,22,25; 14:1,8,9,11–13, 15–17,23–29; 15:1,8,9,11,12,15,17,18, 20,21,23,24,26–29,31,32; 16:3,5,7; 17:1, 2,6–9,13,18–24; 18:1,4,5,9–11; 19:15, 20,22; 21:2,3,7–9,12; 22:15,18; 23:13, 15,19,22,27; 24:13; **1 Chr.** 1:43; 2:7; 4:10; 5:17,26; 6:49(34),64(49); 9:1,2; 10:1,7; 11:1–4,10; 12:32,38,40; 13:2,5, 6,8; 14:2,8; 15:3,12,14,25,28; 16:3,4, 13,17,36,40; 17:5–7,9,10,21,22,24; 18:14; 19:10,16–19; 20:7; 21:1–5, 7,12,14; 22:1,2,6,9,10,12,13,17; 23:1,2,25; 24:19; 26:29,30; 27:1,16, 22–24; 28:1,4,5,8; 29:6,21,23,25–27,30; **2 Chr.** 1:2,13; 2:4(3),12(11),17(16); 5:2–4,6,10; 6:3–7,10–14,16,17,21,24,25, 27,29,32,33; 7:3,6,8,10,18; 8:2,7–9,11; 9:8,30; 10:1,3,16–19; 11:1,3,13,16; 12:1, 6,13; 13:4,5,12,15–18; 15:3,4,9,13,17; 16:1,3,4,11; 17:1,4; 18:3–5,7–9,16,17, 19,25,28–34; 19:8; 20:7,10,19,29,34,35; 21:2,4,6,13; 22:5; 23:2; 24:5,6,9,16; 25:6, 7,9,17,18,21–23,25,26; 27:7; 28:2,3,5, 8,13,19,23,26,27; 29:7,10,24,27; 30:1, 5,21,25,26; 31:1,5,6,8; 32:17,32; 33:2, 7–9,16,18; 34:7,9,21,23,26,33; 35:3, 4,17,18,25,27; 36:8,13; **Ezra** 1:3; 2:2, 59,70; 3:1,2,10,11; 4:1,3; 6:21,22; 7:6 ,7,10,11,28; 8:25,29,35; 9:1,4,15; 10:1, 2,5,10,25; **Neh.** 1:6; 2:10; 7:7,61,73; 8:1,14,17; 9:1,2; 10:33(34),39(40); 11:3,20; 12:47; 13:2,3,18,26; **Ps.** 14:7; 22:3(4),23(24); 25:22; 41:13(14); 50:7; 53:6(7); 59:5(6); 68:8(9),26(27),34(35), 35(36); 69:6(7); 71:22; 72:18; 73:1; 76:1(2); 78:5,21,31,41,55,59,71; 80:1(2); 81:4(5),8(9),11(12),13(14); 83:4(5); 89:18(19); 98:3; 103:7; 105:10,23; 106:48; 114:1,2; 115:9,12; 118:2; 121:4; 122:4; 124:1; 125:5; 128:6; 129:1; 130:7, 8; 131:3; 135:4,12,19; 136:11,14,22; 147:2,19; 148:14; 149:2; **Prov.** 1:1; **Eccl.** 1:12; **Song** 3:7; **Isa.** 1:3,4,24; 4:2; 5:7, 19,24; 7:1; 8:14,18; 9:8(7),12(11),14(13); 10:17,20,22; 11:12,16; 12:6; 14:1,2; 17:3,6,7,9; 19:24,25; 21:10,17; 24:15; 27:6,12; 29:19,23; 30:11,12,15,29; 31:1,6; 37:16,21,23; 40:27; 41:8,14,16, 17,20; 42:24; 43:1,3,14,15,22,28; 44:1, 5,6,21,23; 45:3,4,11,15,17,25; 46:3,13; 47:4; 48:1,2,12,17; 49:3,5–7; 52:12; 54:5; 55:5; 56:8; 60:9,14; 63:7,16; 66:20; **Jer.** 2:3,4,14,26,31; 3:6,8,11,12,18,20,21,23; 4:1; 5:11,15; 6:9; 7:3,12,21; 9:15(14), 26(25); 10:1,16; 11:3,10,17; 12:14; 13:11,12; 14:8; 16:9,14,15; 17:13; 18:6,13; 19:3,15; 21:4; 23:2,6–8,13; 24:5; 25:15,27; 27:4,21; 28:2,14; 29:4,8,21, 23,25; 30:2–4,10; 31:1,2,4,7,9,10,21,23, 27,31,33,36,37; 32:14,15,20,21,30,32,36; 33:4,7,14,17; 34:2,13; 35:13,17–19; 36:2; 37:7; 38:17; 39:16; 41:9; 42:9,15,18; 43:10; 44:2,7,11,25; 45:2; 46:25,27; 48:1,13,27; 49:1,2; 50:4,17–20,29,33; 51:5,33,49; **Lam.** 2:1,3,5; **Ezek.** 2:3; 3:1,4,5,7,17; 4:3–5,13; 5:4; 6:2,3,5,11; 7:2; 8:4,6,10–12; 9:3,8,9; 10:19,20; 11:5,10,11,13,15,17,22; 12:6,9,10,19, 22–24,27; 13:2,4,5,9,16; 14:1,4–7,9,11; 17:2,23; 18:2,3,6,15,25,29–31; 19:1,9; 20:1,3,5,13,27,30,31,38–40,42,44; 21:2(7),3(8),12(17),25(30); 22:6,18; 24:21; 25:3,6,14; 27:17; 28:24,25; 29:6, 16,21; 33:7,10,11,20,24,28; 34:2,13, 14,30; 35:5,12,15; 36:1,4,6,8,10,12, 17,21,22,32,37; 37:11,12,16,19,21,22,28; 38:8,14,16–19; 39:2,4,7,9,11,12,17,22, 23,25,29; 40:2,4; 43:2,7,10; 44:2,6,9,10, 12,15,22,28,29; 45:6,8,9,15–17; 47:13, 18,21,22; 48:11,19,29,31; **Dan.** 1:3; 9:7,11,20; **Hos.** 1:1,4–6,10(2:1),11(2:2); 3:1,4,5; 4:1,15,16; 5:1,3,5,9; 6:10; 7:1,10; 8:2,3,6,8,14; 9:1,7,10; 10:1,6,8,9,15; 11:1,8,12(12:1); 12:12(13),13(14); 13:1,9; 14:1(2),5(6); **Joel** 2:27; 3:2(4:2),16(4:16);

Amos 1:1; 2:6,11; 3:1,12,14; 4:5,12; 5:1–4,25; 6:1,14; 7:8–11,15–17; 8:2; 9:7,9,14; **Obad.** 1:20; **Mic.** 1:5,13–15; 2:12; 3:1,8,9; 5:1(4:14),2(1),3(2); 6:2; **Nah.** 2:2(3); **Zeph.** 2:9; 3:13–15; **Zech.** 1:19(2:2); 8:13; 9:1; 11:14; 12:1; **Mal.** 1:1,5; 2:11,16; 4:4(3:22).

3479. יִשְׂרָאֵל *yiśra'ēl* **Aram. masc. proper noun**
(Israel; corr. to Hebr. 3478,B)
Ezra 5:1,11; 6:14,16,17; 7:13,15.

3480. יְשַׂרְאֵלָה y^e*śar'ēlāh* **masc. proper noun**
(Jesarela)
1 Chr. 25:14.

3481. יִשְׂרְאֵלִי *yiśr*^{e}*'ēliy* **masc. proper noun**
(Israelite)
Lev. 24:10; **2 Sam.** 17:25.

3482. יִשְׂרְאֵלִית *yiśr*^{e}*'ēliyṯ* **fem. proper noun**
(female Israelite)
Lev. 24:10,11.

3483. יִשְׁרָה *yišrāh* **fem. noun**
(uprightness)
1 Kgs. 3:6.

3484. יְשֻׁרוּן y^e*šurûn* **masc. proper noun**
(Jeshurun)
Deut. 32:15; 33:5,26; **Isa.** 44:2.

3485. A. יִשָּׂשכָר *yiśśaśḵār* **masc. proper noun**
(Issachar: son of Jacob)
Gen. 30:18; 35:23; 46:13; 49:14; **Ex.** 1:3; **1 Chr.** 2:1; 7:1.
B. יִשָּׂשכָר *yiśśaśḵār* **masc. proper noun**
(Issachar: tribe or territory of Issachar)
Num. 1:8,28,29; 2:5; 7:18; 10:15; 13:7; 26:23,25; 34:26; **Deut.** 27:12; 33:18; **Josh.** 17:10,11; 19:17,23; 21:6,28; **Judg.** 5:15; 10:1; **1 Kgs.** 4:17; 15:27; **1 Chr.** 6:62(47),72(57); 7:5; 12:32,40; 27:18; **2 Chr.** 30:18; **Ezek.** 48:25,26,33.
C. יִשָּׂשכָר *yiśśaśḵār* **masc. proper noun**
(Issachar: son of Obed-Edom)
1 Chr. 26:5.

3486. יָשֵׁשׁ *yāšēš* **masc. adj.**
(aged, decrepit)
2 Chr. 36:17.

3487. יָת *yāṯ* **Aram. particle**
(sign of the direct object; corr. to Hebr. 853)
Dan. 3:12.

3488. יְתִב y^e*ṯiḇ* **Aram. verb**
(to sit, to dwell, to cause to dwell)
Ezra 4:10,17; **Dan.** 7:9,10,26.

3489. יָתֵד *yaṯēḏ* **fem. noun**
(pin, peg, stake)
Ex. 27:19; 35:18; 38:20,31; 39:40; **Num.** 3:37; 4:32; **Deut.** 23:13(14); **Judg.** 4:21,22; 5:26; 16:14; **Ezra** 9:8; **Isa.** 22:23,25; 33:20; 54:2; **Ezek.** 15:3; **Zech.** 10:4.

3490. יָתוֹם *yāṯôm* **masc. noun**
(an orphan, fatherless child)
Ex. 22:22(21),24(23); **Deut.** 10:18; 14:29; 16:11,14; 24:17,19–21; 26:12,13; 27:19; **Job** 6:27; 22:9; 24:3,9; 29:12; 31:17,21; **Ps.** 10:14,18; 68:5(6); 82:3; 94:6; 109:9,12; 146:9; **Prov.** 23:10; **Isa.** 1:17,23; 9:17(16); 10:2; **Jer.** 5:28; 7:6; 22:3; 49:11; **Lam.** 5:3; **Ezek.** 22:7; **Hos.** 14:3(4); **Zech.** 7:10; **Mal.** 3:5.

3491. יְתוּר y^e*ṯûr* **masc. noun**
(area of ranging, roaming)
Job 39:8(NASB, NIV, *tûr* [8446]).

3492. יַתִּיר *yattiyr,* יַתִּר *yattir* **proper noun**
(Jattir)
Josh. 15:48; 21:14; **1 Sam.** 30:27; **1 Chr.** 6:57(42).

3493. יַתִּיר *yattiyr* **Aram. adj.**
(excellent, outstanding)
Dan. 2:31; 3:22; 4:36(33); 5:12,14; 6:3(4); 7:7,19.

3494. יִתְלָה *yiṯlāh* **proper noun**
(Ithlah)
Josh. 19:42.

3495. יִתְמָה *yiṯmāh* **masc. proper noun**
(Ithmah)
1 Chr. 11:46.

3496. יַתְנִיאֵל *yaṯniy'ēl* **masc. proper noun**
(Jathniel)
1 Chr. 26:2.

3497. יִתְנָן *yiṯnān* **proper noun**
(Ithnan)
Josh. 15:23.

3498. יָתַר *yāṯar* **verb**
(to remain, to be left over)
Gen. 30:36; 32:24(25); 44:20; 49:4; **Ex.** 10:15; 12:10; 16:19,20; 28:10; 29:34; 36:7; **Lev.** 2:3,10; 6:16(9); 7:16,17; 8:32; 10:12,16; 14:18,29; 19:6; 22:30; 27:18; **Num.** 26:65; 33:55; **Deut.** 28:11,54; 30:9; **Josh.** 11:11,22; 17:2,6; 18:2; 21:5, 20,26,34,40(38); **Judg.** 8:10; 9:5; 21:7,16; **Ruth** 2:14,18; **1 Sam.** 2:36; 15:15; 25:34; 30:9; **2 Sam.** 8:4; 9:1; 13:30; 17:12; **1 Kgs.** 9:20,21; 15:18; 17:17; 18:22; 19:10,14; 20:30; **2 Kgs.** 4:7,43,44; 20:17; **1 Chr.** 6:61(46),70(55), 77(62); 18:4; 24:20; **2 Chr.** 8:7,8; 31:10; **Neh.** 6:1; **Ps.** 79:11; 106:11; **Prov.** 2:21; **Isa.** 1:8,9; 4:3; 7:22; 30:17; 39:6; **Jer.** 27:18,19,21; 34:7; 44:7; **Ezek.** 6:8; 12:16; 14:22; 34:18; 39:14,28; 48:15, 18,21; **Dan.** 10:13; **Amos** 6:9; **Zech.** 13:8; 14:16.

3499. I. יֶתֶר *yeṯer* **masc. noun**
(remainder, excess, excellence)
Gen. 49:3; **Ex.** 10:5; 23:11; **Lev.** 14:17; **Num.** 31:32; **Deut.** 3:11,13; 28:54; **Josh.** 12:4; 13:12,27; 23:12; **Judg.** 7:6; **1 Sam.** 13:2; **2 Sam.** 10:10; 12:28; 21:2; **1 Kgs.** 11:41; 12:23; 14:19,29; 15:7,23,31; 16:5,14,20,27; 22:39,45(46),46(47); **2 Kgs.** 1:18; 8:23; 10:34; 12:19(20); 13:8,12; 14:15,18,28; 15:6,11,15,21, 26,31,36; 16:19; 20:20; 21:17,25; 23:28; 24:5; 25:11; **1 Chr.** 19:11; **2 Chr.** 13:22; 20:34; 25:26; 26:22; 27:7; 28:26; 32:32; 33:18; 35:26; 36:8; **Neh.** 2:16; 4:14(8), 19(13); 6:1,14; **Job** 4:21(NASB, NIV, see II); 22:20; **Ps.** 17:14; 31:23(24); **Prov.** 17:7; **Isa.** 38:10; 44:19; 56:12; **Jer.** 27:19; 29:1; 39:9; 52:15; **Ezek.** 34:18; 48:23; **Dan.** 8:9; **Joel** 1:4; **Mic.** 5:3(2); **Hab.** 2:8; **Zeph.** 2:9; **Zech.** 14:2.
II. יֶתֶר *yeṯer* **masc. noun**
(cord, thong, string)
Judg. 16:7–9; **Job** 4:21(KJV, see I); 30:11; **Ps.** 11:2.

3500. A. יֶתֶר *yeṯer* **masc. proper noun**
(Jethro: father of Zipporah)
Ex. 4:18.
B. יֶתֶר *yeṯer* **masc. proper noun**
(Jether: eldest son of Gideon)
Judg. 8:20.
C. יֶתֶר *yeṯer* **masc. proper noun**
(Jether: father of Amasa)
1 Kgs. 2:5,32; **1 Chr.** 2:17.
D. יֶתֶר *yeṯer* **masc. proper noun**
(Jether: son of Jada)
1 Chr. 2:32.
E. יֶתֶר *yeṯer* **masc. proper noun**
(Jether: son of Ezra)
1 Chr. 4:17.
F. יֶתֶר *yeṯer* **masc. proper noun**
(Jether: an Asherite)
1 Chr. 7:38.

3501. יִתְרָא *yiṯrā'* **masc. proper noun**
(Ithra, Jether)
2 Sam. 17:25.

3502. יִתְרָה *yiṯrāh* **fem. noun**
(abundance, wealth)
Isa. 15:7; **Jer.** 48:36.

3503. יִתְרוֹ *yiṯrô* **masc. proper noun**
(Jethro)
Ex. 3:1; 4:18; 18:1,2,5,6,9,10,12.

3504. יִתְרוֹן *yiṯrôn* **fem. noun**
(advantage, profit, gain)
Eccl. 1:3; 2:11,13; 3:9; 5:9(8),16(15); 7:12; 10:10,11.

3505. יִתְרִי *yiṯriy* **masc. proper noun**
(Ithrite)
2 Sam. 23:38; **1 Chr.** 2:53; 11:40.

3506. A. יִתְרָן *yiṯrān* **masc. proper noun**
(Ithran: an Edomite)
Gen. 36:26; **1 Chr.** 1:41.
B. יִתְרָן *yiṯrān* **masc. proper noun**
(Ithran: an Asherite)
1 Chr. 7:37.

3507. יִתְרְעָם *yiṯr*^{e}*'ām* **masc. proper noun**
(Ithream)
2 Sam. 3:5; **1 Chr.** 3:3.

3508. יֹתֶרֶת *yōṯereṯ* **fem. noun**
(caudate lobe of the liver)
Ex. 29:13,22; **Lev.** 3:4,10,15; 4:9; 7:4; 8:16,25; 9:10,19.

3509. יְתֵת *y*^{e}*ṯēṯ* **masc. proper noun**
(Jetheth)
Gen. 36:40; **1 Chr.** 1:51.

כ Kaph

3510. כָּאַב *kā'ab̲* **verb**
(to be sore, to be in pain, to be grieving)
Gen. 34:25; **2 Kgs.** 3:19; **Job** 5:18; 14:22; **Ps.** 69:29(30); **Prov.** 14:13; **Ezek.** 13:22; 28:24.

3511. כְּאֵב *k^e'ēb̲* **masc. noun**
(pain, anguish, sorrow)
Job 2:13; 16:6; **Ps.** 39:2(3); **Isa.** 17:11; 65:14; **Jer.** 15:18.

3512. כָּאָה *kā'āh* **verb**
(to be brokenhearted, to be disheartened)
Ps. 109:16; **Ezek.** 13:22; **Dan.** 11:30.

3513. כָּבֵד *kāb̲ēd̲* **verb**
(to be heavy, to be honorable, to be rich)
Gen. 13:2(NASB, *kāb̲ēd* [3515]); 18:20; 34:19; 48:10; **Ex.** 5:9; 8:15(11),32(28); 9:7,34; 10:1; 14:4,17,18; 20:12; **Lev.** 10:3; **Num.** 22:15,17,37; 24:11; **Deut.** 5:16; 28:58; **Judg.** 1:35; 9:9; 13:17; 20:34; **1 Sam.** 2:29,30; 4:18(NASB, NIV, *kāb̲ēd* [3515]); 5:6,11; 6:6; 9:6; 15:30; 22:14; 31:3; **2 Sam.** 6:20,22; 10:3; 13:25; 14:26; 23:19,23; **1 Kgs.** 12:10,14; **2 Kgs.** 14:10; **1 Chr.** 4:9; 10:3; 11:21,25; 19:3; **2 Chr.** 10:10,14; 25:19; **Neh.** 5:15,18; **Job** 6:3; 14:21; 23:2; 33:7; **Ps.** 15:4; 22:23(24); 32:4; 38:4(5); 50:15,23; 86:9,12; 87:3; 91:15; 149:8; **Prov.** 3:9; 4:8; 8:24; 12:9; 13:18; 14:31; 27:18; **Isa.** 3:5; 6:10; 9:1(8:23); 23:8,9; 24:15,20; 25:3; 26:15; 29:13; 43:4,20,23; 47:6; 49:5; 58:13; 59:1; 60:13; 66:5; **Jer.** 30:19; **Lam.** 1:8; 3:7; **Ezek.** 27:25; 28:22; 39:13; **Dan.** 11:38; **Nah.** 3:10,15; **Hab.** 2:6; **Hag.** 1:8; **Zech.** 7:11; **Mal.** 1:6.

3514. כֹּבֶד *kōb̲ed̲* **masc. noun**
(weight, heaviness, thickness)
Prov. 27:3; **Isa.** 21:15; 30:27; **Nah.** 3:3.

3515. כָּבֵד *kāb̲ēd̲* **adj.**
(heavy, great, grievous)
Gen. 12:10; 13:2(KJV, NIV, *kāb̲ēd* [3513]); 41:31; 43:1; 47:4,13; 50:9–11; **Ex.** 4:10; 7:14; 8:24(20); 9:3,18,24; 10:14; 12:38; 17:12; 18:18; 19:16; **Num.** 11:14; 20:20; **1 Kgs.** 3:9; 10:2; 12:4,11; **2 Kgs.** 6:14; 18:17; **2 Chr.** 9:1; 10:4,11; **Ps.** 38:4(5); **Prov.** 27:3; **Isa.** 1:4; 32:2; 36:2; **Ezek.** 3:5,6.

3516. כָּבֵד *kāb̲ēd̲* **masc. noun**
(liver)
Ex. 29:13,22; **Lev.** 3:4,10,15; 4:9; 7:4; 8:16,25; 9:10,19; **Prov.** 7:23; **Lam.** 2:11; **Ezek.** 21:21(26).

3517. כְּבֵדֻת *k^eb̲ēd̲ut̲* **fem. noun**
(heaviness, difficulty)
Ex. 14:25.

3518. כָּבָה *kāb̲āh* **verb**
(to quench, to put out)
Lev. 6:12(5),13(6); **1 Sam.** 3:3; **2 Sam.** 14:7; 21:17; **2 Kgs.** 22:17; **2 Chr.** 29:7; 34:25; **Prov.** 26:20; 31:18; **Song** 8:7; **Isa.** 1:31; 34:10; 42:3; 43:17; 66:24; **Jer.** 4:4; 7:20; 17:27; 21:12; **Ezek.** 20:47(21:3),48(21:4); 32:7; **Amos** 5:6.

3519. כָּבוֹד *kāb̲ôd̲*, כָּבֹד *kāb̲ōd̲* **masc. noun**
(glory, honor, splendor)
Gen. 31:1; 45:13; 49:6; **Ex.** 16:7,10; 24:16,17; 28:2,40; 29:43; 33:18,22; 40:34,35; **Lev.** 9:6,23; **Num.** 14:10,21,22; 16:19,42(17:7); 20:6; 24:11; **Deut.** 5:24(21); **Josh.** 7:19; **1 Sam.** 2:8;

4:21,22; 6:5; **1 Kgs.** 3:13; 8:11; **1 Chr.** 16:24,28,29; 17:18; 29:12,28; **2 Chr.** 1:11,12; 5:14; 7:1–3; 17:5; 18:1; 26:18; 32:27,33; **Neh.** 9:5; **Esth.** 1:4; 5:11; **Job** 19:9; 29:20; **Ps.** 3:3(4); 4:2(3); 7:5(6); 8:5(6); 16:9; 19:1(2); 21:5(6); 24:7–10; 26:8; 29:1–3,9; 30:12(13); 45:13(14)(KJV, NIV, *kāḇôḏ* [3520,I]); 49:16(17),17(18); 57:5(6),8(9),11(12); 62:7(8); 63:2(3); 66:2; 72:19; 73:24; 79:9; 84:11(12); 85:9(10); 96:3,7,8; 97:6; 102:15(16), 16(17); 104:31; 106:20; 108:1(2),5(6); 112:9; 113:4; 115:1; 138:5; 145:5,11,12; 149:5; **Prov.** 3:16,35; 8:18; 11:16; 15:33; 18:12; 20:3; 21:21; 22:4; 25:2,27; 26:1,8; 29:23; **Eccl.** 6:2; 10:1; **Isa.** 3:8; 4:2,5; 5:13; 6:3; 8:7; 10:3,16,18; 11:10; 14:18; 16:14; 17:3,4; 21:16; 22:18,23,24; 24:23; 35:2; 40:5; 42:8,12; 43:7; 48:11; 58:8; 59:19; 60:1,2,13; 61:6; 62:2; 66:11,12, 18,19; **Jer.** 2:11; 13:16; 14:21; 17:12; 48:18; **Ezek.** 1:28; 3:12,23; 8:4; 9:3; 10:4, 18,19; 11:22,23; 23:41(KJV, NIV, *kāḇôḏ* [3520,I]); 31:18; 39:21; 43:2,4,5; 44:4; **Dan.** 11:39; **Hos.** 4:7; 9:11; 10:5; **Mic.** 1:15; **Nah.** 2:9(10); **Hab.** 2:14,16; **Hag.** 2:3,7,9; **Zech.** 2:5(9),8(12); **Mal.** 1:6; 2:2.

3520. I. כָּבוֹד *kāḇôḏ* **adj.**
(glorious)
Ps. 45:13(14)(NASB, *kāḇôḏ* [3519]); **Ezek.** 23:41(NASB, *kāḇôḏ* [3519]).
II. כְּבוּדָּה *k*^e^*ḇûddāh* **fem. noun**
(abundance, possessions, riches)
Judg. 18:21.

3521. כָּבוּל *kāḇûl* **proper noun**
(Cabul)
Josh. 19:27; **1 Kgs.** 9:13.

3522. כַּבּוֹן *kabbôn* **proper noun**
(Cabbon)
Josh. 15:40.

3523. כָּבִיר *kāḇiyr* **masc. noun**
(garment, pillow, quilt)
1 Sam. 19:13,16.

3524. כַּבִּיר *kabbiyr* **adj.**
(mighty, great)
Job 8:2; 15:10; 31:25; 34:17,24; 36:5; **Isa.** 10:13(NIV, [K^e^] *'abbiyr* [47]); 16:14; 17:12; 28:2.

3525. כֶּבֶל *keḇel* **masc. noun**
(fetters, shackles)
Ps. 105:18; 149:8.

3526. כָּבַס *kāḇas* **verb**
(to wash, to be washed)
Gen. 49:11; **Ex.** 19:10,14; **Lev.** 6:27(20); 11:25,28,40; 13:6,34,54–56,58; 14:8,9,47; 15:5–8,10,11,13,17,21,22,27; 16:26,28; 17:15,16; **Num.** 8:7,21; 19:7, 8,10,19,21; 31:24; **2 Sam.** 19:24(25); **2 Kgs.** 18:17; **Ps.** 51:2(4),7(9); **Isa.** 7:3; 36:2; **Jer.** 2:22; 4:14; **Mal.** 3:2.

3527. כָּבַר *kāḇar* **verb**
(to multiply)
Job 35:16; 36:31(KJV, *makbiyr* [4342]).

3528. כְּבָר *k*^e^*ḇār* **adv.**
(already, long ago)
Eccl. 1:10; 2:12,16; 3:15; 4:2; 6:10; 9:6,7.

3529. כְּבָר *k*^e^*ḇār* **proper noun**
(the river Chebar)
Ezek. 1:1,3; 3:15,23; 10:15,20,22; 43:3.

3530. כִּבְרָה *kiḇrāh* **fem. noun**
(a little distance, some distance)
Gen. 35:16; 48:7; **2 Kgs.** 5:19.

3531. כְּבָרָה *k*^e^*ḇārāh* **fem. noun**
(sieve)
Amos 9:9.

3532. כֶּבֶשׂ *keḇeś* **masc. noun**
(male lamb, sheep)
Ex. 12:5; 29:38–41; **Lev.** 4:32; 9:3; 12:6; 14:10,12,13,21,24,25; 23:12,18–20; **Num.** 6:12,14; 7:15,17,21,23,27,29,33, 35,39,41,45,47,51,53,57,59,63,65,69,71,

75,77,81,83,87,88; 15:5,11; 28:3,4,7–9, 11,13,14,19,21,27,29; 29:2,4,8,10,13, 15,17,18,20,21,23,24,26,27,29,30,32,33, 36,37; **1 Chr.** 29:21; **2 Chr.** 29:21,22,32; 35:7; **Ezra** 8:35; **Job** 31:20; **Prov.** 27:26; **Isa.** 1:11; 5:17; 11:6; **Jer.** 11:19; **Ezek.** 46:4–7,11,13,15; **Hos.** 4:16.

3533. כָּבַשׁ *kāḇaš* **verb**
(to subdue, to bring into subjection, to enslave)
Gen. 1:28; **Num.** 32:22,29; **Josh.** 18:1; **2 Sam.** 8:11; **1 Chr.** 22:18; **2 Chr.** 28:10; **Neh.** 5:5; **Esth.** 7:8; **Jer.** 34:11,16; **Mic.** 7:19; **Zech.** 9:15.

3534. כֶּבֶשׁ *keḇeš* **masc. noun**
(footstool)
2 Chr. 9:18.

3535. כִּבְשָׂה *kiḇśāh*, כַּבְשָׂה *kaḇśāh* **fem. noun**
(ewe lamb, female lamb)
Gen. 21:28–30; **Lev.** 14:10; **Num.** 6:14; **2 Sam.** 12:3,4,6.

3536. כִּבְשָׁן *kiḇšān* **masc. noun**
(furnace, kiln)
Gen. 19:28; **Ex.** 9:8,10; 19:18.

3537. כַּד *kaḏ* **fem. noun**
(jar, pitcher)
Gen. 24:14–18,20,43,45,46; **Judg.** 7:16,19,20; **1 Kgs.** 17:12,14,16; 18:33(34); **Eccl.** 12:6.

3538. כְּדַב *k^e^ḏaḇ* **Aram. adj.**
(misleading, lying)
Dan. 2:9.

3539. כַּדְכֹּד *kaḏkōḏ* **masc. noun**
(ruby, agate)
Isa. 54:12; **Ezek.** 27:16.

3540. כְּדָרְלָעֹמֶר *k^e^ḏārlāʿōmer* **masc. proper noun**
(Chedorlaomer)
Gen. 14:1,4,5,9,17.

3541. כֹּה *kōh* **particle**
(thus, in this way, this is what)
Gen. 15:5; 22:5; 24:30; 31:8,37; 32:4(5); 45:9; 50:17; **Ex.** 2:12; 3:14,15; 4:22; 5:1,10,15; 7:16,17; 8:1(7:26),20(8:16); 9:1,13; 10:3; 11:4; 19:3; 20:22; 32:27; **Num.** 6:23; 8:7; 11:31; 20:14; 22:16,30; 23:5,15,16; 32:8; **Deut.** 7:5; **Josh.** 6:3,14; 7:13; 17:14; 22:16; 24:2; **Judg.** 6:8; 11:15; **Ruth** 1:17; 2:8; **1 Sam.** 2:27; 3:17; 9:9; 10:18; 11:7,9; 14:9,10,44; 15:2; 17:27; 18:25; 20:7,13,22; 25:6,22; 27:11; **2 Sam.** 3:9,35; 7:5,8; 11:25; 12:7,11; 15:26; 16:7,10(NASB, NIV, [K^e^] *kiy* [3588]); 18:30,33(19:1); 19:13(14); 24:12; **1 Kgs.** 2:23,30; 5:11(25); 11:31; 12:10,24; 13:2,21; 14:7; 17:14; 18:45; 19:2; 20:2,5,10,13,14,28,42; 21:19; 22:11,20,27; **2 Kgs.** 1:4,6,11,16; 2:21; 3:16,17; 4:43; 6:31; 7:1; 9:3,6,12,18,19; 18:19,29,31; 19:3,6,10,20,32; 20:1,5; 21:12; 22:15,16,18; **1 Chr.** 17:4,7; 21:10,11; **2 Chr.** 10:10; 11:4; 12:5; 18:10,26; 19:9,10; 20:15; 21:12; 24:11,20; 32:10; 34:23,24,26; 36:23; **Ezra** 1:2; **Neh.** 13:18; **Isa.** 7:7; 8:11; 10:24; 18:4; 20:6; 21:6,16; 22:15; 24:13; 28:16; 29:22; 30:12,15; 31:4; 36:4,14,16; 37:3,6,10,21,33; 38:1,5; 42:5; 43:1,14,16; 44:2,6,24; 45:1,11,14,18; 48:17; 49:7,8, 22,25; 50:1; 51:22; 52:3,4; 56:1,4; 57:15; 65:8,13; 66:1,12; **Jer.** 2:2,5; 4:3,27; 5:13,14; 6:6,9,16,21,22; 7:3,20,21; 8:4; 9:7(6),15(14),17(16),22(21),23(22); 10:2,18; 11:3,11,21,22; 12:14; 13:1,9, 12,13; 14:10,15; 15:2,19; 16:3,5,9; 17:5, 19,21; 18:11,13; 19:1,3,11,15; 20:4; 21:3, 4,8,12; 22:1,3,6,11,18,30; 23:2,15,16, 29,35,37,38; 24:5,8; 25:8,15,27,28,32; 26:2,4,18; 27:2,4,16,19,21; 28:2,11,13, 14,16; 29:4,8,10,16,17,21,25,31,32; 30:2,5,12,18; 31:2,7,15,16,23,35,37; 32:3,14,15,28,36,42; 33:2,4,10,12,17, 20,25; 34:2,4,13,17; 35:13,17,18,19;

36:29,30; 37:7,9; 38:2,3,17; 39:16; 42:9,15,18; 43:10; 44:2,7,11,25,30; 45:2,4; 47:2; 48:1,40; 49:1,7,12,28,35; 50:18,33; 51:1,33,36,58; **Lam.** 2:20; **Ezek.** 2:4; 3:11,27; 5:5,7,8; 6:3,11; 7:2,5; 11:5,7,16,17; 12:10,19,23,28; 13:3,8,13, 18,20; 14:4,6,21; 15:6; 16:3,36,59; 17:3,9, 19,22; 20:3,5,27,30,39,47(21:3); 21:3,9, 24,26,28; 22:3,19,28; 23:22,28,32,35, 39,46; 26:3,6,9,21; 25:3,6,8,12,13,15,16; 26:3,7,15,19; 27:3; 28:2,6,12,22,25; 29:3, 8,13,19; 30:2,6,10,13,22; 31:10,15; 32:3,11; 33:25,27; 34:2,10,11,17,20; 35:3,14; 36:2–7,13,22,33,37; 37:5,9,12, 19,21; 38:3,10,14,17; 39:1,17,25; 43:18; 44:6,9; 45:9,18; 46:1,16; 47:13; **Amos** 1:3,6,9,11,13; 2:1,4,6; 3:11,12; 4:12; 5:3,4,16; 7:1,4,7,11,17; 8:1; **Obad.** 1:1; **Mic.** 2:3; 3:5; **Nah.** 1:12; **Hag.** 1:2,5,7; 2:6,11; **Zech.** 1:3,4,14,16,17; 2:8(12); 3:7; 6:12; 7:9; 8:2–4,6,7,9,14,19,20,23; 11:4; **Mal.** 1:4.

3542. כָּה *kāh* **Aram. adv.**
(at this point, hitherto; corr. to Hebr. 3541)
Dan. 7:28.

3543. I. כָּהָה *kāhāh* **verb**
(to faint, to become expressionless, to become dim)
Gen. 27:1; **Lev.** 13:6(KJV, NASB, *kēheh* [3544]),21(KJV, NASB, *kēheh* [3544]), 26(KJV, NASB, *kēheh* [3544]),28(KJV, NASB, *kēheh* [3544]),39(KJV, NASB, *kēheh* [3544]),56(KJV, NASB, *kēheh* [3544]); **Deut.** 34:7; **Job** 17:7; **Isa.** 42:4; **Ezek.** 21:7(12); **Zech.** 11:17.
II. כָּהָה *kāhāh* **verb**
(to rebuke)
1 Sam. 3:13.

3544. כֵּהֶה *kēheh* **fem. adj.**
(dim, faint, dark)
Lev. 13:6(NIV, *kāhāh* [3543,I]),21(NIV, *kāhāh* [3543,I]),26(NIV, *kāhāh* [3543,I]), 28(NIV, *kāhāh* [3543,I]),39(NIV, *kāhāh* [3543,I]),56(NIV, *kāhāh* [3543,I]); **1 Sam.** 3:2; **Isa.** 42:3; 61:3.

3545. כֵּהָה *kēhāh* **fem. noun**
(healing, relief)
Nah. 3:19.

3546. כְּהַל *k^ehal* **Aram. verb**
(to be able)
Dan. 2:26; 4:18(15); 5:8,15.

3547. כָּהַן *kāhan* **verb**
(to serve as priest)
Ex. 28:1,3,4,41; 29:1,44; 30:30; 31:10; 35:19; 39:41; 40:13,15; **Lev.** 7:35; 16:32; **Num.** 3:3,4; **Deut.** 10:6; **1 Chr.** 6:10 (5:36); 24:2; **2 Chr.** 11:14; **Isa.** 61:10; **Ezek.** 44:13; **Hos.** 4:6.

3548. כֹּהֵן *kōhēn* **masc. noun**
(priest)
Gen. 14:18; 41:45,50; 46:20; 47:22,26; **Ex.** 2:16; 3:1; 18:1; 19:6,22,24; 29:30; 31:10; 35:19; 38:21; 39:41; **Lev.** 1:5, 7–9,11–13,15,17; 2:2,8,9,16; 3:2,11,16; 4:3,5–7,10,16,17,20,25,26,30,31,34,35; 5:6,8,10,12,13,16,18; 6:6(5:25),7(5:26), 10(3),12(5),22(15),23(16),26(19),29(22); 7:5–9,14,31,32,34; 12:6,8; 13:2–13, 15–17,19–23,25–28,30–34,36,37,39, 43,44,49,50,53–56; 14:2–5,11–20,23–29, 31,35,36,38–40,44,48; 15:14,15,29,30; 16:32,33; 17:5,6; 19:22; 21:1,9,10,21; 22:10–14; 23:10,11,20; 27:8,11,12,14, 18,21,23; **Num.** 3:3,6,32; 4:16,28,33; 5:8–10,15–19,21,23,25,26,30; 6:10,11, 16,17,19,20; 7:8; 10:8; 15:25,28; 16:37 (17:2),39(17:4); 18:28; 19:3,4,6,7; 25:7,11; 26:1,3,63,64; 27:2,19,21,22; 31:6,12,13,21,26,29,31,41,51,54; 32:2,28; 33:38; 34:17; 35:25,28,32; **Deut.** 17:9,12,18; 18:1,3; 19:17; 20:2; 21:5; 24:8; 26:3,4; 27:9; 31:9; **Josh.** 3:3,6,8,13–15,17; 4:3,9–11,16–18; 6:4,6, 8,9,12,13,16; 8:33; 14:1; 17:4; 19:51; 20:6; 21:1,4,13,19; 22:13,30–32; **Judg.** 17:5,10,12,13; 18:4,6,17–20,24,27,30;

1 Sam. 1:3,9; 2:11,13–15,28,35; 5:5; 6:2; 14:3,19,36; 21:1(2),2(3),4–6(5–7),9(10); 22:11,17–19,21; 23:9; 30:7; **2 Sam.** 8:17,18; 15:27,35; 17:15; 19:11(12); 20:25,26; **1 Kgs.** 1:7,8,19,25,26,32,34, 38,39,42,44,45; 2:22,26,27,35; 4:2,4,5; 8:3,4,6,10,11; 12:31,32; 13:2,33; **2 Kgs.** 10:11,19; 11:9,10,15,18; 12:2(3),4–10 (5–11),16(17); 16:10,11,15,16; 17:27, 28,32; 19:2; 22:4,8,10,12,14; 23:2,4,8, 9,20,24; 25:18; **1 Chr.** 9:2,10,30; 13:2; 15:11,14,24; 16:6,39; 18:16; 23:2; 24:6,31; 27:5; 28:13,21; 29:22; **2 Chr.** 4:6,9; 5:5,7,11,12,14; 6:41; 7:2,6; 8:14,15; 11:13,15; 13:9,10,12,14; 15:3; 17:8; 19:8,11; 22:11; 23:4,6,8,9,14,17,18; 24:2,5,11,20,25; 26:17–20; 29:4,16,21, 22,24,26,34; 30:3,15,16,21,24,25,27; 31:2,4,9,10,15,17,19; 34:5,9,14,18,30; 35:2,8,10,11,14,18; 36:14; **Ezra** 1:5; 2:36,61,63,69,70; 3:2,8,10,12; 6:20; 7:5,7,11; 8:15,24,29,30,33; 9:1,7; 10:5, 10,16,18; **Neh.** 2:16; 3:1,20,22,28; 5:12; 7:39,63,65,70,72,73; 8:2,9,13; 9:32,34, 38(10:1); 10:8(9),28(29),34(35),36–39 (37–40); 11:3,10,20; 12:1,7,12,22,26,30, 35,41,44; 13:4,5,13,28,30; **Job** 12:19; **Ps.** 78:64; 99:6; 110:4; 132:9,16; **Isa.** 8:2; 24:2; 28:7; 37:2; 61:6; 66:21; **Jer.** 1:1,18; 2:8,26; 4:9; 5:31; 6:13; 8:1,10; 13:13; 14:18; 18:18; 19:1; 20:1; 21:1; 23:11, 33,34; 26:7,8,11,16; 27:16; 28:1,5; 29:1,25,26,29; 31:14; 32:32; 33:18,21; 34:19; 37:3; 48:7; 49:3; 52:24; **Lam.** 1:4,19; 2:6,20; 4:13,16; **Ezek.** 1:3; 7:26; 22:26; 40:45,46; 42:13,14; 43:19,24,27; 44:15,21,22,30,31; 45:4,19; 46:2,19,20; 48:10,11,13; **Hos.** 4:4,9; 5:1; 6:9; **Joel** 1:9,13; 2:17; **Amos** 7:10; **Mic.** 3:11; **Zeph.** 1:4; 3:4; **Hag.** 1:1,12,14; 2:2,4, 11–13; **Zech.** 3:1,8; 6:11,13; 7:3,5; **Mal.** 1:6; 2:1,7.

3549. כָּהֵן *kāhēn* **Aram. masc. noun**
(priest; corr. to Hebr. 3548)
Ezra 6:9,16,18; 7:12,13,16,21,24.

3550. כְּהֻנָּה *k^ehunnāh* **fem. noun**
(priesthood)
Ex. 29:9; 40:15; **Num.** 3:10; 16:10; 18:1,7; 25:13; **Josh.** 18:7; **1 Sam.** 2:36; **Ezra** 2:62; **Neh.** 7:64; 13:29.

3551. כַּוָּה *kawwāh* **Aram. masc. noun**
(window)
Dan. 6:10(11).

3552. כּוּב *kûḇ* **proper noun**
(Chub: possibly another spelling for *lûḇ* [3864], Libya)
Ezek. 30:5.

3553. כּוֹבַע *kôḇa‘* **masc. noun**
(helmet)
1 Sam. 17:5; **2 Chr.** 26:14; **Isa.** 59:17; **Jer.** 46:4; **Ezek.** 27:10; 38:5.

3554. כָּוָה *kāwāh* **verb**
(to burn, to scorch)
Prov. 6:28; **Isa.** 43:2.

3555. כְּוִיָּה *k^ewiyyāh* **fem. noun**
(burn, burning)
Ex. 21:25.

3556. כּוֹכָב *kôḵāḇ* **masc. noun**
(star)
Gen. 1:16; 15:5; 22:17; 26:4; 37:9; **Ex.** 32:13; **Num.** 24:17; **Deut.** 1:10; 4:19; 10:22; 28:62; **Judg.** 5:20; **1 Chr.** 27:23; **Neh.** 4:21(15); 9:23; **Job** 3:9; 9:7; 22:12; 25:5; 38:7; **Ps.** 8:3(4); 136:9; 147:4; 148:3; **Eccl.** 12:2; **Isa.** 13:10; 14:13; 47:13; **Jer.** 31:35; **Ezek.** 32:7; **Dan.** 8:10; 12:3; **Joel** 2:10; 3:15(4:15); **Amos** 5:26; **Obad.** 1:4; **Nah.** 3:16.

3557. כּוּל *kûl* **verb**
(to hold, to contains feed, to supply)
Gen. 45:11; 47:12; 50:21; **Ruth** 4:15; **2 Sam.** 19:32(33),33(34); 20:3; **1 Kgs.** 4:7,27(5:7); 7:26,38; 8:27,64; 17:4,9; 18:4,13; 20:27; **2 Chr.** 2:6(5); 4:5; 6:18; 7:7; **Neh.** 9:21; **Ps.** 55:22(23); 112:5;

Prov. 18:14; **Isa.** 40:12; **Jer.** 2:13; 6:11; 10:10; 20:9; **Ezek.** 23:32; **Joel** 2:11; **Amos** 7:10; **Zech.** 11:16; **Mal.** 3:2.

3558. כּוּמָז *kûmāz* **masc. noun**
(ornament)
Ex. 35:22; **Num.** 31:50.

3559. כּוּן *kûn* **verb**
(to be established, to be prepared, to be firm)
Gen. 41:32; 43:16,25; **Ex.** 8:26(22); 15:17; 16:5; 19:11,15; 23:20; 34:2; **Num.** 21:27; 23:1,29; **Deut.** 13:14(15); 17:4; 19:3; 32:6; **Josh.** 1:11; 3:17; 4:3,4; 8:4; **Judg.** 12:6; 16:26,29; **1 Sam.** 7:3; 13:13; 20:31; 23:22,23; 26:4; **2 Sam.** 5:12; 7:12, 13,16,24,26; **1 Kgs.** 2:12,24,45,46; 5:18(32); 6:19; **1 Chr.** 9:32; 12:39; 14:2; 15:1,3,12; 16:30; 17:11,12,14,24; 22:3,5, 10,14; 28:2,7; 29:2,3,16,18,19; **2 Chr.** 1:4; 2:7(6),9(8); 3:1; 8:16; 12:1,14; 17:5; 19:3; 20:33; 26:14; 27:6; 29:19,35,36; 30:19; 31:11; 35:4,6,10,14–16,20; **Ezra** 3:3; 7:10; **Neh.** 8:10; **Esth.** 6:4; 7:10; **Job** 8:8; 11:13; 12:5; 15:23,35; 18:12; 21:8; 27:16,17; 28:27; 29:7; 31:15; 38:41; 42:7,8; **Ps.** 5:9(10); 7:9(10),12(13),13(14); 8:3(4); 9:7(8); 10:17; 11:2; 21:12(13); 24:2; 37:23; 38:17(18); 40:2(3); 48:8(9); 51:10(12); 57:6(7),7(8); 59:4(5); 65:6(7), 9(10); 68:9(10),10(11); 74:16; 78:8, 20,37; 87:5; 89:2(3),4(5),21(22),37(38); 90:17; 93:1,2; 96:10; 99:4; 101:7; 102:28(29); 103:19; 107:36; 108:1(2); 112:7; 119:5,73,90,133; 140:11(12); 141:2; 147:8; **Prov.** 3:19; 4:18,26; 6:8; 8:27; 12:3,19; 16:3,9,12; 19:29; 20:18; 21:29(NIV, [K^e] *biyn* [995]),31; 22:18; 24:3,27; 25:5; 29:14; 30:25; **Isa.** 2:2; 9:7(6); 14:21; 16:5; 30:33; 40:20; 45:18; 51:13; 54:14; 62:7; **Jer.** 10:12,23; 30:20; 33:2; 46:14; 51:12,15; **Ezek.** 4:3,7; 7:14; 16:7; 28:13; 38:7; 40:43; **Hos.** 6:3; **Amos** 4:12; **Mic.** 4:1; **Nah.** 2:3(4),5(6); **Hab.** 2:12; **Zeph.** 1:7; **Zech.** 5:11.

3560. כּוּן *kûn* **proper noun**
(Cun)
1 Chr. 18:8.

3561. כַּוָּן *kawwān* **masc. noun**
(cake, sacrificial cake)
Jer. 7:18; 44:19.

3562. A. כּוֹנַנְיָהוּ *kônanyāhû* **masc. proper noun**
(Conaniah: a Levite)
2 Chr. 31:12,13.
B. כּוֹנַנְיָהוּ *kônanyāhû* **masc. proper noun**
(Conaniah: a Levite)
2 Chr. 35:9.

3563. I. כּוֹס *kôs* **fem. noun**
(cup, goblet)
Gen. 40:11,13,21; **2 Sam.** 12:3; **1 Kgs.** 7:26; **2 Chr.** 4:5; **Ps.** 11:6; 16:5; 23:5; 75:8(9); 116:13; **Prov.** 23:31(KJV, [K^e] *kiys* [3599]); **Isa.** 51:17,22; **Jer.** 16:7; 25:15,17,28; 35:5; 49:12; 51:7; **Lam.** 4:21; **Ezek.** 23:31–33; **Hab.** 2:16.
II. כּוֹס *kôs* **fem. noun**
(screech owl, pelican)
Lev. 11:17; **Deut.** 14:16; **Ps.** 102:6(7).

3564. I. כּוּר *kûr* **masc. noun**
(furnace)
Deut. 4:20; **1 Kgs.** 8:51; **Prov.** 17:3; 27:21; **Isa.** 48:10; **Jer.** 11:4; **Ezek.** 22:18,20,22.
II. כּוּר *kûr* **verb**
(to pierce)
Ps. 22:16(17)(KJV, *kā'^eriy* [738,III]; NIV, *kārāh* [3738]).

3565. כּוֹר עָשָׁן *kôr 'āšān* **proper noun**
(Chorashan, variant spelling for *bôr* [953] and *'āšān* [6227])
1 Sam. 30:30(NASB, NIV, *bôr 'āšān*).

3566. כּוֹרֶשׁ *kôreš,* כֹּרֶשׁ *kōreš* **masc. proper noun**
(Cyrus)

2 Chr. 36:22,23; **Ezra** 1:1,2,7,8; 3:7; 4:3,5; **Isa.** 44:28; 45:1; **Dan.** 1:21; 10:1.

3567. כּוֹרֶשׁ *kôreš* **Aram. masc. proper noun**
(Cyrus; corr. to Hebr. 3566)
Ezra 5:13,14,17; 6:3,14; **Dan.** 6:28(29).

3568. A. כּוּשׁ *kûš* **masc. proper noun**
(Cush: son of Ham)
Gen. 10:6–8; **1 Chr.** 1:8–10.
B. כּוּשׁ *kûš* **masc. proper noun**
(Cush: land or people of Cush)
Gen. 2:13; **2 Kgs.** 19:9; **Esth.** 1:1; 8:9; **Job** 28:19; **Ps.** 68:31(32); 87:4; **Isa.** 11:11; 18:1; 20:3–5; 37:9; 43:3; 45:14; **Jer.** 46:9; **Ezek.** 29:10; 30:4,5,9; 38:5; **Nah.** 3:9; **Zeph.** 3:10.
C. כּוּשׁ *kûš* **masc. proper noun**
(Cush: a Benjamite)
Ps. 7:[title](1).

3569. A. כּוּשִׁי *kûšiy* **masc. proper noun**
(Cushite [Ethiopian])
Num. 12:1(KJV, NASB, *kûšiyṯ* [3571]); **2 Sam.** 18:21–23(KJV, see B),31(KJV, see B),32(KJV, see B); **2 Chr.** 12:3; 14:9(8),12(11),13(12); 16:8; 21:16; **Jer.** 13:23; 38:7,10,12; 39:16; **Dan.** 11:43; **Amos** 9:7; **Zeph.** 2:12.
B. כּוּשִׁי *kûšiy* **masc. proper noun**
(Cushi: a messenger)
2 Sam. 18:21–23(NASB, NIV, see A),31(NASB, NIV, see A),32(NASB, NIV, see A).

3570. A. כּוּשִׁי *kûšiy* **masc. proper noun**
(Cushi: great-grandfather of Jehudi)
Jer. 36:14.
B. כּוּשִׁי *kûšiy* **masc. proper noun**
(Cushi: father of Zephaniah)
Zeph. 1:1.

3571. כּוּשִׁית *kûšiyṯ* **fem. proper noun**
(Cushite: Ethiopian woman)
Num. 12:1(NIV, *kûšiy* [3569]).

3572. כּוּשָׁן *kûšān* **proper noun**
(Cushan)
Hab. 3:7.

3573. כּוּשַׁן רִשְׁעָתַיִם *kûšan riš'āṯayim* **masc. proper noun**
(Cushan-Rishathaim)
Judg. 3:8,10.

3574. A. כּוֹשָׁרָה *kōshārāh* **fem. noun**
(prosperity)
Ps. 68:6(7)(KJV, see C; NIV, see B).
B. כּוֹשָׁרָה *kōshārāh* **fem. noun**
(singing)
Ps. 68:6(7)(KJV, see C; NASB, see A).
C. כּוֹשָׁרָה *kōshārāh* **fem. noun**
(chains)
Ps. 68:6(7)(NASB, see A; NIV, see B).

3575. כּוּת *kûṯ*, כּוּתָה *kûṯāh* **proper noun**
(Cuthah)
2 Kgs. 17:24,30.

3576. כָּזַב *kāzaḇ* **verb**
(to lie, to be a liar)
Num. 23:19; **2 Kgs.** 4:16; **Job** 6:28; 24:25; 34:6; 41:9(1); **Ps.** 78:36; 89:35(36); 116:11; **Prov.** 14:5; 30:6; **Isa.** 57:11; 58:11; **Ezek.** 13:19; **Mic.** 2:11; **Hab.** 2:3.

3577. כָּזָב *kāzāḇ* **masc. noun**
(lie, falsehood, false god)
Judg. 16:10,13; **Ps.** 4:2(3); 5:6(7); 40:4(5); 58:3(4); 62:4(5),9(10); **Prov.** 6:19; 14:5,25; 19:5,9,22; 21:28; 23:3; 30:8; **Isa.** 28:15,17; **Ezek.** 13:6–9,19; 21:29(34); 22:28; **Dan.** 11:27; **Hos.** 7:13; 12:1(2); **Amos** 2:4; **Zeph.** 3:13.

3578. כֹּזֵבָא *kōzēḇa'* **proper noun**
(Cozeba)
1 Chr. 4:22.

3579. כָּזְבִּי *kozbiy* **fem. proper noun**
(Cozbi)
Num. 25:15,18.

3580. כְּזִיב *k^eziyb̲* **proper noun**
(Chezib)
Gen. 38:5.

3581. I. כֹּחַ *kōaḥ,* כּוֹחַ *kôaḥ* **masc. noun**
(strength, power)
Gen. 4:12; 31:6; 49:3; **Ex.** 9:16; 15:6; 32:11; **Lev.** 26:20; **Num.** 14:13,17; **Deut.** 4:37; 8:17,18; 9:29; **Josh.** 14:11; 17:17; **Judg.** 6:14; 16:5,6,9,15,17,19,30; **1 Sam.** 2:9; 28:20,22; 30:4; **1 Kgs.** 19:8; **2 Kgs.** 17:36; 19:3; **1 Chr.** 26:8; 29:2, 12,14; **2 Chr.** 2:6(5); 13:20; 14:11(10); 20:6,12; 22:9; 25:8; 26:13; **Ezra** 2:69; 10:13; **Neh.** 1:10; 4:10(4); **Job** 3:17; 6:11,12,22; 9:4,19; 23:6; 24:22; 26:2,12; 30:2,18; 31:39; 36:5,19,22; 37:23; 39:11,21; 40:16; **Ps.** 22:15(16); 29:4; 31:10(11); 33:16; 38:10(11); 65:6(7); 71:9; 102:23(24); 103:20; 111:6; 147:5; **Prov.** 5:10; 14:4; 20:29; 24:5,10; **Eccl.** 4:1; 9:10; **Isa.** 10:13; 37:3; 40:9,26,29,31; 41:1; 44:12; 49:4; 50:2; 63:1; **Jer.** 10:12; 27:5; 32:17; 48:45; 51:15; **Lam.** 1:6,14; **Dan.** 1:4; 8:6,7,22,24; 10:8,16,17; 11:6, 15,25; **Hos.** 7:9; **Amos** 2:14; **Mic.** 3:8; **Nah.** 1:3; 2:1(2); **Hab.** 1:11; **Zech.** 4:6.
II. כֹּחַ *kōaḥ* **masc. noun**
(lizard, reptile)
Lev. 11:30.

3582. כָּחַד *kāḥad̲* **verb**
(to hide, to conceal, to cut off, to destroy)
Gen. 47:18; **Ex.** 9:15; 23:23; **Josh.** 7:19; **1 Sam.** 3:17,18; **2 Sam.** 14:18; 18:13; **1 Kgs.** 13:34; **2 Chr.** 32:21; **Job** 4:7; 6:10; 15:18,28; 20:12; 22:20; 27:11; **Ps.** 40:10(11); 69:5(6); 78:4; 83:4(5); 139:15; **Isa.** 3:9; **Jer.** 38:14,25; 50:2; **Hos.** 5:3; **Zech.** 11:8,9,16.

3583. כָּחַל *kāḥal* **verb**
(to paint [one's eyes])
Ezek. 23:40.

3584. כָּחַשׁ *kāḥaš* **verb**
(to lie, to cringe, to deny)
Gen. 18:15; **Lev.** 6:2(5:21),3(5:22); 19:11; **Deut.** 33:29; **Josh.** 7:11; 24:27; **2 Sam.** 22:45; **1 Kgs.** 13:18; **Job** 8:18; 31:28; **Ps.** 18:44(45); 66:3; 81:15(16); 109:24; **Prov.** 30:9; **Isa.** 59:13; **Jer.** 5:12; **Hos.** 4:2; 9:2; **Hab.** 3:17; **Zech.** 13:4.

3585. כַּחַשׁ *kahaš* **masc. noun**
(lying, leanness)
Job 16:8; **Ps.** 59:12(13); **Hos.** 7:3; 10:13; 11:12(12:1); **Nah.** 3:1.

3586. כֶּחָשׁ *keḥāš* **adj.**
(lying, deceptive)
Isa. 30:9.

3587. כִּי *kiy* **masc. noun**
(burning, branding)
Isa. 3:24.

3588. כִּי *kiy* **particle**
(because, for, that)
Gen. 1:4,10,12,18,21,25; 2:3,5,17,23; 3:1,5–7,10,11,14,17,19,20; 4:12,23–25; 5:24; 6:1,2,5–7,12,13; 7:1,4; 8:9,11,21; 9:6; 10:25; 11:9; 12:10–12,14,18; 13:6,8, 10,15,17; 14:14; 15:4,8,13,16; 16:4,5,11, 13; 17:5,15; 18:5,15,19,20; 19:2,8,13,14, 22,30; 20:6,7,9–11,18; 21:7,10,12,13, 16–18,30,31; 22:12,16,17; 24:4,14,41; 25:21,28,30; 26:3,7–9,13,16,20,22,24,28; 27:1,20,23,36; 28:6,8,11,15,17; 29:2,9, 12,15,21,31–34; 30:1,9,13,16,20,26, 30,33; 31:5,6,12,15,16,20,22,30–32, 35–37,42,49; 32:10,11,17,20,25,26,28, 30,32; 33:10,11,13; 34:5,7,14,19; 35:7, 10,17,18; 36:7; 37:3,4,17,26,27,35; 38:9,11,14–16,26; 39:3,6,9,13,15; 40:14–16; 41:21,31,32,49,51,52,57; 42:1,2,4,5,12,15,16,23,33,34,38; 43:5,7, 10,16,18,21,25,30,32; 44:15,18,24,26,27, 31,32,34; 45:3,5,6,8,11,12,20,26; 46:3,

30,32–34; 47:4,13,15,18,20,22; 48:14, 17,18; 49:4,6,7,10,15; 50:3,15,17,19; **Ex.** 1:10,19,21; 2:2,10,12,22; 3:4–7,11,12, 19,21; 4:1,5,10,14,19,25,31; 5:8,11; 6:1,7; 7:5,9,17,24; 8:10,15,21,22,26; 9:2, 11,14,15,29–32,34; 10:1,2,4,7,9–11, 26,28; 12:9,15,17,19,25,26,30,33,39,48; 13:3,5,9,11,14–17,19; 14:4,5,12,13, 18,25; 15:1,19,21,23,26; 16:3,6–9,12,15, 25,29; 17:14,16; 18:1,3,4,11,15,16,18; 19:5,11,13,23; 20:5,7,11,20,22,25; 21:2, 7,14,18,20–22,26,28,33,35,36; 22:1,5–7, 9,10,14,16,21,23,27; 23:4,5,7–9,15, 21–24,31,33; 29:22,28,33,34,46; 30:12; 31:13,14,17; 32:1,7,21–23,25,29; 33:3, 13,16,17,20; 34:9,10,13,14,18,24,27, 29,35; 40:35,38; **Lev.** 1:2; 2:1,4,11; 4:2; 5:1,3–5,11,15,17; 6:2,4; 7:21,25,34; 8:33,35; 9:4; 10:7,12–14,17; 11:4–7,37–39, 42,44,45; 12:2; 13:2,9,11,16,18,24,28,29, 31,38,40,42,47,51,52; 14:13,34,48; 15:2, 8,13,16,19,25; 16:2,30; 17:11,14; 18:10, 13,24,27,29; 19:2,5,8,20,23,33,34; 20:3, 7,9,19,23,26,27; 21:2,6–9,12,14,15, 18,23; 22:6,7,9,11–14,16,20,21,25,27,29; 23:10,28,29,43; 24:9,15,17,19,22; 25:2, 12,14,16,17,20,23,25,26,29,33–35,39,42, 47,55; 26:1,44; 27:2,14; **Num.** 3:13; 5:6, 12,15,20; 6:2,7,9,12; 7:9; 8:16,17; 9:10, 13,14; 10:9,29–32; 11:3,12–14,16,18,20, 29,34; 12:1; 13:28,30,31; 14:9,13,14,22, 30,40,42,43; 15:2,8,14,22,25,26,31,34; 16:3,9,11,13,28,30,34,37,38,46; 17:3; 18:24,26,31; 19:13,14,20; 20:24,29; 21:1,5,7,13,24,26,28,34; 22:3,6,12,13, 17,22,28,29,32–34,36; 23:9,23; 24:1,22; 25:18; 26:33,62,65; 27:3,4,8; 30:2,3,5,14; 32:11,12,15,19; 33:51,53; 34:2,14; 35:10, 28,31,33,34; 36:7,9; **Deut.** 1:17,38,42; 2:5,7,9,19,30; 3:2,11,19,22,27,28; 4:3, 6,7,15,22,24–26,29,31,32,35,37,39; 5:3,5,9,11,15,24–26; 6:10,15,20,25; 7:1,4–9,16,17,21,25,26; 8:3,5,7,18,19; 9:3,5,6,12,19,25; 10:12,17,19; 11:2,7, 10,22,29,31; 12:5,9,12,14,18,20,21,23, 25,28,29,31; 13:1,3,5,6,9,10,12,18; 14:2, 7,8,21,24,27,29; 15:2,4,6–8,10–13,15,16, 18,21; 16:1,3,6,12,15,19; 17:1,2,8,14; 18:5,6,9,12,14,21; 19:1,6,9,11,16; 20:1, 4,10,17,19,20; 21:1,5,9,10,15,17,18, 22,23; 22:5,6,8,13,19,21–23,26–28; 23:5,7,9,10,14,18,21,22,24,25; 24:1, 3–7,10,15,18–22; 25:1,5,11,16; 26:1,3, 12; 27:20; 28:2,9,10,13,38–41,45,57,62; 29:6,15,16,19,20; 30:1,9–11,14,18,20; 31:6,7,17,18,20,21,23,27,29; 32:3,4,9, 20,22,28,30–32,35,36,39,40,43,47,52; 33:9,19,21; 34:9; **Josh.** 1:6,8,9,11; 2:3,5,9–12,15,24; 3:4,5,7,10; 4:6,24; 5:5–7,14,15; 6:16,17,25; 7:3,12,13,15; 8:5,6,14,18,21; 9:9,16,18,24; 10:1,2,4, 6,8,14,19,25,42; 11:6,10,20; 14:3,4,9,12; 15:19; 17:1,3,6,13,15,18; 18:7; 19:9; 20:5; 21:10; 22:7,27,28,31,34; 23:3,8,10, 12–14; 24:17–22,27; **Judg.** 1:15,19,28, 32,34; 2:17,18; 3:12,22,28; 4:3,9,12,14, 17,19; 5:23; 6:5,7,16,22,30–32,37; 7:9,15; 8:1,5,6,15,20–22,24,30; 9:2,3,5,18,28,38,47,55; 10:10; 11:2,12, 13,16,18; 12:3–5; 13:5,7,16,17,21,22; 14:3,4,9,10,17; 15:2,3,6,7,11,13; 16:16–18,20,24,25; 17:13; 18:1,9,10,14,23,26,28; 20:3,6,28,34,36, 39,41; 21:5,15,16,18,22; **Ruth** 1:6,10, 12,13,16–18,20; 2:13,21,22; 3:9,11, 12,14,17,18; 4:4,6,9,15; **1 Sam.** 1:5,6,12, 16,20,22; 2:1–3,8,9,15–17,21,24,25,30; 3:5,6,8–10,13,20,21; 4:6,7,13,18–20,22; 5:7,11; 6:3,4,9,19; 7:7,17; 8:7,9,19; 9:7, 9,12,13,16,20,24; 10:1,7,14,16,19,24; 11:5,13; 12:5,10,12,17,19,21,22,24; 13:6, 11,13,14,19; 14:3,6,10,12,18,22,26,29, 30,39,44,45; 15:11,23,24,26,29,35; 16:1,7,11,12,22; 17:25,26,28,33,36,39, 42,43,46–48,51; 18:12,16,18,25,28; 19:4; 20:1,3,6–9,12,13,17,18,21,22,26,29–31,3 3,34; 21:4–6,8,9,15; 22:6,8,15,17,21–23; 23:3,4,7,9,10,13,15,17,21,22,27; 24:6,10, 11,17,19,20; 25:4,7,8,17,25,28,30,34,39; 26:3,4,9,10,12,15,16,18–21; 27:1,4,8; 28:1,13,14,20–22; 29:6,8,9; 30:6,8,12,13, 17,22,24; 31:4,5,7; **2 Sam.** 1:5,9,10,12, 16,21; 2:7,26,27; 3:9,13,18,22,25,35, 37,38; 4:1,2,10,11; 5:6,12,17,19,24;

6:6,13; 7:1,3,6,11,12,18,22,27,29; 8:9,10; 9:1,7,8,13; 10:3,5,6,9,14,15,19; 11:16, 23,25,26; 12:3,5,10,12,14,18,19,22; 13:2,12,13,15,18,22,28,32,33,39; 14:1, 14–17,19,22,26; 15:8,14,19,21; 16:3, 8,10(KJV, [Q^{e}] *kōh* [3541]),11,18,21; 17:8,10,11,17,21,23,29; 18:3,12,16, 18–20,31; 19:2,6,7,20–22,25,26,28,32, 34,42; 20:12,21; 21:2; 22:5,8,18,20,22, 23,29,30,32; 23:5,6,10,19; 24:10,14,24; **1 Kgs.** 1:11,13,17,25,30,42; 2:7,9,15,17, 20,22–24,26,28–30,37,41,42; 3:2,4,9,10, 22,23,26,28; 4:24; 5:1,3,6; 6:6; 8:7,11,18, 19,27,35–37,39,42–44,46,51,53,60,64; 9:22; 10:22; 11:9,16,21,22,28,31,34; 12:1,15,16,20,24; 13:9,17,21,32; 14:2,4, 5,11,13; 15:4; 16:18; 17:1,7,12,14,24; 18:9,10,15,18,25,27,36,37,41; 19:2,4, 7,10,14,20; 20:5–7,13,22,28,31,41; 21:2, 6,15,16,29; 22:3,8,14,18,31,33,34,48; **2 Kgs.** 1:4,6,16,17; 2:2–6; 3:10,13,14,17, 21,26; 4:1,2,9,24,27,29,39,43; 5:1,7,8,13, 15,17,20; 6:9,12,16,32; 7:10,12; 8:1,10, 12,13,18,27,29; 9:16,20,25,34,35; 10:10, 19,23; 11:1,15; 12:7,10,14,15; 13:4,7; 14:6,26; 15:16; 17:7,21,36,39,40; 18:4, 20,22,26,29,31,32,34–36; 19:3,8,18, 19,31; 20:1,8–10,12; 22:7,13; 23:9,22,23; 24:7,20; 25:23,26; **1 Chr.** 1:19; 2:34; 4:9, 14,40,41; 5:1,2,9,20,22; 6:54; 7:4,21,23; 9:26–28,33; 10:4,5,7; 11:19; 12:18,19,21, 22,39,40; 13:3,4,9,11; 14:2,8,15; 15:2, 13,22; 16:25,26,33,34,41; 17:2,5,11,16, 25,27; 18:9,10; 19:2,3,5,6,10,15,16,19; 21:6,8,13,18,24,28,30; 22:4,8,9,14,18; 23:22,25,27,28; 24:5; 26:5,6,10; 27:23; 28:3–6,9,10,20; 29:1,9,11,14,15,17; **2 Chr.** 1:3,4,9,10; 2:5,6,8,9; 4:18; 5:11, 13,14; 6:8,9,13,18,24,26–28,30,33,34,36; 7:2,3,6,7,9; 8:9,11,14; 9:21; 10:1,15,16; 11:4,14,17,21,22; 12:2,7,8,13,14; 13:5, 11,12,18; 14:6,7,11,13,14; 15:5–7,9,15; 16:9,10,12; 17:3,4; 18:7,13,17,30,32,33; 19:3,6,7; 20:9,10,12,15,21,25–27,29; 21:3,6,10,17; 22:1,3,4,6,9–11; 23:6,8,14; 24:7,11,16,20,24,25; 25:4,7,8,16,20; 26:8,10,15,18,20,21,23; 27:6; 28:11,13, 19,21,23,27; 29:6,11,24,25,34,36; 30:3,5,9,17,18,24,26; 31:10,18; 32:2, 7,14,15,25,29; 33:13,23; 34:21; 35:14, 15,21–23; 36:15; **Ezra** 3:3,11,13; 4:1–3; 6:20,22; 7:9,10; 8:22; 9:2,6,9,10,13,15; 10:1,4,6,13; **Neh.** 2:2,12; 4:1,4,5,7,15; 5:18; 6:1,8–10,12,16,18; 7:2; 8:5,9–12, 17; 9:8,10,18,31,33; 10:39; 11:23; 12:29,43,44,46; 13:2,6,10,13; **Esth.** 1:8,11,13,16,17,20; 2:7,10,12,14,15; 3:2,4–6; 4:2,14; 5:12; 6:13; 7:4,7; 8:1,6,8,17; 9:2–4,24; 10:3; **Job** 1:5,8; 2:3,13; 3:10,12,13,22,24,25; 4:5; 5:2, 6,7,18,21,23–25; 6:3,4,10,11,20–22; 7:7,12,13,16,17,21; 8:6,8,9; 9:2,14,16, 18,28,32,35; 10:3,6,7,9,13; 11:6,11,15, 16,18; 12:2,9; 13:9,16,18,19,26; 14:7,16; 15:5,13,14,16,23,25,27,31,34; 16:3,22; 17:4; 18:8; 19:6,21,28,29; 20:5,19,20; 21:15,21,28,30; 22:2,3,6,12,26,29; 23:10,14,17; 24:17; 25:6; 27:3,8,9; 28:1,24; 29:11,12; 30:11,23,26; 31:11, 12,14,18,21,23,25,26,28,29,34; 32:1, 4,5,16,18,22; 33:12–14,32; 34:3,5, 9,11,19,21,23,31,33,37; 35:3,14,15; 36:2,4,9,10,13,18,21,24,27,31; 37:4,6,20; 38:5,20,21,40,41; 39:11,12,14,15,17, 24,27; 40:14,20,23; 41:10; 42:2,7,8; **Ps.** 1:2,4,6; 2:12; 3:5,7; 4:3,8; 5:2,4,9,10,12; 6:2,5,8; 8:3,4; 9:4,10,12,18; 10:3,14; 11:2,3,7; 12:1; 13:4,6; 14:5,6; 16:1,8,10; 17:6; 18:7,17,19,21,22,27–29,31; 20:6; 21:3,6,7,11,12; 22:8,9,11,16,24,28,31; 23:4; 24:2; 25:5,6,11,15,16,19–21; 26:1,3; 27:5,10,12; 28:5,6; 30:1,5; 31:3, 4,9,10,13,17,21; 32:3,4; 33:4,9,21; 34:8,9; 35:7,20; 36:2,9; 37:2,9,13,17,20, 22,24,28,37,40; 38:2,4,7,15–18; 39:9,12; 40:12; 41:4,11; 42:4,5,11; 43:2,5; 44:3,6, 7,19,21,22,25; 45:11; 46:10; 47:2,7,9; 48:4,14; 49:10,15–18; 50:6,10,12; 51:3,16; 52:9; 53:5; 54:3,6,7; 55:3,9,12, 15,18; 56:1,2,9,13; 57:1,10; 58:10; 59:3, 7,9,13,16,17; 60:2; 61:3,5; 62:5,10–12; 63:3,7,11; 65:9; 66:10; 67:4; 69:1,7,9 ,16,17,26,33,35; 71:3,5,10,11,15,23,24; 72:12; 73:3,4,21,27; 74:20; 75:2,6–8;

76:10; 77:11; 78:22,35,39; 79:7,8; 81:4; 82:8; 83:2,5,18; 84:10,11; 85:8; 86:1–5, 7,10,13,17; 88:3; 89:2,6,17,18; 90:4,7,9, 10; 91:3,9,11,14; 92:4,9,15; 94:11,14,15; 95:3,7; 96:4,5,13; 97:9; 98:1,9; 99:9; 100:3,5; 101:8; 102:3,4,9,10,13,14,16,19; 103:11,14,16; 105:38,42; 106:1,33; 107:1,9,11,16,30; 108:4; 109:2,21,22, 27,31; 112:6; 114:5; 115:1; 116:1,2,7,8, 10,16; 117:2; 118:1–4,10–12,17,21,29; 119:22,32,35,39,42,43,45,50,56,66,71, 74,75,77,78,83,91,93,94,98–100,102, 111,118,131,139,152,153,155,159,168, 171–173,176; 120:5,7; 122:5; 123:3; 125:3; 127:5; 128:2,4; 130:4,7; 132:13,14; 133:3; 135:3–5,14; 136:1–26; 137:3; 138:2,4–6; 139:4,13,14; 140:12; 141:5,6,8; 142:6,7; 143:2,3,8,10,12; 147:1,13; 148:5,13; 149:4; **Prov.** 1:9,16, 17,29,32; 2:3,6,10,18,21; 3:2,12,14,25, 26,32; 4:2,3,8,13,16,17,22,23; 5:3,21; 6:3,23,26,30,34,35; 7:6,19,23,26; 8:6, 7,11,35; 9:11,18; 11:15,31; 15:11; 16:12,26; 17:7; 18:2; 19:7,10,18,19; 20:16; 21:7,25,27; 22:6,9,18,22,23; 23:1, 5,7,9,11,13,17,18,21,22,27,31; 24:2,6, 12,13,16,20,22; 25:7,22; 26:25; 27:1, 13,24; 28:22; 29:19; 30:2,4,22,23,33; 31:18,21; **Eccl.** 1:18; 2:10,12,16,17, 21–26; 3:12,14,17,19,22; 4:4,10,14,16; 5:1–4,6–8,11,18,20; 6:2,4,8,11,12; 7:3,6,7,9,10,12,13,18,20,22; 8:3, 6,7,12,15–17; 9:1,3–5,7,9–12; 10:4,20; 11:1,2,6,8–10; 12:3,5,13,14; **Song** 1:2; 2:5,11,14; 8:6; **Isa.** 1:2,12,15,20,29,30; 2:3,6,12,22; 3:1,6,8–11,16; 4:5; 5:7, 10,24; 6:5; 7:5,8,9,13,16,22,24; 8:4, 6,10,11,19,21; 9:1,4–6,17,18; 10:7, 8,12,13,22,23,25; 11:9; 12:1,2,4–6; 13:6,10; 14:1,20,27,29,31,32; 15:1, 5,6,8,9; 16:4,8,9,12; 17:10; 18:4,5; 19:20; 21:6,15–17; 22:1,5,9,13,16,25; 23:1,4, 14,18; 24:3,5,13,18,23; 25:1,2,4,8,10; 26:3–5,9,12,19,21; 27:10,11; 28:8,10,11, 15,18–22,27,28; 29:10,11,13,16,20,23; 30:4,5,9,15,16,18,19,21,31,33; 31:1,4,7; 32:6,10,13,14; 33:5,21,22; 34:2,5,6,8,16; 35:6; 36:5,7,11,14,16,19–21; 37:3,8,19, 20,32; 38:1,17,18,22; 39:1,8; 40:2,5,7; 41:10,13,20,23; 42:19; 43:1–3,5,10,20, 22; 44:3,17,18,21–23; 45:3,6,18,22,23; 46:9; 47:1,5; 48:2,4,8,11; 49:10,13,18,19, 23,25,26; 50:7; 51:2–4,6,8; 52:1,3–6,8,9, 12,15; 53:8; 54:1,3–6,9,10,14; 55:5,7–12; 56:1,4,7; 57:1,8,11,15,16,20; 58:7,14; 59:2,3,12,14–16,19; 60:1,2,5,9,10,12, 16,20; 61:8–11; 62:4,5,9; 63:4,16; 64:7; 65:5,6,8,16–18,20,22,23; 66:8,12,15, 16,22,24; **Jer.** 1:6–8,12,15,19; 2:5,10, 13,19,20,22,25–28,34,35,37; 3:8,10, 12–14,16,21,22,25; 4:3,6,8,13,15,17–20, 22,27,28,30,31; 5:4–6,10,11,19,26; 6:1,4, 6,11–13,15,19,25,26,30; 7:5,12,16,22, 23,29,30,32,34; 8:10,12,14,17,22; 9:2–4,7,10,19–21,24,26; 10:2,3,5,7,14, 16,18,21,23,25; 11:7,13–15,19,20,23; 12:1,4–6,11,12; 13:11,12,15,17,18,21,22; 14:4–7,12,13,17,18,20,22; 15:2,5,10,14, 16,17,20; 16:3,5,9,10,15,17,21; 17:4,6, 8,13,14; 18:12,15,18,20,22; 19:6,15; 20:3,4,8,10–13; 21:2,10; 22:4–6,10–12, 15,17,20–22,24,30; 23:8,10–12,15,18, 33,36; 24:7,8; 25:14,15,28,29,31,34, 36,38; 26:11,15,16; 27:10,14–16,19,21; 28:4,14,16; 29:7–11,13,15,16,28,32; 30:3,5,7,10–12,14,17,21; 31:6,7,9,11, 15,16,18–20,22,25,30,33,34; 32:4,5, 7,8,15,30,31,42,44; 33:4,11,17,26; 34:3, 5,7; 35:6,7,14,16; 36:7; 37:9,10,15,16,18; 38:4–7,9,15,23,25,27; 39:12,18; 40:3,7, 11,14,16; 41:8,18; 42:2,6,10,11,14, 18–20,22; 43:3,7; 44:14,15,17,19,29; 45:3,5; 46:10,12,14,15,18,19,21–23, 27,28; 47:4; 48:1,5,7,9,18,20,26,27,34, 37,38,40,42,44–46; 49:3,8,10,12,13,15, 16,19,23,30; 50:3,9,11,14,15,20,24,25, 27,29,31,38,44; 51:2,5,6,9,11,12,14,17, 19,26,29,31,33,48,51,53,55,56,62; 52:3; **Lam.** 1:5,8–11,16,18–22; 2:13; 3:8, 22,27,28,31–33; 4:12,15,18; 5:16,22; **Ezek.** 1:20,21; 2:5–7; 3:5,7,9,19–21, 26,27; 5:6,13; 6:7,10,13,14; 7:4,9,12–14, 19,23,27; 8:12,17; 9:9; 10:11,17,20; 11:10,12,16; 12:2,3,6,15,16,20,23–25;

13:9,14,21,23; 14:7–9,13,18,21,23; 15:5,7; 16:14,59,62; 17:21,24; 18:5,11, 18,21,32; 19:5; 20:12,16,20,38,40,42, 44,48; 21:5,7,12,13,21,32; 22:16,22; 23:8,13,28,34,37,40,45,46,49; 24:7,19, 24,27; 25:3,5–7,11,17; 26:5–7,14,19; 28:10,22–24,26; 29:6,9,13,16,21; 30:3,8, 9,19,25,26; 31:7,14; 32:11,15,25–27,32; 33:2,6,9–11,29,31,33; 34:11,27,30; 35:4,6,9,12,15; 36:8,9,11,22,23,36,38; 37:6,13,14,28; 38:23; 39:5–7,10,22, 23,28; 40:4; 41:7; 42:5,6,8,13,14; 44:2,10,22,25; 45:14; 46:9,12,16,17; 47:1,5,9,12; 48:14; **Dan.** 8:17,19,26; 9:9,11,14,16,18,19,23; 10:11,12,14, 19,21; 11:4,25,27,35–37; 12:7,9; **Hos.** 1:2,4,6,9,11; 2:2,4,5,7,8; 3:4; 4:1,6,10, 12–14,16; 5:1,3,4,7,11,14; 6:1,6,9; 7:1,6, 13,14; 8:6,7,9–11; 9:1,4,6,12,15–17; 10:3,5,13; 11:1,3,5,9,10; 13:9,13,15,16; 14:1,4,9; **Joel** 1:5,6,10–13,15,17–20; 2:1,11,13,20–23,27,32; 3:1,8,12–14,17; **Amos** 3:7,14; 4:2,5,12,13; 5:3–5,12,13, 17,22; 6:10–12,14; 7:2,5,11,13,14; 8:11; 9:8,9; **Obad.** 1:15,16,18; **Jon.** 1:2,10–14; 3:10; 4:2,3; **Mic.** 1:3,7,9,12,13,16; 2:1, 3,10; 3:7; 4:2,4,5,9,10,12,13; 5:4–6; 6:2,4,8; 7:1,6,8,9,18; **Nah.** 1:10,14,15; 2:2; 3:19; **Hab.** 1:4–6,16; 2:3,5,8,11,14, 17,18; 3:8,17; **Zeph.** 1:7,11,17,18; 2:4, 7,9–11,14; 3:8,9,11,13,20; **Hag.** 2:4, 6,23; **Zech.** 2:6,8–11,13; 3:8,9; 4:6,9,10; 5:3; 6:15; 7:5,6; 8:6,10,12,14,17,23; 9:1,2,5,8,13,16,17; 10:2,3,5,6,8; 11:2,3, 6,11,16; 13:3,5; 14:5; **Mal.** 1:4,8,11,14; 2:2,4,7,11,14,16; 3:2,6,8,12,14; 4:1,3.

3589. כִּיד *kiyd̲* **masc. noun**
(destruction, decay)
Job 21:20.

3590. כִּידוֹד *kiyd̲ôd̲* **masc. noun**
(spark)
Job 41:19(11).

3591. כִּידוֹן *kiyd̲ôn* **masc. noun**
(javelin, spear)
Josh. 8:18,26; **1 Sam.** 17:6,45; **Job** 39:23; 41:29(21); **Jer.** 6:23; 50:42.

3592. כִּידֹן *kiyd̲ōn* **masc. proper noun**
(Chidon)
1 Chr. 13:9.

3593. כִּידוֹר *kiyd̲ôr* **masc. noun**
(attack, battle)
Job 15:24.

3594. I. כִּיּוּן *kiyyûn* **masc. proper noun**
(Kiyyun, Chiun)
Amos 5:26(NIV, see II).
II. כִּיּוּן *kiyyûn* **masc. noun**
(pedestal, pillar)
Amos 5:26(KJV, NASB, see I).

3595. כִּיּוֹר *kiyyôr* **masc. noun**
(basin, laver, pot)
Ex. 30:18,28; 31:9; 35:16; 38:8; 39:39; 40:7,11,30; **Lev.** 8:11; **1 Sam.** 2:14; **1 Kgs.** 7:30,38,40,43; **2 Kgs.** 16:17; **2 Chr.** 4:6,14; 6:13; **Zech.** 12:6.

3596. כִּילַי *kiylay,* כֵּלַי *kēlay* **masc. noun**
(scoundrel, rogue)
Isa. 32:5,7.

3597. כֵּילַף *kēylap̲* **fem. noun**
(hammer, hatchet)
Ps. 74:6.

3598. כִּימָה *kiymāh* **fem. proper noun**
(Pleiades [a constellation of seven stars])
Job 9:9; 38:31; **Amos** 5:8.

3599. כִּיס *kiys* **masc. noun**
(purse, bag)
Deut. 25:13; **Prov.** 1:14; 16:11; 23:31(NASB, NIV, [Q^e] *kâs* [3563]); **Isa.** 46:6; **Mic.** 6:11.

3600. כִּיר *kiyr* **masc. noun**
(cooking pot, oven)
Lev. 11:35.

3601. כִּישׁוֹר *kiyšôr* **masc. noun**
(spindle, distaff)
Prov. 31:19.

3602. כָּכָה *kāḵāh* **particle**
(in this way, so, thus)
Ex. 12:11; 29:35; **Num.** 8:26; 11:15; 15:11–13; **Deut.** 25:9; 29:24; **Josh.** 10:25; **1 Sam.** 2:14; 19:17; **2 Sam.** 13:4; 17:21; **1 Kgs.** 1:6,48; 9:8; **2 Chr.** 7:21; 18:19; **Neh.** 5:13; **Esth.** 6:9,11; 9:26; **Job** 1:5; **Ps.** 144:15; **Eccl.** 11:5; **Song** 5:9; **Jer.** 13:9; 19:11; 22:8; 28:11; 51:64; **Ezek.** 4:13; 31:18; **Hos.** 10:15.

3603. כִּכָּר *kikkār* **fem. noun**
(something round: talent [coin], district, loaf of bread)
Gen. 13:10–12; 19:17,25,28,29; **Ex.** 25:39; 29:23; 37:24; 38:24,25,27,29; **Deut.** 34:3; **Judg.** 8:5; **1 Sam.** 2:36; 10:3; **2 Sam.** 12:30; 18:23; **1 Kgs.** 7:46; 9:14,28; 10:10,14; 16:24; 20:39; **2 Kgs.** 5:5,22,23; 15:19; 18:14; 23:33; **1 Chr.** 16:3; 19:6; 20:2; 22:14; 29:4,7; **2 Chr.** 3:8; 4:17; 8:18; 9:9,13; 25:6,9; 27:5; 36:3; **Ezra** 8:26; **Neh.** 3:22; 12:28; **Esth.** 3:9; **Prov.** 6:26; **Jer.** 37:21; **Zech.** 5:7.

3604. כַּכַּר *kakkar* **Aram. fem. noun**
(talent [coin, measure of weight]; corr. to Hebr. 3603)
Ezra 7:22.

3605. כֹּל *kōl* **particle**
(all, ever, everything, entire)
Gen. 1:21,25,26,28–31; 2:1–3,5,6,9,11,13,16,19,20; 3:1,14,17,20; 4:14,15,21,22; 5:5,8,11,14,17,20,23, 27,31; 6:2,5,12,13,17,19–22; 7:1–5,8,11, 14–16,19,21–23; 8:1,9,17,19–22; 9:2, 3,5,10–12,15–17,19,29; 10:21,29; 11:1, 4,6,8,9; 12:3,5,20; 13:1,9–11,15; 14:3, 7,11,16,20,23; 15:10; 16:12; 17:8,10, 12,23,27; 18:18,25,26,28; 19:4,12,17, 25,28,31; 20:7,8,13,16,18; 21:6,12,22; 22:18; 23:10,17,18; 24:1,2,10,20,36,66; 25:4,5,18,25; 26:3,4,11,15; 27:33,37; 28:14,15,22; 29:3,8,13,22; 30:32,33, 35,40,41; 31:1,6,8,12,16,18,21,34,37,43; 32:10,19; 33:8,11,13; 34:15,19,22–25,29; 35:2,4,6; 36:6; 37:3,4,35; 39:3–6,8,22,23; 40:17,20; 41:8,19,29,30,35,37,39–41,43, 44,46,48,51,54–57; 42:6,11,29,36; 43:9, 34; 44:32; 45:1,8–11,13,15,20,22,26,27; 46:1,6,7,15,22,25–27,32,34; 47:1,12–15, 17,20; 48:16; 49:28; 50:7,8,14,15; **Ex.** 1:5,6,14,22; 3:20; 4:19,21,28–30; 5:12; 6:29; 7:2,19–21,24; 8:2,4,16,17,24; 9:4,6, 9,11,14,16,19,22,24,25; 10:5,6,12–15,19, 22,23; 11:5–8,10; 12:3,6,12,15,16,19–21, 29,30,33,41–44,47,48,50; 13:2,7,12, 13,15; 14:4,7,9,17,20,21,23,28; 15:15, 20,26; 16:1–3,6,9,10,22,23; 17:1; 18:1, 8,9,11,12,14,21–26; 19:5,7,8,11,12, 16,18; 20:1,4,9–11,17,18,24; 21:30; 22:9,10,19,22; 23:13,17,22,27; 24:3, 4,7,8; 25:2,9,22,36,39; 26:2,17; 27:3, 17,19; 28:3,38; 29:12,13,18,24,35,37; 30:13,14,27–29; 31:3,5–9,11,14,15; 32:3, 13,26; 33:7,8,10,16,19; 34:3,10,19,20,23, 30–32; 35:1–5,10,13,16,20–26,29,31, 33,35; 36:1–4,7–9,22; 37:22,24; 38:3,16, 17,20,22,24,26,30,31; 39:32,33,36,37,39, 40,42,43; 40:9,10,16,36,38; **Lev.** 1:9,13; 2:2,11,13,16; 3:3,9,14,16,17; 4:2,7,8, 11–13,18,19,22,26,30,31,34,35; 5:2–4,17; 6:3,5,7,9,15,18,23,27,29,30; 7:3,6,9,10, 14,19,21,23–27; 8:3,10,11,16,21,25, 27,36; 9:5,23,24; 10:3,6,11; 11:2,3,9,10, 12,15,20,21,23–27,31–35,37,41–44,46; 12:4; 13:12,13,46,48,49,51–53,57–59; 14:8,9,36,45,46,54; 15:4,9–12,16,17, 19–22,24–27; 16:2,16,17,21,22,29,30, 33,34; 17:2,10,12,14,15; 18:6,23,24,26, 27,29; 19:2,23,24,37; 20:5,16,22,23,25; 21:11,18,21,24; 22:3–5,10,13,18,20, 21,25; 23:3,7,8,14,21,25,28–31,35,36, 38,42; 24:14,16,17; 25:7,9,10,24;

26:14,15,34,35; 27:9,11,25,28–30,32; **Num.** 1:2,3,18,20,22,24,26,28,30,32,34, 36,38,40,42,45,46,50,54; 2:9,16,24,31, 32,34; 3:7,8,12,13,15,22,26,28,31,34, 36,39–43,45; 4:3,9,10,12,14–16,23,26, 27,30–33,35,37,39,41,43,46,47; 5:2, 6,9,30; 6:3–6,8; 7:1,85–88; 8:7,9,1 6–18,20; 9:3,5,12,18; 10:3,25; 11:6, 11–14,22,29,32; 12:3,7; 13:2,3,26,32; 14:1,2,5,7,10,11,21–23,29,35,36,39; 15:13,22–26,33,35,36,39,40; 16:3,5,6, 10,11,16,19,22,26,28–34,41; 17:2,6,9, 12,13; 18:3,4,7–15,19,21,28,29,31; 19:11,13–16,18,22; 20:1,14,22,27,29; 21:8,23,25,26,33–35; 22:2,4,17; 23:6, 13,26; 24:17; 25:4,6; 26:2,43,62; 27:2, 16,19–22; 28:18,25,26; 29:1,7,12,35,40; 30:2,4,5,9,11–14; 31:4,7,9–11,13,15, 17–20,23,27,30,35,51,52; 32:13,15,21, 26,27,29; 33:3,4,52; 35:3,7,15,22,23, 29,30; 36:8; **Deut.** 1:1,3,7,18,19,22,30, 31,41; 2:7,14,16,25,32–34,36,37; 3:1–7, 10,13,14,18,21; 4:3,4,6–10,15–19,23,25, 29,30,34,40,49; 5:1,3,8,13,14,21–23, 26–29,31,33; 6:2,5,11,19,22,24,25; 7:6,7, 14–16,18,19; 8:1–3,9,13; 9:10,18; 10:12, 14,15; 11:1,3,6–8,13,22–25,32; 12:1,2,5, 7,8,10,11,13–15,17–21,28,31,32; 13:3,9, 11,15,16,18; 14:2,3,6,9–11,14,19–23, 26,28,29; 15:2,5,10,18,19,21; 16:3,4, 15,16,18,21; 17:1,3,7,10,13,14,19; 18:1, 5–7,12,16,18; 19:3,8,9,15; 20:11,13–16, 18; 21:5,6,17,21; 22:3,5,6,19,29; 23:6, 9,18–20; 24:5,8,19; 25:16,18,19; 26:2, 11–14,16,18,19; 27:1,3,8,9,14–26; 28:1, 2,8,10,12,14,15,20,25,26,29,32,33,37,40, 42,45,47,48,52,55,57,58,60,61,64; 29:2, 9,10,20,21,23,24,27,29; 30:1–3,6–10; 31:1,5,7,9,11–13,18,28,30; 32:4,27, 44–46; 33:3,12; 34:1,2,11,12; **Josh.** 1:2–5,7–9,14,16–18; 2:3,9,13,18,19, 22–24; 3:1,7,11,13,15,17; 4:1,10,11,14, 18,24; 5:1,4–6,8; 6:3,5,17,19,21–25,27; 7:3,9,15,23–25; 8:1,3–5,11,13–16,21, 24–26,33–35; 9:1,5,9–11,18,19,21,24; 10:2,5–7,9,15,21,24,25,28–32,34–43; 11:4–7,10–19,21,23; 12:1,5,24; 13:2, 4–6,9–12,16,17,21,25,30; 15:32,46; 16:9; 17:16; 18:1; 19:8; 20:9; 21:19,26,33, 39–45; 22:2,5,12,14,16,18,20; 23:1–4,6,14,15; 24:1–3,17,18,27,31; **Judg.** 1:25; 2:4,7,10,15,18; 3:1,3,19,29; 4:13,15,16; 5:31; 6:9,13,31,33,35,37, 39,40; 7:1,4–8,12,14,16,18,21–24; 8:10,12,27,34,35; 9:1–3,6,14,25,34, 44–49,51,57; 10:8,15,18; 11:8,11,20–22, 24,26; 12:4; 13:4,7,13,14,23; 14:3; 16:2, 16–18,27,30,31; 18:10,31; 19:19,20,25, 29,30; 20:1,2,6–8,10–12,16,17,25,26, 33–35,37,44,46,48; 21:5,11,13; **Ruth** 1:19; 2:11,21; 3:5,6,11,16; 4:7,9,11; **1 Sam.** 1:4,11,21,28; 2:13,14,22,23,28, 29,32,33,35,36; 3:11,12,17–20; 4:1,5, 8,13; 5:5,8,11; 6:4,18; 7:2,3,5,13,15,16; 8:4,5,7,8,10,20,21; 9:2,6,19–21; 10:9, 11,18–20,23–25; 11:1–4,7,10,15; 12:1, 7,18–20,24; 13:3,4,7,19,20,22; 14:7, 15,20,22,24,25,34,36,38–40,47,52; 15:3,6,8,9,11; 17:11,19,24,46,47; 18:5, 6,14,16,22,29,30; 19:1,5,7,18,24; 20:6, 31; 22:1,2,4,6–8,11,14–16,22; 23:8,14, 20,23; 24:2; 25:1,6,7,9,12,15–17,21, 22,30; 26:12,24; 27:1,11; 28:2–4,20; 29:1; 30:6,16,18–20,22,31; 31:6,12; **2 Sam.** 1:9,11; 2:9,23,28–30,32; 3:12, 18,19,21,23,25,29,31,32,34–37; 4:1,7,9; 5:1,3,5,8,17; 6:1,2,5,11,12,14,15,19,21; 7:1,3,7,9,11,17,21,22; 8:4,6,9,11,14,15; 9:7,9,11,12; 10:7,9,17,19; 11:1,9,18, 19,22; 12:3,12,16,29,31; 13:9,21,23,25, 27,29–33,36,37; 14:7,19,20,25; 15:2,4, 6,10,11,14–18,22–24,30,35,36; 16:4,6, 8,11,14,15,18,21–23; 17:2–4,10–14, 16,22,24; 18:4,5,8,13,17,31,32; 19:2, 5–9,11,13,14,20,28,30,38–42; 20:2,7, 12–15,22,23; 21:5,14; 22:1,23,31; 23:5, 6,39; 24:2,7,8,23; **1 Kgs.** 1:3,9,19,20,25, 29,39–41,49; 2:2–4,15,26,44; 3:13,15,28; 4:1,7,10–12,21,24,25,27,30,31,34; 5:1,6, 8,10,13; 6:7,10,12,18,22,29,38; 7:1,5,9, 14,25,33,37,40,45,47,48,51; 8:1–5,14,16, 22,23,37–40,43,48,50,52–56,58,60,62,63 ,65,66; 9:1,3,4,7–9,11,19,20; 10:2–4,13, 15,20,21,23,24,29; 11:8,13,15,16,25,28,

32,34,36–39,41,42; 12:1,3,7,12,16,18,20, 21,23; 13:11,32; 14:8,9,13,18,21–24,26, 29,30; 15:3,5–7,12,14,16,18,20,22,23, 27,29,31–33; 16:7,11–14,16,17,25,26, 30,33; 18:5,19–21,24,30,36,39; 19:1,18; 20:1,4,6–10,13,15,28; 21:26; 22:10,12, 17,19,22,23,28,39,43,53; **2 Kgs.** 3:6,19, 21,25; 4:2–4,13; 5:12,15; 6:24; 7:13,15; 8:4,6,9,19,21,23; 9:5,7,8,14; 10:5,9,11, 17–19,21,22,30–34; 11:1,7,9,14,18–20; 12:2,4,5,9,12,13,18,19; 13:3,8,11,12,22; 14:3,14,21,24,28; 15:3,6,16,18,20,21,26, 29,31,34; 16:4,10,11,15,16; 17:5,9–11, 13,16,20,22,23,37,39; 18:3,5,7,12,13, 15,21,35; 19:4,11,15,19,24,35; 20:13,15, 17,20; 21:3,5,7,8,11,12,14,17,21,24; 22:2,13,16,17,20; 23:1–5,8,19–22, 24–26,28,32,37; 24:3,5,7,9,13,14,16,19; 25:1,4,5,9,10,14,16,17,23,26,29,30; **1 Chr.** 1:23,33; 2:4,6,23; 3:9; 4:27,33; 5:10,16,17,20; 6:48,49,60; 7:3,5,8,11,40; 8:38,40; 9:1,9,22,29; 10:6,7,11,12; 11:1, 3,4,6,10; 12:15,21,32,33,37,38; 13:1,2, 4–6,8,14; 14:8,17; 15:3,27,28; 16:3,9, 14,23–26,30,32,36,40,43; 17:2,6,8,10,15, 19,20; 18:4,6,9–11,13,14; 19:8,10,17; 20:3; 21:3–5,12,23; 22:5,9,15,17; 23:2, 26,28,29,31; 25:5–7; 26:8,11,26,28,30, 32; 27:1,3,31; 28:1,4,5,8,9,12–14,19–21; 29:1–3,5,10–12,14–17,19–21,23–26,30; **2 Chr.** 1:2,3,17; 2:5,14,16,17; 4:4,16,18, 19; 5:1–6,11,12; 6:3,5,12–14,28–31, 33,38; 7:3–6,8,11,16,17,20–22; 8:4,6, 7,15,16; 9:1,2,12,14,19,20,22,23,26, 28,30; 10:1,3,7,12,16; 11:3,12,13,16, 21,23; 12:1,9,13,15; 13:4,9,15; 14:5,8,14; 15:2,5,6,8,9,12,13,15,17; 16:4,6,9; 17:2, 5,9,10,19; 18:7,9,11,16,18,21,27; 19:5, 10,11; 20:3,4,6,13,15,18,27,29; 21:2,4, 7,9,14,17,18; 22:1,9,10; 23:2,3,5,6,8, 10,13,16,17,19–21; 24:2,5,7,10,14,23; 25:5,7,12,24; 26:1,4,12,14,20; 27:2,7; 28:4,6,14,15,23–26; 29:2,16,18,19,24, 28,29,31,32,34,36; 30:1,2,4–6,14,17,19, 22,23,25; 31:1,5,16,18–21; 32:4,5,7,9, 13–15,21–23,27,28,30,31,33; 33:3,5,7,8, 14,15,19,22,25; 34:7,9,12,13,16,21,24, 25,28–33; 35:3,7,13,16,18,20,24,25; 36:14,17–19,21–23; **Ezra** 1:1–6,11; 2:42,58,64,70; 3:5,8,11; 4:5; 6:20,21; 7:6,28; 8:20–22,25,34,35; 9:4,13; 10:3, 5,7–9,12,14,16,17,44; **Neh.** 4:6,8,12, 15,16; 5:13,16,18,19; 6:9,16; 7:60,66,73; 8:1–3,5,6,9,11–13,15,17; 9:2,5,6,10,25, 32,33,38; 10:28,29,31,33,35,37; 11:2,6, 18,20,24; 12:27,47; 13:3,6,8,12,15,16,18, 20,26,27,30; **Esth.** 1:3,5,8,13,16–18, 20,22; 2:3,11,13,15,17,18; 3:1,2,6,8, 12–14; 4:1,3,7,11,13,16,17; 5:11,13,14; 6:10,13; 8:5,9,11–13,17; 9:2–5,20,21,24, 26–30; 10:2,3; **Job** 1:3,5,10–12,22; 2:4,10,11; 8:12,13; 9:28; 12:9,10; 13:1, 4,27; 14:14; 15:20; 16:2,7; 17:7,10; 19:19; 20:22,26; 21:23,33; 24:24; 27:3, 10,12; 28:3,10,21,24; 30:23; 31:4,12; 33:1,11,13,29; 34:13,15,19,21,27; 36:19,25; 37:3,7,12,24; 38:7,18; 39:8; 40:11,12,20; 41:11,34; 42:2,10,11,15; **Ps.** 1:3; 2:12; 3:7; 5:5,11; 6:6–8,10; 7:1,11; 8:1,6,7,9; 9:1,14,17; 10:4,5; 12:3; 14:3,4; 16:3; 17:15; 18:22,30; 19:4; 20:3–5; 21:8; 22:7,14,17,23,27,29; 23:6; 25:3,5,10, 18,22; 26:7; 27:4; 29:9; 31:11,23,24; 32:3,6,11; 33:4,6,8,13–15; 34:1,4,6,10, 17,19,20,22; 35:10,28; 37:26; 38:6,9,12; 39:5,8,11,12; 40:16; 41:3,7; 42:3,7,10; 44:8,15,17,22; 45:8,13,16,17; 47:1,2,7; 48:2; 49:1,17; 50:10,11; 51:9; 52:1,4; 53:3; 54:7; 56:1,2,5; 57:5,11; 59:5,8; 62:3,8; 63:11; 64:8–10; 65:2,5; 66:1,4,16; 67:2,3,5,7; 69:19,34; 70:4; 71:8,14,15, 18,24; 72:11,15,17,19; 73:14,27,28; 74:3,8,17,22; 75:3,8,10; 76:5,9,11; 77:12; 78:14,32,38,51; 80:12; 82:5,6,8; 83:11,18; 85:2,3; 86:3,5,9,12; 87:2,7; 88:7,9,17; 89:7,16,40–42,47,50; 90:9,14; 91:11; 92:7,9; 94:4,15; 95:3; 96:1,3–5,9,12; 97:5–7,9; 98:3,4; 99:2; 100:1; 101:8; 102:8,15,26; 103:1–3,6,19,21,22; 104:11, 20,24,27; 105:2,7,16,21,31,35,36; 106:2, 3,46,48; 107:18,27,42; 108:5; 109:11; 111:1,2,7,10; 113:4; 115:3,8,17; 116:11, 12,14,18; 117:1; 118:10; 119:2,6, 10,13,14,20,34,58,63,69,86,91,96,97,99,

101,104,118,119,128,133,145,151,160,1
68,172; 121:7; 128:1,5; 129:5; 130:8;
132:1; 134:1; 135:5,6,9,11,18; 136:25;
138:1,2,4; 139:3,4,16; 140:2; 143:2,5,12;
145:2,9,10,13–18,20,21; 146:6; 147:4,20;
148:2,3,7,9–11,14; 149:9; 150:6; **Prov.**
1:13,14,17,19,25,30; 2:9,19; 3:5,6,9,15,
17,31; 4:7,22,23,26; 5:14,19,21; 6:14,29,
31,35; 7:12,26; 8:8,9,11,16,30,36; 10:12;
12:21; 13:7,16; 14:15,23; 15:3,15;
16:2,4,5,11,33; 17:8,17; 18:1; 19:6,7;
20:1,3,8,27; 21:1,2,5,26; 22:2; 23:17;
24:4,31; 26:10; 27:7; 28:5; 29:11,12;
30:4,5,27,30; 31:5,8,12,21,29; **Eccl.**
1:2,3,7–9,13,14,16; 2:5,7,9–11,14,
16–20,22,23; 3:1,11,13,14,17,19,20; 4:1,
4,8,15,16; 5:9,16–19; 6:2,6,7; 7:2,15,18,
21,23,28; 8:3,6,9,17; 9:1–4,6,8–11;
10:3,19; 11:5,8,9; 12:4,8,13,14; **Song**
3:6,8; 4:2,4,7,10,14; 5:16; 6:6; 7:13; 8:7;
Isa. 1:5,23,25; 2:2,12–16; 3:1; 4:3,5;
5:25,28; 6:3; 7:19,22–25; 8:7,9,12;
9:5,9,12,17,21; 10:4,12,14,23; 11:9; 12:5;
13:5,7,15; 14:7,9,10,18,26,29,31; 15:2,3;
16:7,14; 18:3,6; 19:7,8,10,14,17; 21:2,8,
9,16; 22:1,3,24; 23:9,17; 24:7,10,11;
25:6–8; 26:12,14,15; 27:9; 28:8,22,24;
29:7,8,11,20; 30:5,18,25,32; 31:3;
32:13,20; 33:20; 34:1,2,4,12; 36:1,6,20;
37:11,16–18,20,25,36; 38:13,15–17,20;
39:2,4,6; 40:2,4–6,17,26; 41:11,29;
42:15,22; 43:7,9,14; 44:9,11,23,24,28;
45:7,12,13,16,22–25; 46:3,10; 48:6,14;
49:9,11,18,26; 50:9,11; 51:3,13,18,20;
52:5,10; 53:6; 54:5,12,13,17; 55:1,12;
56:2,6,7,9–11; 57:5,13; 58:3,6; 59:8,11;
60:4,6,7,14,21; 61:2,9,11; 62:2,6; 63:3,
7,9; 64:6,8,9,11; 65:2,5,8,12,25; 66:2,
10,16,18,20,23,24; **Jer.** 1:7,14–18;
2:3,4,20,21,24,29,34; 3:6–8,10,13,17;
4:20,24–27,29; 5:6,16,19; 6:6,13,28;
7:2,10,13,15,23,25,27; 8:2,3,6,10,16;
9:2,4,25,26; 10:7,9,14,16,20,21; 11:4,6,8;
12:1,4,9,11,12,14; 13:7,10–13,19; 14:22;
15:4,10,13; 16:10,15–17; 17:3,9,13,19,
20,22,24; 18:16,18,23; 19:3,8,13–15;
20:4–8,10; 21:2,14; 22:20,22; 23:3,8,9,
14,15,17; 24:7,9; 25:1,2,4,9,11,13,15,
17,19,20,22–26,29–31; 26:2,6–9,11,12,
15–21; 27:6,7,12,16,20; 28:1,3–7,11,14;
29:1,4,13,14,16,18,20,22,25,26,31; 30:2,
6,11,14,16,20; 31:1,24,25,30,34,36,
37,40; 32:12,17,19,23,27,32,37,39,41,42;
33:5,8,9,12,18; 34:1,6–8,10,17,19; 35:3,
7,8,10,15,17–19; 36:2–4,6,8–14,16–18,
20,21,23,24,28,31,32; 37:10,21; 38:1,
4,9,22,23,27; 39:1,3,4,6,13; 40:1,4,5,
7,11–13,15; 41:3,9–14,16; 42:1,2,4,5,8,
17,20,21; 43:1,2,4–6; 44:1,2,4,8,11,12,
15,17,18,20,24,26–28; 45:4,5; 46:28;
47:2,4; 48:8,17,24,31,37–39; 49:5,13,
17,26,29,32,36; 50:7,10,13,14,21,23,27,
29,30,32,33,37; 51:3,7,17,19,24,25,28,
41,43,47–49,52,60,61; 52:2,4,7,8,10,13,
14,17,18,20,22,23,30,33,34; **Lam.**
1:2–4,6–8,10–13,15,18,21,22; 2:2–5,
15,16,19; 3:3,14,34,46,51,60–62; 4:1,12;
Ezek. 3:7,10; 5:4,9–12,14; 6:6,9,11,
13,14; 7:3,8,12–14,16–18; 8:10; 9:4,6,
8,11; 10:12; 11:15,18,25; 12:10,14,16,
19,22–24,28; 13:18; 14:5,6,11,22,23;
15:2,3; 16:15,22–25,30,31,33,36,37,43,
44,47,51,54,57,63; 17:9,18,21,23,24;
18:4,11,13,14,19,21,22,24,28,30,31;
20:6,15,26,28,31,40,43,47,48; 21:4,5,
7,10,12,15,24; 22:2,4,18,19; 23:6,7,12,
15,23,29,48; 24:4,24; 25:6,8; 26:11,
16,17; 27:5,9,12,18,21,22,27,29,34,35;
28:3,13,18,19,24,26; 29:2,4–7,18; 30:5,8;
31:4–6,8,9,12–16,18; 32:4,8,12,13,15,
16,20,22–26,29–32; 33:13,16,29;
34:5,6,8,12,13,21; 35:8,12,14,15;
36:5,10,24,25,29,33,34; 37:11,16,22–24;
38:4–9,11,13,15,20,21; 39:4,11,13,17,18,
20,21,23,25,26; 40:4; 41:17,19; 42:11;
43:11,12; 44:5–7,9,13,14,21,24,29–31;
45:1,6,16,17,22; 47:9,12; 48:13,19,20;
Dan. 1:4,15,17,19,20; 8:4,5; 9:6,7,
11–14,16; 11:2,17,36,37,43; 12:1,7,10;
Hos. 2:11; 4:3; 5:2; 7:2,4,6,7,10; 9:1,4,
8,15; 10:14; 12:1,8; 13:2,10,15; 14:2;
Joel 1:2,5,12,14,19; 2:1,6,12,28,32;
3:2,4,9,11,12,18; **Amos** 2:3,8; 3:1,2; 4:6;
5:16,17; 7:10; 8:3,7,8,10; 9:1,5,9,10,

12,13; **Obad.** 1:7,15,16; **Jon.** 2:3; **Mic.** 1:2,5,7; 2:12; 3:7,9; 4:5,13; 5:9,11; 6:16; 7:2,16,19; **Nah.** 1:4,5,15; 2:9,10; 3:1,7, 10,12,19; **Hab.** 1:9,10,15; 2:5,6,8,17, 19,20; **Zeph.** 1:2,4,8,9,11,18; 2:3,11, 14,15; 3:7–9,11,14,19,20; **Hag.** 1:11, 12,14; 2:4,7,12–14,17; **Zech.** 1:11; 2:13; 4:2,10,14; 5:3,6; 6:5; 7:5,14; 8:10,12, 17,23; 9:1; 10:4,11; 11:10; 12:2–4,6,9,14; 13:8; 14:2,5,9,10,12,14–16,19,21; **Mal.** 1:11; 2:9,10,17; 3:9,10,12; 4:1,4.

3606. כֹּל *kōl* **Aram. particle**
(all, any, entire; corr. to Hebr. 3605)
Ezra 4:14,20; 5:7; 6:11,12,17; 7:13,14,16,17,21,23–26; **Dan.** 2:8,10,12, 24,30,35,38–41,44,45,48; 3:2,3,5,7,8,10, 15,22,28,29; 4:1(3:31),6(3),9(6),11(8), 12(9),18(15),20(17),21(18),28(25), 35(32),37(34); 5:7,8,12,19,22,23; 6:1(2), 3–5(4–6),7(8),9(10),10(11),12(13), 15(16),22–26(23–27); 7:7,14,16, 19,23,27.

3607. I. כָּלָא *kālā'* **verb**
(to close, to hinder, to restrain)
Gen. 8:2; 23:6; **Ex.** 36:6; **Num.** 11:28; **1 Sam.** 6:10; 25:33; **Ps.** 40:9(10),11(12); 88:8(9); 119:101; **Eccl.** 8:8; **Isa.** 43:6; **Jer.** 32:2,3; **Ezek.** 31:15; **Hag.** 1:10.
II. כָּלָא *kālā'* **verb**
(to finish)
Dan. 9:24.

3608. כֶּלֶא *kele'* **masc. noun**
(prison)
1 Kgs. 22:27; **2 Kgs.** 17:4; 25:27,29; **2 Chr.** 18:26; **Isa.** 42:7,22; **Jer.** 37:15,18; 52:33.

3609. כִּלְאָב *kil'āḇ* **masc. proper noun**
(Chileab)
2 Sam. 3:3.

3610. כִּלְאַיִם *kil'ayim* **masc. dual noun**
(a mingling of two kinds)
Lev. 19:19; **Deut.** 22:9.

3611. כֶּלֶב *keleḇ* **masc. noun**
(dog, male prostitute)
Ex. 11:7; 22:31(30); **Deut.** 23:18(19); **Judg.** 7:5; **1 Sam.** 17:43; 24:14(15); **2 Sam.** 3:8; 9:8; 16:9; **1 Kgs.** 14:11; 16:4; 21:19,23,24; 22:38; **2 Kgs.** 8:13; 9:10,36; **Job** 30:1; **Ps.** 22:16(17),20(21); 59:6(7),14(15); 68:23(24); **Prov.** 26:11,17; **Eccl.** 9:4; **Isa.** 56:10,11; 66:3; **Jer.** 15:3.

3612. כָּלֵב *kālēḇ* **masc. proper noun**
(Caleb)
Num. 13:6,30; 14:6,24,30,38; 26:65; 32:12; 34:19; **Deut.** 1:36; **Josh.** 14:6, 13,14; 15:13,14,16–18; 21:12; **Judg.** 1:12–15,20; 3:9; **1 Sam.** 30:14; **1 Chr.** 2:18,19,42,46,48–50; 4:15; 6:56(41).

3613. כָּלֵב אֶפְרָתָה *kālēḇ 'eprāṯāh* **proper noun**
(Caleb Ephrathah; from *kālēḇ* [3612] and *'eprāṯāh* [672])
1 Chr. 2:24.

3614. כָּלִבִּי *kālibbiy* **masc. proper noun**
(Calebite)
1 Sam. 25:3.

3615. כָּלָה *kālāh* **verb**
(to finish, to complete, to accomplish, to destroy)
Gen. 2:1,2; 6:16; 17:22; 18:33; 21:15; 24:15,19,22,45; 27:30; 41:30,53; 43:2; 44:12; 49:33; **Ex.** 5:13,14; 31:18; 32:10,12; 33:3,5; 34:33; 39:32; 40:33; **Lev.** 16:20; 19:9; 23:22; 26:16,44; **Num.** 4:15; 7:1; 16:21,31,45(17:10); 17:10(25); 25:11; **Deut.** 7:22; 20:9; 26:12; 28:21; 31:24; 32:23,45; **Josh.** 8:24; 10:20; 19:49,51; 24:20; **Judg.** 3:18; 15:17; **Ruth** 2:21,23; 3:3,18; **1 Sam.** 2:33; 3:12; 10:13; 13:10; 15:18; 18:1; 20:7,9,33;

24:16(17); 25:17; **2 Sam.** 6:18; 11:19; 13:36,39; 21:5; 22:38,39; **1 Kgs.** 1:41; 3:1; 6:9,14,38; 7:1,40; 8:54; 9:1; 17:14,16; 22:11; **2 Kgs.** 10:25; 13:17,19; **1 Chr.** 16:2; 27:24; 28:20; **2 Chr.** 4:11; 7:1,11; 8:8,16; 18:10; 20:23; 24:10,14; 29:17,28,29,34; 31:1,7; 36:22; **Ezra** 1:1; 9:1,14; 10:17; **Neh.** 4:2(3:34); **Esth.** 7:7; **Job** 4:9; 7:6,9; 9:22; 11:20; 17:5; 19:27; 21:13([K^{e}] *bālāh* [1086]); 31:16; 33:21; 36:11; **Ps.** 18:37(38); 31:10(11); 37:20; 39:10(11); 59:13(14); 69:3(4); 71:9,13; 72:20; 73:26; 74:11; 78:33; 84:2(3); 90:7,9; 102:3(4); 119:81,82,87,123; 143:7; **Prov.** 5:11; 16:30; 22:8; **Isa.** 1:28; 10:18,25; 15:6; 16:4; 21:16; 24:13; 27:10; 29:20; 31:3; 32:10; 49:4; **Jer.** 5:3; 8:20; 9:16(15); 10:25; 14:6,12; 16:4; 20:18; 26:8; 43:1; 44:27; 49:37; 51:63; **Lam.** 2:11,22; 3:22; 4:11,17; **Ezek.** 4:6,8; 5:12,13; 6:12; 7:8; 13:14,15; 20:8,13,21; 22:31; 42:15; 43:8(NIV, see *'ākal* [398]),23,27; **Dan.** 11:16(NASB, NIV, *kālāh* [3617]),36; 12:7; **Hos.** 11:6; **Amos** 7:2; **Zech.** 5:4; **Mal.** 3:6.

3616. כָּלֶה *kāleh* **adj.**
(longing, desiring)
Deut. 28:32.

3617. כָּלָה *kālāh* **fem. noun**
(complete destruction, total end)
Gen. 18:21; **Ex.** 11:1; **2 Chr.** 12:12; **Neh.** 9:31; **Isa.** 10:23; 28:22; **Jer.** 4:27; 5:10,18; 30:11; 46:28; **Ezek.** 11:13; 13:13; 20:17; **Dan.** 9:27; 11:16(KJV, *kālāh* [3615]); **Nah.** 1:8,9; **Zeph.** 1:18.

3618. כַּלָּה *kallāh* **fem. noun**
(bride, daughter-in-law)
Gen. 11:31; 38:11,16,24; **Lev.** 18:15; 20:12; **Ruth** 1:6–8,22; 2:20,22; 4:15; **1 Sam.** 4:19; **1 Chr.** 2:4; **Song** 4:8–12; 5:1; **Isa.** 49:18; 61:10; 62:5; **Jer.** 2:32; 7:34; 16:9; 25:10; 33:11; **Ezek.** 22:11; **Hos.** 4:13,14; **Joel** 2:16; **Mic.** 7:6.

3619. כְּלוּב *k^{e}lûḇ* **masc. noun**
(basket, cage)
Jer. 5:27; **Amos** 8:1,2.

3620. A. כְּלוּב *k^{e}lûḇ* **masc. proper noun**
(Chelub: father of Ezri)
1 Chr. 27:26.
B. כְּלוּב *k^{e}lûḇ* **masc. proper noun**
(Chelub: father of Mehir)
1 Chr. 4:11.

3621. כְּלוּבַי *k^{e}lûḇāy* **masc. proper noun**
(Chelubai)
1 Chr. 2:9(NIV, *kālēḇ* [3612]).

3622. כְּלוּהוּ *k^{e}lûhû* **masc. proper noun**
(Chelluh)
Ezra 10:35(NASB, NIV, [K^{e}] *k^{e}lûhiy*).

3623. כְּלוּלָה *k^{e}lûlāh* **fem. noun**
(betrothal, espousal)
Jer. 2:2.

3624. כֶּלַח *kelaḥ* **masc. noun**
(full strength, vigor)
Job 5:26; 30:2.

3625. כֶּלַח *kelaḥ* **proper noun**
(Calah)
Gen. 10:11,12.

3626. A. כָּל־חֹזֶה *kol-ḥōzeh* **masc. proper noun**
(Col-Hozeh: father of Shallun)
Neh. 3:15.
B. כָּל־חֹזֶה *kol-ḥōzeh* **masc. proper noun**
(Col-Hozeh: a Judaite)
Neh. 11:5.

3627. כְּלִי *k^{e}liy* **masc. noun**
(article, vessel, instrument, jewel)
Gen. 24:53; 27:3; 31:37; 42:25; 43:11; 45:20; 49:5; **Ex.** 3:22; 11:2; 12:35;

22:7(6); 25:9,39; 27:3,19; 30:27,28; 31:7–9; 35:13,14,16,22; 37:16,24; 38:3,30; 39:33,36,37,39,40; 40:9,10; **Lev.** 6:28(21); 8:11; 11:32–34; 13:49, 52,53,57–59; 14:5,50; 15:4,6,12,22, 23,26; **Num.** 1:50; 3:8,31,36; 4:9,10, 12,14–16,26,32; 5:17; 7:1,85; 18:3; 19:15,17,18; 31:6,20,50,51; 35:16,18,22; **Deut.** 1:41; 22:5; 23:24(25); **Josh.** 6:19,24; 7:11; **Judg.** 9:54; 18:11,16,17; **Ruth** 2:9; **1 Sam.** 6:8,15; 8:12; 9:7; 10:22; 14:1,6,7,12–14,17; 16:21; 17:22, 40,49,54; 20:40; 21:5(6),8(9); 25:13; 30:24; 31:4–6,9,10; **2 Sam.** 1:27; 8:10; 17:28; 18:15; 23:37; 24:22; **1 Kgs.** 6:7; 7:45,47,48,51; 8:4; 10:21,25; 15:15; 17:10; 19:21; **2 Kgs.** 4:3,4,6; 7:15; 11:8,11; 12:13(14); 14:14; 20:13; 23:4; 24:13; 25:14,16; **1 Chr.** 9:28,29; 10:4,5, 9,10; 11:39; 12:33,37; 15:16; 16:5,42; 18:8,10; 22:19; 23:5,26; 28:13,14; **2 Chr.** 4:16,18,19; 5:1,5,13; 7:6; 9:20,24; 15:18; 20:25; 23:7,13; 24:14; 25:24; 28:24; 29:18,19,26,27; 30:21; 32:27; 34:12; 36:7,10,18,19; **Ezra** 1:6,7,10,11; 8:25–28,30,33; **Neh.** 10:39(40); 12:36; 13:5,8,9; **Esth.** 1:7; **Job** 28:17; **Ps.** 2:9; 7:13(14); 31:12(13); 71:22; **Prov.** 20:15; 25:4; **Eccl.** 9:18; **Isa.** 10:28; 13:5; 18:2; 22:24; 32:7; 39:2; 52:11; 54:16,17; 61:10; 65:4; 66:20; **Jer.** 14:3; 18:4; 19:11; 21:4; 22:7,28; 25:34; 27:16,18,19,21; 28:3,6; 32:14; 40:10; 46:19; 48:11,12,38; 49:29; 50:25; 51:20,34; 52:18,20; **Ezek.** 4:9; 9:1,2; 12:3,4,7; 15:3; 16:17,39; 23:26; 27:13; 32:27; 40:42; **Dan.** 1:2; 11:8; **Hos.** 8:8; 13:15; **Amos** 6:5; **Jon.** 1:5; **Nah.** 2:9(10); **Zech.** 11:15.

3628. כְּלִיא *k^e^liy'*, כְּלוּא *k^e^lû'* **masc. noun**
(prison)
Jer. 37:4; 52:31.

3629. כִּלְיָה *kilyāh* **fem. noun**
(kidney, heart as the seat of emotion)
Ex. 29:13,22; **Lev.** 3:4,10,15; 4:9; 7:4; 8:16,25; 9:10,19; **Deut.** 32:14; **Job** 16:13; 19:27; **Ps.** 7:9(10); 16:7; 26:2; 73:21; 139:13; **Prov.** 23:16; **Isa.** 34:6; **Jer.** 11:20; 12:2; 17:10; 20:12; **Lam.** 3:13.

3630. כִּלְיוֹן *kilyôn* **masc. proper noun**
(Chilion)
Ruth 1:2,5; 4:9.

3631. כִּלָּיוֹן *killāyôn* **masc. noun**
(destruction, failing)
Deut. 28:65; **Isa.** 10:22.

3632. כָּלִיל *kāliyl* **adj.; subst.**
(perfect, complete, whole burnt offering)
Ex. 28:31; 39:22; **Lev.** 6:22(15),23(16); **Num.** 4:6; **Deut.** 13:16(17); 33:10; **Judg.** 20:40; **1 Sam.** 7:9; **Ps.** 51:19(21); **Isa.** 2:18; **Lam.** 2:15; **Ezek.** 16:14; 27:3; 28:12.

3633. כַּלְכֹּל *kalkōl* **masc. proper noun**
(Calcol)
1 Kgs. 4:31(5:11); **1 Chr.** 2:6.

3634. כָּלַל *kālal* **verb**
(to perfect, to bring to perfection)
Ezek. 27:4,11.

3635. כְּלַל *k^e^lal* **Aram. verb**
(to restore, to finish; corr. to Hebr. 3634)
Ezra 4:12,13,16; 5:3,9,11; 6:14.

3636. כְּלָל *k^e^lāl* **masc. proper noun**
(Chelal)
Ezra 10:30.

3637. כָּלַם *kālam* **verb**
(to be disgraced, to be ashamed; to blush)

Num. 12:14; **Judg.** 18:7; **Ruth** 2:15; **1 Sam.** 20:34; 25:7,15; **2 Sam.** 10:5; 19:3(4); **1 Chr.** 19:5; **2 Chr.** 30:15; **Ezra** 9:6; **Job** 11:3; 19:3; **Ps.** 35:4; 40:14(15); 44:9(10); 69:6(7); 70:2(3); 74:21; **Prov.** 25:8; 28:7; **Isa.** 41:11; 45:16,17; 50:7; 54:4; **Jer.** 3:3; 6:15; 8:12; 14:3; 22:22; 31:19; **Ezek.** 16:27,54,61; 36:32; 43:10,11.

3638. כִּלְמַד *kilmad̲* **proper noun**
(Chilmad)
Ezek. 27:23.

3639. כְּלִמָּה *k^e^limmāh* **fem. noun**
(disgrace, shame, humiliation)
Job 20:3; **Ps.** 4:2(3); 35:26; 44:15(16); 69:7(8),19(20); 71:13; 109:29; **Prov.** 18:13; **Isa.** 30:3; 45:16; 50:6; 61:7; **Jer.** 3:25; 20:11; 51:51; **Ezek.** 16:52,54,63; 32:24,25,30; 34:29; 36:6,7,15; 39:26; 44:13; **Mic.** 2:6.

3640. כְּלִמּוּת *k^e^limmût̲* **fem. noun**
(shame, humiliation)
Jer. 23:40.

3641. כַּלְנֶה *kalneh,* כַּלְנֵה *kalnēh,* כַּלְנוֹ *kalnô* **proper noun**
(Calneh, Calno)
Gen. 10:10; **Isa.** 10:9; **Amos** 6:2.

3642. כָּמַהּ *kāmah* **verb**
(to long for, to yearn for)
Ps. 63:1(2).

3643. כִּמְהָם *kimhām,* כִּמְהָן *kimhān* **masc. proper noun**
(Chimham)
2 Sam. 19:37(38),38(39),40(41); **Jer.** 41:17.

3644. כְּמוֹ *k^e^mô* **particle**
(like, as)
Gen. 19:15; 41:39; 44:15,18; **Ex.** 9:14,18,24; 11:6; 15:5,8,11; 30:32,33,38; **Lev.** 19:18,34; **Num.** 23:10; **Deut.** 4:32; 5:14(13),26(25); 7:26; 18:15,18; 33:29; **Judg.** 8:18; 9:48; **1 Sam.** 10:24; 26:15; **2 Sam.** 7:22; 18:3; **1 Kgs.** 3:12,13; 8:23; 22:4; **2 Kgs.** 18:5; 23:25; **1 Chr.** 17:20; **2 Chr.** 6:14; 18:3; 35:18; **Neh.** 6:11; 9:11; 13:26; **Job** 1:8; 2:3; 6:15; 9:32; 10:22; 12:3; 14:9; 19:22; 28:5; 31:37; 35:8; 36:22; 38:14; 40:9,17; 41:24(16); **Ps.** 29:6; 35:10; 50:21; 58:4(5),7–9 (8–10); 61:6(7); 63:5(6); 71:19; 73:15; 78:13,69; 79:5; 86:8; 88:5(6); 89:8(9); 90:9; 92:7(8); 102:3; 115:8; 135:18; 140:3(4); 141:7; **Prov.** 23:7; **Song** 7:1(2); **Isa.** 26:17,18; 30:22; 41:25; 46:9; 51:6; **Jer.** 10:6,7; 13:21; 30:7; 49:19; 50:44; **Lam.** 1:21; 4:6; **Ezek.** 5:9; 16:57; **Hos.** 7:4; 8:12; 13:7; **Joel** 2:2; **Hab.** 3:14; **Mic.** 7:18; **Hag.** 2:3; **Zech.** 5:3; 9:15; 10:2,7,8.

3645. כְּמוֹשׁ *k^e^môš* **masc. proper noun**
(Chemosh)
Num. 21:29; **Judg.** 11:24; **1 Kgs.** 11:7,33; **2 Kgs.** 23:13; **Jer.** 48:7,13,46.

3646. כַּמֹּן *kammōn* **masc. noun**
(cummin)
Isa. 28:25,27.

3647. כָּמַס *kāmas* **verb**
(to store up, to save)
Deut. 32:34.

3648. כָּמַר *kāmar* **verb**
(to be aroused, to be deeply moved)
Gen. 43:30; **1 Kgs.** 3:26; **Lam.** 5:10; **Hos.** 11:8.

3649. כֹּמֶר *kōmer* **masc. noun**
(priest, idolatrous priest)
2 Kgs. 23:5; **Hos.** 10:5; **Zeph.** 1:4.

3650. כִּמְרִיר *kimriyr* **masc. noun**
(blackness)
Job 3:5.

3651. I. כֵּן *kēn* **adv.**
(therefore, so)
Gen. 1:7,9,11,15,24,30; 2:24; 6:4,22; 10:9; 11:9; 15:14; 16:14; 18:5; 19:8,22; 20:6; 21:31; 23:19; 25:22,26,30; 26:33; 29:26,28,34,35; 30:6,15; 31:48; 32:20(21), 32(33); 33:10,17; 34:7; 38:26; 41:13,31; 42:20,21,25; 43:11; 44:10; 45:15,21; 47:22; 48:18; 50:3,11,12; **Ex.** 1:12; 3:20; 5:8,17; 6:6,9; 7:6,10,11,20,22; 8:7(3), 17(13),18(14),24(20),26(22); 10:10,11, 14,29(KJV, NASB, see II); 11:1,8; 12:28,50; 13:15; 14:4; 15:23; 16:17,29; 17:6; 20:11; 22:30; 23:11; 25:9,33; 26:4,17,24; 27:8,11; 34:32; 36:11,22,29; 37:19; 39:32,42,43; 40:16; **Lev.** 4:20; 8:35; 10:13; 14:36; 16:16,26,28; 17:12; 24:19,20; 27:12,14; **Num.** 1:54; 2:17,34; 4:15; 5:4; 6:21; 8:3,4,15,20,22; 9:5,14,16,17; 10:31; 12:7; 13:33; 14:28,43; 15:14,20; 16:11; 17:11(26); 18:24,28; 20:12; 21:14,27; 25:12; 32:23,31; 36:10; **Deut.** 3:21; 4:5; 5:15; 7:19; 8:20; 10:9; 12:4,22,30,31; 15:11,15,17; 18:14; 19:7; 20:15; 21:13; 22:3,26; 24:18,22; 28:63; **Josh.** 1:17; 2:4,21; 4:8; 5:15; 7:26; 8:34; 9:26; 11:15; 14:5,14; 21:42(40); 23:15; **Judg.** 1:7; 2:17; 5:15,31; 6:20,22,38,40; 7:17; 8:7; 10:13; 11:8,10; 14:10; 15:11,19; 16:4; 18:12; 21:14,23; **1 Sam.** 1:7; 2:30; 3:14; 5:5,7; 6:10; 8:8; 9:13; 10:5,12; 15:33; 19:24; 20:29; 23:17,28; 24:5,8; 25:25; 26:24; 27:6; 28:2,18; 30:23; **2 Sam.** 2:1; 3:9,28; 5:8,20,25; 7:17,22,27; 8:1; 9:11; 10:1; 12:31; 13:1,12,18,35; 14:17; 15:1; 16:10,19,23; 18:14; 20:18,21; 21:14,18; 22:50; 23:5; 24:10; **1 Kgs.** 1:30,36,37; 2:7,38; 6:26,33; 7:18,29(KJV, NASB, *kēn* [3653,I]); 9:9; 10:12,20,29; 11:8; 12:32; 13:9; 14:4,10; 20:23,25,40; 22:8,12, 19,22; **2 Kgs.** 1:4,6,16; 2:10; 6:24; 7:20; 15:12; 16:11; 18:21; 19:32; 21:12; 22:20; **1 Chr.** 11:7; 13:4; 14:11; 17:15,25; 18:1; 19:1; 20:3,4; 23:30; **2 Chr.** 1:12,17; 7:22; 8:14; 9:19; 16:7; 18:7,11,18,21; 20:1, 26,35; 24:4; 32:17,23,31; 33:14; 35:12; **Ezra** 10:12,16; **Neh.** 2:16; 5:12,15; 6:6,13; 8:17; **Esth.** 1:8,13; 2:4,12; 3:2; 4:16; 6:10; 7:5; 9:14,19,26; **Job** 3:1; 5:27; 6:3; 7:3,9; 8:13; 9:2,22,35; 17:4; 20:2,21; 22:10; 23:15; 32:6,10; 34:10,25,27; 37:24; 42:3,6; **Ps.** 1:4,5; 16:9; 18:49(50); 25:8; 42:1(2),6(7); 45:2(3),7(8),17(18); 46:2(3); 48:5(6),8(9),10(11); 61:8(9); 63:2(3), 4(5); 65:9(10); 73:6,10; 78:21; 83:15(16); 90:12; 103:15; 110:7; 119:104,119, 127–129; 123:2; 127:2,4; 128:4; 147:20; **Prov.** 1:19; 6:15,29; 7:15; 10:26; 11:19 (NASB, NIV, see II); 15:7; 23:7; 24:14,29; 26:1,2,8,19; 27:8,19; 28:2(NIV, see II); 30:20; **Eccl.** 3:19; 5:2(1),16(15); 7:6; 8:10,11; **Song** 1:3; 2:2,3; **Isa.** 1:24,26; 5:13,14,24,25; 7:14; 8:7; 9:17(16); 10:7,11,16,24; 13:7,13; 14:24; 15:4,7; 16:6(NASB, NIV, see II),7,9,11; 17:10; 20:2,4; 21:3; 22:4; 24:6; 25:3; 26:14,17; 27:9,11; 28:14,16; 29:8,14,22; 30:7, 12,13,16,18; 31:4,5; 33:23(NASB, *kēn* [3653,I]); 36:6; 37:33; 38:13,14; 47:15; 50:7; 51:6(NIV, *kēn* [3654,I]),21; 52:6, 14,15; 53:12; 54:9; 55:9,11; 57:10; 59:9; 61:7,11; 63:14; 65:8,13; 66:13,22; **Jer.** 2:9,26,33; 3:20; 5:2,6,14,19,27,31; 6:7,15,18,21; 7:20,32; 8:6,10,12; 9:7(6), 15(14); 10:21; 11:11,21,22; 12:8; 13:11; 14:10,15; 15:19; 16:14,16,21; 18:6,13,21; 19:6,12; 20:11; 21:7; 22:18; 23:2,7,12, 15,30,38,39; 24:5,8; 25:8; 28:6,16; 29:28,32; 30:16; 31:3,20,28; 32:28,36,42; 33:22; 34:5,11,17; 35:17,19; 36:30; 38:4,12; 39:12; 42:5,15,18,20; 44:11, 23,26; 48:11,12,30,31,36; 49:2,6,20,26; 50:18,30,39,45; 51:7,36,47,52; **Lam.** 1:8; 3:21,24; **Ezek.** 1:28; 5:7,8,10,11; 7:20; 11:4,5,7,16,17; 12:7,11,23,28; 13:8,13, 20,23; 14:4,6; 15:6; 16:35,37; 17:19; 18:30; 20:27,30,36; 21:4(9),12(17), 24(29); 22:4,19,20,22; 23:9,22,35,44; 24:6,9; 25:4,7,9,13,16; 26:3; 28:6,7; 29:8,10,19; 30:22; 31:5,10; 33:10,25; 34:7,9,12,20; 35:6,11,15; 36:3–7,14, 22,38; 37:12; 38:14; 39:25; 40:16; 41:7; 42:6,11; 44:12; 45:20; **Hos.** 2:6(8),9(11), 14(16); 4:3,7,13; 6:5; 11:2; 13:3,6; **Joel**

2:4,28(3:1); **Amos** 3:2,11,12; 4:5,12; 5:11,13,14,16; 6:7; 7:17; **Jon.** 4:2; **Mic.** 1:14; 2:3,5; 3:6,12; 5:3; **Nah.** 1:12; **Hab.** 1:4,15–17; **Zeph.** 2:9; 3:8; **Hag.** 1:10; 2:14; **Zech.** 1:6,16; 7:13; 8:13,15; 10:2; 11:7,11; 14:15.

II. כֵּן *kēn* **adj.**
(right, true)
Gen. 42:11,19,31,33,34; **Ex.** 10:29(NIV, see I); **Num.** 27:7; 36:5; **Judg.** 12:6; **2 Kgs.** 7:9; 17:9; **Prov.** 11:19(KJV, see I); 28:2(KJV, NASB, see I); **Isa.** 16:6(KJV, see I); 33:23(NASB, *kēn* [3653,I]); **Jer.** 23:10.

3652. כֵּן *kēn* **Aram. particle**
(thus, so; corr. to Hebr. 3651,I)
Ezra 5:3; 6:2; **Dan.** 2:24,25; 4:14(11); 6:6(7); 7:5,23.

3653. I. כֵּן *kēn* **masc. noun**
(base, pedestal, stand)
Ex. 30:18,28; 31:9; 35:16; 38:8; 39:39; 40:11; **Lev.** 8:11; **1 Kgs.** 7:29(NIV, *kēn* [3651,I]),31; **Isa.** 33:23(KJV, NIV, *kēn* [3651,II]).

II. כֵּן *kēn* **masc. noun**
(position, office, place)
Gen. 40:13; 41:13; **Dan.** 11:7,20,21,38.

3654. כֵּן *kēn* **masc. noun**
(gnat, louse)
Ex. 8:16–18(12–14); **Ps.** 105:31; **Isa.** 51:6(KJV, NASB *kēn* [3651,I]).

3655. כָּנָה *kānāh* **verb**
(to give a surname, to give a title of flattery or honor)
Job 32:21,22; **Isa.** 44:5; 45:4.

3656. כַּנֵּה *kanneh* **proper noun**
(Canneh)
Ezek. 27:23.

3657. כַּנָּה *kannāh* **fem. noun**
(root, shoot [of a grapevine])
Ps. 80:15(16).

3658. כִּנּוֹר *kinnôr* **masc. noun**
(harp, lyre)
Gen. 4:21; 31:27; **1 Sam.** 10:5; 16:16,23; **2 Sam.** 6:5; **1 Kgs.** 10:12; **1 Chr.** 13:8; 15:16,21,28; 16:5; 25:1,3,6; **2 Chr.** 5:12; 9:11; 20:28; 29:25; **Neh.** 12:27; **Job** 21:12; 30:31; **Ps.** 33:2; 43:4; 49:4(5); 57:8(9); 71:22; 81:2(3); 92:3(4); 98:5; 108:2(3); 137:2; 147:7; 149:3; 150:3; **Isa.** 5:12; 16:11; 23:16; 24:8; 30:32; **Ezek.** 26:13.

3659. כָּנְיָהוּ *konyāhû* **masc. proper noun**
(Coniah, a shortened form of *y^{e}konyāh* [3204])
Jer. 22:24,28; 37:1.

3660. כְּנֵמָא *k^{e}nēmā'* **Aram. adv.**
(thus, so, as follows)
Ezra 4:8; 5:4,9,11; 6:13.

3661. כָּנַן *kānan* **verb**
(to shoot up; probable root of *kannāh* [3657], which see)

3662. כְּנָנִי *k^{e}nāniy* **masc. proper noun**
(Chenani)
Neh. 9:4.

3663. A. כְּנַנְיָהוּ *k^{e}nanyāhû*, כְּנַנְיָה *k^{e}nanyāh* **masc. proper noun**
(Chenaniah: a Levite)
1 Chr. 15:22,27.

B. כְּנַנְיָהוּ *k^{e}nanyāhû* **masc. proper noun**
(Chenaniah: an Izharite)
1 Chr. 26:29.

3664. כָּנַס *kānas* **verb**
(to gather, to gather together)
1 Chr. 22:2; **Neh.** 12:44; **Esth.** 4:16; **Ps.** 33:7; 147:2; **Eccl.** 2:8,26; 3:5; **Isa.** 28:20; **Ezek.** 22:21; 39:28.

3665. כָּנַע *kāna'* **verb**
(to humble, to subdue, to be humble)

Lev. 26:41; **Deut.** 9:3; **Judg.** 3:30; 4:23; 8:28; 11:33; **1 Sam.** 7:13; **2 Sam.** 8:1; **1 Kgs.** 21:29; **2 Kgs.** 22:19; **1 Chr.** 17:10; 18:1; 20:4; **2 Chr.** 7:14; 12:6,7,12; 13:18; 28:19; 30:11; 32:26; 33:12,19,23; 34:27; 36:12; **Neh.** 9:24; **Job** 40:12; **Ps.** 81:14(15); 106:42; 107:12; **Isa.** 25:5.

3666. כִּנְעָה *kin'āh* **fem. noun**
(bundle, bag)
Jer. 10:17.

3667. A. כְּנַעַן *k^{e}na'an* **masc. proper noun**
(Canaan: son of Ham)
1 Chr. 1:8,13.
B. כְּנַעַן *k^{e}na'an* **masc. proper noun**
(Land or people of Canaan)
Gen. 9:18,22,25–27; 10:6,15; 11:31; 12:5; 13:12; 16:3; 17:8; 23:2,19; 28:1,6,8; 31:18; 33:18; 35:6; 36:2,5,6; 37:1; 42:5,7, 13,29,32; 44:8; 45:17,25; 46:6,12,31; 47:1,4,13–15; 48:3,7; 49:30; 50:5,13; **Ex.** 6:4; 15:15; 16:35; **Lev.** 14:34; 18:3; 25:38; **Num.** 13:2,17; 26:19; 32:30,32; 33:40,51; 34:2,29; 35:10,14; **Deut.** 32:49; **Josh.** 5:12; 14:1; 21:2; 22:9–11, 32; 24:3; **Judg.** 3:1; 4:2,23,24; 5:19; 21:12; **1 Chr.** 16:18; **Ps.** 105:11; 106:38; 135:11; **Isa.** 19:18; 23:11; **Ezek.** 16:29 (NASB, NIV, see III); 17:4; **Hos.** 12:7(8); **Zeph.** 1:11(KJV, NIV, see III); 2:5.
C. כְּנַעַן *k^{e}na'an* **masc. noun**
(merchant, tradesman)
Isa. 23:8(KJV, *k^{e}na'^{a}niy* [3669,II]); **Ezek.** 16:29(KJV, see II); 17:4; **Hos.** 12:7(8); **Zeph.** 1:11(NASB, see II).

3668. A. כְּנַעֲנָה *k^{e}na'^{a}nāh* **masc. proper noun**
(Chenaanah: father of the prophet Zedekiah)
1 Kgs. 22:11,24; **2 Chr.** 18:10,23.
B. כְּנַעֲנָה *k^{e}na'^{a}nāh* **masc. proper noun**
(Chenaanah: a Benjamite)
1 Chr. 7:10.

3669. I. כְּנַעֲנִי *k^{e}na'^{a}niy* **masc. proper noun**
(Canaanite)
Gen. 10:18,19; 12:6; 13:7; 15:21; 24:3,37; 34:30; 38:2; 46:10; 50:11; **Ex.** 3:8,17; 6:15; 13:5,11; 23:23,28; 33:2; 34:11; **Num.** 13:29; 14:25,43,45; 21:1,3; 33:40; **Deut.** 1:7; 7:1; 11:30; 20:17; **Josh.** 3:10; 5:1; 7:9; 9:1; 11:3; 12:8; 13:3,4; 16:10; 17:12,13,16,18; 24:11; **Judg.** 1:3–5,9,10,17,27–30,32,33; 3:3,5; **2 Sam.** 24:7; **1 Kgs.** 9:16; **1 Chr.** 2:3; **Ezra** 9:1; **Neh.** 9:8,24; **Prov.** 31:24; **Ezek.** 16:3; **Obad.** 1:20; **Zech.** 14:21.
II. כְּנַעֲנִי *k^{e}na'^{a}niy* **masc. noun**
(merchant, tradesman)
Job 41:6(40:30); **Prov.** 31:24; **Isa.** 23:8(NASB, NIV, *k^{e}na'an* [3667,III]).

3670. כָּנַף *kānap̱* **verb**
(to be put into a corner, to be hidden)
Isa. 30:20.

3671. כָּנָף *kānāp̱* **fem. noun**
(wing, skirt, corner of a garment)
Gen. 1:21; 7:14; **Ex.** 19:4; 25:20; 37:9; **Lev.** 1:17; **Num.** 15:38; **Deut.** 4:17; 22:12,30(23:1); 27:20; 32:11; **Ruth** 2:12; 3:9; **1 Sam.** 15:27; 24:4(5),5(6),11(12); **2 Sam.** 22:11; **1 Kgs.** 6:24,27; 8:6,7; **2 Chr.** 3:11–13; 5:7,8; **Job** 37:3; 38:13; 39:13,26; **Ps.** 17:8; 18:10(11); 36:7(8); 57:1(2); 61:4(5); 63:7(8); 66:13(14); 78:27; 91:4; 104:3; 139:9; 148:10; **Prov.** 1:17; 23:5; **Eccl.** 10:20; **Isa.** 6:2; 8:8; 10:14; 11:12; 18:1; 24:16; **Jer.** 2:34; 48:40; 49:22; **Ezek.** 1:6,8,9,11,23–25; 3:13; 5:3; 7:2; 10:5,8,12,16,19,21; 11:22; 16:8; 17:3,7,23; 39:4,17; **Dan.** 9:27; **Hos.** 4:19; **Hag.** 2:12; **Zech.** 5:9; 8:23; **Mal.** 4:2(3:20).

3672. A. כִּנְּרוֹת *kinn^{e}rôṯ*, כִּנֶּרֶת *kinnereṯ* **proper noun**
(City or region of Chinnereth)
Deut. 3:17; **Josh.** 19:35; **1 Kgs.** 15:20.

B. כִּנְּרוֹת *kinn^e^rôṯ*, כִּנֶּרֶת *kinnereṯ* **proper noun**
(Lake of Chinnereth)
Num. 34:11; **Josh.** 11:2; 12:3; 13:27.

3673. כְּנַשׁ *k^e^naš* **Aram. verb**
(to gather together, to assemble; corr. to Hebr. 3664)
Dan. 3:2,3,27.

3674. כְּנָת *k^e^nāṭ* **masc. noun**
(associate, colleague)
Ezra 4:7.

3675. כְּנָת *k^e^nāṯ* **Aram. masc. noun**
(companion, associate; corr. to Hebr. 3674)
Ezra 4:9,17,23; 5:3,6; 6:6,13.

3676. כֵּס *kēs* **masc. noun**
(throne [fig.], an oath from the one sitting on the throne)
Ex. 17:16(NASB, NIV, kissē' [3678]).

3677. כֶּסֶא *kese'*, כֶּסֶה *keseh* **masc. noun**
(full moon)
Ps. 81:3(4); **Prov.** 7:20.

3678. כִּסֵּא *kissē'*, כִּסֵּה *kissēh* **masc. noun**
(throne, seat of honor)
Gen. 41:40; **Ex.** 11:5; 12:29; 17:16(see *kēs* [3676]); **Deut.** 17:18; **Judg.** 3:20; **1 Sam.** 1:9; 2:8; 4:13,18; **2 Sam.** 3:10; 7:13,16; 14:9; **1 Kgs.** 1:13,17,20,24,27, 30,35,37,46–48; 2:4,12,19,24,33,45; 3:6; 5:5(19); 7:7; 8:20,25; 9:5; 10:9,18,19; 16:11; 22:10,19; **2 Kgs.** 4:10; 10:3,30; 11:19; 13:13; 15:12; 25:28; **1 Chr.** 17:12,14; 22:10; 28:5; 29:23; **2 Chr.** 6:10,16; 7:18; 9:8,17,18; 18:9,18; 23:20; **Neh.** 3:7; **Esth.** 1:2; 3:1; 5:1; **Job** 26:9; 36:7; **Ps.** 9:4(5),7(8); 11:4; 45:6(7); 47:8(9); 89:4(5),14(15),29(30),36(37), 44(45); 93:2; 94:20; 97:2; 103:19; 122:5; 132:11,12; **Prov.** 9:14; 16:12; 20:8,28; 25:5; 29:14; **Isa.** 6:1; 9:7(6); 14:9,13; 16:5; 22:23; 47:1; 66:1; **Jer.** 1:15; 3:17; 13:13; 14:21; 17:12,25; 22:2,4,30; 29:16; 33:17,21; 36:30; 43:10; 49:38; 52:32; **Lam.** 5:19; **Ezek.** 1:26; 10:1; 26:16; 43:7; **Jon.** 3:6; **Hag.** 2:22; **Zech.** 6:13.

3679. כַּסְדָּי *kasdāy* **Aram. masc. proper noun**
(Chaldean; NASB, NIV, var. for *kaśdiym* [3778])
Ezra 5:12.

3680. כָּסָה *kāsāh* **verb**
(to cover, to hide, to conceal)
Gen. 7:19,20; 9:23; 18:17; 24:65; 37:26; 38:14,15; **Ex.** 8:6(2); 10:5,15; 14:28; 15:5,10; 16:13; 21:33; 24:15,16; 26:13; 28:42; 29:13,22; 40:34; **Lev.** 3:3,9,14; 4:8; 7:3; 13:12,13; 16:13; 17:13; **Num.** 4:5,8,9,11,12,15; 9:15,16; 16:33,42(17:7); 22:5,11; **Deut.** 13:8(9); 22:12; 23:13(14); **Josh.** 24:7; **Judg.** 4:18,19; **1 Sam.** 19:13; **1 Kgs.** 1:1; 7:18,41,42; 11:29; **2 Kgs.** 19:1,2; **1 Chr.** 21:16; **2 Chr.** 4:12,13; 5:8; **Neh.** 4:5(3:37); **Job** 9:24; 15:27; 16:18; 21:26; 22:11; 23:17; 31:33; 33:17; 36:30,32; 38:34; **Ps.** 32:1,5; 40:10(11); 44:15(16),19(20); 55:5(6); 69:7(8); 78:53; 80:10(11); 85:2(3); 104:6,9; 106:11,17; 140:9(10); 143:9; 147:8; **Prov.** 10:6,11, 12,18; 11:13; 12:16,23; 17:9; 24:31; 26:26; 28:13; **Eccl.** 6:4; **Isa.** 6:2; 11:9; 26:21; 29:10; 37:1,2; 51:16; 58:7; 59:6; 60:2,6; **Jer.** 3:25; 46:8; 51:42,51; **Ezek.** 1:11,23; 7:18; 12:6,12; 16:8,10,18; 18:7, 16; 24:7,8; 26:10,19; 30:18; 31:15; 32:7; 38:9,16; 41:16; **Hos.** 2:9(11); 10:8; **Obad.** 1:10; **Jon.** 3:6,8; **Mic.** 7:10; **Hab.** 2:14,17; 3:3; **Mal.** 2:13,16.

3681. כָּסוּי *kāsûy* **masc. noun**
(cover, covering)
Num. 4:6,14.

3682. כְּסוּת *k^esûṯ* **fem. noun**
(covering, clothing)
Gen. 20:16; **Ex.** 21:10; 22:27(26); **Deut.** 22:12; **Job** 24:7; 26:6; 31:19; **Isa.** 50:3.

3683. כָּסַח *kāsah* **verb**
(to cut down, to cut up)
Ps. 80:16(17); **Isa.** 33:12.

3684. כְּסִיל *k^esiyl* **masc. noun**
(fool, foolish)
Ps. 49:10(11); 92:6(7); 94:8; **Prov.** 1:22,32; 3:35; 8:5; 10:1,18,23; 12:23; 13:16,19,20; 14:7,8,16,24,33; 15:2,7, 14,20; 17:10,12,16,21,24,25; 18:2,6,7; 19:1,10,13,29; 21:20; 23:9; 26:1,3–12; 28:26; 29:11,20; **Eccl.** 2:14–16; 4:5,13; 5:1(4:17),3(2),4(3); 6:8; 7:4–6,9; 9:17; 10:2,12,15.

3685. כְּסִיל *k^esiyl* **proper noun**
(constellation, espec. the constellation Orion)
Job 9:9; 38:31; **Isa.** 13:10; **Amos** 5:8.

3686. כְּסִיל *k^esiyl* **proper noun**
(Chesil)
Josh. 15:30.

3687. כְּסִילוּת *k^esiylûṯ* **fem. noun**
(foolish)
Prov. 9:13.

3688. כָּסַל *kāsal* **verb**
(to be foolish)
Jer. 10:8.

3689. I. כֶּסֶל *kesel* **masc. noun**
(loins, flank)
Lev. 3:4,10,15; 4:9; 7:4; **Job** 15:27; **Ps.** 38:7(8).
II. כֶּסֶל *kesel* **masc. noun**
(confidence)
Job 8:14; 31:24; **Ps.** 49:13(14)(KJV, NASB, see III); 78:7; **Prov.** 3:26.
III. כֶּסֶל *kesel* **masc. noun**
(folly, stupidity)
Ps. 49:13(14)(NIV, see II); **Eccl.** 7:25.

3690. A. כִּסְלָה *kislāh* **fem. noun**
(confidence)
Job 4:6.
B. כִּסְלָה *kislāh* **fem. noun**
(folly, stupidity)
Ps. 85:8(9).

3691. כִּסְלֵו *kislēw* **proper noun**
(the ninth month Chisleu)
Neh. 1:1; **Zech.** 7:1.

3692. כִּסְלוֹן *kislôn* **masc. proper noun**
(Chislon)
Num. 34:21.

3693. כְּסָלוֹן *k^esālôn* **proper noun**
(Chesalon)
Josh. 15:10.

3694. כְּסוּלּוֹת *k^esûllôṯ* **proper noun**
(Chesulloth)
Josh. 19:18.

3695. כַּסְלֻחִים *kasluhiym* **masc. pl. proper noun**
(Casluhites, Casluhim)
Gen. 10:14; **1 Chr.** 1:12.

3696. כִּסְלֹת תָּבֹר *kislōṯ tāḇōr* **proper noun**
(Chisloth Tabor)
Josh. 19:12.

3697. כָּסַם *kāsam* **verb**
(to trim one's hair)
Ezek. 44:20.

3698. כֻּסֶּמֶת *kussemeṯ* **fem. noun**
(spelt, a species of wheat)
Ex. 9:32; **Isa.** 28:25; **Ezek.** 4:9.

3699. כָּסַס *kāsas* **verb**
(to estimate)
Ex. 12:4.

3700. כָּסַף *kāsap̱* **verb**
(to long for, to desire)
Gen. 31:30; **Job** 14:15; **Ps.** 17:12; 84:2(3); **Zeph.** 2:1.

3701. כֶּסֶף *kesep̱* **masc. noun**
(silver, money)
Gen. 13:2; 17:12,13,23,27; 20:16; 23:9, 13,15,16; 24:35,53; 31:15; 37:28; 42:25, 27,28,35; 43:12,15,18,21–23; 44:1,2,8; 45:22; 47:14–16,18; **Ex.** 3:22; 11:2; 12:35,44; 20:23; 21:11,21,32,34,35; 22:7(6),17(16),25(24); 25:3; 26:19,21,25, 32; 27:10,11,17; 30:16; 31:4; 35:5,24,32; 36:24,26,30,36; 38:10–12,17,19,25,27; **Lev.** 5:15; 22:11; 25:37,50,51; 27:3,6, 15,16,18,19; **Num.** 3:48–51; 7:13,19, 25,31,37,43,49,55,61,67,73,79,84,85; 10:2; 18:16; 22:18; 24:13; 31:22; **Deut.** 2:6,28; 7:25; 8:13; 14:25,26; 17:17; 21:14; 22:19,29; 23:19(20); 29:17(16); **Josh.** 6:19,24; 7:21,22,24; 22:8; **Judg.** 5:19; 9:4; 16:5,18; 17:2–4,10; **1 Sam.** 2:36; 9:8; **2 Sam.** 8:10,11; 18:11,12; 21:4; 24:24; **1 Kgs.** 7:51; 10:21,22,25, 27,29; 15:15,18,19; 16:24; 20:3,5,7,39; 21:2,6,15; **2 Kgs.** 5:5,22,23,26; 6:25; 7:8; 12:4(5),7–11(8–12),13(14),15(16), 16(17); 14:14; 15:19,20; 16:8; 18:14,15; 20:13; 22:4,7,9; 23:33,35; 25:15; **1 Chr.** 18:10,11; 19:6; 21:22,24; 22:14,16; 28:14–17; 29:2–5,7; **2 Chr.** 1:15,17; 2:7(6),14(13); 5:1; 9:14,20,21,24,27; 15:18; 16:2,3; 17:11; 21:3; 24:5,11,14; 25:6,24; 27:5; 32:27; 34:9,14,17; 36:3; **Ezra** 1:4,6,9–11; 2:69; 3:7; 8:25,26,28, 30,33; **Neh.** 5:4,10,11,15; 7:71,72; **Esth.** 1:6; 3:9,11; 4:7; **Job** 3:15; 22:25; 27:16,17; 28:1,15; 31:39; **Ps.** 12:6(7); 15:5; 66:10; 68:13(14),30(31); 105:37; 115:4; 119:72; 135:15; **Prov.** 2:4; 3:14; 7:20; 8:10,19; 10:20; 16:16; 17:3; 22:1; 25:4,11; 26:23; 27:21; **Eccl.** 2:8; 5:10(9); 7:12; 10:19; 12:6; **Song** 1:11; 3:10; 8:9,11; **Isa.** 1:22; 2:7,20; 7:23; 13:17; 30:22; 31:7; 39:2; 40:19; 43:24; 46:6; 48:10; 52:3; 55:1,2; 60:9,17; **Jer.** 6:30; 10:4,9; 32:9,10,25,44; 52:19; **Lam.** 5:4; **Ezek.** 7:19; 16:13,17; 22:18,20,22; 27:12; 28:4; 38:13; **Dan.** 11:8,38,43; **Hos.** 2:8(10); 3:2; 8:4; 9:6; 13:2; **Joel** 3:5(4:5); **Amos** 2:6; 8:6; **Mic.** 3:11; **Nah.** 2:9(10); **Hab.** 2:19; **Zeph.** 1:11,18; **Hag.** 2:8; **Zech.** 6:11; 9:3; 11:12,13; 13:9; 14:14; **Mal.** 3:3.

3702. כְּסַף *k^e^sap̱* **Aram. masc. noun**
(silver, money; corr. to Hebr. 3701)
Ezra 5:14; 6:5; 7:15–18,22; **Dan.** 2:32,35,45; 5:2,4,23.

3703. כָּסִפְיָא *kāsip̱yā'* **proper noun**
(Casiphia)
Ezra 8:17.

3704. כֶּסֶת *keseṯ* **fem. noun**
(wristband)
Ezek. 13:18,20.

3705. כְּעַן *k^e^'an* **Aram. adv.**
(now, now then, furthermore)
Ezra 4:13,14,21; 5:16,17; 6:6; **Dan.** 2:23; 3:15; 4:37(34); 5:12,15,16; 6:8(9).

3706. כְּעֶנֶת *k^e^'eneṯ*, כְּעֶת *k^e^'eṯ* **Aram. particle**
(now, and now)
Ezra 4:10,11,17; 7:12.

3707. כָּעַס *kā'as* **verb**
(to provoke to anger, to be angry)
Deut. 4:25; 9:18; 31:29; 32:16,21; **Judg.** 2:12; **1 Sam.** 1:6,7; **1 Kgs.** 14:9,15; 15:30; 16:2,7,13,26,33; 21:22; 22:53(54); **2 Kgs.** 17:11,17; 21:6,15; 22:17; 23:19,26; **2 Chr.** 16:10; 28:25; 33:6; 34:25; **Neh.** 4:1(3:33),5(3:37); **Ps.** 78:58; 106:29; 112:10; **Eccl.** 5:17(16); 7:9; **Isa.** 65:3; **Jer.** 7:18,19; 8:19; 11:17; 25:6,7; 32:29,

30,32; 44:3,8; **Ezek.** 8:17; 16:26,42; 32:9; **Hos.** 12:14(15).

3708. I. כַּעַס *ka'as* **masc. noun**
(anger, irritation, grief)
Deut. 32:19,27; **1 Sam.** 1:6,16; **1 Kgs.** 15:30; 21:22; **2 Kgs.** 23:26; **Ps.** 6:7(8); 10:14; 31:9(10); 85:4(5); **Prov.** 12:16; 17:25; 21:19; 27:3; **Eccl.** 1:18; 2:23; 7:3,9; 11:10; **Ezek.** 20:28.
II. כַּעַשׂ *ka'aś* **masc. noun**
(anger, irritation, grief)
Job 5:2; 6:2; 10:17; 17:7.

3709. כַּף *kap̱* **fem. noun**
(hand, palm of the hand, sole of the foot; handshaped branch of the palm tree)
Gen. 8:9; 20:5; 31:42; 32:25(26),32(33); 40:11,21; **Ex.** 4:4; 9:29,33; 25:29; 29:24; 33:22,23; 37:16; **Lev.** 8:27,28; 9:17; 11:27; 14:15–18,26–29; 23:40(NIV, *kippah* [3712]); **Num.** 4:7; 5:18; 6:19; 7:14,20,26,32,38,44,50,56,62,68,74,80,84,86; 24:10; **Deut.** 2:5; 11:24; 25:12; 28:35,56,65; **Josh.** 1:3; 3:13; 4:18; **Judg.** 6:13,14; 8:6,15; 12:3; 14:9; **1 Sam.** 4:3; 5:4; 19:5; 25:29; 28:21; **2 Sam.** 14:16,25; 18:12,14; 19:9(10); 22:1; **1 Kgs.** 5:3(17); 7:50; 8:22,38,54; 17:12; 18:44; **2 Kgs.** 4:34; 9:35; 11:12; 16:7; 18:21; 19:24; 20:6; 25:14; **1 Chr.** 12:17; **2 Chr.** 4:22; 6:12,13,29; 24:14; 30:6; 32:11; **Ezra** 8:31; 9:5; **Job** 2:7; 9:30; 10:3; 11:13; 13:14,21; 16:17; 22:30; 27:23; 29:9; 31:7; 36:32; 41:8(40:32); **Ps.** 7:3(4); 9:16(17); 24:4; 26:6; 44:20(21); 47:1(2); 63:4(5); 71:4; 73:13; 78:72; 81:6(7); 88:9(10); 91:12; 98:8; 119:48,109; 128:2; 129:7; 139:5; 141:2; **Prov.** 6:1,3; 10:4; 17:18; 22:26; 31:13,16,19,20; **Eccl.** 4:6; **Song** 5:5; **Isa.** 1:6,15; 28:4; 33:15; 36:6; 37:25; 38:6; 49:16; 55:12; 59:3,6; 60:14; 62:3; **Jer.** 4:31; 12:7; 15:21; 52:18,19; **Lam.** 2:15,19; 3:41; **Ezek.** 1:7; 6:11; 21:11(16),14(19),17(22),24(29); 22:13; 29:7; 43:7; **Dan.** 10:10; **Jon.** 3:8; **Mic.** 4:10; 7:3; **Nah.** 3:19; **Hab.** 2:9; **Hag.** 1:11; **Mal.** 4:3(3:21).

3710. כֵּף *kēp̱* **masc. noun**
(rock)
Job 30:6; **Jer.** 4:29.

3711. כָּפָה *kāp̱āh* **verb**
(to pacify, to soothe)
Prov. 21:14.

3712. כִּפָּה *kippāh* **fem. noun**
(branch, palm branch)
Lev. 23:40(KJV, NASB, *kap̱* [3709]); **Job** 15:32; **Isa.** 9:14(13); 19:15.

3713. I. כְּפוֹר *k^ep̱ôr* **masc. noun**
(bowl)
1 Chr. 28:17; **Ezra** 1:10; 8:27.
II. כְּפוֹר *k^ep̱ôr* **masc. noun**
(hoarfrost)
Ex. 16:14; **Job** 38:29; **Ps.** 147:16.

3714. כָּפִיס *kāp̱iys* **masc. noun**
(beam, rafter)
Hab. 2:11.

3715. I. כְּפִיר *k^ep̱iyr* **masc. noun**
(young lions)
Judg. 14:5; **Job** 4:10; 38:39; **Ps.** 17:12; 34:10(11); 35:17; 58:6(7); 91:13; 104:21; **Prov.** 19:12; 20:2; 28:1; **Isa.** 5:29; 11:6; 31:4; **Jer.** 2:15; 25:38; 51:38; **Ezek.** 19:2,3,5,6; 32:2; 38:13(NASB, NIV, see II); 41:19; **Hos.** 5:14; **Amos** 3:4; **Mic.** 5:8(7); **Nah.** 2:11(12),13(14); **Zech.** 11:3.
II. כְּפִיר *k^ep̱iyr* **masc. noun**
(villages)
Neh. 6:2(NASB, see III); **Ezek.** 38:13(KJV, see I).
III. כְּפִיר *k^ep̱iyr* **masc. noun**
(Chephirim: a village in Benjamin)
Neh. 6:2(KJV, NIV, see II).

3716. כְּפִירָה *k^ep̱iyrāh* **proper noun**
(Chephirah)
Josh. 9:17; 18:26; **Ezra** 2:25; **Neh.** 7:29.

3717. כָּפַל *kāpal* **verb**
(to double, to become double)
Ex. 26:9; 28:16; 39:9; **Ezek.** 21:14(19).

3718. כֶּפֶל *kepel* **masc. noun**
(double, doubled)
Job 11:6; 41:13(5); **Isa.** 40:2.

3719. כָּפַן *kāpan* **verb**
(to bend, to twist)
Ezek. 17:7.

3720. כָּפָן *kāpān* **masc. noun**
(hunger, famine)
Job 5:22; 30:3.

3721. כָּפַף *kāpap* **verb**
(to bow down)
Ps. 57:6(7); 145:14; 146:8; **Isa.** 58:5; **Mic.** 6:6.

3722. כָּפַר *kāpar* **verb**
(to cover, to purge, to make atonement for)
Gen. 6:14; 32:20(21); **Ex.** 29:33,36,37; 30:10,15,16; 32:30; **Lev.** 1:4; 4:20,26, 31,35; 5:6,10,13,16,18; 6:7(5:26),30(23); 7:7; 8:15,34; 9:7; 10:17; 12:7,8; 14:18–21, 29,31,53; 15:15,30; 16:6,10,11,16–18, 20,24,27,30,32–34; 17:11; 19:22; 23:28; **Num.** 5:8; 6:11; 8:12,19,21; 15:25,28; 16:46(17:11),47(17:12); 25:13; 28:22,30; 29:5; 31:50; 35:33; **Deut.** 21:8; 32:43; **1 Sam.** 3:14; **2 Sam.** 21:3; **1 Chr.** 6:49(34); **2 Chr.** 29:24; 30:18; **Neh.** 10:33(34); **Ps.** 65:3(4); 78:38; 79:9; **Prov.** 16:6,14; **Isa.** 6:7; 22:14; 27:9; 28:18; 47:11; **Jer.** 18:23; **Ezek.** 16:63; 43:20,26; 45:15,17,20; **Dan.** 9:24.

3723. כָּפָר *kāpār* **masc. noun**
(village)
1 Chr. 27:25; **Song** 7:11(12).

3724. I. כֹּפֶר *kōper* **masc. noun**
(ransom, bribe)
Ex. 21:30; 30:12; **Num.** 35:31,32; **1 Sam.** 12:3; **Job** 33:24; 36:18; **Ps.** 49:7(8); **Prov.** 6:35; 13:8; 21:18; **Isa.** 43:3; **Amos** 5:12.
II. כֹּפֶר *kōper* **masc. noun**
(bitumen, pitch)
Gen. 6:14.
III. כֹּפֶר *kōper* **masc. noun**
(village)
1 Sam. 6:18.
IV. כֹּפֶר *kōper* **masc. noun**
(camphire, henna)
Song 1:14; 4:13.

3725. כִּפֻּרִים *kippuriym* **masc. pl. noun**
(atonement)
Ex. 29:36; 30:10,16; **Lev.** 23:27,28; 25:9; **Num.** 5:8; 29:11.

3726. כְּפַר הָעַמּוֹנִי *k^e^par ha'ammôniy* **proper noun**
(Chephar-ammoni; from *kāpar* [3723] and *'ammôniy* [5984])
Josh. 18:24.

3727. כַּפֹּרֶת *kappōret* **fem. noun**
(mercy seat, place of atonement)
Ex. 25:17–22; 26:34; 30:6; 31:7; 35:12; 37:6–9; 39:35; 40:20; **Lev.** 16:2,13–15; **Num.** 7:89; **1 Chr.** 28:11.

3728. כָּפַשׁ *kāpaš* **verb**
(to make one cower, to trample)
Lam. 3:16.

3729. כְּפַת *k^e^pat* **Aram. verb**
(to bind, to tie up)
Dan. 3:20,21,23,24.

3730. כַּפְתּוֹר *kaptôr*, כַּפְתֹּר *kaptōr* **masc. noun**
(a bulb, bulge as ornament, capitol on a column)
Ex. 25:31,33–36; 37:17,19–22; **Amos** 9:1; **Zeph.** 2:14.

3731. כַּפְתּוֹר *kaptôr*, כַּפְתֹּר *kaptōr* **proper noun**

(Caphtor)
Deut. 2:23; **Jer.** 47:4; **Amos** 9:7.

3732. כַּפְתֹּרִי *kaptōriy* **masc. proper noun**
(Caphtorite)
Gen. 10:14; **Deut.** 2:23; **1 Chr.** 1:12.

3733. I. כַּר *kar* **masc. noun**
(lamb, ram)
Deut. 32:14; **1 Sam.** 15:9; **2 Kgs.** 3:4; **Ps.** 37:20(NASB, NIV, see II); **Isa.** 16:1; 34:6; **Jer.** 51:40; **Ezek.** 4:2; 21:22(27); 27:21; 39:18; **Amos** 6:4.
II. כַּר *kar* **masc. noun**
(pasture, meadow)
Ps. 37:20(KJV, see I); 65:13(14); **Isa.** 30:23.
III. כַּר *kar* **masc. noun**
(saddle)
Gen. 31:34.

3734. I. כֹּר *kōr* **masc. noun**
(a measure of grain or oil)
1 Kgs. 4:22(5:2); 5:11(25); **2 Chr.** 2:10(9); 27:5; **Ezek.** 45:14.
II. כֹּר *kōr* **Aram. masc. noun**
(a measure of grain)
Ezra 7:22.

3735. כְּרָה *kᵉrāh* **Aram. verb**
(to be troubled, to be grieved)
Dan. 7:15.

3736. כִּרְבֵּל *kirbēl* **verb**
(to be clothed with)
1 Chr. 15:27.

3737. כַּרְבְּלָה *karbᵉlāh* **Aram. fem. noun**
(cap, turban)
Dan. 3:21.

3738. כָּרָה *kārāh* **verb**
(to dig)
Gen. 26:25; 50:5; **Ex.** 21:33; **Num.** 21:18; **2 Chr.** 16:14; **Job** 6:27(NASB, NIV, *kārāh* [3739,I]); **Ps.** 7:15(16); 22:16(17) (KJV, *ʾariy* [738,III]; NASB, *kûr* [3564,II]); 40:6(7); 57:6(7); 94:13; 119:85; **Prov.** 16:27; 26:27; **Jer.** 18:20,22.

3739. I. כָּרָה *kārāh* **verb**
(to buy, to bargain for, to barter for)
Deut. 2:6; **Job** 6:27(KJV, *kārāh* [3738]); 41:6(40:30)(KJV, see II); **Hos.** 3:2.
II. כָּרָה *kārāh* **verb**
(to give a feast or banquet)
2 Kgs. 6:23; **Job** 41:6(40:30)(NASB, NIV, see I).

3740. כֵּרָה *kērāh* **fem. noun**
(feast)
2 Kgs. 6:23.

3741. כָּרָה *kārāh* **fem. noun**
(cottage)
Zeph. 2:6(NIV, *kᵉrēṯiy* [3774]).

3742. כְּרוּב *kᵉrûḇ* **masc. noun**
(cherub)
Gen. 3:24; **Ex.** 25:18–20,22; 26:1,31; 36:8,35; 37:7–9; **Num.** 7:89; **1 Sam.** 4:4; **2 Sam.** 6:2; 22:11; **1 Kgs.** 6:23–29, 32,35; 7:29,36; 8:6,7; **2 Kgs.** 19:15; **1 Chr.** 13:6; 28:18; **2 Chr.** 3:7,10–14; 5:7,8; **Ps.** 18:10(11); 80:1(2); 99:1; **Isa.** 37:16; **Ezek.** 9:3; 10:1–9,14–16,18–20; 11:22; 28:14,16; 41:18,20,25.

3743. כְּרוּב *kᵉrûḇ* **masc. noun**
(Cherub, Kerub)
Ezra 2:59; **Neh.** 7:61.

3744. כָּרוֹז *kārôz* **Aram. masc. noun**
(herald)
Dan. 3:4.

3745. כְּרַז *kᵉraz* **Aram. noun**
(proclamation)
Dan. 5:29.

3746. I. כָּרִי *kāriy* **masc. pl. noun**
(captains)

2 Kgs. 11:4(NASB, NIV, see II),19(NASB, NIV, see II).
II. כָּרִי *kāriy* **masc. pl. noun**
(Carites)
2 Kgs. 11:4(KJV, see I),19(KJV, see I).

3747. כְּרִית k^e*riyṯ* **proper noun**
(Cherith)
1 Kgs. 17:3,5.

3748. כְּרִיתוּת k^e*riyṯûṯ* **fem. noun**
(divorce)
Deut. 24:1,3; **Isa.** 50:1; **Jer.** 3:8.

3749. כַּרְכֹּב *karkōḇ* **masc. noun**
(rim, ledge, edge)
Ex. 27:5; 38:4.

3750. כַּרְכֹּם *karkōm* **masc. noun**
(saffron)
Song 4:14.

3751. כַּרְכְּמִישׁ *kark*^{e}*miyš* **proper noun**
(Carchemish)
2 Chr. 35:20; **Isa.** 10:9; **Jer.** 46:2.

3752. כַּרְכַּס *karkas* **masc. proper noun**
(Carcas)
Esth. 1:10.

3753. כִּרְכָּרָה *kirkārāh* **fem. noun**
(camel)
Isa. 66:20.

3754. כֶּרֶם *kerem* **masc. noun**
(vineyard)
Gen. 9:20; **Ex.** 22:5(4); 23:11; **Lev.** 19:10; 25:3,4; **Num.** 16:14; 20:17; 21:22; 22:24; **Deut.** 6:11; 20:6; 22:9; 23:24(25); 24:21; 28:30,39; **Josh.** 24:13; **Judg.** 9:27; 11:33(NASB, NIV, *'āḇēl k*^{e}*rāmiym* [64,I]); 14:5; 15:5; 21:20,21; **1 Sam.** 8:14,15; 22:7; **1 Kgs.** 21:1,2,6,7,15, 16,18; **2 Kgs.** 5:26; 18:32; 19:29; **1 Chr.** 27:27; **Neh.** 5:3–5,11; 9:25; **Job** 24:6,18; **Ps.** 107:37; **Prov.** 24:30; 31:16; **Eccl.** 2:4; **Song** 1:6,14; 2:15; 7:12(13); 8:11,12; **Isa.** 1:8; 3:14; 5:1,3–5,7,10; 16:10; 27:2; 36:17; 37:30; 65:21; **Jer.** 6:1; 12:10; 31:5; 32:15; 35:7,9; 39:10; **Ezek.** 19:10(KJV, *dām* [1818]); 28:26; **Hos.** 2:15(17); **Amos** 4:9; 5:11,17; 9:14; **Mic.** 1:6; **Zeph.** 1:13.

3755. כֹּרֵם *kōrēm* **masc. noun**
(vinedresser: perh. Qal part. of *kāram*)
2 Kgs. 25:12; **2 Chr.** 26:10; **Isa.** 61:5; **Jer.** 52:16; **Joel** 1:11.

3756. A. כַּרְמִי *karmiy* **masc. proper noun**
(Carmi: son of Reuben)
Gen. 46:9; **Ex.** 6:14; **Num.** 26:6; **1 Chr.** 5:3.
B. כַּרְמִי *karmiy* **masc. proper noun**
(Carmi: a Judaite)
Josh. 7:1,18; **1 Chr.** 2:7; 4:1.

3757. כַּרְמִי *karmiy* **masc. proper noun**
(Carmite)
Num. 26:6.

3758. כַּרְמִיל *karmiyl* **masc. noun**
(crimson, red)
2 Chr. 2:7(6),14(13); 3:14.

3759. I. כַּרְמֶל *karmel* **masc. noun**
(orchard, fertile field)
2 Kgs. 19:23(KJV, *karmel* [3760]); **2 Chr.** 26:10(KJV, *karmel* [3760]); **Isa.** 10:18; 16:10; 29:17; 32:15,16; 37:24; **Jer.** 2:7; 4:26; 48:33; **Amos** 1:2; 9:3; **Mic.** 7:14.
II. כַּרְמֶל *karmel* **masc. noun**
(new grain, fresh corn)
Lev. 2:14; 23:14; **2 Kgs.** 4:42.

3760. A. כַּרְמֶל *karmel* **proper noun**
(Mt. Carmel)

Josh. 12:22; 19:26; **1 Kgs.** 18:19,20,42; **2 Kgs.** 2:25; 4:25; 19:23(NASB, NIV, *karmel* [3759,I]); **2 Chr.** 26:10(NASB, NIV, *karmel* [3759,I]); **Song** 7:5(6); **Isa.** 33:9; 35:2; **Jer.** 4:26; 46:18; 50:19; **Amos** 1:2; 9:3; **Mic.** 7:14; **Nah.** 1:4.

B. כַּרְמֶל *karmel* **proper noun**
(Carmel: city near Hebron)
Josh. 15:55; **1 Sam.** 15:12; 25:2,5, 7,40.

3761. כַּרְמְלִי *karm*^{e}*liy* **masc. proper noun**
(Carmelite)
1 Sam. 30:5; **2 Sam.** 2:2; 3:3; 23:35; **1 Chr.** 11:37.

3762. כַּרְמְלִית *karm*^{e}*liyṯ* **fem. proper noun**
(Carmelitess)
1 Sam. 27:3; **1 Chr.** 3:1.

3763. כְּרָן *k*^{e}*rān* **masc. proper noun**
(Cheran)
Gen. 36:26; **1 Chr.** 1:41.

3764. כָּרְסֵא *korsē'* **Aram. masc. noun**
(throne)
Dan. 5:20; 7:9.

3765. כִּרְסֵם *kirsēm* **verb**
(to ravage, to tear apart)
Ps. 80:13(14).

3766. כָּרַע *kāra'* **verb**
(to bow down, to crouch, to sink)
Gen. 49:9; **Num.** 24:9; **Judg.** 5:27; 7:5,6; 11:35; **1 Sam.** 4:19; **2 Sam.** 22:40; **1 Kgs.** 8:54; 19:18; **2 Kgs.** 1:13; 9:24; **2 Chr.** 7:3; 29:29; **Ezra** 9:5; **Esth.** 3:2,5; **Job** 4:4; 31:10; 39:3; **Ps.** 17:13; 18:39(40); 20:8(9); 22:29(30); 72:9; 78:31; 95:6; **Isa.** 10:4; 45:23; 46:1,2; 65:12.

3767. כְּרַע *k*^{e}*ra'* **masc. noun**
(leg)
Ex. 12:9; 29:17; **Lev.** 1:9,13; 4:11; 8:21; 9:14; 11:21; **Amos** 3:12.

3768. כַּרְפַּס *karpas* **masc. noun**
(linen)
Esth. 1:6.

3769. כָּרַר *kārar* **verb**
(to dance)
2 Sam. 6:14,16.

3770. כָּרֵשׂ *kārēś* **masc. noun**
(stomach)
Jer. 51:34.

3771. כַּרְשְׁנָא *karš*^{e}*nā'* **masc. proper noun**
(Carshena)
Esth. 1:14.

3772. כָּרַת *kāraṯ* **verb**
(to cut off, to cut down, to cut up, with *b*^{e}*riyṯ* [1285] in the sense of to cut a covenant or to make a covenant)
Gen. 9:11; 15:18; 17:14; 21:27,32; 26:28; 31:44; 41:36; **Ex.** 4:25; 8:9(5); 12:15,19; 23:32; 24:8; 30:33,38; 31:14; 34:10,12,13,15,27; **Lev.** 7:20,21,25,27; 17:4,9,10,14; 18:29; 19:8; 20:3,5,6,17,18; 22:3,24; 23:29; 26:22,30; **Num.** 4:18; 9:13; 11:33; 13:23,24; 15:30,31; 19:13,20; **Deut.** 4:23; 5:2,3; 7:2; 9:9; 12:29; 19:1,5; 20:19,20; 23:1(2); 29:1(28:69),12(11), 14(13),25(24); 31:16; **Josh.** 3:13,16; 4:7; 7:9; 9:6,7,11,15,16,23; 11:21; 23:4; 24:25; **Judg.** 2:2; 4:24; 6:25,26,28,30; 9:48,49; **Ruth** 4:10; **1 Sam.** 2:33; 5:4; 11:1,2; 17:51; 18:3; 20:15,16; 22:8; 23:18; 24:4(5),5(6),11(12),21(22); 28:9; 31:9; **2 Sam.** 3:12,13,21,29; 5:3; 7:9; 10:4; 20:22; **1 Kgs.** 2:4; 5:6(20),12(26); 6:36(KJV, NIV, *k*^{e}*ruṯôṯ* [3773]); 7:2(KJV, NIV, *k*^{e}*ruṯôṯ* [3773]),12(KJV, NIV, *k*^{e}*ruṯôṯ* [3773]); 8:9,21,25; 9:5,7; 11:16; 14:10,14; 15:13; 18:4,5; 20:34; 21:21; **2 Kgs.** 9:8;

11:4,17; 17:15,35,38; 18:4; 19:23; 23:3,14; **1 Chr.** 11:3; 16:16; 17:8; 19:4; **2 Chr.** 2:8(7),10(9),16(15); 5:10; 6:11,16; 7:18; 15:16; 21:7; 22:7; 23:3,16; 29:10; 34:31; **Ezra** 10:3; **Neh.** 9:8,38(10:1); **Job** 14:7; 31:1; 41:4(40:28); **Ps.** 12:3(4); 34:16(17); 37:9,22,28,34,38; 50:5; 83:5(6); 89:3(4); 101:8; 105:9; 109:13,15; **Prov.** 2:22; 10:31; 23:13; 24:14; **Isa.** 9:14(13); 10:7; 11:13; 14:8,22; 18:5; 22:25; 28:15; 29:20; 37:24; 44:14; 48:9,19; 55:3,13; 56:5; 57:8; 61:8; **Jer.** 6:6; 7:28; 9:21(20); 10:3; 11:10,19; 22:7; 31:31–33; 32:40; 33:17,18; 34:8,13,15,18; 35:19; 44:7, 8,11; 46:23; 47:4; 48:2; 50:16; 51:62; **Ezek.** 14:8,13,17,19,21; 16:4; 17:13,17; 21:3(8),4(9); 25:7,13,16; 29:8; 30:15; 31:12; 34:25; 35:7; 37:26; **Dan.** 9:26; **Hos.** 2:18(20); 8:4; 10:4; 12:1(2); **Joel** 1:5,9,16; **Amos** 1:5,8; 2:3; **Obad.** 1:9, 10,14; **Mic.** 5:9–13(8–12); **Nah.** 1:14, 15(2:1); 2:13(14); 3:15; **Zeph.** 1:3,4,11; 3:6,7; **Hag.** 2:5; **Zech.** 9:6,10; 11:10; 13:2,8; 14:2; **Mal.** 2:12.

3773. כְּרֻתוֹת k^e*ruṯôṯ* **fem. pl. noun**
(trimmed beams; NASB, *kāraṯ* [3772])
1 Kgs. 6:36; 7:2,12.

3774. כְּרֵתִי k^e*rēṯiy* **masc. proper noun**
(Cheriethite)
1 Sam. 30:14; **2 Sam.** 8:18; 15:18; 20:7,23; **1 Kgs.** 1:38,44; **1 Chr.** 18:17; **Ezek.** 25:16; **Zeph.** 2:5,6(KJV, NASB, *kārāh* [3741]).

3775. כֶּשֶׂב *keśeḇ* **masc. noun**
(lamb, young sheep)
Gen. 30:32,33,35,40; **Lev.** 1:10; 3:7; 4:35; 7:23; 17:3; 22:19,27; **Num.** 18:17; **Deut.** 14:4.

3776. כִּשְׂבָּה *kiśbāh* **fem. noun**
(ewe lamb)
Lev. 5:6.

3777. כֶּשֶׂד *keśeḏ* **masc. proper noun**
(Chesed)
Gen. 22:22.

3778. A. כַּשְׂדִּים *kaśdiym* **masc. proper noun**
(Chaldeans, Babylonians)
Gen. 11:28,31; 15:7; **2 Kgs.** 24:2; 25:4, 5,10,13,24–26; **2 Chr.** 36:17; **Ezra** 5:12(KJV, *kasday* [3679]); **Neh.** 9:7; **Job** 1:17; **Isa.** 13:19; 23:13; 43:14; 47:1,5; 48:14,20; **Jer.** 21:4,9; 22:25; 24:5; 25:12; 32:4,5,24,25,28,29,43; 33:5; 35:11; 37:5, 8–11,13,14; 38:2,18,19,23; 39:5,8; 40:9, 10; 41:3,18; 43:3; 50:1,8,25,35,45; 51:4, 54; 52:7,8,14,17; **Ezek.** 1:3; 12:13; 23:14,15,23; **Dan.** 1:4; 2:2(NIV, see II), 4(NIV, see II); 9:1; **Hab.** 1:6.
B. כַּשְׂדִּים *kaśdiym* **masc. noun**
(astrologers)
Dan. 2:2(KJV, NASB, see I),4(KJV, NASB, see I).
C. כַּשְׂדִּים *kaśdiym* **masc. noun**
(Chaldea, Babylon)
Jer. 50:10; 51:24,35; **Ezek.** 11:24; 16:29; 23:16.

3779. A. כַּשְׂדָּי *kaśdāy* **Aram. masc. proper noun**
(Chaldeans, Babylonians; corr. to Hebr. 3778,I)
Dan. 2:5(NIV, see II),10(NIV, see II); 3:8(NIV, see II); 4:7(4)(NIV, see II); 5:7(NIV, see II),11(NIV, see II),30.
B. כַּשְׂדָּי *kaśdāy* **Aram. masc. noun**
(astrologers; corr. to Hebr. 3778,II)
Dan. 2:5(KJV, NASB, see I),10(KJV, NASB, see I); 3:8(KJV, NASB, see I); 4:7(4)(KJV, NASB, see I); 5:7(KJV, NASB, see I),11(KJV, NASB, see I).

3780. כָּשָׂה *kāśāh* **verb**
(obese, filled with food, sleek)
Deut. 32:15.

3781. כַּשִּׁיל *kaššiyl* **masc. noun**
(ax, hatchet)
Ps. 74:6.

3782. כָּשַׁל *kāšal* **verb**
(to stumble, to fall, to be brought down)
Lev. 26:37; **1 Sam.** 2:4; **2 Chr.** 25:8; 28:15,23; **Neh.** 4:10(4); **Job** 4:4; **Ps.** 9:3(4); 27:2; 31:10(11); 64:8(9); 105:37; 107:12; 109:24; **Prov.** 4:12,16,19; 24:16,17; **Isa.** 3:8; 5:27; 8:15; 28:13; 31:3; 35:3; 40:30; 59:10,14; 63:13; **Jer.** 6:15,21; 8:12; 18:15,23; 20:11; 31:9; 46:6,12,16; 50:32; **Lam.** 1:14; 5:13; **Ezek.** 33:12; 36:14,15; **Dan.** 11:14, 19,33–35,41; **Hos.** 4:5; 5:5; 14:1(2), 9(10); **Nah.** 2:5(6); 3:3; **Zech.** 12:8; **Mal.** 2:8.

3783. כִּשָּׁלוֹן *kiššālôn* **masc. noun**
(a stumbling, fall)
Prov. 16:18.

3784. כָּשַׁף *kāšap̱* **verb**
(to practice sorcery or witchcraft)
Ex. 7:11; 22:18(17); **Deut.** 18:10; **2 Chr.** 33:6; **Dan.** 2:2; **Mal.** 3:5.

3785. כֶּשֶׁף *kešep̱* **masc. noun**
(sorcery, witchcraft)
2 Kgs. 9:22; **Isa.** 47:9,12; **Mic.** 5:12(11); **Nah.** 3:4.

3786. כַּשָּׁף *kaššāp̱* **masc. noun**
(sorcerer)
Jer. 27:9.

3787. כָּשֵׁר *kāšēr* **verb**
(to be right, to prosper)
Esth. 8:5; **Eccl.** 10:10; 11:6.

3788. כִּשְׁרוֹן *kišrôn* **masc. noun**
(skill, advantage, achievement)
Eccl. 2:21; 4:4; 5:11(10).

3789. כָּתַב *kāṯaḇ* **verb**
(to write)
Ex. 17:14; 24:4,12; 31:18; 32:15,32; 34:1,27,28; 39:30; **Num.** 5:23; 11:26; 17:2(17),3(18); 33:2; **Deut.** 4:13; 5:22(19); 6:9; 9:10; 10:2,4; 11:20; 17:18; 24:1,3; 27:3,8; 28:58,61; 29:20(19), 21(20),27(26); 30:10; 31:9,19,22,24; **Josh.** 1:8; 8:31,32,34; 10:13; 18:4,6,8,9; 23:6; 24:26; **Judg.** 8:14; **1 Sam.** 10:25; **2 Sam.** 1:18; 11:14,15; **1 Kgs.** 2:3; 11:41; 14:19,29; 15:7,23,31; 16:5,14, 20,27; 21:8,9,11; 22:39,45(46); **2 Kgs.** 1:18; 8:23; 10:1,6,34; 12:19(20); 13:8,12; 14:6,15,18,28; 15:6,11,15,21,26,31,36; 16:19; 17:37; 20:20; 21:17,25; 22:13; 23:3,21,24,28; 24:5; **1 Chr.** 4:41; 9:1; 16:40; 24:6; 29:29; **2 Chr.** 9:29; 12:15; 13:22; 16:11; 20:34; 23:18; 24:27; 25:4,26; 26:22; 27:7; 28:26; 30:1,5,18; 31:3; 32:17,32; 33:19; 34:21,24,31; 35:12,25–27; 36:8; **Ezra** 3:2,4; 4:6,7; 8:34; **Neh.** 6:6; 7:5; 8:14,15; 9:38(10:1); 10:34(35),36(37); 12:22,23; 13:1; **Esth.** 1:19; 2:23; 3:9,12; 6:2; 8:5,8–10; 9:20, 23,29,32; 10:2; **Job** 13:26; 19:23; 31:35; **Ps.** 40:7(8); 69:28(29); 87:6; 102:18(19); 139:16; 149:9; **Prov.** 3:3; 7:3; 22:20; **Eccl.** 12:10; **Isa.** 4:3; 8:1; 10:1,19; 30:8; 44:5; 65:6; **Jer.** 17:1,13; 22:30; 25:13; 30:2; 31:33; 32:10,12,44; 36:2,4,6,17, 18,27–29,32; 45:1; 51:60; **Ezek.** 2:10; 13:9; 24:2; 37:16,20; 43:11; **Dan.** 9:11,13; 12:1; **Hos.** 8:12; **Hab.** 2:2; **Mal.** 3:16.

3790. כְּתַב $k^e\underline{t}a\underline{b}$ **Aram. verb**
(to write; corr. to Hebr. 3789)
Ezra 4:8; 5:7,10; 6:2; **Dan.** 5:5; 6:25(26); 7:1.

3791. כְּתָב $k^e\underline{t}\bar{a}\underline{b}$ **masc. noun**
(script, writing)
1 Chr. 28:19; **2 Chr.** 2:11(10); 35:4; **Ezra** 2:62; 4:7; **Neh.** 7:64; **Esth.** 1:22; 3:12,14; 4:8; 8:8,9,13; 9:27; **Ezek.** 13:9; **Dan.** 10:21.

3792. כְּתָב $k^e\underline{t}\bar{a}\underline{b}$ **Aram. masc. noun**

(writing, inscription; corr. to Hebr. 3791)
Ezra 6:18; 7:22; **Dan.** 5:7,8,15–17,24,25; 6:8–10(9–11).

3793. כְּתֹבֶת $k^e\underline{t}\bar{o}\underline{b}et$ **fem. noun**
(mark, inscription)
Lev. 19:28.

3794. כִּתִּי *kittiy* **masc. proper noun**
(Kittim)
Gen. 10:4; **Num.** 24:24; **1 Chr.** 1:7; **Isa.** 23:1,12; **Jer.** 2:10; **Ezek.** 27:6; **Dan.** 11:30.

3795. כָּתִית $k\bar{a}\underline{t}iy\underline{t}$ **adj.**
(beaten, pressed)
Ex. 27:20; 29:40; **Lev.** 24:2; **Num.** 28:5; **1 Kgs.** 5:11(25).

3796. כֹּתֶל $k\bar{o}\underline{t}el$ **masc. noun**
(wall)
Song 2:9.

3797. כְּתַל $k^e\underline{t}al$ **Aram. masc. noun**
(wall; corr. to Hebr. 3796)
Ezra 5:8; **Dan.** 5:5.

3798. כִּתְלִישׁ $ki\underline{t}liy\check{s}$ **proper noun**
(Kitlish)
Josh. 15:40.

3799. כָּתַם $k\bar{a}\underline{t}am$ **verb**
(to be stained, to be marked)
Jer. 2:22.

3800. כֶּתֶם $ke\underline{t}em$ **masc. noun**
(gold, pure gold)
Job 28:16,19; 31:24; **Ps.** 45:9(10); **Prov.** 25:12; **Song** 5:11; **Isa.** 13:12; **Lam.** 4:1; **Dan.** 10:5.

3801. כֻּתֹּנֶת $kutt\bar{o}ne\underline{t}$ **fem. noun**
(robe, garment)
Gen. 3:21; 37:3,23,31–33; **Ex.** 28:4, 39,40; 29:5,8; 39:27; 40:14; **Lev.** 8:7,13; 10:5; 16:4; **2 Sam.** 13:18,19; 15:32; **Ezra** 2:69; **Neh.** 7:70,72; **Job** 30:18; **Song** 5:3; **Isa.** 22:21.

3802. כָּתֵף $k\bar{a}\underline{t}\bar{e}\underline{p}$ **fem. noun**
(shoulder, side)
Ex. 27:14,15; 28:7,12,25,27; 38:14,15; 39:4,7,18,20; **Num.** 7:9; 34:11; **Deut.** 33:12; **Josh.** 15:8,10,11; 18:12,13,16, 18,19; **Judg.** 16:3; **1 Sam.** 17:6; **1 Kgs.** 6:8; 7:30,34,39; **2 Kgs.** 11:11; **1 Chr.** 15:15; **2 Chr.** 4:10; 23:10; 35:3; **Neh.** 9:29; **Job** 31:22; **Isa.** 11:14; 30:6; 46:7; 49:22; **Ezek.** 12:6,7,12; 24:4; 25:9; 29:7,18; 34:21; 40:18,40,41,44; 41:2,26; 46:19; 47:1,2; **Zech.** 7:11.

3803. כָּתַר $k\bar{a}\underline{t}ar$ **verb**
(to surround, to enclose; to crown)
Judg. 20:43; **Job** 36:2; **Ps.** 22:12(13); 142:7(8); **Prov.** 14:18; **Hab.** 1:4.

3804. כֶּתֶר $ke\underline{t}er$ **masc. noun**
(crown)
Esth. 1:11; 2:17; 6:8.

3805. כֹּתֶרֶת $k\bar{o}\underline{t}ere\underline{t}$ **fem. noun**
(capital, crown of a pillar)
1 Kgs. 7:16–20,31,41,42; **2 Kgs.** 25:17; **2 Chr.** 4:12,13; **Jer.** 52:22.

3806. כָּתַשׁ $k\bar{a}\underline{t}a\check{s}$ **verb**
(to pound, to grind)
Prov. 27:22.

3807. כָּתַת $k\bar{a}\underline{t}a\underline{t}$ **verb**
(to beat, to crush, to batter)
Lev. 22:24; **Num.** 14:45; **Deut.** 1:44; 9:21; **2 Kgs.** 18:4; **2 Chr.** 15:6; 34:7; **Job** 4:20; **Ps.** 89:23(24); **Isa.** 2:4; 24:12; 30:14; **Jer.** 46:5; **Joel** 3:10(4:10); **Mic.** 1:7; 4:3; **Zech.** 11:6.

ל Lamed

3808. לֹא *lō'*, לוֹא *lô'*, לֹה *lōh* **adv.** (no, not, never)
Gen. 2:5,17,18,20,25; 3:1,3,4,17; 4:5,7, 9,12; 6:3; 7:2; 8:9,12,21,22; 9:4,11,15,23; 11:6,7; 12:18; 13:6,9; 14:23; 15:3,4,10, 13,16; 16:1,10; 17:5,12,14,15; 18:15,21, 24,25,28–32; 19:2,8,19,20,22,33,35; 20:4–6,9,12; 21:10,26; 22:12,16; 23:6,11; 24:3,5,8,16,21,27,33,37–39,41,49,50; 26:22,29; 27:2,12,21,23,36; 28:1,6,15,16; 29:7,8,25,26; 30:1,31,40,42; 31:7,15,27, 28,32–35,38,39,52; 32:12,25,26,28,32; 34:7,14,17,19,23; 35:5,10; 36:7; 37:4,13, 21,32; 38:9,14,16,20–23,26; 39:6,8–10; 40:8,15,23; 41:19,21,31,36,44; 42:2,4, 8,10–12,16,20–23,31,34,37,38; 43:3,5, 8,9,22,32; 44:4,5,15,22,23,26,28,32; 45:1,3,8,26; 47:9,18,19,22,26; 48:10, 11,18; 49:10; **Ex.** 1:8,17,19; 2:3; 3:3, 19,21; 4:1,8–11,14,21; 5:2,7,8,14,18, 19,23; 6:3,9,12; 7:4,13,16,21–24; 8:15, 18,19,26,28,31,32; 9:4,6,7,11,12,18,19, 21,24,26,28,29,32,33,35; 10:5,6,11,14, 15,19,20,23,26,27,29; 11:6,7,9,10; 12:10, 13,16,19,20,22,23,39,43,45,46,48; 13:3, 7,13,17,22; 14:12,13,20,28; 15:22,23,26; 16:4,8,15,18,20,24–27; 18:17,18; 19:13,23; 20:3–5,7,10,13–17,23,25,26; 21:5,7,8,10,11,13,18,21,22,28,29,33,36; 22:8,11,13,15,16,18,21,22,25,28,29,31; 23:1–3,6–9,13,15,18,19,21,24,26,29, 32,33; 24:2,11; 25:15; 28:28,32,35,43; 29:33,34; 30:9,12,15,20,21,32,37; 32:1,23; 33:3,4,11,12,16,20,23; 34:3,7,10,14,17, 20,24–26,28,29; 35:3; 39:21,23; 40:35,37; **Lev.** 1:17; 2:11–13; 3:17; 4:2,13,22,27; 5:1,7,8,11,17,18; 6:12,13,17,23,30; 7:15, 18,19,23,24,26; 8:33,35; 10:1,6,7,9, 17,18; 11:4–8,11,13,41–44,47; 12:4,8; 13:4–6,11,23,28,32–34,36,53,55; 14:32, 36,48; 15:11,25,31; 16:2,13,17,29; 17:4, 7,9,12,14,16; 18:3,6–23,26,28,30; 19:4, 7,9–20,23,26–29,33,35; 20:14,19,22, 23,25; 21:1,3–7,10–12,14,15,17,18, 21,23; 22:2,4,6,8–10,12,13,15,20–25,28, 30,32; 23:3,7,8,14,21,22,25,28,29,31, 35,36; 25:4,5,11,17,20,23,26,28,30,34, 37,39,42,43,46,53,54; 26:1,6,11,14,18, 20,21,23,26,27,31,35,37,44; 27:10,11,20, 22,26–29,33; **Num.** 1:47,49,53; 2:33; 3:4; 4:15,19,20; 5:3,13–15,19,28; 6:3–7; 7:9; 8:19,25,26; 9:6,12,13,19,22; 10:7,30; 11:11,14,17,19,23,25,26; 12:2,7,8,14,15; 13:31; 14:3,11,18,22,23,28,35,41–44; 15:22,34,39; 16:12,14,15,28,29,40; 17:10; 18:3–5,17,20,22–24,32; 19:2,12, 13,20; 20:2,5,12,17,18,20,24; 21:22,23; 22:12,18,30,34,37; 23:8,9,12,13,19–21, 23–26; 24:1,12,13,17; 25:11; 26:11,33, 62,64,65; 27:3,17; 28:18,25,26; 29:1,7, 12,35; 30:2,5,11,12; 31:18,23,35,49; 32:11,18,19,23,30; 33:14,55; 35:12,22, 23,30–34; 36:7,9; **Deut.** 1:9,17,26,29, 37,39,42,43,45; 2:5,7,9,19,27,30,34, 36,37; 3:4,11,22,26,27; 4:2,15,26,28, 31,42; 5:3,5,7–9,11,14,17–22,32; 6:10, 11,14,16; 7:2,3,7,10,14–16,18,21,22, 24–26; 8:2–4,9,16,20; 9:5,6,9,18,23; 10:9,10,16,17; 11:2,10,17,25,28,30; 12:4,8,9,16,17,23–25,31,32; 13:2,3,6, 8,11,13,16,17; 14:1,3,7,8,10,12,19,21, 24,27; 15:2,4,6,7,9–11,13,16,18,19, 21,23; 16:3–5,8,16,19,21,22; 17:1,3,6, 11,13,15–17; 18:1,2,9,10,14,16,19–22; 19:4,6,10,13–15,20,21; 20:1,5–8,12,15, 16,18–20; 21:1,3,4,7,14,16,18,23; 22:1–6,8–11,14,17,19,20,24,26,28–30; 23:1–7,10,14–22,24,25; 24:1,4–6,10,12, 14–17,19–21; 25:3–9,12–14,18,19; 26:13,14; 27:5,26; 28:12–15,27,29–31, 33,35,36,39–41,44,45,47,49–51,56,58,61 ,62,64–66,68; 29:4–6,14,20,23,26; 30:11–13,17,18; 31:2,6,8,13,17,21; 32:5,6,17,20,21,27,30,31,34,47,51,52; 33:9; 34:4,6,7,10; **Josh.** 1:5,8,9,18; 2:4, 5,11,14,22; 3:4; 5:1,5–7,12,14; 6:10;

7:12,13; 8:14,17,20,26,31,35; 9:14, 18–20,23,26; 10:8,13,14,21,28,30,37, 39,40; 11:11,13–15,19,22; 13:13,14,33; 14:3,4,9; 15:63; 16:10; 17:3,12,13,16,17; 18:2; 20:5,9; 21:44,45; 22:3,17,20,24, 26–28,31,33; 23:7,9,13,14; 24:10,12,13, 19,21; **Judg.** 1:19,21,27–34; 2:1–3,10, 14,17,19–23; 3:1,2,22,28,29; 4:6,8,9, 14,16; 5:19,23,30; 6:4,10,13,14,23; 7:4; 8:2,19,20,23,28,34,35; 9:28,38; 10:6, 11,13; 11:2,7,10,15,17,18,20,24,26–28, 35,39; 12:1,2,5,6; 13:2,3,5,6,14,16,21,23; 14:4,6,9,13–16,18; 15:1,2,11,13; 16:7–9, 11,15,17,20; 18:1; 19:10,12,24,25,30; 20:8,13,16,34; 21:1,5,8,12,14,17,18,22; **Ruth** 2:8,9,11,13,15,16,20,22; 3:1,2,13, 18; 4:4,6,10,14; **1 Sam.** 1:7,8,11,13,15, 18,22; 2:9,12,15,16,24,25,32,33; 3:2,5, 6,13,18,19; 4:7,15,20; 5:5,7,11,12; 6:3, 6,7,9,12; 7:13; 8:3,5,7,18,19; 9:4,13, 20,21; 10:1,16,21,27; 11:11,13; 12:4,5, 12,14,15,17,21,22; 13:8,11–14,19,22; 14:1,3,9,24,27,30,34,36,37,45; 15:3,9, 11,17,19,26,29,35; 16:7–11; 17:8,29, 33,39,47; 18:2,26; 19:4; 20:2,9,12,14,15, 26,27,29–31,34,37,39; 21:6,8,11; 22:5, 15,17; 23:14,17,19; 24:7,10–13,18; 25:7, 11,15,19,21,25,28,31,36; 26:1,8,14–16, 21,23; 27:4,9,11; 28:6,15,18,20,23; 29:3–9; 30:2,12,17,19,22,23; 31:4; **2 Sam.** 1:10,14,22,23; 2:19,21,26,28; 3:8,11,13,26,34,37,38; 4:11; 5:6,8,23; 6:10,23; 7:6,7,10,15; 10:3; 11:3,9,10,13, 20,21; 12:6,10,13,17,18,23; 13:4,12–14, 16,22,25,26,28,30; 14:10,11,14,24,25, 28,29; 15:11,14,26,35; 16:17,19; 17:7, 8,12,13,17,19,20,22,23; 18:3,11–14, 20,29; 19:13,21–25,28,43; 20:1,3,10,21; 21:2,10,17; 22:22,23,37–39,42,44; 23:4–6,16,17,19,23; 24:24; **1 Kgs.** 1:1,4, 6,8,10,11,13,18,19,26,27,52; 2:4,6,17,20, 26,28,30,32,36,42,43; 3:2,7,8,11–13, 21–23,26,27; 4:27; 5:3; 6:7,13; 7:31,47; 8:5,8,11,16,19,25,27,35,41,46,56; 9:5, 6,12,20–22; 10:3,5,7,10,12,20,21; 11:2, 4,6,10–13,22,33,34,39,41; 12:15,16,20, 24,31; 13:4,8–10,16,17,21,22,28,33; 14:2,4,8,29; 15:3,5,7,14,23,29,31; 16:5, 11,14,20,27; 17:7,14,16,17; 18:5,10,12, 13,18,21,23,25,44; 19:4,11,12,18; 20:7–9,23,25,28,36; 21:4,6,25,29; 22:8, 16–18,28,31,33,39,43,45,48,49; **2 Kgs.** 1:4,6,16–18; 2:10,12,16–18,21; 3:2,3, 9,17,26; 4:23,27–29,31,39–41; 5:12,13, 17,25,26; 6:10–12,19,22,23,32; 7:2,9,19; 8:19,23; 9:3,18,20,26,35,37; 10:4,5,10, 14,19,21,29,31,34; 11:2; 12:3,6,13,15, 16,19; 13:2,6–8,11,12,23; 14:3,4,6,11,15, 18,24,27,28; 15:4,6,9,16,18,20,21,24,28, 35,36; 16:2,5,19; 17:2,4,9,12,14,18,19, 22,25,26,35,37,38,40; 18:5–7,12,22,27, 29,30,32,36; 19:10,18,25,32,33; 20:1,4, 10,13,15,17,19,20; 21:8,9,17,22,25; 22:2,7,13,17,20; 23:9,22,25,26,28; 24:4,5,7,14; 25:3,16; **1 Chr.** 2:30,32,34; 4:27; 5:1; 10:4,13,14; 11:5,18–21,25; 12:17,19,33; 13:3,13; 14:14; 15:2,13; 16:21; 17:4–6,9,13; 19:3,19; 21:3,6, 17,24,30; 22:8,18; 23:11,17,22; 24:2,28; 26:10; 27:23,24; 28:3,20; 29:1,25; **2 Chr.** 1:11,12; 2:6; 4:18; 5:6,9,14; 6:5,9,16,18, 26,32,36; 7:2,7,13,18; 8:7–9,11,15; 9:2,4, 6,9,11,19,29; 10:15,16; 11:4; 12:7,12, 14,15; 13:5,7,9,10,12,20; 15:3,13,17,19; 16:7,8,12; 17:3,4,10; 18:15–17,27,30,32; 19:6,10; 20:6,7,10,12,15,17,32,33,37; 21:7,12,17,19,20; 22:11; 23:8,14,19; 24:5,6,19,20,22,25; 25:2,4,15,16,20,26; 26:18; 27:2; 28:1,10,13,20,21,27; 29:7,34; 30:3,5,9,17–19,26; 32:11–13, 15,17,25,26; 33:8,10,23; 34:2,21,25, 28,33; 35:18,21,22; 36:12,17; **Ezra** 2:59,62,63; 3:6; 4:3; 8:15; 9:1,9,12,14; 10:6,8,13; **Neh.** 1:7; 2:1,3,12,16,17; 3:5; 4:10,11; 5:8,9,12–16,18; 6:1,3,8,9,11,12; 7:3,61,64,65; 8:17; 9:16,17,19–21,29–31, 34,35; 10:30,31,39; 13:1,2,6,10,18,19, 21,26; **Esth.** 1:15–17,19; 2:10,14,15; 3:2,4; 4:4,11,16; 5:9,12; 6:3,13; 9:2,10, 15,16,27,28; 10:2; **Job** 1:10,11,22; 2:5, 10,12; 3:10,11,16,18,26; 4:6,16,18,21; 5:6,12,19,21,24; 6:10,21,30; 7:1,7–11, 16,19,21; 8:9–12,15,18,20; 9:3,5,7,11,13, 15,16,18,21,24,25,28,32,33,35; 10:7,10,

14,15,18–22; 11:2,11,15; 12:3,9,11,14, 24,25; 13:2,11,16,20; 14:2,4,5,7,12, 16,21; 15:3,6,9,15,18,19,22,28–30,32; 16:6,13,17,22; 17:2,4,10; 18:5,17,19,21; 19:3,7,8,16,22,27; 20:8,9,13,18–21,26; 21:4,9,10,14,16,25,29; 22:5,7,11,12,14, 16,20; 23:6,8,9,11,12,17; 24:1,12,13,15, 16,18,20–22,25; 25:3,5; 26:2,3,8; 27:5,6,11,14,15,19,22; 28:7,8,13–19; 29:12,16,22,24; 30:10,13,17,20,24,25, 27,28; 31:3,4,15,17,20,23,30–32,34,36; 32:3,9,13–16,19,21,22; 33:7,9,12–14, 21,27; 34:9,12,19,20,23,24,27,31–33,35; 35:10,12–15; 36:4–7,12,13,16,19,26; 37:4,5,19,21,23,24; 38:11,26; 39:4,7, 16,17,22,24; 40:5,23; 41:10,12,16,17,28; 42:2,3,7,8,15; **Ps.** 1:1,3–5; 3:6; 5:4,5; 7:12; 9:10,12,18; 10:6,13; 14:4; 15:3–5; 16:10; 17:1; 18:21,22,36–38,41,43; 22:2, 5,6,24,29; 23:1,4; 24:4; 25:3; 26:1,4,5; 27:3; 28:5; 30:1,12; 31:8; 32:2,5,6; 33:16,17; 34:10,20,22; 35:8,11,15,20; 36:4,12; 37:19,21,24,25,28,31,33,36; 38:9,13,14; 39:6,9; 40:4,6,9–12; 41:8,11; 43:1; 44:3,6,9,12,17,18,21; 46:2; 49:7, 9,17,19,20; 50:8,9,12; 51:16,17; 52:7; 53:4–6; 54:3; 55:11,12,19,22,23; 56:4, 8,11,13; 58:5; 59:3,15; 60:10; 62:2,6; 64:4; 66:9,18,20; 69:4,5,20,33; 71:15; 73:5,22,25; 74:9; 75:6; 76:5; 77:2,4,7,19; 78:4,7,8,10,22,30,32,37–39,42,50,53,56, 63,64,67; 79:6; 80:18; 81:5,9,11; 82:5; 83:4; 84:11; 85:6; 86:14; 88:5,8; 89:22, 30,31,33,34,43,48; 91:5,7,10; 92:6,15; 94:7,9,10,14; 95:10; 100:3; 101:3–5,7; 102:17,27; 103:9,10,16; 105:14,28; 106:7,11,13,24,25,34; 107:4,38,40; 108:11; 109:16,17; 110:4; 112:6–8; 115:1,5–7,17; 118:6,17,18; 119:3,6,11, 16,46,51,60,61,80,83,85,87,93,102,109,1 10,136,141,153,155,157,158,176; 121:4,6; 124:6; 125:1,3; 127:1,5; 129:2,7,8; 131:1,2; 132:11; 135:16,17; 137:6; 139:6,12,15, 16,21; 143:2; 147:10,20; 148:6; **Prov.** 1:25,28–30; 2:19; 3:15,23,24,30; 4:12, 16,19; 5:6,13; 6:27–30,33–35; 7:11,23; 8:1,11,26,29; 9:18; 10:2,3,19,22,30; 11:4,21; 12:3,21,27; 13:1,8,23; 14:5, 10,22; 15:7,12; 16:5,8,10,29; 17:5,7, 13,20,21,26; 18:2,5; 19:2,5,7,9,10,24; 20:1,4,19,21,23; 21:10,13,17,26; 22:6, 20,24; 23:13,18; 24:7,12,14,20; 25:10,27; 26:1,2,17,19; 27:1,2,20,22,24; 28:5,13, 20–22; 29:7,19,24; 30:2,3,11,12,15,16, 18,20,21,25,26,30; 31:7,11,12,18,21,27; **Eccl.** 1:8,11,15; 2:10,21,23; 3:11; 4:3,8, 12,13,16; 5:5,10,15,20; 6:2,3,5–7,10; 7:10,14,17,20,21,28; 8:5,8,13,17; 9:11, 12,15; 10:10,11,14,15,17; 11:2,4,5; 12:1,2,6; **Song** 1:6,8; 3:1,2,4; 5:6; 6:12; 8:1,7; **Isa.** 1:3,6,11,13,23; 2:4; 3:7,9; 5:4,6,9,12,25,27; 6:9; 7:1,7,9,12,17,25; 8:10,12,19,20; 9:1,3,12,13,17,19–21; 10:4,7–9,11,14,15,20; 11:3,9,13; 12:2; 13:10,17,18,20,22; 14:8,17,20,24; 15:6; 16:6,10,12,14; 17:8,10; 19:15; 22:2,11; 23:4,12,13,18; 24:9,20; 25:2; 26:21; 27:9,11; 28:12,15,16,18,25,27,28; 29:9, 11,12,16,17,22; 30:1,2,5,6,9,10,14–16, 19,20; 31:1–4,8; 32:3,5; 33:1,8,19,21; 34:10,16; 35:8,9; 36:7,12,14,15,21; 37:10,19,26,33,34; 38:1,11,18; 39:2,4,6; 40:20,21,26,28,31; 41:3,7,9,12,17; 42:2–4,8,16,20,24,25; 43:2,10,19,22–25; 44:8,12,18–21; 45:1,4,5,13,17–21,23; 46:2,7,10,13; 47:1,3,5–8,11,14; 48:1, 6–8,10,11,16,19,21; 49:10,15,23; 50:5–7; 51:6,9,10,14,21,22; 52:1,3,12,15; 53:2, 3,7,9; 54:1,4,10,11,14,17; 55:1,2,5,8, 10,11,13; 56:5,10,11; 57:4,10–12,16,20; 58:2–4,6,7,11; 59:1,6,8,9,14,21; 60:11, 12,18–20; 62:1,4,6,12; 63:8,13,16,19; 64:3,4; 65:1,2,6,12,17,19,20,22,23,25; 66:4,9,19,24; **Jer.** 1:6,19; 2:2,6,8,11,13, 17,19,20,23–25,27,30,31,34,35,37; 3:1–4,7,8,10,12,13,16,17,19,25; 4:1,8, 11,19,22,27,28; 5:3,4,7,9,10,12,15,18,19, 21,22,24,28,29; 6:8,10,15–17,19,20, 23,29; 7:6,9,13,19,20,22,24,26–28,31,32; 8:2,4,6,7,12,20,22; 9:3,5,9,10,13,16; 10:4,5,7,10,14,16,21,23,25; 11:3,8,11, 12,19,21,23; 12:4,13,17; 13:1,7,10–12, 14,17,21,27; 14:3–5,9,10,13–15,18,22; 15:7,10,11,13,14,17–20; 16:2,4,6–8,11,

13,14,17,20; 17:4,6,8,11,16,22,23,27; 18:6,15,17,18; 19:4–6,11; 20:3,9,11,16, 17; 21:7,10; 22:5,6,10–13,15,16,18,21, 26–28,30; 23:2,4,7,10,16,17,20,21,23, 24,29,32,36,38,40; 24:2,3,6,8; 25:3,4, 6–8,27,29,33; 26:4,5,19; 27:8,9,13–15,20; 28:15; 29:9,11,16,17,19,23,27,31,32; 30:8,11,14,19,24; 31:9,12,18,29,32, 34,40; 32:4,5,17,23,33,35,40; 33:3,17, 18,22,24,25; 34:3,4,14,17,18; 35:6,7,9, 13–17,19; 36:5,24,25,30,31; 37:2,4,9,14, 19,20; 38:15,17,18,20,23–25,27; 39:16–18; 40:3,5,7,14,15; 41:4,8; 42:4,5,10,13,14,17,18,21; 43:2,4,7; 44:3, 5,10,14,17,21–23,27; 45:3; 46:5,15,21, 23,28; 47:3,6; 48:8,11,27,30,33; 49:9,10, 12,18,20,23,25,31,33,36; 50:3,5,7,9,13, 20,24,39,40,42,45; 51:5,9,17,19,26,39, 43,44,57,64; 52:6,20; **Lam.** 1:3,6,9,10, 12,14; 2:1,2,8,9,14,17,21,22; 3:2,7,22, 31,33,36–38,42,43,49; 4:6,8,12,14–17, 22; 5:5,12; **Ezek.** 1:9,12,17; 3:5–7,9, 18–21,25,26; 4:8,14; 5:6,7,9,11; 6:10; 7:4,7,9,11,13,19; 8:18; 9:10; 10:11,16; 11:3,11,12; 12:2,6,9,12,13,23–25,28; 13:5–7,9,12,19,21–23; 14:11,18,23; 15:5; 16:4,5,16,22,28,29,31,34,41–43,47,49, 51,56,61,63; 17:9,10,12,16–19; 18:6–8,11–25,28–30,32; 19:9,14; 20:8, 13,16,17,21,24,25,32,33,38,39,44,47–49; 21:5,13,26,27,32; 22:24,26,28–30; 23:8, 27,48; 24:6,7,12–14,16,17,19,22,23, 25,27; 25:10; 26:13–15,19–21; 28:2,3,9, 24; 29:5,11,15,16,18; 30:13,21; 31:8,14; 32:7,9,13,27; 33:4–6,8,9,12,13,15–17, 20,22,27,31; 34:2–4,8,10,22,28,29; 35:6,9; 36:5,7,12,14,15,22,29–32; 37:18, 22,23; 38:14,19; 39:7,10,28,29; 41:6; 42:14; 43:7; 44:2,8,9,13,17–22,25,28,31; 45:8; 46:2,9,18; 47:5,11,12; 48:11,14; **Dan.** 1:8,19; 8:4,7,22,24; 9:6,10,12–14,18; 10:3,7,8,16,17; 11:4,6,12,15,17,19–21, 24,25,27,29,37,38,42; 12:1,8,10; **Hos.** 1:6,7,9,10; 2:2,4,6–8,10,16,17,23; 3:3; 4:10,14; 5:3,4,6,13; 6:6; 7:9,10,14,16; 8:4–6,13; 9:2–4,15,17; 10:3,9; 11:3,5,7,9; 12:8; 13:4,13; 14:3; **Joel** 1:16; 2:2,3,7, 8,19,26,27; 3:17,21; **Amos** 1:3,6,9,11,13; 2:1,4,6,12,14,15; 3:5–8,10; 4:6–11; 5:2,5, 11,18,20–23; 6:6,10,13; 7:3,6,8,10,13,14, 16; 8:2,8,11,12,14; 9:1,4,7–10,15; **Obad.** 1:5,8,16,18; **Jon.** 1:6,13; 3:9,10; 4:2,10,11; **Mic.** 1:5,11; 2:3,5–7,10; 3:1,4,5,11; 4:3,12; 5:7,12,13,15; 6:14,15; 7:18; **Nah.** 1:3,9,12, 14,15; 2:13; 3:1,17,19; **Hab.** 1:2,4–6, 12–14,17; 2:3–7,13; 3:17; **Zeph.** 1:6,12, 13,18; 2:1,2; 3:2,3,5,7,11,13,15; **Hag.** 1:2; 2:3,12,19; **Zech.** 1:4,6,12,21; 3:2; 4:5,6,13; 7:6,7,13,14; 8:10,11,14; 9:5,8; 10:6,10; 11:5,6,9,12,16; 12:7; 13:2–5; 14:2,6,7,11, 17–19,21; **Mal.** 1:2,10; 2:2,6,10,15,16; 3:5–7,10,11,18; 4:1.

3809. לָא *lāʾ* **Aram. particle**
(no, not, never; corr. to Hebr. 3808)
Ezra 4:13,14,16,21; 5:5,16; 6:8,9; 7:22, 24–26; **Jer.** 10:11; **Dan.** 2:5,9–11,18,27, 30,34,35,43–45; 3:6,11,12,14–16,18, 24,25,27–29; 4:7(4),9(6),18(15),30(27), 35(32); 5:8,15,22,23; 6:2(3),4(5),5(6), 8(9),12(13),13(14),15(16),17(18),18(19), 22–24(23–25),26(27); 7:14.

3810. לֹא דְבָר *lōʾ ḏ^{e}ḇār,* לוֹ דְבָר *lô ḏ^{e}ḇār* **masc. proper noun**
(Lo Debar)
2 Sam. 9:4,5; 17:27.

3811. לָאָה *lāʾāh* **verb**
(to be weary, to become weary; to be frustrated)
Gen. 19:11; **Ex.** 7:18; **Job** 4:2,5; 16:7; **Ps.** 68:9(10); **Prov.** 26:15; **Isa.** 1:14; 7:13; 16:12; 47:13; **Jer.** 6:11; 9:5(4); 12:5; 15:6; 20:9; **Ezek.** 24:12; **Mic.** 6:3.

3812. לֵאָה *lēʾāh* **fem. proper noun**
(Leah)
Gen. 29:16,17,23–25,30–32; 30:9–14, 16–20; 31:4,14,33; 33:1,2,7; 34:1; 35:23,26; 46:15,18; 49:31; **Ruth** 4:11.

3813. לָאַט *lāʾaṭ* **verb**
(to cover)
2 Sam. 19:4(5)(NIV, *lûṭ* [3874]).

3814. לָאט *lāʾṭ* **masc. noun**
(softness, silence)
Judg. 4:21(NASB, NIV, see *lāṭ* [3909]).

3815. לָאֵל *lāʾēl* **masc. proper noun**
(Lael)
Num. 3:24.

3816. לְאוֹם *leʾôm,* לְאֹם *leʾōm* **masc. noun**
(people, nation)
Gen. 25:23; 27:29; **Ps.** 2:1; 7:7(8); 9:8(9); 44:2(3),14(15); 47:3(4); 57:9(10); 65:7(8); 67:4(5); 105:44; 108:3(4); 148:11; 149:7; **Prov.** 11:26; 14:28,34; 24:24; **Isa.** 17:12,13; 34:1; 41:1; 43:4,9; 49:1; 51:4; 55:4; 60:2; **Jer.** 51:58; **Hab.** 2:13.

3817. לְאֻמִּים *leʾummiym* **masc. pl. proper noun**
(Leummites)
Gen. 25:3.

3818. לֹא עַמִּי *lōʾ ʿammiy* **masc. proper noun**
(Lo-Ammi)
Hos. 1:9; 2:23(25).

3819. לֹא רֻחָמָה *lōʾ ruḥāmāh* **fem. proper noun**
(Lo-Ruhamah)
Hos. 1:6,8; 2:23(25).

3820. לֵב *lēḇ* **masc. noun**
(heart, mind)
Gen. 6:5,6; 8:21; 17:17; 18:5; 24:45; 27:41; 31:20; 34:3; 42:28; 45:26; 50:21; **Ex.** 4:14,21; 7:3,13,14,22,23; 8:15(11), 19(15),32(28); 9:7,12,14,21,34,35; 10:1,20,27; 11:10; 14:4,8,17; 15:8; 25:2; 28:3,29,30; 31:6; 35:5,10,21,22,25,26,29, 34,35; 36:1,2,8; **Num.** 16:28; 24:13; 32:7,9; **Deut.** 4:11; 28:65; 29:4(3), 19(18); **Josh.** 11:20; 14:8; **Judg.** 5:9,15, 16; 9:3; 16:15,17,18,25; 18:20; 19:3,5, 6,22; **Ruth** 2:13; 3:7; **1 Sam.** 1:13; 2:1; 4:13,20; 6:6; 9:20; 10:9,26; 17:32; 24:5(6); 25:25,31,36,37; 27:1; 28:5; **2 Sam.** 6:16; 7:21,27; 13:20,28,33; 14:1; 15:6,13; 17:10; 18:3,14; 19:7(8),19(20); 24:10; **1 Kgs.** 3:9,12; 4:29(5:9); 8:23,47,66; 9:3; 10:24; 11:3; 12:26,27,33; 18:37; 21:7; **2 Kgs.** 5:26; 6:11; 9:24; 12:4(5); 14:10; 23:3; **1 Chr.** 12:33,38; 15:29; 16:10; 17:19; 28:9; 29:9; **2 Chr.** 6:14,38; 7:10, 11,16; 9:23; 12:14; 17:6; 24:4; 25:19; 26:16; 29:31; 30:12,22; 32:25,26; **Ezra** 6:22; 7:27; **Neh.** 2:2,12; 4:6(3:38); 5:7; 6:8; 7:5; **Esth.** 1:10; 5:9; 6:6; 7:5; **Job** 1:8; 2:3; 7:17; 8:10; 11:13; 12:24; 15:12; 17:4; 23:16; 29:13; 31:7,9,27; 33:3; 34:14; 36:5,13; 37:1,24; 41:24(16); **Ps.** 4:7(8); 7:10(11); 9:1(2); 10:6,11,13,17; 11:2; 12:2(3); 13:5(6); 14:1; 16:9; 17:3; 19:8(9),14(15); 21:2(3); 22:14(15); 26:2; 27:3,8,14; 28:7; 31:12(13); 32:11; 33:11, 15,21; 34:18(19); 35:25; 36:1(2),10(11); 37:4,15,31; 38:8(9),10(11); 39:3(4); 40:10(11),12(13); 41:6(7); 44:18(19), 21(22); 45:1(2),5(6); 46:2(3); 48:13(14); 49:3(4); 51:10(12),17(19); 53:1(2); 55:4(5),21(22); 57:7(8); 58:2(3); 61:2(3); 62:10(11); 64:6(7),10(11); 66:18; 69:20(21); 74:8; 76:5(6); 78:8,37; 81:12(13); 83:5(6); 84:2(3); 94:15; 97:11; 102:4(5); 105:3,25; 107:12; 108:1(2); 109:22; 112:7,8; 119:2,10,11,32,34,36, 58,69,70,80,111,112,145,161; 131:1; 138:1; 140:2(3); 141:4; 143:4; 147:3; **Prov.** 2:2,10; 3:1,3,5; 4:4,23; 5:12; 6:14,18,21,32; 7:3,7,10,25; 8:5; 9:4,16; 10:8,13,20,21; 11:12,20,29; 12:8,11,20, 23,25; 13:12; 14:10,13,14,30,33; 15:7, 13–15,21,28,30,32; 16:1,5,9,21,23; 17:16,18,20,22; 18:2,12,15; 19:3,8,21; 20:5,9; 21:1,4; 22:11,15,17; 23:7,12,15, 17,19,26,33,34; 24:2,17,30,32; 25:3,20; 26:23,25; 27:9,11,19,23; 28:14,26; 30:19; 31:11; **Eccl.** 1:13,16,17; 2:1,3,10,15,20, 22,23; 3:11,17,18; 5:2(1),20(19); 7:2–4, 7,21,22,25,26; 8:5,9,11,16; 9:1,3,7; 10:2,3; 11:9,10; **Song** 3:11; 5:2; 8:6; **Isa.** 6:10; 15:5; 24:7; 29:13; 32:6; 33:18; 35:4;

38:3; 40:2; 41:22; 42:25; 44:19,20; 46:8, 12; 47:7,10; 51:7; 57:1,11,15,17; 59:13; 61:1; 63:4,17; 65:14,17; 66:14; **Jer.** 3:10, 15–17; 4:9,14,18,19; 5:21,23; 7:24,31; 8:18; 9:14(13),26(25); 11:8,20; 12:3,11; 13:10; 14:14; 16:12; 17:1,5,9,10; 18:12; 19:5; 20:9,12; 22:17; 23:9,16,17,20,26; 24:7; 30:21,24; 31:21,33; 32:35,39,41; 44:21; 48:29,36,41; 49:16,22; 51:1(NASB, NIV, *lēb̲ qāmay* [3846,II]); **Lam.** 1:20,22; 2:18,19; 3:21,33,65; 5:15,17; **Ezek.** 2:4; 3:7; 6:9; 11:19,21; 13:2,17,22; 14:3–5,7; 18:31; 20:16; 21:7(12),15(20); 22:14; 27:4,25–27; 28:2,6,8,17; 32:9; 33:31; 36:26; 40:4; 44:5,7,9; **Dan.** 1:8; 10:12; **Hos.** 2:14(16); 4:11; 7:6,11,14; 10:2; 11:8; 13:6,8; **Amos** 2:16; **Obad.** 1:3; **Nah.** 2:10(11); **Zeph.** 3:14; **Zech.** 7:12; 10:7; 12:5; **Mal.** 2:2; 4:6(3:24).

3821. לֵב *lēb̲* **Aram. masc. noun**
(heart, mind; corr. to Hebr. 3820)
Dan. 7:28.

3822. לְבָאוֹת *l^e^b̲ā'ôt̲* **proper noun**
(Lebaoth)
Josh. 15:32.

3823. I. לָבַב *lāb̲ab̲* **verb**
(to become wise, to captivate, to bewitch)
Job 11:12; **Song** 4:9.
II. לָבַב *lāb̲ab̲* **verb**
(to bake cakes, to make bread)
2 Sam. 13:6,8.

3824. לֵבָב *lēb̲āb̲* **masc. noun**
(heart, mind)
Gen. 20:5,6; 31:26; **Ex.** 14:5; **Lev.** 19:17; 26:36,41; **Num.** 15:39; **Deut.** 1:28; 2:30; 4:9,29,39; 5:29(26); 6:5,6; 7:17; 8:2,5,14,17; 9:4,5; 10:12,16; 11:13, 16,18; 13:3(4); 15:7,9,10; 17:17,20; 18:21; 19:6; 20:3,8; 26:16; 28:28,47,67; 29:18(17),19(18); 30:1,2,6,10,14,17; 32:46; **Josh.** 2:11; 5:1; 7:5; 14:7; 22:5; 23:14; 24:23; **Judg.** 19:8,9; **1 Sam.** 1:8; 2:35; 6:6; 7:3; 9:19; 12:20,24; 13:14; 14:7; 16:7; 17:28; 21:12(13); **2 Sam.** 7:3; 19:14(15); **1 Kgs.** 2:4,44; 3:6; 8:17,18, 38,39,48,58,61; 9:4; 10:2; 11:2,4,9; 14:8; 15:3,14; **2 Kgs.** 10:15,30,31; 20:3; 22:19; 23:25; **1 Chr.** 12:17,38; 17:2; 22:7,19; 28:2,9; 29:17–19; **2 Chr.** 1:11; 6:7,8, 30,37; 9:1; 11:16; 13:7; 15:12,15,17; 16:9; 19:3,9; 20:33; 22:9; 25:2; 29:10,34; 30:19; 31:21; 32:6,31; 34:27,31; 36:13; **Ezra** 7:10; **Neh.** 9:8; **Job** 1:5; 9:4; 10:13; 12:3; 17:11; 22:22; 27:6; 34:10,34; **Ps.** 4:4(5); 13:2(3); 15:2; 20:4(5); 22:26(27); 24:4; 25:17; 28:3; 31:24(25); 62:8(9); 69:32(33); 73:1,7,13,21,26; 77:6(7); 78:18,72; 84:5(6); 86:11,12; 90:12; 95:8,10; 101:2,4,5; 104:15; 109:16; 111:1; 119:7; 139:23; **Prov.** 4:21; 6:25; **Eccl.** 9:3; **Isa.** 1:5; 6:10; 7:2,4; 9:9(8); 10:7,12; 13:7; 14:13; 19:1; 21:4; 30:29; 32:4; 47:8; 49:21; 60:5; **Jer.** 4:4; 5:24; 13:22; 15:16; 29:13; 32:40; 51:46,50; **Lam.** 3:41; **Ezek.** 3:10; 28:5,6; 31:10; 36:5; 38:10; **Dan.** 8:25; 11:12,25,27,28; **Hos.** 7:2; **Joel** 2:12,13; **Jon.** 2:3(4); **Nah.** 2:7(8); **Zeph.** 1:12; 2:15; **Hag.** 1:5,7; 2:15,18; **Zech.** 7:10; 8:17.

3825. לְבַב *lēb̲ab̲* **Aram. masc. noun**
(heart, mind; corr. to Hebr. 3824)
Dan. 2:30; 4:16(13); 5:20–22; 7:4.

3826. לִבָּה *libbāh* **fem. noun**
(heart, mind)
Ps. 7:9(10); 125:4; **Prov.** 15:11; 17:3; 21:2; 24:12; **Isa.** 44:18; **Ezek.** 16:30.

3827. לַבָּה *labbāh* **fem. noun**
(flame)
Ex. 3:2.

3828. לְבוֹנָה *l^e^b̲ônah,* לְבֹנָה *l^e^b̲ōnāh* **fem. noun**
(frankincense, incense)
Ex. 30:34; **Lev.** 2:1,2,15,16; 5:11; 6:15(8); 24:7; **Num.** 5:15; **1 Chr.** 9:29;

Neh. 13:5,9; **Song** 3:6; 4:6,14; **Isa.** 43:23; 60:6; 66:3; **Jer.** 6:20; 17:26; 41:5.

3829. לְבוֹנָה *l^e^bônāh* **proper noun**
(Lebonah)
Judg. 21:19.

3830. I. לְבוּשׁ *l^e^bûš*, לְבֻשׁ *l^e^buš* **masc. noun**
(clothing, garments, dress)
Gen. 49:11; **2 Sam.** 1:24; 20:8; **2 Kgs.** 10:22; **Esth.** 4:2; 6:8–11; 8:15; **Job** 24:7,10; 30:18; 31:19; 38:9,14; 41:13(5); **Ps.** 22:18(19); 35:13; 45:13(14); 69:11(12); 102:26(27); 104:6; **Prov.** 27:26; 31:22,25; **Isa.** 14:19(NIV, see II); 63:1,2; **Jer.** 10:9; **Lam.** 4:14; **Mal.** 2:16.
II. לָבוּשׁ *lābûš*, לָבֻשׁ *lābuš* **adj.**
(clothed, dressed; KJV, NASB, Qal. pass. part. of *lābaš* [3847])
1 Sam. 17:5; **Prov.** 31:21; **Isa.** 14:19; **Ezek.** 9:2,3,11; 10:2,6,7; 23:6,12; 38:4; **Dan.** 10:5; 12:6,7; **Zech.** 3:3.

3831. לְבוּשׁ *l^e^bûš* **Aram. masc. noun**
(clothing, garment; corr. to Hebr. 3830,I)
Dan. 3:21; 7:9.

3832. לָבַט *lābaṭ* **verb**
(to be thrown down, to be ruined)
Prov. 10:8,10; **Hos.** 4:14.

3833. I. לְבֶא *lebe'* **masc. noun**
(lion, lioness; only pl. לְבָאִים)
Ps. 57:4(5); **Nah.** 2:12(13).
II. לִבְאָה *lib'āh* **fem. noun**
(lioness)
Ps. 57:4(5); **Nah.** 2:12(13).
III. לְבִיָּא *l^e^biyyā'* **fem. noun**
(lioness)
Ezek. 19:2.
IV. לָבִיא *lābiy'* **masc. noun**
(lion, lioness)
Gen. 49:9; **Num.** 23:24; 24:9; **Deut.** 33:20; **Job** 4:11; 38:39; **Isa.** 5:29; 30:6; **Hos.** 13:8; **Joel** 1:6; **Nah.** 2:11(12).

3834. לְבִבָה *l^e^bibāh* **fem. noun**
(cake, bread)
2 Sam. 13:6,8,10.

3835. I. לָבֵן *lābēn* **verb**
(to make brick)
Gen. 11:3; **Ex.** 5:7,14.
II. לָבֵן *lābēn* **verb**
(to make white, spotless, pure)
Ps. 51:7(9); **Isa.** 1:18; **Dan.** 11:35; 12:10; **Joel** 1:7.

3836. לָבָן *lābān* **adj.**
(white)
Gen. 30:35,37; 49:12; **Ex.** 16:31; **Lev.** 13:3,4,10,13,16,17,19–21,24–26,38,39,42,43; **Eccl.** 9:8; **Zech.** 1:8; 6:3,6.

3837. A. לָבָן *lābān* **masc. proper noun**
(Laban: son of Bethuel)
Gen. 24:29,50; 25:20; 27:43; 28:2,5; 29:5,10,13–16,19,21,22,24–26,29; 30:25,27,34,36,40,42; 31:1,2,12,19,20,22,24–26,31,33,34,36,43,47,48,51,55(32:1); 32:4(5); 46:18,25.
B. לָבָן *lābān* **proper noun**
(Laban: loc. in the Sinai Desert)
Deut. 1:1.

3838. לְבָנָה *l^e^bānāh* **masc. proper noun**
(Lebanah)
Ezra 2:45; **Neh.** 7:48.

3839. לִבְנֶה *libneh* **masc. noun**
(poplar)
Gen. 30:37; **Hos.** 4:13.

3840. לִבְנָה *libnāh* **fem. noun**
(pavement)
Ex. 24:10(NASB, NIV, *l^e^bēnāh* [3843]).

3841. A. לִבְנָה *libnāh* **proper noun**
(Libnah: city in S.W. Judah)
Josh. 10:29,31,32,39; 12:15; 15:42; 21:13; **2 Kgs.** 8:22; 19:8; 23:31; 24:18;

1 Chr. 6:57(42); **2 Chr.** 21:10; **Isa.** 37:8; **Jer.** 52:1.
B. לִבְנָה *li_b_nāh* **proper noun**
(Libnah: wilderness encampment)
Num. 33:20,21.

3842. לְבָנָה *l^e_b_ānāh* **fem. noun**
(moon)
Song 6:10; **Isa.** 24:23; 30:26.

3843. לְבֵנָה *l^e_b_ēnāh* **fem. noun**
(brick)
Gen. 11:3; **Ex.** 1:14; 5:7,8,16,18,19; 24:10(KJV, *li_b_nāh* [3840]); **Isa.** 9:10(9); 65:3; **Ezek.** 4:1.

3844. לְבָנוֹן *l^e_b_ānôn* **proper noun**
(Lebanon)
Deut. 1:7; 3:25; 11:24; **Josh.** 1:4; 9:1; 11:17; 12:7; 13:5,6; **Judg.** 3:3; 9:15; **1 Kgs.** 4:33(5:13); 5:6(20),9(23),14(28); 7:2; 9:19; 10:17,21; **2 Kgs.** 14:9; 19:23; **2 Chr.** 2:8(7),16(15); 8:6; 9:16,20; 25:18; **Ezra** 3:7; **Ps.** 29:5,6; 72:16; 92:12(13); 104:16; **Song** 3:9; 4:8,11,15; 5:15; 7:4(5); **Isa.** 2:13; 10:34; 14:8; 29:17; 33:9; 35:2; 37:24; 40:16; 60:13; **Jer.** 18:14; 22:6,20,23; **Ezek.** 17:3; 27:5; 31:3,15,16; **Hos.** 14:5–7(6–8); **Nah.** 1:4; **Hab.** 2:17; **Zech.** 10:10; 11:1.

3845. לִבְנִי *li_b_niy* **masc. proper noun**
(Libni)
Ex. 6:17; **Num.** 3:18; **1 Chr.** 6:17(2),20(5),29(14).

3846. I. לִבְנִי *li_b_niy* **masc. proper noun**
(Libnite: descendant of Libni)
Num. 3:21; 26:58.
II. לֵב קָמָי *lē_b_ qāmāy* **proper noun**
(Leb Kamai: cryptic name for Babylon)
Jer. 51:1(KJV, *lē_b_* [3820] and *qûm* [6965]).

3847. לָבַשׁ *lā_b_aš*, לָבֵשׁ *lā_b_ēš* **verb**
(to put on clothing, to wear)
Gen. 3:21; 27:15,16; 28:20; 38:19; 41:42; **Ex.** 28:41; 29:5,8,30; 40:13,14; **Lev.** 6:10(3),11(4); 8:7,13; 16:4,23,24, 32; 21:10; **Num.** 20:26,28; **Deut.** 22:5,11; **Judg.** 6:34; **1 Sam.** 17:5(NIV, *lā_b_ûš* [3830,II]),38; 28:8; **2 Sam.** 1:24; 13:18; 14:2; **1 Kgs.** 22:10,30; **1 Chr.** 12:18; **2 Chr.** 5:12; 6:41; 18:9,29; 24:20; 28:15; **Ezra** 3:10; **Esth.** 4:1,4; 5:1; 6:8,9,11; **Job** 7:5; 8:22; 10:11; 27:17; 29:14; 39:19; 40:10; **Ps.** 35:26; 65:13(14); 93:1; 104:1; 109:18,29; 132:9,16,18; **Prov.** 23:21; 31:21(NIV, *lā_b_ûš* [3830,II]); **Song** 5:3; **Isa.** 4:1; 22:21; 49:18; 50:3; 51:9; 52:1; 59:17; 61:10; **Jer.** 4:30; 46:4; **Ezek.** 7:27; 9:2(NIV, *lā_b_ûš* [3830,II]), 3(NIV, *lā_b_ûš* [3830,II]),11(NIV, *lā_b_ûš* [3830,II]); 10:2(NIV, *lā_b_ûš* [3830,II]), 6(NIV, *lā_b_ûš* [3830,II]),7(NIV, *lā_b_ûš* [3830,II]); 16:10; 23:6(NIV, *lā_b_ûš* [3830,II]),12(NIV, *lā_b_ûš* [3830,II]); 26:16; 34:3; 38:4(NIV, *lā_b_ûš* [3830,II]); 42:14; 44:17,19; **Dan.** 10:5(NIV, *lā_b_ûš* [3830,II]); 12:6(NIV, *lā_b_ûš* [3830,II]),7(NIV, *lā_b_ûš* [3830,II]); **Jon.** 3:5; **Zeph.** 1:8; **Hag.** 1:6; **Zech.** 3:3(NIV, *lā_b_ûš* [3830,II]),4,5; 13:4.

3848. לְבַשׁ *l^e_b_aš* **Aram. verb**
(to be clothed; corr. to Hebr. 3847)
Dan. 5:7,16,29.

3849. לֹג *lō_g_* **masc. noun**
(log, a liquid measure of oil)
Lev. 14:10,12,15,21,24.

3850. לֹד *lō_d_* **proper noun**
(Lod)
1 Chr. 8:12; **Ezra** 2:33; **Neh.** 7:37; 11:35.

3851. לַהַב *laha_b_* **masc. noun**
(flame, flashing blade of a sword or spear)
Judg. 3:22; 13:20; **Job** 39:23; 41:21(13); **Isa.** 13:8; 29:6; 30:30; 66:15; **Joel** 2:5; **Nah.** 3:3.

3852. לֶהָבָה *lehāḇāh* **fem. noun**
(flame, tip of a sword or spear)
Num. 21:28; **1 Sam.** 17:7; **Ps.** 29:7; 83:14(15); 105:32; 106:18; **Isa.** 4:5; 5:24; 10:17; 43:2; 47:14; **Jer.** 48:45; **Lam.** 2:3; **Ezek.** 20:47(21:3); **Dan.** 11:33; **Hos.** 7:6; **Joel** 1:19; 2:3; **Obad.** 1:18.

3853. לְהָבִים *l^e^hāḇiym* **masc. pl. proper noun**
(Lehabites)
Gen. 10:13; **1 Chr.** 1:11.

3854. לַהַג *lahag* **masc. noun**
(study, devotion to study)
Eccl. 12:12.

3855. לָהַד *lāhad̲* **masc. proper noun**
(Lahad)
1 Chr. 4:2.

3856. I. לָהַה *lāhah* **verb**
(to behave like a madman)
Prov. 26:18.
II. לָהָה *lāhāh* **verb**
(to languish)
Gen. 47:13.

3857. I. לָהַט *lāhaṭ* **verb**
(to burn, to set on fire, to consume with fire)
Deut. 32:22; **Job** 41:21(13); **Ps.** 57:4(5)(NIV, see II); 83:14(15); 97:3; 104:4; 106:18; **Isa.** 42:25. **Joel** 1:19; 2:3; **Mal.** 4:1(3:19).
II. לָהַט *lāhaṭ* **verb**
(to swallow down, to devour)
Ps. 57:4(5)(KJV, NASB, see I).

3858. I. לַהַט *lahaṭ* **masc. noun**
(flame)
Gen. 3:24.
II. לְהָטִים *l^e^hāṭiym* **masc. pl. noun**
(sorceries, enchantments)
Ex. 7:11.

3859. לָהַם *lāham* **verb**
(to swallow greedily; as a subst.: something to be gulped)
Prov. 18:8; 26:22.

3860. לָהֵן *lāhēn* **particle**
(therefore, on this account)
Ruth 1:13(KJV, NIV, *hēn* [2004]),13(KJV, NIV, *hēn* [2004]).

3861. לָהֵן *lāhēn* **Aram. particle**
(therefore, on this account; corr. to Hebr. 3860)
Ezra 5:12; **Dan.** 2:6,9,11,30; 3:28; 4:27(24); 6:5(6),7(8),12(13).

3862. לַהֲקָה *lah^a^qāh* **fem. noun**
(company, group)
1 Sam. 19:20.

3863. לֻא *lu'*, לוּ *lû*, לוּא *lû'* **particle**
(if, oh that)
Gen. 17:18; 23:13; 30:34; 50:15; **Num.** 14:2; 20:3; 22:29; **Deut.** 32:29; **Josh.** 7:7; **Judg.** 8:19; 13:23; **1 Sam.** 14:30; **2 Sam.** 18:12; 19:6(7); **Job** 6:2; 16:4; **Ps.** 81:13(14); **Isa.** 48:18; 64:1(63:19); **Ezek.** 14:15; **Mic.** 2:11.

3864. לוּבִי *lûḇiy* **masc. proper noun**
(Lubite)
2 Chr. 12:3; 16:8; **Dan.** 11:43; **Nah.** 3:9.

3865. לוּד *lûd̲* **masc. proper noun**
(Lud, Lydia)
Gen. 10:22; **1 Chr.** 1:17; **Isa.** 66:19; **Ezek.** 27:10; 30:5.

3866. לוּדִים *lûd̲iym* **masc. pl. proper noun**
(Ludites; Lydians)
Gen. 10:13; **1 Chr.** 1:11; **Jer.** 46:9.

3867. I. לָוָה *lāwāh* **verb**
(to join, to accompany)

Gen. 29:34; **Num.** 18:2,4; **Esth.** 9:27; **Ps.** 83:8(9); **Eccl.** 8:15; **Isa.** 14:1; 56:3,6; **Jer.** 50:5; **Dan.** 11:34; **Zech.** 2:11(15).
II. לָוָה *lāwāh* **verb**
(to borrow, to lend)
Ex. 22:25(24); **Deut.** 28:12,44; **Neh.** 5:4; **Ps.** 37:21,26; 112:5; **Prov.** 19:17; 22:7; **Isa.** 24:2.

3868. לוּז *lûz* **verb**
(to be devious, to be perverse, to be crooked)
Prov. 2:15; 3:21,32; 4:21; 14:2; **Isa.** 30:12.

3869. לוּז *lûz* **masc. noun**
(almond tree)
Gen. 30:37.

3870. A. לוּז *lûz* **proper noun**
(Luz: another name for Bethel)
Gen. 28:19; 35:6; 48:3; **Josh.** 16:2; 18:13; **Judg.** 1:23.
B. לוּז *lûz* **proper noun**
(Luz: Hittite city)
Judg. 1:26.

3871. לוּחַ *lûaḥ* **masc. noun**
(tablet, slab of stone, board or plank)
Ex. 24:12; 27:8; 31:18; 32:15,16,19; 34:1,4,28,29; 38:7; **Deut.** 4:13; 5:22(19); 9:9–11,15,17; 10:1–5; **1 Kgs.** 7:36; 8:9; **2 Chr.** 5:10; **Prov.** 3:3; 7:3; **Song** 8:9; **Isa.** 30:8; **Jer.** 17:1; **Ezek.** 27:5; **Hab.** 2:2.

3872. לוּחִית *lûḥiyṯ* **proper noun**
(Luhith)
Isa. 15:5; **Jer.** 48:5.

3873. הַלּוֹחֵשׁ *hallôḥēš* **masc. proper noun**
(Hallohesh)
Neh. 3:12; 10:24(25).

3874. לוּט *lûṭ* **verb**
(to wrap, to cover)
1 Sam. 21:9(10); **2 Sam.** 19:4(5) (KJV, NASB, *lā'aṭ* [3813]); **1 Kgs.** 19:13; **Isa.** 25:7.

3875. לוֹט *lôṭ* **masc. noun**
(covering, shroud)
Isa. 25:7.

3876. לוֹט *lôṭ* **masc. proper noun**
(Lot)
Gen. 11:27,31; 12:4,5; 13:1,5,7,8, 10–12,14; 14:12,16; 19:1,5,6,9,10,12, 14,15,18,23,29,30,36; **Deut.** 2:9,19; **Ps.** 83:8(9).

3877. לוֹטָן *lôṭān* **masc. proper noun**
(Lotan)
Gen. 36:20,22,29; **1 Chr.** 1:38,39.

3878. A. לֵוִי *lēwiy* **masc. proper noun**
(Levi: son of Jacob)
Gen. 29:34; 34:25,30; 35:23; 46:11; 49:5; **Ex.** 1:2; 2:1; 6:16; **Num.** 3:17; 16:1; 26:59; **1 Chr.** 2:1; 6:1(5:27), 16(1),38(23),43(28),47(32); **Ezra** 8:18.
B. לֵוִי *lēwiy* **masc. proper noun**
(Levi: tribe of Levi)
Ex. 6:19; 32:26,28; **Num.** 1:49; 3:6,15; 4:2; 16:7,8,10; 17:3(18),8(23); 18:2,21; **Deut.** 10:8,9; 18:1; 21:5; 27:12; 31:9; 33:8; **Josh.** 13:14,33; 21:10; **1 Kgs.** 12:31; **1 Chr.** 9:18; 12:26; 21:6; 23:6, 14,24; 24:6,20; 27:17(KJV, *lēwiy* [3881]); **2 Chr.** 31:12; **Ezra** 8:15; **Neh.** 10:39(40); 12:23; **Ps.** 135:20; **Ezek.** 40:46; 48:31; **Zech.** 12:13; **Mal.** 2:4,8; 3:3.

3879. לֵוָי *lēwāy* **Aram. masc. proper noun**
(Levite; corr. to Hebr. 3881)
Ezra 6:16,18; 7:13,24.

3880. לִוְיָה *liwyāh* **fem. noun**
(wreath, garland)
Prov. 1:9; 4:9.

3881. לֵוִי *lēwiy* **proper noun**
(Levite)
Ex. 4:14; 6:25; 38:21; **Lev.** 25:32,33; **Num.** 1:47,50,51,53; 2:17,33; 3:9,12, 20,32,39,41,45,46,49; 4:18,46; 7:5,6; 8:6,9–15,18–22,24,26; 18:6,23,24,26,30; 26:57,58; 31:30,47; 35:2,4,6–8; **Deut.** 12:12,18,19; 14:27,29; 16:11,14; 17:9,18; 18:1,6,7; 24:8; 26:11,12,13; 27:9,14; 31:25; **Josh.** 3:3; 8:33; 14:3,4; 18:7; 21:1,3,4,8,20,27,34,40(38),41(39); **Judg.** 17:7,9–13; 18:3,15; 19:1; 20:4; **1 Sam.** 6:15; **2 Sam.** 15:24; **1 Kgs.** 8:4; **1 Chr.** 6:19(4),48(33),64(49); 9:2,14,26,31, 33,34; 13:2; 15:2,4,11,12,14–17,22, 26,27; 16:4; 23:2,3,26,27; 24:6,30,31; 26:17,20; 27:17(NASB, NIV, *lēwiy* [3878]); 28:13,21; **2 Chr.** 5:4,5,12; 7:6; 8:14,15; 11:13,14; 13:9,10; 17:8; 19:8,11; 20:14,19; 23:2,4,6–8,18; 24:5,6,11; 29:4,5,12,16,25,26,30,34; 30:15–17,21, 22,25,27; 31:2,4,9,14,17,19; 34:9,12, 13,30; 35:3,5,8–11,14,15,18; **Ezra** 1:5; 2:40,70; 3:8–10,12; 6:20; 7:7; 8:20,29, 30,33; 9:1; 10:5,15,23; **Neh.** 3:17; 7:1,43,73; 8:7,9,11,13; 9:4,5,38(10:1); 10:9(10),28(29),34(35),37(38),38(39); 11:3,15,16,18,20,22,36; 12:1,8,22,24, 27,30,44,47; 13:5,10,13,22,29,30; **Isa.** 66:21; **Jer.** 33:18,21,22; **Ezek.** 43:19; 44:10,15; 45:5; 48:11–13,22.

3882. I. לִוְיָתָן *liwyāṯān* **masc. proper noun**
(Leviathan: mythical sea monster)
Job 3:8(KJV, see II); 41:1(40:25); **Ps.** 74:14; 104:26; **Isa.** 27:1.
II. לִוְיָתָן *liwyāṯān* **masc. noun**
(mourning)
Job 3:8(NASB, NIV, see I).

3883. לוּל *lûl* **masc. noun**
(staircase, winding staircase)
1 Kgs. 6:8.

3884. לוּלֵא *lûlēʾ*, לוּלֵי *lûlēy* **particle**
(unless, if not)
Gen. 31:42; 43:10; **Deut.** 32:27; **Judg.** 14:18; **1 Sam.** 25:34; **2 Sam.** 2:27; **2 Kgs.** 3:14; **Ps.** 27:13; 94:17; 106:23; 119:92; 124:1,2; **Isa.** 1:9.

3885. I. לִין *liyn*, לוּן *lûn* **verb**
(to lodge, to tarry)
Gen. 19:2; 24:23,25,54; 28:11; 31:54; 32:13(14),21(22); **Ex.** 23:18; 34:25; **Lev.** 19:13; **Num.** 22:8; **Deut.** 16:4; 21:23; **Josh.** 3:1; 4:3; 6:11; 8:9; **Judg.** 18:2; 19:4,6,7,9–11,13,15,20; 20:4; **Ruth** 1:16; 3:13; **2 Sam.** 12:16; 17:8,16; 19:7(8); **1 Kgs.** 19:9; **1 Chr.** 9:27; **Neh.** 4:22(16); 13:20,21; **Job** 17:2; 19:4; 24:7; 29:19; 31:32; 39:9,28; 41:22(14); **Ps.** 25:13; 30:5(6); 49:12(13); 55:7(8); 91:1; **Prov.** 15:31; 19:23; **Song** 1:13; 7:11(12); **Isa.** 1:21; 21:13; 65:4; **Jer.** 4:14; 14:8; **Joel** 1:13; **Zeph.** 2:14; **Zech.** 5:4.
II. לוּן *lûn* **verb**
(to murmur, to grumble, to howl)
Ex. 15:24; 16:2,7,8; 17:3; **Num.** 14:2,27,29,36; 16:11,41(17:6); 17:5(20); **Josh.** 9:18; **Ps.** 59:15(16).

3886. I. לָעַע *lāʿaʿ* **verb**
(to devour, to swallow, to drink)
Job 6:3(NASB, NIV, see II); **Obad.** 1:16.
II. לָעַע *lāʿaʿ* **verb**
(to act impetuously, to speak rashly)
Job 6:3(KJV, see I); **Prov.** 20:25(KJV, *yālaʿ* [3216]).

3887. I. לוּץ *lûṣ*, לִיץ *liyṣ* **verb**
(to boast, to mock, to scorn)
Gen. 42:23; **2 Chr.** 32:31; **Job** 16:20; 33:23; **Ps.** 1:1(NIV, see II); 119:51; **Prov.** 1:22(NIV, see II); 3:34(NIV, see II); 9:7(NIV, see II),8(NIV, see II),12; 13:1(NIV, see II); 14:6(NIV, see II),9; 15:12(NIV, see II); 19:25(NIV, see II),28,29(NIV, see II); 20:1(NIV, see II); 21:11(NIV, see II),24(NIV, see II); 22:10(NIV, see II); 24:9(NIV, see II); **Isa.** 28:22; 29:20(NIV, see II); 43:27; **Hos.** 7:5(KJV, NIV, *lāṣaṣ* [3945]; KJV,

NASB, *l^e^ṣaṣiym* [3945,I]; NIV, *l^e^ṣaṣiym* [3945,II]).
II. לֵץ *lēṣ* **masc. noun**
(mocker, scorner; Qal part. of *liyṣ* [3887,I], KJV, NASB, see I)
Ps. 1:1; **Prov.** 1:22; 3:34; 9:7,8; 13:1; 14:6; 15:12; 19:25,29; 20:1; 21:11,24; 22:10; 24:9; **Isa.** 29:20.

3888. לוּשׁ *lûš* **verb**
(to knead [dough])
Gen. 18:6; **1 Sam.** 28:24; **2 Sam.** 13:8; **Jer.** 7:18; **Hos.** 7:4.

3889. לָוִשׁ *lāwiš* **masc. proper noun**
(Laish)
2 Sam. 3:15([Q^e^] לַיִשׁ [3919,B]).

3890. לְוָת *l^e^wāṯ* **Aram. particle**
(beside, from)
Ezra 4:12.

3891. לָזוּת *lāzûṯ* **fem. noun**
(perversity, deceitfulness)
Prov. 4:24.

3892. לַח *laḥ* **adj.**
(green, fresh)
Gen. 30:37; **Num.** 6:3; **Judg.** 16:7,8; **Ezek.** 17:24; 20:47(21:3).

3893. לֵחַ *lēaḥ* **masc. noun**
(vigor, strength)
Deut. 34:7.

3894. לְחוּם *l^e^ḥûm* **masc. noun**
(intestines, bowels)
Job 20:23; **Zeph.** 1:17.

3895. לְחִי *l^e^ḥiy* **masc. noun**
(cheek, jaw)
Deut. 18:3; **Judg.** 15:15–17,19; **1 Kgs.** 22:24; **2 Chr.** 18:23; **Job** 16:10; 41:2 (40:26); **Ps.** 3:7(8); **Song** 1:10; 5:13; **Isa.** 30:28; 50:6; **Lam.** 1:2; 3:30; **Ezek.** 29:4; 38:4; **Hos.** 11:4; **Mic.** 5:1(4:14).

3896. לֶחִי *leḥiy* **proper noun**
(Lehi)
Judg. 15:9,14,19.

3897. לָחַךְ *lāḥak̲* **verb**
(to lick, to lick up)
Num. 22:4; **1 Kgs.** 18:38; **Ps.** 72:9; **Isa.** 49:23; **Mic.** 7:17.

3898. I. לָחַם *lāḥam* **verb**
(to fight, to do battle)
Ex. 1:10; 14:14,25; 17:8–10; **Num.** 21:1,23,26; 22:11; **Deut.** 1:30,41,42; 3:22; 20:4,10,19; **Josh.** 9:2; 10:5,14, 25,29,31,34,36,38,42; 11:5; 19:47; 23:3,10; 24:8,9,11; **Judg.** 1:1,3,5,8,9; 5:19,20; 8:1; 9:17,38,39,45,52; 10:9,18; 11:4–6,8,9,12,20,25,27,32; 12:1,3,4; **1 Sam.** 4:9,10; 8:20; 12:9; 13:5; 14:47; 15:18; 17:9,10,19,32,33; 18:17; 19:8; 23:1,5; 25:28; 28:1,15; 29:8; 31:1; **2 Sam.** 2:28; 8:10; 10:17; 11:17,20; 12:26,27,29; 21:15; **1 Kgs.** 12:21,24; 14:19; 20:1,23,25; 22:31,32,45(46); **2 Kgs.** 3:21; 6:8; 8:29; 9:15; 10:3; 12:17(18); 13:12; 14:15,28; 16:5; 19:8,9; **1 Chr.** 10:1; 18:10; 19:17; **2 Chr.** 11:1,4; 13:12; 17:10; 18:30,31; 20:17,29; 22:6; 26:6; 27:5; 32:8; 35:20,22; **Neh.** 4:8(2), 14(8),20(14); **Ps.** 35:1; 56:1(2),2(3); 109:3; **Isa.** 7:1; 19:2; 20:1; 30:32; 37:8,9; 63:10; **Jer.** 1:19; 15:20; 21:2,4,5; 32:5, 24,29; 33:5; 34:1,7,22; 37:8,10; 41:12; 51:30; **Dan.** 10:20; 11:11; **Zech.** 10:5; 14:3,14.
II. לָחַם *lāḥam* **verb**
(to eat, to taste)
Deut. 32:24; **Ps.** 141:4; **Prov.** 4:17; 9:5; 23:1,6.

3899. לֶחֶם *leḥem* **masc. noun**
(bread, food)
Gen. 3:19; 14:18; 18:5; 21:14; 25:34; 27:17; 28:20; 31:54; 37:25; 39:6; 41:54,55; 43:25,31,32; 45:23; 47:12,13, 15,17,19; 49:20; **Ex.** 2:20; 16:3,4,8,12, 15,22,29,32; 18:12; 23:25; 25:30; 29:2,

23,32,34; 34:28; 35:13; 39:36; 40:23; **Lev.** 3:11,16; 7:13; 8:26,31,32; 21:6,8, 17,21,22; 22:7,11,13,25; 23:14,17,18,20; 24:7; 26:5,26; **Num.** 4:7; 14:9; 15:19; 21:5; 28:2,24; **Deut.** 8:3,9; 9:9,18; 10:18; 16:3; 23:4(5); 29:6(5); **Josh.** 9:5,12; **Judg.** 7:13; 8:5,6,15; 13:16; 19:5,19; **Ruth** 1:6; 2:14; **1 Sam.** 2:5,36; 9:7; 10:3,4; 14:24,28; 16:20; 17:17; 20:24, 27,34; 21:3(4),4(5),6(7); 22:13; 25:11,18; 28:20,22; 30:11,12; **2 Sam.** 3:29,35; 6:19; 9:7,10; 12:17,20,21; 13:5; 16:1,2; **1 Kgs.** 4:22(5:2); 5:9(23); 7:48; 11:18; 13:8,9,15–19,22,23; 14:3; 17:6,11; 18:4,13; 21:4,5,7; 22:27; **2 Kgs.** 4:8,42; 6:22; 18:32; 25:3,29; **1 Chr.** 9:32; 12:40; 16:3; 23:29; **2 Chr.** 4:19; 13:11; 18:26; **Ezra** 10:6; **Neh.** 5:14,15,18; 9:15; 10:33(34); 13:2; **Job** 3:24; 6:7; 15:23; 20:14; 22:7; 24:5; 27:14; 28:5; 30:4; 33:20; 42:11; **Ps.** 14:4; 37:25; 41:9(10); 42:3(4); 53:4(5); 78:20,25; 80:5(6); 102:4(5),9(10); 104:14,15; 105:16,40; 127:2; 132:15; 136:25; 146:7; 147:9; **Prov.** 4:17; 6:8,26; 9:5,17; 12:9,11; 20:13,17; 22:9; 23:3,6; 25:21; 27:27; 28:3,19,21; 30:8,22,25; 31:14,27; **Eccl.** 9:7,11; 10:19; 11:1; **Isa.** 3:1,7; 4:1; 21:14; 28:28; 30:20,23; 33:16; 36:17; 44:15,19; 51:14; 55:2,10; 58:7; 65:25; **Jer.** 5:17; 11:19; 37:21; 38:9; 41:1; 42:14; 44:17; 52:6,33; **Lam.** 1:11; 4:4; 5:6,9; **Ezek.** 4:9,13,15–17; 5:16; 12:18,19; 13:19; 14:13; 16:19,49; 18:7,16; 24:17,22; 44:3,7; 48:18; **Dan.** 10:3; **Hos.** 2:5(7); 9:4; **Amos** 4:6; 7:12; 8:11; **Obad.** 1:7; **Hag.** 2:12; **Mal.** 1:7.

3900. לְחֶם *l^eḥem* **Aram. masc. noun**
(feast, banquet; corr. to Hebr. 3899)
Dan. 5:1.

3901. לָחֶם *lāḥem* **masc. noun**
(war)
Judg. 5:8.

3902. לַחְמִי *laḥmiy* **masc. proper noun**
(Lahmi)
1 Chr. 20:5.

3903. לַחְמָס *laḥmās* **proper noun**
(Lahmas)
Josh. 15:40(KJV, *laḥmām*).

3904. לְחֵנָה *l^eḥēnāh* **Aram. fem. noun**
(concubine)
Dan. 5:2,3,23.

3905. לָחַץ *lāḥaṣ* **verb**
(to oppress, to crush)
Ex. 3:9; 22:21(20); 23:9; **Num.** 22:25; **Judg.** 1:34; 2:18; 4:3; 6:9; 10:12; **1 Sam.** 10:18; **2 Kgs.** 6:32; 13:4,22; **Ps.** 56:1(2); 106:42; **Isa.** 19:20; **Jer.** 30:20; **Amos** 6:14.

3906. לַחַץ *laḥaṣ* **masc. noun**
(oppression, affliction)
Ex. 3:9; **Deut.** 26:7; **1 Kgs.** 22:27; **2 Kgs.** 13:4; **2 Chr.** 18:26; **Job** 36:15; **Ps.** 42:9(10); 43:2; 44:24(25); **Isa.** 30:20.

3907. לָחַשׁ *lāḥaš* **verb**
(to whisper, to whisper as one who conjures)
2 Sam. 12:19; **Ps.** 41:7(8); 58:5(6).

3908. לַחַשׁ *laḥaš* **masc. noun**
(whisper of conjuring, charm, amulet)
Eccl. 10:11; **Isa.** 3:3,20; 26:16; **Jer.** 8:17.

3909. לָט *lāṭ* **masc. noun**
(enchantment, secrecy)
Ex. 7:22; 8:7(3),18(14); **Judg.** 4:21 (KJV, *lā'ṭ* [3814,I]; NASB, *lā'ṭ* [3814,II]); **Ruth** 3:7; **1 Sam.** 18:22; 24:4(5).

3910. לֹט *lōṭ* **masc. noun**
(myrrh)
Gen. 37:25; 43:11.

3911. לְטָאָה *l*^{e}*ṭā'āh* **fem. noun**
(a kind of lizard)
Lev. 11:30.

3912. לְטוּשִׁם *l*^{e}*ṭûšiym* **masc. pl. proper noun**
(Letushites)
Gen. 25:3.

3913. לָטַשׁ *lāṭaš* **verb**
(to sharpen, to hammer, to instruct)
Gen. 4:22; **1 Sam.** 13:20; **Job** 16:9; **Ps.** 7:12(13); 52:2(4).

3914. לֹיָה *lōyāh* **fem. noun**
(wreath, garland, addition)
1 Kgs. 7:29,30,36.

3915. I. לַיְלָה *laylāh*, לָיִל *lāyilā* **masc. noun**
(night, midnight)
Gen. 1:5,14,16,18; 7:4,12; 8:22; 14:15; 19:5,33–35; 20:3; 26:24; 30:15,16; 31:24,39,40; 32:13(14),21(22),22(23); 40:5; 41:11; 46:2; **Ex.** 10:13; 11:4; 12:8,12,29–31,42; 13:21,22; 14:20,21; 24:18; 34:28; 40:38; **Lev.** 6:9(2); 8:35; **Num.** 9:16,21; 11:9,32; 14:1,14; 22:8, 19,20; **Deut.** 1:33; 9:9,11,18,25; 10:10; 16:1; 23:10(11); 28:66; **Josh.** 1:8; 2:2; 4:3; 8:3,9,13; 10:9; **Judg.** 6:25,27,40; 7:9; 9:32,34; 16:2,3; 19:25; 20:5; **Ruth** 1:12; 3:2,8,13; **1 Sam.** 14:34,36; 15:11,16; 19:10,11,24; 25:16; 26:7; 28:8,20,25; 30:12; 31:12; **2 Sam.** 2:29,32; 4:7; 7:4; 17:1,16; 19:7(8); 21:10; **1 Kgs.** 3:5, 19,20; 8:29,59; 19:8; **2 Kgs.** 6:14; 7:12; 8:21; 19:35; 25:4; **1 Chr.** 9:33; 17:3; **2 Chr.** 1:7; 6:20; 7:12; 21:9; 35:14; **Neh.** 1:6; 2:12,13,15; 4:9(3),22(16); 6:10; 9:12,19; **Esth.** 4:16; 6:1; **Job** 2:13; 3:3,6,7; 4:13; 5:14; 7:3; 17:12; 20:8; 24:14; 27:20; 30:17; 33:15; 34:20,25; 35:10; 36:20; **Ps.** 1:2; 6:6(7); 16:7; 17:3; 19:2(3); 22:2(3); 32:4; 42:3(4),8(9); 55:10(11); 74:16; 77:2(3),6(7); 78:14; 88:1(2); 90:4; 91:5; 92:2(3); 104:20; 105:39; 119:55,62; 121:6; 134:1; 136:9; 139:11,12; **Prov.** 7:9; 31:15,18; **Eccl.** 2:23; 8:16; **Song** 3:1,8; 5:2; **Isa.** 4:5; 15:1; 16:3; 21:8,11,12; 26:9; 27:3; 28:19; 29:7; 30:29; 34:10; 38:12,13; 60:11; 62:6; **Jer.** 6:5; 9:1(8:23); 14:17; 16:13; 31:35; 33:20,25; 36:30; 39:4; 49:9; 52:7; **Lam.** 1:2; 2:18,19; **Hos.** 4:5; 7:6; **Amos** 5:8; **Obad.** 1:5; **Jon.** 1:17(2:1); 4:10; **Mic.** 3:6; **Zech.** 1:8; 14:7.
II. לַיִל *layil* **masc. noun**
(night)
Ex. 12:42; **Isa.** 15:1; 16:3; 21:11; 30:29.

3916. לֵילְיָא *lēyl*^{e}*yā'* **Aram. fem. noun**
(night; corr. to Hebr. 3915)
Dan. 2:19; 5:30; 7:2,7,13.

3917. לִילִית *liyliyṯ* **fem. noun**
(night creature, screech owl)
Isa. 34:14.

3918. לַיִשׁ *layiš* **masc. noun**
(lion)
Job 4:11; **Prov.** 30:30; **Isa.** 30:6.

3919. A. לַיִשׁ *layiš* **proper noun**
(Laish: city in northern Israel, later named Dan [see 1835])
Judg. 18:7,14,27,29.
B. לַיִשׁ *layiš* **masc. proper noun**
(Laish: Michal's father-in-law)
1 Sam. 25:44; **2 Sam.** 3:15(*k*^{e}*lûš* [3889]).
C. לַיְשָׁה *lay*^{e}*šāh* **proper noun**
(Laish: village near Jerusalem)
Isa. 10:30.

3920. לָכַד *lāḵaḏ* **verb**
(to capture, to seize)
Num. 21:32; 32:39,41,42; **Deut.** 2:34,35; 3:4; **Josh.** 6:20; 7:14–18; 8:19,21; 10:1,28,32,35,37,39,42; 11:10,12,17; 15:16,17; 19:47; **Judg.** 1:8,12,13,18; 3:28; 7:24,25; 8:12,14; 9:45,50; 12:5; 15:4; **1 Sam.** 10:20,21; 14:41,42,47;

2 Sam. 5:7; 8:4; 12:26–29; **1 Kgs.** 9:16; 16:18; **2 Kgs.** 12:17(18); 17:6; 18:10; **1 Chr.** 11:5; 18:4; **2 Chr.** 12:4; 13:19; 15:8; 17:2; 22:9; 28:18; 32:18; 33:11; **Neh.** 9:25; **Job** 5:13; 36:8; 38:30; 41:17(9); **Ps.** 9:15(16); 35:8; 59:12(13); **Prov.** 5:22; 6:2; 11:6; 16:32; **Eccl.** 7:26; **Isa.** 8:15; 20:1; 24:18; 28:13; **Jer.** 5:26; 6:11; 8:9; 18:22; 32:3,24,28; 34:22; 37:8; 38:3,28; 48:1,7,41,44; 50:2,9,24; 51:31, 41,56; **Lam.** 4:20; **Dan.** 11:15,18; **Amos** 3:4,5; **Hab.** 1:10; **Zech.** 14:2.

3921. לֶכֶד *le<u>k</u>e<u>d</u>* **masc. noun**
(a taking, a capture)
Prov. 3:26.

3922. לֵכָה *lē<u>k</u>āh* **proper noun**
(Lecah)
1 Chr. 4:21.

3923. לָכִישׁ *lā<u>k</u>iyš* **proper noun**
(Lachish)
Josh. 10:3,5,23,31–35; 12:11; 15:39; **2 Kgs.** 14:19; 18:14,17; 19:8; **2 Chr.** 11:9; 25:27; 32:9; **Neh.** 11:30; **Isa.** 36:2; 37:8; **Jer.** 34:7; **Mic.** 1:13.

3924. לֻלָאוֹת *lulā'ō<u>t</u>* **fem. pl. noun**
(loops)
Ex. 26:4,5,10,11; 36:11,12,17.

3925. לָמַד *lāma<u>d</u>* **verb**
(to teach, to learn)
Deut. 4:1,5,10,14; 5:1,31(28); 6:1; 11:19; 14:23; 17:19; 18:9; 20:18; 31:12,13, 19,22; **Judg.** 3:2; **2 Sam.** 1:18; 22:35; **1 Chr.** 5:18; 25:7; **2 Chr.** 17:7,9; **Ezra** 7:10; **Job** 21:22; **Ps.** 18:34(35); 25:4,5,9; 34:11(12); 51:13(15); 60:[title](1); 71:17; 94:10,12; 106:35; 119:7,12,26,64,66,68, 71,73,99,108,124,135,171; 132:12; 143:10; 144:1; **Prov.** 5:13; 30:3; **Eccl.** 12:9; **Song** 3:8; 8:2; **Isa.** 1:17; 2:4; 26:9,10; 29:13,24; 40:14; 48:17; **Jer.** 2:33; 9:5(4),14(13),20(19); 10:2; 12:16; 13:21; 31:18,34; 32:33; **Ezek.** 19:3,6; **Dan.** 1:4; **Hos.** 10:11; **Mic.** 4:3.

3926. לְמוֹ *l^emô* **particle**
(for, at, over)
Job 27:14; 29:21; 38:40; 40:4.

3927. לְמוּאֵל *l^e mû'ēl,* לְמוֹאֵל *l^e mô'ēl* **masc. proper noun**
(Lemuel)
Prov. 31:1,4.

3928. לִמּוּד *limmû<u>d</u>,* לִמֻּד *limmu<u>d</u>* **adj.**
(learned, discipled)
Isa. 8:16; 50:4; 54:13; **Jer.** 2:24; 13:23.

3929. A. לֶמֶךְ *leme<u>k</u>* **masc. proper noun**
(Lamech: son of Methushael)
Gen. 4:18,19,23,24.
B. לֶמֶךְ *leme<u>k</u>* **masc. proper noun**
(Lamech: son of Methuselah)
Gen. 5:25,26,28,30,31; **1 Chr.** 1:3.

3930. לֹעַ *lōa'* **masc. noun**
(throat)
Prov. 23:2.

3931. לָעַב *lā'a<u>b</u>* **verb**
(to mock)
2 Chr. 36:16.

3932. לָעַג *lā'ag* **verb**
(to mock, to deride, to scorn)
2 Kgs. 19:21; **2 Chr.** 30:10; **Neh.** 2:19; 4:1(3:33); **Job** 9:23; 11:3; 21:3; 22:19; **Ps.** 2:4; 22:7(8); 35:16(KJV, NASB, *la'ēg* [3934]); 59:8(9); 80:6(7); **Prov.** 1:26; 17:5; 30:17; **Isa.** 28:11(KJV, NASB, *la'ēg* [3934]); 33:19; 37:22; **Jer.** 20:7.

3933. לַעַג *la'ag* **masc. noun**
(scorn, mocking)
Job 34:7; **Ps.** 44:13(14); 79:4; 123:4; **Ezek.** 23:32; 36:4; **Hos.** 7:16.

3934. לָעֵג *lāʿēg* **adj.**
(mocking, stammering)
Ps. 35:16(NIV, *lāʿag* [3932]); **Isa.** 28:11 (NIV, *lāʿag* [3932]).

3935. לַעְדָּה *laʿdāh* **masc. proper noun**
(Laadah)
1 Chr. 4:21.

3936. A. לַעְדָּן *laʿdān* **masc. proper noun**
(Ladan: an Ephraimite)
1 Chr. 7:26.
B. לַעְדָּן *laʿdān* **masc. proper noun**
(Ladan: a Gershonite)
1 Chr. 23:7–9; 26:21.

3937. לָעַז *lāʿaz* **verb**
(to speak indistinctly, to speak unintelligibly)
Ps. 114:1.

3938. לָעַט *lāʿaṭ* **verb**
(to swallow greedily, to devour)
Gen. 25:30.

3939. לַעֲנָה *laʿᵃnāh* **fem. noun**
(wormwood, bitterness [figuratively])
Deut. 29:18(17); **Prov.** 5:4; **Jer.** 9:15(14); 23:15; **Lam.** 3:15,19; **Amos** 5:7; 6:12.

3940. לַפִּיד *lappiyd̲* **masc. noun**
(torch, lamp)
Gen. 15:17; **Ex.** 20:18; **Judg.** 7:16,20; 15:4,5; **Job** 12:5; 41:19(11); **Isa.** 62:1; **Ezek.** 1:13; **Dan.** 10:6; **Nah.** 2:4(5); **Zech.** 12:6.

3941. לַפִּידוֹת *lappiyd̲ôṯ* **masc. proper noun**
(Lappidoth)
Judg. 4:4.

3942. לִפְנָי *lip̄nāy* **adv.**
(before, in front of)
1 Kgs. 6:17(NASB, NIV, *pānay* [6440]).

3943. לָפַת *lāpaṯ* **verb**
(to take hold, to turn aside)
Judg. 16:29; **Ruth** 3:8; **Job** 6:18.

3944. לָצוֹן *laṣôn* **masc. noun**
(scoffer, mocker, mockery)
Prov. 1:22; 29:8; **Isa.** 28:14.

3945. I. לְצָצִים *leṣaṣiym* **masc. noun**
(scorner, scoffer; Polel pl. part. of *liyṣ* [3887,I])
Hos. 7:5(NIV, see II).
II. לָצַץ *lāṣaṣ* **verb**
(to mock)
Hos. 7:5(KJV, NASB, see I).

3946. לַקּוּם *laqqûm* **proper noun**
(Lakkum)
Josh. 19:33.

3947. לָקַח *lāqaḥ* **verb**
(to take, to get)
Gen. 2:15,21–23; 3:6,19,22,23; 4:11,19; 5:24; 6:2,21; 7:2; 8:9,20; 9:23; 11:29,31; 12:5,15,19; 14:11,12,21,23,24; 15:9,10; 16:3; 17:23; 18:4,5,7,8; 19:14,15; 20:2,3, 14; 21:14,21,27,30; 22:2,3,6,10,13; 23:13; 24:3,4,7,10,22,37,38,40,48,51,61,65,67; 25:1,20; 26:34; 27:9,13–15,35,36,45,46; 28:1,2,6,9,11,18; 29:23; 30:9,15,37; 31:1,23,32,34,45,46,50; 32:13(14),22(23), 23(24); 33:10,11; 34:2,4,9,16,17,21,25, 26,28; 36:2,6; 37:24,31; 38:2,6,20,23,28; 39:20; 40:11; 42:16,24,33,36; 43:11–13, 15,18; 44:29; 45:18,19; 46:6; 47:2; 48:1, 9,13,22; **Ex.** 2:1,3,5,9; 4:9,17,20,25; 5:11; 6:7,20,23,25; 7:9,15,19; 9:8,10,24; 10:26; 12:3–5,7,21,22,32; 13:19; 14:6, 7,11; 15:20; 16:16,33; 17:5,12; 18:2,12; 21:10,14; 22:11(10); 23:8; 24:6–8; 25:2,3; 27:20; 28:5,9; 29:1,5,7,12,13,15,16, 19–22,25,26,31; 30:16,23,34; 32:4,20;

33:7; 34:4,16; 35:5; 36:3; 40:9,20; **Lev.** 4:5,25,30,34; 7:34; 8:2,10,15,16,23,25, 26,28–30; 9:2,3,5,15; 10:1,12; 12:8; 14:4,6,10,12,14,15,21,24,25,42,49,51; 15:14,29; 16:5,7,12,14,18; 18:17,18; 20:14,17,21; 21:7,13,14; 23:40; 24:2,5; 25:36; **Num.** 1:17; 3:12,41,45,47,49,50; 4:9,12; 5:17,25; 6:18,19; 7:5,6; 8:6,8, 16,18; 11:16; 12:1; 13:20; 16:1,6,17,18, 39(17:4),46(17:11),47(17:12); 17:2(17), 9(24); 18:6,26,28; 19:2,4,6,17,18; 20:8,9,25; 21:25,26; 22:41; 23:11,14,20, 27,28; 25:4,7; 27:18,22; 31:11,29,30, 47,51,54; 34:14,15,18; 35:31,32; **Deut.** 1:15,23,25; 3:4,8,14; 4:20,34; 7:3,25; 9:9,21; 10:17; 15:17; 16:19; 19:12; 20:7; 21:3,11; 22:6,7,13–15,18,30(23:1); 24:1,3–5,19; 25:5,7,8; 26:2,4; 27:25; 29:8(7); 30:4,12,13; 31:26; 32:11; **Josh.** 2:4; 3:12; 4:2,20; 6:18; 7:1,11,21,23,24; 8:1,12; 9:4,11,14; 11:16,19,23; 13:8; 18:7; 24:3,26; **Judg.** 3:6,21,25; 4:6,21; 5:19; 6:20,25–27; 7:8; 8:16,21; 9:43,48; 11:5,13,15; 13:19,23; 14:2,3,8,11,19; 15:4,6,15; 16:12; 17:2,4; 18:17,18,20, 24,27; 19:1,28,29; 20:10; 21:22; **Ruth** 4:2,13,16; **1 Sam.** 2:14–16; 4:3,11,17, 19,21,22; 5:1–3; 6:7,8,10; 7:9,12,14; 8:3,11,13,14,16; 9:3,22; 10:1,4,23; 11:7; 12:3,4; 14:32; 15:21; 16:2,11,13,20,23; 17:17,18,31,40,49,51,54,57; 18:2; 19:13, 14,20; 20:21,31; 21:6(7),8(9),9(10); 24:2(3),11(12); 25:11,18,35,39,40,43; 26:11,12,22; 27:9; 28:24; 30:11,16,18–20; 31:4,12,13; **2 Sam.** 1:10; 2:8,21; 3:15; 4:6,7,12; 5:13; 7:8; 8:1,7,8; 9:5; 10:4; 11:4; 12:4,9–11,30; 13:8–10,19; 14:2; 17:19; 18:14,17,18; 19:30(31); 20:3,6; 21:8,10,12; 22:17; 23:6; 24:22; **1 Kgs.** 1:33,39; 3:1,20,24; 4:15; 7:8,13; 9:28; 10:28; 11:18,31,34,35,37; 14:3,26; 15:18; 16:31; 17:10,11,19,23; 18:4,26,31; 19:4,10,14,21; 20:6,33,34; 22:3,26; **2 Kgs.** 2:3,5,8–10,14,20; 3:15,26,27; 4:1,29,41; 5:5,15,16,20,23,24,26; 6:2,7,13; 7:13,14; 8:8,9,15; 9:1,3,13,17; 10:6,7; 11:2,4,9,19; 12:5(6),7–9(8–10), 18(19); 13:15,18,25; 14:14,21; 15:29; 16:8; 18:32; 19:14; 20:7,18; 23:16,30,34; 24:7,12; 25:14,15,18–20; **1 Chr.** 2:19, 21,23; 4:18; 7:15,21; 10:4; 14:3; 17:7; 18:1,7,8; 19:4; 20:2; 21:23; **2 Chr.** 1:16; 8:18; 11:18,20; 12:9; 16:6; 18:25; 22:11; 23:1,8,20; 26:1; 36:1,4; **Ezra** 2:61; **Neh.** 5:2,3,15; 6:18; 7:63; 10:30(31),31(32); **Esth.** 2:7,8,15,16; 6:10,11; **Job** 1:15, 17,21; 2:8; 3:6; 4:12; 5:5; 12:20; 15:12; 22:22; 27:13; 28:2; 35:7; 38:20; 40:24; 41:4(40:28); 42:8; **Ps.** 6:9(10); 15:5; 18:16(17); 31:13(14); 49:15(16),17(18); 50:9; 51:11(13); 68:18(19); 73:24; 75:2(3); 78:70; 109:8; **Prov.** 1:3,19; 2:1; 4:10; 6:25; 7:20; 8:10; 9:7; 10:8; 11:30; 17:23; 20:16; 21:11; 22:25,27; 24:11,32; 27:13; 31:16; **Isa.** 6:6; 8:1; 14:2; 23:16; 28:19; 36:17; 37:14; 39:7; 40:2; 44:14,15; 47:2,3; 49:24,25; 51:22; 52:5; 53:8; 56:12; 57:13; 66:21; **Jer.** 2:30; 3:14; 5:3; 7:28; 9:20(19); 13:4,6,7; 15:15; 16:2; 17:23; 20:5,10; 23:31; 25:9,15,17,28; 27:20; 28:3,10; 29:6,22; 32:11,14,33; 33:26; 35:3,13; 36:2,14,21,26,28,32; 37:17; 38:6,10,11,14; 39:5,12,14; 40:1,2; 41:12,16; 43:5,9,10; 44:12; 46:11; 48:46; 49:29; 51:8,26; 52:18,19,24–26; **Ezek.** 1:4; 3:10,14; 4:1,3,9; 5:1–4; 8:3; 10:6,7; 15:3; 16:16–18,20,32,39,61; 17:3,5,12, 13,22; 18:8,13,17; 19:5; 22:12,25; 23:10, 25,26,29; 24:5,16,25; 27:5; 30:4; 33:2, 4,6; 36:24,30; 37:16,19,21; 38:13; 43:20,21; 44:22; 45:18,19; 46:18; **Hos.** 1:2,3; 2:9(11); 4:11; 10:6; 11:3; 13:11; 14:2(3); **Joel** 3:5(4:5); **Amos** 5:11,12; 6:13; 7:15; 9:2,3; **Jon.** 4:3; **Mic.** 1:11; 2:9; **Zeph.** 3:2,7; **Hag.** 2:23; **Zech.** 6:10,11; 11:7,10,13,15; 14:21; **Mal.** 2:13.

3948. לֶקַח *leqaḥ* **masc. noun** (instruction, teaching, persuasive speech)
Deut. 32:2; **Job** 11:4; **Prov.** 1:5; 4:2; 7:21; 9:9; 16:21,23; **Isa.** 29:24.

3949. לִקְחִי *liqḥiy* **masc. proper noun**
(Likhi)
1 Chr. 7:19.

3950. לָקַט *lāqaṭ* **verb**
(to gather, to pick up, to glean)
Gen. 31:46; 47:14; **Ex.** 16:4,5,16–18, 21,22,26,27; **Lev.** 19:9,10; 23:22; **Num.** 11:8; **Judg.** 1:7; 11:3; **Ruth** 2:2,3,7,8, 15–19,23; **1 Sam.** 20:38; **2 Kgs.** 4:39; **Ps.** 104:28; **Song** 6:2; **Isa.** 17:5; 27:12; **Jer.** 7:18.

3951. לֶקֶט *leqeṭ* **masc. noun**
(gleaning)
Lev. 19:9; 23:22.

3952. לָקַק *lāqaq* **verb**
(to lap up, to lick)
Judg. 7:5–7; **1 Kgs.** 21:19; 22:38.

3953. לָקַשׁ *lāqaš* **verb**
(to gather, to glean)
Job 24:6.

3954. לֶקֶשׁ *leqeš* **masc. noun**
(second crop, spring crop)
Amos 7:1.

3955. לָשָׁד *lāšāḏ* **masc. noun**
(freshness, moisture, vitality)
Num. 11:8; **Ps.** 32:4.

3956. לָשׁוֹן *lāšôn,* לָשֹׁן *lāšōn* **masc. noun**
(tongue, language)
Gen. 10:5,20,31; **Ex.** 4:10; 11:7; **Deut.** 28:49; **Josh.** 7:21,24; 10:21; 15:2,5; 18:19; **Judg.** 7:5; **2 Sam.** 23:2; **Neh.** 13:24; **Esth.** 1:22; 3:12; 8:9; **Job** 5:21; 6:30; 15:5; 20:12,16; 27:4; 29:10; 33:2; 41:1(40:25); **Ps.** 5:9(10); 10:7; 12:3(4), 4(5); 15:3; 22:15(16); 31:20(21); 34:13(14); 35:28; 37:30; 39:1(2),3(4); 45:1(2); 50:19; 51:14(16); 52:2(4),4(6); 55:9(10); 57:4(5); 64:3(4),8(9); 66:17; 68:23(24); 71:24; 73:9; 78:36; 109:2; 119:172; 120:2,3; 126:2; 137:6; 139:4; 140:3(4),11(12); **Prov.** 6:17,24; 10:20,31; 12:18,19; 15:2,4; 16:1; 17:4,20; 18:21; 21:6,23; 25:15,23; 26:28; 28:23; 31:26; **Eccl.** 10:11; **Song** 4:11; **Isa.** 3:8; 5:24; 11:15; 28:11; 30:27; 32:4; 33:19; 35:6; 41:17; 45:23; 50:4; 54:17; 57:4; 59:3; 66:18; **Jer.** 5:15; 9:3(2),5(4),8(7); 18:18; 23:31; **Lam.** 4:4; **Ezek.** 3:5,6,26; 36:3; **Dan.** 1:4; **Hos.** 7:16; **Mic.** 6:12; **Zeph.** 3:13; **Zech.** 8:23; 14:12.

3957. לִשְׁכָּה *liškāh* **fem. noun**
(room, chamber, storeroom)
1 Sam. 9:22; **2 Kgs.** 23:11; **1 Chr.** 9:26,33; 23:28; 28:12; **2 Chr.** 31:11; **Ezra** 8:29; 10:6; **Neh.** 10:37–39(38–40); 13:4,5,8,9; **Jer.** 35:2,4; 36:10,12,20,21; **Ezek.** 40:17,38,44–46; 41:10; 42:1,4, 5,7–13; 44:19; 45:5; 46:19.

3958. לֶשֶׁם *lešem* **masc. noun**
(jacinth, ligure)
Ex. 28:19; 39:12.

3959. לֶשֶׁם *lešem* **proper noun**
(Leshem)
Josh. 19:47.

3960. לָשַׁן *lāšan* **verb**
(to slander)
Ps. 101:5; **Prov.** 30:10.

3961. לִשָּׁן *liššān* **Aram. com. noun**
(language; corr. to Hebr. 3956)
Dan. 3:4,7,29; 4:1(3:31); 5:19; 6:25(26); 7:14.

3962. לֶשַׁע *leša'* **proper noun**
(Lasha)
Gen. 10:19.

3963. לֶתֶךְ *leṯeḵ* **masc. noun**
(a half homer, a dry measure)
Hos. 3:2.

מ Mem

3964. מָא *mā'* **Aram. particle** (what, whatever)
Ezra 6:8.

3965. מַאֲבוּס *ma'ᵃḇûs* **masc. noun** (storehouse, granary)
Jer. 50:26.

3966. מְאֹד *mᵉ'ōḏ* **subst.; adv.; adj.** (very, greatly, great, abundance)
Gen. 1:31; 4:5; 7:18,19; 12:14; 13:2,13; 15:1; 17:2,6,20; 18:20; 19:3,9; 20:8; 21:11; 24:16,35; 26:13,16; 27:33,34; 30:43; 32:7(8); 34:7,12; 41:19,31,49; 47:13,27; 50:9,10; **Ex.** 1:7,20; 9:3,18,24; 10:14,19; 11:3; 12:38; 14:10; 19:16, 18,19; **Num.** 11:10,33; 12:3; 13:28; 14:7,39; 16:15; 22:3,17; 32:1; **Deut.** 2:4; 3:5; 4:9,15; 6:3,5; 9:20; 17:17; 20:15; 24:8; 28:54; 30:14; **Josh.** 1:7; 3:16; 8:4; 9:9,13,22,24; 10:2,20; 11:4; 13:1; 22:5,8; 23:6,11; **Judg.** 2:15; 3:17; 6:6; 10:9; 11:33; 12:2; 13:6; 15:18; 18:9; 19:11; **Ruth** 1:13,20; **1 Sam.** 2:17,22; 4:10; 5:9,11; 11:6,15; 12:18; 14:20,31; 16:21; 17:11,24; 18:8,15,30; 19:2(1),4; 20:19; 21:12(13); 25:2,15,36; 26:21; 28:5,15, 20,21; 30:6; 31:3,4; **2 Sam.** 1:26; 2:17; 3:8; 8:8; 10:5; 11:2; 12:2,5,30; 13:3,15, 21,36; 14:25; 18:17; 19:32(33); 24:10,14; **1 Kgs.** 1:4,6,15; 2:12; 4:29(5:9); 5:7(21); 7:47; 10:2,10,11; 11:19; 17:17; 18:3; 21:26; **2 Kgs.** 10:4; 14:26; 17:18; 21:16; 23:25; **1 Chr.** 10:4; 16:25; 18:8; 19:5; 20:2; 21:8,13; **2 Chr.** 4:18; 7:8; 9:1,9; 11:12; 14:13(12); 16:8,14; 24:24; 25:10; 30:13; 32:27,29; 33:12,14; 35:23; **Ezra** 10:1; **Neh.** 2:2; 4:7(1); 5:6; 6:16; 8:17; 13:8; **Esth.** 1:12; 4:4; **Job** 1:3; 2:13; 8:7; 35:15; **Ps.** 6:3(4),10(11); 21:1(2); 31:11(12); 38:6(7),8(9); 46:1(2); 47:9(10); 48:1(2); 50:3; 78:29,59; 79:8; 92:5(6); 93:5; 96:4; 97:9; 104:1; 105:24; 107:38; 109:30; 112:1; 116:10; 119:4,8,43,51, 96,107,138,140,167; 139:14; 142:6(7); 145:3; **Isa.** 16:6; 31:1; 47:6,9; 52:13; 56:12; 64:9(8),12(11); **Jer.** 2:10,12,36; 9:19(18); 14:17; 18:13; 20:11; 24:2,3; 40:12; 48:16,29; 49:30; 50:12; **Lam.** 5:22; **Ezek.** 9:9; 16:13; 20:13; 27:25; 37:2,10; 40:2; 47:7,9,10; **Dan.** 8:8; 11:25; **Joel** 2:11; **Obad.** 1:2; **Nah.** 2:1(2); **Zeph.** 1:14; **Zech.** 9:2,5,9; 14:4,14.

3967. מֵאָה *mē'āh* **fem. noun** (hundred)
Gen. 5:3–8,10,11,13,14,16–20,22, 23,25–28,30–32; 6:3,15; 7:6,11,24; 8:3,13; 9:28,29; 11:10,11,13,15,17,19, 21,23,25,32; 14:14; 15:13; 17:17; 21:5; 23:1,15,16; 25:7,17; 26:12; 32:6(7), 14(15); 33:1,19; 35:28; 45:22; 47:9,28; 50:22,26; **Ex.** 6:16,18,20; 12:37,40,41; 14:7; 18:21,25; 27:9,11,18; 30:23,24; 38:9,11,24–29; **Lev.** 26:8; **Num.** 1:21, 23,25,27,29,31,33,35,37,39,41,43,46; 2:4,6,8,9,11,13,15,16,19,21,23,24, 26,28,30–32; 3:22,28,34,43,46,50; 4:36,40,44,48; 7:13,19,25,31,37,43,49, 55,61,67,73,79,85,86; 11:21; 16:2,17,35, 49(17:14); 26:7,10,14,18,22,25,27,34,37, 41,43,47,50,51; 31:14,28,32,36,37,39,43, 45,48,52,54; 33:39; **Deut.** 1:15; 22:19; 31:2; 34:7; **Josh.** 7:21; 24:29,32; **Judg.** 2:8; 3:31; 4:3,13; 7:6–8,16,19,22; 8:4, 10,26; 11:26; 15:4; 16:5; 17:2–4; 18:11, 16,17; 20:2,10,15–17,35,47; 21:12; **1 Sam.** 11:8; 13:15; 14:2; 15:4; 17:7; 18:25,27; 22:2,7; 23:13; 25:13,18; 27:2; 29:2; 30:9,10,17,21; **2 Sam.** 2:31; 3:14; 8:4; 10:18; 14:26; 15:11,18; 16:1; 18:1,4; 21:16; 23:8,18; 24:3,9; **1 Kgs.** 4:23(5:3); 5:16(30); 6:1; 7:2,20,42; 8:63; 9:14,23,28;

10:10,14,16,17,26,29; 11:3; 12:21; 18:4, 13,19,22; 20:15,29; 22:6; **2 Kgs.** 3:4,26; 4:43; 11:4,9,10,15,19; 14:13; 18:14; 19:35; 23:33; **1 Chr.** 4:42; 5:18,21; 7:2,9,11; 8:40; 9:6,9,13,22; 11:11,20; 12:14,24–27,30,32,35,37; 13:1; 15:5–8,10; 18:4; 21:3,5,25; 22:14; 25:7; 26:26,30,32; 27:1; 28:1; 29:6,7; **2 Chr.** 1:2,14,17; 2:2(1),17(16),18(17); 3:4,8,16; 4:8,13; 5:12; 7:5; 8:10,18; 9:9,13,15,16; 11:1; 12:3; 13:3,17; 14:8(7),9(8); 15:11; 17:11, 14–18; 18:5; 23:1,9,14,20; 24:15; 25:5,6, 9,23; 26:12,13; 27:5; 28:6,8; 29:32,33; 35:8,9; 36:3; **Ezra** 1:10,11; 2:3–13,15, 17–19,21,23,25–28,30–36,38,41,42,58, 60,64–67,69; 8:3–5,9,10,12,20,26; **Neh.** 5:11,17; 7:8–18,20,22–24,26,27, 29–32,34–39,41,44,45,60,62,66–71; 11:6,8,12–14,18,19; **Esth.** 1:1,4; 8:9; 9:6,12,15,30; **Job** 1:3; 42:16; **Prov.** 17:10; **Eccl.** 6:3; 8:12; **Song** 8:12; **Isa.** 37:36; 65:20; **Jer.** 52:23,29,30; **Ezek.** 4:5,9; 40:19,23,27,47; 41:13–15; 42:2,8, 16(KJV, [K^e] *ʾammāh* [520]),17–20; 45:2,15; 48:16,17,30,32–34; **Dan.** 8:14; 12:11,12; **Amos** 5:3.

3968. מֵאָה *mēʾāh* **proper noun**
(Meah)
Neh. 3:1; 12:39.

3969. מְאָה *m^eʾāh* **Aram. fem. noun**
(hundred; corr. to Hebr. 3967)
Ezra 6:17; 7:22; **Dan.** 6:1(2).

3970. מַאֲוַי *maʾway* **masc. noun**
(desire)
Ps. 140:8(9).

3971. מוּם *mûm,* מאום *mʾûm,* מְאוּם *muʾwm* **masc. noun**
(blemish, defect)
Lev. 21:17,18,21,23; 22:20,21,25; 24:19,20; **Num.** 19:2; **Deut.** 15:21; 17:1; 32:5; **2 Sam.** 14:25; **Job** 11:15; 31:7; **Prov.** 9:7; **Song** 4:7; **Dan.** 1:4.

3972. מְאוּמָה *m^eʾûmāh,* מוּמָה *mûmāh* **indef. pron.**
(anything)
Gen. 22:12; 30:31; 39:6,9,23; 40:15; **Num.** 22:38; **Deut.** 13:17(18); 24:10; **Judg.** 14:6; **1 Sam.** 12:4,5; 20:26,39; 21:2(3); 25:7,15,21; 29:3; **2 Sam.** 3:35; 13:2; **1 Kgs.** 10:21; 18:43; **2 Kgs.** 5:20; **2 Chr.** 9:20; **Eccl.** 5:14(13),15(14); 7:14; 9:5; **Jer.** 39:10,12; **Jon.** 3:7.

3973. מָאוֹס *māʾôs* **masc. noun**
(refuse, trash)
Lam. 3:45.

3974. מָאוֹר *māʾôr,* מָאֹר *māʾōr* **masc. noun**
(light)
Gen. 1:14–16; **Ex.** 25:6; 27:20; 35:8, 14,28; 39:37; **Lev.** 24:2; **Num.** 4:9,16; **Ps.** 74:16; 90:8; **Prov.** 15:30; **Ezek.** 32:8.

3975. מְאוּרָה *m^eʾûrāh* **fem. noun**
(den)
Isa. 11:8.

3976. מֹאזְנַיִם *mōʾz^enayim* **masc. dual noun**
(scales, balance scales)
Lev. 19:36; **Job** 6:2; 31:6; **Ps.** 62:9(10); **Prov.** 11:1; 16:11; 20:23; **Isa.** 40:12,15; **Jer.** 32:10; **Ezek.** 5:1; 45:10; **Hos.** 12:7(8); **Amos** 8:5; **Mic.** 6:11.

3977. מֹאזְנֵא *mōʾz^enēʾ* **Aram. masc. dual noun**
(scales, balance scales; corr. to Hebr. 3976)
Dan. 5:27.

3978. מַאֲכָל *maʾ^akāl* **masc. noun**
(food, meat)
Gen. 2:9; 3:6; 6:21; 40:17; **Lev.** 19:23; **Deut.** 20:20; 28:26; **Judg.** 14:14; **1 Kgs.** 10:5; **1 Chr.** 12:40; **2 Chr.** 9:4; 11:11; **Ezra** 3:7; **Neh.** 9:25; **Job** 33:20; **Ps.**

44:11(12); 74:14; 79:2; **Prov.** 6:8; **Isa.** 62:8; **Jer.** 7:33; 16:4; 19:7; 34:20; **Ezek.** 4:10; 47:12; **Dan.** 1:10; **Hab.** 1:16; **Hag.** 2:12.

3979. מַאֲכֶלֶת *ma'akeleṯ* **fem. noun**
(knife)
Gen. 22:6,10; **Judg.** 19:29; **Prov.** 30:14.

3980. מַאֲכֹלֶת *ma'akōleṯ* **fem. noun**
(fuel)
Isa. 9:5(4),19(18).

3981. מַאֲמָץ *ma'amāṣ* **masc. noun**
(force, effort)
Job 36:19.

3982. מַאֲמַר *ma'amar* **masc. noun**
(command, word)
Esth. 1:15; 2:20; 9:32.

3983. מֵאמַר *mē'mar* **Aram. masc. noun**
(word, request; corr. to Hebr. 3982)
Ezra 6:9; **Dan.** 4:17(14).

3984. מָאן *mā'n* **Aram. masc. noun**
(vessel, utensil)
Ezra 5:14,15; 6:5; 7:19; **Dan.** 5:2,3,23.

3985. מָאַן *mā'an* **verb**
(to refuse)
Gen. 37:35; 39:8; 48:19; **Ex.** 4:23; 7:14; 8:2(7:27)(KJV, NASB, *ma'ēn* [3986]); 9:2 (KJV, NASB, *ma'ēn* [3986]); 10:3,4(KJV, *ma'ēn* [3986]); 16:28; 22:17(16); **Num.** 20:21; 22:13,14; **Deut.** 25:7; **1 Sam.** 8:19; 28:23; **2 Sam.** 2:23; 13:9; **1 Kgs.** 20:35; 21:15; **2 Kgs.** 5:16; **Neh.** 9:17; **Esth.** 1:12; **Job** 6:7; **Ps.** 77:2(3); 78:10; **Prov.** 1:24; 21:7,25; **Isa.** 1:20; **Jer.** 3:3; 5:3; 8:5; 9:6(5); 11:10; 13:10(KJV, NASB, *mē'ēn* [3987]); 15:18; 25:28; 31:15; 38:21 (KJV, *ma'ēn* [3986]); 50:33; **Hos.** 11:5; **Zech.** 7:11.

3986. מָאֵן *mā'ēn* **adj.**
(refusing)
Ex. 8:2(7:27)(NIV, *mā'an* [3985]); 9:2(NIV, *mā'an* [3985]); 10:4(NASB, NIV, *mā'an* [3985]); **Jer.** 38:21(NASB, NIV, *mā'an* [3985]).

3987. מֵאֵן *mē'ēn* **adj.**
(refusing)
Jer. 13:10(NIV, *mē'an* [3985]).

3988. I. מָאַס *mā'as* **verb**
(to reject)
Lev. 26:15,43,44; **Num.** 11:20; 14:31; **Judg.** 9:38; **1 Sam.** 8:7; 10:19; 15:23,26; 16:1,7; **2 Kgs.** 17:15,20; 23:27; **Job** 5:17; 7:5(NASB, NIV, see II),16; 8:20; 9:21; 10:3; 19:18; 30:1; 31:13; 34:33; 36:5; 42:6; **Ps.** 15:4; 36:4(5); 53:5(6); 78:59,67; 89:38(39); 106:24; 118:22; **Prov.** 3:11; 15:32; **Isa.** 5:24; 7:15,16; 8:6; 30:12; 31:7; 33:8,15; 41:9; 54:6; **Jer.** 2:37; 4:30; 6:19,30; 7:29; 8:9; 14:19; 31:37; 33:24,26; **Lam.** 5:22; **Ezek.** 5:6; 20:13,16,24; 21:10(15), 13(18); **Hos.** 4:6; 9:17; **Amos** 2:4; 5:21.
II. מָאַס *mā'as* **verb**
(to vanish, to flow, to ooze, to fester)
Job 7:5(KJV, see I); **Ps.** 58:7(8).

3989. מַאֲפֶה *ma'apeh* **masc. noun**
(something baked)
Lev. 2:4.

3990. מַאֲפֵל *ma'apēl* **masc. noun**
(darkness)
Josh. 24:7.

3991. מַאְפֵּלְיָה *ma'pēlyāh* **fem. noun**
(darkness, thick darkness)
Jer. 2:31.

3992. מָאַר *mā'ar* **verb**
(to prick, to be painful, to be destructive)
Lev. 13:51,52; 14:44; **Ezek.** 28:24.

3993. מַאֲרָב *ma'arāḇ* **masc. noun**
(ambush, hiding place)

Josh. 8:9; Judg. 9:35; 2 Chr. 13:13; Ps. 10:8.

3994. מְאֵרָה m^e'*ērāh* **fem. noun**
(curse)
Deut. 28:20; Prov. 3:33; 28:27; Mal. 2:2; 3:9.

3995. מִבְדָּלָה *mibdālāh* **fem. noun**
(separate place)
Josh. 16:9.

3996. מָבוֹא *mābô'* **masc. noun**
(entrance, going down of the sun, the west)
Deut. 11:30; Josh. 1:4; 23:4; Judg. 1:24,25; 2 Kgs. 11:16; 16:18; 1 Chr. 4:39; 9:19; 2 Chr. 23:13,15; Ps. 50:1; 104:19; 113:3; Prov. 8:3; Jer. 38:14; Ezek. 26:10; 27:3(KJV, *māḇô'āh* [3997]); 33:31; 42:9; 44:5; 46:19; Zech. 8:7; Mal. 1:11.

3997. מְבוֹאָה m^e*ḇô'āh* **fem. noun**
(entrance)
Ezek. 27:3(NASB, NIV, *māḇô'* [3996]).

3998. מְבוּכָה m^e*ḇûkāh* **fem. noun**
(confusion, perplexity)
Isa. 22:5; Mic. 7:4.

3999. מַבּוּל *mabbûl* **masc. noun**
(flood)
Gen. 6:17; 7:6,7,10,17; 9:11,15,28; 10:1,32; 11:10; Ps. 29:10.

4000. מְבוּנִים m^e*ḇûniym* **masc. plural noun**
(teacher, instructor; variant participle of *biyn* [995])
2 Chr. 35:3.

4001. מְבוּסָה m^e*ḇûsāh* **fem. noun**
(downtreading, subjugation)
Isa. 18:2,7; 22:5.

4002. מַבּוּעַ *mabbûa'* **masc. noun**
(spring of water)
Eccl. 12:6; Isa. 35:7; 49:10.

4003. מְבוּקָה m^e*ḇûqāh* **fem. noun**
(emptiness, void)
Nah. 2:10(11).

4004. מָבְחוֹר *māḇḥôr* **masc. noun**
(choice, best, major)
2 Kgs. 3:19; 19:23.

4005. מִבְחָר *miḇḥār* **masc. noun**
(choice, choicest)
Gen. 23:6; Ex. 15:4; Deut. 12:11; 2 Chr. 35:3(KJV, NIV, *miḇrāh* [4015]); Isa. 22:7; 37:24; Jer. 22:7; 48:15; Ezek. 23:7; 24:4,5; 31:16; Dan. 11:15.

4006. מִבְחָר *miḇḥār* **masc. proper noun**
(Mibhar)
1 Chr. 11:38.

4007. מַבָּט *mabbāṭ* **masc. noun**
(expectation, object of hope)
Isa. 20:5,6; Zech. 9:5.

4008. מִבְטָא *miḇṭā'* **masc. noun**
(rash statement, rash promise)
Num. 30:6(7),8(9).

4009. מִבְטָח *miḇṭāḥ* **masc. noun**
(trust, confidence)
Job 8:14; 18:14; 31:24; Ps. 40:4(5); 65:5(6); 71:5; Prov. 14:26; 21:22; 22:19; 25:19; Isa. 32:18; Jer. 2:37; 17:7; 48:13; Ezek. 29:16.

4010. מַבְלִיגִית *mabliygiyt* **fem. noun**
(cheerfulness, comforter)
Jer. 8:18.

4011. מִבְנֶה *miḇneh* **masc. noun**
(structure, building)
Ezek. 40:2.

4012. מְבֻנַּי m^e*ḇunnay* **masc. proper noun**
(Mebunnai)
2 Sam. 23:27.

4013. I. מִבְצָר *mib̲ṣār* **masc. noun**
(fortification)
Num. 13:19; 32:17,36; **Josh.** 10:20; 19:29,35; **1 Sam.** 6:18; **2 Sam.** 24:7; **2 Kgs.** 3:19; 8:12; 10:2; 17:9; 18:8; **2 Chr.** 17:19; **Ps.** 89:40(41); 108:10(11); **Isa.** 17:3; 25:12; 34:13; **Jer.** 1:18; 4:5; 5:17; 6:27(NASB, see II; NIV, see II); 8:14; 34:7; 48:18; **Lam.** 2:2,5; **Dan.** 11:15, 24,39; **Hos.** 10:14; **Amos** 5:9; **Mic.** 5:11(10); **Nah.** 3:12,14; **Hab.** 1:10.
II. מִבְצָר *mib̲ṣār* **masc. noun**
(tester of metals, assayer)
Jer. 6:27(KJV, see I; NIV, see III).
III. מִבְצָר *mib̲ṣār* **masc. noun**
(ore, metal which is tested)
Jer. 6:27(KJV, see I; NASB, see II).

4014. מִבְצָר *mib̲ṣār* **masc. proper noun**
(Mibzar)
Gen. 36:42; **1 Chr.** 1:53.

4015. מִבְרָח *mib̲rāḥ* **masc. noun**
(fugitive, fleeing one)
Ezek. 17:21(NASB, *mib̲ḥar* [4005]).

4016. מְבוּשִׁים *m*e*b̲ûšiym* **masc. pl. noun**
(private parts, male genitals)
Deut. 25:11.

4017. A. מִבְשָׂם *mib̲śām* **masc. proper noun**
(Mibsam: son of Ishmael)
Gen. 25:13; **1 Chr.** 1:29.
B. מִבְשָׂם *mib̲śām* **masc. proper noun**
(Mibsam: descendant of Simeon)
1 Chr. 4:25.

4018. מְבַשְּׁלוֹת *m*e*b̲ašš*e*lôt̲* **fem. pl. noun**
(places for cooking)
Ezek. 46:23.

4019. מַגְבִּישׁ *magbiyš* **masc. proper noun**
(Magbish)
Ezra 2:30.

4020. מִגְבָּלוֹת *migbālôt̲* **fem. pl. noun**
(something braided, twisted)
Ex. 28:14.

4021. מִגְבָּעָה *migbā'āh* **fem. noun**
(turban, headband)
Ex. 28:40; 29:9; 39:28; **Lev.** 8:13.

4022. מֶגֶד *meged̲* **masc. noun**
(choice thing, best thing)
Gen. 24:53(KJV, *migdānāh* [4030]); **Deut.** 33:13–16; **2 Chr.** 21:3(KJV, *migdānāh* [4030]); 32:23(KJV, *migdānāh* [4030]); **Ezra** 1:6(KJV, *migdānāh* [4030]); **Song** 4:13,16; 7:13(14).

4023. מְגִדּוֹ *m*e*giddô,* מְגִדּוֹן *m*e*giddôn* **proper noun**
(Megiddo)
Josh. 12:21; 17:11; **Judg.** 1:27; 5:19; **1 Kgs.** 4:12; 9:15; **2 Kgs.** 9:27; 23:29,30; **1 Chr.** 7:29; **2 Chr.** 35:22; **Zech.** 12:11.

4024. I. מִגְדֹּל *migdōl* **masc. noun**
(tower)
2 Sam. 22:51(NIV, [K^e] *gād̲al* [1431]); **Ezek.** 29:10(NASB, NIV, see II); 30:6(NASB, NIV, see II).
II. מִגְדּוֹל *migdôl,* מִגְדֹּל *migd̲ōl* **proper noun**
(Migdol: city on N.E. border of Egypt)
Ex. 14:2; **Num.** 33:7; **Jer.** 44:1; 46:14; **Ezek.** 29:10(KJV, see I); 30:6(KJV, see I).

4025. מַגְדִּיאֵל *magdiy'ēl* **masc. proper noun**
(Magdiel)
Gen. 36:43; **1 Chr.** 1:54.

4026. מִגְדָּל *migdāl* **masc. noun**
(tower)
Gen. 11:4,5; 35:21(NIV, *migdal-'ēd̲er* [4029]); **Josh.** 15:37; 19:38; **Judg.** 8:9,17;

9:46,47,49,51,52; **2 Kgs.** 9:17; 17:9; 18:8; **1 Chr.** 27:25; **2 Chr.** 14:7(6); 26:9, 10,15; 27:4; 32:5; **Neh.** 3:1,11,25–27; 8:4; 12:38,39; **Ps.** 48:12(13); 61:3(4); **Prov.** 18:10; **Song** 4:4; 5:13; 7:4(5); 8:10; **Isa.** 2:15; 5:2; 30:25; 33:18; **Jer.** 31:38; **Ezek.** 26:4,9; 27:11; **Mic.** 4:8; **Zech.** 14:10.

4027. מִגְדַּל־אֵל *migdal 'ēl* **proper noun**
(Migdal El)
Josh. 19:38.

4028. מִגְדַּל־גָּד *migdal gā<u>d</u>* **proper noun**
(Migdal Gad)
Josh. 15:37.

4029. I. מִגְדַּל־עֵדֶר *migdal-'ē<u>d</u>er* **proper noun**
(Migdal Eder)
Gen. 35:21(KJV, NASB, see II).
II. מִגְדַּל־עֵדֶר *migdal-'ē<u>d</u>er* **masc. noun**
(tower of Edar; from *migdāl* [4026] and *'ē<u>d</u>er* [5740,B])
Gen. 35:21(NIV, see I).

4030. מִגְדָּנָה *migdānāh* **fem. noun**
(precious thing, costly gift)
Gen. 24:53(NIV, *mege<u>d</u>* [4022]); **2 Chr.** 21:3(NIV, *mege<u>d</u>* [4022]); 32:23(NIV, *mege<u>d</u>* [4022]); **Ezra** 1:6(NIV, *mege<u>d</u>* [4022]).

4031. A. מָגוֹג *māgôg* **masc. proper noun**
(Magog: son of Japheth)
Gen. 10:2; **1 Chr.** 1:5.
B. מָגוֹג *māgôg* **proper noun**
(Magog: mountainous region north of Israel)
Ezek. 38:2; 39:6.

4032. מָגוֹר *māgôr* **masc. noun**
(terror, fear)
Ps. 31:13(14); **Isa.** 31:9; **Jer.** 6:25; 20:3,4,10; 46:5; 49:29; **Lam.** 2:22.

4033. מָגוּר *māgûr*, מָגוֹר *magôr* **masc. noun**
(a sojourning, pilgrimage, dwelling place)
Gen. 17:8; 28:4; 36:7; 37:1; 47:9; **Ex.** 6:4; **Job** 18:19; **Ps.** 55:15(16); 119:54; **Ezek.** 20:38.

4034. מְגוֹרָה *m^egôrāh* **fem. noun**
(dread, fear)
Prov. 10:24; **Ps.** 34:4(5)(KJV, *m^egûrāh* [4035,II]); **Isa.** 66:4(KJV, *m^egûrāh* [4035,II]).

4035. I. מְגוּרָה *m^egûrāh* **fem. noun**
(grain pit, barn)
Hag. 2:19.
II. מְגוּרָה *m^egûrāh* **fem. noun**
(fear, dread)
Ps. 34:4(5)(NASB, NIV, *m^egôrāh* [4034]); **Isa.** 66:4(NASB, NIV, *m^egôrāh* [4034]).

4036. מָגוֹר מִסָּבִיב *māgôr missā<u>b</u>iy<u>b</u>* **masc. proper noun**
(Magor-Missabib)
Jer. 20:3.

4037. מַגְזֵרָה *magzērāh* **fem. noun**
(ax)
2 Sam. 12:31.

4038. מַגָּל *maggāl* **fem. noun**
(sickle)
Jer. 50:16; **Joel** 3:13(4:13).

4039. מְגִלָּה *m^egillāh* **fem. noun**
(scroll, roll)
Ps. 40:7(8); **Jer.** 36:2,4,6,14,20,21,23,25,27–29,32; **Ezek.** 2:9; 3:1–3; **Zech.** 5:1,2.

4040. מְגִלָּה *m^egillāh* **Aram. fem. noun**
(scroll, roll; corr. to Hebr. 4039)
Ezra 6:2.

4041. מְגַמָּה *m^egammāh* **fem. noun**
(meaning uncertain, perhaps horde, eagerness)
Hab. 1:9.

4042. מָגַן *māgan* **verb**
(to deliver up, to present)
Gen. 14:20; **Prov.** 4:9; **Hos.** 11:8.

4043. מָגֵן *māgēn* **masc. noun**
(shield, small shield)
Gen. 15:1; **Deut.** 33:29; **Judg.** 5:8; **2 Sam.** 1:21; 22:3,31,36; **1 Kgs.** 10:17; 14:26,27; **2 Kgs.** 19:32; **1 Chr.** 5:18; **2 Chr.** 9:16; 12:9,10; 14:8(7); 17:17; 23:9; 26:14; 32:5,27; **Neh.** 4:16(10); **Job** 15:26; 41:15(7); **Ps.** 3:3(4); 7:10(11); 18:2(3),30(31),35(36); 28:7; 33:20; 35:2; 47:9(10); 59:11(12); 76:3(4); 84:9(10), 11(12); 89:18(19); 115:9–11; 119:114; 144:2; **Prov.** 2:7; 6:11; 24:34; 30:5; **Song** 4:4; **Isa.** 21:5; 22:6; 37:33; **Jer.** 46:3,9; **Ezek.** 23:24; 27:10; 38:4,5; 39:9; **Hos.** 4:18; **Nah.** 2:3(4).

4044. מְגִנָּה *m^eginnāh* **fem. noun**
(sorrow, hardness)
Lam. 3:65.

4045. מִגְעֶרֶת *mig'eret* **fem. noun**
(rebuke)
Deut. 28:20.

4046. מַגֵּפָה *maggēpāh* **fem. noun**
(plague, blow)
Ex. 9:14; **Num.** 14:37; 16:48–50 (17:13–15); 25:8,9,18; 26:1(25:19); 31:16; **1 Sam.** 4:17; 6:4; **2 Sam.** 17:9; 18:7; 24:21,25; **1 Chr.** 21:17,22; **2 Chr.** 21:14; **Ps.** 106:29,30; **Ezek.** 24:16; **Zech.** 14:12,15,18.

4047. מַגְפִּיעָשׁ *magpiy'āš* **masc. proper noun**
(Magpiash)
Neh. 10:20(21).

4048. מָגַר *māgar* **verb**
(to throw, to cast)
Ps. 89:44(45); **Ezek.** 21:12(17).

4049. מְגַר *m^egar* **Aram. verb**
(to overthrow, to destroy; corr. to Hebr. 4048)
Ezra 6:12.

4050. מְגֵרָה *m^egērāh* **fem. noun**
(saw, ax)
2 Sam. 12:31; **1 Kgs.** 7:9; **1 Chr.** 20:3.

4051. מִגְרוֹן *migrôn* **proper noun**
(Migron)
1 Sam. 14:2; **Isa.** 10:28.

4052. מִגְרָעָה *migrā'āh* **fem. noun**
(recess, offset ledge)
1 Kgs. 6:6.

4053. מֶגְרָפָה *megrāpāh* **fem. noun**
(clod of dirt)
Joel 1:17.

4054. מִגְרָשׁ *migrāš* **masc. noun**
(open pastureland)
Lev. 25:34; **Num.** 35:2–5,7; **Josh.** 14:4; 21:2,3,8,11,13–19,21–39,41,42; **1 Chr.** 5:16; 6:55(40),57–60(42–45),64(49),67–81(52–66); 13:2; **2 Chr.** 11:14; 31:19; **Ezek.** 27:28; 36:5(KJV, NASB, *gāruš* [1644]); 45:2; 48:15,17.

4055. מַד *mad* **masc. noun**
(clothes, tunic, robe)
Lev. 6:10(3); **Judg.** 3:16; 5:10; **1 Sam.** 4:12; 17:38,39; 18:4; **2 Sam.** 20:8; 21:20 (KJV, [K^e] *mādôn* [4067]; NIV, [K^e] *middāh* [4060,I]); **Job** 11:9; **Ps.** 109:18; **Jer.** 13:25.

4056. מַדְבַּח *madbaḥ* **Aram. masc. noun**
(altar)
Ezra 7:17.

4057. I. מִדְבָּר *miḏbār* **masc. noun**
(mouth, speech)
Song 4:3.

II. מִדְבָּר *miḏbār* **masc. noun**
(desert, wilderness)
Gen. 14:6; 16:7; 21:14,20,21; 36:24;
37:22; **Ex.** 3:1,18; 4:27; 5:1,3; 7:16;
8:27(23),28(24); 13:18,20; 14:3,11,12;
15:22; 16:1–3,10,14,32; 17:1; 18:5;
19:1,2; 23:31; **Lev.** 7:38; 16:10,21,22;
Num. 1:1,19; 3:4,14; 9:1,5; 10:12,31;
12:16; 13:3,21,26; 14:2,16,22,25,29,32,
33,35; 15:32; 16:13; 20:1,4; 21:5,11,13,
18,23; 24:1; 26:64,65; 27:3,14; 32:13,15;
33:6,8,11,12,15,16,36; 34:3; **Deut.**
1:1,19,31,40; 2:1,7,8,26; 4:43; 8:2,15,16;
9:7,28; 11:5,24; 29:5(4); 32:10,51; **Josh.**
1:4; 5:4–6; 8:15,20,24; 12:8; 14:10;
15:1,61; 16:1; 18:12; 20:8; 24:7; **Judg.**
1:16; 8:7,16; 11:16,18,22; 20:42,45,47;
1 Sam. 4:8; 13:18; 17:28; 23:14,15,
24,25; 24:1(2); 25:1,4,14,21; 26:2,3;
2 Sam. 2:24; 15:23,28; 16:2; 17:16,29;
1 Kgs. 2:34; 9:18; 19:4,15; **2 Kgs.** 3:8;
1 Chr. 5:9; 6:78(63); 12:8; 21:29; **2 Chr.**
1:3; 8:4; 20:16,20,24; 24:9; 26:10; **Neh.**
9:19,21; **Job** 1:19; 24:5; 38:26; **Ps.** 29:8;
55:7(8); 63:[title](1); 65:12(13); 75:6(7);
78:15,19,40,52; 95:8; 102:6(7); 106:9,
14,26; 107:4,33,35; 136:16; **Prov.** 21:19;
Song 3:6; 8:5; **Isa.** 14:17; 16:1,8; 21:1;
27:10; 32:15,16; 35:1,6; 40:3; 41:18,19;
42:11; 43:19,20; 50:2; 51:3; 63:13;
64:10(9); **Jer.** 2:2,6,24,31; 3:2; 4:11,26;
9:2(1),10(9),12(11),26(25); 12:10,12;
13:24; 17:6; 22:6; 23:10; 25:24; 31:2;
48:6; 50:12; **Lam.** 4:3,19; 5:9; **Ezek.**
6:14; 19:13; 20:10,13,15,17,18,21,23,
35,36; 23:42; 29:5; 34:25; **Hos.** 2:3(5),
14(16); 9:10; 13:5,15; **Joel** 1:19,20;
2:3,22; 3:19(4:19); **Amos** 2:10; 5:25;
Zeph. 2:13; **Mal.** 1:3.

4058. מָדַד *māḏaḏ* **verb**
(to measure, to mete out, to stretch)
Ex. 16:18; **Num.** 35:5; **Deut.** 21:2;
Ruth 3:15; **2 Sam.** 8:2; **1 Kgs.** 17:21;
Job 7:4(KJV, *middaḏ* [4059]); **Ps.** 60:6(8);
108:7(8); **Isa.** 40:12; 65:7; **Jer.** 31:37;
33:22; **Ezek.** 40:5,6,8,9,11,13,19,20,23,
24,27,28,32,35,47,48; 41:1–5,13,15;
42:15–20; 43:10; 45:3; 47:3–5,18(NIV,
[Syriac] *tāmār* [8559,D]); **Hos.**
1:10(2:1); **Hab.** 3:6(KJV, *môḏ* [4128,I];
NIV, *môḏ* [4128,II]); **Zech.** 2:2(6).

4059. מִדַּד *middaḏ* **masc. noun**
(flight)
Job 7:4(NASB, NIV, *māḏaḏ* [4058]).

4060. I. מִדָּה *middāh* **fem. noun**
(measure, stature; garment)
Ex. 26:2,8; 36:9,15; **Lev.** 19:35; **Num.**
13:32; **Josh.** 3:4; **2 Sam.** 21:20(KJV, [Qᵉ]
māḏôn [4067]; NASB, [Qᵉ] *maḏ* [4055]);
1 Kgs. 6:25; 7:9,11,37; **1 Chr.** 11:23;
20:6; 23:29; **2 Chr.** 3:3; **Neh.** 3:11,
19–21,24,27,30; **Job** 28:25; **Ps.** 39:4(5);
133:2; **Isa.** 45:14; **Jer.** 22:14; 31:39;
Ezek. 40:3,5,10,21,22,24,28,29,32,
33,35; 41:17; 42:15–19; 43:13; 45:3;
46:22; 48:16,30,33; **Zech.** 2:1(5).

II. מִדָּה *middāh* **fem. noun**
(tax, tribute)
Neh. 5:4.

4061. מִדָּה *middāh*, מִנְדָּה
mindāh **Aram. fem. noun**
(tribute, toll; corr. to Hebr. 4060,I)
Ezra 4:13,20; 6:8; 7:24.

4062. I. מַדְהֵבָה *maḏhēḇāh* **fem. noun**
(fury)
Isa. 14:4(KJV, see II).

II. מַדְהֵבָה *maḏhēḇāh* **fem. noun**
(golden city)
Isa. 14:4(NASB, NIV, see I).

4063. מַדְוֶה *maḏweh* **masc. noun**
(garment)
2 Sam. 10:4; **1 Chr.** 19:4.

4064. מַדְוֶה *maḏweh* **masc. noun**
(sickness, disease)
Deut. 7:15; 28:60.

4065. מַדּוּחַ *maddûaḥ* **masc. noun**
(something misleading)
Lam. 2:14.

4066. מָדוֹן *māḏôn* **masc. noun**
(strife, dissension)
Ps. 80:6(7); **Prov.** 6:14(see *m^{e}ḏāniym* [4090]),19(see *m^{e}ḏāniym* [4090]); 10:12(see *m^{e}ḏāniym* [4090]); 15:18; 16:28; 17:14; 18:18(see *miḏyāniym* [4079]),19(see *miḏyāniym* [4079]); 19:13(see *miḏyāniym* [4079]); 21:9(see *miḏyāniym* [4079]),19(see *miḏyāniym* [4079]); 22:10; 23:29(see *miḏyāniym* [4079]); 25:24(see *miḏyāniym* [4079]); 26:20,21(see *miḏyāniym* [4079]); 27:15 (see *miḏyāniym* [4079]); 28:25; 29:22; **Jer.** 15:10; **Hab.** 1:3.

4067. מָדוֹן *māḏôn* **masc. noun**
(stature, size; form of *middāh* [4060,I])
2 Sam. 21:20(NASB, *māḏ* [4055]; NIV, [K^{e}] *middāh* [4060,I]).

4068. מָדוֹן *māḏôn* **proper noun**
(Madon)
Josh. 11:1; 12:19.

4069. מַדּוּעַ *maddûa'*, מַדֻּעַ *maddūa'* **adv.**
(wherefore, why)
Gen. 26:27; 40:7; **Ex.** 1:18; 2:18; 3:3; 5:14; 18:14; **Lev.** 10:17; **Num.** 12:8; 16:3; **Josh.** 17:14; **Judg.** 5:28; 9:28; 11:7,26; 12:1; **Ruth** 2:10; **1 Sam.** 20:2,27; 21:1(2); **2 Sam.** 3:7; 11:10,20; 12:9; 13:4; 16:10; 18:11; 19:41(42), 43(44); 24:21; **1 Kgs.** 1:6,13,41; 2:43; **2 Kgs.** 4:23; 8:12; 9:11; 12:7(8); **2 Chr.** 24:6; **Neh.** 2:2,3; 13:11,21; **Esth.** 3:3; **Job** 3:12; 18:3; 21:4,7; 24:1; 33:13; **Isa.** 5:4; 50:2; 63:2; **Jer.** 2:14,31; 8:5,19,22; 12:1; 13:22; 14:19; 22:28; 26:9; 30:6; 32:3; 36:29; 46:5,15; 49:1; **Ezek.** 18:19; **Mal.** 2:10.

4070. מְדוֹר *m^{e}ḏôr*, מְדָר *m^{e}ḏār* **Aram. masc. noun**
(dwelling, place)
Dan. 2:11; 4:25(22),32(29); 5:21.

4071. מְדוּרָה *m^{e}ḏûrāh* **fem. noun**
(pile of wood or anything else for burning)
Isa. 30:33; **Ezek.** 24:9.

4072. מִדְחֶה *miḏḥeh* **masc. noun**
(ruin, destruction)
Prov. 26:28.

4073. מַדְחֵפָה *maḏḥēp̄āh* **fem. noun**
(overthrow, destruction)
Ps. 140:11(12).

4074. A. מָדַי *māḏay* **masc. proper noun**
(Madai: descendant of Japheth)
Gen. 10:2; **1 Chr.** 1:5.
B. מָדַי *māḏay* **masc. proper noun**
(Madai: people or land of Media)
2 Kgs. 17:6; 18:11; **Esth.** 1:3,14,18,19; 10:2; **Isa.** 13:17; 21:2; **Jer.** 25:25; 51:11,28; **Dan.** 8:20; 9:1.

4075. מָדִי *māḏiy* **masc. proper noun**
(Mede)
Dan. 11:1.

4076. מָדַי *māḏay* **Aram. masc. proper noun**
(Medes; corr. to Hebr. 4074,B)
Ezra 6:2; **Dan.** 5:28; 6:8(9),12(13),15(16).

4077. מָדָיָא *māḏāy'ā* **Aram. masc. proper noun**
(Mede; corr. to Hebr. 4075)
Dan. 5:31(6:1).

4078. מַדַּי *madday* **adv.**
(enough, sufficiently)
2 Chr. 30:3(NIV, *māh* [4100] and *day* [1767]).

4079. מִדְיָנִים *mi<u>d</u>yāniym* **masc. pl. noun**
(disputes, contentions; pl. of *mā<u>d</u>ôn* [4066])
Prov. 18:18,19; 19:13; 21:9,19; 23:29; 25:24; 26:21; 27:15.

4080. A. מִדְיָן *mi<u>d</u>yān* **masc. proper noun**
(Midian: son of Abraham)
Gen. 25:2,4; **1 Chr.** 1:32,33.
B. מִדְיָן *mi<u>d</u>yān* **masc. proper noun**
(Midian: Arabian tribe)
Gen. 36:35; **Ex.** 2:16; 3:1; 18:1; **Num.** 22:4,7; 25:18; 31:3,7–9; **Josh.** 13:21; **Judg.** 6:1–3,6,7,11,13,14,16,33; 7:1,2,7, 8,12–15,23–25; 8:1,3,5,12,22,26,28; 9:17; **1 Chr.** 1:46; **Ps.** 83:9(10); **Isa.** 9:4(3); 10:26; 60:6; **Hab.** 3:7.
C. מִדְיָן *mi<u>d</u>yān* **masc. proper noun**
(Midian: the land of Midian)
Ex. 2:15; 4:19; **Num.** 25:15; **1 Kgs.** 11:18.

4081. מִדִּין *middiyn* **proper noun**
(Middin)
Josh. 15:61.

4082. מְדִינָה *m^e<u>d</u>iynāh* **fem. noun**
(district, province)
1 Kgs. 20:14,15,17,19; **Ezra** 2:1; **Neh.** 1:3; 7:6; 11:3; **Esth.** 1:1,3,16,22; 2:3,18; 3:8,12–14; 4:3,11; 8:5,9,11–13,17; 9:2–4, 12,16,20,28,30; **Eccl.** 2:8; 5:8(7); **Lam.** 1:1; **Ezek.** 19:8; **Dan.** 8:2; 11:24.

4083. מְדִינָה *m^e<u>d</u>iynāh* **Aram. fem. noun**
(district, province; corr. to Hebr. 4082)
Ezra 4:15; 5:8; 6:2; 7:16; **Dan.** 2:48,49; 3:1–3,12,30.

4084. מִדְיָנִי *mi<u>d</u>yāniy* **masc. proper noun**
(Midianite)
Gen. 37:36(KJV, *m^e<u>d</u>āniy* [4092]); **Num.** 10:29; 25:6,14,15,17; 31:2.

4085. מְדֹכָה *m^e<u>d</u>ō<u>k</u>āh* **fem. noun**
(mortar, bowl)
Num. 11:8.

4086. מַדְמֵן *ma<u>d</u>mēn* **proper noun**
(Madmen)
Jer. 48:2.

4087. מַדְמֵנָה *ma<u>d</u>mēnāh* **fem. noun**
(dunghill, manure pile)
Isa. 25:10.

4088. מַדְמֵנָה *ma<u>d</u>mēnāh* **proper noun**
(Madmenah)
Isa. 10:31.

4089. A. מַדְמַנָּה *ma<u>d</u>mannāh* **proper noun**
(Madmannah: city in Judah)
Josh. 15:31.
B. מַדְמַנָּה *ma<u>d</u>mannāh* **masc. proper noun**
(Madmannah: descendant of Caleb)
1 Chr. 2:49.

4090. מְדָנִים *m^e<u>d</u>āniym* **masc. pl. noun**
(strifes, discords; pl. of *mā<u>d</u>ôn* [4066])
Prov. 6:14,19; 10:12.

4091. מְדָן *m^e<u>d</u>an* **masc. proper noun**
(Medan)
Gen. 25:2; **1 Chr.** 1:32.

4092. מְדָנִי *m^e<u>d</u>āniy* **masc. proper noun**
(Midianite)
Gen. 37:36(NASB, NIV, *mi<u>d</u>yāniy* [4084]).

4093. מַדָּע *maddā'* **masc. noun**
(knowledge, thought)
2 Chr. 1:10–12; **Eccl.** 10:20; **Dan.** 1:4,17.

4094. מַדְקֵרָה *madqērāh* **fem. noun**
(piercing, thrust)
Prov. 12:18.

4095. מַדְרֵגָה *madrēgāh* **fem. noun**
(steep place, mountainside)
Song 2:14; **Ezek.** 38:20.

4096. מִדְרָךְ *midrāk* **masc. noun**
(treading place, footstep)
Deut. 2:5.

4097. מִדְרָשׁ *midrāš* **masc. noun**
(record, treatise)
2 Chr. 13:22; 24:27.

4098. מְדֻשָׁה *m^e dušāh* **fem. noun**
(threshing, that which is threshed)
Isa. 21:10.

4099. הַמְּדָתָא *hamm^e dātā'* **masc. proper noun**
(Hammedatha)
Esth. 3:1,10; 8:5; 9:10,24.

4100. מָה *māh,* מֶה *meh* **interrog. pron.**
(how? what?)
Gen. 2:19; 3:13; 4:6,10; 12:18,19; 15:2,8; 18:13; 20:9,10; 21:17,29; 23:15; 24:31; 25:22,32; 26:10; 27:20,37; 28:17; 29:15,25; 30:31; 31:26,27,30,32,36, 37,43; 32:27(28),29(29); 33:15; 37:10, 15,20,26; 38:16,18,29; 39:8; 42:1,28; 43:6; 44:4,7,15,16; 46:33; 47:3,8,15,19; **Ex.** 2:4,13,20; 3:13; 4:2; 5:4,15,22; 10:26; 12:26; 13:14; 14:5,11,15; 15:24; 16:7,8,15; 17:2–4; 18:14; 22:27(26); 32:1,11,12,21,23; 33:5,16; **Lev.** 25:20; **Num.** 9:7,8; 11:11,20; 13:18–20; 14:3,41; 15:34; 16:11; 20:4,5; 21:5; 22:19,28, 32,37; 23:3,8,11,17,23; 26:5,22; 27:4; 32:7; **Deut.** 5:25(24); 6:20; 10:12; 29:24; 32:20; **Josh.** 4:6,21; 5:14; 7:7–10,19,25; 9:22; 15:18; 22:16,24; **Judg.** 1:14; 2:2; 5:16,17; 6:13,15; 7:11; 8:1–3; 9:2,48; 11:12; 12:3; 13:8,12,18; 14:18; 15:10,11; 16:5,6,10,13,15; 18:3,8,14,18,23,24; 20:12; 21:3,7,16; **Ruth** 1:11,21; **1 Sam.** 1:8; 2:23,29; 3:17; 4:3,6,14,16; 5:8; 6:2–4,6; 9:7,21; 10:2,11,15,27; 11:5; 13:11; 14:38,43; 15:14,19; 17:8,26,28,29; 19:3,5,17; 20:1,4,8,10,32; 21:3(4),14(15); 22:3,13; 24:9; 25:17; 26:15,18; 27:5; 28:9,12–16; 29:3,4,8; **2 Sam.** 1:4,13; 2:22; 3:24; 6:20; 7:7,20; 9:8; 11:21; 12:21,23; 13:26; 14:5,13,31,32; 15:19; 16:2,9,10,17,20; 17:5; 18:22,23,29; 19:10–12(11–13),22(23),25(26),28(29), 29(30),34–36(35–37),42(43); 20:19; 21:3,4; 24:3,13,17; **1 Kgs.** 1:16; 2:22,43; 3:5; 9:8,13; 11:22; 12:9,16; 14:3,6,14; 17:8; 18:9; 19:9,13,20; 21:5; 22:16,22; **2 Kgs.** 1:5,7; 2:9; 3:13; 4:2,13,14,43; 5:8; 6:28,33; 7:3; 8:13,14; 9:18,19,22; 14:10; 18:19; 20:8,14,15; 23:17; **1 Chr.** 12:32; 17:6,18; 21:3,12,17; **2 Chr.** 1:7; 7:21; 10:9,16; 18:15,20; 19:6; 20:12; 24:20; 25:9,15,16,19; 30:3(KJV, NASB, *madday* [4078]); 32:4,10,13; 35:21; **Ezra** 9:10; **Neh.** 2:4,12,16,19; 4:2(3:34); 6:3; 13:17; **Esth.** 1:15; 2:11; 4:5; 5:3,6; 6:3,6; 7:2; 8:1; 9:12,26; **Job** 3:11,12,20; 6:11,24,25; 7:17,19–21; 9:2,12,29; 10:18; 11:8; 13:13,14,23,24; 15:9,12,14; 16:3,6; 19:22,28; 21:15,17,21; 22:13,17; 23:5; 25:4; 26:2,3,14; 27:8,12; 30:2; 31:1,2,14; 34:4,33; 35:3,6,7; 37:19; 38:6; 40:4; **Ps.** 2:1; 3:1(2); 4:2(3); 8:1(2),4(5),9(10); 10:1,13; 11:3; 21:1(2); 22:1(2); 30:9(10); 31:19(20); 35:17; 36:7(8); 39:4(5),7(8); 42:5(6),9(10),11(12); 43:2,5; 44:23(24), 24(25); 49:5(6); 50:16; 52:1(2); 56:4(5), 11(12); 66:3; 68:16(17); 74:1,9,11; 78:40; 79:5,10; 80:12(13); 84:1(2); 85:8(9); 88:14(15); 89:46(47),47(48); 92:5(6); 104:24; 114:5; 115:2; 116:12; 118:6; 119:9,84,97,103; 120:3; 133:1; 139:17; 144:3; **Prov.** 4:19; 5:20; 9:13; 15:23;

16:16; 17:16; 20:24; 22:27; 25:8; 27:1; 30:4,13; 31:2; **Eccl.** 1:3,9; 2:2,12,15,22; 3:9,15,22; 5:6(5),11(10),16(15); 6:8, 10–12; 7:10,16,17,24; 8:4,7; 10:14; 11:2,15; **Song** 1:7; 4:10; 5:8,9; 6:13(7:1); 7:1(2),6(7); 8:4,8; **Isa.** 1:5,11; 2:22; 3:15; 5:4; 10:3; 14:32; 19:12; 21:11; 22:1,16; 36:4; 38:15,22; 39:3,4; 40:6,18,27; 41:22; 45:9,10; 52:5,7; 55:2; 58:3; 63:17; **Jer.** 1:11,13; 2:5,18,23,29,33,36; 4:30; 5:15, 19,31; 6:20; 7:17; 8:6,9,14; 9:12(11); 11:15; 13:21; 14:8,9; 15:18; 16:10; 20:18; 22:8,23; 23:28,33,35,37; 24:3; 27:13,17; 29:27; 30:15; 33:24; 37:18; 38:25; 40:15; 44:7; 48:19; 49:4; **Lam.** 2:13; 3:39; 5:1,20; **Ezek.** 8:6; 12:9,22; 15:2; 16:30; 17:12; 18:2,31; 19:2; 20:29; 21:7(12), 13(18); 24:19; 33:11,30; 37:18; **Dan.** 1:10; 10:20; 12:8; **Hos.** 6:4; 9:5,14; 10:3; 14:8(9); **Joel** 1:18; 2:17; 3:4(4:4); **Amos** 4:13; 5:18; 7:8; 8:2; **Jon.** 1:6,8,10,11; 4:5; **Mic.** 4:9; 6:3,5,6,8; **Nah.** 1:9; **Hab.** 1:3, 13; 2:1,18; **Hag.** 1:9; 2:3; **Zech.** 1:9,19, 21; 2:2(6); 4:2,4,5,11–13; 5:2,5,6; 6:4; 7:3; 9:17; 13:6; **Mal.** 1:2,6,7,13(KJV, *mattᵉlā'āh* [4972]); 2:14,15,17; 3:7,8,13,14.

4101. מָה *māh* **Aram. particle**
(what, why; corr. to Hebr. 4100)
Ezra 4:22; 6:9; 7:18,23; **Dan.** 2:15,22, 28,29,45; 4:3(3:33),35(32).

4102. מָהַהּ *māhah* **verb**
(to tarry, to hesitate, to linger)
Gen. 19:16; 43:10; **Ex.** 12:39; **Judg.** 3:26; 19:8; **2 Sam.** 15:28; **Ps.** 119:60; **Isa.** 29:9; **Hab.** 2:3.

4103. מְהוּמָה *mᵉhûmāh* **fem. noun**
(panic, confusion)
Deut. 7:23; 28:20; **1 Sam.** 5:9,11; 14:20; **2 Chr.** 15:5; **Prov.** 15:16; **Isa.** 22:5; **Ezek.** 7:7; 22:5; **Amos** 3:9; **Zech.** 14:13.

4104. מְהוּמָן *mᵉhûmān* **masc. proper noun**
(Mehuman)
Esth. 1:10.

4105. A. מְהֵיטַבְאֵל *mᵉhēyṭaḇ'ēl* **fem. proper noun**
(Mehetabel: Edomite princess)
Gen. 36:39; **1 Chr.** 1:50.
B. מְהֵיטַבְאֵל *mᵉhēyṭaḇ'ēl* **masc. proper noun**
(Mehetabel: ancestor of Shemaiah)
Neh. 6:10.

4106. מָהִיר *māhiyr* **adj.**
(skilled, well-versed)
Ezra 7:6; **Ps.** 45:1(2); **Prov.** 22:29; **Isa.** 16:5.

4107. מָהַל *māhal* **verb**
(to weaken, to dilute)
Isa. 1:22.

4108. מַהְלְכִים *mahlᵉḵiym* **masc. pl. noun**
(access, places to walk; pl. of *mahᵃlāk* [4109])
Zech. 3:7.

4109. מַהֲלָךְ *mahᵃlāḵ* **masc. noun**
(journey, passageway, access)
Neh. 2:6; **Ezek.** 42:4; **Jon.** 3:3,4; **Zech.** 3:7(see *mahlᵉḵiym* [4108]).

4110. מַהֲלָל *mahᵃlāl* **masc. noun**
(praise)
Prov. 27:21.

4111. A. מַהֲלַלְאֵל *mahᵃlal'ēl* **masc. proper noun**
(Mahalalel: great-grandson of Seth)
Gen. 5:12,13,15–17; **1 Chr.** 1:2.
B. מַהֲלַלְאֵל *mahᵃlal'ēl* **masc. proper noun**
(Mahalalel: a Judaite)
Neh. 11:4.

4112. מַהֲלֻמוֹת *mahᵃlumôṯ* **fem. pl. noun**

(stripes, blows)
Prov. 18:6; 19:29.

4113. מַהֲמֹר *mahamōr* **fem. noun**
(flood, watery pit)
Ps. 140:10(11).

4114. מַהְפֵּכָה *mahpēḵāh* **fem. noun**
(overthrow, destruction)
Deut. 29:23(22); **Isa.** 1:7; 13:19; **Jer.** 49:18; 50:40; **Amos** 4:11.

4115. מַהְפֶּכֶת *mahpeḵeṯ* **fem. noun**
(stocks, prison)
2 Chr. 16:10; **Jer.** 20:2,3; 29:26.

4116. מָהַר *māhar* **verb**
(to hurry, to move quickly)
Gen. 18:6,7; 19:22; 24:18,20,46; 27:20; 41:32; 43:30; 44:11; 45:9,13; **Ex.** 2:18; 10:16; 12:33; 32:8(KJV, NASB, *mahēr* [4118,II]); 34:8; **Deut.** 4:26(KJV, NASB, *mahēr* [4118,II]); 7:4(KJV, NASB, *mahēr* [4118,II]),22(KJV, NASB, *mahēr* [4118,II]); 9:3(KJV, NASB, *mahēr* [4118,II]),12(KJV, NASB, *mahēr* [4118,II]),16(KJV, NASB, *mahēr* [4118,II]); 28:20(KJV, NASB, *mahēr* [4118,II]); **Josh.** 2:5(KJV, NASB, *mahēr* [4118,II]); 4:10; 8:14,19; **Judg.** 2:17(KJV, NASB, *mahēr* [4118,II]),23(KJV, NASB, *mahēr* [4118,II]); 9:48; 13:10; **1 Sam.** 4:14; 9:12; 17:48; 23:27; 25:18, 23,34,42; 28:20,24; **2 Sam.** 15:14; 19:16(17); **1 Kgs.** 20:33,41; 22:9; **2 Kgs.** 9:13; **1 Chr.** 12:8; **2 Chr.** 18:8; 24:5; **Esth.** 5:5; 6:10; **Job** 5:13; **Ps.** 16:4; 69:17(18)(KJV, NASB, *mahēr* [4118,II]); 79:8(KJV, NASB, *mahēr* [4118,II]); 102:2 (3)(KJV, NASB, *mahēr* [4118,II]); 106:13; 143:7(KJV, NASB, *mahēr* [4118,II]); **Prov.** 1:16; 6:18; 7:23; 25:8(KJV, NASB, *mahēr* [4118,II]); **Eccl.** 5:2(1); **Isa.** 5:19; 8:1; 32:4; 35:4; 49:17; 51:14; 59:7; **Jer.** 9:18(17); 48:16; **Nah.** 2:5(6); **Hab.** 1:6; **Zeph.** 1:14(KJV, NASB, *mahēr* [4118,I]); **Mal.** 3:5.

4117. מָהַר *māhar* **verb**
(to give a dowry)
Ex. 22:16(15).

4118. I. מַהֵר *mahēr* **adj.**
(swift; NIV, *māhar* [4116])
Zeph. 1:14; **Isa.** 8:1(KJV, NIV, *mahēr šālāl ḥāš baz* [4122,I]).
II. מַהֵר *mahēr* **adv.**
(quickly; NIV, *māhar* [4116])
Ex. 32:8; **Deut.** 4:26; 7:4,22; 9:3,12,16; 28:20; **Josh.** 2:5; **Judg.** 2:17,23; **Ps.** 69:17(18); 79:8; 102:2(3); 143:7; **Prov.** 25:8.

4119. מֹהַר *mōhar* **masc. noun**
(dowry, purchase price for a wife)
Gen. 34:12; **Ex.** 22:17(16); **1 Sam.** 18:25.

4120. מְהֵרָה *mehērāh* **fem. noun**
(quickly, at once)
Num. 16:46(17:11); **Deut.** 11:17; **Josh.** 8:19; 10:6; 23:16; **Judg.** 9:54; **1 Sam.** 20:38; **2 Sam.** 17:16,18,21; **2 Kgs.** 1:11; **Ps.** 31:2(3); 37:2; 147:15; **Eccl.** 4:12; 8:11; **Isa.** 5:26; 58:8; **Jer.** 27:16; **Joel** 3:4(4:4).

4121. מַהֲרַי *maharay* **masc. proper noun**
(Maharai)
2 Sam. 23:28; **1 Chr.** 11:30; 27:13.

4122. I. מַהֵר שָׁלָל חָשׁ בַּז *mahēr šālāl ḥāš baz* **masc. proper noun**
(Maher-Shalal-Hash-Baz)
Isa. 8:1(NASB, see II),3.
II. מַהֵר שָׁלָל חָשׁ בַּז *mahēr šālāl ḥāš baz* **phrase**
(swift is booty, speedy is prey; from *mahēr* [4118,I], *šālāl* [7998], *ḥûš* [2363,I] and *baz* [957])
Isa. 8:1(KJV, NIV, see I).

4123. מַהֲתַלָּה *mahaṯallāh* **fem. noun**
(illusion, deception)
Isa. 30:10.

4124. A. מוֹאָב *mô'āḇ* **masc. proper noun**
(Moab: son of Lot)
Gen. 19:37.
B. מוֹאָב *mô'āḇ* **masc. proper noun**
(People or territory of Moab)
Gen. 36:35; **Ex.** 15:15; **Num.** 21:11,13, 15,20,26,28,29; 22:1,3,4,7,8,10,14,21,36; 23:6,7,17; 24:17; 25:1; 26:3,63; 31:12; 33:44,48–50; 35:1; 36:13; **Deut.** 1:5; 2:8,9,18; 29:1(28:69); 32:49; 34:1,5,6,8; **Josh.** 13:32; 24:9; **Judg.** 3:12,14,15,17, 28–30; 10:6; 11:15,17,18,25; **Ruth** 1:1,2, 6,22; 2:6; 4:3; **1 Sam.** 12:9; 14:47; 22:3,4; **2 Sam.** 8:2,12; 23:20; **1 Kgs.** 11:7,33; **2 Kgs.** 1:1; 3:4,5,7,10,13,18,21–24,26; 13:20; 23:13; 24:2; **1 Chr.** 1:46; 4:22; 8:8; 11:22; 18:2,11; **2 Chr.** 20:1,10, 22,23; **Ps.** 60:8(10); 83:6(7); 108:9(10); **Isa.** 11:14; 15:1,2,4,5,8,9; 16:2,4,6,7, 11–14; 25:10; **Jer.** 9:26(25); 25:21; 27:3; 40:11; 48:1,2,4,9,11,13,15,16,18,20, 24–26,28,29,31,33,35,36,38–47; **Ezek.** 25:8,9,11; **Dan.** 11:41; **Amos** 2:1,2; **Mic.** 6:5; **Zeph.** 2:8,9.

4125. מוֹאָבִי *mô'āḇiy* **masc. proper noun**
(Moabite)
Deut. 2:11,29; 23:3(4); **Ruth** 1:4,22; 2:2,6,21; 4:5,10; **1 Kgs.** 11:1; **1 Chr.** 11:46; **2 Chr.** 24:26; **Ezra** 9:1; **Neh.** 13:1,23.

4126. מוֹבָא *môḇā'* **masc. noun**
(entrance, entering)
2 Sam. 3:25; **Ezek.** 43:11.

4127. מוּג *mûg* **verb**
(to melt, to melt away, to dissolve)
Ex. 15:15; **Josh.** 2:9,24; **1 Sam.** 14:16; **Job** 30:22; **Ps.** 46:6(7); 65:10(11); 75:3(4); 107:26; **Isa.** 14:31; 64:7(6); **Jer.** 49:23; **Ezek.** 21:15(20); **Amos** 9:5,13; **Nah.** 1:5; 2:6(7).

4128. I. מוֹד *môḏ* **verb**
(to measure)
Hab. 3:6(NASB, *māḏaḏ* [4058]; NIV, see II).
II. מוֹד *môḏ* **verb**
(to shake)
Hab. 3:6(NASB, *māḏaḏ* [4058]; KJV, see I).

4129. מֹדָע *mōḏā'*, מוֹדַע *môḏa'* **masc. noun**
(kinsman, relative)
Ruth 2:1(KJV, [K[e]] *yāḏa'* [3045]); **Prov.** 7:4.

4130. מוֹדַעַת *môḏa'aṯ* **fem. noun**
(kindred, kinship)
Ruth 3:2.

4131. מוֹט *môṭ* **verb**
(to be moved, to be shaken, to be removed, to fall)
Lev. 25:35; **Deut.** 32:35; **1 Chr.** 16:30; **Job** 41:23(15); **Ps.** 10:6; 13:4(5); 15:5; 16:8; 17:5; 21:7(8); 30:6(7); 38:16(17); 46:2(3),5(6),6(7); 55:3(4),22(23); 60:2(4); 62:2(3),6(7); 66:9(KJV, NASB, *môṭ* [4132]); 82:5; 93:1; 94:18; 96:10; 104:5; 112:6; 121:3(KJV, NASB, *môṭ* [4132]); 125:1; 140:10(11); **Prov.** 10:30; 12:3; 24:11; 25:26; **Isa.** 24:19; 40:20; 41:7; 54:10.

4132. מוֹט *môṭ* **masc. noun**
(bar, pole, that which shakes)
Num. 4:10,12; 13:23; **Ps.** 66:9(NIV, *môṭ* [4131]); 121:3(NIV, *môṭ* [4131]); **Nah.** 1:13.

4133. מוֹטָה *môṭāh* **fem. noun**
(yoke, bar)
Lev. 26:13; **1 Chr.** 15:15; **Isa.** 58:6,9; **Jer.** 27:2; 28:10,12,13; **Ezek.** 30:18; 34:27.

4134. מוּךְ *mûḵ* **verb**
(to become poor, to be poor)
Lev. 25:25,35,39,47; 27:8.

4135. מוּל *mûl* **verb**
(to circumcise, to be circumcised)
Gen. 17:10,11(KJV, *nāmal* [5243]),12–14,23–27; 21:4; 34:15,17, 22,24; **Ex.** 12:44,48; **Lev.** 12:3; **Deut.** 10:16; 30:6; **Josh.** 5:2(NIV, *mālal* [4448,II]),3–5,7,8; **Ps.** 58:7(8)(NASB, *mālal* [4448,III]; NIV, *mālal* [4448,III]); 90:6(NASB, NIV, *mālal* [4448,II]); 118:10–12; **Jer.** 4:4; 9:25(24).

4136. מוּל *mûl,* מוֹאל *mô'l,* מוֹל *môl* **prep.**
(against, in front of, toward)
Ex. 18:19; 26:9; 28:25,27,37; 34:3; 39:18,20; **Lev.** 5:8; 8:9; **Num.** 8:2,3; 22:5; **Deut.** 1:1; 2:19; 3:29; 4:46; 11:30; 34:6; **Josh.** 8:33; 9:1; 18:18; 19:46; 22:11; **1 Sam.** 14:5; 17:30; **2 Sam.** 5:23; 11:15; **1 Kgs.** 7:5,39; **1 Chr.** 14:14; **2 Chr.** 4:10; **Neh.** 12:38; **Mic.** 2:8.

4137. מוֹלָדָה *môlāḏāh* **proper noun**
(Moladah)
Josh. 15:26; 19:2; **1 Chr.** 4:28; **Neh.** 11:26.

4138. מוֹלֶדֶת *môleḏeṯ* **fem. noun**
(birth, family background, kindred)
Gen. 11:28; 12:1; 24:4,7; 31:3,13; 32:9(10); 43:7; 48:6; **Lev.** 18:9,11; **Num.** 10:30; **Ruth** 2:11; **Esth.** 2:10,20; 8:6; **Jer.** 22:10; 46:16; **Ezek.** 16:3,4; 23:15.

4139. מוּלָה *mûlāh* **fem. noun**
(circumcision)
Ex. 4:26.

4140. מוֹלִיד *môliyḏ* **masc. proper noun**
(Molid)
1 Chr. 2:29.

4141. מוּסָב *mûsaḇ* **masc. noun**
(circuit)
Ezek. 41:7(NIV, *sāḇaḇ* [5437]).

4142. מוּסַבּוֹת *mûsabbôṯ* **fem. pl. adj.**
(surrounding; NASB, NIV, *sāḇaḇ* [5437])
Ex. 28:11; 39:6,13; **Num.** 32:38; **Ezek.** 41:24.

4143. מוּסָד *mûsāḏ* **masc. noun**
(foundation)
2 Chr. 8:16; **Isa.** 28:16.

4144. מוֹסָד *môsāḏ* **masc. noun**
(foundation)
Deut. 32:22; **2 Sam.** 22:8(KJV, NIV, *môsāḏāh* [4146]),16(KJV, NIV, *môsāḏāh* [4146]); **Ps.** 18:7(8)(KJV, *môsāḏāh* [4146]),15(16)(KJV, NIV, *môsāḏāh* [4146]); 82:5; **Prov.** 8:29; **Isa.** 24:18(KJV, *môsāḏāh* [4146]); 40:21(KJV, NIV, *môsāḏāh* [4146]); 58:12(KJV, *môsāḏāh* [4146]); **Jer.** 31:37(KJV, *môsāḏāh* [4146]); 51:26(KJV, NIV, *môsāḏāh* [4146]); **Mic.** 6:2(KJV, *môsāḏāh* [4146]).

4145. מוּסָדָה *mûsāḏāh* **fem. noun**
(foundation, appointment)
Isa. 30:32; **Ezek.** 41:8(KJV, [K^e] *m^{e}yussāḏāh* [4328]; NASB, [K^e] *yāsaḏ* [3245,I]).

4146. מוֹסָדָה *môsāḏāh* **fem. noun**
(foundation)
2 Sam. 22:8(NASB, *môsāḏ* [4144]),16(NASB, *môsāḏ* [4144]); **Ps.** 18:7(8)(NASB, NIV, *môsāḏ* [4144]), 15(16)(NASB, *môsāḏ* [4144]); **Isa.** 24:18 (NASB, NIV, *môsāḏ* [4144]); 40:21(NASB, *môsāḏ* [4144]); 58:12(NASB, NIV, *môsāḏ* [4144]); **Jer.** 31:37(NASB, NIV, *môsāḏ* [4144]); 51:26(NASB, *môsāḏ* [4144]); **Mic.** 6:2(NASB, NIV, *môsāḏ* [4144]).

4147. I. מוֹסֵר *môsēr* **masc. noun**
(band, chain, fetter)
Ps. 116:16; **Isa.** 28:22; 52:2.
II. מוֹסֵרָה *môsērāh* **masc. noun**
(band, chain, fetter)

Job 39:5; **Ps.** 2:3; 107:14; **Jer.** 2:20; 5:5; 27:2; 30:8; **Nah.** 1:13.

4148. מוּסָר *mûsār* **masc. noun**
(discipline, correction, chastisement)
Deut. 11:2; **Job** 5:17; 12:18; 20:3; 33:16(KJV, *mōsār* [4561]); 36:10; **Ps.** 50:17; **Prov.** 1:2,3,7,8; 3:11; 4:1,13; 5:12,23; 6:23; 7:22; 8:10,33; 10:17; 12:1; 13:1,18,24; 15:5,10,32,33; 16:22; 19:20,27; 22:15; 23:12,13,23; 24:32; **Isa.** 26:16; 53:5; **Jer.** 2:30; 5:3; 7:28; 10:8; 17:23; 30:14; 32:33; 35:13; **Ezek.** 5:15; **Hos.** 5:2; **Zeph.** 3:2,7.

4149. מוֹסֵרָה *môsērāh,* מֹסֵרוֹת *mōsērôṯ* **proper noun**
(Moseroth, Moserah)
Num. 33:30,31; **Deut.** 10:6.

4150. מוֹעֵד *mô'ēḏ* **masc. noun**
(something appointed, place of meeting [congregation], appointed time, appointed feast, appointed season)
Gen. 1:14; 17:21; 18:14; 21:2; **Ex.** 9:5; 13:10; 23:15; 27:21; 28:43; 29:4,10,11, 30,32,42,44; 30:16,18,20,26,36; 31:7; 33:7; 34:18; 35:21; 38:8,30; 39:32,40; 40:2,6,7,12,22,24,26,29,30,32,34,35; **Lev.** 1:1,3,5; 3:2,8,13; 4:4,5,7,14,16,18; 6:16(9),26(19),30(23); 8:3,4,31,33,35; 9:5,23; 10:7,9; 12:6; 14:11,23; 15:14,29; 16:7,16,17,20,23,33; 17:4–6,9; 19:21; 23:2,4,37,44; 24:3; **Num.** 1:1; 2:2,17; 3:7,8,25,38; 4:3,4,15,23,25,28,30,31, 33,35,37,39,41,43,47; 6:10,13,18; 7:5,89; 8:9,15,19,22,24,26; 9:2,3,7,13; 10:3,10; 11:16; 12:4; 14:10; 15:3; 16:2,18,19,42 (17:7),43(17:8),50(17:15); 17:4(19); 18:4,6,21–23,31; 19:4; 20:6; 25:6; 27:2; 28:2; 29:39; 31:54; **Deut.** 16:6; 31:10,14; **Josh.** 8:14; 18:1; 19:51; **Judg.** 20:38; **1 Sam.** 2:22; 9:24; 13:8,11; 20:35; **2 Sam.** 20:5; 24:15; **1 Kgs.** 8:4; **2 Kgs.** 4:16,17; **1 Chr.** 6:32(17); 9:21; 23:31,32; **2 Chr.** 1:3,6,13; 2:4(3); 5:5; 8:13; 30:22; 31:3; **Ezra** 3:5; **Neh.** 10:33(34); **Job** 30:23; **Ps.** 74:4,8; 75:2(3); 102:13(14); 104:19; **Isa.** 1:14; 14:13; 33:20; **Jer.** 8:7; 46:17; **Lam.** 1:4,15; 2:6,7,22; **Ezek.** 36:38; 44:24; 45:17; 46:9,11; **Dan.** 8:19; 11:27,29,35; 12:7; **Hos.** 2:9(11),11(13); 9:5; 12:9(10); **Hab.** 2:3; **Zeph.** 3:18; **Zech.** 8:19.

4151. מוֹעָד *mô'āḏ* **masc. noun**
(appointed place [rank] in army)
Isa. 14:31.

4152. מוּעָדָה *mû'āḏāh* **fem. noun**
(something appointed or designated)
Josh. 20:9.

4153. מוֹעַדְיָה *mô'aḏyāh* **masc. proper noun**
(Moadiah)
Neh. 12:17.

4154. מוּעֶדֶת *mû'eḏeṯ* **fem. noun**
(unsteady, sliding out of joint)
Prov. 25:19(NASB, NIV, *mā'aḏ* [4571]).

4155. מוּעָף *mû'āp̱* **masc. noun**
(gloom, darkness)
Isa. 9:1(8:23).

4156. מוֹעֵצָה *mô'ēṣāh* **fem. noun**
(counsel, intrigue)
Ps. 5:10(11); 81:12(13); **Prov.** 1:31; 22:20; **Jer.** 7:24; **Hos.** 11:6; **Mic.** 6:16.

4157. מוּעָקָה *mû'āqāh* **fem. noun**
(affliction, oppressive burden)
Ps. 66:11.

4158. מֵיפַעַת *mēyp̱a'aṯ,* מוֹפַעַת *môp̱a'aṯ* **proper noun**
(Mephaath)
Josh. 13:18; 21:37; **1 Chr.** 6:79(64); **Jer.** 48:21.

4159. מוֹפֵת *môpēṯ* **masc. noun**
(wonder, sign, miracle)
Ex. 4:21; 7:3,9; 11:9,10; **Deut.** 4:34; 6:22; 7:19; 13:1(2),2(3); 26:8; 28:46; 29:3(2); 34:11; **1 Kgs.** 13:3,5; **1 Chr.** 16:12; **2 Chr.** 32:24,31; **Neh.** 9:10; **Ps.** 71:7; 78:43; 105:5,27; 135:9; **Isa.** 8:18; 20:3; **Jer.** 32:20,21; **Ezek.** 12:6,11; 24:24,27; **Joel** 2:30(3:3); **Zech.** 3:8.

4160. מֵץ *mēṣ* **verb**
(to extort, to oppress)
Isa. 16:4.

4161. מוֹצָא *môṣāʾ* **masc. noun**
(act of going forth, proceeding, a spring)
Num. 30:12(13); 33:2; **Deut.** 8:3; 23:23(24); **2 Sam.** 3:25; **1 Kgs.** 10:28; **2 Kgs.** 2:21; **2 Chr.** 1:16; 32:30; **Job** 28:1; 38:27; **Ps.** 19:6(7); 65:8(9); 75:6(7); 89:34(35); 107:33,35; **Isa.** 41:18; 58:11; **Jer.** 17:16; **Ezek.** 12:4; 42:11; 43:11; 44:5; **Dan.** 9:25; **Hos.** 6:3.

4162. A. מוֹצָא *môṣāʾ* **masc. proper noun**
(Moza: son of Caleb)
1 Chr. 2:46.
B. מוֹצָא *môṣāʾ* **masc. proper noun**
(Moza: descendant of Saul)
1 Chr. 8:36,37; 9:42,43.

4163. מוֹצָאָה *môṣāʾāh* **fem. noun**
(origin, going out or forth, latrine)
Mic. 5:2(1).

4164. מוּצָק *mûṣāq*, מוּצַק *muṣaq* **masc. noun**
(constraint, restriction, frozen [of water])
Job 36:16; 37:10(NIV, *yāṣaq* [3332]); **Isa.** 9:1(8:23).

4165. מוּצָק *mûṣāq* **masc. noun**
(casting, cast metal, hard mass)
1 Kgs. 7:16(KJV, NASB, *yāṣaq* [3332]), 23(KJV, NASB, *yāṣaq* [3332]),33(KJV, NASB, *yāṣaq* [3332]),37; **2 Chr.** 4:2(KJV, NASB, *yāṣaq* [3332]); **Job** 37:18(KJV, NASB, *yāṣaq* [3332]); 38:38.

4166. מוּצָקָה *mûṣāqāh* **fem. noun**
(a casting, pipe, tube)
2 Chr. 4:3; **Zech.** 4:2.

4167. מוּק *mûq* **verb**
(to mock, to scoff)
Ps. 73:8.

4168. מוֹקֵד *môqēḏ* **masc. noun**
(a burning, burning embers, hearth)
Ps. 102:3(4); **Isa.** 33:14.

4169. מוֹקְדָה *môq^{e}ḏāh* **fem. noun**
(hearth, top of the altar)
Lev. 6:9(2).

4170. מוֹקֵשׁ *môqēš* **masc. noun**
(snare, trap, bait)
Ex. 10:7; 23:33; 34:12; **Deut.** 7:16; **Josh.** 23:13; **Judg.** 2:3; 8:27; **1 Sam.** 18:21; **2 Sam.** 22:6; **Job** 34:30; 40:24; **Ps.** 18:5(6); 64:5(6); 69:22(23); 106:36; 140:5(6); 141:9; **Prov.** 12:13; 13:14; 14:27; 18:7; 20:25; 22:25; 29:6,25; **Isa.** 8:14; **Amos** 3:5.

4171. מוּר *mûr* **verb**
(to change, to exchange)
Lev. 27:10,33; **Ps.** 15:4; 46:2(3); 106:20; **Jer.** 2:11(NIV, *yāmar* [3235,II]); 48:11; **Ezek.** 48:14; **Hos.** 4:7; **Mic.** 2:4.

4172. מֹרָא *mōrāʾ* **masc. noun**
(fear, terror)
Gen. 9:2; **Deut.** 4:34; 11:25; 26:8; 34:12; **Ps.** 9:20(21); 76:11(12); **Isa.** 8:12,13; **Jer.** 32:21; **Mal.** 1:6; 2:5.

4173. מוֹרַג *môrag* **masc. noun**
(threshing sledge)
2 Sam. 24:22; **1 Chr.** 21:23; **Isa.** 41:15.

4174. מוֹרָד *môrāḏ* **masc. noun**
(descent, steep slope)
Josh. 7:5; 10:11; **1 Kgs.** 7:29; **Jer.** 48:5; **Mic.** 1:4.

4175. מוֹרֶה *môreh* **masc. noun**
(early rains)
Ps. 84:6(7); **Joel** 2:23.

4176. מוֹרֶה *môreh* **proper noun**
(Moreh)
Gen. 12:6; **Deut.** 11:30; **Judg.** 7:1.

4177. מוֹרָה *môrāh* **masc. noun**
(razor)
Judg. 13:5; 16:17; **1 Sam.** 1:11.

4178. מוֹרָט *môrāṭ* **adj.**
(polished, smooth; Dual part. of *māraṭ* [4803])
Isa. 18:2,7.

4179. מוֹרִיָּה *môriyyāh*, מֹרִיָּה *mōriyyāh* **proper noun**
(Moriah)
Gen. 22:2; **2 Chr.** 3:1.

4180. I. מוֹרָשׁ *môrāš* **masc. noun**
(possession, inheritence)
Isa. 14:23; **Obad.** 1:17.
II. מוֹרָשׁ *môrāš* **masc. noun**
(wish, desire, thought)
Job 17:11.

4181. מוֹרָשָׁה *môrāšāh* **fem. noun**
(possession, inheritance)
Ex. 6:8; **Deut.** 33:4; **Ezek.** 11:15; 25:4,10; 33:24; 36:2,3,5.

4182. מוֹרֶשֶׁת גַּת *môreše*<u>*t*</u> *ga*<u>*t*</u> **proper noun**
(Moresheth Gath)
Mic. 1:14.

4183. מוֹרַשְׁתִּי *môraštiy*, מֹרַשְׁתִּי *mōraštiy* **masc. proper noun**
(Morasthite; inhab. of Moresheth Gath [4182])
Jer. 26:18; **Mic.** 1:1.

4184. מוּשׁ *mûš* **verb**
(to feel)
Gen. 27:21; **Judg.** 16:26([K^{e}] *yāmaš* [3237]); **Ps.** 115:7.

4185. מוּשׁ *mûš* **verb**
(to depart, to remove)
Ex. 13:22; 33:11; **Num.** 14:44; **Josh.** 1:8; **Judg.** 6:18; **Job** 23:12; **Ps.** 55:11(12); **Prov.** 17:13; **Isa.** 22:25; 46:7; 54:10; 59:21; **Jer.** 17:8; 31:36; **Mic.** 2:3,4; **Nah.** 3:1; **Zech.** 3:9; 14:4.

4186. מוֹשָׁב *môšāḇ* **masc. noun**
(habitation, seat, dwelling place)
Gen. 10:30; 27:39; 36:43; **Ex.** 10:23; 12:20,40; 35:3; **Lev.** 3:17; 7:26; 13:46; 23:3,14,17,21,31; 25:29; **Num.** 15:2; 24:21; 31:10; 35:29; **1 Sam.** 20:18,25; **2 Sam.** 9:12; **1 Kgs.** 10:5; **2 Kgs.** 2:19; **1 Chr.** 4:33; 6:54(39); 7:28; **2 Chr.** 9:4; **Job** 29:7; **Ps.** 1:1; 107:4,7,32,36; 132:13; **Ezek.** 6:6,14; 8:3; 28:2; 34:13; 37:23(NIV, *m^{e}šûḇāh* [4878]); 48:15.

4187. מוּשִׁי *mûšiy* **masc. proper noun**
(Mushi)
Ex. 6:19; **Num.** 3:20; **1 Chr.** 6:19(4),47(32); 23:21,23; 24:26,30.

4188. מוּשִׁי *mûšiy* **masc. proper noun**
(Mushite)
Num. 3:33; 26:58.

4189. מוֹשְׁכָה *môš^{e}ḵāh* **fem. noun**
(cord, band)
Job 38:31.

4190. מוֹשָׁעָה *môšā'āh* **fem. noun**
(act of saving, deliverance)
Ps. 68:20(21).

4191. מוּת *mûṯ* **verb**
(to die, to be killed)
Gen. 2:17; 3:3,4; 5:5,8,11,14,17,20,27,31; 7:22; 9:29; 11:28,32; 18:25; 19:19; 20:3,7; 23:2–4, 6,8,11,13,15; 25:8,17,32; 26:9,11; 27:4; 30:1; 33:13; 35:8,18,19,29; 36:33–39; 37:18; 38:7,10–12; 42:2,20,37,38; 43:8; 44:9,20,22,31; 45:28; 46:12,30; 47:15, 19,29; 48:7,21; 50:5,15,24,26; **Ex.** 1:6, 16; 2:23; 4:19,24; 7:18,21; 8:13(9); 9:4, 6,7,19; 10:28; 11:5; 12:30,33; 14:11 ,12,30; 16:3; 17:3; 19:12; 20:19; 21:12, 14–18,20,28,29,34–36; 22:2(1),10(9), 14(13),19(18); 28:35,43; 30:20,21; 31:14,15; 35:2; **Lev.** 8:35; 10:2,6,7,9; 11:39; 15:31; 16:1,2,13; 19:20; 20:2, 4,9–13,15,16,20,27; 21:11; 22:9; 24:16, 17,21; 27:29; **Num.** 1:51; 3:4,10,38; 4:15,19,20; 6:6,7(KJV, NASB, *māweṯ* [4194]),9; 12:12; 14:2,15,35,37; 15:35,36; 16:13,29,41(17:6),48(17:13), 49(17:14); 17:10(25),13(28); 18:3,7, 22,32; 19:11,13,14,16,18; 20:1,4,26,28; 21:5,6; 23:10; 25:9; 26:10(KJV, NASB, *māweṯ* [4194]),11,19,61,65; 27:3,8; 33:38; 35:12,16–21,23,30,31; **Deut.** 2:16; 4:22; 5:25(22); 9:28; 10:6; 13:5(6), 9(10),10(11); 14:1; 17:5–7,12; 18:11, 16,20; 19:5,11,12; 20:5–7; 21:21,22; 22:21,22,24,25; 24:3,7,16; 25:5,6; 26:14; 31:14; 32:39,50; 33:6; 34:5; **Josh.** 1:2,18; 2:14; 5:4; 10:11,26; 11:17; 20:9; 24:12 (KJV, NASB, *m^eṯiym* [4962]),29,33; **Judg.** 1:7; 2:8,19(NASB, NIV, *māweṯ* [4194]),21; 3:11,25; 4:1,21,22; 5:18; 6:23,30,31; 8:32,33; 9:49,54,55; 10:2,5; 12:7,10, 12,15; 13:22,23; 15:13,18; 16:16,30; 20:5,13; 21:5; **Ruth** 1:3,5,8,17; 2:20; 4:5,10; **1 Sam.** 2:6,25,33,34; 4:11,17–20; 5:10–12; 11:12,13; 12:19; 14:13,39, 43–45; 15:3; 17:35,50,51; 19:1,2,5,6,11, 15,17; 20:2,8,14,32,33; 22:16–18; 24:14(15); 25:1,37–39; 26:10; 28:3,9; 30:2,15; 31:5–7; **2 Sam.** 1:4,5,9,10, 15,16; 2:7,23,31; 3:27,30,33,37; 4:1,7,10; 6:7; 8:2; 9:8; 10:1,18; 11:15,17,21,24,26; 12:13,14,18,19,21,23; 13:28,32,33,39; 14:2,5–7,14,32; 16:9; 17:23; 18:3,15,20, 33(19:1); 19:6(7),10(11),21–23(22–24), 37(38); 20:3,10,19; 21:1,4,9,17; 24:15; **1 Kgs.** 1:51,52; 2:1,8,24–26,30,34,37, 42,46; 3:19–23,26,27; 11:21,40; 12:18; 13:24,26,31; 14:11,12,17; 15:28; 16:4, 10,18,22; 17:12,18,20; 18:9; 19:4,17; 21:10,13–16,24; 22:35,37; **2 Kgs.** 1:4, 6,16,17; 4:1,20,32; 5:7; 7:3,4,17,20; 8:5, 10,15; 9:27; 11:1,2,8,15,16,20; 12:21(22); 13:14,20,24; 14:6,19; 15:10,14,25,30; 16:9; 17:26; 18:32; 19:35; 20:1; 21:23; 23:29,30,34; 25:21,25; **1 Chr.** 1:44–51; 2:3,19,30,32; 10:5–7,13,14; 13:10; 19:1, 18; 23:22; 24:2; 29:28; **2 Chr.** 10:18; 13:20; 15:13; 16:13; 18:34; 21:19; 22:9–11; 23:7,14,15,21; 24:15,22(NASB, NIV, *māweṯ* [4194]),25; 25:4,27; 32:11,24; 33:24; 35:24; **Esth.** 4:11; **Job** 1:19; 2:9; 3:11; 4:21; 5:2; 9:23; 12:2; 14:8,10,14; 21:23, 25; 33:22; 34:20; 36:14; 42:17; **Ps.** 31:12(13); 34:21(22); 37:32; 41:5(6); 48:14(15); 49:10(11); 59:[title](1); 82:7; 88:5(6),10(11); 105:29; 106:28; 109:16; 115:17; 118:17; 143:3; **Prov.** 5:23; 10:21; 15:10; 19:16,18; 21:25; 23:13; 30:7; **Eccl.** 2:16; 3:2; 4:2; 7:17; 9:3–5; **Isa.** 8:19; 11:4; 14:30; 22:2,13,14,18; 26:14,19; 37:36; 38:1; 50:2; 51:6,12,14; 59:5,10; 65:15,20; 66:24; **Jer.** 11:21,22; 16:4,6,7; 20:6,17; 21:6,9; 22:10,12,26; 26:8,15,19,21,24; 27:13; 28:16,17; 31:30; 34:4,5; 37:20; 38:2,4,9,10,15,16,24–26; 41:2,4,8; 42:16, 17,22; 43:3; 44:12; 52:27; **Lam.** 3:6; **Ezek.** 3:18–20; 5:12; 6:12; 7:15; 11:13; 12:13; 13:19; 17:16; 18:4,13,17,18,20,21, 24,26,28,31,32; 24:17,18; 28:8,10; 33:8, 9,11,13–15,18,27; 44:25; **Hos.** 2:3(5); 9:16; 13:1; **Amos** 2:2; 6:9; 7:11,17; 9:10; **Jon.** 4:8; **Hab.** 1:12; **Zech.** 11:9.

4192. I. מוּת לַבֵּן *mûṯ labbēn*
proper noun
(Muth-labben; an unknown musical instrument)
Ps. 9:[title](1)(NIV, see II).

II. מוּת לַבֵּן *mûṯ labbēn* **proper noun**
("The Death of the Son"; tune title)
Ps. 9:[title](1)(KJV, NASB, see I).

4193. מוֹת *môṯ* **Aram. masc. noun**
(death; corr. to Hebr. 4194)
Ezra 7:26.

4194. מָוֶת *māweṯ* **masc. noun**
(death)
Gen. 21:16; 25:11; 26:18; 27:2,7,10; 50:16; **Ex.** 10:17; **Lev.** 11:31,32; 16:1; **Num.** 6:7(NIV, *mûṯ* [4191]); 16:29; 23:10; 26:10(NIV, *mûṯ* [4191]); 33:39; 35:25,28,32; **Deut.** 19:6; 21:22; 22:26; 30:15,19; 31:27,29; 33:1; 34:7; **Josh.** 1:1; 2:13; 20:6; **Judg.** 1:1; 2:19(KJV, *mûṯ* [4191]); 13:7; 16:30; **Ruth** 1:17; 2:11; **1 Sam.** 5:11; 15:32,35; 20:3,31; 26:16; **2 Sam.** 1:1,23; 3:33; 6:23; 12:5; 15:21; 19:28(29); 22:5,6; **1 Kgs.** 2:26; 11:40; **2 Kgs.** 1:1; 2:21; 3:5; 4:40; 14:17; 15:5; **1 Chr.** 2:24; 22:5; **2 Chr.** 22:4; 24:15,17; 25:25; 26:21; 32:33; **Esth.** 2:7; **Job** 3:21; 5:20; 7:15; 18:13; 27:15; 28:22; 30:23; 38:17; **Ps.** 6:5(6); 7:13(14); 9:13(14); 13:3(4); 18:4(5),5(6); 22:15(16); 33:19; 49:14(15),17(18); 55:4(5),15(16)([Ke] *yešiyûṯ* [3451]); 56:13(14); 68:20(21); 73:4(NIV, *tām* [8535]); 78:50; 89:48(49); 107:18; 116:3,8,15; 118:18; **Prov.** 2:18; 5:5; 7:27; 8:36; 10:2; 11:4,7,19; 12:28; 13:14; 14:12,27,32; 16:14,25; 18:21; 21:6; 24:11; 26:18; **Eccl.** 3:19; 7:1,26; 8:8; 10:1; **Song** 8:6; **Isa.** 6:1; 14:28; 25:8; 28:15,18; 38:18; 53:9,12; **Jer.** 8:3; 9:21(20); 15:2; 18:21,23; 21:8; 26:11,16; 43:11; 52:11,34; **Lam.** 1:20; **Ezek.** 18:23,32; 28:10; 31:14; 33:11; **Hos.** 13:14; **Jon.** 4:3,8,9; **Hab.** 2:5.

4195. מוֹתָר *môṯār* **masc. noun**
(abundance, advantage)
Prov. 14:23; 21:5; **Eccl.** 3:19.

4196. מִזְבֵּחַ *mizbēaḥ* **masc. noun**
(altar)
Gen. 8:20; 12:7,8; 13:4,18; 22:9; 26:25; 33:20; 35:1,3,7; **Ex.** 17:15; 20:24–26; 21:14; 24:4,6; 27:1,5–7; 28:43; 29:12, 13,16,18,20,21,25,36–38,44; 30:1,18, 20,27,28; 31:8,9; 32:5; 34:13; 35:15,16; 37:25; 38:1,3,4,7,30; 39:38,39; 40:5–7, 10,26,29,30,32,33; **Lev.** 1:5,7–9,11–13, 15–17; 2:2,8,9,12; 3:2,5,8,11,13,16; 4:7, 10,18,19,25,26,30,31,34,35; 5:9,12; 6:9(2), 10(3),12–15(5–8); 7:2,5,31; 8:11,15,16, 19,21,24,28,30; 9:7–10,12–14,17,18, 20,24; 10:12; 14:20; 16:12,18,20,25,33; 17:6,11; 21:23; 22:22; **Num.** 3:26,31; 4:11,13,14,26; 5:25,26; 7:1,10,11,84,88; 16:38(17:3),39(17:4),46(17:11); 18:3,5, 7,17; 23:1,2,4,14,29,30; **Deut.** 7:5; 12:3, 27; 16:21; 26:4; 27:5,6; 33:10; **Josh.** 8:30,31; 9:27; 22:10,11,16,19,23,26,28, 29,34; **Judg.** 2:2; 6:24–26,28,30–32; 13:20; 21:4; **1 Sam.** 2:28,33; 7:17; 14:35; 24:18,21,25; **1 Kgs.** 1:50,51,53; 2:28,29; 3:4; 6:20,22; 7:48; 8:22,31,54,64; 9:25; 12:32,33; 13:1–5,32; 16:32; 18:26,30, 32,35; 19:10,14; **2 Kgs.** 11:11,18; 12:9(10); 16:10–15; 18:22; 21:3–5; 23:9, 12,15–17,20; **1 Chr.** 6:49(34); 16:40; 21:18,22,26,29; 22:1; 28:18; **2 Chr.** 1:5,6; 4:1,19; 5:12; 6:12,22; 7:7,9; 8:12; 14:3(2); 15:8; 23:10,17; 26:16,19; 28:24; 29:18,19, 21,22,24,27; 30:14; 31:1; 32:12; 33:3–5, 15,16; 34:4,5,7; 35:16; **Ezra** 3:2,3; **Neh.** 10:34(35); **Ps.** 26:6; 43:4; 51:19(21); 84:3(4); 118:27; **Isa.** 6:6; 17:8; 19:19; 27:9; 36:7; 56:7; 60:7; **Jer.** 11:13; 17:1,2; **Lam.** 2:7; **Ezek.** 6:4–6,13; 8:5,16; 9:2; 40:46,47; 41:22; 43:13,18,22,26,27; 45:19; 47:1; **Hos.** 8:11; 10:1,2,8; 12:11(12); **Joel** 1:13; 2:17; **Amos** 2:8; 3:14; 9:1; **Zech.** 9:15; 14:20; **Mal.** 1:7,10; 2:13.

4197. מֶזֶג *mezeg* **masc. noun**
(liquor, mixed wine)
Song 7:2(3).

4198. מָזֶה *māzeh* **adj.**
(burned out, wasted)
Deut. 32:24.

4199. מִזָּה *mizzāh* **masc. proper noun**
(Mizzah)
Gen. 36:13,17; **1 Chr.** 1:37.

4200. מָזוּ *māzû* **masc. noun**
(granary, barn)
Ps. 144:13.

4201. מְזוּזָה *m^e^zûzāh* **fem. noun**
(doorpost, gatepost)
Ex. 12:7,22,23; 21:6; **Deut.** 6:9; 11:20; **Judg.** 16:3; **1 Sam.** 1:9; **1 Kgs.** 6:31,33; 7:5; **Prov.** 8:34; **Isa.** 57:8; **Ezek.** 41:21; 43:8; 45:19; 46:2.

4202. מָזוֹן *māzôn* **masc. noun**
(food, provisions)
Gen. 45:23; **2 Chr.** 11:23.

4203. מָזוֹן *māzôn* **Aram. masc. noun**
(food, sustenance; corr. to Hebr. 4202)
Dan. 4:12(9),21(18).

4204. מָזוֹר *māzôr* **masc. noun**
(trap, ambush)
Obad. 1:7.

4205. מָזוֹר *māzôr* **masc. noun**
(sore, wound)
Jer. 30:13; **Hos.** 5:13.

4206. I. מֵזַח *mēzaḥ* **masc. noun**
(belt, girdle, strength)
Job 12:21; **Ps.** 109:19; **Isa.** 23:10 (NIV, see II).
II. מֵזַח *mēzaḥ* **masc. noun**
(dock, harbor)
Isa. 23:10(KJV, NASB, see I).

4207. מַזְלֵג *mazlēg,* מִזְלָגָה *mizlāgāh* **masc./fem. noun**
(a sacrificial utensil)
Ex. 27:3; 38:3; **Num.** 4:14; **1 Sam.** 2:13,14; **1 Chr.** 28:17; **2 Chr.** 4:16.

4208. מַזָּל *mazzāl* **fem. noun**
(constellation, planet)
2 Kgs. 23:5.

4209. מְזִמָּה *m^e^zimmāh* **fem. noun**
(purpose, plot, scheme)
Job 21:27; 42:2; **Ps.** 10:2,4; 21:11(12); 37:7; 139:20; **Prov.** 1:4; 2:11; 3:21; 5:2; 8:12; 12:2; 14:17; 24:8; **Jer.** 11:15; 23:20; 30:24; 51:11.

4210. מִזְמוֹר *mizmôr* **masc. noun**
(psalm, melody)
Ps. 3:[title](1); 4:[title](1); 5:[title](1); 6:[title](1); 8:[title](1); 9:[title](1); 12:[title](1); 13:[title](1); 15:[title](1); 19:[title](1); 20:[title](1); 21:[title](1); 22:[title](1); 23:[title](1); 24:[title](1); 29:[title](1); 30:[title](1); 31:[title](1); 38:[title](1); 39:[title](1); 40:[title](1); 41:[title](1); 47:[title](1); 48:[title](1); 49:[title](1); 50:[title](1); 51:[title](1); 62:[title](1); 63:[title](1); 64:[title](1); 65:[title](1); 66:[title](1); 67:[title](1); 68:[title](1); 73:[title](1); 75:[title](1); 76:[title](1); 77:[title](1); 79:[title](1); 80:[title](1); 82:[title](1); 83:[title](1); 84:[title](1); 85:[title](1); 87:[title](1); 88:[title](1); 92:[title](1); 98:[title](1); 100:[title](1); 101:[title](1); 108:[title](1); 109:[title](1); 110:[title](1); 139:[title](1); 140:[title](1); 141:[title](1); 143:[title](1).

4211. מַזְמֵרָה *mazmērāh* **fem. noun**
(pruning hook, pruning knife)
Isa. 2:4; 18:5; **Joel** 3:10(4:10); **Mic.** 4:3.

4212. מְזַמֶּרֶת *m^e^zammeret* **fem. pl. noun**
(snuffers, wick trimmers)
1 Kgs. 7:50; **2 Kgs.** 12:13(14); 25:14; **2 Chr.** 4:22; **Jer.** 52:18.

4213. מִזְעָר *miz'ār* **masc. noun**
(a short time, a little while, a few)
Isa. 10:25; 16:14; 24:6; 29:17.

4214. מִזְרֶה *mizreh* **masc. noun**
(pitchfork, winnowing fork)
Isa. 30:24; **Jer.** 15:7.

4215. I. מְזָרֶה *m^e^zāreh* **masc. noun**
(north)
Job 37:9(NASB, *zārāh* [2219,I]; NIV, see II).
II. מְזָרֶה *m^e^zāreh* **masc. noun**
(driving wind)
Job 37:9(KJV, see I; NASB, *zārāh* [2219,I]).

4216. מַזָּרוֹת *mazzārôṯ* **fem. pl. noun**
(Mazzaroth: name for a constellation of stars)
Job 38:32.

4217. מִזְרָח *mizrāḥ* **masc. noun**
(place of the sunrise, east, eastward)
Ex. 27:13; 38:13; **Num.** 2:3; 3:38; 21:11; 32:19; 34:15; **Deut.** 3:17,27; 4:41,47,49; **Josh.** 1:15; 4:19; 11:3,8; 12:1,3; 13:5,8, 27,32; 16:1,5,6; 17:10; 18:7; 19:12,13, 27,34; 20:8; **Judg.** 11:18; 20:43; 21:19; **1 Kgs.** 7:25; **2 Kgs.** 10:33; **1 Chr.** 4:39; 5:9,10; 6:78(63); 7:28; 9:18,24; 12:15; 26:14,17; **2 Chr.** 4:4; 5:12; 29:4; 31:14; **Neh.** 3:26,29; 12:37; **Ps.** 50:1; 103:12; 107:3; 113:3; **Isa.** 41:2,25; 43:5; 45:6; 46:11; 59:19; **Jer.** 31:40; **Dan.** 8:9; 11:44; **Amos** 8:12; **Zech.** 8:7; 14:4; **Mal.** 1:11.

4218. מִזְרָע *mizrāʿ* **masc. noun**
(that which is sown, a sown field)
Isa. 19:7.

4219. מִזְרָק *mizrāq* **masc. noun**
(bowl, basin)
Ex. 27:3; 38:3; **Num.** 4:14; 7:13,19,25, 31,37,43,49,55,61,67,73,79,84,85; **1 Kgs.** 7:40,45,50; **2 Kgs.** 12:13(14); 25:15; **1 Chr.** 28:17; **2 Chr.** 4:8,11,22; **Neh.** 7:70; **Jer.** 52:18,19; **Amos** 6:6; **Zech.** 9:15; 14:20.

4220. מֵחַ *mēaḥ* **masc. noun**
(the fat one, fat beast, wealthy one)
Ps. 66:15; **Isa.** 5:17.

4221. מֹחַ *mōaḥ* **masc. noun**
(the marrow of the bone)
Job 21:24.

4222. מָחָא *māḥāʾ* **verb**
(to strike, to clap [the hands])
Ps. 98:8; **Isa.** 55:12; **Ezek.** 25:6.

4223. מְחָא *m^e^ḥāʾ* **Aram. verb**
(to strike, to smite, to kill; corr. to Hebr. 4222)
Ezra 6:11; **Dan.** 2:34,35; 4:35(32).

4224. I. מַחֲבֵא *maḥ^a^ḇēʾ* **masc. noun**
(hiding place)
Isa. 32:2.
II. מַחֲבֹא *maḥ^a^ḇōʾ* **masc. noun**
(hiding place)
1 Sam. 23:23.

4225. מַחְבֶּרֶת *maḥbereṯ* **fem. noun**
(that which is joined, place of joining)
Ex. 26:4,5; 28:27; 36:11,12,17; 39:20.

4226. מְחַבְּרָה *m^e^ḥabb^e^rāh* **fem. noun**
(joint, hinge, joist)
1 Chr. 22:3; **2 Chr.** 34:11.

4227. מַחֲבַת *maḥ^a^ḇaṯ* **fem. noun**
(flat pan, griddle)
Lev. 2:5; 6:21(14); 7:9; **1 Chr.** 23:29; **Ezek.** 4:3.

4228. מַחֲגֹרֶת *maḥ^a^gōreṯ* **fem. noun**
(a wrapping, a girding)
Isa. 3:24.

4229. I. מָחָה *māḥāh* **verb**
(to wipe out)
Gen. 6:7; 7:4,23; **Ex.** 17:14; 32:32,33; **Num.** 5:23; **Deut.** 9:14; 25:6,19;

29:20(19); **Judg.** 21:17; **2 Kgs.** 14:27; 21:13; **Neh.** 4:5(3:37); 13:14; **Ps.** 9:5(6); 51:1(3),9(11); 69:28(29); 109:13,14; **Prov.** 6:33; 30:20; 31:3; **Isa.** 25:8; 43:25; 44:22; **Jer.** 18:23; **Ezek.** 6:6.
II. מָחָה *māḥāh* **verb**
(to be full of marrow)
Isa. 25:6.
III. מָחָה *māḥāh* **verb**
(to reach, to border upon)
Num. 34:11.

4230. מְחוּגָה *m^{e}ḥûgāh* **fem. noun**
(compass, instrument for making circles)
Isa. 44:13.

4231. מָחוֹז *maḥōz* **masc. noun**
(haven, enclosure)
Ps. 107:30.

4232. מְחוּיָאֵל *m^{e}ḥûyā'ēl*, מְחִיָּיאֵל *m^{e}ḥiyyāy'ēl* **masc. proper noun**
(Mehujael)
Gen. 4:18.

4233. מַחֲוִים *maḥªwiym* **masc. proper noun**
(Mahavite)
1 Chr. 11:46.

4234. מָחוֹל *māḥôl* **masc. noun**
(dance, dancing)
Ps. 30:11(12); 149:3; 150:4; **Jer.** 31:4,13; **Lam.** 5:15.

4235. מָחוֹל *māḥôl* **masc. proper noun**
(Mahol)
1 Kgs. 4:31(5:11).

4236. מַחֲזֶה *maḥªzeh* **masc. noun**
(a vision)
Gen. 15:1; **Num.** 24:4,16; **Ezek.** 13:7.

4237. מֶחֱזָה *meḥ^{e}zāh* **fem. noun**
(window)
1 Kgs. 7:4,5.

4238. מַחֲזִיאוֹת *maḥªziy'ôṯ* **masc. proper noun**
(Mahazioth)
1 Chr. 25:4,30.

4239. מְחִי *m^{e}ḥiy* **masc. noun**
(blow [of a battering ram])
Ezek. 26:9.

4240. מְחִידָא *m^{e}ḥiyḏā'* **masc. proper noun**
(Mehida)
Ezra 2:52; **Neh.** 7:54.

4241. מִחְיָה *miḥ^{e}yāh* **fem. noun**
(preservation of life, sustenance)
Gen. 45:5; **Lev.** 13:10,24; **Judg.** 6:4; 17:10; **2 Chr.** 14:13(12); **Ezra** 9:8,9.

4242. מְחִיר *m^{e}ḥiyr* **masc. noun**
(price, wages, cost)
Deut. 23:18(19); **2 Sam.** 24:24; **1 Kgs.** 10:28; 21:2; **2 Chr.** 1:16; **Job** 28:15; **Ps.** 44:12(13); **Prov.** 17:16; 27:26; **Isa.** 45:13; 55:1; **Jer.** 15:13; **Lam.** 5:4; **Dan.** 11:39; **Mic.** 3:11.

4243. מְחִיר *m^{e}ḥiyr* **masc. proper noun**
(Mehir)
1 Chr. 4:11.

4244. A. מַחְלָה *maḥlāh* **fem. proper noun**
(Mahlah: daughter of Zelophehad)
Num. 26:33; 27:1; 36:11; **Josh.** 17:3.
B. מַחְלָה *maḥlāh* **fem. proper noun**
(Mahlah: a Manassite)
1 Chr. 7:18.

4245. I. מַחֲלֶה *maḥªleh* **masc. noun**
(sickness, disease)
2 Chr. 21:15; **Prov.** 18:14.
II. מַחֲלָה *maḥªlāh* **fem. noun**
(sickness, disease)

Ex. 15:26; 23:25; **1 Kgs.** 8:37; **2 Chr.** 6:28.

4246. מְחֹלָה *m*e*ḥōlāh* **fem. noun**
(dancing, dance)
Ex. 15:20; 32:19; **Judg.** 11:34; 21:21; **1 Sam.** 18:6; 21:11(12); 29:5; **Song** 6:13(7:1).

4247. מְחִלָּה *m*e*ḥillāh* **fem. noun**
(hole, cavern)
Isa. 2:19.

4248. מַחְלוֹן *maḥlôn* **masc. proper noun**
(Mahlon)
Ruth 1:2,5; 4:9,10.

4249. A. מַחְלִי *maḥliy* **masc. proper noun**
(Mahli: a Levite)
Ex. 6:19; **Num.** 3:20; **1 Chr.** 6:19(4), 29(14); 23:21; 24:26,28; **Ezra** 8:18.
B. מַחְלִי *maḥliy* **masc. proper noun**
(Mahli: son of Mushi)
1 Chr. 6:47(32); 23:23; 24:30.

4250. מַחְלִי *maḥliy* **masc. proper noun**
(Mahlite)
Num. 3:33; 26:58.

4251. מַחֲלוּ *maḥalû* **masc. noun**
(sickness, disease)
2 Chr. 24:25.

4252. I. מַחֲלָף *maḥalāp̱* **masc. noun**
(knife for slaughter)
Ezra 1:9(NASB, see II; NIV, see II).
II. מַחֲלָף *maḥalāp̱* **masc. noun**
(duplicate)
Ezra 1:9(KJV, see I; NIV, see III).
III. מַחֲלָף *maḥalāp̱* **masc. noun**
(silver pan)
Ezra 1:9(KJV, see I; NASB, see II).

4253. מַחְלָפָה *maḥlāpāh* **fem. noun**
(a lock [of hair], braid [of hair])
Judg. 16:13,19.

4254. מַחֲלָצָה *maḥalāṣāh* **fem. noun**
(festal robe, fine garment)
Isa. 3:22; **Zech.** 3:4.

4255. מַחְלְקָה *maḥleqāh* **Aram. fem. noun**
(a group, division; corr. to Hebr. 4256)
Ezra 6:18.

4256. I. מַחֲלֹקֶת *maḥalōqeṯ* **fem. noun**
(smoothness, slipperiness, escape)
1 Sam. 23:28(KJV, NIV, *sela' hammahleqôṯ* [5555]).
II. מַחֲלֹקֶת *maḥalōqeṯ* **fem. noun**
(group, division)
Josh. 11:23; 12:7; 18:10; **1 Chr.** 23:6; 24:1; 26:1,12,19; 27:1,2,4–15; 28:1, 13,21; **2 Chr.** 5:11; 8:14; 23:8; 31:2, 15–17; 35:4,10; **Neh.** 11:36; **Ezek.** 48:29.

4257. מָחֲלַת *māḥalaṯ* **fem. proper noun**
(Mahalath, mahalath; part of a song title)
Ps. 53:[title](1); 88:[title](1).

4258. A. מָחֲלַת *māḥalaṯ* **fem. proper noun**
(Mahalath: daughter of Ishmael)
Gen. 28:9.
B. מָחֲלַת *māḥalaṯ* **fem. proper noun**
(Mahalath: granddaughter of David)
2 Chr. 11:18.

4259. מְחֹלָתִי *m*e*ḥōlāṯiy* **masc. proper noun**
(Meholathite)
1 Sam. 18:19; **2 Sam.** 21:8.

4260. מַחֲמָאֹת *maḥ^{a}mā'ōṯ* **fem. pl. noun**
(butter)
Ps. 55:21(22).

4261. מַחְמָד *maḥmāḏ* **masc. noun**
(desire, desirable thing, precious thing)
1 Kgs. 20:6; **2 Chr.** 36:19; **Song** 5:16; **Isa.** 64:11(10); **Lam.** 1:7,10,11(KJV, NASB, [K^e] *maḥ^{a}mōḏ* [4262]); 2:4; **Ezek.** 24:16,21,25; **Hos.** 9:6,16; **Joel** 3:5(4:5).

4262. מַחֲמֹד *maḥ^{a}mōḏ* **masc. noun**
(desirable thing, precious thing)
Lam. 1:7,11(NIV, [Q^e] *maḥmāḏ* [4261]).

4263. מַחְמָל *maḥmāl* **masc. noun**
(object of one's love or compassion)
Ezek. 24:21.

4264. מַחֲנֶה *maḥ^{a}neh* **masc./fem. noun**
(camp, encampment)
Gen. 32:2(3),7(8),8(9),10(11),21(22); 33:8; 50:9; **Ex.** 14:19,20,24; 16:13; 19:16,17; 29:14; 32:17,19,26,27; 33:7,11; 36:6; **Lev.** 4:12,21; 6:11(4); 8:17; 9:11; 10:4,5; 13:46; 14:3,8; 16:26–28; 17:3; 24:10,14,23; **Num.** 1:52; 2:3,9,10,16–18, 24,25,31,32; 4:5,15; 5:2–4; 10:2,5,6,14, 18,22,25,34; 11:1,9,26,27,30–32; 12:14,15; 13:19; 14:44; 15:35,36; 19:3, 7,9; 31:12,13,19,24; **Deut.** 2:14,15; 23:9–12(10–13),14(15); 29:11(10); **Josh.** 1:11; 3:2; 5:8; 6:11,14,18,23; 8:13; 9:6; 10:5,6,15,21,43; 11:4; 18:9; **Judg.** 4:15,16; 7:1,8–11,13–15,17–19,21,22; 8:10–12; 13:25; 21:8,12; **1 Sam.** 4:3,5–7; 11:11; 13:17; 14:15,19,21; 17:1,4,17,46,53; 26:6; 28:1,5,19; 29:1,6; **2 Sam.** 1:2,3; 5:24; 23:16; **1 Kgs.** 16:16; 22:34,36; **2 Kgs.** 3:9,24; 5:15; 6:24; 7:4–8,10,12, 14,16; 19:35; **1 Chr.** 9:18,19; 11:15,18; 12:22(23); 14:15,16; **2 Chr.** 14:13(12); 18:33; 22:1; 31:2; 32:21; **Ps.** 27:3; 78:28; 106:16; **Song** 6:13(7:1); **Isa.** 37:36; **Ezek.** 1:24; 4:2; **Joel** 2:11; **Amos** 4:10; **Zech.** 14:15.

4265. מַחֲנֵה־דָן *maḥ^{a}nēh-ḏān* **proper noun**
(Mahaneh Dan)
Judg. 18:12.

4266. מַחֲנַיִם *maḥ^{a}nayim* **proper noun**
(Mahanaim)
Gen. 32:2(3); **Josh.** 13:26,30; 21:38(36); **2 Sam.** 2:8,12,29; 17:24,27; 19:32(33); **1 Kgs.** 2:8; 4:14; **1 Chr.** 6:80(65).

4267. מַחֲנַק *maḥ^{a}naq* **masc. noun**
(strangling, suffocation)
Job 7:15.

4268. מַחְסֶה *maḥseh* **masc. noun**
(refuge, shelter)
Job 24:8; **Ps.** 14:6; 46:1(2); 61:3(4); 62:7(8),8(9); 71:7; 73:28; 91:2,9; 94:22; 104:18; 142:5(6); **Prov.** 14:26; **Isa.** 4:6; 25:4; 28:15,17; **Jer.** 17:17; **Joel** 3:16(4:16).

4269. מַחְסוֹם *maḥsôm* **masc. noun**
(muzzle, bridle)
Ps. 39:1(2).

4270. מַחְסוֹר *maḥsôr*, מַחְסֹר *maḥsōr* **masc. noun**
(lack, need, poverty)
Deut. 15:8; **Judg.** 18:10; 19:19,20; **Ps.** 34:9(10); **Prov.** 6:11; 11:24; 14:23; 21:5,17; 22:16; 24:34; 28:27.

4271. מַחְסֵיָה *maḥsēyāh* **masc. proper noun**
(Mahseiah)
Jer. 32:12; 51:59.

4272. מָחַץ *māḥaṣ* **verb**
(to smite through, to pierce, to shatter, to crush)

Num. 24:8,17; **Deut.** 32:39; 33:11; **Judg.** 5:26; **2 Sam.** 22:39; **Job** 5:18; 26:12; **Ps.** 18:38(39); 68:21(22),23(24); 110:5,6; **Hab.** 3:13.

4273. מַחַץ *maḥaṣ* **masc. noun**
(wound, bruise)
Isa. 30:26.

4274. מַחְצֵב *maḥṣēḇ* **masc. noun**
(something hewed)
2 Kgs. 12:12(13); 22:6; **2 Chr.** 34:11.

4275. מֶחֱצָה *meḥeṣāh* **fem. noun**
(half)
Num. 31:36,43.

4276. מַחֲצִית *maḥaṣiyṯ* **fem. noun**
(half, middle)
Ex. 30:13,15,23; 38:26; **Lev.** 6:20(13); **Num.** 31:29,30,42,47; **Josh.** 21:25; **1 Kgs.** 16:9; **1 Chr.** 6:61(46),70(55); **Neh.** 8:3.

4277. מָחַק *māḥaq* **verb**
(to smash, to crush)
Judg. 5:26.

4278. מֶחְקָר *meḥqār* **masc. noun**
(deep places, depth)
Ps. 95:4.

4279. מָחָר *māḥār* **masc. noun**
(tomorrow, in the future)
Gen. 30:33; **Ex.** 8:10(6),23(19),29(25); 9:5,18; 10:4; 13:14; 16:23; 17:9; 19:10; 32:5; **Num.** 11:18; 14:25; 16:7,16; **Deut.** 6:20; **Josh.** 3:5; 4:6,21; 7:13; 11:6; 22:18, 24,27,28; **Judg.** 19:9; 20:28; **1 Sam.** 9:16; 11:9,10; 19:11; 20:5,12,18; 28:19; **2 Sam.** 11:12; **1 Kgs.** 19:2; 20:6; **2 Kgs.** 6:28; 7:1,18; 10:6; **2 Chr.** 20:16,17; **Esth.** 5:8,12; 9:13; **Prov.** 3:28; 27:1; **Isa.** 22:13; 56:12.

4280. מַחֲרָאָה *maḥarā'āh* **fem. noun**
(latrine)
2 Kgs. 10:27.

4281. מַחֲרֵשָׁה *maḥarēšāh* **fem. noun**
(mattock, sickle, hoe, plowshare)
1 Sam. 13:20(KJV, *maḥarešeṯ* [4282]), 21(NIV, [Sept.] *hermēs* [2770]).

4282. מַחֲרֶשֶׁת *maḥarešeṯ* **fem. noun**
(plowshare)
1 Sam. 13:20(NASB, NIV, *maḥarēšāh* [4281]).

4283. מָחֳרָת *moḥorāṯ* **fem. noun**
(the morrow, next day)
Gen. 19:34; **Ex.** 9:6; 18:13; 32:6,30; **Lev.** 7:16; 19:6; 23:11,15,16; **Num.** 11:32; 16:41(17:6); 17:8(23); 33:3; **Josh.** 5:11,12; **Judg.** 6:38; 9:42; 21:4; **1 Sam.** 5:3,4; 11:11; 18:10; 20:27; 30:17; 31:8; **2 Sam.** 11:12; **2 Kgs.** 8:15; **1 Chr.** 10:8; 29:21; **Jer.** 20:3; **Jon.** 4:7.

4284. מַחֲשָׁבָה *maḥašāḇāh*, מַחֲשֶׁבֶת *maḥašeḇeṯ* **fem. noun**
(thought, purpose, scheme)
Gen. 6:5; **Ex.** 31:4; 35:32,33,35; **2 Sam.** 14:14; **1 Chr.** 28:9; 29:18; **2 Chr.** 2:14(13); 26:15; **Esth.** 8:3,5; 9:25; **Job** 5:12; 21:27; **Ps.** 33:10,11; 40:5(6); 56:5(6); 92:5(6); 94:11; **Prov.** 6:18; 12:5; 15:22,26; 16:3; 19:21; 20:18; 21:5; **Isa.** 55:7–9; 59:7; 65:2; 66:18; **Jer.** 4:14; 6:19; 11:19; 18:11,12,18; 29:11; 49:20,30; 50:45; 51:29; **Lam.** 3:60,61; **Ezek.** 38:10; **Dan.** 11:24,25; **Mic.** 4:12.

4285. מַחְשָׁךְ *maḥšāḵ* **masc. noun**
(darkness, dark place)
Ps. 74:20; 88:6(7),18(19); 143:3; **Isa.** 29:15; 42:16; **Lam.** 3:6.

4286. מַחְשֹׂף *maḥśōp̱* **masc. noun**
(peeling, stripping, as bark from a tree)
Gen. 30:37.

4287. A. מַחַת *maḥaṯ* **masc. proper noun**
(Mahath: son of Amasai)
1 Chr. 6:35(20).
B. מַחַת *maḥaṯ* **masc. proper noun**
(Mahath: chief Levite)
2 Chr. 29:12; 31:13.

4288. מְחִתָּה *m^eḥittāh* **fem. noun**
(ruin, terror, destruction)
Ps. 89:40(41); **Prov.** 10:14,15,29; 13:3; 14:28; 18:7; 21:15; **Isa.** 54:14; **Jer.** 17:17; 48:39.

4289. מַחְתָּה *maḥtāh* **fem. noun**
(censer, firepan)
Ex. 25:38; 27:3; 37:23; 38:3; **Lev.** 10:1; 16:12; **Num.** 4:9,14; 16:6,17,18,37–39(17:2–4),46(17:11); **1 Kgs.** 7:50; **2 Kgs.** 25:15; **2 Chr.** 4:22; **Jer.** 52:19.

4290. מַחְתֶּרֶת *maḥtereṯ* **fem. noun**
(a breaking in, burglary)
Ex. 22:2(1); **Jer.** 2:34.

4291. מְטָא *m^eṭā'*, מְטָה *m^eṭāh* **Aram. verb**
(to reach up to, to attain, to happen)
Dan. 4:11(8),20(17),22(19),24(21), 28(25); 6:24(25); 7:13,22.

4292. מַטְאֲטֵא *maṭ'aṭē'* **masc. noun**
(broom)
Isa. 14:23.

4293. מַטְבֵּחַ *maṭbēaḥ* **masc. noun**
(a slaughtering place)
Isa. 14:21.

4294. מַטֶּה *maṭṭeh*, מַטָּה *maṭṭāh* **masc. and fem. nouns**
(tribe, staff, rod)
Gen. 38:18,25; **Ex.** 4:2,4,17,20; 7:9,10, 12,15,17,19,20; 8:5(1),16(12),17(13); 9:23; 10:13; 14:16; 17:5,9; 31:2,6; 35:30,34; 38:22,23; **Lev.** 24:11; 26:26; **Num.** 1:4,16,21,23,25,27,29,31,33,35, 37,39,41,43,47,49; 2:5,7,12,14,20,22, 27,29; 3:6; 7:2,12; 10:15,16,19,20,23,24, 26,27; 13:2,4–15; 17:2(17),3(18),5–10 (20–25); 18:2; 20:8,9,11; 26:55; 30:1(2); 31:4–6; 32:28; 33:54; 34:13–15,18–28; 36:3–9,12; **Josh.** 7:1,18; 13:15,24,29; 14:1–4; 15:1,20,21; 16:8; 17:1; 18:11,21; 19:1,8,23,24,31,39,40,48,51; 20:8; 21:1,4–7,9,17,20,23,25,27,28,30,32,34, 36,38; 22:1,14; **1 Sam.** 14:27,43; **1 Kgs.** 7:14; 8:1; **1 Chr.** 6:60–63(45–48),65(50), 66(51),70–72(55–57),74(59),76–78(61–63),80(65); 12:31; **2 Chr.** 5:2; **Ps.** 105:16; 110:2; **Isa.** 9:4(3); 10:5,15,24,26; 14:5; 28:27; 30:32; **Jer.** 48:17; **Ezek.** 4:16; 5:16; 7:10,11; 14:13; 19:11,12,14; **Mic.** 6:9; **Hab.** 3:9,14.

4295. מַטָּה *maṭṭāh* **adv.**
(beneath, downward, under)
Ex. 26:24; 27:5; 28:27; 36:29; 38:4; 39:20; **Deut.** 28:13,43; **2 Kgs.** 19:30; **1 Chr.** 27:23; **2 Chr.** 32:30; **Ezra** 9:13; **Prov.** 15:24; **Eccl.** 3:21; **Isa.** 37:31; **Jer.** 31:37; **Ezek.** 1:27; 8:2.

4296. מִטָּה *miṭṭāh* **fem. noun**
(bed, couch, funeral bier)
Gen. 47:31; 48:2; 49:33; **Ex.** 8:3(7:28); **1 Sam.** 19:13,15,16; 28:23; **2 Sam.** 3:31; 4:7; **1 Kgs.** 17:19; 21:4; **2 Kgs.** 1:4,6,16; 4:10,21,32; 11:2; **2 Chr.** 22:11; 24:25; **Esth.** 1:6; 7:8; **Ps.** 6:6(7); **Prov.** 26:14; **Song** 3:7; **Ezek.** 23:41; **Amos** 3:12; 6:4.

4297. מֻטֶּה *muṭṭeh* **masc. noun**
(perversion, injustice)
Ezek. 9:9.

4298. מֻטָּה *muṭṭāh* **fem. noun**
(spreading out, stretching out)
Isa. 8:8(NIV, *nāṭāh* [5186]).

4299. מַטְוֶה *maṭweh* **masc. noun**
(that which is spun)
Ex. 35:25.

4300. מָטִיל *māṭiyl* **masc. noun**
(metal bar, rod)
Job 40:18.

4301. מַטְמוֹן *maṭmôn*, מַטְמֻן *maṭmun* **masc. noun**
(hidden treasure, riches)
Gen. 43:23; **Job** 3:21; **Prov.** 2:4; **Isa.** 45:3; **Jer.** 41:8.

4302. מַטָּע *maṭṭā'* **masc. noun**
(place of planting, act of planting)
Isa. 60:21; 61:3; **Ezek.** 17:7; 31:4; 34:29; **Mic.** 1:6.

4303. מַטְעָם *maṭ'ām* **masc. noun**
(tasty food, delicacy)
Gen. 27:4,7,9,14,17,31; **Prov.** 23:3,6.

4304. מִטְפַּחַת *miṭpaḥaṯ* **fem. noun**
(veil, cloak)
Ruth 3:15; **Isa.** 3:22.

4305. מָטַר *māṭar* **verb**
(to rain)
Gen. 2:5; 7:4; 19:24; **Ex.** 9:18,23; 16:4; **Job** 20:23; 38:26; **Ps.** 11:6; 78:24,27; **Isa.** 5:6; **Ezek.** 38:22; **Amos** 4:7.

4306. מָטָר *māṭār* **masc. noun**
(rain)
Ex. 9:33,34; **Deut.** 11:11,14,17; 28:12,24; 32:2; **1 Sam.** 12:17,18; **2 Sam.** 1:21; 23:4; **1 Kgs.** 8:35,36; 17:1; 18:1; **2 Chr.** 6:26,27; 7:13; **Job** 5:10; 28:26; 29:23; 36:27; 37:6; 38:28; **Ps.** 72:6; 135:7; 147:8; **Prov.** 26:1; 28:3; **Isa.** 4:6; 5:6; 30:23; **Jer.** 10:13; 51:16; **Zech.** 10:1.

4307. מַטָּרָה *maṭṭārāh*, מַטָּרָא *maṭṭārā'* **fem. noun**
(guard, guardhouse, target)
Neh. 3:25; 12:39; **Jer.** 32:2,8,12; 33:1; 37:21; 38:6,13,28; 39:14,15.

4308. מַטְרֵד *maṭrēḏ* **fem. proper noun**
(Matred)
Gen. 36:39; **1 Chr.** 1:50.

4309. מַטְרִי *maṭriy* **masc. proper noun**
(Matri)
1 Sam. 10:21.

4310. מִי *miy* **rel. pron.**
(who, whose, whom)
Gen. 3:11; 19:12; 21:7,26; 24:23,47,65; 27:18,32,33; 32:17(18); 33:5,8; 38:25; 43:22; 48:8; 49:9; **Ex.** 2:14; 3:11; 4:11; 5:2; 10:8; 15:11; 16:3; 24:14; 32:24, 26,33; **Num.** 11:4,18,29; 22:9; 23:10; 24:9,23; **Deut.** 3:24; 4:7,8; 5:26,29; 9:2; 20:5–8; 21:1; 30:12,13; 33:29; **Josh.** 9:8; 24:15; **Judg.** 1:1; 6:29; 7:3; 9:28,29,38; 10:18; 13:17; 15:6; 18:3; 20:18; 21:5,8; **Ruth** 2:5; 3:9,16; **1 Sam.** 2:25; 4:8; 6:20; 9:20; 10:12; 11:12; 12:3; 14:17; 17:26,28, 55,56,58; 18:18; 20:10; 22:14; 23:22; 24:14(15); 25:10; 26:6,9,14,15; 30:13,24; **2 Sam.** 1:8; 3:12; 7:18,25; 11:21; 12:22; 15:4; 16:10,19; 18:33(19:1); 20:11; 22:32; 23:15; **1 Kgs.** 1:20,27; 3:9; 20:14; 22:20; **2 Kgs.** 6:11; 9:5,32; 10:9,13; 18:20,35; 19:22; **1 Chr.** 11:17; 17:16,21; 29:5,14; **2 Chr.** 1:10; 2:6(5); 18:19; 32:14; 36:23; **Ezra** 1:3; **Neh.** 6:11; **Esth.** 4:14; 6:4,6; 7:5; **Job** 4:2,7; 5:1; 6:8; 9:4,12,19,24; 11:5,10; 12:3,9; 13:19; 14:4,13; 17:3,15; 19:23; 21:31; 23:3,13; 24:25; 25:3; 26:4,14; 29:2; 31:31,35; 34:7,13,29; 36:22,23; 38:2,5,6,25,28,29,36,37,41; 39:5; 41:10(2),11(3),13(5),14(6); 42:3; **Ps.** 4:6(7); 6:5(6); 12:4(5); 14:7; 15:1; 18:31(32); 19:12(13); 24:3,8,10; 25:12; 27:1; 34:12(13); 35:10; 39:6(7); 53:6; 55:6; 59:7(8); 60:9(11); 64:5(6); 71:19; 73:25; 76:7(8); 77:13(14); 89:6(7),8(9), 48(49); 90:11; 94:16; 106:2; 107:43; 108:10(11); 113:5; 130:3; 147:17; **Prov.** 9:4,16; 18:14; 20:6,9; 23:29; 24:22; 27:4; 30:4,9; 31:10; **Eccl.** 2:19,25; 3:21,22; 4:8; 5:10; 6:12; 7:13,24; 8:1,4,7; 9:4; 10:14; **Song** 3:6; 6:10; 8:1,5; **Isa.** 1:11;

6:8; 10:3; 14:27; 22:16; 23:8; 27:4; 28:9; 29:15; 33:14; 36:5,20; 37:23; 40:12,13, 14,18,25,26; 41:2,4,26; 42:19,23,24; 43:9,13; 44:7,10,24; 45:21; 46:5; 48:14; 49:21; 50:1,8–10; 51:12,19; 53:1,8; 54:15; 57:4,11; 60:8; 63:1; 66:8; **Jer.** 2:24; 6:10; 9:1(8:23); 10:7; 15:5; 17:9; 18:13; 21:13; 23:18; 30:21; 44:28; 46:7; 49:4,19; 50:44; **Lam.** 2:13,20; 3:37; **Ezek.** 27:32; 31:2,18; 32:19; **Hos.** 14:9(10); **Joel** 2:11,14; **Amos** 3:8; 7:2,5; **Obad.** 1:3; **Jon.** 1:7,8; 3:9; **Mic.** 1:5; 6:9; 7:18; **Nah.** 1:6; 3:7,19; **Hag.** 2:3; **Zech.** 4:7,10; **Mal.** 1:10; 3:2.

4311. מֵידְבָא *mēyḏ^e^ḇā'* **proper noun**
(Medeba)
Num. 21:30; **Josh.** 13:9,16; **1 Chr.** 19:7; **Isa.** 15:2.

4312. מֵידָד *mēyḏāḏ* **masc. proper noun**
(Medad)
Num. 11:26,27.

4313. מֵי הַיַּרְקוֹן *mēy hayyarqôn* **proper noun**
(Me Jarkon)
Josh. 19:46.

4314. מֵי זָהָב *mēy zāhāḇ* **masc. proper noun**
(Mezahab)
Gen. 36:39; **1 Chr.** 1:50.

4315. מֵיטָב *mēyṭāḇ* **masc. noun**
(best)
Gen. 47:6,11; **Ex.** 22:5(4); **1 Sam.** 15:9,15.

4316. A. מִיכָא *miyḵā'* **masc. proper noun**
(Mica: son of Mephibosheth)
2 Sam. 9:12.
B. מִיכָא *miyḵā'* **masc. proper noun**
(Mica: a Levite)
1 Chr. 9:15; **Neh.** 10:11(12).
C. מִיכָא *miyḵā'* **masc. proper noun**
(Mica: a Levite)
Neh. 11:17,22.

4317. A. מִיכָאֵל *miyḵā'ēl* **masc. proper noun**
(Michael: the archangel Michael)
Dan. 10:13,21; 12:1.
B. מִיכָאֵל *miyḵā'ēl* **masc. proper noun**
(Michael: father of a spy)
Num. 13:13.
C. מִיכָאֵל *miyḵā'ēl* **masc. proper noun**
(Michael: a Gadite)
1 Chr. 5:13.
D. מִיכָאֵל *miyḵā'ēl* **masc. proper noun**
(Michael: a Gadite)
1 Chr. 5:14.
E. מִיכָאֵל *miyḵā'ēl* **masc. proper noun**
(Michael: a Levite)
1 Chr. 6:40(25).
F. מִיכָאֵל *miyḵā'ēl* **masc. proper noun**
(Michael: chief of Issachar)
1 Chr. 7:3.
G. מִיכָאֵל *miyḵā'ēl* **masc. proper noun**
(Michael: a Benjamite)
1 Chr. 8:16.
H. מִיכָאֵל *miyḵā'ēl* **masc. proper noun**
(Michael: a Manassite captain)
1 Chr. 12:20.
I. מִיכָאֵל *miyḵā'ēl* **masc. proper noun**
(Michael: a man of Issachar)
1 Chr. 27:18.
J. מִיכָאֵל *miyḵā'ēl* **masc. proper noun**
(Michael: son of Jehoshaphat)
2 Chr. 21:2.

K. מִיכָאֵל *miyḵā'ēl* **masc. proper noun**
(Michael: father of Zebadiah)
Ezra 8:8.

4318. A. מִיכָה *miyḵāh* **masc. proper noun**
(Micah: an Ephraimite; see also *miḵāy^e hû* [4321,A])
Judg. 17:5,8–10,12,13; 18:2–4,13,15,18,22,23,26,27,31.
B. מִיכָה *miyḵāh* **masc. proper noun**
(The prophet Micah of Moresheth)
Jer. 26:18(KJV, [K^e] *miyḵāyāh* [4320,A]); **Mic.** 1:1.
C. מִיכָה *miyḵāh* **masc. proper noun**
(Micah: head of a Reubenite family)
1 Chr. 5:5.
D. מִיכָה *miyḵāh* **masc. proper noun**
(Micah: son of Merib-baal)
1 Chr. 8:34,35; 9:40,41.
E. מִיכָה *miyḵāh* **masc. proper noun**
(Micah: a Kohathite)
1 Chr. 23:20; 24:24,25.
F. מִיכָה *miyḵāh* **masc. proper noun**
(Micaiah: son of Imlah)
2 Chr. 18:14.
G. מִיכָה *miyḵāh* **masc. proper noun**
(Micah: father of Abdon)
2 Chr. 34:20.

4319. מִיכָהוּ *miyḵāhû* **masc. proper noun**
(Micaiah: son of Imlah)
2 Chr. 18:8(NASB, NIV, *miyḵāy^e hû* [4321,B]).

4320. A. מִיכָיָה *miyḵāyāh* **proper noun**
(the prophet Micah of Moresheth)
Jer. 26:18(NASB, NIV, [Q^e] *miyḵāh* [4318,B]).
B. מִיכָיָה *miyḵāyāh* **proper noun**
(Micaiah: ancestor of Zechariah)
Neh. 12:35.
C. מִיכָיָה *miyḵāyāh* **proper noun**
(Micaiah: a priest)
Neh. 12:41.
D. מִיכָיָה *miyḵāyāh* **proper noun**
(Micaiah: father of Achbor)
2 Kgs. 22:12.

4321. A. מִיכָיְהוּ *miyḵāy^e hû* **proper noun**
(Micah: an Ephraimite; same as *miyḵāh* [4318,A])
Judg. 17:1,4.
B. מִיכָיְהוּ *miyḵāy^e hû* **proper noun**
(Micaiah: son of Imlah)
1 Kgs. 22:8,9,13–15,24–26,28; **2 Chr.** 18:7,8(KJV, [Q^e] *miyḵāhû* [4319]),12,13,23–25,27.
C. מִיכָיְהוּ *miyḵāy^e hû*, מִכָיְהוּ *miḵāy^e hû* **proper noun**
(Micaiah: son of Gemariah)
Jer. 36:11,13.

4322. A. מִיכָיָהוּ *miyḵāyāhû* **fem. proper noun**
(Micaiah: mother of Abijah)
2 Chr. 13:2.
B. מִיכָיָהוּ *miyḵāyāhû* **masc. proper noun**
(Micaiah: prince under Jehoshaphat)
2 Chr. 17:7.

4323. מִיכָל *miyḵāl* **masc. noun**
(brook)
2 Sam. 17:20.

4324. מִיכַל *miyḵal* **fem. proper noun**
(Michal)
1 Sam. 14:49; 18:20,27,28; 19:11–13,17; 25:44; **2 Sam.** 3:13,14; 6:16,20,21,23; 21:8; **1 Chr.** 15:29.

4325. מַיִם *mayim* **masc. dual or pl. noun**
(water)

Gen. 1:2,6,7,9,10,20–22; 6:17; 7:6,7,10, 17–20,24; 8:1,3,5,7–9,11,13; 9:11,15; 16:7; 18:4; 21:14,15,19,25; 24:11,13,17,32,43; 26:18–20,32; 30:38; 37:24; 43:24; 49:4; **Ex.** 2:10; 4:9; 7:15,17–21,24; 8:6(2), 20(16); 12:9; 14:21,22,26,28,29; 15:8,10, 19,22,23,25,27; 17:1–3,6; 20:4; 23:25; 29:4; 30:18,20; 32:20; 34:28; 40:7,12,30; **Lev.** 1:9,13; 6:28(21); 8:6,21; 11:9,10,12, 32,34,36,38,46; 14:5,6,8,9,50–52; 15:5–8, 10–13,16–18,21,22,27; 16:4,24,26,28; 17:15; 22:6; **Num.** 5:17–19,22–24,26,27; 8:7; 19:7–9,13,17–21; 20:2,5,8,10,11,13, 17,19,24; 21:5,16,22; 24:6,7; 27:14; 31:23; 33:9,14; **Deut.** 2:6,28; 4:18; 5:8; 8:7,15; 9:9,18; 10:7; 11:4,11; 12:16,24; 14:9; 15:23; 23:4(5),11(12); 29:11(10); 32:51; 33:8; **Josh.** 2:10; 3:8,13,15,16; 4:7,18,23; 5:1; 7:5; 9:21,23,27; 11:5,7; 15:7,9,19; 16:1; 18:15; **Judg.** 1:15; 4:19; 5:4,19,25; 6:38; 7:4–6,24; 15:19; **1 Sam.** 7:6; 9:11; 25:11; 26:11,12,16; 30:11,12; **2 Sam.** 5:20; 12:27; 14:14; 17:20,21; 21:10; 22:12,17; 23:15,16; **1 Kgs.** 13:8,9,16–19,22; 14:15; 17:10; 18:4, 5,13,33(34),35,38; 19:6; 22:27; **2 Kgs.** 2:8, 14,19,21,22; 3:9,11,17,19,20,22,25; 5:12; 6:5,22; 8:15; 18:27,31; 19:24; 20:20; **1 Chr.** 11:17,18; 14:11; **2 Chr.** 18:26; 32:3,4,30; **Ezra** 10:6; **Neh.** 3:26; 4:23(17); 8:1,3,16; 9:11,15,20; 12:37; 13:2; **Job** 3:24; 5:10; 8:11; 9:30([K^e] *b^emû* [1119]); 11:16; 12:15; 14:9,11,19; 15:16; 22:7,11; 24:18,19; 26:5,8,10; 27:20; 28:25; 29:19; 34:7; 36:27; 37:10; 38:30,34; **Ps.** 1:3; 18:11(12),15(16),16(17); 22:14(15); 23:2; 29:3; 32:6; 33:7; 42:1(2); 46:3(4); 58:7(8); 63:1(2); 65:9(10); 66:12; 69:1(2), 2(3),14(15),15(16); 73:10; 74:13; 77:16(17),17(18),19(20); 78:13,16,20; 79:3; 81:7(8); 88:17(18); 93:4; 104:3,6; 105:29,41; 106:11,32; 107:23,33,35; 109:18; 114:8; 119:136; 124:4,5; 136:6; 144:7; 147:18; 148:4; **Prov.** 5:15,16; 8:24,29; 9:17; 17:14; 18:4; 20:5; 21:1; 25:21,25; 27:19; 30:4,16; **Eccl.** 2:6; 11:1; **Song** 4:15; 5:12; 8:7; **Isa.** 1:22,30; 3:1; 8:6,7; 11:9; 12:3; 14:23; 15:6,9; 17:12,13; 18:2; 19:5,8; 21:14; 22:9,11; 23:3; 25:10 (KJV, NIV, [Q^e] *b^emû* [1119]); 28:2,17; 30:14,20,25; 32:2,20; 33:16; 35:6,7; 36:12,16; 37:25; 40:12; 41:17,18; 43:2, 16,20; 44:3,4,12; 48:1,21; 49:10; 50:2; 51:10; 54:9; 55:1; 57:20; 58:11; 63:12; 64:2(1); **Jer.** 2:13,18; 6:7; 8:14; 9:1(8:23), 15(14),18(17); 10:13; 13:1; 14:3; 15:18; 17:8,13; 18:14; 23:15; 31:9; 38:6; 41:12; 46:7,8; 47:2; 48:34; 50:38; 51:13,16,55; **Lam.** 1:16; 2:19; 3:48,54; 5:4; **Ezek.** 1:24; 4:11,16,17; 7:17; 12:18,19; 16:4,9; 17:5,8; 19:10; 21:7(12); 24:3; 26:12,19; 27:26,34; 31:4,5,7,14–16; 32:2,13,14; 34:18; 36:25; 43:2; 47:1–5,8,9,12,19; 48:28; **Dan.** 1:12; 12:6,7; **Hos.** 2:5(7); 5:10; 10:7; **Joel** 1:20; 3:18(4:18); **Amos** 4:8; 5:8,24; 8:11; 9:6; **Jon.** 2:5(6); 3:7; **Mic.** 1:4; **Nah.** 2:8(9); 3:8,14; **Hab.** 2:14; 3:10,15; **Zech.** 9:11; 14:8.

4326. A. מִיָּמִן *miyyāmin* **masc. proper noun**
(Mijamin: descendant of Aaron)
1 Chr. 24:9.
B. מִיָּמִן *miyyāmin* **masc. proper noun**
(Mijamin: postexilic Jew)
Ezra 10:25.
C. מִיָּמִן *miyyāmin* **masc. proper noun**
(Mijamin: a priest)
Neh. 10:7(8).
D. מִיָּמִן *miyyāmin* **masc. proper noun**
(Mijamin: a priest)
Neh. 12:5.

4327. מִין *miyn* **masc. noun**
(kind, species)
Gen. 1:11,12,21,24,25; 6:20; 7:14; **Lev.** 11:14–16,19,22,29; **Deut.** 14:13–15,18; **Ezek.** 47:10.

4328. מְיֻסָּדָה *m^eyussāḏāh* **fem. noun**
(foundation)
Ezek. 41:8(NASB, NIV, [Q^e] *mûsāḏāh* [4145]).

4329. מוּסַךְ *mûsak̲* **masc. noun**
(covered structure, canopy)
2 Kgs. 16:18.

4330. מִיץ *miyṣ* **masc. noun**
(a churning, a twisting, a stirring)
Prov. 30:33.

4331. מֵישָׁא *mēyšā'* **masc. proper noun**
(Mesha)
1 Chr. 8:9.

4332. A. מִישָׁאֵל *miyšā'ēl* **masc. proper noun**
(Mishael: cousin of Moses)
Ex. 6:22; **Lev.** 10:4.
B. מִישָׁאֵל *miyšā'ēl* **masc. proper noun**
(Mishael: companion of Daniel)
Dan. 1:6,7,11,19.
C. מִישָׁאֵל *miyšā'ēl* **masc. proper noun**
(Mishael: postexilic Jew)
Neh. 8:4.

4333. מִישָׁאֵל *miyšā'ēl* **Aram. masc. proper noun**
(Mishael; corr. to Hebr. 4332,B)
Dan. 2:17.

4334. מִישׁוֹר *miyšôr* **masc. noun**
(level place, plain, uprightness)
Deut. 3:10; 4:43; **Josh.** 13:9,16,17,21; 20:8; **1 Kgs.** 20:23,25; **2 Chr.** 26:10; **Ps.** 26:12; 27:11; 45:6(7); 67:4(5); 143:10; **Isa.** 11:4; 40:4; 42:16; **Jer.** 21:13; 48:8,21; **Zech.** 4:7; **Mal.** 2:6.

4335. מֵישַׁךְ *mēyšak̲* **masc. proper noun**
(Meshach)
Dan. 1:7.

4336. מֵישַׁךְ *mēyšak̲* **Aram. masc. proper noun**
(Meshach; corr. to Hebr. 4335)
Dan. 2:49; 3:12–14,16,19,20,22,23,26,28–30.

4337. מֵישָׁע *mēyšā'* **masc. proper noun**
(Mesha: son of Caleb)
1 Chr. 2:42.

4338. מֵישַׁע *mēyša'* **masc. proper noun**
(Mesha: king of Moab)
2 Kgs. 3:4.

4339. מֵישָׁר *mēyšār* **masc. noun**
(rightness, equity, smoothness)
1 Chr. 29:17; **Ps.** 9:8(9); 17:2; 58:1(2); 75:2(3); 96:10; 98:9; 99:4; **Prov.** 1:3; 2:9; 8:6; 23:16,31; **Song** 1:4; 7:9(10); **Isa.** 26:7; 33:15; 45:19; **Dan.** 11:6.

4340. מֵיתָר *mēyt̲ār* **masc. noun**
(cord, string)
Ex. 35:18; 39:40; **Num.** 3:26,37; 4:26,32; **Ps.** 21:12(13); **Isa.** 54:2; **Jer.** 10:20.

4341. מַכְאוֹב *mak̲'ôb̲* **masc. noun**
(pain, suffering, sorrow)
Ex. 3:7; **2 Chr.** 6:29; **Job** 33:19; **Ps.** 32:10; 38:17(18); 69:26(27); **Eccl.** 1:18; 2:23; **Isa.** 53:3,4; **Jer.** 30:15; 45:3; 51:8; **Lam.** 1:12,18.

4342. מַכְבִּיר *mak̲biyr* **masc. noun**
(abundance)
Job 36:31(NASB, NIV, *kāb̲ar* [3527]).

4343. מַכְבֵּנָה *mak̲bēnāh* **masc. proper noun**
(Machbenah)
1 Chr. 2:49.

4344. מַכְבַּנַּי *mak̲bannay* **masc. proper noun**

(Machbannai)
1 Chr. 12:13.

4345. מִכְבָּר *mikbār* **masc. noun**
(grating, cover)
Ex. 27:4; 35:16; 38:4,5,30; 39:39.

4346. מַכְבֵּר *makbēr* **masc. noun**
(thick cloth, light blanket)
2 Kgs. 8:15.

4347. מַכָּה *makkāh* **fem. noun**
(blow, wound, slaughter, plague)
Lev. 26:21; **Num.** 11:33; **Deut.** 25:3; 28:59,61; 29:22(21); **Josh.** 10:10,20; **Judg.** 11:33; 15:8; **1 Sam.** 4:8,10; 6:19; 14:14,30; 19:8; 23:5; **1 Kgs.** 20:21; 22:35; **2 Kgs.** 8:29; 9:15; **2 Chr.** 2:10(9); 13:17; 22:6; 28:5; **Esth.** 9:5; **Ps.** 64:7(8); **Prov.** 20:30; **Isa.** 1:6; 10:26; 14:6; 27:7; 30:26; **Jer.** 6:7; 10:19; 14:17; 15:18; 19:8; 30:12,14,17; 49:17; 50:13; **Mic.** 1:9; **Nah.** 3:19; **Zech.** 13:6.

4348. מִכְוָה *mikwāh* **fem. noun**
(burnt spot)
Lev. 13:24,25,28.

4349. I. מָכוֹן *mākôn* **masc. noun**
(dwelling place, esp. of God)
Ex. 15:17; **1 Kgs.** 8:13,39,43,49; **2 Chr.** 6:2,30,33,39; **Ezra** 2:68; **Ps.** 33:14; **Isa.** 4:5; 18:4; **Dan.** 8:11.
II. מָכוֹן *mākôn* **masc. noun**
(foundation, basis)
Ps. 89:14(15); 97:2; 104:5.

4350. מְכוֹנָה *m*e*kônāh,* מְכֹנָה *m*e*kōnāh* **fem. noun**
(moveable stand, pedestal)
1 Kgs. 7:27,28,30,32,34,35,37–39,43; **2 Kgs.** 16:17; 25:13,16; **2 Chr.** 4:14; **Ezra** 3:3; **Jer.** 27:19; 52:17,20; **Zech.** 5:11(see *m*e*kunāh* [4369]).

4351. מְכוּרָה *m*e*kûrāh,* מְכֹרָה *m*e*kōrāh* **fem. noun**
(birth, origin, ancestry)
Ezek. 16:3; 21:30(35); 29:14.

4352. מָכִי *mākiy* **masc. proper noun**
(Machi)
Num. 13:15.

4353. A. מָכִיר *makiyr* **masc. proper noun**
(Machir: son of Ammiel)
2 Sam. 9:4,5; 17:27.
B. מָכִיר *makiyr* **masc. proper noun**
(Machir: son of Manasseh)
Gen. 50:23; **Num.** 26:29; 27:1; 32:39,40; 36:1; **Deut.** 3:15; **Josh.** 13:31; 17:1,3; **Judg.** 5:14; **1 Chr.** 2:21,23; 7:14–17.

4354. מָכִירִי *mākiyriy* **masc. proper noun**
(Machirite)
Num. 26:29.

4355. מָכַךְ *mākak* **verb**
(to be made low, to sag, to decay)
Job 24:24; **Ps.** 106:43; **Eccl.** 10:18.

4356. מִכְלָאָה *miklā'āh,* מִכְלָה *miklāh* **fem. noun**
(enclosure, pen)
Ps. 50:9; 78:70; **Hab.** 3:17.

4357. מִכְלָה *miklāh* **fem. noun**
(perfection, purity)
2 Chr. 4:21.

4358. מִכְלוֹל *miklôl* **masc. noun**
(perfection, splendor)
Ezek. 23:12; 38:4.

4359. מִכְלָל *miklāl* **masc. noun**
(perfection)
Ps. 50:2.

4360. מַכְלוּל *maklûl* **masc. noun**
(perfection, beauty)
Ezek. 27:24.

4361. מַכֹּלֶת *makkōleṯ* **fem. noun**
(food)
1 Kgs. 5:11(25).

4362. מִכְמָן *mik̲mān* **masc. noun**
(hidden treasure)
Dan. 11:43.

4363. מִכְמָס *mik̲mās,* מִכְמָשׂ *mik̲māś* **proper noun**
(Michmash)
1 Sam. 13:2,5,11,16,23; 14:5,31; **Ezra** 2:27; **Neh.** 7:31; 11:31; **Isa.** 10:28.

4364. מַכְמֹר *mak̲mōr,* מִכְמָר *mik̲mār* **masc. noun**
(net, ensnarement)
Ps. 141:10; **Isa.** 51:20.

4365. מִכְמֶרֶת *mik̲mereṯ,* מִכְמֹרֶת *mik̲mōreṯ* **fem. noun**
(fishing net, dragnet)
Isa. 19:8; **Hab.** 1:15,16.

4366. מִכְמְתָת *mik̲m^{e}ṯāṯ* **proper noun**
(Michmethah)
Josh. 16:6; 17:7.

4367. מַכְנַדְבַי *mak̲nadḇay* **proper noun**
(Machnadebai)
Ezra 10:40.

4368. מְכֹנָה *m^{e}k̲ōnāh* **proper noun**
(Meconah)
Neh. 11:28.

4369. מְכֻנָה *m^{e}k̲unāh* **fem. noun**
(pedestal, base; form of *m^{e}k̲ônāh* [4350])
Zech. 5:11.

4370. מִכְנָס *mik̲nās* **masc. noun**
(underwear, breeches)
Ex. 28:42; 39:28; **Lev.** 6:10(3); 16:4; **Ezek.** 44:18.

4371. מֶכֶס *mek̲es* **masc. noun**
(tribute, tax)
Num. 31:28,37–41.

4372. מִכְסֶה *mik̲seh* **masc. noun**
(covering)
Gen. 8:13; **Ex.** 26:14; 35:11; 36:19; 39:34; 40:19; **Num.** 3:25; 4:8,10–12,25.

4373. מִכְסָה *mik̲sāh* **fem. noun**
(evaluation, number, worth)
Ex. 12:4; **Lev.** 27:23.

4374. מְכַסֶּה *m^{e}k̲asseh* **masc. noun**
(covering, clothes)
Lev. 9:19; **Isa.** 14:11; 23:18; **Ezek.** 27:7.

4375. מַכְפֵּלָה *mak̲pēlāh* **proper noun**
(Machpelah)
Gen. 23:9,17,19; 25:9; 49:30; 50:13.

4376. מָכַר *māk̲ar* **verb**
(to sell)
Gen. 25:31,33; 31:15; 37:27,28,36; 45:4,5; 47:20,22; **Ex.** 21:7,8,16,35; 22:1 (21:37),3(2); **Lev.** 25:14–16,23,25,27,29, 34,39,42,47,48,50; 27:20,27,28; **Deut.** 14:21; 15:12; 21:14; 24:7; 28:68; 32:30; **Judg.** 2:14; 3:8; 4:2,9; 10:7; **Ruth** 4:3; **1 Sam.** 12:9; **1 Kgs.** 21:20,25; **2 Kgs.** 4:7; 17:17; **Neh.** 5:8; 10:31(32); 13:15, 16,20; **Esth.** 7:4; **Ps.** 44:12(13); 105:17; **Prov.** 23:23; 31:24; **Isa.** 24:2; 50:1; 52:3; **Jer.** 34:14; **Ezek.** 7:12,13; 30:12; 48:14; **Joel** 3:3(4:3),6–8(4:6–8); **Amos** 2:6; **Nah.** 3:4; **Zech.** 11:5.

4377. מֶכֶר *mek̲er* **masc. noun**
(merchandise, price, worth)
Num. 20:19; **Neh.** 13:16; **Prov.** 31:10.

4378. I. מַכָּר *makkār* **masc. noun**
(acquaintance, friend)
2 Kgs. 12:5(6)(NIV, see II),7(8)(NIV, see II).
II. מַכָּר *makkār* **masc. noun**
(treasurer)

2 Kgs. 12:5(6)(KJV, NASB, see I),7(8) (KJV, NASB, see I).

4379. מִכְרֶה *mikreh* **masc. noun**
(pit [of salt])
Zeph. 2:9.

4380. I. מְכֵרָה *m^e^kērāh* **fem. noun**
(sword)
Gen. 49:5(KJV, see II).
II. מְכֵרָה *m^e^kērāh* **fem. noun**
(habitation, dwelling)
Gen. 49:5(NASB, NIV, see I).

4381. מִכְרִי *mikriy* **masc. proper noun**
(Michri)
1 Chr. 9:8.

4382. מְכֵרָתִי *m^e^kērātiy* **masc. proper noun**
(Mecherathite)
1 Chr. 11:36.

4383. מִכְשׁוֹל *mikšôl* **masc. noun**
(stumbling, cause of stumbling)
Lev. 19:14; **1 Sam.** 25:31; **Ps.** 119:165; **Isa.** 8:14; 57:14; **Jer.** 6:21; **Ezek.** 3:20; 7:19; 14:3,4,7; 18:30; 21:15(20); 44:12.

4384. מַכְשֵׁלָה *makšēlāh* **fem. noun**
(ruin, heap of rubble)
Isa. 3:6; **Zeph.** 1:3.

4385. מִכְתָּב *miktāb* **masc. noun**
(writing, something written)
Ex. 32:16; 39:30; **Deut.** 10:4; **2 Chr.** 21:12; 35:4; 36:22; **Ezra** 1:1; **Isa.** 38:9.

4386. מְכִתָּה *m^e^kittāh* **fem. noun**
(a bursting, shattering)
Isa. 30:14.

4387. מִכְתָּם *miktām* **masc. noun**
(Michtam: a type of psalm; meaning uncertain)
Ps. 16:[title](1); 56:[title](1); 57:[title](1); 58:[title](1); 59:[title](1); 60:[title](1).

4388. מַכְתֵּשׁ *maktēš* **masc. noun**
(depression, a hollow place in a jawbone or mortar bowl)
Judg. 15:19; **Prov.** 27:22.

4389. I. מַכְתֵּשׁ *maktēš* **proper noun**
(Maktesh)
Zeph. 1:11(NASB, see II; NIV, see III).
II. מַכְתֵּשׁ *maktēš* **proper noun**
(Mortar)
Zeph. 1:11(KJV, see I; NIV, see III).
III. מַכְתֵּשׁ *maktēš* **masc. noun**
(market district)
Zeph. 1:11(KJV, see I; NASB, see II).

4390. מָלֵא *mālēʾ* **verb**
(to fill, to replenish, to fulfill; to be full)
Gen. 1:22,28; 6:11,13; 9:1; 21:19; 24:16; 25:24; 26:15; 29:21,27,28; 42:25; 44:1; 50:3; **Ex.** 1:7; 2:16; 7:25; 8:21(17); 10:6; 15:9; 23:26; 28:3,17,41; 29:9,29,33,35; 31:3,5; 32:29; 35:31,33,35; 39:10; 40:34,35; **Lev.** 8:33; 9:17; 12:4,6; 16:32; 19:29; 21:10; 25:30; **Num.** 3:3; 6:5,13; 14:21,24; 32:11,12; **Deut.** 1:36; 6:11; **Josh.** 3:15; 9:13; 14:8,9,14; **Judg.** 16:27; 17:5,12; **1 Sam.** 16:1; 18:26,27; **2 Sam.** 7:12; 23:7; **1 Kgs.** 1:14; 2:27; 7:14; 8:10, 11,15,24; 11:6; 13:33; 18:33,35; 20:27; **2 Kgs.** 3:17,20,25; 4:6; 6:17; 9:24; 10:21; 21:16; 23:14; 24:4; **1 Chr.** 12:15; 17:11; 29:5; **2 Chr.** 5:13,14; 6:4,15; 7:1,2; 13:9; 16:14; 29:31; 36:21; **Ezra** 9:11; **Esth.** 1:5; 2:12; 3:5; 5:9; 7:5; **Job** 3:15; 8:21; 15:2,32; 16:10; 20:11,22,23; 21:24; 22:18; 23:4; 32:18; 36:16,17; 38:39; 39:2; 41:7 (40:31); **Ps.** 10:7; 17:14; 20:4(5),5(6); 26:10; 33:5; 38:7(8); 48:10(11); 65:9(10); 71:8; 72:19; 74:20; 80:9(10); 81:10(11); 83:16(17); 104:24; 107:9; 110:6; 119:64; 126:2; 127:5; 129:7; **Prov.** 1:13; 3:10; 6:30; 8:21; 12:21; 20:17; 24:4; **Eccl.** 1:8; 6:7; 8:11; 9:3; 11:3; **Song** 5:2,14; **Isa.** 1:15; 2:6–8; 6:4; 11:9; 13:21; 14:21; 15:9; 21:3; 22:7; 23:2; 27:6; 28:8; 30:27; 33:5;

34:6; 40:2; 65:11,20; **Jer.** 4:5; 6:11; 13:12,13; 15:17; 16:18; 19:4; 23:10,24; 25:12,34; 29:10; 31:25; 33:5; 41:9; 44:25; 46:12; 51:5,11,14,34; **Lam.** 4:18; **Ezek.** 3:3; 5:2; 7:19,23; 8:17; 9:7,9; 10:2–4; 11:6; 23:33; 24:4; 26:2; 27:25; 28:16; 30:11; 32:5,6; 35:8; 43:5,26; 44:4; **Dan.** 9:2; 10:3; **Joel** 2:24; 3:13(4:13); **Mic.** 3:8; 6:12; **Nah.** 1:10(NASB, NIV, *mālē'* [4392]); 2:12(13); **Hab.** 2:14; 3:3; **Zeph.** 1:9; **Hag.** 2:7; **Zech.** 8:5; 9:13,15.

4391. מְלָא *m^elā'* **Aram. verb**
(to fill, to be filled; corr. to Hebr. 4390)
Dan. 2:35; 3:19.

4392. מָלֵא *mālē'* **adj.**
(full, filled)
Gen. 23:9; 41:7,22; **Num.** 7:13,14,19, 20,25,26,31,32,37,38,43,44,49,50,55,56, 61,62,67,68,73,74,79,80,86; **Deut.** 6:11; 33:23; 34:9; **Judg.** 6:38(NASB, NIV, *m^elō'* [4393]); **Ruth** 1:21; **2 Sam.** 23:11; **2 Kgs.** 4:4; 7:15; **1 Chr.** 11:13; 21:22,24; **Neh.** 9:25; **Ps.** 73:10; 75:8(9); 144:13; **Prov.** 17:1; **Eccl.** 1:7; 11:5; **Isa.** 1:21; 22:2; 51:20; **Jer.** 4:12; 5:27; 6:11; 12:6; 35:5; **Ezek.** 1:18; 10:12; 17:3; 28:12; 36:38; 37:1; **Amos** 2:13; **Nah.** 1:10 (KJV, *mālē'* [4390]); 3:1.

4393. מְלֹא *m^elō'*, מְלוֹא *m^elô'*, מְלוֹ *m^elô* **masc. noun**
(that which fills something, everything)
Gen. 48:19; **Ex.** 9:8; 16:32,33; **Lev.** 2:2; 5:12; 16:12; **Num.** 22:18; 24:13; **Deut.** 33:16; **Judg.** 6:38(KJV, *mālē'* [4392]); **1 Sam.** 28:20; **2 Sam.** 8:2; **1 Kgs.** 17:12; **2 Kgs.** 4:39; **1 Chr.** 16:32; **Ps.** 24:1; 50:12; 89:11(12); 96:11; 98:7; **Eccl.** 4:6; **Isa.** 6:3; 8:8; 31:4; 34:1; 42:10; **Jer.** 8:16; 47:2; **Ezek.** 12:19; 19:7; 30:12; 32:15; 41:8; **Amos** 6:8; **Mic.** 1:2.

4394. מִלֻּא *millu'*, מִלּוּא *millû'* **masc. noun**
(a setting, mounting; ordination)
Ex. 25:7(NIV, *millu'āh* [4396]); 29:22, 26,27,31,34; 35:9,27; **Lev.** 7:37; 8:22, 28,29,31,33; **1 Chr.** 29:2.

4395. מְלֵאָה *m^elē'āh* **fem. noun**
(full harvest, produce of grain)
Ex. 22:29(28); **Num.** 18:27; **Deut.** 22:9.

4396. מִלֻּאָה *millu'āh* **fem. noun**
(a mounting, setting [of gemstones])
Ex. 25:7(KJV, NASB, *millu'* [4394]); 28:17,20; 39:13.

4397. מַלְאָךְ *mal'āk̲* **masc. noun**
(messenger, angel)
Gen. 16:7,9–11; 19:1,15; 21:17; 22:11,15; 24:7,40; 28:12; 31:11; 32:1(2),3(4),6(7); 48:16; **Ex.** 3:2; 14:19; 23:20,23; 32:34; 33:2; **Num.** 20:14,16; 21:21; 22:5,22–27, 31,32,34,35; 24:12; **Deut.** 2:26; **Josh.** 6:17,25; 7:22; **Judg.** 2:1,4; 5:23; 6:11,12, 20–22,35; 7:24; 9:31; 11:12–14,17,19; 13:3,6,9,13,15–18,20,21; **1 Sam.** 6:21; 11:3,4,7,9; 16:19; 19:11,14–16,20,21; 23:27; 25:14,42; 29:9; **2 Sam.** 2:5; 3:12,14,26; 5:11; 11:4,19,22,23,25; 12:27; 14:17,20; 19:27(28); 24:16,17; **1 Kgs.** 13:18; 19:2,5,7; 20:2,5,9; 22:13; **2 Kgs.** 1:2,3,5,15,16; 5:10; 6:32,33; 7:15; 9:18; 10:8; 14:8; 16:7; 17:4; 19:9,14,23,35; **1 Chr.** 14:1; 19:2,16; 21:12,15,16,18,20, 27,30; **2 Chr.** 18:12; 32:21; 35:21; 36:15,16; **Neh.** 6:3; **Job** 1:14; 4:18; 33:23; **Ps.** 34:7(8); 35:5,6; 78:49; 91:11; 103:20; 104:4; 148:2; **Prov.** 13:17; 16:14; 17:11; **Eccl.** 5:6(5); **Isa.** 14:32; 18:2; 30:4; 33:7; 37:9,14,36; 42:19; 44:26; 63:9; **Jer.** 27:3; **Ezek.** 17:15; 23:16,40; 30:9; **Hos.** 12:4(5); **Nah.** 2:13(14); **Hag.** 1:13; **Zech.** 1:9,11–14,19(2:2); 2:3(7); 3:1,3,5,6; 4:1,4,5; 5:5,10; 6:4,5; 12:8; **Mal.** 2:7; 3:1.

4398. מַלְאַךְ *mal'ak̲* **Aram. masc. noun**
(messenger, angel; corr. to

Hebr. 4397)
Dan. 3:28; 6:22(23).

4399. מְלָאכָה *m^el^ā'<u>k</u>āh* **fem. noun**
(work, task, workmanship)
Gen. 2:2,3; 33:14; 39:11; **Ex.** 12:16; 20:9,10; 22:8(7),11(10); 31:3,5,14,15; 35:2,21,24,29,31,33,35; 36:1–8; 38:24; 39:43; 40:33; **Lev.** 7:24; 11:32; 13:48,51; 16:29; 23:3,7,8,21,25,28,30,31,35,36; **Num.** 4:3; 28:18,25,26; 29:1,7,12,35; **Deut.** 5:13,14; 16:8; **Judg.** 16:11; **1 Sam.** 8:16; 15:9; **1 Kgs.** 5:16(30); 7:14,22,40,51; 9:23; 11:28; **2 Kgs.** 12:11(12),14(15),15(16); 22:5,9; **1 Chr.** 4:23; 6:49(34); 9:13,19,33; 22:15; 23:4,24; 25:1; 26:29,30; 27:26; 28:13,19–21; 29:1, 5,6; **2 Chr.** 4:11; 5:1; 8:9,16; 13:10; 16:5; 17:13; 24:12,13; 29:34; 34:10,12,13,17; **Ezra** 2:69; 3:8,9; 6:22; 10:13; **Neh.** 2:16; 4:11(5),15–17(9–11),19(13),21(15),22(16); 5:16; 6:3,9,16; 7:70,71; 10:33(34); 11:12,16,22; 13:10,30; **Esth.** 3:9; 9:3; **Ps.** 73:28; 107:23; **Prov.** 18:9; 22:29; 24:27; **Jer.** 17:22,24; 18:3; 48:10; 50:25; **Ezek.** 15:3–5; 28:13; **Dan.** 8:27; **Jon.** 1:8; **Hag.** 1:14.

4400. מַלְאָכוּת *mal'ā<u>k</u>û<u>t</u>* **fem. noun**
(message)
Hag. 1:13.

4401. מַלְאָכִי *mal'ā<u>k</u>iy* **masc. proper noun**
(Malachi)
Mal. 1:1.

4402. מִלֵּאת *millē'<u>t</u>* **fem. noun**
(fullness, appropriateness)
Song 5:12.

4403. מַלְבּוּשׁ *malbûš* **masc. proper noun**
(clothing, robes, attire)
1 Kgs. 10:5; **2 Kgs.** 10:22; **2 Chr.** 9:4; **Job** 27:16; **Isa.** 63:3; **Ezek.** 16:13; **Zeph.** 1:8.

4404. מַלְבֵּן *malbēn* **masc. noun**
(brick kiln, brickwork)
2 Sam. 12:31; **Jer.** 43:9; **Nah.** 3:14.

4405. מִלָּה *millāh* **fem. noun**
(word, speech)
2 Sam. 23:2; **Job** 4:2,4; 6:26; 8:10; 12:11; 13:17; 15:3,13; 16:4; 18:2; 19:2,23; 21:2; 23:5; 24:25; 26:4; 29:9,22; 30:9; 32:11, 14,15,18; 33:1,8,32; 34:2,3,16; 35:4,16; 36:2,4; 38:2; **Ps.** 19:4(5); 139:4; **Prov.** 23:9.

4406. מִלָּה *millāh* **Aram. fem. noun**
(word, matter; corr. to Hebr. 4405)
Dan. 2:5,8–11,15,17,23; 3:22,28; 4:31(28),33(30); 5:10,15,26; 6:12(13), 14(15); 7:1,11,16,25,28.

4407. I. מִלּוֹא *millô'* **proper noun**
(citadel in Jerusalem)
2 Sam. 5:9(NIV, see II); **1 Kgs.** 9:15 (NIV, see II),24(NIV, see II); 11:27(NIV, see II); **2 Kgs.** 12:20(21)(NIV, see *bēyt millô'* [1037]); **1 Chr.** 11:8(NIV, see II); **2 Chr.** 32:5(NIV, see II).
II. מִלּוֹא *millô'* **masc. noun**
(supporting terraces; KJV, NASB, see I)
2 Sam. 5:9; **1 Kgs.** 9:15,24; 11:27; **1 Chr.** 11:8; **2 Chr.** 32:5.
III. מִלּוֹא *millô'* **proper noun**
(Millo: loc. near Shechem)
Judg. 9:6(NASB, NIV, see *bēy<u>t</u> millô'* [1037,I]),20(NASB, NIV, see *bēy<u>t</u> millô'* [1037,I]).

4408. מַלּוּחַ *mallûaḥ* **masc. noun**
(mallow, herbs growing in salt marshes)
Job 30:4.

4409. A. מַלּוּךְ *mallû<u>k</u>* **masc. proper noun**
(Malluch: son of Hashabiah)
1 Chr. 6:44(29).

B. מַלּוּךְ *mallûḵ* **masc. proper noun**
(Malluch: a priest)
Neh. 12:2.
C. מַלּוּךְ *mallûḵ* **masc. proper noun**
(Malluch: son of Bani)
Ezra 10:29.
D. מַלּוּךְ *mallûḵ* **masc. proper noun**
(Malluch: son of Harim)
Ezra 10:32.
E. מַלּוּךְ *mallûḵ* **masc. proper noun**
(Malluch: a covenanter)
Neh. 10:4(5).
F. מַלּוּךְ *mallûḵ* **masc. proper noun**
(Malluch: a Jewish leader)
Neh. 10:27(28).
G. מַלּוּכִי *mallûḵiy* **masc. proper noun**
(Malluch: a priest)
Neh. 12:14.

4410. מְלוּכָה *m^{e}lûḵāh* **fem. noun**
(kingdom, royalty)
1 Sam. 10:16,25; 11:14; 14:47; 18:8; **2 Sam.** 12:26; 16:8; **1 Kgs.** 1:46; 2:15,22; 11:35; 12:21; 21:7; **2 Kgs.** 25:25; **1 Chr.** 10:14; **Ps.** 22:28(29); **Isa.** 34:12; 62:3; **Jer.** 41:1; **Ezek.** 16:13; 17:13; **Dan.** 1:3; **Obad.** 1:21.

4411. מָלוֹן *mālôn* **masc. noun**
(lodging place, inn)
Gen. 42:27; 43:21; **Ex.** 4:24; **Josh.** 4:3,8; **2 Kgs.** 19:23; **Isa.** 10:29; **Jer.** 9:2(1).

4412. מְלוּנָה *m^{e}lûnāh* **fem. noun**
(cottage, hut)
Isa. 1:8; 24:20.

4413. מַלּוֹתִי *mallôṯiy* **masc. proper noun**
(Mallothi)
1 Chr. 25:4,26.

4414. I. מָלַח *mālaḥ* **verb**
(to salt, to season)
Ex. 30:35; **Lev.** 2:13; **Ezek.** 16:4.
II. מָלַח *mālaḥ* **verb**
(to tear away, to dissipate, to vanish)
Isa. 51:6.

4415. מְלַח *m^{e}laḥ* **Aram. verb**
(to be in service [to one who pays with salt]; corr. to Hebr. 4414,I)
Ezra 4:14.

4416. מְלַח *m^{e}laḥ* **Aram. masc. noun**
(salt; corr. to Hebr. 4417)
Ezra 4:14; 6:9; 7:22.

4417. מֶלַח *melaḥ* **masc. noun**
(salt)
Gen. 14:3; 19:26; **Lev.** 2:13; **Num.** 18:19; 34:3,12; **Deut.** 3:17; 29:23(22); **Josh.** 3:16; 12:3; 15:2,5; 18:19; **Judg.** 9:45; **2 Sam.** 8:13; **2 Kgs.** 2:20,21; 14:7; **1 Chr.** 18:12; **2 Chr.** 13:5; 25:11; **Job** 6:6; **Ps.** 60:[title](1); **Ezek.** 43:24; 47:11; **Zeph.** 2:9.

4418. מֶלַח *melaḥ* **masc. noun**
(rag)
Jer. 38:11,12.

4419. מַלָּח *mallāḥ* **masc. noun**
(sailor, mariner)
Ezek. 27:9,27,29; **Jon.** 1:5.

4420. מְלֵחָה *m^{e}lēḥāh* **fem. noun**
(barrenness, saltiness)
Job 39:6; **Ps.** 107:34; **Jer.** 17:6.

4421. מִלְחָמָה *milḥāmāh* **fem. noun**
(war, battle)
Gen. 14:2,8; **Ex.** 1:10; 13:17; 15:3; 17:16; 32:17; **Num.** 10:9; 21:14,33; 31:14,21, 27,28,49; 32:6,20,27,29; **Deut.** 1:41; 2:9, 14,16,24,32; 3:1; 4:34; 20:1–3,5–7,12,20; 21:10; 29:7(6); **Josh.** 4:13; 5:4,6; 6:3; 8:1,3,11,14; 10:7,24; 11:7,18–20,23;

14:11,15; 17:1; **Judg.** 3:1,2,10; 8:13; 18:11,16,17; 20:14,17,18,20,22,23,28, 34,39,42; 21:22; **1 Sam.** 4:1,2; 7:10; 8:12,20; 13:22; 14:20,22,23,52; 16:18; 17:1,2,8,13,20,28,33,47; 18:5,17; 19:8; 23:8; 25:28; 26:10; 29:4,9; 30:24; 31:3; **2 Sam.** 1:4,25,27; 2:17; 3:1,6,30; 8:10; 10:8,9,13; 11:7,15,18,19,25; 17:8; 18:6,8; 19:3(4),10(11); 21:15,17–20; 22:35,40; 23:9; **1 Kgs.** 2:5; 5:3(17); 8:44; 9:22; 12:21; 14:30; 15:6,7,16,32; 20:14,18, 26,29,39; 22:1,4,6,15,30,35; **2 Kgs.** 3:7,26; 8:28; 13:25; 14:7; 16:5; 18:20; 24:16; 25:4,19; **1 Chr.** 5:10,18–20,22; 7:4,11,40; 10:3; 11:13; 12:1,8,19,33, 35–38; 14:15; 18:10; 19:7,9,10,14,17; 20:4–6; 22:8; 26:27; 28:3; **2 Chr.** 6:34; 8:9; 11:1; 12:15; 13:2,3,14; 14:6(5),10(9); 15:19; 16:9; 17:13; 18:3,5,14,29,34; 20:1,15; 22:5; 25:8,13; 26:11,13; 27:7; 32:2,6,8; 35:21; **Job** 5:20; 38:23; 39:25; 41:8(40:32); **Ps.** 18:34(35),39(40); 24:8; 27:3; 46:9(10); 76:3(4); 89:43(44); 120:7; 140:2(3); 144:1; **Prov.** 20:18; 21:31; 24:6; **Eccl.** 3:8; 8:8; 9:11; **Song** 3:8; **Isa.** 2:4; 3:2,25; 7:1; 13:4; 21:15; 22:2; 27:4; 28:6; 30:32; 36:5; 41:12; 42:13,25; **Jer.** 4:19; 6:4,23; 8:6; 18:21; 21:4; 28:8; 38:4; 39:4; 41:3,16; 42:14; 46:3; 48:14; 49:2, 14,26; 50:22,30,42; 51:20,32; 52:7,25; **Ezek.** 7:14; 13:5; 17:17; 27:10,27; 32:27; 39:20; **Dan.** 9:26; 11:20,25; **Hos.** 1:7; 2:18(20); 10:9,14; **Joel** 2:5,7; 3:9(4:9); **Amos** 1:14; **Obad.** 1:1; **Mic.** 2:8; 3:5; 4:3; **Zech.** 9:10; 10:3–5; 14:2.

4422. מָלַט *mālaṭ* **verb**
(to escape, to deliver)
Gen. 19:17,19,20,22; **Judg.** 3:26,29; **1 Sam.** 19:10–12,17,18; 20:29; 22:1,20; 23:13; 27:1; 30:17; **2 Sam.** 1:3; 4:6; 19:5(6),9(10); **1 Kgs.** 1:12; 18:40; 19:17; 20:20; **2 Kgs.** 10:24; 19:37; 23:18; **2 Chr.** 16:7; **Esth.** 4:13; **Job** 1:15–17,19; 6:23; 19:20; 20:20; 22:30; 29:12; 41:19(11); **Ps.** 22:5(6); 33:17; 41:1(2); 89:48(49); 107:20; 116:4; 124:7; **Prov.** 11:21; 19:5; 28:26; **Eccl.** 7:26; 8:8; 9:15; **Isa.** 20:6; 31:5; 34:15; 37:38; 46:2,4; 49:24,25; 66:7; **Jer.** 32:4; 34:3; 38:18,23; 39:18; 41:15; 46:6; 48:6,8,19; 51:6,45; **Ezek.** 17:15,18; 33:5; **Dan.** 11:41; 12:1; **Joel** 2:32(3:5); **Amos** 2:14,15; 9:1; **Zech.** 2:7(11); **Mal.** 3:15.

4423. מֶלֶט *meleṭ* **masc. noun**
(clay, mortar)
Jer. 43:9.

4424. מְלַטְיָה *m^e^laṭyāh* **masc. proper noun**
(Melatiah)
Neh. 3:7.

4425. מְלִילָה *m^e^liylāh* **fem. noun**
(kernel, ear [of grain])
Deut. 23:25(26).

4426. מְלִיצָה *m^e^liyṣāh* **fem. noun**
(parable, enigmatic figure of speech; mocking, taunting song)
Prov. 1:6; **Hab.** 2:6.

4427. I. מָלַךְ *mālak* **verb**
(to reign as king)
Gen. 36:31–39; 37:8; **Ex.** 15:18; **Josh.** 13:10,12,21; **Judg.** 4:2; 9:6,8,10,12,14, 16,18; **1 Sam.** 8:7,9,11,22; 11:12,15; 12:1,12,14; 13:1; 15:11,35; 16:1; 23:17; 24:20(21); **2 Sam.** 2:9,10; 3:21; 5:4,5; 8:15; 10:1; 15:10; 16:8; **1 Kgs.** 1:5, 11,13,17,18,24,30,35,43; 2:11,15; 3:7; 6:1; 11:24,25,37,42,43; 12:1,17,20; 14:19–21,31; 15:1,2,8–10,24,25,28, 29,33; 16:6,8,10,11,15,16,21–23,28,29; 22:40–42,50(51),51(52); **2 Kgs.** 1:17; 3:1,27; 8:15–17,20,24–26; 9:13,29; 10:5,35,36; 11:3,12,21(12:1); 12:1(2), 21(22); 13:1,9,10,24; 14:1,2,16,21,23,29; 15:1,2,7,8,10,13,14,17,22,23,25,27,30,32 ,33,38; 16:1,2,20; 17:1,21; 18:1,2; 19:37; 20:21; 21:1,18,19,24,26; 22:1; 23:30,31, 33,34,36; 24:6,8,12,17,18; 25:1,27; **1 Chr.** 1:43–50; 3:4; 4:31; 11:10;

12:31,38; 16:31; 18:14; 19:1; 23:1; 28:4; 29:22,26–28; **2 Chr.** 1:8,9,11,13; 9:30,31; 10:1,17; 11:22; 12:13,16; 13:1,2; 14:1 (13:23); 16:13; 17:1,7; 20:31; 21:1,5,8,20; 22:1,2,12; 23:3,11; 24:1,27; 25:1; 26:1, 3,23; 27:1,8,9; 28:1,27; 29:1,3; 32:33; 33:1,20,21,25; 34:1,3,8; 36:1,2,4,5, 8–11,20; **Esth.** 1:1,3; 2:4,17; **Job** 34:30; **Ps.** 47:8(9); 93:1; 96:10; 97:1; 99:1; 146:10; **Prov.** 8:15; 30:22; **Eccl.** 4:14; **Isa.** 7:6; 24:23; 32:1; 37:38; 52:7; **Jer.** 1:2; 22:11,15; 23:5; 33:21; 37:1; 51:59; 52:1,4; **Ezek.** 17:16; 20:33; **Dan.** 9:1,2; **Hos.** 8:4; **Mic.** 4:7.

II. מָלַךְ *mālak̲* **verb**
(to counsel, to advise)
Neh. 5:7.

4428. מֶלֶךְ *melek̲* **masc. noun**
(king)
Gen. 14:1,2,5,8–10,17,18,21,22; 17:6, 16; 20:2; 26:1,8; 35:11; 36:31; 39:20; 40:1,5; 41:46; 49:20; **Ex.** 1:8,15,17,18; 2:23; 3:18,19; 5:4; 6:11,13,27,29; 14:5,8; **Num.** 20:14,17; 21:1,21,22,26,29,33,34; 22:4,10; 23:7,21; 24:7; 31:8; 32:33; 33:40; **Deut.** 1:4; 2:24,26,30; 3:1–3,6,8,11,21; 4:46,47; 7:8,24; 11:3; 17:14,15; 28:36; 29:7(6); 31:4; 33:5; **Josh.** 2:2,3,10; 5:1; 6:2; 8:1,2,14,23,29; 9:1,10; 10:1,3,5,6, 16,17,22–24,28,30,33,37,39,40,42; 11:1, 2,5,10,12,17,18; 12:1,2,4,5,7,9–24; 13:10,21,27,30; 24:9,12; **Judg.** 1:7; 3:8,10,12,14,15,17,19; 4:2,17,23,24; 5:3,19; 8:5,12,18,26; 9:6,8,15; 11:12–14, 17,19,25,28; 17:6; 18:1; 19:1; 21:25; **1 Sam.** 2:10; 8:5,6,9–11,18–20,22; 10:19,24; 12:1,2,9,12–14,17,19,25; 14:47; 15:1,8,11,17,20,23,26,32; 16:1; 17:25,55,56; 18:6,18,22,23,25–27; 19:4; 20:5,24,25,29; 21:2(3),8(9),10–12 (11–13); 22:3,4,11,14–18; 23:20; 24:8(9), 14(15); 25:36; 26:14–17,19,20,22; 27:2,6; 28:13; 29:3,8; **2 Sam.** 2:4,7,11; 3:3,17, 21,23,24,31–33,36–39; 4:8; 5:2,3,6,11, 12,17; 6:12,16,20; 7:1–3,18; 8:3,5,8–12; 9:2–5,9,11,13; 10:1,5,6,19; 11:1,2,8,9, 19,20,24; 12:7,30; 13:4,6,13,18,21, 23–27,29–33,35–37,39; 14:1,3–5,8–13, 15–19,21,22,24,26,28,29,32,33; 15:2,3, 6,7,9,15–19,21,23,25,27,34,35; 16:2–6, 9,10,14,16; 17:2,16,17,21; 18:2,4,5,12, 13,18–21,25–32,33(19:1); 19:1(2),2(3), 4(5),5(6),8–12(9–13),14–20(15–21), 22–43(23–44); 20:2–4,21,22; 21:2,5–8, 14; 22:51; 24:2–4,9,20–24; **1 Kgs.** 1:1–4, 9,13–16,18–25,27–29,31–34,36–39,43–4 5,47,48,51,53; 2:17–20,22,23,25,26, 29–31,35,36,38,39,42,44–46; 3:1,4,13, 16,22–28; 4:1,5,7,19,24(5:4),27(5:7), 34(5:14); 5:1(15),13(27),17(31); 6:2; 7:13,14,40,45,46,51; 8:1,2,5,14,62–64,66; 9:1,10,11,14–16,26,28; 10:3,6,9,10,12, 13,15–18,21–23,26–29; 11:1,14,18,23, 26,27,37,40; 12:2,6,12,13,15,16,18,23, 27,28; 13:4,6–8,11; 14:2,14,19,25–29; 15:1,7,9,16–20,22,23,25,28,31–33; 16:5,8,10,14–16,18,20,23,27,29,31,33; 19:15,16; 20:1,2,4,7,9,11–13,16,20–24, 28,31,32,38–41,43; 21:1,10,13,18; 22:2–6,8–10,12,13,15,16,18,26,27, 29–35,37,39,41,44(45),45(46),47(48), 51(52); **2 Kgs.** 1:3,6,9,11,15,17,18; 3:1,4–7,9–14,21,23,26; 4:13; 5:1,5–8; 6:8–12,21,24,26,28,30; 7:2,6,9,11,12,14, 15,17,18; 8:3–9,13,16,18,20,23,25,26, 28,29; 9:3,6,12,14–16,18,19,21,27,34; 10:4,6–8,13,34; 11:2,4,5,7,8,10–12,14, 16,17,19,20; 12:6(7),7(8),10(11), 17–19(18–20); 13:1,3,4,7,8,10,12–14,16, 18,22,24; 14:1,5,8,9,11,13–18,22,23, 28,29; 15:1,5,6,8,11,13,15,17,19–21,23, 25–27,29,31,32,36,37; 16:1,3,5–12, 15–19; 17:1–8,24,26,27; 18:1,5,7,9–11, 13–19,21,23,28–31,33,36; 19:1,4–6, 8–11,13,17,20,32,36; 20:6,12,14,18,20; 21:3,11,17,23–25; 22:3,9–12,16,18,20; 23:1–5,11–13,19,21–23,25,28,29; 24:1,5, 7,10–13,15–17,20; 25:1,2,4–6,8,9,11, 19–24,27,28,30; **1 Chr.** 1:43; 3:2; 4:23,41; 5:6,17,26; 9:1,18; 11:2,3; 14:1,2,8; 15:29; 16:21; 17:16; 18:3,5,9–11,17; 19:1,5,7,9; 20:1,2; 21:3,4,6,23,24; 24:6,31; 25:2,5,6; 26:26,30,32; 27:1,24,25,31–34; 28:1,2,4;

29:1,6,9,20,23–25,29; **2 Chr.** 1:12,14–17; 2:3(2),11(10),12(11); 4:11,16,17; 5:3,6; 6:3; 7:4–6,11; 8:10,11,15,18; 9:5,8,9,11, 12,14–17,20–23,25–27; 10:2,6,12,13, 15,16,18; 11:3; 12:2,6,9–11,13; 13:1; 15:16; 16:1–4,6,7,11; 17:19; 18:3–5,7–9, 11,12,14,15,17,19,25,26,28–34; 19:1,2, 11; 20:15,34,35; 21:2,6,8,12,13,17,20; 22:1,5,6,11; 23:3,5,7,9–13,15,16,20; 24:6,8,11,12,14,16,17,21–23,25,27; 25:3, 7,16–18,21,23–26; 26:2,11,13,18,21,23; 27:5,7; 28:2,5,7,16,19–23,26,27; 29:15, 18–20,23–25,27,29,30; 30:2,4,6,12, 24,26; 31:3,13; 32:1,4,7–11,20–23,32; 33:11,18,25; 34:11,16,18–20,22,24,26, 28–31; 35:3,4,7,10,15,16,18,20,21,23,27; 36:3,4,6,8,10,13,17,18,22,23; **Ezra** 1:1,2,7,8; 2:1; 3:7,10; 4:2,3,5,7; 6:22; 7:1,6–8,11,27,28; 8:1,22,25,36; 9:7,9; **Neh.** 1:11; 2:1–9,14,18,19; 3:15,25; 5:4,14; 6:6,7; 7:6; 9:22,24,32,34,37; 11:23,24; 13:6,26; **Esth.** 1:2,5,7–22; 2:1–4,6,8,9,12–19,21–23; 3:1–3,7–13,15; 4:2,3,5–8,11,13,16; 5:1–6,8,9,11–14; 6:1–12,14; 7:1–10; 8:1–5,7–12,14,15,17; 9:1–4,11–14,16,20,25; 10:1–3; **Job** 3:14; 12:18; 15:24; 18:14; 29:25; 34:18; 36:7; 41:34(26); **Ps.** 2:2,6,10; 5:2(3); 10:16; 18:50(51); 20:9(10); 21:1(2),7(8); 24:7–10; 29:10; 33:16; 44:4(5); 45:1(2), 5(6),9(10),11(12),13–15(14–16); 47:2(3), 6(7),7(8); 48:2(3),4(5); 61:6(7); 63:11(12); 68:12(13),14(15),24(25),29(30); 72:1, 10,11; 74:12; 76:12(13); 84:3(4); 89:18(19),27(28); 95:3; 98:6; 99:4; 102:15(16); 105:14,20,30; 110:5; 119:46; 135:10,11; 136:17–20; 138:4; 144:10; 145:1; 148:11; 149:2,8; **Prov.** 1:1; 8:15; 14:28,35; 16:10,12–15; 19:12; 20:2,8, 26,28; 21:1; 22:11,29; 24:21; 25:1–3,5,6; 29:4,14; 30:27,28,31; 31:1,3,4; **Eccl.** 1:1,12; 2:8,12; 4:13; 5:9(8); 8:2,4; 9:14; 10:16,17,20; **Song** 1:4,12; 3:9,11; 7:5(6); **Isa.** 1:1; 6:1,5; 7:1,6,16,17,20; 8:4,7,21; 10:8,12; 14:4,9,18,28; 19:4,11; 20:1,4,6; 23:15; 24:21; 30:33; 32:1; 33:17,22; 36:1, 2,4,6,8,13–16,18,21; 37:1,4–6,8–11,13, 18,21,33,37; 38:6,9; 39:1,3,7; 41:2,21; 43:15; 44:6; 45:1; 49:7,23; 52:15; 57:9 (NIV, *mōlek̲* [4432]); 60:3,10,11,16; 62:2; **Jer.** 1:2,3,18; 2:26; 3:6; 4:9; 8:1,19; 10:7,10; 13:13,18; 15:4; 17:19,20,25; 19:3,4,13; 20:4,5; 21:1,2,4,7,10,11; 22:1, 2,4,6,11,18,24,25; 23:5; 24:1,8; 25:1,3, 9,11,12,14,18–20,22,24–26; 26:1,10, 18,19,21–23; 27:1,3,6–9,11–14,17,18, 20,21; 28:1–4,11,14; 29:2,3,16,21,22; 30:9; 32:1–4,28,32,36; 33:4; 34:1–8,21; 35:1,11; 36:1,9,12,16,20–22,24,25, 26(KJV, *hammelek̲* [4429]),27–30,32; 37:1,3,7,17–21; 38:3–5,6(KJV, *hammelek̲* [4429]),7–11,14,16–19,22,23,25–27; 39:1,3–6,8,11,13; 40:5,7,9,11,14; 41:1,2, 9,10,18; 42:11; 43:6,10; 44:9,17,21,30; 45:1; 46:2,13,17,18,25,26; 48:15; 49:1 (NASB, NIV, *malkām* [4445]),3(NASB, NIV, *malkām* [4445]),28,30,34,38; 50:17,18, 41,43; 51:11,28,31,34,57,59; 52:3–5, 7–13,15,20,25–27,31,32,34; **Lam.** 2:6,9; 4:12; **Ezek.** 1:2; 7:27; 17:12,16; 19:9; 21:19(24),21(26); 24:2; 26:7; 27:33,35; 28:12,17; 29:2,3,18,19; 30:10,21,22, 24,25; 31:2; 32:2,10,11,29; 37:22,24; 43:7,9; **Dan.** 1:1–5,8,10,13,15,18–21; 2:2–4; 8:1,20,21,23,27; 9:6,8; 10:1,13; 11:2,3,5–9,11,13–15,25,27,36,40; **Hos.** 1:1; 3:4,5; 5:1,13; 7:3,5,7; 8:10; 10:3,6,7,15; 11:5; 13:10,11; **Amos** 1:1,15; 2:1; 5:26(KJV, *mōlek̲* [4432]); 7:1,10,13; **Jon.** 3:6,7; **Mic.** 1:1,14; 2:13; 4:9; 6:5; **Nah.** 3:18; **Hab.** 1:10; **Zeph.** 1:1,8; 3:15; **Hag.** 1:1,15; **Zech.** 7:1; 9:5,9; 11:6; 14:5,9,10,16,17; **Mal.** 1:14.

4429. מֶלֶךְ *melek̲*, הַמֶּלֶךְ *hammelek̲* **masc. proper noun**
(Melech, Hammelech)
1 Chr. 8:35; 9:41; **Jer.** 36:26(NASB, NIV, *melek̲* [4428]); 38:6(NASB, NIV, *melek̲* [4428]).

4430. מֶלֶךְ *melek̲* **Aram. masc. noun**
(king, royal; corr. to Hebr. 4428)

Ezra 4:8,11–17,19,20,22–24; 5:6–8, 11–14,17; 6:1,3,4,8,10,12–15; 7:12,14, 15,20,21,23,26; **Dan.** 2:4,5,7,8,10–12, 14–16,21,23–31,36,37,44–49; 3:1–3,5, 7,9,10,12,13,16–18,22,24,27,28,30; 4:1(3:31),18(15),19(16),22–24(19–21),27 (24),28(25),31(28),37(34); 5:1–3,5–13,17, 18,30; 6:2(3),3(4),6–9(7–10),12–25 (13–26); 7:1,17,24.

4431. מְלַךְ *m^{e}lak* **Aram. masc. noun**
(counsel, advice)
Dan. 4:27(24).

4432. מֹלֶךְ *mōlek* **masc. proper noun**
(the false god Molech)
Lev. 18:21; 20:2–5; **1 Kgs.** 11:7; **2 Kgs.** 23:10; **Isa.** 57:9(KJV, NASB, *melek* [4428]); **Jer.** 32:35; **Amos** 5:26(NASB, NIV, *melek* [4428]).

4433. מַלְכָּה *malkāh* **Aram. fem. noun**
(queen; corr. to Hebr. 4336)
Dan. 5:10.

4434. מַלְכֹּדֶת *malkōdet* **fem. noun**
(trap)
Job 18:10.

4435. A. מִלְכָּה *milkāh* **fem. proper noun**
(Milcah: wife of Nahor)
Gen. 11:29; 22:20,23; 24:15,24,47.
B. מִלְכָּה *milkāh* **fem. proper noun**
(Milcah: daughter of Zelophehad)
Num. 26:33; 27:1; 36:11; **Josh.** 17:3.

4436. מַלְכָּה *malkāh* **fem. noun**
(queen)
1 Kgs. 10:1,4,10,13; **2 Chr.** 9:1,3,9,12; **Esth.** 1:9,11,12,15–18; 2:22; 4:4; 5:2, 3,12; 7:1–3,5–8; 8:1,7; 9:12,29,31; **Song** 6:8,9.

4437. מַלְכוּ *malkû* **Aram. fem. noun**
(kingdom, realm, reign; corr. to Hebr. 4438)
Ezra 4:24; 6:15; 7:13,23; **Dan.** 2:37,39–42,44; 4:3(3:33),17(14),18(15), 25(22),26(23),29–32(26–29),34(31), 36(33); 5:7,11,16,18,20,21,26,28,29, 31(6:1); 6:1(2),3(4),4(5),7(8),26(27), 28(29); 7:14,18,22–24,27.

4438. מַלְכוּת *malkût* **fem. noun**
(kingdom, realm, reign)
Num. 24:7; **1 Sam.** 20:31; **1 Kgs.** 2:12; **1 Chr.** 11:10; 12:23(24); 14:2; 17:11,14; 22:10; 26:31; 28:5,7; 29:25,30; **2 Chr.** 1:1; 2:1(1:18),12(11); 3:2; 7:18; 11:17; 12:1; 15:10,19; 16:1,12; 20:30; 29:19; 33:13; 35:19; 36:20,22; **Ezra** 1:1; 4:5,6; 7:1; 8:1; **Neh.** 9:35; 12:22; **Esth.** 1:2, 4,7,9,11,14,19,20; 2:3,16,17; 3:6,8; 4:14; 5:1,3,6; 6:8; 7:2; 8:15; 9:30; **Ps.** 45:6(7); 103:19; 145:11–13; **Eccl.** 4:14; **Jer.** 10:7; 49:34; 52:31; **Dan.** 1:1,20; 2:1; 8:1, 22,23; 9:1; 10:13; 11:2,4,9,17,20,21.

4439. מַלְכִּיאֵל *malkiy'ēl* **masc. proper noun**
(Malchiel)
Gen. 46:17; **Num.** 26:45; **1 Chr.** 7:31.

4440. מַלְכִּיאֵלִי *malkiy'ēliy* **masc. proper noun**
(Malchielites)
Num. 26:45.

4441. A. מַלְכִּיָּה *malkiyyāh* **masc. proper noun**
(Malchijah: son of Ethni)
1 Chr. 6:40(25).
B. לְכִּיָּה *malkiyyāh* **masc. proper noun**
(Malchijah: a priest)
1 Chr. 24:9.
C. מַלְכִּיָּה *malkiyyāh*, מַלְכִּיָּהוּ *malkiyyahû* **masc. proper noun**
(Malchijah: father of Pashhur)
1 Chr. 9:12; **Neh.** 11:12; **Jer.** 21:1; 38:1.

D. מַלְכִּיָּהוּ malkiyyahû **masc. proper noun**
(Malchijah: son of Hammelech)
Jer. 38:6.
E. מַלְכִּיָּה *malkiyyāh* **masc. proper noun**
(Malchijah: a Jew)
Ezra 10:25.
F. מַלְכִּיָּה *malkiyyāh* **masc. proper noun**
(Malchijah: a Jew)
Ezra 10:25.
G. מַלְכִּיָּה *malkiyyāh* **masc. proper noun**
(Malchijah: son of Harim)
Ezra 10:31; **Neh.** 3:11.
H. מַלְכִּיָּה *malkiyyāh* **masc. proper noun**
(Malchijah: son of Rechab)
Neh. 3:14.
I. מַלְכִּיָּה *malkiyyāh* **masc. proper noun**
(Malchijah: repairer of the wall)
Neh. 3:31.
J. מַלְכִּיָּה *malkiyyāh* **masc. proper noun**
(Malchijah: a priest)
Neh. 8:4; 10:3(4); 12:42.

4442. מַלְכִּי־צֶדֶק *malkiy ṣeḏeq* **masc. proper noun**
(Melchizedek)
Gen. 14:18; **Ps.** 110:4.

4443. מַלְכִּירָם *malkiyrām* **masc. proper noun**
(Malchiram)
1 Chr. 3:18.

4444. מַלְכִּישׁוּעַ, מַלְכִּי שׁוּעַ *malkiyšûa'*, *malkiy šûa'* **masc. proper noun**
(Malchi-shua)
1 Sam. 14:49; 31:2; **1 Chr.** 8:33; 9:39; 10:2.

4445. I. מַלְכָּם *malkām* **proper noun**
(Malcham: a Benjamite)
1 Chr. 8:9.
II. מִלְכֹּם *milkōm*, מַלְכָּם *malkām* **masc. proper noun**
(Malcam, Molech a false god)
1 Kgs. 11:5,33; **2 Kgs.** 23:13; **Jer.** 49:1(KJV, *meleḵ* [4428]),3(KJV, *meleḵ* [4428]); **Zeph.** 1:5.

4446. מְלֶכֶת *meleḵeṯ* **fem. noun**
(queen)
Jer. 7:18; 44:17–19,25.

4447. הַמֹּלֶכֶת *hammōleḵeṯ* **fem. proper noun**
(Hamoleketh)
1 Chr. 7:18.

4448. I. מָלַל *mālal* **verb**
(to speak, to utter, to say)
Gen. 21:7; **Job** 8:2; 33:3; **Ps.** 106:2.
II. מָלַל *mālal* **verb**
(to wither, to languish, to melt, to dry up)
Job 14:2(KJV, *nāmal* [5243]); 18:16(KJV, *nāmal* [5243]; NASB, see III); **Ps.** 37:2 (KJV, *nāmal* [5243]); 58:7(8)(KJV, *mûl* [4135]; NASB, see III); 90:6(KJV, *mûl* [4135]).
III. מָלַל *mālal* **verb**
(to cut down, to cut off, to circumcise)
Josh. 5:2(KJV, NASB, *mûl* [4135]); **Job** 18:16(KJV, *nāmal* [5243]; NIV, see II); 24:24(KJV, *nāmal* [5243]); **Ps.** 58:7(8) (KJV, *mûl* [4135]; NIV, see II).
IV. מָלַל *mālal* **verb**
(to signal)
Prov. 6:13.

4449. מְלַל *melal* **Aram. verb**
(to speak, to say; corr. to Hebr. 4448,I)
Dan. 6:21(22); 7:8,11,20,25.

4450. מִלֲלַי *milalay* **masc. proper noun**
(Milalai)
Neh. 12:36.

4451. מַלְמָד *malmā<u>d</u>* **masc. noun**
(goad, prodding stick)
Judg. 3:31.

4452. מָלַץ *mālaṣ* **verb**
(to be sweet, to be smooth)
Ps. 119:103.

4453. מֶלְצַר *melṣar* **masc. proper noun**
(Melzar)
Dan. 1:11,16.

4454. מָלַק *mālaq* **verb**
(to wring off)
Lev. 1:15; 5:8.

4455. I. מַלְקוֹחַ *malqôaḥ* **masc. noun**
(booty, prey)
Num. 31:11,12,26,27,32; **Isa.** 49:24,25.
II. מַלְקוֹחַ *malqôaḥ* **masc. noun**
(jaw, palate)
Ps. 22:15(16).

4456. מַלְקוֹשׁ *malqôš* **masc. noun**
(latter rain, spring rain)
Deut. 11:14; **Job** 29:23; **Prov.** 16:15; **Jer.** 3:3; 5:24; **Hos.** 6:3; **Joel** 2:23; **Zech.** 10:1.

4457. מֶלְקָחַיִם *melqāḥayim,* מַלְקָחַיִם *malqāḥayim* **masc. dual noun**
(tongs, snuffers)
Ex. 25:38; 37:23; **Num.** 4:9; **1 Kgs.** 7:49; **2 Chr.** 4:21; **Isa.** 6:6.

4458. מֶלְתָּחָה *meltāḥāh* **fem. noun**
(wardrobe)
2 Kgs. 10:22.

4459. מַלְתָּעוֹת *maltā'ô<u>t</u>* **fem. pl. noun**
(jaws, jaw teeth, fangs; transposed form of *m*^{e}*<u>t</u>all*^{e}*'ô<u>t</u>* [4973])
Ps. 58:6(7).

4460. מַמְּגוּרָה *mamm*^{e}*gûrāh* **fem. noun**
(barn, granary)
Joel 1:17.

4461. מֵמַד *mēma<u>d</u>* **masc. noun**
(measurement, dimension)
Job 38:5.

4462. מְמוּכָן *m*^{e}*mû<u>k</u>ān* **masc. proper noun**
(Memucan: a chief counselor to Ahasuerus)
Esth. 1:14,16,21.

4463. מָמוֹת *māmô<u>t</u>* **masc. noun**
(death, deadly disease)
Jer. 16:4; **Ezek.** 28:8.

4464. מַמְזֵר *mamzēr* **masc. noun**
(bastard, illegitimate child)
Deut. 23:2(3); **Zech.** 9:6.

4465. מִמְכָּר *mimkār* **masc. noun**
(sale, that which is sold)
Lev. 25:14,25,27–29,33,50; **Deut.** 18:8; **Neh.** 13:20; **Ezek.** 7:13.

4466. מִמְכֶּרֶת *mimkere<u>t</u>* **fem. noun**
(sale)
Lev. 25:42.

4467. מַמְלָכָה *mamlā<u>k</u>āh* **fem. noun**
(kingdom, royalty)
Gen. 10:10; 20:9; **Ex.** 19:6; **Num.** 32:33; **Deut.** 3:4,10,13,21; 17:18,20; 28:25; **Josh.** 10:2; 11:10; **1 Sam.** 10:18; 13:13, 14; 24:20(21); 27:5; 28:17; **2 Sam.** 3:10,28; 5:12; 7:12,13,16; **1 Kgs.** 2:46; 4:21(5:1); 9:5; 10:20; 11:11,13,31,34; 12:26; 14:8; 18:10; **2 Kgs.** 11:1; 14:5; 15:19; 19:15,19; **1 Chr.** 16:20; 29:11,30; **2 Chr.** 9:19; 11:1; 12:8; 13:5,8; 14:5(4); 17:5,10; 20:6,29; 21:3,4; 22:9,10; 23:20; 25:3; 29:21; 32:15; 36:23; **Ezra** 1:2; **Neh.** 9:22; **Ps.** 46:6(7); 68:32(33); 79:6; 102:22(23); 105:13; 135:11; **Isa.** 9:7(6);

10:10; 13:4,19; 14:16; 17:3; 19:2; 23:11,17; 37:16,20; 47:5; 60:12; **Jer.** 1:10,15; 15:4; 18:7,9; 24:9; 25:26; 27:1,8; 28:1,8; 29:18; 34:1,17; 49:28; 51:20,27; **Lam.** 2:2; **Ezek.** 17:14; 29:14,15; 37:22; **Amos** 6:2; 7:13; 9:8; **Mic.** 4:8; **Nah.** 3:5; **Zeph.** 3:8; **Hag.** 2:22.

4468. מַמְלָכוּת *mamlāḵûṯ* **fem. noun**
(kingdom, reign)
Josh. 13:12,21,27,30,31; **1 Sam.** 15:28; **2 Sam.** 16:3; **Jer.** 26:1; **Hos.** 1:4.

4469. מִמְסָךְ *mimsāḵ* **masc. noun**
(mixed wine)
Prov. 23:30; **Isa.** 65:11.

4470. מֶמֶר *memer* **masc. noun**
(bitterness)
Prov. 17:25.

4471. A. מַמְרֵא *mamrē'* **proper noun**
(Mamre: loc. N. of Hebron)
Gen. 13:18; 18:1; 23:17,19; 25:9; 35:27; 49:30; 50:13.
B. מַמְרֵא *mamrē'* **masc. proper noun**
(Mamre: friend of Abram)
Gen. 14:13,24.

4472. מַמְרֹר *mamrōr* **masc. noun**
(bitterness, misery)
Job 9:18.

4473. מִמְשַׁח *mimšaḥ* **masc. noun**
(anointed one)
Ezek. 28:14.

4474. מִמְשָׁל *mimšāl* **masc. noun**
(dominion, authority, rule)
1 Chr. 26:6; **Dan.** 11:3,5.

4475. מֶמְשָׁלָה *memšālāh* **fem. noun**
(dominion, rule)
Gen. 1:16; **1 Kgs.** 9:19; **2 Kgs.** 20:13; **2 Chr.** 8:6; 32:9; **Ps.** 103:22; 114:2; 136:8,9; 145:13; **Isa.** 22:21; 39:2; **Jer.** 34:1; 51:28; **Dan.** 11:5; **Mic.** 4:8.

4476. מִמְשָׁק *mimšāq* **masc. noun**
(possessed, characterized by)
Zeph. 2:9.

4477. מַמְתַקִּים *mamtaqqiym* **masc. pl. noun**
(sweetness)
Neh. 8:10; **Song** 5:16.

4478. I. מָן *mān* **masc. noun**
(manna)
Ex. 16:15(NASB, NIV, see II),31,33,35; **Num.** 11:6,7,9; **Deut.** 8:3,16; **Josh.** 5:12; **Neh.** 9:20; **Ps.** 78:24.
II. מָן *mān* **interrog. pron.**
(what?)
Ex. 16:15(KJV, see I).

4479. מַן *man* **Aram. interrog. pron.**
(who? whoever? what?; corr. to Hebr. 4478,II)
Ezra 5:3,4,9; **Dan.** 3:6,11,15; 4:17(14),25(22),32(29); 5:21.

4480. I. מִן *min* **prep.**
(from, out of, away from; more than; after, since, immediately; because of, since; so that; without; —wards)
Gen. 1:7,9; 2:2,3,6–10,16,17,19,21–23; 3:1–3,5,6,8,11,12,14,17,19,22–24; 4:3,4,10,11,13,14,16; 5:29; 6:2,4,7,13,14,16,17,19–21; 7:2–4,7,8,15–17,20,22,23; 8:2,3,6–8,10,11,13,16,17,19–21; 9:5,10,11,18,19,21,24; 10:5,11,14,19,30,32; 11:2,6,8,9,31; 12:1,4,8; 13:1,3,9,11,14; 14:15,17,20,23; 15:4,7,18; 16:2,3,6,8,10; 17:6,12,14,16,22,27; 18:2,3,14,16,17,22,25; 19:4,9,11,12,14,16,24,26,29,30,32,34,36; 20:1,6,13; 21:15–17,21,30; 22:4,9,11,12,15; 23:3,4,6,8,13,20; 24:3,5,7,8,10,11,17,27,37,40,41,43,46,50,62,64; 25:6,10,18,20,23,29,30; 26:1,16,17,

22,23,26,27,31; 27:1,9,19,25,28,30,31, 33,39,40,45,46; 28:1,2,6,10,11,16; 29:2–4,8,10,19,30,35; 30:2,3,9,14,16,32; 31:1,13,16,24,29,31,33,35,37,39,40,49; 32:10–13; 33:10,15,18,19; 34:7,19,26; 35:1,7–9,11,13,16,21; 36:2,6,7,33,34, 36,37; 37:3,4,14,17,18,21,22,25,28; 38:1, 14,17,19,20,24,26; 39:1,5,9,11; 40:14,15, 17,19; 41:1–3,14,18,31,32,40,42,46; 42:2,3,7,15,16,24,26; 43:2,9,11,34; 44:7–9,17,28,29,32; 45:1,3,19,23,25; 46:3,5,26,34; 47:1,2,10,13,15,18,21, 22,30; 48:7,10,12,13,15–17,19,22; 49:9,10,12,20,24,25,30,32; 50:13,24,25; **Ex.** 1:9,10,12; 2:1,4,6,7,10,11,15,19,23; 3:2,4–8,10–12,17,22; 4:3,7,9,10,26; 5:4,5,8,11,19,20,23; 6:1,6,7,9,11,13, 25–27; 7:2,4,5,18,21,24; 8:8(4),9(5), 11–13(7–9),24(20),29–31(25–27); 9:4,6,7,11,15,18,20,24,25,28,30,33; 10:3,5,6,11,17,18,23,26,28; 11:1,2,5,7, 8,10; 12:4,5,7,9,10,12,15,17,19,22,29,31, 33,35,37,39,41,42,46,51; 13:3,8–10, 14–16,18–20; 14:5,11,12,19,22,25,29,30; 15:22,23; 16:1,4,6,16,19,20,27,29,32; 17:1,3,5,6,12,14,16; 18:1,4,9–11,13, 14,18,21,22,25; 19:1–3,5,14,17,18,21; 20:2,4,18,21,22; 21:14,29,36; 22:4,7, 12,14; 23:5,7,15,16,21,25,28–31; 24:1, 9,16; 25:2,3,11,15,18,19,21,22,31–33, 35,36; 26:4,13,14,24,28,33,35; 27:2,5,21; 28:1,8,10,27,28,42; 29:12,14,20–23, 25–28,30,34,46; 30:2,4,10,14–16,19, 33,36,38; 31:14; 32:1,4,6–8,11,12,15,19, 23,27,28,30,32,33; 33:1,5–7,11,15,16; 34:11,15,16,18,24,29,30,33; 35:5,20; 36:3–6,11,19,29,33; 37:2,7,8,17–19, 21,22,25,27; 38:2,4,15,26; 39:1,5,20, 21,31; 40:19,20,22,31,36; **Lev.** 1:1–3, 10,14; 2:2,3,8–11,13,16; 3:1,3,6,9,14; 4:2,5–8,10,12,13,16–19,21,22,25–27,30, 31,34,35; 5:2–6,8–10,12,13,15–18; 6:3, 5–7,11,15–18,22,27,30; 7:3,14–18,20, 21,25,27,29,32–36; 8:11,12,17,23,24, 26,28–30,33; 9:10,11,17,19,22,24; 10:2, 4,5,7,12–14; 11:2,4,8–11,13,21,22,25, 32–35,37–40,45; 12:7; 13:2–4,12,20, 21,25,26,30–32,34,41,46,56,58; 14:3,7, 8,14–17,19,25–30,37,38,40,41,45,53; 15:2,3,13,15,16,28,30–32; 16:2,5,12, 14–16,18–20,27,30,34; 17:3,4,8–10, 12,13; 18:21,24,26,29,30; 19:6,8,14,22, 32,34,36; 20:2–6,18,23,24,26; 21:7,10, 12,14,17,21,22; 22:2–4,6,7,13,18,22, 25,27,30,33; 23:11,15–17,29,30,32, 38,43; 24:3,8,9,14,23; 25:12,14,15,17, 22,25,33,36,38,41–45,48–51,55; 26:6,8, 10,13,37,43,45; 27:3,5–9,11,16–18,22, 24,28–31; **Num.** 1:1,3,18,20,22,24,26, 28,30,32,34,36,38,40,42,45; 2:2; 3:9, 12,13,15,22,28,34,39,40,43,46,49,50; 4:2,3,6,18,23,25,30,35,39,43,47; 5:2–4, 6,8,13,17,19,20,25,26,31; 6:3,4,11,19,21; 7:5,84,89; 8:6,11,14,16,19,24,25; 9:1,12, 13,17,21; 10:9,11,12,33–35; 11:13,14,16, 17,20,24,25,28,31,35; 12:3,10,12,14–16; 13:3,20,21,23–25,31,33; 14:6,9,12,13,16, 19,29,38,43,44; 15:3,19,21,23,24,30,35, 36,41; 16:2,9,13,15,21,24,26–28,33,35, 37,40,41,45,46,49; 17:2,5,8–10; 18:6, 7,9,16,26–30,32; 19:3,4,9,13,17,20; 20:5, 6,8–10,14,16,21,22,28; 21:1,4–7,11–13, 16,18–20,24,26,28; 22:1,3,5,6,11,15,16, 23,24,30,33,41; 23:7,9,13,22,27; 24:7, 8,11,13,17,19,23,24; 25:4,6–8,11; 26:2, 4,62,64,65; 27:4,11,20; 28:23,31; 29:6, 11,16,19,22,25,28,31,34,38,39; 30:2,14; 31:2,3,5,13,14,19,28–30,35,37,42,43,47, 49,51,52,54; 32:7,8,11,15,17,19,21,22, 24,32; 33:1,3,5–38,41–49,52,55; 34:3–5,7,8,10,11,15,18; 35:2,4,5,8,12, 14,25,27; 36:1,3,4,7–9,12; **Deut.** 1:2, 17,19,23,25,27–29; 2:4–6,8,9,12,14–16, 19,21–23,25,26,36; 3:4,5,8,11,12,16,17; 4:2,3,9,12,15,18,20,26,29,32–39,42,45, 46,48; 5:4–6,8,15,22–24,26; 6:12,14,15, 19,21,23; 7:1,4,6–8,14,15,17–22,24; 8:4, 9,14,15,20; 9:1,4,5,7,10–12,14–17,19,21, 23,24,26,28; 10:4–7,12,15; 11:10,12,17, 23,24,28; 12:3,5,10,21,29,30,32; 13:5,7, 10,13,17; 14:2,7–9,12,24,28; 15:1,7, 11–14,16,18; 16:1,3,4,6,9,13; 17:7,8, 10–12,15,18,20; 18:3,5,6,8,12,15,16,18, 19,22; 19:4–6,12,13,19; 20:1,3,15,16,19;

21:9,13,21; 22:1,3,4,8,21,22,24; 23:4,9, 10,12,14,15,17,21; 24:1–3,7,9,14,18; 25:5,6,9,11,17,19; 26:2,4,8,13–15; 28:10, 14,20,21,24,31,34,35,47,49,55–57,60,63, 64,66,67; 29:1,5,11,18,20–22,25,28; 30:3–5,11,13; 31:3,6,10,17,21,26,29; 32:13,17,19,20,25,26,32,39,42,47,52; 33:2,3,7,11,13–16,22,24,27; 34:1; **Josh.** 1:4,7,8; 2:1,2,4,9–11,13,17,19,20,23,24; 3:1–4,10,12–14,16; 4:2–4,7,8,16–20,23; 5:1,4–6,9,11,12,15; 6:1,10,18,21–23; 7:1,2,4,5,9,11–13,19,23,26; 8:2,4,6,7,9, 11–14,16,19,22,25,29,33,35; 9:6,8,9, 12–14,16,22–24,26; 10:2,6–9,11,20,22, 23,27,29,31,34,36,41; 11:2,3,6,15,17,20, 21,23; 12:1–4,7,9; 13:3–6,9,12,16,26, 27,30,32; 14:3,7,10,15; 15:1–3,5–10,14, 15,18,21,46; 16:1,2,6–8; 17:5,7,9,10; 18:5,7,12–15,17; 19:9,12–14,29,33,34, 47,51; 20:3,4,6,8; 21:3–7,9,10,16,17,20, 23,25,27,28,30,32,34,36,38,40,44,45; 22:9,16–19,23,24,29,31,32; 23:1,3–6, 9,10,13–16; 24:2,3,6,8,10,12,16–18, 30,32; **Judg.** 1:11,13,14,16,20,24,36; 2:1,3,9,12,14,16–19,21; 3:3,9,16,19–22, 27; 4:6,11,13–15; 5:4,5,11,14(see II), 20,22,24; 6:2,6,8,9,11,13,14,18,21,27,38; 7:1,3,5,8,17,23,25; 8:2,3,8,10,11,13,14, 22,24,26,34; 9:4,15,17,20,21,35–37, 40–43; 10:11,12,16; 11:3–5,7,13,16, 18,22–25,29,31,33,34,36,37,39,40; 12:2,6,8,9; 13:2,5–7,13,14,20,23; 14:1–4, 8,9,14,18,19; 15:1–3,5,11,13,14,17,19; 16:12,14,17,19,20,25,28,30; 17:1,3,5, 7–9,11; 18:2,7,11,13,16,22,26,28; 19:1,2, 12,16–18,30; 20:1,13–17,21,25,31–34, 38,40,42–46,48; 21:1,3–10,12,14,16–19, 21,23,24; **Ruth** 1:1,2,5–7,12,13,16,22; 2:1,3,4,6–9,12,14,16,18,20; 3:10,12; 4:2,3,5,9,10,12,15; **1 Sam.** 1:1,3,7,8,14, 16,17,20,27; 2:3,8,15,19,20,23,28,29, 31,33; 3:15,17–20; 4:3,4,8,10,12,16,18, 21,22; 5:1,3,4,9; 6:3,5,7,8,18,20; 7:2,3, 7,8,11,14; 8:7,8,10,18; 9:1–3,5,7,16, 21,25; 10:2–5,9,11–13,18,19,23; 11:5,11; 12:2–4,6,8,10,11,20,23; 13:2,8,11,15,17; 14:1,4,5,11,17,24,28,30,31,39,45,46,48;

15:2,3,6,7,11,15,21–23,26,28,33; 16:1, 13,14,23; 17:3,4,12,15,22–24,26,30, 33–37,39,40,46,49–51,53,57; 18:6, 9–13,15,29,30; 19:8,10; 20:1,2,6,7,9, 15,16,21,22,25,27,28,33,34,37,41; 21:4, 6,7,10,12; 22:1,3,8,19; 23:13,19,23,26, 28,29; 24:1,2,6–8,12,13,15,17,21; 25:10, 11,14,17,21–23,26,28,33–35,37,39,43, 44; 26:11,13,19,20,22,24; 27:1,8; 28:3,9, 13,15–17,20,23; 29:3,6,8; 30:2,10,13,16, 17,19,22,25,26; 31:1,3,8,12; **2 Sam.** 1:1–4,13,15,22,23,26; 2:12,13,15,19, 21–23,26,27,30,31; 3:10,11,13,15,18,22, 26,28,29,37,39; 4:2,4,8,9,11; 5:9,13, 23,25; 6:2–4,12,18,19,21,22; 7:1,6,8,9, 11,12,15,19,23,29; 8:1,4,8,11–13; 9:5,11; 10:9,11,13,14,16,18; 11:2,4,8,10,12,15, 17,20,21,24; 12:3,4,7,10,11,17,20,30; 13:5,6,9,10,13,15–17,22,30,32,34; 14:2, 11,13,14,16,18,19,25,26,32; 15:1,2,7, 11,12,14,18,24,28,34,35; 16:1,5,6,11; 17:11,14,21,27; 18:3,13,16,31; 19:7,9, 16,17,19,24,31,42,43; 20:2,5–7,11–13, 16,21,22; 21:2,5,6,10,12,13; 22:1,3,4,7, 9,13,14,16–18,22–24,32,44,46,49; 23:4, 11,15–17,19–21,23,29,30,36; 24:2,8,12, 15,21,24,25; **1 Kgs.** 1:6,27,29,37,39,45, 47,50,52,53; 2:4,7,8,15,16,20,22,27, 31–33,36,39–41; 3:8,20,28; 4:12,21, 23–25,30,31,33,34; 5:3,4,6,9,13,16; 6:1,8,15,16,19,21,24,29,33; 7:3,7–9,11, 13,14,20,23–25,29–32,34,35,39,47,49; 8:1,5,7–11,16,19,21,23,25,35,41,51,53,5 4,56,64,65; 9:5–7,9,10,12,20,22,24,28; 10:3,11,13,15,19,20,23,28,29; 11:2,9, 11,12,14,17,18,23,26,29,31,32,34,35; 12:2,4,9,10,15,24,25,28,31,33; 13:1,4, 5,12,14,21,26,33,34; 14:4,5,7–9,15,21, 22,24,28; 15:5,12,13,19,21; 16:2,17,24, 25,30,33; 17:1,3,4,6,7,13,19,23; 18:5,12, 13,26,40,44; 19:2,4,7,16,17,19,21; 20:7, 17,19,23–25,33–36,41,42; 21:2,3,13, 26,29; 22:3,7,8,13,19,24,33,34,43,46; **2 Kgs.** 1:2–4,6,10,12,14–16; 2:1,3,5,7, 9,10,13–15,21,23–25; 3:3,6,11,20–22, 24,26,27; 4:1,3,5,8,22,25,27,28,39,40,42; 5:2–4,6,7,12,15,19–22,24–27; 6:1,2,9,11,

12,16,27,30,32,33; 7:2,8,12,13,19; 8:3,6,
8,9,14,15,20,22,29; 9:1,2,5,7,14,15,
24,33; 10:3,10,14,15,23,24,28,29,31,33;
11:2,5,11,15,19; 12:1,5,7,8,13,18; 13:2,5,
6,11,23,25; 14:2,24,25,27; 15:2,9,14,16,
18,24,25,28; 16:3,6,7,11,12,14,17,18;
17:7–9,11,13,18,20–24,27,28,32,33,36,
39; 18:6,8,10,14,17,25,29,33–35; 19:6,8,
14,19,25,31; 20:6,9,14,18; 21:2,7–9,11,
15,16,19; 22:1,4,19; 23:2,4,6,8,11–13,
16–18,22,26,27,30,31,33,36; 24:3,7,8,
13,15,18,20; 25:5,12,19,21,24–28,30;
1 Chr. 1:12,44,45,47,48; 2:3,23,53,55;
3:9; 4:9,10,40,42; 5:2,9,18,22,23,25;
6:31,33,60–63,65,66,70–72,74,76–78,80;
8:8,9,11,40; 9:3–7,10,14,25,28–32; 10:1,
3,8; 11:8,13,15,17–19,21–23,25,26,
31,32; 12:1,2,7,8,14,16,19,20,25,26,
29–37; 13:2,5–7; 14:14,16; 15:13,17,25;
16:2–4,20,23,30,33,35,36; 17:5,7,8,10,
11,13,17,21; 18:1,4,8,11; 19:6,7,10,12,
14–16,18; 20:2,4; 21:2,10,12,14,21,22,
26,30; 22:9,18; 23:3,4,24,27; 24:3–6;
26:1,8,10,27,30; 27:3,10,14,18,23;
28:4,5,19; 29:3,4,10,12,14,16; **2 Chr.**
1:4,13,16,17; 2:5,8,14,16,18; 3:4,17;
4:2,4,6–8,10; 5:2,6,8–11,14; 6:5,9,16,21,
23,25,26,30,32,33,35,39; 7:1,8,14,20,22;
8:1,7–9,11,18; 9:2,10,12,14,18,19,22,
26,28; 10:2,4,9,10,15; 11:4,13,14,16,
21,23; 12:3,5,11–13; 13:2,4,13,16,17,19;
14:5,7,8,13; 15:8,9,11,13,15–17; 16:2,3,
5,7,9,10; 17:6,11,17,19; 18:6,7,12,23,
31–33; 19:2–4,8,10; 20:1,2,4,7,9–11,14,
15,19,27,30,32,37; 21:4,8,10,12,13,15,
19; 22:7,11; 23:2,4,10,14,20; 24:1,5,6,
20,23,25; 25:1,5,6,9,10,12–15,20,23,27;
26:3,11,15,18–21; 28:3,5,8,11,12,15;
29:5,6,10,12–14,34; 30:5,6,8–11,16,18,
25,26; 31:1,3,10,13,16,17; 32:3,7,11,
13–15,17,21–23; 33:2,7–9,12,15,23;
34:3,4,9,12,13,27,30,33; 35:7,11,15,18,
21,22,24; 36:7,12,13,20,23; **Ezra** 1:1,3,
4,7,11; 2:1,59,61–63,65,68,70; 3:3,
6–8,12,13; 4:2; 6:21; 7:6,7,9,28; 8:1–15,
18–24,31,35; 9:1–3,5,7,8,11,13; 10:1–3,
6,8,9,11,14,18,20–30,33,34,43,44; **Neh.**
1:2,3,9; 3:15,19–21,24,25,27,28; 4:2,5,9,
12–14,16,19,21; 5:5,9,12–15,17; 6:8,
9,16; 7:2,6,61,63–65,67,70,71,73; 8:2–5,
17,18; 9:2,5,7,13,15,18–20,27,28,32,35;
10:9,28,31; 11:1,4,10,15–17,22,24,25,
30,31,36; 12:27–29,31,35,37–39,43,46;
13:3,4,6,8,13,19–21,25,28,30; **Esth.**
1:1,5,7,19,20; 2:6,9,12,13,17,21; 3:1,7,
8,10,13; 4:4,5,8,11,13,14; 5:9; 6:2,6,9,
10,13; 7:6–9; 8:2,9,13,15,17; 9:16,22,28;
Job 1:1,3,7,8,10,12,16,19,21; 2:2,3,7,
10–12; 3:4,10,11,19,21; 4:9,11–13,17,20;
5:1,4–6,15,20–22; 6:3,6,13,14,16(see
II),17,22,23,25; 7:6(see II),14–16,19;
8:10,18,19; 9:3(see II),6,25(see II),34;
10:7,14,18–20; 11:6,8,9(see II),15,17,20;
12:3,22(see II); 13:2,13,20,21; 14:4,6,9,
11(see II),12,18; 15:10,11,13,18,22(see
II),30(see II); 16:6,16(see II); 17:4,7,12;
18:4,14–16,17(see II),18; 19:9,13,22,26
,29; 20:3,4(see II),5,15,24,25,29; 21:9,
14,16,20; 22:4,7,17,18,22,23; 23:7,12,
15,17; 24:1,4,7–9,12; 26:4,5,11; 27:5,6,
13,21–23; 28:2,4(see II),5,9,11,12,18,20,
21,28; 29:17; 30:1,5,8,10,11,17,30(see
II); 31:2,7(see II),16–20,22,23,28,31;
32:1,2,4,6,12,15; 33:6,12,17,18(see
II),21,23(see II),24,25,28,30(see II);
34:10,27,30,33; 35:2,3,5,7,9,11,12;
36:3,7,10,16,21,25; 37:1,2,9,10,17,19,22;
38:1,8,12,13,15,29; 39:22,25,26,29; 40:6;
41:19–21,25; 42:2,3,12; **Ps.** 2:3,8,12;
3:4,6; 4:7; 5:10; 6:7,8; 7:1; 8:2,5; 9:3,13;
10:5,16,18; 12:1,5,7; 13:1; 14:2,7; 16:4,8;
17:2,7,9,13–15; 18:3,6,8,12,15–17,
21–23,31,43,45,48; 19:5,6,10,12,13;
20:2,6; 21:4,10; 22:1,9–11,20,21,23–25;
24:5; 25:6,15,17,22; 27:1,4,9; 28:1,7;
30:3; 31:4,11–13,15,20,22; 32:7; 33:8,
13,14,19; 34:4,6,13,14,16,17,19,20;
35:10,17,22; 36:8; 37:8,16,23,27,39,40;
38:3–5,8,9,11,18,21; 39:1,2,8,10,13;
40:2,5,11,12; 41:13; 42:6; 43:1; 44:7,
10(see II),(11),16,18(19); 45:2,7,8,13;
49:14,15; 50:1,2,4,9; 51:2,7,9,11,14;
52:3,5; 53:2,6; 54:7; 55:1,3,8,11,12,
18,21; 56:13; 57:3; 58:3; 59:1,2,12;

60:4,11; 61:2,3; 62:1,4,5,9; 63:3; 64:1,2; 65:3,8; 66:20; 68:1,2,8,22,26,29,31,35; 69:4,5,14,17,23,28,31; 71:4–6,12,17,20; 72:8,14–16; 73:7,8,19,20,27; 74:11,12, 22(see II); 75:6,8; 76:4,6–8; 77:5,11; 78:2(see II),4,16,23,30,42(see II),50, 55,65,70,71; 80:8,13,14,16,18; 81:6, 10,16; 82:4; 83:4; 84:7,10; 85:3,11; 86:13; 87:2; 88:5,8,9(see II)(10),14, 15,18; 89:19,23,33,44,48; 90:2; 91:3,5–7; 93:2,4; 94:12,13; 96:2,9; 97:5,10; 101:4,8; 102:2,4,5,10,19; 103:4,12,17; 104:7,12–15,21,35; 105:13,24; 106:10, 11,23,47,48; 107:2,3,6,13,14,17,19,20, 28,34,39,41; 108:4,12; 109:10,15,17,20, 24,31; 110:2,3,7; 112:7; 113:2,3,7; 114:1,7; 115:18; 116:8; 118:5,8,9,23,26; 119:10,18,19,21,22,28,29,37,43,51–53,7 2,98–104,110,115,116,118,120,127,134, 150,152,155,157,161; 120:2; 121:1,2,7,8; 124:7; 125:2; 127:5; 128:5; 129:1,2; 130:1,6,8; 131:1,3; 132:11; 134:3; 135:5, 7,8,21; 136:11,24; 137:3; 138:6; 139:2, 6,7,12,15,18,19; 140:1,4; 141:9; 142:4, 6,7; 143:5,7,9,11; 144:7,10,11,13; 148:1,4,7; **Prov.** 1:15,31,33; 2:6,12, 16,22; 3:7,9,14,15,21,25–27; 4:5,15,21, 23,24,27; 5:3,7,8,15,18; 6:5,9,24; 7:5,19; 8:10,11,19,22,23,28,35; 10:2; 11:4,8,24; 12:2,9,13,14,26; 13:2,11,14,19; 14:7,14, 16,27; 15:16,17,24,29; 16:1,6,8,16,17, 19,32,33; 17:1,10,13,23; 18:19,20,22,24; 19:1,4,7,14,22,27; 20:3,4,9,24; 21:3,9,13, 16,19,23; 22:1,5,6,9,15,27; 23:4,13,14; 24:18; 25:4,7,17,24,25; 26:7,12,16; 27:3,5,8–10,22; 28:6,9,23; 29:20,21,26; 30:2,7,8,12,14,18,30; 31:10,14,16,21,31; **Eccl.** 1:8,10; 2:6,7,9,10,13,24,25; 3:5, 11,14,19,20,22; 4:1–4,6,8,9,13,14; 5:1,5, 8,15,19; 6:2,3,5,8–10; 7:1–3,5,8,10,18, 19,23,26,28; 8:3,10,12,13; 9:4,16–18; 10:1,5,14; 11:10; 12:5,11,12; **Song** 1:2,4; 2:9; 3:4,6–9; 4:1–3,8–10,15; 5:4,7,9,10; 6:5–7; 8:2,5; **Isa.** 1:6,12,15,16,24,29; 2:2,3,6,10,19,21,22; 3:1; 4:4,6; 5:6,9,13, 23,26; 6:2,4,6,11; 7:2,4,8,11,13,16,17,22; 8:11,17,18; 9:7,12,14; 10:2,3,10,18, 24,27; 11:1,11,12,16; 12:3; 13:5,6,9, 12,13; 14:3,8,9,12,13,19,25,29,31; 16:1,4,10,13; 17:1,3,9,13; 18:1,2,7; 19:1,5,16,17,20,23; 20:2,5,6; 21:1,3, 10,11,15; 22:3,4,11,19,24; 23:1,7,15,17; 24:10,14,16,18,22; 25:1,2,4,8; 26:17,21; 27:12; 28:7,9,19,20,22,29; 29:4,6,13, 15,18; 30:1,6,11,14,17,21,27,31,33; 31:4,8,9; 32:15; 33:3,15,19; 34:3,4, 6,7,10,16; 36:2,10,18–20; 37:6,8,14, 20,26,32; 38:6,7,9,12,13,17; 39:3,7; 40:2,15,17,21,26,27; 41:2,4,9,24–26,28; 42:7,10,11,14,25; 43:4–6,11,13; 44:2, 6–8,11,15,18,24; 45:6,8,21,23; 46:3,6,7, 9–12; 47:12–15; 48:1–8,16,19–21; 49:1, 5,6,12,15,17,19,24; 50:1,2,6,11; 51:4,6, 7,12,13,17,18,21,22; 52:2,11,14; 53:2, 3,5,8,11; 54:1,8–10,14,15,17; 55:9–11; 56:2,3,5,6,11; 57:1,8,9,11,14,16; 58:7, 9,12,13; 59:1,2,5,9,11,13–15,19,21; 60:4,6,9; 62:10; 63:1,3,11,12,15–17,19; 64:1–4,7; 65:9,11(see II),14,16,20; 66:6,11,19–21,23; **Jer.** 1:1,5,8,13,14,17; 2:5,6,15,20,25,35–37; 3:1,4,9,11,14, 18–20,23–25; 4:1,4,6–8,12–17,26,28,29; 5:3,6,15,22,25; 6:1,8,13,20,22,25,29; 7:1,7,12,15,22,25,26,28,32,34; 8:1,3,10, 16,19; 9:2–4,7,10–12,19,21,22; 10:2,3, 5–7,9,10,13,14,17,22; 11:1,4,7,11,15, 19,20; 12:2,4,12–14; 13:6,7,14,17,20,25; 14:16; 15:1,7,8,12,15,17,19,21; 16:5,9, 12–17,19; 17:4,5,8,9,12,16,22,26; 18:1, 8,11,14,18,20,22,23; 19:1,11,14; 20:3, 8,10,12,13,17,18; 21:1,2,4,7,12; 22:3,11, 19–22,24,25,30; 23:3,7–10,14–16,22,23, 30,39; 24:1–3,5,8,10; 25:3,5,10,15–17, 27,28,30,32,33,35,37,38; 26:1,3,9,10,17, 20,23; 27:1,10,16,20; 28:1,3,6,8,10–12, 16; 29:1,2,4,14,17,20,22; 30:1,7,8,10,17, 19,21; 31:3,8,10,11,13,16,20,32,34, 36–38; 32:1,4,9,17,21,24,27,30,31,37, 40,43; 33:5,8,10,12,18,21,24,26; 34:1,3 ,8,12–14,21,22; 35:1,4,11,15; 36:1–4,6, 7,9,11,17,18,21,27,29,32; 37:5,9,11,12, 17,21; 38:8–14,18,23,25,27; 39:4,10, 14,17; 40:1,4,7,9,12; 41:1,5,6,9,14–16, 18; 42:1,2,4,7,8,11,16,17; 43:5,10,12;

44:3,5,7,12,17–19,22,23,28; 45:1; 46:5, 10,16,19,20,23,25,27; 47:2,3; 48:2,3, 9–11,13,18,27,32–34,42,44,45; 49:5,7, 14,16,19,21,29,32,36,38; 50:3,6,8,9, 13,16,26,28,41,44,46; 51:2,5–7,16,17, 25,26,27(see II),29,31,34,37,44,45,48, 50,53–55,62,64; 52:1,3,7,8,15,16,25,27, 29,31,32,34; **Lam.** 1:2–4,6,7,13,16,20; 2:1,3,8,9,17,22; 3:17,18,33,38,44,49–51, 55,66; 4:6–9,13,18,19; 5:8–10,14; **Ezek.** 1:4,5,8,10,11,13,19,21,22,25–27; 2:6; 3:9,12,16–20; 4:8,10,11,14; 5:3,4,6,7; 6:9,14; 7:8,11,15,22,26,27; 8:2,5,6,11, 15,17; 9:2,3,6; 10:2–4,6,7,16,18,19; 11:7,9,15,17–19,22–24; 12:3,16,19; 13:2,17,20–23; 14:1,4–9,11,13,15,17, 19,21; 15:2,3; 16:3,5,9,16,17,20,27,28, 33,34,37,41,42,46,47,51,52,54,57,61,63; 17:5,7,9,13,22; 18:8,10,17,21,23,24, 26–28,30,31; 19:3,5,7,8,10,14; 20:1,6, 9,10,17,34,38,41,47; 21:3–5,19; 22:5, 15,26,30; 23:8,11,17,18,21,22,27,28, 40,42,48; 24:6,12,13,16,25; 25:7,9,13; 26:4,7,10,15–18,20; 27:5–7,12,14,16, 18,29,33,34; 28:3,15,16,18,23–26; 29:4,8,10,13,15,18; 30:6,9,13,22; 31:5, 12,16; 32:4,6,13,15,19,21,27,30; 33:2, 6–9,11,12,14,18,19,21,28,30; 34:5,8, 10,12,13,18,25,27; 35:7,11; 36:3,4,7, 11,20,24–26,29,32,33; 37:9,12,13,21,23; 38:8,12,15,20; 39:2,3,10,14,17,19,22–24, 27–29; 40:2,5,7,10,12,13,19,21,23,26,27, 34,37,39–41,44,46,48,49; 41:1,2,15,17, 19,20,26; 42:5,6,9,14; 43:2,6,9–11,14,15, 19–21,23,25; 44:3,6,10,15,22,30,31; 45:1–4,7,9,13–15,19,20; 46:2,16–18,23; 47:1,2,7,10,12,15,17–20; 48:1–8,11,12, 14,16,19,21–30,35; **Dan.** 1:2,3,5,6,8, 10,12,15,18–20; 8:3–5,7,9–11,22; 9:1, 5,13,15,16,25; 10:12,17; 11:2,4,5,7,8, 13,22,23,31,35,41,44; 12:1,2,6,7,11; **Hos.** 1:2,11; 2:2,7,10,15,17,18; 4:6,12, 19; 5:3,6,13; 6:2,6,8; 7:4,5,13,16; 8:4, 6,10; 9:1,6,11,12,15; 10:5,6,9,15; 11:1, 2,6,10,11; 12:9,13; 13:2–4,14,15; 14:4,8; **Joel** 1:5,9,12,13,15,16; 2:2,6,16,20; 3:6,7,11,12,16,18,19; **Amos** 1:1,2,5,8; 2:3,9–11,14; 3:1,2,4,5,11,12; 4:5,7,11; 5:11,19,23,27; 6:2,4,10,14; 7:11,15,17; 8:12; 9:2–4,7,8,15; **Obad.** 1:1,4,8–11; **Jon.** 1:3,5,8,10–12,15; 2:1,2,4,6; 3:5–10; 4:3,5,6,8,11; **Mic.** 1:2–4,7,11,12,16; 2:3, 8,9,12; 3:2–4,6; 4:1,2,7,10; 5:2,6,7,10, 12–14; 6:4,5,8; 7:2,4,5,12(see II),13, 15–17,20; **Nah.** 1:5,6,11,13,14; 2:8,9,13; 3:4,7,8,11,16; **Hab.** 1:7,8,12,13; 2:8,9, 11,13,16,17,20; 3:3,4,13,17; **Zeph.** 1:2–4,6,7,10; 2:5,11; 3:6,10,11,18; **Hag.** 1:10,12; 2:5,9,15,16,18,19; **Zech.** 1:4,17; 2:4,6,13; 3:2,4; 4:1,3,12; 5:3; 6:1,5,10,12; 7:11,12,14; 8:4,7,9,10,23; 9:5,7,8,10,11; 10:1,4,10; 11:6,13; 13:2,4,5; 14:2,4,5,8, 10,16,17,21; **Mal.** 1:5,9–11,13; 2:5–8, 12,13; 3:7,14.

II. מִנִּי *minniy,* מִנֵּי *minnēy* **prep.** (Poetic form of *min*)
Judg. 5:14; **Job** 6:16; 7:6; 9:3,25; 11:9; 12:22; 14:11; 15:22,30; 16:16; 18:17; 20:4; 28:4; 30:30; 31:7; 33:18,23,30; **Ps.** 44:10(11),18(19); 74:22; 78:2,42; 88:9(10); **Isa.** 65:11; **Jer.** 51:27; **Mic.** 7:12.

4481. מִן *min* **Aram. prep.**
(from, out of, among, more than; corr. to Hebr. 4480)
Ezra 4:12,15,19,21,23; 5:11,12,14,16,17; 6:4–6,8,11,14; 7:13,14,20,21,23,26; **Jer.** 10:11; **Dan.** 2:5,6,8,15,16,18,20,23,25, 30,33,35,39,41,42,45,47,49; 3:15,17,22, 26,29; 4:6(3),12–14(9–11),16(13),23(20), 25(22),26(23),31–33(28–30); 5:2,3,13, 19–21,24; 6:2(3),4(5),7(8),10(11),12(13), 13(14),20(21),23(24),26(27),27(28); 7:3, 4,7,8,10,11,16,17,19,20,23,24.

4482. I. מֵן *mēn* **masc. noun**
(stringed instrument, music of strings)
Ps. 45:8(9)(KJV, see II); 150:4.

II. מֵן *mēn* **masc. noun**
(portion, share; another reading for m^e*nāṯ* [4521])
Ps. 45:8(9)(NASB, NIV, see I); 68:23.

4483. מְנָא *m^e^nā'*, מְנָה *m^e^nāh* **Aram. verb**
(to number, to appoint; corr. to Hebr. 4487)
Ezra 7:25; **Dan.** 2:24,49; 3:12; 5:26.

4484. מְנֵא *m^e^nē'* **Aram. noun**
(Mene; weight of measurement)
Dan. 5:25,26.

4485. מַנְגִּינָה *mangiynāh* **fem. noun**
(a mocking song)
Lam. 3:63.

4486. מַנְדַּע *manda'* **Aram. masc. noun**
(knowledge, reasoning; corr. to Hebr. 4093)
Dan. 2:21; 4:34(31),36(33); 5:12.

4487. מָנָה *mānāh* **verb**
(to count, to number)
Gen. 13:16; **Num.** 23:10; **2 Sam.** 24:1; **1 Kgs.** 3:8; 8:5; 20:25; **2 Kgs.** 12:10(11); **1 Chr.** 9:29; 21:1,17; 27:24; **2 Chr.** 5:6; **Job** 7:3; **Ps.** 61:7(8); 90:12; 147:4; **Eccl.** 1:15; **Isa.** 53:12; 65:12; **Jer.** 33:13; **Dan.** 1:5,10,11; **Jon.** 1:17(2:1); 4:6–8.

4488. מָנֶה *māneh* **masc. noun**
(mina, a weight of money)
1 Kgs. 10:17; **Ezra** 2:69; **Neh.** 7:71,72; **Ezek.** 45:12.

4489. מֹנֶה *mōneh* **masc. noun**
(time, a counted number)
Gen. 31:7,41.

4490. מָנָה *mānāh* **fem. noun**
(portion, one's share)
Ex. 29:26; **Lev.** 7:33; 8:29; **1 Sam.** 1:4,5; 9:23; **2 Chr.** 31:19; **Neh.** 8:10,12; **Esth.** 2:9; 9:19,22; **Ps.** 16:5(NASB, NIV, *m^e^nāṯ* [4521]); **Jer.** 13:25(NASB, NIV, *m^e^nāṯ* [4521]).

4491. מִנְהָג *minhāg* **masc. noun**
(driving [of a chariot])
2 Kgs. 9:20.

4492. מִנְהָרָה *minhārāh* **fem. noun**
(den, shelter)
Judg. 6:2.

4493. מָנוֹד *mānôḏ* **masc. noun**
(a shaking [of the head])
Ps. 44:14(15).

4494. מָנוֹחַ *mānôaḥ* **masc. noun**
(rest, resting place)
Gen. 8:9; **Deut.** 28:65; **Ruth** 3:1; **1 Chr.** 6:31(16); **Ps.** 116:7; **Isa.** 34:14; **Lam.** 1:3.

4495. מָנוֹחַ *mānôaḥ* **masc. proper noun**
(Manoah)
Judg. 13:2,8,9,11–13,15–17,19–22; 16:31.

4496. מְנוּחָה *m^e^nûḥāh*, מְנֻחָה *m^e^nuḥāh* **fem. noun**
(resting place, rest, quiet)
Gen. 49:15; **Num.** 10:33; **Deut.** 12:9; **Judg.** 20:43; **Ruth** 1:9; **2 Sam.** 14:17; **1 Kgs.** 8:56; **1 Chr.** 22:9; 28:2; **Ps.** 23:2; 95:11; 132:8,14; **Isa.** 11:10; 28:12; 32:18; 66:1; **Jer.** 45:3; 51:59; **Mic.** 2:10; **Zech.** 9:1.

4497. I. מָנוֹן *mānôn* **masc. noun**
(son)
Prov. 29:21(NIV, see II).
II. מָנוֹן *mānôn* **masc. noun**
(grief)
Prov. 29:21(KJV, NASB, see I).

4498. מָנוֹס *mānôs* **masc. noun**
(refuge, place of escape, flight)
2 Sam. 22:3; **Job** 11:20; **Ps.** 59:16(17); 142:4(5); **Jer.** 16:19; 25:35; 46:5; **Amos** 2:14.

4499. מְנוּסָה m^e*nûsāh,* מְנֻסָה m^e*nusāh* **fem. noun**
(flight, fleeing)
Lev. 26:36; **Isa.** 52:12.

4500. מָנוֹר *mānôr* **masc. noun**
(beam, rod)
1 Sam. 17:7; **2 Sam.** 21:19; **1 Chr.** 11:23; 20:5.

4501. מְנוֹרָה m^e*nôrāh,* מְנֹרָה m^e*nōrāh* **fem. noun**
(lampstand)
Ex. 25:31–35; 26:35; 30:27; 31:8; 35:14; 37:17–20; 39:37; 40:4,24; **Lev.** 24:4; **Num.** 3:31; 4:9; 8:2–4; **1 Kgs.** 7:49; **2 Kgs.** 4:10; **1 Chr.** 28:15; **2 Chr.** 4:7,20; 13:11; **Jer.** 52:19; **Zech.** 4:2,11.

4502. I. מִנְּזָר *minn*^{e}*zār* **masc. noun**
(consecrated one, anointed one)
Nah. 3:17(NASB, NIV, see II).
II. מִנְּזָר *minn*^{e}*zār* **masc. noun**
(guard, guardsman)
Nah. 3:17(KJV, see I).

4503. מִנְחָה *minḥāh* **fem. noun**
(grain offering, tribute, gift)
Gen. 4:3–5; 32:13(14),18(19),20(21),21(22); 33:10; 43:11,15,25,26; **Ex.** 29:41; 30:9; 40:29; **Lev.** 2:1,3–11,13–15; 5:13; 6:14(7), 15(8),20(13),21(14),23(16); 7:9,10,37; 9:4,17; 10:12; 14:10,20,21,31; 23:13,16, 18,37; **Num.** 4:16; 5:15,18,25,26; 6:15,17; 7:13,19,25,31,37,43,49,55,61 ,67,73,79,87; 8:8; 15:4,6,9,24; 16:15; 18:9; 28:5,8,9,12,13,20,26,28,31; 29:3, 6,9,11,14,16,18,19,21,22,24,25,27,28,30, 31,33,34,37–39; **Josh.** 22:23,29; **Judg.** 3:15,17,18; 6:18; 13:19,23; **1 Sam.** 2:17,29; 3:14; 10:27; 26:19; **2 Sam.** 8:2,6; **1 Kgs.** 4:21(5:1); 8:64; 10:25; 18:29,36; **2 Kgs.** 3:20; 8:8,9; 16:13,15; 17:3,4; 20:12; **1 Chr.** 16:29; 18:2,6; 21:23; 23:29; **2 Chr.** 7:7; 9:24; 17:5,11; 26:8; 32:23; **Ezra** 9:4,5; **Neh.** 10:33(34); 13:5,9; **Ps.** 20:3(4); 40:6(7); 45:12(13); 72:10; 96:8; 141:2; **Isa.** 1:13; 19:21; 39:1; 43:23; 57:6; 66:3,20; **Jer.** 14:12; 17:26; 33:18; 41:5; **Ezek.** 42:13; 44:29; 45:15, 17,24,25; 46:5,7,11,14,15,20; **Dan.** 9:21,27; **Hos.** 10:6; **Joel** 1:9,13; 2:14; **Amos** 5:22,25; **Zeph.** 3:10; **Mal.** 1:10, 11,13; 2:12,13; 3:3,4.

4504. מִנְחָה *minḥāh* **Aram. fem. noun**
(grain offering; corr. to Hebr. 4503)
Ezra 7:17; **Dan.** 2:46.

4505. מְנַחֵם m^e*naḥēm* **masc. proper noun**
(Menahem: son of Gadi)
2 Kgs. 15:14,16,17,19–23.

4506. A. מָנַחַת *mānaḥaṯ* **masc. proper noun**
(Manahath: son of Shobal)
Gen. 36:23; **1 Chr.** 1:40.
B. מָנַחַת *mānaḥaṯ* **proper noun**
(Manahath: loc. in Judah)
1 Chr. 8:6.
C. מָנַחְתִּי *mānaḥtiy* **masc. proper noun**
(Manahathite)
1 Chr. 2:52(KJV, *ḥ*^{a}*ṣiy hamm*^{e}*nuḥôṯ* [2679]),54(KJV, *ḥ*^{a}*ṣiy hamm*^{e}*naḥtiy* [2680]).

4507. I. מְנִי m^e*niy* **masc. noun**
(number)
Isa. 65:11(NASB, NIV, see II).
II. מְנִי m^e*niy* **masc. proper noun**
(a false god)
Isa. 65:11(KJV, see I).

4508. מִנִּי *minniy* **proper noun**
(Minni)
Jer. 51:27.

4509. A. מִנְיָמִין *minyāmiyn* **masc. proper noun**

(Miniamin: priest under Nehemiah)
Neh. 12:17,41.
B. מִנְיָמִין *minyāmiyn* **masc. proper noun**
(Miniamin: priest under Hezekiah)
2 Chr. 31:15.

4510. מִנְיָן *minyān* **Aram. masc. noun**
(number)
Ezra 6:17.

4511. מִנִּית *minniyṯ* **proper noun**
(Minnith)
Judg. 11:33; **Ezek.** 27:17.

4512. I. מִנְלֶה *minleh* **masc. noun**
(perfection)
Job 15:29(NASB, see II; NIV, see III).
II. מִנְלֶה *minleh* **masc. noun**
(grain)
Job 15:29(KJV, see I; NIV, see III).
III. מִנְלֶה *minleh* **masc. noun**
(possession)
Job 15:29(KJV, see I; NASB, see II).

4513. מָנַע *māna'* **verb**
(to withhold, to keep back, to restrain)
Gen. 30:2; **Num.** 22:16; 24:11; **1 Sam.** 25:26,34; **2 Sam.** 13:13; **1 Kgs.** 20:7; **Neh.** 9:20; **Job** 20:13; 22:7; 31:16; 38:15; **Ps.** 21:2(3); 84:11(12); **Prov.** 1:15; 3:27; 11:26; 23:13; 30:7; **Eccl.** 2:10; **Jer.** 2:25; 3:3; 5:25; 31:16; 42:4; 48:10; **Ezek.** 31:15; **Joel** 1:13; **Amos** 4:7.

4514. מַנְעוּל *man'ûl,* מַנְעֻל *man'ul* **masc. noun**
(bolt, lock on a door)
Neh. 3:3,6,13–15; **Song** 5:5.

4515. I. מִנְעָל *min'āl* **masc. noun**
(lock [on a gate or door])
Deut. 33:25(KJV, see II).
II. מִנְעָל *min'āl* **masc. noun**
(shoe)
Deut. 33:25(NASB, NIV, see I).

4516. מַנְעַמִּים *man'ammiym* **masc. pl. noun**
(dainty morsels, delicacies)
Ps. 141:4.

4517. I. מְנַעַנְעִים *m^ena'an'iym* **masc. pl. noun**
(musical rattle; castanet or sistrum)
2 Sam. 6:5(KJV, see II).
II. מְנַעַנְעִים *m^ena'an'iym* **masc. pl. noun**
(musical horn; cornet)
2 Sam. 6:5(NASB, NIV, see I).

4518. מְנַקִּית *m^enaqqiyṯ* **fem. noun**
(bowl, cup)
Ex. 25:29; 37:16; **Num.** 4:7; **Jer.** 52:19.

4519. A. מְנַשֶּׁה *m^enaššeh* **masc. proper noun**
(Manasseh: son of Joseph)
Gen. 41:51; 46:20; 48:1,5,13,14,17,20; 50:23.
B. מְנַשֶּׁה *m^enaššeh* **masc. proper noun**
(tribe or territory of Mannaseh)
Num. 1:10,34,35; 2:20; 7:54; 10:23; 13:11; 26:28,29,34; 27:1; 32:33,39–41; 34:14,23; 36:1,12; **Deut.** 3:13,14; 33:17; 34:2; **Josh.** 1:12; 4:12; 12:6; 13:7,29,31; 14:4; 16:4,9; 17:1–3,5–12,17; 18:7; 20:8; 21:5,6,25,27; 22:1,7,9–11,13,15,21, 30,31; **Judg.** 1:27; 6:15,35; 7:23; 11:29; 12:4; **1 Kgs.** 4:13; **1 Chr.** 5:18,23,26; 6:61(46),62(47),70(55),71(56); 7:14,17, 29; 9:3; 12:19,20,31,37; 27:20,21; **2 Chr.** 15:9; 30:1,10,11,18; 31:1; 34:6,9; **Ps.** 60:7(9); 80:2(3); 108:8(9); **Isa.** 9:21(20); **Ezek.** 48:4,5.
C. מְנַשֶּׁה *m^enaššeh* **masc. proper noun**
(Manasseh: son of Hezekiah)
2 Kgs. 20:21; 21:1,9,11,16–18,20; 23:12,26; 24:3; **1 Chr.** 3:13; **2 Chr.** 32:33; 33:1,9–11,13,18,20,22,23; **Jer.** 15:4.

D. מְנַשֶּׁה *m^e^naššeh* **masc. proper noun**
(Manasseh: son of Pahath-Moab)
Ezra 10:30.
E. מְנַשֶּׁה *m^e^naššeh* **masc. proper noun**
(Manasseh: son of Hashum)
Ezra 10:33.
F. מְנַשֶּׁה *m^e^naššeh* **masc. proper noun**
(Manasseh: father of Gershom)
Judg. 18:30.

4520. מְנַשִּׁי *m^e^naššiy* **masc. proper noun**
(Manassite)
Deut. 4:43; 29:8(7); **2 Kgs.** 10:33; **1 Chr.** 26:32.

4521. מְנָת *m^e^nāṯ* **fem. noun**
(portion)
2 Chr. 31:3,4; **Neh.** 12:44,47; 13:10; **Ps.** 11:6; 16:5(KJV, *mānāh* [4490]); 63:10(11); **Jer.** 13:25(KJV, *mānāh* [4490]).

4522. מַס *mas* **masc. noun**
(forced labor or service, tribute)
Gen. 49:15; **Ex.** 1:11; **Deut.** 20:11; **Josh.** 16:10; 17:13; **Judg.** 1:28,30,33,35; **2 Sam.** 20:24; **1 Kgs.** 4:6; 5:13(27), 14(28); 9:15,21; 12:18; **2 Chr.** 8:8; 10:18; **Esth.** 10:1; **Prov.** 12:24; **Isa.** 31:8; **Lam.** 1:1.

4523. מָס *mās* **adj.**
(afflicted, despairing)
Job 6:14.

4524. I. מֵסַב *mēsaḇ* **masc. noun**
(around, surrounding area)
1 Kgs. 6:29; **2 Kgs.** 23:5; **Ps.** 140:9(10); **Song** 1:12.
II. מְסִבָּה *misbāh* **masc. noun**
(around)
Job 37:12.

4525. I. מַסְגֵּר *masgēr* **masc. noun**
(smith, locksmith)
2 Kgs. 24:14,16; **Jer.** 24:1; 29:2.
II. מַסְגֵּר *masgēr* **masc. noun**
(prison, dungeon)
Ps. 142:7(8); **Isa.** 24:22; 42:7.

4526. מִסְגֶּרֶת *misgereṯ* **fem. noun**
(border, rim, fortress)
Ex. 25:25,27; 37:12,14; **2 Sam.** 22:46; **1 Kgs.** 7:28,29,31,32,35,36; **2 Kgs.** 16:17; **Ps.** 18:45(46); **Mic.** 7:17.

4527. מַסַּד *massaḏ* **masc. noun**
(foundation)
1 Kgs. 7:9.

4528. מִסְדְּרוֹן *misd^e^rôn* **masc. noun**
(porch, vestibule)
Judg. 3:23.

4529. מָסָה *māsāh* **verb**
(to melt, to dissolve, to become water)
Josh. 14:8; **Ps.** 6:6(7); 39:11(12); 147:18.

4530. מִסָּה *missāh* **fem. noun**
(tribute, gift)
Deut. 16:10.

4531. I. מַסָּה *massāh* **fem. noun**
(trial, test, temptation)
Deut. 4:34; 7:19; 29:3(2); **Job** 9:23(NASB, NIV, see II); **Ps.** 95:8(NASB, NIV, *massāh* [4532]).
II. מַסָּה *massāh* **fem. noun**
(despair)
Job 9:23(KJV, see I).

4532. מַסָּה *massāh* **proper noun**
(Massah)
Ex. 17:7; **Deut.** 6:16; 9:22; 33:8; **Ps.** 95:8(KJV, *massāh* [4531,I]).

4533. מַסְוֶה *masweh* **masc. noun**
(veil)
Ex. 34:33–35.

4534. מְסוּכָה *m^e^sûḵāh* **fem. noun**
(hedge, thorn hedge)
Mic. 7:4.

4535. מַסָּח *massāḥ* **masc. noun**
(guard, defense, [lest something be broken down])
2 Kgs. 11:6.

4536. מִסְחָר *misḥār* **masc. noun**
(merchandise, sale of merchandise)
1 Kgs. 10:15.

4537. מָסַךְ *māsaḵ* **verb**
(to mix, to mingle)
Ps. 102:9(10); **Prov.** 9:2,5; **Isa.** 5:22; 19:14.

4538. מֶסֶךְ *meseḵ* **masc. noun**
(something fully mixed)
Ps. 75:8(9).

4539. מָסָךְ *māsāḵ* **masc. noun**
(curtain, covering, screen)
Ex. 26:36,37; 27:16; 35:12,15,17; 36:37; 38:18; 39:34,38,40; 40:5,8,21,28,33; **Num.** 3:25,26,31; 4:5,25,26; **2 Sam.** 17:19; **Ps.** 105:39; **Isa.** 22:8.

4540. מְסֻכָּה *m^e^sukāh* **fem. noun**
(covering, adorning)
Ezek. 28:13.

4541. I. מַסֵּכָה *massēḵāh* **fem. noun**
(cast image; libation)
Ex. 32:4,8; 34:17; **Lev.** 19:4; **Num.** 33:52; **Deut.** 9:12,16; 27:15; **Judg.** 17:3,4; 18:14,17,18; **1 Kgs.** 14:9; **2 Kgs.** 17:16; **2 Chr.** 28:2; 34:3,4; **Neh.** 9:18; **Ps.** 106:19; **Isa.** 30:22; 42:17; **Hos.** 13:2; **Nah.** 1:14; **Hab.** 2:18.
II. מַסֵּכָה *massēḵāh* **fem. noun**
(blanket, covering)
Isa. 25:7; 28:20; 30:1.

4542. מִסְכֵּן *miskēn* **adj.**
(poor)
Eccl. 4:13; 9:15,16.

4543. מִסְכְּנוֹת *misk^e^nôṯ* **fem. pl. noun**
(storage, storehouse)
Ex. 1:11; **1 Kgs.** 9:19; **2 Chr.** 8:4,6; 16:4; 17:12; 32:28.

4544. מִסְכֵּנֻת *miskēnuṯ* **fem. noun**
(scarceness, scarcity)
Deut. 8:9.

4545. מַסֶּכֶת *masseḵeṯ* **fem. noun**
(web [of fabric on a loom])
Judg. 16:13,14.

4546. מְסִלָּה *m^e^sillāh* **fem. noun**
(highway, public road)
Num. 20:19; **Judg.** 5:20; 20:31,32,45; 21:19; **1 Sam.** 6:12; **2 Sam.** 20:12,13; **2 Kgs.** 18:17; **1 Chr.** 26:16,18; **2 Chr.** 9:11; **Ps.** 84:5(6); **Prov.** 16:17; **Isa.** 7:3; 11:16; 19:23; 33:8; 36:2; 40:3; 49:11; 59:7; 62:10; **Jer.** 31:21; **Joel** 2:8.

4547. מַסְלוּל *maslûl* **masc. noun**
(highway)
Isa. 35:8.

4548. מַסְמֵר *masmēr*, מִסְמֵר *mismēr*, מַשְׂמֵר *maśmēr* **masc. noun**
(nail)
1 Chr. 22:3; **2 Chr.** 3:9; **Eccl.** 12:11 (KJV, NIV, *maśmērāh* [4930]); **Isa.** 41:7; **Jer.** 10:4.

4549. מָסַס *māsas* **verb**
(to melt, to dissolve)
Ex. 16:21; **Deut.** 1:28; 20:8; **Josh.** 2:11; 5:1; 7:5; **Judg.** 15:14; **1 Sam.** 15:9; **2 Sam.** 17:10; **Ps.** 22:14(15); 68:2(3); 97:5; 112:10; **Isa.** 10:18; 13:7; 19:1; 34:3; **Ezek.** 21:7(12); **Mic.** 1:4; **Nah.** 2:10(11).

4550. מַסָּע *massa'* **masc. noun**
(journey, moving on)
Gen. 13:3; **Ex.** 17:1; 40:36,38; **Num.** 10:2,6,12,28; 33:1,2; **Deut.** 10:11.

4551. I. מַסָּע *massā‘* **masc. noun**
(missile, dart)
Job 41:26(18).
II. מַסָּע *massā‘* **masc. noun**
(stone quarry)
1 Kgs. 6:7.

4552. מִסְעָד *mis‘āḏ* **masc. noun**
(support, pillar)
1 Kgs. 10:12.

4553. מִסְפֵּד *mispēḏ* **masc. noun**
(wailing, mourning, lamenting)
Gen. 50:10; **Esth.** 4:3; **Ps.** 30:11(12); **Isa.** 22:12; **Jer.** 6:26; 48:38; **Ezek.** 27:31; **Joel** 2:12; **Amos** 5:16,17; **Mic.** 1:8,11; **Zech.** 12:10,11.

4554. מִסְפּוֹא *mispô'* **masc. noun**
(fodder, animal food)
Gen. 24:25,32; 42:27; 43:24; **Judg.** 19:19.

4555. מִסְפָּחָה *mispāḥāh* **fem. noun**
(veil)
Ezek. 13:18,21.

4556. מִסְפַּחַת *mispaḥaṯ* **fem. noun**
(scab, rash)
Lev. 13:6–8.

4557. מִסְפָּר *mispār* **masc. noun**
(number, counts, amount)
Gen. 34:30; 41:49; **Ex.** 16:16; 23:26; **Lev.** 25:15,16,50; **Num.** 1:2,18,20,22, 24,26,28,30,32,34,36,38,40,42; 3:22, 28,34,40,43; 9:20; 14:29,34; 15:12; 23:10; 26:53; 29:18,21,24,27,30,33,37; 31:36; **Deut.** 4:27; 25:2; 32:8; 33:6; **Josh.** 4:5,8; **Judg.** 6:5; 7:6,12,15; 21:23; **1 Sam.** 6:4,18; 27:7; **2 Sam.** 2:11,15; 21:20; 24:2,9; **1 Kgs.** 18:31; **1 Chr.** 7:2,40; 9:28; 11:11; 12:23; 16:19; 21:2,5; 22:4,16; 23:3,24,27,31; 25:1,7; 27:1, 23,24; **2 Chr.** 12:3; 26:11,12; 29:32; 35:7; **Ezra** 1:9; 2:2; 3:4; 8:34; **Neh.** 7:7; **Esth.** 9:11; **Job** 1:5; 3:6; 5:9; 9:10; 14:5; 15:20; 16:22; 21:21,33; 25:3; 31:37; 36:26; 38:21; **Ps.** 40:12(13); 104:25; 105:12,34; 147:4,5; **Eccl.** 2:3; 5:18(17); 6:12; **Song** 6:8; **Isa.** 10:19; 21:17; 40:26; **Jer.** 2:28,32; 11:13; 44:28; 46:23; **Ezek.** 4:4,5,9; 5:3; 12:16; **Dan.** 9:2; **Hos.** 1:10(2:1); **Joel** 1:6.

4558. מִסְפָּר *mispār* **masc. proper noun**
(Mispar)
Ezra 2:2.

4559. מִסְפֶּרֶת *mispereṯ* **masc. proper noun**
(Mispereth)
Neh. 7:7.

4560. מָסַר *māsar* **verb**
(to commit, to deliver up)
Num. 31:5,16.

4561. מֹסָר *mōsār* **masc. noun**
(instruction, warnings)
Job 33:16(NASB, NIV, *mûsār* [4148]).

4562. מָסֹרֶת *māsōreṯ* **fem. noun**
(bond)
Ezek. 20:37.

4563. מִסְתּוֹר *mistôr* **masc. noun**
(hiding place, place of protection)
Isa. 4:6.

4564. מַסְתֵּר *mastēr* **masc. noun**
(the act of hiding)
Isa. 53:3.

4565. מִסְתָּר *mistār* **masc. noun**
(hiding place, place of ambush)
Ps. 10:8,9; 17:12; 64:4(5); **Isa.** 45:3; **Jer.** 13:17; 23:24; 49:10; **Lam.** 3:10; **Hab.** 3:14.

4566. מַעְבָּד *ma‘aḇāḏ* **masc. noun**
(work, deed)
Job 34:25.

4567. מַעֲבָד *ma'ăḇāḏ* **Aram. masc. noun**
(work, deed; corr. to Hebr. 4566)
Dan. 4:37(34).

4568. מַעֲבֶה *ma'ăḇeh* **masc. noun**
(clay)
1 Kgs. 7:46(NIV, [K^e] *'āḇ* [5645,III]).

4569. I. מַעֲבָר *ma'ăḇar* **masc. noun**
(passing)
Gen. 32:22(23); 1 Sam. 13:23; Isa. 30:32.
II. מַעְבָּרָה *ma'ḇārāh* **fem. noun**
(ford, passage)
Josh. 2:7; Judg. 3:28; 12:5,6; 1 Sam. 14:4; Isa. 10:29; 16:2; Jer. 51:32.

4570. I. מַעְגָּל *ma'gāl* **masc. noun**
(encampment, circle of a camp)
1 Sam. 17:20; 26:5,7.
II. מַעְגָּל *ma'gāl* **masc. noun**
(track, course, rut, path)
Ps. 17:5; 23:3; 65:11(12); 140:5(6); Prov. 2:9,15,18; 4:11,26; 5:6,21; Isa. 26:7; 59:8.

4571. מָעַד *mā'aḏ* **verb**
(to slip, to slide, to waver)
2 Sam. 22:37; Job 12:5; Ps. 18:36(37); 26:1; 37:31; 69:23(24); Prov. 25:19(KJV, *mû'eḏeṯ* [4154]); Ezek. 29:7(KJV, NASB, *'āmaḏ* [5976]).

4572. מַעֲדַי *ma'ăḏay* **masc. proper noun**
(Maadai)
Ezra 10:34.

4573. מַעַדְיָה *ma'aḏyāh* **masc. proper noun**
(Maadiah)
Neh. 12:5.

4574. I. מַעֲדָן *ma'ăḏān*, מַעֲדָנָה *ma'ăḏanāh* **fem. noun**
(beauty, delicacy, confidence)
1 Sam. 15:32; Job 38:31(KJV, *ma'ăḏanôṯ* [4575,II]; NASB, *ma'ăḏanôṯ* [4575,I]).
II. מַעֲדַנִּים *ma'ăḏanniym* **masc. pl. noun**
(delicacies, delight)
Gen. 49:20; Prov. 29:17; Lam. 4:5.

4575. I. מַעֲדַנּוֹת *ma'ăḏannôṯ* **fem. pl. noun**
(chains, fetters)
Job 38:31(KJV, see II; NIV, *ma'ăḏān* [4574,I]).
II. מַעֲדַנּוֹת *ma'ăḏannôṯ* **fem. pl. noun**
(sweet influences)
Job 38:31(NASB, see I, NIV, *ma'ăḏān* [4574,I]).

4576. מַעְדֵּר *ma'dēr* **masc. noun**
(hoe, mattock)
Isa. 7:25.

4577. מְעֵה *mə'ēh* **Aram. masc. noun**
(belly; corr. to Hebr. 4578)
Dan. 2:32.

4578. מֵעֶה *mē'eh* **masc. noun**
(body, abdomen, intestines)
Gen. 15:4; 25:23; Num. 5:22; Ruth 1:11; 2 Sam. 7:12; 16:11; 20:10; 2 Chr. 21:15,18,19; 32:21; Job 20:14; 30:27; Ps. 22:14(15); 40:8(9); 71:6; Song 5:4,14; Isa. 16:11; 48:19; 49:1; 63:15; Jer. 4:19; 31:20; Lam. 1:20; 2:11; Ezek. 3:3; 7:19; Jon. 1:17(2:1); 2:1(2).

4579. מֵעָה *mā'āh* **fem. noun**
(grain [of sand], gravel)
Isa. 48:19.

4580. מָעוֹג *mā'ôḡ* **masc. noun**
(cake, bread)
1 Kgs. 17:12; Ps. 35:16.

4581. I. מָעוֹז *mā'ôz* **masc. noun**
(refuge, fortress, shelter)

Judg. 6:26; **2 Sam.** 22:33; **Neh.** 8:10; **Ps.** 27:1; 28:8; 31:2(3),4(5); 37:39; 43:2; 52:7(9); 60:7(9); 108:8(9); **Prov.** 10:29; **Isa.** 17:9,10; 23:4,14; 25:4; 27:5; 30:2,3; **Jer.** 16:19; **Ezek.** 24:25; 30:15; **Dan.** 11:1,7,10,19,31,38,39; **Joel** 3:16(4:16); **Nah.** 1:7; 3:11.
II. מָעוֹזֶן *mā'ôzen* **masc. noun**
(stronghold, fortress)
Isa. 23:11.

4582. מָעוֹךְ *mā'ôḵ* **masc. proper noun**
(Maoch)
1 Sam. 27:2.

4583. מָעוֹן *mā'ôn*, מָעִין *mā'iyn* **masc. noun**
(dwelling, habitation, refuge)
Deut. 26:15; **1 Sam.** 2:29,32; **1 Chr.** 4:41(NASB, NIV, *m^e'ûniym* [4586]); **2 Chr.** 30:27; 36:15; **Ps.** 26:8; 68:5(6); 71:3; 90:1; 91:9; **Jer.** 9:11(10); 10:22; 25:30; 49:33; 51:37; **Nah.** 2:11(12); **Zeph.** 3:7; **Zech.** 2:13(17).

4584. A. מָעוֹן *mā'ôn* **masc. proper noun**
(Maon: son of Shammai)
1 Chr. 2:45.
B. מָעוֹן *mā'ôn* **masc. proper noun**
(Maon: city in Judah)
Josh. 15:55; **1 Sam.** 23:24,25; 25:2.
C. מָעוֹן *mā'ôn* **masc. proper noun**
(Maon: an Arabian tribe)
Judg. 10:12.

4585. מְעוֹנָה *m^e'ônāh*, מְעֹנָה *m^e'ōnāh* **fem. noun**
(dwelling place, refuge)
Deut. 33:27; **Job** 37:8; 38:40; **Ps.** 76:2(3); 104:22; **Song** 4:8; **Jer.** 21:13; **Amos** 3:4; **Nah.** 2:12(13).

4586. מְעוּנִים *m^e'ûniym* **masc. pl. proper noun**
(Meunim, Meunites)
1 Chr. 4:41(KJV, *mā'iyn* [4583]); **2 Chr.** 26:7; **Ezra** 2:50; **Neh.** 7:52.

4587. מְעוֹנֹתַי *m^e'ônōṯay* **?asc. proper noun**
(Meonothai)
1 Chr. 4:14.

4588. מָעוּף *mā'ûp̱* **masc. noun**
(gloom, dimness)
Isa. 8:22.

4589. מָעוֹר *mā'ôr* **masc. noun**
(naked body)
Hab. 2:15.

4590. A. מַעַזְיָה *ma'azyāh* **masc. proper noun**
(Maaziah: priest under Nehemiah)
Neh. 10:8(9).
B. מַעַזְיָהוּ *ma'azyāhû* **masc. proper noun**
(Maaziah: priest under David)
1 Chr. 24:18.

4591. מָעַט *mā'aṭ* **verb**
(to decrease, to become small, to be small)
Ex. 12:4; 16:17,18; 30:15; **Lev.** 25:16; 26:22; **Num.** 11:32; 26:54; 33:54; 35:8; **2 Kgs.** 4:3; **Neh.** 9:32; **Ps.** 107:38,39; **Prov.** 13:11; **Eccl.** 12:3; **Isa.** 21:17; **Jer.** 10:24; 29:6; 30:19; **Ezek.** 29:15.

4592. מְעַט *m^e'aṭ* **masc. noun**
(small amount, few, short time)
Gen. 18:4; 24:17,43; 26:10; 30:15,30; 43:2,11; 44:25; 47:9; **Ex.** 17:4; 23:30; **Lev.** 25:52; **Num.** 13:18; 16:9,13; 26:54,56; 33:54; 35:8; **Deut.** 7:7,22; 26:5; 28:38,62; **Josh.** 7:3; 22:17; **Judg.** 4:19; **Ruth** 2:7; **1 Sam.** 14:6,29,43; 17:28; **2 Sam.** 12:8; 16:1; 19:36(37); **1 Kgs.** 17:10,12; **2 Kgs.** 10:18; **1 Chr.** 16:19; **2 Chr.** 12:7; 29:34; **Ezra** 9:8; **Neh.** 2:12; 7:4; **Job** 10:20; 15:11; 24:24; 32:22; **Ps.** 2:12; 8:5(6); 37:10,16; 73:2;

81:14(15); 94:17; 105:12; 109:8; 119:87; **Prov.** 5:14; 6:10; 10:20; 15:16; 16:8; 24:33; **Eccl.** 5:2(1),12(11); 9:14; 10:1; **Song** 3:4; **Isa.** 1:9; 7:13; 10:7,25; 16:14; 26:20; 29:17; **Jer.** 42:2; 51:33; **Ezek.** 5:3; 11:16; 16:20,47; 34:18; **Dan.** 11:23,34; **Hos.** 1:4; 8:10; **Hag.** 1:6,9; 2:6; **Zech.** 1:15.

4593. מְעֻטָּה *mᵉ'uṭṭāh* **adj.**
(grasped, drawn, wrapped)
Ezek. 21:15(20)(NASB, *'āṭāh* [5844,I]; NIV, *'āṭāh* [5844,II]).

4594. מַעֲטֶה *ma'ᵃṭeh* **masc. noun**
(garment, mantle)
Isa. 61:3.

4595. מַעֲטֶפֶת *ma'ᵃṭepeṯ* **fem. noun**
(outer tunic, cape)
Isa. 3:22.

4596. מְעִי *mᵉ'iy* **masc. noun**
(ruin, heap)
Isa. 17:1.

4597. מָעַי *mā'ay* **masc. proper noun**
(Maai)
Neh. 12:36.

4598. מְעִיל *mᵉ'iyl* **masc. noun**
(robe, cloak)
Ex. 28:4,31,34; 29:5; 39:22–26; **Lev.** 8:7; **1 Sam.** 2:19; 15:27; 18:4; 24:4(5),11(12); 28:14; **2 Sam.** 13:18; **1 Chr.** 15:27; **Ezra** 9:3,5; **Job** 1:20; 2:12; 29:14; **Ps.** 109:29; **Isa.** 59:17; 61:10; **Ezek.** 26:16.

4599. מַעְיָן *ma'yān* **masc. noun**
(spring, fountain)
Gen. 7:11; 8:2; **Lev.** 11:36; **Josh.** 15:9; 18:15; **1 Kgs.** 18:5; **2 Kgs.** 3:19,25; **2 Chr.** 32:4; **Ps.** 74:15; 84:6(7); 87:7; 104:10; 114:8; **Prov.** 5:16; 8:24; 25:26; **Song** 4:12,15; **Isa.** 12:3; 41:18; **Hos.** 13:15; **Joel** 3:18(4:18).

4600. מָעַךְ *mā'aḵ* **verb**
(to squeeze, to crush, to bruise)
Lev. 22:24; **1 Sam.** 26:7; **Ezek.** 23:3,21(KJV, NASB, *ma'an* [4616]).

4601. A. מַעֲכָה *ma'ᵃḵāh* **masc. proper noun**
(Maacah: son of Nahor)
Gen. 22:24.
B. מַעֲכָה *ma'ᵃḵāh* **fem. proper noun**
(Maacah: wife of Machir)
1 Chr. 7:15,16.
C. מַעֲכָה *ma'ᵃḵāh* **fem. proper noun**
(Maacah: a concubine)
1 Chr. 2:48.
D. מַעֲכָה *ma'ᵃḵāh* **fem. proper noun**
(Maacah: wife of Jeiel)
1 Chr. 8:29; 9:35.
E. מַעֲכָה *ma'ᵃḵāh* **fem. proper noun**
(Maacah: daughter of Talmai)
2 Sam. 3:3; **1 Chr.** 3:2.
F. מַעֲכָה *ma'ᵃḵāh* **masc. proper noun**
(Maacah: father of Hanan)
1 Chr. 11:43.
G. מַעֲכָה *ma'ᵃḵāh* **masc. proper noun**
(Maacah: father of Shephatiah)
1 Chr. 27:16.
H. מַעֲכָה *ma'ᵃḵāh* **masc. proper noun**
(Maacah: father of Achish)
1 Kgs. 2:39.
I. מַעֲכָה *ma'ᵃḵāh* **fem. proper noun**
(Maacah: wife of Rehoboam)
1 Kgs. 15:2,10,13; **2 Chr.** 11:20–22; 15:16.
J. מַעֲכָה *ma'ᵃḵāh* **fem. proper noun**
(Maacah: loc. near Mt. Hermon)
2 Sam. 10:6,8; **1 Chr.** 19:6,7.

K. מַעֲכָה *maʿakāh* **masc. proper noun**
(Maacathite: descendant of Maacah)
Josh. 13:13.

4602. מַעֲכָתִי *maʿakātiy* **masc. proper noun**
(Maacathite)
Deut. 3:14; **Josh.** 12:5; 13:11,13; **2 Sam.** 23:34; **2 Kgs.** 25:23; **1 Chr.** 4:19; **Jer.** 40:8.

4603. מָעַל *māʿal* **verb**
(to transgress, to act unfaithfully, to commit [a trespass])
Lev. 5:15; 6:2(5:21); 26:40; **Num.** 5:6,12,27; **Deut.** 32:51; **Josh.** 7:1; 22:16,20,31; **1 Chr.** 2:7; 5:25; 10:13; **2 Chr.** 12:2; 26:16,18; 28:19,22; 29:6; 30:7; 36:14; **Ezra** 10:2,10; **Neh.** 1:8; 13:27; **Prov.** 16:10; **Ezek.** 14:13; 15:8; 17:20; 18:24; 20:27; 39:23,26; **Dan.** 9:7.

4604. מַעַל *maʿal* **masc. noun**
(transgression, trespass)
Lev. 5:15; 6:2(5:21); 26:40; **Num.** 5:6,12,27; 31:16; **Josh.** 7:1; 22:16,20,22,31; **1 Chr.** 9:1; 10:13; **2 Chr.** 28:19; 29:19; 33:19; 36:14; **Ezra** 9:2,4; 10:6; **Job** 21:34; **Ezek.** 14:13; 15:8; 17:20; 18:24; 20:27; 39:26; **Dan.** 9:7.

4605. מַעַל *maʿal* **adv., prep.**
(upward, high; above, over)
Gen. 6:16; 7:20; 22:9; **Ex.** 20:4; 25:20,21; 26:14; 28:27; 30:14; 36:19; 37:9; 38:26; 39:20,31; 40:19,20; **Lev.** 11:21; 27:7; **Num.** 1:3,18,20,22,24,26,28,30,32,34, 36,38,40,42,45; 3:15,22,28,34,39,40,43; 4:3,6,23,25,30,35,39,43,47; 8:24; 14:29; 26:2,4,62; 32:11; **Deut.** 4:39; 5:8; 28:13,43; **Josh.** 2:11; 3:13,16; **Judg.** 1:36; 7:13; **1 Sam.** 9:2; 10:23; 16:13; 30:25; **1 Kgs.** 7:3,11,20,25,29,31; 8:7,23; **2 Kgs.** 3:21; 19:30; **1 Chr.** 14:2; 22:5; 23:3,17,24,27; 29:3,25; **2 Chr.** 1:1; 4:4; 5:8; 16:12; 17:12; 20:19; 25:5; 26:8; 31:16,17; 34:4; **Ezra** 3:8; 9:6; **Job** 3:4; 18:16; 31:2,28; **Ps.** 74:5; 78:23; **Prov.** 8:28; 15:24; **Eccl.** 3:21; **Isa.** 6:2; 7:11; 8:21; 14:13; 37:31; 45:8; **Jer.** 4:28; 31:37; 35:4; 43:10; 52:32; **Ezek.** 1:11,22,26,27; 8:2; 10:19; 11:22; 37:8; 41:7; 43:15; **Dan.** 12:6,7; **Amos** 2:9; **Hag.** 2:15,18.

4606. מֶעָל *meʿāl* **Aram. masc. noun**
(going down, setting [of the sun])
Dan. 6:14(15).

4607. מֹעַל *mōʿal* **masc. noun**
(lifting up)
Neh. 8:6.

4608. I. מַעֲלֶה *maʿaleh* **masc. noun**
(ascent)
Num. 34:4(NIV, *maʿalēh ʿaqrabbiym* [4610]); **Josh.** 10:10; 15:3(KJV, NIV, *maʿalēh ʿaqrabbiym* [4610]),7(NIV, see II); 18:17(NIV, see II); **Judg.** 1:36(NIV, *maʿalēh ʿaqrabbiym* [4610]); 8:13; **1 Sam.** 9:11; **2 Sam.** 15:30; **2 Kgs.** 9:27; **2 Chr.** 20:16; 32:33; **Neh.** 9:4; 12:37; **Isa.** 15:5; **Jer.** 48:5; **Ezek.** 40:31,34,37.
II. מַעֲלֶה *maʿaleh* **masc. proper noun**
(ascent, pass; part of the name Pass of Adummim [see *ʾadummiym* [131])
Josh. 15:7(KJV, NASB, see I); 18:17(KJV, NASB, see I).

4609. I. מַעֲלָה *maʿalāh* **fem. noun**
(step, degree, ascent)
Ex. 20:26; **1 Kgs.** 10:19,20; **2 Kgs.** 9:13; 20:9–11; **1 Chr.** 17:17; **2 Chr.** 9:18,19; **Ezra** 7:9; **Neh.** 3:15; 12:37; **Ps.** 120:[title](1); 121:[title](1); 122:[title](1); 123:[title](1); 124:[title](1); 125:[title](1); 126:[title](1); 127:[title](1); 128:[title](1); 129:[title](1); 130:[title](1); 131:[title](1); 132:[title](1); 133:[title](1); 134:[title](1);

Isa. 38:8; **Ezek.** 40:6,22,26,31,34,37,49; 43:17; **Amos** 9:6.
II. מַעֲלָה *ma'alāh* **fem. noun**
(thought)
Ezek. 11:5; **Num.** 34:4(KJV, NASB, *ma'aleh* [4608,I] and *'aqrāb* [6137]).

4610. A. מַעֲלֵה עַקְרַבִּים *ma'alēh 'aqrabbiym* **masc. proper noun**
(Scorpion Pass; from *ma'aleh* [4608,I] and *'aqrabbiym* [6137,II])
Num. 34:4; **Josh.** 15:3; **Judg.** 1:36.
B. מַעֲלֵה עַקְרַבִּים *ma'alēh 'aqrabbiym* **masc. proper noun**
(Maalehacrabbim)
Josh. 15:3(NIV, see I; NASB, see III).
C. מַעֲלֵה עַקְרַבִּים *ma'alēh 'aqrabbiym* **masc. proper noun**
(Ascent of Akrabbim)
Num. 34:4(KJV, *ma'aleh* [4608,I] and *'aqrabbiym* [6137,II]; NIV, see I); **Josh.** 15:3(KJV, see II, NIV, see I); **Judg.** 1:36 (KJV, *ma'aleh* [4608,I] and *'aqrabbiym* [6137,II]; NIV, see I).

4611. מַעֲלָל *ma'alāl* **masc. noun**
(action, deed, that which is done)
Deut. 28:20; **Judg.** 2:19; **1 Sam.** 25:3; **Neh.** 9:35; **Ps.** 28:4; 77:11(12); 78:7; 106:29,39; **Prov.** 20:11; **Isa.** 1:16; 3:8,10; **Jer.** 4:4,18; 7:3,5; 11:18; 17:10; 18:11; 21:12,14; 23:2,22; 25:5; 26:3,13; 32:19; 35:15; 44:22; **Ezek.** 36:31; **Hos.** 4:9; 5:4; 7:2; 9:15; 12:2(3); **Mic.** 2:7; 3:4; 7:13; **Zech.** 1:4,6.

4612. מַעֲמָד *ma'amād* **masc. noun**
(office, position, place)
1 Kgs. 10:5; **1 Chr.** 23:28; **2 Chr.** 9:4; 35:15; **Isa.** 22:19.

4613. מָעֳמָד *mo'omād* **masc. noun**
(foothold, place to stand)
Ps. 69:2(3).

4614. מַעֲמָסָה *ma'amāsāh* **fem. noun**
(heavy, immoveable)
Zech. 12:3.

4615. מַעֲמַקִּים *ma'amaqqiym* **masc. pl. noun**
(depths [of waters])
Ps. 69:2(3),14(15); 130:1; **Isa.** 51:10; **Ezek.** 27:34.

4616. מַעַן *ma'an* **particle**
(only with prefix prep. *l*: so that, because of, for the sake of)
Gen. 12:13; 18:19,24; 27:25; 37:22; 50:20; **Ex.** 1:11; 4:5; 8:10(6),22(18); 9:16,29; 10:1,2; 11:7,9; 13:9; 16:4,32; 20:12; 23:12; 33:13; **Lev.** 17:5; 20:3; 23:43; **Num.** 15:40; 16:40(17:5); 27:20; 36:8; **Deut.** 2:30; 3:26; 4:1,40; 5:14,16, 29(26),33(30); 6:2,18,23; 8:1–3,16,18; 9:5; 11:8,9,21; 12:25,28; 13:17(18); 14:23,29; 16:3,20; 17:16,19,20; 20:18; 22:7; 23:20(21); 24:19; 25:15; 27:3; 29:6(5),9(8),13(12),19(18); 30:6,19; 31:12,19; **Josh.** 1:7,8; 3:4; 4:6,24; 11:20; **Judg.** 2:22; 3:2; **1 Sam.** 15:15; 17:28; **2 Sam.** 13:5; **1 Kgs.** 2:3,4; 8:40,41, 43,60; 11:12,13,32,34,36,39; 12:15; 15:4; **2 Kgs.** 8:19; 10:19; 13:23; 19:34; 20:6; 22:17; 23:24; **1 Chr.** 28:8; **2 Chr.** 6:31–33; 10:15; 21:7; 25:20; 31:4; 32:18; 34:25; **Ezra** 9:12; **Neh.** 6:13; **Job** 18:4; 19:29; 40:8; **Ps.** 5:8(9); 6:4(5); 8:2(3); 9:14(15); 23:3; 25:7,11; 27:11; 30:12(13); 31:3(4); 44:26(27); 48:11(12),13(14); 51:4(6); 60:5(7); 68:23(24); 69:18(19); 78:6; 79:9; 97:8; 106:8; 108:9; 109:21; 119:11,71,80,101; 122:8,9; 125:3; 130:4; 143:11; **Prov.** 2:20; 15:24; 16:4(NASB, NIV, *ma'an* [4617,II]); **Isa.** 42:21; 43:14,25; 44:9; 45:3,4,6; 48:9,11; 49:7; 55:5; 62:1; 63:17; 65:8; 66:5,11; **Jer.** 4:14; 7:10,18,19,23; 10:18; 11:5; 14:7,21; 25:7; 27:10,15; 32:14,29,35; 35:7; 36:3; 42:6; 43:3; 44:8,29; 50:34; 51:39; **Ezek.** 4:17; 6:6; 11:20; 12:16,19; 14:5,11; 16:54,63; 19:9; 20:9,14,22,26,44; 21:10(15),15(20),28(33); 22:6,9,12,27;

23:21(NIV, *ma'ᵃneh* [4600]); 24:11; 25:10; 26:20; 31:14; 36:5,22,30,32; 38:16; 39:12; 40:4; 46:18; **Dan.** 9:17,19; **Hos.** 8:4; **Joel** 3:6(4:6); **Amos** 1:13; 2:7; 5:14; 9:12; **Obad.** 1:9; **Mic.** 6:5,16; **Hab.** 2:2,15; **Zech.** 12:7; 13:4.

4617. I. מַעֲנֶה *ma'ᵃneh* **masc. noun** (answer, response)
Job 32:3,5; **Prov.** 15:1,23; 16:1; 29:19; **Mic.** 3:7.
II. מַעֲנֶה *ma'ᵃneh* **masc. noun** (end, purpose)
Prov. 16:4.

4618. מַעֲנָה *ma'ᵃnāh* **fem. noun** (furrow, plowed row, place for a furrow)
1 Sam. 14:14; **Ps.** 129:3.

4619. מַעַץ *ma'aṣ* **masc. proper noun** (Maaz: son of Ram)
1 Chr. 2:27.

4620. מַעֲצֵבָה *ma'ᵃṣēḇāh* **fem. noun** (torment, sorrow)
Isa. 50:11.

4621. מַעֲצָד *ma'ᵃṣāḏ* **masc. noun** (ax, tongs)
Isa. 44:12; **Jer.** 10:3.

4622. מַעְצוֹר *ma'ṣôr* **masc. noun** (restraint, hindrance)
1 Sam. 14:6.

4623. מַעְצָר *ma'ṣār* **masc. noun** (control, rule)
Prov. 25:28.

4624. מַעֲקֶה *ma'ᵃqeh* **masc. noun** (parapet, battlement)
Deut. 22:8.

4625. מַעֲקַשִּׁים *ma'ᵃqaššiym* **masc. pl. noun** (crooked places, rough places)
Isa. 42:16.

4626. מַעַר *ma'ar* **masc. noun** (bare place, nakedness)
1 Kgs. 7:36; **Nah.** 3:5.

4627. מַעֲרָב *ma'ᵃrāḇ* **masc. noun** (merchandise, wares)
Ezek. 27:9,13,17,19,25,27,33,34.

4628. מַעֲרָב *ma'ᵃrāḇ* **masc. noun** (west, westward)
Judg. 20:33(KJV, *ma'ᵃreh* [4629,I]; NASB, *ma'ᵃrēh gāḇa'* [4629,II]); **1 Chr.** 7:28; 12:15; 26:16,18,30; **2 Chr.** 32:30; 33:14; **Ps.** 75:6(7); 103:12; 107:3; **Isa.** 43:5; 45:6; 59:19; **Dan.** 8:5.

4629. I. מַעֲרֶה *ma'ᵃreh* **masc. noun** (meadow)
Judg. 20:33(NASB, see II; NIV, *ma'ᵃrāḇ* [4628]).
II. מַעֲרֵה־גָבַע *ma'ᵃrēh gāḇa'* **proper noun** (Maareh-geba; loc. near Geba)
Judg. 20:33(KJV, see I; NIV, *ma'ᵃrāḇ* [4628]).

4630. מַעֲרָה *ma'ᵃrāh* **fem. noun** (army)
1 Sam. 17:23(NASB, NIV, [Qᵉ] *ma'ᵃrāḵāh* [4634]).

4631. I. מְעָרָה *mᵉ'ārāh* **fem. noun** (cave, den)
Gen. 19:30; 23:9,11,17,19,20; 25:9; 49:29,30,32; 50:13; **Josh.** 10:16–18,22, 23,27; **Judg.** 6:2; **1 Sam.** 13:6; 22:1; 24:3(4),7(8),8(9),10(11); **2 Sam.** 23:13; **1 Kgs.** 18:4,13; 19:9,13; **1 Chr.** 11:15; **Ps.** 57:[title](1); 142:[title](1); **Isa.** 2:19; 32:14(NIV, see II); **Jer.** 7:11; **Ezek.** 33:27.
II. מְעָרָה *mᵉ'ārāh* **fem. noun** (wasteland, bare ground)
Isa. 32:14(KJV, NASB, see I).

4632. I. מְעָרָה *mᵉʿārāh* **proper noun**
(Mearah: loc. E. of Sidon)
Josh. 13:4(NIV, see II).
II. עָרָה *ʿārāh* **proper noun**
(Arah: loc. E. of Sidon)
Josh. 13:4(KJV, NASB, see I).

4633. מַעֲרָךְ *maʿᵃrāḵ* **masc. noun**
(plan, preparation)
Prov. 16:1.

4634. מַעֲרָכָה *maʿᵃrāḵāh* **fem. noun**
(an ordered place, a military array)
Ex. 39:37; **Lev.** 24:6; **Judg.** 6:26; **1 Sam.** 4:2,12,16; 17:8,10,20–22,23 (KJV, [Kᵉ] *maʿᵃrāh* [4630]),26,36,45,48; 23:3; **1 Chr.** 12:38.

4635. מַעֲרֶכֶת *maʿᵃreḵeṯ* **fem. noun**
(row, line [especially of the twelve loaves of showbread])
Lev. 24:6,7; **1 Chr.** 9:32; 23:29; 28:16; **2 Chr.** 2:4(3); 13:11; 29:18; **Neh.** 10:33(34).

4636. מַעֲרֹם *maʿᵃrōm* **masc. noun**
(nakedness)
2 Chr. 28:15.

4637. מַעֲרָצָה *maʿᵃraṣāh* **fem. noun**
(great power, terror)
Isa. 10:33.

4638. מַעֲרָת *maʿᵃrāṯ* **proper noun**
(Maarath)
Josh. 15:59.

4639. מַעֲשֶׂה *maʿᵃśeh* **masc. noun**
(work, deed, workmanship)
Gen. 5:29; 20:9; 40:17; 44:15; 46:33; 47:3; **Ex.** 5:4,13; 18:20; 23:12,16,24; 24:10; 26:1,31,36; 27:4,16; 28:6,8,11, 14,15,22,32,39; 30:25,35; 32:16; 34:10; 36:8,35,37; 37:29; 38:4,18; 39:3,5,8,15, 22,27,29; **Lev.** 18:3; **Num.** 8:4; 16:28; 31:20,51; **Deut.** 2:7; 3:24; 4:28; 11:3,7; 14:29; 15:10; 16:15; 24:19; 27:15; 28:12; 30:9; 31:29; **Josh.** 24:31; **Judg.** 2:7,10; 13:12; 19:16; **1 Sam.** 8:8; 19:4; 20:19; 25:2; **1 Kgs.** 7:8,17,19,22,26,28,29, 31,33; 13:11; 16:7; **2 Kgs.** 16:10; 19:18; 22:17; 23:19; **1 Chr.** 9:31; 23:28; **2 Chr.** 3:10; 4:5,6; 16:14; 17:4; 20:37; 31:21; 32:19,30; 34:25; **Ezra** 9:13; **Neh.** 6:14; **Esth.** 10:2; **Job** 1:10; 14:15; 33:17; 34:19; 37:7; **Ps.** 8:3(4),6(7); 19:1(2); 28:4,5; 33:4,15; 45:1(2); 62:12(13); 64:9(10); 66:3; 86:8; 90:17; 92:4(5),5(6); 102:25(26); 103:22; 104:13,24,31; 106:13,35,39; 107:22,24; 111:2,6,7; 115:4; 118:17; 135:15; 138:8; 139:14; 143:5; 145:4,9,10,17; **Prov.** 16:3,11; 31:31; **Eccl.** 1:14; 2:4,11,17; 3:11,17,22; 4:3,4; 5:6(5); 7:13; 8:9,11,14,17; 9:7,10; 11:5; 12:14; **Song** 7:1(2); **Isa.** 2:8; 3:24; 5:12,19; 10:12; 17:8; 19:14,15,25; 26:12; 28:21; 29:15,16,23; 32:17; 37:19; 41:29; 54:16; 57:12; 59:6; 60:21; 64:8(7); 65:22; 66:18; **Jer.** 1:16; 7:13; 10:3,9,15; 25:6,7, 14; 32:30; 44:8; 48:7; 51:10,18; **Lam.** 3:64; 4:2; **Ezek.** 1:16; 6:6; 16:30; 27:16,18; 46:1; **Dan.** 9:14; **Hos.** 13:2; 14:3(4); **Amos** 8:7; **Jon.** 3:10; **Mic.** 5:13(12); 6:16; **Hab.** 3:17; **Hag.** 2:14,17.

4640. מַעְשַׂי *maʿśay* **masc. proper noun**
(Maasai)
1 Chr. 9:12.

4641. A. מַעֲשֵׂיָהוּ *maʿᵃśēyāhû* **masc. proper noun**
(Maaseiah: a Levite)
1 Chr. 15:18,20.
B. מַעֲשֵׂיָהוּ *maʿᵃśēyāhû* **masc. proper noun**
(Maaseiah: son of Adaiah)
2 Chr. 23:1.
C. מַעֲשֵׂיָהוּ *maʿᵃśēyāhû* **masc. proper noun**
(Maaseiah: a ruler)
2 Chr. 26:11.

D. מַעֲשֵׂיָהוּ *ma'ᵃśēyāhû* **masc. proper noun**
(Maaseiah: son of Ahaz)
2 Chr. 28:7.
E. מַעֲשֵׂיָה *ma'ᵃśēyāh* **masc. proper noun**
(Maaseiah: father of Zephaniah)
Jer. 21:1; 29:25; 37:3.
F. מַעֲשֵׂיָהוּ *ma'ᵃśēyāhû* **masc. proper noun**
(Maaseiah: governor of Jerusalem)
2 Chr. 34:8.
G. מַעֲשֵׂיָה *ma'ᵃśēyāh* **proper noun**
(Maaseiah: father of Zedekiah, a false prophet)
Jer. 29:21.
H. מַעֲשֵׂיָהוּ *ma'ᵃśēyāhû* **masc. proper noun**
(Maaseiah: son of Shallum)
Jer. 35:4.
I. מַעֲשֵׂיָה *ma'ᵃśēyāh* **masc. proper noun**
(Maaseiah: son of Ithiel)
Neh. 11:7.
J. מַעֲשֵׂיָה *ma'ᵃśēyāh* **masc. proper noun**
(Maaseiah: father of Azariah)
Neh. 3:23.
K. מַעֲשֵׂיָה *ma'ᵃśēyāh* **masc. proper noun**
(Maaseiah: descendant of Jeshua)
Ezra 10:18.
L. מַעֲשֵׂיָה *ma'ᵃśēyāh* **masc. proper noun**
(Maaseiah: descendant of Harim)
Ezra 10:21.
M. מַעֲשֵׂיָה *ma'ᵃśēyāh* **masc. proper noun**
(Maaseiah: descendant of Pashhur)
Ezra 10:22.
N. מַעֲשֵׂיָה *ma'ᵃśēyāh* **masc. proper noun**
(Maaseiah: son of Pahath-Moab)
Ezra 10:30.
O. מַעֲשֵׂיָה *ma'ᵃśēyāh* **masc. proper noun**
(Maaseiah: a priest)
Neh. 8:4,7.
P. מַעֲשֵׂיָה *ma'ᵃśēyāh* **masc. proper noun**
(Maaseiah: leader under Nehemiah)
Neh. 10:25(26).
Q. מַעֲשֵׂיָה *ma'ᵃśēyāh* **masc. proper noun**
(Maaseiah: son of Baruch)
Neh. 11:5.
R. מַעֲשֵׂיָה *ma'ᵃśēyāh* **masc. proper noun**
(Maaseiah: a priest)
Neh. 12:41.
S. מַעֲשֵׂיָה *ma'ᵃśēyāh* **masc. proper noun**
(Maaseiah: a priest)
Neh. 12:42.

4642. מַעֲשַׁקּוֹת *ma'šaqqôṯ* **fem. pl. noun**
(extortions, oppressions)
Prov. 28:16; **Isa.** 33:15.

4643. מַעֲשֵׂר *ma'ᵃśēr* **masc. noun**
(tithe, tenth part)
Gen. 14:20; **Lev.** 27:30–32; **Num.** 18:21,24,26,28; **Deut.** 12:6,11,17; 14:23,28; 26:12; **2 Chr.** 31:5,6,12; **Neh.** 10:37(38),38(39); 12:44; 13:5,12; **Ezek.** 45:11,14; **Amos** 4:4; **Mal.** 3:8,10.

4644. מֹף *mōp̱* **proper noun**
(Memphis, another name for *nōp̱* [5297])
Hos. 9:6.

4645. מִפְגָּע *mip̱gā'* **masc. noun**
(target, mark)
Job 7:20.

4646. מַפָּח *mappāḥ* **masc. noun**
(breathing out, expiring, dying)
Job 11:20.

4647. מַפֻּחַ *mappuaḥ* **masc. noun**
(bellows)
Jer. 6:29.

4648. A. מְפִיבֹשֶׁת *m*^{e}*p̱iyḇōšeṯ* **masc. proper noun**
(Mephibosheth: son of Saul)
2 Sam. 21:8.
B. מְפִיבֹשֶׁת *m*^{e}*p̱iyḇōšeṯ* **masc. proper noun**
(Mephibosheth: son of Jonathan)
2 Sam. 4:4; 9:6,10–13; 16:1,4; 19:24(25),25(26),30(31); 21:7.

4649. מֻפִּים *muppiym* **masc. proper noun**
(Muppim)
Gen. 46:21.

4650. מֵפִיץ *mep̱iyṣ* **masc. noun**
(club, maul)
Prov. 25:18.

4651. מַפָּל *mappāl* **masc. noun**
(fallen parts, sweeping; folds [of a crocodile])
Job 41:23(15); **Amos** 8:6.

4652. מִפְלָאָה *mip̱lāʾāh* **fem. noun**
(wonderful work)
Job 37:16.

4653. מִפְלַגָּה *mip̱laggāh* **fem. noun**
(a grouping, division [of the priests])
2 Chr. 35:12.

4654. מַפָּלָה *mappālāh* **fem. noun**
(ruin, heap)
Isa. 17:1; 23:13; 25:2.

4655. מִפְלָט *mip̱lāṭ* **masc. noun**
(escape, place of refuge)
Ps. 55:8(9).

4656. מִפְלֶצֶת *mip̱leṣeṯ* **fem. noun**
(a horrible thing [idol], a repulsive thing)
1 Kgs. 15:13; **2 Chr.** 15:16.

4657. מִפְלָשׂ *mip̱laś* **masc. noun**
(hanging, balancing)
Job 37:16.

4658. מַפֶּלֶת *mappeleṯ* **fem. noun**
(fall, overthrow, carcass)
Judg. 14:8; **Prov.** 29:16; **Ezek.** 26:15,18; 27:27; 31:13,16; 32:10.

4659. I. מִפְעָל *mip̱ʿāl* **masc. noun**
(work, deed)
Prov. 8:22.
II. מִפְעָלָה *mip̱ʿālāh* **fem. noun**
(work, deed)
Ps. 46:8(9); 66:5.

4660. מַפָּץ *mappāṣ* **masc. noun**
(shattering, deadly)
Ezek. 9:2.

4661. מַפֵּץ *mappēṣ* **masc. noun**
(war club, battle-ax)
Jer. 51:20.

4662. מִפְקָד *mip̱qāḏ* **masc. noun**
(designated place, appointment, number)
2 Sam. 24:9; **1 Chr.** 21:5; **2 Chr.** 31:13; **Ezek.** 43:21.

4663. מִפְקָד *mip̱qāḏ* **proper noun**
(Miphkad, Inspection Gate with *šaʿar* [8179])
Neh. 3:31.

4664. מִפְרָץ *mip̱raṣ* **masc. noun**
(cove, landing place)
Judg. 5:17.

4665. מַפְרֶקֶת *map̱reqeṯ* **fem. noun**
(neck)
1 Sam. 4:18.

4666. מִפְרָשׂ *mip̱rāś* **masc. noun**
(spreading out)
Job 36:29; **Ezek.** 27:7.

4667. מִפְשָׂעָה *mip̱śāʿāh* **fem. noun**
(hip, buttocks)
1 Chr. 19:4.

4668. מַפְתֵּחַ *mapṯēaḥ* **masc. noun**
(key)
Judg. 3:25; **1 Chr.** 9:27; **Isa.** 22:22.

4669. מִפְתָּח *mipṯāḥ* **masc. noun**
(the act of opening)
Prov. 8:6.

4670. מִפְתָּן *mipṯān* **masc. noun**
(threshold)
1 Sam. 5:4,5; **Ezek.** 9:3; 10:4,18; 46:2; 47:1; **Zeph.** 1:9.

4671. מֹץ *mōts* **masc. noun**
(chaff)
Job 21:18; **Ps.** 1:4; 35:5; **Isa.** 17:13; 29:5; 41:15; **Hos.** 13:3; **Zeph.** 2:2.

4672. מָצָא *māṣā'* **verb**
(to find, to discover)
Gen. 2:20; 4:14,15; 6:8; 8:9; 11:2; 16:7; 18:3,26,28–32; 19:11,15,19; 26:12,19,32; 27:20; 30:14,27; 31:32–35,37; 32:5(6), 19(20); 33:8,10,15; 34:11; 36:24; 37:15, 17,32; 38:20,22,23; 39:4; 41:38; 44:8–10, 12,16,17,34; 47:14,25,29; 50:4; **Ex.** 5:11; 9:19; 12:19; 15:22; 16:25,27; 18:8; 21:16; 22:2(1),4(3),6–8(5–7); 33:12,13,16,17; 34:9; 35:23,24; **Lev.** 6:3(5:22),4(5:23); 9:12,13,18; 12:8; 25:26,28; **Num.** 11:11, 15,22; 15:32,33; 20:14; 31:50; 32:5,23; 35:27; **Deut.** 4:29,30; 17:2; 18:10; 19:5; 20:11; 21:1,17; 22:3,14,17,20,22,23,25, 27,28; 24:1,7; 31:17,21; 32:10; **Josh.** 2:22,23; 10:17; 17:16; **Judg.** 1:5; 5:30; 6:13,17; 9:33; 14:12,18; 15:15; 17:8,9; 20:48; 21:12,14; **Ruth** 1:9; 2:2,10,13; **1 Sam.** 1:18; 9:4,8,11,13,20; 10:2,3,7, 16,21; 12:5; 13:15,16,19,22; 14:30; 16:22; 20:3,21,29,36; 21:3(4); 23:17; 24:19(20); 25:8,28; 27:5; 29:3,6,8; 30:11; 31:3,8; **2 Sam.** 3:8; 7:27; 14:22; 15:25; 16:4; 17:12,13,20; 18:22; 20:6; **1 Kgs.** 1:3,52; 11:19,29; 13:14,24,28; 14:13; 18:5,10,12; 19:19; 20:36,37; 21:20; **2 Kgs.** 2:17; 4:29,39; 7:9; 9:21,35; 10:13,15; 12:5(6),10(11),18(19); 14:14; 16:8; 17:4; 18:15; 19:4,8; 20:13; 22:8, 9,13; 23:2,24; 25:19; **1 Chr.** 4:40,41; 10:3,8; 17:25; 20:2; 24:4; 26:31; 28:9; 29:8,17; **2 Chr.** 2:17(16); 5:11; 15:2, 4,15; 19:3; 20:16,25; 21:17; 22:8; 25:5,24; 29:16,29; 30:21; 31:1; 32:4; 34:14,15, 17,21,30,32,33; 35:7,17,18; 36:8; **Ezra** 2:62; 8:15,25; 10:18; **Neh.** 5:8; 7:5,64; 8:14; 9:8,32; 13:1; **Esth.** 1:5; 2:23; 4:16; 5:8; 6:2; 7:3; 8:5,6; **Job** 3:22; 11:7; 17:10; 19:28; 20:8; 23:3; 28:12,13; 31:25,29; 32:3,13; 33:10,24; 34:11; 37:13,23; 42:15; **Ps.** 10:15; 17:3; 21:8(9); 32:6; 36:2(3); 37:36; 46:1(2); 69:20(21); 76:5(6); 84:3(4); 89:20(21); 107:4; 116:3; 119:143, 162; 132:5,6; **Prov.** 1:13,28; 2:5; 3:4,13; 4:22; 6:31,33; 7:15; 8:9,12,17,35; 10:13; 16:20,31; 17:20; 18:22; 19:8; 20:6; 21:21; 24:14; 25:16; 28:23; 31:10; **Eccl.** 3:11; 7:14,24,26–29; 8:17; 9:10,15; 11:1; 12:10; **Song** 3:1–4; 5:6–8; 8:1,10; **Isa.** 10:10,14; 13:15; 22:3; 30:14; 34:14; 35:9; 37:4,8; 39:2; 41:12; 51:3; 55:6; 57:10; 58:3,13; 65:1,8; **Jer.** 2:5,24,26,34; 5:1,26; 6:16; 10:18; 11:9; 14:3; 15:16; 23:11; 29:13,14; 31:2; 41:3,8,12; 45:3; 48:27; 50:7,20,24; 52:25; **Lam.** 1:3,6; 2:9,16; **Ezek.** 3:1; 22:30; 26:21; 28:15; **Dan.** 1:19,20; 11:19; 12:1; **Hos.** 2:6(8),7(9); 5:6; 9:10; 12:4(5),8(9); 14:8(9); **Amos** 8:12; **Jon.** 1:3; **Mic.** 1:13; **Zeph.** 3:13; **Zech.** 10:10; 11:6; **Mal.** 2:6.

4673. מַצָּב *maṣṣāḇ* **masc. noun**
(garrison, outpost, place of standing)
Josh. 4:3,9; **1 Sam.** 13:23; 14:1,4,6, 11,15; **2 Sam.** 23:14; **Isa.** 22:19.

4674. מֻצָּב *muṣṣāḇ* **masc. noun**
(siege work, tower)
Judg. 9:6(KJV, NASB, *nāṣab* [5324]); **Isa.** 29:3.

4675. מַצָּבָה *maṣṣāḇāh*, מִצָּבָה *miṣṣāḇāh* **fem. noun**
(garrison, army)

1 Sam. 14:12(NASB, *maṣṣāḇ* [4673]); **Zech.** 9:8(NIV, *min* [4480] and *ṣāḇa'* [6635]).

4676. מַצֵּבָה *maṣṣēḇāh* **fem. noun**
(pillar, sacred stone erected as a monument)
Gen. 28:18,22; 31:13,45,51,52; 35:14(see *maṣṣeḇeṯ* [4678,II]),20(see *maṣṣeḇeṯ* [4678,II]); **Ex.** 23:24; 24:4; 34:13; **Lev.** 26:1; **Deut.** 7:5; 12:3; 16:22; **1 Kgs.** 14:23; **2 Kgs.** 3:2; 10:26,27; 17:10; 18:4; 23:14; **2 Chr.** 14:3(2); 31:1; **Isa.** 19:19; **Jer.** 43:13; **Ezek.** 26:11; **Hos.** 3:4; 10:1,2; **Mic.** 5:13(12).

4677. מְצֹבָיָה *m^eṣōḇyāh* **masc. proper noun**
(Mezobaite)
1 Chr. 11:47.

4678. I. מַצֶּבֶת *maṣṣeḇeṯ* **fem. noun**
(pillar, monument)
2 Sam. 18:18.
II. מַצֶּבֶת *maṣṣeḇeṯ* **fem. noun**
(pillar, monument; const. of *maṣṣēḇ* [4676])
Gen. 35:14,20.
III. מַצֶּבֶת *maṣṣeḇeṯ* **fem. noun**
(tree stump)
Isa. 6:13.

4679. מְצָד *m^eṣāḏ*, מְצַד *m^eṣaḏ* **masc. noun**
(stronghold, fortress)
Judg. 6:2; **1 Sam.** 23:14,19,29(24:1); **1 Chr.** 11:7; 12:8,16; **Isa.** 33:16; **Jer.** 48:41; 51:30; **Ezek.** 33:27.

4680. מָצָה *māṣāh* **verb**
(to drain, to drain out, to wring out)
Lev. 1:15; 5:9; **Judg.** 6:38; **Ps.** 73:10; 75:8(9); **Isa.** 51:17; **Ezek.** 23:34.

4681. מֹצָה *mōṣāh* **proper noun**
(Mozah)
Josh. 18:26.

4682. מַצָּה *maṣṣāh* **fem. noun**
(something unleavened, without leaven)
Gen. 19:3; **Ex.** 12:8,15,17,18,20,39; 13:6,7; 23:15; 29:2,23; 34:18; **Lev.** 2:4,5; 6:16(9); 7:12; 8:2,26; 10:12; 23:6; **Num.** 6:15,17,19; 9:11; 28:17; **Deut.** 16:3,8,16; **Josh.** 5:11; **Judg.** 6:19–21; **1 Sam.** 28:24; **2 Kgs.** 23:9; **1 Chr.** 23:29; **2 Chr.** 8:13; 30:13,21; 35:17; **Ezra** 6:22; **Ezek.** 45:21.

4683. מַצָּה *maṣṣāh* **fem. noun**
(strife, contention)
Prov. 13:10; 17:19; **Isa.** 58:4.

4684. מִצְהָלוֹת *miṣhālôṯ* **fem. pl. noun**
(neighing [of a horse])
Jer. 8:16; 13:27.

4685. I. מָצוֹד *māṣôḏ* **masc. noun**
(snare, net, plunder)
Job 19:6; **Prov.** 12:12; **Eccl.** 7:26.
II. מָצוֹד *māṣôḏ* **masc. noun**
(bulwark, siege work)
Eccl. 9:14(NIV, *māṣôr* [4692]).
III. מְצוֹדָה *m^eṣôḏāh* **fem. noun**
(hunting net)
Eccl. 9:12(KJV, *m^eṣûḏāh* [4686,I]); **Ezek.** 19:9(KJV, *m^eṣûḏāh* [4686,II]; NIV, see IV).
IV. מְצוֹדָה *m^eṣôḏāh* **fem. noun**
(prison, fortress, munition)
Isa. 29:7; **Ezek.** 19:9(KJV, *m^eṣûḏāh* [4686,II]; NASB, see III).

4686. I. מְצוּדָה *m^eṣûḏāh* **fem. noun**
(net, prey)
Ps. 66:11(NIV, see II); **Eccl.** 9:12(NASB, NIV, m^eṣûḏāh [4685,III]); **Ezek.** 12:13; 13:21; 17:20.
II. מְצוּדָה *m^eṣûḏāh* **fem. noun**
(stronghold)
1 Sam. 22:4,5; 24:22(23); **2 Sam.** 5:7,9,17; 22:2; 23:14; **1 Chr.** 11:5,16; **Job** 39:28; **Ps.** 18:2(3); 31:2(3),3(4); 66:11(KJV, NASB, see I); 71:3; 91:2; 144:2;

Ezek. 19:9(NASB, *m^e^ṣôḏāh* [4685,III]; NIV, *m^e^ṣôḏāh* [4685,IV]).

4687. מִצְוָה *miṣwāh* **fem. noun**
(command, commandment)
Gen. 26:5; **Ex.** 15:26; 16:28; 20:6; 24:12; **Lev.** 4:2,13,22,27; 5:17; 22:31; 26:3,14, 15; 27:34; **Num.** 15:22,31,39,40; 36:13; **Deut.** 4:2,40; 5:10,29(26),31(28); 6:1,2, 17,25; 7:9,11; 8:1,2,6,11; 10:13; 11:1,8, 13,22,27,28; 13:4(5),18(19); 15:5; 17:20; 19:9; 26:13,17,18; 27:1,10; 28:1,9,13, 15,45; 30:8,10,11,16; 31:5; **Josh.** 22:3,5; **Judg.** 2:17; 3:4; **1 Sam.** 13:13; **1 Kgs.** 2:3,43; 3:14; 6:12; 8:58,61; 9:6; 11:34,38; 13:21; 14:8; 18:18; **2 Kgs.** 17:13,16, 19,34,37; 18:6,36; 23:3; **1 Chr.** 28:7,8; 29:19; **2 Chr.** 7:19; 8:13–15; 14:4(3); 17:4; 19:10; 24:20,21; 29:15,25; 30:6,12; 31:21; 34:31; 35:10,15,16; **Ezra** 7:11; 9:10,14; 10:3; **Neh.** 1:5,7,9; 9:13,14,16, 29,34; 10:29(30),32(33); 11:23; 12:24,45; 13:5; **Esth.** 3:3; **Job** 23:12; **Ps.** 19:8(9); 78:7; 89:31(32); 112:1; 119:6,10,19,21, 32,35,47,48,60,66,73,86,96,98,115,127, 131,143,151,166,172,176; **Prov.** 2:1; 3:1; 4:4; 6:20,23; 7:1,2; 10:8; 13:13; 19:16; **Eccl.** 8:5; 12:13; **Isa.** 29:13; 36:21; 48:18; **Jer.** 32:11; 35:14,16,18; **Dan.** 9:4,5; **Mal.** 2:1,4.

4688. מְצוֹלָה *m^e^ṣôlāh*, מְצוּלָה *m^e^ṣûlāh*, מְצֻלָה *m^e^ṣulāh* **fem. noun**
(depth [of the water])
Ex. 15:5; **Neh.** 9:11; **Job** 41:31(23); **Ps.** 68:22(23); 69:2(3),15(16); 88:6(7); 107:24; **Jon.** 2:3(4); **Mic.** 7:19; **Zech.** 1:8(see *m^e^ṣulāh* [4699]); 10:11.

4689. מָצוֹק *māṣôq* **masc. noun**
(distress, anguish)
Deut. 28:53,55,57; **1 Sam.** 22:2; **Ps.** 119:143; **Jer.** 19:9.

4690. מָצוּק *māṣûq* **masc. noun**
(pillar, foundation, standing like a pillar)
1 Sam. 2:8; 14:5.

4691. מְצוּקָה *m^e^ṣûqāh* **fem. noun**
(distress, anguish)
Job 15:24; **Ps.** 25:17; 107:6,13,19,28; **Zeph.** 1:15.

4692. מָצוֹר *māṣôr* **masc. noun**
(seige, beseiged, fortified area)
Deut. 20:19,20; 28:53,55,57; **2 Kgs.** 19:24(NASB, NIV, *māṣôr* [4693]); 24:10; 25:2; **2 Chr.** 8:5; 11:5; 32:10; **Ps.** 31:21(22); 60:9(11); **Eccl.** 9:14(KJV, NASB, *māṣôr* [4685,II]); **Isa.** 19:6(NASB, NIV, *māṣôr* [4693]); 37:25(NASB, NIV, *māṣôr* [4693]); **Jer.** 10:17; 19:9; 52:5; **Ezek.** 4:2,3,7,8; 5:2; **Mic.** 5:1(4:14); 7:12(NASB, NIV, *māṣôr* [4693]); **Nah.** 3:14; **Hab.** 2:1; **Zech.** 9:3; 12:2.

4693. מָצוֹר *māṣôr* **proper noun**
(Matsor; another name for Egypt)
2 Kgs. 19:24(KJV, *māṣôr* [4692]); **Isa.** 19:6(KJV, *māṣôr* [4692]); 37:25(KJV, *māṣôr* [4692]); **Mic.** 7:12(KJV, *māṣôr* [4692]).

4694. מְצוּרָה *m^e^ṣûrāh*, מְצֻרָה *m^e^ṣurāh* **fem. noun**
(fortified place, fortress)
2 Chr. 11:10,11,23; 12:4; 14:6(5); 21:3; **Isa.** 29:3; **Nah.** 2:1(2).

4695. מַצּוּת *maṣṣûṯ* **fem. noun**
(contention, warfare)
Isa. 41:12.

4696. מֵצַח *meṣaḥ* **masc. noun**
(forehead)
Ex. 28:38; **1 Sam.** 17:49; **2 Chr.** 26:19,20; **Isa.** 48:4; **Jer.** 3:3; **Ezek.** 3:7–9; 9:4.

4697. מִצְחָה *miṣḥāh* **fem. noun**
(greaves [leg armor])
1 Sam. 17:6.

4698. מְצִלָּה *m^e^ṣillāh* **fem. noun**
(bell)
Zech. 14:20.

4699. מְצֻלָה *m^e^ṣulāh* **fem. noun**
(ravine, bottomland, form of *m^e^ṣôlāh* [4688])
Zech. 1:8.

4700. מְצִלְתַּיִם *m^e^ṣiltayim* **fem. dual noun**
(cymbals)
1 Chr. 13:8; 15:16,19,28; 16:5,42; 25:1,6; **2 Chr.** 5:12,13; 29:25; **Ezra** 3:10; **Neh.** 12:27.

4701. מִצְנֶפֶת *miṣnep̱eṯ* **fem. noun**
(turban, miter [of the high priest's wear])
Ex. 28:4,37,39; 29:6; 39:28,31; **Lev.** 8:9; 16:4; **Ezek.** 21:26(31).

4702. מַצָּע *maṣṣā'* **masc. noun**
(bed)
Isa. 28:20.

4703. מִצְעָד *miṣ'āḏ* **masc. noun**
(a step, footstep)
Ps. 37:23; **Prov.** 20:24; **Dan.** 11:43.

4704. מִצְעִירָה *miṣ'iyrāh* **adj.**
(little, small)
Dan. 8:9.

4705. מִצְעָר *miṣ'ār* **masc. noun**
(small thing, little while)
Gen. 19:20; **2 Chr.** 24:24; **Job** 8:7; **Isa.** 63:18.

4706. מִצְעָר *miṣār* **proper noun**
(Mizar)
Ps. 42:6.

4707. מִצְפֶּה *miṣpeh* **masc. noun**
(watchtower)
2 Chr. 20:24; **Isa.** 21:8.

4708. A. מִצְפֶּה *miṣpeh* **proper noun**
(Mizpeh: town in Judah)
Josh. 15:38; **Jer.** 40:6,8,12,13; 41:1.
B. מִצְפֶּה *miṣpeh* **proper noun**
(Mizpeh: city in Moab)
1 Sam. 22:3.
C. מִצְפֶּה *miṣpeh* **proper noun**
(Mizpeh: loc. in Gad)
Judg. 11:29.
D. מִצְפֶּה *miṣpeh* **proper noun**
(Mizpeh: city in Benjamin)
Josh. 18:26.
E. מִצְפֶּה *miṣpeh* **proper noun**
(Mizpeh: valley in Lebanon)
Josh. 11:8.

4709. A. מִצְפָּה *miṣpāh* **proper noun**
(Mizpah: city in Judah)
Josh. 11:3; **Judg.** 10:17; 11:11,34; 20:1,3; 21:1,5,8; **1 Sam.** 7:5–7,11,12,16; 10:17; **2 Kgs.** 25:23,25; **2 Chr.** 16:6; **Jer.** 40:10,15; 41:1,3,6,10,14,16; **Hos.** 5:1.
B. מִצְפָּה *miṣpāh* **proper noun**
(Mizpah: city in Benjamin)
1 Kgs. 15:22; **Neh.** 3:7.
C. מִצְפָּה *miṣpāh* **proper noun**
(Mizpah: heap of stones "watchtower" in Gad)
Gen. 31:49.
D. מִצְפָּה *miṣpāh* **proper noun**
(Mizpah: district under Colhozeh)
Neh. 3:15.
E. מִצְפָּה *miṣpāh* **proper noun**
(Mizpah: town ruled by Jeshua)
Neh. 3:19.

4710. מַצְפּוֹן *maṣpôn* **masc. noun**
(hidden treasure)
Obad. 1:6.

4711. מָצַץ *māṣaṣ* **verb**
(to milk out, to drain out, to nurse)
Isa. 66:11.

4712. מֵצַר *mēṣar* **masc. noun**
(distress, anguish, pain)
Ps. 116:3; 118:5; **Lam.** 1:3.

4713. מִצְרִי *miṣriy* **masc. proper noun**
(Egyptian)
Gen. 12:12,14; 16:1,3; 21:9; 25:12; 39:1,2,5; 43:32; **Ex.** 1:19; 2:11,12,14,19; **Lev.** 24:10; **Deut.** 23:7(8); 26:6; **Josh.** 24:7; **1 Sam.** 30:11,13; **2 Sam.** 23:21; **1 Chr.** 2:34; 11:23; **Ezra** 9:1.

4714. A. מִצְרַיִם *miṣrayim* **masc. proper noun**
(Mizraim: son of Ham)
Gen. 10:6,13; **1 Chr.** 1:8,11.
B. מִצְרַיִם *miṣrayim* **masc. proper noun**
(Egypt)
Gen. 12:10,11,14; 13:1,10; 15:18; 21:21; 25:18; 26:2; 37:25,28,36; 39:1; 40:1,5; 41:8, 19,29,30,33,34,36,41,43–46,48,53–57; 42:1–3; 43:2,15,32; 45:4,8,9,13,18–20, 23,25,26; 46:3,4,6–8,20,26,27; 47:6,11, 13–15,20,21,26–30; 48:5; 50:7,14,22,26; **Ex.** 1:1,5,8,15,17,18; 2:23; 3:7,10–12, 16–20; 4:18–21; 5:4,12; 6:11,13,26–29; 7:3–5,11,19,21,22; 8:5–7(1–3),16(12), 17(13),24(20); 9:4,6,9,18,22–25; 10:2,7, 12–15,19,21,22; 11:1,3–6,9; 12:1,12,13, 17,23,27,29,30,39–42,51; 13:3,8,9, 14–18; 14:5,7,8,11,12; 16:1,3,6,32; 17:3; 18:1; 19:1; 20:2; 22:21(20); 23:9,15; 29:46; 32:1,4,7,8,11,23; 33:1; 34:18; **Lev.** 11:45; 18:3; 19:34,36; 22:33; 23:43; 25:38,42, 55; 26:13,45; **Num.** 1:1; 3:13; 8:17; 9:1; 11:5,18,20; 13:22; 14:2–4,19,22; 15:41; 20:5,15,16; 21:5; 22:5,11; 23:22; 24:8; 26:4,59; 32:11; 33:1,38; 34:5; **Deut.** 1:27, 30; 4:20,34,37,45,46; 5:6,15; 6:12,21,22; 7:8,15,18; 8:14; 9:7,12,26; 10:19,22; 11:3, 4,10; 13:5(6),10(11); 15:15; 16:1,3,6,12; 17:16; 20:1; 23:4(5); 24:9,18,22; 25:17; 26:5,8; 28:27,60,68; 29:2(1),16(15), 25(24); 34:11; **Josh.** 2:10; 5:4–6,9; 9:9; 13:3; 15:4,47; 24:4,5,7,14,17,32; **Judg.** 2:1,12; 6:8,13; 11:13,16; 19:30; **1 Sam.** 2:27; 8:8; 10:18; 12:6,8; 15:2,6,7; 27:8; **2 Sam.** 7:6,23; **1 Kgs.** 3:1; 4:21(5:1), 30(5:10); 6:1; 8:9,16,21,51,53,65; 9:9,16; 10:28,29; 11:17,18,21,40; 12:2,28; 14:25; **2 Kgs.** 17:4,7,36; 18:21,24; 21:15; 23:29, 34; 24:7; 25:26; **1 Chr.** 13:5; 17:21; **2 Chr.** 1:16,17; 5:10; 6:5; 7:8,22; 9:26, 28; 10:2; 12:2,3,9; 20:10; 26:8; 35:20; 36:3,4; **Neh.** 9:9,18; **Ps.** 68:31(32); 78:12, 43,51; 80:8(9); 81:5(6),10(11); 105:23, 38; 106:7,21; 114:1; 135:8,9; 136:10; **Prov.** 7:16; **Isa.** 7:18; 10:24,26; 11:11, 15,16; 19:1,3,12–20,22–25; 20:3–5; 23:5; 27:12,13; 30:2,3; 31:1; 36:6,9; 43:3; 45:14; 52:4; **Jer.** 2:6,18,36; 7:22,25; 9:26(25); 11:4,7; 16:14; 23:7; 24:8; 25:19; 26:21–23; 31:32; 32:20,21; 34:13; 37:5,7; 41:17; 42:14–19; 43:2,7,11–13; 44:1,8,12–15, 24,26–28,30; 46:2,8,11,13,14,17,19, 20,24,25; **Ezek.** 17:15; 19:4; 20:5–10,36; 23:3,8,19,27; 27:7; 29:2,3,6,9,10,20; 30:4,6,8–11,13,15,16,18,19,21,22,25; 31:2; 32:2,12,15,16,18; **Dan.** 9:15; 11:8,42,43; **Hos.** 2:15(17); 7:11,16; 8:13; 9:3,6; 11:1,5,11; 12:1(2),9(10),13(14); 13:4; **Joel** 3:19(4:19); **Amos** 2:10; 3:1,9; 4:10; 8:8; 9:5,7; **Mic.** 6:4; 7:15; **Nah.** 3:9; **Hag.** 2:5; **Zech.** 10:10,11; 14:18,19.
C. מִצְרַיִם *miṣrayim* **masc. proper noun**
(inhabitant of Egypt)
Gen. 41:55,56; 43:32; 45:2; 46:34; 47:15, 20; 50:3,11(NIV, *'āḇēl miṣrayim* [67]); **Ex.** 1:13; 3:8,9,21,22; 6:5–7; 7:5,18,21,24; 8:21,26; 9:11; 10:6; 11:3,7; 12:23,27,30, 33,35,36; 14:4,9,10,12,13,17,18,20, 23–27,30,31; 15:26; 18:8–10; 19:4; 32:12; **Num.** 14:13; 20:15; 33:3,4; **Josh.** 24:6; **Judg.** 6:9; 10:11; **1 Sam.** 4:8; 6:6; 10:18; **2 Kgs.** 7:6; **Isa.** 19:2,4,21,23; 20:4; 30:7; 31:3; **Jer.** 43:13; **Lam.** 5:6; **Ezek.** 16:26; 23:21; 29:12,13; 30:23,26.

4715. מַצְרֵף *maṣrēp̱* **masc. noun**
(crucible, refining pot)
Prov. 17:3; 27:21.

4716. מַק *maq* **masc. noun**
(stench, rottenness)
Isa. 3:24; 5:24.

4717. מַקֶּבֶת *maqqeḇeṯ* **fem. noun**
(hammer)
Judg. 4:21; **1 Kgs.** 6:7; **Isa.** 44:12; **Jer.** 10:4.

4718. מַקֶּבֶת *maqqeḇeṯ* **fem. noun**
(hole, pit, quarry)
Isa. 51:1.

4719. מַקֵּדָה *maqqēḏah* **proper noun**
(Makkedah)
Josh. 10:10,16,17,21,28,29; 12:16; 15:41.

4720. מִקְדָּשׁ *miqdāš* **masc. noun**
(holy place, sanctuary)
Ex. 15:17; 25:8; **Lev.** 12:4; 16:33; 19:30; 20:3; 21:12,23; 26:2,31; **Num.** 3:38; 10:21; 18:1,29; 19:20; **Josh.** 24:26; **1 Chr.** 22:19; 28:10; **2 Chr.** 20:8; 26:18; 29:21; 30:8; 36:17; **Neh.** 10:39(40); **Ps.** 68:35(36); 73:17; 74:7; 78:69; 96:6; **Isa.** 7:24(KJV, NASB, *qāḏaš* [6942]); 8:14; 16:12; 60:13; 63:18; **Jer.** 17:12; 51:51; **Lam.** 1:10; 2:7,20; **Ezek.** 5:11; 8:6; 9:6; 11:16; 21:2(7); 23:38,39; 24:21; 25:3; 28:18; 37:26,28; 43:21; 44:1,5,7–9,11, 15,16; 45:3,4,18; 47:12; 48:8,10,21; **Dan.** 8:11; 9:17; 11:31; **Amos** 7:9,13.

4721. מַקְהֵל *maqhēl* **fem. noun**
(assembly, congregation)
Ps. 26:12; 68:26(27).

4722. מַקְהֵלֹת *maqhēlōṯ* **proper noun**
(Makheloth)
Num. 33:25,26.

4723. I. מִקְוֵא *miqwē',* מִקְוֶה *miqweh* **masc. noun**
(linen yarn)
1 Kgs. 10:28(NASB, NIV, see II); **2 Chr.** 1:16(NASB, NIV, see II).
II. קְוֵא *qᵉwē',* קְוֵה *qᵉweh* **masc. proper noun**
(city of Kue; used with *min* [4480])
1 Kgs. 10:28(KJV, see I); **2 Chr.** 1:16(KJV, see I).
III. מִקְוֶה *miqweh* **masc. noun**
(hope)
1 Chr. 29:15; **Ezra** 10:2; **Jer.** 14:8; 17:13; 50:7.
IV. מִקְוֶה *miqweh* **masc. noun**
(collection, accumulation)
Gen. 1:10; **Ex.** 7:19; **Lev.** 11:36.

4724. מִקְוָה *miqwāh* **fem. noun**
(reservoir, ditch)
Isa. 22:11.

4725. מָקוֹם *māqôm,* מָקֹם *māqōm* **masc. noun**
(place, spot)
Gen. 1:9; 12:6; 13:3,4,14; 18:24,26,33; 19:12–14,27; 20:11,13; 21:31; 22:3,4, 9,14; 24:23,25,31; 26:7; 28:11,16,17,19; 29:3,22,26; 30:25; 31:55(32:1); 32:2(3), 30(31); 33:17; 35:7,13–15; 36:40; 38:21, 22; 39:20; 40:3; **Ex.** 3:5,8; 16:29; 17:7; 18:23; 20:24; 21:13; 23:20; 29:31; 33:21; **Lev.** 1:16; 4:12,24,29,33; 6:11(4),16(9), 25–27(18–20); 7:2,6; 10:13,14,17; 13:19; 14:13,28,40,41,45; 16:24; 24:9; **Num.** 9:17; 10:29; 11:3,34; 13:24; 14:40; 18:31; 19:9; 20:5; 21:3; 22:26; 23:13,27; 24:11, 25; 32:1,17; **Deut.** 1:31,33; 9:7; 11:5,24; 12:2,3,5,11,13,14,18,21,26; 14:23–25; 15:20; 16:2,6,7,11,15,16; 17:8,10; 18:6; 21:19; 23:16(17); 26:2,9; 29:7(6); 31:11; **Josh.** 1:3; 3:3; 4:18; 5:9,15; 7:26; 8:19; 9:27; 20:4; **Judg.** 2:5; 7:7; 9:55; 11:19; 15:17; 18:10,12; 19:13,16,28; 20:22, 33,36; **Ruth** 1:7; 3:4; 4:10; **1 Sam.** 2:20; 3:2,9; 5:3,11; 6:2; 7:16; 9:22; 12:8; 14:46; 20:19,25,27,37; 21:2(3); 23:22,28; 26:5, 13,25; 27:5; 29:4; 30:31; **2 Sam.** 2:16,23; 5:20; 6:8,17; 7:10; 11:16; 15:19,21; 17:9, 12; 19:39(40); **1 Kgs.** 4:28(5:8); 5:9(23); 8:6,7,21,29,30,35; 10:19; 13:8,16,22; 20:24; 21:19; **2 Kgs.** 5:11; 6:1,2,6,8–10; 18:25; 22:16,17,19,20; 23:14; **1 Chr.** 13:11; 14:11; 15:1,3; 16:27; 17:9; 21:22,25; **2 Chr.** 3:1; 5:7,8; 6:20,21,26,40; 7:12,15;

9:18; 20:26; 24:11; 25:10; 33:19; 34:24, 25,27,28; **Ezra** 1:4; 8:17; 9:8; **Neh.** 1:9; 2:14; 4:12(6),13(7),20(14); 12:27; **Esth.** 4:3,14; 8:17; **Job** 2:11; 6:17; 7:10; 8:18; 9:6; 14:18; 16:18; 18:4,21; 20:9; 27:21,23; 28:1,6,12,20,23; 34:26; 37:1; 38:12,19; **Ps.** 24:3; 26:8; 37:10; 44:19(20); 103:16,22; 104:8; 132:5; **Prov.** 15:3; 25:6; 27:8; **Eccl.** 1:5,7; 3:16,20; 6:6; 8:10; 10:4; 11:3; **Isa.** 5:8; 7:23; 13:13; 14:2; 18:7; 22:23,25; 26:21; 28:8; 33:21; 45:19; 46:7; 49:20; 54:2; 60:13; 66:1; **Jer.** 4:7; 7:3,6,7,12,14,20,32; 8:3; 13:7; 14:13; 16:2,3,9; 17:12; 19:3,4,6,7,11–13; 22:3,11,12; 24:5,9; 27:22; 28:3,4,6; 29:10,14; 32:37; 33:10,12; 40:2,12; 42:18,22; 44:29; 45:5; 51:62; **Ezek.** 3:12; 6:13; 10:11; 12:3; 17:16; 21:30(35); 34:12; 38:15; 39:11; 41:11; 42:13; 43:7; 45:4; 46:19,20; **Hos.** 1:10(2:1); 5:15; **Joel** 3:7(4:7); **Amos** 4:6; 8:3; **Mic.** 1:3; **Nah.** 1:8; 3:17; **Zeph.** 1:4; 2:11; **Hag.** 2:9; **Zech.** 14:10; **Mal.** 1:11.

4726. מָקוֹר *māqôr* **masc. noun**
(fountain, spring, flow)
Lev. 12:7; 20:18; **Ps.** 36:9(10); 68:26(27); **Prov.** 5:18; 10:11; 13:14; 14:27; 16:22; 18:4; 25:26; **Jer.** 2:13; 9:1(8:23); 17:13; 51:36; **Hos.** 13:15; **Zech.** 13:1.

4727. מִקָּח *miqqaḥ* **masc. noun**
(taking, accepting)
2 Chr. 19:7.

4728. מַקָּחוֹת *maqqāḥôṯ* **fem. noun**
(merchandise, wares)
Neh. 10:31(32).

4729. מִקְטָר *miqṭār* **masc. noun**
(place for burning)
Ex. 30:1.

4730. מִקְטֶרֶת *miqṭereṯ* **fem. noun**
(censer)
2 Chr. 26:19; **Ezek.** 8:11.

4731. מַקֵּל *maqqēl* **masc. noun**
(rod, stick, staff)
Gen. 30:37–39,41; 32:10(11); **Ex.** 12:11; **Num.** 22:27; **1 Sam.** 17:40,43; **Jer.** 1:11; 48:17; **Ezek.** 39:9; **Hos.** 4:12; **Zech.** 11:7,10,14.

4732. A. מִקְלוֹת *miqlôṯ* **masc. proper noun**
(Mikloth: a Benjamite)
1 Chr. 8:32; 9:37,38.
B. מִקְלוֹת *miqlôṯ* **masc. proper noun**
(Mikloth: officer under David)
1 Chr. 27:4.

4733. מִקְלָט *miqlāṭ* **masc. noun**
(refuge, place of refuge)
Num. 35:6,11–15,25–28,32; **Josh.** 20:2,3; 21:13,21,27,32,38(36); **1 Chr.** 6:57(42),67(52).

4734. מִקְלַעַת *miqla'aṯ* **fem. noun**
(carved, something carved or engraved)
1 Kgs. 6:18,29,32; 7:31.

4735. מִקְנֶה *miqneh* **masc. noun**
(livestock, cattle)
Gen. 4:20; 13:2,7; 26:14; 29:7; 30:29; 31:9,18; 33:17; 34:5,23; 36:6,7; 46:6, 32,34; 47:6,16–18; 49:32; **Ex.** 9:3,4,6, 7,19–21; 10:26; 12:38; 17:3; 34:19; **Num.** 20:19; 31:9; 32:1,4,16,26; **Deut.** 3:19; **Josh.** 1:14; 14:4; 22:8; **Judg.** 6:5; 18:21; **1 Sam.** 23:5; 30:20; **2 Kgs.** 3:17; **1 Chr.** 5:9,21; 7:21; 28:1; **2 Chr.** 14:15(14); 26:10; 32:29; **Job** 1:3,10; 36:33; **Ps.** 78:48; **Eccl.** 2:7; **Isa.** 30:23; **Jer.** 9:10(9); 49:32; **Ezek.** 38:12,13.

4736. מִקְנָה *miqnāh* **fem. noun**
(purchase, possession, price)
Gen. 17:12,13,23,27; 23:18; **Ex.** 12:44; **Lev.** 25:16,51; 27:22; **Jer.** 32:11,12, 14,16.

4737. מִקְנֵיָהוּ *miqnēyāhû* **masc. proper noun**
(Mikneiah)
1 Chr. 15:18,21.

4738. מִקְסָם *miqsām* **masc. noun**
(divination)
Ezek. 12:24; 13:7.

4739. מָקַץ *māqaṣ* **proper noun**
(Makaz)
1 Kgs. 4:9.

4740. מִקְצוֹעַ *miqṣôa'*, מִקְצֹעַ *miqṣōa'* **masc. noun**
(corner, angle)
Ex. 26:23(KJV, *m^equṣ'āh* [4742]; NIV, *qāṣa'* [7106]),24; 36:28(KJV, *m^equṣ'āh* [4742]; NIV, *qāṣa'* [7106]),29; **2 Chr.** 26:9; **Neh.** 3:19,20,24,25; **Ezek.** 41:22; 46:21,22(KJV, *m^equṣ'āh* [4742]),22(KJV, NIV, *qāṣa'* [7106,II]).

4741. מַקְצֻעָה *maqṣu'āh* **fem. noun**
(chisel, planing tool)
Isa. 44:13.

4742. מְקֻצְעָת *m^equṣ'āt* **fem. noun**
(corner, bending)
Ex. 26:23(NASB, *miqṣôa'* [4740]; NIV, *qāṣa'* [7106,II]); 36:28(NASB, *miqṣôa'* [4740]).

4743. מָקַק *māqaq* **verb**
(to waste away, to rot, to rot away)
Lev. 26:39; **Ps.** 38:5(6); **Isa.** 34:4; **Ezek.** 4:17; 24:23; 33:10; **Zech.** 14:12.

4744. מִקְרָא *miqrā'* **masc. noun**
(assembly, convocation)
Ex. 12:16; **Lev.** 23:2–4,7,8,21,24,27,35–37; **Num.** 10:2; 28:18,25,26; 29:1,7,12; **Neh.** 8:8; **Isa.** 1:13; 4:5.

4745. מִקְרֶה *miqreh* **masc. noun**
(chance event, happening, fate)
Ruth 2:3; **1 Sam.** 6:9; 20:26; **Eccl.** 2:14,15; 3:19; 9:2,3.

4746. מְקָרֶה *m^eqāreh* **masc. noun**
(rafter, building)
Eccl. 10:18.

4747. מְקֵרָה *m^eqērāh* **fem. noun**
(summer chamber, cooling room)
Judg. 3:20,24.

4748. מִקְשֶׁה *miqšeh* **masc. noun**
(hair)
Isa. 3:24.

4749. מִקְשָׁה *miqšāh* **fem. noun**
(hammered work)
Ex. 25:18,31,36; 37:7,17,22; **Num.** 8:4; 10:2; **Jer.** 10:5(NASB, NIV, *miqšāh* [4750]).

4750. מִקְשָׁה *miqšāh* **fem. noun**
(field of cucumbers or melons)
Isa. 1:8; **Jer.** 10:5(KJV, *miqšāh* [4749]).

4751. מַר *mar*, מָר *mār* **adj.**
(bitter, distressed)
Gen. 27:34; **Ex.** 15:23; **Num.** 5:18,19, 23,24,27; **Judg.** 18:25; **Ruth** 1:20; **1 Sam.** 1:10; 15:32; 22:2; **2 Sam.** 2:26; 17:8; **Esth.** 4:1; **Job** 3:20; 7:11; 10:1; 21:25; **Ps.** 64:3(4); **Prov.** 5:4; 27:7; 31:6; **Eccl.** 7:26; **Isa.** 5:20; 33:7; 38:15,17; **Jer.** 2:19; 4:18; **Ezek.** 3:14; 27:30,31; **Amos** 8:10; **Hab.** 1:6; **Zeph.** 1:14.

4752. מַר *mar* **masc. noun**
(drop [of water])
Isa. 40:15.

4753. מֹר *mōr*, מוֹר *môr* **masc. noun**
(myrrh)
Ex. 30:23; **Esth.** 2:12; **Ps.** 45:8(9); **Prov.** 7:17; **Song** 1:13; 3:6; 4:6,14; 5:1,5,13.

4754. I. מָרָא *mārā'* **verb**
(to fly, to drive with wings)
Job 39:18.

II. מָרָא *mārā'* **verb**
(filthy)
Zeph. 3:1(NASB, NIV, *mārāh* [4784]).

4755. מָרָא *mārā'* **fem. proper noun**
(Mara)
Ruth 1:20.

4756. מָרֵא *mārē'* **Aram. masc. noun**
(Lord, lord)
Dan. 2:47; 4:19(16),24(21); 5:23.

4757. מְרֹאדַךְ בַּלְאֲדָן *m^e rō'dak bal'^a dān* **masc. proper noun**
(Merodach-Baladan)
Isa. 39:1.

4758. מַרְאֶה *mar'eh* **masc. noun**
(appearance, sight, vision)
Gen. 2:9; 12:11; 24:16; 26:7; 29:17; 39:6; 41:2–4,21; **Ex.** 3:3; 24:17; **Lev.** 13:3,4,12,20,25,30–32,34,43; 14:37; **Num.** 8:4; 9:15,16; 12:8; **Deut.** 28:34,67; **Josh.** 22:10; **Judg.** 13:6; **1 Sam.** 16:7; 17:42; **2 Sam.** 11:2; 14:27; 23:21; **Esth.** 1:11; 2:2,3,7; **Job** 4:16; 41:9(1); **Eccl.** 6:9; 11:9; **Song** 2:14; 5:15; **Isa.** 11:3; 52:14; 53:2; **Ezek.** 1:5,13,14,16,26–28; 8:2,4; 10:1,9,10,22; 11:24; 23:15,16; 40:3; 41:21; 42:11; 43:3; **Dan.** 1:4,13,15; 8:15,16,26,27; 9:23; 10:1,6,18; **Joel** 2:4; **Nah.** 2:4(5).

4759. מַרְאָה *mar'āh* **fem. noun**
(vision [revelation], mirror)
Gen. 46:2; **Ex.** 38:8; **Num.** 12:6; **1 Sam.** 3:15; **Ezek.** 1:1; 8:3; 40:2; 43:3; **Dan.** 10:7,8,16.

4760. מֻרְאָה *mur'āh* **fem. noun**
(crop or craw of a bird)
Lev. 1:16.

4761. מַרְאָשׁוֹת *mar'āšôṯ* **fem. pl. noun**
(heads, principalities)
Jer. 13:18(NASB, NIV, *m^e ra'^a šôṯ* [4763,I]).

4762. A. מָרֵשָׁה *mārēšāh,* מָרֵאשָׁה *mārē'šāh* **proper noun**
(Mareshah: city in Judah)
Josh. 15:44; **2 Chr.** 11:8; 14:9(8),10(9); 20:37; **Mic.** 1:15.
B. מָרֵשָׁה *mārēšāh* **masc. proper noun**
(Mareshah: father of Hebron)
1 Chr. 2:42.
C. מָרֵשָׁה *mārēšāh* **masc. proper noun**
(Mareshah: son of Laadah)
1 Chr. 4:21.

4763. I. מְרַאֲשׁוֹת *m^e ra'^a šôṯ* **fem. noun**
(place at the head)
Gen. 28:11(KJV, see II),18(KJV, see II); **1 Sam.** 19:13(KJV, see II),16(KJV, see II); 26:7(KJV, see II),11(KJV, see II),12(KJV, see II); **1 Kgs.** 19:6; **Jer.** 13:18(KJV, *mar'āšôṯ* [4761]).
II. מְרַאֲשׁוֹת *m^e ra'^a šôṯ* **fem. noun**
(pillow, bolster [for the head])
Gen. 28:11(NASB, NIV, see I),18(NASB, NIV, see I); **1 Sam.** 19:13(NASB, NIV, see I),16(NASB, NIV, see I); 26:7(NASB, NIV, see I),11(NASB, NIV, see I),12(NASB, NIV, see I).

4764. מֵרַב *mēraḇ* **fem. proper noun**
(Merab)
1 Sam. 14:49; 18:17,19.

4765. מַרְבַד *marḇāḏ* **masc. noun**
(covering, spread)
Prov. 7:16; 31:22.

4766. מַרְבֶּה *marbeh* **masc. noun**
(abundance, increase)
Isa. 9:7(6); 33:23.

4767. מִרְבָּה *mirbāh* **fem. noun**
(abundance, much)
Ezek. 23:32.

4768. מַרְבִּית *marbiyṯ* **fem. noun**
(greatness, increase, gain)
Lev. 25:37; **1 Sam.** 2:33; **1 Chr.** 12:29; **2 Chr.** 9:6; 30:18.

4769. מַרְבֵּץ *marbēṣ* **masc. noun**
(resting place)
Ezek. 25:5; **Zeph.** 2:15.

4770. מַרְבֵּק *marbēq* **masc. noun**
(stall, fattened [in the stall])
1 Sam. 28:24; **Jer.** 46:21; **Amos** 6:4; **Mal.** 4:2(3:20).

4771. מַרְגּוֹעַ *margôa'* **masc. noun**
(rest)
Jer. 6:16.

4772. מַרְגְּלוֹת *marg^e^lôṯ* **masc. pl. noun**
(feet, place of the feet)
Ruth 3:4,7,8,14; **Dan.** 10:6.

4773. מַרְגֵּמָה *margēmāh* **fem. noun**
(sling)
Prov. 26:8.

4774. מַרְגֵּעָה *margē'āh* **fem. noun**
(place of rest)
Isa. 28:12.

4775. מָרַד *māraḏ* **verb**
(to rebel, to revolt)
Gen. 14:4; **Num.** 14:9; **Josh.** 22:16,18, 19,29; **2 Kgs.** 18:7,20; 24:1,20; **2 Chr.** 13:6; 36:13; **Neh.** 2:19; 6:6; 9:26; **Job** 24:13; **Isa.** 36:5; **Jer.** 52:3; **Ezek.** 2:3; 17:15; 20:38; **Dan.** 9:5,9.

4776. מְרַד *m^e^raḏ* **Aram. masc. noun**
(rebellion; corr. to Hebr. 4777)
Ezra 4:19.

4777. מֶרֶד *mereḏ* **masc. noun**
(rebellion)
Josh. 22:22.

4778. מֶרֶד *mereḏ* **masc. proper noun**
(Mered)
1 Chr. 4:17,18.

4779. מָרָד *mārāḏ* **Aram. adj.**
(rebellious)
Ezra 4:12,15.

4780. מַרְדּוּת *mardûṯ* **fem. noun**
(rebellion)
1 Sam. 20:30.

4781. מְרֹדָךְ *m^e^rōḏāḵ* **masc. proper noun**
(Merodach, Marduk)
Jer. 50:2.

4782. A. מָרְדֳּכַי *mord^e^ḵay* **masc. proper noun**
(Mordecai: associate of Zerubbabel)
Ezra 2:2; **Neh.** 7:7.
B. מָרְדֳּכַי *mord^e^ḵay* **masc. proper noun**
(Mordecai: cousin of Esther)
Esth. 2:5,7,10,11,15,19–22; 3:2–6; 4:1, 4–7,9,10,12,13,15,17; 5:9,13,14; 6:2–4, 10–13; 7:9,10; 8:1,2,7,9,15; 9:3,4,20,23, 29,31; 10:2,3.

4783. מֻרְדָּף *murdāp̱* **masc. noun**
(persecution, aggression)
Isa. 14:6.

4784. מָרָה *mārāh* **verb**
(to rebel, to be disobedient)
Num. 20:10,24; 27:14; **Deut.** 1:26,43; 9:7,23,24; 21:18,20; 31:27; **Josh.** 1:18; **1 Sam.** 12:14,15; **1 Kgs.** 13:21,26; **2 Kgs.** 14:26; **Neh.** 9:26; **Job** 17:2; **Ps.** 5:10(11); 78:8,17,40,56; 105:28; 106:7,33,43; 107:11; **Isa.** 1:20; 3:8; 50:5; 63:10; **Jer.** 4:17; 5:23; **Lam.** 1:18,20; 3:42; **Ezek.** 5:6; 20:8,13,21; **Hos.**

13:16(14:1); **Zeph.** 3:1(KJV, *mārā'* [4754,II]).

4785. מָרָה *mārāh* **proper noun**
(Marah)
Ex. 15:23; **Num.** 33:8,9.

4786. מֹרָה *mōrāh* **fem. noun**
(grief)
Gen. 26:35; **Prov.** 14:10(KJV, NASB, *morrāh* [4787]).

4787. מָרָּה *morrah* **fem. noun**
(bitterness)
Prov. 14:10(NIV, *mōrāh* [4786]).

4788. מָרוּד *mārûḏ* **masc. noun**
(restlessness, wandering, homelessness)
Isa. 58:7; **Lam.** 1:7; 3:19.

4789. מֵרוֹז *mērôz* **proper noun**
(Meroz)
Judg. 5:23.

4790. מָרוֹחַ *mārôaḥ* **adj.**
(crushed, broken)
Lev. 21:20.

4791. מָרוֹם *mārôm* **masc. noun**
(height, high place, exaltedness)
Judg. 5:18; **2 Sam.** 22:17; **2 Kgs.** 19:22,23; **Job** 5:11; 16:19; 25:2; 31:2; 39:18; **Ps.** 7:7(8); 10:5; 18:16(17); 56:2(3); 68:18(19); 71:19; 73:8; 75:5(6); 92:8(9); 93:4; 102:19(20); 144:7; 148:1; **Prov.** 8:2; 9:3,14; **Eccl.** 10:6; **Isa.** 22:16; 24:4,18,21; 26:5; 32:15; 33:5,16; 37:23,24; 38:14; 40:26; 57:15; 58:4; **Jer.** 17:12; 25:30; 31:12; 49:16; 51:53; **Lam.** 1:13; **Ezek.** 17:23; 20:40; 34:14; **Obad.** 1:3; **Mic.** 6:6; **Hab.** 2:9.

4792. מֵרוֹם *mērôm* **proper noun**
(Merom)
Josh. 11:5,7.

4793. מֵרוֹץ *mērôṣ* **masc. noun**
(running race)
Eccl. 9:11.

4794. מְרוּצָה *m^e^rûṣāh* **fem. noun**
(running, course)
2 Sam. 18:27; **Jer.** 8:6; 23:10.

4795. מָרוּק *mārûq* **masc. noun**
(purification, beautification)
Esth. 2:12.

4796. מָרוֹת *mārôṯ* **proper noun**
(Maroth)
Mic. 1:12.

4797. מִרְזַח *mirzaḥ* **masc. noun**
(banqueting, feasting)
Amos 6:7(NASB, NIV, *marzēaḥ* [4798]).

4798. מַרְזֵחַ *marzēaḥ* **masc. noun**
(mourning, funeral meal)
Jer. 16:5; **Amos** 6:7(KJV, *mirzaḥ* [4797]).

4799. מָרַח *māraḥ* **verb**
(to apply)
Isa. 38:21.

4800. מֶרְחָב *merḥāḇ* **masc. noun**
(large place, spacious place)
2 Sam. 22:20; **Ps.** 18:19(20); 31:8(9); 118:5; **Hos.** 4:16; **Hab.** 1:6.

4801. מֶרְחָק *merḥāq* **masc. noun**
(distant place, faraway place)
2 Sam. 15:17; **Ps.** 138:6; **Prov.** 25:25; 31:14; **Isa.** 8:9; 10:3; 13:5; 17:13; 30:27; 33:17; 46:11; **Jer.** 4:16; 5:15; 6:20; 8:19; 31:10; **Ezek.** 23:40; **Zech.** 10:9.

4802. מַרְחֶשֶׁת *marḥešeṯ* **fem. noun**
(pan, frying pan)
Lev. 2:7; 7:9.

4803. מָרַט *māraṭ* **verb**
(to fall off [of hair], to pluck off [hair], to polish)

Lev. 13:40,41; **1 Kgs.** 7:45; **Ezra** 9:3; **Neh.** 13:25; **Isa.** 18:2(see *môrāṭ* [4178]),7(see *môrāṭ* [4178]); 50:6; **Ezek.** 21:9–11(14–16),28(33); 29:18.

4804. מְרַט *m^{e}raṭ* **Aram. verb**
(to pluck off, to tear off; corr. to Hebr. 4803)
Dan. 7:4.

4805. מְרִי *m^{e}riy* **masc. noun**
(rebellion)
Num. 17:10(25); **Deut.** 31:27; **1 Sam.** 15:23; **Neh.** 9:17; **Job** 23:2; **Prov.** 17:11; **Isa.** 30:9; **Ezek.** 2:5–8; 3:9,26,27; 12:2, 3,9,25; 17:12; 24:3; 44:6.

4806. מְרִיא *m^{e}riy'* **masc. noun**
(fattened calf, fattened animal)
2 Sam. 6:13; **1 Kgs.** 1:9,19,25; **Isa.** 1:11; 11:6; **Ezek.** 39:18; **Amos** 5:22.

4807. מְרִיב בַּעַל *m^{e}riyḇ ba'al* **masc. proper noun**
(Meri-Baal)
1 Chr. 8:34; 9:40.

4808. מְרִיבָה *m^{e}riyḇāh* **fem. noun**
(strife, contention)
Gen. 13:8; **Num.** 27:14; **Ps.** 95:8(NASB, NIV, *m^{e}riyḇāh* [4809,B]); 106:32(NASB, NIV, *m^{e}riyḇāh* [4809,B]); **Ezek.** 47:19 (NASB, NIV, *m^{e}riyḇaṯ qāḏēš* [4809,C]); 48:28(NASB, NIV, *m^{e}riyḇaṯ qāḏēš* [4809,C]).

4809. A. מְרִיבָה *m^{e}riyḇāh* **proper noun**
(Meribah: loc. near Rephidim)
Ex. 17:7.
B. מְרִיבָה *m^{e}riyḇāh* **proper noun**
(Meribah: loc. at Rephidim)
Num. 20:13,24; 27:14(NIV, see C); **Deut.** 33:8; **Ps.** 81:7(8); 95:8(KJV, *m^{e}riyḇāh* [4808] and *qāḏēš* [6946]); 106:32(KJV, *m^{e}riyḇāh* [4808] and *qāḏēš* [6946]).
C. מְרִיבַה קָדֵשׁ *m^{e}riyḇaṯ qāḏēš* **proper noun**
(Meribah Kadesh)
Num. 27:14(KJV, NASB, *m^{e}riyḇāh* [4809,A] and *qāḏēš* [6936]); **Deut.** 32:51; **Ezek.** 47:19,32(KJV, *m^{e}riyḇāh* [4808] and *qāḏēš* [6946]); 48:28(KJV, *m^{e}riyḇāh* [4808] and *qāḏēš* [6946]).

4810. מְרִי בַעַל *m^{e}riy ḇa'al* **masc. proper noun**
(Merib-Baal)
1 Chr. 9:40.

4811. מְרָיָה *m^{e}rāyāh* **masc. proper noun**
(Meraiah)
Neh. 12:12.

4812. A. מְרָיוֹת *m^{e}rāyôṯ* **masc. proper noun**
(Meraioth: a priest)
1 Chr. 6:6(5:32),7(5:33),52(37); **Ezra** 7:3.
B. מְרָיוֹת *m^{e}rāyôṯ* **masc. proper noun**
(Meraioth: son of Ahitub)
1 Chr. 9:11; **Neh.** 11:11.
C. מְרָיוֹת *m^{e}rāyôṯ* **masc. proper noun**
(Meraioth: father of Helkai)
Neh. 12:15(NIV, [Q^e] *m^{e}rēmôṯ* [4822,E]).

4813. A. מִרְיָם *miryām* **fem. proper noun**
(Miriam: sister of Aaron)
Ex. 15:20,21; **Num.** 12:1,4,5,10,15; 20:1; 26:59; **Deut.** 24:9; **1 Chr.** 6:3(5:29); **Mic.** 6:4.
B. מִרְיָם *miryām* **fem. proper noun**
(Miriam: a Judaite)
1 Chr. 4:17.

4814. מְרִירוּת *m^{e}riyrûṯ* **fem. noun**
(bitterness)
Ezek. 21:6(11).

4815. מְרִירִי *m*^{e}*riyriy* **adj.**
(bitter, deadly)
Deut. 32:24.

4816. מֹרֶךְ *mōreḵ* **masc. noun**
(weakness, fearfulness)
Lev. 26:36.

4817. מֶרְכָּב *merkāḇ* **masc. noun**
(covering, saddle, place to ride, chariot)
Lev. 15:9; **1 Kgs.** 4:26(5:6); **Song** 3:10.

4818. מֶרְכָּבָה *merkāḇāh* **fem. noun**
(chariot)
Gen. 41:43; 46:29; **Ex.** 14:25; 15:4; **Josh.** 11:6,9; **Judg.** 4:15; 5:28; **1 Sam.** 8:11; **2 Sam.** 15:1; **1 Kgs.** 7:33; 10:29; 12:18; 20:33; 22:35; **2 Kgs.** 5:21,26; 9:27; 10:15; 23:11; **1 Chr.** 28:18; **2 Chr.** 1:17; 9:25; 10:18; 14:9(8); 18:34; 35:24; **Song** 6:12; **Isa.** 2:7; 22:18; 66:15; **Jer.** 4:13; **Joel** 2:5; **Mic.** 1:13; 5:10(9); **Nah.** 3:2; **Hab.** 3:8; **Hag.** 2:22; **Zech.** 6:1–3.

4819. מַרְכֹּלֶת *markōleṯ* **fem. noun**
(merchandise, marketplace)
Ezek. 27:24.

4820. מִרְמָה *mirmāh* **fem. noun**
(deceit, treachery)
Gen. 27:35; 34:13; **2 Kgs.** 9:23; **Job** 15:35; 31:5; **Ps.** 5:6(7); 10:7; 17:1; 24:4; 34:13(14); 35:20; 36:3(4); 38:12(13); 43:1; 50:19; 52:4(6); 55:11(12),23(24); 109:2; **Prov.** 11:1; 12:5,17,20; 14:8,25; 20:23; 26:24; **Isa.** 53:9; **Jer.** 5:27; 9:6(5),8(7); **Dan.** 8:25; 11:23; **Hos.** 11:12(12:1); 12:7(8); **Amos** 8:5; **Mic.** 6:11; **Zeph.** 1:9.

4821. מִרְמָה *mirmāh* **proper noun**
(Mirmah)
1 Chr. 8:10.

4822. A. מְרֵמוֹת *m*^{e}*rēmôṯ* **masc. proper noun**
(Meremoth: priest under Zerubbabel)
Neh. 12:3.
B. מְרֵמוֹת *m*^{e}*rēmôṯ* **masc. proper noun**
(Meremoth: priest under Ezra)
Ezra 8:33; **Neh.** 3:4,21.
C. מְרֵמוֹת *m*^{e}*rēmôṯ* **masc. proper noun**
(Meremoth: postexilic Jew)
Ezra 10:36.
D. מְרֵמוֹת *m*^{e}*rēmôṯ* **masc. proper noun**
(Meremoth: covenant signer)
Neh. 10:5.
E. מְרֵמוֹת *m*^{e}*rēmôṯ* **masc. proper noun**
(Meremoth: father of Helkai)
Neh. 12:15(KJV, NASB, [K^e] *m*^{e}*rāyôṯ* [4812,C]).

4823. מִרְמָס *mirmās* **masc. noun**
(something trampled, trampled down)
Isa. 5:5; 7:25; 10:6; 28:18; **Ezek.** 34:19; **Dan.** 8:13; **Mic.** 7:10.

4824. מֵרֹנֹתִי *mērōnōṯiy* **masc. proper noun**
(Meronothite)
1 Chr. 27:30; **Neh.** 3:7.

4825. מֶרֶס *meres* **masc. proper noun**
(Meres)
Esth. 1:14.

4826. מַרְסְנָא *mars*^{e}*nā'* **masc. proper noun**
(Marsena)
Esth. 1:14.

4827. מֵרַע *mēra'* **masc. noun**
(evil)
Dan. 11:27(NASB, *rā'a'* [7489]).

4828. מֵרֵעַ *mērēa'* **masc. noun**
(companion, friend)

Gen. 26:26; **Judg.** 14:11,20; 15:2,6; **2 Sam.** 3:8; **Job** 6:14(KJV, NASB, *rēʻ* [7453]); **Prov.** 19:7.

4829. מִרְעֶה *mirʻeh* **masc. noun**
(pasture)
Gen. 47:4; **1 Chr.** 4:39–41; **Job** 39:8; **Isa.** 32:14; **Lam.** 1:6; **Ezek.** 34:14,18; **Joel** 1:18; **Nah.** 2:11(12).

4830. מַרְעִית *marʻiyṯ* **fem. noun**
(pasture, the flock feeding in it)
Ps. 74:1; 79:13; 95:7; 100:3; **Isa.** 49:9; **Jer.** 10:21; 23:1; 25:36; **Ezek.** 34:31; **Hos.** 13:6.

4831. מַרְעֲלָה *marʻalāh* **proper noun**
(Maralah)
Josh. 19:11.

4832. I. מַרְפֵּא *marpēʼ* **masc. noun**
(health, healing, remedy)
2 Chr. 21:18; 36:16; **Prov.** 4:22; 6:15; 12:18; 13:17; 15:4; 16:24; 29:1; **Jer.** 8:15; 14:19; **Mal.** 4:2(3:20).
II. מַרְפֵּא *marpēʼ* **masc. noun**
(peace, composure, calmness)
Prov. 14:30; **Eccl.** 10:4.

4833. מִרְפַּשׂ *mirpaś* **masc. noun**
(to make muddy)
Ex. 34:19.

4834. מָרַץ *māraṣ* **verb**
(to be sick, to be painful)
1 Kgs. 2:8; **Job** 6:25; 16:3; **Mic.** 2:10.

4835. מְרוּצָה m^e*rûṣāh* **fem. noun**
(oppression, violence)
Jer. 22:17.

4836. מַרְצֵעַ *marṣēaʻ* **masc. noun**
(awl, instrument for piercing)
Ex. 21:6; **Deut.** 15:17.

4837. מַרְצֶפֶת *marṣepeṯ* **fem. noun**
(pavement, base)
2 Kgs. 16:17.

4838. מָרַק *māraq* **verb**
(to scour, to polish)
Lev. 6:28(21); **2 Chr.** 4:16; **Prov.** 20:30(KJV, [Q^e] *tamrûq* [8562]); **Jer.** 46:4.

4839. מָרָק *māraq* **masc. noun**
(broth)
Judg. 6:19,20; **Isa.** 65:4(KJV, [K^e] *pārāq* [6564]).

4840. מֶרְקָח *merqāḥ* **masc. noun**
(perfume, sweet scent)
Song 5:13.

4841. מֶרְקָחָה *merqāḥāh* **fem. noun**
(spices, pot of ointment)
Job 41:31(23); **Ezek.** 24:10.

4842. מִרְקַחַת *mirqaḥaṯ* **fem. noun**
(mixture of ointment or perfume)
Ex. 30:25; **1 Chr.** 9:30; **2 Chr.** 16:14.

4843. מָרַר *mārar* **verb**
(to be bitter, to make bitter, to grieve)
Gen. 49:23; **Ex.** 1:14; 23:21; **Ruth** 1:13,20; **1 Sam.** 30:6; **2 Kgs.** 4:27; **Job** 27:2; **Isa.** 22:4; 24:9; 38:17; **Lam.** 1:4; **Dan.** 8:7; 11:11; **Zech.** 12:10.

4844. מָרֹר *mārōr* **masc. noun**
(bitter herb, bitterness)
Ex. 12:8; **Num.** 9:11; **Deut.** 32:32(KJV, NASB, m^e*rōrāh* [4846]); **Job** 13:26(KJV, NASB, m^e*rōrāh* [4846]); **Lam.** 3:15.

4845. מְרֵרָה m^e*rērāh* **fem. noun**
(gall, bile)
Job 16:13; 20:25(KJV, NIV, m^e*rōrāh* [4846]).

4846. מְרֹרָה m^e*rōrāh* **fem. noun**
(gall, liver, bitter thing)
Deut. 32:32(NIV, *mārōr* [4844]); **Job** 13:26(NIV, *mārōr* [4844]); 20:14,25 (NASB, m^e*rērāh* [4845]).

4847. מְרָרִי *m^erāriy* **masc. proper noun**
(Merari)
Gen. 46:11; **Ex.** 6:16,19; **Num.** 3:17,20,33,35,36; 4:29,33,42,45; 7:8; 10:17; 26:57; **Josh.** 21:7,34,40(38); **1 Chr.** 6:1(5:27),16(1),19(4),29(14), 44(29),47(32),63(48),77(62); 9:14; 15:6,17; 23:6,21; 24:26,27; 26:10,19; **2 Chr.** 29:12; 34:12; **Ezra** 8:19.

4848. מְרָרִי *m^erāriy* **masc. proper noun**
(Merarite)
Num. 26:57.

4849. מִרְשַׁעַת *mirša'at̲* **fem. noun**
(wickedness)
2 Chr. 24:7.

4850. מְרָתַיִם *m^erāt̲ayim* **proper noun**
(Merathaim)
Jer. 50:21.

4851. מַשׁ *maš* **masc. proper noun**
(Mash)
Gen. 10:23(NIV, *mešek̲* [4902]).

4852. מֵשָׁא *mēšā'* **proper noun**
(Mesha)
Gen. 10:30.

4853. I. מַשָּׂא *maśśā'* **masc. noun**
(burden, load)
Ex. 23:5; **Num.** 4:15,19,24,27,31,32,47,49; 11:11,17; **Deut.** 1:12; **2 Sam.** 15:33; 19:35(36); **2 Kgs.** 5:17; 8:9; **1 Chr.** 15:22,27; **2 Chr.** 17:11; 20:25; 35:3; **Neh.** 13:15,19; **Job** 7:20; **Ps.** 38:4(5); **Isa.** 22:25; 46:1,2; **Jer.** 17:21,22,24,27; **Ezek.** 24:25; **Hos.** 8:10.
II. מַשָּׂא *maśśā'* **masc. noun**
(prophetic burden, oracle, pronouncement)
2 Kgs. 9:25; **2 Chr.** 24:27; **Prov.** 30:1; 31:1; **Isa.** 13:1; 14:28; 15:1; 17:1; 19:1; 21:1,11,13; 22:1; 23:1; 30:6; **Jer.** 23:33, 34,36,38; **Ezek.** 12:10; **Nah.** 1:1; **Hab.** 1:1; **Zech.** 9:1; 12:1; **Mal.** 1:1.

4854. מַשָּׂא *maśśā'* **masc. proper noun**
(Massa)
Gen. 25:14; **1 Chr.** 1:30.

4855. מַשָּׁא *maššā'* **masc. noun**
(usury)
Neh. 5:7,10; 10:31; **Prov.** 22:26(KJV, NASB, *maššā'āh* [4859]).

4856. מַשֹּׂא *maśśō'* **masc. noun**
(partiality)
2 Chr. 19:7.

4857. מַשְׁאָב *maš'āb̲* **masc. noun**
(watering place, place of drawing water)
Judg. 5:11.

4858. I. מַשָּׂאָה *maśśā'āh* **fem. noun**
(smoke, cloud of smoke)
Isa. 30:27(KJV, see II).
II. מַשָּׂאָה *maśśā'āh* **fem. noun**
(burden)
Isa. 30:27(NASB, NIV, see I).

4859. מַשָּׁאָה *maššā'āh* **fem. noun**
(debt, loan)
Deut. 24:10; **Prov.** 22:26(NIV, *maššāh* [4855]).

4860. מַשָּׁאוֹן *maššā'ôn* **masc. noun**
(guile, deception)
Prov. 26:26.

4861. מִשְׁאָל *miš'āl* **proper noun**
(Mishal; see also *māšal* [4913])
Josh. 19:26; 21:30.

4862. מִשְׁאָלָה *miš'ālāh* **fem. noun**
(petition, request)
Ps. 20:5(6); 37:4.

4863. מִשְׁאֶרֶת *miš'eret̲* **fem. noun**
(kneading trough or bowl)
Ex. 8:3(7:28); 12:34; **Deut.** 28:5,17.

4864. מַשְׂאֵת *maś'ēt̲* **fem. noun**
(tax, gift, portion)
Gen. 43:34; **Judg.** 20:38,40; **2 Sam.** 11:8; **2 Chr.** 24:6,9; **Esth.** 2:18; **Ps.** 141:2; **Jer.** 6:1; 40:5; **Lam.** 2:14; **Ezek.** 20:40; **Amos** 5:11; **Zeph.** 3:18.

4865. מִשְׁבְּצוֹת *mišbᵉṣôt̲* **fem. pl. noun**
(filigree settings [for gems])
Ex. 28:11,13,14,25; 39:6,13,16,18; **Ps.** 45:13(14).

4866. מַשְׁבֵּר *mašbēr* **masc. noun**
(opening of the womb, birth)
2 Kgs. 19:3; **Isa.** 37:3; **Hos.** 13:13.

4867. מִשְׁבָּר *mišbār* **masc. noun**
(waves, breaking waves)
2 Sam. 22:5; **Ps.** 42:7(8); 88:7(8); 93:4; **Jon.** 2:3(4).

4868. מִשְׁבָּת *mišbāt̲* **masc. noun**
(destruction, ruin)
Lam. 1:7.

4869. I. מִשְׂגָּב *miśgāb̲* **masc. noun**
(stronghold)
2 Sam. 22:3; **Ps.** 9:9(10); 18:2(3); 46:7(8),11(12); 48:3(4); 59:9(10),16(17),17(18); 62:2(3),6(7); 94:22; 144:2; **Isa.** 25:12; 33:16; **Jer.** 48:1(KJV, see II).
II. מִשְׂגָּב *miśgāb̲* **proper noun**
(Misgab: loc. in Moab)
Jer. 48:1(NASB, NIV, see I).

4870. מִשְׁגֶּה *mišgeh* **masc. noun**
(mistake, oversight)
Gen. 43:12.

4871. מָשָׁה *māšāh* **verb**
(to draw, to pull)
Ex. 2:10; **2 Sam.** 22:17; **Ps.** 18:16(17).

4872. מֹשֶׁה *mōšeh* **masc. proper noun**
(Moses)
Ex. 2:10,11,14,15,17,21; 3:1,3,4,6,11,13–15; 4:1,3,4,10,14,18–21,27–30; 5:1,4,20,22; 6:1,2,9,10,12,13,20,26–30; 7:1,6–8,10,14,19,20; 8:1(7:26),5(1),8(4),9(5),12(8),13(9),16(12),20(16),25(21),26(22),29–31(25–27); 9:1,8,10–13,22,23,27,29,33,35; 10:1,3,8,9,12,13,16,21,22,24,25,29; 11:1,3,4,9,10; 12:1,21,28,31,35,43,50; 13:1,3,19; 14:1,11,13,15,21,26,27,31; 15:1,22,24; 16:2,4,6,8,9,11,15,19,20,22,24,25,28,32–34; 17:2–6,9–12,14,15; 18:1,2,5–8,12–15,17,24–27; 19:3,7–10,14,17,19–21,23,25; 20:19–22; 24:1–4,6,8,9,12,13,15,16,18; 25:1; 30:11,17,22,34; 31:1,12,18; 32:1,7,9,11,15,17,19,21,23,25,26,28–31,33; 33:1,5,7–9,11,12,17; 34:1,4,8,27,29–31,33–35; 35:1,4,20,29,30; 36:2,3,5,6; 38:21,22; 39:1,5,7,21,26,29,31–33,42,43; 40:1,16,18,19,21,23,25,27,29,31–33,35; **Lev.** 1:1; 4:1; 5:14; 6:1(5:20),8(1),19(12),24(17); 7:22,28,38; 8:1,4–6,9,10,13,15–17,19–21,23,24,28–31,36; 9:1,5–7,10,21,23; 10:3–7,11,12,16,19,20; 11:1; 12:1; 13:1; 14:1,33; 15:1; 16:1,2,34; 17:1; 18:1; 19:1; 20:1; 21:1,16,24; 22:1,17,26; 23:1,9,23,26,33,44; 24:1,11,13,23; 25:1; 26:46; 27:1,34; **Num.** 1:1,17,19,44,48,54; 2:1,33,34; 3:1,5,11,14,16,38–40,42,44,49,51; 4:1,17,21,34,37,41,45,46,49; 5:1,4,5,11; 6:1,22; 7:1,4,6,11,89; 8:1,3–5,20,22,23; 9:1,4–6,8,9,23; 10:1,13,29,35; 11:2,10,11,16,21,23,24,27–30; 12:1–4,7,8,11,13,14; 13:1,3,16,17,26,30; 14:2,5,11,13,26,36,39,41,44; 15:1,17,22,23,33,35–37; 16:2–4,8,12,15,16,18,20,23,25,28,36(17:1),40–44(17:5–9),46(17:11),47(17:12),50(17:15); 17:1(16),6–12(21–27); 18:25; 19:1; 20:2,3,6,7,9–12,14,23,27,28; 21:5,7–9,16,32,34; 25:4–6,10,16; 26:1,3,4,9,52,59,63,64; 27:2,5,6,11,12,15,18,22,23; 28:1; 29:40(30:1); 30:1(2),16(17); 31:1,3,6,7,12–15,21,25,31,41,42,47–49,51,54; 32:2,6,20,25,28,29,33,40; 33:1,2,50;

34:1,13,16; 35:1,9; 36:1,5,10,13; **Deut.** 1:1,3,5; 4:41,44–46; 5:1; 27:1,9,11; 29:1(28:69),2(1); 31:1,7,9,10,14,16,22, 24,25,30; 32:44,45,48; 33:1,4; 34:1,5, 7–10,12; **Josh.** 1:1–3,5,7,13–15,17; 3:7; 4:10,12,14; 8:31–33,35; 9:24; 11:12,15, 20,23; 12:6; 13:8,12,15,21,24,29,32,33; 14:2,3,5–7,9–11; 17:4; 18:7; 20:2; 21:2,8; 22:2,4,5,7,9; 23:6; 24:5; **Judg.** 1:16,20; 3:4; 4:11; **1 Sam.** 12:6,8; **1 Kgs.** 2:3; 8:9,53,56; **2 Kgs.** 14:6; 18:4,6,12; 21:8; 23:25; **1 Chr.** 6:3(5:29),49(34); 15:15; 21:29; 22:13; 23:13–15; 26:24; **2 Chr.** 1:3; 5:10; 8:13; 23:18; 24:6,9; 25:4; 30:16; 33:8; 34:14; 35:6,12; **Ezra** 3:2; 7:6; **Neh.** 1:7,8; 8:1,14; 9:14; 10:29(30); 13:1; **Ps.** 77:20(21); 90:[title](1); 99:6; 103:7; 105:26; 106:16,23,32; **Isa.** 63:11,12; **Jer.** 15:1; **Dan.** 9:11,13; **Mic.** 6:4; **Mal.** 4:4(3:22).

4873. מֹשֶׁה *mōšeh* **Aram. masc. proper noun**
(Moses; corr. to Hebr. 4872)
Ezra 6:18.

4874. מַשֶּׁה *maššeh* **masc. noun**
(loan)
Deut. 15:2.

4875. מְשׁוֹאָה *m^e^šô'āh,* מְשֹׁאָה *m^e^šō'āh* **fem. noun**
(desolation, waste)
Job 30:3; 38:27; **Zeph.** 1:15.

4876. מַשּׁוּאָה *maššû'āh* **fem. noun**
(destruction, ruin, desolation)
Ps. 73:18; 74:3.

4877. מְשׁוֹבָב *m^e^šôḇāḇ* **masc. proper noun**
(Meshobab)
1 Chr. 4:34.

4878. מְשׁוּבָה *m^e^šûḇāh* **fem. noun**
(turning away, apostasy, backsliding)
Prov. 1:32; **Jer.** 2:19; 3:6,8,11,12,22; 5:6; 8:5; 14:7; **Ezek.** 37:23(KJV, NASB, *môšāḇ* [4186]); **Hos.** 11:7; 14:4(5).

4879. מְשׁוּגָה *m^e^šûgāh* **fem. noun**
(error)
Job 19:4.

4880. מָשׁוֹט *māšôṭ,* מִשּׁוֹט *miššôṭ* **masc. noun**
(oar [for rowing])
Ezek. 27:6,29.

4881. מְשׂוּכָה *m^e^śûkāh,* מְשֻׂכָה *m^e^śukāh* **fem. noun**
(hedge of thorns)
Prov. 15:19; **Isa.** 5:5.

4882. מְשׁוּסָה *m^e^šûsāh* **fem. noun**
(loot, spoil)
Isa. 42:24(NASB, NIV, [Q^e^] *m^e^šissāh* [4933]).

4883. מַשּׂוֹר *maśśôr* **masc. noun**
(saw)
Isa. 10:15.

4884. מְשׂוּרָה *m^e^śûrāh* **fem. noun**
(measure, measurement)
Lev. 19:35; **1 Chr.** 23:29; **Ezek.** 4:11,16.

4885. I. מָשׂוֹשׂ *māśôś* **masc. noun**
(joy, rejoicing)
Job 8:19(NIV, see II); **Ps.** 48:2(3); **Isa.** 8:6; 24:8,11; 32:13,14; 60:15; 62:5; 65:18; 66:10; **Jer.** 49:25; **Lam.** 2:15; 5:15; **Ezek.** 24:25; **Hos.** 2:11(13).
II. מָשׂוֹשׂ *māśôś* **masc. noun**
(a rotten thing, something wasted away)
Job 8:19(KJV, NASB, see I).

4886. מָשַׁח *māšaḥ* **verb**
(to anoint)
Gen. 31:13; **Ex.** 28:41; 29:2,7,29,36; 30:26,30; 40:9–11,13,15; **Lev.** 2:4;

6:20(13); 7:12,36; 8:10–12; 16:32; **Num.** 3:3; 6:15; 7:1,10,84,88; 35:25; **Judg.** 9:8,15; **1 Sam.** 9:16; 10:1; 15:1,17; 16:3,12,13; **2 Sam.** 1:21(KJV, NASB, *māšiyaḥ* [4899]); 2:4,7; 3:39; 5:3,17; 12:7; 19:10(11); **1 Kgs.** 1:34,39,45; 5:1(15); 19:15,16; **2 Kgs.** 9:3,6,12; 11:12; 23:30; **1 Chr.** 11:3; 14:8; 29:22; **2 Chr.** 22:7; 23:11; **Ps.** 45:7(8); 89:20(21); **Isa.** 21:5; 61:1; **Jer.** 22:14; **Dan.** 9:24; **Amos** 6:6.

4887. מְשַׁח *m^e^šaḥ* **Aram. masc. noun**
(oil, olive oil)
Ezra 6:9; 7:22.

4888. I. מִשְׁחָה *mišḥāh* **fem. noun**
(portion)
Lev. 7:35.
II. מִשְׁחָה *mišḥāh* **fem. noun**
(anointing)
Ex. 25:6; 29:7,21; 30:25,31; 31:11; 35:8,15,28; 37:29; 39:38; 40:9; **Lev.** 8:2,10,12,30; 10:7; 21:10,12; **Num.** 4:16.
III. מָשְׁחָה *mošḥāh* **fem. noun**
(portion)
Num. 18:8.
IV. מָשְׁחָה *mošḥāh* **fem. noun**
(anointing)
Ex. 40:15.

4889. מַשְׁחִית *mašḥiyṯ* **fem. noun**
(destruction, corruption)
Ex. 12:13(NASB, *šāḥaṯ* [7843]); **2 Kgs.** 23:13; **2 Chr.** 20:23(NIV, *šāḥaṯ* [7843]); 22:4; **Prov.** 18:9(KJV, NASB, *šāḥaṯ* [7843]); 28:24(KJV, NASB, *šāḥaṯ* [7843]); **Isa.** 54:16(KJV, NASB, *šāḥaṯ* [7843]); **Jer.** 5:26; 22:7(KJV, NASB, *šāḥaṯ* [7843]); 51:1(KJV, NASB, *šāḥaṯ* [7843]); **Ezek.** 9:6; 21:31(36); 25:15; **Dan.** 10:8.

4890. מִשְׂחָק *mišḥāq* **masc. noun**
(scorn, object of derision)
Hab. 1:10.

4891. מִשְׁחָר *mišḥār* **masc. noun**
(dawn, morning)
Ps. 110:3.

4892. מַשְׁחֵת *mašḥēṯ* **fem. noun**
(destruction)
Ezek. 9:1.

4893. I. מִשְׁחַת *mišḥaṯ* **masc. noun**
(disfigurement)
Isa. 52:14.
II. מָשְׁחָת *mošḥāṯ* **masc. noun**
(defect)
Lev. 22:25.

4894. מִשְׁטוֹחַ *mišṭôaḥ* **masc. noun**
(place for spreading)
Ezek. 26:5,14; 47:10.

4895. מַשְׂטֵמָה *maśṭēmāh* **fem. noun**
(hostility, hatred)
Hos. 9:7,8.

4896. מִשְׁטָר *mišṭār* **masc. noun**
(rule, dominion)
Job 38:33.

4897. מֶשִׁי *mešiy* **masc. noun**
(silk, costly material)
Ezek. 16:10,13.

4898. מְשֵׁיזַבְאֵל *m^e^šēyzaḇ'ēl* **masc. proper noun**
(Meshezabel)
Neh. 3:4; 10:21(22); 11:24.

4899. מָשִׁיחַ *māšiyaḥ* **masc. noun**
(anointed one, Messiah)
Lev. 4:3,5,16; 6:22(15); **1 Sam.** 2:10,35; 12:3,5; 16:6; 24:6(7),10(11); 26:9,11, 16,23; **2 Sam.** 1:14,16,21(NIV, *māšaḥ* [4886]); 19:21(22); 22:51; 23:1; **1 Chr.** 16:22; **2 Chr.** 6:42; **Ps.** 2:2; 18:50(51); 20:6(7); 28:8; 84:9(10); 89:38(39),51(52); 105:15; 132:10,17; **Isa.** 45:1; **Lam.** 4:20; **Dan.** 9:25,26; **Hab.** 3:13.

4900. מָשַׁךְ *māšak̲* **verb**
(to drag, to draw off, to pull up, to prolong)
Gen. 37:28; **Ex.** 12:21; 19:13; **Deut.** 21:3; **Josh.** 6:5; **Judg.** 4:6,7; 5:14; 20:37; **1 Kgs.** 22:34; **2 Chr.** 18:33; **Neh.** 9:30; **Job** 21:33; 24:22; 41:1(40:25); **Ps.** 10:9; 28:3; 36:10(11); 85:5(6); 109:12; **Prov.** 13:12; **Eccl.** 2:3; **Song** 1:4; **Isa.** 5:18; 13:22; 18:2,7; 66:19; **Jer.** 31:3; 38:13; **Ezek.** 12:25,28; 32:20; **Hos.** 7:5; 11:4; **Amos** 9:13.

4901. I. מֶשֶׁךְ *mešek̲* **masc. noun**
(price, preciousness, acquisition)
Job 28:18; **Ps.** 126:6(NASB, see II; NIV, see III).
II. מֶשֶׁךְ *mešek̲* **masc. noun**
(bag)
Ps. 126:6(KJV, see I; NIV, see III).
III. מֶשֶׁךְ *mešek̲* **masc. noun**
(a trail, a sowing)
Ps. 126:6(KJV, see I; NASB, see II).

4902. מֶשֶׁךְ *mešek̲* **masc. proper noun**
(Meshech)
Gen. 10:2,23(KJV, NASB, *maš* [4851]); **1 Chr.** 1:5,17; **Ps.** 120:5; **Ezek.** 27:13; 32:26; 38:2,3; 39:1.

4903. מִשְׁכַּב *miškab̲* **Aram. masc. noun**
(bed, couch; corr. to Hebr. 4904)
Dan. 2:28,29; 4:5(2),10(7),13(10); 7:1.

4904. מִשְׁכָּב *miškāb̲* **masc. noun**
(bed, couch)
Gen. 49:4; **Ex.** 8:3(7:28); 21:18; **Lev.** 15:4,5,21,23,24,26; 18:22; 20:13; **Num.** 31:17,18,35; **Judg.** 21:11,12; **2 Sam.** 4:5,7,11; 11:2,13; 13:5; 17:28; **1 Kgs.** 1:47; **2 Kgs.** 6:12; **2 Chr.** 16:14; **Job** 7:13; 33:15,19; **Ps.** 4:4(5); 36:4(5); 41:3(4); 149:5; **Prov.** 7:17; 22:27; **Eccl.** 10:20; **Song** 3:1; **Isa.** 57:2,7,8; **Ezek.** 23:17; 32:25; **Hos.** 7:14; **Mic.** 2:1.

4905. מַשְׂכִּיל *maśkiyl* **masc. noun**
(maskil, poem)
Ps. 32:[title](1); 42:[title](1); 44:[title](1); 45:[title](1); 47:7(8)(KJV, *śāk̲al* [7919,I]); 52:[title](1); 53:[title](1); 54:[title](1); 55:[title](1); 74:[title](1); 78:[title](1); 88:[title](1); 89:[title](1); 142:[title](1).

4906. מַשְׂכִּית *maśkiyt̲* **fem. noun**
(imagination, carved image)
Lev. 26:1; **Num.** 33:52; **Ps.** 73:7; **Prov.** 18:11; 25:11; **Ezek.** 8:12.

4907. מִשְׁכַּן *miškan* **Aram. masc. noun**
(habitation, place of dwelling; corr. to Hebr. 4908)
Ezra 7:15.

4908. מִשְׁכָּן *miškān* **masc. noun**
(tabernacle, dwelling place)
Ex. 25:9; 26:1,6,7,12,13,15,17,18,20,22,23,26,27,30,35; 27:9,19; 35:11,15,18; 36:8,13,14, 20,22,23,25,27,28,31,32; 38:20,21,31; 39:32,33,40; 40:2,5,6,9,17–19,21,22,24, 28,29,33–36,38; **Lev.** 8:10; 15:31; 17:4; 26:11; **Num.** 1:50,51,53; 3:7,8,23,25,26, 29,35,36,38; 4:16,25,26,31; 5:17; 7:1,3; 9:15,18–20,22; 10:11,17,21; 16:9,24,27; 17:13(28); 19:13; 24:5; 31:30,47; **Josh.** 22:19,29; **2 Sam.** 7:6; **1 Chr.** 6:32(17), 48(33); 16:39; 17:5; 21:29; 23:26; **2 Chr.** 1:5; 29:6; **Job** 18:21; 21:28; 39:6; **Ps.** 26:8; 43:3; 46:4(5); 49:11(12); 74:7; 78:28,60; 84:1(2); 87:2; 132:5,7; **Song** 1:8; **Isa.** 22:16; 32:18; 54:2; **Jer.** 9:19(18); 30:18; 51:30; **Ezek.** 25:4; 37:27; **Hab.** 1:6.

4909. מַשְׂכֹּרֶת *maśkōret̲* **fem. noun**
(wages)
Gen. 29:15; 31:7,41; **Ruth** 2:12.

4910. מָשַׁל *māšal* **verb**
(to rule, to govern)
Gen. 1:18; 3:16; 4:7; 24:2; 37:8; 45:8,26; **Ex.** 21:8; **Deut.** 15:6; **Josh.** 12:2,5;

Judg. 8:22,23; 9:2; 14:4; 15:11; **2 Sam.** 23:3; **1 Kgs.** 4:21(5:1); **1 Chr.** 29:12; **2 Chr.** 7:18; 9:26; 20:6; 23:20; **Neh.** 9:37; **Job** 25:2; **Ps.** 8:6(7); 19:13(14); 22:28(29); 59:13(14); 66:7; 89:9(10); 103:19; 105:20,21; 106:41; **Prov.** 6:7; 12:24; 16:32; 17:2; 19:10; 22:7; 23:1; 28:15; 29:2,12,26; **Eccl.** 9:17; 10:4; **Isa.** 3:4,12; 14:5; 16:1; 19:4; 28:14; 40:10; 49:7; 52:5; 63:19; **Jer.** 22:30; 30:21; 33:26; 51:46; **Lam.** 5:8; **Ezek.** 19:11,14; **Dan.** 11:3–5, 39,43; **Joel** 2:17; **Mic.** 5:2(1); **Hab.** 1:14; **Zech.** 6:13.

4911. מָשַׁל *māšal* **verb**
(to compare, to be like, to quote a proverb)
Num. 21:27; **Job** 17:6(KJV, NASB, m^e*šōl* [4914]); 30:19; **Ps.** 28:1; 49:12(13), 20(21); 143:7; **Isa.** 14:10; 46:5; **Ezek.** 12:23; 16:44; 17:2; 18:2,3; 20:49(21:5); 24:3.

4912. מָשָׁל *māšāl* **masc. noun**
(proverb, oracle, parable)
Num. 23:7,18; 24:3,15,20,21,23; **Deut.** 28:37; **1 Sam.** 10:12; 24:13(14); **1 Kgs.** 4:32(5:12); 9:7; **2 Chr.** 7:20; **Job** 13:12; 27:1; 29:1; **Ps.** 44:14(15); 49:4(5); 69:11(12); 78:2; **Prov.** 1:1,6; 10:1; 25:1; 26:7,9; **Eccl.** 12:9; **Isa.** 14:4; **Jer.** 24:9; **Ezek.** 12:22,23; 14:8; 17:2; 18:2,3; 20:49(21:5); 24:3; **Mic.** 2:4; **Hab.** 2:6.

4913. מָשָׁל *māšāl* **proper noun**
(Mashal; abbr. form of *miš'āl* [4861])
1 Chr. 6:74(59).

4914. מְשֹׁל m^e*šōl* **masc. noun**
(byword)
Job 17:6(NIV, *māšal* [4911]).

4915. I. מֹשֶׁל *mōšel* **masc. noun**
(similarity, likeness)
Job 41:33(25).

II. מֹשֶׁל *mōšel* **masc. noun**
(dominion)
Dan. 11:4; **Zech.** 9:10.

4916. I. מִשְׁלוֹחַ *mišlôaḥ* **masc. noun**
(sending, stretching forth)
Esth. 9:19,22; **Isa.** 11:14.
II. מִשְׁלָח *mišlāḥ* **masc. noun**
(undertaking; putting forth)
Deut. 12:7,18; 15:10; 23:20(21); 28:8,20; **Isa.** 7:25.

4917. מִשְׁלַחַת *mišlaḥat* **fem. noun**
(release, discharge; a group sent forth)
Ps. 78:49; **Eccl.** 8:8.

4918. A. מְשֻׁלָּם m^e*šullām* **masc. proper noun**
(Meshullam: descendant of Benjamin)
1 Chr. 8:17.
B. מְשֻׁלָּם m^e*šullām* **masc. proper noun**
(Meshullam: descendant of Gad)
1 Chr. 5:13.
C. מְשֻׁלָּם m^e*šullām* **masc. proper noun**
(Meshullam: grandfather of Shaphan)
2 Kgs. 22:3.
D. מְשֻׁלָּם m^e*šullām* **masc. proper noun**
(Meshullam: an overseer in the Temple repair)
2 Chr. 34:12.
E. מְשֻׁלָּם m^e*šullām* **masc. proper noun**
(Meshullam: son of Zerubbabel)
1 Chr. 3:19.
F. מְשֻׁלָּם m^e*šullām* **masc. proper noun**
(Meshullam: son of Shephatiah)
1 Chr. 9:8.
G. מְשֻׁלָּם m^e*šullām* **masc. proper noun**
(Meshullam: son of Zadok)

1 Chr. 9:11; **Neh.** 11:11.
H. מְשֻׁלָּם *m^ešullām* **masc. proper noun**
(Meshullam: son of Joed)
1 Chr. 9:7; **Neh.** 11:7.
I. מְשֻׁלָּם *m^ešullām* **masc. proper noun**
(Meshullam: son of Ezra)
Neh. 12:13,33.
J. מְשֻׁלָּם *m^ešullām* **masc. proper noun**
(Meshullam: son of Meshillemith)
1 Chr. 9:12.
K. מְשֻׁלָּם *m^ešullām* **masc. proper noun**
(Meshullam: Jewish leader)
Ezra 8:16; 10:15; **Neh.** 8:4; 10:20(21).
L. מְשֻׁלָּם *m^ešullām* **masc. proper noun**
(Meshullam: son of Bani)
Ezra 10:29.
M. מְשֻׁלָּם *m^ešullām* **masc. proper noun**
(Meshullam: son of Berechiah)
Neh. 3:4,30; 6:18; 10:7(8).
N. מְשֻׁלָּם *m^ešullām* **masc. proper noun**
(Meshullam: son of Besodeiah)
Neh. 3:6.
O. מְשֻׁלָּם *m^ešullām* **masc. proper noun**
(Meshullam: descendant of Iddo)
Neh. 12:16.
P. מְשֻׁלָּם *m^ešullām* **masc. proper noun**
(Meshullam: a Levite)
Neh. 12:25.

4919. A. מְשִׁלֵּמוֹת *m^ešillēmôṯ* **masc. proper noun**
(Meshillemoth: father of Berechiah)
2 Chr. 28:12.
B. מְשִׁלֵּמוֹת *m^ešillēmôṯ* **masc. proper noun**
(Meshillemoth: son of Immer)
Neh. 11:13.

4920. מְשֶׁלֶמְיָה *m^ešelemyāh,* מְשֶׁלֶמְיָהוּ *m^ešelemyāhû* **masc. proper noun**
(Meshelemiah)
1 Chr. 9:21; 26:1,2,9.

4921. מְשִׁלֵּמִית *m^ešillēmiyṯ* **masc. proper noun**
(Meshillemith)
1 Chr. 9:12.

4922. מְשֻׁלֶּמֶת *m^ešullemeṯ* **fem. proper noun**
(Meshullemeth)
2 Kgs. 21:19.

4923. מְשַׁמָּה *m^ešammāh* **fem. noun**
(desolation, waste)
Isa. 15:6; **Jer.** 48:34; **Ezek.** 5:15; 6:14; 33:28,29; 35:3.

4924. I. מִשְׁמָן *mišmān* **masc. noun**
(fat, fatness)
Gen. 27:28(NASB, NIV, *šāmān* [8082,II]), 39(NASB, NIV, *šāmān* [8082,II]); **Ps.** 78:31; **Isa.** 10:16; 17:4; **Dan.** 11:24.
II. מַשְׁמַנִּים *mašmanniym* **masc. pl. noun**
(festive food)
Neh. 8:10.

4925. מִשְׁמַנָּה *mišmannāh* **masc. proper noun**
(Mishmannah)
1 Chr. 12:10.

4926. מִשְׁמָע *mišmāʿ* **masc. noun**
(that which is heard, rumor)
Isa. 11:3.

4927. A. מִשְׁמָע *mišmāʿ* **masc. proper noun**
(Mishma: son of Ishmael)
Gen. 25:14; **1 Chr.** 1:30.
B. מִשְׁמָע *mišmāʿ* **masc. proper noun**
(Mishma: descendant of Simeon)
1 Chr. 4:25,26.

4928. מִשְׁמַעַת *mišmaʿaṯ* **fem. noun**
(obedient group, bodyguard)
1 Sam. 22:14; **2 Sam.** 23:23; **1 Chr.** 11:25; **Isa.** 11:14.

4929. מִשְׁמָר *mišmār* **masc. noun**
(custody, guard, prison)
Gen. 40:3,4,7; 41:10; 42:17,19; **Lev.** 24:12; **Num.** 15:34; **1 Chr.** 26:16; **Neh.** 4:9(3),22(16),23(17); 7:3; 12:24,25; 13:14; **Job** 7:12; **Prov.** 4:23; **Jer.** 51:12; **Ezek.** 38:7.

4930. מַשְׂמֵרָה *maśmērāh* **fem. noun**
(a nail)
Eccl. 12:11(NASB, *masmēr* [4548]).

4931. מִשְׁמֶרֶת *mišmereṯ* **fem. noun**
(requirement, duty, responsibility)
Gen. 26:5; **Ex.** 12:6; 16:23,32–34; **Lev.** 8:35; 18:30; 22:9; **Num.** 1:53; 3:7,8,25, 28,31,32,36,38; 4:27,28,31,32; 8:26; 9:19,23; 17:10(25); 18:3–5,8; 19:9; 31:30,47; **Deut.** 11:1; **Josh.** 22:3; **1 Sam.** 22:23; **2 Sam.** 20:3; **1 Kgs.** 2:3; **2 Kgs.** 11:5–7; **1 Chr.** 9:23,27; 12:29; 23:32; 25:8; 26:12; **2 Chr.** 7:6; 8:14; 13:11; 23:6; 31:16,17; 35:2; **Neh.** 7:3; 12:9,45; 13:30; **Isa.** 21:8; **Ezek.** 40:45,46; 44:8,14–16; 48:11; **Hab.** 2:1; **Zech.** 3:7; **Mal.** 3:14.

4932. מִשְׁנֶה *mišneh* **masc. noun**
(second place, next in rank, double)
Gen. 41:43; 43:12,15; **Ex.** 16:5,22; **Deut.** 15:18; 17:18; **Josh.** 8:32; **1 Sam.** 8:2; 15:9; 17:13; 23:17; **2 Sam.** 3:3; **2 Kgs.** 22:14; 23:4; 25:18; **1 Chr.** 5:12; 15:18; 16:5; **2 Chr.** 28:7; 31:12; 34:22; 35:24; **Ezra** 1:10; **Neh.** 11:9,17; **Esth.** 10:3; **Job** 42:10; **Isa.** 61:7; **Jer.** 16:18; 17:18; 52:24; **Zeph.** 1:10; **Zech.** 9:12.

4933. מְשִׁסָּה *m^e^šissāh* **fem. noun**
(spoil, plunder)
2 Kgs. 21:14; **Isa.** 42:22,24(KJV, [K^e^] *m^e^šûsāh* [4882]); **Jer.** 30:16; **Hab.** 2:7; **Zeph.** 1:13.

4934. מִשְׁעוֹל *mišʿôl* **masc. noun**
(path)
Num. 22:24.

4935. מִשְׁעִי *mišʿiy* **masc. noun**
(wash)
Ezek. 16:4.

4936. מִשְׁעָם *mišʿām* **masc. proper noun**
(Misham)
1 Chr. 8:12.

4937. I. מִשְׁעָן *mišʿān* **masc. noun**
(staff, support, supply)
2 Sam. 22:19; **Ps.** 18:18(19); **Isa.** 3:1.
II. מַשְׁעֵן *mašʿēn* **masc. noun**
(support, supply)
Isa. 3:1.

4938. I. מַשְׁעֵנָה *mašʿēnāh* **fem. noun**
(support, supply)
Isa. 3:1.
II. מִשְׁעֶנֶת *mišʿeneṯ* **fem. noun**
(pole, staff, support)
Ex. 21:19; **Num.** 21:18; **Judg.** 6:21; **2 Kgs.** 4:29,31; 18:21; **Ps.** 23:4; **Isa.** 36:6; **Ezek.** 29:6; **Zech.** 8:4.

4939. מִשְׂפָּח *miśpāḥ* **masc. noun**
(bloodshed, oppression)
Isa. 5:7.

4940. מִשְׁפָּחָה *mišpāḥāh* **fem. noun**
(clan, family, kind)
Gen. 8:19; 10:5,18,20,31,32; 12:3; 24:38,40,41; 28:14; 36:40; **Ex.** 6:14,15, 17,19,24,25; 12:21; **Lev.** 20:5; 25:10,41, 45,47,49; **Num.** 1:2,18,20,22,24,26,28, 30,32,34,36,38,40,42; 2:34; 3:15,18–21, 23,27,29,30,33,35,39; 4:2,18,22,24,28, 29,33,34,36–38,40–42,44–46; 11:10; 26:5–7,12–18,20–32,34–45,47–50,57,58; 27:1,4,11; 33:54; 36:1,6,8,12; **Deut.** 29:18(17); **Josh.** 6:23; 7:14,17; 13:15, 23,24,28,29,31; 15:1,12,20; 16:5,8; 17:2;

18:11,20,21,28; 19:1,8,10,16,17,23,24, 31,32,39,40,48; 21:4–7,10,20,26,27,33, 34,40(38); **Judg.** 1:25; 9:1; 13:2; 17:7; 18:2,11,19; 21:24; **Ruth** 2:1,3; **1 Sam.** 9:21; 10:21; 18:18; 20:6,29; **2 Sam.** 14:7; 16:5; **1 Chr.** 2:53,55; 4:2,8,21,27,38; 5:7; 6:19(4),54(39),60–63(45–48),66(51), 70(55),71(56); 7:5; 16:28; **Neh.** 4:13(7); **Esth.** 9:28; **Job** 31:34; 32:2; **Ps.** 22:27(28); 96:7; 107:41; **Jer.** 1:15; 2:4; 3:14; 8:3; 10:25; 15:3; 25:9; 31:1; 33:24; **Ezek.** 20:32; **Amos** 3:1,2; **Mic.** 2:3; **Nah.** 3:4; **Zech.** 12:12–14; 14:17,18.

4941. מִשְׁפָּט *mišpāṭ* **masc. noun**
(justice, judgment, ordinance)
Gen. 18:19,25; 40:13; **Ex.** 15:25; 21:1,9,31; 23:6; 24:3; 26:30; 28:15,29,30; **Lev.** 5:10; 9:16; 18:4,5,26; 19:15,35,37; 20:22; 24:22; 25:18; 26:15,43,46; **Num.** 9:3,14; 15:16,24; 27:5,11,21; 29:6,18, 21,24,27,30,33,37; 35:12,24,29; 36:13; **Deut.** 1:17; 4:1,5,8,14,45; 5:1,31(28); 6:1,20; 7:11,12; 8:11; 10:18; 11:1,32; 12:1; 16:18,19; 17:8,9,11; 18:3; 19:6; 21:17,22; 24:17; 25:1; 26:16,17; 27:19; 30:16; 32:4,41; 33:10,21; **Josh.** 6:15; 20:6; 24:25; **Judg.** 4:5; 13:12; 18:7; **1 Sam.** 2:13; 8:3,9,11; 10:25; 27:11; 30:25; **2 Sam.** 8:15; 15:2,4,6; 22:23; **1 Kgs.** 2:3; 3:11,28; 4:28(5:8); 6:12,38; 7:7; 8:45,49,58,59; 9:4; 10:9; 11:33; 18:28; 20:40; **2 Kgs.** 1:7; 11:14; 17:26, 27,33,34,37,40; 25:6; **1 Chr.** 6:32(17); 15:13; 16:12,14; 18:14; 22:13; 23:31; 24:19; 28:7; **2 Chr.** 4:7,20; 6:35,39; 7:17; 8:14; 9:8; 19:6,8,10; 30:16; 33:8; 35:13; **Ezra** 3:4; 7:10; **Neh.** 1:7; 8:18; 9:13,29; 10:29(30); **Job** 8:3; 9:19,32; 13:18; 14:3; 19:7; 22:4; 23:4; 27:2; 29:14; 31:13; 32:9; 34:4–6,12,17,23; 35:2; 36:6,17; 37:23; 40:8; **Ps.** 1:5; 7:6(7); 9:4(5),7(8),16(17); 10:5; 17:2; 18:22(23); 19:9(10); 25:9; 33:5; 35:23; 36:6(7); 37:6,28,30; 48:11(12); 72:1,2; 76:9(10); 81:4(5); 89:14(15),30(31); 94:15; 97:2,8; 99:4; 101:1; 103:6; 105:5,7; 106:3; 111:7; 112:5; 119:7,13,20,30,39,43,52,62,75, 84,91,102,106,108,120,121,132,137,149, 156,160,164,175; 122:5; 140:12(13); 143:2; 146:7; 147:19,20; 149:9; **Prov.** 1:3; 2:8,9; 8:20; 12:5; 13:23; 16:8,10, 11,33; 17:23; 18:5; 19:28; 21:3,7,15; 24:23; 28:5; 29:4,26; **Eccl.** 3:16; 5:8(7); 8:5,6; 11:9; 12:14; **Isa.** 1:17,21,27; 3:14; 4:4; 5:7,16; 9:7(6); 10:2; 16:5; 26:8,9; 28:6,17,26; 30:18; 32:1,7,16; 33:5; 34:5; 40:14,27; 41:1; 42:1,3,4; 49:4; 50:8; 51:4; 53:8; 54:17; 56:1; 58:2; 59:8,9,11,14,15; 61:8; **Jer.** 1:16; 4:2,12; 5:1,4,5,28; 7:5; 8:7; 9:24(23); 10:24; 12:1; 17:11; 21:12; 22:3,13,15; 23:5; 26:11,16; 30:11,18; 32:7,8; 33:15; 39:5; 46:28; 48:21,47; 49:12; 51:9; 52:9; **Lam.** 3:35,59; **Ezek.** 5:6–8; 7:23,27; 11:12,20; 16:38; 18:5,8, 9,17,19,21,27; 20:11,13,16,18,19,21, 24,25; 21:27(32); 22:29; 23:24,45; 33:14,16,19; 34:16; 36:27; 37:24; 39:21; 42:11; 44:24; 45:9; **Dan.** 9:5; **Hos.** 2:19(21); 5:1,11; 6:5; 10:4; 12:6(7); **Amos** 5:7,15,24; 6:12; **Mic.** 3:1,8,9; 6:8; 7:9; **Hab.** 1:4,7,12; **Zeph.** 2:3; 3:5,8,15; **Zech.** 7:9; 8:16; **Mal.** 2:17; 3:5; 4:4(3:22).

4942. I. מִשְׁפְּתַיִם *mišpᵉṯayim* **masc. dual noun**
(burden, saddlebag)
Gen. 49:14.
II. מִשְׁפְּתַיִם *mišpᵉṯayim* **masc. dual noun**
(fireplace, sheepfold)
Judg. 5:16.

4943. מֶשֶׁק *mešeq* **masc. noun**
(heir, steward)
Gen. 15:2.

4944. מַשָּׁק *maššāq* **masc. noun**
(rushing, swarming)
Isa. 33:4.

4945. I. מַשְׁקֶה *mašqeh* **masc. noun**
(cupbearer, butler)
Gen. 40:1,2,5,9,13,20,21,23; 41:9; **1 Kgs.** 10:5; **2 Chr.** 9:4; **Neh.** 1:11.

II. מַשְׁקֶה *mašqeh* **masc. noun**
(liquid, drinking vessel, watering place)
Gen. 13:10; **Lev.** 11:34; **1 Kgs.** 10:21; **2 Chr.** 9:20; **Isa.** 32:6; **Ezek.** 45:15.

4946. מִשְׁקוֹל *mišqôl* **masc. noun**
(weight)
Ezek. 4:10.

4947. מַשְׁקוֹף *mašqôp̱* **masc. noun**
(lintel, top of a door)
Ex. 12:7,22,23.

4948. מִשְׁקָל *mišqāl* **masc. noun**
(weight)
Gen. 24:22; 43:21; **Lev.** 19:35; 26:26; **Num.** 7:13,19,25,31,37,43,49,55,61,67,73,79; **Josh.** 7:21; **Judg.** 8:26; **1 Sam.** 17:5; **2 Sam.** 12:30; 21:16; **1 Kgs.** 7:47; 10:14; **2 Kgs.** 25:16; **1 Chr.** 20:2; 21:25; 22:3,14; 28:14–18; **2 Chr.** 3:9; 4:18; 9:13; **Ezra** 8:30,34; **Job** 28:25; **Jer.** 52:20; **Ezek.** 4:16; 5:1.

4949. מִשְׁקֶלֶת *mišqeleṯ*, מִשְׁקֹלֶת *mišqōleṯ* **fem. noun**
(plumb line, leveling instrument)
2 Kgs. 21:13; **Isa.** 28:17.

4950. מִשְׁקָע *mišqā'* **masc. noun**
(clear, deep)
Ezek. 34:18.

4951. מִשְׂרָה *miśrāh* **fem. noun**
(government)
Isa. 9:6(5),7(6).

4952. מִשְׁרָה *mišrāh* **fem. noun**
(juice [of grapes])
Num. 6:3.

4953. מַשְׁרוֹקִי *mašrôqiy* **Aram. fem. noun**
(flute)
Dan. 3:5,7,10,15.

4954. מִשְׁרָעִי *mišrā'iy* **masc. proper noun**
(Mishraite)
1 Chr. 2:53.

4955. מִשְׂרָפָה *miśrāp̱āh* **fem. noun**
(a burning)
Isa. 33:12; **Jer.** 34:5.

4956. מִשְׂרְפוֹת מַיִם *miśr^ep̱ôṯ mayim* **proper noun**
(Misrephoth Maim)
Josh. 11:8; 13:6.

4957. מַשְׂרֵקָה *maśrēqāh* **proper noun**
(Masrekah)
Gen. 36:36; **1 Chr.** 1:47.

4958. מַשְׂרֵת *maśrēṯ* **fem. noun**
(pan, dish)
2 Sam. 13:9.

4959. מָשַׁשׁ *māšaš* **verb**
(to touch, to feel, to grope)
Gen. 27:12,22; 31:34,37; **Ex.** 10:21; **Deut.** 28:29; **Job** 5:14; 12:25.

4960. מִשְׁתֶּה *mišteh* **masc. noun**
(feast, banquet, meal)
Gen. 19:3; 21:8; 26:30; 29:22; 40:20; **Judg.** 14:10,12,17; **1 Sam.** 25:36; **2 Sam.** 3:20; **1 Kgs.** 3:15; **Ezra** 3:7; **Esth.** 1:3,5,9; 2:18; 5:4–6,8,12,14; 6:14; 7:2,7,8; 8:17; 9:17–19,22; **Job** 1:4,5; **Prov.** 15:15; **Eccl.** 7:2; **Isa.** 5:12; 25:6; **Jer.** 16:8; 51:39; **Dan.** 1:5,8,10,16.

4961. מִשְׁתֵּא *mištē'* **Aram. masc. noun**
(feast, banquet; corr. to Hebr. 4960)
Dan. 5:10.

4962. מַת *maṯ* **masc. noun**
(male, man, few in number)
Gen. 34:30; **Deut.** 2:34; 3:6; 4:27; 26:5; 28:62; 33:6; **1 Chr.** 16:19; **Job** 11:3,11;

19:19; 22:15; 24:12(NIV, מוּת [4191]); 31:31; **Ps.** 17:14; 26:4; 105:12; **Isa.** 3:25; 5:13; 41:14; **Jer.** 44:28.

4963. מַתְבֵּן *maṯbēn* **masc. noun**
(straw)
Isa. 25:10.

4964. מֶתֶג *meṯeg* **masc. noun**
(bridle, bit)
2 Sam. 8:1(see *meṯeg hā'mmāh* [4965,II]); **2 Kgs.** 19:28; **Ps.** 32:9; **Prov.** 26:3; **Isa.** 37:29.

4965. I. מֶתֶג הָאַמָּה *meṯeg hā'ammāh* **proper noun**
(Metheg Ammah; Philistine city)
2 Sam. 8:1(NASB, see II).
II. מֶתֶג הָאַמָּה *meṯeg hā'ammāh* **phrase**
(control of the chief city; *meṯeg* [4964] and *'ammāh* [522,II])
2 Sam. 8:1(KJV, NIV, see I).

4966. מָתוֹק *māṯôq* **adj.**
(sweet)
Judg. 14:14,18; **Ps.** 19:10(11); **Prov.** 16:24; 24:13; 27:7; **Eccl.** 5:12(11); 11:7; **Song** 2:3; **Isa.** 5:20; **Ezek.** 3:3.

4967. מְתוּשָׁאֵל *m^eṯûšā'ēl* **masc. proper noun**
(Methusael)
Gen. 4:18.

4968. מְתוּשֶׁלַח *m^eṯûšelaḥ* **masc. proper noun**
(Methuselah)
Gen. 5:21,22,25–27; **1 Chr.** 1:3.

4969. מָתַח *māṯaḥ* **verb**
(to spread out, to stretch out)
Isa. 40:22.

4970. מָתַי *māṯay* **adv.**
(when, how long)
Gen. 30:30; **Ex.** 8:9(5); 10:3,7; **Num.** 14:27; **1 Sam.** 1:14; **1 Kgs.** 18:21; **Neh.** 2:6; **Job** 7:4; **Ps.** 6:3(4); 41:4(5); 42:2(3); 74:10; 80:4(5); 82:2; 90:13; 94:3,8; 101:2; 119:82,84; **Prov.** 1:22; 6:9; 23:35; **Isa.** 6:1; **Jer.** 4:14,21; 12:4; 23:26; 31:22; 47:5; **Dan.** 8:13; 12:6; **Hos.** 8:5; **Amos** 8:5; **Hab.** 2:6; **Zech.** 1:12.

4971. מַתְכֹּנֶת *maṯkōneṯ* **fem. noun**
(measure, proportion, quota, specifications)
Ex. 5:8; 30:32,37; **2 Chr.** 24:13; **Ezek.** 45:11.

4972. מַתְּלָאָה *matt^elā'āh* **fem. noun**
(weariness)
Mal. 1:13(NASB, NIV; *māh* [4100] and *t^elā'āh* [8513]).

4973. מְתַלְּעוֹת *m^eṯall^e'ôṯ* **fem. pl. noun**
(jaw teeth, fangs)
Job 29:17; **Ps.** 58:6(7)(see *maltā'ôṯ* [4459]); **Prov.** 30:14; **Joel** 1:6.

4974. I. מְתֹם *m^eṯōm* **masc. noun**
(wholeness, soundness)
Judg. 20:48(KJV, see II); **Ps.** 38:3(4),7(8); **Isa.** 1:6.
II. מְתֹם *m^eṯōm* **masc. noun**
(men; pl. of *maṯ* [4962])
Judg. 20:48(NASB, NIV, see I).

4975. I. מָתְנַיִם *moṯnayim* **masc. dual noun**
(loins, waist, body, side)
Gen. 37:34; **Ex.** 12:11; 28:42; **Deut.** 13:11; **2 Sam.** 20:8; **1 Kgs.** 2:5; 12:10; 18:46; 20:31,32; **2 Kgs.** 1:8; 4:29; 9:1; **2 Chr.** 10:10; **Neh.** 4:18(12); **Job** 12:18; 40:16; **Ps.** 66:11; 69:23(24); **Prov.** 30:31; 31:17; **Isa.** 11:5; 20:2; 21:3; 45:1; **Jer.** 1:17; 13:1,2,4,11; 48:37; **Ezek.** 1:27; 8:2; 9:2,3,11; 21:6(11); 23:15; 29:7; 44:18; 47:4; **Dan.** 10:5; **Amos** 8:10; **Nah.** 2:1(2),10(11).

II. מָתְנַיִם *moṯnayim* **masc. dual noun**
(strutting rooster)
Prov. 30:31(KJV, see III).
III. מָתְנַיִם *moṯnayim* **masc. dual noun**
(greyhound)
Prov. 30:31(NASB, NIV, see II).

4976. מַתָּן *mattān* **masc. noun**
(gift)
Gen. 34:12; **Num.** 18:11; **Prov.** 18:16; 19:6; 21:14.

4977. A. מַתָּן *mattān* **masc. proper noun**
(Mattan: priest of Baal)
2 Kgs. 11:18; **2 Chr.** 23:17.
B. מַתָּן *mattān* **masc. proper noun**
(Mattan: father of Shephatiah)
Jer. 38:1.

4978. מַתְּנָה *mattᵉnāh* **Aram. fem. noun**
(gift; corr. to Hebr. 4979)
Dan. 2:6,48; 5:17.

4979. מַתָּנָה *mattānāh* **fem. noun**
(gift)
Gen. 25:6; **Ex.** 28:38; **Lev.** 23:38; **Num.** 18:6,7,29; **Deut.** 16:17; **2 Chr.** 21:3; **Esth.** 9:22; **Ps.** 68:18(19); **Prov.** 15:27; **Eccl.** 7:7; **Ezek.** 20:26,31,39; 46:16,17.

4980. מַתָּנָה *mattānāh* **proper noun**
(Mattanah)
Num. 21:18,19.

4981. מִתְנִי *miṯniy* **masc. proper noun**
(Mithnite)
1 Chr. 11:43.

4982. A. מַתְּנַי *mattᵉnay* **masc. proper noun**
(Mattenai: a priest)
Neh. 12:19.
B. מַתְּנַי *mattᵉnay* **masc. proper noun**
(Mattenai: son of Hashum)
Ezra 10:33.
C. מַתְּנַי *mattᵉnay* **masc. proper noun**
(Mattenai: son of Bani)
Ezra 10:37.

4983. A. מַתַּנְיָה *mattanyāh* **masc. proper noun**
(Mattaniah: a descendant of Asaph)
2 Chr. 20:14.
B. מַתַּנְיָהוּ *mattanyāhû* **masc. proper noun**
(Mattaniah: a Levite)
1 Chr. 25:4,16.
C. מַתַּנְיָהוּ *mattanyāhû* **masc. proper noun**
(Mattaniah: a Levite; possibly same as A)
2 Chr. 29:13.
D. מַתַּנְיָה *mattanyāh* **masc. proper noun**
(Mattaniah: king of Judah)
2 Kgs. 24:17.
E. מַתַּנְיָה *mattanyāh* **masc. proper noun**
(Mattaniah: son of Micah)
1 Chr. 9:15; **Neh.** 11:17,22; 12:8,25,35; 13:13.
F. מַתַּנְיָה *mattanyāh* **masc. proper noun**
(Mattaniah: son of Elam)
Ezra 10:26.
G. מַתַּנְיָה *mattanyāh* **masc. proper noun**
(Mattaniah: son of Zattu)
Ezra 10:27.
H. מַתַּנְיָה *mattanyāh* **masc. proper noun**
(Mattaniah: son of Pahath-Moab)
Ezra 10:30.
I. מַתַּנְיָה *mattanyāh* **masc. proper noun**

(Mattaniah: son of Bani)
Ezra 10:37.

4984. מִתְנַשֵּׂא *miṯnaśēʾ* **masc. noun**
(one who exalts himself; NASB, NIV,
nāśāʾ [5375])
1 Kgs. 1:5; 1 Chr. 29:11.

4985. מָתַק *māṯaq* **verb**
(to be sweet, to be pleasant)
Ex. 15:25; Job 20:12; 21:33; 24:20
(KJV, *māṯāq* [4988]); Ps. 55:14(15);
Prov. 9:17.

4986. מֶתֶק *māṯēq* **masc. noun**
(sweetness)
Prov. 16:21; 27:9.

4987. מֹתֶק *mōṯeq* **masc. noun**
(sweetness)
Judg. 9:11.

4988. מָתָק *māṯāq* **masc. noun**
(one who feeds on a sweet morsel)
Job 24:20(NASB, NIV, *māṯaq* [4985]).

4989. מִתְקָה *miṯqāh* **proper noun**
(Mithcah)
Num. 33:28,29.

4990. A. מִתְרְדָת *miṯrᵉḏāṯ* **masc. proper noun**
(Mithredath: treasurer of Cyrus)
Ezra 1:8.

B. מִתְרְדָת *miṯrᵉḏāṯ* **masc. proper noun**
(Mithredath: Persian governor of Samaria)
Ezra 4:7.

4991. מַתַּת *mattaṯ*, מַתָּת *mattāṯ* **fem. noun**
(gift, reward)
1 Kgs. 13:7; Prov. 25:14; Eccl. 3:13;
5:19(18); Ezek. 46:5,11.

4992. מַתַּתָּה *mattattāh* **masc. proper noun**
(Mattattah)
Ezra 10:33.

4993. A. מַתִּתְיָה *mattityāh,* מַתִּתְיָהוּ *mattityāhû* **masc. proper noun**
(Mattithiah: a Levite)
1 Chr. 9:31; 15:18,21; 16:5.
B. מַתִּתְיָהוּ *mattityāhû* **masc. proper noun**
(Mattithiah: son of Jeduthun)
1 Chr. 25:3,21.
C. מַתִּתְיָה *mattityāh* **masc. proper noun**
(Mattithiah: son of Nebo)
Ezra 10:43.
D. מַתִּתְיָה *mattityāh* **masc. proper noun**
(Mattithiah: postexilic Jew)
Neh. 8:4.

נ Nun

4994. נָא *nā'* **particle**
(I beseech you, now)
Gen. 12:11,13; 13:8,9,14; 15:5; 16:2; 18:3,4,21,27,30–32; 19:2,7,8,18,19,20; 22:2; 24:2,12,14,17,23,42,43,45; 25:30; 26:28; 27:2,3,9,19,21,26; 30:14,27; 31:12; 32:11(12),29(30); 33:10,11,14,15; 34:8; 37:6,14,16,32; 38:16,25; 40:8,14; 44:18,33; 45:4; 47:4,29; 48:9; 50:4,5,17; **Ex.** 3:3,18; 4:6,13,18; 5:3; 10:11,17; 11:2; 32:32; 33:13,18; 34:9; **Num.** 10:31; 11:15; 12:6,11,12,13; 14:17,19; 16:8,26; 20:10,17; 22:6(5),16(15),17(16),19(18); 23:13,27; **Deut.** 3:25; 4:32; **Josh.** 2:12; 7:19; 22:26; **Judg.** 1:24; 4:19; 6:17, 18,39; 7:3; 8:5; 9:2,38; 10:15; 11:17,19; 12:6; 13:3,4,8,15; 14:12; 15:2; 16:6, 10,28; 18:5; 19:6,8,9,11,23,24; **Ruth** 2:2,7; **1 Sam.** 2:36; 3:17; 9:3,6,18; 10:15; 14:17,29; 15:25,30; 16:15–17,22; 17:17; 19:2(1); 20:29,36; 22:3,7,12; 23:11,22; 25:8,24,25,28; 26:8,11,19; 27:5; 28:8,22; 30:7; **2 Sam.** 1:4,9; 2:14; 7:2; 13:5–7,13, 17,24–26,28; 14:2,11,12,15,17,18,21; 15:7,31; 16:9; 17:1,5; 18:19,22; 19:37(38); 20:16; 24:2,10,14,17; **1 Kgs.** 1:12; 2:17; 8:26; 13:6; 14:2; 17:10,11,21; 18:43; 19:20; 20:7,31,32,35,37; 22:5,13; **2 Kgs.** 1:13; 2:2,4,6,9,16,19; 4:9,10,13,22,26; 5:7,8,15,17,18,22; 6:1–3,17,18; 7:12,13; 8:4; 9:12,34; 18:19,21,26; 19:19; 20:3; **1 Chr.** 21:8,13,17; 22:5; 29:20; **2 Chr.** 6:40; 18:4,12; **Ezra** 10:14; **Neh.** 1:6, 8,11; 5:10,11; **Job** 1:11; 2:5; 4:7; 5:1; 6:29; 8:8; 10:9; 12:7; 13:6,18; 17:3,10; 22:21,22; 32:21; 33:1,2; 38:3; 40:7,10, 15,16; 42:4; **Ps.** 7:9(10); 50:22; 80:14(15); 115:2; 116:14,18; 118:2–4,25; 119:76,108; 122:8; 124:1; 129:1; **Eccl.** 2:1; **Song** 3:2; 7:8(9); **Isa.** 1:18; 5:1,3,5; 7:3,13; 19:12; 29:11,12; 36:4,8,11; 38:3; 47:12,13; 51:21; 64:9(8); **Jer.** 4:31; 5:1,21,24; 7:12; 17:15; 18:11,13; 21:2; 25:5; 27:18; 28:7,15; 30:6; 32:8; 35:15; 36:15,17; 37:3,20; 38:4,12,20,25; 40:15; 42:2; 44:4; 45:3; **Lam.** 1:18; 5:16; **Ezek.** 8:5,8; 17:12; 18:25; 33:30; **Dan.** 1:12; 9:16; **Amos** 7:2,5; **Jon.** 1:8,14; 4:3; **Mic.** 3:1,9; **Hag.** 2:2,11,15,18; **Zech.** 1:4; 3:8; 5:5; **Mal.** 1:8,9; 3:10.

4995. נָא *nā'* **adj.**
(raw)
Ex. 12:9.

4996. נֹא *nō'* **proper noun**
(No, another name for Thebes in Egypt)
Jer. 46:25; **Ezek.** 30:14–16; **Nah.** 3:8.

4997. נֹאד *nō'd*, נֹאוד *n^e^ôd* **masc. noun**
(bottle, wineskin)
Josh. 9:4,13; **Judg.** 4:19; **1 Sam.** 16:20; **Ps.** 33:7(KJV, NASB, *nēd* [5067]); 56:8(9); 119:83.

4998. נָאָה *nā'āh* **verb**
(to be beautiful, to be fitting)
Ps. 93:5; **Song** 1:10; **Isa.** 52:7.

4999. נָאָה *nā'āh* **fem. noun**
(pastureland, meadow; NIV, *nāwāh* [5116,II])
Ps. 23:2(NASB, *nāwāh* [5116,II]); 65:12(13); 74:20; 83:12(13); **Jer.** 9:10(9); 23:10; 25:37(NASB, *nāwāh* [5116,II]); **Lam.** 2:2; **Joel** 1:19,20; 2:22; **Amos** 1:2.

5000. נָאוֶה *nā'weh* **adj.**
(beautiful, fitting)
Ps. 33:1; 147:1; **Prov.** 17:7; 19:10; 26:1; **Song** 1:5; 2:14; 4:3; 6:4; **Jer.** 6:2.

5001. נָאַם *nā'am* **verb**
(to declare, to say)
Jer. 23:31.

5002. נְאֻם n^e'*um* **masc. noun**
(oracle, utterance, esp. of a prophet citing God)
Gen. 22:16; **Num.** 14:28; 24:3,4,15,16; **1 Sam.** 2:30; **2 Sam.** 23:1; **2 Kgs.** 9:26; 19:33; 22:19; **2 Chr.** 34:27; **Ps.** 36:1(2); 110:1; **Prov.** 30:1; **Isa.** 1:24; 3:15; 14:22,23; 17:3,6; 19:4; 22:25; 30:1; 31:9; 37:34; 41:14; 43:10,12; 49:18; 52:5; 54:17; 55:8; 56:8; 59:20; 66:2,17,22; **Jer.** 1:8,15,19; 2:3,9,12,19,22,29; 3:1,10, 12–14,16,20; 4:1,9,17; 5:9,11,15,18,22,29; 6:12; 7:11,13,19,30,32; 8:1,3,13,17; 9:3(2),6(5),9(8),22(21),24(23),25(24); 12:17; 13:11,14,25; 15:3,6,9,20; 16:5,11, 14,16; 17:24; 18:6; 19:6,12; 21:7,10, 13,14; 22:5,16,24; 23:1,2,4,5,7,11,12,23, 24,28–33; 25:7,9,12,29,31; 27:8,11,15,22; 28:4; 29:9,11,14,19,23,32; 30:3,8,10,11, 17,21; 31:1,14,16,17,20,27,28,31–34, 36–38; 32:5,30,44; 33:14; 34:5,17,22; 35:13; 39:17,18; 42:11; 44:29; 45:5; 46:5,18,23,26,28; 48:12,15,25,30,35,38, 43,44,47; 49:2,5,6,13,16,26,30–32, 37–39; 50:4,10,20,21,30,31,35,40; 51:24–26,39,48,52,53,57; **Ezek.** 5:11; 11:8,21; 12:25,28; 13:6–8,16; 14:11,14, 16,18,20,23; 15:8; 16:8,14,19,23,30, 43,48,58,63; 17:16; 18:3,9,23,30,32; 20:3,31,33,36,40,44; 21:7(12),13(18); 22:12,31; 23:34; 24:14; 25:14; 26:5, 14,21; 28:10; 29:20; 30:6; 31:18; 32:8,14, 16,31,32; 33:11; 34:8,15,30,31; 35:6,11; 36:14,15,23,32; 37:14; 38:18,21; 39:5,8, 10,13,20,29; 43:19,27; 44:12,15,27; 45:9,15; 47:23; 48:29; **Hos.** 2:13(15), 16(18),21(23); 11:11; **Joel** 2:12; **Amos** 2:11,16; 3:10,13,15; 4:3,5,6,8–11; 6:8,14; 8:3,9,11; 9:7,8,12,13; **Obad.** 1:4,8; **Mic.** 4:6; 5:10(9); **Nah.** 2:13(14); 3:5; **Zeph.** 1:2,3,10; 2:9; 3:8; **Hag.** 1:9,13; 2:4,8, 9,14,17,23; **Zech.** 1:3,4,16; 2:5(9),6(10), 10(14); 3:9,10; 5:4; 8:6,11,17; 10:12; 11:6; 12:1,4; 13:2,7,8; **Mal.** 1:2.

5003. נָאַף *nā'ap̱* **verb**
(to commit adultery)
Ex. 20:14; **Lev.** 20:10; **Deut.** 5:18(17); **Job** 24:15; **Ps.** 50:18; **Prov.** 6:32; 30:20; **Isa.** 57:3; **Jer.** 3:8,9; 5:7; 7:9; 9:2(1); 23:10,14; 29:23; **Ezek.** 16:32,38; 23:37,45; **Hos.** 3:1; 4:2,13,14; 7:4; **Mal.** 3:5.

5004. נִאֻף *ni'up̱* **masc. noun**
(adultery)
Jer. 13:27; **Ezek.** 23:43.

5005. נַאֲפוּף *na'^{a}p̱ûp̱* **masc. noun**
(adultery)
Hos. 2:2(4).

5006. I. נָאַץ *nā'aṣ* **verb**
(to condemn, to spurn)
Num. 14:11,23; 16:30; **Deut.** 31:20; 32:19; **1 Sam.** 2:17; **2 Sam.** 12:14; **Ps.** 10:3,13; 74:10,18; 107:11; **Prov.** 1:30; 5:12; 15:5; **Isa.** 1:4; 5:24; 52:5; 60:14; **Jer.** 14:21; 23:17; 33:24; **Lam.** 2:6.
II. נָאַץ *nā'aṣ* **verb**
(to flourish)
Eccl. 12:5(NASB, NIV, *nāṣaṣ* [5340]).

5007. I. נְאָצָה n^e'*āṣāh* **fem. noun**
(shame, disgrace)
2 Kgs. 19:3; **Isa.** 37:3.
II. נֶאָצָה *ne'āṣāh* **fem. noun**
(blasphemy, aspersion)
Neh. 9:18,26; **Ezek.** 35:12.

5008. נָאַק *nā'aq* **verb**
(to groan)
Job 24:12; **Ezek.** 30:24.

5009. נְאָקָה n^e'*āqāh* **fem. noun**
(a groan, groaning)
Ex. 2:24; 6:5; **Judg.** 2:18; **Ezek.** 30:24.

5010. נָאַר *nā'ar* **verb**
(to renounce, to spurn, to abandon)
Ps. 89:39(40); **Lam.** 2:7.

5011. נֹב *nōḇ* **proper noun**
(Nob)

1 Sam. 21:1(2); 22:9,11,19; **Neh.** 11:32; **Isa.** 10:32.

5012. נָבָא *nāb̲ā'* **verb**
(to prophecy)
Num. 11:25–27; **1 Sam.** 10:5,6,10,11,13; 18:10; 19:20,21,23,24; **1 Kgs.** 18:29; 22:8,10,12,18; **1 Chr.** 25:1–3; **2 Chr.** 18:7,9,11,17; 20:37; **Jer.** 2:8; 5:31; 11:21; 14:14–16; 19:14; 20:1,6; 23:13,16,21,25,26,32; 25:13,30; 26:9,11,12,18,20; 27:10,14–16; 28:6,8,9; 29:9,21,26,27,31; 32:3; 37:19; **Ezek.** 4:7; 6:2; 11:4,13; 12:27; 13:2,16,17; 20:46(21:2); 21:2(7),9(14),14(19),28(33); 25:2; 28:21; 29:2; 30:2; 34:2; 35:2; 36:1, 3,6; 37:4,7,9,10,12; 38:2,14,17; 39:1; **Joel** 2:28(3:1); **Amos** 2:12; 3:8; 7:12, 13,15,16; **Zech.** 13:3,4.

5013. נְבָא *n^e^b̲ā'* **Aram. verb**
(to prophecy; corr. to Hebr. 5012)
Ezra 5:1.

5014. I. נָבַב *nāb̲ab̲* **verb**
(to hollow out; NIV, see II)
Ex. 27:8; 38:7; **Job** 11:12; **Jer.** 52:21.
II. נָבוּב *nāb̲ûb̲* **masc. noun**
(hollow; KJV, NASB, see I)
Ex. 27:8; 38:7; **Job** 11:12; **Jer.** 52:21.

5015. A. נְבוֹ *n^e^b̲ô* **proper noun**
(Nebo: mountain in Moab)
Num. 33:47; **Deut.** 32:49; 34:1.
B. נְבוֹ *n^e^b̲ô* **proper noun**
(Nebo: town in Moab)
Num. 32:3,38; **1 Chr.** 5:8; **Isa.** 15:2; **Jer.** 48:1,22.
C. נְבוֹ *n^e^b̲ô* **proper noun**
(Nebo: city N.W. of Jerusalem)
Ezra 2:29; **Neh.** 7:33.
D. נְבוֹ *n^e^b̲ô* **masc. proper noun**
(Nebo: Jewish ancestor)
Ezra 10:43.
E. נְבוֹ *n^e^b̲ô* **masc. proper noun**
(Nebo: false Babylonian god)
Isa. 46:1.
F. נְבוּ שַׂר־סְכִים *n^e^b̲û śar-s^e^kiym* **masc. proper noun**
(Nebo-Sarsekim)
Jer. 39:3(KJV, NASB, *samgar-n^e^bû* [5562] and *śars^e^k̲iym* [8310]).

5016. נְבוּאָה *n^e^b̲û'āh* **fem. noun**
(prophecy)
2 Chr. 9:29; 15:8; **Neh.** 6:12.

5017. נְבוּאָה *n^e^b̲û'āh* **Aram. fem. noun**
(prophecying, preaching; corr. to Hebr. 5016)
Ezra 6:14.

5018. נְבוּזַרְאֲדָן *n^e^b̲ûzar'^a^d̲ān* **masc. proper noun**
(Nebuzaradan)
2 Kgs. 25:8,11,20; **Jer.** 39:9–11,13; 40:1; 41:10; 43:6; 52:12,15,16,26,30.

5019. נְבוּכַדְנֶאצַּר *n^e^b̲ûkad̲ne'ṣṣar,* נְבוּכַדְרֶאצַּר *n^e^b̲ûk̲ad̲re'ṣṣar* **masc. proper noun**
(Nebuchadnezzar, Nebuchadrezzar)
2 Kgs. 24:1,10,11; 25:1,8,22; **1 Chr.** 6:15(5:41); **2 Chr.** 36:6,7,10,13; **Ezra** 1:7; 2:1; **Neh.** 7:6; **Esth.** 2:6; **Jer.** 21:2,7; 22:25; 24:1; 25:1,9; 27:6,8,20; 28:3,11,14; 29:1,3,21; 32:1,28; 34:1; 35:11; 37:1; 39:1, 5,11; 43:10; 44:30; 46:2,13,26; 49:28,30; 50:17; 51:34; 52:4,12,28–30; **Dan.** 1:1, 18; 2:1; **Ezek.** 26:7; 29:18,19; 30:10.

5020. נְבוּכַדְנֶצַּר *n^e^b̲ûk̲ad̲neṣṣar* **Aram. masc. proper noun**
(Nebuchadnezzar; corr. to Hebr. 5119)
Ezra 5:12,14; 6:5; **Dan.** 2:28,46; 3:1–3, 5,7,9,13,14,16,19,24,26,28; 4:1(3:31), 4(1),18(15),28(25),31(28),33(30),34(31), 37(34); 5:2,11,18.

5021. נְבוּשַׁזְבָּן *n^e^b̲ûšazbān* **masc. proper noun**
(Nebushazban)
Jer. 39:13.

5022. נָבוֹת *nāḇôṯ* **masc. proper noun**
(Naboth)
1 Kgs. 21:1–4,6–9,12–16,18,19; **2 Kgs.** 9:21,25,26.

5023. נְבִזְבָּה *n*e*ḇizbāh* **Aram. fem. noun**
(reward)
Dan. 2:6; 5:17.

5024. נָבַח *nāḇaḥ* **verb**
(to bark)
Isa. 56:10.

5025. A. נֹבַח *nōḇaḥ* **masc. proper noun**
(Nobah: a Manassite)
Num. 32:42.
B. נֹבַח *nōḇah* **proper noun**
(Nobah: loc. in Gilead)
Num. 32:42; **Judg.** 8:11.

5026. נִבְחַז *niḇḥaz* **masc. proper noun**
(Nibhaz: a false god)
2 Kgs. 17:31.

5027. נָבַט *naḇaṭ* **verb**
(to look, to watch, to regard)
Gen. 15:5; 19:17,26; **Ex.** 3:6; 33:8; **Num.** 12:8; 21:9; 23:21; **1 Sam.** 2:32; 16:7; 17:42; 24:8(9); **1 Kgs.** 18:43; 19:6; **2 Kgs.** 3:14; **1 Chr.** 21:21; **Job** 6:19; 28:24; 35:5; 36:25; 39:29; **Ps.** 10:14; 13:3(4); 22:17(18); 33:13; 34:5(6); 74:20; 80:14(15); 84:9(10); 91:8; 92:11(12); 94:9; 102:19(20); 104:32; 119:6,15,18; 142:4(5); **Prov.** 4:25; **Isa.** 5:12,30; 8:22; 18:4; 22:8,11; 38:11; 42:18; 51:1,2,6; 63:5,15; 64:9(8); 66:2; **Lam.** 1:11,12; 2:20; 3:63; 4:16; 5:1; **Amos** 5:22; **Jon.** 2:4(5); **Hab.** 1:3,5,13; 2:15; **Zech.** 12:10.

5028. נְבָט *n*e*ḇāṭ* **masc. proper noun**
(Nebat)
1 Kgs. 11:26; 12:2,15; 15:1; 16:3,26,31; 21:22; 22:52(53); **2 Kgs.** 3:3; 9:9; 10:29; 13:2,11; 14:24; 15:9,18,24,28; 17:21; 23:15; **2 Chr.** 9:29; 10:2,15; 13:6.

5029. נְבִיא *n*e*ḇiy'* **Aram. masc. noun**
(prophet; corr. to Hebr. 5030)
Ezra 5:1,2; 6:14.

5030. נָבִיא *nāḇiy'* **masc. noun**
(prophet)
Gen. 20:7; **Ex.** 7:1; **Num.** 11:29; 12:6; **Deut.** 13:1(2),3(4),5(6); 18:15,18,20,22; 34:10; **Judg.** 6:8; **1 Sam.** 3:20; 9:9; 10:5,10–12; 19:20,24; 22:5; 28:6,15; **2 Sam.** 7:2; 12:25; 24:11; **1 Kgs.** 1:8,10, 22,23,32,34,38,44,45; 11:29; 13:11,18, 20,23,25,26,29; 14:2,18; 16:7,12; 18:4, 13,19,20,22,25,36,40; 19:1,10,14,16; 20:13,22,35,38,41; 22:6,7,10,12,13, 22,23; **2 Kgs.** 2:3,5,7,15; 3:11,13; 4:1,38; 5:3,8,13,22; 6:1,12; 9:1,4,7; 10:19; 14:25; 17:13,23; 19:2; 20:1,11,14; 21:10; 23:2,18; 24:2; **1 Chr.** 16:22; 17:1; 29:29; **2 Chr.** 9:29; 12:5,15; 13:22; 15:8; 18:5,6,9,11, 12,21,22; 20:20; 21:12; 24:19; 25:15,16; 26:22; 28:9; 29:25; 32:20,32; 35:18; 36:12,16; **Ezra** 9:11; **Neh.** 6:7,14; 9:26,30,32; **Ps.** 51:[title](1); 74:9; 105:15; **Isa.** 3:2; 9:15(14); 28:7; 29:10; 37:2; 38:1; 39:3; **Jer.** 1:5; 2:8,26,30; 4:9; 5:13,31; 6:13; 7:25; 8:1,10; 13:13; 14:13–15,18; 18:18; 20:2; 23:9,11,13–16, 21,25,26,28,30,31,33,34,37; 25:2,4; 26:5, 7,8,11,16; 27:9,14–16,18; 28:1,5,6,8–12, 15,17; 29:1,8,15,19,29; 32:2,32; 34:6; 35:15; 36:8,26; 37:2,3,6,13,19; 38:9,10,14; 42:2,4; 43:6; 44:4; 45:1; 46:1,13; 47:1; 49:34; 50:1; 51:59; **Lam.** 2:9,14,20; 4:13; **Ezek.** 2:5; 7:26; 13:2–4,9,16; 14:4,7,9,10; 22:25,28; 33:33; 38:17; **Dan.** 9:2,6,10,24; **Hos.** 4:5; 6:5; 9:7,8; 12:10(11),13(14); **Amos** 2:11,12; 3:7; 7:14; **Mic.** 3:5,6,11;

Hab. 1:1; 3:1; **Zeph.** 3:4; **Hag.** 1:1,3,12; 2:1,10; **Zech.** 1:1,4–7; 7:3,7,12; 8:9; 13:2,4,5; **Mal.** 4:5(3:23).

5031. נְבִיאָה *n^eḇiy'āh* **fem. noun**
(prophetess)
Ex. 15:20; **Judg.** 4:4; **2 Kgs.** 22:14; **2 Chr.** 34:22; **Neh.** 6:14; **Isa.** 8:3.

5032. A. נְבָיוֹת *n^eḇāyôṯ*, נְבָיֹת *n^eḇāyōṯ* **masc. proper noun**
(Nebaioth: son of Ishmael)
Gen. 25:13; 28:9; 36:3; **1 Chr.** 1:29.
B. נְבָיוֹת *n^eḇāyôṯ* **masc. pl. proper noun**
(descendants of Nebaioth)
Isa. 60:7.

5033. נֵבֶךְ *nēḇeḵ* **masc. noun**
(a spring [of water])
Job 38:16.

5034. I. נָבֵל *nāḇēl* **verb**
(to wither, to languish, to fade)
Ex. 18:18; **2 Sam.** 22:46; **Job** 14:18; **Ps.** 1:3; 18:45(46); 37:2; **Isa.** 1:30; 24:4; 28:1,4; 34:4; 40:7,8; 64:6(5); **Jer.** 8:13; **Ezek.** 47:12.
II. נָבֵל *nāḇēl* **verb**
(to be foolish, to act disdainfully)
Deut. 32:15; **Prov.** 30:32; **Jer.** 14:21; **Mic.** 7:6; **Nah.** 3:6.

5035. I. נֵבֶל *nēḇel*, נֶבֶל *neḇel* **masc. noun**
(storage jar, skin bottle)
1 Sam. 1:24; 10:3; 25:18; **2 Sam.** 16:1; **Job** 38:37; **Isa.** 22:24; 30:14; **Jer.** 13:12; 48:12; **Lam.** 4:2.
II. נֵבֶל *nēḇel*, נֶבֶל *neḇel* **masc. noun**
(harp, lyre, stringed instrument)
1 Sam. 10:5; **2 Sam.** 6:5; **1 Kgs.** 10:12; **1 Chr.** 13:8; 15:16,20,28; 16:5; 25:1,6; **2 Chr.** 5:12; 9:11; 20:28; 29:25; **Neh.** 12:27; **Ps.** 33:2; 57:8(9); 71:22; 81:2(3); 92:3(4); 108:2(3); 144:9; 150:3; **Isa.** 5:12; 14:11; **Amos** 5:23; 6:5.

5036. נָבָל *nāḇāl* **adj.; subst.**
(foolish, fool)
Deut. 32:6,21; **2 Sam.** 3:33; 13:13; **Job** 2:10; 30:8; **Ps.** 14:1; 39:8(9); 53:1(2); 74:18,22; **Prov.** 17:7,21; 30:22; **Isa.** 32:5,6; **Jer.** 17:11; **Ezek.** 13:3.

5037. נָבָל *nāḇāl* **masc. proper noun**
(Nabal)
1 Sam. 25:3–5,9,10,14,19,25,26,34,36–39; 27:3; 30:5; **2 Sam.** 2:2; 3:3.

5038. נְבֵלָה *n^eḇēlāh* **fem. noun**
(carcass, corpse, dead body)
Lev. 5:2; 7:24; 11:8,11,24,25,27,28, 35–40; 17:15; 22:8; **Deut.** 14:8,21; 21:23; 28:26; **Josh.** 8:29; **1 Kgs.** 13:22,24,25,28–30; **2 Kgs.** 9:37; **Ps.** 79:2; **Isa.** 5:25; 26:19; **Jer.** 7:33; 9:22(21); 16:4,18; 19:7; 26:23; 34:20; 36:30; **Ezek.** 4:14; 44:31.

5039. נְבָלָה *n^eḇālāh* **fem. noun**
(folly, disgraceful act)
Gen. 34:7; **Deut.** 22:21; **Josh.** 7:15; **Judg.** 19:23,24; 20:6,10; **1 Sam.** 25:25; **2 Sam.** 13:12; **Job** 42:8; **Isa.** 9:17(16); 32:6; **Jer.** 29:23.

5040. נַבְלוּת *naḇlûṯ* **fem. noun**
(lewdness)
Hos. 2:10(12).

5041. נְבַלָּט *n^eḇallaṭ* **proper noun**
(Neballat)
Neh. 11:34.

5042. נָבַע *nāḇa'* **verb**
(to spew out, to pour out, to utter)
Ps. 19:2(3); 59:7(8); 78:2; 94:4; 119:171; 145:7; **Prov.** 1:23; 15:2,28; 18:4; **Eccl.** 10:1.

5043. נֶבְרְשָׁה *nebreshāh* **Aram. fem. noun**
(lampstand)
Dan. 5:5.

5044. נִבְשָׁן *nibshān* **proper noun**
(Nibshan)
Josh. 15:62.

5045. I. נֶגֶב *negeb* **masc. noun**
(the south, south)
Gen. 12:9(NASB, see II); 13:1(NASB, see II),3(NASB, NIV, see II),14; 20:1(NASB, NIV, see II); 24:62(NASB, NIV, see II); 28:14; **Ex.** 26:18; 27:9; 36:23; 38:9; 40:24; **Num.** 13:17(NASB, NIV, see II),22(NASB, NIV, see II),29(NASB, NIV, see II); 21:1 (NASB, NIV, see II); 33:40(NASB, NIV, see II); 34:3,4; 35:5; **Deut.** 1:7(NASB, NIV, see II); 34:3(NASB, see II); **Josh.** 10:40 (NASB, NIV, see II); 11:2,16(NASB, NIV, see II); 12:8(NASB, NIV, see II); 15:1–4, 7,8,19(NASB, NIV, see II),21(NIV, see II); 17:9,10; 18:5,13–16,19; 19:8(NASB, NIV, see II),34; **Judg.** 1:9(NASB, NIV, see II), 15(NASB, NIV, see II),16(NIV, see II); 21:19; **1 Sam.** 14:5; 20:41; 27:10(NASB, NIV, see II); 30:1(NASB, NIV, see II),14 (NASB, NIV, see II),27(NASB, see II); **2 Sam.** 24:7(NIV, see II); **1 Kgs.** 7:25,39; **1 Chr.** 9:24; 26:15,17; **2 Chr.** 4:4,10; 28:18(NASB, NIV, see II); **Ps.** 126:4(NIV, see II); **Isa.** 21:1(NASB, see II); 30:6(NASB, NIV, see II); **Jer.** 13:19(NASB, NIV, see II); 17:26(NASB, NIV, see II); 32:44(NASB, NIV, see II); 33:13(NASB, NIV, see II); **Ezek.** 20:46(21:2),47(21:3)(NASB, see II); 21:4(9); 40:2; 46:9; 47:1,19; 48:10,16,17, 28,33; **Dan.** 8:4,9; 11:5,6,9,11,14,15,25, 29,40; **Obad.** 1:19(NASB, see II),20(NASB, NIV, see II); **Zech.** 7:7; 14:4,10.
II. נֶגֶב *negeb* **proper noun**
(Negev, the southern district of Judah; KJV, see I)
Gen. 12:9(NIV, see I); 13:1(NIV, see I); 20:1; 24:62; **Num.** 13:17,22,29; 21:1; 33:40; 34:3; **Deut.** 1:7; 34:3(NIV, see I); **Josh.** 10:40; 11:16; 12:8; 15:1–19,21 (NASB, see I); 19:8; **Judg.** 1:9,15,16 (NASB, see I); **1 Sam.** 27:10; 30:1,14, 27(NIV, see I); **2 Sam.** 24:7(NASB, see I); **2 Chr.** 28:18; **Ps.** 126:4(NASB, see I); **Isa.** 21:1(NIV, see I); 30:6; **Jer.** 13:19; 17:26; 32:44; 33:13; **Ezek.** 20:47(21:3) (NIV, see I); **Obad.** 1:19(NIV, see I),20; **Zech.** 7:7; 14:4,10.

5046. נָגַד *nāgad* **verb**
(to tell, to declare)
Gen. 3:11; 9:22; 12:18; 14:13; 21:26; 22:20; 24:23,28,49; 26:32; 27:42; 29:12, 15; 31:20,22,27; 32:5(6),29(30); 37:5,16; 38:13,24; 41:24,25; 42:29; 43:6,7; 44:24; 45:13,26; 46:31; 47:1; 48:2; 49:1; **Ex.** 4:28; 13:8; 14:5; 16:22; 19:3,9; **Lev.** 5:1; 14:35; **Num.** 11:27; 23:3; **Deut.** 4:13; 5:5; 17:4,9–11; 26:3; 30:18; 32:7; **Josh.** 2:14,20; 7:19; 9:24; 10:17; **Judg.** 4:12; 9:7,25,42,47; 13:6,10; 14:2,6,9,12–17,19; 16:6,10,13,15,17,18; **Ruth** 2:11,19; 3:4, 16; 4:4; **1 Sam.** 3:13,15,18; 4:13,14; 8:9; 9:6,8,18,19; 10:15,16; 11:9; 14:1,33,43; 15:12,16; 17:31; 18:20,24,26; 19:2,3,7, 11,18,19,21; 20:9,10; 22:21,22; 23:1,7, 11,13,25; 24:1(2),18(19); 25:8,12,14,19, 36,37; 27:4,11; **2 Sam.** 1:4–6,13,20; 2:4; 3:23; 4:10; 6:12; 7:11; 10:5,17; 11:5,10, 18,22; 12:18; 13:4; 14:33; 15:13,28, 31,35; 17:16–18,21; 18:10,11,21,25; 19:1(2),6(7),8(9); 21:11; 24:13; **1 Kgs.** 1:20,23,51; 2:29,39,41; 10:3,7; 14:3; 18:12,13,16; 19:1; 20:17; **2 Kgs.** 4:2,7, 27,31; 5:4; 6:11–13; 7:9–12,15; 8:7; 9:12,15,18,20,36; 10:8; 18:37; 22:10; **1 Chr.** 17:10; 19:5,17; **2 Chr.** 9:2,6; 20:2; 34:18; **Ezra** 2:59; **Neh.** 2:12,16,18; 7:61; **Esth.** 2:10,20,22; 3:4,6; 4:4,7–9,12; 6:2; 8:1; **Job** 1:15–17,19; 11:6; 12:7; 15:18; 17:5; 21:31; 26:4; 31:37; 33:23; 36:9,33; 38:4,18; 42:3; **Ps.** 9:11(12); 19:1(2); 22:31(32); 30:9(10); 38:18(19); 40:5(6); 50:6; 51:15(17); 52:[title](1); 64:9(10); 71:17,18; 75:9(10); 92:2(3), 15(16); 97:6; 111:6; 142:2(3); 145:4;

147:19; **Prov.** 12:17; 29:24; **Eccl.** 6:12; 8:7; 10:14,20; **Song** 1:7; 5:8; **Isa.** 3:9; 7:2; 19:12; 21:2,6,10; 36:22; 40:21; 41:22,23,26; 42:9,12; 43:9,12; 44:7,8; 45:19,21; 46:10; 48:3,5,6,14,20; 57:12; 58:1; 66:19; **Jer.** 4:5,15; 5:20; 9:12(11); 16:10; 20:10; 31:10; 33:3; 36:13,16,17, 20; 38:15,25,27; 42:3,4,20,21; 46:14; 48:20; 50:2,28; 51:31; **Ezek.** 23:36; 24:19; 37:18; 40:4; 43:10; **Dan.** 2:2; 9:23; 10:21; 11:2; **Hos.** 4:12; **Amos** 4:13; **Jon.** 1:8,10; **Mic.** 1:10; 3:8; 6:8; **Zech.** 9:12.

5047. נְגַד *n*^{e}*gaḏ* **Aram. verb**
(to flow, to issue forth)
Dan. 7:10.

5048. נֶגֶד *negeḏ* **prep.**
(before, in front of, opposite)
Gen. 2:18,20; 21:16; 31:32,37; 33:12; 47:15; **Ex.** 10:10; 19:2; 34:10; **Num.** 2:2; 22:32; 25:4; **Deut.** 28:66; 31:11; 32:52; **Josh.** 3:16; 5:13; 6:5,20; 8:11,33,35; **Judg.** 9:17; 20:34; **Ruth** 4:4; **1 Sam.** 12:3; 15:30; 16:6; 26:20; **2 Sam.** 12:12; 18:13; 22:13,23,25; **1 Kgs.** 8:22; 20:27; 21:10,13; **2 Kgs.** 1:13; 2:7,15; 3:22; **1 Chr.** 5:11; 8:32; 9:38; **2 Chr.** 6:12,13; 7:6; 8:14; **Neh.** 3:10,16,19,23,25–31; 4:5(3:37); 7:3; 8:3; 11:22; 12:9,24,37; 13:21; **Job** 4:16; 10:17; 26:6; **Ps.** 5:5(6); 10:5; 16:8; 18:12(13),22(23),24(25); 22:25(26); 23:5; 26:3; 31:19(20),22(23); 36:1(2), 38:9(10),11(10),17(18); 39:1(2), 5(6); 44:15(16); 50:8; 51:3(4); 52:9(11); 54:3(4); 69:19(20); 78:12; 86:14; 88:1(2); 89:36(37); 90:8; 101:3,7; 109:15; 116:14, 18; 119:46,168; 138:1; **Prov.** 4:25; 14:7; 15:11; 21:30; **Eccl.** 4:12; 6:8; **Song** 6:5; **Isa.** 5:21; 24:23; 40:17; 47:14; 49:16; 59:12; 61:11; **Jer.** 16:17; 31:39; **Lam.** 3:35; **Ezek.** 40:13,23; 41:16; 42:1,3; **Dan.** 8:15; 10:13,16; **Hos.** 7:2; **Joel** 1:16; **Amos** 4:3; 9:3; **Obad.** 1:11; **Jon.** 2:4; **Hab.** 1:3.

5049. נֶגֶד *negeḏ* **Aram. prep.**
(toward; corr. to Hebr. 5048)
Dan. 6:10(11).

5050. נָגַהּ *nāgah* **verb**
(to shine, to illuminate)
2 Sam. 22:29; **Job** 18:5; 22:28; **Ps.** 18:28(29); **Isa.** 9:2(1); 13:10.

5051. נֹגַהּ *nōgah* **fem. noun**
(brightness, radiance)
2 Sam. 22:13; 23:4; **Ps.** 18:12(13); **Prov.** 4:18; **Isa.** 4:5; 50:10; 60:3,19; 62:1; **Ezek.** 1:4,13,27,28; 10:4; **Joel** 2:10; 3:15(4:15); **Amos** 5:20; **Hab.** 3:4,11.

5052. נֹגַהּ *nōgah* **masc. proper noun**
(Nogah)
1 Chr. 3:7; 14:6.

5053. נֹגַהּ *nōgah* **Aram. fem. noun**
(morning, daylight; corr. to Hebr. 5051)
Dan. 6:19(20).

5054. נְגֹהָה *n*^{e}*gōhāh* **fem. noun**
(brightness)
Isa. 59:9.

5055. נָגַח *nāgaḥ* **verb**
(to gore, to push)
Ex. 21:28,31,32; **Deut.** 33:17; **1 Kgs.** 22:11; **2 Chr.** 18:10; **Ps.** 44:5(6); **Ezek.** 34:21; **Dan.** 8:4; 11:40.

5056. נַגָּח *naggāḥ* **adj.**
(in the habit of goring)
Ex. 21:29,36.

5057. נָגִיד *nāgiyḏ* **masc. noun**
(leader, ruler, officer)
1 Sam. 9:16; 10:1; 13:14; 25:30; **2 Sam.** 5:2; 6:21; 7:8; **1 Kgs.** 1:35; 14:7; 16:2; **2 Kgs.** 20:5; **1 Chr.** 5:2; 9:11,20; 11:2; 12:27; 13:1; 17:7; 26:24; 27:4,16; 28:4; 29:22; **2 Chr.** 6:5; 11:11,22; 19:11; 28:7; 31:12,13; 32:21; 35:8; **Neh.** 11:11; **Job** 29:10; 31:37; **Ps.** 76:12(13); **Prov.** 8:6; 28:16; **Isa.** 55:4; **Jer.** 20:1; **Ezek.** 28:2; **Dan.** 9:25,26; 11:22.

5058. I. נְגִינָה *n^e^giynāh*, נְגִינַת *n^e^giynaṯ* **fem. noun**
(song, music; sometimes a taunting song)
Job 30:9; **Ps.** 69:12(11); 77:6(7); **Lam.** 3:14; 5:14.
II. נְגִינָה *n^e^giynāh*, נְגִינַת *n^e^giynaṯ* **fem. noun**
(stringed instrument)
Ps. 4:[title](1)(KJV, see III); 6:[title](1)(KJV, see III); 54:[title](1)(KJV, see III); 55:[title](1)(KJV, see III); 61:[title](1)(KJV, see III); 67:[title](1)(KJV, see III); 76:[title](1)(KJV, see III); **Isa.** 38:20; **Hab.** 3:19.
III. נְגִינָה *n^e^giynāh*, נְגִינַת *n^e^giynaṯ* **fem. proper noun**
(Neginah, Neginoth; proper name of a stringed instrument, used only in Psalm titles)
Ps. 4:[title](1)(NASB, NIV, see II); 6:[title](1)(NASB, NIV, see II); 54:[title](1)(NASB, NIV, see II); 55:[title](1)(NASB, NIV, see II); 61:[title](1)(NASB, NIV, see II); 67:[title](1)(NASB, NIV, see II); 76:[title](1)(NASB, NIV, see II).

5059. נָגַן *nāgan* **verb**
(to play a stringed instrument)
1 Sam. 16:16–18,23; 18:10; 19:9; **2 Kgs.** 3:15; **Ps.** 33:3; 68:25(26); **Isa.** 23:16; 38:20; **Ezek.** 33:32.

5060. נָגַע *nāga'* **verb**
(to touch, to strike, to arrive)
Gen. 3:3; 12:17; 20:6; 26:11,29; 28:12; 32:25(26),32(33); **Ex.** 4:25; 12:22; 19:12,13; 29:37; 30:29; **Lev.** 5:2,3,7; 6:18(11),27(20); 7:19,21; 11:8,24,26,27, 31,36,39; 12:4; 15:5,7,10–12,19,21–23, 27; 22:4–6; **Num.** 4:15; 16:26; 19:11,13, 16,18,21,22; 31:19; **Deut.** 14:8; **Josh.** 8:15; 9:19; **Judg.** 6:21; 20:34,41; **Ruth** 2:9; **1 Sam.** 6:9; 10:26; 14:9; **2 Sam.** 5:8; 14:10; 23:7; **1 Kgs.** 6:27; 19:5,7; **2 Kgs.** 13:21; 15:5; **1 Chr.** 16:22; **2 Chr.** 3:11,12; 26:20; 28:9; **Ezra** 3:1; **Neh.** 7:73; **Esth.** 2:12,15; 4:3,14; 5:2; 6:14; 8:17; 9:1,26; **Job** 1:11,19; 2:5; 4:5; 5:19; 6:7; 19:21; 20:6; **Ps.** 32:6; 73:5,14; 88:3(4); 104:32; 105:15; 107:18; 144:5; **Prov.** 6:29; **Eccl.** 8:14; 12:1; **Song** 2:12; **Isa.** 5:8; 6:7; 8:8; 16:8; 25:12; 26:5; 30:4; 52:11; 53:4; **Jer.** 1:9; 4:10,18; 12:14; 48:32; 51:9; **Lam.** 2:2; 4:14,15; **Ezek.** 7:12; 13:14; 17:10; **Dan.** 8:5,7,18; 9:21; 10:10,16,18; 12:12; **Hos.** 4:2; **Amos** 9:5; **Jon.** 3:6; **Mic.** 1:9; **Hag.** 2:12,13; **Zech.** 2:8(12); 14:5.

5061. נֶגַע *nega'* **masc. noun**
(plague, infection, mark [of leprosy], mildew)
Gen. 12:17; **Ex.** 11:1; **Lev.** 13:2–6,9,12, 13,17,20,22,25,27,29–32,42–47,49–59; 14:3,32,34–37,39,40,43,44,48,54; **Deut.** 17:8; 21:5; 24:8; **2 Sam.** 7:14; **1 Kgs.** 8:37,38; **2 Chr.** 6:28,29; **Ps.** 38:11(12); 39:10(11); 89:32(33); 91:10; **Prov.** 6:33; **Isa.** 53:8.

5062. נָגַף *nāgap̱* **verb**
(to strike, to afflict)
Ex. 8:2(7:27); 12:23,27; 21:22,35; 32:35; **Lev.** 26:17; **Num.** 14:42; **Deut.** 1:42; 28:7,25; **Josh.** 24:5; **Judg.** 20:32,35, 36,39; **1 Sam.** 4:2,3,10; 7:10; 25:38; 26:10; **2 Sam.** 2:17; 10:15,19; 12:15; 18:7; **1 Kgs.** 8:33; **2 Kgs.** 14:12; **1 Chr.** 19:16,19; **2 Chr.** 6:24; 13:15,20; 14:12(11); 20:22; 21:14,18; 25:22; **Ps.** 89:23(24); 91:12; **Prov.** 3:23; **Isa.** 19:22; **Jer.** 13:16; **Zech.** 14:12,18.

5063. נֶגֶף *negep̱* **masc. noun**
(plague, cause of stumbling)
Ex. 12:13; 30:12; **Num.** 8:19; 16:46 (17:11),47(17:12); **Josh.** 22:17; **Isa.** 8:14.

5064. נָגַר *nāgar* **verb**
(to pour, to pour out, to spill)
2 Sam. 14:14; **Job** 20:28; **Ps.** 63:10(11); 75:8(9); 77:2(3); **Jer.** 18:21; **Lam.** 3:49; **Ezek.** 35:5; **Mic.** 1:4,6.

5065. נָגַשׂ *nāgaś* **verb**
(to oppress, to require payment)
Ex. 3:7; 5:6,10,13,14; **Deut.** 15:2,3; **1 Sam.** 13:6; 14:24; **2 Kgs.** 23:35; **Job** 3:18; 39:7; **Isa.** 3:5,12; 9:4(3); 14:2,4; 53:7; 58:3; 60:17; **Dan.** 11:20; **Zech.** 9:8; 10:4.

5066. נָגַשׁ *nāgaš* **verb**
(to approach, to come close, to bring)
Gen. 18:23; 19:9; 27:21,22,25–27; 29:10; 33:3,6,7; 43:19; 44:18; 45:4; 48:10,13; **Ex.** 19:15,22; 20:21; 21:6; 24:2,14; 28:43; 30:20; 32:6; 34:30,32; **Lev.** 2:8; 8:14; 21:21,23; **Num.** 4:19; 8:19; 32:16; **Deut.** 20:2; 21:5; 25:1,9; **Josh.** 3:9; 8:11; 14:6; 21:1; **Judg.** 6:19; 9:52; 20:23; **Ruth** 2:14; **1 Sam.** 7:10; 9:18; 13:9; 14:18,34,38; 15:32; 17:16,40; 23:9; 28:25; 30:7,21; **2 Sam.** 1:15; 3:34; 10:13; 11:20,21; 13:11; 17:28(29); **1 Kgs.** 4:21(5:1); 18:21,30,36; 20:13,22,28; 22:24; **2 Kgs.** 2:5; 4:5,6,27; 5:13; **1 Chr.** 19:14; **2 Chr.** 18:23; 29:23,31; **Ezra** 4:2; 9:1; **Job** 40:19; 41:16(8); **Ps.** 91:7; **Isa.** 29:13; 41:1,21,22; 45:20,21; 49:20; 50:8; 65:5; **Jer.** 30:21; 42:1; 46:3; **Ezek.** 9:6; 44:13; **Joel** 3:9(4:9); **Amos** 5:25; 6:3; 9:10,13; **Mal.** 1:7,8,11; 2:12; 3:3.

5067. נֵד *nēd* **masc. noun**
(heap)
Ex. 15:8; **Josh.** 3:13,16; **Ps.** 33:7 (NIV, *nō'd* [4997]); 78:13; **Isa.** 17:11 (NIV, *nādad* [5074]).

5068. נָדַב *nādab* **verb**
(to offer willingly, to offer freely, to give freely)
Ex. 25:2; 35:21,29; **Judg.** 5:2,9; **1 Chr.** 29:5,6,9,14,17; **2 Chr.** 17:16; **Ezra** 1:6; 2:68; 3:5; **Neh.** 11:2.

5069. נְדַב *n^e^dab* **Aram. verb**
(to offer willingly, to do willingly; corr. to Hebr. 5068)
Ezra 7:13,15,16.

5070. A. נָדָב *nādāb* **masc. proper noun**
(Nadab: son of Aaron)
Ex. 6:23; 24:1,9; 28:1; **Lev.** 10:1; **Num.** 3:2,4; 26:60,61; **1 Chr.** 6:3(5:29); 24:1,2.
B. נָדָב *nādāb* **masc. proper noun**
(Nadab: son of Jeroboam)
1 Kgs. 14:20; 15:25,27,31.
C. נָדָב *nādāb* **masc. proper noun**
(Nadab: son of Shammai)
1 Chr. 2:28,30.
D. נָדָב *nādāb* **masc. proper noun**
(Nadab: a Gibeonite)
1 Chr. 8:30; 9:36.

5071. נְדָבָה *n^e^dābāh* **fem. noun**
(freewill offering)
Ex. 35:29; 36:3; **Lev.** 7:16; 22:18,21,23; 23:38; **Num.** 15:3; 29:39; **Deut.** 12:6,17; 16:10; 23:23(24); **2 Chr.** 31:14; 35:8; **Ezra** 1:4; 3:5; 8:28; **Ps.** 54:6(8); 68:9(10); 110:3; 119:108; **Ezek.** 46:12; **Hos.** 14:4(5); **Amos** 4:5.

5072. נְדַבְיָה *n^e^dabyāh* **masc. proper noun**
(Nedabiah)
1 Chr. 3:18.

5073. נִדְבָּךְ *nidbāk* **Aram. masc. noun**
(row, layer)
Ezra 6:4.

5074. נָדַד *nādad* **verb**
(to flee, to wander, to banish)
Gen. 31:40; **2 Sam.** 23:6; **Esth.** 6:1; **Job** 15:23; 18:18; 20:8; **Ps.** 31:11(12); 55:7(8); 64:8(9); 68:12(13); **Prov.** 27:8; **Isa.** 10:14,31; 16:2,3; 17:11(KJV, NASB, *nēd* [5067]); 21:14,15; 22:3; 33:3; **Jer.** 4:25; 9:10(9); 49:5; **Hos.** 7:13; 9:17; **Nah.** 3:7,17.

5075. נְדַד *n^e^dad* **Aram. verb**
(to flee, to go away; corr. to Hebr. 5074)
Dan. 6:18(19).

5076. נְדֻדִים *n^{e}d̲ud̲iym* **masc. pl. noun**
(tossings to and fro)
Job 7:4.

5077. נָדָא *nād̲ā'*, נָדָה *nād̲āh* **verb**
(to separate, to drive away, to disaffect)
2 Kgs. 17:21(NIV, [Q^{e}] *nād̲aḥ* [5080,I]); **Isa.** 66:5; **Amos** 6:3.

5078. נֵדֶה *nēd̲eh* **masc. noun**
(gift, fee)
Ezek. 16:33.

5079. נִדָּה *niddāh* **fem. noun**
(impurity, a woman's menstrual cycle)
Lev. 12:2,5; 15:19,20,24–26,33; 18:19; 20:21; **Num.** 19:9,13,20,21; 31:23; **2 Chr.** 29:5; **Ezra** 9:11; **Lam.** 1:17; **Ezek.** 7:19,20; 18:6; 22:10; 36:17; **Zech.** 13:1.

5080. I. נָדַח *nād̲aḥ* **verb**
(to banish, to drive away, to scatter)
Deut. 4:19; 13:5(6),10(11),13(14); 22:1; 30:1,4,17; **2 Sam.** 14:13,14; **2 Kgs.** 17:21(KJV, NASB, [K^{e}] *nād̲ā'* [5077]); **2 Chr.** 13:9; 21:11; **Neh.** 1:9; **Job** 6:13; **Ps.** 5:10(11); 62:4(5); **Prov.** 7:21; **Isa.** 8:22; 11:12(KJV, *dāḥāh* [1760]); 13:14; 16:3,4; 27:13; **Jer.** 8:3; 16:15; 23:2,3,8; 24:9; 27:10,15; 29:14,18; 30:17; 32:37; 40:12; 43:5; 46:28; 49:5,36; 50:17; **Ezek.** 4:13; 34:4,16; **Dan.** 9:7; **Joel** 2:20; **Mic.** 4:6; **Zeph.** 3:19.
II. נָדַח *nād̲aḥ* **verb**
(to wield, to bring [against])
Deut. 19:5; 20:19; **2 Sam.** 15:14.

5081. נָדִיב *nād̲iyb̲* **adj.**
(willing, generous, noble)
Ex. 35:5,22; **Num.** 21:18; **1 Sam.** 2:8; **1 Chr.** 28:21; **2 Chr.** 29:31; **Job** 12:21; 21:28; 34:18; **Ps.** 47:9(10); 51:12(14) (KJV, NASB, *n^{e}d̲iyb̲āh* [5082]); 83:11(12); 107:40; 113:8; 118:9; 146:3; **Prov.** 8:16; 17:7,26; 19:6; 25:7; **Song** 6:12(KJV, *'ammiy nād̲iyb̲* [5993]); 7:1(2); **Isa.** 13:2; 32:5,8(NASB, NIV, *n^{e}d̲iyb̲āh* [5082]).

5082. נְדִיבָה *n^{e}d̲iyb̲āh* **fem. noun**
(honor, dignity, nobility)
Ps. 51:12(14)(NIV, *nād̲iyb̲* [5081]); **Job** 30:15; **Isa.** 32:8(KJV, *nād̲iyb̲* [5081]).

5083. נָדָן *nād̲ān* **masc. noun**
(gift)
Ezek. 16:33.

5084. נָדָן *nād̲ān* **masc. noun**
(sheath [of a sword])
1 Chr. 21:27.

5085. נִדְנֶה *nid̲neh* **Aram. masc. noun**
(sheath, body)
Dan. 7:15.

5086. נָדַף *nād̲ap̱* **verb**
(to drive away, to be driven about)
Lev. 26:36; **Job** 13:25; 32:13; **Ps.** 1:4; 68:2(3); **Prov.** 21:6; **Isa.** 19:7; 41:2.

5087. נָדַר *nād̲ar* **verb**
(to vow, to make a vow)
Gen. 28:20; 31:13; **Lev.** 27:8; **Num.** 6:2,21; 21:2; 30:2(3),3(4),10(11); **Deut.** 12:11,17; 23:21(22),22(23),23(24); **Judg.** 11:30,39; **1 Sam.** 1:11; **2 Sam.** 15:7,8; **Ps.** 76:11(12); 132:2; **Eccl.** 5:4(3),5(4); **Isa.** 19:21; **Jer.** 44:25; **Jon.** 1:16; 2:9(10); **Mal.** 1:14.

5088. נֵדֶר *nēd̲er*, נֶדֶר *ned̲er* **masc. noun**
(a vow)
Gen. 28:20; 31:13; **Lev.** 7:16; 22:18,21,23; 23:38; 27:2; **Num.** 6:2,5,21; 15:3,8; 21:2; 29:39; 30:2–9(3–10),11–14 (12–15); **Deut.** 12:6,11,17,26; 23:18(19), 21(22); **Judg.** 11:30,39; **1 Sam.** 1:11,21;

2 Sam. 15:7,8; **Job** 22:27; **Ps.** 22:25(26); 50:14; 56:12(13); 61:5(6),8(9); 65:1(2); 66:13; 116:14,18; **Prov.** 7:14; 20:25; 31:2; **Eccl.** 5:4(3); **Isa.** 19:21; **Jer.** 44:25; **Jon.** 1:16; **Nah.** 1:15(2:1).

5089. I. נֹהַ *nōah* **masc. noun**
(something eminent, of value)
Ezek. 7:11(KJV, see II).
II. נֹהַ *nōah* **masc. noun**
(a wailing, lamenting)
Ezek. 7:11(NASB, NIV, see I).

5090. I. נָהַג *nāhag* **verb**
(to drive, to guide)
Gen. 31:18,26; **Ex.** 3:1; 10:13; 14:25; **Deut.** 4:27; 28:37; **1 Sam.** 23:5; 30:2, 20,22; **2 Sam.** 6:3; **2 Kgs.** 4:24; 9:20; **1 Chr.** 13:7; 20:1; **2 Chr.** 25:11; **Job** 24:3; **Ps.** 48:14(15); 78:26,52; 80:1(2); **Eccl.** 2:3; **Song** 8:2; **Isa.** 11:6; 20:4; 49:10; 60:11; 63:14; **Lam.** 3:2.
II. נָהַג *nāhag* **verb**
(to sob, to lament)
Nah. 2:7(8).

5091. נָהָה *nāhāh* **verb**
(to wail, to lament, to mourn)
1 Sam. 7:2; **Ezek.** 32:18; **Mic.** 2:4.

5092. נְהִי *n^{e}hiy* **masc. noun**
(wailing, song of mourning)
Jer. 9:10(9),18–20(17–19); 31:15; **Amos** 5:16; **Mic.** 2:4(KJV, NASB, *nihyāh* [5093]).

5093. נִהְיָה *nihyāh* **fem. noun**
(dolefulness, bitterness)
Mic. 2:4(NIV, *n^{e}hiy* [5092]).

5094. I. נְהִיר *n^{e}hiyr* **Aram. masc. noun**
(light)
Dan. 2:22([Q^{e}] see I).
II. נַהִירוּ *nahiyrû* **Aram. fem. noun**
(illumination, insight)
Dan. 5:11,14.

5095. נָהַל *nāhal* **verb**
(to lead, to guide [to water and rest], to move along)
Gen. 33:14; 47:17; **Ex.** 15:13; **2 Chr.** 28:15; 32:22; **Ps.** 23:2; 31:3(4); **Isa.** 40:11; 49:10; 51:18.

5096. נַהֲלֹל *nah^{a}lōl*, נַהֲלָל *nah^{a}lāl* **proper noun**
(Nahalal, Nahalol)
Josh. 19:15; 21:35; **Judg.** 1:30.

5097. נַהֲלֹל *nah^{a}lōl* **masc. noun**
(bushes, watering places)
Isa. 7:19.

5098. נָהַם *nāham* **verb**
(to groan, to growl, to roar)
Prov. 5:11; 28:15; **Isa.** 5:29,30; **Ezek.** 24:23.

5099. נַהַם *naham* **masc. noun**
(growl, roar [of a lion])
Prov. 19:12; 20:2.

5100. נְהָמָה *n^{e}hāmāh* **fem. noun**
(agitation, roaring)
Ps. 38:8(9); **Isa.** 5:30.

5101. נָהַק *nāhaq* **verb**
(to bray [of donkeys])
Job 6:5; 30:7.

5102. I. נָהַר *nāhar* **verb**
(to flow, to stream)
Isa. 2:2; 60:5(NASB, NIV, see II); **Jer.** 31:12(NASB, NIV, see II); 51:44; **Mic.** 4:1.
II. נָהַר *nāhar* **verb**
(to be radiant)
Ps. 34:5(6); **Isa.** 60:5(KJV, see I); **Jer.** 31:12(KJV, see I).

5103. נְהַר *n*e*har* **Aram. masc. noun**
(river; corr. to 5104)
Ezra 4:10,11,16,17,20; 5:3,6; 6:6,8,13; 7:21,25; **Dan.** 7:10.

5104. נָהָר *nāhār* **masc. noun**
(river)
Gen. 2:10,13,14; 15:18; 24:10; 31:21; 36:37; **Ex.** 7:19; 8:5(1); 23:31; **Num.** 22:5; 24:6; **Deut.** 1:7; 11:24; 23:4(5); **Josh.** 1:4; 24:2,3,14,15; **Judg.** 3:8; **2 Sam.** 8:3; 10:16; **1 Kgs.** 4:21(5:1), 24(5:4); 14:15; **2 Kgs.** 5:12; 17:6; 18:11; 23:29; 24:7; **1 Chr.** 1:48; 5:9,26; 18:3; 19:16; **2 Chr.** 9:26; **Ezra** 8:15,21,31,36; **Neh.** 2:7,9; 3:7; **Job** 14:11; 20:17; 22:16; 28:11; 40:23; **Ps.** 24:2; 46:4(5); 66:6; 72:8; 74:15; 78:16; 80:11(12); 89:25(26); 93:3; 98:8; 105:41; 107:33; 137:1; **Song** 8:7; **Isa.** 7:20; 8:7; 11:15; 18:1,2,7; 19:5,6; 27:12; 33:21; 41:18; 42:15; 43:2, 19,20; 44:27; 47:2; 48:18; 50:2; 59:19; 66:12; **Jer.** 2:18; 46:2,6–8,10; **Ezek.** 1:1,3; 3:15,23; 10:15,20,22; 31:4,15; 32:2,14; 43:3; **Dan.** 10:4; **Jon.** 2:3(4); **Mic.** 7:12; **Nah.** 1:4; 2:6(7); **Hab.** 3:8,9; **Zeph.** 3:10; **Zech.** 9:10.

5105. נְהָרָה *n*e*hārāh* **fem. noun**
(light, light of day)
Job 3:4.

5106. נוּא *nû'* **verb**
(to forbid, to discourage, to thwart)
Num. 30:5(6),8(9),11(12); 32:7,9; **Ps.** 33:10; 141:5.

5107. נוּב *nû*b̲ **verb**
(to flourish, to bear fruit, to bring forth)
Ps. 62:10(11); 92:14(15); **Prov.** 10:31; **Zech.** 9:17.

5108. I. נֹוב *nô*b̲ **masc. noun**
(fruit)
Isa. 57:19(NASB, see II; NIV, see III); **Mal.** 1:12(NASB, NIV, see III).

II. נִיב *niy*b̲ **masc. noun**
(fruit)
Isa. 57:19(KJV, see I; NIV, see III).

III. נִיב *niy*b̲ **masc. noun**
(praise)
Isa. 57:19(KJV, see I; NASB, see II); **Mal.** 1:12(KJV, see I).

5109. נֵיבָי *ne*b̲*āy* **masc. proper noun**
(Nebai)
Neh. 10:19(20).

5110. נוּד *nû*d̲ **verb**
(to flee, to wander, to mourn)
Gen. 4:12,14; **1 Kgs.** 14:15; **2 Kgs.** 21:8; **Job** 2:11; 42:11; **Ps.** 11:1; 36:11(12); 69:20(21); **Prov.** 26:2; **Isa.** 24:20; 51:19; **Jer.** 4:1; 15:5; 16:5; 18:16; 22:10; 31:18; 48:17,27; 49:30; 50:3,8; **Nah.** 3:7.

5111. נוּד *nû*d̲ **Aram. verb**
(to flee)
Dan. 4:14(11).

5112. I. נֹוד *nô*d̲ **masc. noun**
(wandering)
Ps. 56:8(9)(NIV, see II).

II. נֹוד *nô*d̲ **masc. noun**
(lament)
Ps. 56:8(9)(KJV, NASB, see I).

5113. נֹוד *nô*d̲ **proper noun**
(Nod)
Gen. 4:16.

5114. נֹודָב *nô*d̲*ā*b̲ **masc. proper noun**
(Nodab)
1 Chr. 5:19.

5115. I. נָוָה *nāwāh* **verb**
(to dwell, to abide, to rest)
Ex. 15:2(NASB, NIV, see II); **Hab.** 2:5.

II. נָוָה *nāwāh* **verb**
(to beautify; to praise)
Ex. 15:2(KJV, see I).

5116. I. נָוֶה *nāweh* **masc. noun**
(shepherd's abode, flock, camp)
Ex. 15:13; **2 Sam.** 7:8; 15:25; **1 Chr.** 17:7; **Job** 5:3,24; 18:15; **Ps.** 79:7; **Prov.** 3:33; 21:20; 24:15; **Isa.** 27:10; 32:18; 33:20; 34:13; 35:7; 65:10; **Jer.** 10:25; 23:3; 25:30; 31:23; 33:12; 49:19,20; 50:7,19,44,45; **Ezek.** 25:5; 34:14; **Hos.** 9:13.
II. נָוָה *nāwāh* **fem. noun**
(dwelling, habitation, pasturage)
Job 8:6; **Ps.** 23:2(KJV, *nā'āh* [4999]); 65:12(13)(KJV, NASB, *nā'āh* [4999]); 68:12 (13)(KJV, NASB, see III); 74:20(KJV, NASB, *nā'āh* [4999]); 83:12(13)(KJV, NASB, *nā'āh* [4999]); **Jer.** 9:10(9)(KJV, NASB, *nā'āh* [4999]); 23:10(KJV, NASB, *nā'āh* [4999]); 25:37(KJV, *nā'āh* [4999]); **Lam.** 2:2(KJV, NASB, *nā'āh* [4999]); **Joel** 1:19(KJV, NASB, *nā'āh* [4999]),20(KJV, NASB, *nā'āh* [4999]); 2:22(KJV, NASB, *nā'āh* [4999]); **Amos** 1:2(KJV, NASB, *nā'āh* [4999]); **Zeph.** 2:6.
III. נָוֶה *nāweh* **adj.**
(the one dwelling, abiding)
Ps. 68:12(13)(NIV, see II).

5117. I. נוּחַ *nûaḥ* **verb**
(to rest, to pause; includes all references classified under *yānaḥ* [3240] by Strong)
Gen. 2:15; 8:4; 19:16; 39:16; 42:33; **Ex.** 10:14; 16:23,24,33,34; 17:11; 20:11; 23:12; 32:10; 33:14; **Lev.** 7:15; 16:23; 24:12; **Num.** 10:36; 11:25,26; 15:34; 17:4,7; 19:9; 32:15; **Deut.** 3:20; 5:14; 12:10; 14:28; 25:19; 26:4,10; **Josh.** 1:13,15; 3:13; 4:3,8; 6:23; 21:44; 22:4; 23:1; **Judg.** 2:23; 3:1; 6:18,20; 16:26; **1 Sam.** 6:18; 10:25; 25:9; **2 Sam.** 7:1,11; 16:11,21; 17:12; 20:3; 21:10; **1 Kgs.** 5:4; 7:47; 8:9; 13:29–31; 19:3; **2 Kgs.** 2:15; 17:29; 23:18; **1 Chr.** 16:21; 22:9,18; 23:25; **2 Chr.** 1:14; 4:8; 6:41(KJV, NIV, *nûaḥ* [5118]); 9:25; 14:6,7; 15:15; 20:30; **Neh.** 9:28; **Esth.** 3:8; 9:16(KJV, *nûaḥ* [5118]),17(KJV, *nûaḥ* [5118]),18(KJV, *nûaḥ* [5118]),22; **Job** 3:13,17,26; **Ps.** 17:14; 105:14; 119:121; 125:3; **Prov.** 14:33; 21:16; 29:17; **Eccl.** 2:18; 5:12; 7:9,18; 10:4; 11:6; **Isa.** 7:2,19; 11:2; 14:1,3,7; 23:12; 25:10; 28:2,12; 30:32; 46:7; 57:2; 63:14; 65:15; **Jer.** 14:9; 27:11; 43:6; **Lam.** 5:5; **Ezek.** 5:13; 16:39,42; 21:17; 22:20; 24:13; 37:1,14; 40:2,42; 41:9(NIV, see II),11(NIV, see II); 42:13,14; 44:19,30; **Dan.** 12:13; **Hos.** 4:17; **Amos** 5:7; **Hab.** 3:16; **Zech.** 5:11; 6:8.
II. מֻנָּח *munnāḥ* **masc. noun**
(free space, open area)
Ezek. 41:9(KJV, NASB, see I),11(KJV, NASB, see I).

5118. נוּחַ *nûaḥ*, נֹחַ *nôaḥ* **masc. noun**
(rest, resting place)
2 Chr. 6:41(NASB, *nûaḥ* [5117,I]); **Esth.** 9:16(NASB, NIV, *nûaḥ* [5117,I]),17(NASB, NIV, *nûaḥ* [5117,I]),18(NASB, NIV, *nûaḥ* [5117,I]).

5119. נוֹחָה *nôḥāh* **masc. proper noun**
(Nohah)
1 Chr. 8:2.

5120. נוּט *nûṭ* **verb**
(to shake, to move)
Ps. 99:1.

5121. נָיוֹת *nāyôṯ* **proper noun**
(Naioth)
1 Sam. 19:18,19,22,23; 20:1.

5122. נְוָלוּ *n*[e]*wālû*, נְוָלִי *n*[e]*wāliy* **Aram. fem. noun**
(refuse heap, dunghill)
Ezra 6:11; **Dan.** 2:5; 3:29.

5123. נוּם *nûm* **verb**
(to sleep, to slumber)
Ps. 76:5(6); 121:3,4; **Isa.** 5:27; 56:10; **Nah.** 3:18.

5124. נוּמָה *nûmāh* **fem. noun**
(drowsiness)
Prov. 23:21.

5125. נוּן *nûn* **verb**
(to continue, to increase)
Ps. 72:17.

5126. נוּן *nun,* נוֹן *nôn* **masc. proper noun**
(Nun, Non)
Ex. 33:11; **Num.** 11:28; 13:8,16; 14:6, 30,38; 26:65; 27:18; 32:12,28; 34:17; **Deut.** 1:38; 31:23; 32:44; 34:9; **Josh.** 1:1; 2:1,23; 6:6; 14:1; 17:4; 19:49,51; 21:1; 24:29; **Judg.** 2:8; **1 Kgs.** 16:34; **1 Chr.** 7:27; **Neh.** 8:17.

5127. נוּס *nûs* **verb**
(to flee)
Gen. 14:10; 19:20; 39:12,13,15,18; **Ex.** 4:3; 9:20; 14:25,27; 21:13; **Lev.** 26:17,36; **Num.** 10:35; 16:34; 35:6,11,15,25,26,32; **Deut.** 4:42; 19:3–5,11; 28:7,25; 32:30; 34:7; **Josh.** 7:4; 8:5,6,15,20; 10:11,16; 20:3,4,6,9; **Judg.** 1:6; 4:15,17; 6:11; 7:21,22; 8:12; 9:21,40,51; 20:32,45,47; **1 Sam.** 4:10,16,17; 14:22; 17:24,51; 19:8,10; 30:17; 31:1,7; **2 Sam.** 1:4; 4:4; 10:13,14,18; 13:29; 17:2; 18:3,17; 19:3(4),8(9); 23:11; 24:13; **1 Kgs.** 2:28,29; 12:18; 20:20,30; **2 Kgs.** 3:24; 7:7; 8:21; 9:3,10,23,27; 14:12,19; **1 Chr.** 10:1,7; 11:13; 19:14,15,18; **2 Chr.** 10:18; 13:16; 14:12(11); 25:22,27; **Ps.** 60:4(6); 68:1(2); 104:7; 114:3,5; **Prov.** 28:1,17; **Song** 2:17; 4:6; **Isa.** 10:3,29; 13:14; 17:13; 20:6; 24:18; 30:16,17; 31:8; 35:10; 51:11; 59:19; **Jer.** 46:5,6,21; 48:6,19, 44(KJV, [K^{e}] *niys* [5211]),45; 49:8,24,30; 50:16,28; 51:6; **Amos** 2:16; 5:19; 9:1; **Nah.** 2:8(9); **Zech.** 2:6(10); 14:5.

5128. נוּעַ *nûaʻ* **verb**
(to shake, to stagger, to wander)
Gen. 4:12,14; **Ex.** 20:18; **Num.** 32:13; **Judg.** 9:9,11,13; **1 Sam.** 1:13; **2 Sam.** 15:20; **2 Kgs.** 19:21; 23:18; **Job** 16:4; 28:4; **Ps.** 22:7(8); 59:11(12),15(16); 107:27; 109:10,25; **Prov.** 5:6; **Isa.** 6:4; 7:2; 19:1; 24:20; 29:9; 37:22; **Jer.** 14:10; **Lam.** 2:15; 4:14,15; **Dan.** 10:10; **Amos** 4:8; 8:12; 9:9; **Nah.** 3:12; **Zeph.** 2:15.

5129. A. נוֹעַדְיָה *nôʻaḏyāh* **masc. proper noun**
(Noadiah: Levite under Ezra)
Ezra 8:33.
B. נוֹעַדְיָה *nôʻaḏyāh* **fem. proper noun**
(Noadiah: a prophetess)
Neh. 6:14.

5130. I. נוּף *nûp̱* **verb**
(to shake, to wave, to lift up, to offer)
Ex. 20:25; 29:24,26,27; 35:22; **Lev.** 7:30; 8:27,29; 9:21; 10:15; 14:12,24; 23:11, 12,20; **Num.** 5:25; 6:20; 8:11,13,15,21; **Deut.** 23:25(26); 27:5; **Josh.** 8:31; **2 Kgs.** 5:11; **Job** 31:21; **Isa.** 10:15,32; 11:15; 13:2; 19:16(KJV, NIV, *t^{e}nûp̱āh* [8575]); 30:28; **Zech.** 2:9(13).
II. נוּף *nûp̱* **verb**
(to sprinkle, to shed abroad)
Ps. 68:9(10); **Prov.** 7:17.

5131. נוֹף *nôp̱* **masc. noun**
(elevation, height)
Ps. 48:2(3).

5132. I. נוּץ *nûṣ* **verb**
(to bud, to blossom)
Song 6:11(NASB, NIV, *nāṣaṣ* [5340]); 7:12(13)(NASB, NIV, *nāṣaṣ* [5340]).
II. נוּץ *nûṣ* **verb**
(to fly, to wander off)
Lam. 4:15.

5133. I. נוֹצָה *nôṣāh,* נֹצָה *nōṣāh* **fem. noun**
(feathers, plumage)
Lev. 1:16(NIV, see II); **Job** 39:13; **Ezek.** 17:3,7.

II. נֹצָה *nōṣāh* **fem. noun**
(contents)
Lev. 1:16(KJV, NASB, see I).

5134. נוּק *nûq* **verb**
(to nurse)
Ex. 2:9(NIV, *yānaq* [3243]).

5135. נוּר *nûr* **Aram. masc. noun**
(fire)
Dan. 3:6,11,15,17,20–27; 7:9,10.

5136. נוּשׁ *nûš* **verb**
(to be sick, to be helpless)
Ps. 69:20(21).

5137. נָזָה *nāzāh* **verb**
(to sprinkle, to splatter)
Ex. 29:21; **Lev.** 4:6,17; 5:9; 6:27(20); 8:11,30; 14:7,16,27,51; 16:14,15,19; **Num.** 8:7; 19:4,18,19,21; **2 Kgs.** 9:33; **Isa.** 52:15; 63:3.

5138. נָזִיד *nāziyḏ* **masc. noun**
(stew)
Gen. 25:29,34; **2 Kgs.** 4:38–40; **Hag.** 2:12.

5139. נָזִיר *nāziyr* **masc. noun**
(Nazarite, one untrimmed, consecrated)
Gen. 49:26; **Lev.** 25:5,11; **Num.** 6:2, 13,18–21; **Deut.** 33:16; **Judg.** 13:5,7; 16:17; **Lam.** 4:7; **Amos** 2:11,12.

5140. I. נָזַל *nāzal* **verb**
(to flow, to pour down, to drop, to melt)
Ex. 15:8(NIV, see II); **Num.** 24:7; **Deut.** 32:2; **Judg.** 5:5; **Job** 36:28; **Ps.** 78:16 (NIV, see II),44(NIV, see II); 147:18; **Prov.** 5:15(NIV, see II); **Song** 4:15,16; **Isa.** 44:3(NIV, see II); 45:8; 48:21; **Jer.** 9:18(17); 18:14.
II. נֹזֵל *nōzēl* **masc. noun**
(brooks, streaming)
Ex. 15:8(KJV, NASB, see I); **Ps.** 78:16 (KJV, NASB, see I),44(KJV, NASB, see I); **Prov.** 5:15(KJV, NASB, see I); **Isa.** 44:3 (KJV, NASB, see I).

5141. נֶזֶם *nezem* **masc. noun**
(ring, earring, nose ring)
Gen. 24:22,30,47; 35:4; **Ex.** 32:2,3; 35:22; **Judg.** 8:24–26; **Job** 42:11; **Prov.** 11:22; 25:12; **Isa.** 3:21; **Ezek.** 16:12; **Hos.** 2:13(15).

5142. נְזַק *n^ezaq* **Aram. verb**
(to injure, to damage, to cause loss; corr. to Hebr. 5143)
Ezra 4:13,15,22; **Dan.** 6:2(3).

5143. נֵזֶק *nēzeq* **masc. noun**
(damage, disturbance)
Esth. 7:4.

5144. נָזַר *nāzar* **verb**
(to separate oneself, to abstain)
Lev. 15:31; 22:2; **Num.** 6:2,3,5,6,12; **Ezek.** 14:7; **Hos.** 9:10; **Zech.** 7:3.

5145. נֵזֶר *nēzer* **masc. noun**
(crown, separation)
Ex. 29:6; 39:30; **Lev.** 8:9; 21:12; **Num.** 6:4,5,7–9,12,13,18,19,21; **2 Sam.** 1:10; **2 Kgs.** 11:12; **2 Chr.** 23:11; **Ps.** 89:39(40); 132:18; **Prov.** 27:24; **Jer.** 7:29; **Zech.** 9:16.

5146. נֹחַ *nōaḥ* **masc. proper noun**
(Noah)
Gen. 5:29,30,32; 6:8–10,13,22; 7:1,5–7, 9,11,13,15,23; 8:1,6,11,13,15,18,20; 9:1,8,17–20,24,28,29; 10:1,32; **1 Chr.** 1:4; **Isa.** 54:9; **Ezek.** 14:14,20.

5147. נַחְבִּי *naḥbiy* **masc. proper noun**
(Nahbi)
Num. 13:14.

5148. נָחָה *nāḥāh* **verb**
(to lead, to guide)

Gen. 24:27,48; **Ex.** 13:17,21; 15:13; 32:34; **Num.** 23:7; **Deut.** 32:12; **1 Sam.** 22:4; **1 Kgs.** 10:26; **2 Kgs.** 18:11; **Neh.** 9:12,19; **Job** 12:23; 31:18; 38:32; **Ps.** 5:8(9); 23:3; 27:11; 31:3(4); 43:3; 60:9(11); 61:2(3); 67:4(5); 73:24; 77:20(21); 78:14,53,72; 107:30; 108:10(11); 139:10,24; 143:10; **Prov.** 6:22; 11:3; 18:16; **Isa.** 57:18; 58:11.

5149. נְחוּם *n^e ḥûm* **masc. proper noun**
(Nehum)
Neh. 7:7.

5150. נִחוּם *niḥûm*, נִחֻם *niḥum* **masc. noun**
(comfort, compassion)
Isa. 57:18; **Hos.** 11:8; **Zech.** 1:13.

5151. נַחוּם *naḥûm* **masc. proper noun**
(Nahum)
Nah. 1:1.

5152. A. נָחוֹר *nāḥôr* **masc. proper noun**
(Nahor: father of Terah)
Gen. 11:22–25; **1 Chr.** 1:26.
B. נָחוֹר *nāḥôr* **masc. proper noun**
(Nahor: son of Terah)
Gen. 11:26,27,29; 22:20,23; 24:10,15, 24,47; 29:5; 31:53; **Josh.** 24:2.

5153. נָחוּשׁ *nāḥûš* **adj.**
(bronze)
Job 6:12.

5154. נְחוּשָׁה *n^e ḥûšāh* **fem. noun**
(bronze, copper)
Lev. 26:19; **2 Sam.** 22:35; **Job** 20:24; 28:2; 40:18; 41:27(19); **Ps.** 18:34(35); **Isa.** 45:2; 48:4; **Mic.** 4:13.

5155. I. נְחִילָה *n^e ḥiylāh* **fem. proper noun**
(Nehiloth; proper name in Psalm title)
Ps. 5:[title](1)(NASB, NIV, see II).
II. נְחִילָה *n^e ḥiylāh* **fem. noun**
(flute)
Ps. 5:[title](1)(KJV, see I).

5156. נָחִיר *nāḥiyr* **masc. noun**
(nostril)
Job 41:20(12).

5157. נָחַל *nāḥal* **verb**
(to inherit, to possess, to apportion)
Ex. 23:30; 32:13; 34:9; **Lev.** 25:46; **Num.** 18:20,23,24; 26:55; 32:18,19; 33:54; 34:13,17,18,29; 35:8; **Deut.** 1:38; 3:28; 12:10; 19:3,14; 21:16; 31:7; 32:8; **Josh.** 1:6; 13:32; 14:1; 16:4; 17:6; 19:9, 49,51; **Judg.** 11:2; **1 Sam.** 2:8; **1 Chr.** 28:8; **Job** 7:3; **Ps.** 69:36(37); 82:8; 119:111; **Prov.** 3:35; 8:21; 11:29; 13:22; 14:18; 28:10; **Isa.** 14:2; 49:8; 57:13; **Jer.** 3:18; 12:14; 16:19; **Ezek.** 22:16(NASB, NIV, *ḥālal* [2490,I]); 46:18; 47:13,14; **Zeph.** 2:9; **Zech.** 2:12(16); 8:12.

5158. I. נַחֲלָה *naḥ^a lāh* **fem. noun**
(wadi)
Ezek. 47:19; 48:28.
II. נַחַל *naḥal* **masc. noun**
(wadi, stream, torrent)
Gen. 26:17,19; 32:23(24); **Lev.** 11:9,10; 23:40; **Num.** 13:23,24; 21:12,14,15; 24:6; 32:9; 34:5; **Deut.** 1:24; 2:13,14, 24,36,37; 3:8,12,16; 4:48; 8:7; 9:21; 10:7; 21:4,6; **Josh.** 12:1,2; 13:9,16; 15:4,7,47; 16:8; 17:9; 19:11; **Judg.** 4:7,13; 5:21; 16:4; **1 Sam.** 15:5; 17:40; 30:9,10,21; **2 Sam.** 15:23; 17:13; 22:5; 23:30; 24:5; **1 Kgs.** 2:37; 8:65; 15:13; 17:3–7; 18:5,40; **2 Kgs.** 3:16,17; 10:33; 23:6,12; 24:7; **1 Chr.** 11:32; **2 Chr.** 7:8; 15:16; 20:16; 29:16; 30:14; 32:4; 33:14; **Neh.** 2:15; **Job** 6:15; 20:17; 21:33; 22:24; 28:4; 30:6; 40:22; **Ps.** 18:4(5); 36:8(9); 74:15; 78:20; 83:9(10); 104:10; 110:7; 124:4; **Prov.** 18:4; 30:17; **Eccl.** 1:7; **Song** 6:11; **Isa.** 7:19; 11:15; 15:7; 27:12; 30:28,33; 34:9; 35:6; 57:5,6; 66:12; **Jer.** 31:9,40; 47:2;

Lam. 2:18; **Ezek.** 47:5–7,9,12; **Joel** 3:18(4:18); **Amos** 5:24; 6:14; **Mic.** 6:7.

5159. נַחֲלָה *naḥalāh* **fem. noun**
(inheritance, possession)
Gen. 31:14; 48:6; **Ex.** 15:17; **Num.** 16:14; 18:20,21,23,24,26; 26:53,54, 56,62; 27:7–11; 32:18,19,32; 33:54; 34:2,14,15; 35:2,8; 36:2–4,7–9,12; **Deut.** 4:20,21,38; 9:26,29; 10:9; 12:9,12; 14:27,29; 15:4; 18:1,2; 19:10,14; 20:16; 21:23; 24:4; 25:19; 26:1; 29:8(7); 32:9; **Josh.** 11:23; 13:6–8,14,23,28,33; 14:2,3, 9,13,14; 15:20; 16:5,8,9; 17:4,6,14; 18:2, 4,7,20,28; 19:1,2,8–10,16,23,31,39,41, 48,49,51; 21:3; 23:4; 24:28,30,32; **Judg.** 2:6,9; 18:1; 20:6; 21:23,24; **Ruth** 4:5,6,10; **1 Sam.** 10:1; 26:19; **2 Sam.** 14:16; 20:1,19; 21:3; **1 Kgs.** 8:36,51,53; 12:16; 21:3,4; **2 Kgs.** 21:14; **1 Chr.** 16:18; **2 Chr.** 6:27; 10:16; **Neh.** 11:20; **Job** 20:29; 27:13; 31:2; 42:15; **Ps.** 2:8; 16:6; 28:9; 33:12; 37:18; 47:4(5); 68:9(10); 74:2; 78:55,62,71; 79:1; 94:5,14; 105:11; 106:5,40; 111:6; 127:3; 135:12; 136:21,22; **Prov.** 17:2; 19:14; 20:21; **Eccl.** 7:11; **Isa.** 19:25; 47:6; 49:8; 54:17; 58:14; 63:17; **Jer.** 2:7; 3:19; 10:16; 12:7–9,14,15; 16:18; 17:4; 50:11; 51:19; **Lam.** 5:2; **Ezek.** 35:15; 36:12; 44:28; 45:1; 46:16–18; 47:14,22,23; 48:29; **Joel** 2:17; 3:2(4:2); **Mic.** 2:2; 7:14,18; **Mal.** 1:3.

5160. נַחֲלִיאֵל *naḥaliy'ēl* **proper noun**
(Nahaliel)
Num. 21:19.

5161. נֶחֱלָמִי *neḥelāmiy* **masc. proper noun**
(Nehelamite)
Jer. 29:24,31,32.

5162. נָחַם *nāḥam* **verb**
(to comfort, to console; to change one's mind, to regret)
Gen. 5:29; 6:6,7; 24:67; 27:42; 37:35; 38:12; 50:21; **Ex.** 13:17; 32:12,14; **Num.** 23:19; **Deut.** 32:36; **Judg.** 2:18; 21:6,15; **Ruth** 2:13; **1 Sam.** 15:11,29,35; **2 Sam.** 10:2,3; 12:24; 13:39; 24:16; **1 Chr.** 7:22; 19:2,3; 21:15; **Job** 2:11; 7:13; 16:2; 21:34; 29:25; 42:6,11; **Ps.** 23:4; 69:20(21); 71:21; 77:2(3); 86:17; 90:13; 106:45; 110:4; 119:52,76,82; 135:14; **Eccl.** 4:1; **Isa.** 1:24; 12:1; 22:4; 40:1; 49:13; 51:3,12,19; 52:9; 54:11; 57:6; 61:2; 66:13; **Jer.** 4:28; 8:6; 15:6; 16:7; 18:8,10; 20:16; 26:3, 13,19; 31:13,15,19; 42:10; **Lam.** 1:2,9, 16,17,21; 2:13; **Ezek.** 5:13; 14:22,23; 16:54; 24:14; 31:16; 32:31; **Joel** 2:13,14; **Amos** 7:3,6; **Jon.** 3:9,10; 4:2; **Nah.** 3:7; **Zech.** 1:17; 8:14; 10:2.

5163. נַחַם *naḥam* **masc. proper noun**
(Naham)
1 Chr. 4:19.

5164. נֹחַם *nōḥam* **masc. noun**
(repentance, compassion)
Hos. 13:14.

5165. נֶחָמָה *neḥāmāh* **fem. noun**
(consolation, comfort)
Job 6:10; **Ps.** 119:50.

5166. A. נְחֶמְיָה *n^eḥemyāh* **masc. proper noun**
(Nehemiah: rebuilder of Jerusalem)
Neh. 1:1; 8:9; 10:1(2); 12:26,47.
B. נְחֶמְיָה *n^eḥemyāh* **masc. proper noun**
(Nehemiah: postexilic Jew)
Ezra 2:2; **Neh.** 7:7.
C. נְחֶמְיָה *n^eḥemyāh* **masc. proper noun**
(Nehemiah: son of Azbuk)
Neh. 3:16.

5167. נַחֲמָנִי *naḥamāniy* **masc. proper noun**
(Nahamani)
Neh. 7:7.

5168. נַחְנוּ *naḥnû* **1st person pl. pron.**
(we)
Gen. 42:11; **Ex.** 16:7,8; **Num.** 32:32; **Lam.** 3:42.

5169. נָחַץ *nāḥaṣ* **verb**
(to be urgent)
1 Sam. 21:8(9).

5170. I. נַחַר *naḥar* **masc. noun**
(snorting)
Job 39:20.
II. נַחֲרָה *naḥ^a^rāh* **fem. noun**
(snorting)
Jer. 8:16.

5171. נַחֲרַי *naḥ^a^ray,* נַחְרַי *naḥray* **masc. proper noun**
(Naharai: armorbearer of Joab)
2 Sam. 23:37; **1 Chr.** 11:39.

5172. נָחַשׁ *naḥaš* **verb**
(to practice divination, to practice sorcery, to use enchantments)
Gen. 30:27; 44:5,15; **Lev.** 19:26; **Deut.** 18:10; **1 Kgs.** 20:33; **2 Kgs.** 17:17; 21:6; **2 Chr.** 33:6.

5173. נַחַשׁ *naḥaš* **masc. noun**
(enchantment, omen)
Num. 23:23; 24:1.

5174. נְחָשׁ *n^e^ḥāš* **Aram. masc. noun**
(bronze, brass; corr. to Hebr. 5154)
Dan. 2:32,35,39,45; 4:15(12),23(20); 5:4,23; 7:19.

5175. נָחָשׁ *nāḥāš* **masc. noun**
(serpent, snake)
Gen. 3:1,2,4,13,14; 49:17; **Ex.** 4:3; 7:15; **Num.** 21:6,7,9; **Deut.** 8:15; **2 Kgs.** 18:4; **Job** 26:13; **Ps.** 58:4(5); 140:3(4); **Prov.** 23:32; 30:19; **Eccl.** 10:8,11; **Isa.** 14:29; 27:1; 65:25; **Jer.** 8:17; 46:22; **Amos** 5:19; 9:3; **Mic.** 7:17.

5176. A. נָחָשׁ *nāḥāš* **masc. proper noun**
(Nahash: king of Ammon)
1 Sam. 11:1,2; 12:12; **2 Sam.** 10:2; 17:27; **1 Chr.** 19:1,2.
B. נָחָשׁ *nāḥāš* **masc. proper noun**
(Nahash: father of Abigail)
2 Sam. 17:25.

5177. נַחְשׁוֹן *naḥšôn* **masc. proper noun**
(Nahshon)
Ex. 6:23; **Num.** 1:7; 2:3; 7:12,17; 10:14; **Ruth** 4:20; **1 Chr.** 2:10,11.

5178. I. נחשׁת *n^e^ḥōšeṯ* **masc. noun**
(copper, bronze, wealth)
Gen. 4:22; **Ex.** 25:3; 26:11,37; 27:2–4, 6,10,11,17–19; 30:18; 31:4; 35:5,16, 24,32; 36:18,38; 38:2–6,8,10,11,17,19, 20,29,30; 39:39; **Lev.** 6:28(21); **Num.** 16:39(17:4); 21:9; 31:22; **Deut.** 8:9; 28:23; 33:25; **Josh.** 6:19,24; 22:8; **Judg.** 16:21; **1 Sam.** 17:5,6,38; **2 Sam.** 3:34; 8:8,10; 21:16; **1 Kgs.** 4:13; 7:14–16,27, 30,38,45,47; 8:64; 14:27; **2 Kgs.** 16:14, 15,17; 18:4; 25:7,13,14,16,17; **1 Chr.** 15:19; 18:8,10; 22:3,14,16; 29:2,7; **2 Chr.** 1:5,6; 2:7(6),14(13); 4:1,9,16,18; 6:13; 7:7; 12:10; 24:12; 33:11; 36:6; **Ezra** 8:27; **Ps.** 107:16; **Isa.** 60:17; **Jer.** 1:18; 6:28; 15:12,20; 39:7; 52:11,17,18,20,22; **Lam.** 3:7; **Ezek.** 1:7; 9:2; 16:36(KJV, NASB, see II); 22:18,20; 24:11; 27:13; 40:3; **Dan.** 10:6; **Zech.** 6:1.
II. נְחֹשֶׁת *n^e^ḥōšeṯ* **fem. noun**
(lewdness, lust)
Ezek. 16:36(NIV, see I).

5179. נְחֻשְׁתָּא *n^e^ḥuštā'* **fem. proper noun**
(Nehushta)
2 Kgs. 24:8.

5180. נְחֻשְׁתָּן *n^e^ḥuštān* **proper noun**
(Nehushtan)
2 Kgs. 18:4.

5181. נָחַת *nāḥaṯ* **verb**
(to bend, to bring down, to descend)
2 Sam. 22:35; **Job** 21:13; **Ps.** 18:34(35); 38:2(3); 65:10(11); **Prov.** 17:10; **Jer.** 21:13; **Joel** 3:11(4:11).

5182. נְחֵת *n^eḥēṯ* **Aram. verb**
(to bring down, to descend; corr. to Hebr. 5181)
Ezra 5:15; 6:1,5; **Dan.** 4:13(10),23(20); 5:20.

5183. I. נַחַת *naḥaṯ* **masc. noun**
(rest, calmness)
Job 17:16; 36:16; **Prov.** 29:9; **Eccl.** 4:6; 6:5; 9:17; **Isa.** 30:15.
II. נַחַת *naḥaṯ* **masc. noun**
(descent)
Isa. 30:30.

5184. A. נַחַת *naḥaṯ* **masc. proper noun**
(Nahath: son of Reuel)
Gen. 36:13,17; **1 Chr.** 1:37.
B. נַחַת *naḥaṯ* **masc. proper noun**
(Nahath: grandson of Elkanah)
1 Chr. 6:26(11).
C. נַחַת *naḥaṯ* **masc. proper noun**
(Nahath: a Levite)
2 Chr. 31:13.

5185. נָחֵת *nāḥēṯ* **adj.**
(coming down, going down)
2 Kgs. 6:9.

5186. נָטָה *nāṭāh* **verb**
(to stretch out, to extend, to pay attention)
Gen. 12:8; 24:14; 26:25; 33:19; 35:21; 38:1,16; 39:21; 49:15; **Ex.** 6:6; 7:5,19; 8:5(1),6(2),16(12),17(13); 9:22,23; 10:12,13,21,22; 14:16,21,26,27; 15:12; 23:2,6; 33:7; **Num.** 20:17,21; 21:15,22; 22:23,26,33; 24:6; **Deut.** 4:34; 5:15; 7:19; 9:29; 11:2; 16:19; 24:17; 26:8; 27:19; **Josh.** 8:18,19,26; 24:23; **Judg.** 4:11; 9:3; 16:30; 19:8; **1 Sam.** 8:3; 14:7; **2 Sam.** 2:19,21; 3:27; 6:10,17; 16:22; 19:14(15); 21:10; 22:10; **1 Kgs.** 2:28; 8:42,58; 11:2–4,9; **2 Kgs.** 17:36; 19:16; 20:10; 21:13; **1 Chr.** 13:13; 15:1; 16:1; 21:10,16; **2 Chr.** 1:4; 6:32; **Ezra** 7:28; 9:9; **Job** 9:8; 15:25,29; 23:11; 24:4; 26:7; 31:7; 36:18; 38:5; **Ps.** 17:6,11; 18:9(10); 21:11(12); 27:9; 31:2(3); 40:1(2); 44:18(19); 45:10(11); 49:4(5); 62:3(4); 71:2; 73:2; 78:1; 86:1; 88:2(3); 102:2(3), 11(12); 104:2; 109:23; 116:2; 119:36,51, 112,157; 125:5; 136:12; 141:4; 144:5; **Prov.** 1:24; 2:2; 4:5,20,27; 5:1,13; 7:21; 17:23; 18:5; 21:1; 22:17; **Isa.** 3:16; 5:25; 8:8(KJV, NASB, *muṭṭāh* [4298]); 9:12(11), 17(16),21(20); 10:2,4; 14:26,27; 23:11; 29:21; 30:11; 31:3; 34:11; 37:17; 40:22; 42:5; 44:13,20,24; 45:12; 51:13; 54:2; 55:3; 66:12; **Jer.** 5:25; 6:4,12; 7:24,26; 10:12,20; 11:8; 14:8; 15:6; 17:23; 21:5; 25:4; 27:5; 32:17,21; 34:14; 35:15; 43:10; 44:5; 51:15,25; **Lam.** 2:8; 3:35; **Ezek.** 1:22; 6:14; 14:9,13; 16:27; 20:33,34; 25:7,13,16; 30:25; 35:3; **Dan.** 9:18; **Hos.** 11:4; **Amos** 2:7,8; 5:12; **Zeph.** 1:4; 2:13; **Zech.** 1:16; 12:1; **Mal.** 3:5.

5187. נְטִיל *naṭiyl* **adj.**
(to weigh out, trade in something)
Zeph. 1:11.

5188. נְטִיפָה *n^eṭiypāh*, נְטִפָה *n^eṭipāh* **fem. noun**
(pendant, earring)
Judg. 8:26; **Isa.** 3:19.

5189. נְטִישׁוֹת *n^eṭiyšôṯ* **fem. pl. noun**
(branches, tendrils)
Isa. 18:5; **Jer.** 5:10; 48:32.

5190. נָטַל *nāṭal* **verb**
(to lift up, to carry, to offer)
2 Sam. 24:12; **Isa.** 40:15; 63:9; **Lam.** 3:28.

5191. נְטַל *n^{e}ṭal* **Aram. verb**
(to lift up, to raise; corr. to Hebr. 5190)
Dan. 4:34(31); 7:4.

5192. נֵטֶל *nēṭel* **masc. noun**
(weight, burden)
Prov. 27:3.

5193. נָטַע *nāṭa'* **verb**
(to plant, to establish)
Gen. 2:8; 9:20; 21:33; **Ex.** 15:17; **Lev.** 19:23; **Num.** 24:6; **Deut.** 6:11; 16:21; 20:6; 28:30,39; **Josh.** 24:13; **2 Sam.** 7:10; **2 Kgs.** 19:29; **1 Chr.** 17:9; **Ps.** 44:2(3); 80:8(9),15(16); 94:9; 104:16; 107:37; **Prov.** 31:16; **Eccl.** 2:4,5; 3:2; 12:11; **Isa.** 5:2; 17:10; 37:30; 40:24; 44:14; 51:16; 65:21,22; **Jer.** 1:10; 2:21; 11:17; 12:2; 18:9; 24:6; 29:5,28; 31:5,28; 32:41; 35:7; 42:10; 45:4; **Ezek.** 28:26; 36:36; **Dan.** 11:45; **Amos** 5:11; 9:14,15; **Zeph.** 1:13.

5194. נֶטַע *neṭa'* **masc. noun**
(a plant)
1 Chr. 4:23(NASB, NIV, *n^{e}ṭā'iym* [5196]); **Job** 14:9; **Isa.** 5:7; 17:10,11.

5195. נָטִיעַ *nāṭiya'* **masc. noun**
(a plant)
Ps. 144:12.

5196. נְטָעִים *n^{e}ṭā'iym* **proper noun**
(Netaim)
1 Chr. 4:23(KJV, *neṭa'* [5194]).

5197. נָטַף *nāṭap̱* **verb**
(to drip, to drop, to proclaim)
Judg. 5:4; **Job** 29:22; **Ps.** 68:8(9); **Prov.** 5:3; **Song** 4:11; 5:5,13; **Ezek.** 20:46 (21:2); 21:2(7); **Joel** 3:18(4:18); **Amos** 7:16; 9:13; **Mic.** 2:6,11.

5198. I. נָטָף *nāṭāp̱* **masc. noun**
(drops of stacte, resin)
Ex. 30:34.

II. נֶטֶף *neṭep̱* **masc. noun**
(a drop)
Job 36:27.

5199. נְטֹפָה *n^{e}ṭōp̱āh* **proper noun**
(Netophah)
Ezra 2:22; **Neh.** 7:26.

5200. נְטוֹפָתִי *n^{e}ṭôp̱āṯiy* **masc. proper noun**
(Netophathite)
2 Sam. 23:28,29; **2 Kgs.** 25:23; **1 Chr.** 2:54; 9:16; 11:30; 27:13,15; **Neh.** 12:28; **Jer.** 40:8.

5201. נָטַר *nāṭar* **verb**
(to keep, to take care of, to be angry, to maintain a grudge)
Lev. 19:18; **Ps.** 103:9; **Song** 1:6; 8:11,12; **Jer.** 3:5,12; **Nah.** 1:2.

5202. נְטַר *n^{e}ṭar* **Aram. verb**
(to keep; corr. to Hebr. 5201)
Dan. 7:28.

5203. נָטַשׁ *nāṭaš* **verb**
(to abandon, to forsake, to leave, to permit)
Gen. 31:28; **Ex.** 23:11; **Num.** 11:31; **Deut.** 32:15; **Judg.** 6:13; 15:9; **1 Sam.** 4:2; 10:2; 12:22; 17:20,22,28; 30:16; **2 Sam.** 5:18,22; **1 Kgs.** 8:57; **2 Kgs.** 21:14; **Neh.** 10:31(32); **Ps.** 27:9; 78:60; 94:14; **Prov.** 1:8; 6:20; 17:14; **Isa.** 2:6; 16:8; 21:15; 32:14; 33:23; **Jer.** 7:29; 12:7; 15:6; 23:33,39; **Ezek.** 29:5; 31:12; 32:4; **Hos.** 12:14(15); **Amos** 5:2.

5204. נִי *niy* **masc. noun**
(wailing)
Ezek. 27:32.

5205. I. נִיד *niyḏ* **masc. noun**
(comfort, solace)
Job 16:5(KJV, see II).
II. נִיד *niyḏ* **masc. noun**
(moving)
Job 16:5(NASB, NIV, see I).

5206. I. נִידָה *niyḏāh* **fem. noun**
(something unclean)
Lam. 1:8(KJV, see II).
II. נִידָה *niyḏāh* **fem. noun**
(something removed)
Lam. 1:8(NASB, NIV, see I).

5207. נִיחוֹחַ *niyḥôaḥ*, נִיחֹחַ *niyḥōaḥ* **masc. noun**
(something soothing, pleasing)
Gen. 8:21; **Ex.** 29:18,25,41; **Lev.** 1:9, 13,17; 2:2,9,12; 3:5,16; 4:31; 6:15(8), 21(14); 8:21,28; 17:6; 23:13,18; 26:31; **Num.** 15:3,7,10,13,14,24; 18:17; 28:2, 6,8,13,24,27; 29:2,6,8,13,36; **Ezek.** 6:13; 16:19; 20:28,41.

5208. נִיחוֹחַ *niyḥôaḥ*, נִיחֹחַ *niyḥōaḥ* **Aram. masc. noun**
(something fragrant, soothing, pleasing; corr. to Hebr. 5207)
Ezra 6:10; **Dan.** 2:46.

5209. נִין *niyn* **masc. noun**
(offspring, son)
Gen. 21:23; **Job** 18:19; **Isa.** 14:22.

5210. נִינְוֵה *niyn*ᵉ*wēh* **proper noun**
(Ninevah)
Gen. 10:11,12; **2 Kgs.** 19:36; **Isa.** 37:37; **Jon.** 1:2; 3:2–7; 4:11; **Nah.** 1:1; 2:8(9); 3:7; **Zeph.** 2:13.

5211. נִיס *niys* **masc. noun**
(one who flees)
Jer. 48:44(NASB, NIV, [Qᵉ] *nûs* [5127]).

5212. נִיסָן *niysān* **proper noun**
(the month Nisan)
Neh. 2:1; **Esth.** 3:7.

5213. נִיצוֹץ *niyṣôṣ* **masc. noun**
(spark)
Isa. 1:31.

5214. נִיר *niyr* **verb**
(to break up [of ground])
Jer. 4:3; **Hos.** 10:12.

5215. נִיר *niyr* **masc. noun**
(fallow, untilled ground)
Prov. 13:23; 21:4(NASB, NIV, *niyr* [5216,I]); **Jer.** 4:3; **Hos.** 10:12.

5216. I. נִיר *niyr* **masc. noun**
(lamp)
1 Kgs. 11:36; 15:4; **2 Kgs.** 8:19; **2 Chr.** 21:7; **Prov.** 21:4(KJV, *niyr* [5215]).
II. נֵר *nēr*, נֵיר *neyr* **masc. noun**
(lamp)
Ex. 25:37; 27:20; 30:7,8; 35:14; 37:23; 39:37; 40:4,25; **Lev.** 24:2,4; **Num.** 4:9; 8:2,3; **1 Sam.** 3:3; **2 Sam.** 21:17; 22:29; **1 Kgs.** 7:49; **1 Chr.** 28:15; **2 Chr.** 4:20,21; 13:11; 29:7; **Job** 18:6; 21:17; 29:3; **Ps.** 18:28(29); 119:105; 132:17; **Prov.** 6:23; 13:9; 20:20,27; 24:20; 31:18; **Jer.** 25:10; **Zeph.** 1:12; **Zech.** 4:2.

5217. נָכָא *nāḵā'* **verb**
(to drive out)
Job 30:8.

5218. I. נָכֵא *nāḵē'* **adj.**
(broken, beaten, crushed)
Prov. 15:13; 17:22; 18:14.
II. נָכָא *nāḵā'* **adj.**
(stricken, grieved, beaten)
Isa. 16:7.

5219. נְכֹאת *n*ᵉ*ḵō't* **fem. noun**
(spice, aromatic gum)
Gen. 37:25; 43:11.

5220. נֶכֶד *neḵeḏ* **masc. noun**
(descendants)
Gen. 21:23; **Job** 18:19; **Isa.** 14:22.

5221. נָכָה *nāḵāh* **verb**
(to strike, to attack, to kill, to wound)
Gen. 4:15; 8:21; 14:5,7,15,17; 19:11; 32:8(9),11(12); 34:30; 36:35; 37:21; **Ex.** 2:11–13; 3:20; 5:14,16; 7:17,20,25; 8:16(12),17(13); 9:15,25,31,32; 12:12, 13,29; 17:5,6; 21:12,15,18–20,26; 22:2(1);

Lev. 24:17,18,21; 26:24; **Num.** 3:13; 8:17; 11:33; 14:12,45; 20:11; 21:24,35; 22:6,23,25,27,28,32; 25:14,15,17,18; 32:4; 33:4; 35:11,15–18,21,24,30; **Deut.** 1:4; 2:33; 3:3; 4:46; 7:2; 13:15(16); 19:4, 6,11; 20:13; 21:1; 25:2,3,11; 27:24,25; 28:22,27,28,35; 29:7(6); **Josh.** 7:3,5; 8:21,22,24; 9:18; 10:4,10,20,26,28,30, 32,33,35,37,39–41; 11:8,10–12,14,17; 12:1,6,7; 13:12,21; 15:16; 19:47; 20:3, 5,9; **Judg.** 1:4,5,8,10,12,17,25; 3:13, 29,31; 6:16; 7:13; 8:11; 9:43,44; 11:21,33; 12:4; 14:19; 15:8,15,16; 18:27; 20:31,37, 39,45,48; 21:10; **1 Sam.** 2:14; 4:2,8; 5:6, 9,12; 6:19; 7:11; 11:11; 13:3,4; 14:14, 31,48; 15:3,7; 17:9,25–27,35,36,46,49, 50,57; 18:6,7,11,27; 19:5,8,10; 20:33; 21:9(10),11(12); 22:19; 23:2,5; 24:5(6); 26:8; 27:9; 29:5; 30:1,17; 31:2; **2 Sam.** 1:1,15; 2:22,23,31; 3:27; 4:6,7; 5:8,20, 24,25; 6:7; 8:1–3,5,9,10,13; 10:18; 11:15,21; 12:9; 13:28,30; 14:6,7; 15:14; 17:2; 18:11,15; 20:10; 21:2,12,16–19,21; 23:10,12,20,21; 24:10,17; **1 Kgs.** 11:15; 14:15; 15:20,27,29; 16:7,10,11,16; 20:20, 21,29,35–37; 22:24,34; **2 Kgs.** 2:8,14; 3:19,23–25; 6:18,21,22; 8:21,28,29; 9:7, 15,24,27; 10:9,11,17,25,32; 11:12; 12:20(21),21(22); 13:17–19,25; 14:5–7, 10; 15:10,14,16,25,30; 18:8; 19:35,37; 21:24; 25:21,25; **1 Chr.** 1:46; 4:41,43; 10:2; 11:6,14,22,23; 13:10; 14:11,15,16; 18:1–3,5,9,10,12; 20:1,4,5,7; 21:7; **2 Chr.** 13:17; 14:14(13),15(14); 16:4; 18:23,33; 21:9; 22:5,6; 25:3,11,13,14, 16,19; 28:5,17,23; 33:25; **Neh.** 13:25; **Esth.** 9:5; **Job** 1:15,17; 2:7; 16:10; **Ps.** 3:7(8); 60:[title](2); 69:26(27); 78:20, 51,66; 102:4(5); 105:33,36; 121:6; 135:8,10; 136:10,17; **Prov.** 17:10,26; 19:25; 23:13,14,35; **Song** 5:7; **Isa.** 1:5; 5:25; 9:13(12); 10:20,24; 11:4,15; 14:6,29; 27:7; 30:31; 37:36,38; 49:10; 50:6; 53:4; 57:17; 58:4; 60:10; 66:3; **Jer.** 2:30; 5:3,6; 14:19; 18:18,21; 20:2,4; 21:6,7; 26:23; 29:21; 30:14; 33:5; 37:10,15; 40:14,15; 41:2,3,9,16,18; 43:11; 46:2,13; 47:1; 49:28; 52:27; **Lam.** 3:30; **Ezek.** 5:2; 6:11; 7:9; 9:5,7,8; 21:14(19),17(22); 22:13; 32:15; 33:21; 39:3; 40:1; **Dan.** 8:7; **Hos.** 6:1; 9:16; 14:5(6); **Amos** 3:15; 4:9; 6:11; 9:1; **Jon.** 4:7,8; **Mic.** 5:1(4:14); 6:13; **Hag.** 2:17; **Zech.** 9:4; 10:11; 12:4; 13:6,7; **Mal.** 4:6(3:24).

5222. נֵכֶה *nē<u>k</u>eh* **adj.**
(attacking, smiting)
Ps. 35:15.

5223. נָכֶה *nā<u>k</u>eh* **adj.**
(crippled, smitten)
2 Sam. 4:4; 9:3; **Isa.** 66:2.

5224. נְכוֹ *n^e<u>k</u>ô* **masc. proper noun**
(Necho)
2 Chr. 35:20,22; 36:4.

5225. נָכוֹן *nā<u>k</u>ôn* **masc. proper noun**
(Nacon)
2 Sam. 6:6.

5226. נֵכַח *nē<u>k</u>aḥ* **adv.**
(before, against, opposite of; form of *nōkaḥ* [5227])
Ex. 14:2; **Ezek.** 46:9.

5227. נֹכַח *nō<u>k</u>aḥ* **adv.**
(before, directly; with prep. opposite, against, in front of)
Gen. 25:21; 30:38; **Ex.** 14:2(see *nē<u>k</u>aḥ* [5226]); 26:35; 40:24; **Num.** 19:4; **Josh.** 15:7; 18:17; **Judg.** 18:6; 19:10; 20:43; **1 Kgs.** 20:29; 22:35; **2 Chr.** 18:34; **Esth.** 5:1; **Prov.** 4:25; 5:21; **Jer.** 17:16; **Lam.** 2:19; **Ezek.** 14:3,4,7; 46:9(see *ne<u>k</u>aḥ* [5226]); 47:20.

5228. נָכֹחַ *na<u>k</u>ōaḥ* **adj.**
(right, upright)
2 Sam. 15:3; **Prov.** 8:9; 24:26; **Isa.** 26:10(KJV, *n^e<u>k</u>ōḥāh* [5229]); 30:10

(KJV, *n^{e}ḵōḥāh* [5229]); 57:2; 59:14 (KJV, *n^{e}ḵōḥāh* [5229]); **Amos** 3:10 (KJV, *n^{e}ḵōḥāh* [5229]).

5229. נְכֹחָה *n^{e}ḵōḥāh* **adj.**
(right, upright; NASB, NIV, *naḵōaḥ* [5228])
Isa. 26:10; 30:10; 59:14; **Amos** 3:10.

5230. נָכַל *nāḵal* **verb**
(to be deceitful, to cheat)
Gen. 37:18; **Num.** 25:18; **Ps.** 105:25; **Mal.** 1:14.

5231. נֵכֶל *nēḵel* **masc. noun**
(tricks, deceitfulness)
Num. 25:18.

5232. נְכַס *n^{e}ḵas* **Aram. masc. noun**
(goods, property; corr. to Hebr. 5233)
Ezra 6:8; 7:26.

5233. נֶכֶס *neḵes* **masc. noun**
(riches, wealth)
Josh. 22:8; **2 Chr.** 1:11,12; **Eccl.** 5:19(18); 6:2.

5234. I. נָכַר *nāḵar* **verb**
(to know, to recognize)
Gen. 27:23; 31:32; 37:32,33; 38:25,26; 42:8; **Deut.** 1:17; 16:19; 21:17; 33:9; **Judg.** 18:3; **Ruth** 2:10,19; 3:14; **1 Sam.** 26:17; **2 Sam.** 3:36; **1 Kgs.** 18:7; 20:41; **Ezra** 3:13; **Neh.** 6:12; 13:24; **Job** 2:12; 4:16; 7:10; 21:29; 24:13,17; 34:19,25; **Ps.** 103:16; 142:4(5); **Prov.** 20:11; 24:23; 28:21; **Isa.** 61:9; 63:16; **Jer.** 24:5; **Lam.** 4:8; **Dan.** 11:39.
II. נָכַר *nāḵar* **verb**
(to disguise, to make foreign, to misconstrue)
Gen. 42:7; **Deut.** 32:27; **1 Sam.** 23:7; **1 Kgs.** 14:5,6; **Prov.** 26:24; **Jer.** 19:4.

5235. נֶכֶר *neḵer,* נֹכֶר *nōḵer* **masc. noun**
(disaster)
Job 31:3; **Obad.** 1:12.

5236. נֵכָר *nēḵār* **masc. noun**
(foreigner, alien)
Gen. 17:12,27; 35:2,4; **Ex.** 12:43; **Lev.** 22:25; **Deut.** 31:16; 32:12; **Josh.** 24:20,23; **Judg.** 10:16; **1 Sam.** 7:3; **2 Sam.** 22:45,46; **2 Chr.** 14:3(2); 33:15; **Neh.** 9:2; 13:30; **Ps.** 18:44(45),45(46); 81:9(10); 137:4; 144:7,11; **Isa.** 56:3,6; 60:10; 61:5; 62:8; **Jer.** 5:19; 8:19; **Ezek.** 44:7,9; **Dan.** 11:39; **Mal.** 2:11.

5237. נָכְרִי *noḵriy* **adj.**
(foreign, alien, adulterous)
Gen. 31:15; **Ex.** 2:22; 18:3; 21:8; **Deut.** 14:21; 15:3; 17:15; 23:20(21); 29:22(21); **Judg.** 19:12; **Ruth** 2:10; **2 Sam.** 15:19; **1 Kgs.** 8:41,43; 11:1,8; **2 Chr.** 6:32,33; **Ezra** 10:2,10,11,14,17,18,44; **Neh.** 13:26,27; **Job** 19:15; **Ps.** 69:8(9); **Prov.** 2:16; 5:10,20; 6:24; 7:5; 20:16; 23:27; 27:2,13; **Eccl.** 6:2; **Isa.** 2:6; 28:21; **Jer.** 2:21; **Lam.** 5:2; **Obad.** 1:11; **Zeph.** 1:8.

5238. נְכֹת *n^{e}ḵōṯ* **masc. noun**
(treasures, goods)
2 Kgs. 20:13; **Isa.** 39:2.

5239. נָלָה *nālāh* **verb**
(to cease, to stop, to make an end)
Isa. 33:1.

5240. נְמִבְזָה *n^{e}miḇzāh* **adj.**
(vile)
1 Sam. 15:9(NASB, NIV, *bāzāh* [959]).

5241. נְמוּאֵל *n^{e}mû'ēl* **masc. proper noun**
(Nemuel)
Num. 26:9,12; **1 Chr.** 4:24.

5242. נְמוּאֵלִי *n^{e}mû'ēliy* **masc. proper noun**
(Nemuelite)
Num. 26:12.

5243. נָמַל *nāmal* **verb**
(to cut down, to cut off, to circumcise)
Gen. 17:11(NASB, NIV, *mûl* [4135]; **Job** 14:2(NASB, NIV, *mālal* [4448,II]); 18:16(NASB, *mālal* [4448,III]; NIV, *mālal* [4448,II]); 24:24(NASB, NIV, *mālal* [4448,III]); **Ps.** 37:2(NASB, NIV, *mālal* [4448,II]).

5244. נְמָלָה *n^emālāh* **fem. noun**
(ant)
Prov. 6:6; 30:25.

5245. נְמַר *n^emar* **Aram. masc. noun**
(leopard; corr. to Hebr. 5246)
Dan. 7:6.

5246. נָמֵר *nāmēr* **masc. noun**
(leopard)
Song 4:8; **Isa.** 11:6; **Jer.** 5:6; 13:23; **Hos.** 13:7; **Hab.** 1:8.

5247. נִמְרָה *nimrāh* **proper noun**
(Nimrah)
Num. 32:3.

5248. A. נִמְרֹד *nimrōḏ* **masc. proper noun**
(Nimrod: son of Cush)
Gen. 10:8,9; **1 Chr.** 1:10.
B. נִמְרֹד *nimrōḏ* **masc. proper noun**
(Nimrod: another name for Assyria)
Mic. 5:6(5).

5249. נִמְרִים *nimriym* **proper noun**
(Nimrim)
Isa. 15:6; **Jer.** 48:34.

5250. נִמְשִׁי *nimšiy* **masc. proper noun**
(Nimshi)
1 Kgs. 19:16; **2 Kgs.** 9:2,14,20; **2 Chr.** 22:7.

5251. נֵס *nēs* **masc. noun**
(banner, standard)
Ex. 17:15(KJV, see *y^ehōwāh nissiy* [3070]); **Num.** 21:8,9; 26:10; **Ps.** 60:4(6); **Isa.** 5:26; 11:10,12; 13:2; 18:3; 30:17; 31:9; 33:23; 49:22; 62:10; **Jer.** 4:6,21; 50:2; 51:12,27; **Ezek.** 27:7.

5252. נְסִבָּה *n^esibbāh* **fem. noun**
(turn of events, cause)
2 Chr. 10:15.

5253. נָסַג *nāsag* **verb**
(to move away, to be turned; NASB, NIV, *sûg* [5472])
Deut. 19:14; 27:17; **Prov.** 22:28; 23:10; **Isa.** 59:13,14; **Hos.** 5:10; **Mic.** 2:6; 6:14.

5254. נָסָה *nāsāh* **verb**
(to test, to put to the test)
Gen. 22:1; **Ex.** 15:25; 16:4; 17:2,7; 20:20; **Num.** 14:22; **Deut.** 4:34; 6:16; 8:2,16; 13:3(4); 28:56; 33:8; **Judg.** 2:22; 3:1,4; 6:39; **1 Sam.** 17:39; **1 Kgs.** 10:1; **2 Chr.** 9:1; 32:31; **Job** 4:2; **Ps.** 26:2; 78:18,41,56; 95:9; 106:14; **Eccl.** 2:1; 7:23; **Isa.** 7:12; **Dan.** 1:12,14.

5255. נָסַח *nāsah* **verb**
(to be uprooted, to turn away; to tear down)
Deut. 28:63; **Ps.** 52:5(7); **Prov.** 2:22; 15:25.

5256. נְסַח *n^esaḥ* **Aram. verb**
(to pull down; corr. to Hebr. 5255)
Ezra 6:11.

5257. I. נָסִיךְ *nāsiyḵ* **masc. noun**
(libation, molten image)
Deut. 32:38; **Dan.** 11:8(KJV, see II).
II. נָסִיךְ *nāsiyḵ* **masc. noun**
(prince, leader)
Josh. 13:21; **Ps.** 83:11(12); **Ezek.** 32:30; **Dan.** 11:8(NASB, NIV, see I); **Mic.** 5:5(4).

5258. I. נָסַךְ *nāsaḵ* **verb**
(to pour out; to cast metals)

Gen. 35:14; **Ex.** 25:29; 30:9; 37:16; **Num.** 28:7; **2 Sam.** 23:16; **2 Kgs.** 16:13; **1 Chr.** 11:18; **Ps.** 16:4; **Isa.** 29:10; 30:1 (NASB, *nāsak̲* [5259]); 40:19; 44:10; **Jer.** 7:18; 19:13; 32:29; 44:17–19,25; **Ezek.** 20:28; **Hos.** 9:4.
II. נָסַךְ *nāsak̲* **verb**
(to set, to install, to appoint)
Ps. 2:6; **Prov.** 8:23.

5259. נָסַךְ *nāsak̲* **verb**
(to stretch out, to cover)
Isa. 25:7; 30:1(KJV, NIV, *nāsak̲* [5258,I]).

5260. נְסַךְ n^e*sak̲* **Aram. verb**
(to pour out, to offer a liquid sacrifice; corr. to Hebr. 5258,I)
Dan. 2:46.

5261. נְסַךְ n^e*sak̲* **Aram. masc. noun**
(drink offering, liquid sacrifice; corr. to Hebr. 5262)
Ezra 7:17.

5262. נֶסֶךְ *nēsek̲*, נֵסֶךְ *nēsek̲* **masc. noun**
(drink offering, liquid sacrifice)
Gen. 35:14; **Ex.** 29:40,41; 30:9; **Lev.** 23:13,18,37; **Num.** 4:7; 6:15,17; 15:5, 7,10,24; 28:7–10,14,15,24,31; 29:6,11, 16,18,19,21,22,24,25,27,28,30,31,33,34, 37–39; **2 Kgs.** 16:13,15; **1 Chr.** 29:21; **2 Chr.** 29:35; **Ps.** 16:4; **Isa.** 41:29; 48:5; 57:6; **Jer.** 7:18; 10:14; 19:13; 32:29; 44:17–19,25; 51:17; **Ezek.** 20:28; 45:17; **Joel** 1:9,13; 2:14.

5263. I. נָסַס *nāsas* **verb**
(to be sick)
Isa. 10:18(KJV, see II).
II. נָסַס *nāsas* **verb**
(to raise as a beacon)
Isa. 10:18(NASB, NIV, see I).

5264. I. נָסַס *nāsas* **verb**
(to sparkle)
Zech. 9:16(KJV, see II).
II. נָסַס *nāsas* **verb**
(to raise as a beacon)
Zech. 9:16(NASB, NIV, see I).

5265. נָסַע *nāsaʿ* **verb**
(to set out, to travel)
Gen. 11:2; 12:9; 13:11; 20:1; 33:12,17; 35:5,16,21; 37:17; 46:1; **Ex.** 12:37; 13:20; 14:10,15,19; 15:22; 16:1; 17:1; 19:2; 40:36,37; **Num.** 1:51; 2:9,16,17, 24,31,34; 4:5,15; 9:17–23; 10:5,6,12–14, 17,18,21,22,25,28,29,33–35; 11:31,35; 12:15,16; 14:25; 20:22; 21:4,10–13; 22:1; 33:3,5–37,41–48; **Deut.** 1:7,19,40; 2:1,24; 10:6,7; **Josh.** 3:1,3,14; 9:17; **Judg.** 16:3,14; 18:11; **1 Kgs.** 5:17(31); **2 Kgs.** 3:27; 4:4; 19:8,36; **Ezra** 8:31; **Job** 4:21; 19:10; **Ps.** 78:26,52; 80:8(9); **Eccl.** 10:9; **Isa.** 33:20; 37:8,37; 38:12; **Jer.** 4:7; 31:24; **Zech.** 10:2.

5266. נָסַק *nāsaq* **verb**
(to ascend)
Ps. 139:8(NASB, NIV, *sālaq* [5559,I]).

5267. נְסַק n^e*saq* **Aram. verb**
(to take up, to lift)
Dan. 3:22(NASB, NIV, s^e*lēq* [5559,II]); 6:23(24)(NASB, NIV, s^e*lēq* [5559,II]).

5268. נִסְרֹךְ *nisrōk̲* **masc. proper noun**
(Nisroch)
2 Kgs. 19:37; **Isa.** 37:38.

5269. נֵעָה *nēʿāh* **proper noun**
(Neah)
Josh. 19:13.

5270. נֹעָה *nōʿāh* **fem. proper noun**
(Noah: daughter of Zelophehad)
Num. 26:33; 27:1; 36:11; **Josh.** 17:3.

5271. I. נְעוּרִים n^e*ʿûriym* **masc. pl. noun**
(youth, childhood)

Gen. 8:21; 46:34; **Lev.** 22:13; **Num.** 30:3(4),16(17); **1 Sam.** 12:2; 17:33; **2 Sam.** 19:7(8); **1 Kgs.** 18:12; **Job** 13:26; 31:18; **Ps.** 25:7; 71:5,17; 103:5; 127:4; 129:1,2; 144:12; **Prov.** 2:17; 5:18; **Isa.** 47:12,15; 54:6; **Jer.** 2:2; 3:4,24,25; 22:21; 31:19; 48:11; **Lam.** 3:27; **Ezek.** 4:14; 16:22,43,60; 23:3,8,19,21; **Hos.** 2:15(17); **Joel** 1:8; **Zech.** 13:5; **Mal.** 2:14,15.
II. נְעוּרוֹת *n^e'ûrôṯ* **fem. pl. noun**
(youth, childhood)
Jer. 32:30.

5272. נְעִיאֵל *n^e'iy'ēl* **proper noun**
(Neiel)
Josh. 19:27.

5273. I. נָעִים *nā'iym* **adj.**
(pleasant, delightful)
2 Sam. 1:23; **Job** 36:11; **Ps.** 16:6,11; 133:1; 135:3; 147:1; **Prov.** 22:18; 23:8; 24:4; **Song** 1:16.
II. נָעִים *nā'iym* **adj.**
(sweet, sweet-sounding)
2 Sam. 23:1; **Ps.** 81:2(3).

5274. I. נָעַל *nā'al* **verb**
(to bolt, to bar, to lock)
Judg. 3:23,24; **2 Sam.** 13:17,18; **Song** 4:12.
II. נָעַל *nā'al* **verb**
(to shod, to furnish with footwear)
2 Chr. 28:15; **Ezek.** 16:10.

5275. נַעַל *na'al* **fem. noun**
(sandal, shoe)
Gen. 14:23; **Ex.** 3:5; 12:11; **Deut.** 25:9,10; 29:5(4); **Josh.** 5:15; 9:5,13; **Ruth** 4:7,8; **1 Kgs.** 2:5; **Ps.** 60:8(10); 108:9(10); **Song** 7:1(2); **Isa.** 5:27; 11:15; 20:2; **Ezek.** 24:17,23; **Amos** 2:6; 8:6.

5276. נָעֵם *nā'ēm* **verb**
(to be pleasant, to be sweet, to be beautiful)
Gen. 49:15; **2 Sam.** 1:26; **Ps.** 141:6; **Prov.** 2:10; 9:17; 24:25; **Song** 7:6(7); **Ezek.** 32:19.

5277. נַעַם *na'am* **masc. proper noun**
(Naam: son of Caleb)
1 Chr. 4:15.

5278. נֹעַם *nō'am* **masc. noun**
(pleasantness, beauty)
Ps. 27:4; 90:17; **Prov.** 3:17; 15:26; 16:24; **Zech.** 11:7,10.

5279. A. נַעֲמָה *na'^amāh* **fem. proper noun**
(Naamah: sister of Tubal-Cain)
Gen. 4:22.
B. נַעֲמָה *na'^amāh* **fem. proper noun**
(Naamah: mother of Rehoboam)
1 Kgs. 14:21,31; **2 Chr.** 12:13.
C. נַעֲמָה *na'^amāh* **fem. proper noun**
(Naamah: city in Judah)
Josh. 15:41.

5280. נַעֲמִי *na'^amiy* **masc. proper noun**
(Naamite: descendant of Naaman [5283,A])
Num. 26:40.

5281. נָעֳמִי *nā'^omiy* **fem. proper noun**
(Naomi)
Ruth 1:2,3,8,11,19–22; 2:1,2,6,20,22; 3:1; 4:3,5,9,14,16,17.

5282. נַעֲמָן *na'^amān* **masc. noun**
(pleasantness, delightfulness)
Isa. 17:10.

5283. A. נַעֲמָן *na'^amān* **masc. proper noun**
(Naaman: descendant of Benjamin)
Gen. 46:21; **Num.** 26:40; **1 Chr.** 8:4,7.

B. נַעֲמָן *naʿᵃmān* **masc. proper noun**
(Naaman: Syrian general)
2 Kgs. 5:1,2,6,9,11,17,20,21,23,27.

5284. נַעֲמָתִי *naʿᵃmāṯiy* **masc. proper noun**
(Naamathite; inhabitant of Naamah [site unknown])
Job 2:11; 11:1; 20:1; 42:9.

5285. נַעֲצוּץ *naʿᵃṣûṣ* **masc. noun**
(thornbush)
Isa. 7:19; 55:13.

5286. נָעַר *nāʿar* **verb**
(to growl, to yell)
Jer. 51:38.

5287. נָעַר *nāʿar* **verb**
(to shake out, to overthrow, to sweep)
Ex. 14:27; **Judg.** 16:20; **Neh.** 5:13; **Job** 38:13; **Ps.** 109:23; 136:15; **Isa.** 33:9,15; 52:2.

5288. נַעַר *naʿar* **masc. noun**
(boy, young man, servant)
Gen. 14:24; 18:7; 19:4; 21:12,17–20; 22:3,5,12,19; 25:27; 34:19; 37:2; 41:12; 43:8; 44:22,30–34; 48:16; **Ex.** 2:6; 10:9; 24:5; 33:11; **Num.** 11:27; 22:22; **Deut.** 28:50; **Josh.** 6:21,23; **Judg.** 7:10,11; 8:14,20; 9:54; 13:5,7,8,12,24; 16:26; 17:7,11,12; 18:3,15; 19:3,9,11,13,19; **Ruth** 2:5,6,9,15,21; **1 Sam.** 1:22,24, 25,27; 2:11,13,15,17,18,21,26; 3:1,8; 4:21; 9:3,5,7,8,10,22,27; 10:14; 14:1,6; 16:11,18; 17:33,42,55,58; 20:21,35–41; 21:2(3),4(5),5(6); 25:5,8,9,12,14,19, 25,27; 26:22; 30:13,17; **2 Sam.** 1:5,6, 13,15; 2:14,21; 4:12; 9:9; 12:16; 13:17, 28,29,32,34; 14:21; 16:1,2; 17:18; 18:5,12,15,29,32; 19:17(18); 20:11; **1 Kgs.** 3:7; 11:17,28; 14:3,17; 18:43; 19:3; 20:14,15,17,19; **2 Kgs.** 2:23; 4:12,19,22,24,25,29–32,35,38; 5:14,20,22,23; 6:15,17; 8:4; 9:4; 19:6; **1 Chr.** 12:28; 22:5; 29:1; **2 Chr.** 13:7; 34:3; **Neh.** 4:16(10),22(16),23(17); 5:10,15,16; 6:5; 13:19; **Esth.** 2:2; 3:13; 6:3,5; **Job** 1:15–17,19; 24:5; 29:5,8; **Ps.** 37:25; 119:9; 148:12; **Prov.** 1:4; 7:7; 20:11; 22:6,15; 23:13; 29:15; **Eccl.** 10:16; **Isa.** 3:4,5; 7:16; 8:4; 10:19; 11:6; 13:18; 20:4; 37:6; 40:30; 65:20; **Jer.** 1:6,7; 51:22; **Lam.** 2:21; 5:13; **Hos.** 11:1; **Zech.** 2:4(8); 11:16(KJV, *naʿar* [5289,I]; NASB, *naʿar* [5289,II]).

5289. I. נַעַר *naʿar* **masc. noun**
(young one)
Zech. 11:16(NASB, see II).
II. נַעַר *naʿar* **masc. noun**
(scattered)
Zech. 11:16(KJV, see I; NIV, *naʿar* [5288]).

5290. נֹעַר *nōʿar* **masc. noun**
(childhood, youth)
Job 33:25; 36:14; **Ps.** 88:15(16); **Prov.** 29:21.

5291. נַעֲרָה *naʿᵃrāh* **fem. noun**
(girl, young woman, maidservant)
Gen. 24:14,16,28,55,57,61; 34:3,12; **Ex.** 2:5; **Deut.** 22:15,16,19–21,23–29; **Judg.** 19:3–6,8,9; 21:12; **Ruth** 2:5,6,8, 22,23; 3:2; 4:12; **1 Sam.** 9:11; 25:42; **1 Kgs.** 1:2–4; **2 Kgs.** 5:2,4; **Esth.** 2:2–4, 7–9,12,13; 4:4,16; **Job** 41:5(40:29); **Prov.** 9:3; 27:27; 31:15; **Amos** 2:7.

5292. A. נַעֲרָה *naʿᵃrāh* **fem. proper noun**
(Naarah: wife of Ashur)
1 Chr. 4:5,6.
B. נַעֲרָתָה *naʿᵃrāṯāh* **fem. proper noun**
(Naarah: loc. on border of Ephraim)
Josh. 16:7.

5293. נַעֲרַי *naʿᵃray* **masc. proper noun**
(Naarai)
1 Chr. 11:37.

5294. A. נְעַרְיָה *n^eʿaryāh* **masc. proper noun**
(Neariah: descendant of David)
1 Chr. 3:22,23.
B. נְעַרְיָה *n^eʿaryāh* **masc. proper noun**
(Neariah: a Simeonite)
1 Chr. 4:42.

5295. נַעֲרָן *naʿ^{a}rān* **proper noun**
(Naaran)
1 Chr. 7:28.

5296. נְעֹרֶת *n^eʿōre<u>t</u>* **fem. noun**
(string, tow)
Judg. 16:9; **Isa.** 1:31.

5297. נֹף *nō<u>p</u>* **proper noun**
(Memphis, see also *mō<u>p</u>* [4644])
Isa. 19:13; **Jer.** 2:16; 44:1; 46:14,19; **Ezek.** 30:13,16.

5298. A. נֶפֶג *ne<u>p</u>eg* **masc. proper noun**
(Nepheg: a Levite)
Ex. 6:21.
B. נֶפֶג *ne<u>p</u>eg* **masc. proper noun**
(Nepheg: son of David)
2 Sam. 5:15; **1 Chr.** 3:7; 14:6.

5299. I. נָפָה *nāphāh* **fem. noun**
(winnow, sieve)
Isa. 30:28.
II. נָפָה *nāphāh* **fem. noun**
(height, elevation, region, border)
Josh. 11:2(NIV, see III); 12:23(NIV, see III); **1 Kgs.** 4:11(NIV, see III).
III. נָפוֹת *nāpô<u>t</u>* **proper noun**
(Naphoth; part of Naphoth Dor [5299,III] and [1756])
Josh. 11:2(NASB, KJV, see II); 12:23(NASB, KJV, see II); 17:11(see *napô<u>t</u>* [5316,III]; KJV, *ne<u>p</u>e<u>t</u>* [5316,I; NASB, *ne<u>p</u>e<u>t</u>* [5316,II]); **1 Kgs.** 4:11(NASB, KJV, see II).

5300. נְפוּשְׁסִים *n^e<u>p</u>ûš^{e}siym* **proper noun**
(Nephushesim, Nephussim)
Ezra 2:50(NASB, [K^e] *n^e<u>p</u>iyš^{e}siym* [5304]); **Neh.** 7:52(KJV, [Q^e] *n^e<u>p</u>iyš^{e}siym* [5304]).

5301. נָפַח *nā<u>p</u>aḥ* **verb**
(to blow, to breathe; to boil)
Gen. 2:7; **Job** 20:26; 31:39; 41:20(12); **Isa.** 54:16; **Jer.** 1:13; 15:9; **Ezek.** 22:20,21; 37:9; **Hag.** 1:9; **Mal.** 1:13.

5302. נֹפַח *nō<u>p</u>aḥ* **proper noun**
(Nophah)
Num. 21:30.

5303. I. נְפִילִים *n^e<u>p</u>iyliym* **masc. noun**
(giants)
Gen. 6:4(NASB, NIV, see II); **Num.** 13:33(NASB, NIV, see II).
II. נְפִילִים *n^e<u>p</u>iyliym* **masc. proper noun**
(Nephilim)
Gen. 6:4(KJV, see I); **Num.** 13:33(KJV, see I).

5304. נְפִישְׁסִים *n^e<u>p</u>iyš^{e}siym* **proper noun**
(Nephishesim, Nephussim)
Ezra 2:50(KJV, NIV, [Q^e] *n^e<u>p</u>ûš^{e}siym* [5300]); **Neh.** 7:52(NASB, NIV, [K^e] *n^e<u>p</u>ûš^{e}siym*[5300]).

5305. נָפִישׁ *nā<u>p</u>iyš* **masc. proper noun**
(Naphish)
Gen. 25:15; **1 Chr.** 1:31; 5:19.

5306. נֹפֶךְ *nō<u>p</u>e<u>k</u>* **masc. noun**
(precious stone, turquoise or emerald)
Ex. 28:18; 39:11; **Ezek.** 27:16; 28:13.

5307. נָפַל *nā<u>p</u>al* **verb**
(to fall, to collapse, to defect)
Gen. 2:21; 4:5,6; 14:10; 15:12; 17:3,17;

24:64; 25:18; 33:4; 43:18; 44:14; 45:14; 46:29; 49:17; 50:1,18; **Ex.** 15:16; 19:21; 21:18,27,33; 32:28; **Lev.** 9:24; 11:32,33, 35,37,38; 26:7,8,36; **Num.** 5:21,22,27; 6:12; 14:3,5,29,32,43; 16:4,22,45(17:10); 20:6; 24:4,16; 34:2; 35:23; **Deut.** 9:18,25; 21:1; 22:4,8; 25:2; **Josh.** 2:9; 5:14; 6:5,20; 7:6,10; 8:24,25; 11:7; 13:6; 17:5; 21:45(43); 23:4,14; **Judg.** 2:19; 3:25; 4:16,22; 5:27; 7:12,13; 8:10; 9:40; 12:6; 13:20; 15:18; 16:30; 18:1; 19:26,27; 20:44,46; **Ruth** 2:10; 3:18; **1 Sam.** 3:19; 4:10,18; 5:3,4; 11:7; 14:13,42,45; 17:32, 49,52; 18:25; 19:24; 20:41; 25:23,24; 26:12,20; 28:20; 29:3; 31:1,4,5,8; **2 Sam.** 1:2,4,10,12,19,25,27; 2:16,23; 3:29,34,38; 4:4; 9:6; 11:17; 14:4,11,22; 17:9,12; 19:18(19); 20:8,15; 21:9,22; 22:39; 24:14; **1 Kgs.** 1:52; 8:56; 18:7,38,39; 20:25,30; 22:20; **2 Kgs.** 1:2; 2:13,14; 3:19,25; 4:37; 5:21; 6:5,6; 7:4; 10:10; 14:10; 19:7; 25:11; **1 Chr.** 5:10,22; 10:1,4,5,8; 12:19,20; 20:8; 21:13,14,16; 24:31; 25:8; 26:13,14; **2 Chr.** 13:17; 14:13(12); 15:9; 18:19; 20:18,24; 25:19; 29:9; 32:21; **Ezra** 10:1; **Neh.** 6:16; 10:34(35); 11:1; **Esth.** 3:7; 6:10,13; 7:8; 8:3,17; 9:2,3,24; **Job** 1:15, 16,19,20; 4:13; 6:27; 12:3; 13:2,11; 14:18; 29:24; 31:22; 33:15; **Ps.** 5:10(11); 7:15(16); 10:10; 16:6; 18:38(39); 20:8(9); 22:18(19); 27:2; 35:8; 36:12(13); 37:14, 24; 45:5(6); 55:4(5); 57:6(7); 69:9(10); 73:18; 78:28,55,64; 82:7; 91:7; 105:38; 106:26,27; 118:13; 140:10(11); 141:10; 145:14; **Prov.** 1:14; 7:26; 11:5,14,28; 13:17; 17:20; 19:15; 22:14; 24:16,17; 26:27; 28:10,14,18; **Eccl.** 4:10; 9:12; 10:8; 11:3; **Isa.** 3:8,25; 8:15; 9:8(7), 10(9); 10:4,34; 13:15; 14:12; 16:9; 21:9; 22:25; 24:18,20; 26:18,19; 30:13,25; 31:3,8; 34:17; 37:7; 47:11; 54:15; **Jer.** 3:12; 6:15; 8:4,12; 9:22(21); 15:8; 19:7; 20:4; 21:9; 22:7; 23:12; 25:27,34; 36:7; 37:13,14,20; 38:19,26; 39:9,18; 42:2,9; 44:12; 46:6,12,16; 48:32,44; 49:21,26; 50:15,30,32; 51:4,8,44,47,49; 52:15; **Lam.** 1:7; 2:21; 5:16; **Ezek.** 1:28; 3:23; 5:12; 6:4,7,11,12; 8:1; 9:8; 11:5,10,13; 13:11,12,14; 17:21; 23:25; 24:6,21; 25:13; 27:27,34; 28:23; 29:5; 30:4–6,17,22,25; 31:12; 32:12,20,22–24,27; 33:27; 35:8; 38:20; 39:3–5,23; 43:3; 44:4; 45:1; 47:14,22; 48:29; **Dan.** 8:10,17; 9:18,20; 10:7; 11:12,19,26; **Hos.** 7:7,16; 10:8; 13:16(14:1); **Joel** 2:8; **Amos** 3:5,14; 5:2; 7:17; 8:14; 9:9,11; **Jon.** 1:7; **Mic.** 7:8; **Nah.** 3:12; **Zech.** 11:2.

5308. נְפַל *n^e^p̱al* **Aram. verb**
(to fall, to fall down; corr. to Hebr. 5307)
Ezra 7:20; **Dan.** 2:46; 3:5–7,10,11,15,23; 4:31(28); 7:20.

5309. נֵפֶל *nēp̱el,* נֶפֶל *nep̱el* **masc. noun**
(miscarriage, stillbirth)
Job 3:16; **Ps.** 58:8(9); **Eccl.** 6:3.

5310. I. נָפַץ *nāp̱aṣ* **verb**
(to shatter, to break, to smash)
Judg. 7:19; **1 Kgs.** 5:9(23)(KJV, see II); **Ps.** 2:9; 137:9; **Isa.** 11:12(KJV, see II); 27:9; **Jer.** 13:14; 22:28; 48:12; 51:20–23; **Dan.** 12:7(KJV, see II).

II. נָפַץ *nāp̱aṣ* **verb**
(to spread out, to disperse, to scatter)
Gen. 9:19; **1 Sam.** 13:11; **1 Kgs.** 5:9(23)(NASB, NIV, see I); **Isa.** 11:12 (NASB, NIV, see I); 33:3; **Dan.** 12:7 (NASB, NIV, see I).

5311. נֶפֶץ *nep̱eṣ* **masc. noun**
(cloudburst, driving storm)
Isa. 30:30.

5312. נְפַק *n^e^p̱aq* **Aram. verb**
(to go out, to take out)
Ezra 5:14; 6:5; **Dan.** 2:13,14; 3:26; 5:2,3,5; 7:10.

5313. נִפְקָה *nip̱qāh* **Aram. fem. noun**
(cost, expense)
Ezra 6:4,8.

5314. נָפַשׁ *nāp̱aš* **verb**
(to rest, to refresh oneself)
Ex. 23:12; 31:17; **2 Sam.** 16:14.

5315. נֶפֶשׁ *nep̱eš* **fem. noun**
(soul, life, being)
Gen. 1:20,21,24,30; 2:7,19; 9:4,5,10,12, 15,16; 12:5,13; 14:21; 17:14; 19:17, 19,20; 23:8; 27:4,19,25,31; 32:30(31); 34:3,8; 35:18; 36:6; 37:21; 42:21; 44:30; 46:15,18,22,25–27; 49:6; **Ex.** 1:5; 4:19; 12:4,15,16,19; 15:9; 16:16; 21:23,30; 23:9; 30:12,15,16; 31:14; **Lev.** 2:1; 4:2, 27; 5:1,2,4,15,17; 6:2(5:21); 7:18,20, 21,25,27; 11:10,43,44,46; 16:29,31; 17:10–12,14,15; 18:29; 19:8,28; 20:6,25; 21:1,11; 22:3,4,6,11; 23:27,29,30,32; 24:17,18; 26:11,15,16,30,43; 27:2; **Num.** 5:2,6; 6:6,11; 9:6,7,10,13; 11:6; 15:27,28, 30,31; 16:38(17:3); 19:11,13,18,20,22; 21:4,5; 23:10; 29:7; 30:2(3),4–13(5–14); 31:19,28,35,40,46,50; 35:11,15,30,31; **Deut.** 4:9,15,29; 6:5; 10:12,22; 11:13,18; 12:15,20,21,23; 13:3(4),6(7); 14:26; 18:6; 19:6,11,21; 21:14; 22:26; 23:24(25); 24:6,7,15; 26:16; 27:25; 28:65; 30:2,6,10; **Josh.** 2:13,14; 9:24; 10:28,30,32,35, 37,39; 11:11; 20:3,9; 22:5; 23:11,14; **Judg.** 5:18,21; 9:17; 10:16; 12:3; 16:16,30; 18:25; **Ruth** 4:15; **1 Sam.** 1:10,15,26; 2:16,33,35; 17:55; 18:1,3; 19:5,11; 20:1,3,4,17; 22:2,22,23; 23:15,20; 24:11(12); 25:26,29; 26:21,24; 28:9,21; 30:6; **2 Sam.** 1:9; 3:21; 4:8,9; 5:8; 11:11; 14:7,14,19; 16:11; 17:8; 18:13; 19:5(6); 23:17; **1 Kgs.** 1:12,29; 2:4,23; 3:11; 8:48; 11:37; 17:21,22; 19:2–4,10,14; 20:31,32,39,42; **2 Kgs.** 1:13,14; 2:2,4,6; 4:27,30; 7:7; 9:15; 10:24; 12:4(5); 23:3,25; **1 Chr.** 5:21; 11:19; 22:19; 28:9; **2 Chr.** 1:11; 6:38; 15:12; 34:31; **Esth.** 4:13; 7:3,7; 8:11; 9:16,31; **Job** 2:4,6; 3:20; 6:7,11; 7:11,15; 9:21; 10:1; 11:20; 12:10; 13:14; 14:22; 16:4; 18:4; 19:2; 21:25; 23:13; 24:12; 27:2,8; 30:16,25; 31:30,39; 32:2; 33:18, 20,22,28,30; 36:14; 41:21(13); **Ps.** 3:2(3); 6:3(4),4(5); 7:2(3),5(6); 10:3; 11:1,5; 13:2(3); 16:10; 17:9,13; 19:7(8); 22:20(21),29(30); 23:3; 24:4; 25:1, 13,20; 26:9; 27:12; 30:3(4); 31:7(8), 9(10),13(14); 33:19,20; 34:2(3),22(23); 35:3,4,7,9,12,13,17,25; 38:12(13); 40:14(15); 41:2(3),4(5); 42:1(2),2(3), 4–6(5–7),11(12); 43:5; 44:25(26); 49:8(9),15(16),18(19); 54:3(5),4(6); 55:18(19); 56:6(7),13(14); 57:1(2), 4(5),6(7); 59:3(4); 62:1(2),5(6); 63:1(2), 5(6),8(9),9(10); 66:9,16; 69:1(2),10(11), 18(19); 70:2(3); 71:10,13,23; 72:13,14; 74:19; 77:2(3); 78:18,50; 84:2(3); 86:2,4, 13,14; 88:3(4),14(15); 89:48(49); 94:17, 19,21; 97:10; 103:1,2,22; 104:1,35; 105:18,22; 106:15; 107:5,9,18,26; 109:20,31; 116:4,7,8; 119:20,25,28,81, 109,129,167,175; 120:2,6; 121:7; 123:4; 124:4,5,7; 130:5,6; 131:2; 138:3; 139:14; 141:8; 142:4(5),7(8); 143:3,6,8,11,12; 146:1; **Prov.** 1:18,19; 2:10; 3:22; 6:16,26, 30,32; 7:23; 8:36; 10:3; 11:17,25,30; 12:10; 13:2–4,8,19,25; 14:10,25; 15:32; 16:17,24,26; 18:7; 19:2,8,15,16,18; 20:2; 21:10,23; 22:5,23,25; 23:2,7,14; 24:12, 14; 25:13,25; 27:7,9; 28:17,25; 29:10, 17,24; 31:6; **Eccl.** 2:24; 4:8; 6:2,3,7,9; 7:28; **Song** 1:7; 3:1–4; 5:6; 6:12; **Isa.** 1:14; 3:9,20; 5:14; 10:18; 15:4; 19:10; 26:8,9; 29:8; 32:6; 38:15,17; 42:1; 43:4; 44:20; 46:2; 47:14; 49:7; 51:23; 53:10–12; 55:2,3; 56:11; 58:3,5,10,11; 61:10; 66:3; **Jer.** 2:24,34; 3:11; 4:10,19,30,31; 5:9,29; 6:8,16; 9:9(8); 11:21; 12:7; 13:17; 14:19; 15:1,9; 17:21; 18:20; 19:7,9; 20:13; 21:7,9; 22:25,27; 26:19; 31:12,14,25; 32:41; 34:16,20,21; 37:9; 38:2,16,17,20; 39:18; 40:14,15; 42:20; 43:6; 44:7,14,30; 45:5; 46:26; 48:6; 49:37; 50:19; 51:6,14, 45; 52:29,30; **Lam.** 1:11,16,19; 2:12,19; 3:17,20,24,25,51,58; 5:9; **Ezek.** 3:19,21; 4:14; 7:19; 13:18–20; 14:14,20; 16:5,27; 17:17; 18:4,20,27; 22:25,27; 23:17,18,22, 28; 24:21,25; 25:6,15; 27:13,31; 32:10;

33:5,6,9; 36:5; 47:9; **Hos.** 4:8; 9:4; **Amos** 2:14,15; 6:8; **Jon.** 1:14; 2:5(6),7(8); 4:3,8; **Mic.** 6:7; 7:1,3; **Hab.** 2:4,5,10; **Hag.** 2:13; **Zech.** 11:8.

5316. I. נֶפֶת *nepet* **fem. noun**
(Napheth: country, region)
Josh. 17:11(NASB, see II; NIV, see III).
II. נֶפֶת *nepet* **fem. proper noun**
(Napheth: city in Asher)
Josh. 17:11(KJV, see I; NIV, see III).
III. נָפוֹת *nāpôt* **fem. proper noun**
(Naphoth; abbr. form of *nāpôt dō'r* [5299,III])
Josh. 17:11(KJV, see I; NASB, see II).

5317. נֹפֶת *nōpet* **fem. noun**
(honey, honey dripping from the comb)
Ps. 19:10(11); **Prov.** 5:3; 24:13; 27:7; **Song** 4:11.

5318. נֶפְתּוֹחַ *neptôaḥ* **proper noun**
(Nephtoah)
Josh. 15:9; 18:15.

5319. נַפְתּוּלִים *naptûliym* **masc. pl. noun**
(struggles, wrestlings)
Gen. 30:8.

5320. נַפְתֻּחִים *naptuḥiym* **masc. pl. proper noun**
(Naphtuhites, Naphtuhim)
Gen. 10:13; **1 Chr.** 1:11.

5321. A. נַפְתָּלִי *naptāliy* **masc. proper noun**
(Naphtali: son of Jacob)
Gen. 30:8; 35:25; 46:24; 49:21; **1 Chr.** 2:2.
B. נַפְתָּלִי *naptāliy* **masc. proper noun**
(tribe or territory of Naphtali)
Ex. 1:4; **Num.** 1:15,42,43; 2:29; 7:78; 10:27; 13:14; 26:48,50; 34:28; **Deut.** 27:13; 33:23; 34:2; **Josh.** 19:32,39; 20:7; 21:6,32; **Judg.** 1:33; 4:6,10; 5:18; 6:35; 7:23; **1 Kgs.** 4:15; 7:14; 15:20; **2 Kgs.** 15:29; **1 Chr.** 6:62(47),76(61); 7:13; 12:34,40; 27:19; **2 Chr.** 16:4; 34:6; **Ps.** 68:27(28); **Isa.** 9:1(8:23); **Ezek.** 48:3,4,34.

5322. I. נֵץ *nēṣ* **masc. noun**
(blossom, flowers)
Gen. 40:10; **Song** 2:12(KJV, NASB, *niṣṣān* [5339]).
II. נֵץ *nēṣ* **masc. noun**
(hawk)
Lev. 11:16; **Deut.** 14:15; **Job** 39:26.

5323. נָצָא *nāṣā'* **verb**
(to flee)
Jer. 48:9(NIV, *nāṣāh* [5327,II]).

5324. נָצַב *nāṣab* **verb**
(to stand, to set up; to be set up as an official)
Gen. 18:2; 21:28,29; 24:13,43; 28:12,13; 33:20; 35:14,20; 37:7; 45:1; **Ex.** 5:20; 7:15; 15:8; 17:9; 18:14; 33:8,21; 34:2; **Num.** 16:27; 22:23,31,34; 23:6,17; **Deut.** 29:10(9); 32:8; **Josh.** 6:26; **Judg.** 9:6(NIV, *muṣṣāb* [4674]); 18:16,17; **Ruth** 2:5,6; **1 Sam.** 1:26; 4:20; 13:21; 15:12; 19:20; 22:6,7,9,17; **2 Sam.** 13:31; 18:17, 18; **1 Kgs.** 4:5,7,27(5:7); 5:16(30); 9:23; 16:34; 22:47(48); **2 Kgs.** 17:10; **1 Chr.** 18:3; **2 Chr.** 8:10(NASB, [K^{e}] *n^{e}siyb* [5333]); **Ps.** 39:5(6); 41:12(13); 45:9(10); 74:17; 78:13; 82:1; 119:89; **Prov.** 8:2; 15:25; **Isa.** 3:13; 21:8; **Jer.** 5:26; 31:21; **Lam.** 2:4; 3:12; **Amos** 7:7; 9:1; **Nah.** 2:7(8); **Zech.** 11:16.

5325. נִצָּב *niṣṣāb* **masc. noun**
(handle [of a sword or dagger])
Judg. 3:22.

5326. נִצְבָּה *niṣbāh* **Aram. fem. noun**
(strength, toughness)
Dan. 2:41.

5327. I. נָצָה *nāṣāh* **verb**
(to struggle, to quarrel)
Ex. 2:13; 21:22; **Lev.** 24:10; **Num.** 26:9; **Deut.** 25:11; **2 Sam.** 14:6; **Ps.** 60:[title](2).
II. נָצָה *nāṣāh* **verb**
(to fall, to be devastated, to be ruined)
2 Kgs. 19:25; **Isa.** 37:26; **Jer.** 4:7; 48:9(KJV, NASB, *nāṣa'* [5323]).

5328. נִצָּה *niṣṣāh* **fem. noun**
(blossom, flower)
Job 15:33; **Isa.** 18:5.

5329. נָצַח *nāṣaḥ* **verb**
(to lead, to direct, to oversee)
1 Chr. 15:21; 23:4; **2 Chr.** 2:2(1),18(17); 34:12,13; **Ezra** 3:8,9; **Ps.** 4:[title](1); 5:[title](1); 6:[title](1); 8:[title](1); 9:[title](1); 11:[title](1); 12:[title](1); 13:[title](1); 14:[title](1); 18:[title](1); 19:[title](1); 20:[title](1); 21:[title](1); 22:[title](1); 31:[title](1); 36:[title](1); 39:[title](1); 40:[title](1); 41:[title](1); 42:[title](1); 44:[title](1); 45:[title](1); 46:[title](1); 47:[title](1); 49:[title](1); 51:[title](1); 52:[title](1); 53:[title](1); 54:[title](1); 55:[title](1); 56:[title](1); 57:[title](1); 58:[title](1); 59:[title](1); 60:[title](1); 61:[title](1); 62:[title](1); 64:[title](1); 65:[title](1); 66:[title](1); 67:[title](1); 68:[title](1); 69:[title](1); 70:[title](1); 75:[title](1); 76:[title](1); 77:[title](1); 80:[title](1); 81:[title](1); 84:[title](1); 85:[title](1); 88:[title](1); 109:[title](1); 139:[title](1); 140:[title](1); **Jer.** 8:5; **Hab.** 3:19.

5330. נְצַח n^e*ṣaḥ* **Aram. verb**
(to distinguish oneself; corr. to Hebr. 5329)
Dan. 6:3(4).

5331. נֵצַח *nēṣaḥ,* נֶצַח *neṣaḥ* **masc. noun**
(strength, endurance, perpetuity)
1 Sam. 15:29; **2 Sam.** 2:26; **1 Chr.** 29:11; **Job** 4:20; 14:20; 20:7; 23:7; 34:36; 36:7; **Ps.** 9:6(7),18(19); 10:11; 13:1(2); 16:11; 44:23(24); 49:9(10),19(20); 52:5(7); 68:16(17); 74:1,3,10,19; 77:8(9); 79:5; 89:46(47); 103:9; **Prov.** 21:28; **Isa.** 13:20; 25:8; 28:28; 33:20; 34:10; 57:16; **Jer.** 3:5; 15:18; 50:39; **Lam.** 3:18; 5:20; **Amos** 1:11; 8:7; **Hab.** 1:4.

5332. נֵצַח *nēṣaḥ* **masc. noun**
(blood)
Isa. 63:3,6.

5333. נְצִיב n^e*ṣiyḇ* **masc. noun**
(garrison, officer, pillar)
Gen. 19:26; **1 Sam.** 10:5; 13:3,4; **2 Sam.** 8:6,14; **1 Kgs.** 4:19; **1 Chr.** 11:16; 18:13; **2 Chr.** 8:10(KJV, NIV, [Q^e] *nāṣaḇ* [5324]); 17:2.

5334. נְצִיב n^e*ṣiyḇ* **proper noun**
(Nezib)
Josh. 15:43.

5335. נְצִיחַ n^e*ṣiyaḥ* **masc. proper noun**
(Neziah)
Ezra 2:54; **Neh.** 7:56.

5336. נָצִיר *nāṣiyr* **adj.**
(preserved)
Isa. 49:6(NIV, [Q^e] *nāṣar* [5341]).

5337. נָצַל *nāṣal* **verb**
(to rescue, to deliver, to free oneself)
Gen. 31:9,16; 32:11(12),30(31); 37:21,22; **Ex.** 2:19; 3:8,22; 5:23; 6:6; 12:27,36; 18:4,8–10; 33:6; **Num.** 35:25; **Deut.** 23:14(15),15(16); 25:11; 32:39; **Josh.** 2:13; 9:26; 22:31; 24:10; **Judg.** 6:9; 8:34; 9:17; 10:15; 11:26; 18:28; **1 Sam.** 4:8; 7:3,14; 10:18; 12:10,11,21; 14:48; 17:35,37; 26:24; 30:8,18,22; **2 Sam.** 12:7; 14:6,16; 19:9(10); 20:6; 22:1,18,49; 23:12; **2 Kgs.** 17:39; 18:29,30,32–35;

19:11,12; 20:6; **1 Chr.** 11:14; 16:35; **2 Chr.** 20:25; 25:15; 32:11,13–15,17; **Ezra** 8:31; **Neh.** 9:28; **Job** 5:4,19; 10:7; **Ps.** 7:1(2),2(3); 18:[title](1),17(18),48(49); 22:8(9),20(21); 25:20; 31:2(3),15(16); 33:16,19; 34:4(5),17(18),19(20); 35:10; 39:8(9); 40:13(14); 50:22; 51:14(16); 54:7(9); 56:13(14); 59:1(2),2(3); 69:14(15); 70:1(2); 71:2,11; 72:12; 79:9; 82:4; 86:13; 91:3; 97:10; 106:43; 107:6; 109:21; 119:43,170; 120:2; 142:6(7); 143:9; 144:7,11; **Prov.** 2:12,16; 6:3,5; 10:2; 11:4,6; 12:6; 14:25; 19:19; 23:14; 24:11; **Isa.** 5:29; 19:20; 20:6; 31:5; 36:14,15,18–20; 37:11,12; 38:6; 42:22; 43:13; 44:17,20; 47:14; 50:2; 57:13; **Jer.** 1:8,19; 7:10; 15:20,21; 20:13; 21:12; 22:3; 39:17; 42:11; **Ezek.** 3:19,21; 7:19; 13:21,23; 14:14,16,18,20; 33:9,12; 34:10,12,27; **Dan.** 8:4,7; **Hos.** 2:9(11), 10(12); 5:14; **Amos** 3:12; 4:11; **Jon.** 4:6; **Mic.** 4:10; 5:6(5),8(7); **Hab.** 2:9; **Zeph.** 1:18; **Zech.** 3:2; 11:6.

5338. נְצַל *n^e^ṣal* **Aram. verb**
(to deliver, to rescue, to save; corr. to Hebr. 5337)
Dan. 3:29; 6:14(15),27(28).

5339. נִצָּן *niṣṣān* **masc. noun**
(flower, blossom)
Song 2:12(NIV, *nēṣ* [5322,I]).

5340. נָצַץ *nāṣaṣ* **verb**
(to gleam, to sparkle)
Song 6:11(KJV, *nûṣ* [5132,I]); 7:12(13) (KJV, *nûṣ* [5132,I]); **Eccl.** 12:5(KJV, *nā'aṣ* [5006,II]); **Ezek.** 1:7.

5341. נָצַר *nāṣar* **verb**
(to keep, to guard, to preserve)
Ex. 34:7; **Deut.** 32:10; 33:9; **2 Kgs.** 17:9; 18:8; **Job** 7:20; 27:18; **Ps.** 12:7(8); 25:10,21; 31:23(24); 32:7; 34:13(14); 40:11(12); 61:7(8); 64:1(2); 78:7; 105:45; 119:2,22,33,34,56,69,100,115,129,145; 140:1(2),4(5); 141:3; **Prov.** 2:8,11; 3:1,21; 4:6,13,23; 5:2; 6:20; 7:10; 13:3,6; 16:17; 20:28; 22:12; 23:26(NASB, [K^e^] *rāṣāh* [7521,I]); 24:12; 27:18; 28:7; **Isa.** 1:8; 26:3; 27:3; 42:6; 48:6; 49:6 (KJV, NASB, [K^e^] *nāṣiyr* [5336]),8; 65:4; **Jer.** 4:16; 31:6; **Ezek.** 6:12; **Nah.** 2:1(2).

5342. נֵצֶר *nēṣer* **masc. noun**
(branch)
Isa. 11:1; 14:19; 60:21; **Dan.** 11:7.

5343. נְקֵא *n^e^qē'* **Aram. adj.**
(pure, white)
Dan. 7:9.

5344. I. נָקַב *nāqab̲* **verb**
(to pierce; to designate)
Gen. 30:28; **Num.** 1:17; **2 Kgs.** 12:9(10); 18:21; **1 Chr.** 12:31; 16:41; **2 Chr.** 28:15; 31:19; **Ezra** 8:20; **Job** 40:24; 41:2(40:26); **Isa.** 36:6; 62:2; **Amos** 6:1; **Hab.** 3:14; **Hag.** 1:6.
II. נָקַב *nāqab̲* **verb**
(to curse, to blaspheme)
Lev. 24:11(NASB, NIV, *qāb̲ab̲* [6895]),16; 24:11; **Num.** 23:8(NASB, NIV, *qāb̲ab̲* [6895]),25; **Job** 3:8(NASB, NIV, *qāb̲ab̲* [6895]); 5:3(NASB, NIV, *qāb̲ab̲* [6895]); **Prov.** 11:26(NASB, NIV, *qāb̲ab̲* [6895]); 24:24(NASB, NIV, *qāb̲ab̲* [6895]).

5345. I. נֶקֶב *neqeb̲* **masc. noun**
(setting [as for a jewel])
Ezek. 28:13(KJV, see II).
II. נֶקֶב *neqeb̲* **masc. noun**
(pipe)
Ezek. 28:13(NASB, NIV, see I).

5346. I. נֶקֶב *neqeb̲* **proper noun**
(Nekeb; town in Naphtali)
Josh. 19:33(NASB, NIV, see II).
II. נֶקֶב *neqeb̲* **proper noun**
(Nekeb; part of full name Adami Nekeb, [129] and [5346,II])
Josh. 19:33(KJV, see I).

5347. נְקֵבָה $n^e q\bar{e}\underline{b}\bar{a}h$ **fem. noun**
(female, woman)
Gen. 1:27; 5:2; 6:19; 7:3,9,16; **Lev.** 3:1,6; 4:28,32; 5:6; 12:5,7; 15:33; 27:4–7; **Num.** 5:3; 31:15; **Deut.** 4:16; **Jer.** 31:22.

5348. נָקֹד *nāqōḏ* **adj.**
(speckled)
Gen. 30:32,33,35,39; 31:8,10,12.

5349. נֹקֵד *nōqēḏ* **masc. noun**
(shepherd, raiser of sheep)
2 Kgs. 3:4; **Amos** 1:1.

5350. נִקֻּדִים *niqqūḏiym* **masc. pl. noun**
(moldy, crumbly things, crumbling cake)
Josh. 9:5,12; **1 Kgs.** 14:3.

5351. נְקֻדָּה $n^e quddāh$ **fem. noun**
(a stud or bead [of silver])
Song 1:11.

5352. נָקָה *nāqāh* **verb**
(to be innocent, to be guiltless, to go unpunished)
Gen. 24:8,41; **Ex.** 20:7; 21:19; 34:7; **Num.** 5:19,28,31; 14:18; **Deut.** 5:11; **Judg.** 15:3; **1 Sam.** 26:9; **1 Kgs.** 2:9; **Job** 9:28; 10:14; **Ps.** 19:12(13),13(14); **Prov.** 6:29; 11:21; 16:5; 17:5; 19:5,9; 28:20; **Isa.** 3:26; **Jer.** 2:35; 25:29; 30:11; 46:28; 49:12; **Joel** 3:21(4:21); **Nah.** 1:3; **Zech.** 5:3.

5353. A. נְקוֹדָא $n^e q\hat{o}\underline{d}\bar{a}'$ **masc. proper noun**
(Nekoda: head of family of temple slaves returning from Babylonian Exile)
Ezra 2:48; **Neh.** 7:50.
B. נְקוֹדָא $n^e q\hat{o}\underline{d}\bar{a}'$ **masc. proper noun**
(Nekoda: head of an exile family who could not prove Israelite descent)
Ezra 2:60; **Neh.** 7:62.

5354. נָקַט *nāqaṯ* **verb**
(to be weary)
Job 10:1(NASB, NIV, *qûṭ* [6962]).

5355. נָקִי *nāqiy,* נָקִיא *nāqiy'* **adj.**
(innocent, free of blame)
Gen. 24:41; 44:10; **Ex.** 21:28; 23:7; **Num.** 32:22; **Deut.** 19:10,13; 21:8,9; 24:5; 27:25; **Josh.** 2:17,19,20; **1 Sam.** 19:5; **2 Sam.** 3:28; 14:9; **1 Kgs.** 15:22; **2 Kgs.** 21:16; 24:4; **Job** 4:7; 9:23; 17:8; 22:19,30; 27:17; **Ps.** 10:8; 15:5; 24:4; 94:21; 106:38; **Prov.** 1:11; 6:17; **Isa.** 59:7; **Jer.** 2:34; 7:6; 19:4; 22:3,17; 26:15; **Joel** 3:19(4:19); **Jon.** 1:14.

5356. נִקָּיוֹן *niqqāyôn,* נִקָּיֹן *niqqāyōn* **masc. noun**
(innocence, purity)
Gen. 20:5; **Ps.** 26:6; 73:13; **Hos.** 8:5; **Amos** 4:6.

5357. נָקִיק *nāqiyq* **masc. noun**
(cleft, crevice)
Isa. 7:19; **Jer.** 13:4; 16:16.

5358. נָקַם *nāqam* **verb**
(to avenge, to punish)
Gen. 4:15,24; **Ex.** 21:20,21; **Lev.** 19:18; 26:25; **Num.** 31:2; **Deut.** 32:43; **Josh.** 10:13; **Judg.** 15:7; 16:28; **1 Sam.** 14:24; 18:25; 24:12(13); **2 Kgs.** 9:7; **Esth.** 8:13; **Ps.** 8:2(3); 44:16(17); 99:8; **Isa.** 1:24; **Jer.** 5:9,29; 9:9(8); 15:15; 46:10; 50:15; 51:36; **Ezek.** 24:8; 25:12,15; **Nah.** 1:2.

5359. נָקָם *nāqām* **masc. noun**
(vengeance)
Lev. 26:25; **Deut.** 32:35,41,43; **Judg.** 16:28; **Ps.** 58:10(11); **Prov.** 6:34; **Isa.** 34:8; 35:4; 47:3; 59:17; 61:2; 63:4; **Ezek.** 24:8; 25:12,15; **Mic.** 5:15(14).

5360. נְקָמָה $n^e q\bar{a}m\bar{a}h$ **fem. noun**
(vengeance)
Num. 31:2,3; **Judg.** 11:36; **2 Sam.** 4:8; 22:48; **Ps.** 18:47(48); 79:10; 94:1; 149:7; **Jer.** 11:20; 20:10,12; 46:10;

50:15,28; 51:6,11,36; **Lam.** 3:60; **Ezek.** 25:14,15,17.

5361. נָקַע *nāqa'* **verb**
(to turn away in disgust, to be alienated)
Ezek. 23:18,22,28.

5362. I. נָקַף *nāqap̱* **verb**
(to go around, to surround, to compass)
Lev. 19:27; **Josh.** 6:3,11; **1 Kgs.** 7:24; **2 Kgs.** 6:14; 11:8; **2 Chr.** 4:3; 23:7; **Job** 1:5; 19:6; **Ps.** 17:9; 22:16(17); 48:12(13); 88:17(18); **Isa.** 15:8; 29:1(KJV, see II); **Lam.** 3:5.
II. נָקַף *nāqap̱* **verb**
(to cut off, to cut down, to destroy)
Job 19:26; **Isa.** 10:34; 29:1(NASB, NIV, see I).

5363. נֹקֶף *nōqep̱* **masc. noun**
(beating, shaking)
Isa. 17:6; 24:13.

5364. I. נִקְפָּה *niqpāh* **fem. noun**
(rope)
Isa. 3:24(KJV, see II).
II. נִקְפָּה *niqpāh* **fem. noun**
(a rip, a tear)
Isa. 3:24(NASB, NIV, see I).

5365. נָקַר *nāqar* **verb**
(to dig [a well or pit]; to gouge out [the eye])
Num. 16:14; **Judg.** 16:21; **2 Kgs.** 19:24(NASB, NIV, *qûr* [6979,I]); **1 Sam.** 11:2; **Job** 30:17; **Prov.** 30:17; **Isa.** 37:25(NASB, NIV, *qûr* [6979,I]); 51:1.

5366. נְקָרָה *n^eqārāh* **fem. noun**
(cavern, cleft)
Ex. 33:22; **Isa.** 2:21.

5367. נָקַשׁ *nāqaš* **verb**
(to ensnare, to set a trap, to seize)
Deut. 12:30; **1 Sam.** 28:9; **Ps.** 9:16(17) (NIV, *yāqaš* [3369]); 38:12(13); 109:11.

5368. נְקַשׁ *n^eqaš* **Aram. verb**
(to knock [of the knees])
Dan. 5:6.

5369. A. נֵר *nēr* **masc. proper noun**
(Ner: father of Abner)
1 Sam. 14:50,51; 26:5,14; **2 Sam.** 2:8,12; 3:23,25,28,37; **1 Kgs.** 2:5,32; **1 Chr.** 26:28.
B. נֵר *nēr* **masc. proper noun**
(Ner: father of Kish)
1 Chr. 8:33; 9:39.
C. נֵר *nēr* **masc. proper noun**
(Ner: brother of Kish)
1 Chr. 9:36.

5370. נֵרְגַל *nērgal* **masc. proper noun**
(Nergal)
2 Kgs. 17:30.

5371. A. נֵרְגַל שַׂר־אֶצֶר *nērgal śar-'eṣer* **masc. proper noun**
(Nergal-Sharezer: a Babylonian official)
Jer. 39:3,13.
B. נֵרְגַל שַׂר־אֶצֶר *nērgal śar-'eṣer* **masc. proper noun**
(Nergal-Sharezer: another Babylonian official)
Jer. 39:3.

5372. נִרְגָּן *nirgān* **masc. noun**
(gossipper, slanderer; NASB, NIV, *rāgan* [7279])
Prov. 16:28; 18:8; 26:20,22.

5373. נֵרְדְּ *nērd* **masc. noun**
(spikenard, perfume)
Song 1:12; 4:13,14.

5374. נֵרִיָּה *nēriyyāh,* נֵרִיָּהוּ *nēriyyāhû* **masc. proper noun**
(Neriah: father of Baruch)
Jer. 32:12,16; 36:4,8,14,32; 43:3,6; 45:1; 51:59.

5375. נָשָׂא *nāśā'* **verb**
(to carry, to bear up, to lift up)
Gen. 4:13; 7:17; 13:6,10,14; 18:2,24,26; 19:21; 21:16,18; 22:4,13; 24:63,64; 27:3,38; 29:1,11; 31:10,12,17; 32:20(21); 33:1,5; 36:7; 37:25; 39:7; 40:13,19,20; 42:26; 43:29,34; 44:1; 45:19,23,27; 46:5; 47:30; 50:13,17; **Ex.** 6:8; 10:13,17,19; 12:34; 14:10; 18:22; 19:4; 20:7; 23:1,21; 25:14,27,28; 27:7; 28:12,29,30,38,43; 30:4,12; 32:32; 34:7; 35:21,26; 36:2; 37:5,14,15,27; 38:7; **Lev.** 5:1,17; 7:18; 9:22; 10:4,5,17; 11:25,28,40; 15:10; 16:22; 17:16; 19:8,15,17; 20:17,19,20; 22:9,16; 24:15; **Num.** 1:2,49,50; 3:40; 4:2,15,22,25; 5:31; 6:26; 7:9; 9:13; 10:17,21; 11:12,14,17; 13:23; 14:1,18,19, 30,33,34; 16:3,15; 18:1,22,23,32; 23:7, 18,24; 24:2,3,7,15,20,21,23; 26:2; 30:15(16); 31:26,49; **Deut.** 1:9,12,31; 3:27; 4:19; 5:11; 10:8,17; 12:26; 14:24; 24:15; 28:49,50; 31:9,25; 32:11,40; 33:3; **Josh.** 3:3,6,8,13–15,17; 4:3,8–10,16,18; 5:13; 6:4,6,8,12,13; 8:33; 24:19; **Judg.** 2:4; 3:18; 8:28; 9:7,48,54; 16:31; 19:17; 21:2,23; **Ruth** 1:4,9,14; 2:18; **1 Sam.** 2:28; 4:4; 6:13; 10:3; 11:4; 14:1,3,6,7, 12–14,17; 15:25; 16:21; 17:7,20,34,41; 22:18; 24:16(17); 25:28,35; 30:4; 31:4–6; **2 Sam.** 2:22,32; 3:32; 4:4; 5:12,21; 6:3,4,13; 8:2,6; 13:34,36; 14:14; 15:24; 17:13; 18:15,24,28; 19:42(43)(KJV, *niśśē'ṯ* [5379]); 20:21; 23:16,37; **1 Kgs.** 1:5(KJV, *miṯnaśē'* [4984]); 2:26; 5:9(23),15(29); 8:3,31(NASB, NIV, [K^e] *naša'* [5378]); 9:11; 10:2,11,22; 13:29; 14:28; 15:22; 18:12; **2 Kgs.** 2:16; 3:14; 4:19,20,36,37; 5:1,23; 7:8; 9:25,26,32; 14:10,20; 18:14; 19:4,22; 20:17; 23:4; 25:13,27; **1 Chr.** 5:18; 10:4,5,9,12; 11:18,39; 12:24; 14:2; 15:2,15,26,27; 16:29; 18:2,6,11; 21:16,24; 23:22,26; 27:23; 29:11(KJV, *miṯnaśē'* [4984]); **2 Chr.** 5:4; 6:22; 9:1,21; 11:21; 12:11; 13:21; 14:8(7),13(12); 16:6; 24:3,11; 25:19,28; 32:23; **Ezra** 1:4; 8:36; 9:2,12; 10:44; **Neh.** 2:1; 4:17(11); 9:15; 13:25; **Esth.** 2:9,15,17; 3:1; 5:2,11; 9:3; **Job** 2:12; 6:2; 7:13,21; 10:15; 11:15; 13:8,10,14; 21:3,12; 22:8,26; 24:10; 27:1,21; 29:1; 30:22; 31:36; 32:21,22; 34:19,31; 36:3; 40:20; 42:8,9; **Ps.** 4:6(7); 7:6(7); 10:12; 15:3; 16:4; 24:4,5,7,9; 25:1,18; 28:2,9; 32:1,5; 50:16; 55:12(13); 63:4(5); 69:7(8); 72:3; 81:2(3); 82:2; 83:2(3); 85:2(3); 86:4; 88:15(16); 89:9(10) (KJV, *śô'* [7721]),50(51); 91:12; 93:3; 94:2; 96:8; 99:8; 102:10(11); 106:26; 116:13; 119:48; 121:1; 123:1; 126:6; 134:2; 139:9,20; 143:8; **Prov.** 6:35; 9:12; 18:5,14; 19:18,19; 30:13,21,32; **Eccl.** 5:15(14),19(18); **Song** 5:7; **Isa.** 1:14; 2:2,4,9,12–14; 3:3,7; 5:26; 6:1; 8:4; 9:15(14); 10:24,26; 11:12; 13:2; 14:4; 15:7; 18:3; 22:6; 24:14; 30:6,25; 33:10,24; 37:4,23; 38:21; 39:6; 40:4,11,24,26; 41:16; 42:2,11; 45:20; 46:3,4,7; 49:18,22; 51:6; 52:8,11,13; 53:4,12; 57:7,13,15; 60:4,6; 63:9; 64:6(5); 66:12; **Jer.** 3:2; 4:6; 6:1; 7:16,29; 9:10(9),18(17); 10:5,19; 11:14; 13:20; 15:15; 17:21,27; 22:27; 31:19; 44:14,22; 49:29; 50:2; 51:9,12,27; 52:17,31; **Lam.** 2:19; 3:27,41; 4:16; 5:13; **Ezek.** 1:19–21; 3:12,14; 4:4–6; 8:3,5; 10:7,16,19; 11:1,22,24; 12:6,7,12; 14:10; 16:52,54,58; 17:8,9,14,23; 18:6,12,15, 19,20; 19:1; 20:5,6,15,23,28,31,42; 23:27, 35,49; 26:17; 27:2,32; 28:12; 29:15,19; 32:2,24,25,30; 33:25; 34:29; 36:6–8,15; 38:13; 39:10,26; 43:5; 44:10,12,13; 45:11; 47:14; **Dan.** 1:16; 8:3; 10:5; 11:12,14; **Hos.** 1:6; 4:8; 5:14; 13:1; 14:2(3); **Joel** 2:22; **Amos** 4:2; 5:1,26; 6:10; **Jon.** 1:12,15; **Mic.** 2:2,4; 4:1,3; 6:16; 7:9,18; **Nah.** 1:5; **Hab.** 1:3; 2:6; 3:10; **Hag.** 2:12,19; **Zech.** 1:18(2:1), 21(2:4); 2:1(5); 5:1,5,7,9; 6:1,13; **Mal.** 1:8,9; 2:3,9.

5376. נְשָׂא *n^eśā'* **Aram. verb**
(to take, to carry away, to rise up in rebellion)
Ezra 4:19; 5:15; **Dan.** 2:35.

5377. נָשָׁא *nāšā'* **verb**
(to deceive)
Gen. 3:13; **2 Kgs.** 18:29; 19:10; **2 Chr.** 32:15; **Ps.** 55:15(16)(KJV, [K^e^] *y^e^šiymôṯ* [3451]); **Isa.** 19:13; 36:14; 37:10; **Jer.** 4:10; 29:8; 37:9; 49:16; **Obad.** 1:3,7.

5378. נָשָׁא *nāšā'* **verb**
(to lend on interest, to be a creditor)
1 Sam. 22:2; **1 Kgs.** 8:31(KJV, [Q^e^] *nāśa'* [5375]); **Neh.** 5:7; **Ps.** 89:22(23); **Isa.** 24:2.

5379. נִשֵּׂאת *niśśē'ṯ* **verb**
(gift; participle of *nāśā'* [5375])
2 Sam. 19:42(43)(NASB, NIV, *nāśā'* [5375]).

5380. נָשַׁב *nāšaḇ* **verb**
(to blow, to drive [blow] away)
Gen. 15:11; **Ps.** 147:18; **Isa.** 40:7.

5381. נָשַׂג *nāśag* **verb**
(to overtake, to reach, to get)
Gen. 31:25; 44:4,6; 47:9; **Ex.** 14:9; 15:9; **Lev.** 5:11; 14:21,22,30–32; 25:26,47,49; 26:5; 27:8; **Num.** 6:21; **Deut.** 19:6; 28:2,15,45; **Josh.** 2:5; **1 Sam.** 14:26; 30:8; **2 Sam.** 15:14; **2 Kgs.** 25:5; **1 Chr.** 21:12; **Job** 24:2; 27:20; 41:26(18); **Ps.** 7:5(6); 18:37(38); 40:12(13); 69:24(25); **Prov.** 2:19; **Isa.** 35:10; 51:11; 59:9; **Jer.** 39:5; 42:16; 52:8; **Lam.** 1:3; **Ezek.** 46:7; **Hos.** 2:7(9); 10:9; **Zech.** 1:6.

5382. נָשָׁה *nāšāh* **verb**
(to forget)
Gen. 41:51; **Job** 11:6; 39:17; **Isa.** 44:21; **Jer.** 23:39; **Lam.** 3:17.

5383. נָשָׁה *nāšāh*, נָשָׁא *nāšā'* **verb**
(to lend, to borrow)
Ex. 22:25(24); **Deut.** 15:2; 24:10,11; **2 Kgs.** 4:1; **Neh.** 5:10,11; **Ps.** 109:11; **Isa.** 24:2; 50:1; **Jer.** 15:10.

5384. I. נָשֶׁה *nāšeh* **masc. noun**
(that which shrank)
Gen. 32:32(33)(NASB, NIV, see II).
II. נָשֶׁה *nāšeh* **masc. noun**
(tendon, sinew)
Gen. 32:32(33)(KJV, see I).

5385. נְשׂוּאָה *n^e^śû'āh* **fem. noun**
(that which is carried, carriage)
Isa. 46:1.

5386. נְשִׁי *n^e^šiy* **masc. noun**
(debt)
2 Kgs. 4:7.

5387. I. נָשִׂיא *nāśiy'* **masc. noun**
(chief, ruler, prince)
Gen. 17:20; 23:6; 25:16; 34:2; **Ex.** 16:22; 22:28(27); 34:31; 35:27; **Lev.** 4:22; **Num.** 1:16,44; 2:3,5,7,10,12,14,18,20,22,25, 27,29; 3:24,30,32,35; 4:34,46; 7:2,3,10, 11,18,24,30,36,42,48,54,60,66,72,78,84; 10:4; 13:2; 16:2; 17:2(17),6(21); 25:14,18; 27:2; 31:13; 32:2; 34:18,22–28; 36:1; **Josh.** 9:15,18,19,21; 13:21; 17:4; 22:14, 30,32; **1 Kgs.** 8:1; 11:34; **1 Chr.** 2:10; 4:38; 5:6; 7:40; **2 Chr.** 1:2; 5:2; **Ezra** 1:8; **Ezek.** 7:27; 12:10,12; 19:1; 21:12(17),25(30); 22:6; 26:16; 27:21; 30:13; 32:29; 34:24; 37:25; 38:2,3; 39:1,18; 44:3; 45:7–9,16,17,22; 46:2,4,8,10,12,16–18; 48:21,22.
II. נָשִׂיא *nāśiy'* **masc. noun**
(vapor, mist, cloud)
Ps. 135:7; **Prov.** 25:14; **Jer.** 10:13; 51:16.

5388. נְשִׁיָּה *n^e^šiyyāh* **fem. noun**
(forgetfulness, oblivion)
Ps. 88:12(13).

5389. נְשִׁין *n^e^šiyn* **Aram. fem. pl. noun**
(wives)
Dan. 6:24(25).

5390. נְשִׁיקָה *n^e^šiyqāh* **fem. noun**
(kiss)
Prov. 27:6; **Song** 1:2.

5391. I. נָשַׁךְ *nāšak̲* **verb**
(to bite)
Gen. 49:17; **Num.** 21:6,8,9; **Prov.** 23:32; **Eccl.** 10:8,11; **Jer.** 8:17; **Amos** 5:19; 9:3; **Mic.** 3:5; **Hab.** 2:7(NASB, NIV, see II).
II. נָשַׁךְ *nāšak̲* **verb**
(to lend or borrow at interest)
Deut. 23:19(20),20(21); **Hab.** 2:7(KJV, see I).

5392. נֶשֶׁךְ *nešek̲* **masc. noun**
(interest, usury)
Ex. 22:25(24); **Lev.** 25:36,37; **Deut.** 23:19(20); **Ps.** 15:5; **Prov.** 28:8; **Ezek.** 18:8,13,17; 22:12.

5393. נִשְׁכָּה *niškāh* **fem. noun**
(chamber, room, living quarters)
Neh. 3:30; 12:44; 13:7.

5394. נָשַׁל *nāšal* **verb**
(to remove, to drop off, to clear away)
Ex. 3:5; **Deut.** 7:1,22; 19:5; 28:40; **Josh.** 5:15; **2 Kgs.** 16:6.

5395. I. נָשַׁם *nāšam* **verb**
(to gasp)
Isa. 42:14(KJV, see II).
II. נָשַׁם *nāšam* **verb**
(to destroy)
Isa. 42:14(NASB, NIV, see I).

5396. נִשְׁמָה *nišmāh* **Aram. fem. noun**
(breath, life breath; corr. to Hebr. 5397)
Dan. 5:23.

5397. נְשָׁמָה *n^e^šāmāh* **fem. noun**
(breath, spirit)
Gen. 2:7; 7:22; **Deut.** 20:16; **Josh.** 10:40; 11:11,14; **2 Sam.** 22:16; **1 Kgs.** 15:29; 17:17; **Job** 4:9; 26:4; 27:3; 32:8; 33:4; 34:14; 37:10; **Ps.** 18:15(16); 150:6; **Prov.** 20:27; **Isa.** 2:22; 30:33; 42:5; 57:16; **Dan.** 10:17.

5398. נָשַׁף *nāšap̲* **verb**
(to blow)
Ex. 15:10; **Isa.** 40:24.

5399. נֶשֶׁף *nešep̲* **masc. noun**
(twilight, dusk, dawn)
1 Sam. 30:17; **2 Kgs.** 7:5,7; **Job** 3:9; 7:4; 24:15; **Ps.** 119:147; **Prov.** 7:9; **Isa.** 5:11; 21:4; 59:10; **Jer.** 13:16.

5400. נָשַׂק *nāśaq* **verb**
(to kindle, to burn; NASB, *śālaq*)
Ps. 78:21; **Isa.** 44:15; **Ezek.** 39:9.

5401. I. נָשַׁק *nāšaq* **verb**
(to kiss, to touch, to do homage)
Gen. 27:26,27; 29:11,13; 31:28,55(32:1); 33:4; 41:40; 45:15; 48:10; 50:1; **Ex.** 4:27; 18:7; **Ruth** 1:9,14; **1 Sam.** 10:1; 20:41; **2 Sam.** 14:33; 15:5; 19:39(40); 20:9; **1 Kgs.** 19:18,20; **Job** 31:27; **Ps.** 2:12; 85:10(11); **Prov.** 7:13; 24:26; **Song** 1:2; 8:1; **Ezek.** 3:13; **Hos.** 13:2.
II. נָשַׁק *nāšaq* **verb**
(to arm, to equip, to handle)
1 Chr. 12:2; **2 Chr.** 17:17; **Ps.** 78:9.

5402. נֵשֶׁק *nēšeq*, נֶשֶׁק *nešeq* **masc. noun**
(weapon, armor, battle)
1 Kgs. 10:25; **2 Kgs.** 10:2; **2 Chr.** 9:24; **Neh.** 3:19; **Job** 20:24; 39:21; **Ps.** 140:7(8); **Isa.** 22:8; **Ezek.** 39:9,10.

5403. נְשַׁר *n^e^šar* **Aram. masc. noun**
(eagle; corr. to Hebr. 5404)
Dan. 4:33(30); 7:4.

5404. נֶשֶׁר *nešer* **masc. noun**
(eagle)
Ex. 19:4; **Lev.** 11:13; **Deut.** 14:12; 28:49; 32:11; **2 Sam.** 1:23; **Job** 9:26;

39:27; **Ps.** 103:5; **Prov.** 23:5; 30:17,19; **Isa.** 40:31; **Jer.** 4:13; 48:40; 49:16,22; **Lam.** 4:19; **Ezek.** 1:10; 10:14; 17:3,7; **Hos.** 8:1; **Obad.** 1:4; **Mic.** 1:16; **Hab.** 1:8.

5405. נָשַׁת *našat̠* **verb**
(to be dry, to be parched; to dry up, to fail)
Isa. 19:5; 41:17; **Jer.** 18:14(KJV, NASB, *nat̠aš* [5428]); 51:30.

5406. נִשְׁתְּוָן *ništ^{e}wān* **masc. noun**
(letter, correspondence)
Ezra 4:7; 7:11.

5407. נִשְׁתְּוָן *ništ^{e}wān* **Aram. masc. noun**
(letter, correspondence; corr. to Hebr. 5406)
Ezra 4:18,23; 5:5.

5408. נָתַח *nāt̠aḥ* **verb**
(to cut up, to cut into pieces)
Ex. 29:17; **Lev.** 1:6,12; 8:20; **Judg.** 19:29; 20:6; **1 Sam.** 11:7; **1 Kgs.** 18:23,33.

5409. נֵתַח *nēt̠aḥ* **masc. noun**
(pieces [of meat])
Ex. 29:17; **Lev.** 1:6,8,12; 8:20; 9:13; **Judg.** 19:29; **Ezek.** 24:4,6.

5410. I. נָתִיב *nat̠iyb̠* **masc. noun**
(path, pathway, wake)
Job 18:10; 28:7; 41:32(24); **Ps.** 78:50; 119:35; **Prov.** 12:28(KJV, NIV, see II).
II. נְתִיבָה *n^{e}t̠iyb̠āh* **fem. noun**
(path, pathway, wake)
Judg. 5:6; **Job** 19:8; 24:13; 30:13; 38:20; **Ps.** 119:105; 142:3(4); **Prov.** 1:15; 3:17; 7:25; 8:2,20; 12:28(NASB, see I); **Isa.** 42:16; 43:16; 58:12; 59:8; **Jer.** 6:16; 18:15; **Lam.** 3:9; **Hos.** 2:6(8).

5411. נְתִינִים *n^{e}t̠iyniym* **masc. plural noun**
(the Nethinim, temple servants)
1 Chr. 9:2; **Ezra** 2:43,58,70; 7:7; 8:17,20; **Neh.** 3:26,31; 7:46,60,73; 10:28(29); 11:3,21.

5412. נְתִינִין *n^{e}t̠iyniyn* **Aram. masc. plural noun**
(the Nethinim, temple servants; corr. to Hebr. 5411)
Ezra 7:24.

5413. נָתַךְ *nāt̠ak̠* **verb**
(to pour out, be poured out; to melt)
Ex. 9:33; **2 Sam.** 21:10; **2 Kgs.** 22:9; **2 Chr.** 12:7; 34:17,21,25; **Job** 3:24; 10:10; **Jer.** 7:20; 42:18; 44:6; **Ezek.** 22:20–22; 24:11; **Dan.** 9:11,27; **Nah.** 1:6.

5414. נָתַן *nāthan* **verb**
(to give, to grant, to put, to hand over)
Gen. 1:17,29; 3:6,12; 4:12; 9:2,3,12,13; 12:7; 13:15,17; 14:20,21; 15:2,3,7,10,18; 16:3,5; 17:2,5,6,8,16,20; 18:7,8; 20:6,14, 16; 21:14,27; 23:4,9,11,13; 24:7,32,35, 36,41,53; 25:5,6,34; 26:3,4; 27:17,28,37; 28:4,13,20,22; 29:19,24,26–29,33; 30:4,6,9,14,18,26,28,31,35,40; 31:7,9; 32:16(17); 34:8,9,11,12,14,16,21; 35:4,12; 38:9,14,16–18,26,28; 39:4,8,20–22; 40:3, 11,13,21; 41:10,41–43,45,48; 42:25,27, 30,34,37; 43:14,23,24; 45:2,18,21,22; 46:18,25; 47:11,16,17,19,22,24; 48:4, 9,22; 49:20,21; **Ex.** 2:9,21; 3:19,21; 5:7,10,16,18,21; 6:4,8; 7:1,4,9; 9:23; 10:25; 11:3; 12:7,23,25,36; 13:5,11; 16:3,8,15,29,33; 17:2; 18:25; 20:12; 21:4,19,22,23,30,32; 22:7(6),10(9), 17(16),29(28),30(29); 23:27,31; 24:12; 25:12,16,21,26,30; 26:32–35; 27:5; 28:14,23–25,27,30; 29:3,6,12,17,20; 30:6,12–16,18,33,36; 31:6,18; 32:13, 24,29; 33:1; 34:33; 35:34; 36:1,2; 37:13; 39:16–18,20,25,31; 40:5–8,18,20,22, 30,33; **Lev.** 1:7; 2:1,15; 4:7,18,25,30,34;

5:11,16; 6:5(5:24),17(10); 7:32,34,36; 8:7,8,15,23,24,27; 9:9; 10:1,14,17; 11:38; 14:14,17,18,25,28,29,34; 15:14; 16:8,13, 18,21; 17:10,11; 18:20,21,23; 19:14, 20,28; 20:2–4,6,15,24; 22:14,22; 23:10,38; 24:7,19,20; 25:2,19,24,37,38; 26:1,4,6, 11,17,19,20,25,30,31,46; 27:9,23; **Num.** 3:9,48,51; 4:6,7,10,12,14; 5:7,10,15,17, 18,20,21; 6:18,19; 7:5–9; 8:16,19; 10:29; 11:13,18,21,25,29; 13:2; 14:1,4,8; 15:2, 21,38; 16:7,14,17,18,46(17:11),47(17:12); 17:6(21); 18:6–8,11,12,19,21,24,26,28; 19:3,17; 20:8,12,19,21,24; 21:2,3,16,23, 29,34; 22:13,18; 24:13; 25:12; 26:54,62; 27:4,7,9–12,20; 31:3,29,30,41,47; 32:5,7, 9,29,33,40; 33:53; 34:13; 35:2,4,6–8,13, 14; 36:2; **Deut.** 1:8,15,20,21,25,27,35, 36,39; 2:5,9,12,19,24,25,28–31,33,36; 3:2,3,12,13,15,16,18–20; 4:1,8,21,38,40; 5:16,22(19),29(26),31(28); 6:10,22,23; 7:2,3,13,15,16,23,24; 8:10,18; 9:6,10, 11,23; 10:4,11,18; 11:9,14,15,17,21,25, 26,29,31,32; 12:1,9,15,21; 13:1(2), 12(13),17(18); 14:21,25,26; 15:4,7,9,10, 14,17; 16:5,10,17,18,20; 17:2,14,15; 18:3,4,9,14,18; 19:1,2,8,10,12,14; 20:13, 14,16; 21:1,8,10,17,23; 22:16,19,29; 23:14(15),24(25); 24:1,3,4,15; 25:15,19; 26:1–3,6,9–15,19; 27:2,3; 28:1,7,8, 11–13,24,25,31,32,48,52,53,55,65,67; 29:4(3),8(7); 30:1,7,15,19,20; 31:5,7,9; 32:49,52; 34:4; **Josh.** 1:2,3,6,11,13–15; 2:9,12,14,24; 5:6; 6:2,16,24; 7:7,19; 8:1,7,18; 9:24,27; 10:8,12,19,30,32; 11:6,8,23; 12:6,7; 13:8,14,15,24,29,33; 14:3,4,12,13; 15:13,16,17,19; 17:4,13,14; 18:3,7; 19:49,50; 20:2,4,8; 21:2,3,8,9, 11–13,21,43(41),44(42); 22:4,7,25; 23:13,15,16; 24:3,4,8,11,13,33; **Judg.** 1:2,4,12,13,15,20,34; 2:14,23; 3:6,10,28; 4:7,14; 5:11(KJV, NASB, *tānāh* [8567]),25; 6:1,9,13; 7:2,7,9,14–16; 8:3,5–7,15,24, 25; 9:4,29; 11:9,21,30,32; 12:3; 13:1; 14:9,12,13,19; 15:1,2,6,12,13,18; 16:5, 23,24; 17:4,10; 18:10; 20:13,28,36; 21:1, 7,14,18,22; **Ruth** 1:6,9; 2:18; 3:17; 4:7, 11–13; **1 Sam.** 1:4,5,11,16,17,27; 2:10, 15,16,28; 6:5,8; 8:6,14,15; 9:8,22,23; 10:4; 11:12; 12:13,17,18; 14:10,12,37; 15:28; 17:10,25,38,44,46,47; 18:2,4,8,17, 19,21,27; 20:40; 21:3(4),6(7),9(10); 22:7,10,13; 23:4,14; 24:4(5),7(8),10(11); 25:8,11,27,44; 26:23; 27:5,6; 28:17,19; 30:11,12,22,23; **2 Sam.** 3:14; 4:8,10; 5:19; 9:9; 10:10; 11:16; 12:8,11; 14:7; 16:8; 18:9,11,33(19:1); 20:3,21; 21:6, 9,10; 22:14,33(KJV, NASB, *naṯar* [5425,II]), 36,41,48; 24:9,15,23; **1 Kgs.** 1:48; 2:5, 17,21,35; 3:5,6,9,12,13,25–27; 4:29(5:9); 5:3(17),5–7(19–21),9–12(23–26); 6:6,19, 27; 7:16,39,51; 8:32,34,36,39,40,46,48, 50,56; 9:6,7,11–13,16,22; 10:9,10,13,17, 24,27; 11:11,13,18,19,31,35,36,38; 12:4, 9,29; 13:3,5,7,8,26; 14:7,8,15,16; 15:4, 17,18; 16:2,3; 17:14,19,23; 18:1,9,23,26; 19:21; 20:5,13,28; 21:2–4,6,7,15,22; 22:6,12,15,23; **2 Kgs.** 3:10,13,18; 4:42–44; 5:1,17,22,23; 6:28,29; 8:6,19; 9:9; 10:15; 11:10,12; 12:7(8),9(10),11(12), 14(15),15(16); 13:3,5; 14:9; 15:19,20; 16:14,17; 17:20; 18:14–16,23,30; 19:7, 10,18; 21:8,14; 22:5,7–10; 23:5,11,33,35; 25:28,30; **1 Chr.** 2:35; 5:1,20; 6:48(33), 55–57(40–42),64(49),65(50),67(52); 12:18; 14:10,17; 16:4,7,18; 17:22; 19:11; 21:5,14,22,23,25; 22:9,12,18,19; 25:5; 28:5,11; 29:3,7,8,14,19,24,25; **2 Chr.** 1:7,10,12,15; 2:10–12(9–11),14(13); 3:16; 4:6,7,10; 5:1,10; 6:13,23,25,27,30, 31,36,38; 7:19,20; 8:2,9; 9:8,9,12,16, 23,27; 10:4,9; 11:11,16,23; 12:7; 13:5,16; 16:1,8,10; 17:2,5,19; 18:5,11,14,22; 20:3, 7,10,22; 21:3,7; 22:11; 23:9,11; 24:8,9, 12,24; 25:9,16,18,20; 26:8; 27:5; 28:5, 9,21; 29:6,8; 30:7,8,12; 31:4,6,14,15,19; 32:6,11,24,29; 34:9–11,15–18; 35:3,8, 12,25; 36:7,17,23; **Ezra** 1:2,7; 2:69; 3:7; 7:6,11,27; 8:20,36; 9:7–9,12,13; 10:11,19; **Neh.** 1:11; 2:1,6–9,12; 4:4(3:36); 5:7; 7:5,70–72; 9:8,10,13,15,17,20,22,24,27, 29,30,35–37; 10:29(30),30(31),32(33); 12:47; 13:4,5,10,25,26; **Esth.** 1:19,20; 2:3,9,13,18; 3:10,11,14,15; 4:8; 5:3,6,8; 6:8,9; 7:2,3; 8:1,2,7,11,13,14; 19:12–14;

Job 1:21,22; 2:4; 3:20; 5:10; 6:8; 9:18,24; 11:5; 13:5; 14:4,13; 15:19; 19:23; 23:3; 24:23; 28:15; 29:2; 31:30,31,35; 35:7,10; 36:3,6,31; 37:10; 38:36; 39:19; 42:11,15; **Ps.** 1:3; 2:8; 4:7(8); 8:1(2); 10:14; 14:7; 15:5; 16:10; 18:13(14),32(33),35(36), 40(41),47(48); 20:4(5); 21:2(3),4(5); 27:12; 28:4; 29:11; 33:7; 37:4,21; 39:5(6); 40:3(4); 41:2(3); 44:11(12); 46:6(7); 49:7(8); 50:20; 51:16(18); 53:6(7); 55:6(7), 22(23); 60:4(6); 61:5(6); 66:9; 67:6(7); 68:11(12),33–35(34–36); 69:11(12), 21(22),27(28); 72:1,15; 74:14,19; 77:17(18); 78:20,24,46,61,66; 79:2; 81:2(3); 84:11(12); 85:7(8),12(13); 86:16; 89:27(28); 99:7; 104:12,27,28; 105:11, 32,44; 106:15,41,46; 111:5,6; 112:9; 115:1,16; 118:18; 119:110; 120:3; 121:3; 124:6; 127:2; 132:4; 135:12; 136:21,25; 140:8(9); 144:10; 145:15; 146:7; 147:9,16; 148:6; **Prov.** 1:4,20; 2:3,6; 3:28,34; 4:2,9; 5:9; 6:4,31; 8:1; 9:9; 10:10,24; 12:12; 13:10,15; 21:26; 22:9,16; 23:26,31; 26:8; 28:27; 29:15,17,25; 30:8; 31:3,6,15, 24,31; **Eccl.** 1:13,17; 2:21,26; 3:10,11; 5:1(4:17),6(5),18(17),19(18); 6:2; 7:2,21; 8:9,15,16; 9:1,9; 10:6; 11:2; 12:7,11; **Song** 1:12; 2:13; 7:12(13),13(14); 8:1, 7,11; **Isa.** 3:4; 7:14; 8:18; 9:6(5); 22:21, 22; 27:4; 29:11,12; 30:20,23; 33:16; 34:2; 35:2; 36:8,15; 37:7,10,19; 40:23,29; 41:2,19,27; 42:1,5,6,8,24; 43:3,4,6,9,16, 20,28; 45:3; 46:13; 47:6; 48:11; 49:6,8; 50:4,6; 51:12; 53:9; 55:4,10; 56:5; 61:3,8; 62:7,8; **Jer.** 1:5,9,15,18; 2:15; 3:8,15,19; 4:16; 5:14,24; 6:21,27; 7:7,14; 8:10,13; 9:1(8:23),2(1),11(10),13(12); 10:13; 11:5; 12:7,8,10; 13:16,20; 14:13,22; 15:4,9, 13,20; 16:13,15; 17:3,4,10; 18:21; 19:7,12; 20:2,4,5; 21:7,8,10; 22:13,20,25; 23:39,40; 24:7–10; 25:5,18,30,31; 26:4,6,15,24; 27:2,5,6,8; 28:14; 29:6,11,17,18,21,26; 30:3,16; 31:33,35; 32:3,4,12,14,16,19,22, 24,25,28,36,39,40,43; 34:2,3,17,18, 20–22; 35:5,15; 36:32; 37:4,15,17,18,21; 38:3,7,16,18–20; 39:10,14,17; 40:5,11; 42:12; 43:3; 44:10,30; 45:5; 46:24,26; 48:9,34; 49:15; 50:15; 51:16,25,55; 52:11,32,34; **Lam.** 1:11,13,14; 2:7,18; 3:29,30,65; 5:6; **Ezek.** 2:8; 3:3,8,9,17, 20,25; 4:1–3,5,6,8,9,15; 5:14; 6:5,13,14; 7:3,4,8,9,20,21; 9:10; 10:7; 11:9,15,17, 19,21; 12:6; 14:3,8; 15:4,6–8; 16:7,11,12, 17–19,21,27,33,34,36,38,39,41,43,61; 17:5,15,18,19,22; 18:7,8,13,16; 19:8,9; 20:11,12,15,25,28,42; 21:11(16),15(20), 27(32),29(34),31(36); 22:4,31; 23:7,9,24, 25,28,31,42,46,49; 24:8; 25:4,5,7,10, 13,14,17; 26:4,8,9,14,17,19–21; 27:10, 12–14,16,17,19,22; 28:2,6,14,17,18,25; 29:4,5,10,12,19–21; 30:8,12–14,16,21, 24,25; 31:10,11,14; 32:5,8,15,20,23–27, 29,32; 33:2,7,24,27–29; 34:26,27; 35:3,7, 9,12; 36:5,8,26–29; 37:6,14,19,25,26; 38:4; 39:4,11,21,23; 43:8,19,20; 44:14, 28,30; 45:6,8,19; 46:16,17; 47:11,14,23; **Dan.** 1:2,9,12,16,17; 8:12,13; 9:3,10; 10:12,15; 11:6,11,17,21,31; 12:11; **Hos.** 2:5(7),8(10),12(14),15(17); 5:4; 9:14; 11:8; 13:10,11; **Joel** 2:11,17,19,22,23, 30(3:3); 3:3(4:3),16(4:16); **Amos** 1:2; 3:4; 4:6; 9:15; **Obad.** 1:2; **Jon.** 1:3,14; **Mic.** 1:14; 3:5; 5:3(2); 6:7,14,16; 7:20; **Hab.** 3:10; **Zeph.** 3:5,20; **Hag.** 2:9; **Zech.** 3:7,9; 7:11; 8:12; 10:1; **Mal.** 2:2,5,9.

5415. נְתַן *n*^{e}*ṯan* **Aram. verb**
(to give, to bestow; corr. to Hebr. 5414)
Ezra 4:13; 7:20; **Dan.** 2:16; 4:17(14),25(22),32(29).

5416. A. נָתָן *nāṯān* **masc. proper noun**
(Nathan: son of Attai)
1 Chr. 2:36.
B. נָתָן *nāṯān* **masc. proper noun**
(Nathan: father of Igal)
2 Sam. 23:36; **1 Chr.** 11:38.
C. נָתָן *nāṯān* **masc. proper noun**
(Nathan: father of Azariah)
1 Kgs. 4:5.

D. נָתָן *nāt̲ān* **masc. proper noun**
(Nathan: the prophet Nathan)
2 Sam. 7:2–4,17; 12:1,5,7,13,15,25; **1 Kgs.** 1:8,10,11,22–24,32,34,38,44,45; **1 Chr.** 17:1–3,15; 29:29; **2 Chr.** 9:29; 29:25; **Ps.** 51:[title](2).
E. נָתָן *nāt̲ān* **masc. proper noun**
(Nathan: son of David)
2 Sam. 5:14; **1 Chr.** 3:5; 14:4; **Zech.** 12:12.
F. נָתָן *nāt̲ān* **masc. proper noun**
(Nathan: a chief)
Ezra 8:16.
G. נָתָן *nāt̲ān* **masc. proper noun**
(Nathan: son of Binnui)
Ezra 10:39.

5417. A. נְתַנְאֵל *n^e^t̲an'ēl* **masc. proper noun**
(Nethanel: son of Zuar)
Num. 1:8; 2:5; 7:18,23; 10:15.
B. נְתַנְאֵל *n^e^t̲an'ēl* **masc. proper noun**
(Nethanel: father of Shemaiah)
1 Chr. 24:6.
C. נְתַנְאֵל *n^e^t̲an'ēl* **masc. proper noun**
(Nethanel: son of Jesse)
1 Chr. 2:14.
D. נְתַנְאֵל *n^e^t̲an'ēl* **masc. proper noun**
(Nethanel: a priest)
1 Chr. 15:24.
E. נְתַנְאֵל *n^e^t̲an'ēl* **masc. proper noun**
(Nethanel: son of Obed-Edom)
1 Chr. 26:4.
F. נְתַנְאֵל *n^e^t̲an'ēl* **masc. proper noun**
(Nethanel: prince of Judah)
2 Chr. 17:7.
G. נְתַנְאֵל *n^e^t̲an'ēl* **masc. proper noun**
(Nethanel: brother of Cononiah)
2 Chr. 35:9.
H. נְתַנְאֵל *n^e^t̲an'ēl* **masc. proper noun**
(Nethanel: son of Jedaiah)
Neh. 12:21.
I. נְתַנְאֵל *n^e^t̲an'ēl* **masc. proper noun**
(Nethanel: son of Pashur)
Ezra 10:22.
J. נְתַנְאֵל *n^e^t̲an'ēl* **masc. proper noun**
(Nethanel: a priest)
Neh. 12:36.

5418. A. נְתַנְיָה *n^e^t̲anyāh,* נְתַנְיָהוּ *n^e^t̲anyāhû* **masc. proper noun**
(Nethaniah: son of Asaph)
1 Chr. 25:2,12.
B. נְתַנְיָה *n^e^t̲anyāh* **masc. proper noun**
(Nethaniah: a Levite)
2 Chr. 17:8.
C. נְתַנְיָה *n^e^t̲anyāh* **masc. proper noun**
(Nethaniah: father of Jehudi)
Jer. 36:14.
D. נְתַנְיָה *n^e^t̲anyāh,* נְתַנְיָהוּ *n^e^t̲anyāhû* **masc. proper noun**
(Nethaniah: father of Ishmael)
2 Kgs. 25:23,25; **Jer.** 40:8,14,15; 41:1,2,6,7,9–12,15,16,18.

5419. נְתַן־מֶלֶךְ *n^e^t̲an-melek̲* **masc. proper noun**
(Nathan-Melech)
2 Kgs. 23:11.

5420. נָתַס *nāt̲as* **verb**
(to break up, to mar)
Job 30:13.

5421. נָתַע *nāt̲a'* **verb**
(to break)
Job 4:10.

5422. נָתַץ *nāṯaṣ* **verb**
(to break down, to tear down, to destroy)
Ex. 34:13; **Lev.** 11:35; 14:45; **Deut.** 7:5; 12:3; **Judg.** 2:2; 6:28,30–32; 8:9,17; 9:45; **2 Kgs.** 10:27; 11:18; 23:7,8,12,15; 25:10; **2 Chr.** 23:17; 31:1; 33:3; 34:4,7; 36:19; **Job** 19:10; **Ps.** 52:5(7); 58:6(7); **Isa.** 22:10; **Jer.** 1:10; 4:26; 18:7; 31:28; 33:4; 39:8; 52:14; **Ezek.** 16:39; 26:9,12; **Nah.** 1:6.

5423. נָתַק *nāṯaq* **verb**
(to break, to break away, to pull away; to draw away)
Lev. 22:24; **Josh.** 4:18; 8:6,16; **Judg.** 16:9,12; 20:31,32; **Job** 17:11; 18:14; **Ps.** 2:3; 107:14; **Eccl.** 4:12; **Isa.** 5:27; 33:20; 58:6; **Jer.** 2:20; 5:5; 6:29; 10:20; 12:3; 22:24; 30:8; **Ezek.** 17:9; 23:34; **Nah.** 1:13.

5424. נֶתֶק *neṯeq* **masc. noun**
(scab, skin disease, type of leprosy)
Lev. 13:30–37; 14:54.

5425. I. נָתַר *nāṯar* **verb**
(to leap, to jump, to startle, to tremble)
Lev. 11:21; **Job** 37:1; **Hab.** 3:6.
II. נָתַר *nāṯar* **verb**
(to loose, to undo, to set free, to release, to set, to make)
2 Sam. 22:33(NIV, *nāṯan* [5414]); **Job** 6:9; **Ps.** 105:20; 146:7; **Isa.** 58:6.

5426. נְתַר *n^eṯar* **Aram. verb**
(to strip off; corr. to Hebr. 5425,II)
Dan. 4:14(11).

5427. נֶתֶר *neṯer* **masc. noun**
(niter, soda, lye)
Prov. 25:20; **Jer.** 2:22.

5428. נָתַשׁ *nāṯaš* **verb**
(to pluck up, to root out)
Deut. 29:28(27); **1 Kgs.** 14:15; **2 Chr.** 7:20; **Ps.** 9:6(7); **Jer.** 1:10; 12:14,15,17; 18:7,14(NIV, *nāšaṯ* [5405]); 24:6; 31:28,40; 42:10; 45:4; **Ezek.** 19:12; **Dan.** 11:4; **Amos** 9:15; **Mic.** 5:14(13).

ס Samekh

5429. סְאָה *s*[e]*'āh* **fem. noun**
(seah: a measure of flour or grain)
Gen. 18:6; **1 Sam.** 25:18; **1 Kgs.** 18:32; **2 Kgs.** 7:1,16,18.

5430. I. סְאוֹן *s*[e]*'ôn* **masc. noun**
(boot)
Isa. 9:5(4)(KJV, see II).
II. סְאוֹן *s*[e]*'ôn* **masc. noun**
(battle)
Isa. 9:5(4)(NASB, NIV, see I).

5431. סָאַן *sā'an* **verb**
(to be shod, to have boots; to be a warrior)
Isa. 9:5(4).

5432. I. סַאסְּאָה *sa'ss*[e]*'āh* **fem. noun**
(a driving away, warfare)
Isa. 27:8(KJV, see II).
II. סַאסְּאָה *sa'ss*[e]*'āh* **fem. noun**
(moderation, a measured response)
Isa. 27:8(NASB, NIV, see I).

5433. סָבָא *sāḇā'* **verb**
(to imbibe, to carouse, to get drunk)
Deut. 21:20; **Prov.** 23:20,21; **Ezek.** 23:42(KJV, NIV, [Q[e]] *sāḇā'iym* [5436]); **Isa.** 56:12; **Nah.** 1:10.

5434. I. סְבָא *s*[e]*ḇā'* **masc. proper noun**
(Seba)
Gen. 10:7; **1 Chr.** 1:9.
II. סְבָא *s*[e]*ḇā'* **masc. proper noun**
(the land or nation of Seba)
Ps. 72:10; **Isa.** 43:3.

5435. סֹבֶא *sōḇe'* **masc. noun**
(wine, choice wine)
Isa. 1:22; **Hos.** 4:18; **Nah.** 1:10.

5436. סְבָאִים *s*[e]*ḇā'iym,* סָבָאִים *sāḇā'iym* **masc. pl. proper noun**
(Sabeans)
Isa. 45:14; **Ezek.** 23:42(NASB, [K[e]] *sāḇā'* [5433]).

5437. סָבַב *sāḇaḇ* **verb**
(to go around, to surround; to turn around, to turn back, to change)
Gen. 2:11,13; 19:4; 37:7; 42:24; **Ex.** 13:18; 28:11(KJV, *mûsabbôṯ* [4142]); 39:6(KJV, *mûsabbôṯ* [4142]),13(KJV, *mûsabbôṯ* [4142]); **Num.** 21:4; 32:38 (KJV, *mûsabbôṯ* [4142]); 34:4,5; 36:7,9; **Deut.** 2:1,3; 32:10; **Josh.** 6:3,4,7,11, 14,15; 7:9; 15:3,10; 16:6; 18:14; 19:14; **Judg.** 11:18; 16:2; 18:23; 19:22; 20:5; **1 Sam.** 5:8–10; 7:16; 15:12,27; 16:11; 17:30; 18:11; 22:17,18,22; **2 Sam.** 3:12; 5:23; 14:20,24; 18:15,30; 20:12; 22:6; **1 Kgs.** 2:15; 5:3(17); 7:15,23,24; 8:14; 18:37; 21:4; **2 Kgs.** 3:9,25; 6:15; 8:21; 9:18,19; 16:18; 20:2; 23:34; 24:17; **1 Chr.** 10:14; 12:23; 13:3; 14:14; 16:43; **2 Chr.** 4:2,3; 6:3; 13:13; 14:7(6); 17:9; 18:31; 21:9; 23:2; 29:6; 33:14; 35:22; 36:4; **Ezra** 6:22; **Job** 16:13; 40:22; **Ps.** 7:7(8); 17:11; 18:5(6); 22:12(13),16(17); 26:6; 32:7,10; 48:12(13); 49:5(6); 55:10(11); 59:6(7),14(15); 71:21; 88:17(18); 109:3; 114:3,5; 118:10–12; **Prov.** 26:14; **Eccl.** 1:6; 2:20; 7:25; 9:14; 12:5; **Song** 2:17; 3:2,3; 5:7; 6:5; **Isa.** 23:16; 28:27; 38:2; **Jer.** 6:12; 21:4; 31:22,39; 41:14; 52:21; **Ezek.** 1:9,12,17; 7:22; 10:11,16; 26:2; 41:7(KJV, NASB, *mûsaḇ* [4141]),24(KJV, *mûsabbôṯ* [4142]); 42:19; 47:2; **Hos.** 7:2; 11:12(12:1); **Jon.** 2:3(4),5(6); **Hab.** 2:16; **Zech.** 14:10.

5438. סִבָּה *sibbāh* **fem. noun**
(turn of events, cause)
1 Kgs. 12:15.

5439. סָבִיב *sāḇiyḇ* **adv. or prep.** (surrounding, all around, on every side)
Gen. 23:17; 35:5; 41:48; **Ex.** 7:24; 16:13; 19:12; 25:11,24,25; 27:17; 28:32–34; 29:16,20; 30:3; 37:2,11,12,26; 38:16, 20,31; 39:23,25,26; 40:8,33; **Lev.** 1:5,11; 3:2,8,13; 7:2; 8:15,19,24; 9:12,18; 14:41; 16:18; 25:31,44; **Num.** 1:50,53; 2:2; 3:26,37; 4:26,32; 11:24,31,32; 16:24, 27,34; 22:4; 32:33; 34:12; 35:2,4; **Deut.** 6:14; 12:10; 13:7(8); 17:14; 21:2; 25:19; **Josh.** 15:12; 18:20; 19:8; 21:11,42(40), 44(42); 23:1; **Judg.** 2:12,14; 7:18,21; 8:34; 20:29; **1 Sam.** 12:11; 14:21,47; 26:5,7; 31:9; **2 Sam.** 5:9; 7:1; 22:12; 24:6; **1 Kgs.** 3:1; 4:24(5:4),31(5:11); 5:4(18); 6:5,6; 7:12,18,20,23,24,35,36; 18:32,35; **2 Kgs.** 6:17; 11:8,11; 17:15; 25:1,4,10,17; **1 Chr.** 4:33; 6:55(40); 9:27; 10:9; 11:8; 22:9,18; 28:12; **2 Chr.** 4:2,3; 14:7(6),14(13); 15:15; 17:10; 20:30; 23:7,10; 32:22; 34:6; **Ezra** 1:6; **Neh.** 5:17; 6:16; 12:28,29; **Job** 1:10; 10:8; 18:11; 19:10,12; 22:10; 29:5; 41:14(6); **Ps.** 3:6(7); 12:8(9); 18:11(12); 27:6; 31:13(14); 34:7(8); 44:13(14); 50:3; 76:11(12); 78:28; 79:3,4; 89:7(8),8(9); 97:2,3; 125:2; 128:3; **Eccl.** 1:6; **Song** 3:7; **Isa.** 42:25; 49:18; 60:4; **Jer.** 1:15; 4:17; 6:3,25; 12:9; 17:26; 20:3,10; 21:14; 25:9; 32:44; 33:13; 46:5,14; 48:17,39; 49:5,29; 50:14,15,29,32; 51:2; 52:4,7,14, 22,23; **Lam.** 1:17; 2:3,22; **Ezek.** 1:4,18, 27,28; 4:2; 5:2,5–7,12,14,15; 6:5,13; 8:10; 10:12; 11:12; 12:14; 16:33,37,57; 19:8; 23:22,24; 27:11; 28:23,24,26; 31:4; 32:22–26; 34:26; 36:3,4,7,36; 37:2,21; 39:17; 40:5,14,16,17,25,29,30,33,36,43; 41:5–8,10–12,16,17,19; 42:15–17,20; 43:12,13,17,20; 45:1,2; 46:23; 48:35; **Dan.** 9:16; **Joel** 3:11(4:11),12(4:12); **Amos** 3:11; **Nah.** 3:8; **Zech.** 2:5(9); 7:7; 12:2,6; 14:14.

5440. סָבַךְ *sāḇaḵ* **verb** (to wrap around, to intertwine, to become entangled)
Job 8:17; **Nah.** 1:10.

5441. סְבֹךְ *s^eḇōḵ* **masc. noun** (thicket, lair)
Ps. 74:5; **Jer.** 4:7.

5442. סְבַךְ *s^eḇaḵ* **masc. noun** (thicket)
Gen. 22:13; **Isa.** 9:18(17); 10:34.

5443. סַבְּכָא *sabb^eḵā'*, שַׂבְּכָא *śabb^eḵā'* **Aram. fem. noun** (a musical instrument: sackbut, trigon, or harp)
Dan. 3:5,7,10,15.

5444. סִבְּכַי *sibb^eḵai* **masc. proper noun** (Sibbecai)
2 Sam. 21:18; **1 Chr.** 11:29; 20:4; 27:11.

5445. סָבַל *sāḇal* **verb** (to bear a load, to carry)
Gen. 49:15; **Ps.** 144:14; **Eccl.** 12:5; **Isa.** 46:4,7; 53:4,11; **Lam.** 5:7.

5446. סְבַל *s^eḇal* **Aram. verb** (to bear a load; corr. to Hebr. 5445)
Ezra 6:3.

5447. סֵבֶל *sēḇel* **masc. noun** (burden, forced labor)
1 Kgs. 11:28; **Neh.** 4:17(11); **Ps.** 81:6(7).

5448. סֹבֶל *sōḇel* **masc. noun** (burden)
Isa. 9:4(3); 10:27; 14:25.

5449. סַבָּל *sabbāl* **masc. noun** (carrier, burden bearer)
1 Kgs. 5:15(29); **2 Chr.** 2:2(1),18(17); 34:13; **Neh.** 4:10(4).

5450. סְבָלָה *s^eḇālāh* **fem. noun** (burden, hard labor)
Ex. 1:11; 2:11; 5:4,5; 6:6,7.

5451. סִבֹּלֶת *sibbōlet̲* **fem. noun**
(Sibboleth [an ear of grain])
Judg. 12:6.

5452. סְבַר *s^eb̲ar* **Aram. verb**
(to think to do, to try)
Dan. 7:25.

5453. סִבְרַיִם *sib̲rayim* **proper noun**
(the town Sibraim)
Ezek. 47:16.

5454. סַבְתָּא *sab̲tā'*, סַבְתָּה *sab̲tāh* **masc. proper noun**
(Sabta, Sabtah)
Gen. 10:7; **1 Chr.** 1:9.

5455. סַבְתְּכָא *sab̲t^ek̲ā'* **masc. proper noun**
(Sabtecha)
Gen. 10:7; **1 Chr.** 1:9.

5456. סָגַד *sāgad̲* **verb**
(to fall down, to bow down)
Isa. 44:15,17,19; 46:6.

5457. סְגִד *s^eghid̲* **Aram. verb**
(to worship, to do homage; corr. to Hebr. 5456)
Dan. 2:46; 3:5–7,10–12,14,15,18,28.

5458. I. סְגוֹר *s^egôr* **masc. noun**
(gold)
Job 28:15(*sāgar* [5462,II]).
II. סְגוֹר *s^egôr* **masc. noun**
(enclosure, chest)
Hos. 13:8.

5459. סְגֻלָּה *s^egullāh* **fem. noun**
(valued possession, personal treasure)
Ex. 19:5; **Deut.** 7:6; 14:2; 26:18; **1 Chr.** 29:3; **Ps.** 135:4; **Eccl.** 2:8; **Mal.** 3:17.

5460. סְגַן *s^egan* **Aram. masc. noun**
(ruler, prefect; corr. to Hebr. 5461)
Dan. 2:48; 3:2,3,27; 6:7(8).

5461. סֶגֶן *segen*, סָגָן *sāgān* **masc. noun**
(ruler, official)
Ezra 9:2; **Neh.** 2:16; 4:14(8),19(13); 5:7,17; 7:5; 12:40; 13:11; **Isa.** 41:25; **Jer.** 51:23,28,57; **Ezek.** 23:6,12,23.

5462. I. סָגַר *sāgar* **verb**
(to shut, to close)
Gen. 2:21; 7:16; 19:6,10; **Ex.** 14:3; **Lev.** 13:4,5,11,21,26,31,33,50,54; 14:38,46; **Num.** 12:14,15; **Deut.** 23:15(16); 32:30; **Josh.** 2:5,7; 6:1; 20:5; **Judg.** 3:22,23; 9:51; **1 Sam.** 1:5,6; 17:46; 23:7,11,12,20; 24:18(19); 26:8; 30:15; **2 Sam.** 18:28; **1 Kgs.** 6:20(NIV, see II),21(NIV, see II); 7:49(NIV, see II),50(NIV, see II); 10:21 (NIV, see II); 11:27; **2 Kgs.** 4:4,5,21,33; 6:32; **2 Chr.** 4:20,22; 9:20; 28:24; 29:7; **Neh.** 6:10; 13:19; **Job** 3:10; 11:10; 12:14; 16:11; 41:15(7); **Ps.** 17:10; 31:8(9); 35:3; 78:48,50,62; **Eccl.** 12:4; **Isa.** 22:22; 24:10,22; 26:20; 45:1; 60:11; **Jer.** 13:19; **Lam.** 2:7; **Ezek.** 3:24; 44:1,2; 46:1, 2,12; **Amos** 1:6,9; 6:8; **Obad.** 1:14; **Mal.** 1:10.
II. סָגַר *sāgar* **masc. noun**
(finest gold, pure)
1 Kgs. 6:20(KJV, NASB, see I),21(KJV, NASB, see I); 7:49(KJV, NASB, see I),50(KJV, NASB, see I); 10:21(KJV, NASB, see I); **Job** 28:15(KJV, NASB, *s^egôr* [5458,I]).

5463. סְגַר *s^egar* **Aram. verb**
(to shut; corr. to Hebr. 5462,I)
Dan. 6:22(23).

5464. סַגְרִיר *sagriyr* **masc. noun**
(steady rain)
Prov. 27:15.

5465. סַד *sad̲* **masc. noun**
(stocks, shackles [for feet])
Job 13:27; 33:11.

5466. סָדִין *sāḏiyn* **masc. noun**
(sheet, linen garment)
Judg. 14:12,13; **Prov.** 31:24; **Isa.** 3:23.

5467. סְדֹם *s^e^ḏōm* **proper noun**
(Sodom)
Gen. 10:19; 13:10,12,13; 14:2,8,10–12, 17,21,22; 18:16,20,22,26; 19:1,4,24,28; **Deut.** 29:23(22); 32:32; **Isa.** 1:9,10; 3:9; 13:19; **Jer.** 23:14; 49:18; 50:40; **Lam.** 4:6; **Ezek.** 16:46,48,49,53,55,56; **Amos** 4:11; **Zeph.** 2:9.

5468. סֵדֶר *sēḏer* **masc. noun**
(orderliness)
Job 10:22.

5469. סַהַר *sahar* **masc. noun**
(roundness)
Song 7:2(3).

5470. סֹהַר *sōhar* **masc. noun**
(prison, jail)
Gen. 39:20–23; 40:3,5.

5471. סוֹא *sô'* **masc. proper noun**
(So, king of Egypt)
2 Kgs. 17:4.

5472. סוּג *sûg* **verb**
(to turn away, to turn back, to backslide)
Deut. 19:14(KJV, *nāsag* [5253]); 27:17 (KJV, *nāsag* [5253]); **2 Sam.** 1:22(20) (KJV, *śûg* [7734]); **Ps.** 35:4; 40:14(15); 44:18(19); 53:3(4); 70:2(3); 78:57; 80:18(19); 129:5; **Prov.** 14:14; 22:28(KJV, *nāsag* [5253]); 23:10(KJV, *nāsag* [5253]); **Isa.** 42:17; 50:5; 59:13(KJV, *nāsag* [5253]),14(KJV, *nāsag* [5253]); **Jer.** 38:22; 46:5; **Hos.** 5:10(KJV, *nāsag* [5253]); **Mic.** 2:6(KJV, *nāsag* [5253]); 6:14(KJV, *nāsag* [5253]); **Zeph.** 1:6.

5473. סוּג *sûg* **verb**
(to fence in, to encircle)
Song 7:2(3); **Isa.** 17:11(KJV, NIV, *śûg* [7735]).

5474. סוּגַר *sûgar* **masc. noun**
(cage)
Ezek. 19:9.

5475. סוֹד *sôḏ* **masc. noun**
(counsel, secret counsel)
Gen. 49:6; **Job** 15:8; 19:19; 29:4; **Ps.** 25:14; 55:14(15); 64:2(3); 83:3(4); 89:7(8); 111:1; **Prov.** 3:32; 11:13; 15:22; 20:19; 25:9; **Jer.** 6:11; 15:17; 23:18,22; **Ezek.** 13:9; **Amos** 3:7.

5476. סוֹדִי *sôḏiy* **masc. proper noun**
(Sodi)
Num. 13:10.

5477. סוּחַ *sûaḥ* **masc. proper noun**
(Suah)
1 Chr. 7:36.

5478. I. סוּחָה *sûḥāh* **fem. noun**
(refuse, rubbish)
Isa. 5:25(KJV, see II).
II. סוּחָה *sûḥāh* **fem. noun**
(something torn)
Isa. 5:25(NASB, NIV, see I).

5479. סוֹטַי *sôṭay* **masc. proper noun**
(Sotai)
Ezra 2:55; **Neh.** 7:57.

5480. I. סוּךְ *sûk* **verb**
(to pour, to anoint)
Ex. 30:22(KJV, *yāsak* [3251]); **Deut.** 28:40; **Ruth** 3:3; **2 Sam.** 12:20; 14:2; **2 Chr.** 28:15; **Ezek.** 16:9; **Dan.** 10:3; **Mic.** 6:15.
II. סוּךְ *sûk* **verb**
(to enclose, to hedge in)
Job 3:23(KJV, NIV, *sāḵaḵ* [5526]); 38:8(KJV, NIV, *sāḵaḵ* [5526]).

5481. סוּמְפּוֹנְיָה *sûmpônyāh* **Aram. fem. noun**
(bagpipe, dulcimer)
Dan. 3:5,7(KJV, NIV, omit),10,15.

5482. סְוֵנֵה *s^e^wēnēh* **proper noun**
(the town of Syene [the Peshitta has Aswan])
Ezek. 29:10; 30:6.

5483. I. סוּס *sûs* **masc. noun**
(horse)
Gen. 47:17; 49:17; **Ex.** 9:3; 14:9,23; 15:1,19,21; **Deut.** 11:4; 17:16; 20:1; **Josh.** 11:4,6,9; **Judg.** 5:22; **2 Sam.** 15:1; **1 Kgs.** 4:26(5:6),28(5:8); 10:25,28,29; 18:5; 20:1,20,21,25; 22:4; **2 Kgs.** 2:11; 3:7; 5:9; 6:14,15,17; 7:6,7,10,13,14; 9:18,19,33; 10:2; 11:16; 14:20; 18:23; 23:11; **2 Chr.** 1:16,17; 9:24,25,28; 23:15; 25:28; **Ezra** 2:66; **Neh.** 3:28; 7:68; **Esth.** 6:8–11; 8:10; **Job** 39:18,19; **Ps.** 20:7(8); 32:9; 33:17; 76:6(7); 147:10; **Prov.** 21:31; 26:3; **Eccl.** 10:7; **Isa.** 2:7; 5:28; 30:16; 31:1,3; 36:8; 43:17; 63:13; 66:20; **Jer.** 4:13; 5:8; 6:23; 8:6,7,16; 12:5; 17:25; 22:4; 31:40; 46:4,9; 50:37,42; 51:21,27; **Ezek.** 17:15; 23:6,12,20,23; 26:7,10,11; 27:14; 38:4,15; 39:20; **Hos.** 1:7; 14:3(4); **Joel** 2:4; **Amos** 2:15; 4:10; 6:12; **Mic.** 5:10(9); **Nah.** 3:2; **Hab.** 1:8; 3:8,15; **Hag.** 2:22; **Zech.** 1:8; 6:2,3,6; 9:10; 10:3,5; 12:4; 14:15,20.
II. סוּס sûs, סֻס sus **masc. noun**
(swallow, crane, swift)
Isa. 38:14; **Jer.** 8:7.

5484. סוּסָה *sûsāh* **fem. noun**
(mare, female horse)
Song 1:9.

5485. סוּסִי *sûsiy* **masc. proper noun**
(Susi)
Num. 13:11.

5486. סוּף *sûp̱* **verb**
(to come to an end, to perish, to be consumed)
Esth. 9:28; **Ps.** 73:19; **Isa.** 66:17; **Jer.** 8:13; **Amos** 3:15; **Zeph.** 1:2,3.

5487. סוּף *sûp̱* **Aram. verb**
(to bring to an end, to fulfill; corr. to Hebr. 5486)
Dan. 2:44; 4:33(30).

5488. סוּף *sûp̱* **masc. noun**
(reed, red [as in Red Sea, Sea of Reeds])
Ex. 2:3,5; 10:19; 13:18; 15:4,22; 23:31; **Num.** 14:25; 21:4,14; 33:10,11; **Deut.** 1:1(KJV, see *sûp̱* [5489,II]; NASB, NIV, *sûp̱* [5489,I]),40; 2:1; 11:4; **Josh.** 2:10; 4:23; 24:6; **Judg.** 11:16; **1 Kgs.** 9:26; **Neh.** 9:9; **Ps.** 106:7,9,22; 136:13,15; **Isa.** 19:6; **Jer.** 49:21; **Jon.** 2:5(6).

5489. I. סוּף *sûp̱* **proper noun**
(Suph; a place near Mt. Horeb)
Deut. 1:1(KJV, see II).
II. סוּף *sûp̱* **proper noun**
(Red [reed]; a designation for the Red Sea; from *sûp̱* [5488])
Deut. 1:1(NASB, NIV, see I).

5490. סוֹף *sôp̱* **masc. noun**
(end, conclusion)
2 Chr. 20:16; **Eccl.** 3:11; 7:2; 12:13; **Joel** 2:20.

5491. סוֹף *s̱ōph* **Aram. masc. noun**
(end, conclusion)
Dan. 4:11(8),22(19); 6:26(27); 7:26,28.

5492. I. סוּפָה *sûp̱āh* **fem. noun**
(wind, stormy wind)
Job 21:18; 27:20; 37:9; **Ps.** 83:15(16); **Prov.** 1:27; 10:25; **Isa.** 5:28; 17:13; 21:1; 29:6; 66:15; **Jer.** 4:13; **Hos.** 8:7; **Amos** 1:14; **Nah.** 1:3.
II. סוּפָה *sûp̱āh* **proper noun**
(Suphah: loc. in Moab)
Num. 21:14(KJV, see III).
III. סוּפָה *sûp̱āh* **proper noun**
(Red [Reed]; a designation for the Red Sea)
Num. 21:14(NASB, NIV, see II).

5493. I. סוּר *sûr* **verb**
(to turn aside, to remove, to move)
Gen. 8:13; 19:2,3; 30:32,35; 35:2; 38:14,19; 41:42; 48:17; 49:10; **Ex.** 3:3,4; 8:8(4),11(7),29(25),31(27); 10:17; 14:25; 23:25; 25:15; 32:8; 33:23; 34:34; **Lev.** 1:16; 3:4,9,10,15; 4:9,31,35; 7:4; 13:58; **Num.** 12:10; 14:9; 16:26; 21:7; **Deut.** 2:27; 4:9; 5:32(29); 7:4,15; 9:12,16; 11:16,28; 17:11,17,20; 21:13; 28:14; 31:29; **Josh.** 1:7; 7:13; 11:15; 23:6; 24:14,23; **Judg.** 2:17; 4:18; 9:29; 10:16; 14:8; 16:17,19,20; 18:3,15; 19:11,12,15; 20:8; **Ruth** 4:1; **1 Sam.** 1:14; 6:3,12; 7:3,4; 12:20,21; 15:6,32; 16:14,23; 17:26, 39,46; 18:12,13; 21:6(7); 22:14(NASB, NIV, see II); 28:3,15,16; **2 Sam.** 2:21–23; 4:7; 5:6; 6:10; 7:15; 12:10; 16:9; 22:23; **1 Kgs.** 2:31; 15:5,12–14; 20:24,39,41; 22:32,43(44); **2 Kgs.** 3:2,3; 4:8,10,11; 6:32; 10:29,31; 12:3(4); 13:2,6,11; 14:4,24; 15:4,9,18,24,28,35; 16:17; 17:18,22,23; 18:4,6,22; 22:2; 23:19,27; 24:3; **1 Chr.** 13:13; 17:13; **2 Chr.** 8:15; 14:3(2),5(4); 15:16,17; 17:6; 20:10,32,33; 25:27; 30:9,14; 32:12; 33:8,15; 34:2,33; 35:12,15; 36:3; **Neh.** 9:19; **Esth.** 3:10; 4:4; 8:2; **Job** 1:1,8; 2:3; 9:34; 12:20,24; 15:30; 19:9; 21:14; 22:17; 27:2,5; 28:28; 33:17; 34:5,20,27; **Ps.** 6:8(9); 14:3; 18:22(23); 34:14(15); 37:27; 39:10(11); 66:20; 81:6(7); 101:4; 119:29,102,115; 139:19; **Prov.** 3:7; 4:24,27; 5:7; 9:4,16; 11:22; 13:14,19; 14:16,27; 15:24; 16:6, 17; 22:6; 27:22; 28:9; **Eccl.** 11:10; **Isa.** 1:16,25; 3:1,18; 5:5,23; 6:7; 7:17; 10:13,27; 11:13; 14:25; 17:1; 18:5; 25:8; 27:9; 30:11; 31:2; 36:7; 49:21; 52:11; 58:9; 59:15; **Jer.** 2:21(KJV, NIV, *sûr* [5494]); 4:1,4; 5:10,23; 6:28; 15:5; 17:5,13(KJV, [K^e] *yāsûr* [3249]); 32:31,40; **Lam.** 3:11; 4:15; **Ezek.** 6:9; 11:18,19; 16:42,50; 21:26(31); 23:25; 26:16; 36:26; 45:9; **Dan.** 9:5,11; 11:31; 12:11; **Hos.** 2:2(4), 17(19); 4:18; 7:14; 9:12; **Amos** 5:23; 6:7; **Zeph.** 3:11,15; **Zech.** 3:4; 9:7; 10:11; **Mal.** 2:8; 3:7.

II. סָר *sār* **masc. noun**
(captain)
1 Sam. 22:14(KJV, see I).

5494. סוּר *sûr* **masc. noun**
(degenerate)
Jer. 2:21(NASB, sûr [5493,I]).

5495. סוּר *sûr* **proper noun**
(the Temple gate Sur)
2 Kgs. 11:6.

5496. סוּת *sûṯ* **verb**
(to incite, to entice, to mislead)
Deut. 13:6(7); **Josh.** 15:18; **Judg.** 1:14; **1 Sam.** 26:19; **2 Sam.** 24:1; **1 Kgs.** 21:25; **2 Kgs.** 18:32; **1 Chr.** 21:1; **2 Chr.** 18:2,31; 32:11,15; **Job** 2:3; 36:16,18; **Isa.** 36:18; **Jer.** 38:22; 43:3.

5497. סוּת *sûṯ* **masc. noun**
(garment, clothing)
Gen. 49:11.

5498. סָחַב *sāḥaḇ* **verb**
(to drag, to drag off)
2 Sam. 17:13; **Jer.** 15:3; 22:19; 49:20; 50:45.

5499. סְחָבָה *s^eḥāḇāh* **fem. noun**
(old rag, worn-out clothing)
Jer. 38:11,12.

5500. סָחָה *sāḥāh* **verb**
(to scrape)
Ezek. 26:4.

5501. סְחִי *s^eḥiy* **masc. noun**
(scum, offscouring)
Lam. 3:45.

5502. סָחַף *sāḥap̱* **verb**
(to sweep away, to sweep off one's feet)
Prov. 28:3; **Jer.** 46:15.

5503. סָחַר *sāḥar* **verb**
(to travel as merchants, to trade)
Gen. 23:16; 34:10,21; 37:28; 42:34;

1 Kgs. 10:28; **2 Chr.** 1:16; 9:14; **Ps.** 38:10(11); **Prov.** 31:14; **Isa.** 23:2,8; 47:15; **Jer.** 14:18; **Ezek.** 27:12,16,18, 21,36; 38:13.

5504. סַחַר *saḥar* **masc. noun** (merchandise, profit, marketplace) **Prov.** 3:14,14(KJV, *sāḥār* [5505]); 31:18; **Isa.** 23:3(KJV, *sāḥār* [5505]),18; 45:14 (KJV, *sāḥār* [5505]).

5505. סָחָר *sāḥār* **masc. noun** (merchandise; NASB, NIV, same as *saḥar* [5504]) **Prov.** 3:14; **Isa.** 23:3; 45:14.

5506. סְחֹרָה *s^eḥōrāh* **fem. noun** (market, merchandise) **Ezek.** 27:15.

5507. סֹחֵרָה *sōḥērāh* **fem. noun** (small shield, buckler) **Ps.** 91:4.

5508. I. סֹחֶרֶת *sōḥereṯ* **fem. noun** (costly stone used in paving) **Esth.** 1:6(KJV, see II).
II. סֹחֶרֶת *sōḥereṯ* **fem. noun** (black marble used in paving) **Esth.** 1:6(NASB, NIV, see I).

5509. סִיג *siyg*, סוּג *sûg* **masc. noun** (dress) **1 Kgs.** 18:27(KJV, NIV, *śiyg* [7873]); **Ps.** 119:119; **Prov.** 25:4; 26:23; **Isa.** 1:22,25; **Ezek.** 22:18([K^e^] סוּג [5472]),19.

5510. סִיוָן *siywān* **proper noun** (the month Sivan) **Esth.** 8:9.

5511. סִיחוֹן *siyḥôn* **masc. proper noun** (Sihon) **Num.** 21:21,23,26–29,34; 32:33; **Deut.** 1:4; 2:24,26,30–32; 3:2,6; 4:46; 29:7(6); 31:4; **Josh.** 2:10; 9:10; 12:2,5; 13:10, 21,27; **Judg.** 11:19–21; **1 Kgs.** 4:19; **Neh.** 9:22; **Ps.** 135:11; 136:19; **Jer.** 48:45.

5512. A. סִין *siyn* **proper noun** (Sin: city on N.E. border of Egypt) **Ezek.** 30:15,16.
B. סִין *siyn* **proper noun** (Sin: desert W. of Mt. Sinai) **Ex.** 16:1; 17:1; **Num.** 33:11,12.

5513. סִינִי *siyniy* **masc. proper noun** (the Sinite people) **Gen.** 10:17; **1 Chr.** 1:15.

5514. סִינַי *siynay* **proper noun** (Mt. Sinai) **Ex.** 16:1; 19:1,2,11,18,20,23; 24:16; 31:18; 34:2,4,29,32; **Lev.** 7:38; 25:1; 26:46; 27:34; **Num.** 1:1,19; 3:1,4,14; 9:1,5; 10:12; 26:64; 28:6; 33:15,16; **Deut.** 33:2; **Judg.** 5:5; **Neh.** 9:13; **Ps.** 68:8(9),17(18).

5515. I. סִינִים *siyniym* **masc. pl. proper noun** (the Sinim people [perhaps from southern China]) **Isa.** 49:12(NIV, see II).
II. סִינִים *siyniym* **masc. pl. proper noun** (the people of Aswan) **Isa.** 49:12(KJV, NASB, see I).

5516. A. סִיסְרָא *siys^e^rā'* **masc. proper noun** (Sisera: a conquering general of Hazor) **Judg.** 4:2,7,9,12–18,22; 5:20,26,28,30; **1 Sam.** 12:9; **Ps.** 83:9(10).
B. סִיסְרָא *siys^e^rā'* **masc. proper noun** (Sisera: father of a postexilic family) **Ezra** 2:53; **Neh.** 7:55.

5517. סִיעָא *siy'ā'*, סִיעֲהָא *siy'ᵃhā'* **masc. proper noun**
(Siaha)
Ezra 2:44; **Neh.** 7:47.

5518. I. סִיר *siyr* **masc./fem. noun**
(pot)
Ex. 16:3; 27:3; 38:3; **1 Kgs.** 7:45; **2 Kgs.** 4:38–41; 25:14; **2 Chr.** 4:11,16; 35:13; **Job** 41:31(23); **Ps.** 58:9(10); 60:8(10); 108:9(10); **Eccl.** 7:6; **Jer.** 1:13; 52:18,19; **Ezek.** 11:3,7,11; 24:3,6; **Mic.** 3:3; **Zech.** 14:20,21.
II. סִיר *siyr* **masc./fem. noun**
(thorn, hook)
Eccl. 7:6; **Isa.** 34:13; **Hos.** 2:6(8); **Amos** 4:2; **Nah.** 1:10.

5519. סָךְ *sāḵ* **masc. noun**
(multitude, throng)
Ps. 42:4(5).

5520. סֹךְ *sōḵ* **masc. noun**
(cover, hiding place, tent)
Ps. 10:9; 27:5; 76:2(3); **Jer.** 25:38.

5521. סֻכָּה *sukkāh* **fem. noun**
(tent, booth, temporary shelter)
Gen. 33:17; **Lev.** 23:34,42,43; **Deut.** 16:13,16; 31:10; **2 Sam.** 11:11; 22:12; **1 Kgs.** 20:12,16; **2 Chr.** 8:13; **Ezra** 3:4; **Neh.** 8:14–17; **Job** 27:18; 36:29; 38:40; **Ps.** 18:11(12); 31:20(21); **Isa.** 1:8; 4:6; **Amos** 9:11; **Jon.** 4:5; **Zech.** 14:16,18,19.

5522. I. סִכּוּת *sikkûṯ* **fem. noun**
(tent, shrine)
Amos 5:26(NASB, see II).
II. סִכּוּת *sikkûṯ* **masc. proper noun**
(the false god Sikkuth)
Amos 5:26(KJV, NIV, see I).

5523. A. סֻכּוֹת *sukkôṯ* **proper noun**
(Succoth: city in Canaan)
Gen. 33:17; **Josh.** 13:27; **Judg.** 8:5,6,8, 14–16; **1 Kgs.** 7:46; **2 Chr.** 4:17; **Ps.** 60:6(8); 108:7(8).
B. סֻכּוֹת *sukkôṯ* **proper noun**
(Succoth: campsite in Egypt)
Ex. 12:37; 13:20; **Num.** 33:5,6.

5524. סֻכּוֹת בְּנוֹת *sukkôṯ bᵉnôṯ* **proper noun**
(Succoth Benoth)
2 Kgs. 17:30.

5525. סֻכִּיִּים *sukkiyyiym* **masc. pl. proper noun**
(Sukkites)
2 Chr. 12:3.

5526. I. סָכַךְ *sāḵaḵ*, שָׂכַךְ *śaḵaḵ* **verb**
(to cover)
Ex. 25:20; 33:22; 37:9; 40:3,21; **Judg.** 3:24; **1 Sam.** 24:3(4); **1 Kgs.** 8:7; **1 Chr.** 28:18; **Job** 3:23(NASB, *sûḵ* [5480,II]); 38:8; 40:22; **Ps.** 5:11(12); 91:4; 139:11 (KJV, NASB, שׁוּף [7779,III]),13(NASB, NIV, see III); 140:7(8); **Lam.** 3:43,44; **Ezek.** 28:14,16; **Nah.** 2:5(6).
II. סָכַךְ *sāḵaḵ* **verb**
(to stir up, to incite)
Isa. 9:11(10); 19:2.
III. סָכַךְ *sāḵaḵ*, שָׂכַךְ *śāḵaḵ* **verb**
(to weave together)
Job 10:11(KJV, *śûḵ* [7753]); **Ps.** 139:13(KJV, see I).

5527. סְכָכָה *sᵉḵāḵāh* **proper noun**
(Secacah)
Josh. 15:61.

5528. סָכַל *sāḵal* **verb**
(to be foolish, to act foolishly)
Gen. 31:28; **1 Sam.** 13:13; 26:21; **2 Sam.** 15:31; 24:10; **1 Chr.** 21:8; **2 Chr.** 16:9; **Isa.** 44:25.

5529. סֶכֶל *seḵel* **masc. noun**
(folly, foolishness)
Eccl. 10:6.

5530. סָכָל *sāḵāl* **masc. noun**
(fool)
Eccl. 2:19; 7:17; 10:3,14; **Jer.** 4:22; 5:21.

5531. סִכְלוּת *siḵlûṯ*, שִׂכְלוּת *śiḵlûṯ* **fem. noun**

(folly, foolishness)
Eccl. 1:17; 2:3,12,13; 7:25; 10:1,13.

5532. I. סָכַן *sā<u>k</u>an* **verb**
(to be useful, to be profitable, to attend to, to be acquainted with)
Num. 22:30; **1 Kgs.** 1:2(NIV, see II),4 (NIV, see II); **Job** 15:3; 22:2,21; 34:9; 35:3; **Ps.** 139:3; **Isa.** 22:15(NIV, see II).
II. סֹכֵן *sō<u>k</u>ēn* **fem. noun**
(steward, nurse)
1 Kgs. 1:2(KJV, NASB, see I),4(KJV, NASB, see I); **Isa.** 22:15(KJV, NASB, see I).

5533. I. סָכַן *sā<u>k</u>an* **verb**
(to be poor, to be impoverished)
Isa. 40:20.
II. סָכַן *sā<u>k</u>an* **verb**
(to be in danger)
Eccl. 10:9.

5534. I. סָכַר *sā<u>k</u>ar* **verb**
(to stop up, to shut up)
Gen. 8:2; **Ps.** 63:11(12).
II. סָכַר *sā<u>k</u>ar* **verb**
(to hand over, to deliver)
Isa. 19:4.

5535. I. סָכַת *sā<u>k</u>a<u>t</u>* **verb**
(to be silent)
Deut. 27:9(KJV, see II).
II. סָכַת *sā<u>k</u>a<u>t</u>* **verb**
(to take heed)
Deut. 27:9(NASB, NIV, see I).

5536. סַל *sal* **masc. noun**
(basket)
Gen. 40:16–18; **Ex.** 29:3,23,32; **Lev.** 8:2,26,31; **Num.** 6:15,17,19; **Judg.** 6:19.

5537. סָלָא *sālā'* **verb**
(to weigh, to compare)
Lam. 4:2.

5538. סִלָּא *sillā'* **proper noun**
(Silla)
2 Kgs. 12:20(21).

5539. I. סָלַד *sāla<u>d</u>* **verb**
(to rejoice)
Job 6:10(KJV, see II).
II. סָלַד *sāla<u>d</u>* **verb**
(to harden oneself)
Job 6:10(NASB, NIV, see I).

5540. סֶלֶד *sele<u>d</u>* **masc. proper noun**
(Seled)
1 Chr. 2:30.

5541. I. סָלָה *sālāh* **verb**
(to tread down, to reject, to treat as worthless)
Ps. 119:118; **Lam.** 1:15.
II. סָלָה *sālāh* **verb**
(to value, to pay for)
Job 28:16,19.

5542. סֶלָה *selāh* **verb**
(Selah! A technical command in the Psalms, perhaps marking places for pauses in singing. Used by Habakkuk, perhaps as an interjection of praise.)
Ps. 3:2(3),4(5),8(9); 4:2(3),4(5); 7:5(6); 9:16(17),20(21); 20:3(4); 21:2(3); 24:6,10; 32:4,5,7; 39:5(6),11(12); 44:8(9); 46:3(4),7(8),11(12); 47:4(5); 48:8(9); 49:13(14),15(16); 50:6; 52:3(5), 5(7); 54:3(5); 55:7(8),19(20); 57:3(4), 6(7); 59:5(6),13(14); 60:4(6); 61:4(5); 62:4(5),8(9); 66:4,7,15; 67:1(2),4(5); 68:7(8),19(20),32(33); 75:3(4); 76:3(4), 9(10); 77:3(4),9(10),15(16); 81:7(8); 82:2; 83:8(9); 84:4(5),8(9); 85:2(3); 87:3,6; 88:7(8),10(11); 89:4(5),37(38), 45(46),48(49); 140:3(4),5(6),8(9); 143:6; **Hab.** 3:3,9,13.

5543. A. סַלּוּ *sallû,* סַלַּי *sallay* **masc. proper noun**
(Sallu: a priest)
Neh. 12:7,20.
B. סָלוּא *sālû'* **masc. proper noun**
(Salu: a Simeonite)
Num. 25:14.

C. סַלּוּא *sallû'*, סַלֻא *salu'* **masc. proper noun**
(Sallu: postexilic Jew)
1 Chr. 9:7; **Neh.** 11:7.
D. סַלַּי *sallay* **masc. proper noun**
(Sallai: a Benjamite)
Neh. 11:8.

5544. סַלּוֹן *sallôn* **masc. noun**
(brier, thorn)
Ezek. 2:6; 28:24.

5545. סָלַח *sālaḥ* **verb**
(to forgive, to pardon)
Ex. 34:9; **Lev.** 4:20,26,31,35; 5:10,13, 16,18; 6:7(5:26); 19:22; **Num.** 14:19,20; 15:25,26,28; 30:5(6),8(9),12(13); **Deut.** 29:20(19); **1 Kgs.** 8:30,34,36,39,50; **2 Kgs.** 5:18; 24:4; **2 Chr.** 6:21,25,27, 30,39; 7:14; **Ps.** 25:11; 103:3; **Isa.** 55:7; **Jer.** 5:1,7; 31:34; 33:8; 36:3; 50:20; **Lam.** 3:42; **Dan.** 9:19; **Amos** 7:2.

5546. סַלָּח *sallāḥ* **adj.**
(ready to forgive)
Ps. 86:5.

5547. סְלִיחָה *s^e^liyḥāh* **fem. noun**
(forgiveness)
Neh. 9:17; **Ps.** 130:4; **Dan.** 9:9.

5548. סַלְכָה *salḵāh* **proper noun**
(Salecah)
Deut. 3:10; **Josh.** 12:5; 13:11; **1 Chr.** 5:11.

5549. סָלַל *sālal* **verb**
(to build up, to lift up; to exalt)
Ex. 9:17; **Job** 19:12; 30:12; **Ps.** 68:4(5); **Prov.** 4:8; 15:19; **Isa.** 57:14; 62:10; **Jer.** 18:15; 50:26.

5550. סֹלְלָה *sōl^e^lāh*, סוֹלְלָה *sôl^e^lāh* **fem. noun**
(siege mound, siege ramp)
2 Sam. 20:15; **2 Kgs.** 19:32; **Isa.** 37:33; **Jer.** 6:6; 32:24; 33:4; **Ezek.** 4:2; 17:17; 21:22(27); 26:8; **Dan.** 11:15.

5551. סֻלָּם *sullām* **masc. noun**
(ladder, stairway)
Gen. 28:12.

5552. I. סַלְסִלָּה *salsillāh* **fem. noun**
(branch)
Jer. 6:9(KJV, see II).
II. סַלְסִלָּה *salsillāh* **fem. noun**
(basket)
Jer. 6:9(NASB, NIV, see I).

5553. סֶלַע *sela'* **masc. noun**
(rock, cliff)
Num. 20:8,10,11; 24:21; **Deut.** 32:13; **Judg.** 1:36(NASB, NIV, *sela'* [5554]); 6:20; 15:8,11,13; 20:45,47; 21:13; **1 Sam.** 13:6; 14:4; 23:25,28(KJV, NIV, *sela' hammaḥlqôṯ* [5555]); **2 Sam.** 22:2; **1 Kgs.** 19:11; **2 Kgs.** 14:7; **2 Chr.** 25:12; **Neh.** 9:15; **Job** 39:1,28; **Ps.** 18:2(3); 31:3(4); 40:2(3); 42:9(10); 71:3; 78:16; 104:18; 137:9; 141:6; **Prov.** 30:26; **Song** 2:14; **Isa.** 2:21; 7:19; 16:1; 22:16; 31:9; 32:2; 33:16; 42:11(NASB, NIV, *sela'* [5554]); 57:5; **Jer.** 5:3; 13:4; 16:16; 23:29; 48:28; 49:16; 51:25; **Ezek.** 24:7,8; 26:4,14; **Amos** 6:12; **Obad.** 1:3.

5554. סֶלַע *sela'* **proper noun**
(Sela)
Judg. 1:36(KJV, *sela'* [5553]); **2 Kgs.** 14:7; **Isa.** 16:1; 42:11(KJV, *sela'* [5553]).

5555. סֶלַע הַמַּחְלְקוֹת *sela' hammaḥl^e^qôṯ* **proper noun**
(Sela Hammahlekoth)
1 Sam. 23:28(NASB, *sela'* [5553] and *maḥ^a^lōqeṯ* [4256,I]).

5556. סָלְעָם *sol'ām* **masc. noun**
(bald locust, devastating locust)
Lev. 11:22.

5557. סָלַף *sālap̱* **verb**
(to overthrow; to twist; to pervert)

Ex. 23:8; **Deut.** 16:19; **Job** 12:19; **Prov.** 13:6; 19:3; 21:12; 22:12.

5558. סֶלֶף *selep̱* **masc. noun**
(perversion, deceitfulness)
Prov. 11:3; 15:4.

5559. I. סָלַק *sālaq* **verb**
(to ascend, to go up)
Ps. 139:8(KJV, nāsaq [5266]).
II. סְלֵק *s^elēq* **Aram. verb**
(to go up, to ascend)
Ezra 4:12; **Dan.** 2:29; 3:22(KJV, *n^esaq* [5267]); 6:23(24)(KJV, *n^esaq* [5267]); 7:3,8,20.

5560. סֹלֶת *sōleṯ* **fem. noun**
(fine flour)
Gen. 18:6; **Ex.** 29:2,40; **Lev.** 2:1,2,4,5,7; 5:11; 6:15(8),20(13); 7:12; 14:10,21; 23:13,17; 24:5; **Num.** 6:15; 7:13,19, 25,31,37,43,49,55,61,67,73,79; 8:8; 15:4,6,9; 28:5,9,12,13,20,28; 29:3,9,14; **1 Kgs.** 4:22(5:2); **2 Kgs.** 7:1,16,18; **1 Chr.** 9:29; 23:29; **Ezek.** 16:13,19; 46:14.

5561. סַם *sam* **masc. noun**
(fragrant, sweet, fragrant spice)
Ex. 25:6; 30:7,34; 31:11; 35:8,15,28; 37:29; 39:38; 40:27; **Lev.** 4:7; 16:12; **Num.** 4:16; **2 Chr.** 2:4(3); 13:11.

5562. I. סַמְגַּר נְבוֹ *samgar-n^eḇô* **masc. proper noun**
(Samgar-nebu)
Jer. 29:3(NIV, see II).
II. סַמְגַּר *samgar* **masc. proper noun**
(Samgar; NIV, attributes first part of 5562,I as modifier of previous noun and combines second part with next noun, *n^eḇû śar-s^ekiym* [5015,F])
Jer. 29:3(NIV, see II).

5563. סְמָדַר *s^emāḏar* **masc. noun**
(young grapes, grapes in blossom)
Song 2:13,15; 7:12(13).

5564. סָמַךְ *sāmak̲* **verb**
(to lay upon, to uphold, to sustain)
Gen. 27:37; **Ex.** 29:10,15,19; **Lev.** 1:4; 3:2,8,13; 4:4,15,24,29,33; 8:14,18,22; 16:21; 24:14; **Num.** 8:10,12; 27:18,23; **Deut.** 34:9; **Judg.** 16:29; **2 Kgs.** 18:21; **2 Chr.** 29:23; 32:8; **Ps.** 3:5(6); 37:17,24; 51:12(14); 54:4(6); 71:6; 88:7(8); 111:8; 112:8; 119:116; 145:14; **Song** 2:5; **Isa.** 26:3; 36:6; 48:2; 59:16; 63:5; **Ezek.** 24:2; 30:6; **Amos** 5:19.

5565. סְמַכְיָהוּ *s^emak̲yāhû* **masc. proper noun**
(Semachia)
1 Chr. 26:7.

5566. סֵמֶל *sēmel,* סֶמֶל *semel* **masc. noun**
(idol, image, figure)
Deut. 4:16; **2 Chr.** 33:7,15; **Ezek.** 8:3,5.

5567. I. סָמַן *sāman* **verb**
(to appoint)
Isa. 28:25(NIV, see II).
II. סָמַן *sāman* **verb**
(to plot out)
Isa. 28:25(KJV, NASB, see I).

5568. סָמַר *sāmar* **verb**
(to bristle up, to stand up; to shiver)
Job 4:15; **Ps.** 119:120.

5569. I. סָמָר *sāmār* **adj.**
(bristly, rough)
Jer. 51:27(NIV, see II).
II. סָמָר *sāmār* **adj.**
(swarming)
Jer. 51:27(KJV, NASB, see I).

5570. סְנָאָה *s^enā'āh,* הַסְּנָאָה *hass^enā'āh* **masc. proper noun**
(Senaah, Hassenaah)
Ezra 2:35; **Neh.** 3:3; 7:38.

5571. סַנְבַלַּט *sanḇallaṭ* **masc. proper noun**
(Sanballat)
Neh. 2:10,19; 4:1(3:33),7(1); 6:1,2,5,12,14; 13:28.

5572. סְנֶה *s^{e}neh* **masc. noun**
(bush)
Ex. 3:2–4; **Deut.** 33:16.

5573. סֶנֶּה *senneh* **masc. proper noun**
(Seneh)
1 Sam. 14:4.

5574. סְנוּאָה *s^{e}nû'āh,* הַסְּנָאָה *hass^{e}u'āh* **masc. proper noun**
(Senuah, Hassenuah)
1 Chr. 9:7; **Neh.** 11:9.

5575. סַנְוֵרִים *sanwēriym* **masc. pl. noun**
(blindness, sudden blindness)
Gen. 19:11; **2 Kgs.** 6:18.

5576. סַנְחֵרִיב *sanḥēriyḇ* **masc. proper noun**
(Sennacherib)
2 Kgs. 18:13; 19:16,20,36; **2 Chr.** 32:1,2,9,10,22; **Isa.** 36:1; 37:17,21,37.

5577. סַנְסִנָּה *sansinnāh* **masc. noun**
(fruit stalk, bough)
Song 7:8(9).

5578. סַנְסַנָּה *sansannāh* **masc. proper noun**
(Sansannah)
Josh. 15:31.

5579. סְנַפִּיר *s^{e}nappiyr* **masc. noun**
(fin [of a fish])
Lev. 11:9,10,12; **Deut.** 14:9,10.

5580. סָס *sās* **masc. noun**
(grubworm [of a moth])
Isa. 51:8.

5581. סִסְמַי *sismāy* **masc. proper noun**
(Sismai)
1 Chr. 2:40.

5582. סָעַד *sā'aḏ* **verb**
(to support, to sustain, to refresh)
Gen. 18:5; **Judg.** 19:5,8; **1 Kgs.** 13:7; **Ps.** 18:35(36); 20:2(3); 41:3(4); 94:18; 104:15; 119:117; **Prov.** 20:28; **Isa.** 9:7(6).

5583. סְעַד *s^e'aḏ* **Aram. verb**
(to help, to support; corr. to Hebr. 5582)
Ezra 5:2.

5584. סָעָה *sā'āh* **verb**
(to blow strongly [of a storm wind])
Ps. 55:8(9).

5585. I. סָעִיף *sa'iyp̱* **masc. noun**
(cleft, fissure, crack)
Judg. 15:8,11; **Isa.** 2:21; 57:5.
II. סָעִיף *sa'iyp̱* **masc. noun**
(branch, bough)
Isa. 17:6; 27:10.

5586. סָעַף *sā'ap̱* **verb**
(to cut off, to lop off)
Isa. 10:33.

5587. I. סְעִפִּים *s^e'ippiym* **fem. pl. noun**
(opinions)
1 Kgs. 18:21.
II. שְׂעִפִּים *s^e'ippiym* **fem. pl. noun**
(thoughts, disquieting thoughts)
Job 4:13; 20:2.

5588. סֵעֵף *sē'ēp̱* **masc. noun**
(double-mindedness, vanity of thought)
Ps. 119:113.

5589. סְעַפָּה *s^e'appāh* **fem. noun**
(branch, bough)
Ezek. 31:6,8.

5590. סָעַר *sā'ar* **verb**
(to storm, to blow strongly; metaph.: to be enraged)
2 Kgs. 6:11; **Isa.** 54:11; **Hos.** 13:3; **Jon.** 1:11,13; **Hab.** 3:14; **Zech.** 7:14.

5591. I. סַעַר *sa'ar* **masc. noun**
(stormy wind, tempest, whirlwind)
Ps. 55:8(9); 83:15(16); **Jer.** 23:19; 25:32; 30:23; **Amos** 1:14; **Jon.** 1:4,12.
II. סְעָרָה *s^e'ārāh* **fem. noun**
(stormy wind, tempest, whirlwind)
2 Kgs. 2:1,11; **Job** 38:1; 40:6; **Ps.** 107:25,29; 148:8; **Isa.** 29:6; 40:24; 41:16; **Jer.** 23:19; 30:23; **Ezek.** 1:4; 13:11,13; **Zech.** 9:14.

5592. I. סַף *sap̱* **masc. noun**
(basin, bowl)
Ex. 12:22; **2 Sam.** 17:28; **1 Kgs.** 7:50; **2 Kgs.** 12:13(14); **Jer.** 52:19; **Zech.** 12:2.
II. סַף *sap̱* **masc. noun**
(threshold, doorway)
Judg. 19:27; **1 Kgs.** 14:17; **2 Kgs.** 12:9(10); 22:4; 23:4; 25:18; **1 Chr.** 9:19,22; **2 Chr.** 3:7; 23:4; 34:9; **Esth.** 2:21; 6:2; **Isa.** 6:4; **Jer.** 35:4; 52:24; **Ezek.** 40:6,7; 41:16; 43:8; **Amos** 9:1; **Zeph.** 2:14.

5593. סַף *sap̱* **masc. proper noun**
(Saph)
2 Sam. 21:18.

5594. סָפַד *sāp̱aḏ* **verb**
(to mourn, to lament)
Gen. 23:2; 50:10; **1 Sam.** 25:1; 28:3; **2 Sam.** 1:12; 3:31; 11:26; **1 Kgs.** 13:29, 30; 14:13,18; **Eccl.** 3:4; 12:5; **Isa.** 32:12; **Jer.** 4:8; 16:4–6; 22:18; 25:33; 34:5; 49:3; **Ezek.** 24:16,23; **Joel** 1:13; **Mic.** 1:8; **Zech.** 7:5; 12:10,12.

5595. I. סָפָה *sāp̱āh* **verb**
(to sweep away; to gather)
Gen. 18:23,24; 19:15,17; **Num.** 16:26; 32:14; **Deut.** 29:19(18)(KJV, see II); **1 Sam.** 12:25; 26:10; 27:1; **1 Chr.** 21:12; **Ps.** 40:14(15); **Prov.** 13:23; **Isa.** 7:20; 13:15(KJV, see II); **Jer.** 12:4.
II. סָפָה *sāp̱āh* **verb**
(to add, to heap onto)
Deut. 29:19(18)(NASB, NIV, see I); 32:23(NIV, *yāsap̱* [3254]); **Isa.** 13:15 (NASB, NIV, see I); 29:1(NASB, NIV, *yāsap̱* [3254]); 30:1(NIV, *yāsap̱* [3254]); **Jer.** 7:21(NASB, NIV, *yāsap̱* [3254]).

5596. I. סָפַח *sāp̱aḥ* **verb**
(to associate, to join together)
1 Sam. 2:36; 26:19; **Job** 30:7; **Isa.** 14:1; **Hab.** 2:15.
II. שָׂפַח *śāp̱aḥ* **verb**
(to make scabby, to smite with a scab)
Isa. 3:17.

5597. סַפַּחַת *sappaḥaṯ* **fem. noun**
(scab, rash)
Lev. 13:2; 14:56.

5598. סִפַּי *sippay* **masc. proper noun**
(Sippai)
1 Chr. 20:4.

5599. I. סָפִיחַ *sāp̱iyaḥ* **masc. noun**
(aftergrowth, that which grows of itself)
Lev. 25:5,11; **2 Kgs.** 19:29; **Job** 14:19(NASB, NIV, see II); **Isa.** 37:30.
II. סָפִיחַ *sāp̱iyaḥ* **masc. noun**
(torrent)
Job 14:19(KJV, see I).

5600. סְפִינָה *s^e p̱iynāh* **fem. noun**
(ship)
Jon. 1:5.

5601. סַפִּיר *sappiyr* **masc. noun**
(sapphire, lapis lazuli)
Ex. 24:10; 28:18; 39:11; **Job** 28:6,16; **Song** 5:14; **Isa.** 54:11; **Lam.** 4:7; **Ezek.** 1:26; 10:1; 28:13.

5602. סֵפֶל *sēpel* **masc. noun**
(bowl, dish)
Judg. 5:25; 6:38.

5603. I. סָפַן *sāpan* **verb**
(to cover with panels)
1 Kgs. 6:9; 7:3,7; **Jer.** 22:14; **Hag.** 1:4.
II. סָפַן *sāpan* **verb**
(to reserve for seating)
Deut. 33:21.
III. סָפַן *sāpan* **verb**
(to cover as a treasure)
Deut. 33:19(KJV, NIV, *śāpan* [8226]).

5604. סִפֻּן *sippun* **masc. noun**
(ceiling)
1 Kgs. 6:15.

5605. סָפַף *sāpap* **verb**
(to stand guard at the threshold, to be a doorkeeper)
Ps. 84:10(11).

5606. I. סָפַק *sāpaq*, שָׂפַק *śāpaq* **verb**
(to slap, to clap)
Num. 24:10; **Job** 27:23; 34:26,37; **Isa.** 2:6; **Jer.** 31:19; **Lam.** 2:15; **Ezek.** 21:12(17).
II. סָפַק *sāpaq* **verb**
(to wallow, to vomit)
Jer. 48:26.
III. שָׂפַק *śāpaq* **verb**
(to suffice)
1 Kgs. 20:10.

5607. I. סֵפֶק *sēpeq* **masc. noun**
(plenty, abundance, sufficiency)
Job 20:22.
II. שֶׂפֶק *śepeq* **masc. noun**
(riches)
Job 36:18(KJV, NASB, see III).
III. שֶׂפֶק *sepeq* **masc. noun**
(stroke, scoffing, chastisement)
Job 36:18(NIV, see II).

5608. I. סָפַר *sāpar* **verb**
(to recount, to tell, to number, to proclaim)
Gen. 15:5; 16:10; 24:66; 29:13; 32:12(13); 37:9,10; 40:8,9; 41:8,12,49; **Ex.** 9:16; 10:2; 18:8; 24:3; **Lev.** 15:13,28; 23:15,16; 25:8; **Num.** 13:27; **Deut.** 16:9; **Josh.** 2:23; **Judg.** 6:13; 7:13; **1 Sam.** 11:5; **2 Sam.** 24:10; **1 Kgs.** 3:8; 8:5; 13:11; **2 Kgs.** 8:4–6; **1 Chr.** 16:24; 21:2; 23:3; **2 Chr.** 2:2(1),17(16); 5:6; **Ezra** 1:8; **Esth.** 5:11; 6:13; **Job** 12:8; 14:16; 15:17; 28:27; 31:4; 37:20; 38:37; 39:2; **Ps.** 2:7; 9:1(2),14(15); 19:1(2); 22:17(18), 22(23),30(31); 26:7; 40:5(6); 44:1(2); 48:12(13),13(14); 50:16; 56:8(9); 59:12(13); 64:5(6); 66:16; 69:26(27); 71:15; 73:15,28; 75:1(2); 78:3,4,6; 79:13; 87:6; 88:11(12); 96:3; 102:21(22); 107:22; 118:17; 119:13,26; 139:18; 145:6; **Isa.** 22:10; 43:21,26; 52:15; **Jer.** 23:27,28,32; 33:22; 51:10; **Ezek.** 12:16; 44:26; **Hos.** 1:10(2:1); **Joel** 1:3; **Hab.** 1:5.
II. סֹפֵר *sōpēr*, סוֹפֵר *sôpēr* **masc. noun**
(secretary, scribe, writer; KJV, see I)
Judg. 5:14; **2 Sam.** 8:17; 20:25; **1 Kgs.** 4:3; **2 Kgs.** 12:10(11); 18:18,37; 19:2; 22:3,8–10,12; 25:19; **1 Chr.** 2:55; 18:16; 24:6; 27:32; **2 Chr.** 24:11; 26:11; 34:13, 15,18,20; **Ezra** 7:6,11; **Neh.** 8:1,4,9,13; 12:26,36; 13:13; **Esth.** 3:12; 8:9; **Ps.** 45:1(2); **Isa.** 33:18; 36:3,22; 37:2; **Jer.** 8:8; 36:10,12,20,21,23,26,32; 37:15,20; 52:25; **Ezek.** 9:2,3.

5609. סְפַר *s^e^par* **Aram. masc. noun**
(book, record)
Ezra 4:15; 6:1,18; **Dan.** 7:10.

5610. סְפָר *s̱^e^pār* **masc. noun**
(census, numbering)
2 Chr. 2:17(16).

5611. סְפָר *s^e^pār* **proper noun**
(Sephar)
Gen. 10:30.

5612. I. סֵפֶר *sēp̱er* **masc. noun**
(book, writing, scroll)
Gen. 5:1; **Ex.** 17:14; 24:7; 32:32,33; **Num.** 5:23; 21:14; **Deut.** 17:18; 24:1,3; 28:58,61; 29:20(19),21(20),27(26); 30:10; 31:24,26; **Josh.** 1:8; 8:31,34; 10:13; 18:9; 23:6; 24:26; **1 Sam.** 10:25; **2 Sam.** 1:18; 11:14,15; **1 Kgs.** 11:41; 14:19,29; 15:7, 23,31; 16:5,14,20,27; 21:8,9,11; 22:39, 45(46); **2 Kgs.** 1:18; 5:5–7; 8:23; 10:1,2, 6,7,34; 12:19(20); 13:8,12; 14:6,15,18,28; 15:6,11,15,21,26,31,36; 16:19; 19:14; 20:12,20; 21:17,25; 22:8,10,11,13,16; 23:2,3,21,24,28; 24:5; **1 Chr.** 9:1; **2 Chr.** 16:11; 17:9; 20:34; 24:27; 25:4,26; 27:7; 28:26; 32:17,32; 34:14–16,18,21,24, 30,31; 35:12,27; 36:8; **Neh.** 7:5; 8:1,3, 5,8,18; 9:3; 12:23; 13:1; **Esth.** 1:22; 2:23; 3:13; 6:1; 8:5,10; 9:20,25,30,32; 10:2; **Job** 19:23; 31:35; **Ps.** 40:7(8); 69:28(29); 139:16; **Eccl.** 12:12; **Isa.** 29:11,12,18; 30:8; 34:4,16; 37:14; 39:1; 50:1; **Jer.** 3:8; 25:13; 29:1,25,29; 30:2; 32:10–12,14, 16,44; 36:2,4,8,10,11,13,18,32; 45:1; 51:60,63; **Ezek.** 2:9; **Dan.** 1:4,17; 9:2; 12:1,4; **Nah.** 1:1; **Mal.** 3:16.
II. סִפְרָה *siprāh* **fem. noun**
(book)
Ps. 56:8(9).

5613. סָפַר *sāp̱ar* **Aram. masc. noun**
(scribe, secretary)
Ezra 4:8,9,17,23; 7:12,21.

5614. סְפָרַד *s^e^p̱āraḏ* **proper noun**
(Sepharad)
Obad. 1:20.

5615. סְפֹרָה *s^e^p̱ōrāh* **fem. noun**
(sum, number, amount)
Ps. 71:15.

5616. סְפַרְוִי *s^e^p̱arwiy* **masc. proper noun**
(an inhabitant of Sepharvaim)
2 Kgs. 17:31.

5617. סְפַרְוַיִם *s^e^p̱arwayim* **proper noun**
(Sepharvaim)
2 Kgs. 17:24,31,31(word occurs only once in 2 Kgs. 17:31, see 5616); 18:34; 19:13; **Isa.** 36:19; 37:13.

5618. I. סֹפֶרֶת *sōp̱ereṯ* **masc. proper noun**
(Sophereth)
Ezra 2:55(NASB, NIV, see II); **Neh.** 7:57.
II. הַסֹּפֶרֶת *hassōp̱ereṯ* **masc. proper noun**
(Hassophereth)
Ezra 2:55(KJV, see I).

5619. I. סָקַל *sāqal* **verb**
(to stone, to throw stones at, to kill by stoning)
Ex. 8:26(22); 17:4; 19:13; 21:28,29,32; **Deut.** 13:10(11); 17:5; 22:21,24; **Josh.** 7:25; **1 Kgs.** 21:10,13–15; **1 Sam.** 30:6; **2 Sam.** 16:6,13; **Isa.** 5:2; 62:10.
II. סָקַל *sāqal* **verb**
(to remove all stones)
Isa. 5:2; 62:10.

5620. סַר *sar* **adj.**
(sullen, sad)
1 Kgs. 20:43; 21:4,5.

5621. סָרָב *sārāḇ* **masc. noun**
(brier, thistle)
Ezek. 2:6.

5622. סַרְבָּל *sarbāl* **Aram. masc. noun**
(coat, robe, trousers)
Dan. 3:21,27.

5623. סַרְגּוֹן *sargôn* **masc. proper noun**
(Sargon)
Isa. 20:1.

5624. סֶרֶד *sere<u>d</u>* **masc. proper noun**
(Sered)
Gen. 46:14; **Num.** 26:26.

5625. סַרְדִּי *sardiy* **masc. proper noun**
(Seredite, descendant of Sered [5624])
Num. 26:26.

5626. סִרָה *sirāh* **proper noun**
(Sirah)
2 Sam. 3:26.

5627. I. סָרָה *sārāh* **fem. noun**
(revolt, rebellion)
Deut. 13:5(6); 19:16; **Isa.** 1:5; 31:6; 59:13; **Jer.** 28:16; 29:32.
II. סָרָה *sārāh* **fem. noun**
(stopping, ceasing, desisting)
Isa. 14:6.

5628. I. סָרַח *sāraḥ* **verb**
(to spread, to hang over, to sprawl)
Ex. 26:12,13; **Ezek.** 17:6; 23:15; **Amos** 6:4,7.
II. סָרַח *sāraḥ* **verb**
(to decay, to degenerate, to vanish)
Jer. 49:7.

5629. סֶרַח *seraḥ* **masc. noun**
(additional, overlapping)
Ex. 26:12.

5630. סִרְיוֹן *siryôn* **masc. noun**
(armor, scale armor)
Jer. 46:4; 51:3.

5631. סָרִיס *sariys* **masc. noun**
(officer, eunuch)
Gen. 37:36; 39:1; 40:2,7; **1 Sam.** 8:15; **1 Kgs.** 22:9; **2 Kgs.** 8:6; 9:32; 18:17(KJV, NASB, *ra<u>b</u> sariys* [7249]); 20:18; 23:11; 24:12,15; 25:19; **1 Chr.** 28:1; **2 Chr.** 18:8; **Esth.** 1:10,12,15; 2:3,14,15,21; 4:4,5; 6:2,14; 7:9; **Isa.** 39:7; 56:3,4; **Jer.** 29:2; 34:19; 38:7; 39:3(KJV, NASB, *ra<u>b</u> sariys* [7249]),13(KJV, NASB, *ra<u>b</u> sariys* [7249]); 41:16; 52:25; **Dan.** 1:3,7–11,18.

5632. סָרַךְ *sāra<u>k</u>* **Aram. masc. noun**
(overseer, president, administrator)
Dan. 6:2–4(3–5),6(7),7(8).

5633. I. סֶרֶן *seren* **masc. noun**
(lord, prince)
Josh. 13:3; **Judg.** 3:3; 16:5,8,18,23, 27,30; **1 Sam.** 5:8,11; 6:4,12,16,18; 7:7; 29:2,6,7; **1 Chr.** 12:19(20).
II. סֶרֶן *seren* **masc. noun**
(axle)
1 Kgs. 7:30(KJV, see III).
III. סֶרֶן *seren* **masc. noun**
(plate, covering)
1 Kgs. 7:30(NASB, NIV, see II).

5634. סַרְעַפָּה *sar'appāh* **fem. noun**
(bough [of a tree])
Ezek. 31:5.

5635. סָרַף *sārap̱* **verb**
(to burn; NASB, a var. of *śārap̱* [8313])
Amos 6:10.

5636. סִרְפָּד *sirpa<u>d</u>* **masc. noun**
(brier, nettle)
Isa. 55:13.

5637. סָרַר *sārar* **verb**
(to be rebellious, to be stubborn)
Deut. 21:18,20; **Neh.** 9:29; **Ps.** 66:7; 68:6(7),18(19); 78:8; **Prov.** 7:11; **Isa.** 1:23; 30:1; 65:2; **Jer.** 5:23; 6:28; **Hos.** 4:16; 9:15; **Zech.** 7:11.

5638. סְתָו *s^etāw* **masc. noun**
(winter)
Song 2:11.

5639. סְתוּר *s^e^ṯûr* **masc. proper noun**
(Sethur)
Num. 13:13.

5640. סָתַם *sāṯam,* שָׂתַם *śāṯam* **verb**
(to stop, to stop up)
Gen. 26:15,18; **2 Kgs.** 3:19,25; **2 Chr.** 32:3,4,30; **Neh.** 4:7(1); **Ps.** 51:6(8); **Lam.** 3:8; **Ezek.** 28:3; **Dan.** 8:26; 12:4,9.

5641. סָתַר *sāṯar* **verb**
(to hide, to conceal)
Gen. 4:14; 31:49; **Ex.** 3:6; **Num.** 5:13; **Deut.** 7:20; 29:29(28); 31:17,18; 32:20; **1 Sam.** 20:2,5,19,24; 23:19; 26:1; **1 Kgs.** 17:3; **2 Kgs.** 11:2; **2 Chr.** 22:11; **Job** 3:10,23; 13:20,24; 14:13; 28:21; 34:22,29; **Ps.** 10:11; 13:1(2); 17:8; 19:6(7),12(13); 22:24(25); 27:5,9; 30:7(8); 31:20(21); 38:9(10); 44:24(25); 51:9(11); 54:[title](1); 55:12(13); 64:2(3); 69:17(18); 88:14(15); 89:46(47); 102:2(3); 104:29; 119:19; 143:7; **Prov.** 22:3; 25:2; 27:5,12; 28:28; **Isa.** 8:17; 16:3; 28:15; 29:14,15; 40:27; 45:15; 49:2; 50:6; 54:8; 57:17; 59:2; 64:7(6); 65:16; **Jer.** 16:17; 23:24; 33:5; 36:19,26; **Ezek.** 39:23,24,29; **Hos.** 13:14; **Amos** 9:3; **Mic.** 3:4; **Zeph.** 2:3.

5642. I. סְתַר *s^e^ṯar* **Aram. verb**
(to hide, to conceal; corr. to Hebr. 5641)
Dan. 2:22.
II. סְתַר *s^e^ṯar* **Aram. verb**
(to destroy, to demolish)
Ezra 5:12.

5643. I. סֵתֶר *sēṯer* **masc. noun**
(covering, hiding place, secret)
Deut. 13:6(7); 27:15,24; 28:57; **Judg.** 3:19; **1 Sam.** 19:2; 25:20; **2 Sam.** 12:12; **Job** 13:10; 22:14; 24:15; 31:27; 40:21; **Ps.** 18:11(12); 27:5; 31:20(21); 32:7; 61:4(5); 81:7(8); 91:1; 101:5; 119:114; 139:15; **Prov.** 9:17; 21:14; 25:33; **Song** 2:14; **Isa.** 16:4; 28:17; 32:2; 45:19; 48:16; **Jer.** 37:17; 38:16; 40:15.
II. סִתְרָה *siṯrāh* **fem. noun**
(hiding place, shelter, protection)
Deut. 32:38.

5644. סִתְרִי *siṯriy* **masc. proper noun**
(Sithri)
Ex. 6:22.

ע Ayin

5645. I. עָב *'āḇ* **masc. noun**
(thick clouds)
Ex. 19:9; **Judg.** 5:4; **2 Sam.** 22:12; 23:4; **1 Kgs.** 18:44,45; **Job** 20:6; 22:14; 26:8; 30:15; 36:29; 37:11,16; 38:34; **Ps.** 18:11(12),12(13); 77:17(18); 104:3; 147:8; **Prov.** 16:15; **Eccl.** 11:3,4; 12:2; **Isa.** 5:6; 14:14; 18:4; 19:1; 25:5; 44:22; 60:8; **Jer.** 4:29(NIV, see II).
II. עָב *'āḇ* **masc. noun**
(thicket)
Jer. 4:29(KJV, NASB, see I).
III. עָב *'āḇ* **masc. noun**
(clay)
2 Chr. 4:17(KJV, NASB, [Q^e] *ma'^aḇeh* [4568]).

5646. I. עָב *'āḇ*, עֹב *'ōḇ* **masc. noun**
(overhang, thick planks [as covering]; NASB, see II)
1 Kgs. 7:6; **Ezek.** 41:25,26.
II. עָב *'āḇ*, עֹב *'ōḇ* **masc. noun**
(threshold; KJV, NIV, see I)
1 Kgs. 7:6; **Ezek.** 41:25,26.

5647. עָבַד *'āḇaḏ* **verb**
(to serve, to work, to labor; to worship)
Gen. 2:5,15; 3:23; 4:2,12; 14:4; 15:13,14; 25:23; 27:29,40; 29:15,18,20,25,27,30; 30:26,29; 31:6,41; 49:15; **Ex.** 1:13,14; 3:12; 4:23; 5:18; 6:5; 7:16; 8:1(7:26), 20(16); 9:1,13; 10:3,7,8,11,24,26; 12:31; 13:5; 14:5,12; 20:5,9; 21:2,6; 23:24,25, 33; 34:21; **Lev.** 25:39,40,46; **Num.** 3:7,8; 4:23,24,26,30,37,41,47; 7:5; 8:11, 15,19,22,25,26; 16:9; 18:6,7,21,23; **Deut.** 4:19,28; 5:9,13; 6:13; 7:4,16; 8:19; 10:12,20; 11:13,16; 12:2,30; 13:2(3),4(5), 6(7),13(14); 15:12,18,19; 17:3; 20:11; 21:3,4; 28:14,36,39,47,48,64; 29:18(17), 26(25); 30:17; 31:20; **Josh.** 16:10; 22:5,27; 23:7,16; 24:2,14–16,18–22, 24,31; **Judg.** 2:7,11,13,19; 3:6–8,14; 9:28,38; 10:6,10,13,16; **1 Sam.** 4:9; 7:3,4; 8:8; 11:1; 12:10,14,20,24; 17:9; 26:19; **2 Sam.** 9:10; 10:19; 15:8; 16:19; 22:44; **1 Kgs.** 4:21(5:1); 9:6,9,21; 12:4,7; 16:31; 22:53(54); **2 Kgs.** 10:18,19, 21–23; 17:12,16,33,35,41; 18:7; 21:3,21; 25:24; **1 Chr.** 19:19; 28:9; **2 Chr.** 2:18(17); 7:19,22; 10:4; 24:18; 30:8; 33:3,16,22; 34:33; 35:3; **Neh.** 9:35; **Job** 21:15; 36:11; 39:9; **Ps.** 2:11; 18:43(44); 22:30(31); 72:11; 97:7; 100:2; 102:22(23); 106:36; **Prov.** 12:11; 28:19; **Eccl.** 5:9(8),12(11); **Isa.** 14:8; 19:9,21,23; 28:21; 30:24; 43:23,24; 60:12; **Jer.** 2:20(KJV, [Q^e] *'āḇar* [5674,I]); 5:19; 8:2; 11:10; 13:10; 16:11,13; 17:4; 22:9,13; 25:6,11,14; 27:6–9,11–14,17; 28:14; 30:8,9; 34:9,10,14; 35:15; 40:9; 44:3; **Ezek.** 20:39,40; 29:18,20; 34:27; 36:9,34; 48:18,19; **Hos.** 12:12(13); **Zeph.** 3:9; **Zech.** 2:9(13)(NIV, *'eḇeḏ* [5650]); 13:5; **Mal.** 3:14,17,18.

5648. עֲבַד *'^aḇaḏ* **Aram. verb**
(to do, to make, to carry out; corr. to Hebr. 5647)
Ezra 4:15,19,22; 5:8; 6:8,11–13,16; 7:18, 21,23,26; **Jer.** 10:11; **Dan.** 2:5; 3:1,15,29; 4:2(3:32),35(32); 5:1; 6:10(11),22(23), 27(28); 7:21.

5649. עֲבַד *'^aḇaḏ* **Aram. masc. noun**
(servant, slave)
Ezra 4:11; 5:11; **Dan.** 2:4,7; 3:26,28; 6:20(21).

5650. עֶבֶד *'eḇeḏ* **masc. noun**
(servant, slave, official)

Gen. 9:25–27; 12:16; 14:15; 18:3,5; 19:2,19; 20:8,14; 21:25; 24:2,5,9,10,14, 17,34,35,52,53,59,61,65,66; 26:15,19,24, 25,32; 27:37; 30:43; 32:4(5),5(6),10(11), 16(17),18(19),20(21); 33:5,14; 39:17,19; 40:20; 41:10,12,37,38; 42:10,11,13; 43:18,28; 44:7,9,10,16–19,21,23,24, 27,30–33; 45:16; 46:34; 47:3,4,19,25; 50:2,7,17,18; **Ex.** 4:10; 5:15,16,21; 7:10,20; 8:3(7:28),4(7:29),9(5),11(7), 21(17),24(20),29(25),31(27); 9:14,20, 21,30,34; 10:1,6,7; 11:3,8; 12:30,44; 13:3,14; 14:5,31; 20:2,10,17; 21:2,5,7, 20,26,27,32; 32:13; **Lev.** 25:6,39,42, 44,55; 26:13; **Num.** 11:11; 12:7,8; 14:24; 22:18; 31:49; 32:4,5,25,27,31; **Deut.** 3:24; 5:6,14,15,21(18); 6:12,21; 7:8; 8:14; 9:27; 12:12,18; 13:5(6),10(11); 15:15,17; 16:11,12,14; 23:15(16); 24:18,22; 28:68; 29:2(1); 32:36,43; 34:5,11; **Josh.** 1:1,2,7, 13,15; 5:14; 8:31,33; 9:8,9,11,23,24; 10:6; 11:12,15; 12:6; 13:8; 14:7; 18:7; 22:2,4,5; 24:17,29; **Judg.** 2:8; 3:24; 6:8,27; **1 Sam.** 3:9,10; 8:14–17; 12:19; 16:15–17; 17:8,9,32,34,36,58; 18:5,22–24, 26,30; 19:1,4; 20:7,8; 21:7(8),11(12), 14(15); 22:6–9,14,15,17; 23:10,11; 25:8,10,39–41; 26:18,19; 27:5,12; 28:2,7,23,25; 29:3,8,10; 30:13; **2 Sam.** 2:12,13,15,17,30,31; 3:18,22,38; 6:20; 7:5,8,19–21,25–29; 8:2,6,7,14; 9:2,6,8, 10–12; 10:2–4,19; 11:1,9,11,13,17,21,24; 12:18,19,21; 13:24,31,35,36; 14:19,20, 22,30,31; 15:2,8,14,15,18,21,34; 16:6,11; 17:20; 18:7,9,29; 19:5–7(6–8),14(15), 17(18),19(20),20(21),26–28(27–29),35–37(36–38); 20:6; 21:15,22; 24:10,20,21; **1 Kgs.** 1:2,9,19,26,27,33,47,51; 2:38–40; 3:6–9,15; 5:1(15),6(20),9(23); 8:23–26, 28–30,32,36,52,53,56,59,66; 9:22,27; 10:5,8,13; 11:11,13,17,26,32,34,36,38; 12:7; 14:8,18; 15:18,29; 16:9; 18:9,12,36; 20:6,9,12,23,31,32,39,40; 22:3,49(50); **2 Kgs.** 1:13; 2:16; 3:11; 4:1; 5:6,13,15, 17,18,25,26; 6:3,8,11,12; 7:12,13; 8:13,19; 9:7,11,28,36; 10:5,10,23; 12:20(21),21(22); 14:5,25; 16:7; 17:3, 13,23; 18:12,24,26; 19:5,34; 20:6; 21:8, 10,23; 22:9,12; 23:30; 24:1,2,10–12; 25:8,24; **1 Chr.** 2:34,35; 6:49(34); 16:13; 17:4,7,17–19,23–27; 18:2,6,7,13; 19:2–4, 19; 20:8; 21:3,8; **2 Chr.** 1:3; 2:8(7),10(9), 15(14); 6:14–17,19–21,23,27,42; 8:9,18; 9:4,7,10,12,21; 10:7; 12:8; 13:6; 24:6, 9,25; 25:3; 28:10; 32:9,16; 33:24; 34:16,20; 35:23,24; 36:20; **Ezra** 2:55, 58,65; 9:9,11; **Neh.** 1:6–8,10,11; 2:5, 10,19,20; 5:5; 7:57,60,67; 9:10,14,36; 10:29(30); 11:3; **Esth.** 1:3; 2:18; 3:2,3; 4:11; 5:11; 7:4; **Job** 1:8; 2:3; 3:19; 4:18; 7:2; 19:16; 31:13; 41:4(40:28); 42:7,8; **Ps.** 18:[title](1); 19:11(12),13(14); 27:9; 31:16(17); 34:22(23); 35:27; 36:[title](1); 69:17(18),36(37); 78:70; 79:2,10; 86:2, 4,16; 89:3(4),20(21),39(40),50(51); 90:13,16; 102:14(15),28(29); 105:6,17, 25,26,42; 109:28; 113:1; 116:16; 119:17, 23,38,49,65,76,84,91,122,124,125,135,140,176; 123:2; 132:10; 134:1; 135:1,9,14; 136:22; 143:2,12; 144:10; **Prov.** 11:29; 12:9; 14:35; 17:2; 19:10; 22:7; 29:19,21; 30:10,22; **Eccl.** 2:7; 7:21; 10:7; **Isa.** 14:2; 20:3; 22:20; 24:2; 36:9,11; 37:5,24,35; 41:8,9; 42:1,19; 43:10; 44:1,2,21,26; 45:4; 48:20; 49:3,5–7; 50:10; 52:13; 53:11; 54:17; 56:6; 63:17; 65:8,9,13–15; 66:14; **Jer.** 2:14; 7:25; 21:7; 22:2,4; 25:4,9,19; 26:5; 27:6; 29:19; 30:10; 33:21,22,26; 34:9–11,13,16; 35:15; 36:24,31; 37:2,18; 43:10; 44:4; 46:26–28; **Lam.** 5:8; **Ezek.** 28:25; 34:23,24; 37:24,25; 38:17; 46:17; **Dan.** 1:12,13; 9:6,10,11,17; 10:17; **Joel** 2:29(3:2); **Amos** 3:7; **Mic.** 6:4; **Hag.** 2:23; **Zech.** 1:6; 2:9(13)(KJV, NASB, *'āḇaḏ* [5647]); 3:8; **Mal.** 1:6; 4:4(3:22).

5651. A. עֶבֶד *'eḇeḏ* **masc. proper noun**
(Ebed: father of Gaal)
Judg. 9:26,28,30,31,35.
B. עֶבֶד *'eḇeḏ* **masc. proper noun**
(Ebed: companion of Ezra)
Ezra 8:6.

5652. עֲבָד *ᵃḇāḏ* **masc. noun**
(deed, work)
Eccl. 9:1.

5653. A. עַבְדָּא *ʿaḇdāʾ* **masc. proper noun**
(Abda: father of Adoniram)
1 Kgs. 4:6.
B. עַבְדָּא *ʿaḇdāʾ* **masc. proper noun**
(Abda: a Levite)
Neh. 11:17.

5654. A. עֹבֵד אֱדוֹם *ʿōḇēḏ ʾeḏôm* **masc. proper noun**
(Obed-Edom: a Gittite)
2 Sam. 6:10–12; **1 Chr.** 13:13,14; 15:25.
B. עֹבֵד אֱדוֹם *ʿōḇēḏ ʾeḏôm* **masc. proper noun**
(Obed-Edom: a Levite)
1 Chr. 15:18,21,24; 16:5,38; 26:4,8,15; **2 Chr.** 25:24.

5655. עַבְדְּאֵל *ʿaḇdeʾēl* **masc. proper noun**
(Abdeel)
Jer. 36:26.

5656. עֲבוֹדָה *ᵃḇôḏāh*, עֲבֹדָה *ᵃḇōḏāh* **fem. noun**
(work, service, bondage)
Gen. 29:27; 30:26; **Ex.** 1:14; 2:23; 5:9,11; 6:6,9; 12:25,26; 13:5; 27:19; 30:16; 35:21,24; 36:1,3,5; 38:21; 39:32,40,42; **Lev.** 23:7,8,21,25,35,36; 25:39; **Num.** 3:7,8,26,31,36; 4:4,19,23,24,26–28,30–33, 35,39,43,47,49; 7:5,7–9; 8:11,19,22, 24–26; 16:9; 18:4,6,7,21,23,31; 28:18, 25,26; 29:1,12,35; **Deut.** 26:6; **Josh.** 22:27; **1 Kgs.** 12:4; **1 Chr.** 4:21; 6:32(17), 48(33); 9:13,19,28; 23:24,26,28,32; 24:3,19; 25:1,6; 26:8,30; 27:26; 28:13–15, 20,21; 29:7; **2 Chr.** 8:14; 10:4; 12:8; 24:12; 29:35; 31:2,16,21; 34:13; 35:2, 10,15,16; **Ezra** 8:20; **Neh.** 3:5; 5:18; 10:32(33),37(38); **Ps.** 104:14,23; **Isa.** 14:3; 28:21; 32:17; **Lam.** 1:3; **Ezek.** 29:18; 44:14.

5657. עֲבֻדָּה *ᵃḇuddāh* **fem. noun**
(servants, esp. household servants)
Gen. 26:14; **Job** 1:3.

5658. A. עַבְדּוֹן *ʿaḇdôn* **proper noun**
(Abdon: levitical city)
Josh. 21:30; **1 Chr.** 6:74(59).
B. עַבְדּוֹן *ʿaḇdôn* **proper noun**
(Abdon: a judge)
Judg. 12:13,15.
C. עַבְדּוֹן *ʿaḇdôn* **proper noun**
(Abdon: a Benjamite)
1 Chr. 8:23.
D. עַבְדּוֹן *ʿaḇdôn* **proper noun**
(Abdon: son of Jeiel)
1 Chr. 8:30; 9:36.
E. עַבְדּוֹן *ʿaḇdôn* **proper noun**
(Abdon: son of Micah)
2 Chr. 34:20.

5659. עַבְדֻת *ʿaḇduṯ* **fem. noun**
(bondage, slavery)
Ezra 9:8,9; **Neh.** 9:17.

5660. A. עַבְדִּי *ʿaḇdiy* **masc. proper noun**
(Abdi: a Levite)
1 Chr. 6:44(29); **2 Chr.** 29:12.
B. עַבְדִּי *ʿaḇdiy* **masc. proper noun**
(Abdi: postexilic Jew)
Ezra 10:26.

5661. עַבְדִיאֵל *ʿaḇdiyʾēl* **masc. proper noun**
(Abdiel)
1 Chr. 5:15.

5662. A. עֹבַדְיָה *ʿōḇaḏyāh* **masc. proper noun**
(Obadiah: son of Izrahiah)
1 Chr. 7:3.
B. עֹבַדְיָה *ʿōḇaḏyāh* **masc. proper noun**
(Obadiah: a Gadite)
1 Chr. 12:9.

C. עֹבַדְיָהוּ *ōḇadyāhû* **masc. proper noun**
(Obadiah: father of Ishmaiah)
1 Chr. 27:19.

D. עֹבַדְיָהוּ *ōḇadyāhû* **masc. proper noun**
(Obadiah: governor of Ahab's house)
1 Kgs. 18:3–7,16.

E. עֹבַדְיָה *ōḇadyāh* **masc. proper noun**
(Obadiah: prince of Judah)
2 Chr. 17:7.

F. עֹבַדְיָה *ōḇadyāh* **masc. proper noun**
(Obadiah: son of Azel)
1 Chr. 8:38; 9:44.

G. עֹבַדְיָהוּ *ōḇadyāhû* **masc. proper noun**
(Obadiah: Levite)
2 Chr. 34:12.

H. עֹבַדְיָה *ōḇadyāh* **masc. proper noun**
(Obadiah: descendant of David)
1 Chr. 3:21.

I. עֹבַדְיָה *ōḇadyāh* **masc. proper noun**
(Obadiah: son of Jehiel)
Ezra 8:9.

J. עֹבַדְיָה *ōḇadyāh* **masc. proper noun**
(Obadiah: son of Shemaiah)
1 Chr. 9:16.

K. עֹבַדְיָה *ōḇadyāh* **masc. proper noun**
(Obadiah: a covenanter)
Neh. 10:5(6).

L. עֹבַדְיָה *ōḇadyāh* **masc. proper noun**
(Obadiah: a Levite; possibly same as J)
Neh. 12:25.

M. עֹבַדְיָה *ōḇadyāh* **masc. proper noun**
(the prophet Obadiah)
Obad. 1:1.

5663. עֶבֶד מֶלֶךְ *'eḇed melek* **masc. proper noun**
(Ebed-Melech)
Jer. 38:7,8,10–12; 39:16.

5664. עֲבֵד נְגוֹ *'aḇed n^eḡô* **masc. proper noun**
(Abed-nego)
Dan. 1:7.

5665. עֲבֵד נְגוֹא *'aḇēd n^eḡô'* **Aram. masc. proper noun**
(Abed-nego; corr. to Hebr. 5664)
Dan. 2:49;
3:12–14,16,19,20,22,23,26,28–30.

5666. עָבָה *'āḇāh* **verb**
(to be thick, to be fat)
Deut. 32:15; 1 Kgs. 12:10; 2 Chr. 10:10.

5667. עֲבוֹט *'aḇôṭ* **masc. noun**
(a pledge [as security])
Deut. 24:10–13.

5668. עֲבוּר *'aḇûr* **particle**
(for, because, in order to)
Gen. 3:17; 8:21; 12:13,16; 18:26,29,
31,32; 21:30; 26:24; 27:4,10; 27:19,31;
46:34; **Ex.** 9:14,16; 13:8; 19:9; 20:20;
1 Sam. 1:6; 12:22; 23:10; 2 Sam. 5:12;
6:12; 7:21; 9:1,7; 10:3; 12:21,25; 13:2;
14:20; 17:14; 18:18; Job 20:2; 1 Chr.
14:2; 17:19; 19:3; **2 Chr.** 28:19; Ps.
105:45; 106:32; 132:10; Jer. 14:4;
Amos 2:6; 8:6; Mic. 2:10.

5669. עֲבוּר *'aḇûr* **masc. noun**
(produce, food)
Josh. 5:11,12.

5670. I. עָבַט *'āḇaṭ* **verb**
(to borrow or lend, to take a pledge from)
Deut. 15:6,8; 24:10.
II. עָבַט *'āḇaṭ* **verb**
(to deviate, to swerve, to break)
Joel 2:7.

5671. I. עַבְטִיט *ʿaḇṭiyṭ* **masc. noun**
(loans [made on security pledges, as in 5670,I])
Hab. 2:6(KJV, see II).
II. עַבְטִיט *ʿaḇṭiyṭ* **masc. noun**
(thick clay [as a symbol of wealth])
Hab. 2:6(NASB, NIV, see I).

5672. עֲבִי *ʿaḇiy,* עֳבִי *ʿoḇiy* **masc. noun**
(thickness)
1 Kgs. 7:26; **2 Chr.** 4:5; **Job** 15:26; **Jer.** 52:21.

5673. עֲבִידָה *ʿaḇiyḏāh* **Aram. fem. noun**
(work, service, administration; corr. to Hebr. 5656)
Ezra 4:24; 5:8; 6:7,18; **Dan.** 2:49; 3:12.

5674. I. עָבַר *ʿāḇar* **verb**
(to pass over, to cross, to transgress)
Gen. 8:1; 12:6; 15:17; 18:3,5; 23:16; 30:32; 31:21,52; 32:10(11),16(17), 21–23(22–24),31(32); 33:3,14; 37:28; 41:46; 47:21; 50:4; **Ex.** 12:12,23; 13:12; 15:16; 17:5; 30:13,14; 32:27; 33:19,22; 34:6; 36:6; 38:26; **Lev.** 18:21; 25:9; 26:6; 27:32; **Num.** 5:14,30; 6:5; 8:7; 13:32; 14:7,41; 20:17–21; 21:22,23; 22:18,26; 24:13; 27:7,8; 31:23; 32:5,7,21,27,29,30, 32; 33:8,51; 34:4; 35:10; **Deut.** 2:4,8,13, 14,18,24,27–30; 3:18,21,25,27,28; 4:14, 21,22,26; 6:1; 9:1,3; 11:8,11,31; 12:10; 17:2; 18:10; 24:5; 26:13; 27:2–4,12; 29:12(11),16(15); 30:13,18; 31:2,3,13; 32:47; 34:4; **Josh.** 1:2,11,14; 2:23; 3:1,2,4,6,11,14,16,17; 4:1,3,5,7,8,10–13, 22,23; 5:1; 6:7,8; 7:7,11,15; 10:29,31,34; 15:3,4,6,7,10,11; 16:2,6; 18:9,13,18,19; 19:13; 22:19; 23:16; 24:11,17; **Judg.** 2:20; 3:26,28; 6:33; 8:4; 9:25,26; 10:9; 11:17,19,20,29,32; 12:1,3,5; 18:13; 19:12,14,18; **Ruth** 2:8; 4:1; **1 Sam.** 2:24; 9:4,27; 13:7; 14:1,4,6,8,23; 15:12,24; 16:8–10; 20:36; 25:19; 26:13,22; 27:2; 29:2; 30:10; **2 Sam.** 2:8,15,29; 3:10; 10:17; 11:27; 12:13,31; 15:18,22–24,33; 16:1,9; 17:16,20–22,24; 18:9,23; 19:15(16),18(19),31(32),33(34), 36–41(37–42); 20:13,14; 24:5,10,20; **1 Kgs.** 2:37; 6:21; 9:8; 13:25; 15:12; 18:6,29; 19:11,19; 20:39; 22:24,36; **2 Kgs.** 2:8,9,14; 4:8,9,31; 6:9,26,30; 8:21; 12:4(5); 14:9; 16:3; 17:17; 18:12; 21:6; 23:10; **1 Chr.** 12:15; 19:17; 21:8; 29:30; **2 Chr.** 7:21; 15:8; 18:23; 21:9; 24:20; 25:18; 30:5,10; 33:6; 35:23,24; 36:22; **Ezra** 1:1; 10:7; **Neh.** 2:7,14; 8:15; 9:11; **Esth.** 1:19; 3:3; 4:17; 8:2,3; 9:27,28; **Job** 6:15; 7:21; 9:11; 11:16; 13:13; 14:5; 15:19; 17:11; 19:8; 21:10,29; 30:15; 33:18,28; 34:20; 36:12; 37:21; **Ps.** 8:8(9); 17:3; 18:12(13); 37:36; 38:4(5); 42:4(5),7(8); 48:4(5); 57:1(2); 66:6; 73:7; 78:13; 80:12(13); 81:6(7); 84:6(7); 88:16(17); 89:41(42); 90:4; 103:16; 104:9; 119:37,39; 124:4,5; 129:8; 136:14; 141:10; 144:4; 148:6; **Prov.** 4:15; 7:8; 8:29; 9:15; 10:25; 19:11; 22:3; 24:30; 26:10; 27:12; **Eccl.** 11:10; **Song** 2:11; 3:4; 5:5,6,13; **Isa.** 8:8,21; 10:28,29; 16:8; 23:2,6,10,12; 24:5; 26:20; 28:15,18,19; 29:5; 31:9; 33:8,21; 34:10; 35:8; 40:27; 41:3; 43:2; 45:14; 47:2; 51:10,23; 54:9; 60:15; 62:10; **Jer.** 2:6,10,20(NASB, NIV, [K^{e}] *ʿāḇaḏ* [5647]); 5:22,28; 8:13,20; 9:10(9),12(11); 11:15; 13:24; 15:14; 18:16; 19:8; 22:8; 23:9; 32:35; 33:13; 34:18,19; 41:10; 46:17; 48:32; 49:17; 50:13; 51:43; **Lam.** 1:12; 2:15; 3:44; 4:21; **Ezek.** 5:1,14,17; 9:4,5; 14:15,17; 16:6,8,15,21,25; 20:26,31,37; 23:37; 29:11; 33:28; 35:7; 36:34; 37:2; 39:11, 14,15; 46:21; 47:3–5; 48:14; **Dan.** 9:11; 11:10,20,40; **Hos.** 6:7; 8:1; 10:11; **Joel** 3:17(4:17); **Amos** 5:5,17; 6:2; 7:8; 8:2,5; **Jon.** 2:3(4); 3:6; **Mic.** 1:11; 2:8,13; 5:8(7); 7:18; **Nah.** 1:8,12,15(2:1); 3:19; **Hab.** 1:11; 3:10; **Zeph.** 2:2,15; 3:6; **Zech.** 3:4; 7:14; 9:8; 10:11; 13:2.

II. עָבַר *ʿāḇar* **verb**
(to be angry)
Deut. 3:26; **Ps.** 78:21,59,62; 89:38(39); **Prov.** 14:16; 20:2; 26:17.

5675. עֲבַר *ʿaḇar* **Aram. masc. noun**
(region beyond, across from; corr. to Hebr. 5676)
Ezra 4:10,11,16,17,20; 5:3,6; 6:6,8,13; 7:21,25.

5676. I. עֵבֶר *ʿēḇer* **masc. noun**
(side, region beyond, region across from)
Gen. 50:10,11; **Ex.** 25:37; 28:26; 32:15; 39:19; **Num.** 21:13; 22:1; 32:19,32; 34:15; 35:14; **Deut.** 1:1,5; 3:8,20,25; 4:41,46,47,49; 11:30; 30:13; **Josh.** 1:14,15; 2:10; 5:1; 7:7; 9:1,10; 12:1,7; 13:8,27,32; 14:3; 17:5; 18:7; 20:8; 22:4, 7,11(KJV, see II); 24:2,3,8,14,15; **Judg.** 5:17; 7:25; 10:8; 11:18; **1 Sam.** 14:1 ,4,40; 26:13; 31:7; **2 Sam.** 10:16; **1 Kgs.** 4:12,24(5:4); 7:20,30; 14:15; **1 Chr.** 6:78(63); 12:37; 19:16; 26:30; **2 Chr.** 20:2; **Ezra** 8:36; **Neh.** 2:7,9; 3:7; **Job** 1:19; **Isa.** 7:20; 9:1(8:23); 18:1; 47:15; **Jer.** 25:22; 48:28; 49:32; **Ezek.** 1:9,12; 10:22; **Zeph.** 3:10.
II. עֵבֶר *ʿēḇer* **masc. noun**
(passage, place of crossing over)
Josh. 22:11(NASB, NIV, see I); **Jer.** 22:20(NASB, NIV, *ʿaḇariym* [5682]).

5677. A. עֵבֶר *ʿēḇer* **masc. proper noun**
(Eber: son of Shelah)
Gen. 10:21,24,25; 11:14–17; **Num.** 24:24; **1 Chr.** 1:18,19,25.
B. עֵבֶר *ʿēḇer* **masc. proper noun**
(Eber: Gadite chief)
1 Chr. 5:13.
C. עֵבֶר *ʿēḇer* **masc. proper noun**
(Eber: a Benjamite)
1 Chr. 8:12.
D. עֵבֶר *ʿēḇer* **masc. proper noun**
(Eber: a Benjamite)
1 Chr. 8:22.
E. עֵבֶר *ʿēḇer* **masc. proper noun**
(Eber: a priest)
Neh. 12:20.

5678. עֶבְרָה *ʿeḇrāh* **fem. noun**
(wrath, fury, rage)
Gen. 49:7; **Job** 21:30; 40:11; **Ps.** 7:6(7); 78:49; 85:3(4); 90:9,11; **Prov.** 11:4,23; 14:35; 21:24; 22:8; **Isa.** 9:19(18); 10:6; 13:9,13; 14:6; 16:6; **Jer.** 7:29; 48:30; **Lam.** 2:2; 3:1; **Ezek.** 7:19; 21:31(36); 22:21,31; 38:19; **Hos.** 5:10; 13:11; **Amos** 1:11; **Hab.** 3:8; **Zeph.** 1:15,18.

5679. עֲבָרָה *ʿaḇārāh* **fem. noun**
(ford, ferry)
2 Sam. 15:28(KJV, [Qe] *ʿarāḇāh* [6160]); 17:16(KJV, [Ke] *ʿarāḇāh* [6160]); 19:18(19).

5680. עִבְרִי *ʿiḇriy* **masc. proper noun**
(Hebrew)
Gen. 14:13; 39:14,17; 40:15; 41:12; 43:32; **Ex.** 1:15,16,19; 2:6,7,11,13; 3:18; 5:3; 7:16; 9:1,13; 10:3; 21:2; **Deut.** 15:12; **1 Sam.** 4:6,9; 13:3,7,19; 14:11,21; 29:3; **Jer.** 34:9,14; **Jon.** 1:9.

5681. עִבְרִי *ʿiḇriy* **masc. proper noun**
(Ibri)
1 Chr. 24:27.

5682. עֲבָרִים *ʿaḇāriym* **proper noun**
(Abarim)
Num. 27:12; 33:47,48; **Deut.** 32:49; **Jer.** 22:20(KJV, *ēḇer* [5676,II]).

5683. עֶבְרֹן *ʿeḇrōn* **masc. proper noun**
(Hebron)
Josh. 19:28.

5684. עַבְרֹנָה *ʿaḇrōnāh* **proper noun**
(Abronah, Ebronah)
Num. 33:34,35.

5685. עָבַשׁ *ʿāḇaš* **verb**
(to shrivel, to rot)
Joel 1:17.

5686. עָבַת *ʿāḇaṯ* **verb**
(to weave together, to conspire, to wrap up)
Mic. 7:3.

5687. עָבֹת *ʿāḇōṯ* **adj.**
(thick with leaves, dense with leaves; leafy)
Lev. 23:40; **Neh.** 8:15; **Ezek.** 6:13; 20:28.

5688. I. עֲבֹת *ᵃḇōṯ* **masc. noun**
(rope, cord, line)
Ex. 28:14,22,24,25; 39:15,17,18; **Judg.** 15:13,14; 16:11,12; **Job** 39:10; **Ps.** 2:3; 118:27(NIV, see II); 129:4; **Isa.** 5:18; **Ezek.** 3:25; 4:8; **Hos.** 11:4.
II. עֲבוֹת *ᵃḇōṯ* **masc. noun**
(branch, thick foliage, cloud)
Ps. 118:27(KJV, NASB, see I); **Ezek.** 19:11; 31:3,10,14.

5689. עָגַב *ʿāgaḇ* **verb**
(to lust, to love)
Jer. 4:30; **Ezek.** 23:5,7,9,12,16,20.

5690. עָגָב *ʿāgāḇ* **masc. pl. noun**
(love, lust)
Ezek. 33:31,32(NIV, *ᵃgāḇāh* [5691]).

5691. עֲגָבָה *ᵃgāḇāh* **fem. noun**
(lust)
Ezek. 23:11; 33:32(KJV, NASB, *ʿāgāḇ* [5690]).

5692. עֻגָה *ʿugāh* **fem. noun**
(cake of bread)
Gen. 18:6; **Ex.** 12:39; **Num.** 11:8; **1 Kgs.** 17:13; 19:6; **Ezek.** 4:12; **Hos.** 7:8.

5693. עָגוּר *ʿāgûr* **masc. noun**
(a kind of bird: crane or thrush)
Isa. 38:14; **Jer.** 8:7.

5694. עָגִיל *ʿāgiyl* **masc. noun**
(earrings)
Num. 31:50; **Ezek.** 16:12.

5695. עֵגֶל *ʿēgel* **masc. noun**
(calf)
Ex. 32:4,8,19,20,24,35; **Lev.** 9:2,3,8; **Deut.** 9:16,21; **1 Sam.** 28:24; **1 Kgs.** 12:28,32; **2 Kgs.** 10:29; 17:16; **2 Chr.** 11:15; 13:8; **Neh.** 9:18; **Ps.** 29:6; 68:30(31); 106:19; **Isa.** 11:6; 27:10; **Jer.** 31:18; 34:18,19; 46:21; **Ezek.** 1:7; **Hos.** 8:5,6; 13:2; **Amos** 6:4; **Mic.** 6:6; **Mal.** 4:2(3:20).

5696. עָגֹל *ʿāgōl*, עָגוֹל *ʿāgôl* **adj.**
(round, circular)
1 Kgs. 7:23,31,35; 10:19; **2 Chr.** 4:2.

5697. I. עֶגְלָה *ʿeglāh* **fem. noun**
(heifer)
Gen. 15:9; **Deut.** 21:3,4,6; **Judg.** 14:18; **1 Sam.** 16:2; **Isa.** 7:21; 15:5(NASB, NIV, see II); **Jer.** 46:20; 48:34(NASB, NIV, see II); 50:11; **Hos.** 10:5,11.
II. עֶגְלַת שְׁלִשִׁיָּה *ʿeglat šᵉlišiyyāh* **proper noun**
(Eglath Shelishiyah)
Isa. 15:5(KJV, see I and *šᵉliyšiy* [7992,IV]); **Jer.** 48:34(KJV, see I and *šᵉliyšiy* [7992,IV]).

5698. עֶגְלָה *ʿeglāh* **fem. proper noun**
(Eglah)
2 Sam. 3:5; **1 Chr.** 3:3.

5699. עֲגָלָה *ᵃgālāh* **fem. noun**
(cart, wagon)

Gen. 45:19,21,27; 46:5; **Num.** 7:3,6–8; **1 Sam.** 6:7,8,10,11,14; **2 Sam.** 6:3; **1 Chr.** 13:7; **Ps.** 46:9(10); **Isa.** 5:18; 28:27,28; **Amos** 2:13.

5700. A. עֶגְלוֹן *'eglôn* **proper noun**
(Eglon: city in Judah)
Josh. 10:3,5,23,34,36,37; 12:12; 15:39.
B. עֶגְלוֹן *'eglôn* **proper noun**
(Eglon: king of Moab)
Judg. 3:12,14,15,17.

5701. עָגַם *'āgam* **verb**
(to be grieved)
Job 30:25.

5702. עָגַן *'āgan* **verb**
(to shut oneself in, to remain unmarried)
Ruth 1:13.

5703. עַד *'ad̲* **masc. noun**
(perpetuity, eternality, everlastingness)
Ex. 15:18; **Num.** 24:20,24; **1 Chr.** 28:9; **Job** 19:24; 20:4; **Ps.** 9:5(6),18(19); 10:16; 19:9(10); 21:4(5),6(7); 22:26(27); 37:29; 45:6(7),17(18); 48:14(15); 52:8(10); 61:8(9); 83:17(18); 89:29(30); 92:7(8); 104:5; 111:3,8,10; 112:3,9; 119:44; 132:12,14; 145:1,2,21; 148:6; **Prov.** 12:19; 29:14; **Isa.** 9:6(5); 26:4; 30:8; 45:17; 57:15; 64:9(8); 65:18; **Dan.** 12:3; **Amos** 1:11; **Mic.** 4:5; 7:18; **Hab.** 3:6.

5704. עַד *'ad̲* **prep.; adv.**
(as far as, unto, until)
Gen. 3:19; 6:7; 7:23; 8:5,7; 10:19; 11:31; 12:6; 13:3,12,15; 14:6,14,15,23; 15:16,18; 19:4,11,22,37,38; 22:5; 24:19,33; 25:18; 26:13,33; 27:33,34,44,45; 28:15; 29:8; 31:24,29; 32:4(5),24(25),32(33); 33:3,14; 34:5; 35:20; 38:1,11,17; 39:16; 41:49; 43:25; 44:28; 46:34; 47:21,26; 48:5,15; 49:10,26; 50:10; **Ex.** 7:16; 9:7,18,25; 10:3,6,7,26; 11:5,7; 12:6,10,12,15,18,22, 24,29; 13:15; 14:28; 15:16; 16:19,20,23, 24,28,35; 17:12; 18:13,14; 22:4(3),9(8), 26(25); 23:18,30,31; 24:14; 27:5,21; 28:42; 29:34; 32:20; 33:8,22; 34:34,35; 38:4; 40:37; **Lev.** 6:9(2); 7:15; 8:33; 11:24,25,27,28,31,32,39,40,42; 12:4; 13:12; 14:46; 15:5–8,10,11,16–19, 21–23,27; 16:17; 17:15; 19:6,13; 22:4, 6,30; 23:14,16,32; 24:3; 25:22,28,29, 30,40,50,52; 26:18; 27:3,5,6,18,23; **Num.** 3:13; 4:3,23,30,35,39,43,47; 5:3; 6:4,5; 8:4; 9:12,15,21; 10:21; 11:20; 12:15; 13:21–23; 14:11,19,27,33,45; 19:7,8,10,21,22; 20:17; 21:22,24,26, 30,35; 22:30; 23:18,24; 24:22; 32:9,13, 17,18,21; 33:49; 35:12,25,28,32; **Deut.** 1:2,7,19,20,24,31,44; 2:5,14,15,22,23, 29,36; 3:3,8,10,14,16,17,20; 4:11,30,32, 48,49; 7:20,23,24; 9:7,21; 10:8; 11:4,5, 12,24; 12:9,28; 13:7(8); 20:20; 22:2; 23:3(4); 28:20–22,24,35,45,46,48,51, 52,61,64; 29:4(3),11(10),29(28); 30:2; 31:24,30; 32:22; 34:1–3,6; **Josh.** 1:4,15; 2:16,22; 3:1,8,15,17; 4:7,9,10,23; 5:1,6, 8,9; 6:10,21,25; 7:5,6,13,26; 8:6,22, 24–26,28,29; 9:27; 10:10,11,13,20,26, 27,33,41; 11:8,14,17; 12:1–3,5,7; 13:3–6, 9–11,13,25–27; 14:9,14; 15:5,47,63; 16:3,5,10; 17:14; 18:3; 19:8,10,28,29,33; 20:6,9; 22:3,17; 23:8,9,13,15; **Judg.** 1:21,26; 3:3,25,26; 4:11,16,24; 5:7; 6:4,18,24,31; 7:13,22,24; 9:40,52; 10:4; 11:13,16,19,22,33; 13:7; 14:5; 15:5, 14,19; 16:2,3,13; 17:8; 18:1,2,12,13,30; 19:8,10,12,18,25,26,30; 20:1,23,26,43, 45,48; 21:2; **Ruth** 1:13,19; 2:7,17,21,23; 3:3,13,14,18; **1 Sam.** 1:14,15,22,23; 2:5,30; 3:13,14,15,20; 5:5,9; 6:12,18; 7:11,12,14; 8:8; 9:9,13; 10:3,8; 11:11,15; 12:2; 13:13; 14:9,19,20,24,36; 15:3,5, 18,35; 16:1,11; 17:52; 18:4; 19:2(1), 22,23; 20:5,8,15,23,28,37,41,42(21:1); 22:3,19; 25:22,34,36; 27:6,8; 29:3,6,8; 30:2,4,9,17,19,25; **2 Sam.** 1:12; 2:17, 24,26; 3:10,16,28; 4:3,6; 6:6,8,19,23; 7:6,13,16,18,24–26; 10:4,5; 11:23; 12:10;

13:22; 14:25; 15:24,28,32; 16:5; 17:11, 13,22; 18:18; 19:7(8),15(16),24(25); 20:2,3,16; 21:10; 22:38,51; 23:10,19; 24:2,15; **1 Kgs.** 1:4; 2:28,33,45; 3:1,2; 4:12,21(5:1),24(5:4),25(5:5),33(5:13); 5:3(17),9(23); 6:15,16,22,24; 7:7,9,23; 8:8,65; 9:3,13,21; 10:7,12; 11:16,40; 12:19,30; 14:10; 15:29; 17:14,17; 18:21, 26,28,29,45,46; 19:8; 22:11,16,27; **2 Kgs.** 2:2,17,22; 3:25; 4:20,22,35; 6:2,25; 7:3,5,8,9,15; 8:6,7,11,22; 9:18,20,22; 10:8,11,17,25,27; 11:11; 13:17,19,23; 14:7,13,25; 15:5; 16:6,11; 17:9,20,23,34,41; 18:4,8,32; 19:3; 20:17; 21:15,16; 23:2,8; 24:7,20; 25:2,26; **1 Chr.** 4:27,31,33,39,41,43; 5:8,9,11,22, 23,26; 6:32(17); 7:28; 9:18; 11:8,21; 12:16, 22,29,40; 13:5,9,11; 14:16; 15:2,29; 16:3,36; 17:5,12,14,16,22–24; 19:4,5; 21:2,21; 22:10; 23:13,25; 28:7,8,20; 29:10; **2 Chr.** 5:9; 7:8,16; 8:8,16; 9:6,26; 10:19; 12:4; 14:9(8),13(12); 15:13,19; 16:12,14; 17:12; 18:10,15,26,34; 19:4; 20:26; 21:10,15; 23:10; 24:10; 25:13,23; 26:8,15,16,21; 28:9; 29:28,30,34; 30:5,10; 31:1,10; 32:24; 34:6,30; 35:14,25; 36:16, 20,21; **Ezra** 2:63; 3:13; 4:5; 8:29; 9:4, 6,7,12,14; 10:14,17; **Neh.** 2:6,7,16; 3:1,8,13,15,16,20,21,24,26,27,31; 4:6(3:38),11(5),21(15); 5:14; 6:1; 7:3,65; 8:2,3,17,18; 9:5,32; 11:30; 12:23,37–39; 13:1,19; **Esth.** 1:1,5,20; 2:13; 3:13; 4:2; 5:3,6; 7:2; 8:9; **Job** 2:7; 4:5; 5:9; 6:20; 7:4,19; 8:2,21; 9:10; 11:7; 14:6,12–14; 18:2; 19:2; 20:5; 22:23; 23:3; 25:5; 26:10; 27:5; 31:12; 32:11,12; 34:36; 38:11, 16,18; **Ps.** 4:2(3); 6:3(4); 13:1(2),2(3); 18:37(38),50(51); 36:5(6); 38:6(7),8(9); 40:12(13); 41:13(14); 42:4(5); 46:9(10); 48:8(9); 49:19(20); 50:1; 57:1(2),10(11); 60:9(11); 62:3(4); 65:2(3); 69:1(2); 71:17–19; 72:7,8; 73:17; 74:9(10),10(11); 79:5; 80:4(5),11(12); 82:2; 83:17(18); 89:4(5),46(47); 90:2,3,13; 92:7(8); 94:3, 13,15; 100:5; 103:17; 104:23; 105:19; 106:31,48; 107:18; 108:4(5),10(11); 110:1; 112:8; 113:2,3; 115:18; 118:27; 119:8,43,51,107; 121:8; 123:2; 125:2; 131:3; 132:5,12,14; 133:3; 135:8; 137:7; 141:10; 147:6,15; **Prov.** 1:22; 4:18; 6:9,26; 7:18,23; 8:26; 12:19; 28:17; **Eccl.** 2:3; 3:11; 12:1,2,6; **Song** 1:12; 2:7,17; 3:4,5; 4:6; 8:4; **Isa.** 1:6; 5:8; 6:11; 8:8; 9:7(6),13(12); 10:18; 13:20; 15:4,5,8; 16:8; 19:22; 22:14,24; 25:12; 26:5,20; 27:12; 30:8,17; 32:14,15,17; 33:23(KJV, NASB, *'aḏ* [5706]); 34:17; 36:17; 37:3; 38:12,13; 39:6; 42:4; 45:17,24; 46:4; 47:7; 48:20; 49:6; 57:9; 59:21; 62:1,6,7; 64:9(8),12(11); 65:18; **Jer.** 1:3; 3:25; 4:10,14,18,21; 6:13; 7:7,25; 8:10; 9:10(9), 16(15); 11:7; 12:4,12; 17:4; 23:20,26; 24:10; 25:3,5,31,33; 27:7,8,22; 30:24; 31:22,34,40; 32:5,20,31; 33:12,14; 35:6,14; 36:2,23; 37:21; 38:28; 42:1,8; 43:7; 44:10,12,27; 47:5,6; 48:32,34,47; 49:33,37; 50:3,39; 51:9,62,64; 52:3,5, 11,34; **Lam.** 3:40,50; 5:22; **Ezek.** 2:3; 4:8,10,11,14; 10:5; 20:29,31; 21:27(32); 22:4; 24:13; 27:36; 28:15,19; 29:10; 33:22; 34:21; 39:15; 41:16,17,20; 43:14; 46:2,17; 47:10,19,20; 48:2–8,21,23–27; **Dan.** 1:21; 8:6,8,10,11,13,14; 9:25–27; 10:3; 11:10,24,25,35,36,45; 12:1,4,6,9; **Hos.** 5:15; 7:4; 8:5; 10:12; 14:1(2); **Joel** 2:2,12; **Amos** 4:6,8–11; 6:14; 8:12; **Obad.** 1:7,20; **Jon.** 2:5(6); 3:5; 4:2,5,9; **Mic.** 1:7,9,15; 4:3,7,8,10; 5:3,4; 6:5; 7:9,12; **Nah.** 1:10; **Hab.** 1:2; 2:6; 3:13; **Zeph.** 2:9; **Hag.** 2:19; **Zech.** 1:12; 9:10; 14:10; **Mal.** 1:4,11; 3:10.

5705. עַד *'aḏ* **Aram. particle**
(until, unto; corr. to Hebr. 5704)
Ezra 4:21,24; 5:5,16; 6:15; 7:22; **Dan.** 2:9,20,34; 4:8(5),17(14),23(20), 25(22),32(29),33(30); 5:21; 6:7(8), 12(13),14(15),24(25),26(27); 7:4,9, 11–13,18,22,25,26,28.

5706. עַד *'aḏ* **masc. noun**
(prey, booty)
Gen. 49:27; **Isa.** 33:23(NIV, *'aḏ* [5704]); **Zeph.** 3:8(NIV, *'ēḏ* [5707]).

5707. עֵד *ʿēḏ* masc. noun
(witness, testimony)
Gen. 31:44,48,50,52; Ex. 20:16; 22:13(12); 23:1; Lev. 5:1; Num. 5:13; 35:30; Deut. 5:20(17); 17:6,7; 19:15, 16,18; 31:19,21,26; Josh. 22:27,28,34; 24:22; Ruth 4:9–11; 1 Sam. 12:5; Job 10:17; 16:8,19; Ps. 27:12; 35:11; 89:37(38); Prov. 6:19; 12:17; 14:5,25; 19:5,9,28; 21:28; 24:28; 25:18; Isa. 8:2; 19:20; 43:9,10,12; 44:8,9; 55:4; Jer. 29:23; 32:10,12,25,44; 42:5; Mic. 1:2; Zeph. 3:8(KJV, NASB, *ʿaḏ* [5706]); Mal. 3:5.

5708. עֵד, עֵדָה *ʿēḏ, ʿiddāh* masc. noun
(menstruation, filthiness)
Isa. 64:6(5).

5709. עֲדָה *ʿaḏāh* Aram. verb
(to pass away, to pass on; corr. to Hebr. 5710,I)
Dan. 2:21; 3:27; 4:31(28); 5:20; 6:8(9),12(13); 7:12,14,26.

5710. I. עָדָה *ʿāḏāh* verb
(to pass on, to walk; to lay aside)
Job 28:8; Prov. 25:20.
II. עָדָה *ʿāḏāh* verb
(to ornament, to adorn, to deck)
Job 40:10; Isa. 61:10; Jer. 4:30; 31:4; Ezek. 16:11,13; 23:40; Hos. 2:13(15).

5711. A. עָדָה *ʿāḏāh* fem. proper noun
(Adah: wife of Lamech)
Gen. 4:19,20,23.
B. עָדָה *ʿāḏāh* fem. proper noun
(Adah: wife of Esau)
Gen. 36:2,4,10,12,16.

5712. עֵדָה *ʿēḏāh* fem. noun
(congregation; assembly)
Ex. 12:3,6,19,47; 16:1,2,9,10,22; 17:1; 34:31; 35:1,4,20; 38:25; Lev. 4:13,15; 8:3–5; 9:5; 10:6,17; 16:5; 19:2; 24:14,16; Num. 1:2,16,18,53; 3:7; 4:34; 8:9,20; 10:2,3; 13:26; 14:1,2,5,7,10,27,35,36; 15:24–26,33,35,36; 16:2,3,5,6,9,11,16, 19,21,22,24,26,40–42(17:5–7),45(17:10), 46(17:11); 19:9; 20:1,2,8,11,22,27,29; 25:6,7; 26:2,9,10; 27:2,3,14,16,17,19–22; 31:12,13,16,26,27,43; 32:2,4; 35:12, 24,25; Josh. 9:15,18,19,21,27; 18:1; 20:6,9; 22:12,16–18,20,30; Judg. 14:8; 20:1; 21:10,13,16; 1 Kgs. 8:5; 12:20; 2 Chr. 5:6; Job 15:34; 16:7; Ps. 1:5; 7:7(8); 22:16(17); 68:30(31); 74:2; 82:1; 86:14; 106:17,18; 111:1; Prov. 5:14; Jer. 6:18(NIV, *ʿēḏāh* [5713,I]); 30:20; Hos. 7:12.

5713. I. עֵדָה *ʿēḏāh* fem. noun
(witness)
Gen. 21:30; 31:52; Josh. 24:27; Jer. 6:18(KJV, NASB, *ʿēḏāh* [5712]).
II. עֵדָה *ʿēḏāh* fem. noun
(testimony; NIV, *ʿēḏûṯ* [5715])
Deut. 4:45; 6:17,20; Ps. 25:10; 78:56; 93:5; 99:7; 119:2,22,24,46,59,79,95, 119,125,138,146,152,167,168; 132:12.

5714. A. עִדֹּא *ʿiddōʾ* masc. proper noun
(Iddo: father of Ahinadab)
1 Kgs. 4:14.
B. עִדּוֹ, עִדּוֹא *ʿiddô* masc. proper noun
(Iddo: grandfather of Zechariah the prophet)
Neh. 12:4,16([Qe] *ʿiddiy*); Zech. 1:1,7.
C. עִדּוֹא *ʿiddôʾ* Aram. masc. proper noun
(Iddo: grandfather of Zechariah the prophet)
Ezra 5:1; 6:14.
D. עִדּוֹ *ʿiddô* masc. proper noun
(Iddo: a Levite)
1 Chr. 6:21(6).
E. עִדּוֹ *ʿiddô* masc. proper noun
(Iddo: a seer)
2 Chr. 12:15; 13:22.

5715. עֵדוּת ʿēḏûṯ **fem. noun**
(testimony, statute, ordinance)
Ex. 16:34; 25:16,21,22; 26:33,34; 27:21; 30:6,26,36; 31:7,18; 32:15; 34:29; 38:21; 39:35; 40:3,5,20,21; **Lev.** 16:13; 24:3; **Num.** 1:50,53; 4:5; 7:89; 9:15; 10:11; 17:4(19),7(22),8(23),10(25); 18:2; **Deut.** 4:45(KJV, NASB, *ʿeḏāh* [5713,II]); 6:17 (KJV, NASB, *ʿeḏāh* [5713,II]),20(KJV, NASB, *ʿeḏāh* [5713,II]); **Josh.** 4:16; **1 Kgs.** 2:3; **2 Kgs.** 11:12; 17:15; 23:3; **1 Chr.** 29:19; **2 Chr.** 23:11; 24:6; 34:31; **Neh.** 9:34; **Ps.** 19:7(8); 25:10(KJV, NASB, *ʿeḏāh* [5713,II]); 78:5,56(KJV, NASB, *ʿeḏāh* [5713,II]); 81:5(6); 93:5(KJV, NASB, *ʿeḏāh* [5713,II]); 99:7(KJV, NASB, *ʿeḏāh* [5713,II]); 119:2(KJV, NASB, *ʿeḏāh* [5713,II]),14,22(KJV, NASB, *ʿeḏāh* [5713,II]),24(KJV, NASB, *ʿeḏāh* [5713,II]),31,36,46(KJV, NASB, *ʿeḏāh* [5713,II]),59(KJV, NASB, *ʿeḏāh* [5713,II]),79(KJV, NASB, *ʿeḏāh* [5713,II]),88,95(KJV, NASB, *ʿeḏāh* [5713,II]),99,111,119(KJV, NASB, *ʿeḏāh* [5713,II]),125(KJV, NASB, *ʿeḏāh* [5713,II]),129,138(KJV, NASB,*ʿeḏāh* [5713,II]),144,146(KJV, NASB, *ʿeḏāh* [5713,II]),152(KJV, NASB, *ʿeḏāh* [5713,II]),157,167(KJV, NASB, *ʿeḏāh* [5713,II]),168(KJV, NASB, *ʿeḏāh* [5713,II]); 132:12(KJV, NASB, *ʿeḏāh* [5713,II]); 122:4; **Jer.** 44:23.

5716. עֲדִי *ʿaḏiy* **masc. noun**
(ornament, jewelry)
Ex. 33:4–6; **2 Sam.** 1:24; **Ps.** 32:9; 103:5; **Isa.** 49:18; **Jer.** 2:32; 4:30; **Ezek.** 7:20; 16:7,11; 23:40.

5717. A. עֲדִיאֵל *ʿaḏiy'ēl* **masc. proper noun**
(Adiel: a Simeonite)
1 Chr. 4:36.
B. עֲדִיאֵל *ʿaḏiy'ēl* **masc. proper noun**
(Adiel: a priest)
1 Chr. 9:12.
C. עֲדִיאֵל *ʿaḏiy'ēl* **masc. proper noun**
(Adiel: father of officer under David)
1 Chr. 27:25.

5718. A. עֲדָיָהוּ *ʿaḏāyāhû* **masc. proper noun**
(Adaiah: father of Maaseiah)
2 Chr. 23:1.
B. עֲדָיָה *ʿaḏāyāh* **masc. proper noun**
(Adaiah: grandfather of Josiah)
2 Kgs. 22:1.
C. עֲדָיָה *ʿaḏāyāh* **masc. proper noun**
(Adaiah: a Levite)
1 Chr. 6:41(26).
D. עֲדָיָה *ʿaḏāyāh* **masc. proper noun**
(Adaiah: a Benjamite)
1 Chr. 8:21.
E. עֲדָיָה *ʿaḏāyāh* **masc. proper noun**
(Adaiah: a priest)
1 Chr. 9:12; **Neh.** 11:12.
F. עֲדָיָה *ʿaḏāyāh* **masc. proper noun**
(Adaiah: son of Bani)
Ezra 10:29.
G. עֲדָיָה *ʿaḏāyāh* **masc. proper noun**
(Adaiah: son of another Bani)
Ezra 10:39.
H. עֲדָיָה *ʿaḏāyāh* **masc. proper noun**
(Adaiah: a Judaite)
Neh. 11:5.

5719. עָדִין *ʿāḏiyn* **adj.**
(sensuous, wanton)
Isa. 47:8.

5720. A. עָדִין *ʿāḏiyn* **masc. proper noun**
(Adin: ancestor of returning Jewish exiles)
Ezra 2:15; 8:6; **Neh.** 7:20.

B. עָדִין *ʿāḏiyn* **masc. proper noun**
(Adin: covenanter in Nehemiah's day)
Neh. 10:16(17).

5721. עֲדִינָא *ʿaḏiynāʾ* **masc. proper noun**
(Adina)
1 Chr. 11:42.

5722. עֲדִינוֹ הָעֶצְנִי *ʿaḏiynô hāʿeṣniy* **masc. proper noun**
(Adino the Eznite)
2 Sam. 23:8(NIV, omits).

5723. עֲדִיתַיִם *ʿaḏiyṯayim* **proper noun**
(Adithaim)
Josh. 15:36.

5724. עַדְלַי *ʿaḏlay* **masc. proper noun**
(Adlai)
1 Chr. 27:29.

5725. עֲדֻלָּם *ʿaḏullām* **proper noun**
(Adullam)
Josh. 12:15; 15:35; **1 Sam.** 22:1; **2 Sam.** 23:13; **1 Chr.** 11:15; **2 Chr.** 11:7; **Neh.** 11:30; **Mic.** 1:15.

5726. עֲדֻלָּמִי *ʿaḏullāmiy* **masc. proper noun**
(Adullamite: inhabitant of *ʿaḏullām* [5725])
Gen. 38:1,12,20.

5727. עָדַן *ʿāḏan* **verb**
(to revel, to take pleasure in)
Neh. 9:25.

5728. I. עֲדֶן *ʿaḏen* **adv.**
(still, yet)
Eccl. 4:3.
II. עֲדֶנָה *ʿaḏenāh* **adv.**
(still, yet)
Eccl. 4:2.

5729. עֶדֶן *ʿeḏen* **proper noun**
(the town Eden)
2 Kgs. 19:12; **Isa.** 37:12; **Ezek.** 27:23.

5730. I. עֵדֶן *ʿēḏen* **masc. noun**
(luxury, pleasure, delight)
2 Sam. 1:24; **Ps.** 36:8(9); **Jer.** 51:34.
II. עֶדְנָה *ʿeḏnāh* **fem. noun**
(sexual delight, ecstasy)
Gen. 18:12.

5731. A. עֵדֶן *ʿēḏen* **proper noun**
(Garden of Eden)
Gen. 2:8,10,15; 3:23,24; 4:16; **Isa.** 51:3; **Ezek.** 28:13; 31:9,16,18; 36:35; **Joel** 2:3.
B. עֵדֶן *ʿēḏen* **masc. proper noun**
(Eden: a Levite)
2 Chr. 29:12; 31:15.

5732. עִדָּן *ʿiddān* **Aram. masc. noun**
(period of time, moment of time)
Dan. 2:8,9,21; 3:5,15; 4:16(13),23(20), 25(22),32(29); 7:12,25.

5733. A. עַדְנָא *ʿaḏnāʾ* **masc. proper noun**
(Adna: head of a priestly family)
Neh. 12:15.
B. עַדְנָא *ʿaḏnāʾ* **masc. proper noun**
(Adna: postexilic Jew)
Ezra 10:30.

5734. A. עַדְנָה *ʿaḏnāh* **masc. proper noun**
(Adnah: prince of Judah)
2 Chr. 17:14.
B. עַדְנַח *ʿaḏnāh* **masc. proper noun**
(Adnah: a Manassite)
1 Chr. 12:20.

5735. עֲדְעָדָה *ʿaḏʿāḏāh* **proper noun**
(Abadah)
Josh. 15:22.

5736. עָדַף *ʿāḏap̱* **verb**
(to remain over, to be in excess)
Ex. 16:18,23; 26:12,13; **Lev.** 25:27; **Num.** 3:46,48,49.

5737. I. עָדַר *ʿāḏar* **verb**
(to lack, to fail, to remain)
1 Sam. 30:19; **2 Sam.** 17:22; **1 Kgs.** 4:27(5:7); **Isa.** 34:16; 40:26; 59:15; **Zeph.** 3:5.
II. עָדַר *ʿāḏar* **verb**
(to keep rank, to put in order)
1 Chr. 12:33(NASB, NIV, see III),38(39) (NASB, *ʿāraḵ* [6186,I]; NIV, see III).
III. עָדַר *ʿāḏar* **verb**
(to help)
1 Chr. 12:33(KJV, see II),38(39)(KJV, see II; NASB, *ʿāraḵ* [6186,I]).
IV. עָדַר *ʿāḏar* **verb**
(to hoe, to weed, to cultivate)
Isa. 5:6; 7:25.

5738. עֶדֶר *ʿeḏer* **masc. proper noun**
(Eder, Ader)
1 Chr. 8:15.

5739. עֵדֶר *ʿēḏer* **masc. noun**
(flock, herd)
Gen. 29:2,3,8; 30:40; 32:16(17),19(20); **Judg.** 5:16; **1 Sam.** 17:34; **2 Chr.** 32:28; **Job** 24:2; **Ps.** 78:52; **Prov.** 27:23; **Song** 1:7; 4:1,2; 6:5,6; **Isa.** 17:2; 32:14; 40:11; **Jer.** 6:3; 13:17,20; 31:10,24; 51:23; **Ezek.** 34:12; **Joel** 1:18; **Mic.** 2:12; 4:8; 5:8(7); **Zeph.** 2:14; **Zech.** 10:3; **Mal.** 1:14.

5740. A. עֵדֶר *ʿēḏer* **masc. proper noun**
(Eder: a Levite)
1 Chr. 23:23; 24:30.
B. עֵדֶר *ʿēḏer* **masc. proper noun**
(Eder: loc. in S. Judah)
Josh. 15:21.

5741. עַדְרִיאֵל *ʿaḏriyʾēl* **masc. proper noun**
(Adriel)
1 Sam. 18:19; **2 Sam.** 21:8.

5742. עֲדָשִׁים *ʿaḏāšiym* **masc. pl. noun**
(lentils)
Gen. 25:34; **2 Sam.** 17:28; 23:11; **Ezek.** 4:9.

5743. עוּב *ʿûḇ* **verb**
(to cover with a cloud)
Lam. 2:1.

5744. A. עוֹבֵד *ʿôḇēḏ* **masc. proper noun**
(Obed: descendant of Sheshan)
1 Chr. 2:37,38.
B. עוֹבֵד *ʿôḇēḏ*, עֹבֵד *ʿōḇēḏ* **masc. proper noun**
(Obed: son of Boaz)
Ruth 4:17,21,22; **1 Chr.** 2:12.
C. עוֹבֵד *ʿôḇēḏ* **masc. proper noun**
(Obed: one of David's mighty men)
1 Chr. 11:47.
D. עוֹבֵד *ʿôḇēḏ* **masc. proper noun**
(Obed: son of Shemaiah)
1 Chr. 26:7.
E. עוֹבֵד *ʿôḇēḏ* **masc. proper noun**
(Obed: a captain)
2 Chr. 23:1.

5745. עוֹבָל *ʿôḇāl* **masc. proper noun**
(Obal)
Gen. 10:28; **1 Chr.** 1:22(KJV, NASB, *ʿēyḇāl* [5858,B]).

5746. עוּג *ʿûg* **verb**
(to bake)
Ezek. 4:12.

5747. עוֹג *ʿôg*, עֹג *ʿōg* **masc. proper noun**
(Og)
Num. 21:33; 32:33; **Deut.** 1:4; 3:1,3,4, 10,11,13; 4:47; 29:7(6); 31:4; **Josh.** 2:10;

9:10; 12:4; 13:12,30,31; **1 Kgs.** 4:19; **Neh.** 9:22; **Ps.** 135:11; 136:20.

5748. עוּגָב *'ûgāḇ*, עֻגָב *'ugāḇ* **masc. noun**
(flute)
Gen. 4:21; **Job** 21:12; 30:31; **Ps.** 150:4.

5749. I. עוּד *'ûḏ* **verb**
(to witness, to testify, to warn, to protest)
Gen. 43:3; **Ex.** 19:21,23; 21:29; **Deut.** 4:26; 8:19; 30:19; 31:28; 32:46; **1 Sam.** 8:9; **1 Kgs.** 2:42; 21:10,13; **2 Kgs.** 17:13,15; **2 Chr.** 24:19; **Neh.** 9:26,29, 30,34; 13:15,21; **Job** 29:11; **Ps.** 50:7; 81:8(9); **Isa.** 8:2; **Jer.** 6:10; 11:7; 32:10, 25,44; 42:19; **Lam.** 2:13; **Amos** 3:13; **Zech.** 3:6; **Mal.** 2:14.
II. עוּד *'ûḏ* **verb**
(to stand firm, to support, to sustain, to encircle)
Gen. 43:3; **Ex.** 19:21,23; 21:29; **Deut.** 4:26; 8:19; 30:19; 31:28; 32:46; **1 Sam.** 8:9; **1 Kgs.** 2:42; 21:10,13; **2 Kgs.** 17:13,15; **2 Chr.** 24:19; **Neh.** 9:26,29, 30,34; 13:15,21; **Job** 29:11; **Ps.** 20:8(9); 119:61; 146:9; 147:6.

5750. עוֹד *'ôḏ* **adv.**
(again, more, longer, also, yet)
Gen. 4:25; 7:4; 8:10,12,21,22; 9:11,15; 17:5; 18:22,29; 19:12; 24:20; 25:6; 29:7, 9,27,30,33–35; 30:7,19; 31:14; 32:28(29); 35:9,10,16; 37:5,8,9; 38:4,5,26; 40:13,19; 43:6,7,27,28; 44:14; 45:3,6,11,26,28; 46:29,30; 48:7,15; **Ex.** 2:3; 3:15; 4:6,18; 9:2,17,29; 10:29; 11:1; 14:13; 17:4; 36:3,6; **Lev.** 13:57; 17:7; 25:51; 27:20; **Num.** 8:25; 11:33; 18:5,22; 19:13; 22:15,30; 32:14,15; **Deut.** 3:26; 4:35,39; 5:25; 10:16; 13:16(17); 17:13,16; 18:16; 19:9,20; 28:68; 31:2,27; 34:10; **Josh.** 1:11; 2:11; 5:1,12; 14:11; **Judg.** 2:14; 6:24; 7:4; 8:20; 9:37; 11:14; 13:8,9,21; 18:24; 20:25,28; **Ruth** 1:11,14; **1 Sam.** 1:18; 3:6; 7:13; 10:22; 13:7; 16:11; 18:8,29; 20:3,14; 23:4,22; 26:21; 27:1,4; 28:15; **2 Sam.** 1:9; 2:22,28; 3:11,35; 5:13,22; 6:1,22; 7:10,19,20; 9:1,3; 10:19; 12:22,23; 14:10,29,32; 18:14,22; 19:28(29),29(30),35(36); 21:15,17–20; **1 Kgs.** 1:14,22,42; 8:60; 10:5,10; 12:2,5; 20:32; 22:7,8,43; **2 Kgs.** 2:12,21; 4:6; 5:17; 6:23,33; 12:3(4); 14:4; 15:4,35; 24:7; **1 Chr.** 12:1; 14:3,13,14; 17:9,18; 19:19; 20:5,6; 29:3; **2 Chr.** 9:4; 10:5; 13:20; 14:7(6); 17:6; 18:6,7; 20:33; 27:2; 28:17; 32:16; 33:17; 34:3,16; **Neh.** 2:17; **Esth.** 2:14; 6:14; 9:12; **Job** 1:16–18; 2:3,9; 6:10,29; 7:10; 8:12; 14:7; 20:9; 24:20; 27:3; 29:5; 32:15,16; 34:23; 36:2; **Ps.** 10:18; 37:10; 39:1(2); 42:5(6),11(12); 43:5; 49:9(10); 74:9(10); 77:7(8); 78:17, 30,32; 83:4(5); 84:4(5); 88:5(6); 92:14(15); 103:16; 104:33,35; 139:18; 141:5; 146:2; **Prov.** 9:9; 11:24; 19:19; 23:35; 31:7,15; **Eccl.** 3:16; 4:13; 7:28; 9:5,6; 12:9; **Isa.** 1:5; 2:4; 5:4,25; 6:13; 7:8; 8:5; 9:12(11), 17(16),21(20); 10:4,20,25,32; 14:1; 21:16; 23:10,12; 26:21; 28:4; 29:17; 30:20; 32:5; 38:11; 45:5,6,14,18,21,22; 46:9; 47:8,10; 49:20; 51:22; 52:1; 54:4,9; 56:8; 60:18–20; 62:4,8; 65:19,20,24; **Jer.** 2:9,31; 3:1,16,17; 7:32; 10:20; 11:19; 13:27; 15:9; 16:14; 19:6,11; 20:9; 22:10–12,30; 23:4,7,36; 28:3,4; 30:8; 31:4,5,20,23,29,34,39,40; 32:15; 33:1,10,12,13,24; 34:10; 36:32; 38:9; 40:5; 42:18; 44:22,26; 48:2; 49:7; 50:39; 51:33,44; **Lam.** 4:17; **Ezek.** 5:4,9; 7:13; 8:6,13,15; 12:23–25,28; 13:21,23; 14:11; 15:5; 16:41,42,63; 18:3; 19:9; 20:27,39; 21:5(10); 23:27,38; 24:13,27; 26:13, 14,21; 28:24; 29:15,16; 30:13; 32:13; 33:22; 34:10,22,28,29; 36:12,14,15,30, 37; 37:22,23; 39:7,28,29; 43:7; 45:8; **Dan.** 9:20,21; 10:14; 11:2,27,35; **Hos.** 1:4,6; 2:16(18),17(19); 3:1; 11:12(12:1); 12:9(10); 14:3,8; **Joel** 2:19,27; 3:17(4:17); **Amos** 4:7; 6:10; 7:8,13; 8:2,14; 9:15; **Jon.** 3:4; **Mic.** 1:15; 4:3; 5:13(12); 6:10; **Nah.** 1:12,14,15(2:1);

2:13(14); **Hab.** 2:3; **Zeph.** 2:15; 3:11,15; **Hag.** 2:6,19; **Zech.** 1:17; 2:12(16); 8:4,20; 9:8; 11:6,15; 12:6; 13:2,3; 14:11,21; **Mal.** 2:13.

5751. עוֹד *'ôd* **Aram. adv.**
(while, yet; corr. to Hebr. 5750)
Dan. 4:31(28).

5752. A. עֹדֵד *'ōded* **masc. proper noun**
(Oded: father of the prophet Azariah)
2 Chr. 15:1,8.
B. עוֹדֵד *ōded* **masc. proper noun**
(Oded: a prophet)
2 Chr. 28:9.

5753. עָוָה *'āwāh* **verb**
(to do wrong, to be perverted, to be disturbed)
1 Sam. 20:30; **2 Sam.** 7:14; 19:19(20); 24:17; **1 Kgs.** 8:47; **2 Chr.** 6:37; **Esth.** 1:16; **Job** 33:27; **Ps.** 38:6(7); 106:6; **Prov.** 12:8; **Isa.** 21:3; 24:1; **Jer.** 3:21; 9:5(4); **Lam.** 3:9; **Dan.** 9:5.

5754. עַוָּה *'awwāh* **fem. noun**
(ruin, an overturning)
Ezek. 21:27(32).

5755. עַוָּא *'awwā',* עִוָּה *'iwwāh* **proper noun**
(Ivvah, Avva)
2 Kgs. 17:24; 18:34; 19:13; **Isa.** 37:13.

5756. עוּז *'ûz* **verb**
(to seek refuge, to bring to safety)
Ex. 9:19; **Isa.** 10:31; **Jer.** 4:6; 6:1.

5757. A. עַוִּי *'awwiy* **masc. pl. noun**
(Avite: one of a group placed in Israel after the Assyrian deportation)
2 Kgs. 17:31.

B. עַוִּי *'awwiy* **masc. pl. noun**
(Avite: member of one of the original Canaanite nations)
Deut. 2:23; **Josh.** 13:3.

5758. עֲוָיָה *'ᵃwāyāh* **Aram. fem. noun**
(iniquity, wickedness)
Dan. 4:27(24).

5759. עֲוִיל *'ᵃwiyl* **masc. noun**
(young child, little boy)
Job 19:18; 21:11.

5760. עֲוִיל *'ᵃwiyl* **masc. noun**
(ungodly man, evil man)
Job 16:11.

5761. עַוִּים *'awwiym* **masc. proper noun**
(Avvim: city in Benjamin)
Josh. 18:23.

5762. עֲוִית *'ᵃwiyt* **proper noun**
(Avith)
Gen. 36:35; **1 Chr.** 1:46.

5763. עוּל *'ûl* **verb**
(to nurse, to give suck)
Gen. 33:13; **1 Sam.** 6:7,10; **Ps.** 78:71; **Isa.** 40:11.

5764. עוּל *'ûl* **masc. noun**
(infant, child who is still nursing)
Isa. 49:15; 65:20.

5765. עָוַל *'āwal* **verb**
(to act unjustly, to act unrighteously)
Ps. 71:4; **Isa.** 26:10.

5766. I. עָוֶל *'āwel,* עֶוֶל *'ewel* **masc. noun**
(injustice, unrighteousness, iniquity)
Lev. 19:15,35; **Deut.** 25:16; 32:4; **Job** 34:10,32; **Ps.** 7:3(4); 53:1(2); 82:2; **Prov.** 29:27; **Jer.** 2:5; **Ezek.** 3:20; 18:8,24,26; 28:18; 33:13,15,18.

II. עַוְלָה *'awlāh* **fem. noun**
(perversity, wickedness, injustice)
2 Sam. 3:34; 7:10; **1 Chr.** 17:9; **2 Chr.** 19:7; **Job** 6:29,30; 11:14; 13:7; 15:16; 22:23; 24:20; 27:4; 36:23; **Ps.** 37:1; 43:1; 58:2(3); 64:6(7); 89:22(23); 92:15(16)([Ke] see III); 107:42; 119:3; 125:3; **Prov.** 22:8; **Isa.** 59:3; **Ezek.** 28:15; **Hos.** 10:9(KJV, NIV, *'alwāh* [5932]),13; **Mic.** 3:10; **Hab.** 2:12; **Zeph.** 3:5,13; **Mal.** 2:6.

III. עֹלָתָה *'ōlāṯāh* **fem. noun**
(injustice)
Job 5:16; **Ps.** 92:15(16)([Qe] see II).

5767. עַוָּל *'awwāl* **masc. noun**
(wicked one, evil one)
Job 18:21; 27:7; 29:17; 31:3; **Zeph.** 3:5.

5768. I. עוֹלֵל *'ôlēl* **masc. noun**
(child, infant)
1 Sam. 15:3; 22:19; **2 Kgs.** 8:12; **Job** 3:16; **Ps.** 8:2(3); 17:14; **Isa.** 13:16; **Jer.** 44:7; **Lam.** 2:11,20; **Hos.** 13:16(14:1).

II. עוֹלָל *'ôlāl* **masc. noun**
(child, infant)
Ps. 137:9; **Jer.** 6:11; 9:21(20); **Lam.** 1:5; 2:19; 4:4; **Joel** 2:16; **Mic.** 2:9; **Nah.** 3:10.

5769. עוֹלָם *'ôlām* **masc. noun**
(eternity, forever)
Gen. 3:22; 6:3,4; 9:12,16; 13:15; 17:7,8, 13,19; 21:33; 48:4; 49:26; **Ex.** 3:15; 12:14,17,24; 14:13; 15:18; 19:9; 21:6; 27:21; 28:43; 29:9,28; 30:21; 31:16,17; 32:13; 40:15; **Lev.** 3:17; 6:18(11),22(15); 7:34,36; 10:9,15; 16:29,31,34; 17:7; 23:14,21,31,41; 24:3,8,9; 25:32,34,46; **Num.** 10:8; 15:15; 18:8,11,19,23; 19:10,21; 25:13; **Deut.** 5:29(26); 12:28; 13:16(17); 15:17; 23:3(4),6(7); 28:46; 29:29(28); 32:7,40; 33:15,27; **Josh.** 4:7; 8:28; 14:9; 24:2; **Judg.** 2:1; **1 Sam.** 1:22; 2:30; 3:13,14; 13:13; 20:15,23,42; 27:8,12; **2 Sam.** 3:28; 7:13,16,24–26,29; 12:10; 22:51; 23:5; **1 Kgs.** 1:31; 2:33,45; 8:13; 9:3,5; 10:9; **2 Kgs.** 5:27; 21:7; **1 Chr.** 15:2; 16:15,17,34,36,41; 17:12, 14,22–24,27; 22:10; 23:13,25; 28:4,7,8; 29:10,18; **2 Chr.** 2:4(3); 5:13; 6:2; 7:3, 6,16; 9:8; 13:5; 20:7,21; 30:8; 33:4,7 (KJV, *'ēylôm* [5865]); **Ezra** 3:11; 9:12; **Neh.** 2:3; 9:5; 13:1; **Job** 7:16; 22:15; 41:4(40:28); **Ps.** 5:11(12); 9:5(6),7(8); 10:16; 12:7(8); 15:5; 18:50(51); 21:4(5); 24:7,9; 25:6; 28:9; 29:10; 30:6(7),12(13); 31:1(2); 33:11; 37:18,27,28; 41:12(13), 13(14); 44:8(9); 45:2(3),6(7),17(18); 48:8(9),14(15); 49:8(9),11(12); 52:8(10), 9(11); 55:22(23); 61:4(5),7(8); 66:7; 71:1; 72:17,19; 73:12,26; 75:9(10); 77:5(6), 7(8); 78:66,69; 79:13; 81:15(16); 85:5(6); 86:12; 89:1(2),2(3),4(5),28(29),36(37), 37(38),52(53); 90:2; 92:8(9); 93:2; 100:5; 102:12(13); 103:9,17; 104:5,31; 105:8,10; 106:1,31,48; 107:1; 110:4; 111:5,8,9; 112:6; 113:2; 115:18; 117:2; 118:1–4,29; 119:44,52,89,93,98,111,112,142,144, 152,160; 121:8; 125:1,2; 131:3; 133:3; 135:13; 136:1–26; 138:8; 139:24; 143:3; 145:1,2,13,21; 146:6,10; 148:6; **Prov.** 8:23; 10:25,30; 22:28; 23:10; 27:24; **Eccl.** 1:4,10; 2:16; 3:11,14; 9:6; 12:5; **Isa.** 9:7(6); 14:20; 24:5; 25:2; 26:4; 30:8; 32:14,17; 33:14; 34:10,17; 35:10; 40:8,28; 42:14; 44:7; 45:17; 46:9; 47:7; 51:6,8, 9,11; 54:8; 55:3,13; 56:5; 57:11,16; 58:12; 59:21; 60:15,19–21; 61:4,7,8; 63:9,11,12,16,19; 64:4(3),5(4); **Jer.** 2:20; 3:5,12; 5:15,22; 6:16; 7:7; 10:10; 17:4,25; 18:15,16; 20:11,17; 23:40; 25:5,9,12; 28:8; 31:3,40; 32:40; 33:11; 35:6; 49:13, 33; 50:5; 51:26,39,57,62; **Lam.** 3:6,31; 5:19; **Ezek.** 16:60; 25:15; 26:20,21; 27:36; 28:19; 35:5,9; 36:2; 37:25,26,28; 43:7,9; 46:14; **Dan.** 9:24; 12:2,3,7; **Hos.** 2:19(21); **Joel** 2:2,26,27; 3:20(4:20); **Amos** 9:11; **Obad.** 1:10; **Jon.** 2:6(7); **Mic.** 2:9; 4:5,7; 5:2(1); 7:14; **Hab.** 3:6; **Zeph.** 2:9; **Zech.** 1:5; **Mal.** 1:4; 3:4.

5770. עָוַן *'āwan* **verb**
(to look askance, to eye with suspicion)
1 Sam. 18:9.

5771. עָוֺן *ʿāwōn* **masc. noun**
(iniquity, sin, guilt; punishment)
Gen. 4:13; 15:16; 19:15; 44:16; **Ex.** 20:5; 28:38,43; 34:7,9; **Lev.** 5:1,17; 7:18; 10:17; 16:21,22; 17:16; 18:25; 19:8; 20:17,19; 22:16; 26:39–41,43; **Num.** 5:15,31; 14:18,19,34; 15:31; 18:1,23; 30:15(16); **Deut.** 5:9; 19:15; **Josh.** 22:17,20; **1 Sam.** 3:13,14; 20:1,8; 25:24; 28:10; **2 Sam.** 3:8; 14:9,32; 19:19(20); 22:24; 24:10; **1 Kgs.** 17:18; **2 Kgs.** 7:9; **1 Chr.** 21:8; **Ezra** 9:6,7,13; **Neh.** 4:5(3:37); 9:2; **Job** 7:21; 10:6,14; 11:6; 13:23,26; 14:17; 15:5; 19:29; 20:27; 22:5; 31:11,28,33; 33:9; **Ps.** 18:23(24); 25:11; 31:10(11); 32:2,5; 36:2(3); 38:4(5), 18(19); 39:11(12); 40:12(13); 49:5(6); 51:2(4),5(7),9(11); 59:4(5); 65:3(4); 69:27(28); 78:38; 79:8; 85:2(3); 89:32(33); 90:8; 103:3,10; 106:43; 107:17; 109:14; 130:3,8; **Prov.** 5:22; 16:6; **Isa.** 1:4; 5:18; 6:7; 13:11; 14:21; 22:14; 26:21; 27:9; 30:13; 33:24; 40:2; 43:24; 50:1; 53:5, 6,11; 57:17; 59:2,3,12; 64:6(5),7(6),9(8); 65:7; **Jer.** 2:22; 3:13; 5:25; 11:10; 13:22; 14:7,10,20; 16:10,17,18; 18:23; 25:12; 30:14,15; 31:30,34; 32:18; 33:8; 36:3,31; 50:20; 51:6; **Lam.** 2:14; 4:6,13,22; 5:7; **Ezek.** 3:18,19; 4:4–6,17; 7:13,16,19; 9:9; 14:3,4,7,10; 16:49; 18:17–20,30; 21:23–25(28–30),29(34); 24:23; 28:18; 29:16; 32:27; 33:6,8,9; 35:5; 36:31,33; 39:23; 43:10; 44:10,12; **Dan.** 9:13,16,24; **Hos.** 4:8; 5:5; 7:1; 8:13; 9:7,9; 10:10 (KJV, NASB, *ʿônāh* [5772,II]); 12:8(9); 13:12; 14:1(2),2(3); **Amos** 3:2; **Mic.** 7:18,19; **Zech.** 3:4,9; **Mal.** 2:6.

5772. I. עֹנָה *ʿōnāh* **fem. noun**
(conjugal rights, duty of marriage)
Ex. 21:10.
II. עוֹנָה *ʿônāh* **fem. noun**
(sin, guilt)
Hos. 10:10(NIV, *ʿāwōn* [5771]).

5773. עִוְעִים *ʿiwʿiym* **masc. pl. noun**
(distortion, dizziness)
Isa. 19:14.

5774. I. עוּף *ʿûp̱* **verb**
(to fly, to flutter, to flicker, to glow, to shine; to grow weary)
Gen. 1:20; **Deut.** 4:17; **Judg.** 4:21(NASB, NIV, *ʿiyp̱* [5888]); **1 Sam.** 14:28(NASB, NIV, *ʿiyp̱* [5888]),31(NASB, NIV, *ʿiyp̱* [5888]); **2 Sam.** 21:15(NASB, NIV, *ʿiyp̱* [5888]); 22:11; **Job** 5:7; 11:17(NASB, NIV, *t^eʿup̱āh* [8591,II]); 20:8; **Ps.** 18:10(11); 55:6(7); 90:10; 91:5; **Prov.** 23:5; 26:2; **Isa.** 6:2,6; 11:14; 14:29; 30:6; 31:5; 60:8; **Ezek.** 32:10 (NIV, see III); **Hos.** 9:11; **Nah.** 3:16; **Hab.** 1:8; **Zech.** 5:1,2.
II. עוּף *ʿûp̱* **verb**
(to brandish; NIV, *ʿāp̱ap̱*)
Ezek. 32:10.

5775. עוֹף *ʿôp̱* **masc. noun**
(bird, flying creature)
Gen. 1:20–22,26,28,30; 2:19,20; 6:7,20; 7:3,8,14,21,23; 8:17,19,20; 9:2,10; 40:17, 19; **Lev.** 1:14; 7:26; 11:13,20,21,23,46; 17:13; 20:25; **Deut.** 14:19,20; 28:26; **1 Sam.** 17:44,46; **2 Sam.** 21:10; **1 Kgs.** 4:33(5:13); 14:11; 16:4; 21:24; **Job** 12:7; 28:21; 35:11; **Ps.** 50:11; 78:27; 79:2; 104:12; **Eccl.** 10:20; **Isa.** 16:2; **Jer.** 4:25; 5:27; 7:33; 9:10(9); 12:4; 15:3; 16:4; 19:7; 34:20; **Ezek.** 29:5; 31:6,13; 32:4; 38:20; 44:31; **Hos.** 2:18(20); 4:3; 7:12; 9:11; **Zeph.** 1:3.

5776. עוֹף *ʿôp̱* **Aram. masc. noun**
(bird, corr. to Hebr. 5775)
Dan. 2:38; 7:6.

5777. עוֹפֶרֶת *ʿôp̱eret̲*, עֹפֶרֶת *ʿōp̱eret̲* **fem. noun**
(the element lead)
Ex. 15:10; **Num.** 31:22; **Job** 19:24; **Jer.** 6:29; **Ezek.** 22:18,20; 27:12; **Zech.** 5:7,8.

5778. עֵיפַי *'ēyp̱ay* **masc. proper noun**
(Ephai)
Jer. 40:8.

5779. עוּץ *'ûṣ* **verb**
(to devise a plan, to take advice)
Judg. 19:30; **Isa.** 8:10.

5780. A. עוּץ *'ûṣ* **masc. proper noun**
(Uz: son of Nahor)
Gen. 22:21.
B. עוּץ *'ûṣ* **masc. proper noun**
(Uz: grandson of Seir)
Gen. 36:28; **1 Chr.** 1:17,42.
C. עוּץ *'ûṣ* **masc. proper noun**
(Uz: son of Aram)
Gen. 10:23.
D. עוּץ *'ûṣ* **masc. proper noun**
(Uz: land E. of Palestine)
Job 1:1; **Jer.** 25:20; **Lam.** 4:21.

5781. עוּק *'ûq* **verb**
(to be weighed down, to be crushed)
Amos 2:13.

5782. עוּר *'ûr* **verb**
(to stir, to arouse, to awake)
Deut. 32:11; **Judg.** 5:12; **2 Sam.** 23:18; **1 Chr.** 5:26; 11:11,20; **2 Chr.** 21:16; 36:22; **Ezra** 1:1,5; **Job** 3:8; 8:6; 14:12; 17:8; 31:29; 41:10(2); **Ps.** 7:6(7); 35:23; 44:23(24); 57:8(9); 59:4(5); 73:20; 78:38; 80:2(3); 108:2(3); **Prov.** 10:12; **Song** 2:7; 3:5; 4:16; 5:2; 8:4,5; **Isa.** 10:26; 13:17; 14:9; 15:5; 41:2,25; 42:13; 45:13; 50:4; 51:9,17; 52:1; 64:7(6); **Jer.** 6:22; 25:32; 50:9,41; 51:1,11; **Ezek.** 23:22; **Dan.** 11:2,25; **Hos.** 7:4; **Joel** 3:7(4:7),9(4:9),12(4:12); **Hab.** 2:19; **Hag.** 1:14; **Zech.** 2:13(17); 4:1; 9:13; 13:7; **Mal.** 2:12.

5783. עוּר *'ûr* **verb**
(to be exposed, to be uncovered)
Hab. 3:9.

5784. עוּר *'ûr* **Aram. masc. noun**
(chaff)
Dan. 2:35.

5785. עוֹר *'ôr* **masc. noun**
(skin, animal hide)
Gen. 3:21; 27:16; **Ex.** 22:27(26); 25:5; 26:14; 29:14; 34:29,30,35; 35:7,23; 36:19; 39:34; **Lev.** 4:11; 7:8; 8:17; 9:11; 11:32; 13:2–8,10–12,18,20–22,24–28,30–32, 34–36,38,39,43,48,49,51–53,56–59; 15:17; 16:27; **Num.** 4:6,8,10–12,14; 19:5; 31:20; **2 Kgs.** 1:8; **Job** 2:4; 7:5; 10:11; 18:13; 19:20,26; 30:30; 41:7 (40:31); **Jer.** 13:23; **Lam.** 3:4; 4:8; 5:10; **Ezek.** 37:6,8; **Mic.** 3:2,3.

5786. עָוַר *'āwar* **verb**
(to make blind, to put out one's eyes)
Ex. 23:8; **Deut.** 16:19; **2 Kgs.** 25:7; **Jer.** 39:7; 52:11.

5787. עִוֵּר *'iwwēr* **adj.**
(blind)
Ex. 4:11; **Lev.** 19:14; 21:18; **Deut.** 15:21; 27:18; 28:29; **2 Sam.** 5:6,8; **Job** 29:15; **Ps.** 146:8; **Isa.** 29:18; 35:5; 42:7,16,18,19; 43:8; 56:10; 59:10; **Jer.** 31:8; **Lam.** 4:14; **Zeph.** 1:17; **Mal.** 1:8.

5788. I. עִוָּרוֹן *'iwwārôn* **masc. noun**
(blindness)
Deut. 28:28; **Zech.** 12:4.
II. עַוֶּרֶת *'awweret̠* **fem. noun**
(blindness)
Lev. 22:22.

5789. עוּשׁ *'ûš* **verb**
(to hasten, to come quickly; to come together, to assemble)
Joel 3:11(4:11).

5790. I. עוּת *'ût̠* **verb**
(to help, to sustain)
Isa. 50:4(KJV, see II).

II. עוּת *ʿûṯ* **verb**
(to speak)
Isa. 50:4(NASB, NIV, see I).

5791. עָוַת *ʿāwaṯ* **verb**
(to pervert, to twist, to make crooked; to stoop, to bend)
Job 8:3; 19:6; 34:12; **Ps.** 119:78; 146:9; **Eccl.** 1:15; 7:13; 12:3; **Lam.** 3:36; **Amos** 8:5.

5792. עַוָּתָה *ʿawwāṯāh* **fem. noun**
(wrong, oppression)
Lam. 3:59.

5793. A. עוּתַי *ʿûṯay* **masc. proper noun**
(Uthai: son of Ammihud)
1 Chr. 9:4.
B. עוּתַי *ʿûṯay* **masc. proper noun**
(Uthai: son of Bigvai)
Ezra 8:14.

5794. I. עַז *ʿaz* **adj.**
(strong, powerful; insolent)
Gen. 49:7; **Ex.** 14:21; **Num.** 13:28; 21:24; **Deut.** 28:50; **Judg.** 14:14,18; **2 Sam.** 22:18; **Neh.** 9:11; **Ps.** 18:17(18); 59:3(4); **Prov.** 18:23; 21:14; 30:25; **Song** 8:6; **Isa.** 19:4; 25:3; 43:16; 56:11; **Ezek.** 7:24; **Dan.** 8:23; **Amos** 5:9.
II. עַז *ʿaz* **masc. noun**
(power, strength)
Gen. 49:3.

5795. עֵז *ʿēz* **fem. noun**
(a female goat, kid)
Gen. 15:9; 27:9,16; 30:32,33,35; 31:38; 32:14(15); 37:31; 38:17,20; **Ex.** 12:5; 25:4; 26:7; 35:6,23,26; 36:14; **Lev.** 1:10; 3:12; 4:23,28; 5:6; 7:23; 9:3; 16:5; 17:3; 22:19,27; 23:19; **Num.** 7:16,22,28,34, 40,46,52,58,64,70,76,82,87; 15:11,24,27; 18:17; 28:15,30; 29:5,11,16,19,25; 31:20; **Deut.** 14:4; **Judg.** 6:19; 13:15,19; 15:1; **1 Sam.** 16:20; 19:13,16; 25:2; **1 Kgs.** 20:27; **2 Chr.** 29:21; 35:7; **Prov.** 27:27; **Song** 4:1; 6:5; **Ezek.** 43:22; 45:23; **Dan.** 8:5,8.

5796. עֵז *ʿēz* **Aram. fem. noun**
(goat; corr. to Hebr. 5795)
Ezra 6:17.

5797. עֹז *ʿōz*, עוֹז *ʿôz* **masc. noun**
(strength, power)
Ex. 15:2,13; **Lev.** 26:19; **Judg.** 5:21; 9:51; **1 Sam.** 2:10; **2 Sam.** 6:14; **1 Chr.** 13:8; 16:11,27,28; **2 Chr.** 6:41; 30:21; **Ezra** 8:22; **Job** 12:16; 26:2; 37:6; 41:22(14); **Ps.** 8:2(3); 21:1(2),13(14); 28:7,8; 29:1,11; 30:7(8); 46:1(2); 59:9(10), 16(17),17(18); 61:3(4); 62:7(8),11(12); 63:2(3); 66:3; 68:28(29),33–35(34–36); 71:7; 74:13; 77:14(15); 78:26,61; 81:1(2); 84:5(6); 86:16; 89:10(11),17(18); 90:11; 93:1; 96:6,7; 99:4; 105:4; 110:2; 118:14; 132:8; 138:3; 140:7(8); 150:1; **Prov.** 10:15; 14:26; 18:10,11,19; 21:22; 24:5; 31:17,25; **Eccl.** 8:1; **Isa.** 12:2; 26:1; 45:24; 49:5; 51:9; 52:1; 62:8; **Jer.** 16:19; 48:17; 51:53; **Ezek.** 19:11,12,14; 24:21; 26:11; 30:6,18; 33:28; **Amos** 3:11; **Mic.** 5:4(3); **Hab.** 3:4.

5798. A. עֻזָּא *ʿuzzāʾ*, עֻזָּה *ʿuzzāh* **masc. proper noun**
(Uzzah, Uzza: son of Abinadab)
2 Sam. 6:3,6–8; **1 Chr.** 13:7,9–11.
B. עֻזָּא *ʿuzzāʾ* **masc. proper noun**
(Uzzah, Uzza: son of Gera)
1 Chr. 8:7.
C. עֻזָּה *ʿuzzāʾ* **masc. proper noun**
(Uzzah, Uzza: a Levite)
1 Chr. 6:29(14).
D. עֻזָּא *ʿuzzāʾ* **masc. proper noun**
(Uzzah, Uzza: a Jew)
2 Kgs. 21:18,26.
E. עֻזָּא *ʿuzzāʾ* **masc. proper noun**
(Uzzah, Uzza: head of a family)
Ezra 2:49; **Neh.** 7:51.

5799. עֲזָאזֵל *ʿazāʾzēl* **masc. noun**
(scapegoat)
Lev. 16:8,10,26.

5800. I. עָזַב *'āzab̲* **verb**
(to restore, to repair, to fortify, to help)
Ex. 23:5(NASB, see II); **Neh.** 3:8; 4:2(3:34).
II. עָזַב *'āzab̲* **verb**
(to leave, to abandon, to forsake)
Gen. 2:24; 24:27; 28:15; 39:6,12,13, 15,18; 44:22; 50:8; **Ex.** 2:20; 9:21; 23:5 (KJV, NIV, see I); **Lev.** 19:10; 23:22; 26:43; **Num.** 10:31; **Deut.** 12:19; 14:27; 28:20; 29:25(24); 31:6,8,16,17; 32:36; **Josh.** 1:5; 8:17; 22:3; 24:16,20; **Judg.** 2:12,13,21; 10:6,10,13; **Ruth** 1:16; 2:11,16,20; **1 Sam.** 8:8; 12:10; 30:13; 31:7; **2 Sam.** 5:21; 15:16; **1 Kgs.** 6:13; 8:57; 9:9; 11:33; 12:8,13; 14:10; 18:18; 19:10, 14,20; 21:21; **2 Kgs.** 2:2,4,6; 4:30; 7:7; 8:6; 9:8; 14:26; 17:16; 21:22; 22:17; **1 Chr.** 10:7; 14:12; 16:37; 28:9,20; **2 Chr.** 7:19,22; 10:8,13; 11:14; 12:1,5; 13:10,11; 15:2; 21:10; 24:18,20,24,25; 28:6,14; 29:6; 32:31; 34:25; **Ezra** 8:22; 9:9,10; **Neh.** 5:10; 9:17,19,28,31; 10:39(40); 13:11; **Job** 6:14; 9:27; 10:1; 18:4; 20:13,19; 39:11,14; **Ps.** 9:10(11); 10:14; 16:10; 22:1(2); 27:9,10; 37:8,25, 28,33; 38:10(11),21(22); 40:12(13); 49:10(11); 71:9,11,18; 89:30(31); 94:14; 119:8,53,87; **Prov.** 2:13,17; 3:3; 4:2,6; 9:6; 10:17; 15:10; 27:10; 28:4,13; **Isa.** 1:4,28; 6:12(KJV, NASB, *'azûb̲āh* [5805]); 7:16; 10:3,14; 17:2,9(NASB, *'azûb̲āh* [5805]); 18:6; 27:10; 32:14; 41:17; 42:16; 49:14; 54:6,7; 55:7; 58:2; 60:15; 62:4,12; 65:11; **Jer.** 1:16; 2:13,17,19; 4:29; 5:7,19; 9:2(1),13(12),19(18); 12:7; 14:5; 16:11; 17:11,13; 18:14; 19:4; 22:9; 25:38; 48:28; 49:11,25; 51:9; **Lam.** 5:20; **Ezek.** 8:12; 9:9; 20:8; 23:8,29; 24:21; 36:4; **Dan.** 11:30; **Hos.** 4:10; **Jon.** 2:8(9); **Zeph.** 2:4; **Zech.** 11:17; **Mal.** 4:1(3:19).

5801. עִזָּבוֹן *'izzāb̲ôn* **masc. noun**
(wares, merchandise)
Ezek. 27:12,14,16,19,22,27,33.

5802. עַזְבּוּק *'azbûq* **masc. proper noun**
(Azbuk)
Neh. 3:16.

5803. עַזְגָּד *'azgād̲* **masc. proper noun**
(Azgad)
Ezra 2:12; 8:12; **Neh.** 7:17; 10:15(16).

5804. עַזָּה *'azzāh* **proper noun**
(Gaza)
Gen. 10:19; **Deut.** 2:23; **Josh.** 10:41; 11:22; 15:47; **Judg.** 1:18; 6:4; 16:1,21; **1 Sam.** 6:17; **1 Kgs.** 4:24(5:4); **2 Kgs.** 18:8; **1 Chr.** 7:28; **Jer.** 25:20; 47:1,5; **Amos** 1:6,7; **Zeph.** 2:4; **Zech.** 9:5.

5805. עֲזוּבָה *'azûb̲āh* **fem. noun**
(forsakenness)
Isa. 6:12(NIV, *'āzab̲* [5800,II]); 17:9(KJV, NIV, *'āzab̲* [5800,II]).

5806. A. עֲזוּבָה *'azûb̲āh* **fem. proper noun**
(Azubah: mother of Jehoshaphat)
1 Kgs. 22:42; **2 Chr.** 20:31.
B. עֲזוּבָה *'azûb̲āh* **fem. proper noun**
(Azubah: wife of Caleb)
1 Chr. 2:18,19.

5807. עֱזוּז *'ezûz* **masc. noun**
(strength, power, violence)
Ps. 78:4; 145:6; **Isa.** 42:25.

5808. עִזּוּז *'izzûz* **adj.**
(strong, mighty)
Ps. 24:8; **Isa.** 43:17.

5809. A. עַזּוּר *'azzûr* **masc. proper noun**
(Azzur: father of Hananiah)
Jer. 28:1.
B. עַזּוּר *'azzûr* **masc. proper noun**
(Azzur: father of Jaazaniah)
Ezek. 11:1.

C. עַזּוּר *'azzûr* **masc. proper noun**
(Azzur: Jewish leader)
Neh. 10:17(18).

5810. עָזַז *'āzaz* **verb**
(to be strong, to strengthen, to prevail)
Judg. 3:10; 6:2; **Ps.** 9:19(20); 52:7(9); 68:28(29); 89:13(14); **Prov.** 7:13; 8:28; 21:29; **Eccl.** 7:19; **Isa.** 30:2; **Dan.** 11:12.

5811. עָזָז *'āzāz* **masc. proper noun**
(Azaz)
1 Chr. 5:8.

5812. A. עֲזַזְיָהוּ *'azazyāhû* **masc. proper noun**
(Azaziah: a Levite)
1 Chr. 15:21.
B. עֲזַזְיָהוּ *'azazyāhû* **masc. proper noun**
(Azaziah: a Levite)
2 Chr. 31:13.
C. עֲזַזְיָהוּ *'azazyāhû* **masc. proper noun**
(Azaziah: a Benjamite)
1 Chr. 27:20.

5813. עֻזִּי *'uzziy* **masc. proper noun**
(Uzzi)
1 Chr. 6:5(5:31),6(5:32),51(36); 7:2,3,7; 9:8; **Ezra** 7:4; **Neh.** 11:22; 12:19,42.

5814. עֻזִּיָּא *'uziyyā'* **masc. proper noun**
(Uzzia)
1 Chr. 11:44.

5815. עֲזִיאֵל *'Aziy'ēl* **masc. proper noun**
(Aziel; same as *ya'aziy'ēl* [3268])
1 Chr. 15:20.

5816. A. עֻזִּיאֵל *'uzziy'ēl* **masc. proper noun**
(Uzziel: son of Bela)
1 Chr. 7:7.
B. עֻזִּיאֵל *'uzziy'ēl* **masc. proper noun**
(Uzziel: son of Kohath)
Ex. 6:18,22; **Lev.** 10:4; **Num.** 3:19,30; **1 Chr.** 6:2(5:28),18(3); 15:10; 23:12,20; 24:24.
C. עֻזִּיאֵל *'uzziy'ēl* **masc. proper noun**
(Uzziel: son of Heman)
1 Chr. 25:4; **2 Chr.** 29:14.
D. עֻזִּיאֵל *'uzziy'ēl* **masc. proper noun**
(Uzziel: a Simeomite)
1 Chr. 4:42.
E. עֻזִּיאֵל *'uzziy'ēl* **masc. proper noun**
(Uzziel: son of Harhaiah)
Neh. 3:8.

5817. עָזִּיאֵלִי *'ozziy'ēliy* **masc. proper noun**
(Uzzielite)
Num. 3:27; **1 Chr.** 26:23.

5818. A. עֻזִּיָּהוּ *'uzziyyāhû* **masc. proper noun**
(Uzziah: father of Jehonathan)
1 Chr. 27:25.
B. עֻזִּיָּה *'uzziyyāh* **masc. proper noun**
(Uzziah: son of Uriel; see also *'azaryāh* [5838,C])
1 Chr. 6:24(9).
C. עֻזִּיָּה *'uzziyyāh,* עֻזִּיָּהוּ *'uzziyyāhû* **masc. proper noun**
(Uzziah: king of Judah, son of Amaziah; see also *'azaryāh, 'azaryāhû* [5838,N])
2 Kgs. 15:13,30,32,34; **2 Chr.** 26:1,3,8,9,11,14,18,19,21–23; 27:2; **Isa.** 1:1; 6:1; 7:1; **Hos.** 1:1; **Amos** 1:1; **Zech.** 14:5.
D. עֻזִּיָּה *'uzziyyāh* **masc. proper noun**
(Uzziah: son of Zechariah)
Neh. 11:4.

E. עֻזִּיָּה *ʿuzziyyāh* **masc. proper noun**
(Uzziah: son of Harim)
Ezra 10:21.

5819. עֲזִיזָא *ʿaziyzāʾ* **masc. proper noun**
(Aziza)
Ezra 10:27.

5820. A. עַזְמָוֶת *ʿazmāweṯ* **masc. proper noun**
(Azmaveth: one of David's mighty men)
2 Sam. 23:31; **1 Chr.** 11:33; 12:3.
B. עַזְמָוֶת *ʿazmāweṯ* **masc. proper noun**
(Azmaveth: head of a family; possibly same as A)
Ezra 2:24.
C. עַזְמָוֶת *ʿazmāweṯ* **proper noun**
(Azmaveth: village near Jerusalem; same as *bēyṯ ʿazmaweṯ* [1041])
Neh. 12:29.
D. עַזְמָוֶת *ʿazmāweṯ* **masc. proper noun**
(Azmaveth: officer under David)
1 Chr. 27:25.
E. עַזְמָוֶת *ʿazmāweṯ* **masc. proper noun**
(Azmaveth: descendant of Micah)
1 Chr. 8:36; 9:42.

5821. עַזָּן *ʿazzān* **masc. proper noun**
(Azzan)
Num. 34:26.

5822. עָזְנִיָּה *ʿozniyyāh* **fem. noun**
(an unclean bird; perhaps buzzard, black vulture)
Lev. 11:13; **Deut.** 14:12.

5823. עָזַק *ʿāzaq* **verb**
(to dig around, to fence in)
Isa. 5:2.

5824. עִזְקָה *ʿizqāh* **Aram. fem. noun**
(signet ring)
Dan. 6:17(18).

5825. עֲזֵקָה *ʿazēqāh* **proper noun**
(Azekah)
Josh. 10:10,11; 15:35; **1 Sam.** 17:1; **2 Chr.** 11:9; **Neh.** 11:30; **Jer.** 34:7.

5826. עָזַר *ʿāzar* **verb**
(to help, to aid)
Gen. 49:25; **Deut.** 32:38; **Josh.** 1:14; 10:4,6,33; **1 Sam.** 7:12; **2 Sam.** 8:5; 18:3; 21:17; **1 Kgs.** 1:7; 20:16; **2 Kgs.** 14:26; **1 Chr.** 5:20; 12:1,17–19,21,22; 15:26; 18:5; 22:17; **2 Chr.** 14:11(10); 18:31; 19:2; 20:23; 25:8; 26:7,13,15; 28:16,23; 32:3,8; **Ezra** 8:22; 10:15; **Job** 9:13; 26:2; 29:12; 30:13; **Ps.** 10:14; 22:11(12); 28:7; 30:10(11); 37:40; 46:5(6); 54:4(6); 72:12; 79:9; 86:17; 107:12; 109:26; 118:7,13; 119:86,173,175; **Isa.** 30:7; 31:3; 41:6,10,13,14; 44:2; 49:8; 50:7,9; 63:5; **Jer.** 47:4; **Lam.** 1:7; **Ezek.** 30:8; 32:21; **Dan.** 10:13; 11:34,45; **Zech.** 1:15.

5827. A. עֶזֶר *ʿezer* **masc. proper noun**
(Ezer: an Ephraimite)
1 Chr. 7:21.
B. עֶזֶר *ʿezer* **masc. proper noun**
(Ezer: a priest)
Neh. 12:42(KJV, NIV, *ʿēzer* [5829,D].

5828. עֵזֶר *ʿēzer* **masc. noun**
(help, aid, one who helps)
Gen. 2:18,20; **Ex.** 18:4; **Deut.** 33:7, 26,29; **Ps.** 20:2(3); 33:20; 70:5(6); 89:19(20); 115:9–11; 121:1,2; 124:8; 146:5; **Isa.** 30:5; **Ezek.** 12:14; **Dan.** 11:34; **Hos.** 13:9.

5829. A. עֵזֶר *ʿēzer* **masc. proper noun**
(Ezer: builder of the wall)
Neh. 3:19.

B. עֵזֶר ʽēzer **masc. proper noun**
(Ezer: a Judaite)
1 Chr. 4:4.

C. עֵזֶר ʽēzer **masc. proper noun**
(Ezer: one of David's mighty men)
1 Chr. 12:9(10).

D. עֵזֶר ʽēzer **masc. proper noun**
(Ezer: a priest)
Neh. 12:42(NASB, ʽezer [5827,B]).

5830. A. עֶזְרָא ʽezrā' **masc. proper noun**
(Ezra the scribe)
Ezra 7:1,6,10,11; 10:1,2,5,6,10,16;
Neh. 8:1,2,4–6,9,13; 12:26,36.

B. עֶזְרָא ʽezrā' **masc. proper noun**
(Ezra: a priest)
Neh. 12:1,13.

C. עֶזְרָא ʽezrā' **masc. proper noun**
(Ezra: a priest)
Neh. 12:33.

5831. עֶזְרָא ʽezrā' **Aram. masc. proper noun**
(Ezra; corr. to Hebr. 5830)
Ezra 7:12,21,25.

5832. A. עֲזַרְאֵל ʽazar'ēl **masc. proper noun**
(Azarel: a Benjamite warrior)
1 Chr. 12:6.

B. עֲזַרְאֵל ʽazar'ēl **masc. proper noun**
(Azarel: a Levite)
1 Chr. 25:18.

C. עֲזַרְאֵל ʽazar'ēl **masc. proper noun**
(Azarel: a Danite leader)
1 Chr. 27:22.

D. עֲזַרְאֵל ʽazar'ēl **masc. proper noun**
(Azarel: postexilic Jew)
Ezra 10:41.

E. עֲזַרְאֵל ʽazar'ēl **masc. proper noun**
(Azarel: a priest)
Neh. 11:13.

F. עֲזַרְאֵל ʽazar'ēl **masc. proper noun**
(Azarel: a priest)
Neh. 12:36.

5833. עֶזְרָה ʽezrāh, עֶזְרָת ʽezrāth **fem. noun**
(help, assistance)
Judg. 5:23; **2 Chr.** 28:21; **Job** 6:13; 31:21; **Ps.** 22:19(20); 27:9; 35:2; 38:22(23); 40:13(14),17(18); 44:26(27); 46:1(2); 60:11(13); 63:7(8); 70:1(2); 71:12; 94:17; 108:12(13); **Isa.** 10:3; 20:6; 31:1,2; **Jer.** 37:7; **Lam.** 4:17; **Nah.** 3:9.

5834. עֶזְרָה ʽezrāh **masc. proper noun**
(Ezra)
1 Chr. 4:17.

5835. עֲזָרָה ʽazārāh **fem. noun**
(ledge, courtyard)
2 Chr. 4:9; 6:13; **Ezek.** 43:14,17,20; 45:19.

5836. עֶזְרִי ʽezriy **masc. proper noun**
(Ezri)
1 Chr. 27:26.

5837. A. עַזְרִיאֵל ʽazriy'ēl **masc. proper noun**
(Azriel: Manassite chief)
1 Chr. 5:24.

B. עַזְרִיאֵל ʽazriy'ēl **masc. proper noun**
(Azriel: Naphtalite chief)
1 Chr. 27:19.

C. עַזְרִיאֵל ʽazriy'ēl **masc. proper noun**
(Azriel: royal officer)
Jer. 36:26.

5838. A. עֲזַרְיָה ʽazaryāh **masc. proper noun**
(Azariah: son of Ethan)
1 Chr. 2:8.

B. עֲזַרְיָה *ᵃzaryāh* **masc. proper noun**
(Azariah: son of Jehu)
1 Chr. 2:38,39.
C. עֲזַרְיָה *ᵃzaryāh* **masc. proper noun**
(Azariah: another name for *ʿuzziyāh* [5818,B])
1 Chr. 6:36(21).
D. עֲזַרְיָהוּ *ᵃzaryāhû* **masc. proper noun**
(Azariah: son of Zadok)
1 Kgs. 4:2.
E. עֲזַרְיָהוּ *ᵃzaryāhû* **masc. proper noun**
(Azariah: son of Nathan)
1 Kgs. 4:5.
F. עֲזַרְיָהוּ *ᵃzaryāhû* **masc. proper noun**
(Azariah: son of Oded)
2 Chr. 15:1.
G. עֲזַרְיָה *ᵃzaryāh* **masc. proper noun**
(Azariah: son of Ahimaaz)
1 Chr. 6:9(5:35).
H. עֲזַרְיָהוּ *ᵃzaryāhû* **masc. proper noun**
(Azariah: son of Jehoshaphat)
2 Chr. 21:2.
I. עֲזַרְיָה *ᵃzaryāh* **masc. proper noun**
(Azariah: son of Jehoshaphat)
2 Chr. 21:2.
J. עֲזַרְיָה *ᵃzaryāh* **masc. proper noun**
(Azariah: another name for Ahaziah [274,B])
2 Chr. 22:6.
K. עֲזַרְיָה *ᵃzaryāh* **masc. proper noun**
(Azariah: son of Jeroham)
2 Chr. 23:1.
L. עֲזַרְיָהוּ *ᵃzaryāhû* **masc. proper noun**
(Azariah: son of Obed)
2 Chr. 23:1.
M. עֲזַרְיָה *ᵃzaryāh* **masc. proper noun**
(Azariah: son of Johanan)
1 Chr. 6:10(5:36),11(5:37).
N. עֲזַרְיָה *ᵃzaryāh,* עֲזַרְיָהוּ *ᵃzaryāhû* **masc. proper noun**
(Azariah: son of Amaziah, king of Judah; see also *ʿuzziyāh, ʿuzziyāhû* [5818,C])
2 Kgs. 14:21; 15:1,6–8,17,23,27;
1 Chr. 3:12.
O. עֲזַרְיָהוּ *ᵃzaryāhû* **masc. proper noun**
(Azariah: high priest)
2 Chr. 26:17,20.
P. עֲזַרְיָהוּ *ᵃzaryāhû* **masc. proper noun**
(Azariah: son of Johanan the Ephramite)
2 Chr. 28:12.
Q. עֲזַרְיָה *ᵃzaryāh* **masc. proper noun**
(Azariah: high priest)
2 Chr. 31:10,13.
R. עֲזַרְיָה *ᵃzaryāh* **masc. proper noun**
(Azariah: a Kohathite)
2 Chr. 29:12.
S. עֲזַרְיָה *ᵃzaryāh* **masc. proper noun**
(Azariah: a Merarite)
2 Chr. 29:12.
T. עֲזַרְיָה *ᵃzaryāh* **masc. proper noun**
(Azariah: son of Hilkiah)
1 Chr. 6:13(5:39),14(5:40); 9:11;
Ezra 7:1.
U. עֲזַרְיָה *ᵃzaryāh* **masc. proper noun**
(Azariah: enemy of Jeremiah)
Jer. 43:2.
V. עֲזַרְיָה *ᵃzaryāh* **masc. proper noun**
(Azariah: Hebrew name of Abednego)
Dan. 1:6,7,11,19.
W. עֲזַרְיָה *ᵃzaryāh* **masc. proper noun**
(Azariah: son of Maaseiah)

Neh. 3:23,24.
X. עֲזַרְיָה *'ᵃzaryāh* **masc. proper noun**
(Azariah: postexilic Jew; possibly same as W)
Neh. 7:7.
Y. עֲזַרְיָה *'ᵃzaryāh* **masc. proper noun**
(Azariah: a Levite; possibly same as W)
Neh. 8:7.
Z. עֲזַרְיָה *'ᵃzaryāh* **masc. proper noun**
(Azariah: a priest; possibly same as W)
Neh. 10:2(3).
AA. עֲזַרְיָה *'ᵃzaryāh* **masc. proper noun**
(Azariah: Judaite prince; possibly same as W)
Neh. 12:33.
BB. עֲזַרְיָה *'ᵃzaryāh* **masc. proper noun**
(Azariah: son of Meraioth)
Ezra 7:3.

5839. עֲזַרְיָה *'ᵃzaryāh* **Aram. masc. proper noun**
(Azariah)
Dan. 2:17.

5840. A. עַזְרִיקָם *'azriyqām* **masc. proper noun**
(Azrikam: descendant of David)
1 Chr. 3:23.
B. עַזְרִיקָם *'azriyqām* **masc. proper noun**
(Azrikam: prince of Judah)
2 Chr. 28:7.
C. עַזְרִיקָם *'azriyqām* **masc. proper noun**
(Azrikam: a Benjamite)
1 Chr. 8:38; 9:44.
D. עַזְרִיקָם *'azriyqām* **masc. proper noun**
(Azrikam: a Levite)
1 Chr. 9:14; **Neh.** 11:15.

5841. עַזָּתִי *'azzāṯiy* **masc. proper noun**
(Gazite[s], Gazathites)
Josh. 13:3; **Judg.** 16:2.

5842. עֵט *'ēṭ* **masc. noun**
(iron stylus, pen)
Job 19:24; **Ps.** 45:1(2); **Jer.** 8:8; 17:1.

5843. עֵטָה *'ēṭāh* **Aram. fem. noun**
(counsel, discretion)
Dan. 2:14.

5844. I. עָטָה *'āṭāh* **verb**
(to wrap around, to cover)
Lev. 13:45; **1 Sam.** 28:14; **Ps.** 71:13; 84:6(7); 89:45(46); 104:2; 109:19,29; **Song** 1:7; **Isa.** 22:17(NASB, NIV, see II); 59:17; **Jer.** 43:12; **Ezek.** 21:15(20) (KJV, *mᵉ'uṭṭah* [4593] NIV, see II); 24:17,22; **Mic.** 3:7.
II. עָטָה *'āṭāh* **verb**
(to take hold, to grasp)
Isa. 22:17(KJV, see I); **Ezek.** 21:15(20)(KJV, *mᵉ'uṭṭah* [4593] NASB, see I).

5845. עֲטִין *'ᵃṭiyn* **masc. noun**
(body)
Job 21:24.

5846. עֲטִישָׁה *'ᵃṭiyšāh* **fem. noun**
(sneezing, snorting)
Job 41:18(10).

5847. עֲטַלֵּף *'ᵃṭallēp̱* **masc. noun**
(the bird, bat)
Lev. 11:19; **Deut.** 14:18; **Isa.** 2:20.

5848. I. עָטַף *'āṭap̱* **verb**
(to turn, to wrap, to cover)
Job 23:9; **Ps.** 73:6.
II. עָטַף *'āṭap̱* **verb**
(to be feeble, to faint, to be weak)
Gen. 30:42; **Ps.** 61:2(3); 65:13(14); 77:3(4); 102:[title](1); 107:5; 142:3(4); 143:4; **Isa.** 57:16; **Lam.** 2:11,12,19; **Jon.** 2:7(8).

5849. I. עָטַר *'āṭar* **verb**
(to crown)
Ps. 8:5(6); 65:11(12); 103:4; **Song** 3:11; **Isa.** 23:8.
II. עָטַר *'āṭar* **verb**
(to surround, to encompass)
1 Sam. 23:26; **Ps.** 5:12(13).

5850. עֲטָרָה *'ᵃṭārāh* **fem. noun**
(crown, wreath)
2 Sam. 12:30; **1 Chr.** 20:2; **Esth.** 8:15; **Job** 19:9; 31:36; **Ps.** 21:3(4); **Prov.** 4:9; 12:4; 14:24; 16:31; 17:6; **Song** 3:11; **Isa.** 28:1,3,5; 62:3; **Jer.** 13:18; **Lam.** 5:16; **Ezek.** 16:12; 21:26(31); 23:42; **Zech.** 6:11,14.

5851. עֲטָרָה *'ᵃṭārāh* **fem. proper noun**
(Atarah)
1 Chr. 2:26.

5852. A. עֲטָרוֹת *'ᵃṭārôṯ*, עֲטָרֹת *'ᵃṭārōṯ* **proper noun**
(Ataroth: town E. of Jordan)
Num. 32:3,34.
B. עֲטָרוֹת *'ᵃṭārôṯ* **proper noun**
(Ataroth: town on S.W. border of Ephraim)
Josh. 16:2.
C. עֲטָרוֹת *'ᵃṭārôṯ* **proper noun**
(Ataroth: town in N.E. Ephraim)
Josh. 16:7.
D. עֲטָרוֹת *'ᵃṭārôṯ* **proper noun**
(Ataroth: town in Judah; [NASB, NIV, part of the name *'aṭrôṯ-bēṯ-yô'āḇ* [5854])
1 Chr. 2:54.

5853. עַטְרוֹת אַדָּר *'aṭrôṯ 'addār* **proper noun**
(Ataroth-addar)
Josh. 16:5; 18:13.

5854. עַטְרוֹת בֵּית יוֹאָב *'aṭrôṯ-bēṯ-yô'āḇ* **proper noun**
(Atroth-beth-joab)
1 Chr. 2:54(KJV, *'ᵃṭārôṯ* [5852,D], *bayiṯ* [1004], and *yô'āḇ* [3097,A]).

5855. עַטְרוֹת שׁוֹפָן *'aṭrôṯ šôp̄ān* **proper noun**
(Atroth-shophan, Atroth and Shophan)
Num. 32:35.

5856. עִי *'iy* **masc. noun**
(ruins, rubbish heap)
Job 30:24(KJV, *bᵉiy* [1164]); **Ps.** 79:1; **Jer.** 26:18; **Mic.** 1:6; 3:12.

5857. A. עַי *'ay*, עַיָּא *'ayya'*, עַיָּת *'ayyāṯ* **proper noun**
(Ai: Canaanite city)
Gen. 12:8; 13:3; **Josh.** 7:2–5; 8:1–3, 9–12,14,16–18,20,21,23–26,28,29; 9:3; 10:1,2; 12:9; **Ezra** 2:28; **Neh.** 7:32; 11:31; **Isa.** 10:28.
B. עַי *'ay* **proper noun**
(Ai: city in E. Jordan)
Jer. 49:3.

5858. A. עֵיבָל *'ēyḇāl* **proper noun**
(Ebal: an Edomite)
Gen. 36:23.
B. עֵיבָל *'ēyḇāl* **proper noun**
(Ebal: another spelling for *'ôḇāl* [5745])
1 Chr. 1:22(NIV, *'ôḇāl* [5745]),40.
C. עֵיבָל *'ēyḇāl* **proper noun**
(Ebal: mountain in Shechem)
Deut. 11:29; 27:4,13; **Josh.** 8:30,33.

5859. עִיּוֹן *'iyyôn* **proper noun**
(Ijon)
1 Kgs. 15:20; **2 Kgs.** 15:29; **2 Chr.** 16:4.

5860. I. עִיט *'iyṭ* **verb**
(to scorn, to insult)
1 Sam. 14:32([Kᵉ] עָשָׂה [6213]); 15:19; 25:14.
II. עִיט *'iyṭ* **verb**
(to pounce upon, to rush greedily)

1 Sam. 14:32(KJV, [K^{e}] *ʿāśāh* [6213]); 15:19.

5861. עַיִט *ʿayiṭ* **masc. noun**
(bird of prey)
Gen. 15:11; **Job** 28:7; **Isa.** 18:6; 46:11; **Jer.** 12:9; **Ezek.** 39:4.

5862. A. עֵיטָם *ʿēyṭām* **proper noun**
(Etam: town in Simeon)
1 Chr. 4:3,32.
B. עֵיטָם *ʿēyṭām* **proper noun**
(Etam: town near Bethlehem)
2 Chr. 11:6.
C. עֵיטָם *ʿēyṭām* **proper noun**
(Etam: rock formation in Judah)
Judg. 15:8,11.

5863. עִיֵּי הָעֲבָרִים *ʿiyyēy hāʿabāriym* **proper noun**
(Iye Abarim; see also *ʿiyyiym* [5864,A])
Num. 21:11; 33:44.

5864. A. עִיִּים *ʿiyyiym* **proper noun**
(Iyim: another name for *ʿiyyēy hāʿabāriym* [5863])
Num. 33:45.
B. עִיִּים *ʿiyyiym* **proper noun**
(Iim: city in Judah)
Josh. 15:29.

5865. עֵילוֹם *ʿēylôm* **masc. noun**
(eternity; NASB, NIV, var. spelling of *ʿôlām* [5769])
2 Chr. 33:7(NASB, NIV, *ʿôlām* [5769]).

5866. עִילַי *ʿiylay* **masc. proper noun**
(Ilai)
1 Chr. 11:29.

5867. A. עֵילָם *ʿēylām* **masc. proper noun**
(Elam: a people and territory of Elam)
Gen. 10:22; 14:1,9; **1 Chr.** 1:17; **Isa.** 11:11; 21:2; 22:6; **Jer.** 25:25; 49:34–39; **Ezek.** 32:24; **Dan.** 8:2.
B. עֵילָם *ʿēylām* **masc. proper noun**
(Elam: head of a family)
Ezra 2:7; **Neh.** 7:12.
C. עֵילָם *ʿēylām* **masc. proper noun**
(Elam: head of a family)
Ezra 2:31; **Neh.** 7:34.
D. עֵילָם *ʿēylām* **masc. proper noun**
(Elam: head of a family)
Ezra 8:7; 10:2([K^{e}] *ʿôlām*),26.
E. עֵילָם *ʿēylām* **masc. proper noun**
(Elam: Jewish leader)
Neh. 10:14(15).
F. עֵילָם *ʿēylām* **masc. proper noun**
(Elam: a Benjamite)
1 Chr. 8:24.
G. עֵילָם *ʿēylām* **masc. proper noun**
(Elam: a Levite)
1 Chr. 26:3.
H. עֵילָם *ʿēylām* **masc. proper noun**
(Elam: a priest)
Neh. 12:42.

5868. I. עֲיָם *ʿayām* **masc. noun**
(scorching)
Isa. 11:15(KJV, see II).
II. עֲיָם *ʿayām* **masc. noun**
(mighty)
Isa. 11:15(NASB, NIV, see I).

5869. I. עַיִן *ʿayin* **masc./fem. noun**
(eye, sight; appearance)
Gen. 3:5–7; 6:8; 13:10,14; 16:4–6; 18:2,3; 19:8,14,19; 20:15,16; 21:11,12,19; 22:4, 13; 23:11,18; 24:63,64; 27:1,12; 28:8; 29:17,20; 30:27,41; 31:10,12,35,40; 32:5(6); 33:1,5,8,10,15; 34:11,18; 37:25; 38:7,10; 39:4,7,21; 41:37; 42:24; 43:29; 44:21; 45:5,12,16,20; 46:4; 47:19,25,29; 48:10,17; 49:12,22; 50:4; **Ex.** 3:21; 4:30;

5:21; 7:20; 8:26(22); 9:8; 10:5,15; 11:3; 12:36; 13:9,16; 14:10; 15:26; 17:6; 19:11; 21:8,24,26; 24:17; 33:12,13,16,17; 34:9; 40:38; **Lev.** 4:13; 10:19,20; 13:5,12, 37,55; 14:9; 20:4,17; 21:20; 24:20; 25:53; 26:16,45; **Num.** 5:13; 10:31; 11:6,7,10, 11,15; 13:33; 14:14; 15:24,39; 16:14; 19:5; 20:8,12,27; 22:5,11,31,34; 23:27; 24:1–4,15,16; 25:6; 27:14,19; 32:5,13; 33:3,55; 36:6; **Deut.** 1:23,30; 3:21,27; 4:3,6,9,19,25,34; 6:8,18,22; 7:16,19; 9:17,18; 10:21; 11:7,12,18; 12:8,25,28; 13:8(9),18(19); 14:1; 15:9,18; 16:19; 17:2; 19:13,21; 21:7,9; 24:1; 25:3,9,12; 28:31,32,34,54,56,65,67; 29:2–4(1–3); 31:7,29; 32:10; 34:4,7,12; **Josh.** 3:7; 4:14; 5:13; 9:25; 10:12; 22:30,33; 23:13; 24:7,15,17; **Judg.** 2:11; 3:7,12; 4:1; 6:1,17,21; 7:1; 10:6,15; 13:1; 14:3,7; 16:21,28; 17:6; 19:17,24; 21:25; **Ruth** 2:2,9,10,13; **1 Sam.** 1:18,23; 2:33; 3:2,18; 4:15; 6:13; 8:6; 11:2,10; 12:3, 16,17; 14:27,29,36,40; 15:17,19; 16:7, 12,22; 18:5,8,20,23,26; 20:3,29; 21:13(14); 24:4(5),10(11); 25:8; 26:21,24; 27:5; 29:6,7,9; **2 Sam.** 3:19,36; 4:10; 6:20,22; 7:19; 10:3,12; 11:25,27; 12:9,11; 13:2,5, 6,8,34; 14:22; 15:25,26; 17:4; 18:4,24; 19:6(7),18(19),27(28),37(38),38(39); 20:6; 22:25,28; 24:3,22; **1 Kgs.** 1:20,48; 3:10; 8:29,52; 9:3,12; 10:7; 11:6,19,33,38; 14:4,8,22; 15:5,11,26,34; 16:7,19,25,30; 20:6,38,41; 21:2,20,25; 22:43,52(53); **2 Kgs.** 1:13,14; 3:2,18; 4:34,35; 6:17,20; 7:2,19; 8:18,27; 9:30; 10:5,30; 12:2(3); 13:2,11; 14:3,24; 15:3,9,18,24,28,34; 16:2; 17:2,17; 18:3; 19:16,22; 20:3; 21:2,6,15,16,20; 22:2,20; 23:32,37; 24:9,19; 25:7; **1 Chr.** 2:3; 13:4; 17:17; 19:3,13; 21:7,16,23; 28:8; 29:10,25; **2 Chr.** 6:20,40; 7:15,16; 9:6; 14:2(1); 16:9; 20:12,32; 21:6; 22:4; 24:2; 25:2; 26:4; 27:2; 28:1; 29:2,6,8; 30:4; 32:23; 33:2,6,22; 34:2,28; 36:5,9,12; **Ezra** 3:12; 9:8; **Neh.** 1:6; 2:13; 6:16; 8:5; **Esth.** 1:17,21; 2:4,9,15; 3:6,11; 5:2,8; 7:3; 8:5,8; **Job** 2:12; 3:10; 4:16; 7:7,8; 10:4,18; 11:4,20; 13:1; 14:3; 15:12,15; 16:9,20; 17:2,5,7; 18:3; 19:15,27; 20:9; 21:8,20; 22:29; 24:15,23; 25:5; 27:19; 28:7,10,21; 29:11,15; 31:1,7,16; 32:1; 34:21; 36:7; 39:29; 40:24; 41:18(10); 42:5; **Ps.** 5:5(6); 6:7(8); 10:8; 11:4; 13:3(4); 15:4; 17:2,8,11; 18:24(25), 27(28); 19:8(9); 25:15; 26:3; 31:9(10), 22(23); 32:8; 33:18; 34:15(16); 35:19,21; 36:1(2),2(3); 38:10(11); 50:21; 51:4(6); 54:7(9); 66:7; 69:3(4),23(24); 72:14; 73:7,16; 77:4(5); 79:10; 88:9(10); 90:4; 91:8; 92:11(12); 94:9; 98:2; 101:3,5–7; 115:5; 116:8,15; 118:23; 119:18,37,82, 123,136,148; 121:1; 123:1,2; 131:1; 132:4; 135:16; 139:16; 141:8; 145:15; **Prov.** 1:17; 3:4,7,21; 4:21,25; 5:21; 6:4,13,17; 7:2; 10:10,26; 12:15; 15:3,30; 16:2,30; 17:8,24; 20:8,12,13; 21:2,4,10; 22:9,12; 23:5,6,26,29,31,33; 24:18; 25:7; 26:5,12,16; 27:20; 28:11,22,27; 29:13; 30:12,13,17; **Eccl.** 1:8; 2:10,14; 4:8; 5:11(10); 6:9; 8:16; 11:7,9; **Song** 1:15; 4:1,9; 5:12; 6:5; 7:4(5); 8:10; **Isa.** 1:15,16; 2:11; 3:8,16; 5:15,21; 6:5,10; 10:12; 11:3; 13:16,18; 17:7; 29:10,18; 30:20; 32:3; 33:15,17,20; 35:5; 37:17,23; 38:3,14; 40:26; 42:7; 43:4,8; 44:18; 49:5,18; 51:6; 52:8,10; 59:10,15; 60:4; 64:4(3); 65:12,16; 66:4; **Jer.** 3:2; 4:30; 5:3,21; 7:11,30; 9:1(8:23),18(17); 13:17,20; 14:6,17; 16:9,17; 18:4,10; 19:10; 20:4; 22:17; 24:6; 26:14; 27:5; 28:1,5,11; 29:21; 31:16; 32:4,12,13, 19,30; 34:3,15; 39:6,7,12; 40:4,5; 42:2; 43:9; 51:24; 52:2,10,11; **Lam.** 1:16; 2:4,11,18; 3:48,49,51; 4:17; 5:17; **Ezek.** 1:4,7,16,18,22,27; 4:12; 5:8,11,14; 6:9; 7:4,9; 8:2,5,18; 9:5,10; 10:2,9,12,19; 12:2–7,12; 16:5,41; 18:6,12,15; 20:7–9, 14,17,22,24,41; 21:6(11),23(28); 22:16,26; 23:16,27,40; 24:16,21,25; 28:18,25; 33:25; 36:23,34; 37:20; 38:16,23; 39:27; 40:4; 43:11; 44:5; **Dan.** 8:3,5,21; 9:18; 10:5,6; **Hos.** 2:10(12); 10:10; 13:14; **Joel** 1:16; **Amos** 9:3,4,8; **Jon.** 2:4(5); **Mic.** 4:11; 7:10; **Hab.** 1:13;

Zeph. 3:20; **Hag.** 2:3; **Zech.** 1:18(2:1); 2:1(5),8(12); 3:9; 4:10; 5:1,5,6,9; 6:1; 8:6; 9:1,8; 11:12,17; 12:4; 14:12; **Mal.** 1:5; 2:17.

II. עַיִן *'ayin* **masc./fem. noun**
(spring, fountain, well)
Gen. 16:7; 24:13,16,29,30,42,43,45; **Ex.** 15:27; **Num.** 33:9; **Deut.** 8:7; 33:28; **1 Sam.** 29:1; **2 Chr.** 32:3; **Neh.** 2:14; 3:15; 12:37; **Prov.** 8:28.

III. עַיִן *'ayin* **masc. noun**
(open space)
Gen. 38:14(NASB, NIV, see IV),21(NASB, NIV, see IV).

IV. עֵינַיִם *'ēynayim* **proper noun**
(Enaim: dual form of *'ayin* [5869,II])
Gen. 38:14(KJV, see III),21(KJV, see III).

5870. עַיִן *'ayin* **Aram. fem. noun**
(eye; corr. to Hebr. 5869)
Ezra 5:5; **Dan.** 4:34(31); 7:8,20.

5871. A. עַיִן *'ayin* **proper noun**
(Ain: town on N.E. border of Canaan)
Num. 34:11.
B. עַיִן *'ayin* **proper noun**
(Ain: town in the Negev of Judah)
Josh. 15:32; 19:7; 21:16; **1 Chr.** 4:32.

5872. עֵין גֶּדִי *'ēyn gediy* **proper noun**
(En Gedi)
Josh. 15:62; **1 Sam.** 23:29(24:1); 24:1(2); **2 Chr.** 20:2; **Song** 1:14; **Ezek.** 47:10.

5873. A. עֵין גַּנִּים *'ēyn ganniym* **proper noun**
(En Gannim: city in the foothills of Judah)
Josh. 15:34.
B. עֵין גַּנִּים *'ēyn ganniym* **proper noun**
(En Gannim: city in Issachar)
Josh. 19:21; 21:29.

5874. עֵין דֹּאר *'ēyn dō'r* **proper noun**
(Endor)
Josh. 17:11; **1 Sam.** 28:7; **Ps.** 83:10(11).

5875. עֵין הַקּוֹרֵא *'ēyn haqqôrē'* **proper noun**
(En Hakkore)
Judg. 15:19.

5876. עֵין חַדָּה *'ēyn ḥaddāh* **proper noun**
(En Haddah)
Josh. 19:21.

5877. עֵין חָצוֹר *'ēyn ḥāṣôr* **proper noun**
(En Hazor)
Josh. 19:37.

5878. עֵין חֲרֹד *'ēyn ḥ^a^rōd* **proper noun**
(Spring of Harod, Well of Harod)
Judg. 7:1(KJV, NASB, NIV, *'ayin* [5869,II] and *ḥ^a^rōd* [2730,II]).

5879. עֵינָם *'ēnām* **proper noun**
(Enam: city in Judah)
Josh. 15:34.

5880. עֵין מִשְׁפָּט *'ēyn mišpāṭ* **proper noun**
(En Mishpat)
Gen. 14:7.

5881. עֵינָן *'ēynān* **masc. proper noun**
(Enan)
Num. 1:15; 2:29; 7:78,83; 10:27.

5882. עֵין עֶגְלַיִם *'ēyn 'eglayim* **proper noun**
(En Eglaim)
Ezek. 47:10.

5883. עֵין רֹגֵל *'ēyn rōgēl* **proper noun**
(En Rogel)
Josh. 15:7; 18:16; **2 Sam.** 17:17; **1 Kgs.** 1:9.

5884. עֵין רִמּוֹן *ʿēyn rimmôn* **proper noun**
(En Rimmon)
Neh. 11:29.

5885. עֵין שֶׁמֶשׁ *ʿēyn šemeš* **proper noun**
(En Shemesh)
Josh. 15:7; 18:17.

5886. עֵין הַתַּנִּין *ʿēyn hattanniyn* **proper noun**
(Jackal Well)
Neh. 2:13(KJV, NIV, *ʿayin* [5869,II] and *tan* [8565]).

5887. עֵין תַּפּוּחַ *ʿēyn tappûaḥ* **proper noun**
(En Tappuah)
Josh. 17:7.

5888. עִיף *ʿiyp̱* **verb**
(to be faint, to be weary)
Judg. 4:21(KJV, *ʿûp̱* [5774,I]); **1 Sam.** 14:28(KJV, *ʿûp̱* [5774,I]),31(KJV, *ʿûp̱* [5774,I]); **2 Sam.** 21:15(KJV, *ʿûp̱* [5774,I]); **Jer.** 4:31.

5889. עָיֵף *ʿāyēp̱* **adj.**
(faint, weary, exhausted)
Gen. 25:29,30; **Deut.** 25:18; **Judg.** 8:4,5,15(KJV, NASB, *yāʿēp̱* [3287]); **2 Sam.** 16:14; 17:29; **Job** 22:7; **Ps.** 63:1(2); 143:6; **Prov.** 25:25; **Isa.** 5:27; 28:12; 29:8; 32:2; 46:1; **Jer.** 31:25.

5890. עֵיפָה *ʿēyp̱āh* **fem. noun**
(darkness)
Job 10:22; **Amos** 4:13.

5891. A. עֵיפָה *ʿēyp̱āh* **masc. proper noun**
(Ephah: descendants of Midian)
Gen. 25:4; **1 Chr.** 1:33; **Isa.** 60:6.

B. עֵיפָה *ʿēyp̱āh* **masc. proper noun**
(Ephah: a Judaite)
1 Chr. 2:47.

C. עֵיפָה *ʿēyp̱āh* **masc. proper noun**
(Ephah: concubine of Caleb)
1 Chr. 2:46.

5892. I. עִיר *ʿiyr* **fem. noun**
(city, town)
Gen. 4:17; 10:11,12; 11:4,5,8; 13:12; 18:24,26,28; 19:4,12,14–16,20–22,25,29; 23:10,18; 24:10,11,13; 26:33; 28:19; 33:18; 34:20,24,25,27,28; 35:5; 36:32, 35,39; 41:35,48; 44:4,13; 47:21; **Ex.** 1:11; 9:29,33; **Lev.** 14:40,41,45,53; 25:29,30,32–34; 26:25,31,33; **Num.** 13:19,28; 20:16; 21:2,3,25–27; 22:36; 24:19; 31:10; 32:16,17,24,26,33,36,38; 35:2–8,11–15,25–28,32; **Deut.** 1:22,28; 2:34–37; 3:4–7,10,12,19; 4:41,42; 6:10; 9:1; 13:12(13),13(14),15(16),16(17); 19:1,2,5,7,9,11,12; 20:10,14–16,19,20; 21:2–4,6,19–21; 22:15,17,18,21,23,24; 25:8; 28:3,16; 34:3; **Josh.** 3:16; 6:3–5, 7,11,14–17,20,21,24,26; 8:1,2,4–8, 11–14,16–22,27,29; 9:17; 10:2,19,20, 37,39; 11:12–14,19,21; 13:9,10,16,17, 21,23,25,28,30,31; 14:4,12; 15:9,21,32, 36,41,44,51,54,57,59,60,62; 16:9; 17:9,12; 18:9,14,21,24,28; 19:6–8,15,16, 22,23,29–31,35,38,39,48,50; 20:2,4,6,9; 21:2–9,12,13,16,18–22,24–27,29,31–33, 35,37–42; 24:13; **Judg.** 1:8,16,17,23–26; 3:13; 6:27,28,30; 8:16,17,27; 9:30,31,33, 35,43–45,51; 10:4; 11:26,33; 12:7; 14:18; 16:2,3; 17:8; 18:27–29; 19:11,12,15,17,22; 20:11,14,15,31,32,37,38,40,42,48; 21:23; **Ruth** 1:19; 2:18; 3:15; 4:2; **1 Sam.** 1:3; 4:13; 5:9,11,12; 6:18; 7:14; 8:22; 9:6, 10–14,25,27; 10:5; 15:5; 16:4; 18:6; 20:6, 29,40,42(21:1); 22:19; 23:7,10; 27:5; 28:3; 30:3,29; 31:7; **2 Sam.** 2:1,3; 5:7,9; 6:10, 12,16; 8:8; 10:3,12,14; 11:16,17,20,25; 12:1,26–28,30,31; 15:2,12,14,24,25,27, 34,37; 17:13,17,23; 18:3; 19:3(4),37(38);

20:6,15,16,19,21,22; 24:5,7; **1 Kgs.** 2:10; 3:1; 4:13; 8:1,16,44,48; 9:11–13,16,19,24; 10:26; 11:27,32,36,43; 12:17; 13:25,29,32; 14:11,12,21,31; 15:8,20,23,24; 16:4,18,24; 17:10; 20:2,12,19,30,34; 21:8,11,13,24; 22:26,36,39,50(51); **2 Kgs.** 2:19,23; 3:19,25; 6:14,15,19; 7:4,10,12; 8:24; 9:15,28; 10:2,5,6,25; 11:20; 12:21(22); 13:25; 14:20; 15:7,38; 16:20; 17:6,9,24, 26,29; 18:8,11,13,30; 19:13,25,32–34; 20:6,20; 23:5,8,17,19,27; 24:10,11; 25:2–4,11,19; **1 Chr.** 1:43,46,50; 2:22,23; 4:31–33; 6:56(41),57(42),60–67(45–52); 9:2; 10:7; 11:5,7,8; 13:2,13; 15:1,29; 18:8; 19:7,9,13,15; 20:2,3; 27:25; **2 Chr.** 1:14; 5:2; 6:5,34,38; 8:2,4–6,11; 9:25,31; 10:17; 11:5,10,12,23; 12:4,13,16; 13:19; 14:1(13:23),5–7(4–6),14(13); 15:6,8; 16:4,14; 17:2,7,9,12,13,19; 18:25; 19:5,10; 20:4; 21:1,3,20; 23:2,21; 24:5,16,25; 25:13,28; 26:6; 27:4,9; 28:15,18,25,27; 29:20; 30:10; 31:1,6,15,19; 32:1,3,5,6, 18,29,30; 33:14,15; 34:6,8; **Ezra** 2:1,70; 3:1; 10:14; **Neh.** 2:3,5,8; 3:15; 7:4,6,73; 8:15; 9:25; 10:37(38); 11:1,3,9,18,20; 12:37,44; 13:18; **Esth.** 3:15; 4:1,6; 6:9,11; 8:11,15,17; 9:2,19,28; **Job** 15:28; 24:12; **Ps.** 9:6(7); 31:21(22); 46:4(5); 48:1(2),8(9); 55:9(10); 59:6(7),14(15); 60:9(11); 69:35(36); 72:16; 87:3; 101:8; 107:4,7,36; 108:10(11); 122:3; 127:1; **Prov.** 1:21; 16:32; 21:22; 25:28; **Eccl.** 7:19; 8:10; 9:14,15; 10:15; **Song** 3:2,3; 5:7; **Isa.** 1:7,8,26; 6:11; 14:17,21,31; 17:1,2,9; 19:2,18; 22:2,9; 23:16; 24:12; 25:2; 26:1; 27:10; 32:14,19; 33:8; 36:1,15; 37:13,26,33–35; 38:6; 40:9; 42:11; 44:26; 45:13; 48:2; 52:1; 54:3; 60:14; 61:4; 62:12; 64:10(9); 66:6; **Jer.** 1:15,18; 2:15,28; 3:14; 4:5,7,16,26,29; 5:6,17; 6:6; 7:17,34; 8:14,16; 9:11(10); 10:22; 11:6,12,13; 13:19; 14:18; 15:8 (NASB, NIV, see II); 17:24–26; 19:8,11, 12,15; 20:5,16; 21:4,6,7,9,10; 22:6,8; 23:39; 25:18,29; 26:2,6,9,11,12,15,20; 27:17,19; 29:7,16; 30:18; 31:21,23,24,38; 32:3,24,25,28,29,31,36,44; 33:4,5,10, 12,13; 34:1,2,7,22; 36:6,9; 37:8,10,21; 38:2–4,9,17,18,23; 39:2,4,9,16; 40:5,10; 41:7; 44:2,6,17,21; 46:8; 47:2; 48:8,9, 15,24,28; 49:1,13,25; 50:32; 51:31,43; 52:5–7,15,25; **Lam.** 1:1,19; 2:12,15; 3:51; 5:11; **Ezek.** 4:1,3; 5:2; 6:6; 7:15,23; 9:1,4,5,7,9; 10:2; 11:2,6,23; 12:20; 17:4; 19:7; 21:19(24); 22:2,3; 24:6,9; 25:9; 26:10,17,19; 29:12; 30:7; 33:21; 35:4,9; 36:4,10,33,35,38; 39:9,16; 40:1,2; 43:3; 45:6,7; 48:15,17–22,30,31,35; **Dan.** 9:16,18,19,24,26; 11:15; **Hos.** 8:14; 11:6,9(NASB, NIV, see II); 13:10; **Joel** 2:9; **Amos** 3:6; 4:6–8; 5:3; 6:8; 7:17; 9:14; **Obad.** 1:20; **Jon.** 1:2; 3:2–4; 4:5,11; **Mic.** 5:11(10),14(13); 6:9; 7:12; **Nah.** 3:1; **Hab.** 2:12; **Zeph.** 1:16; 2:15; 3:1,6; **Zech.** 1:12,17; 7:7; 8:3,5,20; 14:2.

II. עִיר *ʿiyr* **masc. noun**
(wrath, anguish)
Jer. 15:8(9)(KJV, see I); **Hos.** 11:9(KJV, see I).

5893. עִיר *ʿiyr* **masc. proper noun**
(Ir)
1 Chr. 7:12.

5894. עִיר *ʿiyr* **Aram. masc. noun**
(watcher [NIV, messenger])
Dan. 4:13(10),17(14),23(20).

5895. A. עַיִר *ʿayir* **masc. noun**
(donkey, ass)
Gen. 32:15(16); **Judg.** 10:4; 12:14; **Job** 11:12; **Isa.** 30:6,24; **Zech.** 9:9.
B. עִיר *ʿiyr* **masc. noun**
(donkey, ass)
Gen. 49:11.

5896. A. עִירָא *ʿiyrāʾ* **masc. proper noun**
(Ira: a Jairite)
2 Sam. 20:26.
B. עִירָא *ʿiyrāʾ* **masc. proper noun**
(Ira: son of Ikkesh)
2 Sam. 23:26; **1 Chr.** 11:28; 27:9.

C. עִירָא *ʿiyrāʾ* **masc. proper noun**
(Ira: one of David's mighty men)
2 Sam. 23:38; **1 Chr.** 11:40.

5897. עִירָד *ʿiyrāḏ* **masc. proper noun**
(Irad)
Gen. 4:18.

5898. עִיר הַמֶּלַח *ʿiyr hammelaḥ* **proper noun**
(City of Salt)
Josh. 15:62.

5899. עִיר הַתְּמָרִים *ʿiyr hatt^emāriym* **proper noun**
(City of Palms, city of palm trees; KJV, NASB, NIV, *ʿyir* [5892,I] and *tāmār* [8558])
Deut. 34:3; **Judg.** 1:16; 3:13; **2 Chr.** 28:15.

5900. עִירוּ *ʿiyrû* **masc. proper noun**
(Iru)
1 Chr. 4:15.

5901. עִירִי *ʿiyriy* **masc. proper noun**
(Iri)
1 Chr. 7:7.

5902. עִירָם *ʿiyrām* **masc. proper noun**
(Iram)
Gen. 36:43; **1 Chr.** 1:54.

5903. עֵירֹם *ʿēyrōm,* עֵרֹם *ʿērōm* **adj.**
(naked)
Gen. 3:7,10,11; **Deut.** 28:48; **Ezek.** 16:7,22,39; 18:7,16; 23:29.

5904. עִיר נָחָשׁ *ʿiyr nāḥāš* **masc. proper noun**
(Ir Nahash)
1 Chr. 4:12.

5905. עִיר שֶׁמֶשׁ *ʿiyr šemeš* **proper noun**
(Ir Shemesh)
Josh. 19:41.

5906. I. עַיִשׁ *ʿayiš* **masc. noun**
(Bear [a constellation] or Arcturus [a star])
Job 38:32.
II. עָשׁ *ʿāš* **masc. noun**
(Bear [a constellation] or Arcturus [a star])
Job 9:9.

5907. A. עַכְבּוֹר *ʿaḵbôr* **masc. proper noun**
(Achbor: an Edomite)
Gen. 36:38,39; **1 Chr.** 1:49.
B. עַכְבּוֹר *ʿaḵbôr* **masc. proper noun**
(Achbor: courier of Josiah)
2 Kgs. 22:12,14; **Jer.** 26:22; 36:12.

5908. עַכָּבִישׁ *ʿakkāḇiyš* **masc. noun**
(spider)
Job 8:14; **Isa.** 59:5.

5909. עַכְבָּר *ʿaḵbār* **masc. noun**
(mouse)
Lev. 11:29; **1 Sam.** 6:4,5,11,18; **Isa.** 66:17.

5910. עַכּוֹ *ʿakkô* **proper noun**
(Acco)
Judg. 1:31.

5911. עָכוֹר *ʿāḵôr* **proper noun**
(Achor)
Josh. 7:24,26; 15:7; **Isa.** 65:10; **Hos.** 2:15.

5912. עָכָן *ʿāḵān* **masc. proper noun**
(Achan)
Josh. 7:1,18–20,24; 22:20.

5913. עָכַס *ʿāḵas* **verb**
(to jingle an ornament or bracelet)
Isa. 3:16.

5914. I. עֶכֶס *ʿeḵes* **masc. noun**
(anklet, leg bracelet)
Isa. 3:18.
II. עֶכֶס *ʿeḵes* **masc. noun**
(fetter, noose)
Prov. 7:22.

5915. עַכְסָה *ʿaḵsāh* **fem. proper noun**
(Achsah)
Josh. 15:16,17; **Judg.** 1:12,13; **1 Chr.** 2:49.

5916. עָכַר *ʿāḵar* **verb**
(to cause trouble)
Gen. 34:30; **Josh.** 6:18; 7:25; **Judg.** 11:35; **1 Sam.** 14:29; **1 Kgs.** 18:17,18; **1 Chr.** 2:7; **Ps.** 39:2(3); **Prov.** 11:17,29; 15:6,27.

5917. עָכָר *ʿāḵār* **masc. proper noun**
(Achar)
1 Chr. 2:7.

5918. עָכְרָן *ʿoḵrān* **masc. proper noun**
(Ocran)
Num. 1:13; 2:27; 7:72,77; 10:26.

5919. עַכְשׁוּב *ʿaḵšûḇ* **masc. noun**
(viper, adder)
Ps. 140:3(4).

5920. I. עַל *ʿal* **masc. noun**
(height, from above)
Gen. 27:39(NASB, NIV, *ʿal* [5921]); 49:25(NASB, NIV, *ʿal* [5921]); **2 Sam.** 23:1(NIV, see II); **Ps.** 50:4(NASB, NIV, *ʿal* [5921]); **Hos.** 7:16(KJV, NIV, see II); 11:7(KJV, NIV, see II).
II. עַל *ʿal* **masc. proper noun**
(Most High)
2 Sam. 23:1(KJV, NASB, see I); **Hos.** 7:16(NASB, see I); 11:7(NASB, see I).

5921. עַל *ʿal* **prep.**
(upon, over, against, by, to, for)
Gen. 1:2,7,11,15,17,20,26,28–30; 2:5, 16,21,24; 3:14; 4:14; 6:1,7,12,17; 7:3,4, 6,8,10,12,14,17–19,21,23,24; 8:1,3,4, 7–9,11,13,17,19; 9:2,14,16,17,23; 10:9; 11:4,8,9,28; 12:17,20; 13:9,11; 14:6,15; 15:11,12; 16:5,7,12,14; 17:3,17,22; 18:2,3,5,8,16,19; 19:4,8,16,17,22–24, 28,31; 20:3,6,9,11,18; 21:11,12,14,25,31; 22:2,6,9,17; 23:3,19; 24:9,13,15,18,22, 30,42,43,45–47,49,61,64; 25:6,9,18,30; 26:7,9,10,21,22,32,33; 27:12,13,16, 40,41; 28:6,9,13,18; 29:2,3,8,10,34,35; 30:3,6,28,33,37,40; 31:10,12,17,20,34, 46,48,50; 32:11,21,31,32; 33:1,4,10, 13,17; 34:3,12,25,27,30; 35:5,13,14,20; 37:8,23,34; 38:12,14,19,21,26,28–30; 39:4,5; 40:2,11,13,16,17,19,21; 41:1,3, 10,13,15,17,32–34,40–43,45,56; 42:6, 21,24,26,36,37; 43:7,16,18,19; 44:1,4, 13,21; 45:1,14,15,20,21; 46:4,29; 47:6, 20,22,26,31; 48:2,6,7,14,17,18,22; 49:13,17,22,26,30; 50:1,11,13,20,21,23; **Ex.** 1:8,10,11,16; 2:3,5,6,14,15; 3:5,12, 18,22; 4:20; 5:3,8,9,14,17,21; 6:26; 7:5, 15,17,19; 8:3,5–7,9,12,21,22; 9:9,19, 22,23; 10:6,12–14,17,21,22,28; 11:1,5; 12:4,7–9,13,23,27,29,33,34,51; 13:9, 15,16; 14:2,3,7,9,13,16,21,26,27,30; 15:16,19,23,24,26,27; 16:2,3,5,7,8,14, 20,29; 17:1,3,6,7,9,12,16; 18:8,9,11,13, 14,21–23,25; 19:4,11,16,18,20; 20:3,5, 11,12,20,24–26; 21:14,19,22,30; 22:3, 9,25; 23:2,13,18,29; 24:6,8,16; 25:11,12, 14,19–22,26,30,37; 26:4,7,10,12,13,24, 32,34,35; 27:2,4,7,21; 28:8–12,14,21–30, 33–38,43; 29:3,6,7,10,12,13,15–17, 19–22,24,25,36–38; 30:4,6,7,9,10,13–16, 32,33; 31:7; 32:1,12,14,16,20,21,27, 29,34,35; 33:4,5,16,19,21,22; 34:1,2,6,7, 12,25,27,28,33,35; 35:22; 36:11,14,17; 37:3,5,9,13,16,27; 38:2,7,21,26; 39:4–7, 14–21,24–26,30,31; 40:3,19–24,27,29,

35,36,38; **Lev.** 1:4,5,7,8,11,12,15,17; 2:1,2,5,6,13,15,16; 3:2–5,8–10,13–15; 4:3,4,7–12,14,15,18,20,24–26,28–31,33–35; 5:5,6,9–13,16,18; 6:3,5,7,9,10,12,13, 15,21,27; 7:2,4,9,12,13,20,30; 8:7–9,11, 12,14–16,18,19,22–28,30,34; 9:9,12–14, 17,18,20,24; 10:1,3,6,7,15–17; 11:2,20, 21,27,29,32,34,35,37,38,41,42,44,46; 12:5,7,8; 13:45; 14:5–7,14–21,25–29,31, 50,53; 15:4,6,9,15,17,20,22–26,30; 16:2,4,8–10,12–16,18,19,21,22,30,33,34; 17:5,6,11,12; 18:18,25; 19:16,17,19, 22,26; 21:10–12; 22:3,9,14,22; 23:18, 20,28; 24:4,6,7,12,14; 25:18,19,31; 26:1, 16,18,21,24,25,28,30,32,35; 27:8,13,15, 18,19,27,31; **Num.** 1:18,50,52,53; 2:2,5, 12,17,20,27,34; 3:4,16,26,29,35,39,46, 49,51; 4:6–8,10–14,19,25–27,37,41, 45,49; 5:7,8,14,15,18,30; 6:5–7,9,11, 17–21,27; 7:2,3,9,89; 8:7,10,12,19,21,22; 9:11,15,17–20,22,23; 10:9–11,13–16, 18–20,22–27,29,31,34; 11:9,11–13,17, 25,26,29,31; 12:1,3,10,11; 13:3,18,24,29; 14:2,5,9,14,18,27,29,35,36,43; 15:5,9,25, 28,38; 16:3,4,7,11,13,17,19,22,26,27,29, 33,41,42,45–47,49; 17:2,3,5,10; 18:2, 4,5,17,24,32; 19:2,5,13,15–20; 20:2,6, 21,23,24; 21:7–9,11,14,20,27; 22:5,22, 30,32,36; 23:3,6,15,17,28; 24:2,6; 25:8, 11,13,18; 26:3,9,56,63; 27:3,16,18,20, 21,23; 28:10,15,22,24,30; 29:5; 30:2, 4–11,14; 31:3,7,8,12,14,16,50; 32:14; 33:2,7,10,38,48–50,55; 34:3,11; 35:1,6, 20,22–24; 36:3–5,12,13; **Deut.** 1:11,15; 2:25,36; 3:12,14; 4:2,10,13,21,26,32,36, 39,40,48; 5:7,9,15,16,22; 6:6,8,9,15; 7:6, 13,16,22,25; 8:3,4,10; 9:10,15,17–19; 10:2,4,9; 11:4,9,17,18,20,21,25,29; 12:1, 2,16,19,24,27,32; 13:5,8,10; 14:2; 15:9, 11,15,23; 16:3; 17:6,10,11,14,15,18,20; 18:8; 19:7,9–11,13,15; 20:1,3,10,12, 19,20; 21:5,6,10,13,16,22,23; 22:5,6, 12,14,19,24,26; 23:4,9,13,20,25; 24:5, 15,16,18,22; 25:3,5,6,9,15; 26:6,19; 27:3, 5,6,8,12,13; 28:1,2,7,10,11,15,21,23,24, 35,36,43,45,48,49,56,61,63; 29:5,24,25, 27,28; 30:1,7,9,18,20; 31:13,15,17,18,24; 32:2,11,13,23,36,38,47,49,51; 33:8,10, 12,29; 34:1,5,9; **Josh.** 2:6–9,11; 3:15,16; 4:5,18; 5:1,9,15; 7:6,9,10,26; 8:29,31,32; 9:5,18,20; 10:5,11,13,18,24,26,27,31,34, 36,38; 11:4,7,13; 12:2; 13:3,9,16,25; 14:6,14; 15:8,18,46; 17:7; 18:5,9,13,16; 19:11,12,50; 22:9,10,12,20,23,33; 23:13–16; 24:7; **Judg.** 1:14; 3:10,12,16, 19–21; 4:9,15,24; 5:10,17–19; 6:2–4,7, 22,25,26,28,30,31,37,39,40; 7:1,2,5,6, 12,22; 8:3,26; 9:3,5,8–15,17,18,22,24,25, 31,33,34,43,44,48,49,51,53; 10:4; 11:11, 26,29,37,38; 12:1,14; 13:5,19,20; 14:6, 16,17,19; 15:8,10,14,19; 16:3,9,12,14, 17,19,20,26,27,29,30; 18:5,9,12,19,27; 19:2,3,20,22,27,28,30; 20:5,9,19,34,41; **Ruth** 1:19; 2:5,6,10,13; 3:3,9,15; 4:5, 7,10; **1 Sam.** 1:9–11,13,14; 2:1,8,10, 11,28; 4:1,12,13,18–20; 5:4,5,7; 6:5,7, 12,18,20; 7:10; 8:7,9,11,19; 9:6,16,24,25; 10:1,6,10,12,19; 11:1,2,6,7,12; 12:1, 12–14,19; 13:1,5,8,11,14,18; 14:4,10, 13,25,32,33,47,52; 15:1,3,7,9,15,17,26, 28,35; 16:1,16,23; 17:5,6,15,20,22,26,28, 32,35,38,39,46,49; 18:4,5; 19:20,23,24; 20:8,9,13,15,24,25,29,31,33; 21:13,15; 22:2,6–9,13,17; 23:9,17,21,27,28; 24:3, 5,10,22; 25:8,13,16–18,20,23–25,30, 36,42; 26:1,3,12,13,16; 27:10,11; 28:15, 16,18; 30:6,14,16,17,23,24; 31:4,5; **2 Sam.** 1:2,6,9,10,12,16–19,21,24–26; 2:4,7,9–11,13,19,21,24,25; 3:8,10,17, 29,30,34; 4:2,7,11,12; 5:2,3,5,8,12,17,20; 6:2,7,8,10,21; 7:8,11,22,25–27; 8:10, 15,16; 9:6,7,10,11,13; 10:14; 11:1,2,11, 20,21,23,24,26; 12:6,7,11,17,28,30; 13:5, 9,17–19,22,25,29,32,37,39; 14:1,2,4, 7–9,13,26,33; 15:2,4,14,18,20,23,32,33; 16:1,8,22; 17:2,11,12,19,21,25; 18:1,5, 8,9,11,12,17,18,20,31–33; 19:1,2,7,9, 10,22,26,38,42; 20:8,11,12,15,21–24; 21:1,7,10; 22:11,28,34,50; 23:2,8,18; 24:4,12,20,21,25; **1 Kgs.** 1:13,17,20,23, 24,27,30,33–35,38,44,46–48,53; 2:4,11, 12,15,18,19,24,26,27,31,32,35,43; 3:4,6, 19,26; 4:1,4–7,20,29,33; 5:5,7,14,16; 6:1, 3,5,8,10,32,35; 7:2,3,6,16–20,22,25,29,

31,35,36,38,39,41–43,48; 8:5,7,8,16,20,
23,25,27,36,40,43,44,54,66; 9:5,7–9,23,
25,26; 10:6,9,16,17,20; 11:7,10,11,24,25,
30,37,41,42; 12:4,9–11,14,17,18,20,
32,33; 13:1–4,13,30,32,34; 14:2,7,14,15,
19,23,25,27,29; 15:1,7,17,19,20,23,25,
27,30,31,33; 16:1,2,5,7–9,11,14–20,23,
24,27,29; 17:3,5,14,19–22; 18:1,3,7,12,
21,23,26,28,33,39; 19:15,16; 20:1,12,20,
22,23,30,33,38,41,43; 21:4,7,27,29; 22:6,
8,10,18,19,23,24,32,38,39,41,45,51;
2 Kgs. 1:9,13,18; 2:3,5,7,13–15; 3:1,11,
15,21,22,27; 4:4,9,20,21,29,31,32,34,
35,37; 5:18,21,26; 6:11,14,24–26,30,31;
7:2,6,17; 8:5,13,15,20,23; 9:3,17,25,
29,37; 10:3,5,9,10,22,24,30,31,33,34,36;
11:3,8,11,12,14,18,19; 12:4,11,12,15,
17–19; 13:1,8,10,12–14,16,19,21,23;
14:6,15,18–20,28; 15:5,6,8,10–12,15,
17–21,23,25–27,30,31,36; 16:4,5,7,
12–15,17,19; 17:1,3,5,9,10,18,21,23;
18:9,12–14,18,20,21,23–27,37; 19:2,8,
21,22,32; 20:6,7,13,20; 21:12,13,17,
23–25; 22:5,7–9,13,16,19,20; 23:3,6,8,
12,13,16,17,20,21,24,26–29,33,35; 24:3,
5,11,12,20; 25:1,4,5,11,17,19–22,28;
1 Chr. 5:10,16,20; 6:31,32,39,44,49;
7:4,29; 9:1,19,20,23,26–29,31–33;
10:3–5,13; 11:2,3,7,10,11,15,20,25,42;
12:4,8,15,17,19–23,32,38; 13:2,7,10;
14:2,8,10,11,14,17; 15:15,20,21,27;
16:21,25,40; 17:7,10,17,23,25,26;
18:7,10,14,15,17; 19:2,5; 20:2; 21:1,3,
4,7,10,15,16,22,26; 22:8–14; 23:1,4,14,
28,31; 25:2,3,6; 26:20,22,24,26,28–30,
32; 27:2,4–16,24–31; 28:2,4,5,18,19;
29:8,9,15,23,25–27,29,30; **2 Chr.** 1:1,6,
9,11,13; 2:2,4,11,16; 3:4,5,7,8,13–17;
4:4,12–14,19; 5:6,8,9; 6:5,6,10,13,16,18,
27,31,33,34; 7:3,6,10,11,13,14,20–22;
8:3,12,14,15,17; 9:5,6,8,15,16,18,19,
29,30; 10:4,9–11,14,17,18; 11:13; 12:2,
9,10; 13:1,4–7,11,12,18; 14:11,14; 15:1,
4,5,9,15; 16:1,3,7–11; 17:1,10,15,16,18;
18:7,9,16–18,22,23,31; 19:2,7,9–11;
20:1–3,9–12,14,16,22–24,26,29,31,34,
37; 21:4,8,15,16; 22:5,12; 23:3,10,11,13,
18–20; 24:6,9,13,18,20,21,23,25–27;
25:3,4,26–28; 26:7,9,11,13,15,16,18,
19,21; 27:5,7; 28:4,9,11–13,16,20,26;
29:8,9,21,23,24,27,36; 30:1,9,10,16–18,
22; 31:2,9,12,14,15; 32:1,2,5,6,8–10,12,
16–20,25,26,31,32; 33:8,11,16,18,19,
24,25; 34:4,5,10,12,13,17,21,24,27,
28,31; 35:2,10,15,16,20,21,24,25,27;
36:4,6,8,10,15,17,23; **Ezra** 1:2,6,8;
2:61,68; 3:2,3,7–11; 4:5–7; 6:22; 7:6,
9,11,28; 8:17,18,21–23,26,31,33,35;
9:4,5,9,13,15; 10:2,4,6,9,10,12,15,19;
Neh. 1:2,6; 2:4,5,7,8,18,19; 3:2,4,5,
7–10,12,17,19,28; 4:1,5,9,12,14,18,19;
5:7,15–19; 6:3,6,7,12,17; 7:2,63; 8:4,
5,7,16; 9:1–6,9,10,13,19,30,33,36–38;
10:1,29,32–34; 11:9,14,16,21,23; 12:8,
22,23,31,37–39,44; 13:2,11,13–15,18,19,
22,26,28,29; **Esth.** 1:2,6,8,15–17,19; 2:1,
10,20,23; 3:1,9,10,12; 4:4,5,7,8,16,17;
5:1,4,8,9,11,14; 6:2–4,8,9; 7:3,7–10; 8:2,
3,5,7,8,11,17; 9:2,3,13,16,19,21,24–27,31;
10:1,2; **Job** 1:6,8,11,14,17,19; 2:1,11,12;
3:4,5; 4:13,15; 5:10; 6:3,5,16,27,28; 7:1,
12,20; 8:6,9,15–17; 9:8,11,22,26,33,34;
10:1–3,7; 12:14,21; 13:11,13,14,21,26,27;
14:3,6,16,17,22; 15:27; 16:4,9–11,13–17;
17:4,8,16; 18:6,8–10,15,17,20; 19:5,6,8,
9,11–13,25; 20:4,11,13,21,23,25; 21:5,
9,17,26,27,31,32; 22:2,10,24,26,28;
23:2,15; 24:9,18,23; 25:3; 26:7,9,10;
27:9,10,22,23; 28:8; 29:3,4,7,13,22;
30:1,2,4,5,12,15–17,30; 31:1,5,9,10,21,
36,38; 32:2,3,6; 33:7,10,15,19,23,27;
34:6,13,15,21,23,27–29,36,37; 36:21,
23,28,30,32,33; 37:3,12,15,16,22; 38:5,
6,10,24,26,32; 39:9,14,23,27,28; 41:6,
8,23,30,33,34; 42:6,8,11; **Ps.** 1:3,5; 2:2,6;
3:1,6,8; 4:4,6; 5:11,12; 6:10; 7:7,8,10,
16,17; 8:1,9; 9:19; 10:3,13,14; 11:2,6,7;
13:2,6; 14:2; 15:3,5; 16:2,4,6; 17:9;
18:10,33,41,42,49; 19:6; 21:5,11–13;
22:9,10,13,18; 23:2; 24:2; 25:8; 27:2,3,6;
29:3; 31:13,14,16,18,23; 32:4–6,8;
33:22; 35:13,15,16,20,21,26; 36:4;
37:4,5,10–12,29; 38:2,16; 39:10,11;
40:2,7,12,15; 41:3,7,9,11; 42:1,4–7,11;

43:5; 44:19,22,26; 45:2–4,7,17; 46:2; 47:2,8; 48:10,14; 49:6,11; 50:5,8,16; 51:19; 52:6,9; 53:2; 54:3; 55:3,4,10,12, 15,22,23; 56:5,7,12; 57:2,5,11; 59:3,17; 60:8,12; 61:6,8; 62:3,7; 63:6,10; 64:8; 66:5; 68:29,34,35; 69:7,9,15,24,27; 70:3; 71:6,14; 72:6,13; 74:13; 76:12; 78:24,27; 79:6,9; 80:15,17,19; 81:5,7,14; 83:3,5,18; 86:13,14; 87:7; 88:7,16,17; 89:7,19,45,47; 90:13,16,17; 91:12,13; 92:3,11; 94:2,20, 21,23; 95:3; 96:4; 97:9; 99:2,8; 102:7; 103:10,11,13,17; 104:3,5,6,12,34; 105:14, 16,38; 106:7,17,22,32; 107:40; 108:4,5,9; 109:2,5,6,20; 110:4–7; 113:4; 115:1,14; 116:7,12; 117:2; 119:14,17,22,49,62,69, 104,127–129,136,162,164; 121:5; 124:2, 4,5; 125:3,5; 128:6; 129:3; 131:2; 132:3,18; 133:2,3; 135:14; 136:6; 137:1,2,4,6; 138:2,7; 139:5,14,16; 140:10; 141:3; 142:3,7; 143:4; 145:9; 146:5; 148:4,13; 149:5; **Prov.** 1:27; 2:11; 3:3,29; 4:15; 5:8; 6:15,21,22,28; 7:3,14,15; 8:2,27,34; 9:3,14; 10:12; 13:11; 14:14,19; 16:10,20, 23,26,27; 17:4,26; 19:3,11,12; 20:8,26; 21:1,9; 22:6,18; 23:30; 24:13,18,25,30; 25:11,12,20,22,24,25; 26:11,14,17,23; 27:22; 28:15,21,25; 29:5,12; 30:6,19; 31:26,29; **Eccl.** 1:6,12,13,16; 2:17,20; 3:14,17,18; 5:2,6,8; 6:1; 7:10,14; 8:2,6, 11,14,16; 9:8,12,14; 10:4,7; 11:1–3,9; 12:6,7,14; **Song** 1:3,7,8; 2:4,8,17; 3:1,8; 4:4; 5:4,5,7,12,15; 7:4,5,10,13; 8:5,6, 9,14; **Isa.** 1:1,5,14,25; 2:1,12–16; 4:1,5; 5:6,25,30; 6:1,6,7; 7:1,2,5,17; 8:1,7; 9:2, 6,7,11,17,20,21; 10:3,6,12,15,20,24–28; 11:2,8,15; 13:2,7,11,13,17,18; 14:1,2,4, 8,12,14,22,25,26; 15:2–4,7,9; 16:5,9,12; 17:7,10; 18:2,4,6; 19:1,7,8,12,16,17; 20:2,3; 21:3,8; 22:4,15,22,24,25; 23:8, 11,17; 24:6,11,15,17,20–22; 25:3,7,8; 26:21; 27:1,3,11; 28:1,4,6,22,27; 29:1,3, 7,8,10,12; 30:1,5,6,8,12,16,17,25,28,32; 31:1,2,4,5; 32:8,10–13,15,20; 34:2,5,11, 14,16; 35:10; 36:1,3,5,6,8–12,22; 37:2,8, 9,22,23,33,35; 38:5,6,15,16,20,21; 39:2; 40:2,9,22; 41:18; 42:1,5,13,25; 44:3,4, 16,19; 45:11,12,14; 46:7,8; 47:1,6,7,9, 11,13; 48:2; 49:9,10,16,22; 50:7; 51:11; 52:7,14,15; 53:1,5,9; 54:9,15,17; 56:3, 6–8; 57:1,2,4,6,7,10,11; 58:14; 59:4,9, 18,21; 60:1,2,4,5,7,14; 61:1; 62:5,6,10; 63:3,7,19; 64:12; 65:3,6,7,17; 66:2,10, 12,20; **Jer.** 1:7,9,10,12,14–16,18; 2:5 ,12,15,20,34,35,37; 3:2,6,8,16,18,21; 4:8,16,17,20,28; 5:6,9,12,15,27,29,31; 6:1,3,4,6,7,9–12,14,16,17,19,23,26; 7:8,10,11,14,15,20–22,29–31; 8:2,6,11, 14,18,21; 9:1,4,9,10,12,13,18,22,25,26; 10:1,19,21,25; 11:2,8,10,15–17,19,21,22; 12:8,9,11,12,14; 13:1,2,4,13,16,21,26,27; 14:1,3,6,15,16; 15:1,3–6,8,14–16; 16:3,4, 7,10,11,13,15–18; 17:1,2,8,18,25; 18:3, 7–11,16,18,20–23; 19:3,5,8,13,15; 20:2, 11; 21:2,4,7,9,13,14; 22:2,4,6–9,17,24, 26–28,30; 23:2–4,8,12,15–17,19,30–32, 34,35,39,40; 24:6,10; 25:1,2,5,9,12,13, 26,29,30,33; 26:2,5,13,15,19,20; 27:2,5, 8,10,11,19,21; 28:8,10–12,14–16; 29:10, 11,28,31,32; 30:6,8,14,15,18,20,23; 31:3, 12,15,19,20,26,28,33,37,39; 32:2,19,24, 29,31,32,34,35,40–42; 33:4,5,9,13,17,21; 34:1,4,7,15,21,22; 35:6,7,17,18; 36:2,4, 11,12,18,21,23,28–32; 37:5,8,9,11,14, 15,19; 38:4; 39:9,11,12; 40:4,11; 42:17–19; 43:10; 44:2,13,20,21,23,27,29; 45:1–3,5; 46:1,2,6,21,25; 47:4; 48:2,11,21–24,26, 31,32,36–38,42,43; 49:5,8,11,14,17,19, 20,22,29,30,37; 50:3,9,13–15,21,27,29, 35,42,44,45; 51:1,2,7,8,11,13,14,25, 27–29,35,42,44,46–48,50–52,56,63,64; 52:3,4,7,8,22,23,25,27; **Lam.** 1:2,5,7,8, 10,14–16,22; 2:10,11,14–17,19; 3:5,20, 21,24,28,39,46,48,54,61,62; 4:5,8,19, 21,22; 5:5,17,18,22; **Ezek.** 1:1,3,8, 17,19–22,25,26,28; 2:1,2; 3:14,22–25; 4:1–4,6–9,15; 5:1,8,16,17; 6:3,9,14; 7:2–4,8,9,20,26; 8:1,6,10; 9:3,4,6,8; 10:1,2,4,16,18,19,22; 11:4,5,8,10,13, 15,22–24; 12:6,7,13,22; 13:3,5,17,18,20; 14:3,5,6,9,13,17,19,22; 15:3; 16:5,6,8,9, 11,12,14–16,27,36,37,40,43,44,46; 17:5, 7,10,20,22; 18:2,15,20,26,31; 19:8,10,11; 20:8,13,17,21,32,33; 21:7,15,22,31; 22:3, 4,13,20–22,31; 23:5,7–9,14,16,18,20,22,

24,30,41,42,46,47,49; 24:6–8,11,17,22,23; 25:2,7,10,13,16; 26:2,3,8,16,17,19; 27:2, 3,5,11,30,32,35,36; 28:7,12,17–19, 21–23,25,26; 29:2,3,5,7,8,14,15,18; 30:11,15; 31:5,13,15; 32:2–5,8–10,13, 16,18,27,31; 33:2,3,10,13,19,24–27,29; 34:2,6,23,27; 35:2,3,5,12,13,15; 36:2,3, 5,6,10–12,17,18,21,25,29,31; 37:1,2,4, 6,8,10,14,16,19,20,24,25,27; 38:2,7,8, 10–12,16–22; 39:1,2,4,5,14,17,20,23,26, 28,29; 40:1,2,15; 41:7,15,17,20; 42:6,8; 43:12,18,20,24,27; 44:10,12,13,15,17, 18,24; 45:9,15,17,19; 46:2,14,19; 47:8, 10,12,18; 48:2–8,15,21,24–28,31; **Dan.** 1:1,8,11,20; 2:1; 8:2,5,12,17,18,25,27; 9:1,11–14,17–20,24,27; 10:4,7–11,16,21; 11:5,14,20,21,24,25,27,28,30,34,36–38,40; 12:1; **Hos.** 1:4; 2:13,14; 4:3,9,13,14; 5:1,10; 6:5; 7:12–14; 8:1; 9:1,7,8,15; 10:4, 5,7–11,14; 11:3,4,8,11; 12:2,10,11,14; 13:6,7; 14:3; **Joel** 1:3,5,6,8,11; 2:2,5,13, 17,18,20,28,29; 3:2,4,6; **Amos** 1:1,3,6,8, 9,11,13; 2:1,4,6–8,12; 3:1,2,5,9,14,15; 4:2,7,13; 5:1,2,8,9,11,19,23; 6:4–6,14; 7:3,6,7,9–11,16,17; 8:8,10; 9:1,4,6,8, 12,15; **Obad.** 1:1,11,14–16; **Jon.** 1:2,5, 7,11–14; 2:3,7; 3:6,10; 4:2,6,8–11; **Mic.** 1:1,3,8,14,16; 2:1,3,4,9; 3:2,3,5–7,11; 4:1,7,11; 5:1,3,5,7,9; 6:13; 7:3,13,16,18; **Nah.** 1:11,13–15; 2:1,7; 3:5,6,10,12,18,19; **Hab.** 1:4,15–17; 2:1,2,6,14–16,18; 3:1, 8,19; **Zeph.** 1:2–5,8,9,12,16; 2:2,5,7,8, 10,11,13,15; 3:7,8,17,18; **Hag.** 1:5,7, 10–12; **Zech.** 1:2,8,15,16; 2:9,12; 3:1,4, 5,9; 4:2,3,11,12,14; 5:3,11; 6:5,13; 7:14; 9:8,9,13–16; 10:2,3; 11:5,6,13,17; 12:1–4, 6,7,9,10; 13:7; 14:4,9,12,13,16–18,20; **Mal.** 1:5,7; 2:2,3,14,16; 3:13,17; 4:4,6.

5922. עַל *ʿal* **Aram. prep.**
(upon, to, against, for; corr. to Hebr. 5921)
Ezra 4:8,11,12,14,15,17–20,22,23; 5:1,3,5–7,15,17; 6:7,11,17,18; 7:14,17, 18,23,24; **Dan.** 2:10,15,18,24,28–30,34, 46,48,49; 3:12,16,19,28,29; 4:5(2),10(7), 13(10),16(13),17(14),23–25(20–22), 27–29(24–26),32–34(29–31),36(33); 5:5, 7,9,14,16,21,23,29; 6:1(2),3–6(4–7), 10(11),12–15(13–16),17(18),18(19), 23(24); 7:1,4,6,16,19,20,28.

5923. עֹל *ʿōl* **masc. noun**
(yoke)
Gen. 27:40; **Lev.** 26:13; **Num.** 19:2; **Deut.** 21:3; 28:48; **1 Sam.** 6:7; **1 Kgs.** 12:4,9–11,14; **2 Chr.** 10:4,9–11,14; **Isa.** 9:4(3); 10:27; 14:25; 47:6; **Jer.** 2:20; 5:5; 27:8,11,12; 28:2,4,11,14; 30:8; **Lam.** 1:14; 3:27; **Ezek.** 34:27; **Hos.** 11:4.

5924. עֵלָּא *ʿēllāʾ* **Aram. prep.**
(over)
Dan. 6:2(3).

5925. עֻלָּא *ʿullāʾ* **masc. proper noun**
(Ulla)
1 Chr. 7:39.

5926. עִלֵּג *ʿillēg* **adj.**
(stammering)
Isa. 32:4.

5927. עָלָה *ʿālāh* **verb**
(to go up, to bring up, to offer, to sacrifice)
Gen. 2:6; 8:20; 13:1; 17:22; 19:15,28,30; 22:2,13; 24:16; 26:23; 28:12; 31:10,12; 32:24(25),26(27); 35:1,3,13; 37:28; 38:12,13; 40:10; 41:2,3,5,18,19,22,27; 44:17,24,33,34; 45:9,25; 46:4,29,31; 49:4,9; 50:5–7,9,14,24,25; **Ex.** 1:10; 2:23; 3:8,17; 8:3–7(7:28—8:3); 10:12,14; 12:38; 13:18,19; 16:13,14; 17:3,10; 19:3, 12,13,18,20,23,24; 20:26; 24:1,2,5,9,12, 13,15,18; 25:37; 27:20; 30:8,9; 32:1,4, 6–8,23,30; 33:1,3,5,12,15; 34:2–4,24; 40:4,25,29,36,37; **Lev.** 2:12; 11:3–6, 26,45; 14:20; 16:9,10; 17:8; 19:19; 24:2; **Num.** 8:2,3; 9:17,21,22; 10:11; 13:17,21, 22,30,31; 14:13,40,42,44; 16:12–14, 24,27; 19:2; 20:5,19,25,27; 21:5,17,33; 22:41; 23:2,4,14,30; 27:12; 32:9,11;

33:38; **Deut.** 1:21,22,24,26,28,41–43; 3:1,27; 5:5; 9:9,23; 10:1,3; 12:13,14; 14:6,7; 17:8; 20:1; 25:7; 27:6; 28:43,61; 29:23(22); 30:12; 32:49,50; 34:1; **Josh.** 2:6,8; 4:16–19; 6:5,15,20; 7:2–4,6,24; 8:1,3,10,11,20,21,31; 10:4–7,9,33,36; 11:17; 12:7; 14:8; 15:3,6–8,15; 16:1; 17:15; 18:11,12; 19:10–12,47; 22:12, 23,33; 24:17,32; **Judg.** 1:1–4,16,22; 2:1; 4:5,10,12; 6:3,5,8,13,21,26,28,35; 8:8,11; 9:48,51; 11:13,16,31; 12:3; 13:5,16,19,20; 14:2,19; 15:6,9,10,13; 16:3,5,8,17,18,31; 18:9,12,17; 19:25,30; 20:3,18,23,26,28, 30,31,38,40; 21:4,5,8,19; **Ruth** 4:1; **1 Sam.** 1:3,7,11,21,22,24; 2:6,14,19,28; 5:12; 6:7,9,14,15,20,21; 7:1,7,9,10; 8:8; 9:11,13,14,19,26; 10:3,8,18; 11:1; 12:6; 13:5,9,10,12,15; 14:9,10,12,13,21,46; 15:2,6,34; 17:23,25; 19:15; 23:19,29(24:1); 24:22(23); 25:5,13,35; 27:8; 28:8,11, 13–15; 29:9,11; **2 Sam.** 1:24; 2:1–3,27; 5:17,19,22,23; 6:2,12,15,17,18; 7:6; 11:20; 15:24,30; 17:21; 18:33(19:1); 19:34(35); 20:2; 21:13; 22:9; 23:9; 24:18, 19,22,24,25; **1 Kgs.** 1:35,40,45; 2:34; 3:4,15; 5:13(27); 6:8; 8:1,4; 9:15,16,21, 24,25; 10:5,16,17,29; 11:15; 12:18,24,27, 28,32,33; 14:25; 15:17,19; 16:17; 17:19; 18:29,36,41–44; 20:1,22,26,33; 22:6,12, 15,20,29,35; **2 Kgs.** 1:3,4,6,7,9,13,16; 2:1,11,23; 3:7,8,20,21,27; 4:21,34,35; 6:24; 10:15; 12:4(5),10(11),17(18), 18(19); 14:11; 15:14; 16:5,7,9,12; 17:3–5,7,36; 18:9,13,17,25; 19:14,23,28; 20:5,8; 22:4; 23:2,9,29; 24:1,10; 25:6; **1 Chr.** 11:6; 13:6; 14:8,10,11,14; 15:3, 12,14,25,28; 16:2,40; 17:5; 21:18,19, 24,26; 23:31; 26:16; 27:24; 29:21; **2 Chr.** 1:4,6,17; 2:16(15); 3:5,14; 5:2,5; 8:8, 11–13; 9:4,15,16; 10:18; 11:4; 12:2,9; 16:1,3; 18:2,5,11,14,19,28,34; 20:16,34; 21:17; 23:18; 24:13,14,23; 25:21; 29:7, 20,21,27,29; 32:5; 34:30; 35:14,16,20; 36:6,16,17,23; **Ezra** 1:3,5,11; 2:1,59; 3:2,3,6; 4:2; 7:6,7,28; 8:1; **Neh.** 2:15; 3:19; 4:3(3:35),7(1),21(15); 7:5,6,61; 9:18; 10:38(39); 12:1,31,37; **Job** 1:5; 5:26; 6:18; 7:9; 20:6; 36:20,33; 42:8; **Ps.** 18:8(9); 24:3; 30:3(4); 40:2(3); 47:5(6),9(10); 51:19(21); 62:9(10); 66:15; 68:18(19); 71:20; 74:23; 78:21,31; 81:10(11); 97:9; 102:24(25); 104:8; 107:26; 122:4; 132:3; 135:7; 137:6; **Prov.** 15:1; 21:22; 24:31; 25:7; 26:9; 30:4; 31:29; **Eccl.** 3:21; 10:4; **Song** 3:6; 4:2; 6:6; 7:8(9); 8:5; **Isa.** 2:3; 5:6,24; 7:1,6; 8:7; 11:16; 14:8,13,14; 15:2,5; 21:2; 22:1; 24:18; 32:13; 34:3,10,13; 35:9; 36:1,10; 37:14,24,29; 38:22; 40:9,31; 53:2; 55:13; 57:6–8; 60:7; 63:11; 65:17; 66:3; **Jer.** 2:6; 3:16; 4:7,13,29; 5:10; 6:4,5; 7:31; 8:22; 9:21(20); 10:13; 11:7; 14:2,12; 16:14,15; 19:5; 21:2; 22:20; 23:7,8; 26:10; 27:22; 30:17; 31:6; 32:35; 33:6,18; 34:21; 35:11; 37:5,11; 38:10,13; 39:5; 44:21; 46:4,7–9, 11; 47:2; 48:5,15,18,35,44; 49:19,22, 28,31; 50:3,9,21,44; 51:3,16,27,42,50,53; 52:9; **Lam.** 1:14; 2:10; **Ezek.** 8:11; 9:3; 11:23,24; 13:5; 14:3,4,7; 16:40; 19:3; 20:32; 23:46; 24:8; 26:3,19; 27:30; 29:4; 32:3; 36:3; 37:6,8,12,13; 38:9–11,16,18; 39:2; 40:6,22,40,49; 41:7; 43:18,24; 44:17; 47:12; **Dan.** 8:3,8; 11:23; **Hos.** 1:11(2:2); 2:15(17); 4:15; 8:9; 10:8; 12:13(14); 13:15; **Joel** 1:6; 2:7,9,20; 3:9(4:9),12(4:12); **Amos** 2:10; 3:1,5; 4:10; 5:22; 7:1; 8:8,10; 9:2,5,7; **Obad.** 1:21; **Jon.** 1:2; 2:6(7); 4:6,7; **Mic.** 2:13; 4:2; 6:4; **Nah.** 2:1(2), 7(8); 3:3; **Hab.** 1:15; 3:16; **Hag.** 1:8; **Zech.** 14:13,16–19.

5928. עֲלָה *'alāh* **Aram. fem. noun**
(burnt offering; corr. to Hebr. 5930)
Ezra 6:9.

5929. עָלֶה *'āleh* **masc. noun**
(leaf, branch)
Gen. 3:7; 8:11; **Lev.** 26:36; **Neh.** 8:15; **Job** 13:25; **Ps.** 1:3; **Prov.** 11:28; **Isa.** 1:30; 34:4; 64:6(5); **Jer.** 8:13; 17:8; **Ezek.** 47:12.

5930. עֹלָה *'ōlāh* **fem. noun**
(burnt offering, sacrifice)

Gen. 8:20; 22:2,3,6–8,13; **Ex.** 10:25; 18:12; 20:24; 24:5; 29:18,25,42; 30:9,28; 31:9; 32:6; 35:16; 38:1; 40:6,10,29; **Lev.** 1:3,4,6,9,10,13,14,17; 3:5; 4:7,10,18,24, 25,29,30,33,34; 5:7,10; 6:9(2),10(3), 12(5),25(18); 7:2,8,37; 8:18,21,28; 9:2,3,7,12–14,16,17,22,24; 10:19; 12:6,8; 14:13,19,20,22,31; 15:15,30; 16:3,5,24; 17:8; 22:18; 23:12,18,37; **Num.** 6:11, 14,16; 7:15,21,27,33,39,45,51,57,63, 69,75,81,87; 8:12; 10:10; 15:3,5,8,24; 23:3,6,15,17; 28:3,6,10,11,13–15,19,23, 24,27,31; 29:2,6,8,11,13,16,19,22,25,28, 31,34,36,38,39; **Deut.** 12:6,11,13,14,27; 27:6; **Josh.** 8:31; 22:23,26–29; **Judg.** 6:26; 11:31; 13:16,23; 20:26; 21:4; **1 Sam.** 6:14,15; 7:9,10; 10:8; 13:9,10,12; 15:22; **2 Sam.** 6:17,18; 24:22,24,25; **1 Kgs.** 3:4,15; 8:64; 9:25; 10:5; 18:33(34), 38; **2 Kgs.** 3:27; 5:17; 10:24,25; 16:13,15; **1 Chr.** 6:49(34); 16:1,2,40; 21:23,24, 26,29; 22:1; 23:31; 29:21; **2 Chr.** 1:6; 2:4(3); 4:6; 7:1,7; 8:12; 13:11; 23:18; 24:14; 29:7,18,24,27,28,31,32,34,35; 30:15; 31:2,3; 35:12,14,16; **Ezra** 3:2–6; 8:35; **Neh.** 10:33(34); **Job** 1:5; 42:8; **Ps.** 20:3(4); 40:6(7); 50:8; 51:16(18),19(21); 66:13,15; **Isa.** 1:11; 40:16; 43:23; 56:7; 61:8; **Jer.** 6:20; 7:21,22; 14:12; 17:26; 19:5; 33:18; **Ezek.** 40:26,38,39,42; 43:18,24,27; 44:11; 45:15,17,23,25; 46:2,4,12,13,15; **Hos.** 6:6; **Amos** 5:22; **Mic.** 6:6.

5931. עִלָּה *ʿillāh* **Aram. fem. noun**
(basis for charges)
Dan. 6:4(5),5(6).

5932. עַלְוָה *ʿalwāh* **fem. noun**
(iniquity, evil)
Hos. 10:9(NASB, *ʿawlāh* [5766,II]).

5933. I. עַלְוָה *ʿalwāh* **masc. proper noun**
(Alvah: the same as II)
Gen. 36:40; **1 Chr.** 1:51(KJV, NASB, [Ke] *ʿalyāh* [5933,II]).

II. עַלְיָה *ʿalyāh* **masc. proper noun**
(Alvah: the same as I)
1 Chr. 1:51(NIV, [Qe] *ʿalwāh* [5933,I]).

5934. עֲלוּמִים *ʿalûmiym* **masc. pl. noun**
(youthful times, youth)
Job 20:11; 33:25; **Ps.** 89:45(46); **Isa.** 54:4.

5935. I. עַלְוָן *ʿalwān* **masc. proper noun**
(Alvan: the same as II)
Gen. 36:23; **1 Chr.** 1:40(KJV, NASB, [Ke] *ʿalyān* [5935,II]).

II. עַלְיָן *ʿalyān* **masc. proper noun**
(Alyan: the same as I)
1 Chr. 1:40(NIV, [Qe] *ʿalwān* [5935,I]).

5936. עֲלוּקָה *ʿalûqāh* **fem. noun**
(leech)
Prov. 30:15.

5937. עָלַז *ʿālaz* **verb**
(to rejoice, to exult, to be jubilant)
2 Sam. 1:20; **Ps.** 28:7; 60:6(8); 68:4(5); 94:3; 96:12; 108:7(8); 149:5; **Prov.** 23:16; **Isa.** 23:12; **Jer.** 11:15; 15:17; 50:11; 51:39; **Hab.** 3:18; **Zeph.** 3:14.

5938. עָלֵז *ʿālēz* **adj.**
(exulting, rejoicing)
Isa. 5:14.

5939. עֲלָטָה *ʿalāṭāh* **fem. noun**
(thick darkness)
Gen. 15:17; **Ezek.** 12:6,7,12.

5940. עֱלִי *ʿeliy* **masc. noun**
(pestle)
Prov. 27:22.

5941. עֵלִי *ʿēliy* **masc. proper noun**
(Eli)
1 Sam. 1:3,9,12–14,17,25; 2:11,12,20, 22,27; 3:1,2,5,6,8,9,12,14–16; 4:4,11, 13–16; 14:3; **1 Kgs.** 2:27.

5942. עִלִּי *'illiy* **adj.**
(upper)
Josh. 15:19; **Judg.** 1:15.

5943. עִלָּי *'illāy* **Aram. adj.**
(highest, Most High; corr. to Hebr. 5942)
Dan. 3:26; 4:2(3:32),17(14),24(21), 25(22),32(29),34(31); 5:18,21; 7:25.

5944. עֲלִיָּה *ᵃliyyāh* **fem. noun**
(upper room, chamber, parlor)
Judg. 3:20,23–25; **2 Sam.** 18:33(19:1); **1 Kgs.** 17:19,23; **2 Kgs.** 1:2; 4:10,11; 23:12; **1 Chr.** 28:11; **2 Chr.** 3:9; 9:4; **Neh.** 3:31,32; **Ps.** 104:3,13; **Jer.** 22:13,14.

5945. I. עֶלְיוֹן *'elyôn* **adj.**
(upper, highest)
Gen. 40:17; **Deut.** 26:19; 28:1; **Josh.** 16:5; **1 Kgs.** 9:8; **2 Kgs.** 15:35; 18:17; **1 Chr.** 7:24; **2 Chr.** 7:21; 8:5; 23:20; 27:3; 32:30; **Neh.** 3:25; **Ps.** 89:27(28); **Isa.** 7:3; 36:2; **Jer.** 20:2; 36:10; **Ezek.** 9:2; 41:7; 42:5.
II. עֶלְיוֹן *'elyôn* **adj.**
(Most High as a description of God)
Gen. 14:18–20,22; **Num.** 24:16; **Deut.** 32:8; **2 Sam.** 22:14; **Ps.** 7:17(18); 9:2(3); 18:13(14); 21:7(8); 46:4(5); 47:2(3); 50:14; 57:2(3); 73:11; 77:10(11); 78:17, 35,56; 82:6; 83:18(19); 87:5; 91:1,9; 92:1(2); 97:9; 107:11; **Isa.** 14:14; **Lam.** 3:35,38.

5946. עֶלְיוֹן *'elyôn* **Aram. adj.**
(Most High, as a description of God; corr. to Hebr. 5945,II)
Dan. 7:18,22,25,27.

5947. עַלִּיז *'alliyz* **adj.**
(rejoicing, jubilant)
Isa. 13:3; 22:2; 23:7; 24:8; 32:13; **Zeph.** 2:15; 3:11.

5948. עֲלִיל *ᵃliyl* **masc. noun**
(furnace)
Ps. 12:6(7).

5949. עֲלִילָה *ᵃliylāh* **fem. noun**
(deeds, actions, esp. shameful actions)
Deut. 22:14,17; **1 Sam.** 2:3; **1 Chr.** 16:8; **Ps.** 9:11(12); 14:1; 66:5; 77:12(13); 78:11; 99:8; 103:7; 105:1; 141:4; **Isa.** 12:4; **Ezek.** 14:22,23; 20:43,44; 21:24(29); 24:14; 36:17,19; **Zeph.** 3:7,11.

5950. עֲלִילִיָּה *ᵃliyliyyāh* **fem. noun**
(deed, action)
Jer. 32:19.

5951. עֲלִיצֻת *ᵃliyṣuṯ* **fem. noun**
(gloating, exultation)
Hab. 3:14.

5952. עִלִּי *'illiy* **Aram. fem. noun**
(roof, chamber)
Dan. 6:10(11).

5953. I. עָלַל *'ālal* **verb**
(to do, to deal with, to treat severely, to abuse; to glean)
Ex. 10:2; **Lev.** 19:10; **Num.** 22:29; **Deut.** 24:21; **Judg.** 19:25; 20:45; **1 Sam.** 6:6; 31:4; **1 Chr.** 10:4; **Ps.** 141:4; **Jer.** 6:9; 38:19; **Lam.** 1:12,22; 2:20; 3:51.
II. עָלַל *'ālal* **verb**
(to act childishly, to play the child)
Isa. 3:12.
III. עָלַל *'ālal* **verb**
(to defile)
Job 16:15(NASB, NIV, see IV).
IV. עָלַל *'ālal* **verb**
(to insert, to thrust in, to bury)
Job 16:15(KJV, see III).

5954. עֲלַל *ᵃlal* **Aram. verb**
(to bring in, to enter; corr. to Hebr. 5959,IV)
Dan. 2:16,24,25; 4:6(3),7(4),8(5); 5:7,8, 10,13,15; 6:10(11),18(19).

5955. עֹלֵלוֹת *ʿōlēlôṯ* **fem. pl. noun**
(gleaning)
Judg. 8:2; **Isa.** 17:6; 24:13; **Jer.** 49:9; **Obad.** 1:5; **Mic.** 7:1.

5956. עָלַם *ʿālam* **verb**
(to hide, to conceal, to ignore)
Lev. 4:13; 5:2–4; 20:4; **Num.** 5:13; **Deut.** 22:1,3,4; **1 Sam.** 12:3; **1 Kgs.** 10:3; **2 Kgs.** 4:27; **2 Chr.** 9:2; **Job** 6:16; 28:21; 42:3; **Ps.** 10:1; 26:4; 55:1(2); 90:8; **Prov.** 28:27; **Eccl.** 12:14; **Isa.** 1:15; 58:7; **Lam.** 3:56; **Ezek.** 22:26; **Nah.** 3:11.

5957. עָלַם *ʿālam* **Aram. masc. noun**
(eternity, ancient past)
Ezra 4:15,19; **Dan.** 2:4,20,44; 3:9; 4:3(3:33),34(31); 5:10; 6:6(7),21(22),26(27); 7:14,18,27.

5958. עֶלֶם *ʿelem* **masc. noun**
(young man, youth)
1 Sam. 17:56; 20:22.

5959. עַלְמָה *ʿalmāh* **fem. noun**
(virgin, young woman)
Gen. 24:43; **Ex.** 2:8; **Ps.** 68:25(26); **Prov.** 30:19; **Song** 1:3; 6:8; **Isa.** 7:14.

5960. עַלְמוֹן *ʿalmôn* **proper noun**
(Almon; see also *ʿālemet* [5964,C])
Josh. 21:18.

5961. עֲלָמוֹת *ʿalāmôṯ* **fem. pl. noun**
(alamoth; musical term referring perhaps to a song title or manner of playing)
1 Chr. 15:20; **Ps.** 46:[title](1).

5962. עֵלְמָי *ʿēlmāy* **Aram. masc. proper noun**
(Elamite)
Ezra 4:9.

5963. עַלְמֹן דִּבְלָתָיְמָה *ʿalmon diḇlaṯāyᵉmāh* **proper noun**
(Almon Diblathaim)
Num. 33:46,47.

5964. A. עָלֶמֶת *ʿālemeṯ* **masc. proper noun**
(Alemeth: son of Becher)
1 Chr. 7:8.
B. עָלֶמֶת *ʿālemeṯ* **masc. proper noun**
(Alemeth: son of Jehoadah)
1 Chr. 8:36; 9:42.
C. עָלֶמֶת *ʿālemeṯ* **masc. proper noun**
(Alemeth: town in Benjamin; same as *ʿalmôn* [5960])
1 Chr. 6:60(45).

5965. I. עָלַס *ʿālas* **verb**
(to rejoice, to enjoy)
Job 20:18; **Prov.** 7:18.
II. עָלַס *ʿālas* **verb**
(to flap joyously)
Job 39:13(KJV, see III).
III. נֶעֱלָסָה *neʿᵉlāsāh* **fem. noun**
(to be attractive, to be beautiful)
Job 39:13(NASB, NIV, see II).

5966. עָלַע *ʿālaʿ* **verb**
(to suck up)
Job 39:30.

5967. עֲלַע *ʿalaʿ* **Aram. com. noun**
(rib)
Dan. 7:5.

5968. I. עָלַף *ʿālap̱* **verb**
(to cover, to wrap, to overlay)
Gen. 38:14; **Song** 5:14.
II. עָלַף *ʿālap̱* **verb**
(to faint)
Isa. 51:20; **Amos** 8:13; **Jon.** 4:8.

5969. עֻלְפֶּה *ʿulpeh* **masc. noun**
(something withered)
Ezek. 31:15.

5970. עָלַץ *ʿālaṣ* **verb**
(to rejoice, to be jubilant)

1 Sam. 2:1; **1 Chr.** 16:32; **Ps.** 5:11(12); 9:2(3); 25:2; 68:3(4); **Prov.** 11:10; 28:12.

5971. עַם ʿam, עָם ʿām **masc. noun** (people, throng, army)
Gen. 11:6; 14:16; 17:14,16; 19:4; 23:7, 11–13; 25:8,17; 26:10,11; 27:29; 28:3; 32:7(8); 33:15; 34:16,22; 35:6,29; 41:40, 55; 42:6; 47:21,23; 48:4,19; 49:10,16,29, 33; 50:20; **Ex.** 1:9,20,22; 3:7,10,12,21; 4:16,21,30,31; 5:1,4–7,10,12,16,22,23; 6:7; 7:4,14,16; 8:1(7:26),3(7:28),4(7:29), 8(4),9(5),11(7),20–23(16–19,29(25), 31(27),32(28); 9:1,7,13–15,17,27; 10:3,4; 11:2,3,8; 12:27,31,33,34,36; 13:3,17,18, 22; 14:5,6,13,31; 15:13,14,16,24; 16:4, 27,30; 17:1–6,13; 18:1,10,13–15,18,19, 21–23,25,26; 19:5,7–12,14–17,21,23–25; 20:18,20,21; 21:8; 22:25(24),28(27); 23:11,27; 24:2,3,7,8; 30:33,38; 31:14; 32:1,3,6,7,9,11,12,14,17,21,22,25,28,30, 31,34,35; 33:1,3–5,8,10,12,13,16; 34:9,10; 36:5,6; **Lev.** 4:3,27; 7:20,21,25,27; 9:7, 15,18,22–24; 10:3; 16:15,24,33; 17:4,9, 10; 18:29; 19:8,16,18; 20:2–6,17,18, 24,26; 21:1,4,14,15; 23:29,30; 26:12; **Num.** 5:21,27; 9:13; 11:1,2,8,10–14, 16–18,21,24,29,32–35; 12:15,16; 13:18, 28,30–32; 14:1,9,11,13–16,19,39; 15:26,30; 16:41(17:6),47(17:12); 20:1,3, 20,24; 21:2,4–7,16,18,23,29,33–35; 22:3,5,6,11,12,17,41; 23:9,24; 24:14; 25:1,2,4; 27:13; 31:2,3,32; 32:15; 33:14; **Deut.** 1:28; 2:4,10,16,21,25,32,33; 3:1–3,28; 4:6,10,19,20,27,33; 5:28(25); 6:14; 7:6,7,14,16,19; 9:2,6,12,13,26, 27,29; 10:11,15; 13:7(8),9(10); 14:2,21; 16:18; 17:7,13,16; 18:3; 20:1,2,5,8,9, 11,16; 21:8; 26:15,18,19; 27:1,9,11,12, 15–26; 28:9,10,32,33,37,64; 29:13(12); 30:3; 31:7,12,16; 32:6,8,9,21,36,43, 44,50; 33:3,5,7,17,19,21,29; **Josh.** 1:2, 6,10,11; 3:3,5,6,14,16; 4:2,10,11,19,24; 5:4,5; 6:5,7,8,10,16,20; 7:3–5,7,13; 8:1,3,5,9–11,13,14,16,20,33; 10:7,21,33; 11:4,7; 14:8; 17:14,15,17; 24:2,16–19, 21,22,24,25,27,28; **Judg.** 1:16; 2:4,6,7, 12; 3:18; 4:13; 5:2,9,11,13,14,18; 7:1–8; 8:5; 9:29,32–38,42,43,45,48,49; 10:18; 11:11,20,21,23; 12:2; 14:3,16,17; 16:24,30; 18:7,10,20,27; 20:2,8,10,16,22,26,31; 21:2,4,9,15; **Ruth** 1:6,10,15,16; 2:11; 3:11; 4:4,9,11; **1 Sam.** 2:13,23,24,29; 4:3,4,17; 5:10,11; 6:19; 8:7,10,19,21; 9:2,12,13,16,17,24; 10:11,17,23–25; 11:4,5,7,11,12,14,15; 12:6,18–20,22; 13:2,4–8,11,14–16,22; 14:2,3,15,17,20,24,26–28,30–34,38–41,45; 15:1,4,8,9,15,21,24,30; 17:27,30; 18:5,13; 23:8; 26:5,7,14,15; 27:12; 30:4, 6,21; 31:9; **2 Sam.** 1:4,12; 2:26–28,30; 3:18,31,32,34–37; 5:2,12; 6:2,18,19,21; 7:7,8,10,11,23,24; 8:15; 10:10,12,13; 11:7,17; 12:28,29,31; 13:34; 14:13,15; 15:12,17,23,24,30; 16:6,14,15,18; 17:2, 3,8,9,16,22,29; 18:1–8,16; 19:2(3), 3(4),8(9),9(10),39(40),40(41); 20:12, 15,22; 22:28,44,48; 23:10,11; 24:2–4, 9,10,15–17,21; **1 Kgs.** 1:39,40; 3:2,8,9; 4:34(5:14); 5:7(21),16(30); 6:13; 8:16,30, 33,34,36,38,41,43,44,50–53,56,59,60,66; 9:7,20,23; 12:5–7,9,10,12,13,15,16,23, 27,30,31; 13:33; 14:2,7; 16:2,15,16, 21,22; 18:21,22,24,30,37,39; 19:21; 20:8,10,15,42; 21:9,12,13; 22:4,28, 43(44); **2 Kgs.** 3:7; 4:13,41–43; 6:30; 7:16,17,20; 8:21; 9:6; 10:9,18; 11:13,14, 17–20; 12:3(4),8(9); 13:7; 14:4,21; 15:4, 5,10,35; 16:15; 18:26,36; 20:5; 21:24; 22:4,13; 23:2,3,6,21,30,35; 24:14; 25:3, 11,19,22,26; **1 Chr.** 5:25; 10:9; 11:2,13; 13:4; 14:2; 16:2,8,20,24,26,28,36,43; 17:6,7,9,10,21,22; 18:14; 19:7,11,13,14; 20:3; 21:2,3,5,17,22; 22:18; 23:25; 28:2,21; 29:9,14,17,18; **2 Chr.** 1:9–11; 2:11(10),18(17); 6:5,6,21,24,25,27,29, 32–34,39; 7:4,5,10,13,14,20; 8:7,10; 10:5–7,9,10,12,15,16; 12:3; 13:9,17; 14:13(12); 16:10; 17:9; 18:2,3,27; 19:4; 20:7,21,25,33; 21:14,19; 23:5,6,10,12, 13,16,17,20,21; 24:10,20,23; 25:11,15; 26:1,21; 27:2; 29:36; 30:3,13,18,20,27; 31:4,8,10; 32:4,6,8,13–15,17–19; 33:10, 17,25; 34:30; 35:3,5,7,8,12,13; 36:1,

14–16,23; **Ezra** 1:3; 2:2,70; 3:1,3,11,13; 4:4; 8:15,36; 9:1,2,11,14; 10:1,2,9,11,13; **Neh.** 1:8,10; 4:6(3:38),13(7),14(8), 19(13),22(16); 5:1,13,15,18,19; 7:4,5, 7,72,73; 8:1,3,5–7,9,11–13,16; 9:10,22, 24,30,32; 10:14(15),28(29),30(31), 31(32),34(35); 11:1,2,24; 12:30,38; 13:1,24; **Esth.** 1:5,11,16,22; 2:10,20; 3:6,8,11,12,14; 4:8,11; 7:3,4; 8:6,9,11, 13,17; 9:2; 10:3; **Job** 12:2,24; 17:6; 18:19; 34:20,30; 36:20,31; **Ps.** 3:6(7),8(9); 7:8(9); 9:11(12); 14:4,7; 18:27(28),43(44),47(48); 22:6(7),31(32); 28:9; 29:11; 33:10,12; 35:18; 44:12(13); 45:5(6),10(11),12(13), 17(18); 47:1(2),3(4),9(10); 49:1(2); 50:4,7; 53:4(5),6(7); 56:7(8); 57:9(10); 59:11(12); 60:3(5); 62:8(9); 66:8; 67:3–5(4–6); 68:7(8),30(31),35(36); 72:2–4; 73:10; 74:14,18; 77:14(15), 15(16),20(21); 78:1,20,52,62,71; 79:13; 80:4(5); 81:8(9),11(12),13(14); 83:3(4); 85:2(3),6(7),8(9); 87:6; 89:15(16),19(20), 50(51); 94:5,8,14; 95:7,10; 96:3,5,7,10, 13; 97:6; 98:9; 99:1,2; 100:3; 102:18(19), 22(23); 105:1,13,20,24,25,43; 106:4,34, 40,48; 107:32; 108:3(4); 110:3; 111:6,9; 113:8; 114:1; 116:14,18; 125:2; 135:12, 14; 136:16; 144:2,15; 148:14; 149:4; **Prov.** 11:14; 14:28; 24:24; 28:15; 29:2,18; 30:25,26; **Eccl.** 4:16; 12:9; **Song** 6:12 (KJV, *ʿammiy nāḏiyḇ* [5993]); **Isa.** 1:3,4, 10; 2:3,4,6; 3:5,7,12–15; 5:13,25; 6:5,9, 10; 7:2,8,17; 8:6,9,11,12,19; 9:2(1),9(8), 13(12),16(15),19(18); 10:2,6,13,14,22,24; 11:10,11,16; 12:4; 13:4,14; 14:2,6,20,32; 17:12; 18:2,7; 19:25; 22:4; 23:13; 24:2, 4,13; 25:3,6–8; 26:11,20; 27:11; 28:5,11, 14; 29:13,14; 30:5,6,9,19,26,28; 32:13, 18; 33:3,12,19,24; 34:5; 36:11; 40:1,7; 42:5,6,22; 43:8,20,21; 44:7; 47:6; 49:8, 13,22; 51:4,5,7,16,22; 52:4–6,9; 53:8; 56:3,7; 57:14; 58:1; 60:21; 61:9; 62:10, 12; 63:3,6,8,11,14,18; 64:9(8); 65:2,3,10, 18,19,22; **Jer.** 1:18; 2:11,13,31,32; 4:10, 11,22; 5:14,21,23,26,31; 6:14,19,21,22, 26,27; 7:12,16,23,33; 8:5,7,11,19,21,22; 9:1(8:23),2(1),7(6),15(14); 10:3; 11:4,14; 12:14,16; 13:10,11; 14:10,11,16,17; 15:1, 7,20; 16:5,10; 17:19; 18:15; 19:1,11,14; 21:7,8; 22:2,4; 23:2,13,22,27,32–34; 24:7; 25:1,2,19; 26:7–9,11,12,16–18, 23,24; 27:12,13,16; 28:1,5,7,11,15; 29:1,16,25,32; 30:3,22; 31:1,2,7,14,33; 32:21,38,42; 33:24; 34:1,8,10,19; 35:16; 36:6,7,9,10,13,14; 37:2,4,12,18; 38:1,4; 39:8–10,14; 40:5,6; 41:10,13,14,16; 42:1,8; 43:1,4; 44:15,20,21,24; 46:16,24; 48:42,46; 49:1; 50:6,16,41; 51:45,58; 52:6,15,25,28; **Lam.** 1:1,7,11,18; 2:11; 3:14,45,48; 4:3,6,10; **Ezek.** 3:5,6,11; 7:27; 11:1,17,20; 12:19; 13:9,10,17–19, 21,23; 14:8,9,11; 17:9,15; 18:18; 20:34, 35,41; 21:12(17); 22:29; 23:24; 24:18,19; 25:7,14; 26:2,7,11,20; 27:3,33,36; 28:19,25; 29:13; 30:11; 31:12; 32:3,9,10; 33:2,3,6,12,17,30,31; 34:13,30; 36:3,8, 12,15,20,28; 37:12,13,18,23,27; 38:6, 8,9,12,14,15,16,22; 39:4,7,13,27; 42:14; 44:11,19,23; 45:8,9,16,22; 46:3,9,18, 20,24; **Dan.** 8:24; 9:6,15,16,19,20,24,26; 10:14; 11:14,15,32,33; 12:1,7; **Hos.** 1:9, 10(2:1); 2:1(3),23(25); 4:4,6,8,9,12,14; 6:11; 7:8; 9:1; 10:5,10,14; 11:7; **Joel** 2:2,5,6,16–19,26,27; 3:2(4:2),3(4:3), 16(4:16); **Amos** 1:5; 3:6; 7:8,15; 8:2; 9:10,14; **Obad.** 1:13; **Jon.** 1:8; **Mic.** 1:2,9; 2:4,8,9,11; 3:3,5; 4:1,3,5,13; 5:7(6),8(7); 6:2,3,5,16; 7:14; **Nah.** 3:13,18; **Hab.** 2:5,8,10,13; 3:13,16; **Zeph.** 1:11; 2:8–10; 3:9,12,20; **Hag.** 1:2,12–14; 2:2,4,14; **Zech.** 2:11(15); 7:5; 8:6–8,11,12,20,22; 9:16; 10:9; 11:10; 12:2–4,6; 13:9; 14:2,12; **Mal.** 1:4; 2:9.

5972. עַם *ʿam* **Aram. masc. noun**
(people; corr, to Hebr. 5971)
Ezra 5:12; 6:12; 7:13,16,25; **Dan.** 2:44; 3:4,7,29; 4:1(3:31); 5:19; 6:25(26); 7:14,27.

5973. עִם *ʿim* **prep.**
(with, for, against, toward)
Gen. 3:6,12; 13:1,14; 18:16,23,25; 19:19,30,32,34,35; 20:9,13; 21:10,22,23;

22:5; 23:4; 24:12,14,27,54,58; 25:11; 26:3,16,20,28,29; 27:44; 28:15,20; 29:6, 9,14,19,25,27,30; 30:8,15,16; 31:2,3,5, 23,24,29,31,32,38,50; 32:4,6,9,12,24, 25,28; 33:1,15; 35:2–4,6; 39:7,10,12,14; 40:14; 41:32; 42:38; 43:34; 44:29,32,33; 46:4; 47:29,30; 48:1,12,21; 50:9; **Ex.** 3:12; 4:12,15; 8:12[8],29[25],30[28]; 9:33; 10:6,10,18,24,26; 11:8; 13:19; 14:6; 17:2,8; 18:6,12,18,19; 19:9,24; 20:19,22; 21:3,14; 22:12,14–16,19,25,30; 23:1,5; 24:2,8,14; 33:9,12,16; 34:3,5,10,28; **Lev.** 15:33; 25:6,23,35,36,39–41,45,47,50, 53,54; 26:21,23,24,27,28,40,41; **Num.** 10:32; 11:16,17; 13:31; 14:24,43; 20:3; 22:8,9,12–14,19,21,22,35,39; 23:21; **Deut.** 2:7; 4:23; 5:2,4; 8:5; 9:7,9,10,24; 10:9,12; 12:23; 14:27,29; 15:9,12,13, 16,18; 17:19; 18:1,13,16,19; 20:1,4, 12,20; 22:2,4,22,23,25,28,29; 23:15,16,21; 27:20–23; 29:12[11],15[14],17[16], 18[17],25[24]; 31:6,8,16,23,27; 32:12, 14,24,25; 33:21; **Josh.** 1:5,9,17; 2:12,14; 3:7; 4:3,8; 7:2,12,24; 8:1; 9:2; 10:7,15, 29,31,34,36,38,43; 11:4,5,7,21; 13:8; 14:7,8; 19:46,47; 20:4; 22:7,8,14; 24:27; **Judg.** 1:22,24; 2:18; 3:27; 4:6,8–10; 5:15,20; 6:12,13,16,17; 7:4; 8:10,35; 9:6,16,19,34,37,44,48; 11:3–5,8,11,20, 25; 12:1; 13:9; 15:3; 16:3,13,30; 18:3,7, 19,22,25,28; 19:3,10,11,19; 20:14,18, 20,23,28,38; **Ruth** 1:7,8,11,22; 2:4,6,8, 12,19,21,22; 4:10; **1 Sam.** 1:17,24,26,27; 2:8,21,26,33; 3:19; 4:4; 5:7; 9:5,19,23–25; 10:2,6,7,9,11,26; 12:24; 13:2,5,15,16; 14:2,7,17,21,45; 15:6,25,26,30; 16:12, 14,18; 17:19,23,26,32,33,37,42; 18:12–14,28; 20:5,7–9,13–16,28,33–35; 22:2,4,8,17,23; 23:19; 25:7,16,25; 26:6; 27:2,3,5; 28:8,19; 29:2,4,9; 30:22; 31:5; **2 Sam.** 1:2,24; 2:3,5,6; 3:8,12,15,17,22, 26,28; 5:10; 6:4,7,22; 7:3,9,15; 8:11; 9:1, 3,7; 10:2,13,17; 11:1,4,11,13; 12:3,11,24; 13:11,16,20,22–24,26; 14:17; 15:19,20, 28,31,35,36; 17:24; 18:2; 19:16[17], 17[18],25[26],33[34],37[38],40[41], 41[42]; 20:8; 21:4,15,18,19; 22:26,27; 23:5,9; 24:16,21; **1 Kgs.** 1:7–9,14,21,22, 33,37; 2:8,10,33; 3:6,17; 5:6[20]; 8:9,17, 18,21,57,61,62,65; 9:27; 10:2,22,26; 11:4,9,11,18,21,22,38,43; 12:15,21,24; 13:8; 14:5,20,31; 15:3,8,14,24; 16:6, 17,28; 17:20; 20:26; 22:40,44,49,50; **2 Kgs.** 2:9; 6:33; 8:21,24,28; 9:28; 10:15,23,35; 11:9; 12:21; 13:9,12,13; 14:10,15,16,20,22,29; 15:7,22,25,38; 16:20; 18:7,26,27; 20:21; 21:18; 24:6; **1 Chr.** 4:10,23; 5:10,19,20; 8:32; 9:20, 25,38; 11:9,10,13; 12:18,19,21,27,34,39; 13:1,2,14; 15:18; 16:41,42; 17:2,8,11,13; 18:11; 19:2,6,14,17,19; 20:4; 21:15,20; 22:7,11,15,16,18; 24:5; 25:7,8; 26:16; 27:32; 28:1,2,12,20,21; 29:30; **2 Chr.** 1:1,3,8,9,11,14; 2:3,7,8,14; 5:10,12; 6:7,8,11; 7:8; 8:18; 9:1,21,25,31; 10:15; 11:1,4; 12:1,3,16; 13:3,8,12; 14:1,6,11, 13; 15:2,9; 16:9,10,13; 17:3,8–10,14–18; 18:2,3; 19:3,6,7,11; 20:1,6,17,29,35–37; 21:1,3,9,19; 22:7,8; 23:1,3,8; 24:4,16,22; 25:7,13,19,24,28; 26:2,17,19,23; 27:5,9; 28:10,27; 29:10; 32:3,7–9,33; 33:20; 35:21; 36:10,23; **Ezra** 1:3,4,11; 2:2; 4:2; 7:28; 8:1,3–14,24,33; 10:4,14; **Neh.** 2:9,12; 4:13; 5:18; 7:7; 9:8,13,17; 10:38; 12:1,40; 13:25; **Esth.** 2:6,13; 5:12,14; 6:3,14; 7:1,8; 9:25; **Job** 1:4,12; 3:14,15; 5:23; 9:2,3,14,26; 10:13,17; 11:5; 12:2, 13,16; 14:3; 15:9,11; 16:21; 17:3; 20:11; 21:8; 22:4,21; 23:7,14; 25:2,4; 26:10; 27:11,13; 28:4; 29:18; 30:1; 31:5; 33:29; 34:8,9,33; 35:4; 36:4; 37:18; 40:2,15; 41:4; 42:8,11; **Ps.** 18:23[24],25[26], 26[27]; 26:4,5,9; 28:1,3; 36:9[10]; 39:12[13]; 42:8[9]; 46:7[8],11[12]; 50:11,18; 54:[title](2); 55:18[19]; 66:15; 69:28[29]; 72:5; 73:5,22,23,25; 77:6[7]; 78:37; 81:2[3]; 83:7[8],8[9]; 85:4[5]; 86:17; 87:4; 88:4[5]; 89:13[14],21[22], 24[25],33[34],38[39]; 91:15; 94:16; 104:25; 106:5,6; 113:8; 115:13; 119:65, 124; 120:4–6; 121:2; 126:2,3; 130:4,7; 139:18; 143:7; 148:12; **Prov.** 3:30; 10:22;

18:3; 23:7; 24:21; 29:24; 30:31; 31:23; **Eccl.** 1:11,16; 2:16; 4:15; 6:10; 7:11; 9:9; **Song** 1:11; 4:13,14; 5:1; 6:1; **Isa.** 3:14; 7:11; 8:10,18; 11:6; 25:11; 28:15,29; 29:6; 34:7; 36:12; 38:11; 41:10; **Jer.** 6:11; 32:4; 34:14; 39:12; 41:12; 51:40; **Dan.** 1:13; 8:18; 9:22; 10:7,11,15,17,19–21; 11:8,11,17,39,40; **Hos.** 2:18[20]; 4:1,5, 14; 5:5; 9:8; 11:12[12:1]; 12:1[2],2[3], 4[5]; 14:2; **Joel** 2:26; 3:2[4:2]; **Amos** 2:3; 4:10; 6:10; **Jon.** 1:3; **Mic.** 2:7; 6:2,8; **Nah.** 3:12; **Zeph.** 1:4; **Zech.** 8:23; 10:5; 14:5.

5974. עִם *ʻim* **Aram. prep.**
(with, for; corr. to Hebr. 5973)
Ezra 5:2; 6:8; 7:13,16; **Dan.** 2:11,18, 22,43; 4:2(3:32),3(3:33),15(12),23(20), 25(22),32(29),34(31); 5:21; 6:21(22); 7:2,13,21.

5975. עָמַד *ʻāmad* **verb**
(to stand, to rise up; to take one's stand)
Gen. 18:8,22; 19:17,27; 24:30,31; 29:35; 30:9; 41:1,3,17,46; 43:15; 45:1,9; 47:7; **Ex.** 3:5; 8:22(18); 9:10,11,16,28; 14:19; 17:6; 18:13,23; 20:18,21; 21:21; 26:15; 32:26; 33:9,10; 36:20; **Lev.** 9:5; 13:5,23, 28,37; 14:11; 16:7,10; 18:23; 19:16; 27:8,11; **Num.** 1:5; 3:6; 5:16,18,30; 7:2; 8:13; 9:8; 11:24; 12:5; 14:14; 16:9,18, 48(17:13); 22:24,26; 27:2,19,21,22; 35:12; **Deut.** 1:38; 4:10,11; 5:5,31(28); 10:8,10; 17:12; 18:5,7; 19:17; 24:11; 25:8; 27:12,13; 29:15(14); 31:15; **Josh.** 3:8,13,16,17; 4:10; 5:13,15; 8:33; 10:8, 13,19; 11:13; 18:5; 20:4,6,9; 21:44(42); 23:9; **Judg.** 2:14; 3:19; 4:20; 6:31; 7:21; 9:7,35,44; 16:25; 20:28; **Ruth** 2:7; **1 Sam.** 6:14,20; 9:27; 14:9; 16:21,22; 17:3,8,26,51; 19:3,20; 20:38; 26:13; 30:9,10; **2 Sam.** 1:9,10; 2:23,25,28; 15:2,17; 17:17; 18:4,30; 20:4,11,12,15; 22:34; **1 Kgs.** 1:2,28; 3:15,16; 7:25; 8:11,14,22,55; 10:8,19,20; 12:6,8,32; 13:1,24,25,28; 15:4; 17:1; 18:15; 19:11, 13; 20:38; 22:19,21,35; **2 Kgs.** 2:7,13; 3:14,21; 4:6,12,15; 5:9,11,15,16,25; 6:31; 8:9,11; 9:17; 10:4,6; 11:11,14; 13:6,18; 15:20; 18:17,28; 23:3; **1 Chr.** 6:31(16), 32(17),33(18),39(24); 15:16,17; 16:17; 17:14; 20:4; 21:1,15,16; 22:2; 23:30; **2 Chr.** 3:13; 4:4; 5:12,14; 6:3,12,13; 7:6; 8:14; 9:7,8,18,19; 10:6,8; 11:15,22; 18:18,20,34; 19:5,8; 20:5,9,13,17,20, 21,23; 23:10,13,19; 24:13,20; 25:5,14; 26:18; 29:11,25,26; 30:5,16; 31:2; 33:8,19; 34:31,32; 35:2,5,10; **Ezra** 2:63,68; 3:8–10; 9:9,15; 10:13–15; **Neh.** 3:1,3,6,13–15; 4:9(3),13(7); 6:1,7; 7:1,3,65; 8:4,5; 9:2; 10:32(33); 12:31,39,40,44; 13:11,19,30; **Esth.** 3:4; 4:5,14; 5:1,2; 6:5; 7:7,9; 8:4,11; 9:2,16; **Job** 4:16; 8:15; 14:2; 29:8; 30:20; 32:16; 34:24; 37:14; **Ps.** 1:1; 10:1; 18:33(34); 19:9(10); 26:12; 30:7(8); 31:8(9); 33:9,11; 38:11(12); 76:7(8); 102:26(27); 104:6; 105:10; 106:23,30; 107:25; 109:6,31; 111:3,10; 112:3,9; 119:90,91; 122:2; 130:3; 134:1; 135:2; 147:17; 148:6; **Prov.** 12:7; 25:6; 27:4; 29:4; **Eccl.** 1:4; 2:9; 4:12,15; 8:3; **Song** 2:9; **Isa.** 3:13; 6:2; 10:32; 11:10; 21:6,8; 36:2,13; 44:11; 46:7; 47:12,13; 48:13; 50:8; 59:14; 61:5; 66:22; **Jer.** 4:6; 6:16; 7:2,10; 14:6; 15:1,19; 17:19; 18:20; 19:14; 23:18,22; 26:2; 28:5; 32:14; 35:19; 36:21; 40:10; 44:15; 46:15,21; 48:11,19,45; 49:19; 50:44; 51:50; 52:12; **Ezek.** 1:21,24,25; 2:1,2; 3:23,24; 8:11; 9:2; 10:3,6,17–19; 11:23; 13:5; 17:14; 21:21(26); 22:14,30; 24:11; 27:29; 29:7(KJV, *ʻāmad* [5976]; NIV, *māʻad* [4571]); 31:14; 33:26; 37:10; 40:3; 43:6; 44:11,15,24; 46:2; 47:10; **Dan.** 1:4,5,19; 2:2; 8:3,4,6,7,15,18,22, 23,25; 10:11,13,16,17; 11:1,2–4,6–8,11, 13–17,20,21,25,31; 12:1,5,13; **Hos.** 10:9; 13:13; **Amos** 2:15; **Obad.** 1:11,14; **Jon.** 1:15; **Mic.** 5:4(3); **Nah.** 1:6; 2:8(9); **Hab.** 2:1; 3:6,11; **Hag.** 2:5; **Zech.** 1:8,10,11; 3:1,3–5,7; 4:14; 14:4,12; **Mal.** 3:2.

5976. עָמַד ʿāmad̲ **verb**
(to quake, alternate spelling of
māʿad̲ [4571]; to be at a stand)
Ezek. 29:7(NIV, māʿad̲ [4571]).

5977. עֹמֶד ʿōmed̲ **masc. noun**
(place, standing place)
2 Chr. 30:16; 34:31; 35:10; Neh. 8:7;
9:3; 13:11; Dan. 8:17,18; 10:11; 11:1.

5978. עִמָּד ʿimmād̲ **prep.**
(with, to)
Gen. 21:23; 31:7; Ex. 17:2; Deut. 5:31;
32:34,39; Judg. 17:10; Job 6:4; 9:35;
10:12; 13:19,20; 17:2; 23:6,10; 28:14;
29:5,6,20; 31:13; Ps. 23:4; 50:11; 55:18;
101:6.

5979. עֶמְדָּה ʿemdāh **fem. noun**
(support, protection)
Mic. 1:11.

5980. עֻמָּה ʿummāh **prep.**
(next to, close to, against, alongside)
Ex. 25:27; 28:27; 37:14; 38:18; 39:20;
Lev. 3:9; 2 Sam. 16:13; 1 Kgs. 7:20;
1 Chr. 24:31; 25:8; 26:12,16; Neh.
12:24; Eccl. 5:16(15); 7:14; Ezek.
1:20,21; 3:8,13; 10:19; 11:22; 40:18;
42:7; 45:6,7; 48:13,18,21.

5981. עֻמָּה ʿummāh **proper noun**
(Ummah)
Josh. 19:30.

5982. עַמּוּד ʿammûd̲ **masc. noun**
(pillar, column)
Ex. 13:21,22; 14:19,24; 26:32,37;
27:10–12,14–17; 33:9,10; 35:11,17;
36:36,38; 38:10–12,14,15,17,19,28;
39:33,40; 40:18; Num. 3:36,37; 4:31,32;
12:5; 14:14; Deut. 31:15; Judg. 16:25,
26,29; 20:40; 1 Kgs. 7:2,3,6,15–22,
41,42; 2 Kgs. 11:14; 23:3; 25:13,16,17;
1 Chr. 18:8; 2 Chr. 3:15–17; 4:12,13;
23:13; Neh. 9:12,19; Esth. 1:6; Job 9:6;
26:11; Ps. 75:3(4); 99:7; Prov. 9:1; Song
3:10; 5:15; Jer. 1:18; 27:19; 52:17,20–22;
Ezek. 40:49; 42:6.

5983. עַמּוֹן ʿammôn **masc. proper
noun**
(Ammon)
Gen. 19:38; Num. 21:24; Deut.
2:19,37; 3:11,16; Josh. 12:2; 13:10,25;
Judg. 3:13; 10:6,7,9,11,17,18; 11:4–6,
8,9,12–15,27–33,36; 12:1–3; 1 Sam.
11:11; 12:12; 14:47; 2 Sam. 8:12; 10:1–3,
6,8,10,11,14,19; 11:1; 12:9,26,31; 17:27;
1 Kgs. 11:7,33; 2 Kgs. 23:13; 24:2;
1 Chr. 18:11; 19:1–3,6,7,9,11,12,15,19;
20:1,3; 2 Chr. 20:1,10,22,23; 27:5;
Ps. 83:7(8); Isa. 11:14; Jer. 9:26(25);
25:21; 27:3; 40:11,14; 41:10,15; 49:1,2,6;
Ezek. 21:20(25),28(33); 25:2,3,5,10;
Dan. 11:41; Amos 1:13; Zeph. 2:8,9.

5984. עַמּוֹנִי ʿammôniy **masc.
proper noun**
(Ammonite)
Deut. 2:20; 23:3(4); 1 Sam. 11:1,2;
2 Sam. 23:37; 1 Kgs. 11:1,5; 14:21,31;
1 Chr. 11:39; 2 Chr. 12:13; 20:1; 24:26;
26:8; Ezra 9:1; Neh. 2:10,19; 4:3(3:35),
7(1); 13:1,23.

5985. עַמּוֹנִית ʿammōniyṯ **fem.
proper noun**
(Ammonitess; NIV, ʿammôniy
[5984])
1 Kg. 14:21,31; 2 Chr. 12:13; 24:29.

5986. עָמוֹס ʿāmôs **masc. proper
noun**
(the prophet Amos)
Amos 1:1; 7:8,10–12,14; 8:2.

5987. עָמוֹק ʿāmôq **masc. proper
noun**
(Amok)
Neh. 12:7,20.

5988. עַמִּיאֵל ʿammiyʾēl **masc.
proper noun**

(Ammiel)
Num. 13:12; **2 Sam.** 9:4,5; 17:27; **1 Chr.** 3:5; 26:5.

5989. עַמִּיהוּד *ʿammiyhûḏ* **masc. proper noun**
(Ammihud)
Num. 1:10; 2:18; 7:48,53; 10:22; 34:20, 28; **2 Sam.** 13:37; **1 Chr.** 7:26; 9:4.

5990. עַמִּיזָבָד *ʿammiyzaḇaḏ* **masc. proper noun**
(Ammizabad)
1 Chr. 27:6.

5991. עַמִּיחוּר *ʿammiyḥûr* **masc. proper noun**
(Ammichur)
2 Sam. 13:37(KJV, NASB, NIV, [Qe] *ʿammiyhûḏ* [5989]).

5992. עַמִּינָדָב *ʿammiynāḏaḇ* **masc. proper noun**
(Amminadab)
Ex. 6:23; **Num.** 1:7; 2:3; 7:12,17; 10:14; **Ruth** 4:19,20; **1 Chr.** 2:10; 6:22(7); 15:10,11.

5993. עַמִּי נָדִיב *ʿammiy nāḏiyḇ* **masc. proper noun**
(Ammi-nadib)
Song 6:12(NASB, NIV, *ʿam* [597] and *nāḏiyḇ* [5081]).

5994. עֲמִיק *ᵃmiyq* **Aram. adj.**
(profound, deep)
Dan. 2:22.

5995. עָמִיר *ʿāmiyr* **masc. noun**
(sheaf of grain, fallen grain)
Jer. 9:22(21); **Amos** 2:13; **Mic.** 4:12; **Zech.** 12:6.

5996. עַמִּישַׁדָּי *ʿammiyšaddāy* **masc. proper noun**
(Ammishaddai)
Num. 1:12; 2:25; 7:66,71; 10:25.

5997. עָמִית *ʿāmiyṯ* **masc. noun**
(neighbor, associate)
Lev. 6:2(5:21); 18:20; 19:11,15,17; 24:19; 25:14,15,17; **Zech.** 13:7.

5998. עָמַל *ʿāmal* **verb**
(to labor, to toil)
Ps. 127:1; **Prov.** 16:26; **Eccl.** 1:3; 2:11,19–21; 5:16(15),18(17); 8:17; **Jon.** 4:10.

5999. עָמָל *ʿāmāl* **masc. noun**
(work, labor, trouble, misery)
Gen. 41:51; **Num.** 23:21; **Deut.** 26:7; **Judg.** 10:16; **Job** 3:10; 4:8; 5:6,7; 7:3; 11:16; 15:35; 16:2; **Ps.** 7:14(15),16(17); 10:7,14; 25:18; 55:10(11); 73:5,16; 90:10; 94:20; 105:44; 107:12; 140:9(10); **Prov.** 24:2; 31:7; **Eccl.** 1:3; 2:10,11,18–22,24; 3:13; 4:4,6,8,9; 5:15(14),18(17),19(18); 6:7; 8:15; 9:9; 10:15; **Isa.** 10:1; 53:11; 59:4; **Jer.** 20:18; **Hab.** 1:3,13.

6000. עָמָל *ʿāmāl* **masc. proper noun**
(Amal)
1 Chr. 7:35.

6001. עָמֵל *ʿāmēl* **adj.**
(working, suffering)
Judg. 5:26; **Job** 3:20; 20:22; **Prov.** 16:26; **Eccl.** 2:18,22; 3:9; 4:8; 9:9.

6002. עֲמָלֵק *ᵃmālēq* **masc. proper noun**
(Amalek, Amalekite)
Gen. 36:12,16; **Ex.** 17:8–11,13,14,16; **Num.** 13:29; 24:20; **Deut.** 25:17,19; **Judg.** 3:13; 5:14; 6:3,33; 7:12; 10:12; **1 Sam.** 14:48; 15:2,3,5–8,18,20,32; 28:18; 30:18; **2 Sam.** 1:1; 8:12; **1 Chr.** 1:36; 4:43; 18:11; **Ps.** 83:7(8).

6003. עֲמָלֵקִי *ᵃmālēqiy* **masc. proper noun**
(Amalekite)
Gen. 14:7; **Num.** 14:25,43,45; **Judg.** 12:15; **1 Sam.** 15:6,15; 27:8; 30:1,13; **2 Sam.** 1:8,13.

6004. עָמַם *ʿāmam* **verb**
(to grow dim, to be hidden)
Lam. 4:1; **Ezek.** 28:3; 31:8.

6005. עִמָּנוּאֵל *ʿimmānû'ēl* **masc. proper noun**
(Immanuel)
Isa. 7:14; 8:8.

6006. A. עָמַס *ʿāmas* **verb**
(to load, to carry a load)
Gen. 44:13; **1 Kgs.** 12:11; **2 Chr.** 10:11; **Neh.** 13:15; **Ps.** 68:19(20); **Isa.** 46:1,3; **Zech.** 12:3.
B. עָמַשׂ *ʿāmaś* **verb**
(to load, to carry a load)
Neh. 4:17(11).

6007. עֲמַסְיָה *ʿamasyāh* **masc. proper noun**
(Amasiah)
2 Chr. 17:16.

6008. עַמְעָד *ʿamʿāḏ* **masc. proper noun**
(Amad)
Josh. 19:26.

6009. עָמַק *ʿāmaq* **verb**
(to be profound, to be deep)
Ps. 92:5(6); **Isa.** 7:11; 29:15; 30:33; 31:6; **Jer.** 49:8,30; **Hos.** 5:2; 9:9.

6010. I. עֵמֶק *ʿēmeq* **masc. noun**
(valley, plain)
Gen. 14:3,8,10,17; 37:14; **Num.** 14:25; **Josh.** 7:24,26; 8:13; 10:12; 13:19,27; 15:7,8; 17:16; 18:16,21(NASB, NIV, see I); **Judg.** 1:19,34; 5:15; 6:33; 7:1,8,12; 18:28; **1 Sam.** 6:13; 17:2,19; 21:9(10); 31:7; **2 Sam.** 5:18,22; 18:18; 23:13; **1 Kgs.** 20:28; **1 Chr.** 10:7; 11:15; 12:15; 14:9,13; 27:29; **2 Chr.** 20:26; **Job** 39:10,21; **Ps.** 60:6(8); 65:13(14); 84:6(7); 108:7(8); **Song** 2:1; **Isa.** 17:5; 22:7; 28:21; 65:10; **Jer.** 21:13; 31:40; 47:5; 48:8; 49:4; **Hos.** 1:5; 2:15(17); **Joel** 3:2(4:2),12(4:12),14(4:14); **Mic.** 1:4.
II. עֵמֶק קְצִיץ *ʿēmeq qᵉṣiyṣ* **proper noun**
(Emek Keziz)
Josh. 18:21(KJV, see I).

6011. עֹמֶק *ʿōmeq* **masc. noun**
(depth)
Prov. 25:3.

6012. עָמֵק *ʿāmēq* **adj.**
(deep, unintelligible)
Isa. 33:19; **Ezek.** 3:5,6.

6013. עָמֹק *ʿāmōq* **adj.**
(deep, mysterious)
Lev. 13:3,4,25,30–32,34; **Job** 11:8; 12:22; **Ps.** 64:6(7); **Prov.** 18:4; 20:5; 22:14; 23:27; **Eccl.** 7:24; **Ezek.** 23:32.

6014. עָמַר *ʿāmar* **verb**
(to treat as a slave, to bind)
Deut. 21:14; 24:7; **Ps.** 129:7.

6015. עֲמַר *ʿamar* **Aram. masc. noun**
(wool)
Dan. 7:9.

6016. I. עֹמֶר *ʿōmer* **masc. noun**
(a sheaf of grain)
Lev. 23:10–12,15; **Deut.** 24:19; **Ruth** 2:7,15; **Job** 24:10.
II. עֹמֶר *ʿōmer* **masc. noun**
(an omer; measure of grain)
Ex. 16:16,18,22,32,33,36.

6017. עֲמֹרָה *ʿamōrāh* **proper noun**
(Gomorrah)
Gen. 10:19; 13:10; 14:2,8,10,11; 18:20; 19:24,28; **Deut.** 29:23(22); 32:32; **Isa.** 1:9,10; 13:19; **Jer.** 23:14; 49:18; 50:40; **Amos** 4:11; **Zeph.** 2:9.

6018. עָמְרִי *ʿomriy* **masc. proper noun**
(Omri)

1 **Kgs.** 16:16,17,21–23,25,27–30; **2 Kgs.** 8:26; **1 Chr.** 7:8; 9:4; 27:18; **2 Chr.** 22:2; **Mic.** 6:16.

6019. עַמְרָם *'amrām* **masc. proper noun**
(Amram)
Ex. 6:18,20; **Num.** 3:19; 26:58,59; **1 Chr.** 6:2(5:28),3(5:29),18(3); 23:12,13; 24:20; **Ezra** 10:34.

6020. עַמְרָמִי *'amrāmiy* **masc. proper noun**
(Amramite, descendant of *'amrām* [6019])
Num. 3:27; **1 Chr.** 26:23.

6021. A. עֲמָשָׂא *'amāśā'* **masc. proper noun**
(Amasa: general of Absalom's army)
2 Sam. 17:25; 19:13(14); 20:4,5,8–10, 12; **1 Kgs.** 2:5,32; **1 Chr.** 2:17.
B. עֲמָשָׂא *'amāśā'* **masc. proper noun**
(Amasa: Ephraimite prince)
2 Chr. 28:12.

6022. A. עֲמָשַׂי *'amāśay* **masc. proper noun**
(Amasai: ancestor of Samuel)
1 Chr. 6:25(10),35(20).
B. עֲמָשַׂי *'amāśay* **masc. proper noun**
(Amasai: warrior of David)
1 Chr. 12:18.
C. עֲמָשַׂי *'amāśay* **masc. proper noun**
(Amasai: musician in David's day)
1 Chr. 15:24.
D. עֲמָשַׂי *'amāśay* **masc. proper noun**
(Amasai: Levite in Hezekiah's day)
2 Chr. 29:12.

6023. עֲמַשְׁסַי *'amaššay* **masc. proper noun**
(Amashai)
Neh. 11:13.

6024. עֲנָב *'anāb* **proper noun**
(Anab)
Josh. 11:21; 15:50.

6025. עֵנָב *'ēnāḇ* **masc. noun**
(grape, raisin)
Gen. 40:10,11; 49:11; **Lev.** 25:5; **Num.** 6:3; 13:20,23; **Deut.** 23:24(25); 32:14,32; **Neh.** 13:15; **Isa.** 5:2,4; **Jer.** 8:13; **Hos.** 3:1; 9:10; **Amos** 9:13.

6026. עָנַג *'ānag* **verb**
(to be delicate, to take delight)
Deut. 28:56; **Job** 22:26; 27:10; **Ps.** 37:4,11; **Isa.** 55:2; 57:4; 58:14; 66:11; **Jer.** 6:2.

6027. עֹנֶג *'ōneg* **masc. noun**
(delight, luxury)
Isa. 13:22; 58:13.

6028. עָנֹג *'ānōg* **adj.**
(delicate, sensitive)
Deut. 28:54,56; **Isa.** 47:1.

6029. עָנַד *'ānaḏ* **verb**
(to tie, to bind)
Job 31:36; **Prov.** 6:21.

6030. I. עָנָה *'ānāh* **verb**
(to answer, to respond, to reply, to testify)
Gen. 18:27; 23:5,10,14; 24:50; 27:37,39; 30:33; 31:14,31,36,43; 34:13; 35:3; 40:18; 41:16; 42:22; 45:3; **Ex.** 4:1; 15:21(NIV, see II); 19:8,19; 20:16; 23:2; 24:3; 32:18; **Num.** 11:28; 22:18; 23:12,26; 32:31; 35:30; **Deut.** 1:14,41; 5:20(17); 19:16, 18; 20:11; 21:7; 25:9; 26:5; 27:14,15; 31:21; **Josh.** 1:16; 7:20; 9:24; 22:21; 24:16; **Judg.** 5:29; 7:14; 8:8; 18:14; 19:28; 20:4; **Ruth** 1:21; 2:6,11; **1 Sam.** 1:15,17; 4:17,20; 7:9; 8:18; 9:8,12,17, 19,21; 10:12; 12:3; 14:12,28,37,39; 16:18; 18:7(NASB, NIV, see II); 20:10,28,32; 21:4(5),5(6); 22:9,14; 23:4; 25:10; 26:6,

14,22; 28:6,15; 29:9; 30:22; **2 Sam.** 1:16; 4:9; 13:32; 14:18,19; 15:21; 19:21(22), 42(43),43(44); 20:20; 22:42; **1 Kgs.** 1:28,36,43; 2:22,30; 3:27; 12:7,13; 13:6; 18:21,24,26,29,37; 20:4,11; **2 Kgs.** 1:10–12; 3:11; 4:29; 7:2,13,19; 18:36; **1 Chr.** 12:17; 21:26,28; **2 Chr.** 10:13; 29:31; 34:15; **Ezra** 10:2,12; **Neh.** 8:6; **Esth.** 5:7; 7:3; **Job** 1:7,9; 2:2,4; 3:2; 4:1; 5:1; 6:1; 8:1; 9:1,3,14–16,32; 11:1,2; 12:1,4; 13:22; 14:15; 15:1,2,6; 16:1,3,8; 18:1; 19:1,7,16; 20:1,3; 21:1; 22:1; 23:1,5; 25:1; 26:1; 30:20; 31:35; 32:1,6,12, 15–17,20; 33:12,13; 34:1; 35:1,12; 38:1; 40:1–3,5,6; 42:1; **Ps.** 3:4(5); 4:1(2); 13:3(4); 17:6; 18:41(42); 20:1(2),6(7), 9(10); 22:2(3),21(22); 27:7; 34:4(5); 38:15(16); 55:2(3),19(20)(KJV, NIV, *ʿānāh* [6031,I]); 60:5(7); 65:5(6); 69:13(14), 16(17),17(18); 81:7(8); 86:1,7; 91:15; 99:6,8; 102:2(3); 108:6(7); 118:5,21; 119:26,42,145,172(NASB, NIV, see II); 120:1; 138:3; 143:1,7; **Prov.** 1:28; 15:28; 18:23; 21:13; 25:18; 26:4,5; **Eccl.** 5:20 (19)(NASB, NIV, *ʿānāh* [6031,II]); 10:19; **Song** 2:10; 5:6; **Isa.** 3:9; 14:10,32; 21:9; 25:5; 30:19; 36:21; 41:17; 46:7; 49:8; 50:2; 58:9; 59:12; 65:12,24; 66:4; **Jer.** 7:13,27; 11:5; 14:7; 23:35,37; 25:30; 33:3; 35:17; 42:4; 44:15,20; **Ezek.** 14:4,7; **Hos.** 2:21(23),22(24); 5:5; 7:10; 14:8(9); **Joel** 2:19; **Amos** 7:14; **Jon.** 2:2(3); **Mic.** 3:4; 6:3,5; **Hab.** 2:2,11; **Hag.** 2:12–14; **Zech.** 1:10–13; 3:4; 4:4–6,11,12; 6:4,5; 10:6; 13:9; **Mal.** 2:12.

II. עָנָה *ʿānāh* **verb**
(to sing, to shout, to howl)
Ex. 15:21(KJV, NASB, see I); 32:18; **Num.** 21:17; **1 Sam.** 18:7(KJV, see I); 21:11; 29:5; **Ezra** 3:11; **Ps.** 119:172(KJV, see I); 147:7; **Isa.** 13:22; 27:2; **Jer.** 51:14; **Hos.** 2:15.

III. לְעַנּוֹת *l*ᵉ*ʿannôṯ* **proper noun**
(Leannoth; part of song title Mahalath Leannoth; prep. *l* plus piel partic. of *ʿānāh* [6030,I])
Ps. 88:[title](1).

6031. I. עָנָה *ʿānāh* **verb**
(to be afflicted, to be oppressed, to be humbled)
Gen. 15:13; 16:6,9; 31:50; 34:2; **Ex.** 1:11,12; 10:3; 22:22(21),23(22); **Lev.** 16:29,31; 23:27,29,32; **Num.** 24:24; 29:7; 30:13(14); **Deut.** 8:2,3,16; 21:14; 22:24,29; 26:6; **Judg.** 16:5,6,19; 19:24; 20:5; **2 Sam.** 7:10; 13:12,14,22,32; **1 Kgs.** 2:26; 8:35; 11:39; **2 Kgs.** 17:20; **2 Chr.** 6:26; **Ezra** 8:21; **Job** 30:11; 37:23; **Ps.** 35:13; 55:19(20)(NASB, *ʿānāh* [6030,I]); 88:7(8); 89:22(23); 90:15; 94:5; 102:23(24); 105:18; 107:17; 116:10; 119:67,71,75,107; 132:1; **Eccl.** 1:13(KJV, NIV, see II); **Isa.** 31:4; 53:4,7; 58:3,5,10; 60:14; 64:12(11); **Lam.** 3:33; 5:11; **Ezek.** 22:10,11; **Dan.** 10:12; **Nah.** 1:12; **Zeph.** 3:19; **Zech.** 10:2.

II. עָנָה *ʿānāh* **verb**
(to be occupied, to be exercised)
Eccl. 1:13(NASB, see I); 3:10; 5:20 (KJV, *ʿānāh* [6030,I]).

6032. עֲנָה *ʿᵃnāh* **Aram. verb**
(to answer, to reply; corr. to Hebrew 6030,I)
Dan. 2:5,7,8,10,15,20,26,27,47; 3:9, 14,16,19,24–26,28; 4:19(16),30(27); 5:7,10,13,17; 6:12(13),13(14),16(17), 20(21); 7:2.

6033. עֲנָה *ʿᵃnāh* **Aram. verb**
(to be afflicted, to be poor, to be needy; corr. to Hebr. 6031,I)
Dan. 4:27(24).

6034. עֲנָה *ʿᵃnāh* **masc. proper noun**
(Anah)
Gen. 36:2,14,18,20,24,25,29; **1 Chr.** 1:38,40,41.

6035. עָנָו *ʿānāw* **adj.**
(poor, oppressed, afflicted, humble)
Num. 12:3; **Job** 24:4(NASB, NIV, *ʿāniy* [6041]); **Ps.** 10:12(KJV, [Kᵉ] *ʿāniy*

[6041]),17; 22:26(27); 25:9; 34:2(3); 37:11; 69:32(33); 79:9(10); 147:6; 149:4; **Prov.** 3:34(KJV, [K^e] *ʿāniy* [6041]); 14:21(KJV, [K^e] *ʿāniy* [6041]); 16:19 (KJV, NASB, [K^e] *ʿāniy* [6041]); **Isa.** 11:4; 29:19; 61:1; **Amos** 2:7; **Zeph.** 2:3.

6036. עָנוּב *ʿānûb̲* **masc. proper noun**
(Anub)
1 Chr. 4:8.

6037. עַנְוָה *ʿanwāh* **fem. noun**
(gentleness, meekness, humility)
Ps. 45:4(5)(NASB, NIV, *ʿanāwāh* [6038]).

6038. עֲנָוָה *ʿanāwāh* **fem. noun**
(gentleness, humility)
2 Sam. 22:36; **Ps.** 18:35(36); 45:4(5)(KJV, *ʿanwāh* [6037]); **Prov.** 15:33; 18:12; 22:4; **Zeph.** 2:3.

6039. עֱנוּת *ʿenût̲* **fem. noun**
(affliction)
Ps. 22:24(25).

6040. עֳנִי *ʿoniy* **masc. noun**
(affliction, misery)
Gen. 16:11; 29:32; 31:42; 41:52; **Ex.** 3:7,17; 4:31; **Deut.** 16:3; 26:7; **1 Sam.** 1:11; **2 Sam.** 16:12; **2 Kgs.** 14:26; **1 Chr.** 22:14; **Neh.** 9:9; **Job** 10:15; 30:16,27; 36:8,15,21; **Ps.** 9:13(14); 25:18; 31:7(8); 44:24(25); 88:9(10); 107:10,41; 119:50,92,153; **Prov.** 31:5; **Isa.** 48:10; **Lam.** 1:3,7,9; 3:1,19.

6041. עָנִי *ʿāniy* **adj.**
(poor, afflicted)
Ex. 22:25(24); **Lev.** 19:10; 23:22; **Deut.** 15:11; 24:12,14,15; **2 Sam.** 22:28; **Job** 24:4(KJV, [foll. some Hebr. MSS] *ʿānāw* [6035]),9,14; 29:12; 34:28; 36:6,15; **Ps.** 9:12(13)(NASB, NIV, [Q^e] *ʿānāw* [6035]), 18(19); 10:2,9,12(NASB, NIV, [Q^e] *ʿānāw* [6035]); 12:5(6); 14:6; 18:27(28); 22:24(25); 25:16; 34:6(7); 35:10; 37:14; 40:17(18); 68:10(11); 69:29(30); 70:5(6); 72:2,4,12; 74:19,21; 82:3; 86:1; 88:15(16); 102:[title](1); 109:16,22; 140:12(13); **Prov.** 3:34(NASB, NIV, [Q^e] *ʿānāw* [6035]); 14:21(NASB, NIV, [Q^e] *ʿānāw* [6035]); 15:15; 16:19(NIV, [Q^e] *ʿānāw* [6035]); 22:22; 30:14; 31:9,20; **Eccl.** 6:8; **Isa.** 3:14,15; 10:2,30; 14:32; 26:6; 32:7; 41:17; 49:13; 51:21; 54:11; 58:7; 66:2; **Jer.** 22:16; **Ezek.** 16:49; 18:12,17; 22:29; **Amos** 8:4; **Hab.** 3:14; **Zeph.** 3:12; **Zech.** 7:10; 9:9; 11:7,11.

6042. עֻנִּי *ʿunniy* **masc. proper noun**
(Unni)
1 Chr. 15:18,20; **Neh.** 12:9.

6043. עֲנָיָה *ʿanāyāh* **masc. proper noun**
(Anaiah)
Neh. 8:4; 10:22(23).

6044. עָנִים *ʿāniym* **proper noun**
(Anim)
Josh. 15:50.

6045. עִנְיָן *ʿinyān* **masc. noun**
(task, burden)
Eccl. 1:13; 2:23,26; 3:10; 4:8; 5:3(2), 14(13); 8:16.

6046. עָנֵם *ʿānēm* **proper noun**
(Anem)
1 Chr. 6:73(58).

6047. עֲנָמִים *ʿanāmiym* **masc. pl. proper noun**
(Anamim)
Gen. 10:13; **1 Chr.** 1:11.

6048. עֲנַמֶּלֶךְ *ʿanammelek̲* **masc. proper noun**
(Anammelech)
2 Kgs. 17:31.

6049. I. עָנַן *ʿānan* **verb**
(to bring a cloud, to cause a cloud to appear)
Gen. 9:14.

II. עָנַן *ʿānan* **verb**
(to practice sorcery, to practice witchcraft)
Lev. 19:26; **Deut.** 18:10,14; **Judg.** 9:37; **2 Kgs.** 21:6; **2 Chr.** 33:6; **Isa.** 2:6; 57:3; **Jer.** 27:9; **Mic.** 5:12(11).

6050. עֲנַן *ʿanan* **Aram. masc. noun**
(cloud; corr. to Hebr. 6051)
Dan. 7:13.

6051. עָנָן *ʿānān* **masc. noun**
(cloud)
Gen. 9:13,14,16; **Ex.** 13:21,22; 14:19,20,24; 16:10; 19:9,16; 24:15,16,18; 33:9,10; 34:5; 40:34–38; **Lev.** 16:2,13; **Num.** 9:15–22; 10:11,12,34; 11:25; 12:5,10; 14:14; 16:42(17:7); **Deut.** 1:33; 4:11; 5:22(19); 31:15; **1 Kgs.** 8:10,11; **2 Chr.** 5:13,14; **Neh.** 9:12,19; **Job** 7:9; 26:8,9; 37:11,15; 38:9; **Ps.** 78:14; 97:2; 99:7; 105:39; **Isa.** 4:5; 44:22; **Jer.** 4:13; **Lam.** 3:44; **Ezek.** 1:4,28; 8:11; 10:3,4; 30:3,18; 32:7; 34:12; 38:9,16; **Hos.** 6:4; 13:3; **Joel** 2:2; **Nah.** 1:3; **Zeph.** 1:15.

6052. עָנָן *ʿānān* **masc. proper noun**
(Anan)
Neh. 10:26(27).

6053. עֲנָנָה *ʿanānāh* **fem. noun**
(cloud)
Job 3:5.

6054. עֲנָנִי *ʿanāniy* **masc. proper noun**
(Anani)
1 Chr. 3:24.

6055. A. עֲנַנְיָה *ʿanānᵉyāh* **masc. proper noun**
(Ananiah: grandfather of Azariah)
Neh. 3:23.
B. עֲנַנְיָה *ʿanānᵉyāh* **masc. proper noun**
(Ananiah: city in Nehemiah's day)
Neh. 11:32.

6056. עֲנַף *ʿanap̱* **Aram. masc. noun**
(branch [of a tree]; corr. to Hebr. 6057)
Dan. 4:12(9),14(11),21(18).

6057. עָנָף *ʿānāp̱* **masc. noun**
(branch [of a tree])
Lev. 23:40; **Ps.** 80:10(11); **Ezek.** 17:8,23; 31:3; 36:8; **Mal.** 4:1(3:19).

6058. עָנֵף *ʿānēp̱* **adj.**
(full of branches)
Ezek. 19:10.

6059. עָנַק *ʿānaq* **verb**
(to place around the neck as a necklace; to supply liberally)
Deut. 15:14; **Ps.** 73:6.

6060. עֲנָק *ʿanāq* **masc. noun**
(necklace, chain)
Judg. 8:26; **Prov.** 1:9; **Song** 4:9.

6061. עֲנָק *ʿanāq* **masc. proper noun**
(Anak)
Num. 13:22,28,33; **Deut.** 9:2; **Josh.** 15:13,14; 21:11; **Judg.** 1:20.

6062. עֲנָקִי *ʿanāqiy* **masc. proper noun**
(Anakite, pl. Anakim)
Deut. 1:28; 2:10,11,21; 9:2; **Josh.** 11:21,22; 14:12,15.

6063. A. עָנֵר *ʿānēr* **masc. proper noun**
(Aner: ally of Abraham)
Gen. 14:13,24.
B. עָנֵר *ʿānēr* **masc. proper noun**
(Aner: city in Manasseh)
1 Chr. 6:70(55).

6064. עָנַשׁ *'ānaš* **verb**
(to fine, to punish, to impose a levy)
Ex. 21:22; **Deut.** 22:19; **2 Chr.** 36:3; **Prov.** 17:26; 21:11; 22:3; 27:12; **Amos** 2:8.

6065. עֲנָשׁ *'anāš* **Aram. masc. noun**
(confiscation; corr. to Hebr. 6064)
Ezra 7:26.

6066. עֹנֶשׁ *'ōneš* **masc. noun**
(penalty, fine, levy)
2 Kgs. 23:33; **Prov.** 19:19.

6067. עֲנָת *'anāṯ* **masc. proper noun**
(Anath)
Judg. 3:31; 5:6.

6068. A. עֲנָתוֹת *'anāṯôṯ* **proper noun**
(Anathoth: a city of the Benjamites)
Josh. 21:18; **1 Kgs.** 2:26; **1 Chr.** 6:60(45); **Ezra** 2:23; **Neh.** 7:27; 11:32; **Isa.** 10:30; **Jer.** 1:1; 11:21,23; 32:7–9.
B. עֲנָתוֹת *'anāṯôṯ* **masc. proper noun**
(Anathoth: grandson of Benjamin)
1 Chr. 7:8.
C. עֲנָתוֹת *'anāṯôṯ* **masc. proper noun**
(Anathoth: covenanter in Nehemiah's day)
Neh. 10:19(20).

6069. עַנְּתוֹתִי *'anneṯôṯiy* **masc. proper noun**
(Anathothite)
2 Sam. 23:27; **1 Chr.** 11:28; 12:3; 27:12; **Jer.** 29:27.

6070. עַנְתֹתִיָּה *'anṯōṯiyyāh* **masc. proper noun**
(Anthothijah)
1 Chr. 8:24.

6071. עָסִיס *'āsiys* **masc. noun**
(sweet wine, new wine, nectar)
Song 8:2; **Isa.** 49:26; **Joel** 1:5; 3:18(4:18); **Amos** 9:13.

6072. עָסַס *'āsas* **verb**
(to trample, to tread down)
Mal. 4:3(3:21).

6073. עֳפָאִים *'opa'yim* **masc. pl. noun**
(branches)
Ps. 104:12.

6074. עֳפִי *'opiy* **Aram. masc. noun**
(branches, foliage; corr. to Hebr. 6073)
Dan. 4:12(9),14(11),21(18).

6075. עָפַל *'āpal* **verb**
(to be proud, to presume)
Num. 14:44; **Hab.** 2:4.

6076. I. עֹפֶל *'ōpel* **masc. noun**
(hill, fort, citadel)
2 Kgs. 5:24; **Isa.** 32:14; **Mic.** 4:8.
II. עֹפֶל *'ōpel* **masc. noun**
(tumor)
Deut. 28:27; **1 Sam.** 5:6,9,12; 6:4,5.

6077. עֹפֶל *'ōpel* **proper noun**
(Ophel)
2 Chr. 27:3; 33:14; **Neh.** 3:26,27; 11:21.

6078. עָפְנִי *'opniy* **proper noun**
(Ophni)
Josh. 18:24.

6079. I. עַפְעַף *'ap'ap* **masc. noun**
(eyelid)
Job 16:16; 41:18(10); **Ps.** 11:4; 132:4; **Prov.** 4:25; 6:4,25; 30:13; **Jer.** 9:18(17).
II. עַפְעַף *'ap'ap* **masc. noun**
(first rays of the dawn)
Job 3:9.

6080. עָפַר *'āpar* **verb**
(to throw dust, to throw dirt)
2 Sam. 16:13.

6081. A. עֵפֶר *'ēp̱er* **masc. proper noun**
(Epher: son of Midian)
Gen. 25:4; **1 Chr.** 1:33.
B. עֵפֶר *'ēp̱er* **masc. proper noun**
(Epher: son of Ezra)
1 Chr. 4:17.
C. עֵפֶר *'ēp̱er* **masc. proper noun**
(Epher: head of a family sent into exile)
1 Chr. 5:24.

6082. עֹפֶר *'ōp̱er* **masc. noun**
(young deer, fawn)
Song 2:9,17; 4:5; 7:3(4); 8:14.

6083. עָפָר *'āp̱ār* **masc. noun**
(dust, soil, rubbish)
Gen. 2:7; 3:14,19; 13:16; 18:27; 26:15; 28:14; **Ex.** 8:16(12),17(13); **Lev.** 14:41,42,45; 17:13; **Num.** 5:17; 19:17; 23:10; **Deut.** 9:21; 28:24; 32:24; **Josh.** 7:6; **1 Sam.** 2:8; **2 Sam.** 16:13; 22:43; **1 Kgs.** 16:2; 18:38; 20:10; **2 Kgs.** 13:7; 23:4,6,12,15; **2 Chr.** 1:9; **Neh.** 4:2(3:34), 10(4); **Job** 2:12; 4:19; 5:6; 7:5,21; 8:19; 10:9; 14:8,19; 16:15; 17:16; 19:25; 20:11; 21:26; 22:24; 27:16; 28:2,6; 30:6,19; 34:15; 38:38; 39:14; 40:13; 41:33(25); 42:6; **Ps.** 7:5(6); 18:42(43); 22:15(16), 29(30); 30:9(10); 44:25(26); 72:9; 78:27; 102:14(15); 103:14; 104:29; 113:7; 119:25; **Prov.** 8:26; **Eccl.** 3:20; 12:7; **Isa.** 2:10,19; 25:12; 26:5,19; 29:4; 34:7,9; 40:12; 41:2; 47:1; 49:23; 52:2; 65:25; **Lam.** 2:10; 3:29; **Ezek.** 24:7; 26:4,12; 27:30; **Dan.** 12:2; **Amos** 2:7; **Mic.** 1:10; 7:17; **Hab.** 1:10; **Zeph.** 1:17; **Zech.** 9:3.

6084. A. עָפְרָה *'op̱rāh* **proper noun**
(Ophrah: town of Benjamin)
Josh. 18:23; **1 Sam.** 13:17.
B. עָפְרָה *'op̱rāh* **proper noun**
(Ophrah: town west of the Jordan River, Gideon's hometown)
Judg. 6:11,24; 8:27,32; 9:5.
C. עָפְרָה *'op̱rāh* **masc. proper noun**
(Ophrah: son of Meonothai)
1 Chr. 4:14.

6085. A. עֶפְרוֹן *'ep̱rôn* **masc. proper noun**
(Ephron, a Hittite)
Gen. 23:8,10,13,14,16,17; 25:9; 49:29,30; 50:13.
B. עֶפְרוֹן *'ep̱rôn* **proper noun**
(Mount Ephron)
Josh. 15:9.
C. עֶפְרוֹן *'ep̱rôn* **proper noun**
(the city Ephron)
2 Chr. 13:19.

6086. עֵץ *'ēṣ* **masc. noun**
(tree, wood, timber, stick, plank)
Gen. 1:11,12,29; 2:9,16,17; 3:1–3,6,8, 11,12,17,22,24; 6:14; 18:4,8; 22:3,6,7,9; 23:17; 40:19; **Ex.** 7:19; 9:25; 10:5,15; 15:25; 25:5,10,13,23,28; 26:15,26; 27:1,6; 30:1,5; 31:5; 35:7,24,33; 36:20,31; 37:1,4,10,15,25,28; 38:1,6; **Lev.** 1:7,8, 12,17; 3:5; 4:12; 6:12(5); 11:32; 14:4, 6,45,49,51,52; 15:12; 19:23; 23:40; 26:4, 20; 27:30; **Num.** 13:20; 15:32,33; 19:6; 31:20; 35:18; **Deut.** 4:28; 10:1,3; 12:2; 16:21; 19:5; 20:19,20; 21:22,23; 22:6; 28:36,42,64; 29:11(10),17(16); **Josh.** 2:6; 8:29; 9:21,23,27; 10:26,27; **Judg.** 6:26; 9:8–15,48; **1 Sam.** 6:14; 17:7(KJV, NASB, [K^{e}] *ḥēṣ* [2671]); **2 Sam.** 5:11; 6:5; 21:19; 23:7; 24:22; **1 Kgs.** 4:33(5:13); 5:6(20),8(22),10(24),18(32); 6:10,15,23, 31–34; 9:11; 10:11,12; 14:23; 15:22; 17:10,12; 18:23,33(34),38; **2 Kgs.** 3:19, 25; 6:4,6; 12:11(12),12(13); 16:4; 17:10; 19:18; 22:6; **1 Chr.** 14:1; 16:33; 20:5; 21:23; 22:4,14,15; 29:2; **2 Chr.** 2:8–10(7–9),14(13),16(15); 3:5; 9:10, 11; 16:6; 28:4; 34:11; **Ezra** 3:7; **Neh.** 2:8; 8:4,15; 9:25; 10:34(35),35(36), 37(38); 13:31; **Esth.** 2:23; 5:14; 6:4; 7:9,10; 8:7; 9:13,25; **Job** 14:7; 19:10; 24:20; 41:27(19); **Ps.** 1:3; 74:5; 96:12;

104:16; 105:33; 148:9; **Prov.** 3:18; 11:30; 13:12; 15:4; 26:20,21; **Eccl.** 2:5,6; 10:9; 11:3; **Song** 2:3; 3:9; 4:14; **Isa.** 7:2; 10:15,19; 30:33; 37:19; 40:20; 41:19; 44:13,14,19,23; 45:20; 55:12; 56:3; 57:5; 60:17; 65:22; **Jer.** 2:20,27; 3:6,9,13; 5:14; 7:18,20; 10:3,8; 11:19; 17:2,8; 28:13; 46:22; **Lam.** 4:8; 5:4,13; **Ezek.** 6:13; 15:2, 3,6; 17:24; 20:28,32,47(21:3); 21:10(15); 24:10; 26:12; 31:4,5,8,9,14–16,18; 34:27; 36:30; 37:16,17,19,20; 39:10; 41:16, 22,25; 47:7,12; **Hos.** 4:12; **Joel** 1:12,19; 2:22; **Hab.** 2:11,19; **Hag.** 1:8; 2:19; **Zech.** 5:4; 12:6.

6087. I. עָצַב *ʻāṣab̲* **verb**
(to grieve, to cause pain)
Gen. 6:6; 34:7; 45:5; **1 Sam.** 20:3,34; **2 Sam.** 19:2(3); **1 Kgs.** 1:6; **1 Chr.** 4:10; **Neh.** 8:10,11; **Ps.** 56:5(6); 78:40; **Eccl.** 10:9; **Isa.** 54:6; 63:10.
II. עָצַב *ʻāṣab̲* **verb**
(to fashion, to shape)
Job 10:8; **Jer.** 44:19.

6088. עֲצִיב *ʻaṣiyb̲* **Aram. verb**
(to be grieved, to be troubled; corr. to Hebr. 6087,I)
Dan. 6:20(21).

6089. I. עֶצֶב *ʻeṣeb̲* **masc. noun**
(sorrow, pain, labor)
Gen. 3:16; **Ps.** 127:2; **Prov.** 5:10; 10:22; 14:23; 15:1.
II. עֶצֶב *ʻeṣeb̲* **masc. noun**
(jar, pot)
Jer. 22:28(KJV, see III).
III. עֶצֶב *ʻeṣeb̲* **masc. noun**
(idol, image)
Jer. 22:28(NASB, NIV, see II).

6090. I. עֹצֶב *ʻōṣeb̲* **masc. noun**
(sorrow, pain, hurtfulness)
1 Chr. 4:9; **Ps.** 139:24; **Isa.** 14:3; 48:5.
II. עֹצֶב *ʻōṣeb̲* **masc. noun**
(idol)
Isa. 48:5.

6091. עָצָב *ʻāṣāb̲* **masc. noun**
(idol, image)
1 Sam. 31:9; **2 Sam.** 5:21; **1 Chr.** 10:9; **2 Chr.** 24:18; **Ps.** 106:36,38; 115:4; 135:15; **Isa.** 10:11; 46:1; **Jer.** 50:2; **Hos.** 4:17; 8:4; 13:2; 14:8(9); **Mic.** 1:7; **Zech.** 13:2.

6092. עָצֵב *ʻāṣēb̲* **masc. noun**
(worker, work)
Isa. 58:3.

6093. עִצָּבוֹן *ʻiṣṣāb̲ôn* **masc. noun**
(pain, sorrow, toil)
Gen. 3:16,17; 5:29.

6094. עַצֶּבֶת *ʻaṣṣeb̲et̲* **fem. noun**
(grief, sorrow, wound)
Job 9:28; **Ps.** 16:4; 147:3; **Prov.** 10:10; 15:13.

6095. עָצָה *ʻāṣāh* **verb**
(to shut, to wink [the eye])
Prov. 16:30.

6096. עָצֶה *ʻāṣeh* **masc. noun**
(backbone)
Lev. 3:9.

6097. עֵצָה *ʻēṣāh* **fem. coll. noun**
(trees)
Jer. 6:6.

6098. עֵצָה *ʻēṣāh* **fem. noun**
(counsel, advice, plan)
Deut. 32:28; **Judg.** 20:7; **2 Sam.** 15:31,34; 16:20,23; 17:7,14,23; **1 Kgs.** 1:12; 12:8,13,14; **2 Kgs.** 18:20; **1 Chr.** 12:19; **2 Chr.** 10:8,13,14; 22:5; 25:16; **Ezra** 4:5; 10:3,8; **Neh.** 4:15(9); **Job** 5:13; 10:3; 12:13; 18:7; 21:16; 22:18; 29:21; 38:2; 42:3; **Ps.** 1:1; 13:2(3); 14:6; 20:4(5); 33:10,11; 73:24; 106:13,43; 107:11; 119:24; **Prov.** 1:25,30; 8:14; 12:15; 19:20,21; 20:5,18; 21:30; 27:9; **Isa.** 5:19; 8:10; 11:2; 14:26; 16:3; 19:3,11,17; 25:1; 28:29; 29:15; 30:1;

36:5; 40:13; 44:26; 46:10,11; 47:13; **Jer.** 18:18,23; 19:7; 32:19; 49:7,20,30; 50:45; **Ezek.** 7:26; 11:2; **Hos.** 10:6; **Mic.** 4:12; **Zech.** 6:13.

6099. עָצוּם *'āṣûm* **adj.**
(mighty, strong)
Gen. 18:18; **Ex.** 1:9; **Num.** 14:12; 22:6; 32:1; **Deut.** 4:38; 7:1; 9:1,14; 11:23; 26:5; **Josh.** 23:9; **Ps.** 10:10; 35:18; 135:10; **Prov.** 7:26; 18:18; 30:26; **Isa.** 8:7; 53:12; 60:22; **Dan.** 8:24; 11:25; **Joel** 1:6; 2:2,5,11; **Amos** 5:12; **Mic.** 4:3,7; **Zech.** 8:22.

6100. עֶצְיוֹן גֶּבֶר *'eṣyôn geḇer* **proper noun**
(Ezion Geber)
Num. 33:35,36; **Deut.** 2:8; **1 Kgs.** 9:26; 22:48(49); **2 Chr.** 8:17; 20:36.

6101. עָצַל *'āṣal* **verb**
(to hesitate, to delay)
Judg. 18:9.

6102. עָצֵל *'āṣēl* **adj.**
(sluggish, lazy)
Prov. 6:6,9; 10:26; 13:4; 15:19; 19:24; 20:4; 21:25; 22:13; 24:30; 26:13–16.

6103. עַצְלָה *'aṣlāh* **fem. noun**
(laziness, sluggishness)
Prov. 19:15; **Eccl.** 10:18.

6104. עַצְלוּת *'aṣlûṯ* **fem. noun**
(idleness, sluggishness)
Prov. 31:27.

6105. I. עָצַם *'āṣam* **verb**
(to be numerous, to be mighty)
Gen. 26:16; **Ex.** 1:7,20; **Ps.** 38:19(20); 40:5(6),12(13); 69:4(5); 105:24; 139:17; **Isa.** 31:1; **Jer.** 5:6; 15:8; 30:14,15; 50:17; **Dan.** 8:8,24; 11:23.
II. עָצַם *'āṣam* **verb**
(to shut, to close)
Isa. 29:10; 33:15.

6106. עֶצֶם *'eṣem* **fem. noun**
(bone, body)
Gen. 2:23; 7:13; 17:23,26; 29:14; 50:25; **Ex.** 12:17,41,46,51; 13:19; 24:10; **Lev.** 23:14,21,28–30; **Num.** 9:12; 19:16,18; 24:8; **Deut.** 32:48; **Josh.** 5:11; 10:27; 24:32; **Judg.** 9:2; 19:29; **1 Sam.** 31:13; **2 Sam.** 5:1; 19:12(13),13(14); 21:12–14; **1 Kgs.** 13:2,31; **2 Kgs.** 13:21; 23:14,16, 18,20; **1 Chr.** 10:12; 11:1; **2 Chr.** 34:5; **Job** 2:5; 4:14; 7:15; 10:11; 19:20; 20:11; 21:23,24; 30:17,30; 33:19,21; 40:18; **Ps.** 6:2(3); 22:14(15),17(18); 31:10(11); 32:3; 34:20(21); 35:10; 38:3(4); 42:10(11); 51:8(10); 53:5(6); 102:3(4),5(6); 109:18; 141:7; **Prov.** 3:8; 12:4; 14:30; 15:30; 16:24; **Eccl.** 11:5; **Isa.** 38:13; 58:11; 66:14; **Jer.** 8:1; 20:9; 23:9; **Lam.** 1:13; 3:4; 4:7,8; **Ezek.** 2:3; 6:5; 24:2,4,5,10; 32:27; 37:1,3–5,7,11; 39:15; 40:1; **Amos** 2:1; 6:10; **Mic.** 3:2,3; **Hab.** 3:16.

6107. עֶצֶם *'eṣem* **proper noun**
(Ezem)
Josh. 15:29; 19:3; **1 Chr.** 4:29.

6108. I. עֹצֶם *'ōṣem* **masc. noun**
(strength, might)
Deut. 8:17; **Job** 30:21; **Nah.** 3:9(KJV, NASB, *'oṣmāh* [6109]).
II. עֹצֶם *'ōṣem* **masc. noun**
(frame, substance)
Ps. 139:15.

6109. עָצְמָה *'oṣmāh* **fem. noun**
(strength, potence)
Isa. 40:29; 47:9; **Nah.** 3:9(NIV, *'ōṣem* [6108,I]).

6110. עַצֻמוֹת *'aṣumôṯ* **fem. pl. noun**
(strong reasons, arguments)
Isa. 41:21.

6111. עַצְמוֹן *'aṣmôn* **proper noun**
(Azmon)
Num. 34:4,5; **Josh.** 15:4.

6112. עֵצֶן *'ēṣen* **masc. proper noun**
(Eznite)
2 Sam. 23:8(NIV, does not translate).

6113. עָצַר *'āṣar* **verb**
(to restrain, to shut in, to keep in slavery)
Gen. 16:2; 20:18; **Num.** 16:48(17:13),50(17:15); 25:8; **Deut.** 11:17; 32:36; **Judg.** 13:15,16; **1 Sam.** 9:17; 21:5(6),7(8); **2 Sam.** 24:21,25; **1 Kgs.** 8:35; 14:10; 18:44; 21:21; **2 Kgs.** 4:24; 9:8; 14:26; 17:4; **1 Chr.** 12:1; 21:22; 29:14; **2 Chr.** 2:6(5); 6:26; 7:13; 13:20; 14:11(10); 20:37; 22:9; **Neh.** 6:10; **Job** 4:2; 12:15; 29:9; **Ps.** 106:30; **Isa.** 66:9; **Jer.** 20:9; 33:1; 36:5; 39:15; **Dan.** 10:8,16; 11:6.

6114. I. עֶצֶר *'eṣer* **masc. noun**
(restraint)
Judg. 18:7(NIV, see II).
II. עֶצֶר *'eṣer* **masc. noun**
(prosperity)
Judg. 18:7(KJV, NASB, see I).

6115. עֹצֶר *'ōṣer* **masc. noun**
(oppression, barrenness)
Ps. 107:39; **Prov.** 30:16; **Isa.** 53:8.

6116. עֲצָרָה *'aṣārāh,* עֲצֶרֶת *'aṣeret* **fem. noun**
(assembly, solemn meeting)
Lev. 23:36; **Num.** 29:35; **Deut.** 16:8; **2 Kgs.** 10:20; **2 Chr.** 7:9; **Neh.** 8:18; **Isa.** 1:13; **Jer.** 9:2(1); **Joel** 1:14; 2:15; **Amos** 5:21.

6117. עָקַב *'āqab* **verb**
(to deceive, to take by the heel, to hold back)
Gen. 27:36; **Job** 37:4; **Jer.** 9:4(3); **Hos.** 12:3(4).

6118. עֵקֶב *'ēqeb* **masc. noun**
(consequence, because)
Gen. 22:18; 26:5; **Num.** 14:24; **Deut.** 7:12; 8:20; **2 Sam.** 12:6,10; **Ps.** 19:11(12); 40:15(16); 70:3(4); 119:33,112; **Prov.** 22:4; **Isa.** 5:23; **Amos** 4:12.

6119. עָקֵב *'āqēb* **masc. noun**
(heel, footprint)
Gen. 3:15; 25:26; 49:17,19; **Josh.** 8:13; **Judg.** 5:22; **Job** 18:9; **Ps.** 41:9(10); 49:5(6); 56:6(7); 77:19(20); 89:51(52); **Song** 1:8; **Jer.** 13:22.

6120. I. עָקֵב *'āqēb* **masc. noun**
(heel)
Ps. 49:5(6)(NASB, NIV, see II).
II. עָקֵב *'āqēb* **masc. noun**
(foe, deceiver)
Ps. 49:5(6)(KJV, see I).

6121. I. עָקֹב *'āqōb* **adj.**
(deceitful)
Jer. 17:9.
II. עָקֹב *'āqōb* **adj.**
(covered with footprints)
Hos. 6:8.
III. עָקֹב *'āqōb* **adj.**
(rough ground, hilly)
Isa. 40:4.

6122. עָקְבָה *'oqbāh* **fem. noun**
(deceitfulness)
2 Kgs. 10:19.

6123. עָקַד *'āqad* **verb**
(to bind, to tie up)
Gen. 22:9.

6124. עָקֹד *'āqōd* **adj.**
(streaked, striped)
Gen. 30:35,39,40; 31:8,10,12.

6125. I. עָקָה *'āqāh* **fem. noun**
(oppression, pressure)
Ps. 55:3(4)(NIV, see II).
II. עָקָה *'āqāh* **fem. noun**
(staring)
Ps. 55:3(4)(KJV, NASB, see I).

6126. A. עַקּוּב *ʿaqqûḇ* **masc. proper noun**
(Akkub: descendant of Zerubbabel)
1 Chr. 3:24.
B. עַקּוּב *ʿaqqûḇ* **masc. proper noun**
(Akkub: gatekeeper in Solomon's time and head of a family of gatekeepers)
1 Chr. 9:17; **Ezra** 2:42; **Neh.** 7:45.
C. עַקּוּב *ʿaqqûḇ* **masc. proper noun**
(Akkub: gatekeeper in Nehemiah's time)
Neh. 11:19; 12:25.
D. עַקּוּב *ʿaqqûḇ* **masc. proper noun**
(Akkub: head of a family of temple servants)
Ezra 2:45.
E. עַקּוּב *ʿaqqûḇ* **masc. proper noun**
(Akkub: a Levite who helped Ezra expound the Law)
Neh. 8:7.

6127. עָקַל *ʿāqal* **verb**
(to be perverted, to be made wrong)
Hab. 1:4.

6128. עֲקַלְקַל *ᵃqalqal* **adj.**
(roundabout, winding, crooked [of paths or ways])
Judg. 5:6; **Ps.** 125:5.

6129. עֲקַלָּתוֹן *ᵃqallāṯôn* **adj.**
(crooked, twisted)
Isa. 27:1.

6130. עֲקָן *ᵃqān* **masc. proper noun**
(Akan)
Gen. 36:27.

6131. I. עָקַר *ʿāqar* **verb**
(to cut tendons, to hamstring)
Gen. 49:6(KJV, see II); **Josh.** 11:6,9; **2 Sam.** 8:4; **1 Chr.** 18:4.
II. עָקַר *ʿāqar* **verb**
(to pluck up, to root out)
Gen. 49:6(NASB, NIV, see I); **Eccl.** 3:2; **Zeph.** 2:4.

6132. עֲקַר *ᵃqar* **Aram. verb**
(to pluck up by the roots; corr. to Hebr. 6131,II)
Dan. 7:8.

6133. עֵקֶר *ʿēqer* **masc. noun**
(descendant, member of one's family)
Lev. 25:47.

6134. עֵקֶר *ʿēqer* **masc. proper noun**
(Eker)
1 Chr. 2:27.

6135. עָקָר *ʿāqār* **adj.**
(to be barren, childless)
Gen. 11:30; 25:21; 29:31; **Ex.** 23:26; **Deut.** 7:14; **Judg.** 13:2,3; **1 Sam.** 2:5; **Job** 24:21; **Ps.** 113:9; **Isa.** 54:1.

6136. עִקַּר *ʿiqqar* **Aram. masc. noun**
(root, stump; corr. to Hebr. 6133)
Dan. 4:15(12),23(20),26(23).

6137. I. עַקְרָב *ʿaqrāḇ* **masc. noun**
(scorpion)
Deut. 8:15; **1 Kgs.** 12:11,14; **2 Chr.** 10:11,14; **Ezek.** 2:6.
II. עַקְרַבִּים *ʿaqrabbiym* **proper noun**
(Akrabbim)
Num. 34:4(NIV, see *maᵃlēh ʿaqrabbiym* [4610,I]); **Josh.** 15:3(NIV, see *maᵃlēh ʿaqrabbiym* [4610,I]; KJV, *maᵃlēh ʿaqrabbiym* [4610,II]); **Judg.** 1:36(NIV, see *maᵃlēh ʿaqrabbiym* [4610,I]).

6138. עֶקְרוֹן *ʿeqrôn* **proper noun**
(Ekron)
Josh. 13:3; 15:11,45,46; 19:43; **Judg.** 1:18; **1 Sam.** 5:10; 6:16,17; 7:14; 17:52;

2 Kgs. 1:2,3,6,16; **Jer.** 25:20; **Amos** 1:8; **Zeph.** 2:4; **Zech.** 9:5,7.

6139. עֶקְרוֹנִי *ʿeqrôniy* **masc. proper noun**
(Ekronite)
Josh. 13:3; **1 Sam.** 5:10.

6140. עָקַשׁ *ʿāqaš* **verb**
(to be twisted, to be perverse; to prove something perverted)
Job 9:20; **Prov.** 10:9; 28:18; **Isa.** 59:8; **Mic.** 3:9.

6141. עִקֵּשׁ *ʿiqqēš* **adj.**
(perverse, crooked)
Deut. 32:5; **2 Sam.** 22:27; **Ps.** 18:26(27); 101:4; **Prov.** 2:15; 8:8; 11:20; 17:20; 19:1; 22:5; 28:6.

6142. עִקֵּשׁ *ʿiqqēš* **masc. proper noun**
(Ikkesh)
2 Sam. 23:26; **1 Chr.** 11:28; 27:9.

6143. עִקְּשׁוּת *ʿiqq^{e}šûṯ* **fem. noun**
(perversion, deceitfulness)
Prov. 4:24; 6:12.

6144. עָר *ʿār* **proper noun**
(Ar)
Num. 21:15,28; **Deut.** 2:9,18,29; **Isa.** 15:1.

6145. עָר *ʿār* **masc. noun**
(enemy)
1 Sam. 28:16; **Ps.** 139:20.

6146. עָר *ʿār* **Aram. masc. noun**
(enemy; corr. to Hebr. 6145)
Dan. 4:19(16).

6147. A. עֵר *ʿēr* **masc. proper noun**
(Er; son of Judah)
Gen. 38:3,6,7; 46:12; **Num.** 26:19; **1 Chr.** 2:3.

B. עֵר *ʿēr* **masc. proper noun**
(Er; grandson of Judah)
1 Chr. 4:21.

6148. I. עָרַב *ʿāraḇ* **verb**
(to put up security, to pledge security; to associate with)
Gen. 43:9; 44:32; **2 Kgs.** 18:23; **Neh.** 5:3; **Job** 17:3; **Ps.** 104:34; 106:35; 119:122; **Prov.** 6:1; 11:15; 17:18; 20:16; 22:26; 27:13; **Isa.** 36:8; 38:14; **Jer.** 30:21; **Ezek.** 27:9,27.

II. ערב *ʿāraḇ* **verb**
(to mingle together, to associate)
Ezra 9:2; **Ps.** 106:35; **Prov.** 14:10; 20:19; 24:21.

6149. עָרַב *ʿāraḇ* **verb**
(to be sweet, to be pleasant)
Ps. 104:34; **Prov.** 3:24; 13:19; **Jer.** 6:20; 31:26; **Ezek.** 16:37; **Hos.** 9:4; **Mal.** 3:4.

6150. עָרַב *ʿāraḇ* **verb**
(to become evening; to grow dark)
Judg. 19:9; **1 Sam.** 17:16; **Isa.** 24:11.

6151. עֲרַב *ʿ^{a}raḇ* **Aram. verb**
(to mingle together, to combine; corr. to Hebr. 6148,II)
Dan. 2:41,43.

6152. עֲרָב *ʿ^{a}rāḇ*, עֲרַב *ʿ^{a}raḇ* **proper noun**
(Arabia)
1 Kgs. 10:15; **2 Chr.** 9:14; **Isa.** 21:13; **Jer.** 25:24; **Ezek.** 27:21.

6153. עֶרֶב *ʿereḇ* **masc. noun**
(evening, dusk, night)
Gen. 1:5,8,13,19,23,31; 8:11; 19:1; 24:11,63; 29:23; 30:16; 49:27; **Ex.** 12:6,18; 16:6,8,12,13; 18:13,14; 27:21; 29:39,41; 30:8; **Lev.** 6:20(13); 11:24,25, 27,28,31,32,39,40; 14:46; 15:5–8,10,11, 16–19,21–23,27; 17:15; 22:6; 23:5,32; 24:3; **Num.** 9:3,5,11,15,21; 19:7,8,10,19, 21,22; 28:4,8; **Deut.** 16:4,6; 23:11(12);

28:67; **Josh.** 5:10; 7:6; 8:29; 10:26; **Judg.** 19:16; 20:23,26; 21:2; **Ruth** 2:17; **1 Sam.** 14:24; 20:5; 30:17; **2 Sam.** 1:12; 11:2,13; **1 Kgs.** 17:6; 22:35; **2 Kgs.** 16:15; **1 Chr.** 16:40; 23:30; **2 Chr.** 2:4(3); 13:11; 18:34; 31:3; **Ezra** 3:3; 9:4,5; **Esth.** 2:14; **Job** 4:20; 7:4; **Ps.** 30:5(6); 55:17(18); 59:6(7),14(15); 65:8(9); 90:6; 104:23; 141:2; **Prov.** 7:9; **Eccl.** 11:6; **Isa.** 17:14; **Jer.** 6:4; **Ezek.** 12:4,7; 24:18; 33:22; 46:2; **Dan.** 8:14,26; 9:21; **Hab.** 1:8; **Zeph.** 2:7; 3:3; **Zech.** 14:7.

6154. I. עֶרֶב *ʿēreḇ* **masc. noun**
(knitted material, wool)
Lev. 13:48,49,51–53,56–59.
II. עֶרֶב *ʿēreḇ* **masc. noun**
(foreign people; people who have mingled with Israel)
Ex. 12:38; **Neh.** 13:3; **Jer.** 25:20,24; 50:37; **Ezek.** 30:5(NASB, NIV, untranslated).

6155. עֶרֶב *ʿereḇ* **masc. noun**
(willow tree, poplar tree)
Lev. 23:40; **Job** 40:22; **Ps.** 137:2; **Isa.** 15:7; 44:4.

6156. עָרֵב *ʿārēḇ* **adj.**
(sweet)
Prov. 20:17; **Song** 2:14.

6157. עָרֹב *ʿārōḇ* **masc. noun**
(swarm [of flies])
Ex. 8:21(17),22(18),24(20),29(25), 31(27); **Ps.** 78:45; 105:31.

6158. עֹרֵב *ʿōrēḇ* **masc. noun**
(raven)
Gen. 8:7; **Lev.** 11:15; **Deut.** 14:14; **1 Kgs.** 17:4,6; **Job** 38:41; **Ps.** 147:9; **Prov.** 30:17; **Song** 5:11; **Isa.** 34:11.

6159. עוֹרֵב *ʿôrēḇ* **masc. proper noun**
(Oreb)
Judg. 7:25; 8:3; **Ps.** 83:11(12); **Isa.** 10:26.

6160. I. עֲרָבָה *ʿarāḇāh* **fem. noun**
(plain, desert plain)
Num. 22:1; 26:3,63; 31:12; 33:48–50; 35:1; 36:13; **Deut.** 1:1(NASB, NIV, see II),7(NASB, NIV, see II); 2:8(NASB, NIV, see II); 3:17(NASB, NIV, see II); 4:49 (NASB, NIV, see II); 11:30(NASB, NIV, see II); 34:1,8; **Josh.** 3:16(NASB, NIV, see II); 4:13; 5:10; 8:14(NIV, see II); 11:2(NASB, NIV, see II),16(NASB, NIV, see II); 12:1 (NASB, NIV, see II),3(NASB, NIV, see II), 8(NASB, NIV, see II); 13:32; 18:18; **1 Sam.** 23:24(NASB, NIV, see II); **2 Sam.** 2:29(NASB, NIV, see II); 4:7(NASB, NIV, see II); 15:28; 17:16; **2 Kgs.** 14:25(NASB, NIV, see II); 25:4(NASB, NIV, see II),5; **Job** 24:5; 39:6; **Ps.** 68:4(5)(KJV, see III; NIV, [conj.] *ʿāḇ* [5645]); **Isa.** 33:9(NIV, see II); 35:1(NASB, see II),6(NASB, see II); 40:3; 41:19; 51:3; **Jer.** 2:6; 5:6(KJV, *ʿereḇ* [6153]); 17:6; 39:4(NASB, NIV, see II),5; 50:12; 51:43; 52:7(NASB, NIV, see II),8; **Ezek.** 47:8(NASB, NIV, see II); **Amos** 6:14(NASB, NIV, see II); **Zech.** 14:10(NIV, see II).
II. עֲרָבָה *ʿarāḇāh* **fem. noun**
(the Arabah; technical name for the plains region)
Deut. 1:1(KJV, see I),7(KJV, see I); 2:8(KJV, see I); 3:17(KJV, see I); 4:49(KJV, see I); 11:30(KJV, see I); **Josh.** 3:16(KJV, see I); 8:14(KJV, NASB, see I); 11:2(KJV, see I),16(KJV, see I); 12:1(KJV, see I), 3(KJV, see I),8(KJV, see I); 18:18; **1 Sam.** 23:24(KJV, see I); **2 Sam.** 2:29(KJV, see I); 4:7(KJV, see I); **2 Kgs.** 14:25 (KJV, see I); 25:4(KJV, see I); **Isa.** 33:9 (KJV, NASB, see I); 35:1(KJV, NIV, see I), 6(KJV, NIV, see I); **Jer.** 39:4(KJV, see I); 52:7(KJV, see I); **Ezek.** 47:8(KJV, see I); **Amos** 6:14(KJV, see I); **Zech.** 14:109(KJV, NASB, see I).
III. עֲרָבָה *ʿarāḇāh* **fem. noun**
(heaven)
Ps. 68:4(5)(NASB, see I; NIV, [conj.] *ʿāḇ* [5645]).

6161. עֲרֻבָּה *ʿarubbāh* **fem. noun**
(security pledge, assurance)
1 Sam. 17:18; Prov. 17:18.

6162. עֵרָבוֹן *ʿērāḇôn* **masc. noun**
(security pledge)
Gen. 38:17,18,20.

6163. עַרְבִי *ʿarḇiy*, עֲרָבִי *ʿarāḇiy* **masc. proper noun**
(Arabian: inhabitant of Arabia)
2 Chr. 17:11; 21:16; 22:1; 26:7; **Neh.** 2:19; 4:7(1); 6:1; **Isa.** 13:20; **Jer.** 3:2.

6164. עַרְבָתִי *ʿarḇāṯiy* **masc. proper noun**
(Arbathite: inhabitant of Beth Arabah [1026])
2 Sam. 23:31; 1 Chr. 11:32.

6165. עָרַג *ʿārag* **verb**
(to pant for, to long for)
Ps. 42:1(2); **Joel** 1:20.

6166. A. עֲרָד *ʿarāḏ* **masc. proper noun**
(Arad: Canaanite king)
Num. 21:1(NASB, NIV, see II); 33:40(NASB, NIV, see II).
B. עֲרָד *ʿarāḏ* **masc. proper noun**
(Arad: Canaanite city)
Judg. 1:16.
C. עֲרָד *ʿarāḏ* **masc. proper noun**
(Arad: son of Beriah)
1 Chr. 8:15.

6167. עֲרָד *ʿarāḏ* **Aram. masc. noun**
(wild donkey; corr. to Hebr. 6171)
Dan. 5:21.

6168. עָרָה *ʿārāh* **verb**
(to expose, to uncover, to empty)
Gen. 24:20; Lev. 20:18,19; 2 Chr. 24:11; Ps. 37:35; 137:7; 141:8; Isa. 3:17; 22:6; 32:15; 53:12; **Lam.** 4:21; **Hab.** 3:13; **Zeph.** 2:14.

6169. עָרוֹת *ʿārôṯ* **fem. pl. noun**
(plants, bulrushes)
Isa. 19:7.

6170. עֲרוּגָה *ʿarûḡāh* **fem. noun**
(garden bed, plot)
Song 5:13; 6:2; **Ezek.** 17:7,10.

6171. עָרוֹד *ʿārôḏ* **masc. noun**
(wild donkey)
Job 39:5.

6172. עֶרְוָה *ʿerwāh* **fem. noun**
(nakedness, indecent exposure or behavior)
Gen. 9:22,23; 42:9,12; **Ex.** 20:26; 28:42; **Lev.** 18:6–19; 20:11,17–21; **Deut.** 23:14(15); 24:1; 1 Sam. 20:30; Isa. 20:4; 47:3; **Lam.** 1:8; **Ezek.** 16:8,36,37; 22:10; 23:10,18,29; **Hos.** 2:9(11).

6173. עַרְוָה *ʿarwāh* **Aram. fem. noun**
(dishonor; corr. to Hebr. 6172)
Ezra 4:14.

6174. עָרוֹם *ʿārôm* **adj.**
(naked, exposed)
Gen. 2:25; 1 Sam. 19:24; Job 1:21; 22:6; 24:7,10; 26:6; **Eccl.** 5:15(14); **Isa.** 20:2–4; 58:7; **Hos.** 2:3(5); **Amos** 2:16; **Mic.** 1:8.

6175. עָרוּם *ʿārûm* **adj.**
(prudent, crafty)
Gen. 3:1; **Job** 5:12; 15:5; **Prov.** 12:16,23; 13:16; 14:8,15,18; 22:3; 27:12.

6176. עֲרוֹעֵר *ʿarôʿēr* **masc. noun**
(juniper, health)
Jer. 17:6(NIV, *ʿarʿār* [6199,II]); 48:6.

6177. A. עֲרוֹעֵר *ʿarôʿēr*, עֲרֹעֵר *ʿarōʿēr*, עַרְעוֹר *ʿarʿôr* **proper noun**
(Aroer: city on the Arnon River in Transjordan)

Num. 32:34; **Deut.** 2:36; 3:12; 4:48; **Josh.** 12:2; 13:9,16; **Judg.** 11:26,33; **2 Sam.** 24:5; **2 Kgs.** 10:33; **1 Chr.** 5:8; **Isa.** 17:2; **Jer.** 48:19.
B. עֲרוֹעֵר *ʿărôʿēr* **proper noun**
(Aroer: city near Rabbah)
Josh. 13:25.
C. עֲרֹעֵר *ʿărōʿēr* **proper noun**
(Aroer: city in southern Judah)
1 Sam. 30:28.

6178. I. עָרוּץ *ʿārûṣ* **fem. noun**
(cliff)
Job 30:6(NASB, see II; NIV, see III).
II. עָרוּץ *ʿārûṣ* **adj.**
(dreadful)
Job 30:6(KJV, see II; NIV, see III).
III. עָרוּץ *ʿārûṣ* **adj.**
(dry)
Job 30:6(KJV, see I; NASB, see II).

6179. עֵרִי *ʿēriy* **masc. proper noun**
(Eri)
Gen. 46:16; **Num.** 26:16.

6180. עֵרִי *ʿēriy* **masc. proper noun**
(Erite; descendents of *ʿēriy* [6179])
Num. 26:16.

6181. עֶרְיָה *ʿeryāh* **fem. noun**
(bareness; nakedness)
Ezek. 16:7,22,39; 23:29; **Mic.** 1:11; **Hab.** 3:9.

6182. עֲרִיסָה *ʿărîysāh* **fem. noun**
(dough, ground meal)
Num. 15:20,21; **Neh.** 10:37(38); **Ezek.** 44:30.

6183. עֲרִיפִים *ʿărîyp̱iym* **masc. pl. noun**
(clouds, heavens)
Isa. 5:30.

6184. עָרִיץ *ʿāriyṣ* **adj.**
(ruthless, strong, violent)
Job 6:23; 15:20; 27:13; **Ps.** 37:35; 54:3(5); 86:14; **Prov.** 11:16; **Isa.** 13:11; 25:3–5; 29:5,20; 49:25; **Jer.** 15:21; 20:11; **Ezek.** 28:7; 30:11; 31:12; 32:12.

6185. עֲרִירִי *ʿăriyriy* **adj.**
(childless)
Gen. 15:2; **Lev.** 20:20,21; **Jer.** 22:30.

6186. I. עָרַךְ *ʿārak̲* **verb**
(to arrange, to set in order, to prepare)
Gen. 14:8; 22:9; **Ex.** 27:21; 40:4,23; **Lev.** 1:7,8,12; 6:12(5); 24:3,4,8; **Num.** 23:4; **Josh.** 2:6; **Judg.** 20:20,22,30,33; **1 Sam.** 4:2; 17:2,8,21; **2 Sam.** 10:8–10, 17; 23:5; **1 Kgs.** 18:33; **1 Chr.** 12:8(KJV, *ʿāḏar* [5737,II]),33,35,36,38(39)(KJV, *ʿāḏar* [5737,II]; NIV, *ʿāḏar* [5737,III]); 19:9–11,17; **2 Chr.** 13:3; 14:10(9); **Job** 6:4; 13:18; 23:4; 28:17,19; 32:14; 33:5; 36:19; 37:19; **Ps.** 5:3(4); 23:5; 40:5(6); 50:21; 78:19; 89:6(7); 132:17; **Prov.** 9:2; **Isa.** 21:5; 30:33; 40:18; 44:7; 65:11; **Jer.** 6:23; 46:3; 50:9,14,42; **Ezek.** 23:41; **Joel** 2:5.
II. ערך *ʿārak̲* **verb**
(to set a value, to level a tax)
Lev. 27:8,12,14; **2 Kgs.** 23:35.

6187. עֵרֶךְ *ʿērek̲* **masc. noun**
(estimation, evaluation, value, arrangement in order)
Ex. 40:4,23; **Lev.** 5:15,18; 6:6(5:25); 27:2–8,12,13,15–19,23,25,27; **Num.** 18:16; **Judg.** 17:10; **2 Kgs.** 12:4(5); 23:35; **Job** 28:13; 41:12(4); **Ps.** 55:13(14).

6188. עָרֵל *ʿārēl* **verb**
(to consider uncircumcised, to consider forbidden; to be exposed)
Lev. 19:23; **Hab.** 2:16.

6189. עָרֵל *ʿārēl* **adj.**
(uncircumcised)

Gen. 17:14; **Ex.** 6:12,30; 12:48; **Lev.** 19:23; 26:41; **Josh.** 5:7; **Judg.** 14:3; 15:18; **1 Sam.** 14:6; 17:26,36; 31:4; **2 Sam.** 1:20; **1 Chr.** 10:4; **Isa.** 52:1; **Jer.** 6:10; 9:26(25); **Ezek.** 28:10; 31:18; 32:19,21,24–30,32; 44:7,9.

6190. עָרְלָה *ʿorlāh* **fem. noun**
(foreskin; that which is cut off in circumcision)
Gen. 17:11,14,23–25; 34:14; **Ex.** 4:25; **Lev.** 12:3; 19:23; **Deut.** 10:16; **Josh.** 5:3; **1 Sam.** 18:25,27; **2 Sam.** 3:14; **Jer.** 4:4; 9:25(24).

6191. עָרַם *ʿāram* **verb**
(to be shrewd, to be crafty, to be cunning, to be prudent)
1 Sam. 23:22; **Ps.** 83:3(4); **Prov.** 15:5; 19:25.

6192. עָרַם *ʿāram* **verb**
(to be piled up, to be gathered together)
Ex. 15:8.

6193. עֹרֶם *ʿōrem* **masc. noun**
(craftiness, shrewdness)
Job 5:13.

6194. עֲרֵמָה *ʿarēmāh* **fem. noun**
(heap, pile [of grain, rubble, etc.])
Ruth 3:7; **2 Chr.** 31:6–9; **Neh.** 4:2(3:34); 13:15; **Song** 7:2(3); **Jer.** 50:26; **Hag.** 2:16.

6195. עָרְמָה *ʿormāh* **fem. noun**
(prudence, craftiness, guile)
Ex. 21:14; **Josh.** 9:4; **Prov.** 1:4; 8:5,12.

6196. עַרְמוֹן *ʿarmôn* **masc. noun**
(chestnut tree, plane tree)
Gen. 30:37; **Ezek.** 31:8.

6197. עֵרָן *ʿērān* **masc. proper noun**
(Eran)
Num. 26:36.

6198. עֵרָנִי *ʿērāniy* **masc. proper noun**
(Eranite)
Num. 26:36.

6199. I. עַרְעָר *ʿarʿār* **adj.**
(destitute)
Ps. 102:17(18); **Jer.** 17:6.
II. עַרְעָר *ʿarʿār* **masc. noun**
(bush)
Jer. 17:6(KJV, NASB, *ʿarôʿēr* [6176]).

6200. עֲרֹעֵרִי *ʿarōʿēriy* **masc. proper noun**
(inhabitant of Aroer [6177])
1 Chr. 11:44.

6201. עָרַף *ʿārap̱* **verb**
(to drop down, to drip)
Deut. 32:2; 33:28.

6202. עָרַף *ʿārap̱* **verb**
(to break the neck)
Ex. 13:13; 34:20; **Deut.** 21:4,6; **Isa.** 66:3; **Hos.** 10:2.

6203. עֹרֶף *ʿōrep̱* **masc. noun**
(neck; back)
Gen. 49:8; **Ex.** 23:27; 32:9; 33:3,5; 34:9; **Lev.** 5:8; **Deut.** 9:6,13; 10:16; 31:27; **Josh.** 7:8,12; **2 Sam.** 22:41; **2 Kgs.** 17:14; **2 Chr.** 29:6; 30:8; 36:13; **Neh.** 9:16,17,29; **Job** 16:12; **Ps.** 18:40(41); **Prov.** 29:1; **Isa.** 48:4; **Jer.** 2:27; 7:26; 17:23; 18:17; 19:15; 32:33; 48:39.

6204. עָרְפָּה *ʿorpāh* **fem. proper noun**
(Orpah)
Ruth 1:4,14.

6205. עֲרָפֶל *ʿarāpel* **masc. noun**
(thick darkness, gloom)
Ex. 20:21; **Deut.** 4:11; 5:22(19); **2 Sam.** 22:10; **1 Kgs.** 8:12; **2 Chr.** 6:1; **Job** 22:13; 38:9; **Ps.** 18:9(10); 97:2; **Isa.** 60:2; **Jer.** 13:16; **Ezek.** 34:12; **Joel** 2:2; **Zeph.** 1:15.

6206. עָרַץ *ʿāraṣ* **verb**
(to be afraid, to cause to be afraid)
Deut. 1:29; 7:21; 20:3; 31:6; **Josh.** 1:9; **Job** 13:25; 31:34; **Ps.** 10:18; 89:7(8); **Isa.** 2:19,21; 8:12,13; 29:23; 47:12.

6207. I. עָרַק *ʿāraq* **verb**
(to gnaw)
Job 30:3(KJV, NIV, see II),17(KJV, see III).
II. עָרַק *ʿāraq* **verb**
(to flee, to roam)
Job 30:3(NASB, see I).
III. עָרַק *ʿāraq* **masc. noun**
(that which is gnawed, sinews)
Job 30:17(NASB, NIV, see I).

6208. עַרְקִי *ʿarqiy* **masc. proper noun**
(Arkite)
Gen. 10:17; **1 Chr.** 1:15.

6209. I. עָרַר *ʿārar* **verb**
(to strip off, to undress oneself, to raze [a wall])
Isa. 23:13(KJV, see II); 32:11; **Jer.** 51:58.
II. עָרַר *ʿārar* **verb**
(to raise up [perhaps to raze])
Isa. 23:13(NASB, NIV, see I).

6210. עֶרֶשׂ *ʿereś* **masc. noun**
(couch, bed, bedstead)
Deut. 3:11; **Job** 7:13; **Ps.** 6:6(7); 41:3(4); 132:3; **Prov.** 7:16; **Song** 1:16; **Amos** 3:12; 6:4.

6211. עָשׁ *ʿāš* **masc. noun**
(moth)
Job 4:19; 13:28; 27:18; **Ps.** 39:11(12); **Isa.** 50:9; 51:8; **Hos.** 5:12.

6212. I. עֵשֶׂב *ʿēśeb̲* **masc. noun**
(grass, plants, herbs)
Gen. 1:11,12,29,30; 2:5; 3:18; 9:3; **Ex.** 9:22,25; 10:12,15; **Deut.** 11:15; 29:23(22); 32:2; **2 Kgs.** 19:26; **Job** 5:25; **Ps.** 72:16; 92:7(8); 102:4(5),11(12); 104:14; 105:35; 106:20; **Prov.** 19:12; 27:25; **Isa.** 37:27; 42:15; **Jer.** 12:4; 14:6; **Amos** 7:2; **Mic.** 5:7(6); **Zech.** 10:1.
II. עֲשַׂב *ʿasab̲* **Aram. masc. noun**
(grass; corr. to Hebr. *ʿēśeb̲* [6212,I])
Dan. 4:15(12),25(22),32(29),33(30); 5:21.

6213. עָשָׂה *ʿāśāh* **verb**
(to do, to make)
Gen. 1:7,11,12,16,25,26,31; 2:2–4,18; 3:1,7,13,14,21; 4:10; 5:1; 6:6,7,14–16,22; 7:4,5; 8:6,21; 9:6,24; 11:4,6; 12:2,5,18; 13:4; 14:2; 16:6; 18:5–8,17,19,21,25, 29,30; 19:3,8,19,22; 20:5,6,9,10,13; 21:1, 6,8,22,23,26; 22:12,16; 24:12,14,49,66; 26:10,29,30; 27:4,7,9,14,17,19,31,37,45; 28:6,15; 29:22,25,26,28; 30:30,31; 31:1, 12,16,26,28,29,43,46; 32:10(11); 33:17; 34:7,14,19,31; 35:1,3; 37:3; 38:10; 39:3, 9,11,19,22,23; 40:14,15,20; 41:25,28, 32,34,47,55; 42:18,20,25,28; 43:11,17; 44:2,5,7,15,17; 45:17,19,21; 47:29,30; 50:10,12,20; **Ex.** 1:17,18,21; 2:4; 3:16,20; 4:15,17,21,30; 5:8,9,15,16; 6:1; 7:6,10, 11,20,22; 8:7(3),13(9),17(13),18(14), 24(20),26(22),31(27); 9:5,6; 10:25; 11:10; 12:12,16,28,35,39,47,48,50; 13:8; 14:4,5, 11,13,31; 15:11,26; 16:17; 17:4,6,10; 18:1, 8,9,14,17,18,20,23,24; 19:4,8; 20:4,6, 9–11,23–25; 21:9,11,31; 22:30(29); 23:11,12,22,24; 24:3,7; 25:8–11,13, 17–19,23–26,28,29,31,37,39,40; 26:1, 4–7,10,11,14,15,17–19,22,23,26,29,31, 36,37; 27:1–4,6,8,9; 28:2–4,6,11,13–15, 22,23,26,27,31,33,36,39,40,42; 29:1,2, 35,36,38,39,41; 30:1,3–5,18,25,32,35, 37,38; 31:4–6,11,14–17; 32:1,4,8,10,14, 20,21,23,28,31,35; 33:5,17; 34:10,17,22; 35:1,2,10,29,32,33,35; 36:1–8,11–14, 17–20,22–25,27–29,31,33–37; 37:1,2, 4,6–8,10–12,15–17,23–29; 38:1–4,6–9, 22,24,28,30; 39:1–4,6,8,9,15,16,19,20, 22,24,25,27,30,32,42,43; 40:16; **Lev.** 2:7,8,11; 4:2,13,20,22,27; 5:10,17; 6:3(5:22),7(5:26),21(14),22(15); 7:9,24; 8:4,5,34,36; 9:6,7,16,22; 10:7; 11:32; 13:51; 14:19,30; 15:15,30; 16:9,15,16,

24,29,34; 17:9; 18:3–5,26,27,29,30; 19:4,15,35,37; 20:8,12,13,22,23; 22:3,23, 24,31; 23:3,7,8,12,19,21,25,28,30,31, 35,36; 24:19,23; 25:18,21; 26:1,3,14–16; **Num.** 1:54; 2:34; 4:3,19,26; 5:4,6,7,30; 6:4,11,16,17,21; 8:3,4,7,12,20,22,26; 9:2–6,10–14; 10:2; 11:8,15; 14:11,12,22, 28,35; 15:3,5,6,8,11–14,22,24,29,30, 34,38–40; 16:6,28,38(17:3); 17:11(26); 20:27; 21:8,9,34; 22:2,17,18,20,28,30; 23:2,11,19,26,30; 24:13,14,18; 27:22; 28:4,6,8,15,18,20,21,23–26,31; 29:1,2, 7,12,35,39; 30:2(3); 31:31; 32:8,13,20, 23–25,31; 33:4,56; 36:10; **Deut.** 1:14, 18,30,44; 2:12,22,29; 3:2,6,21,24; 4:1,3, 5,6,13,14,16,23,25,34; 5:1,8,10,13–15, 27(24),31(28),32(29); 6:1,3,18,24,25; 7:5,11,12,18,19; 8:1,17,18; 9:12,14,16, 18,21; 10:1,3,5,18,21; 11:3–7,22,32; 12:1,4,8,14,25,27,28,30,31,32(13:1); 13:11(12),14(15),18(19); 14:29; 15:1, 5,17,18; 16:1,8,10,12,13,21; 17:2,4,5, 10–12,19; 18:9,12; 19:9,19,20; 20:12,15, 18,20; 21:9,12; 22:3,5,8,12,21,26; 23:23(24); 24:8,9,18,22; 25:9,16,17; 26:14,16,19; 27:10,15,26; 28:1,13,15, 20,58; 29:2(1),9(8),24(23),29(28); 30:8, 12–14; 31:4,5,12,18,21,29; 32:6,15,46; 33:21; 34:9,11,12; **Josh.** 1:7,8,16; 2:10, 12,14; 3:5; 4:8,23; 5:2,3,10,15; 6:3,14; 7:9,15,19,20; 8:2,8; 9:3,4,9,10,15,20, 24–26; 10:1,23,25,28,30,32,35,37,39; 11:9,15,18; 14:5; 22:5,23,24,26,28; 23:3, 6,8; 24:5,7,17,31; **Judg.** 1:7,24; 2:2,7,10, 11,17; 3:7,12,16; 4:1; 6:1,2,17,19,20,27, 29,40; 7:17; 8:1–3,27,35; 9:16,19,27,33, 48,56; 10:6,15; 11:10,27,36,37,39; 13:1, 8,15,16,19; 14:6,10; 15:3,6,7,10,11; 16:11; 17:3–6,8; 18:3,4,14,18,24,27,31; 19:23, 24; 20:6,9,10; 21:7,11,15,16,23,25; **Ruth** 1:8,17; 2:11,19; 3:4–6,11,16; 4:11; **1 Sam.** 1:7,23; 2:14,19,22,23,35; 3:11, 17,18; 5:8; 6:2,5,7,9,10; 8:8,12,16; 10:2, 7,8; 11:7,10,13; 12:6,7,16,17,20,22; 13:11,19; 14:6,7,32(NASB, NIV, [Qe] *'iyt* [5860,II]),36,40,43–45,48; 15:2,6,19; 16:3,4; 17:25–27,29; 19:5,18; 20:1,2,4, 8,13,14,32; 22:3; 24:4(5),6(7),18(19), 19(20); 25:17,18,22,28,30; 26:16,18,25; 27:11; 28:2,9,15,17,18; 29:7,8; 30:23; 31:11; **2 Sam.** 2:5,6; 3:8,9,18,20,24,25, 35,36,39; 5:25; 7:3,9,11,21,23,25; 8:13, 15; 9:1,3,7,11; 10:2,12; 11:11,27; 12:4–6, 9,12,18,21,31; 13:2,5,7,10,12,16,29; 14:15,20–22; 15:1,6,26; 16:10,20; 17:6,23; 18:4,13; 19:13(14),18(19),24(25),27(28), 37(38),38(39); 21:3,4,11,14; 22:51; 23:10,12,17,22; 24:10,12,17; **1 Kgs.** 1:5,6,30; 2:3,5–7,9,23,24,31,38,44; 3:6, 12,15,28; 5:8(22),9(23),16(30); 6:4,5,12, 23,31,33; 7:6–8,14,16,18,23,27,37,38, 40,45,48,51; 8:32,39,43,45,49,59,64–66; 9:1,4,8,23,26; 10:9,12,16,18,20; 11:6,8, 12,28,33,38,41; 12:21,27,28,31–33; 13:11,33; 14:4,8,9,15,22,24,26,27,29; 15:3,5,7,11–13,23,26,31,34; 16:5,7,14, 19,25,27,30,33; 17:5,12,13,15; 18:13,23, 25,26,32,36; 19:1,2,20; 20:9,10,22,24, 25,40; 21:7,11,20,25,26; 22:11,22,39,43, 45(46),48(49),52(53),53(54); **2 Kgs.** 1:18; 2:9,19; 3:2,16; 4:2,10,13,14; 5:13,17; 6:2,15,31; 7:2,9,12,19; 8:2,4,12, 13,18,23,27; 10:5,10,19,24,25,30,34; 11:5,9; 12:2(3),11(12),13–15(14–16), 19(20); 13:2,8,11,12; 14:3,15,24,28; 15:3,6,9,18,21,24,26,28,31,34,36; 16:2, 11,16,19; 17:2,8,11,12,15–17,19,22, 29–32,34,37,40,41; 18:3,4,12,31; 19:11, 15,25,30,31; 20:3,9,20; 21:2,3,6–9,11, 15–17,20,25; 22:2,5,7,9,13; 23:4,12,15, 17,19,21–23,28,32,37; 24:3,5,9,13,16,19; 25:16; **1 Chr.** 4:10; 5:10,19; 10:11; 11:19,24; 12:32; 13:4; 14:16; 15:1; 16:12,26; 17:2,8,19,23; 18:8,14; 19:2,13; 20:3; 21:8,10,17,23,29; 22:8,13,15,16; 23:5,24; 27:26; 28:7,10,20; 29:19; **2 Chr.** 1:3,5,8; 2:3(2),7(6),12(11),14(13),18(17); 3:8,10,14–16; 4:1,2,6–9,11,14,16,18,19; 5:1; 6:13,23,33,35,39; 7:6–11,17,21; 9:8,11,15,17,19; 11:1,15; 12:9,10,14; 13:8,9; 14:2(1),4(3); 15:16; 18:10,21; 19:6,7,9–11; 20:12,32,35,36; 21:6,11,19; 22:4; 23:4,8; 24:2,7,8,11–14,16,22,24; 25:2,8,9,16; 26:4,11,13,15; 27:2; 28:1,2,

24,25; 29:2,6; 30:1–3,5,12,13,21,23; 31:20,21; 32:5,13,27,29,33; 33:2,3, 6–9,22; 34:2,10,12,13,16,17,21,31,32; 35:1,6,16–19; 36:5,8,9,12; **Ezra** 3:4,9; 6:19,22; 7:10; 10:3–5,11,12,16; **Neh.** 1:9; 2:12,16,19; 3:16; 4:2(3:34),6(3:38), 8(2),16(10),17(11),21(15); 5:9,12,13, 15,18,19; 6:2,3,9,13,16; 8:4,12,15–18; 9:6,10,17,18,24,26,28,29,31,33,34; 10:29(30); 11:12; 12:27; 13:5,7,10,14, 17,18,27; **Esth.** 1:3,5,8,9,15,20,21; 2:1, 4,11,18,20; 3:8,9,11; 4:1,17; 5:4–6,8,12, 14; 6:3,6,9–11,14; 7:2,5,9; 9:1,3,5,12–14, 17–19,21–23,27,38; **Job** 1:4,5; 4:17; 5:9,12; 9:9,10,12; 10:8,9,12; 12:9; 13:20; 14:5,9; 15:27; 21:31; 23:9,13; 25:2; 27:18; 28:25,26; 31:14,15; 32:22; 33:4; 35:6,10; 37:5; 40:15,19; 41:33(25); 42:8,9; **Ps.** 1:3; 7:3(4); 9:4(5),15(16), 16(17); 14:1,3; 15:3,5; 18:50(51); 22:31(32); 31:23(24); 33:6; 34:14(15), 16(17); 37:1,3,5,7,27; 39:9(10); 40:5(6), 8(9); 50:21; 51:4(6); 52:2(4),9(11); 53:1(2),3(4); 56:4(5),11(12); 60:12(14); 66:15,16; 71:19; 72:18; 77:14(15); 78:4,12; 83:9(10); 86:9,10,17; 88:10(11); 95:5,6; 96:5; 98:1; 99:4; 100:3; 101:3,7; 103:6,10,18,20,21; 104:4,19,24; 105:5; 106:3,19,21; 107:23,37; 108:13(14); 109:16,21,27; 111:4,8,10; 115:3,8,15; 118:6,15,16,24; 119:65,73,84,112,121, 124,126,166; 121:2; 124:8; 126:2,3; 134:3; 135:6,7,18; 136:4,5,7; 139:15; 140:12(13); 143:10; 145:19; 146:6,7; 147:20; 148:8; 149:2,7,9; **Prov.** 2:14; 3:27; 6:3,32; 8:26; 10:4,23; 11:18; 12:22; 13:16; 14:17,31; 16:12; 17:5; 20:12,18; 21:3,7,15,24,25; 22:2,28; 23:5; 24:6,29; 25:8; 26:28; 31:13,22,24,29; **Eccl.** 1:9, 13,14; 2:2,3,5,6,8,11,12,17; 3:9,11,12,14; 4:1,3; 5:1(4:17); 6:12; 7:14,20,29; 8:3,4, 9–12,14,16,17; 9:3,6,10; 10:19; 11:5; 12:12; **Song** 1:11; 3:9,10; 8:8; **Isa.** 2:8,20; 3:11; 5:2,4,5,10; 7:22; 9:7(6); 10:3,11,13,23; 12:5; 15:7; 16:3; 17:7,8; 19:10,15; 20:2; 22:11; 25:1,6; 26:18; 27:5,11; 28:15,21; 29:16; 30:1; 31:7; 32:6; 33:13; 36:16; 37:11,16,26,31,32; 38:3,7,15; 40:23; 41:4,20; 42:16; 43:7,19; 44:2,13,15,17,19,23,24; 45:7,9,12,18; 46:4,6,10,11; 48:3,5,11,14; 51:13; 53:9; 54:5; 55:11; 56:1,2; 57:16; 58:2,13; 63:12,14; 64:3–5(2–4); 65:8,12; 66:2, 4,22; **Jer.** 1:12; 2:13,17,23,28; 3:5–7; 4:18,27,30; 5:1,10,13,18,19,31; 6:13, 15,26; 7:5,10,12–14,17,18,30; 8:6,8, 10,12; 9:7(6),24(23); 10:12,13; 11:4,6, 8,15,17; 12:2,5; 14:7,22; 15:4; 16:12,20; 17:8,11,22,24; 18:3,4,6,8,10,12,13,23; 19:12; 21:2; 22:3,4,8,15,17; 23:5,20; 26:3,14,19; 27:2,5; 28:6,13; 29:23,32; 30:11,15,24; 31:37; 32:17,18,20,23,30, 32,35; 33:2,9,15,18; 34:15; 35:10,18; 36:3,8; 37:15; 38:9,12,16; 39:12; 40:3,16; 41:9,11; 42:3,5,10,20; 44:3,4,7,9,17,19, 22,25; 46:19,28; 48:10,30,36; 50:15,21, 29; 51:12,15,16,24; 52:2,20; **Lam.** 1:21; 2:17; **Ezek.** 3:20; 4:9,15; 5:7–10,15; 6:9,10; 7:20,23,27; 8:6,9,12,13,17,18; 9:4,11; 11:9,12,13,20; 12:3,7,9,11,25,28; 13:18; 14:23; 15:3,5; 16:5,16,17,24,30, 31,41,43,47,48,50,51,54,59,63; 17:6,8, 15,17,18,23,24; 18:5,8–14,17–19,21,22, 24,26–28,31; 20:9,11,13,14,17,19,21,22, 24,43,44; 21:15(20); 22:3,4,7,9,11,13,14; 23:3,8,10,21,25,29,30,38,39,48; 24:14, 17–19,22,24; 25:11,12,14,15,17; 27:5,6; 28:4,22,26; 29:3,9,20; 30:14,19; 31:9,11; 33:13–16,18,19,26,29,31,32; 35:6,11, 14,15; 36:22,27,32,36,37; 37:14,19,22,24; 38:12; 39:21,24; 40:14,17; 41:18–20,25; 43:8,11,18,25,27; 44:13,14; 45:9,17, 20,22–25; 46:2,7,12–15,23; **Dan.** 1:13; 8:4,12,24,27; 9:12,14,15,19; 11:3,6,7,16, 17,23,24,28,30,32,36,39; **Hos.** 2:8(10); 6:4,9; 8:4,6,7,14; 9:5,16; 10:3,15; 11:9; 13:2; **Joel** 2:11,20,21,26; **Amos** 3:6,7,10; 4:12,13; 5:8,26; 9:12,14; **Obad.** 1:15; **Jon.** 1:9–11,14; 3:10; 4:5; **Mic.** 1:8; 2:1; 5:15(14); 6:3,8; 7:9; **Nah.** 1:8,9; **Hab.** 1:14; 2:18; 3:17; **Zeph.** 1:18; 3:5,13,19; **Hag.** 1:14; 2:4; **Zech.** 1:6,21(2:4); 6:11; 7:3,9; 8:16; 10:1; **Mal.** 2:11–13,15,17; 3:15,17; 4:1,3.

6214. A. עֲשָׂהאֵל *ᵃśāh'ēl* **masc. proper noun**
(Asahel: son of Zeriah)
2 Sam. 2:18–23,30,32; 3:27,30; 23:24; **1 Chr.** 2:16; 11:26; 27:7.
B. עֲשָׂהאֵל *ᵃśāh'ēl* **masc. proper noun**
(Asahel: the father of Jonathan)
Ezra 10:15.
C. עֲשָׂהאֵל *ᵃśāh'ēl* **masc. proper noun**
(Asahel: a teacher of the Law)
2 Chr. 17:8.
D. עֲשָׂהאֵל *ᵃśāh'ēl* **masc. proper noun**
(Asahel: a levite)
2 Chr. 31:13.

6215. עֵשָׂו *'ēśāw* **masc. proper noun**
(Esau)
Gen. 25:25–30,32,34; 26:34; 27:1,5,6, 11,15,19,21–24,30,32,34,37,38,41,42; 28:5,6,8,9; 32:3(4),4(5),6(7),8(9), 11(12),13(14),17–19(18–20); 33:1, 4,9,15,16; 35:1,29; 36:1,2,4–6,8–10, 12–15,17–19,40,43; **Deut.** 2:4,5,8, 12,22,29; **Josh.** 24:4; **1 Chr.** 1:34,35; **Jer.** 49:8,10; **Obad.** 1:6,8,9,18,19,21; **Mal.** 1:2,3.

6216. עָשׁוֹק *'āšôq* **masc. noun**
(oppressor)
Jer. 22:3.

6217. עֲשׁוּקִים *ᵃšûqiym* **masc. pl. noun**
(oppressions)
Job 35:9; **Eccl.** 4:1; **Amos** 3:9.

6218. עָשׂוֹר *'āśôr* **masc. noun**
(ten, tenth, ten-stringed instrument)
Gen. 24:55; **Ex.** 12:3; **Lev.** 16:29; 23:27; 25:9; **Num.** 29:7; **Josh.** 4:19; **2 Kgs.** 25:1; **Ps.** 33:2; 92:3(4); 144:9; **Jer.** 52:4,12; **Ezek.** 20:1; 24:1; 40:1.

6219. I. עָשׁוֹת *'āšôṯ* **adj.**
(wrought [iron])
Ezek. 27:19(KJV, see II).
II. עָשׁוֹת *'āšôṯ* **adj.**
(bright)
Ezek. 27:19(NASB, NIV, see I).

6220. עַשְׁוָת *'ašwāṯ* **masc. proper noun**
(Ashvath)
1 Chr. 7:33.

6221. עֲשִׂיאֵל *ᵃśiy'ēl* **masc. proper noun**
(Asiel)
1 Chr. 4:35.

6222. עֲשָׂיָה *ᵃśāyāh* **masc. proper noun**
(Asaiah)
2 Kgs. 22:12,14; **1 Chr.** 4:36; 6:30(15); 9:5; 15:6,11; **2 Chr.** 34:20.

6223. עָשִׁיר *'āšiyr* **masc. noun**
(rich)
Ex. 30:15; **Ruth** 3:10; **2 Sam.** 12:1,2,4; **Job** 27:19; **Ps.** 45:12(13); 49:2(3); **Prov.** 10:15; 14:20; 18:11,23; 22:2,7,16; 28:6,11; **Eccl.** 5:12(11); 10:6,20; **Isa.** 53:9; **Jer.** 9:23(22); **Mic.** 6:12.

6224. עֲשִׂירִי *ᵃśiyriy* **num. adj.**
(tenth, one-tenth)
Gen. 8:5; **Ex.** 16:36; **Lev.** 5:11; 6:20(13); 27:32; **Num.** 5:15; 7:66; 28:5; **Deut.** 23:2(3),3(4); **2 Kgs.** 25:1; **1 Chr.** 12:13; 24:11; 25:17; 27:13; **Ezra** 10:16; **Esth.** 2:16; **Isa.** 6:13; **Jer.** 32:1; 39:1; 52:4; **Ezek.** 24:1; 29:1; 33:21; 45:11; **Zech.** 8:19.

6225. עָשַׁן *'āšan* **verb**
(to smoke, to be angry)
Ex. 19:18; **Deut.** 29:20(19); **Ps.** 74:1; 80:4(5); 104:32; 144:5.

6226. עָשֵׁן *'āšēn* **adj.**
(smoking, smoldering)
Ex. 20:18; **Isa.** 7:4.

6227. עָשָׁן *ʿāšān* **masc. noun**
(smoke)
Gen. 15:17; **Ex.** 19:18; **Josh.** 8:20,21; **Judg.** 20:38,40; **2 Sam.** 22:9; **Job** 41:20(12); **Ps.** 18:8(9); 37:20; 68:2(3); 102:3(4); **Prov.** 10:26; **Song** 3:6; **Isa.** 4:5; 6:4; 9:18(17); 14:31; 34:10; 51:6; 65:5; **Hos.** 13:3; **Joel** 2:30(3:3); **Nah.** 2:13(14).

6228. עָשָׁן *ʿāšān* **proper noun**
(Ashan)
Josh. 15:42; 19:7; **1 Chr.** 4:32; 6:59(44).

6229. עָשַׂק *ʿāśaq* **verb**
(to strive, to contend)
Gen. 26:20.

6230. עֵשֶׂק *ʿēśeq* **proper noun**
(Esek)
Gen. 26:20.

6231. עָשַׁק *ʿāšaq* **verb**
(to oppress, to defraud)
Lev. 6:2(5:21),4(5:23); 19:13; **Deut.** 24:14; 28:29,33; **1 Sam.** 12:3,4; **1 Chr.** 16:21; **Job** 10:3; 40:23; **Ps.** 72:4; 103:6; 105:14; 119:121,122; 146:7; **Prov.** 14:31; 22:16; 28:3,17; **Eccl.** 4:1; **Isa.** 23:12; 52:4; **Jer.** 7:6; 21:12; 50:33; **Ezek.** 18:18; 22:29; **Hos.** 5:11; 12:7(8); **Amos** 4:1; **Mic.** 2:2; **Zech.** 7:10; **Mal.** 3:5.

6232. עֵשֶׁק *ʿēšeq* **masc. proper noun**
(Eshek)
1 Chr. 8:39.

6233. עֹשֶׁק *ʿōšeq* **masc. noun**
(oppression, extortion)
Lev. 6:4(5:23); **Ps.** 62:10(11); 73:8; 119:134; **Eccl.** 5:8(7); 7:7; **Isa.** 30:12; 54:14; 59:13; **Jer.** 6:6; 22:17; **Ezek.** 18:18; 22:7,12,29.

6234. עָשְׁקָה *ʿošqāh* **fem. noun**
(oppression, distress)
Isa. 38:14.

6235. עֶשֶׂר *ʿeśer,* עֲשָׂרָה *ʿaśārāh* **fem., masc. num. adj.**
(ten)
Gen. 5:14; 16:3; 18:32; 24:10,22; 31:7,41; 32:15(16); 42:3; 45:23; 50:22,26; **Ex.** 18:21,25; 26:1,16; 27:12; 34:28; 36:8,21; 38:12; **Lev.** 26:26; 27:5,7; **Num.** 7:14,20,26,32,38,44,50,56, 62,68,74,80,86; 11:19,32; 14:22; 29:23; **Deut.** 1:15; 4:13; 10:4; **Josh.** 15:57; 17:5; 21:5,26; 22:14; 24:29; **Judg.** 1:4; 2:8; 3:29; 4:6,10,14; 6:27; 7:3; 12:11; 17:10; 20:10,34; **Ruth** 1:4; 4:2; **1 Sam.** 1:8; 15:4; 17:17,18; 25:5,38; **2 Sam.** 15:16; 18:3,11,15; 19:43(44); 20:3; **1 Kgs.** 4:23(5:3); 5:14(28); 6:3,23–26; 7:10,23,24,27,37,38,43; 11:31,35; 14:3; **2 Kgs.** 5:5; 13:7; 14:7; 15:17; 20:9–11; 24:14; 25:25; **1 Chr.** 6:61(46); 29:7; **2 Chr.** 4:1–3,6–8; 14:1(13:23); 25:11,12; 27:5; 30:24; 36:9; **Ezra** 1:10; 8:12,24; **Neh.** 4:12(6); 5:18; 11:1; **Esth.** 3:9; 9:10,12–14; **Job** 19:3; **Eccl.** 7:19; **Isa.** 5:10; 38:8; **Jer.** 32:9; 41:1,2,8; 42:7; **Ezek.** 40:11; 41:2; 42:4; 45:1,3, 5,12,14; 48:9,10,13,18; **Dan.** 1:12, 14,15,20; **Amos** 5:3; 6:9; **Hag.** 2:16; **Zech.** 5:2; 8:23.

6236. עֲשַׂר *ʿaśar,* עַשְׂרָה *ʿaśrāh* **fem., masc. Aram. num. adj.**
(ten; corr. to Hebr. 6235)
Ezra 6:17; **Dan.** 4:29(26); 7:7,20,24.

6237. עָשַׂר *ʿāśar* **verb**
(to give a tenth part; to tithe)
Gen. 28:22; **Deut.** 14:22; 26:12; **1 Sam.** 8:15,17; **Neh.** 10:37(38),38(39).

6238. עָשַׁר *ʿāšar* **verb**
(to be rich; to become rich)
Gen. 14:23; **1 Sam.** 2:7; 17:25; **Job** 15:29; **Ps.** 49:16(17); 65:9(10); **Prov.** 10:4,22; 13:7; 21:17; 23:4; 28:20; **Jer.** 5:27; **Ezek.** 27:33; **Dan.** 11:2; **Hos.** 12:8(9); **Zech.** 11:5.

6239. עֹשֶׁר *'ōšer* **masc. noun**
(wealth, riches)
Gen. 31:16; **1 Sam.** 17:25; **1 Kgs.** 3:11,13; 10:23; **1 Chr.** 29:12,28; **2 Chr.** 1:11,12; 9:22; 17:5; 18:1; 32:27; **Esth.** 1:4; 5:11; **Ps.** 49:6(7); 52:7(9); 112:3; **Prov.** 3:16; 8:18; 11:16,28; 13:8; 14:24; 22:1,4; 30:8; **Eccl.** 4:8; 5:13(12),14(13), 19(18); 6:2; 9:11; **Jer.** 9:23(22); 17:11; **Dan.** 11:2.

6240. עָשָׂר *'āśār* **num. adj.**
(ten in combination with other numerals from eleven to nineteen)
Gen. 5:8,10; 7:11,20; 8:4; 11:25; 14:4, 5,14; 17:20,25; 25:16; 31:41; 32:22(23); 35:22; 37:2,9; 42:13,32; 46:18,22; 47:28; 49:28; **Ex.** 12:6,18; 15:27; 16:1; 24:4; 26:7,8,25; 27:14,15; 28:21; 36:14,15,30; 38:14,15; 39:14; **Lev.** 23:5,6,34,39; 24:5; 27:7; **Num.** 1:44; 7:3,72,78,84,86,87; 9:3,5,11; 16:49(17:14); 17:2(17),6(21); 28:16,17; 29:12–15,17,20,23,26,29,32; 31:5,40,46,52; 33:3,9; **Deut.** 1:2,3,23; **Josh.** 3:12; 4:2–4,8,9,20; 5:10; 8:25; 15:36,41,51; 18:24,28; 19:6,15,22,38; 21:4,6,7,19,33,40(38); **Judg.** 3:14; 8:10; 10:8; 19:29; 20:25,44; 21:10; **2 Sam.** 2:15,30; 8:13; 9:10; 10:6; 17:1; 19:17(18); **1 Kgs.** 4:7,26(5:6); 6:38; 7:1,3,15,25,44; 8:65; 10:20,26; 11:30; 12:32,33; 14:21; 15:1; 16:23; 18:31; 19:19; 22:51(52); **2 Kgs.** 3:1; 8:25; 9:29; 13:1,10; 14:17, 21,23; 15:2,33; 16:1,2; 17:1; 18:13; 20:6; 21:1; 22:3; 23:23,36; 24:8,18; 25:2,8, 17,27; **1 Chr.** 4:27; 6:60(45),62(47), 63(48); 7:11; 9:22; 12:13,31; 15:10; 18:12; 24:4,12–16; 25:5,9–31; 26:9,11; 27:14,15; **2 Chr.** 1:14; 4:4,15; 9:19,25; 11:21; 12:13; 13:1,21; 15:10; 25:25; 26:1,3; 27:1,8; 28:1; 29:17; 30:15; 33:1; 34:3,8; 35:1,19; 36:5,11; **Ezra** 2:6,18,39; 6:19; 8:9,18,24,31,35; **Neh.** 5:14; 7:11, 24,42; **Esth.** 2:12; 3:7,12,13; 8:12; 9:1,15,17–19,21; **Job** 42:12; **Ps.** 60:[title](1); **Isa.** 36:1; 38:5; **Jer.** 1:2,3; 25:3; 32:1; 39:2; 52:1,5,12,20,21,29,31; **Ezek.** 26:1; 29:1; 30:20; 31:1; 32:1,17; 33:21; 40:1,11,49; 43:16,17; 45:21,25; 47:13; 48:35; **Hos.** 3:2; **Jon.** 4:11; **Zech.** 1:7.

6241. עִשָּׂרוֹן *'iśśārôn* **masc. noun**
(one-tenth)
Ex. 29:40; **Lev.** 14:10,21; 23:13,17; 24:5; **Num.** 15:4,6,9; 28:9,12,13,20,21,28,29; 29:3,4,9,10,14,15.

6242. עֶשְׂרִים *'eśriym* **num. pl. adj.**
(twenty, twentieth)
Gen. 6:3; 8:14; 11:24; 18:31; 23:1; 31:38,41; 32:14(15),15(16); 37:28; **Ex.** 12:18; 26:2,18–20; 27:10,11,16; 30:13, 14; 36:9,23–25; 38:10,11,18,24,26; **Lev.** 27:3,5,25; **Num.** 1:3,18,20,22,24,26,28, 30,32,34,36,38,40,42,45; 3:39,43,47; 7:86,88; 8:24; 10:11; 11:19; 14:29; 18:16; 25:9; 26:2,4,14,62; 32:11; 33:39; **Deut.** 31:2; 34:7; **Josh.** 15:32; 19:30; **Judg.** 4:3; 7:3; 8:10; 10:2,3; 11:33; 15:20; 16:31; 20:15,21,35,46; **1 Sam.** 7:2; 14:14; **2 Sam.** 3:20; 8:4,5; 9:10; 10:6; 18:7; 19:17(18); 21:20; 24:8; **1 Kgs.** 4:23(5:3); 5:11(25); 6:2,3,16,20; 8:63; 9:10,11,14,28; 10:10; 14:20; 15:9,33; 16:8,10,15,29; 20:30; 22:42; **2 Kgs.** 4:42; 8:26; 10:36; 12:6(7); 13:1; 14:2; 15:1, 27,30,33; 16:2; 18:2; 21:19; 23:31,36; 24:18; 25:27; **1 Chr.** 2:22; 7:2,7,9,40; 12:28,30,35,37; 15:5,6; 18:4,5; 20:6; 23:4,24,27; 24:16–18; 25:27–31; 27:1,2, 4,5,7–15,23; **2 Chr.** 2:10(9); 3:3,4,8, 11,13; 4:1; 5:12; 7:5,10; 8:1; 9:9; 11:21; 13:21; 20:31; 25:1,5; 27:1,8; 28:1,6; 29:1; 31:17; 33:21; 36:2,5,11; **Ezra** 1:9; 2:11, 12,17,19,21,23,26–28,32,33,41,67; 3:8; 8:11,19,20,27; 10:9; **Neh.** 1:1; 2:1; 5:14; 6:15; 7:16,17,22,23,27,30–32,35,37,69; 9:1; 11:8,12,14; **Esth.** 1:1; 8:9; 9:30; **Jer.** 25:3; 52:1,28,30,31; **Ezek.** 4:10; 8:16; 11:1; 29:17; 40:1,13,21,25,29,30,33,36, 49; 41:2,4,10; 42:3; 45:1,3,5,6,12; 48:8–10,13,15,20,21; **Dan.** 10:4,13; **Hag.** 1:15; 2:1,10,16,18,20; **Zech.** 1:7; 5:2.

6243. עֶשְׂרִין *'eśriyn* **Aram. pl. num. adj.**
(twenty; corr. to Hebr. 6242)
Dan. 6:1(2).

6244. עָשֵׁשׁ *'āšēš* **verb**
(to waste away, to become weak)
Ps. 6:7(8); 31:9(10),10(11).

6245. I. עָשַׁת *'āšat̠* **verb**
(to shine, to excel)
Jer. 5:28.
II. עָשַׁת *'āšat̠* **verb**
(to think about, to be concerned about)
Jon. 1:6.

6246. עֲשִׁת *'ašit̠,* עֲשִׁית *'ašiyt̠* **Aram. verb**
(to think about, to plan; corr. to Hebr. 6245,II)
Dan. 6:3(4).

6247. עֶשֶׁת *'ešet̠* **masc. noun**
(a polishing, a carving)
Song 5:14.

6248. עַשְׁתּוֹת *'aštôt̠* **fem. pl. noun**
(thoughts, plans)
Job 12:5.

6249. עַשְׁתֵּי *'aštēy* **num. adj.**
(eleven)
Ex. 26:7,8; 36:14,15; **Num.** 7:72; 29:20; **Deut.** 1:3; **2 Kgs.** 25:2; **1 Chr.** 12:13; 24:12; 25:18; 27:14; **Jer.** 1:3; 39:2; 52:5; **Ezek.** 26:1; 40:49; **Zech.** 1:7.

6250. עֶשְׁתֹּנָה *'eštōnāh* **fem. pl. noun**
(thought, plan)
Ps. 146:4.

6251. I. עַשְׁתְּרוֹת *'aštᵉrôt̠* **fem. pl. noun**
(lambs, young [sheep])
Deut. 7:13(KJV, see II); 28:4(KJV, see II),18(KJV, see II),51(KJV, see II).

II. עַשְׁתְּרוֹת *'aštᵉrôt̠* **fem. pl. noun**
(flocks [of sheep])
Deut. 7:13(NASB, NIV, see I); 28:4(NASB, NIV, see I),18(NASB, NIV, see I),51(NASB, NIV, see I).

6252. A. עַשְׁתָּרוֹת *'aštārôt̠* **fem. proper noun**
(Astaroth: Canaanite false goddess)
Judg. 2:13; 10:6; **1 Sam.** 7:3,4; 12:10.
B. עַשְׁתָּרוֹת *'aštārôt̠* **fem. proper noun**
(Astaroth: city in Manasseh, the same as *'aštᵉrot̠ qarnayim* [6255])
Deut. 1:4; **Josh.** 9:10; 12:4; 13:12,31; **1 Chr.** 6:71(56).

6253. עַשְׁתֹּרֶת *'aštōret̠* **fem. proper noun**
(Ashtoreth; Phoenician goddess)
1 Kgs. 11:5,33; **2 Kgs.** 23:13.

6254. עַשְׁתְּרָתִי *'aštᵉrāt̠iy* **masc. proper noun**
(Ashterathite; inhabitant of Ashtaroth [6252,B])
1 Chr. 11:44.

6255. עַשְׁתְּרֹת קַרְנַיִם *'aštᵉrōt̠ qarnayim* **proper noun**
(Ashteroth Karnaim; city in Manasseh; same as *'aštarôt̠* [6252,B])
Gen. 14:5.

6256. עֵת *'ēt̠* **fem. noun**
(time, season)
Gen. 8:11; 18:10,14; 21:22; 24:11; 29:7; 31:10; 38:1,27; **Ex.** 9:18; 18:22,26; **Lev.** 15:25; 16:2; 26:4; **Num.** 22:4; 23:23; **Deut.** 1:9,16,18; 2:34; 3:4,8,12,18,21,23; 4:14; 5:5; 9:20; 10:1,8; 11:14; 28:12; 32:35; **Josh.** 5:2; 6:26; 8:29; 10:27; 11:6, 10,21; **Judg.** 3:29; 4:4; 10:14; 11:26; 12:6; 13:23; 14:4; 21:14,22,24; **Ruth** 2:14; **1 Sam.** 4:20; 9:16; 18:19; 20:12;

2 Sam. 11:1,2; 24:15; **1 Kgs.** 8:65; 11:4,29; 14:1; 15:23; 19:2; 20:6; **2 Kgs.** 4:16,17; 5:26; 7:1,18; 8:22; 10:6; 16:6; 18:16; 20:12; 24:10; **1 Chr.** 9:25; 12:22,32; 20:1; 21:28,29; 29:30; **2 Chr.** 7:8; 13:18; 15:5; 16:7,10; 18:34; 20:22; 21:10,19; 24:11; 25:27; 28:16,22; 29:27; 30:3; 35:17; **Ezra** 8:34; 10:13,14; **Neh.** 4:22(16); 6:1; 9:27,28; 10:34; 13:21,31; **Esth.** 1:13; 4:14; 5:13; 8:9; **Job** 5:26; 6:17; 22:16; 24:1; 27:10; 38:23,32; 39:1, 2,18; **Ps.** 1:3; 4:7(8); 9:9(10); 10:1,5; 21:9(10); 31:15(16); 32:6; 34:1(2); 37:19,39; 62:8(9); 69:13(14); 71:9; 81:15(16); 102:13(14); 104:27; 105:19; 106:3; 119:20,126; 145:15; **Prov.** 5:19; 6:14; 8:30; 15:23; 17:17; **Eccl.** 3:1–8,11, 17; 7:17; 8:5,6,9; 9:8,11,12; 10:17; **Song** 2:12; **Isa.** 9:1(8:23); 13:22; 17:14; 18:7; 20:2; 33:2,6; 39:1; 48:16; 49:8; 60:22; **Jer.** 2:17,27,28; 3:17; 4:11; 5:24; 6:15; 8:1,7,12,15; 10:15; 11:12,14; 14:8,19; 15:11; 18:23; 20:16; 27:7; 30:7; 31:1; 33:15,20; 46:21; 49:8; 50:4,16,20,27,31; 51:6,18,33; **Ezek.** 4:10,11; 7:7,12; 12:27; 16:8,57; 21:25(30),29(34); 22:3; 27:34; 30:3; 34:26; 35:5; **Dan.** 8:17; 9:21,25; 11:6,13,14,24,35,40; 12:1,4,9,11; **Hos.** 2:9(11); 10:12; 13:13; **Joel** 3:1(4:1); **Amos** 5:13; **Mic.** 2:3; 3:4; 5:3(2); **Zeph.** 1:12; 3:19,20; **Hag.** 1:2,4; **Zech.** 10:1; 14:7.

6257. עָתַד *ʿāṯaḏ* **verb**
(to be ready, to be prepared)
Job 15:28; **Prov.** 24:27.

6258. עַתָּה *ʿattāh* **adv.**
(now, already, then)
Gen. 3:22; 4:11; 11:6; 12:19; 19:9; 20:7; 21:23; 22:12; 24:49; 26:22,29; 27:3,8,36, 43; 29:32,34; 30:30; 31:13,16,28, 30,42,44; 32:4,10; 37:20; 41:33; 43:10; 44:10,30,33; 45:5,8; 46:34; 47:4; 48:5; 50:5,17,21; **Ex.** 3:9,10,18; 4:12; 5:5,18; 6:1; 9:15,18,19; 10:17; 18:11,19; 19:5; 32:10,30,32,34; 33:5,13; **Num.** 11:6,23; 14:17; 22:4,6,11,19,29,33,34,38; 24:11, 14,17; 31:17; **Deut.** 2:13; 4:1; 5:25; 10:12,22; 12:9; 26:10; 31:19; 32:39; **Josh.** 1:2; 2:12; 3:12; 5:14; 9:6,11,12,19, 23,25; 13:7; 14:10–12; 22:4; 24:14,23; **Judg.** 6:13; 7:3; 8:2,6,15; 9:16,32,38; 11:7,8,13,23,25; 13:4,7,12; 14:2; 15:18; 16:10; 17:3,13; 18:14; 20:9,13; **Ruth** 2:7; 3:2,11,12; **1 Sam.** 1:16; 2:16,30; 6:7; 8:5,9; 9:12,13; 10:19; 12:2,7,10,13,16; 13:12–14; 14:30; 15:1,3,25,30; 17:29; 18:22; 19:2; 20:29,31; 21:3; 23:20; 24:20,21; 25:7,17,26,27; 26:8,11,16, 19,20; 27:1; 28:22; 29:7,10; **2 Sam.** 2:6,7; 3:18; 4:11; 7:8,25,28,29; 12:10, 23,28; 13:13,20,33; 14:15,32; 15:34; 16:11; 17:9,16; 18:3; 19:7,9,10; 20:6; 24:10,13,16; **1 Kgs.** 1:12,18; 2:9,16,24; 3:7; 5:4,6; 8:25,26; 12:4,11,16,26; 14:14; 17:24; 18:11,14,19; 19:4; 21:7; 22:23; **2 Kgs.** 1:14; 3:15,23; 4:26; 5:6,15,22; 7:4,9; 8:6; 9:26; 10:2,19; 12:7; 13:19,23; 18:20,21,23,25; 19:19,25; **1 Chr.** 17:7, 23,26,27; 21:8,12,15; 22:11,19; 28:8,10; 29:13,17; **2 Chr.** 1:9,10; 2:7,13,15; 6:16, 17,40,41; 7:15,16; 10:4,11,16; 13:8; 16:9; 18:22; 19:7; 20:10; 25:19; 28:10,11; 29:5, 10,11,31; 30:8; 32:15; 35:3; **Ezra** 9:8, 10,12; 10:2,3,11; **Neh.** 5:5; 6:7,9; 9:32; **Job** 3:13; 4:5; 6:3,21,28; 7:21; 8:6; 13:19; 14:16; 16:7,19; 30:1,9,16; 35:15; 37:21; 42:5,8; **Ps.** 2:10; 12:5; 17:11; 20:6; 27:6; 39:7; 74:6; 113:2; 115:18; 119:67; 121:8; 125:2; 131:3; **Prov.** 5:7; 7:24; 8:32; **Isa.** 1:21; 5:3,5; 9:7; 16:14; 28:22; 29:22; 30:8; 33:10; 36:5,8,10; 37:20,26; 43:1,19; 44:1; 47:8; 48:6,7,16; 49:5,19; 52:5; 59:21; 64:8; **Jer.** 2:18; 3:4; 4:12; 14:10; 18:11; 26:13; 27:6,16; 29:27; 32:36; 37:20; 40:4; 42:15,22; 44:7; **Ezek.** 4:14; 7:3,8; 19:13; 23:43; 26:18; 39:25; 43:9; **Dan.** 9:15, 17,22; 10:11,17,20; 11:2; **Hos.** 2:7,10; 4:16; 5:3,7; 7:2; 8:8,10,13; 10:2,3; 13:2; **Joel** 2:12; **Amos** 6:7; 7:16; **Jon.** 4:3; **Mic.** 4:7,9–11; 5:1,4; 7:4,10; **Nah.** 1:13; **Hag.** 1:5; 2:3,4,15; **Zech.** 8:11; 9:8; **Mal.** 1:9; 2:1; 3:15.

6259. עָתוּד *ʿāṯûḏ* **adj.**
(treasured)
Isa. 10:13(NASB, [K[e]] *ʿāṯiyḏ* [6264,III]).

6260. עַתּוּד *ʿattûḏ* **masc. noun**
(goat, male goat, leader)
Gen. 31:10,12; **Num.** 7:17,23,29,35,41, 47,53,59,65,71,77,83,88; **Deut.** 32:14; **Ps.** 50:9,13; 66:15; **Prov.** 27:26; **Isa.** 1:11; 14:9; 34:6; **Jer.** 50:8; 51:40; **Ezek.** 27:21; 34:17; 39:18; **Zech.** 10:3.

6261. עִתִּי *ʿittiy* **adj.**
(fit, ready to stand)
Lev. 16:21.

6262. A. עַתַּי *ʿattay* **masc. proper noun**
(Attai: descendant of Judah)
1 Chr. 2:35,36.
B. עַתַּי *ʿattay* **masc. proper noun**
(Attai: one of David's warriors)
1 Chr. 12:11.
C. עַתַּי *ʿattay* **masc. proper noun**
(Attai: son of Rehoboam)
2 Chr. 11:20.

6263. עֲתִיד *ʿaṯiyḏ* **Aram. adj.**
(ready; corr. to Hebr. 6264,I)
Dan. 3:15.

6264. I. עָתִיד *ʿāṯiyḏ* **adj.**
(ready, prepared)
Esth. 3:14; 8:13; **Job** 3:8; 15:24.
II. עָתִיד *ʿāṯiyḏ* **adj.**
(impending; about to come)
Deut. 32:35.
III. עָתִיד *ʿāṯiyḏ* **adj.**
(treasures)
Isa. 10:13(KJV, NIV, [Q[e]] *ʿāṯûḏ* [6259]).

6265. עֲתָיָה *ʿaṯāyāh* **masc. proper noun**
(Athaiah)
Neh. 11:4.

6266. I. עָתִיק *ʿāṯiyq* **adj.**
(choice, fine)
Isa. 23:18(KJV, see II).
II. עָתִיק *ʿāṯiyq* **adj.**
(durable)
Isa. 23:18(NASB, NIV, see I).

6267. I. עַתִּיק *ʿattiyq* **adj.**
(ancient)
1 Chr. 4:22; **Isa.** 28:9.
II. עַתִּיק *ʿattiyq* **adj.**
(taken, drawn from)
Isa. 28:9.

6268. עַתִּיק *ʿattiyq* **Aram. adj.**
(ancient; corr. to Hebr. 6267,I)
Dan. 7:9,13,22.

6269. עֲתָךְ *ʿaṯāḵ* **masc. proper noun**
(Athach)
1 Sam. 30:30.

6270. עַתְלַי *ʿaṯlāy* **masc. proper noun**
(Athlai)
Ezra 10:28.

6271. A. עֲתַלְיָה *ʿaṯalyāh,* עֲתַלְיָהוּ *ʿaṯalyāhû* **fem. proper noun**
(Athaliah: daughter of Ahab)
2 Kgs. 8:26; 11:1–3,13,14,20; **2 Chr.** 22:10–12; 23:12,13,21; 24:7.
B. עֲתַלְיָה *ʿaṯalyāh* **masc. proper noun**
(Athaliah: a Benjamite)
1 Chr. 8:26.
C. עֲתַלְיָה *ʿaṯalyāh* **masc. proper noun**
(Athaliah: descendant of Elam)
Ezra 8:7.

6272. עָתַם *ʿāṯam* **verb**
(to scorch, to burn)
Isa. 9:19(18).

6273. עָתְנִי *'oṯniy* **masc. proper noun**
(Othni)
1 Chr. 26:7.

6274. עָתְנִיאֵל *'oṯniy'ēl* **masc. proper noun**
(Othniel)
Josh. 15:17; **Judg.** 1:13; 3:9,11; **1 Chr.** 4:13; 27:15.

6275. עָתַק *'āṯaq* **verb**
(to move, to proceed, to grow old)
Gen. 12:8; 26:22; **Job** 9:5; 14:18; 18:4; 21:7; 32:15; **Ps.** 6:7(8); **Prov.** 25:1.

6276. עָתֵק *'āṯēq* **adj.**
(enduring)
Prov. 8:18.

6277. עָתָק *'āṯāq* **adj.**
(arrogant, insolent)
1 Sam. 2:3; **Ps.** 31:18(19); 75:5(6); 94:4.

6278. I. עִתָּה קָצִין *'ittāh qaṣiyn* **proper noun**
(Ittah Kazin)
Josh. 19:13(NASB, NIV, see II).
II. עֵת קָצִין *'ēṯ qāṣiyn* **proper noun**
(Eth Kazin)
Josh. 19:13(KJV, see I).

6279. עָתַר *'āṯar* **verb**
(to pray to, to entreat)
Gen. 25:21; **Ex.** 8:8(4),9(5),28–30(24–26); 9:28; 10:17,18; **Judg.** 13:8; **2 Sam.** 21:14; 24:25; **1 Chr.** 5:20; **2 Chr.** 33:13,19; **Ezra** 8:23; **Job** 22:27; 33:26; **Isa.** 19:22.

6280. עָתַר *'āthar* **verb**
(to be multiplied [perhaps in deceit])
Prov. 27:6; **Ezek.** 35:13.

6281. עֶתֶר *'ēṯer* **proper noun**
(Ether)
Josh. 15:42; 19:7.

6282. I. עָתָר *'āṯār* **masc. noun**
(worship)
Zeph. 3:10.
II. עָתָר *'āṯār* **masc. noun**
(fragrance)
Ezek. 8:11(KJV, see III).
III. עָתָר *'āṯār* **masc. noun**
(thickness)
Ezek. 8:11(NASB, NIV, see II).

6283. עֲתֶרֶת *ᵃṯereṯ* **fem. noun**
(abundance)
Jer. 33:6.

פּ Pē

6284. פָּאָה *pāʾāh* **verb**
(to divide into pieces or corners)
Deut. 32:26.

6285. פֵּאָה *pēʾāh* **fem. noun**
(side, corner)
Ex. 25:26; 26:18,20; 27:9,11–13; 36:23,25; 37:13; 38:9,11–13; **Lev.** 13:41; 19:9,27; 21:5; 23:22; **Num.** 24:17; 34:3; 35:5; **Josh.** 15:5; 18:12,14,15,20; **Neh.** 9:22; **Jer.** 9:26(25); 25:23; 48:45; 49:32; **Ezek.** 41:12; 45:7; 47:15,17–20; 48:1–8, 16,23–28,30,32–34; **Amos** 3:12.

6286. I. פָּאַר *pāʾar* **verb**
(to glorify, to give honor, to be glorified)
Ex. 8:9(5); **Judg.** 7:2; **Ezra** 7:27; **Ps.** 149:4; **Isa.** 10:15; 44:23; 49:3; 55:5; 60:7,9,13,21; 61:3.
II. פָּאַר *pāʾar* **verb**
(to go over the branches a second time)
Deut. 24:20.

6287. פְּאֵר *pᵉʾēr* **masc. noun**
(headband, turban)
Ex. 39:28; **Isa.** 3:20; 61:3,10; **Ezek.** 24:17,23; 44:18.

6288. A. פֹּארָה *pōʾrāh* **fem. noun**
(bough, branch)
Ezek. 17:6; 31:5,6,8,12,13.
B. פֻּארָה *puʾrāh* **fem. noun**
(bough, branch)
Isa. 10:33.

6289. I. פָּארוּר *pāʾrûr* **masc. noun**
(paleness)
Joel 2:6(KJV, see II); **Nah.** 2:10(11) (KJV, see II).
II. פָּארוּר *pāʾrûr* **masc. noun**
(blackness)
Joel 2:6(NASB, NIV, see I); **Nah.** 2:10(11) (NASB, NIV, see I).

6290. פָּארָן *pāʾrān* **proper noun**
(Paran)
Gen. 21:21; **Num.** 10:12; 12:16; 13:3,26; **Deut.** 1:1; 33:2; **1 Sam.** 25:1; **1 Kgs.** 11:18; **Hab.** 3:3.

6291. פַּג *pag* **masc. noun**
(green fig, early fig)
Song 2:13.

6292. פִּגּוּל *piggûl* **masc. noun**
(impurity, offensive thing)
Lev. 7:18; 19:7; **Isa.** 65:4; **Ezek.** 4:14.

6293. פָּגַע *pāgaʿ* **verb**
(to approach, to make intercession; to reach; to touch, to attack, to strike down)
Gen. 23:8; 28:11; 32:1(2); **Ex.** 5:3,20; 23:4; **Num.** 35:19,21; **Josh.** 2:16; 16:7; 17:10; 19:11,22,26,27,34; **Judg.** 8:21; 15:12; 18:25; **Ruth** 1:16; 2:22; **1 Sam.** 10:5; 22:17,18; **2 Sam.** 1:15; **1 Kgs.** 2:25,29,31,32,34,46; **Job** 21:15; 36:32; **Isa.** 47:3; 53:6,12; 59:16; 64:5(4); **Jer.** 7:16; 15:11; 27:18; 36:25; **Amos** 5:19.

6294. פֶּגַע *pegaʿ* **masc. noun**
(circumstantial event, chance happening)
1 Kgs. 5:4(18); **Eccl.** 9:11.

6295. פַּגְעִיאֵל *pagʿiyʾēl* **masc. proper noun**
(Pagiel)
Num. 1:13; 2:27; 7:72,77; 10:26.

6296. פָּגַר *pāgar* **verb**
(to be exhausted)
1 Sam. 30:10,21.

6297. פֶּגֶר *peger* **masc. noun**
(dead body, corpse, carcass)
Gen. 15:11; **Lev.** 26:30; **Num.** 14:29,32,33; **1 Sam.** 17:46; **2 Kgs.** 19:35; **2 Chr.** 20:24,25; **Isa.** 14:19; 34:3; 37:36; 66:24; **Jer.** 31:40; 33:5; 41:9; **Ezek.** 6:5; 43:7,9; **Amos** 8:3; **Nah.** 3:3.

6298. פָּגַשׁ *pāgaš* **verb**
(to meet, to encounter)
Gen. 32:17(18); 33:8; **Ex.** 4:24,27; **1 Sam.** 25:20; **2 Sam.** 2:13; **Job** 5:14; **Ps.** 85:10(11); **Prov.** 17:12; 22:2; 29:13; **Isa.** 34:14; **Jer.** 41:6; **Hos.** 13:8.

6299. פָּדָה *pā*<u>*d*</u>*āh* **verb**
(to redeem, to ransom, to deliver)
Ex. 13:13,15; 21:8; 34:20; **Lev.** 19:20; 27:27,29; **Num.** 3:46(KJV, *p*^{e}<u>*d*</u>*ûyiym* [6302,I]; NIV, *p*^{e}<u>*d*</u>*ûyiym* [6302,II]), 49(KJV, *pi*<u>*d*</u>*yôm* [6306,A]),51(KJV, *pi*<u>*d*</u>*yôm* [6306,A]; NIV, *p*^{e}*dûyim* [6302]); 18:15–17; **Deut.** 7:8; 9:26; 13:5(6); 15:15; 21:8; 24:18; **1 Sam.** 14:45; **2 Sam.** 4:9; 7:23; **1 Kgs.** 1:29; **1 Chr.** 17:21; **Neh.** 1:10; **Job** 5:20; 6:23; 33:28; **Ps.** 25:22; 26:11; 31:5(6); 34:22(23); 44:26(27); 49:7(8),15(16); 55:18(19); 69:18(19); 71:23; 78:42; 119:134; 130:8; **Isa.** 1:27; 29:22; 35:10; 51:11; **Jer.** 15:21; 31:11; **Hos.** 7:13; 13:14; **Mic.** 6:4; **Zech.** 10:8.

6300. פְּדַהְאֵל *p*^{e}<u>*d*</u>*ah'ēl* **masc. proper noun**
(Pedahel)
Num. 34:28.

6301. פְּדָהצוּר *p*^{e}<u>*d*</u>*āhṣûr* **masc. proper noun**
(Pedahzur)
Num. 1:10; 2:20; 7:54,59; 10:23.

6302. I. פְּדוּיִים *p*^{e}<u>*d*</u>*ûyiym* **masc. pl. noun**
(those who are redeemed)
Num. 3:46(NASB, *pā*<u>*d*</u>*āh* [6299], NIV, see II),48(NASB, NIV, see II).

II. פְּדוּיִים *p*^{e}<u>*d*</u>*ûyiym* **masc. pl. noun**
(redemption, ransom)
Num. 3:46(NASB, *pā*<u>*d*</u>*āh* [6299], KJV, see I),48(KJV, see I),49(KJV, NIV, *pi*<u>*d*</u>*yôm* [6306,A]),51(KJV, *pi*<u>*d*</u>*yôm* [6306,A]; NASB, *pā*<u>*d*</u>*āh* [6299]).

6303. פָּדוֹן *pā*<u>*d*</u>*ôn* **masc. proper noun**
(Padon)
Ezra 2:44; **Neh.** 7:47.

6304. I. פְּדוּת *p*^{e}<u>*d*</u>*û*<u>*t*</u> **fem. noun**
(redemption, ransom)
Ps. 111:9; 130:7; **Isa.** 50:2.
II. פְּדוּת *p*^{e}<u>*d*</u>*û*<u>*t*</u> **fem. noun**
(division)
Ex. 8:23(19).

6305. A. פְּדָיָה *p*^{e}<u>*d*</u>*āyāh* **masc. proper noun**
(Pedaiah: grandfather of Jehoiakim)
2 Kgs. 23:36; **Neh.** 3:25; 8:4; 11:7; 13:13.
B. פְּדָיָהוּ *p*^{e}<u>*d*</u>*āyāhû* **masc. proper noun**
(Pedaiah: son of Jehoiachin)
1 Chr. 3:17,18.
C. פְּדָיָה *p*^{e}<u>*d*</u>*āyāh* **masc. proper noun**
(Pedaiah: son of Parosh)
Neh. 3:25.
D. פְּדָיָה *p*^{e}<u>*d*</u>*āyāh* **masc. proper noun**
(Pedaiah: helper of Ezra)
Neh. 8:4.
E. פְּדָיָה *p*^{e}<u>*d*</u>*āyāh* **masc. proper noun**
(Pedaiah: descendent of Benjamin)
Neh. 11:7.
F. פְּדָיָה *p*^{e}<u>*d*</u>*āyāh* **masc. proper noun**
(Pedaiah: Levite in Nehemiah's day)
Neh. 13:13.
G. פְּדָיָהוּ *p*^{e}<u>*d*</u>*āyāhû* **masc. proper noun**

(Pedaiah: father of Joel)
1 Chr. 27:20.

6306. A. פִּדְיוֹם *piḏyôm* **masc. noun**
(those who are redeemed;
redemption)
Num. 3:49(NASB, *pᵉḏûyiym*
[6302,II]),49(2nd occurrence, NASB, NIV,
pāḏāh [6299]),51(NASB, *pāḏāh* [6299];
NIV, *pᵉḏûyiym* [6302,II]).
B. פִּדְיוֹן *piḏyôn* **masc. noun**
(redemption)
Ex. 21:30; **Ps.** 49:8(9).

6307. A. פַּדָּן *paddān* **proper noun**
(Paddan: shortened form of B)
Gen. 48:7.
B. פַּדַּן אֲרָם *paddan 'ᵃrām* **proper noun**
(Paddan Aram: see also A)
Gen. 25:20; 28:2,5–7; 31:18; 33:18;
35:9,26; 46:15.

6308. פָּדַע *pāḏaʿ* **verb**
(to deliver, to spare)
Job 33:24.

6309. פֶּדֶר *peḏer* **masc. noun**
(fat, suet)
Lev. 1:8,12; 8:20.

6310. פֶּה *peh* **masc. noun**
(mouth)
Gen. 4:11; 8:11; 24:57; 25:28; 29:2,3,
8,10; 34:26; 41:40; 42:27; 43:7,12,21;
44:1,2,8; 45:12,21; 47:12; **Ex.** 4:10–12,
15,16; 12:4; 13:9; 16:16,18,21; 17:1,13;
23:13; 28:32; 34:27; 38:21; 39:23; **Lev.**
24:12; 25:16,51,52; 27:8,16,18; **Num.**
3:16,39,51; 4:27,37,41,45,49; 6:21; 7:5,
7,8; 9:17,18,20,23; 10:13; 12:8; 13:3;
14:41; 16:30,32; 20:24; 21:24; 22:18,
28,38; 23:5,12,16; 24:13; 26:10,54,56;
27:14,21; 30:2(3); 32:24; 33:2,38; 35:8,
30; 36:5; **Deut.** 1:26,43; 8:3; 9:23; 11:6;
13:15(16); 17:6,10,11; 18:18; 19:15;
20:13; 21:5,17; 23:23(24); 30:14;
31:19,21; 32:1; 34:5; **Josh.** 1:8,18;
6:10,21; 8:24; 9:2,14; 10:18,22,27,
28,30,32,35,37,39; 11:11,12,14; 15:13;
17:4; 18:4; 19:47,50; 21:3; 22:9; **Judg.**
1:8,25; 4:15,16; 7:6; 9:38; 11:35,36;
18:19,27; 20:37,48; 21:10; **1 Sam.** 1:12;
2:1,3; 12:14,15; 13:21; 14:26,27; 15:8,24;
17:35; 22:19; **2 Sam.** 1:16; 13:32;
14:3,19; 15:14; 17:5; 18:25; 22:9; **1 Kgs.**
7:31; 8:15,24; 13:21,26; 17:1,24; 19:18;
22:13,22,23; **2 Kgs.** 2:9; 4:34; 10:21,25;
21:16; 23:35; 24:3; **1 Chr.** 12:23,32;
16:12; **2 Chr.** 6:4,15; 18:12,21,22; 31:2;
35:22; 36:12,21,22; **Ezra** 1:1; 8:17; 9:11;
Neh. 9:20; **Esth.** 7:8; **Job** 1:15,17; 3:1;
5:15,16; 7:11; 8:2,21; 9:20; 15:5,6,13,30;
16:5,10; 19:16; 20:12; 21:5; 22:22;
23:4,12; 29:9,23; 30:18; 31:27; 32:5;
33:2,6; 35:16; 36:16; 37:2; 39:27;
40:4,23; 41:19(11),21(13); **Ps.** 5:9(10);
8:2(3); 10:7; 17:3,10; 18:8(9); 19:14(15);
22:13(14),21(22); 33:6; 34:1(2); 35:21;
36:3(4); 37:30; 38:13(14),14(15); 39:1(2),
9(10); 40:3(4); 49:3(4),13(14); 50:16,19;
51:15(17); 54:2(4); 55:21(22); 58:6(7);
59:7(8),12(13); 62:4(5); 63:5(6),11(12);
66:14,17; 69:15(16); 71:8,15; 73:9;
78:1,2,30,36; 81:10(11); 89:1(2); 105:5;
107:42; 109:2,30; 115:5; 119:13,43,72,
88,103,108,131; 126:2; 133:2; 135:16,17;
138:4; 141:3,7; 144:8,11; 145:21; **Prov.**
2:6; 4:5,24; 5:4,7; 6:2,12; 7:24; 8:3,8,
13,29; 10:6,11,14,31,32; 11:9,11; 12:6,
8,14; 13:2,3; 14:3; 15:2,14,23,28; 16:10,
23,26; 18:4,6,7,20; 19:24,28; 20:17;
21:23; 22:6,14; 24:7; 26:7,9,15,28;
27:2,21; 30:20,32; 31:8,9,26; **Eccl.**
5:2(1),6(5); 6:7; 8:2; 10:12,13; **Song** 1:2;
Isa. 1:20; 5:14; 6:7; 9:12(11),17(16);
10:14; 11:4; 19:7; 29:13; 30:2; 34:16;
40:5; 45:23; 48:3; 49:2; 51:16; 52:15;
53:7,9; 55:11; 57:4; 58:14; 59:21; 62:2;
Jer. 1:9; 5:14; 7:28; 9:8(7),12(11),20(19);
12:2; 15:19; 21:7; 23:16; 29:10; 32:4;
34:3; 36:4,6,17,18,27,32; 44:17,25,26;
45:1; 48:28; 51:44; **Lam.** 1:18; 2:16;
3:29,38,46; **Ezek.** 2:8; 3:2,3,17,27; 4:14;

16:56,63; 21:22(27); 24:27; 29:21; 33:7, 22,31; 34:10; 35:13; **Dan.** 10:3,16; **Hos.** 2:17(19); 6:5; 10:12; **Joel** 1:5; **Amos** 3:12; 6:5; **Obad.** 1:12; **Mic.** 3:5; 4:4; 6:12; 7:5,16; **Nah.** 3:12; **Zeph.** 3:13; **Zech.** 1:21(2:4); 5:8; 8:9; 9:7; 13:8; 14:12; **Mal.** 2:6,7,9.

6311. פֹּא *pō'*, פֹּה *pōh*, פוֹ *pô* **adv.**
(here, hither)
Gen. 19:12; 22:5; 40:15; **Num.** 22:8; 32:6,16; **Deut.** 5:3,31; 12:8; 29:15; **Josh.** 18:6,8; **Judg.** 4:20; 18:3; 19:9; **Ruth** 4:1,2; **1 Sam.** 16:11; 21:8; 23:3; **2 Sam.** 20:4; **1 Kgs.** 2:30; 19:9,13; 22:7; **2 Kgs.** 2:2,4,6; 3:11; 7:3,4; 10:23; **1 Chr.** 29:17; **2 Chr.** 18:6; **Ezra** 4:2; **Job** 38:11; **Ps.** 132:14; **Isa.** 22:16; 52:5; **Ezek.** 8:6,9,17; 40:10,12,21,26,34,37,39,41,48,49; 41:1, 2,15,19,26.

6312. A. פּוּאָה *pû'āh*, פֻּוָּה *puwwāh* **masc. proper noun**
(Puah: son of Issachar)
Gen. 46:13; **Num.** 26:23; **1 Chr.** 7:1.
B. פּוּאָה *pû'āh* **masc. proper noun**
(Puah: son of Dodo)
Judg. 10:1.

6313. פּוּג *pûg* **verb**
(to be stunned, to be paralyzed, to be feeble)
Gen. 45:26; **Ps.** 38:8(9); 77:2(3); **Hab.** 1:4.

6314. פּוּגָה *pûgāh* **fem. noun**
(rest, relief)
Lam. 2:18.

6315. פּוּחַ *pûaḥ* **verb**
(to breathe out, to snort, to utter)
Ps. 10:5; 12:5(6); **Prov.** 6:19; 12:17; 14:5,25; 19:5,9; 29:8; **Song** 2:17; 4:6,16; **Ezek.** 21:31(36); **Hab.** 2:3.

6316. פּוּט *pûṭ* **masc. proper noun**
(the nation of Put, probably Libya)
Gen. 10:6; **1 Chr.** 1:8; **Jer.** 46:9; **Ezek.** 27:10; 30:5; 38:5; **Nah.** 3:9.

6317. פּוּטִיאֵל *pûṭiy'ēl* **masc. proper noun**
(Putiel)
Ex. 6:25.

6318. פּוֹטִיפַר *pôṭiyp̱ar* **masc. proper noun**
(Potiphar)
Gen. 37:36; 39:1.

6319. פּוֹטִי פֶרַע *pôṯiy p̱era'* **masc. proper noun**
(Potipherah)
Gen. 41:45,50; 46:20.

6320. I. פּוּךְ *pûḵ* **masc. noun**
(glistening stones, perhaps antimony or turquoise, used in decoration)
1 Chr. 29:2; **Isa.** 54:11.
II. פּוּךְ *pûḵ* **masc. noun**
(glistening pigment used to paint the eyes)
2 Kgs. 9:30; **Jer.** 4:30.

6321. פּוֹל *pôl* **masc. noun**
(beans)
2 Sam. 17:28; **Ezek.** 4:9.

6322. A. פּוּל *pûl* **masc. proper noun**
(Pul, shortened form of *tilgaṯ pil'ēser* [8407])
2 Kgs. 15:19; **1 Chr.** 5:26.
B. פּוּל *pûl* **proper noun**
(the nation of Pul; probably Libya)
Isa. 66:19.

6323. פּוּן *pûn* **verb**
(to be distracted, to be in despair)
Ps. 88:15(16).

6324. פּוּנִי *pûniy* **masc. proper noun**
(Punites, descendants of Puah [6312,A])
Num. 26:23.

6325. פּוּנֹן *pûnōn* **proper noun**
(Punon)
Num. 33:42,43.

6326. פּוּעָה *pûʿāh* **fem. proper noun**
(Puah)
Ex. 1:15.

6327. I. פּוּץ *pûṣ* **verb**
(to scatter, to disperse)
Gen. 10:18; 11:4,8,9; 49:7; **Ex.** 5:12; **Num.** 10:35; **Deut.** 4:27; 28:64; 30:3; **1 Sam.** 11:11; 13:8; 14:34; **2 Sam.** 18:8; 20:22; 22:15; **1 Kgs.** 22:17; **2 Kgs.** 25:5; **2 Chr.** 18:16; **Neh.** 1:8; **Job** 18:11; 37:11; 38:24; 40:11; **Ps.** 18:14(15); 68:1(2); 144:6; **Prov.** 5:16; **Isa.** 24:1; 28:25; 41:16; **Jer.** 9:16(15); 10:21; 13:24; 18:17; 23:1,2; 30:11; 40:15; 52:8; **Ezek.** 11:16,17; 12:15; 20:23,34,41; 22:15; 28:25; 29:12,13; 30:23,26; 34:5,6,12,21; 36:19; 46:18; **Nah.** 2:1(2); **Hab.** 3:14; **Zeph.** 3:10; **Zech.** 1:17; 13:7.
II. פּוּץ *pûṣ* **verb**
(to shatter, to crush, to break in pieces)
Job 16:12(NASB, NIV, *pāṣaṣ* [6483,III]); **Jer.** 23:29(NASB, NIV, *pāṣaṣ* [6483,III]); **Hab.** 3:6(NASB, NIV, *pāṣaṣ* [6483,III]).

6328. פּוּק *pûq* **verb**
(to stumble, to totter)
Isa. 28:7; **Jer.** 10:4.

6329. פּוּק *pûq* **verb**
(to obtain, to bring out)
Ps. 140:8(9); 144:13; **Prov.** 3:13; 8:35; 12:2; 18:22; **Isa.** 58:10.

6330. פּוּקָה *pûqāh* **fem. noun**
(grief, burden on conscience)
1 Sam. 25:31.

6331. פּוּר *pûr* **verb**
(to break, to bring to nought; NASB, NIV, *pārar* [6565])
Ps. 33:10; 89:33(34); **Ezek.** 17:19.

6332. פּוּר *pûr* **masc. noun**
(a lot which is cast to make decisions; in plural, Purim, Jewish feast day)
Esth. 3:7; 9:24,26,28,29,31,32.

6333. פּוּרָה *pûrāh* **fem. noun**
(winepress, wine vat)
Isa. 63:3; **Hag.** 2:16.

6334. פּוֹרָתָה *pôrāṯah* **masc. proper noun**
(Poratha)
Esth. 9:8.

6335. I. פּוּשׁ *pûš* **verb**
(to leap, to spring about, to gallop)
Jer. 50:11(KJV, see II); **Hab.** 1:8(KJV, see II); **Mal.** 4:2(3:20)(KJV, see II).
II. פּוּשׁ *pûš* **verb**
(to scatter; to spread out, to grow fat)
Jer. 50:11(NASB, NIV, see I); **Nah.** 3:18; **Hab.** 1:8(NASB, NIV, see I); **Mal.** 4:2(3:20)(NASB, NIV, see I).

6336. פּוּתִי *pûṯiy* **masc. proper noun**
(Puthites)
1 Chr. 2:53.

6337. פַּז *paz* **masc. noun**
(pure gold, fine gold)
Job 28:17; **Ps.** 19:10(11); 21:3(4); 119:127; **Prov.** 8:19; **Song** 5:11,15; **Isa.** 13:12; **Lam.** 4:2.

6338. פָּזַז *pāzaz* **verb**
(to refine, to be refined [of gold])
1 Kgs. 10:18.

6339. I. פָּזַז *pāzaz* **verb**
(to be agile, to be limber)
Gen. 49:24(KJV, see II).

II. פָּזַז *pāzaz* **verb**
(to be strong)
Gen. 49:24(NASB, NIV, see I).

III. פָּזַז *pāzaz* **verb**
(to leap)
2 Sam. 6:16.

6340. פָּזַר *pāzar* **verb**
(to scatter; to be scattered)
Esth. 3:8; **Ps.** 53:5(6); 89:10(11); 112:9; 141:7; 147:16; **Prov.** 11:24; **Jer.** 3:13; 50:17; **Joel** 3:2(4:2).

6341. I. פַּח *paḥ* **masc. noun**
(snare, trap)
Josh. 23:13; **Job** 18:9; 22:10; **Ps.** 11:6; 69:22(23); 91:3; 119:110; 124:7; 140:5(6); 141:9; 142:3(4); **Prov.** 7:23; 22:5; **Eccl.** 9:12; **Isa.** 8:14; 24:17,18; **Jer.** 18:22; 48:43,44; **Hos.** 5:1; 9:8; **Amos** 3:5.

II. פַּח *paḥ* **masc. noun**
(thin sheet, thin plate [of gold])
Ex. 39:3; **Num.** 16:38(17:3).

6342. פָּחַד *pāḥad̲* **verb**
(to fear, to be afraid, to tremble)
Deut. 28:66,67; **Job** 3:25; 4:14; 23:15; **Ps.** 14:5; 27:1; 53:5(6); 78:53; 119:161; **Prov.** 3:24; 28:14; **Isa.** 12:2; 19:16,17; 33:14; 44:8,11; 51:13; 60:5; **Jer.** 33:9; 36:16,24; **Hos.** 3:5; **Mic.** 7:17.

6343. פַּחַד *paḥad̲* **masc. noun**
(fear, terror, dread)
Gen. 31:42,53; **Ex.** 15:16; **Deut.** 2:25; 11:25; 28:67; **1 Sam.** 11:7; **1 Chr.** 14:17; **2 Chr.** 14:14(13); 17:10; 19:7; 20:29; **Esth.** 8:17; 9:2,3; **Job** 3:25; 4:14; 13:11; 15:21; 21:9; 22:10; 25:2; 31:23; 39:16,22; **Ps.** 14:5; 31:11(12); 36:1(2); 53:5(6); 64:1(2); 91:5; 105:38; 119:120; **Prov.** 1:26,27,33; 3:25; **Song** 3:8; **Isa.** 2:10, 19,21; 24:17,18; **Jer.** 30:5; 48:43,44; 49:5; **Lam.** 3:47.

6344. I. פַּחַד *paḥad̲* **masc. noun**
(thigh)
Job 40:17(KJV, see II).

II. פַּחַד *paḥad̲* **masc. noun**
(testicle)
Job 40:17(NASB, NIV, see I).

6345. פַּחְדָּה *paḥdāh* **fem. noun**
(fear, dread, awe)
Jer. 2:19.

6346. פֶּחָה *peḥāh* **masc. noun**
(governor, official, captain)
1 Kgs. 10:15; 20:24; **2 Kgs.** 18:24; **2 Chr.** 9:14; **Ezra** 8:36; **Neh.** 2:7,9; 3:7; 5:14,15,18; 12:26; **Esth.** 3:12; 8:9; 9:3; **Isa.** 36:9; **Jer.** 51:23,28,57; **Ezek.** 23:6,12,23; **Hag.** 1:1,14; 2:2,21; **Mal.** 1:8.

6347. פֶּחָה *peḥāh* **Aram. masc. noun**
(governor; corr. to Hebr. 6346)
Ezra 5:3,6,14; 6:6,7,13; **Dan.** 3:2,3,27; 6:7(8).

6348. פָּחַז *pāḥaz* **verb**
(to be reckless, to be arrogant)
Judg. 9:4; **Zeph.** 3:4.

6349. פַּחַז *paḥaz* **masc. noun**
(recklessness, uncontrollableness)
Gen. 49:4.

6350. פַּחֲזוּת *paḥᵃzûṯ* **fem. noun**
(recklessness)
Jer. 23:32.

6351. פָּחַח *pāḥaḥ* **verb**
(to ensnare, to trap)
Isa. 42:22.

6352. פֶּחָם *peḥām* **masc. noun**
(pieces of coal, charcoal)
Prov. 26:21; **Isa.** 44:12; 54:16.

6353. פֶּחָר *peḥār* **Aram. masc. noun**
(potter)
Dan. 2:41.

6354. פַּחַת *paḥaṯ* **masc. noun**
(pit, cave)
2 Sam. 17:9; 18:17; **Isa.** 24:17,18; **Jer.** 48:28,43,44; **Lam.** 3:47.

6355. פַּחַת מוֹאָב *paḥaṯ mô'āḇ* **masc. proper noun**
(Pahath-Moab)
Ezra 2:6; 8:4; 10:30; **Neh.** 3:11; 7:11; 10:14(15).

6356. פְּחֶתֶת *p^eḥeṯeṯ* **fem. noun**
(mildew, decay of a fabric)
Lev. 13:55.

6357. פִּטְדָה *piṭḏāh* **fem. noun**
(topaz, a precious stone)
Ex. 28:17; 39:10; **Job** 28:19; **Ezek.** 28:13.

6358. פָּטוּר *pāṭûr* **adj.**
(open; NASB, NIV, pass. part. of *pāṭar* [6362])
1 Kgs. 6:18,29,32,35.

6359. פָּטִיר *pāṭiyr* **adj.**
(free from, exempt from)
1 Chr. 9:33(NASB, NIV, *pāṭar* [6362]).

6360. פַּטִּישׁ *paṭṭiyš* **masc. noun**
(hammer)
Isa. 41:7; **Jer.** 23:29; 50:23.

6361. פַּטִּישׁ *paṭṭiyš* **Aram. masc. noun**
(trousers, hose)
Dan. 3:21.

6362. פָּטַר *pāṭar* **verb**
(to open, to release, to separate)
1 Sam. 19:10; **1 Kgs.** 6:18(KJV, *pāṭûr* [6358]),29(KJV, *pāṭûr* [6358]),32(KJV, *pāṭûr* [6358]),35(KJV, *pāṭûr* [6358]); **1 Chr.** 9:33(KJV, *pāṭiyr* [6359]); **2 Chr.** 23:8; **Ps.** 22:7(8); **Prov.** 17:14.

6363. A. פֶּטֶר *peṭer* **masc. noun**
(firstborn one)
Ex. 13:2,12,13,15; 34:19,20; **Num.** 3:12; 18:15; **Ezek.** 20:26.
B. פִּטְרָה *piṭrāh* **fem. noun**
(firstborn one)
Num. 8:16.

6364. פִּי בֶסֶת *piy ḇeseṯ* **proper noun**
(Pi-beseth; also known as Bubastis)
Ezek. 30:17.

6365. פִּיד *piyḏ* **masc. noun**
(disaster, destruction)
Job 30:24; 31:29; **Prov.** 24:22.

6366. פֵּיָה *pēyāh* **fem. noun**
(edge [of a sword])
Judg. 3:16.

6367. פִּי הַחִירֹת *piy haḥiyrōṯ* **proper noun**
(Pi Hahiroth)
Ex. 14:2,9; **Num.** 33:7,8.

6368. פִּיחַ *piyaḥ* **masc. noun**
(soot, ashes)
Ex. 9:8,10.

6369. פִּיכֹל *piyḵōl* **masc. proper noun**
(Phicol)
Gen. 21:22,32; 26:26.

6370. פִּילֶגֶשׁ *piylegeš* **fem. noun**
(concubine, paramour)
Gen. 22:24; 25:6; 35:22; 36:12; **Judg.** 8:31; 19:1,2,9,10,24,25,27,29; 20:4–6; **2 Sam.** 3:7; 5:13; 15:16; 16:21,22; 19:5(6); 20:3; 21:11; **1 Kgs.** 11:3; **1 Chr.** 1:32; 2:46,48; 3:9; 7:14; **2 Chr.** 11:21; **Esth.** 2:14; **Song** 6:8,9; **Ezek.** 23:20.

6371. פִּימָה *piymāh* **fem. noun**
(bulges of fat)
Job 15:27.

6372. A. פִּינְחָס *piynᵉḥās* **masc. proper noun**
(Phinehas: son of Eleazar)
Ex. 6:25; **Num.** 25:7,11; 31:6; **Josh.** 22:13,30–32; 24:33; **Judg.** 20:28; **1 Chr.** 6:4(5:30),50(35); 9:20; **Ps.** 106:30.
B. פִּינְחָס *piynᵉḥās* **masc. proper noun**
(Phinehas: son of Eli)
1 Sam. 1:3; 2:34; 4:4,11,17,19; 14:3.
C. פִּינְחָס *piynᵉḥās* **masc. proper noun**
(Phinehas: son of a priest)
Ezra 7:5; 8:2,33.

6373. פִּינֹן *piynōn* **masc. proper noun**
(Pinon)
Gen. 36:41; **1 Chr.** 1:52.

6374. פִּיפִיּוֹת *piypiyyôṯ* **fem. pl. noun**
(double-edged)
Ps. 149:6; **Isa.** 41:15.

6375. I. פִּיק *piyq* **masc. noun**
(knocking together [of knees])
Nah. 2:10(11)(NIV, see II).
II. פִּיק *piyq* **masc. noun**
(failing, giving out [of knees])
Nah. 2:10(11)(KJV, NASB, see I).

6376. פִּישׁוֹן *piyšôn* **proper noun**
(Pishon)
Gen. 2:11.

6377. פִּיתוֹן *piyṯôn* **masc. proper noun**
(Pithon)
1 Chr. 8:35; 9:41.

6378. פַּךְ *paḵ* **masc. noun**
(vial, flask)
1 Sam. 10:1; **2 Kgs.** 9:1,3.

6379. פָּכָה *pāḵāh* **verb**
(to trickle, to flow)
Ezek. 47:2.

6380. I. פֹּכֶרֶת הַצְּבָיִים *pōḵereṯ haṣṣᵉḇāyiym* **masc. proper noun**
(Pokereth-Hazzebaim)
Ezra 2:57(KJV, see II); **Neh.** 7:59 (KJV, see II).
II. פֹּכֶרֶת הַצְּבָיִים *pōḵereṯ haṣṣᵉḇāyiym* **masc. proper noun**
(Pochereth of Zebaim)
Ezra 2:57(NASB, NIV, see I); **Neh.** 7:59(NASB, NIV, see I).

6381. פָּלָא *pālā'* **verb**
(to be extraordinary, to be wonderful, to be marvelous)
Gen. 18:14; **Ex.** 3:20; 34:10; **Lev.** 22:21; 27:2; **Num.** 6:2; 15:3,8; **Deut.** 17:8; 28:59; 30:11; **Josh.** 3:5; **Judg.** 6:13; 13:19; **2 Sam.** 1:26; 13:2; **1 Chr.** 16:9, 12,24; **2 Chr.** 2:9(8); 26:15; **Neh.** 9:17; **Job** 5:9; 9:10; 10:16; 37:5,14; 42:3; **Ps.** 9:1(2); 26:7; 31:21(22); 40:5(6); 71:17; 72:18; 75:1(2); 78:4,11,32; 86:10; 96:3; 98:1; 105:2,5; 106:7,22; 107:8,15,21,24,31; 111:4; 118:23; 119:18,27; 131:1; 136:4; 139:14; 145:5; **Prov.** 30:18; **Isa.** 28:29; 29:14; **Jer.** 21:2; 32:17,27; **Dan.** 8:24; 11:36; **Joel** 2:26; **Mic.** 7:15; **Zech.** 8:6.

6382. פֶּלֶא *pele'* **masc. noun**
(wonder, miracle)
Ex. 15:11; **Ps.** 77:11(12),14(15); 78:12; 88:10(11),12(13); 89:5(6); 119:129; **Isa.** 9:6(5); 25:1; 29:14; **Lam.** 1:9; **Dan.** 12:6.

6383. פִּלְאִי *pil'iy*, פֶּלִיא *peliy'* **adj.**
(beyond understanding)
Judg. 13:18; **Ps.** 139:6.

6384. פַּלֻּאִי *pallu'iy* **masc. proper noun**
(Palluites)
Num. 26:5.

6385. פָּלַג *pālag* **verb**
(to divide, to cut)
Gen. 10:25; **1 Chr.** 1:19; **Job** 38:25; **Ps.** 55:9(10).

6386. פְּלַג *p^elag* **Aram. verb**
(to divide; corr. to Hebr. 6385)
Dan. 2:41.

6387. פְּלַג *p^elag* **Aram. masc. noun**
(half)
Dan. 7:25.

6388. פֶּלֶג *peleg* **masc. noun**
(stream, channel)
Job 29:6; **Ps.** 1:3; 46:4(5); 65:9(10); 119:136; **Prov.** 5:16; 21:1; **Isa.** 30:25; 32:2; **Lam.** 3:48.

6389. פֶּלֶג *peleg* **masc. proper noun**
(Peleg)
Gen. 10:25; 11:16–19; **1 Chr.** 1:19,25.

6390. I. פְּלַגָּה *p^elaggāh* **fem. noun**
(division, district)
Judg. 5:15,16.
II. פְּלַגָּה *p^elaggāh* **fem. noun**
(stream, river)
Job 20:17.

6391. פְּלֻגָּה *p^eluggāh* **fem. noun**
(division)
2 Chr. 35:5.

6392. פְּלֻגָּה *p^eluggāh* **Aram. fem. noun**
(division; corr. to Hebr. 6391)
Ezra 6:18.

6393. I. פְּלָדָה *p^elāḏāh* **fem. noun**
(metal, steel)
Nah. 2:3(4)(KJV, see II).
II. פְּלָדָה *p^elāḏāh* **fem. noun**
(torch)
Nah. 2:3(4)(NASB, NIV, see I).

6394. פִּלְדָּשׁ *pildāš* **masc. proper noun**
(Pildash)
Gen. 22:22.

6395. פָּלָה *pālāh* **verb**
(to distinguish, to make a distinction)
Ex. 8:22(18); 9:4; 11:7; 33:16; **Ps.** 4:3(4); 17:7; 139:14.

6396. פַּלּוּא *pallû'* **masc. proper noun**
(Pallu)
Gen. 46:9; **Ex.** 6:14; **Num.** 26:5,8; **1 Chr.** 5:3.

6397. פְּלוֹנִי *p^elôniy* **masc. proper noun**
(Pelonite)
1 Chr. 11:27,36; 27:10.

6398. פָּלַח *pālaḥ* **verb**
(to slice, to cut up, to plow, to pierce through)
2 Kgs. 4:39; **Job** 16:13; 39:3; **Ps.** 141:7; **Prov.** 7:23.

6399. פְּלַח *p^elaḥ* **Aram. verb**
(to serve, to minister)
Ezra 7:24; **Dan.** 3:12,14,17,18,28; 6:16(17),20(21); 7:14,27.

6400. פֶּלַח *pelaḥ* **masc. noun**
(piece [of fruit]; piece [of a millstone])
Judg. 9:53; **1 Sam.** 30:12; **2 Sam.** 11:21; **Job** 41:24(16); **Song** 4:3; 6:7.

6401. פִּלְחָא *pilḥā'* **masc. proper noun**
(Pilha)
Neh. 10:24(25).

6402. פָּלְחַן *polḥan* **Aram. masc. noun**
(service, worship)
Ezra 7:19.

6403. פָּלַט *pālaṭ* **verb**
(to escape, to rescue, to bring to safety)
2 Sam. 22:2,44; **Job** 21:10; 23:7; **Ps.** 17:13; 18:2(3),43(44),48(49); 22:4(5),8(9); 31:1(2); 37:40; 40:17(18); 43:1; 56:7(8)(KJV, NASB, *pallēṭ* [6405,B]); 70:5(6); 71:2,4; 82:4; 91:14; 144:2; **Isa.** 5:29; **Ezek.** 7:16; **Mic.** 6:14.

6404. פֶּלֶט *peleṭ* **masc. proper noun**
(Pelet)
1 Chr. 2:47; 12:3.

6405. I. פָּלֵט *pālēṭ* **masc. noun**
(refugee, fugitive)
Jer. 44:14; 50:28; 51:50.
II. פַּלֵּט *pallēṭ* **masc. noun**
(deliverance, escape)
Ps. 32:7; 56:7(8)(NIV, *pālaṭ* [6403]).

6406. פַּלְטִי *palṭiy* **masc. proper noun**
(Palti)
Num. 13:9; **1 Sam.** 25:44.

6407. פַּלְטִי *palṭiy* **masc. proper noun**
(Paltite)
2 Sam. 23:26.

6408. פִּלְטָי *pilṭāy* **masc. proper noun**
(Piltai)
Neh. 12:17.

6409. פַּלְטִיאֵל *palṭiy'ēl* **masc. proper noun**
(Paltiel)
Num. 34:26; **2 Sam.** 3:15.

6410. A. פְּלַטְיָה *p^e^laṭyāh* **masc. proper noun**
(Pelatiah: son of Hananiah)
1 Chr. 3:21.
B. פְּלַטְיָה *p^e^laṭyāh* **masc. proper noun**
(Pelatiah: son of Ishi)
1 Chr. 4:42.
C. פְּלַטְיָה *p^e^laṭyāh* **masc. proper noun**
(Pelatiah: a leader who signed Nehemiah's covenant)
Neh. 10:22(23).
D. פְּלַטְיָהוּ *p^e^laṭyāhû* **masc. proper noun**
(Pelatiah: son of Benaiah)
Ezek. 11:1,13.

6411. A. פְּלָאיָה *p^e^lā'yāh* **masc. proper noun**
(Pelaiah: descendant of David)
Neh. 8:7; 10:10(11).
B. פְּלָיָה *p^e^lāyāh* **masc. proper noun**
(Pelaiah: postexilic priest)
1 Chr. 3:24.

6412. A. פָּלִיט *pāliyṭ* **masc. noun**
(refugee, survivor)
Gen. 14:13; **Josh.** 8:22; **Judg.** 12:4,5; **2 Kgs.** 9:15; **Isa.** 45:20; **Jer.** 42:17; 44:14,28; 50:28; 51:50; **Lam.** 2:22; **Ezek.** 6:8,9; 7:16; 24:26,27; 33:21,22; **Amos** 9:1; **Obad.** 1:14.
B. פָּלֵיט *pālēṭ* **masc. noun**
(refugee, survivor)
Num. 21:29; **Isa.** 66:19.

6413. פְּלֵיטָה *p^e^lēyṭāh* **fem. noun**
(escape, deliverance, survivor)
Gen. 32:8(9); 45:7; **Ex.** 10:5; **Judg.** 21:17; **2 Sam.** 15:14; **2 Kgs.** 19:30,31; **1 Chr.** 4:43; **2 Chr.** 12:7; 20:24; 30:6; **Ezra** 9:8,13–15; **Neh.** 1:2; **Isa.** 4:2; 10:20; 15:9; 37:31,32; **Jer.** 25:35; 50:29; **Ezek.** 14:22; **Dan.** 11:42; **Joel** 2:3,32(3:5); **Obad.** 1:17.

6414. פָּלִיל *pāliyl* **masc. noun**
(judge, judgment)
Ex. 21:22; **Deut.** 32:31; **Job** 31:11 (NIV, *p^e^liyliy* [6416]).

6415. פְּלִילָה *p^e^liylāh* **fem. noun**
(judgment, judge)
Isa. 16:3.

6416. פְּלִילִי *p^e^liyliy* **adj.**
(liable for judgment)
Job 31:11(KJV, NASB, *pāliyl* [6414]),28.

6417. פְּלִילִיָּה *p^e^liyliyyah* **fem. noun**
(judgment, decision)
Isa. 28:7.

6418. I. פֶּלֶךְ *pelek̲* **masc. noun**
(walking stick, crutch; spindle)
2 Sam. 3:29; **Neh.** 3:9,12,14–18; **Prov.** 31:19.
II. פֶּלֶךְ *pelek̲* **masc. noun**
(district)
Neh. 3:9,12,14–18.

6419. פָּלַל *pālal* **verb**
(to pray, to intervene, to make supplication)
Gen. 20:7,17; 48:11; **Num.** 11:2; 21:7; **Deut.** 9:20,26; **1 Sam.** 1:10,12,26,27; 2:1,25; 7:5; 8:6; 12:19,23; **2 Sam.** 7:27; **1 Kgs.** 8:28–30,33,35,42,44,48,54; 13:6; **2 Kgs.** 4:33; 6:17,18; 19:15,20; 20:2; **1 Chr.** 17:25; **2 Chr.** 6:19–21,24,26,32, 34,38; 7:1,14; 30:18; 32:20,24; 33:13; **Ezra** 10:1; **Neh.** 1:4,6; 2:4; 4:9(3); **Job** 42:8,10; **Ps.** 5:2(3); 32:6; 72:15; 106:30; **Isa.** 16:12; 37:15,21; 38:2; 44:17; 45:14,20; **Jer.** 7:16; 11:14; 14:11; 29:7,12; 32:16; 37:3; 42:2,4,20; **Ezek.** 16:52; **Dan.** 9:4,20; **Jon.** 2:1(2); 4:2.

6420. פָּלָל *pālāl* **masc. proper noun**
(Palal)
Neh. 3:25.

6421. פְּלַלְיָה *p^e^lalyāh* **masc. proper noun**
(Pelaliah)
Neh. 11:12.

6422. פַּלְמוֹנִי *palmôniy* **pron.**
(a certain one)
Dan. 8:13.

6423. פְּלֹנִי *p^e^lōniy* **pron.**
(a certain one)
Ruth 4:1; **1 Sam.** 21:2(3); **2 Kgs.** 6:8.

6424. פָּלַס *pālas* **verb**
(to weigh out, to make level, to ponder)
Ps. 58:2(3); 78:50; **Prov.** 4:26; 5:6,21; **Isa.** 26:7.

6425. פֶּלֶס *peles* **masc. noun**
(balance, scale)
Prov. 16:11; **Isa.** 40:12.

6426. פָּלַץ *pālaṣ* **verb**
(to tremble)
Job 9:6.

6427. פַּלָּצוּת *pallāṣûṯ* **fem. noun**
(horror, fear, trembling)
Job 21:6; **Ps.** 55:5(6); **Isa.** 21:4; **Ezek.** 7:18.

6428. פָּלַשׁ *pālaš* **verb**
(to roll in, to wallow in)
Jer. 6:26; 25:34; **Ezek.** 27:30; **Mic.** 1:10.

6429. פְּלֶשֶׁת *p^e^lešeṯ* **proper noun**
(Philistia, land of the Philistines)
Ex. 15:14; **Ps.** 60:8(10); 83:7(8); 87:4; 108:9(10); **Isa.** 14:29,31; **Joel** 3:4(4:4).

6430. פְּלִשְׁתִּי *p^e^lištiy* **masc. proper noun**
(Philistine)
Gen. 10:14; 21:32,34; 26:1,8,14,15,18; **Ex.** 13:17; 23:31; **Josh.** 13:2,3; **Judg.** 3:3,31; 10:6,7,11; 13:1,5; 14:1–4; 15:3,5, 6,9,11,12,14,20; 16:5,8,9,12,14,18,20, 21,23,27,28,30; **1 Sam.** 4:1–3,6,7,9, 10,17; 5:1,2,8,11; 6:1,2,4,12,16–18,21; 7:3,7,8,10,11,13,14; 9:16; 10:5; 12:9;

13:3–5,11,12,16,17,19,20,23; 14:1,4,11, 19,21,22,30,31,36,37,46,47,52; 17:1–4, 8,10,11,16,19,21,23,26,32,33,36,37,40–4 6,48–55,57; 18:6,17,21,25,27,30; 19:5,8; 21:9(10); 22:10; 23:1–5,27,28; 24:1(2); 27:1,7,11; 28:1,4,5,15,19; 29:1–4,7,9,11; 30:16; 31:1,2,7–9,11; **2 Sam.** 1:20; 3:14, 18; 5:17–19,22,24,25; 8:1,12; 19:9(10); 21:12,15,17–19; 23:9–14,16; **1 Kgs.** 4:21(5:1); 15:27; 16:15; **2 Kgs.** 8:2,3; 18:8; **1 Chr.** 1:12; 10:1,2,7–9,11; 11:13–16,18; 12:19; 14:8–10,13,15,16; 18:1,11; 20:4,5; **2 Chr.** 9:26; 17:11; 21:16; 26:6,7; 28:18; **Ps.** 56:[title](1); **Isa.** 2:6; 9:12(11); 11:14; **Jer.** 25:20; 47:1,4; **Ezek.** 16:27,57; 25:15,16; **Amos** 1:8; 6:2; 9:7; **Obad.** 1:19; **Zeph.** 2:5; **Zech.** 9:6.

6431. פֶּלֶת *pelet̲* **masc. proper noun**
(Peleth)
Num. 16:1; **1 Chr.** 2:33.

6432. פְּלֵתִי *p^elēt̲iy* **masc. proper noun**
(Pelethite)
2 Sam. 8:18; 15:18; 20:7,23; **1 Kgs.** 1:38,44; **1 Chr.** 18:17.

6433. פֻּם *pum* **Aram. masc. noun**
(mouth)
Dan. 4:31(28); 6:17(18),22(23); 7:5, 8,20.

6434. פֵּן *pēn* **masc. noun**
(corner, street corner)
Zech. 14:10(NASB, NIV, *pinnāh* [6438]).

6435. פֶּן *pen* **conj.**
(lest, so that not)
Gen. 3:3,22; 11:4; 19:15,17,19; 24:6; 26:7,9; 31:24,31; 32:11; 38:11,23; 42:4; 44:34; 45:11; **Ex.** 1:10; 5:3; 13:17; 19:21, 22,24; 20:19; 23:29,33; 33:3; 34:12,15; **Lev.** 10:7; **Num.** 16:26,34; 20:18; **Deut.** 4:9,16,19,23; 6:12,15; 7:22,25; 8:11,12; 9:28; 11:16; 12:13,19,30; 15:9; 19:6; 20:5–7; 22:9; 25:3; 29:18; 32:27; **Josh.** 2:16; 6:18; 24:27; **Judg.** 7:2; 9:54; 14:15; 15:12; 18:25; **Ruth** 4:6; **1 Sam.** 9:5; 13:19; 15:6; 20:3; 27:11; 31:4; **2 Sam.** 1:20; 12:28; 15:14; 17:16; 20:6; **2 Kgs.** 2:16; 10:23; **1 Chr.** 10:4; **Job** 32:13; 36:18; **Ps.** 2:12; 7:2; 13:3,4; 28:1; 38:16; 50:22; 59:11; 91:12; **Prov.** 5:6,9,10; 9:8; 20:13; 22:25; 24:18; 25:8,10,16,17; 26:4,5; 30:6,9,10; 31:5; **Isa.** 6:10; 27:3; 28:22; 36:18; 48:5,7; **Jer.** 1:17; 4:4; 6:8; 10:24; 21:12; 38:19; 51:46; **Hos.** 2:3; **Amos** 5:6; **Mal.** 4:6.

6436. I. פַּנַּג *pannag* **masc. noun**
(cake, confection)
Ezek. 27:17(KJV, see II).
II. פַּנַּג *pannag* **proper noun**
(pannag [name of a food])
Ezek. 27:17(NASB, NIV, see I).

6437. פָּנָה *pānāh* **verb**
(to turn away, to turn toward, to consider)
Gen. 18:22; 24:31,49,63; **Ex.** 2:12; 7:23; 10:6; 14:27; 16:10; 32:15; **Lev.** 14:36; 19:4,31; 20:6; 26:9; **Num.** 12:10; 14:25; 16:15,42(17:7); 21:33; **Deut.** 1:7,24, 40; 2:1,3,8; 3:1; 9:15,27; 10:5; 16:7; 23:11(12); 29:18(17); 30:17; 31:18,20; **Josh.** 7:12; 8:20; 15:2,7; 22:4; **Judg.** 6:14; 15:4; 18:21,26; 19:26; 20:40,42, 45,47; **1 Sam.** 10:9; 13:17,18; 14:47; **2 Sam.** 1:7; 2:20; 9:8; **1 Kgs.** 2:3; 7:25; 8:28; 10:13; 17:3; **2 Kgs.** 2:24; 5:12; 13:23; 23:16; **2 Chr.** 4:4; 6:19; 13:14; 20:24; 25:23(NASB, NIV, *pinnāh* [6438]); 26:20; **Job** 5:1; 6:28; 21:5; 24:18; 36:21; **Ps.** 25:16; 40:4(5); 46:5(6); 69:16(17); 80:9(10); 86:16; 90:9; 102:17(18); 119:132; **Prov.** 17:8; **Eccl.** 2:11,12; **Song** 6:1; **Isa.** 8:21; 13:14; 40:3; 45:22; 53:6; 56:11; 57:14; 62:10; **Jer.** 2:27; 6:4; 32:33; 46:5,21; 47:3; 48:39; 49:8,24;

50:16; **Ezek.** 8:3; 9:2; 10:11; 11:1; 17:6; 29:16; 36:9; 43:1,17; 44:1; 46:1,12,19; 47:2; **Hos.** 3:1; **Nah.** 2:8(9); **Zeph.** 3:15; **Hag.** 1:9; **Mal.** 2:13; 3:1.

6438. פִּנָּה *pinnāh* **fem. noun**
(corner, cornerstone, corner tower)
Ex. 27:2; 38:2; **Judg.** 20:2; **1 Sam.** 14:38; **1 Kgs.** 7:34; **2 Kgs.** 14:13; **2 Chr.** 25:23(KJV, *pānāh* [6437]); 26:9,15; 28:24; **Neh.** 3:24,31,32; **Job** 1:19; 38:6; **Ps.** 118:22; **Prov.** 7:8,12; 21:9; 25:24; **Isa.** 19:13; 28:16; **Jer.** 31:38,40; 51:26; **Ezek.** 43:20; 45:19; **Zeph.** 1:16; 3:6; **Zech.** 10:4; 14:10(KJV, *pēn* [6434]).

6439. A. פְּנוּאֵל *p^{e}nû'ēl,* פְּנִיאֵל *p^{e}niy'ēl* **proper noun**
(Penuel: a city on the Jabbok river)
Gen. 32:30(31),31(32); **Judg.** 8:8,9,17; **1 Kgs.** 12:25.
B. פְּנוּאֵל *p^{e}nû'ēl* **masc. proper noun**
(Penuel: descendant of Judah)
1 Chr. 4:4.
C. פְּנוּאֵל *p^{e}nû'ēl* **masc. proper noun**
(Penuel: descendant of Benjamin)
1 Chr. 8:25.

6440. פָּנֶה *pāneh,* פָּנִים *pāniym* **masc. pl. noun**
(face, countenance; position before, in front)
Gen. 1:2,20,29; 2:6; 3:8; 4:5,6,14,16; 6:1,7,11,13; 7:1,3,4,7,18,23; 8:8,9,13; 9:23; 10:9; 11:4,8,9,28; 13:9,10; 16:6, 8,12; 17:1,3,17,18; 18:8,16,22; 19:13, 21,27,28; 20:15; 23:3,4,8,12,17,19; 24:7, 12,33,40,51; 25:9,18; 27:7,10,20,30,46; 29:26; 30:30,33,40; 31:2,5,21,35; 32:3(4), 16(17),17(18),20(21),21(22),30(31); 33:3,10,14,18; 34:10,21; 35:1,7; 36:6, 7,31; 38:15; 40:7,9; 41:31,43,46,56; 43:3,5,9,14,15,31,33,34; 44:14,23,26,29; 45:3,5,7; 46:28,30; 47:2,6,7,10,13,18; 48:11,15,20; 49:30; 50:1,13,16,18; **Ex.** 1:12; 2:15; 3:6,7; 4:3,21; 6:12,30; 7:9,10; 8:20(16),24(20); 9:10,11,13,30; 10:3, 10,11,14,28,29; 11:10; 13:21,22; 14:2, 9,19,25; 16:9,14,33,34; 17:5,6; 18:12; 19:7,18; 20:3,20; 21:1; 23:15,17,20, 21,23,27–31; 25:20,30,37; 26:9; 27:21; 28:12,25,27,29,30,35,37,38; 29:10,11, 23–26,42; 30:6,8,16,36; 32:1,5,11,12, 20,23,34; 33:2,11,14–16,19,20,23; 34:6,11,20,23,24,29,30,33–35; 35:13,20; 36:3; 37:9; 39:18,20,36; 40:5,6,23,25,26; **Lev.** 1:3,5,11; 3:1,7,8,12,13; 4:4,6,7,14, 15,17,18,24; 6:7(5:26),14(7),25(18); 7:30; 8:9,26,27,29; 9:2,4,5,21,24; 10:1–4, 15,17,19; 12:7; 13:41; 14:7,11,12,16,18, 23,24,27,29,31,53; 15:14,15,30; 16:1,2,7, 10,12–15,18,30; 17:4,5,10; 18:23,24,27, 28,30; 19:14,15,22,32; 20:3,5,6,23; 22:3; 23:11,20,28,40; 24:3,4,6,8; 26:7,8,10, 17,37; 27:8,11; **Num.** 3:4,6,7,38; 4:7; 5:16,18,25,30; 6:16,20,25,26; 7:3,10; 8:2,3,9–11,13,21,22; 9:6; 10:9,10,33,35; 11:20,31; 12:3,14; 13:22; 14:5,14,37, 42,43; 15:15,25,28; 16:2,4,7,9,16,17, 22,38(17:3),40(17:5),43(17:8),45(17:10), 46(17:11); 17:4(19),7(22),9(24),10(25); 18:2,19; 19:3,4,16; 20:3,6,9,10; 21:11,20; 22:3,33; 23:28; 24:1; 26:61; 27:2,5,17,19, 21,22; 31:50,54; 32:4,17,20–22,27,29,32; 33:7,8,47,52,55; 35:12; 36:1; **Deut.** 1:8,17,21,22,30,33,38,42,45; 2:10,12, 20–22,25,31,33,36; 3:18,28; 4:8,10,32, 37,38,44; 5:4,5,7; 6:15,19,25; 7:1,2,6,10, 19–24; 8:20; 9:2–5,18,19,25; 10:8,11,17; 11:4,23,25,26,32; 12:7,12,18,29,30; 14:2, 23,26; 15:20; 16:11,16,19; 17:18; 18:7,12; 19:17; 20:3,19; 21:16; 22:6,17; 23:14(15); 24:4,13; 25:2,9; 26:4,5,10,13; 27:7; 28:7,20,25,31,50,60; 29:10(9),15(14); 30:1,15,19; 31:3,5,6,8,11,17,18,21; 32:20,49; 33:1,27; 34:1,10; **Josh.** 1:5,14; 2:9–11,24; 3:6,10,11,14; 4:5,7,11–13,23; 5:1,14; 6:1,4,6–9,13,26; 7:4–6,8,10,12, 13,23; 8:5,6,10,14,15,32; 9:24; 10:8, 10–12,14; 11:6,10; 13:3,6,25; 14:15;

15:8,15; 17:4,7; 18:1,6,8,10,14,16; 19:11,51; 20:6,9; 21:44(42); 22:27,29; 23:3,5,9,13; 24:1,8,12,18; **Judg.** 1:10, 11,23; 2:3,14,18,21; 3:2,27; 4:14,15,23; 5:5; 6:2,6,9,11,18,22; 8:28; 9:21,39,40; 11:3,9,11,23,24,33; 13:15,20; 16:3,25; 18:21,23; 20:23,26,28,32,35,39,42; 21:2; **Ruth** 2:10; 4:7; **1 Sam.** 1:12,15,16,18, 19,22; 2:11,17,18,28,30,35; 3:1; 4:2,3,17; 5:3,4; 6:20; 7:6,7,10; 8:11,18,20; 9:9,12, 15,19,24,27; 10:5,8,19,25; 11:15; 12:2,7; 13:12; 14:13,25; 15:7,33; 16:8,10,16, 21,22; 17:7,24,31,41,49,57; 18:11–13,15, 16,29; 19:7,8,10,24; 20:1,15; 21:6(7), 7(8),10(11),12(13); 22:4; 23:18,24,26; 24:2(3); 25:10,19,23,35; 26:1,3,19,20; 28:22,25; 29:8; 30:16,20; 31:1; **2 Sam.** 2:14,17,22,24; 3:13,31,34,35; 5:3,20,24; 6:4,5,14,16,17,21; 7:9,15,16,18,23,26,29; 9:6; 10:9,13–16,18,19; 11:11,13,15; 13:9; 14:7,20,22,24,28,32,33; 15:1,14,18,23; 16:19; 17:11,19; 18:7–9,14; 19:4(5),5(6), 8(9),13(14),17(18),18(19); 20:8; 21:1,9; 23:11; 24:4,13; **1 Kgs.** 1:2,5,23,25,28, 32,50; 2:4,7,15–17,20,26,45; 3:6,12,15, 16,22,24,28; 5:3(17); 6:3,17(KJV, *lipnāy* [3942]),20,21,29(KJV, NASB, p^e*niymāh* [6441]); 7:6,42,48,49; 8:5,8,11,14,22,23, 25,28,31,33,40,46,50,54,59,62,64,65; 9:3,4,6,7,25; 10:8,24; 11:7,36; 12:2,6, 8,30; 13:6,34; 14:9,24; 15:3; 16:25,30,33; 17:1,3,5,14; 18:1,7,15,39,42,46; 19:11, 13,19; 21:4,26,29; 22:10,21; **2 Kgs.** 1:15; 3:14,24; 4:12,29,31,38,43,44; 5:1–3,15, 16,23,27; 6:1,22,32; 8:9,11,15; 9:14,32, 37; 10:4; 11:2,18; 12:17(18); 13:4,14,23; 14:8,11,12; 16:3,14,18; 17:2,8,11,18, 20,23; 18:5,22,24; 19:6,14,15,26; 20:2,3; 21:2,9,11,13; 22:10,19; 23:3,13,25,27; 24:3,20; 25:19,26,29; **1 Chr.** 1:43; 4:40; 5:10,25; 6:32(17); 9:20; 10:1; 11:3,13; 12:1,8,17; 13:8,10; 14:8,15; 15:24; 16:1, 4,6,11,27,29,30,33,37,39; 17:8,13,16,21, 24,25,27; 19:7,10,14–16,18,19; 21:12, 16,30; 22:5,8,18; 23:13,31; 24:2,6,31; 29:12,15,22,25; **2 Chr.** 1:5,6,10,12,13; 2:4(3),6(5); 3:4,8,13,15,17; 4:13,19,20; 5:6,9,14; 6:3,12,14,16,19,22,24,31,36,42; 7:4,7,14,17,19,20; 8:12; 9:7,11,23; 10:2, 6,8; 12:5; 13:7,8,13–16; 14:5(4),7(6), 10(9),12(11),13(12); 15:2,8; 18:9,20; 19:2,7,11; 20:3,5,7,9,12,13,15–18,21; 22:11; 23:17; 24:14; 25:8,14,17,21,22; 26:19; 27:6; 28:3,9,14; 29:6,11,19,23; 30:9; 31:20; 32:2,7,12,21; 33:2,9,12, 19,23; 34:4,18,24,27,31; 35:22; 36:12; **Ezra** 7:28; 8:21,29; 9:6,7,9,15; 10:1,6; **Neh.** 1:4,6,11; 2:1–3,5,6,13; 4:2(3:34), 5(3:37),9(3),14(8); 5:15; 6:19; 8:1–3; 9:8,11,24,28,32,35; 12:36; 13:4,5,19; **Esth.** 1:3,10,11,13,14,16,17,19; 2:9,11,17,23; 3:7; 4:2,5,6,8; 5:14; 6:1, 9,11,13; 7:6,8,9; 8:1,3–5,15; 9:2,11,25; **Job** 1:11,12; 2:5,7; 3:24; 4:15,19; 5:10; 6:28; 8:12,16; 9:24,27; 11:15,19; 13:8, 10,15,16,20,24; 14:20; 15:4,7,27; 16:8, 14,16; 17:6,12; 18:17; 19:29; 21:8,18, 31,33; 22:8,26; 23:4,15,17; 24:15,18; 26:9,10; 29:24; 30:10,11; 32:21; 33:5,26; 34:19,29; 35:12,14; 37:12,19; 38:30; 39:22; 40:13; 41:10(2),13(5),14(6), 22(14); 42:8,9,11; **Ps.** 3:[title](1); 4:6(7); 5:8(9); 9:3(4),19(20); 10:11; 11:7; 13:1(2); 16:11; 17:2,9,13,15; 18:6(7), 42(43); 19:14(15); 21:6(7),9(10),12(13); 22:24(25),27(28),29(30); 23:5; 24:6; 27:8,9; 30:7(8); 31:16(17),20(21); 34:[title](1),5(6),16(17); 35:5; 38:3(4), 5(6); 41:12(13); 42:2(3),5(6),11(12); 43:5; 44:3(4),15(16),16(17),24(25); 45:12(13); 50:3; 51:9(11),11(13); 55:3(4); 56:13(14); 57:6(7); 60:4(6); 61:3(4),7(8); 62:8(9); 67:1(2); 68:1–4(2–5),7(8),8(9); 69:7(8),17(18),22(23); 72:5,9,17; 76:7(8); 78:55; 79:11; 80:2(3),3(4),7(8),9(10), 16(17),19(20); 82:2; 83:13(14),16(17); 84:9(10); 85:13(14); 86:9; 88:2(3),14(15); 89:14(15),15(16),23(24); 90:8; 95:2,6; 96:6,9,13; 97:3,5; 98:6,9; 100:2; 102:2(3), 10(11),25(26),28(29); 104:15,29,30; 105:4,17; 106:23,46; 114:7; 116:9; 119:58,135,169,170; 132:10; 139:7; 140:13(14); 141:2; 142:2(3); 143:2,7; 147:17; **Prov.** 4:3; 6:35; 7:13,15; 8:25,

27,30; 14:12,19; 15:13,33; 16:15,18,25; 17:14,18,24; 18:5,12,16; 19:6; 21:29; 22:29; 23:1; 24:23,31; 25:5–7,23,26; 27:4,17,19,23; 28:21; 29:26; 30:30; **Eccl.** 1:10,16; 2:7,9,26; 3:14; 4:16; 5:2(1),6(5); 7:3,26; 8:1,3,12,13; 9:1; 10:5,10; 11:1; **Song** 7:4(5); 8:12; **Isa.** 1:12; 2:10,19,21; 3:3,9,15; 5:21; 6:2; 7:2,16; 8:4,17; 9:3(2), 15(14); 10:27; 13:8; 14:21; 16:4; 17:9,13; 18:2,5; 19:1,8,16,17,20; 20:6; 21:15; 23:17,18; 24:1; 25:7,8; 26:17; 27:6; 28:25; 29:22; 30:11,17; 31:8; 36:7,9; 37:6,14,27; 38:2,3; 40:10; 41:2,26; 42:16; 43:10; 45:1,2; 48:7,19; 50:6,7; 51:13; 52:12; 53:2,3,7; 54:8; 55:12; 57:1,16; 58:8; 59:2; 62:11; 63:9,12; 64:1(63:19),2(1), 3(2),7(6); 65:3,6; 66:22,23; **Jer.** 1:8,13,17; 2:22,27; 3:12; 4:1,4,26; 5:3,22; 6:7; 7:10, 12,15,19,24; 8:2; 9:7(6),13(12),22(21); 13:17,26; 14:16; 15:1,9,17,19; 16:4,17; 17:16; 18:17,20,23; 19:7; 21:8,10,12; 22:25; 23:9,10,39; 24:1; 25:16,26,27,33, 37,38; 26:3,4,19; 27:5; 28:8,16; 30:6,20; 31:36; 32:24,31,33; 33:5,18,24; 34:5, 15,18; 35:5,7,11,19; 36:7,9,22; 37:11,20; 38:9,26; 39:16,17; 40:4,10; 41:9,15,18; 42:2,9,11,15,17; 44:3,10–12,22,23; 46:16; 48:44; 49:5,19,37; 50:5,8,16,44; 51:51,64; 52:3,12,25,33; **Lam.** 1:5,6,22; 2:3,19; 3:35; 4:16; 5:9,10,12; **Ezek.** 1:6,8–12,15,28; 2:4,6,10; 3:8,9,20,23; 4:1,3,7; 6:2,4,5,9; 7:18,22; 8:1,11,16; 9:6,8; 10:14,21,22; 11:13; 12:6,12; 13:17; 14:1,3,4,6–8,15; 15:7; 16:5,18,19,50,63; 20:1,35,43,46(21:2),47(21:3); 21:2(7), 16(21); 22:30; 23:24,41; 25:2; 27:35; 28:9,17,21; 29:2,5; 30:9,24; 32:4,10; 33:22,27,31; 34:6; 35:2; 36:17,31; 37:2; 38:2,20; 39:5,14,23,24,29; 40:6,12,15, 19,20,22,26,44–47; 41:4,12,14,15,18, 19,21,22,25; 42:2–4,7,8,10–13,15; 43:3, 4,24; 44:3,4,11,12,15; 45:7; 46:3,9; 47:1; 48:15,21; **Dan.** 1:5,9,10,13,18,19; 2:2; 8:3–7,17,18,23; 9:3,7,8,10,13,17,18,20; 10:6,9,12,15; 11:16–19,22; **Hos.** 2:2(4); 5:5,15; 6:2; 7:2,10; 10:7,15; 11:2; **Joel** 2:3,6,10,11,20,31(3:4); **Amos** 1:1; 2:9; 5:8,19; 9:4,6,8; **Jon.** 1:2,3,10; **Mic.** 1:4; 2:13; 3:4; 6:4; **Nah.** 1:5,6; 2:1(2),10(11); 3:5; **Hab.** 1:9; 2:20; 3:5; **Zeph.** 1:2,3,7; **Hag.** 1:12; 2:14; **Zech.** 2:13(17); 3:1,3, 4,8,9; 4:7; 5:3; 7:2; 8:10,21,22; 12:8; 14:4,5,20; **Mal.** 1:8,9; 2:3,5,9; 3:1,14,16; 4:5(3:23).

6441. פְּנִימָה p^{e}*niymāh* **adv.**
(within, inside, inner)
Lev. 10:18; **1 Kgs.** 6:18,19,21,29(NIV, *pāneh* [6440]),30; **2 Kgs.** 7:11; **2 Chr.** 3:4; 29:16,18; **Ps.** 45:13(14); **Ezek.** 40:16; 41:3.

6442. פְּנִימִי p^{e}*niymiy* **adj.**
(inner, inside)
1 Kgs. 6:27,36; 7:12,50; **1 Chr.** 28:11; **2 Chr.** 4:22; **Esth.** 4:11; 5:1; **Ezek.** 8:3,16; 10:3; 40:15,19,23,27,28,32,44; 41:15,17; 42:3,4,15; 43:5; 44:17,21,27; 45:19; 46:1.

6443. פְּנִינִים p^{e}*niyniym* **masc. pl. noun**
(jewels, rubies)
Prov. 3:15.

6444. פְּנִנָּה p^{e}*ninnāh* **fem. proper noun**
(Peninnah)
1 Sam. 1:2,4.

6445. פָּנַק *pānaq* **verb**
(to pamper)
Prov. 29:21.

6446. I. פַּס *pas* **adj.**
(richly ornamented; made with many colors)
Gen. 37:3,23,32; **2 Sam.** 13:18(NASB, see II),19(NASB, see II).
II. פַּס *pas* **adj.**
(long sleeved)
2 Sam. 13:18(KJV, NIV, see I),19(KJV, NIV, see I).

6447. פַּס *pas* **Aram. masc. noun**
(part [of the hand])
Dan. 5:5,24.

6448. פָּסַג *pāsag* **verb**
(to go through, to view)
Ps. 48:13(14).

6449. פִּסְגָּה *pisgāh* **proper noun**
(Pisgah)
Num. 21:20; 23:14; **Deut.** 3:17,27; 4:49; 34:1; **Josh.** 12:3; 13:20.

6450. פַּס דַּמִּים *pas dammiym* **proper noun**
(Pas Dammim)
1 Chr. 11:13.

6451. I. פִּסָּה *pissāh* **fem. noun**
(abundance, plenty)
Ps. 72:16(KJV, see II).
II. פִּסָּה *pissāh* **fem. noun**
(handful)
Ps. 72:16(NASB, NIV, see I).

6452. I. פָּסַח *pasaḥ* **verb**
(to pass over)
Ex. 12:13,23,27; **Isa.** 31:5.
II. פָּסַח *pasaḥ* **verb**
(to become lame, to limp; to hesitate, to waiver)
2 Sam. 4:4; **1 Kgs.** 18:21.
III. פָּסַח *pasaḥ* **verb**
(to leap, to dance)
1 Kgs. 18:26.

6453. פֶּסַח *pesaḥ* **masc. noun**
(Passover, Passover lamb)
Ex. 12:11,21,27,43,48; 34:25; **Lev.** 23:5; **Num.** 9:2,4–6,10,12–14; 28:16; 33:3; **Deut.** 16:1,2,5,6; **Josh.** 5:10,11; **2 Kgs.** 23:21–23; **2 Chr.** 30:1,2,5,15,17,18; 35:1,6–9,11,13,16–19; **Ezra** 6:19,20; **Ezek.** 45:21.

6454. פָּסֵחַ *pāsēaḥ* **masc. proper noun**
(Paseah)
1 Chr. 4:12; **Ezra** 2:49; **Neh.** 3:6; 7:51.

6455. פִּסֵּחַ *pissēaḥ* **adj.**
(lame, crippled)
Lev. 21:18; **Deut.** 15:21; **2 Sam.** 5:6,8; 9:13; 19:26(27); **Job** 29:15; **Prov.** 26:7; **Isa.** 33:23; 35:6; **Jer.** 31:8; **Mal.** 1:8,13.

6456. I. פָּסִיל *pāsiyl* **masc. noun**
(carved image, idol)
Deut. 7:5,25; 12:3; **Judg.** 3:19(KJV, see II),26(KJV, see II); **2 Kgs.** 17:41; **2 Chr.** 33:19,22; 34:3,4,7; **Ps.** 78:58; **Isa.** 10:10; 21:9; 30:22; 42:8; **Jer.** 8:19; 50:38; 51:47, 52; **Hos.** 11:2; **Mic.** 1:7; 5:13(12).
II. פָּסִיל *pāsiyl* **masc. noun**
(rock quarry)
Judg. 3:19(NASB, NIV, see I),26(NASB, NIV, see I).

6457. פָּסַךְ *pāsak̲* **masc. proper noun**
(Pasach)
1 Chr. 7:33.

6458. פָּסַל *pāsal* **verb**
(to chisel out, to cut out, to carve)
Ex. 34:1,4; **Deut.** 10:1,3; **1 Kgs.** 5:18(32); **Hab.** 2:18.

6459. פֶּסֶל *pesel* **masc. noun**
(carved image, idol)
Ex. 20:4; **Lev.** 26:1; **Deut.** 4:16,23,25; 5:8; 27:15; **Judg.** 17:3,4; 18:14,17,18, 20,30,31; **2 Kgs.** 21:7; **2 Chr.** 33:7; **Ps.** 97:7; **Isa.** 40:19,20; 42:17; 44:9,10,15,17; 45:20; 48:5; **Jer.** 10:14; 51:17; **Nah.** 1:14; **Hab.** 2:18.

6460. פְּסַנְתֵּרִין *p^esanṭēriyn*, פְּסַנְטֵרִין *p^esantēriyn* **Aram. masc. pl. noun**
(stringed musical instrument; harp, psaltery)
Dan. 3:5,7,10,15.

6461. פָּסַס *pāsas* **verb**
(to disappear, to vanish)
Ps. 12:1(2).

6462. פִּסְפָּה *pispāh* **masc. proper noun**

(Pispah)
1 Chr. 7:38.

6463. פָּעָה *pā'āh* **verb**
(to cry out, to groan)
Isa. 42:14.

6464. פָּעוּ *pā'û*, פָּעִי *pā'iy* **proper noun**
(Pau)
Gen. 36:39; **1 Chr.** 1:50.

6465. פְּעוֹר *pᵉ'ôr* **proper noun**
(Peor)
Num. 23:28; 25:18; 31:16; **Josh.** 22:17.

6466. פָּעַל *pā'al* **verb**
(to do, to make)
Ex. 15:17; **Num.** 23:23; **Deut.** 32:27; **Job** 7:20; 11:8; 22:17; 31:3; 33:29; 34:8, 22,32; 35:6; 36:3,23; 37:12(KJV, *pō'al* [6467]); **Ps.** 5:5(6); 6:8(9); 7:13(14), 15(16); 11:3; 14:4; 15:2; 28:3; 31:19(20); 36:12(13); 44:1(2); 53:4(5); 58:2(3); 59:2(3); 64:2(3); 68:28(29); 74:12; 92:7(8),9(10); 94:4,16; 101:8; 119:3; 125:5; 141:4,9; **Prov.** 10:29; 16:4; 21:15; 30:20; **Isa.** 26:12; 31:2; 41:4; 43:13; 44:12,15; **Hos.** 6:8; 7:1; **Mic.** 2:1; **Hab.** 1:5; **Zeph.** 2:3.

6467. פֹּעַל *pō'al* **masc. noun**
(deed, act, work)
Deut. 32:4; 33:11; **Ruth** 2:12; **2 Sam.** 23:20; **1 Chr.** 11:22; **Job** 7:2; 24:5; 34:11; 36:9,24; 37:12(NASB, NIV, *pā'al* [6466]); **Ps.** 9:16(17); 28:4; 44:1(2); 64:9(10); 77:12(13); 90:16; 92:4(5); 95:9; 104:23; 111:3; 143:5; **Prov.** 20:11; 21:6,8; 24:12,29; **Isa.** 1:31; 5:12; 41:24; 45:9,11; 59:6; **Jer.** 22:13; 25:14; 50:29; **Hab.** 1:5; 3:2.

6468. פְּעֻלָּה *pᵉ'ullāh* **fem. noun**
(wages, reward, work)
Lev. 19:13; **2 Chr.** 15:7; **Ps.** 17:4; 28:5; 109:20; **Prov.** 10:16; 11:18; **Isa.** 40:10; 49:4; 61:8; 62:11; 65:7; **Jer.** 31:16; **Ezek.** 29:20.

6469. פְּעֻלְּתַי *pᵉ'ullᵉṯay* **masc. proper noun**
(Peullethai)
1 Chr. 26:5.

6470. פָּעַם *pā'am* **verb**
(to stir, to be stirred, to be troubled)
Gen. 41:8; **Judg.** 13:25; **Ps.** 77:4(5); **Dan.** 2:1,3.

6471. פַּעַם *pa'am* **fem. noun**
(time, occurrence, foot)
Gen. 2:23; 18:32; 27:36; 29:34,35; 30:20; 33:3; 41:32; 43:10; 46:30; **Ex.** 8:32(28); 9:14,17; 10:17; 23:17; 25:12; 34:23,24; 37:3; **Lev.** 4:6,17; 8:11; 14:7, 16,27,51; 16:14,19; 25:8; **Num.** 14:22; 19:4; 20:11; 24:1,10; **Deut.** 1:11; 9:19; 10:10; 16:16; **Josh.** 6:3,4,11,14–16; 10:42; **Judg.** 5:28; 6:39; 15:3; 16:15,18, 20,28; 20:30,31; **1 Sam.** 3:10; 18:11; 20:25,41; 26:8; **2 Sam.** 17:7; 23:8; 24:3; **1 Kgs.** 7:4,5,30; 9:25; 11:9; 17:21; 18:43; 22:16; **2 Kgs.** 4:35; 5:10,14; 13:18,19,25; 19:24; **1 Chr.** 11:11; 21:3; **2 Chr.** 8:13; 18:15; **Neh.** 4:12(6); 6:4,5; 13:20; **Job** 19:3; 33:29; **Ps.** 17:5; 57:6(7); 58:10(11); 74:3; 85:13(14); 106:43; 119:133; 140:4(5); **Prov.** 7:12; 29:5; **Eccl.** 6:6; 7:22; **Song** 7:1(2); **Isa.** 26:6; 37:25; 41:7; 66:8; **Jer.** 10:18; 16:21; **Ezek.** 41:6; **Nah.** 1:9.

6472. פַּעֲמֹן *pa'ᵃmôn* **masc. noun**
(bell [on the high priest's robe])
Ex. 28:33,34; 39:25,26.

6473. פָּעַר *pā'ar* **verb**
(to open one's mouth, to jeer)
Job 16:10; 29:23; **Ps.** 119:131; **Isa.** 5:14.

6474. פַּעֲרַי *pa'ᵃray* **masc. proper noun**
(Paarai)
2 Sam. 23:35.

6475. I. פָּצָה *pāṣāh* **verb**
(to open one's mouth; to utter)
Gen. 4:11; **Num.** 16:30; **Deut.** 11:6; **Judg.** 11:35,36; **Job** 35:16; **Ps.** 22:13 (14); 66:14; **Isa.** 10:14; **Lam.** 2:16; 3:46; **Ezek.** 2:8.
II. פָּצָה *pāṣāh* **verb**
(to rescue, to deliver)
Ps. 144:7,10,11.

6476. I. פָּצַח *pāṣaḥ* **verb**
(to break forth in singing)
Isa. 14:7; 44:23; 49:13; 52:9; 54:1; 55:12.
II. פָּצַח *pāṣaḥ* **verb**
(to break bones)
Mic. 3:3.

6477. I. פְּצִירָה *p*^{e}*ṣiyrāh* **fem. noun**
(price, charge)
1 Sam. 13:21(KJV, see II).
II. פְּצִירָה *p*^{e}*ṣiyrāh* **fem. noun**
(file for sharpening)
1 Sam. 13:21(NASB, NIV, see I).

6478. פָּצַל *pāṣal* **verb**
(to peel or strip back off)
Gen. 30:37,38.

6479. פְּצָלָה *p*^{e}*ṣālāh* **fem. noun**
(peeled spot, stripe)
Gen. 30:37.

6480. פָּצַם *pāṣam* **verb**
(to split open, to tear open)
Ps. 60:2(4).

6481. פָּצַע *pāṣa'* **verb**
(to bruise, to crush [the testicles])
Deut. 23:1(2); **1 Kgs.** 20:37; **Song** 5:7.

6482. פֶּצַע *peṣa'* **masc. noun**
(bruise, wound)
Gen. 4:23; **Ex.** 21:25; **Job** 9:17; **Prov.** 20:30; 23:29; 27:6; **Isa.** 1:6.

6483. I. פִּצֵּץ *piṣṣēṣ* **masc. proper noun**
(Happizzez [including article])
1 Chr. 24:15(KJV, see II).
II. פִּצֵּץ *piṣṣēṣ* **masc. proper noun**
(Aphses)
1 Chr. 24:15(NASB, NIV, see I).
III. פִּצֵּץ *piṣṣēṣ* **verb**
(to shatter, to break in pieces)
Job 16:12(KJV, *pûṣ* [6327,II]); **Jer.** 23:29 (KJV, *pûṣ* [6327,II]); **Hab.** 3:6(KJV, *pûṣ* [6327,II]).

6484. פָּצַר *pāṣar* **verb**
(to urge, to insist, to be arrogant)
Gen. 19:3,9; 33:1; **Judg.** 19:7; **1 Sam.** 15:23; **2 Kgs.** 2:17; 5:16.

6485. פָּקַד *pāqaḏ* **verb**
(to number, to appoint, to punish)
Gen. 21:1; 39:4,5; 40:4; 41:34; 50:24,25; **Ex.** 3:16; 4:31; 13:19; 20:5; 30:12–14; 32:34; 34:7; 38:21(NASB, NIV, *p*^{e}*qûḏiym* [6490,II]),25,26; **Lev.** 6:4(5:23); 18:25; 26:16; **Num.** 1:3,19,21–23,25,27,29, 31,33,35,37,39,41,43–47,49,50; 2:4,6, 8,9,11,13,15,16,19,21,23,24,26,28,30–33 ; 3:10,15,16,22,34,39,40,42,43; 4:23,27, 29,30,32,34,36,–38,40–42,44–46,48,49; 7:2; 14:18,29; 16:29; 26:7,18,22,25,27, 34,37,41,43,47,50,51,54,57,62–64; 27:16; 31:14,48,49; **Deut.** 5:9; 20:9; **Josh.** 8:10; 10:18; **Judg.** 15:1; 20:15,17; 21:3,9; **Ruth** 1:6; **1 Sam.** 2:21; 11:8; 13:15; 14:17; 15:2,4; 17:18; 20:6,18, 25,27; 25:7,15,21; 29:4; **2 Sam.** 2:30; 3:8; 18:1; 24:2,4; **1 Kgs.** 11:28; 14:27; 20:15,26,27,39; **2 Kgs.** 3:6; 5:24; 7:17; 9:34; 10:19; 11:15; 12:11(12); 22:5,9; 25:22,23; **1 Chr.** 21:6; 23:24; 26:32; **2 Chr.** 12:10; 23:14; 25:5; 34:10,12,17; 36:23; **Ezra** 1:2; **Neh.** 7:1; 12:44; **Esth.** 2:3; **Job** 5:24; 7:18; 31:14; 34:13; 35:15; 36:23; **Ps.** 8:4(5); 17:3; 31:5(6); 59:5(6); 65:9(10); 80:14(15); 89:32(33); 106:4; 109:6; **Prov.** 19:23; **Isa.** 10:12,28; 13:4,11; 23:17; 24:21,22; 26:14,16,21; 27:1,3; 29:6; 34:16; 38:10; 62:6; **Jer.** 1:10; 3:16; 5:9,29; 6:6,15; 9:9(8),25(24);

11:22; 13:21; 14:10; 15:3,15; 21:14; 23:2, 4,34; 25:12; 27:8,22; 29:10,32; 30:20; 32:5; 36:20,31; 37:21; 40:5,7,11; 41:2,10, 18; 44:13,29; 46:25; 49:8,19; 50:18,31, 44; 51:27,44,47,52; **Lam.** 4:22; **Ezek.** 23:21; 38:8; **Hos.** 1:4; 2:13(15); 4:9,14; 8:13; 9:9; 12:2(3); **Amos** 3:2,14; **Zeph.** 1:8,9,12; 2:7; 3:7; **Zech.** 10:3; 11:16.

6486. פְּקֻדָּה *p^e^quddāh* **fem. noun**
(oversight, responsibility, punishment)
Num. 3:32,36; 4:16; 16:29; **2 Kgs.** 11:18; **1 Chr.** 23:11; 24:3,19; 26:30; **2 Chr.** 17:14; 23:18; 24:11; 26:11; **Job** 10:12; **Ps.** 109:8; **Isa.** 10:3; 15:7; 60:17; **Jer.** 8:12; 10:15; 11:23; 23:12; 46:21; 48:44; 50:27; 51:18; 52:11; **Ezek.** 9:1; 44:11; **Hos.** 9:7; **Mic.** 7:4.

6487. פִּקָּדוֹן *piqqāḏôn* **masc. noun**
(something deposited, held in reserve)
Gen. 41:36; **Lev.** 6:2(5:21),4(5:23).

6488. פְּקִדֻת *p^e^qiḏuṯ* **fem. noun**
(guard, oversight)
Jer. 37:13.

6489. פְּקוֹד *p^e^qôḏ* **masc. proper noun**
(Pekod)
Jer. 50:21; **Ezek.** 23:23.

6490. I. פִּקּוּד *piqqûḏ* **masc. noun**
(statute, precept)
Ps. 19:8(9); 103:18; 111:7; 119:4,15,27, 40,45,56,63,69,78,87,93,94,100,104,110, 128,134,141,159,168,173.
II. פְּקוּדִים *p^e^qûḏiym* **masc. pl. noun**
(amount, sum, number)
Ex. 38:21(KJV, *pāqaḏ* [6485]).

6491. פָּקַח *pāqaḥ* **verb**
(to open [the eyes or ears])
Gen. 3:5,7; 21:19; **2 Kgs.** 4:35; 6:17,20; 19:16; **Job** 14:3; 27:19; **Ps.** 146:8; **Prov.** 20:13; **Isa.** 35:5; 37:17; 42:7,20; **Jer.** 32:19; **Dan.** 9:18; **Zech.** 12:4.

6492. פֶּקַח *peqaḥ* **masc. proper noun**
(Pekah)
2 Kgs. 15:25,27,29–32,37; 16:1,5; **2 Chr.** 28:6; **Isa.** 7:1.

6493. פִּקֵּחַ *piqqēaḥ* **adj.**
(seeing, clear-sighted)
Ex. 4:11; 23:8.

6494. פְּקַחְיָה *p^e^qaḥyāh* **masc. proper noun**
(Pekahiah)
2 Kgs. 15:22,23,26.

6495. פְּקַח־קוֹחַ *p^e^qaḥ-qôaḥ* **masc. noun**
(opening [of prison]; release from captivity)
Isa. 61:1.

6496. פָּקִיד *pāqiyḏ* **masc. noun**
(officer, overseer, governor)
Gen. 41:34; **Judg.** 9:28; **2 Kgs.** 25:19; **2 Chr.** 24:11; 31:13; **Neh.** 11:9,14,22; 12:42; **Esth.** 2:3; **Jer.** 20:1; 29:26; 52:25.

6497. פְּקָעִים *p^e^qā'iym* **masc. pl. noun**
(gourds, knob-shaped projections)
1 Kgs. 6:18; 7:24.

6498. פַּקֻּעֹת *paqqu'ōṯ* **fem. pl. noun**
(gourds)
2 Kgs. 4:39.

6499. פַּר *par*, פָּר *pār* **masc. noun**
(bull, young bull)
Gen. 32:15(16); **Ex.** 24:5; 29:1,3,10–12, 14,36; **Lev.** 4:3–5,7,8,11,12,14–16,20, 21; 8:2,14,17; 16:3,6,11,14,15,18,27; 23:18; **Num.** 7:15,21,27,33,39,45,51,

57,63,69,75,81,87,88; 8:8,12; 15:24; 23:1,2,4,14,29,30; 28:11,12,14,19,20, 27,28; 29:2,3,8,9,13,14,17,18,20,21, 23,24,26,27,29,30,32,33,36,37; **Judg.** 6:25,26,28; **1 Sam.** 1:24,25; **1 Kgs.** 18:23,25,26,33; **1 Chr.** 15:26; 29:21; **2 Chr.** 13:9; 29:21; 30:24; **Ezra** 8:35; **Job** 42:8; **Ps.** 22:12(13); 50:9; 51:19(21); 69:31(32); **Isa.** 1:11; 34:7; **Jer.** 50:27; **Ezek.** 39:18; 43:19,21–23,25; 45:18, 22–24; 46:6,7,11; **Hos.** 14:2(3).

6500. פָּרָא *pārā'* **verb**
(to be fruitful, to flourish)
Hos. 13:15.

6501. פֶּרֶא *pere'* **masc./fem. noun**
(wild donkey)
Gen. 16:12; **Job** 6:5; 11:12; 24:5; 39:5; **Ps.** 104:11; **Isa.** 32:14; **Jer.** 2:24; 14:6; **Hos.** 8:9.

6502. פִּרְאָם *pir'ām* **masc. proper noun**
(Piram)
Josh. 10:3.

6503. I. פַּרְבָּר *parbār* **masc. noun**
(court area, precinct)
2 Kgs. 23:11; **1 Chr.** 26:18(KJV, NASB, see II).
II. פַּרְבָּר *parbār* **masc. noun**
(Parbar, a court area in Solomon's Temple)
1 Chr. 26:18(NIV, see I).

6504. פָּרַד *pārad̲* **verb**
(to divide, to separate, to disperse, to be separated, to be scattered)
Gen. 2:10; 10:5,32; 13:9,11,14; 25:23; 30:40; **Deut.** 32:8; **Judg.** 4:11; **Ruth** 1:17; **2 Sam.** 1:23; **2 Kgs.** 2:11; **Neh.** 4:19(13); **Esth.** 3:8; **Job** 4:11; 41:17(9); **Ps.** 22:14(15); 92:9(10); **Prov.** 16:28; 17:9; 18:1,18; 19:4; **Ezek.** 1:11; **Hos.** 4:14.

6505. פֶּרֶד *pered̲* **masc. noun**
(mule)
2 Sam. 13:29; 18:9; **1 Kgs.** 10:25; 18:5; **2 Kgs.** 5:17; **1 Chr.** 12:40; **2 Chr.** 9:24; **Ezra** 2:66; **Neh.** 7:68; **Ps.** 32:9; **Isa.** 66:20; **Ezek.** 27:14; **Zech.** 14:15.

6506. פִּרְדָּה *pirdāh* **fem. noun**
(female mule)
1 Kgs. 1:33,38,44.

6507. פְּרֻדֹת *p^e^rud̲ōt̲* **fem. noun**
(seed, grain)
Joel 1:17.

6508. פַּרְדֵּס *pardēs* **masc. noun**
(forest, park, orchard)
Neh. 2:8; **Eccl.** 2:5; **Song** 4:13.

6509. פָּרָה *pārāh* **verb**
(to be fruitful, to flourish)
Gen. 1:22,28; 8:17; 9:1,7; 17:6,20; 26:22; 28:3; 35:11; 41:52; 47:27; 48:4; 49:22; **Ex.** 1:7; 23:30; **Lev.** 26:9; **Deut.** 29:18(17); **Ps.** 105:24; 128:3; **Isa.** 11:1; 17:6; 32:12; 45:8; **Jer.** 3:16; 23:3; **Ezek.** 19:10; 36:11.

6510. פָּרָה *pārāh* **fem. noun**
(cow, heifer)
Gen. 32:15(16); 41:2–4,18–20,26,27; **Num.** 19:2,5,6,9,10; **1 Sam.** 6:7,10,12,14; **Job** 21:10; **Isa.** 11:7; **Hos.** 4:16; **Amos** 4:1.

6511. פָּרָה *pārāh* **proper noun**
(Parah)
Josh. 18:23.

6512. פֵּרָה *pērāh* **fem. noun**
(digging mole, with Qal inf. const. of *ḥāp̲ar* [2658] in the MT)
Isa. 2:20(KJV, NASB, NIV, *ḥ^a^p̲arpārāh* [2661,I]).

6513. פֻּרָה *purāh* **masc. proper noun**

(Purah)
Judg. 7:10,11.

6514. פְּרוּדָא $p^e r\hat{u}\underline{d}\bar{a}'$, פְּרִידָא $p^e riy\underline{d}\bar{a}'$ **masc. proper noun**
(Peruda, Perida)
Ezra 2:55; **Neh.** 7:57.

6515. פָּרוּחַ *pārûaḥ* **masc. proper noun**
(Paruah)
1 Kgs. 4:17.

6516. פַּרְוַיִם *parwayim* **proper noun**
(Parvaim)
2 Chr. 3:6.

6517. פָּרוּר *pārûr* **masc. noun**
(pot, pan)
Num. 11:8; **Judg.** 6:19; **1 Sam.** 2:14.

6518. פָּרָז *pārāz* **masc. noun**
(warrior, throng, village)
Hab. 3:14.

6519. פְּרָזָה $p^e r\bar{a}z\bar{a}h$ **fem. noun**
(unwalled village or town)
Esth. 9:19; **Ezek.** 38:11; **Zech.** 2:4(8).

6520. פְּרָזוֹן $p^e r\bar{a}z\hat{o}n$ **masc. noun**
(village population)
Judg. 5:7,11.

6521. פְּרָזִי $p^e r\bar{a}ziy$ **masc. noun**
(village, unwalled town)
Deut. 3:5; **1 Sam.** 6:18; **Esth.** 9:19.

6522. פְּרִזִּי $p^e rizziy$ **masc. proper noun**
(Perizzite)
Gen. 13:7; 15:20; 34:30; **Ex.** 3:8,17; 23:23; 33:2; 34:11; **Deut.** 7:1; 20:17; **Josh.** 3:10; 9:1; 11:3; 12:8; 17:15; 24:11; **Judg.** 1:4,5; 3:5; **1 Kgs.** 9:20; **2 Chr.** 8:7; **Ezra** 9:1; **Neh.** 9:8.

6523. פַּרְזֶל *parzel* **Aram. masc. noun**
(iron; corr. to Hebr. 1270)
Dan. 2:33–35,40–43,45; 4:15(12), 23(20); 5:4,23; 7:7,19.

6524. I. פָּרַח *pāraḥ* **verb**
(to blossom, to flourish, to break forth, to break out)
Gen. 40:10; **Ex.** 9:9,10; **Lev.** 13:12,20, 25,39,42,57; 14:43; **Num.** 17:5(20), 8(23); **Job** 14:9; **Ps.** 72:7; 92:7(8), 12(13),13(14); **Prov.** 11:28; 14:11; **Song** 6:11; 7:12(13); **Isa.** 17:11; 27:6; 35:1,2; 66:14; **Ezek.** 7:10; 17:24; **Hos.** 10:4; 14:5(6),7(8); **Hab.** 3:17.
II. פָּרַח *pāraḥ* **verb**
(to fly)
Ezek. 13:20.

6525. פֶּרַח *peraḥ* **masc. noun**
(flower, blossom, bud)
Ex. 25:31,33,34; 37:17,19,20; **Num.** 8:4; 17:8(23); **1 Kgs.** 7:26,49; **2 Chr.** 4:5,21; **Isa.** 5:24; 18:5; **Nah.** 1:4.

6526. פִּרְחָח *pirḥāh* **fem. noun**
(a brood, tribe, gang of young people)
Job 30:12.

6527. I. פָּרַט *pāraṭ* **verb**
(to chant, to improvise in singing)
Amos 6:5(KJV, NASB, see II).
II. פָּרַט *pāraṭ* **verb**
(to strum)
Amos 6:5(KJV, NASB, see I).

6528. פֶּרֶט *pereṭ* **masc. noun**
(fallen grape)
Lev. 19:10.

6529. פְּרִי $p^e riy$ **masc. noun**
(fruit, offspring)
Gen. 1:11,12,29; 3:2,3,6; 4:3; 30:2; **Ex.** 10:15; **Lev.** 19:23–25; 23:40; 25:19; 26:4,20; 27:30; **Num.** 13:20,26,27;

Deut. 1:25; 7:13; 26:2,10; 28:4,11,18, 33,42,51,53; 30:9; **2 Kgs.** 19:29,30; **Neh.** 9:36; 10:35(36),37(38); **Ps.** 1:3; 21:10(11); 58:11(12); 72:16; 104:13; 105:35; 107:34,37; 127:3; 132:11; 148:9; **Prov.** 1:31; 8:19; 11:30; 12:14; 13:2; 18:20,21; 27:18; 31:16,31; **Eccl.** 2:5; **Song** 2:3; 4:13,16; 8:11,12; **Isa.** 3:10; 4:2; 10:12; 13:18; 14:29; 27:9; 37:30,31; 65:21; **Jer.** 2:7; 6:19; 7:20; 11:16; 12:2; 17:8,10; 21:14; 29:5,28; 32:19; **Lam.** 2:20; **Ezek.** 17:8,9,23; 19:12,14; 25:4; 34:27; 36:8,30; 47:12; **Hos.** 9:16; 10:1,13; 14:8(9); **Joel** 2:22; **Amos** 2:9; 6:12; 9:14; **Mic.** 6:7; 7:13; **Zech.** 8:12; **Mal.** 3:11.

6530. פָּרִיץ *pariyṣ* **masc. noun**
(robber, violent one)
Ps. 17:4; **Isa.** 35:9; **Jer.** 7:11; **Ezek.** 7:22; 18:10; **Dan.** 11:14.

6531. פֶּרֶךְ *perek̲* **masc. noun**
(ruthlessness, cruelty)
Ex. 1:13,14; **Lev.** 25:43,46,53; **Ezek.** 34:4.

6532. פָּרֹכֶת *pārōk̲et̲* **fem. noun**
(curtain, vail)
Ex. 26:31,33,35; 27:21; 30:6; 35:12; 36:35; 38:27; 39:34; 40:3,21,22,26; **Lev.** 4:6,17; 16:2,12,15; 21:23; 24:3; **Num.** 4:5; 18:7; **2 Chr.** 3:14.

6533. פָּרַם *pāram* **verb**
(to tear, to rend)
Lev. 10:6; 13:45; 21:10.

6534. פַּרְמַשְׁתָּא *parmaštā'* **masc. proper noun**
(Parmashta)
Esth. 9:9.

6535. פַּרְנָךְ *parnāk̲* **masc. proper noun**
(Parnach)
Num. 34:25.

6536. פָּרַס *pāras* **verb**
(to split, to divide)
Lev. 11:3–7,26; **Deut.** 14:6–8; **Ps.** 69:31(32); **Isa.** 58:7; **Jer.** 16:7.

6537. I. פְּרַס *pāras* **Aram. verb**
(to be divided, to be broken in two)
Dan. 5:28.
II. פְּרֵס *p^e^rēs* **masc. proper noun**
(Peres; proper noun in quotation)
Dan. 5:28.
III. וּפַרְסִין *ûp̱arsiyn* **masc. pl. proper noun**
(Upharsin; proper noun in quotation)
Dan. 5:25(NIV, see IV).
IV. פַּרְסִין *parsiyn* **masc. pl. proper noun**
(Parsin; proper noun in quotation, used with conjunction *wû* [and])
Dan. 5:25(KJV, NASB, see III).

6538. פֶּרֶס *peres* **masc. noun**
(vulture, ossifrage)
Lev. 11:13; **Deut.** 14:12.

6539. פָּרַס *pāras* **proper noun**
(Persia)
2 Chr. 36:20,22,23; **Ezra** 1:1,2,8; 3:7; 4:3,5,7; 7:1; 9:9; **Esth.** 1:3,14,18,19; 10:2; **Ezek.** 27:10; 38:5; **Dan.** 8:20; 10:1,13,20; 11:2.

6540. פָּרַס *pāras* **Aram. proper noun**
(Persia; corr. to Hebr. 6539)
Ezra 4:24; 6:14; **Dan.** 5:28; 6:8(9), 12(13),15(16).

6541. פַּרְסָה *parsāh* **fem. noun**
(hoof)
Ex. 10:26; **Lev.** 11:3–7,26; **Deut.** 14:6–8; **Isa.** 5:28; **Jer.** 47:3; **Ezek.** 26:11; 32:13; **Mic.** 4:13; **Zech.** 11:16.

6542. פַּרְסִי *parsiy* **masc. proper noun**

(Persian)
Neh. 12:22.

6543. פַּרְסָיָא *parsāyā'* **Aram. masc. proper noun**
(Persian; corr. to Hebr. 6542)
Dan. 6:28(29).

6544. I. פָּרַע *pāra'* **verb**
(to neglect, to avoid, to uncover)
Ex. 5:4; 32:25; **Lev.** 10:6; 13:45; 21:10; **Num.** 5:18; **2 Chr.** 28:19; **Prov.** 1:25; 4:15; 8:33; 13:18; 15:32; 29:18; **Ezek.** 24:14.
II. פָּרַע *pāra'* **verb**
(to take the lead)
Judg. 5:2.

6545. פֶּרַע *pera'* **masc. noun**
(hair, locks of hair)
Num. 6:5; **Ezek.** 44:20.

6546. I. פֶּרַע *pera'* **masc. noun**
(leader, prince)
Deut. 32:42(KJV, see II; NASB, see III); **Judg.** 5:2(KJV, see II).
II. פֶּרַע *pera'* **masc. noun**
(revenge, vengeance)
Deut. 32:42(NIV, see I; NASB, see III); **Judg.** 5:2(NASB, NIV, see I).
III. פֶּרַע *pera'* **masc. noun**
(the quality of having long hair)
Deut. 32:42(NIV, see I; KJV, see II).

6547. פַּרְעֹה *par'ōh* **masc. proper noun**
(Pharaoh)
Gen. 12:15,17,18,20; 37:36; 39:1; 40:2, 7,11,13,14,17,19–21; 41:1,4,7–10, 14–17,25,28,32–35,37–39,41,42,44–46,5 5; 42:15,16; 44:18; 45:2,8,16,17,21; 46:5, 31,33; 47:1–5,7–11,14,19,20,22–26; 50:4,6,7; **Ex.** 1:11,19,22; 2:5,7–10,15; 3:10,11; 4:21,22; 5:1,2,5,6,10,14,15,20, 21,23; 6:1,11–13,27,29,30; 7:1–4,7,9–11, 13–15,20,22,23; 8:1(7:26),8(4),9(5),12(8), 15(11),19(15),20(16),24(20),25(21),28–3 2(24–28); 9:1,7,8,10,12,13,20,27,33–35; 10:1,3,6–8,11,16,18,20,24,27,28; 11:1,3, 5,8–10; 12:29,30; 13:15,17; 14:3–5, 8–10,17,18,23,28; 15:4,19; 18:4,8,10; **Deut.** 6:21,22; 7:8,18; 11:3; 29:2(1); 34:11; **1 Sam.** 2:27; 6:6; **1 Kgs.** 3:1; 7:8; 9:16,24; 11:1,18–22; **2 Kgs.** 17:7; 18:21; 23:29(KJV, NASB, see *par'ōhn^{e}ḵōh* [6549]),33(KJV, NASB, see *par'ōhn^{e}ḵōh* [6549]),34(KJV, NASB, see *par'ōhn^{e}ḵōh* [6549]),35(KJV, NASB, see *par'ōhn^{e}ḵōh* [6549]); **1 Chr.** 4:18; **2 Chr.** 8:11; **Neh.** 9:10; **Ps.** 135:9; 136:15; **Song** 1:9; **Isa.** 19:11; 30:2,3; 36:6; **Jer.** 25:19; 37:5,7,11; 43:9; 46:2(KJV, NASB, see *par'ōhn^{e}ḵōh* [6549]),17,25; 47:1; **Ezek.** 17:17; 29:2,3; 30:21,22,24,25; 31:2,18; 32:2,31,32.

6548. פַּרְעֹה חָפְרַע *par'ōh ḥop̱ra'* **masc. proper noun**
(Pharaoh Hophra)
Jer. 44:30(NIV, *par'ōh* [6547] and *ḥop̱ra'* [2663,II]).

6549. פַּרְעֹה נְכֹה *par'ōh n^{e}ḵōh* **masc. proper noun**
(Pharaoh Neco)
2 Kgs. 23:29(NIV, *par'ōh* [6547] and *n^{e}ḵô* [5224]),33(NIV, *par'ōh* [6547] and *n^{e}ḵô* [5224]),34(NIV, *par'ōh* [6547] and *n^{e}ḵô* [5224]),35(NIV, *par'ōh* [6547] and *n^{e}ḵô* [5224]); **Jer.** 46:2(NIV, *par'ōh* [6547] and *n^{e}ḵô* [5224]).

6550. פַּרְעֹשׁ *par'ōš* **masc. noun**
(flea)
1 Sam. 24:14(15); 26:20.

6551. פַּרְעֹשׁ *par'ōš* **masc. proper noun**
(Parosh)
Ezra 2:3; 8:3; 10:25; **Neh.** 3:25; 7:8; 10:14(15).

6552. פִּרְעָתוֹן *pir'āṯôn* **proper noun**
(Pirathon)
Judg. 12:15.

6553. פִּרְעָתוֹנִי *pir'āṯôniy* **masc. proper noun**
(Pirathonite)
Judg. 12:13,15; **2 Sam.** 23:30; **1 Chr.** 11:31; 27:14.

6554. פַּרְפַּר *parpar* **proper noun**
(Pharpar)
2 Kgs. 5:12.

6555. פָּרַץ *pāraṣ* **verb**
(to break out, to break down, to burst forth)
Gen. 28:14; 30:30,43; 38:29; **Ex.** 1:12; 19:22,24; **1 Sam.** 3:1; 25:10; 28:23; **2 Sam.** 5:20; 6:8; 13:25,27; **2 Kgs.** 5:23; 14:13; **1 Chr.** 4:38; 13:2,11; 14:11; 15:13; **2 Chr.** 11:23; 20:37; 24:7; 25:23; 26:6; 31:5; 32:5; **Neh.** 1:3; 2:13; 4:3(3:35), 7(1); **Job** 1:10; 16:14; 28:4; **Ps.** 60:1(3); 80:12(13); 89:40(41); 106:29; **Prov.** 3:10; 25:28; **Eccl.** 3:3; 10:8; **Isa.** 5:5; 54:3; **Hos.** 4:2,10; **Mic.** 2:13.

6556. פֶּרֶץ *pereṣ* **masc. noun**
(gap, breach)
Gen. 38:29; **Judg.** 21:15; **2 Sam.** 5:20; 6:8; **1 Kgs.** 11:27; **1 Chr.** 13:11; 14:11; **Neh.** 6:1; **Job** 16:14; 30:14; **Ps.** 106:23; 144:14; **Isa.** 28:21; 30:13; 58:12; **Ezek.** 13:5; 22:30; **Amos** 4:3; 9:11.

6557. פֶּרֶץ *pereṣ* **masc. proper noun**
(Pharez, Perez)
Gen. 38:29; 46:12; **Num.** 26:20,21; **Ruth** 4:12,18; **1 Chr.** 2:4,5; 4:1; 9:4; 27:3; **Neh.** 11:4,6.

6558. פַּרְצִי *parṣiy* **masc. proper noun**
(Pharzite, Perezite)
Num. 26:20.

6559. פְּרָצִים *p^{e}rāṣiym* **proper noun**
(Perazim)
Isa. 28:21.

6560. פֶּרֶץ עֻזָּא *pereṣ 'uzzā'* **proper noun**
(Perez Uzzah)
2 Sam. 6:8; **1 Chr.** 13:11.

6561. פָּרַק *pāraq* **verb**
(to break off, to tear off, to rescue)
Gen. 27:40; **Ex.** 32:2,3,24; **1 Kgs.** 19:11; **Ps.** 7:2(3); 136:24; **Lam.** 5:8; **Ezek.** 19:12; **Zech.** 11:16.

6562. פְּרַק *p^{e}raq* **Aram. verb**
(to break away, to renounce; corr. to Hebr. 6561)
Dan. 4:27(24).

6563. I. פֶּרֶק *pereq* **masc. noun**
(crossroad, fork in the road)
Obad. 1:14.
II. פֶּרֶק *pereq* **masc. noun**
(robbery, plunder)
Nah. 3:1.

6564. פָּרָק *pārāq* **masc. noun**
(broth)
Isa. 65:4(NASB, NIV, [Q^{e}] *māraq* [4839]).

6565. I. פָּרַר *pārar* **verb**
(to break, to frustrate)
Gen. 17:14; **Lev.** 26:15,44; **Num.** 15:31; 30:8(9),12(13),13(14),15(16); **Deut.** 31:16,20; **Judg.** 2:1; **2 Sam.** 15:34; 17:14; **1 Kgs.** 15:19; **2 Chr.** 16:3; **Ezra** 4:5; 9:14; **Neh.** 4:15(9); **Job** 5:12; 15:4; 16:12(NASB, NIV, see II); 40:8; **Ps.** 33:10 (KJV, *pûr* [6331]); 85:4(5); 89:33(34)(KJV, *pûr* [6331]); 119:126; **Prov.** 15:22; **Eccl.** 12:5; **Isa.** 8:10; 14:27; 24:5; 33:8; 44:25; **Jer.** 11:10; 14:21; 31:32; 33:20,21; **Ezek.** 16:59; 17:15,16,18,19(KJV, *pûr* [6331]); 44:7; **Zech.** 11:10,11,14.
II. פָּרַר *pārar* **verb**
(to break, to frustrate)
Job 16:12(KJV, see I); **Ps.** 74:13; **Isa.** 24:19.

6566. פָּרַשׂ *pāraś* **verb**
(to spread out, to stretch out, to spread)
Ex. 9:29,33; 25:20; 37:9; 40:19; **Num.** 4:6–8,11,13,14; **Deut.** 22:17; 32:11; **Judg.** 8:25; **Ruth** 3:9; **2 Sam.** 17:19; **1 Kgs.** 6:27; 8:7,22,38,54; **2 Kgs.** 8:15; 19:14; **1 Chr.** 28:18; **2 Chr.** 3:13; 5:8; 6:12,13,29; **Ezra** 9:5; **Job** 11:13; 36:30; 39:26; **Ps.** 44:20(21); 68:14(15); 105:39; 140:5(6); 143:6; **Prov.** 13:16; 29:5; 31:20; **Isa.** 1:15; 19:8; 25:11; 33:23; 37:14; 65:2; **Jer.** 4:31; 48:40; 49:22; **Lam.** 1:10,13,17; 4:4; **Ezek.** 2:10; 12:13; 16:8; 17:20,21; 19:8; 32:3; 34:12 (KJV, NASB, *paraš* [6567]); **Hos.** 5:1; 7:12; **Joel** 2:2; **Mic.** 3:3; **Zech.** 2:6(10).

6567. I. פָּרַשׁ *pāraš* **verb**
(to show, to make clear, to distinguish)
Lev. 24:12; **Num.** 15:34; **Neh.** 8:8.
II. פָּרַשׁ *pāraš* **verb**
(to sting)
Prov. 23:32.
III. פָּרַשׁ *pāraš* **verb**
(to scatter)
Ezek. 34:12(NIV, *pāraś* [6566]).

6568. פְּרַשׁ *p^{e}raš* **Aram. verb**
(to make clear; corr. to Hebr. 6567,I)
Ezra 4:18.

6569. פֶּרֶשׁ *pereš* **masc. noun**
(dung, refuse, offal)
Ex. 29:14; **Lev.** 4:11; 8:17; 16:27; **Num.** 19:5; **Mal.** 2:3.

6570. פֶּרֶשׁ *pereš* **masc. proper noun**
(Peresh)
1 Chr. 7:16.

6571. פָּרָשׁ *pārāš* **masc. noun**
(horsemen; cavalry)
Gen. 50:9; **Ex.** 14:9,17,18,23,26,28; 15:19; **Josh.** 24:6; **1 Sam.** 8:11; 13:5; **2 Sam.** 8:4; 10:18(NIV, following 1 Chr. 19:18 *ragliy* [7273]); **1 Kgs.** 1:5(NIV, see II); 4:26(5:6)(NIV, see II); 9:19(NIV, see II),22; 10:26(NIV, see II); 20:20; **2 Kgs.** 2:12; 13:7,14; 18:24; **1 Chr.** 18:4; 19:6; **2 Chr.** 1:14(NIV, see II); 8:6(NIV, see II),9; 9:25(NIV, see II); 12:3; 16:8; **Ezra** 8:22; **Neh.** 2:9; **Isa.** 21:7(NIV, see II),9(NIV, see II); 22:6(NIV, see II), 7; 28:28(NASB, NIV, see II); 31:1; 36:9; **Jer.** 4:29; 46:4(NASB, NIV, see II); **Ezek.** 23:6,12; 26:7,10(NIV, see II); 27:14(NASB, NIV, see II); 38:4; **Dan.** 11:40; **Hos.** 1:7; **Joel** 2:4(NASB, NIV, see II); **Nah.** 3:3; **Hab.** 1:8.

6572. A. פַּרְשֶׁגֶן *paršegen* **masc. noun**
(copy)
Ezra 7:11.
B. פַּתְשֶׁגֶן *paṯšegen* **masc. noun**
(copy)
Esth. 3:14; 4:8; 8:13.

6573. פַּרְשֶׁגֶן *paršegen* **Aram. masc. noun**
(copy; corr. to Hebr. 6572,A)
Ezra 4:11,23; 5:6.

6574. פַּרְשְׁדֹנָה *parš^{e}ḏōnāh* **masc. noun**
(refuse, intestines)
Judg. 3:22.

6575. פָּרָשָׁה *pārāšāh* **fem. noun**
(exact amount, sum)
Esth. 4:7; 10:2.

6576. פַּרְשֵׁז *paršēz* **verb**
(to spread)
Job 26:9.

6577. פַּרְשַׁנְדָּתָא *paršandāṯā'* **masc. proper noun**
(Parshandatha)
Esth. 9:7.

6578. I. פְּרָת *p^eraṯ* **proper noun**
(Euphrates [River])
Gen. 2:14; 15:18; **Deut.** 1:7; 11:24; **Josh.** 1:4; **2 Sam.** 8:3; **2 Kgs.** 23:29; 24:7; **1 Chr.** 5:9; 18:3; **2 Chr.** 35:20; **Jer.** 13:4(NIV, see II),5(NIV, see II), 6(NIV, see II),7(NIV, see II); 46:2,6,10; 51:63.
II. פְּרָת *p^eraṯ* **proper noun**
(Perath)
Jer. 13:4(KJV, NASB, see I),5(KJV, NASB, see I),6(KJV, NASB, see I),7(KJV, NASB, see I).

6579. פַּרְתְּמִים *part^{e}miym* **masc. pl. noun**
(nobles, nobility)
Esth. 1:3; 6:9; **Dan.** 1:3.

6580. פַּשׁ *paš* **masc. noun**
(folly, transgression, wickedness)
Job 35:15.

6581. פָּשָׂה *pāśāh* **verb**
(to spread)
Lev. 13:5–8,22,23,27,28,32,34–36,51,53,55; 14:39,44,48.

6582. פָּשַׁח *pāšaḥ* **verb**
(to tear in pieces, to mangle)
Lam. 3:11.

6583. פַּשְׁחוּר *pašḥûr* **masc. proper noun**
(Pashhur)
1 Chr. 9:12; **Ezra** 2:38; 10:22; **Neh.** 7:41; 10:3(4); 11:12; **Jer.** 20:1–3,6; 21:1; 38:1.

6584. פָּשַׁט *pāšaṭ* **verb**
(to strip, to strip off; to raid, to invade)
Gen. 37:23; **Lev.** 1:6; 6:11(4); 16:23; **Num.** 20:26,28; **Judg.** 9:33,44; 20:37; **1 Sam.** 18:4; 19:24; 23:27; 27:8,10; 30:1,14; 31:8,9; **2 Sam.** 23:10; **1 Chr.** 10:8,9; 14:9,13; **2 Chr.** 25:13; 28:18; 29:34; 35:11; **Neh.** 4:23(17); **Job** 1:17; 19:9; 22:6; **Song** 5:3; **Isa.** 32:11; **Ezek.** 16:39; 23:26; 26:16; 44:19; **Hos.** 2:3(5); 7:1; **Mic.** 2:8; 3:3; **Nah.** 3:16.

6585. פָּשַׂע *pāśaʿ* **verb**
(to step, to march)
Isa. 27:4.

6586. פָּשַׁע *pāšaʿ* **verb**
(to rebel, to revolt, to transgress)
1 Kgs. 8:50; 12:19; **2 Kgs.** 1:1; 3:5,7; 8:20,22; **2 Chr.** 10:19; 21:8,10; **Ezra** 10:13; **Ps.** 37:38; 51:13(15); **Prov.** 18:19; 28:21; **Isa.** 1:2,28; 43:27; 46:8; 48:8; 53:12; 59:13; 66:24; **Jer.** 2:8,29; 3:13; 33:8; **Lam.** 3:42; **Ezek.** 2:3; 18:31; 20:38; **Dan.** 8:23; **Hos.** 7:13; 8:1; 14:9(10); **Amos** 4:4; **Zeph.** 3:11.

6587. פֶּשַׂע *peśaʿ* **masc. noun**
(step)
1 Sam. 20:3.

6588. פֶּשַׁע *pešaʿ* **masc. noun**
(trespass, sin, transgression)
Gen. 31:36; 50:17; **Ex.** 22:9(8); 23:21; 34:7; **Lev.** 16:16,21; **Num.** 14:18; **Josh.** 24:19; **1 Sam.** 24:11(12); 25:28; **1 Kgs.** 8:50; **Job** 7:21; 8:4; 13:23; 14:17; 31:33; 33:9; 34:6,37; 35:6; 36:9; **Ps.** 5:10(11); 19:13(14); 25:7; 32:1,5; 36:1(2); 39:8(9); 51:1(3),3(5); 59:3(4); 65:3(4); 89:32(33); 103:12; 107:17; **Prov.** 10:12,19; 12:13; 17:9,19; 19:11; 28:2,13,24; 29:6,16,22; **Isa.** 24:20; 43:25; 44:22; 50:1; 53:5,8; 57:4; 58:1; 59:12,20; **Jer.** 5:6; **Lam.** 1:5,14,22; **Ezek.** 14:11; 18:22,28,30,31; 21:24(29); 33:10,12; 37:23; 39:24; **Dan.** 8:12,13; 9:24; **Amos** 1:3,6,9,11,13; 2:1, 4,6; 3:14; 5:12; **Mic.** 1:5,13; 3:8; 6:7; 7:18.

6589. פָּשַׂק *pāśaq* **verb**
(to open wide, to spread)
Prov. 13:3; **Ezek.** 16:25.

6590. פְּשַׁר *p^e^šar* **Aram. verb**
(to interpret)
Dan. 5:12,16.

6591. פְּשַׁר *p^e^šar* **Aram. masc. noun**
(interpretation; corr. to Hebr. 6592)
Dan. 2:4–7,9,16,24–26,30,36,45; 4:6(3), 7(4),9(6),18(15),19(16),24(21); 5:7,8,12, 15–17,26; 7:16.

6592. פֵּשֶׁר *pēšer* **masc. noun**
(interpretation; explanation)
Eccl. 8:1.

6593. פֵּשֶׁת *pēšeṯ* **masc. noun**
(linen, flax)
Lev. 13:47,48,52,59; **Deut.** 22:11; **Josh.** 2:6; **Judg.** 15:14; **Prov.** 31:13; **Isa.** 19:9; **Jer.** 13:1; **Ezek.** 40:3; 44:17,18; **Hos.** 2:5(7),9(11).

6594. פִּשְׁתָּה *pištāh* **fem. noun**
(flax; wick [of a lamp])
Ex. 9:31; **Isa.** 42:3; 43:17.

6595. A. פַּת *paṯ* **masc. noun**
(piece [usually of bread], morsel)
Gen. 18:5; **Lev.** 2:6; 6:21(14); **Judg.** 19:5; **Ruth** 2:14; **1 Sam.** 2:36; 28:22; **2 Sam.** 12:3; **1 Kgs.** 17:11; **Job** 31:17; **Ps.** 147:17; **Prov.** 17:1; 23:8; 28:21.
B. פְּתוֹת *p^e^ṯôṯ* **masc. noun**
(piece [of bread], morsel)
Ezek. 13:19.

6596. I. פֹּת *pōṯ* **masc. noun**
(hinge [of a door])
1 Kgs. 7:50.
II. פֹּת *pōṯ* **masc. noun**
(private parts [of a woman])
Isa. 3:17(NASB, NIV, see III).
III. פֹּת *pōṯ* **masc. noun**
(forehead, scalp)
Isa. 3:17(KJV, see II).

6597. פִּתְאֹם *piṯ'ōm* **adv.**
(suddenly, unexpectedly)
Num. 6:9; 12:4; **Josh.** 10:9; 11:7; **2 Chr.** 29:36; **Job** 5:3; 9:23; 22:10; **Ps.** 64:4(5),7(8); **Prov.** 3:25; 6:15; 7:22; 24:22; **Eccl.** 9:12; **Isa.** 29:5; 30:13; 47:11; 48:3; **Jer.** 4:20; 6:26; 15:8; 18:22; 51:8; **Mal.** 3:1.

6598. פַּתְבַּג *paṯbag* **masc. noun**
(food, delicacies)
Dan. 1:5,8,13,15,16; 11:26.

6599. פִּתְגָם *piṯgām* **masc. noun**
(decree, edict, sentence for a crime)
Esth. 1:20; **Eccl.** 8:11.

6600. פִּתְגָם *piṯgām* **Aram. masc. noun**
(edict, decision, answer; corr. to Hebr. 6599)
Ezra 4:17; 5:7,11; 6:11; **Dan.** 3:16; 4:17(14).

6601. I. פָּתָה *pāṯāh* **verb**
(to entice, to deceive, to persuade; to be gullible)
Ex. 22:16(15); **Deut.** 11:16; **Judg.** 14:15; 16:5; **2 Sam.** 3:25; **1 Kgs.** 22:20–22; **2 Chr.** 18:19–21; **Job** 5:2; 31:9,27; **Ps.** 78:36; **Prov.** 1:10; 16:29; 20:19; 24:28; 25:15; **Jer.** 20:7,10; **Ezek.** 14:9; **Hos.** 2:14(16); 7:11.
II. פָּתָה *pāṯāh* **verb**
(to enlarge, to extend territory)
Gen. 9:27.

6602. פְּתוּאֵל *p^e^ṯû'ēl* **masc. proper noun**
(Pethuel)
Joel 1:1.

6603. פִּתּוּחַ *pittûaḥ* **masc. noun**
(engraving, carving, inscription)
Ex. 28:11,21,36; 39:6,14,30; **1 Kgs.** 6:29; **2 Chr.** 2:7(6),14(13); **Ps.** 74:6; **Zech.** 3:9.

6604. פְּתוֹר *p^e^ṯôr* **proper noun**
(Pethor)
Num. 22:5; **Deut.** 23:4(5).

6605. I. פָּתַח *pāṯaḥ* **verb**
(to open, to loosen)
Gen. 7:11; 8:6; 24:32; 29:31; 30:22; 41:56; 42:27; 43:21; 44:11; **Ex.** 2:6; 21:33; **Num.** 16:32; 19:15; 22:28; 26:10; **Deut.** 15:8,11; 20:11; 28:12; **Josh.** 8:17; 10:22; **Judg.** 3:25; 4:19; 19:27; **1 Sam.** 3:15; **1 Kgs.** 8:29,52; 20:11; **2 Kgs.** 9:3,10; 13:17; 15:16; **2 Chr.** 6:20,40; 7:15; 29:3; **Neh.** 1:6; 6:5; 7:3; 8:5; 13:19; **Job** 3:1; 11:5; 12:14,18; 29:19; 30:11; 31:32; 32:19,20; 33:2; 38:31; 39:5; 41:14(6); **Ps.** 5:9(10); 30:11(12); 37:14; 38:13(14); 39:9(10); 49:4(5); 51:15(17); 78:2,23; 102:20(21); 104:28; 105:20,41; 106:17; 109:2; 116:16; 118:19; 145:16; **Prov.** 24:7; 31:8,9,26; **Song** 5:2,5,6; 7:12(13); **Isa.** 5:27; 14:17; 20:2; 22:22; 24:18; 26:2; 28:24; 35:5; 41:18; 45:1,8; 48:8; 50:5; 51:14; 52:2; 53:7; 58:6; 60:11; **Jer.** 1:14; 5:16; 13:19; 40:4; 50:25,26; **Ezek.** 1:1; 3:2,27; 21:22(27),28(33); 24:27; 25:9; 33:22; 37:12,13; 44:2; 46:1,12; **Dan.** 10:16; **Amos** 8:5; **Nah.** 2:6(7); 3:13; **Zech.** 11:1; 13:1; **Mal.** 3:10.
II. פָּתַח *pāṯaḥ* **verb**
(to engrave, to carve)
Ex. 28:9,11,36; 39:6; **1 Kgs.** 7:36; **2 Chr.** 2:7(6),14(13); 3:7; **Zech.** 3:9.

6606. פְּתַח *p^eṯaḥ* **Aram. verb**
(to open; corr. to Hebr. 6605,I)
Dan. 6:10(11); 7:10.

6607. פֶּתַח *peṯaḥ* **masc. noun**
(opening, entrance, door, doorway)
Gen. 4:7; 6:16; 18:1,2,10; 19:6,11; 38:14; 43:19; **Ex.** 12:22,23; 26:36; 29:4,11,32,42; 33:8–10; 35:15; 36:37; 38:8,30; 39:38; 40:5,6,12,28,29; **Lev.** 1:3,5; 3:2; 4:4,7,18; 8:3,4,31,33,35; 10:7; 12:6; 14:11,23,38; 15:14,29; 16:7; 17:4–6,9; 19:21; **Num.** 3:25,26; 4:25,26; 6:10,13,18; 10:3; 11:10; 12:5; 16:18,19, 27,50(17:15); 20:6; 25:6; 27:2; **Deut.** 22:21; 31:15; **Josh.** 8:29; 19:51; 20:4; **Judg.** 4:20; 9:35,40,44,52; 18:16,17; 19:26,27; **1 Sam.** 2:22; **2 Sam.** 10:8; 11:9,23; **1 Kgs.** 6:8,31,33; 7:5; 14:6,27; 17:10; 19:13; 22:10; **2 Kgs.** 4:15; 5:9; 7:3; 10:8; 23:8; **1 Chr.** 9:21; 19:9; **2 Chr.** 4:22; 12:10; 18:9; **Neh.** 3:20,21; **Esth.** 5:1; **Job** 31:9,34; **Ps.** 24:7,9; **Prov.** 1:21; 5:8; 8:3,34; 9:14; 17:19; **Song** 7:13(14); **Isa.** 3:26; 13:2; **Jer.** 1:15; 19:2; 26:10; 36:10; 43:9; **Ezek.** 8:3,7,8,14,16; 10:19; 11:1; 33:30; 40:11,13,38,40; 41:2,3,11, 17,20; 42:2,4,11,12; 46:3; 47:1; **Hos.** 2:15(17); **Mic.** 5:6(5); 7:5.

6608. פֵּתַח *pēṯaḥ* **masc. noun**
(entrance, unfolding)
Ps. 119:130.

6609. פְּתִיחָה *p^eṯiyḥāh* **fem. noun**
(drawn sword)
Ps. 55:21(22).

6610. פִּתְחוֹן *piṯḥôn* **masc. noun**
(opening [of the mouth])
Ezek. 16:63; 29:21.

6611. A. פְּתַחְיָה *p^eṯaḥyāh* **masc. proper noun**
(Pethahiah: priest in David's time)
1 Chr. 24:16.
B. פְּתַחְיָה *p^eṯaḥyāh* **masc. proper noun**
(Pethahiah: Levite who assisted Ezra; perhaps same as C)
Neh. 9:5.
C. פְּתַחְיָה *p^eṯaḥyāh* **masc. proper noun**
(Pethahiah: returning exile with foreign wife; perhaps same as B)
Ezra 10:23.
D. פְּתַחְיָה *p^eṯaḥyāh* **masc. proper noun**
(Pethahiah: descendant of Judah, advisor to Zerubbabel)
Neh. 11:24.

6612. פֶּתִי *peṯiy* **adj.**
(foolish, simpleminded)

Ps. 19:7(8); 116:6; 119:130; **Prov.** 1:4, 22,32; 7:7; 8:5; 9:4,6,16; 14:15,18; 19:25; 21:11; 22:3; 27:12; **Ezek.** 45:20.

6613. פְּתָי *p^{e}ṯāy* **Aram. masc. noun**
(width)
Ezra 6:3; **Dan.** 3:1.

6614. I. פְּתִיגִיל *p^{e}ṯiygiyl* **masc. noun**
(rich robe, fine clothes)
Isa. 3:24(KJV, see II).
II. פְּתִיגִיל *p^{e}ṯiygiyl* **masc. noun**
(girdle, stomacher)
Isa. 3:24(NASB, NIV, see I).

6615. פְּתַיּוּת *p^{e}ṯayyûṯ* **fem. noun**
(simplicity, the state of being naïve)
Prov. 9:13.

6616. פָּתִיל *pāṯiyl* **masc. noun**
(cord, piece of string)
Gen. 38:18,25; **Ex.** 28:28,37; 39:3,21,31; **Num.** 15:38; 19:15; **Judg.** 16:9; **Ezek.** 40:3.

6617. פָּתַל *pāṯal* **verb**
(to be shrewd, to be cunning, to be devious; to wrestle)
Gen. 30:8; **2 Sam.** 22:27; **Job** 5:13; **Ps.** 18:26(27); **Prov.** 8:8.

6618. פְּתַלְתֹּל *p^{e}ṯaltōl* **adj.**
(crooked, warped)
Deut. 32:5.

6619. פִּתֹם *piṯōm* **proper noun**
(Pithom)
Ex. 1:11.

6620. פֶּתֶן *peṯen* **masc. noun**
(cobra, poisonous snake)
Deut. 32:33; **Job** 20:14,16; **Ps.** 58:4(5); 91:13; **Isa.** 11:8.

6621. פֶּתַע *peṯa'* **masc. noun**
(suddenness)
Num. 6:9; 35:22; **Prov.** 6:15; 29:1; **Isa.** 29:5; 30:13; **Hab.** 2:7.

6622. פָּתַר *pāṯar* **verb**
(to interpret)
Gen. 40:8,16,22; 41:8,12,13,15.

6623. פִּתְרוֹן *piṯrôn* **masc. noun**
(interpretation, meaning)
Gen. 40:5,8,12,18; 41:11.

6624. פַּתְרוֹס *paṯrôs* **proper noun**
(Pathros)
Isa. 11:11; **Jer.** 44:1,15; **Ezek.** 29:14; 30:14.

6625. פַּתְרֻסִים *paṯrusiym* **masc. pl. proper noun**
(Pathrusites)
Gen. 10:14; **1 Chr.** 1:12.

6626. פָּתַת *pāṯaṯ* **verb**
(to break up, to crumble)
Lev. 2:6.

צ Tsadde

6627. צֵאָה *tṣēʼāh* **fem. noun**
(excrement, dung)
Deut. 23:13(14); **Ezek.** 4:12.

6628. I. צֶאֱלִים *ṣeʼᵉliym* **masc. pl. noun**
(lotus plants)
Job 40:21(KJV, see II),22(KJV, see II).
II. צֶאֱלִים *ṣeʼᵉliym* **masc. pl. noun**
(shady trees)
Job 40:21(NASB, NIV, see I),22(NASB, NIV, see I).

6629. צֹאן *ṣōʼn* **coll. masc./fem. noun**
(sheep, flock)
Gen. 4:2,4; 12:16; 13:5; 20:14; 21:27,28; 24:35; 26:14; 27:9; 29:2,3,6–10; 30:31, 32,36,38–43; 31:4,8,10,12,19,38,41,43; 32:5(6),7(8); 33:13; 34:28; 37:2,12,14; 38:12,13,17; 45:10; 46:32,34; 47:1,3, 4,17; 50:8; **Ex.** 2:16,17,19; 3:1; 9:3; 10:9,24; 12:21,32,38; 20:24; 22:1(21:37), 30(29); 34:3; **Lev.** 1:2,10; 3:6; 5:6,15,18; 6:6(5:25); 22:21; 27:32; **Num.** 11:22; 15:3; 22:40; 27:17; 31:28,30,32,36,37,43; 32:16,24(KJV, NASB, *ṣōneʼ* [6792]),32; **Deut.** 7:13; 8:13; 12:6,17,21; 14:23,26; 15:14,19; 16:2; 18:4; 28:4,18,31,51; 32:14; **Josh.** 7:24; **1 Sam.** 8:17; 14:32; 15:9,14,15,21; 16:11,19; 17:15,20,28,34; 24:3(4); 25:2,4,16,18; 27:9; 30:20; **2 Sam.** 7:8; 12:2,4; 17:29; 24:17; **1 Kgs.** 1:9,19,25; 4:23(5:3); 8:5,63; 22:17; **2 Kgs.** 5:26; **1 Chr.** 4:39,41; 5:21; 12:40; 17:7; 21:17; 27:31; **2 Chr.** 5:6; 7:5; 14:15(14); 15:11; 17:11; 18:2,16; 29:33; 30:24; 31:6; 32:29; 35:7; **Ezra** 10:19; **Neh.** 3:1,32; 5:18; 10:36(37); 12:39; **Job** 1:3,16; 21:11; 30:1; 42:12; **Ps.** 44:11(12), 22(23); 49:14(15); 65:13(14); 74:1; 77:20(21); 78:52,70; 79:13; 80:1(2); 95:7; 100:3; 107:41; 114:4,6; 144:13; **Prov.** 27:23; **Eccl.** 2:7; **Song** 1:8; **Isa.** 7:21; 13:14; 22:13; 53:6; 60:7; 61:5; 63:11; 65:10; **Jer.** 3:24; 5:17; 12:3; 13:20; 23:1–3; 25:34–36; 31:12; 33:12,13; 49:20,29; 50:6,8,45; **Ezek.** 24:5; 25:5; 34:2,3,6,8,10–12,15,17,19,22,31; 36:37,38; 43:23,25; 45:15; **Hos.** 5:6; **Joel** 1:18; **Amos** 6:4; 7:15; **Jon.** 3:7; **Mic.** 2:12; 5:8(7); 7:14; **Hab.** 3:17; **Zeph.** 2:6; **Zech.** 9:16; 10:2; 11:4,7,11,17; 13:7.

6630. צַאֲנָן *ṣaʼănan* **proper noun**
(Zaanan)
Mic. 1:11.

6631. צֶאֱצָא *ṣeʼᵉṣāʼ* **masc. noun**
(offspring, child)
Job 5:25; 21:8; 27:14; 31:8; **Isa.** 22:24; 34:1; 42:5; 44:3; 48:19; 61:9; 65:23.

6632. I. צָב *ṣāḇ* **masc. noun**
(covered wagon, cart)
Num. 7:3; **Isa.** 66:20(KJV, NASB, see II).
II. צָב *ṣāḇ* **masc. noun**
(a litter; burden carried on poles supported on shoulders of men)
Isa. 66:20(NIV, see I).
III. צָב *ṣāḇ* **masc. noun**
(great lizard)
Lev. 11:29(KJV, see IV).
IV. צָב *ṣāḇ* **masc. noun**
(tortoise)
Lev. 11:29(NASB, NIV, see III).

6633. I. צָבָא *ṣāḇāʼ* **verb**
(to muster for war; to fight, to make war)
Num. 4:23; 8:24; 31:7,42; **2 Kgs.** 25:19; **Isa.** 29:7,8; 31:4; **Jer.** 52:25; **Zech.** 14:12.

II. צָבָא *ṣāḇā'* **verb**
(to assemble, to serve [of women at the tabernacle])
Ex. 38:8; **1 Sam.** 2:22.

6634. צְבָא *ṣᵉḇā'* **Aram. verb**
(to wish, to desire, to choose)
Dan. 4:17(14),25(22),32(29),35(32); 5:19,21; 7:19.

6635. צָבָא *ṣāḇā'* **masc. noun**
(army, host; NIV, plural as part of title for God Almighty)
Gen. 2:1; 21:22,32; 26:26; **Ex.** 6:26; 7:4; 12:17,41,51; **Num.** 1:3,20,22,24,26,28, 30,32,34,36,38,40,42,45,52; 2:3,4,6, 8–11,13,15,16,18,19,21,23–26,28,30,32; 4:3,23,30,35,39,43; 8:24,25; 10:14–16, 18–20,22–28; 26:2; 31:3–6,14,21,27,28, 32,36,48,53; 32:27; 33:1; **Deut.** 4:19; 17:3; 20:9; 24:5; **Josh.** 4:13; 5:14,15; 22:12,33; **Judg.** 4:2,7; 8:6; 9:29; **1 Sam.** 1:3,11; 4:4; 12:9; 14:50; 15:2; 17:15,55; 26:5; 28:1; **2 Sam.** 2:8; 3:23; 5:10; 6:2,18; 7:8,26,27; 8:16; 10:7,16,18; 17:25; 19:13(14); 20:23; **1 Kgs.** 1:19,25; 2:5,32,35; 4:4; 11:15,21; 16:16; 18:15; 19:10,14; 22:19; **2 Kgs.** 3:14; 4:13; 5:1; 17:16; 19:31(NASB, [Kᵉ] omits); 21:3,5; 23:4,5; 25:19; **1 Chr.** 5:18; 7:4,11,40; 11:9; 12:8,14,21,23–25,33,36,37; 17:7,24; 18:15; 19:8,16,18; 20:1; 25:1; 26:26; 27:3,5,34; **2 Chr.** 17:18; 18:18; 25:5,7; 26:11,13,14; 28:9,12; 33:3,5,11; **Neh.** 9:6; **Job** 7:1; 10:17; 14:14; **Ps.** 24:10; 33:6; 44:9(10); 46:7(8),11(12); 48:8(9); 59:5(6); 60:10(12); 68:11(12), 12(13); 69:6(7); 80:4(5),7(8),14(15), 19(20); 84:1(2),3(4),8(9),12(13); 89:8(9); 103:21; 108:11(12); 148:2; **Isa.** 1:9,24; 2:12; 3:1,15; 5:7,9,16,24; 6:3,5; 8:13,18; 9:7(6),13(12),19(18); 10:16,23,24,26,33; 13:4,13; 14:22–24,27; 17:3; 18:7; 19:4, 12,16–18,20,25; 21:10; 22:5,12,14,15,25; 23:9; 24:21,23; 25:6; 28:5,22,29; 29:6; 31:4,5; 34:2,4; 37:16,32; 39:5; 40:2,26; 44:6; 45:12,13; 47:4; 48:2; 51:15; 54:5; **Jer.** 2:19; 3:19; 5:14; 6:6,9; 7:3,21; 8:2,3; 9:7(6),15(14),17(16); 10:16; 11:17,20,22; 15:16; 16:9; 19:3,11,13,15; 20:12; 23:15, 16,36; 25:8,27–29,32; 26:18; 27:4,18, 19,21; 28:2,14; 29:4,8,17,21,25; 30:8; 31:23,35; 32:14,15,18; 33:11,12,22; 35:13,17–19; 38:17; 39:16; 42:15,18; 43:10; 44:2,7,11,25; 46:10,18,25; 48:1,15; 49:5,7,26,35; 50:18,25,31,33,34; 51:3,5, 14,19,33,57,58; 52:25; **Dan.** 8:10–13; 10:1; **Hos.** 12:5(6); **Amos** 3:13; 4:13; 5:14–16,27; 6:8,14; 9:5; **Mic.** 4:4; **Nah.** 2:13(14); 3:5; **Hab.** 2:13; **Zeph.** 1:5; 2:9,10; **Hag.** 1:2,5,7,9,14; 2:4,6–9,11,23; **Zech.** 1:3,4,6,12,14,16,17; 2:8(12),9(13), 11(15); 3:7,9,10; 4:6,9; 5:4; 6:12,15; 7:3,4,9,12,13; 8:1–4,6,7,9,11,14,18–23; 9:15; 10:3; 12:5; 13:2,7; 14:16,17,21; **Mal.** 1:4,6,8–11,13,14; 2:2,4,7,8,12,16; 3:1,5,7,10–12,14,17; 4:1(3:19),3(3:21).

6636. צְבֹאִים *ṣᵉḇō'iym,* **צְבֹיִים** *ṣᵉḇōyiym* **proper noun**
(Zeboiim)
Gen. 10:19; 14:2,8; **Deut.** 29:23(22); **Hos.** 11:8.

6637. I. צֹבֵבָה *ṣōḇēḇāh* **masc. proper noun**
(Zobebah; used with def. article)
1 Chr. 4:8(NIV, see II).
II. הַצֹּבֵבָה *haṣṣōḇēḇāh* **masc. proper noun**
(Hazzobebah)
1 Chr. 4:8(KJV, NASB, see I).

6638. צָבָה *ṣāḇāh* **verb**
(to swell up)
Num. 5:22,27.

6639. צָבֶה *ṣāḇeh* **adj.**
(swollen)
Num. 5:21.

6640. צְבוּ *ṣᵉḇû* **Aram. fem. noun**
(situation)
Dan. 6:17(18).

6641. צָבוּעַ *ṣāḇûa'* **adj.**
(speckled)
Jer. 12:9.

6642. צָבַט *ṣāḇaṭ* **verb**
(to reach out, to hand something over)
Ruth 2:14.

6643. I. צְבִי *ṣ*^{e}*ḇiy* **masc. noun**
(beauty, glory)
2 Sam. 1:19; **Isa.** 4:2; 13:19; 23:9; 24:16; 28:1,4,5; **Jer.** 3:19; **Ezek.** 7:20; 20:6,15; 25:9; 26:20; **Dan.** 8:9; 11:16,41,45.
II. צְבִי *ṣ*^{e}*ḇiy* **masc. noun**
(gazelle, roebuck)
Deut. 12:15,22; 14:5; 15:22; **2 Sam.** 2:18; **1 Kgs.** 4:23(5:3); **1 Chr.** 12:8; **Prov.** 6:5; **Song** 2:7,9,17; 3:5; 8:14; **Isa.** 13:14.

6644. צִבְיָא *ṣiḇyā'* **masc. noun**
(Zibia)
1 Chr. 8:9.

6645. צִבְיָה *ṣiḇyāh* **fem. proper noun**
(Zibiah)
2 Kgs. 12:1(2); **2 Chr.** 24:1.

6646. צְבִיָּה *ṣ*^{e}*ḇiyyāh* **fem. noun**
(female gazelle)
Song 4:5; 7:3(4).

6647. צְבַע *ṣ*^{e}*ḇa'* **Aram. verb**
(to be wet, to be drenched)
Dan. 4:15(12),23(20),25(22),33(30); 5:21.

6648. צֶבַע *ṣeḇa'* **masc. noun**
(dyed work, colorful garment)
Judg. 5:30.

6649. צִבְעוֹן *ṣiḇ'ôn* **masc. proper noun**
(Zibeon)
Gen. 36:2,14,20,24,29; **1 Chr.** 1:38,40.

6650. צְבֹעִים *ṣ*^{e}*ḇō'iym* **proper noun**
(Zeboim)
1 Sam. 13:18; **Neh.** 11:34.

6651. צָבַר *ṣāḇar* **verb**
(to heap up, to store up, to gather together)
Gen. 41:35,49; **Ex.** 8:14(10); **Job** 27:16; **Ps.** 39:6(7); **Hab.** 1:10; **Zech.** 9:3.

6652. צִבֻּר *ṣibbur,* צִבּוּר *ṣibbûr* **masc. noun**
(heap, pile)
2 Kgs. 10:8.

6653. צֶבֶת *ṣeḇeṯ* **masc. noun**
(handful)
Ruth 2:16.

6654. צַד *ṣaḏ* **masc. noun**
(side)
Gen. 6:16; **Ex.** 25:32; 26:13; 30:4; 37:18,27; **Num.** 33:55; **Deut.** 31:26; **Josh.** 3:16; 12:9; 23:13; **Judg.** 2:3; **Ruth** 2:14; **1 Sam.** 6:8; 20:20,25; 23:26; **2 Sam.** 2:16; 13:34; **Ps.** 91:7; **Isa.** 60:4; 66:12; **Ezek.** 4:4,6,8,9; 34:21.

6655. צַד *ṣaḏ* **Aram. masc. noun**
(side; used with a preposition against, regarding; corr. to Hebr. 6654)
Dan. 6:4(5); 7:25.

6656. צְדָא *ṣ*^{e}*ḏā'* **Aram. masc. noun**
(truth)
Dan. 3:14.

6657. צְדָד *ṣ*^{e}*ḏāḏ* **proper noun**
(Zedad)
Num. 34:8; **Ezek.** 47:15.

6658. צָדָה *ṣāḏāh* **verb**
(to lie in wait, to hunt down, to destroy)
Ex. 21:13; **1 Sam.** 24:11(12); **Zeph.** 3:6.

6659. A. צָדוֹק *ṣāḏôq* **masc. proper noun**
(Zadok: high priest in David's day)
2 Sam. 8:17; 15:24,25,27,29,35,36; 17:15; 18:19,22,27; 19:11(12); 20:25; **1 Kgs.** 1:8,26,32,34,38,39,44,45; 2:35; 4:2,4; **1 Chr.** 6:8(5:34),53(38); 15:11; 16:39; 18:16; 24:3,6,31; 27:17; 29:22; **2 Chr.** 31:10; **Ezra** 7:2; **Ezek.** 40:46; 43:19; 44:15; 48:11.
B. צָדוֹק *ṣāḏôq* **masc. proper noun**
(Zadok: Levite who joined David at Hebron; possibly the same as A)
1 Chr. 12:28.
C. צָדוֹק *ṣāḏôq* **masc. proper noun**
(Zadok: descendant of original Zadok [A])
1 Chr. 6:12(5:38).
D. צָדוֹק *ṣāḏôq* **masc. proper noun**
(Zadok: priest who was son of Meraioth and father of Meshullam; possibly the same as A)
1 Chr. 9:11; **Neh.** 11:11.
E. צָדוֹק *ṣāḏôq* **masc. proper noun**
(Zadok: grandfather of King Jotham; possibly the same as D)
2 Kgs. 15:33; **2 Chr.** 27:1.
F. צָדוֹק *ṣāḏôq* **masc. proper noun**
(Zadok: a scribe whom Nehemiah appointed treasurer)
Neh. 13:13.
G. צָדוֹק *ṣāḏôq* **masc. proper noun**
(Zadok: signer of covenant in Nehemiah's day; possibly the same as F)
Neh. 10:21(22).
H. צָדוֹק *ṣāḏôq* **masc. proper noun**
(Zadok: son of Baana and repairer of Nehemiah's wall)
Neh. 3:4.
I. צָדוֹק *ṣāḏôq* **masc. proper noun**
(Zadok: son of Immer and repairer of Nehemiah's wall)
Neh. 3:29.

6660. צְדִיָּה *ṣ*^{e}*ḏiyyāh* **fem. noun**
(lying in wait, ambushing)
Num. 35:20,22.

6661. צִדִּים *ṣiddiym* **proper noun**
(Ziddim)
Josh. 19:35.

6662. צַדִּיק *ṣaddiyq* **adj.**
(righteous, just, innocent)
Gen. 6:9; 7:1; 18:23–26,28; 20:4; **Ex.** 9:27; 23:7,8; **Deut.** 4:8; 16:19; 25:1; 32:4; **1 Sam.** 24:17(18); **2 Sam.** 4:11; 23:3; **1 Kgs.** 2:32; 8:32; **2 Kgs.** 10:9; **2 Chr.** 6:23; 12:6; **Ezra** 9:15; **Neh.** 9:8,33; **Job** 12:4; 17:9; 22:19; 27:17; 32:1; 34:17; 36:7; **Ps.** 1:5,6; 5:12(13); 7:9(10),11(12); 11:3,5,7; 14:5; 31:18(19); 32:11; 33:1; 34:15(16),19(20),21(22); 37:12,16,17,21,25,29,30,32,39; 52:6(8); 55:22(23); 58:10(11),11(12); 64:10(11); 68:3(4); 69:28(29); 72:7; 75:10(11); 92:12(13); 94:21; 97:11,12; 112:4,6; 116:5; 118:15,20; 119:137; 125:3; 129:4; 140:13(14); 141:5; 142:7(8); 145:17; 146:8; **Prov.** 2:20; 3:33; 4:18; 9:9; 10:3, 6,7,11,16,20,21,24,25,28,30–32; 11:8–10, 21,23,28,30,31; 12:3,5,7,10,12,13,21,26; 13:5,9,21,22,25; 14:19,32; 15:6,28,29; 17:15,26; 18:5,10,17; 20:7; 21:12,15, 18,26; 23:24; 24:15,16,24; 25:26; 28:1, 12,28; 29:2,6,7,16,27; **Eccl.** 3:17; 7:15,16,20; 8:14; 9:1,2; **Isa.** 3:10; 5:23; 24:16; 26:2,7; 29:21; 41:26; 45:21; 49:24; 53:11; 57:1; 60:21; **Jer.** 12:1; 20:12; 23:5; **Lam.** 1:18; 4:13; **Ezek.** 3:20,21; 13:22; 18:5,9,20,24,26; 21:3(8),4(9); 23:45; 33:12,13,18; **Dan.** 9:14; **Hos.** 14:9(10); **Amos** 2:6; 5:12; **Hab.** 1:4,13; 2:4; **Zeph.** 3:5; **Zech.** 9:9; **Mal.** 3:18.

6663. צָדַק *ṣāḏaq* **verb**
(to justify, to declare innocent, to vindicate)
Gen. 38:26; 44:16; **Ex.** 23:7; **Deut.** 25:1; **2 Sam.** 15:4; **1 Kgs.** 8:32; **2 Chr.** 6:23; **Job** 4:17; 9:2,15,20; 10:15; 11:2;

13:18; 15:14; 22:3; 25:4; 27:5; 32:2; 33:12,32; 34:5; 35:7; 40:8; **Ps.** 19:9(10); 51:4(6); 82:3; 143:2; **Prov.** 17:15; **Isa.** 5:23; 43:9,26; 45:25; 50:8; 53:11; **Jer.** 3:11; **Ezek.** 16:51,52; **Dan.** 8:14; 12:3.

6664. צֶדֶק *ṣed̲eq* **masc. noun**
(righteousness, justice)
Lev. 19:15,36; **Deut.** 1:16; 16:18,20; 25:15; 33:19; **Job** 6:29; 8:3,6; 29:14; 31:6; 35:2; 36:3; **Ps.** 4:1(2),5(6); 7:8(9),17(18); 9:4(5),8(9); 15:2; 17:1,15; 18:20(21), 24(25); 23:3; 35:24,27,28; 37:6; 40:9(10); 45:4(5),7(8); 48:10(11); 50:6; 51:19(21); 52:3(5); 58:1(2); 65:5(6); 72:2; 85:10(11), 11(12),13(14); 89:14(15); 94:15; 96:13; 97:2,6; 98:9; 118:19; 119:7,62,75,106, 121,123,138,142,144,160,164,172; 132:9; **Prov.** 1:3; 2:9; 8:8,15; 12:17; 16:13; 25:5; 31:9; **Eccl.** 3:16; 5:8(7); 7:15; **Isa.** 1:21,26; 11:4,5; 16:5; 26:9,10; 32:1; 41:2,10; 42:6,21; 45:8,13,19; 51:1,5,7; 58:2,8; 59:4; 61:3; 62:1,2; 64:5(4); **Jer.** 11:20; 22:13; 23:6; 31:23; 33:16; 50:7; **Ezek.** 3:20; 45:10; **Dan.** 9:24; **Hos.** 2:19(21); 10:12; **Zeph.** 2:3.

6665. צִדְקָה *ṣid̲qāh* **Aram. fem. noun**
(righteousness; corr. to Hebr. 6666)
Dan. 4:27(24).

6666. צְדָקָה *ṣ^e^d̲āqāh* **fem. noun**
(righteousness, justice)
Gen. 15:6; 18:19; 30:33; **Deut.** 6:25; 9:4–6; 24:13; 33:21; **Judg.** 5:11; **1 Sam.** 12:7; 26:23; **2 Sam.** 8:15; 19:28(29); 22:21,25; **1 Kgs.** 3:6; 8:32; 10:9; **1 Chr.** 18:14; **2 Chr.** 6:23; 9:8; **Neh.** 2:20; **Job** 27:6; 33:26; 35:8; 37:23; **Ps.** 5:8(9); 11:7; 22:31(32); 24:5; 31:1(2); 33:5; 36:6(7), 10(11); 40:10(11); 51:14(16); 69:27(28); 71:2,15,16,19,24; 72:1,3; 88:12(13); 89:16(17); 98:2; 99:4; 103:6,17; 106:3,31; 111:3; 112:3,9; 119:40,142; 143:1,11; 145:7; **Prov.** 8:18,20; 10:2; 11:4,5,6, 18,19; 12:28; 13:6; 14:34; 15:9; 16:8,12, 31; 21:3,21; **Isa.** 1:27; 5:7,16,23; 9:7(6); 10:22; 28:17; 32:16,17; 33:5,15; 45:8, 23,24; 46:12,13; 48:1,18; 51:6,8; 54:14,17; 56:1; 57:12; 58:2; 59:9,14,16,17; 60:17; 61:10,11; 63:1; 64:6(5); **Jer.** 4:2; 9:24(23); 22:3,15; 23:5; 33:15; 51:10; **Ezek.** 3:20; 14:14,20; 18:5,19–22,24,26,27; 33:12–14, 16,18,19; 45:9; **Dan.** 9:7,16,18; **Hos.** 10:12; **Joel** 2:23; **Amos** 5:7,24; 6:12; **Mic.** 6:5; 7:9; **Zech.** 8:8; **Mal.** 3:3; 4:2(3:20).

6667. A. צִדְקִיָּה *ṣid̲qiyyāh,* צִדְקִיָּהוּ *ṣid̲qiyyāhû* **masc. proper noun**
(Zedekiah: false prophet under Ahab)
1 Kgs. 22:11; **2 Chr.** 18:10.
B. צִדְקִיָּה *ṣid̲qiyyāh* **masc. proper noun**
(Zedekiah: the last king of Judah)
2 Kgs. 24:17,18,20; 25:2,7; **1 Chr.** 3:15; **2 Chr.** 36:10,11; **Jer.** 1:3; 21:1,3,7; 24:8; 27:3,12; 28:1; 29:3; 32:1,3–5; 34:2,4,6, 8,21; 37:1,3,17,18,21; 38:5,14–17,19,24; 39:1,2,4–7; 44:30; 49:34; 51:59; 52:1,3, 5,8,10,11.
C. צִדְקִיָּה *ṣid̲qiyyāh* **masc. proper noun**
(Zedekiah: son of Jehoiakim)
1 Chr. 3:16.
D. צִדְקִיָּהוּ *ṣid̲qiyyāhû* **masc. proper noun**
(Zedekiah: false prophet in Jeremiah's day)
Jer. 29:21,22.
E. צִדְקִיָּהוּ *ṣid̲qiyyāhû* **masc. proper noun**
(Zedekiah: prince of Judah; possibly the same as C)
Jer. 36:12.
F. צִדְקִיָּה *ṣid̲qiyyāh* **masc. proper noun**
(Zedekiah: signer of Nehemiah's covenant)
Neh. 10:1(2).

6668. צָהַב *ṣāhab̲* **verb**
(to be shiny, to be fine)
Ezra 8:27.

6669. צָהֹב *ṣāhoḇ* **adj.**
(yellowish)
Lev. 13:30,32,36.

6670. I. צָהַל *ṣāhal* **verb**
(to cry out, to shout, to neigh [as a horse])
Esth. 8:15; **Isa.** 10:30; 12:6; 24:14; 54:1; **Jer.** 5:8; 31:7; 50:11.
II. צָהַל *ṣāhal* **verb**
(to glisten, to shine)
Ps. 104:15.

6671. צָהַר *ṣāhar* **verb**
(to crush olives, produce olive oil)
Job 24:11.

6672. I. צֹהַר *ṣōhar* **masc. noun**
(noon, midday)
Gen. 43:16,25; **Deut.** 28:29; **2 Sam.** 4:5; **1 Kgs.** 18:26,27,29; 20:16; **2 Kgs.** 4:20; **Job** 5:14; 11:17; **Ps.** 37:6; 55:17(18); 91:6; **Song** 1:7; **Isa.** 16:3; 58:10; 59:10; **Jer.** 6:4; 15:8; 20:16; **Amos** 8:9; **Zeph.** 2:4.
II. צֹהַר *ṣōhar* **masc. noun**
(window space)
Gen. 6:16.

6673. I. צַו *ṣaw*, צָו *ṣāw* **masc. noun**
(precept, commandment)
Isa. 28:10,13; **Hos.** 5:11.
II. צַו *ṣaw* **masc. noun**
(idol)
Hos. 5:11(KJV, NASB, see I).

6674. צוֹא *ṣô'*, צוֹאִי *ṣô'iy* **adj.**
(filthy)
Zech. 3:3,4.

6675. צוֹאָה *ṣô'āh* **fem. noun**
(filth, filthiness)
Prov. 30:12; **Isa.** 4:4; 28:8.

6676. צַוַּאר *ṣawwa'r* **Aram. masc. noun**
(neck; corr. to Hebr. 6677)
Dan. 5:7,16,29.

6677. A. צַוָּאר *ṣawwā'r* **masc. noun**
(neck)
Gen. 27:16,40; 33:4; 41:42; 45:14; 46:29; **Deut.** 28:48; **Josh.** 10:24; **Judg.** 5:30; 8:21,26; **Neh.** 3:5; **Job** 15:26; 39:19; 41:22(14); **Ps.** 75:5(6); **Song** 1:10; 4:4,9(NASB, NIV, see II); 7:4(5); **Isa.** 8:8; 10:27; 30:28; 52:2; **Jer.** 27:2,8,11,12; 28:10–12,14; 30:8; **Lam.** 1:14; 5:5; **Ezek.** 21:29(34); **Hos.** 10:11; **Mic.** 2:3; **Hab.** 3:13.
B. צַוְּרֹנִים *ṣawwārōniym* **masc. pl. noun**
(necklaces)
Song 4:9(KJV, see I).

6678. צוֹבָא *ṣôḇā'*, צוֹבָה *ṣôḇāh* **proper noun**
(Zobah: kingdom under Hadadezer)
1 Sam. 14:47; **2 Sam.** 8:3,5,12; 10:6,8; 23:36; **1 Kgs.** 11:23; **1 Chr.** 18:3,5,9; 19:6; **2 Chr.** 8:3.

6679. I. צוּד *ṣûḏ* **verb**
(to hunt, to hunt down, to ensnare)
Gen. 27:3,5,33; **Lev.** 17:13; **Job** 10:16; 38:39; **Ps.** 140:11(12); **Prov.** 6:26; **Lam.** 3:52; 4:18; **Jer.** 16:16; **Ezek.** 13:18,20; **Mic.** 7:2.
II. צוּד *ṣûḏ* **verb**
(to take as provisions)
Josh. 9:12(NASB, NIV, see III).
III. צִיד *ṣiyḏ* **verb**
(to pack, to take as provisions)
Josh. 9:12(KJV, see II).

6680. צָוָה *ṣāwāh* **verb**
(to command, to instruct, to appoint)
Gen. 2:16; 3:11,17; 6:22; 7:5,9,16; 12:20; 18:19; 21:4; 26:11; 27:8; 28:1,6; 32:4(5),17(18),19(20); 42:25; 44:1; 45:19; 47:11; 49:29,33; 50:2,12,16; **Ex.**

1:22; 4:28; 5:6; 6:13; 7:2,6,10,20; 12:28,50; 16:16,24,32,34; 18:23; 19:7; 23:15; 25:22; 27:20; 29:35; 31:6,11; 32:8; 34:4,11,18,32,34; 35:1,4,10,29; 36:1,5,6; 38:22; 39:1,5,7,21,26,29,31,32,42,43; 40:16,19,21,23,25,27,29,32; **Lev.** 6:9(2); 7:36,38; 8:4,5,9,13,17,21,29,31,34–36; 9:5–7,10,21; 10:1,13,15,18; 13:54; 14:4, 5,36,40; 16:34; 17:2; 24:2,23; 25:21; 27:34; **Num.** 1:19,54; 2:33,34; 3:16, 42,51; 4:49; 5:2; 8:3,20,22; 9:5,8; 15:23,36; 17:11(26); 19:2; 20:9,27; 26:4; 27:11,19,22,23; 28:2; 29:40(30:1); 30:1(2), 16(17); 31:7,21,31,41,47; 32:25,28; 34:2, 13,29; 35:2; 36:2,5,6,10,13; **Deut.** 1:3, 16,18,19,41; 2:4,37; 3:18,21,28; 4:2,5, 13,14,23,40; 5:12,15,16,32(29),33(30); 6:1,2,6,17,20,24,25; 7:11; 8:1,11; 9:12,16; 10:5,13; 11:8,13,22,27,28; 12:11,14,21,28,32(13:1); 13:5(6),18(19); 15:5,11,15; 17:3; 18:18,20; 19:7,9; 20:17; 24:8,18,22; 26:13,14,16; 27:1,4,10,11; 28:1,8,13–15,45; 29:1(28:69); 30:2,8, 11,16; 31:5,10,14,23,25,29; 32:46; 33:4; 34:9; **Josh.** 1:7,9–11,13,16,18; 3:3,8; 4:3,8,10,16,17; 6:10; 7:11; 8:4,8,27,29, 31,33,35; 9:24; 10:27,40; 11:12,15,20; 13:6; 14:2,5; 17:4; 18:8; 21:2,8; 22:2,5; 23:16; **Judg.** 2:20; 3:4; 4:6; 13:14; 21:10,20; **Ruth** 2:9,15; 3:6; **1 Sam.** 2:29; 13:13,14; 17:20; 18:22; 20:29; 21:2(3); 25:30; **2 Sam.** 4:12; 5:25; 6:21; 7:7,11; 9:11; 11:19; 13:28,29; 14:8,19; 17:14,23; 18:5,12; 21:14; 24:19; **1 Kgs.** 1:35; 2:1,43,46; 5:6(20),17(31); 8:58; 9:4; 11:10,11,38; 13:9,21; 15:5; 17:4,9; 22:31; **2 Kgs.** 11:5,9,15; 14:6; 16:15,16; 17:13,15,27,34,35; 18:6,12; 20:1; 21:8; 22:12; 23:4,21; **1 Chr.** 6:49(34); 14:16; 15:15; 16:15,40; 17:6,10; 22:6,12,13,17; 24:19; **2 Chr.** 7:13,17; 18:30; 19:9; 23:8; 25:4; 33:8; 34:20; **Ezra** 4:3; 8:17(NASB, [K^{e}] *yāṣāh* [3318]); 9:11; **Neh.** 1:7,8; 5:14; 7:2; 8:1,14; 9:14; **Esth.** 2:10,20; 3:2,12; 4:5,8,10,17; 8:9; **Job** 36:32; 37:12; 38:12; **Ps.** 7:6(7); 33:9; 42:8(9); 44:4(5); 68:28(29); 71:3; 78:5,23; 91:11; 105:8; 111:9; 119:4,138; 133:3; 148:5; **Isa.** 5:6; 10:6; 13:3; 20:10(KJV, NASB, *ṣaw* [6673,I]); 23:11; 28:13(KJV, NASB, *ṣaw* [6673,I]); 34:16; 38:1; 45:11,12; 48:5; 55:4; **Jer.** 1:7,17; 7:22,23,31; 11:4,8; 13:5,6; 14:14; 17:22; 19:5; 23:32; 26:2,8; 27:4; 29:23; 32:13,23,35; 34:22; 35:6,8, 10,14,16,18; 36:5,8,26; 37:21; 38:10,27; 39:11; 47:7; 50:21; 51:59; **Lam.** 1:10,17; 2:17; 3:37; **Ezek.** 9:11; 10:6; 12:7; 24:18; 37:7,10; **Amos** 2:12; 6:11; 9:3,4,9; **Nah.** 1:14; **Zech.** 1:6; **Mal.** 4:4(3:22).

6681. צָוַח *ṣāwaḥ* **verb**
(to shout)
Isa. 42:11.

6682. צְוָחָה *ṣ^{e}wāḥāh* **fem. noun**
(a crying out, a shout)
Ps. 144:14; **Isa.** 24:11; **Jer.** 14:2; 46:12.

6683. צוּלָה *ṣûlāh* **fem. noun**
(depth of the sea)
Isa. 44:27.

6684. צוּם *ṣûm* **verb**
(to abstain from food, to fast)
Judg. 20:26; **1 Sam.** 7:6; 31:13; **2 Sam.** 1:12; 12:16,21–23; **1 Kgs.** 21:27; **1 Chr.** 10:12; **Ezra** 8:23; **Neh.** 1:4; **Esth.** 4:16; **Isa.** 58:3,4; **Jer.** 14:12; **Zech.** 7:5.

6685. צוֹם *ṣôm* **masc. noun**
(a fast, a fasting)
2 Sam. 12:16; **1 Kgs.** 21:9,12; **2 Chr.** 20:3; **Ezra** 8:21; **Neh.** 9:1; **Esth.** 4:3; 9:31; **Ps.** 35:13; 69:10(11); 109:24; **Isa.** 58:3,5,6; **Jer.** 36:6,9; **Dan.** 9:3; **Joel** 1:14; 2:12,15; **Jon.** 3:5; **Zech.** 8:19.

6686. צוּעָר *ṣûʿār* **masc. proper noun**
(Zuar)
Num. 1:8; 2:5; 7:18,23; 10:15.

6687. צוּף *ṣûp̱* **verb**
(to overflow, to engulf; to float)
Deut. 11:4; **2 Kgs.** 6:6; **Lam.** 3:54.

6688. צוּף *ṣûp̱* **masc. noun**
(honeycomb)
Ps. 19:10(11); **Prov.** 16:24.

6689. A. צוּף *ṣûp̱*, צוֹפַי *ṣôp̱ay* **masc. proper noun**
(Zuph: ancestor of Samuel)
1 Sam. 1:1; **1 Chr.** 6:26(11),35(20).
B. צוּף *ṣûp̱* **masc. proper noun**
(Zuph: district in Judah)
1 Sam. 9:5.

6690. צוֹפַח *ṣôp̱aḥ* **masc. proper noun**
(Zophah)
1 Chr. 7:35,36.

6691. צוֹפַר *ṣôp̱ar* **masc. proper noun**
(Zophar)
Job 2:11; 11:1; 20:1; 42:9.

6692. I. צוּץ *ṣûṣ* **verb**
(to blossom, to flourish)
Num. 17:8(23); **Ps.** 72:16; 90:6; 92:7(8); 103:15; 132:18; **Isa.** 27:6; **Ezek.** 7:10.
II. צוּץ *ṣûṣ* **verb**
(to peek, to peer)
Song 2:9.

6693. צוּק *ṣûq* **verb**
(to oppress, to distress, to constrain)
Deut. 28:53,55,57; **Judg.** 14:17; 16:16; **Job** 32:18; **Isa.** 29:2,7; 51:13; **Jer.** 19:9.

6694. צוּק *ṣûq* **verb**
(to pour out, to smelt, to whisper)
Job 28:2; 29:6; **Isa.** 26:16.

6695. A. צוֹק *ṣôq* **masc. noun**
(distress, anguish)
Dan. 9:25.
B. צוּקָה *ṣûqāh* **fem. noun**
(distress, anguish)
Prov. 1:27; **Isa.** 8:22; 30:6.

6696. I. צוּר *ṣûr* **verb**
(to beseige, to lay seige, to bind)
Deut. 14:25; 20:12,19; **Judg.** 9:31; **1 Sam.** 23:8; **2 Sam.** 11:1; 20:15; **1 Kgs.** 15:27; 16:17; 20:1; **2 Kgs.** 5:23; 6:24,25; 12:10(11); 16:5; 17:5; 18:9; 24:11; **1 Chr.** 20:1; **2 Chr.** 28:20; **Ps.** 139:5; **Song** 8:9; **Isa.** 21:2; 29:3; **Jer.** 21:4,9; 32:2; 37:5; 39:1; **Ezek.** 4:3; 5:3; **Dan.** 1:1.
II. צוּר *ṣûr* **verb**
(to attack, to harass, to be an adversary)
Ex. 23:22; **Deut.** 2:9,19; **Esth.** 8:11.
III. צוּר *ṣûr* **verb**
(to fashion)
Ex. 32:4; **1 Kgs.** 7:15.

6697. צוּר *ṣûr* **masc. noun**
(rock)
Ex. 17:6; 33:21,22; **Num.** 23:9; **Deut.** 8:15; 32:4,13,15,18,30,31,37; **Josh.** 5:2(NASB, NIV, *ṣōr* [6864]),3(NASB, NIV, *ṣōr* [6864]); **Judg.** 6:21; 7:25; 13:19; **1 Sam.** 2:2; 24:2(3); **2 Sam.** 2:16; 21:10; 22:3,32,47; 23:3; **1 Chr.** 11:15; **Job** 14:18; 18:4; 19:24; 22:24; 24:8; 28:10; 29:6; **Ps.** 18:2(3),31(32),46(47); 19:14(15); 27:5; 28:1; 31:2(3); 61:2(3); 62:2(3),6(7), 7(8); 71:3; 73:26; 78:15,20,35; 81:16(17); 89:26(27),43(44)(NASB, NIV, *ṣōr* [6864]); 92:15(16); 94:22; 95:1; 105:41; 114:8; 144:1; **Prov.** 30:19; **Isa.** 2:10,19,21; 8:14; 10:26; 17:10; 26:4; 30:29; 44:8; 48:21; 51:1; **Jer.** 18:14; 21:13; **Nah.** 1:6; **Hab.** 1:12.

6698. A. צוּר *ṣûr* **masc. proper noun**
(Zur: Midianite prince)
Num. 25:15; 31:8; **Josh.** 13:21.
B. צוּר *ṣûr* **masc. proper noun**
(Zur: Saul's uncle)
1 Chr. 8:30; 9:36.

6699. צוּרָה *ṣûrāh* **fem. noun**
(design, form)
Ezek. 43:11.

6700. צוּרִיאֵל *ṣûriy'ēl* **masc. proper noun**
(Zuriel)
Num. 3:35.

6701. צוּרִישַׁדָּי *ṣûriyšaddāy* **masc. proper noun**
(Zurishaddai)
Num. 1:6; 2:12; 7:36,41; 10:19.

6702. צוּת *ṣûṯ* **verb**
(to burn, to set on fire)
Isa. 27:4(NASB, *yāṣāt* [3341]).

6703. צַח *ṣaḥ* **adj.**
(dazzling, clear, shimmering)
Song 5:10; **Isa.** 18:4; 32:4; **Jer.** 4:11.

6704. צִחֶה *ṣiḥeh* **adj.**
(parched, dried up)
Isa. 5:13.

6705. צָחַח *ṣāḥaḥ* **verb**
(to be dazzling, to be white)
Lam. 4:7.

6706. צְחִיחַ *ṣ^eḥiyaḥ* **masc. noun**
(bare place [top of a rock], exposed place)
Neh. 4:13(7); **Ezek.** 24:7,8; 26:4,14.

6707. צְחִיחָה *ṣ^eḥiyḥāh* **fem. noun**
(parched, sun-scorched land)
Ps. 68:6(7).

6708. צְחִיחִי *ṣ^eḥiyḥiy* **adj.**
(exposed place)
Neh. 4:13(7)(KJV, NASB, NIV, [Q^e] *ṣ^eḥiyaḥ* [6706]).

6709. צַחֲנָה *ṣaḥ^anāh* **fem. noun**
(stench, foul smell)
Joel 2:20.

6710. צַחְצָחָה *ṣaḥṣāḥāh* **fem. noun**
(sun-scorched land)
Isa. 58:11.

6711. צָחַק *ṣāḥaq* **verb**
(to laugh, to make jokes, to mock)
Gen. 17:17; 18:12,13,15; 19:14; 21:6,9; 26:8; 39:14,17; **Ex.** 32:6; **Judg.** 16:25.

6712. צְחֹק *ṣ^eḥōq* **masc. noun**
(laughter, scorn)
Gen. 21:6; **Ezek.** 23:32.

6713. I. צַחַר *ṣaḥar* **masc. noun**
(white; light-colored)
Ezek. 27:18(NIV, see II).
II. צַחַר *ṣaḥar* **proper noun**
(Zahar)
Ezek. 27:18(KJV, see II).

6714. A. צֹחַר *ṣōḥar* **masc. proper noun**
(Zohar: father of Ephron the Hittite)
Gen. 23:8; 25:9.
B. צֹחַר *ṣōḥar* **masc. proper noun**
(Zohar: son of Simeon; the same as *zeraḥ* [2226,D])
Gen. 46:10; **Ex.** 6:15.
C. צֹחַר *ṣōḥar* **masc. proper noun**
(Zohar: son of Ashur)
1 Chr. 4:7(KJV, NASB, [K^e] *yiṣḥar* [3328]).

6715. צָחֹר *ṣāḥōr* **adj.**
(white; light-colored)
Judg. 5:10.

6716. צִי *ṣiy* **masc. noun**
(ship)
Num. 24:24; **Isa.** 33:21; **Ezek.** 30:9; **Dan.** 11:30.

6717. צִיבָא *ṣiyḇā'* **masc. proper noun**
(Ziba)
2 Sam. 9:2–4,9–12; 16:1–4; 19:17(18),29(30).

6718. I. צַיִד *ṣayiḏ* **masc. noun**
(hunting; that which is caught; game, venison)

Gen. 10:9; 25:27,28; 27:3(KJV, [K[e]] *ṣēyḏāh* [6720]),5,7,19,25,30,31,33; **Lev.** 17:13; **Prov.** 12:27.

II. צַיִד *ṣayiḏ* **masc. noun**
(food, provisions, nourishment)
Josh. 9:5,14; **Neh.** 13:15; **Job** 38:41; **Ps.** 132:15.

6719. צַיָּד *ṣayyāḏ* **masc. noun**
(hunter)
Jer. 16:16.

6720. צֵידָה *ṣēyḏāh* **fem. noun**
(food, provisions, venison)
Gen. 27:3(NASB, NIV, [Q[e]] *ṣayiḏ* [6718,I]); 42:25; 45:21; **Ex.** 12:39; **Josh.** 1:11; 9:11; **Judg.** 7:8; 20:10; **1 Sam.** 22:10; **Ps.** 78:25.

6721. צִידוֹן *ṣiyḏôn*, צִידֹן *ṣiyḏōn* **masc. proper noun**
(Sidon)
Gen. 10:15,19; 49:13; **Josh.** 11:8; 19:28; **Judg.** 1:31; 10:6; 18:28; **2 Sam.** 24:6; **1 Kgs.** 17:9; **1 Chr.** 1:13; **Isa.** 23:2,4,12; **Jer.** 25:22; 27:3; 47:4; **Ezek.** 27:8; 28:21,22; **Joel** 3:4(4:4); **Zech.** 9:2.

6722. צִידֹנִי *ṣiyḏōniy* **masc. proper noun**
(Sidonian)
Deut. 3:9; **Josh.** 13:4,6; **Judg.** 3:3; 10:12; 18:7; **1 Kgs.** 5:6(20); 11:1,5,33; 16:31; **2 Kgs.** 23:13; **1 Chr.** 22:4; **Ezra** 3:7; **Ezek.** 32:30.

6723. צִיָּה *ṣiyyāh* **fem. noun**
(dryness, parched land, desert)
Job 24:19; 30:3; **Ps.** 63:1(2); 78:17; 105:41; 107:35; **Isa.** 35:1; 41:18; 53:2; **Jer.** 2:6; 50:12; 51:43; **Ezek.** 19:13; **Hos.** 2:3(5); **Joel** 2:20; **Zeph.** 2:13.

6724. צָיוֹן *ṣāyôn* **masc. noun**
(dry place, desert)
Isa. 25:5; 32:2.

6725. צִיּוּן *ṣiyyûn* **masc. noun**
(road mark, guidepost, sign, tombstone)
2 Kgs. 23:17; **Jer.** 31:21; **Ezek.** 39:15.

6726. צִיּוֹן *ṣiyyôn* **proper noun**
(Zion)
2 Sam. 5:7; **1 Kgs.** 8:1; **2 Kgs.** 19:21,31; **1 Chr.** 11:5; **2 Chr.** 5:2; **Ps.** 2:6; 9:11(12),14(15); 14:7; 20:2(3); 48:2(3),11(12),12(13); 50:2; 51:18(20); 53:6(7); 65:1(2); 69:35(36); 74:2; 76:2(3); 78:68; 84:7(8); 87:2,5; 97:8; 99:2; 102:13(14),16(17),21(22); 110:2; 125:1; 126:1; 128:5; 129:5; 132:13; 133:3; 134:3; 135:21; 137:1,3; 146:10; 147:12; 149:2; **Song** 3:11; **Isa.** 1:8,27; 2:3; 3:16,17; 4:3–5; 8:18; 10:12,24,32; 12:6; 14:32; 16:1; 18:7; 24:23; 28:16; 29:8; 30:19; 31:4,9; 33:5,14,20; 34:8; 35:10; 37:22,32; 40:9; 41:27; 46:13; 49:14; 51:3,11,16; 52:1,2,7,8; 59:20; 60:14; 61:3; 62:1,11; 64:10(9); 66:8; **Jer.** 3:14; 4:6,31; 6:2,23; 8:19; 9:19(18); 14:19; 26:18; 30:17; 31:6, 12; 50:5,28; 51:10,24,35; **Lam.** 1:4,6,17; 2:1,4,6,8,10,13,18; 4:2,11,22; 5:11,18; **Joel** 2:1,15,23,32(3:5); 3:16(4:16), 17(4:17),21(4:21); **Amos** 1:2; 6:1; **Obad.** 1:17,21; **Mic.** 1:13; 3:10,12; 4:2,7,8,10, 11,13; **Zeph.** 3:14,16; **Zech.** 1:14,17; 2:7(11),10(14); 8:2,3; 9:9,13.

6727. A. צִיחָא *ṣiyḥā'* **masc. proper noun**
(Ziha: ancestor of a family of temple slaves)
Ezra 2:43; **Neh.** 7:46.

B. צִיחָא *ṣiyḥā'* **masc. proper noun**
(Ziha: overseer of temple slaves; possibly the same as A)
Neh. 11:21.

6728. צִיִּים *ṣiyyiym* **masc. pl. noun**
(desert creatures, desert people)
Ps. 72:9; 74:14; **Isa.** 13:21; 23:13; 34:14; **Jer.** 50:39.

6729. I. צִינֹק *ṣiynōq* **masc. noun**
(neck iron; iron collar [for imprisonment])
Jer. 29:26(KJV, see II).
II. צִינֹק *ṣiynōq* **masc. noun**
(stocks [for imprisoning])
Jer. 29:26(NASB, NIV, see I).

6730. צִיעֹר *ṣiy'ōr* **proper noun**
(Zior)
Josh. 15:54.

6731. I. צִיץ *ṣiyṣ* **masc. noun**
(flower, blossom)
Num. 17:8(23); **1 Kgs.** 6:18,29,32,35; **Job** 14:2; **Ps.** 103:15; **Isa.** 28:1,4 (KJV, NIV, *ṣiyṣāh* [6733]); 40:6–8.
II. צִיץ *ṣiyṣ* **masc. noun**
(plate [for the high priest's turban])
Ex. 28:36; 39:30; **Lev.** 8:9.
III. צִיץ *ṣiyṣ* **masc. noun**
(wing)
Jer. 48:9(NIV, see IV).
IV. צִיץ *ṣiyṣ* **masc. noun**
(salt)
Jer. 48:9(KJV, see III).

6732. צִיץ *ṣiyṣ* **proper noun**
(Ziz)
2 Chr. 20:16.

6733. צִיצָה *ṣiyṣāh* **fem. noun**
(flower)
Isa. 28:4(NASB, *ṣiyṣ* [6731,I]).

6734. צִיצִת *ṣiyṣiṯ* **fem. noun**
(tassel, lock [of hair])
Num. 15:38,39; **Ezek.** 8:3.

6735. I. צִיר *ṣiyr* **masc. noun**
(ambassador, envoy, messenger)
Prov. 13:17; 25:13; 26:14; **Isa.** 18:2; 57:9; **Jer.** 49:14; **Obad.** 1:1.
II. צִיר *ṣiyr* **masc. noun**
(pain, labor pain, anguish)
1 Sam. 4:19; **Isa.** 13:8; 21:3; **Dan.** 10:16.
III. צִיר *ṣiyr* **masc. noun**
(hinge)
Prov. 26:14.

6736. צִיר *ṣiyr* **masc. noun**
(idol, image, form)
Ps. 49:14(15); **Isa.** 45:16.

6737. צָיַר *ṣāyar* **verb**
(to act as an ambassador)
Josh. 9:4.

6738. צֵל *ṣēl* **masc. noun**
(shadow, shade, shelter)
Gen. 19:8; **Num.** 14:9; **Judg.** 9:15,36; **2 Kgs.** 20:9–11; **1 Chr.** 29:15; **Job** 7:2; 8:9; 14:2; 17:7; 40:22(KJV, *ṣēlel* [6752]); **Ps.** 17:8; 36:7(8); 57:1(2); 63:7(8); 80:10(11); 91:1; 102:11(12); 109:23; 121:5; 144:4; **Eccl.** 6:12; 7:12; 8:13; **Song** 2:3,17(KJV, *ṣēlel* [6752]); 4:6(KJV, *ṣēlel* [6752]); **Isa.** 4:6; 16:3; 25:4,5; 30:2,3; 32:2; 34:15; 38:8; 49:2; 51:16; **Jer.** 6:4(KJV, *ṣēlel* [6752]); 48:45; **Lam.** 4:20; **Ezek.** 17:23; 31:6,12,17; **Hos.** 4:13; 14:7(8); **Jon.** 4:5,6.

6739. צְלָא *ṣ^{e}lā'* **Aram. verb**
(to pray)
Ezra 6:10; **Dan.** 6:10(11).

6740. צָלָה *ṣālāh* **verb**
(to roast)
1 Sam. 2:15; **Isa.** 44:16,19.

6741. צִלָּה *ṣillāh* **fem. proper noun**
(Zillah)
Gen. 4:19,22,23.

6742. צְלוּל *ṣ^{e}lûl*, צְלִיל *ṣ^{e}liyl* **masc. noun**
(round loaf of bread)
Judg. 7:13.

6743. I. צָלַח *ṣālaḥ* **verb**
(to rush, to break forth, to come mightily)

Judg. 14:6,9; 15:14; **1 Sam.** 10:6,10; 11:6; 16:13; 18:10; **2 Sam.** 19:17(18); **Amos** 5:6.

II. צָלַח *ṣālaḥ*, צָלֵחַ *ṣālēaḥ* **verb**
(to prosper, to succeed, to be victorious)
Gen. 24:21,40,42,56; 39:2,3,23; **Num.** 14:41; **Deut.** 28:29; **Josh.** 1:8; **Judg.** 18:5; **1 Kgs.** 22:12,15; **1 Chr.** 22:11,13; 29:23; **2 Chr.** 7:11; 13:12; 14:7(6); 18:11,14; 20:20; 24:20; 26:5; 31:21; 32:30; **Neh.** 1:11; 2:20; **Ps.** 1:3; 37:7; 45:4(5); 118:25; **Prov.** 28:13; **Isa.** 48:15; 53:10; 54:17; 55:11; **Jer.** 2:37; 5:28; 12:1; 13:7,10; 22:30; 32:5; **Ezek.** 15:4; 16:13; 17:9,10,15; **Dan.** 8:12,24,25; 11:27,36.

6744. צְלַח *ṣ^e^laḥ* **Aram. verb**
(to prosper, to succeed; corr. to Hebr. 6743,II)
Ezra 5:8; 6:14; **Dan.** 3:30; 6:28(29).

6745. צֵלָחָה *ṣēlāḥāh* **fem. noun**
(cooking pan)
2 Chr. 35:13(NIV, *ṣallaḥaṯ* [6747,I]).

6746. צְלֹחִית *ṣ^e^lōḥiyṯ* **fem. noun**
(jar, bowl)
2 Kgs. 2:20.

6747. I. צַלַּחַת *ṣallaḥaṯ* **fem. noun**
(dish, pan)
2 Kgs. 21:13; **2 Chr.** 35:13(KJV, NASB, *ṣēlāḥah* [6745]); **Prov.** 19:24(KJV, see II); 26:15(KJV, see II).

II. צַלַּחַת *ṣallaḥaṯ* **fem. noun**
(bosom)
Prov. 19:24(NASB, NIV, see I); 26:15(NASB, NIV, see I).

6748. צָלִי *ṣāliy* **adj.**
(roasted)
Ex. 12:8,9; **Isa.** 44:16.

6749. צָלַל *ṣālal* **verb**
(to sink)
Ex. 15:10.

6750. צָלַל *ṣālal* **verb**
(to tingle, to quiver)
1 Sam. 3:11; **2 Kgs.** 21:12; **Jer.** 19:3; **Hab.** 3:16.

6751. צָלַל *ṣālal* **verb**
(to become dark, to overshadow)
Neh. 13:19; **Ezek.** 31:3.

6752. צֵלֶל *ṣēlel* **masc. noun**
(shadow; NASB, NIV, *ṣēl* [6738])
Job 40:22; **Song** 2:17; 4:6; **Jer.** 6:4.

6753. צְלֶלְפּוֹנִי *ṣ^e^lelpôniy*, הַצְלֶלְפּוֹנִי *haṣṣ^e^lelpôniy* **fem. proper noun**
(Hazzelelponi)
1 Chr. 4:3.

6754. I. צֶלֶם *ṣelem* **masc. noun**
(likeness, image, idol)
Gen. 1:26,27; 5:3; 9:6; **Num.** 33:52; **1 Sam.** 6:5,11; **2 Kgs.** 11:18; **2 Chr.** 23:17; **Ps.** 73:20(NIV, see II); **Ezek.** 7:20; 16:17; 23:14; **Amos** 5:26.

II. צֶלֶם *ṣelem* **masc. noun**
(fantasy, phantom)
Ps. 39:6(7); 73:20(KJV, NASB, see I).

6755. צֶלֶם *ṣelem*, צְלֵם *ṣ^e^lēm* **Aram. masc. noun**
(image, form, idol)
Dan. 2:31,32,34,35; 3:1–3,5,7,10,12,14,15,18,19.

6756. A. צַלְמוֹן *ṣalmôn* **masc. proper noun**
(Zalmon: wooded place near Shechem)
Judg. 9:48; **Ps.** 68:14(15).

B. צַלְמוֹן *ṣalmôn* **masc. proper noun**
(Zalmon: one of David's warriors)
2 Sam. 23:28.

6757. צַלְמָוֶת *ṣalmāweṯ* **fem. noun**
(deep darkness, shadow of death)
Job 3:5; 10:21,22; 12:22; 16:16; 24:17;

28:3; 34:22; 38:17; **Ps.** 23:4; 44:19(20); 107:10,14; **Isa.** 9:2(1); **Jer.** 2:6; 13:16; **Amos** 5:8.

6758. צַלְמֹנָה *ṣalmōnāh* **proper noun**
(Zalmonah)
Num. 33:41,42.

6759. צַלְמֻנָּע *ṣalmunnā'* **masc. proper noun**
(Zalmunna)
Judg. 8:5–7,10,12,15,18,21; **Ps.** 83:11(12).

6760. צָלַע *ṣāla'* **verb**
(to limp, to be lame)
Gen. 32:31(32); **Mic.** 4:6,7; **Zeph.** 3:19.

6761. צֶלַע *ṣela'* **masc. noun**
(a stumbling, a fall, a slip)
Job 18:12(KJV, NASB, *ṣēlā'* [6763]); **Ps.** 35:15; 38:17(18); **Jer.** 20:10.

6762. צֶלַע *ṣēla'* **proper noun**
(Zelah)
Josh. 18:28; **2 Sam.** 21:14.

6763. צֵלָע *ṣēlā'* **fem. noun**
(side, side room [chamber], hillside, wall)
Gen. 2:21,22; **Ex.** 25:12,14; 26:20,26,27,35; 27:7; 30:4; 36:25,31,32; 37:3,5,27; 38:7; **2 Sam.** 16:13; **1 Kgs.** 6:5,8,15,16,34; 7:3; **Job** 18:12(NIV, *ṣela'* [6761]); **Ezek.** 41:5–9,11,26.

6764. צָלָף *ṣālāp̱* **masc. proper noun**
(Zalaph)
Neh. 3:30.

6765. צְלָפְחָד *ṣ^elāp̱^eḥād* **masc. proper noun**
(Zelophehad)
Num. 26:33; 27:1,7; 36:2,6,10,11; **Josh.** 17:3; **1 Chr.** 7:15.

6766. צֶלְצַח *ṣelṣaḥ* **proper noun**
(Zelzah)
1 Sam. 10:2.

6767. I. צִלְצָל *ṣilṣāl* **masc. noun**
(whirring)
Isa. 18:1.
II. צִלְצָל *ṣilṣāl* **masc. noun**
(spear)
Job 41:7(40:31).
III. צְלָצַל *ṣ^elāṣal* **masc. noun**
(locust, cricket)
Deut. 28:42.
IV. צֶלְצְלִים *ṣelṣ^eliym* **masc. pl. noun**
(cymbals)
2 Sam. 6:5; **Ps.** 150:5.

6768. צֶלֶק *ṣeleq* **masc. proper noun**
(Zelek)
2 Sam. 23:37; **1 Chr.** 11:39.

6769. צִלְּתַי *ṣill^eṯay* **masc. proper noun**
(Zillethai)
1 Chr. 8:20; 12:20.

6770. צָמֵא *ṣāmē'* **verb**
(to be thirsty)
Ex. 17:3; **Judg.** 4:19; 15:18; **Ruth** 2:9; **Job** 5:5(KJV, NASB, *ṣammiym* [6782]); 24:11; **Ps.** 42:2(3); 63:1(2); **Isa.** 48:21; 49:10; 65:13.

6771. צָמֵא *ṣāmē'* **adj.**
(thirsty)
Deut. 29:19(18); **2 Sam.** 17:29; **Ps.** 107:5; **Prov.** 25:21(NIV, *ṣāmē'* [6770]); **Isa.** 21:14; 29:8; 32:6; 44:3; 55:1.

6772. צָמָא *ṣāmā'* **masc. noun**
(thirst)
Ex. 17:3; **Deut.** 28:48; **Judg.** 15:18; **2 Chr.** 32:11; **Neh.** 9:15,20; **Ps.** 69:21(22); 104:11; **Isa.** 5:13; 41:17; 50:2; **Jer.** 48:18; **Lam.** 4:4; **Ezek.** 19:13; **Hos.** 2:3(5); **Amos** 8:11,13.

6773. צִמְאָה ṣim'āh **fem. noun**
(thirst, dryness)
Jer. 2:25.

6774. צִמָּאוֹן ṣimmā'ôn **masc. noun**
(thirsty ground, drought)
Deut. 8:15; Ps. 107:33; Isa. 35:7.

6775. צָמַד ṣāmaḏ **verb**
(to join, to yoke, to harness)
Num. 25:3,5; 2 Sam. 20:8; Ps. 50:19; 106:28.

6776. I. צֶמֶד ṣemeḏ **masc. noun**
(a couple, yoke, team of two, pair)
Judg. 19:3,10; 1 Sam. 11:7; 14:14 (NASB, NIV, see II); 2 Sam. 16:1; 1 Kgs. 19:19,21; 2 Kgs. 5:17; 9:25; Job 1:3; 42:12; Isa. 21:7,9; Jer. 51:23.
II. צֶמֶד ṣemeḏ **masc. noun**
(acre; the amount of land plowed by two oxen in a day)
1 Sam. 14:14(KJV, see I); Isa. 5:10.

6777. I. צַמָּה ṣammāh **fem. noun**
(veil)
Song 4:1,3; 6:7; Isa. 47:2.
II. צַמָּה ṣammāh **fem. noun**
(lock of hair)
Song 4:1(NASB, NIV, see I),3(NASB, NIV, see I); 6:7(NASB, NIV, see I); Isa. 47:2 (NASB, NIV, see I).

6778. צִמּוּק ṣimmûq **masc. noun**
(cluster of raisins, cake of raisins)
1 Sam. 25:18; 30:12; 2 Sam. 16:1; 1 Chr. 12:40.

6779. צָמַח ṣāmaḥ **verb**
(to grow, to spring forth, to sprout)
Gen. 2:5,9; 3:18; 41:6,23; Ex. 10:5; Lev. 13:37; Deut. 29:23(22); Judg. 16:22; 2 Sam. 10:5; 23:5; 1 Chr. 19:5; Job 5:6; 8:19; 38:27; Ps. 85:11(12); 104:14; 132:17; 147:8; Eccl. 2:6; Isa. 42:9; 43:19; 44:4; 45:8; 55:10; 58:8; 61:11; Jer. 33:15; Ezek. 16:7; 17:6; 29:21; Zech. 6:12.

6780. צֶמַח ṣemaḥ **masc. noun**
(a branch, growth, crop)
Gen. 19:25; Ps. 65:10(11); Isa. 4:2; 61:11; Jer. 23:5; 33:15; Ezek. 16:7; 17:9,10; Hos. 8:7; Zech. 3:8; 6:12.

6781. I. צָמִיד ṣāmiyḏ **masc. noun**
(bracelet)
Gen. 24:22,30,47; Num. 31:50; Ezek. 16:11; 23:42.
II. צָמִיד ṣāmiyḏ **masc. noun**
(covering, lid)
Num. 19:15.

6782. צַמִּים ṣammiym **masc. noun**
(snare, trap, robber)
Job 5:5(NIV, ṣāme' [6771]); 18:9.

6783. צְמִיתֻת ṣᵉmiyṯuṯ **fem. noun**
(permanence)
Lev. 25:23,30.

6784. צָמַק ṣāmaq **verb**
(to dry up [of women's breasts])
Hos. 9:14.

6785. צֶמֶר ṣemer **masc. noun**
(wool)
Lev. 13:47,48,52,59; Deut. 22:11; Judg. 6:37; 2 Kgs. 3:4; Ps. 147:16; Prov. 31:13; Isa. 1:18; 51:8; Ezek. 27:18; 34:3; 44:17; Hos. 2:5(7),9(11).

6786. צְמָרִי ṣᵉmāriy **masc. proper noun**
(Zemarite)
Gen. 10:18; 1 Chr. 1:16.

6787. צְמָרַיִם ṣᵉmārayim **proper noun**
(Zemaraim)
Josh. 18:22; 2 Chr. 13:4.

6788. צַמֶּרֶת ṣammereṯ **fem. noun**
(top, highest branch)
Ezek. 17:3,22; 31:3,10,14.

6789. צָמַת *ṣāmaṯ* **verb**
(to destroy, to consume, to cut off)
2 Sam. 22:41; **Job** 6:17; 23:17; **Ps.** 18:40(41); 54:5(7); 69:4(5); 73:27; 88:16(17); 94:23; 101:5,8; 119:139; 143:12; **Lam.** 3:53.

6790. צִן *ṣin* **proper noun**
(Zin)
Num. 13:21; 20:1; 27:14; 33:36; 34:3,4; **Deut.** 32:51; **Josh.** 15:1,3.

6791. צֵן *ṣēn* **masc. noun**
(thorn, hook)
Job 5:5; **Prov.** 22:5; **Amos** 4:2(KJV, NASB, *ṣinnāh* [6793,I]).

6792. צֹנֵא *ṣōnēʾ*, צֹנֶה *ṣōneh* **masc. noun**
(flock, sheep)
Num. 32:24(NIV, *ṣōʾn* [6629]); **Ps.** 8:7(8).

6793. I. צִנָּה *ṣinnāh* **fem. noun**
(hook)
Amos 4:2(NIV, *ṣēn* [6791]).
II. צִנָּה *ṣinnāh* **fem. noun**
(shield, large shield, buckler)
1 Sam. 17:7,41; **1 Kgs.** 10:16; **1 Chr.** 12:8,24,34; **2 Chr.** 9:15; 11:12; 14:8(7); 25:5; **Ps.** 5:12(13); 35:2; 91:4; **Jer.** 46:3; **Ezek.** 23:24; 26:8; 38:4; 39:9.
III. צִנָּה *ṣinnāh* **fem. noun**
(cold, coolness)
Prov. 25:13.

6794. צִנּוֹר *ṣinnôr* **masc. noun**
(water shaft, waterfalls)
2 Sam. 5:8; **Ps.** 42:7(8).

6795. I. צָנַח *ṣānaḥ* **verb**
(to get off an animal)
Josh. 15:18; **Judg.** 1:14.
II. צָנַח *ṣānaḥ* **verb**
(to go through)
Judg. 4:21.

6796. צָנִין *ṣāniyn* **masc. noun**
(thorn)
Num. 33:55; **Josh.** 23:13.

6797. I. צָנִיף *ṣāniyp̱* **masc. noun**
(turban, hood)
Job 29:14(KJV, see II); **Isa.** 3:23; 62:3; **Zech.** 3:5(KJV, see III).
II. צָנִיף *ṣāniyp̱* **masc. noun**
(diadem)
Job 29:14(NASB, NIV, see I); **Isa.** 62:3.
III. צָנִיף *ṣāniyp̱* **masc. noun**
(mitre)
Zech. 3:5(NASB, NIV, see I).

6798. צָנַם *ṣānam* **verb**
(to be withered, to be dried up)
Gen. 41:23.

6799. צְנָן *ṣ^{e}nān* **proper noun**
(Zenan)
Josh. 15:37.

6800. I. צָנַע *ṣānaʿ* **verb**
(to be humble)
Prov. 11:2; **Mic.** 6:8.
II. צָנוּעַ *ṣānûaʿ* **masc. noun**
(humility)
Prov. 11:2; **Mic.** 6:8.

6801. צָנַף *ṣānap̱* **verb**
(to wrap around, to roll up tightly)
Lev. 16:4; **Isa.** 22:18(KJV, *ṣ^{e}nēp̱āh* [6802,I]; NIV, *ṣ^{e}nēp̱āh* [6802,II]).

6802. I. צְנֵפָה *ṣ^{e}nēp̱āh* **fem. noun**
(a tossing)
Isa. 22:18(NASB, *ṣānap̱* [6801]; NIV, see II).
II. צְנֵפָה *ṣ^{e}nēp̱āh* **fem. noun**
(a tightness)
Isa. 22:18(KJV, see I; NASB, *ṣānap̱* [6801]).

6803. צִנְצֶנֶת *ṣinṣeneṯ* **fem. noun**
(jar, pot)
Ex. 16:33.

6804. צַנְתָּרוֹת *ṣantārôṯ* **fem. pl. noun**
(pipes)
Zech. 4:12.

6805. צָעַד *ṣā'aḏ* **verb**
(to march, to walk, to run)
Gen. 49:22; **Judg.** 5:4; **2 Sam.** 6:13; **Job** 18:14; **Ps.** 68:7(8); **Prov.** 7:8; **Jer.** 10:5; **Hab.** 3:12.

6806. צַעַד *ṣa'aḏ* **masc. noun**
(a step, a stride)
2 Sam. 6:13; 22:37; **Job** 14:16; 18:7; 31:4,37; 34:21; **Ps.** 18:36(37); **Prov.** 4:12; 5:5; 16:9; 30:29; **Jer.** 10:23; **Lam.** 4:18.

6807. I. צְעָדָה *ṣ^e'āḏāh* **fem. noun**
(a marching)
2 Sam. 5:24; **1 Chr.** 14:15.
II. צְעָדָה *ṣ^e'āḏāh* **fem. noun**
(ankle bracelet, ankle chain)
Isa. 3:20.

6808. I. צָעָה *ṣā'āh* **verb**
(to imprison, to take captive)
Isa. 51:14.
II. צָעָה *ṣā'āh* **verb**
(to travel, to wander)
Isa. 63:1(NASB, NIV, see III); **Jer.** 2:20 (NASB, NIV, see IV); 48:12(NASB, NIV, see V).
III. צָעָה *ṣā'āh* **verb**
(to march, to stride)
Isa. 63:1(KJV, see II).
IV. צָעָה *ṣā'āh* **verb**
(to lay down)
Jer. 2:20(KJV, see II).
V. צָעָה *ṣā'āh* **verb**
(to tip over, to pour out)
Jer. 48:12(KJV, see II).

6809. צָעִיף *ṣa'iyp̱* **masc. noun**
(veil, shawl)
Gen. 24:65; 38:14,19.

6810. צָעִיר *ṣā'iyr* **adj.**
(young, younger, little, small)
Gen. 19:31,34,35,38; 25:23; 29:26; 43:33; 48:14; **Josh.** 6:26; **Judg.** 6:15; **1 Sam.** 9:21; **1 Kgs.** 16:34; **Job** 30:1; 32:6; **Ps.** 68:27(28); 119:141; **Isa.** 60:22; **Jer.** 14:3; 48:4; 49:20; 50:45; **Mic.** 5:2(1).

6811. צָעִירָה *ṣā'iyrāh* **proper noun**
(Zair)
2 Kgs. 8:21.

6812. צְעִירָה *ṣ^e'iyrāh* **fem. noun**
(youth)
Gen. 43:33.

6813. צָעַן *ṣā'an* **verb**
(to travel; to fold a tent for moving)
Isa. 33:20.

6814. צֹעַן *ṣō'an* **proper noun**
(Zoan)
Num. 13:22; **Ps.** 78:12,43; **Isa.** 19:11,13; 30:4; **Ezek.** 30:14.

6815. צַעֲנַנִּים *ṣa'^{a}nanniym* **proper noun**
(Zaanannim)
Josh. 19:33; **Judg.** 4:11.

6816. צַעֲצֻעִים *ṣa'^{a}ṣu'iym* **masc. pl. noun**
(sculptured)
2 Chr. 3:10.

6817. צָעַק *ṣā'aq* **verb**
(to cry out, to summons)
Gen. 4:10; 27:34; 41:55; **Ex.** 5:8,15; 8:12(8); 14:10,15; 15:25; 17:4; 22:23(22), 27(26); **Num.** 11:2; 12:13; 20:16; **Deut.** 22:24,27; 26:7; **Josh.** 24:7; **Judg.** 4:3; 7:23,24; 10:12,17; 12:1; **1 Sam.** 10:17; 13:4; **1 Kgs.** 20:39; **2 Kgs.** 2:12; 3:21; 4:1,40; 6:5,26; 8:3,5; **2 Chr.** 13:14; **Neh.** 9:27; **Job** 19:7; 35:12; **Ps.** 34:17(18); 77:1(2); 88:1(2); 107:6,28; **Isa.** 19:20; 33:7; 42:2; 46:7; 65:14; **Jer.** 22:20; 49:3; **Lam.** 2:18.

6818. צְעָקָה *ṣᵉ'āqāh* **fem. noun**
(cry, outcry)
Gen. 18:21; 19:13; 27:34; **Ex.** 3:7,9; 11:6; 12:30; 22:23(22); **1 Sam.** 4:14; 9:16; **Neh.** 5:1; **Job** 27:9; 34:28; **Ps.** 9:12(13); **Isa.** 5:7; **Jer.** 25:36; 48:3,5; 49:21; **Zeph.** 1:10.

6819. צָעַר *ṣā'ar* **verb**
(to be brought low, to be insignificant)
Job 14:21; **Jer.** 30:19; **Zech.** 13:7.

6820. צוֹעַר *ṣô'ar* **proper noun**
(Zoar)
Gen. 13:10; 14:2,8; 19:22,23,30; **Deut.** 34:3; **Isa.** 15:5; **Jer.** 48:34.

6821. צָפַד *ṣāp̱aḏ* **verb**
(to be shriveled up)
Lam. 4:8.

6822. צָפָה *ṣāp̱āh* **verb**
(to wait for, to be a lookout)
Gen. 31:49; **1 Sam.** 14:13,16; **2 Sam.** 13:34; 18:24–27; **2 Kgs.** 9:17,18,20; **Job** 15:22; **Ps.** 5:3(4); 37:32; 66:7; **Prov.** 15:3; 31:27; **Song** 7:4(5); **Isa.** 21:5,6; 52:8; 56:10; **Jer.** 6:17; 48:19; **Lam.** 4:17; **Ezek.** 3:17; 33:2,6,7; **Hos.** 9:8; **Mic.** 7:4,7; **Nah.** 2:1(2); **Hab.** 2:1.

6823. צָפָה *ṣāp̱āh* **verb**
(to overlay, to cover)
Ex. 25:11,13,24,28; 26:29,32,37; 27:2,6; 30:3,5; 36:34,36,38; 37:2,4,11,15,26,28; 38:2,6,28; **1 Kgs.** 6:15,20–22,28,30, 32,35; 10:18; **2 Kgs.** 18:16; **2 Chr.** 3:4,6,10; 4:9; 9:17; **Prov.** 26:23.

6824. I. צָפָה *ṣāp̱āh* **fem. noun**
(a flow, a discharge)
Ezek. 32:6(KJV, see II).
II. צָפָה *ṣāp̱āh* **fem. noun**
(a swimming)
Ezek. 32:6(NASB, NIV, see I).

6825. צְפוֹ *ṣᵉp̱ô*, צְפִי *ṣᵉp̱iy* **masc. proper noun**
(Zepho, Zephi: son of Eliphaz)
Gen. 36:11,15; **1 Chr.** 1:36.

6826. צִפּוּי *ṣippûy* **masc. noun**
(overlay, plating)
Ex. 38:17,19; **Num.** 16:38(17:3),39(17:4); **Isa.** 30:22.

6827. צְפוֹן *ṣᵉp̱ôn* **masc. proper noun**
(Zephon; the same as *ṣip̱yôn* [6837])
Num. 26:15.

6828. צָפוֹן *ṣāp̱ôn* **fem. noun**
(north; northward)
Gen. 13:14; 28:14; **Ex.** 26:20,35; 27:11; 36:25; 38:11; 40:22; **Lev.** 1:11; **Num.** 2:25; 3:35; 34:7,9; 35:5; **Deut.** 2:3; 3:27; **Josh.** 8:11,13; 11:2; 13:3; 15:5–8,10,11; 16:6; 17:9,10; 18:5,12,16–19; 19:14,27; 24:30; **Judg.** 2:9; 7:1; 12:1(NASB, NIV, *ṣāp̱ôn* [6829]); 21:19; **1 Sam.** 14:5; **1 Kgs.** 7:25; **2 Kgs.** 16:14; **1 Chr.** 9:24; 26:14,17; **2 Chr.** 4:4; **Job** 26:7; 37:22; **Ps.** 48:2(3)(NIV, *ṣap̱ôn* [6829]); 89:12(13); 107:3; **Prov.** 25:23; **Eccl.** 1:6; 11:3; **Song** 4:16; **Isa.** 14:13,31; 41:25; 43:6; 49:12; **Jer.** 1:13–15; 3:12,18; 4:6; 6:1,22; 10:22; 13:20; 15:12; 16:15; 23:8; 25:9,26; 31:8; 46:6,10,20,24; 47:2; 50:3,9,41; 51:48; **Ezek.** 1:4; 8:3,5,14; 9:2; 20:47 (21:3); 21:4(9); 26:7; 32:30; 38:6,15; 39:2; 40:19,20,23,35,40,44,46; 41:11; 42:1,2,4,11,13,17; 44:4; 46:9,19; 47:2, 15,17; 48:1,10,16,17,30,31; **Dan.** 8:4; 11:6–8,11,13,15,40,44; **Amos** 8:12; **Zeph.** 2:13; **Zech.** 2:6(10); 6:6,8; 14:4.

6829. צָפוֹן *ṣāp̱ôn* **proper noun**
(Zaphon)
Josh. 13:27; **Judg.** 12:1(KJV, *ṣāp̱ôn* [6828]); **Ps.** 48:2(3)(KJV, NASB, *ṣāp̱ôn* [6828]).

6830. צְפוֹנִי *ṣᵉp̱ôniy* **adj.**
(northern)
Joel 2:20.

6831. צְפוֹנִי *ṣ^{e}p̱ôniy* **masc. proper noun**
(Zephonite)
Num. 26:15.

6832. צְפִיעַ *ṣ^{e}p̱iya‘* **masc. noun**
(manure, dung)
Ezek. 4:15.

6833. צִפּוֹר *ṣippôr* **masc./fem. noun**
(bird, fowl)
Gen. 7:14; 15:10; **Lev.** 14:4–7,49–53; **Deut.** 4:17; 14:11; 22:6; **Neh.** 5:18; **Job** 41:5(40:29); **Ps.** 8:8(9); 11:1; 84:3(4); 102:7(8); 104:17; 124:7; 148:10; **Prov.** 6:5; 7:23; 26:2; 27:8; **Eccl.** 9:12; 12:4; **Isa.** 31:5; **Lam.** 3:52; **Ezek.** 17:23; 39:4,17; **Hos.** 11:11; **Amos** 3:5.

6834. צִפּוֹר *ṣippôr* **masc. proper noun**
(Zippor)
Num. 22:2,4,10,16; 23:18; **Josh.** 24:9; **Judg.** 11:25.

6835. צַפַּחַת *ṣappaḥaṯ* **fem. noun**
(jar, jug)
1 Sam. 26:11,12,16; **1 Kgs.** 17:12,14,16; 19:6.

6836. צְפִיָּה *ṣ^{e}p̱iyyāh* **fem. noun**
(watchtower)
Lam. 4:17.

6837. צִפְיוֹן *ṣip̱yôn* **masc. proper noun**
(Ziphion; the same as *ṣ^{e}p̱ôn* [6827])
Gen. 46:16.

6838. צַפִּיחִת *ṣap̱iyḥiṯ* **fem. noun**
(wafer)
Ex. 16:31.

6839. צֹפִים *ṣōp̱iym* **proper noun**
(Zophim)
Num. 23:14.

6840. צָפִין *ṣāp̱iyn* **adj.**
(hidden [treasure])
Ps. 17:14.

6841. צְפִיר *ṣ^{e}p̱iyr* **Aram. masc. noun**
(male [goat]; corr. to Hebr. 6842)
Ezra 6:17.

6842. צָפִיר *ṣāp̱iyr* **masc. noun**
(male [goat])
2 Chr. 29:21; **Ezra** 8:35; **Dan.** 8:5,8,21.

6843. I. צְפִירָה *ṣ^{e}p̱iyrāh* **fem. noun**
(diadem, crown)
Isa. 28:5.
II. צְפִירָה *ṣ^{e}p̱iyrāh* **fem. noun**
(doom)
Ezek. 7:7(KJV, see III),10(KJV, see III).
III. צְפִירָה *ṣ^{e}p̱iyrāh* **fem. noun**
(morning)
Ezek. 7:7(NASB, NIV, see II),10(NASB, NIV, see II).

6844. I. צָפִית *ṣāp̱iyṯ* **fem. noun**
(rug, tablecloth)
Isa. 21:5(KJV, see II).
II. צָפִית *ṣāp̱iyṯ* **fem. noun**
(watchtower)
Isa. 21:5(NASB, NIV, see I).

6845. צָפַן *ṣāp̱an* **verb**
(to hide, to keep secret)
Ex. 2:2,3; **Josh.** 2:4; **Job** 10:13; 14:13; 15:20; 17:4; 20:26; 21:19; 23:12; 24:1; **Ps.** 10:8; 17:14; 27:5; 31:19(20),20(21); 56:6(7); 83:3(4); 119:11; **Prov.** 1:11,18; 2:1,7; 7:1; 10:14; 13:22; 27:16; **Song** 7:13(14); **Jer.** 16:17; **Ezek.** 7:22; **Hos.** 13:12.

6846. A. צְפַנְיָה *ṣ^{e}p̱anyāh* **masc. proper noun**
(Zephaniah: the prophet)
Zeph. 1:1.
B. צְפַנְיָה *ṣ^{e}p̱anyāh,* צְפַנְיָהוּ *ṣ^{e}p̱anyāhû* **masc. proper noun**
(Zephaniah: priest in Jeremiah's day)

2 Kgs. 25:18; **Jer.** 21:1; 29:25,29; 37:3; 52:24.
C. צְפַנְיָה *ṣ^{e}p̱anyāh* **masc. proper noun**
(Zephaniah: ancestor of Heman)
1 Chr. 6:36(21).
D. צְפַנְיָה *ṣ^{e}p̱anyāh* **masc. proper noun**
(Zephaniah: father of Josiah and Hen in Zechariah's day; possibly the same as A or B)
Zech. 6:10,14.

6847. צָפְנַת פַּעְנֵחַ *ṣāp̱naṯ pa'nēaḥ* **masc. proper noun**
(Zaphnath-Paneah; another name for Joseph [3130,A])
Gen. 41:45.

6848. I. צֶפַע *ṣepa'* **masc. noun**
(viper, a poisonous serpent)
Isa. 14:29.
II. צִפְעֹנִי *ṣip̱'ôniy* **masc. noun**
(viper, a poisonous serpent)
Prov. 23:32; **Isa.** 11:8; 59:5; **Jer.** 8:17.

6849. צְפִיעָה *ṣ^{e}p̱iy'āh* **fem. noun**
(offshoot, issue)
Isa. 22:24.

6850. צָפַף *ṣāp̱ap̱* **verb**
(to chirp, to whisper)
Isa. 8:19; 10:14; 29:4; 38:14.

6851. צַפְצָפָה *ṣapṣāp̱āh* **fem. noun**
(willow tree)
Ezek. 17:5.

6852. צָפַר *ṣāp̱ar* **verb**
(to leave, to depart)
Judg. 7:3.

6853. צִפַּר *ṣippar* **Aram. masc. noun**
(bird, fowl; corr. to Hebr. 6833)
Dan. 4:12(9),14(11),21(18),33(30).

6854. צְפַרְדֵּעַ *ṣ^{e}p̱ardēa'* **masc. noun**
(frog)
Ex. 8:2–9(7:27—8:5),11–13(7–9);
Ps. 78:45; 105:30.

6855. צִפֹּרָה *ṣippōrāh* **fem. proper noun**
(Zipporah)
Ex. 2:21; 4:25; 18:2.

6856. צִפֹּרֶן *ṣippōren* **masc. noun**
(point, fingernail, toenail)
Deut. 21:12; **Jer.** 17:1.

6857. צְפַת *ṣ^{e}p̱aṯ* **proper noun**
(Zephath)
Judg. 1:17.

6858. צֶפֶת *ṣep̱eṯ* **fem. noun**
(capital [top of a pillar])
2 Chr. 3:15.

6859. צְפָתָה *ṣ^{e}p̱āṯāh* **proper noun**
(Zephathah)
2 Chr. 14:10(9).

6860. צִיקְלַג *ṣiyqlag* **proper noun**
(Ziklag)
Josh. 15:31; 19:5; **1 Sam.** 27:6; 30:1, 14,26; **2 Sam.** 1:1; 4:10; **1 Chr.** 4:30; 12:1,20; **Neh.** 11:28.

6861. I. צִקְלוֹן *ṣiqlôn* **masc. noun**
(sack)
2 Kgs. 4:42(KJV, see II; NIV, untranslated).
II. צִקְלוֹן *ṣiqlôn* **masc. noun**
(husk [of an ear of corn])
2 Kgs. 4:42(NASB, see I; NIV, untranslated).

6862. I. צַר *ṣar* **masc. noun**
(narrowness, tightness, distress, affliction, misery)
Num. 22:26; **Deut.** 4:30; **Judg.** 11:7(KJV, NASB, *ṣārar* [6887,I]); **1 Sam.** 2:32(KJV, see II); **2 Sam.** 22:7; 24:14

(KJV, NASB, *ṣārar* [6887,I]); **2 Kgs.** 6:1; **2 Chr.** 15:4; **Esth.** 7:4(KJV, see II); **Job** 7:11; 15:24; 36:16; 38:23; 41:15(7); **Ps.** 4:1(2); 18:6(7); 31:9(10)(KJV, NASB, *ṣārar* [6887,I]); 32:7; 59:16(17); 60:11(13)(NASB, NIV, see II); 66:14; 69:17(18)(KJV, NASB, *ṣārar* [6887,I]); 102:2(3); 106:44; 107:6,13,19,28; 108:12(13)(NASB, NIV, see II); 119:143; **Prov.** 23:27; 24:10; **Isa.** 5:30; 25:4; 26:16; 30:20; 49:20; 59:19(KJV, see II); 63:9; **Jer.** 48:5(KJV, see II); **Lam.** 1:20 (KJV, NASB, *ṣārar* [6887,I]); **Ezek.** 30:16; **Hos.** 5:15; **Zech.** 8:10(NASB, NIV, see II).

II. צַר *ṣar* **masc. noun**
(enemy, foe, adversary, oppressor)
Gen. 14:20; **Num.** 10:9; 24:8; **Deut.** 32:27,41,43; 33:7; **Josh.** 5:13; **1 Sam.** 2:32(NASB, NIV, see I); **2 Sam.** 24:13; **1 Chr.** 12:17(18); 21:12; **Ezra** 4:1; **Neh.** 4:11; 9:27; **Esth.** 7:4(NASB, NIV, see I),6; **Job** 6:23; 16:9; 19:11; **Ps.** 3:1(2); 13:4; 27:2,12; 44:5(6),7(8),10(11); 60:11(13)(KJV, see I),12(14); 69:17; 74:10; 78:42,61,66; 81:14(15); 89:23,42; 97:3; 105:24; 106:11; 107:2; 108:12(13) (KJV, see I),13(14); 112:8; 119:139,157; 136:24; **Isa.** 1:24; 9:11; 26:11; 59:18,19 (NASB, NIV, see I); 63:18; 64:2(1); **Jer.** 30:16; 46:10; 48:5(NASB, NIV, see I); 50:7; **Lam.** 1:5,7,10,17,20; 2:4,17; 4:12; **Ezek.** 39:23; **Amos** 3:11; **Mic.** 5:9; **Nah.** 1:2; **Zech.** 8:10(KJV, see I).

III. צַר *ṣar* **masc. noun**
(flint)
Isa. 5:28(KJV, *ṣōr* [6864]).

6863. צֵר *ṣēr* **proper noun**
(Zer)
Josh. 19:35.

6864. צֹר *ṣōr* **masc. noun**
(flint, flint knife, edge)
Ex. 4:25; **Josh.** 5:2(KJV, *ṣûr* [6697]),3(KJV, *ṣûr* [6697]); **Ps.** 89:43(44) (KJV, *ṣûr* [6697]); **Isa.** 5:28(KJV, NASB, *ṣur* [6862,III]); **Ezek.** 3:9.

6865. צֹר *ṣōr,* צוֹר *ṣôr* **proper noun**
(Tyre)
Josh. 19:29; **2 Sam.** 5:11; 24:7; **1 Kgs.** 5:1(15); 7:13; 9:11,12; **1 Chr.** 14:1; **2 Chr.** 2:3(2),11(10); **Ps.** 45:12(13); 83:7(8); 87:4; **Isa.** 23:1,5,8,15,17; **Jer.** 25:22; 27:3; 47:4; **Ezek.** 26:2–4,7,15; 27:2,3,8,32; 28:2,12; 29:18; **Hos.** 9:13; **Joel** 3:4(4:4); **Amos** 1:9,10; **Zech.** 9:2,3.

6866. צָרַב *ṣāraḇ* **verb**
(to burn, to scorch)
Ezek. 20:47(21:3).

6867. I. צָרָב *ṣārāḇ* **adj.**
(burning, scorching)
Lev. 13:23,28; **Prov.** 16:27.

II. צָרֶבֶת *ṣāreḇeṯ* **fem. noun**
(scar, scab, inflammation)
Lev. 13:23,28.

6868. I. צְרֵדָה *ṣᵉrēḏāh* **proper noun**
(Zereda)
1 Kgs. 11:26.

II. צְרֵדָתָה *ṣᵉrēḏaṯah* **proper noun**
(Zeredah, Zeredathah)
2 Chr. 4:17(NIV, *ṣārṯān* [6891]).

6869. I. צָרָה *ṣārāh* **fem. noun**
(trouble, distress, anguish)
Gen. 35:3; 42:21; **Deut.** 31:17,21; **Judg.** 10:14; **1 Sam.** 10:19; 26:24; **2 Sam.** 4:9; **1 Kgs.** 1:29; **2 Kgs.** 19:3; **2 Chr.** 15:6; 20:9; **Neh.** 9:27,37; **Job** 5:19; 27:9; **Ps.** 9:9; 10:1; 20:1; 22:11(12); 25:17,22; 31:7(8); 34:6(7),17(18); 37:39; 46:1; 50:15; 54:7(9); 71:20; 77:2(3); 78:49; 81:7(8); 86:7; 91:15; 116:3; 120:1; 138:7; 142:2(3); 143:11; **Prov.** 1:27; 11:8; 12:13; 17:17; 21:23; 24:10; 25:19; **Isa.** 8:22; 30:6; 33:2; 37:3; 46:7(8); 63:9; 65:16; **Jer.** 4:31; 6:24; 14:8; 15:11; 16:19; 30:7; 49:24; 50:43; **Dan.** 12:1; **Obad.** 1:12,14; **Jon.** 2:2(3); **Nah.** 1:7,9; **Hab.** 3:16; **Zeph.** 1:15; **Zech.** 10:11.

II. צָרָה *ṣārāh* **fem. noun**
(rival)
1 Sam. 1:6.

6870. צְרוּיָה *ṣᵉrûyāh* **fem. proper noun**
(Zeruiah)
1 Sam. 26:6; **2 Sam.** 2:13,18; 3:39; 8:16; 14:1; 16:9,10; 17:25; 18:2; 19:21,22; 21:17; 23:18,37; **1 Kgs.** 1:7; 2:5,22; **1 Chr.** 2:16; 11:6,39; 18:12,15; 26:28; 27:24.

6871. צְרוּעָה *ṣᵉrûʿāh* **fem. proper noun**
(Zeruah)
1 Kgs. 11:26.

6872. I. צְרוֹר *ṣᵉrôr* **masc. noun**
(bag, bundle, pouch, purse)
Gen. 42:35; **1 Sam.** 25:29; **Job** 14:17; **Prov.** 7:20; **Song** 1:13; **Hag.** 1:6.
II. צְרוֹר *ṣᵉrôr* **masc. noun**
(pebble, piece of grain)
2 Sam. 17:13; **Amos** 9:9.
III. צְרוֹר *ṣᵉrôr* **masc. proper noun**
(Zeror)
1 Sam. 9:1.

6873. צָרַח *ṣāraḥ* **verb**
(to roar, to give a war cry)
Isa. 42:13; **Zeph.** 1:14.

6874. צְרִי *ṣᵉriy* **masc. proper noun**
(Zeri)
1 Chr. 25:3.

6875. צֳרִי *ṣᵒriy,* צְרִי *ṣᵉriy* **masc. noun**
(balm)
Gen. 37:25; 43:11; **Jer.** 8:22; 46:11; 51:8; **Ezek.** 27:17.

6876. צֹרִי *ṣōriy* **masc. proper noun**
(Tyrian, from Tyre)
1 Kgs. 7:14; **1 Chr.** 22:4; **2 Chr.** 2:14(13); **Ezra** 3:7; **Neh.** 13:16.

6877. I. צְרִיחַ *ṣᵉriyaḥ* **masc. noun**
(cellar, inner chamber, stronghold)
Judg. 9:46,49; **1 Sam.** 13:6(KJV, see II).
II. צְרִיחַ *ṣᵉriyaḥ* **masc. noun**
(high place)
1 Sam. 13:6(NASB, NIV, see I).

6878. צֹרֶךְ *ṣōreḵ* **masc. noun**
(that which is needed)
2 Chr. 2:16(15).

6879. צָרַע *ṣāraʿ* **verb**
(to have leprosy, to be a leper)
Ex. 4:6; **Lev.** 13:44,45; 14:2,3; 22:4; **Num.** 5:2; 12:10; **2 Sam.** 3:29; **2 Kgs.** 5:1,11,27; 7:3,8; 15:5; **2 Chr.** 26:20, 21,23.

6880. צִרְעָה *ṣirʿāh* **coll. fem. noun**
(hornets)
Ex. 23:28; **Deut.** 7:20; **Josh.** 24:12.

6881. צָרְעָה *ṣorʿāh* **proper noun**
(Zorah)
Josh. 15:33; 19:41; **Judg.** 13:2,25; 16:31; 18:2,8,11; **2 Chr.** 11:10; **Neh.** 11:29.

6882. צָרְעִי *ṣorʿiy,* צָרְעָתִי *ṣorʿāṯiy* **proper noun**
(Zorite, Zorathite)
1 Chr. 2:53,54; 4:2.

6883. צָרַעַת *ṣarʿaṯ* **fem. noun**
(leprosy, skin disease)
Lev. 13:2,3,8,9,11–13,15,20,25,27,30,42,43,47,49,51,52,59; 14:3,7,32,34,44,54,55,57; **Deut.** 24:8; **2 Kgs.** 5:3,6,7,27; **2 Chr.** 26:19.

6884. צָרַף *ṣārap̱* **verb**
(to smelt, to refine, to test)
Judg. 7:4; 17:4; **2 Sam.** 22:31; **Neh.** 3:8,32; **Ps.** 12:6(7); 17:3; 18:30(31); 26:2; 66:10; 105:19; 119:140; **Prov.** 25:4; 30:5; **Isa.** 1:25; 40:19; 41:7; 46:6; 48:10;

Jer. 6:29; 9:7(6); 10:9,14; 51:17; **Dan.** 11:35; 12:10; **Zech.** 13:9; **Mal.** 3:2,3.

6885. צֹרְפִי *ṣōrpiy* **masc. noun**
(goldsmith)
Neh. 3:31.

6886. צָרְפַת *ṣārᵉpaṯ* **proper noun**
(Zarephath)
1 Kgs. 17:9,10; **Obad.** 1:20.

6887. I. צָרַר *ṣārar* **verb**
(to bind up, to tie up, to be distressed, to be troubled, to be oppressed, to be cramped)
Gen. 32:7(8)(KJV, *yāṣar* [3334]); **Ex.** 12:34; **Deut.** 28:52; **Josh.** 9:4; **Judg.** 2:15(KJV, *yāṣar* [3334]); 10:9(KJV, *yāṣar* [3334]); **1 Sam.** 13:6; 25:29; 28:15; 30:6(KJV, *yāṣar* [3334]); **2 Sam.** 1:26; 13:2(KJV, *yāṣar* [3334]); 20:3; 24:14(KJV, *ṣar* [6862,I]); **1 Kgs.** 8:37; **1 Chr.** 21:13; **2 Chr.** 6:28; 28:22; 33:12; **Job** 18:7(KJV, *yāṣar* [3334]); 20:22(KJV, *yāṣar* [3334]); 26:8; **Ps.** 31:9(10)(KJV, *ṣar* [6862,I]); 69:17(18)(KJV, *ṣar* [6862,I]); **Prov.** 4:12(KJV, *yāṣar* [3334]); 26:8; 30:4; **Isa.** 8:16; 28:20; 49:19(KJV, *yāṣar* [3334]); **Jer.** 10:18; 48:41; 49:22; **Lam.** 1:20(KJV, *ṣar* [6862,I]); **Hos.** 4:19; 13:12; **Zeph.** 1:17.

II. צָרַר *ṣārar* **verb**
(to be an enemy, to be an adversary, to be an oppressor, to be a rival)
Ex. 23:22; **Lev.** 18:18; **Num.** 10:9; 25:17,18; 33:55; **Neh.** 9:27; **Esth.** 3:10; 8:1; 9:10,24; **Ps.** 6:7(8); 7:4(5),6(7); 8:2(3); 10:5; 23:5; 31:11(12); 42:10(11); 69:19(20); 74:4,23; 129:1,2; 143:12; **Isa.** 11:13; **Amos** 5:12.

6888. צְרֵרָה *ṣᵉrērāh* **proper noun**
(Zererah)
Judg. 7:22.

6889. צֶרֶת *ṣereṯ* **masc. proper noun**
(Zereth)
1 Chr. 4:7.

6890. צֶרֶת הַשַּׁחַר *ṣereṯ haššaḥar* **proper noun**
(Zereth Shahar)
Josh. 13:19.

6891. צָרְתָן *ṣārᵉṯān* **proper noun**
(Zarethan, Zaretan)
Josh. 3:16; **1 Kgs.** 4:12; 7:46; **2 Chr.** 4:17(KJV, NASB, *ṣᵉrēḏāh* [6868,B]).

ק Qoph

6892. A. קֵא *qē'* **masc. noun**
(vomit)
Prov. 26:11.
B. קֵיא *qēy'* **masc. noun**
(vomit; NASB, NIV, *qiy'* [7006,II])
Isa. 19:14; 28:8; **Jer.** 48:26.

6893. קָאַת *qā'aṯ* **fem. noun**
(pelican, desert owl, cormorant)
Lev. 11:18; **Deut.** 14:17; **Ps.** 102:6(7); **Isa.** 34:11; **Zeph.** 2:14.

6894. קַב *qaḇ* **masc. noun**
(a cab or kab; dry measure equal to about two quarts)
2 Kgs. 6:25.

6895. קָבַב *qāḇaḇ* **verb**
(to curse, to blaspheme)
Lev. 24:11(KJV, *nāqaḇ* [5344,II]); **Num.** 22:11,17; 23:8(KJV, *nāqaḇ* [5344,II]), 11,13,25,27; 24:10; **Job** 3:8(KJV, *nāqaḇ* [5344,II]); 5:3(KJV, *nāqaḇ* [5344,II]); **Prov.** 11:26(KJV, *nāqaḇ* [5344,II]); 24:24(KJV, *nāqaḇ* [5344,II]).

6896. קֵבָה *qēḇāh* **fem. noun**
(stomach, belly)
Num. 25:8(KJV, *qōḇāh* [6897]); **Deut.** 18:3.

6897. קֹבָה *qōḇāh* **fem. noun**
(belly)
Num. 25:8(NASB, NIV, *qēḇāh* [6896]).

6898. קֻבָּה *qubbāh* **fem. noun**
(tent)
Num. 25:8.

6899. קִבּוּץ *qibbûṣ* **masc. noun**
(collection, assembly)
Isa. 57:13.

6900. קְבוּרָה *q^{e}ḇûrāh*, קְבֻרָה *q^{e}burāh* **fem. noun**
(tomb, grave, burial)
Gen. 35:20; 47:30; **Deut.** 34:6; **1 Sam.** 10:2; **2 Kgs.** 9:28; 21:26; 23:30; **2 Chr.** 26:23; **Eccl.** 6:3; **Isa.** 14:20; **Jer.** 22:19; **Ezek.** 32:23,24.

6901. קָבַל *qāḇal* **verb**
(to accept, to receive, to take, to undertake, to choose)
Ex. 26:5; 36:12; **1 Chr.** 12:18; 21:11; **2 Chr.** 29:16,22; **Ezra** 8:30; **Esth.** 4:4; 9:23,27; **Job** 2:10; **Prov.** 19:20.

6902. קָבַל *qāḇal* **Aram. verb**
(to receive, to take over; corr. to Hebr. 6901)
Dan. 2:6; 5:31(6:1); 7:18.

6903. קֳבֵל *q^{e}ḇēl* **Aram. conj.**
(because, inasmuch as; before)
Ezra 4:14,16; 6:13; 7:14,17; **Dan.** 2:8,10,12,24,31,40,41,45; 3:3,7,8,22,29; 4:18(15); 5:1,5,10,12,22; 6:3(4),4(5), 9(10),10(11),22(23).

6904. I. קֹבֶל *qōḇel*, קְבֹל *q^{e}ḇōl* **masc. noun**
(battering ram)
Ezek. 26:9(KJV, see II).
II. קֹבֶל *qōḇel*, קְבֹל *q^{e}ḇōl* **masc. noun**
(war)
Ezek. 26:9(NASB, NIV, see I).
III. קְבֹל *q^{e}ḇōl* **masc. noun**
(something before)
2 Kgs. 15:10(KJV, *qāḇāl* [6905]).

6905. קָבָל *qāḇāl* **masc. noun**
(something before, in front of)
2 Kgs. 15:10(NASB, NIV, *q^{e}ḇōl* [6904,III]).

6906. קָבַע *qāḇa'* **verb**
(to rob, to plunder)
Prov. 22:23; **Mal.** 3:8,9.

6907. קֻבַּעַת *qubba'aṯ* **fem. noun**
(goblet, chalice, dregs [of the cup])
Isa. 51:17,22.

6908. קָבַץ *qāḇaṣ* **verb**
(to gather, to assemble, to call together)
Gen. 41:35,48; 49:2; **Deut.** 13:16(17); 30:3,4; **Josh.** 9:2; 10:6; **Judg.** 9:47; 12:4; **1 Sam.** 7:5–7; 8:4; 22:2; 25:1; 28:1,4; 29:1; **2 Sam.** 2:25,30; 3:21; **1 Kgs.** 11:24; 18:19,20; 20:1; 22:6; **2 Kgs.** 6:24; 10:18; **1 Chr.** 11:1; 13:2; 16:35; **2 Chr.** 13:7; 15:9,10; 18:5; 20:4; 23:2; 24:5; 25:5; 32:4,6; **Ezra** 7:28; 8:15; 10:1,7,9; **Neh.** 1:9; 4:20(14); 5:16; 7:5; 13:11; **Esth.** 2:3,8,19; **Ps.** 41:6; 102:22(23); 106:47; 107:3; **Prov.** 13:11; 28:8; **Isa.** 11:12; 13:14; 22:9; 34:15,16; 40:11; 43:5,9; 44:11; 45:20; 48:14; 49:18; 54:7; 56:8; 60:4,7; 62:9; 66:18; **Jer.** 23:3; 29:14; 31:8,10; 32:37; 40:15; 49:5,14; **Ezek.** 11:17; 16:37; 20:34,41; 22:19,20; 28:25; 29:5,13; 34:13; 36:24; 37:21; 38:8; 39:17,27; **Hos.** 1:11(2:2); 8:10; 9:6; **Joel** 2:6,16; 3:2(4:2),11(4:11); **Mic.** 1:7; 2:12; 4:6,12; **Nah.** 2:10(11); 3:18; **Hab.** 2:5; **Zeph.** 3:8,19,20; **Zech.** 10:8,10.

6909. קַבְצְאֵל *qaḇṣᵉ'ēl* **proper noun**
(Kabzeel)
Josh. 15:21; **2 Sam.** 23:20; **1 Chr.** 11:22.

6910. קְבֻצָה *qᵉḇuṣāh* **fem. noun**
(a gathering)
Ezek. 22:20.

6911. קִבְצַיִם *qiḇṣayim* **proper noun**
(Kibzaim)
Josh. 21:22.

6912. קָבַר *qāḇar* **verb**
(to bury)
Gen. 15:15; 23:4,6,8,11,13,15,19; 25:9,10; 35:8,19,29; 47:29,30; 48:7; 49:29,31; 50:5–7,13,14; **Num.** 11:34; 20:1; 33:4; **Deut.** 10:6; 21:23; 34:6; **Josh.** 24:30,32,33; **Judg.** 2:9; 8:32; 10:2,5; 12:7,10,12,15; 16:31; **Ruth** 1:17; **1 Sam.** 25:1; 28:3; 31:13; **2 Sam.** 2:4, 5,32; 3:32; 4:12; 17:23; 21:14; **1 Kgs.** 2:10,31,34; 11:15,43; 13:29,31; 14:13, 18,31; 15:8,24; 16:6,28; 22:37,50; **2 Kgs.** 8:24; 9:10,28,34,35; 10:35; 12:21; 13:9, 13,20,21; 14:16,20; 15:7,38; 16:20; 21:18,26; 23:30; **1 Chr.** 10:12; **2 Chr.** 9:31; 12:16; 14:1; 16:14; 21:1,20; 22:9; 24:16,25; 25:28; 26:23; 27:9; 28:27; 32:33; 33:20; 35:24; **Job** 27:15; **Ps.** 79:3; **Eccl.** 8:10; **Jer.** 7:32; 8:2; 14:16; 16:4,6; 19:11; 20:6; 22:19; 25:33; **Ezek.** 39:11–15; **Hos.** 9:6.

6913. קֶבֶר *qeḇer* **masc. noun**
(grave, tomb)
Gen. 23:4,6,9,20; 49:30; 50:5,13; **Ex.** 14:11; **Num.** 19:16,18; **Judg.** 8:32; 16:31; **2 Sam.** 2:32; 3:32; 4:12; 17:23; 19:37(38); 21:14; **1 Kgs.** 13:22,30,31; 14:13; **2 Kgs.** 13:21; 22:20; 23:6,16,17; **2 Chr.** 16:14; 21:20; 24:25; 28:27; 32:33; 34:4,28; 35:24; **Neh.** 2:3,5; 3:16; **Job** 3:22; 5:26; 10:19; 17:1; 21:32; **Ps.** 5:9(10); 88:5 (6),11(12); **Isa.** 14:19; 22:16; 53:9; 65:4; **Jer.** 5:16; 8:1; 20:17; 26:23; **Ezek.** 32:22, 23,25,26; 37:12,13; 39:11; **Nah.** 1:14.

6914. קִבְרוֹת הַתַּאֲוָה *qiḇrôṯ hatta'ᵃwāh* **proper noun**
(Kibroth Hattaavah)
Num. 11:34,35; 33:16,17; **Deut.** 9:22.

6915. קָדַד *qāḏaḏ* **verb**
(to bow down)
Gen. 24:26,48; 43:28; **Ex.** 4:31; 12:27; 34:8; **Num.** 22:31; **1 Sam.** 24:8; 28:14; **1 Kgs.** 1:16,31; **1 Chr.** 29:20; **2 Chr.** 20:18; 29:30; **Neh.** 8:6.

6916. קִדָּה *qiddāh* **fem. noun**
(cassiah [a spice])
Ex. 30:24; **Ezek.** 27:19.

6917. קְדוּמִים $q^e\underline{d}\hat{u}miym$ **masc. noun**
(ancient, age-old)
Judg. 5:21.

6918. קָדוֹשׁ *qā*<u>d</u>*ôš* **adj.**
(holy, holy one, sacred)
Ex. 19:6; 29:31; **Lev.** 6:16(9),26(19), 27(20); 7:6; 10:13; 11:44,45; 16:24; 19:2; 20:7,26; 21:6–8; 24:9; **Num.** 5:17; 6:5,8; 15:40; 16:3,5,7; **Deut.** 7:6; 14:2,21; 23:14(15); 26:19; 28:9; 33:3; **Josh.** 24:19; **1 Sam.** 2:2; 6:20; **2 Kgs.** 4:9; 19:22; **2 Chr.** 35:3; **Neh.** 8:9–11; **Job** 5:1; 6:10; 15:15; **Ps.** 16:3; 22:3(4); 34:9(10); 46:4(5); 65:4(5); 71:22; 78:41; 89:5(6),7(8),18(19); 99:3,5,9; 106:16; 111:9; **Prov.** 9:10; 30:3; **Eccl.** 8:10; **Isa.** 1:4; 4:3; 5:16,19,24; 6:3; 10:17,20; 12:6; 17:7; 29:19,23; 30:11,12,15; 31:1; 37:23; 40:25; 41:14,16,20; 43:3,14,15; 45:11; 47:4; 48:17; 49:7; 54:5; 55:5; 57:15; 58:13; 60:9,14; **Jer.** 50:29; 51:5; **Ezek.** 39:7; 42:13; **Dan.** 8:13,24; **Hos.** 11:9,12; **Hab.** 1:12; 3:3; **Zech.** 14:5.

6919. קָדַח *qā*<u>d</u>*aḥ* **verb**
(to kindle, to set on fire)
Deut. 32:22; **Isa.** 50:11; 64:2(1); **Jer.** 15:14; 17:4.

6920. קַדַּחַת *qaddaḥa*<u>t</u> **fem. noun**
(fever)
Lev. 26:16; **Deut.** 28:22.

6921. קָדִים *qā*<u>d</u>*iym* **masc. noun**
(east, east wind)
Gen. 41:6,23,27; **Ex.** 10:13; 14:21; **Job** 15:2; 27:21; 38:24; **Ps.** 48:7(8); 78:26; **Isa.** 27:8; **Jer.** 18:17; **Ezek.** 11:1; 17:10; 19:12; 27:26; 40:6,10,19,22,23,32,44; 41:14; 42:9,10,12,15,16; 43:1,2,4,17; 44:1; 45:7; 46:1,12; 47:1–3,18; 48:1–8, 10,16–18,21,23–27,32; **Hos.** 12:1(2); 13:15; **Jon.** 4:8; **Hab.** 1:9.

6922. קַדִּישׁ *qaddiš* **Aram. adj.**
(holy, saintly; corr. to Hebr. 6918)
Dan.
4:8(5),9(6),13(10),17(14),18(15),23(20); 5:11; 7:18,21,22,25,27.

6923. קָדַם *qādam* **verb**
(to come before, to meet, to confront)
Deut. 23:4(5); **2 Sam.** 22:6,19; **2 Kgs.** 19:32; **Neh.** 13:2; **Job** 3:12; 30:27; 41:11(3); **Ps.** 17:13; 18:5(6),18(19); 21:3(4); 59:10(11); 68:25(26); 79:8; 88:13(14); 89:14(15); 95:2; 119:147,148; **Isa.** 21:14; 37:33; **Amos** 9:10; **Jon.** 4:2; **Mic.** 6:6.

6924. I. קֶדֶם *qe*<u>d</u>*em* **masc. noun**
(east, east side; former times)
Gen. 2:8; 3:24; 10:30; 11:2; 12:8; 13:11; 29:1; **Num.** 23:7; **Deut.** 33:15,27; **Josh.** 7:2; **Judg.** 6:3,33; 7:12; 8:10,11; **1 Kgs.** 4:3(5:10); **2 Kgs.** 19:25; **Neh.** 12:46; **Job** 1:3; 23:8; 29:2; **Ps.** 44:1(2); 55:19(20); 68:33(34); 74:2,12; 77:5(6),11(12); 78:2; 119:152; 139:5; 143:5; **Prov.** 8:22,23; **Isa.** 2:6; 9:12; 11:14; 19:11; 23:7; 37:26; 45:21; 46:10; 51:9; **Jer.** 30:20; 46:26; 49:28; **Lam.** 1:7; 2:17; 5:21; **Ezek.** 11:23; 25:4,10; **Jon.** 4:5; **Mic.** 5:2(1); 7:20; **Hab.** 1:12; **Zech.** 14:4.
II. קֶדֶם *qe*<u>d</u>*em* **adv.**
(eastward, eastern)
Gen. 13:14; 25:6; 28:14; **Ex.** 27:13; 38:13; **Lev.** 1:16; 16:14; **Num.** 2:3; 3:38; 10:5; 34:3,10,11,15; 35:5; **Josh.** 15:5; 18:20; 19:12,13; **1 Kgs.** 7:39; 17:3; **2 Kgs.** 13:17; **2 Chr.** 4:10; **Ezek.** 8:16; 45:7.

6925. קֳדָם $q^o\underline{d}\bar{a}m$ **Aram. prep.**
(before, in the presence of)
Ezra 4:18,23; 7:14,19; **Dan.** 2:6,9–11,15,18,24,25,27,36; 3:13; 4:2 (3:32),6(3),7(4),8(5); 5:13,15,17,19,

23,24; 6:1(2),10–13(11–14),18(19), 22(23),26(27); 7:7,8,10,13,20.

6926. קִדְמָה *qiḏmāh* **fem. noun**
(east)
Gen. 2:14; 4:16; **1 Sam.** 13:5; **Ezek.** 39:11.

6927. קַדְמָה *qaḏmāh* **fem. noun**
(antiquity, former time)
Ps. 129:6; **Isa.** 23:7; **Ezek.** 16:55; 36:11.

6928. קַדְמָה *qaḏmāh* **Aram. fem. noun**
(former time, former situation; corr. to Hebr. 6927)
Ezra 5:11; **Dan.** 6:10(11).

6929. קֵדְמָה *qēḏ^{e}māh* **masc. proper noun**
(Kedemah)
Gen. 25:15; **1 Chr.** 1:31.

6930. קַדְמוֹן *qaḏmôn* **adj.**
(eastern)
Ezek. 47:8.

6931. I. קַדְמוֹנִי *qaḏmôniy*, קַדְמֹנִי *qaḏmōniy* **adj.**
(eastern)
Job 18:20(KJV, see II); **Ezek.** 10:19; 11:1; 47:18; **Joel** 2:20; **Zech.** 14:8.
II. קַדְמוֹנִי *qaḏmôniy*, קַדְמֹנִי *qaḏmōniy* **adj.**
(former, previous)
1 Sam. 24:13(14); **Job** 18:20(NASB, NIV, see I); **Isa.** 43:18; **Ezek.** 38:17; **Mal.** 3:4.

6932. קְדֵמוֹת *q^{e}ḏēmôṯ* **proper noun**
(Kedemoth)
Deut. 2:26; **Josh.** 13:18; 21:37; **1 Chr.** 6:79(64).

6933. קַדְמָי *qaḏmāy* **Aram. adj.**
(first, former; corr. to Hebr. 6923)
Dan. 7:4,8,24.

6934. קַדְמִיאֵל *qaḏmiy'ēl* **masc. proper noun**
(Kadmiel)
Ezra 2:40; 3:9; **Neh.** 7:43; 9:4,5; 10:9; 12:8,24.

6935. קַדְמֹנִי *qaḏmōniy* **masc. proper noun**
(Kadmonite)
Gen. 15:19.

6936. קָדְקֹד *qoḏqōḏ* **masc. noun**
(top of the head, crown of the head)
Gen. 49:26; **Num.** 24:17(KJV, [Hebr.] *qûr* [6979,I]; NASB, [Hebr.] *qārar* [6979,IV]); **Deut.** 28:35; 33:16,20; **2 Sam.** 14:25; **Job** 2:7; **Ps.** 7:16(17); 68:21(22); **Isa.** 3:17; **Jer.** 2:16; 48:45.

6937. קָדַר *qāḏar* **verb**
(to make dark; to become dark; to be black; to mourn)
1 Kgs. 18:45; **Job** 5:11; 6:16; 30:28; **Ps.** 35:14; 38:6(7); 42:9(10); 43:2; **Jer.** 4:28; 8:21; 14:2; **Ezek.** 31:15; 32:7,8; **Joel** 2:10; 3:15(4:15); **Mic.** 3:6.

6938. קֵדָר *qēḏār* **masc. proper noun**
(Kedar)
Gen. 25:13; **1 Chr.** 1:29; **Ps.** 120:5; **Song** 1:5; **Isa.** 21:16,17; 42:11; 60:7; **Jer.** 2:10; 49:28; **Ezek.** 27:21.

6939. קִדְרוֹן *qiḏrôn* **proper noun**
(the brook Kidron)
2 Sam. 15:23; **1 Kgs.** 2:37; 15:13; **2 Kgs.** 23:4,6,12; **2 Chr.** 15:16; 29:16; 30:14; **Jer.** 31:40.

6940. קַדְרוּת *qaḏrûṯ* **fem. noun**
(blackness, darkness)
Isa. 50:3.

6941. קְדֹרַנִּית *q^{e}ḏōranniyṯ* **adv.**
(mournfully, in mourning)
Mal. 3:14.

6942. קָדַשׁ **qāḏaš verb**
(to sanctify, to consecrate, to dedicate; to show oneself holy)
Gen. 2:3; **Ex.** 13:2; 19:10,14,22,23; 20:8,11; 28:3,38,41; 29:1,21,27,33,36, 37,43,44; 30:29,30; 31:13; 40:9–11,13; **Lev.** 6:18(11),27(20); 8:10–12,15,30; 10:3; 11:44; 16:19; 20:7,8; 21:8,15,23; 22:2,3,9,16,32; 25:10; 27:14–19,22,26; **Num.** 3:13; 6:11; 7:1; 8:17; 11:18; 16:37(17:2),38(17:3); 20:12,13; 27:14; **Deut.** 5:12; 15:19; 22:9; 32:51; **Josh.** 3:5; 7:13; 20:7; **Judg.** 17:3; **1 Sam.** 7:1; 16:5; 21:5(6); **2 Sam.** 8:11; 11:4; **1 Kgs.** 8:64; 9:3,7; **2 Kgs.** 10:20; 12:18(19); **1 Chr.** 15:12,14; 18:11; 23:13; 26:26–28; **2 Chr.** 2:4(3); 5:11; 7:7,16,20; 26:18; 29:5, 15,17,19,34; 30:3,8,15,17,24; 31:6,18; 35:6; 36:14; **Ezra** 3:5; **Neh.** 3:1; 12:47; 13:22; **Job** 1:5; **Isa.** 5:16; 8:13; 13:3; 29:23; 30:29; 65:5; 66:17; **Jer.** 1:5; 6:4; 12:3; 17:22,24,27; 22:7; 51:27,28; **Ezek.** 7:24(NIV, *miqdāš* [4720]); 20:12,20,41; 28:22,25; 36:23; 37:28; 38:16,23; 39:27; 44:19,24; 46:20; 48:11; **Joel** 1:14; 2:15, 16; 3:9(4:9); **Mic.** 3:5; **Zeph.** 1:7; **Hag.** 2:12.

6943. A. קֶדֶשׁ **qeḏeš proper noun**
(Kedesh: city in Naphtali)
Josh. 12:22; 19:37; 20:7; 21:32; **Judg.** 4:6,9–11; **2 Kgs.** 15:29; **1 Chr.** 6:76(61).
B. קֶדֶשׁ **qeḏeš proper noun**
(Kedesh: town in Judah; possibly the same as Kadesh [6946,A] and Kadesh Barnea [6947])
Josh. 15:23.
C. קֶדֶשׁ **qeḏeš proper noun**
(Kedesh: a town in Issachar)
1 Chr. 6:72(57).

6944. קֹדֶשׁ **qōḏeš masc. noun**
(holiness, sanctuary)
Ex. 3:5; 12:16; 15:11,13; 16:23; 22:31(30); 26:33,34; 28:2,4,29,35,36,38,43; 29:6,29, 30,33,34,37; 30:10,13,24,25,29,31,32, 35–37; 31:10,11,14,15; 35:2,19,21; 36:1, 3,4,6; 37:29; 38:24–27; 39:1,30,41; 40:9, 10,13; **Lev.** 2:3,10; 4:6; 5:15,16; 6:17(10), 25(18),29(22),30(23); 7:1,6; 8:9; 10:4,10, 12,17,18; 12:4; 14:13; 16:2–4,16,17,20, 23,27,32,33; 19:8,24; 20:3; 21:6,22; 22:2–4,6,7,10,12,14–16,32; 23:2–4,7, 8,20,21,24,27,35–37; 24:9; 25:12; 27:3, 9,10,14,21,23,25,28,30,32,33; **Num.** 3:28,31,32,47,50; 4:4,12,15,16,19,20; 5:9,10; 6:20; 7:9,13,19,25,31,37,43,49, 55,61,67,73,79,85,86; 8:19; 18:3,5,8–10, 16,17,19,32; 28:7,18,25,26; 29:1,7,12; 31:6; 35:25; **Deut.** 12:26; 26:13,15; 33:2; **Josh.** 5:15; 6:19; **1 Sam.** 21:4(5),5(6), 6(7); **1 Kgs.** 6:16; 7:50,51; 8:4,6,8,10; 15:15; **2 Kgs.** 12:4(5),18(19); **1 Chr.** 6:49(34); 9:29; 16:10,29,35; 22:19; 23:13,28,32; 24:5; 26:20,26; 28:12; 29:3,16; **2 Chr.** 3:8,10; 4:22; 5:1,5,7,11; 8:11; 15:18; 20:21; 23:6; 24:7; 29:5,7,33; 30:19,27; 31:6,12,14,18; 35:3,5,13; **Ezra** 2:63; 8:28; 9:2,8; **Neh.** 7:65; 9:14; 10:31 (32),33(34); 11:1,18; **Ps.** 2:6; 3:4(5); 5:7(8); 11:4; 15:1; 20:2(3),6(7); 24:3; 28:2; 29:2; 30:4(5); 33:21; 43:3; 47:8(9); 48:1; 51:11(13); 60:6(8); 63:2(3); 68:5(6), 17(18),24(25); 74:3; 77:13(14); 78:54; 79:1; 87:1; 89:20(21),35(36); 93:5; 96:9; 97:12; 98:1; 99:9; 102:19(20); 103:1; 105:3,42; 106:47; 108:7; 110:3; 114:2; 134:2; 138:2; 145:21; 150:1; **Prov.** 20:25; **Isa.** 6:13; 11:9; 23:18; 27:13; 35:8; 43:28; 48:2; 52:1,10; 56:7; 57:13; 58:13; 62:9, 12; 63:10,11,15,18; 64:10(9),11(10); 65:11,25; 66:20; **Jer.** 2:3; 11:15; 23:9; 25:30; 31:23,40; **Lam.** 4:1; **Ezek.** 20:39,40; 22:8,26; 28:14; 36:20–22,38; 39:7,25; 41:4,21,23; 42:13,14,20; 43:7,8, 12; 44:8,13,19,23,27; 45:1–4,6,7; 46:19; 48:10,12,14,18,20,21; **Dan.** 8:13,14; 9:16,20,24,26; 11:28,30,45; 12:7; **Joel** 2:1; 3:17(4:17); **Amos** 2:7; 4:2; **Obad.** 1:16,17; **Jon.** 2:4(5),7(8); **Mic.** 1:2; **Hab.** 2:20; **Zeph.** 3:4,11; **Hag.** 2:12; **Zech.** 2:12(16),13(17); 8:3; 14:20,21; **Mal.** 2:11.

6945. קָדֵשׁ *qāḏēš* **masc. noun**
(male temple prostitute; sodomite; NASB, NIV, see also *q^eḏēšāh* [6948])
Deut. 23:17(18); **1 Kgs.** 14:24; 15:12; 22:46(47); **2 Kgs.** 23:7; **Job** 36:14.

6946. קָדֵשׁ *qāḏēš* **proper noun**
(Kadesh; the same as Kadesh Barnea [6947], and possibly the same as Kedesh [6943,B])
Gen. 14:7; 16:14; 20:1; **Num.** 13:26; 20:1,14,16,22; 27:14(NASB, NIV, *m^eriyḇaṯ qāḏēš* [4809,C]); 33:36,37; **Deut.** 1:46; **Judg.** 11:16,17; **Ps.** 29:8; **Ezek.** 47:19 (NASB, NIV, *m^eriyḇaṯ qāḏēš* [4809,C]); 48:28(NASB, NIV, *m^eriyḇaṯ qāḏēš* [4809,C]).

6947. קָדֵשׁ בַּרְנֵעַ *qāḏēš barnēa'* **proper noun**
(Kadesh Barnea; the same as Kadesh [6946] and possibly the same as Kedesh [6947])
Num. 32:8; 34:4; **Deut.** 1:2,19; 2:14; 9:23; **Josh.** 10:41; 14:6,7; 15:3.

6948. קְדֵשָׁה *q^eḏēšāh* **fem. noun**
(female cult prostitute; NASB, NIV, fem. of *qāḏēš* [6945])
Gen. 38:21,22; **Deut.** 23:17(18); **Hos.** 4:14.

6949. I. קָהָה *qāhāh* **verb**
(to be blunt, to be dull)
Eccl. 10:10.
II. קָהָה *qāhāh* **verb**
(to be set on edge [of teeth])
Jer. 31:29,30; **Ezek.** 18:2.

6950. קָהַל *qāhal* **verb**
(to gather together, to assemble)
Ex. 32:1; 35:1; **Lev.** 8:3,4; **Num.** 1:18; 8:9; 10:7; 16:3,19,42(17:7); 20:2,8,10; **Deut.** 4:10; 31:12,28; **Josh.** 18:1; 22:12; **Judg.** 20:1; **2 Sam.** 20:14(KJV, [K^e] *qālāh* [7035]); **1 Kgs.** 8:1,2; 12:21; **1 Chr.** 13:5; 15:3; 28:1; **2 Chr.** 5:2,3; 11:1; 20:26; **Esth.** 8:11; 9:2,15,16,18; **Job** 11:10; **Jer.** 26:9; **Ezek.** 38:7,13.

6951. קָהָל *qāhāl* **masc. noun**
(assembly, congregation, company, horde)
Gen. 28:3; 35:11; 48:4; 49:6; **Ex.** 12:6; 16:3; **Lev.** 4:13,14,21; 16:17,33; **Num.** 10:7; 14:5; 15:15; 16:3,33,47(17:12); 19:20; 20:4,6,10,12; 22:4; **Deut.** 5:22; 9:10; 10:4; 18:16; 23:1(2),2(3),3(4),8(9); 31:30; **Josh.** 8:35; **Judg.** 20:2; 21:5,8; **1 Sam.** 17:47; **1 Kgs.** 8:14,22,55,65; 12:3; **1 Chr.** 13:2,4; 28:8; 29:1,10,20; **2 Chr.** 1:3,5; 6:3,12,13; 7:8; 20:5,14; 23:3; 24:6; 28:14; 29:23,28,31,32; 30:2,4,13,17,23–25; 31:18; **Ezra** 2:64; 10:1,8,12,14; **Neh.** 5:13; 7:66; 8:2,17; 13:1; **Job** 30:28; **Ps.** 22:22(23),25(26); 26:5; 35:18; 40:9(10),10(11); 89:5(6); 107:32; 149:1; **Prov.** 5:14; 21:16; 26:26; **Jer.** 26:17; 31:8; 44:15; 50:9; **Lam.** 1:10; **Ezek.** 16:40; 17:17; 23:24,46,47; 26:7; 27:27,34; 32:3,22,23; 38:4,7,13,15; **Joel** 2:16; **Mic.** 2:5.

6952. קְהִלָּה *q^ehillāh* **fem. noun**
(assembly, congregation)
Deut. 33:4; **Neh.** 5:7.

6953. קֹהֶלֶת *qōheleṯ* **masc. noun**
(preacher, teacher)
Eccl. 1:1,2,12; 7:27; 12:8–10.

6954. קְהֵלָתָה *q^ehēlāṯāh* **proper noun**
(Kehelathah)
Num. 33:22,23.

6955. קְהָת *q^ehāṯ* **masc. proper noun**
(Kohath)
Gen. 46:11; **Ex.** 6:16,18; **Num.** 3:17,19,27,29; 4:2,4,15; 7:9; 16:1; 26:57,58; **Josh.** 21:5,20,26; **1 Chr.** 6:1(5:27),2(5:28),16(1),18(3),22(7),38(23),61(46),66(51),70(55); 15:5; 23:6,12.

6956. קְהָתִי *q^e^hāṯiy* **masc. proper noun**
(Kohathite)
Num. 3:27,30; 4:18,34,37; 10:21; 26:57; **Josh.** 21:4,10; **1 Chr.** 6:33(18),54(39); 9:32; **2 Chr.** 20:19; 29:12; 34:12.

6957. קַו *qaw,* קָו *qāw* **masc. noun**
(line, measuring line)
1 Kgs. 7:23(NASB, [K^e^] *qāweh* [6961]); **2 Kgs.** 21:13; **2 Chr.** 4:2; **Job** 38:5; **Ps.** 19:4; **Isa.** 28:10,13,17; 34:11,17; 44:13; **Jer.** 31:39; **Lam.** 2:8; **Ezek.** 47:3; **Zech.** 1:16.

6958. I. קוֹה *qôh* **verb**
(to vomit; NASB, NIV, *qiy'* [7006,I])
Lev. 18:25,28; 20:22; **Job** 20:15; **Prov.** 23:8; 25:16; **Jon.** 2:10(11).
II. קָיָה *qāyāh* **verb**
(to vomit)
Jer. 25:27.

6959. קוֹבַע *qôḇa'* **masc. noun**
(helmet)
1 Sam. 17:38; **Ezek.** 23:24.

6960. I. קָוָה *qāwāh* **verb**
(to wait for, to look for, to expect)
Gen. 49:18; **Job** 3:9; 6:19; 7:2; 17:13; 30:26; **Ps.** 25:3,5,21; 27:14; 37:9,34; 39:7(8); 40:1; 52:9(11); 56:6(7); 69:6(7), 20(21); 119:95; 130:5; **Prov.** 20:22; **Isa.** 5:2,4,7; 8:17; 25:9; 26:8; 33:2; 40:31; 49:23; 51:5; 59:9,11; 60:9; 64:3(2); **Jer.** 8:15; 13:16; 14:19,22; **Lam.** 2:16; 3:25; **Hos.** 12:6(7); **Mic.** 5:7(6).
II. קָוָה *qāwāh* **verb**
(to gather)
Gen. 1:9; **Jer.** 3:17.

6961. קָוֶה *qāweh* **masc. noun**
(line, measuring line)
1 Kgs. 7:23(NIV, KJV, [Q^e^] *qāw* [6957]);

6962. קוּט *qûṭ* **verb**
(to loathe, to abhor)
Job 10:1(KJV, *nāqaṭ* [5354]); **Ps.** 95:10; 119:158; 139:21; **Ezek.** 6:9; 20:43; 36:31.

6963. קוֹל *qôl* **masc. noun**
(voice, sound, noise, cry)
Gen. 3:8,10,17; 4:10,23; 16:2; 21:12, 16,17; 22:18; 26:5; 27:8,13,22,38,43; 29:11; 30:6; 39:14,15,18; 45:2,16; **Ex.** 3:18; 4:1,8,9; 5:2; 9:23,28,29,33,34; 15:26; 18:19,24; 19:5,16,19; 20:18; 23:21,22; 24:3; 28:35; 32:17,18; 36:6; **Lev.** 5:1; 26:36; **Num.** 7:89; 14:1,22; 16:34; 20:16; 21:3; **Deut.** 1:34,45; 4:12,30,33,36; 5:22–26,28; 8:20; 9:23; 13:4(5),18(19); 15:5; 18:16; 21:18,20; 26:7,14,17; 27:10,14; 28:1,2,15,45,62; 30:2,8,10,20; 33:7; **Josh.** 5:6; 6:5,10,20; 10:14; 22:2; 24:24; **Judg.** 2:2,4,20; 5:11; 6:10; 9:7; 13:9; 18:3,25; 20:13; 21:2; **Ruth** 1:9,14; **1 Sam.** 1:13; 2:25; 4:6,14; 7:10; 8:7,9,19,22; 11:4; 12:1,14,15,17,18; 15:1,14,19,20,22,24; 19:6; 24:16(17); 25:35; 26:17; 28:12,18,21–23; 30:4; **2 Sam.** 3:32; 5:24; 6:15; 12:18; 13:14,36; 15:10,23; 19:4(5),35(36); 22:7,14; **1 Kgs.** 1:40,41,45; 8:55; 14:6; 17:22; 18:26–29, 41; 19:12,13; 20:25,36; **2 Kgs.** 4:31; 6:32; 7:6,10; 10:6; 11:13; 18:12,28; 19:22; **1 Chr.** 14:15; 15:16,28; **2 Chr.** 5:13; 15:14; 20:19; 23:12; 24:9; 30:5,27; 32:18; 36:22; **Ezra** 1:1; 3:12,13; 10:7,12; **Neh.** 4:20; 8:15; 9:4; **Job** 2:12; 3:18; 4:10,16; 9:16; 15:21; 21:12; 28:26; 29:10; 30:31; 33:8; 34:16; 37:2,4,5; 38:25,34; 39:24; 40:9; **Ps.** 3:4(5); 5:2(3),3(4); 6:8(9); 18:6(7),13(14); 19:3(4); 26:7; 27:7; 28:2,6; 29:3–5,7–9; 31:22(23); 42:4(5),7(8); 44:16(17); 46:6(7); 47:1(2), 5(6); 55:3(4),17(18); 58:5(6); 64:1; 66:8,19; 68:33(34); 74:23; 77:1(2),17(18), 18(19); 81:11(12); 86:6; 93:3,4; 95:7; 98:5,6; 102:5(6); 103:20; 104:7,12; 106:25; 116:1; 118:15; 119:149; 130:2; 140:6(7); 141:1; 142:1; **Prov.** 1:20; 2:3; 5:13; 8:1,4; 26:25; 27:14; **Eccl.** 5:3(2), 6(5); 7:6; 10:20; 12:4; **Song** 2:8,12,14;

5:2; 8:13; **Isa.** 6:4,8; 10:30; 13:2,4; 15:4; 24:14,18; 28:23; 29:4,6; 30:19,30,31; 31:4; 32:9; 33:3; 36:13; 37:23; 40:3,6,9; 42:2; 48:20; 50:10; 51:3; 52:8; 58:1,4; 65:19; 66:6; **Jer.** 2:15; 3:9,13,21,25; 4:15,16,19,21,29,31; 6:17,23; 7:23,28,34; 8:16,19; 9:10(9),13(12),19(18); 10:13,22; 11:4,7,16; 12:8; 16:9; 18:10,19; 22:20,21; 25:10,30,36; 26:13; 30:5,19; 31:15,16; 32:23; 33:11; 35:8; 38:20; 40:3; 42:6,13, 14,21; 43:4,7; 44:23; 46:22; 47:3; 48:3,34; 49:21; 50:22,28,42,46; 51:16,54,55; **Lam.** 2:7; 3:56; **Ezek.** 1:24,25,28; 3:12,13; 8:18; 9:1; 10:5; 11:13; 19:7,9; 21:22(27); 23:42; 26:10,13,15; 27:28,30; 31:16; 33:4,5,32; 37:7; 43:2; **Dan.** 8:16; 9:10,11,14; 10:6,9; **Joel** 2:5,11; 3:16 (4:16); **Amos** 1:2; 2:2; 3:4; **Jon.** 2:2(3), 9(10); **Mic.** 6:1,9; **Nah.** 2:7(8),13(14); 3:2; **Hab.** 3:10,16; **Zeph.** 1:10,14; 2:14; 3:2; **Hag.** 1:12; **Zech.** 6:15; 11:3.

6964. A. קוֹלָיָה *qôlāyāh* **masc. proper noun**
(Kolaiah: a Benjamite)
Neh. 11:7.
B. קוֹלָיָה *qôlāyāh* **masc. proper noun**
(Kolaiah: father of the false prophet Ahab)
Jer. 29:21.

6965. קוּם *qûm* **verb**
(to rise up, to stand; to raise up, to establish)
Gen. 4:8; 6:18; 9:9,11,17; 13:17; 17:7, 19,21; 18:16; 19:1,14,15,33,35; 21:18,32; 22:3,19; 23:3,7,17,20; 24:10,54,61; 25:34; 26:3; 27:19,31,43; 28:2; 31:13,17,21,35; 32:22(23); 35:1,3; 37:7,35; 38:8,19; 41:30; 43:8,13,15; 44:4; 46:5; 49:9; **Ex.** 1:8; 2:17; 6:4; 10:23; 12:30,31; 15:7; 21:19; 24:13; 26:30; 32:1,6,25; 33:8,10; 40:2,17,18,33; **Lev.** 19:32; 25:30; 26:1,9; 27:14,17,19; **Num.** 1:51; 7:1; 9:15; 10:21,35; 11:32; 16:2,25; 22:13,14,20,21; 23:18,19,24; 24:9,17,25; 25:7; 30:4(5), 5(6),7(8),9(10),11–14(12–15); 32:14; **Deut.** 2:13,24; 6:7; 8:18; 9:5,12; 10:11; 11:19; 13:1(2); 16:22; 17:8; 18:15,18; 19:11,15,16; 22:4,26; 25:6,7; 27:2,4,26; 28:7,9,36; 29:13(12),22(21); 31:16; 32:38; 33:11; 34:10; **Josh.** 1:2; 2:11; 3:16; 4:9,20; 5:7; 6:26; 7:10,12,13,26; 8:1,3,7,19,29; 18:4,8; 24:9,26; **Judg.** 2:10,16,18; 3:9,15,20; 4:9,14; 5:7,12; 7:9,15,19; 8:20,21; 9:18,32,34,35,43; 10:1,3; 13:11; 16:3; 18:9,30; 19:3,5,7,9, 10,27,28; 20:5,8,18,19,33; **Ruth** 1:6; 2:15; 3:14; 4:5,7,10; **1 Sam.** 1:9,23; 2:8,35; 3:6,8,12; 4:15; 9:3,26; 13:14,15; 15:11,13; 16:12,13; 17:35,48,52; 18:27; 20:25,34,41,42(21:1); 21:10(11); 22:8,13; 23:4,13,16,24; 24:4(5),7(8),8(9),20(21); 25:1,29,41,42; 26:2,5; 27:2; 28:23,25; 31:12; **2 Sam.** 2:14,15; 3:10,21; 6:2; 7:12,25; 11:2; 12:11,17,20,21; 13:15, 29,31; 14:7,23,31; 15:9,14; 17:1,21–23; 18:31,32; 19:7(8),8(9); 22:39,40,49; 23:1, 10; 24:11,18; **1 Kgs.** 1:49,50; 2:4,19,40; 3:12,20,21; 6:12; 7:21; 8:20,54; 9:5; 11:14,18,23,40; 12:15; 14:2,4,12,14,17; 15:4; 16:32; 17:9,10; 19:3,5,7,8,21; 21:7, 15,16,18; **2 Kgs.** 1:3,15; 3:24; 4:30; 6:15; 7:5,7,12; 8:1,2,21; 9:2,6; 10:12; 11:1; 12:20(21); 13:21; 16:7; 19:26(KJV, NASB, *qāmāh* [7054]); 21:3; 23:3,24,25; 25:26; **1 Chr.** 10:12; 17:11; 21:18; 22:16,19; 28:2; **2 Chr.** 3:17; 6:10,41; 7:18; 10:15; 13:4,6; 20:19; 21:4,9; 22:10; 28:12,15; 29:12; 30:14,27; 33:3; **Ezra** 1:5; 3:2; 9:5; 10:4–6,10; **Neh.** 2:12,18,20; 3:1; 4:14; 5:13; 9:3–5,8; **Esth.** 5:9; 7:7; 8:4; 9:21, 27,29,31,32; **Job** 1:20; 4:4; 7:4; 8:15; 11:17; 14:12; 15:29; 16:8,12; 19:18,25; 20:27; 22:28; 24:14,22; 25:3; 27:7; 29:8; 30:12,28; 31:14; 41:26(18); **Ps.** 1:5; 3:1(2),7(8); 7:6(7); 9:19(20); 10:12; 12:5(6); 17:7,13; 18:38(39),39(40), 48(49); 20:8(9); 24:3; 27:3,12; 35:2,11; 36:12(13); 40:2(3); 41:8(9),10(11); 44:5(6),26(27); 54:3(5); 59:1; 68:1; 74:22,23; 76:9(10); 78:5,6; 82:8; 86:14; 88:10(11); 89:43(44); 92:11(12); 94:16;

102:13(14); 107:29; 109:28; 113:7; 119:28,38,62,106; 124:2; 127:2; 132:8; 139:2,21(KJV, *t*[e]*qômēm* [8618]); 140:10(11); **Prov.** 6:9; 15:22; 19:21; 24:16,22; 28:12,28; 30:4,31; 31:15,28; **Eccl.** 4:10; 12:4; **Song** 2:10,13; 3:2; 5:5; **Isa.** 2:19,21; 7:7; 8:10; 14:9,21,22,24; 21:5; 23:12,13; 24:20; 26:14,19; 27:9; 28:18,21; 29:3; 31:2; 32:8,9; 33:10; 40:8; 43:17; 44:26; 46:10; 49:6–8; 51:17; 52:2; 54:17; 58:12; 60:1; 61:4; **Jer.** 1:17; 2:27,28; 6:4,5,17; 8:4; 10:20; 11:5; 13:4,6; 18:2; 23:4,5,20; 25:27; 26:17; 28:6; 29:10,15; 30:9,24; 31:6; 33:14; 34:18; 35:14,16; 37:10; 41:2; 44:25, 28,29; 46:16; 49:14,28,31; 50:32; 51:1, 12,29,64; **Lam.** 1:14; 2:19; 3:62; **Ezek.** 3:22,23; 7:11; 13:6; 16:60,62; 26:8; 34:23,29; **Dan.** 8:27; 9:12; **Hos.** 6:2; 10:14; **Amos** 2:11; 5:2; 6:14; 7:2,5,9; 8:14; 9:11; **Obad.** 1:1; **Jon.** 1:2,3,6; 3:2,3,6; **Mic.** 2:8,10; 4:13; 5:5(4); 6:1; 7:6,8; **Nah.** 1:6,9; **Hab.** 1:6; 2:7; **Zeph.** 3:8; **Zech.** 11:16.

6966. קוּם *qûm* **Aram. verb**
(to stand, to arise, to set up, to establish; corr. to Hebr. 6565)
Ezra 5:2; 6:18; **Dan.** 2:21,31,39,44; 3:1–3,5,7,12,14,18,24; 4:17(14); 5:11,21; 6:1(2),3(4),7(8),8(9),15(16),19(20); 7:4, 5,10,16,17,24.

6967. קוֹמָה *qômāh* **fem. noun**
(height, stature, length)
Gen. 6:15; **Ex.** 25:10,23; 27:1,18; 30:2; 37:1,10,25; 38:1,18; **1 Sam.** 16:7; 28:20; **1 Kgs.** 6:2,10,20,23,26; 7:2,15,16,23,27, 32,35; **2 Kgs.** 19:23; 25:17; **2 Chr.** 4:1,2; 6:13; **Song** 7:7(8); **Isa.** 10:33; 37:24; **Jer.** 52:21,22; **Ezek.** 13:18; 17:6; 19:11; 31:3,5,10,14; 40:5.

6968. קוֹמְמִיּוּת *qôm*[e]*miyyûṯ* **fem. noun**
(uprightness, erectness)
Lev. 26:13.

6969. קוּן *qûn*, קִין *qiyn*, קוֹנֵן *qônēn* **verb**
(to chant, to lament, to mourn)
2 Sam. 1:17; 3:33; **2 Chr.** 35:25; **Jer.** 9:17(16); **Ezek.** 27:32; 32:16.

6970. קוֹעַ *qôa'* **proper noun**
(Koa)
Ezek. 23:23.

6971. קוֹף *qôp̱* **masc. noun**
(ape)
1 Kgs. 10:22; **2 Chr.** 9:21.

6972. קוּץ *qûṣ*, קִיץ *qiyṣ* **verb**
(to spend the summer)
Isa. 18:6.

6973. I. קוּץ *qûṣ* **verb**
(to abhor, to detest, to dread, to grow weary of)
Gen. 27:46; **Ex.** 1:12; **Lev.** 20:23; **Num.** 21:5; 22:3; **1 Kgs.** 11:25; **Prov.** 3:11; **Isa.** 7:16.
II. קוּץ *qûṣ* **verb**
(to vex, to terrorize, to tear apart)
Isa. 7:6.

6974. קוּץ *qûṣ*, קִיץ *qiyṣ* **verb**
(to wake up, to arouse)
1 Sam. 26:12; **2 Kgs.** 4:31; **Job** 14:12; **Ps.** 3:5(6); 17:15; 35:23; 44:23(24); 59:5(6); 73:20; 139:18; **Prov.** 6:22; 23:35; **Isa.** 26:19; 29:8; **Jer.** 31:26; 51:39,57; **Ezek.** 7:6; **Dan.** 12:2; **Joel** 1:5; **Hab.** 2:19.

6975. קוֹץ *qôṣ* **masc. noun**
(thorn, thornbush)
Gen. 3:18; **Ex.** 22:6; **Judg.** 8:7,16; **2 Sam.** 23:6; **Ps.** 118:12; **Isa.** 32:13; 33:12; **Jer.** 4:3; 12:13; **Ezek.** 28:24; **Hos.** 10:8.

6976. I. קוֹץ *qôṣ* **masc. proper noun**
(Koz: a descendant of Caleb)
1 Chr. 4:8.

II. הַקּוֹץ *haqqôṣ* **masc. proper noun**
(Hakkoz: a priest returning from Babylonian exile)
1 Chr. 24:10; **Ezra** 2:61; **Neh.** 3:4,21; 7:63.

6977. קְוֻצָּה *q^e^wuṣṣāh* **fem. noun**
(hair, lock of hair)
Song 5:2,11.

6978. I. קַו *qaw* **masc. noun**
(might, power)
Isa. 18:2(KJV, see II; NIV, see III), 7(KJV, see II; NIV, see III).
II. קַו־קַו *qaw-qaw* **masc. noun**
(measure, a meting out)
Isa. 18:2(NASB, see I; NIV, see III),7(NASB, see I; NIV, see III).
III. קָו *qāw* **masc. noun**
(strange speech)
Isa. 18:2(NASB, see I; KJV, see II),7(NASB, see I; KJV, see II).

6979. I. קוּר *qûr* **verb**
(to dig)
2 Kgs. 19:24(KJV, *nāqar* [5365]);
Isa. 37:25(KJV, *nāqar* [5365]).
II. קוּר *qûr* **verb**
(to break down, to destroy)
Num. 24:17(NIV, *qoḏqōḏ* [6936]);
Isa. 22:5.
III. קוּר *qûr* **verb**
(to cast out; to pour out)
Jer. 6:7.

6980. קוּר *qûr* **masc. noun**
(spider's web)
Isa. 59:5,6.

6981. A. קוֹרֵא *qôrē'*, קֹרֵא *qōrē'* **masc. proper noun**
(Kore, ancestor of gatekeepers in David's day)
1 Chr. 9:19; 26:1.
B. קוֹרֵא *qôrē'* **masc. proper noun**
(Kore: a Levite under Hezekiah)
2 Chr. 31:14.

6982. קוֹרָה *qôrāh* **fem. noun**
(beam, pole, roof)
Gen. 19:8; **2 Kgs.** 6:2,5; **2 Chr.** 3:7; **Song** 1:17.

6983. קוּשׁ *qûš* **verb**
(to ensnare)
Isa. 29:21.

6984. קוּשָׁיָהוּ *qûšāyāhû* **masc. proper noun**
(Kushaiah)
1 Chr. 15:17.

6985. קָט *qāṭ* **adj.**
(little, very little; soon)
Ezek. 16:47.

6986. קֶטֶב *qeṭeḇ* **masc. noun**
(destruction)
Deut. 32:24; **Ps.** 91:6; **Isa.** 28:2; **Hos.** 13:14(KJV).

6987. קֹטֶב *qōṭeḇ* **masc. noun**
(destruction)
Hos. 13:14(NASB, NIV, *qeṭeḇ* [6986]).

6988. קְטוֹרָה *q^e^ṭôrāh* **masc. noun**
(incense)
Deut. 33:10.

6989. קְטוּרָה *q^e^ṭûrāh* **fem. proper noun**
(Keturah)
Gen. 25:1,4; **1 Chr.** 1:32,33.

6990. I. קָטַט *qāṭaṭ* **verb**
(to be cut off)
Job 8:14(NASB, see II; NIV, see III).
II. קָטַט *qāṭaṭ* **verb**
(to be fragile)
Job 8:14(NASB, see II; NIV, see III).

6991. קָטַל *qāṭal* **verb**
(to slay, to kill)
Job 13:15; 24:14; **Ps.** 139:19.

6992. קְטַל *q^eṭal* **Aram. verb**
(to slay, to kill; corr. to Hebr. 6991)
Dan. 2:13,14; 3:22; 5:19,30; 7:11.

6993. קֶטֶל *qeṭel* **masc. noun**
(slaughter)
Obad. 1:9.

6994. קָטֹן *qāṭan* **verb**
(to be small)
Gen. 32:10(11); **2 Sam.** 7:19; **1 Chr.** 17:17; **Amos** 8:5.

6995. קֹטֶן *qōṭen* **masc. noun**
(little finger)
1 Kgs. 12:10; **2 Chr.** 10:10.

6996. I. קָטָן *qāṭān* **adj.**
(small, little, insignificant)
Gen. 9:24; 27:15,42; 29:16,18; 44:20; **Num.** 22:18; **Deut.** 25:13,14; **Judg.** 15:2; **1 Sam.** 9:21; 14:49; 16:11; 17:14; **2 Sam.** 9:12; 12:3; **1 Kgs.** 2:20; 11:17; 17:13; 18:44; **2 Kgs.** 2:23; 4:10; 5:2; 18:24; **1 Chr.** 12:14(15); 24:31; **2 Chr.** 31:15; 34:30; 36:18; **Esth.** 1:5,20; **Ps.** 104:25; 115:13; **Prov.** 30:24; **Eccl.** 9:14; **Song** 2:15; 8:8; **Isa.** 22:24; **Jer.** 6:13; 8:10; 16:6; 31:34; **Ezek.** 16:46,61; **Zech.** 4:10.
II. קָטֹן *qāṭōn* **adj.**
(small, little, insignificant)
Gen. 1:16; 19:11; 42:13,15,20,32,34; 43:29; 44:2,12,23,26; 48:19; **Ex.** 18:22,26; **Deut.** 1:17; **Judg.** 1:13; 3:9; 9:5; **1 Sam.** 2:19; 5:9; 15:17; 20:2,35; 22:15; 25:36; 30:2,19; **1 Kgs.** 3:7; 8:64; 22:31; **2 Kgs.** 5:14; 23:2; 25:26; **1 Chr.** 25:8; 26:13; **2 Chr.** 15:13; 18:30; 21:17; 22:1; **Job** 3:19; **Isa.** 11:6; 54:7; 60:22; **Jer.** 42:1,8; 44:12; 49:15; **Ezek.** 43:14; **Amos** 6:11; 7:2,5; **Obad.** 1:2; **Jon.** 3:5.

6997. קָטָן *qāṭān*, הַקָּטָן *haqqāṭan* **masc. proper noun**
(Hakkatan)
Ezra 8:12.

6998. קָטַף *qāṭap̱* **verb**
(to break off, to pluck off, to cut off)
Deut. 23:25(26); **Job** 8:12; 30:4; **Ezek.** 17:4,22.

6999. קָטַר *qāṭar* **verb**
(to burn incense, to burn sacrifices)
Ex. 29:13,18,25; 30:7,8,20; 40:27; **Lev.** 1:9,13,15,17; 2:2,9,11,16; 3:5,11,16; 4:10,19,26,31,35; 5:12; 6:12(5),15(8), 22(15); 7:5,31; 8:16,20,21,28; 9:10,13, 14,17,20; 16:25; 17:6; **Num.** 5:26; 16:40; 18:17; **1 Sam.** 2:15,16,28; **1 Kgs.** 3:3; 9:25; 11:8; 12:33; 13:1,2; 22:43; **2 Kgs.** 12:3(4); 14:4; 15:4,35; 16:4,13,15; 17:11; 18:4; 22:17; 23:5,8; **1 Chr.** 6:49(34); 23:13; **2 Chr.** 2:4(3),6(5); 13:11; 25:14; 26:16,18,19; 28:3,4,25; 29:7,11; 30:14; 32:12; 34:25; **Song** 3:6; **Isa.** 65:3,7; **Jer.** 1:16; 7:9; 11:12,13,17; 18:15; 19:4,13; 32:29; 33:18; 44:3,5,8,15,17–19,21, 23,25; 48:35; **Hos.** 2:13; 4:13; 11:2; **Amos** 4:5; **Hab.** 1:16; **Mal.** 1:11.

7000. קָטַר *qāṭar* **verb**
(to enclose, to be joined to)
Ezek. 46:22.

7001. I. קְטַר *q^eṭar* **Aram. masc. noun**
(hip joint)
Dan. 5:6.
II. קְטַר *q^eṭar* **Aram. masc. noun**
(difficult problem)
Dan. 5:12,16.

7002. קִטֵּר *qiṭṭēr* **fem. noun**
(incense)
Jer. 44:21.

7003. קִטְרוֹן *qiṭrôn* **proper noun**
(Kitron)
Judg. 1:30.

7004. קְטֹרֶת *q^eṭōreṯ* **fem. noun**
(incense, perfume)
Ex. 25:6; 30:1,7–9,27,35,37; 31:8,11; 35:8,15,28; 37:25,29; 39:38; 40:5,27;

Lev. 4:7; 10:1; 16:12,13; **Num.** 4:16; 7:14,20,26,32,38,44,50,56,62,68,74,80, 86; 16:7,17,18,35,40(17:5),46(17:11), 47(17:12); **1 Sam.** 2:28; **1 Chr.** 6:49(34); 28:18; **2 Chr.** 2:4(3); 13:11; 26:16,19; 29:7; **Ps.** 66:15; 141:2; **Prov.** 27:9; **Isa.** 1:13; **Ezek.** 8:11; 16:18; 23:41.

7005. קַטָּת *qaṭṭāṯ* **proper noun**
(Kattath, Kattah)
Josh. 19:15.

7006. I. קִיא *qiy'* **verb**
(to vomit; KJV, *qôh* [6958,I])
Lev. 18:25,28; 20:22; **Job** 20:15; **Prov.** 23:8; 25:16; **Jon.** 2:10(11).
II. קִיא *qiy'* **masc. noun**
(to vomit; KJV, *qēy'* [6892,B])
Isa. 19:14; 28:8; **Jer.** 48:26.

7007. קַיִט *qayiṭ* **Aram. masc. noun**
(summer; corr. to Hebr. 7019)
Dan. 2:35.

7008. קִיטוֹר *qiyṭôr*, קִיטֹר *qiyṭōr* **masc. noun**
(smoke, dense smoke)
Gen. 19:28; **Ps.** 119:83; 148:8.

7009. I. קִים *qiym* **masc. noun**
(adversary, foe)
Job 22:20(KJV, see II).
II. קִים *qiym* **masc. noun**
(substance)
Job 22:20(NASB, NIV, see I).

7010. קְיָם *q^{e}yām* **Aram. masc. noun**
(statute, edict)
Dan. 6:7(8),15(16).

7011. קַיָּם *qayyām* **Aram. adj.**
(assured, enduring)
Dan. 4:26(23); 6:26(27).

7012. קִימָה *qiymāh* **fem. noun**
(a rising up, standing)
Lam. 3:63.

7013. קַיִן *qayin* **masc. noun**
(spear, spearhead)
2 Sam. 21:16.

7014. I. קַיִן *qayin* **masc. proper noun**
(Cain; first son of Adam)
Gen. 4:1–3,5,6,8,9,13,15–17,24,25.
II. קַיִן *qayin* **masc. proper noun**
(Kain; city in Judah)
Num. 24:22(KJV, NIV, see III); **Josh.** 15:57.
III. קַיִן *qayin* **masc. proper noun**
(Kenite)
Num. 24:22(NASB, see II); **Judg.** 4:11.

7015. קִינָה *qiynāh* **fem. noun**
(lament, funeral lamentation)
2 Sam. 1:17; **2 Chr.** 35:25; **Jer.** 7:29; 9:10(9),20(19); **Ezek.** 2:10; 19:1,14; 26:17; 27:2,32; 28:12; 32:2,16; **Amos** 5:1; 8:10.

7016. קִינָה *qiynāh* **proper noun**
(Kinah)
Josh. 15:22.

7017. קֵינִי *qēyniy* **masc. proper noun**
(Kenite)
Gen. 15:19; **Num.** 24:21; **Judg.** 1:16; 4:11,17; 5:24; **1 Sam.** 15:6; 27:10; 30:29; **1 Chr.** 2:55.

7018. קֵינָן *qēynān* **masc. proper noun**
(Kenan, Cainan)
Gen. 5:9,10,12–14; **1 Chr.** 1:2.

7019. קַיִץ *qayiṣ* **masc. noun**
(summer, summer fruit)
Gen. 8:22; **2 Sam.** 16:1,2; **Ps.** 32:4; 74:17; **Prov.** 6:8; 10:5; 26:1; 30:25; **Isa.** 16:9; 28:4; **Jer.** 8:20; 40:10,12; 48:32; **Amos** 3:15; 8:1,2; **Mic.** 7:1; **Zech.** 14:8.

7020. קִיצוֹן *qiyṣôn* **adj.**
(outermost, at the end)
Ex. 26:4,10; 36:11,17.

7021. קִיקָיוֹן *qiyqāyôn* **masc. noun**
(plant, vine, gourd)
Jon. 4:6,7,9,10.

7022. קִיקָלוֹן *qiyqālôn* **masc. noun**
(disgrace)
Hab. 2:16.

7023. קִיר *qiyr,* קִר *qir,* קִירָה *qiyrāh* **masc. noun**
(wall, side)
Ex. 30:3; 37:26; **Lev.** 1:15; 5:9; 14:37,39; **Num.** 22:25; 35:4; **Josh.** 2:15; **1 Sam.** 18:11; 19:10; 20:25; 25:22,34; **2 Sam.** 5:11; **1 Kgs.** 4:33(5:13); 6:5,6, 15,16,27,29; 14:10; 16:11; 21:21; **2 Kgs.** 4:10; 9:8,33; 20:2; **1 Chr.** 14:1; 29:4; **2 Chr.** 3:7,11,12; **Ps.** 62:3(4); **Isa.** 22:5; 25:4; 38:2; 59:10; **Jer.** 4:19; 48:31,36; **Ezek.** 4:3; 8:7,8,10; 12:5,7,12; 13:12, 14,15; 23:14; 33:30; 41:5,6,9,12,13,17, 20,22,25; 43:8; **Amos** 5:19; **Hab.** 2:11.

7024. A. קִיר *qiyr* **proper noun**
(Kir: a city in Mesopotamia)
2 Kgs. 16:9; **Isa.** 22:6; **Amos** 1:5; 9:7.
B. קִיר *qiyr* **proper noun**
(Kir: a city in Moab; possibly the same as Kir Hareseth [7025])
Isa. 15:1.

7025. קִיר חֲרֶשֶׂת *qiyr ḥ^a^reśet,* קִיר חֶרֶשׂ *qiyr ḥereś* **proper noun**
(Kir Hareseth, Kir Heres: a city in Moab)
2 Kgs. 3:25; **Isa.** 16:7,11; **Jer.** 48:31,36.

7026. קֵירֹס *qēyrōs,* קֵרֹס *qērōs* **masc. proper noun**
(Keros)
Ezra 2:44; **Neh.** 7:47.

7027. קִישׁ *qiyš* **masc. proper noun**
(Kish)
1 Sam. 9:1,3; 10:11,21; 14:51; **2 Sam.** 21:14; **1 Chr.** 8:30,33; 9:36,39; 12:1; 23:21,22; 24:29; 26:28; **2 Chr.** 29:12; **Esth.** 2:5.

7028. קִישׁוֹן *qiyšôn* **proper noun**
(Kishon)
Judg. 4:7,13; 5:21; **1 Kgs.** 18:40; **Ps.** 83:9(10).

7029. קִישִׁי *qiyšiy* **masc. proper noun**
(Kishi)
1 Chr. 6:44(29).

7030. קִיתָרֹס *qiyṯārōs* **Aram. masc. noun**
(zither, lyre, harp)
Dan. 3:5,7,10,15.

7031. קַל *qal* **adj.**
(swift, speedy)
2 Sam. 2:18; **Job** 24:18; **Eccl.** 9:11; **Isa.** 5:26; 18:2; 19:1; 30:16; **Jer.** 2:23; 46:6; **Lam.** 4:19; **Joel** 3:4(4:4); **Amos** 2:14,15.

7032. קָל *qāl* **Aram. masc. noun**
(sound, voice; corr. to Hebr. 6963)
Dan. 3:5,7,10,15; 4:31[28]; 6:20(21); 7:11.

7033. I. קָלָה *qālāh* **verb**
(to roast, to parch, to dry)
Lev. 2:14; **Josh.** 5:11; **Jer.** 29:22.
II. קָלָה *qālāh* **verb**
(to be burning, to be searing [of pain])
Ps. 38:7(8)(KJV, see III).
III. קָלָה *qālāh* **verb**
(to be loathsome)
Ps. 38:7(8)(NASB, NIV, see II).

7034. קָלָה *qālāh* **verb**
(to be lightly esteemed, to despised)

Deut. 25:3; 27:16; **1 Sam.** 18:23 (KJV, NASB, *qālal* [7043]); **Prov.** 12:9; **Isa.** 3:5; 16:14.

7035. קָלָה *qālāh* **verb**
(to assemble, to be gathered together)
2 Sam. 20:14(NASB, NIV, [Q^{e}] *qāhal* [6950]).

7036. קָלוֹן *qālôn* **masc. noun**
(shame, disgrace)
Job 10:15; **Ps.** 83:16(17); **Prov.** 3:35; 6:33; 9:7; 11:2; 12:16; 13:18; 18:3; 22:10; **Isa.** 22:18; **Jer.** 13:26; 46:12; **Hos.** 4:7,18; **Nah.** 3:5; **Hab.** 2:16.

7037. קַלַּחַת *qallaḥaṯ* **fem. noun**
(cauldron, kettle)
1 Sam. 2:14; **Mic.** 3:3.

7038. קָלַט *qālaṭ* **verb**
(to be stunted, to be deformed)
Lev. 22:23.

7039. קָלִי *qāliy,* קָלִיא *qāliy'* **masc. noun**
(parched or roasted grain)
Lev. 23:14; **Ruth** 2:14; **1 Sam.** 17:17; 25:18; **2 Sam.** 17:28.

7040. קַלָּי *qallāy* **masc. proper noun**
(Kallai)
Neh. 12:20.

7041. קֵלָיָה *qēlāyāh* **masc. proper noun**
(Kelaiah)
Ezra 10:23.

7042. קְלִיטָא *qeliyṭā'* **masc. proper noun**
(Kelita)
Ezra 10:23; **Neh.** 8:7; 10:10(11).

7043. קָלַל *qālal* **verb**
(to curse, to blaspheme, to consider trivial or insignificant, to be trivial, to be insignificant)
Gen. 8:8,11,21; 12:3; 16:4,5; **Ex.** 18:22; 21:17; 22:28(27); **Lev.** 19:14; 20:9; 24:11,14,15,23; **Deut.** 23:4(5); **Josh.** 24:9; **Judg.** 9:27; **1 Sam.** 2:30; 3:13; 6:5; 17:43; 18:23(NIV, *qālāh* [7034]); **2 Sam.** 1:23; 6:22; 16:5,7,9–11,13; 19:21(22), 43(44); **1 Kgs.** 2:8; 12:4,9,10; 16:31; **2 Kgs.** 2:24; 3:18; 20:10; **2 Chr.** 10:4,9,10; **Neh.** 13:2,25; **Job** 3:1; 7:6; 9:25; 24:18; 40:4; **Ps.** 37:22; 62:4(5); 109:28; **Prov.** 14:6; 20:20; 30:10,11; **Eccl.** 7:21,22; 10:10,20; **Isa.** 8:21; 9:1(8:23); 23:9; 30:16; 49:6; 65:20; **Jer.** 4:13,24; 6:14; 8:11; 15:10; **Ezek.** 8:17; 21:21(26); 22:7; **Jon.** 1:5; **Nah.** 1:14; **Hab.** 1:8.

7044. קָלָל *qālal* **adj.**
(polished, burnished)
Ezek. 1:7; **Dan.** 10:6.

7045. קְלָלָה *q^{e}lālāh* **fem. noun**
(curse, cursing)
Gen. 27:12,13; **Deut.** 11:26,28,29; 21:23; 23:5(6); 27:13; 28:15,45; 29:27(26); 30:1,19; **Josh.** 8:34; **Judg.** 9:57; **2 Sam.** 16:12; **1 Kgs.** 2:8; **2 Kgs.** 22:19; **Neh.** 13:2; **Ps.** 109:17,18; **Prov.** 26:2; 27:14; **Jer.** 24:9; 25:18; 26:6; 29:22; 42:18; 44:8,12,22; 49:13; **Zech.** 8:13.

7046. קָלַס *qālas* **verb**
(to mock, to deride, to scorn)
2 Kgs. 2:23; **Ezek.** 16:31; 22:5; **Hab.** 1:10.

7047. קֶלֶס *qeles* **masc. noun**
(derision, reproach)
Ps. 44:13(14); 79:4; **Jer.** 20:8.

7048. קַלָּסָה *qallāsāh* **fem. noun**
(mocking, laughingstock)
Ezek. 22:4.

7049. I. קָלַע *qāla'* **verb**
(to sling, to hurl)

Judg. 20:16; **1 Sam.** 17:49; 25:29; **Jer.** 10:18.

II. קָלַע *qāla'* **verb**
(to carve)
1 Kgs. 6:29,32,35.

7050. I. קֶלַע *qela'* **masc. noun**
(sling, sling stone)
1 Sam. 17:40,50; 25:29; **2 Chr.** 26:14; **Job** 41:28(20); **Zech.** 9:15.

II. קֶלַע *qela'* **masc. noun**
(curtain, drape, hanging)
Ex. 27:9,11,12,14,15; 35:17; 38:9,12, 14–16,18; 39:40; **Num.** 3:26; 4:26; **1 Kgs.** 6:34.

7051. קַלָּע *qallā'* **masc. noun**
(slinger, man armed with a sling)
2 Kgs. 3:25.

7052. קְלֹקֵל *qᵉlōqēl* **adj.**
(miserable, worthless)
Num. 21:5.

7053. קִלְּשׁוֹן *qillᵉšôn* **masc. noun**
(pitchfork)
1 Sam. 13:21.

7054. קָמָה *qāmāh* **fem. noun**
(standing grain, stalk)
Ex. 22:6(5); **Deut.** 16:9; 23:25(26); **Judg.** 15:5; **2 Kgs.** 19:26(NIV, *qûm* [6965]); **Isa.** 17:5; 37:27(NIV, *qûm* [6965]); **Hos.** 8:7.

7055. A. קְמוּאֵל *qᵉmû'ēl* **masc. proper noun**
(Kemuel: nephew of Abraham)
Gen. 22:21.

B. קְמוּאֵל *qᵉmû'ēl* **masc. proper noun**
(Kemuel: an Ephraimite)
Num. 34:24.

C. קְמוּאֵל *qᵉmû'ēl* **masc. proper noun**
(Kemuel: a Levite)
1 Chr. 27:17.

7056. קָמוֹן *qāmôn* **proper noun**
(Kamon)
Judg. 10:5.

7057. קִמּוֹשׂ *qimmôś* **masc. coll. noun**
(thistles, nettles)
Isa. 34:13; **Prov.** 24:31(KJV, *qimmāśôn* [7063]); **Hos.** 9:6.

7058. קֶמַח *qemaḥ* **masc. noun**
(flour, meal)
Gen. 18:6; **Num.** 5:15; **Judg.** 6:19; **1 Sam.** 1:24; 28:24; **2 Sam.** 17:28; **1 Kgs.** 4:22; 17:12,14,16; **2 Kgs.** 4:41; **1 Chr.** 12:40(41); **Isa.** 47:2; **Hos.** 8:7.

7059. I. קָמַט *qāmaṭ* **verb**
(to cause to shrivel; to fill with wrinkles)
Job 16:8(NIV, see II).

II. קָמַט *qāmaṭ* **verb**
(to bind)
Job 16:8(KJV, NASB, see I).

III. קָמַט *qāmaṭ* **verb**
(to snatch away; to cut down)
Job 22:16.

7060. I. קָמַל *qāmal* **verb**
(to wither, to rot away)
Isa. 19:6; 33:9(KJV, see II).

II. קָמַל *qāmal* **verb**
(to wither, to rot away)
Isa. 33:9(NASB, NIV, see I).

7061. קָמַץ *qāmaṣ* **verb**
(to take [a handful])
Lev. 2:2; 5:12; **Num.** 5:26.

7062. קֹמֶץ *qōmeṣ* **masc. noun**
(handful; abundance)
Gen. 41:47; **Lev.** 2:2; 5:12; 6:15(8).

7063. קִמָּשׂוֹן *qimmaśôn* **masc. coll. noun**
(thorns)
Prov. 24:31(NASB, NIV, *qimmôś* [7057]).

7064. I. קֵן *qēn* **masc. noun**
(a nest [of a bird])
Num. 24:21; **Deut.** 22:6; 32:11; **Job** 29:18; 39:27; **Ps.** 84:3(4); **Prov.** 27:8; **Isa.** 10:14; 16:2; **Jer.** 49:16; **Obad.** 1:4; **Hab.** 2:9.
II. קֵן *qēn* **masc. noun**
(a nest [of a bird])
Gen. 6:14.

7065. קָנָא *qānā'* **verb**
(to be jealous, to be envious, to be zealous)
Gen. 26:14; 30:1; 37:11; **Num.** 5:14,30; 11:29; 25:11,13; **Deut.** 32:16,21; **2 Sam.** 21:2; **1 Kgs.** 14:22; 19:10,14; **Ps.** 37:1; 73:3; 78:58; 106:16; **Prov.** 3:31; 23:17; 24:1,19; **Isa.** 11:13; **Ezek.** 8:3; 31:9; 39:25; **Joel** 2:18; **Zech.** 1:14; 8:2.

7066. קְנָא *q^e^nā'* **Aram. verb**
(to buy; corr. to Hebr. 7069)
Ezra 7:17.

7067. קַנָּא *qannā'* **adj.**
(jealous)
Ex. 20:5; 34:14; **Deut.** 4:24; 5:9; 6:15.

7068. קִנְאָה *qin'āh* **fem. noun**
(jealousy, envy, zeal)
Num. 5:14,15,18,25,29,30; 25:11; **Deut.** 29:20(19); **2 Kgs.** 10:16; 19:31; **Job** 5:2; **Ps.** 69:9(10); 79:5; 119:139; **Prov.** 6:34; 14:30; 27:4; **Eccl.** 4:4; 9:6; **Song** 8:6; **Isa.** 9:7(6); 11:13; 26:11; 37:32; 42:13; 59:17; 63:15; **Ezek.** 5:13; 8:3,5; 16:38, 42; 23:25; 35:11; 36:5,6; 38:19; **Zeph.** 1:18; 3:8; **Zech.** 1:14; 8:2.

7069. I. קָנָה *qānāh* **verb**
(to buy, to purchase, to acquire, to possess)
Gen. 4:1(NIV, see II); 14:19(NIV, see II),22(NIV, see II); 25:10; 33:19; 39:1; 47:19,20,22,23; 49:30; 50:13; **Ex.** 15:16; 21:2; **Lev.** 22:11; 25:14,15,28,30,44, 45,50; 27:24; **Deut.** 28:68; 32:6 (NIV, see II); **Josh.** 24:32; **Ruth** 4:4,5,8–10; **2 Sam.** 12:3; 24:21,24; **1 Kgs.** 16:24; **2 Kgs.** 12:12(13); 22:6; **1 Chr.** 21:24; **2 Chr.** 34:11; **Neh.** 5:8,16; **Ps.** 74:2; 78:54; 139:13(NASB, NIV, see II); **Prov.** 1:5; 4:5,7; 8:22(NIV, see II); 15:32; 16:16; 17:16; 18:15; 19:8; 20:14; 23:23; **Eccl.** 2:7; **Isa.** 1:3; 11:11; 24:2; 43:24; **Jer.** 13:1,2,4; 19:1; 32:7–9, 15,25,43,44; **Ezek.** 7:12; **Amos** 8:6; **Zech.** 11:5; 13:5(NIV, *qinyān* [7075]).
II. קָנָה *qānāh* **verb**
(to create, to bring forth)
Gen. 4:1(KJV, NASB, see I); 14:19(KJV, NASB, see I),22(KJV, NASB, see I); **Deut.** 32:6(KJV, NASB, see I); **Ps.** 139:13(KJV, see I); **Prov.** 8:22(KJV, NASB, see I).

7070. קָנֶה *qāneh* **masc. noun**
(red, stalk, reed, calamus reed; beam of scales)
Gen. 41:5,22; **Ex.** 25:31–33,35,36; 30:23; 37:17–19,21,22; **1 Kgs.** 14:15; **2 Kgs.** 18:21; **Job** 31:22; 40:21; **Ps.** 68:30(31); **Song** 4:14; **Isa.** 19:6; 35:7; 36:6; 42:3; 43:24; 46:6; **Jer.** 6:20; **Ezek.** 27:19; 29:6; 40:3,5–8; 41:8; 42:16–19.

7071. A. קָנָה *qānāh* **proper noun**
(Kanah: stream between Ephraim and Manasseh)
Josh. 16:8; 17:9.
B. קָנָה *qānāh* **proper noun**
(Kanah: city on Asher's border)
Josh. 19:28.

7072. קַנּוֹא *qannô'* **adj.**
(jealous)
Josh. 24:19; **Nah.** 1:2.

7073. A. קְנַז *q^e^naz* **masc. proper noun**
(Kenaz: grandson of Esau)
Gen. 36:11,15,42; **1 Chr.** 1:36,53.
B. קְנַז *q^e^naz* **masc. proper noun**
(Kenaz: father of Othniel)
Josh. 15:17; **Judg.** 1:13; 3:9,11; **1 Chr.** 4:13.

C. קְנַז *q^e^naz* **masc. proper noun**
(Kenaz: grandson of Caleb)
1 Chr. 4:15.

7074. קְנִזִּי *q^e^nizziy* **masc. proper noun**
(Kenizzite)
Gen. 15:19; **Num.** 32:12; **Josh.** 14:6,14.

7075. קִנְיָן *qinyān* **masc. noun**
(goods, possessions, property)
Gen. 31:18; 34:23; 36:6; **Lev.** 22:11; **Josh.** 14:4; **Ps.** 104:24; 105:21; **Prov.** 4:7; **Ezek.** 38:12,13; **Zech.** 13:5(KJV, NASB, *qānāh* [7069]).

7076. קִנָּמוֹן *qinnāmôn* **masc. noun**
(cinnamon)
Ex. 30:23; **Prov.** 7:17; **Song** 4:14.

7077. קָנַן *qānan* **verb**
(to make a nest; to build a nest)
Ps. 104:17; **Isa.** 34:15; **Jer.** 22:23; 48:28; **Ezek.** 31:6.

7078. I. קֶנֶץ *qenes̱* **masc. noun**
(snare for hunting)
Job 18:2(KJV, NIV, see II).
II. קֶנֶץ *qenes̱* **masc. noun**
(an ending)
Job 18:2(NASB, see I).

7079. קְנָת *q^e^nāṯ* **proper noun**
(Kenath)
Num. 32:42; **1 Chr.** 2:23.

7080. קָסַם *qāsam* **verb**
(to practice divination, to seek omens)
Deut. 18:10,14; **Josh.** 13:22; **1 Sam.** 6:2; 28:8; **2 Kgs.** 17:17; **Isa.** 3:2; 44:25; **Jer.** 27:9; 29:8; **Ezek.** 13:9,23; 21:21(26), 23(28),29(34); 22:28; **Mic.** 3:6,7,11; **Zech.** 10:2.

7081. קֶסֶם *qesem* **masc. noun**
(divination; witchcraft)
Num. 22:7; 23:23; **Deut.** 18:10; **1 Sam.** 15:23; **2 Kgs.** 17:17; **Prov.** 16:10; **Jer.** 14:14; **Ezek.** 13:6,23; 21:21(26),22(27).

7082. קָסַס *qāsas* **verb**
(to cut off, to strip off)
Ezek. 17:9.

7083. קֶסֶת *qeseṯ* **fem. noun**
(inkhorn; writing kit)
Ezek. 9:2,3,11.

7084. קְעִילָה *q^e^ʿiylāh* **proper noun**
(Keilah)
Josh. 15:44; **1 Sam.** 23:1–8,10–13; **1 Chr.** 4:19; **Neh.** 3:17,18.

7085. קַעֲקַע *qaʿ^a^qaʿ* **masc. noun**
(tattoo, mark)
Lev. 19:28.

7086. קְעָרָה *q^e^ʿārāh* **fem. noun**
(plate, dish)
Ex. 25:29; 37:16; **Num.** 4:7; 7:13,19,25, 31,37,43,49,55,61,67,73,79,84,85.

7087. קָפָא *qāp̱āʾ* **verb**
(to curdle, to congeal; to become settled, to become stagnant)
Ex. 15:8; **Job** 10:10; **Zeph.** 1:12; **Zech.** 14:6.

7088. I. קָפַד *qāp̱aḏ* **verb**
(to roll up)
Isa. 38:12(KJV, see II).
II. קָפַד *qāp̱aḏ* **verb**
(to cut off)
Isa. 38:12(NASB, NIV, see I).

7089. קְפָדָה *q^e^p̱āḏāh* **fem. noun**
(destruction, anguish, terror)
Ezek. 7:25.

7090. I. קִפּוֹד *qippôḏ*, קִפֹּד *qippōḏ* **masc. noun**
(porcupine)

7091. I. קִפֹּז *qippôz*

Isa. 14:23(NIV, see II; KJV, see III); 34:11(NIV, see II; KJV, see III); **Zeph.** 2:14(NIV, see II; KJV, see III).
II. קִפּוֹד *qippôḏ,* קִפֹּד *qippōḏ* **masc. noun**
(owl)
Isa. 14:23(NASB, see I; KJV, see III); 34:11(NASB, see I; KJV, see III); **Zeph.** 2:14(NASB, see I; KJV, see III).
III. קִפּוֹד *qippôḏ,* קִפֹּד *qippōḏ* **masc. noun**
(bittern: a wading marsh bird)
Isa. 14:23(NASB, see I; KJV, see II); 34:11(NASB, see I; KJV, see II); **Zeph.** 2:14(NASB, see I; KJV, see II).

7091. I. קִפֹּז *qippôz* **masc. noun**
(owl, great owl)
Isa. 34:15(NASB, see II).
II. קִפֹּז *qippôz* **masc. noun**
(tree snake)
Isa. 34:15(KJV, NIV, see I).

7092. קָפַץ *qāpaṣ* **verb**
(to gather up, to shut, to close)
Deut. 15:7; **Job** 5:16; 24:24; **Ps.** 77:9(10); 107:42; **Song** 2:8; **Isa.** 52:15.

7093. קֵץ *qēṣ* **masc. noun**
(end [of a time or space])
Gen. 4:3; 6:13; 8:6; 16:3; 41:1; **Ex.** 12:41; **Num.** 13:25; **Deut.** 9:11; 15:1; 31:10; **Judg.** 11:39; **2 Sam.** 14:26; 15:7; **1 Kgs.** 2:39; 17:7; **2 Kgs.** 19:23; **2 Chr.** 8:1; 18:2; 21:19; **Neh.** 13:6; **Esth.** 2:12; **Job** 6:11; 16:3; 22:5; 28:3; **Ps.** 39:4(5); 119:96; **Eccl.** 4:8,16; 12:12; **Isa.** 9:7(6); 23:15,17; 37:24; **Jer.** 13:6; 34:14; 42:7; 50:26; 51:13; **Lam.** 4:18; **Ezek.** 7:2,3,6; 21:25(30),29(34); 29:13; 35:5; **Dan.** 8:17,19; 9:26; 11:6,13,27,35,40,45; 12:4, 6,9,13; **Amos** 8:2; **Hab.** 2:3.

7094. קָצַב *qāṣaḇ* **verb**
(to cut down; to cut off, to shear)
2 Kgs. 6:6; **Song** 4:2.

7095. I. קֶצֶב *qeṣeḇ* **masc. noun**
(shape, form, size)
1 Kgs. 6:25; 7:37.
II. קֶצֶב *qeṣeḇ* **masc. noun**
(base, root, bottom)
Jon. 2:6(7).

7096. קָצָה *qāṣāh* **verb**
(to cut off; to scrape)
Lev. 14:41,43; **2 Kgs.** 10:32; **Prov.** 26:6; **Hab.** 2:10(NIV, *qāṣāh* [7098]).

7097. I. קָצֶה *qāṣeh* **masc. noun**
(end, extremity, border, edge)
Gen. 8:3; 19:4; 23:9; 47:2,21; **Ex.** 13:20; 16:35; 19:12; 26:5,28; 36:12,33; **Num.** 11:1; 20:16; 22:36,41; 23:13; 33:6,37; 34:3; **Deut.** 4:32; 13:7; 14:28; 28:49,64; 30:4; **Josh.** 3:2,8,15; 4:19; 9:16; 13:27; 15:1,2,5,8,21; 18:15,16,19; **Judg.** 6:21; 7:11,17,19; **Ruth** 3:7; **1 Sam.** 9:27; 14:2,27,43; **2 Sam.** 24:8; **1 Kgs.** 9:10; **2 Kgs.** 7:5,8; 8:3; 18:10; **Neh.** 1:9; **Ps.** 19:4(5),6(7); 46:9(10); 61:2(3); 135:7; **Prov.** 17:24; **Isa.** 5:26; 7:3,18; 13:5; 26:15(NASB, NIV, *qāṣû* [7099]); 42:10; 43:6; 48:20; 49:6; 56:11; 62:11; **Jer.** 10:13; 12:12; 25:31,33; 51:16,31; **Ezek.** 3:16; 25:9; 33:2; 39:14; 48:1.
II. קָצֶה *qēṣeh* **masc. noun**
(end, limit [used only in negatives])
Isa. 2:7; **Nah.** 2:9(10); 3:3,9.

7098. קָצָה *qāṣāh* **fem. noun**
(end, edge, extremity)
Ex. 25:18,19; 26:4; 27:4; 28:7,23–26; 36:11; 37:7,8(KJV, *qāṣû* [7099]); 39:4 (KJV, *qāṣû* [7099]; NIV, *qᵉsāṯ* [7117]), 16–19; **Judg.** 18:2; **1 Kgs.** 6:24; 12:31; 13:33; **2 Kgs.** 17:32; **Job** 26:14; 28:24; **Ps.** 19:6(7); 65:8(NASB, NIV, *qᵉsāṯ* [7117]); **Isa.** 40:28; 41:5,9; **Jer.** 49:36; **Ezek.** 15:4; **Hab.** 2:10(KJV, NASB, *qāṣāh* [7096]).

7099. קָצוּ *qāṣû,* קִצְוָה *qiṣwāh* **masc. noun**

(end, extremity, corner)
Ex. 37:8(NASB, NIV, *qāṣāh* [7098]); 38:5(NASB, NIV, *q^esāṯ* [7117]); 39:4(NASB, *q^esāṯ* [7117]; NIV, *qāṣāh* [7098]); **Ps.** 48:10(11); 65:5(6); **Isa.** 26:15(KJV, *qāṣeh* [7097,I]).

7100. קֶצַח *qeṣaḥ* **masc. noun**
(a seasoning plant: dill, caraway, fitch)
Isa. 28:25,27.

7101. קָצִין *qāṣiyn* **masc. noun**
(commander, ruler, chief)
Josh. 10:24; **Judg.** 11:6,11; **Prov.** 6:7; 25:15; **Isa.** 1:10; 3:6,7; 22:3; **Dan.** 11:18; **Mic.** 3:1,9.

7102. קְצִיעָה *q^eṣiy'āh* **fem. noun**
(cassia: a spice)
Ps. 45:8(9).

7103. קְצִיעָה *q^eṣiy'āh* **fem. proper noun**
(Keziah)
Job 42:14.

7104. קְצִיץ *q^eṣiyṣ* **proper noun**
(Keziz)
Josh. 18:21(NASB, NIV, *'ēmeq q^eṣiyṣ* [6010,II]).

7105. I. קָצִיר *qāṣiyr* **masc. noun**
(harvest, reaping)
Gen. 8:22; 30:14; 45:6; **Ex.** 23:16; 34:21,22; **Lev.** 19:9; 23:10,22; 25:5; **Deut.** 24:19; **Josh.** 3:15; **Judg.** 15:1; **Ruth** 1:22; 2:21,23; **1 Sam.** 6:13; 8:12; 12:17; **2 Sam.** 21:9,10; 23:13; **Job** 5:5; **Prov.** 6:8; 10:5; 20:4; 25:13; 26:1; **Isa.** 9:3(2); 16:9; 17:5,11; 18:4,5; 23:3; **Jer.** 5:17,24; 8:20; 50:16; 51:33; **Hos.** 6:11; **Joel** 1:11; 3:13(4:13); **Amos** 4:7.
II. קָצִיר *qāṣiyr* **masc. noun**
(bough, branch)
Job 14:9; 18:16; 29:19; **Ps.** 80:11(12); **Isa.** 27:11.

7106. I. קָצַע *qāṣa'* **verb**
(to scrape)
Lev. 14:41.
II. קָצַע *qāṣa'* **verb**
(to form a bend or corner)
Ex. 26:23(KJV, *m^equṣ'āh* [4742]; NASB, *miqṣôa'* [4740]); 36:28; **Ezek.** 46:22(NASB, *miqṣôa'* [4740]).

7107. קָצַף *qāṣaṗ* **verb**
(to be angry)
Gen. 40:2; 41:10; **Ex.** 16:20; **Lev.** 10:6,16; **Num.** 16:22; 31:14; **Deut.** 1:34; 9:7,8,19,22; **Josh.** 22:18; **1 Sam.** 29:4; **2 Kgs.** 5:11; 13:19; **Esth.** 1:12; 2:21; **Ps.** 106:32; **Eccl.** 5:6(5); **Isa.** 8:21; 47:6; 54:9; 57:16,17; 64:5(4),9(8); **Jer.** 37:15; **Lam.** 5:22; **Zech.** 1:2,15; 8:14.

7108. קְצַף *q^eṣaṗ* **Aram. verb**
(to be angry; corr. to Hebr. 7107)
Dan. 2:12.

7109. קְצַף *q^eṣaṗ* **Aram. masc. noun**
(wrath; corr. to Hebr. 7110)
Ezra 7:23.

7110. I. קֶצֶף *qeṣeṗ* **masc. noun**
(wrath; anger)
Num. 1:53; 16:46(17:11); 18:5; **Deut.** 29:28; **Josh.** 9:20; 22:20; **2 Kgs.** 3:27; **1 Chr.** 27:24; **2 Chr.** 19:2,10; 24:18; 29:8; 32:25,26; **Esth.** 1:18; **Ps.** 38:1; 102:10; **Eccl.** 5:17(16); **Isa.** 34:2; 54:8; 60:10; **Jer.** 10:10; 21:5; 32:37; 50:13; **Zech.** 1:2,15; 7:12.
II. קֶצֶף *qeṣeṗ* **masc. noun**
(stick, twig)
Hos. 10:7(KJV, see III).
III. קֶצֶף *qeṣeṗ* **masc. noun**
(foam)
Hos. 10:7(NASB, NIV, see II).

7111. קְצָפָה *q^eṣāṗāh* **fem. noun**
(a splintering, peeling of bark)
Joel 1:7.

7112. I. קָצַץ *qāṣaṣ* **verb**
(to cut off, to cut in pieces)
Ex. 39:3; **Deut.** 25:12; **Judg.** 1:6,7; **2 Sam.** 4:12; **2 Kgs.** 16:17; 18:16; 24:13; **2 Chr.** 28:24; **Ps.** 46:9(10); 129:4; **Jer.** 9:26(KJV, see II; NIV, see III); 25:23(KJV, see II; NIV, see III); 49:32(KJV, see II; NIV, see III).
II. קָצַץ *qāṣaṣ* **verb**
(to be at the end, to be at the utmost)
Jer. 9:26(NASB, see I; NIV, see III); 25:23(NASB, see I; NIV, see III); 49:32(NASB, see I; NIV, see III).
III. קָצוּץ *qāṣûṣ* **adj.**
(distant)
Jer. 9:26(NASB, see I; KJV, see II); 25:23(NASB, see I; KJV, see II); 49:32(NASB, see I; KJV, see II).

7113. קְצַץ *q^eṣaṣ* **Aram. verb**
(to cut off, to trim off; corr. to Hebr. 7112,I)
Dan. 4:14(11).

7114. I. קָצַר *qāṣar* **verb**
(to reap, to harvest)
Lev. 19:9; 23:10,22; 25:5,11; **Deut.** 24:19; **Ruth** 2:3–7,9,14; **1 Sam.** 6:13; 8:12; **2 Kgs.** 4:18; 19:29; **Job** 4:8; 24:6; **Ps.** 126:5; 129:7; **Prov.** 22:8; **Eccl.** 11:4; **Isa.** 17:5; 37:30; **Jer.** 9:22(21); 12:13; **Hos.** 8:7; 10:12,13; **Amos** 9:13; **Mic.** 6:15.
II. קָצַר *qāṣar* **verb**
(to shorten; to become impatient)
Num. 11:23; 21:4; **Judg.** 10:16; 16:16; **Job** 21:4; **Ps.** 89:45(46); 102:23(24); **Prov.** 10:27; **Isa.** 28:20; 50:2; 59:1; **Ezek.** 42:5; **Mic.** 2:7; **Zech.** 11:8.

7115. קוֹצֶר *qôṣer* **masc. noun**
(despair, discouragement, anguish)
Ex. 6:9.

7116. קָצֵר *qāṣār* **adj.**
(weak, few, hasty)
2 Kgs. 19:26; **Job** 14:1; **Prov.** 14:17,29; **Isa.** 37:27.

7117. קְצָת *q^eṣāṯ* **fem. noun**
(end, corner, part)
Ex. 38:5(KJV, *qāṣû* [7099]); 39:4(KJV, *qāṣû* [7099]; NIV, *qāṣāh* [7098]); **Neh.** 7:70(69); **Ps.** 65:8(9)(KJV, *qāṣāh* [7098]); **Dan.** 1:2,5,15,18.

7118. קְצָת *q^eṣāṯ* **fem. noun**
(end, part)
Dan. 2:42; 4:29(26),34(31).

7119. קַר *qar* **adj.**
(cold, cool; even-tempered)
Prov. 25:25; **Jer.** 18:14.

7120. קֹר *qōr* **masc. noun**
(cold)
Gen. 8:22.

7121. קָרָא *qārā'* **verb**
(to call, to cry out, to proclaim, to read)
Gen. 1:5,8,10; 2:19,20,23; 3:9,20; 4:17,25,26; 5:2,3,29; 11:9; 12:8,18; 13:4; 16:11,13–15; 17:5,15,19; 19:5,22,37,38; 20:8,9; 21:3,12,17,31,33; 22:11,14,15; 24:57,58; 25:25,26,30; 26:9,18,20–22, 25,33; 27:1,36,42; 28:1,19; 29:32–35; 30:6,8,11,13,18,20,21,24; 31:4,47,48,54; 32:2(3),30(31); 33:17,20; 35:7,8,10, 15,18; 38:3–5,29,30; 39:14,15,18; 41:8, 14,43,45,51,52; 45:1; 46:33; 47:29; 48:6,16; 49:1; 50:11; **Ex.** 1:18; 2:7,8,10, 20,22; 3:4; 7:11; 8:8(4),25(21); 9:27; 10:16,24; 12:21,31; 15:23; 16:31; 17:7,15; 19:3,7,20; 24:7,16; 31:2; 32:5; 33:7,19; 34:5,6,15,31; 35:30; 36:2; **Lev.** 1:1; 9:1; 10:4; 13:45; 23:2,4,21,37; 25:10; **Num.** 1:16(NASB, [K^e] *qāniy'* [7148]); 11:3,34; 12:5; 13:16,24; 16:12; 21:3; 22:5,20,37; 24:10; 25:2; 26:9(NASB, NIV, [Q^e] *qāriy'* [7148]); 32:38,41,42; **Deut.** 2:11,20; 3:9,13,14; 4:7; 5:1; 15:2,9; 17:19; 20:10; 24:15; 25:8,10; 28:10;

29:2(1); 31:7,11,14; 32:3; 33:19; **Josh.** 4:4; 5:9; 6:6; 7:26; 8:34,35; 9:22; 10:24; 19:47; 21:9; 22:1,34; 23:2; 24:1,9; **Judg.** 1:17,26; 2:5; 4:6; 6:24,32; 7:3,20; 8:1; 9:7,54; 10:4; 12:1; 13:24; 14:15; 15:17–19; 16:18,19,25,28; 18:12,23,29; 21:13; **Ruth** 1:20,21; 4:11,14,17; **1 Sam.** 1:20; 3:4–6,8–10,16; 4:21; 6:2; 7:12; 9:9,13, 22,24,26; 12:17,18; 16:3,5,8; 17:8; 19:7; 20:37,38; 22:11; 23:28; 24:8(9); 26:14; 28:15; 29:6; **2 Sam.** 1:7,15; 2:16,26; 5:9,20; 6:2,8; 9:2,9; 11:13; 12:24,25,28; 13:17,23; 14:33; 15:2,11; 17:5; 18:18, 25,26,28; 20:16; 21:2; 22:4,7; **1 Kgs.** 1:9,10,19,25,26,28,32,41,49; 2:36,42; 7:21; 8:43,52; 9:13; 12:3,20; 13:2,4, 21,32; 16:24; 17:10,11,20,21; 18:3, 24–28; 20:7; 21:9,12; 22:9,13; **2 Kgs.** 3:10,13; 4:12,15,22,36; 5:7,11; 6:11; 7:10,11; 8:1; 9:1; 10:19,20; 11:14; 12:7(8); 14:7; 18:4,18,28; 19:14; 20:11; 22:8,10,16; 23:2,16,17; **1 Chr.** 4:9,10; 6:65(50); 7:16,23; 11:7; 13:6,11; 14:11; 15:11; 16:8; 21:26; 22:6; 23:14; **2 Chr.** 3:17; 6:33; 7:14; 10:3; 14:11(10); 18:8,12; 20:3,26; 24:6; 32:18; 34:18,24,30; **Ezra** 2:61; 8:21; **Neh.** 5:12; 6:7; 7:63; 8:3, 8,18; 9:3; 13:1; **Esth.** 2:14; 3:12; 4:5,11; 5:12; 6:1,9,11; 8:9; 9:26; **Job** 1:4; 5:1; 9:16; 12:4; 13:22; 14:15; 17:14; 19:16; 27:10; 42:14; **Ps.** 3:4(5); 4:1(2),3(4); 14:4; 17:6; 18:3(4),6(7); 20:9(10); 22:2(3); 27:7; 28:1; 30:8(9); 31:17(18); 34:6(7); 42:7(8); 49:1(2); 50:1,4,15; 53:4(5); 55:16(17); 56:9(10); 57:2(3); 61:2(3); 66:17; 69:3(4); 79:6; 80:18(19); 81:7(8); 86:3,5,7; 88:9(10); 89:26(27); 91:15; 99:6; 102:2(3); 105:1,16; 116:2, 4,13,17; 118:5; 119:145,146; 120:1; 130:1; 138:3; 141:1; 145:18; 147:4,9; **Prov.** 1:21,24,28; 2:3; 7:4; 8:1,4; 9:3, 15,18; 12:23; 16:21; 18:6; 20:6; 21:13; 24:8; 27:16; **Eccl.** 6:10; **Song** 5:6; **Isa.** 1:13,26; 4:1; 6:3,4; 7:14; 8:3,4; 9:6(5); 12:4; 13:3; 14:20; 21:8,11; 22:12,20; 29:11,12; 30:7; 31:4; 32:5; 34:12,14,16; 35:8; 36:13; 37:14; 40:2,3,6,26; 41:2,4, 9,25; 42:6; 43:1,7,22; 44:5,7; 45:3,4; 46:11; 47:1,5; 48:1,2,8,12,13,15; 49:1; 50:2; 51:2; 54:5,6; 55:5,6; 56:7; 58:1,5, 9,12,13; 59:4; 60:14,18; 61:1–3,6; 62:2, 4,12; 63:19; 64:7(6); 65:1,12,15,24; 66:4; **Jer.** 1:15; 2:2; 3:4,12,17,19; 4:5,20; 6:30; 7:2,10,11,13,14,27,30; 9:17(16); 10:25; 11:6,14,16; 12:6; 14:9; 15:16; 19:2,6; 20:3,8; 23:6; 25:29; 29:12,29; 30:17; 31:6; 32:34; 33:3,16; 34:8,15,17; 35:17; 36:4,6,8–10,13–15,18,21,23; 42:8; 44:26; 46:17; 49:29; 51:61,63; **Lam.** 1:15,19,21; 2:22; 3:55,57; 4:15; **Ezek.** 8:18; 9:1,3; 10:13; 20:29; 23:23; 36:29; 38:21; 39:11; **Dan.** 2:2; 8:16; 9:18,19; 10:1; **Hos.** 1:4, 6,9; 2:16; 7:7,11; 11:1,2,7; **Joel** 1:14,19; 2:15,32; 3:9(4:9); **Amos** 4:5; 5:8,16; 7:4; 9:6,12; **Jon.** 1:2,6,14; 2:2(3); 3:2,4,5,8; **Mic.** 3:5; 6:9; **Hab.** 2:2; **Zeph.** 1:7; 3:9; **Hag.** 1:11; **Zech.** 1:4,14,17; 3:10; 7:7, 13; 8:3; 11:7; 13:9; **Mal.** 1:4.

7122. קָרָא *qārā'* **verb**
(to meet, to encounter, to come across; NASB, NIV, see also *qir'āh* [7125])
Gen. 42:4,38; 49:1; **Ex.** 1:10; 5:3; **Lev.** 10:19; **Deut.** 22:6; 31:29; **2 Sam.** 1:6; 18:9; 20:1; **Job** 4:14; **Isa.** 51:19; **Jer.** 13:22; 32:23; 44:23.

7123. קְרָא *q^erā'* **Aram. verb**
(to read; to call, to shout; corr. to Hebr. 7121)
Ezra 4:18,23; **Dan.** 3:4; 4:14(11); 5:7,8,12,15–17.

7124. קֹרֵא *qōrē'* **masc. noun**
(partridge)
1 Sam. 26:20; **Jer.** 17:11.

7125. קִרְאָה *qir'āh* **masc. noun**
(a meeting, encounter; NASB, NIV, Qal inf. constr. of *qārā'* [7122])
Gen. 14:17; 15:10; 18:2; 19:1; 24:17,65; 29:13; 30:16; 32:6(7); 33:4; 46:29; **Ex.** 4:14,27; 5:20; 7:15; 14:27; 18:7; 19:17;

Num. 20:18,20; 21:23,33; 22:34,36; 23:3; 24:1; 31:13; **Deut.** 1:44; 2:32; 3:1; 29:7(6); **Josh.** 8:5,14,22; 9:11; 11:20; **Judg.** 4:18,22; 6:35; 7:24; 11:31,34; 14:5; 15:14; 19:3; 20:25,31; **1 Sam.** 4:1,2; 9:14; 10:10; 13:10; 15:12; 16:4; 17:2,21, 48,55; 18:6; 21:1(2); 23:28; 25:20,32,34; 30:21; **2 Sam.** 6:20; 10:5,9,10,17; 15:32; 16:1; 18:6; 19:15(16),16(17),20(21), 24(25),25(26); **1 Kgs.** 2:8,19; 18:7,16; 20:27; 21:18; **2 Kgs.** 1:3,6,7; 2:15; 4:26,31; 5:21,26; 8:8,9; 9:17,18,21; 10:15; 16:10; 23:29; **1 Chr.** 19:5,10, 11,17; **2 Chr.** 35:20; **Job** 39:21; **Ps.** 35:3; 59:4(5); **Prov.** 7:10,15; **Isa.** 7:3; 14:9; 21:14; **Jer.** 41:6; 51:31; **Amos** 4:12; **Zech.** 2:3(7).

7126. קָרַב *qāraḇ* **verb**
(to bring near, to offer, to approach)
Gen. 12:11; 20:4; 27:41; 37:18; 47:29; **Ex.** 3:5; 12:48; 14:10,20; 16:9; 22:8(7); 28:1; 29:3,4,8,10; 32:19; 36:2; 40:12, 14,32; **Lev.** 1:2,3,5,10,13–15; 2:1,4,8, 11–14; 3:1,3,6,7,9,12,14; 4:3,14; 5:8; 6:14(7),20(13),21(14); 7:3,8,9,11–14, 16,18,25,29,33,35,38; 8:6,13,18,22,24; 9:2,5,7–9,15–17; 10:1,4,5,19; 12:7; 14:12; 16:1,6,9,11,20; 17:4; 18:6,14,19; 20:16; 21:6,8,17,18,21; 22:3,18,20–22,24,25; 23:8,16,18,25,27,36,37; 27:9,11; **Num.** 3:4,6; 5:9,16,25; 6:14,16; 7:2,3,10–12,18, 19; 8:9,10; 9:6,7,13; 15:4,7,9,10,13, 27,33; 16:5,9,10,17,35,38–40(17:3–5); 18:2–4,15,22; 25:6; 26:61; 27:1,5; 28:2,3,11,19,26,27; 29:8,13,36; 31:48,50; 36:1; **Deut.** 1:17,22; 2:19,37; 4:11; 5:23,27; 15:9; 20:2,10; 22:14; 25:11; 31:14; **Josh.** 3:4; 7:14,16–18; 8:5,23; 10:24; 17:4; **Judg.** 3:17,18; 5:25; 19:13; 20:24; **1 Sam.** 10:20,21; 14:36; 17:48; **2 Sam.** 15:5; 20:16,17; **1 Kgs.** 2:1,7; 20:29; **2 Kgs.** 16:12,14; **1 Chr.** 16:1; **2 Chr.** 35:12; **Ezra** 8:35; **Esth.** 5:2; **Job** 31:37; 33:22; **Ps.** 27:2; 32:9; 65:4(5); 69:18(19); 72:10; 91:10; 119:150,169; **Prov.** 5:8; **Eccl.** 5:1(4:17)(KJV, *qārûḇ* [7138]); **Isa.** 5:8,19; 8:3; 26:17; 34:1; 41:1,5,21; 46:13; 48:16; 54:14; 57:3; 65:5; **Jer.** 30:21; **Lam.** 3:57; 4:18; **Ezek.** 9:1; 12:23; 18:6; 22:4; 36:8; 37:7,17; 42:14; 43:22–24; 44:7,15,16,27; 46:4; **Hos.** 7:6; **Jon.** 1:6; **Zeph.** 3:2; **Hag.** 2:14; **Mal.** 1:8; 3:5.

7127. קְרֵב *qᵉrēḇ* **Aram. verb**
(to approach; to bring near, to offer; corr. to Hebr. 7126)
Ezra 6:10,17; 7:17; **Dan.** 3:8,26; 6:12(13),20(21); 7:13,16.

7128. קְרָב *qᵉrāḇ* **masc. noun**
(battle, war)
2 Sam. 17:11; **Job** 38:23; **Ps.** 55:18(19), 21(22); 68:30(31); 78:9; 144:1; **Eccl.** 9:18; **Zech.** 14:3.

7129. קְרָב *qᵉrāḇ* **Aram. masc. noun**
(war; corr. to Hebr. 7128)
Dan. 7:21.

7130. קֶרֶב *qereḇ* **masc. noun**
(midst, that which is within, among)
Gen. 18:12,24; 24:3; 25:22; 41:21; 45:6; 48:16; **Ex.** 3:20; 8:22(18); 10:1; 12:9; 17:7; 23:21,25; 29:13,17,22; 31:14; 33:3,5; 34:9,10,12; **Lev.** 1:9,13; 3:3,9,14; 4:8,11; 7:3; 8:16,21,25; 9:14; 17:4,10; 18:29; 20:3,5,6,18; 23:30; **Num.** 5:27; 11:4,20,21; 14:11,13,14,42,44; 15:30; **Deut.** 1:42; 2:14–16; 4:3,5,34; 6:15; 7:21; 11:6; 13:1(2),5(6),11(12),13(14), 14(15); 15:11; 16:11; 17:2,7,15,20; 18:2,15,18; 19:10,19,20; 21:8,9,21; 22:21,24; 23:14(15),16(17); 24:7; 26:11; 28:43; 29:11(10),16(15); 31:16,17; **Josh.** 1:11; 3:2,5,10; 4:6; 6:25; 7:12,13; 8:35; 9:7,16,22; 10:1; 13:13; 16:10; 18:7; 24:5,17,23; **Judg.** 1:29,30,32,33; 3:5; 10:16; 18:7,20; **1 Sam.** 4:3; 16:13; 25:37; **1 Kgs.** 3:28; 17:21,22; 20:39; **Job** 20:14; **Ps.** 5:9(10); 36:1; 39:3(4); 46:5(6); 48:9(10); 49:11(12); 51:10(12); 55:4(5),

10(11),11(12),15(16); 62:4(5); 64:6(7); 74:4,11,12; 78:28; 82:1; 94:19; 101:2,7; 103:1; 109:18,22; 110:2; 138:7; 147:13; **Prov.** 14:33; 15:31; 26:24; **Isa.** 4:4; 5:8,25; 6:12; 7:22; 10:23; 12:6; 16:11; 19:1,3,14,24; 24:13; 25:11; 26:9; 29:23; 63:11; **Jer.** 4:14; 6:1,6; 9:8(7); 14:9; 23:9; 29:8; 30:21; 31:33; 46:21; **Lam.** 1:15,20; 3:45; 4:13; **Ezek.** 11:19; 22:27; 36:26,27; **Hos.** 5:4; 11:9; **Joel** 2:27; **Amos** 2:3; 3:9; 5:17; 7:8,10; **Mic.** 3:11; 5:7(6),8(7), 10(9),13(12),14(13); 6:14; **Nah.** 3:13; **Hab.** 2:19; 3:2; **Zeph.** 3:3,5,11,12,15,17; **Zech.** 12:1; 14:1.

7131. קָרֵב *qāre͟b* **adj.**
(approaching, drawing near)
Num. 1:51; 3:10,38; 17:13(28); 18:7; **Deut.** 20:3; **1 Sam.** 17:41; **2 Sam.** 18:25; **1 Kgs.** 4:27(5:7); **Ezek.** 40:46; 45:4.

7132. קִרְבָה *qir͟bāh* **fem. noun**
(an approach; a drawing near, being near)
Ps. 73:28; **Isa.** 58:2.

7133. I. קָרְבָּן *qorbān* **masc. noun**
(offering, oblation)
Lev. 1:2,3,10,14; 2:1,4,5,7,12,13; 3:1,2,6–8,12,14; 4:23,28,32; 5:11; 6:20(13); 7:13–16,29,38; 9:7,15; 17:4; 22:18,27; 23:14; 27:9,11; **Num.** 5:15; 6:14,21; 7:3,10–13,17,19,23,25,29,31, 35,37,41,43,47,49,53,55,59,61,65,67,71, 73,77,79,83; 9:7,13; 15:4,25; 18:9; 28:2; 31:50; **Ezek.** 20:28; 40:43.
II. קֻרְבָּן *qurbān* **masc. noun**
(contribution, offering)
Neh. 10:34(35); 13:31.

7134. קַרְדֹּם *qardōm* **masc. noun**
(ax)
Judg. 9:48; **1 Sam.** 13:20,21; **Ps.** 74:5; **Jer.** 46:22.

7135. קָרָה *qārāh* **fem. noun**
(cold)
Job 24:7; 37:9; **Ps.** 147:17; **Prov.** 25:20; **Nah.** 3:17; **Zech.** 14:6(KJV, NASB, [Hebr.], *yāqār* [3368]).

7136. I. קָרָה *qārāh* **verb**
(to meet; to occur, to happen)
Gen. 24:12; 27:20; 42:29; 44:29; **Ex.** 3:18; **Num.** 11:23; 23:3,4,15,16; 35:11; **Deut.** 25:18; **Ruth** 2:3; **1 Sam.** 28:10; **2 Sam.** 1:6; **Esth.** 4:7; 6:13; **Eccl.** 2:14,15; 9:11; **Isa.** 41:22; **Dan.** 10:14.
II. קָרָה *qārāh* **verb**
(to lay beams of wood)
2 Chr. 34:11; **Neh.** 2:8; 3:3,6; **Ps.** 104:3.

7137. קָרֶה *qāreh* **masc. noun**
(temporary sickness)
Deut. 23:10.

7138. קָרוֹב *qārô͟b*, קָרֹב *qārō͟b* **adj.**
(near, close by, closely related)
Gen. 19:20; 45:10; **Ex.** 12:4; 13:17; 32:27; **Lev.** 10:3; 21:2,3; 25:25; **Num.** 24:17; 27:11; **Deut.** 4:7; 13:7(8); 21:3,6; 22:2; 30:14; 32:17,35; **Josh.** 9:16; **Ruth** 2:20; 3:12; **2 Sam.** 19:42(43); **1 Kgs.** 8:46,59; 21:2; **1 Chr.** 12:40(41); **2 Chr.** 6:36; **Neh.** 13:4; **Esth.** 1:14; 9:20; **Job** 17:12; 19:14; 20:5; **Ps.** 15:3; 22:11(12); 34:18(19); 38:11(12); 75:1; 85:9(10); 119:151; 145:18; 148:14; **Prov.** 10:14; 27:10; **Eccl**. 5:1(4:17)(NASB, NIV, *qāra͟b* [7126]); **Isa.** 13:6,22; 33:13; 50:8; 51:5; 55:6; 56:1; 57:19; **Jer.** 12:2; 23:23; 25:26; 48:16,24; **Ezek.** 6:12; 7:7,8; 11:3; 22:5; 23:5,12; 30:3; 42:13; 43:19; **Dan.** 9:7; **Joel** 1:15; 2:1; 3:14(4:14); **Obad.** 1:15; **Zeph.** 1:7,14.

7139. קָרַח *qāraḥ* **verb**
(to shave the head, to make bald)
Lev. 21:5; **Jer.** 16:6; **Ezek.** 27:31; 29:18; **Mic.** 1:16.

7140. קֶרַח *qeraḥ* **masc. noun**
(frost, ice)
Gen. 31:40; **Job** 6:16; 37:10; 38:29; **Ps.** 147:17; **Jer.** 36:30; **Ezek.** 1:22.

7141. A. קֹרַח *qōraḥ* **masc. proper noun**
(Korah: son of Esau through Oholibamah)
Gen. 36:5,14,18; **1 Chr.** 1:35.
B. קֹרַח *qōraḥ* **masc. proper noun**
(Korah: son of Esau through Adah)
Gen. 36:16.
C. קֹרַח *qōraḥ* **masc. proper noun**
(Korah: Levite who rebelled against Moses)
Ex. 6:21,24; **Num.** 16:1,5,6,8,16,19,24,27,32,40,49; 26:9–11; 27:3; **1 Chr.** 6:22,37; 9:19; **Ps.** 42:[title]1; 44:[title]1; 45:[title]1; 46:[title]1; 47:[title]1; 48:[title]1; 49:[title]1; 84:[title]1; 85:[title]1; 87:[title]1; 88:[title]1.
D. קֹרַח *qōraḥ* **masc. proper noun**
(Korah: descendant of Caleb)
1 Chr. 2:43.

7142. קֵרֵחַ *qērēaḥ* **adj.**
(bald)
Lev. 13:40; **2 Kgs.** 2:23.

7143. קָרֵחַ *qārēaḥ* **masc. proper noun**
(Kareah)
2 Kgs. 25:23; **Jer.** 40:8,13,15,16; 41:11,13,14,16; 42:1,8; 43:2,4,5.

7144. קָרְחָה *qorḥāh*, קָרְחָא *qorḥā'* **fem. noun**
(baldness, shaved head)
Lev. 21:5; **Deut.** 14:1; **Isa.** 3:24; 15:2; 22:12; **Jer.** 47:5; 48:37; **Ezek.** 7:18; 27:31; **Amos** 8:10; **Mic.** 1:16.

7145. קָרְחִי *qorḥiy* **masc. proper noun**
(Korahites)
Ex. 6:24; **Num.** 26:58; **1 Chr.** 9:19,31; 12:6; 26:1,19; **2 Chr.** 20:19.

7146. קָרַחַת *qārḥaṯ* **fem. noun**
(bald head, bald spot)
Lev. 13:42,43,55.

7147. קְרִי *qeriy* **masc. noun**
(hostility, contrariness)
Lev. 26:21,23,24,27,28,40,41.

7148. קָרִיא *qāriy'* **adj.**
(appointed, called)
Num. 1:16(KJV, NIV, [Q^{e}] *qārā'* [7121]); 16:2; 26:9(KJV, [K^{e}] *qārā'* [7121]).

7149. קִרְיָא *qiryā'*, קִרְיָה *qiryāh* **Aram. fem. noun**
(city; corr. to Hebr. 7151)
Ezra 4:10,12,13,15,16,19,21.

7150. קְרִיאָה *q^{e}riy'āh* **fem. noun**
(message, proclamation)
Jon. 3:2.

7151. קִרְיָה *qiryāh* **fem. noun**
(city, town)
Num. 21:28; **Deut.** 2:36; 3:4; **Josh.** 15:13(NASB, NIV, *qiryaṯ 'arba'* [7153]); 21:11(NASB, NIV, *qiryaṯ 'arba'* [7153]); **1 Kgs.** 1:41,45; **Job** 39:7; **Ps.** 48:2(3); **Prov.** 10:15; 11:10; 18:11,19; 29:8; **Isa.** 1:21,26; 22:2; 24:10; 25:2,3; 26:5; 29:1; 32:13; 33:20; **Jer.** 49:25; **Lam.** 2:11; **Hos.** 6:8; **Mic.** 4:10; **Hab.** 2:8,12,17.

7152. I. קְרִיּוֹת *q^{e}riyyôṯ* **proper noun**
(Kerioth)
Josh. 15:25(NASB, NIV, see II); **Jer.** 48:24,41; **Amos** 2:2.
II. קְרִיּוֹת חֶצְרוֹן *q^{e}riyyôṯ ḥeṣrôn* **proper noun**
(Kerioth Hezron)
Josh. 15:25(KJV, *q^{e}riyyôṯ* [7152,I] and *q^{e}riyyôṯ* [2696,C]).

7153. קִרְיַת אַרְבַּע *qiryaṯ 'arba'*, קִרְיַת הָאַרְבַּע *qiryaṯ hā'arba'* **proper noun**
(Kiriath Arba)
Gen. 23:2; 35:27; **Josh.** 14:15; 15:13 (KJV, *qiryāh* [7151] and *'arba'* [704]),54; 20:7; 21:11(KJV, *qiryāh* [7151] and *'arba'* [704]); **Judg.** 1:10; **Neh.** 11:25.

7154. קִרְיַת בַּעַל *qiryaṯ baʻal* **proper noun**
(Kiriath Baal)
Josh. 15:60; 18:14.

7155. קִרְיַת חֻצוֹת *qiryaṯ ḥuṣôṯ* **proper noun**
(Kiriath Huzoth)
Num. 22:39.

7156. A. קִרְיָתַיִם *qiryāṯayim* **proper noun**
(Kiriathaim: a city east of the Jordan River)
Num. 32:37; **Josh.** 13:19; **Jer.** 48:1,23; **Ezek.** 25:9.
B. קִרְיָתַיִם *qiryāṯayim* **proper noun**
(Kiriathaim: a town in Naphtali)
1 Chr. 6:76(61).

7157. I. קִרְיַת יְעָרִים *qiryaṯ yᵉʻāriym,* קִרְיַת עָרִים *qiryaṯ ʻāriym* **proper noun**
(Kiriath Jearim)
Josh. 9:17; 15:9,60; 18:14,15; **Judg.** 18:12; **1 Sam.** 6:21; 7:1,2; **1 Chr.** 2:50,52,53; 13:5,6; **2 Chr.** 1:4; **Ezra** 2:25; **Neh.** 7:29; **Jer.** 26:20.
II. קִרְיַת *qiryaṯ* **proper noun**
(Kiriath)
Josh. 18:28.

7158. I. קִרְיַת סֵפֶר *qiryaṯ sēp̱er* **proper noun**
(Kiriath Sepher)
Josh. 15:15,16; **Judg.** 1:11,12.
II. קִרְיַת סַנָּה *qiryath sannāh* **proper noun**
(Kiriath Sannah)
Josh. 15:49.

7159. קָרַם *qāram* **verb**
(to cover)
Ezek. 37:6,8.

7160. I. קָרַן *qāran* **verb**
(to radiate light; to shine)
Ex. 34:29,30,35.
II. קָרַן *qāran* **verb**
(to have horns)
Ps. 69:31(32)(NASB, *qeren* [7161]).

7161. I. קֶרֶן *qeren* **fem. noun**
(horn, hill)
Gen. 22:13; **Ex.** 27:2; 29:12; 30:2,3,10; 37:25,26; 38:2; **Lev.** 4:7,18,25,30,34; 8:15; 9:9; 16:18; **Deut.** 33:17; **Josh.** 6:5; **1 Sam.** 2:1,10; 16:1,13; **2 Sam.** 22:3; **1 Kgs.** 1:39,50,51; 2:28; 22:11; **1 Chr.** 25:5; **2 Chr.** 18:10; **Job** 16:15; **Ps.** 18:2(3); 22:21(22); 69:31(32)(KJV, NIV, *qāran* [7160,II]); 75:4(5),5(6),10(11); 89:17(18),24(25); 92:10(11); 112:9; 118:27; 132:17; 148:14; **Isa.** 5:1; **Jer.** 17:1; 48:25; **Lam.** 2:3,17; **Ezek.** 27:15; 29:21; 34:21; 43:15,20; **Dan.** 8:3,5–9, 20,21; **Amos** 3:14; 6:13(NASB, NIV, see II); **Mic.** 4:13; **Hab.** 3:4; **Zech.** 1:18(2:1),19(2:2),21(2:4).
II. קַרְנַיִם *qarnayim* **proper noun**
(Karnaim)
Amos 6:13(KJV, see I).

7162. קֶרֶן *qeren* **Aram. fem. noun**
(horn, cornet; corr. to Hebr. 7161)
Dan. 3:5,7,10,15; 7:7,8,11,20,21,24.

7163. קֶרֶן הַפּוּךְ *qeren happûḵ* **fem. proper noun**
(Keren-Happuch)
Job 42:14.

7164. קָרַס *qāras* **verb**
(to stoop, to bend low)
Isa. 46:1,2.

7165. קֶרֶס *qeres* **masc. noun**
(clasp, hook)
Ex. 26:6,11,33; 35:11; 36:13,18; 39:33.

7166. קַרְסֹל *qarsōl* **fem. noun**
(ankle, foot)
2 Sam. 22:37; **Ps.** 18:36(37).

7167. קָרַע *qāra‘* **verb**
(to tear, to rend)
Gen. 37:29,34; 44:13; **Ex.** 28:32; 39:23; **Lev.** 13:56; **Num.** 14:6; **Josh.** 7:6; **Judg.** 11:35; **1 Sam.** 4:12; 15:27,28; 28:17; **2 Sam.** 1:2,11; 3:31; 13:19,31; 15:32; **1 Kgs.** 11:11–13,30,31; 13:3,5; 14:8; 21:27; **2 Kgs.** 2:12; 5:7,8; 6:30; 11:14; 17:21; 18:37; 19:1; 22:11,19; **2 Chr.** 23:13; 34:19,27; **Ezra** 9:3,5; **Esth.** 4:1; **Job** 1:20; 2:12; **Ps.** 35:15; **Eccl.** 3:7; **Isa.** 36:22; 37:1; 64:1(63:19); **Jer.** 4:30; 22:14; 36:23,24; 41:5; **Ezek.** 13:20,21; **Hos.** 13:8; **Joel** 2:13.

7168. קֶרַע *qera‘* **masc. noun**
(piece [of cloth]; rag)
1 Kgs. 11:30,31; **2 Kgs.** 2:12; **Prov.** 23:21.

7169. I. קָרַץ *qāraṣ* **verb**
(to wink; to compress the lips)
Ps. 35:19; **Prov.** 6:13; 10:10; 16:30.
II. קָרַץ *qāraṣ* **verb**
(to form)
Job 33:6.

7170. קְרַץ *q^e^raṣ* **Aram. verb**
(to accuse, to denounce)
Dan. 3:8; 6:24(25).

7171. I. קֶרֶץ *qereṣ* **masc. noun**
(gadfly)
Jer. 46:20(KJV, see II).
II. קֶרֶץ *qereṣ* **masc. noun**
(destruction)
Jer. 46:20(NASB, NIV, see I).

7172. קַרְקַע *qarqa‘* **masc. noun**
(floor, bottom)
Num. 5:17; **1 Kgs.** 6:15,16,30; 7:7; **Amos** 9:3.

7173. קַרְקַע *qarqa‘* **proper noun**
(Karka)
Josh. 15:3.

7174. קַרְקֹר *qarqōr* **proper noun**
(Karkor)
Judg. 8:10.

7175. קֶרֶשׁ *qereš* **masc. noun**
(board, frame)
Ex. 26:15–23,25–29; 35:11; 36:20–28,30–34; 39:33; 40:18; **Num.** 3:36; 4:31; **Ezek.** 27:6.

7176. קֶרֶת *qereṯ* **fem. noun**
(city)
Job 29:7; **Prov.** 8:3; 9:3,14; 11:11.

7177. קַרְתָּה *qartāh* **proper noun**
(Kartah)
Josh. 21:34; **I Chr.** 6:77(62)(in NIV, only, following some Greek and some Hebr. MSS).

7178. קַרְתָּן *qartān* **proper noun**
(Kartan)
Josh. 21:32.

7179. קַשׁ *qaš* **masc. noun**
(stubble, chaff)
Ex. 5:12; 15:7; **Job** 13:25; 41:28(20),29(21); **Ps.** 83:13(14); **Isa.** 5:24; 33:11; 40:24; 41:2; 47:14; **Jer.** 13:24; **Joel** 2:5; **Obad.** 1:18; **Nah.** 1:10; **Mal.** 4:1(3:19).

7180. קִשֻּׁאָה *qiššu’āh* **fem. noun**
(cucumber)
Num. 11:5.

7181. קָשַׁב *qāšaḇ* **verb**
(to hear, to listen, to pay attention)
1 Sam. 15:22; **2 Chr.** 20:15; 33:10; **Neh.** 9:34; **Job** 13:6; 33:31; **Ps.** 5:2(3); 10:17; 17:1; 55:2(3); 61:1(2); 66:19; 86:6; 142:6(7); **Prov.** 1:24; 2:2; 4:1,20; 5:1; 7:24; 17:4; 29:12; **Song** 8:13; **Isa.** 10:30; 21:7; 28:23; 32:3; 34:1; 42:23; 48:18; 49:1; 51:4; **Jer.** 6:10,17,19; 8:6; 18:18,19; 23:18; **Dan.** 9:19; **Hos.** 5:1; **Mic.** 1:2; **Zech.** 1:4; 7:11; **Mal.** 3:16.

7182. קֶשֶׁב *qešeḇ* **masc. noun**
(attentiveness, response)
1 Kgs. 18:29; **2 Kgs.** 4:31; **Isa.** 21:7.

7183. I. קַשָּׁב *qaššāḇ* **adj.**
(attentive)
Neh. 1:6,11.
II. קַשֻּׁב *qaššuḇ* **adj.**
(attentive)
2 Chr. 6:40; 7:15; **Ps.** 130:2.

7184. I. קַשָׂה *qaśāh,* קַשְׂוָה *qaśwāh* **fem. noun**
(jar, cup)
Ex. 25:29(KJV, see II); 37:16(KJV, see II); **Num.** 4:7(KJV, see II); **1 Chr.** 28:17.
II. קַשָׂה *qaśāh,* קַשְׂוָה *qaśwāh* **fem. noun**
(cover)
Ex. 25:29(NASB, NIV, see I); 37:16(NASB, NIV, see I); **Num.** 4:7(NASB, NIV, see I).

7185. קָשָׁה *qāšāh* **verb**
(to be hard; to be hardened, to be stiffnecked)
Gen. 35:16,17; 49:7; **Ex.** 7:3; 13:15; **Deut.** 1:17; 2:30; 10:16; 15:18; **1 Sam.** 5:7; **2 Sam.** 19:43(44); **1 Kgs.** 12:4; **2 Kgs.** 2:10; 17:14; **2 Chr.** 10:4; 30:8; 36:13; **Neh.** 9:16,17,29; **Job** 9:4; **Ps.** 95:8; **Prov.** 28:14; 29:1; **Isa.** 8:21; **Jer.** 7:26; 17:23; 19:15.

7186. קָשֶׁה *qāšeh* **adj.**
(stiffnecked, harsh, cruel, stubborn)
Gen. 42:7,30; **Ex.** 1:14; 6:9; 18:26; 32:9; 33:3,5; 34:9; **Deut.** 9:6,13; 26:6; 31:27; **Judg.** 2:19; 4:24; **1 Sam.** 1:15; 20:10; 25:3; **2 Sam.** 2:17; 3:39; **1 Kgs.** 12:4,13; 14:6; **2 Chr.** 10:4,13; **Job** 30:25; 39:16 (KJV, NASB, *qāsah* [7188]); **Ps.** 60:3(5); **Song** 8:6; **Isa.** 14:3; 19:4; 21:2; 27:1,8; 48:4; **Ezek.** 2:4; 3:7.

7187. קְשׁוֹט *qāšôṭ,* קְשֹׁט *q^ešōṭ* **Aram. masc. noun**
(truth)
Dan. 2:47; 4:37(34).

7188. קָשַׁח *qāšaḥ* **verb**
(to harden the heart; to treat cruelly)
Job 39:16(NIV, *qāsāh* [7185]); **Isa.** 63:17.

7189. I. קֹשֶׁט *qōšeṭ,* קֹשְׁטְ *qōš^eṭ* **masc. noun**
(truth, certainty)
Ps. 60:4(6)(NIV, see II); **Prov.** 22:21.
II. קֹשֶׁט *qōšeṭ* **masc. noun**
(bow)
Ps. 60:4(6)(KJV, NASB, see I); **Prov.** 22:21.

7190. קְשִׁי *q^ešiy* **masc. noun**
(stubbornness)
Deut. 9:27.

7191. קִשְׁיוֹן *qišyôn* **proper noun**
(Kishion)
Josh. 19:20; 21:28.

7192. קְשִׂיטָה *q^eśiyṭāh* **fem. noun**
(piece of money, piece of silver)
Gen. 33:19; **Josh.** 24:32; **Job** 42:11.

7193. קַשְׂקֶשֶׂת *qaśqeśeṯ* **fem. noun**
(scales [of a fish]; scale armor)
Lev. 11:9,10,12; **Deut.** 14:9,10; **1 Sam.** 17:5; **Ezek.** 29:4.

7194. קָשַׁר *qāšar* **verb**
(to conspire, to plot; to bind)
Gen. 30:41,42; 38:28; 44:30; **Deut.** 6:8; 11:18; **Josh.** 2:18,21; **1 Sam.** 18:1; 22:8,13; **2 Sam.** 15:31; **1 Kgs.** 15:27; 16:9,16,20; **2 Kgs.** 9:14; 10:9; 12:20(21); 14:19; 15:10,15,25,30; 21:23,24; **2 Chr.** 24:21,25,26; 25:27; 33:24,25; **Neh.** 4:6(3:38),8(2); **Job** 38:31; 39:10; 41:5 (40:29); **Prov.** 3:3; 6:21; 7:3; 22:15; **Isa.** 49:18; **Jer.** 51:63; **Amos** 7:10.

7195. קֶשֶׁר *qešer* **masc. noun**
(conspiracy; treason)
2 Sam. 15:12; **1 Kgs.** 16:20; **2 Kgs.** 11:14; 12:20(21); 14:19; 15:15,30; 17:4;

2 Chr. 23:13; 25:27; **Isa.** 8:12; **Jer.** 11:9; **Ezek.** 22:25.

7196. קִשֻּׁרִים *qiššuriym* **masc. pl. noun**
(headbands, sashes, attire)
Isa. 3:20; **Jer.** 2:32.

7197. קָשַׁשׁ *qāšaš* **verb**
(to gather things; to assemble together)
Ex. 5:7,12; **Num.** 15:32,33; **1 Kgs.** 17:10,12; **Zeph.** 2:1.

7198. קֶשֶׁת *qešeṯ* **fem. noun**
(bow [of archery]; rainbow)
Gen. 9:13,14,16; 21:16; 27:3; 48:22; 49:24; **Josh.** 24:12; **1 Sam.** 2:4; 18:4; 31:3; **2 Sam.** 1:18,22; 22:35; **1 Kgs.** 22:34; **2 Kgs.** 6:22; 9:24; 13:15,16; **1 Chr.** 5:18; 8:40; 10:3; 12:2; **2 Chr.** 14:8(7); 17:17; 18:33; 26:14; **Neh.** 4:13(7),16(10); **Job** 20:24; 29:20; 41:28(20); **Ps.** 7:12(13); 11:2; 18:34(35); 37:14,15; 44:6(7); 46:9(10); 76:3(4); 78:9,57; **Isa.** 5:28; 7:24; 13:18; 21:15,17; 22:3; 41:2; 66:19; **Jer.** 4:29; 6:23; 9:3(2); 46:9; 49:35; 50:14,29,42; 51:3,56; **Lam.** 2:4; 3:12; **Ezek.** 1:28; 39:3,9; **Hos.** 1:5,7; 2:18(20); 7:16; **Amos** 2:15; **Hab.** 3:9; **Zech.** 9:10,13; 10:4.

7199. קַשָּׁת *qaššāṯ* **masc. noun**
(archer)
Gen. 21:20.

ר Resh

7200. I. רָאָה *rā'āh* **verb** (to see, to look, to examine; to appear)
Gen. 1:4,9,10,12,18,21,25,31; 2:19; 3:6; 6:2,5,12; 7:1; 8:5,8,13; 9:14,16,22,23; 11:5; 12:1,7,12,14,15; 13:10,14,15; 16:4, 5,13; 17:1; 18:1,2,21; 19:1,28; 20:10; 21:9,16,19; 22:4,8,13,14; 24:30,63,64; 26:2,8,24,28; 27:1,27; 28:6,8; 29:2,10, 31,32; 30:1,9; 31:2,5,10,12,42,43,50; 32:2(3),20(21),25(26),30(31); 33:1,5,10; 34:1,2; 35:1,9; 37:4,14,18,20,25; 38:2, 14,15; 39:3,13,14,23; 40:6,16; 41:19,22, 28,33,41; 42:1,7,9,12,21,27,35; 43:3,5, 16,29; 44:23,26,28,31,34; 45:12,13, 27,28; 46:29,30; 48:3,8,10,11,17; 49:15; 50:11,15,23; **Ex.** 1:16; 2:2,5,6,11,12,25; 3:2–4,7,9,16; 4:1,5,14,18,21,31; 5:19,21; 6:1,3; 7:1; 8:15(11); 9:16,34; 10:5,6,10, 23,28,29; 12:13,23; 13:7,17; 14:13,30,31; 16:7,10,15,29,32; 18:14; 19:4,21; 20:18,22; 22:10(9); 23:5,15,17; 24:10; 25:9,40; 26:30; 27:8; 31:2; 32:1,5,9,19,25; 33:10, 12,13,18,20,23; 34:3,10,20,23,24,30,35; 35:30; 39:43; **Lev.** 5:1; 9:4,6,23,24; 13:3, 5–8,10,13–15,17,19–21,25–27,30–32,34, 36,39,43,49–51,53,55–57; 14:3,35–37, 39,44,48; 16:2; 20:17; **Num.** 4:20; 8:4; 11:15,23; 13:18,26,28,32,33; 14:10,14, 22,23; 15:39; 16:19,42(17:7); 17:9(24); 20:6,29; 21:8; 22:2,23,25,27,31,33,41; 23:3,9,13,21; 24:1,2,17,20,21; 25:7; 27:12,13; 32:1,8,9,11; 35:23; **Deut.** 1:8, 19,21,28,31,33,35,36; 2:24,31; 3:21,24, 25,27,28; 4:3,5,9,12,15,19,28,35,36; 5:24; 7:19; 9:13,16; 10:21; 11:2,7,26; 12:13; 16:4,16; 18:16; 20:1; 21:7,11; 22:1,4; 23:14(15); 26:7; 28:10,32,34, 67,68; 29:2–4(1–3),17(16),22(21); 30:15; 31:11,15; 32:19,20,36,39,49,52; 33:9,21; 34:1,4; **Josh.** 2:1; 3:3; 5:6,13; 6:2; 7:21; 8:1,4,8,14,20,21; 22:28; 23:3,4; 24:7; **Judg.** 1:24,25; 2:7; 3:24; 4:22; 5:8; 6:12,22; 7:17; 9:36,43,48,55; 11:35; 12:3; 13:3,10,19–23; 14:1,2,8,11; 16:1,5, 18,24,27; 18:7,9,26; 19:3,17,30; 20:36,41; 21:21; **Ruth** 1:18; 2:18; **1 Sam.** 1:11,22; 3:2,21; 4:15; 5:7; 6:9,13,16,19; 10:11, 14,24; 12:12,16,17,24; 13:6,11; 14:16,17, 29,38,52; 15:35; 16:1,6,7,17,18; 17:24, 25,28,42,51,55; 18:15,28; 19:3,5,15,20; 20:29; 21:14; 22:9; 23:15,22,23; 24:10, 11,15; 25:17,23,25,35; 26:3,5,12,16; 28:5,12,13,21; 31:5,7; **2 Sam.** 1:7; 3:13; 6:16; 7:2; 10:6,9,14,15,19; 11:2; 12:19; 13:5,6,28,34; 14:24,28,30,32; 15:3,25,27 (NASB, NIV, see II),28; 16:12; 17:17, 18,23; 18:10,11,21,24,26,27,29; 20:12; 22:11,16; 24:3,13,17,20,22; **1 Kgs.** 1:48; 3:5,28; 6:18; 8:8; 9:2,12; 10:4,7,12; 11:9,28; 12:16; 13:12,25; 14:4; 16:18; 17:23; 18:1,2,15,17,39; 19:3; 20:7,13,22; 21:29; 22:17,19,25,32,33; **2 Kgs.** 2:10, 12,15,19,24; 3:14,17,22,26; 4:25; 5:7,21; 6:6,13,17,20,21,30,32; 7:2,13,14,19; 8:10,13,29; 9:2,16,17,22,26,27; 10:3, 16,23; 11:1,4,14; 12:10(11); 13:4,21; 14:8,11,26; 16:10,12; 19:16; 20:5,13,15; 22:20; 23:16,17,24,29; 25:19; **1 Chr.** 9:22(NASB, NIV, see II); 10:5,7; 12:17(18); 15:29; 17:17; 19:6,10,15,16,19; 21:12, 15,16,20,21,23,28; 26:28(NASB, NIV, see II); 28:10; 29:17,29(NASB, NIV, see II); **2 Chr.** 1:7; 3:1; 5:9; 7:3,12; 9:3,6,11; 10:16; 12:7; 15:9; 16:7(NASB, NIV, see II), 10(NASB, NIV, see II); 18:16,18,24,31,32; 19:6; 20:17; 22:6,10; 23:13; 24:11,22; 25:17,21; 26:5; 29:8; 30:7; 31:8; 32:2; 34:28; **Ezra** 3:12; **Neh.** 2:17; 4:11(4), 14(8); 6:16; 9:9; 13:15,23; **Esth.** 1:4, 11,14; 2:9,15; 3:4,5; 4:8; 5:2,9,13; 7:7; 8:6; 9:26; **Job** 2:13; 3:9,16; 4:8; 5:3; 6:21; 7:7; 8:18; 9:11,25; 10:4,15,18; 11:11; 13:1; 19:27; 20:7,17; 21:20; 22:11,12,14,19;

23:9; 28:10,24,27; 29:8,11; 31:4,19, 21,26; 32:5; 33:21,26,28; 34:21,26; 35:5; 37:21,24; 38:17,22; 40:11,12; 41:34(26); 42:5,16; **Ps.** 4:6(7); 8:3(4); 9:13(14); 10:11,14; 14:2; 16:10; 18:15(16); 22:7(8), 17(18); 25:18,19; 27:13; 31:7(8),11(12); 33:13; 34:8(9),12(13); 35:17,21,22; 36:9(10); 37:13,25,34,35,37; 40:3(4), 12(13); 41:6(7); 42:2(3); 45:10(11); 48:5(6),8(9); 49:9(10),10(11),19(20); 50:18,23; 52:6(8); 53:2(3); 54:7(9); 55:9(10); 59:4(5),10(11); 60:3(5); 63:2(3); 64:5(6),8(9); 66:5,18; 68:24(25); 69:23(24),32(33); 71:20; 73:3; 74:9; 77:16(17); 78:11; 80:14(15); 84:7(8), 9(10); 85:7(8); 86:17; 89:48(49); 90:15,16; 91:8,16; 94:7; 95:9; 97:4,6; 98:3; 102:16 (17); 106:5,44; 107:24,42; 109:25; 112:8,10; 113:6; 114:3; 115:5; 118:7; 119:37,74,96,153,158,159; 128:5,6; 135:16; 138:6; 139:16,24; 142:4(5); **Prov.** 6:6; 7:7; 20:12; 22:3; 23:31,33; 24:18,32; 25:7; 26:12; 27:12,25; 29:16; **Eccl.** 1:8,10,14,16; 2:1,3,12,13,24; 3:10, 13,16,18,22; 4:1,3,4,7,15; 5:8(7),13(12), 18(17); 6:1,5,6; 7:11,13–15,27,29; 8:9, 10,16,17; 9:9,11,13; 10:5,7; 11:4,7; 12:3; **Song** 1:6; 2:12,14; 3:3,11; 6:9,11; 7:12(13); **Isa.** 1:12; 5:12,19; 6:1,5,9,10; 9:2(1); 14:16; 16:12; 17:7,8; 18:3; 21:3, 6,7; 22:9,11; 26:10; 28:4; 29:15,18,23; 30:10(NASB, NIV, see II),20,30; 32:3; 33:15,17,19,20; 35:2; 37:17; 38:5,11; 39:2,4; 40:5,26; 41:5,20,23,28; 42:18,20; 44:9,16,18; 47:3,10; 49:7,18; 52:8,10,15; 53:2,10,11; 57:18; 58:3,7; 59:15,16; 60:2, 4,5; 61:9; 62:2; 63:15; 64:4(3); 66:5,8, 14,18,19,24; **Jer.** 1:10–13; 2:10,19,23,31; 3:2,6–8; 4:21,23–26; 5:1,12,21; 6:16; 7:11,12,17; 11:18,20; 12:3,4; 13:20, 26,27; 14:13; 17:6,8; 18:17; 20:4,12,18; 22:10,12; 23:13,14,18,24; 24:1,3; 29:32; 30:6; 31:3,26; 32:4,24; 33:24; 34:3; 38:21; 39:4; 40:4; 41:13; 42:2,14,18; 44:2,17; 46:5; 51:61; 52:25; **Lam.** 1:7–12,18,20; 2:16,20; 3:1,36,50,59,60; 5:1; **Ezek.** 1:1, 4,15,27,28; 2:9; 3:23; 4:15; 8:2,4,6,7,9, 10,12,13,15,17; 9:9; 10:1,8,9,15,20,22; 11:1,24,25; 12:2,3,6,12,13; 13:3; 14:22,23; 16:6,8,37,50; 18:14,28; 19:5,11; 20:28, 48(21:4); 21:21(26),24(29); 23:11,13,14; 28:17,18; 32:31; 33:3,6; 37:8; 39:15,21; 40:4; 41:8; 43:3; 44:4,5; 47:6; **Dan.** 1:10, 13,15; 8:1–4,6,7,15,20; 9:18,21; 10:5,7,8; 12:5; **Hos.** 5:13; 6:10; 9:10,13; **Joel** 2:28(3:1); **Amos** 3:9; 6:2; 7:1,4,7,8; 8:1,2; 9:1; **Obad.** 1:12,13; **Jon.** 3:10; 4:5; **Mic.** 6:9; 7:9,10,15,16; **Nah.** 3:5,7; **Hab.** 1:3,5,13; 2:1; 3:6,7,10; **Zeph.** 3:15; **Hag.** 2:3; **Zech.** 1:8,9,18(2:1),20(2:3); 2:1(5),2(6); 3:1,4; 4:2,10; 5:1,2,5,9; 6:1,8; 9:5,8,14; 10:7; **Mal.** 1:5; 3:2,18.

II. רֹאֶה *rō'eh* **masc. noun**
(seer, one who sees)
1 Sam. 9:9(KJV, see I),11(KJV, see I),18(KJV, see I),19(KJV, see I); **2 Sam.** 15:27(KJV, see I); **1 Chr.** 9:22(KJV, see I); 26:28(KJV, see I); 29:29(KJV, see I); **2 Chr.** 16:7(KJV, see I),10(KJV, see I); **Isa.** 30:10(KJV, see I).

7201. רָאָה *rā'āh* **fem. noun**
(bird of prey; red kite, glede)
Deut. 14:13(NASB, *dā'āh* [1676]).

7202. רָאֶה *rā'eh* **adj.**
(conscious)
Job 10:15(NIV, [speculation] *rāwāh* [7302]).

7203. רֹאֶה *rō'eh* **masc. noun**
(vision)
Isa. 28:7.

7204. רֹאֶה *rō'eh,* הָרֹאֶה *hārō'eh* **masc. proper noun**
(Haroeh)
1 Chr. 2:52.

7205. רְאוּבֵן *r^e'ûbēn* **masc. proper noun**
(Reuben)
Gen. 29:32; 30:14; 35:22,23; 37:21, 22,29; 42:22,37; 46:8,9; 48:5; 49:3;

Ex. 1:2; 6:14; **Num.** 1:5,20,21; 2:10,16; 7:30; 10:18; 13:4; 16:1; 26:5; 32:1,2,6, 25,29,31,33,37; **Deut.** 11:6; 27:13; 33:6; **Josh.** 4:12; 13:15,23; 15:6; 18:7,17; 20:8; 21:7,36; 22:9–11,13,15,21,25,30–34; **Judg.** 5:15,16; **1 Chr.** 2:1; 5:1,3,18; 6:63(48),78(63); **Ezek.** 48:6,7,31.

7206. רְאוּבֵנִי *r*[e]*ʾûḇēniy* **masc. proper noun**
(Reubenite)
Num. 26:7; 34:14; **Deut.** 3:12,16; 4:43; 29:8(7); **Josh.** 1:12; 12:6; 13:8; 22:1; **2 Kgs.** 10:33; **1 Chr.** 5:6,26; 11:42; 12:37(38); 26:32; 27:16.

7207. רַאֲוָה *raʾ*[a]*wāh* **masc. noun**
(beholding)
Eccl. 5:11(10)(NASB, NIV, [K[e]] *r*[e]*ʾiyt* [7212]).

7208. רְאוּמָה *r*[e]*ʾûmāh* **fem. proper noun**
(Reumah)
Gen. 22:24.

7209. רְאִי *r*[e]*ʾiy* **masc. noun**
(mirror)
Job 37:18.

7210. רֳאִי *r*[o]*ʾiy* **masc. noun**
(appearance, sight, spectacle)
Gen. 16:13(NIV, *rāʾāh* [7200]); **1 Sam.** 16:12; **Job** 7:8; 33:21(NIV, *rāʾāh* [7200]); **Nah.** 3:6.

7211. רְאָיָה *r*[e]*ʾāyāh* **masc. proper noun**
(Reaiah)
1 Chr. 4:2; 5:5; **Ezra** 2:47; **Neh.** 7:50.

7212. רְאִית *r*[e]*ʾiyṯ*, רְאוּת *r*[e]*ʾûṯ* **masc. noun**
(a looking, a feasting of the eyes)
Eccl. 5:11(10)(KJV, [Q[e]] *raʾ*[a]*wāh* [7207]).

7213. רָאַם *rāʾam* **verb**
(to rise; to be lifted up)
Zech. 14:10.

7214. רְאֵם *r*[e]*ʾēm*, רְאֵים *r*[e]*ʾēym*, רֵים *rēym*, רֵם *rēm* **masc. noun**
(wild ox)
Num. 23:22; 24:8; **Deut.** 33:17; **Job** 39:9,10; **Ps.** 22:21(22); 29:6; 92:10(11); **Isa.** 34:7.

7215. רָאמוֹת *rāʾmôṯ* **fem. pl. noun**
(coral)
Job 28:18; **Ezek.** 27:16.

7216. A. רָאמוֹת *rāʾmôṯ*, רָאמֹת *rāʾmōṯ* **proper noun**
(Ramoth: city in Gilead; see also *rāmōṯ gilʿāḏ* [7433])
Deut. 4:43; **Josh.** 20:8; 21:38(KJV, *rāmôṯ gilʿāḏ* [7433]); **1 Chr.** 6:80(65).
B. רָאמוֹת *rāʾmôṯ* **proper noun**
(Ramoth: a city in Issachar)
1 Chr. 6:73(58).

7217. רֵאשׁ *r*[e]*ʾēš* **Aram. masc. noun**
(head, mind; corr. to Hebr. 7218)
Ezra 5:10; **Dan.** 2:28,32,38; 3:27; 4:5(2),10(7),13(10); 7:1,6,9,15,20.

7218. ראשׁ *rōʾš* **masc. noun**
(head, chief, top)
Gen. 2:10; 3:15; 8:5; 11:4; 28:12,18; 40:13,16,17,19,20; 47:31; 48:14,17,18; 49:26; **Ex.** 6:14,25; 12:2,9; 17:9,10; 18:25; 19:20; 24:17; 26:24; 28:32; 29:6, 7,10,15,17,19; 30:12,23; 34:2; 36:29,38; 38:17,19,28; **Lev.** 1:4,8,12,15; 3:2,8,13; 4:4,11,15,24,29,33; 5:8; 6:5; 8:9,12,14, 18,20,22; 9:13; 10:6; 13:12,29,30,40, 41,44,45; 14:9,18,29; 16:21; 19:27; 21:5,10; 24:14; **Num.** 1:2,4,16,49; 4:2,22; 5:7,18; 6:5,7,9,11,18; 7:2; 8:12; 10:4,10; 13:3; 14:4,40,44; 17:3; 20:28; 21:20; 23:9,14,28; 25:4,15; 26:2; 28:11; 30:1(2); 31:26,49; 32:28; 36:1; **Deut.** 1:13,15; 3:27; 5:23; 20:9; 21:12; 28:13, 23,44; 29:10; 32:42; 33:5,15,16,21; 34:1; **Josh.** 2:19; 7:6; 11:10; 14:1; 15:8,9;

19:51; 21:1; 22:14,21,30; 23:2; 24:1; **Judg.** 5:26,30; 6:26; 7:16,19,20,25; 8:28; 9:7,25,34,36,37,43,44,53,57; 10:18; 11:8,9,11; 13:5; 16:3,13,17,19,22; **1 Sam.** 1:11; 4:12; 5:4; 9:22; 10:1; 11:11; 13:17,18; 14:45; 15:17; 17:5,38, 46,51,54,57; 25:39; 26:13; 28:2; 29:4; 31:9; **2 Sam.** 1:2,10,16; 2:16,25; 3:8,29; 4:7,8,12; 5:24; 12:30; 13:19; 14:26; 15:30,32; 16:1,9; 18:9; 20:21,22; 22:44; 23:8,13,18; **1 Kgs.** 2:32,33,37,44; 7:16–19,22,35,41; 8:1,8,32; 10:19; 18:42; 20:31,32; 21:9,12; **2 Kgs.** 1:9; 2:3,5; 4:19; 6:25,31,32; 9:3,6,30; 10:6–8; 19:21; 25:18,27; **1 Chr.** 4:42; 5:7,12, 15,24; 7:2,3,7,9,11,40; 8:6,10,13,28; 9:9, 13,17,33,34; 10:9; 11:6,10,11,15,20,42; 12:9(10),14(15),18–20(19–21),23(24),32 (33); 14:15; 15:12; 16:5,7; 20:2; 23:8,9, 11,16–20,24; 24:4,6,21,31; 26:10,12,21, 26,31,32; 27:1,3,5; 29:11; **2 Chr.** 1:2; 3:15,16; 4:12; 5:2,9; 6:23; 11:22; 13:12; 19:8,11; 20:27; 23:2; 24:6,11; 25:12; 26:12,20; 28:12; 31:10; **Ezra** 1:5; 2:68; 3:12; 4:2,3; 7:5,28; 8:1,16,17; 9:3,6; 10:16; **Neh.** 4:4(3:36); 7:70(69),71(70); 8:13; 9:17; 10:14(15); 11:3,13,16,17; 12:7,12,22–24,46; **Esth.** 2:17; 5:2; 6:8,12; 9:25; **Job** 1:17,20; 2:12; 10:15; 12:24; 16:4; 19:9; 20:6; 22:12; 24:24; 29:3,25; 41:7(40:31); **Ps.** 3:3(4); 7:16(17); 18:43(44); 21:3(4); 22:7(8); 23:5; 24:7,9; 27:6; 38:4(5); 40:12(13); 44:14(15); 60:7(9); 66:12; 68:21(22); 69:4(5); 72:16; 74:13,14; 83:2(3); 108:8(9); 109:25; 110:6,7; 118:22; 119:160; 133:2; 137:6; 139:17; 140:7(8), 9(10); 141:5; **Prov.** 1:9,21; 4:9; 8:2, 23,26; 10:6; 11:26; 23:34; 25:22; **Eccl.** 2:14; 3:11; 9:8; **Song** 2:6; 4:8,14; 5:2,11; 7:5(6); 8:3; **Isa.** 1:5,6; 2:2; 7:8,9,20; 9:14(13),15(14); 15:2; 17:6; 19:15; 28:1, 4; 29:10; 30:17; 35:10; 37:22; 40:21; 41:4,26; 42:11; 48:16; 51:11,20; 58:5; 59:17; **Jer.** 2:37; 9:1(8:23); 13:21; 14:3,4; 18:16; 22:6; 23:19; 30:23; 31:7; 48:37; 52:24,31; **Lam.** 1:5; 2:10,15,19; 3:54; 4:1; 5:16; **Ezek.** 1:22,25,26; 5:1; 6:13; 7:18; 8:3; 9:10; 10:1,11; 11:21; 13:18; 16:12,25,31,43; 17:4,19,22; 21:19(24), 21(26); 22:31; 23:15,42; 24:23; 27:22,30; 29:18; 32:27; 33:4; 38:2(NASB, *rō'š* [7220,B]),3(NASB, *rō'š* [7220,B]); 39:1(NASB, *rō'š* [7220,B]); 40:1; 42:12; 43:12; 44:18,20; **Dan.** 1:10; **Hos.** 1:11 (2:2); 4:13; **Joel** 2:5; 3:4(4:4),7(4:7); **Amos** 1:2; 2:7; 6:7; 8:10; 9:1,3; **Obad.** 1:15; **Jon.** 2:5; 4:6,8; **Mic.** 2:13; 3:1,9,11; 4:1; **Nah.** 3:10; **Hab.** 3:13,14; **Zech.** 1:21(2:4); 3:5; 4:2; 6:11.

7219. ראשׁ רושׁ *rō'š, rôš* **masc. noun**
(poison, bitterness, gall)
Deut. 29:18(17); 32:32,33; **Job** 20:16; **Ps.** 69:21(22); **Jer.** 8:14; 9:15(14); 23:15; **Lam.** 3:5,19; **Hos.** 10:4; **Amos** 6:12.

7220. A. ראשׁ *rō'š* **masc. proper noun**
(Rosh)
Gen. 46:21.
B. ראשׁ *rō'š* **proper noun**
(Rosh)
Isa. 66:19(not in KJV, or NIV); **Ezek.** 38:2(KJV, NIV, *rō'š* [7218]),3(KJV, NIV, *rō'š* [7218]); 39:1(KJV, NIV, *rō'š* [7218]).

7221. רִאשָׁה *ri'šāh* **fem. noun**
(beginning)
Ezek. 36:11.

7222. רֹאשָׁה *rō'šāh* **fem. noun**
(top [as in capstone])
Zech. 4:7.

7223. רִאשׁוֹן *ri'šôn,* רִאשֹׁן *ri'šōn* **adj.**
(first, beginning, former)
Gen. 8:13; 13:4; 25:25; 26:1; 28:19; 32:17(18); 33:2; 38:28; 40:13; 41:20; **Ex.** 4:8; 12:2,15,16,18; 34:1,4; 40:2,17; **Lev.** 4:21; 5:8; 9:15; 23:5,7,35,39,40; 26:45; **Num.** 2:9; 6:12; 7:12; 9:1,5; 10:13,14;

20:1; 21:26; 28:16,18; 33:3; **Deut.** 4:32; 9:18; 10:1–4,10; 13:9(10); 16:4; 17:7; 19:14; 24:4; **Josh.** 4:19; 8:5,6,33; 21:10; **Judg.** 18:29; 20:22,32,39; **Ruth** 3:10; **1 Sam.** 14:14; 17:30; **2 Sam.** 7:10; 18:27; 19:20(21),43(44); 20:18; 21:9; **1 Kgs.** 13:6; 17:13; 18:25; 20:9,17; **2 Kgs.** 1:14; 17:34,40; **1 Chr.** 9:2; 11:6; 12:15(16); 15:13; 17:9; 18:17; 24:7; 25:9; 27:2,3; 29:29; **2 Chr.** 3:3; 9:29; 12:15; 16:11; 17:3; 20:34; 22:1; 25:26; 26:22; 28:26; 29:3,17; 35:1,27; **Ezra** 3:12; 6:19; 7:9; 8:31; 9:2; 10:17; **Neh.** 5:15; 7:5; 8:18; **Esth.** 1:14; 3:7,12; **Job** 8:8; 15:7; **Ps.** 79:8; 89:49(50); **Prov.** 18:17; 20:21; **Eccl.** 1:11; 7:10; **Isa.** 1:26; 9:1(8:23); 41:4,22,27; 42:9; 43:9,18,27; 44:6; 46:9; 48:3,12; 52:4; 60:9; 61:4; 65:7,16,17; **Jer.** 7:12; 11:10; 16:18; 17:12; 33:7,11; 34:5; 36:28; 50:17; **Ezek.** 29:17; 30:20; 40:21; 45:18,21; **Dan.** 8:21; 10:4,12,13; 11:13,29; **Hos.** 2:7(9); **Joel** 2:23; **Mic.** 4:8; **Hag.** 2:3,9; **Zech.** 1:4; 6:2; 7:7,12; 8:11; 12:7; 14:10.

7224. רִאשֹׁנִי *ri'šôniy* **adj.**
(first)
Jer. 25:1.

7225. רֵאשִׁית *rē'šiyt̲* **fem. noun**
(beginning, firstfruits; best)
Gen. 1:1; 10:10; 49:3; **Ex.** 23:19; 34:26; **Lev.** 2:12; 23:10; **Num.** 15:20,21; 18:12; 24:20; **Deut.** 11:12; 18:4; 21:17; 26:2,10; 33:21; **1 Sam.** 2:29; 15:21; **2 Chr.** 31:5; **Neh.** 10:37(38); 12:44; **Job** 8:7; 40:19; 42:12; **Ps.** 78:51; 105:36; 111:10; **Prov.** 1:7; 3:9; 4:7; 8:22; 17:14; **Eccl.** 7:8; **Isa.** 46:10; **Jer.** 2:3; 26:1; 27:1; 28:1; 49:34,35; **Ezek.** 20:40; 44:30; 48:14; **Dan.** 11:41; **Hos.** 9:10; **Amos** 6:1,6; **Mic.** 1:13.

7226. רַאֲשֹׁת *ra'ᵃšōt̲* **noun**
(bolster; not a known Hebrew form, see *mᵉra'ᵃšôt̲* [4763])
1 Sam. 26:12.

7227. I. רַב *rab̲* **adj.**
(many, much, great, long, mighty)
Gen. 6:5; 7:11; 13:6; 18:20(NASB, NIV, *rāḇab̲* [7231]); 21:34; 24:25; 25:23; 26:14; 30:43; 33:9; 36:7; 37:34; 45:28; 50:20; **Ex.** 1:9; 2:23; 5:5; 9:28; 12:38; 19:21; 23:2,29; 34:6; **Lev.** 15:25; 25:51; **Num.** 9:19; 11:33; 13:18; 14:18; 16:3,7; 20:11,15; 21:6; 22:3,15; 24:7; 26:54,56; 32:1; 33:54; 35:8; **Deut.** 1:6,46; 2:1,3, 10,21; 3:19,26; 7:1,17; 9:14; 15:6; 20:1,19; 25:3; 26:5; 28:12,38; 31:17,21; 33:7; **Josh.** 10:11; 11:4,8,18; 17:14, 15,17; 19:9,28; 22:3,8; 23:1; 24:7; **Judg.** 7:2,4; 8:30; 9:40; 16:30; **1 Sam.** 2:5; 12:17; 14:6,19; 26:13; **2 Sam.** 3:22; 13:34; 14:2; 15:12; 22:17; 23:20; 24:14,16; **1 Kgs.** 2:38; 3:8,11; 4:20; 5:7(21); 10:2; 11:1; 12:28; 18:1,25; 19:4,7; **2 Kgs.** 6:16; 9:22; 12:10(11); **1 Chr.** 4:27; 5:22; 7:22; 11:22; 18:8; 21:13,15; 22:8; 24:4; 28:5; **2 Chr.** 1:9,11; 13:8,17; 14:11,14; 15:3,5; 17:13; 20:2,12, 15,25; 21:3,15; 24:11,25; 25:13; 26:10; 28:8,13; 30:13,17,18; 32:4,7,23,29; **Ezra** 3:12; 10:1,13; **Neh.** 5:2; 6:18; 7:2; 9:17, 19,27,28,30,31,35; 13:26; **Esth.** 1:4,7, 8,20; 2:8; 4:3; 8:17; **Job** 1:3; 4:3; 5:25; 11:19; 16:2; 22:5; 23:14; 31:25,34; 32:9; 35:9; 36:18(NASB, NIV, *rōb̲* [7230]),28; 38:21; 39:11; **Ps.** 3:1(2),2(3); 4:6(7); 18:14(15)(KJV, *rab̲ab̲* [7231]),16(17); 19:10(11),11(12),13(14); 22:12(13), 25(26); 25:11; 29:3; 31:13(14),19(20); 32:6,10; 34:19(20); 35:18; 36:6(7); 37:16; 40:3(4),5(6),9(10),10(11); 48:2(3); 55:18(19); 56:2(3); 62:2(3); 65:9(10); 68:11(12); 71:7,20; 77:19(20); 78:15; 86:5,15; 89:7(8),50(51); 93:4; 97:1; 103:8; 106:43; 107:23; 109:30; 110:6; 119:156,157,162,165; 120:6; 123:3,4; 129:1,2; 135:10; 144:7; 145:7; 147:5; **Prov.** 7:26; 10:21; 13:7; 14:20,29; 15:6,16; 19:4,6,21; 22:1; 26:10(NASB, NIV, *rab̲* [7228]); 28:2,12,16,20,27; 29:22,26; 31:29; **Eccl.** 2:21; 6:1,3; 7:22,29; 8:6; 10:6; **Song** 8:7; **Isa.** 2:3,4; 5:9; 6:12;

8:7,15; 13:4; 16:14; 17:12,13; 21:7; 23:3; 30:25; 31:1; 42:20; 51:10; 52:14,15; 53:11,12; 54:1,13; 63:1,7; **Jer.** 3:1; 11:15; 12:10; 13:6,9; 16:16; 20:10; 22:8; 25:14; 27:7; 28:8; 32:14,19; 35:7; 36:32; 37:16; 41:12; 50:29(KJV, NIV, *rab̲* [7228]),41; 51:13,55; **Lam.** 1:1,22; 3:23; **Ezek.** 1:24; 3:6; 12:27; 16:41; 17:5,7–9,15,17; 19:10; 22:5; 24:12; 26:3,7,19; 27:3,15, 26,33; 31:5–7,15; 32:3,9,10,13; 33:24; 37:2; 38:4,6,8,9,15,22,23; 39:27; 43:2; 44:6; 45:9; 47:7,9,10; **Dan.** 8:25,26; 9:18,27; 11:3,5,10,11,13,14,18,26,33, 34,39–41,44; 12:2–4,10; **Hos.** 3:3,4; 9:7; **Joel** 2:2,11,13; 3:13(4:14); **Amos** 3:9,15; 5:12; 6:2; 7:4; 8:3; **Jon.** 4:2,11; **Mic.** 4:2, 3,11,13; 5:7,8; **Nah.** 1:12; **Hab.** 2:8,10; 3:15; **Zech.** 2:11(15); 8:20,22; 14:13; **Mal.** 2:6,8.

II. רַב *rab̲* **adj.**
(chief, captain, high official)
2 Kgs. 18:17(KJV, NASB, *rab̲-sariys* [7249]); 25:8,10–12,15,18–20; **Esth.** 1:8; **Isa.** 19:20; **Jer.** 39:3(KJV, NASB, *rab̲-sariys* [7249]),9–11,13(KJV, NASB, *rab̲-sariys* [7249]); 40:1,2,5; 41:1,10; 43:6; 52:12,14–16,19,24,26,30; **Dan.** 1:3; **Jon.** 1:6.

7228. רַב *rab̲* **masc. noun**
(archer, arrow)
Job 16:13; **Prov.** 2:10(MT, *rab̲* [7227]); **Jer.** 50:29(NASB, *rab̲* [7227]).

7229. רַב *rab̲* **Aram. adj.**
(great, boastful, large; NASB, NIV, see also *rab̲ rab̲* [7260])
Ezra 4:10; 5:8,11; **Dan.** 2:10,31,35, 45,48; 4:9(6),30(27); 5:1,11; 7:2,20.

7230. רֹב *rōb̲* **masc. noun**
(large number, great number, abundance)
Gen. 16:10; 27:28; 30:30; 32:12(13); 48:16; **Ex.** 15:7; **Lev.** 25:16; **Deut.** 1:10; 7:7; 10:22; 28:47,62; **Josh.** 9:13; 11:4; **Judg.** 6:5; 7:12; **1 Sam.** 1:16; 13:5; **2 Sam.** 17:11; **1 Kgs.** 1:19,25; 3:8; 4:20; 7:47; 8:5; 10:10,27; **2 Kgs.** 19:23; **1 Chr.** 4:38; 12:40(41); 22:3–5,8,14,15; 29:2,21; **2 Chr.** 1:15; 2:9(8); 4:18; 5:6; 9:1,9,27; 11:23; 14:15(14); 15:9; 16:8; 17:5; 18:1,2; 20:25; 24:11,24,27; 27:3; 29:35; 30:5, 13,24; 31:5,10; 32:5,29; **Neh.** 9:25; 13:22; **Esth.** 5:11; 10:3; **Job** 4:14; 11:2; 23:6; 26:3; 30:18; 32:7; 33:19(NASB, NIV, [K^{e}] *riyb̲* [7379]); 35:9; 36:18(KJV, *rab̲* [7271,I]); 37:23; **Ps.** 5:7(8),10(11); 33:16,17; 37:11; 49:6(7); 51:1; 52:7(9); 66:3; 69:13(14),16(17); 72:7; 94:19; 106:7,45; 150:2; **Prov.** 5:23; 7:21; 10:19; 11:14; 13:23; 14:4,28; 15:22; 16:8; 20:6,15; 24:6; **Eccl.** 1:18; 5:3(2),7(6); 11:1; **Isa.** 1:11; 7:22; 24:22; 37:24; 40:26; 47:9,12,13; 57:10; 63:1,7; **Jer.** 13:22; 30:14,15; **Lam.** 1:3,5; 3:32; **Ezek.** 14:4; 19:11; 23:42; 27:12,16,18,33; 28:5,16,18; 31:9; **Hos.** 4:7(NASB, NIV, *rāb̲ab̲* [7231]); 8:12(NASB, [K^{e}] *ribbô* [7239]); 9:7; 10:1, 13; **Nah.** 3:3,4; **Zech.** 2:4(8); 8:4; 14:14.

7231. רָבַב *rāb̲ab̲* **verb**
(to be many; to be increased or multiplied)
Gen. 6:1; 18:20(KJV, *rab̲* [7227,I]); **1 Sam.** 25:10; **Job** 35:6; **Ps.** 3:1; 4:7(8); 25:19; 38:19(20); 69:4(5); 104:24; 144:13; **Eccl.** 5:11(10); **Isa.** 22:9; 59:12; 66:16; **Jer.** 5:6; 14:7; 46:23; **Hos.** 4:7 (KJV, *rōb̲* [7230]).

7232. רָבַב *rāb̲ab̲* **verb**
(to shoot, to shoot out)
Gen. 49:23; **Ps.** 18:14(15)(NASB, NIV, *rab̲* [7227,I]).

7233. רְבָבָה *r^{e}b̲āb̲āh* **fem. noun**
(ten thousand, myriad, countless)
Gen. 24:60; **Lev.** 26:8; **Num.** 10:36; **Deut.** 32:30; 33:2,17; **Judg.** 20:10; **1 Sam.** 18:7,8; 21:11(12); 29:5; **Ps.** 3:6(7); 91:7; **Song** 5:10; **Ezek.** 16:7; **Mic.** 6:7.

7234. רָבַד *rāḇaḏ* **verb**
(to spread a covering over something)
Prov. 7:16.

7235. I. רָבָה *rāḇāh* **verb**
(to be many or become many; to be abundant; KJV, NASB, see also II)
Gen. 1:22,28; 3:16; 7:17,18; 8:17; 9:1,7; 16:10; 17:2,20; 22:17; 26:4,24; 28:3; 34:12; 35:11; 38:12; 43:34; 47:27; 48:4; **Ex.** 1:7,10,12,20; 7:3; 11:9; 16:17,18; 30:15; 32:13; 36:5; **Lev.** 11:42; 25:16; 26:9; **Num.** 26:54; 33:54; 35:8; **Deut.** 1:10; 6:3; 7:13,22; 8:1,13; 11:21; 13:17(18); 14:24; 17:16,17; 19:6; 28:63; 30:5,16; **Josh.** 24:3; **Judg.** 9:29; 16:24; 20:38; **1 Sam.** 1:12; 2:3; 7:2; 14:30; **2 Sam.** 14:11; 18:8; 22:36; **1 Kgs.** 4:30(5:10); **2 Kgs.** 21:6; **1 Chr.** 4:10,27; 5:9,23; 7:4; 8:40; 23:11,17; 27:23; **2 Chr.** 31:5; 33:6,23; 36:14; **Ezra** 9:6; 10:13; **Neh.** 6:17; 9:23,37; **Job** 9:17; 10:17; 27:14; 29:18; 33:12; 34:37; 39:4; 41:3 (40:27); **Ps.** 16:4; 18:35(36); 44:12(13); 49:16(17); 71:21; 78:38; 107:38; 139:18; **Prov.** 4:10; 6:35; 9:11; 13:11; 22:16; 25:27; 28:8,28; 29:2,16; **Eccl.** 5:11(10); 10:14; 11:8; **Isa.** 1:15; 9:3(2); 23:16; 40:29; 51:2; 55:7; 57:9; **Jer.** 2:22; 3:16; 23:3; 29:6; 30:19; 33:22; 46:11,16; **Lam.** 2:5,22; **Ezek.** 11:6; 16:7,25,26,29,51; 19:2; 21:15(20); 22:25; 23:19; 24:10; 28:5; 31:5; 36:10,11,29,30,37; 37:26; **Dan.** 11:39; 12:4; **Hos.** 2:8(10); 8:11,14; 10:1; 12:1(2),10(11); **Amos** 4:4,9; **Nah.** 3:16; **Hab.** 2:6; **Zech.** 10:8.
II. הַרְבֵּה *harbēh* **adj.**
(to be much or many; to be abundant)
Gen. 15:1; 41:49; **Deut.** 3:5; **Josh.** 13:1; 22:8; **1 Sam.** 26:21; **2 Sam.** 1:4; 8:8; 12:2,30; **1 Kgs.** 4:29(5:9); 10:10,11; **2 Kgs.** 10:18; 21:16; **1 Chr.** 20:2; **2 Chr.** 11:12; 14:13(12); 16:8; 25:9; 32:27; **Ezra** 10:1; **Neh.** 2:2; 4:1(3:33), 10(4),19(13); 5:18; **Ps.** 51:2(4); 130:7; **Eccl.** 1:16; 2:7; 5:7(6),12(11),17(16), 20(19); 6:11; 7:16,17; 9:18; 12:9,12; **Isa.** 30:33; **Jer.** 40:12; 42:2; **Jon.** 4:11; **Hag.** 1:6,9.
III. רָבָה *rāḇāh* **verb**
(to shoot an arrow)
Gen. 21:20.

7236. רְבָה *r^eḇāh* **Aram. verb**
(to become large; to become great; corr. to Hebr. 7235)
Dan. 2:48; 4:11(8),20(17),22(19),33(30).

7237. רַבָּה *rabbāh* **proper noun**
(Rabbah)
Deut. 3:11; **Josh.** 13:25; 15:60; **2 Sam.** 11:1; 12:26,27,29; 17:27; **1 Chr.** 20:1; **Jer.** 49:2,3; **Ezek.** 21:20(25); 25:5; **Amos** 1:14.

7238. רְבוּ *r^eḇû* **Aram. fem. noun**
(greatness; majesty)
Dan. 4:22(19),36(33); 5:18,19; 7:27.

7239. רִבּוֹ *ribbô* **fem. noun**
(ten thousand, myriad)
1 Chr. 29:7; **Ezra** 2:64,69; **Neh.** 7:66, 71(70),72(71); **Ps.** 68:17(18); **Dan.** 11:12; **Hos.** 8:12(KJV, NIV, [Q^e] *rōḇ* [7230]); **Jon.** 4:11.

7240. רִבּוֹ *ribbô* **Aram. fem. noun**
(ten thousand, myriad; corr. to Hebr. 7239)
Dan. 7:10.

7241. רָבִיב *rāḇiyḇ* **masc. noun**
(rain shower)
Deut. 32:2; **Ps.** 65:10(11); 72:6; **Jer.** 3:3; 14:22; **Mic.** 5:7(6).

7242. רָבִיד *rāḇiyḏ* **masc. noun**
(chain, necklace)
Gen. 41:42; **2 Chr.** 3:16(KJV, NASB, *d^eḇiyḏ* [1687]); **Ezek.** 16:11.

7243. רְבִיעִי *r^e^b̲iy'iy*, רְבִעִי *r^e^b̲i'iy* **adj.**
(fourth, fourth part)
Gen. 1:19; 2:14; 15:16; **Ex.** 28:20; 29:40; 39:13; **Lev.** 19:24; 23:13; **Num.** 7:30; 15:4,5; 28:5,7,14; 29:23; **Josh.** 19:17; **Judg.** 14:15(KJV, [Hebr.] *š^e^b̲iy'iy* [7637]); 19:5; **2 Sam.** 3:4; **1 Kgs.** 6:1,33,37; **2 Kgs.** 10:30; 15:12; 18:9; **1 Chr.** 2:14; 3:2,15; 8:2; 12:10(11); 23:19; 24:8,23; 25:11; 26:2,4,11; 27:7; **2 Chr.** 20:26; **Ezra** 8:33; **Neh.** 9:3; **Jer.** 25:1; 28:1; 36:1; 39:2; 45:1; 46:2; 51:59; 52:6; **Ezek.** 1:1; 10:14; 48:20; **Dan.** 11:2; **Zech.** 6:3; 8:19.

7244. רְבִיעִי *r^e^b̲iy'iy*, רְבִעִי *r^e^b̲i'iy* **adj.**
(fourth, fourth part)
Dan. 2:40; 3:25; 7:7,19,23.

7245. רַבִּית *rabbiyṯ* **proper noun**
(Rabbith)
Josh. 19:20.

7246. I. רָבַךְ *rāb̲ak̲* **verb**
(to mix, to stir)
Lev. 6:21(14)(KJV, see II); 7:12(KJV, see II); **1 Chr.** 23:29(KJV, see II).
II. רָבַךְ *rāb̲ak̲* **verb**
(to bake, to fry)
Lev. 6:21(14)(NASB, NIV, see I); 7:12(NASB, NIV, see I); **1 Chr.** 23:29(NASB, NIV, see I).

7247. רִבְלָה *rib̲lāh* **proper noun**
(Riblah)
Num. 34:11; **2 Kgs.** 23:33; 25:6,20,21; **Jer.** 39:5,6; 52:9,10,26,27.

7248. I. רַב־מָג *rab̲-māg* **proper noun**
(Rab-mag; a position in Babylon)
Jer. 39:3(NIV, see II),13(NIV, see II).
II. רַב־מָג *rab̲-māg* **masc. noun**
(high official; from *rāb̲* [7227,II] and *māg*, official)
Jer. 39:3(KJV, NASB, see I),13(KJV, NASB, see I).

7249. I. רַב־סָרִיס *rab̲-sāriys* **masc. proper noun**
(Rab-saris)
2 Kgs. 18:17(NIV; *rab̲* [7227,II] and *sariys* [5631]); **Jer.** 39:3(NASB, see II; NIV, *rab̲* [7227,II] and *sariys* [5631]), 13(NASB, see II; NIV, *rab̲* [7227,II] and *sariys* [5631]).
II. רַב־סָרִיס *rab̲-sāriys* **masc. noun**
(Rab-saris; a military title for Babylon's chief officer)
Jer. 39:3(KJV, see I; NIV, *rab̲* [7227,II] and *sariys* [5631]); 13(KJV, see I; NIV, *rab̲* [7227,II] and *sariys* [5631]).

7250. רָבַע *rāb̲a'* **verb**
(to lie down, to mate with an animal or a person, to breed animals)
Lev. 18:23; 19:19; 20:16; **Ps.** 139:3 (KJV, *reb̲a'* [7252]).

7251. רָבַע *rāb̲a'* **verb**
(to be square)
Ex. 27:1; 28:16; 30:2; 37:25; 38:1; 39:9; **1 Kgs.** 7:5,31; **Ezek.** 40:47; 41:21; 43:16; 45:2.

7252. רֶבַע *reb̲a'* **verb**
(to lie down)
Ps. 139:3(NASB, NIV, *rāb̲a'* [7250]).

7253. רֶבַע *reb̲a'* **masc. noun**
(a fourth part, quarter; four sides)
Ex. 29:40; **1 Sam.** 9:8; **Ezek.** 1:8,17; 10:11; 43:16,17.

7254. רֶבַע *reb̲a'* **masc. proper noun**
(Reba)
Num. 31:8; **Josh.** 13:21.

7255. רֹבַע *rōb̲a'* **masc. noun**
(fourth part; quarter)
Num. 23:10; **2 Kgs.** 6:25.

7256. רִבֵּעַ *ribbēa‘* **adj.**
(fourth [generation])
Ex. 20:5; 34:7; **Num.** 14:18; **Deut.** 5:9.

7257. רָבַץ *rāḇaṣ* **verb**
(to lie down, to rest; to lay down something)
Gen. 4:7; 29:2; 49:9,14,25; **Ex.** 23:5; **Num.** 22:27; **Deut.** 22:6; 29:20(19); 33:13; **Job** 11:19; **Ps.** 23:2; 104:22; **Song** 1:7; **Isa.** 11:6,7; 13:20,21; 14:30; 17:2; 27:10; 54:11; **Jer.** 33:12; **Ezek.** 19:2; 29:3; 34:14,15; **Zeph.** 2:7,14; 3:13.

7258. רֵבֶץ *rēḇeṣ* **masc. noun**
(resting place, dwelling place)
Prov. 24:15; **Isa.** 35:7; 65:10; **Jer.** 50:6.

7259. רִבְקָה *riḇqāh* **fem. proper noun**
(Rebekah)
Gen. 22:23; 24:15,29,30,45,51,53, 58–61,64,67; 25:20,21,28; 26:7,8,35; 27:5,6,11,15,42,46; 28:5; 29:12; 35:8; 49:31.

7260. רַבְרַב *raḇraḇ* **Aram. adj.**
(great, great things; NASB, NIV, *raḇ* [7229])
Dan. 2:48; 4:3(3:33); 7:3,7,8,11,17,20.

7261. רַבְרְבָן *raḇrᵉḇān* **Aram. masc. noun**
(a noble, prince)
Dan. 4:36(33); 5:1–3,9,10,23; 6:17(18).

7262. I. רַב־שָׁקֵה *raḇ-šāqēh* **masc. proper noun**
(Rabshakeh; NIV, see II)
2 Kgs. 18:17,19,26–28,37; 19:4,8; **Isa.** 36:2,4,11–13,22; 37:4,8.
II. רַב־שָׁקֵה *raḇ-šāqēh* **masc. noun**
(field commander of the Assyrian army; KJV, NASB, see I)
2 Kgs. 18:17,19,26–28,37; 19:4,8; **Isa.** 36:2,4,11–13,22; 37:4,8.

7263. רֶגֶב *regeḇ* **masc. noun**
(clod of soil)
Job 21:33; 38:38.

7264. רָגַז *rāgaz* **verb**
(to tremble, to shake, to be disturbed)
Gen. 45:24; **Ex.** 15:14; **Deut.** 2:25; **1 Sam.** 14:15; 28:15; **2 Sam.** 7:10; 18:33(19:1); 22:8; **2 Kgs.** 19:27,28; **1 Chr.** 17:9; **Job** 9:6; 12:6; **Ps.** 4:4(5); 18:7(8); 77:16(17),18(19); 99:1; **Prov.** 29:9; 30:21; **Isa.** 5:25; 13:13; 14:9,16; 23:11; 28:21; 32:10,11; 37:28,29; 64:2(1); **Jer.** 33:9; 50:34; **Ezek.** 16:43; **Joel** 2:1,10; **Amos** 8:8; **Mic.** 7:17; **Hab.** 3:7,16.

7265. רְגַז *rᵉgaz* **Aram. verb**
(to be angered; corr. to Hebr. 7264)
Ezra 5:12.

7266. רְגַז *rᵉgaz* **Aram. masc. noun**
(rage)
Dan. 3:13.

7267. רֹגֶז *rōgez* **masc. noun**
(turmoil, excitement, rage)
Job 3:17,26; 14:1; 37:2; 39:24; **Isa.** 14:3; **Hab.** 3:2.

7268. רַגָּז *raggāz* **adj.**
(trembling, anxious)
Deut. 28:65.

7269. רָגְזָה *rogzāh* **fem. noun**
(trembling, quivering)
Ezek. 12:18.

7270. I. רָגַל *rāgal* **verb**
(to spy out)
Gen. 42:9,11,14,16,30,31,34; **Num.** 21:32; **Deut.** 1:24; **Josh.** 2:1; 6:22,23, 25; 7:2; 14:7; **Judg.** 18:2,14,17; **1 Sam.** 26:4; **2 Sam.** 10:3; 15:10; **1 Chr.** 19:3.

II. רָגַל *rāgal* **verb**
(to slander)
2 Sam. 19:27(28); **Ps.** 15:3.
III. רָגַל *rāgal* **verb**
(to walk; to teach to walk)
Hos. 11:3(KJV, *tirgal* [8637]).

7271. רְגַל *r^e gal* **Aram. fem. noun**
(foot; corr. to Hebr. 7272)
Dan. 2:33,34,41,42; 7:4,7,19.

7272. רֶגֶל *regel* **fem. noun**
(foot)
Gen. 8:9; 18:4; 19:2; 24:32; 29:1; 30:30; 33:14; 41:44; 43:24; 49:10,33; **Ex.** 3:5; 4:25; 11:8; 12:11; 21:24; 23:14; 24:10; 25:26; 29:20; 30:19,21; 37:13; 40:31; **Lev.** 8:23,24; 11:21,23,42; 13:12; 14:14, 17,25,28; 21:19; **Num.** 20:19; 22:25,28, 32,33; **Deut.** 2:5,28; 8:4; 11:6,10,24; 19:21; 25:9; 28:35,56,57,65; 29:5(6); 32:35; 33:3,24; **Josh.** 1:3; 3:13,15; 4:3, 9,18; 5:15; 9:5; 10:24; 14:9; **Judg.** 1:6,7; 3:24; 4:10,15,17; 5:15,27; 8:5; 19:21; **1 Sam.** 2:9; 14:13; 17:6; 23:22; 24:3(4); 25:24,27,41,42; **2 Sam.** 2:18; 3:34; 4:4,12; 9:3,13; 11:8; 14:25; 15:16–18; 19:24(25); 21:20; 22:10,34,39; **1 Kgs.** 2:5; 5:3(17); 14:6,12; 15:23; 20:10; **2 Kgs.** 3:9; 4:27,37; 6:32; 9:35; 13:21; 18:27; 21:8; **1 Chr.** 28:2; **2 Chr.** 3:13; 16:12; 33:8; **Neh.** 9:21; **Esth.** 8:3; **Job** 2:7; 12:5; 13:27; 18:8,11; 23:11; 28:4; 29:15; 30:12; 31:5; 33:11; 39:15; **Ps.** 8:6(7); 9:15(16); 18:9(10),33(34),38(39); 22:16(17); 25:15; 26:12; 31:8(9); 36:11(12); 38:16(17); 40:2(3); 47:3(4); 56:13(14); 66:6,9; 68:23; 73:2; 91:12; 94:18; 99:5; 105:18; 110:1; 115:7; 116:8; 119:59,101,105; 121:3; 122:2; 132:7; **Prov.** 1:15,16; 3:23,26; 4:26,27; 5:5; 6:13,18,28; 7:11; 19:2; 25:17,19; 26:6; **Eccl.** 5:1(4:17); **Song** 5:3; **Isa.** 1:6; 3:16; 6:2; 7:20; 20:2; 23:7; 26:6; 28:3; 32:20; 36:12; 41:2,3; 49:23; 52:7; 58:13; 59:7; 60:13,14; 66:1; **Jer.** 2:25; 13:16; 14:10; 18:22; 38:22; **Lam.** 1:13; 2:1; 3:34; **Ezek.** 1:7; 2:1,2; 3:24; 6:11; 16:25; 24:17,23; 25:6; 29:11; 32:2,13; 34:18,19; 37:10; 43:7; **Amos** 2:15; **Nah.** 1:3,15 (2:1); **Hab.** 3:5,19; **Zech.** 14:4,12; **Mal.** 4:3(3:21).

7273. רַגְלִי *ragliy* **masc. noun**
(foot soldiers, footmen)
Ex. 12:37; **Num.** 11:21; **Judg.** 20:2; **1 Sam.** 4:10; 15:4; **2 Sam.** 8:4; 10:6,18 (KJV, NASB, Hebr. *paraš* [5671]); **1 Kgs.** 20:29; **2 Kgs.** 13:7; **1 Chr.** 18:4; 19:18; **Jer.** 12:5.

7274. רֹגְלִים *rōgliym* **proper noun**
(Rogelim)
2 Sam. 17:27; 19:31(32).

7275. רָגַם *rāgam* **verb**
(to stone, to kill by stoning)
Lev. 20:2,27; 24:14,16,23; **Num.** 14:10; 15:35,36; **Deut.** 21:21; **Josh.** 7:25; **1 Kgs.** 12:18; **2 Chr.** 10:18; 24:21; **Ezek.** 16:40; 23:47.

7276. רֶגֶם *regem* **masc. proper noun**
(Regem)
1 Chr. 2:47.

7277. I. רִגְמָה *rigmāh* **fem. noun**
(throng, crowd)
Ps. 68:27(28)(KJV, see II).
II. רִגְמָה *rigmāh* **fem. noun**
(council)
Ps. 68:27(28)(NASB, NIV, see I).

7278. רֶגֶם מֶלֶךְ *regem melek̲* **masc. proper noun**
(Regem-melech)
Zech. 7:2.

7279. רָגַן *rāgan* **verb**
(to gossip, to complain)
Deut. 1:27; **Ps.** 106:25; **Prov.** 16:28(KJV, *nirgān* [5372]); 18:8(KJV, *nirgān* [5372]); 26:20(KJV, *nirgān*

[5372]),22(KJV, *nirgān* [5372]); **Isa.** 29:24.

7280. I. רָגַע *rāga'* **verb**
(to do instantaneously, to do in a moment; to endure only for a moment)
Prov. 12:19; **Jer.** 49:19; 50:44.
II. רָגַע *rāga'* **verb**
(to stir up, to churn up)
Job 26:12(NASB, see III); **Isa.** 51:15; **Jer.** 31:35.
III. רָגַע *rāga'* **verb**
(to be at rest; to cease struggles; to bring rest)
Deut. 28:65; **Job** 26:12(KJV, NIV, see II); **Isa.** 34:14; 51:4; **Jer.** 31:2; 47:6; 50:34.
IV. רָגַע *rāga'* **verb**
(to break upon [of skin])
Job 7:5(NASB, see V).
V. רָגַע *rāga'* **verb**
(to harden; to become crusty [of skin])
Job 7:5(KJV, NIV, see IV).

7281. רֶגַע *rega'* **masc. noun**
(moment, instant)
Ex. 33:5; **Num.** 16:21,45(17:10); **Ezra** 9:8; **Job** 7:18; 20:5; 21:13; 34:20; **Ps.** 6:10(11); 30:5(6); 73:19; **Isa.** 26:20; 27:3; 47:9; 54:7,8; **Jer.** 4:20; 18:7,9; **Lam.** 4:6; **Ezek.** 26:16; 32:10.

7282. רָגֵעַ *rāgēa'* **adj.**
(quiet)
Ps. 35:20.

7283. I. רָגַשׁ *rāgaš* **verb**
(to be in a rage)
Ps. 2:1(NIV, see II).
II. רָגַשׁ *rāgaš* **verb**
(to conspire)
Ps. 2:1(KJV, NASB, see I).

7284. רְגַשׁ *r^egaš* **Aram. verb**
(to come together as a group; to conspire; corr. to Hebr. 7283,II)
Dan. 6:6(7),11(12),15(16).

7285. I. רֶגֶשׁ *regeš* **masc. noun**
(throng, company)
Ps. 55:14(15).
II. רֶגֶשׁ *regeš* **masc. noun**
(tumult, noisy crowd)
Ps. 64:2(3).

7286. רָדַד *rāḏaḏ* **verb**
(to subdue; to beat down [of gold]; to be almost gone)
Judg. 19:11(NIV, *yāraḏ* [3381]); **1 Kgs.** 6:32; **Ps.** 144:2; **Isa.** 45:1(NIV, *yāraḏ* [3381]).

7287. I. רָדָה *rāḏāh* **verb**
(to dominate, to rule, to prevail)
Gen. 1:26,28; **Lev.** 25:43,46,53; 26:17; **Num.** 24:19; **Judg.** 5:13(NASB, NIV, *yāraḏ* [3381]); **1 Kgs.** 4:24(5:4); 5:16(30); 9:23; **2 Chr.** 8:10; **Neh.** 9:28; **Ps.** 49:14(15); 68:27(28); 72:8; 110:2; **Isa.** 14:2,6; 41:2; **Jer.** 5:31; **Lam.** 1:13; **Ezek.** 29:15; 34:4.
II. רָדָה *rāḏāh* **verb**
(to scrape out)
Judg. 14:9(KJV, see III).
III. רָדָה *rāḏāh* **verb**
(to take [in one's hands])
Judg. 14:9(NASB, NIV, see II).

7288. רַדַּי *radday* **masc. proper noun**
(Raddai)
1 Chr. 2:14.

7289. רְדִיד *r^eḏiyḏ* **masc. noun**
(cloak, shawl, veil)
Song 5:7; **Isa.** 3:23.

7290. רָדַם *rāḏam* **verb**
(to be asleep; to fall asleep)
Judg. 4:21; **Ps.** 76:6(7); **Prov.** 10:5; **Dan.** 8:18; 10:9; **Jon.** 1:5,6.

7291. רָדַף *rāḏap* **verb**
(to pursue, to chase, to persecute)
Gen. 14:14,15; 31:23; 35:5; 44:4; **Ex.**

14:4,8,9,23; 15:9; **Lev.** 26:7,8,17,36,37; **Deut.** 1:44; 11:4; 16:20; 19:6; 28:22,45; 30:7; 32:30; **Josh.** 2:5,7,16,22; 7:5; 8:16,17,20,24; 10:10,19; 11:8; 20:5; 23:10; 24:6; **Judg.** 1:6; 3:28; 4:16,22; 7:23,25; 8:4,5,12; 9:40; 20:43; **1 Sam.** 7:11; 17:52; 23:25,28; 24:14; 25:29; 26:18,20; 30:8,10; **2 Sam.** 2:19,24,28; 17:1; 18:16; 20:6,7,10,13; 22:38; 24:13; **1 Kgs.** 20:20; **2 Kgs.** 5:21; 9:27; 25:5; **2 Chr.** 13:19; 14:13(12); **Neh.** 9:11; **Job** 13:25; 19:22,28; 30:15; **Ps.** 7:1(2), 5(6); 18:37(38); 23:6; 31:15(16); 34:14(15); 35:3,6; 38:20(21); 69:26(27); 71:11; 83:15(16); 109:16; 119:84,86,150, 157,161; 142:6(7); 143:3; **Prov.** 11:19; 12:11; 13:21; 15:9; 19:7; 21:21; 28:1,19; **Eccl.** 3:15; **Isa.** 1:23; 5:11; 17:13; 30:16; 41:3; 51:1; **Jer.** 15:15; 17:18; 20:11; 29:18; 39:5; 52:8; **Lam.** 1:3,6; 3:43,66; 4:19; 5:5; **Ezek.** 35:6; **Hos.** 2:7(9); 6:3; 8:3; 12:1(2); **Amos** 1:11; **Nah.** 1:8.

7292. רָהַב *rāhab̲* **verb**
(to be bold, proud; to overwhelm)
Ps. 138:3; **Prov.** 6:3; **Song** 6:5; **Isa.** 3:5.

7293. רַהַב *rahab̲* **masc. noun**
(pride, strength)
Job 9:13(NASB, NIV, *rahab̲* [7294,B]); 26:12(NASB, NIV, *rahab̲* [7294,B]); **Isa.** 30:7(NASB, NIV, *rahab̲* [7294,A]).

7294. A. רַהַב *rahab̲* **masc. proper noun**
(Rahab: a poetic name for Egypt)
Ps. 87:4; **Isa.** 30:7(KJV, *rahab̲* [7293]); 51:9.
B. רַהַב *rahab̲* **masc. proper noun**
(Rahab: a mythical sea monster)
Job 9:13(KJV, *rahab̲* [7293]); 26:12 (KJV, *rahab̲* [7293]); **Ps.** 89:10(11).

7295. רָהָב *rāhāb̲* **adj.**
(proud)
Ps. 40:4(5).

7296. רֹהַב *rōhab̲* **masc. noun**
(strength)
Ps. 90:10(NIV, *rōḥab̲* [7341]).

7297. רָהָה *rāhāh* **verb**
(to fear)
Isa. 44:8(NASB, NIV, *yārah* [3384,VII]).

7298. I. רַהַט *rahaṭ* **masc. noun**
(trough, gutter)
Gen. 30:38,41; **Ex.** 2:16.
II. רַהַט *rahaṭ* **masc. noun**
(tress, lock of hair)
Song 7:5(6)(KJV, see III).
III. רַהַט *rahaṭ* **masc. noun**
(gallery)
Song 7:5(6)(NASB, NIV, see II).

7299. רֵו *rēw* **Aram. masc. noun**
(form, appearance)
Dan. 2:31; 3:25.

7300. I. רוּד *rûd̲* **verb**
(to roam; to be restless)
Gen. 27:40(KJV, see III); **Ps.** 55:2(3)(KJV, see IV); **Jer.** 2:31(KJV, see III).
II. רוּד *rûd̲* **verb**
(to be unruly)
Hos. 11:12(12:1)(KJV, see III).
III. רוּד *rûd̲* **verb**
(to have dominion; to rule)
Gen. 27:40(NASB, NIV, see I); **Jer.** 2:31 (NASB, NIV, see I); **Hos.** 11:12(12:1)(NASB, NIV, see II).
IV. רוּד *rûd̲* **verb**
(to mourn)
Ps. 55:2(3)(NASB, NIV, see I).

7301. רָוָה *rāwāh* **verb**
(to give water, to drench; to drink one's fill)
Ps. 36:8(9); 65:10(11); **Prov.** 5:19; 7:18; 11:25; **Isa.** 16:9; 34:5,7; 43:24; 55:10; **Jer.** 31:14,25; 46:10; **Lam.** 3:15.

7302. רָוֶה *rāweh* **adj.**
(watered, well-watered)
Deut. 29:19(18); **Job** 10:15(KJV, NASB, [Hebr] *rā'eh* [7202]); **Isa.** 58:11; **Jer.** 31:12.

7303. רוֹהֲגָה *rôh*^{a}*gāh,* רָהְגָּה *rohgāh* **masc. proper noun**
(Rohgah)
1 Chr. 7:34.

7304. רָוַח *rāwaḥ* **verb**
(to find relief; to be spacious)
1 Sam. 16:23; **Job** 32:20; **Jer.** 22:14.

7305. רֶוַח *rewaḥ* **masc. noun**
(relief; space)
Gen. 32:16(17); **Esth.** 4:14.

7306. רוּחַ *rûaḥ,* רִיחַ *riyaḥ* **verb**
(to smell, to enjoy a fragrance; to accept; to touch)
Gen. 8:21; 27:27; **Ex.** 30:38; **Lev.** 26:31; **Deut.** 4:28; **Judg.** 16:9; **1 Sam.** 26:19; **Job** 39:25; **Ps.** 115:6; **Isa.** 11:3; **Amos** 5:21.

7307. רוּחַ *rûaḥ* **fem. noun**
(spirit, wind, breath)
Gen. 1:2; 3:8; 6:3,17; 7:15,22; 8:1; 26:35; 41:8,38; 45:27; **Ex.** 6:9; 10:13,19; 14:21; 15:8,10; 28:3; 31:3; 35:21,31; **Num.** 5:14,30; 11:17,25,26,29,31; 14:24; 16:22; 24:2; 27:16,18; **Deut.** 2:30; 34:9; **Josh.** 2:11; 5:1; **Judg.** 3:10; 6:34; 8:3; 9:23; 11:29; 13:25; 14:6,19; 15:14,19; **1 Sam.** 1:15; 10:6,10; 11:6; 16:13–16,23; 18:10; 19:9,20,23; 30:12; **2 Sam.** 22:11,16; 23:2; **1 Kgs.** 10:5; 18:12,45; 19:11; 21:5; 22:21–24; **2 Kgs.** 2:9,15,16; 3:17; 19:7; **1 Chr.** 5:26; 9:24; 12:18(19); 28:12; **2 Chr.** 9:4; 15:1; 18:20–23; 20:14; 21:16; 24:20; 36:22; **Ezra** 1:1,5; **Neh.** 9:20,30; **Job** 1:19; 4:9,15; 6:4,26; 7:7,11; 8:2; 9:18; 10:12; 12:10; 15:2,13,30; 16:3; 17:1; 19:17; 20:3; 21:4,18; 26:13; 27:3; 28:25; 30:15,22; 32:8,18; 33:4; 34:14; 37:21; 41:16(8); **Ps.** 1:4; 11:6; 18:10(11), 15(16),42(43); 31:5(6); 32:2; 33:6; 34:18(19); 35:5; 48:7(8); 51:10–12 (12–14),17(19); 55:8(9); 76:12(13); 77:3(4),6(7); 78:8,39; 83:13(14); 103:16; 104:3,4,29,30; 106:33; 107:25; 135:7,17; 139:7; 142:3(4); 143:4,7,10; 146:4; 147:18; 148:8; **Prov.** 1:23; 11:13,29; 14:29; 15:4,13; 16:2,18,19,32; 17:22,27; 18:14; 25:14,23,28; 27:16; 29:11,23; 30:4; **Eccl.** 1:6,14,17; 2:11,17,26; 3:19,21; 4:4,6,16; 5:16(15); 6:9; 7:8,9; 8:8; 10:4; 11:4,5; 12:7; **Isa.** 4:4; 7:2; 11:2,4,15; 17:13; 19:3,14; 25:4; 26:9,18; 27:8; 28:6; 29:10,24; 30:1,28; 31:3; 32:2,15; 33:11; 34:16; 37:7; 38:16; 40:7,13; 41:16,29; 42:1,5; 44:3; 48:16; 54:6; 57:13,15,16; 59:19,21; 61:1,3; 63:10,11,14; 64:6(5); 65:14; 66:2; **Jer.** 2:24; 4:11,12; 5:13; 10:13,14; 13:24; 14:6; 18:17; 22:22; 49:32,36; 51:1,11, 16,17; 52:23; **Lam.** 4:20; **Ezek.** 1:4,12, 20,21; 2:2; 3:12,14,24; 5:2,10,12; 8:3; 10:17; 11:1,5,19,24; 12:14; 13:3,11,13; 17:10,21; 18:31; 19:12; 20:32; 21:7(12); 27:26; 36:26,27; 37:1,5,6,8–10,14; 39:29; 42:16–20; 43:5; **Dan.** 2:1,3; 8:8; 11:4; **Hos.** 4:12,19; 5:4; 8:7; 9:7; 12:1; 13:15; **Joel** 2:28(3:1),29(3:2); **Amos** 4:13; **Jon.** 1:4; 4:8; **Mic.** 2:7,11; 3:8; **Hab.** 1:11; 2:19; **Hag.** 1:14; 2:5; **Zech.** 2:6(10); 4:6; 5:9; 6:5,8; 7:12; 12:1,10; 13:2; **Mal.** 2:15,16.

7308. רוּחַ *rûaḥ* **Aram. fem. noun**
(spirit; wind)
Dan. 2:35; 4:8(5),9(6),18(15); 5:11,12, 14,20; 6:3(4); 7:2,15.

7309. רְוָחָה r^e*wāḥāh* **fem. noun**
(respite, relief)
Ex. 8:15(11); **Lam.** 3:56.

7310. רְוָיָה r^e*wāyāh* **fem. noun**
(abundance; state of overflowing)
Ps. 23:5; 66:12.

7311. רוּם *rûm* **verb**
(to raise, to lift up; to be exalted)
Gen. 7:17; 14:22; 31:45; 39:15,18; 41:44; **Ex.** 7:20; 14:8,16; 15:2; 16:20(NASB, NIV, *rāmam* [7426,II]); 17:11; 29:27; 35:24; **Lev.** 2:9; 4:8,10,19; 6:10(3),15(8); 22:15; **Num.** 15:19,20,30; 16:37(17:2); 18:19, 24,26,28–30,32; 20:11; 24:7; 31:28,52; 33:3; **Deut.** 1:28; 2:10,21; 8:14; 9:2; 12:2; 17:20; 27:14; 32:27; **Josh.** 4:5; **1 Sam.** 2:1,7,8,10; 9:24; **2 Sam.** 22:28, 47,49; **1 Kgs.** 11:26,27; 14:7; 16:2; **2 Kgs.** 2:13; 6:7; 19:22; **1 Chr.** 15:16; 25:5; **2 Chr.** 5:13; 30:24; 35:7–9; **Ezra** 3:12; 8:25; 9:6,9; **Neh.** 9:5; **Job** 17:4; 21:22; 22:12; 38:15,34; 39:27; **Ps.** 3:3(4); 9:13(14); 12:8(9); 13:2(3); 18:27(28), 46(47),48(49); 21:13(14); 27:5,6; 30:1(2), 5(6); 34:3(4); 37:34; 46:10(11); 57:5(6), 11(12); 61:2(3); 66:7,17(KJV, NIV, *rômām* [7318]); 74:3; 75:4–7(5–8),10(11); 78:69; 89:13(14),16(17),17(18),19(20),24(25), 42(43); 92:10(11); 99:2,5,9; 107:25,32; 108:5; 110:7; 112:9; 113:4,7; 118:16 (KJV, *rāmam* [7426]),28; 131:1; 138:6; 140:8(9); 145:1; 148:14; **Prov.** 3:35; 4:8; 6:17; 11:11; 14:29,34; 24:7; 30:13; **Isa.** 1:2; 2:12–14; 6:1; 10:15,33; 13:2; 14:13; 23:4; 25:1; 26:11; 30:18; 33:10 (NASB, *rāmem* [7426]); 37:23; 40:9; 49:11,22; 52:13; 57:14,15; 58:1; 62:10; **Lam.** 2:17; **Ezek.** 6:13; 10:4,16,17; 17:22; 20:28; 21:22(27),26(31); 31:4,10; 34:6; 45:1,9,13; 48:8,9,20; **Dan.** 8:11; 11:12,36; 12:7; **Hos.** 11:4,7; 13:6; **Mic.** 5:9(8).

7312. רוּם *rûm*, רֻם *rum* **masc. noun**
(height, haughtiness, pride)
Prov. 21:4; 25:3; **Isa.** 2:11,17; 10:12; **Jer.** 48:29.

7313. רוּם *rûm* **Aram. verb**
(to lift up, to exalt; corr. to Hebr. 7311)
Dan. 4:37(34); 5:19,20,23.

7314. רוּם *rûm* **Aram. masc. noun**
(height)
Ezra 6:3; **Dan.** 3:1; 4:10(7),11(8), 20(17).

7315. רוֹם *rôm* **adv.**
(high)
Hab. 3:10.

7316. רוּמָה *rûmāh* **proper noun**
(Rumah)
2 Kgs. 23:36.

7317. רוֹמָה *rômāh* **adv.**
(haughtily, proudly)
Mic. 2:3.

7318. רוֹמָם *rômam* **masc. noun**
(praise, high praise)
Ps. 66:17(NASB, *rûm* [7311]); 149:6(KJV, *rôm*ᵉ*māh* [7319]).

7319. רוֹמְמָה *rôm*ᵉ*māh* **fem. noun**
(high praise)
Ps. 149:6(NASB, NIV, *rômām* [7318]).

7320. רוֹמַמְתִּי עֶזֶר *rômamtiy ʿezer*, רֹמַמְתִּי עֶזֶר *rōmamtiy ʿezer* **masc. proper noun**
(Romamti-Ezer)
1 Chr. 25:4,31.

7321. I. רוּעַ *rûaʿ* **verb**
(to shout, to cry out, to raise a battle cry)
Num. 10:7,9; **Josh.** 6:5,10,16,20; **Judg.** 7:21; 15:14; **1 Sam.** 4:5; 10:24; 17:20,52; **2 Chr.** 13:12,15; **Ezra** 3:11,13; **Job** 30:5; 38:7; **Ps.** 41:11(12); 47:1(2); 60:8(10); 65:13(14); 66:1; 81:1; 95:1,2; 98:4,6; 100:1; 108:9(10); **Prov.** 11:15(NASB, NIV, *rāʿaʿ* [7489,I]); **Isa.** 8:9(KJV, *rāʿaʿ* [7489, III]; NASB, *rāʿaʿ* [7489,II]); 15:4; 16:10; 42:13; 44:23; **Jer.** 50:15; **Hos.** 5:8; **Joel** 2:1; **Mic.** 4:9; **Zeph.** 3:14; **Zech.** 9:9.
II. רוּעַ *rûaʿ* **verb**
(to suffer evil; to be destroyed)

Prov. 11:15(NASB, NIV, *rā'a'* [7489,I]); 13:20(NASB, NIV, *rā'a'* [7489,I]).

7322. I. רוּף *rûp̱* **verb**
(to tremble; to quake)
Job 26:11(NASB, NIV, see II).
II. רָפַף *rāp̱ap̱* **verb**
(to tremble; to quake)
Job 26:11(KJV, see I).

7323. I. רוּץ *rûṣ* **verb**
(to run, to guard)
Gen. 18:2,7; 24:17,20,28,29; 29:12,13; 33:4; 41:14; **Num.** 11:27; 16:47(17:12); **Josh.** 7:22; 8:19; **Judg.** 7:21; 13:10; **1 Sam.** 3:5; 4:12; 8:11; 10:23; 17:17,22, 48,51; 20:6,36; 22:17; **2 Sam.** 15:1; 18:19,21–24,26; 22:30; **1 Kgs.** 1:5; 14:27,28; 18:46; 19:20; **2 Kgs.** 4:22,26; 5:20,21; 10:25; 11:4,6,11,13,19; **2 Chr.** 12:10,11; 23:12; 30:6,10; 35:13; **Esth.** 3:13,15; 8:10,14; **Job** 9:25; 15:26; 16:14; **Ps.** 18:29(30); 19:5(6); 59:4(5); 68:31(32); 119:32; 147:15; **Prov.** 1:16; 4:12; 6:18; 18:10; **Song** 1:4; **Isa.** 40:31; 55:5; 59:7; **Jer.** 12:5; 23:21; 49:19; 50:44; 51:31; **Dan.** 8:6; **Joel** 2:4,7,9; **Amos** 6:12; **Nah.** 2:4(5); **Hab.** 2:2; **Hag.** 1:9; **Zech.** 2:4(8).
II. רוּץ *rûṣ* **verb**
(to smash, to break down)
2 Kgs. 23:12(NIV, *rāṣaṣ* [7533]).

7324. רוּק *rûq*, רִיק *riyq* **verb**
(to empty, to pour out, to draw out [a sword])
Gen. 14:14; 42:35; **Ex.** 15:9; **Lev.** 26:33; **Ps.** 18:42(43); 35:3; **Eccl.** 11:3; **Song** 1:3; **Isa.** 32:6; **Jer.** 48:11,12; **Ezek.** 5:2,12; 12:14; 28:7; 30:11; **Hab.** 1:17; **Zech.** 4:12; **Mal.** 3:10.

7325. רוּק *rûq*, רִיק *riyq* **verb**
(to flow [of a running sore])
Lev. 15:3.

7326. רוּשׁ *rûš* **verb**
(to be poor)
1 Sam. 18:23; **2 Sam.** 12:1,3,4; **Ps.** 34:10(11); 82:3; **Prov.** 10:4; 13:7,8,23; 14:20; 17:5; 18:23; 19:1,7,22; 22:2,7; 28:3,6,27; 29:13; **Eccl.** 4:14; 5:8(7).

7327. רוּת *rûṯ* **fem. proper noun**
(Ruth)
Ruth 1:4,14,16,22; 2:2,8,21,22; 3:9; 4:5,10,13.

7328. רָז *raz* **Aram. masc. noun**
(secret, mystery)
Dan. 2:18,19,27–30,47; 4:9(6).

7329. רָזָה *rāzāh* **verb**
(to starve, to waste away)
Isa. 17:4; **Zeph.** 2:11.

7330. רָזֶה *rāzeh* **adj.**
(lean, skinny)
Num. 13:20; **Ezek.** 34:20.

7331. רְזוֹן *r^ezôn* **masc. proper noun**
(Rezon)
1 Kgs. 11:23.

7332. רָזוֹן *rāzôn* **masc. noun**
(leanness, skimpiness)
Ps. 106:15; **Isa.** 10:16; **Mic.** 6:10.

7333. רָזוֹן *rāzôn* **masc. noun**
(prince)
Prov. 14:28.

7334. רָזִי *rāziy* **masc. noun**
(wasting away, leanness)
Isa. 24:16.

7335. רָזַם *rāzam* **verb**
(to wink, to flash the eyes)
Job 15:12.

7336. רָזַן *rāzan* **verb**
(to rule; to be a prince)
Judg. 5:3; **Ps.** 2:2; **Prov.** 8:15; 31:4; **Isa.** 40:23; **Hab.** 1:10.

7337. רָחַב *rāḥab̲* **verb**
(to enlarge, to extend; to open wide)
Gen. 26:22; **Ex.** 34:24; **Deut.** 12:20; 19:8; 33:20; **1 Sam.** 2:1; **2 Sam.** 22:37; **Ps.** 4:1; 18:36(37); 25:17; 35:21; 81:10(11); 119:32; **Prov.** 18:16; **Isa.** 5:14; 30:23,33; 54:2; 57:4,8; 60:5; **Ezek.** 41:7; **Amos** 1:13; **Mic.** 1:16; **Hab.** 2:5.

7338. רַחַב *rāḥab̲* **masc. noun**
(broad place, expanse)
Job 36:16; 38:18.

7339. רְחֹב *r^eḥōb̲*, רְחוֹב *r^eḥôb̲* **fem. noun**
(street, public square, open place)
Gen. 19:2; **Deut.** 13:16(17); **Judg.** 19:15,17,20; **2 Sam.** 21:12; **2 Chr.** 29:4; 32:6; **Ezra** 10:9; **Neh.** 8:1,3,16; **Esth.** 4:6; 6:9,11; **Job** 29:7; **Ps.** 55:11(12); 144:14; **Prov.** 1:20; 5:16; 7:12; 22:13; 26:13; **Song** 3:2; **Isa.** 15:3; 59:14; **Jer.** 5:1; 9:21(20); 48:38; 49:26; 50:30; **Lam.** 2:11,12; 4:18; **Ezek.** 16:24,31; **Dan.** 9:25; **Amos** 5:16; **Nah.** 2:4; **Zech.** 8:4,5.

7340. A. רְחֹב *r^eḥōb̲* **proper noun**
(Rehob: town near Hamath)
Num. 13:21.
B. רְחֹב *r^eḥōb̲* **proper noun**
(Rehob: town in Asher)
Josh. 19:28,30; 21:31; **Judg.** 1:31; **1 Chr.** 6:75(60).
C. רְחוֹב *r^eḥôb̲* **proper noun**
(Rehob: Aramean town)
2 Sam. 10:8.
D. רְחֹב *r^eḥōb̲* **masc. proper noun**
(Rehob: father of Hadadezer)
2 Sam. 8:3,12.
E. רְחוֹב *r^eḥôb̲* **masc. proper noun**
(Rehob: covenanter in Nehemiah's day)
Neh. 10:11(12).

7341. רֹחַב *rōḥab̲* **masc. noun**
(breadth, width)
Gen. 6:15; 13:17; **Ex.** 25:10,17,23; 26:2,8,16; 27:1,12,13,18; 28:16; 30:2; 36:9,15,21; 37:1,6,10,25; 38:1,18; 39:9; **Deut.** 3:11; **1 Kgs.** 4:29(5:9); 6:2,3,6,20; 7:2,6,27; **2 Chr.** 3:3,4,8; 4:1; 6:13; **Job** 37:10; **Ps.** 91:10(KJV, NASB, *rōhab̲* [7296]); **Isa.** 8:8; **Ezek.** 40:5–7,11,13, 19–21,25,29,30,33,36,42,47–49; 41:1–5,7,9–12,14; 42:2,4,10,11,20; 43:13,14,16,17; 45:1,3,5,6; 46:22; 48:8–10,13,15; **Zech.** 2:2(6); 5:2.

7342. רָחָב *rāḥāb̲* **adj.**
(broad, wide, spacious, large)
Gen. 34:21; **Ex.** 3:8; **Judg.** 18:10; **1 Chr.** 4:40; **Neh.** 3:8; 4:19(13); 7:4; 9:35; 12:38; **Job** 11:9; 30:14; **Ps.** 101:5; 104:25; 119:45,96; **Prov.** 21:4; 28:25; **Isa.** 22:18; 33:21; **Jer.** 51:58; **Ezek.** 23:32.

7343. רָחָב *rāḥab̲* **fem. proper noun**
(Rahab)
Josh. 2:1,3; 6:17,23,25.

7344. A. רְחֹבוֹת *r^eḥōb̲ôt̲* **proper noun**
(Rehoboth: well dug by Isaac)
Gen. 26:22.
B. רְחֹבוֹת *r^eḥōb̲ôt̲* **proper noun**
(Rehoboth: city on the Euphrates River; see also C and D)
Gen. 36:37; **1 Chr.** 1:48.
C. רְחֹבוֹת *r^eḥōb̲ôt̲* **proper noun**
(Rehoboth: city of Shaul, king of Edom; possibly the same as B)
Gen. 10:11(NASB, NIV, see D).
D. רְחֹבוֹת עִיר *r^eḥōb̲ôt̲ 'iyr* **proper noun**
(Rehoboth-Ir: *r^eḥōb̲ôt̲* [7344,B] and *'iyr* [5892]; possibly the same as B)
Gen. 10:11(KJV, see C).

7345. רְחַבְיָה *r^eḥab̲yāh*, רְחַבְיָהוּ *r^eḥab̲yāhû* **masc. proper noun**
(Rehabiah)
1 Chr. 23:17; 24:21; 26:25.

7346. רְחַבְעָם *r^eḥaḇ'ām* **masc. proper noun**
(Rehoboam)
1 Kgs. 11:43; 12:1,3,6,12,17,18,21, 23,27; 14:21,25,27,29–31; 15:6; **1 Chr.** 3:10; **2 Chr.** 9:31; 10:1,3,6,12,13,17,18; 11:1,3,5,17,18,21,22; 12:1,2,5,10,13, 15,16; 13:7.

7347. רֵחֶה *rēḥeh,* רֵחַיִם *rēḥayim* **masc. noun**
(handmill, millstones)
Ex. 11:5; **Num.** 11:8; **Deut.** 24:6; **Isa.** 47:2; **Jer.** 25:10.

7348. A. רְחוּם *r^eḥûm* **masc. proper noun**
(Rehum: leader returning with Zerubbabel)
Ezra 2:2; **Neh.** 12:3.
B. רְחוּם *r^eḥûm* **masc. proper noun**
(Rehum: Jewish builder of Nehemiah's wall)
Neh. 3:17.
C. רְחוּם *r^eḥûm* **masc. proper noun**
(Rehum: a covenanter in Nehemiah's day; possibly the same as B)
Neh. 10:25(26).
D. רְחוּם *r^eḥûm* **Aram. masc. proper noun**
(Rehum: commanding officer who opposed the rebuilding of Jerusalem)
Ezra 4:8,9,17,23.

7349. רַחוּם *raḥûm* **adj.**
(compassionate, merciful)
Ex. 34:6; **Deut.** 4:31; **2 Chr.** 30:9; **Neh.** 9:17,31; **Ps.** 78:38; 86:15; 103:8; 111:4; 112:4; 145:8; **Joel** 2:13; **Jon.** 4:2.

7350. רָחוֹק *rāḥôq,* רָחֹק *rāḥōq* **adj.**
(far off, faraway, distant)
Gen. 22:4; 37:18; **Ex.** 2:4; 20:18,21; 24:1; **Num.** 9:10; **Deut.** 13:7(8); 20:15; 28:49; 29:22(21); 30:11; **Josh.** 3:4; 9:6,9,22; **Judg.** 18:7,28; **1 Sam.** 26:13; **2 Sam.** 7:19; **1 Kgs.** 8:41,46; **2 Kgs.** 2:7; 19:25; 20:14; **1 Chr.** 17:17; **2 Chr.** 6:32,36; 26:15; **Ezra** 3:13; **Neh.** 4:19(13); 12:43; **Esth.** 9:20; **Job** 2:12; 36:3,25; 39:25,29; **Ps.** 10:1; 22:1; 38:11(12); 65:5(6); 103:12; 119:155; 139:2; **Prov.** 7:19; 15:29; 27:10; 31:10; **Eccl.** 7:23,24; **Isa.** 5:26; 22:3,11; 23:7; 25:1; 33:13; 37:26; 39:3; 43:6; 46:12; 49:1,12; 57:9,19; 59:14; 60:4,9; 66:19; **Jer.** 12:2; 23:23; 25:26; 30:10; 31:3; 46:27; 48:24; 51:50; **Ezek.** 6:12; 12:27; 22:5; **Dan.** 9:7; **Joel** 3:8(4:8); **Mic.** 4:3; **Hab.** 1:8; **Zech.** 6:15.

7351. רָחִיט *rāḥiyt,* רָהִיט *rāhiyṭ* **masc. coll. noun**
(rafters)
Song 1:17.

7352. רַחִיק *raḥiyq* **Aram. adj.**
(faraway, distant; corr. to Hebr. 7350)
Ezra 6:6.

7353. רָחֵל *rāḥēl* **fem. noun**
(ewe, female sheep)
Gen. 31:38; 32:14(15); **Song** 6:6; **Isa.** 53:7.

7354. רָחֵל *rāḥēl* **fem. proper noun**
(Rachel)
Gen. 29:6,9–12,16–18,20,25,28–31; 30:1,2,6–8,14,15,22,25; 31:4,14,19, 32–34; 33:1,2,7; 35:16,19,20,24,25; 46:19,22,25; 48:7; **Ruth** 4:11; **1 Sam.** 10:2; **Jer.** 31:15.

7355. I. רָחַם *rāḥam* **verb**
(to have mercy, to have compassion; to be loved)
Ex. 33:19; **Deut.** 13:17(18); 30:3; **1 Kgs.** 8:50; **2 Kgs.** 13:23; **Ps.** 18:1;

102:13(14); 103:13; 116:5; **Prov.** 28:13; **Isa.** 9:17(16); 13:18; 14:1; 27:11; 30:18; 49:10,13,15; 54:8,10; 55:7; 60:10; **Jer.** 6:23; 12:15; 13:14; 21:7; 30:18; 31:20; 33:26; 42:12; 50:42; **Lam.** 3:32; **Ezek.** 39:25; **Hos.** 1:6,7; 2:1(3)(KJV, NASB, see II),4(6),23(25); 14:3(4); **Mic.** 7:19; **Hab.** 3:2; **Zech.** 1:12; 10:6.

II. רֻחָמָה *ruḥāmāh* **fem. proper noun**
(Ruhamah [lit.: loved one])
Hos. 2:1(3)(NIV, see I).

7356. I. רַחַם *raḥam* **masc. noun**
(compassion, mercy)
Gen. 43:14,30; **Deut.** 13:17(18); **2 Sam.** 24:14; **1 Kgs.** 3:26; 8:50; **1 Chr.** 21:13; **2 Chr.** 30:9; **Neh.** 1:11; 9:19,27,28,31; **Ps.** 25:6; 40:11(12); 51:1; 69:16(17); 77:9(10); 79:8; 103:4; 106:46; 119:77,156; 145:9; **Prov.** 12:10; **Isa.** 47:6; 54:7; 63:7,15; **Jer.** 16:5; 42:12; **Lam.** 3:22; **Dan.** 1:9; 9:9,18; **Hos.** 2:19(21); **Amos** 1:11; **Zech.** 1:16; 7:9.

II. רַחַם *raḥam* **masc. noun**
(womb)
Gen. 49:25(NASB, NIV, *reḥem* [7358]); **Prov.** 30:16(NASB, NIV, *reḥem* [7358]); **Isa.** 46:3(NASB, NIV, *reḥem* [7358]); **Ezek.** 20:26(NASB, NIV, *reḥem* [7358]).

7357. רַחַם *raḥam* **masc. proper noun**
(Raham)
1 Chr. 2:44.

7358. רֶחֶם *reḥem* **masc. noun**
(womb, matrix)
Gen. 20:18; 29:31; 30:22; 49:25(KJV, *raḥam* [7356,II]); **Ex.** 13:2,12,15; 34:19; **Num.** 3:12; 8:16; 12:12; 18:15; **Judg.** 5:30(KJV, NIV, *raḥamāh* [7361]); **1 Sam.** 1:5,6; **Job** 3:11; 10:18; 24:20; 31:15; 38:8; **Ps.** 22:10; 58:3; 110:3; **Prov.** 30:16(KJV, *raḥam* [7356,II]); **Isa.** 46:3(KJV, *raḥam* [7356,II]); **Jer.** 1:5; 20:17,18; **Ezek.** 20:26(KJV, *raḥam* [7356,II]); **Hos.** 9:14.

7359. רַחֲמִין *raḥ^a^miyn* **Aram. masc. noun**
(mercy, compassion; corr. to Hebr. 7356,I)
Dan. 2:18.

7360. רָחָם *rāḥām*, רָחָמָה *rāḥāmāh* **masc. noun**
(carrion vulture, osprey, gier-eagle)
Lev. 11:18; **Deut.** 14:17.

7361. רַחֲמָה *raḥ^a^māh* **fem. noun**
(maiden, girl)
Judg. 5:30(NASB, *reḥem* [7358]).

7362. רַחֲמָנִי *raḥ^a^māniy* **adj.**
(compassionate, characterized by pity)
Lam. 4:10.

7363. רָחַף *rāḥap̱* **verb**
(to move, to hover, to tremble)
Gen. 1:2; **Deut.** 32:11; **Jer.** 23:9.

7364. רָחַץ *rāḥaṣ* **verb**
(to wash, to bathe)
Gen. 18:4; 19:2; 24:32; 43:24,31; **Ex.** 2:5; 29:4,17; 30:18–21; 40:12,30–32; **Lev.** 1:9,13; 8:6,21; 9:14; 14:8,9; 15:5–8,10,11,13,16,18,21,22,27; 16:4,24,26,28; 17:15,16; 22:6; **Num.** 19:7,8,19; **Deut.** 21:6; 23:11(12); **Judg.** 19:21; **Ruth** 3:3; **1 Sam.** 25:41; **2 Sam.** 11:2,8; 12:20; **1 Kgs.** 22:38; **2 Kgs.** 5:10,12,13; **2 Chr.** 4:6; **Job** 9:30; 29:6; **Ps.** 26:6; 58:10(11); 73:13; **Prov.** 30:12; **Song** 5:3,12; **Isa.** 1:16; 4:4; **Ezek.** 16:4,9; 23:40.

7365. רְחַץ *r^e^ḥaṣ* **Aram. verb**
(to trust)
Dan. 3:28.

7366. רַחַץ *raḥaṣ* **masc. noun**
(washbowl, washbasin)
Ps. 60:8(10); 108:9(10).

7367. רַחְצָה *raḥṣāh* **fem. noun**
(washing)
Song 4:2; 6:6.

7368. רָחַק *rāḥaq* **verb**
(to be faraway; to become faraway)
Gen. 21:16; 44:4; **Ex.** 8:28; 23:7; 33:7; **Deut.** 12:21; 14:24; **Josh.** 3:16; 8:4; **Judg.** 18:22; **Job** 5:4; 11:14; 13:21; 19:13; 21:16; 22:18,23; 30:10; **Ps.** 22:11(12), 19(20); 35:22; 38:21(22); 55:7(8); 71:12; 88:8(9),18(19); 103:12; 109:17; 119:150; **Prov.** 4:24; 5:8; 19:7; 22:5,15; 30:8; **Eccl.** 3:5; 12:6(NASB, [Qe] *rāṯaḥ* [7576]); **Isa.** 6:12; 26:15; 29:13; 46:13; 49:19; 54:14; 59:9,11; **Jer.** 2:5; 27:10; **Lam.** 1:16; **Ezek.** 8:6; 11:15,16; 43:9; 44:10; **Joel** 2:20; 3:6(4:6); **Mic.** 7:11.

7369. רָחֵק *rāḥēq* **adj.**
(faraway)
Ps. 73:27.

7370. I. רחשׁ *rāḥaš* **verb**
(to be stirred, to overflow)
Ps. 45:1(KJV, see II).
II. רָחַשׁ *rāḥaš* **verb**
(to indite; to put in words)
Ps. 45:1(NASB, NIV, see I).

7371. רַחַת *raḥaṯ* **fem. noun**
(shovel, pitchfork)
Isa. 30:24.

7372. רָטַב *rāṭaḇ* **verb**
(to be wet, drenched)
Job 24:8.

7373. רָטֹב *rāṭōḇ* **adj.**
(well-watered, thriving)
Job 8:16.

7374. רֶטֶט *reṭeṭ* **masc. noun**
(panic, fear)
Jer. 49:24.

7375. רֻטֲפַשׁ *ruṭapaš* **verb**
(to become fresh, to be renewed)
Job 33:25.

7376. רָטַשׁ *rāṭaš* **verb**
(to dash to pieces; to strike down)
2 Kgs. 8:12; **Isa.** 13:16,18; **Hos.** 10:14; 13:16(14:1); **Nah.** 3:10.

7377. רִי *riy* **masc. noun**
(moisture; watering)
Job 37:11.

7378. רִיב *riyḇ*, רוּב *rûḇ* **verb**
(to strive, to contend, to quarrel; to plead)
Gen. 26:20–22; 31:36; **Ex.** 17:2,7(KJV, NASB, *riyḇ* [7379]); 21:18; **Num.** 20:3,13; **Deut.** 33:8; **Judg.** 6:31,32; 8:1; 11:25; 21:22; **1 Sam.** 2:10; 24:15(16); 25:39; **Neh.** 5:7; 13:11,17,25; **Job** 9:3; 10:2; 13:8,19; 23:6; 31:13(NASB, NIV, *riyḇ* [7379]); 33:13; 40:2; **Ps.** 35:1; 43:1; 74:22; 103:9; 119:154; **Prov.** 3:30; 22:23; 23:11; 25:8,9; **Isa.** 1:17; 3:13; 27:8; 45:9; 49:25; 50:8; 51:22; 57:16; **Jer.** 2:9,29; 12:1; 50:34; 51:36; **Lam.** 3:58; **Hos.** 2:2(4); 4:4; **Amos** 7:4; **Mic.** 6:1; 7:9.

7379. I. רִיב *riyḇ*, רִב *riḇ* **masc. noun**
(dispute, strife, quarrel, cause, case)
Gen. 13:7; **Ex.** 17:7(NIV, *riyḇ* [7378]); 23:2,3,6; **Deut.** 1:12; 17:8(NIV, see II); 19:17; 21:5; 25:1; **Judg.** 12:2; **1 Sam.** 24:15(16); 25:39; **2 Sam.** 15:2,4; 22:44; **2 Chr.** 19:8,10; **Job** 13:6(NIV, see II); 29:16; 31:35; 33:19(KJV, [Qe] *rōḇ* [7230]); **Ps.** 18:43(44); 31:20(21); 35:23; 43:1; 55:9(10); 74:22; 119:154; **Prov.** 15:18; 17:1,14; 18:6,17; 20:3; 22:23; 23:11; 25:9; 26:17,21; 30:33; **Isa.** 1:23; 34:8; 41:11,21; 58:4; **Jer.** 11:20; 15:10; 20:12; 25:31; 50:34; 51:36; **Lam.** 3:36,58; **Ezek.** 44:24; **Hos.** 4:1; 12:2(3); **Mic.** 6:2; 7:9; **Hab.** 1:3.
II. רִיבָה *riyḇāh* **masc. noun**
(cause, plea)
Deut. 17:8(KJV, NASB, see I); **Job** 13:6(KJV, NASB, see I).

7380. רִיבַי *riybay* **masc. proper noun**
(Ribai)
2 Sam. 23:29; **1 Chr.** 11:31.

7381. רֵיחַ *rēyaḥ* **masc. noun**
(aroma, fragrance, odor)
Gen. 8:21; 27:27; **Ex.** 5:21; 29:18,25,41; **Lev.** 1:9,13,17; 2:2,9,12; 3:5,16; 4:31; 6:15(8),21(14); 8:21,28; 17:6; 23:13,18; 26:31; **Num.** 15:3,7,10,13,14,24; 18:17; 28:2,6,8,13,24,27; 29:2,6,8,13,36; **Job** 14:9; **Song** 1:3,12; 2:13; 4:10,11; 7:8(9), 13(14); **Jer.** 48:11; **Ezek.** 6:13; 16:19; 20:28,41; **Hos.** 14:6(7).

7382. רֵיחַ *rēyaḥ* **Aram. fem. noun**
(smell, odor; corr. to Hebr. 7381)
Dan. 3:27.

7383. רִיפָה *riypāh*, רִפָה *ripāh* **fem. noun**
(grain)
2 Sam. 17:19; **Prov.** 27:22.

7384. I. רִיפַת *riypat* **masc. proper noun**
(Riphath, see also II)
Gen. 10:3.
II. דִיפַת *diypat* **masc. proper noun**
(Diphath, Riphath, same as I)
1 Chr. 1:6.

7385. רִיק *riyq* **masc. noun**
(emptiness, vanity, delusion)
Lev. 26:16,20; **Job** 39:16; **Ps.** 2:1; 4:2(3); 73:13; **Isa.** 30:7; 49:4; 65:23; **Jer.** 51:34(NASB, *rēyq* [7386]),58; **Hab.** 2:13.

7386. רֵיק *rēyq*, רֵק *rēq* **adj.**
(empty, worthless, vain)
Gen. 37:24; 41:27(NASB, *rāq* [7534]); **Deut.** 32:47; **Judg.** 7:16; 9:4; 11:3; **2 Sam.** 6:20; **2 Kgs.** 4:3; **2 Chr.** 13:7; **Neh.** 5:13; **Prov.** 12:11; 28:19; **Isa.** 29:8; **Ezek.** 24:11.

7387. רֵיקָם *rēyqām* **adv.**
(empty-handed, empty)
Gen. 31:42; **Ex.** 3:21; 23:15; 34:20; **Deut.** 15:13; 16:16; **Ruth** 1:21; 3:17; **1 Sam.** 6:3; **2 Sam.** 1:22; **Job** 22:9; **Ps.** 7:4(5); 25:3; **Isa.** 55:11; **Jer.** 14:3; 50:9.

7388. I. רִיר *riyr* **masc. noun**
(saliva)
1 Sam. 21:13(14).
II. רִיר *riyr* **masc. noun**
(white of an egg)
Job 6:6.

7389. רֵישׁ *rēyš*, רֵאשׁ *rē'š*, רִישׁ *riyš* **masc. noun**
(poverty)
Prov. 6:11; 10:15; 13:18; 24:34; 28:19; 30:8; 31:7.

7390. רַךְ *rak* **adj.**
(gentle, tender, weak, indecisive)
Gen. 18:7; 29:17; 33:13; **Deut.** 20:8(NASB, *rākak* [7401]); 28:54,56; **2 Sam.** 3:39; **2 Kgs.** 22:19(KJV, NASB, *rākak* [7401]); **1 Chr.** 22:5; 29:1; **2 Chr.** 13:7; 24:27(KJV, NASB, *rākak* [7401]); **Job** 41:3(40:27); **Prov.** 4:3; 15:1; 25:15; **Isa.** 47:1; **Ezek.** 17:22.

7391. רֹךְ *rōk* **masc. noun**
(gentleness, refinement)
Deut. 28:56.

7392. רָכַב *rākab* **verb**
(to ride a horse; to ride in a chariot)
Gen. 24:61; 41:43; 49:17; **Ex.** 4:20; 15:1,21; **Lev.** 15:9; **Num.** 22:22,30; **Deut.** 32:13; 33:26; **Judg.** 5:10; 10:4; 12:14; **1 Sam.** 25:20,42; 30:17; **2 Sam.** 6:3; 13:29; 16:2; 18:9; 19:26(27); 22:11; **1 Kgs.** 1:33,38,44; 13:13; 18:45; **2 Kgs.** 4:24; 9:16,18,19,25,28; 10:16; 13:16; 18:23; 23:30; **1 Chr.** 13:7; **2 Chr.** 35:24; **Neh.** 2:12; **Esth.** 6:8,9,11; 8:10,14; **Job** 30:22; 39:18; **Ps.** 18:10(11); 45:4(5); 66:12; 68:4(5),33(34); **Isa.** 19:1; 30:16;

36:8; 58:14; **Jer.** 6:23; 17:25; 22:4; 50:42; 51:21; **Ezek.** 23:6,12,23; 38:15; **Hos.** 10:11; 14:3(4); **Amos** 2:15; **Hab.** 3:8; **Hag.** 2:22; **Zech.** 1:8; 9:9; 10:5; 12:4.

7393. I. רֶכֶב *rek̲eb̲* **masc. noun**
(chariot)
Gen. 50:9; **Ex.** 14:6,7,9,17,18,23,26,28; 15:19; **Deut.** 11:4; 20:1; **Josh.** 11:4; 17:16,18; 24:6; **Judg.** 1:19; 4:3,7,13, 15,16; 5:28; **1 Sam.** 8:12; 13:5; **2 Sam.** 1:6; 8:4; 10:18; **1 Kgs.** 1:5; 9:19,22; 10:26; 16:9; 20:1,21,25; 22:31–33,35,38; **2 Kgs.** 2:11,12; 5:9; 6:14,15,17; 7:6,14; 8:21; 9:21,24; 10:2,16; 13:7,14; 18:24; 19:23; **1 Chr.** 18:4; 19:6,7,18; **2 Chr.** 1:14; 8:6,9; 9:25; 12:3; 16:8; 18:30–32; 21:9; 35:24; **Ps.** 20:7(8); 68:17(18); 76:6(7); **Song** 1:9; **Isa.** 21:7,9; 22:6,7; 31:1; 36:9; 37:24; 43:17; 66:20; **Jer.** 17:25; 22:4; 46:9; 47:3; 50:37; 51:21; **Ezek.** 23:24; 26:7,10; 39:20; **Dan.** 11:40; **Nah.** 2:3(4),4(5),13(14); **Zech.** 9:10.
II. רֶכֶב *rek̲eb̲* **masc. noun**
(upper millstone)
Deut. 24:6; **Judg.** 9:53; **2 Sam.** 11:21.

7394. A. רֵכָב *rēk̲āb̲* **masc. proper noun**
(Rechab: one of the assassins of Ishbosheth)
2 Sam. 4:2,5,6,9.
B. רֵכָב *rēk̲āb̲* **masc. proper noun**
(Rechab: father of Jehonadab; reference also to his descendants)
2 Kgs. 10:15,23; **1 Chr.** 2:55; **Neh.** 3:14; **Jer.** 35:6,8,14,16,19.

7395. רַכָּב *rakkāb̲* **masc. noun**
(chariot driver, horseman)
1 Kgs. 22:34; **2 Kgs.** 9:17; **2 Chr.** 18:33.

7396. I. רִכְבָּה *rik̲bāh* **fem. noun**
(saddle)
Ezek. 27:20(KJV, see II).
II. רִכְבָּה *rik̲bāh* **fem. noun**
(chariot)
Ezek. 27:20(NASB, NIV, see I).

7397. I. רֵכָה *rēk̲āh* **proper noun**
(Recah, Rechah)
1 Chr. 4:12.
II. רֵכָבִי *rēk̲āb̲iy* **masc. proper noun**
(Rechabite)
Jer. 35:2,3,5,18.

7398. רְכוּב *rᵉk̲ûb̲* **masc. noun**
(chariot)
Ps. 104:3.

7399. רְכוּשׁ *rᵉk̲ûš*, רְכֻשׁ *rᵉk̲uš* **masc. noun**
(possessions; property, goods)
Gen. 12:5; 13:6; 14:11,12,16,21; 15:14; 31:18; 36:7; 46:6; **Num.** 16:32; 35:3; **1 Chr.** 27:31; 28:1; **2 Chr.** 20:25; 21:14,17; 31:3; 32:29; 35:7; **Ezra** 1:4,6; 8:21; 10:8; **Dan.** 11:13,24,28.

7400. רָכִיל *rāk̲iyl* **masc. noun**
(gossip, slander; talebearer)
Lev. 19:16; **Prov.** 11:13; 20:19; **Jer.** 6:28; 9:4(3); **Ezek.** 22:9.

7401. רָכַךְ *rākak* **verb**
(to be tender, fainthearted, faint, weak, soft)
Deut. 20:3,8(KJV, NIV, *rak̲* [7390]); **2 Kgs.** 22:19(NIV, *rak̲* [7390]); **2 Chr.** 34:27(NIV, *rak̲* [7390]); **Job** 23:16; **Ps.** 55:21(22); **Isa.** 1:6; 7:4; **Jer.** 51:46.

7402. רָכַל *rāk̲al* **verb**
(to sell merchandise, to trade)
1 Kgs. 10:15; **Neh.** 3:31,32; 13:20; **Song** 3:6; **Ezek.** 17:4; 27:3,13,15,17, 20,22–24; **Nah.** 3:16.

7403. רָכָל *rāk̲āl* **proper noun**
(Racal, Rachal)
1 Sam. 30:29.

7404. רְכֻלָּה *r^e^k̲ullāh* **fem. noun**
(merchandise, trading)
Ezek. 26:12; 28:5,16,18.

7405. רָכַס *rāk̲as* **verb**
(to bind, to tie)
Ex. 28:28; 39:21.

7406. רֶכֶס *rek̲es* **masc. noun**
(rugged terrain)
Isa. 40:4.

7407. I. רֹכֶס *rōk̲es* **masc. noun**
(conspiracy, intrigue)
Ps. 31:20(21)(KJV, see II).
II. רֹכֶס *rōk̲es* **masc. noun**
(pride)
Ps. 31:20(21)(NASB, NIV, see I).

7408. רָכַשׁ *rāk̲aš* **verb**
(to accumulate, to acquire)
Gen. 12:5; 31:18; 36:6; 46:6.

7409. I. רֶכֶשׁ *rek̲eš* **masc. noun**
(horse, steed)
1 Kgs. 4:28(5:8)(KJV, see II); **Esth.** 8:10(KJV, see III),14(KJV, see III); **Mic.** 1:13(KJV, see IV).
II. רֶכֶשׁ *rek̲eš* **masc. noun**
(camel, dromedary)
1 Kgs. 4:28(5:8)(NASB, NIV, see I).
III. רֶכֶשׁ *rek̲eš* **masc. noun**
(mule)
Esth. 8:10(NASB, NIV, see I),14(NASB, NIV, see I).
IV. רֶכֶשׁ *rek̲eš* **masc. noun**
(swift beast)
Mic. 1:13)(NASB, NIV, see I).

7410. A. רָם *rām* **masc. proper noun**
(Ram: son of Hezron)
Ruth 4:19; **1 Chr.** 2:9.
B. רָם *rām* **masc. proper noun**
(Ram: son of Jerahmeel)
1 Chr. 2:25,27.
C. רָם *rām* **masc. proper noun**
(Ram: relative of Elihu)
Job 32:2.

7411. I. רָמָה *rāmāh* **verb**
(to throw; to shoot [an arrow])
Ex. 15:1,21; **Ps.** 78:9; **Jer.** 4:29.
II. רָמָה *rāmāh* **verb**
(to betray; to deceive)
Gen. 29:25; **Josh.** 9:22; **1 Sam.** 19:17; 28:12; **2 Sam.** 19:26; **1 Chr.** 12:17; **Prov.** 26:19; **Lam.** 1:19.

7412. רְמָה *r^e^māh* **Aram. verb**
(to cast down, to throw; to impose a tribute)
Ezra 7:24; **Dan.** 3:6,11,15,20,21,24; 6:7(8),12(13),16(17),24(25); 7:9.

7413. רָמָה *rāmāh* **fem. noun**
(height, hill, high place [of worship])
1 Sam. 22:6(KJV, *rāmāh* [7414,B]); **Ezek.** 16:24,25,31,39.

7414. A. רָמָה *rāmāh* **proper noun**
(Ramah: town in Benjamin)
Josh. 18:25; **Judg.** 4:5; 19:13; **1 Kgs.** 15:17,21,22; **2 Chr.** 16:1,5,6; **Ezra** 2:26; **Neh.** 7:30; 11:33; **Isa.** 10:29; **Jer.** 31:15; 40:1; **Hos.** 5:8.
B. רָמָה *rāmāh* **proper noun**
(Ramah: Samuel's home town in Ephraim; the same as *rāmāt̲ayim ṣôp̲iym* [7436])
1 Sam. 1:19; 2:11; 7:17; 8:4; 15:34; 16:13; 19:18,19,22,23; 20:1; 22:6(NASB, NIV, *rāmāh* [7413]); 25:1; 28:3.
C. רָמָה *rāmāh* **proper noun**
(Ramah: town on border of Asher)
Josh. 19:29.
D. רָמָה *rāmāh* **proper noun**
(Ramah: town in Naphtali)
Josh. 19:36.
E. רָמָה *rāmāh* **proper noun**
(Ramah, Ramath; town in Simeon; the same as *rāmôt̲ negeb̲* [7418])
Josh. 19:8.

F. רָמָה *rāmāh* **proper noun**
(Ramah: short for *rāmôt̲ gil^{e}ʿād̲* [7433])
2 Kgs. 8:29; **2 Chr.** 22:6.

7415. רִמָּה *rimmāh* **fem. noun**
(worm, maggot)
Ex. 16:24; **Job** 7:5; 17:14; 21:26; 24:20; 25:6; **Isa.** 14:11.

7416. רִמּוֹן *rimmôn,* רִמֹּן *rimmōn* **masc. noun**
(pomegranate)
Ex. 28:33,34; 39:24–26; **Num.** 13:23; 20:5; **Deut.** 8:8; **1 Sam.** 14:2; **1 Kgs.** 7:18,20,42; **2 Kgs.** 25:17; **2 Chr.** 3:16; 4:13; **Song** 4:3,13; 6:7,11; 7:12(13); 8:2; **Jer.** 52:22,23; **Joel** 1:12; **Hag.** 2:19.

7417. A. רִמּוֹן *rimmôn* **masc. proper noun**
(Rimmon: a Syrian god)
2 Kgs. 5:18.
B. רִמּוֹן *rimmôn* **masc. proper noun**
(Rimmon: a Benjaminite)
2 Sam. 4:2,5,9.
C. רִמּוֹן *rimmôn* **proper noun**
(Rimmon: a rock in the wilderness of Benjamin)
Judg. 20:45,47; 21:13.
D. רִמּוֹן *rimmôn* **proper noun**
(Rimmon: a town in Judah)
Josh. 15:32; 19:7; **1 Chr.** 4:32; **Zech.** 14:10.
E. רִמּוֹן *rimmôn,* רִמּוֹנוֹ *rimmônô* **proper noun**
(Rimmon: a town in Zebulun)
Josh. 19:13(KJV, see F); **1 Chr.** 6:77(62).
F. רִמּוֹן הַמְּתֹאָר *rimmôn hamm^{e}tōʾār* **proper noun**
(Remmon-methoar: *rimmôn* [7417,E] and *t̲āʾar* [8388,I])
Josh. 19:13.

7418. רָמוֹת נֶגֶב *rāmôt̲ negeb̲* **proper noun**
(Ramoth Negev; Ramoth of the south; the same as *rāmāh* [7414,E])
1 Sam. 30:27.

7419. I. רָמוּת *rāmût̲* **fem. noun**
(remains; refuse)
Ezek. 32:5(KJV, see II).
II. רָמוּת *rāmût̲* **fem. noun**
(height)
Ezek. 32:5(NASB, NIV, see I).

7420. רֹמַח *rōmaḥ* **masc. noun**
(spear, javelin)
Num. 25:7; **Judg.** 5:8; **1 Kgs.** 18:28; **1 Chr.** 12:8(9),24(25); **2 Chr.** 11:12; 14:8(7); 25:5; 26:14; **Neh.** 4:13(7), 16(10),21(15); **Jer.** 46:4; **Ezek.** 39:9; **Joel** 3:10(4:10).

7421. רַמִּי *rammiy* **masc. proper noun**
(Syrian)
2 Chr. 22:5(NASB, NIV, *ʾ^{a}rammiy* [761]).

7422. רַמְיָה *ramyāh* **masc. proper noun**
(Ramiah)
Ezra 10:25.

7423. I. רְמִיָּה *r^{e}miyyāh* **fem. noun**
(deceit, treachery, fault)
Job 13:7; 27:4; **Ps.** 32:2; 52:2(4); 78:57; 101:7; 120:2,3; **Jer.** 48:10(NASB, NIV, see II); **Hos.** 7:16; **Mic.** 6:12.
II. רְמִיָּה *r^{e}miyyāh* **fem. noun**
(laziness, negligence, sloth)
Prov. 10:4; 12:24,27; 19:15; **Jer.** 48:10 (KJV, see I).

7424. I. רַמָּךְ *rammāk̲* **fem. noun**
(royal horse)
Esth. 8:10(KJV, see II).
II. רַמָּךְ *rammāk̲* **fem. noun**
(camel, dromedary)
Esth. 8:10(NASB, NIV, see I).

7425. רְמַלְיָהוּ *r*^{e}*malyāhû* **masc. proper noun**
(Remaliah)
2 Kgs. 15:25,27,30,32,37; 16:1,5; **2 Chr.** 28:6; **Isa.** 7:1,4,5,9; 8:6.

7426. I. רָמַם *rāmam* **verb**
(to be exalted, to be lifted up)
Num. 16:45(17:10); **Job** 24:24; **Ps.** 118:16(NASB, NIV, *rûm* [7311]); **Isa.** 33:10(NASB, NIV, *rûm* [7311]); **Ezek.** 10:15,17,19.
II. רָמַם *rāmam* **verb**
(to be full)
Ex. 16:20(KJV, *rûm* [7311]).

7427. רֹמֵמֻת *rōmēmuṯ,* רוֹמֵמֻת *rômēmuṯ* **masc. noun**
(a lifting up; a rising up)
Isa. 33:3.

7428. רִמּוֹן פֶּרֶץ *rimmôn pereṣ* **proper noun**
(Rimmon Perez)
Num. 33:19,20.

7429. רָמַס *rāmas* **verb**
(to trample underfoot; to tread down)
2 Kgs. 7:17,20; 9:33; 14:9; **2 Chr.** 25:18; **Ps.** 7:5(6); 91:13; **Isa.** 1:12; 16:4; 26:6; 28:3; 41:25; 63:3; **Ezek.** 26:11; 34:18; **Dan.** 8:7,10; **Mic.** 5:8(7); **Nah.** 3:14.

7430. רָמַשׂ *rāmaś* **verb**
(to creep, to move lightly)
Gen. 1:21,26,28,30; 7:8,14,21; 8:17,19; 9:2; **Lev.** 11:44,46; 20:25; **Deut.** 4:18; **Ps.** 69:34(35); 104:20; **Ezek.** 38:20.

7431. רֶמֶשׂ *remeś* **masc. coll. noun**
(creeping things, moving things)
Gen. 1:24–26; 6:7,20; 7:14,23; 8:17,19; 9:3; **1 Kgs.** 4:33(5:13); **Ps.** 104:25; 148:10; **Ezek.** 8:10; 38:20; **Hos.** 2:18(20); **Hab.** 1:14.

7432. רֶמֶת *remeṯ* **proper noun**
(Remeth)
Josh. 19:21.

7433. A. רָמוֹת *rāmôṯ,* רָמוֹת גִּלְעָד *rāmôt gil'āḏ* **proper noun**
(Ramoth, Ramoth Gilead; the same as *rāmāh* [7414,F])
Josh. 21:38(NASB, NIV, *rā'môth* [7216] and *gil'āḏ* [1568]); **1 Kgs.** 4:13; 22:3, 4,6,12,15,20,29; **2 Kgs.** 8:28; 9:1,4,14; **2 Chr.** 18:2,3,5,11,14,19,28; 22:5.
B. רָמוֹת *rāmôṯ* **masc. proper noun**
(Ramoth: a covenanter in Ezra's day)
Ezra 10:29(NASB, NIV, [K^{e}] *y*^{e}*rēmôṯ* [3406,N]).

7434. רָמַת הַמִּצְפֶּה *rāmaṯ hammiṣpeh* **proper noun**
(Ramath Mizpeh)
Josh. 13:26.

7435. רָמָתִי *rāmāṯiy* **masc. proper noun**
(Ramathite)
1 Chr. 27:27.

7436. I. רָמָתַיִם צוֹפִים *rāmāṯayim ṣôp̱iym* **proper noun**
(Ramathaim-zophim; the same as B and *rāmāh* [7414,B])
1 Sam. 1:1(NIV, see B).
II. רָמָתַיִם *rāmāṯayim* **proper noun**
(Ramathaim; used with *ṣûp̱iy* [6689])
1 Sam. 1:1(KJV, NASB, see A).

7437. רָמַת לְחִי *rāmāṯ l*^{e}*ḥiy* **proper noun**
(Ramath Lehi)
Judg. 15:17.

7438. רֹן *rōn* **masc. noun**
(song)
Ps. 32:7.

7439. רָנָה *rānāh* **verb**
(to rattle)
Job 39:23.

7440. רִנָּה *rinnāh* **fem. noun**
(glad shouting, joyful singing, crying out)
1 Kgs. 8:28; 22:36; **2 Chr.** 6:19; 20:22; **Ps.** 17:1; 30:5; 42:4; 47:1; 61:1; 88:2; 105:43; 106:44; 107:22; 118:15; 119:169; 126:2,5,6; 142:6; **Prov.** 11:10; **Isa.** 14:7; 35:10; 43:14; 44:23; 48:20; 49:13; 51:11; 54:1; 55:12; **Jer.** 7:16; 11:14; 14:12; **Zeph.** 3:17.

7441. רִנָּה *rinnāh* **masc. proper noun**
(Rinnah)
1 Chr. 4:20.

7442. I. רָנַן *rānan* **verb**
(to shout for joy, to sing joyfully)
Lev. 9:24; **Deut.** 32:43; **1 Chr.** 16:33; **Job** 29:13; 38:7; **Ps.** 5:11(12); 20:5(6); 32:11; 33:1; 35:27; 51:14(16); 59:16(17); 63:7(8); 65:8(9); 67:4(5); 71:23; 78:65 (NASB, see II; NIV, see III); 81:1(2); 84:2(3); 89:12(13); 90:14; 92:4(5); 95:1; 96:12; 98:4,8; 132:9,16; 145:7; 149:5; **Prov.** 1:20; 8:3; 29:6; **Isa.** 12:6; 16:10; 24:14; 26:19; 35:2(KJV, *rannēn* [7444]),6; 42:11; 44:23; 49:13; 52:8,9; 54:1; 61:7; 65:14; **Jer.** 31:7,12; 51:48; **Lam.** 2:19; **Zeph.** 3:14; **Zech.** 2:10(14).
II. רוּן *rûn* **verb**
(to be overcome)
Ps. 78:65(KJV, see I; NIV, see III).
III. רוּן *rûn* **verb**
(to wake out of stupor)
Ps. 78:65(KJV, see I; NASB, see II).

7443. I. רֶנֶן *renen* **masc. noun**
(ostrich)
Job 39:13(KJV, see II).
II. רֶנֶן *renen* **masc. noun**
(peacock)
Job 39:13(NASB, NIV, see I).

7444. רַנֵּן *rannēn* **verb**
(to shout, to sing)
Isa. 35:2(NASB, NIV, *rānan* [7442]).

7445. רְנָנָה *r^enānāh* **fem. noun**
(joyful shout, singing)
Job 3:7; 20:5; **Ps.** 63:5(6); 100:2.

7446. רִסָּה *rissāh* **proper noun**
(Rissah)
Num. 33:21,22.

7447. I. רָסִיס *rāsiys* **masc. noun**
(drop [of dew]; dampness)
Song 5:2; **Amos** 6:11.
II. רָסִיס *rāsiys* **masc. noun**
(piece, fragment)
Amos 6:11(KJV, see III).
III. רָסִיס *rāsiys* **masc. noun**
(breach, break in the walls)
Amos 6:11(NASB, NIV, see II).

7448. I. רֶסֶן *resen* **masc. noun**
(bridle, restraint)
Job 30:11; 41:13(5)(NASB, see II); **Ps.** 32:9; **Isa.** 30:28.
II. רֶסֶן *resen* **masc. noun**
(mail, armor)
Job 41:13(5)(KJV, NIV, see I).

7449. רֶסֶן *resen* **proper noun**
(Resen)
Gen. 10:12.

7450. רָסַס *rāsas* **verb**
(to moisten)
Ezek. 46:14.

7451. רַע *ra'*, רָעָה *rā'āh* **adj.; masc. noun**
(bad, disastrous; evil, wicked)
Gen. 2:9,17; 3:5,22; 6:5; 8:21; 13:13; 19:19; 24:50; 26:29; 28:8; 31:24,29,52; 37:2,20,33; 38:7; 39:9; 40:7; 41:3,4, 19–21,27; 44:4,29,34; 47:9; 48:16; 50:15, 17,20; **Ex.** 5:19; 10:10; 21:8; 23:2; 32:12, 14,22; 33:4; **Lev.** 26:6; 27:10,12,14,33;

Num. 11:1,10(NASB, *rāʿaʿ* [7489]),15; 13:19; 14:27,35,37; 20:5; 24:13; 32:13; 35:23; **Deut.** 1:35,39; 4:25; 6:22; 7:15; 9:18; 13:5(6),11(12); 15:21; 17:1,2,5, 7,12; 19:19,20; 21:21; 22:14,19,21,22,24; 23:9(10); 24:7; 28:35,59; 29:21(20); 30:15; 31:17,18,21,29; 32:23; **Josh.** 23:15; **Judg.** 2:11,15; 3:7,12; 4:1; 6:1; 9:23,56,57; 10:6; 11:27; 13:1; 15:3; 20:3, 12,13,34,41; **1 Sam.** 2:23; 6:9; 10:19; 12:17,19,20; 15:19; 16:14–16,23; 18:10; 19:9; 20:7,9,13; 23:9; 24:9(10),11(12), 17(18); 25:3,17,21,26,28,39; 26:18; 29:6,7; 30:22; **2 Sam.** 3:39; 12:9,11,18; 13:16,22; 14:17; 15:14; 16:8; 17:14; 18:32; 19:7,35; 24:16; **1 Kgs.** 1:52; 2:44; 3:9; 5:4(18); 9:9; 11:6,25; 13:33; 14:10,22; 15:26,34; 16:7,19,25,30; 20:7; 21:20,21, 25,29; 22:8,18,23,52(53); **2 Kgs.** 2:19; 3:2; 4:41; 6:33; 8:12,18,27; 13:2,11; 14:10,24; 15:9,18,24,28; 17:2,11,13,17; 21:2,6,9,12,15,16,20; 22:16,20; 23:32,37; 24:9,19; **1 Chr.** 2:3; 4:10; 7:23; 21:15; **2 Chr.** 7:14,22; 12:14; 18:7,17,22; 20:9; 21:6,19; 22:4; 25:19; 29:6; 33:2,6,9,22; 34:24,28; 36:5,9,12; **Ezra** 9:13; **Neh.** 1:3; 2:1,2,10,17; 6:2,13; 9:28,35; 13:7, 17,18,27; **Esth.** 7:6,7; 8:3,6; 9:2,25; **Job** 1:1,8; 2:3,7,10,11; 5:19; 20:12; 21:30; 22:5; 28:28; 30:26; 31:29; 35:12; 42:11; **Ps.** 5:4(5); 7:4(5),9(10); 10:6,15; 15:3; 21:11(12); 23:4; 27:5; 28:3; 34:13(14), 14(15),16(17),19(20),21(22); 35:4,12,26; 36:4(5); 37:19,27; 38:12(13),20(21); 40:12(13),14(15); 41:1(2),5(6),7(8); 49:5(6); 50:19; 51:4(6); 52:1(3),3(5); 54:5(7); 55:15(16); 56:5(6); 70:2(3); 71:13,20,24; 73:8; 78:49; 88:3(4); 90:15; 91:10; 94:13,23; 97:10; 101:4; 107:26, 34,39; 109:5,20; 112:7; 119:101; 121:7; 140:1(2),2(3),11(12); 141:4,5; 144:10; **Prov.** 1:16,33; 2:12,14; 3:7,29,30; 4:14,27; 5:14; 6:14,18,24; 8:13; 11:15 (NASB, NIV, *rāʿaʿ* [7489]),19,21,27; 12:12, 13,20,21; 13:17,19,21; 14:16,19,22,32; 15:3,10,15,26,28; 16:4,6,17,27,30; 17:11,13,20; 19:23; 20:8,14,22,30; 21:10,12; 22:3; 23:6; 24:1,16,20; 25:20; 26:23,26; 27:12; 28:5,10,14,22; 29:6; 31:12; **Eccl.** 1:13; 2:17,21; 4:3,8; 5:1(4:17),13(12),14(13),16(15); 6:1,2; 7:14,15; 8:3,5,6,9,11,12; 9:3,12; 10:5,13; 11:2,10; 12:1,14; **Isa.** 3:9,11; 5:20; 7:5,15,16; 13:11; 31:2; 32:7; 33:15; 45:7; 47:10,11; 56:2; 57:1; 59:7,15; 65:12; 66:4; **Jer.** 1:14,16; 2:3,13,19,27,28,33; 3:2,5,17; 4:6,14,18; 5:12,28; 6:1,7,19,29; 7:6,12,24,30; 8:3,6; 9:3(2); 11:8,11,12, 14,15,17,23; 12:4,14; 13:10; 14:16; 15:11,21; 16:10,12; 17:17,18; 18:8, 10–12,20; 19:3,15; 21:10; 22:22; 23:10–12,14,17,22; 24:2,3,8,9; 25:5, 7,32; 26:3,13,19; 28:8; 29:11; 32:23, 30,32,42; 33:5; 35:15,17; 36:3,7,31; 38:4; 39:12,16; 40:2; 41:11; 42:6,10,17; 44:2,3, 5,7,9,11,17,23,27,29; 45:5; 48:2,16; 49:23,37; 51:2,24,60,64; 52:2; **Lam.** 1:21,22; 3:38; **Ezek.** 5:16,17; 6:9–11; 7:5,24; 8:9; 11:2; 13:22; 14:15,21,22; 16:23,57; 20:43,44; 30:12; 33:11; 34:25; 36:31; 38:10; **Dan.** 9:12–14; **Hos.** 7:1–3,15; 9:15; 10:15; **Joel** 2:13; 3:13(4:13); **Amos** 3:6; 5:13–15; 6:3; 9:4,10; **Obad.** 1:13; **Jon.** 1:2,7,8; 3:8,10; 4:1,2,6; **Mic.** 1:12; 2:1,3; 3:2,11; 7:3; **Nah.** 1:11; 3:19; **Hab.** 1:13; 2:9; **Zeph.** 3:15; **Zech.** 1:4,15; 7:10; 8:17; **Mal.** 1:8; 2:17.

7452. רֵעַ *rēaʿ* **masc. noun**
(a loud shout, a roar, thunder)
Ex. 32:17; **Job** 36:33; **Mic.** 4:9.

7453. רֵעַ *rēaʿ*, רֵיעַ *rēyaʿ* **masc. noun**
(neighbor, friend, companion, another person)
Gen. 11:3,7; 15:10; 31:49; 38:12,20; 43:33; **Ex.** 2:13; 11:2; 18:7,16; 20:16,17; 21:14,18,35; 22:7–11(6–10),14(13), 26(25); 32:27; 33:11; **Lev.** 19:13,16,18; 20:10; **Deut.** 4:42; 5:20,21; 13:6(7); 15:2; 19:4,5,11,14; 22:24,26; 23:24(25), 25(26); 24:10; 27:17,24; **Josh.** 20:5;

Judg. 6:29; 7:13,14,22; 10:18; **Ruth** 3:14; 4:7; **1 Sam.** 10:11; 14:20; 15:28; 20:41; 28:17; 30:26; **2 Sam.** 2:16; 12:11; 13:3; 16:17; **1 Kgs.** 8:31; 16:11; 20:35; **2 Kgs.** 3:23; 7:3,9; **1 Chr.** 27:33; **2 Chr.** 6:22; 20:23; **Esth.** 9:19,22; **Job** 2:11; 6:14(NIV, *mērēa'* [4828]),27; 12:4; 16:20,21; 17:5; 19:21; 30:29; 31:9; 32:3; 35:4; 42:7,10; **Ps.** 12:2; 15:3; 28:3; 35:14; 38:11(12); 88:18(19); 101:5; 122:8; **Prov.** 3:28,29; 6:1,3,29; 11:9,12; 12:26; 14:20, 21; 16:29; 17:17,18; 18:17,24; 19:4,6; 21:10; 22:11; 24:28; 25:8,9,17,18; 26:19; 27:9,10,14,17; 29:5; **Eccl.** 4:4; **Song** 5:1,16; **Isa.** 3:5; 13:8; 19:2; 34:14; 41:6; **Jer.** 3:1,20; 5:8; 6:21; 7:5; 9:4(3),5(4), 8(7); 19:9; 22:8,13; 23:27,30,35; 29:23; 31:34; 34:15,17; 36:16; 46:16; **Lam.** 1:2; **Ezek.** 18:6,11,15; 22:11,12; 33:26; **Hos.** 3:1; **Jon.** 1:7; **Mic.** 7:5; **Hab.** 2:15; **Zech.** 3:8,10; 8:10,16,17; 11:6; 14:13; **Mal.** 3:16.

7454. רֵעַ *rēa'* **masc. noun**
(thought, purpose)
Ps. 139:2,17.

7455. רֹעַ *rōa'* **masc. noun**
(evil, wickedness, rottenness)
Gen. 41:19; **Deut.** 28:20; **1 Sam.** 17:28; **Neh.** 2:2; **Ps.** 28:4; **Eccl.** 7:3; **Isa.** 1:16; **Jer.** 4:4; 21:12; 23:2,22; 24:2,3,8; 25:5; 26:3; 29:17; 44:22; **Hos.** 9:15.

7456. רָעֵב *rā'ēḇ* **verb**
(to be hungry, to be famished)
Gen. 41:55; **Deut.** 8:3; **Ps.** 34:10(11); 50:12; **Prov.** 6:30; 10:3; 19:15; **Isa.** 8:21; 9:20; 44:12; 49:10; 65:13; **Jer.** 42:14.

7457. רָעֵב *rā'ēḇ* **adj.**
(hungry, famished)
1 Sam. 2:5; **2 Sam.** 17:29; **2 Kgs.** 7:12; **Job** 5:5; 18:12; 22:7; 24:10; **Ps.** 107:5, 9,36; 146:7; **Prov.** 25:21; 27:7; **Isa.** 29:8; 32:6; 58:7,10; **Ezek.** 18:7,16.

7458. רָעָב *rā'āḇ* **masc. noun**
(famine, hunger)
Gen. 12:10; 26:1; 41:27,30,31,36,50,54,56,57; 42:5; 43:1; 45:6,11; 47:4,13,20; **Ex.** 16:3; **Deut.** 28:48; 32:24; **Ruth** 1:1; **2 Sam.** 21:1; 24:13; **1 Kgs.** 8:37; 18:2; **2 Kgs.** 4:38; 6:25; 7:4; 8:1; 25:3; **1 Chr.** 21:12; **2 Chr.** 6:28; 20:9; 32:11; **Neh.** 5:3; 9:15; **Job** 5:20; **Ps.** 33:19; 105:16; **Isa.** 5:13; 14:30; 51:19; **Jer.** 5:12; 11:22; 14:12,13,15, 16,18; 15:2; 16:4; 18:21; 21:7,9; 24:10; 27:8,13; 29:17,18; 32:24,36; 34:17; 38:2,9; 42:16,17,22; 44:12,13,18,27; 52:6; **Lam.** 2:19; 4:9; 5:10; **Ezek.** 5:12,16,17; 6:11,12; 7:15; 12:16; 14:13,21; 34:29; 36:29,30; **Amos** 8:11.

7459. רְעָבוֹן *r^e'āḇôn* **masc. noun**
(famine, starving)
Gen. 42:19,33; **Ps.** 37:19.

7460. רָעַד *rā'aḏ* **verb**
(to tremble, to be distressed)
Ezra 10:9; **Ps.** 104:32; **Dan.** 10:11.

7461. I. רַעַד *ra'aḏ* **masc. noun**
(trembling, fear)
Ex. 15:15; **Ps.** 2:11; 48:6; 55:5; **Isa.** 33:14.
II. רְעָדָה *r^e'āḏāh* **fem. noun**
(trembling, fear)
Ex. 15:15; **Ps.** 2:11; 48:6; 55:5; **Isa.** 33:14.

7462. I. רָעָה *rā'āh* **verb**
(to feed, to tend; to be a shepherd)
Gen. 4:2; 13:7,8; 26:20; 29:7,9; 30:31,36; 36:24; 37:2,12,13,16; 41:2,18; 46:32,34; 47:3; 48:15; 49:24; **Ex.** 2:17,19; 3:1; 34:3; **Num.** 14:33; 27:17; **1 Sam.** 16:11; 17:15,34,40; 21:7; 25:7,16; **2 Sam.** 5:2; 7:7; **1 Kgs.** 22:17; **2 Kgs.** 10:32; **1 Chr.** 11:2; 17:6; 27:29; **2 Chr.** 18:16; **Job** 1:14; 24:2,21; **Ps.** 2:9(KJV, NIV, *rā'a'* [749,II]); 23:1; 28:9; 37:3(NASB, see II); 49:14(15); 78:71,72; 80:1(2),13(14);

Prov. 10:21; 15:14; **Eccl.** 12:11; **Song** 1:7,8; 2:16; 4:5; 6:2,3; **Isa.** 5:17; 11:7; 13:20; 14:30; 27:10; 30:23; 31:4; 38:12 (KJV, NASB, *rō'iy* [7473]); 40:11; 44:20,28; 49:9; 56:11; 61:5; 63:11; 65:25; **Jer.** 2:8,16; 3:15; 6:3; 10:21; 12:10; 17:16; 22:22; 23:1,2,4; 25:34–36; 31:10; 33:12; 43:12; 49:19; 50:6,19,44; 51:23; **Ezek.** 34:2,3,5,7–10,12–16,18,19,23; 37:24; **Hos.** 4:16; 9:2; 12:1(2); **Amos** 1:2; 3:12; **Jon.** 3:7; **Mic.** 5:4(3),5(4),6(5)(KJV, *rā'a'* [7489]); 7:14; **Nah.** 3:18; **Zeph.** 2:6,7; 3:13; **Zech.** 10:2,3; 11:3–5,7–9,15, 16,17(KJV, NASB, *rō'iy* [7473]); 13:7.

II. רָעָה *rā'āh* **verb**
(to associate with, to be a companion, to be a friend)
Judg. 14:20; **Ps.** 37:3(KJV, NIV, see I); **Prov.** 13:20; 22:24; 28:7; 29:3.

7463. רֵעֶה *rē'eh* **masc. noun**
(friend, friend of the king as personal advisor)
2 Sam. 15:37; 16:16; **1 Kgs.** 4:5.

7464. רֵעָה *rē'āh* **fem. noun**
(female friend)
Judg. 11:37,38; **Ps.** 45:14(15).

7465. רֹעָה *rō'āh* **adj.**
(broken)
Prov. 25:19(NASB, NIV, *rā'a'* [7489,II]).

7466. רְעוּ *r^e'û* **masc. proper noun**
(Reu)
Gen. 11:18–21; **1 Chr.** 1:25.

7467. A. רְעוּאֵל *r^e'û'ēl* **masc. proper noun**
(Reuel: son of Esau)
Gen. 36:4,10,13,17; **1 Chr.** 1:35,37.

B. רְעוּאֵל *r^e'û'ēl* **masc. proper noun**
(Reuel: Moses' father-in-law)
Ex. 2:18; **Num.** 10:29.

C. רְעוּאֵל *r^e'û'ēl* **masc. proper noun**
(Reuel: father of Eliasaph; the same as *d^e'û'ēl* [1845])
Num. 2:14(NASB, NIV, *d^e'û'ēl* [1845]).

D. רְעוּאֵל *r^e'û'ēl* **masc. proper noun**
(Reuel: father of Shephatiah)
1 Chr. 9:8.

7468. רְעוּת *r^e'ûṯ* **fem. noun**
(companion, neighbor woman)
Ex. 11:2; **Esth.** 1:19; **Isa.** 34:15,16; **Jer.** 9:20(19); **Zech.** 11:9.

7469. רְעוּת *r^e'ûṯ* **masc. noun**
(striving, vexation)
Eccl. 1:14; 2:11,17,26; 4:4,6; 6:9.

7470. רְעוּ *r^e'û*, רְעוּת *r^e'ûṯ* **Aram. fem. noun**
(decision, will)
Ezra 5:17; 7:18.

7471. רְעִי *r^e'iy* **masc. noun**
(pasture, pasture-fed)
1 Kgs. 4:23(5:3).

7472. רֵעִי *rē'iy* **masc. proper noun**
(Rei)
1 Kgs. 1:8.

7473. רֹעִי *rō'iy* **masc. noun**
(shepherd)
Isa. 38:12(NIV, *rā'āh* [7462,I]); **Zech.** 11:17(NIV, *rā'āh* [7462,I]).

7474. רַעְיָה *ra'yāh* **fem. noun**
(lover, darling)
Song 1:9,15; 2:2,10,13; 4:1,7; 5:2; 6:4.

7475. רַעְיוֹן *ra'yôn* **masc. noun**
(striving, chasing)
Eccl. 1:17; 2:22; 4:16.

7476. רַעְיוֹן *raʿyôn* **Aram. masc. noun**
(a thought)
Dan. 2:29,30; 4:19(16); 5:6,10; 7:28.

7477. רעַל *rāʿal* **verb**
(to shake, to brandish)
Nah. 2:3(4).

7478. רַעַל *raʿal* **masc. noun**
(trembling, reeling)
Zech. 12:2.

7479. רְעָלָה *rᵉʿālāh* **fem. noun**
(veil, muffler)
Isa. 3:19.

7480. רְעֵלָיָה *rᵉʿēlāyāh* **masc. proper noun**
(Reelaiah, the same as *raʿamyāh* [7485])
Ezra 2:2.

7481. I. רָעַם *rāʿam* **verb**
(to thunder, to roar)
1 Sam. 2:10; 7:10; **2 Sam.** 22:14; **1 Chr.** 16:32; **Job** 37:4,5; 40:9; **Ps.** 18:13(14); 29:3; 96:11; 98:7.
II. רָעַם *rāʿam* **verb**
(to irritate, to trouble)
1 Sam. 1:6; **Ezek.** 27:35.

7482. רַעַם *raʿam* **masc. noun**
(thunder)
Job 26:14; 39:25; **Ps.** 77:18(19); 81:7(8); 104:7; **Isa.** 29:6.

7483. I. רַעְמָה *raʿmāh* **fem. noun**
(flowing mane [of a horse])
Job 39:19(KJV, see II).
II. רַעְמָה *raʿmāh* **fem. noun**
(thunder)
Job 39:19(NASB, NIV, see I).

7484. A. רַעְמָה *raʿmāh*, רַעְמָא *raʿmāʾ* **masc. proper noun**
(Raamah: a son of Cush)
Gen. 10:7; **1 Chr.** 1:9.
B. רַעְמָה *raʿmāh*, רַעְמָא *raʿmāʾ* **proper noun**
(Raamah: a home of traders)
Ezek. 27:22.

7485. רַעַמְיָה *raʿamyāh* **masc. proper noun**
(Raamiah; the same as *rᵉʿēlāyāh* [7480])
Neh. 7:7.

7486. רַעְמְסֵס *raʿamsēs*, רַעְמְסֵס *raʿmᵉsēs* **proper noun**
(Rameses, Raamses)
Gen. 47:11; **Ex.** 1:11; 12:37; **Num.** 33:3,5.

7487. I. רָעַן *rāʿan* **verb**
(to grow luxurious; to be green)
Job 15:32(KJV, *raʿᵃnān* [7488]).
II. רַעֲנַן *raʿᵃnan* **Aram. adj.**
(flourishing; corr. to Hebr. 7488)
Dan. 4:4(1).

7488. רַעֲנָן *raʿᵃnān* **adj.**
(green, flourishing)
Deut. 12:2; **1 Kgs.** 14:23; **2 Kgs.** 16:4; 17:10; **2 Chr.** 28:4; **Job** 15:32(NASB, NIV, *rāʿan* [7487,I]); **Ps.** 37:35; 52:8(10); 92:10(11),14(15); **Song** 1:16; **Isa.** 57:5; **Jer.** 2:20; 3:6,13; 11:16; 17:2,8; **Ezek.** 6:13; **Hos.** 14:8(9).

7489. I. רָעַע *rāʿaʿ* **verb**
(to be evil, to be wicked; to harm; to be displeased; to be distressed)
Gen. 19:7,9; 21:11,12; 31:7; 38:10; 43:6; 44:5; 48:17; **Ex.** 5:22,23; **Lev.** 5:4; **Num.** 11:11; 16:15; 20:15; 22:34; **Deut.** 15:9,10; 26:6; 28:54,56; **Josh.** 24:15,20; **Judg.** 19:23; **Ruth** 1:21; **1 Sam.** 1:8; 8:6; 18:8; 25:34; 26:21; **2 Sam.** 19:7(8); 11:25,27; 20:6; 21:7; **1 Kgs.** 14:9; 16:25;

17:20; **2 Kgs.** 21:11; **1 Chr.** 16:22; 21:17; **Neh.** 2:3,10; 13:8; **Job** 8:20; 20:26; 34:24; **Ps.** 2:9; 15:4; 22:16(17); 26:5; 27:2; 37:1,8,9; 44:2(3); 64:2(3); 74:3; 92:11(12); 94:16; 105:15; 106:32; 119:115; **Prov.** 4:16; 11:15(KJV, *rûaʿ* [7321]); 13:20(KJV, *rûaʿ* [7321]); 17:4; 18:24; 24:8,18,19; **Isa.** 1:4,16; 8:9; 9:17; 11:9; 14:20; 24:19; 31:2; 41:23; 59:15; 65:25; **Jer.** 4:22; 7:26; 10:5; 11:16; 13:23; 15:12; 16:12; 20:13; 23:14; 25:6,29; 31:28; 38:9; 40:4; **Dan.** 11:27(KJV, NIV, *mēraʿ* [4827]); **Jon.** 4:1; **Mic.** 3:4; 4:6; 5:6(5)(NASB, NIV, *raʿāh* [7462,I]); **Zeph.** 1:12; **Zech.** 8:14.

II. רָעַע *rāʿaʿ* **verb**
(to break, to shatter, to come to ruin)
Job 34:24; **Ps.** 2:9(NASB, *rāʿāh* [7462,I]); **Prov.** 18:24; **Isa.** 8:9(KJV, see III; NIV, *rûaʿ* [7321]); 24:19; **Jer.** 11:16; 15:12; **Ezek.** 19:7(KJV, *yāḏaʿ* [3045]; NIV, *gaḏaʿ* [1438]).

III. רָעַע *rāʿaʿ* **verb**
(to associate with; to be friends with)
Isa. 8:9(NASB, see II; NIV, *rûaʿ* [7321]).

7490. רְעַע *r^eʿaʿ* **Aram. verb**
(to break in pieces, to crush; corr. to Hebr. 7489,II)
Dan. 2:40.

7491. רָעַף *rāʿap̱* **verb**
(to overflow, to drip down [of rain])
Job 36:28; **Ps.** 65:11(12),12(13); **Prov.** 3:20; **Isa.** 45:8.

7492. רָעַץ *rāʿaṣ* **verb**
(to shatter, to afflict)
Ex. 15:6; **Judg.** 10:8.

7493. רָעַשׁ *rāʿaš* **verb**
(to quake, to tremble; to shake)
Judg. 5:4; **2 Sam.** 22:8; **Job** 39:20; **Ps.** 18:7(8); 46:3(4); 60:2(4); 68:8(9); 72:16; 77:18(19); **Isa.** 13:13; 14:16; 24:18; **Jer.** 4:24; 8:16; 10:10; 49:21; 50:46; 51:29; **Ezek.** 26:10,15; 27:28; 31:16; 38:20; **Joel** 2:10; 3:16(4:16); **Amos** 9:1; **Nah.** 1:5; **Hag.** 2:6,7,21.

7494. רַעַשׁ *raʿaš* **masc. noun**
(earthquake, shaking, rumbling, commotion)
1 Kgs. 19:11,12; **Job** 39:24; 41:29(21); **Isa.** 9:5(4); 29:6; **Jer.** 10:22; 47:3; **Ezek.** 3:12,13; 12:18; 37:7; 38:19; **Amos** 1:1; **Nah.** 3:2; **Zech.** 14:5.

7495. רָפָא *rāp̱aʾ* **verb**
(to heal; to make fresh)
Gen. 20:17; 50:2; **Ex.** 15:26; 21:19; **Lev.** 13:18,37; 14:3,48; **Num.** 12:13; **Deut.** 28:27,35; 32:39; **1 Sam.** 6:3; **1 Kgs.** 18:30; **2 Kgs.** 2:21,22; 6:11; 8:29; 9:15; 20:5,8; **2 Chr.** 7:14; 16:12; 22:6; 30:20; **Job** 5:18; 13:4; **Ps.** 6:2(3); 30:2(3); 41:4(5); 60:2(4); 103:3; 107:20; 147:3; **Eccl.** 3:3; **Isa.** 6:10; 19:22; 30:26; 53:5; 57:18,19; **Jer.** 3:22; 6:14; 8:11,22; 15:18; 17:14; 19:11; 30:17; 33:6; 51:8,9; **Lam.** 2:13; **Ezek.** 34:4; 47:8,9,11; **Hos.** 5:13; 6:1; 7:1; 11:3; 14:4(5); **Zech.** 11:16.

7496. רָפָא *rāp̱āʾ* **masc. noun**
(dead one)
Job 26:5; **Ps.** 88:10(11); **Prov.** 2:18; 9:18; 21:16; **Isa.** 14:9; 26:14,19.

7497. I. רְפָאִים *r^ep̱āʾiym* **proper noun**
(Rephaim)
Josh. 15:8(KJV, see III); 18:16(KJV, see III); **2 Sam.** 5:18,22; 23:13; **1 Chr.** 11:15; 14:9; **Isa.** 17:5.

II. רְפָאִים *r^ep̱āʾiym* **masc. proper noun**
(Rephaites; inhabitants of *r^ep̱āʾiym* [7497,I])
Gen. 14:5; 15:20; **Deut.** 2:11(KJV, see III),20(KJV, see III); 3:11(KJV, see III), 13(KJV, see III); **Josh.** 12:4(KJV, see III); 13:12(KJV, see III); 17:15(KJV, see III); **1 Chr.** 20:4(KJV, see III).

III. רָפָא *rāp̱a'*, רָפָה *rāp̱ah* **masc. noun**
(giant)
Deut. 2:11(NASB, NIV, see II),20(NASB, NIV, see II); 3:11(NASB, NIV, see II), 13(NASB, NIV, see II); **Josh.** 12:4(NASB, NIV, see II); 13:12(NASB, NIV, see II); 15:8(NASB, NIV, see I); 17:15(NASB, NIV, see II); 18:16(NASB, NIV, see I); **2 Sam.** 21:16(NIV, *rāp̱ā'* [7498,A]),18(NIV, *rāp̱ā'* [7498,A]),20(NIV, *rāp̱ā'* [7498,A]), 22(NIV, *rāp̱ā'* [7498,A]); **1 Chr.** 20:4(NASB, NIV, see II),6(NIV, *rāp̱ā'* [7498,A]),8(NIV, *rāp̱ā'* [7498,A]).

7498. A. רָפָא *rāp̱a'*, רָפָה *rāp̱āh* **masc. proper noun**
(Rapha: the father of several giants among David's enemies; KJV, NASB, *rāp̱a'* [7497,III])
1 Sam. 21:16,18,20,22; **1 Chr.** 20:6,8.
B. רָפָה *rāp̱āh* **masc. proper noun**
(Rapha: son of Benjamin)
1 Chr. 8:2.
C. רָפָה *rāp̱āh* **masc. proper noun**
(Rapha: son of Binea; the same as Rephaiah [7509,D])
1 Chr. 8:37.

7499. רְפוּאָה *r^ep̱û'āh* **fem. noun**
(remedy, healing)
Jer. 30:13; 46:11; **Ezek.** 30:21.

7500. רִפְאוּת *rip̱'ûṯ* **fem. noun**
(health, healing)
Prov. 3:8.

7501. רְפָאֵל *r^ep̱ā'ēl* **masc. proper noun**
(Rephael)
1 Chr. 26:7.

7502. I. רָפַד *rāp̱aḏ* **verb**
(to spread out; to spread a blanket)
Job 17:13; 41:30(22).
II. רָפַד *rāp̱aḏ* **verb**
(to comfort, to refresh)
Song 2:5.

7503. רָפָה *rāp̱āh* **verb**
(to relax, to become limp; to be feeble, to be weak; to leave alone)
Ex. 4:26; 5:8,17; **Deut.** 4:31; 9:14; 31:6,8; **Josh.** 1:5; 10:6; 18:3; **Judg.** 8:3; 11:37; 19:9; **1 Sam.** 11:3; 15:16; **2 Sam.** 4:1; 24:16; **2 Kgs.** 4:27; **1 Chr.** 21:15; 28:20; **2 Chr.** 15:7; **Ezra** 4:4; **Neh.** 6:3,9; **Job** 7:19; 12:21; 27:6; **Ps.** 37:8; 46:10(11); 138:8; **Prov.** 4:13; 18:9; 24:10; **Song** 3:4; **Isa.** 5:24; 13:7; **Jer.** 6:24; 38:4; 49:24; 50:43; **Ezek.** 1:24,25; 7:17; 21:7(12); **Zeph.** 3:16.

7504. רָפֶה *rāp̱eh* **adj.**
(weak, feeble)
Num. 13:18; **2 Sam.** 17:2; **Job** 4:3; **Isa.** 35:3.

7505. רָפוּא *rāp̱û'* **masc. proper noun**
(Raphu)
Num. 13:9.

7506. רֶפַח *rep̱āḥ* **masc. proper noun**
(Rephah)
1 Chr. 7:25.

7507. רְפִידָה *r^ep̱iyḏāh* **fem. noun**
(the bottom or back [of a sedan chair])
Song 3:10.

7508. רְפִידִים *r^ep̱iyḏiym* **proper noun**
(Rephidim)
Ex. 17:1,8; 19:2; **Num.** 33:14,15.

7509. A. רְפָיָה *r^ep̱āyāh* **masc. proper noun**
(Rephaiah: son of Jeshaiah)
1 Chr. 3:21.
B. רְפָיָה *r^ep̱āyāh* **masc. proper noun**
(Rephaiah: a Simeonite)
1 Chr. 4:42.

C. רְפָיָה *r*[e]*pāyāh* **masc. proper noun**
(Rephaiah: grandson of Issachar)
1 Chr. 7:2.
D. רְפָיָה *r*[e]*pāyāh* **masc. proper noun**
(Rephaiah: descendant of Saul; the same as Rapha [7498,C])
1 Chr. 9:43.
E. רְפָיָה *r*[e]*pāyāh* **masc. proper noun**
(Rephaiah: son of Hur)
Neh. 3:9.

7510. רִפְיוֹן *ripyôn* **masc. noun**
(limpness, feebleness)
Jer. 47:3.

7511. רָפַס *rāpas* **verb**
(to submit, to humble oneself; NASB, NIV, see also *rāpaś* [7515])
Ps. 68:30(31); **Prov.** 6:3.

7512. רְפַס *rāpas* **Aram. verb**
(to trample, to tread down; corr. to Hebr. 7511)
Dan. 7:7,19.

7513. רַפְסֹדָה *rapsôdāh* **fem. noun**
(raft)
2 Chr. 2:16.

7514. רָפַק *rāpaq* **verb**
(to support oneself; to lean on)
Song 8:5.

7515. רָפַשׂ *rāpaś* **verb**
(to trample down, to foul water or to make muddy by trampling; NASB, NIV, the same as *rāpas* [7511])
Prov. 25:26; **Ezek.** 32:2; 34:18.

7516. רֶפֶשׁ *repeś* **masc. noun**
(mire, mud, refuse)
Isa. 57:20.

7517. רֶפֶת *repet* **masc. noun**
(stall [of a stable])
Hab. 3:17.

7518. רַץ *raṣ* **masc. noun**
(piece or bar [of silver])
Ps. 68:30(31).

7519. רָצָא *rāṣāʾ* **verb**
(to run, to speed forth)
Ezek. 1:14.

7520. I. רָצַד *rāṣad* **verb**
(to look with envy)
Ps. 68:16(17)(KJV, see II).
II. רָצַד *rāṣad* **verb**
(to leap)
Ps. 68:16(17)(NASB, NIV, see I).

7521. I. רָצָה *rāṣāh* **verb**
(to accept with pleasure; to be pleased with; to enjoy)
Gen. 33:10; **Lev.** 1:4; 7:18; 19:7; 22:23,25,27; 26:34,41,43; **Deut.** 33:11,24; **1 Sam.** 29:4; **2 Sam.** 24:23; **1 Chr.** 28:4; 29:3,17; **2 Chr.** 10:7; 36:21; **Esth.** 10:3; **Job** 14:6; 20:10; 33:26; 34:9; **Ps.** 40:13(14); 44:3(4); 49:13(14); 50:18; 51:16(18); 62:4(5); 77:7(8); 85:1; 102:14(15); 119:108; 147:10,11; 149:4; **Prov.** 3:12; 16:7; 23:26(KJV, NIV, [Q[e]] *nāṣar* [5341]); **Eccl.** 9:7; **Isa.** 40:2; 42:1; **Jer.** 14:10,12; **Ezek.** 20:40,41; 43:27; **Hos.** 8:13; **Amos** 5:22; **Mic.** 6:7; **Hag.** 1:8; **Mal.** 1:8,10,13.
II. רָצָה *rāṣāh* **verb**
(to make amends; to pay for)
Lev. 26:41(KJV, see I),43(KJV, see I); **Job** 20:10(KJV, NASB, see I); **Isa.** 40:2 (KJV, NASB, see I).

7522. רָצוֹן *rāṣôn,* רָצֹן *raṣōn* **masc. noun**
(to make amends; to pay for)
Gen. 49:6; **Ex.** 28:38; **Lev.** 1:3; 19:5; 22:19–21,29; 23:11; **Deut.** 33:16,23; **2 Chr.** 15:15; **Ezra** 10:11; **Neh.**

9:24,37; **Esth.** 1:8; 9:5; **Ps.** 5:12(13); 19:14; 30:5,7; 40:8(9); 51:18; 69:13(14); 89:17; 103:21; 106:4; 143:10; 145:16,19; **Prov.** 8:35; 10:32; 11:1,20,27; 12:2,22; 14:9,35; 15:8; 16:13,15; 18:22; 19:12; **Isa.** 49:8; 56:7; 58:5; 60:7,10; 61:2; **Jer.** 6:20; **Dan.** 8:4; 11:3,16,36; **Mal.** 2:13.

7523. רָצַח *rāṣaḥ* **verb**
(to kill, to murder)
Ex. 20:13; **Num.** 35:6,11,12,16–19,21, 25–28,30,31; **Deut.** 4:42; 5:17; 19:3, 4,6; 22:26; **Josh.** 20:3,5,6; 21:13,21,27, 32,38; **Judg.** 20:4; **1 Kgs.** 21:19; **2 Kgs.** 6:32; **Job** 24:14; **Ps.** 62:3(4); 94:6; **Prov.** 22:13; **Isa.** 1:21; **Jer.** 7:9; **Hos.** 4:2; 6:9.

7524. רֶצַח *reṣaḥ* **masc. noun**
(slaughter; shattering)
Ps. 42:10(11); **Ezek.** 21:22(27).

7525. רִצְיָא *riṣyāʾ* **masc. proper noun**
(Rizia)
1 Chr. 7:39.

7526. A. רְצִין *r^eṣiyn* **masc. proper noun**
(Rezin: king of Damascus)
2 Kgs. 15:37; 16:5,6,9; **Isa.** 7:1,4,8; 8:6; 9:11(10).
B. רְצִין *r^eṣiyn* **masc. proper noun**
(Rezin: head of family of temple servants)
Ezra 2:48; **Neh.** 7:50.

7527. רָצַע *rāṣaʿ* **verb**
(to bore; to pierce)
Ex. 21:6.

7528. רָצַף *rāṣap̱* **verb**
(to fit out; to inlay)
Song 3:10.

7529. רֶצֶף *reṣep̱* **masc. noun**
(something baked on hot coals)
1 Kgs. 19:6(NASB, *riṣpāh* [7531,II]).

7530. רֶצֶף *reṣep̱* **proper noun**
(Rezeph)
2 Kgs. 19:12; **Isa.** 37:12.

7531. I. רִצְפָּה *riṣpāh* **fem. noun**
(pavement)
2 Chr. 7:3; **Esth.** 1:6; **Ezek.** 40:17,18; 42:3.
II. רִצְפָּה *riṣpāh* **fem. noun**
(live coal, hot coal)
1 Kgs. 19:6(KJV, NIV, *reṣep̱* [7529]); **Isa.** 6:6.

7532. רִצְפָּה *riṣpāh* **fem. proper noun**
(Rizpah)
2 Sam. 3:7; 21:8,10,11.

7533. רָצַץ *rāṣāṣ* **verb**
(to break; to crush; to oppress)
Gen. 25:22; **Deut.** 28:33; **Judg.** 9:53; 10:8; **1 Sam.** 12:3,4; **2 Kgs.** 18:21; 23:12(KJV, NASB, *rûṣ* [7323,II]); **2 Chr.** 16:10; **Job** 20:19; **Ps.** 74:14; **Eccl.** 12:6; **Isa.** 36:6; 42:3,4; 58:6; **Ezek.** 29:7; **Hos.** 5:11; **Amos** 4:1.

7534. רַק *raq* **adj.**
(lean, thin, gaunt)
Gen. 41:19,20,27.

7535. רַק *raq* **adv.**
(nevertheless, only, but, except)
Gen. 6:5; 14:24; 19:8; 20:11; 24:8; 26:29; 41:40; 47:22,26; 50:8; **Ex.** 8:9(5),11(7),28(24),29(25); 9:26; 10:17,24; 21:19; **Num.** 12:2; 20:19; **Deut.** 2:28,35,37; 3:11,19; 4:6,9; 10:15; 12:15,16,23,26; 15:5,23; 17:16; 20:14, 16,20; 28:13,33; **Josh.** 1:7,17,18; 6:15, 17,24; 8:2,27; 11:13,14,22; 13:6,14; 22:5; **Judg.** 3:2; 6:39; 11:34; 14:16; 19:20; **1 Sam.** 1:13; 5:4; **1 Kgs.** 3:2,3; 8:9, 19,25; 11:13; 14:8; 15:5,14,23; 21:25; 22:16; **2 Kgs.** 3:2,3; 10:29; 12:3(4); 14:3,4; 15:4,35; 17:2,18; 21:8; **2 Chr.** 5:10; 6:9,16; 15:17; 18:15; 25:2; 27:2;

28:10; 29:34; 33:8,17; **Job** 1:12,15–17, 19; **Ps.** 32:6; 91:8; **Prov.** 13:10; **Isa.** 4:1; 28:19; **Amos** 3:2.

7536. רֹק *rōq* **masc. noun**
(spit, saliva)
Job 7:19; 30:10; **Isa.** 50:6.

7537. רָקַב *rāqab̲* **verb**
(to rot)
Prov. 10:7; **Isa.** 40:20.

7538. רָקָב *rāqāb̲* **masc. noun**
(rottenness, decay)
Job 13:28; **Prov.** 12:4; 14:30; **Hos.** 5:12; **Hab.** 3:16.

7539. רִקָּבוֹן *riqqāb̲ôn* **masc. noun**
(rottenness, decay)
Job 41:27.

7540. רָקַד *rāqad̲* **verb**
(to skip, to leap, to dance)
1 Chr. 15:29; **Job** 21:11; **Ps.** 29:6; 114:4,6; **Eccl.** 3:4; **Isa.** 13:21; **Joel** 2:5; **Nah.** 3:2.

7541. רַקָּה *raqqāh* **fem. noun**
(temple [of the head])
Judg. 4:21,22; 5:26; **Song** 4:3; 6:7.

7542. רַקּוֹן *raqqôn* **proper noun**
(Rakkon)
Josh. 19:46.

7543. רָקַח *rāqaḥ* **verb**
(to mix perfume; to mix ointment)
Ex. 30:25,33,35; 37:29; **1 Chr.** 9:30; **2 Chr.** 16:14; **Eccl.** 10:1; **Ezek.** 24:10.

7544. רֶקַח *reqaḥ* **masc. noun**
(that which is spicy, that which is spiced)
Song 8:2.

7545. רֹקַח *rōqaḥ* **masc. noun**
(ointment, perfume)
Ex. 30:25,35.

7546. רַקָּח *raqqāḥ* **masc. noun**
(perfume maker)
Neh. 3:8.

7547. רִקֻּחַ *riquaḥ*, רִקּוּחַ *riqûaḥ* **masc. noun**
(perfume)
Isa. 57:9.

7548. רַקָּחָה *raqqāḥāh* **fem. noun**
(perfume maker; confectionary)
1 Sam. 8:13.

7549. רָקִיעַ *rāqiya'* **masc. noun**
(expanse, firmament)
Gen. 1:6–8,14,15,17,20; **Ps.** 19:1; 150:1; **Ezek.** 1:22,23,25,26; 10:1; **Dan.** 12:3.

7550. רָקִיק *rāqiyq* **masc. noun**
(wafer, thin cake)
Ex. 29:2,23; **Lev.** 2:4; 7:12; 8:26; **Num.** 6:15,19; **1 Chr.** 23:29.

7551. רָקַם *rāqam* **verb**
(to embroider, to weave, to do needlework)
Ex. 26:36; 27:16; 28:39; 35:35; 36:37; 38:18,23; 39:29; **Ps.** 139:15.

7552. A. רֶקֶם *reqem* **masc. proper noun**
(Rekem: a Midianite king)
Num. 31:8; **Josh.** 13:21.
B. רֶקֶם *reqem* **masc. proper noun**
(Rekem: descendant of Caleb)
1 Chr. 2:43,44.
C. רֶקֶם *reqem* **masc. proper noun**
(Rakem: descendant of Manasseh)
1 Chr. 7:16.
D. רֶקֶם *reqem* **proper noun**
(Rekem: city of Benjamin)
Josh. 18:27.

7553. רִקְמָה *riqmāh* **fem. noun**
(embroidery work; stones of various colors)
Judg. 5:30; **1 Chr.** 29:2; **Ps.** 45:14(15); **Ezek.** 16:10,13,18; 17:3; 26:16; 27:7, 16,24.

7554. רָקַע *rāqa'* **verb**
(to hammer out, to bend out, to spread out; to overlay)
Ex. 39:3; **Num.** 16:39(17:4); **2 Sam.** 22:43; **Job** 37:18; **Ps.** 136:6; **Isa.** 40:19; 42:5; 44:24; **Jer.** 10:9; **Ezek.** 6:11; 25:6.

7555. רִקּוּעַ *riqqûa'*, רִקֻּעַ *riqqua'* **masc. noun**
(something hammered out)
Num. 16:38(17:3).

7556. רָקַק *rāqaq* **verb**
(to spit)
Lev. 15:8.

7557. רַקַּת *rāqqat* **proper noun**
(Rakkath)
Josh. 19:35.

7558. רִשְׁיוֹן *rišyôn* **masc. noun**
(permission; authority)
Ezra 3:7.

7559. רָשַׁם *rāšam* **verb**
(to inscribe, to write)
Dan. 10:21.

7560. רְשַׁם *r^e^šam* **Aram. verb**
(to write; to sign; corr. to Hebr. 7559)
Dan. 5:24,25; 6:8–10(9–11),12(13), 13(14).

7561. רָשַׁע *rāša'* **verb**
(to be wicked; to act wickedly; to be guilty, to be condemned)
Ex. 22:9(8); **Deut.** 25:1; **1 Sam.** 14:47; **2 Sam.** 22:22; **1 Kgs.** 8:32,47; **2 Chr.** 6:37; 20:35; 22:3; **Neh.** 9:33; **Job** 9:20,29; 10:2,7,15; 15:6; 32:3; 34:12, 17,29; 40:8; **Ps.** 18:21(22); 37:33; 94:21; 106:6; **Prov.** 12:2; 17:15; **Eccl.** 7:17; **Isa.** 50:9; 54:17; **Dan.** 9:5,15; 11:32; 12:10.

7562. רֶשַׁע *reša'* **masc. noun**
(wickedness; iniquity)
Deut. 9:27; **1 Sam.** 24:13; **Job** 34:8,10; 35:8; **Ps.** 5:4(5); 10:15; 45:7(8); 84:10(11); 125:3; 141:4; **Prov.** 4:17; 8:7; 10:2; 12:3; 16:12; **Eccl.** 3:16; 7:25; 8:8; **Isa.** 58:4,6; **Jer.** 14:20; **Ezek.** 3:19; 7:11; 31:11; 33:12; **Hos.** 10:13; **Mic.** 6:10,11; **Mal.** 1:4(KJV, NIV, *riš'āh* [7564]).

7563. רָשָׁע *rāšā'* **adj.**
(wicked, guilty, ungodly)
Gen. 18:23,25; **Ex.** 2:13; 9:27; 23:1,7; **Num.** 16:26; 35:31; **Deut.** 25:1,2; **1 Sam.** 2:9; 24:13(14); **2 Sam.** 4:11; **1 Kgs.** 8:32; **2 Chr.** 6:23; 19:2; **Job** 3:17; 8:22; 9:22,24; 10:3; 11:20; 15:20; 16:11; 18:5; 20:5,29; 21:7,16,17,28; 22:18; 24:6; 27:7,13; 34:18,26; 36:6,17; 38:13,15; 40:12; **Ps.** 1:1,4–6; 3:7(8); 7:9(10); 9:5(6),16(17),17(18); 10:2–4, 13,15; 11:2,5,6; 12:8; 17:9,13; 26:5; 28:3; 31:17(18); 32:10; 34:21(22); 36:1(2), 11(12); 37:10,12,14,16,17,20,21,28,32, 34,35,38,40; 39:1(2); 50:16; 55:3(4); 58:3(4),10(11); 68:2(3); 71:4; 73:3,12; 75:4(5),8(9),10(11); 82:2,4; 91:8; 92:7(8); 94:3,13; 97:10; 101:8; 104:35; 106:18; 109:2,6,7; 112:10; 119:53,61,95,110, 119,155; 129:4; 139:19; 140:4(5),8(9); 141:10; 145:20; 146:9; 147:6; **Prov.** 2:22; 3:25,33; 4:14,19; 5:22; 9:7; 10:3,6,7,11, 16,20,24,25,27,28,30,32; 11:5,7,8,10,11, 18,23,31; 12:5–7,10,12,21,26; 13:5,9, 17,25; 14:11,19,32; 15:6,8,9,28,29; 16:4; 17:15,23; 18:3,5; 19:28; 20:26; 21:4,7,10, 12,18,27,29; 24:15,16,19,20,24; 25:5,26; 28:1,4,12,15,28; 29:2,7,12,16,27; **Eccl.** 3:17; 7:15; 8:10,13,14; 9:2; **Isa.** 3:11; 5:23; 11:4; 13:11; 14:5; 26:10; 48:22; 53:9; 55:7; 57:20,21; **Jer.** 5:26; 12:1; 23:19; 25:31; 30:23; **Ezek.** 3:18,19; 7:21; 13:22; 18:20,21,23,24,27; 21:3(8),4(9), 25(30),29(34); 33:8,9,11,12,14,15,19; **Dan.** 12:10; **Mic.** 6:10; **Hab.** 1:4,13; 3:13; **Zeph.** 1:3; **Mal.** 3:18; 4:3(3:21).

7564. רִשְׁעָה *riš'āh* **fem. noun**
(wickedness, guilt)

Deut. 9:4,5; 25:2; **Prov.** 11:5; 13:6; **Isa.** 9:18(17); **Ezek.** 5:6; 18:20,27; 33:12,19; **Zech.** 5:8; **Mal.** 1:4(NASB, *reša'* [7562]); 3:15; 4:1(3:19).

7565. רֶשֶׁף *rešep̱* **masc. noun**
(flame, flash, lightning bolt, burning pestilence)
Deut. 32:24; **Job** 5:7; **Ps.** 76:3(4); 78:48; **Song** 8:6; **Hab.** 3:5.

7566. רֶשֶׁף *rešep̱* **masc. proper noun**
(Resheph)
1 Chr. 7:25.

7567. רָשַׁשׁ *rāšaš* **verb**
(to beat down; to demolish)
Jer. 5:17; **Mal.** 1:4.

7568. רֶשֶׁת *rešet̠* **fem. noun**
(net, network)
Ex. 27:4,5; 38:4; **Job** 18:8; **Ps.** 9:15(16); 10:9; 25:15; 31:4(5); 35:7,8; 57:6(7); 140:5(6); **Prov.** 1:17; 29:5; **Lam.** 1:13; **Ezek.** 12:13; 17:20; 19:8; 32:3; **Hos.** 5:1; 7:12.

7569. רַתּוֹק *rattôq* **masc. noun**
(chain)
1 Kgs. 6:21(NIV, [K^{e}] *rattiyqāh* [7572]); **Ezek.** 7:23.

7570. רָתַח *rāt̠ah̩* **verb**
(to boil, [fig.] to seethe)
Job 30:27; 41:31(23); **Ezek.** 24:5.

7571. רֶתַח *ret̠ah̩* **masc. noun**
(a boiling)
Ezek. 24:5.

7572. רַתִּיקָה *rattiyqāh* **fem. noun**
(chain)
1 Kgs. 6:21(KJV, NASB, [Q^{e}] *rattôq* [7569]).

7573. רָתַם *rāt̠am* **verb**
(to bind, to harness)
Mic. 1:13.

7574. רֶתֶם *ret̠em*, רֹתֶם *rōt̠em* **masc. noun**
(broom tree, juniper tree)
1 Kgs. 19:4,5; **Job** 30:4; **Ps.** 120:4.

7575. רִתְמָה *rit̠māh* **proper noun**
(Rithmah)
Num. 33:18,19.

7576. רָתַק *rāt̠aq* **verb**
(to bind, to tie up)
Eccl. 12:6(KJV, NIV, [K^{e}] *rāh̩aq* [7368]); **Nah.** 3:10.

7577. רְתוּקָה *r^{e}t̠ûqāh* **fem. noun**
(chain)
Isa. 40:19.

7578. רְתֵת *r^{e}t̠ēt̠* **masc. noun**
(trembling)
Hos. 13:1.

שׂ, שׁ Sin, Shin

7579. שָׁאַב *šā'aḇ* **verb**
(to draw [water])
Gen. 24:11,13,19,20,43–45; **Deut.** 29:11(10); **Josh.** 9:21,23,27; **Ruth** 2:9; **1 Sam.** 7:6; 9:11; **2 Sam.** 23:16; **1 Chr.** 11:18; **Isa.** 12:3; **Nah.** 3:14.

7580. שָׁאַג *šā'ag* **verb**
(to roar [in victory or distress])
Judg. 14:5; **Job** 37:4; **Ps.** 22:13; 38:8; 74:4; 104:21; **Isa.** 5:29; **Jer.** 2:15; 25:30; 51:38; **Ezek.** 22:25; **Hos.** 11:10; **Joel** 3:16; **Amos** 1:2; 3:4,8; **Zeph.** 3:3.

7581. שְׁאָגָה *šᵉ'āgāh* **fem. noun**
(roaring [of a lion]; roaring in distress)
Job 3:24; 4:10; **Ps.** 22:1(2); 32:3; **Isa.** 5:29; **Ezek.** 19:7; **Zech.** 11:3.

7582. I. שָׁאָה *šā'āh* **verb**
(to lay waste; to turn into ruins)
2 Kgs. 19:25; **Isa.** 6:11; 37:26.
II. שָׁאָה *šā'āh* **verb**
(to roar)
Isa. 17:12,13.

7583. שָׁאָה *šā'āh* **verb**
(to gaze)
Gen. 24:21.

7584. שַׁאֲוָה *ša'ᵃwāh* **fem. noun**
(storm, desolation)
Prov. 1:27(NIV, [Qᵉ] *šô'āh* [7722,II]).

7585. שְׁאוֹל *šᵉ'ôl*, שְׁאֹל *šᵉ'ōl* **fem. noun**
(grave, hell; Sheol, death)
Gen. 37:35; 42:38; 44:29,31; **Num.** 16:30,33; **Deut.** 32:22; **1 Sam.** 2:6; **2 Sam.** 22:6; **1 Kgs.** 2:6,9; **Job** 7:9; 11:8; 14:13; 17:13,16; 21:13; 24:19; 26:6; 33:18(KJV, NIV, *šelaḥ* [7973,I]); **Ps.** 6:5(6); 9:17(18); 16:10; 18:5(6); 30:3(4); 31:17(18); 49:14(15),15(16); 55:15(16); 86:13; 88:3(4); 89:48(49); 116:3; 139:8; 141:7; **Prov.** 1:12; 5:5; 7:27; 9:18; 15:11,24; 23:14; 27:20; 30:16; **Eccl.** 9:10; **Song** 8:6; **Isa.** 5:14; 7:11(KJV, *šā'al* [7592]); 14:9,11,15; 28:15,18; 38:10,18; 57:9; **Ezek.** 31:15–17; 32:21,27; **Hos.** 13:14; **Amos** 9:2; **Jon.** 2:2(3); **Hab.** 2:5.

7586. A. שָׁאוּל *šā'ûl* **masc. proper noun**
(Saul: first king of Israel)
1 Sam. 9:2,3,5,7,8,10,15,17–19,21,22,24–27; 10:11,12,14–16,21,26; 11:4–7,11–13,15; 13:1–4,7,9–11,13,15,16,22; 14:1,2,16–21, 24,33–38,40–47,49–52; 15:1,4–7,9, 11–13,15,16,20,24,26,31,34,35; 16:1,2, 14,15,17,19–23; 17:2,8,11–15,19, 31–34,37–39,55,57,58; 18:1,2,5–13,15, 17–25,27–30; 19:1,2,4,6,7,9–11,14,15, 17–21,24; 20:25–28,30,32,33; 21:7(8), 10(11),11(12); 22:6,7,9,12,13,21,22; 23:7–17,19,21,24–28; 24:1–5(2–6), 7–9(8–10),16(17),22(23); 25:44; 26:1–7, 12,17,21,25; 27:1,4; 28:3–10,12–15, 20,21,25; 29:3,5; 31:2–8,11,12; **2 Sam.** 1:1,2,4–6,12,17,21–24; 2:4,5,7,8,10, 12,15; 3:1,6–8,10,13,14; 4:1,2,4,8,10; 5:2; 6:16,20,23; 7:15; 9:1–3,6,7,9; 12:7; 16:5,8; 19:17(18),24(25); 21:1,2,4,6–8, 11–14; 22:1; **1 Chr.** 5:10; 8:33; 9:39; 10:2–8,11–13; 11:2; 12:1,2,19(20), 23(24),29(30); 13:3; 15:29; 26:28; **Ps.** 18:[title](1); 52:[title](1); 54:[title](1); 57:[title](1); 59:[title](1); **Isa.** 10:29.
B. שָׁאוּל *šā'ûl* **masc. proper noun**
(Shaul: king of Edom)
Gen. 36:37,38; **1 Chr.** 1:48,49.

C. שָׁאוּל *šā'ûl* **masc. proper noun**
(Shaul: son of Simeon)
Gen. 46:10; **Ex.** 6:15; **Num.** 26:13; **1 Chr.** 4:24.

D. שָׁאוּל *šā'ûl* **masc. proper noun**
(Shaul: a Levite)
1 Chr. 6:24(9).

7587. שָׁאוּלִי *šā'ûliy* **masc. proper noun**
(Shaulite, descendant of Simeon [7586,C])
Num. 26:13.

7588. שָׁאוֹן *šā'ôn* **masc. noun**
(uproar; tumult; loud noise)
Ps. 40:2(3); 65:7(8); 74:23; **Isa.** 5:14; 13:4; 17:12,13; 24:8; 25:5; 66:6; **Jer.** 25:31; 46:17; 48:45; 51:55; **Hos.** 10:14; **Amos** 2:2.

7589. שְׁאָט *s^e'āṭ* **masc. noun**
(malice, scorn, contempt)
Ezek. 25:6,15; 36:5.

7590. שָׁאט *šā'ṭ,* שׁוּט *šûṭ* **verb**
(to despise, to scorn, to malign)
Ezek. 16:57; 28:24,26.

7591. שְׁאִיָּה *s^e'iyyāh* **fem. noun**
(destruction, ruin)
Isa. 24:12.

7592. שָׁאַל *šā'al* **verb**
(to ask, inquire; to request, to greet)
Gen. 24:47,57; 26:7; 32:17(18),29(30); 37:15; 38:21; 40:7; 43:7,27; 44:19; **Ex.** 3:22; 11:2; 12:35,36; 13:14; 18:7; 22:14(13); **Num.** 27:21; **Deut.** 4:32; 6:20; 10:12; 13:14(15); 14:26; 18:11,16; 32:7; **Josh.** 4:6,21; 9:14; 15:18; 19:50; **Judg.** 1:1,14; 4:20; 5:25; 8:14,24,26; 13:6,18; 18:5,15; 20:18,23,27; **1 Sam.** 1:17,20,27,28; 2:20; 8:10; 10:4,22; 12:13,17,19; 14:37; 17:22,56; 19:22; 20:6,28; 22:10,13,15; 23:2,4; 25:5,8; 28:6,16; 30:8,21; **2 Sam.** 2:1; 3:13; 5:19,23; 8:10; 11:7; 12:20; 14:18; 16:23; 20:18; **1 Kgs.** 2:16,20,22; 3:5,10,11,13; 10:13; 19:4; **2 Kgs.** 2:9,10; 4:3,28; 6:5; 8:6; **1 Chr.** 4:10; 10:13; 14:10,14; 18:10; **2 Chr.** 1:7,11; 9:12; 11:23; **Ezra** 8:22; **Neh.** 1:2; 13:6; **Job** 8:8; 12:7; 21:29; 31:30; 38:3; 40:7; 42:4; **Ps.** 2:8; 21:4(5); 27:4; 35:11; 40:6(7); 78:18; 105:40; 109:10; 122:6; 137:3; **Prov.** 20:4; 30:7; **Eccl.** 2:10; 7:10; **Isa.** 7:11(NASB, NIV, *s^e'ôl* [7585]),12; 30:2; 41:28; 45:11; 65:1; **Jer.** 6:16; 15:5; 18:13; 23:33; 30:6; 36:17; 37:17; 38:14,27; 48:19; 50:5; **Lam.** 4:4; **Ezek.** 21:21(26); **Hos.** 4:12; **Jon.** 4:8; **Mic.** 7:3; **Hag.** 2:11; **Zech.** 10:1.

7593. שְׁאֵל *s^e'ēl* **Aram. verb**
(to ask, to require; corr. to Hebr. 7592)
Ezra 5:9,10; 7:21; **Dan.** 2:10,11,27.

7594. שְׁאָל *s^e'āl* **masc. proper noun**
(Sheal)
Ezra 10:29.

7595. שְׁאֵלָה *s^e'ēlāh* **Aram. fem. noun**
(decision, verdict)
Dan. 4:17(14).

7596. שְׁאֵלָה *s^e'ēlāh,* שֵׁלָה *šēlāh* **fem. noun**
(petition, request)
Judg. 8:24; **1 Sam.** 1:17,27; 2:20; **1 Kgs.** 2:16,20; **Esth.** 5:6–8; 7:2,3; 9:12; **Job** 6:8; **Ps.** 106:15.

7597. I. שְׁאַלְתִּיאֵל *s^e'altiy'ēl* **masc. proper noun**
(Shealtiel)
1 Chr. 3:17; **Ezra** 3:2,8; **Neh.** 12:1; **Hag.** 1:1; 2:23.

II. שַׁלְתִּיאֵל *šaltiy'ēl* **masc. proper noun**
(Shealtiel)
Hag. 1:12,14; 2:2.

7598. שְׁאַלְתִּיאֵל *še'altiy'ēl* **Aram. masc. proper noun**
(Shealtiel)
Ezra 5:2.

7599. שָׁאַן *šā'an* **verb**
(to be at ease; to be secure)
Job 3:18; **Prov.** 1:33; **Jer.** 30:10; 46:27; 48:11.

7600. I. שַׁאֲנָן *ša'ᵃnān* **adj.**
(at ease, quiet, complacent)
Job 12:5; 21:23(KJV, NIV, *šal'ᵃnān* [7946]); **Ps.** 123:4(NIV, see II); **Isa.** 32:9, 11,18; 33:20; **Amos** 6:1; **Zech.** 1:15.
II. שַׁאֲנָן *ša'ᵃnān* **adj.**
(arrogant, proud, insolent)
2 Kgs. 19:28; **Ps.** 123:4(KJV, NASB, see I); **Isa.** 37:29.

7601. שָׁאַס *šā'as* **verb**
(to plunder spoil)
Jer. 30:16(NASB, NIV, [Qᵉ] *šāsas* [8155]).

7602. I. שָׁאַף *šā'ap̱* **verb**
(to gasp, to pant; to wait eagerly for, to hurry for)
Job 5:5(KJV, see III); 7:2; 36:20; **Ps.** 119:131; **Eccl.** 1:5; **Isa.** 42:14(KJV, see III); **Jer.** 2:24; 14:6; **Amos** 2:7 (NIV, see IV).
II. שָׁאַף *šā'ap̱* **verb**
(to pursue, to chase)
Ps. 56:1(2)(KJV, see III; NASB, see IV), 2(3)(KJV, see III; NASB, see IV); 57:3(4) (KJV, see III; NASB, see IV).
III. שָׁאַף *šā'ap̱* **verb**
(to swallow up)
Job 5:5(NASB, NIV, see I); **Ps.** 56:1(2) (NASB, see IV, NIV, see II),2(3)(NASB, see IV, NIV, see II); 57:3(4)(NASB, see IV, NIV, see II); **Isa.** 42:14(NASB, NIV, see I); **Ezek.** 36:3(NASB, NIV, see IV).
IV. שָׁאַף *šā'ap̱* **verb**
(to trample on; to crush)
Ps. 56:1(2)(KJV, see III; NIV, see II),2(3) (KJV, see III; NIV, see II); 57:3(4)(KJV, see III; NIV, see II); **Ezek.** 36:3(KJV, see III); **Amos** 2:7(KJV, NASB, see I).

7603. שְׂאֹר *śᵉ'ōr* **masc. noun**
(leaven, yeast)
Ex. 12:15,19; 13:7; **Lev.** 2:11; **Deut.** 16:4.

7604. שָׁאַר *šā'ar* **verb**
(to leave behind; to be left, to remain)
Gen. 7:23; 14:10; 32:8(9); 42:38; 47:18; **Ex.** 8:9(5),11(7),31(27); 10:5,12,19,26; 14:28; **Lev.** 5:9; 25:52; 26:36,39; **Num.** 9:12; 11:26; 21:35; **Deut.** 2:34; 3:3,11; 4:27; 7:20; 19:20; 28:51,55,62; **Josh.** 8:17,22; 10:28,30,33,37,39,40; 11:8, 14,22; 13:1,2,12; 23:4,7,12; **Judg.** 4:16; 6:4; 7:3; **Ruth** 1:3,5; **1 Sam.** 5:4; 9:24; 11:11; 14:36; 16:11; 25:22; **2 Sam.** 14:7; **1 Kgs.** 15:29; 16:11; 19:18; 22:46(47); **2 Kgs.** 3:25; 7:13; 10:11,14,17,21; 13:7; 17:18; 19:30; 24:14; 25:11,12,22; **1 Chr.** 13:2; **2 Chr.** 21:17; 30:6; 34:21; **Ezra** 1:4; 9:8,15; **Neh.** 1:2,3; **Job** 21:34; **Isa.** 4:3; 11:11,16; 17:6; 24:6,12; 37:31; 49:21; **Jer.** 8:3; 21:7; 24:8; 34:7; 37:10; 38:4,22; 39:9,10; 40:6; 41:10; 42:2; 49:9; 50:20; 52:15,16; **Ezek.** 6:12; 9:8; 17:21; 36:36; **Dan.** 10:8,17; **Joel** 2:14; **Amos** 5:3; **Obad.** 1:5; **Zeph.** 3:12; **Hag.** 2:3; **Zech.** 9:7; 11:9; 12:14.

7605. שְׁאָר *šᵉ'ār* **masc. noun**
(remnant, remainder, rest)
1 Chr. 11:8; 16:41; **2 Chr.** 9:29; 24:14; **Ezra** 3:8; 4:3,7; **Neh.** 10:28(29); 11:1,20; **Esth.** 9:12,16; **Isa.** 10:19–22; 11:11,16; 14:22; 16:14; 17:3; 21:17; 28:5; **Zeph.** 1:4; **Mal.** 2:15(NIV, *šᵉ'ēr* [7607]).

7606. שְׁאָר *šᵉ'ār* **Aram. masc. noun**
(remnant, remainder, rest; corr. to Hebr. 7605)
Ezra 4:9,10,17; 6:16; 7:18,20; **Dan.** 2:18; 7:7,12,19.

7607. שְׁאֵר *šᵉʾēr* **masc. noun**
(flesh, meat; fig.: relative, kinsman)
Ex. 21:10; **Lev.** 18:6,12,13,17(KJV, *šaʾᵃrāh* [7608]); 20:19; 21:2; 25:49; **Num.** 27:11; **Ps.** 73:26; 78:20,27; **Prov.** 5:11; 11:17; **Jer.** 51:35; **Mic.** 3:2,3; **Mal.** 2:15(KJV, NASB, *šᵉʾār* [7605]).

7608. שַׁאֲרָה *šaʾᵃrāh* **fem. noun**
(kinswoman)
Lev. 18:17(NASB, NIV, *šᵉʾēr* [7607]).

7609. שֶׁאֱרָה *šeʾᵉrāh* **fem. proper noun**
(Sheerah)
1 Chr. 7:24.

7610. שְׁאָר יָשׁוּב *šᵉʾār yāšûḇ* **masc. proper noun**
(Shear-Jashub)
Isa. 7:3.

7611. שְׁאֵרִית *šᵉʾēriyṯ* **fem. noun**
(remnant, survivors, the rest)
Gen. 45:7; **2 Sam.** 14:7; **2 Kgs.** 19:4,31; 21:14; **1 Chr.** 4:43; 12:38(39); **2 Chr.** 34:9; 36:20; **Ezra** 9:14; **Neh.** 7:72; **Ps.** 76:10(11); **Isa.** 14:30; 15:9; 37:4,32; 44:17; 46:3; **Jer.** 6:9; 8:3; 11:23; 15:9,11; 23:3; 24:8; 25:20; 31:7; 39:3; 40:11,15; 41:10,16; 42:2,15,19; 43:5; 44:7,12, 14,28; 47:4,5; 50:26; **Ezek.** 5:10; 9:8; 11:13; 25:16; 36:3–5; **Amos** 1:8; 5:15; 9:12; **Mic.** 2:12; 4:7; 5:7(6),8(7); 7:18; **Zeph.** 2:7,9; 3:13; **Hag.** 1:12,14; 2:2; **Zech.** 8:6,11,12.

7612. שֵׁאת *šēʾṯ* **fem. noun**
(desolation, ruin)
Lam. 3:47.

7613. I. שְׂאֵת *śᵉʾēṯ* **fem. noun**
(elevation, honoring, dignity)
Gen. 4:7; 49:3; **Lev.** 13:2(NASB, NIV, see II),10(NASB, NIV, see II),19(NASB, NIV, see II),28(NASB, NIV, see II),43(NASB, NIV, see II); 14:56(NASB, NIV, see II); **Job** 13:11; 31:23; 41:25(17); **Ps.** 62:4; **Hab.** 1:7.
II. שְׂאֵת *śᵉʾēṯ* **fem. noun**
(swelling)
Lev. 13:2(KJV, see I),10(KJV, see I),19(KJV, see I),28(KJV, see I),43(KJV, see I); 14:56(KJV, see I).

7614. A. שְׁבָא *šᵉḇāʾ* **masc. proper noun**
(Sheba: descendant of Seth through Joktan)
Gen. 10:28; **1 Chr.** 1:22.
B. שְׁבָא *šᵉḇāʾ* **masc. proper noun**
(Sheba: descendant of Ham)
Gen. 10:7; **1 Chr.** 1:9.
C. שְׁבָא *šᵉḇāʾ* **masc. proper noun**
(Sheba: grandson of Abraham through Keturah)
Gen. 25:3; **1 Chr.** 1:32.
D. שְׁבָא *šᵉḇāʾ* **proper noun**
(Sheba: nation in Arabia)
1 Kgs. 10:1,4,10,13; **2 Chr.** 9:1,3,9,12; **Job** 1:15; 6:19; **Ps.** 72:10,15; **Isa.** 60:6; **Jer.** 6:20; **Ezek.** 27:22,23; 38:13.

7615. שְׁבָאִי *šᵉḇāʾiy* **masc. proper noun**
(Sabean: citizen of Sheba [7614,D])
Joel 3:8(4:8).

7616. שְׁבָבִים *šᵉḇaḇiym* **masc. pl. noun**
(broken pieces)
Hos. 8:6.

7617. שָׁבָה *šāḇāh* **verb**
(to take captive, to carry off)
Gen. 14:14; 31:26; 34:29; **Ex.** 22:10(9); **Num.** 21:1; 24:22(NASB, *šᵉḇiy* [7628]); 31:9; **Deut.** 21:10; **Judg.** 5:12(NASB, *šᵉḇiy* [7628]); **1 Sam.** 30:2,3,5; **1 Kgs.** 8:46(NASB, *šᵉḇiy* [7628]),47,48,50; **2 Kgs.** 5:2; 6:22; **1 Chr.** 5:21; **2 Chr.** 6:36–38; 14:15(14); 21:17; 25:12; 28:5,8,11,17; 30:9; **Ps.** 68:18(19); 106:46;

137:3; **Isa.** 14:2; 61:1; **Jer.** 13:17; 41:10,14; 43:12; 50:33; **Ezek.** 6:9; **Obad.** 1:11.

7618. שְׁבוֹ *šᵉḇô* **fem. noun**
(agate, a precious stone)
Ex. 28:19; 39:12.

7619. A. שְׁבוּאֵל *šᵉḇû'ēl*, שׁוּבָאֵל *šûḇā'ēl* **masc. proper noun**
(Shebuel, Shubael: levitical official descended from Gershom)
1 Chr. 23:16; 24:20; 26:24.
B. שְׁבוּאֵל *šᵉḇû'ēl*, שׁוּבָאֵל *šûḇā'ēl* **masc. proper noun**
(Shebuel, Shubael: levitical musician, son of Heman)
1 Chr. 25:4,20.

7620. שָׁבוּעַ *šāḇûaʿ* **masc. noun**
(seven, week; group of seven days or years)
Gen. 29:27,28; **Ex.** 34:22; **Lev.** 12:5; **Num.** 28:26; **Deut.** 16:9,10,16; **2 Chr.** 8:13; **Jer.** 5:24; **Ezek.** 45:21(KJV, *šiḇʿāh* [7651]); **Dan.** 9:24–27; 10:2,3.

7621. שְׁבוּעָה *šᵉḇûʿāh* **fem. noun**
(oath, curse)
Gen. 24:8; 26:3; **Ex.** 22:11(10); **Lev.** 5:4; **Num.** 5:21; 30:2(3),10(11),13(14); **Deut.** 7:8; **Josh.** 2:17,20; 9:20; **Judg.** 21:5; **1 Sam.** 14:26; **2 Sam.** 21:7; **1 Kgs.** 2:43; **1 Chr.** 16:16; **2 Chr.** 15:15; **Neh.** 6:18; 10:29(30); **Ps.** 105:9; **Eccl.** 8:2; 9:2; **Isa.** 65:15; **Jer.** 11:5; **Ezek.** 21:23(28); **Dan.** 9:11; **Hab.** 3:9(NIV, *šeḇaʿ* [7651]); **Zech.** 8:17.

7622. שְׁבוּת *šᵉḇûṯ*, שְׁבִית *šᵉḇiyṯ* **fem. noun**
(captivity; with *šûḇ* [7725], lit., "turning back of captivity": "restoration to favor")
Num. 21:29(KJV, *šᵉḇiy* [7628]); **Deut.** 30:3; **Job** 42:10; **Ps.** 14:7; 53:6(7); 85:1(2); 126:1(KJV, NIV, *šiyḇāh* [7870]),4;

Jer. 29:14; 30:3,18; 31:23; 32:44; 33:7, 11,26; 48:47; 49:6,39; **Lam.** 2:14; **Ezek.** 16:53; 29:14; 39:25; **Hos.** 6:11; **Joel** 3:1(4:1); **Amos** 9:14; **Zeph.** 2:7; 3:20.

7623. I. שָׁבַח *šāḇaḥ* **verb**
(to praise, to extol, to laud)
1 Chr. 16:35; **Ps.** 63:3(4); 106:47; 117:1; 145:4; 147:12; **Eccl.** 4:2; 8:10(KJV, NASB, *šāḵaḥ* [7911]),15.
II. שָׁבַח *šāḇaḥ* **verb**
(to quiet, to still, to hold)
Ps. 65:7(8); 89:9(10); **Prov.** 29:11.

7624. שְׁבַח *šᵉḇaḥ* **Aram. verb**
(to praise; to honor)
Dan. 2:23; 4:34(31),37(34); 5:4,23.

7625. שְׁבַט *šᵉḇaṭ* **Aram. masc. noun**
(tribe)
Ezra 6:17.

7626. שֵׁבֶט *šēḇeṭ* **masc. noun**
(rod, scepter; [by extension] tribe)
Gen. 49:10,16,28; **Ex.** 21:20; 24:4; 28:21; 39:14; **Lev.** 27:32; **Num.** 4:18; 18:2; 24:2,17; 32:33; 36:3; **Deut.** 1:13,15,23; 3:13; 5:23; 10:8; 12:5,14; 16:18; 18:1,5; 29:8,10,18,21; 31:28; 33:5; **Josh.** 1:12; 3:12; 4:2,4,5,8,12; 7:14,16; 11:23; 12:6,7; 13:7,14,29,33; 18:2,4,7; 21:16; 22:7,9–11,13,15,21; 23:4; 24:1; **Judg.** 5:14; 18:1,19,30; 20:2,10,12; 21:3,5,6,8,15,17,24; **1 Sam.** 2:28; 9:21; 10:19–21; 15:17; **2 Sam.** 5:1; 7:7,14; 15:2,10; 18:14; 19:9(10); 20:14; 23:21; 24:2; **1 Kgs.** 8:16; 11:13,31,32,35,36; 12:20,21; 14:21; 18:31; **2 Kgs.** 17:18; 21:7; **1 Chr.** 5:18,23,26; 11:23; 12:37(38); 23:14; 26:32; 27:16,20,22; 28:1; 29:6; **2 Chr.** 6:5; 11:16; 12:13; 33:7; **Job** 9:34; 21:9; 37:13; **Ps.** 2:9; 23:4; 45:6(7); 74:2; 78:55,67,68; 89:32(33); 105:37; 122:4; 125:3; **Prov.** 10:13; 13:24; 22:8,15; 23:13,14; 26:3; 29:15; **Isa.** 9:4(3); 10:5, 15,24; 11:4; 14:5,29; 19:13; 28:27; 30:31;

49:6; 63:17; **Jer.** 10:16; 51:19; **Lam.** 3:1; **Ezek.** 19:11,14; 20:37; 21:10(15),13(18); 37:19; 45:8; 47:13,21–23; 48:1,19,23, 29,31; **Hos.** 5:9; **Amos** 1:5,8; **Mic.** 5:1(4:14); 7:14; **Zech.** 9:1; 10:11.

7627. שְׁבָט *šᵉḇāṭ* **proper noun**
(Shebat)
Zech. 1:7.

7628. שְׁבִי *šᵉḇiy* **masc. noun**
(captivity, prisoner)
Ex. 12:29; **Num.** 21:1,29(NASB, NIV, *šᵉḇiyṯ* [7622]); 31:12,19,26; **Deut.** 21:10,13; 28:41; **Judg.** 5:12; **2 Chr.** 6:37,38; 28:17; 29:9; **Ezra** 2:1; 3:8; 8:35; 9:7; **Neh.** 1:2,3; 7:6; 8:17; **Ps.** 68:18(19); 78:61; **Isa.** 20:4; 46:2; 49:24,25; 52:2; **Jer.** 15:2; 20:6; 22:22; 30:10,16; 43:11; 46:27; 48:46; **Lam.** 1:5,18; **Ezek.** 12:11; 30:17,18; **Dan.** 11:8,33; **Amos** 4:10; 9:4; **Nah.** 3:10; **Hab.** 1:9.

7629. שֹׁבִי *šōḇiy* **masc. proper noun**
(Shobi)
2 Sam. 17:27.

7630. שֹׁבָי *šōḇāy* **masc. proper noun**
(Shobai)
Ezra 2:42; **Neh.** 7:45.

7631. שְׁבִיב *šᵉḇiyḇ* **Aram. masc. noun**
(flame, fire; corr. to Hebr. 7632)
Dan. 3:22; 7:9.

7632. שָׁבִיב *šāḇiyḇ* **masc. noun**
(spark, flame)
Job 18:5.

7633. שִׁבְיָה *šiḇyāh* **fem. noun**
(captive, prisoner; captivity)
Deut. 21:11; 32:42; **2 Chr.** 28:5,11, 13–15; **Neh.** 4:4(3:36); **Jer.** 48:46.

7634. שָׁבְיָה *šoḇyāh* **masc. proper noun**
(Shobyah: alternate form for *śāḵyāh* [7914,III], which see)

7635. שְׁבִיל *šāḇiyl,* שָׁבוּל *šāḇûl* **masc. noun**
(path, way)
Ps. 77:19(20); **Jer.** 18:15.

7636. שָׁבִיס *šaḇiys* **masc. noun**
(headband)
Isa. 3:18.

7637. שְׁבִיעִי *šᵉḇiy'iy,* שְׁבִיעִית *šᵉḇiy'iṯ* **masc., fem. adj.**
(seventh)
Gen. 2:2,3; 8:4; **Ex.** 12:15,16; 13:6; 16:26,27,29,30; 20:10,11; 21:2; 23:11,12; 24:16; 31:15,17; 34:21; 35:2; **Lev.** 13:5, 6,27,32,34,51; 14:9,39; 16:29; 23:3,8, 16,24,27,34,39,41; 25:4,9,20; **Num.** 6:9; 7:48; 19:12,19; 21:29; 28:25; 29:1,7, 12,32; 31:19,24; **Deut.** 5:14; 15:12; 16:8; **Josh.** 6:4,15,16; 19:40; **Judg.** 14:15 (NASB, NIV, [some versions] *rᵉḇiy'iy* [7243]),17,18; **2 Sam.** 12:18; **1 Kgs.** 8:2; 18:44; 20:29; **2 Kgs.** 11:4; 18:9; 25:25; **1 Chr.** 2:15; 12:11(12); 24:10; 25:14; 26:3,5; 27:10; **2 Chr.** 5:3; 7:10; 23:1; 31:7; **Ezra** 3:1,6; 7:8; **Neh.** 7:73(72); 8:2,14; 10:31(32); **Esth.** 1:10; **Jer.** 28:17; 41:1; **Ezek.** 20:1; 39:25; 45:25; **Hag.** 2:1; **Zech.** 7:5; 8:19.

7638. שָׂבָךְ *śāḇāḵ* **masc. noun**
(net, network)
1 Kgs. 7:17(NASB, NIV, *śᵉḇāḵāh* [7639]).

7639. שְׂבָכָה *śᵉḇāḵāh* **fem. noun**
(network, lattice, webbing)
1 Kgs. 7:17(KJV, *śāḇāḵ* [7638]),18,20,41,42; **2 Kgs.** 1:2; 25:17; **2 Chr.** 4:12,13; **Job** 18:8; **Jer.** 52:22,23.

7640. שֹׁבֶל *šōḇel* **masc. noun**
(skirt)
Isa. 47:2.

7641. I. שִׁבֹּלֶת *šibbōleṯ* **fem. noun**
(head of grain)
Gen. 41:5,6,7,22–24,26,27; **Judg.** 12:6; **Ruth** 2:2; **Job** 24:24; **Isa.** 17:5; **Zech.** 4:12.
II. שִׁבֹּלֶת *šibbōleṯ* **fem. noun**
(stream, torrent, flood; branch, twig-bundle)
Ps. 69:2(3),15(16); **Isa.** 27:12.

7642. שַׁבְּלוּל *šablûl* **masc. noun**
(snail, slug)
Ps. 58:8(9).

7643. שְׂבָם *śᵉḇām*, שִׂבְמָה *śiḇmāh* **proper noun**
(Sebam, Sibmah)
Num. 32:3,38; **Josh.** 13:19; **Isa.** 16,8,9; **Jer.** 48:32.

7644. שֶׁבְנָא *šeḇnā'*, שֶׁבְנָה *šeḇnāh* **masc. proper noun**
(Shebna, Shebnah)
2 Kgs. 18:18,26,37; 19:2; **Isa.** 22:15; 36:3,11,22; 37:2.

7645. A. שְׁבַנְיָהוּ *šᵉḇanyāhû* **masc. proper noun**
(Shebaniah: a priest in David's day)
1 Chr. 15:24.
B. שְׁבַנְיָה *šᵉḇanyāh* **masc. proper noun**
(Shebaniah: a Levite who led worship in Nehemiah's day; possibly the same as D or E)
Neh. 9:4,5; 10:10(11).
C. שְׁבַנְיָה *šᵉḇanyāh* **masc. proper noun**
(Shebaniah: a priest in Ezra's day)
Neh. 10:4(5); 12:14(15)(NIV, *šᵉkanyāh* [7935,C]).
D. שְׁבַנְיָה *šᵉḇanyāh* **masc. proper noun**
(Shebaniah: a Levite who signed Ezra's covenant; possibly the same as B)
Neh. 10:10(11).
E. שְׁבַנְיָה *šᵉḇanyāh* **masc. proper noun**
(Shebaniah: another Levite who signed Ezra's covenant; possibly the same as B)
Neh. 10:12(13).

7646. שָׂבַע ,שָׂבֵעַ *śāḇa'*, *śābēa'* **verb**
(to be satisfied, to be filled, to be full)
Ex. 16:8,12; **Lev.** 26:26; **Deut.** 6:11; 8:10,12; 11:15; 14:29; 26:12; 31:20; **Ruth** 2:14,18(KJV, NASB, *śōḇa'* [7648]); **1 Chr.** 23:1; **2 Chr.** 24:15; 31:10; **Neh.** 9:25; **Job** 7:4; 9:18; 19:22; 27:14; 31:31; 38:27; **Ps.** 17:14,15; 22:26(27); 37:19; 59:15(16); 63:5(6); 65:4(5); 78:29; 81:16(17); 88:3(4); 90:14; 91:16; 103:5; 104:13,16,28; 105:40; 107:9; 123:3,4; 132:15; 145:16; 147:14; **Prov.** 1:31; 5:10; 12:11,14; 14:14; 18:20; 20:13; 25:16,17; 27:20; 28:19; 30:9,15,16,22; **Eccl.** 1:8; 4:8; 5:10(9); 6:3; **Isa.** 1:11; 9:20; 44:16; 50:19; 53:11; 58:10,11; 66:11; **Jer.** 5:7; 31:14; 44:17; 46:10; 50:10,19; **Lam.** 3:15,30; 5:6; **Ezek.** 7:19; 16:28(KJV, NASB, *śāḇ'āh* [7654]); 27:33; 32:4; 39:20; **Hos.** 4:10; 13:6; **Joel** 2:19,26; **Amos** 4:8; **Mic.** 6:14; **Hab.** 2:5,16; **Hag.** 1:6(KJV, NASB, *śāb'āh* [7654]).

7647. שָׂבָע *śāḇā'* **masc. noun**
(abundance, plenty, overflow)
Gen. 41:29–31,34,47,53; **Prov.** 3:10; **Eccl.** 5:12(11).

7648. שֹׂבַע *śōḇa'* **masc. noun**
(abundance, satisfaction, fulness)
Ex. 16:3; **Lev.** 25:19; 26:5; **Deut.** 23:24(25); **Ruth** 2:18(NIV, *śāḇa'* [7646]); **Ps.** 16:11; 78:25; **Prov.** 13:25.

7649. שָׂבֵעַ *śaḇēa'* **adj.**
(full, satisfied, abounding)
Gen. 25:8; 35:29; **Deut.** 33:23; **1 Sam.** 2:5; **1 Chr.** 29:28; **Job** 10:15; 14:1; 42:17; **Prov.** 19:23; 27:7.

7650. שָׁבַע *šaḇa'* **verb**
(to swear, to promise on oath)
Gen. 21:23,24,31; 22:16; 24:3,7,9,37; 25:33; 26:3,31; 31:53; 47:31; 50:5,6, 24,25; **Ex.** 13:5,11,19; 32:13; 33:1; **Lev.** 5:4; 6:3(5:22),5(5:24); 19:12; **Num.** 5:19,21; 11:12; 14:16,23; 30:2(3); 32:10, 11; **Deut.** 1:8,34,35; 2:14; 4:21,31; 6:10, 13,18,23; 7:8,12,13; 8:1,18; 9:5; 10:11,20; 11:9,21; 13:17(18); 19:8; 26:3,15; 28:9,11; 29:13(12); 30:20; 31:7,20,21,23; 34:4; **Josh.** 1:6; 2:12,17,20; 5:6; 6:22,26; 9:15,18,19,20; 14:9; 21:43,44; 23:7; **Judg.** 2:1,15; 15:12; 21:1,7,18; **1 Sam.** 3:14; 14:27,28; 19:6; 20:3,17,35,42; 24:21(22),22(23); 28:10; 30:15; **2 Sam.** 3:9,35; 19:7(8),23(24); 21:2,17; **1 Kgs.** 1:13,17,29,30,51; 2:8,23,42; 18:10; 22:16; **2 Kgs.** 11:4; 25:24; **2 Chr.** 15:14,15; 18:15; 36:13; **Ezra** 10:5; **Neh.** 5:12; 13:25; **Ps.** 15:4; 24:4; 63:11(12); 89:3(4),35(36),49(50); 95:11; 102:8(9); 110:4; 119:106; 132:2,11; **Eccl.** 9:2; **Song** 2:7; 3:5; 5:8,9; 8:4; **Isa.** 14:24; 19:18; 45:23; 48:1; 54:9; 62:8; 65:16; **Jer.** 4:2; 5:2,7; 7:9; 11:5,12,16; 12:16; 22:5; 32:22; 38:16; 40:9; 44:26; 49:13; 51:14; **Ezek.** 16:8; 21:23(28); **Dan.** 12:7; **Hos.** 4:15; **Amos** 4:2; 6:8; 8:7,14; **Mic.** 7:20; **Zeph.** 1:5; **Zech.** 5:3,4; **Mal.** 3:5.

7651. שֶׁבַע *šeḇa'*, שִׁבְעָה *šiḇ'āh* **masc., fem. noun**
(seven [NIV, see also *šiḇ'iym* [7657] and *šiḇ'ātayim* [7658])
Gen. 5:7,25,26,31; 7:2,3,4,10,11; 8:4, 10,12,14; 11:21; 21:28–30; 23:1; 25:17; 29:18,20,27,30; 31:23; 33:3; 37:2; 41:2–7, 18–20,22–24,26,27,29,30,34,36,47,48, 53,54; 46:25; 47:28; 50:10; **Ex.** 2:16; 6:16,20; 7:25; 12:15,19; 13:6,7; 22:30(29); 23:15; 25:37; 29:30,35,37; 34:18; 37:23; 38:24,25,28; **Lev.** 4:6,17; 8:11,33,35; 12:2; 13:4,5,21,26,31,33,50,54; 14:7,8, 16,27,38,51; 15:13,19,24,28; 16:14,19; 22:27; 23:6,8,15,18,34,36,39–42; 25:8; 26:18,21,24,28; **Num.** 1:31,39; 2:8, 26,31; 3:22; 4:36; 8:2; 12:14,15; 13:22; 16:49(17:14); 19:4,11,14,16; 23:1,4,14,29; 26:7,34,51; 28:11,17,19,21,24,27,29; 29:2,4,8,10,12,32,36; 31:19,36,43,52; **Deut.** 7:1; 15:1,9; 16:3,4,9,13,15; 28:7,25; 31:10; **Josh.** 6:4,6,8,13,15; 18:2,5,6,9; **Judg.** 6:1,25; 8:14,26; 12:9; 14:12,17; 16:7,8,13,19; 20:15,16; **Ruth** 4:15; **1 Sam.** 2:5; 6:1; 10:8; 11:3; 13:8; 16:10; 31:13; **2 Sam.** 2:11; 5:5; 8:4; 10:18; 21:6,9; 23:39; 24:13; **1 Kgs.** 2:11; 6:6,38; 7:17; 8:65; 11:3; 14:21; 16:10,15; 18:43; 19:18; 20:15,29,30; 22:51(52); **2 Kgs.** 3:9,26; 4:35; 5:10,14; 8:1–3; 11:21(12:1); 12:1(2); 13:1,10; 15:1; 16:1; 24:16; 25:8,27; **1 Chr.** 3:4,24; 5:13,18; 7:5,11; 9:13,25; 10:12; 12:25(26),27(28),34(35); 15:26; 18:4; 19:18; 24:15; 25:24; 26:30,32; 29:4,27; **2 Chr.** 7:8,9; 12:13; 13:9; 15:11; 17:11; 24:1; 26:13; 29:21; 30:21–24; 35:17; **Ezra** 2:5,9,25,33,38,39,65–67; 6:22; 7:7; 8:25; **Neh.** 7:14,18,19,29,37,41,42,67–69, 72; 8:18; **Esth.** 1:1,5,10,14; 2:9,16; 8:9; 9:30; **Job** 1:2,3; 2:13; 5:19; 42:8; **Ps.** 119:164; **Prov.** 6:16; 9:1; 24:16; 26:16,25; **Eccl.** 11:2; **Isa.** 4:1; 11:15; 30:26; **Jer.** 15:9; 32:9; 34:14; 52:25,28,30,31; **Ezek.** 3:15,16; 29:17; 30:20; 39:9,12,14; 40:22,26; 41:3; 43:25,26; 44:26; 45:20,21 (NASB, NIV, *šāḇûa'* [7620]),23,25; **Dan.** 9:25; **Mic.** 5:5(4); **Hab.** 3:9(KJV, NASB, *šᵉḇû'āh* [7621]); **Zech.** 3:9; 4:2,10.

7652. A. שֶׁבַע *šeḇa'* **masc. proper noun**
(Sheba: a Benjamite)
2 Sam. 20:1,2,6,7,10,13,21,22.
B. שֶׁבַע *šeḇa'* **masc. proper noun**
(Sheba: a Gadite)
1 Chr. 5:13.
C. שֶׁבַע *šeḇa'* **masc. proper noun**
(Sheba: town in Simeon)
Josh. 19:2.

7653. שִׂבְעָה *śiḇ'āh* **fem. noun**
(abundance, fulness, satiety)
Ezek. 16:49(NASB, *śoḇ'āh* [7654]).

7654. שָׂבְעָה *śo<u>b</u>'āh* **fem. noun**
(abundance, satisfaction)
Isa. 23:18; 55:2; 56:11; **Ezek.** 16:28(NIV, *śō<u>b</u>a'* [7646]),49(KJV, NIV, *śi<u>b</u>'āh* [7653]); 39:19; **Hag.** 1:6(NIV, *śō<u>b</u>a'* [7646]).

7655. שִׁבְעָה *ši<u>b</u>'āh,* שְׁבַע *š^e ba'* **Aram. masc., fem. noun**
(seven)
Ezra 7:14; **Dan.** 3:19; 4:16(13),23(20),25(22),32(29).

7656. שִׁבְעָה *ši<u>b</u>'āh* **proper noun**
(Shibah)
Gen. 26:33.

7657. שִׁבְעִים *ši<u>b</u>'iym* **pl. noun**
(seventy [NIV, plural of *še<u>b</u>a'* [7651])
Gen. 4:24; 5:12,31; 11:26; 12:4; 25:7; 46:27; 50:3; **Ex.** 1:5; 15:27; 24:1,9; 38:25,28,29; **Num.** 1:27; 2:4; 3:43,46; 7:13,19,25,31,37,43,49,55,61,67,73,79,85; 11:16,24,25; 26:22; 31:32,33,37,38; 33:9; **Deut.** 10:22; **Judg.** 1:7; 8:14,30; 14:30; 9:2,4,5,18,24,56; 12:14; **1 Sam.** 6:19; **2 Sam.** 24:15; **1 Kgs.** 5:15(29); **2 Kgs.** 10:1,6,7; **1 Chr.** 21:5,14; **2 Chr.** 2:2(1),18(17); 29:32; 36:21; **Ezra** 2:3–5, 36,40; 8:7,14,35; **Neh.** 7:8,9,39,43; 11:19; **Esth.** 9:16; **Ps.** 90:10; **Isa.** 23:15, 17; **Jer.** 25:11,12; 29:10; **Ezek.** 8:11; 41:12; **Dan.** 9:2,24; **Zech.** 1:12; 7:5.

7658. שִׁבְעָנָה *ši<u>b</u>'ānāh* **masc. noun**
(seven)
Job 42:13.

7659. שִׁבְעָתַיִם *ši<u>b</u>'ā<u>t</u>ayim* **fem. noun**
(sevenfold, seven times [NIV, dual form of *še<u>b</u>a'* [7651]; often used adverbially)
Gen. 4:15,24; **Ps.** 12:6(7); 79:12; **Prov.** 6:31; **Isa.** 30:26.

7660. שָׁבַץ *šā<u>b</u>aṣ* **verb**
(to weave in; to set [a gem])
Ex. 28:20,39.

7661. שָׁבָץ *šā<u>b</u>āṣ* **masc. noun**
(anguish, agony)
2 Sam. 1:9.

7662. שְׁבַק *š^e<u>b</u>aq* **Aram. verb**
(to leave, to let alone)
Ezra 6:7; **Dan.** 2:44; 4:15(12),23(20),26(23).

7663. I. שָׂבַר *śā<u>b</u>ar* **verb**
(to inspect, to examine)
Neh. 2:13,15.
II. שָׂבַר *śā<u>b</u>ar* **verb**
(to wait, to hope, to anticipate)
Ruth 1:13; **Esth.** 9:1; **Ps.** 104:27; 119:166; 145:15; **Isa.** 38:18.

7664. שֵׂבֶר *śē<u>b</u>er* **masc. noun**
(hope)
Ps. 119:116; 146:5.

7665. שָׁבַר *šā<u>b</u>ar* **verb**
(to break, to smash, to injure)
Gen. 19:9; **Ex.** 9:25; 12:46; 22:10(9), 14(13); 23:24; 32:19; 34:1,13; **Lev.** 6:28(21); 11:33; 15:12; 22:22; 26:13, 19,26; **Num.** 9:12; **Deut.** 7:5; 9:17; 10:2; 12:3; **Judg.** 7:20; **1 Sam.** 4:18; **1 Kgs.** 13:26,28; 19:11; 22:48(49); **2 Kgs.** 11:18; 18:4; 23:14; 25:13; **2 Chr.** 14:3(2),13(12); 20:37; 23:17; 31:1; 34:4; **Job** 24:20; 29:17; 31:22; 38:10,15; **Ps.** 3:7(8); 10:15; 29:5; 34:18(19),20(21); 37:15,17; 46:9(10); 48:7(8); 51:17(19); 69:20(21); 74:13; 76:3(4); 104:11; 105:16,33; 107:16; 124:7; 147:3; **Prov.** 6:15; 25:15; 29:1; **Eccl.** 12:6; **Isa.** 8:15; 14:5,25,29; 21:9; 24:10; 27:11; 28:13; 30:14; 38:13; 42:3; 45:2; 61:1; 66:9; **Jer.** 2:13,20; 5:5; 8:21; 14:17; 17:18; 19:10,11; 22:20; 23:9; 28:2,4,10,11,12,13; 30:8; 43:13; 48:4,17,25,38; 49:35; 50:23; 51:8,30; 52:17; **Lam.** 1:15; 2:9; 3:4; **Ezek.** 4:16; 5:16; 6:4,6,9; 14:13; 26:2; 27:26,34; 29:7; 30:8,18,21,22,24; 31:12; 32:28; 34:4,27; **Dan.** 8:7,8,22,25; 11:4, 20,22,26; **Hos.** 1:5; 2:18(20); **Amos** 1:5; **Jon.** 1:4; **Nah.** 1:13; **Zech.** 11:16.

7666. שָׁבַר *šāḇar* **verb**
(to buy; to sell)
Gen. 41:56,57; 42:2,3,5–7,10; 43:2,4, 20,22; 44:25; 47:14; **Deut.** 2:6,28; **Prov.** 11:26; **Isa.** 55:1; **Amos** 8:5,6.

7667. I. שֶׁבֶר *šeḇer* **masc. noun**
(destruction, crushing, breaking)
Lev. 21:19; 24:20; **Job** 41:25(17); **Ps.** 60:2(4); **Prov.** 15:4; 16:18; 17:19; 18:12; **Isa.** 1:28; 15:5; 30:13,14,26; 51:19; 59:7; 60:18; 65:14; **Jer.** 4:6,20; 6:1,14; 8:11,21; 10:19; 14:17; 30:12,15; 48:3,5; 50:22; 51:54; **Lam.** 2:11,13; 3:47,48; 4:10; **Ezek.** 32:9; **Amos** 6:6; **Nah.** 3:19; **Zeph.** 1:10.
II. שֵׁבֶר *šēḇer* **masc. noun**
(interpretation)
Judg. 7:15.

7668. שֶׁבֶר *šeḇer* **masc. noun**
(grain)
Gen. 42:1,2,19,26; 43:2; 44:2; 47:14; **Neh.** 10:31(32); **Amos** 8:5.

7669. שֶׁבֶר *šeḇer* **masc. proper noun**
(Sheber)
1 Chr. 2:48.

7670. שִׁבְרוֹן *šiḇrôn* **masc. noun**
(breaking, destruction)
Jer. 17:18; **Ezek.** 21:6(11).

7671. I. שְׁבָרִים *šᵉḇāriym* **masc. proper noun**
(Shebarim)
Josh. 7:5(NIV, see II).
II. שְׁבָרִים *šᵉḇāriym* **masc. pl. noun**
(stone quarries)
Josh. 7:5(KJV, NASB, see I).

7672. שְׁבַשׁ *šᵉḇaš* **Aram. verb**
(to be astonished, to be perplexed)
Dan. 5:9.

7673. שָׁבַת *šaḇaṯ* **verb**
(to rest; to cease; to put to an end)
Gen. 2:2,3; 8:22; **Ex.** 5:5; 12:15; 16:30; 23:12; 31:17; 34:21; **Lev.** 2:13; 23:32; 25:2; 26:6,34,35; **Deut.** 32:26; **Josh.** 5:12; 22:25; **Ruth** 4:14; **2 Kgs.** 23:5,11; **2 Chr.** 16:5; 36:21; **Neh.** 4:11(5); 6:3; **Job** 32:1; **Ps.** 8:2(3); 46:9(10); 89:44(5); 119:119; **Prov.** 18:18; 22:10; **Isa.** 13:11; 14:4; 16:10; 17:3; 21:2; 24:8; 30:11; 33:8; **Jer.** 7:34; 16:9; 31:36; 36:29; 48:33,35; **Lam.** 5:14,15; **Ezek.** 6:6; 7:24; 12:23; 16:41; 23:27,48; 26:13; 30:10,13,18; 33:28; 34:10,25; **Dan.** 9:27; 11:18; **Hos.** 1:4; 2:11(13); 7:4; **Amos** 8:4.

7674. שֶׁבֶת *šeḇeṯ* **masc. noun**
(a ceasing, loss of time)
Ex. 21:19; **Prov.** 20:3(NIV, *yāšaḇ* [3427]); **Isa.** 30:7.

7675. שֶׁבֶת *šeḇeṯ* **fem. noun**
(seat, dwelling place, site)
Num. 21:15(KJV, *yāšaḇ* [3427]); **2 Sam.** 23:7,8(NASB, NIV, *yōšēḇ baššeḇeṯ* [3429,II]); **1 Kgs.** 10:19; **2 Chr.** 9:18 (KJV, *yāšaḇ* [3427]); **Amos** 6:3; **Obad.** 1:3(KJV, *yāšaḇ* [3427]).

7676. שַׁבָּת *šabbāṯ* **masc. noun**
(Sabbath)
Ex. 16:23,25,26,29; 20:8,10,11; 31:13–16; 35:2,3; **Lev.** 16:31; 19:3,30; 23:3,11,15, 16,32,38; 24:8; 25:2,4,6,8; 26:2,34,35,43; **Num.** 15:32; 28:9,10; **Deut.** 5:12,14,15; **2 Kgs.** 4:23; 11:5,7,9; 16:18; **1 Chr.** 9:32; 23:31; **2 Chr.** 2:4(3); 8:13; 23:4,8; 31:3; 36:21; **Neh.** 9:14; 10:31(32), 33(34); 13:15–19,21,22; **Ps.** 92:1; **Isa.** 1:13; 56:2,4,6; 58:13; 66:23; **Jer.** 17:21, 22,24,27; **Lam.** 2:6; **Ezek.** 20:12,13,16, 20,21,24; 22:8,26; 23:38; 44:24; 45:17; 46:1,3,4,12; **Hos.** 2:11(13); **Amos** 8:5.

7677. שַׁבָּתוֹן *šabbāṯôn* **masc. noun**
(rest, esp. Sabbath rest)
Ex. 16:23; 31:15; 35:2; **Lev.** 16:31; 23:3,24,32,39; 25:4,5.

7678. שַׁבְּתַי *šabb^e^tay* **masc. proper noun**
(Shabbethai: a levite)
Ezra 10:15; **Neh.** 8:7; 11:10.

7679. שָׂגָא *śāgā'* **verb**
(to magnify, to make great, to extol)
Job 12:23; 36:24.

7680. שְׂגָא *ś^e^gā'* **Aram. verb**
(to increase, to grow; corr. to Hebr. 7679)
Ezra 4:22; **Dan.** 4:1(3:31); 6:25(26).

7681. שָׁגֵה *šāgēh* **masc. proper noun**
(Shagee)
1 Chr. 11:34.

7682. שָׂגַב *śagab̲* **verb**
(to be raised, to be exalted; to be high; to defend)
Deut. 2:36; **Job** 5:11; 36:22; **Ps.** 20:1(2); 59:1(2); 69:29(30); 91:14; 107:41; 139:6; 148:13; **Prov.** 18:10,11; 29:25; **Isa.** 2:11, 17; 9:11(10); 12:4; 26:5; 30:13; 33:5.

7683. I. שָׁגַג *šāgag* **verb**
(to go astray, to err; to be deceived)
Lev. 5:18; **Num.** 15:28; **Job** 12:16; **Ps.** 119:67.
II. שָׁגַג *šāgag* **conj.**
(because [as an apology])
Gen. 6:3(NIV, *še* [7945] and *gam* [1751]).

7684. שְׁגָגָה *š^e^gāgāh* **fem. noun**
(unintentionally; in ignorance)
Lev. 4:2,22,27; 5:15,18; 22:14; **Num.** 15:24–29; 35:11,15; **Josh.** 20:3,9; **Eccl.** 5:6(5); 10:5.

7685. שָׂגָה *śāgāh* **verb**
(to grow, to increase; to thrive)
Job 8:7,11; **Ps.** 73:12; 92:12(13).

7686. שָׁגָה *šagāh* **verb**
(to sin unintentionally; to go astray, to stagger)
Lev. 4:13; **Num.** 15:22; **Deut.** 27:18; **1 Sam.** 26:21; **Job** 6:24; 12:16; 19:4; **Ps.** 119:10,21,118; **Prov.** 5:19,20,23; 19:27; 20:1; 28:10; **Isa.** 28:7; **Ezek.** 34:6; 45:20.

7687. A. שְׂגוּב *ś^e^gûb̲* **masc. proper noun**
(Segub: son of Hiel)
1 Kgs. 16:34.
B. שְׂגוּב *ś^e^gûb̲* **masc. proper noun**
(Segub: son of Hezron)
1 Chr. 2:21,22.

7688. שָׁגַח *šāgāḥ* **verb**
(to gaze, to watch, to stare)
Ps. 33:14; **Song** 2:9; **Isa.** 14:16.

7689. שַׂגִּיא *śaggiy'* **adj.**
(great, exalted)
Job 36:26; 37:23.

7690. שַׂגִּיא *śaggiy'* **Aram. adj.**
(great, abundant, many, much)
Ezra 5:11; **Dan.** 2:6,12,31,48; 4:10(7), 12(9),21(18); 5:9; 6:14(15),23(24); 7:5,28.

7691. שְׁגִיאָה *š^e^giy'āh* **fem. noun**
(error)
Ps. 19:12(13).

7692. שִׁגָּיוֹן *šiggāyôn,* שִׁגְיֹנָה *šiggāyōnāh* **proper noun**
(shiggaion: musical term of uncertain meaning)
Ps. 7:[title](1); **Hab.** 3:1.

7693. שָׁגַל *šāgal* **verb**
(to rape, to violate sexually)
Deut. 28:30; **Isa.** 13:16; **Jer.** 3:2; **Zech.** 14:2.

7694. שֵׁגַל *šēgal* **fem. noun**
(queen, royal bride)
Neh. 2:6; **Ps.** 45:9(10).

7695. שֵׁגַל *šēgal* **Aram. fem. noun**
(king's wife; corr. to Hebr. 7694)
Dan. 5:2,3,23.

7696. שָׁגַע *šaga'* **verb**
(to be insane, to be demented, to be mad)
Deut. 28:34; **1 Sam.** 21:14(15),15(16); 21:15(16); **2 Kgs.** 9:11; **Jer.** 29:26; **Hos.** 9:7.

7697. שִׁגָּעוֹן *šiggā'ôn* **masc. noun**
(insanity, madness)
Deut. 28:28; **2 Kgs.** 9:20; **Zech.** 12:4.

7698. שֶׁגֶר *šeger* **masc. noun**
(offspring of an animal)
Ex. 13:12; **Deut.** 7:13; 28:4,18,51.

7699. I. שַׁד *šad* **masc. noun**
(breast)
Gen. 49:25; **Job** 3:12; **Ps.** 22:9(10); **Song** 1:13; 4:5; 7:3(4),7(8),8(9); 8:1, 8,10; **Isa.** 28:9; 32:12; **Lam.** 4:3; **Ezek.** 16:7; 23:3,21,34; **Hos.** 2:2(4); 9:14; **Joel** 2:16.
II. שֹׁד *šōḏ* **masc. noun**
(breast)
Job 24:9; **Isa.** 60:16; 66:11.

7700. שֵׁד *šēḏ* **masc. noun**
(demon)
Deut. 32:17; **Ps.** 106:37.

7701. שֹׁד *šōḏ*, שׁוֹד *šôḏ* **masc. noun**
(destruction, desolation, violence)
Job 5:21,22; **Ps.** 12:5(6); **Prov.** 21:7; 24:2; **Isa.** 13:6; 16:4; 22:4; 51:19; 59:7; 60:18; **Jer.** 6:7; 20:8; 48:3; **Ezek.** 45:9; **Hos.** 7:13; 9:6; 10:14; 12:1(2); **Joel** 1:15; **Amos** 3:10; 5:9; **Hab.** 1:3; 2:17.

7702. שָׂדַד *śāḏaḏ* **verb**
(to break up the ground; to harrow)
Job 39:10; **Isa.** 28:24; **Hos.** 10:11.

7703. שָׁדַד *šāḏaḏ* **verb**
(to destroy, to lay waste, to devastate)
Judg. 5:27; **Job** 12:6; 15:21; **Ps.** 17:9; 91:6(KJV, *šûḏ* [7736]); 137:8; **Prov.** 11:3; 19:26; 24:15; **Isa.** 15:1; 16:4; 21:2; 23:1, 14; 33:1; **Jer.** 4:13,20,30; 5:6; 6:26; 9:19(18); 10:20; 12:12; 15:8; 25:36; 47:4; 48:1,8,15,18,20,32; 49:3,10,28; 51:48,53, 55,56; **Ezek.** 32:12; **Hos.** 10:2,14; **Joel** 1:10; **Obad.** 1:5; **Mic.** 2:4; **Nah.** 3:7; **Zech.** 11:2,3.

7704. I. שָׂדַי *śaḏay* **masc. noun**
(field)
Deut. 32:13; **Ps.** 8:7(8); 50:11; 80:13(14); 96:12; 104:11; **Isa.** 56:9; **Jer.** 4:17; 18:14; **Lam.** 4:9; **Hos.** 10:4; 12:11(12); **Joel** 2:22.
II. שָׂדֶה *śāḏeh* **masc. noun**
(field, country, region)
Gen. 2:5,19,20; 3:1,14,18; 4:8; 14:7; 23:9,11,13,17,19,20; 24:63,65; 25:9,10, 27,29; 27:3,5,27; 29:2; 30:14; 32:3(4); 33:19; 34:5,7,28; 36:35; 37:7,15; 39:5; 41:48; 47:20,24; 49:29,30,32; 50:13; **Ex.** 1:14; 8:13(9); 9:3,19,21,22,25; 10:5,15; 16:25; 22:5(4),6(5),31(30); 23:11,16,29; **Lev.** 14:7,53; 17:5; 19:9,19; 23:22; 25:3, 4,12,31,34; 26:4,22; 27:16–22,24,28; **Num.** 16:14; 19:16; 20:17; 21:20,22; 22:4,23; 23:14; **Deut.** 5:21; 7:22; 11:15; 14:22; 20:19; 21:1; 22:25,27; 24:19; 28:3,16,38; **Josh.** 8:24; 15:18; 21:12; 24:32; **Judg.** 1:14; 5:4,18; 9:27,32, 42–44; 13:9; 19:16; 20:6,31; **Ruth** 1:1,2,6,22; 2:2,3,6,8,9,17,22; 4:3,5; **1 Sam.** 4:2; 6:1,14,18; 8:14; 11:5; 14:14,15,25; 17:44; 19:3; 20:5,11,24,35; 22:7; 25:15; 27:5,7,11; 30:11; **2 Sam.** 1:21; 2:18; 9:7; 10:8; 11:11,23; 14:6; 17:8; 18:6; 19:29(30); 20:12; 21:10; 23:11; **1 Kgs.** 2:26; 11:29; 14:11; 16:4; 21:24; **2 Kgs.** 4:39; 7:12; 8:3,5,6; 9:25, 37; 14:9; 18:17; 19:26; **1 Chr.** 1:46; 6:56(41); 8:8; 11:13; 16:32; 19:9; 27:25, 26; **2 Chr.** 25:18; 26:23; 31:5,19; **Neh.** 5:3–5,11,16; 11:25,30; 12:29,44; 13:10; **Job** 5:23; 24:6; 39:15; 40:20; **Ps.** 78:12, 43; 103:15; 107:37; 132:6; **Prov.** 23:10;

24:27,30; 27:26; 31:16; **Eccl.** 5:9(8); **Song** 2:7; 3:5; 7:11(12); **Isa.** 5:8; 7:3; 32:12; 36:2; 37:27; 40:6; 43:20; 55:12; **Jer.** 6:12,25; 7:20; 8:10; 9:22(21); 12:4,9; 13:27; 14:5,18; 17:3; 26:18; 27:6; 28:14; 32:7–9,15,25,43,44; 35:9; 40:7,13; 41:8; **Ezek.** 7:15; 16:5,7; 17:5,8,24; 20:46(21:2); 26:6,8; 29:5; 31:4–6,13,15; 32:4; 33:27; 34:5,8,27; 36:30; 38:20; 39:4,5,10,17; **Hos.** 2:12(14),18(20); 4:3; 12:11(13); 13:8; **Joel** 1:10–12,19,20; **Obad.** 1:19; **Mic.** 1:6; 2:2,4; 3:12; 4:10; **Zech.** 10:1; **Mal.** 3:11.

7705. I. שִׁדָּה *šiddāh* **fem. noun**
(concubine; member of harem)
Eccl. 2:8(KJV, see II).
II. שִׁדָּה *šiddāh* **fem. noun**
(musical instrument)
Eccl. 2:8(NASB, NIV, see I).

7706. שַׁדַּי *šadday* **masc. noun**
(Shaddai; the Almighty [spoken only of God])
Gen. 17:1; 28:3; 35:11; 43:14; 48:3; 49:25; **Ex.** 6:3; **Num.** 24:4,16; **Ruth** 1:20,21; **Job** 5:17; 6:4,14; 8:3,5; 11:7; 13:3; 15:25; 21:15,20; 22:3,17,23,25,26; 23:16; 24:1; 27:2,10,11,13; 29:5; 31:2,35; 32:8; 33:4; 34:10,12; 35:13; 37:23; 40:2; **Ps.** 68:14(15); 91:1; **Isa.** 13:6; **Ezek.** 1:24; 10:5; **Joel** 1:15.

7707. שְׁדֵיאוּר *še̱dēy'ûr* **masc. proper noun**
(Shedeur)
Num. 1:5; 2:10; 7:30,35; 10:18.

7708. שִׂדִּים *śiddiym* **masc. proper noun**
(Siddim)
Gen. 14:3,8,10.

7709. I. שְׁדֵמָה *šedēmāh* **fem. noun**
(field)
Deut. 32:32; **2 Kgs.** 23:4; **Isa.** 16:8; **Jer.** 31:40(KJV, [K^e] *šerēmāh* [8309]); **Hab.** 3:17.

II. שְׁדֵמָה *šedēmāh* **fem. noun**
(blasted)
Isa. 37:27(NASB, NIV, [conjecture] *šedēpāh* [7711,I]).

7710. שָׁדַף *šādap* **verb**
(to scorch, to blight)
Gen. 41:6,23,27.

7711. I. שְׁדֵפָה *šedēpāh* **fem. noun**
(something scorched)
Isa. 37:27(KJV, [Hebr.] *šedēmāh* [7709,II]); **2 Kgs.** 19:26.
II. שִׁדָּפוֹן *šiddāpôn* **masc. noun**
(a blight, scorching)
Deut. 28:22; **1 Kgs.** 8:37; **2 Chr.** 6:28; **Amos** 4:9; **Hag.** 2:17.

7712. שְׁדַר *šedar* **Aram. verb**
(to exert oneself; to labor)
Dan. 6:14(15).

7713. I. שְׂדֵרָה *śedērāh* **fem. noun**
(row [rank] of soldiers)
2 Kgs. 11:8,15; **2 Chr.** 23:14.
II. שְׂדֵרָה *śedērāh* **fem. noun**
(board or plank of wood)
1 Kgs. 6:9.

7714. שַׁדְרַךְ *šadrak* **masc. proper noun**
(Shadrach)
Dan. 1:7.

7715. שַׁדְרַךְ *šadrak* **Aram. masc. proper noun**
(Shadrach; corr. to Hebr. 7714)
Dan. 2:49; 3:12–14,16,19,20,22,23,26, 28,29,30.

7716. שֶׂה *śeh* **masc./fem. noun**
(sheep, lamb)
Gen. 22:7,8; 30:32; **Ex.** 12:3–5; 13:13; 22:1(21:37),4(3),9(8),10(9); 34:19,20; **Lev.** 5:7; 12:8; 22:23,28; 27:26; **Num.** 15:11; **Deut.** 14:4; 17:1; 18:3; 22:1; **Josh.** 6:21; **Judg.** 6:4; **1 Sam.** 14:34;

15:3; 17:34(KJV, *zeh* [2089]); 22:19; **Ps.** 119:176; **Isa.** 7:25; 43:23; 53:7; 66:3; **Jer.** 50:17; **Ezek.** 34:17,20,22; 45:15.

7717. שָׂהֵד *śāhēḏ* **masc. noun**
(advocate, witness)
Job 16:19.

7718. שֹׁהַם *šōham* **masc. noun**
(onyx)
Gen. 2:12; **Ex.** 25:7; 28:9,20; 35:9,27; 39:6,13; **1 Chr.** 29:2; **Job** 28:16; **Ezek.** 28:13.

7719. שֹׁהַם *šōham* **masc. proper noun**
(Shoham)
1 Chr. 24:27.

7720. שַׂהֲרֹון *śahₐrôn* **masc. noun**
(ornament)
Judg. 8:21,26; **Isa.** 3:18.

7721. שׂוֹא *śô'* **verb**
(to arise)
Ps. 89:9(10)(NASB, NIV, *nāśā'* [5375]).

7722. I. שׁוֹא *shō'* **masc. noun**
(ravaging, destruction)
Ps. 35:17.
II. שׁוֹאָה *šô'āh,* שֹׁאָה *šō'āh* **fem. noun**
(destruction, ruin, storm)
Job 30:3,14; 38:27; **Ps.** 35:8; 63:9(10); **Prov.** 1:27(KJV, NASB, [Ke] *ša'ₐwāh* [7584]); 3:25; **Isa.** 10:3; 47:11; **Ezek.** 38:9; **Zeph.** 1:15.

7723. שָׁוְא *šāw'* **masc. noun**
(vanity, falsehood, emptiness)
Ex. 20:7; 23:1; **Deut.** 5:11,20; **Job** 7:3; 11:11; 15:31; 31:5; 35:13; **Ps.** 12:2(3); 24:4; 26:4; 31:6(7); 41:6(7); 60:11(13); 89:47(48); 108:12(13); 119:37; 127:1,2; 139:20; 144:8,11; **Prov.** 30:8; **Isa.** 1:13; 5:18; 30:28; 59:4; **Jer.** 2:30; 4:30; 6:29; 18:15; 46:11; **Lam.** 2:14; **Ezek.** 12:24; 13:6–9,23; 21:23(28),29(34); 22:28; **Hos.** 10:4; 12:11(12); **Jon.** 2:8(9); **Zech.** 10:2; **Mal.** 3:14.

7724. A. שְׁוָא *šewā'* **masc. proper noun**
(Sheva: a scribe)
2 Sam. 20:25.
B. שְׁוָא *šewā'* **masc. proper noun**
(Sheva: descendant of Caleb)
1 Chr. 2:49.

7725. שׁוּב *šûḇ* **verb**
(to turn back; to return, to go back; to restore; to send back)
Gen. 3:19; 8:3,7,9,12; 14:7,16,17; 15:16; 16:9; 18:10,14,33; 20:7,14; 21:32; 22:5,19; 24:5,6,8; 26:18; 27:44,45; 28:15,21; 29:3; 30:31; 31:3,13,55(32:1); 32:6(7),9(10); 33:16; 37:14,22,29,30; 38:22,29; 40:13,21; 41:13; 42:24,25,28,37; 43:2,10,12,13, 18,21; 44:8,13,25; 48:21; 50:5,14,15; **Ex.** 4:7,18–21; 5:22; 10:8; 13:17; 14:2,26–28; 15:19; 19:8; 21:34; 22:26(25); 23:4,14; 32:12,27,31; 33:11; 34:31,35; **Lev.** 6:4(5:23); 13:16; 14:39,43; 22:13; 25:10, 13,27,28,41,51,52; 26:26; 27:24; **Num.** 5:7,8; 8:25; 10:36; 11:4; 13:25,26; 14:3, 4,36,43; 16:50(17:15); 17:10(25); 18:9; 22:8,34; 23:5,6,16,20; 24:25; 25:4,11; 32:15,18,22; 33:7; 35:25,28,32; **Deut.** 1:22,25,45; 3:20; 4:30,39; 5:30; 13:17(18); 17:16; 20:5–8; 22:1,2; 23:13(14),14(15); 24:4,13,19; 28:31,60,68; 30:1–3,8–10; 32:41,43; **Josh.** 1:15; 2:16,22,23; 4:18; 5:2; 6:14; 7:3,26; 8:21,24,26; 10:15,21, 38,43; 11:10; 14:7; 18:8; 19:12,27,29,34; 20:6; 22:8,9,16,18,23,29,32; 23:12; 24:20; **Judg.** 2:19; 3:19; 5:29; 6:18; 7:3,15; 8:9, 13,33; 9:56,57; 11:8,9,13,31,35,39; 14:8; 15:19; 17:3,4; 18:26; 19:3,7; 20:48; 21:14,23; **Ruth** 1:6–8,10–12,15,16, 21,22; 2:6; 4:3,15; **1 Sam.** 1:19; 3:5,6; 5:3,11; 6:3,4,7,8,16,17,21; 7:3,14; 9:5; 12:3; 14:27; 15:11,25,26,30,31; 17:15,30, 53,57; 18:2,6; 23:23,28; 24:1(2); 25:12, 21,39; 26:21,23,25; 27:9; 29:4,7,11; 30:12,19; **2 Sam.** 1:1,22; 2:26,30; 3:11,

16,26,27; 6:20; 8:3,13; 9:7; 10:5,14; 11:4,15; 12:23,31; 14:13,21; 15:8,19, 20,25,27,29,34; 16:3,8,12; 17:3,20; 18:16; 19:10–12(11–13),14(15),15(16), 37(38),39(40),43(44); 20:22; 22:21,25,38; 23:10; 24:13; **1 Kgs.** 2:16,17,20,30,32, 33,41,44; 8:33–35,47,48; 9:6; 12:5,6,9, 12,16,20,21,24,26,27; 13:4,6,9,10,16–20, 22,23,26,29,33; 14:28; 17:21,22; 18:43; 19:6,7,15,20,21; 20:5,9,34; 22:17,26, 28,33; **2 Kgs.** 1:5,6,11,13; 2:13,18,25; 3:4,27; 4:22,31,35,38; 5:10,14,15; 7:8,15; 8:3,6,29; 9:15,18,20,36; 13:25; 14:14,22, 25,28; 15:20; 16:6; 17:3,13; 18:14,24; 19:7–9,28,33,36; 20:5,9–11; 21:3; 22:9,20; 23:20,25,26; **1 Chr.** 19:5; 20:3; 21:12,20,27; **2 Chr.** 6:23–26,37,38,42; 7:14,19; 10:2,5,6,9,12,16; 11:1,4; 12:11,12; 14:15; 15:4; 18:16,25–27,32; 19:1,4,8; 20:27; 22:6; 24:11,19; 25:10, 13,24; 26:2; 27:5; 28:11,15; 29:10; 30:6, 8,9; 31:1; 32:21,25; 33:3,13; 34:7,9,16,28; 36:13; **Ezra** 2:1; 6:21; 9:14; 10:14; **Neh.** 1:9; 2:6,15,20; 4:4(3:36),12(6),15(9); 5:11,12; 6:4; 7:6; 8:17; 9:17,26,28,29,35; 13:9; **Esth.** 2:14; 4:13,15; 6:12; 7:8; 8:5,8; 9:25; **Job** 1:21; 6:29; 7:7,10; 9:12,13,18; 10:9,16,21; 11:10; 13:22; 14:13; 15:13,22; 16:22; 17:10; 20:2,10, 18; 22:23; 23:13; 30:23; 31:14; 32:14; 33:5,25,26,30,32; 34:15; 35:4; 36:10; 39:4,12,22; 40:4; 42:10; **Ps.** 6:4(5),10(11); 7:7(8),12(13),16(17); 9:3(4),17(18); 14:7; 18:20(21),24(25),37(38); 19:7(8); 22:27(28); 23:3; 28:4; 35:13,17; 44:10(11); 51:12(14),13(15); 53:6(7); 54:5(7); 56:9(10); 59:6(7),14(15); 60:1; 68:22(23); 69:4(5); 70:3(4); 71:20; 72:10; 73:10; 74:11,21; 78:34,38,39; 78:41; 79:12; 80:3(4),7(8),14(15),19(20); 81:14; 85:1(2),3(4),4(5),6(7),8(9); 89:43(44); 90:3,13; 94:2,15,23; 104:9,23; 106:23; 116:7,12; 119:59,79; 126:1,4; 132:10,11; 146:4; **Prov.** 1:23; 2:19; 3:28; 12:14; 15:1; 17:13; 18:13; 19:24; 20:26; 22:21; 24:12,18,26,29; 25:10,13; 26:11,15, 16,27; 27:11; 29:8; 30:30; **Eccl.** 1:6,7; 3:20; 4:1,7; 5:15(14); 9:11; 12:2,7; **Song** 6:13(7:1); **Isa.** 1:25–27; 5:25; 6:10,13; 9:12(11),13(12),17(16),21(20); 10:4, 21,22; 12:1; 14:27; 19:22; 21:12; 23:17; 28:6; 29:17; 31:6; 35:10; 36:9; 37:7,8, 29,34,37; 38:8; 41:28; 42:22; 43:13; 44:19,22,25; 45:23; 46:8; 47:10; 49:5,6; 51:11; 52:8; 55:7,10,11; 58:12,13; 59:20; 63:17; 66:15; **Jer.** 2:24,35; 3:1,7,10,12, 14,19,22; 4:1,8,28; 5:3; 6:9; 8:4–6; 11:10; 12:15; 14:3; 15:7,19; 16:15; 18:4,8,11,20; 22:10,11,27; 23:3,14,20,22; 24:6,7; 25:5; 26:3; 27:16,22; 28:3,4,6; 29:10,14; 30:3, 10,18,24; 31:8,16–19,21,23; 32:37,40,44; 33:7,11,26; 34:11,15,16,22; 35:15; 36:3, 7,28; 37:7,8,20; 38:26; 40:5,12; 41:14,16; 42:10,12; 43:5; 44:5,14,28; 46:16,27; 48:47; 49:6,39; 50:6,9,19; **Lam.** 1:8,11, 13,16,19; 2:3,8,14; 3:3,21,40,64; 5:21; **Ezek.** 1:14; 3:19,20; 7:13; 8:6,13,15,17; 9:11; 13:22; 14:6; 16:53,55; 18:7,8,12,17, 21,23,24,26–28,30,32; 20:22; 21:5(10), 30(35); 27:15; 29:14; 33:9,11,12,14,15, 18,19; 34:4,16; 35:7; 38:4,8,12; 39:2,25, 27; 44:1; 46:9,17; 47:1,6,7; **Dan.** 9:13, 16,25; 10:20; 11:9,10,13,18,19,28–30; **Hos.** 2:7(9),9(11); 3:5; 4:9; 5:4,15; 6:1, 11; 7:10,16; 8:13; 9:3; 11:5,9; 12:2(3), 6(7),14(15); 14:1(2),2(3),4(5),7(8); **Joel** 2:12–14; 3:1(4:1),4(4:4),7(4:7); **Amos** 1:3,6,8,9,11,13; 2:1,4,6; 4:6,8–11; 9:14; **Obad.** 1:15; **Jon.** 1:13; 3:8–10; **Mic.** 1:7; 2:4(NASB, NIV, *šôḇēḇ* [7728]),8; 5:3(2); 7:19; **Nah.** 2:2(3); **Hab.** 2:1; **Zeph.** 2:7; 3:20; **Zech.** 1:3,4,6; 4:1; 5:1; 6:1; 7:14; 8:3,15; 9:8,12; 10:6(NIV, *yāšaḇ* [3427]), 9,10; 13:7; **Mal.** 1:4; 2:6; 3:7,18; 4:6(3:24).

7726. שׁוֹבָב *šôḇāḇ* **adj.**
(faithless, backsliding)
Isa. 57:17; **Jer.** 3:14,22.

7727. A. שׁוֹבָב *šôḇāḇ* **masc. proper noun**
(Shobab: son of David)
2 Sam. 5:14; **1 Chr.** 3:5; 14:4.

B. שׁוֹבָב *šôḇāḇ* **masc. proper noun**
(Shobab: son of Caleb)
1 Chr. 2:18.

7728. שׁוֹבֵב *šôḇēḇ* **adj.**
(unfaithful, apostate)
Jer. 31:22; 49:4; **Mic.** 2:4(KJV, *šûḇ* [7725]).

7729. שׁוּבָה *šûḇāh* **fem. noun**
(repentance, returning)
Isa. 30:15.

7730. שׂוֹבֶךְ *śôḇeḵ* **masc. noun**
(thick branch [of a tree])
2 Sam. 18:9.

7731. שׁוֹבָךְ *šôḇāḵ* **masc. proper noun**
(Shobach; the same as *šôp̄āḵ* [7780])
2 Sam. 10:16,18.

7732. A. שׁוֹבָל *šôḇal* **masc. proper noun**
(Shobal: an Edomite leader)
Gen. 36:20,23,29; **1 Chr.** 1:38,40.
B. שׁוֹבָל *šôḇal* **masc. proper noun**
(Shobal: son of Caleb)
1 Chr. 2:50,52.
C. שׁוֹבָל *šôḇal* **masc. proper noun**
(Shobal: son of Judah)
1 Chr. 4:1,2.

7733. שׁוֹבֵק *šôḇēq* **masc. proper noun**
(Shobek)
Neh. 10:24(25).

7734. שׂוּג *śûg* **verb**
(to turn)
2 Sam. 1:22(NASB, NIV, regard as another spelling for *sûg* [5472]).

7735. שׂוּג *śûg* **verb**
(to grow, to raise)
Isa. 17:11(NASB, alternate spelling for *sûg* [5473]).

7736. שׁוּד *šûḏ* **verb**
(to destroy, to lay waste)
Ps. 91:6(NASB, NIV, *šāḏaḏ* [7703]).

7737. I. שָׁוָה *šāwāh* **verb**
(to be or become like or equal, to match, to suffice)
2 Sam. 22:34; **Esth.** 3:8; 5:13; 7:4; **Job** 33:27; **Ps.** 18:33(34); **Prov.** 3:15; 8:11; 26:4; 27:15; **Isa.** 28:25; 38:13; 40:25; 46:5; **Lam.** 2:13.
II. שָׁוָה *šāwāh* **verb**
(to set, to place, to put, to lay)
Ps. 16:8; 21:5(6); 89:19(20); 119:30; 131:2; **Hos.** 10:1.

7738. שָׁוָה *šāwāh* **fem. noun**
(substance)
Job 30:22(NASB, NIV, [Kᵉ] *tᵉšû'āh* [8663]).

7739. שְׁוָה *šᵉwāh* **Aram. verb**
(to become like; to be made like; corr. to Hebr. 7737,I)
Dan. 3:29; 5:21.

7740. שָׁוֵה *šāwēh* **proper noun**
(Shaveh)
Gen. 14:17.

7741. שָׁוֵה קִרְיָתַיִם *šāwēh qiryāṯayim* **proper noun**
(Shaveh Kiriathaim)
Gen. 14:5.

7742. שׂוּחַ *śûaḥ* **verb**
(to meditate)
Gen. 24:63.

7743. I. שׁוּחַ *šûaḥ* **verb**
(to sink down; to be bowed down)
Ps. 44:25(26)(NIV, see II); **Prov.** 2:18; **Lam.** 3:20(NIV, *šāḥaḥ* [7817]).
II. שִׁיחַ *šiyaḥ* **verb**
(to be bowed down; to be downcast)
Ps. 42:5(6)(KJV, NASB, *šāḥaḥ*),6(7)(KJV, NASB, *šāḥaḥ*),11(12)(KJV, NASB, *šāḥaḥ*);

43:5(KJV, NASB, šāḥah); 44:25(26)(KJV, NASB, see I).

7744. שׁוּחַ *šûaḥ* **masc. proper noun**
(Shuah)
Gen. 25:2; **1 Chr.** 1:32.

7745. שׁוּחָה *šûḥāh* **fem. noun**
(pit, ditch)
Prov. 22:14; 23:27; **Jer**. 2:6; 18:20,22(KJV, [K^e] *šiyḥāh* [7882]).

7746. שׁוּחָה *šûḥāh* **masc. proper noun**
(Shuhah)
1 Chr. 4:11.

7747. שׁוּחִי *šûḥiy* **masc. proper noun**
(Shuhite)
Job 2:11; 8:1; 18:1; 25:1; 42:9.

7748. שׁוּחָם *šûḥām* **masc. proper noun**
(Shuham)
Num. 26:42.

7749. שׁוּחָמִי *šûḥāmiy* **masc. proper noun**
(Shuhamite)
Num. 26:42,43.

7750. שׂוּט *śûṭ*, סוּט *sûṭ* **verb**
(to turn aside; to fall back)
Ps. 40:4(5); 101:3(NASB, NIV, *sēṭ* [7846,II]).

7751. I. שׁוּט *šûṭ* **verb**
(to roam, to move to and fro, to wander)
Num. 11:8; **2 Sam.** 24:2,8; **2 Chr.** 16:9; **Job** 1:7; 2:2; **Jer**. 5:1; 49:3; **Ezek**. 27:8, 26; **Dan**. 12:4; **Amos** 8:12; **Zech**. 4:10.
II. שׁוּט *šûṭ* **verb**
(to row [a boat])
Ezek. 27:8,26.

7752. שׁוֹט *šôṭ* **masc. noun**
(whip, scourge)
1 Kgs. 12:11,14; **2 Chr.** 10:11,14; **Job** 5:21; 9:23; **Prov**. 26:3; **Isa**. 10:26; 28:15([K^e] *šayiṭ* [7885]),18; **Nah**. 3:2.

7753. שׂוּךְ *śûḵ* **verb**
(to hedge in, to fence in)
Job 1:10; 10:11(NASB, NIV, *śāḵak* [5526,III]); **Hos**. 2:6(8).

7754. I. שׂוֹךְ *śôḵ* **masc. noun**
(branch, bough)
Judg. 9:48.
II. שׂוֹכָה *śôḵāh* **masc. noun**
(branch, bough)
Judg. 9:49.

7755. A. שׂוֹכוֹ *śôḵô* **masc. proper noun**
(Soco: son of Heber)
1 Chr. 4:18.
B. שׂוֹכֹה *śôḵōh* **proper noun**
(Socoh: city in Judah)
Josh. 15:48.
C. שׂוֹכֹה *śôkōh*, שׂוֹכוֹ *śôḵô* **proper noun**
(Socoh: city in Judah-Shephelah)
Josh. 15:35; **1 Sam.** 17:1; **1 Kgs.** 4:10; **2 Chr.** 11:7; 28:18.

7756. שׂוּכָתִים *śûḵāṯiym* **masc. proper noun**
(Sucathites)
1 Chr. 2:55.

7757. שׁוּל *šûl* **masc. noun**
(hem, skirt, or train of a robe)
Ex. 28:33,34; 39:24–26; **Isa**. 6:1; **Jer**. 13:22,26; **Lam**. 1:9; **Nah**. 3:5.

7758. שׁוֹלָל *šôlāl* **adj.**
(barefoot, stripped)
Job 12:17,19; **Mic**. 1:8.

7759. שׁוּלַמִּית *šûlammiyṯ* **fem. proper noun**
(Shulamite)
Song 6:13(7:1).

7760. שׂוּם *śûm,* שִׂים *śiym* **verb**
(to put, to place, to set, to fix in position, to establish, to ordain, to constitute)
Gen. 2:8; 4:15; 6:16; 9:23; 13:16; 21:13, 14,18; 22:6,9; 24:2,9,33,47; 27:37; 28:11, 18,22; 30:36,41,42; 31:21,34,37; 32:12(13), 16(17); 33:2; 37:34; 40:15; 41:42; 43:22, 31,32; 44:1,2,21; 45:7–9; 46:3; 47:6, 26,29; 48:18,20; 50:26(KJV, [K^{e}] *yāśam* [3455]); **Ex.** 1:11; 2:3,14; 3:22; 4:11, 15,21; 5:8,14; 8:12(8),23(19); 9:5,21; 10:2; 14:21; 15:25,26; 17:12,14; 18:21; 19:7; 21:1,13; 22:25(24); 24:6; 26:35; 28:12,26,37; 29:6,24; 32:27; 33:22; 39:7,19; 40:3,5,8,18–21,24,26,28–30; **Lev.** 2:15; 5:11; 6:10(3); 8:8,9,26; 9:20; 10:1; 20:5; 24:6; **Num.** 4:6,8,11,14,19; 6:26,27; 11:11,17; 16:7,18,46(17:11); 21:8,9; 22:38; 23:5,12,16; 24:21,23; **Deut.** 1:13; 4:44; 7:15; 10:2,5,22; 11:18; 12:5,21; 14:1,24; 17:14,15; 22:8,14,17; 26:2; 27:15; 31:19,26; 32:46; 33:10; **Josh.** 6:18; 7:11,19; 8:2,12,13,28; 10:24,27; 24:7,25; **Judg.** 1:28; 4:21; 6:19; 7:22; 8:31,33; 9:24,25,48,49; 11:11; 12:3; 15:4; 16:3; 18:19,21,31; 19:30; 20:29,36; **Ruth** 3:3; **1 Sam.** 2:20; 6:8,11,15; 7:12; 8:1,5, 11,12; 9:20,23,24; 10:19; 11:2,11; 13:32; 15:2; 17:40,54; 18:5,13; 19:5,13; 21:6(7), 12(13); 22:7,15; 25:18,25; 28:2,21,22; 30:25; 31:10; **2 Sam.** 7:10,23; 8:6,14; 12:20,31; 13:19,32,33; 14:3,7,19; 15:4; 17:25; 18:1,3; 19:19(20); 23:5,23; **1 Kgs.** 2:5,15,19; 5:9(23); 8:21; 9:3; 10:9; 11:36; 12:29; 14:21; 18:23,25,33,42; 19:2; 20:6, 12,24,31,34; 21:27; 22:27; **2 Kgs.** 2:20; 4:10,29,31,34; 6:22; 8:11; 9:13,30; 10:3, 7,24,27; 11:16,18; 12:17(18); 13:7,16; 17:34; 18:14; 19:28; 20:7; 21:4,7; **1 Chr.** 10:10; 11:25; 17:9,21; 18:6,13; 20:3(KJV, NASB, *śûr* [7787]); 26:10; **2 Chr.** 1:5; 6:11,20; 12:13; 18:26; 23:15,18; 33:7,14; **Ezra** 8:17; 10:44; **Neh.** 8:8; 9:7; **Esth.** 2:17; 3:1; 8:2; 10:1; **Job** 1:8,17; 2:3; 4:18,20; 5:8,11; 7:12,20; 13:14,27; 17:3, 12; 18:2; 19:8; 20:4; 21:5; 22:22; 23:6; 24:12,15,25; 28:3; 29:9; 31:24; 33:11; 34:13,14,23; 36:13; 37:15; 38:5,9,10,33; 39:6; 40:4; 41:2(40:26),8(40:32),31(23); **Ps.** 18:43(44); 19:4(5); 39:8(9); 40:4(5); 44:13(14),14(15); 46:8(9); 50:23; 52:7(9); 54:3(5); 56:8(9); 66:2,9,11; 74:4; 78:5,7, 43; 79:1; 80:6(7); 81:5(6); 85:13(14); 86:14; 89:25(26),29(30),40(41); 91:9; 104:3,9; 105:21,27; 107:33,35,41; 109:5; 147:14; **Prov.** 8:29; 23:2; 30:26; **Song** 1:6; 6:12; 8:6; **Isa.** 3:7; 5:20; 10:6; 13:9; 14:17,23; 21:4; 23:13; 25:2; 27:9; 28:15,17,25; 37:29; 41:15,18–20,22; 42:4,12,15,16,25; 43:19; 44:7; 47:6,7; 49:2,11; 50:2,3,7; 51:3,10, 16,23; 53:10; 54:12; 57:1,7,8,11; 59:21; 60:15,17; 61:3; 62:7; 63:11; 66:19; **Jer.** 2:7; 4:7; 5:22; 6:8; 7:30; 9:8(7); 10:22; 11:13; 12:11; 13:1,2,16; 17:5; 18:16; 19:8; 21:10; 24:6; 25:9,12; 29:22; 31:21; 32:20,34; 33:25; 38:12; 39:12; 40:4,10; 42:15,17; 43:10; 44:11,12; 49:38; 51:29; **Lam.** 3:11,45; **Ezek.** 4:2,4; 5:5; 6:2; 7:20; 11:7; 13:17; 14:4,7; 15:7; 16:14; 17:4,5; 19:5; 20:28,46(21:2); 21:2(7),16(21), 19(24),20(25),22(27),27(32); 23:24,41; 24:7,17; 25:2; 26:12; 28:21; 29:2; 30:21; 32:20; 35:2,4; 38:2; 39:21; 40:4; 44:5,8; **Dan.** 1:7,8; 11:17; **Hos.** 1:11(2:2); 2:3(5), 12(14); 11:8; **Joel** 1:7; **Amos** 7:8; 8:10; 9:4; **Obad.** 1:4,7; **Mic.** 1:6,7; 2:12; 4:7, 13; 5:1(4:14); 7:16; **Nah.** 1:14; 3:6; **Hab.** 1:12; 2:9; 3:19; **Zeph.** 2:13; 3:19; **Hag.** 1:5,7; 2:15,18,23; **Zech.** 3:5; 6:11; 7:12, 14; 9:13; 10:3; 12:2,3,6; **Mal.** 1:3; 2:2.

7761. שׂוּם *śûm,* שִׂים *śiym* **Aram. verb**
(to issue [a decree], to appoint, to place)
Ezra 4:19,21; 5:3,8,9,13,14,17; 6:1,3,8, 11,12; 7:13,21; **Dan.** 2:5; 3:10,12,29; 4:6(3); 5:12; 6:13(14),14(15),17(18), 26(27).

7762. שׁוּם *šûm* **masc. noun**
(garlic)
Num. 11:5.

7763. A. שׁוֹמֵר *šômēr*, שֹׁמֵר *šōmēr* **fem. proper noun**
(Shomer: mother of Jehozabad; the same as *šimriyṯ* [8116])
2 Kgs. 12:21(22).
B. שׁוֹמֵר *šômēr*, שֹׁמֵר *šōmēr* **masc. proper noun**
(Shomer: an Asherite; same person as *šemer* [8106,C])
1 Chr. 7:32,34(KJV, NASB, *šemer* [8106,C]).

7764. שׁוּנִי *šûniy* **masc. proper noun**
(Shuni)
Gen. 46:16; **Num.** 26:15.

7765. שׁוּנִי *šûniy* **masc. proper noun**
(Shunite)
Num. 26:15.

7766. שׁוּנֵם *šûnēm* **masc. proper noun**
(Shunem)
Josh. 19:18; **1 Sam.** 28:4; **2 Kgs.** 4:8.

7767. שׁוּנַמִּית *šûnammiyṯ* **fem. proper noun**
(Shunammite)
1 Kgs. 1:3,15; 2:17,21,22; **2 Kgs.** 4:12,25,36.

7768. שָׁוַע *šāwaʿ* **verb**
(to cry out for help, to cry out)
2 Sam. 22:42(KJV, NASB, *šāʾāh* [8159]); **Job** 19:7; 24:12; 29:12; 30:20,28; 35:19; 36:13; 38:41; **Ps.** 18:6(7),41(42); 22:24(25); 28:2; 30:2(3); 31:22(23); 72:12; 88:13(14); 119:147; **Isa.** 58:9; **Lam.** 3:8; **Jon.** 2:2(3); **Hab.** 1:2.

7769. I. שׁוּעַ *šûaʿ* **masc. noun**
(cry for help, passionate plea)
Job 30:24; **Ps.** 5:2(3)(KJV, NIV, *šewaʿ* [7773]).
II. שׁוּעַ *shūaʿ* **masc. noun**
(riches, wealth)
Job 36:19;.

7770. שׁוּעַ *šûaʿ* **masc. proper noun**
(Shua)
Gen. 38:2,12; **1 Chr.** 2:3(NASB, see *baṯ šûaʿ* [1340,A]).

7771. I. שׁוֹעַ *šôaʿ* **masc. noun**
(noble, distinguished, wealthy)
Job 34:19; **Isa.** 32:5.
II. שׁוֹעַ *šôaʿ* **masc. noun**
(cry for help, passionate plea)
Isa. 22:5.

7772. שׁוֹעַ *šôaʿ* **masc. proper noun**
(Shoa)
Ezek. 23:23.

7773. שֶׁוַע *šewaʿ* **masc. noun**
(cry for help)
Ps. 5:2(3)(NASB, *šûaʿ* [7769,I]).

7774. שׁוּעָא *šûʿāʾ* **fem. proper noun**
(Shua)
1 Chr. 7:32.

7775. שַׁוְעָה *šaw^{e}ʿāh* **fem. noun**
(cry for help)
Ex. 2:23; **1 Sam.** 5:12; **2 Sam.** 22:7; **Ps.** 18:6(7); 34:15(16); 39:12(13); 40:1(2); 102:1(2); 145:19; **Jer.** 8:19; **Lam.** 3:56.

7776. שׁוּעָל *šûʿāl* **masc. noun**
(fox; jackal)
Judg. 15:4; **Neh**. 4:3(3:35); **Ps.** 63:10(11); **Song** 2:15; **Lam**. 5:18; **Ezek**. 13:4.

7777. A. שׁוּעָל *šûʿāl* **masc. proper noun**
(Shual: an Asherite)
1 Chr. 7:36.
B. שׁוּעָל *šûʿāl* **proper noun**
(Shual: district in Benjamin)
1 Sam. 13:17.

7778. שׁוֹעֵר *šô'ēr,* שֹׁעֵר *šō'ēr*
masc. noun
(gatekeeper; porter)
2 Sam. 18:26; **2 Kgs.** 7:10,11; **1 Chr.** 9:17,18,21,22,24,26; 15:18,23,24; 16:38; 23:5; 26:1,12,19; **2 Chr.** 8:14; 23:4,19; 31:14; 34:13; 35:15; **Ezra** 2:42,70; 7:7; 10:24; **Neh.** 7:1,45,73(72); 10:28(29), 39(40); 11:19; 12:25,45,47; 13:5.

7779. I. שׁוּף *šûp̱* **verb**
(to crush, to bruise)
Gen. 3:15(NIV, see II); **Job** 9:17; **Ps.** 139:11.
II. שׁוּף *šûp̱* **verb**
(to strike, to snap at)
Gen. 3:15(KJV, NASB, see I).
III. שׁוּף *šûp̱* **verb**
(to cover, to envelop, to overwhelm)
Ps. 139:11(NIV, [conjec.] *śāḵak* [5526,I]).

7780. שׁוֹפָךְ *šôp̱āḵ* **masc. proper noun**
(Shophach: another name for *šôḇāḵ* [7731])
1 Chr. 19:16,18.

7781. שׁוּפָמִי *šûp̱āmiy* **masc. proper noun**
(Shuphamite; descendant of *š*^{e}*p̱ûp̱am* [8197])
Num. 26:39.

7782. שׁוֹפָר *šôp̱ār,* שֹׁפָר *šōp̱ār* **masc. noun**
(trumpet, ram's horn)
Ex. 19:16,19; 20:18; **Lev.** 25:9; **Josh.** 6:4–6,8,9,13,16,20; **Judg.** 3:27; 6:34; 7:8,16,18–20,22; **1 Sam.** 13:3; **2 Sam.** 2:28; 6:15; 15:10; 18:16; 20:1,22; **1 Kgs.** 1:34,39,41; **2 Kgs.** 9:13; **1 Chr.** 15:28; **2 Chr.** 15:14; **Neh.** 4:18(12),20(14); **Job** 39:24,25; **Ps.** 47:5(6); 81:3(4); 98:6; 150:3; **Isa.** 18:3; 27:13; 58:1; **Jer.** 4:5,19 ,21; 6:1,17; 42:14; 51:27; **Ezek.** 33:3–6; **Hos.** 5:8; 8:1; **Joel** 2:1,15; **Amos** 2:2; 3:6; **Zeph.** 1:16; **Zech.** 9:14.

7783. שׁוּק *šûq* **verb**
(to water; to overflow)
Ps. 65:9(10); **Joel** 2:24; 3:13(4:13).

7784. שׁוּק *šûq* **masc. noun**
(street)
Prov. 7:8; **Eccl.** 12:4,5; **Song** 3:2.

7785. שׁוֹק *šôq* **masc. noun**
(leg, hip; thigh [or shoulder] of a sacrificial animal)
Ex. 29:22,27; **Lev.** 7:32–34; 8:25,26; 9:21; 10:14,15; **Num.** 6:20; 18:18; **Deut.** 28:35; **Judg.** 15:8; **1 Sam.** 9:24; **Ps.** 147:10; **Prov.** 26:7; **Isa.** 47:2.

7786. שׂוּר *śûr* **verb**
(to reign, to rule; to establish a ruler)
Judg. 9:22(NASB, NIV, *śārar* [8323]); **Hos.** 8:4(NASB, NIV, *śārar* [8323]).

7787. שׂוּר *śûr* **verb**
(to cut)
1 Chr. 20:3(NIV, *śûm* [7760,II]).

7788. שׁוּר *šûr* **verb**
(to journey; to go)
Job 33:27(KJV, *šûr* [7789]; NASB, *šiyr* [7891]); **Song** 4:8(KJV, *šûr* [7789]); **Isa.** 57:9; **Ezek.** 27:25(KJV, *šiyr* [7891]).

7789. שׁוּר *šûr* **verb**
(to see, to look on, to regard)
Num. 23:9; 24:17; **Job** 7:8; 17:15; 20:9; 24:15; 33:14,27(NASB, *šiyr* [7891]; NIV, *šûr* [7788]); 34:29; 35:5,13,14; 36:24 (NASB, NIV, *šiyr* [7891]); **Song** 4:8(NASB, NIV, *šûr* [7788]); **Jer.** 5:26; **Hos.** 13:7; 14:8(9).

7790. שׁוּר *šûr* **masc. noun**
(enemy, foe)
Ps. 92:11(12)(NIV, *šārar* [8324]).

7791. I. שׁוּר *šûr* **masc. noun**
(wall)

Gen. 49:6(NASB, NIV, *šôr* [7794]),22; **2 Sam.** 22:30; **Ps.** 18:29(30).
II. שׁוּרָה *šûrāh* **fem. noun**
(terrace, supporting wall)
Job 24:11.

7792. שׁוּר *šûr* **Aram. masc. noun**
(wall; corr. to Hebr. 7791,I)
Ezra 4:12,13,16.

7793. שׁוּר *šûr* **proper noun**
(Shur)
Gen. 16:7; 20:1; 25:18; **Ex.** 15:22; **1 Sam.** 15:7; 27:8.

7794. שׁוֹר *šôr* **masc. noun**
(ox, bull, cow)
Gen. 32:5(6); 49:6(KJV, *šûr* [7791,I]); **Ex.** 20:17; 21:28,29,32,33,35,36; 22:1 (21:37),4(3),9(8),10(9),30(29); 23:4,12; 34:19; 49:6; **Lev.** 4:10; 7:23; 9:4,18,19; 17:3; 22:23,27,28; 27:26; **Num.** 7:3; 15:11; 18:17; 22:4; **Deut.** 5:14,21; 14:4; 15:19; 17:1; 18:3; 22:1,4,10; 25:4; 28:31; 33:17; **Josh.** 6:21; 7:24; **Judg.** 6:4,25; **1 Sam.** 12:3; 14:34; 15:3; 22:19; **2 Sam.** 6:13; **1 Kgs.** 1:19,25; **Neh.** 5:18; **Job** 6:5; 21:10; 24:3; **Ps.** 69:31(32); 106:20; **Prov.** 7:22; 14:4; 15:17; **Isa.** 1:3; 7:25; 32:20; 66:3; **Ezek.** 1:10; **Hos.** 12:11(12).

7795. I. שׂוֹרָה *śôrah* **fem. noun**
(row, order)
Isa. 28:25(KJV, see II).
II. שׂוֹרָה *śôrah* **fem. noun**
(millet, chief grain or wheat)
Isa. 28:25(NASB, NIV, see I).

7796. שׂוֹרֵק *śôrēq*, שֹׂרֵק *śōrēq* **proper noun**
(Sorek)
Judg. 16:4.

7797. שׂוּשׂ *śûś*, שִׂישׂ *śiyś* **verb**
(to rejoice, to exalt; to be glad)
Deut. 28:63; 30:9; **Job** 3:22; 39:21; **Ps.** 19:5(6); 35:9; 40:16(17); 68:3(4); 70:4(5); 119:14,162; **Isa.** 35:1; 61:10; 62:5; 64:5(4); 65:18,19; 66:10,14; **Jer.** 32:41; **Lam.** 1:21; 4:21; **Ezek.** 21:10(15); **Zeph.** 3:17.

7798. שַׁוְשָׁא *šawšā'* **masc. proper noun**
(Shavsha)
1 Chr. 18:16.

7799. I. שׁוּשַׁן *šûšan*, שׁוֹשָׁן *šôšān*, שׁוֹשַׁנָּה *šôšannāh* **masc. and fem. noun**
(lily)
1 Kgs. 7:19,22,26; **2 Chr.** 4:5; **Ps.** 45:[title](1)(KJV, NASB, see II); 60:[title](1)(KJV, NASB, *šûšan 'ēḏûṯ* [7802,I]); 69:[title](1)(KJV, NASB, see II); 80:[title](1)(KJV, NASB, *šôšanniym 'ēḏûṯ* [7802,I]); **Song** 2:1,2,16; 4:5; 5:13; 6:2,3; 7:2(3); **Hos.** 14:5(6).
II. שׁוֹשַׁנִּים *šôšanniym* **proper noun**
(Shoshannim: song title [lit. Lilies])
Ps. 45:[title](1)(NIV, see I); 69:[title](1)(NIV, see I).

7800. שׁוּשַׁן *šûšan* **proper noun**
(Shushan, Susa)
Neh. 1:1; **Esth.** 1:5; 2:3,5,8; 3:15; 4:8,16; 8:14,15; 9:6,11–15,18; **Dan.** 8:2.

7801. שׁוּשַׁנְכִי *šûšanḵiy* **Aram. masc. proper noun**
(Susanchites: inhabitants of Susa, Shushan [7800])
Ezra 4:9.

7802. I. שׁוּשַׁן עֵדוּת *šûšan 'ēḏûṯ* **proper noun**
(Shushan Eduth: song title [lit.: Lily of the Covenant])
Ps. 60:[title](1)(NIV, *šûšan* [7799,I] and *'ēḏûṯ* [5715]).
II. שׁוֹשַׁנִּים עֵדוּת *šôšanniym 'ēḏûṯ* **proper noun**
(Shoshanniym Eduth: song title [lit.: Lilies of the Covenant])
Ps. 80:[title](1)(NIV, *šûšan* [7799,I] and *'ēḏûṯ* [5715]).

7803. שׁוּתֶלַח *šûṯelaḥ* **masc. proper noun**
(Shuthelah)
Num. 26:35,36; **1 Chr.** 7:20,21.

7804. שְׁזַב *š^{e}zaḇ*, שֵׁיזִב *šēyziḇ*
Aram. verb
(to deliver, to rescue)
Dan. 3:15,17,28; 6:14(15),16(17),20(21),27(28).

7805. I. שָׁזַף *šāzap̱* **verb**
(to look at, to see)
Job 20:9; 28:7; **Song** 1:6(NASB, NIV, see II).
II. שָׁזַף *šāzap̱* **verb**
(to burn, to darken [the result of the sun looking on one])
Song 1:6(KJV, see I).

7806. שָׁזַר *šāzar* **verb**
(to be finely twisted)
Ex. 26:1,31,36; 27:9,16,18; 28:6,8,15; 36:8,35,37; 38:9,16,18; 39:2,5,8,24,28,29.

7807. שַׁח *šaḥ* **adj.**
(humble, downcast)
Job 22:29.

7808. שֵׂחַ *śēaḥ* **masc. noun**
(thought)
Amos 4:13.

7809. שָׁחַד *šāḥaḏ* **verb**
(to give a reward, to bribe)
Job 6:22; **Ezek.** 16:33.

7810. שֹׁחַד *šōḥaḏ* **masc. noun**
(bribe, reward, gift)
Ex. 23:8; **Deut.** 10:17; 16:19; 27:25; **1 Sam.** 8:3; **1 Kgs.** 15:19; **2 Kgs.** 16:8; **2 Chr.** 19:7; **Job** 15:34; **Ps.** 15:5; 26:10; **Prov.** 6:35; 17:8,23; 21:14; **Isa.** 1:23; 5:23; 33:15; 45:13; **Ezek.** 22:12; **Mic.** 3:11.

7811. שָׂחָה *śāḥāh* **verb**
(to swim, to cause to swim, to flood)
Ps. 6:6(7); **Isa.** 25:11.

7812. שָׁחָה *shāchāh* **verb**
(to bow down, to prostrate oneself)
Gen. 18:2; 19:1; 22:5; 23:7,12; 24:26, 48,52; 27:29; 33:3,6,7; 37:7,9,10; 42:6; 43:26,28; 47:31; 48:12; 49:8; **Ex.** 4:31; 11:8; 12:27; 18:7; 20:5; 23:24; 32:8; 33:10; 34:8,14; **Lev.** 26:1; **Num.** 22:31; 25:2; **Deut.** 4:19; 5:9; 8:19; 11:16; 17:3; 26:10; 29:26(25); 30:17; **Josh.** 5:14; 23:7,16; **Judg.** 2:12,17,19; 7:15; **Ruth** 2:10; **1 Sam.** 1:3,19,28; 2:36; 15:25, 30,31; 20:41; 24:8(9); 25:23,41; 28:14; **2 Sam.** 1:2; 9:6,8; 12:20; 14:4,22,33; 15:5,32; 16:4; 18:21,28; 24:20; **1 Kgs.** 1:16,23,31,47,53; 2:19; 9:6,9; 11:33; 16:31; 22:53(54); **2 Kgs.** 2:15; 4:37; 5:18; 17:16,35,36; 18:22; 19:37; 21:3,21; **1 Chr.** 16:29; 21:21; 29:20; **2 Chr.** 7:3,19,22; 20:18; 24:17; 25:14; 29:28–30; 32:12; 33:3; **Neh.** 8:6; 9:3,6; **Esth.** 3:2,5; **Job** 1:20; **Ps.** 5:7(8); 22:27(28),29(30); 29:2; 45:11(12); 66:4; 72:11; 81:9(10); 86:9; 95:6; 96:9; 97:7; 99:5,9; 106:19; 132:7; 138:2; **Prov.** 12:25; **Isa.** 2:8,20; 27:13; 36:7; 37:38; 44:15,17; 45:14; 46:6; 49:7,23; 51:23; 60:14; 66:23; **Jer.** 1:16; 7:2; 8:2; 13:10; 16:11; 22:9; 25:6; 26:2; **Ezek.** 8:16; 46:2,3,9; **Mic.** 5:13(12); **Zeph.** 1:5; 2:11; **Zech.** 14:16,17.

7813. שָׂחוּ *śāḥû* **masc. noun**
(swimming)
Ezek. 47:5.

7814. שְׂחוֹק *ś^{e}ḥôq*, שְׂחֹק *ś^{e}ḥōq* **masc. noun**
(laughter, ridicule, derision)
Job 8:21; 12:4; **Ps.** 126:2; **Prov.** 10:23; 14:13; **Eccl.** 2:2; 7:3,6; 10:19; **Jer.** 20:7; 48:26,27,39; **Lam.** 3:14.

7815. שְׁחוֹר *š^{e}ḥôr* **masc. noun**
(soot, coal)
Lam. 4:8.

7816. שְׁחוּת *š^{e}ḥûṯ* **fem. noun**
(pit, trap)
Prov. 28:10.

7817. שָׁחַח *šāḥaḥ* **verb**
(to bow down, to stoop, to crouch, to sink low)
Job 9:13; 38:40; **Ps.** 10:10; 35:14; 38:6(7); 42:5(6)(NIV, *šiyaḥ* [7743,II]), 6(7)(NIV, *šiyaḥ* [7743,II]),11(12)(NIV, *šiyaḥ* [7743,II]); 43:5(NIV, *šiyaḥ* [7743,II]); 107:39; **Prov.** 14:19; **Eccl.** 12:4; **Isa.** 2:9,11,17; 5:15; 25:12; 26:5; 29:4; 60:14; **Lam.** 3:20(KJV, NASB, *šûaḥ*[7743,I]); **Hab.** 3:6.

7818. שָׂחַט *śāḥaṭ* **verb**
(to squeeze, to press)
Gen. 40:11.

7819. I. שָׁחַט *šāḥaṭ* **verb**
(to kill, to slaughter)
Gen. 22:10; 37:31; **Ex.** 12:6,21; 29:11, 16,20; 34:25; **Lev.** 1:5,11; 3:2,8,13; 4:4, 15,24,29,33; 6:25(18); 7:2; 8:15,19,23; 9:8,12,15,18; 14:5,6,13,19,25,50,51; 16:11,15; 17:3; 22:28; **Num.** 11:22; 14:16; 19:3; **Judg.** 12:6; **1 Sam.** 1:25; 14:32,34; **1 Kgs.** 18:40; **2 Kgs.** 10:7,14; 25:7; **2 Chr.** 29:22,24; 30:15; 35:1,6,11; **Ezra** 6:20; **Isa.** 22:13; 57:5; 66:3; **Jer.** 9:8(7)(KJV, see II); 39:6; 41:7; 52:10; **Ezek.** 16:21; 23:39; 40:39,41,42; 44:11; **Hos.** 5:2(NASB, *šaḥᵃṭāh* [7821,II]).
II. שָׁחַט *šāḥaṭ* **verb**
(to shoot out)
Jer. 9:8(7)(NASB, NIV, see I).

7820. שָׁחַט *šāḥaṭ* **verb**
(to beat, to hammer)
1 Kgs. 10:16,17; **2 Chr.** 9:15,16.

7821. I. שְׁחִיטָה *šᵉḥiyṭāh* **fem. noun**
(slaughter, killing)
2 Chr. 30:17.
II. שַׁחֲטָה *šaḥᵃṭāh* **fem. noun**
(depravity)
Hos. 5:2(KJV, NIV, *šāḥaṭ* [7819,I]).

7822. שְׁחִין *šᵉḥiyn* **masc. noun**
(a boil)
Ex. 9:9–11; **Lev.** 13:18–20,23; **Deut.** 28:27,35; **2 Kgs.** 20:7; **Job** 2:7; **Isa.** 38:21.

7823. I. שָׁחִיס *šāḥiys* **masc. noun**
(aftergrowth, that which grows of itself)
Isa. 37:30.
II. סָחִישׁ *sāḥiyš* **masc. noun**
(aftergrowth, that which grows of itself)
2 Kgs. 19:29.

7824. שָׂחִיף *śaḥiyp̱* **masc. noun**
(paneled, ceiled)
Ezek. 41:16.

7825. שְׁחִית *šᵉḥiyṯ* **fem. noun**
(pit, grave, destruction)
Ps. 107:20; **Lam.** 4:20.

7826. שַׁחַל *šaḥal* **masc. noun**
(lion)
Job 4:10; 10:16; 28:8; **Ps.** 91:13; **Prov.** 26:13; **Hos.** 5:14; 13:7.

7827. שְׁחֵלֶת *šᵉḥēleṯ* **fem. noun**
(onycha; an ingredient in the holy incense)
Ex. 30:34.

7828. שַׁחַף *šaḥap̱* **masc. noun**
(seagull)
Lev. 11:16; **Deut.** 14:15.

7829. שַׁחֶפֶת *šaḥep̱eṯ* **fem. noun**
(consumption; wasting disease)
Lev. 26:16; **Deut.** 28:22.

7830. I. שַׁחַץ *šaḥaṣ* **masc. noun**
(pride)
Job 41:34(26).
II. שַׁחַץ *šaḥaṣ* **masc. noun**
(lion[as a proud beast])
Job 28:8.

7831. I. שַׁחֲצוּם *šaḥᵃṣûm* **proper noun**
(Shahazumah [with directional *h*])
Josh. 19:22(KJV, [Kᵉ] see II).
II. שַׁחֲצִים *šaḥᵃṣiym* **proper noun**
(Shahazimah [with directional *h*])
Josh. 19:22(NASB, NIV, [Qᵉ] see I).

7832. שָׂחַק *śāḥaq* **verb**
(to laugh; to celebrate; to rejoice; to mock)
Judg. 16:25,27; **1 Sam.** 18:7; **2 Sam.** 2:14; 6:5,21; **1 Chr.** 13:8; 15:29; **2 Chr.** 30:10; **Job** 5:22; 29:24; 30:1; 39:7,18,22; 40:20; 41:5(40:29),29(21); **Ps.** 2:4; 37:13; 52:6(8); 59:8(9); 104:26; **Prov.** 1:26; 8:30,31; 26:19; 29:9; 31:25; **Eccl.** 3:4; **Jer.** 15:17; 30:19; 31:4; **Lam.** 1:7; **Hab.** 1:10; **Zech.** 8:5.

7833. שָׁחַק *šāḥaq* **verb**
(to beat fine, to pulverize; to wear away)
Ex. 30:36; **2 Sam.** 22:43; **Job** 14:19; **Ps.** 18:42(43).

7834. שַׁחַק *šaḥaq* **masc. noun**
(sky, cloud, speck of dust)
Deut. 33:26; **2 Sam.** 22:12; **Job** 35:5; 36:28; 37:18,21; 38:37; **Ps.** 18:11(12); 36:5(6); 57:10(11); 68:34(35); 77:17(18); 78:23; 89:6(7),37(38); 108:4(5); **Prov.** 3:20; 8:28; **Isa.** 40:15; 45:8; **Jer.** 51:9.

7835. שָׁחַר *šāḥar* **verb**
(to be black, to turn black)
Job 30:30.

7836. I. שָׁחַר *šāḥar* **verb**
(to diligently seek; to search for)
Job 7:21; 8:5; 24:5; **Ps.** 63:1(2); 78:34; **Prov.** 1:28; 7:15; 8:17; 11:27; 13:24; **Isa.** 26:9; **Hos.** 5:15.
II. שָׁחַר *šāḥar* **verb**
(to conjure away; to charm away)
Isa. 47:11(KJV, *šaḥar* [7837]); **Hos.** 5:15.

7837. I. שַׁחַר *šaḥar* **masc. noun**
(morning, dawn, rising up)
Gen. 19:15; 32:24(25),26(27); **Josh.** 6:15; **Judg.** 19:25; **1 Sam.** 9:26; **Neh.** 4:21(15); **Job** 3:9; 38:12; 41:18(10); **Ps.** 22:[title](1)(KJV, NASB, see II); 57:8(9); 108:2(3); 139:9; **Song** 6:10; **Isa.** 8:20; 14:12; 47:11(NASB, NIV, *šāḥar* [7836,II]); 58:8; **Hos.** 6:3; 10:15; **Joel** 2:2; **Amos** 4:13; **Jon.** 4:7.
II. שַׁחַר *šaḥar* **proper noun**
(Shahar, Hashshahar; part of a song title)
Ps. 22:[title](1)(NIV, see I).

7838. שָׁחֹר *šāḥōr* **adj.**
(black)
Lev. 13:31,37; **Song** 1:5; 5:11; **Zech.** 6:2,6.

7839. שַׁחֲרוּת *šaḥᵃrûṯ* **fem. noun**
(youth, prime of life)
Eccl. 11:10.

7840. שְׁחַרְחֹר *šᵉḥarḥōr* **adj.**
(dark, black [of a suntanned skin])
Song 1:6.

7841. שְׁחַרְיָה *šᵉḥaryāh* **masc. proper noun**
(Sheheriah)
1 Chr. 8:26.

7842. שַׁחֲרַיִם *šaḥᵃrayim* **masc. proper noun**
(Shaharaim)
1 Chr. 8:8.

7843. שָׁחַת *šāḥaṯ* **verb**
(to destroy, to mar, to corrupt)
Gen. 6:11–13,17; 9:11,15; 13:10; 18:28, 31,32; 19:13,14,29; 38:9; **Ex.** 8:24(20); 12:23(NIV, *mašḥiyṯ* [4889]); 21:26; 32:7; **Lev.** 19:27; **Num.** 32:15; **Deut.** 4:16, 25,31; 9:12,26; 10:10; 20:19,20; 31:29; 32:5; **Josh.** 22:33; **Judg.** 2:19; 6:4,5; 20:21,25,35,42; **Ruth** 4:6; **1 Sam.** 6:5; 13:17; 14:15; 23:10; 26:9,15; **2 Sam.** 1:14; 11:1; 14:11; 20:15,20; 24:16; **2 Kgs.** 8:19; 13:23; 18:25; 19:12;

1 Chr. 20:1; 21:12,15; **2 Chr.** 12:7,12; 20:23(KJV, NASB, *mašḥiyṯ* [4889]); 21:7; 24:23; 25:16; 26:16; 27:2; 34:11; 35:21; 36:19; **Ps.** 14:1; 53:1(2); 57:[title](1) (see *'al tašḥēṯ* [516]); 58:[title](1)(see *'al tašḥēṯ* [516]); 59:[title](1)(see *'al tašḥēṯ* [516]); 75:[title](1)(see *'al tašḥēṯ* [516]); 78:38,45; 106:23; **Prov.** 6:32; 11:9; 18:9 (NIV, *mašḥiyṯ* [4889]); 23:8; 25:26; 28:24 (KJV, NASB, *mašḥiyṯ* [4889]); **Isa.** 1:4; 11:9; 14:20; 36:10; 37:12; 51:13; 54:16(NIV, *mašḥiyṯ* [4889]); 65:8,25; **Jer.** 2:30; 4:7; 5:10; 6:5,28; 11:19; 12:10; 13:7,9,14; 15:3,6; 18:4; 22:7(NIV, *mašḥiyṯ* [4889]); 36:29; 48:18; 49:9; 51:1(NIV, *mašḥiyṯ* [4889]),11,20,25; **Lam.** 2:5,6,8; **Ezek.** 5:16; 9:8; 16:47; 20:17,44; 22:30; 23:11; 26:4; 28:17; 30:11; 43:3; **Dan.** 8:24,25; 9:26; 11:17; **Hos.** 9:9; 11:9; 13:9; **Amos** 1:11; **Nah.** 2:2(3); **Zeph.** 3:7; **Mal.** 1:14; 2:8; 3:11.

7844. שְׁחַת *šᵉḥaṯ* **Aram. verb**
(to corrupt; corr. to Hebr. 7843)
Dan. 2:9; 6:4(5).

7845. שַׁחַת *šaḥaṯ* **fem. noun**
(pit; destruction)
Job 9:31; 17:14; 33:18,22,24,28,30; **Ps.** 7:15(16); 9:15(16); 16:10; 30:9(10); 35:7; 49:9(10); 55:23(24); 94:13; 103:4; **Prov.** 26:27; **Isa.** 38:17; 51:14; **Ezek.** 19:4,8; 28:8; **Jon.** 2:6(7).

7846. I. שֵׂט *śēṭ* **masc. noun**
(defection, deviation, revolt)
Hos. 5:2.
II. סֵט *sēṭ* **masc. noun**
(defection, deviation, revolt)
Ps. 101:3(KJV, *sûṭ* [7750]).

7847. שָׂטָה *śāṭāh* **verb**
(to turn aside; to go astray)
Num. 5:12,19,20,29; **Prov.** 4:15; 7:25.

7848. שִׁטָּה *šiṭṭāh* **fem. noun**
(acacia wood, acacia tree; shittim wood)
Ex. 25:5,10,13,23,28; 26:15,26,32,37; 27:1,6; 30:1,5; 35:7,24; 36:20,31,36; 37:1,4,10,15,25,28; 38:1,6; **Deut.** 10:3; **Isa.** 41:19; **Joel** 3:18(4:18)(KJV, NASB, *šittiym* [7851,B]).

7849. שָׁטַח *šāṭaḥ* **verb**
(to spread out; to stretch out; to enlarge)
Num. 11:32; **2 Sam.** 17:19; **Job** 12:23; **Ps.** 88:9(10); **Jer.** 8:2.

7850. שֹׁטֵט *šōṭēṭ* **masc. noun**
(whip, scourge)
Josh. 23:13.

7851. A. שִׁטִּים *šiṭṭiym* **proper noun**
(Shittim: loc. in the plains of Moab; shortened form of *'āḇēl haššiṭṭiym* [63])
Num. 25:1; **Josh.** 2:1; 3:1; **Mic.** 6:5.
B. שִׁטִּים *šiṭṭiym* **proper noun**
(Shittim: valley NW of Dead Sea)
Joel 3:18(4:18)(NIV, *šiṭṭāh* [7848]).

7852. שָׂטַם *śāṭam* **verb**
(to hate, to bear a grudge against, to harrass)
Gen. 27:41; 49:23; 50:15; **Job** 16:9; 30:21; **Ps.** 55:3(4).

7853. שָׂטַן *śāṭan* **verb**
(to accuse; to act as an adversary)
Ps. 38:20(21); 71:13; 109:4,20,29; **Zech.** 3:1.

7854. I. שָׂטָן *śāṭān* **masc. proper noun**
(Satan, the Devil)
1 Chr. 21:1; **Job** 1:6–9,12; 2:1–4,6,7; **Ps.** 109:6(NASB, NIV, see II); **Zech.** 3:1,2.
II. שָׂטָן *śāṭān* **masc. noun**
(adversary, accuser)
Num. 22:22,32; **1 Sam.** 29:4; **2 Sam.** 19:22(23); **1 Kgs.** 5:4(18); 11:14,23,25; **Ps.** 109:6(KJV, see I).

7855. שִׂטְנָה *śiṭnāh* **fem. noun**
(accusation)
Ezra 4:6.

7856. שִׂטְנָה *śiṭnāh* **proper noun**
(Sitnah)
Gen. 26:21.

7857. שָׁטַף *šāṭap̱* **verb**
(to overflow; to wash away, to rinse)
Lev. 6:28(29); 15:11,12; **1 Kgs.** 22:38; **2 Chr.** 32:4; **Job** 14:19; **Ps.** 69:2(3), 15(16); 78:20; 124:4; **Song** 8:7; **Isa.** 8:8; 10:22; 28:2,15,17,18; 30:28; 43:2; 66:12; **Jer.** 8:6; 47:2; **Ezek.** 13:11,13; 16:9; 38:22; **Dan.** 11:10,22,26,40.

7858. שֶׁטֶף *šeṭep̱* **masc. noun**
(flood, overflow, torrent of rain)
Job 38:25; **Ps.** 32:6; **Prov.** 27:4; **Isa.** 54:8(KJV, *šeṣep̱* [8241,II]; NIV, *šeṣep̱* [8241,I]); **Dan.** 9:26; 11:22; **Nah.** 1:8.

7859. שְׁטַר *š^eṭar* **Aram. masc. noun**
(side)
Dan. 7:5.

7860. שֹׁטֵר *šōṭēr* **masc. noun**
(official, officer, foreman)
Ex. 5:6,10,14,15,19; **Num.** 11:16; **Deut.** 1:15; 16:18; 20:5,8,9; 29:10(9); 31:28; **Josh.** 1:10; 3:2; 8:33; 23:2; 24:1; **1 Chr.** 23:4; 26:29; 27:1; **2 Chr.** 19:11; 26:11; 34:13; **Prov.** 6:7.

7861. שִׁטְרַי *šiṭray* **masc. proper noun**
(Shitrai)
1 Chr. 27:29.

7862. שַׁי *šay* **masc. noun**
(gift, present)
Ps. 68:29(30); 76:11(12); **Isa.** 18:7.

7863. שִׂיא *śiy'* **masc. noun**
(pride, loftiness)
Job 20:6.

7864. שְׁיָא *š^eyā'* **masc. proper noun**
(Sheja; [K^e] for [Q^e] *š^ewā'*, "Sheva" [7724,A] in 2 Sam. 20:25)

7865. שִׂיאֹן *śiy'ōn* **proper noun**
(Sion, another name for Mt. Hermon)
Deut. 4:48.

7866. שִׁיאֹן *šiy'ōn* **proper noun**
(Shion)
Josh. 19:19.

7867. שִׂיב *śiyḇ* **verb**
(to be gray-headed)
1 Sam. 12:2; **Job** 15:10.

7868. שִׂיב *śiyḇ*, שָׂב *śāḇ* **Aram. verb**
(to be gray-headed, elderly; corr. to Hebr. 7867)
Ezra 5:5,9; 6:7,8,14.

7869. שֵׂיב *śeyḇ* **masc. noun**
(old age, gray-headed age)
1 Kgs. 14:4.

7870. שִׁיבָה *šiyḇāh* **fem. noun**
(captivity)
Ps. 126:1(NASB, *š^eḇûṯ* [7622]).

7871. שִׁיבָה *šiyḇāh* **fem. noun**
(sojourn, stay)
2 Sam. 19:32(33).

7872. שֵׂיבָה *śeyḇāh* **fem. noun**
(old age, state of being gray-headed)
Gen. 15:15; 25:8; 42:38; 44:29,31; **Lev.** 19:32; **Deut.** 32:25; **Judg.** 8:32; **Ruth** 4:15; **1 Kgs.** 2:6,9; **1 Chr.** 29:28; **Job** 41:32(24); **Ps.** 71:18; 92:14(15); **Prov.** 16:31; 20:29; **Isa.** 46:4; **Hos.** 7:9.

7873. שִׂיג *śiyg* **masc. noun**
(pursuit, a moving away)
1 Kgs. 18:27(NASB, *siyg* [5509]).

7874. שִׂיד *śiyd* **verb**
(to plaster; to coat [with lime])
Deut. 27:2,4.

7875. שִׂיד *śiyd* **masc. noun**
(plaster, lime)
Deut. 27:2,4; **Isa.** 33:12; **Amos** 2:1.

7876. שָׁיָה *šāyāh* **verb**
(to neglect, to desert)
Deut. 32:18.

7877. שִׁיזָא *šiyzā'* **masc. proper noun**
(Shiza)
1 Chr. 11:42.

7878. שִׂיחַ *śiyaḥ* **verb**
(to meditate, to consider; to speak, to complain)
Judg. 5:10; **1 Kgs.** 18:27(KJV, NASB, *śiyaḥ* [7879]); **1 Chr.** 16:9; **Job** 7:11; 12:8; **Ps.** 55:17(18); 69:12(13); 77:3(4), 6(7),12(13); 105:2; 119:15,23,27,48,78, 148; 143:5; 145:5; **Prov.** 6:22; **Isa.** 53:8.

7879. שִׂיחַ *śiyaḥ* **masc. noun**
(complaint, concern, meditation)
1 Sam. 1:16; **1 Kgs.** 18:27(NIV, *śiyaḥ* [7878]); **2 Kgs.** 9:11; **Job** 7:13; 9:27; 10:1; 21:4; 23:2; **Ps.** 55:2(3); 64:1(2); 102:[title](1); 104:34; 142:2(3); **Prov.** 23:29.

7880. שִׂיחַ *śiyaḥ* **masc. noun**
(bush, shrub)
Gen. 2:5; 21:15; **Job** 30:4,7.

7881. שִׂיחָה *śiyḥāh* **fem. noun**
(meditation, prayer)
Job 15:4; **Ps.** 119:97,99.

7882. שִׁיחָה *šiyḥāh* **fem. noun**
(pit)
Ps. 57:6(7); 119:85; **Jer.** 18:22(NASB, NIV, [Qe] *šûḥāh* [7745]).

7883. שִׁיחוֹר *šiyḥôr* **proper noun**
(Shihor; a river that was a branch of the Nile)
Josh. 13:3; **1 Chr.** 13:5; **Isa.** 23:3; **Jer.** 2:18.

7884. שִׁיחוֹר לִבְנָת *šiyḥôr libnat* **proper noun**
(Shihor Libnath)
Josh. 19:26.

7885. שַׁיִט *šayiṭ* **masc. noun**
(oar)
Isa. 33:21.

7886. שִׁילֹה *šiylōh* **masc. proper noun**
(Shiloh)
Gen. 49:10(NIV, *še* [7945]).

7887. שִׁילֹה *šiylōh,* שִׁלֹה *šilōh,* שִׁילוֹ *šiylô,* שִׁלוֹ *šilô* **proper noun**
(Shiloh)
Josh. 18:1,8–10; 19:51; 21:2; 22:9,12; **Judg.** 18:31; 21:12,19,21; **1 Sam.** 1:3, 9,24; 2:14; 3:21; 4:3,4,12; 14:3; **1 Kgs.** 2:27; 14:2,4; **Ps.** 78:60; **Jer.** 7:12,14; 26:6,9; 41:5.

7888. שִׁילֹנִי *šiylōniy,* שִׁילוֹנִי *šiylôniy,* שִׁלֹנִי *šilōniy* **masc. proper noun**
(Shilonite)
1 Kgs. 11:29; 12:15; 15:29; **1 Chr.** 9:5; **2 Chr.** 9:29; 10:15; **Neh.** 11:5(KJV, *šilōniy* [8023]; NIV, *šēlāniy* [8024]).

7889. שִׁימוֹן *šiymôn* **masc. proper noun**
(Shimon)
1 Chr. 4:20.

7890. שַׁיִן *šayin* **masc. noun**
(urine)
2 Kgs. 18:27; **Isa.** 36:12.

7891. שִׁיר *šiyr* **verb**
(to sing)

Ex. 15:1,21; **Num.** 21:17; **Judg.** 5:1,3; **1 Sam.** 18:6; **2 Sam.** 6:5(KJV, NASB, *b^{e}rûš* [1265]); 19:35(36); **1 Kgs.** 10:12; **1 Chr.** 6:33(18); 9:33; 15:16,19,27; 16:9,23; **2 Chr.** 5:12,13; 9:11; 20:21; 23:13; 29:28; 35:15,25; **Ezra** 2:41,65, 70; 7:7; 10:24; **Neh.** 7:1,44,67,73(72); 10:28(29),39(40); 11:22,23; 12:28,29, 42,45–47; 13:5,10; **Job** 33:27(KJV, *šûr* [7789]; NIV, *šûr* [7788]); 36:24(KJV, *šûr* [7789]); **Ps.** 7:[title]:(1); 13:6; 21:13(14); 27:6; 33:3; 57:7(8); 59:16(17); 65:13(14); 68:4(5),25(26),32(33); 87:7; 89:1(2); 96:1,2; 98:1; 101:1; 104:33; 105:2; 106:12; 108:1(2); 137:3,4; 138:5; 144:9; 149:1; **Prov.** 25:20; **Eccl.** 2:8; **Isa.** 5:1; 26:1; 42:10; **Jer.** 20:13; **Ezek.** 27:25 (NASB, NIV, *šûr* [7788]); 40:44(NIV, *š^{e}nayim* [8147]); **Zeph.** 2:14.

7892. I. שִׁירָה *šiyrāh* **fem. noun**
(song)
Ex. 15:1; **Num.** 21:17; **Deut.** 31:19,21,22,30; 32:44; **2 Sam.** 22:1; **Ps.** 18:[title]:(1); **Isa.** 5:1; 23:15; **Amos** 8:3.
II. שִׁיר *šiyr* **masc. noun**
(song)
Gen. 31:27; **Judg.** 5:12; **1 Kgs.** 4:32(5:12); **1 Chr.** 6:31(16),32(17); 13:8; 15:16; 16:42; 25:6,7; **2 Chr.** 5:13; 7:6; 23:13,18; 29:27,28; 34:12; **Neh.** 12:27, 36,46; **Ps.** 28:7; 30:[title](1); 33:3; 40:3(4); 42:8(9); 45:[title](1); 46:[title](1); 48:[title](1); 65:[title](1); 66:[title](1); 67:[title](1); 68:[title](1); 69:30(31); 75:[title](1); 76:[title](1); 83:[title](1); 87:[title](1); 88:[title](1); 92:[title](1); 96:1; 98:1; 108:[title](1); 120:[title](1); 121:[title](1); 122:[title](1); 123:[title](1); 124:[title](1); 125:[title](1); 126:[title](1); 127:[title](1); 128:[title](1); 129:[title](1); 130:[title](1); 131:[title](1); 132:[title](1); 133:[title](1); 134:[title](1); 137:3,4; 144:9; 149:1; **Prov.** 25:20; **Eccl.** 7:5; 12:4; **Song** 1:1; **Isa.** 23:16; 24:9; 26:1; 30:29; 42:10; **Ezek.** 26:13; 33:32; **Amos** 5:23; 6:5; 8:10.

7893. שַׁיִשׁ *šayiš* **masc. noun**
(marble, alabaster)
1 Chr. 29:2.

7894. שִׁישָׁא *šiyšā'* **masc. proper noun**
(Shisha)
1 Kgs. 4:3.

7895. שִׁישַׁק *šiyšaq* **masc. proper noun**
(Shishak)
1 Kgs. 11:40; 14:25; **2 Chr.** 12:2,5–7,9.

7896. שִׁית *šiyṯ* **verb**
(to set, to put, to lay)
Gen. 3:15; 4:25; 30:40; 41:33; 46:4; 48:14,17; **Ex.** 7:23; 10:1; 21:22,30; 23:1, 31; 33:4; **Num.** 12:11; 24:1; **Ruth** 3:15; 4:16; **1 Sam.** 2:8; 4:20; **2 Sam.** 13:20; 19:28(29); 22:12; **1 Kgs.** 11:34; **Job** 7:17; 9:33; 10:20; 14:13; 22:24; 30:1; 38:11,36; **Ps.** 3:6(7); 8:6(7); 9:20(21); 12:5(6); 13:2(3); 17:11; 18:11(12); 21:3(4),6(7),9(10),12(13); 45:16(17); 48:13(14); 62:10(11); 73:9(KJV, NIV, *šāṯaṯ* [8371]),18,28; 83:11(12),13(14); 84:3(4), 6(7); 88:6(7),8(9); 90:8; 101:3; 104:20; 110:1; 132:11; 139:5; 140:5(6); 141:3; **Prov.** 22:17; 24:32; 26:24; 27:23; **Isa.** 5:6; 15:9; 16:3; 22:7; 26:1; **Jer.** 2:15; 3:19; 13:16; 22:6; 31:21; 50:3; 51:39; **Hos.** 2:3(5); 6:11.

7897. שִׁית *šiyṯ* **masc. noun**
(garment)
Ps. 73:6; **Prov.** 7:10.

7898. שַׁיִת *šayiṯ* **masc. noun**
(thorn)
Isa. 5:6; 7:23–25; 9:18(17); 10:17; 27:4.

7899. שֵׂךְ *śēḵ* **masc. noun**
(barb, prick)
Num. 33:55.

7900. שֹׂךְ *śōḵ* **masc. noun**
(tabernacle, dwelling)
Lam. 2:6.

7901. שָׁכַב *šāḵaḇ* **verb**
(to lie down, to sleep)
Gen. 19:4,32–35; 26:10; 28:11,13; 30:15,16; 34:2,7; 35:22; 39:7,10,12,14; 47:30; **Ex.** 22:16(15),19(18),27(26); **Lev.** 14:47; 15:4,18,20,24,26,33; 18:22; 19:20; 20:11–13,18,20; 26:6; **Num.** 5:13,19; 23:24; 24:9; **Deut.** 6:7; 11:19; 22:22,23, 25,28,29; 24:12,13; 27:20,23; 31:16; **Josh.** 2:1,8; **Judg.** 5:27; 16:3; **Ruth** 3:4, 7,8,13,14; **1 Sam.** 2:22; 3:2,3,5,6,9,15; 26:5,7; **2 Sam.** 4:5,7; 7:12; 8:2; 11:4,9, 11,13; 12:3,11,16,24; 13:5,6,8,11,14,31; **1 Kgs.** 1:2,21; 2:10; 3:19,20; 11:21,43; 14:20,31; 15:8,24; 16:6,28; 17:19; 19:5,6; 21:4,27; 22:40,50; **2 Kgs.** 4:11,21,32,34; 8:24; 9:16; 10:35; 13:9,13; 14:16,22,29; 15:7,22,38; 16:20; 20:21; 21:18; 24:6; **2 Chr.** 9:31; 12:16; 14:1(13:23); 16:13,14; 21:1; 26:2,23; 27:9; 28:27; 32:33; 33:20; **Job** 3:13; 7:4,21; 11:18; 14:12; 20:11; 21:26; 27:19; 30:17; 38:37; 40:21; **Ps.** 3:5(6); 4:8(9); 41:8(9); 57:4(5); 68:13(14); 88:5(6); **Prov.** 3:24; 6:9,10,22; 23:24; 24:33; **Eccl.** 2:23; 4:11; **Isa.** 14:8,18; 43:17; 50:11; 51:20; 56:10; **Jer.** 3:25; **Lam.** 2:21; **Ezek.** 4:4,6,9; 23:8; 31:18; 32:19,21,27–30,32; **Hos.** 2:18(20); **Amos** 6:4; **Jon.** 1:5; **Mic.** 7:5.

7902. I. שְׁכָבָה *šᵉḵāḇāh* **fem. noun**
(a layer or coating [as of dew])
Ex. 16:13,14.
II. שְׁכָבָה *šᵉḵāḇāh* **fem. noun**
(a lying with sexually; semen)
Lev. 15:16–18,32; 19:20; 22:4; **Num.** 5:13.

7903. שְׁכֹבֶת *šᵉḵōḇeṯ* **fem. noun**
(intercourse; copulation)
Lev. 18:20,23; **Lev.** 20:15; **Num.** 5:20.

7904. I. שָׁכָה *šāḵāh* **verb**
(to be full of lust)
Jer. 5:8(KJV, see II).
II. שָׁכָה *šāḵāh* **verb**
(to arise in the morning)
Jer. 5:8(NASB, NIV, see I).

7905. שֻׂכָּה *śukkāh* **fem. noun**
(spear, harpoon)
Job 41:7(40:31).

7906. שֵׂכוּ *śēḵû* **proper noun**
(Secu, Sechu)
1 Sam. 19:22.

7907. שֶׂכְוִי *śeḵwiy* **masc. noun**
(mind, heart)
Job 38:36.

7908. שְׁכוֹל *šᵉḵôl* **masc. noun**
(bereavement; loss of children)
Ps. 35:12; **Isa.** 47:8,9.

7909. I. שַׁכּוּל *šakkûl* **adj.**
(bereaved [of children])
2 Sam. 17:8; **Prov.** 17:12; **Song** 4:2; 6:6; **Jer.** 18:21; **Hos.** 13:8.
II. שְׁכוּלָה *šᵉḵûlāh* **adj.**
(bereaved [of children])
Isa. 49:21.

7910. שִׁכּוֹר *šikkôr,* שִׁכֹּר *šikkor* **adj.**
(drunk, drunken)
1 Sam. 1:13; 25:36; **1 Kgs.** 16:9; 20:16; **Job** 12:25; **Ps.** 107:27; **Prov.** 26:9; **Isa.** 19:14; 24:20; 28:1,3; **Jer.** 23:9; **Joel** 1:5.

7911. שָׁכַח *šāḵaḥ* **verb**
(to forget)
Gen. 27:45; 40:23; 41:30; **Deut.** 4:9, 23,31; 6:12; 8:11,14,19; 9:7; 24:19; 25:19; 26:13; 31:21; 32:18; **Judg.** 3:7; **1 Sam.** 1:11; 12:9; **2 Kgs.** 17:38; **Job** 8:13; 9:27; 11:16; 19:14; 24:20; 28:4; 39:15; **Ps.** 9:12(13),18(19); 10:11,12; 13:1; 31:12(13); 42:9(10); 44:17(18), 20(21),24(25); 45:10(11); 50:22; 59:11(12); 74:19,23; 77:9(10); 78:7,11; 102:4(5); 103:2; 106:13,21; 119:16,61, 83,93,109,139,141,153,176; 137:5; **Prov.** 2:17; 3:1; 4:5; 31:5,7; **Eccl.** 2:16; 8:10; 9:5; **Isa.** 17:10; 23:15,16; 49:14,15; 51:13; 54:4; 65:16; **Jer.** 2:32; 3:21; 13:25; 18:15; 20:11; 23:27,40; 30:14; 44:9; 50:5,6; **Lam.**

2:6; 5:20; **Ezek.** 22:12; 23:35; **Hos.** 2:13(15); 4:6; 8:14; 13:6; **Amos** 8:7.

7912. שְׂכַח *śᵉkaḥ* **Aram. verb**
(to find)
Ezra 4:15,19; 6:2; 7:16; **Dan.** 2:25,35; 5:11,12,14,27; 6:4(5),5(6),11(12),22(23), 23(24).

7913. שָׂכֵחַ *śākēaḥ* **adj.**
(forgetting, forgetful)
Ps. 9:17(18); **Isa.** 65:11.

7914. I. שְׂכִיָּה *śᵉkiyyāh* **fem. noun**
(ship, vessel)
Isa. 2:16(KJV, see II).
II. שְׂכִיָּה *śᵉkiyyāh* **fem. noun**
(picture)
Isa. 2:16(NASB, NIV, see I).
III. שָׂכְיָה *śākᵉyāh* **masc. proper noun**
(Sachia)
1 Chr. 8:10.

7915. שַׂכִּין *śakkiyn* **masc. noun**
(knife)
Prov. 23:2.

7916. שָׂכִיר *śakiyr* **masc. adj.**
(hired)
Ex. 12:45; 22:15(14); **Lev.** 19:13; 22:10; 25:6,40,50,53; **Deut.** 15:18; 24:14; **Job** 7:1,2; 14:6; **Isa.** 7:20(KJV, NASB, *śakiyrāh* [7917]); 16:14; 21:16; **Jer.** 46:21; **Mal.** 3:5.

7917. שְׂכִירָה *śᵉkiyrāh* **fem. adj.**
(hired)
Isa. 7:20(NIV, *śakiyr* [7916]).

7918. שָׂכַךְ *šākak* **verb**
(to abate, to cause to cease)
Gen. 8:1; **Num.** 17:5(20); **Esth.** 2:1; 7:10; **Jer.** 5:26.

7919. I. שָׂכַל *śākal* **verb**
(to be prudent, to be wise, to be successful)
Gen. 3:6; **Deut.** 29:9(8); 32:29; **Josh.** 1:7,8; **1 Sam.** 18:5,14,15,30; **1 Kgs.** 2:3; **2 Kgs.** 18:7; **1 Chr.** 28:19; **2 Chr.** 30:22; **Neh.** 8:13; 9:20; **Job** 22:2; 34:27,35; **Ps.** 2:10; 14:2; 32:8; 36:3(4); 41:1(2); 47:7(8) (NASB, NIV, *maśkiyl* [4905]); 53:2(3); 64:9(10); 94:8; 101:2; 106:7; 119:99; **Prov.** 1:3; 10:5,19; 14:35; 15:24; 16:20, 23; 17:2,8; 19:14; 21:11,12,16; **Isa.** 41:20; 44:18; 52:13; **Jer.** 3:15; 9:24(23); 10:21; 20:11; 23:5; 50:9; **Dan.** 1:4,17; 9:13, 22,25; 11:33,35; 12:3,10; **Amos** 5:13.
II. שָׂכַל *sākhal* **verb**
(to cross one's hands deliberately)
Gen. 48:14.

7920. שְׂכַל *śᵉkal* **Aram. verb**
(to consider, to contemplate; corr. to Hebr. 7919)
Dan. 7:8.

7921. שָׁכֹל *šākōl* **verb**
(to be bereaved, to be childless, to make childless, to miscarry)
Gen. 27:45; 31:38; 42:36; 43:14; **Ex.** 23:26; **Lev.** 26:22; **Deut.** 32:25; **1 Sam.** 15:33; **2 Kgs.** 2:19,21; **Job** 21:10; **Jer.** 15:7; **Lam.** 1:20; **Ezek.** 5:17; 14:15; 36:12–14; **Hos.** 9:12,14; **Mal.** 3:11.

7922. שֶׂכֶל *śekel,* שֵׂכֶל *śēkel* **masc. noun**
(understanding, discretion, prudence)
1 Sam. 25:3; **1 Chr.** 22:12; 26:14; **2 Chr.** 2:12(11); 30:22; **Ezra** 8:18; **Neh.** 8:8; **Job** 17:4; **Ps.** 111:10; **Prov.** 3:4; 12:8; 13:15; 16:22; 19:11; 23:9; **Dan.** 8:25.

7923. שִׁכֻּלִים *šikkuliym* **masc. noun**
(bereavement; childlessness)
Isa. 49:20.

7924. שָׂכְלְתָנוּ *śoklᵉtānû* **Aram. fem. noun**
(insight)
Dan. 5:11,12,14.

7925. שָׁכַם *šāḵam* **verb**
(to rise early)
Gen. 19:2,27; 20:8; 21:14; 22:3; 26:31; 28:18; 31:55(32:1); **Ex.** 8:20(16); 9:13; 24:4; 32:6; 34:4; **Num.** 14:40; **Josh.** 3:1; 6:12,15; 7:16; 8:10,14; **Judg.** 6:28,38; 7:1; 9:33; 19:5,8,9; 21:4; **1 Sam.** 1:19; 5:3,4; 9:26; 15:12; 17:16,20; 29:10,11; **2 Sam.** 15:2; **2 Kgs.** 3:22; 6:15; 19:35; **2 Chr.** 20:20; 29:20; 36:15; **Job** 1:5; **Ps.** 127:2; **Prov.** 27:14; **Song** 7:12(13); **Isa.** 5:11; 37:36; **Jer.** 7:13,25; 11:7; 25:3,4; 26:5; 29:19; 32:33; 35:14,15; 44:4; **Hos.** 6:4; 13:3; **Zeph.** 3:7.

7926. I. שְׁכֶם *šᵉḵem* **masc. noun**
(shoulder, upper back)
Gen. 9:23; 21:14; 24:15,45; 48:22; 49:15; **Ex.** 12:34; **Josh.** 4:5; **Judg.** 9:48; **1 Sam.** 9:2; 10:9,23; **Job** 31:22(KJV, *šiḵmāh* [7929]),36; **Ps.** 21:12(13); 81:6(7); **Isa.** 9:4(3),6(5); 10:27; 14:25; 22:22.
II. שְׁכֶם *šᵉḵem* **masc. noun**
(in consent [shoulder to shoulder])
Hos. 6:9(NASB, NIV, *šeḵem* [7927]); **Zeph.** 3:9.

7927. שְׁכֶם *šeḵem* **proper noun**
(Shechem)
Gen. 12:6; 33:18; 35:4; 37:12,13,14; **Josh.** 17:7; 20:7; 21:21; 24:1,25,32; **Judg.** 8:31; 9:1–3,6,7,18,20,23–26,31, 34,39,41,46,47,49,57; 21:19; **1 Kgs.** 12:1,25; **1 Chr.** 6:67(52); 7:28; **2 Chr.** 10:1; **Ps.** 60:6(8); 108:7(8); **Jer.** 41:5; **Hos.** 6:9(KJV, *šeḵem* [7926,II]).

7928. A. שֶׁכֶם *šeḵem* **masc. proper noun**
(Shechem: a Manassite)
Num. 26:31; **Josh.** 17:2.
B. שְׁכֶם *šeḵem* **masc. proper noun**
(Shechem: son of Hamor)
Gen. 33:19; 34:2,4,6,8,11,13,18,20,24, 26; **Josh.** 24:32; **Judg.** 9:25(KJV, NASB, *šeḵem* [7927]),28.
C. שֶׁכֶם *šeḵem* **masc. proper noun**
(Shechem: son of Shemidah)
1 Chr. 7:19.

7929. שִׁכְמָה *šiḵmāh* **fem. noun**
(shoulder blade; socket)
Job 31:22(NASB, NIV, *šeḵem* [7926]).

7930. שִׁכְמִי *šiḵmiy* **masc. proper noun**
(Shechemite)
Num. 26:31.

7931. שָׁכַן *šāḵan* **verb**
(to dwell, to live at a certain place; to cause to dwell)
Gen. 3:24; 9:27; 14:13; 16:12; 25:18; 26:2; 35:22; 49:13; **Ex.** 24:16; 25:8; 29:45,46; 40:35; **Lev.** 16:16; **Num.** 5:3; 9:17,18,22; 10:12; 14:30; 23:9; 24:2; 35:34; **Deut.** 12:5(KJV, *šēḵen* [7933]),11; 14:23; 16:2,6,11; 26:2; 33:12,16,20,28; **Josh.** 18:1; 22:19; **Judg.** 5:17; 8:11; **2 Sam.** 7:10; **1 Kgs.** 6:13; 8:12; **1 Chr.** 17:9; 23:25; **2 Chr.** 6:1; **Neh.** 1:9; **Job** 3:5; 4:19; 11:14; 15:28; 18:15; 26:5; 29:25; 30:6; 37:8; 38:19; 39:28; **Ps.** 7:5(6); 15:1; 16:9; 37:3,27,29; 55:6(7); 65:4(5); 68:6(7),16(17),18(19); 69:36(37); 74:2; 78:55,60; 85:9(10); 94:17; 102:28(29); 104:12; 120:5,6; 135:21; 139:9; **Prov.** 1:33; 2:21; 7:11; 8:12; 10:30; **Isa.** 8:18; 13:20,21; 18:3; 26:19; 32:16; 33:5,16; 34:11,17; 57:15; 65:9; **Jer.** 7:3,7,12; 17:6; 23:6; 25:24; 33:16; 46:26; 48:28; 49:16,31; 50:39; 51:13; **Ezek.** 17:23; 31:13; 32:4; 43:7,9; **Joel** 3:17(4:17),21(4:21); **Obad.** 1:3; **Mic.** 4:10; 7:14; **Nah.** 3:18; **Zech.** 2:10(14),11(15); 8:3,8.

7932. שְׁכַן *šᵉḵan* **Aram. verb**
(to dwell, to lodge)
Ezra 6:12; **Dan.** 4:21(18).

7933. שֵׁכֶן *šēḵen* **masc. noun**
(dwelling, habitation)
Deut. 12:5(NASB, NIV, *šāḵan* [7931]).

7934. שָׁכֵן *šāḵēn* **adj.**
(neighboring)
Ex. 3:22; 12:4; **Deut.** 1:7; **Ruth** 4:17; **2 Kgs.** 4:3; **Ps.** 31:11(12); 44:13(14); 79:4,12; 80:6(7); 89:41(42); **Prov.** 27:10; **Isa.** 33:24; **Jer.** 6:21; 12:14; 49:10,18; 50:40; **Ezek.** 16:26; **Hos.** 10:5.

7935. A. שְׁכַנְיָהוּ *šᵉḵanyāhû* **masc. proper noun**
(Shecaniah: a priest)
1 Chr. 24:11.
B. שְׁכַנְיָה *šᵉḵanyāh* **masc. proper noun**
(Shecaniah: a Levite)
2 Chr. 31:15.
C. שְׁכַנְיָה *šᵉḵanyāh* **masc. proper noun**
(Shechaniah: a priest)
Neh. 12:3,14(KJV, NASB, שְׁבַנְיָה [7645,C]).
D. שְׁכַנְיָה *šᵉḵanyāh* **masc. proper noun**
(Shechaniah: descendant of Zerubbabel)
1 Chr. 3:21,22; **Ezra** 8:3; **Neh.** 3:29.
E. שְׁכַנְיָה *šᵉḵanyāh* **masc. proper noun**
(Shechaniah: son of Jahaziel)
Ezra 8:5.
F. שְׁכַנְיָה *šᵉḵanyāh* **masc. proper noun**
(Shechaniah: son of Jehiel)
Ezra 10:2.
G. שְׁכַנְיָה *šᵉḵanyāh* **masc. proper noun**
(Shechaniah: son of Arah)
Neh. 6:18.

7936. שָׂכַר *śāḵar*, סָכַר *sāḵar* **verb**
(to hire)
Gen. 30:16; **Deut.** 23:4(5); **Judg.** 9:4; 18:4; **1 Sam.** 2:5; **2 Sam.** 10:6; **2 Kgs.** 7:6; **1 Chr.** 19:6,7; **2 Chr.** 24:12; 25:6; **Ezra** 4:5; **Neh.** 6:12,13; 13:2; **Prov.** 26:10; **Isa.** 46:6; **Hag.** 1:6.

7937. I. שָׁכֻר *šāḵur* **adj.**
(drunken, made drunk)
Isa. 51:21(KJV, NASB, see II).
II. שָׁכַר *šāḵar* **verb**
(to be or to become drunk, to be intoxicated)
Gen. 9:21; 43:34; **Deut.** 32:42; **1 Sam.** 1:14; **2 Sam.** 11:13; **Song** 5:1; **Isa.** 29:9; 49:26; 51:21(NIV, see I); 63:6; **Jer.** 25:27; 48:26; 51:7,39,57; **Lam.** 4:21; **Nah.** 3:11; **Hab.** 2:15; **Hag.** 1:6.

7938. I. שֶׂכֶר *śeḵer* **masc. noun**
(wages, reward)
Prov. 11:18; **Isa.** 19:10(KJV, see II).
II. שֶׂכֶר *śeḵer* **masc. noun**
(sluice)
Isa. 19:10(NASB, NIV, see I).

7939. שָׂכָר *śāḵār* **masc. noun**
(wages, reward, pay)
Gen. 15:1; 30:18,28,32,33; 31:8; **Ex.** 2:9; 22:15(14); **Num.** 18:31; **Deut.** 15:18; 24:15; **1 Kgs.** 5:6(20); **2 Chr.** 15:7; **Ps.** 127:3; **Eccl.** 4:9; 9:5; **Isa.** 40:10; 62:11; **Jer.** 31:16; **Ezek.** 29:18,19; **Jon.** 1:3; **Zech.** 8:10; 11:12; **Mal.** 3:5.

7940. A. שָׂכָר *śāḵār* **masc. proper noun**
(Sacar: father of Ahiam; the same as *šāḵār* [8325])
1 Chr. 11:35.
B. שָׂכָר *śāḵār* **masc. proper noun**
(Sacar: a Korahite gatekeeper)
1 Chr. 26:4.

7941. שֵׁכָר *šēḵār* **masc. noun**
(strong drink; beer)
Lev. 10:9; **Num.** 6:3; 28:7; **Deut.** 14:26; 29:6(5); **Judg.** 13:4,7,14; **1 Sam.** 1:15; **Ps.** 69:12(13); **Prov.** 20:1; 31:4,6; **Isa.** 5:11,22; 24:9; 28:7; 29:9; 56:12; **Mic.** 2:11.

7942. שִׁכְּרוֹן *šikkᵉrôn* **proper noun**
(Shikkeron, Shicron)
Josh. 15:11.

7943. שִׁכָּרוֹן *šikkārôn* **masc. noun**
(drunkenness)
Ezek. 23:33; 39:19; **Jer.** 13:13.

7944. I. שַׁל *šal* **masc. noun**
(irreverence)
2 Sam. 6:7(KJV, see II).
II. שַׁל *šal* **masc. noun**
(error)
2 Sam. 6:7(NASB, NIV, see I).

7945. שָׁ *ša,* שֶׁ *še,* שְׁ *š^e^* **rel. pron.**
(who, which, what)
Gen. 6:3(KJV, NASB, *šāgag* [7683,II]); 49:10(KJV, NASB, *šiylōh* [7886]); **Judg.** 5:7; 6:17; 7:12; 8:26; **1 Chr.** 5:20; 27:27; **Ezra** 8:20; **Job** 19:29; **Ps.** 122:3,4; 123:2; 124:1,2,6; 129:6,7; 133:2,3; 135:2,8,10; 136:23; 137:8,9; 144:15; 146:3,5; **Eccl.** 1:3,7,9–11,14,17; 2:7,9,11–22,24,26; 3:13–15,18,22; 4:2,10; 5:5(4),15(14), 16(15),18(17); 6:3,10; 7:10,14,24; 8:7, 14,17; 9:5,12; 10:3,5,14,16,17; 11:3,8; 12:3,7,9; **Song** 1:6,7,12; 2:7,17; 3:1–5, 7,11; 4:1,2,6; 5:2,8,9; 6:5,6; 8:4,8,12; **Lam.** 2:15,16; 4:9; 5:18; **Ezek.** 20:47 (21:3)(KJV, NIV, *šalhebet* [7957,I]); **Jon.** 1:7,12; 4:10.

7946. שַׁלְאֲנָן *šal'ănan* **adj.**
(secure, at ease)
Job 21:23(NASB, *ša'ănān* [7600,I]).

7947. שָׁלַב *šālab* **verb**
(to set parallel)
Ex. 26:17; 36:22.

7948. שָׁלָב *šālāb* **masc. noun**
(upright, frame)
1 Kgs. 7:28,29.

7949. שָׁלַג *šālag* **verb**
(to snow; to be as snow)
Ps. 68:14(15).

7950. I. שֶׁלֶג *šeleg* **masc. noun**
(snow)
Ex. 4:6; **Num.** 12:10; **2 Sam.** 23:20; **2 Kgs.** 5:27; **1 Chr.** 11:22; **Job** 6:16; 9:30(NIV, see II); 24:19; 37:6; 38:22; **Ps.** 51:7(9); 147:16; 148:8; **Prov.** 25:13; 26:1; 31:21; **Isa.** 1:18; 55:10; **Jer.** 18:14; **Lam.** 4:7.
II. שֶׁלֶג *šeleg* **masc. noun**
(soap, soapwort)
Job 9:30(KJV, NASB, see I).

7951. I. שָׁלָה *šālāh,* שָׁלַו *šālaw* **verb**
(to be at ease, to be safe, to prosper)
Job 3:26; 12:6; **Ps.** 122:6; **Jer.** 12:1; **Lam.** 1:5.
II. שָׁלָה *šālāh* **verb**
(to deceive; to be negligent)
2 Kgs. 4:28(KJV, *šālāh* [7952]); **2 Chr.** 29:11(KJV, *šālāh* [7952]).

7952. שָׁלָה *šālāh* **verb**
(to deceive; to be negligent)
2 Kgs. 4:28(NASB, NIV, *šālāh* [7951,II]); **2 Chr.** 29:11(NASB, NIV, *šālāh* [7951,II]).

7953. שָׁלָה *šālāh* **verb**
(to take away; to require)
Job 27:8.

7954. שְׁלֵה *š^e^lēh* **Aram. verb**
(to be at ease; corr. to Hebr. 7951,I)
Dan. 4:4(1).

7955. שָׁלָה *šālūh* **Aram. fem. noun**
(anything amiss, offensive)
Dan. 3:29(NASB, NIV, [Q^e^] *šālû* [7960]).

7956. שֵׁלָה *šēlāh* **masc. proper noun**
(Shelah: son of Judah)
Gen. 38:5,11,14,26; 46:12; **Num.** 26:20; **1 Chr.** 2:3; 4:21.

7957. I. שַׁלְהֶבֶת *šalhebet* **fem. noun**
(flame)
Job 15:30; **Ezek.** 20:47(21:3)(NASB, *še* [7945] and *lehābāh* [3052]).

II. שַׁלְהֶבֶתְיָה *šalhebetyāh* **fem. noun**
(mighty flame)
Song 8:6(NASB, see I and *yāh* [3050]).

7958. שְׂלָו *śᵉlāw* **masc. noun**
(quail)
Ex. 16:13; **Num.** 11:31,32; **Ps.** 105:40.

7959. שָׁלוּ *šālû* **masc. noun**
(security, prosperity)
Ps. 30:6(7).

7960. שָׁלוּ *šālû* **Aram. fem. noun**
(error, failure, neglect, offense)
Ezra 4:22; 6:9; **Dan.** 3:29(KJV, [Kᵉ] *šāluh* [7955]); 6:4(5).

7961. שָׁלֵו *šālēw,* שָׁלֵיו *šālēyw,* שְׁלֵיו *šᵉlēyw* **adj.**
(at ease, peaceable, prosperous, carefree)
1 Chr. 4:40; **Job** 16:12; 20:20; 21:23; **Ps.** 73:12; **Jer.** 49:31; **Ezek.** 23:42; **Zech.** 7:7.

7962. שַׁלְוָה *šalwāh* **fem. noun**
(security, prosperity, quietness)
Ps. 122:7; **Prov.** 1:32; 17:1; **Jer.** 22:21; **Ezek.** 16:49; **Dan.** 8:25; 11:21,24.

7963. שְׁלֵוָה *šᵉlēwāh* **Aram. fem. noun**
(prosperity, tranquility)
Dan. 4:27(24).

7964. שִׁלּוּחִים *šillûḥiym* **masc. pl. noun**
(parting gifts, dowry)
Ex. 18:2(NASB, *šālaḥ* [7971]); **1 Kgs.** 9:16; **Mic.** 1:14.

7965. שָׁלוֹם *šālôm* **masc. noun**
(peace, prosperity, good health)
Gen. 15:15; 26:29,31; 28:21; 29:6; 37:4,14; 41:16; 43:23,27,28; 44:17; **Ex.** 4:18; 18:7,23; **Lev.** 26:6; **Num.** 6:26; 25:12; **Deut.** 2:26; 20:10,11; 23:6(7); 29:19(18); **Josh.** 9:15; 10:21; **Judg.** 4:17; 6:23,24(KJV, *yᵉhōwāh šālôm* [3073]); 8:9; 11:13,31; 18:6,15; 19:20; 21:13; **1 Sam.** 1:17; 7:14; 10:4; 16:4,5; 17:18,22; 20:7, 13,21,42; 25:5,6,35; 29:7; 30:21; **2 Sam.** 3:21–23; 8:10; 11:7; 15:9,27; 17:3; 18:28, 29,32; 19:24(25),30(31); 20:9; **1 Kgs.** 2:5,6,13,33; 4:24(5:4); 5:12(26); 20:18; 22:17,27,28; **2 Kgs.** 4:23,26; 5:19,21,22; 9:11,17–19,22,31; 10:13; 20:19; 22:20; **1 Chr.** 12:17,18; 18:10; 22:9; **2 Chr.** 15:5; 18:16,26,27; 19:1; 34:28; **Ezra** 9:12; **Esth.** 2:11; 9:30; 10:3; **Job** 5:24; 15:21; 21:9; 25:2; **Ps.** 4:8(9); 28:3; 29:11; 34:14(15); 35:20,27; 37:11,37; 38:3(4); 41:9(10); 55:18(19),20(21); 69:22(23) (NIV, *šillûm* [7966]); 72:3,7; 73:3; 85:8(9), 10(11); 119:165; 120:6,7; 122:6–8; 125:5; 128:6; 147:14; **Prov.** 3:2,17; 12:20; **Eccl.** 3:8; **Song** 8:10; **Isa.** 9:6(5),7(6); 26:3,12; 27:5; 32:17,18; 33:7; 38:17; 39:8; 41:3; 45:7; 48:18,22; 52:7; 53:5; 54:10,13; 55:12; 57:2,19,21; 59:8; 60:17; 66:12; **Jer.** 4:10; 6:14; 8:11,15; 9:8(7); 12:5,12; 13:19; 14:13,19; 15:5; 16:5; 20:10; 23:17; 25:37; 28:9; 29:7,11; 30:5; 33:6,9; 34:5; 38:4,22; 43:12; **Lam.** 3:17; **Ezek.** 7:25; 13:10,16; 34:25; 37:26; **Dan.** 10:19; **Obad.** 1:7; **Mic.** 3:5; 5:5(4); **Nah.** 1:15(2:1); **Hag.** 2:9; **Zech.** 6:13; 8:10,12,16,19; 9:10; **Mal.** 2:5,6.

7966. שִׁלּוּם *šillûm,* שִׁלֻּם *šillum* **masc. noun**
(retribution, recompense, bribe)
Ps. 69:22(23)(KJV, NASB, *šālôm* [7965]); **Isa.** 34:8; **Hos.** 9:7; **Mic.** 7:3.

7967. A. שַׁלּוּם *šallûm,* שַׁלֻּם *šallum* **masc. proper noun**
(Shallum: king of Israel)
2 Kgs. 15:10,13–15.
B. שַׁלּוּם *šallûm* **masc. proper noun**
(Shallum: husband of Huldah the prophetess)

2 Kgs. 22:14; **2 Chr.** 34:22.
C. שַׁלֻּם *šallum* **masc. proper noun**
(Shallum: father of Jekamiah)
1 Chr. 2:40,41.
D. שַׁלּוּם *šallûm,* שַׁלֻּם *šallum* **masc. proper noun**
(Shallum: king of Judah, fourth son of Josiah)
1 Chr. 3:15; **Jer.** 22:11.
E. שַׁלֻּם *šallum* **masc. proper noun**
(Shallum: descendant of Jacob)
1 Chr. 4:25.
F. שַׁלּוּם *šallûm* **masc. proper noun**
(Shallum: a priest, father of Hilkiah)
1 Chr. 6:12(5:38),13(5:39); **Ezra** 7:2.
G. שַׁלּוּם *šallûm* **masc. proper noun**
(Shallum: son of Naphtali; also called Shillem [8006])
1 Chr. 7:13(NIV, *šillēm* [8006]).
H. שַׁלּוּם *šallûm,* שַׁלֻּם *šallum* **masc. proper noun**
(Shallum: a Levite)
1 Chr. 9:17,19,31; **Ezra** 2:42; **Neh.** 7:45.
I. שַׁלֻּם *šallum* **masc. proper noun**
(Shallum: Ephramite chief)
2 Chr. 28:12.
J. שַׁלֻּם *šallum* **masc. proper noun**
(Shallum: a Levite)
Ezra 10:24.
K. שַׁלּוּם *šallûm* **masc. proper noun**
(Shallum: son of Bani)
Ezra 10:42.
L. שַׁלּוּם *šallûm* **masc. proper noun**
(Shallum: repairer of Jerusalem's wall, son of Halohesh)
Neh. 3:12.
M. שַׁלֻּם *šallum* **masc. proper noun**
(Shallum: uncle of Jeremiah the prophet)
Jer. 32:7.
N. שַׁלּוּם *šallûm,* שַׁלֻּם *šallum* **masc. proper noun**
(Shallum: father of Maaseiah)
Jer. 35:4.

7968. שַׁלּוּן *šallûn* **masc. proper noun**
(Shallun)
Neh. 3:15.

7969. שָׁלוֹשׁ *šālôš,* שָׁלֹשׁ *šālōš,* שְׁלֹשָׁה *šᵉlōšāh* **masc./fem. noun**
(three; NIV, see also *šᵉlôšiym* [7970])
Gen. 5:22,23; 6:10,15; 7:13; 9:19,28; 11:13,15; 14:4,14; 17:25; 18:2,6; 29:2,34; 30:36; 38:24; 40:10,12,13,16,18,19; 42:17; 45:22; 46:15; **Ex.** 2:2; 3:18; 5:3; 6:18; 7:7; 8:27(23); 10:22,23; 15:22; 19:15; 21:11; 23:14,17; 25:32,33; 27:1,14,15; 32:28; 34:23,24; 37:18,19; 38:1,14,15,26; **Lev.** 12:4; 14:10; 19:23; 25:21; 27:6; **Num.** 1:23,43,46; 2:13,30,32; 3:43,46, 50; 4:44; 10:33; 12:4; 15:9; 22:28,32,33; 24:10; 26:7,25,47,62; 28:12,20,28; 29:3, 9,13,14; 31:36,43; 33:8,39; 35:14; **Deut.** 4:41; 14:28; 16:16; 17:6; 19:2,7,9,15; **Josh.** 1:11; 2:16,22; 3:2; 7:3,4; 9:16; 15:14; 17:11; 18:4; 19:6; 21:4,6,19,32,33; **Judg.** 1:20; 7:6–8,16,20,22; 8:4; 9:22,43; 10:2; 11:26; 14:14; 15:4,11; 16:15,27; 19:4; **1 Sam.** 1:24(NIV, *šālaš* [8027]); 2:13,21; 9:20; 10:3; 11:8,11; 13:2,17,21; 17:13,14; 20:20,41; 24:2(3); 25:2; 26:2; 30:12,13; 31:6,8; **2 Sam.** 2:18,31; 5:5; 6:11; 13:38; 14:27; 18:14; 20:4; 21:1,16; 23:9,13,16–19,22,23; 24:12,13; **1 Kgs.** 2:11,39; 4:32(5:12); 5:16(30); 6:36; 7:1, 4,5,12,25,27; 9:25; 10:17,22; 11:3; 12:5; 15:2,28,33; 17:21; 22:1; **2 Kgs.** 2:17; 3:10,13; 9:32; 12:6(7); 13:1,18,19,25; 17:5; 18:1,10,24; 23:31; 24:1,8; 25:17,18; **1 Chr.** 2:3,16,22; 3:4,23; 6:60(45),62(47); 7:6; 10:6; 11:11,12,15,18–21,24,25; 12:27(28),29(30),39(40); 13:14; 21:10,12; 23:8,9,23; 24:13,18; 25:5,20,30; 26:11; 29:4,27; **2 Chr.** 2:2(1),17(16),18(17); 4:4,5; 6:13; 7:10; 8:13; 9:16,21; 10:5; 11:17; 13:2; 14:8(7),9(8); 17:7,14; 20:25;

25:5,13; 26:13; 29:33; 31:16; 35:7,8; 36:2,9; **Ezra** 2:4,11,17,19,21,25,28,32, 34–36,58,64,65; 8:5,15,32; 10:8,9; **Neh.** 2:11; 7:9,17,22,23,29,32,35,36,38,39, 60,66,67; **Esth.** 1:3; 3:12,13; 4:16; 8:9,12; 9:1,15,17,18; **Job** 1:2–4,17; 2:11; 32:1,3,5; 33:29; 42:13; **Prov.** 30:15,18, 21,29; **Isa.** 16:14; 17:6; 20:3; **Jer.** 1:2; 25:3; 36:23; 52:24,28,30; **Ezek.** 4:5,9; 14:14,16,18; 40:10,11,21,48; 41:6,16,22; 48:31–34; **Dan.** 1:1,5; 8:1,14; 10:1–3; 11:2; 12:12; **Amos** 1:3,6,9,11,13; 2:1,4,6; 4:4,7,8; **Jon.** 1:17(2:1); 3:3; **Zech.** 11:8.

7970. שְׁלוֹשִׁים *šᵉlôšiym,* שְׁלֹשִׁים *šᵉlōšiym* **masc. pl. noun**
(thirty; NIV, considers this as the plural of *šālôš* [7969])
Gen. 5:3,5,16; 11:12,14,16–18,20,22; 18:30; 25:17; 32:15(16); 41:46; 46:15; 47:9; **Ex.** 6:16,18,20; 12:40,41; 21:32; 26:8; 36:15; 38:24; **Lev.** 12:4; 27:4; **Num.** 1:35,37; 2:21,23; 4:3,23,30,35,39, 40,43,47; 7:13,19,25,31,37,43,49,55,61, 67,73,79,85; 20:29; 26:7,37,51; 31:35,36, 38–40,43–45; **Deut.** 2:14; 34:8; **Josh.** 7:5; 8:3; 12:24; **Judg.** 10:4; 12:9,14; 14:11–13,19; 20:31,39; **1 Sam.** 4:10; 9:22; 11:8; 13:5; **2 Sam.** 5:4,5; 6:1; 23:13,23, 24,39; **1 Kgs.** 2:11; 4:22(5:2); 5:13(27); 6:2; 7:2,6,23; 16:23,29; 20:1,15,16; 22:31,42; **2 Kgs.** 8:17; 13:10; 15:8,13,17; 18:14; 22:1; 25:27; **1 Chr.** 3:4; 7:4,7; 11:11(KJV, NIV, [Qᵉ] *šāliyš* [7991,III]), 15,25,42; 12:4,18(19)(KJV, [Qᵉ] *šāiyš* [7991,III]),34; 15:7; 19:7; 23:3; 27:6; 29:27; **2 Chr.** 3:15; 4:2; 15:19; 16:1,12; 20:31; 21:5,20; 24:15; 34:1; 35:7; **Ezra** 1:9,10; 2:35,42,65–67; **Neh.** 5:14; 7:38, 45,67–70; 13:6; **Esth.** 4:11; **Prov.** 22:20 (KJV, NASB, [Qᵉ] *šaliyš* [7991,III]); **Jer.** 38:10; 52:29,31; **Ezek.** 1:1; 40:17; 41:6; 46:22; **Dan.** 12:12; **Zech.** 11:12,13.

7971. שָׁלַח *šālaḥ* **verb**
(to send forth, to send away; to let go; to put)
Gen. 3:22,23; 8:7–10,12; 12:20; 18:16; 19:10,13,29; 20:2; 21:14; 22:10,12; 24:7, 40,54,56,59; 25:6; 26:27,29,31; 27:42,45; 28:5,6; 30:25; 31:4,27,42; 32:3(4),5(6), 18(19),26(27); 37:13,14,22,32; 38:17,20, 23,25; 41:8,14; 42:4,16; 43:4,5,8,14; 44:3; 45:5,7,8,23,24,27; 46:5,28; 48:14; 49:21; **Ex.** 2:5; 3:10,12–15,20; 4:4,13, 21,23,28; 5:1,2,22; 6:1,11; 7:2,14,16; 8:1(7:26),2(7:27),8(4),20(16),21(17), 28(24),29(25),32(28); 9:1,2,7,13–15,17, 19,27,28,35; 10:3,4,7,10,20,27; 11:1,10; 12:33; 13:15,17; 14:5; 15:7; 18:2(KJV, NIV, *šillûḥiym* [7964]),27; 21:26,27; 22:5(4), 8(7),11(10); 23:20,27,28; 24:5,11; 33:2, 12; **Lev.** 14:7,53; 16:10,21,22,26; 18:24; 20:23; 26:22,25; **Num.** 5:2–4; 13:2,3,16, 17,27; 14:36; 16:12,28,29; 20:14,16; 21:6,21,32; 22:5,10,15,37,40; 24:12; 31:4,6; 32:8; **Deut.** 1:22; 2:26; 7:20; 9:23; 15:12,13,18; 19:12; 21:14; 22:7, 19,29; 24:1,3,4; 25:11; 28:20,48; 32:24; 34:11; **Josh.** 1:16; 2:1,3,21; 6:17,25; 7:2,22; 8:3,9; 10:3,6; 11:1; 14:7,11; 18:4; 22:6,7,13; 24:5,9,12,28; **Judg.** 1:8,25; 2:6; 3:15,18,21; 4:6; 5:15,26; 6:8,14,21, 35; 7:8,24; 9:23,31; 11:12,14,17,19,28, 38; 12:9; 13:8; 15:5,15; 16:18; 18:2; 19:25,29; 20:6,12,48; 21:10,13; **1 Sam.** 4:4; 5:8,10,11; 6:2,3,6,8,21; 9:16,19,26; 10:25; 11:3,7; 12:8,11; 13:2; 14:27; 15:1, 18,20; 16:1,11,12,19,20,22; 17:49; 18:5; 19:11,14,15,17,20,21; 20:5,12,13,20–22, 29,31; 21:2(3); 22:11,17; 24:6(7),10(11), 19(20); 25:5,14,25,32,39,40; 26:4,9,11,23; 30:26; 31:9; **2 Sam.** 1:14; 2:5; 3:12,14, 15,21–24,26; 5:11; 6:6; 8:10; 9:5; 10:2–7, 16; 11:1,3–6,12,14,18,22,27; 12:1,25,27; 13:7,16,17,27; 14:2,29,32; 15:5,10,12, 36; 17:16; 18:2,12,29; 19:11(12),14(15), 31(32); 22:15,17; 24:13,16; **1 Kgs.** 1:44, 53; 2:25,29,36,42; 5:1(5),2(16),8(22), 9(23),14(28); 7:13; 8:44,66; 9:7,14,27; 11:21,22; 12:3,18,20; 13:4; 14:6; 15:18–20; 18:10,19,20; 19:2; 20:2,5–7,9,10,17,34, 42; 21:8,11,14; **2 Kgs.** 1:2,6,9,11,13,16; 2:2,4,6,16,17; 3:7; 4:22; 5:5–8,10,22,24;

6:7,9,10,13,14,23,32; 7:13,14; 8:9,12; 9:17,19; 10:1,5,7,21; 11:4; 12:18(19); 14:8,9,19; 15:37; 16:7,8,10,11; 17:4, 13,25,26; 18:14,17,27; 19:2,4,9,16,20; 20:12; 22:3,15,18; 23:1,16; 24:2; **1 Chr.** 8:8; 10:9; 12:19(20); 13:2,9,10; 14:1; 18:10; 19:2–6,8,16; 21:12,15; **2 Chr.** 2:3(2),7(6),8(7),11(10),13(12),15(14); 6:34; 7:10,13; 8:18; 10:3,18; 16:2–4; 17:7; 24:19,23; 25:15,17,18,27; 28:16; 30:1; 32:9,21,31; 34:8,23,26,29; 35:21; 36:10,15; **Ezra** 8:16; **Neh.** 2:5,6,9; 4:23(17)(NASB, NIV, *šelaḥ* [7973,I]); 6:2–5,8,12,19; 8:10,12; 13:21; **Esth.** 1:22; 2:21; 3:6,13; 4:4; 5:10; 6:2; 8:7,10; 9:2,10,15,16,20,30; **Job** 1:4,5,11,12; 2:5; 5:10; 8:4; 12:15; 14:20; 18:18; 20:23; 21:11; 22:9; 28:9; 30:11,12,24; 38:35; 39:3,5; **Ps.** 18:14(15),16(17); 20:2(3); 43:3; 44:2(3); 50:19; 55:20(21); 57:3(4); 59:[title](1); 74:7; 78:25,45,49; 80:11(12); 81:12(13); 104:10,30; 105:17,20,26,28; 106:15; 107:20; 110:2; 111:9; 125:3; 135:9; 138:7; 144:6,7; 147:15,18; **Prov.** 6:14,19; 9:3; 10:26; 16:28; 17:11; 22:21; 25:13; 26:6; 29:15; 31:19,20; **Eccl.** 11:1; **Song** 5:4; **Isa.** 6:8; 9:8(7); 10:6,16; 16:1,2; 18:2; 19:20; 20:1; 27:8,10; 32:20; 36:2,12; 37:2,4,9,17,21; 39:1; 42:19; 43:14; 45:13; 48:16; 50:1; 55:11; 57:9; 58:6,9; 61:1; 66:19; **Jer.** 1:7,9; 2:10; 3:1,8; 7:25; 8:17; 9:16(15),17(16); 14:3,14,15; 15:1; 16:16; 17:8; 19:14; 21:1; 23:21,32,38; 24:5,10; 25:4,9,15–17, 27; 26:5,12,15,22; 27:3,15; 28:9,15,16; 29:1,3,9,17,19,20,25,28,31; 34:9–11,14, 16; 35:15; 36:14,21; 37:3,7,17; 38:6,11, 14; 39:13,14; 40:1,5,14; 42:5,6,9,20,21; 43:1,2,10; 44:4; 48:12; 49:14,37; 50:33; 51:2; **Lam.** 1:13; **Ezek.** 2:3,4,9; 3:5,6; 5:16,17; 7:3; 8:3,17; 10:7; 13:6,20; 14:13, 19,21; 17:6,7,15; 23:16,40; 28:23; 31:4,5; 39:6; 44:20; **Dan.** 10:11; 11:42; **Hos.** 5:13; 8:14; **Joel** 2:19,25; 3:13(4:13); **Amos** 1:4,7,10,12; 2:2,5; 4:10; 7:10; 8:11; **Obad.** 1:1,7,13; **Mic.** 6:4; **Hag.** 1:12; **Zech.** 1:10; 2:8(12),9(13),11(15); 4:9; 6:15; 7:2,12; 8:10; 9:11; **Mal.** 2:2,4, 16; 3:1; 4:5(3:23).

7972. שְׁלַח *šᵉlaḥ* **Aram. verb**
(to send; to be sent; corr. to Hebr. 7971)
Ezra 4:11,14,17,18; 5:6,7,17; 6:12,13; 7:14; **Dan.** 3:2,28; 5:24; 6:22(23).

7973. I. שֶׁלַח *šelaḥ* **masc. noun**
(weapon, sword, dart)
2 Chr. 23:10; 32:5; **Neh.** 4:17(11),23(17) (KJV, *šālaḥ* [7971]); **Job** 33:18(NASB, *šᵉʼôl* [7585]); 36:12; **Joel** 2:8.
II. שֶׁלַח *šelaḥ* **masc. noun**
(shoots, tendrils, plants)
Song 4:13.

7974. שֶׁלַח *šelaḥ* **masc. proper noun**
(Shelah)
Gen. 10:24; 11:12–15; **1 Chr.** 1:18,24.

7975. I. שִׁלֹחַ šilōaḥ **proper noun**
(Shiloah: a pool in SE Jerusalem)
Isa. 8:6.
II. שֶׁלַח *šelaḥ* **proper noun**
(Shelah; another name for I [NIV, Shiloam])
Neh. 3:15.

7976. שִׁלֻּחָה *šilluḥāh* **fem. noun**
(branch, tendril, shoot)
Isa. 16:8.

7977. שִׁלְחִי *šilḥiy* **masc. proper noun**
(Shilhi)
1 Kgs. 22:42; **2 Chr.** 20:31.

7978. שִׁלְחִים *šilḥiym* **masc. proper noun**
(Shilhim)
Josh. 15:32.

7979. שֻׁלְחָן *šulḥān* **masc. noun**
(table)

Ex. 25:23,27,28,30; 26:35; 30:27; 31:8; 35:13; 37:10,14–16; 39:36; 40:4,22,24; **Lev.** 24:6; **Num.** 3:31; 4:7; **Judg.** 1:7; **1 Sam.** 20:29,34; **2 Sam.** 9:7,10,11,13; 19:28(29); **1 Kgs.** 2:7; 4:27(5:7); 7:48; 10:5; 13:20; 18:19; **2 Kgs.** 4:10; **1 Chr.** 28:16; **2 Chr.** 4:8,19; 9:4; 13:11; 29:18; **Neh.** 5:17; **Job** 36:16; **Ps.** 23:5; 69:22(23); 78:19; 128:3; **Prov.** 9:2; **Isa.** 21:5; 28:8; 65:11; **Ezek.** 23:41; 39:20; 40:39–43; 41:22; 44:16; **Dan.** 11:27; **Mal.** 1:7,12.

7980. שָׁלַט *šālaṭ* **verb**
(to rule; to exercise power over; to dominate)
Neh. 5:15; **Esth.** 9:1; **Ps.** 119:133; **Eccl.** 2:19; 5:19(18); 6:2; 8:9.

7981. שְׁלֵט *š^elaṭ* **Aram. verb**
(to rule, to exercise power over; corr. to Hebr. 7980)
Dan. 2:38,39,48; 3:27; 5:7,16; 6:24(25).

7982. I. שֶׁלֶט *šeleṭ* **masc. noun**
(shield, small shield)
2 Sam. 8:7; **2 Kgs.** 11:10; **1 Chr.** 18:7; **2 Chr.** 23:9; **Song** 4:4; **Jer.** 5:11(NASB, see II); **Ezek.** 27:11.
II. שֶׁלֶט *šeleṭ* **masc. noun**
(quiver)
Jer. 51:11(KJV, NIV, see I).

7983. שִׁלְטוֹן *šilṭôn* **masc. noun**
(power, authority)
Eccl. 8:4,8.

7984. שִׁלְטוֹן *šilṭôn* **Aram. masc. noun**
(ruler, official; corr. to Hebr. 7983)
Dan. 3:2,3.

7985. שָׁלְטָן *šoltān* **Aram. masc. noun**
(dominion; authority)
Dan. 4:3(3:33),22(19),34(31); 6:26(27); 7:6,12,14,26,27.

7986. שַׁלֶּטֶת *šalleṭeṯ* **adj.**
(impudent, brazen, domineering)
Ezek. 16:30(NASB, *šalliyṭ* [7989]).

7987. שְׁלִי *š^eliy* **masc. noun**
(quietness, privacy)
2 Sam. 3:27.

7988. I. שִׁלְיָה *šilyāh* **fem. noun**
(afterbirth; placenta)
Deut. 28:57(KJV, see II).
II. שִׁלְיָה *šilyāh* **fem. noun**
(young one; child)
Deut. 28:57(NASB, NIV, see I).

7989. שַׁלִּיט *šalliyṭ* **adj.**
(having authority; ruling)
Gen. 42:6; **Eccl.** 7:19; 8:8; 10:5; **Ezek.** 16:30(KJV, NIV, *šalleṭeṯ* [7986]).

7990. שַׁלִּיט *šalliyṭ* **Aram. adj.**
(having authority; ruling; corr. to Hebr. 7989)
Ezra 4:20; 7:24; **Dan.** 2:10,15; 4:17(14), 25(22),26(23),32(29); 5:21,29.

7991. I. שָׁלִישׁ *šāliyš* **masc. noun**
(third [part], a measure)
Ps. 80:5(6); **Isa.** 40:12.
II. שָׁלִישׁ *šāliyš* **masc. noun**
(lute, triangle, trichord sistrum, musical instrument)
1 Sam. 18:6.
III. שָׁלִישׁ *šāliyš* **masc. noun**
(captain, chariot officer, adjutant chief; excellent way)
Ex. 14:7; 15:4; **2 Sam.** 23:8(NIV, *šālišiy* [7969,II]); **1 Kgs.** 9:22; **2 Kgs.** 7:2,17, 19; 9:25; 10:25; 15:25; **1 Chr.** 11:11 (NASB, [K^e] *š^elōšiym* [7970]); 12:18(19) (NASB, NIV, [K^e] *š^elōšiym* [7970]); **2 Chr.** 8:9; **Prov.** 22:20(NIV, [K^e] *š^elōšiym* [7970]); **Ezek.** 23:15,23.

7992. I. שְׁלִישִׁי *š^eliyšiy* **adj.**
(third [in a series, or a third part of)
Gen. 1:13; 2:14; 6:16; 22:4; 31:22;

32:19(20); 34:25; 40:20; 42:18; **Ex.** 19:1, 11,16; 28:19; 39:12; **Lev.** 7:17,18; 19:6,7; **Num.** 2:24; 7:24; 15:6,7; 19:12,19; 28:14; 29:20; 31:19; **Deut.** 23:8(9); 26:12; **Josh.** 9:17; 19:10; **Judg.** 20:30; **1 Sam.** 3:8; 17:13; 19:21; 20:5,12; 30:1; **2 Sam.** 1:2; 3:3; 18:2; 23:18; **1 Kgs.** 3:18; 6:6,8; 12:12; 18:1; 22:2; **2 Kgs.** 1:13; 11:5,6; 19:29; 20:5,8; **1 Chr.** 2:13; 3:2,15; 8:1, 39; 12:9(10); 23:19; 24:8,23; 25:10; 26:2,4,11; 27:5; **2 Chr.** 10:12; 15:10; 23:4,5; 27:5; 31:7; **Neh.** 10:32(33); **Esth.** 5:1; 8:9; **Job** 42:14; **Isa.** 19:24; 37:30; **Jer.** 28:14; **Ezek.** 5:2,12; 10:14; 21:14(19); 31:1; 46:14; **Hos.** 6:2; **Zech.** 6:3; 13:8,9.

II. שְׁלִישִׁי *šᵉliyšiy*, שָׁלִשִׁי *šališiy* **adj.**
(third [in a series, or a third part of)
2 Sam. 23:8(KJV, NASB, *šāliyš* [7991,III]), 18(NASB, see III); **Ezek.** 42:3.

III. שְׁלִישִׁי *šᵉliyšiy* **adj.**
(thirty)
2 Sam. 23:18(KJV, NIV, see II).

IV. שְׁלִישִׁי *šᵉliyšiy* **adj.**
(three years old)
Isa. 15:5(NASB, NIV, see *ʿeglaṯ šᵉlišyāh* [5697,II]); **Jer.** 48:34(NASB, NIV, see *ʿeglaṯ šᵉlišyāh* [5697,II]).

7993. שָׁלַךְ *šālak̲* **verb**
(to throw, to throw away; to cast down)
Gen. 21:15; 37:20,22,24; **Ex.** 1:22; 4:3; 7:9,10,12; 15:25; 22:31(30); 32:19,24; **Lev.** 1:16; 14:40; **Num.** 19:6; 35:20,22; **Deut.** 9:17,21; 29:28(27); **Josh.** 8:29; 10:11,27; 18:8,10; **Judg.** 8:25; 9:17,53; 15:17; **2 Sam.** 11:21; 18:17; 20:12,22; **1 Kgs.** 13:24,25,28; 14:9; 19:19; **2 Kgs.** 2:16,21; 3:25; 4:41; 6:6; 7:15; 9:25,26; 10:25; 13:21,23; 17:20; 23:6,12; 24:20; **2 Chr.** 7:20; 24:10; 25:12; 30:14; 33:15; **Neh.** 9:11,26; 13:8; **Job** 15:33; 18:7; 27:22; 29:17; **Ps.** 2:3; 22:10(11); 50:17; 51:11(13); 55:22(23); 60:8(10); 71:9; 102:10(11); 108:9(10); 147:17; **Eccl.** 3:5,6; **Isa.** 2:20; 14:19; 19:8; 34:3; 38:17; **Jer.** 7:15,29; 9:19(18); 14:16; 22:19,28; 26:23; 36:23,30; 38:6,9; 41:9; 51:63; 52:3; **Lam.** 2:1; **Ezek.** 5:4; 7:19; 16:5; 18:31; 19:12; 20:7,8; 23:35; 28:17; 43:24; **Dan.** 8:7,11,12; **Joel** 1:7; **Amos** 4:3; 8:3; **Jon.** 2:3(4); **Mic.** 2:5; 7:19; **Nah.** 3:6; **Zech.** 5:8; 11:13.

7994. שָׁלָךְ *šālak̲* **masc. noun**
(cormorant)
Lev. 11:17; **Deut.** 14:17.

7995. I. שַׁלֶּכֶת *šalleḵeṯ* **fem. noun**
(a cutting down of a tree)
Isa. 6:13(KJV, see II).

II. שַׁלֶּכֶת *šalleḵeṯ* **fem. noun**
(a casting of leaves)
Isa. 6:13(NASB, NIV, see I).

7996. שַׁלֶּכֶת *šalleḵeṯ* **proper noun**
(Shallecheth)
1 Chr. 26:16.

7997. I. שָׁלַל *šālal* **verb**
(to pull or to draw out)
Ruth 2:16.

II. שָׁלַל *šālal* **verb**
(to despoil, to plunder)
Ps. 76:5(6); **Isa.** 10:6; 59:15; **Jer.** 50:10; **Ezek.** 26:12; 29:19; 38:12,13; 39:10; **Hab.** 2:8; **Zech.** 2:8(12).

7998. שָׁלָל *šālāl* **masc. noun**
(plunder, loot, spoils)
Gen. 49:27; **Ex.** 15:9; **Num.** 31:11,12; **Deut.** 2:35; 3:7; 13:16(17); 20:14; **Josh.** 7:21; 8:2,27; 11:14; 22:8; **Judg.** 5:30; 8:24,25; **1 Sam.** 14:30,32; 15:19,21; 30:16,19,20,22,26; **2 Sam.** 3:22; 8:12; 12:30; **2 Kgs.** 3:23; **1 Chr.** 20:2; 26:27; **2 Chr.** 14:13(12); 15:11; 20:25; 24:23; 28:8,15; **Esth.** 3:13; 8:11; **Ps.** 68:12(13); 119:162; **Prov.** 1:13; 16:19; 31:11; **Isa.** 8:1(KJV, NIV, see *māhēr šālāl ḥaš baz* [4122,I]),4; 9:3(2); 10:2,6; 33:4,23; 53:12; **Jer.** 21:9; 38:2; 39:18; 45:5; 49:32; 50:10; **Ezek.** 7:21; 29:19; 38:12,13; **Dan.** 11:24; **Zech.** 2:9(13); 14:1.

7999. שָׁלַם *šālam* **verb**
(to restore, to repay, to make restitution; to reward; to make a covenant of peace)
Gen. 44:4; **Ex.** 21:34,36; 22:1(21:37), 3(2),4(3),5(4),6(5),7(6),9(8),11(10), 12(11),13(12),14(13),15(14); **Lev.** 5:16; 6:5(5:24); 24:18,21; **Deut.** 7:10; 20:12; 23:21(22); 32:35(KJV, NASB, *šillēm* [8005]), 41; **Josh.** 10:1,4; 11:19; **Judg.** 1:7; **Ruth** 2:12; **1 Sam.** 24:19(20); **2 Sam.** 3:39; 10:19; 12:6; 15:7; 20:19; **1 Kgs.** 7:51; 9:25; 22:44(45); **2 Kgs.** 4:7; 9:26; **1 Chr.** 19:19; **2 Chr.** 5:1; **Neh.** 6:15; **Job** 5:23; 8:6; 9:4; 21:19,31; 22:21,27; 23:14; 34:11,33; 41:11(3); **Ps.** 7:4(5); 22:25(26); 31:23(24); 35:12; 37:21; 38:20(21); 41:10(11); 50:14; 56:12(13); 61:8(9); 62:12(13); 65:1(2); 66:13; 76:11(12); 116:14,18; 137:8; **Prov.** 6:31; 7:14; 11:31; 13:13,21; 16:7; 19:17; 20:22; 22:27; 25:22; **Eccl.** 5:4(3),5(4); **Isa.** 19:21; 38:12,13; 42:19; 44:26,28; 57:18; 59:18; 60:20; 65:6; 66:6; **Jer.** 16:18; 18:20; 25:14; 32:18; 50:29; 51:6,24,56; **Ezek.** 33:15; **Hos.** 14:2(3); **Joel** 2:25; 3:4(4:4); **Jon.** 2:9(10); **Nah.** 1:5(2:1).

8000. שְׁלֵם *š^e^lēm* **Aram. verb**
(to finish, to bring to an end; to deliver; corr. to Hebr. 7999)
Ezra 5:16; 7:19; **Dan.** 5:26.

8001. שְׁלָם *š^e^lām* **Aram. masc. noun**
(peace [as a greeting: peace be to you])
Ezra 4:17; 5:7; **Dan.** 4:1(3:31); 6:25(26).

8002. שֶׁלֶם *šelem* **masc. noun**
(peace offering; fellowship offering)
Ex. 20:24; 24:5; 29:28; 32:6; **Lev.** 3:1,3, 6,9; 4:10,26,31,35; 6:12(5); 7:11,13–15, 18,20,21,29,32–34,37; 9:4,18,22; 10:14; 17:5; 19:5; 22:21; 23:19; **Num.** 6:14, 17,18; 7:17,23,29,35,41,47,53,59,65, 71,77,83,88; 10:10; 15:8; 29:39; **Deut.** 27:7; **Josh.** 8:31; 22:23,27; **Judg.** 20:26; 21:4; **1 Sam.** 10:8; 11:15; 13:9; **2 Sam.** 6:17,18; 24:25; **1 Kgs.** 3:15; 8:63,64; 9:25; **2 Kgs.** 16:13; **1 Chr.** 16:1,2; 21:26; **2 Chr.** 7:7; 29:35; 30:22; 31:2; 33:16; **Prov.** 7:14; **Ezek.** 43:27; 45:15,17; 46:2,12; **Amos** 5:22.

8003. שָׁלֵם *šālēm* **adj.**
(complete, wholehearted, perfect)
Gen. 15:16; 33:18(KJV, *šālēm* [8004]); 34:21; **Deut.** 25:15; 27:6; **Josh.** 8:31; **Ruth** 2:12; **1 Kgs.** 6:7; 8:61; 11:4; 15:3, 14; **2 Kgs.** 20:3; **1 Chr.** 12:38; 28:9; 29:9,19; **2 Chr.** 8:16; 15:17; 16:9; 19:9; 25:2; **Prov.** 11:1; **Isa.** 38:3; **Amos** 1:6,9; **Nah.** 1:12.

8004. שָׁלֵם *šālēm* **proper noun**
(Salem)
Gen. 14:18; 33:18(NASB, NIV, *šālēm* [8003]); **Ps.** 76:2(3).

8005. שִׁלֵּם *šillēm* **masc. noun**
(retribution)
Deut. 32:35(NIV, *šālam* [7999]).

8006. שִׁלֵּם *šillēm* **masc. proper noun**
(Shillem)
Gen. 46:24; **Num.** 26:49; **1 Chr.** 7:13 (KJV, NASB, *šallûm* [7967,G]).

8007. שַׂלְמָא *śalmā'* **masc. proper noun**
(Salma; the same as *śalmāh* [8009])
1 Chr. 2:11(NIV, *śalmôn* [8012]),51,54.

8008. שַׂלְמָה *śalmāh* **fem. noun**
(cloak, clothes, robe)
Ex. 22:9(8),26(25); **Deut.** 24:13; 29:5(4); **Josh.** 9:5,13; 22:8; **1 Kgs.** 10:25; 11:29,30; **2 Chr.** 9:24; **Neh.** 9:21; **Job** 9:31; **Ps.** 104:2; **Song** 4:11; **Mic.** 2:8.

8009. שַׂלְמָה *śalmāh* **masc. proper noun**
(Salmon; the same as *śalmā'* [8007] and *śalmôn* [8012])
Ruth 4:20.

8010. שְׁלֹמֹה *š^{e}lōmōh* **masc. proper noun**
(Solomon)
2 Sam. 5:14; 12:24; **1 Kgs.** 1:10–13, 17,19,21,26,30,33,34,37–39,43,46,47, 50–53; 2:1,12,13,17,19,22,23,25,27,29, 41,45,46; 3:1,3–6,10,15; 4:1,7,11,15, 21(5:1),22(5:2),25–27(5:5–7),29(5:9),30: (5:10),34(5:14); 5:1(15),2(16),7(21), 8(22),10–13(24–27),15(29),16(30),18(32); 6:1,2,11,14,21; 7:1,8,13,14,40,45,47, 48,51; 8:1,2,5,12,22,54,63,65; 9:1,2, 10–12,15–17,19,21–23,25–28; 10:1–4, 10,13,14,16,21,23,24,26,28; 11:1,2,4–7, 9,11,14,25–28,31,40–43; 12:2,6,21,23; 14:21,26; **2 Kgs.** 21:7; 23:13; 24:13; 25:16; **1 Chr.** 3:5,10; 6:10(5:36),32(17); 14:4; 18:8; 22:5–7,9,17; 23:1; 28:5,6,9, 11,20; 29:1,19,22–25,28; **2 Chr.** 1:1–3, 5–8,11,13,14,16; 2:1–3,5–8,11(10),17(16); 3:1,3; 4:11,16,18,19; 5:1,2,6; 6:1,13; 7:1,5,7,8,10–12; 8:1–3,6,8–12,16–18; 9:1–3,9,10,12–15,20,22,23,25,28–31; 10:2,6; 11:3,17; 12:9; 13:6,7; 30:26; 33:7; 35:3,4; **Ezra** 2:55,58; **Neh.** 7:57,60; 11:3; 12:45; 13:26; **Ps.** 72:[title](1); 127:[title](1); **Prov.** 1:1; 10:1; 25:1; **Song** 1:1,5; 3:7,9,11; 8:11,12; **Jer.** 52:20.

8011. שִׁלֻּמָה *šillumāh* **fem. noun**
(punishment, recompense)
Ps. 91:8.

8012. שַׂלְמוֹן *śalmôn* **masc. proper noun**
(Salmon; the same as *śalma'* [8007] and *śalmāh* [8009])
Ruth 4:21.

8013. A. שְׁלֹמוֹת *š^{e}lōmôṯ* **masc. proper noun**
(Shelomoth: a Levite, son of Izhar; same as *š^{e}lōmiyṯ* [8019,D])
1 Chr. 24:22.
B. שְׁלֹמוֹת *š^{e}lōmôṯ* **masc. proper noun**
(Shelomith: a Gershonite Levite; the same as *š^{e}lōmiyṯ* [8019,C])
1 Chr. 23:9(KJV, [Q^{e}] *š^{e}lōmiyṯ* [8019,C]).
C. שְׁלֹמוֹת *š^{e}lōmôṯ* **masc. proper noun**
(Shelomith: a Levite descended from Eliezer; the same as *š^{e}lōmiyṯ* [8019,E])
1 Chr. 26:25(KJV, NIV, [Q^{e}] *š^{e}lōmiyṯ* [8019,E]),26(KJV, NIV, *š^{e}lōmiyṯ* [8019,E]), 28(KJV, NIV, *š^{e}lōmiyṯ* [8019,E]).

8014. שַׂלְמַי *śalmay,* שַׁלְמַי *šalmay* **masc. proper noun**
(Shalmai)
Ezra 2:46; **Neh.** 7:48.

8015. שְׁלֹמִי *š^{e}lōmiy* **masc. proper noun**
(Shelomi)
Num. 34:27.

8016. שִׁלֵּמִי *šillēmiy* **masc. proper noun**
(Shillemite)
Num. 26:49.

8017. שְׁלֻמִיאֵל *š^{e}lumiy'ēl* **masc. proper noun**
(Shelumiel)
Num. 1:6; 2:12; 7:36,41; 10:19.

8018. A. שֶׁלֶמְיָהוּ *šelemyāhû* **masc. proper noun**
(Shelemiah: a gatekeeper)
1 Chr. 26:14.
B. שֶׁלֶמְיָהוּ *šelemyāhû* **masc. proper noun**
(Shelemiah: son of Cushi)
Jer. 36:14.
C. שֶׁלֶמְיָהוּ *šelemyāhû* **masc. proper noun**
(Shelemiah: son of Abdeel)
Jer. 36:26(Sept. omits).

D. שֶׁלֶמְיָה *šelemyāh*, שֶׁלֶמְיָהוּ *šelemyāhû* **masc. proper noun**
(Shelemiah: father of Jehucal)
Jer. 37:3; 38:1.
E. שֶׁלֶמְיָה *šelemyāh* **masc. proper noun**
(Shelemiah: father of Irijah)
Jer. 37:13.
F. שֶׁלֶמְיָה *šelemyāh* **masc. proper noun**
(Shelemiah: son of Bani)
Ezra 10:39.
G. שֶׁלֶמְיָהוּ *šelemyāhû* **masc. proper noun**
(Shelemiah: another son of Bani)
Ezra 10:41.
H. שֶׁלֶמְיָה *šelemyāh* **masc. proper noun**
(Shelemiah: father of Hananiah)
Neh. 3:30.
I. שֶׁלֶמְיָהוּ *šelemyāhû* **masc. proper noun**
(Shelemiah: a priest in Nehemiah's day)
Neh. 13:13.

8019. A. שְׁלֹמִית *šᵉlōmiyṯ* **fem. proper noun**
(Shelomith: a Danite woman)
Lev. 24:11.
B. שְׁלֹמִית *šᵉlōmiyṯ* **fem. proper noun**
(Shelomith: daughter of Zerubbabel)
1 Chr. 3:19.
C. שְׁלֹמִית *šᵉlōmiyṯ* **fem. proper noun**
(Shelomith: a Gershonite Levite; the same as *šᵉlōmôṯ* [8013,B])
1 Chr. 23:9(NASB, NIV, [Kᵉ] *šᵉlōmôṯ* [8013,B]).
D. שְׁלֹמִית *šᵉlōmiyṯ* **fem. proper noun**
(Shelomith: a Levite, son of Izhar; the same as *šᵉlōmôṯ* [8013,A])
1 Chr. 23:18.
E. שְׁלֹמִית *šᵉlōmiyṯ* **fem. proper noun**
(Shelomith: a Levite descended from Eliezer; the same as *šᵉlōmôṯ* [8013,C])
1 Chr. 26:25(NASB, [Kᵉ] *šᵉlōmôṯ* [8013,C]),26(NASB, *šᵉlōmôṯ* [8013,C]), 28(NASB, *šᵉlōmôṯ* [8013,C]).
F. שְׁלֹמִית *šᵉlōmiyṯ* **fem. proper noun**
(Shelomith: son of Rehoboam)
2 Chr. 11:20.
G. שְׁלוֹמִית *šᵉlōmiyṯ* **fem. proper noun**
(Shelomith: a head of a family)
Ezra 8:10.

8020. שַׁלְמַן *šalman* **masc. proper noun**
(Shalman)
Hos. 10:14.

8021. שַׁלְמֹן *šalmon* **masc. noun**
(reward, gift)
Isa. 1:23.

8022. שַׁלְמַנְאֶסֶר *šalman'eser* **masc. proper noun**
(Shalmaneser)
2 Kgs. 17:3; 18:9.

8023. שִׁלֹנִי *šilōniy* **masc. proper noun**
(Shiloni)
Neh. 11:5(NASB, *šiylōniy* [7888]; NIV, *šēlāniy* [8024]).

8024. שֵׁלָנִי *šēlāniy* **masc. proper noun**
(Shelanite; descendant of Shelah [7956])
Num. 26:20; **Neh.** 11:5(KJV, *šilōniy* [8023]; NASB, *šiylôniy* [7888]).

8025. שָׁלַף *šālap̱* **verb**
(to draw out [a sword]; to take off [a shoe])

Num. 22:23,31; **Josh.** 5:13; **Judg.** 3:22; 8:10,20; 9:54; 20:2,15,17,25,35,46; **Ruth** 4:7,8; **1 Sam.** 17:51; 31:4; **2 Sam.** 24:9; **2 Kgs.** 3:26; **1 Chr.** 10:4; 21:5,16; **Job** 20:25; **Ps.** 129:6.

8026. שֶׁלֶף *šelep̱* **masc. proper noun**
(Sheleph)
Gen. 10:26; **1 Chr.** 1:20.

8027. שָׁלַשׁ *šālaš* **verb**
(to do a third time; to divide into three parts, to be three years old)
Gen. 15:9; **Deut.** 19:3; **1 Sam.** 1:24(KJV, NASB, *šālōš* [7969]); 20:19; **1 Kgs.** 18:34; **Eccl.** 4:12; **Ezek.** 42:6.

8028. שֵׁלֶשׁ *šēleš* **masc. proper noun**
(Shelesh)
1 Chr. 7:35.

8029. שִׁלֵּשׁ *šillēš* **adj.**
(third [generation])
Gen. 50:23; **Ex.** 20:5; 34:7; **Num.** 14:18; **Deut.** 5:9.

8030. שִׁלְשָׁה *šilšāh* **masc. proper noun**
(Shilshah)
1 Chr. 7:37.

8031. שָׁלִשָׁה *šālišāh* **masc. proper noun**
(Shalisha)
1 Sam. 9:4.

8032. שִׁלְשׁוֹם *šilšôm,* שִׁלְשֹׁם *šilšōm* **adv.**
(before, in times past, formerly)
Gen. 31:2,5; **Ex.** 4:10; 5:7,8,14; 21:29, 36; **Deut.** 4:42; 19:4,6; **Josh.** 3:4; 4:18; 20:5; **Ruth** 2:11; **1 Sam.** 4:7; 10:11; 14:21; 19:7; 21:5(6); **2 Sam.** 3:17; 5:2; **2 Kgs.** 13:5; **1 Chr.** 11:2.

8033. שָׁם *šām* **adv.**
(there, where, in that direction)
Gen. 2:8,10–12; 3:23; 10:14; 11:2,7–9, 31; 12:7,8,10; 13:3,4,14,18; 14:10; 18:16,22,28–32; 19:20,22,27; 20:1,13; 21:17,31,33; 22:2,9; 23:13; 24:5–8; 25:10; 26:8,17,19,22,23,25; 27:9,45; 28:2, 6,11; 29:2,3; 30:32; 31:13,46; 32:13(14), 29(30); 33:19,20; 35:1,3,7,15,27; 38:2; 39:1,11,20,22; 40:3; 41:12; 42:2,26; 43:25,30; 44:14; 45:11; 46:3; 48:7; 49:24,31; 50:5,10; **Ex.** 8:22(18); 9:26; 10:26; 12:13,30; 15:25,27; 16:33; 17:3,6; 18:5; 19:2; 20:21; 21:13,33; 24:12; 25:22; 26:33; 29:42,43; 30:6,18,36; 34:2,5,28; 40:3,7,30; **Lev.** 2:2; 8:31; 16:23; 18:3; 20:22; **Num.** 9:17; 11:16,17,34; 13:22–24, 28,33; 14:24,35,43; 15:18; 17:4(19); 19:18; 20:1,4,26,28; 21:12,13,16,32; 22:41; 23:13,27; 32:26; 33:9,14,38,54; 35:6,11,15,25,26; **Deut.** 1:28,37–39; 3:21; 4:5,14,26–29,42; 5:15; 6:1,23; 7:1; 9:28; 10:5–7; 11:8,10,11,29; 12:2,5–7,11, 14,21,29; 13:12(13); 14:23,24,26; 16:2, 6,11; 17:12; 18:6,7; 19:3,4,12; 21:4; 23:12(13),20(21); 24:18; 26:2,5; 27:5,7; 28:21,36,37,63–65,68; 30:1,3,4,16,18; 31:13,16,26; 32:47,50,52; 33:19,21; 34:4,5; **Josh.** 2:1,16,22; 3:1; 4:8,9; 6:22; 7:3,4; 8:32; 10:27; 14:12; 15:14,15; 17:15; 18:1,10,13; 19:13,34; 20:3,6,9; 22:10,19; 24:26; **Judg.** 1:7,11,20; 2:5; 5:11,27; 6:24; 7:4; 8:8,25,27; 9:21,51; 14:10; 16:1,27; 17:7; 18:2,3,10,11,13,15,17; 19:2,4,7,15, 18,26; 20:22,26,27; 21:2,4,9,10,24; **Ruth** 1:2,4,7,17; 3:4; 4:1; **1 Sam.** 1:3,22,28; 2:14; 3:3; 4:4; 5:11; 6:14; 7:6,17; 9:6,10; 10:3,5,10,12,23; 11:14,15; 14:11,34; 17:49; 19:3,23; 20:6,19; 21:6(7),7(8); 22:1,3,22; 23:22,23,29(24:1); 24:3(4); 26:5; 27:5; 29:4; 30:31; 31:12; **2 Sam.** 1:21; 2:2,4,18,23; 3:27; 4:3; 5:20,21; 6:2,7; 10:18; 11:16; 13:38; 14:2,30,32; 15:21,29,32,35,36; 16:5,14; 17:12,13,18; 18:7,8,11; 20:1; 21:12,13; 23:9,11; 24:25; **1 Kgs.** 1:14,34,45; 2:3,36; 3:4; 4:28(5:8); 5:9(23); 6:19; 7:7,8; 8:8,9,16,21,29,47,64;

9:3,28; 10:20; 11:16,36; 12:25; 13:17; 14:2,21; 17:4,9,10,13,19; 18:10,40; 19:3, 9,19; 21:18; **2 Kgs.** 1:4,6,16; 2:20,21, 23,25; 4:8,10,11; 5:18; 6:1,2,6,9,10,14; 7:2,4,5,8,10,19; 9:2,16,27; 10:15; 11:16; 12:5(6),9(10); 14:19; 15:20; 16:6; 17:11, 25,27,29,33; 19:32; 23:7,8,12,16,20, 27,34; 24:13; **1 Chr.** 1:12; 3:4; 4:23, 40,41,43; 11:4,13; 12:39(40); 13:6,10; 14:11,12; 16:37; 21:26,28; **2 Chr.** 1:3,6; 5:9; 6:5,6,11,20,37; 7:7,16; 8:2,18; 9:19; 12:13; 20:26; 23:15; 25:27; 26:20; 28:9, 18; 32:21; **Ezra** 1:4; 8:15,21,32; 10:6; **Neh.** 1:3,9; 2:11; 4:20(14); 5:16; 10:39(40); 13:5,9; **Job** 1:21; 3:17,19; 23:7; 34:22; 35:12; 39:29,30; 40:20; **Ps.** 14:5; 36:12(13); 48:6(7); 53:5(6); 66:6; 68:27(28); 69:35(36); 76:3(4); 87:4,6; 104:17,25,26; 107:36; 122:4,5; 132:17; 133:3; 137:1,3; 139:8,10; **Prov.** 8:27; 9:18; 15:17; 22:14; **Eccl.** 1:5,7; 3:16,17; 9:10; 11:3; **Song** 7:12(13); 8:5; **Isa.** 7:23–25; 13:20,21; 20:6; 22:18; 23:12; 27:10; 28:10,13; 33:21; 34:12,14,15; 35:8,9; 37:33; 48:16; 52:4,11; 55:10; 57:7; 65:9,20; **Jer.** 2:6; 3:6; 7:2,12; 8:3,14,22; 13:4,6,7; 16:13,15; 18:2; 19:2,14; 20:6; 22:1,11,12,24,26,27; 23:3,8; 24:9; 27:22; 29:6,7,14,18; 30:11; 32:5,37; 35:7; 36:12; 37:12,13,16,20; 38:11,26; 40:4,12; 41:1,3,9; 42:14–17,22; 43:2,5,12; 44:8,12,14,28; 45:5; 46:17,28; 47:7; 49:16,18,33,36,38; 50:9,40; **Ezek.** 1:3,12,20; 3:15,22,23; 4:13; 5:3; 6:9,13; 8:1,3,4,14; 11:16,18; 12:13,16; 13:20; 17:20; 20:28,29,35,40,43; 23:3; 29:13,14; 30:18; 32:22,24,26,29,30; 34:12,14; 35:10; 36:20–22; 37:21; 39:11,28; 40:1,3,38; 42:13,14; 43:7; 46:19,20,24; 47:9,23; 48:35; **Dan.** 9:7; 10:13; **Hos.** 2:15(17); 6:7,10; 9:15; 10:9; 12:4(5); 13:8; **Joel** 3:2(4:2),7(4:7),11(4:11), 12(4:12); **Amos** 6:2; 7:12; 9:2–4; **Obad.** 1:4; **Jon.** 4:5; **Mic.** 2:3; 4:10; **Nah.** 2:11(12); 3:15; **Hab.** 3:4; **Zeph.** 1:14; **Hag.** 2:14; **Zech.** 5:11.

8034. שֵׁם *šēm* **masc. noun** (name, fame)

Gen. 2:11,13,14,19,20; 3:20; 4:17,19, 21,25,26; 5:2,3,29; 6:4; 10:25; 11:4,9,29; 12:2,8; 13:4; 16:1,11,13,15; 17:5,15,19; 19:22,37,38; 21:3,33; 22:14,24; 24:29; 25:1,13,16,25,26,30; 26:18,20–22,25,33; 27:36; 28:19; 29:16,32–35; 30:6,8,11,13, 18,20,21,24; 31:48; 32:2(3),27–30(28–31); 33:17; 35:8,10,15,18; 36:10,32,35,39,40; 38:1–6,29,30; 41:45,51,52; 46:8; 48:6,16; 50:11; **Ex.** 1:1,15; 2:10,22; 3:13,15; 5:23; 6:3,16; 9:16; 15:3,23; 16:31; 17:7,15; 18:3,4; 20:7,24; 23:13,21; 28:9–12,21,29; 31:2; 33:12,17,19; 34:5,14; 35:30; 39:6, 14; **Lev.** 18:21; 19:12; 20:3; 21:6; 22:2, 32; 24:11,16; **Num.** 1:2,5,17,18,20,22, 24,26,28,30,32,34,36,38,40,42; 3:2,3,17, 18,40,43; 4:32; 6:27; 11:3,26,34; 13:4,16; 16:2; 17:2(17),3(18); 21:3; 25:14,15; 26:33,46,53,55,59; 27:1,4; 32:38,42; 34:17,19; **Deut.** 3:14; 5:11; 6:13; 7:24; 9:14; 10:8,20; 12:3,5,11,21; 14:23,24; 16:2,6,11; 18:5,7,19,20,22; 21:5; 22:14, 19; 25:6,7,10; 26:2,19; 28:10,58; 29:20(19); 32:3; **Josh.** 2:1; 5:9; 7:9,26; 9:9; 14:15; 15:15; 17:3; 19:47; 21:9; 23:7; **Judg.** 1:10,11,17,23,26; 2:5; 8:31; 13:2, 6,17,18,24; 15:19; 16:4; 17:1; 18:29; **Ruth** 1:2,4; 2:1,19; 4:5,10,11,14,17; **1 Sam.** 1:1,2,20; 7:12; 8:2; 9:1,2; 12:22; 14:4,49,50; 17:4,12,13,23,45; 18:30; 20:42; 21:7(8); 22:20; 24:21(22); 25:3,5, 9,25; **2 Sam.** 3:7; 4:2,4; 5:14,20; 6:2,18; 7:9,13,23,26; 8:13; 9:2,12; 12:24,25,28; 13:1,3; 14:7,27; 16:5; 17:25; 18:18; 20:1,21; 22:50; 23:8,18,22; **1 Kgs.** 1:47; 3:2; 4:8,31(5:11); 5:3(17),5(19),7,21; 8:16–20,29,33,35,41–44,48; 9:3,7; 10:1; 11:26,36; 13:2; 14:21,31; 15:2,10; 16:24; 18:24–26,31,32; 21:8; 22:16,42; **2 Kgs.** 2:24; 5:11; 8:26; 12:1(2); 14:2,7,27; 15:2, 33; 17:34; 18:2; 21:1,4,7,19; 22:1; 23:27, 31,34,36; 24:8,17,18; **1 Chr.** 1:19,43,46, 50; 2:26,29,34; 4:3,9,38,41; 5:24; 6:17(2), 65(50); 7:15,16,23; 8:29,38; 9:35,44;

11:20,24; 12:30(31),31(32); 13:6; 14:4,11,17; 16:2,8,10,29,35,41; 17:8,21, 24; 21:19; 22:5,7–10,19; 23:13,24; 28:3; 29:13,16; **2 Chr.** 2:1(1:18),4(3); 3:17; 6:5–10,20,24,26,32–34,38; 7:14,16,20; 12:13; 13:2; 14:11(10); 18:15; 20:8,9, 26,31; 22:2; 24:1; 25:1; 26:3,8,15; 27:1; 28:9,15; 29:1; 31:19; 33:4,7,18; 36:4; **Ezra** 2:61; 8:13,20; 10:16; **Neh.** 1:9,11; 6:13; 7:63; 9:5,7,10; **Esth.** 2:5,14,22; 3:12; 8:8,10; 9:26; **Job** 1:1,21; 18:17; 30:8; 42:14; **Ps.** 5:11(12); 7:17(18); 8:1(2),9(10); 9:2(3),5(6),10(11); 16:4; 18:49(50); 20:1(2),5(6),7(8); 22:22(23); 23:3; 25:11; 29:2; 31:3(4); 33:21; 34:3(4); 41:5(6); 44:5(6),8(9),20(21); 45:17(18); 48:10(11); 49:11(12); 52:9(11); 54:1(3), 6(8); 61:5(6),8(9); 63:4(5); 66:2,4; 68:4(5); 69:30(31),36(37); 72:17,19; 74:7,10,18,21; 75:1(2); 76:1(2); 79:6,9; 80:18(19); 83:4(5),16(17),18(19); 86:9, 11,12; 89:12(13),16(17),24(25); 91:14; 92:1(2); 96:2,8; 99:3,6; 100:4; 102:15(16), 21(22); 103:1; 105:1,3; 106:8,47; 109:13, 21; 111:9; 113:1–3; 115:1; 116:4,13,17; 118:10–12,26; 119:55,132; 122:4; 124:8; 129:8; 135:1,3,13; 138:2; 140:13(14); 142:7(8); 143:11; 145:1,2,21; 147:4; 148:5,13; 149:3; **Prov.** 10:7; 18:10; 21:24; 22:1; 30:4,9; **Eccl.** 6:4,10; 7:1; **Song** 1:3; **Isa.** 4:1; 7:14; 8:3; 9:6(5); 12:4; 14:22; 18:7; 24:15; 25:1; 26:8,13; 29:23; 30:27; 40:26; 41:25; 42:8; 43:1,7; 44:5; 45:3,4; 47:4; 48:1,2,9,19; 49:1; 50:10; 51:15; 52:5,6; 54:5; 55:13; 56:5,6; 57:15; 59:19; 60:9; 62:2; 63:12,14,16,19; 64:2(1),7(6); 65:1,15; 66:5,22; **Jer.** 3:17; 7:10–12,14, 30; 10:6,16,25; 11:16,19,21; 12:16; 13:11; 14:7,9,14,15,21; 15:16; 16:21; 20:3,9; 23:6,25,27; 25:29; 26:9,16,20; 27:15; 29:9,21,23,25; 31:35; 32:18,20,34; 33:2,9; 34:15,16; 37:13; 44:16,26; 46:18; 48:15,17; 50:34; 51:19,57; 52:1; **Lam.** 3:55; **Ezek.** 16:14,15; 20:9,14,22,29, 39,44; 22:5; 23:4,10; 24:2; 34:29; 36:20–23; 39:7,13,16,25; 43:7,8; 48:1, 31,35; **Dan.** 1:7; 9:6,15,18,19; 10:1; **Hos.** 1:4,6,9; 2:17(19); **Joel** 2:26, 32(3:5); **Amos** 2:7; 4:13; 5:8,27; 6:10; 9:6,12; **Mic.** 4:5; 5:4(3); 6:9; **Nah.** 1:14; **Zeph**. 1:4; 3:9,12,19,20; **Zech.** 5:4; 6:12; 10:12; 13:2,3,9; 14:9; **Mal.** 1:6,11,14; 2:2,5; 3:16; 4:2(3:20).

8035. שֵׁם *šēm* **masc. proper noun**
(Shem)
Gen. 5:32; 6:10; 7:13; 9:18,23,26,27; 10:1,21,22,31; 11:10,11; **1 Chr.** 1:4, 17,24.

8036. שֻׁם *šum* **Aram. masc. noun**
(name; corr. to Hebr. 8034)
Ezra 5:1,4,10,14; 6:12; **Dan.** 2:20,26; 4:8(5),19(16); 5:12.

8037. שַׁמָּא *šammā'* **masc. proper noun**
(Shamma)
1 Chr. 7:37.

8038. שֶׁמְאֵבֶר *šem'ēḇer* **masc. proper noun**
(Shemeber)
Gen. 14:2.

8039. שִׁמְאָה *šim'āh* **masc. proper noun**
(Shimeah; the same as *šim'ām* [8043])
1 Chr. 8:32.

8040. שְׂמֹאוּל *śᵉmō'wl,* שְׂמֹאל *śᵉmō'l* **masc. noun**
(left hand, left side, north)
Gen. 13:9; 14:15; 24:49; 48:13,14; **Ex.** 14:22,29; **Num.** 20:17; 22:26; **Deut.** 2:27; 5:32; 17:11,20; 28:14; **Josh.** 1:7; 19:27; 23:6; **Judg.** 3:21; 7:20; 16:29; **1 Sam.** 6:12; **2 Sam.** 2:19,21; 16:6; **1 Kgs.** 7:39,49; 22:19; **2 Kgs.** 22:2; 23:8; **1 Chr.** 6:44(29); **2 Chr.** 3:17; 4:6–8; 18:18; 34:2; **Neh.** 8:4; **Job** 23:9; **Prov.**

3:16; 4:27; **Eccl.** 10:2; **Song** 2:6; 8:3; **Isa.** 9:20(19); 54:3; **Ezek.** 1:10; 16:46; 39:3; **Dan.** 12:7; **Jon.** 4:11; **Zech.** 4:3,11; 12:6.

8041. שִׂמְאֵל *śim'ēl* **verb**
(to go to the left; to use the left hand)
Gen. 13:9; **2 Sam.** 14:19; **1 Chr.** 12:2; **Isa.** 30:21; **Ezek.** 21:16(21).

8042. שְׂמָאלִי *śemā'liy* **adj.**
(on the left; on the north)
Lev. 14:15,16,26,27; **1 Kgs.** 7:21; **2 Kgs.** 11:11; **2 Chr.** 3:17; 23:10; **Ezek.** 4:4.

8043. שִׁמְאָם *šim'ām* **masc. proper noun**
(Shimeam; the same as *šim'āh* [8039])
1 Chr. 9:38.

8044. שַׁמְגַּר *šamgar* **masc. proper noun**
(Shamgar)
Judg. 3:31; 5:6.

8045. שָׁמַד *šāmad̠* **verb**
(to destroy, to demolish)
Gen. 34:30; **Lev.** 26:30; **Num.** 33:52; **Deut.** 1:27; 2:12,21–23; 4:3,26; 6:15; 7:4,23,24; 9:3,8,14,19,20,25; 12:30; 28:20,24,45,48,51,61,63; 31:3,4; 33:27; **Josh.** 7:12; 9:24; 11:14,20; 23:15; 24:8; **Judg.** 21:16; **1 Sam.** 24:21(22); **2 Sam.** 14:7,11,16; 21:5; 22:38; **1 Kgs.** 13:34; 15:29; 16:12; **2 Kgs.** 10:17,28; 21:9; **1 Chr.** 5:25; **2 Chr.** 20:10,23; 33:9; **Esth.** 3:6,13; 4:8; 7:4; 8:11; **Ps.** 37:38; 83:10(11); 92:7(8); 106:23,34; 145:20; **Prov.** 14:11; **Isa.** 10:7; 13:9; 14:23; 23:11; 26:14; 48:19; **Jer.** 48:8,42; **Lam.** 3:66; **Ezek.** 14:9; 25:7; 32:12; 34:16; **Dan.** 11:44; **Hos.** 10:8; **Amos** 2:9; 9:8; **Mic.** 5:14(13); **Hag.** 2:22; **Zech.** 12:9.

8046. שְׁמַד *šemad̠* **Aram. verb**
(to destroy, to annihilate; corr. to Hebr. 8045)
Dan. 7:26.

8047. שַׁמָּה *šāmmāh* **fem. noun**
(desolation, waste, horror)
Deut. 28:37; **2 Kgs.** 22:19; **2 Chr.** 29:8; 30:7; 36:21(KJV, NASB, *šāmēm* [8074]); **Ps.** 46:8(9); 73:19; **Isa.** 5:9; 13:9; 24:12; **Jer.** 2:15; 4:7; 5:30; 8:21; 18:16; 19:8; 25:9,11,18,38; 29:18; 42:18; 44:12,22; 46:19; 48:9; 49:13,17; 50:3,23; 51:29,37, 41,43; **Ezek.** 23:33; **Hos.** 5:9; **Joel** 1:7; **Mic.** 6:16; **Zeph.** 2:15; **Zech.** 7:14.

8048. A. שַׁמָּה *šammāh* **masc. proper noun**
(Shammah: Edomite chief, son of Reuel)
Gen. 36:13,17; **1 Chr.** 1:37.
B. שַׁמָּה *šammāh* **masc. proper noun**
(Shammah: third son of Jesse)
1 Sam. 16:9; 17:13.
C. שַׁמָּה *šammāh* **masc. proper noun**
(Shammah: son of Agee the Hararite)
2 Sam. 23:11,33.
D. שַׁמָּה *šammāh* **masc. proper noun**
(Shammah: one of David's mighty men)
2 Sam. 23:25.

8049. שַׁמְהוּת *šamhûṯ* **masc. proper noun**
(Shamhuth)
1 Chr. 27:8.

8050. A. שְׁמוּאֵל *šemû'ēl* **masc. proper noun**
(Samuel, Shemuel: a Simeonite)
Num. 34:20.
B. שְׁמוּאֵל *šemû'ēl* **masc. proper noun**

(Samuel, Shemuel: an Issacharite)
1 Chr. 7:2.
C. שְׁמוּאֵל *š^e mû'ēl* **masc. proper noun**
(the prophet Samuel)
1 Sam. 1:20; 2:18,21,26; 3:1,3,4,6–11, 15,16,18–21; 4:1; 7:3,5,6,8–10,12,13,15; 8:1,4,6,7,10,19,21,22; 9:14,15,17–19, 22–24,26,27; 10:1,9,14–17,20,24,25; 11:7,12,14; 12:1,6,11,18–20; 13:8,9,10, 11,13,15; 15:1,10–14,16,17,20,22,24, 26–28,31–35; 16:1,2,4,7,8,10,11,13; 19:18,20,22,24; 25:1; 28:3,11,12,14–16, 20; **1 Chr.** 6:28(13),33(18); 9:22; 11:3; 26:28; 29:29; **2 Chr.** 35:18; **Ps.** 99:6; **Jer.** 15:1.

8051. A. שַׁמּוּעַ *šammûa'* **masc. proper noun**
(Shammua: son of David)
2 Sam. 5:14; **1 Chr.** 14:4.
B. שַׁמּוּעַ *šammûa'* **masc. proper noun**
(Shammua: a Reubenite)
Num. 13:4.
C. שַׁמּוּעַ *šammûa'* **masc. proper noun**
(Shammua: a Levite)
Neh. 11:17.
D. שַׁמּוּעַ *šammûa'* **masc. proper noun**
(Shammua: head of a Levite family)
Neh. 12:18.

8052. שְׁמוּעָה *š^e mû'āh* **fem. noun**
(report; news; rumor)
1 Sam. 2:24; 4:19; **2 Sam.** 4:4; 13:30; **1 Kgs.** 2:28; 10:7; **2 Kgs.** 19:7; **2 Chr.** 9:6; **Ps.** 112:7; **Prov.** 15:30; 25:25; **Isa.** 28:9,19; 37:7; 53:1; **Jer.** 10:22; 49:14,23; 51:46; **Ezek.** 7:26; 16:56; 21:7(12); **Dan.** 11:44; **Obad.** 1.

8053. שָׁמוּר *šāmûr* **masc. proper noun**
(Shamur: [K^e] for [Q^e] *šāmiyr* [8069,III], which see)

8054. שַׁמּוֹת *šammôṯ* **masc. proper noun**
(Shammoth)
1 Chr. 11:27.

8055. שָׂמַח *śāmaḥ* **verb**
(to rejoice; to be joyful, to be glad; to gloat)
Ex. 4:14; **Lev.** 23:40; **Deut.** 12:7,12,18; 14:26; 16:11,14; 24:5; 26:11; 27:7; 33:18; **Judg.** 9:13,19; 19:3; **1 Sam.** 2:1; 6:13; 11:9,15; 19:5; **2 Sam.** 1:20; **1 Kgs.** 5:7(21); **2 Kgs.** 11:20; **1 Chr.** 16:10,31; 29:9; **2 Chr.** 6:41; 15:15; 20:27; 23:21; 24:10; 29:36; 30:25; **Ezra** 6:22; **Neh.** 12:43; **Esth.** 8:15(KJV, *śāmēḥ* [8056]); **Job** 21:12; 22:19; 31:25,29; **Ps.** 5:11(12); 9:2(3); 14:7; 16:9; 19:8(9); 21:1(2); 30:1; 31:7(8); 32:11; 33:21; 34:2(3); 35:15,19, 24,27; 38:16(17); 40:16(17); 45:8(9); 46:4(5); 48:11(12); 53:6(7); 58:10(11); 63:11(12); 64:10(11); 66:6; 67:4(5); 68:3(4); 69:32(33); 70:4(5); 85:6(7); 86:4; 89:42(43); 90:14,15; 92:4(5); 96:11; 97:1, 8,12; 104:15,31,34; 105:3,38; 106:5; 107:30,42; 109:28; 118:24; 119:74; 122:1; 149:2; **Prov.** 5:18; 10:1; 12:25; 13:9; 15:20,30; 17:5(KJV, NASB, *śāmēḥ* [8056]),21; 23:15,24,25; 24:17; 27:9,11; 29:2,3,6; **Eccl.** 3:12,22; 4:16; 5:19(18); 8:15; 10:19; 11:8,9; **Song** 1:4; **Isa.** 9:3(2),17(16); 14:8,29; 25:9; 39:2; 56:7; 65:13; 66:10; **Jer.** 20:15; 31:13; 41:13; 50:11; **Lam.** 2:17; 4:21; **Ezek.** 7:12; 26:6; 35:14; **Hos.** 7:3; 9:1; **Joel** 2:21,23; **Amos** 6:13(NASB, NIV, *śāmēḥ* [8056]); **Obad.** 1:12; **Jon.** 4:6; **Mic.** 7:8; **Hab.** 1:15; **Zeph.** 3:14; **Zech.** 2:10(14); 4:10; 10:7.

8056. שָׂמֵחַ *śāmēaḥ* **adj.**
(glad, happy, merry, joyful)
Deut. 16:15; **1 Kgs.** 1:40,45; 4:20; 8:66; **2 Kgs.** 11:14; **2 Chr.** 7:10; 23:13; **Esth.** 5:9,14; 8:15(NASB, NIV, *śāmaḥ* [8055]); **Job** 3:22; **Ps.** 35:26; 113:9; 126:3; **Prov.** 2:14; 15:13; 17:5(NIV, *śāmaḥ* [8055]),22;

Eccl. 2:10; **Isa.** 24:7; **Amos** 6:13(KJV, *śāmaḥ* [8055]).

8057. שִׂמְחָה *śimḥāh* **fem. noun**
(joy, rejoicing, gladness, pleasure)
Gen. 31:27; **Num.** 10:10; **Deut.** 28:47; **Judg.** 16:23; **1 Sam.** 18:6; **2 Sam.** 6:12; **1 Kgs.** 1:40; **1 Chr.** 12:40(41); 15:16,25; 29:9,17,22; **2 Chr.** 20:27; 23:18; 29:30; 30:21,23,26; **Ezra** 3:12,13; 6:22; **Neh.** 8:12,17; 12:27,43,44; **Esth.** 8:16,17; 9:17–19,22; **Job** 20:5; **Ps.** 4:7(8); 16:11; 21:6(7); 30:11(12); 43:4; 45:15(16); 51:8(10); 68:3(4); 97:11; 100:2; 106:5; 137:3,6; **Prov.** 10:28; 12:20; 14:10,13; 15:21,23; 21:15,17; **Eccl.** 2:1,2,10,26; 5:20(19); 7:4; 8:15; 9:7; **Song** 3:11; **Isa.** 9:3(2); 16:10; 22:13; 24:11; 29:19; 30:29; 35:10; 51:3,11; 55:12; 61:7; 66:5; **Jer.** 7:34; 15:16; 16:9; 25:10; 31:7; 33:11; 48:33; **Ezek.** 35:15; 36:5; **Joel** 1:16; **Jon.** 4:6; **Zeph.** 3:17; **Zech.** 8:19.

8058. שָׁמַט *šāmaṭ* **verb**
(to throw down, to cancel, to release; to stumble)
Ex. 23:11; **Deut.** 15:2,3; **2 Sam.** 6:6; **2 Kgs.** 9:33; **1 Chr.** 13:9; **Ps.** 141:6; **Jer.** 17:4.

8059. שְׁמִטָּה *šᵉmiṭṭāh* **fem. noun**
(release, cancelling of debt)
Deut. 15:1,2,9; 31:10.

8060. A. שַׁמַּי *šammay* **masc. proper noun**
(Shammai: son of Onam)
1 Chr. 2:28,32.
B. שַׁמַּי *šammay* **masc. proper noun**
(Shammai: son of Rekem)
1 Chr. 2:44,45.
C. שַׁמַּי *šammay* **masc. proper noun**
(Shammai: son of Mered)
1 Chr. 4:17.

8061. שְׁמִידָע *šᵉmiyḏāʿ* **masc. proper noun**
(Shemida)
Num. 26:32; **Josh.** 17:2; **1 Chr.** 7:19.

8062. שְׁמִידָעִי *šᵉmiyḏāʿiy* **masc. proper noun**
(Shemidaite)
Num. 26:32.

8063. I. שְׂמִיכָה *śᵉmiyḵāh* **fem. noun**
(mantle, covering)
Judg. 4:18(NASB, see II).
II. שְׂמִיכָה *śᵉmiyḵāh* **fem. noun**
(rug)
Judg. 4:18(KJV, NIV, see I).

8064. שָׁמַיִם *šāmayim* **masc. dual noun**
(heaven, sky)
Gen. 1:1,8,9,14,15,17,20,26,28,30; 2:1,4,19,20; 6:7,17; 7:3,11,19,23; 8:2; 9:2; 11:4; 14:19,22; 15:5; 19:24; 21:17; 22:11,15,17; 24:3,7; 26:4; 27:28,39; 28:12,17; 49:25; **Ex.** 9:8,10,22,23; 10:21, 22; 16:4; 17:14; 20:4,11,22; 24:10; 31:17; 32:13; **Lev.** 26:19; **Deut.** 1:10,28; 2:25; 3:24; 4:11,17,19,26,32,36,39; 5:8; 7:24; 9:1,14; 10:14,22; 11:11,17,21; 17:3; 25:19; 26:15; 28:12,23,24,26,62; 29:20(19); 30:4,12,19; 31:28; 32:1,40; 33:13,26,28; **Josh.** 2:11; 8:20; 10:11,13; **Judg.** 5:4,20; 13:20; 20:40; **1 Sam.** 2:10; 5:12; 17:44,46; **2 Sam.** 18:9; 21:10; 22:8,10,14; **1 Kgs.** 8:22,23,27,30,32,34–36,39,43,45,49,54; 14:11; 16:4; 18:45; 21:24; 22:19; **2 Kgs.** 1:10,12,14; 2:1,11; 7:2,19; 14:27; 17:16; 19:15; 21:3,5; 23:4,5; **1 Chr.** 16:26,31; 21:16,26; 27:23; 29:11; **2 Chr.** 2:6(5), 12(11); 6:13,14,18,21,23,25–27,30,33, 35,39; 7:1,13,14; 18:18; 20:6; 28:9; 30:27; 32:20; 33:3,5; 36:23; **Ezra** 1:2; 9:6; **Neh.** 1:4,5,9; 2:4,20; 9:6,13,15,23, 27,28; **Job** 1:16; 2:12; 9:8; 11:8; 12:7; 14:12; 15:15; 16:19; 20:6,27; 22:12,14; 26:11,13; 28:21,24; 35:5,11; 37:3; 38:29,

33,37; 41:11(3); **Ps.** 2:4; 8:1(2),3(4),8(9); 11:4; 14:2; 18:9(10),13(14); 19:1(2),6(7); 20:6(7); 33:6,13; 36:5(6); 50:4,6; 53:2(3); 57:3(4),5(6),10(11),11(12); 68:8(9), 33(34); 69:34(35); 73:9,25; 76:8(9); 78:23,24,26; 79:2; 80:14(15); 85:11(12); 89:2(3),5(6),11(12),29(30); 96:5,11; 97:6; 102:19(20),25(26); 103:11,19; 104:2,12; 105:40; 107:26; 108:4(5),5(6); 113:4,6; 115:3,15,16; 119:89; 121:2; 123:1; 124:8; 134:3; 135:6; 136:5,26; 139:8; 144:5; 146:6; 147:8; 148:1,4,13; **Prov.** 3:19; 8:27; 23:5; 25:3; 30:4,19; **Eccl.** 1:13; 2:3; 3:1; 5:2(1); 10:20; **Isa.** 1:2; 13:5,10,13; 14:12,13; 34:4,5; 37:16; 40:12,22; 42:5; 44:23,24; 45:8,12,18; 47:13; 48:13; 49:13; 50:3; 51:6,13,16; 55:9,10; 63:15; 64:1 (63:19); 65:17; 66:1,22; **Jer.** 2:12; 4:23, 25,28; 7:18,33; 8:2,7; 9:10(9); 10:2,12,13; 14:22; 15:3; 16:4; 19:7,13; 23:24; 31:37; 32:17; 33:22,25; 34:20; 44:17–19,25; 49:36; 51:9,15,16,48,53; **Lam.** 2:1; 3:41, 50,66; 4:19; **Ezek.** 1:1; 8:3; 29:5; 31:6,13; 32:4,7,8; 38:20; **Dan.** 8:8,10; 9:12; 11:4; 12:7; **Hos.** 2:18(20),21(23); 4:3; 7:12; **Joel** 2:10,30(3:3); 3:16(4:16); **Amos** 9:2,6; **Jon.** 1:9; **Nah.** 3:16; **Hab.** 3:3; **Zeph.** 1:3,5; **Hag.** 1:10; 2:6,21; **Zech.** 2:6(10); 5:9; 6:5; 8:12; 12:1; **Mal.** 3:10.

8065. שְׁמַיִן *šemayin* **Aram. masc. dual noun**
(heaven, sky; corr. to Hebr. 8064)
Ezra 5:11,12; 6:9,10; 7:12,21,23; **Jer.** 10:11; **Dan.** 2:18,19,28,37,38,44; 4:11–13(8–10),15(12),20–23(17–20), 25(22),26(23),31(28),33–35(30–32), 37(34); 5:21,23; 6:27(28); 7:2,13,27.

8066. שְׁמִינִי *š^e^miyniy* **adj.**
(eighth)
Ex. 22:30(29); **Lev.** 9:1; 12:3; 14:10,23; 15:14,29; 22:27; 23:36,39; 25:22; **Num.** 6:10; 7:54; 29:35; **1 Kgs.** 6:38; 8:66; 12:32,33; **1 Chr.** 12:12; 24:10; 25:15; 26:5; 27:11; **2 Chr.** 7:9; **Neh.** 8:18; **Ezek.** 43:27; **Zech.** 1:1.

8067. שְׁמִינִית *š^e^miyniyṯ* **fem. noun**
(musical term; perhaps signifying an instrument or an octave)
1 Chr. 15:21; **Ps.** 6:[title](1); 12:[title](1).

8068. I. שָׁמִיר *šāmiyr* **masc. noun**
(brier)
Isa. 5:6; 7:23–25; 9:18(17); 10:17; 27:4; 32:13.
II. שָׁמִיר *šāmiyr* **masc. noun**
(flint stone, diamond)
Jer. 17:1; **Ezek.** 3:9; **Zech.** 7:12.

8069. I. שָׁמִיר *šāmiyr* **proper noun**
(Shamir: a town in Judah)
Josh. 15:48.
II. שָׁמִיר *šāmiyr* **proper noun**
(Shamir: a town in Ephraim)
Judg. 10:1,2.
III. שָׁמִיר *šāmiyr* **masc. proper noun**
(Shamir: a Levite in David's day)
1 Chr. 24:24.

8070. A. שְׁמִירָמוֹת *š^e^miyrāmôṯ* **masc. proper noun**
(Shemiramoth: Levite harpist in David's day)
1 Chr. 15:18,20; 16:5.
B. שְׁמִירָמוֹת *š^e^miyrāmôṯ* **masc. proper noun**
(Shemiramoth: Levite teacher in Jehoshaphat's day)
2 Chr. 17:8.

8071. שִׂמְלָה *śimlāh* **fem. noun**
(clothing, garment)
Gen. 9:23; 35:2; 37:34; 41:14; 44:13; 45:22; **Ex.** 3:22; 12:34,35; 19:10,14; 22:27(26); **Deut.** 8:4; 10:18; 21:13; 22:3,5,17; **Josh.** 7:6; **Judg.** 8:25; **Ruth** 3:3; **1 Sam.** 21:9(10); **2 Sam.** 12:20; **Prov.** 30:4; **Isa.** 3:6,7; 4:1; 9:5(4).

8072. שַׂמְלָה *śamlāh* **masc. proper noun**
(Samlah)
Gen. 36:36,37; **1 Chr.** 1:47,48.

8073. שַׁמְלַי *šamlay* **masc. proper noun**
("Shamlai," the [K^{e}] for the [Q^{e}] *šalmay* [8014] in Ezra 2:46; see *šalmay* [8014])

8074. שָׁמֵם *šāmēm* **verb**
(to be desolate; to be astonished, to be appalled)
Gen. 47:19(KJV, NASB, *yāšam* [3456]); **Lev.** 26:22,31,32,34,35,43; **Num.** 21:30; **1 Sam.** 5:6; **2 Sam.** 13:20; **1 Kgs.** 9:8; **2 Chr.** 7:21; 36:21(NIV, *šāmāh* [8047]); **Ezra** 9:3,4; **Job** 16:7; 17:8; 18:20; 21:5; **Ps.** 40:15(16); 69:25(26); 79:7; 143:4; **Eccl.** 7:16; **Isa.** 33:8; 49:8,19; 52:14; 54:1,3; 59:16; 61:4; 63:5; **Jer.** 2:12; 4:9; 10:25; 12:11; 18:16; 19:8; 33:10; 49:17, 20; 50:13,45; **Lam.** 1:4,13,16; 3:11; 4:5; 5:18; **Ezek.** 3:15; 4:17; 6:4,6(KJV, *yāšam* [3456]); 12:19(KJV, NASB, *yāšam* [3456]); 19:7(KJV, NASB, *yāšam* [3456]); 20:26; 25:3; 26:16; 27:35; 28:19; 29:12; 30:7,12, 14; 32:10,15; 33:28; 35:12,15; 36:3,4, 34–36; **Dan.** 8:13,27; 9:18,26,27(KJV, *šāmēm* [8076]); 11:31; 12:11; **Hos.** 2:12(14); **Joel** 1:17; **Amos** 7:9; 9:14; **Mic.** 6:13; **Zeph.** 3:6; **Zech.** 7:14.

8075. שְׁמַם *š^{e}mam* **Aram. verb**
(to be astonished, to be appalled; corr. to Hebr. 8074)
Dan. 4:19(16).

8076. שָׁמֵם *šāmēm* **adj.**
(desolate)
Jer. 12:11; **Dan.** 9:17,27(NASB, NIV, *šāmam* [8074]).

8077. I. שִׁמָּמָה *šimmāh* **fem. noun**
(desolation, dismay, horror)
Ezek. 35:7.
II. שְׁמָמָה *š^{e}māmāh* **fem. noun**
(waste, desolation, devastation)
Ex. 23:29; **Lev.** 26:33; **Josh.** 8:28; **Isa.** 1:7; 6:11; 17:9; 62:4; 64:10(9); **Jer.** 4:27; 6:8; 9:11(10); 10:22; 12:10,11; 25:12; 32:43; 34:22; 44:6; 49:2,33; 50:13; 51:26, 62; **Ezek.** 6:14; 7:27; 12:20; 14:15,16; 15:8; 23:33; 29:9,10,12; 32:15; 33:28,29; 35:3,4,7,9,14,15; 36:34; **Joel** 2:3,20; 3:19(4:19); **Mic.** 1:7; 7:13; **Zeph.** 1:13; 2:4,9,13; **Mal.** 1:3.

8078. שִׁמָּמוֹן *šimmāmôn* **masc. noun**
(astonishment, horror, despair)
Ezek. 4:16; 12:19.

8079. I. שְׂמָמִית *ś^{e}māmiyṯ* **fem. noun**
(lizard)
Prov. 30:28(KJV, see II).
II. שְׂמָמִית *ś^{e}māmiyṯ* **fem. noun**
(spider)
Prov. 30:28(NASB, NIV, see I).

8080. שָׁמַן *šāman*, שָׁמֵן *šāmēn* **verb**
(to be fat; to become fat)
Deut. 32:15; **Neh.** 9:25; **Isa.** 6:10(KJV, *šamēn* [8082,I]); **Jer.** 5:28.

8081. שֶׁמֶן *šemen* **masc. noun**
(oil, fat; olive; ointment, perfume)
Gen. 28:18; 35:14; **Ex.** 25:6; 27:20; 29:2, 7,21,23,40; 30:24,25,31; 31:11; 35:8,14, 15,28; 37:29; 39:37,38; 40:9; **Lev.** 2:1, 2,4–7,15,16; 5:11; 6:15(8),21(14); 7:10, 12; 8:2,10,12,26,30; 9:4; 10:7; 14:10, 12,15–18,21,24,26–29; 21:10,12; 23:13; 24:2; **Num.** 4:9,16; 5:15; 6:15; 7:13,19, 25,31,37,43,49,55,61,67,73,79; 8:8; 11:8; 15:4,6,9; 28:5,9,12,13,20,28; 29:3,9,14; 35:25; **Deut.** 8:8; 28:40; 32:13; 33:24; **1 Sam.** 10:1; 16:1,13; **2 Sam.** 1:21; 14:2; **1 Kgs.** 1:39; 5:11(25); 6:23,31–33; 17:12,14,16; **2 Kgs.** 4:2,6,7; 9:1,3,6; 20:13; **1 Chr.** 9:29; 12:40(41); 27:28; **2 Chr.** 2:10(9),15(14); 11:11; **Ezra** 3:7; **Neh.** 8:15; **Esth.** 2:12; **Job** 29:6; **Ps.** 23:5; 45:7(8); 55:21(22); 89:20(21);

92:10(11); 104:15; 109:18,24; 133:2; 141:5; **Prov.** 5:3; 21:17,20; 27:9,16; **Eccl.** 7:1; 9:8; 10:1; **Song** 1:3; 4:10; **Isa.** 1:6; 5:1; 10:27; 25:6; 28:1,4; 39:2; 41:19; 57:9; 61:3; **Jer.** 40:10; 41:8; **Ezek.** 16:9,13,18,19; 23:41; 27:17; 32:14; 45:14,24,25; 46:5,7,11,14,15; **Hos.** 2:5(7); 12:1(2); **Amos** 6:6; **Mic.** 6:7,15; **Hag.** 2:12.

8082. I. שָׁמֵן *šāmēn* **adj.**
(fat, rich, plentiful; robust)
Gen. 49:20; **Num.** 13:20; **Judg.** 3:29; **1 Chr.** 4:40; **Neh.** 9:25,35; **Isa.** 6:10 (NASB, NIV, *šāman* [8080]); 30:23; **Ezek.** 34:14,16; **Hab.** 1:16.
II. שָׁמָן *šāmān* **masc. noun**
(richness [of earth])
Gen. 27:28(KJV, *mišmān* [4924]),39(KJV, *mišmān* [4924]).

8083. שְׁמֹנֶה *š^{e}mōneh,* שְׁמֹנָה *š^{e}mōnāh* **fem. noun**
(eight, eighth; NIV, see also *š^{e}mōniym* [8084])
Gen. 5:4,7,10,13,16,17,19; 14:14; 17:12; 21:4; 22:23; **Ex.** 26:2,25; 36:9,30; **Num.** 2:24; 3:28; 4:48; 7:8; 29:29; 35:7; **Deut.** 2:14; **Josh.** 21:41; **Judg.** 3:8,14; 10:8; 12:14; 20:25,44; **1 Sam.** 4:15; 17:12; **2 Sam.** 8:13; 23:8; 24:9; **1 Kgs.** 7:10,15; 15:1; 16:29; **2 Kgs.** 3:1; 8:17; 10:36; 15:8; 22:1,3; 23:23; 24:8,12; 25:17; **1 Chr.** 12:24(25),30(31),31(32),35(36); 16:38; 18:12; 23:3; 24:4,15; 25:7,25; 26:9; 29:7; **2 Chr.** 11:21; 13:1,3; 21:5,20; 29:17; 34:1,3,8; 35:19; 36:9; **Ezra** 2:6,16, 23,41; 8:9,11,18; **Neh.** 7:11,13,15,16, 21,22,26,27,44,45; 11:6,8,12,14; **Eccl.** 11:2; **Jer.** 32:1; 41:15; 52:21,29; **Ezek.** 40:9,31,34,37,41; 48:35; **Mic.** 5:5(4).

8084. שְׁמֹנִים *š^{e}mōniym,* שְׁמוֹנִים *š^{e}môniym* **pl. adj.**
(eighty, eightieth; NIV, regards as the plural of *š^{e}mōneh* [8083])
Gen. 5:25,26,28; 16:16; 35:28; **Ex.** 7:7; **Num.** 2:9; 4:48; **Josh.** 14:10; **Judg.** 3:30; **1 Sam.** 22:18; **2 Sam.** 19:32(33), 35(36); **1 Kgs.** 5:15(29); 6:1; 12:21; **2 Kgs.** 6:25; 10:24; 19:35; **1 Chr.** 7:5; 15:9; 25:7; **2 Chr.** 2:2(1),18(17); 11:1; 14:8(7); 17:15,18; 26:17; **Ezra** 8:8; **Neh.** 7:26; 11:18; **Esth.** 1:4; **Ps.** 90:10; **Song** 6:8; **Isa.** 37:36; **Jer.** 41:5.

8085. שָׁמַע *šāma'* **verb**
(to hear, to listen, to obey; to publish [cause to be heard])
Gen. 3:8,10,17; 4:23; 11:7; 14:14; 16:2,11; 17:20; 18:10; 21:6,12,17,26; 22:18; 23:6,8,11,13,15,16; 24:30,52; 26:5; 27:5,6,8,13,34,43; 28:7; 29:13,33; 30:6,17,22; 31:1; 34:5,7,17,24; 35:22; 37:6,17,21,27; 39:10,15,19; 41:15; 42:2, 21–23; 43:25; 45:2,16; 49:2; **Ex.** 2:15,24; 3:7,18; 4:1,8,9,31; 5:2; 6:5,9,12,30; 7:4, 13,16,22; 8:15(11),19(15); 9:12; 11:9; 15:14,26; 16:7–9,12,20; 18:1,19,24; 19:5,9; 20:19; 22:23(22),27(26); 23:13, 21,22; 24:7; 28:35; 32:17,18; 33:4; **Lev.** 5:1; 10:20; 24:14; 26:14,18,21,27; **Num.** 7:89; 9:8; 11:1,10; 12:2,6; 14:13–15,22,27; 16:4,8; 20:10,16; 21:1,3; 22:36; 23:18; 24:4,16; 27:20; 30:4(5),5(6),7(8),8(9), 11(12),12(13),14(15),15(16); 33:40; **Deut.** 1:16,17,34,43,45; 2:25; 3:26; 4:1,6,10,12,28,30,32,33,36; 5:1, 23–28(20–25); 6:3,4; 7:12; 8:20; 9:1,2,19,23; 10:10; 11:13,27,28; 12:28; 13:3(4),4(5),8(9),11(12),12(13),18(19); 15:5; 17:4,12,13; 18:14–16,19; 19:20; 20:3; 21:18,20,21; 23:5(6); 26:7,14,17; 27:9,10; 28:1,2,13,15,45,49,62; 29:4(3), 19(18); 30:2,8,10,12,13,17,20; 31:12,13; 32:1; 33:7; 34:9; **Josh.** 1:17,18; 2:10,11; 3:9; 5:1,6; 6:5,10,20; 7:9; 9:1,3,9,16; 10:1,14; 11:1; 14:12; 22:2,11,12,30; 24:10,24,27; **Judg.** 2:2,17,20; 3:4; 5:3, 16; 6:10; 7:11,15; 9:7,30,46; 11:10,17,28; 13:9,23; 14:13; 18:25; 19:25; 20:3,13; **Ruth** 1:6; 2:8; **1 Sam.** 1:13; 2:22–25; 3:9–11; 4:6,14,19; 7:7; 8:7,9,19,21,22; 9:27; 11:6; 12:1,14,15; 13:3,4; 14:22,27;

15:1,4,14,19,20,22,24; 16:2; 17:11,23, 28,31; 19:6; 22:1,6,7,12; 23:8,10,11,25; 24:9(10); 25:4,7,24,35,39; 26:19; 28:18, 21–23; 30:24; 31:11; **2 Sam.** 3:28; 4:1; 5:17,24; 7:22; 8:9; 10:7; 11:26; 12:18; 13:14,16,21; 14:16,17; 15:3,10,35,36; 16:21; 17:5,9; 18:5; 19:2(3),35(36); 20:16,17; 22:7,45; **1 Kgs.** 1:11,41,45; 2:42; 3:9,11,28; 4:34(5:14); 5:1(15), 7(21),8(22); 6:7; 8:28–30,32,34,36,39, 42,43,45,49,52; 9:3; 10:1,6–8,24; 11:21,38; 12:2,15,16,20,24; 13:4,26; 14:6; 15:20–22; 16:16; 17:22; 19:13; 20:8,12,25,31,36; 21:15,16,17; 22:19,28; **2 Kgs.** 3:21; 5:8; 6:30; 7:1,6; 9:30; 10:6; 11:13; 13:4; 14:11; 16:9; 17:14,40; 18:12, 26,28,31,32; 19:1,4,6–9,11,16,20,25; 20:5,12,13,16; 21:9,12; 22:11,13,18,19; 25:23; **1 Chr.** 10:11; 14:8,15; 15:16, 19,28; 16:5,42; 17:20; 18:9; 19:8; 28:2; 29:23; **2 Chr.** 5:13; 6:19–21,23,25,27,30, 33,35,39; 7:12,14; 9:1,5–7,23; 10:2, 15,16; 11:4; 13:4; 15:2,8; 16:4,5; 18:18,27; 20:9,20,29; 23:12; 24:17; 25:16,20; 28:11; 29:5; 30:20,27; 33:13; 34:19,26,27; 35:22; **Ezra** 3:13; 4:1; 9:3; **Neh.** 1:4,6; 2:10,19; 4:1(3:33),4(3:36), 7(1),15(9),20(14); 5:6; 6:1,6,7,16; 8:2,9,15; 9:9,16,17,27–29; 12:42,43; 13:3,27; **Esth.** 1:18,20; 2:8; 3:4; **Job** 2:11; 3:18; 4:16; 5:27; 13:1,6,17; 15:8,17; 16:2; 20:3; 21:2; 22:27; 26:14; 27:9; 28:22; 29:11,21; 31:35; 32:10; 33:1,8, 31,33; 34:2,10,16,28,34; 35:13; 36:11,12; 37:2,4; 39:7; 42:4,5; **Ps.** 4:1(12),3(4); 5:3(4); 6:8(9),9(10); 10:17; 17:1,6; 18:6(7),44(45); 19:3(4); 22:24(25); 26:7; 27:7; 28:2,6; 30:10(11); 31:13(14), 22(23); 34:2(3),6(7),11(12),17(18); 38:13(14),14(15); 39:12(13); 40:1(2); 44:1(2); 45:10(11); 48:8(9); 49:1(2); 50:7; 51:8(10); 54:2(4); 55:17(18),19(20); 58:5(6); 59:7(8); 61:1(2),5(6); 62:11(12); 64:1(2); 65:2(3); 66:8,16,18,19; 69:33(34); 76:8(9); 78:3,21,59; 81:5(6),8(9),11(12), 13(14); 84:8(9); 85:8(9); 92:11(12); 94:9; 95:7; 97:8; 102:1(2),20(21); 103:20; 106:2,25,44; 115:6; 116:1; 119:149; 130:2; 132:6; 138:4; 141:6; 143:1,8; 145:19; **Prov.** 1:5,18,33; 4:1,10; 5:7,13; 7:24; 8:6,32–34; 12:15; 13:1,8; 15:29, 31,32; 18:13; 19:20,27; 20:12; 21:28; 22:17; 23:19,22; 25:10,12; 28:9; 29:24; **Eccl.** 1:8; 5:1(4:17); 7:5,21; 9:16,17; 12:13; **Song** 2:12,14; 8:13; **Isa.** 1:2,10, 15,19; 6:8–10; 7:13; 15:4; 16:6; 18:3; 21:3,10; 24:16; 28:12,14,22,23; 29:18; 30:9,19,21,30; 32:3,9; 33:13,15,19; 34:1; 36:11,13,16; 37:1,4,6–9,11,17,26; 38:5; 39:1,5; 40:21,28; 41:22,26; 42:2,9,18,20, 23,24; 43:9,12; 44:1,8; 45:21; 46:3,12; 47:8; 48:1,3,5–8,12,14,16,20; 49:1; 50:4, 10; 51:1,7,21; 52:7,15; 55:2,3; 58:4; 59:1, 2; 60:18; 62:11; 64:4(3); 65:12,19,24; 66:4,5,8,19; **Jer.** 2:4; 3:13,21,25; 4:5,15, 16,19,21,31; 5:15,20,21; 6:7,10,18,19,24; 7:2,13,16,23,24,26–28; 8:6,16; 9:10(9), 13(12),19(18),20(19); 10:1; 11:2–4,6–8, 10,11,14; 12:17; 13:10,11,15,17; 14:12; 16:12; 17:20,23,24,27; 18:2,10,13,19,22; 19:3,15; 20:1,10,16; 21:11; 22:2,5,21,29; 23:16,18,22,25; 25:3,4,7,8; 26:3–5,7, 10–13,21; 27:9,14,16,17; 28:7,15; 29:8, 12,19,20; 30:5; 31:7,10,15,18; 32:23,33; 33:9,10; 34:4,10,14,17; 35:8,10,13–18; 36:3,11,13,16,24,25,31; 37:2,5,14,20; 38:1,7,15,20,25,27; 40:3,7,11; 41:11; 42:4,6,13–15,21; 43:4,7; 44:5,16,23,24,26; 46:12,14; 48:4,5,29; 49:2,14,20,21,23; 50:2,29,43,45,46; 51:27,46,51; **Lam.** 1:18,21; 3:56,61; **Ezek.** 1:24,28; 2:2,5, 7,8; 3:6,7,10–12,17,27; 6:3; 8:18; 10:5; 12:2; 13:2,19; 16:35; 18:25; 19:4,9; 20:8,39,47(21:3); 25:3; 26:13; 27:30; 33:4,5,7,30–32; 34:7,9; 35:12,13; 36:1, 4,15; 37:4; 40:4; 43:6; 44:5; **Dan.** 1:14; 8:13,16; 9:6,10,11,14,17–19; 10:9,12; 12:7,8; **Hos.** 4:1; 5:1; 9:17; **Joel** 1:2; **Amos** 3:1,9,13; 4:1,5; 5:1,23; 7:16; 8:4,11; **Obad.** 1:1; **Jon.** 2:2(3); **Mic.** 1:2; 3:1,9; 5:15; 6:1,2,9; 7:7; **Nah.** 1:15(2:1), 2:13(14); 3:19; **Hab.** 1:2; 3:2,16; **Zeph.** 2:8; 3:2; **Hag.** 1:12; **Zech.** 1:4; 3:8; 6:15; 7:11–13; 8:9,23; **Mal.** 2:2; 3:16.

8086. שְׁמַע *š^ema'* **Aram. verb**
(to hear, to obey; corr. to Hebr. 8085)
Dan. 3:5,7,10,15; 5:14,16,23; 6:14(15); 7:27.

8087. A. שֶׁמַע *šema'* **masc. proper noun**
(Shema: son of Hebron)
1 Chr. 2:43,44.
B. שֶׁמַע *šema'* **masc. proper noun**
(Shema: a Reubenite)
1 Chr. 5:8.
C. שֶׁמַע *šema'* **masc. proper noun**
(Shema: a Benjamite)
1 Chr. 8:13.
D. שֶׁמַע *šema'* **masc. proper noun**
(Shema: a postexilic Jew)
Neh. 8:4.

8088. I. שֶׁמַע *šema'* **masc. noun**
(sound, loud noise, clash, musical noise)
Ps. 150:5.
II. שֵׁמַע *šēma'* **masc. noun**
(sound, report, news, fame; hearing)
Gen. 29:13; **Ex.** 23:1; **Num.** 14:15; **Deut.** 2:25; **1 Kgs.** 10:1; **2 Chr.** 9:1; **Job** 28:22; 42:5; **Ps.** 18:44(45); **Isa.** 23:5; 66:19; **Jer.** 37:5; 50:43; **Hos.** 7:12; **Nah.** 3:19; **Hab.** 3:2.

8089. שֹׁמַע *šōma'* **masc. noun**
(fame, report, reputation)
Josh. 6:27; 9:9; **Esth.** 9:4; **Jer.** 6:24.

8090. שְׁמַע *š^ema'* **proper noun**
(Shema)
Josh. 15:26.

8091. שָׁמָע *šāmā'* **masc. proper noun**
(Shama)
1 Chr. 11:44.

8092. A. שִׁמְעָא *šim'ā'* **masc. proper noun**
(Shimea: brother of David; the same as *šim'āh* [8093])
1 Chr. 2:13; 20:7.
B. שִׁמְעָא *šim'ā'* **masc. proper noun**
(Shimea: son of David)
1 Chr. 3:5.
C. שִׁמְעָא *šim'ā'* **masc. proper noun**
(Shimea: a Merarite Levite)
1 Chr. 6:30(15).
D. שִׁמְעָא *šim'ā'* **masc. proper noun**
(Shimea: a Kohathite Levite)
1 Chr. 6:39(24).

8093. שִׁמְעָה *šim'āh* **masc. proper noun**
(Shimeah: brother of David; the same as *šim'a'* [8092,A])
2 Sam. 13:3,32; 21:21(NASB, [K^e] *šim'iy* [8096,C]).

8094. שְׁמָעָה *š^emā'āh* **masc. proper noun**
(Shemaah)
1 Chr. 12:3.

8095. A. שִׁמְעוֹן *šim'ôn* **masc. proper noun**
(Simeon: son of Jacob)
Gen. 29:33; 34:25,30; 35:23; 42:24,26; 43:23; 46:10; 48:5; 49:5; **Ex.** 1:2; 6:15; **Num.** 1:6,22,23; 2:12; 7:36; 10:19; 13:5; 26:12; 34:20; **Deut.** 27:12; **Josh.** 19:1, 8,9; 21:9; **Judg.** 1:3,17; **1 Chr.** 2:1; 4:24,42; 6:65(50); 12:25; **2 Chr.** 15:9; 34:6; **Ezek.** 48:24,25,33.
B. שִׁמְעוֹן *šim'ôn* **masc. proper noun**
(Simeon: a layman with a foreign wife in Ezra's day)
Ezra 10:31.

8096. A. שִׁמְעִי *šim'iy* **masc. proper noun**
(Shimei: grandson of Levi)
Ex. 6:17; **Num.** 3:18; **1 Chr.** 6:17(2), 42(29); 23:7,9,10.

B. שִׁמְעִי *šim'iy* **masc. proper noun**
(Shimei: descendant of Saul; possibly the same as R)
2 Sam. 16:5,7,13; 19:16(17),18(19),21(22),23(24); **1 Kgs.** 2:8,36,38–42,44.
C. שִׁמְעִי *šim'iy* **masc. proper noun**
(Shimei: brother of David; the same as *šim'a'* [8092,A] and *šim'āh* [8093])
2 Sam. 21:21(KJV, NIV, [Q^e] *šim'āh* [8093].
D. שִׁמְעִי *šim'iy* **masc. proper noun**
(Shimei: supporter of Solomon; possibly the same as E)
1 Kgs. 1:8.
E. שִׁמְעִי *šim'iy* **masc. proper noun**
(Shimei: officer of Solomon; possibly the same as D)
1 Kgs. 4:18.
F. שִׁמְעִי *šim'iy* **masc. proper noun**
(Shimei: brother of Zerubbabel)
1 Chr. 3:19.
G. שִׁמְעִי *šim'iy* **masc. proper noun**
(Shimei: head of a Simeonite family)
1 Chr. 4:26,27.
H. שִׁמְעִי *šim'iy* **masc. proper noun**
(Shimei: head of a Reubenite family)
1 Chr. 5:4.
I. שִׁמְעִי *šim'iy* **masc. proper noun**
(Shimei: Levite descended from Merari)
1 Chr. 6:29(14).
J. שִׁמְעִי *šim'iy* **masc. proper noun**
(Shimei: head of a Benjamite family)
1 Chr. 8:21.
K. שִׁמְעִי *šim'iy* **masc. proper noun**
(Shimei: a levitical singer under David)
1 Chr. 25:3(not in Hebr. or KJV; supplied in NASB, NIV, from some Sept. MSS),27.
L. שִׁמְעִי *šim'iy* **masc. proper noun**
(Shimei: officer under David)
1 Chr. 27:27.
M. שִׁמְעִי *šim'iy* **masc. proper noun**
(Shimei: a levitical official descended from Heman in Hezekiah's day; possibly the same as N)
2 Chr. 29:14.
N. שִׁמְעִי *šim'iy* **masc. proper noun**
(Shimei: Levite in charge of contributions in Hezekiah's day; possibly the same as M)
2 Chr. 31:12,13.
O. שִׁמְעִי *šim'iy* **masc. proper noun**
(Shimei: a Levite who divorced a foreign wife in Ezra's day)
Ezra 10:23.
P. שִׁמְעִי *šim'iy* **masc. proper noun**
(Shimei: a layman who divorced a foreign wife in Ezra's day)
Ezra 10:33.
Q. שִׁמְעִי *šim'iy* **masc. proper noun**
(Shimei: another layman who divorced a foreign wife in Ezra's day)
Ezra 10:38.
R. שִׁמְעִי *šim'iy* **masc. proper noun**
(Shimei: a Benjamite ancestor of Mordecai; possibly the same as B)
Esth. 2:5.

8097. שִׁמְעִי *šim'iy* **masc. proper noun**
(Shimeites: descendants of Shimei [8096,A])
Num. 3:21; **Zech.** 12:13.

8098. A. שְׁמַעְיָה *š^ema'yāh* **masc. proper noun**
(Shemaiah: a Reubenite)
1 Chr. 5:4.
B. שְׁמַעְיָה *š^ema'yāh* **masc. proper noun**
(Shemaiah: a Simeonite chief)
1 Chr. 4:37.

C. שְׁמַעְיָה *šᵉmaʿyāh* **masc. proper noun**
(Shemaiah: a Levite in David's day)
1 Chr. 15:8,11.
D. שְׁמַעְיָה *šᵉmaʿyāh* **masc. proper noun**
(Shemaiah: a Levite scribe in David's day)
1 Chr. 24:6.
E. שְׁמַעְיָה *šᵉmaʿyāh* **masc. proper noun**
(Shemaiah: a Levite gatekeeper in David's day)
1 Chr. 26:4,6,7.
F. שְׁמַעְיָה *šᵉmaʿyāh*, שְׁמַעְיָהוּ *šᵉmāyāhû* **masc. proper noun**
(Shemaiah: a prophet)
1 Kgs. 12:22; **2 Chr.** 11:2; 12:5,7,15.
G. שְׁמַעְיָהוּ *šᵉmāyāhû* **masc. proper noun**
(Shemaiah: a Levite in Jehoshaphat's day)
2 Chr. 17:8.
H. שְׁמַעְיָה *šᵉmaʿyāh* **masc. proper noun**
(Shemaiah: a Levite in Hezekiah's day; possibly the same as I)
2 Chr. 29:14.
I. שְׁמַעְיָהוּ *šᵉmāyāhû* **masc. proper noun**
(Shemaiah: another Levite in Hezekiah's day; possibly the same as H)
2 Chr. 31:15.
J. שְׁמַעְיָהוּ *šᵉmāyāhû* **masc. proper noun**
(Shemaiah: a chief Levite in Josiah's day)
2 Chr. 35:9.
K. שְׁמַעְיָהוּ *šᵉmāyāhû* **masc. proper noun**
(Shemaiah: father of the prophet Uriah; possibly the same as L or M)
Jer. 26:20.
L. שְׁמַעְיָהוּ *šᵉmāyāhû* **masc. proper noun**
(Shemaiah: father of Prince Delaiah; possibly the same as K or M)
Jer. 36:12.
M. שְׁמַעְיָה *šᵉmaʿyāh*, שְׁמַעְיָהוּ *šᵉmāyāhû* **masc. proper noun**
(Shemaiah: opponent of Jeremiah in exile; possibly the same as K or L)
Jer. 29:24,31,32.
N. שְׁמַעְיָה *šᵉmaʿyāh* **masc. proper noun**
(Shemaiah: priestly ancestor of Babylonian returnees; possibly the same as O)
Neh. 10:8(9); 12:6,18.
O. שְׁמַעְיָה *šᵉmaʿyāh* **masc. proper noun**
(Shemaiah: a Levite among first returnees from Babylon)
1 Chr. 9:14; **Neh.** 11:15.
P. שְׁמַעְיָה *šᵉmaʿyāh* **masc. proper noun**
(Shemaiah: another Levite among first returnees from Babylon)
1 Chr. 9:16.
Q. שְׁמַעְיָה *šᵉmaʿyāh* **masc. proper noun**
(Shemaiah: a Babylonian lay exile returning with Ezra)
Ezra 8:13,16.
R. שְׁמַעְיָה *šᵉmaʿyāh* **masc. proper noun**
(Shemaiah: a priest who divorced a foreign wife in Ezra's day)
Ezra 10:21.
S. שְׁמַעְיָה *šᵉmaʿyāh* **masc. proper noun**
(Shemaiah: a layman who divorced a foreign wife in Ezra's day)
Ezra 10:31.
T. שְׁמַעְיָה *šᵉmaʿyāh* **masc. proper noun**
(Shemaiah: a descendant of Zerubbabel)
1 Chr. 3:22; **Neh.** 3:29.
U. שְׁמַעְיָה *šᵉmaʿyāh* **masc. proper noun**

(Shemaiah: a false prophet in Nehemiah's day)
Neh. 6:10.
V. שְׁמַעְיָה *š^ema'yāh* **masc. proper noun**
(Shemaiah: an official in Nehemiah's day; possibly the same as W)
Neh. 12:34.
W. שְׁמַעְיָה *š^ema'yāh* **masc. proper noun**
(Shemaiah: grandfather of the priest Zechariah in Nehemiah's day; possibly the same as V or X)
Neh. 12:35,42.
X. שְׁמַעְיָה *š^ema'yāh* **masc. proper noun**
(Shemaiah: a Levite musician in Nehemiah's day; possibly the same as W)
Neh. 12:36.

8099. שִׁמְעֹנִי *šim'ōniy* **masc. proper noun**
(Simeonite: descendant of Simeon [8095,A])
Num. 25:14; 26:14; **Josh.** 21:4; **1 Chr.** 27:16.

8100. שִׁמְעַת *šim'at* **fem. proper noun**
(Shimeath; mother of Jozachar or Zabad)
2 Kgs. 12:21(22); **2 Chr.** 24:26.

8101. שִׁמְעָתִים *šim'ātiym* **masc. pl. proper noun**
(Shimeathites)
1 Chr. 2:55.

8102. שֶׁמֶץ *šēmeṣ* **masc. noun**
(whisper, faint sound)
Job 4:12; 26:14.

8103. שִׁמְצָה *šimṣāh* **fem. noun**
(derision; laughingstock)
Ex. 32:25.

8104. שָׁמַר *šāmar* **verb**
(to keep, to obey, to observe)
Gen. 2:15; 3:24; 4:9; 17:9,10; 18:19; 24:6; 26:5; 28:15,20; 30:31; 31:24,29; 37:11; 41:35; **Ex.** 10:28; 12:17,24,25; 13:10; 15:26; 16:28; 19:5,12; 20:6; 21:29,36; 22:7(6),10(9); 23:13,15,20,21; 31:13,14,16; 34:11,12,18; **Lev.** 8:35; 18:4,5,26,30; 19:3,19,30,37; 20:8,22; 22:9,31; 25:18; 26:2,3; **Num.** 1:53; 3:7,8, 10,28,32,38; 6:24; 8:26; 9:19,23; 18:3–5, 7; 23:12; 28:2; 31:30,47; **Deut.** 2:4; 4:2, 6,9,15,23,40; 5:1,10,12,29,32; 6:2,3,12, 17,25; 7:8,9,11,12; 8:1,2,6,11; 10:13; 11:1,8,16,22,32; 12:1,13,19,28,30, 32(13:1); 13:4(5),18(19); 15:5,9; 16:1,12; 17:10,19; 19:9; 23:9(10),23(24); 24:8; 26:16–18; 27:1; 28:1,9,13,15,45,58; 29:9; 30:10,16; 31:12; 32:46; 33:9; **Josh.** 1:7,8; 6:18; 10:18; 22:2,3,5; 23:6,11; 24:17; **Judg.** 1:24; 2:22; 7:19; 13:4,13,14; **1 Sam.** 1:12; 2:9; 7:1; 9:24; 13:13,14; 17:20,22; 19:2,11; 21:4(5); 25:21; 26:15, 16; 28:2; 30:23; **2 Sam.** 11:16; 15:16; 16:21; 18:12; 20:3,10; 22:22,24,44; 23:5; **1 Kgs.** 2:3,4,43; 3:6,14; 6:12; 8:23–25, 58,61; 9:4,6; 11:10,11,34,38; 13:21; 14:8,27; 20:39; **2 Kgs.** 6:9,10; 9:14; 10:31; 11:5–7; 12:9(10); 17:13,19,37; 18:6; 21:8; 22:4,14; 23:3,4; 25:18; **1 Chr.** 9:19; 10:13; 12:29(30); 22:12,13; 23:32; 28:8; 29:18,19; **2 Chr.** 5:11; 6:14–16; 7:17; 12:10; 13:11; 19:7; 23:6; 33:8; 34:9, 21,22,31; **Ezra** 8:29; **Neh.** 1:5,7,9; 2:8; 3:29; 9:32; 10:29(30); 11:19; 12:25,45; 13:22; **Esth.** 2:3,8,14,15,21; 6:2; **Job** 2:6; 10:12,14; 13:27; 14:16; 22:15; 23:11; 24:15; 29:2; 33:11; 36:21; 39:1; **Ps.** 12:7(8),8; 16:1; 17:4,8; 18:21(22),23(24); 19:11(12); 25:20; 31:6(7); 34:20(21); 37:28,34,37; 39:1(2); 41:2(3); 56:6(7); 59:[title](1),9(10); 71:10; 78:10,56; 86:2; 89:28(29),31(32); 91:11; 97:10; 99:7; 103:18; 105:45; 106:3; 107:43; 116:6; 119:4,5,8,9,17,34,44,55,57,60,63,67,88, 101,106,134,136,146,158,167,168; 121:3–5,7,8; 127:1; 130:3,6; 132:12;

140:4(5); 141:9; 145:20; 146:6,9; **Prov.** 2:8,11,20; 3:26; 4:4,6,21; 5:2; 6:22,24; 7:1,2,5; 8:32,34; 10:17; 13:3,18; 14:3; 15:5; 16:17; 19:8,16; 21:23; 22:5,18; 27:18; 28:4; 29:18; **Eccl.** 3:6; 5:1(4:17), 8(7),13(12); 8:2,5; 11:4; 12:3,13; **Song** 3:3; 5:7; **Isa.** 7:4; 21:11,12; 26:2; 42:20; 56:1,2,4,6; 62:6; **Jer.** 3:5; 4:17; 5:24; 8:7; 9:4; 16:11; 17:21; 20:10; 31:10; 35:4,18; 51:12; 52:24; **Ezek.** 11:20; 17:14; 18:9, 19,21; 20:18,19,21; 36:27; 37:24; 40:45, 46; 43:11; 44:8,14–16,24; 48:11; **Dan.** 9:4; **Hos.** 4:10; 12:6(7),12(13),13(14); **Amos** 1:11; 2:4; 8:11; **Jon.** 2:8(9); **Mic.** 6:16; 7:5; **Zech.** 3:7; 11:11; **Mal.** 2:7,9,15,16; 3:7,14.

8105. שֶׁמֶר *šemer* **masc. pl. noun**
(dregs, aged wine)
Ps. 75:8(9); **Isa.** 25:6; **Jer.** 48:11; **Zeph.** 1:12.

8106. A. שֶׁמֶר *šemer* **masc. proper noun**
(Shemer: owner of the hill where Samaria was built)
1 Kgs. 16:24.
B. שֶׁמֶר *šemer* **masc. proper noun**
(Shemer: a Levite)
1 Chr. 6:46(31).
C. שֶׁמֶר *šemer* **masc. proper noun**
(Shamer: an Asherite; same person as *šōmer* [7763,B])
1 Chr. 7:34(NIV, *šōmer* [7763,B]).
D. שָׁמֶד *šāmed* **masc. proper noun**
(Shamed: a Benjamite)
1 Chr. 8:12.

8107. שִׁמֻּר *šimmur* **masc. noun**
(vigil, observation)
Ex. 12:42.

8108. שָׁמְרָה *šāmrāh* **fem. noun**
(guard, watch)
Ps. 141:3.

8109. שְׁמֻרָה *š^e^murāh* **fem. noun**
(openness, watchfulness)
Ps. 77:4(5).

8110. A. שִׁמְרוֹן *šimrôn* **masc. proper noun**
(Shimron: son of Issachar)
Gen. 46:13; **Num.** 26:24; **1 Chr.** 7:1.
B. שִׁמְרוֹן *šimrôn* **proper noun**
(Shimron: Canaanite city)
Josh. 11:1; 19:15.

8111. שֹׁמְרוֹן *šōm^e^rôn* **proper noun**
(Samaria)
1 Kgs. 13:32; 16:24,28,29,32; 18:2; 20:1, 10,17,34,43; 21:1,18; 22:10,37,38,51(52); **2 Kgs.** 1:2,3; 2:25; 3:1,6; 5:3; 6:19,20, 24,25; 7:1,18; 10:1,12,17,35,36; 13:1,6,9, 10,13; 14:14,16,23; 15:8,13,14,17,23, 25,27; 17:1,5,6,24,26,28; 18:9,10,34; 21:13; 23:18,19; **2 Chr.** 18:2,9; 22:9; 25:13,24; 28:8,9,15; **Neh.** 4:2(3:34); **Isa.** 7:9; 8:4; 9:9(8); 10:9–11; 36:19; **Jer.** 23:13; 31:5; 41:5; **Ezek.** 16:46,51, 53,55; 23:4,33; **Hos.** 7:1; 8:5,6; 10:5,7; 13:16(14:1); **Amos** 3:9,12; 4:1; 6:1; 8:14; **Obad.** 1:19; **Mic.** 1:1,5,6.

8112. שִׁמְרוֹן מְרוֹן *šimrôn m^e^rôn* **proper noun**
(Shimron Meron)
Josh. 12:20.

8113. A. שִׁמְרִי *šimriy* **masc. proper noun**
(Shimri: a Simeonite)
1 Chr. 4:37.
B. שִׁמְרִי *šimriy* **masc. proper noun**
(Shimri: father of Jediael and Joha)
1 Chr. 11:45.
C. שִׁמְרִי *šimriy* **masc. proper noun**
(Shimri: a Levite gatekeeper in David's day)
1 Chr. 26:10.
D. שִׁמְרִי *šimriy* **masc. proper noun**

(Shimri: a Levite in Hezekiah's day)
2 Chr. 29:13.

8114. A. שְׁמַרְיָהוּ *šᵉmaryāhû* **masc. proper noun**
(Shemariah: a Benjamite warrior)
1 Chr. 12:5(6).
B. שְׁמַרְיָה *šᵉmaryāh* **masc. proper noun**
(Shemariah: son of King Rehoboam)
2 Chr. 11:19.
C. שְׁמַרְיָה *šᵉmaryāh* **masc. proper noun**
(Shemariah: a man who divorced a foreign wife in the time of Ezra)
Ezra 10:32.
D. שְׁמַרְיָה *šᵉmaryāh* **masc. proper noun**
(Shemariah: another man who divorced a foreign wife in the time of Ezra)
Ezra 10:41.

8115. שָׁמְרַיִן *šāmᵉrayin* **Aram. proper noun**
(Samaria; corr. to Hebr. 8111)
Ezra 4:10,17.

8116. שִׁמְרִית *šimriyṯ* **fem. proper noun**
(Shimrith; the same as *šōmēr* [7763,A])
2 Chr. 24:26.

8117. שִׁמְרֹנִי *šimrōniy* **masc. proper noun**
(Shimronite; descendant of Shimron [8110,A])
Num. 26:24.

8118. שֹׁמְרֹנִי *šōmᵉrōniy* **masc. proper noun**
(Samaritan: an inhabitant of Samariah [8111])
2 Kgs. 17:29.

8119. שִׁמְרָת *šimrāṯ* **masc. proper noun**
(Shimrath)
1 Chr. 8:21.

8120. שְׁמַשׁ *šᵉmaš* **Aram. verb**
(to attend)
Dan. 7:10.

8121. שֶׁמֶשׁ *šemeš* **masc./fem. noun**
(sun, daylight)
Gen. 15:12,17; 19:23; 28:11; 32:31(32); 37:9; **Ex.** 16:21; 17:12; 22:3(2),26(25); **Lev.** 22:7; **Num.** 21:11; 25:4; **Deut.** 4:19,41,47; 11:30; 16:6; 17:3; 23:11(12); 24:13,15; 33:14; **Josh.** 1:4,15; 8:29; 10:12,13,27; 12:1; 13:5; 19:12,27,34; 23:4; **Judg.** 5:31; 9:33; 11:18; 19:14; 20:43; 21:19; **1 Sam.** 11:9; **2 Sam.** 2:24; 3:35; 12:11,12; 23:4; **1 Kgs.** 22:36; **2 Kgs.** 3:22; 10:33; 23:5,11; **2 Chr.** 18:34; **Neh.** 7:3; **Job** 8:16; **Ps.** 19:4(5); 50:1; 58:8(9); 72:5,17; 74:16; 84:11(12); 89:36(37); 104:19,22; 113:3; 121:6; 136:8; 148:3; **Eccl.** 1:3,5,9,14; 2:11,17–20,22; 3:16; 4:1,3,7,15; 5:13(12),18(17); 6:1, 5,12; 7:11; 8:9,15,17; 9:3,6,9,11,13; 10:5; 11:7; 12:2; **Song** 1:6; **Isa.** 13:10; 38:8; 41:25; 45:6; 49:10; 54:12; 59:19; 60:19,20; **Jer.** 8:2; 15:9; 31:35; **Ezek.** 8:16; 32:7; **Joel** 2:10,31(3:4); 3:15(4:15); **Amos** 8:9; **Jon.** 4:8; **Mic.** 3:6; **Nah.** 3:17; **Hab.** 3:11; **Zech.** 8:7; **Mal.** 1:11; 4:2(3:20).

8122. שֶׁמֶשׁ *šemeš* **Aram. com. noun**
(sun; corr. to Hebr. 8121)
Dan. 6:14(15).

8123. שִׁמְשׁוֹן *šimšôn* **masc. proper noun**
(Samson)
Judg. 13:24; 14:1,3,5,7,10,12,15,16,20; 15:1,3,4,6,7,10–12,16; 16:1–3,6,7,9,10, 12–14,20,23,25–30.

8124. שִׁמְשַׁי *šimšay* **Aram. masc. proper noun**

(Shimshai)
Ezra 4:8,9,17,23.

8125. שַׁמְשְׁרַי *šamšᵉray* **masc. proper noun**
(Shamsherai)
1 Chr. 8:26.

8126. שֻׁמָתִי *šumāṯiy* **masc. proper noun**
(Shumathite)
1 Chr. 2:53.

8127. שֵׁן *šēn* **masc./fem. noun**
(tooth, ivory, fang, sharp projecting rock)
Gen. 49:12; **Ex.** 21:24,27; **Lev.** 24:20; **Num.** 11:33; **Deut.** 19:21; 32:24; **1 Sam.** 2:13; 14:4,5; **1 Kgs.** 10:18; 22:39; **2 Chr.** 9:17; **Job** 4:10; 13:14; 16:9; 19:20; 29:17; 39:28; 41:14(6); **Ps.** 3:7(8); 35:16; 37:12; 45:8(9); 57:4(5); 58:6(7); 112:10; 124:6; **Prov.** 10:26; 25:19; 30:14; **Song** 4:2; 5:14; 6:6; 7:4; **Jer.** 31:29,30; **Lam.** 2:16; 3:16; **Ezek.** 18:2; 27:6,15; **Joel** 1:6; **Amos** 3:15; 4:6; 6:4; **Mic.** 3:5; **Zech.** 9:7.

8128. שֵׁן *šēn* **Aram. masc. noun**
(tooth; corr. to Hebr. 8127)
Dan. 7:5,7,19.

8129. שֵׁן *šēn* **proper noun**
(Shen)
1 Sam. 7:12.

8130. שָׂנֵא *śānē'* **verb**
(to hate, to dislike; to be in enmity)
Gen. 24:60; 26:27; 29:31,33; 37:4,5,8; **Ex.** 1:10; 18:21; 20:5; 23:5; **Lev.** 19:17; 26:17; **Num.** 10:35; **Deut.** 4:42; 5:9; 7:10,15; 12:31; 16:22; 19:4,6,11; 21:15–17; 22:13,16; 24:3; 30:7; 32:41; 33:11; **Josh.** 20:5; **Judg.** 11:7; 14:16; 15:2; **2 Sam.** 5:8; 13:15,22; 19:6(7); 22:18,41; **1 Kgs.** 22:8; **2 Chr.** 1:11; 18:7; 19:2; **Esth.** 9:1,5,16; **Job** 8:22; 31:29; 34:17; **Ps.** 5:5(6); 9:13(14); 11:5; 18:17(18),40(41); 21:8(9); 25:19; 26:5; 31:6(7); 34:21(22); 35:19; 36:2(3); 38:19(20); 41:7(8); 44:7(8),10(11); 45:7(8); 50:17; 55:12(13); 68:1(2); 69:4(5),14(15); 81:15(16); 83:2(3); 86:17; 89:23(24); 97:10; 101:3; 105:25; 106:10,41; 118:7; 119:104,113,128,163; 120:6; 129:5; 139:21,22; **Prov.** 1:22,29; 5:12; 6:16; 8:13,36; 9:8; 11:15; 12:1; 13:5,24; 14:17,20; 15:10,27; 19:7; 25:17, 21; 26:24,28; 27:6; 28:16; 29:10,24; 30:23; **Eccl.** 2:17,18; 3:8; **Isa.** 1:14; 60:15; 61:8; 66:5; **Jer.** 12:8; 44:4; **Ezek.** 16:27,37; 23:28; 35:6; **Hos.** 9:15; **Amos** 5:10,15,21; 6:8; **Mic.** 3:2; **Zech.** 8:17; **Mal.** 1:3; 2:16.

8131. שְׂנֵא *śᵉnē'* **Aram. verb**
(to hate; corr. to Hebr. 8130)
Dan. 4:19(16).

8132. I. שָׁנָא *šānā'* **verb**
(to change)
2 Kgs. 25:29; **Eccl.** 8:1; **Lam.** 4:1(NIV, see II).
II. שָׁנָא *šānā'* **verb**
(to become dull)
Lam. 4:1(KJV, NASB, see I).

8133. שְׁנָא *šᵉnā'* **Aram. verb**
(to change; to be different; corr. to Hebr. 8132,A)
Ezra 6:11,12; **Dan.** 2:9,21; 3:19,27,28; 4:16(13); 5:6,9,10; 6:8(9),15(16),17(18); 7:3,7,19,23–25,28.

8134. שִׁנְאָב *šin'āḇ* **masc. proper noun**
(Shinab)
Gen. 14:2.

8135. שִׂנְאָה *śin'āh* **fem. noun**
(hatred)
Num. 35:20; **Deut.** 1:27; 9:28; **2 Sam.** 13:15; **Ps.** 25:19; 109:3,5; 139:22; **Prov.** 10:12,18; 15:17; 26:26; **Eccl.** 9:1,6; **Ezek.** 23:29; 35:11.

8136. I. שִׁנְאָן *šin'ān* **masc. noun** (thousand)
Ps. 68:17(18)(KJV, see II).
II. שִׁנְאָן *šin'ān* **masc. noun** (angel)
Ps. 68:17(18)(NASB, NIV, see I).

8137. שֶׁנְאַצַּר *šen'aṣṣar* **masc. proper noun** (Shenazzar)
1 Chr. 3:18.

8138. I. שָׁנָה *šānāh* **verb** (to change; to disguise; to be different)
1 Sam. 21:13(14); **1 Kgs.** 14:2; **Esth.** 1:7; 2:9; 3:8; **Job** 14:20; **Ps.** 34:[title](1); 77:10(11)(KJV, NIV, *šānāh* [3141]); 89:34(35); **Prov.** 24:21; 31:5; **Jer.** 2:36; 52:33; **Mal.** 3:6.
II. שָׁנָה *šānāh* **verb** (to repeat; to do again)
Gen. 41:32; **1 Sam.** 26:8; **2 Sam.** 20:10; **1 Kgs.** 18:34; **Neh.** 13:21; **Job** 29:22; **Prov.** 17:9; 26:11.

8139. שְׁנָה *s^enāh* **Aram. fem. noun** (sleep; corr. to Hebr. 8142)
Dan. 6:18(19).

8140. שְׁנָה *s^enāh* **Aram. fem. noun** (year; corr. to Hebr. 8141)
Ezra 4:24; 5:11,13; 6:3,15; **Dan.** 5:31(6:1); 7:1.

8141. שָׁנָה *šānāh* **fem. noun** (year)
Gen. 1:14; 5:3–23,25–28,30–32; 6:3; 7:6,11; 8:13; 9:28,29; 11:10–26,32; 12:4; 14:4,5; 15:13; 16:3,16; 17:1,17,21,24,25; 21:5; 23:1; 25:7,17,20,26; 26:12,34; 29:18,20,27,30; 31:38,41; 35:28; 37:2; 41:1,26,27,29,30,34– 36,46–48,50,53,54; 45:6,11; 47:8,9,17,18,28; 50:22,26; **Ex.** 6:16,18,20; 7:7; 12:2,5,40,41; 16:35; 21:2; 23:10,14,16,17,29; 29:38; 30:10,14; 34:22–24; 38:26; 40:17; **Lev.** 9:3; 12:6; 14:10; 16:34; 19:23–25; 23:12,18,19,41; 25:3–5,8,10,11,13,15,16,20–22,27–30, 40,50–54; 27:3,5–7,17,18,23,24; **Num.** 1:1,3,18,20,22,24,26,28,30,32,34,36,38, 40,42,45; 4:3,23,30,35,39,43,47; 6:12,14; 7:15,17,21,23,27,29,33,35,39,41,45,47, 51,53,57,59,63,65,69,71,75,77,81,83, 87,88; 8:24,25; 9:1; 10:11; 13:22; 14:29, 33,34; 15:27; 26:2,4; 28:3,9,11,14,19,27; 29:2,8,13,17,20,23,26,29,32,36; 32:11, 13; 33:38,39; **Deut.** 1:3; 2:7,14; 8:2,4; 11:12; 14:22,28; 15:1,9,12,18,20; 16:16; 24:5; 26:12; 29:5(4); 31:2,10; 32:7; 34:7; **Josh.** 5:6,12; 14:7,10; 24:29; **Judg.** 2:8; 3:8,11,14,30; 4:3; 5:31; 6:1,25; 8:28; 9:22; 10:2,3,8; 11:26,40; 12:7,9,11,14; 13:1; 15:20; 16:31; **Ruth** 1:4; **1 Sam.** 1:7; 4:15,18; 7:2,16; 13:1; 29:3; **2 Sam.** 2:10,11; 4:4; 5:4,5; 11:1; 13:23,38; 14:28; 15:7; 19:32(33),34(35),35(36); 21:1; 24:13; **1 Kgs.** 2:11,39; 4:7; 5:11(25); 6:1,37,38; 7:1; 9:10,25; 10:14,22,25; 11:42; 14:20,21,25; 15:1,2,9,10,25,28,33; 16:8,10,15,23,29; 17:1; 18:1; 20:22,26; 22:1,2,41,42,51(52); **2 Kgs.** 1:17; 3:1; 8:1–3,16,17,25,26; 9:29; 10:36; 11:3,4, 21(12:1); 12:1(2),6(7); 13:1,10,20; 14:1, 2,17,21,23; 15:1,2,8,13,17,23,27,30, 32,33; 16:1,2; 17:1,4–6; 18:1,2,9,10,13; 19:29; 20:6; 21:1,19; 22:1,3; 23:23,31, 36; 24:1,8,12,18; 25:1,2,8,27; **1 Chr.** 2:21; 3:4; 20:1; 21:12; 23:3,24,27; 26:1,3; 27:1,23; 29:27; **2 Chr.** 3:2; 8:1,13; 9:13, 21,24,30; 11:17; 12:2,13; 13:1,2; 14:1 (13:23),6(5); 15:10,19; 16:1,12,13; 17:7; 18:2; 20:31; 21:5,20; 22:2,12; 23:1; 24:1, 5,15,23; 25:1,5,25; 26:1,3; 27:1,5,8; 28:1; 29:1,3; 31:16,17; 33:1,21; 34:1,3,8; 35:19; 36:2,5,9–11,21,22; **Ezra** 1:1; 3:8; 7:7,8; **Neh.** 1:1; 2:1; 5:14; 9:21,30; 10:31(32), 32(33),34(35),35(36); 13:6; **Esth.** 1:3; 2:16; 3:7; 9:21,27; **Job** 3:6; 10:5; 15:20; 16:22; 32:7; 36:11,26; 42:16; **Ps.** 31:10(11); 61:6(7); 65:11(12); 77:5(6),10(11)(NASB, *šānāh* [8138,I]); 78:33; 90:4,9,10,15; 95:10; 102:24(25),27(28); **Prov.** 3:2; 4:10; 5:9; 9:11; 10:27; **Eccl.** 6:3,6; 11:8;

12:1; **Isa.** 6:1; 7:8; 14:28; 16:14; 20:1,3; 21:16; 23:15,17; 29:1; 32:10; 34:8; 36:1; 37:30; 38:5,10,15; 61:2; 63:4; 65:20; **Jer.** 1:2,3; 11:23; 17:8; 23:12; 25:1,3,11,12; 28:1,3(NASB, *šēniy* [8145]),11(NASB, *šēniy* [8145]),16,17; 29:10; 32:1; 34:14; 36:1,9; 39:1,2; 45:1; 46:2; 48:44; 51:46, 59; 52:1,4,5,12,28–31; **Ezek.** 1:1,2; 4:5,6; 8:1; 20:1; 22:4; 24:1; 26:1; 29:1,11–13,17; 30:20; 31:1; 32:1,17; 33:21; 38:8,17; 39:9; 40:1; 46:13,17; **Dan.** 1:1,5,21; 2:1; 8:1; 9:1,2; 10:1; 11:1,6,8,13; **Joel** 2:2,25; **Amos** 1:1; 2:10; 5:25; **Mic.** 6:6; **Hab.** 3:2; **Hag.** 1:1,15; 2:10; **Zech.** 1:1,7,12; 7:1,3,5; 14:16; **Mal.** 3:4.

8142. שֵׁנָא *šēnā',* שֵׁנָה *šēnāh*
fem. noun
(sleep)
Gen. 28:16; 31:40; **Judg.** 16:14,20; **Esth.** 6:1; **Job** 14:12; **Ps.** 76:5(6); 90:5; 127:2; 132:4(KJV, *š^{e}nat* [8153]); **Prov.** 3:24; 4:16; 6:4,9,10; 20:13; 24:33; **Eccl.** 5:12(11); 8:16; **Jer.** 31:26; 51:39,57; **Dan.** 2:1; **Zech.** 4:1.

8143. שֶׁנְהַבִּים *šenhabbiym* **masc. pl. noun**
(ivory)
1 Kgs. 10:22; **2 Chr.** 9:21.

8144. שָׁנִי *šāniy* **masc. noun**
(scarlet)
Gen. 38:28,30; **Ex.** 25:4; 26:1,31,36; 27:16; 28:5,6,8,15,33; 35:6,23,25,35; 36:8,35,37; 38:18,23; 39:1–3,5,8,24,29; **Lev.** 14:4,6,49,51,52; **Num.** 4:8; 19:6; **Josh.** 2:18,21; **2 Sam.** 1:24; **Prov.** 31:21; **Song** 4:3; **Isa.** 1:18; **Jer.** 4:30.

8145. שֵׁנִי *šēniy* **adj.**
(second, another, again)
Gen. 1:8; 2:13; 4:19; 6:16; 7:11; 8:14; 22:15; 30:7,12; 32:19(20); 41:5,52; 47:18; **Ex.** 1:15; 2:13; 16:1; 25:12,32; 26:4,5, 10,20,27; 27:15; 28:10,18; 29:19,39,41; 36:11,12,17,25,32; 37:3,18; 38:15; 39:11; 40:17; **Lev.** 5:10; 8:22; 13:5–7,33,54,58; **Num.** 1:1,18; 2:16; 7:18; 8:8; 9:1,11; 10:6,11; 11:26; 28:4,8; 29:17; **Josh.** 5:2; 6:14; 10:32; 19:1; **Judg.** 6:25,26,28; 20:24,25; **Ruth** 1:4; **1 Sam.** 1:2; 20:27, 34; **2 Sam.** 4:2; 14:29; 16:19; **1 Kgs.** 6:1,24–27,34; 7:15–18,20; 9:2; 19:7; **2 Kgs.** 9:19; 10:6; 19:29; 25:17; **1 Chr.** 2:13; 3:1,15; 6:28(13)(KJV, *wašniy* [2059]); 7:15; 8:1,39; 12:9(10); 23:11,19,20; 24:7,23; 25:9; 26:2,4,11; 27:4; 29:22; **2 Chr.** 3:2; 27:5; 30:2,13,15; **Ezra** 3:8; **Neh.** 3:11,19–21,24,27,30; 8:13; 12:38; **Esth.** 2:14,19; 7:2; 9:29; **Job** 42:14; **Eccl.** 4:8,10,15; **Isa.** 11:11; 37:30; **Jer.** 1:13; 13:3; 28:3(KJV, NIV, *šānāh* [8141]); 33:1; 41:4; 52:22; **Ezek.** 4:6; 10:14; 43:22; **Dan.** 8:3; **Jon.** 3:1; **Hag.** 2:20; **Zech.** 4:12; 6:2; 11:14; **Mal.** 2:13.

8146. שָׂנִיא *śāniy'* **adj.**
(unloved, hated)
Deut. 21:15.

8147. שְׁנַיִם *š^{e}nayim,* שְׁתַּיִם *š^{e}ttayim*
adj., dual adj.
(two, both, pair)
Gen. 1:16; 2:25; 3:7; 4:19; 5:8,18,20, 26,28; 6:19,20; 7:2,9,15; 9:22,23; 10:25; 11:20; 14:4; 17:20; 19:1,8,15,16,30,36; 21:27,31; 22:3,6,8; 24:22; 25:16,23; 27:9, 45; 29:16; 31:33,37,41; 32:7(8),10(11), 22(23); 33:1; 34:25; 35:22; 40:2,5; 41:50; 42:13,32,37; 44:27; 46:27; 48:1,5,13; 49:28; **Ex.** 2:13; 4:9; 12:7,22,23; 15:27; 16:22; 18:3,6; 21:21; 22:4(3),7(6),9(8), 11(10); 24:4; 25:12,18,19,22,35; 26:17, 19,21,23–25; 27:7; 28:7,9,11,12,14,21, 23–27; 29:1,3,13,22,38; 30:4; 31:18; 32:15; 34:1,4,29; 36:22,24,26,28–30; 37:3,7,8,21,27; 39:4,14,16–20; **Lev.** 3:4,10,15; 4:9; 5:7,11; 7:4; 8:2,16,25; 12:8; 14:4,10,22,49; 15:14,29; 16:1,5, 7,8,21; 20:11–13,18; 23:13,17–20; 24:5,6; **Num.** 1:35,39,44; 2:21,26; 3:39,43; 6:10; 7:3,7,13,17,19,23,25,29, 31,35,37,41,43,47,49,53,55,59,61,65,67,

71,73,77–79,83,84,86,87,89; 10:2; 11:26; 12:5; 13:23; 15:6; 17:2(17),6(21); 22:22; 25:8; 26:14,34,37; 28:3,9,11,12,19,20, 27,28; 29:3,9,13,14,17,20,23,26,29,32; 31:5,33,35,38,40; 33:9; 34:15; 35:6; **Deut.** 1:23; 3:8,21; 4:13,47; 5:22; 9:10, 11,15,17; 10:1,3; 14:6; 17:6; 19:15,17; 21:15,17; 22:22,24; 23:18(19); 32:30; **Josh.** 2:1,4,10,23; 3:12; 4:2–4,8,9,20; 6:22; 8:25; 9:10; 14:3,4; 15:60; 18:24; 19:15,30; 21:7,16,25,27,40; 24:12; **Judg.** 3:16; 7:3,25; 8:12; 9:44; 10:3; 11:37–39; 12:6; 15:4,13; 16:3,28,29; 19:6,8,29; 20:21; 21:10; **Ruth** 1:1–3,5,7,8,19; 4:11; **1 Sam.** 1:2,3; 2:21,34; 3:11; 4:4,11,17; 5:4; 6:7,10; 9:26; 10:2,4; 11:11; 13:1; 14:11,49; 18:21; 20:11,42; 23:18; 25:18, 43; 27:3; 28:8; 30:5,12,18; **2 Sam.** 1:1; 2:2,10,15; 4:2; 8:2,5; 9:13; 10:6; 12:1; 13:6; 14:6; 15:27,36; 17:1,18; 18:24; 21:8; 23:20; **1 Kgs.** 2:5,32,29; 3:16, 18,25; 4:7,26(5:6); 5:12(26),14(28); 6:23,25,32,34; 7:15,16,18,20,24,25, 41,42,44; 8:9,63; 9:10; 10:19,20,26; 11:29,30; 12:28; 14:20; 15:25; 16:23,29; 17:12; 18:21,23,31; 19:19; 20:1,15,16,27; 21:10,13; 22:31; **2 Kgs.** 1:14,17; 2:6–9, 11,12,24; 3:1; 4:1,33; 5:22,23; 6:10; 7:14; 8:17,25,26; 9:32; 10:4,8,14; 11:7; 14:1; 15:2,27,32; 17:1,16; 21:1,5,12,19; 23:12; 25:16,27; **1 Chr.** 1:19; 4:5; 6:63(48); 7:2,7; 9:22; 11:21,22; 12:28(29); 15:10; 18:5; 19:7; 24:12,17; 25:9–31; 26:8, 17,18; 27:15; **2 Chr.** 1:14; 3:10,15; 4:3,4,12,13,15; 5:10; 7:5; 9:18,19,25; 13:21; 21:5,19,20; 22:2; 24:3; 26:3; 33:1,5,21; 34:3; **Ezra** 2:3,4,6,10,12,18, 24,27,29,37,58,60; 8:24,27,31,35; 10:13; **Neh.** 5:14; 6:15; 7:8–10,17,24,28,31,33, 40,60,62,71,72; 11:12,13,19; 12:31,40; 13:6,20; **Esth.** 2:12,21,23; 3:7,13; 6:2; 8:12; 9:1,27; **Job** 9:33; 13:20; 33:14; 40:5; 42:7; **Ps.** 60:[title](2); 62:11(12); **Prov.** 17:15; 20:10,12; 24:22; 27:3; 29:13; 30:7,15; **Eccl.** 4:3,9,11,12; 11:6; **Song** 4:5; 7:3(4); **Isa.** 1:31; 6:2; 7:4, 16,21; 8:14; 17:6; 47:9; 51:19; **Jer.** 2:13; 3:14; 24:1; 33:24; 34:18; 46:12; 52:20, 21,29,31; **Ezek.** 1:11,23; 15:4; 21:19(24), 21(26); 23:2,13; 29:1; 32:1,17; 33:21; 35:10; 37:22; 40:9,39,40,44(KJV, NASB, *šiyr* [7891]); 41:3,18,22–24; 43:14,16; 47:13; **Dan.** 2:1; 8:7; 9:25,26; 11:27; 12:5; **Hos.** 10:10; **Amos** 3:3,12; 4:8; **Jon.** 4:11; **Hag.** 1:1,15; 2:10; **Zech.** 1:1,7; 4:3,11, 12,14; 5:9; 6:1,13; 11:7; 13:8.

8148. שְׁנִינָה *š^eniynāh* **fem. noun**
(a byword; a taunt)
Deut. 28:37; **1 Kgs.** 9:7; **2 Chr.** 7:20; **Jer.** 24:9.

8149. שְׂנִיר *ś^eniyr*, שְׁנִיר *š^eniyr* **proper noun**
(Senir, Shenir)
Deut. 3:9; **1 Chr.** 5:23; **Song** 4:8; **Ezek.** 27:5.

8150. I. שָׁנַן *šānan* **verb**
(to sharpen, to be sharp)
Deut. 32:41; **Ps.** 45:5(6); 64:3(4); 73:21; 120:4; 140:3(4); **Prov.** 25:18; **Isa.** 5:28.
II. שָׁנַן *šānan* **verb**
(to teach diligently)
Deut. 6:7.

8151. שָׁנַס *šānas* **verb**
(to gird up)
1 Kgs. 18:46.

8152. שִׁנְעָר *šin'ār* **proper noun**
(Shinar, another name for Babylon)
Gen. 10:10; 11:2; 14:1,9; **Josh.** 7:21; **Isa.** 11:11; **Dan.** 1:2; **Zech.** 5:11.

8153. שְׁנָת *š^enat̠* **fem. noun**
(sleep)
Ps. 132:4(NASB, NIV, *šēnāh* [8142]).

8154. שָׁסָה *šāsāh*, שָׂשָׂה *šāśāh* **verb**
(to plunder, to loot, to pillage)
Judg. 2:14,16; **1 Sam.** 14:48; 23:1; **2 Kgs.** 17:20; **Ps.** 44:10(11); **Isa.** 10:13; 17:14; 42:22; **Jer.** 50:11; **Hos.** 13:15.

8155. שָׂסַס *šāsas* **verb**
(to plunder, to loot)
Judg. 2:14; **1 Sam.** 17:53; **Ps.** 89:41(42); **Isa.** 13:16; **Jer.** 30:16(KJV, [K^e] *šā'as* [7601]); **Zech.** 14:2.

8156. שָׂסַע *šāsa'* **verb**
(to split, to divide, to tear)
Lev. 1:17; 11:3,7,26; **Deut.** 14:6,7; **Judg.** 14:6; **1 Sam.** 24:7(8).

8157. שֶׂסַע *šesa'* **masc. noun**
(dividedness)
Lev. 11:3,7,26; **Deut.** 14:6.

8158. שָׂסַף *šāsap̱* **verb**
(to hew in pieces; to put to death)
1 Sam. 15:33.

8159. I. שָׁעָה *šā'āh* **verb**
(to look [with favor, or in dismay])
Gen. 4:4,5; **Ex.** 5:9; **2 Sam.** 22:42(NIV, *šāwa'* [7768]); **Job** 7:19; 14:6; **Ps.** 39:13,(14); 119:117; **Isa.** 17:7,8; 22:4; 31:1; 32:3(NASB, NIV, *šā'a'* [8173,A]); 41:10(NIV, see II),23(NIV, see II).
II. שָׁתַע *šāṯa'* **verb**
(to look with dismay)
Isa. 41:10(KJV, NASB, see I),23(KJV, NASB, see I).

8160. שָׁעָה *šā'āh* **Aram. fem. noun**
(a short time, the same hour)
Dan. 3:6,15; 4:19(16),33(30); 5:5.

8161. שַׁעֲטָה *ša'ăṭāh* **fem. noun**
(stamping [of hooves]; galloping)
Jer. 47:3.

8162. שַׁעַטְנֵז *ša'aṭnēz* **masc. noun**
(mixed material; material of more than one kind [e.g., wool and linen])
Lev. 19:19; **Deut.** 22:11.

8163. I. שָׂעִיר *śā'iyr*, שָׂעִר *śā'ir* **masc. noun**
(hairy, shaggy)
Gen. 27:11,23; **Isa.** 13:21(KJV, see III; NIV, see II); **Dan.** 8:21.
II. שָׂעִיר *śā'iyr* **masc. noun**
(goat, male goat)
Gen. 37:31; **Lev.** 4:23,24; 9:3,15; 10:16; 16:5,7–10,15,18,20–22,26,27; 23:19; **Num.** 7:16,22,28,34,40,46,52,58,64,70, 76,82,87; 15:24; 28:15,22,30; 29:5,11,16, 19,22,25,28,31,34,38; **2 Chr.** 29:23; **Isa.** 13:21(NASB, see I; KJV, see III); 34:14 (KJV, see III); **Ezek.** 43:22,25; 45:23.
III. שָׂעִיר *śā'iyr* **masc. noun**
(satyr, goat demon, goat idol)
Lev. 17:7; **2 Chr.** 11:15; **Isa.** 13:21(NASB, see I; NIV, see II); 34:14(NASB, NIV, see II).

8164. שָׂעִיר *śā'iyr* **masc. noun**
(raindrop)
Deut. 32:2.

8165. A. שֵׂעִיר *śē'iyr* **proper noun**
(Seir: mountain, and mountain range in Edom)
Gen. 14:6; 32:3(4); 33:14,16; 36:8,9,30; **Num.** 24:18; **Deut.** 1:2,44; 2:1,4,5,8,12, 22,29; 33:2; **Josh.** 11:17; 12:7; 24:4; **Judg.** 5:4; **1 Chr.** 4:42; **2 Chr.** 20:10, 22,23; 25:11,14; **Isa.** 21:11; **Ezek.** 25:8; 35:2,3,7,15.
B. שֵׂעִיר *śē'iyr* **masc. proper noun**
(Seir: ancestor of those who settled in Mt. Seir)
Gen. 36:20,21; **1 Chr.** 1:38.
C. שֵׂעִיר *śē'iyr* **proper noun**
(Seir: mountain in northern Judah)
Josh. 15:10.

8166. שְׂעִירָה *s^e'iyrāh* **fem. noun**
(a female goat)
Lev. 4:28; 5:6.

8167. שְׂעִירָה *s^e'iyrāh* **proper noun**
(Seirah)
Judg. 3:26.

8168. שֹׁעַל *šōʻal* **masc. noun**
(hollow of the hand; handful)
1 Kgs. 20:10; **Isa.** 40:12; **Ezek.** 13:19.

8169. שַׁעַלְבִים *šaʻal̲biym*, שַׁעֲלַבִּין *šaʻalabbiyn* **proper noun**
(Shaalbim, Shallabbin)
Josh. 19:42; **Judg.** 1:35; **1 Kgs.** 4:9.

8170. שַׁעַלְבֹנִי *šaʻal̲bōniy* **masc. proper noun**
(Shaalbonite; an inhabitant of Shaalbim [8169,A])
2 Sam. 23:32; **1 Chr.** 11:33.

8171. שַׁעֲלִים *šaʻaliym* **proper noun**
(Shaalim)
1 Sam. 9:4.

8172. שָׁעַן *šāʻan* **verb**
(to lean on, to rely on, to rest)
Gen. 18:4; **Num.** 21:15; **Judg.** 16:26; **2 Sam.** 1:6; **2 Kgs.** 5:18; 7:2,17; **2 Chr.** 13:18; 14:11(10); 16:7,8; **Job** 8:15; 24:23; **Prov.** 3:5; **Isa.** 10:20; 30:12; 31:1; 50:10; **Ezek.** 29:7; **Mic.** 3:11.

8173. I. שָׁעַע *šāʻaʻ* **verb**
(to close one's eyes, to be blinded)
Isa. 6:10; 29:9(KJV, see III); 32:3(KJV, *šāʻāh* [8159,I]).
II. שָׁעַע *šāʻaʻ* **verb**
(to take delight in; to fondle)
Ps. 94:19; 119:16,47,70; **Isa.** 11:8; 66:12.
III. שָׁעַע *šāʻaʻ* **verb**
(to cry out)
Isa. 29:9(NASB, NIV, see I).

8174. A. שָׁעַף *šāʻap̲* **masc. proper noun**
(Shaaph: son of Caleb, the brother of Jerahmeel)
1 Chr. 2:49.
B. שָׁעַף *šāʻap̲* **masc. proper noun**
(Shaaph: another descendant of Caleb, the brother of Jerahmeel)
1 Chr. 2:47.

8175. I. שָׂעַר *śāʻar* **verb**
(to sweep away, to storm, to whirl away)
Job 27:21; **Ps.** 50:3; 58:9(10); **Dan.** 11:40.
II. שָׂעַר *śāʻar* **verb**
(to dread, to be horribly afraid)
Deut. 32:17; **Jer.** 2:12; **Ezek.** 27:35; 32:10.

8176. שָׁעַר *šāʻar* **verb**
(to think)
Prov. 23:7.

8177. שְׂעַר *śeʻar* **Aram. masc. noun**
(hair; corr. to Hebr. 8181)
Dan. 3:27; 4:33(30); 7:9.

8178. I. שַׂעַר *śaʻar* **masc. noun**
(horror; fear)
Job 18:20; **Ezek.** 27:35; 32:10.
II. שַׂעַר *śaʻar* **masc. noun**
(storm)
Isa. 28:2.

8179. שַׁעַר *šaʻar* **masc. noun**
(gate, entrance; city, town)
Gen. 19:1; 22:17; 23:10,18; 24:60; 28:17; 34:20,24; **Ex.** 20:10; 27:16; 32:26,27; 35:17; 38:15,18,31; 39:40; 40:8,33; **Num.** 4:26; **Deut.** 5:14; 6:9; 11:20; 12:12,15,17,18,21; 14:21,27–29; 15:7,22; 16:5,11,14,18; 17:2,5,8; 18:6; 21:19; 22:15,24; 23:16(17); 24:14; 25:7; 26:12; 28:52,55,57; 31:12; **Josh.** 2:5,7; 7:5; 8:29; 20:4; **Judg.** 5:8,11; 9:35,40,44; 16:2,3; 18:16,17; **Ruth** 3:11; 4:1,10,11; **1 Sam.** 4:18; 9:18; 17:52; 21:13(14); **2 Sam.** 3:27; 10:8; 11:23; 15:2; 18:4,24,33(19:1); 19:8(9); 23:15,16; **1 Kgs.** 8:37; 22:10; **2 Kgs.** 7:1,3,17, 18,20; 9:31; 10:8; 11:6,19; 14:13; 15:35;

23:8; 25:4; **1 Chr.** 9:18,23; 11:17,18; 16:42; 22:3; 26:13,16; **2 Chr.** 6:28; 8:14; 18:9; 23:5,15,19,20; 24:8; 25:23; 26:9; 27:3; 31:2; 32:6; 33:14; 35:15; **Neh.** 1:3; 2:3,8,13–15,17; 3:1,3,6,13–15,26,28,29, 31,32; 6:1; 7:3; 8:1,3,16; 11:19; 12:25, 30,31,37,39; 13:19,22; **Esth.** 2:19,21; 3:2,3; 4:2,6; 5:9,13; 6:10,12; **Job** 5:4; 29:7; 31:21; 38:17; **Ps.** 9:13(14),14(15); 24:7,9; 69:12(13); 87:2; 100:4; 107:18; 118:19,20; 122:2; 127:5; 147:13; **Prov.** 1:21; 8:3; 14:19; 22:22; 24:7; 31:23,31; **Song** 7:4; **Isa.** 14:31; 22:7; 24:12; 26:2; 28:6; 29:21; 38:10; 45:1; 54:12; 60:11, 18; 62:10; **Jer.** 1:15; 7:2; 14:2; 15:7; 17:19–21,24,25,27; 19:2; 20:2; 22:2,4,19; 26:10; 31:38,40; 36:10; 37:13; 38:7; 39:3,4; 51:58; 52:7; **Lam.** 1:4; 2:9; 4:12; 5:14; **Ezek.** 8:3,5,14; 9:2; 10:19; 11:1; 21:15(20),22(27); 26:10; 40:3,6–11, 13–16,18–24,27,28,32,35,38–41,44,48; 42:15; 43:1,4; 44:1–4,11,17; 45:19; 46:1–3,8,9,12,19; 47:2; 48:31–34; **Amos** 5:10,12,15; **Obad.** 1:11,13; **Mic.** 1:9,12; 2:13; **Nah.** 2:6(7); 3:13; **Zeph.** 1:10; **Zech.** 8:16; 14:10.

8180. שַׁעַר *ša'ar* **masc. noun**
(hundredfold)
Gen. 26:12.

8181. שֵׂעָר *śē'ār* **masc. noun**
(hair)
Gen. 25:25; **Lev.** 13:3,4,10,20,21,25,26,30–32,36,37; 14:8,9; **Num.** 6:5,18; **Judg.** 16:22; **2 Sam.** 14:26; **2 Kgs.** 1:8; **Ezra** 9:3; **Ps.** 68:21(22); **Song** 4:1; 6:5; **Isa.** 7:20; **Ezek.** 16:7; **Zech.** 13:4.

8182. שֹׁעָר *šō'ār* **adj.**
(split open, poor, vile)
Jer. 29:17.

8183. שְׂעָרָה *śe'ārāh* **fem. noun**
(storm, tempest)
Job 9:17; **Nah.** 1:3.

8184. שְׂעֹרָה *śe'ōrāh* **fem. noun**
(barley)
Ex. 9:31; **Lev.** 27:16; **Num.** 5:15; **Deut.** 8:8; **Judg.** 7:13; **Ruth** 1:22; 2:17,23; 3:2,15,17; **2 Sam.** 14:30; 17:28; 21:9; **1 Kgs.** 4:28(5:8); **2 Kgs.** 4:42; 7:1,16,18; **1 Chr.** 11:13; **2 Chr.** 2:10(9),15(14); 27:5; **Job** 31:40; **Isa.** 28:25; **Jer.** 41:8; **Ezek.** 4:9,12; 13:19; 45:13; **Hos.** 3:2; **Joel** 1:11.

8185. שַׂעֲרָה *śa'arāh* **fem. noun**
(hair)
Judg. 20:16; **1 Sam.** 14:45; **2 Sam.** 14:11; **1 Kgs.** 1:52; **Job** 4:15; **Ps.** 40:12(13); 69:4(5).

8186. I. שַׁעֲרוּר *ša'arûr*, שַׁעֲרוּרָה *ša'arûrāh* **fem. noun**
(horrible thing)
Jer. 5:30; 23:14.
II. שַׁעֲרוּרִי *ša'arûriy*, שַׁעֲרוּרִיָּה *ša'arûriyyāh* **fem. noun**
(horrible thing)
Jer. 18:13; **Hos.** 6:10.

8187. שְׁעַרְיָה *še'aryāh* **masc. proper noun**
(Sheariah)
1 Chr. 8:38; 9:44.

8188. שְׂעֹרִים *śe'ōriym* **masc. proper noun**
(Seorim)
1 Chr. 24:8.

8189. A. שַׁעֲרַיִם *ša'arayim* **proper noun**
(Shaaraim: a town in Judah)
Josh. 15:36; **1 Sam.** 17:52.
B. שַׁעֲרַיִם *ša'arayim* **proper noun**
(Shaaraim: a town in Simeon)
1 Chr. 4:31.

8190. שַׁעַשְׁגַז *ša'ašgaz* **masc. proper noun**
(Shaashgaz)
Esth. 2:14.

8191. שַׁעֲשֻׁעִים *ša'ᵃšu'iym* **masc. pl. noun**
(delight)
Ps. 119:24,77,92,143,174; **Prov.** 8:30,31; **Isa.** 5:7; **Jer.** 31:20.

8192. שָׁפָה *šāp̱āh* **verb**
(to be bare; to stick out)
Job 33:21(KJV, [Kᵉ] *šᵉp̱iy* [8205]); **Isa.** 13:2.

8193. שָׂפָה *śap̱āh* **fem. noun**
(lip; language; brim, edge)
Gen. 11:1,6,7,9; 22:17; 41:3,17; **Ex.** 2:3; 6:12,30; 7:15; 14:30; 26:4,10; 28:26,32; 36:11,17; 39:19,23; **Lev.** 5:4; **Num.** 30:6(7),8(9),12(13); **Deut.** 2:36; 4:48; 23:23(24); **Josh.** 11:4; 12:2; 13:9,16; **Judg.** 7:12,22; **1 Sam.** 1:13; 13:5; **1 Kgs.** 4:29(5:9); 7:23,24,26; 9:26; **2 Kgs.** 2:13; 18:20; 19:28; **2 Chr.** 4:2,5; 8:17; **Job** 2:10; 8:21; 11:2,5; 12:20; 13:6; 15:6; 16:5; 23:12; 27:4; 32:20; 33:3; **Ps.** 12:2–4(3–5); 16:4; 17:1,4; 21:2(3); 22:7(8); 31:18(19); 34:13(14); 40:9(10); 45:2(3); 51:15(17); 59:7(8),12(13); 63:3(4),5(6); 66:14; 71:23; 81:5(6); 89:34(35); 106:33; 119:13,171; 120:2; 140:3(4),9(10); 141:3; **Prov.** 4:24; 5:2,3; 7:21; 8:6,7; 10:8,10,13,18,19,21,32; 12:13,19,22; 13:3; 14:3,7,23; 15:7; 16:10, 13,21,23,27,30; 17:4,7,28; 18:6,7,20; 19:1; 20:15,19; 22:11,18; 23:16; 24:2, 26,28; 26:23,24; 27:2; **Eccl.** 10:12; **Song** 4:3,11; 5:13; 7:9(10); **Isa.** 6:5,7; 11:4; 19:18; 28:11; 29:13; 30:27; 33:19; 36:5; 37:29; 57:19; 59:3; **Jer.** 17:16; **Lam.** 3:62; **Ezek.** 3:5,6; 36:3; 43:13; 47:6,7,12; **Dan.** 10:16; 12:5; **Hos.** 14:2(3); **Hab.** 3:16; **Zeph.** 3:9; **Mal.** 2:6,7.

8194. שָׁפָה *šāp̱āh,* שְׁפוֹת *šᵉp̱ôṯ* **fem. noun**
(cheese)
2 Sam. 17:29.

8195. שְׁפוֹ *šᵉp̱ô,* שְׁפִי *šᵉp̱iy* **masc. proper noun**
(Shepho, Shephi)
Gen. 36:23; **1 Chr.** 1:40.

8196. שְׁפוֹט *šᵉp̱ôṭ* **masc. noun**
(judgment, punishment)
2 Chr. 20:9; **Ezek.** 23:10.

8197. I. שְׁפוּפָם *šᵉp̱ûp̱am* **masc. proper noun**
(Shephupham: descendant of Benjamin)
Num. 26:39(KJV, NIV, [following some MSS and versions] *šûp̱ām*).
II. שְׁפוּפָן *šᵉp̱ûp̱ān* **masc. proper noun**
(Shephuphan: son of Bela [perhaps the same as A])
1 Chr. 8:5.

8198. שִׁפְחָה *šip̱ḥāh* **fem. noun**
(maidservant, female slave)
Gen. 12:16; 16:1–3,5,6,8; 20:14; 24:35; 25:12; 29:24,29; 30:4,7,9,10,12,18,43; 32:5(6),22(23); 33:1,2,6; 35:25,26; **Ex.** 11:5; **Lev.** 19:20; **Deut.** 28:68; **Ruth** 2:13; **1 Sam.** 1:18; 8:16; 25:27,41; 28:21,22; **2 Sam.** 14:6,7,12,15,17,19; 17:17; **2 Kgs.** 4:2,16; 5:26; **2 Chr.** 28:10; **Esth.** 7:4; **Ps.** 123:2; **Prov.** 30:23; **Eccl.** 2:7; **Isa.** 14:2; 24:2; **Jer.** 34:9–11,16; **Joel** 2:29(3:2).

8199. שָׁפַט *šāp̱aṭ* **verb**
(to judge, to execute judgment; to rule)
Gen. 16:5; 18:25; 19:9; 31:53; **Ex.** 2:14; 5:21; 18:13,16,22,26; **Lev.** 19:15; **Num.** 25:5; 35:24; **Deut.** 1:16; 16:18; 17:9,12; 19:17,18; 21:2; 25:1,2; **Josh.** 8:33; 23:2; 24:1; **Judg.** 2:16–19; 3:10; 4:4; 10:2,3; 11:27; 12:7–9,11,13,14; 15:20; 16:31; **Ruth** 1:1; **1 Sam.** 3:13; 4:18; 7:6,15–17; 8:1,2,5,6,20; 12:7; 24:12(13),15(16); **2 Sam.** 7:11; 15:4; 18:19,31; **1 Kgs.** 3:9,28; 7:7; 8:32; **2 Kgs.** 15:5; 23:22; **1 Chr.** 16:33; 17:6,10; 23:4; 26:29; **2 Chr.** 1:2,10,11; 6:23; 19:5,6; 20:12;

22:8; 26:21; **Ezra** 10:14; **Job** 9:15,24; 12:17; 21:22; 22:13; 23:7; **Ps.** 2:10; 7:8(9),11(12); 9:4(5),8(9),19(20); 10:18; 26:1; 35:24; 37:33; 43:1; 50:6; 51:4(6); 58:1(2),11(12); 67:4(5); 72:4; 75:2(3), 7(8); 82:1–3,8; 94:2; 96:13; 98:9; 109:7, 31; 141:6; 148:11; **Prov.** 8:16; 29:9,14; 31:9; **Eccl.** 3:17; **Isa.** 1:17,23,26; 2:4; 3:2; 5:3; 11:3,4; 16:5; 33:22; 40:23; 43:26; 51:5; 59:4; 66:16; **Jer.** 2:35; 5:28; 11:20; 25:31; **Lam.** 3:59; **Ezek.** 7:3, 8,27; 11:10,11; 16:38; 17:20; 18:30; 20:4,35,36; 21:30(35); 22:2; 23:24,36,45; 24:14; 33:20; 34:17,20,22; 35:11; 36:19; 38:22; 44:24; **Dan.** 9:12; **Hos.** 7:7; 13:10; **Joel** 3:12(4:12); **Amos** 2:3; **Obad.** 1:21; **Mic.** 3:11; 4:3; 5:1(4:14); 7:3; **Zeph.** 3:3; **Zech.** 7:9; 8:16.

8200. שְׁפַט *š^{e}p̱aṭ* **Aram. verb**
(to judge; corr. to Hebr. 8199)
Ezra 7:25.

8201. שֶׁפֶט *šep̱eṭ* **masc. noun**
(judgment; punishment)
Ex. 6:6; 7:4; 12:12; **Num.** 33:4; **2 Chr.** 24:24; **Prov.** 19:29; **Ezek.** 5:10,15; 11:9; 14:21; 16:41; 25:11; 28:22,26; 30:14,19.

8202. A. שָׁפָט *šāp̱āṭ* **masc. proper noun**
(Shaphat: a Simeonite)
Num. 13:5.
B. שָׁפָט *šāp̱āṭ* **masc. proper noun**
(Shaphat: father of the prophet Elisha)
1 Kgs. 19:16,19; **2 Kgs.** 3:11; 6:31.
C. שָׁפָט *šāp̱āṭ* **masc. proper noun**
(Shaphat: descendant of David)
1 Chr. 3:22.
D. שָׁפָט *šāp̱āṭ* **masc. proper noun**
(Shaphat: a Gadite)
1 Chr. 5:12.
E. שָׁפָט *šāp̱āṭ* **masc. proper noun**
(Shaphat: son of Adlai)
1 Chr. 27:29.

8203. A. שְׁפַטְיָהוּ *š^{e}p̱aṭyāhû* **masc. proper noun**
(Shephatiah: a Benjamite warrior)
1 Chr. 12:5(6).
B. שְׁפַטְיָהוּ *š^{e}p̱aṭyāhû* **masc. proper noun**
(Shephatiah: a Simeonite official)
1 Chr. 27:16.
C. שְׁפַטְיָה *š^{e}p̱aṭyāh* **masc. proper noun**
(Shephatiah: a son of David)
2 Sam. 3:4; **1 Chr.** 3:3.
D. שְׁפַטְיָהוּ *š^{e}p̱aṭyāhû* **masc. proper noun**
(Shephatiah: a son of Jehoshaphat)
2 Chr. 21:2.
E. שְׁפַטְיָה *š^{e}p̱aṭyāh* **masc. proper noun**
(Shephatiah: prince who opposed Jeremiah)
Jer. 38:1.
F. שְׁפַטְיָה *š^{e}p̱aṭyāh* **masc. proper noun**
(Shephatiah: head of a family returning from exile with Zerubbabel)
Ezra 2:4; 8:8; **Neh.** 7:9.
G. שְׁפַטְיָה *š^{e}p̱aṭyāh* **masc. proper noun**
(Shephatiah: a descendant of one of Solomon's servants)
Ezra 2:57; **Neh.** 7:59.
H. שְׁפַטְיָה *š^{e}p̱aṭyāh* **masc. proper noun**
(Shephatiah: ancestor of Meshullam)
1 Chr. 9:8.
I. שְׁפַטְיָה *š^{e}p̱aṭyāh* **masc. proper noun**
(Shephatiah: descendant of Perez)
Neh. 11:4.

8204. שִׁפְטָן *šip̱ṭān* **masc. proper noun**
(Shiphtan: father of Kemuel)
Num. 34:24.

8205. שְׁפִי *šᵉp̱iy* **masc. noun**
(barren hill; high place)
Num. 23:3; **Job** 33:21(NASB, NIV, [Qᵉ] *šāp̱āh* [8192]); **Isa.** 41:18; 49:9; **Jer.** 3:2,21; 4:11; 7:29; 12:12; 14:6.

8206. A. שֻׁפִּים *šuppiym* **masc. proper noun**
(Shuppim: a Benjamite)
1 Chr. 7:12,15.
B. שֻׁפִּים *šuppiym* **masc. proper noun**
(Shuppim: a Levite gatekeeper)
1 Chr. 26:16.

8207. שְׁפִיפֹן *šᵉp̱iyp̱ōn* **masc. noun**
(a snake, viper, adder)
Gen. 49:17.

8208. שָׁפִיר *šāp̱iyr* **masc. proper noun**
(Shaphir)
Mic. 1:11.

8209. שַׁפִּיר *šap̱iyr* **Aram. adj.**
(beautiful)
Dan. 4:12(9),21(18).

8210. שָׁפַךְ *šāp̱ak̲* **verb**
(to pour out, to spill; to shed [blood])
Gen. 9:6; 37:22; **Ex.** 4:9; 29:12; **Lev.** 4:7,18,25,30,34; 14:41; 17:4,13; **Num.** 35:33; **Deut.** 12:16,24,27; 15:23; 19:10; 21:7; **Judg.** 6:20; **1 Sam.** 1:15; 7:6; 25:31; **2 Sam.** 20:10,15; **1 Kgs.** 2:31; 13:3,5; 18:28; **2 Kgs.** 19:32; 21:16; 24:4; **1 Chr.** 22:8; 28:3; **Job** 12:21; 16:13; 30:16; **Ps.** 22:14; 42:4(5); 62:8(9); 69:24(25); 73:2; 79:3,6,10; 102:[title](1); 106:38; 107:40; 142:2(3); **Prov.** 1:16; 6:17; **Isa.** 37:33; 42:25; 57:6; 59:7; **Jer.** 6:6,11; 7:6; 10:25; 14:16; 22:3,17; **Lam.** 2:4,11,12,19; 4:1, 11,13; **Ezek.** 4:2; 7:8; 9:8; 14:19; 16:15, 36,38; 17:17; 18:10; 20:8,13,21,33,34; 21:22(27),31(36); 22:3,4,6,9,12,22,27,31; 23:8,45; 24:7; 26:8; 30:15; 33:25; 36:18; 39:29; **Dan.** 11:15; **Hos.** 5:10; **Joel** 2:28(3:1),29(3:2); 3:19(4:19); **Amos** 5:8; 9:6; **Zeph.** 1:17; 3:8; **Zech.** 12:10.

8211. שֶׁפֶךְ *šep̱ek̲* **masc. noun**
(place of pouring out; act of pouring out)
Lev. 4:12.

8212. שָׁפְכָה *šop̱kāh* **fem. noun**
(male penis)
Deut. 23:1(2).

8213. שָׁפֵל *šāp̱al* **verb**
(to make humble, to humiliate; to bring down)
1 Sam. 2:7; **2 Sam.** 22:28; **Job** 22:29; 40:11; **Ps.** 18:27(28); 75:7(8); 113:6; 147:6; **Prov.** 25:7; 29:23; **Eccl.** 12:4(KJV, NASB, *šāp̱āl* [8217]); **Isa.** 2:9,11,12,17; 5:15; 10:33; 13:11; 25:11,12; 26:5; 29:4; 32:19; 40:4; 57:9; **Jer.** 13:18; **Ezek.** 17:24; 21:26(31).

8214. שְׁפַל *šᵉp̱al* **Aram. verb**
(to humble; to subdue; corr. to Hebr. 8213)
Dan. 4:37(34); 5:19,22; 7:24.

8215. שְׁפַל *šᵉp̱al* **Aram. adj.**
(lowliest)
Dan. 4:17(14).

8216. שֵׁפֶל *šēp̱el* **masc. noun**
(low place, low estate)
Ps. 136:23; **Eccl.** 10:6.

8217. שָׁפָל *šāp̱āl* **adj.**
(low, humble; lower)
Lev. 13:20,21,26; 14:37; **2 Sam.** 6:22; **Job** 5:11; **Ps.** 138:6; **Prov.** 16:19; 29:23; **Eccl.** 12:4(NIV, *šāp̱al* [8213]); **Isa.** 57:15; **Ezek.** 17:6,14,24; 21:26(31); 29:14,15; **Mal.** 2:9.

8218. שִׁפְלָה *šip̱lāh* **fem. noun**
(lowliness)
Isa. 32:19.

8219. I. שְׁפֵלָה *š^e^p̱ēlāh* **fem. noun**
(low country; foothill; valley)
Deut. 1:7; **Josh.** 9:1; 10:40; 11:2,16; 12:8; 15:33; **Judg.** 1:9; **1 Kgs.** 10:27; **1 Chr.** 27:28(NASB, see II); **2 Chr.** 1:15; 9:27; 26:10; 28:18; **Jer.** 17:26; 32:44; 33:13; **Obad.** 1:19(NASB, see II); **Zech.** 7:7.
II. שְׁפֵלָה *š^e^p̱ēlāh* **proper noun**
(Shephelah)
1 Chr. 27:28(KJV, NIV, see I); **Obad.** 1:19(KJV, NIV, see I).

8220. שִׁפְלוּת *šip̱lûṯ* **fem. noun**
(idleness)
Eccl. 10:18.

8221. שְׁפָם *š^e^p̱ām* **proper noun**
(Shepham)
Num. 34:10,11.

8222. שָׂפָם *śāp̱ām* **masc. noun**
(upper lip; mustache; lower face)
Lev. 13:45; **2 Sam.** 19:24(25); **Ezek.** 24:17,22; **Mic.** 3:7.

8223. שָׁפָם *šāp̱ām* **masc. proper noun**
(Shapham)
1 Chr. 5:12.

8224. שִׂפְמוֹת *śip̱môṯ* **proper noun**
(Siphmoth)
1 Sam. 30:28.

8225. שִׁפְמִי *šip̱miy* **masc. proper noun**
(Shiphmite)
1 Chr. 27:27.

8226. שָׂפַן *śāp̱an* **verb**
(to cover as a treasure)
Deut. 33:19(NASB, *sāp̱an* [5603,III]).

8227. I. שָׁפָן *šāp̱ān* **masc. noun**
(coney, badger)
Lev. 11:5; **Deut.** 14:7; **Ps.** 104:18; **Prov.** 30:26.
II. שָׁפָן *šāp̱ān* **masc. proper noun**
(Shaphan: secretary of Josiah)
2 Kgs. 22:3,8–10,12,14; 25:22; **2 Chr.** 34:8,15,16,18,20.
III. שָׁפָן *šāp̱ān* **masc. proper noun**
(Shaphan: father of Ahikam; perhaps the same as II)
2 Kgs. 25:22; **2 Chr.** 34:20; **Jer.** 26:24; 39:14; 40:5,9,11; 41:2; 43:6.
IV. שָׁפָן *šāp̱ān* **masc. proper noun**
(Shaphan: father of Elasah; perhaps the same as II)
Jer. 29:3.
V. שָׁפָן *šāp̱ān* **masc. proper noun**
(Shaphan: father of Gemariah; perhaps the same as II)
Jer. 36:10–12.
VI. שָׁפָן *šāp̱ān* **masc. proper noun**
(Shaphan: father of Jaazaniah; perhaps the same as II)
Ezek. 8:11.

8228. שֶׁפַע *šepa'* **masc. noun**
(abundance)
Deut. 33:19.

8229. שִׁפְעָה *šip̱'āh* **fem. noun**
(abundance, multitude, company)
2 Kgs. 9:17; **Job** 22:11; 38:34; **Isa.** 60:6; **Ezek.** 26:10.

8230. שִׁפְעִי *šip̱'iy* **masc. proper noun**
(Shiphi)
1 Chr. 4:37.

8231. שָׁפַר *šāp̱ar* **verb**
(to be beautiful)
Ps. 16:6.

8232. שְׁפַר *š^e^p̱ar* **Aram. verb**
(to be good; to be pleasing; corr. to Hebr. 8231)
Dan. 4:2(3:32),27(24); 6:1(2).

8233. שֶׁפֶר *šep̱er* **masc. noun**
(beauty, goodness)
Gen. 49:21.

8234. שֶׁפֶר *šeper* **proper noun**
(Shepher)
Num. 33:23,24.

8235. שִׁפְרָה *šiprāh* **fem. noun**
(brightness, clearness)
Job 26:13.

8236. שִׁפְרָה *šiprāh* **fem. proper noun**
(Shiphrah)
Ex. 1:15.

8237. שַׁפְרִיר *šapriyr* **masc. noun**
(canopy; pavilion)
Jer. 43:10.

8238. שְׁפַרְפָּר *š^e^parpār* **Aram. masc. noun**
(dawn; early morning)
Dan. 6:19(20).

8239. שָׁפַת *šāpaṯ* **verb**
(to place on; to establish)
2 Kgs. 4:38; **Ps.** 22:15(16); **Isa.** 26:12; **Ezek.** 24:3.

8240. I. שְׁפַתַּיִם *š^e^pattayim* **masc. dual noun**
(double-pronged hooks)
Ezek. 40:43.
II. שְׁפַתַּיִם *š^e^pattayim* **masc. dual noun**
(campfires)
Ps. 68:13(KJV, see III; NASB, see IV).
III. שְׁפַתַּיִם *š^e^pattayim* **masc. dual noun**
(pots)
Ps. 68:13(NIV, see II; NASB, see IV).
IV. שְׁפַתַּיִם *š^e^pattayim* **masc. dual noun**
(sheepfolds)
Ps. 68:13(NIV, see II; KJV, see III).

8241. I. שֶׁצֶף *šeṣep* **masc. noun**
(a surge)
Isa. 54:8(KJV, see II; NASB, *šeṭep* [7858]).
II. שֶׁצֶף *šeṣep* **masc. noun**
(a little)
Isa. 54:8(NASB, *šeṭep* [7858]; NIV, see I).

8242. שַׂק *śaq* **masc. noun**
(sackcloth; sack)
Gen. 37:34; 42:25,27,35; **Lev.** 11:32; **Josh.** 9:4; **2 Sam.** 3:31; 21:10; **1 Kgs.** 20:31,32; 21:27; **2 Kgs.** 6:30; 19:1,2; **1 Chr.** 21:16; **Neh.** 9:1; **Esth.** 4:1–4; **Job** 16:15; **Ps.** 30:11(12); 35:13; 69:11(12); **Isa.** 3:24; 15:3; 20:2; 22:12; 37:1,2; 50:3; 58:5; **Jer.** 4:8; 6:26; 48:37; 49:3; **Lam.** 2:10; **Ezek.** 7:18; 27:31; **Dan.** 9:3; **Joel** 1:8,13; **Amos** 8:10; **Jon.** 3:5,6,8.

8243. שָׁק *šāq* **Aram. masc. noun**
(leg; corr. to Hebr. 7785)
Dan. 2:33.

8244. שָׂקַד *śāqaḏ* **verb**
(to bind)
Lam. 1:14.

8245. שָׁקַד *šāqaḏ* **verb**
(to watch; to guard)
Ezra 8:29; **Job** 21:32; **Ps.** 102:7(8); 127:1; **Prov.** 8:34; **Isa.** 29:20; **Jer.** 1:12; 5:6; 31:28; 44:27; **Dan.** 9:14.

8246. שָׁקַד *šāqaḏ* **verb**
(shaped like an almond; NIV, *m^e^šuqqāḏ* as a noun)
Ex. 25:33,34; 37:19,20.

8247. שָׁקֵד *šāqēḏ* **masc. noun**
(almond, almond tree)
Gen. 43:11; **Num.** 17:8(23); **Eccl.** 12:5; **Jer.** 1:11.

8248. שָׁקָה *šāqāh* **verb**
(to give water; to cause one to drink)
Gen. 2:6,10; 19:32–35; 21:19; 24:14, 18,19,43,45,46; 29:2,3,7,8,10; **Ex.** 2:16, 17,19; 32:20; **Num.** 5:24,26,27; 20:8; **Deut.** 11:10; **Judg.** 4:19; **1 Sam.** 30:11;

2 Sam. 23:15; **1 Chr.** 11:17; **2 Chr.** 28:15; **Esth.** 1:7; **Job** 21:24; 22:7; **Ps.** 36:8(9); 60:3(5); 69:21(22); 78:15; 80:5(6); 104:11,13; **Prov.** 25:21; **Eccl.** 2:6; **Song** 8:2; **Isa.** 27:3; 43:20; **Jer.** 8:14; 9:15(14); 16:7; 23:15; 25:15,17; 35:2; **Ezek.** 17:7; 32:6; **Joel** 3:18(4:18); **Amos** 2:12; 8:8; **Hab.** 2:15.

8249. שִׁקּוּ *šiqquw* **masc. noun**
(a drink)
Ps. 102:9(10)(NASB, NIV, *šiqqûy* [8250]).

8250. שִׁקּוּי *šiqqûy* **masc. noun**
(a drink; moisture)
Ps. 102:9(10)(KJV, *šiqquw* [8249]); **Prov.** 3:8; **Hos.** 2:5(7).

8251. שִׁקּוּץ *šiqqûṣ*, שִׁקֻּץ *šiqquṣ* **masc. noun**
(abominable idol, detestable thing)
Deut. 29:17(16); **1 Kgs.** 11:5,7; **2 Kgs.** 23:13,24; **2 Chr.** 15:8; **Isa.** 66:3; **Jer.** 4:1; 7:30; 13:27; 16:18; 32:34; **Ezek.** 5:11; 7:20; 11:18,21; 20:7,8,30; 37:23; **Dan.** 9:27; 11:31; 12:11; **Hos.** 9:10; **Nah.** 3:6; **Zech.** 9:7.

8252. שָׁקַט *šāqaṭ* **verb**
(to rest; to be quiet, to be peaceful)
Josh. 11:23; 14:15; **Judg.** 3:11,30; 5:31; 8:28; 18:7,27; **Ruth** 3:18; **2 Kgs.** 11:20; **1 Chr.** 4:40; **2 Chr.** 14:1(13:23),5(4), 6(5); 20:30; 23:21; **Job** 3:13,26; 34:29; 37:17; **Ps.** 76:8(9); 83:1(2); 94:13; **Prov.** 15:18; **Isa.** 7:4; 14:7; 18:4; 30:15; 32:17; 57:20; 62:1; **Jer.** 30:10; 46:27; 47:6,7; 48:11; 49:23; **Ezek.** 16:42,49; 38:11; **Zech.** 1:11.

8253. שֶׁקֶט *šeqeṭ* **masc. noun**
(quietness)
1 Chr. 22:9.

8254. שָׁקַל *šāqal* **verb**
(to weigh; to weigh out money, to pay)
Gen. 23:16; **Ex.** 22:17(16); **2 Sam.** 14:26; 18:12; **1 Kgs.** 20:39; **Ezra** 8:25,26,29,33; **Esth.** 3:9; 4:7; **Job** 6:2; 28:15; 31:6; **Isa.** 33:18; 40:12; 46:6; 55:2; **Jer.** 32:9,10; **Zech.** 11:12.

8255. שֶׁקֶל *šeqel* **masc. noun**
(shekel; unit of weight for metals)
Gen. 23:15,16; **Ex.** 21:32; 30:13,15,24; 38:24–26,29; **Lev.** 5:15; 27:3–7,16,25; **Num.** 3:47,50; 7:13,19,25,31,37,43,49, 55,61,67,73,79,85,86; 18:16; 31:52; **Josh.** 7:21; **1 Sam.** 9:8; 17:5,7; **2 Sam.** 14:26; 24:24; **2 Kgs.** 7:1,16,18; 15:20; **1 Chr.** 21:25; **2 Chr.** 3:9; **Neh.** 5:15; 10:32(33); **Jer.** 32:9; **Ezek.** 4:10; 45:12; **Amos** 8:5.

8256. שִׁקְמָה *šiqmāh* **fem. noun**
(sycamore tree; sycamore fig)
1 Kgs. 10:27; **1 Chr.** 27:28; **2 Chr.** 1:15; 9:27; **Ps.** 78:47; **Isa.** 9:10(9); **Amos** 7:14.

8257. שָׁקַע *šāqaʿ* **verb**
(to sink down, to settle)
Num. 11:2; **Job** 41:1(40:25); **Jer.** 51:64; **Ezek.** 32:14; **Amos** 8:8; 9:5.

8258. שְׁקַעֲרוּרָה *$š^e$qa$ʿ^a$rûrāh* **fem. noun**
(depression; hollow streak on a branch)
Lev. 14:37.

8259. שָׁקַף *šāqaḇ* **verb**
(to look down on, to overlook)
Gen. 18:16; 19:28; 26:8; **Ex.** 14:24; **Num.** 21:20; 23:28; **Deut.** 26:15; **Judg.** 5:28; **1 Sam.** 13:18; **2 Sam.** 6:16; 24:20; **2 Kgs.** 9:30,32; **1 Chr.** 15:29; **Ps.** 14:2; 53:2(3); 85:11(12); 102:19(20); **Prov.** 7:6; **Song** 6:10; **Jer.** 6:1; **Lam.** 3:50.

8260. I. שֶׁקֶף *šeqeḇ* **masc. noun**
(squared frame)
1 Kgs. 7:5(KJV, see II).

8261. I. שָׁקוּף šāqûp̱, שָׁקֻף šāqup̱

II. שֶׁקֶף šeqep̱ **masc. noun**
(window)
1 Kgs. 7:5(NASB, NIV, see I).

8261. I. שָׁקוּף šāqûp̱, שָׁקֻף šāqup̱
masc. noun
(squared frames)
1 Kgs. 6:4(KJV, NIV, see II).

II. שָׁקוּף šāqûp̱, שָׁקֻף šāqup̱ **masc. noun**
(windows)
1 Kgs. 6:4(NASB, see I).

8262. שָׁקַץ šāqaṣ **verb**
(to detest; to consider defiled)
Lev. 11:11,13,43; 20:25; **Deut.** 7:26;
Ps. 22:24(25).

8263. שֶׁקֶץ šeqeṣ **masc. noun**
(something detested; something considered defiled)
Lev. 7:21; 11:10–13,20,23,41,42;
Isa. 66:17; **Ezek.** 8:10.

8264. I. שָׁקַק šāqaq **verb**
(to rush about; to charge)
Prov. 28:15; **Isa.** 33:4; **Joel** 2:9;
Nah. 2:4(5).

II. שָׁקַק šāqaq **verb**
(to thirst; to long for)
Ps. 107:9(NIV, see III); **Isa.** 29:8(NIV, see III).

III. שֹׁקֵק šôqēq **adj.**
(thirsty)
Ps. 107:9(KJV, NASB, see II); **Isa.** 29:8(KJV, NASB, see II).

8265. שָׂקַר śāqar **verb**
(to flirt)
Isa. 3:16.

8266. שָׁקַר šāqar **verb**
(to deal falsely; to lie)
Gen. 21:23; **Lev.** 19:11; **1 Sam.** 15:29;
Ps. 44:17(18); 89:33(34); **Isa.** 63:8.

8267. שֶׁקֶר šeqer **masc. noun**
(a lie; falsehood)

Ex. 5:9; 20:16; 23:7; **Lev.** 6:3(5:22),
5(5:24); 19:12; **Deut.** 19:18; **1 Sam.**
25:21; **2 Sam.** 18:13; **1 Kgs.** 22:22,23;
2 Kgs. 9:12; **2 Chr.** 18:21,22; **Job** 13:4;
36:4; **Ps.** 7:14(15); 27:12; 31:18(19); 33:17;
35:19; 38:19(20); 52:3(5); 63:11(12);
69:4(5); 101:7; 109:2; 119:29,69,78,86,
104,118,128,163; 120:2; 144:8,11;
Prov. 6:17,19; 10:18; 11:18; 12:17,19,
22; 13:5; 14:5; 17:4,7; 19:5,9; 20:17;
21:6; 25:14,18; 26:28; 29:12; 31:30;
Isa. 9:15(14); 28:15; 32:7; 44:20; 57:4;
59:3,13; **Jer.** 3:10,23; 5:2,31; 6:13; 7:4,
8,9; 8:8,10; 9:3(2),5(4); 10:14; 13:25;
14:14; 16:19; 20:6; 23:14,25,26,32;
27:10,14–16; 28:15; 29:9,21,23,31; 37:14;
40:16; 43:2; 51:17; **Ezek.** 13:22; **Hos.** 7:1;
Mic. 2:11; 6:12; **Hab.** 2:18; **Zech.** 5:4;
8:17; 10:2; 13:3; **Mal.** 3:5.

8268. שֹׁקֶת šōqet̠ **fem. noun**
(water trough)
Gen. 24:20; 30:38.

8269. שַׂר śar **masc. noun**
(leader, captain, prince)
Gen. 12:15; 21:22,32; 26:26; 37:36;
39:1,21–23; 40:2–4,9,16,20–23; 41:9,
10,12; 47:6; **Ex.** 1:11; 2:14; 18:21,25;
Num. 21:18; 22:3,13–15,21,35,40;
23:6,17; 31:14,18,52,54; **Deut.** 1:15;
20:9; **Josh.** 5:14,15; **Judg.** 4:2,7; 5:15;
7:25; 8:3,6,14; 9:30; 10:18; **1 Sam.** 8:12;
12:9; 14:50; 17:18,55; 18:13,30; 22:2,7;
26:5; 29:3,4,9; **2 Sam.** 2:8; 3:38; 4:2;
10:3,16,18; 18:1,5; 19:6(7),13(14); 23:19;
24:2,4; **1 Kgs.** 1:19,25; 2:5,32; 4:2;
5:16(30); 9:22,23; 11:15,21,24; 14:27;
15:20; 16:9,16; 20:14,15,17,19; 22:26,
31–33; **2 Kgs.** 1:9–11,13,14; 4:13; 5:1;
8:21; 9:5; 10:1; 11:4,9,10,14,15,19; 23:8;
24:12,14; 25:19,23,26; **1 Chr.** 11:6,21;
12:21(22),28(29),34(35); 13:1; 15:5–10,
16,22,25,27; 19:3,16,18; 21:2; 22:17;
23:2; 24:5,6; 25:1; 26:26; 27:1,3,5,8,22,
31,34; 28:1,21; 29:6,24; **2 Chr.** 1:2;
8:9,10; 12:5,6,10; 16:4; 17:7,14,15;

18:25,30,31,32; 21:4,9; 22:8; 23:1,9,13, 14,20; 24:10,17,23; 25:5; 26:11; 28:14,21; 29:20,30; 30:2,6,12,24; 31:8; 32:3,6, 21,31; 33:11,14; 34:8; 35:8,9; 36:14,18; **Ezra** 7:28; 8:20,24,25,29; 9:1,2; 10:5, 8,14; **Neh.** 2:9; 3:9,12,14,15–19; 4:16(10); 7:2; 9:32,34,38(10:1); 11:1; 12:31,32; **Esth.** 1:3,11,14,16,18,21; 2:18; 3:1,12; 5:11; 6:9; 8:9; 9:3; **Job** 3:15; 29:9; 34:19; 39:25; **Ps.** 45:16(17); 68:27(28); 82:7; 105:22; 119:23,161; 148:11; **Prov.** 8:16; 19:10; 28:2; **Eccl.** 10:7,16,17; **Isa.** 1:23; 3:3,4,14; 9:6(5); 10:8; 19:11,13; 21:5; 23:8; 30:4; 31:9; 32:1; 34:12; 43:28; 49:7; **Jer.** 1:18; 2:26; 4:9; 8:1; 17:25; 24:1,8; 25:18,19; 26:10–12,16,21; 29:2; 32:32; 34:10,19,21; 35:4; 36:12,14,19,21; 37:14,15; 38:4,17,18,22,25,27; 39:3; 40:7,13; 41:11,13,16; 42:1,8; 43:4,5; 44:17,21; 48:7; 49:3,38; 50:35; 51:57,59; 52:10,25; **Lam.** 1:6; 2:2,9; 5:12; **Ezek.** 11:1; 17:12; 22:27; **Dan.** 1:7–11,18; 8:11,25; 9:6,8; 10:13,20,21; 11:5; 12:1; **Hos.** 3:4; 5:10; 7:3,5,16; 8:10; 9:15; 13:10; **Amos** 1:15; 2:3; **Mic.** 7:3; **Zeph.** 1:8; 3:3.

8270. שֹׁר *šōr* **masc. noun**
(navel, navel cord)
Prov. 3:8; **Song** 7:2(KJV, *šōrer* [8326]); **Ezek.** 16:4.

8271. שְׁרֵא *šᵉrēʾ* **Aram. verb**
(to loosen, to dissolve; to solve [problems])
Ezra 5:2; **Dan.** 2:22; 3:25; 5:6,12,16.

8272. A. שַׁרְאֶצֶר *šarʾeṣer,* שַׂרְאֶצֶר *śarʾeṣer* **masc. proper noun**
(Sharezer: son of Sennacherib)
2 Kgs. 19:37; **Isa.** 37:38.
B. שַׁרְאֶצֶר *šarʾeṣer,* שַׂרְאֶצֶר *śarʾeṣer* **masc. proper noun**
(Sharezer: an Israelite in Zechariah's day)
Zech. 7:2.

8273. שָׁרָב *šārāb̲* **masc. noun**
(scorched ground; scorching heat)
Isa. 35:7; 49:10.

8274. A. שֵׁרֵבְיָה *šērēb̲yāh* **masc. proper noun**
(Sherebiah: a Levite returning from exile with Ezra; possibly the same as B)
Ezra 8:18,24.
B. שֵׁרֵבְיָה *šērēb̲yāh* **masc. proper noun**
(Sherebiah: a Levite who assisted Ezra; possibly the same as A or C)
Neh. 8:7; 9:4,5; 10:12(13).
C. שֵׁרֵבְיָה *šērēb̲yāh* **masc. proper noun**
(Sherebiah: a Levite who returned with Zerubbabel; possibly the same as B)
Neh. 12:8,24.

8275. שַׁרְבִיט *šarb̲iyṭ* **masc. noun**
(scepter)
Esth. 4:11; 5:2; 8:4.

8276. שָׂרַג *śārag* **verb**
(to be woven together)
Job 40:17; **Lam.** 1:14.

8277. שָׂרַד *śārad̲* **verb**
(to remain, to be left)
Josh. 10:20.

8278. I. שְׂרָד *śᵉrād̲* **masc. noun**
(woven work)
Ex. 31:10(KJV, see II); 35:19(KJV, see II); 39:1(KJV, see II),41(KJV, see II).
II. שְׂרָד *śᵉrād̲* **masc. noun**
(service, work)
Ex. 31:10(NASB, NIV, see I); 35:19(NASB, NIV, see I); 39:1(NASB, NIV, see I),41(NASB, NIV, see I).

8279. I. שֶׂרֶד *śered̲* **masc. noun**
(marking tool)
Isa. 44:13(KJV, see II; NASB, see III).

II. שֶׂרֶד *śered* **masc. noun**
(line)
Isa. 44:13(NIV, see I; NASB, see III).
III. שֶׂרֶד *śered* **masc. noun**
(chalk)
Isa. 44:13(NIV, see I; KJV, see II).

8280. שָׂרָה *śārāh* **verb**
(to wrestle, to struggle; to have power)
Gen. 32:28(29); **Hos.** 12:3(4),4(5).

8281. שָׁרָה *šārāh* **verb**
(to set free, to unleash)
Job 37:3(KJV, *yāšar* [3474]); **Jer.** 15:11(KJV, [Q^e] *šērûṯ* [8293]).

8282. שָׂרָה *śārāh* **fem. noun**
(woman of nobility, princess, queen)
Judg. 5:29; **1 Kgs.** 11:3; **Esth.** 1:18; **Isa.** 49:23; **Lam.** 1:1.

8283. שָׂרָה *śārāh* **fem. proper noun**
(Sarah)
Gen. 17:15,17,19,21; 18:6,9–15; 20:2, 14,16,18; 21:1–3,6,7,9,12; 23:1,2,19; 24:36,67; 25:10,12; 49:31; **Isa.** 51:2.

8284. I. שָׂרָה *śārāh,* שׁוּרָה *šûrāh* **fem. noun**
(vineyard, vinerow)
Jer. 5:10(KJV, see II; NASB).
II. שׁוּרָה *šûrāh* **fem. noun**
(wall)
Jer. 5:10(NASB, NIV, see I).

8285. שֵׁרָה *šērāh* **fem. noun**
(bracelet)
Isa. 3:19.

8286. שְׂרוּג *ś^e rûg* **masc. proper noun**
(Serug)
Gen. 11:20–23; **1 Chr.** 1:26.

8287. שָׁרוּחֶן *šārûḥen* **masc. proper noun**
(Sharuhen)
Josh. 19:6.

8288. שְׂרוֹךְ *ś^e rûḵ* **masc. noun**
(strap, thong)
Gen. 14:23; **Isa.** 5:27.

8289. A. שָׁרוֹן *šārôn* **proper noun**
(Lasharon: early Canaanite city)
Josh. 12:18(NIV, see D).
B. שָׁרוֹן *šārôn* **proper noun**
(Sharon: coastal plain)
1 Chr. 27:29; **Song** 2:1; **Isa.** 33:9; 35:2; 65:10.
C. שָׁרוֹן *šārôn* **proper noun**
(Sharon: plain east of the Jordan)
1 Chr. 5:16.
D. לַשָּׁרוֹן *laššārôn* **proper noun**
(Lasharon: early Canaanite city)
Josh. 12:18(KJV, NASB, see A).

8290. שָׁרוֹנִי *šarôniy* **masc. proper noun**
(Sharonite)
1 Chr. 27:29.

8291. שָׂרֹק *śārōq* **masc. noun**
(choice vine, principal plant)
Isa. 16:8.

8292. שְׁרוּקָה *š^e riyqāh,* שְׁרִקָה *š^e riqāh* **fem. noun**
(hissing, whistling, playing a pipe or flute)
Judg. 5:16; **Jer.** 18:16.

8293. שֵׁרוּת *š^e rûṯ* **fem. noun**
(remnant)
Jer. 15:11(NASB, NIV, [Q^e] *šārāh* [8281]).

8294. שֶׂרַח *śeraḥ* **fem. proper noun**
(Serah)
Gen. 46:17; **Num.** 26:46; **1 Chr.** 7:30.

8295. שָׂרַט *śāraṭ* **verb**
(to cut oneself; to injure oneself)
Lev. 21:5; **Zech.** 12:3.

8296. שֶׂרֶט *śereṭ,* שָׂרֶטֶת *śāreṭeṯ* **masc./fem. noun**
(a cutting [of one's body])
Lev. 19:28; 21:5.

8297. שָׂרַי *śāray* **fem. proper noun**
(Sarai)
Gen. 11:29–31; 12:5,11,17; 16:1–3,5, 6,8; 17:15.

8298. שָׂרַי *śāray* **masc. proper noun**
(Sharai)
Ezra 10:40.

8299. שָׂרִיג *śāriyg* **masc. noun**
(branch)
Gen. 40:10,12; **Joel** 1:7.

8300. שָׂרִיד *śāriyḏ* **masc. noun**
(survivor, remaining one)
Num. 21:35; 24:19; **Deut.** 2:34; 3:3; **Josh.** 8:22; 10:20,28,30,33,37,39,40; 11:8; **Judg.** 5:13; **2 Kgs.** 10:11; **Job** 18:19; 20:21,26; 27:15; **Isa.** 1:9; **Jer.** 31:2; 42:17; 44:14; 47:4; **Lam.** 2:22; **Joel** 2:32(3:5); **Obad.** 1:14,18.

8301. שָׂרִיד *śāriyḏ* **proper noun**
(Sarid)
Josh. 19:10,12.

8302. I. שִׁרְיוֹן *širyôn,* שִׁרְיָן *širyān* **masc. noun**
(body armor; breastplate)
1 Sam. 17:5,38; **1 Kgs.** 22:34; **2 Chr.** 18:33; 26:14; **Neh.** 4:16(10); **Isa.** 59:17.
II. שִׁרְיָה *širyāh* **fem. noun**
(body armor)
Job 41:26(18)(NASB, NIV, see III).
III. שִׁרְיוֹן *širyôn,* שִׁרְיָן *širyān* **masc. noun**
(javelin)
Job 41:26(18)(KJV, see II).

8303. שִׂרְיֹן *śiryōn* **proper noun**
(Sirion)
Deut. 3:9; **Ps.** 29:6.

8304. A. שְׂרָיָה *śᵉrāyāh* **masc. proper noun**
(Seraiah: secretary of David)
2 Sam. 8:17.
B. שְׂרָיָה *śᵉrāyāh* **masc. proper noun**
(Seraiah: a Judaite, father of Joab)
1 Chr. 4:13,14.
C. שְׂרָיָה *śᵉrāyāh* **masc. proper noun**
(Seraiah: a Simeonite)
1 Chr. 4:35.
D. שְׂרָיָהוּ *śᵉrāyāhû* **masc. proper noun**
(Seraiah: an officer of King Jehoiakim)
Jer. 36:26.
E. שְׂרָיָה *śᵉrāyāh* **masc. proper noun**
(Seraiah: friend and associate of Jeremiah)
Jer. 51:59,61.
F. שְׂרָיָה *śᵉrāyāh* **masc. proper noun**
(Seraiah: associate of Gedaliah)
2 Kgs. 25:23; **Jer.** 40:8.
G. שְׂרָיָה *śᵉrāyāh* **masc. proper noun**
(Seraiah: chief priest when Jerusalem fell; possibly the same as H)
2 Kgs. 25:18; **1 Chr.** 6:14(5:40); **Jer.** 52:24.
H. שְׂרָיָה *śᵉrāyāh* **masc. proper noun**
(Seraiah: the father or ancestor of Ezra; possibly the same as G)
Ezra 7:1.
I. שְׂרָיָה *śᵉrāyāh* **masc. proper noun**

(Seraiah: one who returned from exile with Zerubbabel)
Ezra 2:2.
J. שְׂרָיָה *ś^e^rāyāh* **masc. proper noun**
(Seraiah: one who signed a covenant with Nehemiah; possibly the same as K)
Neh. 10:2(3).
K. שְׂרָיָה *ś^e^rāyāh* **masc. proper noun**
(Seraiah: priest in restored temple; possibly the same as J)
Neh. 11:11; 12:1,12.

8305. שָׂרִיק *śāriyq* **adj.**
(combed [of flax])
Isa. 19:9.

8306. שָׁרִיר *šāriyr* **masc. noun**
(muscles, navel)
Job 40:16.

8307. שְׁרִירוּת *š^e^riyrûṯ*, שְׁררוּת *š^e^rirûṯ* **fem. noun**
(stubbornness)
Deut. 29:19(18); **Ps.** 81:12(13); **Jer.** 3:17; 7:24; 9:14(13); 11:8; 13:10; 16:12; 18:12; 23:17.

8308. שָׂרַךְ *śāraḵ* **verb**
(to criss-cross; to traverse)
Jer. 2:23.

8309. שְׁרֵמָה *š^e^rēmāh* **fem. noun**
(field)
Jer. 31:40(NASB, NIV, [Q^e^] *š^e^ḏēmāh* [7709,I]).

8310. שַׂרְסְכִים *śars^e^ḵiym* **masc. proper noun**
(Sar-sekim)
Jer. 39:3(NIV, *n^e^bû śar-s^e^kiym* [5015,F]).

8311. I. שָׂרַע *śāra'* **verb**
(to stretch out)
Isa. 28:20.
II. שָׂרַע *śāra'* **verb**
(to be superfluous, to be deformed)
Lev. 21:18; 22:23.

8312. שַׂרְעַפִּים *śar'appiym* **masc. pl. noun**
(anxious thoughts)
Ps. 94:19; 139:23.

8313. שָׂרַף *śārap̱* **verb**
(to burn, to burn up; to be set on fire)
Gen. 11:3; 38:24; **Ex.** 12:10; 29:14,34; 32:20; **Lev.** 4:12,21; 6:30(23); 7:17,19; 8:17,32; 9:11; 10:6,16; 13:52,55,57; 16:27,28; 19:6; 20:14; 21:9; **Num.** 16:39(17:4); 19:5,8; 31:10; **Deut.** 7:5,25; 9:21; 12:3,31; 13:16(17); **Josh.** 6:24; 7:15,25; 8:28; 11:6,9,11,13; **Judg.** 9:52; 12:1; 14:15; 15:6; 18:27; **1 Sam.** 30:1,3, 14; 31:12; **2 Sam.** 23:7; **1 Kgs.** 9:16; 13:2; 15:13; 16:18; **2 Kgs.** 10:26; 17:31; 23:4,6,11,15,16,20; 25:9; **1 Chr.** 14:12; **2 Chr.** 15:16; 16:14; 34:5; 36:19; **Neh.** 4:2(3:34); **Ps.** 46:9(10); 74:8; 80:16(17); **Prov.** 6:27; **Isa.** 1:7; 44:16,19; 47:14; **Jer.** 7:31; 19:5; 21:10; 32:29; 34:2,5,22; 36:25,27–29,32; 37:8,10; 38:17,18,23; 39:8; 43:12,13; 51:32; 52:13; **Ezek.** 5:4; 16:41; 23:47; 43:21; **Amos** 2:1; **Mic.** 1:7.

8314. I. שָׂרָף *śārāp̱* **masc. noun**
(fiery serpent, fiery)
Num. 21:6,8; **Deut.** 8:15; **Isa.** 14:29; 30:6.
II. שָׂרָף *śārāp̱* **masc. noun**
(seraph; an angelic being)
Isa. 6:2,6.

8315. שָׂרָף *śārāp̱* **masc. proper noun**
(Saraph)
1 Chr. 4:22.

8316. שְׂרֵפָה *ś^e^rēp̱āh* **fem. noun**
(fire, burning)

Gen. 11:3; **Lev.** 10:6; **Num.** 16:37(17:2); 19:6,17; **Deut.** 29:23(22); **2 Chr.** 16:14; 21:19; **Isa.** 9:5(4); 64:11(10); **Jer.** 51:25; **Amos** 4:11.

8317. I. שָׁרַץ *šāraṣ* **verb**
(to swarm; to breed abundantly; to multiply)
Gen. 1:20,21; 7:21(KJV, see II); 8:17; 9:7; **Ex.** 1:7; 8:3(7:28); **Lev.** 11:29(KJV, see II),41(KJV, see II),42(KJV, see II),43(KJV, see II),46(KJV, see II); **Ps.** 105:30; **Ezek.** 47:9.
II. שָׁרַץ *šāraṣ* **verb**
(to creep)
Gen. 7:21(NASB, NIV, see I); **Lev.** 11:29(NASB, NIV, see I),41(NASB, NIV, see I),42(NASB, NIV, see I),43(NASB, NIV, see I),46(NASB, NIV, see I).

8318. שֶׁרֶץ *šereṣ* **masc. noun**
(creature that crawls or swarms; insect or small animal)
Gen. 1:20; 7:21; **Lev.** 5:2; 11:10,20,21,23,29,31,41–44; 22:5; **Deut.** 14:19.

8319. שָׁרַק *šāraq* **verb**
(to hiss; to whistle; to scorn)
1 Kgs. 9:8; **Job** 27:23; **Isa.** 5:26; 7:18; **Jer.** 19:8; 49:17; 50:13; **Lam.** 2:15,16; **Ezek.** 27:36; **Zeph.** 2:15; **Zech.** 10:8.

8320. I. שָׂרֹק *śārōq* **masc. noun**
(sorrel or brown [of horses])
Zech. 1:8(KJV, see II).
II. שָׂרֹק *śārōq* **masc. noun**
(speckled [of horses])
Zech. 1:8(NASB, NIV, see I).

8321. שֹׂרֵק *śōrēq*, שֹׂרֵקָה *śōrēqāh* **masc./fem. noun**
(choice vine)
Gen. 49:11; **Isa.** 5:2; **Jer.** 2:21.

8322. שְׁרֵקָה *šᵉrēqāh* **fem. noun**
(hissing as derision or scorn)
2 Chr. 29:8; **Jer.** 19:8; 25:9,18; 29:18; 51:37; **Mic.** 6:16.

8323. שָׂרַר *śārar* **verb**
(to govern, to rule, to lord it over)
Num. 16:13; **Judg.** 9:22(KJV, *śûr* [7786]); **Esth.** 1:22; **Prov.** 8:16; **Isa.** 32:1; **Hos.** 8:4(KJV, *śûr* [7786]).

8324. שֹׁרֵר *šôrēr*, שׁוֹרֵר *šôrēr* **masc. noun**
(enemy, foe; slanderer)
Ps. 5:8(9); 27:11; 54:5(7); 56:2(3); 59:10(11); 92:11(12)(KJV, NASB, *šûr* [7790]).

8325. שָׁרָר *šārār* **masc. proper noun**
(Sharar; the same as *śāḵār* [7940,A])
2 Sam. 23:33.

8326. שֹׁרֶר *šōrer* **masc. noun**
(navel)
Song 7:2(3)(NASB, NIV, *šōr* [8270]).

8327. שָׁרַשׁ *šāraš* **verb**
(to take root; to uproot)
Job 5:3; 31:8,12; **Ps.** 52:5(7); 80:9(10); **Isa.** 27:6; 40:24; **Jer.** 12:2.

8328. שֶׁרֶשׁ *šereš* **masc. noun**
(root, depth)
Deut. 29:18(17); **Judg.** 5:14; **2 Kgs.** 19:30; **Job** 8:17; 13:27; 14:8; 18:16; 19:28; 28:9; 29:19; 30:4; 36:30; **Ps.** 80:9(10); **Prov.** 12:3,12; **Isa.** 5:24; 11:1,10; 14:29,30; 37:31; 53:2; **Jer.** 17:8; **Ezek.** 17:6,7,9; 31:7; **Dan.** 11:7; **Hos.** 9:16; 14:5(6); **Amos** 2:9; **Mal.** 4:1(3:19).

8329. שֶׁרֶשׁ *šereš* **masc. proper noun**
(Sheresh)
1 Chr. 7:16.

8330. שֹׁרֶשׁ *šōreš* **Aram. masc. noun**
(root; corr. to Hebr. 8328)
Dan. 4:15(12),23(20),26(23).

8331. שַׁרְשָׁה *šaršāh* **fem. noun**
(chain)
Ex. 28:22(NASB, NIV, *šarš^{e}rāh* [8333]).

8332. שְׁרֹשׁוּ *š^{e}rōšû* **Aram. fem. noun**
(banishment)
Ezra 7:26.

8333. שַׁרְשְׁרָה *šarš^{e}rāh* **fem. noun**
(chain)
Ex. 28:14,22(KJV, *šaršāh* [8331]); 39:15; **1 Kgs.** 7:17; **2 Chr.** 3:5,16.

8334. שָׁרַת *šārat̲* **verb**
(to serve; to minister)
Gen. 39:4; 40:4; **Ex.** 24:13; 28:35,43; 29:30; 30:20; 33:11; 35:19; 39:1,26,41; **Num.** 1:50; 3:6,31; 4:9,12,14; 8:26; 11:28; 16:9; 18:2; **Deut.** 10:8; 17:12; 18:5,7; 21:5; **Josh.** 1:1; **1 Sam.** 2:11,18; 3:1; **2 Sam.** 13:17,18; **1 Kgs.** 1:4,15; 8:11; 10:5; 19:21; **2 Kgs.** 4:43; 6:15; 25:14; **1 Chr.** 6:32(17); 15:2; 16:4,37; 23:13; 26:12; 27:1; 28:1; **2 Chr.** 5:14; 8:14; 9:4; 13:10; 17:19; 22:8; 23:6; 24:14(KJV, NASB, *šārēt̲* [8335]); 29:11; 31:2; **Ezra** 8:17; **Neh.** 10:36(37),39(40); **Esth.** 1:10; 2:2; 6:3; **Ps.** 101:6; 103:21; 104:4; **Prov.** 29:12; **Isa.** 56:6; 60:7,10; 61:6; **Jer.** 33:21,22; 52:18; **Ezek.** 20:32; 40:46; 42:14; 43:19; 44:11,12,15–17, 19,27; 45:4,5; 46:24; **Joel** 1:9,13; 2:17.

8335. שָׁרֵת *šārēt̲* **masc. noun**
(ministry)
Num. 4:12; **2 Chr.** 24:14(NIV, *šārat* [8334]).

8336. I. שֵׁשׁ *šēš* **masc. noun**
(linen, fine linen)
Gen. 41:42; **Ex.** 25:4; 26:1,31; 27:9, 16,18; 28:5,6,15,39; 35:6,23,25,35; 36:8, 35,37; 38:9,16,18,23; 39:2,3,5,8,27–29; **Prov.** 31:22; **Ezek.** 16:10,13; 27:7.
II. שֵׁשׁ *šēš* **masc. noun**
(marble)
Esth. 1:6; **Song** 5:15.

8337. שֵׁשׁ *šēš*, שִׁשָּׁה *šiššāh* **fem. noun**
(six; NIV, see also *šiššim* [8346])
Gen. 7:6,11; 8:13; 16:16; 30:20; 31:41; 46:18,26; **Ex.** 12:37; 14:7; 16:26; 20:9,11; 21:2; 23:10,12; 24:16; 25:32,33,35; 26:9, 22,25; 28:10; 31:15,17; 34:21; 35:2; 36:16, 27,30; 37:18,19,21; 38:26; **Lev.** 12:5; 23:3; 24:6; 25:3; **Num.** 1:21,25,27,46; 2:4,9, 11,15,31,32; 3:28,34; 4:40; 7:3; 11:21; 26:22,41,51; 31:32,37,38,40,44,46,52; 35:6,13,15; **Deut.** 5:13; 15:12,18; 16:8; **Josh.** 6:3,14; 7:5; 15:41,59,62; 19:22; **Judg.** 3:31; 12:7; 18:11,16,17; 20:15,47; **Ruth** 3:15,17; **1 Sam.** 13:5,15; 14:2; 17:4,7; 23:13; 27:2; 30:9; **2 Sam.** 2:11; 5:5; 6:13; 15:18; 21:20; **1 Kgs.** 6:6; 10:14, 16,19,20,29; 11:16; 16:8,23; **2 Kgs.** 5:5; 11:3; 13:10,19; 14:21; 15:2,8,33; 16:2; 18:10; **1 Chr.** 3:4,22; 4:27; 7:2,4,40; 8:38; 9:6,9,44; 12:24(25),26(27),35(36); 20:6; 21:25; 23:4; 24:4,14; 25:3,23; 26:17; **2 Chr.** 1:17; 2:2(1),17(16),18(17); 3:8; 9:13,15,18,19; 13:21; 16:1; 22:12; 26:1, 3,12; 27:1,8; 28:1; 29:17,33; 35:8; **Ezra** 2:10,11,13,14,22,26,30,35,60,66,67,69; 8:26,35; **Neh.** 5:18; 7:10,15,16,18,20, 30,62,68,69; **Esth.** 2:12; **Job** 5:19; 42:12; **Prov.** 6:16; **Isa.** 6:2; **Jer.** 34:14; 52:23,30; **Ezek.** 9:2; 40:5,12; 41:1,3,5,8; 46:1,4,6.

8338. I. שָׁשָׁא *šāšā'* **verb**
(to drive; to drag along)
Ezek. 39:2(KJV, see II).
II. שָׁשָׁא *šāšā'* **verb**
(to leave a sixth part)
Ezek. 39:2(NASB, NIV, see I).

8339. שֵׁשְׁבַּצַּר *šēšbaṣṣar* **masc. proper noun**
(Sheshbazzar)
Ezra 1:8,11.

8340. שֵׁשְׁבַּצַּר *šēšbaṣṣār* **Aram. masc. proper noun**
(Sheshbazzar)
Ezra 5:14,16.

8341. שָׁשָׁה *šāšāh* **verb**
(to give a sixth part)
Ezek. 45:13.

8342. שָׂשׂוֹן *śāśôn* **masc. noun**
(joy, gladness)
Esth. 8:16,17; **Ps.** 45:7(8); 51:8(10), 12(14); 105:43; 119:111; **Isa.** 12:3; 22:13; 35:10; 51:3,11; 61:3; **Jer.** 7:34; 15:16; 16:9; 25:10; 31:13; 33:9,11; **Joel** 1:12; **Zech.** 8:19.

8343. שָׁשַׁי *šāšay* **masc. proper noun**
(Shashai)
Ezra 10:40.

8344. שֵׁשַׁי *šēšai* **masc. proper noun**
(Sheshai)
Num. 13:22; **Josh.** 15:14; **Judg.** 1:10.

8345. שִׁשִּׁי *šiššiy* **ord. num. adj.**
(sixth)
Gen. 1:31; 30:19; **Ex.** 16:5,22,29; 26:9; **Lev.** 25:21; **Num.** 7:42; 29:29; **Josh.** 19:32; **2 Sam.** 3:5; **1 Chr.** 2:15; 3:3; 12:11(12); 24:9; 25:13; 26:3,5; 27:9; **Neh.** 3:30; **Ezek.** 4:11; 8:1; 45:13; 46:14; **Hag.** 1:1,15.

8346. שִׁשִּׁים *šiššiym* **pl. num. adj.**
(sixty; [NIV, pl. of šēš [8337])
Gen. 5:15,18,20,21,23,27; 25:26; 46:26; **Lev.** 12:5; 27:3,7; **Num.** 1:39; 2:26; 3:50; 7:88; 26:25,27,43; 31:34,39; **Deut.** 3:4; **Josh.** 13:30; **2 Sam.** 2:31; **1 Kgs.** 4:13,22(5:2); 6:2; 10:14; **2 Kgs.** 25:19; **1 Chr.** 2:21,23; 5:18; 9:13; 16:38; 26:8; **2 Chr.** 3:3; 9:13; 11:21; 12:3; **Ezra** 2:9, 13,64; 8:10,13; **Neh.** 7:14,18,19,66, 72(71); 11:6; **Song** 3:7; 6:8; **Isa.** 7:8; **Jer.** 52:25; **Ezek.** 40:14; **Dan.** 9:25,26.

8347. שֵׁשַׁךְ *šēšaḵ* **proper noun**
(Sheshach)
Jer. 25:26; 51:41.

8348. שֵׁשָׁן *šēšān* **masc. proper noun**
(Sheshan)
1 Chr. 2:31,34,35.

8349. שָׁשָׁק *šāšāq* **masc. proper noun**
(Shashak)
1 Chr. 8:14,25.

8350. שָׁשֵׁר *šāšēr* **masc. noun**
(red, vermillion)
Jer. 22:14; **Ezek.** 23:14.

8351. I. שֵׁת *šēṯ* **masc. noun**
(buttocks, hip)
2 Sam. 10:4(KJV, *šēṯāh* [8357]); **Isa.** 20:4 (KJV, *šēṯāh* [8357]).
II. שֵׁת *šēṯ* **masc. noun**
(foundation)
Ps. 11:3(KJV, NASB, *šāṯāh* [8356]).

8352. A. שֵׁת *šēṯ* **masc. proper noun**
(Seth, Sheth: son of Adam and Eve)
Gen. 4:25,26; 5:3,4,6–8; **1 Chr.** 1:1.
B. שֵׁת *šēṯ* **masc. proper noun**
(Sheth: poetic name for Moab)
Num. 24:17.

8353. שֵׁת *šēṯ*, שִׁת *šiṯ* **Aram. num. adj.**
(six, sixth; corr. to Hebr. 8337)
Ezra 6:15; **Dan.** 3:1.

8354. שָׁתָה *šāṯāh* **verb**
(to drink)
Gen. 9:21; 24:14,18,19,22,44,46,54; 25:34; 26:30; 27:25; 30:38; 43:34; 44:5; **Ex.** 7:18,21,24; 15:23,24; 17:1,2,6; 24:11; 32:6; 34:28; **Lev.** 10:9; 11:34; **Num.** 6:3, 20; 20:5,11,17,19; 21:22; 23:24; 33:14; **Deut.** 2:6,28; 9:9,18; 11:11; 28:39; 29:6(5); 32:14,38; **Judg.** 7:5,6; 9:27; 13:4,7,14; 15:19; 19:4,6,21; **Ruth** 2:9; 3:3,7; **1 Sam.** 1:9,15; 30:12,16; **2 Sam.**

11:11,13; 12:3; 16:2; 19:35(36); 23:16,17; **1 Kgs.** 1:25; 4:20; 13:8,9,16–19,22,23; 16:9; 17:4,6,10; 18:41,42; 19:6,8; 20:12, 16; **2 Kgs.** 3:17; 6:22,23; 7:8; 9:34; 18:27, 31; 19:24; **1 Chr.** 11:18,19; 12:39(40); 29:22; **Ezra** 10:6; **Neh.** 8:10,12; **Esth.** 3:15; 4:16; 17:1; **Job** 1:4,13,18; 6:4; 15:16; 21:20; 34:7; **Ps.** 50:13; 69:12(13); 75:8(9); 78:44; 110:7; **Prov.** 4:17; 5:15; 9:5; 23:7; 26:6; 31:4,5,7; **Eccl.** 2:24; 3:13; 5:18(17); 8:15; 9:7; **Song** 5:1; **Isa.** 5:22; 21:5; 22:13; 24:9; 29:8; 36:12,16; 37:25; 44:12; 51:17, 22; 62:8,9; 65:13; **Jer.** 2:18; 16:8; 22:15; 25:16,26–28; 35:5,6,8,14; 49:12; 51:7; **Lam.** 5:4; **Ezek.** 4:11,16; 12:18,19; 23:32, 34; 25:4; 31:14,16; 34:18,19; 39:17–19; 44:21; **Dan.** 1:12; **Joel** 1:5; 3:3(4:3); **Amos** 2:8; 4:1,8; 5:11; 6:6; 9:14; **Obad.** 1:16; **Jon.** 3:7; **Mic.** 6:15; **Hab.** 2:16; **Zeph.** 1:13; **Hag.** 1:6; **Zech.** 7:6; 9:15.

8355. שְׁתָה *šeṯāh* **Aram. verb**
(to drink; corr. to Hebr. 8354)
Dan. 5:1–4,23.

8356. I. שָׁתָה *šāṯāh* **masc. noun**
(foundation, pillar)
Ps. 11:3(NIV, *šēṯ* [8351,II]); **Isa.** 19:10(KJV, see II; NIV, see III).
II. שָׁתָה *šāṯāh* **masc. noun**
(purpose, goal)
Isa. 19:10(NASB, see I; NIV, see III).
III. שָׁתָה *šāṯāh* **masc. noun**
(worker in cloth)
Isa. 19:10(NASB, see I; KJV, see II).

8357. שֵׁתָה *šēṯāh* **masc. noun**
(buttocks, hip)
2 Sam. 10:4(NASB, NIV, *šēṯ* [8351,I]); **Isa.** 20:4(NASB, NIV, *šēṯ* [8351,I]).

8358. שְׁתִי *šeṯiy* **masc. noun**
(drunkenness)
Eccl. 10:17.

8359. שְׁתִי *šeṯiy* **masc. noun**
(warp, woven material)
Lev. 13:48,49,51–53,56–59.

8360. שְׁתִיָּה *šeṯiyyāh* **fem. noun**
(drinking)
Esth. 1:8.

8361. שִׁתִּין *šittiyn* **Aram. num. pl. adj.**
(sixty; corr. to Hebr. 8346)
Ezra 6:3; **Dan.** 3:1; 5:31(6:1).

8362. שָׁתַל *šāṯal* **verb**
(to plant; to transplant)
Ps. 1:3; 92:13(14); **Jer.** 17:8; **Ezek.** 17:8, 10,22,23; 19:10,13; **Hos.** 9:13.

8363. שְׁתִל *šeṯil,* שָׁתִיל *šāṯiyl* **masc. noun**
(plant, shoot [of a plant])
Ps. 128:3.

8364. שֻׁתַלְחִי *šuṯalḥiy* **masc. proper noun**
(Shuthelahite)
Num. 26:35.

8365. שָׁתַם *šāṯam* **verb**
(to open; to be open)
Num. 24:3,15.

8366. שָׁתַן *šaṯan* **verb**
(to urinate: used in the phrase: "to urinate against the wall" as describing a male)
1 Sam. 25:22,34; **1 Kgs.** 14:10; 16:11; 21:21; **2 Kgs.** 9:8.

8367. שָׁתַק *šāṯaq* **verb**
(to be calm; to be quiet)
Ps. 107:30; **Prov.** 26:20; **Jon.** 1:11,12.

8368. שָׁתַר *šāṯar* **verb**
(to break out [spoken of tumors or hemorrhoids])
1 Sam. 5:9.

8369. שֵׁתָר *šēṯar* **masc. proper noun**
(Shethar)
Esth. 1:14.

8370. שְׁתַר בּוֹזְנַי *š^{e}ṯar bôz^{e}nay* **Aram. masc. proper noun**
(Shethar-Bozenai)
Ezra 5:3,6; 6:6,13.

8371. I. שָׁתַת *šāṯaṯ* **verb**
(to set; to lay)
Ps. 49:14(15)(NASB, NIV, see II); 73:9 (NASB, *šiyṯ* [7896], NIV, see III).

II. שָׁתַת *šāṯaṯ* **verb**
(to be appointed; to be destined)
Ps. 49:14(15)(KJV, see I); 73:9)(KJV, see I; NASB, *šiyṯ* [7896]).

III. שָׁתַת *šāṯaṯ* **verb**
(to claim something)
Ps. 73:9)(KJV, see I; NASB, *šiyṯ* [7896]).

ת Tau

8372. תָּא *tā'* **masc. noun**
(room, chamber, guardroom)
1 Kgs. 14:28; **2 Chr.** 12:11; **Ezek.** 40:7, 10,12,13,16,21,29,33,36.

8373. תָּאַב *tā'aḇ* **verb**
(to long for)
Ps. 119:40,174.

8374. תָּאַב *tā'aḇ* **verb**
(to abhor; to loathe)
Amos 6:8.

8375. תַּאֲבָה *ta'ᵃḇāh* **fem. noun**
(longing, desire)
Ps. 119:20.

8376. תָּאָה *tā'āh* **verb**
(to mark out; to draw a line [as a boundary])
Num. 34:7,8.

8377. I. תְּאוֹ *tᵉ'ô* **masc. noun**
(antelope)
Deut. 14:5(KJV, see II); **Isa.** 51:20 (KJV, see II).
II. תְּאוֹ *tᵉ'ô* **masc. noun**
(wild ox)
Deut. 14:5(NASB, NIV, see I); **Isa.** 14:5(NASB, NIV, see I).

8378. תַּאֲוָה *ta'ᵃwāh* **fem. noun**
(desire, delight, bounty; craving, greed)
Gen. 3:6; 49:26(KJV, NASB, *ta'ᵃwāh* [8379]); **Job** 33:20; **Ps.** 10:3,17; 21:2(3); 38:9(10); 78:29,30; 106:14; 112:10; **Prov.** 10:24; 11:23; 13:12,19; 18:1; 19:22; 21:25,26; **Isa.** 26:8.

8379. תַּאֲוָה *ta'ᵃwāh* **fem. noun**
(outer boundary)
Gen. 49:26(NIV, *ta'ᵃwāh* [8378]).

8380. תָּאוֹם *tā'ôm,* תּוֹאָם *tô'ām* **masc. noun**
(a twin, a double; pl. twins)
Gen. 25:24; 38:27; **Ex.** 26:24(KJV, NASB, *tā'am* [8382]); 36:29(KJV, NASB, *tā'am* [8382]); **Song** 4:5; 7:3(4).

8381. תַּאֲלָה *ta'ᵃlāh* **fem. noun**
(curse)
Lam. 3:65.

8382. תָּאַם *tā'am* **verb**
(to be double, to bear twins)
Ex. 26:24(NIV, *tô'ām* [8380]); 36:29 (NIV, *tô'ām* [8380]); **Song** 4:2; 6:6.

8383. I. תְּאֻן *tᵉ'un* **masc. noun**
(toil, effort)
Ezek. 24:12(KJV, see II).
II. תְּאֻן *tᵉ'un* **masc. noun**
(a lie)
Ezek. 24:12(NASB, NIV, see I).

8384. תְּאֵנָה *tᵉ'ēnāh* **fem. noun**
(fig, fig tree)
Gen. 3:7; **Num.** 13:23; 20:5; **Deut.** 8:8; **Judg.** 9:10,11; **1 Kgs.** 4:25(5:5); **2 Kgs.** 18:31; 20:7; **Neh.** 13:15; **Ps.** 105:33; **Prov.** 27:18; **Song** 2:13; **Isa.** 34:4; 36:16; 38:21; **Jer.** 5:17; 8:13; 24:1–3,5,8; 29:17; **Hos.** 2:12(14); 9:10; **Joel** 1:7,12; 2:22; **Amos** 4:9; **Mic.** 4:4; **Nah.** 3:12; **Hab.** 3:17; **Hag.** 2:19; **Zech.** 3:10.

8385. I. תַּאֲנָה *ta'ᵃnāh* **fem. noun**
(occasion or time of copulation; heat)
Jer. 2:24.
II. תֹּאֲנָה *ta'ᵃnāh* **fem. noun**
(occasion, opportunity)
Judg. 14:4.

8386. תַּאֲנִיָּה *ta'aniyyāh* **fem. noun**
(to mourn, to lament)
Isa. 29:2; **Lam.** 2:5.

8387. תַּאֲנַת שִׁלֹה *ta'anat̲ šilōh*
proper noun
(Taanath Shiloh)
Josh. 16:6.

8388. I. תָּאַר *tā'ar* **verb**
(to incline; to stretch out)
Josh. 15:9,11; 18:14,17; 19:13(KJV, part of *rimmôn hammetō'ār* [7417,F]).
II. תָּאַר *tā'ar* **verb**
(to trace an outline)
Isa. 44:13.

8389. תֹּאַר *tō'ar* **masc. noun**
(form, appearance, beauty)
Gen. 29:17; 39:6; 41:18,19; **Deut.** 21:11; **Judg.** 8:18; **1 Sam.** 16:18; 25:3; 28:14; **1 Kgs.** 1:6; **Esth.** 2:7; **Isa.** 52:14; 53:2; **Jer.** 11:16; **Lam.** 4:8.

8390. תַּאֲרֵעַ *ta'arēa'* **masc. proper noun**
(Tarea)
1 Chr. 8:35.

8391. תְּאַשּׁוּר *te'aššûr* **masc. noun**
(cypress, box tree; cypress wood)
Isa. 41:19; 60:13; **Ezek.** 27:6(KJV, *bat* [1323] and *'aššuriym* [839]).

8392. תֵּבָה *tēḇāh* **fem. noun**
(ark [Noah's boat]; basket [in which Moses was placed)
Gen. 6:14–16,18,19; 7:1,7,9,13,15,17, 18,23; 8:1,4,6,9,10,13,16,19; 9:10,18; **Ex.** 2:3,5.

8393. תְּבוּאָה *teḇû'āh* **fem. noun**
(crop, harvest, increase, revenue)
Gen. 47:24; **Ex.** 23:10; **Lev.** 19:25; 23:39; 25:3,7,12,15,16,20–22; **Num.** 18:30; **Deut.** 14:22,28; 16:15; 22:9; 26:12; 33:14; **Josh.** 5:12; **2 Kgs.** 8:6; **2 Chr.** 31:5; 32:28; **Neh.** 9:37; **Job** 31:12; **Ps.** 107:37; **Prov.** 3:9,14; 8:19; 10:16; 14:4; 15:6; 16:8; 18:20; **Eccl.** 5:10(9); **Isa.** 23:3; 30:23; **Jer.** 2:3; 12:13; **Ezek.** 48:18.

8394. תְּבוּנָה *teḇûnāh* **masc. noun**
(understanding; discernment)
Ex. 31:3; 35:31; 36:1; **Deut.** 32:28; **1 Kgs.** 4:29(5:9); 7:14; **Job** 12:12,13; 26:12; 32:11; **Ps.** 49:3(4); 78:72; 136:5; 147:5; **Prov.** 2:2,3,6,11; 3:13,19; 5:1; 8:1; 10:23; 11:12; 14:29; 15:21; 17:27; 18:2; 19:8; 20:5; 21:30; 24:3; 28:16; **Isa.** 40:14,28; 44:19; **Jer.** 10:12; 51:15; **Ezek.** 28:4; **Hos.** 13:2; **Obad.** 1:7,8.

8395. תְּבוּסָה *teḇûsāh* **fem. noun**
(destruction, downfall)
2 Chr. 22:7.

8396. A. תָּבוֹר *tāḇôr* **proper noun**
(Mt. Tabor)
Josh. 19:22; **Judg.** 4:6,12,14; 8:18; **Ps.** 89:12(13); **Jer.** 46:18; **Hos.** 5:1.
B. תָּבוֹר *tāḇôr* **proper noun**
(Tabor: city in Zebulun)
1 Chr. 6:77(62).
C. תָּבוֹר *tāḇôr* **proper noun**
(Tabor: near Bethel)
1 Sam. 10:3.

8397. תֶּבֶל *teḇel* **masc. noun**
(perversion; incest)
Lev. 18:23; 20:12.

8398. תֵּבֵל *tēḇēl* **fem. noun**
(world, inhabited world)
1 Sam. 2:8; **2 Sam.** 22:16; **1 Chr.** 16:30; **Job** 18:18; 34:13; 37:12; **Ps.** 9:8(9); 18:15(16); 19:4(5); 24:1; 33:8; 50:12; 77:18(19); 89:11(12); 90:2; 93:1; 96:10,13; 97:4; 98:7,9; **Prov.** 8:26,31; **Isa.** 13:11; 14:17,21; 18:3; 24:4; 26:9,18; 27:6; 34:1; **Jer.** 10:12; 51:15; **Lam.** 4:12; **Nah.** 1:5.

8399. תַּבְלִית *ta<u>b</u>liy<u>t</u>* **fem. noun**
(destruction)
Isa. 10:25.

8400. תְּבַלֻּל *t^e^<u>b</u>allul* **masc. noun**
(defect; blemish)
Lev. 21:20.

8401. תֶּבֶן *te<u>b</u>en* **masc. noun**
(straw)
Gen. 24:25,32; **Ex.** 5:7,10–13,16,18; **Judg.** 19:19; **1 Kgs.** 4:28(5:8); **Job** 21:18; 41:27(19); **Isa.** 11:7; 65:25; **Jer.** 23:28.

8402. תִּבְנִי *ti<u>b</u>niy* **masc. proper noun**
(Tibni)
1 Kgs. 16:21,22.

8403. תַּבְנִית *ta<u>b</u>niy<u>t</u>* **fem. noun**
(pattern; form; likeness)
Ex. 25:9,40; **Deut.** 4:16–18; **Josh.** 22:28; **2 Kgs.** 16:10; **1 Chr.** 28:11,12, 18,19; **Ps.** 106:20; 144:12; **Isa.** 44:13; **Ezek.** 8:3,10; 10:8.

8404. תַּבְעֵרָה *ta<u>b</u>'ērāh* **masc. proper noun**
(Taberah)
Num. 11:3; **Deut.** 9:22.

8405. תֵּבֵץ *tē<u>b</u>ēṣ* **proper noun**
(Thebez)
Judg. 9:50; **2 Sam.** 11:21.

8406. תְּבַר *t^e^<u>b</u>ar* **Aram. verb**
(to break; to be brittle)
Dan. 2:42.

8407. A. תִּגְלַת פִּלְאֶסֶר *tigla<u>t</u> pil'eser* **masc. proper noun**
(Tiglath-Pileser; the same as B)
2 Kgs. 15:29; 16:7,10; **1 Chr.** 5:6,26; **2 Chr.** 28:20.
B. תִּלְגַת פִּלְנֶסֶר *tilga<u>t</u> pilneser*, תִּלְּגַת פִּלְנְאֶסֶר *tilga<u>t</u> piln^e^'eser* **masc. proper noun**
(Tilgath-Pilneser; the same as A)
1 Chr. 5:6,26; **2 Chr.** 28:20.

8408. תַּגְמוּל *tagmûl* **masc. noun**
(benefit; goodness)
Ps. 116:12.

8409. תִּגְרָה *tigrāh* **fem. noun**
(blow [of the hand]; opposition)
Ps. 39:10(11).

8410. תִּדְהָר *ti<u>d</u>hār* **masc. noun**
(fir tree, pine tree)
Isa. 41:19; 60:13.

8411. תְּדִירָה *t^e^<u>d</u>iyr*, תְּדִירָא *t^e^<u>d</u>iyrā'* **Aram. fem. noun**
(continuance)
Dan. 6:16(17),20(21).

8412. תַּדְמֹר *ta<u>d</u>mōr* **proper noun**
(Tadmor)
1 Kgs. 9:18(NASB, [K^e^] *tāmār* [8559]); **2 Chr.** 8:4.

8413. תִּדְעָל *ti<u>d</u>'āl* **masc. proper noun**
(Tidal: king of Goiim [nations])
Gen. 14:1,9.

8414. תֹּהוּ *tōhû* **masc. noun**
(chaos, formlessness; emptiness, vanity, waste)
Gen. 1:2; **Deut.** 32:10; **1 Sam.** 12:21; **Job** 6:18; 12:24; 26:7; **Ps.** 107:40; **Isa.** 24:10; 29:21; 34:11; 40:17,23; 41:29; 44:9; 45:18,19; 49:4; 59:4; **Jer.** 4:23.

8415. תְּהוֹם *t^e^hôm*, תְּהֹם *t^e^hōm* **masc. noun**
(depth, deep place)
Gen. 1:2; 7:11; 8:2; 49:25; **Ex.** 15:5,8; **Deut.** 8:7; 33:13; **Job** 28:14; 38:16,30; 41:32(24); **Ps.** 33:7; 36:6(7); 42:7(8); 71:20; 77:16(17); 78:15; 104:6; 106:9; 107:26; 135:6; 148:7; **Prov.** 3:20; 8:24,

27,28; **Isa.** 51:10; 63:13; **Ezek.** 26:19; 31:4,15; **Amos** 7:4; **Jon.** 2:5(6); **Hab.** 3:10.

8416. תְּהִלָּה *t^ehillāh* **fem. noun**
(praise)
Ex. 15:11; **Deut.** 10:21; 26:19; **1 Chr.** 16:35; **2 Chr.** 20:22; **Neh.** 9:5; 12:46; **Ps.** 9:14(15); 22:3(4),25(26); 33:1; 34:1(2); 35:28; 40:3(4); 48:10(11); 51:15(17); 65:1(2); 66:2,8; 71:6,8,14; 78:4; 79:13; 100:4; 102:21(22); 106:2, 12,47; 109:1; 111:10; 119:171; 145:[title](1),21; 147:1; 148:14; 149:1; **Isa.** 42:8, 10,12; 43:21; 48:9; 60:6,18; 61:3,11; 62:7; 63:7; **Jer.** 13:11; 17:14; 33:9; 48:2; 49:25; 51:41; **Hab.** 3:3; **Zeph.** 3:19,20.

8417. תָּהֳלָה *tāh^{o}lāh* **fem. noun**
(error, folly)
Job 4:18.

8418. תַּהֲלֻכָה *tah^{a}lukāh* **fem. noun**
(procession, proceeding)
Neh. 12:31(NIV, *hālak* [1980]).

8419. תַּהְפֻּכָה *tahpukāh* **fem. noun**
(perversity)
Deut. 32:20; **Prov.** 2:12,14; 6:14; 8:13; 10:31,32; 16:28,30; 23:33.

8420. תָּו *tāw* **masc. noun**
(mark, signature)
Job 31:35; **Ezek.** 9:4,6.

8421. תּוּב *tûb* **Aram. verb**
(to return; to answer)
Ezra 5:5,11; 6:5; **Dan.** 2:14; 3:16; 4:34(31),36(33).

8422. תּוּבַל *tûbal*, תֻּבַל *tubal* **masc. proper noun**
(Tubal)
Gen. 10:2; **1 Chr.** 1:5; **Isa.** 66:19; **Ezek.** 27:13; 32:26; 38:2,3; 39:1.

8423. תּוּבַל קַיִן *tûbal qayin* **masc. proper noun**
(Tubal-Cain)
Gen. 4:22.

8424. תּוּגָה *tûgāh* **fem. noun**
(grief, sorrow)
Ps. 119:28; **Prov.** 10:1; 14:13; 17:21.

8425. I. תּוֹגַרְמָה *tôgarmāh*, תֹּגַרְמָה *tōgarmāh* **masc. proper noun**
(Togarmah: son of Gomer)
Gen. 10:3; **1 Chr.** 1:6; **Ezek.** 27:14 (NASB, NIV, see B); 38:6(NASB, NIV, see B).
II. בֵּית תּוֹגַרְמָה *bēyt tôgarmāh* **proper noun**
(Beth Togarmah)
Ezek. 27:14(KJV, see I); 38:6(KJV, see I).

8426. תּוֹדָה *tôdāh* **fem. noun**
(thanksgiving, thanks offering; praise)
Lev. 7:12,13,15; 22:29; **Josh.** 7:19; **2 Chr.** 29:31; 33:16; **Ezra** 10:11; **Neh.** 12:27,31,38,40; **Ps.** 26:7; 42:4(5); 50:14,23; 56:12(13); 69:30(31); 95:2; 100:[title](1),4; 107:22; 116:17; 147:7; **Isa.** 51:3; **Jer.** 17:26; 30:19; 33:11; **Amos** 4:5; **Jon.** 2:9(10).

8427. תָּוָה *tāwāh* **verb**
(to scribble; to make a mark)
1 Sam. 21:13(14); **Ezek.** 9:4.

8428. I. תָּוָה *tāwāh* **verb**
(to vex; to cause pain)
Ps. 78:41(KJV, see II).
II. תָּוָה *tāwāh* **verb**
(to limit)
Ps. 78:41(NASB, NIV, see I).

8429. תְּוַהּ *t^ewah* **Aram. verb**
(to be astonished; to be amazed)
Dan. 3:24.

8430. תּוֹחַ *tôaḥ* **masc. proper noun**
(Toah; the same as *tōḥû* [8459])
1 Chr. 6:34(19).

8431. תּוֹחֶלֶת *tôḥelet̲* **fem. noun**
(hope, expectation)
Job 41:9(1); **Ps.** 39:7(8); **Prov.** 10:28; 11:7; 13:12; **Lam.** 3:18.

8432. תָּוֶךְ *tāwek̲* **masc. noun**
(midst, middle [place among])
Gen. 1:6; 2:9; 3:3,8; 9:21; 15:10; 18:24,26; 19:29; 23:6,9,10; 35:2; 37:7; 40:20; 41:48; 42:5; **Ex.** 2:5; 3:2,4; 7:5; 9:24; 11:4; 12:31,49; 14:16,22,23,27,29; 15:19; 24:16,18; 25:8; 26:28; 28:1,32,33; 29:45,46; 33:11; 36:33; 39:3,23,25; **Lev.** 11:33; 15:31; 16:16,29; 17:8,10,12,13; 18:26; 20:14; 22:32; 24:10; 25:33; 26:11, 12,25; **Num.** 1:47,49; 2:17,33; 3:12; 4:2,18; 5:3,21; 8:6,14,16,19; 9:7; 13:32; 15:14,26,29; 16:3,21,33,45(17:10), 47(17:12); 17:6(21); 18:6,20,23,24; 19:6,10,20; 25:7,11; 26:62; 27:3,4,7; 32:30; 33:8; 35:5,15,34; **Deut.** 3:16; 4:12,15,33,36; 5:4,22–24,26; 9:10; 10:4; 11:3; 13:16(17); 19:2; 21:12; 22:2; 23:10(11),11(12); 32:51; **Josh.** 3:17; 4:3,5,8–10,18; 7:21,23; 8:9,13,22; 12:2; 13:9,16; 14:3; 15:13; 16:9; 17:4,6,9; 19:1,9,49; 20:9; 21:41; 22:19,31; **Judg.** 7:16; 9:51; 12:4; 15:4; 16:29; 18:1; 20:42; **1 Sam.** 7:3; 9:14,18; 10:10,23; 11:11; 15:6; 18:10; 25:29; **2 Sam.** 1:25; 3:27; 4:6; 6:17; 7:2; 20:12; 23:12,20; 24:5; **1 Kgs.** 3:8,20; 6:13,19,27; 8:51,64; 11:20; 14:7; **2 Kgs.** 4:13; 6:20; 9:2; 11:2; 23:9; **1 Chr.** 11:14,22; 16:1; 21:6; **2 Chr.** 6:13; 7:7; 20:14; 22:11; 23:20; 32:4; **Neh.** 4:11(5),22(16); 6:10; 7:4; 9:11; **Esth.** 4:1; 9:28; **Job** 1:6; 2:1,8; 15:19; 20:13; 42:15; **Ps.** 22:14(15),22(23); 40:8(9),10(11); 57:4(5),6(7); 68:25(26); 109:30; 116:19; 135:9; 136:11,14; 137:2; 143:4; **Prov.** 1:14; 4:21; 5:14,15; 8:20; 17:2; 22:13; 27:22; **Song** 3:10; **Isa.** 5:2; 6:5; 7:6; 16:3; 19:19; 24:13,18; 41:18; 52:11; 58:9; 61:9; 66:17; **Jer.** 9:6(5); 12:14,16; 21:4; 29:32; 37:4,12; 39:3,14; 40:1,5,6; 41:7,8; 44:7; 50:8,37; 51:6,45, 47,63; 52:25; **Ezek.** 1:1,4,5,16; 2:5; 3:15, 24,25; 5:2,4,5,8,10,12; 6:7,13; 7:4,9; 8:11; 9:2,4; 10:10; 11:1,7,9,11,23; 12:2, 10,12,24; 13:14; 14:8,9,14,16,18,20; 15:4; 16:53; 17:16; 18:18; 19:2,6; 20:8,9; 21:32(37); 22:3,7,9,13,18–22,25,26; 23:39; 24:5,7,11; 26:5,12,15; 27:27, 32,34; 28:14,16,18,22,23; 29:3,4,12,21; 30:7; 31:14,17,18; 32:20,21,25,28,32; 33:33; 34:12,24; 36:23; 37:1,26,28; 39:7; 43:7,9; 44:9; 46:10; 47:22; 48:8,10,15, 21,22; **Amos** 3:9; 6:4; **Mic.** 2:12; 3:3; 7:14; **Zeph.** 2:14; **Hag.** 2:5; **Zech.** 2:4(8),5(9),10(14),11(15); 5:4,7,8; 8:3,8.

8433. I. תּוֹכֵחָה *tôk̲ēḥāh* **fem. noun**
(rebuke, punishment)
2 Kgs. 19:3; **Ps.** 149:7; **Isa.** 37:3; **Hos.** 5:9.
II. תּוֹכַחַת *tôk̲aḥat̲* **fem. noun**
(rebuke, punishment, correction)
Job 13:6; 23:4; **Ps.** 38:14(15); 39:11(12); 73:14; **Prov.** 1:23,25,30; 3:11; 5:12; 6:23; 10:17; 12:1; 13:18; 15:5,10,31,32; 27:5; 29:1,15; **Ezek.** 5:15; 25:17; **Hab.** 2:1.

8434. תּוֹלָד *tôlād̲* **proper noun**
(Tolad)
1 Chr. 4:29.

8435. תּוֹלְדוֹת *tôlēd̲ôt̲* **fem. pl. noun**
(genealogical records, lines of descent)
Gen. 2:4; 5:1; 6:9; 10:1,32; 11:10,27; 25:12,13,19; 36:1,9; 37:2; **Ex.** 6:16,19; 28:10; **Num.** 1:20,22,24,26,28,30,32, 34,36,38,40,42; 3:1; **Ruth** 4:18; **1 Chr.** 1:29; 5:7; 7:2,4,9; 8:28; 9:9,34; 26:31.

8436. תִּילוֹן *tiylôn* **masc. proper noun**
(Tilon)
1 Chr. 4:20.

8437. תּוֹלָל *tôlāl* **masc. noun**
(tormentor)
Ps. 137:3.

8438. I. תּוֹלָע *tôlāʻ* **masc. noun**
(crimson, purple, scarlet)
Isa. 1:18; **Lam.** 4:5.
II. תּוֹלָע *tôlāʻ* **masc. noun**
(worm)
Ex. 16:20(KJV, NIV, see IV).
III. תּוֹלֵעָה *tôlēʻāh*, תּוֹלַעַת *tôlaʻat* **masc. noun**
(crimson, purple, scarlet)
Ex. 25:4; 26:1,31,36; 27:16; 28:5,6,8, 15,33; 35:6,23,25,35; 36:8,35,37; 38:18,23; 39:1–3,5,8,24,29; **Lev.** 14:4 (NASB, see V),6(NASB, see V),49(NASB, see V),51(NASB, see V),52(NASB, see V); **Num.** 4:8; 19:6.
IV. תּוֹלָע *tôlāʻ* **masc. noun**
(worm)
Ex. 16:20(NASB, see II); **Deut.** 28:39; **Job** 25:6; **Ps.** 22:6(7); **Isa.** 14:11; 41:14; 66:24; **Jon.** 4:7.
V. תּוֹלָע *tôlāʻ* **masc. noun**
(string)
Lev. 14:4(KJV, NIV, see III),6(KJV, NIV, see III),49(KJV, NIV, see III),51(KJV, NIV, see III),52(KJV, NIV, see III).

8439. A. תּוֹלָע *tôlāʻ* **masc. proper noun**
(Tola: son of Issachar)
Gen. 46:13; **Num.** 26:23; **1 Chr.** 7:1,2.
B. תּוֹלָע *tôlāʻ* **masc. proper noun**
(Tola: a later judge from the tribe of Issachar)
Judg. 10:1.

8440. תּוֹלָעִי *tôlāʻiy* **masc. proper noun**
(Tolaite)
Num. 26:23.

8441. תּוֹעֵבָה *tôʻēḇāh*, תֹּעֵבָה *tōʻēḇāh* **fem. noun**
(abominable thing, detestable thing or practice)
Gen. 43:32; 46:34; **Ex.** 8:26(22); **Lev.** 18:22,26,27,29,30; 20:13; **Deut.** 7:25,26; 12:31; 13:14(15); 14:3; 17:1,4; 18:9,12; 20:18; 22:5; 23:18(19); 24:4; 25:16; 27:15; 32:16; **1 Kgs.** 14:24; **2 Kgs.** 16:3; 21:2,11; 23:13; **2 Chr.** 28:3; 33:2; 34:33; 36:8,14; **Ezra** 9:1,11,14; **Ps.** 88:8(9); **Prov.** 3:32; 6:16; 8:7; 11:1,20; 12:22; 13:19; 15:8,9,26; 16:5,12; 17:15; 20:10,23; 21:27; 24:9; 26:25; 28:9; 29:27; **Isa.** 1:13; 41:24; 44:19; **Jer.** 2:7; 6:15; 7:10; 8:12; 16:18; 32:35; 44:4,22; **Ezek.** 5:9,11; 6:9,11; 7:3,4,8,9,20; 8:6,9,13,15,17; 9:4; 11:18,21; 12:16; 14:6; 16:2,22,36,43,47, 50,51,58; 18:12,13,24; 20:4; 22:2,11; 23:26; 33:26,29; 36:31; 43:8; 44:6,7,13; **Mal.** 2:11.

8442. תּוֹעָה *tōʻāh* **fem. noun**
(error; disturbance, trouble)
Neh. 4:8(2); **Isa.** 32:6.

8443. I. תּוֹעָפָה *tôʻāp̱āh* **fem. noun**
(strength)
Num. 23:22(NASB, see II); 24:8(NASB, see II); **Ps.** 95:4(NASB, NIV, see III).
II. תּוֹעָפָה *tôʻāp̱āh* **fem. noun**
(horn [of a wild ox])
Num. 23:22(KJV, NIV, see I); 24:8 (KJV, NIV, see I).
III. תּוֹעָפָה *tôʻāp̱āh* **fem. noun**
(peak [of a mountain])
Ps. 95:4(KJV, see I).
IV. תּוֹעָפָה *tôʻāp̱āh* **fem. noun**
(choice; abundance)
Job 22:25.

8444. תּוֹצָאָה *tôṣāʼāh*, תֹּצָאָה *tōṣāʼāh* **fem. noun**
(border, extremity, end point)
Num. 34:4,5,8,9,12; **Josh.** 15:4,7,11; 16:3,8; 17:9,18; 18:12,14,19; 19:14, 22,29,33; **1 Chr.** 5:16; **Ps.** 68:20(21); **Prov.** 4:23; **Ezek.** 48:30.

8445. תָּוקְהַת *towq^{e}haṯ*, תָּקְהַת *toqhaṯ* **masc. proper noun**

(Tokhath; the same as *tiqwah* [8616,A])
2 Chr. 34:22(KJV, [foll. Sept.] *tiqwah* [8616,A]).

8446. תּוּר *tûr* **verb**
(to explore; to seek out; to spy out)
Num. 10:33; 13:2,16,17,21,25,32; 14:6,7,34,36,38; 15:39; **Deut.** 1:33; **Judg.** 1:23; **1 Kgs.** 10:15; **2 Chr.** 9:14; **Job** 39:8(KJV, *y^e^ṯûr* [3491]); **Prov.** 12:26; **Eccl.** 1:13; 2:3; 7:25; **Ezek.** 20:6.

8447. I. תֹּר *tōr* **masc. noun**
(turn, opportunity)
Esth. 2:12,15.
II. תּוֹר *tôr,* תֹּר *tōr* **masc. noun**
(ornaments, earrings)
Song 1:10(KJV, see III),11(KJV, see III).
III. תּוֹר *tôr,* תֹּר *tōr* **masc. noun**
(row, border)
Song 1:10(NASB, NIV, see II),11(NASB, NIV, see II).
IV. תּוֹר *tôr* **masc. noun**
(standard, manner)
2 Sam. 7:19(KJV, *tôrāh* [8452]; NIV, *tôrāh* [8451]); **1 Chr.** 17:17(KJV, *tôr* [8448]).

8448. תּוֹר *tôr* **masc. noun**
(standard, manner)
1 Chr. 17:17(NASB, NIV, *tôr*[8447,IV]).

8449. תּוֹר *tôr,* תֹּר *tōr* **masc. noun**
(dove, turtledove)
Gen. 15:9; **Lev.** 1:14; 5:7,11; 12:6,8; 14:22,30; 15:14,29; **Num.** 6:10; **Ps.** 74:19; **Song** 2:12; **Jer.** 8:7.

8450. תּוֹר *tôr* **Aram. masc. noun**
(bull, ox)
Ezra 6:9,17; 7:17; **Dan.** 4:25(22),32(29), 33(30); 5:21.

8451. תּוֹרָה *tôrāh,* תֹּרָה *tōrāh* **fem. noun**
(law, regulation, teaching)
Gen. 26:5; **Ex.** 12:49; 13:9; 16:4,28; 18:16,20; 24:12; **Lev.** 6:9(2),14(7), 25(18); 7:1,7,11,37; 11:46; 12:7; 13:59; 14:2,32,54,57; 15:32; 26:46; **Num.** 5:29,30; 6:13,21; 15:16,29; 19:2,14; 31:21; **Deut.** 1:5; 4:8,44; 17:11,18,19; 27:3,8,26; 28:58,61; 29:21(20),29(28); 30:10; 31:9,11,12,24,26; 32:46; 33:4,10; **Josh.** 1:7,8; 8:31,32,34; 22:5; 23:6; 24:26; **2 Sam.** 7:19(KJV, *tôrāh* [8452]; NASB, *tôr* [8447,IV]); **1 Kgs.** 2:3; **2 Kgs.** 10:31; 14:6; 17:13,34,37; 21:8; 22:8,11; 23:24,25; **1 Chr.** 16:40; 22:12; **2 Chr.** 6:16; 12:1; 14:4(3); 15:3; 17:9; 19:10; 23:18; 25:4; 30:16; 31:3,4,21; 33:8; 34:14,15,19; 35:26; **Ezra** 3:2; 7:6,10; 10:3; **Neh.** 8:1–3,7–9,13,14,18; 9:3,13, 14,26,29,34; 10:28(29),29(30),34(35), 36(37); 12:44; 13:3; **Job** 22:22; **Ps.** 1:2; 19:7(8); 37:31; 40:8(9); 78:1,5,10; 89:30(31); 94:12; 105:45; 119:1,18,29,34, 44,51,53,55,61,70,72,77,85,92,97,109,113,126,136,142,150,153,163,165,174; **Prov.** 1:8; 3:1; 4:2; 6:20,23; 7:2; 13:14; 28:4,7,9; 29:18; 31:26; **Isa.** 1:10; 2:3; 5:24; 8:16,20; 24:5; 30:9; 42:4,21,24; 51:4,7; **Jer.** 2:8; 6:19; 8:8; 9:13(12); 16:11; 18:18; 26:4; 31:33; 32:23; 44:10,23; **Lam.** 2:9; **Ezek.** 7:26; 22:26; 43:11,12; 44:5,24; **Dan.** 9:10,11,13; **Hos.** 4:6; 8:1,12; **Amos** 2:4; **Mic.** 4:2; **Hab.** 1:4; **Zeph.** 3:4; **Hag.** 2:11; **Zech.** 7:12; **Mal.** 2:6–9; 4:4(3:22).

8452. תּוֹרָה *tôrāh* **fem. noun**
(custom, manner)
2 Sam. 7:19(NASB, *tôr* [8447,IV]; NIV, *tôrāh* [8451]).

8453. I. תּוֹשָׁב *tôšāḇ,* תֹּשָׁב *tōšāḇ* **masc. noun**
(sojourner, temporary resident, foreigner)
Gen. 23:4; **Ex.** 12:45; **Lev.** 22:10; 25:6,23,35,40,45,47; **Num.** 35:15; **1 Kgs.** 17:1(NIV, see II); **1 Chr.** 29:15; **Ps.** 39:12(13).

II. תִּשְׁבֵּי *tišbēy* **proper noun**
(Tishbe)
1 Kgs. 17:1(KJV, NASB, see I).

8454. תּוּשִׁיָּה *tûšiyyāh* **fem. noun**
(sound, judgment, wisdom, insight)
Job 5:12; 6:13; 11:6; 12:16; 26:3; **Prov.** 2:7; 3:21; 8:14; 18:1; **Isa.** 28:29; **Mic.** 6:9.

8455. I. תּוֹתָח *tôṯāḥ* **masc. noun**
(club)
Job 41:29(21)(KJV, see II).
II. תּוֹתָח *tôṯāḥ* **masc. noun**
(dart)
Job 41:29(21)(NASB, NIV, see I).

8456. תָּזַז *tāzaz* **verb**
(to cut down; to cut away)
Isa. 18:5.

8457. תַּזְנוּת *taznûṯ* **fem. noun**
(prostitution, harlotry, promiscuity)
Ezek. 16:15,20,22,25,26,29,33,34,36; 23:7,8,11,14,17–19,29,35,43.

8458. תַּחְבֻּלָה *taḥbulāh* **fem. noun**
(counsel, advice)
Job 37:12; **Prov.** 1:5; 11:14; 12:5; 20:18; 24:6.

8459. תֹּחוּ *tōḥû* **masc. proper noun**
(Tohu: the same as tôaḥ [8430])
1 Sam. 1:1.

8460. תְּחוֹת *t^eḥôṯ* **Aram. prep.**
(under)
Jer. 10:11; **Dan.** 4:12(9),14(11)(KJV, *taḥaṯ* [8479]),21(18); 7:27.

8461. תַּחְכְּמֹנִי *taḥk^emōniy* **masc. proper noun**
(Tahkemonite: the same as *ḥaḵmôniy* [2453,II])
2 Sam. 23:8.

8462. תְּחִלָּה *t^eḥillāh* **fem. noun**
(beginning, first time)
Gen. 13:3; 41:21; 43:18,20; **Judg.** 1:1; 20:18; **Ruth** 1:22; **2 Sam.** 17:9; 21:9,10; **2 Kgs.** 17:25; **Ezra** 4:6; **Neh.** 11:17; **Prov.** 9:10; **Eccl.** 10:13; **Isa.** 1:26; **Dan.** 8:1; 9:21,23; **Hos.** 1:2; **Amos** 7:1.

8463. תַּחֲלוּא *taḥ^alû'*, תַּחֲלֻא *taḥ^alu'* **masc. noun**
(disease, sickness, pain)
Deut. 29:22(21); **2 Chr.** 21:19; **Ps.** 103:3; **Jer.** 14:18; 16:4.

8464. I. תַּחְמָס *taḥmās* **masc. noun**
(owl, screech owl)
Lev. 11:16(KJV, see II); **Deut.** 14:15(KJV, see II).
II. תַּחְמָס *taḥmās* **masc. noun**
(night hawk)
Lev. 11:16(NASB, NIV, see I); **Deut.** 14:15(NASB, NIV, see I).

8465. תַּחַן *taḥan* **masc. proper noun**
(Tahan)
Num. 26:35; **1 Chr.** 7:25.

8466. תַּחֲנָה *taḥ^anāh* **fem. noun**
(camp)
2 Kgs. 6:8.

8467. תְּחִנָּה *t^eḥinnāh* **fem. noun**
(supplication, plea, cry for mercy)
Josh. 11:20; **1 Kgs.** 8:28,30,38,45,49, 52,54; 9:3; **2 Chr.** 6:19,29,35,39; 33:13; **Ezra** 9:8; **Ps.** 6:9(10); 55:1(2); 119:170; **Jer.** 36:7; 37:20; 38:26; 42:2,9; **Dan.** 9:20.

8468. תְּחִנָּה *t^eḥinnāh* **masc. proper noun**
(Tehinnah)
1 Chr. 4:12.

8469. תַּחֲנוּן *taḥ^anûn* **masc. noun**
(supplication, cry for mercy)

2 Chr. 6:21; **Job** 41:3(40:27); **Ps.** 28:2,6; 31:22(23); 86:6; 116:1; 130:2; 140:6(7); 143:1; **Prov.** 18:23; **Jer.** 3:21; 31:9; **Dan.** 9:3,17,18,23; **Zech.** 12:10.

8470. תַּחֲנִי *taḥ^a^niy* **masc. proper noun**
(Tahanite)
Num. 26:35.

8471. תַּחְפַּנְחֵס *taḥpanḥēs,* תְּחַפְנְחֵס *t^e^ḥap̱n^e^ḥēs* **proper noun**
(Tahpanhes: an Egyptian outpost)
Jer. 2:16; 43:7,8,9; 44:1; 46:14; **Ezek.** 30:18.

8472. תַּחְפְּנֵיס *taḥp^e^nēys* **fem. proper noun**
(Tahpenes)
1 Kgs. 11:19,20.

8473. I. תַּחְרָא *taḥrā'* **fem. noun**
(coat of mail; habergeon)
Ex. 28:32(NIV, see II); 39:23(NIV, see II).
II. תַּחְרָא *taḥrā'* **fem. noun**
(collar)
Ex. 28:32(KJV, NASB, see I); 39:23 (KJV, NASB, see I).

8474. I. תַּחֲרָה *taḥārāh* **verb**
(to contend; to compete; derived from *ḥārāh* [2734])
Jer. 12:5(NASB, NIV, *ḥārāh* [2734]).
II. תַּחֲרָה *taḥārāh* **verb**
(to close oneself in; derived from *ḥārāh* [2734])
Jer. 22:15(NASB, NIV, *ḥārāh* [2734]).

8475. תַּחְרֵעַ *taḥrēa'* **masc. proper noun**
(Tahrea)
1 Chr. 9:41.

8476. תַּחַשׁ *tāḥaš* **masc. noun**
(an unknown animal or the skin of some unknown animal; KJV: badger; NASB: dolphin; NIV: sea cow)
Ex. 25:5; 26:14; 35:7,23; 36:19; 39:34; **Num.** 4:6,8,10,11,12,14,25; **Ezek.** 16:10.

8477. תַּחַשׁ *taḥaš* **masc. proper noun**
(Tahash; Thahash)
Gen. 22:24.

8478. תַּחַת *taḥaṯ* **prep.**
(under, beneath; in place of)
Gen. 1:7,9; 2:21; 4:25; 6:17; 7:19; 16:9; 18:4,8; 21:15; 22:13; 24:2,9; 30:2,15; 35:4,8; 36:33–39; 41:35; 44:4,33; 47:29; 49:25; 50:19; **Ex.** 6:6,7; 10:23; 16:29; 17:12,14; 18:10; 20:4; 21:20,23–27,36; 22:1(21:37); 23:5; 24:4,10; 25:35; 26:19, 21,25,33; 27:5; 29:30; 30:4; 32:19; 36:24, 26,30; 37:21,27; 38:4; **Lev.** 6:22(15); 13:23,28; 14:42; 15:10; 16:32; 22:27; 24:18,20; 27:32; **Num.** 3:12,41,45; 5:19,20,29; 6:18; 8:16,18; 16:31; 22:27; 25:13; 32:14; **Deut.** 2:12,21–23,25; 3:17; 4:11,18,19,37,39,49; 5:8; 7:24; 9:14; 10:6; 12:2; 21:14; 22:29; 25:19; 28:23, 47,62; 29:20(19); 33:13,27; **Josh.** 2:11,14; 4:9; 5:7,8; 6:5,20; 7:21,22; 11:3,17; 12:3; 13:5; 24:26; **Judg.** 1:17; 3:16,30; 4:5; 6:11,19; 7:8,21; 15:2; **Ruth** 2:12; **1 Sam.** 2:20; 7:11; 14:2,9; 21:3(4), 4(5),8(9); 22:6; 24:19(20); 25:21; 26:21; 31:13; **2 Sam.** 2:23; 3:12; 7:10; 10:1; 16:8,12; 17:25; 18:9,33(19:1); 19:13(14), 21(22); 22:10,37,39,40,48; **1 Kgs.** 1:30,35; 2:35; 3:7; 4:12,25(5:5); 5:1(15),3(17), 5(19); 7:24,29,30,32,44; 8:6,20,23; 11:43; 13:14; 14:20,23,27,31; 15:8,24,28; 16:6, 10,28; 19:4,5,16; 20:24,39,42; 21:2,6; 22:40,50(51); **2 Kgs.** 1:17; 3:27; 8:15, 20,22,24; 9:13; 10:24,35; 12:21(22); 13:5,9,24; 14:16,21,27,29; 15:7,10,14, 22,25,30,38; 16:4,17,20; 17:7,10,24; 19:37; 20:21; 21:18,24,26; 22:17; 23:30,34; 24:6,17; **1 Chr.** 1:44–50; 4:41; 5:22; 10:12; 17:1,9; 19:1; 29:23,24,28; **2 Chr.** 1:8; 4:3,15; 5:7; 6:10; 9:31;

12:10,16; 14:1(13:23); 17:1; 21:1,8,10, 12; 22:1; 24:27; 26:1,23; 27:9; 28:4,27; 32:33; 33:20,25; 34:25; 36:1,8; **Neh.** 2:14; **Esth.** 2:4,17; **Job** 9:13; 16:4; 18:16; 20:12; 26:5,8; 28:5,15,24; 30:7,14; 31:40; 34:24,26; 36:16,20; 37:3; 40:12,21; 41:11(3),30(22); **Ps.** 8:6(7); 10:7; 18:9(10), 36(37),38(39),39(40),47(48); 35:12; 38:20(21); 45:5(6),16(17); 47:3(4); 144:2; **Prov.** 1:29; 11:8; 17:13; 21:18; 22:27; 30:21–23; **Eccl.** 1:3,9,13,14; 2:3,11, 17–20,22; 3:1,16; 4:1,3,7,15; 5:13(12), 18(17); 6:1,12; 7:6; 8:9,15,17; 9:3,6,9, 11,13; 10:5; **Song** 2:6; 4:11; 8:3,5; **Isa.** 3:6,24; 10:4,16; 14:9,11; 24:5; 25:10; 37:38; 43:3,4; 46:7; 51:6; 53:12; 55:13; 57:5; 60:15,17; 61:3,7; **Jer.** 2:20; 3:6,13; 5:19; 18:20; 22:11; 28:13; 29:19,26; 37:1; 38:9,11,12; 50:7; 52:20; **Lam.** 3:34,66; **Ezek.** 1:8,23; 4:15; 6:13; 10:2,8,20,21; 16:32; 17:6,23; 20:37; 23:5; 24:5; 31:6; 32:27; 36:34; 42:9; 46:23; 47:1; **Dan.** 8:8,22; 9:12; **Hos.** 4:12,13; **Joel** 1:17; **Amos** 2:9,13; **Obad.** 1:7; **Jon.** 4:5; **Mic.** 1:4; 4:4; **Hab.** 3:7,16; **Zeph.** 2:10; **Zech.** 3:10; 6:12; 12:6; 14:10; **Mal.** 4:3(3:21).

8479. תַּחַת *taḥaṯ* **Aram. prep.**
(under; corr. to Hebr. 8478)
Dan. 4:14(11)(NASB, NIV, *t^eḥôṯ* [8460]).

8480. A. תַּחַת *taḥaṯ* **masc. proper noun**
(Tahath: a Kohathite)
1 Chr. 6:24(9),37(22).
B. תַּחַת *taḥaṯ* **masc. proper noun**
(Tahath: son of Ephraim)
1 Chr. 7:20.
C. תַּחַת *taḥaṯ* **masc. proper noun**
(Tahath: grandson of B)
1 Chr. 7:20.
D. תַּחַת *taḥaṯ* **proper noun**
(Tahath: a wilderness location)
Num. 33:26,27.

8481. תַּחְתּוֹן *taḥtôn* **adj.**
(lower, lowest)
Josh. 16:3; 18:13; **1 Kgs.** 6:6,8(KJV, *tiyḵōn* [8484,I]; NASB, *tiyḵōn* [8484,I]); 9:17; **1 Chr.** 7:24; **2 Chr.** 8:5; **Isa.** 22:9; **Ezek.** 40:18,19; 41:7; 42:5,6; 43:14.

8482. תַּחְתִּי *taḥtiy* **adj.**
(lower, below)
Gen. 6:16; **Ex.** 19:17; **Deut.** 32:22; **Josh.** 15:19; **Judg.** 1:15; **Neh.** 4:13(7); **Job** 41:24(16); **Ps.** 63:9(10); 86:13; 88:6(7); 139:15; **Isa.** 44:23; **Lam.** 3:55; **Ezek.** 26:20; 31:14,16,18; 32:18,24.

8483. תַּחְתִּים חָדְשִׁי *taḥtiym ḥoḏšiy* **proper noun**
(Tahtim-Hodshi)
2 Sam. 24:6.

8484. I. תִּיכוֹן *tiyḵôn*, תִּיכֹן *tiyḵōn* **adj.**
(middle)
Ex. 26:28; 36:33; **Judg.** 7:19; **1 Kgs.** 6:6,8(NASB, see II; NIV, [Greek and Aramaic] *taḥtôn* [8481]); **2 Kgs.** 20:4; **Ezek.** 41:7; 42:5,6.
II. תִּיכֹן *tiyḵōn* **adj.**
(lower, lowest)
1 Kgs. 6:8(KJV, see I; NIV, [Greek and Aramaic] *taḥtôn* [8481]).

8485. תֵּימָא *tēymā'* **masc. proper noun**
(Tema)
Gen. 25:15; **1 Chr.** 1:30; **Job** 6:19; **Isa.** 21:14; **Jer.** 25:23.

8486. תֵּימָן *tēymān* **fem. noun**
(south)
Ex. 26:18,35; 27:9; 36:23; 38:9; **Num.** 2:10; 3:29; 10:6; **Deut.** 3:27; **Josh.** 12:3; 13:4; 15:1; **Job** 9:9; 39:26; **Ps.** 78:26; **Song** 4:16; **Isa.** 43:6; **Ezek.** 20:46

(21:2)(NASB, *tēymān* [8487,B]); 47:19; 48:28; **Zech.** 6:6; 9:14.

8487. A. תֵּימָן *tēymān* **masc. proper noun**
(Teman: grandson of Esau)
Gen. 36:11,15,42; **1 Chr.** 1:36,53.
B. תֵּימָן *tēymān* **proper noun**
(Teman: the area in Edom occupied by descendants of A)
Jer. 49:7,20; **Ezek.** 20:46(21:2)(KJV, NIV, *tēymān* [8486]); 25:13; **Amos** 1:12; **Obad.** 1:9; **Hab.** 3:3.

8488. תֵּימְנִי *tēym^{e}niy* **masc. proper noun**
(Temeni, Temani)
1 Chr. 4:6.

8489. תֵּימָנִי *tēymāniy* **masc. proper noun**
(Temanite, Temani)
Gen. 36:34(KJV, see II); **1 Chr.** 1:45; **Job** 2:11; 4:1; 15:1; 22:1; 42:7,9.

8490. תִּימָרָה *tiymārāh* **fem. noun**
(column, pillar)
Song 3:6; **Joel** 2:30(3:3).

8491. תִּיצִי *tiyṣiy* **masc. proper noun**
(Tizite)
1 Chr. 11:45.

8492. תִּירוֹשׁ *tiyrôš* **masc. noun**
(new wine)
Gen. 27:28,37; **Num.** 18:12; **Deut.** 7:13; 11:14; 12:17; 14:23; 18:4; 28:51; 33:28; **Judg.** 9:13; **2 Kgs.** 18:32; **2 Chr.** 31:5; 32:28; **Neh.** 5:11; 10:37(38),39(40); 13:5,12; **Ps.** 4:7(8); **Prov.** 3:10; **Isa.** 24:7; 36:17; 62:8; 65:8; **Jer.** 31:12; **Hos.** 2:8(10),9(11),22(24); 4:11; 7:14; 9:2; **Joel** 1:10; 2:19,24; **Mic.** 6:15; **Hag.** 1:11; **Zech.** 9:17.

8493. תִּירְיָא *tiyryāʾ* **masc. proper noun**
(Tiria)
1 Chr. 4:16.

8494. תִּירָס *tiyrās* **masc. proper noun**
(Tiras)
Gen. 10:2; **1 Chr.** 1:5.

8495. תַּיִשׁ *tayiš* **masc. noun**
(male goat)
Gen. 30:35; 32:14(15); **2 Chr.** 17:11; **Prov.** 30:31.

8496. תֹּךְ *tōk̲*, תּוֹךְ *tôk̲* **masc. noun**
(oppression)
Ps. 10:7; 55:11(12); 72:14; **Prov.** 29:13(KJV, *tāk̲ak̲* [8501]).

8497. I. תָּכָה *tāk̲āh* **verb**
(to bow down, to sit down)
Deut. 33:3(NASB, see II).
II. תָּכָה *tāk̲āh* **verb**
(to follow)
Deut. 33:3(KJV, NIV, see I).

8498. I. תְּכוּנָה *t^{e}k̲ûnāh* **fem. noun**
(arrangement, pattern)
Ezek. 43:11; **Nah.** 2:9(10).
II. תְּכוּנָה *t^{e}k̲ûnāh* **fem. noun**
(seat; place of dwelling)
Job 23:3(KJV, *t^{e}k̲ûnāh* [8499]).

8499. תְּכוּנָה *t^{e}khūnāh* **fem. noun**
(seat; place of dwelling)
Job 23:3(NASB, NIV, *t^{e}kûnāh* [8498,II]).

8500. I. תֻּכִּיִּים *tukkiyyiym* **masc. pl. noun**
(peacocks)
1 Kgs. 10:22(NIV, see II); **2 Chr.** 9:21(NIV, see II).
II. תֻּכִּיִּים *tukkiyyiym* **masc. pl. noun**
(baboons)
1 Kgs. 10:22(KJV, NASB, see I); **2 Chr.** 9:21(KJV, NASB, see I).

8501. תָּכָךְ *tāḵak* **masc. noun**
(deceit)
Prov. 29:13(NASB, NIV, *tōḵ* [8496]).

8502. תִּכְלָה *tiḵlāh* **fem. noun**
(perfection)
Ps. 119:96.

8503. תַּכְלִית *taḵliyt* **fem. noun**
(boundary, limit)
Neh. 3:21; **Job** 11:7; 26:10; 28:3; **Ps.** 139:22.

8504. תְּכֵלֶת *t*[e]*ḵēleṯ* **fem. noun**
(blue, violet)
Ex. 25:4; 26:1,4,31,36; 27:16; 28:5,6,8, 15,28,31,33,37; 35:6,23,25,35; 36:8,11, 35,37; 38:18,23; 39:1–3,5,8,21,22,24, 29,31; **Num.** 4:6,7,9,11,12; 15:38; **2 Chr.** 2:7(6),14(13); 3:14; **Esth.** 1:6; 8:15; **Jer.** 10:9; **Ezek.** 23:6; 27:7,24.

8505. תָּכַן *tāḵan* **verb**
(to weigh; to be equal)
1 Sam. 2:3; **2 Kgs.** 12:11(12); **Job** 28:25; **Ps.** 75:3(4); **Prov.** 16:2; 21:2; 24:12; **Isa.** 40:12,13; **Ezek.** 18:25,29; 33:17,20.

8506. תֹּכֶן *tōḵen* **masc. noun**
(quantity, quota)
Ex. 5:18; **Ezek.** 45:11.

8507. תֹּכֶן *tōḵen* **proper noun**
(Token)
1 Chr. 4:32.

8508. תָּכְנִית *toḵniyṯ* **fem. noun**
(perfection; plan, pattern)
Ezek. 28:12; 43:10.

8509. תַּכְרִיךְ *taḵriyḵ* **masc. noun**
(garment, robe)
Esth. 8:15.

8510. תֵּל *tēl* **masc. noun**
(mound, heap, ruins)
Deut. 13:16(17); **Josh.** 8:28; 11:13; **Jer.** 30:18; 49:2.

8511. תָּלָא *tālā'* **verb**
(to hang; to be determined)
Deut. 28:66; **2 Sam.** 21:12(NASB, [K[e]] *tālāh* [8518]); **Hos.** 11:7.

8512. תֵּל אָבִיב *tēl 'āḇiyḇ* **proper noun**
(Tel Abib)
Ezek. 3:15.

8513. תְּלָאָה *t*[e]*lā'āh* **fem. noun**
(hardship)
Ex. 18:8; **Num.** 20:14; **Neh.** 9:32; **Lam.** 3:5; **Mal.** 1:13(KJV, *matt*[e]*lā'āh* [4972]).

8514. תַּלְאוּבָה *tal'ûḇāh* **fem. noun**
(drought, burning heat)
Hos. 13:5.

8515. תְּלַאשָּׂר *t*[e]*la'śśār* **proper noun**
(Tel Assar)
2 Kgs. 19:12; **Isa.** 37:12.

8516. תִּלְבֹּשֶׁת *tilbōšeṯ* **fem. noun**
(clothing, garment)
Isa. 59:17.

8517. תְּלַג *t*[e]*lag* **Aram. masc. noun**
(snow)
Dan. 7:9.

8518. תָּלָה *tālāh* **verb**
(to hang)
Gen. 40:19,22; 41:13; **Deut.** 21:22,23; **Josh.** 8:29; 10:26; **2 Sam.** 4:12; 18:10; 21:12(KJV, NIV, [Q[e]] *tālā'* [8511]); **Esth.** 2:23; 5:14; 6:4; 7:9,10; 8:7; 9:13,14,25; **Job** 26:7; **Ps.** 137:2; **Song** 4:4; **Isa.** 22:24; **Lam.** 5:12; **Ezek.** 15:3; 27:10,11.

8519. תְּלֻנָּה *t*[e]*lunāh* **fem. noun**
(grumbling; murmuring)
Ex. 16:7–9,12; **Num.** 14:27; 17:5(20),10(25).

8520. תֶּלַח *telaḥ* masc. proper noun
(Telah)
1 Chr. 7:25.

8521. תֵּל חַרְשָׁא *tel ḥaršaʾ* masc. proper noun
(Tel Harsha)
Ezra 2:59; Neh. 7:61.

8522. תְּלִי *tᵉliy* masc. noun
(quiver)
Gen. 27:3.

8523. תְּלִיתָי *tᵉliytāy*, תַּלְתַּי *taltay* Aram. ord. num.
(third)
Dan. 2:39; 5:7(NIV, *taltāʾ* [8531]).

8524. תָּלוּל *tālûl* adj.
(lofty)
Ezek. 17:22.

8525. תֶּלֶם *telem* masc. noun
(furrow)
Job 31:38; 39:10; Ps. 65:10(11); Hos. 10:4; 12:11(12).

8526. A. תַּלְמַי *talmay* masc. proper noun
(Talmai: descendant of the giant Anak)
Num. 13:22; Josh. 15:14; Judg. 1:10.
B. תַּלְמַי *talmay* masc. proper noun
(Talmai: grandfather of Absalom)
2 Sam. 3:3; 13:37; 1 Chr. 3:2.

8527. תַּלְמִיד *talmiyd* masc. noun
(student, pupil)
1 Chr. 25:8.

8528. תֵּל מֶלַח *tēl mᵉlaḥ* proper noun
(Tel Melah)
Ezra 2:59; Neh. 7:61.

8529. תָּלַע *tālaʿ* verb
(to dress in scarlet)
Nah. 2:3(4).

8530. I. תַּלְפִּיּוֹת *talpiyyôṯ* fem. pl. noun
(rows of stones)
Song 4:4(KJV, see II; NIV, see III).
II. תַּלְפִּיּוֹת *talpiyyôṯ* fem. pl. noun
(armories)
Song 4:4(NASB, see I; NIV, see III).
III. תַּלְפִּיּוֹת *talpiyyôṯ* fem. pl. noun
(an array of stones; fig., something done in order, elegance)
Song 4:4(NASB, see I; KJV, see II).

8531. תְּלַת *tᵉlaṯ*, תַּלְתָּא *taltāʾ* Aram. ord. num.
(third highest)
Dan. 5:7(KJV, NASB, *tᵉliytay* [8523]),16,29.

8532. תְּלָת *tᵉlāṯ*, תְּלָתָה *tᵉlāṯāh* Aram. num. noun
(three; third)
Ezra 6:4,15; Dan. 3:23,24; 6:2(3), 10(11),13(14); 7:5,8,20,24.

8533. תְּלָתִין *tᵉlāṯiyn* Aram. pl. num.
(thirty)
Dan. 6:7(8),12(13).

8534. I. תַּלְתַּל *taltal* adj.
(wavy, bushy [of hair])
Song 5:11(NASB, see II).
II. תַּלְתַּל *taltal* fem. noun
(cluster of dates)
Song 5:11(KJV, NIV, see I).

8535. תָּם *tām* adj.
(blameless, peaceful; perfect, complete)
Gen. 25:27; Ex. 26:24(KJV, *tāʾam* [8382]); 36:29(KJV, *tāʾam* [8382]); Job 1:1,8; 2:3; 8:20; 9:20–22; Ps. 37:37; 64:4(5); 73:4(KJV, NASB, *māweṯ* [4194]); Prov. 29:10; Song 5:2; 6:9.

8536. תָּם *tām,* תַּמָּה *tammāh* **Aram. adv.**
(there)
Ezra 5:17; 6:1,6,12.

8537. תֹּם *tōm* **masc. noun**
(integrity; blamelessness; completeness)
Gen. 20:5,6; **Lev.** 25:29(KJV, NASB, *tāmam* [8552]); **Num.** 14:33(KJV, NASB, *tāmam* [8552]); **2 Sam.** 15:11; **1 Kgs.** 9:4; 22:34; **2 Chr.** 18:33; **Job** 4:6; 21:23; **Ps.** 7:8(9); 25:21; 26:1,11; 41:12(13); 78:72; 101:2; **Prov.** 2:7; 10:9,29; 13:6; 19:1; 20:7; 28:6; **Isa.** 47:9.

8538. תֻּמָּה *tummāh* **fem. noun**
(integrity)
Job 2:3,9; 27:5; 31:6; **Prov.** 11:3.

8539. תָּמַהּ *tāmah* **verb**
(to be amazed; to be astounded)
Gen. 43:33; **Job** 26:11; **Ps.** 48:5(6); **Eccl.** 5:8(7); **Isa.** 13:8; 29:9; **Jer.** 4:9; **Hab.** 1:5.

8540. תְּמַהּ *t^e^mah* **Aram. masc. noun**
(a wonder)
Dan. 4:2(3:32),3(3:33); 6:27(28).

8541. תִּמָּהוֹן *timmāhôn* **masc. noun**
(bewilderment, confusion)
Deut. 28:28; **Zech.** 12:4.

8542. תַּמּוּז *tāmmûz* **masc. proper noun**
(Tammuz)
Ezek. 8:14.

8543. תְּמוֹל *t^e^môl,* תְּמֹל *t^e^mōl* **adv.**
(before; previously; yesterday)
Gen. 31:2,5; **Ex.** 4:10; 5:7,8,14; 21:29,36; **Deut.** 4:42; 19:4,6; **Josh.** 3:4; 4:18; 20:5; **Ruth** 2:11; **1 Sam.** 4:7(KJV, NIV, *'etmôl* [865]); 20:27; 21:5(6); **2 Sam.** 3:17; 15:20; **2 Kgs.** 13:5; **1 Chr.** 11:2; **Job** 8:9; **Ps.** 90:4(KJV, NIV, *'etmôl* [865]).

8544. תְּמוּנָה *t^e^mûnāh* **fem. noun**
(form, likeness)
Ex. 20:4; **Num.** 12:8; **Deut.** 4:12,15,16, 23,25; 5:8; **Job** 4:16; **Ps.** 17:15.

8545. תְּמוּרָה *t^e^mûrāh* **fem. noun**
(substitution; exchange; reward)
Lev. 27:10,33; **Ruth** 4:7; **Job** 15:31; 20:18; 28:17.

8546. תְּמוּתָה *t^e^mûtāh* **fem. noun**
(death)
Ps. 79:11; 102:20(21).

8547. תֶּמַח *temah* **masc. proper noun**
(Temah)
Ezra 2:53; **Neh.** 7:55.

8548. תָּמִיד *tāmiyd* **masc. noun/adv.**
(continuity, perpetuity; continually, always)
Ex. 25:30; 27:20; 28:29,30,38; 29:38,42; 30:8; **Lev.** 6:13(6),20(13); 24:2–4,8; **Num.** 4:7,16; 9:16; 28:3,6,10,15,23, 24,31; 29:6,11,16,19,22,25,28,31,34,38; **Deut.** 11:12; **2 Sam.** 9:7,10,13; **1 Kgs.** 10:8; **2 Kgs.** 4:9; 25:29,30; **1 Chr.** 16:6, 11,37,40; 23:31; **2 Chr.** 2:4(3); 9:7; 24:14; **Ezra** 3:5; **Neh.** 10:33,(34); **Ps.** 16:8; 25:15; 34:1(2); 35:27; 38:17(18); 40:11(12),16(17); 50:8; 51:3(5); 69:23(24); 70:4(5); 71:3,6,14; 72:15; 73:23; 74:23; 105:4; 109:15,19; 119:44, 109,117; **Prov.** 5:19; 6:21; 15:15; 28:14; **Isa.** 21:8; 49:16; 51:13; 52:5; 58:11; 60:11; 62:6; 65:3; **Jer.** 6:7; 52:33,34; **Ezek.** 38:8; 39:14; 46:14,15; **Dan.** 8:11–13; 11:31; 12:11; **Hos.** 12:6(7); **Obad.** 1:16; **Nah.** 3:19; **Hab.** 1:17.

8549. תָּמִים *tāmiym* **adj.**
(without defect; blameless)
Gen. 6:9; 17:1; **Ex.** 12:5; 29:1; **Lev.** 1:3,10; 3:1,6,9; 4:3,23,28,32; 5:15,18; 6:6(5:25); 9:2,3; 14:10; 22:19,21; 23:12,

15,18; 25:30; **Num.** 6:14; 19:2; 28:3,9, 11,19,31; 29:2,8,13,17,20,23,26,29, 32,36; **Deut.** 18:13; 32:4; **Josh.** 10:13; 24:14; **Judg.** 9:16,19; **1 Sam.** 14:41; **2 Sam.** 22:24,26,31,33; **Job** 12:4; 36:4; 37:16; **Ps.** 15:2; 18:23(24),25(26),30(31), 32(33); 19:7(8); 37:18; 84:11(12); 101:2,6; 119:1,80; **Prov.** 1:12; 2:21; 11:5,20; 28:10,18; **Ezek.** 15:5; 28:15; 43:22,23,25; 45:18,23; 46:4,6,13; **Amos** 5:10.

8550. תֻּמִּים *tummiym* **proper noun**
(Thummim)
Ex. 28:30; **Lev.** 8:8; **Deut.** 33:8; **Ezra** 2:63; **Neh.** 7:65.

8551. תָּמַךְ *tāmak̲* **verb**
(to grasp, to hold; to support)
Gen. 48:17; **Ex.** 17:12; **Job** 36:17; **Ps.** 16:5; 17:5; 41:12(13); 63:8(9); **Prov.** 3:18; 4:4; 5:5,22; 11:16; 28:17; 29:23; 31:19; **Isa.** 33:15; 41:10; 42:1; **Amos** 1:5,8.

8552. תָּמַם *tāmam* **verb**
(to be complete; to be consumed; to be finished; to perish)
Gen. 47:15,18; **Lev.** 25:29(NIV, *tōm* [8537]); 26:20; **Num.** 14:33(NIV, *tōm* [8537]),35; 17:13(28); 32:13; **Deut.** 2:14–16; 31:24,30; 34:8; **Josh.** 3:16,17; 4:1,10,11; 5:6,8; 8:24; 10:20; **1 Sam.** 16:11; **2 Sam.** 15:24; 20:18; 22:26; **1 Kgs.** 6:22; 7:22; 14:10; **2 Kgs.** 7:13; 22:4; **Job** 22:3; 31:40; **Ps.** 9:6(7); 18:25(26); 19:13(14); 64:6(7); 73:19; 102:27(28); 104:35; **Isa.** 16:4; 18:5; 33:1; **Jer.** 1:3; 6:29; 14:15; 24:10; 27:8; 36:23; 37:21; 44:12,18,27; **Lam.** 3:22; 4:22; **Ezek.** 22:15; 24:10,11; 47:12; **Dan.** 8:23; 9:24(KJV, [K^{e}] *ḥāt̲am* [2856]).

8553. A. תִּמְנָה *timnāh* **proper noun**
(Timnah: a city in northern Judah)
Gen. 38:12–14; **Josh.** 15:10; 19:43; **Judg.** 14:1,2,5; **2 Chr.** 28:18.
B. תִּמְנָה *timnāh* **proper noun**
(Timnah: a city in southern Judah)
Josh. 15:57.

8554. תִּמְנִי *timniy* **masc. proper noun**
(Timnite)
Judg. 15:6.

8555. A. תִּמְנָע *timnāʿ* **fem. proper noun**
(Timna: concubine of Eliphaz)
Gen. 36:12,22; **1 Chr.** 1:39.
B. תִּמְנָע *timnāʿ* **masc. proper noun**
(Timna: a chief of Edom)
Gen. 36:40; **1 Chr.** 1:51.
C. תִּמְנָע *timnāʿ* **masc. proper noun**
(Timna: son of Eliphaz)
1 Chr. 1:36.

8556. I. תִּמְנַת חֶרֶס *timnat̲ ḥeres* **proper noun**
(Timnath Heres: the same as II)
Judg. 2:9.
II. תִּמְנַת סֶרַח *timnat̲ seraḥ* **proper noun**
(Timnath Serah: the same as I)
Josh. 19:50; 24:30.

8557. תֶּמֶס *temes* **masc. noun**
(a melting away)
Ps. 58:8(9).

8558. תָּמָר *tāmār* **masc. noun**
(palm tree)
Ex. 15:27; **Lev.** 23:40; **Num.** 33:9; **Deut.** 34:3; **Judg.** 1:16; 3:13; **2 Chr.** 28:15; **Neh.** 8:15; **Ps.** 92:12(13); **Song** 7:7(8),8(9); **Joel** 1:12.

8559. A. תָּמָר *tāmār* **fem. proper noun**
(Tamar: daughter-in-law of Judah)
Gen. 38:6,11,13,24; **Ruth** 4:12; **1 Chr.** 2:4.
B. תָּמָר *tāmār* **fem. proper noun**
(Tamar: daughter of David)

2 Sam. 13:1,2,4–8,10,19,20,22,32; **1 Chr.** 3:9.
C. תָּמָר *tāmār* **fem. proper noun**
(Tamar: daughter of Absalom)
2 Sam. 14:27.
D. תָּמָר *tāmār* **proper noun**
(Tamar: city on the border of Gad)
1 Kgs. 9:18(KJV, NIV, [Qe] *taḏmōr* [8412]); **Ezek.** 47:18(KJV, NASB, [Hebr.] *māḏaḏ* [4058]); 48:28.

8560. I. תֹּמֶר *tōmer* **masc. noun**
(palm tree)
Judg. 4:5; **Jer.** 10:5(NASB, NIV, see II).
II. תֹּמֶר *tōmer* **masc. noun**
(scarecrow)
Jer. 10:5(KJV, see I).

8561. תִּמֹרָה *timōrāh* **fem. noun**
(palm tree, palm tree ornament)
1 Kgs. 6:29,32,35; 7:36; **2 Chr.** 3:5; **Ezek.** 40:16,22,26,31,34,37; 41:18–20,25,26.

8562. תַּמְרוּק *tamrûq* **masc. noun**
(beauty treatment; cosmetics)
Esth. 2:3,9,12; **Prov.** 20:30(NASB, NIV, [Ke] *māraq* [4838]).

8563. תַּמְרוּר *tamrûr* **masc. noun**
(bitterness)
Jer. 6:26; 31:15; **Hos.** 12:14(15).

8564. I. תַּמְרוּר *tamrûr* **masc. noun**
(guide post, road mark)
Jer. 31:21(KJV, see II).
II. תַּמְרוּר *tamrûr* **masc. noun**
(high heap)
Jer. 31:21(NASB, NIV, see I).

8565. תַּן *tān* **masc. noun**
(jackal; KJV, dragon)
Neh. 2:13(NASB, *'ēyn hatanniyn* [5886]); **Job** 30:29; **Ps.** 44:19(20); **Isa.** 13:22; 34:13; 35:7; 43:20; **Jer.** 9:11(10); 10:22; 14:6; 49:33; 51:37; **Lam.** 4:3(KJV, *tanniyn* [8577]); **Mic.** 1:8; **Mal.** 1:3.

8566. תָּנָה *tānāh* **verb**
(to hire; to sell oneself)
Hos. 8:9,10.

8567. תָּנָה *tānāh* **verb**
(to commemorate; to rehearse)
Judg. 5:11(NIV, *nāṯan* [5414]); 11:40.

8568. תַּנָּה *tānnāh* **fem. noun**
(dragon)
Mal. 1:3(NASB, NIV, *tan* [8565]).

8569. תְּנוּאָה *tenû'āh* **fem. noun**
(opposition; pretext)
Num. 14:34; **Job** 33:10.

8570. תְּנוּבָה *tenûḇāh* **fem. noun**
(fruit, crop)
Deut. 32:13; **Judg.** 9:11; **Isa.** 27:6; **Lam.** 4:9; **Ezek.** 36:30.

8571. תְּנוּךְ *tenûḵ* **masc. noun**
(lobe, tip of the ear)
Ex. 29:20; **Lev.** 8:23,24; 14:14,17,25,28.

8572. תְּנוּמָה *tenûmāh* **fem. noun**
(slumber)
Job 33:15; **Ps.** 132:4; **Prov.** 6:4,10; 24:33.

8573. תְּנוּפָה *tenûp̱āh* **fem. noun**
(a waving; a wave offering)
Ex. 29:24,26,27; 35:22; 38:24,29; **Lev.** 7:30,34; 8:27,29; 9:21; 10:14,15; 14:12,21,24; 23:15,17,20; **Num.** 6:20; 8:11,13,15,21; 18:11,18; **Isa.** 19:16(NASB, *nûp̱* [5130,I]); 30:32.

8574. תַּנּוּר *tannûr* **masc. noun**
(oven, furnace)
Gen. 15:17; **Ex.** 8:3(7:28); **Lev.** 2:4; 7:9; 11:35; 26:26; **Neh.** 3:11; 12:38; **Ps.** 21:9(10); **Isa.** 31:9; **Lam.** 5:10; **Hos.** 7:4,6,7; **Mal.** 4:1(3:19).

8575. תַּנְחוּם *tanḥûm* **masc./fem. noun**

(consolation)
Job 15:11; 21:2; **Ps.** 94:19; **Isa.** 66:11; **Jer.** 16:7.

8576. תַּנְחֻמֶת *tanhumeṯ* **masc. proper noun**
(Tanhumeth)
2 Kgs. 25:23; **Jer.** 40:8.

8577. תַּנִּין *tanniyn* **masc. noun**
(dragon, sea monster)
Gen. 1:21; **Ex.** 7:9,10,12; **Deut.** 32:33; **Neh.** 2:13(NIV, *tan* [8565]); **Job** 7:12; **Ps.** 74:13; 91:13; 148:7; **Isa.** 27:1; 51:9; **Jer.** 51:34; **Lam.** 4:3; **Ezek.** 29:3.

8578. תִּנְיָן *tinyān* **Aram. ord. num.**
(second)
Dan. 7:5.

8579. תִּנְיָנוּת *tinyānûṯ* **Aram. adv.**
(again, a second time)
Dan. 2:7.

8580. I. תִּנְשֶׁמֶת *tinšemeṯ* **fem. noun**
(white owl)
Lev. 11:18(KJV, see III); **Deut.** 14:16(KJV, see III).
II. תִּנְשֶׁמֶת *tinšemeṯ* **fem. noun**
(chameleon)
Lev. 11:30(KJV, see IV).
III. תִּנְשֶׁמֶת *tinšemeṯ* **fem. noun**
(swan)
Lev. 11:18(NASB, NIV, see I); **Deut.** 14:16(NASB, NIV, see I).
IV. תִּנְשֶׁמֶת *tinšemeṯ* **fem. noun**
(mole)
Lev. 11:30(NASB, NIV, see II).

8581. תָּעַב *ta'aḇ* **verb**
(to abhor, to detest; to be vile, to be detestable)
Deut. 7:26; 23:7(8); **1 Kgs.** 21:26; **1 Chr.** 21:6; **Job** 9:31; 15:16; 19:19; 30:10; **Ps.** 5:6(7); 14:1; 53:1(2); 106:40; 107:18; 119:163; **Isa.** 14:19; 49:7; **Ezek.** 16:25,52; **Amos** 5:10; **Mic.** 3:9.

8582. תָּעָה *tā'āh* **verb**
(to wander, to be led astray; to stagger)
Gen. 20:13; 21:14; 37:15; **Ex.** 23:4; **2 Kgs.** 21:9; **2 Chr.** 33:9; **Job** 12:24,25; 15:31; 38:41; **Ps.** 58:3(4); 95:10; 107:4,40; 119:110,176; **Prov.** 7:25; 10:17; 12:26; 14:22; 21:16; **Isa.** 3:12; 9:16(15); 16:8; 19:13,14; 21:4; 28:7; 29:24; 30:28; 35:8; 47:15; 53:6; 63:17; **Jer.** 23:13,32; 42:20; 50:6; **Ezek.** 14:11; 44:10,15; 48:11; **Hos.** 4:12; **Amos** 2:4; **Mic.** 3:5.

8583. I. תֹּעוּ *tō'û* **masc. proper noun**
(Tou; the same as II)
1 Chr. 18:9,10.
II. תֹּעִי *tō'iy* **masc. proper noun**
(Toi [NIV; Tou]; the same as I)
2 Sam. 8:9,10.

8584. תְּעוּדָה *tᵉ'ûḏāh* **fem. noun**
(testimony; method of legalizing transactions)
Ruth 4:7; **Isa.** 8:16,20.

8585. I. תְּעָלָה *tᵉ'ālāh* **fem. noun**
(trench, channel, aquaduct)
1 Kgs. 18:32,35,38; **2 Kgs.** 18:17; 20:20; **Job** 38:25; **Isa.** 7:3; 36:2; **Ezek.** 31:4.
II. תְּעָלָה *tᵉ'ālāh* **fem. noun**
(remedy, healing)
Jer. 30:13; 46:11.

8586. תַּעֲלוּלִים *ta'ᵃlûliym* **masc. pl. noun**
(punishments; capricious ones [children])
Isa. 3:4; 66:4.

8587. תַּעֲלֻמָה *ta'ᵃlumāh* **fem. noun**
(secret; hidden thing)
Job 11:6; 28:11; **Ps.** 44:21(22).

8588. תַּעֲנוּג *ta'ᵃnûg* **masc. noun**
(delight, pleasure)
Prov. 19:10; **Eccl.** 2:8; **Song** 7:6(7); **Mic.** 1:16; 2:9.

8589. תַּעֲנִית *ta'ᵃniyṯ* **fem. noun**
(fasting, humiliation)
Ezra 9:5.

8590. תַּעְנָךְ *ta'nāḵ*, תַּעְנַךְ *ta'naḵ* **proper noun**
(Taanach)
Josh. 12:21; 17:11; 21:25; **Judg.** 1:27; 5:19; **1 Kgs.** 4:12; **1 Chr.** 7:29.

8591. I. תָּעַע *tā'a'* **verb**
(to deceive, to scoff)
Gen. 27:12; **2 Chr.** 36:16.
II. תְּעוּפָה *tᵉ'ûp̱āh* **fem. noun**
(darkness)
Job 11:17(KJV, *'ûp̱* [5774,I]).

8592. תַּעֲצֻמָה *ta'ᵃṣumāh* **fem. noun**
(power, strength)
Ps. 68:35(36).

8593. תַּעַר *ta'ar̠* **masc. noun**
(razor, knife; sheath)
Num. 6:5; 8:7; **1 Sam.** 17:51; **2 Sam.** 20:8; **Ps.** 52:2(4); **Isa.** 7:20; **Jer.** 36:23; 47:6; **Ezek.** 5:1; 21:3(8),4(9),5(10),30(35).

8594. תַּעֲרוּבָה *ta'ᵃrûḇāh* **fem. noun**
(hostage)
2 Kgs. 14:14; **2 Chr.** 25:24.

8595. תַּעְתֻּעִים *ta'tu'iym* **masc. pl. noun**
(mockery, error)
Jer. 10:15; 51:18.

8596. I. תֹּף *tōp̱* **masc. noun**
(tambourine)
Gen. 31:27; **Ex.** 15:20; **Judg.** 11:34; **1 Sam.** 10:5; 18:6; **2 Sam.** 6:5; **1 Chr.** 13:8; **Job** 21:12; **Ps.** 81:2(3); 149:3; 150:4; **Isa.** 5:12; 24:8; 30:32; **Jer.** 31:4; **Ezek.** 28:13(NASB, NIV, see II).
II. תֹּף *tōp̱* **masc. noun**
(setting [of a jewel])
Ezek. 28:13(KJV, see I).

8597. תִּפְאָרָה *tiph'ārāh* **fem. noun**
(glory, beauty, splendor)
Ex. 28:2,40; **Deut.** 26:19; **Judg.** 4:9; **1 Chr.** 22:5; 29:11,13; **2 Chr.** 3:6; **Esth.** 1:4; **Ps.** 71:8; 78:61; 89:17(18); 96:6; **Prov.** 4:9; 16:31; 17:6; 19:11; 20:29; 28:12; **Isa.** 3:18; 4:2; 10:12; 13:19; 20:5; 28:1,4,5; 44:13; 46:13; 52:1; 60:7,19; 62:3; 63:12,14,15; 64:11(10); **Jer.** 13:11, 18,20; 33:9; 48:17; **Lam.** 2:1; **Ezek.** 16:12,17,39; 23:26,42; 24:25; **Zech.** 12:7.

8598. תַּפּוּחַ *tappûaḥ* **masc. noun**
(apple tree, apple)
Prov. 25:11; **Song** 2:3,5; 7:8(9); 8:5; **Joel** 1:12.

8599. A. תַּפּוּחַ *tappûaḥ* **masc. proper noun**
(Tappuah: descendant of Caleb)
1 Chr. 2:43.
B. תַּפּוּחַ *tappûaḥ* **proper noun**
(Tappuah: city in Judah)
Josh. 15:34.
C. תַּפּוּחַ *tappûaḥ* **proper noun**
(Tappuah: city on the border of Ephraim)
Josh. 12:17; 16:8; 17:8.

8600. I. תְּפוֹצָה *tᵉp̱ôṣāh* **fem. noun**
(a dispersing)
Jer. 25:34(NIV, see II).
II. תְּפוֹצָה *tᵉp̱ôṣāh* **fem. noun**
(a shattering)
Jer. 25:34(KJV, NASB, see I).

8601. I. תֻּפִּינִים *tuppiyniym* **masc. pl. noun**
(baked pieces)
Lev. 6:21(14)(NIV, see II).
II. תֻּפִּינִים *tuppiyniym* **masc. pl. noun**
(broken pieces)
Lev. 6:21(14)(KJV, NASB, see I).

8602. I. תָּפֵל *tāpēl* **adj.**
(foolish, tasteless)
Job 6:6; **Lam.** 2:14.
II. תָּפֵל *tāpēl* **masc. noun**
(whitewash)
Ezek. 13:10(KJV, see III),11(KJV, see III),14(KJV, see III),15(KJV, see III); 22:28(KJV, see III).
III. תָּפֵל *tāpēl* **masc. noun**
(untempered mortar)
Ezek. 13:10(NASB, NIV, see II),11(NASB, NIV, see II),14(NASB, NIV, see II),15(NASB, NIV, see II); 22:28(NASB, NIV, see II).

8603. תֹּפֶל *tōpel* **proper noun**
(Tophel)
Deut. 1:1.

8604. תִּפְלָה *tiplāh* **fem. noun**
(folly, wrongdoing)
Job 1:22; 24:12; **Jer.** 23:13.

8605. תְּפִלָּה *t^e^pillāh* **fem. noun**
(prayer)
2 Sam. 7:27; **1 Kgs.** 8:28,29,38,45, 49,54; 9:3; **2 Kgs.** 19:4; 20:5; **2 Chr.** 6:19,20,29,35,39,40; 7:12,15; 30:27; 33:18,19; **Neh.** 1:6,11; 11:17; **Job** 16:17; **Ps.** 4:1(2); 6:9(10); 17:[title](1),1(2); 35:13; 39:12(13); 42:8(9); 54:2(4); 55:1(2); 61:1(2); 65:2(3); 66:19,20; 69:13(14); 72:20; 80:4(5); 84:8(9); 86:[title](1),6(7); 88:2(3),13(14); 90:[title](1); 102:[title](1), 1(2),17(18); 109:4,7; 141:2,5; 142:[title](1); 143:1; **Prov.** 15:8,29; 28:9; **Isa.** 1:15; 37:4; 38:5; 56:7; **Jer.** 7:16; 11:14; **Lam.** 3:8,44; **Dan.** 9:3,17,21; **Jon.** 2:7(8); **Hab.** 3:1.

8606. תִּפְלֶצֶת *tipleṣet* **fem. noun**
(terror)
Jer. 49:16.

8607. A. תִּפְסַח *tipsaḥ* **proper noun**
(Tiphsah: a city in northern Syria)
1 Kgs. 4:24.
B. תִּפְסַח *tipsaḥ* **proper noun**
(Tiphsah: a city in northern Israel)
2 Kgs. 15:16.

8608. תָּפַף *tāpap* **verb**
(to play tambourines)
Ps. 68:25(26); **Nah.** 2:7(8).

8609. תָּפַר *tāpar* **verb**
(to sew; to mend)
Gen. 3:7; **Job** 16:15; **Eccl.** 3:7; **Ezek.** 13:18.

8610. תָּפַשׂ *tāpaś* **verb**
(to seize, to catch, to capture; to play [an instrument])
Gen. 4:21; 39:12; **Num.** 5:13; 31:27; **Deut.** 9:17; 20:19; 21:19; 22:28; **Josh.** 8:8,23; **1 Sam.** 15:8; 23:26; **1 Kgs.** 11:30; 13:4; 18:40; 20:18; **2 Kgs.** 7:12; 10:14; 14:7,13; 16:9; 18:13; 25:6; **2 Chr.** 25:23; **Josh.** 87:8,23; **Ps.** 10:2; 71:11; **Prov.** 30:9,28; **Isa.** 3:6; 36:1; **Jer.** 2:8; 26:8; 34:3; 37:13,14; 38:23; 40:10; 46:9; 48:41; 49:16; 50:16,24,46; 51:32,41; 52:9; **Ezek.** 12:13; 14:5; 17:20; 19:4,8; 21:11(16),23(28),24(29); 27:29; 29:7; 30:21; 38:4; **Amos** 2:15; **Hab.** 2:19.

8611. I. תֹּפֶת *tōpet* **fem. noun**
(object of spitting)
Job 17:6(KJV, see II).
II. תֹּפֶת *tōpet* **fem. noun**
(tabret [drum])
Job 17:6(NASB, NIV, see I).

8612. תֹּפֶת *tōpet* **proper noun**
(Topheth)
2 Kgs. 23:10; **Jer.** 7:31,32; 19:6,11–14.

8613. תָּפְתֶּה *topteh* **proper noun**
(Topheth)
Isa. 30:33.

8614. תִּפְתָּי *tiptāy* **Aram. masc. noun**
(magistrate; sheriff)
Dan. 3:2,3.

8615. I. תִּקְוָה *tiqwāh* **fem. noun**
(cord, line)
Josh. 2:18,21.
II. תִּקְוָה *tiqwāh* **fem. noun**
(hope, expectation)
Ruth 1:12; **Job** 4:6; 5:16; 6:8; 7:6; 8:13; 11:18,20; 14:7,19; 17:15; 19:10; 27:8; **Ps.** 9:18(19); 62:5(6); 71:5; **Prov.** 10:28; 11:7,23; 19:18; 23:18; 24:14; 26:12; 29:20; **Jer.** 29:11; 31:17; **Lam.** 3:29; **Ezek.** 19:5; 37:11; **Hos.** 2:15(17); **Zech.** 9:12.

8616. A. תִּקְוָה *tiqwāh* **masc. proper noun**
(Tikvah: father-in-law of the prophetess Huldah; the same as *towqhaṯ* [8445])
2 Kgs. 22:14; **2 Chr.** 34:22(NASB, NIV, [Hebr.] *towqhaṯ* [8445]).
B. תִּקְוָה *tiqwāh* **masc. proper noun**
(Tikvah: father of Jahaziah)
Ezra 10:15.

8617. תְּקוּמָה *tᵉqûmāh* **fem. noun**
(ability to stand)
Lev. 26:37.

8618. תְּקוֹמֵם *tᵉqômēm* **masc. noun**
(one who rises up)
Ps. 139:21(NASB, NIV, *qûm* [6965]).

8619. תָּקוֹעַ *tāqôaʿ* **masc. noun**
(trumpet)
Ezek. 7:14.

8620. תְּקוֹעַ *tᵉqôaʿ* **proper noun**
(Tekoa)
2 Sam. 14:2; **1 Chr.** 2:24; 4:5; **2 Chr.** 11:6; 20:20; **Jer.** 6:1; **Amos** 1:1.

8621. תְּקוֹעִי *tᵉqôʿiy*, תִּקְעִי *tᵉqōʿiy* **masc. proper noun**
(Tekoite; one from Tekoah [8620])
2 Sam. 14:4,9; 23:26; **1 Chr.** 11:28; 27:9; **Neh.** 3:5,27.

8622. תְּקוּפָה *tᵉqûpāh* **fem. noun**
(a turning around; a circuit)
Ex. 34:22; **1 Sam.** 1:20; **2 Chr.** 24:23; **Ps.** 19:6(7).

8623. תַּקִּיף *taqqiyp̱* **adj.**
(mighty; strong)
Eccl. 6:10.

8624. תַּקִּיף *taqqiyp̱* **Aram. adj.**
(mighty, strong; corr. to Hebr. 8623)
Ezra 4:20; **Dan.** 2:40,42; 4:3(3:33); 7:7.

8625. I. תְּקַל *tᵉqal* **Aram. verb**
(to weigh)
Dan. 5:27.
II. תְּקֵל *tᵉqēl* **proper noun**
(Tekel; a unit of weight, shekel)
Dan. 5:25,27.

8626. תָּקַן *tāqan* **verb**
(to make straight; to set in order)
Eccl. 1:15; 7:13; 12:9.

8627. תְּקַן *tᵉqan* **Aram. verb**
(to be set in order; to be established; corr. to Hebr. [8626])
Dan. 4:36(33).

8628. תָּקַע *tāqaʿ* **verb**
(to blow a trumpet; to thrust, to fasten, to drive in; to clap; to pitch a tent)
Gen. 31:25; **Ex.** 10:19; **Num.** 10:3–8, 10; **Josh.** 6:4,8,9,13,16,20; **Judg.** 3:21, 27; 4:21; 6:34; 7:18–20,22; 16:14; **1 Sam.** 13:3; 31:10; **2 Sam.** 2:28; 18:14,16; 20:1,22; **1 Kgs.** 1:34,39; **2 Kgs.** 9:13; 11:14; **1 Chr.** 10:10; **2 Chr.** 23:13; **Neh.** 4:18(12); **Job** 17:3; **Ps.** 47:1(2); 81:3(4); **Prov.** 6:1; 11:15; 17:18; 22:26; **Isa.** 18:3; 22:23,25; 27:13; **Jer.** 4:5; 6:1,3; 51:27; **Ezek.** 7:14; 33:3,6; **Hos.** 5:8; **Joel**

2:1,15; **Amos** 3:6; **Nah.** 3:19; **Zech.** 9:14.

8629. תֵּקַע *tēqaʻ* **masc. noun**
(the sounding [of a trumpet])
Ps. 150:3.

8630. תָּקֵף *tāqēp̱* **verb**
(to overpower; to prevail)
Job 14:20; 15:24; **Eccl.** 4:12.

8631. תְּקֵף *t^eqēp̱* **Aram. verb**
(to be powerful; to become strong; corr. to Hebr. 8630)
Dan. 4:11(8),20(17),22(19); 5:20; 6:7(8).

8632. I. תְּקָף *t^eqāp̱* **Aram. masc. noun**
(strength, might)
Dan. 4:30(27).
II. תְּקֹף *t^eqōp̱* **masc. noun**
(strength, might)
Dan. 2:37.

8633. תֹּקֶף *tōqep̱* **masc. noun**
(authority, strength, power)
Esth. 9:29; 10:2; **Dan.** 11:17.

8634. תַּרְאֲלָה *tar'alāh* **proper noun**
(Taralah)
Josh. 18:27.

8635. תַּרְבּוּת *tarbûṯ* **fem. noun**
(offspring, generation)
Num. 32:14.

8636. תַּרְבִּית *tarbiyṯ* **fem. noun**
(increase, excessive interest, usury)
Lev. 25:36; **Prov.** 28:8; **Ezek.** 18:8,13,17; 22:12.

8637. תִּרְגַּל *tirgal* **verb**
(to teach to walk)
Hos. 11:3(NASB, NIV, *rāgal* [7270,III]).

8638. תִּרְגֵּם *tirgam* **verb**
(to interpret; to translate)
Ezra 4:7.

8639. תַּרְדֵּמָה *tardēmāh* **fem. noun**
(deep sleep; sound sleep)
Gen. 2:21; 15:12; **1 Sam.** 26:12; **Job** 4:13; 33:15; **Prov.** 19:15; **Isa.** 29:10.

8640. תִּרְהָקָה *tirhāqāh* **masc. noun**
(Tirhakah)
2 Kgs. 19:9; **Isa.** 37:9.

8641. תְּרוּמָה *t^erûmāh* **fem. noun**
(offering; contribution)
Ex. 25:2,3; 29:27,28; 30:13–15; 35:5, 21,24; 36:3,6; **Lev.** 7:14,32,34; 10:14,15; 22:12; **Num.** 5:9; 6:20; 15:19–21; 18:8, 11,19,24,26–29; 31:29,41,52; **Deut.** 12:6,11,17; **2 Sam.** 1:21; **2 Chr.** 31:10, 12,14; **Ezra** 8:25; **Neh.** 10:37(38), 39(40); 12:44; 13:5; **Prov.** 29:4; **Isa.** 40:20; **Ezek.** 20:40; 44:30; 45:1,6,7, 13,16; 48:8–10,12,18,20,21; **Mal.** 3:8.

8642. תְּרוּמִיָּה *t^erûmiyyāh* **fem. noun**
(special gift, allotment)
Ezek. 48:12.

8643. תְּרוּעָה *t^erûʻāh* **fem. noun**
(shout of joy; shout of alarm, battle cry)
Lev. 23:24; 25:9; **Num.** 10:5,6; 23:21; 29:1; 31:6; **Josh.** 6:5,20; **1 Sam.** 4:5,6; **2 Sam.** 6:15; **1 Chr.** 15:28; **2 Chr.** 13:12; 15:14; **Ezra** 3:11–13; **Job** 8:21; 33:26; 39:25; **Ps.** 27:6; 33:3; 47:5(6); 89:15(16); 150:5; **Jer.** 4:19; 20:16; 49:2; **Ezek.** 21:22(27); **Amos** 1:14; 2:2; **Zeph.** 1:16.

8644. תְּרוּפָה *t^erûp̱āh* **fem. noun**
(healing, medicine)
Ezek. 47:12.

8645. תִּרְזָה *tirzāh* **fem. noun**
(cypress tree)
Isa. 44:14.

8646. A. תֶּרַח *teraḥ* **masc. proper noun**
(Terah: the father of Abraham)
Gen. 11:24–28,31,32; **Josh.** 24:2; **1 Chr.** 1:26.
B. תֶּרַח *teraḥ* **proper noun**
(Terah: a place in the wilderness)
Num. 33:27,28.

8647. תִּרְחֲנָה *tirḥ*ᵃ*nāh* **masc. proper noun**
(Tirhanah)
1 Chr. 2:48.

8648. תְּרֵין *t*ᵉ*rēyn* **Aram. num.**
(two, second)
Ezra 4:24; 6:17; **Dan.** 4:29(26); 5:31(6:1).

8649. I. תָּרְמָה *tarmāh* **fem. noun**
(deceitfulness; under cover)
Judg. 9:31.
II. תַּרְמִית *tarmiyṯ* **fem. noun**
(deceitfulness; deception; delusion)
Ps. 119:118; **Jer.** 8:5; 14:14; 23:26; **Zeph.** 3:13.

8650. תֹּרֶן *tōren* **masc. noun**
(mast; flagstaff)
Isa. 30:17; 33:23; **Ezek.** 27:5.

8651. תְּרַע *t*ᵉ*ra'* **Aram. masc. noun**
(door; court [as held at the gate])
Dan. 2:49; 3:26.

8652. תָּרָע *tārā'* **Aram. masc. noun**
(doorkeeper; gatekeeper)
Ezra 7:24.

8653. תַּרְעֵלָה *tar'ēlāh* **fem. noun**
(staggering; reeling)
Ps. 60:3(5); **Isa.** 51:17,22.

8654. תִּרְעָתִים *tir'āṯiym* **masc. pl. proper noun**
(Tirathites)
1 Chr. 2:55.

8655. תְּרָפִים *t*ᵉ*rāpiym* **masc. pl. noun**
(household gods, idols)
Gen. 31:19,34,35; **Judg.** 17:5; 18:14,17, 18,20; **1 Sam.** 15:23; 19:13,16; **2 Kgs.** 23:24; **Ezek.** 21:21(26); **Hos.** 3:4; **Zech.** 10:2.

8656. A. תִּרְצָה *tirṣāh* **fem. proper noun**
(Tirzah: daughter of Zelophehad)
Num. 26:33; 27:1; 36:11; **Josh.** 17:3.
B. תִּרְצָה *tirṣāh* **proper noun**
(Tirzah: Canaanite city and later capital of the Northern Kingdom)
Josh. 12:24; **1 Kgs.** 14:17; 15:21,33; 16:6,8,9,15,17,23; **2 Kgs.** 15:14,16; **Song** 6:4.

8657. תֶּרֶשׁ *tereš* **masc. proper noun**
(Teresh)
Esth. 2:21; 6:2.

8658. I. תַּרְשִׁישׁ *taršiyš* **masc. noun**
(a gemstone: either beryl [KJV, NASB] or chrysolite [NIV])
Ex. 28:20; 39:13; **Song** 5:14; **Ezek.** 1:16; 10:9(NASB, see II); 28:13; **Dan.** 10:6.
II. תַּרְשִׁישׁ *taršiyš* **proper noun**
(Tarshish: proper name for the gemstone in I, perhaps referring to origin [8659,D])
Ezek. 10:9(KJV, NIV, see I).

8659. I. תַּרְשִׁישׁ *taršiyš* **masc. proper noun**
(Tarshish: son of Javan)
Gen. 10:4; **1 Chr.** 1:7.
II. תַּרְשִׁישׁ *taršiyš* **masc. proper noun**
(Tarshish: descendant of Benjamin)
1 Chr. 7:10.
III. תַּרְשִׁישׁ *taršiyš* **masc. proper noun**
(Tarshish: a Persian advisor)
Esth. 1:14.

8660. I. תִּרְשָׁתָא *tiršāṯāʾ* **masc. noun**
(governor)
Ezra 2:63(KJV, see II); **Neh.** 7:65(NASB, NIV, see I),70(69)(NASB, NIV, see I); 8:9(NASB, NIV, see I); 10:1(NASB, NIV, see I).
II. תִּרְשָׁתָא *tiršāṯāʾ* **proper noun**
(Tirshatha: title of the Persian governor of Judah)
Ezra 2:63(NASB, NIV, see I); **Neh.** 7:65 (NASB, NIV, see I),70(69)(NASB, NIV, see I); 8:9(NASB, NIV, see I); 10:1(NASB, NIV, see I).

8661. I. תַּרְתָּן *tartān* **masc. proper noun**
(Tartan: an Assyrian general)
2 Kgs. 18:17(NIV, see II); **Isa.** 20:1(NASB, NIV, see II).
II. תַּרְתָּן *tartān* **masc. noun**
(supreme commander)
2 Kgs. 18:17(KJV, NASB, see I); **Isa.** 20:1 (KJV, see II).

8662. תַּרְתָּק *tartāq* **masc. proper noun**
(Tartak: an Avite deity)
2 Kgs. 17:31.

8663. תְּשֻׁאָה t^e*shuʾāh*, תְּשֻׁוָה t^e*shūwāh* **fem. noun**
(shouting, loud noise, thundering)
Job 30:22(KJV, [Q^e] *šāwāh* [7738]); 36:29; 39:7; **Isa.** 22:2; **Zech.** 4:7.

8664. תִּשְׁבִּי *tišbey* **masc. proper noun**
(Tishbite)
1 Kgs. 17:1; 21:17,28; **2 Kgs.** 1:3,8; 9:36.

8665. תַּשְׁבֵּץ *tašbēṣ* **masc. noun**
(checkered, woven, embroidered)
Ex. 28:4.

8666. I. תְּשׁוּבָה t^e*šûḇāh* **fem. noun**
(return; answer)
1 Sam. 7:17; **Job** 21:34; 34:36.
II. תְּשׁוּבָה t^e*šûḇāh* **fem. noun**
(return [of the year]; spring)
2 Sam. 11:1(KJV, see III); **1 Kgs.** 20:22(KJV, see III),26;(KJV, see III); **1 Chr.** 20:1(KJV, see III); **2 Chr.** 36:10(KJV, see III).
III. תְּשׁוּבָה t^e*šûḇāh* **fem. noun**
(turn of the year; end of the year)
2 Sam. 11:1(NASB, NIV, see II); **1 Kgs.** 20:22(NASB, NIV, see II),26;(NASB, NIV, see II); **1 Chr.** 20:1(NASB, NIV, see II); **2 Chr.** 36:10(NASB, NIV, see II).

8667. תְּשׂוּמֶת t^e*śûmeṯ* **fem. noun**
(something left in security [as a pledge])
Lev. 6:2(5:21).

8668. תְּשׁוּעָה t^e*šûʿāh* **fem. noun**
(salvation, deliverance, victory)
Judg. 15:18; **1 Sam.** 11:9,13; 19:5; **2 Sam.** 19:2(3); 23:10,12; **2 Kgs.** 5:1; 13:17; **1 Chr.** 11:14; 19:12; **2 Chr.** 6:41; **Ps.** 33:17; 37:39; 38:22(23); 40:10(11), 16(17); 51:14(16); 60:11(13); 71:15; 108:12(13); 119:41,81; 144:10; 146:3; **Prov.** 11:14; 21:31; 24:6; **Isa.** 45:17; 46:13; **Jer.** 3:23; **Lam.** 3:26.

8669. תְּשׁוּקָה t^e*šûqāh* **fem. noun**
(desire, longing)
Gen. 3:16; 4:7; **Song** 7:10(11).

8670. תְּשׁוּרָה t^e*šûrāh* **fem. noun**
(gift, present)
1 Sam. 9:7.

8671. תְּשִׁיעִי t^e*šiyʿiy* **ord. num.**
(ninth)
Lev. 25:22; **Num.** 7:60; **2 Kgs.** 17:6; 25:1; **1 Chr.** 12:12(13); 24:11; 25:16; 27:12; **Ezra** 10:9; **Jer.** 36:9,22; 39:1; 52:4; **Ezek.** 24:1; **Hag.** 2:10,18; **Zech.** 7:1.

8672. תֵּשַׁע *tēša'* **masc. num.**
(nine [NIV, see also *tiš'iym* [8673])
Gen. 5:5,8,11,14,20,27; 9:29; 11:19, 24,25; 17:1,24; **Ex.** 38:24; **Lev.** 23:32; 25:8; **Num.** 1:23; 2:13; 29:26; 34:13; **Deut.** 3:11; **Josh.** 13:7; 14:2; 15:32, 44,54; 19:38; 21:16; **Judg.** 4:3,13; **2 Sam.** 2:30; 24:8; **2 Kgs.** 14:2; 15:13,17; 17:1; 18:2,10; 25:3,8; **1 Chr.** 3:8; 9:9; 24:16; 25:26; **2 Chr.** 16:12; 25:1; 29:1; **Ezra** 1:9; 2:8,36,42; **Neh.** 7:38,39; 11:1,8; **Jer.** 39:2; 52:6,12.

8673. תִּשְׁעִים *tiš'iym* **masc. pl. num.**
(ninety; regarded by NIV, as the plural of *tēša'* [8672])
Gen. 5:9,17,30; 17:1,17,24; **1 Sam.** 4:15; **1 Chr.** 9:6; **Ezra** 2:16,20,58; 8:35; **Neh.** 7:21,25,60; **Jer.** 52:23; **Ezek.** 4:5,9; 41:12; **Dan.** 12:11.

8674. תַּתְּנַי *tatt^{e}nay* **Aram. masc. proper noun**
(Tattenai, Tatnai)
Ezra 5:3,6; 6:6,13.